THE
SOURCEBOOK
To Public Record Information

The Comprehensive Guide to County, State, & Federal
Public Records Sources

Fourth Edition

BRB Publications, Inc.
www.brbpub.com

Dedicated to the Searching & Understanding of Public Records

Public Record Research Library

THE
SOURCEBOOK
TO PUBLIC RECORD INFORMATION - *Fourth Edition*

Edited by: Peter J. Weber and Michael Sankey

©2002 By BRB Publications, Inc.
206 West Julie Dr, Suite 2
Tempe, AZ 85283
800-929-3811   Fax 800-929-4981

www.brbpub.com

ISBN 1-879792-68-0

The sourcebook to public record information : the
comprehensive guide to county, state, & federal public
records sources / [edited by Peter J. Weber and Michael L.
Sankey]. – 4th ed.
  p. cm.
  ISBN: 1-879792-68-0

  1. Public records--United States--States--Information
Services--Directories. 2. Courts--United States--States
--Directories. 3. Public records--United States--States
--Computer network resources. I. Weber, Peter J.
(Peter Julius), 1952- II. Sankey, Michael L., 1949-
1949- II. Weber, Peter J.

JK468.P76S68 2002   352.3'87
                               QBI02-864

Contents

Section II: Public Records by State   63

51 State Chapters   Page 65 and forward

Each State Chapter is Organized as Follows:

1. State Agencies
2. State Licensing Boards
3. Federal Courts
4. County Courts
5. Recording Offices
6. County Locator

Limited information about Guam, Puerto Rico and The Virgin Islands is located on pages 1651-1653

Introduction

Complex and Mysterious?

> *The access to and use of current public records is one of the fundamental pillars of our democratic society.*
>
> *Yet, the words "Public Records" often convey a complex, almost mysterious source of information that is perceived as difficult to access, hard to decipher, and likely to be of interest only to private investigators and reporters.*
>
> *This view could not be further from the truth!*

Your Access to Over 20,000 Government Agencies

Herein, we will examine these paper trails that begin or are maintained at the federal, state, county, and in certain instances, the city and town level. This *Sourcebook* is especially useful for these applications:

- Legal Research
- Background Investigation
- Pre-Employment and Tenant Screening
- Locating People
- Locating Assets
- Skiptracing
- Genealogy

This *Sourcebook* reveals where records are kept, outlines the access requirements and gives searching hints, tells which agencies are online. Over 20,000 government agencies are profiled so you can explore the depths of the public record industry.

Public records are meant to be used for the benefit of society. As a member of the public, you or someone in authority is entitled to review the public records held by government agencies. Whether you are a business owner, a reporter, an investigator, or even a father trying to check on your daughter's first date, you can access public records to meet your needs.

Equipped with the information contained in these pages, you can find the facts, gain access to the information you need, and even track your own "information trail!"

Special Note From the Editors

The Fourth Edition of *The Sourcebook to Public Record Information* represents thousands of hours of research right up to the day of printing. We have compiled what we feel is the most up-to-date and unique compendium of its kind.

The research for this year's edition has led to an enormous amount of new information. Extra importance was placed in these areas:

- Online access
- Web addresses
- Area code changes
- Access procedure changes
- New ZIP Codes

For those of you who need to know more or need to have this information constantly updated, we recommend two expanded versions of this product. *The Public Records Research System* (PRRS) is available on CD-ROM with semi-annual updates, and as a subscription service on the Internet at www.publicrecordsources.com.

BRB Publications is 100% devoted to the understanding of public records. We hope you find *The Sourcebook* a valuable asset for your business or use.

The research and editorial staff at BRB Publications—

Helen Doornbos

William Roberts

Annette Talley

Peter J. Weber

Michael Sankey

How This Book Is Organized

General Layout

The Sourcebook is organized into two Sections--

1. Public Record Primer
2. 51 Individual State Chapters

The Public Record Primer

The purpose of *The Public Record Primer* section is to assist the reader in knowing *where categories of records can be found* and *how to search*. An important segment of this section is the discussion of privacy issues including public information vs. personal information and how records enter the public domain.

The Primer contains many searching hints and is an excellent overall source of information that will especially help those not familiar with searching government records.

The **Searching Federal Court Records** chapter (page 25) contains an excellent article (on page 35) contributed by Alan Schlein, author of *Find it Online! The Complete Guide to Online Research* (Facts on Demand Press). Mr. Schlein presents a unique dissertation about the best federal government Internet sites for finding usual information quickly and efficiently.

Another important chapter is **Using a Public Record Vendor** (page 57). This chapter contains a wealth of information about commercial public record vendors, especially those who offer online access to records.

The State Chapters

The individual state chapters in the *Sourcebook* have been compiled into an easy to use format.

Six sub-chapters or sections are presented in this order:

1. State Public Record Agencies
2. State Licensing and Regulatory Boards
3. Federal Courts (US District and Bankruptcy)
4. County Courts
5. County Recorder Offices
6. County Locator

Information Found in the Agency Profiles

The depth of knowledge presented about each government agency is what separates this *Sourcebook* from a typical address and phone listing reference book. The beginning of each state and/or county sub-chapter has an overall discussion of the public records policies, with important characteristics and searching hints.

The following details are have been researched and presented (when applicable) within each profile:

- **Agency Facts**: office hours; time zone; web sites.

- **Searching Facts**: methods of access; indexing; search requirements; if records are available online; when free public access terminals are at the counter; turnaround times, how far back (years) records are kept.

- **Privacy Facts**: restrictions that the agencies impose on searchers or types of searchers; when signed releases or notarized statements are required.

- **Fees**: access fees, copy fees; certification fees; expedited fees, if credit cards accepted; what types of checks accepted; to whom to make the check payable.

- **Misc:** how to purchase databases or customized lists; if the more than one agency must be visited in the county to get all records; if results will or will not be returned by fax, etc.

Using The County Locator

The County Locator portion of each state chapter is extremely useful when it is unclear which county to perform a localized record search. This section contains two cross-reference indices. The City/County Cross Reference will indicate what county(s) in which a "place" (city or town) is located. There are over 40,000 places referenced. The ZIP Code/City Cross Reference assists those people who have an address with ZIP Code, but are unsure in which county the ZIP in located.

Keep in mind that over 8,000 ZIP Codes cross county lines.

Section I

Public Record Primer

Public Records Unveiled

Definition of Public Records

The strict **definition** of **public records** is—

> *"Those records maintained by government agencies*
> *that are open without restriction to public inspection,*
> *either by statute or by tradition."*

If access to a record that is held by a government agency is restricted in some way, then it is not a public record.

Accessibility Paradox

Adding to the mystique of government records is the accessibility paradox. For example, in some states a specific category of records is severely restricted, and therefore those records are not "public," while the very same category of records may be 100% open in other states. Among these categories are criminal histories, vehicle ownership records and worker's compensation records.

At times, you will see the following box printed on pages throughout the *Sourcebook*. We are not trying to fill up space. As your public record searching takes you from state-to-state, this is the one important adage to keep in mind.

> "Just because records are maintained in a certain way in
> your state or county, do not assume that any other county or
> state does things the same way you are used to."

Public vs. Private vs. Personal

Before reading further, let's define types of records held by government or by private industry. Of course, not all information about a company or individual is public. The boundaries between public and private information are not well understood, and continually undergo intense scrutiny. The following is an introduction to the subject from a viewpoint of a professional record searcher.

Public Record

Public records are records of **incidents** or **actions** filed or recorded with a government agency for the purpose of notifying others about the matter—the "public." The **deed** to your house recorded at the county recorder's office is a public record—it is a legal requirement that you record with the county recorder. Anyone requiring details about your property may review or copy the documents.

Public Information

Your **telephone listing** in the phone book is public information; that is, you freely furnished the information to ease the flow of commercial and private communications.

Personal Information

Any information about a person or business that the person or business might consider private and confidential in nature, such as your **Social Security Number**, is personal information. Such information will remain private to a limited extent unless it is disclosed to some outside entity that could make it public. **Personal information may be found in either public records or in public information.**

How Personal Information Enters the Public Domain

Many people confuse the three categories above, lump them into one and wonder how "big brother" accumulated so much information about them. Therefore, these distinctions are important. The reality is that **much of this information is given willingly**.

Actually, there are two ways that personal information can enter the public domain—statutory and voluntary. In a **voluntary** transaction, you **share** personal information of your own free will. In a **statutory** transaction, you **disclose** personal information because the law requires you to.

The confusion of terms used today feeds the increasing conflict between privacy advocates and commercial interests. This, in turn, is driving legislation towards more and more **restrictions** on the **dissemination of personal information**—the same personal information that, in fact, is willingly shared by most people and companies in order to participate in our market economy.

Where Public Records are Held

There are two places you can find public records—

1. at a government agency
2. within the database of a private company

Government agencies maintain records in a variety of ways. While many state agencies and highly populated county agencies are computerized, many others use microfiche, microfilm, and paper to store files and indexes. Agencies that have converted to computer will not necessarily place complete file records on their system; they are more apt to include only an index, pointer or summary data to the files.

Private enterprises develop their databases in one of two ways: they buy the records in bulk from government agencies; or they send personnel to the agencies and compile this information by using a copy machine or keying information into a laptop computer. The database is then available for internal use or for resale purposes. An example of such a company is *Superior Information* (800 848-0489). Superior maintains a very comprehensive database of civil judgments, tax liens, Uniform Commercial Code filings and bankruptcy data gathered from the Mid-Atlantic States.

The Common Methods Used to Access Public Records

The following is a look at the various methods available to access public records.

Visit in Person

This is easy if you live close by. Many courthouses and recorders offices have free access terminals open to the public. Certain records, such as corporate or UCC records generally found at the Secretary of State, can be viewed or pulled for free, but will incur a fee for copies. A signed release is a common requirement for accessing motor vehicle and criminal records.

Mail, Fax, or Telephone

Although some agencies permit phone or fax requests, the majority of agencies prefer mail requests. Some agencies consider fax requesting to be an expedited service that incurs higher fees. Agencies that permit telephone requests may merely answer "Yes" or "No" to questions such as "Does John Doe have a civil court case in his name?" We have indicated when telephone and fax requesting is available, as well as the extent of the service.

Online and the Internet

The Internet may be a free means to certain agency records or may be the conduit to a subscription or commercial site. This commercial online access method of public records is much more prevalent at the state level compared to the county level. Many agencies, such as DMVs, make the information available to pre-approved, high volume, ongoing accounts. Typically, this access involves fees and a specified, minimum amount of usage.

However, there is a definite trend of certain agencies posting public record data on the Internet for free. Two examples are Secretary of State offices (whose records include corporation, UCC and tax liens) and county/city tax assessor offices (whose records reveal property ownership). Usually this information is limited to name indexes and summary data, rather than document images. In addition, a growing number of state licensing boards are posting their membership lists on the net (although addresses and phone numbers of the licensed individuals typically are not listed).

Also, the Internet is a good place to find *general* information about government agencies. Many web sites enable one to download, read and/or print current forms, policies and regulations.

Hire Someone Else

As mentioned previously, one method to access public records is from a vendor. These companies must comply with state and federal laws, thus if the government agency will not a release a record, chances are a vendor company will not either. There are a variety of types of companies that can be hired to perform record searches. An excellent, quick source to find the right vendor for a particular need is www.publicrecordsources.com or *The National Directory of Public Record Vendors*.

Bulk or Database Purchases

Many agencies offer programs to purchase all or parts of their database for statistical or commercial purposes. The restrictions vary widely from state to state, even within the same record type or category. Typically, records are available (to those who qualify) in the following media types; magnetic tapes, FTP, cartridges, paper printouts, labels, disks, CDs, microfiche and/or microfilm. Throughout the individual state chapters, we have indicated where these bulk purchases are available, to whom, and for what purposes as well as the costs involved.

Using the Freedom of Information Act and Other Acts

The Federal Freedom of Information Act has no bearing on state, county or local government agencies because these agencies are subject to that state's individual act. Further, the government agencies profiled in this book generally already have systems in place to release information and the act is not needed. However, if you are trying to obtain records from agencies beyond the scope of this book, there are many useful Internet sites that will give you the information you need to complete such a request. We can recommend these sites:

www.epic.org/open_gov/rights.html

www.usdoj.gov/04foia/

Fees, Charges, and Usage

Public records are not necessarily free of charge, certainly not if they are maintained by private industry. Remember that **public records are records of incidents or transactions**. These incidents can be civil or criminal court actions, recordings, filings or occurrences such as speeding tickets or accidents. **It costs money** (time, salaries, supplies, etc.) **to record and track these events**. Common charges found at the government level include copy fees (to make copies of the document), search fees (for clerical personnel to search for the record), and certification fees (to certify that a document as being accurate and coming from the particular agency). Fees can vary from $.10 per page for copies to a $25.00 search fee for government personnel to do the actual look-up. Some government agencies will allow you to walk in and view records at no charge. Fewer will release information over the phone for no fee.

If a private enterprise is in the business of maintaining a public records database, it generally does so to offer these records for resale. Typical clients include financial institutions, the legal industry, the insurance industry, and pre-employment screening firms among others. Usually, records are sold via online access or on a CD-ROM.

Also, there are a number of public record search firms—companies that will do a name search—for a fee. These companies do not warehouse the records, but search on demand for a specific name.

Private companies usually offer different price levels based on volume of usage, while government agencies have one price per category, regardless of the amount of requests.

The Myth of Searching Public Records Online

The availability of online public records is not as widespread as one might think. According to our research, only *20% of public records can be found online*. Most of the county agencies offering online access are recorders' offices and tax assessors. At the state level, UCC Filing and corporation and business ownership records are frequently found online. However, you will not find an abundance of criminal and civil court records, except at the federal court level.

A strong word of caution—many government online sources should not be used as the sole search for true due diligence needs, such as compliance with the Fair Credit Reporting Act. Many government web sites offering online record access include a warning or disclosure statement that the data can have errors and/or should be used for informational purposes only.

Keep in mind the 200+ private companies offering online access to their proprietary databases of public record information present many records that may not be otherwise found online via the government online sources.

Public Record & Public Information Categories

The following descriptions of the record categories fall into our definitions of either "public records" or "public information."

In considering these definitions, keep the following points in mind:

♦ Very little government record information is truly open to the public. Even presumably harmless information is subject to restrictions somewhere in the US. Likewise items that you believe should be highly confidential are probably considered "public information" in one or more states.

♦ Just because your state or county has certain rules, regulations and practices regarding the accessibility and content of public records does not mean that any other state or county follows the same rules.

Business Records

Corporation Records (found at the state level)

Checking to see if a corporation is incorporated is considered a **"status check."** The information that results from a status check typically includes the date of incorporation, status, type, registered agent and, sometimes, officers or directors. This is a good way to find the start of a paper trail and/or to find affiliates of the subject of your search. Some states permit status checks over the telephone.

If available, articles of incorporation (or amendments to them) as well as copies of annual reports may also provide useful information about a business or business owner. However, corporate records may *not* be a good source for a business address because most states allow corporations to use a registered agent as their address for service of process.

Partnership Records (found at the state level)

Some state statutes require registration of certain kinds of partnerships at the state level. Sometimes, these partner names and addresses may be available from the same office that handles corporation records. Some states have a department created specifically to administer limited partnerships and the records associated with them. These filings provide a wealth of information about other partners. Such information can be used to uncover other businesses that may be registered as well.

Limited Liability Companies (found at state level)

A newer form of business entity, similar to a corporation but has the favorable tax characteristics of a partnership, is known as the Limited Liability Company (LLC). An LLC is legal in most every state. An offspring of this, which many states now permit, is the Limited Liability Partnership (LLP).

Trademark & Trade Name (found at state or county levels)

"Trade names" and "trademarks" are relative terms. A trademark may be known as a "service mark." Trade names may be referred to as "fictitious names," "assumed names," or "DBAs." States (or counties) will not let two entities register and use the same (or close to the same) name or trademark

Typically, the agency that oversees corporation records usually maintains the files for trademarks and/or trade names. Most states will allow verbal status checks of names or worded marks. Some states will administer "fictitious names" at the state level while county agencies administer "trade names," or vice versa.

Sales Tax Registrations (found at state level)

Any individual or firm that sells applicable goods or services to an end-user, is required to register with the appropriate state agency. Such registration is necessary to collect applicable sales tax on the goods and services, and to ensure remittance of those taxes to the state.

45 states collect some sort of sales tax on a variety of goods and services. Of these, 38 will at the very least confirm that a tax permit exists. Each sales tax registrant is given a special state tax permit number, which may be called by various names, including tax ID number or seller's permit number. These numbers are not to be confused with the federal employer identification number.

SEC & Other Financial Data

The Federal Securities and Exchange Commission (SEC) is the public repository for information about publicly held companies. These companies are required to share their material facts with existing and prospective stockholders. See page 33 for information about the SEC database EDGAR.

Private companies, on the other hand, are not subject to public scrutiny. Their financial information is public information only to the extent that the company itself decides to disclose information.

Lien and Security Interest Records

Uniform Commercial Code (found at state and county or city levels)

All 50 states and the District of Columbia have passed a version of the model Uniform Commercial Code (UCC). UCC filings are used to record liens in financing transactions such as equipment loans, leases, inventory loans, and accounts receivable financing. The Code allows potential lenders to be notified that certain assets of a debtor are already used to secure a loan or lease. *Therefore, examining UCC filings is an excellent way to find bank accounts, security interests, financiers, and assets.*

Revised Article 9 **(see pages 49-51)** of the Code made significant changes to the location of filings and records. Prior to July 2001, of the 7.5 million new UCC financing statements filed annually, 2.5 million were filed at the state level; 5 million were filed at the local level. Now, less than 3% of filings are done so at the local level. Although there are significant variations among state statutes, the state level is usually a good starting place to uncover liens filed against an individual or business.

Tax Liens (found at state and county or city levels)

The federal government and every state have some sort of taxes, such as those associated with sales, income, withholding, unemployment, and/or personal property. When these taxes go unpaid, the appropriate state agency can file a lien on the real or personal property of the subject. *Normally, the state agency that maintains UCC records also maintains tax liens.*

Individuals vs. Businesses

Tax liens filed against individuals are frequently maintained at separate locations from those liens filed against businesses. For example, a large number of states require liens filed against businesses to be filed at a central state location (i.e., Secretary of State's office) and liens against individuals to be filed at the county level (i.e., Recorder, Register of Deeds, Clerk of Court, etc.).

State vs. Federal Liens

Liens on a company may not all be filed in the same location. A federal tax lien will not necessarily be filed (recorded) at the same location/jurisdiction as a lien filed by the state. This holds true for both individual liens and as well as business liens filed against personal property. Typically, state tax liens on personal property will be found where UCCs are filed. *Tax liens on real property will be found where real property deeds are recorded*, with few exceptions. Unsatisfied state and federal tax liens may be renewed if prescribed by individual state statutes. However, once satisfied, the time the record will remain in the repository before removal varies by jurisdiction.

Real Estate and Tax Assessor (found at county and local levels)

Traditionally, real estate records are public so that everyone can know who owns what property. Liens on real estate must be public so a buyer knows all the facts. The county (or parish) recorder's office is the record source. However, many private companies purchase entire county record databases and create their own database for commercial purposes.

This category of public record is perhaps the fastest growing in regards to freely accessible over the Internet. We have indicated all the recorder offices that offer web **name queries;** many more offer location searches (using maps and parcel numbers to locate an address).

Bankruptcies (found at federal court level)

This entails case information about people and businesses that have filed for protection under the bankruptcy laws of the United States. Only federal courts handle bankruptcy cases. Many types of financial records maintained by government agencies are considered public records; bankruptcy records, unlike some other court records, are in this class of fully open court records. There are several private companies that compile databases with names and dates of these records.

Important Individual Records

Criminal Records (found at state level, county courts, and federal courts)

Every state has a central repository of major misdemeanor, felony arrest records and convictions. States submit criminal record activity to the National Crime Information Center (which is not open to the public). *Not all states open their criminal records to the public*. Of those states that *will* release records to the public, many require fingerprints or signed release forms. The information that *could be* disclosed on the report includes the arrest record, criminal charges, fines, sentencing and incarceration information.

In states where records are not released, the best places to search for criminal record activity is at the city or county level with the county or district court clerk. Many of these searches can be done with a phone call. For detailed information about criminal records, see BRB's *Criminal RecordsBook*.

Litigation & Civil Judgments (found at county, local, and federal courts)

Actions under federal laws are found at US District Courts. Actions under state laws are found within the state court system at the county level. Municipalities also have courts. Records of civil litigation case and records about judgments are often collected by commercial database vendors. For more information, please refer to the **County Court Records** chapter.

Motor Vehicle Records (found at state level, but, on occasion, accessible at county level)

The retrieval industry often refers to driving records as "MVRs." Typical information on an MVR might include full name, address, Social Security Number, physical description and date of birth along with the conviction and accident history. Also, the license type, restrictions and/or endorsements can provide background data on an individual.

In recent years there have been major changes regarding the release of motor vehicle data to the public. This is a direct result of the Driver's Privacy Protection Act (DPPA). States must differentiate between *permissible users* (14 are designated in DPPA) and *casual requesters* to determine who may receive a record and/or how much personal information is reported on the record. For example, if a state DMV chooses to sell a record to a "casual requester," the record can contain personal information (address, etc.) only with the consent of the subject.

Pay particular attention to the restriction requirements mentioned in this category throughout this publication. Refer to pages 55-56 for more about this subject. Also, for those interested in extensive, detailed information about either driver or vehicle records, refer to BRB Publication's *The MVR Book*.

Vehicle & Vessel Ownership, Registration, VINs, Titles, & Liens (found at state and, on occasion, at county level)

State repositories of vehicle/vessel registration and ownership records hold a wide range of information. Generally, record requesters submit a name to uncover vehicle(s) owned or submit vehicle information to obtain an owner's name and address. However, this category of record information is also subject to the DPPA as described above.

The original language of DPPA required the states to offer an "opt out" option to drivers and vehicle owners, if they (the states) sold marketing lists or individual records to casual requesters (those requesters not specifically mentioned in DPPA). Public Law 106-69 reversed this. Effective June 1, 2000, states automatically opt out all individuals, unless the individual specifically asks to be included. While nearly all states have this "opt in" procedure in place, very few individuals request to be placed on marketing lists and such.

Passage of Public Law 106-69 was dramatic since it essentially did away with sales of:

* marketing lists;
* records (with addresses and other personal information) to "casual" requesters;
* record databases to information vendors and database compilers (except for vehicle recall purposes, etc.)

Accident Reports (found at state level or local level)

The State Police or Department of Public Safety usually maintains accident reports. For the purposes of this publication, "accident records" are designated as those prepared by the investigating officer. Copies of a *citizen's* accident report are not usually available to the public and are not reviewed herein. Typical information found on a state accident report includes drivers' addresses and license numbers as well as a description of the incident. Accidents investigated by local officials or minor accidents where the damage does not exceed a reporting limit (such as $1,000), are not available from state agencies. When state DMV's hold accident reports, they follow the DPPA guidelines with regards to record requests.

Occupational Licensing & Business Registration (found at state boards)

Occupational licenses and business registrations contain a plethora of information readily available from various state agencies. A common reason to call these agencies is to corroborate professional or industry credentials. Often, a telephone call to the agency may secure an address and phone number.

GED Records (found at state level)

By contacting the state offices that oversee GED Records, one can verify whether someone truly received a GED certificate for the high school education equivalency. These records are useful for pre-employment screening or background checking purposes. Most state agencies will verify over the phone the existence of a GED certificate. Many even offer copies of transcripts free-of-charge. When doing a record search, you must know the name of the student at the time of the test and a general idea of the year and test location. GED Records are *not* useful when trying to locate an individual.

Hunting & Fishing Licenses (found at state, county & local levels)

We have singled out one type of state license that merits a closer look. When trying to locate an individual, state hunting and fishing license information can be very informative. Currently 44 states maintain a central repository of fishing and/or hunting license records and 31 states permit access in some capacity by the public. Although some of these record repositories are literally "in boxes in the basement," more and more are becoming computerized.

Effects of Cooperative State-Federal Program on Hunting/Fishing License Databases

In 1992, the US Fish and Wildlife Service implemented a Migratory Bird Harvest Information Program that changed state hunting licensing procedures. Under this cooperative program, that helps biologists better manage the Nation's migratory bird populations, hunters provide their names and addresses when buying state licenses to hunt migratory birds. The states then must provide the name and address information to the US Fish and Wildlife Service on a timely basis. As of today, all states except Hawaii participate. Each state has several options for how they provide the US Fish and Wildlife Service with the names and address of their hunters.

The policy of the US Service is to use the names and addresses only for conducting hunter surveys. All records of hunters' names and addresses are after the surveys, and no permanent records are maintained.

However, since the states collect these names and addresses under state authority, the state may decide not to delete the information. Therefore, as states began or continue to maintain new automated record repositories, the release of these records for investigative or search purposes depends upon individual "state sunshine laws." For more information about the federal program, contact the Office of Migratory Bird Management in Laurel, MD at 301-497-5980.

Workers' Compensation Records (found at state level)

Research at state workers' compensation boards is generally limited to determining if an employee has filed a claim and/or obtaining copies of the claim records themselves. With the passage of the Americans with Disabilities Act (ADA) in the early 1990s, using information from workers' compensation boards for pre-employment screening was virtually eliminated. However, *a review of workers' compensation histories may be conducted after a conditional job offer has been made* and when medical information is reviewed. The legality of performing this review is subject to individual state statutes, which vary widely.

Voter Registration (found at state & county levels)

Voting Registration Records are a good place to find addresses and voting history, and can generally be viewed at the local level.

Every state has a central election agency or commission, and most have a central repository of voter information collected from the county level agencies. The degree or level of accessibility to these records varies widely from state to state. Over half of the states will sell portions of the registered voter database, but only 10 states permit individual searching by name. Most states only allow access for political purposes such as "Get Out the Vote" campaigns or compilation of campaign contribution lists. Nearly every state and local agency blocks the release of Social Security Numbers and telephone numbers found on these records.

Vital Records: Birth, Death, Marriage, & Divorce Records (found at state & county levels)

Copies of vital record certificates are needed for a variety of reasons—social security, jobs, passports, family history, litigation, lost heir searching, proof of identity, etc. Most states understand the urgency of these requests, and many offer an expedited service. ***A number of states will take requests over the phone if you use a credit card.*** Searchers must also be aware that in many instances certain vital records are *not* kept at the state level. The searcher must then turn to city and county record repositories to find the information needed.

Most states offer expedited fax ordering, requiring the use of a credit card, through the services of an outside vendor known as VitalChek. This independent company maintains individual fax order telephone lines at each state office they service. Whether it is behind the scenes or not, ordering vital records by fax typically involves VitalChek in some manner. Their web site www.vitalchek.com is also a good place to order vital records online from many states the states (results are still mailed.)

Older vital records are usually found in the state archives. There is an excellent web site of extensive historical genealogy-related databases at http://ancestry.com/mainv.htm. Another source of historical vital record information is the Family History Library of the Church of Jesus Christ of Latter Day Saints (located at 35 North West Temple, Salt Lake City 84150). They have millions of microfilmed records from church and civil registers from all over the world.

Credit Information and Social Security Numbers

Social Security Numbers

The Social Security Number (SSN) is the subject of a persistent struggle between privacy rights groups and various business interests. The truth is that many individuals gave up the privacy of their number by writing it on a voter registration form, product registration form, or any of a myriad of other voluntary disclosures made over the years. It is probable that a good researcher can still legally find the SSN of anyone (along with at least an approximate birth date) with some ease. In the past, a major source of finding a SSN was in the "header" of a credit report. But not any more, see below.

Credit Information

Credit data is derived from financial transactions of people or businesses. **Private companies maintain this information; government only regulates access.** Certain credit information about individuals is restricted by law, such as the Fair Credit Reporting Act, at the federal level and by even more restrictive laws in many states. Credit information about businesses is not restricted by law and is fully open to anyone who requests (pays for) it.

A credit report essentially has two parts—the credit header and the credit history. A credit header is essentially the upper portion of a credit report containing the Social Security Number, age, phone number, last several addresses, and any AKAs. Recently, access to credit header information (see below) has been closed to most business entities.

Credit Header Ban Went Into Effect July 1st, 2001

July 1st, 2001 was an important date for skiptracers, fraud investigators, and other businesses that rely on "credit headers." This information has always been available without the consent of the individual (subject). Per a federal court ruling, beginning July 1st 2001, access to credit header information was treated in the same manner as access to credit reports—there has to be permission granted by the individual.

The basis of this ban is traced to the Gramm-Leach-Bliley Act (GLB). Section 502 of this act prohibits a financial institution from disclosing nonpublic personal information about a consumer to non-affiliated third parties, unless a consumer has elected not to opt out from disclosure. Trans Union and other members of the Individual References Services Group (IRSG), among others, filed suit in an effort to keep this information open for "appropriate commercial purposes." The ruling, dated April 30th, denied this argument. The sale of credit headers seemed to be on borrowed time anyway—originally, the ban was to begin November 2000. However, due to the lawsuits and action involving the FTC, a provision changed the start of the ban until July 1st, 2001.

Impact of Changes

The impact of the ruling (and an FTC opinion) was far ranging. The ruling restricted credit bureaus from selling the above-mentioned data to information vendors who compile their own proprietary databases. But there are some alternatives to those business entities that rely on this type of public record information. The data is grandfathered. Provider companies that purchased files from the credit bureaus can continue to sell the data to their customers. Although data will never be updated from the credit bureaus, the existing data can still be used without the restrictions imposed by the ruling.

According to our friends at Merlin Information Services, TransUnion has created the only IRSG compliant "Super File" known as the TUCS file. This file contains identifying information such as Social Security Numbers and dates of birth, obtained from financial institutions before GLB went into effect on July 1, 2001. Since that date, the file has been updated from public record sources, phone listings and postal change of address information.

The Gramm-Leach-Bliley Act did not deny access to public record sources or databases that may contain age, SSN, phone, prior addresses, and AKAs. The Act only forbid financial institutions from disclosing this data. Therefore, those businesses that were shut-off from credit headers, had to investigate alternative sources of public records. For example, there are over 150 private companies in the US that maintain a proprietary database of public records, see BRB Publication's *National Directory of Public Record Vendors*.

Additional Record Sources Worth Reviewing

State Legislation & Regulations

Telephone numbers, costs and procedures for obtaining copies of passed and pending bills are listed under the heading "Legislation." Most state legislative bodies offer free Internet access to bill text and status, some even offer subject queries. Notwithstanding federal guidelines, the state legislatures and legislators control the policies and provisions for the release of state held information. Every year there is a multitude of bills introduced in state legislatures that would, if passed, create major changes in the access and retrieval of records and personal information.

Education & Employment

Information about an employee's or prospective employee's schooling, training, education, and jobs is important to any employer. Learning institutions maintain their own records of attendance, completion and degree/certification granted. Also, employers will confirm certain information about former employees. This is an example of private information that becomes public by voluntary disclosure. As part of your credit record, this information would be considered restricted. If, however, you disclose this information to Who's Who, or to a credit card company, it becomes public information.

Environmental

Information about hazards to the environment is critical. There is little tradition and less law regarding how open or restricted information is at the state and local (recorder's office) levels. Most information on hazardous materials, soil composition, even OSHA inspection reports is public record. But many federal web sites have removed information since 9-11.

OSHA stands for Occupational Safety & Health Administration, which is part of the US Department of Labor. Their web site is www.osha.gov/.

Another federal government source is the US Environmental Protection Agency found at www.epa.gov/records/. According to Author Alan Schlein (Find it Online) the EPA "…no longer allows direct access to the Envirofacts databases, which explain what toxic chemicals are found in water, hazardous waste, toxic waste, and Superfund sites, and is broken down by community. The EPA had originally created the database to provide the public with direct access to the wealth of information contained in its databases. The public is no longer able to access the information."

The same can be said for the US Geological Survey (www.usgs.gov/); this agency has removed a number of its reports on water resources.

Medical

Medical record Information about an individual's medical status and history are summarized in various repositories that are accessible only to authorized insurance and other private company employees. Medical information is neither public information nor closed record. Like credit information, it is not meant to be shared with anyone, unless you give authorization.

Military

Each branch maintains its own records. Much of this, such as years of service and rank, is open public record. However, some details in the file of an individual may be subject to restrictions on access—approval by the subject may be required.

For more information about military records, including, turn to page 34.

More About Searching State Agency Records

The previous chapter includes a wealth of knowledge about the various types of public records found at the state level. This chapter in the Primer explains how to use the State Agencies Sections found in each state chapter in the body of this *Sourcebook*.

Major State Offices

Each state chapter begins with a list of four important state offices that may be helpful to your record searching needs. This is followed by several helpful web sites.

Governor's Office

The office of the Governor is a good place to start if you are looking for an obscure agency, phone number or address. We have found that typically the person who answers the phone will point you in the right direction if he or she cannot answer your question.

Attorney General's Office

This is another excellent starting point. For example, if you are looking for a non-profit organization, the Attorney General's Office may be able to help you out.

State Archives

The state archives contain an abundance of historical documents and records, especially useful to those interested in genealogy.

State Court Administrator

The court administrator oversees the state court system, which is also known as the county court system. This office can inform you of the structure of that system (i.e. the courts of general and limited jurisdiction and the types of cases they handle). The state judicial web site is a good place to find opinions from the state supreme court and for appeals court opinions.

In some states, the state court administration office oversees a statewide online access system to court records. Some of these systems are commercial fee-based. Other systems offer free access, but are usually very limited in comparison. With *The Sourcebook*, each state's County Court Record Section includes a summary of online access that is available from that particular State Court Administrator's office.

Understanding the State Agency Profiles

After the preceding four state offices mentioned, the various state agency profiles are presented, starting with the state criminal records agency. Each of these state agency profiles is broken into distinct segments that create a total picture of record searching, including access methods and privacy restrictions.

Indexing & Storage

This segment examines the following—

- How many years of records are accessible
- How long before new records are available
- How records are indexed and in what format are they maintained.

Searching

This segment looks in depth at the searching requirements and when privacy restrictions are in place. For example, here you learn what the agencies requirements are for doing a search, such as if a signed release is needed from the subject, or if a certain state form must be used.

Access Methods

The following access methods are both listed and described in a detailed paragraph—

- Mail
- Phone
- In person
- Fax
- Online

Here you will learn the turnaround time for mail requests, or if there is free Internet access, or if the agency will release any information over the phone. In addition, there is a section describing expedited services or bulk database purchases, when applicable.

Fee & Payments

Fee coverage includes search fees, copy fees, certification fees, and expedite fees. Also covered if credit cards are accepted, if personal checks (many agencies only accept business checks) are accepted and who to make the check payable to.

Special Situations in State Records

We won't waste your time reading about agencies if the record data is truly unavailable. The following special situations are noted—

- If the state agency does not release any information period, except to government personnel.
- If the records are not maintained by a state level agency…and where to find these records if they are held at the local level.

Searching State Occupational Licensing Boards

The Privacy Question

While some agencies consider this information private and confidential, most agencies freely release at least some basic data over the phone or by mail.

Our research indicates that many agencies appear to make their own judgments regarding what specifically is private and confidential in their files. For example, approximately 45% of the agencies indicate that they will disclose adverse information about a registrant, and many others will only disclose selected portions of the information or merely verify a credential.

In any event, the basic rule to follow when you contact a licensing agency is to **ask for the specific kinds of information available.**

What Information May Be Available

An agency may be willing to release part or all of the following—

- Field of Certification
- Status of License/Certificate
- Date License/Certificate Issued
- Date License/Certificate Expires
- Current or Most Recent Employer
- Social Security Number
- Address of Subject
- Complaints, Violations or Disciplinary Actions

How to Use the State Licenses Section

Each *State Licenses* section is separated into three parts—

1. Licenses Searchable Online
2. Licensing Quick Finder
3. Licensing Agency Information

A "Key Number" ties the sections together.

The License Searchable Online List

This is a list of boards and their corresponding URLs that offer **free Internet access** to their records. This means that you can do a name search or query from this web site.

Using the Quick Finder

The place to start a verification search is in the **Licensing Quick Finder.** Here you will find, licenses, registrations or occupations listed in alphabetical order.

Although we reflect the official name used in a state for most items, names of some of the major license types have been standardized to make them easier to locate. For example, some states use the word "Physician" rather than "Medical Doctor." We have chosen to use the latter.

Agency Information

This section gives the address and telephone number of the agency or board where the records are maintained.

Use the "Key Number"

The **Key Number** is the *identifying number* for the agency that maintains information about this license. By matching the Key Number found in the Quick Finder to the profile in the Agency Information, you will have the address and other details about how this agency operates. The key number follows the "#" sign in the Quick Finder Section.

An Example of How to Use the Sections

Let's say the following appears in the *Quick Finder Section*:

Beautician #03   216-123-4536

As stated above, the Key Number, which follows the # sign, leads you to the Agency Information Section, where you will find the Agency or Board's address and phone number. For example, "#3" refers to the following:

(3) Department of Health & Social Services, Division of Public Health, 123 Sesame Street, Mapletown, OH 44414, 216-123-4536

State Records Search Fees

Several trends are observed when verifying search fees of the various licensing agencies. They are—

1. There is no charge to verify if a particular person is licensed; this can usually be done by phone.

2. The fee for copies or faxes ranges from $.25 to $2.00.

3. A fee of $5 to $20 usually applies to written requests. This is due to the fact that written certifications give more information than verbal inquiries, i.e. disciplinary action, exam scores.

4. A fee that is $25 or more is typically for a list of licensed professionals. For example, a hospital might need a roster of registered nurses in a certain geographic area.

Searching Tip—Distinguish the Type of Agency

Within the agency category listings, it is important to note that there are five general types of agencies. When you are verifying credentials, you should be aware of what distinguishes each type, which in turn could alter the questions you ask.

Private Certification

Private Licensing and Certification—requires a proven level of minimum competence before license is granted. These professional licenses separate the true "professions" from the third category below. In many of these professions, the certification body, such as the American Institute of Certified Public Accountants, is a private association whereas the licensing body, such as the New York State Education Department, is the licensing agency. Also, many professions may provide additional certifications in specialty areas.

State Certification

State Licensing & Certification—requires certification through an *examination* and/or other *requirements supervised* directly *by the state* rather than by a private association.

By Individual

Individual Registration—required if an individual intends to offer specified products or services in the designated area, but does not require certification that the person has met minimum requirements. An everyday example would be registering a handgun in a state that does not require passing a gun safety course.

By Business

Business Registration—required if a business intends to do business or offer specified products or services in a designated area, such as registering a liquor license. Some business license agencies require testing or a background check. Others merely charge a fee after a cursory review of the application.

Special Permits

Permits—give the grantee specific permission to do something, whether it is to sell hot-dogs on the corner or to put up a three story sign. Permits are usually granted at the local level rather than the state level of government.

Other Forms of Licensing & Registration

Although the state level is where much of the licensing and registration occurs, you should be aware of other places you may want to search.

Local Government Agencies

Local government agencies at both the **county** and **municipal levels** require a myriad of business registrations and permits in order to do business (construction, signage, etc.) within their borders. Even where you think a business or person, such as a remodeling contractor, should have local registrations you want to check out, it is still best to start at the state level.

County Recording Office and City Hall

If you decide to check on local registrations and permits, call the offices at both the county—try the **county recording office**—and municipal level—try **city hall**—to find out what type of registrations may be required for the person or business you are checking out.

Like the state level, you should expect that receiving basic information will only involve a phone call and that you will not be charged for obtaining a status summary.

Professional Associations

As mentioned above, many professional licenses are based on completion of the requirements of professional associations. In addition, there are *many professional designations* from such associations that *are not recognized as official licenses by government*. Other designations are basic certifications in fields that are so specialized that they are not of interest to the states, but rather only to the professionals within an industry. For example, if your company needs to hire an investigator to check out a potential fraud against you, you might want to hire a CFE—Certified Fraud Examiner—who has met the minimum requirements for that title from the Association of Certified Fraud Examiners.

Other Available State Public Record Information

Mail Lists & Databases

Many agencies make their lists available in reprinted or computer form, and a few maintain online access to their files. If you are interested in the availability of licensing agency information in bulk (e.g. mailing lists, magnetic tapes, disks) or online, call the agency and ask about formats that are available.

Online Searching & CD-ROMS

A number of private vendors also compile lists from these agencies and make them available online or on CD-ROM. We do not suggest these databases for credential searching because they may not be complete, may not be up to date and may not contain all the information you can obtain directly from the licensing agency. However, these databases are extremely valuable as a general source of background information on an individual or company that you wish to do business with.

Searching Federal Court Records

First published in May 1993, the BRB Publication The Sourcebook of Federal Courts *provided the first truly complete coverage of where and how to search for case records in the US Federal Courts. Now, this information is fully revised and integrated into* The Sourcebook.

In addition to detailing how to obtain Federal Court information, another objective of this publication is to show searchers how the Federal Court system has evolved during the past few years. One problem searchers encounter is that older records may be in a different form or in a different location from newer records. For example, a searcher can go astray trying to find bankruptcy cases in Ohio unless they know about changes in Dayton.

One development that continues to change the fundamental nature of Federal Courts case record access is, of course, computerization. Now, every Federal Court in the United States has converted to a computerized index.

Federal Court Structure

The Federal Court system includes three levels of courts, plus some special courts, described as follows—

Supreme Court of the United States

The Supreme Court of the United States is the court of last resort in the United States. It is located in Washington, DC, where it hears appeals from the United States Courts of Appeals and from the highest courts of each state.

United States Court of Appeals

The United States Court of Appeals consists of thirteen appellate courts that hear appeals of verdicts from the courts of general jurisdiction. They are designated as follows:

The Federal Circuit Court of Appeals hears appeals from the US Claims Court and the US Court of International Trade. It is located in Washington, DC.

The District of Columbia Circuit Court of Appeals hears appeals from the district courts in Washington, DC as well as from the Tax Court.

Eleven geographic **Courts of Appeals**—each of these appeal scourts covers a designated number of states and territories. The chart on the pages 30-31 lists the circuit numbers (1 through 11) and location of the Court of Appeals for each state.

United States District Courts

The United States District Courts are the courts of general jurisdiction, or trial courts, and are subdivided into two categories—

The District Courts are courts of general jurisdiction, or trial courts, for federal matters, excluding bankruptcy. Essentially, this means they hear cases involving federal law and cases where there is diversity of citizenship. Both **civil** and **criminal** cases come before these courts.

The Bankruptcy Courts generally follow the same geographic boundaries as the US District Courts. There is at least one bankruptcy court for each state; within a state there may be one or more judicial districts and within a judicial district there may be more than one location (division) where the courts hear cases. While civil lawsuits may be filed in either state or federal courts depending upon the applicable law, all bankruptcy actions are filed with the US Bankruptcy Courts.

Special Courts/Separate Courts

The Special Courts/Separate Courts have been created to hear cases or appeals for certain areas of litigation demanding special expertise. Examples include the US Tax Court, the Court of International Trade and the US Claims Court.

How Federal Trial Courts are Organized

At the federal level, all cases involve federal or US constitutional law or interstate commerce. The task of locating the right court is seemingly simplified by the nature of the federal system—

- All court locations are based upon the plaintiff's county of domicile.

- All civil and criminal cases go to the US District Courts.

- All bankruptcy cases go to the US Bankruptcy Courts.

However, a plaintiff or defendant may have cases in any of the 500 court locations, so it is really not all that simple to find them.

There is at least one District and one Bankruptcy Court in each state. In many states there is more than one court, often divided further into judicial districts—e.g., the State of New York consists of four judicial districts, the Northern, Southern, Eastern and Western. Further, many judicial districts contain more than one court location (usually called a division).

The Bankruptcy Courts generally use the same hearing locations as the District Courts. If court locations differ, the usual variance is to have fewer Bankruptcy Court locations.

Case Numbering

When a case is filed with a federal court, a case number is assigned. This is the primary indexing method. Therefore, in searching for case records, you will need to know or find the applicable case number. If you have the number in good form already, your search should be fast and reasonably inexpensive.

You should be aware that case numbering procedures are not consistent throughout the Federal Court system: one judicial district may assign numbers by district while another may assign numbers by location (division) within the judicial district or by judge. Remember that case numbers appearing in legal text citations may not be adequate for searching unless they appear in the proper form for the particular court.

All the basic civil case information that is entered onto docket sheets, and into computerized systems like PACER (see below), starts with standard form JS-44, the Civil Cover Sheet, or the equivalent.

Docket Sheet

As in the state court system, information from cover sheets, and from documents filed as a case goes forward, is recorded on the **docket sheet**, which then contains the case history from initial filing to its current status. While docket sheets differ somewhat in format, the basic information contained on a docket sheet is consistent from court to court. As noted earlier in the state court section, all docket sheets contain:

- Name of court, including location (division) and the judge assigned;

- Case number and case name;

- Names of all plaintiffs and defendants/debtors;

- Names and addresses of attorneys for the plaintiff or debtor;

- Nature and cause (e.g., US civil statute) of action;

- Listing of documents filed in the case, including docket entry number, the date and a short description (e.g., 12-2-92, #1, Complaint).

Assignment of Cases and Computerization

Traditionally, cases were assigned within a district by county. Although this is still true in most states, the introduction of computer systems to track dockets has led to a more flexible approach to case assignment, as is the case in Minnesota and Connecticut. Rather than blindly assigning all cases from a county to one judge, their districts are using random numbers and other logical methods to balance caseloads among their judges.

This trend may appear to confuse the case search process. Actually, the only problem that the searcher may face is to figure out where the case records themselves are located. Finding cases has become significantly easier with the wide availability of PACER from remote access and on-site terminals in each court location with the same district-wide information base.

Computerized Indexes are Available

Computerized courts generally index each case record by the names of some or all the parties to the case—the plaintiffs and defendants (debtors and creditors in Bankruptcy Court) as well as by case number. Therefore, when you search by name you will first receive a listing of all cases in which the name appears, both as plaintiff and defendant.

Electronic Access to Federal Courts

Numerous programs have been developed for electronic access to Federal Court records. In recent years the Administrative Office of the United States Courts in Washington, DC has developed three innovative public access programs: VCIS, PACER, and the Case Management/ Electronic Case Files (CM/ECF) project. The most useful program for online searching is PACER.

PACER

PACER, the acronym for **P**ublic **A**ccess to **E**lectronic **C**ourt **R**ecords, provides docket information online for open cases at **all US Bankruptcy courts** and **most US District courts**. Access is via either a commercial dial-up system (user fee of $.60 a minute) or through the Internet (user fee is $.07 per page. Cases for the US Court of Federal Claims are also available.

Each court controls its own computer system and case information database; therefore, there are some variations among jurisdictions as to the information offered.

Sign-up and technical support is handled at the PACER Service Center in San Antonio, Texas (800) 676-6856. You can sign up for all or multiple districts at once. In many judicial districts, when you sign up for PACER access, you will receive a PACER Primer that has been customized for each district. The primer contains a summary of how to access PACER, how to select cases, how to read case numbers and docket sheets, some searching tips, who to call for problem resolution, and district specific program variations.

A continuing problem with PACER is that each court determines when records will be purged and how records will be indexed, leaving you to guess how a name is spelled or abbreviated and how much information about closed cases your search will uncover. A PACER search for anything but open cases **cannot** take the place of a full seven-year search of the federal court records available by written request from the court itself or through a local document retrieval company. Many districts report that they have closed records back a number of years, but at the same time indicate they purge docket items every six months.

Before Accessing PACER, Search the "National" US Party/Case Index

It is no longer necessary to call each court in every state and district to determine where a debtor has filed bankruptcy, or if someone is a defendant in Federal litigation. National and regional searches of district and bankruptcy filings can be made with one call (via modem) to the US Party/Case Index.

The **US Party/Case Index** is a national index for U.S. district, bankruptcy, and appellate courts. This index allows searches to determine whether or not a party is involved in federal litigation almost anywhere in the nation.

The US Party/Case Index provides the capability to perform national or regional searches on party name and Social Security Number in the bankruptcy index, party name and nature of suit in the civil index, and party name in the criminal and appellate indices.

The search will provide a list of case numbers, filing locations and filing dates for those cases matching the search criteria. If you need more information about the case, you must obtain it from the court directly or through that court's individual PACER system.

You may access the US Party/Case Index by dialup connection or via the Internet. The Internet site for the US Party/Case Index is http://pacer.uspci.uscourts.gov. The toll-free dial-up number for the US Party/Case Index is 800-974-8896. For more information, call the PACER service center at 800-676-6856.

In accordance with Judicial Conference policy, most courts charge a $.60 per minute access fee for the traditional dial-up service or $.07 per page for Internet service.

RACER

RACER stands for Remote Access to Court Electronic Records. Accessed through the Internet, RACER offers access to the same records as PACER. At present, searching RACER is free in a few courts, but normally the fee structure is $.07 per page.

Miscellaneous Online Systems

Some courts have developed their own online systems. In addition to RACER, Idaho's Bankruptcy and District Courts have other searching options available on their web site. Likewise, the Southern District Court of New York offers CourtWeb, which provides information to the public on selected recent rulings of those judges who have elected to make information available in electronic form.

Case Management/Electronic Case Files (CM/ECF)

Electronic Case Files (ECF) is a prototype system for the filing of cases electronically. This service, initially introduced in January 1996, enables participating attorneys and litigants to electronically submit pleadings and corresponding docket entries to the court via the Internet thereby eliminating substantial paper handling and processing time. ECF permits any interested parties to instantaneously access the entire official case docket and documents on the Internet of selective civil and bankruptcy cases within these jurisdictions.

The federal judiciary's *Case management/Electronic Case Files (CM/ECF)* project is designed to replace the aging electronic docketing and case management systems in more than 200 bankruptcy, district and appellate courts by 2005. CM/ECF will provide the capability for courts to have case file documents in electronic format and to accept filings over the Internet. Forty-seven federal courts are currently operational as we go to press, and another group of courts are in the process of implementing CM/ECF.

It is important to note that when you search ECF, you are ONLY searching cases that have been filed electronically. A case may not have been filed electronically through CM-ECF, so you must still conduct a search using PACER if you want to know if a case exists.

One important feature of this system is their *National Locator*, known as the *United States Party Index*. This is a name search, used to locate the specific court where records are available.

For further information about CM/ECF visit http://pacer.psc.uscourts.gov/cmecf./index.html.

VCIS

Another important system is **VCIS** (Voice Case Information System). Nearly all of the US Bankruptcy Court judicial districts provide **VCIS**, a means of accessing information regarding open bankruptcy cases by merely using a touch-tone telephone. There is no charge. Individual names are entered last name first with as much of the first name as you wish to include. For example, Carl R. Ernst could be entered as ERNSTC or ERNSTCARL. Do not enter the middle initial. Business names are entered as they are written, without blanks.

The VCIS System, like the PACER System, has become pervasive and now covers open cases for all but a few US Bankruptcy Court locations. **Each Bankruptcy Court profile includes that court's VCIS phone number.**

Federal Courts Searching Hints

- VCIS should *only* be used to locate information about open cases. Do not attempt to use VCIS as a substitute for a PACER search.

- Since this publication includes the counties of jurisdiction for each court, the list of counties in each Court's profile is a good starting point for determining where case records may or may not be found.

- Before performing a general PACER search to determine whether cases exist under a particular plaintiff, debtor, or defendant name, first be certain to review that Court's profile, which will show the earliest dates of case records available on the PACER. Also, searchers need to be sure that the Court's case index includes all cases, open and closed, for that particular period. Be aware that some courts purge older, closed cases after a period of time, making such a PACER search incomplete. (Wherever known, this publication indicates within the court profiles the purge timeframe for PACER records. Times vary from court to court and state to state.)

- Experience shows that court personnel are typically not aware of — nor concerned about — the types of searches performed by readers of this publication. Court personnel often focus on only open cases, whereas a searcher may want to know as much about closed cases as open ones. Thus, court personnel are sometimes fuzzy in answering questions about how far back case records go on PACER, and whether closed cases have been purged. If you are looking for cases older than a year or two, there is no substitute for a real, on-site search performed by the court itself or by a local search expert (if the court allows full access to its indexes).

- Some courts may be more willing than others to give out information by telephone. This is because most courts have converted from the old card index system to fully computerized indexes, which are easily accessible, while on the phone.

Federal Records Centers and the National Archives

After a federal case is closed, the documents are held by Federal Courts themselves for a number of years, then stored at a designated Federal Records Center (FRC). After 20 to 30 years, the records are then transferred from the FRC to the regional archives offices of the National Archives and Records Administration (NARA). The length of time between a case being closed and its being moved to an FRC varies widely by district. Each court has its own transfer cycle and determines access procedures to its case records, even after they have been sent to the FRC.

When case records are sent to an FRC, the boxes of records are assigned accession, location and box numbers. These numbers, which are called case locator information, **must be obtained from the originating court in order to retrieve documents from the FRC.** Some courts will provide such information over the telephone, but others require a written request. This information is now available on PACER in certain judicial districts. The Federal Records Center for each state is listed as follows:

State	Circuit	Appeals Court	Federal Records Center
AK	9	San Francisco, CA	Anchorage (Some records are in temporary storage in Seattle)
AL	11	Atlanta, GA	Atlanta
AR	8	St. Louis, MO	Fort Worth
AZ	9	San Francisco, CA	Los Angeles
CA	9	San Francisco, CA	Los Angeles (Central & Southern CA) San Francisco (Eastern & Northern CA)
CO	10	Denver, CO	Denver
CT	2	New York, NY	Boston
DC		Washington, DC	Washington, DC
DE	3	Philadelphia, PA	Philadelphia
FL	11	Atlanta, GA	Atlanta
GA	11	Atlanta, GA	Atlanta
GU	9	San Francisco, CA	San Francisco
HI	9	San Francisco, CA	San Francisco
IA	8	St. Louis, MO	Kansas City, MO
ID	9	San Francisco, CA	Seattle
IL	7	Chicago, IL	Chicago
IN	7	Chicago, IL	Chicago
KS	10	Denver, CO	Kansas City, MO
KY	6	Cincinnati, OH	Atlanta
LA	5	New Orleans, LA	Fort Worth
MA	1	Boston, MA	Boston
MD	4	Richmond, VA	Philadelphia
ME	1	Boston, MA	Boston
MI	6	Cincinnati, OH	Chicago

State	Circuit	Appeals Court	Federal Records Center
MN	8	St. Louis, MO	Chicago
MO	8	St. Louis, MO	Kansas City, MO
MS	5	New Orleans, LA	Atlanta
MT	9	San Francisco, CA	Denver
NC	4	Richmond, VA	Atlanta
ND	8	St. Louis, MO	Denver
NE	8	St. Louis, MO	Kansas City, MO
NH	1	Boston, MA	Boston
NJ	3	Philadelphia, PA	New York
NM	10	Denver, CO	Denver
NV	9	San Francisco, CA	Los Angeles (Clark County, NV) / San Francisco (Other NV counties)
NY	2	New York, NY	New York
OH	6	Cincinnati, OH	Chicago; Dayton has some bankruptcy
OK	10	Denver, CO	Fort Worth
OR	9	San Francisco, CA	Seattle
PA	3	Philadelphia, PA	Philadelphia
PR	1	Boston, MA	New York
RI	1	Boston, MA	Boston
SC	4	Richmond, VA	Atlanta
SD	8	St. Louis, MO	Denver
TN	6	Cincinnati, OH	Atlanta
TX	5	New Orleans, LA	Fort Worth
UT	10	Denver, CO	Denver
VA	4	Richmond, VA	Philadelphia
VI	3	Philadelphia, PA	New York
VT	2	New York, NY	Boston
WA	9	San Francisco, CA	Seattle
WI	7	Chicago, IL	Chicago
WV	4	Richmond, VA	Philadelphia
WY	10	Denver, CO	Denver

Notes to the Chart:

GU is Guam, PR is Puerto Rico, and VI is the Virgin Islands.

According to some odd logic, the following Federal Records Centers are not located in the city named above, but are actually somewhere else. Below are the exceptions:

Atlanta—in East Point, GA; Boston—in Waltham, MA; Los Angeles—in Laguna Niguel, CA; New York—in Bayonne, NJ; San Francisco—in San Bruno, CA

Searching Other Federal Records Online

EDGAR

EDGAR, the Electronic Data Gathering Analysis, and Retrieval system was established by the Securities and Exchange Commission (SEC) to allow companies to make required filing to the SEC by direct transmission. As of May 6, 1996, all public domestic companies are required to make their filings on EDGAR, except for filings made to the Commission's regional offices and those filings made on paper due to a hardship exemption.

EDGAR is an extensive repository of US corporation information and it is available online.

What Information is Available on EDGAR?

Companies must file the following reports with the SEC:

- 10-K, an annual financial report, which includes audited year-end financial statements.

- 10-Q, a quarterly report, unaudited.

- 8K - a report detailing significant or unscheduled corporate changes or events.

- Securities offering and trading registrations and the final prospectus.

The list above is not conclusive. There are other miscellaneous reports filed, including those dealing with security holdings by institutions and insiders. Access to these documents provides a wealth on information.

How to Access EDGAR Online

EDGAR is searchable online at: www.sec.gov/edgar.shmtl. A number of private vendors offer access to EDGAR records. LEXIS/NEXIS acts as the data wholesaler or distributor on behalf of the government. LEXIS/NEXIS sells data to information retailers, including it's own NEXIS service.

Aviation Records

The Federal Aviation Association (FAA) is the US government agency with the responsibility of all matters related to the safety of civil aviation. The FAA, among other functions, provides the system that registers aircraft, and documents showing title or interest in aircraft. Their web site, at www.faa.gov, is the ultimate source of aviation records, airports and facilities, safety regulations, and civil research and engineering.

The Aircraft Owners and Pilots Association is the largest organization of its kind with a 340,000 members. Their web site is www.aopa.org and is an excellent source of information regarding the aviation industry.

Another excellent source of aircraft information is *Jane's World Airlines* at www.janes.com.

Military Records

This topic is so broad that there can be a book written about it, and in fact there is! *The Armed Forces Locator Directory* from MIE Publishing (800-937-2133) is an excellent source. The book, now in its 8th edition, covers every conceivable topic regarding military records. Their web site www.militaryusa.com offers free access to some useful databases.

The Privacy Act of 1974 (5 U.S.C. 552a) and the Department of Defense directives require a written request, signed and dated, to access military personnel records. For further details, visit the NPRC site listed below.

Military Internet Sources

There are a number of great Internet sites that provide valuable information on obtaining military and military personnel records. The National Personnel Records Center (NPRC), maintained by the National Archives and Records Administration is www.nara.gov/regional/mpr.html. This site is full of useful information and links. Other excellent sites include:

www.army.mil	The official site of the US Army
www.af.mil	The official site of the US Air Force
www.navy.mil	The official site of the US Navy
www.usmc.mil	The official site of the US Marine Corps
www.ngb.dtic.mil	The official site of the National Guard
www.uscg.mil	The official site of the US Coast Guard

US Government Gateways

The remainder of this Chapter was written and contributed by online pioneer and award winning journalist Alan M. Schlein, author of Find It Online.

We sincerely thank Alan for permitting the use of his material in The Sourcebook. *Alan can be reached at his* www.deadlineonline.com. *Check out his web site—it is a great source with lots of useful links!*

In the U.S., almost every federal government agency is online. There's a nationwide network of depository libraries, including the enormous resources of the National Archives (www.nara.gov), the twelve presidential libraries, and four national libraries (the Library of Congress, the National Agricultural Library, the National Library of Education and the National Library of Medicine). There are almost 5000 government web sites from more than forty-two U.S. departments and agencies.

Because there are so many government web sites, you may need to turn to the hundreds of web sites, called *government gateways*, that organize and link government sites, in order to find the starting point for your research. Some gateways are simply collections of links. Others provide access to bulletin boards of specific government agencies so that you find and contact employees with specific knowledge. Guides are becoming increasingly important in light of the growing number of reports and publications that aren't printed any more, but simply posted online.

Best Government Gateways (listed alphabetically)

Documents Center
www.lib.umich.edu/govdocs/index.html

Documents Center is a clearinghouse for local, state, federal, foreign, and international government information. It is one of the more comprehensive online searching aids for all kinds of government information on the Internet. It's especially useful as a meta-site of meta-sites.

Federal Web Locators
www.infoctr.edu/fwl/

This web locator is really two sites in one: a federal government web site at www.infoctr.edu/fwl and a separate site that tracks federal courts at www.infoctr.edu/fwl/fedweb.juris.htm, both of which are browsable by category or by keyword. Together they provide links to thousands of government agencies and departments.

FedLaw
http://fedlaw.gsa.gov

FedLaw is an extremely broad resource for federal legal and regulatory research containing 1,600+ links to law-related information. It has very good topical and title indices that group web links into hundreds of subjects. It is operated by the General Services Administration (GSA).

Fedstats

www.fedstats.gov

A terrific collection of statistical sites from the federal government and a good central clearinghouse for other federal statistics sites.

FedWorld Information Network

www.fedworld.gov

FedWorld helps you search over thirty million U.S. government pages. It is a massive collection of 15,000 files and databases of government sites, including bulletin boards that can help you identify government employees with expertise in a broad range of subjects. A surprising number of these experts will take the time to discuss questions from the general public.

FirstGov

www.firstgov.gov

Responding to the need for a central clearinghouse of U.S. federal government sites, the U.S. government developed FirstGov and linked every federal agency to its site as well as every state government. It has an easy-to-use search tool, allowing you to specify if you want federal or state agencies and to easily locate business regulations and vital records. It also lets you look for federal government phone numbers and email addresses. This is an easy-to-use starting point, powered by the FAST/AllTheWeb search engine. Also, check out the FAQs of the U.S. government for questions and answers about the U.S. government at www.faq.gov.

Google's Uncle Sam

www.google.com/unclesam

Google's Uncle Sam site is a search engine geared to looking at U.S. government sites. It's an easy-to-use tool if you know what you are looking for.

Govbot – Government Search Engine

http://ciir.cs.umass.edu/ciirdemo/Govbot

Developed by the Center for Intelligent Information Retrieval, Govbot's searchable keyword index of government web sites is limited to sites with a top-level domain name ending in.gov or.mil.

Healthfinder

www.healthfinder.gov

This is a great starting point for health-related government information.

InfoMine: Scholarly Internet Resource Collections

http://lib-www.ucr.edu

InfoMine provides collections of scholarly Internet resources, best for academics. It is one of the best academic resources anywhere, from the librarians at the University of California Riverside. Its Government Information section is easily searchable by subject. It has detailed headings and its resource listings are very specific. Since it's run by a university, some of its references are limited to student use only.

SearchGov.com

www.searchgov.com

A private company that has an effective search for U.S. government sites.

Speech & Transcript Center

http://gwis2.circ.gwu.edu/~gprice/speech.htm

This site links directly to web sites containing transcripts of speeches. Pulled together by former George Washington University reference librarian and Invisible Web author Gary Price, it encompasses government resources, business leaders, and real audio. A large section is devoted to U.S. and international government speech transcripts – including Congressional hearings, testimony and transcripts.

U.S. Federal Government Agencies Directory

www.lib.lsu.edu/gov/fedgov.html

This directory of federal agencies is maintained by Louisiana State University and links to hundreds of federal government Internet sites. It's divided by branch and agency and is very thorough, but focus on your target because it's easy to lose your way or become overwhelmed en route.

U.S. Government Information

www-libraries.colorado.edu/ps/gov/us/federal.htm

This is a gem of a site from the University of Colorado and a good starting point. It's not as thorough as the LSU site above, but still very valuable.

Best US Federal Government Web Sites

U.S. tax dollars are put to good and visible use here. A few of the government's web pages are excellent. Some can be used in lieu of commercial tools, but only if you have the time to invest.

A few of the top government sites – the Census and the Securities and Exchange Commission – are models of content and presentation. They are very deep, very thorough, and easy to use. If only the rest of the federal government would follow suit. Unfortunately, the best of the federal government is just that: the best. Not all agencies maintain such detailed and relevant resources.

Following are the crown jewels of the government's collection, in ranked order:

U.S. Census Bureau

www.census.gov

Without question, this is the U.S. government's top site. It's saturated with information and census publications – at times overwhelmingly so – but worth every minute of your time. A few hours spent here is a worthwhile investment for almost anyone seeking to background a community, learn about business, or find any kind of demographic information. You can search several ways: alphabetically by subject, by word, by location, and by geographic map. The only problem is the sheer volume of data.

One feature, the Thematic Mapping System, allows users to extract data from Census CD-ROMs and display them in maps by state or county. You can create maps on all kinds of subjects – for example, tracking violent crime to farm income by region. The site also features the Statistical Abstract of the U.S. with a searchable index at www.census.gov/statab/www/stateabs.html.

The potential uses of census data are infinite. Marketers use it to find community information.

Reporters search out trends by block, neighborhood or region. Educators conduct research. Businesses evaluate new business prospects. Genealogists trace family trees – though full census data isn't available for seventy-two years from the date the census is taken. You can even use it to identify ideal communities in which to raise a family. Jennifer LaFleur, now at The St. Louis Post-Dispatch did a story while at The San Jose Mercury News using the census site to find eligible bachelors in specific areas of San Jose. Additional census resources include:

1990 U.S. Census LOOKUP
http://venus.census.gov/cdrom/lookup/

Census Tract Street Locator
http://tier2.census.gov/ctsl/ctsl.htm

Census FactFinder
http://factfinder.census.gov

Census Industry Statistics
www.censusgov/main/www/industries.html

U.S. Securities and Exchange Commission (SEC)
www.sec.gov

Only the Census site is better than the SEC site, which is a first-rate, must-stop place for information shopping on U.S. companies. Its EDGAR database search site at www.sec.gov/edaux/searches.htm is easy to use and provides access to documents that companies and corporations are required to file under regulatory laws.

The SEC site is a great starting point for information about specific companies and industry trends. The SEC requires all publicly-held corporations and some large privately-held corporations to disclose detailed financial information about their activities, plans, holdings, executives' salaries and stakes, legal problems and so forth.

Library of Congress (LOC)
www.loc.gov

This site is an extraordinary collection of documents. Thomas, the Library's Congressional online center site at http://thomas.loc.gov provides an exhaustive collection of congressional documents, including bill summaries, voting records and the full Congressional Record, which is the official record of Congressional action. This LOC site also links to many international, federal, state and local government sites. You can also access the library's more than five million records online, some versions in full-text and some in abstract form. Though the library's entire 121 million item collection is not yet available online, the amount online increases daily. In addition to books and papers, it includes an extensive images collection ranging from Frank Lloyd Wright's designs to the Dead Sea Scrolls to the world's largest online collection of baseball cards. The Library of Congress also has a terrific collection of international information on its web site at www.loc.gov/rr/international/portals.html.

Superintendent of Documents Home Page (GPO)
www.access.gpo.gov/su_docs

The GPO is the federal government's primary information printer and distributor. All federally funded information from every agency is sent here, which makes the GPO's holdings priceless. Luckily, the GPO site is well-constructed and easy to use. For example, it has the full text of the Federal Register, which lists all federal regulations and proposals, and full-text access to the Congressional Record. The GPO also produces an online version of the Congressional Directory, providing details on every congressional district, profiles of members, staff profiles, maps of every district and historical documents about Congress. This site will expand exponentially over the next few years, as the number of materials go out of print and online. GPO Access also allows you to electronically retrieve much of the bureaucratic paper in Washington, electronically, from the Government Printing Office including searching more than seventy databases and indices. If you need some help finding things, use the topic-specific finder at this site.

National Technical Information Service (NTIS)
www.ntis.gov

The best place to find federal government reports related to technology and science. NTIS is the nation's clearinghouse for unclassified technical reports of government-sponsored research. NTIS collects, indexes, abstracts, and sells U.S. and foreign research – mostly in science, technology, behavioral, and social science data.

IGnet
www.ignet.gov

This is a truly marvelous collection of reports and information from the Inspector Generals of about sixty federal agency departments. They find waste and abuse within government agencies. It is well worth checking when starting research on government-related matters.

General Accounting Office GAO Reports
www.gao.gov/decisions/decision.htm

The Comptroller General Opinions from the last sixty days are posted on this GAO web site. These reports and opinions are excellent references. For historical opinions back to 1996 go to www.access.gpo.gov/su_docs/aces/aces170.shtml.

White House
www.whitehouse.gov

This site wouldn't make this list if not for its economic statistics page and the transcript of every official action the U.S. President takes at www.whitehouse.gov/news/. Unfortunately, as with many government sites, its primary focus is in promoting itself.

DefenseLINK – U.S. Department of Defense (DOD)
www.defenselink.mil

This is the brand-name site for Pentagon-related information. There's a tremendous amount of data here – categorized by branch of service – including U.S. troop deployments worldwide. And to the Pentagon's credit they've made this a very easy site to use.

Defense Technical Information Center (DTIC)
www.dtic.mil

The DTIC site is loaded with links and defense information – everything from contractors to weapon systems. It even includes de-classified information about the Gulf War. It is the best place to start for defense information. You can even find a list of all military-related contracts, including beneficiary communities and the kinds of contracts awarded. The only problem with the site is there's no search engine to make it easy to find information.

Bureau of Transportation Statistics
www.bts.gov

The U.S. Department of Transportation's enormous collection of information about every facet of transportation. There's a lot of valuable material here including the Transportation Statistics Annual Report. It also holds financial data for airlines and searchable databases containing information about fatal accidents and on-time statistics for airlines, which can be narrowed to your local airport.

National Archives And Records Administration

www.nara.gov

A breathtaking collection of research online, for example the National Archives has descriptions of more than 170,000 documents related to the Kennedy assassination. It also contains a world-class database holding descriptions of more than 95,000 records held by the Still Picture and Motion Picture, Sound and Video Branches. This site also links to the twelve Presidential Archives with their records of every person ever mentioned in Executive Branch correspondence. You can view an image of the original document. The Archives Research Center Online has great collections of family history/genealogy research and veteran's service records.

usgovsearch

www.usgovsearch.com

This site may be retooling under a new URL. In conjunction with the National Technical Information Service, search engine company Northern Light has created one of the most thorough search tools for finding government-related information. Usgovsearch is a strong rival to the U.S. government run FirstGov.gov. With Divines Inc.'s recent purchase of Northern Light, it is unclear how long this will stay an inexpensive site. You can search the Web using usgovsearch but you can also get information from Northern Light's low-cost Special Collections resources. It allows you to run searches and find out the inter-relationships among agencies. Most of the material can be found elsewhere for free, but for speed and thoroughness usgovsearch is excellent. With the special collections between US$1 and US$4 per article, it is a very useful and inexpensive tool.

Federal Consumer Information Center National Contact Center

www.info.gov

While this is largely a telephone service that gets more than a million calls a year, this web site tries to provide a way through the maze of federal agencies. It includes a clearinghouse of phone numbers for all federal agencies, state, and local government sites as well.

SciTechResources.gov

www.scitechresources.gov

This is a tremendous directory of about 700 science and technology resources on U.S. government sites from the U.S. Department of Commerce, National Technical and Information Service.

Searching County Court Records

The County Court Records Sections

The purpose of the County Court Records Sections is to provide quick yet detailed access information on the more than 6,400 major courts that have jurisdiction over significant criminal and civil cases under state law.

Included in *The Sourcebook* are all state felony courts, larger claim civil courts, and probate courts in the United States. Since most courts have jurisdiction over a number of categories of cases, we also include many of the courts that hear misdemeanor, eviction, and small claims court cases. In addition, each County Court Records Section begins with an introduction that summarizes where other major categories of court cases—DUI, preliminary hearings, and juvenile cases—can be found.

The term "County Courts," as used in this publication, refers to those courts of original jurisdiction (trial courts) within each state's court system that handle…

- **Felonies**   -- Generally defined as crimes punishable by one year or more of jail time

- **Civil Actions**   -- For money damages (usually greater than $3,000)

- **Probate**   -- Estate matters

- **Misdemeanors**   -- Generally defined as minor infractions with a fine or minimal jail time

- **Evictions**   -- Landlord/tenant actions

- **Small Claims**   -- Actions for minor money damages (generally under $3,000)

Useful Applications

The County Court Record Sections are especially useful for four kinds of applications—

General litigation searching/background searching…Combined with the *Federal Court section*, you have complete coverage of all the important courts in the United States.

Employment background checking…Included is full coverage of local criminal courts at the felony level, and many misdemeanor courts as well.

Tenant background checking…Courts where landlord/tenant cases are filed are indicated in the state introduction charts, and most of the courts handling such cases are profiled.

Asset searching…The probate courts have records of wills and estate matters that can be used to determine assets, related parties, and useful addresses.

Reading the State Court Charts

On the first page of each County Court Records Section are three charts. Together, they present that state's court structure.

When searching for case records, keep in mind that many of the higher level courts also handle appeals from lower courts.

The First Chart

The chart at the top of the page summarizes the structure of the court system, listing the court of general jurisdiction, followed underneath by the courts of limited, municipal, and special jurisdiction. Court types with an asterisk (*) after their names are profiled in *The Sourcebook*.

The number of case record locations is indicated for each court. Where two classifications of courts are combined into one location and only one entry appears in the profiles, the number of combined courts is noted. The number of locations for courts not profiled in *The Sourcebook* are estimates.

Where useful, the number and type of organization of each of the classifications of court are indicated under the "How Organized" column.

The Civil and Criminal Charts

The other two charts consolidate information about what types of cases each court hears, i.e. the "jurisdiction" of the type of court.

Where more than one court has jurisdiction for a particular kind of civil case, the minimum and maximum claim fields clarify whether there is overlapping jurisdiction in the state. In most states, the lower and upper court civil claim limits dovetail nicely between the court levels, so you can readily tell which court has the type of civil case you are concerned about.

Although these charts oversimplify complex sets of state statues, their purpose is to provide you with a practical starting point to help you decide where to search for case records.

Beyond the Charts

When you cannot make a determination to your satisfaction where to search, we suggest you contact that state's administrator of courts by telephone or visit their Internet site.

The address, telephone number, and Internet address of the administrative office in each state are listed under the heading "Administration."

Reading the Court Profiles

Basic Information

The 3,140 US counties (and where applicable—parishes, towns, cities, etc.) are listed in alphabetical order, within each state. When a county has more than one court profiled, the courts appear in order beginning with the court of general jurisdiction, then proceeding down to more limited jurisdictions. Each profile specifically lists the types of cases handled by that court. If a level of court has divisions, civil courts are listed before criminal courts. Where more than one court of the same type is located in a county, they are listed in alphabetical order by the name of the city where they are located.

All city/ZIP Code combinations have been verified against our latest version of *The County Locator* database for accuracy. In addition to the address and telephone number, the time zone is indicated (see below for an explanation of the abbreviations used). Fax numbers are given for most courts.

Watch for Name Variations From State to State

Do not assume that the structure of the court system in another state is anything like your own. In one state, the Circuit Court may be the highest trial court whereas in another it is a limited jurisdiction court. Examples are: (1) New York, where the Supreme Court is not very "supreme," and the downstate court structure varies from upstate; and (2) Tennessee, where circuit courts are in districts.

Access and Searching Details

Each court profile indicates acceptable searching methods including phone, fax mail, in person, and online. The profiles also indicate all fees (including search, copy and certification) and acceptable payment methods. For example, some courts accept credit cards, some do not accept personal checks, and some may bill for copies.

Here are some searching hints to keep in mind:

- When a county has multiple courts of the same level, general information is provided to help determine which office to search in, depending upon the subject's address.

- In many instances two types of courts within a county (e.g., circuit and district) are combined. When phoning or writing these courts, we recommend that your request specifically state in your request that you want both courts included in the search.

- Be aware that the number of courts that no longer conduct name searches has risen. For these courts, you must hire a local retriever, directly or through a search company, to search for you. It should be noted that usually these courts still take specific document copy requests by mail. Because of long mail turnaround times and court fees, local retrievers are frequently used even when the court will honor a request by mail. A court's entry indicates if it is one of the many to offer a public access terminal, free of charge, to view case documents or indexes.

Index & Record Systems

Most profiles of the civil courts indicate whether the plaintiffs as well as the defendants are indexed. A plaintiff search is useful, for example, to determine if someone is especially litigious.

During the past decade, thousands of courts have installed computerized indexing systems. The year when computer indexing started in each of these courts is indicated in the profile of most of the automated courts. Computerized systems are considerably faster and easier to search, allowing for more indexing capability than the microfilm and card indexes that preceded them.

Search Requirements

There is a strong tendency for courts to overstate their search requirements. For civil cases, the usual reasonable requirement is a defendant (or plaintiff) name—full name if it is a common name—and the time frame to search—e.g., 1993-2002. For criminal cases, the court may require more identification, such as date of birth (DOB), to ascertain the correct individual. Other information "required" by courts— such as Social Security Number (SSN)—is often just "helpful" to narrow the search on a common name. Further, we have indicated when certain pieces of information may be helpful but are not required.

Restricted Records

Most courts have a number of types of case records, such as juvenile and adoptions, which are not released without a court order. These types are indicated in each profile.

Fees & Other Requirements

As mentioned above, search, copy, and certification fees are given for most courts, as well as fax fees if known. Where specified, we indicate whether the court requires a self-addressed stamped envelope (SASE) to accompany a written search request. Even where it is not indicated, we recommend including a SASE to make sure the results are returned to you.

Some Court Basics

Before trudging into a courthouse and demanding to view a document, you should first be aware of some basic court procedures. Whether the case is filed in a state, municipal, or federal court, each case follows a similar process.

A **civil case** usually commences when a plaintiff files a complaint with a court against defendants. The defendants respond to the complaint with an answer. After this initial round, there may be literally hundreds of activities before the court issues a judgment. These activities can include revised complaints and their answers, motions of various kinds, discovery proceedings (including depositions) to establish the documentation and facts involved in the case. All of these activities are listed on a **docket sheet**, which may be a piece of paper or a computerized index.

Once the court issues a judgment, either party may appeal the ruling to an appellate division or court. In the case of a money judgment, the winning side can usually file it as a judgment lien with the county recorder. Appellate divisions usually deal only with legal issues and not the facts of the case.

In a **criminal case**, the plaintiff is a government jurisdiction. The Government brings the action against the defendant for violation of one or more of its statutes.

In a **bankruptcy case,** which can be heard only in federal courts, there is neither defendant nor plaintiff. Instead, the debtor files voluntarily for bankruptcy protection against creditors, or the creditors file against the debtor in order to force the debtor into involuntary bankruptcy.

State Court Structure

The secret to determining where a state court case is located is to understand how the court system is structured in that particular state. The general structure of all state court systems has four parts:

Appellate courts	Limited jurisdiction trial courts
Intermediate appellate courts	General jurisdiction trial courts

The two highest levels, appellate and intermediate appellate courts, only hear cases on appeal from the trial courts. Opinions of these appellate courts are of interest primarily to attorneys seeking legal precedents for new cases.

General jurisdiction trial courts usually handle a full range of civil and criminal litigation. These courts usually handle felonies and larger civil cases.

Limited jurisdiction trial courts come in two varieties. First, many limited jurisdiction courts handle smaller civil claims (usually $10,000 or less), misdemeanors, and pretrial hearing for felonies. Second, some of these courts, sometimes called special jurisdiction courts, are limited to one type of litigation, for example the Court of Claims in New York, which only handles liability cases against the state.

Some states, for instance Iowa, have consolidated their general and limited jurisdiction court structure into one combined court system. In other states there may be a further distinction between state-supported courts and municipal courts. In New York, for example, nearly 1,300 Justice Courts handle local ordinance and traffic violations, including DWI.

Generalizations should not be made about where specific types of cases are handled in the various states. Misdemeanors, probate, landlord/tenant (eviction), domestic relations, and juvenile cases may be handled in either or both the general and limited jurisdiction courts. To help you locate the correct court to perform your search in, this publication specifically lists the types of cases handled by each court.

Types of Litigation in Trial Courts

Criminal

Criminal cases are categorized as *felonies* or *misdemeanors*. A general rule, a felony involves a jail term of one year or more, whereas a misdemeanor may only involve a monetary *fine*.

Civil

Civil cases are categorized as *tort*, *contract*, and *real property* rights. Torts can include *automobile accidents*, *medical malpractice*, and *product liability* cases. Actions for small money damages, typically under $3,000, are known as *small claims*.

Other

Other types of cases that frequently are handled by separate courts or specialized divisions of courts include *juvenile*, *probate* (wills and estates), and *domestic relations.*

How Courts Maintain Records

Case Numbering

When a case is filed, it is assigned a case number. This is the primary indexing method in every court. Therefore, in searching for case records, you will need to know—or find—the applicable case number. If you have the number in good form already, your search should be fast and reasonably inexpensive.

You should be aware that case numbering procedures are not consistent throughout a state court system. One district may assign numbers by district while another may assign numbers by location (division) within the district, or by judge. Remember: case numbers appearing in legal text citations may not be adequate for searching unless they appear in the proper form for the particular court in which you are searching.

All basic civil case information is entered onto docket sheets.

Docket Sheet

Information from cover sheets and from documents filed as a case goes forward is recorded on the docket sheet. The docket sheet then contains an outline of the case history from initial filing to its current status. While docket sheets differ somewhat in format, the basic information contained on a docket sheet is consistent from court to court. All docket sheets contain:

- Name of court, including location (division) and the judge assigned;
- Case number and case name;
- Names of all plaintiffs and defendants/debtors;
- Names and addresses of attorneys for the plaintiff or debtor;
- Nature and cause (e.g., statute) of action.

Computerization

Most courts are computerized, which means that the docket sheet data is entered into a computer system. Within a state or judicial district, the courts *may* be linked together via a single computer system.

Docket sheets from cases closed before the advent of computerization may not be in the computer system. For pre-computer cases, most courts keep summary case information on microfilm, microfiche, or index cards.

Case documents are not generally available on computer because courts are still experimenting with and developing electronic filing and imaging of court documents. Generally, documents are only available to be copied by contacting the court where the case records are located.

Additional State Court Resources

The National Center for State Courts

www.ncsconline.org

NASCIO State Search

https://www.nascio.org/stateSearch/

Searching Recording Office Records

Combined, the Recording Offices section for each state section contains 4,266 local recording offices where Uniform Commercial Code and real estate records are maintained.

The Lowdown on Recorded Documents

Documents filed and record at local county, parish, city or town offices represent some of the best opportunities to gain access to open public records, especially if you are searching online. If you are lucky enough to live in close proximity, you can visit your local office and, for free, view records. Recorded documents are also one of the most available types of public records that can be viewed or obtain via online and through the Internet.

Real Estate

As mentioned previously, real estate records are public so that everyone can know who owns what property. Liens on real estate must be public so a buyer knows all the facts. The county (or parish or city) recorder's office is the source. Also, access is also available from many private companies that purchase entire county record databases and create their own database for commercial purposes.

Uniform Commercial Code (UCC)

UCC filings are to personal property what mortgages are to real estate property. UCCs are in the category of financial records that must be fully open to public scrutiny so that other potential lenders are on notice about which assets of the borrower have been pledged as collateral.

As with tax liens, UCC recordings are filed, according to state law, either at the state or local (county, town, parish) level. Until June 30, 2001, liens on certain types of companies required dual filing (must file at BOTH locations, thus records can be searched at BOTH locations). As of July 1, 2001, UCC filings other than those that go into real estate records are no longer filed at the local filing offices in most states, but older filings can still be located there until 2008. As with real estate records, there are a number of private companies who have created their own databases for commercial resale.

A Great Source of Information

Although recorded documents are a necessity to making an informed business-related decision, they are also a virtual treasure trove of data. UCC filing documents will you the names and addresses of creditors and debtors, describe the asset offered for collateral, the date of the filing, and whether or note the loan has been satisfied. This information contained on the statements can lead an experience investigator to other roads done the information trail. For example, if the collateral is a plane or a vessel, this will lead to registration records or if the debtor is a business, other names on the filing may lead to other traceable business partners or ventures.

EDITOR'S NOTE: An excellent book that gives great insight on how to use these and other public records to find information about any person or business in Dennis King's *Get the Facts on Anyone* published by Peterson's.

How the Recording Offices Section is Organized

General Organization

The mailing address, telephone, time zone and fax number are listed for each office. If online access is available from the agencies, a detailed profile is provided. Included are other categories of information offered online from this or a related agency, such as tax assessor information and vital records, licenses, etc. Searching fees are listed. Other important phone numbers in the county are listed to the extent that we have researched and verified these numbers. Examples are telephone numbers for the assessor, treasure, vital records and elections offices.

An introduction to each state Recording Offices section contains a summary of the facts about where and how real estate records are maintained, as well as indicating information about Uniform Commercial Code and tax lien filings. It mentions any unusual conditions pertaining to real estate, tax lien and UCC searching in that state. A list of some of the other liens that are filed at the local level is also included.

Recording Office Searching Rules

The general rules for background searching of UCC records are as follows:

- *Except in local filing states, a search at the state level is adequate to locate all UCC records on a subject.*

- *Mortgage record searches will include any real estate related UCC filings.*

See the sections below for discussions of special collateral rules.

Due diligence searching, however, usually demands searching the local records in dual filing states as well.

Special Categories of Collateral

Real Estate Related UCC Collateral

A specific purpose of lien statutes under both the UCC and real estate laws is to put a buyer or potential secured creditor on notice that someone has a prior security interest in real or personal property. UCC financing statements are to personal property what mortgages or deeds of trust are to real property.

One problem addressed by the UCC is that certain types of property have the characteristics of both real and personal property. In those instances, it is necessary to have a way to provide lien notice to two different categories of interested parties: those who deal with the real estate aspect of the property and those who deal with the "personal" aspect of the property.

In general, our definition of real estate related UCC collateral is any property that in one form is attached to land, but that in another form is not attached. For the sake of simplicity, we can define the characteristics of two broad types of property that meet this definition:

Property that is initially attached to real property, but then is separated. Three specific types of collateral have this characteristic: *minerals* (including oil and gas), *timber*, and *crops*. These things are grown on or extracted from land. While they are on or in the ground they are thought of as real property, but once they are harvested or extracted they become personal property. Some states have a separate central filing system for crops.

*Property that is initially personal property, but then is attached to land, generally called **fixtures**.* Equipment such as telephone systems or heavy industrial equipment permanently affixed to a building are examples of fixtures. It is important to realize that what is a fixture, like beauty, is in the eye of the beholder, since it is a vague concept at best.

UCC financing statements applicable to real estate related collateral must be filed where the real estate and mortgage records are kept, which is generally at the county level—except in Connecticut, Rhode Island and Vermont, where the Town/City Clerk maintains these records. The chart gives the titles of the local official who maintains these records.

Consumer Goods

Among the state-to-state variations, some states required filing where real estate is filed for certain consumer goods. However, as of July 1, 2001 all non-realty related UCC filings in most states, including consumer goods, now go only to the central filing office in the state.

Equipment Used in Farming Operations

33 states required only local filing for equipment used in farming operations. However as of July 1, 2001, all non-realty-related UCC filing has been centralized.

Searching Note

If you are looking for information on subjects that might have these types of filings against them, a search of county records may still be revealing even if you would normally search only at the state level.

The Importance of Revised Article 9

Revised Article 9

On July 1, 2001, Revised Article 9 became law in 46 states and the District of Columbia, with 4 states adopting the law later; Alabama (January 1, 2002), Connecticut (October 1, 2001), Florida (January 1, 2002) and Mississippi (January 1, 2002). Under this new law, most UCC filings will go to the state where a business is organized, not where the collateral or chief executive offices are located. Thus, you will find new filings against IBM only in Delaware (IBM and many other public companies are Delaware corporations), and not in New York or in any other states where it has branch offices. Therefore, you will need to know where a company is organized in order to know where to find new UCC filings against it.

The place to file against individuals is the state where the person resides.

However, the new law does not apply to federal tax liens, which are still generally filed where the chief executive office is located. IBM's chief executive offices, for example, may still be in New York State.

As stated above, realty-related UCC filings continue to go to land recording offices where the property is located.

Old Article 9

Under old Article 9, Uniform Commercial Code financing statements and changes to them might be filed at two or three government agencies in each state, depending upon the type of collateral involved in the transaction. Each state's UCC statute contained variations on a nationally recommended Model Act. Each variation is explained below. The charts appear at the end of this chapter.

You will still need to know about where UCC filings are located under old Article 9 because the transition period to Revised Article 9 is five years long. UCC filings on record before July 1, 2001 remain effective until they lapse, which is generally five years from initial filing date.

A lot of UCC filings against IBM, for example, made before July 1, 2001 will still be on record in New York's central filing office, and may also be found in county filing offices since New York was a dual filing state, as explained below.

Under old Article 9, 33 states were central filing states. Central filing states are those where most types of personal property collateral require filing of a UCC financing statement only at a central filing location within that state.

Under old Article 9, five states had statewide UCC database systems. Some of these systems are still in effect under Revised Article 9. Minnesota and **Wisconsin** were central filing states with a difference: UCC financing statements filed at the county level are also entered into a statewide database. In **North Dakota** UCC financing statements may be filed at either the state or county level, and all filings are entered into a statewide database. In **Louisiana**, **Nebraska**, and **Georgia**, UCC financing statements may be filed with **any** county (parish). Under Revised Article 9, Minnesota has established a county/state system like North Dakota in all but six county offices, and Nebraska is now a central filing state. In each of these six states the records are entered into a central, statewide database that is available for searching in each county, as well as at the state agency (no state agency in Louisiana or Georgia).

Under old Article 9, eight states required dual filing of certain types of UCC financing statements. The usual definition of a dual filing state is one in which financing statements containing collateral such as inventory, equipment or receivables *must* be filed in *both* a central filing office, usually with the Secretary of State, and in a local (county) office where the collateral or business is located. The three states below were also dual filing states, with a difference. Under Revised Article 9, no dual filing is required within a state

Under old Article 9, the filing systems in three states, MA, NH, and PA, can be described as triple filing because the real estate portion of the filings goes to an office separate from the UCC filing offices. In Massachusetts and New Hampshire, UCC filings were submitted to the town/city while real estate filings go to the county. In Pennsylvania, county government was separated into the Prothonotary for UCC filings and the Recorder for real estate filings. The local filing offices for non-realty-related UCC filings no longer take filings under Revised Article 9, but they will continue to perform searches of the old records.

Some counties in other states do have separate addresses for real estate recording, but this is usually just a matter of local departmentalization.

Under old Article 9, Kentucky and Wyoming were the only *local filing only* states. In both of these states a few filings were also found at the state level because filings for out of state debtors went to the Secretary of State. And in Wyoming, filings for Wyoming debtor accounts receivable and farm products require dual filing. However, under Revised Article 9, all filings have been centralized.

The Old Article 9 UCC Locator Chart

This handy chart will tell you at a glance where UCC and real estate records are filed under old Article 9 on a state-by-state basis. Under Revised Article 9, effective July 1, 2001 except as noted later for Alabama, Connecticut, Florida and Mississippi, all new personal property filings go to the central filing office.

State	Most Personal Property Central Filing Office	Local Filing Office	All Real Property Filing Office
AK	Department of Natural Resources		District Recorder
AL	Secretary of State		Judge of Probate
AR	Secretary of State	and Circuit Clerk	Circuit Clerk
AZ	Secretary of State		County Recorder
CA	Secretary of State		County Recorder
CO	Secretary of State	or any County Recorder (as of July 1, 1996)	County Clerk & Recorder
CT	Secretary of State		Town/City Clerk
DC	County Recorder		County Recorder
DE	Secretary of State		County Recorder
FL	Secretary of State		Clerk of Circuit Court
GA	None	Clerk Superior Court	Clerk of Superior Court
HI	Bureau of Conveyances		Bureau of Conveyances
IA	Secretary of State		County Recorder
ID	Secretary of State		County Recorder
IL	Secretary of State		County Recorder
IN	Secretary of State		County Recorder
KS	Secretary of State		Register
KY	Secretary of State (Out of state only)	County Clerk	County Clerk
LA	None	Clerk of Court	Clerk of Court
MA	Secretary of the Commonwealth	and Town/City Clerk	Register of Deeds
MD	Department of Assessments & Taxation	and Clerk of Circuit Court (until 7/1/95)	Clerk of Circuit Court
ME	Secretary of State		County Register
MI	Secretary of State		County Register
MN	Secretary of State or Recorder		County Recorder
MO	Secretary of State	and County Recorder	County Recorder
MS	Secretary of State	and Chancery Clerk	Chancery Clerk

| State | Most Personal Property | | All Real Property |
	Central Filing Office	Local Filing Office	Filing Office
MT	Secretary of State		Clerk & Recorder
NC	Secretary of State	and Register of Deeds	Register of Deeds
ND	Secretary of State or County Register		County Register
NE	Secretary of State (Out of state only)	County Clerk	County Register
NH	Secretary of State	and Town/City Clerk	County Register
NJ	Secretary of State		County Clerk/Register
NM	Secretary of State		County Clerk
NV	Secretary of State		County Recorder
NY	Secretary of State	and County Clerk (Register)	County Clerk (Register)
OH	Secretary of State	and County Recorder	County Recorder
OK	Oklahoma County Clerk		County Clerk
OR	Secretary of State		County Clerk
PA	Department of State	and Prothonotary	County Recorder
RI	Secretary of State		County Clerk & Recorder
SC	Secretary of State		County Register/Clerk
SD	Secretary of State		County Register
TN	Secretary of State		County Register
TX	Secretary of State		County Clerk
UT	Division of Corporations & Commercial Code		County Recorder
VA	Corporation Commission	and Clerk of Circuit Court	Clerk of Circuit Court
VT	Secretary of State	and Town/City Clerk (until 7/1/95)	Town/City Clerk
WA	Department of Licensing		County Auditor
WI	Dept. of Financial Institutions		County Register
WV	Secretary of State		County Clerk
WY	Secretary of State (Out of state and A/R only)	County Clerk	County Clerk

Using the County Locator Section

A list at the end of each state section cross references place names to counties. Comprised of every official US Postal Service place name, the city/county cross references contain more that 40,000 entries. This information is summarized from the BRB publication The County Locator.

The cross references contain a special feature that identifies ZIP Codes that cross county lines.

Using ZIP Codes When Searching For Public Records

A place name (capitalized type) may be listed more than once in the city/county cross-references. For example,

> LOS GATOS (95030) Santa Clara (88), Santa Cruz (12)
> LOS GATOS Santa Clara

This duplicate listing indicates that the bulk of LOS GATOS addresses is in Santa Clara county, but those addresses with the ZIP Code 95030 may be in Santa Cruz county. Specifically, ZIP Code 95030 is approximately 88% in Santa Clara and 12% in Santa Cruz.

Note: county names are listed in upper and lower case type, and place names are always capitalized.

10,000 Problems Pointed Out

Multiple county ZIP Codes always appear, as in the above example, before the main entry for a place name. The percentages may not always add up to 100% because of rounding off. Counties that represent less than 1% of the addresses in a ZIP Code have also been eliminated. In all, there are almost 10,000 ZIP Codes shown in this *Sourcebook* that cross county lines.

Using Multiple County Information

The special multiple county entries put you on notice that addresses within a ZIP Code may not be in the county usually associated with that place name. This information can be crucial to finding public records, including court cases that are filed based on the location of property or residence. Remember, if you search in the wrong county, then you may get a false "no hit" response.

Non-Geographic Zip Codes

When trying to locate public records based upon place names and ZIP Codes, be aware that 10,000 ZIP Codes are useless in determining county of residence because they are assigned exclusively to post office boxes or rural routes. Anyone can have a post office box in any county. Never use an address containing one of these non-geographic ZIP Codes to determine where to search.

For More Extensive Information

BRB Publications has several products take a deeper look at counties, place names and ZIP Codes. The Public Record Research System on CD and on the Web each contain an additional 40,000 place names, as well as information about the characteristics of each ZIP Code. For example, these products indicate whether the ZIP Code only contains post office boxes, high rise building, or general delivery.

For more information, visit www.publicrecordsources.com or www.brbpub.com

Motor Vehicle Records and the Driver's Privacy Protection Act

The Driver's Privacy Protection Act Title XXXI—Protection of Privacy of Information in State Motor Vehicle Records—was attached as an amendment to the Violent Crime Control Act of 1994 and was signed by President Clinton late in that summer. The intent of the DPPA is to protect the personal privacy of persons licensed to drive by prohibiting certain disclosures of information maintained by the states. This federal mandate declared that the federal government had the right to restrict or prohibit the release of personal information of persons licensed to drive or own motor vehicles. States were given three years to comply.

The profiles of the state motor vehicle departments throughout this book often refer to DPPA and permissible users. Therefore, we are printing a copy of the Act's permissible uses.

Personal Information and the Permissible Uses

The Act prohibits disclosure of personal information from the driver history, vehicle registration, title files held by state DMVs, except for 14 specific "permissible uses." The Act's definition of Personal Information is..

"..information that identifies an individual, including an individual's photograph, social security number, driver identification number, name, address (but not the 5-digit zip code), telephone number, and medical or disability information, but does not include information on vehicular accidents, driving violations, and driver's status."

The permissible uses do, in general, permit ongoing, legitimate businesses and individuals to obtain full record data, but with added compliance procedures. The following text, taken directly from the Act, details these 14 Permissible Uses—

§2721. Prohibition on release and use of certain personal information from State motor vehicle records

"(a) IN GENERAL.--Except as provided in subsection (b), a State department of motor vehicles, and any officer, employee, or contractor, thereof, shall not knowingly disclose or otherwise make available to any person or entity personal information about any individual obtained by the department in connection with a motor vehicle record.

"(b) PERMISSIBLE USES.--Personal information referred to in subsection (a) shall be disclosed for use in connection with matters of motor vehicle or driver safety and theft, motor vehicle emissions, motor vehicle product alterations, recalls, or advisories, performance monitoring of motor vehicles and dealers by motor vehicle manufacturers, and removal of non-owners records from the original owner records of motor vehicle manufacturers to carry out the purposes of the Automobile Information Disclosure Act, the Motor Vehicle Information and Cost Saving Act, the National Traffic and Motor Vehicle Safety Act of 1966, the Anti-Car Theft Act of 1992, and the Clean Air Act, and may be disclosed as follows:

"(1) For use by **any government agency**, including any court or law enforcement agency, in carrying out its functions, or any private person or entity acting on behalf of a Federal, State, or local agency in carrying out its functions.

"(2) For use in connection with matters of motor vehicle or **driver safety** and **theft**; motor vehicle emissions; motor vehicle product alterations, recalls, or advisories; performance monitoring of motor vehicles, motor vehicle parts and dealers; motor vehicle **market**

research activities, including survey research; and removal of non-owner records from the original owner records of motor vehicle manufacturers.

"(3) For use in the normal course of business by a legitimate business or its agents, employees, or contractors, but only--

"(A) to **verify the accuracy of personal information submitted** by the individual to the business or its agents, employees, or contractors; and

"(B) if such information as so submitted is not correct or is no longer correct, to obtain the correct information, but only for the purposes of preventing fraud by, **pursuing legal remedies** against, or **recovering on a debt** or security interest against, the individual.

"(4) For use in connection with any civil, criminal, administrative, or arbitral proceeding in any Federal, State, or local court or agency or before any self-regulatory body, including the service of process, **investigation in anticipation of litigation**, and the execution or enforcement of judgments and orders, or pursuant to an order of a Federal, State, or local court.

"(5) For use in **research activities**, and for use in producing statistical reports, so long as the personal information is not published, redisclosed, or used to contact individuals.

"(6) For use by **any insurer or insurance support organization**, or by a self-insured entity, or its agents, employees, or contractors, in connection with claims investigation activities, antifraud activities, rating or underwriting.

"(7) For use in providing notice to the owners of towed or impounded vehicles.

"(8) For use by any **licensed private investigative agency** or licensed security service for any purpose permitted under this subsection.

"(9) For use by an employer or its agent or insurer to obtain or verify information relating to a holder of a commercial driver's license that is required under the Commercial Motor Vehicle Safety Act of 1986 (49 U.S.C. App. 2710 et seq.)

"(10) For use in connection with the operation of private toll transportation facilities.

"(11) For any other use in response to requests for individual motor vehicle records if the State has obtained the express consent of the person to whom such personal information pertains.

"(12) For bulk distribution for surveys, marketing or solicitations if if the State has obtained the express consent of the person to whom such personal information pertains.

"(13) For use by any requester, if the requester demonstrates it has obtained the written consent of the individual to whom the information pertains.

"(14) For any other use specifically authorized under the law of the State that holds the record, if such use is related to the operation of a motor vehicle or public safety.

"(c) RESALE OR REDISCLOSURE.--An authorized recipient of personal information (except a recipient under subsection (b)(11) or (12) may resell or redisclose the information only for a use permitted under subsection (b) (but not for uses under subsection (b) (11) or (12). An authorized recipient under subsection (b)(11) may resell or redisclose personal information for any purpose. An authorized recipient under subsection (b)(12) may resell or redisclose personal information pursuant to subsection (b)(12). Any authorized recipient (except a recipient under subsection (b)(11)) that resells or rediscloses personal information covered by this title must keep for a period of 5 years records identifying each person or entity that receives information and the permitted purpose for which the information will be used and must make such records available to the motor vehicle department upon request.

"(d) WAIVER PROCEDURES.--A State motor vehicle department may establish and carry out procedures under which the department or its agents, upon receiving a request for personal information that does not fall within one of the exceptions in subsection (b), may mail a copy of the request to the individual about whom the information was requested, informing such individual of the request, together with a statement to the effect that the information will not be released unless the individual waives such individual's right to privacy under this section.

Using a Public Record Vendor

Hiring Someone to Obtain the Record

There are five main categories of public record professionals: distributors and gateways; search firms; local document retrievers; investigative firms; and information brokers.

Distributors and Gateways (Proprietary Database Vendors)

Distributors are automated public record firms who combine public sources of bulk data and/or online access to develop their own database product(s). Primary Distributors include companies that collect or buy public record information from its original source and reformat the information in some useful way. They tend to focus on one or a limited number of types of information, although a few firms have branched into multiple information categories.

Gateways are companies that either compile data from or provide an automated gateway to Primary Distributors. Gateways thus provide "one-stop shopping" for multiple geographic areas and/or categories of information.

Companies can be *both* Primary Distributors and Gateways. For example, a number of online database companies are both primary distributors of corporate information and also gateways to real estate information from other Primary Distributors

Search Firms

Search firms are companies that furnish public record search and document retrieval services through outside online services and/or through a network of specialists, including their own employees or correspondents (see Retrievers below). There are three types of Search Firms.

Search Generalists offer a full range of search capabilities in many public record categories over a wide geographic region. They may rely on gateways, primary distributors and/or networks of retrievers. They combine online proficiency with document retrieval expertise.

Search Specialists focus either on one geographic region—like Ohio—or on one specific type of public record information—like driver/vehicle records.

Application Specialists focus on one or two types of services geared to specific needs. In this category are pre-employment screening firms and tenant screening firms. Like investigators, they search many of the public record categories in order to prepare an overall report about a person or business.

Local Document Retrievers

Local document retrievers use their own personnel to search specific requested categories of public records usually in order to obtain documentation for legal compliance (e.g., incorporations), for lending, and for litigation. They do not usually review or interpret the results or issue reports in the sense that investigators do, but rather return documents with the results of searches. They tend to be localized, but there are companies that offer a national network of retrievers and/or correspondents. The retriever or his/her personnel goes directly to the agency to look up the information. A retriever may be relied upon for strong knowledge in a local area, whereas a search generalist has a breadth of knowledge and experience in a wider geographic range.

The 725+ members of the **Public Record Retriever Network (PRRN)** can be found, by state and counties served, at www.brbpub.com/PRRN. This organization has set industry standards for the retrieval of public record documents and operates under a Code of Professional Conduct. Using one of these record retrievers is an excellent way to access records in those jurisdictions that do not offer online access.

Private Investigation Firms

Investigators use public records as tools rather than as ends in themselves, in order to create an overall, comprehensive "picture" of an individual or company for a particular purpose. They interpret the information they have gathered in order to identify further investigation tracks. They summarize their results in a report compiled from all the sources used.

Many investigators also act as Search Firms, especially as tenant or pre-employment screeners, but this is a different role from the role of Investigator per se, and screening firms act very much like investigators in their approach to a project. In addition, an investigator may be licensed, and may perform the types of services traditionally thought of as detective work, such as surveillance.

Information Brokers

There is one additional type of firm that occasionally utilizes public records. **Information Brokers** (IB) gather information that will help their clients make informed business decisions. Their work is usually done on a custom basis with each project being unique. IBs are extremely knowledgeable in online research of full text databases and most specialize in a particular subject area, such as patent searching or competitive intelligence. The Association of Independent Information Professionals (AIIP), at www.aiip.org, has over 700 experienced professional information specialist members from 21 countries.

Which Type of Vendor is Right for You?

With all the variations of vendors and the categories of information, the obvious question is; "How do I find the right vendor to go to for the public record information I need?" Before you start calling every interesting online vendor that catches your eye, you need to narrow your search to the **type** of vendor for your needs. To do this, ask yourself the following questions—

What is the Frequency of Usage?

If you have on-going, recurring requests for a particular type of information, it is probably best to choose a different vendor then if you have infrequent requests. Setting up an account with a primary distributor, such as LEXIS or Westlaw will give you an inexpensive per search fee, but the monthly minimum requirements will be prohibitive to the casual requester, who would be better off finding a vendor who accesses or is a gateway to one of these vendors. **EDITOR'S NOTE**: Check out LEXIS, Westlaw and similar vendors in the *National Directory of Public Record Vendors*.

What is the Complexity of the Search?

The importance of hiring a vendor who understands and can interpret the information in the final format increases with the complexity of the search. Pulling a corporation record in Maryland is not difficult, but doing an online criminal record search in Maryland, when only a portion of the felony records are online, is not so easy.

Thus, part of the answer to determining which vendor or type of vendor to use is to become conversant with what is (and is not) available from government agencies. Without knowing what is available (and what restrictions apply), you cannot guide the search process effectively. Once you are comfortable knowing the kinds of information available in the public record, you are in a position to find the best method to access needed information.

What are the Geographic Boundaries of the Search?

A search of local records close to you may require little assistance, but a search of records nationally or in a state 2,000 miles away will require seeking a vendor who covers the area you need to search. Many national primary distributors and gateways combine various local and state databases into one large comprehensive system available for searching. However, if your record searching is narrowed by a region or locality, then an online source that specializes in a specific geographic region (like Superior Information Services in NJ) may be an alternative to a national vendor. Keep in mind that many national firms allow you to order a search online, even though results cannot be delivered immediately and some hands-on local searching is required.

Of course, you may want to use the government agency online system if available for the kind of information you need.

10 Questions to Ask a Public Records Vendor

(Or a Vendor Who Uses Online Sources)

The following discussion focuses specifically on automated sources of information because many valuable types of public records have been entered into a computer and, therefore, require a computer search to obtain reliable results. The original version of the text to follow was written by **Mr. Leroy Cook**. Mr. Cook is the founder and Director of ION and The Investigators Anywhere Resource Line (800-338-3463, http://ioninc.com). Mr. Cook has graciously allowed us to edit the article and reprint it for our readers.

1. Where does he or she get the information?

You may feel awkward asking a vendor where he or she obtained the information you are purchasing. The fake Rolex watch is a reminder that even buying physical things based on looks alone—without knowing where they come from—is dangerous.

Reliable information vendors *will* provide verification material such as the name of the database or service accessed, when it was last updated, and how complete it is.

It is important that you know the gathering process in order to better judge the reliability of the information being purchased. There *are* certain investigative sources that a vendor will not be willing to disclose to you. However, that type of source should not be confused with the information that is being sold item by item. Information technology has changed so rapidly that some information vendors may still confuse "items of information" with "investigative reports." Items of information sold as units are *not* investigative reports. The professional reputation of an information vendor is a guarantee of sorts. Still, because information as a commodity is so new, there is little in the way of an implied warranty of fitness.

2. How long does it take for the new information or changes to get into the system?

Any answer *except* a clear, concise date and time or the vendor's personal knowledge of an ongoing system's methods of maintaining information currency is a reason to keep probing. In view of the preceding question, this one might seem repetitive, but it *really* is a different issue. Microfiche or a database of records may have been updated last week at a courthouse or a DMV, but the department's computer section may also be working with a three-month backlog. In this case, a critical incident occurring one month ago would *not* show up in the information updated last week. The importance of timeliness is a variable to be determined by you, but to be truly informed you need to know how "fresh" the information is. Ideally, the mechanism by which you purchase items of information *should* include an update or statement of accuracy—as a part of the reply—*without* having to ask.

3. What are the searchable fields? Which fields are mandatory?

If your knowledge of "fields" and "records" is limited to the places where cattle graze and those flat, round things that play music, you *could* have a problem telling a good database from a bad one. An MVR vendor, for example, should be able to tell you that a subject's middle initial is critical when pulling an Arizona driving record. You don't have to become a programmer to use a computer and you needn't know a database management language to benefit from databases, *but* it is very helpful to understand how databases are constructed and (*at the least*) what fields, records, and indexing procedures are used.

As a general rule, the computerized, public-record information world is not standardized from county to county or from state to state; in the same way, there is little standardization within or between information vendors. Look at the system documentation from the vendor. The manual should include this sort of information.

4. How much latitude is there for error (misspellings or inappropriate punctuation) in a data request?

If the vendor's requirements for search data appear to be concise and meticulous, then you're probably on the right track. Some computer systems will tell (or "flag") an operator when they make a mistake such as omitting important punctuation or using an unnecessary comma. Other systems allow you to make inquiries by whatever means or in whatever format you like—and then tell you the requested information has *not* been found. In this instance, the desired information may *actually* be there, but the computer didn't understand the question because of the way in which it was asked. It is easy to misinterpret "no record found" as "there is no record." Please take note that the meanings of these two phrases are quite different.

5. What method is used to place the information in the repository and what error control or edit process is used?

In some databases, information may be scanned in or may be entered by a single operator as it is received and, in others, information may be entered *twice* to allow the computer to catch input errors by searching for non-duplicate entries. You don't have to know *everything* about all the options, but the vendor selling information in quantity *should*.

6. How many different databases or sources does the vendor access *and* how often?

The chance of obtaining an accurate search of a database increases with the frequency of access and the vendor's/searcher's level of knowledge. If he or she only makes inquiries once a month—and the results are important—you may need to find someone who sells data at higher volume. The point here is that it is better to find someone who specializes in the type of information you are seeking than it is to utilize a vendor who *can* get the information, but actually specializes in another type of data.

7. Does the price include assistance in interpreting the data received?

A report that includes coding and ambiguous abbreviations may look impressive in your file, but may not be too meaningful. For all reports, except those you deal with regularly, interpretation assistance can be *very* important. Some information vendors offer searches for information they really don't know much about through sources that they only use occasionally. Professional pride sometimes prohibits them from disclosing their limitations—until *you* ask the right questions.

8. Do vendors "keep track" of requesters and the information they seek (usage records)?

This may not seem like a serious concern when you are requesting information you're legally entitled to; however, there *is* a possibility that your usage records could be made available to a competitor. Most probably, the information itself is *already* being (or will be) sold to someone else, but you may not necessarily want *everyone* to know what you are requesting and how often. If the vendor keeps records of who-asks-what, the confidentiality of that information should be addressed in your agreement with the vendor.

9. Will the subject of the inquiry be notified of the request?

If your inquiry is sub rosa or if the subject's discovery of the search could lead to embarrassment, double check! There are laws that mandate the notification of subjects when certain types of inquires are made into their files. If notification is required, the way it is accomplished could be critical.

10. Is the turnaround time and cost of the search made clear at the outset?

You should be crystal clear about what you expect and/or need; the vendor should be succinct when conveying exactly what will be provided and how much it will cost. Failure to address these issues can lead to disputes and hard feelings.

These are excellent questions and concepts to keep in mind when searching for the right public record vendor to meet your needs.

Section II

Public Records by State

Alabama

General Help Numbers:

Governor's Office
600 Dexter Ave, #N-104
Montgomery, AL 36130
www.governor.state.al.us

334-242-7100
Fax 334-242-0937
8AM-5PM

Attorney General's Office
State House
11 S. Union Street, 3rd Fl
Montgomery, AL 36130
www.ago.state.al.us

334-242-7300
Fax 334-242-4891
8AM-5PM

State Court Administrator
300 Dexter Ave
Montgomery, AL 36104-3741
www.alacourt.org

334-242-0300
Fax 334-242-2099
8AM-5PM

State Archives
Archives & History Department
Reference Room, PO Box 300100
Montgomery, AL 36130-0100
www.archives.state.al.us

334-242-4435
Fax 334-240-3433
8AM-5PM T-F,
9AM-5PM SA

State Specifics:

Capital:

Montgomery
Montgomery County

Time Zone:

CST

Number of Counties:

67

Population:

4,464,356

Web Site:

www.alabama.gov

State Agencies

Criminal Records

Alabama Department of Public Safety, A.B.I., Identification Unit, PO Box 1511, Montgomery, AL 36102-1511 (Courier: 2720 A Gunter PK Dr W, Montgomery, AL 36109); 334-395-4340, 334-395-4350 (Fax), 8AM-5PM.

www.dps.state.al.us

Note: Sex offender data and felony fugitive list is available online at www.gsiweb.net . The Alabama State Court Administration provides criminal

records online via a state designated vendor. Visit www.alacourt.com for details.

Indexing & Storage: Records are available from 1942 on. It takes about 7 days before new records are available for inquiry. 40% of arrests in database have final dispositions recorded, 65% for those arrests in last 5 years.

Searching: The request must be on a state form (call to have copy sent). Include the following in your request: notarized release from subject, date of birth, Social Security Number, full name, race, sex. Fingerprints optional. 100% of the record files

have fingerprints. The following data is not released: juvenile records. All records or arrests are released, including those without dispositions.

Access by: mail, in person, online.

Fee & Payment: The fee is $25.00 per name. For a fingerprint search of both the state and FBI records, the fee is $49.00 per name. Prepayment is required. Fee payee: Alabama Bureau of Investigation. Cashier checks and money orders accepted. No personal checks accepted. No credit cards accepted.

Mail search: Turnaround time: 7 days. No self addressed stamped envelope is required.

In person search: You may bring in the required release and request form.

Online search: The State Court Administration provides records over its State Judicial Online System (SJIS) at www.alacourt.org. The SJIS contains criminal records from all county courthouses. Access to this statewide system, which is used by the courts as well as the public, requires a $150 setup fee plus a $50 per month for unlimited access. The system is open 24 hours daily. Call Cheryl Lenoir at 334-242-0300 for more information.

Corporation Records
Limited Partnership Records
Limited Liability Company Records
Limited Liability Partnerships
Trade Names
Trademarks/Servicemarks

Secretary of State, Corporations Division, PO Box 5616, Montgomery, AL 36103-5616 (Courier: 11 S Union St, Ste 207, Montgomery, AL 36104); 334-242-5324, 334-242-5325 (Trademarks), 334-240-3138 (Fax), 8AM-5PM.

www.sos.state.al.us

Indexing & Storage: Records are available for all corporations, active or inactive. All information here on file is considered public information. Formal registration of trademarks and service marks was codified in 1981, and trade name registration in 1989. It takes 1 month before new records are available for inquiry. Records are indexed on images and on inhouse computer.

Searching: Include the following in your request: full name of business. In addition to the articles of incorporation, corporation records include the following information: Annual Reports, Officers, Directors, Prior (Merged) names, Inactive and Reserved names.

Access by: mail, phone, in person, online.

Fee & Payment: There is no search fee, but copies are $1.00 per page. Prepayment is required. Fee payee: Secretary of State. The agency will invoice members of the AL state bar. Personal checks accepted.

Mail search: Turnaround time: 1 week. A self addressed stamped envelope is requested.

Phone search: There is a limit of 3 inquiries per call.

In person search: Call first for page amount before going to their office.

Online search: The web site has free searches of corporate and UCC records. Search individual files for Active Names at http://arc-sos.state.al.us/CGI/SOSCRP01.MBR/INPUT

Expedited service: Expedited service is available for mail and phone searches, call for fees. Turnaround time: 24 to 48 hours. Expedited service ends at 2PM each day.

Uniform Commercial Code
Federal Tax Liens
State Tax Liens

UCC Division, Secretary of State, PO Box 5616, Montgomery, AL 36103-5616 (Courier: 11 South Union St, Suite 207, Montgomery, AL 36104); 334-242-5231, 8AM-5PM.

www.sos.state.al.us/sosinfo/inquiry.cfm

Indexing & Storage: Records are indexed on inhouse computer.

Searching: Use search request form UCC-11. The search includes tax liens. Federal and state tax liens on individuals may also be filed at the county level. All tax liens on businesses are filed here. Include the following in your request: debtor name.

Access by: mail, in person, online.

Fee & Payment: In addition to the $20.00 search fee per debter name, this agency charges $1.00 for each page (financing statement or assignment) searched plus $1.00 for each listing. The copy fee is $1.00 per page. Certification is $5.00. Fee payee: Secretary of State. Prepayment required. Personal checks accepted. No credit cards accepted.

Mail search: Turnaround time: 1 to 2 weeks.

In person search: Searching is available in person.

Online search: The agency has UCC information available to search at the web address, there is no fee. Corporation data is also available. You can search by name or file number.

Expedited service: This service is available for an additional $100.00, usually same day service.

Sales Tax Registrations
Access to Records is Restricted

Alabama Department of Revenue, Sales, Use and Business Tax Division, 4303 Gordon Persons Bldg, 50 N Ripley St, Montgomery, AL 36104; 334-242-1490, 334-242-8916 (Fax), 8AM-5PM.

www.ador.state.al.us

Note: According to state law 40-2A-10, Code of Alabama 1975, this agency is unable to release any information about tax registrations. Note, their web site has motor vehicle dealer regulatory license information.

Birth Certificates

Center for Health Statistics, Record Services Division, PO Box 5625, Montgomery, AL 36103-5625 (Courier: RSA Tower Suite 1150, 201 Monroe St, Montgomery, AL 36104); 334-206-5418, 334-262-9563 (Fax), 8AM-5PM.

www.adph.org

Note: Certificates can, also, be delivered in any County Health Department for any vital record event occurring in AL. Delivery time is usually 15-30 minutes.

Indexing & Storage: Records are available from 1908 to present. New records are available for inquiry immediately. Records are indexed on microfiche, inhouse computer.

Searching: Birth certificates under 125 years old may be requested by an immediate family member or person with legal right to certificate. Include the following in your request: full name, names of father, mother's maiden name, date of birth, county or city of birth, reason for information request. Include a daytime phone number and a signature.

Access by: mail, phone, fax, in person.

Fee & Payment: Fee is $12.00, add $4.00 per name for each additional copy. Fee payee: State Board of Health Prepayment required. Credit cards accepted for phone, fax and expedited requests only. Personal checks accepted. Credit cards accepted: MasterCard, Visa, AmEx, Discover.

Mail search: Turnaround time: 5 to 10 days. No self addressed stamped envelope is required.

Phone search: Telephone requests allowed using a credit card, see expedited service.

Fax search: Same criteria as phone searching.

In person search: Also, go to the nearest County Health Department.

Expedited service: Expedited service is available for mail, phone and fax searches. Additional expedite fee is $10.00, use of credit card is $5.50. Turnaround time: 1 day. Include overnight shipping if desired.

Death Records

Center for Health Statistics, Record Services Division, PO Box 5625, Montgomery, AL 36103-5625 (Courier: RSA Tower Suite 1150, 201 Monroe St, Montgomery, AL 36104); 334-206-5418, 334-262-9563 (Fax), 8AM-5PM.

www.adph.org

Note: Certificates can, also, be delivered in any County Health Department for any vital record event occurring in AL. Delivery time is usually 15-30 minutes.

Indexing & Storage: Records are available from 1908 on. New records are available for inquiry immediately. Records are indexed on microfiche, inhouse computer.

Searching: Must be immediate family or have leagl right to certificate for ordering death records less than 25 years old. Include the following in your request: full name, date of death, names of parents including mother's maiden name, county or city of death, reason for information request, and signature of requester. Include a daytime phone number.

Access by: mail, phone, fax, in person.

Fee & Payment: Fee is $12.00, add $4.00 per copy for each additional copy. Fee payee: State Board of Health. Prepayment required. Personal checks accepted. Credit cards accepted: MasterCard, Visa, AmEx, Discover.

Mail search: Turnaround time: 2 to 3 weeks. No self addressed stamped envelope is required.

Phone search: Telephone requests allowed using a credit card, see expedited service.

Fax search: Same criteria as phone searching.

In person search: Also, you can go to the nearest County Health Department.

Other access: Some indexes are available on microfiche for $40.00 per roll. Rolls are available for records for 1908 through 1959.

Expedited service: Expedited service is available for mail, phone and fax searches. Additional expedite fee is $10.00, use of credit card is $5.50. Include overnight shipping fee if desired.

Marriage Certificates

Center for Health Statistics, Record Services Division, PO Box 5625, Montgomery, AL 36103-5625 (Courier: RSA Tower Suite 1150, 201 Monroe St, Montgomery, AL 36104); 334-206-5418, 334-262-9563 (Fax), 8AM-5PM.

www.adph.org

Note: Certificates can, also, be delivered in any County Health Department for any vital record event occurring in AL. Delivery time is usually 15-30 minutes.

Indexing & Storage: Records are available from 1936 to present. New records are available for inquiry immediately. Records are indexed on microfiche, inhouse computer.

Searching: Include the following in your request: names of husband and wife, date of marriage, county of license issue. Include a daytime phone number and signature of requester.

Access by: mail, phone, fax, in person.

Fee & Payment: Fee is $12.00, add $4.00 per copy for additional copies. Fee payee: State Board of Health. Prepayment required. Personal checks accepted. Credit cards accepted: MasterCard, Visa, AmEx, Discover.

Mail search: Turnaround time: 2 to 3 weeks. No self addressed stamped envelope is required.

Phone search: Telephone requests allowed using a credit card, see expedited service.

Fax search: Same criteria as phone searches.

In person search: Also, you can go to the nearest County Health Department.

Other access: Microfilm rolls are available for purchase at $40.00 each. There are 11 rolls available which includes records from 1936 to 1969.

Expedited service: Expedited service is available for mail, phone and fax searches. Turnaround time: 1 to 2 days. Include a $40.00 expedite fee and a $5.50 credit card fee, and overnight shipping if desired.

Divorce Records

Center for Health Statistics, Record Services Division, PO Box 5625, Montgomery, AL 36103-5625 (Courier: RSA Tower Suite 1150, 201 Monroe St, Montgomery, AL 36104); 334-206-5418, 334-206-2659 (Fax), 8AM-5PM.

www.adph.org

Note: Certificates can, also, be delivered in any County Health Department for any vital record event occurring in AL. Delivery time is usually 15-30 minutes.

Indexing & Storage: Records are available from 1950 to present. New records are available for inquiry immediately. Records are indexed on inhouse computer, microfiche.

Searching: Include the following in your request: names of husband and wife including maiden name, date of divorce, county. Include a daytime phone number, all requests must have signature of the requester.

Access by: mail, phone, fax, in person.

Fee & Payment: Fee is $12.00, add $4.00 per copy for additional copies. Fee payee: State Board of Health. Prepayment required. Personal checks accepted. Credit cards accepted: MasterCard, Visa, AmEx, Discover.

Mail search: Turnaround time: 5 to 10 days. No self addressed stamped envelope is required.

Phone search: Telephone requests allowed using a credit card, see expedited service.

Fax search: Same criteria as phone searches.

In person search: Also, you can go to the nearest County Health Department.

Other access: There are microfilm rolls of records for 1950-59 available for $40.00 per roll.

Expedited service: Expedited service is available for mail, phone and fax searches. Turnaround time: 1 to 2 days. Include the $10.00 expedite fee and $5.50 credit card fee, and overnight shipping fee if desired.

Workers' Compensation Records

Department of Industrial Relations, Disclosure Unit, 649 Monroe Street, Rm. 276, Montgomery, AL 36131; 334-242-8980, 334-261-2304 (Fax), 8AM-4:30PM.

www.dir.state.al.us/uc.htm

Indexing & Storage: Records are available from 1986 on computer (index). Actual file copies are placed on microfilm after 6 months. Older records (pre 1986) are on microfiche and must be searched by SSN.

Searching: Must have a written, notarized release from claimant. Include the following in your request: claimant name, Social Security Number.

Access by: mail, in person.

Fee & Payment: The fee is $8.00 per record. Fee payee: Department of Industrial Relations, Workers Compensation. Prepayment required. Personal checks accepted. No credit cards accepted.

Mail search: Turnaround time: 1 week. No self addressed stamped envelope is required.

In person search: A notarized release form is required.

Driver Records

Department of Public Safety, Driver Records-License Division, PO Box 1471, Montgomery, AL 36102-1471 (Courier: 502 Dexter Ave, Montgomery, AL 36104); 334-242-4400, 334-242-4639 (Fax), 8AM-5PM.

www.dps.state.al.us/

Note: Ticket information must be secured at the local level.

Indexing & Storage: Records are available for convictions in last five years for moving violations, surrendered licenses, DWI and suspensions. It takes 2 weeks before new records are available for inquiry.

Searching: Some juvenile records are considered confidential and are not released. The driver's address and personal information is not included, even if the requester is a DPPA permissible user. Need full name, DOB and license number to obtain a record. Use Form MV-DPPA1 if you are a permissible user.

Access by: mail, in person, online.

Fee & Payment: The fee is $5.75 per record for all access modes. Fee payee: Alabama DPS, Drivers License Division. Prepayment required. No credit cards accepted.

Mail search: Turnaround time: 3 to 5 days. Providing a self-addressed return envelope usually means quicker service.

In person search: Walk-in requesters are not charged for a no record found report.

Online search: Alabama offers real time processing access via the AAMVAnet 3270 Terminal Connection. There is a minimum order requirement of 500 requests per month. Fee is $5.75 per record. Requesters must provide their own connection device and terminal emulation software.

Vehicle Ownership
Vehicle Identification

Motor Vehicle Division, Records & Registration Unit, PO Box 327630, Montgomery, AL 36132-7630 (Courier: 50 North Ripley St, 1202 Gordon Persons Bldg, Montgomery, AL 36140); 334-242-9000, 334-242-9102 (Title Inquiry), 334-242-0312 (Fax), 8AM-5PM.

www.ador.state.al.us/motorvehicle

Indexing & Storage: Records are available from 1975 for title records and 10 years for registration records. It takes 2 weeks before new records are available for inquiry.

Searching: The restrictions specified under the DPPA (Driver's Privacy Protection Act) apply. Access is restricted to permissible users who must use Form MV-DPPA1. Non-permissible users must have notarized release of subject. The address of the title or registration holder must be included as part of the request. The following data is not released: bulk information or lists for commercial purposes.

Access by: mail.

Fee & Payment: Fees are $3.00 per record per year for registration records and $15.00 for title searches (includes lien data). Fee payee: Alabama Department of Revenue. Prepayment required. Only certified funds are accepted. No credit cards accepted.

Mail search: Turnaround time: 3 to 4 weeks. No self addressed stamped envelope is required.

Accident Reports

Alabama Department of Public Safety, Accident Records, PO Box 1471, Montgomery, AL 36102-1471 (Courier: 502 Washington Ave, Montgomery, 36104); 334-242-4241, 8AM-5PM.

Indexing & Storage: Records are available for a minimum of 10 years. After 2 years, they put reports on microfiche. It takes 2 weeks before new records are available for inquiry.

Searching: Include the following in your request: date of accident, location of accident, county. Also, submit names of drivers.

Access by: mail, phone, in person.

Fee & Payment: The fee is $15.00 and prepayment is required. Fee payee: Alabama DPS, Accident Reports. Only certified funds or cash is accepted. No credit cards accepted.

Mail search: Turnaround time: within 2 weeks. A self addressed stamped envelope is requested.

Phone search: No fee for telephone request. They will search to see if a report exists, but will not give any information over the phone.

In person search: Turnaround time is while you wait.

Vessel Ownership
Vessel Registration

Dept of Conservation & Natural Resources, Marine Police Div. Boat Reg. Records, PO Box 301451, Montgomery, AL 36130 (Courier: 64 N Union St, Montgomery, AL 36104); 334-242-3673, 334-242-0336 (Fax), 8AM-5PM.

www.dcnr.state.al.us

Indexing & Storage: Records are available from 1985 to the present. Records are indexed on computer. All mechanically propelled, sail or rental boats must be registered. It takes 2 months before new records are available for inquiry.

Searching: Vessels that have been commercially documented by the Coast Guard are not required to register with Alabama. Liens are not recorded here, but at the central state locations for UCC filings. To search, at least one of the following is required: owner's name, hull id #, current decal #, or registration #. For purged records, the registration # is required to search.

Access by: mail, phone, fax, in person.

Fee & Payment: There is no search fee, except for bulk searches (see below) or lengthy lists ($1.00 per record). Fee payee: Department of Conservation. Prepayment required. No credit cards accepted.

Mail search: Turnaround time: 1 to 2 days. No self addressed stamped envelope is required.

Phone search: Records are available by phone.

Fax search: Turnaround time is within 1 day.

In person search: Searching is available in person.

Other access: The state accepts e-mail requests for records at rthornell@dcnr.state.al.us. The state will sell all or parts of its database. Fees start at $100.00 for the first 2,500 records.

Legislation Records

Alabama Legislature, State House, 11 S Union St, Montgomery, AL 36130-4600; 334-242-7826 (Senate), 334-242-7637 (House), 334-242-8819 (Fax), 8:30AM-4:30PM.

www.legislature.state.al.us

Note: Use Room 716 for the Senate, Room 512 for the House. Fax number above is for Senate only.

Indexing & Storage: Records are available from 1995 to present on computer and from 1819 in journal books. Records are indexed on inhouse computer, books (volumes).

Searching: Include the following in your request: bill number. You may also request bills by subject or sponsor.

Access by: mail, phone, fax, in person, online.

Fee & Payment: The search fee is $1.00 per page with a $25.00 maximum. Computer printouts are $1.00 per page. The state will charge postage for large print runs. Fee payee: Either to the Senate or the House. Personal checks accepted. No credit cards accepted.

Mail search: Turnaround time: 1 day. No self addressed stamped envelope is required.

Phone search: Records are available by phone.

Fax search: The fax fee is $5.00.

In person search: You may make copies at $.25 per page. This is the preferred request method.

Online search: There is a free service on the Internet for bill text, status, history, voting, audio of Senate, and Code of Alabama.

Voter Registration
Access to Records is Restricted

Alabama State House, Voter Registration, 11 S Union, Rm 236, Montgomery, AL 36130; 334-242-4337, 334-242-2940 (Fax), 8AM-5PM.

Note: Individual name requests must be done at the county level, there are no restrictions.

GED Certificates

State Dept of Education, GED Testing Office, PO Box 302101, Montgomery, AL 36130-2101 (Courier: Gordon Persons Bldg Rm 5345, 50 N Ripley St, Montgomery, AL 36104); 334-242-8181 (Main Number), 334-242-2236 (Fax), 8AM-5PM.

Searching: Requests should be writing. Only the name is needed to verify. All of the following is required for a transcript: a signed release, name, year of test, date of birth, Social Security Number, and city of testing.

Access by: mail, fax, in person.

Fee & Payment: There is no verification or search fee, but there is a $5.00 certification fee. If transcript is needed, fee is $5.00 plus $5.00 for certification. Fee payee: GED Testing. Only cashier's checks and money orders are accepted. No credit cards accepted.

Mail search: Turnaround time is 1-2 days. No self addressed stamped envelope is required.

Fax search: Turnaround time is same day. Results will be called or faxed.

In person search: No fee for request. Turnaround time is a few minutes.

Hunting License Information
Fishing License Information
Access to Records is Restricted

Conservation & Natural Resources Department, Division of Wildlife & Freshwater Fisheries, 64 N Union Street, Room 559, Montgomery, AL 36130-1456; 334-242-3829, 334-353-5239, 334-242-3032 (Fax), 8AM-5PM.

Note: They do not have a central computerized database. Records must be hand searched and are grouped by issuing agent. This makes searching very time consuming and thus it is discouraged.

Alabama State Licensing Agencies

Licenses Searchable Online

Abortion/Reproductive Health Center #31 ...www.adph.org/providers/
Ambulatory Surgery Center #31 ....www.adph.org/providers/
Architect #8...www.alarchbd.state.al.us/rostersearch/rostersearch.asp
Assisted Living Facility/Unit #31 ....www.adph.org/providers/
Attorney #3 ....www.alabar.org/page.cfm?page=im_include/im_dirSearch.cfm
Birthing Center #31 ....www.adph.org/providers/
Cerebral Palsy Center #31 ....www.adph.org/providers/
Electrical Contractor #14 ....www.aecb.state.al.us/Search/new_search.asp
Electrician, Journeyman #14.......................www.aecb.state.al.us/Search/new_search.asp
Engineer/Engineer in Training #27 ....www.bels.state.al.us/LicenseeSearch/searchmenu.asp
Forester #26 ....http://home.earthlink.net/~pbsears/foresters.html
Home Builder #53......................................www.hblb.state.al.us/Lic_Search/search.asp
Home Health Agency #31 ....www.adph.org/providers/
Home Inspector #42 ....www.sos.state.al.us/sosinfo/inquiry.cfm
Hospice #31...www.adph.org/providers/
Hospital #31..www.adph.org/providers/
Hospital, Rural Primary Care #31 ....www.adph.org/providers/
Independent Clinical/Physiological Lab #31.www.adph.org/providers/
Insurance Adjuster #39..............................www.aldoi.org/licenseesearch.htm
Insurance Agent #39..................................www.aldoi.org/licenseesearch.htm
Insurance Broker/Producer #39 ....www.aldoi.org/licenseesearch.htm
Insurance Company #39.............................www.aldoi.org/companysearch.htm
Insurance Corporation/Partnership #39 ....www.aldoi.org/companysearch.htm
Massage Therapist #56 ....www.adeca.state.al.us/soicc/soicc/WebSTAR3.0/SOICC/LicOcc/massage.html
Medical Doctor #19....................................www.albme.org/verification.htm
Mental Health Center #31 ....www.adph.org/providers/
Notary Public #42 ....www.sos.state.al.us/sosinfo/inquiry.cfm
Nursing Home #31......................................www.adph.org/providers/
Nursing Home Administrator #22.................www.alboenha.state.al.us/logon.html
Optometrist #20 ....www.odfinder.org/LicSearch.asp
Physical Therapist/Therapist Asst #24.........www.pt.state.al.us/License/searchform.asp
Preneed Sales Agent #39...........................www.aldoi.org/licenseesearch.htm
Public Accountant-CPA #25........................www.asbpa.state.al.us/register/register.asp
Real Estate Appraiser #43 ....http://reab.state.al.us/appraisers/searchform.asp
Real Estate Broker #2................................www.arec.state.al.us/search.asp
Real Estate Salesperson/Agent #2 ....www.arec.state.al.us/search.asp
Rehabilitation Center #31 ....www.adph.org/providers/
Reinsurance Intermediary #39....................www.aldoi.org/licenseesearch.htm
Renal Disease (End Stage) Treatment Ctr. #31 .....www.adph.org/providers/
Sleep Disorder Center #31 ....www.adph.org/providers/
Social Worker #58 ....www.abswe.state.al.us/Lic_Search/search.asp
Surplus Line Broker #39 ....www.aldoi.org/licenseesearch.htm
Surveyor, Land #27 ....www.bels.state.al.us/LicenseeSearch/searchmenu.asp
X-ray (Portable) Supplier #31 ....www.adph.org/providers/

Licensing Quick Finder

Abortion/Reproductive Health Ctr #31...334-206-5175
Aircraft Personnel #51 205-731-1557
Ambulatory Surgery Center #31 334-206-5175
Anesthesiologist Assistant #19.............334-242-4116
Architect #8...334-242-4179
Assisted Living Facility/Unit #31 334-206-5175
Attorney #3 334-269-1515
Auctioneer #9..334-269-9990
Bank #5 334-242-3452
Bear Creek Recreation #6 256-332-4392
Beauty Shop/Booth Rental #11 334-242-1918
Beauty Shop/Salon #11.........................334-242-1918
Birthing Center #31...............................334-206-5175
Boxer/Wrestler - not regulated #52 334-242-1380
Broker/Dealer Agent #48 334-242-2984
Cerebral Palsy Center #31 334-206-5175

Chiropractor #10....................................205-755-8000
Clinical Nurse Specialist #21................334-242-0767
Consumer Finance Company #5 334-242-3452
Contractor, General #7..........................334-242-2839
Cosmetic Studio #11 334-242-1918
Cosmetologist & Cosmetology Instructor #11.............
....334-242-1918
Cosmetologist Manager Pending Exam #11.............
....334-242-1918
Cosmetologist Student/Apprentice #11.334-242-1918
Cosmetologist, Restricted Managing #11 ....
....334-242-1918
Cosmetologist/Esthetician/Manicurist Manager #11
....334-242-1918
Cosmetologist/Esthetician/Manicurist Master #11 .....
....334-242-1918

Cosmetology School/Instructor/Pending Exam #11 ...
....334-242-1918
Counselor, Professional #15................205-458-8716
Dental Hygienist #12 256-533-4638
Dental Scholarship Award #13.............205-934-4384
Dentist #12 256-533-4638
Dietitian/Nutritionist #33 334-242-4505
Education Administrator #49 334-242-9977
Electrical Contractor #14......................334-269-9990
Electrician, Journeyman #14................334-269-9990
Embalmer #17..334-242-4049
Emergency Medical Technician #50....334-206-5383
Engineer/Engineer in Training #27 334-242-5568
Esthetician School/Salon #11 334-242-1918
Esthetician Student/Instr./School/Pending Exam #11 .
....334-242-1918

Esthetician/Esthetician Apprentice #11.334-242-1918
Firefighter #36...205-391-3776
Forester #26 334-240-9368
Funeral Director #17.............................334-242-4049
Gas Fitter #46...205-945-4857
Geologist #37.............................334-269-9990 x10
Hearing Instrument Dealer #35 334-242-1925
Heating/Air Conditioning Contractor #38................
....334-242-5550
Home Builder #53....................................334-242-2230
Home Health Agency #31.......................334-206-5175
Home Inspector #42................................334-242-7205
Hospice #31...334-206-5175
Hospital #31...334-206-5175
Hospital, Rural Primary Care #31.........334-206-5175
Independent Clinical/Physiological Lab #31..............
....334-206-5175
Insurance Adjuster #39..........................334-241-4126
Insurance Agent #39...............................334-241-4126
Insurance Broker/Producer #39.............334-241-4126
Insurance Company #39..........................334-241-4126
Insurance Corporation/Partnership #39 334-241-4126
Interior Designer #54..............................205-669-0542
Investment Advisor #48..........................334-242-2984
Investment Advisor Rep. #48..................334-242-2984
Landscape Architect #18.........................334-262-1351
Landscape Design #55.............................334-240-7241
Landscape Planter #55............................334-240-7241
Law Enforcement Personnel #44 334-242-4047
Legal/Dental Svc. Representative #39...334-241-4126
Livestock Market Operator #30 334-240-7208
LPG-Liquified Petroleum Gas Broker #40 ....
....334-242-5649

Manicurist Salon/School/Student/Instructor #11.........
....334-242-1918
Manicurist/Manicurist Apprentice/Pending Exam #11
....334-242-1918
Massage Therapist #56......................334-263-3407
Medical Doctor #19..............................334-242-4116
Medical Gas #46....................................205-945-4857
Mental Health Center #31 334-206-5175
Midwife Nurse #21................................334-242-0767
Mine Safety and Inspection #32...........205-254-1275
Mobile Home Manufacturer #41............334-242-4036
Mobile Home Set-up/Installer #41........334-242-4036
Motor Club Representative #39 334-241-4126
Notary Public #42.................................334-242-7205
Nurse #21...334-242-0767
Nurse Anesthetist #21..........................334-242-0767
Nurse-LPN/RN #21...............................334-242-0767
Nursing Home #31.................................334-206-5175
Nursing Home Administrator #22...........334-271-6214
Occup. Therapist Assistant #57............334-353-4466
Occupational Therapist #57...................334-353-4466
Optometrist #20......................................256-538-9903
Osteopathic Physician #19.....................334-242-4116
Pawn Shop #5...334-242-3452
Pest Control #30.....................................334-240-7239
Pesticide Applicator/Dealer #30 334-240-7239
Pharmacist #23.......................................205-967-0130
Physical Therapist/Therapist Asst #24..334-242-4064
Physician Assistant #19.........................334-242-4116
Pilot/Bar Pilot #45..................................251-432-2639
Plumber #46 205-945-4857
Podiatrist #4..205-995-8537
Polygraph Examiner #47 334-260-1182

Preneed Sales Agent #39 334-241-4126
Psychological Technician #16...............334-242-4127
Psychologist #16....................................334-242-4127
Public Accountant-CPA #25...................334-242-5700
Real Estate Appraiser #43 334-242-8747
Real Estate Broker #2............................334-242-5544
Real Estate Salesperson/Agent #2 334-242-5544
Rehabilitation Center #31......................334-206-5175
Reinsurance Intermediary #39..............334-241-4126
Renal Disease (End Stage) Treatment Ctr. #31..........
....334-206-5175
School Bus Driver #49............................334-242-9730
School Counselor #49.............................334-242-9977
Securities Broker/Dealer #48................334-242-2984
Shampoo Assistant #11 334-242-1918
Sleep Disorder Center #31....................334-206-5175
Social Worker #58.................................334-242-5860
Soil Classifier #1....................................334-242-2620
Speech Pathologist/Audiologist #28 334-269-1434
Subcontractor #7....................................334-242-2839
Surface Mining #32................................334-242-8265
Surplus Line Broker #39.........................334-241-4126
Surveyor, Land #27................................334-242-5568
Teacher #49..334-242-9977
Teacher, Elementary School #49..........334-242-9977
Timeshare Real Estate Seller #43 334-242-8747
Timeshare Seller #2...............................334-242-5544
Tree Surgeon #55...................................334-240-7241
Veterinarian #29.....................................256-353-3544
Veterinary Premise Permit #29.............256-353-3544
Veterinary Technician #29 256-353-3544
Water Transportation Personnel #45....251-432-2639
X-ray (Portable) Supplier #31 334-206-5175

Licensing Agency Information

#1 Soil and Water Conservation Committee, 100 N Union St #334, Montgomery, AL 36104-3702; 334-242-2620, Fax: 334-242-0551.

#2 Real Estate Commission, 1201 Carmichael Way, Montgomery, AL 36106; 334-242-5544, Fax: 334-270-9118.
www.arec.state.al.us
Agency email: arec@arec.state.al.us.
Search database at www.arec.state.al.us/search.asp

#3 Alabama State Bar Association, 415 Dexter Ave (36104), Montgomery, AL 36106; 334-269-1515, Fax: 334-261-6310.
www.alabar.org. Agency email: info@alabar.org.
Search database at
www.alabar.org/page.cfm?page=im_include/im_dirSearch.cfm

#4 Board of Podiatry, 13 Innisbrook Ln, Birmingham, AL 35242; 205-995-8537, Fax: 205-995-8537.
www.alabamapodiatryboard.org.

#5 State Banking Department, Licensing and Registration, 401 Adams St, #680, Montgomery, AL 36130; 334-242-3452, Fax: 334-353-5961.
www.bank.state.al.us

#6 Bear Creek Development Authority, PO Box 670, Russellville, AL 35653; 256-332-4392, Fax: 256-332-4372.
www.bearcreeklakes.com/about.html
Agency email: contactus@bearcreeklakes.com.

#7 Board for General Contractors, 2525 Fairlane Drive, Montgomery, AL 36116; 334-272-5030, Fax: 334-395-5336.
http://agencies.state.al.us/gencontrbd/2k-welcome

#8 Board for Registration of Architects, 770 Washington Ave, #150, Montgomery, AL 36130-4450; 334-242-4179, Fax: 334-242-4531.
www.alarchbd.state.al.us
Agency email: cgainey@dsmd.dsmd.state.al.us.
Search database at
www.alarchbd.state.al.us/rostersearch/rostersearch.asp

#9 Board of Auctioneers, 610 S McDonough St, Montgomery, AL 36104-5612; 334-269-9990, Fax: 334-263-6115
Agency email: alaucbd@aol.com.

#10 Board of Chiropractic Examiners, 737 Logan Road, Clanton, AL 35045; 205-755-8000, Fax: 205-755-0081.
http://chiro.state.al.us
Agency email: sbolton@chiro.state.al.us.

#11 Board of Cosmetology, RSA Union Bldg, 100 N Union St #320, Montgomery, AL 36130; 334-242-1918, Fax: 334-242-1926.
www.aboc.state.al.us. Agency email: cosmetology@aboc.state.al.us.

#12 Board of Dental Examiners, 2327-B Pansy St, Huntsville, AL 35801; 256-533-4638, Fax: 256-533-4690.

#13 Board of Dental Scholarship Awards, 1600 University, Volker P115, Birmingham, AL 35294; 205-934-4384, Fax: 205-975-6066.
www.uab.edu/uasom

#14 Board of Electrical Contractors, 660 Adams Ave #301, Montgomery, AL 36104; 334-269-9990, Fax: 334-263-6115.

www.aecb.state.al.us
Agency email: alelectricalbd@aol.com.
Search database at
www.aecb.state.al.us/Search/new_search.asp

#15 Board of Examiners in Counseling, 950 22nd St N. #670, Birmingham, AL 35203; 205-458-8716, Fax: 205-458-8718.
www.abec.state.al.us
Agency email: fhemphill@abec.state.al.us.

#16 Board of Examiners in Psychology, 660 Adams Ave, #360, Mongomery, AL 36104; 334-242-4127.
www.psychology.state.al.us
Agency email: albdpsychology@mindspring.com.

#17 Board of Funeral Service, 11 South Union #219, Montgomery, AL 36130; 334-242-4049, Fax: 334-353-7988.

#18 Board of Landscape Architects, 908 S Hull St, Montgomery, AL 36104; 334-262-1351, Fax: 334-262-1351.

#19 Board of Medical Examiners, 848 Washington Ave, Montgomery, AL 36104; 334-242-4116, Fax: 334-242-4155.
www.albme.org. Agency email: webmaster@albme.org. You can download ASCII and dbf files of currently licensed physicians.

#20 Board of Optometry, 1431 2nd Ave, Bessemer, AL 35020; 205-481-9993, Fax: 205-481-9959.
www.al-optometry.org
Agency email: rpp@al-optometry.com.
Search database at
www.odfinder.org/LicSearch.asp

#21 Board of Nursing, 770 Washington Ave #250, Montgomery, AL 36130-3900; 334-242-4060, Fax: 334-242-4360.
www.abn.state.al.us
Agency email: abn@abn.state.al.us.

#22 Board of Nursing Home Administrators, 4156 Carmichael Road, Montgomery, AL 36106; 334-271-6214, Fax: 334-244-6509.
www.alboenha.state.al.us
Search database at
www.alboenha.state.al.us/logon.html

#23 Board of Pharmacy, 1 Perimeter Park S, #425, Birmingham, AL 35243; 205-967-0130, Fax: 205-967-1009.
www.albop.com

#24 Board of Physical Therapy, 100 N Union St, #627, Montgomery, AL 36130-5040; 334-242-4064, Fax: 334-240-3288.
www.pt.state.al.us
Agency email: kbrown@pt.state.al.us.
Search database at
www.pt.state.al.us/License/searchform.asp

#25 Board of Public Accountancy, PO Box 300375 (770 Washington Ave, #236), Montgomery, AL 36130-0375; 334-242-5700, Fax: 334-240-2711.
www.asbpa.state.al.us
Search database at www.asbpa.state.al.us

#26 Board of Registration for Foresters, 513 Madison Ave, Montgomery, AL 36130; 334-353-3640, Fax: 334-353-3641.
http://home.earthlink.net/~pbsears
Agency email: pbsears@earthlink.net.
Search database at
http://home.earthlink.net/~pbsears/foresters.html

#27 Board of Licensure for Professional Engineers & Land Surveyors, PO Box 304451 (100 North Union St #382), Montgomery, AL 36130-4451; 334-242-5568, Fax: 334-242-5105.
www.bels.state.al.us
Agency email: engineer@bels.state.al.us.
Search database at www.bels.state.al.us/LicenseeSearch/searchmenu.asp

#28 Board of Examiners for Speech-Language Pathology & Audiology, PO Box 304760 (400 S Union St #225), Montgomery, AL 36130-4760; 334-269-1434, Fax: 334-269-6379.
www.mindspring.net/~abespa
Agency email: abespa@mindspring.com.

#29 Board of Veterinary Medical Examiners, PO Box 1968, Decatur, AL 35602; 256-353-3544, Fax: 256-350-5629. Agency email: asbvme@mindspring.com.

#30 Department of Agriculture & Industries, PO Box 3336 (1445 Federal Dr), Montgomery, AL 36109; 334-240-7282, Fax: 334-240-7168.
www.agi.state.al.us

#31 Department of Health, Division of Licensing, 434 Monroe St, Montgomery, AL 36130-3017; 334-206-5175, Fax: 334-206-5219.
www.adph.org
Search database at www.adph.org/providers. The search site is new; enter by clicking on "Facility Directory."

#32 Department of Industrial Relations, State Programs Division, 649 Monroe St, Rm 2211, Montgomery, AL 36131-5200; 334-242-8265, Fax: 334-242-8403.
www.dir.state.al.us/sp
Agency email: wcartwright@dir.state.al.us.

#33 Dietetic/Nutrition Examiners Board, 400 S Union St #445, Montgomery, AL 36104; 334-242-4505, Fax: 334-834-6398.

#35 Hearing Aid Dealers, Executive Secretary, 400 S Union St, #445, Montgomery, AL 36130-3010; 334-242-1925, Fax: 334-834-6389.

#36 Fire College & Personnel Standards Commission, 2501 Phoenix Dr, Tuscaloosa, AL 35405; 205-391-3750, Fax: 205-391-3747.
www.alabamafirecollege.cc.al.us

#37 Board of Licensure of Professional Geologists, 610 S McDonough St, Montgomery, AL 36104; 334-269-9990 x10, Fax: 334-263-6115.
www.algeobd.state.al.us
Agency email: ALGEOBD@aol.com.

#38 Heating & Air Conditioning Contractors Board, 100 N Union St, #630, Montgomery, AL 36130; 334-242-5550, Fax: 334-353-7050.
www.hvacboard.state.al.us

#39 Department of Insurance, Agent Licensing Division, 201 Monroe St #1700, Mongomery, AL 36104; 334-269-3550, Fax: 334-240-3282.
www.aldoi.org
Search database at
www.aldoi.org/licenseesearch.htm

#40 Liquefied Petroleum Gas Board, 818 S Perry St, Montgomery, AL 36104; 334-242-5649, Fax: 334-240-3255.

#41 Manufactured Housing Commission, 350 S Decator St, Montgomery, AL 36104; 334-242-4036, Fax: 334-240-3178.
www.amac.state.al.us

#42 Office of the Secretary of State, PO Box 5616, Montgomery, AL 36104; 334-242-7205, Fax: 334-242-4993.
www.sos.state.al.us.
Agency email: glsecst@glalinc.net.
Search database at
www.sos.state.al.us/sosinfo/inquiry.cfm

#43 Office of the Secretary of State, Real Estate Appraisers Licensing, PO Box 304355 (100 North Union St #370, RSA Bldg), Montgomery, AL 36130; 334-242-8747, Fax: 334-242-8749.
http://reab.state.al.us. Agency email: lbrooks@reab.state.al.us.

#44 Peace Officers Standards & Training Commission, 100 Union St, RSA Union Bldg, #600, Montgomery, AL 36130-0075; 334-242-4045, Fax: 334-242-4633.
www.apostc.state.al.us

#45 Pilotage Commission, PO Box 273, Mobile, AL 36601; 251-432-2639, Fax: 251-432-9964.

#46 Plumbers & Gas Fitters Examining Board, 11 W Oxmoor, #104, Birmingham, AL 35209; 205-945-4857, Fax: 205-945-9915.

www.pgfb.state.al.us
Agency email: staff@pgfb.state.al.us.

#47 Polygraph Examiners Board, 2720-A W Gunter Park Dr, Montgomery, AL 36109; 344-260-1182, Fax: 344-260-8788. Agency email: joanbeck@gsiweb.net.

#48 Securities Division, 770 Washington Ave, #570, Montgomery, AL 36130; 334-242-2984, Fax: 334-242-0240.
www.asc.state.al.us
Agency email: asc@asc.state.al.us.

#49 Department of Education, 50 N Ripley St, Montgomery, AL 36104; 334-242-9977, Fax: 334-242-2818.
www.alsde.edu
Agency email: jmabry@sdenet.alsde.edu.

#50 Department of Health, Emergency Medical Services Division, PO Box 303017, Birmingham, AL 36130-3017; 334-206-5383, Fax: 334-206-5260.
www.alabamafirecollege.cc.al.us/pages/emsdiv.html

#51 Department of Transportation, Flight Standards District Office, 1500 Urban Center Dr #250, Vestavia Hills, AL 35242; 205-731-1557, Fax: 205-731-0939.
www.faa.gov/fsdo/bhm/

#52 Department of Revenue, Athletic Commission - Inactive, 50 N Ripley St Rm 4131, Montgomery, AL 36132; 334-242-1380.

#53 Home Builders Licensure Board, 400 S Union St #195, Montgomery, AL 36130; 334-242-2230, Fax: 334-263-1397.
www.agencies.state.al.us/homebuilders
Search database at
www.hblb.state.al.us/Lic_Search/search.asp

#54 Board of Registration for Interior Designers, PO Box 11026 (65 Bagby Dr #3B), Birmingham, AL 53202; 205-942-6487. Agency email: intdespd@bellsouth.net.

#55 Department of Agriculture & Industries, Plant Protection & Pesticide Management Division, PO Box 3336 - Beard Building, Montgomery, AL 36109-0336; 334-240-7171, Fax: 334-240-7168.

#56 Board of Massage Therapy, 660 Adams Ave #301, Montgomery, AL 36104; 334-269-9990, Fax: 334-263-6115.
www.adeca.state.al.us
Search database at
www.adeca.state.al.us/soicc/soicc/WebSTAR3.0/SOICC/LicOcc/massage.html

#57 Board of Occupational Therapy, 64 N Union St #734, PO Box 304510, Montgomery, AL 36130-4510; 334-353-4466, Fax: 334-353-4465. Agency email: acosby@asbot.state.al.us.

#58 Board of Social Work Examiners, 64 N Union St #129, Montgomery, AL 36130; 334-242-5860, Fax: 334-242-0280.
www.abswe.state.al.us

Alabama Federal Courts

The following list indicates the district and division name for each county in the state. If the bankruptcy court location is different from the district court, then the location of the bankruptcy court appears in parentheses.

County/Court Cross Reference

County	District	Division
Autauga	Middle	Montgomery
Baldwin	Southern	Mobile
Barbour	Middle	Montgomery
Bibb	Northern	Birmingham (Tuscaloosa)
Blount	Northern	Birmingham
Bullock	Middle	Montgomery
Butler	Middle	Montgomery
Calhoun	Northern	Birmingham (Anniston)
Chambers	Middle	Opelika (Montgomery)
Cherokee	Northern	Gadsden (Anniston)
Chilton	Middle	Montgomery
Choctaw	Southern	Mobile
Clarke	Southern	Mobile
Clay	Northern	Birmingham (Anniston)
Cleburne	Northern	Birmingham (Anniston)
Coffee	Middle	Dothan (Montgomery)
Colbert	Northern	Florence (Decatur)
Conecuh	Southern	Mobile
Coosa	Middle	Montgomery
Covington	Middle	Montgomery
Crenshaw	Middle	Montgomery
Cullman	Northern	Huntsville (Decatur)
Dale	Middle	Dothan (Montgomery)
Dallas	Southern	Selma (Mobile)
De Kalb	Northern	Gadsden (Anniston)
Elmore	Middle	Montgomery
Escambia	Southern	Mobile
Etowah	Northern	Gadsden (Anniston)
Fayette	Northern	Jasper (Tuscaloosa)
Franklin	Northern	Florence (Decatur)
Geneva	Middle	Dothan (Montgomery)
Greene	Northern	Birmingham (Tuscaloosa)
Hale	Southern	Selma (Mobile)
Henry	Middle	Dothan (Montgomery)
Houston	Middle	Dothan (Montgomery)
Jackson	Northern	Huntsville (Decatur)
Jefferson	Northern	Birmingham
Lamar	Northern	Jasper (Tuscaloosa)
Lauderdale	Northern	Florence (Decatur)
Lawrence	Northern	Huntsville (Decatur)
Lee	Middle	Opelika (Montgomery)
Limestone	Northern	Huntsville (Decatur)
Lowndes	Middle	Montgomery
Macon	Middle	Opelika (Montgomery)
Madison	Northern	Huntsville (Decatur)
Marengo	Southern	Selma (Mobile)
Marion	Northern	Jasper (Tuscaloosa)
Marshall	Northern	Gadsden (Anniston)
Mobile	Southern	Mobile
Monroe	Southern	Mobile
Montgomery	Middle	Montgomery
Morgan	Northern	Huntsville (Decatur)
Perry	Southern	Selma (Mobile)
Pickens	Northern	Birmingham (Tuscaloosa)
Pike	Middle	Montgomery
Randolph	Middle	Opelika (Montgomery)
Russell	Middle	Opelika (Montgomery)
Shelby	Northern	Birmingham
St. Clair	Northern	Gadsden (Anniston)
Sumter	Northern	Birmingham (Tuscaloosa)
Talladega	Northern	Birmingham (Anniston)
Tallapoosa	Middle	Opelika (Montgomery)
Tuscaloosa	Northern	Birmingham (Tuscaloosa)
Walker	Northern	Jasper (Tuscaloosa)
Washington	Southern	Mobile
Wilcox	Southern	Selma (Mobile)
Winston	Northern	Jasper (Tuscaloosa)

Standards for Federal Courts: The search fee is $20.00 per item (one party name or case number). Certification fee is $7.00 per document. Copy fee is $.50 per page. All fees standard unless noted in profile. Mail Search: always enclose a stamped self addressed envelope unless otherwise noted. Before releasing records, all courts require prepayment unless noted in profile.

Open records are located at the court unless otherwise noted. District courts index by defendant and plaintiff as well as by case number. Bankruptcy courts usually index by debtor and case number. While most courts now have their indexes on computer, many still maintain index card files as well.

The universal PACER sign-up number is 800-676-6856. Find PACER and the Party/Case Index on the Web at http://pacer.psc.uscourts.gov. PACER dial-up access is $.60 per minute. Courts offering internet access via RACER, PACER, Web-PACER or the new CM-ECF charge $.07 per page fee unless noted as free.

US District Court

Middle District of Alabama

Dothan Division c/o Montgomery Division, PO Box 711, Montgomery, AL 36101 (Courier Address: 15 Lee St, Montgomery, AL 36104), 334-223-7308.

www.almd.uscourts.gov

Counties: Coffee, Dale, Geneva, Henry, Houston.

Indexing & Storage: Cases are indexed by defendant, plaintiff, and case number. New cases are available in the index immediately after filing date. Open records are located at the Montgomery Division.

Fee & Payment Notes: Payment may be made by money order, cashier check. Business checks are not accepted. Personal checks are not accepted.

Phone Search: Searching is not available by phone.

In Person Search: In person searching available.

PACER: Local dial-up access: 334-954-3942. Case records are available back to 1994. New records are available online after 1 day.

Montgomery Division Records Search, PO Box 711, Montgomery, AL 36101-0711 (Courier Address: 15 Lee St, Montgomery, AL 36104), 334-223-7308.

www.almd.uscourts.gov

Counties: Autauga, Barbour, Bullock, Butler, Chilton, Coosa, Covington, Crenshaw, Elmore, Lowndes, Montgomery, Pike.

Indexing & Storage: Cases are indexed by defendant, plaintiff, and case number. New cases are available in the index immediately after filing date. Records are also indexed on microfiche. Open records are located at this court.

Fee & Payment Notes: Payment may be made by money order, cashier check, business check. Personal checks are not accepted. Payee: Clerk, US District Court.

Phone Search: Searching is not available by phone.

In Person Search: In person searching available.

PACER: Local dial-up access: 334-954-3942. Case records are available back to 1994. New records are available online after 1 day.

Opelika Division c/o Montgomery Division, PO Box 711, Montgomery, AL 36101 (Courier Address: 15 Lee St, Montgomery, AL 36104), 334-223-7308.

www.almd.uscourts.gov

Counties: Chambers, Lee, Macon, Randolph, Russell, Tallapoosa.

Indexing & Storage: Cases are indexed by defendant, plaintiff, and case number. New cases are available in the index immediately after filing date. Open records are located at the Montgomery Division.

Fee & Payment Notes: Payment may be made by money order, cashier check. Business checks are not accepted. Personal checks are not accepted.

Phone Search: Searching is not available by phone.

Mail Search: A stamped self addressed envelope is not required.

In Person Search: In person searching available.

PACER: Local dial-up access: 334-954-3942. Case records are available back to 1994. New records are available online after 1 day.

US Bankruptcy Court

Middle District of Alabama

Montgomery Division PO Box 1248, Montgomery, AL 36102-1248 (Courier Address: 1 Church St, Montgomery, AL 36104), 334-954-3800, Fax: 334-954-3819.

www.almb.uscourts.gov

Counties: Autauga, Barbour, Bullock, Butler, Chambers, Chilton, Coffee, Coosa, Covington, Crenshaw, Dale, Elmore, Geneva, Henry, Houston, Lee, Lowndes, Macon, Montgomery, Pike, Randolph, Russell, Tallapoosa.

Indexing & Storage: Cases are indexed by debtor as well as by case number. New cases are available in the index 3 days after filing date. Open records are located at this court.

Fee & Payment Notes: Payment may be made by money order, cashier check, business check. Personal checks are not accepted. Court may bill on request. Payee: Clerk of Court.

Phone Search: Docket information is available by phone. An automated voice case information service (VCIS) is available. Call VCIS at 334-206-6359.

Fax Search: The fee is $1.50 per page to fax back.

In Person Search: In person searching available.

PACER: NIBS court. Use of PC Anywhere V4.0 recommended. Case records are available back to case 89-02000. Records are purged every 6 months. New civil records are available online after 2-3 days. WebPacer is available online at https://ecf.almb.uscourts.gov. Document images available.

Electronic Filing: Electronic filing information is available online at https://ecf.almb.uscourts.gov

US District Court

Northern District of Alabama

Birmingham Division Room 104, US Courthouse, 1729 5th Ave N, Birmingham, AL 35203 (Courier Address: Use mail address for courier delivery), 205-278-1700.

www.alnd.uscourts.gov

Counties: Bibb, Blount, Calhoun, Clay, Cleburne, Greene, Jefferson, Pickens, Shelby, Sumter, Talladega, Tuscaloosa.

Indexing & Storage: Cases are indexed by defendant, plaintiff, and case number. New cases are available in the index 2-3 days after filing date. Records are also indexed on microfiche. Open records are located at this court.

Fee & Payment Notes: Payment may be made by money order, cashier check, personal check. Payee: Clerk of Court. You are allowed to make your own copies. These copies cost - current fee is not known - per page.

Phone Search: All public information will be released over the phone.

In Person Search: In person searching available.

PACER: Local dial-up access: 205-731-3502, 205-731-2055. Case records are available back to 1994. Records are purged every 18 months. New records are available online after 1 day. PACER is available online at http://pacer.alnd.uscourts.gov. Document images available.

Florence Division PO Box 776, Florence, AL 35630 (Courier Address: 210 Court St, Florence, AL 35631), 205-760-5815, Fax: 205-760-5727.

www.alnd.uscourts.gov

Counties: Colbert, Franklin, Lauderdale.

Indexing & Storage: Cases are indexed by defendant, plaintiff, and case number. New cases are available in the index 2-3 days after filing date. Records are also indexed on microfiche. Some case files may be held in Birmingham if a Birmingham judge is assigned.

Fee & Payment Notes: Payment may be made by money order, cashier check, personal check. Payee: US District Court.

Phone Search: Only docket information is available by phone.

Mail Search: A stamped self addressed envelope is not required.

In Person Search: In person searching available.

PACER: Local dial-up access: 205-731-3502, 205-731-2055. Case records are available back to 1994. Records are purged every 18 months. New records are available online after 1 day. PACER is available online at http://pacer.alnd.uscourts.gov. Document images available.

Gadsden Division c/o Birmingham Division, Room 140, US Courthouse, 1729 5th Ave N, Birmingham, AL 35203 (Courier Address: Use mail address for courier delivery), 205-278-1700.

www.alnd.uscourts.gov

Counties: Cherokee, De Kalb, Etowah, Marshall, St. Clair.

Indexing & Storage: Cases are indexed by defendant, plaintiff, and case number. New cases are available in the index 2-3 days after filing date. Open records are located at the Birmingham Division.

Fee & Payment Notes: Payment may be made by money order, cashier check. Business checks are not accepted. Personal checks are not accepted.

Phone Search: Searching is not available by phone.

In Person Search: In person searching available.

PACER: Local dial-up access: 205-731-3502, 205-731-2055. Case records are available back to 1994. Records are purged every 18 months. New records are available online after 1 day. PACER is available online at http://pacer.alnd.uscourts.gov. Document images available.

Huntsville Division Clerk's Office, US Post Office & Courthouse, 101 Holmes Ave NE, Huntsville, AL 35801 (Courier Address: Use mail address for courier delivery), 205-534-6495.

www.alnd.uscourts.gov

Counties: Cullman, Jackson, Lawrence, Limestone, Madison, Morgan.

Indexing & Storage: Cases are indexed by defendant, plaintiff, and case number. New cases are available in the index 2 days after filing date. Records are also indexed on microfiche. Open records are located at this court.

Fee & Payment Notes: Payment may be made by money order, cashier check, personal check. Payee: US District Court Clerk.

Phone Search: All public information will be released over the phone.

Mail Search: All requests for criminal searches will be sent to Birmingham. Always enclose a stamped self addressed envelope.

In Person Search: In person searching available.

PACER: Local dial-up access: 205-731-3502, 205-731-2055. Case records are available back to 1994. Records are purged every 18 months. New records are available online after 1 day. PACER is available online at http://pacer.alnd.uscourts.gov. Document images available.

Jasper Division c/o Birmingham Division, Room 140, US Courthouse, 1729 5th Ave N, Birmingham, AL 35203 (Courier Address: Use mail address for courier delivery), 205-278-1700.

www.alnd.uscourts.gov

Counties: Fayette, Lamar, Marion, Walker, Winston.

Indexing & Storage: Cases are indexed by defendant, plaintiff, and case number. New cases are available in the index 2-3 days after filing date. Open records are located at the Birmingham Division. Some. Case records may be held in Florence, depending upon the judge assigned.

Fee & Payment Notes: Payment may be made by money order, cashier check. Business checks are not accepted. Personal checks are not accepted.

Phone Search: Searching is not available by phone.

In Person Search: In person searching available.

PACER: Local dial-up access: 205-731-3502, 205-731-2055. Case records are available back to 1994. Records are purged every 18 months. New records are available online after 1 day. PACER is available online at http://pacer.alnd.uscourts.gov. Document images available.

US Bankruptcy Court

Northern District of Alabama

Anniston Division 914 Noble St, Anniston, AL 36201 (Courier Address: Use mail address for courier delivery), 256-741-1500, Fax: 256-741-1503.

www.alnb.uscourts.gov

Counties: Calhoun, Cherokee, Clay, Cleburne, De Kalb, Etowah, Marshall, St. Clair, Talladega.

Indexing & Storage: Cases are indexed by debtor as well as by case number. New cases are available in the index immediately after filing date. Open records are located at this court.

Fee & Payment Notes: Payment may be made by money order, cashier check, personal check. Payee: Clerk, US Bankruptcy Court, Northern District.

Phone Search: An automated voice case information service (VCIS) is available. Call VCIS at 877-466-8879.

In Person Search: In person searching available.

PACER: Use of PC Anywhere v4.0 suggested. Case records are available back to October 31, 1976. New civil records are available online after 1 day. PACER is available online at http://pacer.alnb.uscourts.gov.

Birmingham Division Room 120, 1800 5th Ave N, Birmingham, AL 35203 (Courier: Use mail address for courier delivery), 205-714-4000.

www.alnb.uscourts.gov

Counties: Blount, Jefferson, Shelby.

Indexing & Storage: Cases are indexed by debtor as well as by case number. New cases are available in the index immediately after filing date. Along with the debtor's name and the case number, the searcher must provide the year the case was closed and the location where the case was filed. Open records are located at this court.

Fee & Payment Notes: Payment may be made by money order, cashier check, personal check. Payee: Clerk, US Bankruptcy Court.

Phone Search: Only docket information is available by phone. An automated voice case information service (VCIS) is available. Call VCIS at 877-466-0795.

In Person Search: In person searching available.

PACER: Use of PC Anywhere v4.0 suggested. Case records are available back to 1992. Records are purged every six months. New civil records are available online after 1 day. PACER is available online at http://pacer.alnb.uscourts.gov.

Decatur Division PO Box 1289, Decatur, AL 35602 (Courier: Room 220, 400 Well St, Decatur, AL 35601), 256-353-2817, Fax: 256-350-7334.

www.alnb.uscourts.gov

Counties: Colbert, Cullman, Franklin, Jackson, Lauderdale, Lawrence, Limestone, Madison, Morgan. The part of Winston County North of Double Springs is handled by this division.

Indexing & Storage: Cases are indexed by debtor as well as by case number. New cases are available in the index immediately after filing date. Along with the debtor's name and the case number, the searcher must provide the year the case was closed and the location where the case was filed. Open records are located at this court.

Fee & Payment Notes: Payment may be made by money order, cashier check, personal check. Payee: Clerk, US Bankruptcy Court.

Phone Search: If a searcher calls, the court will indicate charges but not release information. An automated voice case information service (VCIS) is available. Call VCIS at 877-466-0796 or 256-353-2817.

In Person Search: In person searching available.

PACER: Use of PC Anywhere v4.0 suggested. Case records are available back to 1992. Records are purged every six months. New civil records are available online after 1 day. PACER is available online at http://pacer.alnb.uscourts.gov.

Tuscaloosa Division PO Box 3226, Tuscaloosa, AL 35403 (Courier Address: 1118 Greensboro Ave, Tuscaloosa, AL 35401), 205-752-0426, Fax: 205-752-6468.

www.alnb.uscourts.gov

Counties: Bibb, Fayette, Greene, Lamar, Marion, Pickens, Sumter, Tuscaloosa, Walker, Winston. The part of Winston County North of Double Springs is handled by Decatur Division.

Indexing & Storage: Cases are indexed by debtor as well as by case number. New cases are available in the index 2 days after filing date. Card indexes are maintained on cases filed prior to October 1, 1979. Computer indexes only on cases filed commencing October 1, 1979. Open records are located at this court.

Fee & Payment Notes: Payment may be made by money order, cashier check, business check. Personal checks are not accepted. Payee: Clerk, US Bankruptcy Court.

Phone Search: An automated voice case information service (VCIS) is available. Call VCIS at 877-466-9267 or 205-752-0426.

In Person Search: In person searching available.

PACER: Use of PC Anywhere v4.0 suggested. Case records are available back to 1990. Records are never purged. New civil records are available online after 1 day. PACER is available online at http://pacer.alnb.uscourts.gov.

US District Court

Southern District of Alabama

Mobile Division Clerk, 113 St Joseph St, Mobile, AL 36602 (Courier Address: Use mail address for courier delivery), 251-690-2371.

www.als.uscourts.gov

Counties: Baldwin, Choctaw, Clarke, Conecuh, Escambia, Mobile, Monroe, Washington.

Indexing & Storage: Cases are indexed by defendant, plaintiff, and case number. New cases are available in the index immediately after filing date. Open records are located at this court.

Fee & Payment Notes: Payment may be made by money order, cashier check, personal check. Payee: Clerk, US District Court. You are allowed to make your own copies. These copies cost $.25 per page.

Phone Search: Will only check docket information for a case number over the phone.

In Person Search: In person searching available.

PACER: Toll-free dial-up access: 800-622-9392. Local dial-up access: 334-694-4672. Case records

are available back to 1993. New records are available online after 1 day. PACER is available online at http://pacer.alsd.uscourts.gov.

Other Online Access: Search records on the Internet using RACER; connect via the link at www.als.uscourts.gov.

Selma Division c/o Mobile Division, 113 St Joseph St, Mobile, AL 36602 (Courier: Use mail address for courier delivery), 251-690-2371.

www.als.uscourts.gov

Counties: Dallas, Hale, Marengo, Perry, Wilcox.

Indexing & Storage: Cases are indexed by defendant, plaintiff, and case number. New cases are available in the index immediately after filing date. Open records are located at the Mobile Division.

Fee & Payment Notes: Payment may be made by money order, cashier check. Business checks are not accepted. Personal checks are not accepted.

Phone Search: Searching is not available by phone.

In Person Search: In person searching available.

PACER: Toll-free dial-up access: 800-622-9392. Local dial-up access: 334-694-4672. Case records are available back to 1993. New records are available online after 1 day. PACER is available online at http://pacer.alsd.uscourts.gov.

Other Online Access: Search records on the Internet using RACER; connect via the link at www.als.uscourts.gov.

US Bankruptcy Court

Southern District of Alabama

Mobile Division Clerk, 201 St. Louis St, Mobile, AL 36602 (Courier Address: Use mail address for courier delivery), 251-441-5391, Fax: 251-441-6286.

www.alsb.uscourts.gov

Counties: Baldwin, Choctaw, Clarke, Conecuh, Dallas, Escambia, Hale, Marengo, Mobile, Monroe, Perry, Washington, Wilcox.

Indexing & Storage: Cases are indexed by debtor as well as by case number. New cases are available in the index immediately after filing date. District wide computer searches are available for information from 1985 for this court.

Fee & Payment Notes: Payment may be made by money order, cashier check, business check. Personal checks are not accepted. Payee: Clerk, US Bankruptcy Court. You are allowed to make your own copies. These copies cost $.25 per page.

Phone Search: Only the name and case number is released over the phone. An automated voice case information service (VCIS) is available. Call VCIS at 334-441-5637.

Mail Search: A stamped self addressed envelope is not required.

In Person Search: In person searching available.

PACER: Case records are available back to 1993. New civil records are available online after 1 day.

Electronic Filing: Electronic filing information is available online at https://ecf.alsb.uscourts.gov.

Other Online Access: Check www.alsb.uscourts.gov/EFiling.htm for latest ECF updates.

Alabama County Courts

Court	Jurisdiction	No. of Courts	How Organized
Circuit Courts*	General	17	40 Circuits
District Courts*	Limited	15	67 Districts
Combined Courts*		61	
Municipal Courts	Municipal	253	
Probate Courts*	Probate	68	

* Profiled in this Sourcebook.

Court	CIVIL								
	Tort	Contract	Real Estate	Min. Claim	Max. Claim	Small Claims	Estate	Eviction	Domestic Relations
Circuit Courts*	X	X	X	$3000	No Max				X
District Courts*	X	X	X	$3000	$10,000	$3000		X	
Municipal Courts									
Probate Courts*							X		

Court	CRIMINAL				
	Felony	Misdemeanor	DWI/DUI	Preliminary Hearing	Juvenile
Circuit Courts*	X				
District Courts*		X	X	X	X
Municipal Courts		X	X		
Probate Courts*					

ADMINISTRATION   Director of Courts, 300 Dexter Ave, Montgomery, AL, 36104; 334-242-0300, Fax: 334-242-2099. www.alacourt.org

COURT STRUCTURE   Circuit Courts are the courts of general jurisdiction; District Courts have limited jurisdiction in civil matters. These courts are combined in all but eight larger counties. Barbour, Coffee, Jefferson, St. Clair, Talladega, and Tallapoosa Counties have two court locations within the county.

Jefferson County (Birmingham), Madison (Huntsville), Marshall, and Tuscaloosa Counties have separate criminal divisions for Circuit and/or District Courts. Misdemeanors committed with felonies are tried with the felony. The Circuit Courts are appeals courts for misdemeanors.

District Courts can receive guilty pleas in felony cases.

ONLINE ACCESS   In the past, the state offered a commercial remote access to the State Judicial Information System (SJIS), but they are no longer adding new users. Instead, they are reccommending new users to contact a designated private vendor. For more information, visit their web site at www.alacourt.com, note that fees are involved.

State Supreme Court and Appellette decisions are available at www.alalinc.net.

ADDITIONAL INFORMATION   Although in most counties Circuit and District courts are combined, each index may be separate. Therefore, when you request a search of both courts, be sure to state that the search is to cover "both the Circuit and District Court records." Several offices do not perform searches. Some offices do not have public access computer terminals.

Autauga County

Circuit & District Court 134 N Court St, #114, Prattville, AL 36067-3049; 334-361-3737. Hours: 8AM-5PM (CST). *Felony, Misdemeanor, Civil, Eviction, Small Claims.*

Civil Records: Access: Mail, online, in person. Both court and visitors may perform in person searches. No search fee. Required to search: name, years to search. Civil cases indexed by defendant, plaintiff. Civil records on computer since 1977 and in books from 1950. Online access available through SJIS. See state introduction.

Criminal Records: Access: Mail, online, in person. Both court and visitors may perform in person searches. No search fee. Required to search: name, years to search; also helpful: DOB, SSN. Criminal records on computer since 1977 and in books from 1950. Online access available through SJIS. See state introduction.

General Information: Public access terminal is available. No sealed, adoptions, youthful offenders or juvenile records released. Turnaround time 1-2 weeks. Copy fee: $.25 per page. Certification fee: $2.25. Fee payee: Circuit Court. Only cashiers checks and money orders accepted. Prepayment is required.

Probate Court 176 W 5th, Prattville, AL 36067; 334-361-3728/4842; Fax: 334-361-3740. Hours: 8:30AM-5PM (CST). *Probate.*

Baldwin County

Circuit & District Court 312 Courthouse Sq #10, Bay Minette, AL 36507; 251-937-0370; Civil phone: 251-937-0277; Criminal phone: 251-937-0280. Hours: 8AM-4:30PM (CST). *Felony, Misdemeanor, Civil, Eviction, Small Claims.*

Civil Records: Access: Online, in person. Visitors must perform in person searches for themselves. Search fee: No search fee. Required to search: name, years to search. Civil cases indexed by defendant, plaintiff. Civil records indexed on computer from 1977, index books by case # to early 1900s. Online access available through SJIS. See state introduction.

Criminal Records: Access: Online, in person. Visitors must perform in person searches for themselves. Search fee: No search fee. Required to search: name, years to search, DOB. Criminal records indexed on computer from 1977, index books by case # to early 1900s. Online access available through SJIS. See state introduction.

General Information: Public access terminal is available. No sealed, adoptions, youthful offenders or juvenile records released. Certification fee: $1.25 per page. Fee payee: Circuit Court Clerk. Only cashiers checks and money orders accepted. Prepayment is required.

Probate Court PO Box 459, Bay Minette, AL 36507; 251-937-9561. Hours: 8AM-4:30PM (CST). *Probate.*

Note: Online access to probate property records is available free at www.deltacomputersystems.com/al/al05/probatea.html.

Barbour County

Circuit & District Court - Clayton Division PO Box 219, Clayton, AL 36016; 334-775-8366; Probate phone: 334-775-8371; Fax: 334-775-1125. Hours: 8AM-5PM (CST). *Felony, Misdemeanor, Civil, Eviction, Small Claims, Probate.*

Note: Probate court is separate from this court, and can be contacted at the telephone number above.

Civil Records: Access: Phone, mail, online, in person. Both court and visitors may perform in person searches. Search fee: $5.00 per name. Fee is per division. Required to search: name, years to search. Civil cases indexed by defendant. Civil records on computer back

to 1993; books from 1977; archives back to 1920. Online access available through SJIS. See state introduction.

Criminal Records: Access: Mail, online, in person. Both court and visitors may perform in person searches. Search fee: $5.00 per name. $5.00 per division. Required to search: name, years to search, DOB; also helpful: SSN. Criminal records on computer back to 1993, books from 1977; archives back to 1920. Online access available through SJIS. See state introduction.

General Information: Public access terminal is available. No sealed, adoptions, youthful offenders records released. SASE required. Turnaround time 2-3 days. Fax notes: Fee to fax results is $.50 per page. Copy fee: $.50 per page. Certification fee: $1.50. Fee payee: David S Nix. Business checks accepted.

Circuit & District Court - Eufaula Division

303 E Broad St, Rm 201, Eufaula, AL 36027; 334-687-1513/1516; Probate phone: 334-687-1530; Fax: 334-687-1599. Hours: 8AM-4:30PM (CST). *Misdemeanor, Civil, Eviction, Small Claims, Probate.*

Note: Probate court is separate from this court, and can be contacted at the telephone number above.

Civil Records: Access: Online, in person. Visitors must perform in person searches for themselves. No search fee. Required to search: name, years to search. Civil cases indexed by defendant, plaintiff. Civil records on computer from 1993. Index from 1977 to present, records are easily searched, prior to 1977 more difficult to search. Online access available through SJIS. See state introduction.

Criminal Records: Access: Online, in person. Visitors must perform in person searches for themselves. No search fee. Required to search: name, years to search; also helpful: DOB, SSN. Criminal records on computer from 1993. Index from 1977 to present, records are easily searched, prior to 1977 more difficult to search. Online access available through SJIS. See state introduction.

General Information: Public access terminal is available. No sealed, adoptions, youthful offenders or juvenile records released. Copy fee: $.25 per page. Certification fee: $3.00. Fee payee: Clerk of Courts. Personal checks accepted. Prepayment is required.

Bibb County

Circuit & District Court Bibb County Courthouse, PO Box 185, Centreville, AL 35042; 205-926-3103 Civil (Circuit); Civil phone: 205-926-3100 (Dist); Criminal phone: 205-926-3107; Probate phone: 205-926-3108; Fax: 205-926-3132. Hours: 8AM-5PM (CST). *Felony, Misdemeanor, Civil, Eviction, Small Claims, Probate.*

Note: Probate court is separate from this court, and can be contacted at the telephone number above.

Civil Records: Access: Mail, online, in person. Both court and visitors may perform in person searches. No search fee. Required to search: name, years to search. Civil cases indexed by defendant. Civil records on index book back to 1940s. Online access available through SJIS. See state introduction.

Criminal Records: Access: Mail, online, in person. Both court and visitors may perform in person searches. No search fee. Required to search: name, years to search, DOB; also helpful: SSN. Criminal records on computer from 1988, on index books back to 1940s. Online access available through SJIS. See state introduction.

General Information: Public access terminal is available. No sealed, adoptions, youthful offenders or juvenile records released. SASE required. Turnaround time 3-4 days. Copy fee: $.25 per page. Certification fee: $1.00 plus $.25 per page. Fee payee: John H Stacy, Clerk. Business checks accepted. Prepayment required.

Blount County

Circuit & District Court 220 2nd Ave East Room 208, Oneonta, AL 35121; 205-625-4153. Hours: 8AM-5PM (CST). *Felony, Misdemeanor, Civil, Eviction, Small Claims.*

Civil Records: Access: Mail, online, in person. Both court and visitors may perform in person searches. Search fee: $10.00 per name. Required to search: name, years to search. Civil cases indexed by defendant, plaintiff. Civil records on computer from March 1994, on index books from 1977. Online access available through SJIS. See state introduction.

Criminal Records: Access: Mail, online, in person. Both court and visitors may perform in person searches. Search fee: $10.00 per name. Required to search: name, years to search, DOB; also helpful: SSN. Criminal records on computer from March 1994, on index books from 1977. Online access available through SJIS. See state introduction.

General Information: Public access terminal is available. No sealed, adoptions, youthful offenders or juvenile records released. SASE required. Turnaround time up to 1 month. Copy fee: $.25 per page. Certification fee: $1.25. Fee payee: Mike Chriswell. No personal checks accepted. Prepayment is required.

Probate Court 220 2nd Ave E, Oneonta, AL 35121; 205-625-4191/4180; Fax: 205-625-4206. Hours: 8AM-5PM (CST). *Probate.*

Bullock County

Circuit & District Court PO Box 230, Union Springs, AL 36089; 334-738-2280; Probate phone: 334-738-2250; Fax: 334-738-2282. Hours: 8AM-4:30PM (CST). *Felony, Misdemeanor, Civil, Eviction, Small Claims, Probate.*

Note: Probate court is separate from this court, and can be contacted at the telephone number above.

Civil Records: Access: Phone, fax, mail, online, in person. Both court and visitors may perform in person searches. No search fee. Required to search: name, years to search. Civil cases indexed by defendant, plaintiff. Civil records on index books back to 1930s; on computer back to 1995. Online access available through SJIS. See state introduction.

Criminal Records: Access: Phone, fax, mail, online, in person. Only the court performs in person searches; visitors may not. No search fee. Required to search: name, years to search, DOB; also helpful: SSN, signed release. Criminal records on index books back to 1930s; on computer back to 1995. Online access available through SJIS. See state introduction.

General Information: Public access terminal is available. (Terminal for civil records only) No sealed, adoptions, youthful offenders or juvenile records released. SASE required. Turnaround time depends on clerk availability. Fax notes: No fee to fax results.

Butler County

Circuit & District Court PO Box 236, Greenville, AL 36037; 334-382-3521; Probate phone: 334-382-3512. Hours: 8AM-4PM (CST). *Felony, Misdemeanor, Civil, Eviction, Small Claims, Probate.*

Note: Probate court is separate from this court, and can be contacted at the telephone number above.

Civil Records: Access: Mail, online, in person. Both court and visitors may perform in person searches. Search fee: $5.00 per name. Fee is for first 2-3 years. Required to search: name, years to search. Civil cases indexed by defendant, plaintiff. Civil records on computer from 1992, books to 1979. Online access available through SJIS. See state introduction.

Criminal Records: Access: Mail, online, in person. Both court and visitors may perform in person searches. Search fee: $5.00 per name. Fee for first 2-3 years.

Required to search: name, years to search; also helpful: SSN, DOB. Criminal records on computer from 1992, books to 1979. Online access available through SJIS. See state introduction.

General Information: Public access terminal is available. No sealed, adoptions, youthful offenders or juvenile records released. SASE requested. Turnaround time 1-2 weeks. Fax notes: Fee to fax results is $.50 per page. Copy fee: $.50 per page. Certification fee: $1.50 per page. Fee payee: Butler County District Court. Business checks accepted. Prepayment is required.

Calhoun County

Circuit Court 25 W 11th St, #300, Anniston, AL 36201; 256-231-1750; Fax: 256-231-1826. Hours: 8AM-4:30PM (CST). *Felony, Civil Actions Over $10,000.*

Civil Records: Access: Online, in person. Visitors must perform in person searches for themselves. No search fee. Required to search: name, years to search. Civil cases indexed by defendant, plaintiff. Civil records indexed on computer from 1970s, prior in books. Online access available through SJIS. See state introduction.

Criminal Records: Access: Online, mail, in person. Visitors must perform in person searches for themselves. No search fee. Required to search: name, years to search, DOB; also helpful: SSN. Criminal records indexed on computer from 1970s, prior on books. Online access available through SJIS. See state introduction. The County sex offender registry is available online at www.calhouncountysheriff.org/html/Framsex.html. From Sept. 1999 forward only.

General Information: Public access terminal is available. No sealed, adoptions, youthful offenders or juvenile records released. Turnaround time 2-4 days. Copy fee: $.25 per page. Certification fee: $1.00. Personal checks accepted. Prepayment is required.

District Court 25 W 11th St, Box 9, Anniston, AL 36201; 256-231-1850; Fax: 256-231-1826. Hours: 8AM-4:30PM (CST). *Misdemeanor, Civil Actions Under $10,000, Eviction, Small Claims.*

Civil Records: Access: Online, in person. Visitors must perform in person searches for themselves. No search fee. Required to search: name, years to search. Civil cases indexed by defendant, plaintiff. Civil records on computer from 1989, books from 1977 to 1989. Online access available through SJIS. See state introduction.

Criminal Records: Access: Online, in person. Visitors must perform in person searches for themselves. No search fee. Required to search: name, years to search; also helpful: SSN. Criminal records on computer from 1989, books from 1977 to 1989. Online access available through SJIS. See state introduction.

General Information: Public access terminal is available. No sealed, adoptions, youthful offenders or juvenile records released. Copy fee: $.25 per page. Certification fee: $1.25. Fee payee: District Court. Personal checks accepted. Prepayment is required.

Probate Court 1702 Noble St, #102, Anniston, AL 36201; 256-241-2825. *Probate.*

Chambers County

Circuit & District Court Chambers County Courthouse - Clerks Office, Lafayette, AL 36862; 334-864-4348; Probate phone: 334-864-4372. Hours: 8AM-4:30PM (CST). *Felony, Misdemeanor, Civil, Eviction, Small Claims, Probate.*

Note: Probate court is separate from this court, and can be contacted at the telephone number above.

Civil Records: Access: Mail, online, in person. Both court and visitors may perform in person searches. Search fee: None for mail. Required to search: name, years to search. Civil cases indexed by defendant, plaintiff. Civil records on computer from 4/93, on index

books to early 1900s. Online access available through SJIS. See state introduction.

Criminal Records: Access: Mail, online, in person. Both court and visitors may perform in person searches. Search fee: None for mail. Required to search: name, years to search; also helpful: DOB, SSN. Criminal records are computerized since 1993. Online access available through SJIS. See state introduction.

General Information: Public access terminal is available. No sealed, adoptions, youthful offenders or juvenile records released. Turnaround time 1 week. Copy fee: $.25 per page. Certification fee: $1.00. Business checks accepted.

Cherokee County

Circuit & District Court 100 Main St, Rm 203, Centre, AL 35960-1532; 256-927-3340. Hours: 8AM-4:30PM (CST). *Felony, Misdemeanor, Civil, Eviction, Small Claims.*

Civil Records: Access: Mail, online, in person. Both court and visitors may perform in person searches. No search fee. Required to search: name, years to search. Civil cases indexed by defendant, plaintiff. Civil records on books from 1977. Online access available through SJIS. See state introduction.

Criminal Records: Access: Mail, online, in person. Both court and visitors may perform in person searches. No search fee. Required to search: name, years to search; also helpful: DOB, SSN. Criminal records on books from 1977. Online access available through SJIS. See state introduction.

General Information: Public access terminal is available. No sealed, adoptions, youthful offenders or juvenile records released. Turnaround time up to 2 wks. Copy fee: $.25 per page. Certification fee: $1.00. Fee payee: Circuit Clerk. Business checks accepted. Prepayment is required.

Probate Court 100 Main St, Rm 204, Centre, AL 35960; 256-927-3363; Fax: 256-927-6949. Hours: 8AM-4PM M-F, 8AM-Noon Sat (CST). *Probate.*

Chilton County

Circuit & District Court PO Box 1946, Clanton, AL 35046; 205-755-4275; Probate phone: 205-755-1555. Hours: 8AM-5PM (CST). *Felony, Misdemeanor, Civil, Eviction, Small Claims, Probate.*

Note: Probate court is separate from this court, and can be contacted at the telephone number above.

Civil Records: Access: Online, in person. Visitors must perform in person searches for themselves. No search fee. Required to search: name, years to search. Civil cases indexed by defendant, plaintiff. Civil records on computer from 9/93, on books from 1950s. Online access available through SJIS. See state introduction.

Criminal Records: Access: Online, in person. Visitors must perform in person searches for themselves. No search fee. Required to search: name, years to search; also helpful: DOB, SSN. Criminal records on computer since 1977. Online access available through SJIS. See state introduction.

General Information: Public access terminal is available. No sealed, adoptions, youthful offenders or juvenile records released. Copy fee: $.25 per page. Certification fee: $1.00. Fee payee: Clerk. Business checks accepted. Prepayment is required.

Choctaw County

Circuit & District Court Choctaw County Courthouse, Ste 10, PO Box 428, Butler, AL 36904; 205-459-2155; Probate phone: 205-459-2417. Hours: 8AM-4:30PM (CST). *Felony, Misdemeanor, Civil, Eviction, Small Claims, Probate.*

Note: Probate court is separate from this court, and can be contacted at the telephone number above.

Civil Records: Access: Mail, online, in person. Both court and visitors may perform in person searches. No search fee. Required to search: name, years to search. Civil cases indexed by defendant, plaintiff. Civil records on index books from 1940. Putting records on computer starting September 1994. Online access available through SJIS. See state introduction.

Criminal Records: Access: Mail, online, in person. Both court and visitors may perform in person searches. No search fee. Required to search: name, years to search; also helpful: DOB, SSN. Criminal records on index books from 1940. Putting records on computer starting September 1994. Online access available through SJIS. See state introduction.

General Information: Public access terminal is available. No sealed, adoptions, youthful offenders or juvenile records released. Copy fee: $.25 per page. Certification fee: $1.00. Fee payee: Circuit Clerk. Business checks accepted. Prepayment is required.

Clarke County

Circuit & District Court PO Box 921, Grove Hill, AL 36451; 251-275-3363; Probate phone: 251-275-3251. Hours: 8AM-5PM (CST). *Felony, Misdemeanor, Civil, Eviction, Small Claims, Probate.*

Note: Probate court is separate from this court, and can be contacted at the telephone number above.

Civil Records: Access: Mail, online, in person. Both court and visitors may perform in person searches. Search fee: $5.00 per name. Required to search: name, years to search. Civil cases indexed by defendant, plaintiff. Civil records on index cards from 1977. Online access available through SJIS. See state introduction.

Criminal Records: Access: Mail, online, in person. Both court and visitors may perform in person searches. Search fee: $5.00 per name. Required to search: name, years to search; also helpful: DOB, SSN. Criminal records on index cards from 1977. Online access available through SJIS. See state introduction.

General Information: No sealed, adoptions, youthful offenders or juvenile records released. Turnaround time 1 week. Copy fee: $.40 per page. Certification fee: $2.50. Fee payee: Circuit Clerk. Business checks accepted.

Clay County

Circuit & District Court PO Box 816, Ashland, AL 36251; 256-354-7926; Probate phone: 256-354-2198. Hours: 8AM-4:30PM (CST). *Felony, Misdemeanor, Civil, Eviction, Small Claims, Probate.*

Note: Probate court is separate from this court, and can be reached at the telephone number given above.

Civil Records: Access: Mail, online, in person. Visitors must perform in person searches for themselves. No search fee. Required to search: name, years to search. Civil cases indexed by defendant, plaintiff. Overall records go back to 1977; computerized records go back to 1994. Online access available through SJIS. See state introduction.

Criminal Records: Access: Mail, online, in person. Visitors must perform in person searches for themselves. No search fee. Required to search: name, years to search; also helpful: SSN, DOB, signed release. Overall records go back to 1977; computerized records go back to 1994. Online access available through SJIS. See state introduction.

General Information: Public access terminal is available. No sealed, adoptions, youthful offenders or juvenile records released. Fax notes: Fee to fax results is $1.00 per page. Copy fee: $.25 per page. Certification fee: $1.25. Fee payee: Circuit Clerk. Business checks accepted.

Cleburne County

Circuit & District Court 120 Vickery St Room 202, Heflin, AL 36264; 256-463-2651; Probate phone: 256-463-5655; Fax: 256-463-2257. Hours: 8AM-4:30PM (CST). *Felony, Misdemeanor, Civil, Eviction, Small Claims, Probate.*

Note: Probate court is separate from this court, and can be contacted at the telephone number above.

Civil Records: Access: Phone, mail, online, in person. Both court and visitors may perform in person searches. No search fee. Required to search: name, years to search. Civil cases indexed by defendant, plaintiff. Civil records on computer from 1993, on books and cards from 1900. Online access available through SJIS. See state introduction.

Criminal Records: Access: Phone, mail, online, in person. Both court and visitors may perform in person searches. No search fee. Required to search: name, years to search, DOB; also helpful: SSN. Criminal records on computer from 1993, on books and cards from 1900. Online access available through SJIS. See state introduction.

General Information: Public access terminal is available. No sealed, adoptions, youthful offenders or juvenile records released. SASE required. Turnaround time 1-2 days. Copy fee: $.25 per page. Certification fee: $1.00. Fee payee: Clerk. Only cashiers checks and money orders accepted.

Coffee County

Circuit & District Court - Elba Division 230 M Court Ave, Elba, AL 36323; 334-897-2954. Hours: 8AM-noon, 1-5PM (CST). *Felony, Misdemeanor, Civil, Eviction, Small Claims, Probate.*

Civil Records: Access: Mail, online, in person. Both court and visitors may perform in person searches. No search fee. Required to search: name, years to search. Civil cases indexed by defendant. Civil records on computer back to 8/1993. Online access available through SJIS. See state introduction.

Criminal Records: Access: Mail, online, in person. Both court and visitors may perform in person searches. No search fee. Required to search: name, years to search; also helpful: DOB. Criminal records on computer back to 8/1993. Online access available through SJIS. See state introduction.

General Information: Public access terminal is available. No sealed, adoptions, youthful offenders or juvenile records released. SASE required. Turnaround time 3-4 days. Copy fee: $.25 per page. Certification fee: $1.25. Fee payee: Circuit Clerk. Business checks accepted.

Circuit & District Court - Enterprise Division PO Box 1294, Enterprise, AL 36331; 334-347-2519. Hours: 8AM-5PM (CST). *Felony, Misdemeanor, Civil, Eviction, Small Claims.*

Civil Records: Access: Mail, fax, online, in person. Both court and visitors may perform in person searches. No search fee. Required to search: name, years to search. Civil cases indexed by defendant, plaintiff. Civil records on computer since 8/1993. Online access available through SJIS. See state introduction.

Criminal Records: Access: Mail, fax, online, in person. Both court and visitors may perform in person searches. No search fee. Required to search: name, years to search, DOB; also helpful: SSN. Criminal records on computer since 8/1993. Online access available through SJIS. See state introduction.

General Information: No sealed, adoptions, youthful offenders or juvenile records released. Turnaround time up to 1 week. Copy fee: $.25 per page. Certification fee: $1.25. Fee payee: Clerk of Courts. Only cashiers checks and money orders accepted. Prepayment is required.

Probate Court - Enterprise Division PO Box 311247, Enterprise, AL 36331; 334-347-2688; Fax: 334-347-2095. Hours: 8AM-4:30PM (CST). *Probate.*

Colbert County

Circuit Court Colbert County Courthouse, 201 N Main Street, Tuscumbia, AL 35674; 256-386-8512; Probate phone: 256-386-8542. Hours: 8AM-4:30PM (CST). *Felony, Civil Actions Over $10,000, Probate.*

Note: Probate court is separate from this court, and can be contacted at the telephone number above.

Civil Records: Access: Online, in person. Visitors must perform in person searches for themselves. No search fee. Required to search: name, years to search. Civil cases indexed by defendant, plaintiff. Civil records on computer from 1993, books from 1959. Online access available through SJIS. See state introduction.

Criminal Records: Access: Online, in person. Visitors must perform in person searches for themselves. No search fee. Required to search: name, years to search; also helpful: DOB, SSN. Criminal records on computer from 1993, books prior. Online access available through SJIS. See state introduction.

General Information: Public access terminal is available. No sealed, youthful offenders or juvenile records released. Copy fee: $.25 per page. Certification fee: $1.00. Fee payee: Circuit Court Clerk. Business checks accepted. Prepayment is required.

District Court Colbert County Courthouse, 201 N Main Street, Tuscumbia, AL 35674; 256-386-8518. Hours: 8AM-Noon; 1PM-4:30PM (CST). *Misdemeanor, Civil Actions Under $10,000, Eviction, Small Claims.*

Civil Records: Access: Online, in person. Visitors must perform in person searches for themselves. No search fee. Required to search: name, years to search. Civil cases indexed by defendant, plaintiff. Civil records on computer from 1993, prior on books. Online access available through SJIS. See state introduction.

Criminal Records: Access: Online, in person. Visitors must perform in person searches for themselves. No search fee. Required to search: name, years to search; also helpful: SSN. Criminal records on computer from 1993, prior on books. Online access available through SJIS. See state introduction.

General Information: Public access terminal is available. No sealed, adoptions, youthful offenders or juvenile records released. Copy fee: $.25 per page. Certification fee: $1.00. Fee payee: Circuit Clerk. Only cashiers checks and money orders accepted. Prepayment is required.

Conecuh County

Circuit & District Court PO Box 107, Evergreen, AL 36401; 251-578-2066; Probate phone: 251-578-1221. Hours: 8AM-4:30PM (CST). *Felony, Misdemeanor, Civil, Eviction, Small Claims, Probate.*

Note: Probate court is separate from this court, and can be contacted at the telephone number above.

Civil Records: Access: Mail, online, in person. Both court and visitors may perform in person searches. No search fee. Required to search: name, years to search. Civil cases indexed by defendant, plaintiff. Civil records on index cards from 1977, on computer back to 12/1994. Online access available through SJIS. See state introduction.

Criminal Records: Access: Mail, online, in person. Both court and visitors may perform in person searches. No search fee. Required to search: name, years to search, DOB; also helpful: SSN. Criminal records on index cards from 1977, on computer back to 1994. Online access available through SJIS. See state introduction.

General Information: Public access terminal is available. No sealed, adoptions, youthful offenders or juvenile records released. Turnaround time 1 week. Fax notes: Fee to fax results is $1.00 per page. Copy fee: $.50 per page. Certification fee: $2.50. Fee payee: Circuit Clerk, George Hendrix. Business checks accepted. Prepayment is required.

Coosa County

Circuit & District Court PO Box 98, Rockford, AL 35136; 256-377-4988; Probate phone: 256-377-4919. Hours: 8AM-4:30PM (CST). *Felony, Misdemeanor, Civil, Eviction, Small Claims, Probate.*

Note: Probate court is separate from this court, and can be contacted at the telephone number above.

Civil Records: Access: Online, in person. Visitors must perform in person searches for themselves. No search fee. Required to search: name, years to search. Civil cases indexed by plaintiff. Civil records on books from the late 1800s, computerized records go back to July 1994. Online access available through SJIS. See state introduction.

Criminal Records: Access: Online, in person. Visitors must perform in person searches for themselves. No search fee. Required to search: name, years to search; also helpful: DOB, SSN. Criminal records on books from the late 1800s, computerized records go back to July 1994. Online access available through SJIS. See state introduction.

General Information: No sealed, adoptions, youthful offenders or juvenile records released. Copy fee: $.25 per page. Certification fee: $1.00. Fee payee: Clerk of Court. Business checks accepted.

Covington County

Circuit & District Court Covington County Courthouse, Andalusia, AL 36420; 334-428-2520; Probate phone: 334-428-2510. Hours: 8AM-5PM (CST). *Felony, Misdemeanor, Civil, Eviction, Small Claims, Probate.*

Note: Probate court is separate from this court, and can be contacted at the telephone number above.

Civil Records: Access: Online, in person. Both the court and visitors may perform in person searches. Search fee: $.25 per copy. Required to search: name, years to search. Civil cases indexed by defendant, plaintiff. Civil records on computer from 3/94; prior on books to 1920. Online access available through SJIS. See state introduction. Also, online access to probate records is available by subscription at www.recordsusa.com/Alabama/CovingtonCnAl.htm. Credit card, username and password is required; choose either monthly or per-use plan. Visit the web site or call Lisa at 601-264-7701 for information.

Criminal Records: Access: Online, in person. Both the court and visitors may perform in person searches. Search fee: $.25 per copy. Required to search: name, years to search, DOB; also helpful: SSN. Criminal records on computer from 3/94; prior on books to 1920. Online access available through SJIS. See state introduction.

General Information: Public access terminal is available. No sealed, adoptions, youthful offenders or juvenile records released. Copy fee: $.25 per page. Certification fee: $1.00. Fee payee: Circuit Clerk. Business checks accepted.

Crenshaw County

Circuit & District Court PO Box 167, Luverne, AL 36049; 334-335-6575; Probate phone: 334-335-6568; Fax: 334-335-2076. Hours: 8AM-4:30PM (CST). *Felony, Misdemeanor, Civil, Eviction, Small Claims, Probate.*

Note: Probate court is separate from this court, and can be contacted at the telephone number above. Their address is PO Box 328, Luverne 36049.

Civil Records: Access: Mail, online, in person. Both court and visitors may perform in person searches. No search fee. Required to search: name, years to search. Civil cases indexed by defendant, plaintiff. Civil records on computer from 1993, on book from 1977. Online access available through SJIS. See state introduction.

Criminal Records: Access: Mail, online, in person. Both court and visitors may perform in person searches. No search fee. Required to search: name, years to search, DOB; also helpful: SSN. Criminal records on computer from 1993, on book from 1977. Online access available through SJIS. See state introduction.

General Information: Public access terminal is available. No sealed, adoptions, youthful offenders or juvenile records released. SASE requested. Turnaround time 2-3 days. Copy fee: $.50 per page. Certification fee: $1.00. Only cashiers checks and money orders accepted.

Cullman County

Circuit Court Cullman County Courthouse, Rm 303, 500 2nd Ave SW, Cullman, AL 35055; 256-775-4654; Probate phone: 256-775-4652. Hours: 8AM-4:30PM (CST). *Felony, Civil Actions Over $10,000, Probate.*

Civil Records: Access: Phone, mail, online, in person. Both court and visitors may perform in person searches. No search fee. Required to search: name, years to search. Civil cases indexed by defendant, plaintiff. Civil records on computer back to 1993, index back to 1977; books from 1900s. Online access available through SJIS. See state introduction.

Criminal Records: Access: Mail, online, in person. Both court and visitors may perform in person searches. No search fee. Required to search: name, years to search, DOB; also helpful: SSN. Criminal records on computer back to 1993; index back to 1977; prior in books. Online access available through SJIS. See state introduction.

General Information: Public access terminal is available. No sealed, adoptions, youthful offenders or juvenile records released. SASE not required. Turnaround time 10 days. Copy fee: $.25 per page. Add postage costs if by mail. Certification fee: $1.00 per document. Fee payee: Robert Bates, Circuit Clerk. Business checks accepted. Prepayment is required.

District Court 500 2nd Ave SW, Courthouse Rm 211, Cullman, AL 35055-4197; 256-775-4660. Hours: 8AM-4:30PM (CST). *Misdemeanor, Civil Actions Under $10,000, Eviction, Small Claims.*

Civil Records: Access: Mail, online, in person. Visitors must perform in person searches for themselves. No search fee. Required to search: name, years to search. Civil cases indexed by defendant. Civil records on computer from 11/92, on books 10 yrs back. Online access available through SJIS. See state introduction.

Criminal Records: Access: Mail, online, in person. Visitors must perform in person searches for themselves. No search fee. Required to search: name, years to search, DOB; also helpful: SSN. Criminal records on computer from 11/92, on books 10 yrs back. Online access available through SJIS. See state introduction.

General Information: Public access terminal is available. No sealed, adoptions, youthful offenders or juvenile records released. SASE required. Turnaround time 1 week. Copy fee: $.25 per page. Certification fee: $1.25. Fee payee: District Clerk. Only cashiers checks and money orders accepted. Prepayment is required.

Dale County

Circuit & District Court PO Box 1350, Ozark, AL 36361; 334-774-5003; Probate phone: 334-774-2754. Hours: 8AM-4:30PM (CST). *Felony, Misdemeanor, Civil, Eviction, Small Claims, Probate.*

Note: Probate court is separate from this court, and can be contacted at the telephone number above.

Civil Records: Access: Online, in person. Visitors must perform in person searches for themselves. No search fee. Required to search: name, years to search. Civil cases indexed by defendant, plaintiff. Civil records on computer from 8/92, on books and index cards from the 1920s. Online access available through SJIS. See state introduction.

Criminal Records: Access: Online, in person. Visitors must perform in person searches for themselves. No search fee. Required to search: name, years to search, DOB; also helpful: SSN. Criminal records on computer from 8/92, on books and index cards from the 1920s. Online access available through SJIS. See state introduction.

General Information: Public access terminal is available. No sealed, adoptions, youthful offenders or juvenile records released. Copy fee: $.25 per page. Certification fee: $1.00. Fee payee: Dale County Circuit Clerk. Only cashiers checks and money orders accepted.

Dallas County

Circuit Court PO Box 1148, Selma, AL 36702; 334-874-2523; Probate phone: 334-874-2597. Hours: 8AM-5PM (CST). *Felony, Civil Actions Over $10,000, Probate.*

Note: Probate court is separate from this court, and can be contacted at the telephone number above.

Civil Records: Access: Mail, online, in person. Both court and visitors may perform in person searches. No search fee. Required to search: name, years to search. Civil cases indexed by defendant, plaintiff. Civil records on computer from 1980, on microfiche from the late 1800s, index books prior. Online access available through SJIS. See state introduction.

Criminal Records: Access: Phone, mail, online, in person. Both court and visitors may perform in person searches. No search fee. Required to search: name, years to search, DOB; also helpful: SSN. Criminal records on computer from 1980, on microfiche from the late 1800s, index books prior. Online access available through SJIS. See state introduction.

General Information: Public access terminal is available. No sealed, adoptions, youthful offenders or juvenile records released. SASE required. Turnaround time less than 1 week for civil cases. Copy fee: $.25 per page. Certification fee: $1.00. Fee payee: Dallas County Circuit Court. Personal checks accepted. Prepayment is required.

District Court PO Box 1148, Selma, AL 36702; 334-874-2526. Hours: 8AM-5PM (CST). *Misdemeanor, Civil Actions Under $10,000, Eviction, Small Claims.*

Civil Records: Access: Phone, mail, online, in person. Visitors must perform in person searches for themselves. No search fee. Required to search: name, years to search. Civil cases indexed by defendant. Civil records on books from 1967, on computer since 1993. Online access available through SJIS. See state introduction.

Criminal Records: Access: Mail, online, in person. Visitors must perform in person searches for themselves. No search fee. Required to search: name, years to search; also helpful: DOB, SSN. Criminal records on books from 1967, on computer since 1993. Online access available through SJIS. See state introduction.

General Information: Public access terminal is available. No sealed, adoptions, youthful offenders or juvenile records released. Copy fee: $.25 per page. Certification fee: $1.00. Fee payee: District Clerk. Personal checks accepted. Prepayment is required.

De Kalb County

Circuit & District Court PO Box 681149, Fort Payne, AL 35968; 256-845-8525; Probate phone: 256-845-8510. Hours: 8AM-4PM (CST). *Felony, Misdemeanor, Civil, Eviction, Small Claims, Probate.*

Note: Probate court is separate from this court, and can be contacted at the telephone number above.

Civil Records: Access: Mail, online, in person. Both court and visitors may perform in person searches. No search fee. Required to search: name, years to search. Civil cases indexed by defendant. Civil records on computer from August 1991, on books from 1959. Online access available through SJIS. See state introduction.

Criminal Records: Access: Mail, online, in person. Both court and visitors may perform in person searches. No search fee. Required to search: name, years to search; also helpful: DOB, SSN. Criminal records on computer from August 1991, on books from 1959. Online access available through SJIS. See state introduction.

General Information: Public access terminal is available. No sealed, adoptions, youthful offenders or juvenile records released. Turnaround time 1 week. Copy fee: $.25 per page. Certification fee: $1.25. Business checks accepted.

Elmore County

Circuit & District Court - Civil Division PO Box 310, Wetumpka, AL 36092; 334-567-1123; Probate phone: 334-567-1139; Fax: 334-567-5957. Hours: 8AM-4:30PM (CST). *Civil, Probate.*

Note: Probate court is separate from this court, and can be contacted at the telephone number above.

Civil Records: Access: Online, in person. Visitors must perform in person searches for themselves. No search fee. Required to search: name, years to search. Civil cases indexed by defendant, plaintiff. Civil records on computer from 1983, books from 1930. Online access available through SJIS. See state introduction.

General Information: Public access terminal is available. No sealed, adoptions, youthful offenders or juvenile records released. Copy fee: $.25 per page. Certification fee: $1.25. Fee payee: Circuit Court Clerk. Business checks accepted. Prepayment is required.

Circuit Court - Criminal Division PO Box 310, 8935 US Hwy 23, Wetumpka, AL 36092; 334-567-1123; Fax: 334-567-5957. Hours: 8AM-4:30PM (CST). *Felony, Misdemeanor.*

Criminal Records: Access: Online, in person. Visitors must perform in person searches for themselves. No search fee. Required to search: name, years to search, DOB, SSN. Criminal records on computer from mid 1991, books from 1960-1992. Online access available through SJIS. See state introduction.

General Information: Public access terminal is available. No sealed, adoptions, youthful offenders or juvenile records released. Copy fee: $.25 per page. Certification fee: $1.25. Fee payee: Circuit Court Clerk. Only cashiers checks and money orders accepted. Prepayment is required.

Escambia, County

Circuit & District Court PO Box 856, Brewton, AL 36427; 251-867-0305; Probate phone: 251-867-0201; Fax: 251-867-0365. Hours: 8AM-4:30PM (CST). *Felony, Misdemeanor, Civil, Eviction, Small Claims, Probate.*

Note: Probate court is separate from this court, and can be contacted at the telephone number above.

Civil Records: Access: Mail, fax, online, in person. Both court and visitors may perform in person searches. No search fee. Required to search: name, years to search. Civil cases indexed by defendant, plaintiff. Civil records on computer from 10/93, books and cards back to 1990. Online access available through SJIS. See state introduction.

Criminal Records: Access: Mail, fax, online, in person. Both court and visitors may perform in person searches. No search fee. Required to search: name, years to search, DOB. Criminal records on computer from 10/93, books and cards back to 1950. Online access available through SJIS. See state introduction.

General Information: No sealed, adoptions, youthful offenders or juvenile records released. SASE required. Turnaround time 2-3 days. Fax notes: Fee to fax results is $1.00 per document and $.25 per page. Copy fee: $.25 per page. Certification fee: $1.00. Business checks accepted.

Etowah County

Circuit & District Court 801 Forrest Ave #202, Gadsden, AL 35901; 256-549-5437/5430; Probate phone: 256-549-8135. Hours: 8AM-5PM (CST). *Felony, Misdemeanor, Civil, Eviction, Small Claims.*

Note: Probate court is separate from this court.

Civil Records: Access: Mail, online, in person. Both court and visitors may perform in person searches. No search fee. Required to search: name, years to search. Civil cases indexed by defendant, plaintiff. Civil records on computer from 1984, index on computer since 1977, books prior to 1977. Online access available through SJIS. See state introduction.

Criminal Records: Access: Mail, online, in person. Both court and visitors may perform in person searches. No search fee. Required to search: name, years to search; also helpful: DOB, SSN. Criminal records on computer from 1984, index on computer since 1977, books prior to 1977. Online access available through SJIS. See state introduction.

General Information: Public access terminal is available. No sealed, adoptions, youthful offenders or juvenile records released. SASE requested. Turnaround time 4-6 weeks. Copy fee: $.25 per page. Certification fee: $1.25. Fee payee: Clerk of Court. Only cashiers checks and money orders accepted.

Probate Court PO Box 187, Gadsden, AL 35901; 256-549-2150; Fax: 256-546-1149. *Probate.*

Fayette County

Circuit & District Court PO Box 906, Fayette, AL 35555; 205-932-4617; Probate phone: 205-932-4519. Hours: 8AM-4:30PM (CST). *Felony, Misdemeanor, Civil, Eviction, Small Claims, Probate.*

Note: Probate court is separate from this court, and can be contacted at the telephone number above.

Civil Records: Access: Online, mail, fax, in person. Visitors must perform in person searches for themselves. No search fee. Required to search: name, years to search. Civil cases indexed by defendant. Civil records on computer from 3/94, on books and cards from 1977. Online access available through SJIS. See state introduction.

Criminal Records: Access: Online, mail, fax, in person. Visitors must perform in person searches for themselves. No search fee. Required to search: name, years to search, DOB; also helpful: SSN. Criminal records on computer from 3/94, on books and cards from 1977. Online access available through SJIS. See state introduction.

General Information: Public access terminal is available. No sealed, adoptions, youthful offenders or juvenile records released. Copy fee: $.25 per page. Certification fee: $1.00. Fee payee: Circuit Clerk. Business checks accepted.

Franklin County

Circuit & District Court PO Box 160, Russellville, AL 35653; 256-332-8861; Probate phone: 256-332-8801. Hours: 8AM-4:30PM (CST). *Felony, Misdemeanor, Civil, Eviction, Small Claims, Probate.*

Note: Note: Probate court is separate from this court, and can be contacted at the telephone number above or PO Box 70.

Civil Records: Access: Mail, online, in person. Both court and visitors may perform in person searches. Search fee: $5.00 per five years searched per name. Required to search: name, years to search; also helpful: address. Civil cases indexed by defendant, plaintiff. Civil records on computer from 1993, on index books prior. SSN and DOB helpful, but records are not indexed by SSN. Online access available through SJIS. See state introduction.

Criminal Records: Access: Mail, online, in person. Both court and visitors may perform in person searches. Search fee: $5.00 per five years searched per name. Required to search: name, years to search, DOB; also helpful: SSN. Criminal records on computer from 1993, on index books prior. SSN and DOB helpful, but records are not indexed by SSN. Online access available through SJIS. See state introduction.

General Information: Public access terminal is available. No sealed, youthful offenders or juvenile released. SASE required. Turnaround time 3-4 days. Copy fee: $.25 per page. Certification fee: $1.00. Fee payee: Circuit Court Clerk. Business checks accepted. Prepayment is required.

Geneva County

Circuit & District Court PO Box 86, Geneva, AL 36340; 334-684-5620; Probate phone: 334-684-2276; Fax: 334-684-5605. Hours: 8AM-5PM (CST). *Felony, Misdemeanor, Civil, Eviction, Small Claims, Probate.*

Note: Probate court is separate from this court, and can be contacted at the telephone number above.

Civil Records: Access: Mail, online, in person. Both court and visitors may perform in person searches. Search fee: $5.00 per name. Required to search: name, years to search; also helpful: address. Civil cases indexed by defendant, plaintiff. Civil records on computer from 1992, index cards from the 1950s. Online access available through SJIS. See state introduction.

Criminal Records: Access: Mail, online, in person. Both court and visitors may perform in person searches. Search fee: $5.00 per name. Required to search: name, years to search, DOB; also helpful: SSN. Criminal records on computer from 1992, index cards from the 1950s. Online access available through SJIS. See state introduction.

General Information: Public access terminal is available. No sealed, adoptions, youthful offenders or juvenile records released. Turnaround time 1 week. Copy fee: $.25 per page. Certification fee: $1.50. Fee payee: Circuit Clerk Valerie Thomley. Business checks accepted. Out of state personal checks not accepted. Prepayment is required.

Greene County

Circuit & District Court PO Box 307, Eutaw, AL 35462; 205-372-3598; Probate phone: 205-372-3340. Hours: 8AM-4PM (CST). *Felony, Misdemeanor, Civil, Eviction, Small Claims, Probate.*

Note: Probate court is separate from this court, and can be contacted at the telephone number above.

Civil Records: Access: Mail, online, in person. Both court and visitors may perform in person searches. No search fee. Required to search: name, years to search; also helpful: DOB, SSN and signed release. Civil cases indexed by defendant, plaintiff. Civil records on books from 1984. Online access available through SJIS. See state introduction.

Criminal Records: Access: Mail, online, in person. Both court and visitors may perform in person searches. No search fee. Required to search: name, years to search; also helpful: DOB, SSN and signed release. Criminal records on books from 1984. Online access available through SJIS. See state introduction.

General Information: Public access terminal is available. No sealed, adoptions, youthful offenders or juvenile records released. SASE required. Turnaround time 1 week. Copy fee: $.25 per page. Certification fee: $1.25. Fee payee: Circuit Clerk. Business checks accepted. Prepayment is required.

Hale County

Circuit & District Court Hale County Courthouse, Rm 8, PO Drawer 99, Greensboro, AL 36744; 334-624-4334; Probate phone: 334-624-7391. Hours: 8AM-5PM (CST). *Felony, Misdemeanor, Civil, Eviction, Small Claims, Probate.*

Note: Probate court is separate from this court, and can be contacted at the telephone number above.

Civil Records: Access: Mail, online, in person. Both court and visitors may perform in person searches. No search fee. Required to search: name, years to search. Civil cases indexed by defendant, plaintiff. Civil records on books from 1985. Online access available through SJIS. See state introduction.

Criminal Records: Access: Mail, online, in person. Both court and visitors may perform in person searches. No search fee. Required to search: name, years to search; also helpful: DOB, SSN. Criminal records on books from 1985. Online access available through SJIS. See state introduction.

General Information: Public access terminal is available. No sealed, adoptions, youthful offenders or juvenile records released. Turnaround time 1 week. Copy fee: $.25 per page. Certification fee: $1.00. Fee payee: Clerk of the Court. Business checks accepted. No personal checks accepted.b. Prepayment is required.

Henry County

Circuit & District Court 101 W Court St, #J, Abbeville, AL 36310-2135; 334-585-2753; Probate phone: 334-585-3257; Fax: 334-585-5006. Hours: 8AM-4:30PM (CST). *Felony, Misdemeanor, Civil, Eviction, Small Claims, Probate.*

Note: Probate court is separate from this court, and can be contacted at the telephone number above.

Civil Records: Access: Mail, online, in person. Both court and visitors may perform in person searches. Search fee: $3.00 per name. Required to search: name, years to search. Civil cases indexed by defendant. Civil records on computer from 1994, index cards 10 yrs back. Online access available through SJIS. See state introduction.

Criminal Records: Access: Mail, online, in person. Both court and visitors may perform in person searches. Search fee: $3.00 per name. Required to search: name, years to search, DOB; also helpful: SSN. Criminal records on computer from 5/93, index cards 10 yrs back. Online access available through SJIS. See state introduction.

General Information: No sealed, adoptions, youthful offenders or juvenile records released. SASE required. Turnaround time 2-3 day. Copy fee: $.25 per page. Certification fee: $1.00. Fee payee: Circuit Clerk. Personal checks accepted. Prepayment is required.

Houston County

Circuit & District Court PO Drawer 6406, Dothan, AL 36302; 334-677-4800/4872; Civil phone: Circ-334-677-4858; Dist-334-677-4868; Criminal phone: Circ-334-677-4863; Dist-334-677-4872; Probate phone: 334-677-4719. Hours: 7:30AM-4:30PM (CST). *Felony, Misdemeanor, Civil, Eviction, Small Claims, Probate.*

Note: Probate court is separate from this court, and can be contacted at the telephone number above.

Civil Records: Access: Mail, online, in person. Both court and visitors may perform in person searches. No search fee. Required to search: name, years to search. Civil cases indexed by defendant. Civil records on computer from 1977, index books from 1950s. Online access available through SJIS. See state introduction.

Criminal Records: Access: Mail, online, in person. Both court and visitors may perform in person searches. No search fee. Required to search: name, years to search; also helpful: DOB, SSN. Criminal records on computer from 1977, index books from 1950s. Online access available through SJIS. See state introduction.

General Information: Public access terminal is available. No sealed, adoptions, youthful offenders or juvenile records released. Turnaround time 1 week. Copy fee: $.25 per page. Certification fee: $1.00. Fee payee: Judy Byrd. Business checks accepted. Prepayment is required.

Jackson County

Circuit & District Court PO Box 397, Scottsboro, AL 35768; Civil phone: 256-574-9320; Criminal phone: 256-574-9323; Probate phone: 256-574-9290; Fax: 256-259-9981. Hours: 8AM-4:30PM (CST). *Felony, Misdemeanor, Civil, Eviction, Small Claims, Probate.*

Note: Probate court is at a separate office at the courthouse (PO Box 128) and can be contacted at the telephone number above or 256-574-9295.

Civil Records: Access: Mail, fax, online, in person. Both court and visitors may perform in person searches. No search fee. Required to search: name, years to search. Civil cases indexed by defendant. Civil records on computer from 5/1993, on cards from 1977. Online access available through SJIS. See state introduction.

Criminal Records: Access: Mail, fax, online, in person. Both court and visitors may perform in person searches. No search fee. Required to search: name, years to search, DOB; also helpful: SSN. Criminal records on computer from 5/1993, on cards from 1977. Online access available through SJIS. See state introduction.

General Information: Public access terminal is available. No sealed, adoptions, youthful offenders or juvenile records released. SASE required. Turnaround time 1-2 days. Copy fee: $.25 per page. Certification fee: $2.00. Fee payee: Circuit Court Clerk. Only cashiers checks and money orders accepted. Prepayment is required.

Jefferson County

Circuit Court - Bessemer Division Rm 606, Courthouse Annex, Bessemer, AL 35020; 205-481-4165. Hours: 8AM-5PM (CST). *Felony, Civil Actions Over $10,000.*

Civil Records: Access: Online, in person. Visitors must perform in person searches for themselves. No search fee. Required to search: name, years to search. Civil

cases indexed by defendant, plaintiff. Civil records on computer from 1988, on index books from 1930s to 1977. Online access available through SJIS. See state introduction.

Criminal Records: Access: Online, in person. Visitors must perform in person searches for themselves. No search fee. Required to search: name, years to search, DOB; also helpful: SSN. Criminal records on computer from 1988, on index books from 1930s to 1977. Online access available through SJIS. See state introduction.

General Information: Public access terminal is available. No sealed, adoptions, youthful offenders or juvenile records released. Copy fee: $.25 per page. Certification fee: $1.25. Fee payee: Clerk of Circuit Court. Business checks accepted. Prepayment is required.

District Court - Bessemer Division Rm 506, Courthouse Annex, Bessemer, AL 35020; 205-481-4187. Hours: 8AM-5PM (CST). *Misdemeanor, Civil Actions Under $10,000, Eviction, Small Claims.*

Civil Records: Access: Online, in person. Visitors must perform in person searches for themselves. No search fee. Required to search: name, years to search. Civil cases indexed by defendant, plaintiff. Civil records on computer from 1986, on index cards from 1977, prior on docket books. Online access available through SJIS. See state introduction.

Criminal Records: Access: Online, in person. Visitors must perform in person searches for themselves. No search fee. Required to search: name, years to search, DOB; also helpful: SSN. Criminal records on computer from 1986, on index cards from 1977, prior on docket books. Online access available through SJIS. See state introduction.

General Information: Public access terminal is available. No sealed, adoptions, youthful offenders or juvenile records released. Copy fee: $.25 per page. Certification fee: $1.00. Fee payee: Bessemer District Court. Business checks accepted. Prepayment is required.

Circuit Court - Birmingham Civil Division 716 N 21st St, Rm 400, Birmingham, AL 35263; 205-325-5355. Hours: 8AM-5PM (CST). *Civil Actions Over $10,000 (Over $5,000 if jury trial).*

Civil Records: Access: Phone, mail, online, in person. Both court and visitors may perform in person searches. No search fee. Required to search: name, years to search. Civil cases indexed by defendant, plaintiff. Civil records on computer from 1976, on index books from 1976 to 1986, prior to 1976 archived. Online access available through SJIS. See state introduction.

General Information: Public access terminal is available. No sealed, adoptions, youthful offenders or juvenile records released. Turnaround time 1-2 weeks. Copy fee: $.25 per page. Certification fee: $1.25. Fee payee: Clerk of Circuit Court. Business checks accepted. Prepayment is required. Under $10.00 need not prepay.

Circuit Court - Birmingham Criminal Division 801 Richard Arrington Blvd, Room 901, Birmingham, AL 35263; 205-325-5285. Hours: 8AM-4:55PM (CST). *Felony.*

Criminal Records: Access: Online, in person. Visitors must perform in person searches for themselves. No search fee. Required to search: name, years to search, DOB, signed release; also helpful: address, SSN. Criminal records on computer from 1960s, index books prior. Online access available through SJIS. See state introduction.

General Information: Public access terminal is available. No sealed, adoptions, youthful offenders, sex offender cases or juvenile records released. Copy fee: $.25 per page. Certification fee: $1.00. Fee payee: Clerk

of Court. Only cashiers checks and money orders accepted. Prepayment is required.

District Court - Birmingham Civil Division 716 Richard Arrington BLVD N, Birmingham, AL 35203; 205-325-5331. Hours: 8AM-5PM (CST). *Civil Actions Under $10,000, Eviction, Small Claims.*

Civil Records: Access: Phone, mail, online, in person. Both court and visitors may perform in person searches. No search fee. Required to search: name, years to search. Civil cases indexed by defendant, plaintiff. Civil records on computer from 1977, index books stored in warehouse. Online access available through SJIS. See state introduction.

General Information: Public access terminal is available. No sealed, adoptions, youthful offenders or juvenile records released. SASE required. Turnaround time 1-2 days. Copy fee: $.25 per page. Certification fee: $1.00. Fee payee: District Court. Only cashiers checks and money orders accepted. Prepayment is required.

District Court - Birmingham Criminal Division 801 Richard Arrington Blvd N, Rm 207, Birmingham, AL 35203; 205-325-5309. Hours: 8AM-5PM (CST). *Misdemeanor.*

Criminal Records: Access: Mail, online, in person. Both court and visitors may perform in person searches. Search fee: $1.25. Required to search: name, DOB; also helpful: years to search, SSN, sex, date of arrest. Criminal records on computer from 1986. To search for records prior to 1987, require arrest date. Online access available through SJIS. See state introduction.

General Information: Public access terminal is available. No sealed, sexual abuse, adoptions, youthful offenders or juvenile records released. Turnaround time 5-10 days. Copy fee: $.25 per page. Certification fee: $1.25. Fee payee: District Court. Only cashiers checks and money orders accepted. Prepayment is required.

Probate Court 716 Richard Arrington Jr Blvd N., Birmingham, AL 35203; 205-325-5420/5411; Fax: 205-325-4885. Hours: 8AM-4:45PM (CST). *Probate.*

Lamar County

Circuit & District Court PO Box 434, Vernon, AL 35592; 205-695-7193; Probate phone: 205-695-9119; Fax: 205-695-1871. Hours: 8AM-4:30PM (CST). *Felony, Misdemeanor, Civil, Eviction, Small Claims, Probate.*

Note: Probate court is separate from this court, and can be contacted at the telephone number above.

Civil Records: Access: Mail, online, in person. Only visitors may perform in person searches. No search fee. Required to search: name, years to search; also helpful: address. Civil cases indexed by defendant, plaintiff. Civil records on books from 1900; computerized records go back to 1995. Online access available through SJIS. See state introduction.

Criminal Records: Access: Mail, fax, online, in person. Only visitors may perform in person searches. No search fee. Required to search: name, years to search, DOB, signed release; also helpful: SSN. Criminal records on books from 1900; computerized records go back to 1995. Online access available through SJIS. See state introduction.

General Information: Public access terminal is available. No sealed, adoptions, youthful offenders or juvenile records released. SASE required. Turnaround time 1-2 days. Copy fee: $.25 per page. Certification fee: $2.25. Fee payee: Circuit Clerk. Only cashiers checks and money orders accepted. Will bill copy fees.

Lauderdale County

Circuit Court PO Box 795, Florence, AL 35631; 256-760-5710; Probate phone: 256-760-5800. Hours: 8AM-Noon, 1-5PM (CST). *Felony, Civil Actions Over $10,000, Probate.*

Note: Probate court is separate from this court, and can be contacted at the telephone number above.

Civil Records: Access: Online, in person. Visitors must perform in person searches for themselves. No search fee. Required to search: name, years to search. Civil cases indexed by defendant, plaintiff. Civil records on computer from 1977, index books from the 1930s. Online access available through SJIS. See state introduction.

Criminal Records: Access: Online, in person. Visitors must perform in person searches for themselves. No search fee. Required to search: name, years to search, DOB; also helpful: SSN. Criminal records on computer from 1977, index books from the 1930s. Online access available through SJIS. See state introduction.

General Information: Public access terminal is available. No sealed, adoptions, youthful offenders or juvenile records released. Copy fee: $.25 per page. Certification fee: $1.00. Fee payee: Circuit Court Clerk. Personal checks accepted. Prepayment is required.

District Court PO Box 776, Florence, AL 35631; 256-760-5726; Fax: 256-760-5727. Hours: 8AM-Noon, 1-5PM (CST). *Misdemeanor, Civil Actions Under $10,000, Eviction, Small Claims.*

Civil Records: Access: Mail, fax, online, in person. Both court and visitors may perform in person searches. No search fee. Required to search: name, years to search. Civil cases indexed by defendant, plaintiff. Civil records on computer from 1986, books from the 1930s. Online access available through SJIS. See state introduction.

Criminal Records: Access: Mail, fax, online, in person. Both court and visitors may perform in person searches. No search fee. Required to search: name, years to search, DOB; also helpful: SSN. Criminal records on computer from 1986, books from the 1930s. Online access available through SJIS. See state introduction.

General Information: Public access terminal is available. No sealed, adoptions, youthful offenders or juvenile records released. Turnaround time 1 week. Fax notes: No fee to fax results. Copy fee: $.25 per page. Certification fee: $1.00. Fee payee: Circuit Clerk. Personal checks accepted. Prepayment is required.

Lawrence County

Circuit & District Court PO Box 249, Moulton, AL 35650; 256-974-2432; Probate phone: 256-974-2439. Hours: 8AM-5PM (CST). *Felony, Misdemeanor, Civil, Eviction, Small Claims, Probate.*

Note: Probate court is separate from this court, and can be contacted at the telephone number above.

Civil Records: Access: Online, in person. Visitors must perform in person searches for themselves. No search fee. Required to search: name, years to search. Civil cases indexed by defendant. Civil records on computer from mid-1994, on books and index cards from 1920s. Online access available through SJIS. See state introduction.

Criminal Records: Access: Online, in person. Visitors must perform in person searches for themselves. No search fee. Required to search: name, years to search; also helpful: DOB, SSN. Criminal records on computer from mid-1994, on books and index cards from 1920s. Online access available through SJIS. See state introduction.

General Information: Public access terminal is available. No sealed, adoption, youthful offender, juvenile records released. Copy fee: $.25 per page.

Certification fee: $1.00. Fee payee: Clerk. Business checks accepted. Prepayment is required.

Lee County

Circuit & District Court 2311 Gateway Dr, Rm 104, Opelika, AL 36801; 334-749-7141; Fax: 334-737-3520. Hours: 8:30AM-4:30PM (CST). *Felony, Misdemeanor, Civil, Eviction, Small Claims.*

Note: Probate court is separate from this court, and can be contacted at 334-745-9761 or at Lee County Courthouse, 215 S 9 St, Opelika, AL 36801.

Civil Records: Access: Phone, mail, online, in person. Only the court performs in person searches; visitors may not. No search fee. Required to search: name, years to search. Civil cases indexed by defendant, plaintiff. Civil records on computer from 1980s, on index cards from 1988. Online access available through SJIS. See state introduction.

Criminal Records: Access: Phone, mail, online, in person. Only the court performs in person searches; visitors may not. No search fee. Required to search: name, years to search; also helpful: DOB, SSN. Criminal records on computer from 1980s, on index cards from 1988. Online access available through SJIS. See state introduction.

General Information: No sealed, adoptions, youthful offenders or juvenile records released. Turnaround time 1 week. Copy fee: $.50 per page. Certification fee: $1.00. Fee payee: Clerk's Office. Business checks accepted.

Limestone County

Circuit & District Court 200 Washington St West, Athens, AL 35611; 256-233-6406; Probate phone: 256-233-6427. Hours: 8AM-4:30PM (CST). *Felony, Misdemeanor, Civil, Eviction, Small Claims, Probate.*

Note: Probate court is separate from this court, and can be contacted at the telephone number above.

Civil Records: Access: Mail, online, in person. Both court and visitors may perform in person searches. No search fee. Required to search: name, years to search. Civil cases indexed by defendant, plaintiff. Civil records on computer since 1992; prior in docket books. Online access available through SJIS. See state introduction.

Criminal Records: Access: Mail, online, in person. Both court and visitors may perform in person searches. No search fee. Required to search: name, years to search, DOB; also helpful: SSN, sex. Criminal records on computer since 1992, prior in docket books. Online access available through SJIS. See state introduction.

General Information: Public access terminal is available. No juvenile, youthful offender records released. SASE required. Turnaround time 2 weeks. Copy fee: $.25 per page. Certification fee: $1.00. Fee payee: Clerk of Court. Personal checks accepted.

Lowndes County

Circuit & District Court PO Box 876, Hayneville, AL 36040; 334-548-2252; Probate phone: 334-548-2365. Hours: 8AM-4:30PM (CST). *Felony, Misdemeanor, Civil, Eviction, Small Claims, Probate.*

Note: Probate court is separate from this court, and can be contacted at the telephone number above.

Civil Records: Access: Mail, online, in person. Both court and visitors may perform in person searches. Search fee: $10.00 per name. Required to search: name, years to search. Civil cases indexed by defendant, plaintiff. Civil records on index cards from 1977; computerized since 1996. Online access available through SJIS. See state introduction.

Criminal Records: Access: Mail, online, in person. Both court and visitors may perform in person searches. Search fee: $10.00 per name. Required to search: name, years to search; also helpful: DOB, SSN. Criminal records on index cards from 1977; computerized since

1996. Online access available through SJIS. See state introduction.

General Information: Public access terminal is available. No sealed, adoptions, youthful offenders or juvenile records released. SASE required. Turnaround time up to 1 week. Copy fee: $.25 per page. Certification fee: $1.00. Fee payee: District Court Clerk. Business checks accepted.

Macon County

Circuit & District Court PO Box 830723, Tuskegee, AL 36083; 334-724-2614; Probate phone: 334-724-2611. Hours: 8AM-4:30PM (CST). *Felony, Misdemeanor, Civil, Eviction, Small Claims, Probate.*

Note: Probate court is separate from this court, and can be contacted at the telephone number above.

Civil Records: Access: Mail, online, in person. Both court and visitors may perform in person searches. Search fee: $10.00 per name. Required to search: name, years to search. Civil cases indexed by defendant, plaintiff. Civil records on index books from 1977; on computer back to 1993. Online access available through SJIS. See state introduction.

Criminal Records: Access: Mail, online, in person. Both court and visitors may perform in person searches. Search fee: $10.00 per name. Required to search: name, years to search; also helpful: DOB, SSN. Criminal records go back to 1977; on computer back to 1993. Online access available through SJIS. See state introduction.

General Information: No sealed, adoption, youthful offender, juvenile records released. SASE not required. Turnaround time 1-2 days. Copy fee: $.25 per page. Certification fee: $2.50 per page. Fee payee: Office of Circuit Clerk. Business checks accepted.

Madison County

Circuit Court- Civil 100 N Side Square, Courthouse, Huntsville, AL 35801; 256-532-3381; Probate phone: 256-532-3330. Hours: 8AM-5PM (CST). *Civil Actions Over $10,000, Probate.*

Note: Probate court is separate from this court, and can be contacted at the telephone number above

Civil Records: Access: Online, in person. Visitors must perform in person searches for themselves. No search fee. Required to search: name, years to search; also helpful: address. Civil cases indexed by defendant, plaintiff. Civil records on computer from 1977, index books from 1937. Online access available through SJIS. See state introduction.

General Information: Public access terminal is available. No sealed, adoptions, youthful offenders or juvenile records released. Copy fee: $.25 per page. Certification fee: $1.00. Personal checks accepted. Prepayment is required. Cost bill will be sent for search and copies.

Circuit Court - Criminal 100 N Side Square, Courthouse, Huntsville, AL 35801-4820; 256-532-3389. Hours: 8AM-5PM (CST). *Felony.*

Criminal Records: Access: Online, in person. Visitors must perform in person searches for themselves. No search fee. Required to search: name, years to search; also helpful: DOB, SSN. Criminal records on computer from 1977, books from 1937. Online access available through SJIS. See state introduction.

General Information: Public access terminal is available. No sealed, adoptions, youthful offenders or juvenile records released. Copy fee: $.25 per page. Certification fee: $1.25. Fee payee: Circuit Court Clerk. Personal checks accepted. Prepayment is required.

District Court 100 N Side Square, Rm 822 Courthouse, Huntsville, AL 35801; Civil phone: 256-532-3622; Criminal phone: 256-532-3373; Fax: 256-532-6972. Hours: 8:30AM-5PM (CST). *Misdemeanor, Civil Actions Under $10,000, Eviction, Small Claims.*

Civil Records: Access: Online, in person. Visitors must perform in person searches for themselves. No search fee. Required to search: name, years to search. Civil cases indexed by defendant, plaintiff. Civil records on computer from 1982, index books prior. Online access available through SJIS. See state introduction.

Criminal Records: Access: Online, in person. Visitors must perform in person searches for themselves. No search fee. Required to search: name, years to search; also helpful: DOB, SSN. Criminal records on computer from 1982, index books prior since 1979. Online access available through SJIS. See state introduction.

General Information: Public access terminal is available. No sealed, adoptions, youthful offenders or juvenile records released. Copy fee: $.25 per page. Certification fee: $1.25. Fee payee: District Court. Business checks accepted. Prepayment is required.

Marengo County

Circuit & District Court PO Box 480566, Linden, AL 36748; 334-295-2223. Hours: 8AM-4:30PM (CST). *Felony, Misdemeanor, Civil, Eviction, Small Claims, Probate.*

Civil Records: Access: Mail, online, in person. Both court and visitors may perform in person searches. No search fee. Required to search: name, years to search. Civil cases indexed by defendant, plaintiff. Civil records on computer from 6/94, on books and index cards from 1965. Online access available through SJIS. See state introduction.

Criminal Records: Access: Mail, online, in person. Both court and visitors may perform in person searches. No search fee. Required to search: name, years to search; also helpful: DOB, SSN. Criminal records on computer from 6/94, on books and index cards from 1965. Online access available through SJIS. See state introduction.

General Information: Public access terminal is available. No sealed, adoptions, youthful offenders or juvenile records released. Turnaround time 1 week. Copy fee: $.25 per page. Certification fee: $1.00. Fee payee: Circuit Clerk. Business checks accepted. Prepayment is required.

Marion County

Circuit & District Court PO Box 1595, Hamilton, AL 35570; 205-921-7451; Probate phone: 205-921-2471. Hours: 8AM-5PM (CST). *Felony, Misdemeanor, Civil, Eviction, Small Claims, Probate.*

Note: Probate court is separate from this court, and can be contacted at the telephone number above.

Civil Records: Access: Mail, online, in person. Both court and visitors may perform in person searches. No search fee. Required to search: name, years to search. Civil cases indexed by defendant, plaintiff. Civil records on computer from 5/94, on books from 1950s. Online access available through SJIS. See state introduction.

Criminal Records: Access: Mail, online, in person. Both court and visitors may perform in person searches. No search fee. Required to search: name, years to search; also helpful: DOB, SSN. Criminal records on computer from 5/94, on books from 1950s. Online access available through SJIS. See state introduction.

General Information: Public access terminal is available. No sealed, adoptions, youthful offenders or juvenile records released. SASE required. Turnaround time 2 days. Copy fee: $.50 per page. Certification fee: $1.50. Fee payee: Circuit Clerk. Only cashiers checks and money orders accepted.

Marshall County

Circuit & District Court - Albertville Division 200 W Main, Albertville, AL 35950; 256-878-4522/4521/4515. Hours: 8AM-4:30PM (CST). *Felony, Misdemeanor, Civil, Eviction, Small Claims.*

Civil Records: Access: Mail, online, in person. Both court and visitors may perform in person searches. No search fee. Required to search: name, years to search. Civil cases indexed by defendant. Civil records on computer from 8/92, on index books from 1974. Online access available through SJIS. See state introduction.

Criminal Records: Access: Mail, online, in person. Both court and visitors may perform in person searches. No search fee. Required to search: name, years to search, DOB; also helpful: SSN. Criminal records on computer from 8/92, on index books from 1974. Online access available through SJIS. See state introduction.

General Information: Public access terminal is available. No sealed, adoptions, youthful offenders or juvenile records released. SASE required. Turnaround time 2-3 days for criminal, 1-2 weeks civil. Copy fee: $.25 per page. Certification fee: $1.25. Fee payee: Clerk of Courts. Business checks accepted. Prepayment is required.

Circuit Court - Guntersville Civil Division

PO Box 248, Guntersville, AL 35976; 256-571-7788; Probate phone: 256-571-7764. Hours: 8AM-4:30PM (CST). *Civil Actions Over $10,000, Small Claims, Probate.*

Note: Probate court is separate from this court, and can be contacted at the telephone number above

Civil Records: Access: Online, in person. Visitors must perform in person searches for themselves. No search fee. Required to search: name, years to search. Civil cases indexed by defendant, plaintiff. Civil records on computer for past 3 years, on index books early 1900s. Online access available through SJIS. See state introduction.

General Information: Public access terminal is available. No sealed, adoptions, youthful offenders or juvenile records released. SASE required. Copy fee: $.25 per page. Certification fee: $1.00. Fee payee: Circuit Clerk. Business checks accepted. Prepayment is required.

Circuit Court - Guntersville Criminal Division

425 Gunter Ave, PO Box 248, Guntersville, AL 35976; 256-571-7791. Hours: 8AM-4:30PM (CST). *Felony, Misdemeanor.*

Criminal Records: Access: Online, mail, in person. Visitors must perform in person searches for themselves. No search fee. Required to search: name, years to search; also helpful: DOB, SSN. Criminal records on computer from 1992, on index books from 1984, prior back to 1930s. Online access available through SJIS. See state introduction.

General Information: Public access terminal is available. No sealed, adoptions, youthful offenders or juvenile records released. SASE required. Turnaround time 2 or more weeks. Copy fee: $.25 per page. Certification fee: $1.00. Fee payee: Circuit Clerk. Business checks accepted. Prepayment is required.

Mobile County

Circuit Court 205 Government St #C-913, Mobile, AL 36644-2913; 251-574-8786. Hours: 8AM-5PM (CST). *Felony, Civil Actions Over $10,000.*

Civil Records: Access: Online, in person. Visitors must perform in person searches for themselves. No search fee. Required to search: name, years to search. Civil cases indexed by defendant. Civil records on computer from 1977, microfiche from early 1900s. Online access available through SJIS. See state introduction.

Criminal Records: Access: Online, in person. Visitors must perform in person searches for themselves. No

search fee. Required to search: name, years to search; also helpful: DOB, SSN. Criminal records on computer from 1977, microfiche from early 1900s. Online access available through SJIS. See state introduction.

General Information: Public access terminal is available. No sealed, adoptions, youthful offenders or juvenile records released. Copy fee: $.25 per page. Certification fee: $1.00. Fee payee: Circuit Clerk. Only cashiers checks and money orders accepted. Prepayment is required. Exact change for payments is required.

District Court 205 Government St, Mobile, AL 36644; 251-574-8520, 251-690-8525 (small claims); Civil phone: 251-574-8526; Criminal phone: 251-574-8511; Probate phone: 251-574-8502; Fax: 251-574-4840. Hours: 8AM-5PM (CST). *Misdemeanor, Civil Actions Under $10,000, Eviction, Small Claims, Probate.*

Note: Probate court is a separate court, and can be reached at the telephone number given above.

Civil Records: Access: Phone, fax, mail, online, in person. Both court and visitors may perform in person searches. No search fee. Required to search: name, years to search. Civil cases indexed by defendant, plaintiff. Civil records on computer from 1977, index books from 1950s. Online access available through SJIS. See state introduction.

Criminal Records: Access: Phone, fax, mail, online, in person. Both court and visitors may perform in person searches. No search fee. Required to search: name, years to search, DOB; also helpful: SSN. Criminal records on computer from 1977, index books from 1950s. Online access available through SJIS. See state introduction.

General Information: Public access terminal is available. No sealed, youthful offenders, protected files or juvenile records released. Turnaround time 2-3 days. Copy fee: $.25 per page. Certification fee: $1.25. Fee payee: Clerk, District Court. Business checks accepted. Business checks must be approved. Prepayment is required.

Monroe County

Circuit & District Court County Courthouse, 65 North Alabama Ave, Monroeville, AL 36460; 251-743-2283; Probate phone: 251-743-4107. Hours: 8AM-5PM (CST). *Felony, Misdemeanor, Civil, Eviction, Small Claims, Probate.*

Note: Probate court is separate from this court, and can be contacted at the telephone number above.

Civil Records: Access: Mail, online, in person. Both court and visitors may perform in person searches. No search fee. Required to search: name, years to search. Civil cases indexed by defendant. Civil records on index cards from 1977 and on computer since July 1994. Online access available through SJIS. See state introduction.

Criminal Records: Access: Mail, online, in person. Both court and visitors may perform in person searches. No search fee. Required to search: name, years to search; also helpful: DOB, SSN. Criminal records on index cards from 1977 and on computer since July 1994. Online access available through SJIS. See state introduction.

General Information: Public access terminal is available. No sealed, adoptions, youthful offenders or juvenile records released. SASE required. Turnaround time 1 wk. Copy fee: $.25 per page. Certification fee: $1.25 per page. Fee payee: John Sawyer, Circuit Clerk. Business checks accepted. Prepayment is required.

Montgomery County

Circuit Court PO Box 1667, Montgomery, AL 36102-1667; 334-832-1260; Probate phone: 334-832-1237. Hours: 8AM-5PM (CST). *Felony, Civil Actions Over $10,000, Probate.*

Note: Probate court is separate from this court, and can be contacted at the telephone number above.

Civil Records: Access: Mail, online, in person. Both court and visitors may perform in person searches. No search fee. Required to search: name, years to search. Civil cases indexed by defendant, plaintiff. Civil records on computer from 1982, microfiche from 1976. Online access available through SJIS. See state introduction.

Criminal Records: Access: Mail, online, in person. Both court and visitors may perform in person searches. No search fee. Required to search: name, years to search; also helpful: DOB, SSN. Criminal records on computer from 1982, microfiche from 1976. Online access available through SJIS. See state introduction.

General Information: Public access terminal is available. No sealed, youthful offenders or juvenile records released. SASE required. Turnaround time 3-4 days. Copy fee: $.25 per page. Certification fee: $1.00. Fee payee: Circuit Clerk. Business checks accepted. Prepayment is required.

District Court PO Box 1667, Montgomery, AL 36102; 334-832-4950. Hours: 8AM-5PM (CST). *Misdemeanor, Civil Actions Under $10,000, Eviction, Small Claims.*

Civil Records: Access: Mail, online, in person. Both court and visitors may perform in person searches. No search fee. Required to search: name, years to search. Civil cases indexed by defendant. Civil records on computer from the 1980s, index books from 1977. Online access available through SJIS. See state introduction.

Criminal Records: Access: Mail, online, in person. Both court and visitors may perform in person searches. No search fee. Required to search: name, years to search; also helpful: DOB, SSN. Criminal records on computer from the 1980s, index books from 1977. Online access available through SJIS. See state introduction.

General Information: Public access terminal is available. No sealed, youthful offender, juvenile records released. SASE required. Turnaround time 3-4 days. Copy fee: $.25 per page. Certification fee: $1.00. Fee payee: District Court. Only cashiers checks and money orders accepted.

Morgan County

Circuit Court PO Box 848, Decatur, AL 35602; 256-351-4790; Probate phone: 256-351-4675. Hours: 8AM-4:30PM (CST). *Felony, Civil Actions Over $10,000, Probate.*

Note: Probate court is separate from this court, and can be contacted at the telephone number above.

Civil Records: Access: Online, in person. Visitors must perform in person searches for themselves. No search fee. Required to search: name, years to search. Civil cases indexed by defendant, plaintiff. Civil records on computer from 1994, on microfiche from 1950s, books from 1965. Online access available through SJIS. See state introduction.

Criminal Records: Access: Online, in person. Visitors must perform in person searches for themselves. No search fee. Required to search: name, years to search; also helpful: DOB, SSN. Criminal records on computer from 1992. Online access available through SJIS. See state introduction.

General Information: Public access terminal is available. No sealed, adoption, youthful offender, juvenile records released. Copy fee: $.25 per page. Certification fee: $1.25 per page. Fee payee: John Pat

Orr, Circuit Clerk. Personal checks accepted. Prepayment is required.

District Court PO Box 668, Decatur, AL 35602; 256-351-4649. Hours: 8:30AM-4:30PM (CST). *Misdemeanor, Civil Actions Under $10,000, Eviction, Small Claims.*

Civil Records: Access: Online, in person. Visitors must perform in person searches for themselves. No search fee. Required to search: name, years to search. Civil cases indexed by defendant. Civil records on computer from 1992, books from 1960. Online access available through SJIS. See state introduction.

Criminal Records: Access: Online, in person. Visitors must perform in person searches for themselves. No search fee. Required to search: name, years to search; also helpful: DOB, SSN. Criminal records on computer from 1992, books from 1960. Online access available through SJIS. See state introduction.

General Information: Public access terminal is available. No sealed, adoption, youthful offender, juvenile records released. Copy fee: $.25 per page. Certification fee: $1.50. Fee payee: District Court. Business checks accepted. Prepayment is required.

Perry County

Circuit & District Court PO Box 505, Marion, AL 36756; 334-683-6106; Probate phone: 334-683-2210. Hours: 8AM-4:30PM (CST). *Felony, Misdemeanor, Civil, Eviction, Small Claims, Probate.*

Note: Probate court is separate from this court, and can be contacted at the telephone number above.

Civil Records: Access: Mail, online, in person. Both court and visitors may perform in person searches. No search fee. Required to search: name, years to search. Civil cases indexed by defendant, plaintiff. Civil records on books from 1900's, on computer back to 1990. Online access available through SJIS. See state introduction.

Criminal Records: Access: Mail, online, in person. Both court and visitors may perform in person searches. No search fee. Required to search: name, years to search; also helpful: DOB, SSN. Criminal records on index cards back to 1900, computerized back to 1990. Online access available through SJIS. See state introduction.

General Information: No sealed, adoption, youthful offender, juvenile records released. SASE required. Turnaround time 2-3 days. Copy fee: $.25 per page. Certification fee: $1.25 per page. Fee payee: District Court Clerk. Business checks accepted. Prepayment is required.

Pickens County

Circuit & District Court PO Box 418, Carrollton, AL 35447; 205-367-2050; Probate phone: 205-367-2010. Hours: 8AM-4:30PM (CST). *Felony, Misdemeanor, Civil, Eviction, Small Claims, Probate.*

Civil Records: Access: Mail, online, in person. Only the court may perform in person searches. No search fee. Required to search: name, years to search. Civil cases indexed by defendant, plaintiff. Civil records on computer from 10/93, on books and index cards from 1840s. Online access available through SJIS. See state introduction.

Criminal Records: Access: Mail, online, in person. Only the court may perform in person searches. No search fee. Required to search: name, years to search; also helpful: DOB, SSN. Criminal records on computer, on books and index cards from 1840s. Online access available through SJIS. See state introduction.

General Information: No sealed, adoption, youthful offender, juvenile records released. SASE required. Turnaround time 1-2 weeks. Copy fee: $.25 per page. Certification fee: $1.00. Fee payee: District Court. Business checks accepted. Prepayment is required.

Pike County

Circuit & District Court PO Box 948, Troy, AL 36081; 334-566-4622; Probate phone: 334-566-1246. Hours: 8AM-5PM (CST). *Felony, Misdemeanor, Civil, Eviction, Small Claims, Probate.*

Note: Probate court is separate from this court, and can be contacted at the telephone number above.

Civil Records: Access: Mail, online, in person. Both court and visitors may perform in person searches. Search fee: $5.00 per name. Required to search: name, years to search. Civil cases indexed by defendant, plaintiff. Civil records on computer from 1977, on books from 1938. Online access available through SJIS. See state introduction.

Criminal Records: Access: Mail, online, in person. Both court and visitors may perform in person searches. Search fee: $5.00 per name. Required to search: name, years to search, DOB, SSN. Criminal records on computer from 1977, on books from 1938. Online access available through SJIS. See state introduction.

General Information: Public access terminal is available. No sealed, adoption, youthful offender, juvenile records released. SASE required. Turnaround time same day. Copy fee: $.25 per page. Certification fee: $1.00. Fee payee: Pike County Circuit/District Court. Only cashiers checks and money orders accepted. Prepayment is required.

Randolph County

Circuit & District Court PO Box 328, Wedowee, AL 36278; 256-357-4551; Probate phone: 256-357-4933. Hours: 8AM-Noon, 1-5PM (CST). *Felony, Misdemeanor, Civil, Eviction, Small Claims, Probate.*

Note: Probate court is separate from this court, and can be contacted at the telephone number above.

Civil Records: Access: Online, in person. Visitors must perform in person searches for themselves. No search fee. Required to search: name, years to search. Civil cases indexed by defendant, plaintiff. Civil records on computer from 1994. Online access available through SJIS. See state introduction.

Criminal Records: Access: Online, in person. Visitors must perform in person searches for themselves. No search fee. Required to search: name, years to search; also helpful: DOB, SSN. Criminal records on computer from 1977. Online access available through SJIS. See state introduction.

General Information: Public access terminal is available. No sealed, adoption, youthful offender, juvenile records released. Copy fee: $.25 per page. Certification fee: $1.50. Fee payee: Kim S Benefield. Business checks accepted. Prepayment is required.

Russell County

Circuit & District Court PO Box 518, Phenix City, AL 36868; 334-298-0516; Probate phone: 334-298-7979; Fax: 334-297-6250. Hours: 8:30AM-4:30PM (EST). *Felony, Misdemeanor, Civil, Eviction, Small Claims, Probate.*

Civil Records: Access: Mail, online, in person. Both court and visitors may perform in person searches. No search fee. Required to search: name, years to search. Civil cases indexed by defendant, plaintiff. Civil records on computer from 1988, books from 1800s (prior to 1940 extremely difficult to find). Online access available through SJIS. See state introduction.

Criminal Records: Access: Mail, online, in person. Both court and visitors may perform in person searches. No search fee. Required to search: name, years to search; also helpful: DOB, SSN. Criminal records on computer from 1988, books from 1800s (prior to 1940 extremely difficult to find). Online access available through SJIS. See state introduction. The county sex offender registry if available free at www.rcso.org/sex2.htm.

General Information: Public access terminal is available. No sealed, adoption, youthful offender, juvenile records released. Turnaround time 2 days. Copy fee: $.25 per page. Certification fee: $1.00. Fee payee: Clerk of Circuit Court. Business checks accepted.

Shelby County

Circuit & District Court PO Box 1810, Columbiana, AL 35051; 205-669-3760; Probate phone: 205-669-3711. Hours: 8AM-4:30PM (CST). *Felony, Misdemeanor, Civil, Eviction, Small Claims, Probate.*

Note: Probate court is separate from this court, and can be contacted at the telephone number above.

Civil Records: Access: Mail, fax, online, in person. Visitors must perform in person searches for themselves. No search fee. Required to search: name, years to search. Civil cases indexed by defendant, plaintiff. Civil records on computer from 1993, on index books from 1820s. Online access available through SJIS. See state introduction.

Criminal Records: Access: Mail, fax, online, in person. Visitors must perform in person searches for themselves. No search fee. Required to search: name, years to search, DOB; also helpful: SSN. Criminal records on computer from 1993, on index books from 1820s. Online access available through SJIS. See state introduction.

General Information: Public access terminal is available. No sealed, adoption, youthful offender, juvenile records released. Copy fee: $.25 per page. Certification fee: $1.00. Fee payee: Mary Harris, Circuit Clerk. Only cashiers checks and money orders accepted.

St. Clair County

Circuit & District Court - Ashville Division PO Box 1569, Ashville, AL 35953; 205-594-2184; Probate phone: 205-594-2120. Hours: 8AM-5PM (CST). *Felony, Misdemeanor, Civil, Eviction, Small Claims, Probate.*

www.stclairco.com/

Note: Probate court is separate from this court and can be contacted at the telephone number above.

Civil Records: Access: Mail, online, in person. Both court and visitors may perform in person searches. No search fee. Required to search: name, years to search. Civil cases indexed by defendant, plaintiff. Civil records on computer from 1/94, in books from 1800s, no index before 1940. Online access available through SJIS. See state introduction. Also, online access to probate records is available by subscription at www.recordsusa.com/Alabama/StClairCnAl.htm. Credit card, username and password is required; choose either monthly or per-use plan. Visit the web site or call Lisa at 601-264-7701 for information.

Criminal Records: Access: Mail, online, in person. Both court and visitors may perform in person searches. No search fee. Required to search: name, years to search, DOB; also helpful: SSN. Criminal records on computer from 1/94, in books from 1800s, no index before 1940. Online access available through SJIS. See state introduction.

General Information: Public access terminal is available. No sealed, adoption, youthful offender, juvenile records released. SASE required. Turnaround time 10 days. Copy fee: $.25 per page. Certification fee: $1.25. Fee payee: Jeff Wyatt Circuit Clerk. Business checks accepted.

Circuit & District Court - Pell City Division 1815 Cogswell Ave, #217, Pell City, AL 35125; 205-338-2511; Circuit: 205-338-7224 District; Probate phone: 205-338-9449. Hours: 8AM-5PM (CST). *Felony, Misdemeanor, Civil, Eviction, Small Claims, Probate.*

Note: Probate court is separate from this court, and can be contacted at the telephone number above.

Civil Records: Access: Mail, online, in person. Both court and visitors may perform in person searches. No search fee. Required to search: name, years to search. Civil cases indexed by defendant, plaintiff. Civil records on computer from 11/93, on books from early 1940s. Online access available through SJIS. See state introduction. Also, online access to probate records is available by subscription at www.recordsusa.com/Alabama/StClairCnAl.htm. Credit card, username and password is required; choose either monthly or per-use plan. Visit the web site or call Lisa at 601-264-7701 for information.

Criminal Records: Access: Mail, online, in person. Both court and visitors may perform in person searches. No search fee. Required to search: name, years to search, DOB; also helpful: SSN. Criminal records on computer from 11/93, on books from early 1940s. Online access available through SJIS. See state introduction.

General Information: Public access terminal is available. No sealed, adoption, youthful offender, juvenile records released. SASE required. Turnaround time 7-14 days. Copy fee: $.25 per page. Certification fee: $1.25. Fee payee: Clerk of Courts. Business checks accepted. Prepayment is required.

Sumter County

Circuit & District Court PO Box 936, Livingston, AL 35470; 205-652-2291; Probate phone: 205-652-7281. Hours: 8AM-4:30PM (CST). *Felony, Misdemeanor, Civil, Eviction, Small Claims.*

Civil Records: Access: Mail, online, in person. Both court and visitors may perform in person searches. No search fee. Required to search: name, years to search. Civil cases indexed by defendant, plaintiff. Civil records on computer from early 1995, on index books from 1962. Online access available through SJIS. See state introduction.

Criminal Records: Access: Mail, online, in person. Both court and visitors may perform in person searches. No search fee. Required to search: name, years to search; also helpful: DOB, SSN. Criminal records on computer from early 1995, on index books from 1962. Online access available through SJIS. See state introduction.

General Information: Public access terminal is available. No sealed, adoption, youthful offender, juvenile records released. SASE required. Turnaround time 2 wks. Copy fee: $.50 per page. Certification fee: $1.50. Fee payee: Circuit Court Clerk. Business checks accepted. Prepayment is required.

Probate Court PO Box 1040, Livingston, AL 35470; 205-652-7281; Fax: 205-652-2606. Hours: 8AM-4PM (CST). *Probate.*

Talladega County

Circuit & District Court - Northern Division PO 6137, Talladega, AL 35161; 256-761-2102. Hours: 8AM-5PM (CST). *Felony, Misdemeanor, Civil, Eviction, Small Claims.*

Civil Records: Access: Online, in person. Visitors must perform in person searches for themselves. No search fee. Required to search: name, years to search. Civil cases indexed by defendant, plaintiff. Civil records on computer from 1989, index books from 1970s. Online access available through SJIS. See state introduction.

Criminal Records: Access: Online, in person. Visitors must perform in person searches for themselves. No search fee. Required to search: name, years to search; also helpful: DOB, SSN. Criminal records on computer from 1989, index books from 1970s. Online access available through SJIS. See state introduction.

General Information: Public access terminal is available. No sealed, adoption, youthful offender, juvenile records released. Copy fee: $.25 per page. Certification fee: $1.25. Fee payee: Circuit Court Clerk. Business checks accepted.

District Court - Southern Division PO Box 183, Sylacauga, AL 35150; 256-245-4352. Hours: 7:30AM-4:30AM (CST). *Misdemeanor, Civil Actions Under $10,000, Eviction, Small Claims.*

Civil Records: Access: Mail, online, in person. Visitors must perform in person searches. No search fee. Required to search: name, years to search. Civil cases indexed by defendant. Civil records on computer from 1977, on index books and cards prior to 1982 at the Northern Division District Court. Online access available through SJIS. See state introduction.

Criminal Records: Access: Mail, online, in person. Visitors must perform in person searches. No search fee. Required to search: name, years to search; also helpful: DOB, SSN. Criminal records on computer from 1977, on index books and cards prior to 1982 at the Northern Division District Court. Online access available through SJIS. See state introduction.

General Information: No juvenile, youthful offender records released. SASE required. Turnaround time up to 7-10 days. Copy fee: $.25 per page. Certification fee: $1.25. Fee payee: Clerk of District Court. Business checks accepted. Prepayment is required.

Probate Court PO Box 737, Talladega, AL 35161; 256-362-4175. *Probate.*

Tallapoosa County

Circuit & District Court - Eastern Division Tallapoosa County Courthouse, Dadeville, AL 36853; 256-825-1098; Probate phone: 256-825-4266. Hours: 8AM-5PM (CST). *Felony, Misdemeanor, Civil, Eviction, Small Claims, Probate.*

Note: Probate court is separate from this court, and can be contacted at the telephone number above.

Civil Records: Access: Mail, online, in person. Only the court performs in person searches; visitors may not. Search fee: $3.00 per name. Required to search: name, years to search. Civil cases indexed by defendant, plaintiff. Civil records on computer from 1993, on index books from 1977. Online access available through SJIS. See state introduction.

Criminal Records: Access: Mail, online, in person. Only the court performs in person searches; visitors may not. Search fee: $3.00 per name. Required to search: name, years to search, DOB; also helpful: SSN. Criminal records on computer from 1993, on index books from 1977. Online access available through SJIS. See state introduction.

General Information: No sealed, adoption, youthful offender, juvenile records released. SASE required. Turnaround time 1-2 weeks. Copy fee: $.50 per page. Certification fee: $1.00. Fee payee: Circuit Clerk. Business checks accepted. Prepayment is required.

Circuit & District Court - Western Division PO Box 189, Alexander City, AL 35011; 256-329-8123/234-4361. Hours: 8AM-5PM (CST). *Felony, Misdemeanor, Civil, Eviction, Small Claims.*

Civil Records: Access: Mail, online, in person. Both court and visitors may perform in person searches. Search fee: $3.00 per name. Required to search: name, years to search. Civil cases indexed by defendant, plaintiff. Civil records on index books from 1977, prior in docket books; on computer back to 1994. Online access available through SJIS. See state introduction.

Criminal Records: Access: Mail, online, in person. Both court and visitors may perform in person searches. Search fee: $3.00 per name. Required to search: name, years to search, DOB; also helpful: SSN, signed release. Criminal records on index books from 1977, prior in docket books; on computer back to 1994. Online access available through SJIS. See state introduction.

General Information: No sealed, adoption, youthful offender, juvenile records released. SASE requested. Turnaround time up to 2 weeks. Copy fee: $.50 per page. Certification fee: $1.00. Fee payee: Clerk of Courts. Business checks accepted. Prepayment is required.

Tuscaloosa County

Circuit & District Courts - Civil 714 Greensboro Ave, Tuscaloosa, AL 35401; 205-349-3870; Civil phone: Circ-205-349-3870 X260; Dist: X357; Probate phone: 205-349-3870 X203. Hours: 8:30AM-5PM (CST). *Civil, Probate.*

Note: The District Court civil records are concurrent with the District Court Probate court is separate from this court, and can be contacted at the telephone number above

Civil Records: Access: Online, in person. Visitors must perform in person searches for themselves. No search fee. Required to search: name, years to search. Civil cases indexed by defendant, plaintiff. Civil records on computer from 1977, index books early 1900s. Online access available through SJIS. See state introduction.

General Information: Public access terminal is available. No sealed, adoption, youthful offender, juvenile records released. Copy fee: $.25 per page. Certification fee: $1.00. Fee payee: Doris Turner, Circuit Clerk. Business checks accepted. Prepayment is required.

Circuit Court - Criminal 714 Greensboro Ave, Tuscaloosa, AL 35401; 205-349-3870 X326. Hours: 8AM-5PM (CST). *Felony.*

Criminal Records: Access: Mail, online, in person. Both court and visitors may perform in person searches. No search fee. Required to search: name, years to search, DOB; also helpful: SSN. Criminal records on computer and index books back to 1977. Online access available through SJIS. See state introduction.

General Information: Public access terminal is available. No sealed, adoption, youthful offender, juvenile records released. SASE required. Turnaround time 1-2 days. Fax notes: Will not fax results. Copy fee: $.25 per page. Certification fee: $1.00. Fee payee: Circuit Clerk. Business checks accepted. Prepayment is required.

District Court - Criminal Division PO Box 1687, Tuscaloosa, AL 35403; 205-349-3870 X357. Hours: 8:30AM-5PM (CST). *Misdemeanor.*

Criminal Records: Access: Phone, mail, online, in person. Both court and visitors may perform in person searches. No search fee. Required to search: name, years to search, signed release; also helpful: DOB, SSN.

Criminal records on computer from 1985, books in storage from early 1965. Online access available through SJIS. See state introduction.

General Information: Public access terminal is available. No sealed, youthful offender records released. SASE preferred. Turnaround time 5 days. Copy fee: $.25 per page. Certification fee: $1.25. Business checks accepted. Prepayment is required.

Walker County

Circuit & District Court PO Box 749, Jasper, AL 35502; 205-384-7268; Fax: 205-384-7271. Hours: 8AM-4:30PM (CST). *Felony, Misdemeanor, Civil, Eviction, Small Claims, Probate.*

Note: Probate court is separate from this court, and can be contacted at PO Box 502 or at 205-384-7281.

Civil Records: Access: Online, in person. Visitors must perform in person searches for themselves. No search fee. Required to search: name, years to search. Civil cases indexed by defendant, plaintiff. Civil records on computer from 3/93, on index books from 1920s. Online access available through SJIS. See state introduction.

Criminal Records: Access: Online, in person. Visitors must perform in person searches for themselves. No search fee. Required to search: name, years to search. Criminal records on computer from 3/93, on index books from 1920s. Online access available through SJIS. See state introduction.

General Information: Public access terminal is available. No sealed, adoption, youthful offender, juvenile records released. Copy fee: $.25 per page. Certification fee: $1.00. Fee payee: Vinita Thomspon, Circuit Clerk. Only cashiers checks and money orders accepted. Prepayment is required.

Washington County

Circuit & District Court PO Box 548, Chatom, AL 36518; 251-847-2239. Hours: 8AM-4:30PM (CST). *Felony, Misdemeanor, Civil, Eviction, Small Claims, Probate.*

www.millry.net/~spgrimes

Civil Records: Access: Online, in person. Visitors must perform in person searches for themselves. No search fee. Required to search: name, years to search. Civil cases indexed by defendant. Civil records on computer since September 1994; prior 7 years on index cards. Online access available through SJIS. See state introduction. Also, online access to probate records is available by subscription at www.recordsusa.com/ Alabama/WashingtonCnAl.htm. Credit card, username and password is required; choose either monthly or per-use plan. Visit the web site or call Lisa at 601-264-7701 for information.

Criminal Records: Access: Online, in person. Visitors must perform in person searches for themselves. No search fee. Required to search: name, years to search, DOB; also helpful: SSN. Criminal records on computer since September 1994; prior 7 years on index cards. Online access available through SJIS. See state introduction.

General Information: Public access terminal is available. No sealed, adoption, youthful offender, juvenile records released. Copy fee: $.25 per page. Certification fee: $1.00. Fee payee: Circuit Clerk. Only cashiers checks and money orders accepted. Prepayment is required.

Wilcox County

Circuit & District Court PO Box 608, Camden, AL 36726; 334-682-4126; Probate phone: 334-682-4883. Hours: 8AM-Noon, 1-5PM (CST). *Felony, Misdemeanor, Civil, Eviction, Small Claims, Probate.*

Note: Probate court is separate from this court, and can be contacted at the telephone number above.

Civil Records: Access: Online, in person. Visitors must perform in person searches for themselves. No search fee. Required to search: name, years to search, address. Civil cases indexed by defendant, plaintiff. Civil records on computer since 1995; prior records on index books from 1970s, prior to 1970s in vault. Online access available through SJIS. See state introduction.

Criminal Records: Access: Online, in person. Visitors must perform in person searches for themselves. No search fee. Required to search: name, years to search; also helpful: DOB. Criminal records on computer since 1995; prior records on index books from 1970s, prior to 1970s in vault. Online access available through SJIS. See state introduction.

General Information: Public access terminal is available. No sealed, adoption, youthful offender, juvenile records released. Copy fee: $.25 per page. Certification fee: $1.50. Fee payee: Circuit Clerk. Business checks accepted.

Winston County

Circuit & District Court PO Box 309, Double Springs, AL 35553; 205-489-5533; Probate phone: 205-489-5219. Hours: 8AM-4:30PM (CST). *Felony, Misdemeanor, Civil, Eviction, Small Claims, Probate.*

Note: Probate court is separate from this court, and can be contacted at the telephone number above.

Civil Records: Access: Online, in person. Visitors must perform in person searches for themselves. No search fee. Required to search: name, years to search. Civil cases indexed by defendant, plaintiff. Civil records on index books from 1977, on computer since June 1994 including pending cases. Online access available through SJIS. See state introduction.

Criminal Records: Access: Online, in person. Visitors must perform in person searches for themselves. No search fee. Required to search: name, years to search, DOB; also helpful: SSN. Criminal records on index books from 1977, on computer since June 1994 including pending cases. Online access available through SJIS. See state introduction.

General Information: Public access terminal is available. No sealed, adoption, youthful offender, juvenile records released. Copy fee: $.25 per page. Certification fee: $1.00. Fee payee: Circuit Clerk. Business checks accepted. Prepayment is required.

Alabama Recording Offices

ORGANIZATION: 67 counties, 71 recording offices. The recording officer is Judge of Probate. Four counties have two recording offices-Barbour, Coffee, Jefferson, and St. Clair. See the notes under each county regarding how to determine which office is appropriate to search. The state is in the Central Time Zone (CST).

REAL ESTATE RECORDS: Most counties do not perform real estate searches. Copy fees vary. Certification fees vary. Tax records are located at the Assessor's Office.

UCC RECORDS: Alabama has adopted Revised Article 9 effective 01/01/2002. Financing statements are filed at the state level; real estate related collateral with the County Judge of Probate. Prior to 01/01/2002, consumer goods and farm collateral were filed with the county Judge of Probate. Only one-third of counties will perform UCC searches. Use search request form UCC-11. Search fees vary from $5.00 to $12.00 per debtor name. Copies usually cost $1.00 per page.

TAX LIEN RECORDS: Federal and state tax liens on personal property of businesses are filed with the Secretary of State. Other federal and state tax liens are filed with the county Judge of Probate. Counties do not perform separate tax lien searches although the liens are usually filed in the same index with UCC financing statements.

OTHER LIENS: Mechanics, judgment, lis pendens, hospital, vendor.

ONLINE ACCESS: There is no statewide system, but a limited number of counties offer free online access to recorded documents.

Autauga County

County Judge of Probate, 176 W. 5th St., Prattville, AL 36067-3041. 334-361-3731 R/E Recording: 334-361-3732; UCC Recording: 334-361-3732; Fax 334-361-3740.
This agency will not perform searches. **Other Phone Numbers:** Elections 334-361-3728.

Baldwin County

County Judge of Probate, PO Box 459, Bay Minette, AL 36507. County Judge of Probate, R/E and UCC Recording 251-937-0230; Fax 251-580-2563. www.probate.co.baldwin.al.us
Will search UCC records. This agency will not do a tax lien search. Will not search real estate records. **Online Access:** Property, Deed, Recording, UCC Records. Access to recordings, deeds, and UCCs is available at the web site, see the "Recording" box. Also, Online access to probate's property information is available at www.deltacomputersystems.com/al/al05/probatea.html.
Other Phone Numbers: Assessor 251-937-0245; Treasurer 251-937-0282; Appraiser/Auditor 251-937-0245; Elections 251-937-0399.

Barbour County (Clayton Division)

County Judge of Probate, PO Box 158, Clayton, AL 36016. 334-775-8371; Fax 334-775-1126.
File and search here for addresses in Clayton. File and search for Eufaula addresses there. For other addresses in the county, call for where to file. Will not search UCC records. Tax liens not included in UCC search. Will not search real estate records. **Other Phones:** Assessor 334-775-1110; Treasurer 334-775-3203.

Barbour County (Eufaula Division)

County Judge of Probate, PO Box 758, Eufaula, AL 36072. 334-687-1530; Fax 334-687-0921.
File and search for Eufaula addresses here. File and search for Clayton addresses there. For other addresses in the county, call for where to file. This agency will not perform searches. **Other Phone Numbers:** Assessor 334-687-1575; Treasurer 334-775-3203.

Bibb County

County Judge of Probate, 8 Court Square W, #A, 455 Walnut St, Centerville, AL 35042. 205-926-3104; Fax 205-926-1131.
This agency will not perform searches. **Other Phones:** Assessor 205-926-3105; Treasurer 205-926-3114.

Blount County

County Judge of Probate, 220 2nd Ave East, Oneonta, AL 35121. 205-625-4180; Fax 205-625-4206.
This agency will not perform searches. **Other Phones:** Assessor 205-625-4117; Treasurer 205-625-4117.

Bullock County

County Judge of Probate, PO Box 71, Union Springs, AL 36089. 334-738-2250; Fax 334-738-3839.
Will search UCC records. This agency will not do a tax lien search. Will not search real estate records. **Other Phone Numbers:** Assessor 334-738-2888.

Butler County

County Judge of Probate, PO Box 756, Greenville, AL 36037. 334-382-3512; Fax 334-382-5489.
This agency will not perform searches. **Other Phone Numbers:** Assessor 334-382-3221.

Calhoun County

County Judge of Probate, 1702 Noble St, Suite 102, Anniston, AL 36201. 256-241-2834 R/E Recording: 256-241-2825; Fax 256-231-1728.
Will not search UCC records. This agency will not do a tax lien search. Will help look for a specific property. **Other Phone Numbers:** Assessor 256-241-2855.

Chambers County

County Judge of Probate, Courthouse, Lafayette, AL 36862. 334-864-4384 R/E Recording: 334-864-4397 UCC Recording: 334-864-4393; Fax 334-864-4394.
Will search UCC records. This agency will not do a tax lien search. Will not search real estate records. **Other Phones:** Assessor 334-864-4389; Appraiser 334-864-4379; Elections 864-4380; Vital Records 864-4393.

Cherokee County

County Judge of Probate, 100 Main St #204, Centre, AL 35960. 256-927-3363; Fax 256-927-6949.
This agency will not perform searches. **Other Phone Numbers:** Assessor 256-927-5527.

Chilton County

County Judge of Probate, PO Box 270, Clanton, AL 35046. County Judge of Probate, R/E and UCC Recording 205-755-1555; Fax 205-280-7204.
This agency will not perform searches. **Other Phone Numbers:** Assessor 205-755-0155; Appraiser/Auditor 205-755-0160.

Choctaw County

County Judge of Probate, 117 S. Mulberry, Courthouse, Butler, AL 36904. 205-459-2417; Fax 205-459-4248.
Will search UCC records. This agency will not do a tax lien search. Will not search real estate records. **Other Phones:** Assessor 205-459-2412; Treasurer 205-459-2411.

Clarke County

County Judge of Probate, PO Box 10, Grove Hill, AL 36451. County Judge of Probate, R/E and UCC Recording 251-275-3251; Fax 251-275-8517.
Will search UCC records. This agency will not do a tax lien search. Will not search real estate records. **Other Phone Numbers:** Assessor 251-275-3376; Treasurer 251-275-3507; Appraiser/Auditor 251-275-3010; Elections 251-275-3251; Vital Records 251-275-3251.

Clay County

County Judge of Probate, PO Box 1120, Ashland, AL 36251. 256-354-3006; Fax 256-354-4778.
This agency will not perform searches. **Other Phone Numbers:** Assessor 256-354-2454.

Cleburne County

County Judge of Probate, 120 Vickery St, Room 101, Heflin, AL 36264. 256-463-5655; Fax 256-463-1044.
Will search UCC records. This agency will not do a tax lien search. Will not search real estate records. **Other Phone Numbers:** Assessor 256-463-5419; Treasurer 205-463-2873.

Coffee County (Elba Division)

County Judge of Probate, 230-P N. Court Ave, Elba, AL 36323. 334-897-2211; Fax 334-897-2028.
Will search UCC records. This agency will not do a tax lien search. Will not search real estate records.

Coffee County (Enterprise Div.)

County Judge of Probate, PO Box 311247, Enterprise, AL 36331. 334-347-2688; Fax 334-347-2095.
Will search UCC records. This agency will not do a tax lien search. Will not search real estate records. **Other Phone Numbers:** Assessor 334-347-8734.

Colbert County

County Judge of Probate, PO Box 47, Tuscumbia, AL 35674. 256-386-8546; Fax 256-386-8547.
This agency will not perform searches. **Other Phone Numbers:** Assessor 256-386-8530.

Conecuh County

County Judge of Probate, PO Box 149, Evergreen, AL 36401. 251-578-1221; Fax 251-578-7021.
Will not search real estate records. **Other Phone Numbers:** Assessor 251-578-7019.

Coosa County

County Judge of Probate, PO Box 218, Rockford, AL 35136. 256-377-4919; Fax 256-377-1549.
Will search UCC records. This agency will not do a tax lien search. Will look up specific real estate book and page number. **Other Phone Numbers:** Assessor 256-377-4919; Appraiser/Auditor 256-377-2684.

Covington County

County Judge of Probate, PO Box 789, Andalusia, AL 36420-0789. 334-428-2510 R/E Recording: 334-428-2518 UCC Recording: 334-428-2519; Fax 334-428-2536.
This agency will not perform searches. **Other Phone Numbers:** Assessor 334-428-2540.

Crenshaw County

County Judge of Probate, PO Box 328, Luverne, AL 36049-0328. 334-335-6568 R/E Recording: 334-335-6568 x227 UCC Recording: 334-335-6568 x227; Fax 334-335-3616.
This agency will not perform searches. **Other Phone Numbers:** Assessor 334-335-6568 x115; Treasurer 334-335-6568 x222; Appraiser/Auditor 334-335-6568 x236; Elections 334-335-6568 x254; Vital Records 334-335-2471.

Cullman County

County Judge of Probate, PO Box 970, Cullman, AL 35055. County Judge of Probate, R/E and UCC Recording 256-775-4807; Fax 256-775-4813.
Will search UCC records. This agency will not do a tax lien search. Will not search real estate records. **Other Phones:** Assessor 256-775-4844; Appraiser/Auditor 256-775-4825; Elections 256-775-4815.

Dale County

County Judge of Probate, PO Box 580, Ozark, AL 36361-0580. County Judge of Probate, R/E and UCC Recording 334-774-2754; Fax 334-774-0468.
Will search UCC records. This agency will not do a tax lien search. Will not search real estate records. **Other Phone Numbers:** Assessor 334-774-8100; Appraiser/Auditor 334-774-7208; Elections 334-774-9038; Vital Records 334-774-5146.

Dallas County

County Judge of Probate, PO Box 987, Selma, AL 36702-0987. 334-874-2516.
Will search UCC records. UCC search includes tax liens if requested. Will not search real estate records. **Other Phone Numbers:** Assessor 334-874-2520; Tax Collector 334-874-2519.

De Kalb County

County Judge of Probate, 300 Grand SW #100, Courthouse, Fort Payne, AL 35967. 256-845-8510; Fax 256-845-8514.
This agency will not perform searches. **Other Phone s:** Assessor 256-845-8515; Treasurer 256-845-8520.

Elmore County

County Judge of Probate, PO Box 280, Wetumpka, AL 36092. County Judge of Probate, R/E and UCC Recording 334-567-1143 UCC Recording: 334-567-1143 or 1145; Fax 334-567-1144.
This agency will not perform searches. **Other Phone Numbers:** Assessor 334-567-1118; Treasurer 334-567-1156; Appraiser/Auditor 334-567-1117; Vital Records 334-567-1145.

Escambia County

County Judge of Probate, PO Box 557, Brewton, AL 36427. 251-867-0206; Fax 251-867-0284. www.clerk.co.escambia.fl.us
Will search UCC records. This agency will not do a tax lien search. Will not search real estate records. **Other Phone Numbers:** Assessor 251-867-0214; Appraiser/Auditor 251-867-9168.

Etowah County

County Judge of Probate, PO Box 187, Gadsden, AL 35902. 256-549-5341; Fax 256-546-1149.
Will search UCC records. This agency will not do a tax lien search. Will not search real estate records. **Other Phone Numbers:** Assessor 256-549-5341 x121.

Fayette County

County Judge of Probate, PO Box 509, Fayette, AL 35555. 205-932-4519; Fax 205-932-7600.
This agency will not perform searches. **Other Phone Numbers:** Assessor 205-932-6081.

Franklin County

County Judge of Probate, PO Box 70, Russellville, AL 35653. 256-332-8801; Fax 256-332-8855.
This agency will not perform searches. **Other Phone Numbers:** Assessor 256-332-8831; Treasurer 256-332-8850.

Geneva County

County Judge of Probate, PO Box 430, Geneva, AL 36340-0430. County Judge of Probate, R/E and UCC Recording 334-684-5647; Fax 334-684-5602.
Will search UCC records. This agency will not do a tax lien search. Will not search real estate records. **Other Phone Numbers:** Assessor 334-684-3119; Appraiser/Auditor 334-684-5713; Elections 334-684-5655; Main Number 334-684-5600.

Greene County

County Judge of Probate, PO Box 790, Eutaw, AL 35462-0790. 205-372-3340; Fax 205-372-0499.
Will search UCC records. This agency will not do a tax lien search. Will not search real estate records. **Other Phone Numbers:** Assessor 205-372-3202.

Hale County

County Judge of Probate, 1001 Main St, Courthouse, Greensboro, AL 36744. 334-624-8740; Fax 334-624-8725.
Will search UCC records. Tax liens not included in UCC search. Will not search real estate records. **Other Phone Numbers:** Assessor 334-624-3854; Treasurer 334-624-4257; Appraiser/Auditor 334-624-0705.

Henry County

County Judge of Probate, 101 Court Square, Ste A, 101 W. Court Square, Abbeville, AL 36310. County Judge of Probate, R/E and UCC Recording 334-585-3257; Fax 334-585-3610.
Will search UCC records. This agency will not do a tax lien search. Will not search real estate records. **Other Phone Numbers:** Assessor 334-585-3043.

Houston County

County Judge of Probate, PO Drawer 6406, Dothan, AL 36302. County Judge of Probate, R/E and UCC Recording 334-677-4723; Fax 334-677-4733.
Will search UCC records. This agency will not do a tax lien search. Will not search real estate records. **Other Phone Numbers:** Assessor 334-677-4714.

Jackson County

County Judge of Probate, PO Box 128, Scottsboro, AL 35768. 256-574-9292; Fax 256-574-9318.

Will search UCC records. This agency will not do a tax lien search. Will not search real estate records. **Other Phone Numbers:** Assessor 256-574-9270.

Jefferson County (Bessemer Div.)

County Judge of Probate, 1801 3rd Ave., Bessemer, AL 35020. 205-481-4100.
Will search UCC records. This agency will not do a tax lien search. Will not search real estate records. **Other Phone Numbers:** Assessor 205-481-4125.

Jefferson County (Birmingham Div.)

County Judge of Probate, 716 N. 21st St, Courthouse, Birmingham, AL 35203. 205-325-5112 R/E Recording: 205-325-5411 UCC Recording: 205-325-5411; Fax 205-325-1437.
Will not search UCC records. Will search tax liens, including federal tax liens. Will not search real estate records. **Online Access:** Property Tax, Unclaimed Property Records. Access to the property tax due database is available free at http://tc.jeffcointouch.com/taxcollection/HTML/index.asp. No name searching. Also, access to the unclaimed property list is available free at www.jeffcointouch.com/unclaimed/alpha.asp?section=directory. **Other Phones:** Assessor 205-325-5505; Treasurer 205-325-5372; Vital Records 205-325-5182.

Lamar County

County Judge of Probate, PO Box 338, Vernon, AL 35592. 205-695-9119; Fax 205-695-9253.
Will search UCC records. This agency will not do a tax lien search. Will not search real estate records. **Other Phone Numbers:** Assessor 205-695-9139; Treasurer 205-695-7151.

Lauderdale County

County Judge of Probate, PO Box 1059, Florence, AL 35631-1059. 256-760-5800; Fax 256-760-5807.
This agency will not perform searches. **Other Phone Numbers:** Assessor 256-760-5785.

Lawrence County

County Judge of Probate, PO Box 310, Moulton, AL 35650. County Judge of Probate, R/E and UCC Recording 256-974-2440; Fax 256-974-3188.
This agency will not perform searches. **Other Phone Numbers:** Assessor 256-974-2476; Appraiser/Auditor 256-974-2546.

Lee County

County Judge of Probate, PO Drawer 2266, Opelika, AL 36803. 334-745-9761; Fax 334-745-5082.
This agency will not perform searches. **Other Phone Numbers:** Assessor 334-745-9786.

Limestone County

County Judge of Probate, PO Box 1145, Athens, AL 35612. 256-233-6427; Fax 256-233-6474.
This agency will not perform searches. **Other Phones:** Assessor 256-233-6435; Appraiser 256-233-6437.

Lowndes County

County Judge of Probate, PO Box 5, Hayneville, AL 36040-0005. 334-548-2365; Fax 334-548-5398.
Will search UCC records. UCC search includes tax liens if requested. Real estate owner, mortgage, and property transfer searches available. **Other Phone Numbers:** Assessor 334-548-2271.

Macon County

County Judge of Probate, 101 E. Northside St., Suite 101, Tuskegee, AL 36083-1731. 334-724-2611 R/E Recording: 334-724-2508 UCC Recording: 334-724-2508; Fax 334-724-2512.
Will search UCC records. This agency will not do a tax lien search. Will search real estate records. **Other**

Phone Numbers: Assessor 334-724-2603; Treasurer 334-724-5120; Appraiser/Auditor 334-724-2607; Elections 334-724-2611; Vital Records 334-724-2611.

Madison County

County Judge of Probate, 100 Northside Square, Room 101, Huntsville, AL 35801-4820. County Judge of Probate, R/E and UCC Recording 256-532-3339; Fax 256-532-3338.

Will search UCC records. This agency will not do a tax lien search. Will not search real estate records. **Other Phone Numbers:** Assessor 256-532-3350; Treasurer 256-532-3370; Appraiser/Auditor 256-532-3350.

Marengo County

County Judge of Probate, PO Box 480668, Linden, AL 36748. 334-295-2210; Fax 334-295-2254.

This agency will not perform searches. **Other Phone Numbers:** Assessor 334-295-2215.

Marion County

County Judge of Probate, PO Box 1687, Hamilton, AL 35570. County Judge of Probate, R/E and UCC Recording 205-921-2471; Fax 205-921-5109.

This agency will not perform searches. **Other Phone Numbers:** Assessor 205-921-2606; Treasurer 205-921-3561; Appraiser/Auditor 205-921-2606; Elections 205-921-2471; Vital Records 205-921-2471.

Marshall County

County Judge of Probate, 425 Gunter Ave, Guntersville, AL 35976. 256-571-7767 R/E Recording: 256-571-7764 x208 UCC Recording: 256-571-7764 x208; Fax 256-571-7732.

Will search UCC records. This agency will not do a tax lien search. Will not search real estate records. **Other Phone Numbers:** Assessor 256-571-5733; Treasurer 256-571-7758; Elections 256-571-7764 x202.

Mobile County

County Judge of Probate, PO Box 7, Mobile, AL 36601. 251-574-8497 R/E Recording: 251-690-8497 UCC Recording: 251-690-8497; Fax 251-690-4939. http://mobile-county.net/probate

Will search UCC records. This agency will not do a tax lien search. Will not search real estate records. **Online Access:** Deed, UCC, Property, Incs, Marriage Records. Access to the Probate court's recordings database are available free at www.mobilecounty.org/probatecourt/recordssearch.htm. Marriages are in a separate index. **Other Phone Numbers:** Assessor 251-574-8530; Treasurer 251-690-8585; Appraiser/Auditor 251-690-8531; Elections 251-574-8480.

Monroe County

County Judge of Probate, PO Box 665, Monroeville, AL 36461-0665. 251-743-4107 R/E Recording: 251-743-4107 x121 UCC Recording: 251-743-4107 x121; Fax 251-575-7934.

This agency will not perform searches. **Other Phone Numbers:** Assessor 251-743-4107 x124; Appraiser/Auditor 251-743-4107 x124; Elections 251-743-4107 x120; Vital Records 251-743-4107 x121.

Montgomery County

County Judge of Probate, PO Box 223, Montgomery, AL 36195. 334-832-1237 R/E Recording: 334-832-1236/1237.

This agency will not perform searches. **Other Phone Numbers:** Assessor 334-832-4950.

Morgan County

County Judge of Probate, PO Box 848, Decatur, AL 35602-0848. County Judge of Probate, R/E and UCC Recording 256-351-4680.

Will search UCC records. This agency will not do a tax lien search. Will not search real estate records. **Online**

Access: Property, Appraisal Records. Access is available free at www.deltacomputersystems.com/AL/AL52/INDEX.html. **Other Phone Numbers:** Assessor 256-351-4690.

Perry County

County Judge of Probate, PO Box 478, Marion, AL 36756. County Judge of Probate, R/E and UCC Recording 334-683-2210; Fax 334-683-2201.

Will search UCC records. This agency will not do a tax lien search. Will not search real estate records. **Other Phone Numbers:** Assessor 334-683-2219; Appraiser/Auditor 334-683-2221; Elections 334-683-2210; Collector 334-683-2220.

Pickens County

County Judge of Probate, PO Box 370, Carrollton, AL 35447. County Judge of Probate, R/E and UCC Recording 205-367-2010; Fax 205-367-2011.

Will search UCC records. This agency will not do a tax lien search. Will not search real estate records. **Other Phone Numbers:** Assessor 205-367-2041; Elections 205-367-2010.

Pike County

County Judge of Probate, PO Drawer 1008, Troy, AL 36081. 334-566-1246; Fax 334-566-8585.

This agency will not perform searches. **Other Phone Numbers:** Assessor 334-566-1792.

Randolph County

County Judge of Probate, PO Box 249, Wedowee, AL 36278. 256-357-4933; Fax 256-357-9053.

Will search UCC records. This agency will not do a tax lien search. Will not search real estate records. **Other Phone Numbers:** Assessor 256-357-4343.

Russell County

County Judge of Probate, PO Box 700, Phenix City, AL 36868-0700. 334-298-7979; Fax 334-298-7979.

Will search UCC records. This agency will not do a tax lien search. Will not search real estate records. **Other Phone Numbers:** Assessor 334-298-4441; Treasurer 334-298-6426; Appraiser/Auditor 334-297-8996.

Shelby County

County Judge of Probate, PO Box 825, Columbiana, AL 35051. 205-669-3720; Fax 205-669-3714.

Will search UCC records. This agency will not do a tax lien search. Will not search real estate records. **Other Phone Numbers:** Assessor 205-669-3902; Appraiser/Auditor 205-669-3902.

St. Clair County (Northern Congressional District)

County Judge of Probate, PO Box 220, Ashville, AL 35953. County Judge of Probate, R/E and UCC Recording 205-594-2124; Fax 205-594-2125. www.stclairco.com/sections/probate_office/index.htm

This agency will not perform searches. **Other Phone Numbers:** Assessor 205-594-2160; Appraiser/Auditor 205-594-2168; Vital Records 334-206-5418.

St. Clair County (Southern Congressional District)

County Judge of Probate, 1815 Cogswell Ave, Suite 212, 1815 Cogswell Ave., Pell City, AL 35125. County Judge of Probate, R/E and UCC Recording 205-338-9449; Fax 205-884-1182.

Will search UCC records. This agency will not do a tax lien search. Will not search real estate records. **Online Access:** Property, Appraisal Records. Access is available free at www.deltacomputersystems.com/AL/AL59/INDEX.html. **Other Phone Numbers:** Assessor 205-884-2395; Appraiser/Auditor 205-884-2395.

Sumter County

County Judge of Probate, PO Box 1040, Livingston, AL 35470-1040. County Judge of Probate, R/E and UCC Recording 205-652-7281; Fax 205-652-6206.

Will search UCC records. This agency will not do a tax lien search. Will not search real estate records. **Other Phone Numbers:** Assessor 205-652-2424; Treasurer 205-652-2731; Elections 205-652-7281; Vital Records 205-652-7281.

Talladega County

County Judge of Probate, PO Box 737, Talladega, AL 35161. 256-362-4175; Fax 256-761-2128.

This agency will not perform searches. **Other Phone Numbers:** Assessor 256-761-2123.

Tallapoosa County

County Judge of Probate, Courthouse, Room 126, 125 N. Broadnax St., Dadeville, AL 36853. County Judge of Probate, R/E and UCC Recording 256-825-1090; Fax 256-825-1604.

Will search UCC records. This agency will not do a tax lien search. Will not search real estate records. **Other Phone Numbers:** Assessor 256-825-7831; Appraiser/Auditor 256-825-1090.

Tuscaloosa County

County Judge of Probate, PO Box 20067, Tuscaloosa, AL 35402-0067. 205-349-3870 x205/6; www.tuscco.com

Will not search UCC records. This agency will not do a tax lien search. Will search real estate names as time permits. **Online Access:** Real Estate, Lien, UCC, Grantor/Grantee, Probate, Marriage Records. Access to the records database is available free at www.tuscco.com/RecordsRoom/Records.htm. Also included are searches for mortgages, incorporations, bonds, discharges, exemptions. **Other Phone Numbers:** Assessor 205-349-3870 x370.

Walker County

County Judge of Probate, PO Box 502, Jasper, AL 35502-0502. 205-384-7282 R/E Recording: 205-384-7281; Fax 205-384-7005.

Will search UCC records. This agency will not do a tax lien search. Will not search real estate records. **Other Phone Numbers:** Assessor 205-384-7265; Treasurer 205-384-7276.

Washington County

County Judge of Probate, PO Box 549, Chatom, AL 36518. County Judge of Probate, R/E and UCC Recording 251-847-2201; Fax 251-847-3677. www.recordsusa.com

Will search UCC records. This agency will not do a tax lien search. Will not search real estate records. **Other Phone Numbers:** Assessor 251-847-2780; Treasurer 251-847-2208.

Wilcox County

County Judge of Probate, PO Box 668, Camden, AL 36726. 334-682-4883; Fax 334-682-9484.

Will search UCC records. This agency will not do a tax lien search. Will not search real estate records. **Other Phone Numbers:** Assessor 334-682-4625; Treasurer 334-682-9112.

Winston County

County Judge of Probate, PO Box 27, Double Springs, AL 35553. County Judge of Probate, R/E and UCC Recording 205-489-5219; Fax 205-489-5135.

This agency will not perform searches. **Other Phones:** Assessor 205-489-5166; Appraiser/Auditor 205-489-5166; Vital Records 205-489-5219 (marriages).

Alabama County Locator

You will usually be able to find the city name in the City/County Cross Reference below. In that case, it is a simple matter to determine the county from the cross reference. However, only the official US Postal Service city names are included in this index. There are an additional 40,000 place names that people use in their addresses. Therefore, we have also included a ZIP/City Cross Reference immediately following the City/County Cross Reference.

If you know the ZIP Code but the city name does not appear in the City/County Cross Reference index, look up the ZIP Code in the ZIP/City Cross Reference, find the city name, then look up the city name in the City/County Cross Reference. For example, you want to know the county for an address of Menands, NY 12204. There is no "Menands" in the City/County Cross Reference. The ZIP/City Cross Reference shows that ZIP Codes 12201-12288 are for the city of Albany. Looking back in the City/County Cross Reference, Albany is in Albany County.

City/County Cross Reference

ABBEVILLE Henry
ABERNANT Tuscaloosa
ADAMSVILLE Jefferson
ADDISON (35540) Winston(95),
   Cullman(4)
ADGER (35006) Jefferson(91),
   Walker(5), Tuscaloosa(2)
AKRON Hale
ALABASTER Shelby
ALBERTA Wilcox
ALBERTVILLE (35951) Marshall(72), De
   Kalb(27)
ALEXANDER CITY Tallapoosa
ALEXANDRIA Calhoun
ALICEVILLE (35442) Pickens(88),
   Sumter(11)
ALLEN Clarke
ALLGOOD Blount
ALMA Clarke
ALPINE Talladega
ALTON Jefferson
ALTOONA (35952) Etowah(57),
   Blount(42)
ANDALUSIA (36420) Covington(96),
   Escambia(2), Conecuh(1)
ANDERSON (35610) Lauderdale(74),
   Limestone(25)
ANNEMANIE Wilcox
ANNISTON Calhoun
ARAB (35016) Marshall(82),
   Cullman(14), Blount(2)
ARDMORE (35739) Limestone(77),
   Madison(22)
ARITON (36311) Dale(68), Barbour(21),
   Coffee(9)
ARLEY Winston
ARLINGTON (36722) Wilcox(97),
   Marengo(2)
ASHFORD Houston
ASHLAND Clay
ASHVILLE St. Clair
ATHENS Limestone
ATMORE Escambia
ATTALLA Etowah
AUBURN Lee
AUBURN UNIVERSITY Lee
AUTAUGAVILLE Autauga
AXIS Mobile
BAILEYTON (35019) Cullman(73),
   Morgan(26)
BANKS (36005) Pike(42), Barbour(34),
   Bullock(22)
BANKSTON Fayette
BAY MINETTE Baldwin
BAYOU LA BATRE Mobile
BEAR CREEK Marion
BEATRICE Monroe
BEAVERTON Lamar

BELK Fayette
BELLAMY Sumter
BELLE MINA Limestone
BELLWOOD Geneva
BERRY (35546) Fayette(65),
   Tuscaloosa(31), Walker(3)
BESSEMER Jefferson
BIGBEE Washington
BILLINGSLEY (36006) Autauga(59),
   Chilton(40)
BIRMINGHAM Jefferson
BLACK Geneva
BLOUNTSVILLE Blount
BOAZ (35957) Marshall(77), De
   Kalb(18), Blount(3)
BOLIGEE Greene
BOLINGER Choctaw
BON AIR Talladega
BON SECOUR Baldwin
BOOTH Autauga
BOYKIN Wilcox
BRANTLEY (36009) Crenshaw(94),
   Coffee(5)
BREMEN (35033) Cullman(90),
   Walker(9)
BRENT Bibb
BREWTON Escambia
BRIDGEPORT Jackson
BRIERFIELD (35035) Bibb(97),
   Shelby(1)
BRILLIANT Marion
BROOKLYN Conecuh
BROOKSIDE Jefferson
BROOKWOOD (35444) Tuscaloosa(96),
   Jefferson(3)
BROWNSBORO Madison
BRUNDIDGE (36010) Pike(65),
   Coffee(34)
BRYANT Jackson
BUCKS Mobile
BUHL Tuscaloosa
BURNT CORN Monroe
BURNWELL Walker
BUTLER Choctaw
BYNUM Calhoun
CALERA (35040) Shelby(86),
   Chilton(13)
CALVERT Washington
CAMDEN Wilcox
CAMP HILL (36850) Tallapoosa(76),
   Chambers(20), Lee(3)
CAMPBELL Clarke
CAPSHAW Limestone
CARBON HILL (35549) Walker(82),
   Fayette(17)
CARDIFF Jefferson
CARLTON Clarke
CARROLLTON Pickens

CASTLEBERRY (36432) Conecuh(66),
   Escambia(33)
CATHERINE Wilcox
CECIL (36013) Montgomery(94),
   Macon(5)
CEDAR BLUFF Cherokee
CENTRE Cherokee
CENTREVILLE Bibb
CHANCELLOR (36316) Geneva(53),
   Coffee(46)
CHAPMAN Butler
CHATOM Washington
CHELSEA Shelby
CHEROKEE Colbert
CHILDERSBURG Talladega
CHOCCOLOCCO Calhoun
CHUNCHULA Mobile
CITRONELLE (36522) Mobile(95),
   Washington(4)
CLANTON (35046) Chilton(97),
   Coosa(2)
CLAY Jefferson
CLAYTON Barbour
CLEVELAND Blount
CLINTON Greene
CLIO Barbour
CLOPTON (36317) Henry(90),
   Barbour(6), Dale(3)
CLOVERDALE Lauderdale
COALING Tuscaloosa
CODEN Mobile
COFFEE SPRINGS (36318)
   Geneva(70), Coffee(29)
COFFEEVILLE Clarke
COKER Tuscaloosa
COLLINSVILLE (35961) De Kalb(78),
   Etowah(10), Cherokee(10)
COLUMBIA (36319) Henry(53),
   Houston(46)
COLUMBIANA Shelby
COOK SPRINGS St. Clair
COOSADA Elmore
CORDOVA Walker
COTTONDALE Tuscaloosa
COTTONTON Russell
COTTONWOOD Houston
COURTLAND Lawrence
COWARTS Houston
COY Wilcox
CRAGFORD (36255) Clay(97),
   Tallapoosa(2)
CRANE HILL Cullman
CREOLA Mobile
CROMWELL Choctaw
CROPWELL St. Clair
CROSSVILLE (35962) De Kalb(93),
   Marshall(6)
CUBA Sumter

CULLMAN Cullman
CUSSETA (36852) Lee(74),
   Chambers(25)
DADEVILLE Tallapoosa
DALEVILLE (36322) Dale(97),
   Geneva(1), Coffee(1)
DANVILLE (35619) Morgan(49),
   Lawrence(49)
DAPHNE Baldwin
DAUPHIN ISLAND Mobile
DAVISTON (36256) Tallapoosa(94),
   Clay(5)
DAWSON De Kalb
DAYTON Marengo
DE ARMANVILLE Calhoun
DEATSVILLE (36022) Elmore(82),
   Autauga(17)
DECATUR Morgan
DEER PARK Washington
DELMAR Winston
DELTA (36258) Clay(53), Cleburne(29),
   Randolph(17)
DEMOPOLIS Marengo
DETROIT (35552) Marion(56),
   Lamar(43)
DICKINSON Clarke
DIXONS MILLS Marengo
DOCENA Jefferson
DOLOMITE Jefferson
DORA (35062) Jefferson(54),
   Walker(45)
DOTHAN (36305) Houston(86),
   Geneva(13)
DOUBLE SPRINGS Winston
DOUGLAS Marshall
DOZIER (36028) Crenshaw(64),
   Covington(35)
DUNCANVILLE Tuscaloosa
DUTTON Jackson
EAST TALLASSEE Tallapoosa
EASTABOGA (36260) Calhoun(63),
   Talladega(36)
ECHOLA Tuscaloosa
ECLECTIC Elmore
EDWARDSVILLE Cleburne
EIGHT MILE Mobile
ELBA Coffee
ELBERTA Baldwin
ELDRIDGE (35554) Fayette(65),
   Walker(28), Marion(5)
ELKMONT Limestone
ELMORE Elmore
ELROD Tuscaloosa
EMELLE Sumter
EMPIRE (35063) Walker(71), Blount(19),
   Jefferson(9)
ENTERPRISE Coffee
EPES Sumter

EQUALITY (36026) Elmore(61), Coosa(38)
ESTILLFORK Jackson
ETHELSVILLE Pickens
EUFAULA Barbour
EUTAW Greene
EVA (35621) Morgan(92), Cullman(7)
EVERGREEN Conecuh
EXCEL Monroe
FACKLER Jackson
FAIRFIELD Jefferson
FAIRHOPE Baldwin
FALKVILLE (35622) Morgan(79), Cullman(20)
FAUNSDALE Marengo
FAYETTE (35555) Fayette(92), Tuscaloosa(5), Lamar(1)
FITZPATRICK (36029) Macon(47), Bullock(33), Montgomery(19)
FIVE POINTS Chambers
FLAT ROCK (35966) Jackson(64), De Kalb(35)
FLOMATON Escambia
FLORALA Covington
FLORENCE Lauderdale
FOLEY Baldwin
FOREST HOME (36030) Butler(96), Wilcox(3)
FORKLAND Greene
FORT DAVIS Macon
FORT DEPOSIT (36032) Lowndes(75), Butler(24)
FORT MITCHELL Russell
FORT PAYNE De Kalb
FORT RUCKER Dale
FOSTERS Tuscaloosa
FRANKLIN Monroe
FRANKVILLE Washington
FRISCO CITY Monroe
FRUITDALE Washington
FRUITHURST Cleburne
FULTON Clarke
FULTONDALE Jefferson
FURMAN Wilcox
FYFFE De Kalb
GADSDEN Etowah
GAINESTOWN Clarke
GAINESVILLE (35464) Sumter(96), Greene(3)
GALLANT (35972) Etowah(74), St. Clair(25)
GALLION (36742) Marengo(95), Hale(4)
GANTT Covington
GARDEN CITY Cullman
GARDENDALE Jefferson
GAYLESVILLE Cherokee
GENEVA Geneva
GEORGIANA (36033) Butler(98), Conecuh(1)
GERALDINE De Kalb
GILBERTOWN Choctaw
GLEN ALLEN Fayette
GLENWOOD (36034) Pike(51), Crenshaw(48)
GOODSPRINGS Walker
GOODWATER (35072) Clay(51), Coosa(27), Tallapoosa(20)
GOODWAY Monroe
GORDO (35466) Pickens(93), Tuscaloosa(6)
GORDON Houston
GOSHEN (36035) Pike(56), Crenshaw(43)
GRADY (36036) Montgomery(75), Crenshaw(24)
GRAHAM Randolph
GRAND BAY Mobile

GRANT Marshall
GRAYSVILLE Jefferson
GREEN POND Bibb
GREENSBORO Hale
GREENVILLE Butler
GROVE HILL Clarke
GROVEOAK (35975) De Kalb(92), Marshall(7)
GUIN (35563) Marion(91), Fayette(4), Lamar(3)
GULF SHORES Baldwin
GUNTERSVILLE (35976) Marshall(97), Blount(2)
GURLEY (35748) Madison(95), Jackson(4)
HACKLEBURG Marion
HALEYVILLE (35565) Winston(66), Marion(29), Franklin(4)
HAMILTON Marion
HANCEVILLE Cullman
HARDAWAY Macon
HARPERSVILLE Shelby
HARTFORD Geneva
HARTSELLE Morgan
HARVEST (35749) Madison(74), Limestone(25)
HATCHECHUBBEE Russell
HAYDEN Blount
HAYNEVILLE Lowndes
HAZEL GREEN Madison
HEADLAND (36345) Henry(81), Houston(11), Dale(6)
HEFLIN (36264) Cleburne(92), Randolph(7)
HELENA Shelby
HENAGAR (35978) De Kalb(79), Jackson(20)
HIGDON (35979) De Kalb(67), Jackson(32)
HIGHLAND HOME (36041) Crenshaw(96), Montgomery(3)
HILLSBORO Lawrence
HODGES (35571) Franklin(69), Marion(30)
HOLLINS Clay
HOLLY POND Cullman
HOLLYTREE Jackson
HOLLYWOOD Jackson
HOLY TRINITY Russell
HONORAVILLE (36042) Crenshaw(54), Butler(45)
HOPE HULL (36043) Montgomery(65), Lowndes(34)
HORTON (35980) Marshall(66), Blount(33)
HOUSTON Winston
HUNTSVILLE Madison
HURTSBORO (36860) Russell(86), Bullock(8), Macon(4)
HUXFORD Escambia
IDER De Kalb
IRVINGTON Mobile
JACHIN Choctaw
JACK Coffee
JACKSON Clarke
JACKSONS GAP Tallapoosa
JACKSONVILLE Calhoun
JASPER Walker
JEFFERSON Marengo
JEMISON Chilton
JONES (36749) Dallas(53), Autauga(46)
JOPPA (35087) Cullman(50), Morgan(38), Marshall(11)
KANSAS Walker
KELLERMAN Tuscaloosa
KELLYTON (35089) Tallapoosa(61), Coosa(38)

KENNEDY (35574) Lamar(55), Pickens(33), Fayette(10)
KENT Elmore
KILLEN Lauderdale
KIMBERLY Jefferson
KINSTON (36453) Coffee(53), Geneva(45), Covington(1)
KNOXVILLE (35469) Tuscaloosa(50), Greene(49)
LACEYS SPRING (35754) Morgan(98), Marshall(1)
LAFAYETTE Chambers
LAMISON Wilcox
LANETT Chambers
LANGSTON (35755) Marshall(58), Jackson(41)
LAPINE (36046) Crenshaw(52), Montgomery(47)
LAVACA Choctaw
LAWLEY (36793) Bibb(67), Chilton(24), Perry(7)
LEEDS (35094) Jefferson(69), Shelby(19), St. Clair(10)
LEESBURG (35983) Cherokee(98), De Kalb(1)
LEIGHTON Colbert
LENOX Conecuh
LEROY Washington
LESTER Limestone
LETOHATCHEE (36047) Lowndes(68), Montgomery(31)
LEXINGTON Lauderdale
LILLIAN Baldwin
LINCOLN (35096) Talladega(89), Calhoun(10)
LINDEN Marengo
LINEVILLE (36266) Clay(83), Randolph(16)
LISMAN Choctaw
LITTLE RIVER Baldwin
LIVINGSTON Sumter
LOACHAPOKA Lee
LOCKHART Covington
LOCUST FORK Blount
LOGAN (35098) Cullman(89), Winston(10)
LOUISVILLE Barbour
LOWER PEACH TREE (36751) Monroe(47), Wilcox(28), Clarke(24)
LOWNDESBORO Lowndes
LOXLEY Baldwin
LUVERNE Crenshaw
LYNN Winston
MADISON Madison
MAGNOLIA Marengo
MAGNOLIA SPRINGS Baldwin
MALCOLM Washington
MALVERN Geneva
MAPLESVILLE (36750) Chilton(93), Bibb(6)
MARBURY (36051) Autauga(43), Elmore(30), Chilton(26)
MARGARET St. Clair
MARION Perry
MARION JUNCTION (36759) Dallas(94), Perry(5)
MATHEWS (36052) Montgomery(93), Bullock(6)
MAYLENE Shelby
MC CALLA (35111) Tuscaloosa(63), Jefferson(35), Bibb(1)
MC INTOSH Washington
MC KENZIE (36456) Butler(80), Conecuh(14), Covington(4)
MC SHAN Pickens
MC WILLIAMS Wilcox
MEGARGEL Monroe

MELVIN Choctaw
MENTONE (35984) De Kalb(79), Cherokee(20)
MERIDIANVILLE Madison
MEXIA Monroe
MIDLAND CITY (36350) Dale(91), Houston(8)
MIDWAY (36053) Barbour(78), Bullock(21)
MILLBROOK Elmore
MILLERS FERRY Wilcox
MILLERVILLE Clay
MILLPORT (35576) Lamar(88), Pickens(11)
MILLRY (36558) Washington(80), Choctaw(19)
MINTER (36761) Dallas(59), Lowndes(39), Wilcox(1)
MOBILE Mobile
MONROEVILLE Monroe
MONTEVALLO (35115) Shelby(83), Chilton(14), Bibb(1)
MONTGOMERY Montgomery
MONTROSE Baldwin
MOODY St. Clair
MOORESVILLE Limestone
MORRIS Jefferson
MORVIN Clarke
MOULTON Lawrence
MOUNDVILLE (35474) Hale(87), Tuscaloosa(12)
MOUNT HOPE (35651) Lawrence(98), Franklin(1)
MOUNT MEIGS Montgomery
MOUNT OLIVE Jefferson
MOUNT VERNON Mobile
MULGA Jefferson
MUNFORD Talladega
MUSCADINE Cleburne
MUSCLE SHOALS Colbert
MYRTLEWOOD Marengo
NANAFALIA Marengo
NATURAL BRIDGE Winston
NAUVOO (35578) Walker(79), Winston(20)
NEEDHAM Choctaw
NEW BROCKTON (36351) Coffee(96), Henry(3)
NEW CASTLE Jefferson
NEW HOPE (35760) Madison(88), Marshall(11)
NEW MARKET Madison
NEWBERN (36765) Hale(85), Perry(14)
NEWELL Randolph
NEWTON (36352) Houston(63), Dale(33), Geneva(3)
NEWVILLE (36353) Henry(76), Dale(23)
NORMAL Madison
NORTHPORT Tuscaloosa
NOTASULGA (36866) Macon(73), Tallapoosa(20), Lee(5)
OAK HILL Wilcox
OAKMAN (35579) Walker(97), Tuscaloosa(1)
ODENVILLE St. Clair
OHATCHEE Calhoun
ONEONTA (35121) Blount(98), St. Clair(1)
OPELIKA (36804) Lee(97), Macon(1), Russell(1)
OPP (36467) Covington(94), Coffee(5)
ORANGE BEACH Baldwin
ORRVILLE Dallas
OWENS CROSS ROADS Madison
OZARK Dale
PAINT ROCK Jackson
PALMERDALE Jefferson

PANOLA Sumter
PANSEY Houston
PARRISH Walker
PAUL Conecuh
PELHAM Shelby
PELL CITY St. Clair
PENNINGTON Choctaw
PERDIDO (36562) Baldwin(90),
    Escambia(9)
PERDUE HILL Monroe
PEROTE Bullock
PETERMAN (36471) Monroe(96),
    Conecuh(3)
PETERSON Tuscaloosa
PETREY Crenshaw
PHENIX CITY (36870) Lee(71),
    Russell(28)
PHIL CAMPBELL (35581) Franklin(87),
    Marion(12)
PIEDMONT (36272) Calhoun(60),
    Cherokee(25), Etowah(9), Cleburne(3)
PIKE ROAD Montgomery
PINCKARD Dale
PINE APPLE Wilcox
PINE HILL Wilcox
PINE LEVEL Montgomery
PINSON (35126) Jefferson(95),
    Blount(4)
PISGAH (35765) Jackson(92), De
    Kalb(7)
PITTSVIEW Russell
PLANTERSVILLE (36758) Dallas(90),
    Autauga(7), Chilton(1)
PLEASANT GROVE Jefferson
POINT CLEAR Baldwin
PRAIRIE Wilcox
PRATTVILLE Autauga
PRINCETON Jackson
QUINTON (35130) Walker(64),
    Jefferson(35)
RAGLAND St. Clair
RAINBOW CITY Etowah
RAINSVILLE De Kalb
RALPH (35480) Tuscaloosa(97),
    Greene(2)
RAMER Montgomery
RANBURNE Cleburne
RANDOLPH (36792) Bibb(72),
    Chilton(27)
RANGE Conecuh
RED BAY Franklin
RED LEVEL (36474) Covington(92),
    Conecuh(6), Butler(1)
REFORM Pickens
REMLAP (35133) Blount(93), St. Clair(6)

REPTON (36475) Conecuh(64),
    Monroe(35)
RIVER FALLS Covington
RIVERSIDE St. Clair
ROANOKE (36274) Randolph(92),
    Chambers(7)
ROBERTSDALE Baldwin
ROCKFORD Coosa
ROGERSVILLE (35652) Lauderdale(98),
    Limestone(1)
RUSSELLVILLE (35654) Franklin(80),
    Colbert(14), Lawrence(5)
RUTLEDGE (36071) Crenshaw(97),
    Butler(2)
RYLAND Madison
SAFFORD (36773) Dallas(89),
    Marengo(10)
SAGINAW Shelby
SAINT ELMO Mobile
SAINT STEPHENS Washington
SALEM (36874) Lee(95), Russell(4)
SALITPA Clarke
SAMANTHA Tuscaloosa
SAMSON (36477) Geneva(92),
    Coffee(7)
SARALAND Mobile
SARDIS (36775) Dallas(81),
    Lowndes(18)
SATSUMA Mobile
SAWYERVILLE Hale
SAYRE Jefferson
SCOTTSBORO (35769) Jackson(70),
    Marshall(29)
SEALE Russell
SECTION (35771) Jackson(96), De
    Kalb(3)
SELMA (36703) Dallas(97), Autauga(2)
SEMINOLE Baldwin
SEMMES Mobile
SHANNON Jefferson
SHEFFIELD Colbert
SHELBY Shelby
SHORTER Macon
SHORTERVILLE Henry
SILAS Choctaw
SILURIA Shelby
SILVERHILL Baldwin
SIPSEY Walker
SKIPPERVILLE (36374) Barbour(60),
    Dale(39)
SLOCOMB (36375) Geneva(87),
    Houston(12)
SMITHS Lee
SMITHS STATION Lee
SNOW HILL Wilcox
SOMERVILLE Morgan

SPANISH FORT Baldwin
SPRING GARDEN Cherokee
SPRINGVILLE (35146) St. Clair(80),
    Blount(17), Jefferson(1)
SPROTT Perry
SPRUCE PINE Franklin
STANTON Chilton
STAPLETON Baldwin
STEELE St. Clair
STERRETT Shelby
STEVENSON Jackson
STOCKTON Baldwin
SULLIGENT Lamar
SUMITON Walker
SUMMERDALE Baldwin
SUNFLOWER Washington
SWEET WATER Marengo
SYCAMORE Talladega
SYLACAUGA (35151) Talladega(67),
    Coosa(32)
SYLVANIA De Kalb
TALLADEGA Talladega
TALLASSEE (36078) Elmore(81),
    Tallapoosa(18)
TANNER Limestone
THEODORE Mobile
THOMASTON Marengo
THOMASVILLE (36784) Clarke(80),
    Marengo(16), Wilcox(3)
THORSBY Chilton
TIBBIE Washington
TITUS (36080) Elmore(98), Coosa(1)
TONEY (35773) Madison(72),
    Limestone(27)
TOWN CREEK (35672) Lawrence(97),
    Colbert(2)
TOWNLEY Walker
TOXEY Choctaw
TRAFFORD (35172) Blount(83),
    Jefferson(16)
TRENTON Jackson
TRINITY (35673) Lawrence(78),
    Morgan(21)
TROY Pike
TRUSSVILLE (35173) Jefferson(82), St.
    Clair(17)
TUSCALOOSA Tuscaloosa
TUSCUMBIA Colbert
TUSKEGEE Macon
TUSKEGEE INSTITUTE Macon
TYLER (36785) Lowndes(74), Dallas(25)
UNION GROVE (35175) Marshall(89),
    Morgan(10)
UNION SPRINGS Bullock
UNIONTOWN (36786) Perry(89),
    Hale(6), Marengo(4)

URIAH Monroe
VALHERMOSO SPRINGS Morgan
VALLEY Lee
VALLEY HEAD De Kalb
VANCE Tuscaloosa
VANDIVER Shelby
VERBENA (36091) Chilton(95),
    Autauga(3)
VERNON Lamar
VINA (35593) Franklin(86), Marion(13)
VINCENT (35178) Shelby(70), St.
    Clair(29)
VINEGAR BEND Washington
VINEMONT (35179) Cullman(98),
    Morgan(1)
VREDENBURGH Monroe
WADLEY (36276) Randolph(66),
    Chambers(16), Clay(12),
    Tallapoosa(4)
WAGARVILLE Washington
WALKER SPRINGS Clarke
WALNUT GROVE Etowah
WARD (36922) Choctaw(91), Sumter(8)
WARRIOR (35180) Jefferson(55),
    Blount(44)
WATERLOO Lauderdale
WATSON Jefferson
WATTSVILLE St. Clair
WAVERLY (36879) Lee(50),
    Chambers(49)
WEAVER Calhoun
WEBB Houston
WEDOWEE Randolph
WELLINGTON Calhoun
WEOGUFKA Coosa
WEST BLOCTON (35184) Bibb(98),
    Tuscaloosa(1)
WEST GREENE Greene
WESTOVER Shelby
WETUMPKA Elmore
WHATLEY (36482) Clarke(98),
    Monroe(1)
WILMER Mobile
WILSONVILLE Shelby
WILTON Shelby
WINFIELD (35594) Fayette(55),
    Marion(44)
WING (36483) Escambia(64),
    Covington(35)
WOODLAND Randolph
WOODSTOCK (35188) Bibb(88),
    Tuscaloosa(11)
WOODVILLE (35776) Jackson(83),
    Marshall(14), Madison(1)
YORK Sumter

ZIP/City Cross Reference

35004-35004 MOODY	35143-35143 SHELBY	35563-35563 GUIN	35768-35769 SCOTTSBORO
35005-35005 ADAMSVILLE	35144-35144 SILURIA	35564-35564 HACKLEBURG	35771-35771 SECTION
35006-35006 ADGER	35146-35146 SPRINGVILLE	35565-35565 HALEYVILLE	35772-35772 STEVENSON
35007-35007 ALABASTER	35147-35147 STERRETT	35570-35570 HAMILTON	35773-35773 TONEY
35010-35011 ALEXANDER CITY	35148-35148 SUMITON	35571-35571 HODGES	35774-35774 TRENTON
35013-35013 ALLGOOD	35149-35149 SYCAMORE	35572-35572 HOUSTON	35775-35775 VALHERMOSO SPRINGS
35014-35014 ALPINE	35150-35151 SYLACAUGA	35573-35573 KANSAS	35776-35776 WOODVILLE
35015-35015 ALTON	35160-35161 TALLADEGA	35574-35574 KENNEDY	35800-35899 HUNTSVILLE
35016-35016 ARAB	35171-35171 THORSBY	35575-35575 LYNN	35901-35905 GADSDEN
35019-35019 BAILEYTON	35172-35172 TRAFFORD	35576-35576 MILLPORT	35906-35906 RAINBOW CITY
35020-35023 BESSEMER	35173-35173 TRUSSVILLE	35577-35577 NATURAL BRIDGE	35907-35907 GADSDEN
35031-35031 BLOUNTSVILLE	35175-35175 UNION GROVE	35578-35578 NAUVOO	35950-35951 ALBERTVILLE
35032-35032 BON AIR	35176-35176 VANDIVER	35579-35579 OAKMAN	35952-35952 ALTOONA
35033-35033 BREMEN	35178-35178 VINCENT	35580-35580 PARRISH	35953-35953 ASHVILLE
35034-35034 BRENT	35179-35179 VINEMONT	35581-35581 PHIL CAMPBELL	35954-35954 ATTALLA
35035-35035 BRIERFIELD	35180-35180 WARRIOR	35582-35582 RED BAY	35956-35957 BOAZ
35036-35036 BROOKSIDE	35181-35181 WATSON	35584-35584 SIPSEY	35958-35958 BRYANT
35038-35038 BURNWELL	35182-35182 WATTSVILLE	35585-35585 SPRUCE PINE	35959-35959 CEDAR BLUFF
35040-35040 CALERA	35183-35183 WEOGUFKA	35586-35586 SULLIGENT	35960-35960 CENTRE
35041-35041 CARDIFF	35184-35184 WEST BLOCTON	35587-35587 TOWNLEY	35961-35961 COLLINSVILLE
35042-35042 CENTREVILLE	35185-35185 WESTOVER	35592-35592 VERNON	35962-35962 CROSSVILLE
35043-35043 CHELSEA	35186-35186 WILSONVILLE	35593-35593 VINA	35963-35963 DAWSON
35044-35044 CHILDERSBURG	35187-35187 WILTON	35594-35594 WINFIELD	35964-35964 DOUGLAS
35045-35046 CLANTON	35188-35188 WOODSTOCK	35601-35609 DECATUR	35966-35966 FLAT ROCK
35048-35048 CLAY	35200-35299 BIRMINGHAM	35610-35610 ANDERSON	35967-35968 FORT PAYNE
35049-35049 CLEVELAND	35401-35407 TUSCALOOSA	35611-35614 ATHENS	35971-35971 FYFFE
35051-35051 COLUMBIANA	35440-35440 ABERNANT	35615-35615 BELLE MINA	35972-35972 GALLANT
35052-35052 COOK SPRINGS	35441-35441 AKRON	35616-35616 CHEROKEE	35973-35973 GAYLESVILLE
35053-35053 CRANE HILL	35442-35442 ALICEVILLE	35617-35617 CLOVERDALE	35974-35974 GERALDINE
35054-35054 CROPWELL	35443-35443 BOLIGEE	35618-35618 COURTLAND	35975-35975 GROVEOAK
35055-35058 CULLMAN	35444-35444 BROOKWOOD	35619-35619 DANVILLE	35976-35976 GUNTERSVILLE
35060-35060 DOCENA	35446-35446 BUHL	35620-35620 ELKMONT	35978-35978 HENAGAR
35061-35061 DOLOMITE	35447-35447 CARROLLTON	35621-35621 EVA	35979-35979 HIGDON
35062-35062 DORA	35448-35448 CLINTON	35622-35622 FALKVILLE	35980-35980 HORTON
35063-35063 EMPIRE	35449-35449 COALING	35630-35634 FLORENCE	35981-35981 IDER
35064-35064 FAIRFIELD	35452-35452 COKER	35640-35640 HARTSELLE	35983-35983 LEESBURG
35068-35068 FULTONDALE	35453-35453 COTTONDALE	35643-35643 HILLSBORO	35984-35984 MENTONE
35070-35070 GARDEN CITY	35456-35456 DUNCANVILLE	35645-35645 KILLEN	35986-35986 RAINSVILLE
35071-35071 GARDENDALE	35457-35457 ECHOLA	35646-35646 LEIGHTON	35987-35987 STEELE
35072-35072 GOODWATER	35458-35458 ELROD	35647-35647 LESTER	35988-35988 SYLVANIA
35073-35073 GRAYSVILLE	35459-35459 EMELLE	35648-35648 LEXINGTON	35989-35989 VALLEY HEAD
35074-35074 GREEN POND	35460-35460 EPES	35649-35649 MOORESVILLE	35990-35990 WALNUT GROVE
35077-35077 HANCEVILLE	35461-35461 ETHELSVILLE	35650-35650 MOULTON	35999-35999 GADSDEN
35078-35078 HARPERSVILLE	35462-35462 EUTAW	35651-35651 MOUNT HOPE	36003-36003 AUTAUGAVILLE
35079-35079 HAYDEN	35463-35463 FOSTERS	35652-35652 ROGERSVILLE	36004-36004 EUFAULA
35080-35080 HELENA	35464-35464 GAINESVILLE	35653-35654 RUSSELLVILLE	36005-36005 BANKS
35082-35082 HOLLINS	35466-35466 GORDO	35660-35660 SHEFFIELD	36006-36006 BILLINGSLEY
35083-35083 HOLLY POND	35468-35468 KELLERMAN	35661-35662 MUSCLE SHOALS	36008-36008 BOOTH
35085-35085 JEMISON	35469-35469 KNOXVILLE	35670-35670 SOMERVILLE	36009-36009 BRANTLEY
35087-35087 JOPPA	35470-35470 LIVINGSTON	35671-35671 TANNER	36010-36010 BRUNDIDGE
35089-35089 KELLYTON	35471-35471 MC SHAN	35672-35672 TOWN CREEK	36013-36013 CECIL
35091-35091 KIMBERLY	35473-35473 NORTHPORT	35673-35673 TRINITY	36015-36015 CHAPMAN
35094-35094 LEEDS	35474-35474 MOUNDVILLE	35674-35674 TUSCUMBIA	36016-36016 CLAYTON
35096-35096 LINCOLN	35475-35476 NORTHPORT	35677-35677 WATERLOO	36017-36017 CLIO
35097-35097 LOCUST FORK	35477-35477 PANOLA	35699-35699 DECATUR	36020-36020 COOSADA
35098-35098 LOGAN	35478-35478 PETERSON	35739-35739 ARDMORE	36022-36022 DEATSVILLE
35111-35111 MC CALLA	35480-35480 RALPH	35740-35740 BRIDGEPORT	36023-36023 EAST TALLASSEE
35112-35112 MARGARET	35481-35481 REFORM	35741-35741 BROWNSBORO	36024-36024 ECLECTIC
35114-35114 MAYLENE	35482-35482 SAMANTHA	35742-35742 CAPSHAW	36025-36025 ELMORE
35115-35115 MONTEVALLO	35485-35487 TUSCALOOSA	35744-35744 DUTTON	36026-36026 EQUALITY
35116-35116 MORRIS	35490-35490 VANCE	35745-35745 ESTILLFORK	36027-36027 EUFAULA
35117-35117 MOUNT OLIVE	35491-35491 WEST GREENE	35746-35746 FACKLER	36028-36028 DOZIER
35118-35118 MULGA	35501-35504 JASPER	35747-35747 GRANT	36029-36029 FITZPATRICK
35119-35119 NEW CASTLE	35540-35540 ADDISON	35748-35748 GURLEY	36030-36030 FOREST HOME
35120-35120 ODENVILLE	35541-35541 ARLEY	35749-35749 HARVEST	36031-36031 FORT DAVIS
35121-35121 ONEONTA	35542-35542 BANKSTON	35750-35750 HAZEL GREEN	36032-36032 FORT DEPOSIT
35123-35123 PALMERDALE	35543-35543 BEAR CREEK	35751-35751 HOLLYTREE	36033-36033 GEORGIANA
35124-35124 PELHAM	35544-35544 BEAVERTON	35752-35752 HOLLYWOOD	36034-36034 GLENWOOD
35125-35125 PELL CITY	35545-35545 BELK	35754-35754 LACEYS SPRING	36035-36035 GOSHEN
35126-35126 PINSON	35546-35546 BERRY	35755-35755 LANGSTON	36036-36036 GRADY
35127-35127 PLEASANT GROVE	35548-35548 BRILLIANT	35756-35758 MADISON	36037-36037 GREENVILLE
35128-35128 PELL CITY	35549-35549 CARBON HILL	35759-35759 MERIDIANVILLE	36038-36038 GANTT
35130-35130 QUINTON	35550-35550 CORDOVA	35760-35760 NEW HOPE	36039-36039 HARDAWAY
35131-35131 RAGLAND	35551-35551 DELMAR	35761-35761 NEW MARKET	36040-36040 HAYNEVILLE
35133-35133 REMLAP	35552-35552 DETROIT	35762-35762 NORMAL	36041-36041 HIGHLAND HOME
35135-35135 RIVERSIDE	35553-35553 DOUBLE SPRINGS	35763-35763 OWENS CROSS ROADS	36042-36042 HONORAVILLE
35136-35136 ROCKFORD	35554-35554 ELDRIDGE	35764-35764 PAINT ROCK	36043-36043 HOPE HULL
35137-35137 SAGINAW	35555-35555 FAYETTE	35765-35765 PISGAH	36045-36045 KENT
35139-35139 SAYRE	35559-35559 GLEN ALLEN	35766-35766 PRINCETON	36046-36046 LAPINE
35142-35142 SHANNON	35560-35560 GOODSPRINGS	35767-35767 RYLAND	36047-36047 LETOHATCHEE

ZIP Range	City	ZIP Range	City	ZIP Range	City	ZIP Range	City
36048-36048	LOUISVILLE	36344-36344	HARTFORD	36528-36528	DAUPHIN ISLAND	36752-36752	LOWNDESBORO
36049-36049	LUVERNE	36345-36345	HEADLAND	36529-36529	DEER PARK	36753-36753	MC WILLIAMS
36051-36051	MARBURY	36346-36346	JACK	36530-36530	ELBERTA	36754-36754	MAGNOLIA
36052-36052	MATHEWS	36349-36349	MALVERN	36532-36533	FAIRHOPE	36756-36756	MARION
36053-36053	MIDWAY	36350-36350	MIDLAND CITY	36535-36536	FOLEY	36758-36758	PLANTERSVILLE
36054-36054	MILLBROOK	36351-36351	NEW BROCKTON	36538-36538	FRANKVILLE	36759-36759	MARION JUNCTION
36057-36057	MOUNT MEIGS	36352-36352	NEWTON	36539-36539	FRUITDALE	36760-36760	MILLERS FERRY
36061-36061	PEROTE	36353-36353	NEWVILLE	36540-36540	GAINESTOWN	36761-36761	MINTER
36062-36062	PETREY	36360-36361	OZARK	36541-36541	GRAND BAY	36762-36762	MORVIN
36064-36064	PIKE ROAD	36362-36362	FORT RUCKER	36542-36542	GULF SHORES	36763-36763	MYRTLEWOOD
36065-36065	PINE LEVEL	36370-36370	PANSEY	36543-36543	HUXFORD	36764-36764	NANAFALIA
36066-36068	PRATTVILLE	36371-36371	PINCKARD	36544-36544	IRVINGTON	36765-36765	NEWBERN
36069-36069	RAMER	36373-36373	SHORTERVILLE	36545-36545	JACKSON	36766-36766	OAK HILL
36071-36071	RUTLEDGE	36374-36374	SKIPPERVILLE	36547-36547	GULF SHORES	36767-36767	ORRVILLE
36072-36072	EUFAULA	36375-36375	SLOCOMB	36548-36548	LEROY	36768-36768	PINE APPLE
36075-36075	SHORTER	36376-36376	WEBB	36549-36549	LILLIAN	36769-36769	PINE HILL
36078-36078	TALLASSEE	36401-36401	EVERGREEN	36550-36550	LITTLE RIVER	36771-36771	PRAIRIE
36079-36079	TROY	36419-36419	ALLEN	36551-36551	LOXLEY	36773-36775	SAFFORD
36080-36080	TITUS	36420-36420	ANDALUSIA	36553-36553	MC INTOSH	36775-36775	SARDIS
36081-36082	TROY	36425-36425	BEATRICE	36555-36555	MAGNOLIA SPRINGS	36776-36776	SAWYERVILLE
36083-36083	TUSKEGEE	36426-36427	BREWTON	36556-36556	MALCOLM	36778-36778	SNOW HILL
36087-36088	TUSKEGEE INSTITUTE	36429-36429	BROOKLYN	36558-36558	MILLRY	36779-36779	SPROTT
36089-36089	UNION SPRINGS	36431-36431	BURNT CORN	36559-36559	MONTROSE	36782-36782	SWEET WATER
36091-36091	VERBENA	36432-36432	CASTLEBERRY	36560-36560	MOUNT VERNON	36783-36783	THOMASTON
36092-36093	WETUMPKA	36435-36435	COY	36561-36561	ORANGE BEACH	36784-36784	THOMASVILLE
36100-36199	MONTGOMERY	36436-36436	DICKINSON	36562-36562	PERDIDO	36785-36785	TYLER
36201-36207	ANNISTON	36439-36439	EXCEL	36564-36564	POINT CLEAR	36786-36786	UNIONTOWN
36250-36250	ALEXANDRIA	36441-36441	FLOMATON	36567-36567	ROBERTSDALE	36790-36790	STANTON
36251-36251	ASHLAND	36442-36442	FLORALA	36568-36568	SAINT ELMO	36792-36792	RANDOLPH
36253-36253	BYNUM	36444-36444	FRANKLIN	36569-36569	SAINT STEPHENS	36793-36793	LAWLEY
36254-36254	CHOCCOLOCCO	36445-36445	FRISCO CITY	36570-36570	SALITPA	36801-36804	OPELIKA
36255-36255	CRAGFORD	36446-36446	FULTON	36571-36571	SARALAND	36830-36832	AUBURN
36256-36256	DAVISTON	36449-36449	GOODWAY	36572-36572	SATSUMA	36849-36849	AUBURN UNIVERSITY
36257-36257	DE ARMANVILLE	36451-36451	GROVE HILL	36574-36574	SEMINOLE	36850-36850	CAMP HILL
36258-36258	DELTA	36453-36453	KINSTON	36575-36575	SEMMES	36851-36851	COTTONTON
36260-36260	EASTABOGA	36454-36454	LENOX	36576-36576	SILVERHILL	36852-36852	CUSSETA
36261-36261	EDWARDSVILLE	36455-36455	LOCKHART	36577-36577	SPANISH FORT	36853-36853	DADEVILLE
36262-36262	FRUITHURST	36456-36456	MC KENZIE	36578-36578	STAPLETON	36854-36854	VALLEY
36263-36263	GRAHAM	36457-36457	MEGARGEL	36579-36579	STOCKTON	36855-36855	FIVE POINTS
36264-36264	HEFLIN	36458-36458	MEXIA	36580-36580	SUMMERDALE	36856-36856	FORT MITCHELL
36265-36265	JACKSONVILLE	36460-36462	MONROEVILLE	36581-36581	SUNFLOWER	36858-36858	HATCHECHUBBEE
36266-36266	LINEVILLE	36467-36467	OPP	36582-36582	THEODORE	36859-36859	HOLY TRINITY
36267-36267	MILLERVILLE	36469-36469	EVERGREEN	36583-36583	TIBBIE	36860-36860	HURTSBORO
36268-36268	MUNFORD	36469-36469	PAUL	36584-36584	VINEGAR BEND	36861-36861	JACKSONS GAP
36269-36269	MUSCADINE	36470-36470	PERDUE HILL	36585-36585	WAGARVILLE	36862-36862	LAFAYETTE
36270-36270	NEWELL	36471-36471	PETERMAN	36586-36586	WALKER SPRINGS	36863-36863	LANETT
36271-36271	OHATCHEE	36473-36473	RANGE	36587-36587	WILMER	36865-36865	LOACHAPOKA
36272-36272	PIEDMONT	36474-36474	RED LEVEL	36590-36590	THEODORE	36866-36866	NOTASULGA
36273-36273	RANBURNE	36475-36475	REPTON	36600-36612	MOBILE	36867-36870	PHENIX CITY
36274-36274	ROANOKE	36476-36476	RIVER FALLS	36613-36613	EIGHT MILE	36871-36871	PITTSVIEW
36275-36275	SPRING GARDEN	36477-36477	SAMSON	36614-36695	MOBILE	36872-36872	VALLEY
36276-36276	WADLEY	36480-36480	URIAH	36701-36703	SELMA	36874-36874	SALEM
36277-36277	WEAVER	36481-36481	VREDENBURGH	36720-36720	ALBERTA	36875-36875	SEALE
36278-36278	WEDOWEE	36482-36482	WHATLEY	36721-36721	ANNEMANIE	36877-36877	SMITHS
36279-36279	WELLINGTON	36483-36483	WING	36722-36722	ARLINGTON	36877-36877	SMITHS STATION
36280-36280	WOODLAND	36501-36501	ALMA	36723-36723	BOYKIN	36879-36879	WAVERLY
36301-36305	DOTHAN	36502-36504	ATMORE	36726-36726	CAMDEN	36901-36901	BELLAMY
36310-36310	ABBEVILLE	36505-36505	AXIS	36727-36727	CAMPBELL	36903-36903	BOLINGER
36311-36311	ARITON	36507-36507	BAY MINETTE	36728-36728	CATHERINE	36904-36904	BUTLER
36312-36312	ASHFORD	36509-36509	BAYOU LA BATRE	36731-36731	DAYTON	36906-36906	CROMWELL
36313-36313	BELLWOOD	36510-36510	BIGBEE	36732-36732	DEMOPOLIS	36907-36907	CUBA
36314-36314	BLACK	36511-36511	BON SECOUR	36736-36736	DIXONS MILLS	36908-36908	GILBERTOWN
36316-36316	CHANCELLOR	36512-36512	BUCKS	36738-36738	FAUNSDALE	36910-36910	JACHIN
36317-36317	CLOPTON	36513-36513	CALVERT	36740-36740	FORKLAND	36911-36911	LAVACA
36318-36318	COFFEE SPRINGS	36515-36515	CARLTON	36741-36741	FURMAN	36912-36912	LISMAN
36319-36319	COLUMBIA	36518-36518	CHATOM	36742-36742	GALLION	36913-36913	MELVIN
36320-36320	COTTONWOOD	36521-36521	CHUNCHULA	36744-36744	GREENSBORO	36915-36915	NEEDHAM
36321-36321	COWARTS	36522-36522	CITRONELLE	36745-36745	JEFFERSON	36916-36916	PENNINGTON
36322-36322	DALEVILLE	36523-36523	CODEN	36747-36747	LAMISON	36919-36919	SILAS
36323-36323	ELBA	36524-36524	COFFEEVILLE	36748-36748	LINDEN	36921-36921	TOXEY
36330-36331	ENTERPRISE	36525-36525	CREOLA	36749-36749	JONES	36922-36922	WARD
36340-36340	GENEVA	36526-36526	DAPHNE	36750-36750	MAPLESVILLE	36925-36925	YORK
36343-36343	GORDON	36527-36527	SPANISH FORT	36751-36751	LOWER PEACH TREE		

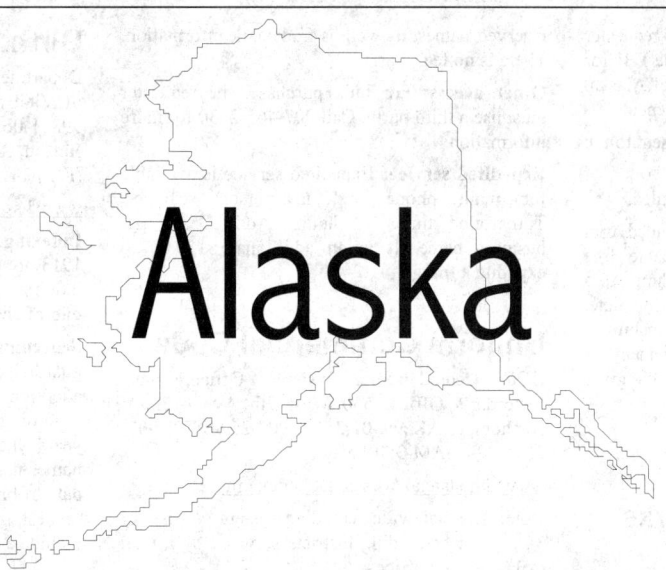

Alaska

General Help Numbers:

Governor's Office
PO Box 110001
Juneau, AK 99811-0001
www.gov.state.ak.us

907-465-3500
Fax 907-465-3532
8AM-5PM

Attorney General's Office
Law Department
PO Box 110300
Juneau, AK 99811-0300
www.law.state.ak.us

907-465-3600
Fax 907-465-2075
8AM-4:30PM

State Court Administrator
303 K St
Anchorage, AK 99501
www.alaska.net/~akctlib/
homepage.htm

907-264-0547
Fax 907-264-0881
8AM-4:30PM

State Archives
Alaska State Archives
141 Willoughby Ave
Juneau, AK 99801-1720
www.archives.state.ak.us

907-465-2270
Fax 907-465-2465
9AM-5PM

State Specifics:

Capital:

Juneau
Juneau Borough

Time Zone: AK (Alaska Standard Time)*
* Alaska's Aleutian Islands are HT (Hawaii Standard Time)

Number of Counties: 23

Population: 634,892

Web Site: www.state.ak.us

State Agencies

Criminal Records

Department of Public Safety, Records and Identification, 5700 E Tudor Rd, Anchorage, AK 99507; 907-269-5765, 907-269-5091 (Fax), 8AM-4:30PM.

www.dps.state.ak.us

Note: Sex offender data is available online at www.dps.state.ak.us/nSorcr/asp

Indexing & Storage: Records are available for 10 years from the unconditional discharge date of the

incident. 86% of arrests in database have final dispositions recorded; 85% for those arrests in last 5 years.

Searching: To receive full record, requester must provide verification of status as "Interested Party" defined as person who employs, appoints or permits the subject to have supervisory power over others, primarily in the child care industry. Include the following in your request: set of fingerprints, full name. "Any Person" reports are processed for those who are not "Interested Person" qualified

and who have a proper letter of explanation and fingerprints. Approximately 62% of records are fingerprint-supported. The following data is not released: sealed records. All records are released, including those without dispositions to "Interested Person" requesters. "Any Person" requesters receive criminal records only with dispositions.

Access by: mail, in person, online.

Fee & Payment: The fee is $35.00 per search. The subject may - in person - request a search for $20.00, without fingerprints. This also applies to government agencies. If authorized, a requester may also request a national check by the FBI for an additional $24.00. Fee payee: State of Alaska. Prepayment required. No credit cards accepted.

Mail search: Results of search are also sent to the subject.

In person search: Results are usually mailed.

Online search: Name searching of limited trial court records and calendars are available free online at www.state.ak.us/courts/names.htm. As a pilot program, the records are not complete, though all courts with electronic capabilities contribute some records. This excludes many of the smaller outlying courts. Name search gives case number only.

Corporation Records
Trademarks/Servicemarks
Fictitious Name
Assumed Name
Limited Partnership Records
Limited Liability Company Records
Limited Liability Partnership Records

Corporation Section, Department of Community & Econ Dev, PO Box 110808, Juneau, AK 99811-0808 (Courier: 150 Third Street Rm 217, Juneau, AK 99801); 907-465-2530, 907-465-3257 (Fax), 8AM-5PM.

www.dced.state.ak.us/bsc/corps.htm

Indexing & Storage: Records are available from early 1900's on. Prior to 1960, the records are kept at the State Archives. You must go through this office in order to get records. New records are available for inquiry immediately. Records are indexed on microfiche, inhouse computer.

Searching: All information contained is considered public record. Include the following in your request: full name of business. In addition to the articles of incorporation, corporation records include the following information: Annual Reports, Officers, Directors, DBAs, Prior (Merged) names, Inactive and Reserved names.

Access by: mail, phone, fax, in person, online.

Fee & Payment: Fees are $10.00 for articles and amendments and $30.00 for everything on file. The fee is $5.00 to certify a document and $10.00 for a good standing. A copy of a one page document is $1.00 and a print of a computer screen is $1.00. Fee payee: State of Alaska. Prepayment required. Personal checks accepted. Credit cards accepted: MasterCard, Visa.

Mail search: Turnaround time: 2 weeks.

Phone search: You can make a search request only if you are local and you plan to pick-up.

Fax search: Typical fax searches involve use of a credit card.

In person search: All results are mailed unless request is being processed using expedited service. The agency will call the requester when his/her request has been processed and is ready for pick-up, if it is a local call.

Online search: At the web site, one can access status information on corps, LLCs, LLP, LP (all both foreign and domestic), registered and reserved names, as well as trademark information. There is no fee.

Other access: For bulk purchase, the requester must use a third party. Call 907-465-2530 for more information.

Expedited service: Expedited service is available for mail, phone and in person searches. Turnaround time: 48 hours. Add $35.00 per business name. It is an additional $150.00 to expedite a filing.

Uniform Commercial Code

UCC Central File Systems Office, State Recorder's Office, 550 West 7th Ave #1200A, Anchorage, AK 99501-3564; 907-269-8873, 907-269-8899, 8AM-3:30PM.

www.dnr.state.ak.us/ssd/ucc/index.cfm

Note: The statewide recording system consists of 34 separate recording districts serviced by a total of 14 separate offices.

Indexing & Storage: Records are available from 1961 when the UCC system was established. Records are computerized since October 20, 1986 or earlier if with continuations. Records are kept on microfiche since 1981 or prior if continuations filed.

Searching: Use search request form UCC-11. Search results include all filings up to one year after lapse. All tax liens are filed at the local District Recorder offices. Include the following in your request: debtor name. All requests must be in writing.

Access by: mail, in person, online.

Fee & Payment: Fee to search by name is $5.00 per debtor name. For information and copies, fee is $15.00 per debtor name. Certification costs an additional $5.00. Single page copies are $2.00 each. Also, see In Person searching for those fees. Fee payee: Alaska Department of Revenue. Prepayment required. Personal checks accepted. Credit cards accepted: MasterCard, Visa.

Mail search: Turnaround time: 1 to 2 days. No self addressed stamped envelope is required.

In person search: A public access terminal is available. There is no fee to use the terminal, and a $2.00 per document (not page) when requesting copies in person.

Online search: One can search by granter-grantee name, date, document number or dcoument type at www.dnr.state.ak.us/ucc/search. There is no fee.

Other access: Bulkmedia of the entire UCC database can be purchased from the State Recorder's Office (907-269-8881).

Federal Tax Liens
State Tax Liens

Records not maintained by a state level agency.

Note: All tax liens are filed at local District Recorder Offices.

Sales Tax Registrations

State does not impose sales tax.

Birth Certificates

Department of Health & Social Services, Bureau of Vital Statistics, PO Box 110675, Juneau, AK 99811-0675 (Courier: 350 Main, Room 114, Juneau, AK 99811); 907-465-3392, 907-465-3618 (Fax), 8AM-4:30PM.

www.hss.state.ak.us/dph/bvs/bvs_home.htm

Indexing & Storage: Records are available from 1913 to present. New records are available for inquiry immediately. Records are indexed on microfiche, inhouse computer.

Searching: Person requesting must be a parent or guardian or give a justifying reason for request. No adoption information will be given except according to statute. Records are public after 100 years. Include the following in your request: full name, names of parents, mother's maiden name, date of birth, place of birth, reason for information request, relationship to person of record. Also, include a day time phone number.

Access by: mail, phone, fax, in person.

Fee & Payment: The $15.00 search fee includes a 3 year search; add $1.00 per year for each additional year searched. Fee payee: Bureau of Vital Statistics. Prepayment required. Personal checks accepted. Credit cards accepted: MasterCard, Visa, AmEx, Discover.

Mail search: Turnaround time: 2 weeks. No self addressed stamped envelope is required.

Phone search: Credit card requests require an additional $10.00.

Fax search: Same criteria as phone searching.

In person search: Turnaround time 10 minutes.

Expedited service: Expedited service is available for mail, phone and fax searches. Turnaround time: 2 days. Add $10.00 if using a credit card and $15.50 for Fed Ex or $11.75 for Express Mail.

Death Records

Department of Health & Social Services, Bureau of Vital Statistics, PO Box 110675, Juneau, AK 99811-0675 (Courier: 350 Main, Room 114, Juneau, AK 99811); 907-465-3392, 907-465-3618 (Fax), 8AM-4:30PM.

www.hss.state.ak.us/dph/bvs/bvs_home.htm

Indexing & Storage: Records are available from 1913 to present. New records are available for inquiry immediately. Records are indexed on microfiche, inhouse computer.

Searching: You must be next of kin or have a notarized release statement from immediate family. Records are public after 50 years. Include the following in your request: full name, date of death, place of death, names of parents, reason for information request, relationship to person of record. Also, include a daytime phone number.

Access by: mail, phone, fax, in person.

Fee & Payment: The $15.00 search fee includes a 3 year search. Add $1.00 per year searched for each year over 3 years. Fee payee: Bureau of Vital Statistics. Prepayment required. Personal checks accepted. Credit cards accepted: MasterCard, Visa, AmEx, Discover.

Mail search: Turnaround time: 2 weeks.

Phone search: Add $10.00 for using a credit card.

Fax search: Same criteria as phone searching.

In person search: Turnaround time 10 minutes.

Expedited service: Expedited service is available for mail, phone and fax searches. Turnaround time: 2 days. Add $10.00 if using a credit card and add $15.50 for Fed Ex or $11.75 for Express Mail.

Marriage Certificates

Department of Health & Social Services, Bureau of Vital Statistics, PO Box 110675, Juneau, AK 99811-0675 (Courier: 350 Main, Room 114, Juneau, AK 99811); 907-465-3392, 907-465-3618 (Fax), 8AM-4:30PM.

www.hss.state.ak.us/dph/bvs/bvs_home.htm

Indexing & Storage: Records are available from 1913 to present. New records are available for inquiry immediately. Records are indexed on microfiche, inhouse computer.

Searching: Person requesting must be one of the registrants or an attorney representing one of them. Records are public after 50 years. Include the following in your request: names of husband and wife, date of marriage, place or county of marriage. Include wife's maiden name and a daytime phone number.

Access by: mail, phone, fax, in person.

Fee & Payment: The $15.00 search fee includes a 3 year search. Add $1.00 per year searched for each year over 3 years. Fee payee: Bureau of Vital Statistics. Prepayment required. Personal checks accepted. Credit cards accepted: MasterCard, Visa.

Mail search: Turnaround time: 2 weeks.

Phone search: Add $10.00 for using a credit card.

Fax search: Same criteria as phone searches.

In person search: Turnaround time 10 minutes.

Expedited service: Expedited service is available for mail, phone and fax searches. Turnaround time: 2 days. Add $10.00 if using a credit card and add $15.50 for Fed Ex or $11.75 for Express Mail.

Divorce Records

Department of Health & Social Services, Bureau of Vital Statistics, PO Box 110675, Juneau, AK 99811-0675 (Courier: 350 Main, Room 114, Juneau, AK 99811); 907-465-3392, 907-465-3618 (Fax), 8AM-4:30PM.

www.hss.state.ak.us/dph/bvs/bvs_home.htm

Indexing & Storage: Records are available from 1950 to present. New records are available for inquiry immediately. Records are indexed on microfiche, inhouse computer.

Searching: Person requesting must be one of the registrants or an attorney representing a registrant. Records are public after 50 years. Include the following in your request: names of husband and wife, date of divorce, place of divorce. Also, include a daytime phone number.

Access by: mail, phone, fax, in person.

Fee & Payment: The $15.00 search fee includes a 3 year search. Add $1.00 per year searched for each year over 3 years. Fee payee: Bureau of Vital Statistics. Prepayment required. Personal checks accepted. Credit cards accepted: MasterCard, Visa, AmEx, Discover.

Mail search: Turnaround time: 2 weeks. No self addressed stamped envelope is required.

Phone search: Add $10.00 for use of a credit card.

Fax search: Same criteria as phone searches.

In person search: Turnaround time 10 minutes.

Expedited service: Expedited service is available for mail, phone and fax searches. Turnaround time: 2 days. Add $10.00 if using a credit card and add $15.50 for Fed Ex or $11.75 for Express Mail.

Workers' Compensation Records

Workers' Compensation, PO Box 25512, Juneau, AK 99802 (Courier: 1111 W Eighth St, Room 307, Juneau, AK 99802); 907-465-2790, 907-465-2797 (Fax), 8AM-4:30PM.

www.labor.state.ak.us/wc/wc.htm

Indexing & Storage: Records are available from 1982 on the computer and prior to 1982 the records are on microfilm and/or microfiche to the 1960s. It takes one week before new records are available for inquiry.

Searching: All requests must be in writing. To receive a copy of a file, a signed medical release from claimant is required. Include the following in your request: claimant name, Social Security Number, date of accident.

Access by: mail, fax, in person.

Fee & Payment: Copies cost $.35 per page for active files and $.75 per page for microfilmed files. A computer printout costs $.50 per screen. There is no search fee. Fee payee: State of Alaska. Large orders require prepayment. Personal checks accepted. No credit cards accepted.

Mail search: Turnaround time: 2 to 3 weeks. No self addressed stamped envelope is required.

Fax search: Fax searching available.

In person search: Searching is available in person.

Driver Records

Division of Motor Vehicles, Driver's Records, 2760 Sherwood Lane #B, Juneau, AK 99801; 907-465-4361 (Motor Vehicle Reports Desk), 907-465-4363 (Licensing), 907-465-5509 (Fax), 8AM-5PM.

www.state.ak.us/dmv

Note: Copies of tickets are only released, in writing, to the participant, legal representative, or insurance representative.

Indexing & Storage: Records are available for minor moving violations and suspensions for three years, major moving violations for five years. Convictions are automatically purged from public record by conviction date. Accidents are reported only if action is taken.

Searching: Records are considered confidential. Any private company or individual requester must have a signed release from the licensee or a subpoena. High volume requesters may maintain these forms rather than send in with requests. Include the following in your request: name, driver's license number, date of birth. Driver's residence and mailing address are included as part of the search report.

Access by: mail, in person, online.

Fee & Payment: The fee is $5.00 per record. Prepayment required. Fee payee: State of Alaska. Personal checks accepted. No credit cards accepted.

Mail search: Turnaround time: 3 to 4 working days. No self addressed stamped envelope is required.

In person search: Turnaround time is while you wait.

Online search: Online access costs $5.00 per record. Inquiries may be made at any time, 24 hours a day. Batch inquiries may call back within thirty minutes for responses. Search by the first four letters of driver's name, license number and date of birth. At present, there is only one phone line available for users; you may experience a busy signal.

Vehicle Ownership
Vehicle Identification
Vessel Registration

Division of Motor Vehicles, Research, 1300 W Benson Blvd #200, Anchorage, AK 99503-3600; 907-269-5551, 8AM-5PM.

www.state.ak.us/dmv

Note: All powered boats, and all non-powered boats over 10 ft or with auxiliary power units used on any water of the state must be registered.

Indexing & Storage: Records are available for 7 years to present. However, until Jan. 1, 2001, all boat registrations were done through the US Coast Guard.

Searching: Record requests are honored for employment, insurance, court or impound purposes. Otherwise, a signed release is required, signed by requester, attesting to purpose of request. Use of Form 851-Request for Vehicle Record is recommended.

Access by: mail, in person.

Fee & Payment: The fee is $5.00 per record. There is no fee to do a vessel search. Fee payee: State of Alaska. Prepayment required. No credit cards accepted.

Mail search: Turnaround time: 2 to 3 weeks. No self addressed stamped envelope is required.

In person search: Turnaround time depends on workload and complexity of request. Typically, requests are processed within 5 to 10 days, but can extend to 5 weeks or more.

Other access: The entire master tape file of registration information is available at a cost of approximately $50 per 1,000 records. Call the Director's Office (907-269-5551) for more information.

Accident Reports

Department of Public Safety, Driver Services, 2760 Sherwood Lane #B, Juneau, AK 99801; 907-465-4361, 907-463-5509 (Fax), 8AM-5PM.

www.state.ak.us/dmv

Indexing & Storage: Records are available from seven years.

Searching: Only legal representatives and insurance agents of the participants, or the participant him/herself may obtain copies. The lawyer or legal representative must have a notarized request, an insurance agent a signed request with reason. Items required for search include names, date of incident, city, physical location of the accident.

Access by: mail, in person.

Fee & Payment: The cost of obtaining an accident report is $1.00 for the first page and $.25 for each additional page. Fee payee: State of Alaska, Department of Public Safety. Prepayment required. Personal checks accepted. No credit cards accepted.

Mail search: Turnaround time: 1 to 2 weeks. No self addressed stamped envelope is required.

In person search: Turnaround time is while you wait.

Vessel Ownership

Records not maintained by a state level agency.

Note: Alaska is not a title state. Liens are filed with the Department of Natural Resources at 907-269-8882. Also, until Jan. 1, 2001 all boat registrations were done through the US Coast Guard (970-463-2294).

Legislation Records

Alaska State Legislative Affairs Agency, Legislative Information Office, 120 4th St #111-State Capitol, Juneau, AK 99801-1182; 907-465-4648, 907-465-2864 (Fax), 8AM-5PM.

www.legis.state.ak.us

Indexing & Storage: Records are available from 1982 to present. Records are indexed on inhouse computer.

Searching: Include the following in your request: bill number, year.

Access by: mail, phone, in person, online.

Fee & Payment: There is no search fee nor is there a fee for one copy of a bill. Copy fees vary; therefore, call for fees, if you need more than one copy. Fee payee: State of Alaska. Prepayment required. Personal checks accepted. No credit cards accepted.

Mail search: Turnaround time: 1 day. No self addressed stamped envelope is required.

Phone search: You may call for copies.

In person search: Turnaround time is while you wait.

Online search: All information, including statutes, is available from the Internet site.

Voter Registration

Division of Elections, PO Box 110017, Juneau, AK 99811-0017 (Courier: Court Plaza Building, 4th Floor, 240 Main Street, Juneau, AK 99801); 907-465-4611, 8AM-4:30PM.

www.elections.state.ak.us

Note: There are four regional Elections Offices, each has access to the election records database.

Indexing & Storage: Records are available from 1968. It takes 1 day before new records are available for inquiry.

Searching: Searching by name is permitted. The following data is not released: Social Security Numbers, place or date of birth, and phone numbers.

Access by: mail, phone, fax, in person.

Fee & Payment: There is no fee.

Mail search: Turnaround time: 1 day.

Phone search: Records are available by phone.

Fax search: Fax searching available.

In person search: Turnaround time is immediate unless extensive lists or requests for older records are presented.

Other access: The agency offers the complete record database on CD-ROM for $178. Individual districts (there are 40) can be purchased on disk for $20.00 each.

GED Certificates

Department of Labor, Employment Security Division, PO Box 25509, Juneau, AK 99802-5509 (Courier: 1111 8th Street #210, Juneau, AK 99801); 907-465-4685, 907-465-8753 (Fax), 8AM-4:30PM.

www.eed.state.ak.us

Searching: Include the full name, DOB, SSN, year of test and city of test. Fax requesters must include a signed release.

Access by: mail, fax, in person.

Fee & Payment: There is no fee for a verification or a transcript copy. There is a $10.00 fee for a copy of a diploma.

Mail search: Turnaround time: 1 to 2 weeks. No self addressed stamped envelope is required.

Fax search: A written release form is required.

In person search: Searching is available in person.

Hunting License Information
Fishing License Information

Department of Fish & Game, Licensing Section, PO Box 25525, Juneau, AK 99802-5525 (Courier: 1255 W 8th St, Juneau, AK 99802); 907-465-2376, 907-465-2440 (Fax), 8AM-5PM.

www.state.ak.us/local/akpages/FISH.GAME/adfgh ome.htm

Indexing & Storage: Records are available from 10 years to present. Records since 1994 are computerized, older records are on microfiche. It takes 4 weeks before new records are available for inquiry.

Searching: Information used to search includes SSN, DOB, address, driver's license number, or year license issued. The following data is not released: Social Security Numbers or telephone numbers.

Access by: mail, phone, fax, in person.

Fee & Payment: No fee unless you request a large list. For certified copies the turnaround time is 6 weeks. Fee payee: State of Alaska. Prepayment required. Personal checks accepted. Credit cards accepted.

Mail search: Turnaround time: within 3 weeks. No self addressed stamped envelope is required.

Phone search: Limited number of requests given over the phone.

Fax search: Same criteria as phone searches.

In person search: Large lists will not be processed immediately.

Other access: The vendor file is available for $25 on paper or disk. The entire license file is available for $350 on CD-ROM.

Alaska State Licensing Agencies

Licenses Searchable Online

Acupuncturist #20	www.dced.state.ak.us/occ/search3.htm
Alcohol Establishment #21	www.abc.revenue.state.ak.us/Feb%2002%20Operating.xls
Anesthetist (Dental), General/Permit #20	www.dced.state.ak.us/occ/search3.htm
Architect #20	www.dced.state.ak.us/occ/search3.htm
Athletic Promoter #20	www.dced.state.ak.us/occ/search3.htm
Athletic Trainer #20	www.dced.state.ak.us/occ/search3.htm
Audiologist/Hearing Aid Dealer #20	www.dced.state.ak.us/occ/search3.htm
Bail Bondsman #13	www.dced.state.ak.us/ins/apps/InsLicStart.cfm
Barber #20	www.dced.state.ak.us/occ/search3.htm
Barber Shop Owner/School/Instructor #20	www.dced.state.ak.us/occ/search3.htm
Big Game Guide/Assistant/Transporter #20	www.dced.state.ak.us/occ/search3.htm
Boxer #20	www.dced.state.ak.us/occ/search3.htm
Boxing Physician #20	www.dced.state.ak.us/occ/search3.htm
Boxing/Wrestling Personnel #20	www.dced.state.ak.us/occ/search3.htm
Chiropractor #20	www.dced.state.ak.us/occ/search3.htm
Collection Agency/Operator #20	www.dced.state.ak.us/occ/search3.htm
Concert Promoter #20	www.dced.state.ak.us/occ/search3.htm
Construction Contractor #20	www.dced.state.ak.us/occ/search3.htm
Contractor, Civil/Elect./Mech./Mining/Petrol. #20	www.dced.state.ak.us/occ/search3.htm
Contractor, Residential #20	www.dced.state.ak.us/occ/search3.htm
Cosmetologist/Hairdresser #20	www.dced.state.ak.us/occ/search3.htm
Cosmetology Shop Owner/School/Instructor #20	www.dced.state.ak.us/occ/search3.htm
Counselor, Professional #20	www.dced.state.ak.us/occ/OccStart.cfm
Dental Hygienist #20	www.dced.state.ak.us/occ/search3.htm
Dentist/Dental Examiner #20	www.dced.state.ak.us/occ/search3.htm
Dietitian/Nutritionist #20	www.dced.state.ak.us/occ/OccStart.cfm
Drug Distributor/Drug Room #20	www.dced.state.ak.us/occ/search3.htm
Electrical Administrator #20	www.dced.state.ak.us/occ/search3.htm
Employment Agency Oper./Agency Permit #5	www.dced.state.ak.us/occ/search3.htm
Engineer #20	www.dced.state.ak.us/occ/search3.htm
Esthetician #20	www.dced.state.ak.us/occ/search3.htm
Funeral Director/Establishment #20	www.dced.state.ak.us/occ/search3.htm
Geologist #20	www.dced.state.ak.us/occ/search3.htm
Guide Outfitter, Hunting #20	www.dced.state.ak.us/occ/search3.htm
Hearing Aid Dealer #20	www.dced.state.ak.us/occ/search3.htm
Independent Adjuster #13	www.dced.state.ak.us/ins/apps/InsLicStart.cfm
Insurance Agent, Managing General #13	www.dced.state.ak.us/ins/apps/InsLicStart.cfm
Insurance Occupation #13	www.dced.state.ak.us/ins/apps/InsLicStart.cfm
Insurance Producer #13	www.dced.state.ak.us/ins/apps/InsLicStart.cfm
Lobbyist/Lobbyist Employer #9	www.state.ak.us/local/akpages/ADMIN/apoc/lobcov.htm
Marine Pilot #20	www.dced.state.ak.us/occ/search3.htm
Marriage & Family Therapist #20	www.dced.state.ak.us/occ/OccStart.cfm
Mechanical Administrator #20	www.dced.state.ak.us/occ/search3.htm
Medical Doctor/Surgeon #20	www.dced.state.ak.us/occ/search3.htm
Midwife #20	www.dced.state.ak.us/occ/OccStart.cfm
Mortician/Embalmer #20	www.dced.state.ak.us/occ/search3.htm
Naturopathic Physician #20	www.dced.state.ak.us/occ/search3.htm
Nurse (names A-K) #20	www.dced.state.ak.us/occ/search3.htm
Nurse (names L-Z) #20	www.dced.state.ak.us/occ/search3.htm
Nurse Anesthetist #20	www.dced.state.ak.us/occ/search3.htm
Nurse-RN/LPN #20	www.dced.state.ak.us/occ/search3.htm
Nurses' Aide #20	www.dced.state.ak.us/occ/search3.htm

Nursing Home Administrator #20	www.dced.state.ak.us/occ/search3.htm
Occupational Therapist/Assistant #20	www.dced.state.ak.us/occ/search3.htm
Occupational Therapist/Assistant #20	www.dced.state.ak.us/occ/search3.htm
Optician, Dispensing #20	www.dced.state.ak.us/occ/search3.htm
Optometrist #20	www.dced.state.ak.us/occ/search3.htm
Osteopathic Physician #20	www.dced.state.ak.us/occ/search3.htm
Paramedic #20	www.dced.state.ak.us/occ/search3.htm
Parenteral Sedation (Dental) #20	www.dced.state.ak.us/occ/search3.htm
Pharmacist/Pharmacist Intern #20	www.dced.state.ak.us/occ/search3.htm
Pharmacy #20	www.dced.state.ak.us/occ/search3.htm
Physical Therapist/Assistant #20	www.dced.state.ak.us/occ/search3.htm
Physician Assistant #20	www.dced.state.ak.us/occ/search3.htm
Podiatrist #20	www.dced.state.ak.us/occ/search3.htm
Psychologist/Psychological Assistant #20	www.dced.state.ak.us/occ/search3.htm
Public Accountant-CPA #20	www.dced.state.ak.us/occ/OccStart.cfm
Real Estate Agent/Broker/Assoc. #20	www.dced.state.ak.us/occ/search3.htm
Real Estate Appraiser #20	www.dced.state.ak.us/occ/search3.htm
Referee #20	www.dced.state.ak.us/occ/OccStart.cfm
Reinsurance Intermediary Broker/Mgr. #13	www.dced.state.ak.us/ins/apps/InsLicStart.cfm
Social Worker #20	www.dced.state.ak.us/occ/OccStart.cfm
Social Worker, Clinical #20	www.dced.state.ak.us/occ/OccStart.cfm
Surplus Line Broker #13	www.dced.state.ak.us/ins/apps/InsLicStart.cfm
Surveyor, Land #20	www.dced.state.ak.us/occ/search3.htm
Underground Storage Tank Worker/Contr. #20	www.dced.state.ak.us/occ/search3.htm
Vessel Agent #20	www.dced.state.ak.us/occ/search3.htm
Veterinarian/Veterinary Technician #20	www.dced.state.ak.us/occ/search3.htm
Wrestler #20	www.dced.state.ak.us/occ/OccStart.cfm

Licensing Quick Finder

Acupuncturist #20 907-465-2695	Dentist/Dental Examiner #20 907-465-2542	Nursing Home Administrator #20 907-465-2695
Aircraft-related Occupation #18 907-271-2000	Dietitian/Nutritionist #20 907-465-2534	Occupational Therapist/Assistant #20 .. 907-465-2580
Alcohol Establishment #21 907-929-8477	Drug Distributor/Drug Room #20 907-465-2589	Optician, Dispensing #20 907-465-5470
Alcohol Server #21 907-929-8477	Electrical Administrator #20 907-465-2589	Optometrist #20 907-465-2580
Anesthetist (Dental), General/Permit #20	Electrician #7 907-269-4925	Osteopathic Physician #20 907-465-2541
.... 907-465-2542	Emergency Medical Technician #17 907-465-3029	Painter #7 907-269-4925
Architect #20 907-465-2540	Employment Agency Operator/Agency Permit #5	Paramedic #20 907-465-2541
Asbestos Worker #7 907-269-4925	 907-269-8160	Parenteral Sedation (Dental) #20 907-465-2542
Asbestos Removal Worker #7 907-269-4925	Engineer #20 907-465-2540	Pesticide Applicator #2 907-745-3236
Athletic Promoter #20 907-465-2695	Esthetician #20 907-465-2547	Pharmacist/Pharmacist Intern #20 907-465-2589
Athletic Trainer #20 907-465-2695	Explosives Handler #7 907-269-4925	Pharmacy #20 907-465-2589
Attorney #11 907-272-7469	Fishing Operation #8 907-260-4882	Physical Therapist/Assistant #20 907-465-2580
Audiologist/Hearing Aid Dealer #20 907-465-2695	Funeral Director/Establishment #20 607-465-2695	Physician Assistant #20 907-269-8163
Bail Bondsman #13 907-465-2515	Geologist #20 907-465-2695	Pilot, Marine #20 907-465-2548
Barber #20 907-465-2547	Guide Outfitter, Hunting #20 907-465-2543	Plumber #7 907-269-4925
Barber Shop Owner/School/Instructor #20	Guide, Sport Fishing #8 907-260-4882	Podiatrist #20 907-465-2541
.... 907-465-2547	Hearing Aid Dealer #20 907-465-2695	Process Server #10 907-269-0392
Big Game Guide/Assistant/Transporter #20	Hunting Guide #20 907-465-2543	Psychologist/Psychological Assistant #20
.... 907-465-2543	Independent Adjuster #13 907-465-2515	 907-465-3811
Boiler Operator #7 907-269-4925	Insurance Agent, Managing General #13	Public Accountant-CPA #20 907-465-3817
Boxer #20 907-465-2695	 907-465-2515	Real Estate Agent/Broker/Assoc. #20.. 907-269-8162
Boxing Physician #20 907-465-2695	Insurance Occupation #13 907-465-2515	Real Estate Appraiser #20 907-465-2542
Boxing/Wrestling Personnel #20 907-465-2695	Insurance Producer #13 907-465-2515	Referee #20 907-465-2695
Broker/Dealer #12 907-465-2521	Investment Advisor #12 907-465-2521	Reinsurance Intermediary Broker/Mgr. #13
Child Care Provider (Home or Center) #16	Investment Broker/Dealer/Related Occupation #12	 907-465-2515
.... 907-465-3207	 907-465-2521	Securities Agent #12 907-465-2521
Chiropractor #20 907-465-2589	Lobbyist/Lobbyist Employer #9 907-465-4864	Security Guard #10 907-269-0393
Collection Agency/Operator #20 907-465-2695	Marriage & Family Therapist #20 907-465-2551	Social Worker #20 907-465-2551
Concert Promoter #20 907-465-2534	Mechanical Administrator #20 907-465-2589	Social Worker, Clinical #20 907-465-2551
Construction Contractor #20 907-465-2546	Medical Doctor/Surgeon #20 907-465-2541	Surplus Line Broker #13 907-465-2515
Contractor, Civil/Elect./Mech./Mining/Petroleum #20	Midwife #20 907-465-2580	Surveyor, Land #20 907-465-2540
.... 907-465-2546	Mobile Home Dealer #20 907-465-2547	Taxidermist #4 907-465-2376
Contractor, Residential #20 907-465-2546	Mortician/Embalmer #20 607-465-2695	Teacher #1 907-465-2831
Cosmetologist/Hairdresser #20 907-465-2547	Naturopathic Physician #20 907-465-2695	Underground Storage Tank Worker/Contractor #20
Cosmetology Shop Owner/School/Instructor #20	Notary Public #19 907-465-3509	 907-465-5470
.... 907-465-2547	Nurse (names A-K) #20 907-465-2544	Vessel Agent #20 907-465-2548
Counselor, Professional #20 907-465-2551	Nurse (names L-Z) #20 907-465-2648	Veterinarian/Veterinary Technician #20 907-465-5470
Crewmember (Fishing Boat) #4 907-465-2376	Nurse Anesthetist #20 907-465-2544	Waste Water System Operator #3 907-465-5140
Defibillator Technician #17 907-465-3029	Nurse-RN/LPN #20 907-465-2544	Wrestler #20 907-465-2695
Dental Hygienist #20 907-465-2542	Nurses' Aide #20 907-269-8169	

Licensing Agency Information

#1 Department of Education & Early Development, Teacher Education & Certification, 801 W 10th St, #200, Juneau, AK 99801-1894; 907-465-2831, Fax: 907-465-2441. www.eed.state.ak.us Agency email: certify@eed.State.ak.us.

#2 Department of Environmental Conservation, Division of Environmental Health, 500 S Alaska St, Palmer, AK 99645; 907-745-3236, Fax: 907-745-8125. www.state.ak.us/dec Agency email: WebSite@envircon.state.ak.us.

#3 Department of Environmental Conservation, Facility Construction & Operation, 410 Willoughby Ave, Juneau, AK 99801-1795; 907-465-5140, Fax: 907-465-5177. www.state.ak.us/local/akpages/ENV.CONSERV/home.htm

#4 Department of Fish & Game, Licensing Section, PO Box 25525, Juneau, AK 99802-5525; 907-465-2376, Fax: 907-265-2440. www.state.ak.us/local/akpages/FISH.GAME/admin/license/crew.htm. Agency email: Kris_Wright@fishgame.state.ak.us.

#5 Department of Labor, Department of Commerce, Div of Occupational Licensing, 13601 C St, #722, Anchorage, AK 99503; 907-269-8160, Fax: 907-261-8156. www.dced.state.ak.us/occ Search database at www.dced.state.ak.us/occ/search3.htm

#7 Department of Labor, Labor Standards & Safety, Mechanical Inspection Section, PO Box 107020, Anchorage, AK 99510; 907-269-4925, Fax: 907-269-4932.

#8 Department of Natural Resources, Division of Parks & Outdoor Recreation, 514 Funny River Rd, Soldotna, AK 99669; 907-260-4882, Fax: 907-260-5992.

#9 Public Offices Commission, PO Box 110222, Juneau, AK 99811-0222; 907-465-4864, Fax: 907-465-4832. www.state.ak.us/local/akpages/ADMIN/apoc/lobcov.htm Search database at www.state.ak.us/local/akpages/ADMIN/apoc/lobcov.htm. Download directories of licensed lobbyists at the web site.

#10 Alaska State Troopers, ASPIN Permits & Licensing Unit, 5700 E Tudor Rd, Anchorage, AK 99507-1225; 907-269-0391, Fax: 907-269-0394. www.dps.state.ak.us Agency email: margaret_simmons@dps.state.ak.

#11 Alaska Bar Association, Board of Governors, PO Box 100279 (550 W 7th Ave #1900), Anchorage, AK 99510-0279; 907-272-7469, Fax: 907-272-2932. www.alaskabar.org Agency email: alaskabar@alaskabar.org. Recent yearly bar exam name results are available at www.alaskabar.org/ada.cfm?id=5239

#12 Department of Commerce & Economic Development, Division of Banking; Securities & Corporations, PO Box 110807, Juneau, AK 99811-0807; 907-465-2521, Fax: 907-465-2549. www.dced.state.ak.us/bsc/secur.htm Agency email: dbsc@dced.state.ak.us.

#13 Department of Community & Economic Development, Division of Insurance, PO Box 110805, Juneau, AK 99811-0805; 907-465-2816, Fax: 907-465-3422. www.dced.state.ak.us/insurance Agency email: insurance@dced.state.ak.us.

#16 Department of Health & Social Services, Division of Family & Youth Services, 3025 Clinton Dr, 2nd Fl, Juneau, AK 99801; 907-465-3207, Fax: 907-465-3397. www.hss.state.ak.us/dfys

#17 Department of Health & Social Services, Division of Public Health/Section of Community Health and EMS, 410 Willoughby Rm 109 Box 110616, Juneau, AK 99811-0616; 907-465-3027, Fax: 907-465-4101. www.chems.alaska.gov Agency email: matt_anderson@health.state.ak.us. Search database at http://chems.alaska.gov/emsdata

#18 Federal Aviation Administration, Flight Standards Regional Office, 222 W 7th Ave, AAL 200, #14, Anchorage, AK 99513-7587; 907-271-5514, Fax: 907-271-1665.

#19 Office of Lieutenant Governor, PO Box 110015, State Capitol, Juneau, AK 99811-0015; 907-465-3520, Fax: 907-465-5400. www.gov.state.ak.us/ltgov

#20 Department of Community & Economic Development, Div of Occupational Licensing, PO Box 110806, Juneau, AK 99811-0806; 907-465-2534, Fax: 907-465-2974. www.dced.state.ak.us/occ Agency email: license@dced.state.ak.us. Search database at www.dced.state.ak.us/occ/search3.htm

#21 Department of Revenue, Alcholic Beverage Control Board, 550 W 7th Ave #540, Anchorage, AK 99501-3556; 907-929-4242, Fax: 907-272-9412. www.4aha.org/directors.html

Alaska Federal Courts

The following list indicates the district and division name for each county in the state. If the bankruptcy court location is different from the district court, then the location of the bankruptcy court appears in parentheses.

County/Court Cross Reference

Aleutian Islands, East..Anchorage
Aleutian Islands, West...Anchorage
Anchorage Borough Borough ....Anchorage
Bethel..Fairbanks (Anchorage)
Bristol Bay Borough Borough....................................Anchorage
Fairbanks North Star Borough Borough ....Fairbanks (Anchorage)
Haines. Borough Borough ....Juneau (Anchorage)
Juneau Borough Borough ....Juneau (Anchorage)
Kenai Peninsula Borough Borough ....Anchorage
Ketchikan Gateway Borough Borough ....Ketchikan (Anchorage)
Kodiak Island Borough Borough ....Anchorage
Matanuska-Susitna Borough Borough........................Anchorage

Nome ....Nome (Anchorage)
North Slope Borough Borough.....................Fairbanks (Anchorage)
Northwest Arctic Borough..........................Fairbanks (Anchorage)
Prince of Wales-Outer Ketchikan ....Juneau (Anchorage)
Sitka Borough Borough ....Juneau (Anchorage)
Southeast Fairbanks....................................Fairbanks (Anchorage)
Valdez-Cordova ....Anchorage
Wade Hampton ....Fairbanks (Anchorage)
Wrangell-Petersburg....................................Juneau (Anchorage)
Yakutat ....Juneau (Anchorage)
Yukon-Koyukuk ....Fairbanks (Anchorage)

Standards for Federal Courts: The search fee is $20.00 per item (one party name or case number). Certification fee is $7.00 per document. Copy fee is $.50 per page. All fees standard unless noted in profile. Mail Search: always enclose a stamped self addressed envelope unless otherwise noted. Before releasing records, all courts require prepayment unless noted in profile.

Open records are located at the court unless otherwise noted. District courts index by defendant and plaintiff as well as by case number. Bankruptcy courts usually index by debtor and case number. While most courts now have their indexes on computer, many still maintain index card files as well.

The universal PACER sign-up number is 800-676-6856. Find PACER and the Party/Case Index on the Web at http://pacer.psc.uscourts.gov. PACER dial-up access is $.60 per minute. Also courts offering internet access via RACER, PACER, Web-PACER or the new CM-ECF charge $.07 per page fee unless noted as free.

US District Court

District of Alaska

Anchorage Division Box 4, 222 W 7th Ave, Anchorage, AK 99513-7564 (Courier Address: Use mail address for courier delivery), 907-677-6100.

www.akd.uscourts.gov

Counties: Aleutian Islands-East, Aleutian Islands-West, Anchorage Borough, Bristol Bay Borough, Kenai Peninsula Borough, Kodiak Island Borough, Matanuska-Susitna Borough, Valdez-Cordova.

Indexing & Storage: Cases are indexed by defendant, plaintiff, and case number. New cases are available in the index immediately after filing date. An index card system was used to index files prior to May 1987. Records after May 1987 are on computer. If a case was tried, the file will be sent to the Anchorage Federal Records Center. If the case did not go to trial, the file will be sent to the

Seattle Federal Records Center. Case records are sent to a Center after the case is closed.

Fee & Payment Notes: Payment may be made by money order, cashier check, personal check. Payee: Clerk, US District Court. You are allowed to make your own copies. These copies cost $.50 per page.

Phone Search: Only docket information is available by phone.

In Person Search: In person searching available.

PACER: Toll-free dial-up access: 888-271-6212. Local dial-up access: 907-677-6178. Case records are available back to 1987. Records are purged every 6 months. New records are available online after 1 day.

Other Online Access: Court does not participate in the U.S. party case index.

Fairbanks Division Box 1, 101 12th Ave, Fairbanks, AK 99701 (Courier Address: Use mail address for courier delivery), 907-451-5791.

www.akd.uscourts.gov

Counties: Bethel, Fairbanks North Star Borough, North Slope Borough, Northwest Arctic Borough, Southeast Fairbanks, Wade Hampton, Yukon-Koyukuk.

Indexing & Storage: Cases are indexed by defendant, plaintiff, and case number. New cases are available in the index 1-2 days after filing date. Open records are located at this court.

Fee & Payment Notes: Payment may be made by money order, cashier check, personal check. Prepayment is required unless other arrangements have been made. Payee: US District Court.

Phone Search: Only docket information is available by phone.

In Person Search: In person searching available.

PACER: Toll-free dial-up access: 888-271-6212. Local dial-up access: 907-677-6178. Case records are available back to 1987. Records are purged every 6 months. New records are available online after 1 day.

Other Online Access: Court does not participate in the U.S. party case index.

Juneau Division PO Box 020349, Juneau, AK 99802-0349 (Courier Address: Room 979, Federal Bldg-US Courthouse, 709 W 9th, Juneau, AK 99802), 907-586-7458.

www.akd.uscourts.gov

Counties: Haines Borough, Juneau Borough, Prince of Wales-Outer Ketchikan, Sitka Borough, Skagway-Hoonah-Angoon, Wrangell-Petersburg.

Indexing & Storage: Cases are indexed by defendant, plaintiff, and case number. New cases are available in the index immediately after filing date. Case files are indexed on computer and then stored in file cabinets. If the case was tried, the file will be sent to the divison where it was filed. If the case did not go to trial, it will be sent to the Seattle Federal Records Center some time after the case is closed.

Fee & Payment Notes: Payment may be made by money order, cashier check, personal check. Payee: Clerk, US District Court.

Phone Search: Only docket information is available by phone.

In Person Search: In person searching available.

PACER: Toll-free dial-up access: 888-271-6212. Local dial-up access: 907-677-6178. Case records are available back to 1987. Records are purged every 6 months. New records are available online after 1 day.

Other Online Access: Court does not participate in the U.S. party case index.

Ketchikan Division 648 Mission St, Room 507, Ketchikan, AK 99901 (Courier Address: Use mail address for courier delivery), 907-247-7576.

www.akd.uscourts.gov

Counties: Ketchikan Gateway Borough.

Indexing & Storage: Cases are indexed by defendant, plaintiff, and case number. New cases are available in the index immediately after filing date. Case files are indexed on computer and then stored in file cabinets. If the case was tried, the file will be sent to the Anchorage Division. If the case did not go to trial, it will be sent to the Seattle

Federal Records Center. Case records are sent to a Center after the case is closed.

Fee & Payment Notes: Payment may be made by money order, cashier check, business check. Personal checks are not accepted. Payee: Clerk, US District Court.

Phone Search: Only docket information is available by phone.

In Person Search: In person searching available.

PACER: Toll-free dial-up access: 888-271-6212. Local dial-up access: 907-677-6178. Case records are available back to 1987. Records are purged every 6 months. New records are available online after 1 day.

Other Online Access: Court does not participate in the U.S. party case index.

Nome Division PO Box 130, Nome, AK 99762 (Courier Address: 2nd Floor, Federal Bldg, Front St, Nome, AK 99762), 907-443-5216, Fax: 907-443-2192.

www.akd.uscourts.gov

Counties: Nome.

Indexing & Storage: Cases are indexed by defendant, plaintiff, and case number. New cases are available in the index immediately after filing date. Records have been retained at this court since 1960. No records have been sent to the repository.

Fee & Payment Notes: Payment may be made by money order, cashier check, personal check. Prepayment is not required, but is preferred. For copies, make checks payable to Alaska Court System. For searches and certified copies, make checks payable to US District Court. Copy fee:

$.25 per page. The fee for copies made by court personnel is $.50 per page.

Phone Search: Only docket information is available by phone. The court prefers that requests be submitted in writing.

Fax Search: Will bill for fax search like a mail search. Fax requests should be sent AFTER hours. Prefer not to fax results, but will in expedited cases at cost of fax, search and copies. Fax copies cannot be certified.

Mail Search: A stamped self addressed envelope is not required.

In Person Search: In person searching available.

PACER: Toll-free dial-up access: 888-271-6212. Local dial-up access: 907-677-6178. Case records are available back to 1987. Records are purged every 6 months. New records are available online after 1 day.

Other Online Access: Court does not participate in the U.S. party case index.

US Bankruptcy Court

District of Alaska

Anchorage Division Historic Courthouse, Suite 138, 605 W 4th Ave, Anchorage, AK 99501-2296 (Courier Address: Use mail address for courier delivery), 907-271-2655.

http://www2.akb.uscourts.gov/mainpage.htm

Counties: All boroughs and districts in Alaska.

Indexing & Storage: Cases are indexed by debtor as well as by case number. New cases are available in the index 1-2 days after filing date. To insure

accuracy, the court advises including a social security number or tax ID number. If the case was tried, it will be sent to Anchorage Federal Records Center. If the case did not go to trial, it will be sent to Seattle Federal Records Center. Case records are sent to a Center 60 days after the case is closed.

Fee & Payment Notes: Payment may be made by money order, cashier check, personal check. Payee: Clerk, US Bankruptcy Court. You are allowed to make your own copies. These copies cost $.15 per page. The copy machine works on a debit card system. The cards may be purchased through the State Law Library. The card costs $.50 and can be credited with $1.00, $5.00, $10.00 or $20.00 amounts.

Phone Search: Accession numbers will be released over the phone if a case number is provided. If the case number is unknown, the information must be requested in writing with the $20.00 search fee. An automated voice case information service (VCIS) is available. Call VCIS at 888-878-3110 or 907-271-2658.

In Person Search: In person searching available.

PACER:. Case records are available back to July 1991. Records are purged 6 months. New civil records are available online after 2 days. PACER is available online at http://pacer.akb.uscourts.gov. Document images available.

Electronic Filing: Electronic filing information is available online at https://ecf.akb.uscourts.gov

Other Online Access: The RACER system has been replaced by the ECF/PACER system.

Alaska Local Courts

Court	Jurisdiction	No. of Courts	How Organized
Superior Courts*	General		4 Districts
District Courts*	Limited	6	4 Districts
Combined Courts*		16	
Magistrate Courts*	Limited	40	4 Districts

* Profiled in this Sourcebook

Court	CIVIL								
	Tort	Contract	Real Estate	Min. Claim	Max. Claim	Small Claims	Estate	Eviction	Domestic Relations
Superior Courts*	X	X	X	$0	No Max		X	X	X
District Courts*	X	X		$0	$50,000	$7500		X	X
Magistrate Courts*	X	X		$0	$7500	$7500			

Court	CRIMINAL				
	Felony	Misdemeanor	DWI/DUI	Preliminary Hearing	Juvenile
Superior Courts*	X				X
District Courts*		X	X	X	X
Magistrate Courts*		X	X	X	

ADMINISTRATION

Office of the Administrative Director, 303 K St, Anchorage, AK, 99501; 907-264-0547, Fax: 907-264-0881. www.state.ak.us/courts

COURT STRUCTURE

Alaska is not organized into counties, but rather into 15 boroughs (3 unified home rule municipalities that are combination borough and city, and 12 boroughs) and 12 home rule cities, which do not directly coincide with the 4 Judicial Districts into which the judicial system is divided, that is, judicial boundaries cross borough boundaries. We have listed the courts by their borough or home rule city in keeping with the format of this book. You should search through the city court location names to determine the correct court for your search. Probate is handled by the Superior Courts.

The First District encompasses all of S.E. Alaska. Magistrates act as judicial officers. This 1st District has five trial/Superior courts: Ketchikan, Wrangell, Petersburg, Sitka and Juneau. District Magistrate Courts are Haines, Skagway, Yakutat, Angoon, Kake, Hoona, Craig.

ONLINE ACCESS

You may name search the nearly statewide Alaska Trial Courts database at www.state.ak.us/courts/names.htm. This includes all courts with electronic indexing and access. Search results give case number and court only. Data is updated quarterly; records do not go back beyond 1990. The home web page also gives access to Supreme Court and Appellate opinions.

ADDITIONAL INFORMATION

Documents may not be filed by fax in any Alaska court location without prior authorization of a judge.

The fees established by court rules for Alaska courts are: search fee - $15.00 per hour or fraction thereof; certification fee - $5.00 per document and $2.00 per additional copy of the document; copy fee - $.25 per page.

Magistrate Courts vary widely in how records are maintained and in the hours of operation (some are open only a few hours per week)

📖 📖 📖 📖 📖 📖 📖

Aleutian Islands Borough

Unalaska District Court (3rd District) PO Box 245, Unalaska, AK 99685-0245; 907-581-1266; Fax: 907-581-2809. Hours: 8AM-4:30PM (AK). *Felony, Misdemeanor, Civil Actions Under $7,500, Small Claims.*

www.state.ak.us/courts

Civil Records: Access: In person, mail, online. Only the court performs in person searches; visitors may not. Search fee: $15.00 per hour. Civil records on computer back to 1992. Search names on the Alaska Trial Courts database at www.state.ak.us/courts/names.htm. Search gives basic info.

Criminal Records: Access: In person, mail, online. Only the court performs in person searches; visitors may not. Search fee: $15.00 per hour. Required to

search: name, years to search, DOB. Criminal records on computer back to 1992. Online access to criminal records is the same as civil.

General Information: Turnaround time 1-2 weeks. Certification fee: $5.00. Fee payee: State of Alaska. Prepayment is required.

Sand Point Magistrate Court (3rd District) c/o Cordova Court, PO Box 898, Seward, AK 99574; 907-424-3378; Fax: 907-424-7581. *Felony, Misdemeanor, Civil Actions Under $7,500, Small Claims.*

Note: Court closed; records at Cordova Court, address and phone here. Limited trial court records and calendars available free online at www.state.ak.us/courts/names.htm.

St Paul Island Magistrate Court (3rd District) c/o Seward Magistrate Court, PO Box 1929, Seward, AK 99664; 907-224-3075; Fax: 907-227-7192. *Misdemeanor, Civil Actions Under $7,500, Small Claims.*

Note: Court closed. See Seward Magistrate Court, address and phone here.

Anchorage Borough

Superior & District Court (3rd District) 825 West 4th, Anchorage, AK 99501-2004; 907-264-0444; Probate phone: 907-264-0435; Fax: 907-264-0873. Hours: 8AM-4:30PM (AK). *Felony, Misdemeanor, Civil, Eviction, Small Claims, Probate.*

www.state.ak.us/courts

Civil Records: Access: Phone, fax, mail, in person, online. Both court and visitors may perform in person searches. Search fee: $15.00 per hour. Required to search: name, years to search; also helpful: address. Civil cases indexed by defendant, plaintiff. Civil records on computer from 1990, on microfiche and archived from 1977 to 1989, on roll index from 1940s. Search names on the Alaska Trial Courts database at www.state.ak.us/courts/names.htm. Search gives case number only.

Criminal Records: Access: Phone, fax, mail, in person, online. Both court and visitors may perform in person searches. Search fee: $15.00 per hour. Required to search: name, years to search; also helpful: address, DOB, SSN. Criminal records on computer from 1990, on microfiche and archived from 1977 to 1989, on roll index from 1940s. Online access to criminal records is the same as civil.

General Information: Public access terminal is available. No adoption, juvenile, sealed or mental records released. SASE required. Turnaround time 1-3 days. Fax notes: No fee to fax results. Local fax only. Copy fee: $.25 per page. Certification fee: $5.00. Fee payee: Alaska Court System. Personal checks accepted. Prepayment is required.

Bethel

Superior & District Court (4th District) PO Box 130, Bethel, AK 99559-0130; 907-543-2298; Fax: 907-543-4419. Hours: 8AM-4:30PM (AK). *Felony, Misdemeanor, Civil, Eviction, Small Claims, Probate.*

www.state.ak.us/courts

Civil Records: Access: Fax, mail, in person, online. Visitors must perform in person searches for themselves. Search fee: $15.00 per name. Required to search: name, years to search. Civil cases indexed by defendant, plaintiff. Civil records on computer back to 1983, on microfiche, archived and on index from 1977. Search names on the Alaska Trial Courts database at www.state.ak.us/courts/names.htm. Search gives case number only.

Criminal Records: Access: Fax, mail, in person, online. Visitors must perform in person searches for themselves. Search fee: $15.00 per name. Required to search: name, years to search, DOB; also helpful- case number. Criminal records on computer back to 1983, on microfiche, archived and on index from 1977. Online access to criminal records is the same as civil.

General Information: Public access terminal is available. No adoption, juvenile, guardianship or mental

records released. SASE required. Turnaround time 2 weeks. Fax notes: Fee to fax results is $.25 per page. Copy fee: $.25 per page. Certification fee: $5.00 plus $2.00 per page after first. Fee payee: Clerk of Court. Personal checks accepted. Prepayment is required.

Aniak District Court (4th District) PO Box 147, Aniak, AK 99557-0147; 907-675-4325; Fax: 907-675-4278. Hours: 8AM-4:30PM (AK). *Misdemeanor, Civil Actions Under $7,500, Small Claims.*

Civil Records: Access: Phone, mail, fax, in person. Both court and visitors may perform in person searches. Search fee: $15.00 per search. Civil records go back to 1960; on computer back to 1998.

Criminal Records: Access: Phone, mail, fax, in person. Both court and visitors may perform in person searches. Search fee: $15.00 per search. Required to search: name, years to search, DOB. Civil records go back to 1960; on computer back to 1998.

General Information: Turnaround time 1-2 weeks. Copy fee: $.25 per page. Certification fee: $5.00 per document. Fee payee: Aniak District Court. Prepayment is required.

Quinhagak Magistrate Court (Bethel Area) c/o Bethel Clerk, PO Box 130, Bethel, AK 99559-0130; 907-543-1105. *Misdemeanor, Civil Actions Under $7,500, Small Claims.*

Note: Court closed; records at Bethel Clerk of Courts at address and phone here.

Bristol Bay Borough

Naknek Magistrate Court (3rd District) PO Box 229, Naknek, AK 99633-0229; 907-246-6151; Fax: 907-246-7418. Hours: 8:30AM-4PM (AK). *Misdemeanor, Civil Actions Under $7,500, Small Claims.*

www.state.ak.us/courts

Note: Call Dillingham Superior Court for felony case location.

Civil Records: Access: Mail, in person, online. Only the court performs in person searches; visitors may not. Search fee: $15.00 per hour. Records go back to 1970's; computerized from 1993. Search names on the Alaska Trial Courts database at www.state.ak.us/courts/names.htm. Search gives case number only.

Criminal Records: Access: Mail, in person, online. Only the court performs in person searches; visitors may not. Search fee: $15.00 per hour. Required to search: name, years to search. Records go back to 1970's; computerized from 1993. Online access to criminal records is the same as civil.

General Information: Turnaround time same day. Certification fee: $10.00. Fee payee: Alaska Court System. Prepayment is required.

Denali Borough

Healy Magistrate Court (4th District) PO Box 298, Healy, AK 99743-0298; 907-683-2213; Fax: 907-683-1383. Hours: 8AM-4:30PM (AK). *Misdemeanor, Civil Actions Under $7,500, Small Claims.*

www.state.ak.us/courts

Note: Felony cases are at Fairbanks Superior & District Court.

Civil Records: Access: Phone, mail, fax, in person, online. Both court and visitors may perform in person searches. Search fee: $15.00 per hour. Required to search: name, years to search, DOB. Records on computer back to 1972. Search names on the Alaska Trial Courts database at www.state.ak.us/courts/names.htm. Search gives case number only.

Criminal Records: Access: Phone, mail, fax, in person, online. Both court and visitors may perform in person searches. Search fee: $15.00 per hour. Required to search: name, years to search, DOB. Records on

computer back to 1972. Online access to criminal records is the same as civil.

General Information: Public access terminal is available. Turnaround time 1-2 weeks. Fax notes: Will only fax to a toll-free when no record is found. Certification fee: $5.00. Fee payee: State of Alaska. Prepayment is required.

Dillingham

Dillingham Superior Court (3rd District) PO Box 909, Dillingham, AK 99576-0909; 907-842-5215; Fax: 907-842-5746. Hours: 8AM-4:30PM (AK). *Felony, Misdemeanor, Civil, Small Claims.*

www.state.ak.us/courts

Civil Records: Access: In person, mail, online. Only the court performs in person searches; visitors may not. Search fee: $15.00. Search names on the Alaska Trial Courts database at www.state.ak.us/courts/names.htm. Search gives case number only.

Criminal Records: Access: In person, mail, online. Only the court performs in person searches; visitors may not. Search fee: $15.00 per hour. Required to search: name, years to search, DOB. Online access to criminal records is the same as civil.

General Information: Turnaround time 1-2 weeks. Fee payee: State of Alaska. Prepayment is required.

Fairbanks North Star Borough

Superior & District Court (4th District) 101 Lacey St, Fairbanks, AK 99701-4761; 907-452-9277; Fax: 907-452-9392. Hours: 8AM-4:30PM (AK). *Felony, Misdemeanor, Civil, Eviction, Small Claims, Probate.*

www.statc.ak.us/courts/courtdir.htm

Civil Records: Access: In person, online. Visitors must perform in person searches for themselves. No search fee. Required to search: name, years to search. Civil cases indexed by defendant, plaintiff. Civil records on computer from 1988, on microfiche, archived and on index from 1900s. Search names on the Alaska Trial Courts database at www.state.ak.us/courts/names.htm. Search gives case number only. Access to the previous 6 months of Fairbanks civil court records are available free at www.state.ak.us/courts/akct.htm. Click on "trial courts.". Access to the previous 3 months of Fairbanks eviction, divorce, and probate cases are also available.

Criminal Records: Access: In person only, online. Visitors must perform in person searches for themselves. No search fee. Required to search: name, years to search, DOB. Criminal records on computer from 1988, on microfiche, archived and on index from 1900s. Online access to criminal records is the same as civil.

General Information: Public access terminal is available. No adoption, juvenile, guardianship or mental records released. Copy fee: $.25 per page. Certification fee: $5.00 plus $2.00 per copy after first. Fee payee: Clerk of Court. Personal checks accepted. In person only. Prepayment is required.

Haines Borough

District Court (1st District) PO Box 169, Haines, AK 99827-0169; 907-766-2801; Fax: 907-766-3148. Hours: 8AM-N, 1-4:30PM (AK). *Misdemeanor, Civil Actions Under $50,000, Small Claims.*

www.state.ak.us/courts

Note: Felony cases are at Juneau Superior & District Court.

Civil Records: Access: Phone, fax, mail, in person, online. Only the court performs in person searches; visitors may not. Search fee: $15.00 per hour. Required to search: name, years to search; also helpful: address. Civil cases indexed by defendant, plaintiff. Civil records on computer since 1993, index from 1960s. Search names on the Alaska Trial Courts database at www.state.ak.us/courts/names.htm. Search gives case number only. Limited information is available by phone.

Criminal Records: Access: Phone, fax, mail, in person, online. Only the court performs in person searches; visitors may not. Search fee: $15.00 per hour. Required to search: name, years to search; also helpful: address, DOB, SSN. Criminal records on computer since 1993, index from 1960s. Online access to criminal records is the same as civil.

General Information: No juvenile records released. SASE required. Turnaround time 1-2 days. Copy fee: $.25 per page. Certification fee: $5.00 plus $2.00 per each additional document requested at same time. Fee payee: Alaska Court System. Personal checks accepted. Prepayment is required.

Juneau Borough

Superior & District Court (1st District) Dimond Courthouse, PO Box 114100, Juneau, AK 99811-4100; 907-463-4700; Fax: 907-463-3788. Hours: 8AM-4:30PM (AK). *Felony, Misdemeanor, Civil, Eviction, Small Claims, Probate.*

www.state.ak.us/courts/courtdir.htm

Civil Records: Access: Fax, mail, in person, online. Both court and visitors may perform in person searches. Search fee: $15.00 per hour. Required to search: name, years to search. Civil cases indexed by defendant. Civil records on computer back to 1987, on microfiche from 1960 to 1986, on index from 1959 to 1987. Search names on the Alaska Trial Courts database at www.state.ak.us/courts/names.htm. Search gives case number only.

Criminal Records: Access: Fax, mail, in person, online. Both court and visitors may perform in person searches. Search fee: $15.00 per hour. Required to search: name, years to search. Criminal records on computer back to 1987, on microfiche from 1960 to 1986, on index from 1959 to 1987. Online access to criminal records is the same as civil.

General Information: Public access terminal is available. No adoption, juvenile, guardianship or mental records released. SASE required. Turnaround time 2-5 days. Copy fee: $.25 per page. Certification fee: $5.00 plus $2.00 per page after first. Fee payee: Juneau Trial Court. Personal checks accepted. Prepayment is required.

Kenai Peninsula Borough

Superior & District Court (3rd District) 125 Trading Bay Dr, Ste 100, Kenai, AK 99611; 907-283-3110; Fax: 907-283-8535. Hours: 8AM-4:30PM (AK). *Felony, Misdemeanor, Civil, Eviction, Small Claims, Probate.*

www.state.ak.us/courts

Civil Records: Access: Mail, in person, online. Both court and visitors may perform in person searches. Search fee: $15.00 per hour. Required to search: name, years to search. Civil cases indexed by defendant, plaintiff. Civil records on computer from 1983, on microfiche, archived and on index from 1959. Search names on the Alaska Trial Courts database at www.state.ak.us/courts/names.htm. Search gives case number only.

Criminal Records: Access: Mail, in person, online. Both court and visitors may perform in person searches. Search fee: $15.00 per hour. Required to search: name, years to search, DOB. Criminal records on computer from 1983, on microfiche, archived and on index from 1959. Online access to criminal records is the same as civil.

General Information: Public access terminal is available. No adoption, guardianship, children's, conservatorship or coroner records released. SASE required. Turnaround time 1 week. Copy fee: $.25 per page. Certification fee: $5.00 plus $2.00 per page after first. Fee payee: Clerk of Court. Personal checks accepted. Prepayment is required.

District Court (3rd District) 3670 Lake St, Ste 400, Homer, AK 99603-9647; 907-235-8171; Fax: 907-235-4257. Hours: 8AM-4:30PM (AK). *Misdemeanor, Civil Actions Under $50,000, Small Claims.*

www.state.ak.us/courts/courtdir.htm

Civil Records: Access: Phone, fax, mail, in person, online. Both court and visitors may perform in person searches. Search fee: $15.00 per hour. Required to search: name, years to search. Civil cases indexed by defendant, plaintiff. Civil records on computer back to 1984. Search names on the Alaska Trial Courts database at www.state.ak.us/courts/names.htm. Search gives case number only. Phone access limited to name searches.

Criminal Records: Access: Phone, fax, mail, in person, online. Both court and visitors may perform in person searches. Search fee: $15.00 per hour. Required to search: name, years to search. Criminal records on computer back to 1984. Online access to criminal records is the same as civil.

General Information: Public access terminal is available. No confidential or sealed records released. SASE required. Turnaround time 5 days. Copy fee: $.25 per page. Certification fee: $5.00. Fee payee: Alaska Court System. Personal checks accepted. Prepayment is required.

Seward Magistrate Court (3rd District) PO Box 1929, Seward, AK 99664-1929; 907-224-3075; Fax: 907-227-7192. Hours: 8AM-4:30PM (AK). *Misdemeanor, Civil Actions Under $7,500, Small Claims.*

www.state.ak.us/courts

Civil Records: Access: In person, mail, online. Both court and visitors may perform in person searches. Search fee: $15.00 per name; may do for free is time permits. Civil records on computer since 1983. Search names on the Alaska Trial Courts database at www.state.ak.us/courts/names.htm. Search gives case number only.

Criminal Records: Access: In person, mail, online. Only the court may perform in person searches. Search fee: $15.00 per name. Required to search: name, years to search, DOB. Criminal records on computer since 1983. Online access to criminal records is the same as civil.

General Information: Turnaround time 1-2 weeks. Fee payee: State of Alaska. Prepayment is required.

Ketchikan Gateway Borough

Superior & District Court (1st District) 415 Main, Rm 400, Ketchikan, AK 99901-6399; 907-225-3195; Fax: 907-225-7849. Hours: 8AM-4:30PM M-Th, 9AM-4:30PM Fridays (AK). *Felony, Misdemeanor, Civil, Eviction, Small Claims, Probate.*

www.state.ak.us/courts/names.htm.

Civil Records: Access: Fax, mail, in person, online. Both court and visitors may perform in person searches. Search fee: $15.00 per hour. Required to search: name, years to search. Civil cases indexed by defendant, plaintiff. Civil records on computer from 1983, on microfiche from 1972 to 1989, index from 1972. Search names on the Alaska Trial Courts database at www.state.ak.us/courts/names.htm. Search gives case number only.

Criminal Records: Access: Fax, mail, in person, online. Both court and visitors may perform in person searches. Search fee: $15.00 per hour. Required to search: name, years to search, DOB. Criminal records on computer from 1983, on microfiche from 1972 to 1989, index from 1972. Online access to criminal records is the same as civil.

General Information: Public access terminal is available. No confidential probate or children's records released. SASE required. Turnaround time 2 weeks. Fax notes: No fee to fax results. Copy fee: $.25 per page. Certification fee: $5.00. Fee payee: Alaska Court System. Personal checks accepted. Prepayment is required.

Kodiak Island Borough

Superior & District Court (3rd District) 204 Mission Road, Rm 10, Kodiak, AK 99615-7312; 907-486-1600; Fax: 907-486-1660. Hours: 8AM-4:30PM M,T,Th,F; 9AM-4:30PM W (AK). *Felony, Misdemeanor, Civil, Eviction, Small Claims, Probate.*

www.state.ak.us/courts

Civil Records: Access: Mail, fax, in person, online. Both court and visitors may perform in person searches. Search fee: $15.00 per hour. Required to search: name, years to search; also helpful: address. Civil cases indexed by defendant, plaintiff. Civil records on computer from 1982, on microfiche, index and archived from 1959. Search names on the Alaska Trial Courts database at www.state.ak.us/courts/names.htm. Search gives case number only.

Criminal Records: Access: Mail, fax, in person, online. Both court and visitors may perform in person searches. Search fee: $15.00 per hour. Required to search: name, years to search; also helpful: address, DOB, SSN. Criminal records on computer from 1982, on microfiche, index and archived from 1959. Online access to criminal records is the same as civil.

General Information: Public access terminal is available. No adoption, juvenile, guardianship or mental records released. SASE required. Turnaround time 1-3 weeks. Copy fee: $.25 per page. Certification fee: $5.00 plus $2.00 per add'l copy. Fee payee: Clerk of Court. Personal checks accepted. Prepayment is required.

Matanuska-Susitna Borough

Superior & District Court (3rd District) 435 S Denali, Palmer, AK 99645-6437; Civil phone: 907-746-8108; Criminal phone: 907-746-8104; Fax: 907-746-4151. Hours: 8AM-4:30PM (AK). *Felony, Misdemeanor, Civil, Eviction, Small Claims, Probate.*

www.state.ak.us/courts

Civil Records: Access: Mail, in person, online. Both court and visitors may perform in person searches. Search fee: $15.00 per hour. Required to search: name, years to search; also helpful: address. Civil cases indexed by defendant, plaintiff. Civil records on computer from 1988, on microfiche, archived and index from 1974. Search names on the Alaska Trial Courts database at www.state.ak.us/courts/names.htm. Search gives case number only.

Criminal Records: Access: Mail, in person, online. Both court and visitors may perform in person searches. Search fee: $15.00 per hour. Required to search: name, years to search; also helpful: address, DOB, SSN. Criminal records on computer from 1988, on microfiche, archived and index from 1974. Online access to criminal records is the same as civil.

General Information: Public access terminal is available. No adoption, juvenile, guardianship or mental records released. SASE required. Turnaround time 1-3 weeks. Copy fee: $.25 per page. Certification fee: $5.00. A second copy is $2.00 per document. Fee payee: State of Alaska. Personal checks accepted. Prepayment is required.

first. Fee payee: Clerk of Court. Personal checks accepted. Prepayment is required.

Nome

Superior & District Court (2nd District) PO Box 1110, Nome, AK 99762-1110; 907-443-5216; Fax: 907-443-2192. Hours: 8AM-4:30PM (AK). *Felony, Misdemeanor, Civil, Eviction, Small Claims, Probate.*

www.state.ak.us/courts/courtdir.htm

Civil Records: Access: Fax, mail, in person, online. Both court and visitors may perform in person searches. Search fee: $15.00 per hour or fraction of. Required to search: name, years to search; also helpful: DOB. Civil cases indexed by defendant, plaintiff. Civil records on computer from 1983, on microfiche from 1960 to 1983, on index and archived from 1960. Search names on the Alaska Trial Courts database at www.state.ak.us/courts/names.htm. Search gives case number only.

Criminal Records: Access: Fax, mail, in person, online. Both court and visitors may perform in person searches. Search fee: $15.00 per hour or fraction of. Required to search: name, years to search; also helpful: DOB, SSN. Criminal records on computer from 1983, on microfiche from 1960 to 1983, on index and archived from 1960. Online access to criminal records is the same as civil.

General Information: Public access terminal is available. No adoption, juvenile, guardianship or mental records released. SASE required. Turnaround time 5 days. Fax notes: Will fax results to toll-free numbers only. Copy fee: $.25 per page. Certification fee: $5.00 plus $2.00 per copy after first. Fee payee: Nome Trial Courts. Personal checks accepted. Prepayment is required.

Gambell Magistrate Court (2nd District) PO Box 1110, Nome, AK 99762-1110; 907-443-5216. *Misdemeanor, Civil Actions Under $7,500, Small Claims.*

Note: Court is vacant; records at Superior Court in Nome at address and phone here.

Unalakleet Magistrate Court (2nd District) PO Box 250, Unalakleet, AK 99684-0250; 907-624-3015; Fax: 907-624-3118. Hours: 8AM-1:30PM (AK). *Misdemeanor, Civil Actions Under $7,500, Small Claims.*

Civil Records: Access: In person, mail. Only the court performs in person searches; visitors may not. Search fee: $15.00 per hour. Required to search: name, years to search.

Criminal Records: Access: In person, mail. Only the court performs in person searches; visitors may not. Search fee: $15.00 per hour. Required to search: name, years to search.

General Information: Turnaround time 1-2 weeks. Fee payee: Magistrate Court. Prepayment is required.

North Slope Borough

Superior & District Court (2nd District) PO Box 270, Barrow, AK 99723-0270; 907-852-4800 X80; Fax: 907-852-4804. Hours: 8AM-4:30PM (AK). *Felony, Misdemeanor, Civil, Eviction, Small Claims, Probate.*

www.state.ak.us/courts

Civil Records: Access: Fax, mail, in person, online. Both the court and visitors may perform in person searches. Search fee: $15.00 per name. Required to search: name, years to search; also helpful: address. Civil cases indexed by defendant, plaintiff. Civil records on computer from 1983, prior on microfiche. Search names on the Alaska Trial Courts database at www.state.ak.us/courts/names.htm. Search gives case number only.

Criminal Records: Access: Fax, mail, in person, online. Both the court and visitors may performs in

person searches. Search fee: $15.00 per hour. Required to search: name, years to search; also helpful: address, DOB, SSN. Criminal records on computer from 1983, prior on microfiche. Online access to criminal records is the same as civil.

General Information: Public access terminal is available. No confidential records released. SASE required. Turnaround time 1-2 weeks. Fax notes: No fee to fax results. Copy fee: $.25 per page. Certification fee: $5.00 plus $2.00 per page after first. Fee payee: Alaska Court System. Personal checks accepted. Prepayment is required.

Northwest Arctic Borough

Superior & District Court (2nd District) PO Box 317, Kotzebue, AK 99752-0317; 907-442-3208; Fax: 907-442-3974. Hours: 8AM-4:30PM (AK). *Felony, Misdemeanor, Civil, Eviction, Small Claims, Probate.*

www.state.ak.us/courts

Civil Records: Access: Phone, fax, mail, in person, online. Both court and visitors may perform in person searches. Search fee: $15.00. Required to search: name, years to search. Civil cases indexed by defendant and plaintiff. Civil records on computer from 1983, prior records on microfilm, archived and index from 1966. Search names on the Alaska Trial Courts database at www.state.ak.us/courts/names.htm. Search gives case number only. Copy of check required for fax access.

Criminal Records: Access: Mail, fax, in person, online. Both court and visitors may perform in person searches. Search fee: $15.00. Required to search: name, years to search, DOB;. Criminal records on computer from 1983, prior records on microfilm, archived and index from 1966. Online access to criminal records is the same as civil.

General Information: Public access terminal is available. No adoption, juvenile, guardianship or mental records released. Turnaround time 2-3 days. Copy fee: $.25 per page. Certification fee: $5.00 plus $2.00 per page after first. Notary fee is $3.00. Fee payee: Alaska Court System. Personal checks accepted. Prepayment is required.

Ambler Magistrate Court (2nd District) PO Box 317, Kotzebue, AK 99752; 907-442-3208; Fax: 907-442-3974. Hours: 9AM-2PM (AK). *Misdemeanor, Civil Actions Under $7,500, Small Claims.*

Note: Court is closed; for records, contact Kotzebue Court at the phone number and address here.

Kiana Magistrate Court (2nd District) PO Box 317, Kotzebue, AK 99752-0317; 907-442-3208. Hours: 10AM-3PM M,W,F (AK). *Misdemeanor, Civil Actions Under $7,500, Small Claims.*

Note: Court is temporarily vacant; for records, contact Kotzebue Court at address and phone here.

Selawik Magistrate Court (2nd District) PO Box 231, Selawik, AK 99770. Hours: variable (AK). *Misdemeanor, Civil Actions Under $7,500, Small Claims.*

Note: Information about this court is incomplete; contact the Kotzebue Court.

General Information: Fee payee: Magistrate Court.

Prince of Wales-Outer Ketchikan

Craig Magistrate Court (1st District) PO Box 646, Craig, AK 99921-0646; 907-826-3316/3306; Fax: 907-826-3904. Hours: 8AM-4:30PM (AK). *Misdemeanor, Civil Actions Under $7,500, Small Claims.*

www.state.ak.us/courts

Note: Felony cases are at Ketchikan Superior & District Court.

Civil Records: Access: In person, phone, mail, online. Only the court performs in person searches; visitors may not. Search fee: $15.00 per name. Required to search: name, years to search; also helpful: DOB. Search names on the Alaska Trial Courts database at www.state.ak.us/courts/names.htm. Search gives case number only.

Criminal Records: Access: In person, phone, mail, online. Only the court performs in person searches; visitors may not. Search fee: $15.00 per name. Required to search: name, years to search; also helpful: DOB. Online access to criminal records is the same as civil.

General Information: Turnaround time 2 weeks. Copy fee: $.25. Certification fee: $5.00. Fee payee: Alaska Court System. Prepayment is required.

Sitka Borough

Superior & District Court (1st District) 304 Lake St, Rm 203, Sitka, AK 99835-7759; 907-747-3291; Fax: 907-747-6690. Hours: 8AM-4:30PM (AK). *Felony, Misdemeanor, Civil, Eviction, Small Claims, Probate.*

www.state.ak.us/courts

Civil Records: Access: Phone, fax, mail, in person, online. Both court and visitors may perform in person searches. Search fee: $15.00 per hour. Required to search: name. Civil cases indexed by defendant, plaintiff. Civil records on computer from 1983, on microfilm and archived from 1970 to 1987, on index from 1960. Search names on the Alaska Trial Courts database at www.state.ak.us/courts/names.htm. Search gives case number only.

Criminal Records: Access: Phone, fax, mail, in person, online. Both court and visitors may perform in person searches. Search fee: $15.00 per hour. Required to search: name. Criminal records on computer from 1983, on microfilm and archived from 1970 to 1987, on index from 1960. Online access to criminal records is the same as civil.

General Information: Public access terminal is available. No adoption, juvenile, guardianship or mental records released. SASE required. Turnaround time 1 week. Fax notes: No fee to fax results. Will fax collect. Copy fee: $.25 per page. Certification fee: $5.00. Fee payee: Alaska Court System. Personal checks accepted. Prepayment is required.

Skagway-Yakutat-Angoon (Yakutat Borough)

Hoonah District Court (1st District) PO Box 430, Hoonah, AK 99829-0430; 907-945-3668; Fax: 907-945-3637. Hours: 8AM-Noon, 1-4:30PM (AK). *Misdemeanor, Civil Actions Under $50,000, Small Claims.*

www.alaska.net/~akctlib/homepage.htm

Note: Felony cases are at Juneau Superior & District Court.

Civil Records: Access: Mail, in person. Only the court performs in person searches; visitors may not. No search fee. Required to search: name, years to search. Civil cases indexed by defendant, plaintiff. Civil records on index from 1971 to present.

Criminal Records: Access: Mail, in person. Only the court performs in person searches; visitors may not. No search fee. Required to search: name, years to search; also helpful: DOB. Criminal records on index from 1971 to present.

General Information: No confidential, juvenile or sex related records released. SASE not required. Turnaround time 2-3 days. Copy fee: $.25 per page. Certification fee: $5.00 plus $2.00 per page after first. Fee payee: Alaska Court System. Personal checks accepted. Prepayment is required.

Angoon Magistrate Court (1st District) PO
Box 250, Angoon, AK 99820-0123; 907-788-3229; Fax: 907-788-3108. Hours: 1PM-4:30PM (AK). *Misdemeanor, Civil Actions Under $7,500, Small Claims.*

Note: Felony cases are at Sitka Superior & District Court.

Civil Records: Access: Phone, mail, fax, in person. Only the court performs in person searches; visitors may not. Search fee: $15.00 per hour. Required to search: name, years to search. Records go back to 1994.

Criminal Records: Access: Phone, mail, fax, in person. Only the court performs in person searches; visitors may not. Search fee: $15.00 per hour. Required to search: name, years to search, date of birth. Records go back to 1994.

General Information: Turnaround time 1 week. Fax notes: Fee to fax results is $5.00 per page or $15.00 per document. Fee payee: Alaska Court System. Prepayment is required.

Pelican Magistrate Court (1st District) 304
Lake St number203, Sitka, AK 99835; 907-747-3291; Fax: 907-747-6690. *Misdemeanor, Civil Actions Under $7,500, Small Claims.*

Note: This Pelican court closed permanently on 12/31/99. All records are at the Sitka court, address and phone given here.

Skagway Magistrate Court (1st District)
PO Box 495, Skagway, AK 99840-0495; 907-983-2368; Fax: 907-983-3801. Hours: 9AM-12M-F; 1PM-4PM Tue-Fri (AK). *Misdemeanor, Civil Actions Under $7,500, Small Claims.*

Note: Hours will vary from Summer to Winter. Felony cases are at Juneau Superior & District Court.

Civil Records: Access: Phone, mail, fax, in person. No search fee. Civil records go back to 1970; on computer back to 1998.

Criminal Records: Access: In person, mail. Only the court performs in person searches; visitors may not. Search fee: $15.00 per hour. Required to search: name, years to search, DOB. Criminal records go back to 1970; on computer back to 1998. No charge for a simple name search.

General Information: Turnaround time 1-2 weeks. Fax notes: Will fax back to toll-free numbers no charge. Certification fee: $3.00 per document. Fee payee: Magistrate Court. Prepayment is required.

Yakutat Magistrate Court (1st District) PO
Box 426, Yakutat, AK 99689-0426; 907-784-3274; Fax: 907-784-3257. Hours: 9AM-4:30PM M-Th (AK). *Misdemeanor, Civil Actions Under $7,500, Small Claims.*

Note: Felony cases are at Juneau Superior & District Court.

Civil Records: Access: Phone, mail, fax, in person, email. Only the court performs in person searches; visitors may not. Search fee: $15.00 per hour or a fraction of. Required to search: name. Civil records go back to 1998; on computer back to 1976.

Criminal Records: Access: Mail, fax, in person, email. Only the court performs in person searches; visitors may not. Search fee: $15.00 per hour or a fraction of. Required to search: name, DOB. Criminal records go back to 1959; on computer back to 1998.

General Information: Certification fee: $5.00. Fee payee: Alaska Court System. Prepayment is required.

Southeast Fairbanks

Delta Junction Magistrate Court (4th District) PO Box 401, Delta Junction, AK 99737-0401; 907-895-4211; Fax: 907-895-4204. Hours: 8AM-Noon, 1-4:30PM (AK). *Misdemeanor, Civil Actions Under $7,500, Small Claims.*

www.state.ak.us/courts

Note: Felony cases are at Fairbanks Superior & District Court.

Civil Records: Access: In person, mail, online. Only the court performs in person searches; visitors may not. No search fee. Search names on the Alaska Trial Courts database at www.state.ak.us/courts/names.htm. Search gives case number only.

Criminal Records: Access: phone, mail, fax, in person, online. Only the court performs in person searches; visitors may not. Search fee: $15.00 per hour. Required to search: name, years to search. Criminal records computerized go back to 1980; prior records go back to mid-70's. Online access to criminal records is the same as civil.

General Information: Turnaround time 1 week. Certification fee: $5.00. Fee payee: District Court. Prepayment is required.

Tok Magistrate Court (4th District) PO Box 187, Tok, AK 99780-0187; 907-883-5171; Fax: 907-883-4367. Hours: 8AM-4:30PM (AK). *Misdemeanor, Civil Actions Under $7,500, Small Claims.*

www.state.ak.us/courts

Note: Felony cases are at Fairbanks Superior & District Court.

Civil Records: Access: In person, phone, mail, online. Only the visitors may perform in person searches. No search fee. Civil records computerized since 1994. Search names on the Alaska Trial Courts database at www.state.ak.us/courts/names.htm. Search gives case number only.

Criminal Records: Access: In person, phone, mail, online. Only visitors may perform in person searches. No search fee. Required to search: name, years to search, DOB. Criminal records computerized since 1994. Online access to criminal records is the same as civil.

General Information: Public access terminal is available. Turnaround time 5 days.

Valdez-Cordova

Superior & District Court (3rd District) PO Box 127, Valdez, AK 99686-0127; 907-835-2266; Fax: 907-835-3764. Hours: 8AM-4:30PM (AK). *Felony, Misdemeanor, Civil, Eviction, Small Claims, Probate.*

www.state.ak.us/courts

Civil Records: Access: Fax, mail, in person, online. Both court and visitors may perform in person searches. No search fee. Required to search: name, years to search; also helpful: address. Civil cases indexed by defendant, plaintiff. Civil records on computer from 1984, on microfiche, archived and index from 1960. Search names on the Alaska Trial Courts database at www.state.ak.us/courts/names.htm. Search gives case number only.

Criminal Records: Access: Fax, mail, in person, online. Both court and visitors may perform in person searches. No search fee. Required to search: name, years to search; also helpful: address, DOB, SSN. Criminal records on computer from 1984, on microfiche, archived and index from 1960. Online access to criminal records is the same as civil.

General Information: No adoption, juvenile, guardianship or mental records released. SASE required. Turnaround time 1-3 weeks. Copy fee: $.25 per page. Certification fee: $5.00. Fee payee: Valdez Trial Court of Alaska. Personal checks accepted. Prepayment is required.

Cordova Court (3rd District) PO Box 898,
Cordova, AK 99574-0898; 907-424-3378; Fax: 907-424-7581. Hours: 8AM-4:30PM (AK). *Felony, Misdemeanor, Civil, Small Claims, Probate.*

www.state.ak.us/courts

Civil Records: Access: Phone, mail, fax, in person, online. Both court and visitors may perform in person searches. No search fee. Civil records on computer back to 1993; other records back to 1975. Search names on the Alaska Trial Courts database at www.state.ak.us/courts/names.htm. Search gives case number only. Access by phone if time allows.

Criminal Records: Access: Phone, mail, fax, in person, online. Both court and visitors may perform in person searches. Search fee: $15.00 per hour. Required to search: name, years to search, DOB. Criminal records on computer back to 1993; other records back to 1975. Online access to criminal records is the same as civil. Will take phone requests if time allows.

General Information: Public access terminal is available. Turnaround time 1 week. Certification fee: $5.00. Fee payee: State of Alaska. Prepayment is required.

Glennallen District Court (3rd District) PO
Box 86, Glennallen, AK 99588-0086; 907-822-3405; Fax: 907-822-3601. Hours: 8AM-4:30PM (AK). *Misdemeanor, Civil, Small Claims.*

www.state.ak.us/courts

Civil Records: Access: Mail, fax, in person, online. Visitors must perform in person searches for themselves Search fee: $15.00 per hour. Records go back to 1960; on computer back to 1992. Search names on the Alaska Trial Courts database at www.state.ak.us/courts/names.htm. Search gives case number only.

Criminal Records: Access: Mail, fax, in person, online. Both court and visitors may perform in person searches. Search fee: $15.00 per hour. Required to search: name, years to search, DOB. Records go back to 1960; on computer back to 1992. Online access to criminal records is the same as civil.

General Information: Turnaround time 1-2 weeks. Fax notes: Will not fax results. Copy fee: $.25 per page. Certification fee: $5.00 per document. Fee payee: Alaska Court System. Prepayment is required.

Whittier Magistrate Court (3rd District),
825 W 4th Ave, Anchorage, AK 99501-2004; 907-264-514. *Misdemeanor, Civil Actions Under $7,500, Small Claims.*

Note: Court closed; records available at the address and phone here.

Wade Hampton

Chevak Magistrate Court (Bethel Area)
PO Box 238, Chevak, AK 99563-0238; 907-858-7231; Fax: 907-858-7230. Hours: 8AM-4:30PM (AK). *Misdemeanor, Civil Actions Under $7,500, Small Claims.*

Note: Felony cases are at Bethel Superior & District Court.

Civil Records: Access: Mail, fax, in person. Only the court performs in person searches; visitors may not. No search fee. Required to search: name, years to search. Civil records go back to 1993; on computer back to 1997.

Criminal Records: Access: Mail, fax, in person. Both court and visitors may perform in person searches. Search fee: $15.00 per hour. Required to search: name, years to search, address, DOB, SSN, signed release. Criminal records go back to 1993; on computer back to 1997.

General Information: Turnaround time 1-2 weeks. Certification fee: $3.00. Fee payee: Magistrate Court. Prepayment is required.

Emmonak Magistrate Court (Bethel Area)
PO Box 176, Emmonak, AK 99581-0176; 907-949-1748; Fax: 907-949-1535. Hours: 8AM-4:30PM (AK). *Misdemeanor, Civil Actions Under $7,500, Small Claims.*

Note: Felony cases are at Bethel Superior & District Court.
Civil Records: Access: In person, mail. Only the court performs in person searches; visitors may not. No search fee. Required to search: years to search, DOB, SSN, signed release. Overall records go back to 1995. Computerized records go back to 2000.
Criminal Records: Access: In person, mail. Only the court performs in person searches; visitors may not. Search fee: $15.00 per hour. Required to search: name, years to search, address, DOB, signed release; also helpful: SSN. Overall records go back to 1995. Computerized records go back to 2000.
General Information: Turnaround time 1-2 weeks. Fee payee: Magistrate Court. Prepayment is required.

St Mary's Magistrate Court (Bethel Area)
PO Box 183, St Mary's, AK 99658-0183; 907-438-2912; Fax: 907-438-2819. Hours: 8AM-4:30PM (AK). *Misdemeanor, Civil Actions Under $7,500, Small Claims.*

Note: Felony cases are at Bethel Superior & District Court.
Civil Records: Access: In person, mail. Only the court performs in person searches; visitors may not. No search fee. Required to search: $15.00 per hour. Civil records computerized go back to 1996.
Criminal Records: Access: In person, mail. Only the court performs in person searches; visitors may not. Search fee: $15.00 per hour. Required to search: name, years to search; also helpful: DOB. Criminal records computerized go back to 1996.
General Information: Turnaround time 3 weeks. Copy fee: $.25 per page.

Wrangell-Petersburg

Petersburg Superior & District Court (1st District) PO Box 1009, Petersburg, AK 99833-1009; 907-772-3824; Fax: 907-772-3018. Hours: 8AM-4:30PM (AK). *Felony, Misdemeanor, Civil, Eviction, Small Claims, Probate.*
www.state.ak.us/courts

Civil Records: Access: Phone, fax, mail, in person, online. Both court and visitors may perform in person searches. No search fee. Required to search: name, years to search; also helpful: address. Civil cases indexed by defendant, plaintiff. Civil records on computer from 1988, on microfiche and index from 1960s, archived from 1920s. Search names on the Alaska Trial Courts database at www.state.ak.us/courts/names.htm. Search gives case number only.
Criminal Records: Access: Phone, fax, mail, in person, online. Both court and visitors may perform in person searches. No search fee. Required to search: name, years to search; also helpful: address, DOB, SSN. Criminal records on computer from 1988, on microfiche and index from 1960s, archived from 1920s. Online access to criminal records is the same as civil.
General Information: No adoption, juvenile, guardianship or mental records released. SASE required. Turnaround time 1 week. Fax notes: Outgoing fax limited to 10 pages; call for fee. Copy fee: $.25 per page. Certification fee: $5.00. Fee payee: Alaska Court System. Personal checks accepted. Prepayment is required.

Wrangell Superior & District Court (1st District) PO Box 869, Wrangell, AK 99929-0869; 907-874-2311; Fax: 907-874-3509. Hours: 8AM-4:30PM (AK). *Felony, Misdemeanor, Civil, Eviction, Small Claims, Probate.*
www.state.ak.us/courts

Civil Records: Access: Phone, fax, mail, in person, online. Only the court performs in person searches; visitors may not. Search fee: $15.00 per hour. Search fee is charged for all written requests. Required to search: name, years to search. Civil cases indexed by defendant, plaintiff. Civil records on computer from 1988, on microfiche and card files from 1959, archived from 1900s. Search names on the Alaska Trial Courts database at www.state.ak.us/courts/names.htm. Search gives case number and court location only.
Criminal Records: Access: Phone, fax, mail, in person, online. Only the court performs in person searches; visitors may not. Search fee: $15.00 per hour. Required to search: name, years to search, DOB. Criminal records on computer from 1988, on microfiche and card files from 1959, archived from 1900s. Online access to criminal records is the same as civil.
General Information: No adoption, juvenile, guardianship or mental records released. SASE required. Turnaround time 3 days. Fax notes: Fee to fax results is $15.00 per document. Copy fee: $.25 per page. Certification fee: $5.00 plus $2.00 per copy after first. Fee payee: Alaska Court System or State of Alaska. Personal checks accepted. Prepayment is required.

Kake Magistrate Court (1st District) PO Box 100, Kake, AK 99830-0100; 907-785-3651; Fax: 907-785-3152. Hours: 8AM-Noon (AK). *Misdemeanor, Civil Actions Under $7,500, Small Claims.*

Civil Records: Access: In person, mail. Only the court performs in person searches; visitors may not. No search fee.
Criminal Records: Access: In person, mail. Only the court performs in person searches; visitors may not. No search fee. Required to search: name, years to search, DOB, SSN, signed release.
General Information: Turnaround time 1-2 weeks. Fee payee: Alaska Court System. Prepayment is required.

Yukon-Koyukuk

Fort Yukon Magistrate Court (4th District) PO Box 211, Fort Yukon, AK 99740-0211; 907-662-2336; Fax: 907-662-2824. Hours: 9:30AM-3PM (AK). *Misdemeanor, Civil Actions Under $7,500, Small Claims.*

Note: Felony cases are at Fairbanks Superior & District Court.
Civil Records: Access: Fax, mail, in person. Only the court performs in person searches; visitors may not. No search fee. Required to search: name, DOB. Records go back to 1960s.
Criminal Records: Access: Fax, mail, in person. Only the court performs in person searches; visitors may not. Search fee: $15.00 per hour. Required to search: name, years to search, DOB. Records go back to 1960s.
General Information: Turnaround time 1-2 weeks. Fee payee: District Court. Prepayment is required.

Galena Magistrate Court (4th District) PO Box 167, Galena, AK 99741-0167; 907-656-1322; Fax: 907-656-1546. Hours: 8AM-4:30PM (AK). *Misdemeanor, Civil Actions Under $7,500, Small Claims.*

Note: Felony cases are at Fairbanks Superior & District Court.
Civil Records: Access: In person, mail. Only the court performs in person searches; visitors may not. No search fee. Civil record computerized since 1995.
Criminal Records: Access: In person, mail. Only the court performs in person searches; visitors may not. Search fee: $15.00 per hour. Required to search: name, years to search. Criminal records computerized since 1995.
General Information: Turnaround time 1-2 weeks. Fee payee: Magistrate Court. Prepayment is required.

McGrath Magistrate Court (4th District) PO Box 167, Galena, AK 99741-0167; 907-656-1322; Fax: 907-656-1546. Hours: 8:30AM-4:30PM (AK). *Misdemeanor, Civil Actions Under $7,500, Small Claims.*

Note: McGrath Court is vacant. Court records at Galena Magistrate Court, address and phone here.

Nenana Magistrate Court (4th District) PO Box 449, Nenana, AK 99760-0449; 907-832-5430; Fax: 907-832-5841. Hours: 8:30AM-4PM (AK). *Misdemeanor, Civil Actions Under $7,500, Small Claims.*
www.state.ak.us/courts/names.htm

Note: Felony cases are at Fairbanks Superior & District Court.
Civil Records: Access: In person, phone, online. Both the court and visitors may perform in person searches. No search fee. Required to search: name, years to search, DOB. Search names on the Alaska Trial Courts database at www.state.ak.us/courts/names.htm. Search gives case number only.
Criminal Records: Access: In person, phone, online. Both the court and visitors may perform in person searches. No search fee. Required to search: name, years to search, DOB. Criminal records on computer back to 1995. Online access to criminal records is the same as civil.
General Information: Public access terminal is available. Copy fee is $.25 per page.

Tanana Magistrate Court (4th District) PO Box 449, Nenana, AK 99777; 907-366-7243; Fax: 907-832-5841. Hours: Th-F 2nd full week each month (AK). *Misdemeanor, Civil Actions Under $7,500, Small Claims.*
www.state.ak.us/courts

Note: Magistrate may also be contacted by phone at 907-832-5430. Felony cases are at Fairbanks Superior & District Court.
Civil Records: Access: In person, phone, mail. Both court and visitors may perform in person searches. No search fee. There is no search fee.
Criminal Records: Access: In person, phone, mail. Both court and visitors may perform in person searches. No search fee. Required to search: name, years to search, DOB, signed release. There is no search fee.
General Information: Public access terminal is available. Copy fee-$.25 per page. Turnaround time 1-2 weeks. Fee payee: Magistrate Court. Prepayment is required.

Alaska Recording Offices

ORGANIZATION: The 23 Alaskan counties are called boroughs. However, real estate recording is done under a system that was established at the time of the Gold Rush (whenever that was) of 34 Recording Districts. Some of the Districts are identical in geography to boroughs, such as the Aleutian Islands, but other boroughs and districts overlap. Therefore, you need to know which recording district any given town or city is located in. A helpful web site www.dnr.state.ak.us/recorders/findYourDistrict.htm

The entire state except the Aleutian Islands is in the Alaska Time Zone (AK).

REAL ESTATE RECORDS: Districts do not perform real estate searches. Certification fees are usually $5.00 per document. Copies usually cost $1.25 for the first page, $.25 per additional page.

UCC RECORDS: Financing statements are filed at the state level, except for real estate related collateral, which are filed with the District Recorder. However, prior to 07/2001, consumer goods and farm collateral were filed at the District Recorder and can be searched there. All districts will perform UCC searches at $5.00 per debtor name for information and $15.00 with copies. Use search request form UCC-11. Copies ordered separately usually cost $2.00 per financing statement.

TAX LIEN RECORDS: All state and federal tax liens are filed with the District Recorder. Districts do not perform separate tax lien searches.

ONLINE ACCESS: Online access to the state recorder's office database from the Dept. of Natural Resources is available free at www.dnr.state.ak.us/recorders/search. This includes property information, liens, deeds, bankruptcies and more. Images go back to 6/2001; index to 2000. Also, a DNR "land records" database is searchable at www.dnr.state.ak.us/cgi-bin/lris/landrecords. Finally, UCCs may be searched at www.dnr.state.ak.us/ucc/search

Aleutian Islands District

District Recorder, 550 W 7th Ave, #1200, Suite 1140, Anchorage, AK 99501. 907-269-8899 R/E Recording: 907-762-2444.
Will search UCC records. This agency will not do a tax lien search. Will not search real estate records. **Online Access:** Real Estate, UCC Records. Access is available on the statewide DNR system at www.dnr.state.ak.us/recorders/search. **Other Phone Numbers:** Assessor 907-343-6770.

Anchorage District

District Recorder, 550 W 7th Ave, #1200, Suite 1140, Anchorage, AK 99501. 907-269-8899 R/E Recording: 907-762-2443.
Will search UCC records. This agency will not do a tax lien search. Will not search real estate records. **Online Access:** Real Estate, UCC Records. Access is available on the statewide DNR system at www.dnr.state.ak.us/recorders/search. **Other Phone Numbers:** Assessor 907-343-6770.

Barrow District

District Recorder, 1648 S Cushman St. #201, Fairbanks, AK 99701-6206. 907-452-3521; Fax 907-452-2951.
Will search UCC records. This agency will not do a tax lien search. Will not search real estate records. **Online Access:** Real Estate, UCC Records. Access is available on the statewide DNR system at www.dnr.state.ak.us/recorders/search. **Other Phone Numbers:** Assessor 907-459-1000.

Bethel District

District Recorder, PO Box 426, Bethel, AK 99559. 907-543-3391; Fax 907-543-7053.
Will search UCC records. This agency will not do a tax lien search. Will not search real estate records. **Online Access:** Real Estate, UCC Records. Access is available on the statewide DNR system at www.dnr.state.ak.us/recorders/search. **Other Phone Numbers:** Assessor 907-543-2296; Treasurer 907-543-2298.

Bristol Bay District

District Recorder, 550 W 7th Ave, #1200, Suite 1140, Anchorage, AK 99501. 907-269-8899 R/E Recording: 907-762-2443.
Will search UCC records. This agency will not do a tax lien search. Will not search real estate records. **Online Access:** Real Estate, UCC Records. Access is available on the statewide DNR system at www.dnr.state.ak.us/recorders/search. **Other Phone Numbers:** Assessor 907-343-6770.

Cape Nome District

District Recorder, Box 431, Nome, AK 99762. 907-443-5178.
Will search UCC records. This agency will not do a tax lien search. Will not search real estate records. **Online Access:** Real Estate, UCC Records. Access is available on the statewide DNR system at www.dnr.state.ak.us/recorders/search.

Chitina District

District Recorder, Box 86, Glennallen, AK 99588. 907-822-3726 R/E Recording: 907-745-9683 UCC Recording: 907-269-8899; www.dnr.state.ak.us/recorders
This agency will not perform searches. **Online Access:** Real Estate, UCC Records. Access is available on the statewide DNR system at www.dnr.state.ak.us/recorders/search. **Other Phone Numbers:** Elections 907-451-2835; Vital Records 907-465-8606.

Cordova District

District Recorder, 550 W 7th Ave, #1200, Suite 1140, Anchorage, AK 99501. 907-269-8899 R/E Recording: 907-762-2443.
Will search UCC records. This agency will not do a tax lien search. Will not search real estate records. **Online Access:** Real Estate, UCC Records. Access is available on the statewide DNR system at www.dnr.state.ak.us/recorders/search. **Other Phone Numbers:** Assessor 907-343-6770.

Fairbanks District

District Recorder, 1648 S Cushman St. #201, Fairbanks, AK 99701-6206. 907-452-3521; Fax 907-269-8912. www.co.fairbanks.ak.us
Will search UCC records. This agency will not do a tax lien search. Will not search real estate records. **Online Access:** Real Estate, UCC Records. Access to the City of Fairbanks Property database is available for free at www.co.fairbanks.ak.us/database/aurora/default.asp. Also, online access is available on the statewide DNR system at www.dnr.state.ak.us/recorders/search. **Other Phone Numbers:** Assessor 907-459-1000.

Fort Gibbon District

District Recorder, 1648 S Cushman St. #201, Fairbanks, AK 99701-6206. 907-452-3521.
Will search UCC records. This agency will not do a tax lien search. Will not search real estate records. **Online Access:** Real Estate, UCC Records. Access is available on the statewide DNR system at www.dnr.state.ak.us/recorders/search. **Other Phone Numbers:** Assessor 907-459-1000.

Haines District

District Recorder, 400 Willoughby, 3rd Floor, Juneau, AK 99801. 907-465-3449.
Will search UCC records. This agency will not do a tax lien search. Will not search real estate records. **Online Access:** Real Estate, UCC Records. Access is available on the statewide DNR system at www.dnr.state.ak.us/recorders/search. **Other Phone Numbers:** Assessor 907-586-5220.

Homer District

District Recorder, 195 E. Bunnell Ave., Suite A, Homer, AK 99603. 907-235-8136.
Will search UCC records. This agency will not do a tax lien search. Will not search real estate records. **Online Access:** Real Estate, UCC Records. Access is available on the statewide DNR system at www.dnr.state.ak.us/recorders/search.

Iliamna District

District Recorder, 550 W 7th Ave, #1200, Suite 1140, Anchorage, AK 99501. 907-269-8899 R/E Recording: 907-762-2443.
Will search UCC records. This agency will not do a tax lien search. Will not search real estate records. **Online Access:** Real Estate, UCC Records. Access is available on the statewide DNR system at www.dnr.state.ak.us/recorders/search. **Other Phone Numbers:** Assessor 907-343-6770.

Juneau District

District Recorder, 400 Willoughby, 3rd Floor, Juneau, AK 99801. 907-465-3449;
www.juneau.org/cbj/index.php
Will search UCC records. This agency will not do a tax lien search. Will not search real estate records. **Online Access:** Real Estate, UCC Records. Access to City of Juneau Property Records database is available free at www.juneau.lib.ak.us/assessordata/assessor.asp. Also includes link access to Juneau rentals data and the Records home page. Also, online access is available on the statewide DNR system at www.dnr.state.ak.us/recorders/search. **Other Phone Numbers:** Assessor 907-586-5220.

Kenai District

District Recorder, 120 Trading Bay Road #230, Suite 230, Kenai, AK 99611. 907-283-3118 R/E Recording: 907-225-3142;
www.dnr.state.ak.us/ssd/recoff/default.htm
Will search UCC records. This agency will not do a tax lien search. Will not search real estate records. **Online Access:** Assessor, Real Estate, UCC Records. Access to Kenai Peninsula Borough Assessing Dept. Public Information Search Page is available free at www.borough.kenai.ak.us/assessingdept/Parcel/SEAR CH.htm. Also, online access is available on the statewide DNR system at www.dnr.state.ak.us/recorders/search. **Other Phone Numbers:** Assessor 907-343-6770.

Ketchikan District

District Recorder, 415 Main St, Room 320, Ketchikan, AK 99901. 907-225-3142; Fax 907-247-3142.
Will search UCC records. This agency will not do a tax lien search. Will not search real estate records. **Online Access:** Real Estate, UCC Records. Access is available on the statewide DNR system at www.dnr.state.ak.us/recorders/search. **Other Phone Numbers:** Assessor 907-225-0277.

Kodiak District

District Recorder, 204 Mission Road, Room 16, Kodiak, AK 99615. 907-486-9432; Fax 907-486-9432.
This agency will not perform searches. **Online Access:** Real Estate, UCC Records. Access is available on the statewide DNR system at www.dnr.state.ak.us/recorders/search. **Other Phone Numbers:** Assessor 907-486-9310.

Kotzebue District

District Recorder, 1648 S. Cushman St. #201, Fairbanks, AK 99701-6206. 907-452-3521.
Will search UCC records. This agency will not do a tax lien search. Will not search real estate records. **Online Access:** Real Estate, UCC Records. Access is available on the statewide DNR system at www.dnr.state.ak.us/recorders/search. **Other Phone Numbers:** Assessor 907-459-1000.

Kuskokwim District

District Recorder, PO Box 426, Bethel, AK 99559. 907-543-3391; Fax 907-543-7053.
Will search UCC records. This agency will not do a tax lien search. Will not search real estate records. **Online**

Access: Real Estate, UCC Records. Access is available on the statewide DNR system at www.dnr.state.ak.us/recorders/search.

Kvichak District

District Recorder, 550 W 7th Ave, #1200, Suite 1140, Anchorage, AK 99501. 907-269-8899 R/E Recording: 907-762-2443.
Will search UCC records. This agency will not do a tax lien search. Will not search real estate records. **Online Access:** Real Estate, UCC Records. Access is available on the statewide DNR system at www.dnr.state.ak.us/recorders/search. **Other Phone Numbers:** Assessor 907-343-6770.

Manley Hot Springs District

District Recorder, 1648 S Cushman St. #201, Fairbanks, AK 99701-6206. 907-452-3521.
Will search UCC records. This agency will not do a tax lien search. Will not search real estate records. **Online Access:** Real Estate, UCC Records. Access is available on the statewide DNR system at www.dnr.state.ak.us/recorders/search. **Other Phone Numbers:** Assessor 907-459-1000.

Mount McKinley District

District Recorder, 1648 S Cushman St. #201, Fairbanks, AK 99701-6206. 907-452-3521.
Will search UCC records. This agency will not do a tax lien search. Will not search real estate records. **Online Access:** Real Estate, UCC Records. Access is available on the statewide DNR system at www.dnr.state.ak.us/recorders/search. **Other Phone Numbers:** Assessor 907459-1000.

Nenana District

District Recorder, 1648 S Cushman St. #201, Fairbanks, AK 99701-6206. 907-452-3521.
Will search UCC records. This agency will not do a tax lien search. Will not search real estate records. **Online Access:** Real Estate, UCC Records. Access is available on the statewide DNR system at www.dnr.state.ak.us/recorders/search. **Other Phone Numbers:** Assessor 907-459-1000.

Nulato District

District Recorder, 1648 S Cushman St. #201, Fairbanks, AK 99701-6206. 907-452-3521.
Will search UCC records. This agency will not do a tax lien search. Will not search real estate records. **Online Access:** Real Estate, UCC Records. Access is available on the statewide DNR system at www.dnr.state.ak.us/recorders/search. **Other Phone Numbers:** Assessor 907-459-1000.

Palmer District

District Recorder, 1800 Glenn Hwy #7, Palmer, AK 99645. 907-745-3080.
Will search UCC records. This agency will not do a tax lien search. Will not search real estate records. **Online Access:** Real Estate, UCC Records. Access is available on the statewide DNR system at www.dnr.state.ak.us/recorders/search.

Petersburg District

District Recorder, 415 Main St, Room 320, Ketchikan, AK 99901. 907-225-3142; Fax 907-247-3142.
Will search UCC records. This agency will not do a tax lien search. Will not search real estate records. **Online Access:** Real Estate, UCC Records. Access is available on the statewide DNR system at www.dnr.state.ak.us/recorders/search. **Other Phone Numbers:** Assessor 907-225-0277.

Rampart District

District Recorder, 1648 S. Cushman St. #201, Fairbanks, AK 99701-6206. 907-452-3521.
Will search UCC records. This agency will not do a tax lien search. Will not search real estate records. **Online Access:** Real Estate, UCC Records. Access is available on the statewide DNR system at www.dnr.state.ak.us/recorders/search. **Other Phone Numbers:** Assessor 907-459-1000.

Seldovia District

District Recorder, 195 E. Bunnell Ave., Suite A, Homer, AK 99603. 907-235-8136.
Will search UCC records. This agency will not do a tax lien search. Will not search real estate records. **Online Access:** Real Estate, UCC Records. Access is available on the statewide DNR system at www.dnr.state.ak.us/recorders/search.

Seward District

District Recorder, Box 1929, Seward, AK 99664. 907-224-3075; Fax 907-224-7192.
www.dnr.state.ak.us/recorders
Will not search real estate records. **Online Access:** Real Estate, UCC Records. Access is available free on the system at www.dnr.state.ak.us/recorders/search.

Sitka District

District Recorder, 210C Lake St, Sitka, AK 99835. 907-747-3275.
Will search UCC records. This agency will not do a tax lien search. Will not search real estate records. **Online Access:** Real Estate, UCC Records. Access is available on the statewide DNR system at www.dnr.state.ak.us/recorders/search. **Other Phone Numbers:** Assessor 907-343-6770.

Skagway District

District Recorder, 400 Willoughby, 3rd Floor, Juneau, AK 99801. 907-269-8899 R/E Recording: 907-465-3449.
Will search UCC records. This agency will not do a tax lien search. Will not search real estate records. **Online Access:** Real Estate, UCC Records. Access is available on the statewide DNR system at www.dnr.state.ak.us/recorders/search. **Other Phone Numbers:** Assessor 907-343-6770.

Talkeetna District

District Recorder, 1800 Glenn Hwy #7, Palmer, AK 99645. 907-745-3080.
Will search UCC records. This agency will not do a tax lien search. Will not search real estate records. **Online Access:** Real Estate, UCC Records. Access is available on the statewide DNR system at www.dnr.state.ak.us/recorders/search.

Valdez District

District Recorder, Box 127, Valdez, AK 99686. 907-835-2266.
Will search UCC records. This agency will not do a tax lien search. Will not search real estate records. **Online Access:** Real Estate, UCC Records. Access is available on the statewide DNR system at www.dnr.state.ak.us/recorders/search.

Wrangell District

District Recorder, 415 Main St, Room 320, Ketchikan, AK 99901. 907-225-3142; Fax 907-247-3142.
Will search UCC records. This agency will not do a tax lien search. Will not search real estate records. **Online Access:** Real Estate, UCC Records. Access is available on the statewide DNR system at www.dnr.state.ak.us/recorders/search. **Other Phone Numbers:** Assessor 907-225-0277.

Alaska County Locator

You will usually be able to find the city name in the City/County Cross Reference below. In that case, it is a simple matter to determine the county from the cross reference. However, only the official US Postal Service city names are included in this index. There are an additional 40,000 place names that people use in their addresses. Therefore, we have also included a ZIP/City Cross Reference immediately following the City/County Cross Reference.

If you know the ZIP Code but the city name does not appear in the City/County Cross Reference index, look up the ZIP Code in the ZIP/City Cross Reference, find the city name, then look up the city name in the City/County Cross Reference. For example, you want to know the county for an address of Menands, NY 12204. There is no "Menands" in the City/County Cross Reference. The ZIP/City Cross Reference shows that ZIP Codes 12201-12288 are for the city of Albany. Looking back in the City/County Cross Reference, Albany is in Albany County.

City/County Cross Reference

ADAK Aleutian Islands, West
AKIACHAK Bethel
AKIAK Bethel
AKUTAN Aleutian Islands, East
ALAKANUK Wade Hampton
ALEKNAGIK Dillingham
ALLAKAKET Yukon-Koyukuk
AMBLER Northwest Arctic
ANAKTUVUK PASS North Slope Borough
ANCHOR POINT Kenai Peninsula Borough
ANCHORAGE Anchorage Borough
ANDERSON Denali
ANGOON Yakutat
ANIAK Bethel
ANVIK Yukon-Koyukuk
ARCTIC VILLAGE Yukon-Koyukuk
ATKA Aleutian Islands, West
ATQASUK North Slope Borough
AUKE BAY Juneau Borough
BARROW North Slope Borough
BEAVER Yukon-Koyukuk
BETHEL Bethel
BETTLES FIELD Yukon-Koyukuk
BIG LAKE Matanuska-Susitna Borough
BREVIG MISSION Nome
BUCKLAND Northwest Arctic
CANTWELL Denali
CENTRAL Yukon-Koyukuk
CHALKYITSIK Yukon-Koyukuk
CHEFORNAK Bethel
CHEVAK Wade Hampton
CHICKEN Southeast Fairbanks
CHIGNIK Lake & Peninsula
CHIGNIK LAGOON Lake & Peninsula
CHIGNIK LAKE Lake & Peninsula
CHITINA Valdez-Cordova
CHUGIAK Anchorage Borough
CIRCLE Yukon-Koyukuk
CLAM GULCH Kenai Peninsula Borough
CLARKS POINT Dillingham
CLEAR Denali
COFFMAN COVE Prince of Wales-Outer
  Ketchikan
COLD BAY Aleutian Islands, East
COOPER LANDING Kenai Peninsula
  Borough
COPPER CENTER Valdez-Cordova
CORDOVA Valdez-Cordova
CRAIG Prince of Wales-Outer Ketchikan
CROOKED CREEK Bethel
DEERING Northwest Arctic
DELTA JUNCTION Southeast Fairbanks
DENALI NATIONAL PARK Denali
DILLINGHAM Dillingham
DOUGLAS Juneau Borough
DUTCH HARBOR Aleutian Islands, West
EAGLE Southeast Fairbanks
EAGLE RIVER Anchorage Borough
EEK Bethel
EGEGIK Lake & Peninsula
EIELSON AFB Fairbanks North Star
  Borough

EKWOK Dillingham
ELFIN COVE Yakutat
ELIM Nome
ELMENDORF AFB Anchorage Borough
EMMONAK Wade Hampton
ESTER Fairbanks North Star Borough
FAIRBANKS Fairbanks North Star Borough
FALSE PASS Aleutian Islands, East
FLAT Yukon-Koyukuk
FORT RICHARDSON Anchorage Borough
FORT WAINWRIGHT Fairbanks North Star
  Borough
FORT YUKON Yukon-Koyukuk
GAKONA Valdez-Cordova
GALENA Yukon-Koyukuk
GAMBELL Nome
GIRDWOOD Anchorage Borough
GLENNALLEN Valdez-Cordova
GOODNEWS BAY Bethel
GRAYLING Yukon-Koyukuk
GUSTAVUS Yakutat
HAINES Haines Borough
HEALY Denali
HOLY CROSS Yukon-Koyukuk
HOMER Kenai Peninsula Borough
HOONAH Yakutat
HOOPER BAY Wade Hampton
HOPE Kenai Peninsula Borough
HOUSTON Matanuska-Susitna Borough
HUGHES Yukon-Koyukuk
HUSLIA Yukon-Koyukuk
HYDABURG Prince of Wales-Outer
  Ketchikan
HYDER Prince of Wales-Outer Ketchikan
ILIAMNA Lake & Peninsula
INDIAN Anchorage Borough
JUNEAU Juneau Borough
KAKE Wrangell-Petersburg
KAKTOVIK North Slope Borough
KALSKAG Bethel
KALTAG Yukon-Koyukuk
KARLUK Kodiak Island Borough
KASIGLUK Bethel
KASILOF Kenai Peninsula Borough
KENAI Kenai Peninsula Borough
KETCHIKAN Ketchikan Gateway Borough
KIANA Northwest Arctic
KING COVE Aleutian Islands, East
KING SALMON Bristol Bay Borough
KIPNUK Bethel
KIVALINA Northwest Arctic
KLAWOCK Prince of Wales-Outer
  Ketchikan
KOBUK Northwest Arctic
KODIAK Kodiak Island Borough
KOTLIK Wade Hampton
KOTZEBUE Northwest Arctic
KOYUK Nome
KOYUKUK Yukon-Koyukuk
KWETHLUK Bethel
KWIGILLINGOK Bethel
LAKE MINCHUMINA Yukon-Koyukuk

LARSEN BAY Kodiak Island Borough
LEVELOCK Lake & Peninsula
LOWER KALSKAG Bethel
MANLEY HOT SPRINGS Yukon-Koyukuk
MANOKOTAK Dillingham
MARSHALL Wade Hampton
MC GRATH Yukon-Koyukuk
MEKORYUK Bethel
METLAKATLA Prince of Wales-Outer
  Ketchikan
MEYERS CHUCK Prince of Wales-Outer
  Ketchikan
MINTO Yukon-Koyukuk
MOOSE PASS Kenai Peninsula Borough
MOUNTAIN VILLAGE Wade Hampton
NAKNEK Bristol Bay Borough
NAPAKIAK Bethel
NENANA Yukon-Koyukuk
NEW STUYAHOK Dillingham
NIGHTMUTE Bethel
NIKISKI Kenai Peninsula Borough
NIKOLAI Yukon-Koyukuk
NIKOLSKI Aleutian Islands, West
NINILCHIK Kenai Peninsula Borough
NOATAK Northwest Arctic
NOME Nome
NONDALTON Lake & Peninsula
NOORVIK Northwest Arctic
NORTH POLE Fairbanks North Star
  Borough
NORTHWAY Southeast Fairbanks
NUIQSUT North Slope Borough
NULATO Yukon-Koyukuk
NUNAM IQUA Wade Hampton
NUNAPITCHUK Bethel
OLD HARBOR Kodiak Island Borough
OUZINKIE Kodiak Island Borough
PALMER Matanuska-Susitna Borough
PEDRO BAY Lake & Peninsula
PELICAN Yakutat
PERRYVILLE Lake & Peninsula
PETERSBURG Wrangell-Petersburg
PILOT POINT Lake & Peninsula
PILOT STATION Wade Hampton
PLATINUM Bethel
POINT BAKER Prince of Wales-Outer
  Ketchikan
POINT HOPE North Slope Borough
POINT LAY North Slope Borough
PORT ALEXANDER Wrangell-Petersburg
PORT ALSWORTH Lake & Peninsula
PORT HEIDEN Lake & Peninsula
PORT LIONS Kodiak Island Borough
PRUDHOE BAY North Slope Borough
QUINHAGAK Bethel
RAMPART Yukon-Koyukuk
RED DEVIL Bethel
RUBY Yukon-Koyukuk
RUSSIAN MISSION Wade Hampton
SAINT GEORGE ISLAND Aleutian Islands,
  West
SAINT MARYS Wade Hampton

SAINT MICHAEL Nome
SAINT PAUL ISLAND Aleutian Islands,
  West
SALCHA Fairbanks North Star Borough
SAND POINT Aleutian Islands, East
SAVOONGA Nome
SCAMMON BAY Wade Hampton
SELAWIK Northwest Arctic
SELDOVIA Kenai Peninsula Borough
SEWARD Kenai Peninsula Borough
SHAGELUK Yukon-Koyukuk
SHAKTOOLIK Nome
SHELDON POINT Wade Hampton
SHISHMAREF Nome
SHUNGNAK Northwest Arctic
SITKA Sitka Borough
SKAGWAY Yakutat
SKWENTNA Matanuska-Susitna Borough
SLEETMUTE Bethel
SOLDOTNA Kenai Peninsula Borough
SOUTH NAKNEK Bristol Bay Borough
STEBBINS Nome
STERLING Kenai Peninsula Borough
STEVENS VILLAGE Yukon-Koyukuk
SUTTON Matanuska-Susitna Borough
TAKOTNA Yukon-Koyukuk
TALKEETNA Matanuska-Susitna Borough
TANACROSS Southeast Fairbanks
TANANA Yukon-Koyukuk
TATITLEK Valdez-Cordova
TELLER Nome
TENAKEE SPRINGS Yakutat
TETLIN Southeast Fairbanks
THORNE BAY Prince of Wales-Outer
  Ketchikan
TOGIAK Dillingham
TOK Southeast Fairbanks
TOKSOOK BAY Bethel
TRAPPER CREEK Matanuska-Susitna
  Borough
TULUKSAK Bethel
TUNTUTULIAK Bethel
TUNUNAK Bethel
TWO RIVERS Fairbanks North Star
  Borough
TYONEK Kenai Peninsula Borough
UNALAKLEET Nome
UNALASKA Aleutian Islands, West
VALDEZ Valdez-Cordova
VENETIE Yukon-Koyukuk
WAINWRIGHT North Slope Borough
WALES Nome
WARD COVE Ketchikan Gateway Borough
WASILLA Matanuska-Susitna Borough
WHITE MOUNTAIN Nome
WHITTIER Valdez-Cordova
WILLOW Matanuska-Susitna Borough
WRANGELL Wrangell-Petersburg
YAKUTAT Yakutat-Not Used

ZIP/City Cross Reference

99500-99504 ANCHORAGE	99614-99614 KIPNUK	99682-99682 TYONEK	99760-99760 NENANA
99505-99505 FORT RICHARDSON	99615-99619 KODIAK	99683-99683 TRAPPER CREEK	99761-99761 NOATAK
99506-99506 ELMENDORF AFB	99620-99620 KOTLIK	99684-99684 UNALAKLEET	99762-99762 NOME
99507-99524 ANCHORAGE	99621-99621 KWETHLUK	99685-99685 UNALASKA	99763-99763 NOORVIK
99540-99540 INDIAN	99622-99622 KWIGILLINGOK	99686-99686 VALDEZ	99764-99764 NORTHWAY
99546-99546 ADAK	99624-99624 LARSEN BAY	99687-99687 WASILLA	99765-99765 NULATO
99547-99547 ATKA	99625-99625 LEVELOCK	99688-99688 WILLOW	99766-99766 POINT HOPE
99548-99548 CHIGNIK LAKE	99626-99626 LOWER KALSKAG	99689-99689 YAKUTAT	99767-99767 RAMPART
99549-99549 PORT HEIDEN	99627-99627 MC GRATH	99690-99690 NIGHTMUTE	99768-99768 RUBY
99550-99550 PORT LIONS	99628-99628 MANOKOTAK	99691-99691 NIKOLAI	99769-99769 SAVOONGA
99551-99551 AKIACHAK	99630-99630 MEKORYUK	99692-99692 DUTCH HARBOR	99770-99770 SELAWIK
99552-99552 AKIAK	99631-99631 MOOSE PASS	99693-99693 WHITTIER	99771-99771 SHAKTOOLIK
99553-99553 AKUTAN	99632-99632 MOUNTAIN VILLAGE	99694-99694 HOUSTON	99772-99772 SHISHMAREF
99554-99554 ALAKANUK	99633-99633 NAKNEK	99695-99695 ANCHORAGE	99773-99773 SHUNGNAK
99555-99555 ALEKNAGIK	99634-99634 NAPAKIAK	99697-99697 KODIAK	99774-99774 STEVENS VILLAGE
99556-99556 ANCHOR POINT	99635-99635 NIKISKI	99701-99701 FAIRBANKS	99775-99775 FAIRBANKS
99557-99557 ANIAK	99636-99636 NEW STUYAHOK	99702-99702 EIELSON AFB	99776-99776 TANACROSS
99558-99558 ANVIK	99637-99637 TOKSOOK BAY	99703-99703 FORT WAINWRIGHT	99777-99777 TANANA
99559-99559 BETHEL	99638-99638 NIKOLSKI	99704-99704 CLEAR	99778-99778 TELLER
99561-99561 CHEFORNAK	99639-99639 NINILCHIK	99705-99705 NORTH POLE	99779-99779 TETLIN
99563-99563 CHEVAK	99640-99640 NONDALTON	99706-99712 FAIRBANKS	99780-99780 TOK
99564-99564 CHIGNIK	99641-99641 NUNAPITCHUK	99714-99714 SALCHA	99781-99781 VENETIE
99565-99565 CHIGNIK LAGOON	99643-99643 OLD HARBOR	99716-99716 TWO RIVERS	99782-99782 WAINWRIGHT
99566-99566 CHITINA	99644-99644 OUZINKIE	99720-99720 ALLAKAKET	99783-99783 WALES
99567-99567 CHUGIAK	99645-99645 PALMER	99721-99721 ANAKTUVUK PASS	99784-99784 WHITE MOUNTAIN
99568-99568 CLAM GULCH	99647-99647 PEDRO BAY	99722-99722 ARCTIC VILLAGE	99785-99785 BREVIG MISSION
99569-99569 CLARKS POINT	99648-99648 PERRYVILLE	99723-99723 BARROW	99786-99786 AMBLER
99571-99571 COLD BAY	99649-99649 PILOT POINT	99724-99724 BEAVER	99788-99788 CHALKYITSIK
99572-99572 COOPER LANDING	99650-99650 PILOT STATION	99725-99725 ESTER	99789-99789 NUIQSUT
99573-99573 COPPER CENTER	99651-99651 PLATINUM	99726-99726 BETTLES FIELD	99790-99790 FAIRBANKS
99574-99574 CORDOVA	99652-99652 BIG LAKE	99727-99727 BUCKLAND	99791-99791 ATQASUK
99575-99575 CROOKED CREEK	99653-99653 PORT ALSWORTH	99729-99729 CANTWELL	99801-99811 JUNEAU
99576-99576 DILLINGHAM	99654-99654 WASILLA	99730-99730 CENTRAL	99820-99820 ANGOON
99577-99577 EAGLE RIVER	99655-99655 QUINHAGAK	99732-99732 CHICKEN	99821-99821 AUKE BAY
99578-99578 EEK	99656-99656 RED DEVIL	99733-99733 CIRCLE	99824-99824 DOUGLAS
99579-99579 EGEGIK	99657-99657 RUSSIAN MISSION	99734-99734 PRUDHOE BAY	99825-99825 ELFIN COVE
99580-99580 EKWOK	99658-99658 SAINT MARYS	99736-99736 DEERING	99826-99826 GUSTAVUS
99581-99581 EMMONAK	99659-99659 SAINT MICHAEL	99737-99737 DELTA JUNCTION	99827-99827 HAINES
99583-99583 FALSE PASS	99660-99660 SAINT PAUL ISLAND	99738-99738 EAGLE	99829-99829 HOONAH
99584-99584 FLAT	99661-99661 SAND POINT	99739-99739 ELIM	99830-99830 KAKE
99585-99585 MARSHALL	99662-99662 SCAMMON BAY	99740-99740 FORT YUKON	99832-99832 PELICAN
99586-99586 GAKONA	99663-99663 SELDOVIA	99741-99741 GALENA	99833-99833 PETERSBURG
99587-99587 GIRDWOOD	99664-99664 SEWARD	99742-99742 GAMBELL	99835-99835 SITKA
99588-99588 GLENNALLEN	99665-99665 SHAGELUK	99743-99743 HEALY	99836-99836 PORT ALEXANDER
99589-99589 GOODNEWS BAY	99666-99666 SHELDON POINT	99744-99744 ANDERSON	99840-99840 SKAGWAY
99590-99590 GRAYLING	99666-99666 NUNAM IQUA	99745-99745 HUGHES	99841-99841 TENAKEE SPRINGS
99591-99591 SAINT GEORGE ISLAND	99667-99667 SKWENTNA	99746-99746 HUSLIA	99850-99850 JUNEAU
99599-99599 ANCHORAGE	99668-99668 SLEETMUTE	99747-99747 KAKTOVIK	99901-99901 KETCHIKAN
99602-99602 HOLY CROSS	99669-99669 SOLDOTNA	99748-99748 KALTAG	99903-99903 MEYERS CHUCK
99603-99603 HOMER	99670-99670 SOUTH NAKNEK	99749-99749 KIANA	99918-99918 COFFMAN COVE
99604-99604 HOOPER BAY	99671-99671 STEBBINS	99750-99750 KIVALINA	99919-99919 THORNE BAY
99605-99605 HOPE	99672-99672 STERLING	99751-99751 KOBUK	99921-99921 CRAIG
99606-99606 ILIAMNA	99674-99674 SUTTON	99752-99752 KOTZEBUE	99922-99922 HYDABURG
99607-99607 KALSKAG	99675-99675 TAKOTNA	99753-99753 KOYUK	99923-99923 HYDER
99608-99608 KARLUK	99676-99676 TALKEETNA	99754-99754 KOYUKUK	99925-99925 KLAWOCK
99609-99609 KASIGLUK	99677-99677 TATITLEK	99755-99755 DENALI NATIONAL PARK	99926-99926 METLAKATLA
99610-99610 KASILOF	99678-99678 TOGIAK	99756-99756 MANLEY HOT SPRINGS	99927-99927 POINT BAKER
99611-99611 KENAI	99679-99679 TULUKSAK	99757-99757 LAKE MINCHUMINA	99928-99928 WARD COVE
99612-99612 KING COVE	99680-99680 TUNTUTULIAK	99758-99758 MINTO	99929-99929 WRANGELL
99613-99613 KING SALMON	99681-99681 TUNUNAK	99759-99759 POINT LAY	99950-99950 KETCHIKAN

Arizona

General Help Numbers:

Governor's Office
S1700 W Washington
Phoenix, AZ 85007
www.governor.state.az.us

602-542-4331
Fax 602-542-1381
8AM-5PM

Attorney General's Office
1275 W Washington
Phoenix, AZ 85007
www.attorneygeneral.state.az.us

602-542-5025
Fax 602-542-4085
8AM-5PM

State Court Administrator
Arizona Supreme Court Bldg
1501 W Washington
Phoenix, AZ 85007-3231
www.supreme.state.az.us/nav2/aoc.htm

602-542-9301
Fax 602-542-9484
8AM-5PM

State Archives
1700 W Washington, Room 342
Phoenix, AZ 85007
www.dlapr.lib.az.us/archives

602-542-4159
Fax 602-542-4402
8AM-5PM

State Specifics:

Capital:
Phoenix
Maricopa County

Time Zone:
MST

Number of Counties:
15

Population:
5,397,331

Web Site: http://azportal.clearlake.ibm.com/webapp/portal

State Agencies

Criminal Records

Department of Public Safety, Applicant Team One, PO Box 18430//Mail Code 2250, Phoenix, AZ 85005-8430 (Courier: 2320 N 20th Ave, Phoenix, AZ 85005); 602-223-2223, 8AM-5PM.

www.dps.state.az.us

Note: Sex offender data is available online at www.azsexoffender.com.

Indexing & Storage: Records are available from 1988. It takes about 14 days before new records are available for inquiry. Records are indexed on computer back to 1983; non-automated records may go back as far as 1960's, depending on charge. 50% of arrests in database have final dispositions recorded.

Searching: Record access is limited to agencies that have specific authorization by law including employers or pre-employment search firms located in AZ. Fingerprints are required for a search. Include the following in your request: full set of fingerprints plus demographic information on the applicant. Be sure to address requests to Applicant Team One. All records are released, including those without dispositions.

Access by: mail.

Fee & Payment: The fee is $6.00 per name. Fee payee: Department of Public Safety. Only cashier's checks and money orders accepted. No credit cards accepted.

Mail search: Turnaround time: 2 to 3 days. Arizona employers may call 602-223-2223 to request fingerprint cards and forms. No self addressed stamped envelope is required.

Fictitious Name
Assumed Name

Records not maintained by a state level agency.

Note: Records are found at the county level.

Corporation Records
Limited Liability Company Records

Corporation Commission, 1300 W Washington, Phoenix, AZ 85007; 602-542-3026 (Status), 602-542-3285 (Annual Reports), 602-542-3414 (Fax), 8AM-5PM.

www.cc.state.az.us

Note: Fictitious Name & Assumed Name records are found at the county level.

Indexing & Storage: Records are available from 1809 on. You must go through this office for records. If copies are needed for historical records, it can take as long as 4 to 6 weeks due to the filming process. It takes after 2-3 months before new records are available for inquiry. Records are indexed on microfiche, inhouse computer, microfilm.

Searching: Include the following in your request: full name of business, specific records that you need copies of. In addition to the articles of incorporation, corporation records include the following information: Annual Reports, Officers, Directors, Prior (Merged) Names, Inactive and Reserved Names.

Access by: mail, phone, fax, in person, online.

Fee & Payment: There is no charge for a search. Copies cost $.50 per page. Fee payee: Arizona Corporation Commission. Prepayment required. Phone and fax orders require deposit accounts. Personal checks accepted. No credit cards accepted.

Mail search: Turnaround time: 3 to 5 days. Enclose a check marked "Not to exceed $20." A self addressed stamped envelope is requested.

Phone search: Phone requests are limited to 3 inquiries per call.

Fax search: Established accounts may fax multiple requests per day. There is an additional charge of $.50 per page.

In person search: Turnaround time is while you wait for up to 5 corporate names.

Online search: The web site provides free access to all corporation information. Also, a commercial online system, called STARPAS, functions 24 hours a day, 7 days a week. The initial set-up fee is $36.00 and access costs $.30 per minute. Call 602-542-0685 for a sign-up package.

Expedited service: Expedited service is available for mail, phone and in person searches. Turnaround time: 24 hours. Add $35.00 per request. The fee applies to large orders that must be completed within 24 hours. Generally, smaller orders or single document orders do not require this fee.

Trademarks/Servicemarks
Trade Names
Limited Partnership Records

Secretary of State, Trademarks/Tradenames/Limited Partnership Division, 1700 W Washington, 7th Floor, Phoenix, AZ 85007; 602-542-6187, 602-542-7386 (Fax), 8AM-5PM.

www.sosaz.com

Indexing & Storage: Records are available from 1984 to present on computer. It takes 1 to 3 days before new records are available for inquiry.

Searching: Provide the entity name, owner name or file number to search.

Access by: mail, phone, in person.

Fee & Payment: There is no search fee, but certification is $3.00 plus the copy fee of $.10 per page. Fee payee: Secretary of State. Prepayment required. Personal checks accepted. No credit cards accepted.

Mail search: Turnaround time: 1 to 3 days. Trademarks may take longer. A self addressed stamped envelope is requested.

Phone search: They will give general information at no charge over the phone for up to 3 searches, such as owner's name, date of application, mailing address & expiration date.

In person search: If there are more than 5 pages of copy, service is overnight. You may view microfiche at no charge.

Online search: Search registered Trade Names, Trademarks and Registered Name (partnerhips) databases for free at www.sosaz.com/scripts/TNT_Search_engine.dll

Other access: Bulk purchase is available on microfiche.

Expedited service: Expedited service is available for mail, phone and in person searches. Add $25.00 per filing.

Uniform Commercial Code
Federal Tax Liens
State Tax Liens

UCC Division, Secretary of State, 1700 W Washington, 7th Floor, Phoenix, AZ 85007 (Courier: Customer Service Center, 14 North 18th Ave, Phoenix, AZ 85007); 602-542-6178, 602-542-7386 (Fax), 8AM - 5PM.

www.sosaz.com

Indexing & Storage: Records are available from 3/80 to present on microfiche and from 06/95 to present on the Internet.

Searching: Use search request form UCC-11. The search includes tax liens recorded here. Please note that tax liens recorded on individuals may be filed at the county level and not here. Include the following in your request: debtor name.

Access by: mail, phone, fax, in person, online.

Fee & Payment: The search fee is $6.00 per debtor name, except via the web which is no charge. Copies are $.10 each. Certification is an additional $3.00. Fee payee: Secretary of State. Prepayment required. Personal checks accepted. No credit cards accepted.

Mail search: Turnaround time: 5 days.

Phone search: Records are available by phone.

Fax search: Records are available by fax.

In person search: Searching is available in person.

Online search: UCC records can be searched for free at www.sosaz.com/scripts/UCC_Search.dll. Searching can be done by debtor, secured party name, or file number. From this site you can also pull down a weekly microfiche file of filings (about 10 megabytes). Note there are 2 searches - a pre 07/01/01 search of the old database, and a strict Revised Article 9 which is current up within 4 days of present.

Other access: E-mail requests are accepted. Microfilm of filings is available for purchase.

Expedited service: Expedited service is available for mail and phone searches. Turnaround time: same day if possible. Add $25.00 per package.

Sales Tax Registrations

Revenue Department, Taxpayer Assistance, 1600 W Monroe, Phoenix, AZ 85007; 602-542-4565, 602-542-4772 (Fax), 8AM-5PM.

www.revenue.state.az.us

Indexing & Storage: Records are available from 1980.

Searching: This agency will only confirm that a business is registered and whether it is active. It will provide no other information without a power of attorney. Include the following in your request: business name. The tax permit number is very helpful.

Access by: mail, phone, in person.

Mail search: A self addressed stamped envelope is requested. No fee for mail request.

Phone search: They will confirm license on phone, if given permit #.

In person search: No fee for request.

Birth Certificates

Department of Health Services, Vital Records Section, PO Box 3887, Phoenix, AZ 85030 (Courier: 2727 W Glendale Ave, Phoenix, AZ 85051); 602-255-3260, 602-364-1300 (Recording), 602-249-3040 (Fax), 8AM-5PM.

www.hs.state.az.us/vitalrcd/index.htm

Note: A certificate of birth resulting in stillbirth is available as of 08/09/2001.

Indexing & Storage: Records are available from late 1800's to present. Records are computerized from 1950 to present. Records are indexed on file folders.

Searching: Must by 18 years of age or older to request a record and be the person named or that person's parent or legal guardian. Records 75 years or older available to the public for a $2.00 fee. Include the following in your request: full name, names of parents, mother's maiden name, date of birth, place of birth, relationship to person of record, reason for information request. Bring a government issued picture ID (or send a copy) with signature.

Access by: mail, fax, in person.

Fee & Payment: For birth records prior to 1950, the fee for a certified photo copy is $15.00. For birth records after 1950, the fee for a certified computerized copy is $14.00. The search fee is $4.00 for the 1st 10 years and $3.00 each add'l year. The service fee for using a credit card is $5.50. Fee payee: Vital Records Section. Prepayment required. Credit cards accepted: MasterCard, Visa, AmEx, Discover.

Mail search: Turnaround time: 2 weeks. No self addressed stamped envelope is required.

Fax search: Include the following additional information on the request: copy of government ID with your signature, return address, phone #, credit card #, and expiration date. Fee is $5.00 plus cost of copy. Turnaround time is 2 days.

In person search: Turnaround time is usually less than 1 hour.

Expedited service: Expedited service is available for mail, fax, and phone searches. Turnaround time: 1 day. The agency will not accept expedited requests over the phone. They must be sent by fax. There is $13.00 fee to have the results returned by Federal Express. Use of credit card required.

Death Records

Department of Health Services, Vital Records Section, PO Box 3887, Phoenix, AZ 85030 (Courier: 2727 W Glendale Ave, Phoenix, AZ 85051); 602-255-3260, 602-364-1300 (Recording), 602-249-3040 (Fax), 8AM-5PM.

www.hs.state.az.us/vitalrcd/index.htm

Indexing & Storage: Records are available from late 1800's to present. New records are available for inquiry immediately. Records are indexed on file folders.

Searching: Must have notarized release from immediate family. Only immediate family, attorney or funeral director acting for immediate family can get records. Records 50 years or older are available to the public for a $2.00 fee. Include the following in your request: full name, date of death, place of death, relationship to person of record, reason for information request. Send a copy of your ID or your signature must be notarized.

Access by: mail, fax, in person.

Fee & Payment: There is a $4.00 fee for the 1st 10 years and $3.00 each add'l year. A certified photo copy is $10.00. The fee for use of a credit card is $5.50. Fee payee: Vital Records Section. Prepayment required. Personal checks accepted. Credit cards accepted: MC, Visa, AmEx, Discover.

Mail search: Turnaround time: 2 weeks. A self addressed stamped envelope is requested.

Fax search: Include the following additional information on the request: copy of government ID with signature, return address, phone #, credit card #, and expiration date. Fee is $5.00 for processing/handling. Certification fee is $6.00.

In person search: Turnaround time is usually 30-50 minutes.

Expedited service: Expedited service is available for fax searches. Include your Fed Ex number. Expedited service is by fax only (must use credit card), the agency will not accept phone requests. Use of credit card required. Add $13.00 for express delivery.

Marriage Certificates
Divorce Records

Records not maintained by a state level agency.

Note: These records are not available from the state they must be requested from the county or court of issue.

Workers' Compensation Records

State Compensation Fund, 3031 N Second St, Phoenix, AZ 85012; 602-631-2000, 602-631-2213 (Fax), 8AM-5PM.

www.statefund.com

Indexing & Storage: Records are available from 1926 on. New records are available for inquiry immediately. Records are indexed on microfilm, inhouse computer.

Searching: Records that are closed or inactive are stored on microfilm. All active records are on the in-house computer. Claim and policy records are confidential, but you can get claim records with release form from claimant. Most other records are public. Include the following in your request: claimant name, Social Security Number, claim number. Requester must have signed release from claimant or policyholder prior to obtaining confidential records. Copies of legal, claims, and policy working files are not released otherwise.

Access by: mail, in person.

Fee & Payment: Copies are $.25 per page. There is no search fee. Fee payee: State Compensation Fund. Requesters will be billed. Personal checks accepted. No credit cards accepted.

Mail search: Turnaround time: 1 to 2 weeks. No self addressed stamped envelope is required.

In person search: Searching is available in person.

Driver Records

Motor Vehicle Division, Record Services Section, PO Box 2100, Mail Drop 539M, Phoenix, AZ 85001-2100 (Courier: Customer Records Services, 1801 W Jefferson, Rm 111, Phoenix, AZ 85007); 602-255-0072, 8AM-5PM.

www.dot.state.az.us/MVD/mvd.htm

Note: Arizona will suspend the license for unpaid out-of-state tickets.

Indexing & Storage: Records are available for either a thirty-nine month record or for a five-year record. CDL records may be available for ten years. It takes 2 weeks before new records are available for inquiry.

Searching: Any person requesting a motor vehicle record shall identify himself and state the reason for the request. ID may be required. Certain requesters, identified by law, are labeled as "exempt" (generally, in line with DPPA requirements). Include the following in your request: full name, date of birth, driver's license number. Exempt requesters need only supply 2 out of the 3 items required to search. The driver's mailing address is provided as part of the record to exempt requesters.

Access by: mail, in person, online.

Fee & Payment: The current fees are $3.00 for 39 month records and $5.00 for certified 5 year records. Insurers may only receive the 39 month record. All non-exempt requests must be signed and notarized. Fee payee: Motor Vehicle Division, Record Services. Prepayment required. Personal checks accepted. No credit cards accepted.

Mail search: Turnaround time: 1 week to 10 days. If express mail is requested, then envelope must be pre-paid. If mail requester is not DPPA permissible, the requester's signature must be notarized. No self addressed stamped envelope is required.

In person search: Records are available at any of the MVD field offices. There is a limit of 4 requests for immediate service.

Online search: Arizona's online system is interactive and open 24 hours daily. Fee is $3.00 per record. This system is primarily for those requesters who are exempt. For more information call 602-712-7235.

Other access: Overnight magnetic tape-to-tape ordering is available.

Vehicle Ownership
Vehicle Identification

Motor Vehicle Division - Director's Office, Record Services Section, PO Box 2100, Mail Drop 504M, Phoenix, AZ 85001-2100 (Courier: Customer Records Services, 1801 W Jefferson, Rm 111, Phoenix, AZ 85007); 602-712-8420, 8AM-5PM.

www.dot.state.az.us/MVD/mvd.htm

Indexing & Storage: Records are available for 5 years to present. It takes 2 weeks before new records are available for inquiry.

Searching: The record searcher must state the reason for the request and have his/her signature notarized. Records are not given by merely giving a plate license number or a name for ownership searches. The vehicle's owner, VIN, and plate number must be submitted to receive a vehicle history. If not a permissible use, need notarized release form.

Access by: mail, fax, in person, online.

Fee & Payment: The fee is $3.00, $2.00 if walk-in is willing to pick up the next day, and $5.00 if the record is certified. Fee payee: Motor Vehicle Division. Prepayment required. Money orders and checks are accepted through the mail. Walk-ins may pay with cash. Personal checks accepted. No credit cards accepted.

Mail search: Turnaround time: 1 week to 10 days. A self addressed stamped envelope is requested.

Fax search: Ongoing, permissible users may have requests returned by fax, usually next day service, for an additional fee of $4.00 per record.

In person search: You may request information in person.

Online search: Online access is offered only to permissible users. Fee is $3.00 per record. The system is open 24 hours a day, seven days a week. For more information, call 602-712-7235.

Accident Reports

Department of Public Safety, Accident Reports, PO Box 6638, Phoenix, AZ 85005 (Courier: 2102 W Encanto, 1st Floor, Phoenix, AZ 85005-6638), 602-223-2230, 8AM-5PM.

Indexing & Storage: It takes 2 weeks before new records are available for inquiry. Records are indexed on inhouse computer.

Searching: A written request is required and the requester must state his/her connection to the incident. Include the following in your request: relationship to person of record, date of accident, location of accident, full name, report number.

Access by: mail, in person.

Fee & Payment: The fee is $9.00 per record. Fee payee: Department of Public Safety. Prepayment required; business check or money order. No credit cards or personal checks accepted.

Mail search: Turnaround time: 1 week to 14 days. A self addressed stamped envelope is requested. No fee for mail request.

In person search: Turnaround time is while you wait, provided record is on file.

Vessel Ownership
Vessel Registration

Game & Fish Dept, 2222 W Greenway Rd, Phoenix, AZ 85023-4399; 602-942-3000, 602-789-3729 (Fax), 8AM-5PM M-F.

www.azgf.com

Note: Lien information is recorded at the county level. Maricopa County has some liens from other counties.

Indexing & Storage: Records are available from 1977 to present. Records are indexed on computer for the last 5 years. No titles are issued. All watercraft must be registered unless they are non-motorized.

Searching: To search, the following information is required: Arizona #, hull ID, owner's name, and a picture ID.

Access by: mail, phone, fax, in person.

Fee & Payment: There is no search fee.

Mail search: Turnaround time is within 30 days. No self addressed stamped envelope is required.

Phone search: Only lawyers, private investigators, boat owners, and government representatives can search by phone or fax.

Fax search: Same criteria as phone searching.

In person search: Turnaround time is normally immediate.

Legislation Records

Arizona Legislature, State Senate - Room 203, 1700 W Washington, Phoenix, AZ 85007 (Courier: Senate Wing or, House Wing, Phoenix, AZ 85007); 602-542-3559 (Senate Information), 602-542-4221 (House Information), 602-542-3429 (Senate Fax), 602-542-3550 (Senate Resource Ctr), 602-542-4099 (Fax), 8AM-5PM.

www.azleg.state.az.us

Note: The phone number provides information on current session bills and on some previous bills.

Indexing & Storage: Records are available from 1969 to 1994 on microfilm for bill files. Committee minutes are available from 1967 to present on hard copy.

Searching: Include the following in your request: bill number, year.

Access by: mail, fax, in person, online.

Fee & Payment: Copies are $.10 per page. Fee payee: State Senate or House of Representatives. Prepayment is requested for large photocopying projects. Personal checks accepted. No credit cards accepted.

Mail search: Turnaround time: 1 day. All research requests are processed ASAP, determined by the demands of the legislative sessions on the staff. No self addressed stamped envelope is required. No fee for mail request.

Fax search: Fee is $.10 per page, with a turnaround time of 1 day or sooner.

In person search: No fee for request. A desk is provided for reviewing files, reading minutes, etc. Staff will assist if time and workload permits.

Online search: Most information, beginning with 1997, is available through the Internet (i.e. bill text, committee minutes, committee assignments, member bios, etc.). There is no fee.

Other access: Name, address, and office # lists are available at no charge. Roll call vote histories of individuals per year are available at $.10 per page.

Voter Registration
Access to Records is Restricted

Secretary of State, Election Division, 1700 W Washington, 7th Floor, Phoenix, AZ 85007.

www.sosaz.com

Note: Records are maintained at the county recorder offices. Records are permitted to be sold in bulk only for political related purposes. Go to the county level to can confirm names on a single inquiry basis.

GED Certificates

Department of Education, GED Testing, 1535 W Jefferson, Phoenix, AZ 85007; 602-542-5802, 602-542-1161 (Fax), 8AM-5PM.

www.ade.az.gov/adult-ed

Indexing & Storage: Records are available from 1945 to present. It takes 3 to 4 weeks before new records are available for inquiry.

Searching: Include the following in your request: date of birth, Social Security Number, signed release, year of test and test site. All requests must be in writing, all require student signature.

Access by: mail, fax, in person.

Fee & Payment: There is no fee for either a verification or a copy of transcript.

Mail search: Turnaround time: 5 to 7 days. No self addressed stamped envelope is required. No fee for mail request.

Fax search: Same criteria as mail searching.

In person search: No fee for request.

Hunting License Information
Fishing License Information

Game & Fish Department, Information & Licensing Division, 2221 W Greenway Rd, Phoenix, AZ 85023-4399; 602-942-3000, 602-789-3924 (Fax), 8AM-5PM.

www.azgfd.com

Note: This agency will also release watercraft registration information within specific legal constraints.

Indexing & Storage: Records are available for past 3 years.

Searching: Records are not available to the public except as a mailing list. They will release certain data to attorneys for pending litigation.

Access by: mail.

Fee & Payment: Prepayment required. Fee payee: Arizona Game & Fish. Personal checks accepted. Credit cards accepted: MasterCard, Visa.

Mail search: Turnaround time: variable. Must complete a request form. No self addressed stamped envelope is required.

Other access: There is a program to purchase the database or portions of. You can get 3 years of approximately 160,000 to 190,000 names for $.05 per name, which includes addresses. This is available for commercial purposes only. Lists are completed within 30 days.

Arizona State Licensing Agencies

Licenses Searchable Online

Advance Fee Loan Broker #5	www.azbanking.com/Lists/Lists.htm
Appraiser, Real/Personal Property #56	www.asc.gov/content/category1/appr_by_state.asp
Architect #29	www.btr.state.az.us
Assayer #29	www.btr.state.az.us
Attorney #30	www.azbar.org/MemberFinder/MF_Search.cfm
Bank #5	www.azbanking.com/Lists/Lists.htm
Bank #0	www.azbanking.com/Lists/BA_List.HTML
Behavioral Health Emergency/Resi. Svc #47	www.hs.state.az.us/als/databases/index.html
Behavioral Outpatient Clinic #47	www.hs.state.az.us/als/databases/index.html
Behavioral Outpatient Rehab Center #47	www.hs.state.az.us/als/databases/index.html
Charity #71	www.sosaz.com/scripts/Charity_Search.dll
Chiropractor #11	www.azchiroboard.com/dir.html
Collection Agency #5	www.azbanking.com/Lists/Lists.htm
Consumer Lender #5	www.azbanking.com/Lists/Lists.htm
Contractor #70	www.rc.state.az.us/clsc/AZROCLicenseQuery
Counselor, Professional #10	http://aspin.asu.edu/~azbbhe/directory/listing.html
Court Reporter #0	www.supreme.state.az.us/cr/CRcertlist2001.htm
Credit Union #5	www.azbanking.com/Lists/Lists.htm
Day Care Establishment #45	www.hs.state.az.us/als/databases/index.html
Debt Management #5	www.azbanking.com/Lists/Lists.htm
Degree Program (Vocational) #6	http://azppse.state.az.us/directory.html
Engineer #29	www.btr.state.az.us
Escrow Agent #5	www.azbanking.com/Lists/Lists.htm
Funeral Preneed Trust Company #5	www.azbanking.com/Lists/Lists.htm
Geologist #29	www.btr.state.az.us
Hearing Aid Dispenser #49	www.hs.state.az.us/als/databases/index.html
Home Inspector #29	www.btr.state.az.us
Landscape Architect #29	www.btr.state.az.us
Liquor Producer #52	www.azll.com/query.htm
Liquor Retail Co-OpAgent/Mgr. (Retail) #52	www.azll.com/query.htm
Liquor Wholesaler #52	www.azll.com/query.htm
Lobbyist #71	www.sos.state.az.us/scripts/Lobbyist_Search.dll
Marriage & Family Therapist #10	http://aspin.asu.edu/~azbbhe/directory/listing.html
Medical Doctor, Intern/Resident #17	www.bomex.org/getlicense.asp
Money Transmitter #5	www.azbanking.com/Lists/Lists.htm
Mortgage Banker, Commercial #5	www.azbanking.com/Lists/Lists.htm
Mortgage Banker/Broker #5	www.azbanking.com/Lists/Lists.htm
Motor Vehicle Dealer/Sales Finance #5	www.azbanking.com/Lists/Lists.htm
Naturopathic Physician #19	www.npbomex.az.gov/lic.html
Notary Public #71	www.sosaz.com/scripts/Notary_Search.dll
Optometrist #22	www.asbo.state.az.us
Pawn Shop #0	www.azbanking.com/Lists/DPC_List.HTML
Pesticide Company #72	www.sb.state.az.us/pdf/codir.pdf
Physician Assistant #17	www.bomex.org/getlicense.asp
Physician Assistant #18	www.docboard.org/az/df/azsearch.htm
Post-Secondary Education Institution #6	http://azppse.state.az.us/directory.html
Post-Secondary Voca. Program, Private #6	http://azppse.state.az.us/directory.html
Premium Finance Company #5	www.azbanking.com/Lists/Lists.htm
Property Tax Agent #8	www.appraisal.state.az.us/Directory/taxagent.html
Psychologist #27	http://psychboard.az.gov/dir.html
Public Accountant-CPA #7	www.accountancy.state.az.us
Public Accounting Firm-CPA/PA #7	www.accountancy.state.az.us
Real Estate Appraiser #8	www.appraisal.state.az.us/Directory/appr1.html
Real Estate Broker/Salesperson #55	www.re.state.az.us/db.html
Real Estate Firm #55	www.re.state.az.us/db.html
Sales Finance Company #5	www.azbanking.com/Lists/Lists.htm
Social Worker #10	http://aspin.asu.edu/~azbbhe/directory/listing.html
Substance Abuse Counselor #10	http://aspin.asu.edu/~azbbhe/directory/listing.html
Surveyor, Land #29	www.btr.state.az.us
Telemarketing Firm #71	www.sosaz.com/scripts/TS_Search_engine.cgi
Trust Company #5	www.azbanking.com/Lists/Lists.htm
Trust Division of Chartered Fin. Inst. #5	www.azbanking.com/Lists/Lists.htm

Licensing Quick Finder

Acupuncturist #11 602-542-3095	Denturist #13 602-242-1492	Minnow Dealer #59 602-942-3000
Advance Fee Loan Broker #5 602-255-4421	Detoxification Service #47 602-674-4300	Mobile Home Dealer/Broker/Salesperson #36
Aesthetician #12 480-784-4539	Developmentally Disabled Group Home #49	....602-255-4072 x251
Aesthetics Instructor #12 480-784-4539	602-674-4340	Mobile Home Installer/Mfg. #36 .. 602-255-4072 x251
Agricultural Aircraft Pilot #33 602-542-0904	Dog Racing Kennel #54 602-277-1704	Money Transmitter #5 602-255-4421
Agricultural Grower Permit #33 602-542-0904	Drug Mfg/Wholesaler #24...................602-255-5125	Mortgage Banker, Commercial #5 602-255-4421
Agricultural Grower/Seller #33 602-542-0904	Dry Well Registration #41...................602-207-4696	Mortgage Banker/Broker #5 602-255-4421
Agricultural Pest Control Advisor #33...602-542-0904	DUI Education Agency #47 602-674-4300	Motor Vehicle Dealer/Sales Finance #5 602-255-4421
Agricultural Seller Permit #33 602-542-0904	DUI Screening/Treatment Agency #47 602-674-4300	MRI License #66 ....602-255-4845 x237
Air Pollution Source #39 602-207-2338	Embalmer #15 602-542-3095	Nail Technician #12...........................480-784-4539
Air Quality Permit #65........................602-506-6970	Emergency Medical Technician #48 602-861-1188	Nail Technology Instructor #12 480-784-4539
Aircraft Dealer for Wreckers or Salvage #57	Emergency Medical Technician Instructor #48	Naturopathic Physician #19 602-542-8242
....602-294-9144	602-861-1188	Notary Public #71 602-542-4086
Aircraft Dealer/Retail #57 602-294-9144	Emergency Response Div. #66.. 602-255-4845 x239	Nuclear Medicine Tech. #66 ....602-255-4845x242
Aircraft Mfg/Importer/Dist./Transporter #57	Engineer #29 602-255-4053	Nurse-LPN #20 602-331-8111
....602-294-9144	Environmental Laboratory #44 602-255-3454	Nurse-RN #20 602-331-8111
Aircraft Owner #57............................602-294-9144	Escrow Agent #5 602-255-4421	Nurses' Aide #20 602-331-8111
Aircraft Pilot Trainer School/Instructor #57	Falconer #59....................................602-942-3000	Occupational Therapist/Assistant #21 . 602-589-8352
....602-294-9144	Feed & Fertilizer #33 602-542-0904	Oil & Gas Production #56....................602-542-4565
Aircraft Use Fuel Dealer/Mfg #56 602-542-4565	Feed Distribution, Commercial #34..... 602-242-0814	Optical Establishment #14 602-542-3095
Ambulance Service #48.......................602-861-0809	Feed, Wholesale #56 602-542-4565	Optician #14 602-542-3095
Ambulatory Surgical Center #43 602-674-9750	Fertilizer Distribution, Commercial #34 . 602-253-0949	Optometrist #22................................602-542-3095
Amusement Park #56 602-542-4565	Field Trial License #59 602-942-3000	Osteopathic Physician #23............ 480-657-7703 x21
Amusement Printing & Advertising #56.602-542-4565	Food Establishment #65.....................602-506-6970	Out-Patient Surgical Ctr./Treatment Clinic #43
Appraiser, Real/Personal Property #56.602-542-4565	Food Packer/Grower/Shipper, Contract #35	602-674-9750
Aquifer Protection Permit #41..............602-207-4743	602-542-0943	P & C Broker #51 602-912-8470
Architect #29....................................602-255-4053	Foster Care Home #49 602-674-4340	P & C Managing Agent, also Life/Disability #51
Assayer #29.....................................602-255-4053	Fruit/Vegetable Broker/Dealer #35......602-542-0943	602-912-8470
Assisted Living Facility #49 602-674-4340	Funeral Director #15..........................602-542-3095	Pesticide Appl./Supv./Advisor #72.......602-255-3664
Attorney #30....................................602-252-4804	Funeral Preneed Trust Company #5.... 602-255-4421	Pesticide Applicator #33.....................602-542-0904
Audiologist #49 602-674-4340	Fur Dealer #59.................................602-942-3000	Pesticide Company #72 602-255-3664
Bank #5...602-255-4421	Game Farm, Private #59 602-942-3000	Pesticide Distribution #34...................602-253-0949
Barber School/Instruction #9 602-542-4498	Game Resident Guide #59 602-942-3000	Pesticide Qualifying Party #72 602-255-3664
Barber/Barber Shop #9.......................602-542-4498	Geologist #29 602-255-4053	Pharmacist #24 602-255-5125
Bathing Place #65.............................602-506-6970	Groom #54.......................................602-277-1704	Pharmacy Intern #24 602-255-5125
Bedding/Furniture Manufacturer #65....602-506-6970	Guidance Counselor #38....................602-542-4368	Physical Therapist #25.......................602-542-3095
Behavioral Health Emergency/Residential Service #47	Hazardous Waste Facility #40 602-207-4197	Physical Therapist Assistant #25.........602-542-3095
....602-674-4300	Headstart Facility #45.......................602-674-4220	Physician Assistant #17 480-551-2700
Behavioral Outpatient Clinic #47 602-674-4300	Hearing Aid Dispenser #49 602-674-4340	Physiotherapist #11...........................602-864-5088
Behavioral Outpatient Rehab Center #47	Home Health Agency #43 602-674-9750	Pipeline #56.....................................602-542-4565
....602-674-4300	Home Inspector #29 602-255-4053	Plant Operator #41............................602-207-4643
Bingo Operation #56..........................602-542-4565	Homeopathic Physician #16................602-542-3095	Pollutant Discharge Permit #41 602-207-4665
Bondsman (Insurance) #51 602-912-8470	Horse or Greyhound Racing #54 602-277-1704	Post-Secondary Education Inst. #6....602-542-5709
Bone Densitometer Operator #66 602-255-4845 x242	Horse Owner/Trainer #54...................602-277-1704	Post-Secondary Vocational Program, Private #6
Bottled Water Processor #65................602-506-6970	Hospice #43.....................................602-674-9750	602-542-5709
Boxer #3...602-542-1417	Hospital #43.....................................602-674-9750	Premium Finance Company #5 602-255-4421
Boxing Physician #3 602-542-1417	Hotel/Motel/Tourist Court #65 602-506-6970	Preschool #45 602-674-4220
Boxing Professional #3.......................602-542-1417	Hunting & Fishing License Dealer #59..602-942-3000	Private Car, Rail & Aircraft #56 602-542-4565
Campground Membership Broker/Salesman #55	Industrial Laser #66 ....602-255-4845 x237	Private Investigator #53 602-223-2361
....602-468-1414	Infirmary #43....................................602-674-9750	Property Broker #51 602-912-8470
Cannabis & Controlled Substance Dealer #56	Insurance Agent #51.........................602-912-8470	Property Tax Agent #8 602-542-1539
....602-542-4565	Insurance Broker P&C only #51...........602-912-8470	Psychiatric Unit #47 602-674-4300
Cemetery Broker/Salesman #55 602-468-1414	Investment Advisor #32......................602-542-0678	Psychologist #27...............................602-542-8162
Charity #71......................................602-542-6670	Investment Advisor Rep. #32...............602-542-0678	Public Accountant-CPA #7 602-255-3648
Chiropractor #11...............................602-864-5088	Jockey #54 602-277-1704	Public Accounting Firm-CPA/PA #7......602-255-3648
Citrus Fruit Broker/Dealer/Packer/Shipper #35	Landscape Architect #29 602-255-4053	Publishing #56..................................602-542-4565
....602-542-0943	Laser Light Show #56........................602-255-4845	Radiation Machine Possession Facility #66
Clinical Laboratory #44 602-255-3454	Laser, Medical #66 ....602-255-4845 x237	....602-255-4845 x231
Collection Agency #5.........................602-255-4421	Lay Midwife #50................................602-364-1400	Radiation Therapy Tech. #66.......602-255-4845 x242
Commercial Leasing #56.....................602-542-4565	Liquor Producer #52..........................602-542-5141	Radioactive Material Possessor #66....602-255-4845
Concealed Weapon Permit #53 602-256-6280	Liquor Retail Co-Operative/Agent/Mgr. (Retail) #52	Radioactive Materials Lab #66....602-255-4845 x246
Consumer Lender #5..........................602-255-4421	602-542-5141	Radiologic Technologist #66.......602-255-4845 x242
Contractor #70..................................602-542-1525	Liquor Wholesaler #52 602-542-5141	Radiology Practical Tech. #66 ....602-255-4845 x242
Cosmetologist #12 480-784-4539	Lobbyist #71....................................602-542-0229	Radon Mitigation Specialist #66...602-255-4845 x244
Cosmetology Instructor #12.................480-784-4539	Long Term Care Facility #49...............602-674-4340	Real Estate Appraiser #8 602-542-1539
Cosmetology or Nail Technology Salon or School #12	Lottery Retailer #4 480-921-4400	Real Estate Broker/Salesperson #55...602-468-1414
....480-784-4539	LPG Service Agency/Rep #2...............602-255-5211	Real Estate Division #62....................602-542-1704
Counselor, Professional #10 602-542-1851	Marriage & Family Therapist #10 602-542-1851	Real Estate Firm #55 602-468-1414
Credit Union #5.................................602-255-4421	Medical Doctor, Intern/Resident #17....480-551-2700	Real Estate School/Inst./Course #55 . 602-468-1414
Day Care Establishment #45................602-674-4220	Medical Facility #49 602-674-4340	Rehabilitation Agency #43 602-674-9750
Debt Management #5 602-255-4421	Mental Health Screening/Evaluation/Treatment #47	Rehabilitation Unit #47 602-674-4300
Degree Program (Vocational) #6.........602-542-5709	602-674-4300	Renal Disease Facility #43................602-674-9750
Dental Assistant #13..........................602-242-1492	Mining #56......................................602-542-4565	Rental of Personal Property #56 602-542-4565
Dental Hygienist #13 602-242-1492	Mining Elevator/Diesel #67.................602-542-5971	Respiratory Therapist #28..................602-542-5995
Dentist #13.......................................602-242-1492	Mining Operator/Start-up #67..............602-542-5971	

Restaurant/Bar #56 602-542-4565
Retail Sales Outlet #56 602-542-4565
Risk Management Company #51 602-912-8470
Sales Finance Company #5 602-255-4421
Sanitarian #46 602-230-5911
School Bus Driver/Instructor #1 602-223-2646
School Librarian #38 602-542-4368
School Psychologist/Psychometrist #38
.... 602-542-4368
School Superintendent #38 602-542-4368
School Supervisor #38 602-542-4368
Scientific Collector #59 602-942-3000
Securities Dealer/Salesperson #32 602-542-0678
Security Guard #53 602-223-2361
Self Insured Employer #60 602-542-1836
Sewage, Sludge & Septic Pumping Vehicle #40 ....
.... 602-207-4123
Shooting Preserve License #59 602-942-3000
Social Worker #10 602-542-1851
Solid Waste Facility #40 602-207-4123
Speech-Language Pathologist #49 602-674-4340
Spray Process Applicator/Sterilizer/Renovator #65
.... 602-506-6970
Subdivision Public Report #55 602-468-1414

Substance Abuse Counselor #10 602-542-1851
Substance Abuse Treatment Svc. #47 .. 602-674-4300
Surety #51 602-912-8470
Surplus Line Broker #51 602-912-8470
Surveyor, Land #29 602-255-4053
Tanning Facility #66 .... 602-255-4845 x237
Taxidermist #59 602-942-3000
Teacher, Community College #31 602-255-5582
Teacher, Elementary/Special Edu. #38. 602-542-4368
Telemarketing Firm #71 602-542-6670
Timbering #56 602-542-4565
Timeshare Public Report #55 602-468-1414
Tobacco Product Distributor #56 602-542-4565
Trailer Coach Park #65 602-506-6970
Transporting & Towing Company #56 .. 602-542-4565
Travel Agent, Limited #51 602-912-8470
Trust Company #5 602-255-4421
Trust Division of Chartered Financial Inst. #5
.... 602-255-4421
Vehicle Emission Fleet Inspector #42 .. 602-207-7007
Vendor/Concession on State Park Land #69
.... 602-542-2155
Veterinary Medicine/Surgery #73 602-542-3095
Veterinary Premise (Hospital) #73 602-542-3095

Veterinary Technician #73 602-542-3095
Vocational Rehabilitation #61 602-542-3294
Waste Water Collection/Treatment/Construction #41
.... 602-207-4692
Waste Water Facility Operator #41 602-207-4625
Waste Water Reuse #41 602-207-4464
Water Distribution System Operator #41
.... 602-207-4643
Water Quality Certification #41 602-207-4625
Water Rights Assignment #58 602-417-2405
Water Transporter, out of state #58 602-417-2405
Watercraft Registration Agent #59 602-942-3000
Weighmaster, Public #2 602-255-5211
Weights & Measures Rep./Svc. Agency #2
.... 602-255-5211
Well Drilling Firm #58 .... 602-417-2470 x 7141
Well Registration/Construction #58 602-417-2405
White Amor Stocking License #59 602-942-3000
Wildlife Hobby License #59 602-942-3000
Wildlife Holding Permit #59 602-942-3000
Wildlife Rehab/Service License #59 602-942-3000
X-ray Supplier #66 .... 602-255-4845 x231
Zoo #59 602-942-3000

Licensing Agency Information

#1 Department of Public Safety, Student Transportation, PO Box 6638 - Mail Drop 1250, Phoenix, AZ 85005-6638; 602-223-2646, Fax: 602-223-2923. www.dps.state.az.us

#2 Department of Weights & Measures, 4425 W Olive Av #134, Glendale, AZ 85302-3844; 602-255-5211, Fax: 602-255-1950. www.weights.az.gov

#3 Boxing Commission, 1400 W Washington, #210, Phoenix, AZ 85007; 602-542-1417, Fax: 602-542-1458.

#4 Arizona State Lottery, 4740 E University Dr, Phoenix, AZ 85034; 800-921-4400, Fax: 480-921-4512.
www.arizonalottery.com.
Agency email: feedback@arizonalottery.com.

#5 Banking Department, 2910 N 44th St, #310, Phoenix, AZ 85018; 602-255-4421, Fax: 602-381-1225.
www.azbanking.com
Agency email: mailbox@azbanking.com.
Search database at
www.azbanking.com/Lists/Lists.htm

#6 Board for Private Postsecondary Education, 1400 W Washington, Rm 260, Phoenix, AZ 85007; 602-542-5709, Fax: 602-542-1253.
http://azppse.state.az.us
Search database at
http://azppse.state.az.us/directory.html

#7 Board of Accountancy, 3877 N Seventh St, #106, Phoenix, AZ 85014; 602-255-3648, Fax: 602-255-1283.
www.accountancy.state.az.us
Agency email: info@mail.accountancy.state.az.us
Search database at www.accountancy.state.az.us

#8 Board of Appraisal, 1400 W Washington, #360, Phoenix, AZ 85007; 602-542-1539, Fax: 602-542-1598.
www.appraisal.state.az.us
Agency email: logan_edward@pop.state.az.us.
Search database at www.appraisal.state.az.us/ Directory/directory.html

#9 Board of Barbers, 1400 W Washington, Rm 220, Phoenix, AZ 85007; 602-542-4498.

#10 Board of Behavioral Health Examiners, 1400 E Washington St #320, Phoenix, AZ 85007; 602-542-1882, Fax: 602-542-1830.
www.aspin.asu/~azbbhe
Agency email: behavioral_health@pop.state.az.us.
Search database at
http://aspin.asu.edu/~azbbhe/directory/listing.html

#11 Board of Chiropractic Examiners, 5060 N 19th Ave #416, Phoenix, AZ 85015; 602-864-5088, Fax: 602-864-5099.
www.azchiroboard.com. Agency email: merriejoh@earthlink.net.
Search database at
www.azchiroboard.com/dir.html. Accupuncture and physiotherapy are certifications under a Chiropractic license.

#12 Information Services, Board of Cosmetology, 1721 E Broadway Rd, Tempe, AZ 85282; 480-784-4539, Fax: 480-255-3680.

#13 Board of Dental Examiners, 5060 N 19th Ave, #406, Phoenix, AZ 85015; 602-242-1492, Fax: 602-242-1445.
www.azdentalboard.org

#14 Board of Dispensing Opticians, 1400 W Washington, Rm 230, Phoenix, AZ 85007; 602-542-3095, Fax: 602-542-3093.

#15 Board of Funeral Directors & Embalmers, 1400 W Washington, Room 230, Phoenix, AZ 85007; 602-542-3095, Fax: 602-542-3093.

#16 Board of Homeopathic Medical Examiners, 1400 W Washington, Rm 230, Phoenix, AZ 85007; 602-542-3095, Fax: 602-542-3093.
www.goodnet.com/~bhme. Agency email: bhme@goodnet.com.

#17 Board of Medical Examiners, 9545 E Doubletree Ranch Dr, Scottsdale, AZ 85258-5514; 480-551-2700, Fax: 480-551-2704.
www.bomex.org
Agency email: questions@bomex.org.
Search database at www.bomex.org/getlicense.asp

#19 Board of Naturopathic Physicians Examiners, 1400 W Washington, Rm 230, Phoenix, AZ 85007; 602-542-8242, Fax: 602-542-3093.
www.npbomex.az.gov

Search database at www.npbomex.az.gov/lic.html. Licensing lookup may be under construction.

#20 Board of Nursing, 1651 E Morton, #210, Phoenix, AZ 85020-7605; 602-331-8111, Fax: 602-906-9365.
www.azboardofnursing.org
Agency email: jridenour@azbn.org.

#21 Board of Occupational Therapy Examiners, 5060 N 19th Av #209, Phoenix, AZ 85015-3212; 602-589-8352, Fax: 602-589-8354. Agency email: azot@primenet.com.

#22 Board of Optometry, 1400 W Washington, Rm 230, Phoenix, AZ 85007; 602-542-3095, Fax: 602-542-3093.
www.asbo.state.az.us
Agency email: jconfez@webmail.state.az.us.
Search database at www.asbo.state.az.us

#23 Board of Osteopathic Medicine & Surgery Examiners, 9535 E Doubletree Ranch Rd, Scottsdale, AZ 85258-5539; 480-657-7703 x21, Fax: 480-657-7715.
www.azosteoboard.org
Agency email: azosteo@goodnet.com.

#24 Board of Pharmacy, 4425 W Olive #140, Glendale, AZ 85302-3844; 623-463-2727, Fax: 623-934-0583.
www.pharmacy.state.az.us
Agency email: info@azsbp.com.

#25 Board of Physical Therapy, 1400 W Washington, Rm 230, Phoenix, AZ 85007; 602-542-3095, Fax: 602-542-3093.
www.ptboard.state.az.us.
Agency email: carol.lopez@ptboard.state.az.us.
Online searching will be available 1/1/2003.

#26 Board of Podiatry Examiners, 1400 W Washington, Rm 230, Phoenix, AZ 85007; 602-542-3095, Fax: 602-542-3093.

#27 Board of Psychologist Examiners, 1400 W Washington St, Rm 235, Phoenix, AZ 85007; 602-542-8162, Fax: 602-542-8279.
http://psychboard.az.gov
Agency email: info@psychboard.az.gov.
Search database at
http://psychboard.az.gov/dir.html

#28 Board of Respiratory Care Examiners, 1400 W Washington, #200, Phoenix, AZ 85007; 602-542-5995, Fax: 602-542-5900.
www.rb.state.az.us
Agency email: recept@rb.state.az.us.

#29 Board of Technical Registration, 1110 W Washington #240, Phoenix, AZ 85007; 602-364-4930, Fax: 602-364-4931.
www.btr.state.az.us
Agency email: azbtrweb@yahoo.com.
Search database at www.btr.state.az.us

#30 State Bar of Arizona, 111 W Monroe, #1800, Phoenix, AZ 85003-1742; 602-252-4804, Fax: 602-271-4930.
www.azbar.org. Agency email: azbar@azbar.org.
Search database at
www.azbar.org/MemberFinder/MF_Search.cfm

#31 Community College Board of Directors, 2020 N Central Ave. #570, Phoenix, AZ 85004-4578; 602-255-5582, Fax: 602-279-3464.
www.stbd.cc.az.us
Agency email: collins@stbd.cc.az.us.

#32 Registration Department, Securities Division, Corporation Commission, 1300 W Washington, 3rd Fl, Phoenix, AZ 85007; 602-542-4242, Fax: 602-594-7470.
www.ccsd.cc.state.az.us/licensing_and_registratio n/index.asp
Agency email: accsec@ccsd.cc.state.az.us.

#33 Department of Agriculture, Environmental Services Division, 1688 W Adams St, Phoenix, AZ 85007; 602-542-0904, Fax: 602-542-5420; 602-542-0466.
www.agriculture.state.az.us
Agency email: adaweb@getnet.com.

#34 Department of Agriculture, Environmental Services Division, 1688 W Adams St, 1st Fl, Phoenix, AZ 85007; 602-542-4373, Fax: 602-542-0466.
www.agriculture.state.az.us
Agency email: adaweb@getnet.com.

#35 Department of Agriculture, Plant Services, Citrus, Fruit & Vegetable Standardization, 1688 W Adams, Phoenix, AZ 85007; 602-542-0947, Fax: 602-542-0898.
www.agriculture.state.az.us
Agency email: cfv@agriculture.state.az.us.

#36 Department of Building & Fire Safety, 99 E Virginia, Wildlife & Parks Bldg, #100, Phoenix, AZ 85004; 602-255-4072, Fax: 602-255-4962.

#38 Department of Education, Teacher Certification Unit, PO Box 6490 (1535 W Jefferson St, Bin 34), Phoenix, AZ 85005; 602-542-4367, Fax: 602-542-5388.
www.ade.state.az.us
Agency email: webmaster@mail1.ade.state.az.us.

#39 Department of Environmental Quality, Office of Air Quality, 3033 N Central T5109B, Phoenix, AZ 85012; 602-207-2338, Fax: 602-207-2366.
www.adeq.state.az.us

#40 Department of Environmental Quality, Office of Waste Programs, 3033 N Central Ave, 6th Fl, Phoenix, AZ 85012; 602-207-2300, Fax: 602-207-4138.
www.adeq.state.az.us

#41 Department of Environmental Quality, Office of Water Quality, 3033 N Central, 2nd Fl, Phoenix, AZ 85012; 602-207-2300, Fax: 602-207-4674. www.adeq.state.az.us

#42 Department of Environmental Quality, Vehicle Emissions Section, 600 N 40th St, Phoenix, AZ 85008; 602-207-7007, Fax: 602-207-7020.
www.adeq.state.az.us/environ/air/vei/index.html.
Agency email: gibbons.john@ev.state.az.us.

#43 Department of Health Services, 1740 W Adams, Phoenix, AZ 85007; 602-542-1001, Fax: 602-542-0883.
www.hs.state.az.us
Agency email: webmaster@hs.state.az.us.

#44 Department of Health Services, Bureau of State Lab Services/Licensure/Cert, 1740 W Adams St, Phoenix, AZ 85007; 602-255-3454, Fax: 602-255-3462. www.hs.state.az.us

#45 Department of Health Services, Division of Child Care, 1647 E Morten, #230, Phoenix, AZ 85020; 602-674-4220, Fax: 602-861-0674.
www.hs.state.az.us

#46 Department of Health Services, Food Protection & Institutional Sanitation Section, 3815 N Black Canyon Hwy, Phoenix, AZ 85015; 602-230-5911, Fax: 602-230-5817.
www.hs.state.az.us

#47 Department of Health Services, Office of Behavioral Health Licensure, 1647 E Morten, #240, Phoenix, AZ 85020; 602-674-4300, Fax: 602-861-0643. www.hs.state.az.us
Search database at
www.hs.state.az.us/als/databases/index.html

#48 Department of Health Services, Bureau of EMS, 1651 E Morten, #120, Phoenix, AZ 85020; 602-861-0708, Fax: 602-861-9812.
www.hs.state.az.us

#49 Department of Health Services, Office of Health Care Licensure, 1647 E Morten Ave, #110, Phoenix, AZ 85020; 602-674-4340, Fax: 602-861-0463.
www.hs.state.az.us

#50 Department of Health Services, Office of Women & Children, 2927 N 35th Ave, Phoenix, AZ 85017-5253; 602-364-1400, Fax: 602-364-1496.
www.hs.state.az.us

#51 Department of Insurance, Licensing Section, 2910 N 44th St, #210, Phoenix, AZ 85018-7256; 602-912-8470, Fax: 602-912-8453.
www.state.az.us/id
Agency email: mcatalioto@azdoi.e-mail.com.

#52 Department of Liquor License & Control, 800 W Washington, 5th Fl, Phoenix, AZ 85007; 602-542-5141, Fax: 602-542-5707.
www.azll.com
Search database at www.azll.com/query.htm.
Search recently issued, expired, closed, suspended and inactive licenses at the web site.

#53 Department of Public Safety, Security Guard & Private Investigator Licensing, PO Box 6638 (2102 W Encanto Blvd, 85009), Phoenix, AZ 85005; 602-223-2361, Fax: 602-223-2938.
www.dps.state.az.us/dpsphone.htm

#54 Department of Racing, Licensing Division, 3877 N 7th St, #201, Phoenix, AZ 85014; 602-277-1704, Fax: 602-277-1165.
www.raccom.state.az.us
Agency email: racing@state.az.us.

#55 Department of Real Estate, 2910 N 44th St, Phoenix, AZ 85018; 602-468-1414, Fax: 602-468-0562.

www.re.state.az.us
Agency email: cdowns@adre.org.
Search database at www.re.state.az.us/db.html

#56 Department of Revenue, License & Registration, PO Box 29002, Phoenix, AZ 85038-9069; 602-542-4565.
www.revenue.state.az.us

#57 Department of Transportation, Aeronautics Division, 255 E Osborn #101, Phoenix, AZ 85012; 602-294-9144, Fax: 602-294-9141.
www.dot.state.az.us/ABOUT/aero/index.htm.
Agency email: info@dot.state.az.us.

#58 Department of Water Resources, 500 N 3rd St (PO Box 458, 85001-0458), Phoenix, AZ 85004-3903; 602-417-2400, Fax: 602-417-2421.
http://water.az.gov

#59 Game & Fish Department, 2222 W Greenway Rd, Phoenix, AZ 85023; 602-942-3000, Fax: 602-789-3921.
www.gf.state.az.us

#60 Division of Administration, Industrial Commission of Arizona, 800 W Washington, 3rd Fl, Phoenix, AZ 85007; 602-542-4653, Fax: 602-542-3070.
www.ica.state.az.us

#61 Special Fund Division, Industrial Commission of Arizona, 800 W Washington, 4th Fl, Rm 401, Phoenix, AZ 85007; 602-542-3294, Fax: 602-542-3696.

#65 Maricopa Environmental Services, 1001 N Central, #550, Phoenix, AZ 85004; 602-506-6970, Fax: 602-506-5141.
www.maricopa.gov/envsvc/default.asp

#66 Medical Radiologic Technology Board of Examiners, 4814 S 40th St, Phoenix, AZ 85040-2940; 602-255-4845, Fax: 602-437-0705. Agency email: agodwin@arra.state.az.us.

#67 Mine Inspector, 1700 W Washington, #400, Phoenix, AZ 85007-2805; 602-542-5971, Fax: 602-542-5335. www.asmi.state.az.us
Agency email: admin@mi.state.az.us.

#69 Parks Board, 1300 W Washington, #221, Phoenix, AZ 85007; 602-542-2155, Fax: 602-542-4180.

#70 Registrar of Contractors, 800 W Washington, 6th Fl, Phoenix, AZ 85007; 602-542-1525, Fax: 602-542-1599.
www.rc.state.az.us
Agency email: webmaster@roc1.rc.state.az.us.
Search database at
www.rc.state.az.us/clsc/AZROCLicenseQuery.

#71 Secretary of State, 1700 W Washington St, Exec Towers, 7th Fl, Phoenix, AZ 85007; 602-542-4285, Fax: 602-542-6172.
www.sosaz.com
Search database at www.sosaz.com. Search lobbyists using the public body's name, the lobbyist's name or the lobbyist's employee's name.

#72 Structural Pest Control Commission, 9535 E Doubletree Ranch Rd, Scottsdale, AZ 85258-5514; 602-255-3664.
www.sb.state.az.us

#73 Veterinary Medical Examining Board, 1400 W Washington, #230, Phoenix, AZ 85007; 602-542-3095, Fax: 602-542-3093.

Arizona Federal Courts

The following list indicates the district and division name for each county in the state. If the bankruptcy court location is different from the district court, then the location of the bankruptcy court appears in parentheses.

County/Court Cross Reference

Apache .... Prescott (Phoenix)
Cochise .... Tucson
Coconino .... Prescott (Phoenix)
Gila .... Phoenix (Tucson)
Graham .... Tucson
Greenlee .... Tucson
La Paz .... Phoenix (Yuma)
Maricopa .... Phoenix

Mohave .... Prescott (Yuma)
Navajo .... Prescott (Phoenix)
Pima .... Tucson
Pinal .... Phoenix (Tucson)
Santa Cruz .... Tucson
Yavapai .... Prescott (Phoenix)
Yuma .... Phoenix (Yuma)

Standards for Federal Courts: The search fee is $20.00 per item (one party name or case number). Certification fee is $7.00 per document. Copy fee is $.50 per page. All fees standard unless noted in profile. Mail Search: always enclose a stamped self addressed envelope unless otherwise noted. Before releasing records, all courts require prepayment unless noted in profile.

Open records are located at the court unless otherwise noted. District courts index by defendant and plaintiff as well as by case number. Bankruptcy courts usually index by debtor and case number. While most courts now have their indexes on computer, many still maintain index card files as well.

The universal PACER sign-up number is 800-676-6856. Find PACER and the Party/Case Index on the Web at http://pacer.psc.uscourts.gov. PACER dial-up access is $.60 per minute. Also, courts offering internet access via RACER, PACER, Web-PACER or the new CM-ECF charge $.07 per page fee unless noted as free.

US District Court

District of Arizona

Phoenix Division Room 1400, 230 N 1st Ave, Phoenix, AZ 85025-0093 (Courier Address: Use mail address for courier delivery), 602-514-7101.

www.azd.uscourts.gov

Counties: Gila, La Paz, Maricopa, Pinal, Yuma. Some Yuma cases handled by San Diego Division of the Southern District of California.

Indexing & Storage: Cases are indexed by defendant, plaintiff, and case number. New cases are available in the index 2-3 weeks after filing date. Records are also indexed on microfiche. Open records are located at this court.

Fee & Payment Notes: Payment may be made by money order, cashier check, business check, Mastercard. In state personal checks are also accepted. Payee: Clerk, US District Court.

Phone Search: Searching is not available by phone. If case number is known by the caller, basic information will be released over the phone.

Mail Search: All information is public unless the file is sealed. Always enclose a stamped self addressed envelope.

In Person Search: In person searching available.
PACER: Toll-free dial-up access: 888-372-5707. Local dial-up access: 602-322-7194. Case records are available back to 1992. Records are purged every 12 months. New records are available online after 1-3 days. PACER is available online at http://pacer.azd.uscourts.gov.

Prescott Division c/o Phoenix Division, Room 1400, 230 N 1st Ave, Phoenix, AZ 85025-0093 (Courier Address: Use mail address for courier delivery), 602-514-7101.

www.azd.uscourts.gov

Counties: Apache, Coconino, Mohave, Navajo, Yavapai.

Indexing & Storage: New cases are available in the index after filing date. Open records are located at the Phoenix Division.

Fee & Payment Notes: Payment may be made by money order, cashier check. Business checks are not accepted. Personal checks are not accepted.

Phone Search: Searching is not available by phone.

Mail Search: A stamped self addressed envelope is not required.

In Person Search: In person searching available.
PACER: Toll-free dial-up access: 888-372-5707. Local dial-up access: 602-322-7194. Case records are available back to 1992. Records are purged every 12 months. New records are available online after 1-3 days. PACER is available online at http://pacer.azd.uscourts.gov.

Tucson Division %%AZ503%%, 405 W. Congress, Tucson, AZ 85701-1711 (Courier Address: Use mail address for courier delivery), 520-205-4200, Fax: 520-205-4209.

www.azd.uscourts.gov

Counties: Cochise, Graham, Greelee, Pima, Santa Cruz. The Globe Division was closed effective January 1994, and all. Case records for that division are now found here.

Indexing & Storage: Cases are indexed by defendant, plaintiff, and case number. New cases are available in the index immediately after filing date. Open records are located at this court.

Fee & Payment Notes: Payment may be made by money order, cashier check, business check. In state personal checks are also accepted. A copy

service at a much lower rate (currently $.07 per page) may be used in lieu of court staff. The copy service has a one day turnaround time. Payee: Clerk, US District Court.

Phone Search: Only docket information is available by phone.

Mail Search: A stamped self addressed envelope is not required.

In Person Search: In person searching available.
PACER: Toll-free dial-up access: 888-372-5707. Local dial-up access: 602-322-7194. Case records are available back to 1992. Records are purged every 12 months. New records are available online after 1-3 days. PACER is available online at http://pacer.azd.uscourts.gov.

US Bankruptcy Court

District of Arizona

Phoenix Division PO Box 34151, Phoenix, AZ 85067-4151 (Courier Address: Use mail address for courier delivery), 602-640-5800.

www.azb.uscourts.gov

Counties: Apache, Coconino, Maricopa, Navajo, Yavapai.

Indexing & Storage: Cases are indexed by debtor as well as by case number. New cases are available in the index immediately after filing date. Creditors are also indexed from case # 95-1668 forward. Case files are stored alphabetically. Individuals cannot request files from the Federal Records Center themselves.

Fee & Payment Notes: Payment may be made by money order, cashier check, business check. Personal checks are not accepted. Payee: Clerk, US Bankruptcy Court.

Phone Search: Only docket information is available by phone. An automated voice case information service (VCIS) is available. Call VCIS at 602-640-5820.

In Person Search: In person searching available.
PACER: Toll-free dial-up access: 800-556-9230. Local dial-up access: 602-640-5832. Use of PC Anywhere v4.0 suggested. Additional password is bkc. Case records are available back to 1986. Records are purged every six months. New civil records are available online after 1 week. PACER is available online at http://pacer.azb.uscourts.gov.

Electronic Filing: Information is available online at http://pacer.psc.uscourts.gov/bk/azbh.html

Tucson Division
Suite 8112, 110 S Church Ave, Tucson, AZ 85701-1608 (Courier Address: Use mail address for courier delivery), 520-620-7500.

www.azb.uscourts.gov

Counties: Cochise, Gila, Graham, Greenlee, Pima, Pinal, Santa Cruz.

Indexing & Storage: Cases are indexed by debtor as well as by case number. New cases are available in the index immediately after filing date. Records are also indexed by adversary case number if applicable. A master list of creditors is available for each case from 1995 on. Open records are located at this court.

Fee & Payment Notes: Payment may be made by money order, cashier check, business check. Personal checks are not accepted. Payee: Clerk, US Bankruptcy Court.

Phone Search: Only docket and cover sheet information will be released over the phone. An automated voice case information service (VCIS) is available. Call VCIS at 520-620-7475.

In Person Search: In person searching available.

PACER: Toll-free dial-up access: 800-556-9224. Local dial-up access: 520-620-7470. Use of PC Anywhere v4.0 suggested. Additional password is bkc. Case records are available back to 1914. Records are purged every six months. New civil records are available online after 1 week. PACER is available online at http://pacer.azb.uscourts.gov.

Electronic Filing: Searching of electronically filed cases requires registration and password with the court. Information is available online at http://pacer.psc.uscourts.gov/bk/azbh.html

Other Online Access: Use your PACER password to access ECF cases back to 2001 at https://ecf.azb.uscourts.gov.

Yuma Division
Suite D, 325 W 19th St, Yuma, AZ 85364 (Courier Address: Use mail address for courier delivery), 928-783-2288.

www.azb.uscourts.gov

Counties: La Paz, Mohave, Yuma.

Indexing & Storage: Cases are indexed by debtor as well as by case number. New cases are available in the index immediately after filing date. Open records are located at this court.

Fee & Payment Notes: Payment may be made by money order, cashier check, business check. Personal checks are not accepted. Payee: Clerk, US Bankruptcy Court.

Phone Search: Docket information is available by phone.

In Person Search: In person searching available.

PACER: Toll-free dial-up access: 800-556-9227. Local dial-up access: 520-783-9535. Use of PC Anywhere v4.0 suggested. Additional password is bkc. Case records are available back to the mid 1980's. Records are purged every six months. New civil records are available online after 1 day. PACER is available online at http://pacer.azb.uscourts.gov.

Electronic Filing: Information is available online at http://pacer.psc.uscourts.gov/bk/azbh.html

Arizona County Courts

Court	Jurisdiction	No. of Courts	How Organized
Superior Courts*	General	15	15 Counties
Justice of the Peace Courts*	Limited	79	79 Precincts
Municipal Courts	Municipal	85	

* Profiled in this Sourcebook.

Court	CIVIL								
	Tort	Contract	Real Estate	Min. Claim	Max. Claim	Small Claims	Estate	Eviction	Domestic Relations
Superior Courts*	X	X	X	$5000	No Max			X	
Justice of the Peace Courts*	X	X	X	$0	$10,000	$2500		X	X
Municipal Courts									X

Court	CRIMINAL				
	Felony	Misdemeanor	DWI/DUI	Preliminary Hearing	Juvenile
Superior Courts*	X	X			X
Justice of the Peace Courts*		X	X	X	
Municipal Courts		X	X		

ADMINISTRATION

Administrative Office of the Courts, Arizona Supreme Court Bldg, 1501 W Washington, Phoenix, AZ, 85007; 602-542-9301, Fax: 602-542-9484.

www.supreme.state.az.us

COURT STRUCTURE

The Superior is the court of general jurisdiction. Justice, and Municipal courts generally have separate jurisdiction over case types as indicated in the text. Most courts will search their records by plaintiff or defendant. Estate cases are handled by Superior Court. Fees are the same as for civil and criminal case searching.

ONLINE ACCESS

The Arizona Judicial Branch offers Public Access to Court Case Information, a valuable on-line service providing a resource for information about court cases from 137 out of 180 superior, justice, and municipal courts in Arizona. Access information includes: detailed case information, i.e., case type, charges, filing and disposition dates; the parties in the case, not including victims and witnesses; and the court mailing address and location. Go to www.supreme.state.az.us/publicaccess

The Maricopa and Pima county courts maintain their own systems, but will also, under current planning, be part of ACAP. These two counties provide ever-increasing online access to the public.

ADDITIONAL INFORMATION

Public access to all Maricopa County court case indexes is available at a central location - 1 W Madison Ave in downtown Phoenix. Copies, however, must be obtained from the court where the case is heard.

As of Fall, 2001, Justice Courts accept civil actions up to $10.000; the increase is due to higher value claims in landlord/tenant cases. Civil cases between $5,000 and $10,000 may be filed at either Justice or Superior Courts.

Many offices do not perform searches due to personnel and/or budget constraints. As computerization of record offices increases across the state, more record offices are providing public access computer terminals.

Fees across all jurisdictions, as established by the Arizona Supreme Court and State Legislature, are as follows as of August 9, 2001: search - Superior Court: $18.00 per name; lower courts: $17.00 per name; certification - Superior Court: $18.00 per document; lower courts: $17.00 per document; copies - $.50 per page. Courts may choose to charge no fees.

Apache County

Superior Court PO Box 365, St John's, AZ 85936; 928-337-7550; Fax: 928-337-2771. Hours: 8AM-5PM (MST). *Felony, Civil Actions Over $5,000, Probate.*

Civil Records: Access: Mail, in person, online. Both court and visitors may perform in person searches. Search fee: $18.00 per name. Required to search: name, years to search; also helpful: address. Civil cases indexed by defendant, plaintiff. Civil records on computer and docket books. Online access to records is free at www.supreme.state.az.us/publicaccess.

Criminal Records: Access: Mail, in person, online. Both court and visitors may perform in person searches. Search fee: $18.00 per name. Required to search: name, years to search, DOB; also helpful: address, SSN. Criminal records on computer and docket books. Online access to records is free at www.supreme.state.az.us/publicaccess.

General Information: Public access terminal is available. No juvenile dependencies, mental health, victims, sealed or adoption records released. SASE required. Copy fee: $.50 per page. Certification fee: $18.00. Fee payee: Clerk of the Courts. Business checks accepted. Prepayment is required.

Chinle Justice Court PO Box 888, Chinle, AZ 86503; 928-674-5922; Fax: 928-674-5926. Hours: 8AM-5PM (MST). *Misdemeanor, Civil Actions Under $10,000, Eviction, Small Claims.*

Civil Records: Access: Fax, mail, in person, online. Only the court performs in person searches; visitors may not. Search fee: $17.00 per name. Required to search: name, years to search; also helpful: address. Civil cases indexed by defendant. Civil records on docket books from 1977, computerized back to 2000. Online access to records is free at www.supreme.state.az.us/publicaccess.

Criminal Records: Access: Fax, mail, in person, online. Only the court performs in person searches; visitors may not. Search fee: $17.00 per name. Required to search: name, years to search; also helpful: address, DOB, SSN. Criminal records on docket books from 1977, computerized back to 2000. Online access to records is free www.supreme.state.az.us/publicaccess. Phone access is discouraged.

General Information: No juvenile, mental health, victims, sealed or adoption records released. SASE required. Turnaround time 1-2 days. Fax notes: Fee to fax results is $1.25 per page. Copy fee: $1.25 per page. Certification fee: $17.00. Fee payee: Chinle Justice Court. Business checks accepted. Prepayment is required.

Puerco Justice Court PO Box 610, Sanders, AZ 86512; 928-688-2954. Hours: 8AM-Noon, 1-5PM (MST). *Misdemeanor, Civil Actions Under $10,000, Eviction, Small Claims.*

Civil Records: Access: Mail, in person, online. Only the court performs in person searches; visitors may not. Search fee: $17.00 per name. Required to search: name, years to search; also helpful: address. Civil cases indexed by defendant. Civil records on docket books. Online access to records is free at www.supreme.state.az.us/publicaccess.

Criminal Records: Access: Mail, in person, online. Only the court performs in person searches; visitors may not. Search fee: $17.00 per name. Required to search: name, years to search, DOB; also helpful: address, SSN. Criminal records on docket books. Online access to records is free at www.supreme.state.az.us/publicaccess.

General Information: No juvenile, mental health, victims, sealed or adoption records released. SASE required. Turnaround time as soon as possible. Copy fee: $.50 per page. Certification fee: $17.00. Fee payee:

Sanders Justice Court. Only cashiers checks and money orders accepted. Prepayment is required.

Round Valley Justice Court PO Box 1356, Springerville, AZ 85938; 928-333-4613; Fax: 928-333-4205. Hours: 8AM-Noon, 1-5PM (MST). *Misdemeanor, Civil Actions Under $10,000, Eviction, Small Claims.*

Civil Records: Access: Phone, fax, mail, in person, online. Both court and visitors may perform in person searches. Search fee: $17.00 per name. Required to search: name, years to search; also helpful: address. Civil cases indexed by defendant, plaintiff. Civil records on docket books, computerized since 02/96. Online access to records is free at www.supreme.state.az.us/publicaccess.

Criminal Records: Access: Phone, fax, mail, in person, online. Both court and visitors may perform in person searches. Search fee: $17.00 per name. Required to search: name, years to search; also helpful: address, DOB, SSN. Criminal records on docket books, computerized since 02/96. Online access to records is free at www.supreme.state.az.us/publicaccess.

General Information: Public access terminal is available. No juvenile, mental health, victims, sealed or adoption records released. SASE required. Turnaround time 5 working days. Copy fee: $.50 per page. Certification fee: $17.00. Fee payee: Round Valley Justice Court. Only cashiers checks and money orders accepted. Prepayment is required.

St John's Justice Court PO Box 308, St John's, AZ 85936; 928-337-7558; Fax: 928-337-2683. Hours: 8AM-5PM (MST). *Misdemeanor, Civil Actions Under $10,000, Eviction, Small Claims.*

Civil Records: Access: Mail, in person, online. Both court and visitors may perform in person searches. Search fee: $17.00 per name. Required to search: name, years to search; also helpful: address. Civil cases indexed by defendant. Civil records on docket books since 1972; on computer since 1996. Online access to records is free www.supreme.state.az.us/publicaccess.

Criminal Records: Access: Mail, in person, online. Both court and visitors may perform in person searches. Search fee: $17.00 per name. Required to search: name, years to search, DOB; also helpful: address, SSN. Criminal records on docket books since 1972; on computer since 1996. Online access to records is free at www.supreme.state.az.us/publicaccess.

General Information: No juvenile, mental health, victims, sealed or adoption records released. SASE required. Turnaround time 48 hours. Copy fee: $.50 per page. Certification fee: $17.00. Fee payee: St John's Justice Court. Only cashiers checks and money orders accepted. Prepayment is required.

Cochise County

Superior Court PO Box CK, Bisbee, AZ 85603; 520-432-9364; Fax: 520-432-4850. Hours: 8AM-5PM (MST). *Felony, Civil Actions Over $5,000, Probate.*

www.co.cochise.az.us/Court/Crtclerk.htm

Civil Records: Access: Fax, mail, in person, email, online. Both court and visitors may perform in person searches. Search fee: $18.00 per name per year. Required to search: name, years to search. Civil cases indexed by defendant, plaintiff. Civil records on computer since 1996 and on index books from 1881 to present. Online access to records is free at www.supreme.state.az.us/publicaccess.

Criminal Records: Access: Fax, mail, in person, email, online. Both court and visitors may perform in person searches. Search fee: $18.00 per name. Per every 5 years. Required to search: name, years to search; also helpful: DOB, SSN. Criminal records on computer since 1996; prior records on index books. Online access to records is free at www.supreme.state.az.us/publicaccess.

General Information: Public access terminal is available. (Records after 1/1/96 are available.) No juvenile, mental health, victims, sealed or adoption records released. SASE required. Turnaround time 7-14 days. Fax notes: Fee to fax results is $.50 per page. Copy fee: $.50 per page. Certification fee: $18.00. Fee payee: Clerk of Superior Court. Only cashiers checks and money orders accepted. Prepayment is required.

Benson Justice Court PO Box 2167, Benson, AZ 85602; 520-586-2247; Fax: 520-586-9647. Hours: 8AM-5PM (MST). *Misdemeanor, Civil Actions Under $10,000, Eviction, Small Claims.*

Civil Records: Access: Fax, mail, in person, online. Only the court performs in person searches; visitors may not. Search fee: $17.00 per name. Required to search: name, years to search; also helpful: address. Civil cases indexed by defendant. Online access to records is free www.supreme.state.az.us/publicaccess.

Criminal Records: Access: Fax, mail, in person, online. Only the court performs in person searches; visitors may not. Search fee: $17.00 per name. Required to search: name, years to search; also helpful: address, DOB, SSN. Online access to records is free at www.supreme.state.az.us/publicaccess.

General Information: No juvenile, mental health, victims, sealed records released. SASE required. Turnaround time 1-3 days. Fax notes: No fee to fax results. Copy fee: $.50 per page. Certification fee: $17.00. Fee payee: Benson Justice Court. Only cashiers checks and money orders accepted. Prepayment is required.

Bisbee Justice Court 207 N Judd Dr, Bisbee, AZ 85603; 520-432-9542; Fax: 520-432-9594. Hours: 8AM-5PM (MST). *Misdemeanor, Civil Actions Under $10,000, Eviction, Small Claims.*

Civil Records: Access: Fax, mail, in person, online. Only the court performs in person searches; visitors may not. Search fee: $17.00 per name. Required to search: name, years to search; also helpful: address. Civil cases indexed by defendant, plaintiff. Civil records on computer from 1992. Some records on dockets. Online access to records is free at www.supreme.state.az.us/publicaccess.

Criminal Records: Access: Fax, mail, in person, online. Only the court performs in person searches; visitors may not. Search fee: $17.00 per name. Required to search: name, years to search; also helpful: address, DOB, SSN. Criminal records on computer from 7/92. Some records on dockets; computerized records since 1992. Online access to records is free at www.supreme.state.az.us/publicaccess.

General Information: No juvenile, mental health, victims, sealed or adoption records released. SASE required. Turnaround time 1-7 days. Fax notes: No fee to fax results. Copy fee: $.25 per page. Certification fee: $17.00. Fee payee: Bisbee Justice Court #1. Personal checks accepted. Prepayment is required.

Bowie Justice Court PO Box 317, Bowie, AZ 85605; 520-847-2303; Fax: 520-847-2242. Hours: 8AM-5PM (MST). *Misdemeanor, Civil Actions Under $10,000, Eviction, Small Claims.*

Civil Records: Access: Phone, fax, mail, in person, online. Only the court performs in person searches; visitors may not. Search fee: $17.00 per name. Required to search: name, years to search; also helpful: address. Civil cases indexed by defendant. Civil records on computer from 7/85. Some records on dockets. Online access to records is free at www.supreme.state.az.us/publicaccess.

Criminal Records: Access: Phone, fax, mail, in person, online. Only the court performs in person searches; visitors may not. Search fee: $17.00 per name. Required to search: name, years to search, DOB; also helpful: address, SSN. Criminal records on computer from 1989. Some records on dockets. Online access to records is free www.supreme.state.az.us/publicaccess.

General Information: No juvenile, mental health, victims, sealed or adoption records released. SASE required. Turnaround time 1-3 days. Fax notes: $2.00 per page. Copy fee: $1.25 per page. Certification fee: $17.00. Fee payee: Bowie Justice Court. Only cashiers checks and money orders accepted. Credit cards accepted: Visa, MasterCard. Prepayment is required.

Douglas Justice Court 661 G Ave, Douglas, AZ 85607; 520-364-3561; Fax: 520-364-3684. Hours: 8AM-5PM (MST). *Misdemeanor, Civil Actions Under $10,000, Eviction, Small Claims.*

Civil Records: Access: Fax, mail, in person, online. Only the court performs in person searches; visitors may not. Search fee: $17.00 per name. Required to search: name, years to search; also helpful: address. Civil cases indexed by defendant, plaintiff. Civil records on computer from 1990. Some records on dockets. Online access to records is free at www.supreme.state.az.us/publicaccess.

Criminal Records: Access: Fax, mail, in person, online. Only the court performs in person searches; visitors may not. Search fee: $17.00 per name. Required to search: name, years to search, DOB; also helpful: address, SSN. Criminal records on computer from 1990. Some records on dockets. Online access to records is free www.supreme.state.az.us/publicaccess.

General Information: No juvenile, mental health, victims, sealed or adoption records released. SASE required. Turnaround time 1-7 days. Fax notes: Fee to fax certified search results is $.50 per page. Copy fee: $.50 per page. Certification fee: $17.00. Fee payee: Douglas Justice Court. Personal checks accepted. Prepayment is required.

Sierra Vista Justice Court 4001 E Foothills Dr, Sierra Vista, AZ 85635; 520-803-3801; Fax: 520-439-9106. Hours: 8AM-5PM (MST). *Misdemeanor, Civil Actions Under $10,000, Eviction, Small Claims.*

Civil Records: Access: Fax, mail, in person, online. Only the court performs in person searches; visitors may not. Search fee: $17.00 per name. Required to search: name, years to search; also helpful: address. Civil cases indexed by plaintiff and defendant. Civil records on computer since 08/96. Online access to records is free www.supreme.state.az.us/publicaccess. In person access requires a written request.

Criminal Records: Access: Fax, mail, in person, onlone. Only the court performs in person searches; visitors may not. Search fee: $17.00 per name. Required to search: name, years to search; also helpful: address, DOB, SSN. Criminal records by case number, traffic alphabetically; on computer back to 8/1996. Online access to records is free at www.supreme.state.az.us/publicaccess. In person access requires a written request.

General Information: No juvenile, mental health, victims, sealed, financial, or adoption records released. SASE required. Turnaround time 3-7 days. Copy fee: $.50 per page. Certification fee: $17.00. Fee payee: Cochise County Treasurer. Personal checks accepted. Credit cards accepted: Visa, MasterCard. Prepayment is required.

Willcox Justice Court 450 S Haskell, Willcox, AZ 85643; 520-384-2105; Fax: 520-384-4305. Hours: 8AM-5PM (MST). *Misdemeanor, Civil Actions Under $10,000, Eviction, Small Claims.*

Civil Records: Access: Phone, fax, mail, in person, online. Only the court performs in person searches; visitors may not. Search fee: $17.00. Required to search: name; also helpful: years to search, address. Civil cases indexed by defendant, plaintiff. Civil records on computer from 1996. Some records on dockets. Online access to records is free at www.supreme.state.az.us/publicaccess.

Criminal Records: Access: Phone, fax, mail, in person, online. Only the court performs in person searches; visitors may not. Search fee: $17.00. Required to search: name, DOB; also helpful: years to search, address, SSN. Criminal records on computer from 1996. Some records on dockets. Online access to records is free www.supreme.state.az.us/publicaccess.

General Information: No juvenile, mental health, victims, sealed or adoption records released. SASE required. Turnaround time usually 1-3 days. Fax notes: No fee to fax results. Copy fee: $.50 per page. Certification fee: $17.00. Fee payee: Willcox Justice Court. Only cashiers checks and money orders accepted. Prepayment is required.

Coconino County

Superior Court 200 N San Francisco St, Flagstaff, AZ 86001; 928-779-6535. Hours: 8AM-5PM (MST). *Felony, Civil Actions Over $5,000, Probate.*

Civil Records: Access: Mail, in person, online. Both court and visitors may perform in person searches. Search fee: $18.00 per name per year. Required to search: name, years to search; also helpful: address. Civil cases indexed by defendant. Civil records on handwritten ledger books from 1890. Some records on microfiche and dockets; computer from 1994. Online access to records is free at www.supreme.state.az.us/publicaccess.

Criminal Records: Access: Mail, in person, online. Both court and visitors may perform in person searches. Search fee: $18.00 per name per year. Required to search: name, years to search, DOB; also helpful: address, SSN. Criminal records on handwritten ledger books from 1890. Some records on microfiche and dockets; computer from 1994. Online access to records is free at www.supreme.state.az.us/publicaccess.

General Information: No mental health, victims, sealed or adoption records released. SASE required. Turnaround time 2 weeks. Copy fee: $.50 per page. Certification fee: $18.00. Fee payee: Clerk of Superior Court. Business checks accepted. Prepayment is required.

Flagstaff Justice Court 200 N San Franciso St., Flagstaff, AZ 86001; 928-779-6806. Hours: 8AM-5PM (MST). *Misdemeanor, Civil Actions Under $10,000, Eviction, Small Claims.*

Civil Records: Access: Mail, in person, online. Only the court performs in person searches; visitors may not. Search fee: $17.00 per name. Required to search: name, years to search; also helpful: address. Civil records on docket books. Will only maintain records for 5 years. Online access to records is free at www.supreme.state.az.us/publicaccess.

Criminal Records: Access: Mail, in person, online. Only the court performs in person searches; visitors may not. Search fee: $17.00 per name per year. Required to search: name, years to search, DOB; also helpful: address, SSN. Criminal records on computer since 1987. Will only maintain records for 5 years. Online access to records is free at www.supreme.state.az.us/publicaccess.

General Information: No juvenile, mental health, victims, sealed or adoption records released. SASE required. Turnaround time 10 days. Copy fee: $.50 per page. Certification fee: $17.00. Fee payee: Flagstaff Justice Court. Only cashiers checks and money orders accepted. Prepayment is required.

Fredonia Justice Court PO Box 559, 100 N Main, Fredonia, AZ 86022; 928-643-7472; Fax: 928-643-7491. Hours: 8AM-5PM (MST). *Misdemeanor, Civil Actions Under $10,000, Eviction, Small Claims.*

Civil Records: Access: Mail, in person, online. Only the court performs in person searches; visitors may not. Search fee: $17.00 per name. Required to search: name, years to search; also helpful: address. Civil cases

indexed by number. Civil records on docket books. Will only maintain records for 5 years. Online access to records is free www.supreme.state.az.us/publicaccess.

Criminal Records: Access: Mail, in person, online. Only the court performs in person searches; visitors may not. Search fee: $17.00 per name. Required to search: name, years to search, DOB; also helpful: address, SSN. Criminal records for misdemeanors on computer from 1992, all others on docket books. Online access to records is free at www.supreme.state.az.us/publicaccess.

General Information: No juvenile, mental health, victims, sealed or adoption records released. SASE required. Turnaround time 5 days from date request/receive. Copy fee: $.50 per page. Certification fee: $17.00. Fee payee: Justice Court. Only cashiers checks and money orders accepted.

Page Justice Court PO Box 1565, Page, AZ 86040; 928-645-8871; Fax: 928-645-1869. Hours: 8AM-5PM (MST). *Misdemeanor, Civil Actions Under $10,000, Eviction, Small Claims.*

Civil Records: Access: Mail, in person, online. Only the court performs in person searches; visitors may not. Search fee: $17.00 per name. Required to search: name, years to search; also helpful: address. Civil cases indexed by defendant. Civil records on computer since 9/96; prior on docket books. Will only maintain records for 5 years. Online access to records is free at www.supreme.state.az.us/publicaccess.

Criminal Records: Access: Mail, in person, online. Only the court performs in person searches; visitors may not. Search fee: $17.00 per name. Required to search: name, years to search, DOB; also helpful: address, SSN. Criminal records for misdemeanors on computer from 1987, felony since 1991, all others on docket books. Online access to records is free at www.supreme.state.az.us/publicaccess.

General Information: No juvenile, mental health, victims, sealed or adoption records released. SASE required. Turnaround time 5 days. Copy fee: $.50 per page. Certification fee: $17.00. Fee payee: Page Justice Court. Only cashiers checks and money orders accepted. Credit cards accepted: Visa, MasterCard. Prepayment is required.

Williams Justice Court 117 W Route 66 #180, Williams, AZ 86046; 928-635-2691. Hours: 8AM-5PM (MST). *Misdemeanor, Civil Actions Under $10,000, Eviction, Small Claims.*

Civil Records: Access: Mail, in person, online. Both court and visitors may perform in person searches. Search fee: $17.00 per name. Required to search: name, years to search; also helpful: address. Civil cases indexed by defendant, plaintiff. Civil records on docket books. Will only maintain records for 5 years. Online access to records is free at www.supreme.state.az.us/publicaccess.

Criminal Records: Access: Mail, in person, online. Both court and visitors may perform in person searches. Search fee: $17.00 per name. Required to search: name, years to search, DOB; also helpful: address, SSN. Criminal records on docket books. Online access to records is free www.supreme.state.az.us/publicaccess.

General Information: No juvenile, mental health, victims, sealed or adoption records released. SASE required. Turnaround time 2-3 weeks. Copy fee: $1.25 per page. Certification fee: $17.00. Fee payee: Williams Justice Court. Only cashiers checks and money orders accepted. Prepayment is required.

Gila County

Superior Court 1400 E Ash, Globe, AZ 85501; 928-425-3231 X241. Hours: 8AM-5PM (MST). *Felony, Civil Actions Over $5,000, Probate.*

Civil Records: Access: Mail, in person, online. Both court and visitors may perform in person searches.

Search fee: $18.00 per name per year. Required to search: name, years to search; also helpful: address. Civil cases indexed by defendant, plaintiff. Civil records indexed on computer from 1982. On microfiche from 1913 to 1982. Some records on docket books and index cards. Online access to records is free at www.supreme.state.az.us/publicaccess.

Criminal Records: Access: Mail, in person, online. Both court and visitors may perform in person searches. Search fee: $18.00 per name. Required to search: name, years to search, DOB; also helpful: address, SSN. Criminal records on computer from 1913. Online access to records is free at www.supreme.state.az.us/publicaccess.

General Information: No juvenile prior to June 1996, mental health, victims, sealed or adoption records released. SASE Required. Turnaround time 10 days to 2 weeks. Copy fee: $.50 per page. Certification fee: $18.00. Fee payee: Clerk of Superior Court. Personal checks accepted. Prepayment is required.

Globe Regional Justice Court 1400 E Ash, Globe, AZ 85501; 928-425-3231; Fax: 928-425-4773. Hours: 8AM-5PM (MST). *Misdemeanor, Civil Actions Under $10,000, Eviction, Small Claims.*

Note: This courts holds the records for the justice courts formally located in Miami and Hayden/Winkelman.

Civil Records: Access: Mail, fax, in person, online. Only the court performs in person searches; visitors may not. Search fee: $17.00 per name. Required to search: name, years to search. Civil cases indexed by defendant, plaintiff. Civil records on computer from 1995. Some records on dockets. Will retain criminal and civil for 5 years. Online access to records is free at www.supreme.state.az.us/publicaccess.

Criminal Records: Access: Mail, fax, in person, online. Only the court performs in person searches; visitors may not. Search fee: $17.00 per name. Required to search: name, years to search; also helpful: SSN, DOB, signed release. Criminal records on computer from 1995. Some records on dockets. Will retain criminal and civil for 5 years. Online access to records is free at www.supreme.state.az.us/publicaccess.

General Information: No juvenile, mental health, victims, sealed or adoption records released. SASE required. Turnaround time 2-4 days. Copy fee: $.50 per page. Certification fee: $17.00. Fee payee: Globe Justice Court. Business checks accepted. Prepayment is required.

Payson Justice Court 714 S Beeline Hwy #103, Payson, AZ 85541; 928-474-5267; Fax: 928-474-6214. Hours: 8AM-5PM (MST). *Misdemeanor, Civil Actions Under $10,000, Eviction, Small Claims.*

Note: This court holds the records for the Pine Justice Court which is closed.

Civil Records: Access: Fax, mail, in person, online. Only the court performs in person searches; visitors may not. Search fee: $17.00 per name. Required to search: name, years to search; also helpful: address. Civil cases indexed by defendant. Civil records on computer since 1990. Records on dockets. Will retain criminal and civil for 5 years. Online access to records is free at www.supreme.state.az.us/publicaccess.

Criminal Records: Access: Phone, fax, mail, in person, online. Only the court performs in person searches; visitors may not. Search fee: $17.00 per name. Required to search: name, years to search, DOB; also helpful: address, SSN. Criminal records on computer since 1990. Records on dockets. Will retain criminal and civil for 5 years. Online access to records is free at www.supreme.state.az.us/publicaccess.

General Information: No juvenile, mental health, victims, sealed or adoption records released. SASE required. Turnaround time 10 days. Copy fee: $.50 per page. Certification fee: $17.00. Fee payee: Payson

Justice Court. No personal checks accepted. Prepayment is required.

Winkleman Justice Court 1400 E Ash St, c/o Globe Regional Justice Court, Globe, AZ 85501-1414. *Misdemeanor, Civil Actions Under $10,000, Eviction, Small Claims.*

Note: Now part of the Globe Regional Justice Court.

Graham County

Superior Court 800 Main St, Safford, AZ 85546-3803; 928-428-3100; Fax: 928-428-0061. Hours: 8AM-5PM (MST). *Felony, Civil Actions Over $5,000, Probate.*

Civil Records: Access: Fax, mail, in person, online. Both court and visitors may perform in person searches. Search fee: $18.00 per name. Required to search: name, years to search. Civil cases indexed by defendant, plaintiff. Civil records on dockets. Online access to records is free www.supreme.state.az.us/publicaccess.

Criminal Records: Access: Phone, fax, mail, in person, online. Both court and visitors may perform in person searches. Search fee: $18.00 per name per year. Required to search: name, years to search. Criminal records on dockets. Online access to records is free at www.supreme.state.az.us/publicaccess.

General Information: No mental health, victims, sealed or adoption records released. SASE required. Turnaround time 3 days minimum. Copy fee: $.50 per page. Certification fee: $18.00. Fee payee: Clerk of Superior Court. Personal checks accepted. Prepayment is required.

Justice Court Precinct #1 800 W Main St, Safford, AZ 85546; 928-428-1210; Fax: 928-428-3523. Hours: 8AM-5PM (MST). *Misdemeanor, Civil Actions Under $10,000, Eviction.*

Civil Records: Access: Mail, in person, online. Both court and visitors may perform in person searches. Search fee: $17.00 per name. Required to search: name, years to search; also helpful: address. Civil cases indexed by case number. Civil records on computer from 1995, on dockets prior. Online access to records is free at www.supreme.state.az.us/publicaccess.

Criminal Records: Access: Mail, in person, online. Both court and visitors may perform in person searches. Search fee: $17.00 per name. Required to search: name, years to search, DOB; also helpful: address, SSN. Criminal records on computer from 1995, on dockets prior. Online access to records is free at www.supreme.state.az.us/publicaccess.

General Information: No juvenile, mental health, victims, sealed or adoption records released. SASE required. Turnaround time 2 days. Copy fee: $.50 per page. Certification fee: $17.00. Fee payee: Safford Justice Court. Only cashiers checks and money orders accepted. Prepayment is required.

Pima Justice Court Precinct #2 PO Box 1159, 136 W Center St, Pima, AZ 85543; 928-485-2771; Fax: 928-485-9961. Hours: 8AM-5PM (MST). *Misdemeanor, Civil Actions Under $10,000, Eviction, Small Claims.*

Civil Records: Access: Fax, mail, in person, online. Both court and visitors may perform in person searches. Search fee: $17.00 per name. Required to search: name, years to search; also helpful: address, docket number. Civil cases indexed by defendant. Civil records on dockets back to 1985; on computer back to 1995. Retained for 5 years. Online access to records is free at www.supreme.state.az.us/publicaccess.

Criminal Records: Access: Fax, mail, in person, online. Both court and visitors may perform in person searches. Search fee: $17.00 per name. Required to search: name, years to search, DOB; also helpful: address, SSN, docket number. Criminal records on dockets back to 1985; on computer back to 1995.

Retained for 5 years. Online access to records is free at www.supreme.state.az.us/publicaccess.

General Information: No juvenile, mental health, victims, sealed or adoption records released. SASE required. Turnaround time 2 weeks. Fax notes: $17.00 per document. Copy fee: $5.00 per document. Certification fee: $17.00. Fee payee: Graham Justice Court. Only cashiers checks and money orders accepted. Prepayment is required.

Greenlee County

Superior Court PO Box 1027, Clifton, AZ 85533; 928-865-4242; Fax: 928-865-5358. Hours: 8AM-5PM (MST). *Felony, Civil Actions Over $5,000, Probate.*

Civil Records: Access: Mail, in person, online. Both court and visitors may perform in person searches. Search fee: $18.00 per name per year. Required to search: name, years to search. Civil cases indexed by defendant, plaintiff. Civil records in docket books from 1911; on computer from 12/97. Online access to records is free at www.supreme.state.az.us/publicaccess.

Criminal Records: Access: Mail, in person, online. Both court and visitors may perform in person searches. Search fee: $18.00 per name per year. Required to search: name, years to search. Criminal records on computer since 12/97; on books from 1911. Online access to records is free at www.supreme.state.az.us/publicaccess.

General Information: No juvenile or adoptions released. SASE required. Turnaround time 7 days. Copy fee: $.50 per page. Certification fee: $18.00. Fee payee: Clerk of Superior Court. Personal checks accepted. Prepayment is required.

Justice Court Precinct #1 PO Box 517, Clifton, AZ 85533; 928-865-4312; Fax: 928-865-4417. Hours: 9AM-5PM (MST). *Misdemeanor, Civil Actions Under $10,000, Eviction, Small Claims.*

Civil Records: Access: Mail, in person, online. Only the court performs in person searches; visitors may not. Search fee: $17.00 per name. Required to search: name, years to search. Civil cases indexed by defendant, plaintiff. Civil records in docket books. Online access to records is free www.supreme.state.az.us/publicaccess.

Criminal Records: Access: Mail, in person, online. Only the court performs in person searches; visitors may not. Search fee: $17.00 per name. Required to search: name, years to search; also helpful: DOB, SSN. Criminal records in docket books. Online access to records is free www.supreme.state.az.us/publicaccess.

General Information: No juvenile, sealed, victims, mental health or adoption records released. SASE not required. Turnaround time 1 week. No copy fee. Certification fee: $17.00. Fee payee: Justice of the Peace. Only cashiers checks and money orders accepted.

Justice Court Precinct #2 PO Box 208, Duncan, AZ 85534; 928-359-2536; Fax: 928-359-2079. Hours: 9AM-5PM (MST). *Misdemeanor, Civil Actions Under $10,000, Eviction, Small Claims.*

Civil Records: Access: Mail, in person, online. Both court and visitors may perform in person searches. Search fee: $17.00 per name. Required to search: name, years to search. Civil cases indexed by defendant, plaintiff. Civil records on computer since 1996. Documents retained for 5 years. Online access to records is free www.supreme.state.az.us/publicaccess.

Criminal Records: Access: Mail, in person, online. Both court and visitors may perform in person searches. Search fee: $17.00 per name. Required to search: name, years to search. Criminal Records computerized since 1996. Online access to records is free at www.supreme.state.az.us/publicaccess.

General Information: Public access terminal is available. No juvenile, victims, sealed, mental health or adoption records released. Turnaround time 2 days.

Copy fee: $.50 per page. Certification fee: $17.00. Fee payee: Justice Court. Personal checks accepted. Prepayment is required.

La Paz County

Superior Court 1316 Kofa Ave, #607, Parker, AZ 85344; 928-669-6131; Fax: 928-669-2186. Hours: 8AM-5PM (MST). *Felony, Civil Actions Over $5,000, Probate.*

www.co.la-paz.az.us/courts.htm

Civil Records: Access: Mail, in person, online. Both court and visitors may perform in person searches. Search fee: $18.00 per name per year. Required to search: name, years to search; also helpful: address. Civil cases indexed by defendant, plaintiff. Civil records computerized since 1996, to 1983 on docket books. For records prior to 1983, check with Yuma County Superior Court. Online access to records is free at www.supreme.state.az.us/publicaccess.

Criminal Records: Access: Mail, in person, online. Both court and visitors may perform in person searches. Search fee: $18.00 per name per year. Required to search: name, years to search; also helpful: address, DOB, SSN. Criminal records computerized since 1993, to 1983 on docket books. For records prior to 1983, check with Yuma County Superior Court. Online access to records is free at www.supreme.state.az.us/publicaccess.

General Information: No dependency or adoption records released. SASE required. Turnaround time 2-3 days. Copy fee: $.50 per page. Certification fee: $18.00. Fee payee: Clerk of Superior Court. Business checks accepted. Prepayment is required.

Parker Justice Court 1105 Arizona Ave, Parker, AZ 85344; 928-669-2504; Fax: 928-669-2915. Hours: 8AM-5PM (MST). *Misdemeanor, Civil Actions Under $10,000, Eviction, Small Claims.*

Civil Records: Access: Mail, in person, online. Visitors must perform in person searches for themselves. Search fee: $17.00. Required to search: name, years to search; also helpful: address. Civil cases indexed by defendant. Civil records on dockets back to 1800s, computerized since 1996. Online access to records is free at www.supreme.state.az.us/publicaccess.

Criminal Records: Access: Mail, in person, online. Visitors must perform in person searches for themselves. Search fee: $17.00. Required to search: name, years to search, DOB; also helpful: address, SSN. Criminal records on dockets back to 1800s, computerized since 1996. Online access to records is free at www.supreme.state.az.us/publicaccess.

General Information: No juvenile, mental health, victims or sealed records released. SASE required. Turnaround time 2-3 weeks. Copy fee: $1.25 per page. Certification fee: $17.50. Fee payee: Clerk of Justice Court. Only cashiers checks and money orders accepted.

Quartzsite Justice Court PO Box 580, Quartzsite, AZ 85346; 928-927-6313; Fax: 928-927-4842. Hours: 8AM-5PM (MST). *Misdemeanor, Civil Actions Under $10,000, Eviction, Small Claims.*

Civil Records: Access: Fax, mail, in person, online. Both court and visitors may perform in person searches. Search fee: $17.00 per name/year. Required to search: name, years to search. Civil cases indexed by defendant, plaintiff. Civil records on dockets and computer. Retained for 5 yrs after final disposition. Online access to records is free at www.supreme.state.az.us/publicaccess.

Criminal Records: Access: Fax, mail, in person, online. Both court and visitors may perform in person searches. Search fee: $17.00 per name. Required to search: name, years to search, date of offense; also helpful: DOB, SSN, offense. Criminal records on dockets and computer. Retained for 5 yrs after final

disposition. Online access to records is free at www.supreme.state.az.us/publicaccess.

General Information: No juvenile, mental health, victims, sealed or adoption records released. SASE required. Turnaround time within 3 weeks. Copy fee: $.50 per page. Certification fee: $17.00. Fee payee: Quartsite Justice Court. Only cashiers checks and money orders accepted. Prepayment is required.

Salome Justice Court PO Box 661, Salome, AZ 85348; 928-859-3871; Fax: 928-859-3709. Hours: 8AM-5PM (MST). *Misdemeanor, Civil Actions Under $10,000, Eviction, Small Claims.*

Civil Records: Access: Mail, in person, online. Only the court performs in person searches; visitors may not. No search fee. Required to search: name, years to search; also helpful: address. Civil cases indexed by defendant. Civil records on dockets from mid-1960s. Records destroyed after 5 years. Computerized back to 1996. Online access to records is free at www.supreme.state.az.us/publicaccess.

Criminal Records: Access: Mail, in person, online. Only the court performs in person searches; visitors may not. No search fee. Required to search: name, years to search, DOB; also helpful: address, SSN. Criminal records on dockets from mid-1960s. Records destroyed after 5 years. Computerized back to 1996. Online access to records is free at www.supreme.state.az.us/publicaccess.

General Information: No juvenile, mental health, victims, sealed or adoption records released. SASE not required. Turnaround time 2-3 days. Copy fee: $.50 per page. Certification fee: $17.00. Fee payee: Salome Justice Court. Only cashiers checks and money orders accepted. Prepayment is required.

Maricopa County

Superior Court 601 W. Jackson St., Phoenix, AZ 85003; 602-506-3360; Fax: 602-506-7619. Hours: 8AM-5PM (MST). *Felony, Civil Actions Over $5,000, Probate.*

www.superiorcourt.maricopa.gov

Note: Address for in person searches is 601 W Jackson St, Phoenix, AZ 85003.

Civil Records: Access: Fax, mail, online, in person. Both court and visitors may perform in person searches. Search fee: $18.00 per name. Required to search: name, years to search. Civil cases indexed by defendant, plaintiff. Civil records on computer from 7/87, on microfiche from 1969 to present. Some records on docket books. Online access is available free at www.superiorcourt.maricopa.gov/docket/public_new.html. Case file can be printed.

Criminal Records: Access: Fax, mail, online, in person. Both court and visitors may perform in person searches. Search fee: $18.00 per name. Required to search: name, years to search; also helpful: DOB. Criminal records on computer from 7/87, on microfiche from 1969 to present. Some records on docket books. Online access to criminal records is the same as civil.

General Information: No mental health, victims, sealed or adoption records released. Turnaround time 4 weeks. Fax notes: $18.50 for first page, $.50 each add'l. Copy fee: $.50 per page. Certification fee: $18.00. Fee payee: Clerk of Superior Court. Personal checks accepted.

Buckeye Justice Court 100 N Apache Rd, Buckeye, AZ 85326; 623-386-4289; Fax: 623-386-5796. Hours: 8AM-5PM (MST). *Misdemeanor, Civil Actions Under $10,000, Eviction, Small Claims.*

http://justicecourts.maricopa.gov/precincts/Buckeye.htm

Civil Records: Access: Mail, in person, online. Only the court performs in person searches; visitors may not. Search fee: $17.00 per name. Required to search: name, years to search. Civil cases indexed by defendant,

plaintiff. Civil records on dockets by number, computerized since 1992. Online access to records is free at www.supreme.state.az.us/publicaccess.

Criminal Records: Access: Mail, in person, online. Only the court performs in person searches; visitors may not. Search fee: $17.00 per name. Required to search: name, years to search, DOB. Criminal records on dockets by number, computerized since 1992. Online access to records is free at www.supreme.state.az.us/publicaccess.

General Information: No juvenile, mental health, victims, sealed or adoption records released. SASE required. Turnaround time 1-2 weeks. Copy fee: $.50 per page. Certification fee: $17.00. Fee payee: Buckeye Justice Court. Personal checks accepted. Credit cards accepted: Visa, MasterCard.

Central Phoenix Justice Court 1 W Madison St, Phoenix, AZ 85003; 602-254-1488; Fax: 602-254-1496. Hours: 8AM-5PM (MST). *Misdemeanor, Civil Actions Under $10,000, Eviction, Small Claims.*

http://justicecourts.maricopa.gov/precincts/Central_Phoenix.htm

Civil Records: Access: Phone, fax, mail, in person. Only the court performs in person searches; visitors may not. Search fee: $17.00 per name. Required to search: name, years to search. Civil cases indexed by defendant, plaintiff. Civil records on computer since 1985.

Criminal Records: Access: Mail, fax, in person. Only the court performs in person searches; visitors may not. Search fee: $17.00 per name. Required to search: name, years to search, DOB, SSN. Criminal records on computer since 1985.

General Information: Public access terminal is available. No sealed records released. SASE required. Turnaround time 1-2 weeks. Copy fee: $.50 per page. Certification fee: $17.00. Fee payee: Central Phoenix Justice Court. Personal checks accepted. Personal checks accepted with DL. Credit cards accepted: Visa, MasterCard. Visa, MC.

Chandler Justice Court 2051 W Warner Rd, #20, Chandler, AZ 85224; 480-963-6691; Fax: 480-786-6210. Hours: 8AM-5PM (MST). *Misdemeanor, Civil Actions Under $10,000, Eviction, Small Claims.*

http://justicecourts.maricopa.gov/precincts/Chandler.htm

Civil Records: Access: Mail, in person. Only the court performs in person searches; visitors may not. Search fee: $17.00 per name. Required to search: name, years to search; also helpful: address. Civil records on dockets by number; records go back 5 years; on computer back to 1991.

Criminal Records: Access: Mail, in person. Only the court performs in person searches; visitors may not. Search fee: $17.00 per name. Required to search: name, years to search, DOB; also helpful: address, SSN. Criminal records on dockets by number; records on computer go back to 1991.

General Information: No juvenile, mental health, victims, sealed or adoption records released. SASE required. Turnaround time 1-2 weeks. Copy fee: $.50 per page. Certification fee: $17.00. Fee payee: Clerk of Justice Court. Personal checks accepted. Credit cards accepted: Visa, MasterCard. Prepayment is required.

East Mesa Justice Court 4811 E Julep #128, Mesa, AZ 85205; 480-985-0188; Fax: 480-396-6327. Hours: 7AM-5PM (MST). *Misdemeanor, Civil Actions Under $10,000, Eviction, Small Claims.*

http://justicecourts.maricopa.gov/precincts/East_Mesa.htm

Civil Records: Access: Mail, in person. Only the court performs in person searches; visitors may not. Search fee: $17.00 per name. Required to search: name, years to search; also helpful: address. Civil cases indexed by defendant, plaintiff. Civil records on computer since 1990. Prior records in docket books by number.

Criminal Records: Access: Mail, in person. Only the court performs in person searches; visitors may not. Search fee: $17.00 per name. Required to search: name, years to search, DOB; also helpful: address, SSN. Criminal records on computer since 1990. Prior records in docket books by number.

General Information: No juvenile, mental health, victims, sealed or adoption records released. SASE required. Turnaround time 1-2 weeks. Copy fee: $.50 per page. Certification fee: $17.00. Fee payee: East Mesa Justice Court. Personal checks accepted. Credit cards accepted: Visa, MasterCard. Prepayment is required.

East Phoenix Justice Court #1 1 W Madison St #1, Phoenix, AZ 85003; 602-254-1599; Fax: 602-254-1603. Hours: 8AM-5PM (MST). *Misdemeanor, Civil Actions Under $10,000, Eviction, Small Claims.*

http://justicecourts.maricopa.gov/precincts/East_Phoenix1.htm

Civil Records: Access: Phone, mail, in person. Only the court performs in person searches; visitors may not. Search fee: $17.00 per name. Required to search: name, years to search. Civil cases indexed by defendant, plaintiff. Civil records on dockets by number; computerized records since 1990's.

Criminal Records: Access: Phone, mail, in person. Only the court performs in person searches; visitors may not. Search fee: $17.00 per name. Required to search: name, years to search, DOB. Criminal records on dockets by number; computerized records since 1990's.

General Information: Public access terminal is available. No mental health, victims or sealed records released. SASE required. Turnaround time 1-2 weeks. Copy fee: $.50 per page. Certification fee: $17.00. Fee payee: East Phoenix #1 Justice Court. Personal checks accepted. Credit cards accepted: Visa, MasterCard. Credit cards only if paid in person.

East Phoenix Justice Court #2 4109 N 12th St, Phoenix, AZ 85014; 602-266-3741; Fax: 602-277-9442. Hours: 8AM-4:30PM (MST). *Misdemeanor, Civil Actions Under $10,000, Eviction, Small Claims.*

http://justicecourts.maricopa.gov/precincts/East_Phoenix2.htm

Civil Records: Access: Mail, in person. Both court and visitors may perform in person searches. Search fee: $17.00 per name. Required to search: name, years to search. Civil cases indexed by defendant, plaintiff. Civil records on computer since 1981.

Criminal Records: Access: Mail, in person. Both court and visitors may perform in person searches. Search fee: $17.00 per name. Required to search: name, years to search, DOB. Criminal records computerized since 1991.

General Information: Public access terminal is available. No juvenile, mental health, victims, sealed or adoption records released. SASE required. Turnaround time immediate. Copy fee: $.50 per page. Certification fee: $17.00. Fee payee: East Phoenix #2 Justice Court. Personal checks accepted. Credit cards accepted: Visa, MasterCard. Prepayment is required.

East Tempe Justice Court 1845 E Broadway #8, Tempe, AZ 85282; 480-967-8856; Fax: 480-921-7413. Hours: 8AM-5PM (MST). *Misdemeanor, Civil Actions Under $10,000, Eviction, Small Claims.*

http://justicecourts.maricopa.gov/precincts/East_Tempe.htm

Civil Records: Access: Mail, in person. Only the court performs in person searches; visitors may not. No search fee. Required to search: name, years to search. Civil cases indexed by defendant, plaintiff. Civil records on computer by case number.

Criminal Records: Access: Mail, in person. Only the court performs in person searches; visitors may not. No search fee. Required to search: name, years to search, DOB. Criminal records on computer by case number.

General Information: No juvenile, mental health, victims, sealed records released. SASE required. Copy fee: $.50 per page. Certification fee: $17.00. Fee payee: Tempe Justice Court. Personal checks accepted. Credit cards accepted: Visa, MasterCard. Prepayment is required.

Gila Bend Justice Court PO Box 648 (209 E. Pima Street), Gila Bend, AZ 85337; 928-683-2651; Fax: 928-683-6412. Hours: 8AM-5PM (MST). *Misdemeanor, Civil Actions Under $10,000, Eviction, Small Claims.*

http://justicecourts.maricopa.gov/precincts/GilaBend.htm

Civil Records: Access: Mail, in person, online. Only the court performs in person searches; visitors may not. Search fee: $17.00 per name. Required to search: name, years to search. Civil cases indexed by defendant, plaintiff. Civil records on computer since 1987. Online access to records is free at www.supreme.state.az.us/publicaccess.

Criminal Records: Access: Mail, in person, online. Only the court performs in person searches; visitors may not. Search fee: $17.00 per name. Required to search: name, years to search; also helpful: DOB. Criminal records on computer since 1987. Online access to records is free at www.supreme.state.az.us/publicaccess.

General Information: Public access terminal is available. (Public access terminal available only in main Phoenix court.) No juvenile, mental health, victims, sealed or adoption records released. SASE required. Turnaround time 1-2 weeks. Copy fee: $.50 per page. Certification fee: Included in search fee. Fee payee: Gila Bend Justice Court. Personal checks accepted. Credit cards accepted: Visa, MasterCard. Prepayment is required.

Glendale Justice Court 5222 W Glendale, Glendale, AZ 85301; 623-939-9477; Fax: 623-842-2260. Hours: 8AM-5PM (MST). *Misdemeanor, Civil Actions Under $10,000, Eviction, Small Claims.*

http://justicecourts.maricopa.gov/precincts/Glendale.htm

Civil Records: Access: Mail, in person, online. Only the court performs in person searches; visitors may not. Search fee: $17.00 per name. Required to search: name, years to search. Civil records on dockets by case number. Online access to records is free at www.supreme.state.az.us/publicaccess.

Criminal Records: Access: Mail, in person, online. Only the court performs in person searches; visitors may not. Search fee: $17.00 per name. Required to search: name, years to search, DOB; also helpful: SSN. Criminal records on dockets by case number. Online access to records is free at www.supreme.state.az.us/publicaccess.

General Information: No juvenile, mental health, victims, sealed or adoption records released. SASE required. Turnaround time 1-2 weeks. Copy fee: $1.25 per page. Certification fee: $17.00. Fee payee: Glendale Justice Court. Personal checks accepted. Credit cards accepted: Visa, MasterCard. Prepayment is required.

Maryvale Justice Court 4622 W Indian School Rd Bldg D, Phoenix, AZ 85031; 623-245-0432; Fax: 623-245-1216. Hours: 8AM-5PM (MST). *Misdemeanor, Civil Actions Under $10,000, Eviction, Small Claims.*

http://justicecourts.maricopa.gov/precincts/Maryvale.htm

Civil Records: Access: Mail, in person, online. Only the court performs in person searches; visitors may not.

Search fee: $17.00 per name. Required to search: name, years to search, address. Civil records on dockets by number. Online access to records is free at www.supreme.state.az.us/publicaccess.

Criminal Records: Access: Mail, in person, online. Only the court performs in person searches; visitors may not. Search fee: $17.00 per name. Required to search: name, years to search, address, DOB; also helpful: SSN, aliases. Criminal records on dockets by number. Online access to records is free at www.supreme.state.az.us/publicaccess.

General Information: No juvenile, mental health, victims, sealed or adoption records released. SASE required. Turnaround time 2-4 weeks. Copy fee: $.50 per page. Certification fee: $17.00. Fee payee: Maryvale Justice Court. Personal checks accepted. Credit cards accepted: Visa, MasterCard. Prepayment is required.

North Mesa Justice Court 1837 S Mesa Dr #A-201, Mesa, AZ 85210; 480-926-9731; Fax: 480-926-7763. Hours: 8AM-5PM (MST). *Misdemeanor, Civil Actions Under $10,000, Eviction, Small Claims.*

http://justicecourts.maricopa.gov/precincts/NorthMesa.htm

Civil Records: Access: Fax, mail, in person. Visitors must perform in person searches for themselves. No search fee. Required to search: name, years to search. Civil cases indexed by defendant, plaintiff. Civil records on computer by case number.

Criminal Records: Access: Fax, mail, in person. Visitors must perform in person searches for themselves. No search fee. Required to search: name, years to search, offense; also helpful: DOB. Criminal records on computer by case number.

General Information: Public access terminal is available. (Public access terminal available only in main Phoenix court.) No juvenile, mental health, victims or sealed records released. SASE required. Turnaround time 1-2 weeks. Fax notes: No fee to fax results. Copy fee: $.50 per page. Certification fee: $17.00. Fee payee: North Mesa Justice Court. Personal checks accepted. Credit cards accepted: Visa, MasterCard. Prepayment is required.

North Valley Justice Court 5222 W Glendale, Glendale, AZ 85301; 623-915-2877; Fax: 623-463-0670. Hours: 8AM-5PM (MST). *Misdemeanor, Civil Actions Under $10,000, Eviction, Small Claims.*

http://justicecourts.maricopa.gov/precincts/NorthValley.htm

Civil Records: Access: Mail, in person, online. Only the court performs in person searches; visitors may not. Search fee: $17.00 per name. Required to search: name, years to search. Civil records on dockets by case number; on computer back to 1999. Online access to records is free www.supreme.state.az.us/publicaccess.

Criminal Records: Access: Mail, in person, online. Only the court performs in person searches; visitors may not. Search fee: $17.00 per name. Required to search: name, years to search, DOB; also helpful: SSN. Criminal records on dockets by case number; on computer back to 1999. Online access to records is free at www.supreme.state.az.us/publicaccess.

General Information: No juvenile, mental health, victims, sealed or adoption records released. SASE required. Turnaround time 1-2 weeks. Copy fee: $.50 per page. Certification fee: $17.00. Fee payee: North Valley Justice Court. Personal checks accepted. Credit cards accepted: Visa, MasterCard. Prepayment is required.

Northeast Phoenix Justice Court 10255 N 32nd St, Phoenix, AZ 85028; 602-494-0620; Fax: 602-952-2315. Hours: 8AM-5PM (MST). *Misdemeanor, Civil Actions Under $10,000, Eviction, Small Claims.*

http://justicecourts.maricopa.gov/precincts/NorthEastPhoenix.htm

Civil Records: Access: Mail, in person. Only the court performs in person searches; visitors may not. Search fee: $17.00 per name; no fee if records are on-site. Required to search: name, years to search; also helpful: address. Civil cases indexed by defendant, plaintiff. Civil records on computer since 1993. Records on dockets by name and case number.
Criminal Records: Access: Mail, in person. Only the court performs in person searches; visitors may not. Search fee: $17.00 per name; no fee if records are on-site. Required to search: name, years to search, DOB; also helpful: address, SSN. Criminal records on dockets by name and case number.
General Information: No juvenile, mental health, victims, sealed or adoption records released. SASE required. Turnaround time 1-2 weeks. Copy fee: $.50 per page. Certification fee: $17.00. Fee payee: Clerk of Justice Court-Northeast. Personal checks accepted. Checks accepted for civil filings, for traffic-cashier's check or MO only. Credit cards accepted: Visa, MasterCard.

Northwest Phoenix Justice Court 11601 N 19th Ave, Phoenix, AZ 85029; 602-395-0293; Fax: 602-678-4508. Hours: 8AM-5PM (MST). *Misdemeanor, Civil Actions Under $10,000, Eviction, Small Claims.*

http://justicecourts.maricopa.gov/precincts/NorthWestPhoenix.htm

Civil Records: Access: Mail, in person. Both court and visitors may perform in person searches. Search fee: $17.00 per name. Required to search: name, years to search. Civil cases indexed by defendant, plaintiff. Civil records on dockets. Will retain criminal and civil for 5 years; computerized records since 1987.
Criminal Records: Access: Mail, in person. Both court and visitors may perform in person searches. Search fee: $17.00 per name. Required to search: name, years to search. Criminal records on dockets. Will retain criminal and civil for 5 years; computerized records since 1987.
General Information: SASE required. Turnaround time 1 week. Copy fee: $.50 per page. Certification fee: $17.00. Fee payee: Northwest Phoenix Justice Court. Personal checks accepted. Credit cards accepted: Visa, MasterCard.

Peoria Justice Court 7420 W Cactus Rd, Peoria, AZ 85381; 623-979-3234; Fax: 623-979-1194. Hours: 8AM-5PM (MST). *Misdemeanor, Civil Actions Under $10,000, Eviction, Small Claims.*

http://justicecourts.maricopa.gov/precincts/Peoria.htm

Civil Records: Access: Phone, fax, mail, in person, online. Both court and visitors may perform in person searches. Search fee: $17.00 per name. Required to search: name, years to search. Civil cases indexed by defendant, plaintiff. Civil records on computer by case number. Online access to records is free at www.supreme.state.az.us/publicaccess.
Criminal Records: Access: Phone, fax, mail, in person, online. Both court and visitors may perform in person searches. Search fee: $17.00 per name. Required to search: name, years to search; also helpful: DOB. Criminal records on computer by case number. Online access to records is free at www.supreme.state.az.us/publicaccess.
General Information: No juvenile, mental health, victims, sealed or adoption records released. SASE required. Turnaround time 1-2 weeks. Fax notes: $1.25 per page. Will only fax to 602 area code. Copy fee: $.50 per page. Certification fee: $17.00. Fee payee: Peoria Justice Court. Personal checks accepted. Credit cards accepted: Visa, MasterCard.

Scottsdale Justice Court 8250 E Butherus Dr, Scottsdale, AZ 85260; 480-443-6600; Fax: 480-443-5980. Hours: 8AM-5PM (MST). *Misdemeanor, Civil Actions Under $10,000, Eviction, Small Claims.*

http://justicecourts.maricopa.gov/precincts/Scottsdale.htm

Civil Records: Access: Phone, mail, in person, online. Only the court performs in person searches; visitors may not. Search fee: $17.00 per name. Required to search: name, years to search. Civil cases indexed by defendant, plaintiff. Civil records on computer since 1985. Records kept for 5 years on closed cases. Online access to records is free at www.supreme.state.az.us/publicaccess.
Criminal Records: Access: Phone, mail, in person, online. Only the court performs in person searches; visitors may not. Search fee: $17.00 per name. Required to search: name, years to search. Criminal records on computer since 1985. Records kept for 5 years on closed cases. Online access to records is free at www.supreme.state.az.us/publicaccess.
General Information: No juvenile, mental health, victims, sealed or adoption records released. SASE required. Turnaround time 2-3 weeks. Copy fee: $.50 per page. Certification fee: $17.00. Fee payee: Scottsdale Justice Court. Personal checks accepted. Credit cards accepted: Visa, MasterCard. Prepayment is required.

South Mesa/Gilbert Justice Court 1837 S Mesa Dr #B103, Mesa, AZ 85210; 480-926-3051; Fax: 480-545-1638. Hours: 8AM-5PM (MST). *Misdemeanor, Civil Actions Under $10,000, Eviction, Small Claims.*

http://justicecourts.maricopa.gov/precincts/SouthMesa.htm

Civil Records: Access: Mail, in person. Only the court performs in person searches; visitors may not. Search fee: $17.00 per name. Required to search: name, years to search, DOB, SSN, signed release. Civil cases indexed by defendant, plaintiff. Civil records on computer by case number back to 1994.
Criminal Records: Access: Mail, in person. Only the court performs in person searches; visitors may not. Search fee: $17.00 per name. Required to search: name, years to search, DOB, SSN, signed release. Criminal records on computer by case number; computerized back to 1994.
General Information: No juvenile, mental health, victims, sealed or adoption records released. SASE required. Turnaround time 1-2 weeks. Copy fee: $.50 per page. Certification fee: $17.00. Fee payee: South Mesa/Gilbert Justice Court. Only cashiers checks and money orders accepted. Prepayment is required.

South Phoenix Justice Court 217 E Olympic Dr, Phoenix, AZ 85040; 602-243-0318; Fax: 602-243-6389. Hours: 8AM-5PM (MST). *Misdemeanor, Civil Actions Under $10,000, Eviction, Small Claims.*

http://justicecourts.maricopa.gov/precincts/SouthPhoenix.htm

Civil Records: Access: In person only. Only the court performs in person searches; visitors may not. No search fee. Required to search: name, years to search; also helpful: address. Civil cases indexed by defendant, plaintiff. Civil records on computer since 1990, on dockets by number.
Criminal Records: Access: In person only. Only the court performs in person searches; visitors may not. No search fee. Required to search: name, years to search; also helpful: DOB. Criminal records on dockets by number.
General Information: No juvenile, mental health, victims, sealed or adoption records released. Copy fee: $.50 per page. Certification fee: $17.00. Fee payee:

South Phoenix Justice Court. Personal checks accepted. Credit cards accepted: Visa, MasterCard.

Tolleson Justice Court 9550 W Van Buren #6, Tolleson, AZ 85353; 623-936-1449; Fax: 623-936-4859. Hours: 8AM-5PM (MST). *Misdemeanor, Civil Actions Under $10,000, Eviction, Small Claims.*

http://justicecourts.maricopa.gov/precincts/Tolleson.htm

Civil Records: Access: Mail, in person, online. No search fee. Required to search: name, years to search; also helpful: address. Civil cases indexed by defendant, plaintiff. Civil records in docket books by number prior to 1992, on computer since 1993. Online access to records is free www.supreme.state.az.us/publicaccess.
Criminal Records: Access: Mail, in person, online. Only the court performs in person searches; visitors may not. No search fee. Required to search: name, years to search, DOB; also helpful: address, SSN. Criminal records in docket books by number prior to 1992, on computer since 1993. Online access to records is free at www.supreme.state.az.us/publicaccess.
General Information: No juvenile, mental health, victims, sealed or adoption records released. SASE required. Turnaround time 1-2 weeks. Copy fee: $.50 per page. Certification fee: $17.00. Fee payee: Tolleson Justice Court. Personal checks accepted. Credit cards accepted: Visa, MasterCard.

West Mesa Justice Court 2050 W University Dr, Mesa, AZ 85201; 480-964-2958; Fax: 480-969-1098. Hours: 8AM-5PM (MST). *Misdemeanor, Civil Actions Under $10,000, Eviction, Small Claims.*

http://justicecourts.maricopa.gov/precincts/WestMesa.htm

Civil Records: Access: In person only. Visitors must perform in person searches for themselves. No search fee. Required to search: name, years to search. Civil cases indexed by defendant, plaintiff. Civil records on computer since 1990 by case number.
Criminal Records: Access: In person only. Visitors must perform in person searches for themselves. No search fee. Required to search: name, years to search, DOB; also helpful: SSN. Criminal records on computer since 1990 by case number.
General Information: No juvenile, mental health, victims, sealed or adoption records released. Copy fee: $.50 per page. Certification fee: $17.00. Fee payee: West Mesa Justice Court. Personal checks accepted. Credit cards accepted: Visa, MasterCard. Prepayment is required.

West Phoenix Justice Court 1 W Madison St, Phoenix, AZ 85003; 602-256-0292; Fax: 602-256-7959. Hours: 8AM-5PM (MST). *Misdemeanor, Civil Actions Under $10,000, Eviction, Small Claims.*

http://justicecourts.maricopa.gov/precincts/West_Phoenix.htm

Civil Records: Access: Mail, in person. Both court and visitors may perform in person searches. Search fee: $17.00 per name. Required to search: name, years to search. Civil cases indexed by defendant, plaintiff. Civil records on computer since 1993.
Criminal Records: Access: In person only. Both court and visitors may perform in person searches. Search fee: $17.00 per name. Required to search: name, years to search, DOB. Criminal records on computer by case number.
General Information: Public access terminal is available. No juvenile, mental health, victims, sealed or adoption records released. SASE required. Turnaround time is 1-2 days. Copy fee: $.50 per page. Certification fee: $17.00. Fee payee: West Phoenix Justice Court. Personal checks accepted. Credit cards accepted: Visa, MasterCard.

West Tempe Justice Court 1845 E Broadway #109, Tempe, AZ 85282; 480-705-7349; Fax: 480-785-4577. Hours: 8AM-5PM (MST). *Misdemeanor, Civil Actions Under $10,000, Eviction, Small Claims.*

http://justicecourts.maricopa.gov/precincts/WestTempe.htm

Civil Records: Access: Mail, in person. Only the court performs in person searches; visitors may not. No search fee. Required to search: name, years to search. Civil cases indexed by defendant, plaintiff. Civil records on computer by case number.

Criminal Records: Access: Mail, in person. Only the court performs in person searches; visitors may not. No search fee. Required to search: name, years to search, DOB. Criminal records on computer by case number.

General Information: No juvenile, mental health, victims, sealed records released. SASE required. Copy fee: $.50 per page. Certification fee: $17.00. Fee payee: Tempe Justice Court. Personal checks accepted. Credit cards accepted: Visa, MasterCard. Prepayment is required.

Wickenburg Justice Court 155 N Tegner, #D, Wickenburg, AZ 85390; 928-506-1554; Fax: 928-684-9639. Hours: 8AM-5PM (MST). *Misdemeanor, Civil Actions Under $10,000, Eviction, Small Claims.*

http://justicecourts.maricopa.gov/precincts/Wickenburg.htm

Civil Records: Access: Mail, in person, online. Both court and visitors may perform in person searches. Search fee: $17.00 per name. Required to search: name, years to search; also helpful: address. Civil cases indexed by defendant, plaintiff. Civil records on computer since 1994. Online access to records is free at www.supreme.state.az.us/publicaccess.

Criminal Records: Access: Mail, in person, online. Both court and visitors may perform in person searches. Search fee: $17.00 per name. Required to search: name, years to search, DOB; also helpful: SSN. Criminal records on computer by name and case number. Online access to records is free at www.supreme.state.az.us/publicaccess.

General Information: No juvenile, mental health, victims, sealed records released. SASE required. Turnaround time 1-2 weeks. Copy fee: $.50 per page. Certification fee: $17.00. Fee payee: Wickenburg Justice Court. Personal checks accepted. Credit cards accepted: Visa, MasterCard. Prepayment is required.

Mohave County

Superior Court PO Box 7000, Kingman, AZ 86402-7000; 928-753-0713; Fax: 928-753-0781. Hours: 8AM-5PM (MST). *Felony, Civil Actions Over $5,000, Probate.*

www.mohavecourts.com

Civil Records: Access: Phone, fax, mail, in person. Both court and visitors may perform in person searches. Search fee: $18.00 per name. Fee is per source. Required to search: name, years to search. Civil cases indexed by defendant, plaintiff. Civil records on computer since 11/95; prior records on microfiche and index books.

Criminal Records: Access: Phone, fax, mail, in person. Both court and visitors may perform in person searches. Search fee: $18.00 per name. Fee is per source. Required to search: name, years to search; also helpful: DOB, SSN. Criminal records on computer since 11/95; prior records on microfiche and index books.

General Information: No juvenile, mental health, victims, sealed or adoption records released. SASE required. Turnaround time 3 days. Fax notes: Fee to fax results is $.50 per page. Copy fee: $.50 per page. Certification fee: $18.00. Fee payee: Clerk of Superior Court. Business checks accepted. Prepayment is required.

Bullhead City Justice Court 2225 Trane Rd, Bullhead City, AZ 86442; 928-758-0709; Fax: 928-758-2644. Hours: 8AM-5PM (MST). *Misdemeanor, Civil Actions Under $10,000, Eviction, Small Claims.*

Civil Records: Access: Phone, mail, in person. Only the court performs in person searches; visitors may not. No search fee. Required to search: name, years to search. Civil cases indexed by defendant, plaintiff. Civil records on computer from 1988. Some records on docket books. Records retained for 5 years. Will only search back to 1988 unless w/docket number.

Criminal Records: Access: Phone, mail, in person. Only the court performs in person searches; visitors may not. No search fee. Required to search: name, years to search; also helpful: DOB, SSN. Criminal records on computer from 1988. Some records on docket books. Records retained for 5 years. Will only search back to 1988 unless w/docket number.

General Information: No juvenile, mental health, victims, sealed or adoption records released. SASE required. Turnaround time 2-3 days. Copy fee: $.50 per page. Certification fee: $17.00. Fee payee: Bullhead City Justice Court. Personal checks accepted. Prepayment is required.

Kingman/Cerbat Justice Court 524 W Beale St, PO Box 29, Kingman, AZ 86401-0029; 928-753-0710; Fax: 928-753-7840. Hours: 8AM-5PM (MST). *Misdemeanor, Civil Actions Under $10,000, Eviction, Small Claims.*

Civil Records: Access: Phone, fax, mail, in person. Only the court performs in person searches; visitors may not. Search fee: $17.00 per name. Required to search: name, years to search. Civil cases indexed by defendant, plaintiff. Civil records on computer from 1988. Some records on docket books. Records retained for 5 years.

Criminal Records: Access: Phone, fax, mail, in person. Only the court performs in person searches; visitors may not. Search fee: $17.00 per name. Required to search: name, years to search; also helpful: DOB, SSN. Criminal records on computer from 1988. Some records on docket books. Records retained for 5 years.

General Information: No juvenile, mental health, victims, sealed or adoption records released. SASE required. Turnaround time 2-3 days. Fax notes: $.50 per page. Copy fee: $.50 per page. Certification fee: $17.00. Fee payee: Kingman/Cerbat Justice Court. Personal checks accepted. Credit cards accepted: Visa, MasterCard. Prepayment is required.

Lake Havasu City Justice Court 2001 College Dr #148, Lake Havasu City, AZ 86403; 928-453-0705; Fax: 928-680-0193. Hours: 8AM-5PM (MST). *Misdemeanor, Civil Actions Under $10,000, Eviction, Small Claims.*

Civil Records: Access: Mail, fax, in person. Only the court performs in person searches; visitors may not. Search fee: $17.00 per name. Required to search: name, years to search. Civil cases indexed by defendant, plaintiff. Civil records on computer from 1988. Some records on docket books. Records retained for 5 years after closed/satisfied.

Criminal Records: Access: Fax, mail, in person. Only the court performs in person searches; visitors may not. Search fee: $17.00 per name. Required to search: name, years to search; also helpful: DOB. Criminal records on computer from 1988. Some records on docket books. Records retained for 5 years after closed/satisfied.

General Information: No juvenile or victims records released. SASE required. Turnaround time 2-3 days. Copy fee: $.50 per page. Certification fee: $17.00. Fee payee: Lake Havasu City Justice Court. Personal checks accepted. Prepayment is required.

Moccasin Justice Court HC-65 PO Box 90, Moccasin, AZ 86022; 928-643-7104; Fax: 928-643-6206. Hours: 8AM-5PM (MST). *Misdemeanor, Civil Actions Under $10,000, Eviction, Small Claims.*

Note: This court is also the Justice of Peace Court for Colorado City, and Municipal Court for Moccasin.

Civil Records: Access: Mail, in person, online. Only the court performs in person searches; visitors may not. Search fee: $17.00 per name. Required to search: name, years to search. Civil cases indexed by defendant, plaintiff. Civil records on docket books. Records retained for 5 years. Online access to records is free at www.supreme.state.az.us/publicaccess.

Criminal Records: Access: Mail, in person, online. Only the court performs in person searches; visitors may not. Search fee: $17.00 per name. Required to search: name, years to search. Criminal records on docket books. Records retained for 5 years. Online access to records is free at www.supreme.state.az.us/publicaccess.

General Information: No juvenile, mental health, victims, sealed or adoption records released. SASE required. Turnaround time 2-3 days. Copy fee: $.50 per page. Certification fee: $17.00. Fee payee: Moccasin Justice Court. Personal checks accepted. Prepayment is required.

Navajo County

Superior Court PO Box 668, Holbrook, AZ 86025; 928-524-4188; Fax: 928-524-4261. Hours: 8AM-5PM (MST). *Felony, Civil Actions Over $5,000, Probate.*

Civil Records: Access: Phone, fax, mail, in person, online. Both court and visitors may perform in person searches. Search fee: $18.00 per document. Required to search: name, years to search. Civil cases indexed by defendant, plaintiff. Civil records on docket books, index cards and microfiche back to 1890; computerized back to 1994. Online access to records is free at www.supreme.state.az.us/publicaccess.

Criminal Records: Access: Phone, fax, mail, in person, online. Only the court performs in person searches; visitors may not. Search fee: $18.00 per document. Required to search: name, years to search; also helpful: DOB, SSN. Criminal records on docket books, index cards and microfiche back to 1890; computerized back to 1994. Online access to records is free at www.supreme.state.az.us/publicaccess.

General Information: No juvenile, mental health, victims, sealed or adoption records released. SASE required. Turnaround time 3 days. Fax notes: Fee to fax is $18.00. Copy fee: $.50 per page. Certification fee: $18.00. Fee payee: Clerk of Superior Court. Only cashiers checks and money orders accepted. Prepayment is required.

Holbrook Justice Court PO Box 366, Holbrook, AZ 86025; 928-524-4720; Fax: 928-524-4725. Hours: 8AM-5PM (MST). *Misdemeanor, Civil Actions Under $10,000, Eviction, Small Claims.*

www.supreme.state.az.us

Civil Records: Access: Mail, in person, online. Both the court and visitors may perform in person searches. Search fee: $17.00 per name. Required to search: name, years to search. Civil cases indexed by defendant, plaintiff. Civil records on computer since 1994. Records on dockets and index cards back for 5 years. Online access to records is free at www.supreme.state.az.us/publicaccess.

Criminal Records: Access: Mail, in person, online. Both the court and visitors may perform in person searches. Search fee: $17.00 per name. Required to search: name, years to search. Criminal records on computer since 1992. Records on dockets and stat books back for 5 years. Online access to records is free at www.supreme.state.az.us/publicaccess.

133   *The Sourcebook to Public Record Information*   County Courts - Arizona

General Information: Public access terminal is available. No victim names or sealed records released. SASE required. Turnaround time 1 week. Copy fee: $.50 per page. Certification fee: $17.00. Fee payee: Holbrook Justice Court. Business checks accepted. Prepayment is required.

Kayenta Justice Court Box 38, Kayenta, AZ 86033; 928-697-3522; Fax: 928-697-3528. Hours: 8AM-Noon,1-5PM (MST). *Misdemeanor, Civil Actions Under $10,000, Eviction, Small Claims.*

Note: If planning to make an in-person search, call to make an appointment.

Civil Records: Access: Mail, in person, online. Only the court performs in person searches; visitors may not. Search fee: $17.00 per name. Required to search: name, years to search, address. Civil cases indexed by defendant, plaintiff. Civil records on docket books and index cards; on computer back to 1994. Online access to records is free at www.supreme.state.az.us/publicaccess.

Criminal Records: Access: Mail, in person, online. Only the court performs in person searches; visitors may not. Search fee: $17.00 per name. Required to search: name, years to search, address, DOB, SSN, signed release. Criminal records on docket books and index cards; on computer back to 1994. Online access to records is free at www.supreme.state.az.us/publicaccess.

General Information: No victim's names released. SASE required. Turnaround time 1 week. Copy fee: $.50 per page. Certification fee: $17.00. Fee payee: Kayenta Justice Court. Only cashiers checks and money orders accepted. Prepayment is required.

Pinetop-Lakeside Justice Court Box 2020, Lakeside, AZ 85929; 928-368-6200; Fax: 928-368-8674. Hours: 8AM-5PM (MST). *Misdemeanor, Civil Actions Under $10,000, Eviction, Small Claims.*

Civil Records: Access: Fax, mail, in person, online. Only the court performs in person searches; visitors may not. Search fee: $17.00 per name. Required to search: name, years to search. Civil cases indexed by case #. Civil records on electronic dockets by case number and case files by numeric. Online access to records is free at www.supreme.state.az.us/publicaccess.

Criminal Records: Access: Fax, mail, in person, online. Only the court performs in person searches; visitors may not. Search fee: $17.00 per name. Required to search: name, years to search. Criminal records on electronic dockets by case number and case files by alpha back to 1970. Computerized back to 1996. Online access to records is free at www.supreme.state.az.us/publicaccess.

General Information: Public access terminal is available. No victim's names released. SASE required. Turnaround time 7-10 days. Fax notes: No fee to fax results. Copy fee: $.50 per page. Certification fee: $17.00. Fee payee: Pinetop-Lakeside Justice Court. Personal checks accepted. Prepayment is required.

Show Low Justice Court PO Box 3085, Show Low, AZ 85902-3085; 928-532-6030; Fax: 928-532-6035. Hours: 8AM-5PM (MST). *Misdemeanor, Civil Actions Under $10,000, Eviction, Small Claims.*

Civil Records: Access: Fax, mail, in person, online. Only the court performs in person searches; visitors may not. Search fee: $17.00 per name. Required to search: name, years to search. Civil cases indexed by defendant, plaintiff. Civil records on computer. Online access to records is free at www.supreme.state.az.us/publicaccess. In person access requires a written request.

Criminal Records: Access: Fax, mail, in person, online. Only the court performs in person searches; visitors may not. Search fee: $17.00 per name per year. Required to search: name, years to search; also helpful:

DOB, SSN. Criminal records on computer for five years. Online access to records is free at www.supreme.state.az.us/publicaccess. In person access requires a written request.

General Information: No victim's names released. SASE required. Turnaround time 1 week. Copy fee: $.50 per page. Certification fee: $17.00. Fee payee: Show Low Justice Court. Personal checks accepted. Prepayment is required.

Snowflake Justice Court 145 S Main St #D, Snowflake, AZ 85937; 928-536-4141; Fax: 928-536-3511. Hours: 8AM-5PM (MST). *Misdemeanor, Civil Actions Under $10,000, Eviction, Small Claims.*

Civil Records: Access: Phone, fax, mail, in person, online. Only the court performs in person searches; visitors may not. Search fee: $17.00 per name per year. No charge if search is for two years or less. Required to search: name, years to search. Civil cases indexed by defendant, plaintiff. Civil records on computer back to 6/96, prior on docket books and index cards. Misdemeanors, DUI's and traffic records kept for 3 years, others held for 5 years. Online access to records is free at www.supreme.state.az.us/publicaccess.

Criminal Records: Access: Fax, mail, in person, online. Only the court performs in person searches; visitors may not. Search fee: $17.00 per name per year. No charge if search is for two years or less. Required to search: name, years to search; also helpful: DOB, SSN. Criminal records on computer back to 6/96, prior on docket books and index cards. Misdemeanors, DUI's and traffic records kept for 3 years, others held for 5 years. Online access to records is free at www.supreme.state.az.us/publicaccess.

General Information: No victim's names or search warrants released, no juvenile records released. SASE required. Turnaround time 2 weeks. Copy fee: $1.25 per page. Certification fee: $17.00. Fee payee: Snowflake Justice Court. Only cashiers checks and money orders accepted. Prepayment is required.

Winslow Justice Court Box 808, Winslow, AZ 86047; 928-289-6840; Fax: 928-289-2197. Hours: 8AM-5PM (MST). *Misdemeanor, Civil Actions Under $10,000, Eviction, Small Claims.*

Civil Records: Access: Fax, mail, in person, online. Only the court performs in person searches; visitors may not. No search fee. Required to search: name, years to search. Civil cases indexed by defendant, plaintiff. Civil records on docket books; on computer since 1994. Online access to records is free at www.supreme.state.az.us/publicaccess.

Criminal Records: Access: Fax, mail, in person, online. Only the court performs in person searches; visitors may not. No search fee. Required to search: name, years to search; also helpful: DOB, SSN. Criminal records on docket books; on computer since 1995. Online access to records is free at www.supreme.state.az.us/publicaccess.

General Information: No victim's names released. SASE required. Turnaround time 1 week. Copy fee: $.50 per page. Certification fee: $18.00. Fee payee: Winslow Justice Court. Personal checks accepted. Prepayment is required.

Pima County

Superior Court 110 W Congress, Tucson, AZ 85701; 520-740-3240; Fax: 520-798-3531. Hours: 8AM-5PM (MST). *Felony, Civil Actions Over $5,000, Probate.*

www.cosc.co.pima.az.us

Note: Address correspondence to attention of civil or criminal section.

Civil Records: Access: Phone, mail, in person, online. Both court and visitors may perform in person searches. Search fee: $18.00 per name. Required to search: name, years to search, DOB. Civil cases indexed by defendant,

plaintiff. Civil records on computer since 1980s, on microfilm since late 1800s. Online access to superior court records is available free at www.cosc.co.pima.az.us/record_search.

Criminal Records: Access: Mail, in person, online. Both court and visitors may perform in person searches. Search fee: $18.00 per name. Add $5.00 for postage and handling. Required to search: name, years to search, DOB. Criminal records on computer since 1980s, on microfilm since late 1800s. Online access to superior court records is available free at www.cosc.co.pima.az.us/record_search. Cases without dispositions are not included online.

General Information: Public access terminal is available. No juvenile, mental health, adoption, victims or sealed records released. SASE required. Turnaround time 2 days. Plus $5.00 mailing fee. Fax notes: Fee to fax results is $5.00 plus $.50 per page. Copy fee: $.50 per page. Certification fee: $18.00. Fee payee: Clerk of Superior Court. Only cashiers checks and money orders accepted. Credit cards accepted: Visa, MasterCard. In person only. Prepayment is required.

Ajo Justice Court 111 La Mina, Ajo, AZ 85321; 520-387-7684. Hours: 8AM-5PM (MST). *Misdemeanor, Civil Actions Under $10,000, Eviction, Small Claims.*

Civil Records: Access: Mail, in person, online. Only the court performs in person searches; visitors may not. No search fee. Required to search: name, years to search. Civil cases indexed by defendant, plaintiff. Civil records on computer since 1987, prior in docket books. Online access to records is free at http://geronimo.jp.co.pima.az.us/casesearch/.

Criminal Records: Access: Mail, in person, online. Only the court performs in person searches; visitors may not. No search fee. Required to search: name, years to search. Criminal records on computer since 1987, prior in docket books. Online access to records is free at http://geronimo.jp.co.pima.az.us/casesearch/.

General Information: No juvenile, sealed, victim records released. Turnaround time 1 week. Copy fee: $.50 per page. Certification fee: $17.00. Fee payee: Ajo Justice Court. Personal checks accepted. Prepayment is required.

Green Valley Justice Court 601 N LaCanada, Green Valley, AZ 85614; 520-648-0658; Fax: 520-648-2235. Hours: 8AM-5PM (MST). *Misdemeanor, Civil Actions Under $10,000, Eviction, Small Claims.*

Civil Records: Access: Mail, in person, online. Only the court performs in person searches; visitors may not. Search fee: $17.00 per name. Required to search: name, years to search. Civil cases indexed by defendant, plaintiff. Civil records on computer back to 1996; card files prior. Online access to records is free at http://geronimo.jp.co.pima.az.us/casesearch/. Clerk will only search computerized records.

Criminal Records: Access: Mail, in person, online. Only the court performs in person searches; visitors may not. Search fee: $17.00 per name. Required to search: name, years to search, DOB. Criminal records on computer back to 1996; card files prior. Online access to records is free at http://geronimo.jp.co.pima.az.us/casesearch/. Clerk will only search computerized records.

General Information: No juvenile, mental health, victims, sealed or adoption records released. SASE required. Turnaround time 5 days. Copy fee: $.50 per page. Certification fee: $17.00. Fee payee: Green Valley Justice Court. Personal checks accepted. Prepayment is required.

Pima County Consolidated Justice Court

115 N Church Ave, Tucson, AZ 85701; 520-740-3171; Fax: 520-884-0346. Hours: 8AM-5PM (MST). *Misdemeanor, Civil Actions Under $10,000, Eviction, Small Claims.*

http://jp.co.pima.az.us

Civil Records: Access: Fax, mail, online, in person. Both court and visitors may perform in person searches. Search fee: $10.00 per name. Required to search: name, years to search. Civil cases indexed by defendant, plaintiff. Civil records on computer since 1988, on docket books prior. Online access is free at http://geronimo.jp.co.pima.az.us/casesearch/. You can search docket information for civil, criminal or traffic cases by name, docket or citation number.

Criminal Records: Access: Fax, mail, online, in person. Both court and visitors may perform in person searches. Search fee: $10.00 per name. Required to search: name, years to search, DOB, SSN. Criminal records on computer since 1988, on docket books prior. Online access to criminal records is the same as civil.

General Information: Public access terminal is available. No information about set-aside judgments, unserved search warrants or felony warrants released. SASE required. Turnaround time 10 days. Copy fee: $1.25 per page. Certification fee: $17.00. Fee is per page. Fee payee: Pima County Justice Court. Personal checks accepted. Credit cards accepted: Visa, MasterCard. Visa, MC. Prepayment is required.

Pinal County

Superior Court PO Box 2730, Florence, AZ 85232-2730; 520-868-6296; Fax: 520-868-6252. Hours: 8AM-5PM (MST). *Felony, Civil Actions Over $5,000, Probate.*

www.co.pinal.az.us/clerksc

Civil Records: Access: Phone, mail, in person, online. Both court and visitors may perform in person searches. Search fee: $18.00 per name. Required to search: name, years to search. Civil cases indexed by defendant, plaintiff. Civil records on computer from 1987. Some records on docket books back to 1775. Online access to records is free www.supreme.state.az.us/publicaccess.

Criminal Records: Access: Phone, mail, in person, online. Both court and visitors may perform in person searches. Search fee: $18.00 per name. Required to search: name, years to search. Criminal records on computer from 1987. Some records on docket books back to 1775. Online access to records is free at www.supreme.state.az.us/publicaccess.

General Information: Public access terminal is available. No victim names, adoption records released. SASE required. Turnaround time 2 days. Fax notes: Fee to fax results is $.50 per page. Copy fee: $.50 per page. Certification fee: $18.00. Fee payee: Clerk of Superior Court. Business checks accepted. Prepayment is required.

Apache Junction Justice Court 575 N Idaho, #200, Apache Junction, AZ 85219; 480-982-2921; Fax: 480-982-9472. Hours: 8AM-Noon, 1-5PM (MST). *Misdemeanor, Civil Actions Under $10,000, Eviction, Small Claims.*

http://co.pinal.az.us/JusticeCourts

Civil Records: Access: Fax, mail, in person, online. Both court and visitors may perform in person searches. Search fee: $17.00. Required to search: name, years to search. Civil cases indexed by defendant, plaintiff. Civil records on computer since 1993. Records retained for 5 years. Online access to records is free at www.supreme.state.az.us/publicaccess.

Criminal Records: Access: Fax, mail, in person, online. Only the court performs in person searches; visitors may not. Search fee: $17.00. Required to search: name, years to search. Criminal records on computer since 1993. Records retained for 7 years.

Online access to records is free at www.supreme.state.az.us/publicaccess.

General Information: Turnaround time varies. Fax notes: $1.25 per page. Copy fee: $.50 per page. Certification fee: $17.00. Fee payee: Apache Junction Justice Court. Personal checks accepted. Prepayment is required.

Casa Grande Justice Court 820 E Cottonwood Lane, Bldg B, Casa Grande, AZ 85222; 520-836-5471; Fax: 520-868-7404. Hours: 8AM-5PM (MST). *Misdemeanor, Civil Actions Under $10,000, Eviction, Small Claims.*

http://co.pinal.az.us/JusticeCourts

Civil Records: Access: Mail, in person, online. Only the court performs in person searches; visitors may not. No search fee. Required to search: name, years to search. Civil cases indexed by defendant, plaintiff. Civil records on computer since 1999, index back to 1995. Online access to records is free at www.supreme.state.az.us/publicaccess.

Criminal Records: Access: Mail, in person, online. Only the court performs in person searches; visitors may not. No search fee. Required to search: name, years to search, DOB; also helpful: SSN. Criminal records on computer since 1999, index back to 1995. Online access to records is free at www.supreme.state.az.us/publicaccess.

General Information: No juvenile, mental health, victims, sealed or adoption records released. SASE required. Turnaround time 1 day. Copy fee: $.50. Certification fee: $17.00. Fee payee: Casa Grande Justice Court. Business checks accepted. Credit cards accepted: Visa, MasterCard. Prepayment is required.

Eloy Justice Court PO Box 586, Eloy, AZ 85231; 520-466-9221; Fax: 520-466-4473. Hours: 8AM-Noon, 1-5PM (MST). *Misdemeanor, Civil Actions Under $10,000, Eviction, Small Claims.*

http://co.pinal.az.us/JusticeCourts

Civil Records: Access: Mail, in person, online. Only the court performs in person searches; visitors may not. No search fee. Required to search: name, years to search. Civil cases indexed by defendant, plaintiff. Civil records on computer since 8/92. On docket books and index cards from 1981. Online access to records is free at www.supreme.state.az.us/publicaccess.

Criminal Records: Access: Mail, in person, online. Only the court performs in person searches; visitors may not. No search fee. Required to search: name, years to search, DOB. Criminal records on computer since 8/92. On docket books and index cards from 1981. Online access to records is free at www.supreme.state.az.us/publicaccess.

General Information: No juvenile, mental health, victims, sealed or adoption records released. SASE required. Turnaround time 1-2 weeks. Copy fee: $.50 per page. Certification fee: $17.00. Fee payee: Eloy Justice Court. Business checks accepted. Prepayment is required.

Florence Justice Court PO Box 1818, Florence, AZ 85232; 520-868-7194; Fax: 520-868-7190. Hours: 8AM-5PM (MST). *Misdemeanor, Civil Actions Under $10,000, Eviction, Small Claims.*

http://co.pinal.az.us/JusticeCourts

Civil Records: Access: Mail, in person, online. Only the court performs in person searches; visitors may not. Search fee: $17.00 per name. Required to search: name, years to search. Civil cases indexed by defendant, plaintiff. Civil records are on computer since January 1999. Online access to records is free at www.supreme.state.az.us/publicaccess.

Criminal Records: Access: Mail, in person, online. Only the court performs in person searches; visitors may not. Search fee: $17.00 per name. Required to search: name, years to search. Criminal records are on

computer since January 1999. Online access to records is free at www.supreme.state.az.us/publicaccess.

General Information: No juvenile, mental health, victims, sealed or adoption records released. SASE required. Turnaround time 1 week. Copy fee: $.50 per page. Certification fee: $17.00. Fee payee: Florence Justice Court. Only cashiers checks and money orders accepted. Prepayment is required.

Mammoth Justice Court PO Box 777, Mammoth, AZ 85618; 520-487-2262; Fax: 520-487-2585. Hours: 8AM-5PM (MST). *Misdemeanor, Civil Actions Under $10,000, Eviction, Small Claims.*

http://co.pinal.az.us/JusticeCourts

Civil Records: Access: Mail, in person, online. Both court and visitors may perform in person searches. Search fee: $17.00 per name. Required to search: name, years to search. Civil cases indexed by defendant, plaintiff. Civil records on docket books. Misdemeanor and civil records retained for 7 years; on computer back 4 years. Online access to records is free at www.supreme.state.az.us/publicaccess.

Criminal Records: Access: Mail, in person, online. Both court and visitors may perform in person searches. Search fee: $17.00 per name. Required to search: name, years to search, DOB. Criminal records on docket books. Misdemeanor and civil records retained for 7 years; on computer back 4 years. Online access to records is free www.supreme.state.az.us/publicaccess.

General Information: Public access terminal is available. No juvenile, mental health, victims, sealed or adoption records released. SASE required. Turnaround time 2 days. Copy fee: $.50 per page. Certification fee: $7.00. Fee payee: Mammoth Justice Court. Personal checks accepted. Prepayment is required.

Maricopa Justice Court 44625 W Garvey Rd, Maricopa, AZ 85239; 520-568-2451; Fax: 520-568-2924. Hours: 8AM-4PM (MST). *Misdemeanor, Civil Actions Under $10,000, Eviction, Small Claims.*

http://co.pinal.az.us/JusticeCourts

Civil Records: Access: Fax, mail, in person, online. Only the court performs in person searches; visitors may not. Search fee: $17.00 per name. Required to search: name, years to search. Civil cases indexed by defendant. Civil records on computer since 1999; on dockets to 1993. Online access to records is free at www.supreme.state.az.us/publicaccess.

Criminal Records: Access: Fax, mail, in person, online. Only the court performs in person searches; visitors may not. Search fee: $17.00 per name. Required to search: name, years to search. Criminal records on computer since 1999; on dockets to 1993. Online access to records is free at www.supreme.state.az.us/publicaccess.

General Information: No juvenile, mental health, victims, sealed or adoption records released. SASE required. Turnaround time 2 days. Copy fee: $.50 per page. Certification fee: $17.00. Fee payee: Maricopa Justice Court. Personal checks accepted. Prepayment is required.

Oracle Justice Court PO Box 3924, Oracle, AZ 85623; 520-896-9250; Fax: 520-868-7812. Hours: 8AM-5PM (MST). *Misdemeanor, Civil Actions Under $10,000, Eviction, Small Claims.*

http://co.pinal.az.us/JusticeCourts

Civil Records: Access: Mail, in person, online. Both court and visitors may perform in person searches. Search fee: $17.00 per name. Required to search: name, years to search; also helpful: address. Civil cases indexed by defendant. Civil records on docket books and computer back to 1991. Online access to records is free at www.supreme.state.az.us/publicaccess.

Criminal Records: Access: Mail, in person, online. Both court and visitors may perform in person searches. Search fee: $17.00 per name. Required to search: name, years to search, DOB; also helpful: address, SSN. Criminal records on docket books and computer back to 1991. Online access to records is free at www.supreme.state.az.us/publicaccess.

General Information: Public access terminal is available. No juvenile, mental health, victims, sealed, adoption records released. SASE required. Fax notes: Fee to fax results is $1.00 per page. Copy fee: $1.50 per page. Certification fee: $17.00. Fee payee: Oracle Justice Court. Personal checks accepted. Prepayment is required.

Superior/Kearny Justice Court 60 E Main St, Superior, AZ 85273; 520-689-5871; Fax: 520-689-2369. Hours: 8AM-Noon, 1-5PM (MST). *Misdemeanor, Civil Actions Under $10,000, Eviction, Small Claims.*

http://co.pinal.az.us/JusticeCourts

Civil Records: Access: Fax, mail, in person. Only the court performs in person searches; visitors may not. Search fee: $17.00 per name. Required to search: name, years to search. Civil cases indexed by defendant, plaintiff. Civil records go back 5 years; computerized records go back 5 years. Online access to records is free at www.supreme.state.az.us/publicaccess.

Criminal Records: Access: Fax, mail, in person, online. Only the court performs in person searches; visitors may not. Search fee: $17.00 per name. Required to search: name, years to search, DOB; also helpful: SSN. Criminal recordsgo back 5 years; computerized records go back 5 years. Online access to records is free at www.supreme.state.az.us/publicaccess.

General Information: No juvenile, mental health, victims, sealed or adoption records released. SASE required. Turnaround time 3 days. Fax notes: No fee to fax results. Copy fee: $1.25 per page. Certification fee: $17.00. Fee payee: Superior/Kearny Justice Court. Personal checks accepted. Prepayment is required.

Santa Cruz County

Superior Court PO Box 1265, Nogales, AZ 85628; 520-375-7700; Fax: 520-761-7857. Hours: 8AM-5PM (MST). *Felony, Civil Actions Over $5,000, Probate.*

http://sccazcourts.org

Civil Records: Access: Mail, fax, in person, online. Both court and visitors may perform in person searches. Search fee: $18.00 per year/source. Required to search: name, years to search. Civil cases indexed by defendant, plaintiff. Civil records on microfiche from 1898 to 1950. Records on docket books from 1950 to 1996; on computer after 1996. Online access to records is free at www.supreme.state.az.us/publicaccess.

Criminal Records: Access: Mail, fax, in person, online. Both court and visitors may perform in person searches. Search fee: $18.00 per year/source. Required to search: name, years to search, DOB; also helpful: SSN. Criminal records archived on microfiche from 1898 to 1989. Records on docket books from 1977 to 1996; on computer after 1996. Online access to records is free at www.supreme.state.az.us/publicaccess.

General Information: No mental health, victims, sealed or adoption records released. SASE required. Turnaround time 1 1/2 weeks. Fax notes: Fee to fax results is $.50 per page. Copy fee: $.50 per page. Certification fee: $18.00. Fee payee: Clerk of Superior Court. Personal checks accepted. Prepayment is required.

East Santa Cruz County Justice Court - Precinct #2 PO Box 100, Patagonia, AZ 85624; 520-455-5796; Fax: 520-455-5517 (Attn: Justice Court). Hours: 8:30AM-4:30PM (MST). *Misdemeanor, Civil Actions Under $10,000, Eviction, Small Claims.*

Civil Records: Access: Mail, in person, online. Only the court performs in person searches; visitors may not. Search fee: $17.00 per name. Required to search: name, years to search; also helpful: address. Civil cases indexed by plaintiff. Civil records on docket books. Online access to records is free at www.supreme.state.az.us/publicaccess.

Criminal Records: Access: Mail, in person, online. Only the court performs in person searches; visitors may not. Search fee: $17.00 per name. Required to search: name, years to search, DOB, SSN, signed release; also helpful: address. Criminal records on docket books. Online access to records is free at www.supreme.state.az.us/publicaccess.

General Information: No juvenile, mental health, victims, sealed or adoption records released. SASE not required. Turnaround time 3-5 days. Copy fee: $.50 per page. Certification fee: $17.00. Fee payee: East Santa Cruz County Justice Court. Personal checks accepted. Prepayment is required.

Santa Cruz Justice Court PO Box 1150, Nogales, AZ 85628; 520-761-7853; Fax: 520-761-7929. Hours: 8AM-5PM (MST). *Misdemeanor, Civil Actions Under $10,000, Eviction, Small Claims.*

Civil Records: Access: Fax, mail, in person, online. Both court and visitors may perform in person searches. Search fee: $17.00 per name. Required to search: name, years to search; also helpful: address. Civil cases indexed by defendant, plaintiff. Civil records go back to 1975; on computer back to 2/96. Online access to records is free www.supreme.state.az.us/publicaccess.

Criminal Records: Access: Fax, mail, in person, online. Both court and visitors may perform in person searches. Search fee: $17.00 per name. Required to search: name, years to search, DOB; also helpful: address, SSN. Criminal records go back to 1975; on computer back to 2/96. Online access to records is free at www.supreme.state.az.us/publicaccess.

General Information: Public access terminal is available. No juvenile, mental health, victims, sealed or adoption records released. SASE required. Turnaround time 1-3 weeks. Copy fee: $.50 per page. Certification fee: $17.00. Fee payee: Santa Cruz Justice Court. Personal checks accepted.

Yavapai County

Superior Court Yavapai County Courthouse, Prescott, AZ 86301; 928-771-3313; Fax: 928-771-3111. Hours: 8AM-5PM (MST). *Felony, Civil Actions Over $5,000, Probate.*

Civil Records: Access: Fax, mail, in person, online. Both court and visitors may perform in person searches. Search fee: $18.00 per name. Required to search: name, years to search. Civil cases indexed by defendant, plaintiff. Civil records archived from 1900s. Some records on handwritten index book. Free access to Superior Court records at www.supreme.state.az.us/publicaccess.

Criminal Records: Access: Fax, mail, in person, online. Both court and visitors may perform in person searches. Search fee: $18.00 per name per year. Required to search: name, years to search, offense. Criminal records archived from 1900s. Some records on handwritten index book. Free access to Superior Court records at www.supreme.state.az.us/publicaccess.

General Information: Public access terminal is available. No juvenile, mental health, victims, sealed or adoption records released. SASE required. Turnaround time 10 days. Fax notes: $.50 per page. Copy fee: $.50 per page. Certification fee: $18.00. Fee payee: Clerk of Superior Court. Personal checks accepted. Prepayment is required.

Bagdad Justice Court PO Box 243, Bagdad, AZ 86321; 928-633-2141; Fax: 928-633-4451. Hours: 8AM-5PM M; 8:00AM-4:00PM T-Th (MST). (MST). *Misdemeanor, Civil Actions Under $10,000, Eviction, Small Claims.*

Civil Records: Access: Mail, in person, online. Only the court performs in person searches; visitors may not. Search fee: $17.00 per name. Required to search: name, years to search; also helpful: address. Civil records on computer since 3/94. Records on docket books and index cards. Records purged after 10 years. Online access to records is free at www.supreme.state.az.us/publicaccess.

Criminal Records: Access: Mail, in person, online. Only the court performs in person searches; visitors may not. Search fee: $17.00 per name. Required to search: name, years to search, DOB; also helpful: address, SSN. Criminal records on computer since 3/94. Records on docket books and index cards. Records purged after 5 years. Online access to records is free at www.supreme.state.az.us/publicaccess.

General Information: No juvenile, mental health, victims, sealed or adoption records released. SASE required. Turnaround time 2 days. Copy fee: $.50 per page. Certification fee: $17.00. Fee payee: Bagdad Justice Court. Only cashiers checks and money orders accepted.

Bagdad-Yarnell Justice Court PO Box 65, Yarnell, AZ 85362; 928-427-3318; Fax: 928-771-3362. Hours: 8AM-5PM (MST). *Misdemeanor, Civil Actions Under $10,000, Eviction, Small Claims.*

Civil Records: Access: Mail, in person, online. Only the court performs in person searches; visitors may not. Search fee: $17.00 per name. Required to search: name, years to search. Civil cases indexed by defendant, plaintiff. Civil records on computer from 1989. Prior records on docket books. Records purged after 10 years. Online access to records is free at www.supreme.state.az.us/publicaccess.

Criminal Records: Access: Mail, in person, online. Only the court performs in person searches; visitors may not. Search fee: $17.00 per name. Required to search: name, years to search. Criminal records on computer from 1989. prior on docket books. Records purged after 5 years. Online access to records is free at www.supreme.state.az.us/publicaccess.

General Information: No juvenile, mental health, victims, sealed or adoption records released. SASE required. Turnaround time 5 days. Copy fee: $.50 per page. Certification fee: $17.00. Fee payee: Yarnell Justice Court. Only cashiers checks and money orders accepted. Prepayment is required.

Mayer Justice Court PO Box 245, Mayer, AZ 86333; 928-771-3355. Hours: 8AM-5PM (MST). *Misdemeanor, Civil Actions Under $10,000, Eviction, Small Claims.*

Civil Records: Access: Mail, in person, online. Only the court performs in person searches; visitors may not. Search fee: $17.00 per name. Required to search: name, years to search. Civil cases indexed by defendant, plaintiff. Civil records on computer back to 1989. Records purged after 5 years. Online access to records is free at www.supreme.state.az.us/publicaccess.

Criminal Records: Access: Mail, in person, online. Only the court performs in person searches; visitors may not. Search fee: $17.00 per name. Required to search: name, years to search; also helpful: DOB. Criminal records on computer back to 1989. Records purged after 5 years. Online access to records is free at www.supreme.state.az.us/publicaccess.

General Information: No juvenile, mental health, victims, sealed or adoption records released. SASE required. Turnaround time 4 days. Copy fee: $.50 per page. Certification fee: $17.00. Fee payee: Mayer

Justice Court. Only cashiers checks and money orders accepted. Prepayment is required.

Prescott Justice Court Yavapai County Courthouse, Room 103, Prescott, AZ 86301; 928-771-3300; Fax: 928-771-3302. Hours: 8AM-5PM (MST). *Misdemeanor, Civil Actions Under $10,000, Eviction, Small Claims.*

Civil Records: Access: Fax, mail, in person. Both court and visitors may perform in person searches. No search fee. Required to search: name, years to search; also helpful: address. Civil cases indexed by defendant, plaintiff. Civil records are indexed on computer then purged after 5 years. Searches only available for past 5 years.

Criminal Records: Access: Fax, mail, in person. Both court and visitors may perform in person searches. No search fee. Required to search: name, years to search, DOB; also helpful: address, SSN. Criminal records are indexed on computer then purged after 5 years. Searches only available for past 5 years.

General Information: Public access terminal is available. No juvenile, victims or sealed records released. SASE required. Turnaround time 2 days. Fax notes: $17.00 per document. Copy fee: $.50 per page. Certification fee: $17.00 per document. Fee payee: City of Prescott. Personal checks accepted. No two party checks. Credit cards accepted: Visa, MasterCard. Prepayment is required.

Seligman Justice Court PO Box 56, Seligman, AZ 86337-0056; 928-422-3281; Fax: 928-422-3282. Hours: 8AM-5PM (MST). *Misdemeanor, Civil Actions Under $10,000, Eviction, Small Claims.*

Civil Records: Access: Phone, fax, mail, in person, online. Both court and visitors may perform in person searches. No search fee. Required to search: name, years to search; also helpful: address. Civil cases indexed by defendant, plaintiff. Civil records on computer. Records purged after 5 years. Online access to records is free at www.supreme.state.az.us/publicaccess.

Criminal Records: Access: Phone, fax, mail, in person, online. Both court and visitors may perform in person searches. No search fee. Required to search: name, years to search, DOB; also helpful: address, SSN. Criminal records on computer. Records purged after 5 years. Online access to records is free at www.supreme.state.az.us/publicaccess.

General Information: No juvenile or victims records released. SASE required. Turnaround time 2 days. Fax notes: No fee to fax results. Copy fee: $1.25 per page. Certification fee: $17.00. Fee payee: Seligman Justice Court. Business checks accepted.

Verde Valley Justice Court 10 S 6th St, Cottonwood, AZ 86326; 928-639-5820; Fax: 928-639-5828. Hours: 8AM-5PM (MST). *Misdemeanor, Civil Actions Under $10,000, Eviction, Small Claims.*

Civil Records: Access: Mail, in person, online. Both court and visitors may perform in person searches. Search fee: $17.00. Required to search: name, years to

search; also helpful: address. Civil cases indexed by defendant, plaintiff. Civil records on computer from 1994. Records purged after 5 years. Online access to records is free at www.supreme.state.az.us/publicaccess.

Criminal Records: Access: Mail, in person, online. Both court and visitors may perform in person searches. Search fee: $17.00. Required to search: name, years to search, DOB; also helpful: address, SSN. Criminal records on docket books and index cards. Records purged after 5 years. Online access to records is free at www.supreme.state.az.us/publicaccess.

General Information: No juvenile, mental health, victims, sealed or adoption records released. SASE required. Turnaround time 2 days. Copy fee: $.50 per page. Certification fee: $17.00. Fee payee: Verde Valley Justice Court.

Yuma County

Superior Court 168 S 2nd Ave, Yuma, AZ 85364; 928-329-2164; Fax: 928-329-2007. Hours: 8AM-5PM (MST). *Felony, Civil Actions Over $5,000, Probate.*

Civil Records: Access: Fax, mail, in person, online. Both court and visitors may perform in person searches. Search fee: $18.00 per name. Required to search: name, years to search. Civil cases indexed by defendant. Civil records on docket books from 1900s, new and pending cases from November 1994 on computer. Online access to records is free at www.supreme.state.az.us/publicaccess.

Criminal Records: Access: Fax, mail, in person, online. Both court and visitors may perform in person searches. Search fee: $18.00 per name. Required to search: name, years to search. Criminal records on docket books from 1900s, new and pending cases from November 1994 on computer. Online access to records is free at www.supreme.state.az.us/publicaccess.

General Information: No adoption, mental health records released. SASE required. Turnaround time 1 week. Fax notes: $18.00 per document. Copy fee: $.50 per page. Certification fee: $18.00. Fee payee: Clerk of Superior Court. Business checks accepted. Credit cards accepted: Visa, MasterCard. Prepayment is required.

Somerton Justice Court PO Box 458, Somerton, AZ 85350; 928-627-2722; Fax: 928-627-1076. Hours: 8AM-5PM (MST). *Misdemeanor, Civil Actions Under $10,000, Eviction, Small Claims.*

Civil Records: Access: Phone, fax, mail, in person, online. Both court and visitors may perform in person searches. No search fee. Required to search: name, years to search. Civil cases indexed by defendant. Civil records on computer. Online access to records is free at www.supreme.state.az.us/publicaccess.

Criminal Records: Access: Phone, fax, mail, in person, online. Only the court performs in person searches; visitors may not. No search fee. Required to search: name, years to search, DOB, SSN, offense, date of offense. Criminal records on computer. Online access to records is free at www.supreme.state.az.us/publicaccess.

General Information: No set aside judgment records released. SASE required. Turnaround time 2-4 days. Fax notes: $1.25 per page. Copy fee: $1.25 per page. Certification fee: $17.00. Fee payee: Somerton Justice Court. Business checks accepted. Prepayment is required.

Wellton Justice Court PO Box 384, Wellton, AZ 85356; 928-785-3321; Fax: 928-785-4933. Hours: 8AM-5PM (MST). *Misdemeanor, Civil Actions Under $10,000, Eviction, Small Claims.*

Civil Records: Access: Phone, fax, mail, in person, online. Only the court performs in person searches; visitors may not. No search fee. Required to search: name, years to search. Civil cases indexed by defendant, plaintiff. Civil records on computer to 1992. Online access to records is free at www.supreme.state.az.us/publicaccess.

Criminal Records: Access: Phone, fax, mail, in person, online. Only the court performs in person searches; visitors may not. No search fee. Required to search: name, years to search, offense, date of offense. Criminal records on computer to 1992. Online access to records is free www.supreme.state.az.us/publicaccess.

General Information: No set aside judgment records released. SASE not required. Turnaround time same day. Copy fee: $.50 per page. Fee payee: Wellton Justice Court. Personal checks accepted. Credit cards accepted: Visa, MasterCard, Discover, American Express.

Yuma Justice Court 168 S 2nd Ave, Yuma, AZ 85364; 928-329-2180; Fax: 928-329-2005. Hours: 8AM-5PM (MST). *Misdemeanor, Civil Actions Under $10,000, Eviction, Small Claims.*

Civil Records: Access: Mail, in person, online. Both court and visitors may perform in person searches. Search fee: $17.00 per name. Required to search: name, years to search. Civil cases indexed by defendant. Civil records on computer. Purged after 5 years. Info available only for cases after 09/01/97; computerized records since 1997. Online access to records is free at www.supreme.state.az.us/publicaccess.

Criminal Records: Access: Mail, in person, online. Only the court performs in person searches; visitors may not. Search fee: $17.00 per name. Required to search: name, years to search. Criminal records on computer. Purged after 5 years. Info available only for cases after 09/01/97; computerized records since 1997. Online access to records is free at www.supreme.state.az.us/publicaccess.

General Information: Public access terminal is available for civil only. Will not release victim's names. SASE required. Turnaround time 2-4 days. Copy fee: $.50 per page. Certification fee: $17.00. Fee payee: Justice Court #1. Personal checks accepted. Credit cards accepted: Visa, MasterCard. Visa, MC. Prepayment is required.

Arizona Recording Offices

ORGANIZATION: 15 counties, 16 recording offices. The Navajo Nation is profiled here. The recording officer is County Recorder. Recordings are usually placed in a Grantor/Grantee index. The entire state is in the Mountain Time Zone (MST), and does not change to daylight savings time. Note that no less than four new zip codes have added in recent years: 480 and 623 for east and west Phoenix Metro area respectively, 520 for south and southeastern state, 924 for west and north of state.

REAL ESTATE RECORDS: Counties do not perform real estate searches. Copy fees are usually $1.00 per page. Certification fees are usually $3.00 per document.

UCC RECORDS: Financing statements are filed at the state level, except for real estate related collateral, which are filed with the County Recorder. However, prior to 07/2001, consumer goods and farm collateral were filed at the County Recorder and these older records can be searched there. All counties will perform UCC searches. Use search request form UCC-3. Search fees are generally $10.00 per debtor name. Copies usually cost $1.00 per page.

TAX LIEN RECORDS: Federal and state tax liens on personal property of businesses are filed with the Secretary of State. Other federal and state tax liens are filed with the County Recorder. Several counties will do a separate tax lien search.

OTHER LIENS: Executions, judgments, labor.

ONLINE ACCESS: A number of county assessor offices offer online access:. The Secretary of State offers online access to UCC records at www.sosaz.com/scripts/UCC_Search.dll

Apache County

County Recorder, PO Box 425, St. Johns, AZ 85936. 928-337-4364 R/E Recording: 928-337-7515 UCC Recording: 928-337-7515; Fax 928-337-2003. www.co.apache.az.us/Recorder/index.htm
Will search UCC records. UCC search does not include tax liens. Separate combined tax lien search available. Will not search real estate records. **Online Access:** Real Estate, Recording Records. Access to the Apache County Recorder Query Index are available free at www.co.apache.az.us/Recorder/index/query.asp. **Other Phone Numbers:** Assessor 928-337-7521; Treasurer 928-337-7515; Elections 928-337-7515.

Cochise County

County Recorder, PO Box 184, Bisbee, AZ 85603. County Recorder, R/E and UCC Recording 520-432-9270; Fax 520-432-9274. www.co.cochise.az.us
Will search UCC records. This agency will not do a tax lien search. Will not search real estate records. **Other Phone Numbers:** Assessor 520-432-9329; Treasurer 520-432-9222; Elections 520-432-9236.

Coconino County

County Recorder, 110 E. Cherry Ave, Flagstaff, AZ 86001. County Recorder, R/E and UCC Recording 928-779-6585; Fax 928-779-6739. http://co.coconino.az.us/recorder/
Will search UCC records. Tax liens included in UCC search if requested with extra $2.00 fee. Real estate record owner searches available. **Online Access:** Recording, Grantor/Grantee, Real Estate Records. Access to county iCRIS system is available free at http://coco-criswf.infomagic.net/splash.jsp. Registration is required. Documents are $1.00 to print, signup and request documents at 800-793-6181. Online records go back to 1983; images back to 3/1999. **Other Phone Numbers:** Assessor 928-779-6502; Treasurer 928-779-6615; Appraiser/Auditor 928-779-6502; Elections 928-779-6589; Vital Records 602-364-1300.

Gila County

County Recorder, 1400 E. Ash St, Globe, AZ 85501. 928-425-3231 R/E Recording: 928-425-3231 x238 UCC Recording: 928-425-3231 x238; Fax 928-425-9270.
Will search UCC records. This agency will do a federal or state tax lien search. Will search real estate records. **Other Phone Numbers:** Assessor 928-425-3231 x238; Treasurer 928-425-3231 x201; Elections 928-425-3231 x441.

Graham County

County Recorder, 921 Thatcher Blvd., Safford, AZ 85546. County Recorder, R/E and UCC Recording 928-428-3560; Fax 928-428-5951. www.graham.az.gov
Will search UCC records. UCC search includes tax liens if requested. Will not search real estate records. **Other Phone Numbers:** Assessor 928-428-2828; Treasurer 928-428-3440; Elections 928-428-3930.

Greenlee County

County Recorder, PO Box 1625, Clifton, AZ 85533-1625. 928-865-2632 UCC Recording: 928-865-2632 or 928-865-1717; Fax 928-865-4417.
Will search UCC records. This agency will not do a tax lien search. Will not search real estate records. **Other Phone Numbers:** Assessor 928-865-5302; Treasurer 928-865-3422; Elections 928-865-1717.

La Paz County

County Recorder, Suite 201, 1112 Joshua Ave., Parker, AZ 85344. 928-669-6136; Fax 928-669-5638. www.co.la-paz.az.us/recorder.htm
Will search UCC records. This agency will not do a tax lien search. Will not search real estate records. **Other Phone Numbers:** Assessor 928-669-6165; Treasurer 928-669-6145.

Maricopa County

County Recorder, 111 S. 3rd Ave, Phoenix, AZ 85003. 602-506-3535; Fax 602-506-3069. http://recorder.maricopa.gov
Will search UCC records. This agency will not do a tax lien search. Will not search real estate records. **Online Access:** Real Estate, Lien Records. Access is available by direct dial-up or on the Internet. Dial-up access requires one-time set-up fee of $300 plus $.06 per minute. Dial-up hours are 8am-10pm M-F, 8-5 S-S. Records date back to 1983. For additional information, contact Linda Kinchloe at 602-506-3637. Also, access to the County Recorder's database is available free at http://recorder.maricopa.gov/recdocdata. Records go back to 1983. Also, access to the Assessor database is available free at www.maricopa.gov/assessor/default.asp. Residential data is available. Also, perform name/parcel/property tax appeal lookups free on the SBOE site at www.sboe.state.az.us/cgi-bin/name_lookup.pl. **Other Phone Numbers:** Assessor 602-506-3406.

Mohave County

County Recorder, PO Box 70, Kingman, AZ 86402-0070. County Recorder, R/E and UCC Recording 928-753-0701; Fax 928-753-0727. www.co.mohave.az.us
Will search UCC records. This agency will not do a tax lien search. Will not search real estate records. **Online Access:** Real Estate, Grantor/Grantee, Lien, Assessor Records. Access to the Recorder's System is available at http://icris.co.mohave.az.us/splash.jsp. Registration and password is required. Also, online access to the Assessor's property database is available free (no registration) at www.co.mohave.az.us/1moweb/depts_files/assessor_files/assessdata.asp. A sales history database is also here. Also, the treasurer's tax sale parcel search is available at www.co.mohave.az.us/1moweb/depts_files/treasure_files/about_treasure.htm. Also, search restaurant inspections at the main web site. **Other Phone Numbers:** Assessor 928-753-0703; Treasurer 928-753-0737; Appraiser/Auditor 928-753-0703; Elections 928-753-0733.

Navajo County

County Recorder, PO Box 668, Holbrook, AZ 86025-0668. 928-524-4194; Fax 928-524-4308. www.co.navajo.az.us
Will search UCC records. UCC search includes tax liens if requested. Will not search real estate records. **Online Access:** Property, Assessor, Grantor/Grantee, Recording, UCC Records. Access to the recorder's database of land inormation, UCCs and Grantor/Grantee indexes is available free at http://iris.co.navajo.az.us/irisonweb. Also, access to the property assessor database if available free at www.co.mohave.az.us/navajo/assessor/assessdatalink.asp. **Other Phone Numbers:** Assessor 928-524-4086.

Navajo Nation

County Recorder, PO Box 663, Window Rock, AZ 86515. 928-871-7365; Fax 928-871-7381.
Will search UCC records. This agency will not do a tax lien search. Will not search real estate records.

Pima County

County Recorder, 115 N. Church Ave, Tucson, AZ 85701. 520-740-4350; Fax 520-623-1785. www.recorder.co.pima.az.us
Will search UCC records. Tax liens not included in UCC search. Will not search real estate records. **Online Access:** Assessor, Real Estate, Lien, Recording Records. Access to the recorder's Research Records database is available free at www.recorder .co.pima.az.us/research.html. Click "Enter Here" and use the word "public" for user name and password. Also, records on the Pima County Tax Assessor database are available free online at www.asr.co.pima.az.us/apiq/index.html. Also, a name/parcel/property tax lookup may be performed free on the SBOE site at www.sboe.state.az.us/cgi-bin/name_lookup.pl. Also, search by parcel number on the Treasurer's tax inquiry database at www.to.co.pima.az.us/inquiry.html. **Other Phone Numbers:** Assessor 520-740-8630.

Pinal County

County Recorder, PO Box 848, Florence, AZ 85232-0848. County Recorder, R/E and UCC Recording 520-868-7100 UCC Recording: 520-868-6179; Fax 520-868-7170. http://co.pinal.az.us
Will search UCC records. Will do state tax lien search. Real estate record owner searches available. The Recorder's office does inquiries by grantor/grantee name. **Online Access:** Grantor/Grantee, Tax Bill, Tax Lien, Tax Sales Records. Access to the county recorder's index is available free at http://co.pinal.az.us/recorder/docsearch.asp. Also, online access to the county treasurer's database of tax liens, tax bills, and tax sales is available free at http://co.pinal.az.us/treasurer. Click on appropriate "Tax Searches" button. **Other Phone Numbers:** Assessor 520-868-6361; Treasurer 520-868-6425; Elections 520-868-6236.

Santa Cruz County

County Recorder, 2150 N. Congress, County Complex, Nogales, AZ 85621. 520-761-7800 x3037; Fax 520-761-7938.
Will search UCC records. This agency will not do a tax lien search. Will not search real estate records. **Other Phone Numbers:** Assessor 520-761-7938 x3008.

Yavapai County

County Recorder, 1015 Fair St, Room 228, Prescott, AZ 86305. 928-771-3244; Fax 928-771-3258. www.co.yavapai.az.us/departments/recorder/RecorderMain.asp
A second office is located at 10 S 6th St, Cottonwood AZ 86326, phone 928-639-5807, fax: 928-639-5812. Will search UCC records. Will not perform "open-ended" real estate records searches. **Online Access:** Assessor, Real Estate, Recording Records. Access to the recording office iCRIS database is available free at http://icris.co.yavapai.az.us/splash.jsp. Records from 1976 to present; images from 1986 to present. Also, assessor and land records on the County Geographic Information Systems (GIS) database are available free online at www.co.yavapai.az.us/departments/gis/gisOnlineApps.asp. To search, choose a "session" in the "Locate Property Information" box. **Other Phone Numbers:** Assessor 520-771-3220; Treasurer 928-771-3233; Elections 928-771-3250; Voter Registration 928-771-3248.

Yuma County

County Recorder, 410 S Maiden Lane, Yuma, AZ 85364-2311. 928-373-6020 R/E Recording: 928-373-6029 UCC Recording: 928-373-6028; Fax 928-373-6024.
Will search UCC records. This agency will not do a tax lien search. Will not search real estate records. **Other Phone Numbers:** Assessor 928-373-6040; Treasurer 928-539-7781; Elections 928-329-2119; Vital Records 928-317-4530.

Arizona County Locator

You will usually be able to find the city name in the City/County Cross Reference below. In that case, it is a simple matter to determine the county from the cross reference. However, only the official US Postal Service city names are included in this index. There are an additional 40,000 place names that people use in their addresses. Therefore, we have also included a ZIP/City Cross Reference immediately following the City/County Cross Reference.

If you know the ZIP Code but the city name does not appear in the City/County Cross Reference index, look up the ZIP Code in the ZIP/City Cross Reference, find the city name, then look up the city name in the City/County Cross Reference. For example, you want to know the county for an address of Menands, NY 12204. There is no "Menands" in the City/County Cross Reference. The ZIP/City Cross Reference shows that ZIP Codes 12201-12288 are for the city of Albany. Looking back in the City/County Cross Reference, Albany is in Albany County.

City/County Cross Reference

AGUILA Maricopa
AJO Pima
ALPINE Apache
AMADO (85645) Pima(85), Santa Cruz(14)
ANTHEM Maricopa
APACHE JUNCTION Pinal
ARIVACA Pima
ARIZONA CITY Pinal
ARLINGTON Maricopa
ASH FORK Yavapai
AVONDALE Maricopa
BAGDAD Yavapai
BAPCHULE Pinal
BELLEMONT Coconino
BENSON (85602) Cochise(93), Pima(6)
BISBEE Cochise
BLACK CANYON CITY Yavapai
BLUE Greenlee
BLUE GAP Navajo
BOUSE La Paz
BOWIE Cochise
BUCKEYE Maricopa
BULLHEAD CITY Mohave
BYLAS Graham
CAMERON Coconino
CAMP VERDE Yavapai
CAREFREE Maricopa
CASA GRANDE Pinal
CASHION Maricopa
CATALINA Pima
CAVE CREEK Maricopa
CENTRAL Graham
CHAMBERS Apache
CHANDLER Maricopa
CHANDLER HEIGHTS Maricopa
CHINLE Apache
CHINO VALLEY Yavapai
CHLORIDE Mohave
CIBICUE Navajo
CIBOLA La Paz
CLARKDALE Yavapai
CLAY SPRINGS Navajo
CLAYPOOL Gila
CLIFTON Greenlee
COCHISE Cochise
COLORADO CITY Mohave
CONCHO Apache
CONGRESS Yavapai
COOLIDGE Pinal
CORNVILLE Yavapai
CORTARO Pima
COTTONWOOD Yavapai
CROWN KING Yavapai
DATELAND Yuma
DENNEHOTSO Apache
DEWEY Yavapai
DOLAN SPRINGS Mohave
DOUGLAS Cochise
DRAGOON Cochise
DUNCAN Greenlee
EAGAR Apache
EDEN Graham
EHRENBERG La Paz
EL MIRAGE Maricopa
ELFRIDA Cochise
ELGIN Santa Cruz

ELOY Pinal
FLAGSTAFF Coconino
FLORENCE Pinal
FOREST LAKES Coconino
FORT APACHE Navajo
FORT DEFIANCE Apache
FORT HUACHUCA Cochise
FORT MCDOWELL Maricopa
FORT MOHAVE Mohave
FORT THOMAS Graham
FOUNTAIN HILLS Maricopa
FREDONIA Coconino
GADSDEN Yuma
GANADO Apache
GILA BEND Maricopa
GILBERT Maricopa
GLENDALE Maricopa
GLOBE Gila
GOLDEN VALLEY Mohave
GOODYEAR Maricopa
GRAND CANYON Coconino
GRAY MOUNTAIN Coconino
GREEN VALLEY Pima
GREER Apache
HACKBERRY Mohave
HAPPY JACK Coconino
HAYDEN Gila
HEBER Navajo
HEREFORD Cochise
HIGLEY Maricopa
HOLBROOK Navajo
HOTEVILLA Navajo
HOUCK Apache
HUACHUCA CITY Cochise
HUALAPAI Mohave
HUMBOLDT Yavapai
INDIAN WELLS Navajo
IRON SPRINGS Yavapai
JEROME Yavapai
JOSEPH CITY Navajo
KAIBITO Coconino
KAYENTA Navajo
KEAMS CANYON Navajo
KEARNY Pinal
KINGMAN Mohave
KIRKLAND Yavapai
KYKOTSMOVI VILLAGE Navajo
LAKE HAVASU CITY Mohave
LAKE MONTEZUMA Yavapai
LAKESIDE Navajo
LAVEEN Maricopa
LEUPP Coconino
LITCHFIELD PARK Maricopa
LITTLEFIELD Mohave
LUKACHUKAI Apache
LUKE AFB Maricopa
LUKEVILLE Pima
LUPTON Apache
MAMMOTH Pinal
MANY FARMS Apache
MARANA (85653) Pima(87), Pinal(12)
MARBLE CANYON Coconino
MARICOPA Pinal
MAYER Yavapai
MC NARY Apache
MC NEAL Cochise

MEADVIEW Mohave
MESA Maricopa
MIAMI Gila
MOHAVE VALLEY Mohave
MORENCI Greenlee
MORMON LAKE Coconino
MORRISTOWN Maricopa
MOUNT LEMMON Pima
MUNDS PARK Coconino
NACO Cochise
NAZLINI Apache
NEW RIVER Maricopa
NOGALES Santa Cruz
NORTH RIM Coconino
NUTRIOSO Apache
OATMAN Mohave
ORACLE Pinal
OVERGAARD Navajo
PAGE Coconino
PALO VERDE Maricopa
PARADISE VALLEY Maricopa
PARKER La Paz
PARKS Coconino
PATAGONIA Santa Cruz
PAULDEN Yavapai
PAYSON Gila
PEACH SPRINGS Mohave
PEARCE Cochise
PEORIA Maricopa
PERIDOT Gila
PETRIFIED FOREST NATL PK Apache
PHOENIX Maricopa
PICACHO Pinal
PIMA Graham
PINE Gila
PINEDALE Navajo
PINETOP Navajo
PINON Navajo
PIRTLEVILLE Cochise
POLACCA Navajo
POMERENE Cochise
POSTON La Paz
PRESCOTT Yavapai
PRESCOTT VALLEY Yavapai
QUARTZSITE La Paz
QUEEN CREEK (85242) Pinal(52), Maricopa(47)
RED ROCK Pinal
RED VALLEY Apache
RILLITO Pima
RIMROCK Yavapai
RIO RICO Santa Cruz
RIO VERDE Maricopa
ROCK POINT Apache
ROLL Yuma
ROOSEVELT Gila
ROUND ROCK Apache
SACATON Pinal
SAFFORD Graham
SAHUARITA Pima
SAINT DAVID Cochise
SAINT JOHNS Apache
SAINT MICHAELS Apache
SALOME La Paz
SAN CARLOS Gila
SAN LUIS Yuma

SAN MANUEL Pinal
SAN SIMON Cochise
SANDERS Apache
SASABE Pima
SAWMILL Apache
SCOTTSDALE Maricopa
SECOND MESA Navajo
SEDONA (86351) Yavapai(96), Coconino(3)
SELIGMAN Yavapai
SELLS Pima
SHONTO Navajo
SHOW LOW Navajo
SIERRA VISTA Cochise
SKULL VALLEY Yavapai
SNOWFLAKE Navajo
SOLOMON Graham
SOMERTON Yuma
SONOITA (85637) Santa Cruz(80), Pima(20)
SPRINGERVILLE Apache
STANFIELD Pinal
SUN CITY Maricopa
SUN CITY WEST Maricopa
SUN VALLEY Navajo
SUPAI Coconino
SUPERIOR Pinal
SURPRISE Maricopa
TACNA (85352) Maricopa(90), Yuma(9)
TAYLOR Navajo
TEEC NOS POS Apache
TEMPE Maricopa
TEMPLE BAR MARINA Mohave
THATCHER Graham
TOLLESON Maricopa
TOMBSTONE Cochise
TONALEA Coconino
TONOPAH Maricopa
TONTO BASIN Gila
TOPAWA Pima
TOPOCK Mohave
TORTILLA FLAT Maricopa
TSAILE Apache
TUBA CITY Coconino
TUBAC Santa Cruz
TUCSON Pima
TUMACACORI Santa Cruz
VAIL Pima
VALENTINE Mohave
VALLEY FARMS Pinal
VERNON Apache
WADDELL Maricopa
WELLTON Yuma
WENDEN La Paz
WHITE MOUNTAIN LAKE Navajo
WHITERIVER Navajo
WICKENBURG Maricopa
WIKIEUP Mohave
WILLCOX Cochise
WILLIAMS Coconino
WILLOW BEACH Mohave
WINDOW ROCK Apache
WINKELMAN (85292) Pinal(71), Gila(28)
WINSLOW Navajo
WITTMANN Maricopa
WOODRUFF Navajo

YARNELL Yavapai   YOUNGTOWN Maricopa   YUMA Yuma
YOUNG Gila   YUCCA Mohave

ZIP/City Cross Reference

ZIP	City	ZIP	City	ZIP	City	ZIP	City
85000-85086	PHOENIX	85349-85349	SAN LUIS	85633-85633	SASABE	86052-86052	NORTH RIM
85086-85086	ANTHEM	85350-85350	SOMERTON	85634-85634	SELLS	86053-86053	KAIBITO
85087-85087	NEW RIVER	85351-85351	SUN CITY	85635-85636	SIERRA VISTA	86054-86054	SHONTO
85098-85099	PHOENIX	85352-85352	TACNA	85637-85637	SONOITA	86301-86305	PRESCOTT
85201-85216	MESA	85353-85353	TOLLESON	85638-85638	TOMBSTONE	86312-86312	PRESCOTT VALLEY
85217-85220	APACHE JUNCTION	85354-85354	TONOPAH	85639-85639	TOPAWA	86313-86313	PRESCOTT
85221-85221	BAPCHULE	85355-85355	WADDELL	85640-85640	TUMACACORI	86314-86314	PRESCOTT VALLEY
85222-85222	CASA GRANDE	85356-85356	WELLTON	85641-85641	VAIL	86320-86320	ASH FORK
85223-85223	ARIZONA CITY	85357-85357	WENDEN	85643-85644	WILLCOX	86321-86321	BAGDAD
85224-85226	CHANDLER	85358-85358	WICKENBURG	85645-85645	AMADO	86322-86322	CAMP VERDE
85227-85227	CHANDLER HEIGHTS	85359-85359	QUARTZSITE	85646-85646	TUBAC	86323-86323	CHINO VALLEY
85228-85228	COOLIDGE	85360-85360	WIKIEUP	85648-85648	RIO RICO	86324-86324	CLARKDALE
85230-85230	CASA GRANDE	85361-85361	WITTMANN	85650-85650	SIERRA VISTA	86325-86325	CORNVILLE
85231-85231	ELOY	85362-85362	YARNELL	85652-85652	CORTARO	86326-86326	COTTONWOOD
85232-85232	FLORENCE	85363-85363	YOUNGTOWN	85653-85653	MARANA	86327-86327	DEWEY
85233-85234	GILBERT	85364-85369	YUMA	85654-85654	RILLITO	86329-86329	HUMBOLDT
85235-85235	HAYDEN	85371-85371	POSTON	85655-85655	DOUGLAS	86330-86330	IRON SPRINGS
85236-85236	HIGLEY	85372-85373	SUN CITY	85662-85662	NOGALES	86331-86331	JEROME
85237-85237	KEARNY	85374-85374	SURPRISE	85670-85670	FORT HUACHUCA	86332-86332	KIRKLAND
85239-85239	MARICOPA	85375-85376	SUN CITY WEST	85671-85671	SIERRA VISTA	86333-86333	MAYER
85240-85240	MESA	85377-85377	CAREFREE	85700-85737	TUCSON	86334-86334	PAULDEN
85241-85241	PICACHO	85378-85379	SURPRISE	85738-85738	CATALINA	86335-86335	RIMROCK
85242-85242	QUEEN CREEK	85380-85385	PEORIA	85739-85777	TUCSON	86336-86336	SEDONA
85244-85244	CHANDLER	85387-85387	SURPRISE	85901-85902	SHOW LOW	86337-86337	SELIGMAN
85245-85245	RED ROCK	85390-85390	WICKENBURG	85911-85911	CIBICUE	86338-86338	SKULL VALLEY
85246-85246	CHANDLER	85501-85502	GLOBE	85912-85912	WHITE MOUNTAIN LAKE	86339-86341	SEDONA
85247-85247	SACATON	85530-85530	BYLAS	85920-85920	ALPINE	86342-86342	LAKE MONTEZUMA
85248-85249	CHANDLER	85531-85531	CENTRAL	85922-85922	BLUE	86343-86343	CROWN KING
85250-85252	SCOTTSDALE	85532-85532	CLAYPOOL	85923-85923	CLAY SPRINGS	86351-86351	SEDONA
85253-85253	PARADISE VALLEY	85533-85533	CLIFTON	85924-85924	CONCHO	86401-86402	KINGMAN
85254-85262	SCOTTSDALE	85534-85534	DUNCAN	85925-85925	EAGAR	86403-86406	LAKE HAVASU CITY
85263-85263	RIO VERDE	85535-85535	EDEN	85926-85926	FORT APACHE	86411-86411	HACKBERRY
85264-85264	FORT MCDOWELL	85536-85536	FORT THOMAS	85927-85927	GREER	86412-86412	HUALAPAI
85266-85267	SCOTTSDALE	85539-85539	MIAMI	85928-85928	HEBER	86413-86413	GOLDEN VALLEY
85268-85269	FOUNTAIN HILLS	85540-85540	MORENCI	85929-85929	LAKESIDE	86426-86427	FORT MOHAVE
85271-85271	SCOTTSDALE	85541-85541	PAYSON	85930-85930	MC NARY	86429-86430	BULLHEAD CITY
85272-85272	STANFIELD	85542-85542	PERIDOT	85931-85931	FOREST LAKES	86431-86431	CHLORIDE
85273-85273	SUPERIOR	85543-85543	PIMA	85932-85932	NUTRIOSO	86432-86432	LITTLEFIELD
85274-85277	MESA	85544-85544	PINE	85933-85933	OVERGAARD	86433-86433	OATMAN
85278-85278	APACHE JUNCTION	85545-85545	ROOSEVELT	85934-85934	PINEDALE	86434-86434	PEACH SPRINGS
85279-85279	FLORENCE	85546-85546	SAFFORD	85935-85935	PINETOP	86435-86435	SUPAI
85280-85289	TEMPE	85547-85547	PAYSON	85936-85936	SAINT JOHNS	86436-86436	TOPOCK
85290-85290	TORTILLA FLAT	85548-85548	SAFFORD	85937-85937	SNOWFLAKE	86437-86437	VALENTINE
85291-85291	VALLEY FARMS	85550-85550	SAN CARLOS	85938-85938	SPRINGERVILLE	86438-86438	YUCCA
85292-85292	WINKELMAN	85551-85551	SOLOMON	85939-85939	TAYLOR	86439-86439	BULLHEAD CITY
85296-85299	GILBERT	85552-85552	THATCHER	85940-85940	VERNON	86440-86440	MOHAVE VALLEY
85301-85308	GLENDALE	85553-85553	TONTO BASIN	85941-85941	WHITERIVER	86441-86441	DOLAN SPRINGS
85309-85309	LUKE AFB	85554-85554	YOUNG	85942-85942	WOODRUFF	86442-86442	BULLHEAD CITY
85310-85318	GLENDALE	85601-85601	ARIVACA	86001-86011	FLAGSTAFF	86443-86443	TEMPLE BAR MARINA
85320-85320	AGUILA	85602-85602	BENSON	86015-86015	BELLEMONT	86444-86444	MEADVIEW
85321-85321	AJO	85603-85603	BISBEE	86016-86016	GRAY MOUNTAIN	86445-86445	WILLOW BEACH
85322-85322	ARLINGTON	85605-85605	BOWIE	86017-86017	MUNDS PARK	86446-86446	MOHAVE VALLEY
85323-85323	AVONDALE	85606-85606	COCHISE	86018-86018	PARKS	86502-86502	CHAMBERS
85324-85324	BLACK CANYON CITY	85607-85608	DOUGLAS	86020-86020	CAMERON	86503-86503	CHINLE
85325-85325	BOUSE	85609-85609	DRAGOON	86021-86021	COLORADO CITY	86504-86504	FORT DEFIANCE
85326-85326	BUCKEYE	85610-85610	ELFRIDA	86022-86022	FREDONIA	86505-86505	GANADO
85327-85327	CAVE CREEK	85611-85611	ELGIN	86023-86023	GRAND CANYON	86506-86506	HOUCK
85328-85328	CIBOLA	85613-85613	FORT HUACHUCA	86024-86024	HAPPY JACK	86507-86507	LUKACHUKAI
85329-85329	CASHION	85614-85614	GREEN VALLEY	86025-86025	HOLBROOK	86508-86508	LUPTON
85331-85331	CAVE CREEK	85615-85615	HEREFORD	86028-86028	PETRIFIED FOR, NATL PK	86509-86509	CHAMBERS
85332-85332	CONGRESS	85616-85616	HUACHUCA CITY	86029-86029	SUN VALLEY	86510-86510	PINON
85333-85333	DATELAND	85617-85617	MC NEAL	86030-86030	HOTEVILLA	86511-86511	SAINT MICHAELS
85334-85334	EHRENBERG	85618-85618	MAMMOTH	86031-86031	INDIAN WELLS	86512-86512	SANDERS
85335-85335	EL MIRAGE	85619-85619	MOUNT LEMMON	86032-86032	JOSEPH CITY	86514-86514	TEEC NOS POS
85336-85336	GADSDEN	85620-85620	NACO	86033-86033	KAYENTA	86515-86515	WINDOW ROCK
85337-85337	GILA BEND	85621-85621	NOGALES	86034-86034	KEAMS CANYON	86520-86520	BLUE GAP
85338-85338	GOODYEAR	85622-85622	GREEN VALLEY	86035-86035	LEUPP	86535-86535	DENNEHOTSO
85339-85339	LAVEEN	85623-85623	ORACLE	86036-86036	MARBLE CANYON	86538-86538	MANY FARMS
85340-85340	LITCHFIELD PARK	85624-85624	PATAGONIA	86038-86038	MORMON LAKE	86540-86540	NAZLINI
85341-85341	LUKEVILLE	85625-85625	PEARCE	86039-86039	KYKOTSMOVI VILLAGE	86544-86544	RED VALLEY
85342-85342	MORRISTOWN	85626-85626	PIRTLEVILLE	86040-86040	PAGE	86545-86545	ROCK POINT
85343-85343	PALO VERDE	85627-85627	POMERENE	86042-86042	POLACCA	86547-86547	ROUND ROCK
85344-85344	PARKER	85628-85628	NOGALES	86043-86043	SECOND MESA	86549-86549	SAWMILL
85345-85345	PEORIA	85629-85629	SAHUARITA	86044-86044	TONALEA	86556-86556	TSAILE
85346-85346	QUARTZSITE	85630-85630	SAINT DAVID	86045-86045	TUBA CITY		
85347-85347	ROLL	85631-85631	SAN MANUEL	86046-86046	WILLIAMS		
85348-85348	SALOME	85632-85632	SAN SIMON	86047-86047	WINSLOW		

Arkansas

General Help Numbers:

Governor's Office
State Capitol, #250   501-682-2345
Little Rock, AR 72201   Fax 501-682-3597
www.accessarkansas.org/governor   8AM-5PM

Attorney General's Office
323 Center St #200   501-682-2007
Little Rock, AR 72201   Fax 501-682-8084
www.ag.state.ar.us   8AM-5PM

State Court Administrator
625 Marshall Street, 1100 Justice Bldg   501-682-9400
Little Rock, AR 72201-1078   Fax 501-682-9410
www.courts.state.ar.us/courts/aoc.html   8AM-5PM

State Archives
State Archives   501-682-6900
One Capitol Mall
Little Rock, AR 72201   8AM-4:30PM M-SA
www.ark-ives.com/

State Specifics:

Capital: Little Rock
                                  Pulaski County

Time Zone: CST

Number of Counties: 75

Population: 2,692,090

Web Site: www.state.ar.us

State Agencies

Criminal Records

Arkansas State Police, Identification Bureau, #1 State Police Plaza Dr, Little Rock, AR 72209; 501-618-8500, 501-618-8404 (Fax), 8AM-4:30PM.

www.asp.state.ar.us

Note: A sexual offender registrant list is not available online.

Indexing & Storage: Records are available for the past 25 years. Older records are located in the off-site State Archives. It takes 2-3 weeks before new records are available for inquiry. Records are indexed on fingerprint cards. 58% of arrests in database have final dispositions recorded, 77% for those arrests in last 5 years.

Searching: You must use the Bureau's request form. Include the following in your request: notarized release from subject, name, date of birth, sex, Social Security Number, driver's license number. Fingerprints are not required, but may be included. 100% of the arrest records are fingerprint-supported. Records without dispositions are not released.

Access by: mail, in person.

Fee & Payment: The fee is $15.00 per record. Fee payee: Arkansas State Police. Prepayment required. Personal checks accepted, credit cards are not.

Mail search: Turnaround time: 5 to 7 days. A self addressed stamped envelope is requested.

In person search: Bring in signed, notarized release. If applicant is subject, record is released immediately, otherwise it is mailed back.

Corporation Records
Fictitious Name
Limited Liability Company Records
Limited Partnerships

Secretary of State, Corporation Department-Aegon Bldg, 501 Woodlane, Rm 310, Little Rock, AR

72201-1094; 501-682-3409, 888-233-0325, 501-682-3437 (Fax), 8AM-5PM.

www.sosweb.state.ar.us/corps

Indexing & Storage: Records are available from late 1800's on. Corporation records are on computer from 1987 on. Prior records, such as dissolved corporations, may be in paper files. New records are available for inquiry immediately. Records are indexed on inhouse computer, file folders.

Searching: Franchise tax information is not released except for names and addressees of parties involved and certain information about the shares of stock. Include the following in your request: full name of business. In addition to the articles of incorporation, corporation records include the following information: Prior (Merged) names, Reserved names, Good standing. Officers listed on franchise tax form is now public information.

Access by: mail, phone, in person, online.

Fee & Payment: There are no search fees. Certification of records costs $5.00. Fee payee: Secretary of State. Prepayment required. Personal checks accepted. No credit cards accepted.

Mail search: Turnaround time: same day if possible. Call first for copy fees. Records prior to 1988 will take longer to search. No self addressed stamped envelope is required. Copies cost $.50 per page.

Phone search: They will give incorporation dates, history, agent name, and status over the phone.

In person search: Copies cost $.50 per page.

Online search: The Internet site permits free searching of corporation records. You can search by name, registered agent, or filing number.

Other access: Bulk release of records is available for $.50 per page. Contact Julie Butler at 501-682-3409 for details.

Trademarks/Servicemarks

Secretary of State, Trademarks Section-Aegon Bldg, 501 Woodlane, #310, Little Rock, AR 72201; 501-682-3409, 888-233-0325, 501-682-3437 (Fax), 8AM-5PM.

www.sosweb.state.ar.us/corps/trademk

Indexing & Storage: Records are available from the 1950s. It takes 2 to 3 days before new records are available for inquiry. Records are indexed on inhouse computer.

Searching: Include the following in your request: name.

Access by: mail, phone, in person, online.

Fee & Payment: There is no search fee, copy fees are $.50 per copy. Fee payee: Secretary of State. Prepayment required. Personal checks accepted. No credit cards accepted.

Mail search: Turnaround time: 3 to 4 working days. No self addressed stamped envelope is required.

Phone search: They will give information over the phone.

In person search: Turnaround time is within a few minutes, there is an in-house terminal available to the public.

Online search: Searching is available at no fee over the Internet site. Search by name, owner, city, or filing number. You can also search via e-mail at corprequest@sosmail.state.ar.us.

Other access: Records can be provided in bulk for $.50 per page. Contact Julie Butler at 501-682-3409 for details.

Uniform Commercial Code Federal Tax Liens

UCC Division, Secretary of State-Aegon Bldg, 501 Woodlane, Rm 310, Little Rock, AR 72201-1094; 501-682-5078, 501-682-3500 (Fax), 8AM-5PM.

www.sosweb.state.ar.us

Indexing & Storage: Records are available from 1962. Records are indexed on cards. You can make requests by fax, but they will be returned by mail. Records are not searched by phone, but they will inform if there is anything on file.

Searching: Use search request form UCC-11. A search includes tax liens on businesses, via a lien search certificate. Federal tax liens on individuals and all state tax liens (AKA municipal judgments before 1978) are filed at the county. Include the following in your request: debtor name.

Access by: mail, fax, in person.

Fee & Payment: A lien search certificate is $10.00. Photostat copies of financing statements are $10.00 for the first page, $.50 each additional, maximum $100.00. The fee for certification of a copy of a filed financing statement is $1.00. Fee payee: Secretary of State. Prepayment required. Personal checks accepted. No credit cards accepted.

Mail search: Turnaround time: 1 to 2 days. No self addressed stamped envelope is required.

Fax search: There is an additional fee of $5.00 plus $.50 per page.

In person search: Walk-in customers may view the index cards for no charge.

State Tax Liens

Records not maintained by a state level agency.

Note: Records are at the county level.

Sales Tax Registrations

Finance & Administration Department, Sales & Use Tax Office, PO Box 1272, Little Rock, AR 72203; 501-682-7104, 501-682-7900 (Fax), 8AM-4:30PM.

www.state.ar.us/dfa/taxes/salestax

Indexing & Storage: Records are available from the 1940s.

Searching: This agency will only confirm that a business is registered. They will provide no other information. All searches are based upon tax permit number

Access by: mail, phone, fax, in person.

Mail search: Turnaround time: 3 to 5 days. A self addressed stamped envelope is requested. No fee for mail request.

Phone search: No fee for telephone request. This is the recommended search request method.

Fax search: Fax searching available.

In person search: No fee for request.

Birth Certificates

Arkansas Department of Health, Division of Vital Records, 4815 W Markham St, Slot 44, Little Rock, AR 72205; 501-661-2174, 501-661-2336 (Message Number), 506-661-2726 (Credit Card Line), 800-637-9314 (Toll Free), 501-663-2832 (Fax), 8AM-4:30PM.

www.healthyarkansas.com

Note: Thre types of records are available; certification copy, actual copy, and wallet size copy.

Indexing & Storage: Records are available from 1914 on. New records are available for inquiry immediately. Records are indexed on microfiche, inhouse computer.

Searching: Must have a signed release from person of record if requester is not a member of parents, grandparents or spouse. Include your name, address and signature on the request. Include the following in your request: full name, names of parents, mother's maiden name, date of birth, place of birth, relationship to person of record, reason for information request. Also include your phone number.

Access by: mail, phone, fax, in person.

Fee & Payment: The fee is $8.00 for the first copy and $5.00 for each add'l of same record. Add $5.00 if you use a credit card. Fee payee: Division of Vital Records. Prepayment required. Personal checks accepted. Credit cards accepted: MasterCard, Visa, AmEx, Discover.

Mail search: Turnaround time: 3 weeks. No self addressed stamped envelope is required.

Phone search: You must use a credit card. Turnaround time is 1 week.

Fax search: Fax requests require the use of a credit card or prepayment. No certificates may be faxed back. Turnaround time is 1 week.

In person search: Turnaround time: While you wait.

Other access: Research projects require the approval of the director.

Expedited service: Expedited service is available for mail, phone and fax searches. Turnaround time: next day. Add $21.25 for use of credit card and for express delivery. Overnight express is available.

Death Records

Arkansas Department of Health, Division of Vital Records, 4815 W Markham St, Slot 44, Little Rock, AR 72205; 501-661-2174, 501-661-2336 (Message number), 501-661-2726 (Credit Card Line), 501-663-2832 (Fax), 8AM-4:30PM.

www.healthyarkansas.com

Note: This agency does not hold the actual records, but does have an index of all deaths since 1914 and some death index records for Fort Smith and Little Rock prior to 1914.

Indexing & Storage: Records are available from 1914 on. New records are available for inquiry immediately. Records are indexed on microfiche, inhouse computer.

Searching: Must have a signed release from immediate family member if requester is not a member of family. Include the following in your request: full name, date of death, place of death, relationship to person of record, reason for information request, wife's maiden name. Include requester's signature and phone number.

Access by: mail, phone, fax, in person.

Fee & Payment: The fee is $8.00 for the first copy and $3.00 for each add'l of same record. Add $5.00 if you use a credit card. Fee payee: Division of Vital Records. Prepayment required. Personal checks accepted. Credit cards accepted: MasterCard, Visa, AmEx, Discover.

Mail search: Turnaround time: 3 weeks. Turnaround time with a credit card is 1 week. No self addressed stamped envelope is required.

Phone search: You must use a credit card.

Fax search: You must use a credit card or prepay before record is sent.

In person search: Turnaround time is usually 1 to 2 hours.

Expedited service: Expedited service is available for mail, phone and fax searches. Turnaround time: overnight delivery. Add $21.25 for delivery and use of credit card.

Marriage Certificates

Arkansas Department of Health, Division of Vital Records, 4815 W Markham St, Slot 44, Little Rock, AR 72205; 501-661-2174, 501-661-2336 (Message Number), 501-661-2726 (Credit Card Line), 501-663-2832 (Fax), 8AM-4:30PM.

www.healthyarkansas.com

Indexing & Storage: Records are available from 1917 on. New records are available for inquiry immediately. Records are indexed on microfiche, inhouse computer.

Searching: Must have a signed release from person of record if requester is not a member of immediate family. Include the following in your request: full names of husband and wife, registration number, date of marriage, place or county of marriage, wife's maiden name. Requester must sign request and provide phone number.

Access by: mail, phone, fax, in person.

Fee & Payment: The fee is $8.00 for the first copy and $5.00 for each add'l of same record. Add $5.00 if you use a credit card. Fee payee: Division of Vital Records. Prepayment required. Personal checks accepted. Credit cards accepted: MasterCard, Visa, AmEx, Discover.

Mail search: Turnaround time: 3 weeks. Turnaround time with a credit card is 1 week. No self addressed stamped envelope is required.

Phone search: You may call in your request, but you must use a credit card. Turnaround time is 1 week.

Fax search: A credit card is required or must prepay before records sent.

In person search: Turnaround time is 30 minutes to an hour.

Expedited service: Expedited service is available for mail, phone and fax searches. Turnaround time: overnight delivery. Add $21.25 for use of credit card and express delivery.

Divorce Records

Arkansas Department of Health, Department of Vital Records, 4815 W Markham St, Slot 44, Little Rock, AR 72205; 501-661-2174, 501-661-2336 (Message Number), 501-661-2726 (Credit Card Line), 800-637-9314, 501-663-2832 (Fax), 8AM-4:30PM.

www.healthyarkansas.com

Indexing & Storage: Records are available from 1914 to present. New records are available for inquiry immediately.

Searching: Must have a signed release from person of record if requester is not a member of the immediate family. Include the following in your request: names of husband and wife, date of divorce, place of divorce. Signature of requester required.

Access by: mail, phone, fax, in person.

Fee & Payment: The fee is $8.00 for the first copy and $5.00 for each add'l of same record. Add $5.00 if you use a credit card. Fee payee: Division of Public Records. Prepayment required. Personal checks accepted. Credit cards accepted: MasterCard, Visa, AmEx, Discover.

Mail search: Turnaround time: 3 weeks. Turnaround time with a credit card is 1 week. No self addressed stamped envelope is required.

Phone search: You must use a credit card. Turnaround time is 1 week.

Fax search: A credit card or prepayment is required.

In person search: Turnaround time is within 1 hour.

Expedited service: Expedited service is available for mail, phone and fax searches. Turnaround time: overnight delivery. The fee of $21.25 includes the $5.00 credit card fee and express delivery.

Workers' Compensation Records

Workers Compensation Department, 324 Spring Street, PO Box 950, Little Rock, AR 72203-0950; 501-682-3930, 800-622-4472, 501-682-6761 (Fax), 8AM-4:30PM M-F.

www.awcc.state.ar.us

Indexing & Storage: Records are available from 1940's on. New records are available for inquiry immediately. Records are indexed on microfilm, index cards, inhouse computer.

Searching: Only written requests are accepted. You may fax a request, but it is returned by mail. Include the following in your request: claimant name, Social Security Number, place of employment at time of accident, file number (if known). The following data is not released: Social Security Numbers or medical information.

Access by: mail, phone, fax, in person, online.

Fee & Payment: The fee is $5.00 per name searched and $.50 per page for copies. Fee payee: Workers' Compensation Commission. An invoice is mailed with the results of the request. Personal checks accepted. No credit cards accepted.

Mail search: Turnaround time: 10 days. No self addressed stamped envelope is required.

Phone search: Records are available by phone.

Fax search: Same criteria as mail searching.

In person search: You may make copies at $.50 per page. You are allowed to look through the files without charge.

Online search: To perform an online claim search, one must be a subscriber to the Information Network of Arkansas (INA). Records are from May 1, 1997 forward. There is an annual $50 subscriber fee to INA. For more information, visit the web site at www.state.ar.us/ina.html.

Driver Records

Department of Driver Services, Driving Records Division, PO Box 1272, Room 1130, Little Rock, AR 72203-1272 (Courier: 1900 W 7th, #1130, Little Rock, AR 72201); 501-682-7207, 501-682-7908, 501-682-2075 (Fax), 8AM-4:30PM.

www.accessarkansas.org/dfa/driverservices

Note: Copies of tickets must be requested from the local jurisdiction where the ticket was issued.

Indexing & Storage: Records are available for 3 years for moving violations, 3 years for employment or insurance purposes and are retained indefinitely for departmental purposes. DWI and suspensions show until all requirements are met. Records are indexed on inhouse computer.

Searching: Arkansas requires signed authorization by the driver to obtain a driving record. Volume requesters must have these authorizations on file. Violations on an interstate highway not exceeding 75 mph won't show on records requested for insurance purposes. Include the following in your request: full name, driver's license number, date of birth. Driver's address is included as part of the search report for permissible requesters.

Access by: mail, in person, online.

Fee & Payment: Fees are $7.00 for insurance record and $10.00 for CDLs. There is a full charge for a "no record found." Fee payee: State of Arkansas, Driver Services. Prepayment required. Personal checks accepted. No credit cards accepted.

Mail search: Turnaround time: 24 hours. Requester must enclose written release, full name, DOB, driver's license number, and proper fees. No self addressed stamped envelope is required.

In person search: The state will process up to 5 requests while you wait.

Online search: Access is available through the Information Network of Arkansas (INA). The system offers both batch and interactive service. The system is only available to INA subscribers who have statutory rights to the data. The record fee is $8.00, or $11.00 for commercial drivers. Visit www.state.ar.us/ina.html.

Other access: High volume requesters use magnetic tape-to-tape for overnight access.

Vehicle Ownership
Vehicle Identification

Office of Motor Vehicles, MV Title Records, PO Box 1272, Room 1100, Little Rock, AR 72203 (Courier: 7th & Battery Sts, Ragland Bldg, Room 1100, Little Rock, AR 72201); 501-682-4692, 800-662-8247, 8AM-4:30PM.

www.accessarkansas.org/dfa

Indexing & Storage: Records are available from 1950 for titles; license plate records from 1968 on microfilm; plate number and name from 1981 on microfiche. It takes 4 to 6 weeks before new records are available for inquiry.

Searching: Vehicle registration information cannot be sold or used for solicitation purposes. Requesters that do not have DPPA approved purpose, cannot receive records with personal information, unless consent of subject is given. The following data is not released: Social Security Numbers or date of birth.

Access by: mail, phone, in person.

Fee & Payment: The fee for vehicle and/or ownership searches is $1.00 per copy and $1.00 per search. Fee payee: Department of Finance and Administration. Prepayment required. If mailing a check to open a new account, place "Attn: Search Account" on the request. If mailing an information request, place "Attn: Correspondence Desk" on the request. Personal checks accepted. No credit cards accepted.

Mail search: Turnaround time: 24 hours. No self addressed stamped envelope is required.

Phone search: Searching by phone is available for established accounts. A $25.00 deposit is required.

In person search: Turnaround time: while you wait.

Other access: The bulk purchase of records, except for recall or statistical purposes, is prohibited.

Accident Reports

Arkansas State Police, Accident Records Section, 1 State Police Plaza Drive, Little Rock, AR 72209; 501-618-8130, 501-618-8131 (Fax), 8AM-5PM.

www.asp.state.ar.us/ar/ar.html

Indexing & Storage: Records are available from 1958 to present. Records are on microfilm from 1958 to 1982, off-line storage 1982-1994, and on computer 1994 to present. It takes 5 to 10 days before new records are available for inquiry.

Searching: Include the following in your request: date of accident, location, name of at least on driver.

Access by: mail, phone, fax, in person.

Fee & Payment: The fee is $10.00 per record. There is no charge for a "no record found." Payment will be refunded. Fee payee: Arkansas State Police, Accident Records. Prepayment required. Personal checks accepted. No credit cards accepted.

Mail search: Turnaround time: 1 to 2 weeks. A self addressed stamped envelope is requested.

Phone search: Limited information is available.

Fax search: Records are available by fax.

In person search: Turnaround time is while you wait if 1994 or newer, otherwise 1-2 weeks.

Vessel Ownership
Vessel Registration

Office of Motor Vehicles, Boat Registration, PO Box 1272, Little Rock, AR 72203; 501-682-4692, 8AM-4:30PM.

www.accessarkansas.org/dfa

Note: Lien information may be filed at the Secretary of State.

Indexing & Storage: Records are available from 1980. All boats propelled by sail or machinery must be registered. Vessels are not titled in this state. New records are available for inquiry immediately.

Searching: This state considers that requests for boat information does not fall under DPPA, records are open to the public. Search by name or registration number or hull number.

Access by: mail, in person.

Fee & Payment: The search fee is $1.00 per search and $1.00 per copy of a record. Fee payee: Office of Motor Vehicles. Prepayment required. No credit cards accepted.

Mail search: Turnaround time: 2 weeks. No self addressed stamped envelope is required.

In person search: Records are usually obtained at once, unless they require extensive research.

Legislation Records

Elections Department, State Capitol, Room 026, Little Rock, AR 72201; 501-682-5070, 501-682-3408 (Fax), 8AM-5PM.

www.arkleg.state.ar.us

Note: This agency will not do any research; they will only respond to requests by act number.

Indexing & Storage: Records are available from 1909 to present.

Access by: mail, fax, in person, online.

Fee & Payment: You can purchase copies of bills for $.25 per page. They will return copies by Federal Express if you give your billing number. Fee payee: Secretary of State. Prepayment required. Personal checks accepted. No credit cards accepted.

Mail search: No self addressed stamped envelope is required.

Fax search: Fax searching available.

In person search: Searching is available in person.

Online search: Probably the best way to search is through the Internet site listed above. You may also search by subject matter.

Voter Registration
Access to Records is Restricted

Secretary of State, Voter Services, State Capitol, Room 026, Little Rock, AR 72201; 501-682-3526, 501-682-3548 (Fax), 8AM-5PM.

www.sosweb.state.ar.us/elect.html

Note: The state will sell the voter database for voting or election purposes. All individual search requests must be at the local County Clerk's office. The SSN will not be released.

GED Certificates

GED Testing, Dept of Workforce Education, #3 Capitol mall, Room 305D, Little Rock, AR 72201; 501-682-1978 (Main Number), 501-682-1982 (Fax).

www.work-ed.state.ar.us

Indexing & Storage: Records are available from 1980 forward. It takes on month before new records are available for inquiry.

Searching: For verification or for a copy of a transcript, all of the following is required: a signed release, name, year of test, date of birth, and Social Security Number.

Access by: mail, fax, in person.

Fee & Payment: There is no fee.

Mail search: Turnaround time is within a week. No self addressed stamped envelope is required.

Fax search: Turnaround time is next day, but results returned by mail.

In person search: Records can be accessed immediately.

Hunting License Information
Fishing License Information

Game & Fish Commission, Two Natural Resources Dr, Little Rock, AR 72205; 501-223-6300, 501-223-6425 (Fax), 8AM-4:30PM.

www.agfc.com

Note: Lists maintained here include fish farmers, put & take pay lakes, shell buyers, commercial game breeders, commercial shooting resorts, fur dealers, and bull frog permits.

Indexing & Storage: Records are available for 2 to 3 years then purged. It takes 4 days before new records are available for inquiry. Records are indexed on inhouse computer.

Searching: Must mention request is under the Freedom of Information Act. Include the following in your request: full name. Addresses are given and telephone numbers, if available.

Access by: mail, in person.

Fee & Payment: The search and copy fee is $2.00. Fee payee: Game & Fish Commission. Personal checks accepted. No credit cards accepted.

Mail search: Turnaround time: 1 to 2 days. No self addressed stamped envelope is required.

In person search: Some searches require 1 to 2 days to process.

Arkansas State Licensing Agencies

Licenses Searchable Online

Agriculture Education #32	www.as-is.org/directory/search_lic.html
Architect #6	www.state.ar.us/arch/search.html
Asbestos Abatement Inspector #28	www.adeq.state.ar.us/compsvs/webmaster/databases.htm
Asbestos Abatement Mgmt. Planner #28	www.adeq.state.ar.us/compsvs/webmaster/databases.htm
Asbestos Abatement Training Provider #28	www.adeq.state.ar.us/compsvs/webmaster/databases.htm
Asbestos Removal Worker #28	www.adeq.state.ar.us/compsvs/webmaster/databases.htm
Attorney #43	http://courts.state.ar.us/attylist/new/
Bank #38	www.sosweb.state.ar.us/corps/bkin
Business Education Teacher #32	www.as-is.org/directory/search_lic.html
Career Education Coordinator #32	www.as-is.org/directory/search_lic.html
Career Orientation Teacher #32	www.as-is.org/directory/search_lic.html
Cemetery, Perpetual Care #39	www.ark.org/arsec/database/dbsearch.cgi?dbname=7&LIMIT=20&LISTALL=ON
Child Care Provider #26	www.state.ar.us/childcare/search.html
Chiropractor #9	www.accessarkansas.org/asbce/search.html
Contractor #23	www.state.ar.us/clb/search.html
Cosmetologist #49	www.accessarkansas.org/cos/search.php
Cosmetology Instructor #49	www.accessarkansas.org/cos/search.php
Counselor, Professional #51	www.state.ar.us/abec/search.php
Dental Hygienist #11	www.asbde.org
Dentist #11	www.asbde.org
Electrologist #49	www.accessarkansas.org/cos/search.php
Electrolysis Instructor #49	www.accessarkansas.org/cos/search.php
Embalmer/Embalmer Apprentice #12	www.accessarkansas.org/fdemb/
Engineer/Engineer in Training #19	www.accessarkansas.org/pels/search.html
Fire Equipment Inspector #56	www.arfireprotection.org/roster/index.html
Fire Extinguisher Repairer #56	www.arfireprotection.org/roster/index.html
Fire Extinguisher Sprinkler Inspector #56	www.arfireprotection.org/roster/index.html
Funeral Director/Apprentice #12	www.accessarkansas.org/fdemb/
Funeral Home/Crematory #12	www.accessarkansas.org/fdemb/
Home Inspector #38	www.sosweb.state.ar.us/corps/homeinsp
Insurance Agency #38	www.sosweb.state.ar.us/corps/bkin
Insurance Sales Agent #2	www.accessarkansas.org/insurance/license/search.php
Investment Advisor #39	www.ark.org/arsec/database/search.html
Landscape Architect #6	www.state.ar.us/arch/search.html
Lobbyist #38	www.sosweb.state.ar.us/elect.html
Manicurist #49	www.accessarkansas.org/cos/search.php
Marriage & Family Therapist #51	www.state.ar.us/abec/search.php
Midwife Nurse #15	www.accessarkansas.org/nurse/registry/index.html
Mortgage Loan Broker/Company #39	www.ark.org/arsec/database/search.html
Motor Vehicle Dealer/Salesperson #55	www.armvc.com/mfg_dist/search.php
Motor Vehicle Mfg/Rep, New #55	www.armvc.com/mfg_dist/search.php
Notary Public #38	www.sosweb.state.ar.us/corps/notary
Nurse #15	www.accessarkansas.org/nurse/registry/index.html
Nurse Anesthetist #15	www.accessarkansas.org/nurse/registry/index.html
Nurse-LPN #15	www.accessarkansas.org/nurse/registry/index.html
Optician #50	www.ark.org/directory/detail2.cgi?ID-1050
Optometrist #16	www.odfinder.org/LicSearch.asp
Public Accountant-CPA #18	www.accessarkansas.org/asbpa
Real Estate Appraiser #37	www.asc.gov/content/category1/appr_by_state.asp
Real Estate Broker #37	www.accessarkansas.org/arec/db/
Real Estate Sales Agent #37	www.accessarkansas.org/arec/db/
School Counselor #32	www.as-is.org/directory/search_lic.html
School Principal/Admin/Super #32	www.as-is.org/directory/search_lic.html
Securities Agent #39	www.ark.org/arsec/database/search.html
Securities Broker/Dealer #39	www.ark.org/arsec/database/search.html
Social Worker #40	www.state.ar.us/swlb/search/index.html
Solid Waste Facility Operator #28	www.adeq.state.ar.us/compsvs/webmaster/databases.htm
Surveyor, Land #19	www.accessarkansas.org/pels/search.html
Surveyor-in-Training #19	www.accessarkansas.org/pels/search.html
Teacher #32	www.as-is.org/directory/search_lic.html
Waste Water Treatment Plant Oper. #28	www.adeq.state.ar.us/compsvs/webmaster/databases.htm

Licensing Quick Finder

Abstractor #48 870-942-8064
Acupuncturist #46 501-228-0644
Agricultural Consultant #33 501-225-1598
Agriculture Education #32 501-682-4695
Alcohol/Drug Abuse Treatment Program #25
....501-280-4504
Anesthetician #15 501-686-2200
Announcer, Athletic Event (Ring) #4 ...501-666-5544
Architect #6 501-682-3171
Armored Car Guard #42 501-618-8600
Asbestos Abatement Inspector #28 501-682-0718
Asbestos Abatement Management Planner #28
....501-682-0718
Asbestos Abatement Training Provider #28
....501-682-0718
Asbestos Removal Worker #28 501-682-0718
Athletic Manager #4 501-666-5544
Athletic Promoter/Matchmaker #4 501-666-5544
Attorney #43 501-682-6849
Auctioneer #5 501-682-1156
Audiologist #41 501-320-4319
Bail Bondsman #2 501-686-9050
Bank #38 501-682-3409
Barber Instructor #7 501-682-4035
Barber/Barber Technician #7 501-682-4035
Birthing Center #25 501-661-2518
Boiler Inspector/Installer/Repairer #27 ..501-682-4513
Boiler Operator #27 501-682-4513
Boxer #4 501-666-5544
Boxing/Wrestling Referee #4 501-666-5544
Burglar Alarm Systems Agent/Manager #42
....501-618-8600
Business Education Teacher #32 501-682-4695
Career Education Coordinator #32 501-682-4695
Career Orientation Teacher #32 501-682-4695
Cemetery, Perpetual Care #39 501-324-9260
Check Casher #10 501-244-9194
Child Care Provider #26 501-682-9699
Chiropractor #9 501-682-9015
Claims Adjuster #2 501-371-2750
Clinics, Health #25 501-661-2518
Collection Agency #10 501-376-9814
Collection Agency Collector/Mgr. #10 ..501-376-9814
Contractor #23 501-372-4661
Cosmetologist #49 501-682-2168
Cosmetology Instructor #49 501-682-2168
Counselor, Professional #51 870-235-4131
Court Reporter #8 501-682-6850
Dental Assistant #11 501-682-2085
Dental Hygienist #11 501-682-2085
Dentist #11 501-682-2085
Dietitian #29 ....501-221-0566 or 501-580-9294
Egg Grader #53 501-907-2400
Electrical Contractor #27 501-682-4549
Electrologist #49 501-682-2168

Electrolysis Instructor #49 501-682-2168
Elevator/Lifting Device Inspector #27 ...501-682-4531
Embalmer/Embalmer Apprentice #12 ..501-682-0574
Emergency Medical Technician #25 501-661-2262
Emergency Medical Technician-Paramedic #25
....501-661-2262
Employment Agency Manager #27 501-682-4505
Employment Agent/Counselor #27 501-682-4505
Engineer/Engineer in Training #19 501-682-2824
Exterminator #33 501-225-1598
Fire Equipment Inspector #56 501-661-7903
Fire Extinguisher Repairer #56 501-661-7903
Fire Extinguisher Sprinkler Inspector #56
....501-661-7903
Forester #20 501-296-1998
Funeral Director/Apprentice #12 501-682-0574
Funeral Home/Crematory #12 501-682-0574
Gas Fitter/Trainee #25 501-661-2242
Geologist #21 501-296-1877
Grain Warehouseman #33 501-225-1598
Greyhound Racing #36 501-682-1467
Handgun, Concealed #42 501-618-8600
Health Facility #25 501-661-2518
Hearing Instrument Dispenser #14 501-663-5869
HMO #25 501-661-2518
Home Health Agency #25 501-661-2518
Home Inspector #38 501-682-3409
Homebuilders #23 501-372-4661
Horse Racing #36 501-682-1467
Hospice Facility #25 501-661-2518
Hospital Maintenance Plumber #25 501-661-2242
Industrial Maintenance Electrician #27 .501-682-4549
Insurance Agency #38 501-682-3409
Insurance Sales Agent #2 501-371-2750
Investment Advisor #39 501-324-9260
Laboratory #25 501-661-2191
Landscape Architect #6 501-682-3393
Liquor Distributor #1 501-682-1105
Livestock Brand #53 501-907-2400
Livestock Dealer #53 501-907-2400
Lobbyist #38 501-682-1010
LPG Safety Supervisor #30 501-683-4100
Manicurist #49 501-682-2168
Manufactured Home Dealer/Mfg #54 ...501-324-9032
Manufactured Home Installer #54 501-324-9032
Manufactured Home Salesperson #54 ..501-324-9032
Marriage & Family Therapist #51 870-235-4131
Martial Arts #4 501-666-5544
Massage Therapy Technician (Masseur/Masseuse)
#22 501-534-4734
Medical Doctor/Surgeon #31 501-296-1802
Medicare Certified Facility #25 501-661-2201
Midwife Nurse #15 501-686-2200
Mortgage Loan Broker/Company #39 ..501-324-9260

Motor Vehicle Dealer/Salesperson, New #55
....501-682-1428
Motor Vehicle Dealer/Salesperson, Used #42
....501-618-8600
Motor Vehicle Mfg/Rep, New #55 501-682-1428
Notary Public #38 501-682-3409
Nurse #15 501-686-2200
Nurse Anesthetist #15 501-686-2200
Nurse-LPN #15 501-686-2200
Nurseryman #33 501-225-1598
Nursing Home Administrator #52 501-682-1873
Occupational Therapist/Assistant #31 .501-296-1802
Optician #50 870-572-2847
Optometrist #16 501-268-4351
Osteopathic Physician #31 501-296-1802
Permanent Cosmetic/Tattoo Artist #25 .501-661-2242
Pesticide Applicator #33 501-225-1598
Petroleum Dealer #30 501-683-4100
Pharmacist #17 501-682-0190
Pharmacist Intern #17 501-682-0190
Physical Therapist #3 501-228-7100
Podiatrist #34 501-664-3668
Polygraph Examiner #42 501-618-8600
Precious Metals Dealer #42 501-618-8600
Private Investigator #42 501-618-8600
Psychological Examiner #13 501-682-6167
Psychologist #13 501-682-6167
Public Accountant-CPA #18 501-682-1520
Pump Installer #45 501-682-1025
Radiologic Technician #25 501-661-2301
Real Estate Appraiser #37 501-683-8010
Real Estate Broker #37 501-683-8010
Real Estate Sales Agent #37 501-683-8010
Respiratory Care Practitioner #31 501-296-1802
School Counselor #32 501-682-4344
School Principal/Admin/Super #32 501-682-4344
Securities Agent #39 501-324-9260
Securities Broker/Dealer #39 501-324-9260
Security Guard #42 501-618-8600
Seed Dealer #33 501-225-1598
Septic Tank Cleaner #25 501-661-2242
Social Worker #40 501-372-5071
Solid Waste Facility Operator #28 501-682-0585
Speech Pathologist #41 501-320-4319
State Trooper #42 501-618-8600
Surveyor, Land #19 501-682-2824
Surveyor-in-Training #19 501-682-2824
Teacher #32 501-682-4695
Veterinarian #44 501-224-2836
Veterinary Technician #44 501-224-2836
Waste Water Treatment Plant Operator #28
....501-682-0998
Water Supply Operator #25 501-661-2242
Water Well Driller #45 501-682-1025
Wrestler #4 501-666-5544

Licensing Agency Information

#1 Alcoholic Beverage Control Division, 100 Main St, #503, Little Rock, AR 72201; 501-682-1105, Fax: 501-682-2221.

#2 Department of Insurance, Licensing Division, 1200 W 3rd St, Little Rock, AR 72201; 800-282-9134, Fax: 501-371-2618. www.accessarkansas.org/insurance/index.html. Email: Insurance.License@mail.state.ar.us. Search database at www.accessarkansas.org/ insurance/license/search.php

#3 Board of Physical Therapy, 9 Shackelford Plaza, #3, Little Rock, AR 72211; 501-228-7100, Fax: 501-228-5535.

#4 Athletic Com., 809 N Palm St, Little Rock, AR 72205-1946; 501-666-5544, Fax: 501-666-5546.

#5 Auctioneers Licensing Board, 101 E Capital, #112B, Little Rock, AR 72201; 501-682-1156, Fax: 501-682-1158. www.state.ar.us/directory/detail2.cgi?ID=962. Agency email: betty.king@mail.state.ar.us.

#6 Board of Architecture, 101 E Capitol, #208, Little Rock, AR 72201; 501-682-3171, Fax: 501-682-3172. www.accessarkansas.org/arch Agency email: arch@mac.state.ar.us. Search database: www.state.ar.us/arch/search.html

#7 Board of Barber Examiners, 103 E 7th St Rm 212, Little Rock, AR 72201-4512; 501-682-4035, Fax: 501-682-2806. www.state.ar.us/directory/detail2.cgi?ID=1044. Email: charles.kirkpatrick@mail.state.ar.us.

#8 Board of Certified Court Reporter Examiners, 625 Marshall St, Justice Bldg, Little Rock, AR 72201; 501-682-6850, Fax: 501-682-6877 c/o Renee Agency email: renee.herndon@mail.state.ar.us.

#9 Board of Chiropractic Examiners, 101 E Capital, #209, Little Rock, AR 72201; 501-682-9015, Fax: 501-682-9016. www.accessarkansas.org/asbce Agency email: ann.gates@mail.state.ar.us. Search database at www.accessarkansas.org/asbce/search.html

#10 Board of Collection Agencies, 523 S Louisiana St, #460, Little Rock, AR 72201; 501-376-9814, Fax: 501-372-5383.

#11 Board of Dental Examiners, 101 E Capitol Ave, #111, Little Rock, AR 72201; 501-682-2085, Fax: 501-682-3543. www.asbde.org Agency email: asbde@mail.state.ar.us. Search database at www.asbde.org

#12 Board of Embalmers & Funeral Directors, 101 E Capitol Ave, #113, Little Rock, AR 72201; 501-682-0574, Fax: 501-682-0575. www.accessarkansas.org/fdemb Search database at www.accessarkansas.org/fdemb

#13 Board of Examiners in Psychology, 101 E Capitol Ave, #415, Little Rock, AR 72201; 501-682-6167, Fax: 501-682-6165. www.accessarkansas.org/abep Agency email: janet.welsh@mail.state.ar.us.

#14 Board of Hearing Instrument Dispensers, 305 N Monroe, Little Rock, AR 72205; 501-663-5869, Fax: 501-663-6359.

#15 Board of Nursing, 1123 S University, University Tower Bldg, #800, Little Rock, AR 72204-1619; 501-686-2700, Fax: 501-686-2714. www.accessarkansas.org/nurse/ Search database at www.accessarkansas.org/nurse/registry/index.html

#16 Board of Optometry, 410 W Race St, Searcy, AR 72143; 501-268-4351, Fax: 501-268-5631. www.state.ar.us/opt/arkopt.html Agency email: hflippin@cswnet.com. Search database at www.odfinder.org/LicSearch.asp

#17 Board of Pharmacy, 101 E Capitol, #218, Little Rock, AR 72201; 501-682-0190, Fax: 501-682-0195. www.accessarkansas.org/asbp Agency email: sheila.castin@mail.state.ar.us.

#18 Board of Public Accountancy, 101 E Capitol, #430, Little Rock, AR 72201; 501-682-1520, Fax: 501-682-5538. www.accessarkansas.org/asbpa/

#19 Board of Registration for Engineers/Land Surveyors, PO Box 3750, Little Rock, AR 72203; 501-682-2824, Fax: 501-682-2827. www.state.ar.us/pels Agency email: joseph.clement@mail.state.ar.us. Search database at www.accessarkansas.org/pels/search.html

#20 Board of Registration for Foresters, PO Box 7424, Little Rock, AR 72217; 501-296-1998, Fax: 501-296-1949. http://members.aol.com/JOSTNIX/rf.htm. Agency email: robert.mcfarland@mail.state.ar.us.

#21 Board of Registration for Professional Geologists, 3815 W Roosevelt Rd, Little Rock, AR 72204; 501-296-1877, Fax: 501-663-7360. www.state.ar.us/agc/BOR.htm. Agency email: connie.rape@mail.state.ar.us.

#22 Board of Massage Therapy, 103 Airways (PO Box 20739), Hot Springs, AR 71903-0739; 501-623-0444, Fax: 501-623-4130.

#23 Contractors Licensing Board, 4100 Richards Road, North Little Rock, AR 72117; 501-372-4661, Fax: 501-372-2247. www.accessarkansas.org/clb/ Search database at www.state.ar.us/clb/search.html

#25 Department of Health, Bureau of Health Resources; Administration/Licencing, 5800 W. Tenth St, #400, Little Rock, AR 72205-3867; 501-661-2242, Fax: 501-280-4901.

#26 Department of Human Services, Division of Child Care & Early Childhood Education, PO Box 1437 Slot S140, Little Rock, AR 72203; 501-682-4891, Fax: 501-682-4897. www.accessarkansas.org/childcare. Agency email: Jennifer.Spriggs@mail.state.ar.us. Search database at www.state.ar.us/childcare/search.html

#27 Department of Labor, 10421 W Markham, Little Rock, AR 72205; 501-682-4500, Fax: 501-682-4535. www.accessarkansas.org/labor Agency email: becky.bryant@mail.state.ar.us.

#28 Department of Environmental Quality, 8001 National Dr, Little Rock, AR 72209; 501-682-0744, Fax: 501-682-0798. www.adeq.state.ar.us Agency email: hansen@adeq.state.ar.us. Search database at www.adeq.state.ar.us/compsvs/webmaster/databases.htm

#29 Dietetics Licensing Board, PO Box 1016, Little Rock, AR 72115; 501-221-0566, Fax: 501-843-0878.

#30 Liquefied Petroleum Gas Board, 3800 Richards Rd, North Little Rock, AR 72117; 501-683-4100.

#31 Medical Board, 2100 Riverside, Little Rock, AR 72202-1435; 501-296-1802, Fax: 501-296-1805. www.armedicalboard.org Agency email: asmb@mail.state.ar.us. They offer online verification using a modem system. To obtain more information on the program, fax a request including a contact name to the fax number listed above.

#32 Department of Education, Office of Teacher Education & Licensure, State Education Bldg, Rm 106, Capitol Mall #4, Little Rock, AR 72201; 501-682-4695, Fax: 501-682-4898. http://arkedu.state.ar.us/teachers Agency email: gmorris@arkedu.k12.ar.us. Search database at www.as-is.org/directory/search_lic.html

#33 Plant Board, PO Box 1069 (One Natural Resources Dr), Little Rock, AR 72203; 501-225-1598, Fax: 501-225-3590. www.plantboard.org

#34 Board of Podiatrical Medicine, 2001 Georgia Ave, Little Rock, AR 72207-5014; 501-664-3668, Fax: 501-666-3338.

#36 Racing Commission, PO Box 3076, Little Rock, AR 72203-3076; 501-682-1467, Fax: 501-682-5273. Agency email: bob.cohen@dfa.state.ar.us

#37 Real Estate Commission, 612 Summit St, Little Rock, AR 72201; 501-683-8010, Fax: 501-682-2729. www.state.ar.us/arec/frmain.htm Search database at www.accessarkansas.org/arec/db

#38 Secretary of State, 256 State Capitol, Little Rock, AR 72201; 501-682-3409, Fax: 501-682-3437. www.sosweb.state.ar.us/corps/ Search database at www.sosweb.state.ar.us/corps

#39 Securities Department, 201 W Markham, Heritage West Bldg, 3rd Fl, Little Rock, AR 72201; 501-324-9260, Fax: 501-324-9268. www.accessarkansas.org/arsec/ Search database at www.accessarkansas.org/asbce/search.html

#40 Social Work Licensing Board, 2020 W 3rd St #503, POB 2560381, Little Rock, AR 72225; 501-372-5071, Fax: 501-372-6301. www.accessarkansas.org/swlb. Agency email: swlb@mail.state.ar.us. Search database at www.state.ar.us/swlb/search/index.html.

#41 Speech Pathology & Audiology, Arkansas Children's Hospital, 800 Marshall St., Little Rock, AR 72202; 501-320-4319, Fax: 501-320-6881.
www.archildrens.org

#42 Regulartory Service Section, State Police Admin. Svcs. Section, #1 State Police Plaza Drive, Little Rock, AR 72209; 501-618-8608.
www.asp.state.ar.us

#43 Supreme Court, 625 Marshall, Justice Bldg, Little Rock, AR 72201; 501-682-6849, Fax: 501-682-6877.
http://courts.state.ar.us
Search data at http://courts.state.ar.us/attylist/new

#44 Veterinary Medical Examining Board, PO Box 8505, Little Rock, AR 72215; 501-224-2836, Fax: 501-224-1100.

#45 Waterwell Construction Commission, 101 E Capitol #350, Little Rock, AR 72201; 501-682-1025, Fax: 501-682-3991.
www.accessarkansas.org/aswcc

#46 Board of Acupuncture & Related Techniques, 5110 Kavanaugh Blvd, Little Rock, AR 72207; 501-228-0644.
www.state.ar.us/directory/detail2.cgi?ID=1254

#48 Abstractor's Board of Examiners, #5 Pinecrest Circle, Sheridan, AR 72150; 870-942-8064, Fax: 870-942-3101.
www.ark.org
Search database at
www.ark.org/directory/detail2.cgi?ID-1014

#49 Board of Cosmetology, 101 E Capitol #108, Little Rock, AR 72201; 501-682-2168.
www.accessarkansas.org/cos

#50 Board of Dispensing Opticians, Box 627, Helena, AR 72342; 870-572-2847, Fax: 870-572-2847.
www.ark.org
Search database at
www.ark.org/directory/detail2.cgi?ID-1050

#51 Board of Examiners for Counselors & Marriage/Family Therapists, 124 South Jackson #312 (PO Box 90), Magnolia, AR 71753; 870-901-7055, Fax: 870-234-1842.
www.accessarkansas.org/abec
Agency email: arboec@ipa.net.
Search database at
www.state.ar.us/abec/search.php

#52 Department of Human Services, 7th & Main Streets, Little Rock, AR 72203; 501-682-1001.
www.medicaid.state.ar.us/general/units/OLTC/index.htm

#53 Livestock & Poultry Commission, 1 Natural Resources Dr, PO Box 8505, Little Rock, AR 72215; 501-907-2400, Fax: 501-907-2425.

#54 Manufactured Home Commission, 523 S Louisiana #500, Little Rock, AR 72201; 501-324-9032, Fax: 501-324-9032.

#55 Motor Vehicle Commission, 101 E Capitol #210, Little Rock, AR 72201; 501-682-1428, Fax: 501-682-5573.
www.armvc.com
Agency email: amvc@mail.state.ar.us.
Search database at
www.armvc.com/mfg_dist/search.php

#56 Fire Protection Licensing Board, 7509 Cantrell Rd #103-A, Little Rock, AR 72207; 501-661-7903, Fax: 501-603-3540.
www.arfireprotection.org
Agency email: afplb@aristotle.net.
Search database at
www.arfireprotection.org/roster/index.html

Arkansas Federal Courts

The following list indicates the district and division name for each county in the state. If the bankruptcy court location is different from the district court, then the location of the bankruptcy court appears in parentheses.

County/Court Cross Reference

County	District	Division
Arkansas	Eastern	Pine Bluff (Little Rock)
Ashley	Western (Eastern)	El Dorado (Little Rock)
Baxter	Western	Harrison (Fayetteville)
Benton	Western	Fayetteville
Boone	Western	Harrison (Fayetteville)
Bradley	Western (Eastern)	El Dorado (Little Rock)
Calhoun	Western (Eastern)	El Dorado (Little Rock)
Carroll	Western	Harrison (Fayetteville)
Chicot	Eastern	Pine Bluff (Little Rock)
Clark	Western (Eastern)	Hot Springs (Little Rock)
Clay	Eastern	Jonesboro (Little Rock)
Cleburne	Eastern	Batesville (Little Rock)
Cleveland	Eastern	Pine Bluff (Little Rock)
Columbia	Western (Eastern)	El Dorado (Little Rock)
Conway	Eastern	Little Rock
Craighead	Eastern	Jonesboro (Little Rock)
Crawford	Western	Fort Smith (Fayetteville)
Crittenden	Eastern	Jonesboro (Little Rock)
Cross	Eastern	Helena (Little Rock)
Dallas	Eastern	Pine Bluff (Little Rock)
Desha	Eastern	Pine Bluff (Little Rock)
Drew	Eastern	Pine Bluff (Little Rock)
Faulkner	Eastern	Little Rock
Franklin	Western	Fort Smith (Fayetteville)
Fulton	Eastern	Batesville (Little Rock)
Garland	Western (Eastern)	Hot Springs (Little Rock)
Grant	Eastern	Pine Bluff (Little Rock)
Greene	Eastern	Jonesboro (Little Rock)
Hempstead	Western (Eastern)	Texarkana (Little Rock)
Hot Spring	Western (Eastern)	Hot Springs (Little Rock)
Howard	Western (Eastern)	Texarkana (Little Rock)
Independence	Eastern	Batesville (Little Rock)
Izard	Eastern	Batesville (Little Rock)
Jackson	Eastern	Batesville (Little Rock)
Jefferson	Eastern	Pine Bluff (Little Rock)
Johnson	Western	Fort Smith (Fayetteville)
Lafayette	Western (Eastern)	Texarkana (Little Rock)
Lawrence	Eastern	Jonesboro (Little Rock)
Lee	Eastern	Helena (Little Rock)
Lincoln	Eastern	Pine Bluff (Little Rock)
Little River	Western (Eastern)	Texarkana (Little Rock)
Logan	Western	Fort Smith (Fayetteville)
Lonoke	Eastern	Little Rock
Madison	Western	Fayetteville
Marion	Western	Harrison (Fayetteville)
Miller	Western (Eastern)	Texarkana (Little Rock)
Mississippi	Eastern	Jonesboro (Little Rock)
Monroe	Eastern	Helena (Little Rock)
Montgomery	Western (Eastern)	Hot Springs (Little Rock)
Nevada	Western (Eastern)	Texarkana (Little Rock)
Newton	Western	Harrison (Fayetteville)
Ouachita	Western (Eastern)	El Dorado (Little Rock)
Perry	Eastern	Little Rock
Phillips	Eastern	Helena (Little Rock)
Pike	Western (Eastern)	Hot Springs (Little Rock)
Poinsett	Eastern	Jonesboro (Little Rock)
Polk	Western	Fort Smith (Fayetteville)
Pope	Eastern	Little Rock
Prairie	Eastern	Little Rock
Pulaski	Eastern	Little Rock
Randolph	Eastern	Jonesboro (Little Rock)
Saline	Eastern	Little Rock
Scott	Western	Fort Smith (Fayetteville)
Searcy	Western	Harrison (Fayetteville)
Sebastian	Western	Fort Smith (Fayetteville)
Sevier	Western (Eastern)	Texarkana (Little Rock)
Sharp	Eastern	Batesville (Little Rock)
St. Francis	Eastern	Helena (Little Rock)
Stone	Eastern	Batesville (Little Rock)
Union	Western (Eastern)	El Dorado (Little Rock)
Van Buren	Eastern	Little Rock
Washington	Western	Fayetteville
White	Eastern	Little Rock
Woodruff	Eastern	Helena (Little Rock)
Yell	Eastern	Little Rock

Standards for Federal Courts: The search fee is $20.00 per item (one party name or case number). Certification fee is $7.00 per document. Copy fee is $.50 per page. All fees standard unless noted in profile. Mail Search: always enclose a stamped self addressed envelope unless otherwise noted. Before releasing records, all courts require prepayment unless noted in profile.

Open records are located at the court unless otherwise noted. District courts index by defendant and plaintiff as well as by case number. Bankruptcy courts usually index by debtor and case number. While most courts now have their indexes on computer, many maintain card indices.

The universal PACER sign-up number is 800-676-6856. Find PACER and the Party/Case Index on the Web at http://pacer.psc.uscourts.gov. PACER dial-up access is $.60 per minute. Also, courts offering internet access via RACER, PACER,

Web-PACER or the new CM-ECF charge $.07 per page fee unless noted as free.

US District Court

Eastern District of Arkansas

Batesville Division c/o Little Rock Division, PO Box 869, Little Rock, AR 72201-3325 (Courier Address: 600 W Capital, Room 402, Little Rock, AR 72201), 501-604-5351.

www.are.uscourts.gov

Counties: Cleburne, Fulton, Independence, Izard, Jackson, Sharp, Stone.

Indexing & Storage: New cases are available in the index after filing date. Open records are located at the Little Rock Division.

Fee & Payment Notes: Payment may be made by money order, cashier check. Business checks are not accepted. Personal checks are not accepted.

Phone Search: Will search name.

In Person Search: In person searching available.

PACER: Toll-free dial-up access: 800-371-8842. Local dial-up access: 501-324-6190. Case records are available back to 1987-89. Records are purged every five years. New records are available online after 1 day.

Other Online Access: on Internet using RACER at www.are.uscourts.gov/perl/bkplog.html.

Helena Division c/o Little Rock Division, 600 W Capital Rm 402, Little Rock, AR 72201-3325 (Courier Address: 600 W Capital, Room 402, Little Rock, AR 72201), 501-604-5351.

www.are.uscourts.gov

Counties: Cross, Lee, Monroe, Phillips, St. Francis, Woodruff.

Indexing & Storage: New cases are available in the index after filing date. Open records are located at the Little Rock Division.

Fee & Payment Notes: Payment may be made by money order, cashier check. Business checks are not accepted. Personal checks are not accepted.

Phone Search: Will search name.

In Person Search: In person searching available.

PACER: Toll-free dial-up access: 800-371-8842. Local dial-up access: 501-324-6190. Case records are available back to 1987-89. Records are purged every five years. New records are available online after 1 day.

Other Online Access: on Internet using RACER at www.are.uscourts.gov/perl/bkplog.html.

Jonesboro Division PO Box 7080, Jonesboro, AR 72403 (Courier Address: Federal Office Bldg, Room 312, 615 S Main St, Jonesboro, AR 72401), 870-972-4610, Fax: 870-972-4612.

www.are.uscourts.gov

Counties: Clay, Craighead, Crittenden, Greene, Lawrence, Mississippi, Poinsett, Randolph.

Indexing & Storage: Cases are indexed by defendant, plaintiff, and case number. New cases are available in the index immediately after filing date. Open records are located at this court.

Fee & Payment Notes: Payment may be made by money order, cashier check, personal check. Payee: Clerk, US District Court.

Phone Search: Docket information available.

Fax Search: Fax requests accepted on same basis as mail requests.

Mail Search: A stamped self addressed envelope is not required.

In Person Search: In person searching available.

PACER: Toll-free dial-up access: 800-371-8842. Local dial-up access: 501-324-6190. Case records are available back to 1987-89. Records are purged every five years. New records are available online after 1 day.

Other Online Access: on Internet using RACER at www.are.uscourts.gov/perl/bkplog.html.

Little Rock Division Room 402, 600 W Capitol, Little Rock, AR 72201 (Courier: Use mail address for courier delivery), 501-324-5351.

www.are.uscourts.gov

Counties: Conway, Faulkner, Lonoke, Perry, Pope, Prairie, Pulaski, Saline, Van Buren, White, Yell.

Indexing & Storage: Cases are indexed by defendant, plaintiff, and case number. New cases are available in the index immediately after filing date. Records are also indexed on microfiche. Open records are located at this court.

Fee & Payment Notes: Payment may be made by money order, cashier check, personal check, Visa, Mastercard. Payee: Clerk, US District Court.

Phone Search: Docket information available by phone.

In Person Search: In person searching available.

PACER: Toll-free dial-up access: 800-371-8842. Local dial-up access: 501-324-6190. Case records are available back to 1987-89. Records are purged every five years. New records are available online after 1 day.

Other Online Access: on Internet using RACER at www.are.uscourts.gov/perl/bkplog.html.

Pine Bluff Division PO Box 8307, Pine Bluff, AR 71611-8307 (Courier Address: US Post Office & Courthouse, 100 E 8th St, Room 3103, Pine Bluff, AR 71601), 870-536-1190, Fax: 870-536-6330.

www.are.uscourts.gov

Counties: Arkansas, Chicot, Cleveland, Dallas, Desha, Drew, Grant, Jefferson, Lincoln.

Indexing & Storage: Cases are indexed by defendant, plaintiff, and case number. New cases are available in the index immediately after filing date. Records are on the computer from 1989. Records are also indexed on microfiche. Open records are located at this court.

Fee & Payment Notes: Payment may be made by money order, cashier check, personal check. Prepayment is required for copies and certification. Payee: US District Clerk.

Phone Search: Searching is not available by phone.

In Person Search: In person searching available.

PACER: Toll-free dial-up access: 800-371-8842. Local dial-up access: 501-324-6190. Case records are available back to 1987-89. Records are purged every five years. New records are available online after 1 day.

Other Online Access: on Internet using RACER at www.are.uscourts.gov/perl/bkplog.html.

US Bankruptcy Court

Eastern District of Arkansas

Little Rock Division PO Drawer 3777, Little Rock, AR 72203 (Courier Address: Room 101, 600 W Capitol, Little Rock, AR 72201), 501-918-5500, Fax: 501-918-5520.

www.areb.uscourts.gov

Counties: Same counties as included in Eastern District of Arkansas, plus the counties included in the Western District divisions of El Dorado, Hot Springs and Texarkana. All bankruptcy cases in Arkansas prior to mid-1993 were heard here.

Indexing & Storage: Cases are indexed by debtor and creditors as well as by case number. New cases are available in the index immediately after filing date. Records are also indexed on microfiche. Open records are located at this court.

Fee & Payment Notes: Payment may be made by money order, cashier check, personal check, Visa or Mastercard. Debtor's checks are not accepted. Payee: Clerk, US Bankruptcy Court.

Phone Search: Only the basic information not provided on the VCIS will be released over the phone. This includes the case number, chapter, judge, attorney, trustee, date if case closed, etc. An automated voice case information service (VCIS) is available. Call VCIS at 800-891-6741 or 501-918-5555.

In Person Search: In person searching available.

PACER: Case records are available back to May 1989. Records are purged every six months. New civil records are available online after 1 day. PACER is available online at http://pacer.areb.uscourts.gov.

Electronic Filing: Information is available online at https://ecf.areb.uscourts.gov

US District Court

Western District of Arkansas

El Dorado Division PO Box 1566, El Dorado, AR 71731 (Courier: Room 205, 101 S Jackson, El Dorado, AR 71731), 870-862-1202.

www.arwd.uscourts.gov

Counties: Ashley, Bradley, Calhoun, Columbia, Ouachita, Union.

Indexing & Storage: Cases are indexed by defendant, plaintiff, and case number. New cases are available in the index immediately after filing date. Files are maintained numerically by year. Open records are located at this court.

Fee & Payment Notes: Payment may be made by money order, cashier check, personal check, Visa, Mastercard. Prepayment is required for out of state searchers. Payee: Clerk, US District Court.

Phone Search: Only docket information is available by phone.

Fax Search: Will accept fax request usually at no cost as long as results do not have to be in writing. Call for more information.

In Person Search: In person searching available.

PACER: Sign-up number is 501-783-6833. Local dial-up access: 501-783-3538. Case records are available back to September 1990. Records are purged every five years. New records are available online after 1 day.

Other Online Access: PACER via E-mail offers case information directly to your e-mailbox. Visit www.arwd.uscourts.gov/mailform.html and input the information you are looking for; results sent to you by email. Court does not participate in the U.S. party case index.

Fayetteville Division PO Box 6420, Fayetteville, AR 72702 (Courier Address: Room 510, 35 E Mountain, Fayetteville, AR 72701), 479-521-6980, Fax: 479-575-0774.

www.arwd.uscourts.gov

Counties: Benton, Madison, Washington.

Indexing & Storage: Cases are indexed by defendant, plaintiff, and case number. New cases are available in the index immediately after filing date. Files are maintained numerically by year. Open records are located at this court.

Fee & Payment Notes: Payment may be made by money order, cashier check, personal check, Visa, Mastercard. Prepayment is required for out of state searchers. Payee: Clerk, Western District of Arkansas. You are allowed to make your own copies. These copies cost $.50 per page. Searches can be done in person at no charge to the searcher if no written record is furnished.

Phone Search: Only docket information is available by phone.

Fax Search: Will accept fax request on same basis as mail request. Call for information regarding fax results.

Mail Search: A stamped self addressed envelope is not required.

In Person Search: In person searching available.

PACER: Sign-up number is 479-783-6833. Local dial-up access: 479-783-3538. Case records are available back to September 1990. Records are purged every five years. New records are available online after 1 day.

Other Online Access: PACER via E-mail offers case information directly to your e-mailbox. Visit www.arwd.uscourts.gov/mailform.html and input the information you are looking for; results sent to you by email. Court does not participate in the U.S. party case index.

Fort Smith Division
PO Box 1547, Fort Smith, AR 72902 (Courier Address: Judge Isaac C. Parker Federal Bldg #1038, 6th & Rogers Ave, Fort Smith, AR 72901), 479-783-6833, Fax: 479-783-6308.

www.arwd.uscourts.gov

Counties: Crawford, Franklin, Johnson, Logan, Polk, Scott, Sebastian.

Indexing & Storage: Cases are indexed by defendant, plaintiff, and case number. New cases are available in the index immediately after filing date. Files are maintained numerically by year. Open records are located at this court.

Fee & Payment Notes: Payment may be made by money order, cashier check, personal check, Visa, Mastercard. Prepayment is required for out of state searchers. Payee: Clerk of Court. You are allowed to make your own copies. These copies cost $.50 per page.

Phone Search: Only docket information is available by phone.

Mail Search: A stamped self addressed envelope is not required.

In Person Search: In person searching available.

PACER: Sign-up number is 479-783-6833. Local dial-up access: 479-783-3538. Case records are available back to September 1990. Records are purged every five years. New records are available online after 1 day.

Other Online Access: PACER via E-mail offers case information directly to your e-mailbox. Visit www.arwd.uscourts.gov/mailform.html and input the information you are looking for; results sent to you by email. Court does not participate in the U.S. party case index.

Hot Springs Division
PO Drawer I, Hot Springs, AR 71902 (Courier Address: Federal Bldg Room 347, 100 Reserve, Hot Springs, AR 71901), 501-623-6411.

www.arwd.uscourts.gov

Counties: Clark, Garland, Hot Springs, Montgomery, Pike.

Indexing & Storage: Cases are indexed by defendant, plaintiff, and case number. New cases are available in the index immediately after filing date. Files are maintained numerically by year. Open records are located at this court.

Fee & Payment Notes: Payment may be made by money order, cashier check, personal check, Visa, Mastercard. Prepayment is required for out of state searchers. Payee: Clerk, Western District of Arkansas.

Phone Search: Searching is not available by phone.

In Person Search: In person searching available.

PACER: Sign-up number is 501-783-6833. Local dial-up access: 501-783-3538. Case records are available back to September 1990. Records are purged every five years. New records are available online after 1 day.

Other Online Access: PACER via E-mail offers case information directly to your e-mailbox. Visit www.arwd.uscourts.gov/mailform.html and input the information you are looking for; results sent to you by email. Court does not participate in the U.S. party case index.

Texarkana Division
PO Box 2746, Texarkana, AR 75504-2746 (Courier: 500 State Line Ave, Texarkana, AR 71854), 870-773-3381.

www.arwd.uscourts.gov

Counties: Hempstead, Howard, Lafayette, Little River, Miller, Nevada, Sevier.

Indexing & Storage: Cases are indexed by defendant, plaintiff, and case number. New cases are available in the index immediately after filing date. Files are maintained numerically by year. Records are also indexed by microfiche. Open records are located at this court.

Fee & Payment Notes: Payment may be made by money order, cashier check, personal check, Visa, Mastercard. Prepayment is required for out of state searchers. Payee: Clerk of the Court. You are allowed to make your own copies. These copies cost $.50 per page.

Phone Search: Case numbers are released by phone. Anything else will depend on workload of deputy clerk.

Mail Search: A stamped self addressed envelope is not required.

In Person Search: In person searching available.

PACER: Sign-up number is 501-783-6833. Local dial-up access: 501-783-3538. Case records are available back to September 1990. Records are purged every five years. New records are available online after 1 day.

Other Online Access: PACER via E-mail offers case information directly to your e-mailbox. Visit www.arwd.uscourts.gov/mailform.html and input the information you are looking for; results sent to you by email. Court does not participate in the U.S. party case index.

US Bankruptcy Court
Western District of Arkansas

Fayetteville Division PO Box 3097, Fayetteville, AR 72702-3097 (Courier Address: 35 E Mountain, Room 316, Fayetteville, AR 72701), 479-582-9800, Fax: 479-582-9825.

www.arb.uscourts.gov

Counties: Same counties as included in the Western District of Arkansas except that counties included in the divisions of El Dorado and Texarkana are heard in Little Rock.

Indexing & Storage: Cases are indexed by debtor and creditors as well as by case number. New cases are available in the index immediately after filing date. Open records are located at this court.

Fee & Payment Notes: Payment may be made by money order, cashier check, personal check, Visa. Personal checks are not accepted from debtors. Licensed attorneys may be invoiced for copywork. Payee: Clerk, US Bankruptcy Court.

Phone Search: Only the basic information not provided on the VCIS will be released over the phone. This includes the case number, chapter, judge, attorney, and trustee. An automated voice case information service (VCIS) is available. Call VCIS at 800-891-6741 or 501-918-5555.

In Person Search: In person searching available.

PACER: Case records are available back to May 1989. Records are purged every six months. New civil records are available online after 1 day.

Electronic Filing: Information is available online at https://ecf.arwb.uscourts.gov

Arkansas County Courts

Court	Jurisdiction	No. of Courts	How Organized
Circuit Courts*	General	38	28 Circuits
County Courts*	Limited	Comb	
Circuit & County Courts*		47	
District (Municipal) Courts*	Limited	126	
City Courts	Limited	1084	
Court of Common Pleas	Limited	4	
Justice of the Peace Courts	Limited	55	
Police Courts	Limited	5	

* Profiled in this Sourcebook.

Court	CIVIL								
	Tort	Contract	Real Estate	Min. Claim	Max. Claim	Small Claims	Estate	Eviction	Domestic Relations
Circuit Courts*	X	X	X	$5000	No Max		X		X
County Courts*			X						
District (Munici-pal) Courts*		X	X	$0	$5000	$5000		X	
City Courts		X	X	$0	$300				
Court of Common Pleas		X		$500	$1000				
Justice of the Peace Courts						$300			
Police Courts		X	X	$0	$300				

Court	CRIMINAL				
	Felony	Misdemeanor	DWI/DUI	Preliminary Hearing	Juvenile
Circuit Courts*	X				
County Courts*					
District (Munici-pal) Courts*		X	X	X	
City Courts		X	X	X	
Court of Common Pleas					
Justice of the Peace Courts		X			
Police Courts		X	X		

ADMINISTRATION
Administrative Office of Courts, 625 Marshall St, Justice Bldg, Little Rock, AR, 72201; 501-682-9400, Fax: 501-682-9410. http://courts.state.ar.us

COURT STRUCTURE
Circuit Courts are the courts of general jurisdiction and are arranged in 28 circuits. County Courts are, fundamentally, administrative courts dealing with county fiscal issues. For all intents and purposes, Circuit and County courts are combined. By abolishing the distriction between law and equity case types, the legislature allowed the former Chancery courts to be absorbed into the Circuit courts as of 1/2002. As of 8/2/97, the civil limit raised to $5000 in limited jurisidiction District Courts. As of 7/1/2001, Municipal Courts are known as District Courts.

ONLINE ACCESS
There is a very limited internal online computer system at the Administrative Office of Courts. The home web page gives online access to Supreme and Appellate opinions.

ADDITIONAL INFORMATION
Most courts that allow written search requests require an SASE. Fees vary widely across jurisdictions as do prepayment requirements.

Arkansas County

Circuit Court - Northern District 302 S College St, Stuttgart, AR 72160; 870-673-2056; Fax: 870-673-3869. Hours: 8AM-5PM (CST). *Felony, Civil Actions, Probate.*

Note: The court is not bonded to search Civil or Chancery records.

Civil Records: Access: In person only. Visitors must perform in person searches for themselves. No search fee. Required to search: name, years to search. Civil cases indexed by defendant, plaintiff. Civil records on files from 1923, prior to 1923 records located in DeWitt (946-4219).

Criminal Records: Access: In person only. Visitors must perform in person searches for themselves. No search fee. Required to search: name, years to search, DOB. Criminal records in files from 1923, prior to 1923 records located in DeWitt (946-4219).

General Information: No juvenile records released. Fax notes: Fee to fax results is $1.00 per page. Copy fee: $.50 per page. Certification fee: $4.00. Personal checks accepted. Prepayment is required.

Circuit Court - Southern District 101 Courthouse Sq, De Witt, AR 72042; 870-946-4219; Fax: 870-946-1394. Hours: 8AM-4:30PM (closed btw12 & 12:30) (CST). *Felony, Civil Actions Over $5,000.*

Civil Records: Access: Fax, mail, in person. Both court and visitors may perform in person searches. Search fee: $6.00 per name. Required to search: name, years to search. Civil cases indexed by defendant, plaintiff. Civil records in files from 1923, computerized since 1995, prior records (the two other courts in this county also) located at this court.

Criminal Records: Access: Fax, mail, in person. Both court and visitors may perform in person searches. Search fee: $6.00 per name. Required to search: name, DOB; also helpful: SSN. Criminal records in files from 1923, computerized since 1995, prior records (the two other courts in this county also) located at this court. Search request must be in writing.

General Information: No juvenile, expunged records released. SASE requested. Turnaround time 1-2 days. Fax notes: Fax fee $1.00 per copy; $6.00 per search. Copy fee: $.50 per page. Certification fee: $4.00. Fee payee: Arkansas County Circuit Clerk. Personal checks accepted. Prepayment is required.

Stuttgart District Court PO Box 819, Stuttgart, AR 72160; 870-673-7951; Fax: 870-673-6522. Hours: 8AM-5PM (CST). *Misdemeanor, Civil Actions Under $5,000, Eviction, Small Claims.*

Civil Records: Access: Phone, mail, fax, in person. Both court and visitors may perform in person searches. No search fee. Required to search: name plus SSN. Records go back to 1990; on computer back to 1991.

Criminal Records: Access: Phone, mail, fax, in person. Both court and visitors may perform in person searches. No search fee. Required to search: name, years to search, SSN; also helpful: DOB. Records go back to 1990; on computer back to 1991.

General Information: Turnaround time 3 days.

Ashley County

Circuit Court Ashley County Courthouse, 205 E Jefferson, Hamburg, AR 71646; 870-853-2030; Fax: 870-853-2034. Hours: 8AM-4:30PM (CST). *Felony, Civil Actions Over $5,000, Probate.*

Civil Records: Access: Mail, in person. Visitors must perform in person searches for themselves. No search fee. Required to search: name, years to search. Civil cases indexed by defendant, plaintiff. Civil records on files and index cards from 1950s.

Criminal Records: Access: Mail, in person. Visitors must perform in person searches for themselves. No

search fee. Required to search: name, years to search; also helpful: DOB, SSN. Criminal records on files and index cards from 1950s. No name searches by mail, must have case numbers. Mail requests must have case numbers.

General Information: No juvenile records released. SASE required. Fax notes: Fee to fax results is $1.00 per page. Copy fee: $.50 per page. Certification fee: $2.50. Fee payee: Circuit Clerk's Office. Personal checks accepted. Prepayment is required.

Hamburg District Court PO Box 558, City Hall, Hamburg, AR 71646; 870-853-8326; Fax: 870-853-8600. Hours: 8AM-4:30PM (CST). *Misdemeanor, Civil Actions Under $5,000, Eviction, Small Claims.*

Civil Records: Access: Mail, in person. Both court and visitors may perform in person searches. Search fee: $5.00. Civil records go back 10 years; on computer back to 1989.

Criminal Records: Access: Mail, in person. Both court and visitors may perform in person searches. Search fee: $5.00. Required to search: name, years to search, DOB. Criminal records go back to 1976; on computer back to 1989.

General Information: Public access terminal is available. Turnaround time 1-2 days. Certification fee: $10.00. Fee payee: District Court.

Baxter County

Circuit Court 1 E 7th St Courthouse Square, Mountain Home, AR 72653; 870-425-3475; Fax: 870-424-5105. Hours: 8AM-4:30PM (CST). *Felony, Civil Actions Over $5,000, Probate.*

Civil Records: Access: Fax, mail, in person. Both court and visitors may perform in person searches. Search fee: $6.00 per name. Required to search: name, years to search. Civil cases indexed by defendant, plaintiff. Civil records on computer from 1982, on criminal fee book from early 1900s.

Criminal Records: Access: Mail, in person. Both court and visitors may perform in person searches. Search fee: $6.00 per name. Required to search: name, years to search, SSN. Criminal records on computer from 1982, on criminal fee book from early 1900s.

General Information: Public access terminal is available. No adoption or juvenile records released. SASE required. Turnaround time 1-2 days. Copy fee: $.25 per page. Certification fee: $3.00. Fee payee: Baxter County Clerk. Personal checks accepted. Prepayment is required. Fee to fax results is $5.00 per page.

District Court 720 S Hickory, Mountain Home, AR 72653; 870-425-3140; Fax: 870-425-9290. Hours: 8AM-4:30PM (CST). *Misdemeanor, Civil Actions Under $5,000, Eviction, Small Claims.*

Civil Records: Access: In person, mail. Only the court performs in person searches; visitors may not. No search fee. Civil records go back to 1980's; computerized records since 1995.

Criminal Records: Access: In person, mail. Only the court performs in person searches; visitors may not. No search fee. Required to search: name, years to search, DOB, SSN. Criminal records go back to 1980's; computerized since 1995.

General Information: Turnaround time 1-2 days.

Benton County

Circuit Court 102 NE "A" St, Bentonville, AR 72712; 479-271-1015; Fax: 479-271-5719. Hours: 8AM-4:30PM (CST). *Felony, Civil Actions Over $5,000, Probate.*

www.co.benton.ar.us

Civil Records: Access: Online, in person. Visitors must perform in person searches for themselves. No search fee. Required to search: name, years to search. Civil

cases indexed by defendant, plaintiff. Civil records on computer from 1991, on dockets from 1880s.

Criminal Records: Access: Online, in person. Visitors must perform in person searches for themselves. No search fee. Required to search: name, years to search. Criminal records on computer from 1991, on dockets from 1880s. Online access to criminal records is the same as civil.

General Information: Public access terminal is available. No juvenile records released. Copy fee: $.50 per page. Certification fee: $2.00. Fee payee: Benton County Circuit Clerk. Personal checks accepted. Prepayment is required.

District Court 117 W Central, Bentonville, AR 72712; 479-271-3120; Fax: 479-271-3134. Hours: 8AM-4:30PM (CST). *Misdemeanor, Civil Actions Under $5,000, Small Claims.*

Civil Records: Access: In person, mail. Both court and visitors may perform in person searches. No search fee. Civil records on computer back to 1992; other records go back to 1982.

Criminal Records: Access: In person, mail. Both court and visitors may perform in person searches. No search fee. Required to search: name, years to search, DOB. Civil records on computer back to 1992; other records go back to 1982.

General Information: Public access terminal is available. Turnaround time 5 days. Copy fee: $.25 per page. Fee payee: Bentonville District Court. Prepayment is required.

Boone County

Circuit Court 100 N Main St #200, Harrison, AR 72601; 870-741-5560; Fax: 870-741-4335. Hours: 8AM-4:30PM (CST). *Felony, Civil Actions Over $5,000.*

Note: Probate records are in the County Clerk's office, 870-741-8428.

Civil Records: Access: Mail, in person. Both court and visitors may perform in person searches Search fee: $5.00. Required to search: name, years to search. Civil cases indexed by defendant, plaintiff. Civil records archived from 1940, index from 1977, computerized from 1990.

Criminal Records: Access: Mail, in person. Both court and visitors may perform in person searches Search fee: $5.00. Required to search: name, years to search. Criminal records archived from 1940, index from 1977, computerized from 1990.

General Information: Public access terminal is available. No indictments or juvenile records released. SASE required. Turnaround time 1 day. Fax notes: Fee to fax results is $5.00 per document. Copy fee: $.25 per page. Certification fee: $5.00. Fee payee: Circuit Clerk. Personal checks accepted. Prepayment is required.

District Court PO Box 968, Harrison, AR 72602; 870-741-2788; Fax: 870-741-4329. Hours: 8AM-4:30PM (CST). *Misdemeanor, Civil Actions Under $5,000, Eviction, Small Claims.*

Civil Records: Access: In person, mail. Both court and visitors may perform in person searches. No search fee.

Criminal Records: Access: In person, mail. Both court and visitors may perform in person searches. No search fee. Required to search: name, years to search; also helpful: DOB.

General Information: Turnaround time 2 weeks.

Bradley County

Circuit Court Bradley County Courthouse - Records, 101 E Cedar, Warren, AR 71671; 870-226-2272; Probate phone: 870-226-3464; Fax: 870-226-8401. Hours: 8AM-4:30PM (CST). *Felony, Civil Actions Over $5,000, Probate.*

Civil Records: Access: In person only. Visitors must perform in person searches for themselves. No search fee. Required to search: name, years to search. Civil cases indexed by defendant, plaintiff. Civil records (active cases) on dockets, retired cases on indexes from 1850, no computerization.

Criminal Records: Access: Mail, in person. Both court and visitors may perform in person searches. Search fee: $6.00. Required to search: name, years to search; also helpful: DOB, SSN. Criminal records (active cases) on dockets, retired cases on indexes from 1850, no computerization.

General Information: No juvenile released. SASE required. Turnaround time 1 week. Copy fee: $.50per page. Certification fee: $3.00. Fee payee: Circuit Court. Personal checks accepted. Prepayment is required.

District Court PO Box 352, Warren, AR 71671; 870-226-2567; Fax: 870-226-2567. Hours: 8AM-5PM (CST). *Misdemeanor, Civil Actions Under $5,000, Eviction, Small Claims.*

Civil Records: Access: In person, mail. Only the court performs in person searches; visitors may not. No search fee. Required to search: $6.00 per name. Computerized records since 1993.

Criminal Records: Access: In person, mail. Only the court performs in person searches; visitors may not. Search fee: $6.00 per name. Required to search: name, years to search, SSN. Computerized records since 1993.

General Information: Turnaround time 1 week. Fee payee: District Court.

Calhoun County

Circuit & County Courts PO Box 1175, Hampton, AR 71744; 870-798-2517. Hours: 8:30AM-4:30PM (CST). *Felony, Civil Actions Over $5,000, Probate.*

Civil Records: Access: Mail, in person. Both court and visitors may perform in person searches. Search fee: $6.00. Required to search: name, years to search. Civil cases indexed by defendant, plaintiff. Civil records on dockets from 1851.

Criminal Records: Access: Mail, in person. Visitors must perform in person searches for themselves. Search fee: $6.00. Required to search: name, years to search, DOB; also helpful: SSN. Criminal records on dockets from 1851.

General Information: No juvenile or adoption released. SASE required. Turnaround time 1-3 days. Copy fee: $.25 per page. Certification fee: $5.00. Fee payee: Calhoun County Clerk. Personal checks accepted. Prepayment is required.

District Court PO Box 783, Hampton, AR 71744; 870-798-2753; Fax: 870-798-3665. Hours: 8AM-4:30PM (CST). *Misdemeanor, Civil Actions Under $5,000, Eviction, Small Claims.*

Civil Records: Access: In person, mail. Both court and visitors may perform in person searches. No search fee.

Criminal Records: Access: In person, mail. Both court and visitors may perform in person searches. No search fee. Required to search: name, years to search, SSN.

General Information: Turnaround time 2 days.

Carroll County

Berryville Circuit Court - Eastern District Carroll County Circuit Court, PO Box 71, Berryville, AR 72616; 870-423-2422; Fax: 870-423-4796. Hours: 8:30AM-4:30PM (CST). *Felony, Civil Actions Over $5,000, Eviction, Probate.*

Civil Records: Access: Mail, in person. Both court and visitors may perform in person searches. Search fee: $6.00 per name. Required to search: name, years to search. Civil cases indexed by defendant, plaintiff. Civil records on computer from 1997, on index books since 1869.

Criminal Records: Access: Fax, mail, in person. Both court and visitors may perform in person searches. Search fee: $6.00 per name. Required to search: name,

years to search, DOB, SSN. Criminal records on computer back to 1997, on index books since 1869.

General Information: Public access terminal is available. No juvenile records released. SASE required. Turnaround time 1-2 days. Fax notes: Fee to fax results is $1.00 per page. Copy fee: $.25 per page. Certification fee: $2.00 per document. Fee payee: Circuit Clerk of Carroll County. Personal checks accepted. Prepayment is required.

Eureka Springs Circuit & County Courts - Western District 44 S Main, PO Box 109, Eureka Springs, AR 72632; 479-253-8646. Hours: 8:30AM-4:30PM (CST). *Felony, Civil Actions Over $5,000, Eviction, Probate.*

Civil Records: Access: In person only. Visitors must perform in person searches for themselves. No search fee. Required to search: name, years to search. Civil cases indexed by defendant, plaintiff. Civil records on indexes from 1883.

Criminal Records: Access: Phone, mail, in person. Both court and visitors may perform in person searches. Search fee: $6.00 per name. Required to search: name, years to search; also helpful: DOB. Criminal records on indexes from 1883.

General Information: No expunged criminal records released. SASE required. Turnaround time varies. Fax notes: Fee to fax results is $1.00 per page. Copy fee: $.50 by mail or $.25 in person. Certification fee: $2.00; $5.00 for Probate records. Fee payee: Circuit Clerk of Carroll County or County Clerk. Personal checks accepted. Prepayment is required.

Berryville District Court 103 S Springs, Berryville, AR 72616; 870-423-6247; Fax: 870-423-7069. Hours: 8AM-4:30PM (CST). *Misdemeanor, Civil Actions Under $5,000, Small Claims.*

Civil Records: Both court and visitors may perform in person searches. No search fee. Records computerized since 1987.

Criminal Records: Access: In person, mail. Both court and visitors may perform in person searches. No search fee. Required to search: name, years to search; also helpful: DOB. Records computerized since 1987.

General Information: Turnaround time 1-2 days.

Eureka Springs District Court Courthouse, 44 S Main, Eureka Springs, AR 72632; 479-253-8574; Fax: 479-253-6887. Hours: 8AM-5PM (CST). *Misdemeanor, Civil Actions Under $5,000, Small Claims.*

www.cityofeurekasprings.org/muncourt.html

Civil Records: Access: Phone, mail, in person. Both court and visitors may perform in person searches. Search fee: No search fee. Records on computer back to 1990.

Criminal Records: Access: Phone, mail, in person. Both court and visitors may perform in person searches. No search fee. Required to search: name, years to search. Criminal records on computer back to 1990.

General Information: Turnaround time 1 week.

Chicot County

Circuit Court 108 Main St, County Courthouse, Lake Village, AR 71653; 870-265-8010; Fax: 870-265-5102. Hours: 8AM-4:30PM (CST). *Felony, Civil Actions Over $5,000, Probate.*

Civil Records: Access: Mail, in person. Both court and visitors may perform in person searches. Search fee: $6.00 per name. Required to search: name, years to search. Civil cases indexed by defendant, plaintiff. Civil records on dockets and files from 1900s; computerized since 1999.

Criminal Records: Access: Mail, in person. Both court and visitors may perform in person searches. Search fee: $6.00 per name. Required to search: name, years to

search. Criminal records on dockets and files from 1900s; computerized records since 1999.

General Information: No juvenile records released. SASE required. Turnaround time 1-2 days. Copy fee: $.50 per page. Certification fee: $2.00. Fee payee: Circuit Clerk. Personal checks accepted. Prepayment is required.

Lake Village District Court PO Box 832, Lake Village, AR 71653; 870-265-3283. Hours: 9AM-5PM (CST). *Misdemeanor, Civil Actions Under $5,000, Eviction, Small Claims.*

Civil Records: Access: Phone, mail, fax, in person. Both court and visitors may perform in person searches. Search fee: $5.00 per name. Civil records on computer go back to 8/2000; other records go back to 1977.

Criminal Records: Access: Phone, mail, fax, in person. Both court and visitors may perform in person searches. Search fee: $5.00 per name. Required to search: name, years to search; also helpful: DOB, SSN. Criminal records on computer go back to 8/2000; other records go back to 1977.

General Information: Turnaround time ASAP. Fee payee: Lake Village District Court.

Clark County

Circuit Court PO Box 576, Arkadelphia, AR 71923; 870-246-4281. Hours: 8:30AM-4:30PM (CST). *Felony, Civil Actions Over $5,000, Probate.*

Civil Records: Access: Mail, in person. Both court and visitors may perform in person searches. Search fee: $5.00 per name. Required to search: name, years to search. Civil cases indexed by defendant, plaintiff. Civil records on computer since 1985.

Criminal Records: Access: Mail, in person. Both court and visitors may perform in person searches. Search fee: $5.00 per name. Required to search: name, years to search. Criminal records on computer since 1980.

General Information: No juvenile records released. SASE required. Turnaround time 1-2 days. Copy fee: $.50 per page. Certification fee: $5.00. Fee payee: Pamela King Circuit Clerk. Personal checks accepted. Prepayment is required.

District Court PO Box 449, Arkadelphia, AR 71923; 870-246-9552. Hours: 8:30AM-4:30PM (CST). *Misdemeanor, Civil Actions Under $5,000, Eviction, Small Claims.*

Civil Records: Access: Phone, mail, fax, in person. Both court and visitors may perform in person searches. No search fee. Records go back to 1980; on computer since 1990.

Criminal Records: Access: Phone, mail, fax, in person. Both court and visitors may perform in person searches. No search fee. Required to search: name, years to search; also helpful: DOB. Records go back to 1980; on computer since 1990.

General Information: Turnaround time same day.

Clay County

Corning Circuit & County Courts PO Box 176, Corning, AR 72422; 870-857-3271; Fax: 870-857-9201. Hours: 8AM-4:30PM (CST). *Felony, Civil Actions Over $5,000, Probate.*

Civil Records: Access: Mail, in person. Both court and visitors may perform in person searches. Search fee: $6.00 per name. Required to search: name, years to search. Civil cases indexed by defendant, plaintiff. Civil records on books from 1893.

Criminal Records: Access: Mail, in person. Both court and visitors may perform in person searches. Search fee: $6.00 per name. Required to search: name, years to search; also helpful: DOB, SSN. Criminal records on books from 1893.

General Information: No juvenile records released. Turnaround time 1-2 days. Copy fee: $1.00 per page.

Certification fee: $5.00. Fee payee: Circuit Clerk. Personal checks accepted. Prepayment is required.

Piggott Circuit & County Courts PO Box 29, Piggott, AR 72454; 870-598-2524; Fax: 870-598-2524. Hours: 8AM-4:30PM (CST). *Felony, Civil Actions Over $5,000.*

Civil Records: Access: Mail, in person. Both court and visitors may perform in person searches. Search fee: $6.00 per name. Required to search: name, years to search. Civil cases indexed by defendant, plaintiff. Civil records on books from 1893.
Criminal Records: Access: Mail, in person. Both court and visitors may perform in person searches. Search fee: $6.00 per name. Required to search: name, years to search, DOB, SSN. Criminal records on books from 1893.
General Information: No expunged criminal records released. SASE required. Turnaround time 1-2 days. Fax notes: $5.00 per document. Copy fee: $1.00 per page. Certification fee: $5.00 per page. Fee payee: Circuit Clerk. Personal checks accepted. Prepayment is required.

District Court 121 W Main St, Piggott, AR 72454; 870-598-2265. Hours: 8AM-4:30PM (CST). *Misdemeanor, Civil Actions Under $5,000, Eviction, Small Claims.*

Note: Office is open 20 hours per week only. For eviction information the court says to contact Clay County Sheriff, 151 S 2nd St, Piggott, AR 72454, 870-598-2266.
Civil Records: Access: Mail, in person. Both court and visitors may perform in person searches. Search fee: $8.00. Records on computer back to 1998.
Criminal Records: Access: Mail, in person. Both court and visitors may perform in person searches. No search fee. Required to search: name, years to search, SSN; also helpful: DOB. Records on computer back to 1998.
General Information: Turnaround time 3-4 days. Fee payee: District Court. Prepayment is required.

Cleburne County

Circuit & County Courts PO Box 543, Heber Springs, AR 72543; 501-362-8149; Fax: 501-362-4650. Hours: 8:30AM-4:30PM (CST). *Felony, Civil Actions Over $5,000, Probate, Eviction.*

Civil Records: Access: Phone, mail, in person. Both court and visitors may perform in person searches. Search fee: $6.00 per name. Required to search: name, years to search. Civil cases indexed by defendant, plaintiff. Civil records on dockets from 1883.
Criminal Records: Access: Phone, mail, in person. Both court and visitors may perform in person searches. Search fee: $6.00 per name. Required to search: name, years to search. Criminal records on dockets from 1883.
General Information: No juvenile records released. SASE required. Turnaround time 1-2 days. Copy fee: $.25 per page. Certification fee: $1.00 per document. Fee payee: Circuit Clerk. Personal checks accepted. Prepayment is required.

District Court 102 E Main, Heber Springs, AR 72543; 501-362-6585; Fax: 501-362-4661. Hours: 8:30AM-4:30PM (CST). *Misdemeanor, Civil Actions Under $5,000, Small Claims.*

Civil Records: Access: Phone, mail, fax, in person. Both court and visitors may perform in person searches. No search fee. Civil records on computer back to 1989.
Criminal Records: Access: Phone, mail, fax, in person. Both court and visitors may perform in person searches. No search fee. Required to search: name, years to search, offense, DOB. Criminal records on computer back to 1989.
General Information: Public access terminal is available. Turnaround time 10 working days.

Cleveland County

Circuit & County Courts PO Box 368, Rison, AR 71665; 870-325-6521; Fax: 870-325-6144. Hours: 8AM-4:30PM (CST). *Felony, Civil Actions Over $5,000, Probate.*

Civil Records: Access: Mail, in person. Visitors must perform in person searches for themselves. Search fee: $6.00. Required to search: name, years to search. Civil cases indexed by defendant, plaintiff. Civil records from 1980.
Criminal Records: Access: Mail, in person. Both court and visitors may perform in person searches. Search fee: $6.00. Required to search: name, years to search, DOB. Criminal records from 1980.
General Information: No juvenile or adoption records released. Fax notes: Fee to fax results is $1.00 per document. Copy fee: $.25 per page. Certification fee: $3.00. Fee payee: Clerk of Circuit Court. Personal checks accepted. Prepayment is required.

District Court PO Box 405, City Hall, Rison, AR 71665; 870-325-7382; Fax: 870-325-6152. Hours: 8AM-4PM (CST). *Misdemeanor, Civil Actions Under $5,000, Eviction, Small Claims.*

Civil Records: Access: In person only. Both court and visitors may perform in person searches. No search fee. Computerized records go back 3 years.
Criminal Records: Access: In person only. Both court and visitors may perform in person searches. No search fee. Required to search: name, years to search, SSN. Computerized records go back 3 years.

Columbia County

Circuit & County Courts 1 Court Square Ste 3, Magnolia, AR 71753-3595; 870-235-3700; Fax: 870-235-3786. Hours: 8AM-4:30PM (CST). *Felony, Civil Actions Over $5,000, Probate.*

Civil Records: Access: Mail, in person. Both court and visitors may perform in person searches. Search fee: $10.00 per name. Required to search: name, years to search. Civil cases indexed by defendant, plaintiff. Civil records on dockets and index cards; computerized records since 8/97.
Criminal Records: Access: Mail, in person. Both court and visitors may perform in person searches. Search fee: $10.00 per name. Required to search: name, years to search, DOB, SSN. Criminal records on dockets and index cards; computerized records since 8/97.
General Information: No juvenile or adoption. SASE required. Turnaround time 2-4 days. Copy fee: $1.00 per page. Certification fee: $3.00. Fee payee: Circuit Clerk. Personal checks accepted. Prepayment is required.

Magnolia District Court 121 S Jefferson, Magnolia, AR 71753; 870-234-7312. Hours: 8AM-5PM (CST). *Misdemeanor, Civil Actions Under $5,000, Eviction, Small Claims.*

Civil Records: Access: Mail, in person. Both court and visitors may perform in person searches. No search fee.
Criminal Records: Access: Mail, in person. Only the court performs in person searches; visitors may not. Search fee: $1.00 per name. Required to search: name, years to search; also helpful: address.
General Information: SASE is required. Turnaround time 3 days. Copy fee: $1.00 per page. Fee payee: District Court Clerk. Prepayment is required.

Conway County

Circuit Court Conway County Courthouse, Rm 206, Morrilton, AR 72110; 501-354-9617; Probate phone: 501-354-9621; Fax: 501-354-9612. Hours: 8AM-5PM (CST). *Felony, Civil Actions Over $5,000, Probate.*

Civil Records: Access: Phone, fax, mail, in person. Both court and visitors may perform in person searches.

Search fee: $8.00 per name. Required to search: name, years to search. Civil cases indexed by defendant, plaintiff. Civil records (child support) on computer. All others on dockets from 1900s.
Criminal Records: Access: Phone, mail, in person. Both court and visitors may perform in person searches. Search fee: $8.00 per name. Required to search: name, years to search, DOB; also helpful: sex, SSN. Criminal records indexed in books back to 1900's.
General Information: No juvenile records released. SASE required. Turnaround time 1-2 days. Fax notes: Fee to fax results is $1.00 per page. Copy fee: $1.00 per page. Certification fee: $5.00. Fee payee: Circuit Clerk. Personal checks accepted. Prepayment is required.

District Court Conway County Courthouse, PO Box 127, Morrilton, AR 72110; 501-354-9615; Fax: 501-354-9633. Hours: 8AM-4:30PM (CST). *Misdemeanor, Civil Actions Under $5,000, Eviction, Small Claims.*

Civil Records: Access: In person, mail. Both court and visitors may perform in person searches. No search fee. Computerized records since 1994.
Criminal Records: Access: In person, mail. Only the court performs in person searches; visitors may not. No search fee. Required to search: name, years to search; also helpful: DOB. Computerized records since 1994.
General Information: Public access terminal is available. Turnaround time 1-2 days. Copy fee: $1.00. Certification fee: $5.00. Fee payee: District Court Clerk. Prepayment is required.

Craighead County

Jonesboro Circuit Court PO Box 120, Jonesboro, AR 72403; 870-933-4530; Fax: 870-933-4534. Hours: 8AM-5PM (CST). *Felony, Civil Actions Over $5,000, Probate.*

Civil Records: Access: Fax, mail, in person. Both court and visitors may perform in person searches. Search fee: $6.00 per name. Required to search: name, years to search. Civil cases indexed by defendant, plaintiff. Civil records on computer from 1972, on microfiche from 1800s.
Criminal Records: Access: Fax, mail, in person. Both court and visitors may perform in person searches. Search fee: $6.00 per name. Required to search: name, years to search, DOB; also helpful: address, SSN. Criminal records on computer from 1972, on microfiche from 1800s.
General Information: Public access terminal is available. No juvenile records released. SASE required. Turnaround time 1-2 days. Fax notes: $1.00 per page. Copy fee: $.50 per page. Certification fee: $3.00. Fee payee: Circuit Clerk. Personal checks accepted. Prepayment is required.

Lake City Circuit & County Courts PO Box 537, Lake City, AR 72437; 870-237-4342; Fax: 870-237-8174. Hours: 8AM-5PM (CST). *Felony, Civil Actions Over $5,000, Probate.*

Civil Records: Access: Mail, fax, in person. Both court and visitors may perform in person searches. Search fee: $6.00 per name. Required to search: name, years to search, address. Civil cases indexed by defendant, plaintiff. Civil records on computer from 1972, on microfiche from 1800s.
Criminal Records: Access: Mail, fax, in person. Both court and visitors may perform in person searches. Search fee: $6.00 per name. Required to search: name, years to search, address, DOB; also helpful: SSN. Criminal records on computer from 1972, on microfiche from 1800s.
General Information: Public access terminal is available. No adoption records released. SASE required. Turnaround time 1-2 days. Copy fee: $.50 per page. Certification fee: $3.00 per page. Fee payee: Circuit

Clerk. Business checks accepted. Prepayment is required.

District Court 410 W Washington, Jonesboro, AR 72401; 870-933-4508; Fax: 870-933-4582. Hours: 8AM-5PM (CST). *Misdemeanor, Civil Actions Under $5,000, Eviction, Small Claims.*

Civil Records: Access: In person, mail. Only the court may perform in person searches. Search fee: $4.00 per name. Required to search: name, DOB. Computerized records go back 10 years.

Criminal Records: Access: In person, mail. Only the court may perform in person searches. No search fee. Required to search: name, years to search, SSN. Computerized records go back 10 years.

General Information: Turnaround time 1-2 days. Certification fee: $2.00 each.

Crawford County

Circuit Court County Courthouse, 300 Main St, Rm 22, Van Buren, AR 72956; 479-474-1821; Fax: 479-471-0622. Hours: 8AM-5PM (CST). *Felony, Civil Actions Over $5,000, Probate.*

Civil Records: Access: Mail, in person. Both court and visitors may perform in person searches. Search fee: $6.00 per name. Required to search: name, years to search. Civil cases indexed by defendant, plaintiff. Civil records on computer from 1993, on dockets from 1877.

Criminal Records: Access: In person only. Both court and visitors may perform in person searches. Search fee: $6.00 per name. Required to search: name, years to search. Criminal records on computer from 1993, on dockets from 1877.

General Information: Public access terminal is available. (Starting 1/2003, no court records available.) No juvenile records released. SASE required. Turnaround time 1-2 days. Copy fee: $1.00 per page. Certification fee: $2.00. Fee payee: Circuit Clerk. Personal checks accepted. Prepayment is required.

District Court 1003 Broadway, Van Buren, AR 72956; 479-474-1671; Fax: 479-471-5010. Hours: 8AM-5PM (CST). *Misdemeanor, Civil Actions Under $5,000, Eviction, Small Claims.*

Civil Records: Access: In person, mail. Both court and visitors may perform in person searches. No search fee. Records available from 1975, computerized from 2000.

Criminal Records: Access: In person, mail. Both court and visitors may perform in person searches. Search fee: $10.00 per name. Required to search: name, years to search; also helpful: DOB, SSN. Specific court cases prior to 2000 need the conviction date. Records available from 1975, computerized from 2000.

General Information: Public access terminal is available. (However, the terminal is only available on Fridays.) Turnaround time 2-3 days. Copy fee: $.50. Certification fee: $10.00 per document. Fee payee: Van Buren District Court. Prepayment is required.

Crittenden County

Circuit Court 100 Court St, Marion, AR 72364; 870-739-3248; Fax: 870-739-3287. Hours: 8AM-4:30PM (CST). *Felony, Civil Actions Over $5,000, Probate.*

Civil Records: Access: Mail, in person. Both court and visitors may perform in person searches. Search fee: $6.00 per name. Required to search: name, years to search. Civil cases indexed by plaintiff. Civil records on dockets or microfiche from 1930s.

Criminal Records: Access: Mail, in person. Visitors must perform in person searches for themselves. Search fee: $6.00 per name. Required to search: name, case number. Criminal records on dockets or microfiche from 1930s. Case number required for mail search. Criminal record inquires must be sent to Ark. State Police, 501-681-8100.

General Information: Public access terminal is available. No juvenile records released. SASE required. Turnaround time 1-2 days. Fax notes: Fee to fax results is $4.50 per document. Copy fee: $.25 per page. Certification fee: $3.00. Fee payee: Circuit Court. Personal checks accepted. Prepayment is required.

District Court PO Box 766, West Memphis, AR 72303; 870-732-7560; Fax: 870-732-7538/7566. Hours: 8AM-5PM (CST). *Misdemeanor, Civil Actions Under $5,000, Eviction, Small Claims.*

Civil Records: Access: Phone, fax, mail, in person. Both court and visitors may perform in person searches. No search fee. Civil records on computer back to 1989; other records go back to 1945.

Criminal Records: Access: Phone, mail, in person. Both court and visitors may perform in person searches. No search fee. Required to search: name, years to search; also helpful: SSN, race, sex, DOB. Criminal records on computer back to 1989; other records go back to 1945.

General Information: Public access terminal is available. Turnaround time 2-3 days. Fax notes: No fee to fax results. Copy fee: $1 per page if over 5 pages.

Cross County

Circuit & County Courts County Courthouse, 705 E Union, Rm 9, Wynne, AR 72396; 870-238-5720. Hours: 8AM-4PM (CST). *Felony, Civil Actions Over $5,000, Probate.*

Civil Records: Access: Mail, in person. Search fee: $6.00 per name. Required to search: name, years to search. Civil cases indexed by defendant. Civil records (child support) on computer. All on dockets from 1800s.

Criminal Records: Access: Mail, in person. Both court and visitors may perform in person searches. Search fee: $6.00 per name. Required to search: name, years to search; also helpful: SSN. Criminal records (child support) on computer. All on dockets from 1800s.

General Information: No juvenile records released. SASE required. Turnaround time same day. Copy fee: $.25 per page. Certification fee: $3.00. Fee payee: Cross County Circuit Court. Personal checks accepted. Prepayment is required.

District Court 205 Mississippi St, Wynne, AR 72396; 870-238-9171; Fax: 870-238-3930. Hours: 8AM-4PM (CST). *Misdemeanor, Civil Actions Under $5,000, Eviction, Small Claims.*

Civil Records: Access: Mail, in person. Both court and visitors may perform in person searches. Search fee: $2.00. Required to search: name, years to search. Records on computer back to 1986.

Criminal Records: Access: Mail, in person. Both court and visitors may perform in person searches. Search fee: $2.00. Required to search: name, years to search, signed release; also helpful: SSN. Records on computer back to 1986.

General Information: Public access terminal is available. Turnaround time 1-2 days. Fax notes: Fee to fax results is $2.00 per document. Certification fee: $2.00. Fee payee: Wynne District Court. Prepayment is required.

Dallas County

Circuit & County Courts Dallas County Courthouse, Fordyce, AR 71742; 870-352-2307; Fax: 870-352-7179. Hours: 8:30AM-4:30PM (CST). *Felony, Civil Actions Over $5,000, Probate.*

Civil Records: Access: Phone, fax, mail, in person. Both court and visitors may perform in person searches. Search fee: $6.00. Required to search: name, years to search. Civil cases indexed by defendant, plaintiff. Civil records go back to 1863; on computer back to 8/1997.

Criminal Records: Access: In person only. Visitors must perform in person searches for themselves.

Required to search: name, years to search, DOB; also helpful: SSN. Criminal records go back to 1863; on computer back to 8/1997.

General Information: Public access terminal is available. No juvenile records released. SASE required. Turnaround time 1-2 days. Fax notes: $2.00 fax fee plus $.25 per page. Copy fee: $.50 per page. Certification fee: $3.00. Fee payee: Circuit Clerk. Business checks accepted. Law firm accounts, money orders and cashier checks allowed. Prepayment is required.

District Court 202 W 3rd St, Fordyce, AR 71742; 870-352-2332; Fax: 870-352-3414. Hours: 8AM-4PM (CST). *Misdemeanor, Civil Actions Under $5,000, Eviction, Small Claims.*

Civil Records: Access: In person, mail. Only the court performs in person searches; visitors may not. No search fee. Required to search: No search fee. Computerized records since 1997.

Criminal Records: Access: In person, mail. Only the court performs in person searches; visitors may not. No search fee. Required to search: name, years to search, SSN; also helpful: DOB. Computerized records since 1997.

General Information: Turnaround time 1-2 days.

Desha County

Circuit Court PO Box 309, Arkansas City, AR 71630; 870-877-2411; Probate phone: 870-877-2323; Fax: 870-877-3407. Hours: 8AM-4PM (CST). *Felony, Civil Actions Over $5,000, Probate.*

Civil Records: Access: Fax, mail, in person. Both court and visitors may perform in person searches. Search fee: $5.00 per name. Required to search: name, years to search. Civil cases indexed by defendant, plaintiff. Civil records on dockets from 1920s; on computer back to 1997.

Criminal Records: Access: Fax, mail, in person. Both court and visitors may perform in person searches. Search fee: $5.00 per name. Required to search: name, years to search, SSN. Criminal records on dockets from 1920s, on computer back to 1997.

General Information: No juvenile records released. SASE required. Turnaround time 1-2 days. Fax notes: No fee to fax results. Copy fee: $.50 per page. Certification fee: $3.50. Fee payee: Skippy Leek, Circuit Court Clerk. Personal checks accepted. Prepayment is required.

District Court PO Box 157, Dumas, AR 71639-2226; 870-382-6972; Fax: 870-382-1106. Hours: 8AM-4:30PM (CST). *Misdemeanor, Civil Actions Under $5,000, Eviction, Small Claims.*

Civil Records: Access: In person, mail. Only the court performs in person searches; visitors may not. Search fee: $5.00 per name. Required to search: name, years to search, signed release; also helpful: address.

Criminal Records: Access: In person, mail. Only the court performs in person searches; visitors may not. Search fee: $5.00 per name. Required to search: name, years to search, signed release; also helpful: address.

General Information: Turnaround time 1-2 days. Fee payee: Dumas District Court. Prepayment is required.

Drew County

Circuit & County Courts 210 S Main, Monticello, AR 71655; 870-460-6250; Fax: 870-460-6246. Hours: 8AM-4:30PM (CST). *Felony, Civil Actions Over $5,000, Probate.*

Civil Records: Access: Phone, fax, mail, in person. Both court and visitors may perform in person searches. No search fee. Required to search: name, years to search. Civil cases indexed by defendant, plaintiff. Civil records on dockets from 1846; on computer back to 1992 approx.

Criminal Records: Access: In person only. Visitors must perform in person searches for themselves. No

search fee. Required to search: name, years to search. Criminal records on dockets from 1846; on computer back to 1992 approx.

General Information: No juvenile or expunged records released. SASE required. Turnaround time 1-2 days. Fax notes: $1.25 for first page, $1.00 each add'l. Copy fee: $.50 per page. Certification fee: $,50 per page or $2.00 per document. Fee payee: Drew County Circuit Clerk. Personal checks accepted. Prepayment is required.

District Court PO Box 505, Monticello, AR 71655; 870-367-4420; Fax: 870-460-9056. Hours: 8:30AM-5PM (CST). *Misdemeanor, Civil Actions Under $5,000, Eviction, Small Claims.*

Civil Records: Access: Mail, fax, in person. Only the court performs in person searches; visitors may not. Search fee: No search fee. Required to search: name, years to search, DOB, SSN, signed release. Records overall since 1980, on computer since 1987.

Criminal Records: Access: Mail, fax, in person. Only the court performs in person searches; visitors may not. No search fee. Required to search: name, years to search, DOB; also helpful: sex, signed release. Records overall since 1980, on computer since 1987.

General Information: Turnaround time 1-2 days.

Faulkner County

Circuit Court PO Box 9, Conway, AR 72033; 501-450-4911; Fax: 501-450-4948. Hours: 8AM-4:30PM (CST). *Felony, Civil Actions Over $5,000, Probate.*

Civil Records: Access: Fax, mail, in person. Both court and visitors may perform in person searches. Search fee: $6.00 per name. Required to search: name, years to search. Civil cases indexed by defendant, plaintiff. Civil records on computer back to 1987; on docket from 1800s.

Criminal Records: Access: Fax, mail, in person. Both court and visitors may perform in person searches. Search fee: $6.00 per name. Required to search: name, years to search. Criminal records on computer back to 1987; on docket from 1800s.

General Information: Public access terminal is available. No juvenile records released. SASE required. Turnaround time 1-2 days. Fax notes: $1.00 if local, $3.50 plus $.25 per page if long distance. Copy fee: $.25 per page. Certification fee: $3.00. Fee payee: Faulkner County Circuit Clerk. Personal checks accepted. Prepayment is required.

District Court 810 Parkway, Conway, AR 72032; 501-450-6112; Fax: 501-450-6184. Hours: 8AM-4:30PM (CST). *Misdemeanor, Civil Actions Under $5,000, Small Claims.*

Civil Records: Access: Mail, fax, in person, online. Both court and visitors may perform in person searches. Search fee: $10.00 for 3 years; $20.00 more than 3 years. Required to search: name, years to search, DOB, signed release; also helpful: address, SSN. Computerized records go back to 1993.

Criminal Records: Access: Mail, fax, in person, online. Both court and visitors may perform in person searches. Search fee: $10.00 for 3 years; $20.00 more than 3 years. Required to search: name, years to search, DOB, signed release; also helpful: address, SSN. Computerized records go back to 1993.

General Information: Public access terminal is available. Turnaround time 2 days. Certification fee: $5.00. Fee payee: Conway District Court.

Franklin County

Charleston Circuit Court PO Box 387, Charleston, AR 72933; 479-965-7332. Hours: 8AM-4:30PM (CST). *Felony, Civil Actions Over $5,000, Probate.*

Civil Records: Access: Mail, in person. Both court and visitors may perform in person searches. Search fee:

$6.00 per name. Required to search: name, years to search, DOB. Civil cases indexed by defendant, plaintiff. Civil records on dockets from 1900s.

Criminal Records: Access: Mail, in person. Both court and visitors may perform in person searches. Search fee: $6.00 per name. Required to search: name, years to search, DOB. Criminal records on dockets from 1900s.

General Information: No juvenile records released. SASE required. Turnaround time 1-2 days. Fax notes: $1.00 per page to fax back. Copy fee: $.25 per page. Certification fee: $5.00. Fee payee: Franklin County. Personal checks accepted. Prepayment is required.

Ozark Circuit Court PO Box 1112, 211 W Commercial, Ozark, AR 72949; 479-667-3818; Probate phone: 479-667-3607; Fax: 479-667-5174. Hours: 8AM-4:30PM (CST). *Felony, Civil Actions Over $5,000, Probate.*

Note: Probate is maintained at the County Clerk's Office.

Civil Records: Access: Fax, mail, in person. Both court and visitors may perform in person searches. Search fee: $6.00 per name. Required to search: name, years to search. Civil cases indexed by plaintiff. Civil records on dockets from 1900s.

Criminal Records: Access: Fax, mail, in person. Both court and visitors may perform in person searches. Search fee: $6.00 per name. Required to search: name, years to search. Criminal records on dockets from 1900s.

General Information: No juvenile records released. SASE required. Turnaround time 1-2 days. Fax notes: $1.00 per page. Copy fee: $.25 per page. Certification fee: $2.00. Fee payee: Circuit Clerk. Personal checks accepted. Prepayment is required.

District Court PO Box 426, Charleston, AR 72933; 479-965-7455; Fax: 479-965-2231. Hours: 8AM-5PM (CST). *Misdemeanor, Civil Actions Under $5,000, Small Claims.*

Civil Records: Access: Mail, fax, in person. Both court and visitors may perform in person searches. No search fee. Civil records on computer back to 1/2000.

Criminal Records: Access: Mail, fax, in person. Both court and visitors may perform in person searches. No search fee. Required to search: name, years to search, DOB; also helpful-SSN, signed release. Criminal records on computer back to 1/2000.

General Information: Turnaround time 1-2 days.

Fulton County

Circuit Court PO Box 485, Salem, AR 72576; 870-895-3310; Fax: 870-895-3383. Hours: 8AM-4:30PM (CST). *Felony, Civil Actions Over $5,000, Probate.*

Civil Records: Access: Mail, in person. Both court and visitors may perform in person searches. Search fee: $6.00 per name. Required to search: name, years to search. Civil cases indexed by defendant, plaintiff. Civil records on dockets from 1900s; on computer back to 2000.

Criminal Records: Access: Mail, in person. Both court and visitors may perform in person searches. Search fee: $6.00 per name. Required to search: name, years to search. Criminal records on dockets from 1900s; on computer back to 2000.

General Information: No juvenile records released. SASE required. Turnaround time 1-2 days. Copy fee: $.20 per page. Fee payee: Fulton County Clerks. Personal checks accepted. Prepayment is required.

District Court PO Box 928, Salem, AR 72576; 870-895-4136; Fax: 870-895-4114. Hours: 8AM-4:30PM (CST). *Misdemeanor, Civil Actions Under $5,000, Eviction, Small Claims.*

Civil Records: Access: In person, mail. Only the court may perform in person searches. No search fee. Computerized records since 1995.

Criminal Records: Access: In person, mail. Both court and visitors may perform in person searches. No search fee. Required to search: name, years to search, DOB. Computerized records since 1995.

General Information: Turnaround time 1 week.

Garland County

Circuit Court Garland County Courthouse, 501 Ouachita Ave, Room 207, Hot Springs, AR 71901; Civil phone: 501-622-3630; Criminal phone: 501-622-3640; Probate phone: 501-622-3610; Fax: 501-609-9043. Hours: 8AM-5PM (CST). *Felony, Civil Actions Over $5,000, Probate.*

Note: Probate records are handled by the County Clerk, phone number above.

Civil Records: Access: In person only. Visitors must perform in person searches for themselves. No search fee. Required to search: name; also helpful: years to search. Civil cases indexed by defendant, plaintiff. Civil records on microfiche and docket from 1900s; on computer back to 1989.

Criminal Records: Access: Fax, mail, in person. Both court and visitors may perform in person searches. No search fee. Required to search: name, years to search; also helpful: DOB, SSN, maiden name, race, aliases, sex. Criminal records on microfiche and docket from 1900s; on computer back to 1989.

General Information: Public access terminal is available. No expunged, sealed records released. SASE required. Turnaround time 1-2 days. Fax notes: Fee to fax results is $2.00 plus $.25 per page. Copy fee: $.25 per page. Certification fee: $.50. Fee payee: Garland County Circuit Clerk. Personal checks accepted. Prepayment is required.

District Court PO Box 700, Hot Springs, AR 71902; 501-321-6765; Fax: 501-321-6764. Hours: 8AM-5PM (CST). *Misdemeanor, Civil Actions Under $5,000, Eviction, Small Claims.*

Civil Records: Access: In person, mail. Both court and visitors may perform in person searches. No search fee. Civil record on computer back to 2000.

Criminal Records: Access: In person, mail. Both court and visitors may perform in person searches. No search fee. Required to search: name, years to search, offense. Criminal records on computer back to 1990.

General Information: Turnaround time 1-2 days. Copy fee: $.25 per page. Certification fee: $5.00 per document.

Grant County

Circuit & County Courts Grant County Courthouse, 101 W Center, Rm 106, Sheridan, AR 72150; 870-942-2631; Fax: 870-942-3564. Hours: 8AM-4:30PM (CST). *Felony, Civil Actions Over $5,000, Probate.*

Civil Records: Access: In person only. Visitors must perform in person searches for themselves. No search fee. Required to search: name, years to search. Civil cases indexed by defendant, plaintiff. Civil records on dockets and index from 1982.

Criminal Records: Access: In person only. Visitors must perform in person searches for themselves. No search fee. Required to search: name, years to search. Criminal records on dockets and index from 1982.

General Information: No juvenile, probate or adoption records released. Copy fee: $.25 per page. Certification fee: $3.00. Fee payee: Circuit Clerk. Personal checks accepted. Prepayment is required.

District Court PO Box 603, Sheridan, AR 72150; 870-942-3464; Fax: 870-942-8885. Hours: 8AM-4:30PM (CST). *Misdemeanor, Civil Actions Under $5,000, Eviction, Small Claims.*

Civil Records: Access: In person, mail. Both court and visitors may perform in person searches. No search fee. Computerized records since 1992.

Criminal Records: Access: In person, mail. Both court and visitors may perform in person searches. No search fee. Required to search: name, years to search. Computerized records since 1992.

General Information: Turnaround time 1-2 days. Copy fee: $.25.

Greene County

Circuit & County Courts 320 W Court #124, Paragould, AR 72450; 870-239-6330; Fax: 870-239-3550. Hours: 8AM-4:30PM (CST). *Felony, Civil Actions Over $5,000, Probate.*

Civil Records: Access: Fax, mail, in person. Both court and visitors may perform in person searches. Search fee: $6.00 per name. Required to search: name, years to search. Civil cases indexed by plaintiff. Civil records on computer from 1986, on index from 1930s.

Criminal Records: Access: Fax, mail, in person. Both court and visitors may perform in person searches. Search fee: $6.00 per name. Required to search: name, years to search; also helpful: DOB, SSN. Criminal records computerized since 1990.

General Information: Public access terminal is available. No juvenile records released. SASE required. Turnaround time 1-2 days. Fax notes: For fax back, $1.00 for first 3 pages then $.25 per page. Copy fee: $.50 per page. Certification fee: $3.00. Fee payee: Green County Circuit Clerk. Personal checks accepted. Prepayment is required.

District Court 320 W Court, Rm 227, Paragould, AR 72450; 870-239-7507; Fax: 870-239-7506. Hours: 8AM-4:30PM (CST). *Misdemeanor, Civil Actions Under $5,000, Eviction, Small Claims.*

www.gccourt.com

Civil Records: Access: In person, mail. Only the court performs in person searches; visitors may not. No search fee. Required to search: name, years to search, DOB or SSN. Records on computer back to 1989.

Criminal Records: Access: In person, mail. Only the court performs in person searches; visitors may not. Search fee: $5.00 per name. Required to search: name, years to search, DOB or SSN. Records on computer back to 1989.

General Information: Turnaround time 2 days. Copy fee: $.50 per page. Fee payee: District Clerk. Prepayment is required.

Hempstead County

Circuit Court PO Box 1420, Hope, AR 71802; 870-777-2384; Probate phone: 870-777-2241; Fax: 870-777-7827. Hours: 8AM-4PM (CST). *Felony, Civil Actions Over $5,000, Probate.*

Note: Probate is handled by the County Clerk at same address.

Civil Records: Access: Phone, fax, mail, in person. Both court and visitors may perform in person searches. Search fee: $6.00 per name. Required to search: name, years to search. Civil cases indexed by defendant, plaintiff. Civil records on dockets from 1910.

Criminal Records: Access: Phone, fax, mail, in person. Both court and visitors may perform in person searches. Search fee: $6.00 per name. Required to search: name, years to search, DOB, SSN. Criminal records on dockets from 1910; computerized since 198.

General Information: No juvenile records released. SASE required. Turnaround time 1-2 days. Copy fee: $.50 per page. Certification fee: $5.00. Fee payee: Circuit Clerk. Personal checks accepted. Prepayment is required.

District Court PO Box 1420, Hope, AR 71802-1420; 870-777-2525; Fax: 870-777-7830. Hours: 8AM-4PM (CST). *Misdemeanor, Civil Actions Under $5,000, Eviction, Small Claims.*

Civil Records: Access: Mail, in person. Both court and visitors may perform in person searches. Search fee: $5.00 per name. Required to search: name, years to search. Civil records not computerized.

Criminal Records: Access: Mail, in person. Both court and visitors may perform in person searches. Search fee: $5.00 per name. Required to search: name, years to search, SSN, DOB. Criminal records on computer back to 1987.

General Information: Turnaround time less than 1 week. Fee payee: District Court. Prepayment required.

Hot Spring County

Circuit Court 210 Locust St, PO Box 1200, Malvern, AR 72104; 501-332-2281. Hours: 8:00AM-4:30PM (CST). *Felony, Civil Actions Over $5,000.*

Civil Records: Access: Mail, in person. Both court and visitors may perform in person searches. Search fee: $5.00 per name. Required to search: name, years to search. Civil cases indexed by plaintiff. Civil records on dockets from 1800s.

Criminal Records: Access: Mail, in person. Both court and visitors may perform in person searches. Search fee: $5.00 per name. Required to search: name, years to search, DOB or SSN. Criminal records on dockets from 1800s.

General Information: No juvenile records released. SASE required. Turnaround time 1-2 days. Copy fee: $.50 per page. Certification fee: $5.00. Fee payee: Circuit Clerk. Personal checks accepted. Prepayment is required.

Malvern District Court 305 Locust St, Rm 201, Malvern, AR 72104; 501-332-7604; Fax: 501-332-3144. Hours: 8AM-4:30PM (CST). *Misdemeanor, Civil Actions Under $5,000, Eviction, Small Claims.*

Note: Formerly known as Malvern Municipal Court before 7/1/01.

Civil Records: Access: Mail, fax, in person. Visitors must perform in person searches for themselves. No search fee. Required to search: name, years to search and DOB or SSN. Records computerized back to 1994.

Criminal Records: Access: mail, fax, in person. Visitors must perform in person searches for themselves. No search fee. Required to search: name, years to search, DOB; also helpful: address, SSN. Records computerized back to 1994.

General Information: Turnaround time 3 days.

Howard County

Circuit & County Courts 421 N Main, Rm 7, Nashville, AR 71852; 870-845-7506; Probate phone: 870-845-7503. Hours: 8AM-4:30PM (CST). *Felony, Civil Actions Over $5,000, Probate.*

Note: Probate is handled by the County Clerk at this address.

Civil Records: Access: Phone, mail, in person. Both court and visitors may perform in person searches. No search fee. Required to search: name, years to search. Civil cases indexed by defendant, plaintiff. Civil records on dockets from 1873.

Criminal Records: Access: In person only. Visitors must perform in person searches for themselves. No search fee. Required to search: name, years to search, DOB. Criminal records on dockets from 1873.

General Information: No juvenile or sealed records released. SASE required. Turnaround time 1 week. Copy fee: $.25 per page. Certification fee: $2.00. Fee payee: Circuit Clerk. Personal checks accepted. Prepayment is required.

District Court 426 N Main, ##7, Nashville, AR 71852-2009; 870-845-7522; Fax: 870-845-3705. Hours: 8AM-4:30PM (CST). *Misdemeanor, Civil Actions Under $5,000, Eviction, Small Claims.*

Civil Records: Access: In person, mail. Visitors must perform in person searches for themselves. No search fee.

Criminal Records: Access: In person, mail. Both court and visitors may perform in person searches. No search fee. Required to search: name, years to search, DOB; also helpful: address, SSN.

General Information: Turnaround time 1-3 days.

Independence County

Circuit & County Courts Main and Broad St, Batesville, AR 72501; 870-793-8833; Fax: 870-793-8888. Hours: 8AM-4:30PM (CST). *Felony, Civil Actions Over $5,000.*

Civil Records: Access: In person only. Visitors must perform in person searches for themselves. Required to search: name, years to search; also helpful: address. Civil cases indexed by defendant, plaintiff. Civil judgments on computer from 1980, all others on index books from 1970s.

Criminal Records: Access: Mail, in person. Both court and visitors may perform in person searches. Search fee: $6.00 per name. Required to search: name, years to search, DOB; also helpful: address. Criminal records on index books from 1970s.

General Information: No juvenile records released. SASE required. Turnaround time varies, but usually same day. Copy fee: $.50 per page. Fee payee: Circuit Clerk. Personal checks accepted. Prepayment is required.

District Court 368 E Main, Rm 205, Batesville, AR 72501; 870-793-8817; Fax: 870-793-8875. Hours: 8AM-4:30PM (CST). *Misdemeanor, Civil Actions Under $5,000, Eviction, Small Claims.*

Civil Records: Access: In person, mail. Both court and visitors may perform in person searches. No search fee.

Criminal Records: Access: In person, mail. Both court and visitors may perform in person searches. No search fee. Required to search: name, years to search.

General Information: Turnaround time 1-2 days.

Izard County

Circuit & County Courts PO Box 95, Melbourne, AR 72556; 870-368-4316; Fax: 870-368-4748. Hours: 8:30AM-4:30PM (CST). *Felony, Civil Actions Over $5,000, Probate.*

Civil Records: Access: Fax, mail, in person. Both court and visitors may perform in person searches. Search fee: $6.00 per name. Required to search: name, years to search, address. Civil cases indexed by plaintiff. Civil records on judgment books from 1889; computerized records since 2002.

Criminal Records: Access: Fax, mail, in person. Both court and visitors may perform in person searches. Search fee: $6.00 per name. Required to search: name, years to search, DOB; also helpful: address. Criminal records on judgment books from 1889; computerized records since 2002.

General Information: No juvenile records released. SASE required. Turnaround time 2 weeks. Fax notes: No fee to fax results. Copy fee: $.20 per page. Certification fee: $3.00. Fee payee: Izard County and Circuit Clerk. Personal checks accepted. Prepayment is required.

District Court PO Box 337, Melbourne, AR 72556; 870-368-4390; Fax: 870-368-5042. Hours: 8:30AM-4:30PM (CST). *Misdemeanor, Civil Actions Under $5,000, Small Claims.*

Civil Records: Access: Mail, fax, in person. Both court and visitors may perform in person searches. No search fee. Civil records go back to 1977; on computer back to 1993.

Criminal Records: Access: Mail, fax, in person. Both court and visitors may perform in person searches. No search fee. Required to search: name, years to search, DOB. Criminal records go back to 1977; on computer back to 1993.

General Information: Turnaround time varies.

Jackson County

Circuit Court Jackson County Courthouse, 208 Main St, Newport, AR 72112; 870-523-7423; Fax: 870-523-7404. Hours: 8AM-4:30PM (CST). *Felony, Civil Actions Over $5,000, Probate.*

Civil Records: Access: In person only. Visitors must perform in person searches for themselves. No search fee. Required to search: name, years to search. Civil cases indexed by defendant, plaintiff. Civil records on dockets from 1800s.

Criminal Records: Access: In person only. Visitors must perform in person searches for themselves. No search fee. Required to search: name, years to search. Criminal records on dockets from 1800s.

General Information: No juvenile records released. Copy fee: $.25 per page. Certification fee: $3.00. Fee payee: Circuit Clerk. Personal checks accepted. Prepayment is required.

District Court 615 3rd St, Newport, AR 72112; 870-523-9555; Fax: 870-523-4365. Hours: 8AM-4:30PM (CST). *Misdemeanor, Civil Actions Under $5,000, Eviction, Small Claims.*

Civil Records: Access: Phone, mail, fax, in person. Both court and visitors may perform in person searches. Search fee: No search fee. Civil records go back to 1987.

Criminal Records: Access: Mail, fax, in person. Both court and visitors may perform in person searches. No search fee. Required to search: name, years to search, DOB. Criminal records go back to 1987 on computer, searchable to 1950.

General Information: Turnaround time 5-7 days. Certification fee: $3.00. Fee payee: Newport District Court. Prepayment is required.

Jefferson County

Circuit Court PO Box 7433, Pine Bluff, AR 71611; Civil phone: 870-541-5307; Criminal phone: 870-541-5306. Hours: 8:30PM-5PM (CST). *Felony, Civil Actions Over $5,000, Probate.*

Civil Records: Access: In person only. Visitors must perform in person searches for themselves. No search fee. Required to search: name, years to search. Civil cases indexed by defendant, plaintiff. Civil records on dockets from 1950.

Criminal Records: Access: In person only. Visitors must perform in person searches for themselves. No search fee. Required to search: name, years to search, DOB. Criminal records on dockets from 1950.

General Information: Public access terminal is available. No juvenile records released. Copy fee: $.50 per page. Certification fee: $2.00. Fee payee: Circuit Clerk. Personal checks accepted. Prepayment is required.

District Court 200 E 8th Ave, Pine Bluff, AR 71601; 870-543-1860; Fax: 870-543-1889. Hours: 8AM-5PM (CST). *Misdemeanor, Civil Actions Under $5,000, Eviction, Small Claims.*

Civil Records: Access: In person, mail. Both court and visitors may perform in person searches. Search fee: $5.00.

Criminal Records: Access: In person, mail. Both court and visitors may perform in person searches. Search fee: $5.00. Required to search: name, years to search; also helpful: DOB, SSN. Criminal records go back to 1989; computerized records since 1997.

General Information: Turnaround time 1-2 days.

Johnson County

Circuit Court PO Box 217, Clarksville, AR 72830; 501-754-2977; Probate phone: 501-754-3967. Hours: 8AM-4:30PM (CST). *Felony, Civil Actions Over $5,000, Probate.*

Note: Probate is handled by County Clerk, PO Box 57.

Civil Records: Access: Fax, mail, in person. Both court and visitors may perform in person searches. No search fee. Required to search: name, years to search. Civil cases indexed by defendant, plaintiff. Civil records on index from 1900s. Fax access limited to 800#'s.

Criminal Records: Access: Fax, mail, in person. Both court and visitors may perform in person searches. No search fee. Required to search: name, years to search, DOB; also helpful: SSN. Criminal records on index from 1900s. Fax access limited to 800#'s.

General Information: No juvenile records released. SASE required. Turnaround time 1-2 days. Fax notes: No fee to fax results. Will fax to 800 numbers only. Copy fee: $.50 per page. Certification fee: $1.00. Fee payee: Circuit. Personal checks accepted. Draft or two party checks not allowed.

District Court PO Box 581, Clarksville, AR 72830; 479-754-8533; Fax: 479-754-6014. Hours: 8AM-4PM (CST). *Misdemeanor, Civil Actions Under $5,000, Eviction, Small Claims.*

Civil Records: Access: In person, mail. Both court and visitors may perform in person searches. No search fee.

Criminal Records: Access: In person, mail. Both court and visitors may perform in person searches. No search fee. Required to search: name, years to search; also helpful: DOB, SSN.

General Information: Turnaround time 1-2 days.

Lafayette County

Circuit Court #3 Courthouse Square, Lewisville, AR 71845; 870-921-4878; Probate phone: 870-921-4633; Fax: 870-921-4505. Hours: 8AM-4:30PM (CST). *Felony, Civil Actions Over $5,000, Probate.*

Civil Records: Access: Phone, mail, in person. Both court and visitors may perform in person searches. Search fee: $6.00 per name. Required to search: name, years to search. Civil cases indexed by defendant, plaintiff. Civil records on dockets from 1950s.

Criminal Records: Access: Mail, in person. Both court and visitors may perform in person searches. Search fee: $6.00 per name. Required to search: name, years to search. Criminal records on dockets from 1950s.

General Information: No juvenile records released without written order form the judge. SASE required. Turnaround time 2 days. Copy fee: $.50 per page. Certification fee: $3.00. Fee payee: Circuit Clerk. Personal checks accepted. Prepayment is required.

District Court 110 E Fourth, #1, Lewisville, AR 71845; 870-921-5555; Fax: 870-921-4256. Hours: 8AM-4:30PM (CST). *Misdemeanor, Civil Actions Under $5,000, Eviction, Small Claims.*

Civil Records: Access: In person only. Both court and visitors may perform in person searches. No search fee.

Criminal Records: Access: In person only. Both court and visitors may perform in person searches. No search fee. Required to search: name, years to search, DOB, SSN.

Lawrence County

Circuit Court PO Box 581 (W. Main St.), Walnut Ridge, AR 72476; 870-886-1112; Fax: 870-886-1128. Hours: 8AM-4:30PM (CST). *Felony, Civil Actions Over $5,000, Probate.*

Civil Records: Access: Phone, fax, mail, in person. Visitors must perform in person searches for themselves. No search fee. Required to search: name,

years to search. Civil cases indexed by defendant, plaintiff. Civil records on index from 1981, on docket sheets from 1960s.

Criminal Records: Access: Phone, fax, mail, in person. Visitors must perform in person searches for themselves. Search fee: $6.00. Required to search: name, years to search. Criminal records on index from 1981, on docket sheets from 1960s.

General Information: No juvenile records released. SASE required. Turnaround time 1 day. Fax notes: $1.00 per page. Copy fee: $.50 per page. Certification fee: $3.00 per document. Fee payee: Circuit Clerk. Personal checks accepted. Prepayment is required.

Walnut Ridge District Court 201 SW 2nd St, Walnut Ridge, AR 72476; 870-886-3905. Hours: 8AM-4:30PM (CST). *Misdemeanor, Civil Actions Under $5,000, Eviction, Small Claims.*

Civil Records: Access: In person, mail. Both court and visitors may perform in person searches. No search fee. Computerized records since 1992.

Criminal Records: Access: In person, mail. Both court and visitors may perform in person searches. No search fee. Required to search: name, years to search, offense. Computerized records since 1992.

General Information: Turnaround time 2-3 days.

Lee County

Circuit Court 15 E Chestnut, Marianna, AR 72360; 870-295-7710; Fax: 870-295-7766. Hours: 8:30AM-4:30PM (CST). *Felony, Civil Actions Over $5,000, Probate.*

Civil Records: Access: In person only. Visitors must perform in person searches for themselves. No search fee. Required to search: name, years to search. Civil cases indexed by defendant, plaintiff. Civil records on index books from 1873; computerized records since 1/2002.

Criminal Records: Access: In person only. Only the court performs in person searches; visitors may not. No search fee. Required to search: name, years to search, DOB. Criminal records on index books from 1873; computerized records since 1/2002.

General Information: No juvenile records released. Copy fee: $.25 per page. Certification fee: $2.50. Fee payee: Circuit Court. Personal checks accepted. Prepayment is required.

District Court 45 W Mississippi, Marianna, AR 72360; 870-295-3813; Fax: 870-295-5726. Hours: 8AM-Noon; 1-5PM (CST). *Misdemeanor, Civil Actions Under $5,000, Eviction, Small Claims.*

Civil Records: Access: In person, mail. Only the court performs in person searches; visitors may not. No search fee. Computerized records since 1994.

Criminal Records: Access: In person, mail. Only the court performs in person searches; visitors may not. No search fee. Required to search: name, years to search. Computerized records since 1994.

General Information: Turnaround time 5 days. Certification fee: $2.00 per document.

Lincoln County

Circuit & County Courts Courthouse, 300 S Drew, Star City, AR 71667; 870-628-3154; Probate phone: 870-628-5114; Fax: 870-628-5546. Hours: 8AM-5PM (CST). *Felony, Civil Actions Over $5,000, Probate.*

Civil Records: Access: In person only. Both court and visitors may perform in person searches. No search fee. Required to search: name, years to search. Civil cases indexed by defendant, plaintiff. Civil records on index from 1920, archived from 1920.

Criminal Records: Access: In person only. Visitors must perform in person searches for themselves. No search fee. Criminal records on index from 1920, archived from 1920.

General Information: No sealed records released. Copy fee: $.50 per page. Certification fee: $3.00. Fee payee: Lincoln County Circuit Court. Personal checks accepted. Prepayment is required.

Lincoln County District Court 300 S Drew St, Star City, AR 71667; 870-628-4904. Hours: 8AM-4:30PM (CST). *Misdemeanor, Civil Actions Under $5,000, Eviction, Small Claims.*

Civil Records: Access: Mail, in person. Both court and visitors may perform in person searches. Search fee: $6.00 per name. Required to search: name, years to search, DOB. Civil records go back to 1980.

Criminal Records: Access: Mail, in person. Both court and visitors may perform in person searches. Search fee: $6.00 per name. Required to search: name, years to search, DOB, signed release; also helpful: address, SSN, DL#. Criminal records go back to 1980; on computer back to 1991.

General Information: Turnaround time 3-5 days. Fax notes: No fee to fax back 5 pages or less; if 6 or more, $.50 per page. Copy fee: $.50 per page. Certification fee: $25.00. Fee payee: District Court of Star City. Prepayment is required.

Little River County

Circuit & County Courts PO Box 575, Ashdown, AR 71822; 870-898-7211; Fax: 870-898-7207. Hours: 8:30AM-4:30PM (CST). *Felony, Civil Actions Over $5,000, Probate.*

Civil Records: Access: Phone, mail, in person. Both court and visitors may perform in person searches. Search fee: $6.00 per name. Required to search: name, years to search. Civil cases indexed by plaintiff. Civil records docket books from early 1900s.

Criminal Records: Access: Phone, mail, in person. Both court and visitors may perform in person searches. Search fee: $6.00 per name. Required to search: name, years to search, address, DOB, signed release. Criminal records on docket books back to 1868.

General Information: No juvenile records released. SASE required. Turnaround time 1 day. Copy fee: $.50 per page. Certification fee: $5.00. Fee payee: Circuit Clerk. Personal checks accepted. Prepayment is required.

District Court 351 N 2nd St, #8, Ashdown, AR 71822; 870-898-7230; Fax: 870-898-7262. Hours: 8:30AM-4:30PM (CST). *Misdemeanor, Civil Actions Under $5,000, Eviction, Small Claims.*

Civil Records: Access: In person, mail. Both court and visitors may perform in person searches. No search fee. Civil records on computer since 1987.

Criminal Records: Access: In person, mail. Both court and visitors may perform in person searches. No search fee. Required to search: name, years to search; also helpful: DOB, SSN. Criminal records on computer since 1987.

General Information: Turnaround time 1 week. Copy fee: $.50 per page. Certification fee: $5.00 per document.

Logan County

Circuit Court Courthouse, 25 W Walnut, Paris, AR 72855; 479-963-2164; Fax: 479-963-3304. Hours: 8AM-4:30PM (CST). *Felony, Civil Actions Over $5,000, Probate.*

Civil Records: Access: Fax, mail, in person. Visitors must perform in person searches. Search fee: $6.00 per name. Required to search: name, years to search. Civil cases indexed by defendant, plaintiff. Civil records on criminal index from 1901.

Criminal Records: Access: Fax, mail, in person. Visitors must perform in person searches. Search fee: $6.00 per name. Required to search: name, years to search. Criminal records on criminal index from 1901.

General Information: No adoption or probate records released. SASE required. Turnaround time 1 days. Fax notes: $1.00 per page. Copy fee: $.50 per page. Certification fee: $5.00. Fee payee: Circuit Clerk. Personal checks accepted. Prepayment is required.

Paris District Court Paris Courthouse, Paris, AR 72855; 479-963-3792; Fax: 479-963-2590. Hours: 8:30AM-4:30PM (CST). *Misdemeanor, Civil Actions Under $5,000, Eviction, Small Claims.*

Civil Records: Access: In person, mail. Both court and visitors may perform in person searches. No search fee. Civil records go back to the 1970's; computerized records since 1994.

Criminal Records: Access: In person, mail. Both court and visitors may perform in person searches. No search fee. Required to search: name, years to search; also helpful: DOB. Criminal records go back to 1970's; computerized records since 1994.

General Information: Public access terminal is available. Turnaround time 1-2 days.

Lonoke County

Circuit Court PO Box 218 Attn: Circuit Clerk, Lonoke, AR 72086; 501-676-2316. Hours: 8AM-4:30PM (CST). *Felony, Civil Actions Over $5,000, Probate.*

Civil Records: Access: in person. Visitors must perform in person searches for themselves. No search fee. Required to search: name, years to search. Civil cases indexed by defendant. Civil records on computer from 1989, on dockets from 1918's.

Criminal Records: Access: Mail, in person. Both court and visitors may perform in person searches. Search fee: $6.00 per name. Required to search: name, years to search, SSN. Criminal records on computer from 1989, on dockets from 1918's (not for public use).

General Information: No juvenile records released. SASE required. Turnaround time 1-2 days. Copy fee: $.25 per page. Certification fee: $6.00. Fee payee: Circuit Clerk. Personal checks accepted. Prepayment is required.

Lonoke District Court 107 W 2nd St, Lonoke, AR 72086-2701; 501-676-3585; Fax: 501-676-2500. Hours: 8AM-4:30PM (CST). *Misdemeanor, Civil Actions Under $5,000, Eviction, Small Claims.*

Civil Records: Access: Mail, in person. Both court and visitors may perform in person searches. Search fee: $5.00. Computerized records since 1999.

Criminal Records: Access: Mal, in person. Both court and visitors may perform in person searches. Search fee: $5.00 per name. Required to search: name, years to search. Computerized records since 1999.

General Information: Fee payee: District Court. Prepayment is required.

Madison County

Circuit Court PO Box 416 (Courthouse), Huntsville, AR 72740; 479-738-2215; Probate phone: 479-738-2747; Fax: 479-738-1544. Hours: 8AM-4:30PM (CST). *Felony, Civil Actions Over $5,000, Probate.*

Note: Probate is in the County Clerk's office, PO Box 37.

Civil Records: Access: In person only. Visitors must perform in person searches for themselves. No search fee. Required to search: name, years to search; also helpful: address. Civil cases indexed by defendant, plaintiff. Civil records on dockets back to 1892.

Criminal Records: Access: In person only. Visitors must perform in person searches for themselves. No search fee. Required to search: name, years to search; also helpful: address, DOB, SSN. Criminal records on dockets back to 1906.

General Information: Public access terminal is available. No juvenile records released. Copy fee: $.25

per page. Certification fee: $5.00. Fee payee: Circuit Clerk. Personal checks accepted. Prepayment is required.

District Court PO Box 549, Huntsville, AR 72740; 479-738-2911; Fax: 479-738-6846. Hours: 8AM-4:30PM (CST). *Misdemeanor, Civil Actions Under $5,000, Eviction, Small Claims.*

Civil Records: Access: Mail, fax, in person. Both court and visitors may perform in person searches, but court will search only if time permits. Search fee: No search fee. Records go back to 1991; computerized records since 1999.

Criminal Records: Access: In person, mail. Both court and visitors may perform in person searches, but court will search only if time permits. No search fee. Required to search: name, years to search, DOB, SSN. Criminal records go back to 1991; on computer back to 1999.

General Information: Turnaround time 1 week. No copy fee. Certification fee: $5.00.

Marion County

Circuit & County Courts PO Box 385, Yellville, AR 72687; 870-449-6226; Fax: 870-449-5143. Hours: 8AM-5PM (CST). *Felony, Civil Actions Over $5,000, Probate.*

Civil Records: Access: In person only. Visitors must perform in person searches for themselves. No search fee. Required to search: name, years to search. Civil cases indexed by plaintiff. Civil records on dockets from 1956, records are not computerized.

Criminal Records: Access: Mail, in person. Both court and visitors may perform in person searches. Search fee: $6.00 per name. Required to search: name, years to search. Criminal records on dockets from 1956, records are not computerized.

General Information: Public access terminal is available. No juvenile or adoption records released. SASE required. Turnaround time 1 day. Copy fee: $.50 per page. Certification fee: $3.00. Fee payee: Marion County Circuit Clerk. Personal checks accepted. Prepayment is required.

District Court PO Box 301, Yellville, AR 72687; 870-449-6030. Hours: 8AM-4:30PM (CST). *Misdemeanor, Civil Actions Under $5,000, Small Claims, Eviction.*

Civil Records: Access: Mail, in person. Both court and visitors may perform in person searches. No search fee. Civil records go back to 1985; on computer back to 1996.

Criminal Records: Access: Mail, in person. Both court and visitors may perform in person searches. No search fee. Required to search: name, years to search, DOB. Criminal records go back to 1985; on computer back to 1996.

General Information: Copy fee: $.25 per page.

Miller County

Circuit & County Courts 412 Laurel St Rm 109, Texarkana, AR 71854; 870-774-4501; Fax: 870-772-5293. Hours: 8AM-4:30PM (CST). *Felony, Civil Actions Over $5,000, Probate.*

Note: Probate is at the County Clerk's office.

Civil Records: Access: Phone, mail, in person. Both court and visitors may perform in person searches. Search fee: $6.00 per name. Required to search: name, years to search. Civil cases indexed by defendant, plaintiff. Civil records on index from 1850s.

Criminal Records: Access: Phone, mail, in person. Both court and visitors may perform in person searches. Search fee: $6.00 per name. Required to search: name, years to search. Criminal records on index from 1850s; computerized records since 2000.

General Information: No expunged records released. SASE required. Turnaround time 1-2 days. Copy fee:

$1.00 per page. Certification fee: $3.50. Fee payee: Miller County Circuit Clerk. Personal checks accepted. Prepayment is required.

District Court 400 Laurel #101, Texarkana, AR 71854; 870-772-2780; Fax: 870-773-3595. Hours: 8AM-4:30PM (CST). *Misdemeanor, Eviction.*

Civil Records: Access: Mail, in person. Both court and visitors may perform in person searches. Search fee: $25.00 per search. Civil records on computer back to 1997.
Criminal Records: Access: In person, mail. Both court and visitors may perform in person searches. Search fee: $25.00 per search. Required to search: name, years to search, DOB. Criminal records on computer back to 1997.
General Information: Turnaround time 2 days. Copy fee: $1.00. Fee payee: Miller County Court. Prepayment is required.

Mississippi County

Blytheville Circuit Court PO Box 1498, Blytheville, AR 72316; 870-762-2332; Fax: 870-763-0150. Hours: 9AM-4:30PM (CST). *Felony, Civil Actions Over $5,000, Probate.*

Civil Records: Access: In person only. Visitors must perform in person searches for themselves. No search fee. Required to search: name, years to search. Civil cases indexed by plaintiff. Civil records prior on index from 1940.
Criminal Records: Access: Phone, fax, mail, in person. Both court and visitors may perform in person searches. Search fee: $6.00 per name. Required to search: name, years to search, DOB, SSN. Criminal records prior on index from 1940. Court will search 7 years only.
General Information: No juvenile records released. SASE required. Turnaround time 1-2 days. Fax notes: $5.00 per document. Copy fee: $.25 per page. Certification fee: $3.00. Fee payee: Circuit Clerk. Personal checks accepted. Prepayment is required.

Osceola Circuit Court County Courthouse, PO Box 466 (200 W Hale), Osceola, AR 72370; 870-563-6471. Hours: 9AM-4:30PM (CST). *Felony, Civil Actions Over $5,000, Probate.*

Civil Records: Access: Mail, in person. Visitors must perform in person searches for themselves. No search fee. Required to search: name, years to search. Civil cases indexed by defendant, plaintiff. Civil records computerized since 1992, on index from 1940.
Criminal Records: Access: Mail, in person. Visitors must perform in person searches for themselves. No search fee. Required to search: name, years to search, DOB, SSN. Criminal records on computer (not for public use) since 1992.
General Information: Public access terminal is available. No juvenile records released. SASE required. Turnaround time 1-2 days. Copy fee: $.50 per page. Certification fee: $3.00. Fee payee: Circuit Clerk. Personal checks accepted. Prepayment is required.

Blytheville District Court 121 N 2nd St, #104, Blytheville, AR 72315; 870-763-7513; Fax: 870-762-0443. Hours: 8AM-5PM (CST). *Misdemeanor, Civil Actions Under $5,000, Small Claims.*

Civil Records: Access: Mail, fax, in person. Both court and visitors may perform in person searches. Search fee: $4.00 per name. Civil records go back to 1960; on computer back to 1987.
Criminal Records: Access: Mail, fax, in person. Both court and visitors may perform in person searches. Search fee: $4.00 per name. Required to search: name, years to search; also helpful: DOB, SSN. Criminal records go back to 1960; on computer back to 1987.

General Information: Turnaround time 1-2 days. Copy fee: $.50 per page. Certification fee: $2.50. Fee payee: City of Blytheville.

Osceola District Court 397 W Keiser, Osceola, AR 72370; 870-563-1303; Fax: 870-563-8439. Hours: 8AM-4PM (CST). *Misdemeanor, Civil Actions Under $5,000, Eviction, Small Claims.*

Civil Records: Access: Mail, in person, fax. Only the court may perform in person searches. Search fee: $5.00. Required to search: name, DOB and SSN. Records computerized for at least 7 years.
Criminal Records: Access: Mail, in person. Only the court may perform in person searches. Search fee: $5.00. Required to search: name, years to search; also helpful: address, DOB, SSN. Records computerized for at least 7 years.
General Information: Turnaround time 1-2 days.

Monroe County

Circuit Court 123 Madison St, Courthouse, Clarendon, AR 72029; 870-747-3615; Fax: 870-747-3710. Hours: 8AM-4:30PM (CST). *Felony, Civil Actions Over $5,000, Probate.*

Civil Records: Access: Fax, mail, in person. Both court and visitors may perform in person searches. No search fee. Required to search: name, years to search. Civil cases indexed by defendant, plaintiff. Civil records on index books from 1931.
Criminal Records: Access: In person only. Visitors must perform in person searches for themselves. No search fee. Required to search: name, years to search. Criminal records on index books from 1933.
General Information: No juvenile records released. SASE required. Turnaround time 1-2 days. Fax notes: $2.50 per document. Additional fee of $.50 if more than 10 pages. Copy fee: $.50 per page. Certification fee: $2.50. Fee payee: Monroe County Circuit Clerk. Personal checks accepted. Prepayment is required.

District Court City Hall, 270 Madison St, Clarendon, AR 72029; 870-747-5200; Fax: 870-747-9969. Hours: 8AM-5PM (CST). *Misdemeanor, Civil Actions Under $5,000, Small Claims.*

Civil Records: Access: In person only. Both court and visitors may perform in person searches. No search fee. Required to search: name, years to search, DOB. Records go back to 1988, on computer since 1994.
Criminal Records: Access: In person only. Both court and visitors may perform in person searches. No search fee. Required to search: name, years to search, DOB, SSN. Records go back to 1988, on computer since 1994.
General Information: Certification fee: $1.00. Fee payee: Clarendon District Court.

Montgomery County

Circuit & County Courts PO Box 369, Courthouse, Mount Ida, AR 71957; 870-867-3521; Fax: 870-867-2177. Hours: 8AM-4:30PM (CST). *Felony, Civil Actions Over $5,000, Probate.*

Civil Records: Access: Phone, fax, mail, in person. Both court and visitors may perform in person searches. No search fee. Required to search: name, years to search; also helpful: address. Civil cases indexed by defendant, plaintiff. Civil records on card files from 1960s.
Criminal Records: Access: In person only. Visitors must perform in person searches for themselves. No search fee. Required to search: name, years to search; also helpful: address, DOB, SSN. Criminal records on card files from 1960s.
General Information: No juvenile or adoption records released. SASE required. Turnaround time 1 day. Copy fee: $.50 per page. Certification fee: $5.00. Fee payee: Circuit Clerk. Personal checks accepted. Prepayment is required.

District Court PO Box 548, Mount Ida, AR 71957; 870-867-2221. Hours: 8AM-4:30PM M-Th, other days hours may vary (CST). *Misdemeanor, Civil Actions Under $5,000, Eviction, Small Claims.*

Civil Records: Access: In person, mail. Both court and visitors may perform in person searches. No search fee. Required to search: name, years to search, DOB, SSN. Records go back to 1973; computerized records go back to 1993.
Criminal Records: Access: In person, mail. Both court and visitors may perform in person searches. No search fee. Required to search: name, years to search, DOB, SSN. Records go back to 1973; computerized records go back to 1993.
General Information: Turnaround time 1-2 days. Fax notes: No fee to fax results. Copy fee: No search fee.

Nevada County

Circuit Court PO Box 204, Prescott, AR 71857; 870-887-2511; Fax: 870-887-5795. Hours: 8AM-5PM (CST). *Felony, Civil Actions Over $5,000, Probate.*

Civil Records: Access: Phone, fax, mail, in person. Both court and visitors may perform in person searches. Search fee: $6.00 per name. Required to search: name, years to search. Civil cases indexed by defendant, plaintiff. Civil records on index since 1850.
Criminal Records: Access: Phone, fax, mail, in person. Both court and visitors may perform in person searches. Search fee: $6.00 per name. Required to search: name, years to search, DOB. Criminal records on index since 1850.
General Information: No juvenile records released. SASE required. Turnaround time 1-2 days. Fax notes: $.25 per page. Copy fee: $.25 per page. Certification fee: $2.00. Fee payee: Nevada County Circuit Clerk. Personal checks accepted. Prepayment is required.

District Court PO Box 22, Prescott, AR 71857; 870-887-6016; Fax: 870-887-3244. Hours: 8AM-5PM (CST). *Misdemeanor, Civil Actions Under $5,000, Eviction, Small Claims.*

Civil Records: Access: Phone, mail, fax, in person. Both court and visitors may perform in person searches. Search fee: No search fee. Records on computer go back to 1994.
Criminal Records: Access: Phone, mail, fax, in person. Both court and visitors may perform in person searches. No search fee. Required to search: name, years to search, DOB, SSN. Records on computer go back to 1994.
General Information: Turnaround time 2-5 days. Fax notes: Will not fax results.

Newton County

Circuit Court PO Box 410, Jasper, AR 72641; 870-446-5125; Fax: 870-446-5155. Hours: 8AM-4:30PM (CST). *Felony, Civil Actions Over $5,000, Probate.*

Civil Records: Access: Fax, mail, in person. Both court and visitors may perform in person searches. Search fee: $5.00 per name. Required to search: name, years to search. Civil cases indexed by defendant, plaintiff. Civil records on dockets.
Criminal Records: Access: Fax, mail, in person. Both court and visitors may perform in person searches. Search fee: $5.00 per name. Required to search: name, years to search, DOB. Criminal records on dockets.
General Information: No juvenile records released. SASE required. Turnaround time varies. Fax notes: $2.50 for first page, $.50 each add'l. Copy fee: $.25 per page. Certification fee: $5.00. Fee payee: Circuit Clerk. Personal checks accepted. Prepayment is required.

District Court PO Box 550, Jasper, AR 72641; 870-446-5335; Fax: 870-446-2234. Hours: 8AM-4:30PM (CST). *Misdemeanor, Civil Actions Under $5,000, Eviction, Small Claims.*

Civil Records: Access: Phone, mail, fax, in person. Only the court performs in person searches; visitors may not. No search fee. Required to search: name plus years to search, and DOB or SSN. Records go back to 1972, civil records not computerized.

Criminal Records: Access: Phone, mail, fax, in person. Only the court performs in person searches; visitors may not. No search fee. Required to search: name plus years to search, and DOB or SSN. Records go back to 1972, on computer back to 1993.

General Information: Copy fee: $.25 per page. Certification fee: $10.00. Fee payee: District Court.

Ouachita County

Circuit Court PO Box 667, Camden, AR 71701; 870-837-2230 (Circuit); Probate phone: 870-837-2220; Fax: 870-837-2252. Hours: 8AM-4:30PM (CST). *Felony, Civil Actions Over $5,000, Probate.*

Civil Records: Access: In person only. Visitors must perform in person searches for themselves. No search fee. Required to search: name, years to search. Civil cases indexed by defendant, plaintiff. Civil records archived from 1950s; on computer back to 3/1999.

Criminal Records: Access: In person only. Visitors must perform in person searches for themselves. No search fee. Required to search: name, years to search; also helpful: DOB, SSN. Criminal records archived from 1950s; on computer back to 3/1999.

General Information: Public access terminal is available. No juvenile records released. Copy fee: $1.00 per page. Certification fee: $2.50. Fee payee: Circuit Clerk of Ouachita County. Personal checks accepted. Prepayment is required.

District Court 213 Madison St, Camden, AR 71701; 870-836-0331; Fax: 870-837-5530. Hours: 8AM-4:30PM (CST). *Misdemeanor, Civil Actions Under $5,000, Eviction, Small Claims.*

Civil Records: Access: Mail, fax, in person. Both court and visitors may perform in person searches. Search fee: $5.00 per name. Required to search: name, years to search. Records go back to 1950; computerized since 1987.

Criminal Records: Access: Mail, fax, in person. Both court and visitors may perform in person searches. Search fee: $5.00 per name. Required to search: name, years to search, DOB; also helpful: SSN. Records go back to 1950; computerized since 1987.

General Information: Turnaround time 1-2 days. Certification fee: $5.00. Fee payee: District Court. Prepayment is required.

Perry County

Circuit Court PO Box 358, Perryville, AR 72126; 501-889-5126; Fax: 501-889-5759. Hours: 8AM-4:30PM (CST). *Felony, Civil Actions Over $5,000, Probate.*

Civil Records: Access: In person only. Visitors must perform in person searches for themselves. No search fee. Required to search: name, years to search. Civil cases indexed by defendant, plaintiff. Civil records on computer from 1997, on dockets from 1974.

Criminal Records: Access: In person only. Visitors must perform in person searches for themselves. No search fee. Required to search: name, years to search, DOB. Criminal records on computer from 1997, on dockets from 1974.

General Information: Public access terminal is available. No juvenile or adoption records released. Copy fee: $.50 for first page, $.25 each add'l. Certification fee: $5.00. Fee payee: Circuit Clerk. Personal checks accepted. Prepayment is required.

District Court PO Box 186, Perryville, AR 72126; 501-889-5296; Fax: 501-889-5835. Hours: 8AM-4:30PM (CST). *Misdemeanor, Civil Actions Under $5,000, Eviction, Small Claims.*

Civil Records: Access: Mail, fax, in person. Only the court performs in person searches; visitors may not Search fee: $2.00. Records back to 1993.

Criminal Records: Access: In person, mail. Only the court performs in person searches; visitors may not Search fee: $2.00. Required to search: name, years to search, DOB, SSN. Computerized records back to 1997, prior on hard copy back to 1993.

General Information: Turnaround time 3-5 days. Fee payee: District Court. Prepayment is required.

Phillips County

Circuit Court Courthouse, 620 Cherry St #206, Helena, AR 72342; 870-338-5515; Probate phone: 870-338-5505; Fax: 870-338-5513. Hours: 8AM-4:30PM (CST). *Felony, Civil Actions Over $5,000, Probate.*

Civil Records: Access: Mail, in person. Visitors must perform in person searches for themselves. Search fee: $6.00 per name. Required to search: name, years to search, DOB. Civil cases indexed by plaintiff. Civil records on fee books from 1970; on computer back to 1998.

Criminal Records: Access: Mail, in person. Visitors must perform in person searches for themselves. Search fee: $6.00 per name. Required to search: name, years to search; also helpful-DOB, SSN. Criminal records on fee books from 1970; on computer back to 1998.

General Information: No juvenile records released. Fax notes: Fee to fax results is $2.00 per document. Copy fee: $.25 per page. Certification fee: $3.00. Fee payee: Circuit Clerk Wanda McIntosh. Personal checks accepted. Prepayment is required.

District Court 226 Perry ST, City Hall, Helena, AR 72342; 870-338-9831; Fax: 870-338-9832. Hours: 8AM-4:30PM (CST). *Misdemeanor, Civil Actions Under $5,000, Eviction, Small Claims.*

Civil Records: Access: In person, mail. Both court and visitors may perform in person searches. Search fee: $9.00. Computerized from 1993-2000.

Criminal Records: Access: In person, mail. Both court and visitors may perform in person searches. Search fee: $5.00 per name. Required to search: name, years to search, address, DOB, SSN. Computerized back to 1993.

General Information: Turnaround time 3 days. Copy fee: $.25 per page. Certification fee: $2.50 per page. Fee payee: City of Helena District Court. Prepayment is required.

Pike County

Circuit Court PO Box 219, Murfreesboro, AR 71958; 870-285-2231; Fax: 870-285-3281. Hours: 8AM-4:30PM (CST). *Felony, Civil Actions Over $5,000, Probate.*

Civil Records: Access: Fax, mail, in person. Both court and visitors may perform in person searches. Search fee: $6.00 per name. Required to search: name, years to search. Civil cases indexed by defendant. Civil records archived from 1895. Some records on dockets, fee books and computer.

Criminal Records: Access: Fax, mail, in person. Both court and visitors may perform in person searches. Search fee: $6.00 per name. Required to search: name, years to search, DOB. Criminal records archived from 1895. Some records on dockets, fee books. Computerized records from 1992.

General Information: No juvenile or adoption records released. Turnaround time 1 week. Fax notes: Fax fee $1.50 1st 3 pages, $.50 each additional page. Copy fee: $.50 per page. Certification fee: $5.00. Fee payee: Pike County Clerk. Prepayment is required.

District Court PO Box 197, Murfreesboro, AR 71958; 870-285-3865; Fax: 870-285-2660. Hours: 8:30AM-4:30PM (CST). *Misdemeanor, Civil Actions Under $5,000, Eviction, Small Claims.*

Civil Records: Access: In person, mail. Both court and visitors may perform in person searches. No search fee.

Criminal Records: Access: In person, mail. Both court and visitors may perform in person searches. Search fee: $6.00 per name. Required to search: name, years to search, offense.

General Information: Turnaround time 2-3 days. Fee payee: Pike County District Court. Prepayment is required.

Poinsett County

Circuit Court PO Box 46, Harrisburg, AR 72432; 870-578-4420; Fax: 870-578-2441. Hours: 8:30AM-4:30PM (CST). *Felony, Civil Actions Over $5,000, Probate.*

Civil Records: Access: Mail, in person. Both court and visitors may perform in person searches. Search fee: $6.00 per name. Required to search: name, years to search. Civil cases indexed by defendant, plaintiff. Civil records on computer from 1985. Some records on dockets.

Criminal Records: Access: Mail, in person. Both court and visitors may perform in person searches. Search fee: $6.00 per name. Required to search: name, years to search, DOB. Criminal records on computer from 1985. Some records on dockets.

General Information: No juvenile records released. SASE required. Turnaround time 1-2 days. Copy fee: $.25 per page. Certification fee: $2.00. Fee payee: Circuit Clerk. Personal checks accepted. Prepayment is required.

Harrisburg District Court 202 N East St, Harrisburg, AR 72432; 870-578-4110; Fax: 870-578-4123. Hours: 8AM-4:30PM (CST). *Misdemeanor, Civil Actions Under $5,000, Eviction, Small Claims.*

Civil Records: Access: In person only. Both court and visitors may perform in person searches. Search fee: $2.00. Required to search: name, DOB, SSN, signed release. Civil records go back to 1987.

Criminal Records: Access: In person only. Both court and visitors may perform in person searches. No search fee. Required to search: name, years to search; also helpful: DOB, SSN, signed release. Criminal records on computer back to 1987. Court does not allow public access to computer index.

General Information: Copy fee: $.25 per page. Certification fee: $5.00. Fee payee: Harrisburg District Court. Prepayment is required.

Polk County

Circuit Court 507 Church St, Mena, AR 71953; 479-394-8100; Probate phone: 479-394-8123. Hours: 8AM-4:30PM (CST). *Felony, Civil Actions Over $5,000, Probate.*

Note: Probate is handled separately from the court.

Civil Records: Access: Mail, in person. Both court and visitors may perform in person searches. Search fee: $6.00 per name. Required to search: name, years to search. Civil cases indexed by defendant, plaintiff. Civil records on dockets and index from late 1800s.

Criminal Records: Access: Mail, in person. Both court and visitors may perform in person searches. Search fee: $6.00 per name. Required to search: name, years to search, DOB. Criminal records on dockets and index from late 1800s.

General Information: No juvenile records released. SASE required. Turnaround time 1-2 days. Copy fee: $.25 per page. $.50 for legal size copies. Certification fee: $2.00. Fee payee: Circuit Clerk. Personal checks accepted. Prepayment is required.

District Court Courthouse, 507 Church St, Mena, AR 71953; 479-394-8140; Fax: 479-394-6199. Hours: 8AM-4:30PM (CST). *Misdemeanor, Civil Actions Under $5,000, Eviction, Small Claims.*

Civil Records: Access: In person. Visitors must perform in person searches for themselves. No search fee. Civil records go back 10 years; computerized records go back 8 years.

Criminal Records: Access: In person. Visitors must perform in person searches for themselves. No search fee. Required to search: name, years to search, DOB; also helpful: SSN. Criminal records go back 10 years; computerized records go back 8 years.

Pope County

Circuit Court 100 W Main, Russellville, AR 72801; 479-968-7499. Hours: 8AM-5PM (CST). *Felony, Civil Actions Over $5,000.*

Civil Records: Access: In person only. Visitors must perform in person searches for themselves. No search fee. Required to search: name, years to search. Civil cases indexed by defendant, plaintiff. Civil records on dockets from early 1900s; on computer back to 1998.

Criminal Records: Access: In person only. Visitors must perform in person searches for themselves. No search fee. Required to search: name, years to search, DOB; also helpful: SSN. Criminal records on dockets from early 1900s; on computer back to 1998.

General Information: Public access terminal is available. No juvenile records released. Copy fee: If the court makes the copy, the fee is $1.00 per page, otherwise $.15. Certification fee: $3.00. Fee payee: Pope County. Personal checks accepted.

District Court 205 W Second, Russellville, AR 72801; 479-968-1393; Fax: 479-968-4166. Hours: 8:30AM-5PM (CST). *Misdemeanor, Civil Actions Under $5,000, Small Claims.*

Civil Records: Access: Phone, fax, mail, in person. Both court and visitors may perform in person searches. No search fee. Civil records go back to 1970s; on computer back to 1991.

Criminal Records: Access: Phone, fax, mail, in person. Both court and visitors may perform in person searches. No search fee. Required to search: name, years to search; also helpful: DOB. Criminal records go back to 1970s; on computer back to 1991.

General Information: Turnaround time 2-3 days. Copy fee: $.25 per page. Certification fee: $5.00. Fee payee: District Court. Prepayment is required.

Prairie County

Circuit Court - Southern District PO Box 283, De Valls Bluff, AR 72041; 870-998-2314; Fax: 870-998-2314. Hours: 8AM-4:30PM (CST). *Felony, Civil Actions Over $5,000, Probate.*

Civil Records: Access: Phone, fax, mail, in person. Both court and visitors may perform in person searches. Search fee: $6.00. Required to search: name, years to search. Civil cases indexed by defendant, plaintiff. Civil records on dockets from 1800s.

Criminal Records: Access: Phone, fax, mail, in person. Both court and visitors may perform in person searches. Search fee: $6.00. Required to search: name, years to search, DOB, SSN. Criminal records on dockets from 1800s.

General Information: No juvenile or adoption records released. SASE required. Turnaround time 1 day. Fax notes: $1.00 per page. Copy fee: $.25 per page. Certification fee: $6.00. Fee payee: Circuit Clerk. Personal checks accepted. Prepayment is required.

Circuit & County Courts - Northern District PO Box 1011, Des Arc, AR 72040; 870-256-4434; Fax: 870-256-4434. Hours: 8AM-4:30PM (CST). *Felony, Civil Actions Over $5,000, Probate.*

Civil Records: Access: Mail, in person. Both court and visitors may perform in person searches. Search fee: $6.00 per name. Required to search: name, years to search. Civil cases indexed by defendant, plaintiff. Civil records on dockets from 1800s; limited records on computer.

Criminal Records: Access: Mail, in person. Both court and visitors may perform in person searches. Search fee: $6.00 per name. Required to search: name, years to search. Criminal records on dockets from 1800s; limited records on computer.

General Information: No juvenile, adoption records released. SASE required. Turnaround time 1 day. Fax notes: Fee to fax results is $.25 per page. Copy fee: $.25 per page. Certification fee: $6.00. Fee payee: Circuit Clerk. Personal checks accepted. Prepayment is required.

Des Arc District Court PO Box 389, Des Arc, AR 72040; 870-256-3011; Fax: 870-256-4612. Hours: 8AM-4:30PM (CST). *Misdemeanor, Civil Actions Under $5,000, Eviction, Small Claims.*

Civil Records: Access: In person, mail. Both court and visitors may perform in person searches. No search fee.

Criminal Records: Access: In person, mail. Both court and visitors may perform in person searches. No search fee. Required to search: name, years to search.

General Information: Turnaround time 1-2 days.

Pulaski County

Circuit Court Courthouse, Rm 102, 401 W Markham St, Ste 102, Little Rock, AR 72201; 501-340-8431; Probate phone: 501-340-8411; Fax: 501-340-8420. Hours: 8:30AM-4:30PM (CST). *Felony, Civil Actions Over $5,000, Probate.*

Note: Probate is handled by the Chancery Court #120 until July 1, 2001.

Civil Records: Access: In person only. Visitors must perform in person searches for themselves. No search fee. Required to search: name, years to search. Civil cases indexed by defendant, plaintiff. Civil records on computer from 1982, on microfiche from 1974 to 1982, archived from 1900.

Criminal Records: Access: In person only. Visitors must perform in person searches for themselves. No search fee. Required to search: name, years to search, DOB, SSN. Criminal records on computer from 1982, on microfiche from 1974 to 1982, archived from 1900.

General Information: Public access terminal is available. No expunged records released. Copy fee: $.25 per page. Certification fee: $2.50. Fee payee: Circuit Clerk. Personal checks accepted. Prepayment is required.

District Court 3001 W Roosevelt, Little Rock, AR 72204; 501-340-6824; Fax: 501-340-6899. Hours: 8AM-4:30PM (CST). *Misdemeanor, Civil Actions Under $5,000, Eviction, Small Claims.*

Civil Records: Access: In person, mail. Both court and visitors may perform in person searches. No search fee. Required to search: DOB, SNS, case number. Overall records and computerized records go to 1988.

Criminal Records: Access: In person, mail. Both court and visitors may perform in person searches. No search fee. Required to search: name, years to search; also helpful: SSN.

General Information: Turnaround time 2-3 days.

Randolph County

Circuit Court 107 West Broadway, Pocahontas, AR 72455; 870-892-5522; Fax: 870-892-8794. Hours: 8AM-4:30PM (CST). *Felony, Civil Actions Over $5,000, Probate.*

Civil Records: Access: Mail, in person. Both court and visitors may perform in person searches. Search fee: $6.00 per name. Required to search: name, years to search. Civil cases indexed by defendant, plaintiff. Civil records on criminal index from 1836.

Criminal Records: Access: Mail, in person. Both court and visitors may perform in person searches. Search fee: $6.00 per name. Required to search: name, years to search, DOB. Criminal records on criminal index from 1836.

General Information: No juvenile records released. SASE required. Turnaround time same day. Copy fee: $.25 per page. Certification fee: $2.00. Fee payee: Circuit Clerk. Personal checks accepted.

District Court 1510 Pace Rd, Pocahontas, AR 72455; 870-892-4033; Fax: 870-892-4392. Hours: 8:00AM-4:30PM (CST). *Misdemeanor, Civil Actions Under $5,000, Eviction, Small Claims.*

Civil Records: Access: In person, mail. Both court and visitors may perform in person searches. Search fee: $6.00. Required to search: name, years to search, DOB, SSN.

Criminal Records: Access: In person, mail. Both court and visitors may perform in person searches. Search fee: $6.00. Required to search: name, years to search, DOB, SSN.

General Information: Turnaround time 1 day. Fee payee: District Court. Prepayment is required.

Saline County

Circuit Court 200 North Main St, Benton, AR 72018; 501-303-5615; Fax: 501-303-5675. Hours: 8AM-4:30PM (CST). *Felony, Civil Actions Over $5,000, Probate.*

www.salinecounty.org

Civil Records: Access: In person only. Visitors must perform in person searches for themselves. No search fee. Required to search: name, years to search. Civil cases indexed by defendant, plaintiff. Civil records on computer since 9/94, prior on docket books.

Criminal Records: Access: In person only. Visitors must perform in person searches for themselves. No search fee. Required to search: name, years to search, DOB, SSN. Criminal records on computer since 9/94, prior on docket books.

General Information: No juvenile records released. Copy fee: $.25 per page. Certification fee: $3.00. Fee payee: Circuit Court. Personal checks accepted. Prepayment is required.

Benton District Court 1605 Edison Ave, Benton, AR 72015; 501-303-5670/1 & 5975; Fax: 501-776-5696. Hours: 8AM-4:30PM (CST). *Misdemeanor, Civil Actions Under $5,000, Eviction, Small Claims.*

Civil Records: Access: In person, mail. Both court and visitors may perform in person searches. Search fee: $5.00 per name.

Criminal Records: Access: In person, mail. Both court and visitors may perform in person searches. Search fee: $5.00 per name. Required to search: name, years to search; also helpful: DOB, SSN.

General Information: Turnaround time 1 day.

Scott County

Circuit Court PO Box 2165, 100 W First St Box 10, Waldron, AR 72958; 479-637-2642. Hours: 8AM-4:30PM (CST). *Felony, Civil Actions Over $5,000, Probate.*

Civil Records: Access: Phone, mail, fax, in person. Both court and visitors may perform in person searches. No search fee. Required to search: name, years to search. Civil cases indexed by defendant, plaintiff. Civil records on index books from 1882.

Criminal Records: Access: Phone, mail, fax, in person. Both court and visitors may perform in person searches. No search fee. Required to search: name, years to search, DOB, SSN. Criminal records on index books from 1882.

General Information: No juvenile or adoption records released. SASE required. Turnaround time 1 week. Copy fee: $.25 per page. Certification fee: $5.00. Fee payee: Scott County. Personal checks accepted. Prepayment is required.

District Court 100 W 1st St, Box 15, Waldron, AR 72958; 479-637-4694; Fax: 479-437-4199. Hours: 8AM-4:30PM (CST). *Misdemeanor, Civil Actions Under $5,000, Eviction, Small Claims.*

Civil Records: Access: In person, mail. Both court and visitors may perform in person searches. No search fee. Records on computer go back to 1998.

Criminal Records: Access: In person, mail. Both court and visitors may perform in person searches. No search fee. Required to search: name, years to search. Records go back to 1998; on computer back to 10/1998.

General Information: Turnaround time 1-2 days. Certification fee: No certification fee.

Searcy County

Circuit Court PO Box 998, Marshall, AR 72650; 870-448-3807. Hours: 8AM-4:30PM (CST). *Felony, Civil Actions Over $5,000, Probate.*

Civil Records: Access: Mail, in person. Visitors must perform in person searches for themselves No search fee. Required to search: name, years to search. Civil cases indexed by defendant, plaintiff. Civil records archived from 1881. Some records on dockets.

Criminal Records: Access: In person only. Visitors must perform in person searches for themselves. No search fee. Required to search: name, years to search, offense; also helpful: DOB, SSN. Criminal records archived from 1881. Some records on dockets.

General Information: No juvenile or adoption records released. SASE required. Turnaround time 1-2 days. Copy fee: $.25 per page. Fee is for civil division only. Certification fee: $3.00 per doc. Fee payee: Searcy County Clerk. Personal checks accepted. Prepayment is required.

District Court PO Box 885, Marshall, AR 72650; 870-448-5411; Fax: 870-448-5692. Hours: 9AM-5PM (CST). *Misdemeanor, Civil Actions Under $5,000, Eviction, Small Claims.*

Civil Records: Access: In person, mail. Both court and visitors may perform in person searches. No search fee.

Criminal Records: Access: In person, mail. Both court and visitors may perform in person searches. No search fee. Required to search: name, years to search, DOB, SSN.

General Information: Turnaround time 1 week. Certification fee: $5.00 per document.

Sebastian County

Circuit Court - Greenwood Division PO Box 310, County Courthouse, Greenwood, AR 72936; 479-996-4175; Fax: 479-996-6885. Hours: 8AM-5PM (CST). *Felony, Civil Actions Over $5,000, Probate.*

Civil Records: Access: Mail, in person. Both court and visitors may perform in person searches. Search fee: $6.00 per name. Required to search: name, years to search. Civil cases indexed by defendant, plaintiff. Civil records on computer from 10/87, on dockets from 1900.

Criminal Records: Access: Mail, in person. Both court and visitors may perform in person searches. Search fee: $6.00 per name. Required to search: name, years to search; also helpful: SSN. Criminal records on computer from 10/87, on dockets from 1900.

General Information: Public access terminal is available. No juvenile records released. SASE required. Turnaround time 1-2 weeks. Fax notes: $1.00 per page. Copy fee: $1.00 per page. Certification fee: $2.50. Fee payee: Circuit Clerk. Personal checks accepted. Prepayment is required.

Circuit Court - Fort Smith 35 S 6th St, PO Box 1179, Fort Smith, AR 72902; 479-782-1046. Hours: 8AM-5PM (CST). *Felony, Civil Actions Over $5,000, Probate.*

Civil Records: Access: Fax, mail, in person. Both court and visitors may perform in person searches. Search fee: $6.00 per name. Required to search: name, years to search; also helpful: address. Civil cases indexed by defendant, plaintiff. Civil records on computer from 1988, on dockets from 1900.

Criminal Records: Access: Fax, mail, in person. Both court and visitors may perform in person searches. Search fee: $6.00 per name. Required to search: name, years to search; also helpful: address, DOB, SSN. Criminal records on computer from 1988, on dockets from 1900. Court will only perform searches for criminal justice purposes.

General Information: Public access terminal is available. No juvenile records released. SASE required. Turnaround time 1-2 weeks. Fax notes: $1.00 per page. Copy fee: $1.00 per page. The fee is $.50 if in person, $1.00 for mail requesters. Certification fee: $2.50. Fee payee: Circuit Clerk. Personal checks accepted. Prepayment is required.

Fort Smith District Court Courthouse, 35 S 6th St, Fort Smith, AR 72901; 479-784-2420; Fax: 479-784-2438. Hours: 8:30AM-5PM (CST). *Misdemeanor, Civil Actions Under $5,000, Eviction, Small Claims.*

Note: Area code will change to 479 in July 2002.

Civil Records: Access: Phone, fax, mail, in person. Both court and visitors may perform in person searches. No search fee. If copies are reuqired, then your request must be in writing.

Criminal Records: Access: Phone, fax, mail, in person. Both court and visitors may perform in person searches. No search fee. Required to search: name, years to search, DOB; also helpful: SSN. Records are computerized since 1984. If copies are reuqired, then your request must be in writing.

General Information: Public access terminal is available. Turnaround time 1-2 days. Fax notes: Fee to fax results is $.50 per page. Copy fee: $.50 per page. Certification fee: $5.00.

Sevier County

Circuit Court 115 N 3rd, Courthouse, De Queen, AR 71832; 870-584-3055; Probate phone: 870-642-2852; Fax: 870-642-9119. Hours: 8AM-4:30PM (CST). *Felony, Civil Actions Over $5,000, Probate.*

Note: Probate court is located in the same building at County Clerk; probate phone is above.

Civil Records: Access: Phone, mail, fax, in person. Visitors must perform in person searches for themselves. Search fee: No search fee. Required to search: name, years to search. Civil cases indexed by defendant, plaintiff. Civil records archived from 1900.

Criminal Records: Access: In person only. Visitors must perform in person searches for themselves. Search fee: No search fee. Required to search: name, years to search, DOB. Criminal records index goes back to 1961, prior back to 1912.

General Information: No juvenile records released. SASE required. Turnaround time 3 days. Fax notes: Fee to fax is $5.00 per document; free if to a toll-free number. Copy fee: $.50 per page. Certification fee: $5.00 per document. Fee payee: Circuit Clerk. Personal checks accepted. Prepayment is required.

District Court 115 N 3rd St, Rm 215, De Queen, AR 71832; 870-584-7311; Fax: 870-642-6651. Hours: 8AM-4:30PM (CST). *Misdemeanor, Civil Actions Under $5,000, Eviction, Small Claims.*

Civil Records: Access: In person, mail. Both court and visitors may perform in person searches. No search fee.

Criminal Records: Access: In person, mail. Both court and visitors may perform in person searches. No search fee. Required to search: name, years to search, DOB.

General Information: Turnaround time 1-2 weeks. Fee payee: District Court.

Sharp County

Circuit & County Courts PO Box 307, Ash Flat, AR 72513; 870-994-7361; Fax: 870-994-7712. Hours: 8AM-4PM (CST). *Felony, Civil Actions Over $5,000, Probate.*

Civil Records: Access: Fax, mail, in person, online. Both court and visitors may perform in person searches. Search fee: $6.00 per name. Required to search: name, years to search. Civil cases indexed by defendant, plaintiff. Civil records on card files from 1970s. Some records on dockets. The court has outsourced online access to civil, probate, criminal, and all recordings to www.ecourtstor.com. Fees are involved.

Criminal Records: Access: In person, online. Visitors must perform in person searches for themselves. No search fee. Required to search: name, years to search; also helpful: DOB, SSN. Criminal records on card files from 1970s. Some records on dockets. The court has outsourced online access to civil, probate, criminal, and all recordings to www.ecourtstor.com. Fees are involved.

General Information: No juvenile or expunged records released. SASE required. Turnaround time 1 day. Fax notes: No fee to fax results. Will only fax to 800 numbers. Copy fee: $.15 per page. Certification fee: $5.00. Fee payee: Sharp County Clerk. Personal checks accepted. Prepayment is required.

District Court PO Box 2, Ash Flat, AR 72513; 870-994-2745; Fax: 870-994-7901. Hours: 8AM-4PM (CST). *Misdemeanor, Civil Actions Under $5,000, Eviction, Small Claims.*

Civil Records: Access: In person, mail. Both court and visitors may perform in person searches. No search fee.

Criminal Records: Access: In person, mail. Both court and visitors may perform in person searches. No search fee. Required to search: name, years to search; also helpful: DOB, SSN.

General Information: Turnaround time 1 day.

St. Francis County

Circuit & County Courts PO Box 1775, Forrest City, AR 72335; 870-261-1715; Fax: 870-261-1723. Hours: 8AM-4:30PM (CST). *Felony, Civil Actions Over $5,000, Probate.*

Civil Records: Access: Fax, mail, in person. Both court and visitors may perform in person searches. Search fee: $5.00 per name. Required to search: name, years to search. Civil cases indexed by defendant, plaintiff. Civil records on index from 1982, archived from 1920s.

Criminal Records: Access: Fax, mail, in person. Both court and visitors may perform in person searches. Search fee: $5.00 per name. Required to search: name, years to search, DOB, SSN. Criminal records on index from 1982, archived from 1920s.

General Information: No juvenile records released. SASE required. Turnaround time 2-3 days. Fax notes: No fee to fax results. Local or toll free calls only. Copy fee: $.25 per page. Certification fee: $3.00. Fee payee: Circuit Clerk. Personal checks accepted.

District Court 615 East Cross, Forrest City, AR 72335; 870-261-1410; Fax: 870-261-1411. Hours: 8AM-4:30PM (CST). *Misdemeanor, Civil Actions Under $5,000, Eviction, Small Claims.*

Civil Records: Access: In person, mail. Only the court performs in person searches; visitors may not. No search fee. Civil records on computer since 1990.

Criminal Records: Access: In person, mail. Only the court performs in person searches; visitors may not. Search fee: $5.00 per name. Required to search: name, years to search. Criminal records on computer since 1994.

General Information: Turnaround time 5 days. Copy fee: $.25 per page. Certification fee: $5.00 per page. Fee payee: District Court. Prepayment is required.

Stone County

Circuit Court 107 W Mail #d, Mountain View, AR 72560; 870-269-3271; Fax: 870-269-2303. Hours: 8AM-4:30PM (CST). *Felony, Civil Actions Over $5,000, Probate.*

Civil Records: Access: In person only. Visitors must perform in person searches for themselves. No search fee. Required to search: name, years to search. Civil cases indexed by defendant, plaintiff. Civil records on dockets from 1960s; computerized records since 1992. Mountain View Abstract Corp does searches by mail. Call 870-269-3470.

Criminal Records: Access: In person only. Visitors must perform in person searches for themselves. No search fee. Required to search: name, years to search, DOB; also helpful: SSN. Criminal records on dockets from 1960s; computerized records since 1992.

General Information: Public access terminal is available. No juvenile or adoption records released. Copy fee: $.25 per page. Certification fee: $3.00. Fee payee: Stone County Clerk. Personal checks accepted. Prepayment is required.

District Court HC 71 Box 4, Mountain View, AR 72560; 870-269-3465. Hours: 8AM-4:30PM (CST). *Misdemeanor, Civil Actions Under $5,000, Eviction, Small Claims.*

Civil Records: Access: Phone, fax, mail, in person. Both court and visitors may perform in person searches. No search fee. Required to search: names, years to search. Records on computer since 1990.

Criminal Records: Access: Phone, fax, mail, in person. Both court and visitors may perform in person searches. No search fee. Required to search: name, years to search; also helpful: DOB, SSN. Records on computer since 1990.

General Information: Turnaround time varies. Certification fee: $3.00. Fee payee: District Court.

Union County

Circuit Court PO Box 1626, El Dorado, AR 71730; 870-864-1940. Hours: 8:30AM-5PM (CST). *Felony, Civil Actions Over $5,000, Probate.*

Civil Records: Access: Mail, in person, online. Both court and visitors may perform in person searches. Search fee: $6.00 per name. Required to search: name, years to search. Civil cases indexed by defendant, plaintiff. Civil records on computer back to 1980, on dockets from 1800s. Online access to circuit court dockets available by subscription through

RecordsUSA.com. Credit card, username and password is required; choose either monthly or per-use plan. Visit the web site for sign-up or call Lisa at 601-264-7701 for information.

Criminal Records: Access: Mail, in person, online. Both court and visitors may perform in person searches. Search fee: $6.00 per name. Required to search: name, years to search, DOB; also helpful: SSN. Criminal records on computer back to 1980, on dockets from 1800s. Online access to criminal dockets is the same as civil.

General Information: Public access terminal is available. No juvenile records released. SASE required. Turnaround time 2 days. Fax notes: Fee to fax results is $1.00 per page. Copy fee: $.50 per page. Certification fee: $3.00. Fee payee: Circuit Clerk. Personal checks accepted. Prepayment is required.

District Court 250 American Ste A, El Dorado, AR 71730; 870-864-1950; Fax: 870-864-1955. Hours: 8:30AM-5PM (CST). *Misdemeanor, Civil Actions Under $5,000, Eviction, Small Claims.*

Civil Records: Access: In person, fax, mail. Both court and visitors may perform in person searches. No search fee. Computerized records since 1987.

Criminal Records: Access: In person, fax, mail. Both court and visitors may perform in person searches. No search fee. Required to search: name, years to search, DOB; also helpful: SSN. Computerized records since 1987.

General Information: Turnaround time 1-2 days.

Van Buren County

Circuit & County Courts 451 Main St, Clinton, AR 72031; 501-745-4140. Hours: 8AM-5PM (CST). *Felony, Civil Actions Over $5,000, Probate.*

Civil Records: Access: Mail, in person. Visitors must perform in person searches for themselves. Search fee: $1.00. Required to search: name, years to search; also helpful: address. Civil cases indexed by defendant, plaintiff. Civil records on computer from 1987, archived from 1900s.

Criminal Records: Access: Mail, in person. Both court and visitors may perform in person searches. Search fee: $1.00 per name. Required to search: name, years to search; also helpful: address, DOB, SSN. Criminal records on computer from 1987, archived from 1900s.

General Information: Public access terminal is available. No juvenile or adoption records released. SASE required. Turnaround time 7-10 days. Copy fee: $1.00 per page. $.50 for microfilm copies. Certification fee: $5.00. Fee payee: Van Buren County Clerk's Office. Personal checks accepted. Prepayment is required.

District Court PO Box 181, Clinton, AR 72031; 501-745-8894; Fax: 501-745-5810. Hours: 8:30AM-4:30PM (CST). *Misdemeanor, Civil Actions Under $5,000, Small Claims.*

Civil Records: Access: Phone, mail, fax, in person. Visitors must perform in person searches for themselves. No search fee. Civil records on computer back to 1988; in books back to 1993.

Criminal Records: Access: Phone, mail, fax, in person. Both court and visitors may perform in person searches. Search fee: $5.00 per name. Required to search: name, years to search, DOB, SSN; also helpful-docket or ticket number. Criminal records on computer back to 1988; in books back to 1993; computerized sincee 1993.

General Information: Certification fee: $5.00. Fee payee: Clinton District Court. Prepayment is required.

Washington County

Circuit Court 280 N College, #320, Fayetteville, AR 72701; 479-444-1542; Fax: 479-444-1537. Hours: 8AM-4:30PM (CST). *Felony, Civil Actions Over $5,000, Probate.*

Civil Records: Access: Fax, mail, in person. Both court and visitors may perform in person searches. Search fee: $6.00. Required to search: name, years to search. Civil cases indexed by defendant, plaintiff. Civil records on computer from 1992, on index from 1950.

Criminal Records: Access: Fax, mail, in person. Both court and visitors may perform in person searches. Search fee: $6.00. Required to search: name, years to search; also helpful: address, DOB, SSN. Criminal records on computer from 1992, on index from 1950.

General Information: Public access terminal is available. No juvenile records released. Turnaround time 1-2 days. Fax notes: $5.00 per document. Copy fee: $.15 per page. Certification fee: $2.00. Fee payee: Circuit Clerk. Personal checks accepted. Prepayment is required.

Fayetteville District Court 100 B West Rock, Fayetteville, AR 72701; 479-587-3596; Fax: 479-444-3480. Hours: 8AM-5PM (CST). *Misdemeanor, Civil Actions Under $5,000, Small Claims.*

Civil Records: Access: Phone, mail, fax, in person. Both court and visitors may perform in person searches. Search fee: $5.00 per name. Required to search: name, years to search. Civil records on computer go back to 1984.

Criminal Records: Access: In person, mail. Only the court may perform in person searches. Search fee: $5.00 per name. Required to search: name, years to search, DOB, SSN, signed release; also helpful: address. Criminal records on computer go back to 1984.

General Information: Turnaround time 1 week. Copy fee: $5.00 per document. Fee payee: City of Fayetteville. Prepayment is required.

White County

Circuit Court 301 W Arch, Searcy, AR 72143; 501-279-6223; Probate phone: 501-279-6204; Fax: 501-279-6218. Hours: 8AM-4:30PM (CST). *Felony, Civil Actions Over $5,000, Probate.*

Civil Records: Access: Phone, mail, in person. Both court and visitors may perform in person searches. Search fee: $6.00 per name. Required to search: name, years to search; also helpful: address. Civil cases indexed by plaintiff. Civil records on dockets from 1982.

Criminal Records: Access: Phone, mail, in person. Both court and visitors may perform in person searches. Search fee: $6.00 per name. Required to search: name, years to search, DOB, SSN; also helpful: address. Criminal records on dockets from 1982.

General Information: Public access terminal is available. No juvenile records released. SASE required. Turnaround time 1 day. Fax notes: $1.00 per page to fax results. Copy fee: $.50 per page. Certification fee: $2.50. Fee payee: Chancery Clerk. Personal checks accepted. Prepayment is required.

Searcy District Court 311 N Gum, Searcy, AR 72143; 501-268-7622/279-1040; Fax: 501-279-1042. Hours: 8:00AM-4:30PM (CST). *Misdemeanor, Civil Actions Under $5,000, Small Claims.*

Civil Records: Access: Mail, fax, phone, in person. Only the court performs in person searches; visitors may not. Search fee: $6.00. Records go back to 1990; on computer since 6/1995.

Criminal Records: Access: In person, phone, fax, mail. Only the court performs in person searches; visitors may not. Search fee: $6.00 if after 6/1995; $10.00 if before and $15.00 is record found. Required to search: name, years to search, DOB, SSN. Records go back since 1993; on computer since 6/1995.

General Information: Turnaround time 5 days. Copy fee: $.50 per page. Fee payee: Searcy District Court.

Woodruff County

Circuit & County Courts PO Box 492, Augusta, AR 72006; 870-347-2391; Probate phone: 870-347-2871; Fax: 870-347-2915. Hours: 8AM-4PM (CST). *Felony, Civil Actions Over $5,000.*

Note: Probate is handled by the County Clerk.

Civil Records: Access: Phone, mail, in person, fax. Both court and visitors may perform in person searches. No search fee. Required to search: name, years to search. Civil cases indexed by defendant, plaintiff. Civil records on dockets from 1982.

Criminal Records: Access: Phone, mail, in person. Both court and visitors may perform in person searches. No search fee. Required to search: name, years to search, DOB. Criminal records on dockets from 1980.

General Information: No juvenile records released. SASE required. Turnaround time 1-2 days. Copy fee: $.50 per page. Certification fee: $3.00. Fee payee: Circuit Clerk. Personal checks accepted. Prepayment is required.

District Court PO Box 381, Augusta, AR 72006; 870-347-2790; Fax: 870-347-2436. Hours: 8:30AM-5PM (CST). *Misdemeanor, Civil Actions Under $5,000, Eviction, Small Claims.*

Civil Records: Access: In person, mail. Only the court may perform in person searches. No search fee. Computerized records go back to 1995.

Criminal Records: Access: In person, mail. Only the court may perform in person searches. Search fee: $5.00 per name. Required to search: name, years to search, DOB, signed release. Computerized records go back to 1995.

General Information: Turnaround time 10 days. Fax notes: No fee to fax results. Certification fee: $.25. Fee payee: Augusta District Court. Prepayment is required.

Yell County

Danville Circuit & County Courts PO Box 219, Danville, AR 72833; 479-495-4850; Fax: 479-495-4875. Hours: 8AM-4PM (CST). *Felony, Civil Actions Over $5,000, Probate.*

Civil Records: Access: Mail, fax, in person. Both court and visitors may perform in person searches. Search fee: $6.00 per name. Required to search: name, years to search; also helpful: address. Civil cases indexed by defendant. Civil records on dockets from 1865.

Criminal Records: Access: Mail, fax, in person. Both court and visitors may perform in person searches. Search fee: $6.00 per name. Required to search: name, years to search, DOB; also helpful: address. Criminal records on dockets from 1865.

General Information: No juvenile or adoption records released. SASE required. Turnaround time 1 day. Copy fee: $.25 per page. Certification fee: $5.00. Fee payee: Circuit Clerk of Yell County. Personal checks accepted. Prepayment is required.

Dardanelle Circuit & County Courts County Courthouse, PO Box 457, Dardanelle, AR 72834; 501-229-4404. Hours: 8AM-4PM (CST). *Felony, Civil Actions Over $5,000, Probate.*

Civil Records: Access: Mail, in person. Both court and visitors may perform in person searches. Search fee: $6.00 per name. Required to search: name, years to search. Civil cases indexed by defendant. Civil records on dockets from 1800s.

Criminal Records: Access: Mail, in person. Both court and visitors may perform in person searches. Search fee: $6.00 per name. Required to search: name, years to search; also helpful: DOB. Criminal records on dockets from 1800s.

General Information: No adoption or juvenile records released. SASE required. Turnaround time 1 day. Copy fee: $.25 per page. Certification fee: $3.00. Fee payee: Circuit Clerk of Yell County. Personal checks accepted. Prepayment is required.

District Court County Courthouse, Dardanelle, AR 72834; 501-229-1389. Hours: 8AM-4PM (CST). *Misdemeanor, Civil Actions Under $5,000, Eviction, Small Claims.*

Civil Records: Access: In person, mail. Both court and visitors may perform in person searches. Search fee: $3.00 per name.

Criminal Records: Access: In person, mail. Both court and visitors may perform in person searches. Search fee: $3.00 per name. Required to search: name, years to search, signed release; also helpful: address, DOB, SSN. Criminal records go back to 1982, on computer back to 1994.

General Information: Turnaround time 2-4 days. No certification fee. Fee payee: District Court. Prepayment is required.

Arkansas Recording Offices

ORGANIZATION: 75 counties, 85 recording offices. The recording officer is the Clerk of Circuit Court, who is Ex Officio Recorder. Ten counties have two recording offices - Arkansas, Carroll, Clay, Craighead, Franklin, Logan, Mississippi, Prairie, Sebastian, and Yell. See the notes under each county for how to determine which office is appropriate to search. The entire state is in the Central Time Zone (CST).

REAL ESTATE RECORDS: Most counties do not perform real estate searches. Copy fees and certification fees vary.

UCC RECORDS: Prior to 07/01 this was a dual filing state. Financing statements were filed at the state level and with the Circuit Clerk, except for consumer goods, farm and real estate related collateral, which were filed only with the Circuit Clerk. Now all financing statements are filed at the state level, except for real estate related collateral, which is still filed with the Circuit Clerk. Most counties will perform UCC searches. Use search request form UCC-11. Search fees are usually $10.00 per debtor name. Copy fees vary.

TAX LIEN RECORDS: Federal tax liens on personal property of businesses are filed with the Secretary of State. Other federal and all state tax liens are filed with the Circuit Clerk. Many counties will perform separate tax lien searches. Search fees are usually $6.00 per name.

OTHER LIENS: Mechanics, lis pendens, judgments, hospital, child support, materialman.

ONLINE ACCESS: There is no statewide access. Benton county offers records via their web site. Also, there is a commercial system available for a limited number of participating counties. Registration and logon is required, the signup fee is $200 minimum plus $.10 per minute usage. For signup or information call 479-631-8054 or visit www.arcountydata.com.

Arkansas County (Northern District)

County Circuit Clerk, PO Box 719, Stuttgart, AR 72160. County Circuit Clerk, R/E and UCC Recording 870-673-2056; Fax 870-673-3869.
Will search UCC records. This agency will not do a tax lien search. Will not search real estate records. **Other Phone Numbers:** Assessor 870-673-6586.

Arkansas County (Southern District)

County Circuit Clerk, 101 Court Square, De Witt, AR 72042. 870-946-4219; Fax 870-946-1394.
Will search UCC records. This agency will not do a tax lien search. Will not search real estate records. **Other Phone Numbers:** Assessor 870-946-1795; Tax Collector 870-946-4210.

Ashley County

County Circuit Clerk, 205 E. Jefferson St, Courthouse, Hamburg, AR 71646. County Circuit Clerk, R/E and UCC Recording 870-853-2030; Fax 870-853-2034.
Will search UCC records. This agency will not do a tax lien search. Will not search real estate records. **Other Phone Numbers:** Assessor 870-853-2060; Treasurer 870-853-2010; Elections 870-853-2020; Tax Collector 870-853-2050.

Baxter County

County Circuit Clerk, Courthouse Square, 1 E. 7th St, Mountain Home, AR 72653. 870-425-3475; Fax 870-425-5105.
Will search UCC records. UCC search includes tax liens. Property transfer searches available. **Online Access:** Assessor, Property Records. Registration and logon is required to search all participating counties at www.arcountydata.com. Signup fee is $200 minimum plus $.10 per minute usage. For signup or information call 479-631-8054 or visit www.arcountydata.com. **Other Phone Numbers:** Assessor 870-425-3453; Tax Collector 870-425-3444.

Benton County

County Circuit Clerk, 215 E. Central St, Suite 6, Bentonville, AR 72712. County Circuit Clerk, R/E and UCC Recording 479-271-1017; Fax 479-271-5719. www.co.benton.ar.us
This agency will not perform searches. **Online Access:** Real Estate, Lien, Property Tax Records. Benton County Assessor, tax collector, and circuit court information is available free online at http://64.217.42.130:5061. Also, registration and logon is required to search all participating counties at www.arcountydata.com. Signup fee is $200 minimum plus $.10 per minute usage. For signup or information call 479-631-8054 or visit www.arcountydata.com. Also, online access to property records is available by subscription at www.recordsusa.com. Credit card, username and password is required; choose either monthly or per-use plan. Visit the web site or call Lisa at 601-264-7701 for information. **Other Phone Numbers:** Assessor 479-271-1037; Elections 479-271-1013; Tax Collector 479-271-1037.

Boone County

County Circuit Clerk, Courthouse, Suite 200, 100 N. Main, Harrison, AR 72601. County Circuit Clerk, R/E and UCC Recording 870-741-5560; Fax 870-741-4335.
Will search UCC records. This agency will not do a tax lien search. Will not search real estate records. **Other Phones:** Assessor 870-741-3783; Elections 741-8428; Tax Collector 741-6646; Marriages 870-741-8428;

Bradley County

County Circuit Clerk, 101 E. Cedar St, Courthouse, Warren, AR 71671. County Circuit Clerk, R/E and UCC Recording 870-226-2272; Fax 870-226-8401.
This agency will not perform searches. **Other Phone Numbers:** Assessor 870-226-2211; Treasurer 870-226-8402; Elections 870-226-3464.

Calhoun County

County Circuit Clerk, PO Box 626, Hampton, AR 71744. 870-798-2517 R/E Recording: 870-423-2422; Fax 870-798-2428.
Will search UCC records. This agency will not do a tax lien search. Will not search real estate records. **Other Phones:** Assessor 798-2740; Tax Collector 798-2827.

Carroll County (Eastern District)

County Circuit Clerk, PO Box 71, Berryville, AR 72616. County Circuit Clerk, R/E and UCC Recording 870-423-2422; Fax 870-423-4796.
Will search UCC records. UCC search includes tax liens if requested. Will not search real estate records. **Online Access:** Assessor, Property Records. Registration and logon is required to search all participating counties at www.arcountydata.com. Signup fee is $200 minimum plus $.10 per minute usage. For signup or information call 479-631-8054 or visit www.arcountydata.com. **Other Phone Numbers:** Assessor 870-423-2388; Tax Collector 870-423-3189.

Carroll County (Western District)

County Circuit Clerk, PO Box 109, Eureka Springs, AR 72632. 479-253-8646 R/E Recording: 870-423-2422; Fax 479-253-6013.
Will search UCC records. UCC search includes tax liens if requested. Will not search real estate records. **Online Access:** Assessor, Property Records. Registration and logon is required to search all participating counties at www.arcountydata.com. Signup fee is $200 minimum plus $.10 per minute usage. For signup or information call 479-631-8054 or visit www.arcountydata.com. **Other Phone Numbers:** Assessor 870-423-2388.

Chicot County

County Circuit Clerk, Courthouse, 108 Main St., Lake Village, AR 71653. 870-265-8010 R/E Recording: 870-265-236; Fax 870-265-8012.
Will search UCC records. Tax lien search is included in the UCC search. Will not search real estate records. **Other Phone Numbers:** Assessor 870-265-8025; Tax Collector 870-265-8040.

Clark County

County Circuit Clerk, PO Box 576, Arkadelphia, AR 71923. 870-246-4281; Fax 870-846-1416.
Will search UCC records. This agency will not do a tax lien search. Will not search real estate records. **Other Phone Numbers:** Assessor 870-246-4431; Tax Collector 870-246-2211.

Clay County
(Eastern District)

County Circuit Clerk, PO Box 29, Piggott, AR 72454. 870-598-2524; Fax 870-598-2524.
Will search UCC records. UCC search includes tax liens. Will not search real estate records. **Other Phone Numbers:** Assessor 870-598-3870.

Clay County
(Western District)

County Circuit Clerk, PO Box 176, Corning, AR 72422. 870-857-3271; Fax 870-857-9201.
Will search UCC records. UCC search includes tax liens. Will not search real estate records. **Other Phone Numbers:** Assessor 870-857-3133; Tax Collector 870-855-3011.

Cleburne County

County Circuit Clerk, PO Box 543, Heber Springs, AR 72543. County Circuit Clerk, R/E and UCC Recording 501-362-8149; Fax 501-362-4650.
Will search UCC records. UCC search includes tax liens if requested. Will not search real estate records. **Other Phone Numbers:** Assessor 501-362-8147; Tax Collector 501-362-8124.

Cleveland County

County Circuit Clerk, PO Box 368, Rison, AR 71665. County Circuit Clerk, R/E and UCC Recording 870-325-6521; Fax 870-325-6144.
Will search UCC records. This agency will not do a tax lien search. Will not search real estate records. **Other Phone Numbers:** Assessor 870-325-6695; Tax Collector 870-325-6681.

Columbia County

County Circuit Clerk, PO Box 327, Magnolia, AR 71753. County Circuit Clerk, R/E and UCC Recording 870-235-3700; Fax 870-235-3778.
Will search UCC records. This agency will not do a tax lien search. Will search real estate records. **Other Phone Numbers:** Assessor 870-235-4380; Appraiser/Auditor 870-235-4380; Elections 870-235-3774; Tax Collector 870-235-3704.

Conway County

County Circuit Clerk, 115 S. Moose St, County Courthouse - Room 206, Morrilton, AR 72110. 501-354-9617; Fax 501-354-9612.
Will search UCC records. This agency will not do a tax lien search. Will not search real estate records. **Other Phone Numbers:** Assessor 501-354-9622; Tax Collector 501-354-9623.

Craighead County
(Eastern District)

County Circuit Clerk, PO Box 537, Lake City, AR 72437. 870-237-4342; Fax 870-237-8174.
Will search UCC records. This agency will not do a tax lien search. Will not search real estate records.

Craighead County
(Western District)

County Circuit Clerk, PO Box 120, Jonesboro, AR 72401. 870-933-4530; Fax 870-933-4534.
Will search UCC records. This agency will not do a tax lien search. Will search real estate records. **Online Access:** Assessor, Property Records. Registration and logon is required to search all participating counties at www.arcountydata.com. Signup fee is $200 minimum plus $.10 per minute usage. For signup or information call 479-631-8054 or visit www.arcountydata.com. **Other Phone Numbers:** Assessor 870-933-4570; Tax Collector 870-933-4540.

Crawford County

County Circuit Clerk, 300 Main, Courthouse Room 22, Van Buren, AR 72956-5799. County Circuit Clerk, R/E and UCC Recording 479-474-1821.
Will search UCC records. This agency will not do a tax lien search. Will not search real estate records. **Other Phone Numbers:** Assessor 479-471-1751; Tax Collector 479-474-6641.

Crittenden County

County Circuit Clerk, 100 Court St., Marion, AR 72364. County Circuit Clerk, R/E and UCC Recording 870-739-3248; Fax 870-739-3072.
Will search UCC records. Will not search real estate records. **Online Access:** Assessor, Property Records. May be online. Registration and logon is required to search all participating counties at www.arcountydata.com. Signup fee is $200 minimum plus $.10 per minute usage. For signup or information call 479-631-8054 or visit www.arcountydata.com. **Other Phone Numbers:** Assessor 870-739-3606; Treasurer 870-739-4112; Appraiser/Auditor 870-739-3606; Elections 870-739-4434.

Cross County

County Circuit Clerk, 705 East Union, Room 9, Wynne, AR 72396. 870-238-5720 R/E Recording: 870-238-5735; Fax 870-238-5739.
Will search UCC records. UCC search includes tax liens if requested. Will not search real estate records. **Other Phone Numbers:** Assessor 870-238-5720; Tax Collector 870-238-5720.

Dallas County

County Circuit Clerk, Courthouse, 206 W. 3rd St, Fordyce, AR 71742-3299. County Circuit Clerk, R/E and UCC Recording 870-352-2307; Fax 870-352-7179.
Will search UCC records. UCC search includes tax liens. Will not search real estate records. **Other Phone Numbers:** Assessor 870-352-2232; Tax Collector 870-352-7983.

Desha County

County Circuit Clerk, PO Box 309, Arkansas City, AR 71630. 870-877-2411; Fax 870-877-3407.
Will search UCC records. Will not search real estate records. **Online Access:** Real Estate, Recording Records. Access to county recorder records is available by subscription at www.recordsusa.com. Credit card, username and password is required; choose either monthly or per-use plan. Visit the web site or call Lisa at 601-264-7701 for information. **Other Phone Numbers:** Assessor 870-877-2431; Tax Collector 870-877-2353.

Drew County

County Circuit Clerk, 210 S. Main, Monticello, AR 71655. 870-460-6250 R/E Recording: 870-367-2446; Fax 870-460-6246.
Will search UCC records. Real estate owner, mortgage, and property transfer searches available. **Online Access:** UCC, Land Records. UCC and Land Records are available by subscription at www.recordsusa.com. Credit card, username and password is required; choose either monthly or per-use plan. Visit the web site or call Lisa at 601-264-7701 for information. **Other Phone Numbers:** Assessor 870-460-6240; Tax Collector 870-460-6225.

Faulkner County

Faulkner County Circuit Clerk, PO Box 9, Conway, AR 72033. Faulkner County Circuit Clerk, R/E and UCC Recording 501-450-4911; Fax 501-450-4948.
Will search UCC records. This agency will not do a tax lien search. Will not search real estate records. **Online Access:** Assessor, Property Records. Registration and logon is required to search all participating counties at www.arcountydata.com. Signup fee is $200 minimum plus $.10 per minute usage. For signup or information call 479-631-8054 or visit www.arcountydata.com. **Other Phone Numbers:** Assessor 501-450-4905; Tax Collector 501-450-4902.

Franklin County
(Charleston District)

County Circuit Clerk, PO Box 387, Charleston, AR 72933. County Circuit Clerk, R/E and UCC Recording 479-965-7332; Fax 479-965-9322.
Will search UCC records. UCC search includes tax liens if requested. Will not search real estate records. **Other Phone Numbers:** Assessor 479-965-7797.

Franklin County
(Ozark District)

County Circuit Clerk, PO Box 1112, Ozark, AR 72949. 479-667-3818; Fax 479-667-5174.
Will search UCC records. Tax liens not included in UCC search. Will not search real estate records. **Other Phone Numbers:** Assessor 479-667-2415.

Fulton County

County Circuit Clerk, PO Box 485, Salem, AR 72576-0485. 870-895-3310; Fax 870-895-3362.
Will search UCC records. UCC search includes tax liens. Will not search real estate records. **Online Access:** Assessor, Property Records. Registration and logon is required to search all participating counties at www.arcountydata.com. Signup fee is $200 minimum plus $.10 per minute usage. For signup or information call 479-631-8054 or visit www.arcountydata.com. **Other Phone Numbers:** Assessor 870-895-3592; Treasurer 870-895-3522; Vital Records 501-661-2336; Tax Collector 870-895-3522.

Garland County

County Circuit Clerk, Courthouse - Room 207, Quachita and Hawthorn Streets, Hot Springs, AR 71901. County Circuit Clerk, R/E and UCC Recording 501-622-3630.
Will search UCC records. This agency will not do a tax lien search. Will not search real estate records. **Other Phone Numbers:** Assessor 501-622-3730; Elections 501-622-3610; Tax Collector 501-622-3710.

Grant County

County Circuit Clerk, Courthouse, 101 W. Center, Room 106, Sheridan, AR 72150. 870-942-2631; Fax 870-942-3564.
Will search UCC records. UCC search includes tax liens if requested. Real estate owner, mortgage, and property transfer searches available. **Other Phone Numbers:** Assessor 870-942-3711; Tax Collector 870-942-4315.

Greene County

County Circuit Clerk, 320 W. Court St., Room 124, Paragould, AR 72450. 870-239-6330; Fax 870-239-3550.
Will search UCC records. Tax liens not included in UCC search. **Other Phone Numbers:** Assessor 870-239-6303.

Hempstead County

County Circuit Clerk, PO Box 1420, Hope, AR 71802. County Circuit Clerk, R/E and UCC Recording 870-777-2384; Fax 870-777-7827.
Will search UCC records. This agency will not do a tax lien search. Will not search real estate records. **Other Phone Numbers:** Assessor 870-777-6190; Tax Collector 870-777-4103.

Hot Spring County

Circuit Clerk, PO Box 1220, Malvern, AR 72104. 501-332-2281.
Will search UCC records. This agency will not do a tax lien search. Will not search real estate records. **Other Phone Numbers:** Assessor 501-332-2461; Treasurer 501-337-7411; Elections 501-332-2291; Tax Collector 501-332-7211.

Howard County

County Circuit Clerk, 421 N. Main St, Rm 7, Room 7, Nashville, AR 71852. 870-845-7506.
Will search UCC records. UCC search includes tax liens if requested. Will not search real estate records. **Other Phone Numbers:** Assessor 870-845-7511.

Independence County

County Circuit Clerk, PO Box 2155, Batesville, AR 72503. 870-793-8865 R/E Recording: 870-793-8833; Fax 870-793-8888.
Will search UCC records. UCC search includes tax liens if requested. Will not search real estate records. **Other Phone Numbers:** Assessor 870-793-8842.

Izard County

County Circuit Clerk, PO Box 95, Melbourne, AR 72556. 870-368-4316; Fax 870-368-4748.
Will search UCC records. Will not search real estate records. **Online Access:** Assessor, Property Records. Registration and logon is required to search all participating counties at www.arcountydata.com. Signup fee is $200 minimum plus $.10 per minute usage. For signup or information call 479-631-8054 or visit www.arcountydata.com. **Other Phone Numbers:** Assessor 870-368-7810; Tax Collector 870-368-4394.

Jackson County

County Circuit Clerk, Courthouse, 208 Main St, Newport, AR 72112. 870-523-7423 R/E Recording: 870-523-3826; Fax 870-523-3682.
Will search UCC records. this agency will not do a tax lien search. Will not search real estate records. **Other Phone Numbers:** Assessor 870-523-7410; Tax Collector 870-523-7401.

Jefferson County

County Circuit Clerk, PO Box 7433, Pine Bluff, AR 71611. 870-541-5309 R/E Recording: 870-541-5360; Fax none.
Will search UCC records. Will not search real estate records. **Other Phone Numbers:** Assessor 870-541-5338; Tax Collector 870-541-5302.

Johnson County

County Circuit Clerk, PO Box 217, Clarksville, AR 72830. County Circuit Clerk, R/E and UCC Recording 479-754-2977; Fax 479-754-4235.
Will not search UCC records. Will not search real estate records. **Online Access:** Assessor, Property Records. May be online. Registration and logon is required to search all participating counties at www.arcountydata.com. Signup fee is $200 minimum plus $.10 per minute usage. For signup or information call 479-631-8054 or visit www.arcountydata.com. **Other Phone Numbers:** Assessor 479-754-8839; Appraiser/Auditor 479-754-8839; Tax Collector 479-754-3056.

Lafayette County

County Circuit Clerk, 3 Courthouse Square, Third & Spruce, Lewisville, AR 71845. County Circuit Clerk, R/E and UCC Recording 870-921-4878; Fax 870-421-4879.
Will search UCC records. This agency will not do a tax lien search. Will search real estate records. **Other**

Phone Numbers: Assessor 870-921-4808; Treasurer 870-921-4755; Tax Collector 870-921-4755.

Lawrence County

County Circuit Clerk, PO Box 581, Walnut Ridge, AR 72476. 870-886-1112 R/E Recording: 870-886-3421; Fax 870-886-1128.
Will search UCC records. This agency will not do a tax lien search. Will search for deed with a date or book and page. **Other Phone Numbers:** Assessor 870-886-1113; Tax Collector 870-886-1116.

Lee County

County Circuit Clerk, 15 E. Chestnut St, Courthouse, Marianna, AR 72360. 870-295-7710; Fax 870-295-7712.
Will search UCC records. This agency will not do a tax lien search. Will not search real estate records. **Other Phone Numbers:** Assessor 870-295-7750; Tax Collector 870-295-5296.

Lincoln County

County Circuit Clerk, 300 S. Drew St, Star City, AR 71667. County Circuit Clerk, R/E and UCC Recording 870-628-3154; Fax 870-628-5546.
Will search UCC records. UCC search includes tax liens. Will not search real estate records. **Other Phone Numbers:** Assessor 870-628-4401; Tax Collector 870-628-4816.

Little River County

County Circuit Clerk, PO Box 575, Ashdown, AR 71822-0575. 870-898-7211; Fax 870-898-7207.
Will search UCC records. Will not search real estate records. **Other Phone Numbers:** Assessor 870-898-7204.

Logan County
(Northern District)

County Circuit Clerk, Courthouse, Paris, AR 72855. 479-963-2164 R/E Recording: 479-963-2618; Fax 479-963-3304.
Will search UCC records. This agency will not do a tax lien search. Will not search real estate records. **Other Phone Numbers:** Assessor 479-963-2716; Tax Collector 479-963-2038.

Logan County
(Southern District)

County Circuit Clerk, Courthouse, 366 N Broadway #2, Booneville, AR 72927. 479-675-2894; Fax 479-675-0577.
Will search UCC records. Will not search real estate records. **Other Phone Numbers:** Assessor 479-675-3942; Tax Collector 479-675-5131.

Lonoke County

County Circuit Clerk, PO Box 219, Lonoke, AR 72086-0219. County Circuit Clerk, R/E and UCC Recording 501-676-2316.
Will search UCC records. This agency will not do a tax lien search. Will not search real estate records. **Online Access:** Assessor, Property Records. Registration and logon is required to search all participating counties at www.arcountydata.com. Signup fee is $200 minimum plus $.10 per minute usage. For signup or information call 479-631-8054 or visit www.arcountydata.com. **Other Phone Numbers:** Assessor 501-676-6938.

Madison County

County Circuit Clerk, PO Box 416, Huntsville, AR 72740. 479-738-2215 R/E Recording: 479-738-2747; Fax 479-738-1544.
Will search UCC records. This agency will not do a tax lien search. Will search real estate records. **Other**

Phone Numbers: Assessor 479-738-2325; Tax Collector 479-738-6514.

Marion County

County Circuit Clerk, PO Box 385, Yellville, AR 72687. County Circuit Clerk, R/E and UCC Recording 870-449-6226; Fax 870-449-4979.
Will search UCC records. This agency will not do a tax lien search. Will not search real estate records. **Other Phone Numbers:** Assessor 870-449-4113; Treasurer 870-449-6331; Tax Collector 870-449-6253.

Miller County

County Circuit Clerk, County Courthouse-Suite 109, 412 Laurel St., Texarkana, AR 71854. 870-774-4501; Fax 870-772-5293.
Will search UCC records. Tax liens not included in UCC search. Mortgage searches available. **Other Phone Numbers:** Assessor 870-772-1502; Tax Collector 870-772-0003.

Mississippi County
(Chickasawba District)

County Circuit Clerk, PO Box 1498, Blytheville, AR 72316-1498. 870-762-2332; Fax 870-762-8148.
Will search UCC records. This agency will not do a tax lien search. Will not search real estate records. **Other Phone Numbers:** Assessor 870-763-6860; Tax Collector 870-762-2152.

Mississippi County
(Osceola District)

County Circuit Clerk, PO Box 466, Osceola, AR 72370. 870-563-6471; Fax 870-563-2543.
Will search UCC records. Will not search real estate records. **Other Phone Numbers:** Assessor 870-563-2682; Tax Collector 870-762-2152.

Monroe County

County Circuit Clerk, 123 Madison St, Clarendon, AR 72029. 870-747-3615; Fax 870-747-3710.
Will search UCC records. This agency will not do a tax lien search. Will not search real estate records. **Other Phone Numbers:** Assessor 870-747-3847; Tax Collector 870-747-3722.

Montgomery County

County Circuit Clerk, PO Box 369, Mount Ida, AR 71957-0369. 870-867-3521; Fax 870-867-2177.
Will search UCC records. UCC search includes tax liens. Will not search real estate records. **Other Phone Numbers:** Assessor 870-867-3271; Tax Collector 870-867-3411.

Nevada County

County Circuit Clerk, PO Box 204, Prescott, AR 71857. 870-887-2511; Fax 870-887-1911.
Will search UCC records. UCC search includes tax liens if requested. Real estate record owner and mortgage searches available. **Other Phone Numbers:** Assessor 870-887-3410; Tax Collector 870-887-2811.

Newton County

County Circuit Clerk, PO Box 410, Jasper, AR 72641. 870-446-5125; Fax 870-446-5755.
Will search UCC records. This agency will not do a tax lien search. Will not search real estate records. **Other Phone Numbers:** Assessor 870-446-2937; Treasurer 870-446-2936; Tax Collector 870-446-2936.

Ouachita County

County Circuit Clerk, PO Box 667, Camden, AR 71701. County Circuit Clerk, R/E and UCC Recording 870-837-2230; Fax 870-837-2252.
Will search UCC records. This agency will not do a tax lien search. Will not search real estate records. **Other**

Phone Numbers: Assessor 870-837-2240; Treasurer 870-837-2250; Appraiser/Auditor 870-837-2240; Elections 870-837-2220; Vital Records 501-661-2336.

Perry County

County Circuit Clerk, PO Box 358, Perryville, AR 72126. 501-889-5126; Fax 501-889-5759.
Will search UCC records. This agency will not do a tax lien search. Will not search real estate records. **Other Phone Numbers:** Assessor 501-889-2865; Treasurer 501-889-5285; Tax Collector 501-889-2710.

Phillips County

County Circuit Clerk, Courthouse, Suite 206, 620 Cherry St., Helena, AR 72342. County Circuit Clerk, R/E and UCC Recording 870-338-5515; Fax 870-338-5513.
Will search UCC records. This agency will not do a tax lien search. Will not search real estate records. **Other Phone Numbers:** Assessor 870-338-5535; Treasurer 870-338-5510; Tax Collector 870-338-5510.

Pike County

County Circuit Clerk, PO Box 219, Murfreesboro, AR 71958. County Circuit Clerk, R/E and UCC Recording 870-285-2231; Fax 870-285-3281.
Will search UCC records. Will not search real estate records. **Other Phone Numbers:** Assessor 870-285-3316; Treasurer 870-285-2422; Tax Collector 870-285-2422.

Poinsett County

County Circuit Clerk, PO Box 46, Harrisburg, AR 72432-0046. 870-578-4420; Fax 870-578-2441.
Will search UCC records. This agency will not do a tax lien search. Will not search real estate records. **Other Phone Numbers:** Assessor 870-578-4430; Treasurer 870-578-4405; Tax Collector 870-578-4405.

Polk County

County Circuit Clerk, 507 Church, Courthouse, Mena, AR 71953. County Circuit Clerk, R/E and UCC Recording 479-394-8100.
Will search UCC records. Tax liens not included in UCC search. Will not search real estate records. **Other Phone Numbers:** Assessor 479-394-8121; Treasurer 479-394-8150; Tax Collector 479-394-8150.

Pope County

County Circuit Clerk, 100 W. Main, 3rd Floor, County Courthouse, Russellville, AR 72801. 479-968-7499; Fax none.
This agency will not perform searches. **Online Access:** Assessor, Property Records. Registration and logon is required to search all participating counties at www.arcountydata.com. Signup fee is $200 minimum plus $.10 per minute usage. For signup or information call 479-631-8054 or visit www.arcountydata.com. **Other Phone Numbers:** Assessor 479-968-7418; Treasurer 479-968-7016; Tax Collector 479-968-7016.

Prairie County
(Northern District)

County Circuit Clerk, PO Box 1011, Des Arc, AR 72040. 870-256-4434; Fax 870-256-4434.
Will search UCC records. This agency will not do a tax lien search Will not search real estate records. **Other Phone Numbers:** Assessor 870-256-4692; Treasurer 870-256-4137; Tax Collector 870-256-4137.

Prairie County
(Southern District)

County Circuit Clerk, PO Box 283, De Valls Bluff, AR 72041-0283. County Circuit Clerk, R/E and UCC Recording 870-998-2314; Fax 870-998-2314.

Will search UCC records. UCC search includes tax liens. Will not search real estate records. **Other Phone Numbers:** Assessor 870-256-4692; Treasurer 870-998-4786; Tax Collector 870-998-4786.

Pulaski County

County Circuit Clerk, Room S216, 401 W. Markham St., Little Rock, AR 72201. 501-340-8433; Fax 501-340-8420.
Will search UCC records. Tax liens not included in UCC search. Will not search real estate records. **Online Access:** Assessor, Property Records. Registration and logon is required to search all participating counties at www.arcountydata.com. Signup fee is $200 minimum plus $.10 per minute usage. For signup or information call 479-631-8054 or visit www.arcountydata.com. **Other Phone Numbers:** Assessor 501-340-6170; Treasurer 501-340-8345; Elections 501-340-8683 (Vote); Tax Collector 501-340-8345.

Randolph County

County Circuit Clerk, 107 W. Broadway, Pocahontas, AR 72455. 870-892-5522 R/E Recording: 870-372-8433; Fax 870-892-8794.
Will search UCC records. Tax liens not included in UCC search. Will not search real estate records. **Other Phone Numbers:** Assessor 870-892-3200; Treasurer 870-892-5238; Tax Collector 870-892-5238.

Saline County

County Circuit Clerk, 200 N. Main St. #113, Benton, AR 72018. 501-303-5615 R/E Recording: 501-776-5615; Fax 501-303-5675.
Will search UCC records. Will not search real estate records. **Online Access:** Assessor, Property Records. Registration and logon is required to search all participating counties at www.arcountydata.com. Signup fee is $200 minimum plus $.10 per minute usage. For signup or information call 479-631-8054 or visit www.arcountydata.com. **Other Phone Numbers:** Assessor 501-776-5622; Treasurer 501-776-5633; Tax Collector 501-776-5633.

Scott County

County Circuit Clerk, PO Box 2165, Waldron, AR 72958. County Circuit Clerk, R/E and UCC Recording 479-637-2642; Fax 479-637-0124.
Will search UCC records. Will not search real estate records. **Other Phone Numbers:** Assessor 479-637-2666; Treasurer 479-637-2780; Tax Collector 479-637-2780.

Searcy County

County Circuit Clerk, PO Box 935, Marshall, AR 72650. 870-448-3807; Fax 870-448-5005.
Will search UCC records. This agency will do a tax lien search. Will not search real estate records. **Other Phone Numbers:** Assessor 870-448-2464; Treasurer 870-448-3828; Appraiser/Auditor 870-448-2464; Tax Collector 870-448-5050.

Sebastian County
(Fort Smith District)

County Clerk and Recorder, PO Box 1089, Fort Smith, AR 72902-1089. 479-782-5065 R/E Recording: 479-782-1046 UCC Recording: 479-782-1546; Fax 479-784-1567.
Will search UCC records. This agency will not do a tax lien search. Will not search real estate records. **Online Access:** Assessor, Property Records. Registration and logon is required to search all participating counties at www.arcountydata.com. Signup fee is $200 minimum plus $.10 per minute usage. For signup or information call 479-631-8054 or visit www.arcountydata.com. **Other Phone Numbers:** Assessor 479-783-8948; Elections 479-782-5065.

Sebastian County
(Southern District)

County Clerk, PO Box 428, Greenwood, AR 72936. 479-996-4195 R/E Recording: 479-996-4175; Fax 479-996-4165.
Will search UCC records. This agency will not do a tax lien search. Will not search real estate records. **Online Access:** Assessor, Property Records. Registration and logon is required to search all participating counties at www.arcountydata.com. Signup fee is $200 minimum plus $.10 per minute usage. For signup or information call 479-631-8054 or visit www.arcountydata.com. **Other Phone Numbers:** Assessor 479-996-6591.

Sevier County

County Circuit Clerk, 115 N. 3rd St, De Queen, AR 71832. 870-584-3055; Fax 870-642-9638.
Will search UCC records. This agency will not do a tax lien search. Will not search real estate records. **Other Phone Numbers:** Assessor 870-584-3182; Treasurer 870-642-2358; Tax Collector 870-642-2358.

Sharp County

County Circuit Clerk, PO Box 307, Ash Flat, AR 72513. 870-994-7361 R/E Recording: 501-994-7361; Fax 870-994-7712.
Will search UCC records. Will not search real estate records. **Online Access:** Assessor, Property Records. Registration and logon is required to search all participating counties at www.arcountydata.com. Signup fee is $200 minimum plus $.10 per minute usage. For signup or information call 479-631-8054 or visit www.arcountydata.com. **Other Phone Numbers:** Assessor 501-994-7328; Treasurer 501-994-7347; Tax Collector 501-994-7347.

St. Francis County

County Circuit Clerk, PO Box 1775, Forrest City, AR 72336-1775. County Circuit Clerk, R/E and UCC Recording 870-261-1715 UCC Recording: 870-261-1721; Fax 870-261-1723.
Will search UCC records. Will not search real estate records. **Online Access:** Assessor, Property Records. May be online. Registration and logon is required to search all participating counties at www.arcountydata.com. Signup fee is $200 minimum plus $.10 per minute usage. For signup or information call 479-631-8054 or visit www.arcountydata.com. **Other Phone Numbers:** Assessor 870-261-1710; Treasurer 870-261-1705; Tax Collector 870-261-1792.

Stone County

County Circuit Clerk, Courthouse, HC 71 Box 1, Mountain View, AR 72560. County Circuit Clerk, R/E and UCC Recording 870-269-3271; Fax 870-269-2303.
Will search UCC records. UCC search includes tax liens if requested. Will not search real estate records. **Online Access:** Assessor, Property Records. Registration and logon is required to search all participating counties at www.arcountydata.com. Signup fee is $200 minimum plus $.10 per minute usage. For signup or information call 479-631-8054 or visit www.arcountydata.com. **Other Phone Numbers:** Assessor 870-269-3524; Treasurer 870-269-8426; Elections 870-269-5550; Tax Collector 870-269-8426.

Union County

County Circuit Clerk, PO Box 1626, El Dorado, AR 71731-1626. 870-864-1940; Fax 870-864-1994.
Will search UCC records. UCC search includes tax liens if requested. Will not search real estate records. **Other Phone Numbers:** Assessor 870-864-1920; Treasurer 870-864-1928; Tax Collector - 870-864-1928.

Van Buren County

County Circuit Clerk, RR6 Box 254-9, Clinton, AR 72031-9806. County Circuit Clerk, R/E and UCC Recording 501-745-4140; Fax 501-745-7400.
Will search UCC records. UCC search includes tax liens. Real estate owner, mortgage, and property transfer searches available. **Other Phone Numbers:** Assessor 501-745-2464; Treasurer 501-745-2400; Appraiser/Auditor 501-745-2474; Elections 501-745-4140.

Washington County

County Circuit Clerk, Courthouse, 280 N. College, Suite 302, Fayetteville, AR 72701. 479-444-1538; Fax 479-444-1537.
Will search UCC records. Tax liens not included in UCC search. Will not search real estate records. **Other Phone Numbers:** Assessor 479-444-1520; Treasurer 479-444-1526; Tax Collector 479-444-1526.

White County

County Circuit Clerk, White County Courthouse, Spring St./East Entrance/Courthouse Sq., Searcy, AR 72143. 501-279-6203; Fax 501-279-6233.
Will search UCC records. Will not search real estate records. **Online Access:** Assessor, Property Records. Registration and logon is required to search all participating counties at www.arcountydata.com. Signup fee is $200 minimum plus $.10 per minute usage. For signup or information call 479-631-8054 or visit www.arcountydata.com. **Other Phone Numbers:** Assessor 501-279-6205; Treasurer 501-279-6206; Tax Collector 501-279-6206.

Woodruff County

County Circuit Clerk, PO Box 492, Augusta, AR 72006. 870-347-2391.
Will search UCC records. Tax liens not included in UCC search. Will not search real estate records. **Other Phone Numbers:** Assessor 870-347-5151; Treasurer 870-347-5416; Tax Collector 870-347-5416.

Yell County (Danville District)

County Circuit Clerk, PO Box 219, Danville, AR 72833. County Circuit Clerk, R/E and UCC Recording 479-495-4850; Fax 479-495-4875.
Will search UCC records. Tax liens not included in UCC search. Will not search real estate records. **Other Phone Numbers:** Assessor 479-495-2940; Treasurer 479-495-2933; Elections 479-495-4850; Vital Records 479-495-4850.

Yell County (Dardanelle District)

County Circuit Clerk, PO Box 457, Dardanelle, AR 72834. 479-229-4404; Fax 479-229-1130.
Will search UCC records. Tax liens not included in UCC search. Will not search real estate records. **Other Phone Numbers:** Assessor 479-229-2693.

Arkansas County Locator

You will usually be able to find the city name in the City/County Cross Reference below. In that case, it is a simple matter to determine the county from the cross reference. However, only the official US Postal Service city names are included in this index. There are an additional 40,000 place names that people use in their addresses. Therefore, we have also included a ZIP/City Cross Reference immediately following the City/County Cross Reference.

If you know the ZIP Code but the city name does not appear in the City/County Cross Reference index, look up the ZIP Code in the ZIP/City Cross Reference, find the city name, then look up the city name in the City/County Cross Reference. For example, you want to know the county for an address of Menands, NY 12204. There is no "Menands" in the City/County Cross Reference. The ZIP/City Cross Reference shows that ZIP Codes 12201-12288 are for the city of Albany. Looking back in the City/County Cross Reference, Albany is in Albany County.

City/County Cross Reference

ADONA (72001) Perry(56), Conway(43)
ALCO (72610) Stone(95), Searcy(4)
ALEXANDER (72002) Saline(90), Pulaski(9)
ALICIA Lawrence
ALIX Franklin
ALLEENE Little River
ALMA Crawford
ALMYRA Arkansas
ALPENA (72611) Carroll(50), Boone(49)
ALPINE Clark
ALTHEIMER Jefferson
ALTUS (72821) Franklin(90), Johnson(9)
AMAGON Jackson
AMITY (71921) Clark(53), Pike(29), Hot Spring(16)
ANTOINE Pike
ARKADELPHIA Clark
ARKANSAS CITY Desha
ARMOREL Mississippi
ASH FLAT (72513) Fulton(52), Sharp(42), Izard(5)
ASHDOWN Little River
ATKINS (72823) Pope(97), Conway(2)
AUBREY Lee
AUGUSTA Woodruff
AUSTIN Lonoke
AVOCA Benton
BALCH Jackson
BALD KNOB White
BANKS Bradley
BARLING Sebastian
BARTON Phillips
BASS Newton
BASSETT Mississippi
BATES Scott
BATESVILLE Independence
BAUXITE Saline
BAY Craighead
BEARDEN (71720) Ouachita(85), Dallas(11), Calhoun(3)
BEAVER Carroll
BEE BRANCH (72013) Van Buren(98), Conway(1)
BEEBE White
BEECH GROVE Greene
BEEDEVILLE Jackson
BEIRNE Clark
BELLA VISTA Benton
BELLEVILLE Yell
BEN LOMOND Sevier
BENTON Saline
BENTONVILLE Benton
BERGMAN Boone
BERRYVILLE Carroll
BEXAR Fulton
BIG FLAT (72617) Baxter(75), Searcy(20), Stone(3)
BIGELOW (72016) Perry(52), Pulaski(47)
BIGGERS (72413) Randolph(92), Clay(7)
BIRDEYE Cross
BISCOE Prairie

BISMARCK Hot Spring
BLACK OAK Craighead
BLACK ROCK Lawrence
BLAKELY Garland
BLEVINS Hempstead
BLUE MOUNTAIN Logan
BLUFF CITY Nevada
BLUFFTON (72827) Yell(96), Scott(4)
BLYTHEVILLE Mississippi
BOARD CAMP Polk
BOLES Scott
BONNERDALE (71933) Hot Spring(45), Garland(37), Montgomery(17)
BONO (72416) Craighead(76), Greene(23)
BOONEVILLE (72927) Logan(92), Sebastian(6), Scott(1)
BOSWELL Izard
BRADFORD (72020) Jackson(49), White(36), Independence(14)
BRADLEY Lafayette
BRANCH Franklin
BRICKEYS Lee
BRIGGSVILLE Yell
BRINKLEY (72021) Monroe(98), Woodruff(1)
BROCKWELL Izard
BROOKLAND Craighead
BRUNO Marion
BRYANT Saline
BUCKNER (71827) Lafayette(75), Nevada(24)
BULL SHOALS Marion
BURDETTE Mississippi
CABOT (72023) Lonoke(75), Pulaski(24)
CADDO GAP Montgomery
CALDWELL St. Francis
CALE Nevada
CALICO ROCK (72519) Baxter(64), Stone(19), Izard(16)
CALION Union
CAMDEN Ouachita
CAMP Fulton
CANEHILL Washington
CARAWAY (72419) Craighead(93), Poinsett(5)
CARLISLE (72024) Lonoke(96), Prairie(3)
CARTHAGE (71725) Dallas(92), Cleveland(7)
CASA (72025) Conway(56), Perry(41), Yell(2)
CASH (72421) Craighead(76), Poinsett(20), Jackson(3)
CASSCOE Arkansas
CAVE CITY (72521) Sharp(70), Independence(29)
CAVE SPRINGS Benton
CECIL (72930) Franklin(79), Sebastian(20)
CEDARVILLE Crawford
CENTER RIDGE (72027) Conway(97), Faulkner(2)
CENTERTON Benton
CENTERVILLE Yell

CHARLESTON (72933) Franklin(83), Sebastian(16)
CHARLOTTE Independence
CHATFIELD Crittenden
CHEROKEE VILLAGE (72529) Sharp(77), Fulton(22)
CHERRY VALLEY (72324) Cross(90), Poinsett(9)
CHESTER Crawford
CHIDESTER Ouachita
CHOCTAW Van Buren
CLARENDON Monroe
CLARKEDALE Crittenden
CLARKRIDGE Baxter
CLARKSVILLE Johnson
CLEVELAND (72030) Conway(51), Van Buren(48)
CLINTON (72031) Van Buren(96), Stone(2), Conway(1)
COAL HILL Johnson
COLLEGE STATION Pulaski
COLLINS Drew
COLT (72326) St. Francis(88), Cross(11)
COLUMBUS (71831) Hempstead(58), Howard(41)
COMBS Madison
COMPTON (72624) Newton(83), Carroll(16)
CONCORD (72523) Cleburne(86), Independence(13)
CONWAY Faulkner
CORD Independence
CORNING Clay
COTTER Baxter
COTTON PLANT (72036) Woodruff(87), Monroe(12)
COVE Polk
COY Lonoke
CRAWFORDSVILLE Crittenden
CROCKETTS BLUFF Arkansas
CROSSETT Ashley
CRUMROD Phillips
CURTIS Clark
CUSHMAN Independence
DAMASCUS (72039) Van Buren(69), Faulkner(30)
DANVILLE (72833) Yell(98), Scott(1)
DARDANELLE (72834) Yell(97), Logan(2)
DATTO Clay
DE QUEEN Sevier
DE VALLS BLUFF Prairie
DE WITT Arkansas
DECATUR Benton
DEER Newton
DELAPLAINE Greene
DELAWARE Logan
DELIGHT Pike
DELL Mississippi
DENNARD Van Buren
DERMOTT (71638) Chicot(84), Drew(12), Desha(3)
DES ARC (72040) Prairie(98), Woodruff(1)

DESHA Independence
DIAMOND CITY Boone
DIAZ Jackson
DIERKS (71833) Howard(94), Sevier(5)
DODDRIDGE Miller
DOLPH Izard
DONALDSON Hot Spring
DOVER Pope
DRASCO (72530) Cleburne(94), Stone(5)
DRIVER Mississippi
DUMAS (71639) Desha(97), Lincoln(2)
DYER Crawford
DYESS Mississippi
EARLE (72331) Crittenden(95), Cross(4)
EDGEMONT (72044) Cleburne(84), Stone(15)
EDMONDSON Crittenden
EGYPT Craighead
EL DORADO Union
EL PASO White
ELAINE Phillips
ELIZABETH (72531) Baxter(52), Fulton(47)
ELKINS (72727) Washington(93), Madison(6)
ELM SPRINGS Washington
EMERSON Columbia
EMMET (71835) Nevada(78), Hempstead(21)
ENGLAND (72046) Lonoke(81), Pulaski(10), Jefferson(7)
ENOLA Faulkner
ETHEL Arkansas
ETOWAH Mississippi
EUDORA Chicot
EUREKA SPRINGS Carroll
EVANSVILLE Washington
EVENING SHADE Sharp
EVERTON (72633) Boone(60), Marion(36), Searcy(3)
FAIRFIELD BAY (72088) Van Buren(91), Cleburne(8)
FARMINGTON Washington
FAYETTEVILLE Washington
FERNDALE Pulaski
FIFTY SIX Stone
FISHER (72429) Poinsett(96), Cross(3)
FLIPPIN Marion
FLORAL (72534) Independence(86), Cleburne(13)
FORDYCE (71742) Dallas(96), Calhoun(3)
FOREMAN Little River
FORREST CITY St. Francis
FORT SMITH Sebastian
FOUKE Miller
FOUNTAIN HILL (71642) Ashley(82), Drew(17)
FOX Stone
FRANKLIN Izard
FRENCHMANS BAYOU Mississippi
FRIENDSHIP Hot Spring
FULTON Hempstead
GAMALIEL Baxter

GARFIELD Benton
GARLAND CITY (71839) Miller(92), Lafayette(7)
GARNER White
GASSVILLE Baxter
GATEWAY Benton
GENOA Miller
GENTRY Benton
GEPP (72538) Fulton(93), Baxter(6)
GILBERT Searcy
GILLETT (72055) Arkansas(89), Jefferson(10)
GILLHAM (71841) Sevier(88), Polk(11)
GILMORE Crittenden
GLENCOE Fulton
GLENWOOD (71943) Pike(55), Montgomery(39), Hot Spring(4)
GOODWIN St. Francis
GOSHEN Washington
GOSNELL Mississippi
GOULD (71643) Lincoln(88), Desha(11)
GRADY (71644) Jefferson(65), Lincoln(34)
GRANNIS Polk
GRAPEVINE Grant
GRAVELLY (72838) Yell(75), Scott(25)
GRAVETTE Benton
GREEN FOREST Carroll
GREENBRIER Faulkner
GREENLAND Washington
GREENWAY Clay
GREENWOOD Sebastian
GREGORY Woodruff
GRIFFITHVILLE (72060) White(79), Prairie(20)
GRUBBS Jackson
GUION Izard
GURDON Clark
GUY Faulkner
HACKETT Sebastian
HAGARVILLE (72839) Johnson(93), Pope(6)
HAMBURG Ashley
HAMPTON Calhoun
HARDY (72542) Sharp(87), Fulton(12)
HARRELL Calhoun
HARRIET (72639) Searcy(95), Marion(4)
HARRISBURG Poinsett
HARRISON Boone
HARTFORD Sebastian
HARTMAN Johnson
HARVEY (72841) Scott(82), Yell(17)
HASTY Newton
HATFIELD Polk
HATTIEVILLE (72063) Conway(94), Pope(5)
HATTON Polk
HAVANA (72842) Yell(94), Logan(5)
HAYNES Lee
HAZEN Prairie
HEBER SPRINGS Cleburne
HECTOR Pope
HELENA Phillips
HENDERSON Baxter
HENSLEY (72065) Saline(83), Pulaski(11), Grant(5)
HERMITAGE Bradley
HETH (72346) St. Francis(95), Cross(4)
HICKORY PLAINS Prairie
HICKORY RIDGE (72347) Cross(80), Jackson(18)
HIGDEN (72067) Cleburne(90), Van Buren(9)
HIGGINSON White
HINDSVILLE (72738) Madison(81), Washington(11), Benton(6)
HIWASSE Benton
HOLLY GROVE (72069) Monroe(91), Phillips(8)
HOPE Hempstead
HORATIO Sevier
HORSESHOE BEND Izard
HOT SPRINGS NATIONAL PARK Garland

HOT SPRINGS VILLAGE Garland
HOUSTON Perry
HOWELL Woodruff
HOXIE Lawrence
HUGHES (72348) Crittenden(47), St. Francis(47), Lee(5)
HUMNOKE (72072) Lonoke(91), Jefferson(8)
HUMPHREY (72073) Arkansas(75), Jefferson(24)
HUNT Johnson
HUNTER Woodruff
HUNTINGTON Sebastian
HUNTSVILLE (72740) Madison(98), Carroll(1)
HUTTIG Union
IDA Cleburne
IMBODEN (72434) Randolph(72), Lawrence(27)
IVAN Dallas
JACKSONPORT Jackson
JACKSONVILLE Pulaski
JASPER Newton
JEFFERSON (72079) Jefferson(78), Grant(21)
JENNIE Chicot
JEROME Drew
JERSEY Bradley
JERUSALEM (72080) Van Buren(50), Conway(40), Pope(9)
JESSIEVILLE Garland
JOHNSON Washington
JOINER Mississippi
JONES MILLS Hot Spring
JONESBORO Craighead
JUDSONIA White
JUNCTION CITY Union
KEISER Mississippi
KENSETT White
KEO Lonoke
KINGSLAND Cleveland
KINGSTON (72742) Madison(92), Newton(7)
KIRBY Pike
KNOBEL (72435) Clay(97), Greene(2)
KNOXVILLE Johnson
LA GRANGE Lee
LAFE (72436) Greene(84), Clay(15)
LAKE CITY Craighead
LAKE VILLAGE Chicot
LAKEVIEW Baxter
LAMAR (72846) Johnson(95), Pope(4)
LAMBROOK Phillips
LANEBURG Nevada
LANGLEY Pike
LAVACA Sebastian
LAWSON Union
LEACHVILLE (72438) Mississippi(88), Craighead(11)
LEAD HILL (72644) Boone(89), Marion(10)
LEOLA (72084) Grant(52), Hot Spring(28), Dallas(19)
LEPANTO (72354) Poinsett(77), Mississippi(22)
LESLIE (72645) Van Buren(43), Searcy(34), Stone(21)
LETONA White
LEWISVILLE Lafayette
LEXA (72355) Phillips(88), Lee(11)
LIGHT Greene
LINCOLN Washington
LITTLE ROCK Pulaski
LITTLE ROCK AIR FORCE BASE Pulaski
LOCKESBURG Sevier
LOCUST GROVE (72550) Independence(60), Cleburne(29), Stone(9)
LONDON (72847) Pope(87), Johnson(12)
LONOKE Lonoke
LONSDALE (72087) Saline(57), Garland(42)
LOUANN Ouachita

LOWELL Benton
LUXORA Mississippi
LYNN Lawrence
MABELVALE (72103) Saline(79), Pulaski(20)
MADISON St. Francis
MAGAZINE Logan
MAGNESS Independence
MAGNOLIA Columbia
MALVERN (72104) Hot Spring(98), Saline(1)
MAMMOTH SPRING (72554) Fulton(70), Sharp(29)
MANILA Mississippi
MANSFIELD (72944) Sebastian(56), Scott(43)
MARBLE FALLS Newton
MARCELLA Stone
MARIANNA Lee
MARION Crittenden
MARKED TREE Poinsett
MARMADUKE Greene
MARSHALL (72650) Searcy(90), Stone(9)
MARVELL (72366) Phillips(95), Lee(2), Monroe(1)
MAUMELLE Pulaski
MAYFLOWER Faulkner
MAYNARD Randolph
MAYSVILLE Benton
MC CASKILL Hempstead
MC CRORY Cross
MC DOUGAL Clay
MC GEHEE Desha
MC NEIL Columbia
MC RAE White
MELBOURNE Izard
MELLWOOD Phillips
MENA Polk
MENIFEE Conway
MIDLAND Sebastian
MIDWAY Baxter
MINERAL SPRINGS Howard
MINTURN Lawrence
MOKO Fulton
MONETTE Craighead
MONROE Monroe
MONTICELLO Drew
MONTROSE Ashley
MORO (72368) Lee(91), Monroe(8)
MORRILTON Conway
MORROW Washington
MOSCOW Jefferson
MOUNT HOLLY Union
MOUNT IDA Montgomery
MOUNT JUDEA Newton
MOUNT PLEASANT Izard
MOUNT VERNON (72111) Faulkner(64), White(35)
MOUNTAIN HOME Baxter
MOUNTAIN PINE Garland
MOUNTAIN VIEW Stone
MOUNTAINBURG Crawford
MULBERRY (72947) Crawford(61), Franklin(38)
MURFREESBORO Pike
NASHVILLE (71852) Howard(87), Hempstead(6), Pike(6)
NATURAL DAM (72948) Crawford(95), Washington(4)
NEW BLAINE Logan
NEW EDINBURG (71660) Cleveland(94), Bradley(5)
NEWARK Independence
NEWHOPE (71959) Pike(62), Howard(37)
NEWPORT Jackson
NORFORK Baxter
NORMAN Montgomery
NORPHLET Union
NORTH LITTLE ROCK Pulaski
O KEAN Randolph
OAK GROVE Carroll
OAKLAND Marion

OARK (72852) Johnson(59), Newton(22), Madison(18)
ODEN Montgomery
OGDEN Little River
OIL TROUGH Independence
OKOLONA Clark
OLA (72853) Yell(80), Perry(19)
OMAHA (72662) Boone(98), Carroll(1)
ONEIDA Phillips
ONIA Stone
OSCEOLA Mississippi
OXFORD Izard
OZAN Hempstead
OZARK (72949) Franklin(97), Logan(1), Johnson(1)
OZONE (72854) Johnson(75), Newton(24)
PALESTINE (72372) St. Francis(84), Lee(15)
PANGBURN (72121) White(68), Cleburne(31)
PARAGOULD Greene
PARIS Logan
PARKDALE (71661) Ashley(87), Chicot(12)
PARKIN Cross
PARKS Scott
PARON (72122) Saline(66), Pulaski(33)
PARTHENON Newton
PATTERSON Woodruff
PEA RIDGE Benton
PEACH ORCHARD (72453) Greene(90), Clay(9)
PEARCY (71964) Garland(89), Hot Spring(10)
PEEL Marion
PELSOR (72856) Pope(58), Newton(41)
PENCIL BLUFF Montgomery
PERRY (72125) Perry(61), Conway(38)
PERRYVILLE (72126) Perry(96), Pulaski(3)
PETTIGREW (72752) Madison(97), Johnson(1), Newton(1)
PICKENS (71662) Lincoln(53), Desha(46)
PIGGOTT Clay
PINDALL Searcy
PINE BLUFF Jefferson
PINEVILLE Izard
PLAINVIEW (72857) Perry(63), Yell(36)
PLEASANT GROVE Stone
PLEASANT PLAINS (72568) Independence(93), White(6)
PLUMERVILLE Conway
POCAHONTAS Randolph
POLLARD Clay
PONCA Newton
POPLAR GROVE (72374) Phillips(98), Lee(1)
PORTIA Lawrence
PORTLAND (71663) Ashley(66), Chicot(33)
POTTSVILLE Pope
POUGHKEEPSIE Sharp
POWHATAN Lawrence
POYEN (72128) Grant(98), Hot Spring(1)
PRAIRIE GROVE Washington
PRATTSVILLE Grant
PRESCOTT Nevada
PRIM Cleburne
PROCTOR (72376) Crittenden(98), St. Francis(1)
PYATT Marion
QUITMAN (72131) Cleburne(83), Faulkner(8), Van Buren(7)
RATCLIFF (72951) Logan(58), Franklin(41)
RAVENDEN (72459) Lawrence(49), Randolph(36), Sharp(14)
RAVENDEN SPRINGS Randolph
RECTOR (72461) Clay(91), Greene(8)
REDFIELD (72132) Jefferson(84), Grant(15)
REYDELL Jefferson
REYNO Randolph
RISON (71665) Cleveland(98), Jefferson(1)
RIVERVALE Poinsett

ROE (72134) Monroe(82), Arkansas(14), Prairie(3)
ROGERS Benton
ROLAND Pulaski
ROMANCE White
ROSE BUD (72137) White(59), Cleburne(40)
ROSIE Independence
ROSSTON Nevada
ROUND POND St. Francis
ROVER Yell
ROYAL Garland
RUDY Crawford
RUSSELL White
RUSSELLVILLE Pope
SAFFELL (72572) Lawrence(65), Independence(34)
SAGE Izard
SAINT CHARLES Arkansas
SAINT FRANCIS Clay
SAINT JOE (72675) Marion(59), Searcy(40)
SAINT PAUL Madison
SALADO Independence
SALEM Fulton
SARATOGA (71859) Hempstead(59), Howard(40)
SCOTLAND Van Buren
SCOTT (72142) Pulaski(61), Lonoke(38)
SCRANTON Logan
SEARCY White
SEDGWICK Lawrence
SHERIDAN (72150) Grant(98), Jefferson(1)
SHERRILL Jefferson
SHERWOOD (72120) Pulaski(96), Faulkner(3)
SHIRLEY (72153) Van Buren(93), Stone(6)
SIDNEY (72577) Sharp(73), Izard(26)
SILOAM SPRINGS Benton
SIMS Montgomery
SMACKOVER (71762) Union(96), Ouachita(3)
SMITHVILLE (72466) Lawrence(64), Sharp(35)

SNOW LAKE Desha
SOLGOHACHIA Conway
SPARKMAN (71763) Dallas(92), Ouachita(4), Clark(2)
SPRINGDALE Washington
SPRINGFIELD Conway
SPRINGTOWN Benton
STAMPS (71860) Lafayette(95), Columbia(4)
STAR CITY (71667) Lincoln(97), Cleveland(2)
STATE UNIVERSITY Craighead
STEPHENS (71764) Ouachita(57), Columbia(36), Nevada(4), Union(1)
STEPROCK White
STORY Montgomery
STRAWBERRY (72469) Lawrence(80), Sharp(19)
STRONG Union
STURKIE Fulton
STUTTGART (72160) Arkansas(96), Prairie(1)
SUBIACO Logan
SUCCESS Clay
SULPHUR ROCK (72579) Independence(94), Sharp(5)
SULPHUR SPRINGS Benton
SUMMERS Washington
SUMMIT Marion
SWEET HOME Pulaski
SWIFTON Jackson
TAYLOR (71861) Columbia(62), Lafayette(37)
TEXARKANA Miller
THIDA Independence
THORNTON (71766) Calhoun(96), Ouachita(3)
TICHNOR Arkansas
TILLAR (71670) Desha(80), Drew(19)
TILLY (72679) Pope(76), Van Buren(21), Searcy(1)
TIMBO Stone
TOMATO Mississippi
TONTITOWN Washington

TRASKWOOD (72167) Saline(80), Hot Spring(14), Grant(4)
TRUMANN Poinsett
TUCKER Jefferson
TUCKERMAN Jackson
TUMBLING SHOALS Cleburne
TUPELO Jackson
TURNER Phillips
TURRELL Crittenden
TWIST Cross
TYRONZA (72386) Poinsett(64), Mississippi(18), Crittenden(16)
ULM Prairie
UMPIRE (71971) Howard(78), Pike(21)
UNIONTOWN Crawford
URBANA Union
VALLEY SPRINGS (72682) Marion(81), Boone(18)
VAN BUREN Crawford
VANDERVOORT Polk
VANNDALE Cross
VENDOR Newton
VILLAGE Columbia
VILONIA Faulkner
VIOLA Fulton
VIOLET HILL Izard
WABASH Phillips
WABBASEKA (72175) Jefferson(98), Arkansas(1)
WALCOTT Greene
WALDENBURG Poinsett
WALDO (71770) Columbia(88), Nevada(11)
WALDRON Scott
WALNUT RIDGE (72476) Lawrence(91), Randolph(4), Craighead(2), Greene(1)
WARD (72176) Lonoke(97), Prairie(2)
WARM SPRINGS Randolph
WARREN (71671) Bradley(97), Cleveland(2)
WASHINGTON Hempstead
WATSON Desha
WAVELAND Yell

WEINER (72479) Poinsett(84), Jackson(11), Craighead(4)
WESLEY (72773) Madison(98), Washington(1)
WEST FORK Washington
WEST HELENA Phillips
WEST MEMPHIS Crittenden
WEST POINT White
WEST RIDGE Mississippi
WESTERN GROVE (72685) Newton(92), Searcy(4), Boone(2)
WHEATLEY (72392) St. Francis(82), Monroe(14), Lee(1), Woodruff(1)
WHEELER Washington
WHELEN SPRINGS Clark
WHITE HALL Jefferson
WICKES (71973) Polk(97), Howard(2)
WIDEMAN Izard
WIDENER St. Francis
WILBURN Cleburne
WILLIFORD Sharp
WILLISVILLE Nevada
WILMAR (71675) Drew(92), Bradley(6)
WILMOT (71676) Ashley(94), Chicot(5)
WILSON Mississippi
WILTON Little River
WINCHESTER Drew
WINSLOW (72959) Washington(87), Crawford(12)
WINTHROP Little River
WISEMAN (72587) Izard(93), Fulton(6)
WITTER Madison
WITTS SPRINGS (72686) Searcy(87), Pope(12)
WOODSON Pulaski
WOOSTER Faulkner
WRIGHT Jefferson
WRIGHTSVILLE Pulaski
WYNNE Cross
YELLVILLE Marion
YORKTOWN Lincoln

ZIP/City Cross Reference

71601-71612	PINE BLUFF	
71612-71612	WHITE HALL	
71613-71613	PINE BLUFF	
71630-71630	ARKANSAS CITY	
71631-71631	BANKS	
71634-71634	COLLINS	
71635-71635	CROSSETT	
71638-71638	DERMOTT	
71639-71639	DUMAS	
71640-71640	EUDORA	
71642-71642	FOUNTAIN HILL	
71643-71643	GOULD	
71644-71644	GRADY	
71646-71646	HAMBURG	
71647-71647	HERMITAGE	
71649-71649	JENNIE	
71650-71650	JEROME	
71651-71651	JERSEY	
71652-71652	KINGSLAND	
71653-71653	LAKE VILLAGE	
71654-71654	MC GEHEE	
71655-71657	MONTICELLO	
71658-71658	MONTROSE	
71659-71659	MOSCOW	
71660-71660	NEW EDINBURG	
71661-71661	PARKDALE	
71662-71662	PICKENS	
71663-71663	PORTLAND	
71665-71665	RISON	
71666-71666	MC GEHEE	
71667-71667	STAR CITY	
71670-71670	TILLAR	
71671-71671	WARREN	
71674-71674	WATSON	
71675-71675	WILMAR	
71676-71676	WILMOT	
71677-71677	WINCHESTER	
71678-71678	YORKTOWN	
71701-71711	CAMDEN	
71720-71720	BEARDEN	
71721-71721	BEIRNE	
71722-71722	BLUFF CITY	
71724-71724	CALION	
71725-71725	CARTHAGE	
71726-71726	CHIDESTER	
71728-71728	CURTIS	
71730-71731	EL DORADO	
71740-71740	EMERSON	
71742-71742	FORDYCE	
71743-71743	GURDON	
71744-71744	HAMPTON	
71745-71745	HARRELL	
71747-71747	HUTTIG	
71748-71748	IVAN	
71749-71749	JUNCTION CITY	
71750-71750	LAWSON	
71751-71751	LOUANN	
71752-71752	MC NEIL	
71753-71754	MAGNOLIA	
71758-71758	MOUNT HOLLY	
71759-71759	NORPHLET	
71762-71762	SMACKOVER	
71763-71763	SPARKMAN	
71764-71764	STEPHENS	
71765-71765	STRONG	
71766-71766	THORNTON	
71767-71767	HAMPTON	
71768-71768	URBANA	
71769-71769	VILLAGE	
71770-71770	WALDO	
71772-71772	WHELEN SPRINGS	
71801-71802	HOPE	
71820-71820	ALLEENE	
71822-71822	ASHDOWN	
71823-71823	BEN LOMOND	
71825-71825	BLEVINS	
71826-71826	BRADLEY	
71827-71827	BUCKNER	
71828-71828	CALE	
71831-71831	COLUMBUS	
71832-71832	DE QUEEN	
71833-71833	DIERKS	
71834-71834	DODDRIDGE	
71835-71835	EMMET	
71836-71836	FOREMAN	
71837-71837	FOUKE	
71838-71838	FULTON	
71839-71839	GARLAND CITY	
71840-71840	GENOA	
71841-71841	GILLHAM	
71842-71842	HORATIO	
71844-71844	LANEBURG	
71845-71845	LEWISVILLE	
71846-71846	LOCKESBURG	
71847-71847	MC CASKILL	
71851-71851	MINERAL SPRINGS	
71852-71852	NASHVILLE	
71853-71853	OGDEN	
71854-71854	TEXARKANA	
71855-71855	OZAN	
71857-71857	PRESCOTT	
71858-71858	ROSSTON	
71859-71859	SARATOGA	
71860-71860	STAMPS	
71861-71861	TAYLOR	
71862-71862	WASHINGTON	
71864-71864	WILLISVILLE	
71865-71865	WILTON	
71866-71866	WINTHROP	
71901-71903	HOT SPRINGS NATIONAL PARK	
71909-71910	HOT SPRINGS VILLAGE	
71913-71914	HOT SPRINGS NATIONAL PARK	
71920-71920	ALPINE	
71921-71921	AMITY	
71922-71922	ANTOINE	
71923-71923	ARKADELPHIA	
71929-71929	BISMARCK	
71931-71931	BLAKELY	
71932-71932	BOARD CAMP	
71933-71933	BONNERDALE	
71935-71935	CADDO GAP	
71937-71937	COVE	
71940-71940	DELIGHT	
71941-71941	DONALDSON	
71942-71942	FRIENDSHIP	
71943-71943	GLENWOOD	
71944-71944	GRANNIS	
71945-71945	HATFIELD	
71946-71946	HATTON	
71949-71949	JESSIEVILLE	

ZIP Range	Place	ZIP Range	Place	ZIP Range	Place	ZIP Range	Place
71950-71950	KIRBY	72071-72071	HOWELL	72200-72207	LITTLE ROCK	72422-72422	CORNING
71951-71951	HOT SPRINGS NATIONAL PARK	72072-72072	HUMNOKE	72208-72208	FERNDALE	72424-72424	DATTO
71952-71952	LANGLEY	72073-72073	HUMPHREY	72209-72297	LITTLE ROCK	72425-72425	DELAPLAINE
71953-71953	MENA	72074-72074	HUNTER	72301-72303	WEST MEMPHIS	72426-72426	DELL
71956-71956	MOUNTAIN PINE	72075-72075	JACKSONPORT	72310-72310	ARMOREL	72427-72427	EGYPT
71957-71957	MOUNT IDA	72076-72078	JACKSONVILLE	72311-72311	AUBREY	72428-72428	ETOWAH
71958-71958	MURFREESBORO	72079-72079	JEFFERSON	72312-72312	BARTON	72429-72429	FISHER
71959-71959	NEWHOPE	72080-72080	JERUSALEM	72313-72313	BASSETT	72430-72430	GREENWAY
71960-71960	NORMAN	72081-72081	JUDSONIA	72314-72314	BIRDEYE	72431-72431	GRUBBS
71961-71961	ODEN	72082-72082	KENSETT	72315-72317	BLYTHEVILLE	72432-72432	HARRISBURG
71962-71962	OKOLONA	72083-72083	KEO	72319-72319	GOSNELL	72433-72433	HOXIE
71964-71964	PEARCY	72084-72084	LEOLA	72320-72320	BRICKEYS	72434-72434	IMBODEN
71965-71965	PENCIL BLUFF	72085-72085	LETONA	72321-72321	BURDETTE	72435-72435	KNOBEL
71966-71966	ODEN	72086-72086	LONOKE	72322-72322	CALDWELL	72436-72436	LAFE
71968-71968	ROYAL	72087-72087	LONSDALE	72323-72323	CHATFIELD	72437-72437	LAKE CITY
71969-71969	SIMS	72088-72088	FAIRFIELD BAY	72324-72324	CHERRY VALLEY	72438-72438	LEACHVILLE
71970-71970	STORY	72089-72089	BRYANT	72325-72325	CLARKEDALE	72439-72439	LIGHT
71971-71971	UMPIRE	72099-72099	LITTLE ROCK AIR FORCE BASE	72326-72326	COLT	72440-72440	LYNN
71972-71972	VANDERVOORT	72100-72100	NORTH LITTLE ROCK	72327-72327	CRAWFORDSVILLE	72441-72441	MC DOUGAL
71973-71973	WICKES	72101-72101	MC CRORY	72328-72328	CRUMROD	72442-72442	MANILA
71998-71999	ARKADELPHIA	72102-72102	MC RAE	72329-72329	DRIVER	72443-72443	MARMADUKE
72001-72001	ADONA	72103-72103	MABELVALE	72330-72330	DYESS	72444-72444	MAYNARD
72002-72002	ALEXANDER	72104-72104	MALVERN	72331-72331	EARLE	72445-72445	MINTURN
72003-72003	ALMYRA	72105-72105	JONES MILLS	72332-72332	EDMONDSON	72447-72447	MONETTE
72004-72004	ALTHEIMER	72106-72106	MAYFLOWER	72333-72333	ELAINE	72449-72449	O KEAN
72005-72005	AMAGON	72107-72107	MENIFEE	72335-72336	FORREST CITY	72450-72451	PARAGOULD
72006-72006	AUGUSTA	72108-72108	MONROE	72338-72338	FRENCHMANS BAYOU	72453-72453	PEACH ORCHARD
72007-72007	AUSTIN	72110-72110	MORRILTON	72339-72339	GILMORE	72454-72454	PIGGOTT
72009-72009	BALCH	72111-72111	MOUNT VERNON	72340-72340	GOODWIN	72455-72455	POCAHONTAS
72010-72010	BALD KNOB	72112-72112	NEWPORT	72341-72341	HAYNES	72456-72456	POLLARD
72011-72011	BAUXITE	72113-72113	MAUMELLE	72342-72342	HELENA	72457-72457	PORTIA
72012-72012	BEEBE	72114-72119	NORTH LITTLE ROCK	72346-72346	HETH	72458-72458	POWHATAN
72013-72013	BEE BRANCH	72120-72120	SHERWOOD	72347-72347	HICKORY RIDGE	72459-72459	RAVENDEN
72014-72014	BEEDEVILLE	72121-72121	PANGBURN	72348-72348	HUGHES	72460-72460	RAVENDEN SPRINGS
72015-72015	BENTON	72122-72122	PARON	72350-72350	JOINER	72461-72461	RECTOR
72016-72016	BIGELOW	72123-72123	PATTERSON	72351-72351	KEISER	72462-72462	REYNO
72017-72017	BISCOE	72124-72124	NORTH LITTLE ROCK	72352-72352	LA GRANGE	72464-72464	SAINT FRANCIS
72018-72018	BENTON	72125-72125	PERRY	72353-72353	LAMBROOK	72465-72465	SEDGWICK
72020-72020	BRADFORD	72126-72126	PERRYVILLE	72354-72354	LEPANTO	72466-72466	SMITHVILLE
72021-72021	BRINKLEY	72127-72127	PLUMERVILLE	72355-72355	LEXA	72467-72467	STATE UNIVERSITY
72022-72022	BRYANT	72128-72128	POYEN	72358-72358	LUXORA	72469-72469	STRAWBERRY
72023-72023	CABOT	72129-72129	PRATTSVILLE	72359-72359	MADISON	72470-72470	SUCCESS
72024-72024	CARLISLE	72130-72130	PRIM	72360-72360	MARIANNA	72471-72471	SWIFTON
72025-72025	CASA	72131-72131	QUITMAN	72364-72364	MARION	72472-72472	TRUMANN
72026-72026	CASSCOE	72132-72132	REDFIELD	72365-72365	MARKED TREE	72473-72473	TUCKERMAN
72027-72027	CENTER RIDGE	72133-72133	REYDELL	72366-72366	MARVELL	72474-72474	WALCOTT
72028-72028	CHOCTAW	72134-72134	ROE	72367-72367	MELLWOOD	72475-72475	WALDENBURG
72029-72029	CLARENDON	72135-72135	ROLAND	72368-72368	MORO	72476-72476	WALNUT RIDGE
72030-72030	CLEVELAND	72136-72136	ROMANCE	72369-72369	ONEIDA	72478-72478	WARM SPRINGS
72031-72031	CLINTON	72137-72137	ROSE BUD	72370-72370	OSCEOLA	72479-72479	WEINER
72032-72035	CONWAY	72139-72139	RUSSELL	72372-72372	PALESTINE	72482-72482	WILLIFORD
72036-72036	COTTON PLANT	72140-72140	SAINT CHARLES	72373-72373	PARKIN	72501-72503	BATESVILLE
72037-72037	COY	72141-72141	SCOTLAND	72374-72374	POPLAR GROVE	72512-72512	HORSESHOE BEND
72038-72038	CROCKETTS BLUFF	72142-72142	SCOTT	72376-72376	PROCTOR	72513-72513	ASH FLAT
72039-72039	DAMASCUS	72143-72149	SEARCY	72377-72377	RIVERVALE	72515-72515	BEXAR
72040-72040	DES ARC	72150-72150	SHERIDAN	72378-72378	ROUND POND	72516-72516	BOSWELL
72041-72041	DE VALLS BLUFF	72152-72152	SHERRILL	72379-72379	SNOW LAKE	72517-72517	BROCKWELL
72042-72042	DE WITT	72153-72153	SHIRLEY	72381-72381	TOMATO	72519-72519	CALICO ROCK
72043-72043	DIAZ	72156-72156	SOLGOHACHIA	72383-72383	TURNER	72520-72520	CAMP
72044-72044	EDGEMONT	72157-72157	SPRINGFIELD	72384-72384	TURRELL	72521-72521	CAVE CITY
72045-72045	EL PASO	72158-72158	BENTON	72385-72385	TWIST	72522-72522	CHARLOTTE
72046-72046	ENGLAND	72159-72159	STEPROCK	72386-72386	TYRONZA	72523-72523	CONCORD
72047-72047	ENOLA	72160-72160	STUTTGART	72387-72387	VANNDALE	72524-72524	CORD
72048-72048	ETHEL	72164-72164	SWEET HOME	72389-72389	WABASH	72525-72525	CHEROKEE VILLAGE
72051-72051	FOX	72165-72165	THIDA	72390-72390	WEST HELENA	72526-72526	CUSHMAN
72052-72052	GARNER	72166-72166	TICHNOR	72391-72391	WEST RIDGE	72527-72527	DESHA
72053-72053	COLLEGE STATION	72167-72167	TRASKWOOD	72392-72392	WHEATLEY	72528-72528	DOLPH
72055-72055	GILLETT	72168-72168	TUCKER	72394-72394	WIDENER	72529-72529	CHEROKEE VILLAGE
72057-72057	GRAPEVINE	72169-72169	TUPELO	72395-72395	WILSON	72530-72530	DRASCO
72058-72058	GREENBRIER	72170-72170	ULM	72396-72397	WYNNE	72531-72531	ELIZABETH
72059-72059	GREGORY	72173-72173	VILONIA	72397-72397	MC CRORY	72532-72532	EVENING SHADE
72060-72060	GRIFFITHVILLE	72175-72175	WABBASEKA	72401-72404	JONESBORO	72533-72533	FIFTY SIX
72061-72061	GUY	72176-72176	WARD	72410-72410	ALICIA	72534-72534	FLORAL
72063-72063	HATTIEVILLE	72178-72178	WEST POINT	72411-72411	BAY	72536-72536	FRANKLIN
72064-72064	HAZEN	72179-72179	WILBURN	72412-72412	BEECH GROVE	72537-72537	GAMALIEL
72065-72065	HENSLEY	72180-72180	WOODSON	72413-72413	BIGGERS	72538-72538	GEPP
72066-72066	HICKORY PLAINS	72181-72181	WOOSTER	72414-72414	BLACK OAK	72539-72539	GLENCOE
72067-72067	HIGDEN	72182-72182	WRIGHT	72415-72415	BLACK ROCK	72540-72540	GUION
72068-72068	HIGGINSON	72183-72183	WRIGHTSVILLE	72416-72416	BONO	72542-72542	HARDY
72069-72069	HOLLY GROVE	72189-72189	MC CRORY	72417-72417	BROOKLAND	72543-72543	HEBER SPRINGS
72070-72070	HOUSTON	72190-72199	NORTH LITTLE ROCK	72419-72419	CARAWAY	72544-72544	HENDERSON
				72421-72421	CASH	72545-72545	HEBER SPRINGS

72546-72546	IDA	72636-72636	GILBERT	72734-72734	GENTRY	72844-72844	HUNT
72550-72550	LOCUST GROVE	72638-72638	GREEN FOREST	72735-72735	GOSHEN	72845-72845	KNOXVILLE
72553-72553	MAGNESS	72639-72639	HARRIET	72736-72736	GRAVETTE	72846-72846	LAMAR
72554-72554	MAMMOTH SPRING	72640-72640	HASTY	72737-72737	GREENLAND	72847-72847	LONDON
72555-72555	MARCELLA	72641-72641	JASPER	72738-72738	HINDSVILLE	72851-72851	NEW BLAINE
72556-72556	MELBOURNE	72642-72642	LAKEVIEW	72739-72739	HIWASSE	72852-72852	OARK
72557-72557	MOKO	72644-72644	LEAD HILL	72740-72740	HUNTSVILLE	72853-72853	OLA
72560-72560	MOUNTAIN VIEW	72645-72645	LESLIE	72741-72741	JOHNSON	72854-72854	OZONE
72561-72561	MOUNT PLEASANT	72648-72648	MARBLE FALLS	72742-72742	KINGSTON	72855-72855	PARIS
72562-72562	NEWARK	72650-72650	MARSHALL	72744-72744	LINCOLN	72856-72856	PELSOR
72564-72564	OIL TROUGH	72651-72651	MIDWAY	72745-72745	LOWELL	72857-72857	PLAINVIEW
72565-72565	OXFORD	72653-72654	MOUNTAIN HOME	72747-72747	MAYSVILLE	72858-72858	POTTSVILLE
72566-72566	PINEVILLE	72655-72655	MOUNT JUDEA	72749-72749	MORROW	72860-72860	ROVER
72567-72567	PLEASANT GROVE	72657-72657	TIMBO	72751-72751	PEA RIDGE	72863-72863	SCRANTON
72568-72568	PLEASANT PLAINS	72658-72659	NORFORK	72752-72752	PETTIGREW	72865-72865	SUBIACO
72569-72569	POUGHKEEPSIE	72660-72660	OAK GROVE	72753-72753	PRAIRIE GROVE	72867-72867	WAVELAND
72571-72571	ROSIE	72661-72661	OAKLAND	72756-72758	ROGERS	72901-72919	FORT SMITH
72572-72572	SAFFELL	72662-72662	OMAHA	72760-72760	SAINT PAUL	72921-72921	ALMA
72573-72573	SAGE	72663-72663	ONIA	72761-72761	SILOAM SPRINGS	72923-72923	BARLING
72575-72575	SALADO	72666-72666	PARTHENON	72762-72766	SPRINGDALE	72924-72924	BATES
72576-72576	SALEM	72668-72668	PEEL	72767-72767	SPRINGTOWN	72926-72926	BOLES
72577-72577	SIDNEY	72669-72669	PINDALL	72768-72768	SULPHUR SPRINGS	72927-72927	BOONEVILLE
72578-72578	STURKIE	72670-72670	PONCA	72769-72769	SUMMERS	72928-72928	BRANCH
72579-72579	SULPHUR ROCK	72672-72672	PYATT	72770-72770	TONTITOWN	72930-72930	CECIL
72581-72581	TUMBLING SHOALS	72675-72675	SAINT JOE	72773-72773	WESLEY	72932-72932	CEDARVILLE
72583-72583	VIOLA	72677-72677	SUMMIT	72774-72774	WEST FORK	72933-72933	CHARLESTON
72584-72584	VIOLET HILL	72679-72679	TILLY	72775-72775	WHEELER	72934-72934	CHESTER
72585-72585	WIDEMAN	72680-72680	TIMBO	72776-72776	WITTER	72935-72935	DYER
72587-72587	WISEMAN	72682-72682	VALLEY SPRINGS	72801-72812	RUSSELLVILLE	72936-72936	GREENWOOD
72601-72602	HARRISON	72683-72683	VENDOR	72820-72820	ALIX	72937-72937	HACKETT
72610-72610	ALCO	72685-72685	WESTERN GROVE	72821-72821	ALTUS	72938-72938	HARTFORD
72611-72611	ALPENA	72686-72686	WITTS SPRINGS	72822-72823	ATKINS	72940-72940	HUNTINGTON
72612-72612	BASS	72687-72687	YELLVILLE	72824-72824	BELLEVILLE	72941-72941	LAVACA
72613-72613	BEAVER	72701-72704	FAYETTEVILLE	72826-72826	BLUE MOUNTAIN	72943-72943	MAGAZINE
72615-72615	BERGMAN	72711-72711	AVOCA	72827-72827	BLUFFTON	72944-72944	MANSFIELD
72616-72616	BERRYVILLE	72712-72712	BENTONVILLE	72828-72828	BRIGGSVILLE	72945-72945	MIDLAND
72617-72617	BIG FLAT	72714-72715	BELLA VISTA	72829-72829	CENTERVILLE	72946-72946	MOUNTAINBURG
72618-72618	BRUNO	72716-72716	BENTONVILLE	72830-72830	CLARKSVILLE	72947-72947	MULBERRY
72619-72619	BULL SHOALS	72717-72717	CANEHILL	72832-72832	COAL HILL	72948-72948	NATURAL DAM
72623-72623	CLARKRIDGE	72718-72718	CAVE SPRINGS	72833-72833	DANVILLE	72949-72949	OZARK
72624-72624	COMPTON	72719-72719	CENTERTON	72834-72834	DARDANELLE	72950-72950	PARKS
72626-72626	COTTER	72721-72721	COMBS	72835-72835	DELAWARE	72951-72951	RATCLIFF
72628-72628	DEER	72722-72722	DECATUR	72837-72837	DOVER	72952-72952	RUDY
72629-72629	DENNARD	72727-72727	ELKINS	72838-72838	GRAVELLY	72955-72955	UNIONTOWN
72630-72630	DIAMOND CITY	72728-72728	ELM SPRINGS	72839-72839	HAGARVILLE	72956-72957	VAN BUREN
72631-72632	EUREKA SPRINGS	72729-72729	EVANSVILLE	72840-72840	HARTMAN	72958-72958	WALDRON
72633-72633	EVERTON	72730-72730	FARMINGTON	72841-72841	HARVEY	72959-72959	WINSLOW
72634-72634	FLIPPIN	72732-72732	GARFIELD	72842-72842	HAVANA		
72635-72635	GASSVILLE	72733-72733	GATEWAY	72843-72843	HECTOR		

California

General Help Numbers:

Governor's Office
State Capitol, 1st Floor
Sacramento, CA 95814
www.governor.ca.gov/state
/govsite/gov_homepage.jsp

916-445-2841
Fax 916-445-4633
8:30AM-5PM

Attorney General's Office
Justice Department
PO Box 944255
Sacramento, CA 94244-2550
http://caag.state.ca.us

916-445-9555
Fax 916-324-5205
8AM-5PM

State Court Administrator
455 Golden Gate Ave
San Francisco, CA 94102-3660
www.courtinfo.ca.gov

415-865-4200
Fax 415-865-4205
8AM-5PM

State Archives
1020 "O" St
Sacramento, CA 95814
www.ss.ca.gov/archives/
archives.htm

916-653-7715
Fax 916-653-7363
9:30AM-4PM

State Specifics:

Capital:	Sacramento
	Sacramento County
Time Zone:	PST
Number of Counties:	58
Population:	34,501,130
Web Site:	www.state.ca.us/state/ portal/myca_homepage.jsp

State Agencies

Criminal Records
Access to Records is Restricted
Department of Justice, Records Search Section, PO Box 903417, Sacramento, CA 94203-4170 (Courier: 4949 Broadway, Sacramento, CA 95820); 916-227-3460 (Dept of Justice), 916-227-3849 (General Information), 916-227-3812 (Sealing & Dismissal), 8AM-5PM.

www.caag.state.ca.us

Note: Penal Code Sec. 11105.3 limits criminal records access to searches involving child care, education, the handicaped and mentally impaired. The report subject can obtain their own copy. Sexual Offender data on CD-rom can be viewed in person at agency offices. Entities must be pre-appoved before records can be ordered.

Corporation Records
Limited Liability Company
   Records
Limited Partnerships
Limited Liability
   Partnerships,
Secretary of State, Information Retrieval/ Certification Unit, 1500 11th Street, 3rd Fl,

Sacramento, CA 95814; 916-657-5448 (Corps), 916-653-3794 (LLCs), 916-653-3365 (Partnerships), 8AM-4:30PM.

www.ss.ca.gov

Indexing & Storage: New records are available for inquiry immediately. Records are indexed on microfiche, inhouse computer.

Searching: Include the following in your request: full name of business. In addition to the articles of incorporation, corporation records include the following information: Statement of Officers (up to 2), Prior (merged) or amended names, Inactive and Reserved names. Reserved names are not available on the online search.

Access by: mail, phone, fax, in person, online.

Fee & Payment: Statement of Officers or rticles of incorporation and amendments is $1.00 first page, $.50 each add'l; status report is $4.00. Add $5.00 for certification for any document. Fee payee: Secretary of State. Prepayment required. Personal checks accepted. No credit cards accepted.

Mail search: Turnaround time: 2 to 3 weeks. A self addressed stamped envelope is requested.

Phone search: Only pre-paid accounts have telephone access to corporate status and name availability/reservation. Fee is $4.00 per name searched.

Fax search: Return of documents and/or status information is $5.00 per name, $10.00.

In person search: Turnaround time is while you wait if search not extensive.

Online search: The web site offers access to more than 2 million records including corporation, LLC, LP and LLP. Information available includes status, file number, date of filing and agent for service of process. Please note the file is updated weekly (not daily).

Assumed Name
Fictitious Name

Records not maintained by a state level agency.

Note: Records are found at the county level.

Trademarks/Servicemarks
Limited Partnership Records

Secretary of State, Trademark Unit, PO Box 944225, Sacramento, CA 94244-2250 (Courier: 1500 11th Street, Rm 345, Sacramento, CA 95814); 916-653-4984 (Trademark/Servicemarks), 916-653-3365 (Partnership Information), 8AM-5PM.

www.ss.ca.gov

Indexing & Storage: Records are available for active and expired records. Records are indexed on index cards.

Searching: Include the following in your request: trademark/servicemark name. Information returned includes name of trademark, name of owner and address, and date of filing.

Access by: mail, phone, in person.

Fee & Payment: Copies are $1.00 per page and $.50 each add'l. Certification is $5.00 per document. A Certificate of Status is $5.00. Fee payee: Secretary of State. Prepayment required. Personal checks accepted. No credit cards accepted.

Mail search: Turnaround time: 2 to 3 weeks. A self addressed stamped envelope is requested. No fee for mail request.

Phone search: No fee for telephone request of a name search. There is a limit of 2 searches per call.

In person search: You can wait for results. If lists are presented, then the results are returned by mail.

Uniform Commercial Code
Federal Tax Liens
State Tax Liens

UCC Division, Secretary of State, PO Box 942835, Sacramento, CA 94235-0001 (Courier: 1500 11th St, 2nd Fl, Sacramento, CA 95814); 916-653-3516, 8AM-5PM.

www.ss.ca.gov

Note: This office does not currently offer fax service, but may make it available in the near future.

Indexing & Storage: Records are available for current records and expired records up to 1 year after lapse. There is an index on computer dating back to 1965. Records are indexed on inhouse computer.

Searching: Use search request form UCC-11; one form per debtor name. The search includes federal and some state tax liens on businesses. Federal tax liens on individuals are filed at the county level, state tax liens are filed at either location. Include the following in your request: debtor name.

Access by: mail, in person, online.

Fee & Payment: The search fee is $10.00 per debtor name. The copy fee is $1.00 for the first page of the document and $.50 each additional page. Fee payee: Secretary of State. Prepayment required. Credit cards are only for over-the-counter services. Those conducting business frequently with this office may utilize a prepaid account option. Personal checks accepted. Credit cards accepted: MasterCard, Visa.

Mail search: Records are available by mail.

In person search: There is an additional $6.00 special handling fee for each document received over the counter.

Online search: Direct Access provides dial-up searching via PC and modem. This provides limited search capabilities, it's primary use is to verify filings. The data available conatins names and file dates, but not colateral. Fees range from $1-3 dollars, depending on type of search. Each page scroll is $.25. Requesters operate from a prepaid account.

Sales Tax Registrations

Board of Equalization, Sales and Use Tax Department, PO Box 942879, Sacramento, CA 94279-0001; 916-445-6362, 800-400-7115 (In California Only), 916-324-4433 (Fax), 8AM-5PM.

www.boe.ca.gov

Note: District Offices are: Oakland, 510-286-0347; Sacramento, 916-255-3350; San Diego, 619-525-4526; San Jose, 408-277-1231; Orange Cty, 714-558-4059; Van Nuys, 818-904-2300; Norwalk, 562-466-1694; Torrance, 310-516-4300; Riverside, 909-680-6400.

Searching: This Board will provide owners' name, firm name, business address, account number, starting date, whether account is active or closed and, if closed, the closing date. The responsibility of assisting taxpayers in verifying the validity of resale certificates is primarily at the District level, but this office will provide search services. Requesters must provide the name of the business, its location, and the permit #.

Access by: mail, phone, fax.

Fee & Payment: No charge is required for verification of resale certificates and permits. However, a fee for other requests, such as those received from attorneys and collection agencies, is $3.00 per name searched. Fee payee: Board of Equalization. Prepayment required. Monthly billing is available for ongoing requesters. Personal checks accepted. No credit cards accepted.

Mail search: Turnaround time: 2 weeks. A self addressed stamped envelope is requested.

Phone search: No fee for telephone request. Phone service is offered to verify a seller's permit is valid. Calls are limited to three requests.

Fax search: Generally, turnaround time is 2 weeks.

Other access: Lists are available for a fee sorted in a number of ways, including CA Industry Code. For further information and fees, call the Technical Services Division at 916-323-1088.

Birth Certificates

State Department of Health Svcs, Office of Vital Records, PO Box 730241, Sacramento, CA 94244-0241 (Courier: 304 S Street, Sacramento, CA 95814); 916-445-2684 (Recording), 916-445-1719 (Attendant), 800-858-5553 (Fax), 8AM-4:30PM.

www.dhs.ca.gov/chs

Indexing & Storage: Records are available from July 1905 on. It takes 1 to 3 months before new records are available for inquiry. Records are indexed on microfiche, inhouse computer.

Searching: Include the following in your request: full name, mother's full maiden name, date of birth, place of birth, father's full name is optional. If you do not use their form, the search can take up to 7 weeks.

Access by: mail, in person, online.

Fee & Payment: The fee for a certified copy is $13.00, if the birth date is not known, a fee of $12.00 is charged for each decade searched. Fee payee: Office of Vital Records. Prepayment required. Personal checks and money orders accepted.

Mail search: Turnaround time: within 1 month. Always include your daytime phone number. No self addressed stamped envelope is required.

In person search: Turnaround time is 3 weeks.

Online search: Birth records from 1905-1995 can be accessed at http://userdb.rootsweb.com/ca/birth/search.cgi. The site is maintained by a private entity, but the data is provided by this agency.

Expedited service: Expedited service is available for mail, phone and fax searches. Turnaround time: 1 day. Add $7.00 per event for express mail delivery service. You may send request by special mail (express, registered, etc.) and mark "urgent."

Death Records

State Department of Health Svcs, Office of Vital Records, PO Box 730241, Sacramento, CA 94244-0241 (Courier: 304 S Street, Sacramento, CA 95814); 916-445-2684, 916-445-1719 (Attendant), 800-858-5553 (Fax), 8AM-4:30PM.

www.dhs.ca.gov/chs

Indexing & Storage: Records are available from July 1905 to present. It takes 1 to 2 months before new records are available for inquiry. Records are indexed on microfiche, inhouse computer.

Searching: Include the following in your request: full name, date of death, date of birth, place of death, Social Security Number. There will be a 2-3 week delay if you do not use their form.

Access by: mail, in person.

Fee & Payment: Search fee is $11.00 per name for each decade searched. Fee payee: Office of Vital Records. Prepayment required. Personal checks accepted.

Mail search: Turnaround time: within 1 month.

In person search: Turnaround time is 3 weeks.

Expedited service: Expedited service is available for mail, phone and fax searches. Turnaround time: 1 day. Add $7.00 per event for express delivery service. Send request by special mail (express, registered, etc.) and mark "urgent."

Marriage Certificates

State Department of Health Svcs, Office of Vital Records, PO Box 730241, Sacramento, CA 94244-0241 (Courier: 304 S Street, Sacramento, CA 95814); 916-445-2684, 916-445-1719 (Attendant), 800-858-5553 (Fax), 8AM-4:30PM.

www.dhs.ca.gov/chs

Note: Records between 1986 and 1997 must be searched at the county level (state does not have access to these records).

Indexing & Storage: Records are available from July 1905 to March 1986 and 1998 forward. Records are indexed on microfiche.

Searching: Include the following in your request: names of husband and wife, date of marriage, place or county of marriage.

Access by: mail, in person.

Fee & Payment: Search fee is $13.00 per name for each decade searched. Fee payee: Office of Vital Records. Prepayment required. Personal checks & money orders accepted.

Mail search: Turnaround time: within 1 month. No self addressed stamped envelope is required.

In person search: Turnaround time 3 weeks.

Expedited service: Expedited service is available for mail, phone and fax searches. Turnaround time: 1 day. Add $7.00 per event for express delivery service. Send request by special mail (express, registered, etc.) and mark "urgent."

Divorce Records

State Department of Health Svcs, Office of Vital Records, PO Box 730241, Sacramento, CA 94244-0241 (Courier: 304 S Street, Sacramento, CA 95814); 916-445-2684, 916-445-1719 (Attendant), 800-858-5553 (Fax), 8AM-4:30PM.

www.dhs.ca.gov/chs

Indexing & Storage: Records are available from 1962 to 1984 for certificate of record only. All divorce records are found at the country court issuing the decree. Records are indexed on microfiche.

Searching: Include the following in your request: names of husband and wife, place of divorce, date of divorce.

Access by: mail, in person.

Fee & Payment: Search fee is $13.00 per name for decade searched. Fee payee: Office of Vital Records. Prepayment required. Personal checks accepted.

Mail search: Turnaround time: within 1 month. No self addressed stamped envelope is required.

In person search: Searching is available in person.

Expedited service: Expedited service is available for mail and phone searches. Turnaround time: 1 day. Add $7.00 per event for express delivery service. Send request by special mail (express, registered, etc.) and mark "urgent."

Workers' Compensation Records

Division of Workers' Compensation, Headquarters, PO Box 429003, San Francisco, CA 94142-9003 (Courier: 455 Golden Gate Ave, 9th Fl, San Francisco, CA 94102); 415-703-4600, 415-703-4717 (Fax), 8AM-5PM.

www.dir.ca.gov/dwc/dwc_home_page.htm

Note: Per law, no addresses of any injured workers are given out.

Indexing & Storage: Records are available for varying periods depending on injury.

Searching: Using the proper forms, one can either view a file or ask if records exist. This authorization process does not require the signature or approval of the claimant. Forms may be faxed. All forms must be obtained from this agency and require approval before a searcher can present a request at the district office.

Access by: mail, fax, in person.

Fee & Payment: There is no search fee.

Mail search: Turnaround time: variable. You must use "Request for WCAB Case # Search Form" and the agency will let you know if there is a record. The state suggests that out-of-state requesters use a local CA retriever who already has the necessary authorization to search. No self addressed stamped envelope is required.

Fax search: Turnaround is usually 1 week.

In person search: Requester must be authorized first (by this office) with either the "Request to View a WCAB Case File" or "Request for DWC Authorization # for Access to Index Cards." Then, with a case number, requester can visit any of the 25 district offices.

Driver Records

Department of Motor Vehicles, Information Services Branch, PO Box 944247, Mail Station G199, Sacramento, CA 94244-2470; 916-657-8098, 916-657-6525 (Driver Licensing), 916-657-5564 (Requester Accounts), 8AM-5PM.

www.dmv.ca.gov

Note: The public counter is closed for record access by walk-in requesters. Copies of tickets are not available at the state level.

Indexing & Storage: Records are available for 3 years for accidents and minor moving violations, 4 years for fatal accidents and major violations, and 10 years for DWIs. It takes 10 days or more before new records are available for inquiry. Records are normally destroyed after the Director determines they are no longer necessary to retain.

Searching: Commercial requesters/users who meet certain criteria must maintain a Commercial Requester Account, which may require a $50,000 bond if confidential address information is released. For more information about a Requester Account call (916) 657-5564. Include the following in your request: driver's license number, full name, date of birth. Non-commercial requesters are known as "casual requesters." These requests are held for 10 days while the state notifies the licensee who can then deny the release. If released, address is shielded. The following data is not released: mental health records, medical records, pending records, residence addresses and Social Security Numbers.

Access by: mail, phone, online.

Fee & Payment: Searches-driver record by name and license #, full name and DOB-$5.00; Driver record by magnetic tape-name and license #-$2.00; full name and DOB-$4.00; guarantor's signature-$20.00; license status only $1.00. Fee payee: California Department of Motor Vehicles. Prepayment required. Personal checks accepted. No credit cards accepted.

Mail search: Turnaround time: 2 to 3 days. Individuals mailing any request forms may be subject to a 10 day delay due to a notice to subject(s) of the record request.

Phone search: However, records are only released to the subject. Call 916-657-6525.

Online search: The department offers online access, but a $10,000 one-time setup fee is required. The system is open 24 hours, 7 days a week. For more information call 916-657-5582.

Other access: Employers and regulatory agencies may monitor their drivers in the Pull Notic Program. The DMV informs the organization when there is activity on enrolled drivers. Call 916-657-6346 for details.

Vehicle Ownership & Registration
Vessel Ownership & Registration

Department of Motor Vehicle, Office of Information Services, PO Box 944247, MS-G199, Sacramento, CA 94244-2470; 916-657-8098 (Walk-in/Mail-in Phone), 916-657-7914 (Commercial Accounts), 916-657-6739 (Vessel Registration), 916-657-5583 (Fax), 8AM-5PM.

www.dmv.ca.gov

Indexing & Storage: Records are available for three years. Beyond that, a subpoena is required. Hardcopy and microfilmed records date back to 1976. All watercraft must be registered if over 8 ft (except rowboats).

Searching: It is suggested to use departmental forms, which can be obtained from the Forms Management Unit, PO Box 932382, Sacramento, 94232-3820 or fax request to 916-657-7243. There are two types of requesters: "casual requesters" and "requester account holders." For those businesses and entities who need to access on a regular basis, call 916-657-5564.

Access by: mail, phone, online.

Fee & Payment: Current record by license, VIN or CR#, by registration owner name and address-$5.00; magnetic tape inquiry-$2.00; owner as of data by license, VIN or CR#-$5.00; current automated history data-$5.00; photocopies-$20.00. Fee payee: California Department of Motor Vehicles. Prepayment required. Personal checks accepted. No credit cards accepted.

Mail search: Turnaround time: 1 to 3 days. A self addressed stamped envelope is requested.

Phone search: Phone requesters must be pre-approved and are limited to 7 verbal responses. Hours of operation are 7 AM to 6 PM. The phone number is 916- 657-7914.

Online search: 24 hour online access is limited to certain Authorized Vendors. Requesters are may not use the data for direct marketing, solicitation, nor resell for those purposes. A bond is required and very high fees are involved. For more information, call Sue Jefferson at 916-657-5582.

Other access: California offers delivery of registration information on magnetic tape, disk or paper within special parameters. Release of information is denied for commercial marketing purposes.

Accident Reports

Department of Motor Vehicles, Accident Reports, PO Box 942884, Sacramento, CA 94284.

www.dmv.ca.gov

Note: Most accident reports are held by the California Highway Patrol or local law enforcement agency that filed the report. There are 115 area offices of the California Highway Patrol. Fees vary. Limited reports are held by this office.

Searching: Copies of SR-1 accident reports are provided to limited requesters by the Department of Motor Vehicles.

Access by: mail.

Fee & Payment: The fee is $20.00.

Mail search: SR-1 accident reports are available by mail from this office.

Legislation Records

California State Legislature, State Capitol, Room B-32 (Legislative Bill Room), Sacramento, CA 95814, 916-445-2323 (Current/Pending Bills), 916-653-7715 (State Archives), 8AM-5PM.

www.leginfo.ca.gov

Note: This office carries only latest amended versions (last 2 years). The agency recommends that any California law library would have complete copies of all bills for other years and may be easier to search.

Searching: Include the following in your request: bill number, year.

Access by: mail, phone, in person, online.

Fee & Payment: There is no charge for up to 5 bills. They will compute copy charges, if needed. Fee payee: Legislative Bill Room. Personal checks accepted. No credit cards accepted.

Mail search: Turnaround time: 5 to 7 days. You must first know what the copies will be prior to ordering.

Phone search: You may call for bill copies.

In person search: You may request copies in person.

Online search: The Internet site has all legislative information back to 1993. The site also gives access to state laws.

Voter Registration
Access to Records is Restricted

Secretary of State, Elections Division, 1500 11th Street, Sacramento, CA 95814; 916-657-2166, 916-653-3214 (Fax), 8AM-5PM.

Note: Records are not open and cannot be viewed at this agency. Individual verification must be done at the local level. The state will sell all or portions of the statewide database for political or pre-approved purposes. Call 916-653-6224 for details.

GED Certificates

Dept of Education, State GED Office, PO Box 710273, Sacramento, CA 94244-0273; 916-651-6623, 800-331-6316.

www.cde.ca.gov/ged

Indexing & Storage: Records are available from July 1990, prior are archived. It takes 2 months before new records are available for inquiry.

Searching: To verify or to obtain a copy of a transcript, all of the following is required: a signed release, name, date of birth, date/year of test, Social Security Number, and city of test.

Access by: mail.

Fee & Payment: There is no fee for verifications or transcripts.

Mail search: Turnaround time is 7-10 working days or 2-3 weeks if the information is older than 1990. No self addressed stamped envelope is required.

Hunting License Information
Fishing License Information
Access to Records is Restricted

Department of Fish & Game, License & Revenue Branch, 3211 "S" St, Sacramento, CA 95816; 916-227-2245, 916-227-2261 (Fax), 8AM-5PM.

www.dfg.ca.gov

Note: Records are not available to the public.

California State Licensing Agencies

Licenses Searchable Online

Acupuncturist #1 ....www.acupuncture.ca.gov
Air Conditioning Contractor #28 ....http://www2.cslb.ca.gov/CSLB_LIBRARY/Name+Request.asp
Alarm Company #22 ....www.dca.ca.gov/bsis/lookup.htm
Alarm Company Employee/Manager #22 ....www.dca.ca.gov/bsis/lookup.htm
Animal Health Technician #40 ....www.vmb.ca.gov/2licensg/lic1list.htm
Architect #7..www.cab.ca.gov/Templates/querysearch.cfm
Athletic Event Mgr./Promo./Matchmaker #3 .www.dca.ca.gov/csac/directories.htm
Attorney #23 ....www.calsb.org/MM/SBMBRSHP.HTM
Automobile Dealer/Repair #19.....................www.smogcheck.ca.gov/stdPage.asp?Body=/Consumer/verify_a_license.htm
Bank #11 ....www.sbd.ca.gov/directry/db.asp
Baton Training Facility/Instructor #22 ....www.dca.ca.gov/bsis/lookup.htm
Boxer #3 ....www.dca.ca.gov/csac/directories.htm
Brake & Lamp Adjuster #19...........................www.smogcheck.ca.gov/stdPage.asp?Body=/Consumer/verify_a_license.htm
Brake Station #19 ....www.smogcheck.ca.gov/stdPage.asp?Body=/Consumer/verify_a_license.htm
Building Contractor, General-Class B #28 ...http://www2.cslb.ca.gov/CSLB_LIBRARY/Name+Request.asp
Cabinet & Millwork #28 ....http://www2.cslb.ca.gov/CSLB_LIBRARY/Name+Request.asp
Cemetery, Cemetery Broker/Agent #25 ....www.dca.ca.gov/cemetery/lookup.htm
Clinic Pharmaceutical Permit #13 ....www.pharmacy.ca.gov/license_lookup.htm
Concrete Contractor/Company #28 ....http://www2.cslb.ca.gov/CSLB_LIBRARY/Name+Request.asp
Continuing Education Provider #8 ....www.bbs.ca.gov/weblokup.htm
Contractor #46..www.cslb.ca.gov
Court Reporter (Shorthand Reporter) #29 ....www.courtreportersboard.ca.gov
Credit Union #11...www.sbd.ca.gov/directry/cu.asp
Cremated Remains Disposer #25.................www.dca.ca.gov/cemetery/lookup.htm
Crematory #25 ....www.dca.ca.gov/cemetery/lookup.htm
Dental Assistant #27......................................www.comda.ca.gov/licensestatus.html
Dental Assistant, Extended Function #27 ....www.comda.ca.gov/licensestatus.html
Dental Hygienist #27 ....www.comda.ca.gov/licensestatus.html
Dentist #9 ....www.dbc.ca.gov/License.html
Drug Wholesaler/Drug Room #13 ....www.pharmacy.ca.gov/license_lookup.htm
Drywall #28 ....http://www2.cslb.ca.gov/CSLB_LIBRARY/Name+Request.asp
Earthwork & Paving #28 ....http://www2.cslb.ca.gov/CSLB_LIBRARY/Name+Request.asp
Educational Psychologist #8 ....www.bbs.ca.gov/weblokup.htm
Electrical (General) & Electric Sign #28 ......http://www2.cslb.ca.gov/CSLB_LIBRARY/Name+Request.asp
Electronics & Appliance Repair #20.............http://www2.dca.ca.gov/pls/wllpub/wllquery$.startup
Elevator Installation #28 ....http://www2.cslb.ca.gov/CSLB_LIBRARY/Name+Request.asp
Embalmer/Embalmer Apprentice #25 ....www.dca.ca.gov/cemetery/lookup.htm
Engineer (Various) #10 ....www.dca.ca.gov/pels/l_lookup.htm
Fencing #28..http://www2.cslb.ca.gov/CSLB_LIBRARY/Name+Request.asp
Firearm Permit #22 ....www.dca.ca.gov/bsis/lookup.htm
Firearm Training Facility/Instructor #22 ....www.dca.ca.gov/bsis/lookup.htm
Flooring & Floor Covering #28 ....http://www2.cslb.ca.gov/CSLB_LIBRARY/Name+Request.asp
Fumigation #44...www.dca.ca.gov/pestboard/lookup.htm
Funeral Director/Establishment #25.............www.dca.ca.gov/cemetery/lookup.htm
Funerary Training Estbl./Appren. #25 ....www.dca.ca.gov/cemetery/lookup.htm
Geologist #18..www.dca.ca.gov/geology/lookup/
Geologist, Engineering #18............................www.dca.ca.gov/geology/lookup/
Geophysicist #18 ....www.dca.ca.gov/geology/lookup/
Glazier #28 ....http://www2.cslb.ca.gov/CSLB_LIBRARY/Name+Request.asp
Hearing Aid Dispenser #34 ....www.dca.ca.gov/hearingaid/
Heating & Warm-Air Ventilating #28 ....http://www2.cslb.ca.gov/CSLB_LIBRARY/Name+Request.asp
Horse Racing Entity #24 ....www.chrb.ca.gov/license_search.htm
Horse Racing Occupation #24 ....www.chrb.ca.gov/license_search.htm
Hospital Exemptees #13................................www.pharmacy.ca.gov/license_lookup.htm
Hydrogeologist #18..www.dca.ca.gov/geology/lookup/
Hypodermic Needle & Syringe Dist. #13......www.pharmacy.ca.gov/license_lookup.htm
Industrial Loan Company, Premium #11......www.sbd.ca.gov/directry/pf.asp
Insulation & Accoustical Contractor #28 ......http://www2.cslb.ca.gov/CSLB_LIBRARY/Name+Request.asp
Insurance Adjuster #32..................................www.insurance.ca.gov/LIC/Licensestatus.htm
Insurance Agent/Broker #32 ....www.insurance.ca.gov/LIC/Licensestatus.htm
Insurance Company #32.................................www.insurance.ca.gov/docs/FS-CompanyProfiles.htm
Lamp Station #19..www.smogcheck.ca.gov/stdPage.asp?Body=/Consumer/verify_a_license.htm

Landscape Architect #35 ....www.latc.dca.ca.gov/Licensee/search.htm
Landscaping #28 ....http://www2.cslb.ca.gov/CSLB_LIBRARY/Name+Request.asp
Lobbyist/Lobbyist Firm/Employer #47 ....http://cal-access.ss.ca.gov/Lobbying/
Locksmith/Locksmith Company #22 ....www.dca.ca.gov/bsis/lookup.htm
Marriage & Family Therapist #8..................www.bbs.ca.gov/weblokup.htm
Masonry #28 ....http://www2.cslb.ca.gov/CSLB_LIBRARY/Name+Request.asp
Medical Doctor/Surgeon #36 ....www.docboard.org/ca/df/casearch.htm
Money Orders/Payment Instru. Issuer #11 ..www.sbd.ca.gov/directry/pi.asp
Nurse #16 ....www.rn.ca.gov/online/online.htm
Optometrist #12 ....www.optometry.ca.gov/search.asp
Optometry Branch Office #12 ....www.optometry.ca.gov/search.asp
Optometry Fictitious Name Practice #12......www.optometry.ca.gov/search.asp
Ornamental Metal #28 ....http://www2.cslb.ca.gov/CSLB_LIBRARY/Name+Request.asp
Painting & Decorating #28 ....http://www2.cslb.ca.gov/CSLB_LIBRARY/Name+Request.asp
Parking & Highway Improvement #28..........http://www2.cslb.ca.gov/CSLB_LIBRARY/Name+Request.asp
Patrol Operator, Private #22 ....www.dca.ca.gov/bsis/lookup.htm
Pest Control Field Rep./Operator #44..........www.dca.ca.gov/pestboard/lookup.htm
Pesticide Applicator #44 ....www.dca.ca.gov/pestboard/lookup.htm
Pharmacist/Pharmacist Intern #13..............www.pharmacy.ca.gov/license_lookup.htm
Pharmacy #13...www.pharmacy.ca.gov/license_lookup.htm
Pharmacy Technician #13 ....www.pharmacy.ca.gov/license_lookup.htm
Physician Assistant #39 ....www.docboard.org/ca/df/casearch.htm
Plastering #28 ....http://www2.cslb.ca.gov/CSLB_LIBRARY/Name+Request.asp
Plumber #28 ....http://www2.cslb.ca.gov/CSLB_LIBRARY/Name+Request.asp
Podiatrist #14..www.docboard.org/ca/df/casearch.htm
Private Investigator #22 ....www.dca.ca.gov/bsis/lookup.htm
Psychiatric Technician #17 ....www.bvnpt.ca.gov/licverif.htm
Psychological Assistant #15 ....www.psychboard.ca.gov
Psychologist #15..www.psychboard.ca.gov
Real Estate Broker/Corporation #33 ....www.dre.ca.gov/licstats.htm
Real Estate Sales Agent #33 ....www.dre.ca.gov/licstats.htm
Refrigeration #28 ....http://www2.cslb.ca.gov/CSLB_LIBRARY/Name+Request.asp
Repossessor Agency/Mgr./Employee #22 ...www.dca.ca.gov/bsis/lookup.htm
Respiratory Care Practitioner #41................www.rcb.ca.gov/activercps.htm
Roofing Contractor #28...............................http://www2.cslb.ca.gov/CSLB_LIBRARY/Name+Request.asp
Sanitation System #28................................http://www2.cslb.ca.gov/CSLB_LIBRARY/Name+Request.asp
Savings & Loan Association #11 ....www.sbd.ca.gov/directry/sl.asp
Security Guard/Armored Car Guard #22.....www.dca.ca.gov/bsis/lookup.htm
Service Contract Seller (Appliance) #20 ......http://www2.dca.ca.gov/pls/wllpub/wllquery$.startup
Sheet Metal #28..http://www2.cslb.ca.gov/CSLB_LIBRARY/Name+Request.asp
Smog Check Station #19 ....www.smogcheck.ca.gov/stdPage.asp?Body=/Consumer/verify_a_license.htm
Smog Check Technician #19 ....www.smogcheck.ca.gov/stdPage.asp?Body=/Consumer/verify_a_license.htm
Social Worker, Clinical #8...........................www.bbs.ca.gov/weblokup.htm
Social Worker, Clinical Associate #8 ....www.bbs.ca.gov/weblokup.htm
Solar Energy #28 ....http://www2.cslb.ca.gov/CSLB_LIBRARY/Name+Request.asp
Specialty Contractor-Class C #28...............http://www2.cslb.ca.gov/CSLB_LIBRARY/Name+Request.asp
Steel, Reinforcing & Structural #28..............http://www2.cslb.ca.gov/CSLB_LIBRARY/Name+Request.asp
Supervising Physician #39..........................www.docboard.org/ca/df/casearch.htm
Surveyor, Land #10 ....www.dca.ca.gov/pels/l_lookup.htm
Swimming Pool #28 ....http://www2.cslb.ca.gov/CSLB_LIBRARY/Name+Request.asp
Tax Education Provider #45.........................www.ctec.org/html/approved_education_providers_.html
Teacher #26 ....https://teachercred.ctc.ca.gov/teachers/index.jsp
Termite Control #44 ....www.dca.ca.gov/pestboard/lookup.htm
Thrift & Loan Company #11 ....www.sbd.ca.gov/directry/tl.asp
Tile Contractor, Ceramic & Mosaic #28 ....http://www2.cslb.ca.gov/CSLB_LIBRARY/Name+Request.asp
Travelers Checks Issuer #11 ....www.sbd.ca.gov/directry/tc.asp
Trust Company #11 ....www.sbd.ca.gov/directry/trust.asp
Veterinarian #40 ....www.vmb.ca.gov/2licensg/lic1list.htm
Veterinary Food/Animal Drug Retailer #13 ...www.pharmacy.ca.gov/license_lookup.htm
Veterinary Hospital #40...............................www.vmb.ca.gov/2licensg/lic1list.htm
Vocational Nurse #17 ....www.bvnpt.ca.gov/licverif.htm
Water Well Driller #28.................................http://www2.cslb.ca.gov/CSLB_LIBRARY/Name+Request.asp

Licensing Quick Finder

Acupuncturist #1	916-263-2680	
Agricultural Engineer #10	916-263-2222	
Air Conditioning Contractor #28	916-255-3985	
Alarm Company #22	800-952-5210	
Alarm Company Employee/Mgr. #22	800-952-5210	
Animal Health Technician #40	916-263-2613	
Announcer, Athletic Event (Ring) #3	916-263-2195	
Architect #7	916-445-3393	
Athletic Event Box Office Employee/Ticket Seller #3	916-263-2195	
Athletic Event Manager/Promoter/Matchmaker #3	916-263-2195	
Athletic Event Referee/Judge/Timekeeper/Doorperson #3	916-263-2195	
Athletic Gym #3	916-263-2195	
Athletic Trainer/Second #3	916-263-2195	
Attorney #23	415-538-2303	
Audiologist #42	916-263-2666	
Automobile Dealer/Repair #19	916-322-4010	
Automobile Manufacturer Arbitration Program #2	916-323-3406	
Bank #11	800-622-0620	
Barber Instructor/School #4	916-445-7061	
Barber Shop/Barber/Barber Appre. #4	916-445-7061	
Baton Training Facility/Instructor #22	800-952-5210	
Bedding Mfg./Renovator/Retailer/Whlse. #21	800-952-5210	
Boiler, Hot Water & Steam Fitting #28	916-255-3985	
Boxer #3	916-263-2195	
Boxing Second #3	916-263-2195	
Brake & Lamp Adjuster #19	916-322-4010	
Brake Station #19	916-322-4010	
Building Contractor, General-Class B #28	916-255-3985	
Building Moving/Demolition #28	916-255-3985	
Cabinet & Millwork #28	916-255-3985	
Cemetery, Cemetery Broker/Sales Agent #25	916-322-7737	
Clinic Pharmaceutical Permit #13	916-445-5014	
Clinical Nurse Specialist #16	800-838-6828	
Collection Agency Manager/Collector/Bookkeeper #22	800-952-5210	
Concrete Contractor/Company #28	916-255-3985	
Continuing Education Provider #8	916-445-4933	
Contractor #46	800-321-2752	
Cosmetician/Cosmetologist #4	916-445-7061	
Cosmetology Estbl./Inst./School #4	916-445-7061	
Court Reporter (Certified Shorthand Reporter) #29	916-263-3660	
CPA #6	916-263-3680	
Credit Union #11	800-622-0620	
Cremated Remains Disposer #25	916-322-7737	
Crematory #25	916-322-7737	
Dental Assistant #27	916-263-2595	
Dental Assist, Extended Function #27	916-263-2595	
Dental Hygienist #27	916-263-2595	
Dentist #9	916-263-2300	
Diagnostic Pharmaceutical #12	916-323-8720	
Drug Wholesaler/Drug Room #13	916-445-5014	
Dry Cleaning Plant #21	916-574-0280	
Drywall #28	916-255-3985	
Earthwork & Paving #28	916-255-3985	
Educational Psychologist #8	916-445-4933	
Electrical (General) & Electric Sign #28	916-255-3985	
Electrologist #4	916-445-7061	
Electrology Estbl./Instructor/School #4	916-445-7061	
Electroneuromyographer #38	916-263-2550	
Electronics & Appliance Repair #20	916-574-2067	
Elevator Installation #28	916-255-3985	
Embalmer/Embalmer Apprentice #25	916-322-7737	
Engineer (Various) #10	916-263-2222	
Esthetician #4	916-445-7061	
Fencing #28	916-255-3985	
Fire Protection #28	916-255-3985	
Firearm Permit #22	800-952-5210	

Firearm Training Facility/Instructor #22	800-952-5210	
Flooring & Floor Covering #28	916-255-3985	
Fumigation #44	916-263-2540	
Fund Raiser to Establish Training School #43	916-324-9328	
Funeral Director/Establishment #25	916-322-7737	
Funerary Training Establishment/Apprentice #25	916-322-7737	
Furniture & Bedding Retailer #21	916-574-0280	
Furniture Mfg./Retailer/Whlse. #21	916-574-0280	
Geologist #18	916-263-2113	
Geologist, Engineering #18	916-263-2113	
Geophysicist #18	916-263-2113	
Glazier #28	916-255-3985	
Guard/Protection Dog Operator #22	800-952-5210	
Healing Art Supervisor #31	916-445-6430	
Hearing Aid Dispenser #34	916-263-2288	
Heating & Warm-Air Ventilating #28	916-255-3985	
Home Furnishings/Thermal Insulation Importer/Headquarters/Supply Dealer #21	916-574-0280	
Horse Racing Entity #24	916-263-6000	
Horse Racing Occupation #24	916-263-6000	
Hospital Exemptee #13	916-445-5014	
Hydrogeologist #18	916-263-2113	
Hygienist #9	916-263-2300	
Hypodermic Needle & Syringe Distributor #13	916-445-5014	
Industrial Loan Company, Premium #11	800-622-0620	
Insulation & Accoustical Contractor #28	916-255-3985	
Insurance Adjuster #32	916-322-3555	
Insurance Agent/Broker #32	916-322-3555	
Insurance Company #32	916-322-3555	
Investment Advisors #30	916-445-3062	
Kickboxer, Amateur #3	916-263-2195	
Kickboxer/Full Contact Karate #3	916-263-2195	
Kinesiological Electromyographer #38	916-263-2550	
Lamp Station #19	916-322-4010	
Landscape Architect #35	916-445-4954	
Landscaping #28	916-255-3985	
Lathing #28	916-255-3985	
Lobbyist/Lobbyist Firm/Employer #47	916-653-6224	
Locksmith/Locksmith Company #22	800-952-5210	
Mammographic Facility #31	916-323-2772	
Manicurist #4	916-445-7061	
Manufactured Housing #28	916-255-3985	
Marriage & Family Therapist #8	916-445-4933	
Masonry #28	916-255-3985	
Medical Doctor/Surgeon #36	916-263-2635	
Medical Provider Consultant #22	800-952-5210	
Midwife #36	916-263-2393	
Midwife Nurse #16	800-838-6828	
Money Orders/Payment Instruments Issuer #11	800-622-0620	
Notary Public #37	916-653-3595	
Nuclear Medicine Technologist #31	916-445-8820	
Nurse #16	800-838-6828	
Nurse Anesthetist #16	800-838-6828	
Nursing Home Administrator #5	916-323-6838	
Optician, Dispensing #36	916-263-2634	
Optometric Corporation #12	916-323-8720	
Optometrist #12	916-323-8720	
Optometry Branch Office #12	916-323-8720	
Optometry Fictitious Name Practice #12	916-323-8720	
Ornamental Metal #28	916-255-3985	
Painting & Decorating #28	916-255-3985	
Parking & Highway Improvement #28	916-255-3985	
Patrol Operator, Private #22	800-952-5210	
Pest Control Field Rep./Operator #44	916-263-2540	
Pesticide Applicator #44	916-263-2540	
Pharmaceutical Dist., Out-of-State #13	916-445-5014	
Pharmaceutical Whlse./Exemptee #13	916-445-5014	
Pharmacist/Pharmacist Intern #13	916-445-5014	
Pharmacy #13	916-445-5014	
Pharmacy Cont. Edu. Provider #13	916-445-5014	
Pharmacy Technician #13	916-445-5014	

Pharmacy, Non-resident #13	916-445-5014	
Photogrammetrist #10	916-263-2222	
Physical Therapist/Assistant #38	916-263-2550	
Physician Assistant #39	916-263-2323	
Pipeline #28	916-255-3985	
Plastering #28	916-255-3985	
Plumber #28	916-255-3985	
Podiatrist #14	916-263-2382	
Polygraph Examiner #48	800-593-8598	
Polygraph Examiner of Sex Offenders #48	800-593-8598	
Private Investigator #22	800-952-5210	
Psychiatric Mental Health Nurse #16	800-838-6828	
Psychiatric Technician #17	916-263-7800	
Psychological Assistant #15	916-263-2699	
Psychologist #15	916-263-2699	
Public Accountant-CPA #6	916-263-3680	
Public Health Nurse #16	800-838-6828	
Radioactive Material Licensee #31	916-445-0931	
Radiologic Technologist #31	916-445-8820	
Real Estate Broker/Corporation #33	916-227-0931	
Real Estate Sales Agent #33	916-227-0931	
Refrigeration #28	916-255-3985	
Repossessor Agency/Mgr./Employee #22	800-952-5210	
Research Psychoanalyst #36	916-263-2370	
Respiratory Care Practitioner #41	916-323-9983	
Roofing Contractor #28	916-255-3985	
Sanitation System #28	916-255-3985	
Sanitizer of Home Furnishing Products #21	916-574-0280	
Savings & Loan Association #11	800-622-0620	
School Administrator #26	916-445-7254	
School Library Media Specialist #26	916-445-7254	
Securities Broker/Dealer #30	916-445-3062	
Security Guard/Armored Car Guard #22	800-952-5210	
Service Contract Seller (Appliance) #20	916-574-2067	
Sheet Metal #28	916-255-3985	
Smog Check Station #19	916-322-4010	
Smog Check Technician #19	916-322-4010	
Social Worker, Clinical #8	916-445-4933	
Social Worker, Clinical Associate #8	916-445-4933	
Solar Energy #28	916-255-3985	
Sparring Permit #3	916-263-2195	
Specialty Contractor-Class C #28	916-255-3985	
Specialty Sublicenses, Limited #28	916-255-3985	
Speech Pathologist/Audiologist Aide #42	916-263-2666	
Speech-Language Pathologist #42	916-263-2666	
Steel, Reinforcing & Structural #28	916-255-3985	
Supervising Physician #39	916-263-2323	
Surgical Clinic, Nonprofit #13	916-445-5014	
Surveyor, Land #10	916-263-2222	
Surveyor-in-Training #10	916-263-2222	
Swimming Pool #28	916-255-3985	
Tax Education Provider #45	916-492-0457	
Tax Interviewer #45	916-492-0457	
Tax Preparer #45	916-492-0457	
Teacher #26	916-445-7254	
Termite Control #44	916-263-2540	
Thermal Insulation Manufacturer #21	916-574-0280	
Thrift & Loan Company #11	800-622-0620	
Tile Contractor, Ceramic & Mosaic #28	916-255-3985	
Travelers Checks Issuer #11	800-622-0620	
Trust Company #11	800-622-0620	
Upholsterer, Custom #21	800-952-5210	
Veterinarian #40	916-263-2610	
Veterinary Food/Animal Drug Retailer #13	916-445-5014	
Veterinary Hospital #40	916-263-2610	
Vocational Nurse #17	916-263-7800	
Water Well Driller #28	916-255-3985	
X-ray Machine Registration #31	916-445-0931	
X-ray Technician #31	916-323-2775	

Licensing Agency Information

#1 Acupuncture Board, 1424 Howe Ave, #37, Sacramento, CA 95825-3233; 916-263-2680, Fax: 916-263-2654.
www.acupuncture.ca.gov
Search database at www.acupuncture.ca.gov

#2 Arbitration Review Program, 401 S St #201, Sacramento, CA 95814; 916-323-3406, Fax: 916-323-3968.
www.dca.ca.gov/acp/acp_resp.htm

#3 Athletic Commission, 1424 Howe Ave, #33, Sacramento, CA 95825; 916-263-2195, Fax: 916-263-2197.
www.dca.ca.gov/csac/
Search database at
www.dca.ca.gov/csac/directories.htm

#4 Barber & Cosmetology Program, 400 R St, #5100, Sacramento, CA 95814-6200; 916-445-1254, Fax: 916-445-8893.
www.dca.ca.gov/barber

#5 Nursing Home Administrator Program, PO Box 942732 (1800 3rd St #162), Sacramento, CA 95234-7320; 916-323-6838, Fax: 916-323-6845.
www.dca.ca.gov/r_r/nursehol.htm
Agency email: nhap@dhs.ca.gov.

#6 Board of Accountancy, 2000 Evergreen St, #250, Sacramento, CA 95815-3832; 916-263-7777, Fax: 916-263-3675.
www.dca.ca.gov/cba
Agency email: pagemaster@cba.ca.gov.

#7 Architects Board, 400 R St, #4000, Sacramento, CA 95814-6238; 916-445-3393, Fax: 916-445-8524.
www.cab.ca.gov
Agency email: cab@dca.ca.gov.
Search database at
www.cab.ca.gov/Templates/querysearch.cfm

#8 Board of Behavioral Sciences, 400 R St, #3150, Sacramento, CA 95814-6200; 916-445-4933, Fax: 916-323-0707.
www.bbs.ca.gov
Agency email: BBSWebMaster@bbs.ca.gov.
Search database at www.bbs.ca.gov/weblokup.htm

#9 Dental Board, 1432 Howe Ave, #85-B, Sacramento, CA 95825-3241; 916-263-2300, Fax: 916-263-2140.
www.dca.ca.gov

#10 Board of Professional Engineers & Land Surveyors, PO Box 349002, (2535 Capitol Oaks Dr, #300), Sacramento, CA 95834-9002; 916-263-2222, Fax: 916-263-2246.
www.dca.ca.gov/pels. Agency email: bpels-license-verifications@dca.ca.gov.
Search database at
www.dca.ca.gov/pels/l_lookup.htm. Member lists may be downloaded. Engineers include: civil, fire protection, electrical, mechanical, geotechnical, structural, traffic, oil, nuclear, control system, chemical, industrial, manufacturing, metallurgical, petroleum, corrosion, quality, safety.

#11 Department of Financial Institutions, Consumer Affairs, 801 Street #2124, Sacramento, CA 95814; 916-322-5966.
www.sbd.ca.gov
Search database at
www.sbd.ca.gov/directry/directry.asp

#12 Board of Optometry, 400 R St, #4090, Sacramento, CA 95814-6200; 916-323-8720, Fax: 916-445-8711.
www.optometry.ca.gov. Agency email: boardemail@optometry.ca.gov.
Search database at
www.odfinder.org/LicSearch.asp

#13 Board of Pharmacy, 400 R St, #4070, Sacramento, CA 95814-6200; 916-445-5014, Fax: 916-327-6308.
www.pharmacy.ca.gov
Search database at
www.pharmacy.ca.gov/license_lookup.htm

#14 Board of Podiatric Medicine, 1420 Howe Ave, #8, Sacramento, CA 95825-3229; 916-263-2647, Fax: 916-263-2651.
www.dca.ca.gov/bpm
Agency email: bpm@dca.ca.gov.
Search database at
www.docboard.org/ca/df/casearch.htm

#15 Board of Psychology, 1422 Howe Ave, #22, Sacramento, CA 95825-3200; 916-263-2699.
www.psychboard.ca.gov
Agency email: bopmail@dca.ca.gov.
Search database at www.psychboard.ca.gov

#16 Board of Registered Nursing, 400 R St, #4030, Sacramento, CA 95814-6200; 916-322-3350, Fax: 916-327-4402.
www.rn.ca.gov. Agency email: webmaster@rn.ca.gov.
Search database at
www.rn.ca.gov/online/online.htm

#17 Board of Vocational Nursing & Psychiatric Treatment, 2535 Capitol Oaks Dr, #205, Sacramento, CA 95833; 916-263-7800, Fax: 916-263-7859.
www.bvnpt.ca.gov
Agency email: webmaster@bvnpt.ca.gov.
Search database at www.bvnpt.ca.gov/licverif.htm

#18 Board of Registration for Geologists & Geophysicists, 2535 Capitol Oaks Dr, #300A, Sacramento, CA 95833; 916-263-2113, Fax: 916-263-2099.
www.dca.ca.gov/geology
Agency email: geology@dca.ca.gov
Search database at
www.dca.ca.gov/geology/lookup

#19 Bureau of Automotive Repair, PO Box 989001, West Sacramento, CA 95798-9001; 916-322-4000, Fax: 916-322-4274.
www.smogcheck.ca.gov/stdhome.asp
Search database at
www.smogcheck.ca.gov/stdPage.asp?Body=/Consumer/verify_a_license.htm

#20 Department of Consumer Affairs, Bureau of Electronic & Appliance Repair, 400 R St, #3080, Sacramento, CA 95814; 916-574-2067, Fax: 916-574-2043.
www.dca.ca.gov/r_r/electron.htm
Search database at
http://www2.dca.ca.gov/pls/wllpub/wllquery$.startup

#21 Department of Consumer Affairs, Bureau of Home Furnishings & Thermal Insulation, 3485 Orange Grove Ave, North Highlands, CA 95660; 916-574-0280, Fax: 916-574-2449.
www.dca.ca.gov/bhfti/

#22 Bureau of Security & Investigative Services, 400 R St, #3080, Sacramento, CA 95814; 800-952-5210, Fax: 916-445-1694.
www.dca.ca.gov/bsis. Agency email: webmaster@dca.ca.gov.
Search database at
www.dca.ca.gov/bsis/lookup.htm

#23 State Bar of California, California Committee of Bar Examiners, 180 Howard St, San Francisco, CA 94105; 415-538-2577, Fax: 415-538-2361.
www.calbar.org
Search database at
www.calsb.org/MM/SBMBRSHP.HTM. The member records online database does not include judges or deceased former members.

#24 Horse Racing Board, 1010 Hurley Way, #300, Sacramento, CA 95825; 916-263-6000, Fax: 916-263-6042.
www.chrb.ca.gov
Search database at
www.chrb.ca.gov/license_search.htm.

#25 Cemetery and Funeral Bureau, 400 R St, #3040, Sacramento, CA 95814; 916-327-3219.
www.dca.ca.gov/cemetery/
Search database at
www.dca.ca.gov/cemetery/lookup.htm

#26 Commission on Teacher Credentialing, 1900 Capitol Ave (95814-4213), Sacramento, CA 95814-7000; 916-445-7254, Fax: 916-445-7255.
www.ctc.ca.gov
Agency email: credentials@ctc.ca.gov.
Search database at
https://teachercred.ctc.ca.gov/teachers/index.jsp

#27 Committee on Dental Auxiliaries, 1428 Howe Ave, #58, Sacramento, CA 95825; 916-263-2595, Fax: 916-263-2709.
www.comda.ca.gov
Search database at
www.comda.ca.gov/licensestatus.html

#28 Contractors License Board, PO Box 26000, Sacramento, CA 95826; 916-255-3900, Fax: 916-361-7497 or 800-321-2752.
www.cslb.ca.gov. Agency email: Licensing@dca.cslb.ca.gov.
Search database at
http://www2.cslb.ca.gov/CSLB_LIBRARY/Name+Request.asp

#29 Court Reporters Board of California, 2535 Capitol Oaks Dr, #230, Sacramento, CA 95833; 916-263-3660, Fax: 916-263-3664.
www.courtreportersboard.ca.gov
Search database at www.courtreportersboard.ca.gov. To search, click on "License Verification."

#30 Department of Corporations, 1515 K St #200, Sacramento, CA 95814; 916-445-7205.
www.corp.ca.gov. Agency email: Webmaster@corp.ca.gov. Old address: 980 9th St #500. Did not give a time when office will be moved.

#31 Department of Health Services, Radiological Health Branch, 601 N 7th ST, Mail Stop #178, Sacramento, CA 95814; 916-445-6695, Fax: 916-324-3610.

#32 Department of Insurance, License Bureau, 320 Capitol Mall, Sacramento, CA 95814; 916-322-3555, Fax: 916327-6907.

www.insurance.ca.gov. Agency email:
license.bureau@insurance.ca.gov.
Search database at www.insurance.ca.gov
/LIC/Licensestatus.htm

#33 Department of Real Estate, 2201 Broadway,
Sacramento, CA 95826; 916-227-0931, Fax: 916-
227-0925.
www.dre.ca.gov
Search database at www.dre.ca.gov/licstats.htm

#34 Hearing Aid Dispensers Examining
Committee, 1422 Howe Ave #5, Sacramento, CA
95825-3204; 916-327-3433, Fax: 916-445-1696.
www.dca.ca.gov/hearingaid
Agency email: hearingaid@dca.ca.gov.
Search database at www.dca.ca.gov/hearingaid

#35 Landscape Architects Technical Committee,
400 R St, #4000, Sacramento, CA 95814-6200;
916-445-4954, Fax: 916-324-2333.
www.latc.dca.ca.gov
Agency email: latc@dca.ca.gov.
Search database at
www.latc.dca.ca.gov/Licensee/search.htm

#36 Medical Board of California, 1426 Howe Ave,
#54, Sacramento, CA 95825-3236; 916-263-2382,
Fax: 916-263-2567.
www.medbd.ca.gov

#37 Office of the Secretary of State, 1500 11th St,
2nd Fl, Sacramento, CA 95814; 916-653-3595,
Fax: 916-653-9580.
www.ss.ca.gov/business/notary/notary.htm.
Agency email: notaries@ss.ca.gov.

#38 Physical Therapy Examining Committee,
1418 Howe Ave #16, Sacramento, CA 95825-
3204; 916-263-2550, Fax: 916-263-2560.
www.ptb.ca.gov

#39 Department of Consumer Affairs, Physician
Assistant Committee, 1424 Howe Ave, #54,
Sacramento, CA 95825-3237; 916-263-2323, Fax:
916-263-2671.
www.medbd.ca.gov
Agency email: webmaster@dca.ca.gov.
Search database at
www.docboard.org/ca/df/casearch.htm

#40 Veterinary Medical Board, 1420 Howe Ave,
#6, Sacramento, CA 95825-3228; 916-263-2610,
Fax: 916-263-2621.
www.vmb.ca.gov
Agency email: webmaster@vmb.ca.gov.
Search database at
www.vmb.ca.gov/2licensg/lic1list.htm

#41 Respiratory Care Board of California, 444 N
3rd St #270, Sacramento, CA 95814; 916-323-
9983, Fax: 916-323-9999.
www.rcb.ca.gov
Agency email: rcbinfo@dca.ca.gov.
Search database at www.rcb.ca.gov/activercps.htm

#42 Speech Language Pathology & Audiology
Board, 1422 Howe Ave, #3, Sacramento, CA
95825; 916-263-2666, Fax: 916-263-2668.
www.dca.ca.gov/slpab
Agency email: slpab@dca.ca.gov.

#43 Board of Guide Dogs for the Blind, 400 R St
#5100-A, Sacramento, CA 95814; 916-324-9328,
Fax: 916-324-9340.
www.dca.ca.gov/guidedogboard. Agency email:
guidedogboard@dca.ca.gov.

#44 Structural Pest Control Board, 1418 Howe
Ave #18, Sacramento, CA 95825-3280; 916-263-
8700, Fax: 916-263-2469.
www.dca.ca.gov/pestboard/
Search database at
www.dca.ca.gov/pestboard/lookup.htm

#45 Tax Preparer Program, CA Tax Education
Council, PO Box 2890, Sacramento, CA 95812-
2840; 916-492-0457.
www.ctec.org

#46 Contractors State License Board, 9821
Business Park Drive, Sacramento, CA 95826; 800-
321-2752, Fax: 916-366-9130.
www.cslb.ca.gov

#47 Secretary of State, Political Reform Division,
1500 11th Street, Room 495, Sacramento, CA
95814; 916-653-6224, Fax: 916-653-5045.
http://cal-access.ss.ca.gov
Agency email: PoliticalReform@ss.ca.gov.
Search database at http://cal-
access.ss.ca.gov/Lobbying

#48 Association of Polygraph Examiners, 969-G
Edgewater Blvd #330, Foster City, CA 94404-
Agency email: DMoody1@aol.com.

California Federal Courts

The following list indicates the district and division name for each county in the state. If the district or division name of the bankruptcy court is different from the civil/criminal court, it appears in parentheses.

Please note: For counties of Alameda, Contra Costa, Del Norte, Humboldt, Lake, Marin, Mendocino, Napa, San Francisco, San Mateo, and Sonoma in the Northern District of California District Court, cases may be filed at the San Francisco Division or Oakland Division. From there a case may be assigned to either division. Records are available electronically or on public access terminals at either Division, and at the San Jose Division. To find the actual locations of records, first search by name to find case numbers; the first number of the case number indicates the file location: 3~=San Francisco, 4~=Oakland., 5~=San Jose.

County/Court Cross Reference

County	District	Division
Alameda	Northern	Oakland/SF (Oakland)
Alpine	Eastern	Sacramento
Amador	Eastern	Sacramento
Butte	Eastern	Sacramento
Calaveras	Eastern	Sacramento (Modesto)
Colusa	Eastern	Sacramento
Contra Costa	Northern	Oakland/SF (Oakland)
Del Norte	Northern	San Francisco/Oakland (Santa Rosa)
El Dorado	Eastern	Sacramento
Fresno	Eastern	Fresno
Glenn	Eastern	Sacramento
Humboldt	Northern	San Francisco/Oakland (Santa Rosa)
Imperial	Southern	San Diego
Inyo	Eastern	Fresno
Kern	Eastern	Fresno
Kings	Eastern	Fresno
Lake	Northern	San Francisco/Oakland (Santa Rosa)
Lassen	Eastern	Sacramento
Los Angeles	Central	Los Angeles (Western)
Madera	Eastern	Fresno
Marin	Northern	San Francisco/Oakland (Santa Rosa)
Mariposa	Eastern	Fresno
Mendocino	Northern	San Francisco/Oakland (Santa Rosa)
Merced	Eastern	Fresno
Modoc	Eastern	Sacramento
Mono	Eastern	Sacramento
Monterey	Northern	San Jose
Napa	Northern	San Francisco/Oakland (Santa Rosa)
Nevada	Eastern	Sacramento
Orange	Central	Santa Ana (Southern)
Placer	Eastern	Sacramento
Plumas	Eastern	Sacramento
Riverside	Central	Riverside (Eastern)
Sacramento	Eastern	Sacramento
San Benito	Northern	San Jose
San Bernardino	Central	Riverside (Eastern)
San Diego	Southern	San Diego
San Francisco	Northern	San Francisco/Oakland (San Francisco)
San Joaquin	Eastern	Sacramento (Modesto)
San Luis Obispo	Central	Los Angeles (Western)
San Mateo	Northern	San Francisco/Oakland (San Francisco)
Santa Barbara	Central	Los Angeles (Western)
Santa Clara	Northern	San Jose
Santa Cruz	Northern	San Jose
Shasta	Eastern	Sacramento
Sierra	Eastern	Sacramento
Siskiyou	Eastern	Sacramento
Solano	Eastern	Sacramento
Sonoma	Northern	San Francisco/Oakland (Santa Rosa)
Stanislaus	Eastern	Fresno (Modesto)
Sutter	Eastern	Sacramento
Tehama	Eastern	Sacramento
Trinity	Eastern	Sacramento
Tulare	Eastern	Fresno
Tuolumne	Eastern	Fresno (Modesto)
Ventura	Central	Los Angeles (Western)
Yolo	Eastern	Sacramento
Yuba	Eastern	Sacramento

Standards for Federal Courts: The search fee is $20.00 per item (one party name or case number). Certification fee is $7.00 per document. Copy fee is $.50 per page. All fees standard unless noted in profile. Mail Search: always enclose a stamped self addressed envelope unless otherwise noted. Before releasing records, all courts require prepayment unless noted in profile.

Open records are located at the court unless otherwise noted. District courts index by defendant and plaintiff as well as by case number. Bankruptcy courts usually index by debtor and case number. While most courts now have their indexes on computer, many still maintain index card files as well.

The universal PACER sign-up number is 800-676-6856. Find PACER and the Party/Case Index on the Web at http://pacer.psc.uscourts.gov. PACER dial-up access is $.60 per minute. Also, courts offering internet access via RACER, PACER, Web-PACER or the new CM-ECF charge $.07 per page fee unless noted as free.

US District Court

Central District of California

Los Angeles (Western) Division US Courthouse, Attn: Correspondence, 312 N Spring St, Room G-8, Los Angeles, CA 90012 (Courier Address: Use mail address for courier delivery), 213-894-5261.

www.cacd.uscourts.gov

Counties: Los Angeles, San Luis Obispo, Santa Barbara, Ventura.

Indexing & Storage: Cases are indexed by defendant, plaintiff, and case number. New cases are available in the index 3 days after filing date. In general, criminal. Case records from 1989 back and civil cases from 1992 back have been sent to the Federal Records Center.

Fee & Payment Notes: Payment may be made by money order, cashier check, business check. Personal checks are not accepted. Payee: Clerk, US District Court.

Phone Search: Searching not available by phone.

Fax Search: Fax search allowed for the urgent matters of attorneys with approval of Supervisor. An account must be established first. Call 213-894-3649.

In Person Search: In person searching available.

PACER: Access fee is. Case records are available back to 1993. New records are available online after 2 days. PACER is available online at http://pacer.cacd.uscourts.gov. Document images available.

Electronic Filing: (CM/ECF available late 2002)

Opinions Online: Court opinions are available online at www.cacd.uscourts.gov

Riverside (Eastern) Division US District Court, PO Box 13000, Riverside, CA 92502-3000 (Courier Address: 3470 12th St., Riverside, CA 92501), 909-328-4450.

www.cacd.uscourts.gov

Counties: Riverside, San Bernardino.

Indexing & Storage: Cases are indexed by defendant, plaintiff, and case number. New cases are available in the index 3 days after filing date. Open records are located at this court.

Fee & Payment Notes: Payment may be made by money order, cashier check, business check. Personal checks are not accepted. Payee: Clerk, US District Court.

Phone Search: Searching not available by phone.

In Person Search: In person searching available.

PACER: Access fee is. Case records are available back to 1993. New records are available online after 2 days. PACER is available online at http://pacer.cacd.uscourts.gov. Document images available.

Electronic Filing: (CM/ECF available late 2002)

Opinions Online: Court opinions are available online at www.cacd.uscourts.gov

Santa Ana (Southern) Division 411 W 4th St Rm 1053, Santa Ana, CA 92701-4516 (Courier Address: Use mail address for courier delivery), 714-338-4750.

www.cacd.uscourts.gov

Counties: Orange.

Indexing & Storage: Cases are indexed by defendant, plaintiff, and case number. New cases are available in the index 3 days after filing date. Open records are located at this court.

Fee & Payment Notes: Payment may be made by money order, cashier check, business check. Personal checks are not accepted. Prepayment is required unless a deposit account is set up with the court. Payee: Clerk, US District Court.

Phone Search: Only docket information is available by phone.

In Person Search: In person searching available.

PACER: Access fee is. Case records are available back to 1993. New records are available online after 2 days. PACER is available online at http://pacer.cacd.uscourts.gov. Document images available.

Electronic Filing: (CM/ECF available late 2002)

Opinions Online: Court opinions are available online at www.cacd.uscourts.gov

US Bankruptcy Court

Central District of California

Los Angeles Division 255 E Temple St, Roybal Bldg, #945, Los Angeles, CA 90012 (Courier Address: Use mail address for courier delivery), 213-894-3118, Fax: 213-894-1261.

www.cacb.uscourts.gov

Counties: Los Angeles (certain Los Angeles ZIP Codes are shared with San Fernando Valley Division.).

Indexing & Storage: Cases are indexed by debtor as well as by case number. New cases are available in the index immediately after filing date. Records are indexed on microfiche. Open records are located at this court.

Fee & Payment Notes: Payment may be made by money order, cashier check. Business checks are not accepted. Personal checks are not accepted. Payee: Clerk, US Bankruptcy Court.

Phone Search: An automated voice case information service (VCIS) is available. Call VCIS at 213-894-4111.

Fax Search: Handled like mail searches.

In Person Search: In person searching available.

PACER: Toll-free dial-up access: 800-257-3887. Local dial-up access: 213-620-0031. Case records are available back to 1992. Records are purged once a year. New civil records are available online after 1 day. PACER is available online at http://pacerla.cacb.uscourts.gov. Document images available.

Other Online Access: WebPACER Dial-up Networking is available at IP address of 156.131.137.252.

Riverside (East) Division 3420 12th St #125, Riverside, CA 92501-3819 (Courier Address: Use mail address for courier delivery), 909-774-1000.

www.cacb.uscourts.gov

Counties: Riverside, San Bernardino.

Indexing & Storage: Cases are indexed by debtor as well as by case number. New cases are available in the index immediately after filing date. Files are stored in numerical sequence. The time that records are kept at the Riverside court is varied. There is no set time limit before they are sent to the Los Angeles Federal Records Center.

Fee & Payment Notes: Payment may be made by money order, cashier check. Business checks are not accepted, Visa or Mastercard. Personal checks are not accepted. Payee: US Bankruptcy Court.

Phone Search: Only docket information is available by phone. An automated voice case information service (VCIS) is available. Call VCIS at 909-774-1150.

Mail Search: Include the case number, document title, document number (if available), your phone number, and any applicable fees. Always enclose a stamped self addressed envelope.

In Person Search: In person searching available.

PACER: Toll-free dial-up access: 888-819-0233. Local dial-up access: 909-276-2914. Case records are available back to 1992. Records are purged once a year. New civil records are available online after 1 day. PACER is available online at http://pacerrs.cacb.uscourts.gov. Document images available.

Other Online Access: WebPACER Dial-up Networking is available at IP address of 156.131.137.252.

San Fernando Valley Division 21041 Burbank Blvd, Woodland Hills, CA 91367 (Courier Address: Use mail address for courier delivery), 818-587-2900.

www.cacb.uscourts.gov

Counties: Los Angeles (certain Los Angeles ZIP Codes are shared with Los Angeles Division), Ventura.

Indexing & Storage: Cases are indexed by debtor as well as by case number. New cases are available in the index immediately after filing date. Open records are located at this court.

Fee & Payment Notes: Payment may be made by money order, cashier check. Business checks are not accepted. Personal checks are not accepted. Payee: Clerk, US Bankruptcy Court.

Phone Search: An automated voice case information service (VCIS) is available. Call VCIS at 818-587-2936.

Fax Search: Handled like mail searches.

Mail Search: Include SASE.

In Person Search: In person searching available.

PACER: Toll-free dial-up access: 800-838-2479. Local dial-up access: 818-587-2802. Case records are available back to 1992. Records are purged once a year. New civil records are available online after 1 day. PACER is available online at http://pacersv.cacb.uscourts.gov. Document images available.

Other Online Access: WebPACER Dial-up Networking is available at IP address of 156.131.137.252.

Santa Ana Division Ronald Reagan Federal Bldg & US Courthouse, 411 W 4th St #2030, Santa Ana, CA 92701-4593 (Courier Address: Use mail address for courier delivery), 714-836-5300.

www.cacb.uscourts.gov

Counties: Orange.

Indexing & Storage: Cases are indexed by debtor and creditors as well as by case number. New cases are available in the index 24-48 hours after filing date. Open records are located at this court.

Fee & Payment Notes: Payment may be made by money order, cashier check, business check. Personal checks are not accepted. Prepayment is required unless prior arrangements have been made. Payee: US Bankruptcy Court.

Phone Search: Docket information available by phone. An automated voice case information service (VCIS) is available. Call VCIS at 714-338-5401.

In Person Search: In person searching available.

PACER: Toll-free dial-up access: 888-819-0232. Local dial-up access: 714-338-5406. Case records are available back to June 3, 1991. New civil records are available online after 1 day. PACER available at http://pacersa.cacb.uscourts.gov. Document images available.

Other Online Access: WebPACER Dial-up Networking is available at IP address of 156.131.137.252.

Santa Barbara (Northern) Division 1415 State St, Santa Barbara, CA 93101 (Courier Address: Use mail address for courier delivery), 805-884-4800.

www.cacb.uscourts.gov

Counties: San Luis Obispo, Santa Barbara, Ventura. Certain Ventura ZIP Codes are assigned to the new office in San Fernando Valley.

Indexing & Storage: Cases are indexed by debtor as well as by case number. New cases are available in the index immediately after filing date. There is no set time for sending records to the repository.

Fee & Payment Notes: Payment may be made by money order, cashier check. Business checks are not accepted. Personal checks are not accepted. Payee: US Bankruptcy Court.

Phone Search: An automated voice case information service (VCIS) is available. Call VCIS at 805-884-4805.

Mail Search: Include case number, document title, document number (if available), your phone number and applicable fees. Always enclose a stamped self addressed envelope.

In Person Search: In person searching available.

PACER: Toll-free dial-up access: 888-819-0231. Case records are available back to June 1992. New civil records are available online after 1 day. PACER is available online at http://pacernd.cacb.uscourts.gov. Document images available.

Other Online Access: WebPACER Dial-up Networking is available at IP address of 156.131.137.252.

US District Court
Eastern District of California

Fresno Division US Courthouse, Room 5000, 1130 "O" St, Fresno, CA 93721-2201 (Courier Address: Use mail address for courier delivery), 559-498-7483.

www.caed.uscourts.gov

Counties: Fresno, Inyo, Kern, Kings, Madera, Mariposa, Merced, Stanislaus, Tulare, Tuolumne.

Indexing & Storage: Cases are indexed by defendant, plaintiff, and case number. New cases are available in the index 24 hours after filing date. Records are stored by case type and case number. Open records are located at this court.

Fee & Payment Notes: Payment may be made by money order, cashier check, personal check. Payee: Clerk, US District Court.

Phone Search: Only docket information is available by phone.

Mail Search: A stamped self addressed envelope is not required.

In Person Search: In person searching available.

PACER: Toll-free dial-up access: 800-530-7682. Local dial-up access: 916-498-6567. Case records are available back to 1990 (some earlier). Records are purged at varying intervals. New records are available online after 1 day. PACER is available online at http://pacer.caed.uscourts.gov. Document images available.

Opinions Online: Court opinions are available online at www.caed.uscourts.gov

Other Online Access: Search records using RACER at https://racer.caed.uscourts.gov.

Sacramento Division 501 I St, Sacramento, CA 95814 (Courier: Use mail address for courier delivery), 916-930-4000, Fax: 916-930-4015.

www.caed.uscourts.gov

Counties: Alpine, Amador, Butte, Calaveras, Colusa, El Dorado, Glenn, Lassen, Modoc, Mono, Nevada, Placer, Plumas, Sacramento, San Joaquin, Shasta, Sierra, Siskiyou, Solano, Sutter, Tehama, Trinity, Yolo, Yuba.

Indexing & Storage: Cases are indexed by defendant, plaintiff, and case number. New cases are available in the index immediately after filing date. Archived records are stored by case number. A case number can be researched by the plaintiff's or defendant's name. Archived. Case records are indexed on microfiche. Open records are located at this court.

Fee & Payment Notes: Payment may be made by money order, cashier check, business check. Personal checks are not accepted. Payee: Clerk, US District Court. You are allowed to make your own copies. These copies cost $.15 per page. For copy service, call 916-448-8875. A 24-hour drop box is located on the premises.

Phone Search: Only docket information is available by phone.

In Person Search: In person searching available.

PACER: Toll-free dial-up access: 800-530-7682. Local dial-up access: 916-498-6567. Case records are available back to 1990 (some earlier). Records are purged at varying intervals. New records are

available online after 1 day. PACER is available online at http://pacer.caed.uscourts.gov. Document images available.

Opinions Online: Court opinions are available online at www.caed.uscourts.gov

Other Online Access: Search records on the Internet using RACER at https://racer.caed.uscourts.gov.

US Bankruptcy Court
Eastern District of California

Fresno Division Room 2656, 1130 O Street, Fresno, CA 93721 (Courier Address: Use mail address for courier delivery), 559-498-7217.

www.caeb.uscourts.gov

Counties: Fresno, Inyo, Kern, Kings, Madera, Mariposa, Merced, Tulare. Three Kern ZIP Codes, 93243 and 93523-24, are handled by San Fernando Valley in the Central District.

Indexing & Storage: Cases are indexed by debtor as well as by case number. New cases are available in the index immediately after filing date. Open records are located at this court.

Fee & Payment Notes: Payment may be made by money order, cashier check, business check. Personal checks are not accepted. Payee: Clerk, US Bankruptcy Court. You are allowed to make your own copies. These copies cost $.15 per page.

Phone Search: Only docket information is available by phone. An automated voice case information service (VCIS) is available. Call VCIS at 916-551-2989.

In Person Search: In person searching available.

PACER: Access fee is. Case records are available back to August 1990. Records are purged every six months. New civil records are available online after 1 day. PACER is available online at http://pacer.caeb.uscourts.gov/pacerhome.html.

Modesto Division PO Box 5276, Modesto, CA 95352 (Courier Address: Suite C, 1130 12th St, Modesto, CA 95354), 209-521-5160.

www.caeb.uscourts.gov

Counties: Calaveras, San Joaquin, Stanislaus, Tuolumne. The following ZIP Codes in San Joaquin County are handled by the Sacramento Division: 95220, 95227, 95234, 95237, 95240-95242, 95253, 95258, and 95686. Mariposa and Merced counties were transferred to the Fresno Division as of January 1, 1995.

Indexing & Storage: Cases are indexed by debtor as well as by case number. New cases are available in the index 1 day after filing date. Case numbers can be researched by using the debtor's name. Open records are located at this court.

Fee & Payment Notes: Payment may be made by money order, cashier check, personal check. Payee: Clerk, US Bankruptcy Court. You are allowed to make your own copies. These copies cost $.25 per page.

Phone Search: Only docket information is available by phone. An automated voice case information service (VCIS) is available. Call VCIS at 916-551-2989.

Mail Search: A stamped self addressed envelope is not required.

In Person Search: In person searching available.

PACER: Case records are available back to August 1990. Records are purged every six months. New civil records are available online after 1 day. PACER is available online at http://pacer.caeb.uscourts.gov/pacerhome.html.

Sacramento Division US Courthouse, 501 I St, Rm 3-200, Sacramento, CA 95814 (Courier Address: Use mail address for courier delivery), 916-930-4400.

www.caeb.uscourts.gov

Counties: Alpine, Amador, Butte, Colusa, El Dorado, Glenn, Lassen, Modoc, Mono, Nevada, Placer, Plumas, Sacramento, Shasta, Sierra, Siskiyou, Solano, Sutter, Tehama, Trinity, Yolo, Yuba. This court also handles the following ZIP Codes in San Joaquin County:95220, 95227, 95234, 95237, 95240-95242, 95253, 95258 and 95686.

Indexing & Storage: Cases are indexed by debtor as well as by case number. New cases are available in the index immediately after filing date. Open records are located at this court.

Fee & Payment Notes: Payment may be made by money order, cashier check, business check. Personal checks are not accepted. Payee: Clerk, US Bankruptcy Court. You are allowed to make your own copies. These copies cost $.15 per page. You must make an appointment in order to conduct a search yourself.

Phone Search: Only docket information is available by phone. An automated voice case information service (VCIS) is available. Call VCIS at 916-551-2989.

In Person Search: In person searching available.

PACER:. Case records are available back to August 1990. Records are purged every six months. New civil records are available online after 1 day. PACER is available online at http://pacer.caeb.uscourts.gov/pacerhome.html.

US District Court

Northern District of California

Oakland Division 1301 Clay St, Ste 400S, Oakland, CA 94612-5212 (Courier Address: Use mail address for courier delivery), 510-637-3530.

www.cand.uscourts.gov

Counties: Alameda, Contra Costa(Note: Cases may be filed here or at San Francisco Div.; records available electronically at either; the 1st number of the case number indicates the file location: 3=SF, 4=Oak., 5=SJ.

Indexing & Storage: Cases are indexed by defendant, plaintiff, and case number. New cases are available in the index immediately after filing date. Records are stored by case number, however, a case number can be researched by using the plaintiff's or the defendant's name. Records on computer since 1994. Records are also indexed on microfiche. Open records are located at this court.

Fee & Payment Notes: Payment may be made by money order, cashier check, personal check. Payee: Clerk, US District Court. You are allowed to make your own copies. These copies cost - current fee is not known - per page. Use public pay copier for copies.

Phone Search: Only docket information is available by phone.

In Person Search: In person searching available.

PACER: Toll-free dial-up access: 888-877-5883. Local dial-up access: 415-522-2144. Case records are available back to 1984. Records are purged

every six months. New records are available online after 1 day. PACER is available online at http://pacer.cand.uscourts.gov.

Electronic Filing: Information is available online at https://ecf.cand.uscourts.gov. ECF cases data back to 4/2001.

San Francisco Division 450 Golden Gate Ave, 16th Fl, San Francisco, CA 94102 (Courier Address: Use mail address for courier delivery), 415-522-2000.

www.cand.uscourts.gov

Counties: Del Norte, Humboldt, Lake, Marin, Mendocino, Napa, San Francisco, San Mateo, Sonoma(Note: Cases may be filed here or at Oakland Div; records available electronically at either; the 1st number of the case number indicates the file location: 3=SF, 4=Oak. 5=SJ.

Indexing & Storage: Cases are indexed by defendant, plaintiff, and case number. New cases are available in the index immediately after filing date. Records are stored by case number, however, a case number can be researched by using the plaintiff's or the defendant's name. Records on computer since 1994. Records are also indexed on microfiche. Open records are located at this court.

Fee & Payment Notes: Payment may be made by money order, cashier check, personal check. Payee: Clerk, US District Court. You are allowed to make your own copies. These copies cost - current fee is not known - per page. Use public pay copier for copies.

Phone Search: Only docket information is available by phone.

In Person Search: In person searching available.

PACER: Toll-free dial-up access: 888-877-5883. Local dial-up access: 415-522-2144. Case records are available back to 1984. Records are purged every six months. New records are available online after 1 day. PACER is available online at http://pacer.cand.uscourts.gov.

Electronic Filing: Information is available online at https://ecf.cand.uscourts.gov. ECF cases data back to 4/2001.

San Jose Division Room 2112, 280 S 1st St, San Jose, CA 95113 (Courier Address: Use mail address for courier delivery), 408-535-5364.

www.cand.uscourts.gov

Counties: Monterey, San Benito, Santa Clara, Santa Cruz.

Indexing & Storage: Cases are indexed by defendant, plaintiff, and case number. New cases are available in the index immediately after filing date. Records are stored by case number, however, a case number can be researched by using the plaintiff's or the defendant's name. Records are also indexed on microfiche. Open records are located at this court.

Fee & Payment Notes: Payment may be made by money order, cashier check, personal check. Payee: Clerk, US District Court. You are allowed to make your own copies. These copies cost - current fee is not known - per page. Use public pay copier for copies.

Phone Search: Only docket information is available by phone.

In Person Search: In person searching available.

PACER: Toll-free dial-up access: 888-877-5883. Local dial-up access: 415-522-2144. Case records are available back to 1984. Records are purged every six months. New civil records are available online

after 1 day. PACER is available online at http://pacer.cand.uscourts.gov.

Electronic Filing: ECF cases data back to 4/2001. Information is available online at https://ecf.cand.uscourts.gov

US Bankruptcy Court

Northern District of California

Oakland Division PO Box 2070, Oakland, CA 94604 (Courier Address: 1300 Clay St, Rm 300, Oakland, CA 94612), 510-879-3600.

www.canb.uscourts.gov

Counties: Alameda, Contra Costa.

Indexing & Storage: Cases are indexed by debtor as well as by case number. New cases are available in the index 2 days after filing date. Open records are located at this court.

Fee & Payment Notes: Payment may be made by money order, cashier check, business check. Personal checks are not accepted. Payee: Clerk, US Bankruptcy Court. You are allowed to make your own copies. These copies cost $.25 per page.

Phone Search: An automated voice case information service (VCIS) is available. Call VCIS at 800-570-9819 or 415-705-3160.

In Person Search: In person searching available.

PACER: Toll-free dial-up access: 888-773-8548. Local dial-up access: 415-268-4832. Case records are available back to 1993. Records are purged every six months to one year. New civil records are available online after 1 day. PACER is available online at http://pacer.canb.uscourts.gov.

Electronic Filing: (Currently in the process of implementing CM/ECF.)

San Francisco Division PO Box 7341, San Francisco, CA 94120-7341 (Courier Address: 235 Pine St, 19th Fl, San Francisco, CA 94104), 415-268-2300.

www.canb.uscourts.gov

Counties: San Francisco, San Mateo.

Indexing & Storage: Cases are indexed by debtor as well as by case number. New cases are available in the index 3-4 working days after filing date. All searches are conducted by a copy service. To reach them, call 415-781-4910. Records are also indexed on microfiche. Open records are located at this court.

Fee & Payment Notes: Payment may be made by money order, cashier check, business check. Personal checks are not accepted. Payee: Clerk of the Court. You are allowed to make your own copies. These copies cost $.25 per page.

Phone Search: Only information available from dockets of open cases is released over the phone. An automated voice case information service (VCIS) is available. Call VCIS at 800-570-9819 or 415-705-3160.

Mail Search: A stamped self addressed envelope is not required.

In Person Search: In person searching available.

PACER: Toll-free dial-up access: 888-773-8548. Local dial-up access: 415-268-4832. Case records are available back to 1993. Records are purged every six months to one year. New civil records are available online after 1 day. PACER is available online at http://pacer.canb.uscourts.gov.

Electronic Filing: (Currently in the process of implementing CM/ECF.)

San Jose Division Room 3035, 3rd Fl, 280 S 1st St, San Jose, CA 95113-3099 (Courier Address: Use mail address for courier delivery), 408-535-5118.

www.canb.uscourts.gov

Counties: Monterey, San Benito, Santa Clara, Santa Cruz.

Indexing & Storage: Cases are indexed by debtor as well as by case number. New cases are available in the index 1-2 days after filing date. Open records are located at this court.

Fee & Payment Notes: Payment may be made by money order, cashier check, business check. Personal checks are not accepted. Payee: Clerk, US Bankruptcy Court. Copy fee: $1.00 per page. The fee for copies made by court personnel is $.50 per page.

Phone Search: Only basic information, such as date of filing is released over the phone. An automated voice case information service (VCIS) is available. Call VCIS at 800-570-9819, 888-457-0604 or 415-705-3160.

In Person Search: In person searching available.

PACER: Toll-free dial-up access: 888-773-8548. Local dial-up access: 415-268-4832. Case records are available back to 1993. Records are purged every six months to one year. New civil records are available online after 1 day. PACER is available online at http://pacer.canb.uscourts.gov.

Electronic Filing: (Currently in the process of implementing CM/ECF.)

Santa Rosa Division 99 South E St, Santa Rosa, CA 95404 (Courier Address: Use mail address for courier delivery), 369-525-8539, Fax: 369-579-0374.

www.canb.uscourts.gov

Counties: Del Norte, Humboldt, Lake, Marin, Mendocino, Napa, Sonoma.

Indexing & Storage: Cases are indexed by debtor as well as by case number. New cases are available in the index immediately after filing date. Open records are located at this court.

Fee & Payment Notes: Payment may be made by money order, cashier check, business check. Personal checks are not accepted. This court will

not bill. Payee: Clerk - US Bankruptcy Court. You are allowed to make your own copies. These copies cost $.20 per page. This court urges use of their contracted copy service, Attorney's Diversified (707-545-5455).

Phone Search: Names and accession numbers will be released over the phone. An automated voice case information service (VCIS) is available. Call VCIS at 800-570-9819, 888-457-0604 or 415-705-3160.

In Person Search: In person searching available.

PACER: Toll-free dial-up access: 888-773-8548. Local dial-up access: 415-268-4832. Case records are available back to 1993. Records are purged every six months to one year. New civil records are available online after 1 day. PACER is available online at http://pacer.canb.uscourts.gov.

Electronic Filing: (Currently in the process of implementing CM/ECF.)

US District Court

Southern District of California

San Diego Division Room 4290, 880 Front St, San Diego, CA 92101-8900 (Courier Address: Use mail address for courier delivery), 619-557-5600, Fax: 619-557-6684.

www.casd.uscourts.gov

Counties: Imperial, San Diego. Court also handles some cases from Yuma County, AZ.

Indexing & Storage: Cases are indexed by defendant, plaintiff, and case number. New cases are available in the index 24 hours after filing date. Open records are located at this court.

Fee & Payment Notes: Payment may be made by money order, cashier check, personal check. Contract copy service makes copies at $.24 per page. Payee: US District Court.

Phone Search: Searching not available by phone.

Mail Search: A stamped self addressed envelope is not required.

In Person Search: In person searching available.

PACER: Toll-free dial-up access: 888-241-9760. Local dial-up access: 619-557-7138. Case records

are available back to 1990. New records are available online after 1 day. PACER is available online at http://pacer.casd.uscourts.gov. Document images available.

Other Online Access: A computer bulletin board is accessible at 619-557-6779.

US Bankruptcy Court

Southern District of California

San Diego Division Office of the Clerk, US Courthouse, 325 West "F" St., San Diego, CA 92101 (Courier Address: Use mail address for courier delivery), 619-557-5620.

www.casb.uscourts.gov

Counties: Imperial, San Diego.

Indexing & Storage: Cases are indexed by debtor as well as by case number. New cases are available in the index 3 days after filing date. Open records are located at this court.

Fee & Payment Notes: Payment may be made by money order, cashier check, personal check. Payee: Clerk, US Bankruptcy Court.

Phone Search: Only docket information is available by phone. An automated voice case information service (VCIS) is available. Call VCIS at 619-557-6521.

Fax Search: The court has contracted Court Copy Ltd to handle copies and fax requests. To make arrangements for a fax transaction, call Court Copy Ltd at 619-234-4425. They will accept credit cards.

Mail Search: A stamped self addressed envelope is not required.

In Person Search: In person searching available.

PACER: Toll-free dial-up access: 800-870-9972. Local dial-up access: 619-557-6875. Case records are available back to 1989. Records are purged every six months. New civil records are available online after 3 days. PACER is available online at http://pacer.casb.uscourts.gov. Document images available.

Electronic Filing: Information is available online at http://ecf.casb.uscourts.gov

California County Courts

Court	Jurisdiction	No. of Courts	How Organized
Superior Courts*	General	29	
Limited Superior Courts*	Limited	122	
Combined Superior Courts*	Limited & General	58	

* Profiled in this Sourcebook.

Court	CIVIL								
	Tort	Contract	Real Estate	Min. Claim	Max. Claim	Small Claims	Estate	Eviction	Domestic Relations
General Jurisdiction	X	X	X	$25,000	No Max		X		X
Limited Jurisdiction	X	X	X	$0	$25,000	$5000		X	

Court	CRIMINAL				
	Felony	Misdemeanor	DWI/DUI	Preliminary Hearing	Juvenile
General Jurisdiction*	X	X	X		X
Limited Jurisdiction*		X	X	X	

ADMINISTRATION

Administrative Office of Courts, 455 Golden Gate Ave, San Francisco, CA, 94102; 415-865-4200, Fax: 415-865-4205. www.courtinfo.ca.gov

COURT STRUCTURE

In July, 1998, the judges in individual counties were given the opportunity to vote on unification of superior and municipal courts within their respective counties. By late 2000, all counties had voted to unify these courts. Courts that were formally Municipal Courts are now known as Limited Jurisdiction Superior Courts. In some counties, superior and municipal courts were combined into one superior court. Civil under $25,000 is a Limited Civil Court, over $25,000 is an Unlimited Civil Court, and if both are over and under, then the court is a Combined Civil Court.

It is important to note that Limited Courts may try minor felonies not included under our felony definition.

Due to its large number of courts, the Los Angeles County section is arranged uniquely in this book. Each Branch or Division of the Los Angeles Superior Court is given by name, which usually indicates a court's general jurisdictional and geographic boundary (the actual jurisdiction area is noted in the text). The court name is followed by the District it is located in - South Central, West, Northeast, Central, etc. Also, a court name may mention whether its jurisdiction is "Civil" only or "Criminal" only.

ONLINE ACCESS

There is no statewide online computer access available, internal or external. However, a number of counties have developed their own online access sytems and provide Internet access at no fee. Also, www.courtinfo.ca.gov contains very useful information about the state court system.

ADDITIONAL INFORMATION

If there is more than one court of a type within a county, where the case is tried and where the record is held depends on how a citation is written, where the infraction occurred, or where the filer chose to file the case.

Some courts now require signed releases from the subject in order to perform criminal searches and will no longer allow the public to conduct such searches.

Personal checks are acceptable by state law.

Although fees are set by statute, courts interpret them differently. For example, the search fee is supposed to be $5.00 per name per year searched, but many courts charge only $5.00 per name. Generally, certification is $6.00 per document and copies are $.50 per page, in some counties $.75 each, and in Los Angeles County, $.57 each.

Alameda County

Superior Court - Criminal 1225 Fallon St Rm 107, Oakland, CA 94612; 510-272-6777; Fax: 510-835-4850. Hours: 8:30AM-4:30PM (PST). *Felony.*
www.co.alameda.ca.us/courts/index.shtml

Note: Located at the Rene C Davidson Alameda County Courthouse.
Criminal Records: Access: Mail, in person. Both court and visitors may perform in person searches. Search fee: $5.00 per name per year. There is no fee if you do the search. Required to search: name, years to search; also helpful: DOB, SSN. Criminal records on computer from 1975, on microfiche from 1940, archived and indexed from 1880.
General Information: No probation, medical, adoption, juvenile or sealed records released. SASE required. Turnaround time 1 week. Copy fee: $.75 per page. Certification fee: $6.00. Fee payee: Clerk of Superior Court. Personal checks accepted. Prepayment is required.

Superior Court North Branch - Civil 1225 Fallon St Rm 109, Oakland, CA 94612; 510-272-6799. Hours: 8:30AM-4:30PM (PST). *Civil Actions Over $25,000, Probate.*
www.co.alameda.ca.us/courts/index.shtml

Note: Located at the Rene C Davidson Alameda County Courthouse.
Civil Records: Access: Mail, in person, online. Both court and visitors may perform in person searches. Search fee: $5.00 per name per year. Additional $5.00 fee for years prior to 1974. Required to search: name, years to search. Civil cases indexed by defendant, plaintiff. Civil records on computer from 1974, on microfiche and archived from 1900s. Online access to calendars, limited civil case summaries and complex litigations are available free from Register of Actions/Domain Web at the web site. Search limited cases by number; litigations by case name or number.
General Information: No sealed records nor adoption records released unless court ordered. SASE required. Turnaround time 2 weeks. Copy fee: $.75 per page. Certification fee: $6.00. Fee payee: Superior Court. Personal checks accepted. Prepayment is required.

Superior Court Pleasanton Branch - Civil 5672 Stoneridge Dr 1st Fl, Pleasanton, CA 94588; 925-803-7123. Hours: 8:30AM-5:00PM (PST). *Civil Actions, Probate.*
www.co.alameda.ca.us/courts/index.shtml

Note: Located at the Schenone Hall of Justice.
Civil Records: Access: Mail, in person, online. Both court and visitors may perform in person searches. Search fee: $5.00 per name per year. Required to search: name, years to search. Civil cases indexed by defendant, plaintiff. Civil records on computer from 1976, on microfiche and archived from 1900s. Online access to calendars and civil case summaries and complex litigations are available free from Register of Actions/Domain Web at the web site. Search limited cases by number; litigations by case name or number.
General Information: Public access terminal is available. No sealed or confidential records released. SASE required. Turnaround time 2 weeks. Copy fee: $.75 per page. Certification fee: $6.00. Fee payee: Alameda County Superior Court. Personal checks accepted. Prepayment is required.

Superior Court South Branch/Hayward - Civil 24405 Amador St Rm 108, Hayward, CA 94544; 510-670-5060; Fax: 510-783-9456. Hours: 8:30AM-5PM (PST). *Civil Actions Over $25,000, Probate.*
www.co.alameda.ca.us/courts/index.shtml

Note: Located at the Hayward Hall of Justice.

Civil Records: Access: Mail, in person, online. Visitors must perform in person searches Search fee: $5.00 per name. Required to search: name, years to search. Civil cases indexed by defendant, plaintiff. Civil records on computer from 1976, on microfiche and archived from 1900s. Online access to calendars, limited civil case summaries and complex litigations are available free from Register of Actions/Domain Web at the web site. Search limited cases by number; litigations by case name or number.
General Information: Public access terminal is available. No sealed files, paternity or adoption records released. SASE required. Turnaround time 4-6 weeks. Copy fee: $.75 per page. Certification fee: $6.00. Fee payee: Clerk of Superior Court. Personal checks accepted. Prepayment is required.

Alameda Branch Superior Court 2233 Shoreline Dr, Alameda, CA 94501; 510-268-4209; Civil phone: 510-268-7484; Criminal phone: 510-268-4293; Fax: 510-268-4219. Hours: 8:30AM-5:00PM (PST). *Misdemeanor, Civil Actions Under $25,000, Eviction, Small Claims.*
www.co.alameda.ca.us/courts/index.shtml

Note: Co-extensive with the city limits of Alameda only. Located at the George E McDonald Hall of Justice.
Civil Records: Access: Mail, in person, online. Both court and visitors may perform in person searches. Search fee: $5.00 per name. Required to search: name, years to search. Civil cases indexed by defendant, plaintiff. Civil records on computer since 1987. Online access to calendars, limited civil case summaries and complex litigations are available free from Register of Actions/Domain Web at the web site. Search limited cases by number; litigations by case name or number.
Criminal Records: Access: Mail, in person. Both court and visitors may perform in person searches. Search fee: $5.00 per name. Required to search: name, years to search, DOB, signed release; also helpful: SSN. Criminal records on computer 7 years back. Only seven year search available.
General Information: No confidential records released. SASE required. Turnaround time 1 week. Copy fee: $.75 per page. Certification fee: $6.00. Fee payee: Alameda Superior Court. Personal checks accepted. Credit cards accepted. Accepted in person only. Prepayment is required.

Berkeley/Albany Superior Court - Civil 2000 Center St, Room 202, Berkeley, CA 94704; 510-644-6423. Hours: 8:30AM-4:30PM (PST). *Civil Actions Under $25,000, Eviction, Small Claims.*
www.co.alameda.ca.us/courts/index.shtml

Note: Co-extensive with the city limits of Berkeley and Albany.
Civil Records: Access: Mail, in person, online. Both court and visitors may perform in person searches. Search fee: $5.00 per name. Required to search: name, years to search. Civil cases indexed by defendant, plaintiff. Civil records on computer from 1986. Online access to calendars, limited civil case summaries and complex litigations are available free from Register of Actions/Domain Web at the web site. Search limited cases by number; litigations by case name or number.
General Information: Public access terminal is available. No sealed, judge's notes or confidential records released. SASE required. Turnaround time 1 week. Copy fee: $.75 per page. Certification fee: $6.00. Fee payee: Berkeley Superior Court. Personal checks accepted. Prepayment is required.

Berkeley/Albany Superior Court - Criminal 2120 Martin Luther King Jr Way, Berkeley, CA 94704; 510-644-6917; Fax: 510-848-6916. Hours: 8:30AM-4:30PM (PST). *Misdemeanor.*
www.co.alameda.ca.us/courts/index.shtml

Note: Co-extensive with the city limits of Berkeley and Albany. Located at the Berkeley Courthouse.
Criminal Records: Access: Mail, in person. Only the court performs in person searches; visitors may not. Search fee: $5.00 per name. Required to search: name, signed release, years to search (within 3-7 years), DOB; also helpful: SSN. Criminal records on computer from 1984.
General Information: No sealed or confidential records released. SASE required. Turnaround time 1 week. Copy fee: $.75 per page. Certification fee: $6.00 per document. Fee payee: Superior Court. Personal checks accepted. Prepayment is required.

Fremont Superior Court 39439 Paseo Padre Pky, Fremont, CA 94538; Civil phone: 510-795-2360; Criminal phone: 510-795-2300; Fax: 510-795-2349. Hours: 8:30AM-5PM (PST). *Misdemeanor, Civil Actions Under $25,000, Eviction, Small Claims.*
www.co.alameda.ca.us/courts/index.shtml

Note: Jurisdiction includes Fremont, Newark and Union City. Located at the Fremont Hall of Justice.
Civil Records: Access: Fax, mail, in person, online. Both court and visitors may perform in person searches. Search fee: $5.00 per name. Required to search: name, years to search. Civil cases indexed by defendant, plaintiff. Civil records on computer from 1990. Online access to calendars, limited civil case summaries and complex litigations are available free from Register of Actions/Domain Web at the web site. Search limited cases by number; litigations by case name or number.
Criminal Records: Access: Fax, mail, in person. Both court and visitors may perform in person searches. Search fee: $5.00 per name. Required to search: name, years to search, DOB, signed release. Criminal records on computer only go back 7 years.
General Information: Public access terminal is available. (Public access terminal for civil only.) No sealed or confidential records released. SASE required. Turnaround time 1 week. Fax notes: Will fax civil results only, $1.00 per page. Copy fee: $.75 per page. Certification fee: $6.75. Fee payee: Fremont Superior Court. Personal checks accepted. Prepayment required.

Hayward Superior Court 24405 Amador St, Hayward, CA 94544; Civil phone: 510-670-6432; Criminal phone: 510-670-6434; Fax: 510-670-5522. Hours: 8:30AM-4:30PM (PST). *Misdemeanor, Civil Actions Under $25,000, Eviction, Small Claims.*
www.co.alameda.ca.us/courts/index.shtml

Note: Formerly San Leandro/Hayward Superior Ct. Includes the cities of San Leandro, Hayward and adjoining unincorporated areas of Castro Valley and San Lorenzo. Located at the Hayward Hall of Justice.
Civil Records: Access: Fax, mail, in person, online. Both court and visitors may perform in person searches. Search fee: $5.00 per name. Required to search: name, years to search. Civil cases indexed by defendant, plaintiff. Civil records on computer back 20 years; also on paper index. Online access to calendars, limited civil case summaries and complex litigations are available free from Register of Actions/Domain Web at the web site. Search limited cases by number; litigations by case name or number.
Criminal Records: Access: Fax, mail, in person. Both court and visitors may perform in person searches. Search fee: $5.00 per name. Fee is per case. Required to search: name, years to search, DOB, signed release; also helpful: SSN. Criminal records on computer back 20 years; also on paper index.
General Information: Public access terminal is available. No sealed or confidential records released. SASE required. Turnaround time 2 weeks. Fax notes: No fee to fax results. Copy fee: $.75 per page. Certification fee: $6.00. Fee payee: Clerk of the Court. Personal checks accepted. Credit cards accepted: Visa,

MasterCard. ATM card accepted. Prepayment is required.

Livermore/Pleasanton/Dublin Superior Court
5672 Stoneridge Dr, Hall of Justice, Pleasanton, CA 94588; 925-803-7123; Civil phone: 925-803-7207; Criminal phone: 925-803-7995; Fax: 925-803-7979 (civ) 803-7989 (crim). Hours: 8:30AM-5PM (PST). *Misdemeanor, Civil Actions Under $25,000, Eviction, Small Claims.*

www.co.alameda.ca.us/courts/index.shtml

Note: Includes the cities of Livermore, Dublin, Sunol and Pleasanton and all areas east to San Joaquin County line, north of Highway 580 to Contra Costa line. Located at the Gale/Schenone Hall of Justice.
Civil Records: Access: Mail, in person, online. Both court and visitors may perform in person searches. Search fee: $5.00 per name. Required to search: name, years to search. Civil cases indexed by defendant, plaintiff. Civil records on computer from 1990. Online access to calendars, limited civil case summaries and complex litigations are available free from Register of Actions/Domain Web at the web site. Search limited cases by number; litigations by case name or number.
Criminal Records: Access: Mail, in person. Both court and visitors may perform in person searches. Search fee: $5.00 per name. Required to search: name, years to search; also helpful: address, DOB. Criminal records on computer from 1990.
General Information: No records older than 10 years are released. SASE required. Turnaround time 1 week. Copy fee: $.75 per page. Certification fee: $6.00. Fee payee: Alameda County Superior Court. Personal checks accepted. Credit cards accepted: Visa, MasterCard. Prepayment is required.

Oakland/Piedmont/Emeryville Superior Court - Civil
600 Washington St, 4th Floor, Oakland, CA 94607; 510-268-7724; Fax: 510-268-7807. Hours: 8:30AM-4:30PM (PST). *Civil Actions Under $25,000, Eviction, Small Claims.*

www.co.alameda.ca.us/courts/index.shtml

Note: Comprises the cities of Oakland, Piedmont and Emeryville. Located at the Allen E Broussard Justice Center.
Civil Records: Access: Mail, in person, online. Both court and visitors may perform in person searches. Search fee: $5.00 per name. Required to search: name, years to search. Civil cases indexed by defendant, plaintiff. Civil records on computer from 1990. Online access to calendars, limited civil case summaries and complex litigations are available free from Register of Actions/Domain Web at the web site. Search limited cases by number; litigations by case name or number.
General Information: No sealed or confidential records released. SASE required. Turnaround time 1 week. Copy fee: $.75 per page. Certification fee: $6.00. Fee payee: Oakland Superior Court. Personal checks accepted. Prepayment is required.

Oakland/Piedmont/Emeryville Superior Court - Criminal
661 Washington St, 2nd Floor, Oakland, CA 94607; 510-268-7700; Fax: 510-268-7705. Hours: 8:30AM-5PM (PST). *Misdemeano, Felonies.*

www.co.alameda.ca.us/courts/index.shtml

Note: Comprises the cities of Oakland, Piedmont and Emeryville, Albany and Berkeley. Located at the Wiley W Manuel Courthouse.
Criminal Records: Access: Mail, in person. Both court and visitors may perform in person searches. Search fee: $5.00 per name. Required to search: name, years to search. Criminal records on computer from 1990.
General Information: No sealed or confidential records released. SASE required. Turnaround time 1 week. Copy fee: $.75 per page. Certification fee: $6.00.

Fee payee: Oakland Superior Court. Personal checks accepted. Prepayment is required.

Alpine County

Superior Court PO Box 518, Markleeville, CA 96120; 530-694-2113; Fax: 530-694-2119. Hours: 8AM-Noon, 1-5PM (PST). *Felony, Misdemeanor, Civil, Eviction, Small Claims, Probate.*

www.alpine.courts.ca.gov

Civil Records: Access: Mail, in person. Both court and visitors may perform in person searches. Search fee: $5.00 per name per year. Required to search: name, years to search. Civil cases indexed by defendant, plaintiff. Civil records on index file from 1981, archived from 1800s. Computer records go back 10 years.
Criminal Records: Access: Mail, in person. Both court and visitors may perform in person searches. Search fee: $5.00 per name per year. Required to search: name, years to search; also helpful-SSN. Criminal records on index file from 1981, archived from 1800s. Computer records go back 10 years.
General Information: No juvenile, paternity, adoption or sealed released. SASE required. Turnaround time 1 week. Fax notes: Fee to fax results is $1.00 per page. Copy fee: $.50 per page. Certification fee: $6.00 per page. Fee payee: Alpine County Superior Court. Personal checks accepted. Prepayment is required.

Amador County

Superior Court 108 Court St, Jackson, CA 95642; 209-223-6463. Hours: 8AM-4PM (PST). *Felony, Misdemeanor, Civil, Eviction, Small Claims, Probate.*
Civil Records: Access: Mail, in person. Both court and visitors may perform in person searches. Search fee: $5.00 per name. Required to search: name, years to search. Civil cases indexed by defendant, plaintiff. Civil records on computer from 1989, archived and indexed from 1800s.
Criminal Records: Access: Phone, fax, mail, in person. Only the court performs in person searches; visitors may not. Search fee: $5.00 per name. $5.00 for search by case number. Required to search: name, years to search. Criminal records on computer from 1989, archived and indexed from 1800s. Phone & fax access limited to short searches.
General Information: No adoption, juvenile or paternity records released. SASE required. Turnaround time 7-14 days. Fax notes: Will fax results to 800 numbers only. Copy fee: $1.00 for first page, $.20 each add'l. Certification fee: $6.00. Fee payee: Superior Court Clerk. Personal checks accepted. Prepayment is required.

Butte County

Superior Court One Court St, Oroville, CA 95965; 530-538-7551; Fax: 530-538-2112. Hours: 8:30AM-4PM (PST). *Felony, Misdemeanor, Civil, Probate.*

www.courtinfo.ca.gov/courts/trial/butte

Note: This courthouse physically holds most court files for the county; however, one can search the countywide computer index at any court. Closed Probate cases are archived in the court's basement; Active case records are at Chico court, 530-891-2988.
Civil Records: Access: Fax, mail, in person. Both court and visitors may perform in person searches. Search fee: $5.00 per name. Required to search: name, years to search; also helpful: address. Civil cases indexed by defendant, plaintiff. Civil records on computer from 1988, on microfiche from 1983 thru 1988.
Criminal Records: Access: Mail, in person. Both court and visitors may perform in person searches. Search fee: $5.00 per name. Required to search: name, years to search; also helpful: DOB. Criminal records on computer from 1988, on microfiche from 1983 thru 1988.

General Information: Public access terminal is available. No juvenile, paternity or adoption records released. SASE required. Turnaround time 1 week. Fax notes: $5.00 for first page, $1.00 each add'l. Copy fee: $.50 per page. $1.00 minimum. Certification fee: $6.00 per document. Fee payee: Butte County Superior Court. Personal checks accepted. Credit cards accepted: Visa, MasterCard. Prepayment is required.

Chico Branch - Superior Court
655 Oleander Ave, Chico, CA 95926; 530-891-2716 (Traffic); Civil phone: 530-891-2702; Criminal phone: 530-891-2703. Hours: 8:30AM-4PM (PST). *Misdemeanor, Civil Actions Under $25,000, Eviction, Small Claims, Probate.*

Note: Active county Probate case records are located here; closed cases are archived in the basement at the main Superior Court in Oroville.
Civil Records: Access: Mail, in person. Only the court performs in person searches; visitors may not. Search fee: $5.00 per name. Required to search: name, years to search. Civil cases indexed by defendant, plaintiff. Civil records in index files. Records destroyed after 10 years.
Criminal Records: Access: Mail, in person. Only the court performs in person searches; visitors may not. Search fee: $5.00 per name. Required to search: name, years to search; also helpful: DOB. Criminal records in index files. Records destroyed after 10 years.
General Information: No sealed records released. SASE required. Turnaround time 2-3 days. Copy fee: $1.00 for first page, $.50 each add'l. Certification fee: $6.00. Fee payee: Superior Court. Personal checks accepted. Prepayment is required.

Gridley Branch - Superior Court
c/o One Court St, Oroville, CA 95965; 530-846-5701 or 538-7551. Hours: 8AM-1PM 2 days a month (PST). *Misdemeanor, Eviction, Small Claims.*

Note: Open the first "full week" Thursday and 3rd Thursday. The court's physical address is 239 Sycamore, Gridley, CA.
Criminal Records: Access: In person, mail. Only the court performs in person searches; visitors may not. Search fee: $5.00 per name. Required to search: name, years to search.
General Information: Turnaround time 2 days. Fee payee: Butte County Superior Court. Prepayment is required.

Paradise Branch - Superior Court
747 Elliott Rd, Paradise, CA 95969; 530-872-6347. Hours: 8AM-1PM M-W & F; 8AM-Noon, 1-5PM Th; Phone Hours: 9AM-Noon M-F (PST). *Misdemeanor, Eviction, Small Claims.*

Civil Records: Access: Mail, in person. Only the court performs in person searches; visitors may not. Search fee: $5.00 per name. Required to search: name; also helpful: years to search. Civil cases indexed by defendant, plaintiff. Civil records are located in North Butte County Superior Court. Records go back to 1980; on computer back to 1997.
Criminal Records: Access: Mail, in person. Only the court performs in person searches; visitors may not. Search fee: $5.00 per name. Required to search: name, years to search. Criminal records are located in North Butte County Superior Court. Records go back to 1980; on computer back to 1997.
General Information: No sealed records released. SASE required. Turnaround time 2-3 days. Copy fee: $1.00 for first page, $.50 each add'l. Certification fee: $6.00. Fee payee: Superior Court. Personal checks accepted. Prepayment is required.

Calaveras County

Superior Court 891 Mt Ranch Rd, San Andreas, CA 95249; 209-754-6310/6311/6338; Fax: 209-754-6689. Hours: 8AM-4PM (PST). *Misdemeanor, Civil, Small Claims, Probate.*

www.co.calaveras.ca.us/departments/courts.html

Civil Records: Access: Phone, mail, in person. Both court and visitors may perform in person searches. Search fee: $5.00 per name. Fee is for each 15 year period. Required to search: name, years to search. Civil cases indexed by defendant, plaintiff. Civil records on computer since 6/96; in index books and microfiche from 1975.

Criminal Records: Access: Mail, in person. Both court and visitors may perform in person searches. Search fee: $5.00 per name. Fee is for each 15 year period. Required to search: name, years to search, DOB; also helpful: aliases. Criminal records on computer since 6/96; in index books and microfiche from 1975.

General Information: No juvenile or confidential records released. SASE required. Turnaround time 2-3 weeks. Copy fee: $.50 per page. Certification fee: $6.00. Fee payee: Calaveras Superior Court. Personal checks accepted. Prepayment is required.

Colusa County

Superior Court 532 Oak St - Dept. 1, Colusa, CA 95932; 530-458-0507; Fax: 530-458-2230. Hours: 8:30AM-5PM (PST). *Felony, Civil Actions Over $25,000, Probate.*

Note: Since 1995, the records have been combined for both courts in this county; prior records must be searched at the individual courts. Dept. 1's courtroom is at 547 Market St.

Civil Records: Access: Mail, in person. Both court and visitors may perform in person searches. Search fee: $5.00 per name. Required to search: name, years to search. Civil cases indexed by defendant, plaintiff. Civil records on computer from 1986, in index files from 1800s.

Criminal Records: Access: Mail, in person. Both court and visitors may perform in person searches. Search fee: $5.00 per name. Required to search: name, years to search. Criminal records on computer from 1986, in index files from 1800s.

General Information: Public access terminal is available. No juvenile, paternity (except Judgment) or adoption records released. SASE required. Turnaround time 2 days. Copy fee: $.50 per page. Certification fee: $6.00. Fee payee: Colusa County Superior Court. Personal checks accepted. Prepayment is required.

Colusa Superior Court 532 Oak St - Dept. 2, Colusa, CA 95932; 530-458-5149; Fax: 530-458-2230. Hours: 8:30AM-5PM (PST). *Misdemeanor, Civil Actions Under $25,000, Eviction, Small Claims.*

Note: Since 1995, records from both courts in this county have been combined; prior records must be searched at the individual courts.

Civil Records: Access: Mail, in person. Both court and visitors may perform in person searches. Search fee: $5.00 per name per year. Required to search: name, years to search. Civil cases indexed by defendant, plaintiff. Civil records on computer from 1994, index books prior.

Criminal Records: Access: Mail, in person. Both court and visitors may perform in person searches. Search fee: $5.00 per name per year. Required to search: name, years to search, DOB. Criminal records on computer from 1994, index books prior.

General Information: Public access terminal is available. No sealed records released. SASE required. Turnaround time 1-2 days. Copy fee: $.50 per page. Certification fee: $6.00. Fee payee: Colusa Superior

Court. Personal checks accepted. Prepayment is required.

Contra Costa County

Superior Court 725 Court St Rm 103, Martinez, CA 94553; 925-646-2950; Civil phone: 925-646-2951; Criminal phone: 925-646-2440. Hours: 8AM-4PM (PST). *Felony, Civil Actions Over $25,000, Probate.*

www.co.contra-costa.ca.us

Civil Records: Access: Mail, online, in person. Both court and visitors may perform in person searches. Search fee: $5.00 per name. Required to search: name, years to search. Civil cases indexed by defendant, plaintiff. Civil records on computer from 1987, on microfiche from 1900s. There is a free remote dial-up system for civil, probate and county law records. Call 925-646-2479 for details.

Criminal Records: Access: Mail, in person. Both court and visitors may perform in person searches. Search fee: $5.00 per name. Required to search: name, years to search; also helpful: DOB. Criminal records on computer from 1987, on microfiche from 1900s.

General Information: No adoption, juvenile or sealed records released. SASE required. Turnaround time 1 week. Copy fee: $1.00 per page. Certification fee: $6.00. Fee payee: Clerk of the Superior Court. Business checks accepted. Prepayment is required.

Walnut Creek Branch - Superior Court 640 Ygnacio Valley Rd (PO Box 5128), Walnut Creek, CA 94596-1128; 925-646-6769; Civil phone: 925-646-6060; Criminal phone: 925-646-6572. Hours: 8AM-4PM M, T, W, F; 8AM-5PM Th (PST). *Felony, Misdemeanor, Civil Actions Under $25,000, Eviction, Small Claims.*

www.co.contra-costa.ca.us

Note: Includes Alamo, Canyon, Danville, Lafayette, Moraga, Orinda, Rheem, San Ramon, St Mary's College, Walnut Creek and Ygnacio Valley. Effective 01/01/99, this court has all civil records formally at the municipal court in Concord.

Civil Records: Access: Phone, mail, online, in person. Both court and visitors may perform in person searches. Search fee: $5.00 per name. Add $5.00 archive retrieval fee for older cases. In person searching of microfiche is free. Required to search: name; also helpful: years to search. Civil cases indexed by defendant, plaintiff. Civil records on computer from 1991. Records are destroyed after 10 years. There is a subscription online dial-up system for civil, probate and family law records. Call 925-646-2479 for sign-up.

Criminal Records: Access: Mail, in person. Both court and visitors may perform in person searches. Search fee: $5.00 per name. Add $5.00 archive retrieval fee for older cases. Required to search: name, years to search, DOB.

General Information: No probation reports or sealed case records released. SASE required. Turnaround time 2 days. Fax notes: Will not fax results. Copy fee: $1.00 per page. Certification fee: $6.00. Fee payee: Walnut Creek Superior Court. Personal checks accepted. Prepayment is required.

Pittsburg Branch - Superior Court 45 Civic Ave, Pittsburg, CA 94565-0431; Civil phone: 925-427-8159; Criminal phone: 925-427-8173. Hours: 8AM-4PM; 8AM-5PM Tues. (PST). *Felony, Misdemeanor, Civil Actions $25,000 and under, Eviction, Small Claims.*

www.co.contra-costa.ca.us

Note: Includes Antioch, Bay Pt., Bradford Island, Brentwood, Byron, Discovery Bay, Knightsen, Oakley, Pittsburg.

Civil Records: Access: Mail, online, in person. Both court and visitors may perform in person searches. Search fee: $5.00 per name. Required to search: name,

years to search. Civil cases indexed by defendant, plaintiff. Civil records on computer from 1991. Records are destroyed after 10 years. There is a free remote dial-up system for civil, probate and family law records. Call 925-646-2479 for sign-up.

Criminal Records: Access: Mail, in person. Both court and visitors may perform in person searches. Search fee: $5.00 per name. Required to search: name, years to search, DOB. Criminal records on computer from 1991, index files for 10 years. Records are destroyed after 10 years. Visitor may search microfiche only.

General Information: No probation reports released. SASE required. Turnaround time 2 days. Copy fee: $1.00 per page. Certification fee: $6.00. Fee payee: Superior Court. Personal checks accepted. Prepayment is required.

Richmond Superior Court 100 37th St Rm 185, Richmond, CA 94805; Civil phone: 510-374-3137; Criminal phone: 510-374-3158. Hours: 8AM-4PM (PST). *Misdemeanor, Civil Actions Under $25,000, Eviction, Small Claims.*

www.co.contra-costa.ca.us

Note: Includes Crockett, El Cerrito, El Sobrante, Hercules, Kensington, North Richmond, Pinole, Point Richmond, Port Costa, Richmond, Rodeo, Rollingwood and San Pablo.

Civil Records: Access: Mail, in person. Both court and visitors may perform in person searches. Search fee: $5.00 per name. Required to search: name. Civil cases indexed by defendant, plaintiff. Civil records on computer from 1991. Records are destroyed after 10 years. There is a free remote dial-up service for civil, probate and family law records. Call 925-646-2479 for sign-up and fee information.

Criminal Records: Access: Mail, in person. Only the court performs in person searches; visitors may not. Search fee: $5.00 per name. There is an additional fee for retrieval of archive files. Required to search: name, years to search; also helpful: address, DOB, SSN. Criminal records on computer from 1991, index files from 1983. Records are destroyed after 10 years.

General Information: No probation reports released. SASE required. Turnaround time 5 days. Copy fee: $1.00 per page. Certification fee: $6.00. Fee payee: Richmond Superior Court. Personal checks accepted. Prepayment is required.

Del Norte County

Superior Court 450 "H" St, Rm 209, Crescent City, CA 95531; 707-464-8115; Fax: 707-465-4005. Hours: 8AM-5PM (PST). *Felony, Misdemeanor, Civil, Eviction, Small Claims, Probate.*

Civil Records: Access: Phone, fax, mail, in person. Both court and visitors may perform in person searches. Search fee: $5.00 per name per year. Required to search: name, years to search. Civil cases indexed by defendant, plaintiff. Civil records archived and in index files.

Criminal Records: Access: Mail, fax, in person. Both court and visitors may perform in person searches. Search fee: $5.00 per name per year. Required to search: name, years to search, DOB, middle name; also helpful-SSN. Criminal records archived and in index files.

General Information: No adoption, juvenile, probate, LPS conservatorship released. SASE required. Turnaround time 1-2 days. Copy fee: $.50 per page. Certification fee: $6.00. Plus $.50 per page. Fee payee: Superior Court. Personal checks accepted. Prepayment is required.

El Dorado County

Placerville Branch - Superior Court 495 Main St, Placerville, CA 95667; 530-621-6426; Fax: 530-622-9774. Hours: 8AM-4PM (PST). *Felony, Civil, Probate.*

http://co.el-dorado.ca.us/superiorcourts

Civil Records: Access: Mail, in person. Both court and visitors may perform in person searches. Search fee: $5.00 per name. Required to search: name, years to search. Civil cases indexed by defendant, plaintiff. Civil records on computer from 1989, in hardbound books from 1979 to 1989, prior archived in Placerville. Judge's weekly tentative rulings may be available free online at the web site.

Criminal Records: Access: Mail, fax, in person. Both court and visitors may perform in person searches. Search fee: $5.00 per name. Required to search: name, years to search. Criminal records on computer from 1989, in hardbound books from 1979 to 1989, prior archived in Placerville. Judge's weekly tentative rulings may be available free online at the web site.

General Information: No adoption, juvenile, mental or confidential released. SASE required. Turnaround time 2 weeks. Copy fee: $.50 per page. Certification fee: $6.00. Fee payee: Clerk of Court. Personal checks accepted. Prepayment is required.

South Lake Tahoe Branch - Superior Court - Civil 1354 Johnson Blvd #2, South Lake Tahoe, CA 96150; 530-573-3075/3069; Fax: 530-544-6532. Hours: 8AM-4PM (PST). *Civil, Eviction, Probate.*

http://co.el-dorado.ca.us/superiorcourts

Civil Records: Access: Phone, mail, in person. Both court and visitors may perform in person searches. Search fee: $5.00 per name. Required to search: name, years to search. Civil cases indexed by defendant, plaintiff. Civil records on computer from 1989, in hardbound books from 1979 to 1989, prior archived in Placerville. Judge's weekly tentative rulings may be available free online at the web site.

General Information: No adoption, juvenile, mental or confidential released. SASE required. Turnaround time 2 weeks. Copy fee: $.50 per page. Certification fee: $6.00. Fee payee: Superior Court. Personal checks accepted. Prepayment is required.

South Lake Tahoe Branch - Superior Court - Criminal 1354 Johnson Blvd #1, South Lake Tahoe, CA 96150; 530-573-3047; Fax: 530-542-9102. Hours: 8AM-4PM (PST). *Felony, Misdemeanor.*

www.co.el-dorado.ca.us/superiorcourts

Criminal Records: Access: Mail, in person. Both court and visitors may perform in person searches. Search fee: $5.00 per name. Required to search: name, years to search; also helpful: DOB, SSN. Criminal records on computer from 1991, index files from 1983. Records are destroyed after 10 years. Judge's weekly tentative rulings may be available free online at the web site.

General Information: No probation reports released. SASE required. Turnaround time 2 days. Copy fee: $.50 per page. Certification fee: $6.00. Fee payee: El Dorado Superior Court. Personal checks accepted. Prepayment is required.

Cameron Park Branch - Superior Court 3321 Cameron Park Dr, Cameron Park, CA 95682; 530-621-5867; Fax: 530-672-2413. Hours: 8AM-4PM (PST). *Felony, Misdemeanor.*

http://co.el-dorado.ca.us/superiorcourts/index.html

Note: This is a trial court only. Only records prior to 1995 are housed here. Records from 1995 and after are available at the Placerville Branch Superior Court. Civil cases are handled in Placerville.

Criminal Records: Access: Mail, in person. Both court and visitors may perform in person searches. Search fee: $5.00 per name. Required to search: name, years to search; also helpful: address, DOB. Criminal records on computer from 1991, index files from 1983. Records are destroyed after 10 years. Judge's weekly tentative rulings may be available free online at the web site.

General Information: No probation reports released. SASE required. Turnaround time 1 week. Copy fee: $.50 per page. Certification fee: $6.00. Fee payee: Superior Court. Personal checks accepted. Prepayment is required.

Fairlane Branch Superior Court 2850 Fairlane Ct, Placerville, CA 95667; Civil phone: 530-621-7470; Criminal phone: 530-621-7464. Hours: 8AM-4PM (PST). *Misdemeanor, Small Claims, Traffic.*

http://co.el-dorado.ca.us/superiorcourts

Note: Also hears felony arraignments.

Civil Records: Access: Mail, in person. Both court and visitors may perform in person searches. Search fee: $5.00 per name per year. Required to search: name, years to search. Civil cases indexed by defendant, plaintiff. Civil records on computer from 1991. Actual records after 1996 are kept at the main Superior Court in Placerville. Judge's weekly tentative rulings may be available free online at the web site. Address search requests to Dept. 8.

Criminal Records: Access: Mail, in person. Both court and visitors may perform in person searches. Search fee: $5.00 per name. Required to search: name, years to search; also helpful: DOB. Criminal records on computer from 1994, prior on index books, index files from 1983. Records are destroyed after 10 years. Judge's weekly tentative rulings may be available free at the web site. Address search requests to Dept 7.

General Information: No probation reports released. SASE required. Turnaround time 2 weeks. Copy fee: $.50 per page. Certification fee: $6.00. Fee payee: El Dorado County Superior Courts. Personal checks accepted. Prepayment is required.

Fresno County

Superior Court 1100 Van Ness Ave, #401, Fresno, CA 93724; Civil phone: 559-448-3352; Criminal phone: 559-488-3142; Probate phone: 559-488-3618; Fax: 559-488-1976. Hours: 8AM-4PM (PST). *Felony, Misdemeanor, Civil, Small Claims, Probate.*

www.fresno.ca.gov/2810/default.htm

Note: The telephone number for the Limited Civil clerk is 559-488-3453.

Civil Records: Access: Phone, fax, mail, in person, online. Both court and visitors may perform in person searches. Search fee: $5.00 per name. Required to search: name, years to search. Civil cases indexed by defendant, plaintiff. Civil records on computer back to 1976, on microfiche, index files and archived from 1800s. Online access to civil, probate, family, small claims cases is available free at www.fresno.ca.gov/2810/SJVAP/CourtConnect.asp. You must enter a Fresno county zip code to enter.

Criminal Records: Access: Phone, fax, mail, in person. Both court and visitors may perform in person searches. Search fee: $5.00 per name. Required to search: name, years to search. Criminal records on computer back to 1976, microfiche, index files and archived from 1800s.

General Information: Public access terminal is available. No confidential, adoption or juvenile records released. SASE required. Turnaround time 3-5 days. Copy fee: $.50 per page. Certification fee: $6.00. Fee payee: Superior Court Clerk's Office. Personal checks accepted. Prepayment is required.

Clovis Division - Superior Court 1011 5th St, Clovis, CA 93612; 559-299-4964; Fax: 559-299-2595. Hours: 8AM-4PM (PST). *Misdemeanor, Civil Actions Under $25,000, Eviction, Small Claims.*

www.fresno.ca.gov/2810/default.htm

Note: Includes Alder Springs, Auberry, Big Creek, Burroughs Valley, Clovis, friant, Huntington Lake, Millerton Lake, Pine Ridge, Prather, Shaver, Tollhouse, and Watts. Does felony, welfare, and fraud cases.

Civil Records: Access: Mail, in person, online. Only the court performs in person searches; visitors may not. Search fee: $5.00. Required to search: name, years to search. Civil cases indexed by defendant, plaintiff. Civil records on computer and index files from 1983. Records destroyed after 10 years. Online access to civil, probate, family, small claims cases is available free at www.fresno.ca.gov/2810/SJVAP/CourtConnect.asp. You must enter a Fresno county zip code to enter.

Criminal Records: Access: Mail, in person. Only the court performs in person searches; visitors may not. Search fee: $5.00. Required to search: name, years to search, DOB. Criminal records on computer and index files from 1983. Records destroyed after 10 years.

General Information: No probation reports released. SASE required. Turnaround time 1 week. Copy fee: $.50 per page. Certification fee: $6.00. Fee payee: Clovis Superior Court. Personal checks accepted. Prepayment is required.

Coalinga Division - Superior Court 160 West Elm St, Coalinga, CA 93210; 559-935-2017/2018; Fax: 559-935-5324. Hours: 8AM-Noon, 1-4PM (PST). *Misdemeanor, Civil Actions Under $25,000, Eviction, Small Claims.*

www.fresno.ca.gov/2810/default.htm

Note: Includes Coalinga and Huron.

Civil Records: Access: Mail, in person, online. Only the court performs in person searches; visitors may not. No search fee. Required to search: name, years to search; also helpful: address. Civil cases indexed by defendant, plaintiff. Civil records on index cards and are computerized since 1990. Will only search back 10 years. Online access to civil, probate, family, small claims cases is available free at www.fresno.ca.gov/2810/SJVAP/CourtConnect.asp. You must enter a Fresno county zip code to enter.

Criminal Records: Access: Mail, in person. Only the court performs in person searches; visitors may not. No search fee. Required to search: name, years to search, DOB; also helpful: address, SSN. Criminal records on computer from 1990, on index cards prior. Will only search back 10 years, Traffic 10 years.

General Information: No confidential records or cases not finished released. SASE required. Turnaround time 1 week. Copy fee: $.50 per page. Certification fee: $6.00. Fee payee: Superior Court. Personal checks accepted. Prepayment is required.

Firebaugh Division - Superior Court 1325 "O" St, Firebaugh, CA 93622; 559-659-2011/2012; Fax: 559-659-6228. Hours: 8AM-4:30 M; 8AM-4PM T-F (PST). *Misdemeanor, Civil Actions Under $25,000, Eviction, Small Claims.*

www.fresno.ca.gov/2810/default.htm

Note: Includes Dos Palos, Firebaugh, Mendota, Ora Loma, and Three Rocks.

Civil Records: Access: Phone, fax, mail, in person, online. Only the court performs in person searches; visitors may not. Search fee: $5.00 per name. Required to search: name, years to search. Civil cases indexed by defendant, plaintiff. Civil records on computer from 1990, index cards prior. Will only search back 7 years. Online access to civil, probate, family, small claims cases is available free at www.fresno.ca.gov/2810/SJVAP/CourtConnect.asp. You must enter a Fresno county zip code to enter.

Criminal Records: Access: Phone, fax, mail, in person. Only the court performs in person searches; visitors may not. Search fee: $5.00 per name. Required to search: name, years to search, DOB. Criminal records on computer from 1990, index cards prior. Will only search back 7 years.

General Information: No confidential records released. SASE required. Turnaround time 1 week. Copy fee: $.50 per page. Certification fee: $6.00. Fee payee: Firebaugh Superior Court. Personal checks accepted. Prepayment is required.

Fowler Division - Superior Court PO Box 400, Fowler, CA 93625; 559-834-3215; Fax: 559-834-1645. Hours: 8AM-4PM (PST). *Misdemeanor, Civil Actions Under $25,000, Eviction, Small Claims.*

www.fresno.ca.gov/2810/default.htm

Note: This court holds the records for the closed courts in Caruthers and Parlier, as well as the cities of Bowles, Del Rey, Fowler, Monmouth, and Raisin City.

Civil Records: Access: Mail, in person, online. Only the court performs in person searches; visitors may not. Search fee: $5.00 per name. Required to search: name, years to search. Civil cases indexed by defendant, plaintiff. Civil records on index cards. Will only search back 7 years. Online access to civil, probate, family, small claims cases is available free at www.fresno.ca.gov/2810/SJVAP/CourtConnect.asp. You must enter a Fresno county zip code to enter.

Criminal Records: Access: Mail, in person. Only the court performs in person searches; visitors may not. Search fee: $5.00 per name. Required to search: name, years to search; also helpful: DOB, SSN. Criminal records on computer from 1990, index cards prior. Will only search back 7 years.

General Information: No confidential records released. SASE required. Turnaround time 1 week. Copy fee: $.50 per page. Certification fee: $6.00. Fee payee: Fowler Superior Court. Personal checks accepted. Prepayment is required.

Kerman Division - Superior Court 719 S Madera Ave, Kerman, CA 93630; 559-846-7371/7372; Fax: 559-846-5751. Hours: 8AM-4PM M-F (2-4 for phone calls) (PST). *Misdemeanor, Civil Actions Under $25,000, Eviction, Small Claims.*

www.fresno.ca.gov/2810/default.htm

Includes Biola, Biola Junction, Cantua, Five Points, Helm, Kerman, Rolinda, San Joaquin, and Tranquility.

Note: The court holds preliminary hearings for felonies.
Civil Records: Access: Phone, mail, in person, online. Both court and visitors may perform in person searches. No search fee. Required to search: name, years to search. Civil cases indexed by defendant, plaintiff. Civil records on index cards. Will only search back 7 years. Online access to civil, probate, family, small claims cases is available free at www.fresno.ca.gov/2810/SJVAP/CourtConnect.asp. You must enter a Fresno county zip code to enter.

Criminal Records: Access: Phone, mail, in person. Both court and visitors may perform in person searches. No search fee. Required to search: name, years to search. Criminal records on computer from 1990, index cards prior. Will only search back 7 years.

General Information: No confidential records released. SASE required. Turnaround time 1 week. Copy fee: $.50 per page. Certification fee: $6.00. Fee payee: Superior Court. Personal checks accepted. Prepayment is required.

Kingsburg Division - Superior Court 1600 California St, Kingsburg, CA 93631; 559-897-2241; Fax: 559-897-1419. Hours: 8AM-Noon, 1-4PM (PST). *Misdemeanor, Civil Actions Under $25,000, Eviction, Small Claims.*

www.fresno.ca.gov/2810/default.htm

Note: This court includes records from the branch court closed in Riverdale. Includes Burrel, Camden, Kingsburg, Lanare, Laton, Riverdale.
Civil Records: Access: Mail, in person, online. Only the court performs in person searches; visitors may not. Search fee: $5.00 per name. Required to search: name, years to search. Online access to civil, probate, family, small claims cases is available free at www.fresno.ca.gov/2810/SJVAP/CourtConnect.asp. You must enter a Fresno county zip code to enter.
Criminal Records: Access: Mail, in person. Only the court performs in person searches; visitors may not. Search fee: $5.00 per name. Required to search: name, years to search, DOB. Criminal records on computer from April, 1994, index cards prior.
General Information: No confidential records released. SASE required. Turnaround time 1 week. Copy fee: $.50 per page. Certification fee: $6.00. Fee payee: Superior Court. Personal checks accepted. Prepayment is required.

Reedley Division - Superior Court 815 "G" St, Reedley, CA 93654; 559-638-3114; Fax: 559-637-1534. Hours: 8AM-Noon, 1-4PM (1-4 for phone calls) (PST). *Misdemeanor, Civil Actions Under $25,000, Eviction, Small Claims.*

www.fresno.ca.gov/2810/default.htm

Note: Includes Badger, Cedarbrook, Cedar Pines, Dunlap, Hume, Kings River Canyon, Navalencia, Minkler, Miramonte, Orange Cove, Reedley, Squaw Valley, and Wahtoke.

Civil Records: Access: Mail, in person, online. Both court and visitors may perform in person searches. Search fee: $5.00 per name. Required to search: name, years to search. Civil cases indexed by defendant, plaintiff. Civil records on computer back 10 years, index cards prior. Will only search back 7 years. Online access to civil, probate, family, small claims cases is available free at www.fresno.ca.gov/2810/SJVAP/CourtConnect.asp. You must enter a Fresno county zip code to enter.
Criminal Records: Access: Mail, in person. Both court and visitors may perform in person searches. Search fee: $5.00 per name. Required to search: name, years to search, DOB. Criminal records on computer back 10 years, index cards prior. Will only search back 7 years.
General Information: No confidential records released. SASE required. Turnaround time 1 week. Copy fee: $.50 per page. Certification fee: $6.00. Fee payee: Reedley Superior Court. Personal checks accepted. Prepayment is required.

Sanger Division - Superior Court 619 "N" St, Sanger, CA 93657; 559-875-7158/7159; Fax: 559-875-0002. Hours: 8AM-Noon, 1-4PM (PST). *Misdemeanor, Civil Actions Under $25,000, Eviction, Small Claims.*

www.fresno.ca.gov/2810/default.htm

Note: The clerk's office answers telephone calls from 1-4pm. Includes Centerville, Piedra, Sanger, and Trimmer Springs.
Civil Records: Access: Mail, in person, online. Only the court performs in person searches; visitors may not. Search fee: $5.00 per name. Required to search: name, years to search. Civil cases indexed by defendant, plaintiff. Will only search back 10 years. Online access to civil, probate, family, small claims cases is available at www.fresno.ca.gov/2810/SJVAP/CourtConnect.asp. You must enter a Fresno county zip code to enter.
Criminal Records: Access: Mail, in person. Only the court performs in person searches; visitors may not. Search fee: $5.00 per name. Required to search: name, years to search, DOB, signed release. Criminal records on computer from 1990, index cards prior. Will only search back 10 years.
General Information: No confidential records released. SASE required. Turnaround time 1 week.

Copy fee: $.50 per page. Certification fee: $6.00. Fee payee: Superior Court. Personal checks accepted.

Selma Division - Superior Court 2117 Selma St, Selma, CA 93662; 559-896-2123; Fax: 559-896-4465. Hours: 8AM-Noon, 1-4PM (PST). *Misdemeanor, Civil Actions Under $25,000, Eviction, Small Claims.*

www.fresno.ca.gov/2810/default.htm

Note: Includes Conejo and Selma.

Civil Records: Access: Mail, in person, online. Only the court performs in person searches; visitors may not. No search fee. Required to search: name, years to search. Civil cases indexed by defendant, plaintiff. Civil records on index cards. Will only search back 7 years. Online access to civil, probate, family, small claims cases is available free at www.fresno.ca.gov/2810/SJVAP/CourtConnect.asp. You must enter a Fresno county zip code to enter.
Criminal Records: Access: Mail, in person. Only the court performs in person searches; visitors may not. No search fee. Required to search: name, years to search, DOB. Criminal records on computer back to 1990, index cards prior. Will only search back 7 years.
General Information: No confidential records released. SASE required. Turnaround time 1 week. Copy fee: $.50 per page. Certification fee: $6.00. Fee payee: Selma Superior Court. Personal checks accepted. Prepayment is required.

Glenn County

Superior Court 526 W Sycamore, Willows, CA 95988; 530-934-6446; Fax: 530-934-6406. Hours: 8AM-5PM (PST). *Felony, Misdemeanor, Civil, Small Claims, Probate.*

Note: Records from the municipal court were combined with this court when the courts were consolidated.
Civil Records: Access: Mail, in person. Both court and visitors may perform in person searches. Search fee: $5.00 per search. Required to search: name, years to search. Civil cases indexed by defendant, plaintiff. Civil records on computer back to 1996, on microfiche, archived and in index file from 1894.
Criminal Records: Access: Mail, in person. Both court and visitors may perform in person searches. Search fee: $5.00 per search. Required to search: name, years to search; also helpful: DOB. Criminal records on computer back to 1996, on microfiche, archived and in index file from 1894.
General Information: No adoption, juvenile or paternity released. SASE required. Turnaround time 1 day. Copy fee: $.50 per page. Certification fee: $6.00. Fee payee: Superior Court. Personal checks accepted. Prepayment is required.

Humboldt County

Superior Court 825 5th Street, Eureka, CA 95501; 707-445-7256. Hours: 8:30AM-Noon, 1-4PM (PST). *Felony, Civil, Probate.*

Note: Countywide searching can be done from this court, records computerized for 10 years. The former Eureka, Eel River, and North Humboldt Municipal Court Divisions have been combined with this court. Physical address is at 421 I Street.
Civil Records: Access: Mail, in person. Both court and visitors may perform in person searches. Search fee: $5.00 per name. Required to search: name, years to search. Civil cases indexed by defendant, plaintiff. Civil records on computer back to 1993; on microfiche and archived from 1964.
Criminal Records: Access: Mail, in person. Both court and visitors may perform in person searches. Search fee: $5.00 per name. Required to search: name, years to search; also helpful: DOB. Criminal records on computer back to 1985; on microfiche and archived from 1964.

General Information: No probation, medical, adoption, juvenile or sealed records released. SASE required. Turnaround time 3 weeks. Copy fee: $.50 per page. Certification fee: $6.00. Fee payee: Humboldt Superior Court. Personal checks accepted. Prepayment is required.

Garberville Branch - Superior Court 483
Conger St, Garberville, CA 95542; 707-923-2141; Fax: 707-923-3133. Hours: 8:30AM-Noon, 1-4PM (PST). *Misdemeanor, Civil Actions Under $25,000, Eviction, Small Claims.*

Note: Court no longer opens new civil cases.

Klamath/Trinity Branch - Superior Court
825 5th St, Eureka, CA 95501; 707-445-7256. Hours: 8:30AM-Noon, 1-5PM (PST). *Misdemeanor, Civil Actions Under $25,000, Eviction, Small Claims.*

Note: Records for this branch are housed at the main court in Eureka.
Civil Records: Access: Mail, in person. Both court and visitors may perform in person searches. Search fee: $5.00 per name. Required to search: name, years to search. Civil cases indexed by defendant, plaintiff. Civil records in index files from 1983. Records destroyed after 10 yrs. Records on computer go back to 1997.
Criminal Records: Access: Mail, in person. Both court and visitors may perform in person searches. Search fee: $5.00 per name. Required to search: name, years to search, DOB. Criminal records on computer back to 1987, index and dockets kept for 10 years, files kept for 5 years.
General Information: No probation reports released. SASE required. Turnaround time 2 days. Copy fee: $.50 per page. Certification fee: $6.00 per document. Fee payee: Humboldt Superior Court. Personal checks accepted. Prepayment is required.

Imperial County

Imperial Branch - Superior Court 939 W
Main St, El Centro, CA 92243; Civil phone: 760-482-4217; Criminal phone: 760-482-4219; Fax: 760-482-4219. Hours: 8AM-4PM (PST). *Felony, Misdemeanor, Civil, Eviction, Small Claims, Probate.*

Note: All record searching for Imperial county must be done at each location.
Civil Records: Access: Mail, in person. Both court and visitors may perform in person searches. Search fee: $5.00 per name. Required to search: name, years to search. Civil cases indexed by defendant, plaintiff. Civil records on microfiche from 1972, in index file from 1917.
Criminal Records: Access: Mail, in person. Both court and visitors may perform in person searches. Search fee: $5.00 per name. Required to search: name, years to search. Criminal records on microfiche from 1972, index file from 1917.
General Information: No adoptions, juvenile, medical, probation or sealed records released. SASE required. Turnaround time 2 weeks. Copy fee: $1.00 for first page, $.50 each add'l. Certification fee: $6.00. Fee payee: Imperial County Superior Court. Personal checks accepted. Prepayment is required.

Brawley Branch - Superior Court 383 Main
St, Brawley, CA 92227; 760-344-0710; Fax: 760-344-9231. Hours: 8AM-4PM (PST). *Misdemeanor, Civil Actions Under $25,000, Eviction, Small Claims.*

Note: There is no countywide database in this county.
Civil Records: Access: Phone, fax, mail, in person. Both court and visitors may perform in person searches. Search fee: $5.00 per name. Required to search: name, years to search. Civil cases indexed by defendant, plaintiff. Civil records on computer back 2 years (traffic from 1991), in index files from 1983. Records destroyed after 10 years.

Criminal Records: Access: Phone, fax, mail, in person. Only the court performs in person searches; visitors may not. Search fee: $5.00 per name. Required to search: name, years to search, DOB. Criminal records on computer back 2 years (traffic only from 1991), in index files from 1983. Records destroyed after 10 years.
General Information: No probation reports released. SASE required. Turnaround time 1 week. Copy fee: $1.00 for first page, $.50 each add'l. Certification fee: $6.00. Fee payee: Brawley Superior Court. Personal checks accepted. Prepayment is required.

Calexico Branch - Superior Court 415 4th
St, Calexico, CA 92231; 760-357-3726; Fax: 760-357-6571. Hours: 8AM-4PM (PST). *Misdemeanor, Civil Actions Under $25,000, Eviction, Small Claims.*

Note: There is no countywide database in this county.
Civil Records: Access: Fax, mail, in person. Both court and visitors may perform in person searches. Search fee: $5.00 per name. Required to search: name, years to search. Civil cases indexed by defendant, plaintiff. Civil records on computer from 1991, index files from 1983. Records destroyed after 10 years.
Criminal Records: Access: Fax, mail, in person. Only the court performs in person searches; visitors may not. Search fee: $5.00 per name. Required to search: name, years to search. Criminal records on computer from 1991, index files from 1983. Records destroyed after 10 years.
General Information: No probation reports released. SASE required. Turnaround time within 2 weeks. Copy fee: $.50 per page. Certification fee: $6.00. Fee payee: Superior Court. Personal checks accepted. Write case # on check. Prepayment is required.

Winterhaven Branch - Superior Court PO
Box 1087, Winterhaven, CA 92283-1087; 760-572-0354; Fax: 760-572-2683. Hours: 8AM-Noon, 1-4PM (PST). *Eviction, Small Claims.*

Note: Misdemeanor and civil records have been moved to the Calexico Branch. Only small claims and traffic records remain here

Inyo County

Superior Court 168 N Edwards St (PO Drawer 4),
Independence, CA 93526; 760-878-0218. Hours: 9AM-5PM (PST). *Felony, Civil Actions Over $25,000, Probate.*

Note: There is no central record database, each court in the county has its own records.
Civil Records: Access: Mail, in person. Both court and visitors may perform in person searches. Search fee: $5.00 per name. Required to search: name, years to search. Civil cases indexed by defendant, plaintiff. Civil records on computer to mid-1999, on microfiche and in index files from 1800s.
Criminal Records: Access: Mail, in person. Both court and visitors may perform in person searches. Search fee: $5.00 per name. Required to search: name, years to search. Criminal records on computer back to 1992, on microfiche and in index files from 1800s.
General Information: No adoptions, juvenile, medical, probation or sealed records released. SASE required. Turnaround time 2-3 business days. Copy fee: $1.00 per page. Certification fee: $6.00. Fee payee: Inyo Superior Court. Personal checks accepted. Prepayment is required.

Bishop Branch - Superior Court 301 W Line
St, Bishop, CA 93514; 760-872-4971. Hours: 9AM-Noon, 1-5PM; Phone: 2-5PM (PST). *Misdemeanor, Civil Actions Under $25,000, Eviction, Small Claims.*

Note: There is no countywide database, each branch court must be searched.
Civil Records: Access: Mail, in person. Only the court performs in person searches; visitors may not. Search fee: $5.00 per name. Required to search: name, years to

search. Civil cases indexed by defendant, plaintiff. Civil records on index cards. Will only search back 7 years.
Criminal Records: Access: Mail, in person. Only the court performs in person searches; visitors may not. Search fee: $5.00 per name. Required to search: name, years to search. Criminal records on computer from 1993, index cards prior. Will only search back 7 years.
General Information: No confidential records released. SASE required. Turnaround time 1 week. Copy fee: $1.00 per page. Certification fee: $6.00. Fee payee: Superior Court. Personal checks accepted. Prepayment is required.

Independence Limited Branch - Superior
Court 168 N Edwards St (PO Box 518), Independence, CA 93526; 760-878-0319; Fax: 760-872-1060. Hours: 9AM-Noon, 1-5PM (PST). *Misdemeanor, Civil Actions Under $25,000, Eviction, Small Claims.*

Note: There is no countywide database, each branch court must be searched.
Civil Records: Access: Mail, in person. Both court and visitors may perform in person searches. Search fee: $5.00 per name. Required to search: name, years to search. Civil cases indexed by defendant, plaintiff. Civil records on computer back to 1999, in index books and index cards. Will only search back 7 years.
Criminal Records: Access: Mail, in person. Both court and visitors may perform in person searches. Search fee: $5.00 per name. Required to search: name, years to search, DOB. Criminal records on computer from 2/1993, index books and index cards prior. Will only search back 7 years.
General Information: No confidential records released. SASE required. Turnaround time 1 week. Fax notes: Fee to fax results is $1.00 per page. Copy fee: $1.00 per page. Certification fee: $7.00. Fee payee: Inyo County Court. Personal checks accepted. Prepayment is required.

Kern County

Superior Court 1415 Truxtun Ave, Bakersfield,
CA 93301; 661-868-5393. Hours: 8AM-5PM (PST). *Felony, Civil Actions Over $25,000, Probate.*

www.co.kern.ca.us/courts

Civil Records: Access: Mail, in person. Visitors must perform in person searches for themselves. No search fee. Required to search: name, years to search. Civil cases indexed by defendant, plaintiff. Civil records on microfiche from 1964, archived and in index file from 1800s.
Criminal Records: Access: Mail, in person. Visitors must perform in person searches for themselves. No search fee. Required to search: name, years to search, DOB. Criminal records on computer from 1989, on microfiche, archived, and in index files.
General Information: No adoptions, juvenile, medical, probation or sealed records released. SASE required. Turnaround time 1 day to 1 week. Copy fee: $.75 per page. Certification fee: $6.00. Fee payee: Kern County Superior Court. Personal checks accepted. Prepayment is required.

Delano/McFarland Branch Superior
Court - North Division 1122 Jefferson St, Delano, CA 93215; 661-720-5800; Fax: 661-721-1237. Hours: 8AM-5PM (PST). *Misdemeanor, Civil Actions Under $25,000, Eviction, Small Claims.*

www.co.kern.ca.us/courts

Civil Records: Access: Phone, fax, mail, in person. Both court and visitors may perform in person searches. Search fee: $5.00 per name per year. Required to search: name, years to search. Civil cases indexed by defendant, plaintiff. Civil records in index files from 1983. Records destroyed after 10 years.

Criminal Records: Access: Phone, fax, mail, in person. Both court and visitors may perform in person searches. Search fee: $5.00 per name per year. Required to search: name, years to search; also helpful: DOB. Criminal records on computer from 1988, in index files from 1983. Records destroyed after 10 years.

General Information: Public access terminal is available. (For criminal records only.) No probation reports released. SASE required. Turnaround time 2 days. Copy fee: $.75 per page. Certification fee: $6.00. Fee payee: Superior Court Kern County-Delano/McFarland Branch. Personal checks accepted. Prepayment is required.

Kern River Branch Superior Court - East Division 7046 Lake Isabella Blvd, Lake Isabella, CA 93240; 760-379-3635; Fax: 760-379-4544. Hours: 8AM-4PM M-Th 8AM-5PM F (PST). *Misdemeanor, Civil Actions Under $25,000, Eviction, Small Claims.*

www.co.kern.ca.us/courts

Civil Records: Access: Phone, fax, mail, in person. Only the court performs in person searches; visitors may not. No search fee. Required to search: name, years to search. Civil cases indexed by defendant, plaintiff. Civil records on computer from 1991, in index files from 1983. Records destroyed after 10 years.

Criminal Records: Access: Phone, mail, in person. Only the court performs in person searches; visitors may not. No search fee. Required to search: name, years to search. Criminal records on computer from 1991, in index files from 1983. Records destroyed after 10 years.

General Information: No probation reports released. SASE required. Turnaround time 2 days. Copy fee: $.75 per page. Certification fee: $6.00. Fee payee: East Kern Superior Court. Personal checks accepted. Credit cards accepted: Visa, AmEx. Prepayment is required.

Lamont/Arvin Branch Superior Court - South Division 12022 Main St, Lamont, CA 93241; 661-845-3741 or 868-5700; Fax: 661-845-9142. Hours: 8AM-4PM (PST). *Misdemeanor, Civil Actions Under $25,000, Eviction, Small Claims.*

www.co.kern.ca.us/courts

Civil Records: Access: Fax, mail, in person. Only the court performs in person searches; visitors may not. Search fee: $5.00 per name. Required to search: name, years to search. Civil cases indexed by defendant, plaintiff. Civil records on computer from 1989. Records destroyed after 10 years. Current court calendars are available free online at www.co.kern.ca.us/apps/courtcal/courtcalendar.asp.

Criminal Records: Access: Fax, mail, in person. Only the court performs in person searches; visitors may not. Search fee: $5.00 per name. Required to search: name, years to search, DOB; also helpful CA DL#, SSN, signed release. Criminal records on computer from 1989. Records destroyed after 10 years. Current court calendars are available free online at www.co.kern.ca.us/apps/courtcal/courtcalendar.asp.

General Information: No probation reports released. SASE required. Turnaround time 2 days. Fax notes: No fee to fax results. Copy fee: $.75 per page. Certification fee: $6.00. Fee payee: Superior Court Lamont Branch. Personal checks accepted. Credit cards accepted: Visa, AmEx. Prepayment is required.

Mojave Branch Superior Court - East Division 1773 Hwy 58, Mojave, CA 93501; 661-824-7100. Hours: 8AM-5PM (PST). *Misdemeanor, Civil Actions Under $25,000, Eviction, Small Claims.*

www.co.kern.ca.us/courts

Civil Records: Access: Mail, in person. Only the court performs in person searches; visitors may not. Search fee: $5.00 per name. Required to search: name, years to search. Civil cases indexed by defendant, plaintiff. Civil records on computer from 1991, in index files from 1983. Records destroyed after 10 years.

Criminal Records: Access: Mail, in person. Only the court performs in person searches; visitors may not. Search fee: $5.00. Required to search: name, years to search, DOB. Criminal records on computer from 1991, in index files from 1983.

General Information: No probation reports released. SASE required. Turnaround time up to 1 week. Copy fee: $6.75 per page (certified). Certification fee: $6.75 per page. Fee payee: East Kern Superior Court. Personal checks accepted. Credit cards accepted: Visa, AmEx. Additional fee charged for use of credit card. Prepayment is required.

Ridgecrest Branch Superior Court - East Division 132 E Coso St, Ridgecrest, CA 93555; 760-375-1397; Fax: 760-375-2112. Hours: 8AM-4PM M-T, 8AM-5PM F (PST). *Misdemeanor, Civil Actions Under $25,000, Eviction, Small Claims.*

www.co.kern.ca.us/courts

Note: Includes Eastern Kern County, including Edwards Air Force Base, Lake Isabella, Kernville, China Lake NWC, California City, Ridgecrest, Mojave and Tehachapi.

Civil Records: Access: Mail, in person. Both court and visitors may perform in person searches. Search fee: $5.00 per name. Required to search: name, years to search. Civil cases indexed by defendant, plaintiff. Civil records on computer from 1990, in index files from 1983. Records destroyed after 10 years.

Criminal Records: Access: Mail, in person. Both court and visitors may perform in person searches. Search fee: $5.00 per name. Required to search: name, years to search; also helpful: DOB, SSN. Criminal records on computer from 1990, in index files from 1983. Records destroyed after 10 years.

General Information: No probation reports released. SASE required. Turnaround time 2 days. Copy fee: $.75 per page. Certification fee: $6.00. Fee payee: Kern County Superior Court. Personal checks accepted. Credit cards accepted: Visa, AmEx. Prepayment is required.

Shafter/Wasco Branch Superior Court - North Division 325 Central Valley Hwy, Shafter, CA 93263; 661-746-7500; Fax: 661-746-0545. Hours: 8AM-5PM (PST). *Misdemeanor, Civil Actions Under $25,000, Eviction, Small Claims.*

www.co.kern.ca.us/courts

Civil Records: Access: Phone, fax, mail, in person. Both court and visitors may perform in person searches. Visitors may search counter index; court searches electronically. Search fee: $5.00 per name per year. Required to search: name, years to search; also helpful: address. Civil cases indexed by defendant, plaintiff. Civil records go back to 1994.

Criminal Records: Access: Phone, fax, mail, in person. Both court and visitors may perform in person searches. Search fee: $5.00 per name per year. Required to search: name, years to search, DOB; also helpful: address, SSN. Criminal records on computer since 1988, traffic since 1991.

General Information: Public access terminal is available. (Terminal available for criminal only.) No probation reports released. SASE required. Turnaround time 2 days. Fax notes: No fee to fax results. Copy fee: $.75 per page. Certification fee: $6.00 or $10.00 if a dissolution. Fee payee: Superior Court North Division. Personal checks accepted. Prepayment is required.

Superior Court Metropolitan Division 1215 Truxtun Ave, Bakersfield, CA 93301; Civil phone: 661-868-2456; Criminal phone: 661-868-2482; Fax: 800-487-45675 (civ); 661-868-2695 (crim). Hours: 8AM-5PM (PST). *Misdemeanor, Civil Actions Under $25,000, Eviction, Small Claims.*

www.co.kern.ca.us/courts

Note: Formerly Bakersfield Municipal Court. Includes Bakersfield, Oildale, Edison, Glenville, Woody.

Civil Records: Access: Fax, in person. Both court and visitors may perform in person searches. Search fee: $5.00 per name per year. Required to search: name, years to search. Civil cases indexed by defendant, plaintiff. Civil records on index files from 1977 on microfilm. Records destroyed after 10 years.

Criminal Records: Access: Fax, in person. Both court and visitors may perform in person searches. Search fee: $5.00 per name per year. Required to search: name, years to search. Criminal records on computer since 1988, microfilm since 1952.

General Information: Public access terminal is available. No probation reports, rap sheets, medical or financial released. Mail requests not accepted. Fax notes: No fee to fax results. Fax fee varies by quantity. Copy fee: $.75 per page. Certification fee: $6.00. Fee payee: Superior Court of California. Personal checks accepted. Prepayment is required.

Taft/Maricopa Branch Superior Court - South Division 311 N Lincoln St, Taft, CA 93268; 661-763-8531; Fax: 661-763-2439. Hours: 8AM-Noon,1-4PM (PST). *Misdemeanor, Civil Actions Under $25,000, Eviction, Small Claims.*

www.co.kern.ca.us/courts

Civil Records: Access: Phone, mail, in person. Only the court performs in person searches; visitors may not. Search fee: $5.00 per name. Required to search: name, years to search; also helpful: address. Civil cases indexed by defendant, plaintiff. Civil records on computer from 1988, in index files from 1983. Records destroyed after 10 years.

Criminal Records: Access: Phone, mail, in person. Only the court performs in person searches; visitors may not. Search fee: $5.00 per name. Purchase of complaint and docket required. Required to search: name, years to search, DOB; also helpful: address, SSN. Criminal records on computer from 1988, in index files from 1983. Records destroyed after 10 years.

General Information: No probation reports released. SASE required. Turnaround time 2 days. Copy fee: $.75 per page. Certification fee: $6.00. Fee payee: South Taft Court. Personal checks accepted. Credit cards accepted: Visa, Discover. Prepayment is required.

Kings County

Superior Court 1400 W Lacey Blvd, Hanford, CA 93230; 559-582-3211 X2430; Fax: 559-584-0319. Hours: 8AM-5PM (PST). *Felony, Misdemeanor, Civil Actions, Probate.*

Civil Records: Access: Mail, in person. Both court and visitors may perform in person searches. Search fee: $5.00 per name. Required to search: name, years to search. Civil cases indexed by defendant, plaintiff. Civil records on computer from 1989, on microfiche and archived from 1970s, in index file from 1914.

Criminal Records: Access: Mail, in person. Both court and visitors may perform in person searches. Search fee: $5.00 per name. Required to search: name, years to search. Criminal records on computer from 1989, on microfiche and archived from 1970s, in index file from 1914.

General Information: Public access terminal is available. No adoptions, juvenile, medical, probation or sealed records released. SASE required. Turnaround time 1 week. Copy fee: $.50 per page. Certification fee: $6.00. Fee payee: Superior Court of the State of California. Business checks accepted. Checks accepted with proper identification. Prepayment is required.

Avenal Division Superior Court 501 E Kings St, Avenal, CA 93204; 559-386-5225; Fax: 559-386-9452. Hours: 8AM-5PM (PST). *Misdemeanor, Civil Actions Under $25,000, Eviction, Small Claims.*

Civil Records: Access: Phone, fax, mail, in person. Both court and visitors may perform in person searches. No search fee. Required to search: name, years to search. Civil records on index cards. Will only search back to 1993.

Criminal Records: Access: Phone, fax, mail, in person. Both court and visitors may perform in person searches. No search fee. Required to search: name, years to search, DOB. Criminal records on computer from 1990, index cards prior. Will only search back 3 years.

General Information: Public access terminal is available. No juvenile or adoption records released. SASE required. Turnaround time 1 week. Copy fee: $.50 per page. Certification fee: $1.50. Fee payee: Avenal Superior Court. Personal checks accepted. Prepayment is required.

Corcoran Division Superior Court 1000
Chittenden Ave, Corcoran, CA 93212; 559-992-5193/5194; Fax: 559-992-5933. Hours: 8AM-5PM (PST). *Misdemeanor, Civil Actions Under $25,000, Eviction, Small Claims.*

Civil Records: Access: Fax, mail, in person. Only the court performs in person searches; visitors may not. Search fee: $1.75 per name per year. Required to search: name, years to search; also helpful: address. Civil cases indexed by defendant, plaintiff. Civil records on computer from 1990, index cards to 1974. Will only search back 7 years.

Criminal Records: Access: Mail, in person. Only the court performs in person searches; visitors may not. Search fee: $1.75 per name per year. Required to search: name, years to search, DOB; also helpful: address, aka's. Criminal records on computer from 1990, index cards to 1974. Will only search back 7 years.

General Information: No juvenile or adoption records released. SASE required. Turnaround time 1 week. Fax notes: No fee to fax results. Copy fee: $.50 per page. Certification fee: $6.00. Fee payee: Kings County Superior Court. Personal checks accepted. Prepayment is required.

Hanford Division Superior Court 1400 W
Lacey Blvd, Hanford, CA 93230; Civil phone: 559-582-4379; Criminal phone: 559-582-4370; Fax: 559-584-7054. Hours: 8AM-5PM (PST). *Misdemeanor, Civil Actions Under $25,000, Eviction, Small Claims.*

Civil Records: Access: Fax, mail, in person. Both court and visitors may perform in person searches. Search fee: $5.00 per name per year. Required to search: name, years to search. Civil cases indexed by defendant, plaintiff. Civil records on computer from 1991, in index files from 1983. Records destroyed after 10 years.

Criminal Records: Access: Mail, in person. Both court and visitors may perform in person searches. Search fee: $5.00 per name per year. Required to search: name, years to search, DOB. Criminal records on computer from 1991, in index files from 1983. Records destroyed after 10 years.

General Information: Public access terminal is available. No probation or police reports released. SASE required. Turnaround time 1 week. Fax notes: $1.00 per page. Copy fee: $.50 per page. Certification fee: $6.00. Fee payee: Kings County Superior Court. Personal checks accepted. Prepayment is required.

Lemoore Division Superior Court 449 "C"
St, Lemoore, CA 93245; 559-924-7757; Fax: 559-925-0319. Hours: 8AM-5PM (PST). *Misdemeanor, Civil Actions Under $25,000, Eviction, Small Claims.*

Civil Records: Access: Mail, in person. Both court and visitors may perform in person searches. Search fee: $5.00 per name. Required to search: name, years to search. Civil cases indexed by defendant, plaintiff. Civil records computerized since 1990, on index cards back to 1977. In person access limited.

Criminal Records: Access: Mail, in person. Both court and visitors may perform in person searches. Search fee: $5.00 per name. Required to search: name, years to search, date of birth. Criminal records on computer since 1990, index cards back to 1977.

General Information: SASE required. Turnaround time 10 days. Fax notes: Fee to fax results is $1.00 per page. Copy fee: $.50 per page. Certification fee: $6.00. Fee payee: Clerk of Courts. Personal checks accepted. Prepayment is required.

Lake County

Superior Court 255 N Forbes St, Lakeport, CA
95453; 707-263-2374; Fax: 707-262-1327. Hours: 8AM-5PM (PST). *Felony, Misdemeanor, Civil, Eviction, Small Claims, Probate.*

www.courtinfo.ca.gov/courts/trial/lake/lakeport.htm

Note: This court holds the records for the former Northlake Municipal Court.

Civil Records: Access: Mail, in person. Only the court performs in person searches; visitors may not. Search fee: $5.00 per name. Required to search: name, years to search. Civil cases indexed by defendant, plaintiff. Civil records on computer from 1991, on microfiche, archived, and in index files from 1800s.

Criminal Records: Access: Mail, in person. Only the court performs in person searches; visitors may not. Search fee: $5.00 per name. Required to search: name, years to search, DOB. Criminal records on computer from 1991, on microfiche, archived, and in index files from 1800s.

General Information: No adoptions, juvenile, medical, probation or sealed records released. SASE required. Turnaround time 1-3 weeks. Copy fee: $.25 per page. Certification fee: $6.00. Fee payee: Lake County Superior Court. Personal checks accepted. Prepayment is required.

South Lake Division - Superior Court 7000
S Center Dr, Clearlake, CA 95422; 707-994-4859; Civil phone: 707-994-8262; Criminal phone: 707-994-6598; Fax: 707-994-1625. Hours: 8AM-4:30PM; Phone hours 8:30AM-12:30PM (PST). *Misdemeanor, Civil Actions Under $25,000, Eviction, Small Claims.*

www.co.lake.ca.us

Civil Records: Access: Mail, in person. Visitors must perform in person searches for themselves. Search fee: $5.00 per name. Required to search: name, years to search. Civil cases indexed by defendant, plaintiff. Civil records on index books.

Criminal Records: Access: Mail, in person. Only the court performs in person searches; visitors may not. Search fee: $5.00 per name. Required to search: name, years to search, DOB. Criminal records on computer from 1990, index books prior.

General Information: No police reports or sealed records released. SASE required. Turnaround time 1 week (civil) or 30 days (criminal). Copy fee: $.25 per page. Certification fee: $6.00. Fee payee: Lake County Superior Court. Personal checks accepted. Prepayment is required.

Lassen County

Superior Court 220 S Lassen St, #2, Susanville,
CA 96130; 530-251-8189 (dept 1);251-8205 (dept 2). Hours: 8AM-5PM (PST). *Felony, Misdemeanor, Civil, Eviction, Small Claims, Probate.*

www.lassencourt.org

Civil Records: Access: Phone, mail, in person. Both court and visitors may perform in person searches. Search fee: $5.00 per name. Required to search: name, years to search. Civil cases indexed by defendant, plaintiff. Civil records on computer from 11/89, archived and in index files from 1900s.

Criminal Records: Access: Phone, mail, in person. Both court and visitors may perform in person searches.

Search fee: $5.00 per name. Required to search: name, years to search. Criminal records on computer from 11/89, archived and in index files from 1900s.

General Information: No adoptions, juvenile, medical, probation or sealed records released. SASE required. Turnaround time 1-5 days. Copy fee: $1.50 for first page, $.50 each add'l. Certification fee: $6.00. Fee payee: Lassen County Superior Court. Business checks accepted. Prepayment is required.

Los Angeles County

Los Angeles Superior Court - Central
District - Civil 110 N Grand Ave, Rm 426, Los Angeles, CA 90012; 213-974-6135 (974-5171 if over $25,000); Fax: 213-621-2701. Hours: 8:30AM-4:30PM (PST). *Civil Actions, Eviction, Small Claims.*

www.lasuperiorcourt.org

Note: Any civil cases here under $25,000 are co-extensive with the city limits of Los Angeles and includes the City of San Fernando and sections designated as San Pedro, West Los Angeles, Van Nuys, Venice and the unincorporated area of the county known as Florence.

Civil Records: Access: Phone, mail, online, in person. Both court and visitors may perform in person searches. Search fee: $5.00 per name. Required to search: name, years to search. Civil cases indexed by defendant, plaintiff. Civil records on computer from 1991, index files from 1983. Records destroyed after 10 years. Online access is available for free at www.lasuperiorcourt.org. Court location, case number required to search. Available for civil, small claims, probate and unlawful detainer records. Three other Courts in Los Angeles County handle civil cases over $25,000; they are Norwalk, Palmdale, and Van Nuys.

General Information: Public access terminal is available. No probation reports released. SASE required. Turnaround time 24 hours, more if busy. Copy fee: $.57 per page. Certification fee: $6.00. Fee payee: Los Angeles Superior Court. Personal checks accepted. Credit cards accepted: Visa, MasterCard. Prepayment is required.

Los Angeles Superior Court - Central
District - Felony 210 W Temple St Rm M-6, Los Angeles, CA 90012; 213-974-5259; Fax: 213-617-1224. Hours: 8:30AM-4:30PM (PST). *Felony.*

www.lasuperiorcourt.org

Criminal Records: Access: Mail, in person. Only the court performs in person searches; visitors may not. Search fee: $5.00 per name. Required to search: name, years to search, DOB, sex. Criminal records on microfiche and index files since 1956, computerized misdemeanors since 1988; felonies since 1996. Court suggests to include full spelling of middle name.

General Information: No adoptions, juvenile, medical, probation or sealed records released. SASE required. Turnaround time 24 hours; up to 3 weeks if busy. Copy fee: $.57 per page. Certification fee: $6.00. Fee payee: Los Angeles Superior Court. Personal checks accepted. Prepayment is required.

Los Angeles Superior Court - Probate
Department 111 N. Hill St, Rm 112, Los Angeles, CA 90012; 213-974-5471. Hours: 8AM-4PM (PST). *Probate.*

www.lasuperiorcourt.org/probate

Note: Case summaries available free at web site. Also, probate available for current cases in Central Dist., Burbank, Compton, Glendale, Lancaster, Long Beach, Pasadena, Pomona, San Fernando, Santa Monica, Torrance District Courts. Search by case number.

Airport Superior Court - West District

11701 S La Cienega Blvd, Los Angeles, CA 90045; 310-727-6020; Criminal phone: 310-727-6100. Hours: 8:30AM-4:30PM (PST). *Felony, Misdemeanor.*

www.lasuperiorcourt.org/Locations/LAX.htm

Note: New Court in 2000, includes the areas of Palms, Mar Vista, Rancho Park, Marina del Rey, Venice, Playa del Rey and Sawtelle. Holds records for the former Robertson branch.

Criminal Records: Access: Mail, in person. Only the court performs in person searches; visitors may not. Search fee: $5.00 per name. Required to search: name, years to search; also helpful: DOB, address. Criminal records index goes back to.

General Information: No probation reports released. SASE required. Turnaround time 3-5 days. Copy fee: $.57 per page. Certification fee: $6.00. Fee payee: Los Angeles Superior Court. Personal checks accepted. Prepayment is required.

Alhambra Superior Court - Northeast District

150 W Commonwealth Ave, Alhambra, CA 91801; 626-308-5521. Hours: 8AM-4:30PM (PST). *Misdemeanor, Civil Actions Under $25,000, Eviction, Small Claims.*

www.lasuperiorcourt.org

Note: Includes cities of Alhambra, Monterey Park, San Gabriel, Temple City and the unincorporated County area known as South San Gabriel. Address the specific division (criminal, civil, small claims) in correspondence.

Civil Records: Access: Mail, online, in person. Only the court performs in person searches; visitors may not. Search fee: $5.00 per name. Required to search: name, years to search. Civil cases indexed by defendant, plaintiff. Civil records on computer back to 1991, index files from 1983. Records destroyed after 10 years. Online access available free at www.lasuperiorcourt.org. Court location, case number required to search. Available for civil, small claims, probate and unlawful detainer records.

Criminal Records: Access: Mail, in person. Only the court performs in person searches; visitors may not. Search fee: $5.00 per name. Required to search: name, years to search, DOB; also helpful: SSN. Criminal records on computer from 1996, index files from 1991. Records destroyed after 10 years.

General Information: No probation records released. SASE required. Turnaround time 2 days. Copy fee: $.57 per page. Certification fee: $6.00. Fee payee: Los Angeles Superior Court. Personal checks accepted. Prepayment is required.

Beverly Hills Superior Court - West District

9355 Burton Way, Beverly Hills, CA 90210; 310-860-0070. Hours: 8:30AM-4:30PM (PST). *Misdemeanor, Civil Actions Under $25,000, Eviction, Small Claims.*

www.lasuperiorcourt.org

Note: Includes cities of Beverly Hills and West Hollywood.

Criminal Records: Access: Phone, mail, in person. Only the court performs in person searches; visitors may not. Search fee: $5.00 per name. Fee is per data bank per year. Required to search: name, years to search, DOB; also helpful: address, SSN, sex, signed release. Criminal records on computer from 1991, index files from 1983. Records destroyed after 10 years.

General Information: No probation, arrest records released. SASE required. Turnaround time 3 days. Copy fee: $.57 per page. Certification fee: $6.00. Court location, case number, and last name are all required to search. Available for civil, small claims, and unlawful detainer records. Fee payee: Los Angeles Superior Court. Personal checks accepted. Credit cards accepted:

Visa, MasterCard, Discover. Visa, Dicover plus user fees. Prepayment is required.

Burbank Superior Court - North Central District

300 E Olive, PO Box 750, Burbank, CA 91503; Civil phone: 818-557-3461; Criminal phone: 818-557-3466. Hours: 8AM-4:30PM (PST). *Misdemeanor, Civil Actions, Eviction, Small Claims.*

www.lasuperiorcourt.org

Civil Records: Access: Mail, online, in person. Both court and visitors may perform in person searches. Search fee: $5.00 per name. Required to search: name, years to search. Civil cases indexed by defendant, plaintiff. Civil records on computer from 1991, index files from 1983. Records destroyed after ten years. Online access available free at www.lasuperiorcourt.org. Court location, case number required to search. Available for civil, small claims, probate and unlawful detainer records.

Criminal Records: Access: Mail, in person. Only the court performs in person searches; visitors may not. Search fee: $5.00 per name. Required to search: name, years to search, DOB. Criminal records on computer from 1991, index files from 1983. Records destroyed after ten years.

General Information: No probation reports released. SASE required. Turnaround time 3-5 days. Copy fee: $.57 per page. Certification fee: $6.00. Fee payee: Los Angeles Superior Court. Personal checks accepted. Prepayment is required.

Citrus Superior Court - East District

1427 W Covina Pky, West Covina, CA 91790; Civil phone: 626-813-3236; Criminal phone: 626-813-3239; Fax: 626-338-7364. Hours: 8AM-4:30PM (PST). *Misdemeanor, Civil Actions Under $25,000, Eviction, Small Claims.*

www.lasuperiorcourt.org

Note: Includes cities of Azusa, Baldwin Park, Covina, Glendora, Industry, Irwindale, Valinda, West Covina and surrounding unincorporated County area.

Civil Records: Access: Mail, online, in person. Both court and visitors may perform in person searches. Search fee: $5.00 per name. Required to search: name, years to search. Civil cases indexed by defendant, plaintiff. Civil records on computer from 1991, index files from 1983. Records destroyed after 10 years. Online access available free at www.lasuperiorcourt.org. Court location, case number required to search. Available for civil, small claims, probate and unlawful detainer records.

Criminal Records: Access: Mail, in person. Both court and visitors may perform in person searches. Search fee: $5.00 per name. Required to search: name, years to search. Criminal records on computer from 1991, index files from 1983. Records destroyed after 10 years. Court may choose not to run lists of names.

General Information: Public access terminal is available. No probation reports released. SASE required. Turnaround time 1 week. Copy fee: $.57 per page. Certification fee: $6.00. Fee payee: Los Angeles Superior Court. Personal checks accepted. Prepayment is required.

Compton Superior Court - South Central District

200 W Compton Blvd, Compton, CA 90220; Civil phone: 310-603-7812/7842; Criminal phone: 310-603-7112; Fax: 310-223-5941. Hours: 8AM-4:30PM (PST). *Felony, Misdemeanor, Civil Actions, Eviction, Small Claims.*

www.lasuperiorcourt.org

Note: Includes cities of Carson, Compton, Lynwood and Paramount and the unincorporated portions of county that surround them. There is a branch in Lynwood (323-357-5200) that handles pretrials only.

Civil Records: Access: Mail, online, in person. Both court and visitors may perform in person searches.

Search fee: $5.00 per name. Fee is per year prior to 1991. Required to search: name, years to search. Civil cases indexed by defendant, plaintiff. Civil records on computer from 1991, index files from 1983. Records destroyed after 10 years. Online access available free at www.lasuperiorcourt.org. Court location, case number required to search. Available for civil, small claims, probate and unlawful detainer records.

Criminal Records: Access: Mail, in person. Only the court performs in person searches; visitors may not. Search fee: $5.00 per name. Required to search: name, years to search, DOB. Criminal records maintained per G.C. 68152(E).

General Information: No complaint records released. SASE required. Turnaround time 2 days. Copy fee: $.57 per page. Certification fee: $6.00. Fee payee: Los Angeles Superior Court-Compton. Personal checks accepted. Credit cards accepted: Visa, MasterCard, Discover. Prepayment is required.

Culver City Superior Court - West District

4130 Overland Ave, Culver City, CA 90230; 310-202-3181; Civil phone: 310-202-3160; Criminal phone: 310-202-3158; Fax: 310-836-8345. Hours: 8:30AM-4:30PM (PST). *Misdemeanor, Civil Actions Under $25,000, Eviction, Small Claims.*

www.lasuperiorcourt.org

Note: Includes Culver City and surrounding unincorporated areas including Angelus Vista, portions of Marina del Rey, View Park and Windsor Hills, all surrounded by the City of Los Angeles, on south bounded by Inglewood.

Civil Records: Access: Mail, online, in person. Only the court performs in person searches; visitors may not. Search fee: $5.00 per name. Required to search: name, years to search. Civil cases indexed by defendant, plaintiff. Civil records on computer from 1987, index files from 1983. Records destroyed after 10 years. Online access available free at www.lasuperiorcourt.org. Court location, case number required to search. Available for civil, small claims, probate and unlawful detainer records.

Criminal Records: Access: Mail, in person. Only the court performs in person searches; visitors may not. Search fee: $5.00 per name. Required to search: name, years to search. Criminal records computerized since 1987. Closed cases over 10 years old are destroyed. Court may choose not to run lists of names.

General Information: No probation reports released. SASE required. Turnaround time 2 days. Copy fee: $.57 per page. Certification fee: $6.00. Fee payee: Los Angeles Superior Court. Personal checks accepted. Prepayment is required.

Downey Superior Court - Southeast District

7500 E Imperial Hwy, Downey, CA 90242; Civil phone: 562-803-7052; Criminal phone: 562-803-7049. Hours: 8:30AM-4:30PM T-F; 8:30AM-6PM M (PST). *Misdemeanor, Civil Actions Under $25,000, Eviction, Small Claims.*

www.lasuperiorcourt.org

Note: Comprises the cities of Downey, Norwalk and La Mirada.

Civil Records: Access: Mail, online, in person. Both court and visitors may perform in person searches. Search fee: $5.00 per name. Required to search: name, years to search. Civil cases indexed by defendant, plaintiff. Civil records on microfiche from 1964, archived and index file from 1800s. Online access available free at www.lasuperiorcourt.org. Court location, case number required to search. Available for civil, small claims, probate and unlawful detainer records.

Criminal Records: Access: Mail, in person. Only the court performs in person searches; visitors may not. Search fee: $5.00 per name. Required to search: name, years to search; also helpful: DOB. Criminal records on computer from 1989, on microfiche, archived, and index files. Court may choose not to run lists of names.

General Information: No adoptions, juvenile, medical, probation or sealed records released. SASE required. Turnaround time 5 days. Copy fee: $.57 per page. Certification fee: $6.00. Fee payee: Los Angeles Superior Court. Personal checks accepted. Credit cards accepted: Discover. Prepayment is required.

East Los Angeles Superior Court - Central District

214 S Fetterly Ave, Los Angeles, CA 90022; Civil phone: 323-780-2017; Criminal phone: 323-780-2025. Hours: 8AM-4:30PM (PST). *Misdemeanor, Civil Actions Under $25,000, Eviction, Small Claims.*

www.lasuperiorcourt.org

Note: Includes cities of Montebello and Commerce and adjacent unincorporated territory bordering Monterey Park on the north and Los Angeles on the west.

Civil Records: Access: Mail, online, in person. Only the court performs in person searches; visitors may not. Search fee: $5.00 per name. Required to search: name, years to search. Civil cases indexed by defendant, plaintiff. Civil records on computer from 1991, index files from 1983. Records destroyed after 10 years. Online access available free at www.lasuperiorcourt.org. Court location, case number required to search. Available for civil, small claims, probate and unlawful detainer records.

Criminal Records: Access: Mail, in person. Only the court performs in person searches; visitors may not. Search fee: $5.00 per name. Required to search: name, years to search, DOB; also helpful: SSN. Criminal records on computer from 1991, index files from 1983. Records destroyed after 10 years.

General Information: No probation reports released. SASE required. Turnaround time 2 days. Copy fee: $.57 per page. Certification fee: $6.00. Fee payee: Superior Court of East Los Angeles. Personal checks accepted. Credit cards accepted: Discover. Prepayment is required.

Glendale Superior Court - NorthCentral District

Los Angeles Superior Court, 600 E Broadway, Glendale, CA 91206; 818-500-5840; Civil phone: 818-500-3538; Criminal phone: 818-500-3541; Fax: 818-548-0486 Civ; 0236 Crim. Hours: 8:30AM-4:30PM (PST). *Misdemeanor, Civil Actions Under $25,000, Eviction, Small Claims.*

www.lasuperiorcourt.org

Note: Includes cities of Glendale, LaCanada-Flintridge and unincorporated county are known as Montrose, La Crescenta, Verdugo City, Highway Highlands, and Kogel Canyon.

Civil Records: Access: Mail, online, in person. Only the court performs in person searches; visitors may not. Search fee: $5.00 per name. Required to search: name, years to search. Civil cases indexed by defendant, plaintiff. Civil records on computer from 1990, small claims from 07/92, index files from 1983. Records destroyed after 10 years. Online access available free at www.lasuperiorcourt.org. Court location, case number required to search. Available for civil, small claims, probate and unlawful detainer records.

Criminal Records: Access: Mail, in person. Only the court performs in person searches; visitors may not. Search fee: $5.00 per name. Required to search: name, years to search. Criminal records on computer from 1990, microfilm past 10 years.

General Information: No probation reports, police reports, CII records released. SASE required. Turnaround time 2 days. Copy fee: $.57 per page. Certification fee: $6.00. Fee payee: Los Angeles Superior Court. Personal checks accepted. Credit cards accepted: Visa, MasterCard. Prepayment is required.

Hollywood Superior Court - Central District

5925 Hollywood Blvd, Los Angeles, CA 90028; 323-856-5747. Hours: 8:30AM-4:30PM (PST). *Misdemeanor.*

www.lasuperiorcourt.org

Note: High-grade and low-grade Misdemeanors for the Hollywood area.

Criminal Records: Access: Mail, in person. Only the court performs in person searches; visitors may not. Search fee: $5.00 per name. Required to search: name, years to search, DOB. Criminal records on computer go back 10 years, prior on books.

General Information: No probation, driver's license, medical, arrest report or confidential reports released. SASE required. Turnaround time 2-3 days. Copy fee: $.57 per page. Certification fee: $6.00. Fee payee: Los Angeles Superior Court. Personal checks accepted. Credit cards accepted. Prepayment is required.

Huntington Park Superior Court - Southeast District

6548 Miles Ave, Huntington Park, CA 90255; Civil phone: 323-586-6365; Criminal phone: 323-586-6362; Fax: 323-589-6769. Hours: 8AM-4:30PM (PST). *Misdemeanor, Civil Actions Under $25,000, Eviction, Small Claims.*

www.lasuperiorcourt.org

Note: Includes cities of Bell, Bell Gardens, Cudahy, Huntington Park, Maywood and Vernon.

Civil Records: Access: Mail, online, in person. Only the court performs in person searches; visitors may not. Search fee: $5.00 per name. Required to search: name, years to search. Civil cases indexed by defendant, plaintiff. Civil records on computer from 1991, index files from 1983. Records destroyed after 10 years. Online access available free at www.lasuperiorcourt.org. Court location, case number required to search. Available for civil, small claims, probate and unlawful detainer records.

Criminal Records: Access: Phone, mail, in person. Only the court performs in person searches; visitors may not. Search fee: $5.00 per name. Required to search: name, years to search; also helpful: DOB. Criminal records on computer from 1991, index files from 1983. Records destroyed after 10 years.

General Information: No probation reports released. SASE required. Turnaround time 2 days. Copy fee: $.57 per page. Certification fee: $6.00. Fee payee: Los Angeles Superior Court. Personal checks accepted. Credit cards accepted: Visa, MasterCard, Discover. Prepayment is required.

Inglewood Superior Court - Southwest District

1 Regent St, Inglewood, CA 90301; 310-419-5132; Civil phone: 310-419-5125; Criminal phone: 310-419-5128; Fax: 310-674-4862. Hours: 8AM-4:30PM (PST). *Misdemeanor, Civil Actions Under $25,000, Eviction, Small Claims.*

www.lasuperiorcourt.org

Note: Includes cities of Inglewood, Hawthorne, El Segundo, Lennox and adjoining unincorporated area.

Civil Records: Access: Mail, online, in person. Only the court performs in person searches; visitors may not. Search fee: $5.00 per name. Required to search: name, years to search. Civil cases indexed by defendant, plaintiff. Civil records on computer from 1991, index files from 1983. Records destroyed after 10 years. Online access available free at www.lasuperiorcourt.org. Court location, case number required to search. Available for civil, small claims, probate and unlawful detainer records.

Criminal Records: Access: Mail, in person. Only the court performs in person searches; visitors may not. Search fee: $5.00 per name. Required to search: name, years to search; also helpful: DOB. Criminal records on computer from 1991, index files from 1983. Records destroyed after 10 years.

General Information: No probation reports released. SASE required. Turnaround time 2 days. Copy fee: $.57 per page. Certification fee: $6.00. Fee payee: Los Angeles Superior Court. Personal checks accepted. Credit cards accepted: Visa, MasterCard, Discover, AmEx. Visa, Discover. Prepayment is required.

Lancaster Superior Court - North District

1040 W Ave J, #107, Lancaster, CA 93534; 661-945-6355. 8AM-4:30PM (PST). *Felony, Misdemeanor.*

www.lasuperiorcourt.org

Note: Formerly Antelope; includes Lancaster, City of Palmdale, and unincorporated County territory including Acton, Agua Dulce, Fairmont, Lake Hughes, Llano, Leona Valley, Littlerock, Pearblossom, Quartz Hill, Roosevelt, Green Valley Big Pines, Lake Elizabeth

Criminal Records: Access: Mail, in person. Only the court performs in person searches; visitors may not. Search fee: $5.00 per name. Required to search: name, years to search; also helpful: case number. Criminal records on computer since 1989, index books since 1983. Records destroyed after 10 years. Court may choose not to run lists of names.

General Information: No probation reports released. SASE required. Turnaround time 2 days. Copy fee: $.57 per page. Certification fee: $6.00. Fee payee: Los Angeles Superior Court. Personal checks accepted. Checks accepted (must be pre-imprinted). Prepayment is required.

Long Beach Superior Court - South District

415 W Ocean Blvd, Long Beach, CA 90801; 562-491-6201; Civil phone: 562-491-6234; Criminal phone: 562-491-6226; Fax: 562-437-0147 (Criminal). Hours: 8:30AM-4:30PM (PST). *Misdemeanor, Civil Actions Under $25,000, Eviction, Small Claims.*

www.lasuperiorcourt.org

Note: Includes cities of Long Beach and Signal Hill and adjoining unincorporated area. Address requests to civil or criminal division.

Civil Records: Access: Mail, online, in person. Both court and visitors may perform in person searches. Search fee: $5.00 per name. Required to search: name, years to search. Civil cases indexed by defendant, plaintiff. Civil records on computer from 1991, index files from 1983. Records destroyed after 10 years. Online access available free at www.lasuperiorcourt.org. Court location, case number required to search. Available for civil, small claims, probate and unlawful detainer records.

Criminal Records: Access: Mail, in person. Both court and visitors may perform in person searches. Search fee: $5.00 per name. Required to search: name, years to search, DOB. Criminal records on computer from 1991, index files from 1983. Records destroyed after 10 years.

General Information: No probation reports released. SASE required. Turnaround time 2 days. Copy fee: $.57 per page. Certification fee: $6.00. Fee payee: Los Angeles Superior Court. Personal checks accepted. Credit cards accepted: Discover. Accepted in person only. Prepayment is required.

Los Angeles Superior Court - Central District - Misdemeanor

210 W Temple St Rm 5-305, Los Angeles, CA 90012; 213-974-6151. Hours: 8:30AM-4:30PM (PST). *Misdemeanor.*

www.lasuperiorcourt.org

Note: Includes incorporated City of Los Angeles excluding communities of San Pedro, West Los Angeles, Hollywood and San Fernando Valley

Criminal Records: Access: Phone, mail, in person. Only the court performs in person searches; however, visitors may search michrofiche index free. Search fee: $5.00 per name. Required to search: name, years to search; also helpful: address, DOB. Criminal records are kept back to 1985. Search request phone: 213-974-6141.

General Information: No probation reports released. SASE required. Turnaround time 24 hours to 1 week. Copy fee: $.57 per page. Certification fee: $6.00. Fee payee: Los Angeles Superior Court. Personal checks accepted. Credit cards accepted: Visa, MasterCard. Accepted in person only. Prepayment is required.

Los Cerritos (Bellflower) Superior Court - Southeast District
10025 E Flower St, Bellflower, CA 90706; 562-804-8025; Civil phone: 562-804-8009; Criminal phone: 562-804-8018. Hours: 8AM-4:30PM (PST). *Misdemeanor, Civil Actions Under $25,000, Eviction, Small Claims.*

www.lasuperiorcourt.org/Locations/LosCerritos.htm

Note: Includes Artesia, Bellflower, Hawaiian Gardens, Lakewood and Cerritos. Specify civil or criminal search request. Small claims phone is 562-804-8011.

Civil Records: Access: Mail, online, in person. Only the court performs in person searches; visitors may not. Search fee: $5.00 per name. Required to search: name, years to search. Civil cases indexed by defendant, plaintiff. Civil records on computer from 1991, index files from 1983. Records destroyed after 10 years. Online access available free at www.lasuperiorcourt.org. Court location, case number required to search. Available for civil, small claims, probate and unlawful detainer records. Always specify that it is a "civil records" search request.

Criminal Records: Access: Mail, in person. Only the court performs in person searches; visitors may not. Search fee: $5.00 per name. Required to search: name, years to search, DOB; also helpful: SSN, sex. Criminal records on computer from 1991, index files from 1983. Records destroyed after 10 years. Always specify that it is a "criminal records" search request.

General Information: No probation reports released. SASE required. Turnaround time 2-3 days. Copy fee: $.57 per page. Certification fee: $6.00. Fee payee: Los Angeles Superior Court. Personal checks accepted. Credit cards accepted: Visa, MasterCard, Discover. Prepayment is required.

Malibu Superior Court - West District
23525 W Civic Center Way, Malibu, CA 90265; 310-317-1312; Fax: 310-456-7415. Hours: 8AM-4:30PM (PST). *Misdemeanor, Civil Actions Under $25,000, Eviction, Small Claims.*

www.lasuperiorcourt.org

Note: Includes Malibu, Agoura Hills, Calabasas, Westlake Village, Hidden Hills and unincorporated areas known as Topanga and Chatsworth Lake, bounded by Ventura County on the west and north, Pacific Ocean on the south and City of Los Angeles on the east.

Civil Records: Access: Mail, online, in person. Only the court performs in person searches; visitors may not. Search fee: $5.00 per name. Required to search: name, years to search. Civil cases indexed by defendant, plaintiff. Civil records on computer from 1991, index files from 1983. Records destroyed after 10 years. Online access available free at www.lasuperiorcourt.org. Court location, case number required to search. Available for civil, small claims, probate and unlawful detainer records.

Criminal Records: Access: Mail, in person. Only the court performs in person searches; visitors may not. Search fee: $5.00 per name. Required to search: name, years to search; also helpful: DOB. Criminal records on computer from 1991, index files from 1983. Records destroyed after 10 years.

General Information: No probation reports released. SASE required. Turnaround time 1-5 days. Copy fee: $.57 per page. Certification fee: $6.00. Court location, case number, and last name are all required to search. Available for civil, small claims, and unlawful detainer records. Fee payee: Los Angeles Superior Court. Personal checks accepted. Prepayment is required.

Metropolitan Los Angeles Superior Court - Central District
1945 S Hill St Rm 200, Los Angeles, CA 90007; 213-744-1884; Fax: 213-744-1879. Hours: 8AM-4:30PM (PST). *Misdemeanor.*

www.lasuperiorcourt.org

Note: Vehicle Code misdemeanor and traffic citations for the incorporated City of Los Angeles excluding the areas known as San Pedro, West Los Angeles and communities of San Fernando Valley and the unincorporated County area more commonly known as Florence

Criminal Records: Access: Phone, mail, in person. Only the court performs in person searches; visitors may not. Search fee: $5.00 per name. Required to search: name, years to search, DOB. Criminal records on computer from 1991, index files from 1983. Records destroyed after 10 years.

General Information: No probation, driver's license, medical, arrest report or confidential reports released. SASE required. Turnaround time 2-3 days. Copy fee: $.57 per page. Certification fee: $6.00. Fee payee: Los Angeles Superior Court. Personal checks accepted. Credit cards accepted. Prepayment is required.

Norwalk Superior Court - Southeast District
12720 Norwalk Blvd, Norwalk, CA 90650; 562-807-7340. Hours: 8:30AM-4PM (PST). *Felony, Civil Actions Over $25,000, Probate.*

www.lasuperiorcourt.org

Civil Records: Access: Mail, online, in person. Only the court performs in person searches; visitors may only use public access terminal only to find case numbers. Search fee: $5.00 per name. Required to search: name, years to search. Civil cases indexed by defendant, plaintiff. Civil records on computer from 1991, index files from 1983. Online access available free at www.lasuperiorcourt.org. Court location, case number required to search. Available for civil, small claims, probate and unlawful detainer records.

Criminal Records: Access: Mail, in person. Only the court performs in person searches; visitors may only use public access terminal only to find case numbers. Search fee: $5.00 per name. Required to search: name, years to search, DOB; also helpful: SSN, sex. Criminal records on computer from 1991, index files from 1983.

General Information: Public access terminal is available. (Public access terminal to find case number only.) No probation reports released. SASE required. Turnaround time 2-10 days. Copy fee: $.57 per page. Certification fee: $6.00. Fee payee: Los Angeles Superior Court. Personal checks accepted. Credit cards accepted. Prepayment is required.

Palmdale Superior Court - North District
38256 Sierra Highway, Palmdale, CA 93550; 661-537-2714. Hours: 8AM-4:30PM (PST). *Civil Actions, Eviction, Small Claims, Probate.*

www.lasuperiorcourt.org

Note: Includes City of Lancaster, City of Palmdale, and unincorporated County territory including Acton, Agua Dulce, Fairmont, Lake Hughes, Llano, Leona Valley, Littlerock, Pearblossom, Quartz Hill, Roosevelt, Green Valley Big Pines, Lake Elizabeth

Civil Records: Access: Phone, mail, online, in person. Only the court performs in person searches; visitors may not. Search fee: $5.00 per name. Required to search: name, years to search. Civil cases indexed by defendant, plaintiff. Civil records on computer since 1989, index books since 1983. Records destroyed after 10 years. Online access available free at www.lasuperiorcourt.org. Court location, case number required to search. Available for civil, small claims, probate and unlawful detainer records.

General Information: No probation reports released. SASE required. Turnaround time 2-10 days. Copy fee: $.57 per page. Certification fee: $6.00. Fee payee: Los

Angeles Superior Court. Personal checks accepted. Prepayment is required.

Pasadena Superior Court - Northeast District
300 E Walnut, Pasadena, CA 91101; Civil phone: 626-356-5695; Criminal phone: 626-356-5254; Fax: 626-568-3903. Hours: 8:30AM-4:30PM (PST). *Misdemeanor, Civil Actions Under $25,000, Eviction, Small Claims.*

www.lasuperiorcourt.org

Note: Includes cities of Pasadena, South Pasadena, San Marino, Sierra Madre and the area of Altadena and East Pasadena.

Civil Records: Access: Mail, online, in person. Both court and visitors may perform in person searches. Search fee: $5.00 per name. Required to search: name, years to search. Civil cases indexed by defendant, plaintiff. Civil records on computer from 1991, index files from 1983. Records destroyed after 10 years. Online access available free at www.lasuperiorcourt.org. Court location, case number required to search. Available for civil, small claims, probate and unlawful detainer records.

Criminal Records: Access: Mail, in person. Only the court performs in person searches; visitors may not. Search fee: $5.00 per name. Required to search: name, years to search. Criminal records on computer from 1991, index files from 1983. Records destroyed after 10 years.

General Information: No probation reports released. SASE required. Turnaround time 2 days. Copy fee: $.57 per page. Certification fee: $6.00. Fee payee: Los Angeles Superior Court. Personal checks accepted. Prepayment is required.

Pomona Superior Court - East District
350 W Mission Blvd, Pomona, CA 91766; 909-620-3201; Fax: 909-865-6767. Hours: 8AM-4:30PM; Phone Hours: 8AM-Noon, 2-4PM (PST). *Misdemeanor, Civil Actions Under $25,000, Eviction, Small Claims.*

www.lasuperiorcourt.org

Note: Includes cities of Pomona, Claremont, La Verne, Walnut, San Dimas and unincorporated area including Diamond Bar. Also, 909-802-9944 is good phone number.

Civil Records: Access: Fax, mail, online, in person. Both court and visitors may perform in person searches. Search fee: $5.00 per name. Required to search: name, years to search. Civil cases indexed by defendant, plaintiff. Civil records on computer from 1990, index files from 1983. Records destroyed after 10 years. Online access available free at www.lasuperiorcourt.org. Court location, case number required to search. Available for civil, small claims, probate and unlawful detainer records.

Criminal Records: Access: Mail, in person. Only the court performs in person searches; visitors may not. Search fee: $5.00 per name. Required to search: name, years to search, DOB. Criminal records on computer from 1990, index files from 1983. Records destroyed after 10 years. Drop box available.

General Information: No probation, mental health or police reports released. SASE required. Turnaround time 2-4 days. Copy fee: $.57 per page. Certification fee: $6.00. Court location, case number, and last name are all required to search. Available for civil, small claims, and unlawful detainer records. Fee payee: Los Angeles Superior Court. Personal checks accepted. Prepayment is required.

Redondo Beach Superior Court - Southwest District
117 W Torrance Blvd, Redondo Beach, CA 90277-3638; 310-798-6875; Fax: 310-376-4051. Hours: 8:15AM-4:30PM (PST). *Civil Actions Under $25,000, Eviction, Small Claims.*

www.lasuperiorcourt.org

Note: Also known as the Southwest District South Bay Court - Beach Cities Branch

Civil Records: Access: Mail, online, in person. Only the court performs in person searches; visitors may not. Search fee: $5.00 per name. Required to search: name, years to search. Civil cases indexed by defendant, plaintiff. Civil records on computer from 1991, index files from 1983. Records destroyed after 10 years. Online access available free at www.lasuperiorcourt.org. Court location, case number required to search. Available for civil, small claims, probate and unlawful detainer records.

General Information: Unlawful detainers held for 60 days. SASE required. Turnaround time 3-4 days. Copy fee: $.57 for first page, $.20 each add'l. Certification fee: $6.00. Fee payee: Los Angeles Superior Court. Personal checks accepted. Prepayment is required.

Rio Hondo Superior Court - East District

11234 E Valley Blvd, El Monte, CA 91731; Civil phone: 626-575-4117; Criminal phone: 626-575-4121; Fax: 626-444-9029. Hours: 8AM-4:30PM (PST). *Misdemeanor, Civil Actions Under $25,000, Eviction, Small Claims.*

www.lasuperiorcourt.org

Note: Includes cities of El Monte, South El Monte, La Puente, Rosemead and adjacent unincorporated county area.

Civil Records: Access: Mail, online, in person. Only the court performs in person searches; visitors may not. No search fee. Required to search: name, years to search. Civil cases indexed by defendant, plaintiff. Civil records on computer since 1989, microfiche since 1980. Records destroyed after 10 years. Online access available free at www.lasuperiorcourt.org. Court location, case number required to search. Available for civil, small claims, probate and unlawful detainer records.

Criminal Records: Access: Phone, mail, in person. Only the court performs in person searches; visitors may not. Search fee: $5.00 per name. Required to search: name, years to search; also helpful: DOB. Criminal records on computer since 1985, microfiche since 1980.

General Information: Will not release unlawful detainer for 60 days. No probation reports, medical records, search warrants, rap sheet, CLETS report, transcripts or sealed records released. SASE required. Turnaround time 5 days. Copy fee: $.57 per page. Certification fee: $6.00. Fee payee: Los Angeles Superior Court. Personal checks accepted. Two-party checks not accepted. Write "not to exceed $x.xx" on check.

San Fernando Superior Court - North Valley District

900 Third St, #1137, San Fernando, CA 91340; 818-898-2401. Hours: 8AM-4:30PM (PST). *Misdemeanor, Small Claims.*

www.lasuperiorcourt.org

Note: Includes Granada Hills, Northridge, Chatsworth, Sunland, Tujunga, Pacoima, Mission Hills, Sylmar, Arleta, Lake View Terrace, Sun Valley and City of San Fernando. They merged with the Newhall Court to form the North Valley District Court

Criminal Records: Access: Mail, online, in person. Only the court performs in person searches; visitors may not. Search fee: $5.00 per name. Required to search: name, years to search; also helpful: DOB. Criminal records on computer from 1988. Records destroyed after 10 years. Limited criminal records are available online.

General Information: No probation reports or arrest reports released. SASE required. Turnaround time 2 days. Copy fee: $.57 per page. Certification fee: $6.00. Fee payee: Los Angeles Superior Court. Personal checks accepted. Checks accepted (no 3 party checks). Credit cards accepted. Prepayment is required.

San Pedro Superior Court - South District

505 S Centre St Rm 202, San Pedro, CA 90731; 310-519-6014 Sm Claims; 519-6016 Traffic; Civil phone: 310-519-6015; Criminal phone: 310-519-6018. Hours: 8:30AM-4:30PM (civ, sm claims & criminal); 8AM-4:30PM (traffic) (PST). *Misdemeanor, Civil Actions Under $25,000, Eviction, Small Claims.*

www.lasuperiorcourt.org

Note: Includes San Pedro, Wilmington and a county strip in Torrance extending up to Western Avenue. Holds records for Catalina Branch.

Civil Records: Access: Mail, online, in person. Only the court performs in person searches; visitors may not. Search fee: $5.00 per name. Required to search: name, years to search. Civil cases indexed by defendant, plaintiff. Civil records on computer go back 10 years; on index files from 1984. Records destroyed after 10 years. Online access available for free at www.lasuperiorcourt.org. Court location, case number required to search. Available for civil, small claims, probate and unlawful detainer records.

Criminal Records: Access: Mail, in person. Only the court performs in person searches; visitors may not. Search fee: $5.00 per name. Required to search: name, years to search, DOB. Criminal records on computer go back 10 years; on index files from 1984. Records destroyed after 10 years.

General Information: No probation, arrest, records released. SASE required. Turnaround time 2 days. Copy fee: $.57 per page. Certification fee: $6.00. Fee payee: Los Angeles Superior Court. Personal checks accepted. Credit cards accepted: Visa. Visa-additional 6% fee charged. Prepayment is required.

Santa Anita Superior Court - Northeast District

300 W Maple Ave, Monrovia, CA 91016; 626-301-4056; Civil phone: 626-301-4050; Criminal phone: 626-301-4051; Fax: 626-357-7825. Hours: 8AM-4:30PM (PST). *Misdemeanor, Civil Actions Under $25,000, Eviction, Small Claims.*

www.lasuperiorcourt.org

Note: Includes cities of Monrovia, Arcadia, Duarte, Bradbury and unincorporated county territory in surrounding area.

Civil Records: Access: Mail, online, in person. Only the court performs in person searches; visitors may not. Search fee: $5.00 per name. Required to search: name, years to search. Civil cases indexed by defendant, plaintiff. Civil records on computer from 1991, ion microfiche from 1983. Records destroyed after 10 years. Online access available free at www.lasuperiorcourt.org. Court location, case number required to search. Available for civil, small claims, probate and unlawful detainer records.

Criminal Records: Access: Mail, in person. Only the court performs in person searches; visitors may not. Search fee: $5.00 per name. Required to search: name, years to search; also helpful: DOB. Criminal records on computer from 1991, index files from 1983. Records destroyed after 10 years.

General Information: Will not release unlawful detainers less than 60 days old. No sealed, criminal history information, arrest reports or any documents containing witness information records released. SASE required. Turnaround time 2 days. Copy fee: $.57 per page. Certification fee: $6.00. Fee payee: Los Angeles Superior Court. Personal checks accepted. Credit cards accepted: Visa, MasterCard, Discover. Prepayment is required.

Santa Clarita Superior Court - North Valley District

23747 W Valencia Blvd, Valencia, CA 91355; 661-253-7316; Civil phone: 661-253-7313; Criminal phone: 661-253-7384; Fax: 661-254-4107. Hours: 8:30AM-4:30PM (PST). *Misdemeanor, Civil Actions Under $25,000, Eviction, Small Claims.*

www.lasuperiorcourt.org

Note: Formerly known as Newhall Sup. Court, it includes Saugus, Valencia, Santa Clarita and unincorporated area bound by Ventura County line (west), Kern County line (north), Agua Dulce on the east, and Glendale and Los Angeles city limits (south).

Civil Records: Access: Mail, online, in person. Only the court performs in person searches; visitors may not. Search fee: $5.00 per name. There is no fee to view records on microfiche or for first 3 records searched in person. Required to search: name, years to search. Civil cases indexed by defendant, plaintiff. Civil records on computer from 1991, index files from 1983. Records destroyed after 10 years, many records on microfiche. Online access available for free at www.lasuperiorcourt.org. Court location, case number required to search. Available for civil, small claims, probate and unlawful detainer records. Call first for permission to fax request.

Criminal Records: Access: Mail, in person. Only the court performs in person searches; visitors may not. Search fee: $5.00 per name. Required to search: name, years to search; also helpful: DOB, SSN. Criminal records on computer from 1991, index files from 1983. Records destroyed after 10 years, many records on microfiche.

General Information: No probation, or police reports w/out court approval released. SASE required. Turnaround time 7-10 days. Copy fee: $.57 per page. Certification fee: $6.00. Court location, case number, and last name are all required to search. Available for civil, small claims, and unlawful detainer records. Fee payee: Los Angeles Superior Court. Personal checks accepted. Prepayment is required.

Santa Monica Superior Court - West District

1725 Main St Rm 224, Santa Monica, CA 90401; Civil phone: 310-260-3706; Criminal phone: 310-260-3517. Hours: 8:30AM-4:30PM (PST). *Misdemeanor, Civil Actions Under $25,000, Eviction, Small Claims.*

www.lasuperiorcourt.org

Note: Includes City of Santa Monica and the unincorporated territory of the Veteran's Administration facilities located at West Los Angeles.

Civil Records: Access: Mail, online, in person. Both court and visitors may perform in person searches. Search fee: $5.00 per name. Required to search: name, years to search. Civil cases indexed by defendant, plaintiff. Civil records on computer from 1991, index files from 1983. Records destroyed after 10 years. Online access available for free at www.lasuperiorcourt.org. Court location, case number required to search. Available for civil, small claims, probate and unlawful detainer records.

Criminal Records: Access: Mail, in person. Only the court performs in person searches; visitors may not. Search fee: $5.00 per name. Required to search: name, years to search. Criminal records on computer from 1991, index files from 1983. Records destroyed after 10 years.

General Information: No probation reports or unlawful detainer records released. SASE required. Turnaround time 1-2 days. Copy fee: $.57 per page. Certification fee: $6.00. Fee payee: Los Angeles Superior Court. Personal checks accepted. Prepayment is required.

South Gate Superior Court - Southeast District

8640 California Ave, South Gate, CA 90280; Civil phone: 323-563-4037; Criminal phone: 323-563-4012; Fax: 323-569-4840. Hours: 8AM-4PM T-F; 8AM-7PM M traffic (PST). *Misdemeanor, Civil Actions Under $25,000, Eviction, Small Claims.*

www.lasuperiorcourt.org

Note: Includes city of South Gate, Hollydale and unincorporated area of Walnut Park.

Civil Records: Access: Mail, online, in person. Only the court performs in person searches; visitors may not. Search fee: $5.00 per name. Required to search: name, years to search. Civil cases indexed by defendant, plaintiff. Civil records on computer from 1991, index files from 1983. Records destroyed after 10 years. Online access available for free at www.lasuperiorcourt.org. Court location, case number required to search. Available for civil, small claims, probate and unlawful detainer records.

Criminal Records: Access: Mail, in person. Only the court performs in person searches; visitors may not. Search fee: $5.00 per name. Required to search: name, years to search. Criminal records on computer from 1991, index files from 1983. Records destroyed after 10 years.

General Information: No probation reports released. SASE required. Turnaround time 2 days. Copy fee: $.57 per page. Certification fee: $6.00. Fee payee: Los Angeles Superior Court. Personal checks accepted. Credit cards accepted: Visa, MasterCard, Discover. Prepayment is required.

Torrance Superior Court - Southwest District 825 Maple Ave, Torrance, CA 90503-5058; 310-222-6501; Civil phone: 310-222-6400; Criminal phone: 310-222-6505; Fax: 310-222-7277. Hours: 8:30AM-4PM (PST). *Misdemeanor, Traffic, Eviction, Small Claims.*

www.lasuperiorcourt.org

Note: Includes cities of Torrance, Gardena, Rolling Hills, Rolling Hills Estates, Manhattan Beach, Lomita, Redondo Beach, Hermosa Beach, Palos Verdes Estates, Rancho Palos Verdes and Lawndale.

Civil Records: Access: Mail, online, in person. Only the court performs in person searches; visitors may not. Search fee: $5.00 per name. Required to search: name, years to search. Civil cases indexed by defendant, plaintiff. Civil records on computer from 1991, index files from 1983. Records destroyed after 10 years. Online access available for free at www.lasuperiorcourt.org. Court location, case number required to search. Available for civil, small claims, probate and unlawful detainer records.

Criminal Records: Access: Mail, in person. Only the court performs in person searches; visitors may not. Search fee: $5.00 per name. Required to search: name, years to search, DOB. Criminal records on computer from 1991, index files from 1983. Records destroyed after 10 years.

General Information: No probation reports, medical or psychiatric reports, criminal history rap sheets released. SASE required. Turnaround time 5 days. Copy fee: $.57 per page. Certification fee: $6.00. Fee payee: Los Angeles Superior Court. Personal checks accepted. Prepayment is required.

Van Nuys Superior Court - Northwest District - Civil 6230 Sylmar St, Van Nuys, CA 91401; 818-374-3060. Hours: 8:30AM-4:30PM (PST). *Civil Actions, Eviction, Small Claims, Family Law.*

www.lasuperiorcourt.org

Note: Small Claims and Civil for that part of city known as Sherman Oaks, Van Nuys, Reseda, North Hollywood, Woodland Hills, Canoga Park, Tarzana, Proter Ranch, Winnetka and Panorama City

Civil Records: Access: Mail, online, in person. Both court and visitors may perform in person searches. Search fee: $5.00 per name. Required to search: name, years to search. Civil cases indexed by defendant, plaintiff. Civil records on computer from 1991, index files from 1983. Records destroyed after 10 years. Online access available for free at www.lasuperiorcourt.org. Court location, case number

required to search. Available for civil, small claims, probate and unlawful detainer records.

General Information: No probation reports or arrest reports released. SASE required. Turnaround time 2-3 days. Copy fee: $.57 per page. Certification fee: $6.00. Fee payee: Los Angeles Superior Court or LASC. Personal checks and credit cards accepted. Prepayment is required.

Van Nuys Superior Court - Northwest District - Criminal 14400 Erwin St Mall 2nd Fl, Van Nuys, CA 91401; 818-374-2628. Hours: 8:30AM-4:30PM (PST). *Misdemeanor, felony.*

www.lasuperiorcourt.org

Note: Misdemeanors for that part of city known as Sherman Oaks, Van Nuys, Reseda, North Hollywood, Woodland Hills, Canoga Park, Tarzana, Proter Ranch, Winnetka and Panorama City

Criminal Records: Access: Phone, mail, in person. Only the court performs in person searches; visitors may not. Search fee: $5.00 per name. Required to search: name, years to search, sex; also helpful: DOB. Criminal records on computer from 1991, index files from 1983. Records destroyed after 10 years.

General Information: No probation reports or arrest reports released. SASE required. Turnaround time 2-3 days. Copy fee: $.57 per page. Certification fee: $6.00. Fee payee: Los Angeles Superior Court. Personal checks accepted. Prepayment is required.

West Los Angeles Superior Court - West District 1633 Purdue Ave, Los Angeles, CA 90025; 310-914-7477; Fax: 310-312-2902. Hours: 8:30AM-4:30PM (PST). *Civil Actions Under $25,000, Eviction, Small Claims.*

www.lasuperiorcourt.org

Note: Includes the areas of Palms, Mar Vista, Rancho Park, Marina del Rey, Venice, Playa del Rey and Sawtelle. Holds records for the former Robertson branch. Criminal felony and misdemeanors are at the new Airport Court.

Civil Records: Access: Phone, mail, online, in person. Only the court performs in person searches; visitors may not. Search fee: $5.00 per name. Required to search: name, years to search. Civil cases indexed by defendant, plaintiff. Online access available free at www.lasuperiorcourt.org. Court location, case number required to search. Available for civil, small claims, probate and unlawful detainer records.

Criminal Records: Access: Mail, in person. Search fee: $5.00 per name. Required to search: name, years to search; also helpful: DOB. Felony and misdemeanor records have been moved to the Airport Court.

General Information: SASE required. Turnaround time 1-5 days. Copy fee: $.57 per page. Certification fee: $6.00. Fee payee: Los Angeles Superior Court. Personal checks accepted. Prepayment is required.

Whittier Superior Court - Southeast District 7339 S Painter Ave, Whittier, CA 90602; Civil phone: 562-907-3127; Criminal phone: 562-907-3113. Hours: 8AM-4:30PM (PST). *Misdemeanor, Civil Actions Under $25,000, Eviction, Small Claims.*

www.lasuperiorcourt.org

Note: Includes cities of Whittier, Santa Fe Springs, Pico Rivera, La Habra Heights plus unincorporated territory in the Whittier area including areas designated as Los Nietos and South Whittier.

Civil Records: Access: Mail, online, in person. Both court and visitors may perform in person searches. No search fee. Required to search: name, years to search. Civil cases indexed by defendant, plaintiff. Civil records on computer from 1991, index files from 1983. Records destroyed after 10 years. Online access available free at www.lasuperiorcourt.org. Court location, case number

required to search. Available for civil, small claims, probate and unlawful detainer records.

Criminal Records: Access: Mail, in person. Only the court performs in person searches; visitors may not. Search fee: $5.00 per name. Required to search: name, years to search; also helpful: DOB. Criminal records computerized since 1987.

General Information: No probation reports released. SASE required. Turnaround time 2 days. Copy fee: $.57 per page. Certification fee: $6.00. Fee payee: Los Angeles Superior Court. Personal checks accepted. Credit cards accepted: Visa, MasterCard, Discover. Prepayment is required.

Madera County

Superior Court 209 W Yosemite Ave, Madera, CA 93637; 559-675-7995; Civil phone: 559-675-7996; Criminal phone: 559-675-7334; Fax: 559-675-0701. Hours: 8AM-5PM (PST). *Felony, Civil, Probate, Eviction.*

Note: The Superior and Municipal courts located in the city of Madera have combined into a consolidated court. There is no countywide database of records; each court must be searched.

Civil Records: Access: Mail, fax, in person. Both court and visitors may perform in person searches. Search fee: $5.00 per name. There is no fee if searcher comes to court and does search. Required to search: name, years to search. Civil cases indexed by defendant, plaintiff. Civil records on microfiche, archived and index file from 1893.

Criminal Records: Access: Mail, fax, in person. Both court and visitors may perform in person searches. Search fee: $5.00 per name. There is no fee if searcher comes to court and does search. Required to search: name, years to search; also helpful: DOB, signed release. Criminal records on microfiche, archived and index file from 1893.

General Information: No adoptions, juvenile, medical, probation or sealed records released. SASE required. Turnaround time 2 days. Copy fee: $.50 per page. Certification fee: $6.00. Fee payee: Madera Superior Court. Personal checks accepted. Prepayment is required.

Borden Division - Superior Court 14241 Road 28, Madera, CA 93638; 559-675-7930; Fax: 559-673-0542. Hours: 8AM-5PM (PST). *Small Claims.*

Note: There is no countywide database of records; each court must be searched.

Civil Records: Access: Mail, in person. Only the court performs in person searches; visitors may not. Search fee: $5.00 plus $1.00 per name per year. Required to search: name, years to search. Cases indexed by defendant, plaintiff. Records on index cards since 1986, on computer back to 10/98. Will only search back 7 years.

General Information: SASE required. Turnaround time 1 week. Copy fee: $.50 per page. Certification fee: $6.00. Fee payee: Madera Superior Court. Personal checks accepted. Prepayment is required.

Sierra Division - Superior Court 40601 Road 274, Bass Lake, CA 93604; 559-642-3235; Fax: 559-642-3445. Hours: 8AM-5PM (PST). *Felony, Misdemeanor, Civil Actions Under $25,000, Eviction, Small Claims, Probate.*

Civil Records: Access: Mail, in person. Only the court performs in person searches; visitors may not. Search fee: $5.00 per name. Required to search: name, years to search. Civil cases indexed by defendant, plaintiff. Civil records on index cards. Will only search back 7 years.

Criminal Records: Access: Mail, in person. Only the court performs in person searches; visitors may not. Search fee: $5.00 per name. Required to search: name, years to search; also helpful: DOB. Criminal records on computer (traffic only), index cards for criminal.

General Information: No adoptions, juvenile, medical, probation or sealed records released. SASE required. Turnaround time 1-2 weeks. Copy fee: $.50 per page. Certification fee: $6.00. Fee payee: Madera Superior Court. Personal checks accepted. Prepayment is required.

Marin County

Superior Court PO Box 4988, San Rafael, CA 94913-4988; Civil phone: 415-499-6407; Criminal phone: 415-499-6225. Hours: 8:30AM-4PM (PST). *Felony, Misdemeanor, Civil, Eviction, Small Claims, Probate.*

www.co.marin.ca.us/courts

Civil Records: Access: Phone, mail, in person, online. Both court and visitors may perform in person searches. Search fee: $5.00 per name per year. Required to search: name, years to search. Civil cases indexed by defendant, plaintiff. Civil records on computer from 1986, on microfiche from 1973 to 1985, archived from 1900 to 1972, on reel from 1900. Online access to the current court calendar is available free at www.co.marin.ca.us/depts/MC/main/courtcal/name.cfm. Phone requests are limited to one name.

Criminal Records: Access: Phone, mail, in person, online. Both court and visitors may perform in person searches. Search fee: $5.00 per name per year. Required to search: name, years to search. Criminal records on computer from 1986, on microfiche from 1973 to 1985, archived from 1900 to 1972, on reel from 1900. Online Access to the active criminal calendar is the same as civil. Phone requests are limited to one name.

General Information: Public access terminal is available. No adoptions, paternity, sole custody, juvenile, medical, probation or sealed records released. SASE required. Turnaround time 3 weeks. Copy fee: $1.00 per page. Certification fee: $6.00. Fee payee: Marin County Superior Court. Personal checks accepted. Out-of-state checks not accepted. Write "not to exceed $x.xx" on check. Call first. Prepayment is required.

Mariposa County

Superior Court 5088 Bullion St (PO Box 28), Mariposa, CA 95338; Civil phone: 209-966-6599; Criminal phone: 209-966-2005; Probate phone: 209-966-6599; Fax: 209-742-6860. Hours: 8AM-5PM (PST). *Felony, Misdemeanor, Civil, Small Claims, Eviction, Probate.*

www.mariposacourts.org

Note: This former municipal court is now known as Department 2.

Civil Records: Access: Phone, fax, mail, in person. Only the court performs in person searches; visitors may not. Search fee: $5.00 per name. Fee applies to years prior to 1990. No fee for computer records search. Required to search: name, years to search. Civil records on computer from 1989, on microfiche and index files from 1800s. Phone access limited to short searches.

Criminal Records: Access: Phone, fax, mail, in person. Only the court performs in person searches; visitors may not. Search fee: $5.00 per name per year. Required to search: name, years to search. Criminal records on computer from 1989, on microfiche and index files from 1800s.

General Information: No adoptions, juvenile, medical, probation or sealed records released. SASE required. Turnaround time 2-3 days. Copy fee: $.50 per page. Certification fee: $6.00. Fee payee: Mariposa Superior Court. Personal checks accepted. Prepayment is required.

Mendocino County

Superior Court State & Perkins Sts (PO Box 996 Civ; PO Box 337 Crim), Ukiah, CA 95482; Civil phone: 707-463-4481; Criminal phone: 707-463-4486; Fax: 707-468-3459. Hours: 8AM-4PM (PST). *Felony, Civil Actions Over $25,000, Probate.*

www.co.mendocino.ca.us/courts/ukiah.html

Civil Records: Access: Mail, in person. Both court and visitors may perform in person searches. Search fee: $5.00 per name. Fee for mail search only. Required to search: name, years to search. Civil cases indexed by defendant, plaintiff. Civil records on computer from 1990s, on microfilm from 1800 to 1940.

Criminal Records: Access: Mail, in person. Both court and visitors may perform in person searches. Search fee: $5.00 per name. Required to search: name, years to search. Criminal records on computer from 1990s, on microfilm from 1800 to 1940.

General Information: No adoptions, juvenile, medical, probation or sealed records released. SASE required. Turnaround time 1 week. Copy fee: $1.00 for first page, $.50 each add'l. Certification fee: $6.00. Fee payee: Mendocino Superior Court. Personal checks accepted. Prepayment is required.

Ten Mile Branch - Superior Court 700 S Franklin St, Fort Bragg, CA 95437; 707-964-3192; Fax: 707-961-2611. Hours: 8AM-Noon, 1-4PM (PST). *Felony, Misdemeanor, Civil Actions, Eviction, Small Claims.*

www.co.mendocino.ca.us/courts/fortbragg.html

Civil Records: Access: Mail, in person. Both the court and visitors may perform in person searches Search fee: $5.00 per name. Required to search: name, years to search. Civil cases indexed by defendant, plaintiff. Civil records on index cards back to 1990. Will only search back 7 years.

Criminal Records: Access: Mail, in person. Both the court and visitors may perform in person searches Search fee: $5.00 per name. Required to search: name, years to search, DOB. Criminal records go back to 1990; on computer back 1995.

General Information: No juvenile or probation records released. SASE required. Turnaround time 2 weeks. Copy fee: $1.00 for first page, $.50 each add'l. Certification fee: $6.00. Fee payee: Superior Court. Personal checks accepted. Prepayment is required.

Willits Branch - Superior Court 125 E Commercial St, Rm 100, Willits, CA 95490; 707-459-7800; Fax: 707-459-7818. Hours: 8AM-4PM (PST). *Felony, Misdemeanor, Civil Actions Under $25,000, Eviction, Small Claims.*

www.co.mendocino.ca.us/courts/willits.html

Civil Records: Access: Mail, in person. Only the court performs in person searches; visitors may not Search fee: $5.00 per name. Required to search: name, years to search. Civil cases indexed by defendant, plaintiff. Civil records on computer since 1992, index files prior.

Criminal Records: Access: Mail, in person. Both court and visitors may perform in person searches. Search fee: $5.00 per name. Required to search: name, years to search, DOB. Criminal records on computer since 1992, index files prior.

General Information: No probation reports released. SASE required. Turnaround time 1 week. Copy fee: $1.00 for 1st page & $.50 per additional page. Certification fee: $6.00. Fee payee: MCSC. Personal checks accepted. Prepayment is required.

Anderson Branch - Superior Court PO Box 336 (14470 Hwy 128, Veteran Bldg), Boonville, CA 95415; 707-895-3329; Fax: 707-895-2349. Hours: 8AM-Noon, 2-4PM (PST). *Misdemeanor, Civil Actions Under $25,000, Eviction, Small Claims.*

www.co.mendocino.ca.us/courts/boon.html

Note: Court is open on Friday only.

Civil Records: Access: Phone, fax, mail, in person. Only the court performs in person searches; visitors may not. Search fee: $5.00 per name. Required to search: name, years to search. Civil cases indexed by defendant, plaintiff. Civil records on computer back to 1996; prior on index cards. Will only search back 7 years.

Criminal Records: Access: Phone, fax, mail, in person. Both court and visitors may perform in person searches. Search fee: $5.00 per name. Required to search: name, years to search, DOB. Criminal records on computer back to 1996, index books prior.

General Information: No juvenile records released. SASE required. Turnaround time 1-2 weeks. Fax notes: Fax Fee: Local $1.00 per pg; Long Distance or out of county $1.50 per pg. Copy fee: $1.00 for first page, $.50 each add'l. Certification fee: $6.00. Fee payee: Superior Court. Personal checks accepted. Prepayment is required.

Arena Branch - Superior Court 24000 S Hwy 1 (PO Box 153), Point Arena, CA 95468; 707-882-2116. Hours: 8AM-Noon, 1-4PM, M, T, W, TH (PST). *Misdemeanor, Civil Actions Under $25,000, Eviction, Small Claims.*

www.co.mendocino.ca.us/courts/ptarena.html

Civil Records: Access: Mail, in person. Both court and visitors may perform in person searches. Search fee: $5.00 per name. Required to search: name, years to search. Civil cases indexed by defendant, plaintiff. Civil records on index cards back to 1985, computerized since 07/98. Will search back 10 years.

Criminal Records: Access: Mail, in person. Only the court performs in person searches; visitors may not. Search fee: $5.00 per name. Required to search: name, years to search, DOB. Criminal records indexed on cards back to 1985, computerized since 07/98.

General Information: No juvenile records released. SASE required. Turnaround time 1 week. Copy fee: $1.00 for first page, $.50 each add'l. $2.00 minimum. Certification fee: $6.00. Fee payee: Arena Court. Personal checks accepted. Prepayment is required.

Long Valley Branch - Superior Court PO Box 157, Drive Thru Tree Rd, Leggett, CA 95585; 707-925-6460; Fax: 707-925-6225. Hours: 8AM-Noon, 1-4PM (PST). *Misdemeanor, Civil Actions Under $25,000, Eviction, Small Claims.*

www.co.mendocino.ca.us/courts/leggett.html

Civil Records: Access: Mail, fax, in person. Both court and visitors may perform in person searches. Search fee: $5.00 per name. Required to search: name, years to search. Civil cases indexed by defendant, plaintiff. Civil records on computer (DMV only) back 2 to 3 years, index cards back 7 years. Will only search back 7 years.

Criminal Records: Access: Mail, fax, in person. Both court and visitors may perform in person searches. Search fee: $5.00 per name. Required to search: name, years to search. Criminal records on index cards back 7 years. Will only search back 7 years. Computer records go back 5 years.

General Information: No probation records released. SASE required. Turnaround time 1 week. Copy fee: $1.00 per page. Certification fee: $6.00. Fee payee: Mendocino Superior Court. Personal checks accepted. Prepayment is required.

Round Valley Branch - Superior Court 76091 Covelo Rd (PO Box 25), Covelo, CA 95428; 707-983-6446; Fax: 707-983-6996. Hours: 9AM-4PM Fri (PST). *Misdemeanor, Civil Actions Under $25,000, Eviction, Small Claims.*

www.co.mendocino.ca.us/courts/covelo.html

Note: Court is open on Friday only.

Civil Records: Access: Mail, in person. Only the court may perform in person searches. Search fee: $5.00 per name. Required to search: name, years to search. Civil cases indexed by defendant, plaintiff. Civil records on computer back to 1997, on index cards back to 1989. Will only search back 7 years.

Criminal Records: Access: Mail, in person. Only the court may perform in person searches. Search fee: $5.00 per name. Required to search: name, years to search, DOB. Criminal records on computer from 1997, index cards back to 1993. Will only search back 7 years.

General Information: No juvenile or probation records released. SASE required. Turnaround time 1 week. Copy fee: $1.00 per page. Certification fee: $6.00 per page. Fee payee: Superior Court. Personal checks accepted. Prepayment is required.

Merced County

Superior Court 627 W 21st St, Merced, CA 95340; 209-385-7531; Fax: 209-725-9223. Hours: 8AM-4PM (PST). *Felony, Civil Actions Over $25,000, Probate.*

Civil Records: Access: Mail, in person. Both court and visitors may perform in person searches. Search fee: $5.00 per name. Required to search: name, years to search. Civil cases indexed by defendant, plaintiff. Civil records in index files from 1900s, computer from 1979, on microfiche from 1900s.

Criminal Records: Access: Mail, in person. Both court and visitors may perform in person searches. Search fee: $5.00 per name. Required to search: name, years to search. Criminal records in index files from 1900s, computer from 1979, on microfiche from 1900s.

General Information: Public access terminal is available. No juvenile nor adoption records released. SASE required. Turnaround time 1 week. Copy fee: $.50 per page. Certification fee: $6.00. Fee payee: Merced County Superior Court. Business checks accepted. Prepayment is required.

4, 5, 7 & 8 Divisions - Merced Limited Superior Court 670 W 22nd St, Merced, CA 95340; Civil phone: 209-385-7337; Criminal phone: 209-385-7335; Fax: 209-725-0323 (civil) 209-725-3599 (criminal). Hours: 8AM-4PM M-F (civil); Noon-4PM M-F (civ only) (PST). *Misdemeanor, Civil Actions Under $25,000, Eviction, Small Claims.*

Civil Records: Access: Mail, in person. Search fee: $5.00 per name. Required to search: name, years to search. Civil cases indexed by defendant, plaintiff. Civil records on computer from 1992, index cards prior. Will only search back 7 years.

Criminal Records: Access: Mail, in person. Both court and visitors may perform in person searches. Search fee: $5.00 per name. Required to search: name, years to search. Criminal records on computer from 1992; prior on microfiche. Will only search back 7 years.

General Information: No juvenile or probation records released. SASE required. Turnaround time 2-5 days. Copy fee: $.50 per page. Certification fee: $6.00. Fee payee: Merced County Superior Court. Personal checks accepted. Prepayment is required.

Los Banos Branch - Superior Court 445 "I" St, Los Banos, CA 93635; 209-826-6500; Fax: 209-826-8108. Hours: 8AM-4PM (PST). *Misdemeanor, Civil Actions Under $25,000, Eviction, Small Claims.*

Note: This court was combined with the old Dos Palos and Gustine Municipal Courts.

Civil Records: Access: Mail, in person. Only the court may perform in person searches. Search fee: $5.00 per name. Required to search: name, years to search. Civil cases indexed by defendant, plaintiff. Civil records on microfiche.

Criminal Records: Access: Mail, in person. Only the court may perform in person searches. Search fee: $5.00 per name. Required to search: name, years to search; also helpful: DOB. Criminal records on microfiche.

General Information: No juvenile or probation records released. SASE required. Turnaround time 2-3 days. Copy fee: $.50 per page. Certification fee: $6.00. Fee payee: Merced Superior Court. Personal checks accepted. Prepayment is required.

Modoc County

Superior Court 205 S East St, Alturas, CA 96101; 530-233-6515/6; Fax: 530-233-6500. Hours: 8:30AM-5PM (PST). *Felony, Misdemeanor, Civil, Small Claims, Eviction, Probate.*

Civil Records: Access: Mail, in person. Only the court performs in person searches; visitors may not. Search fee: $5.00 per name. Required to search: name, years to search. Civil cases indexed by plaintiff. Civil records in index file from 1874, computerized since 07/25/95.

Criminal Records: Access: Fax, mail, in person. Only the court performs in person searches; visitors may not. Search fee: $5.00 per name. Required to search: name, years to search; also helpful: DOB. Criminal records computerized since 1991.

General Information: No adoptions, juvenile, medical, probation or sealed records released. SASE required. Turnaround time 1-2 weeks. Copy fee: $.50 per page. Certification fee: $7.00. Fee payee: Modoc County Superior Courts. Personal checks accepted. Prepayment is required.

Mono County

Superior Court - Bridgeport Branch PO Box 537, Bridgeport, CA 93517; 760-932-5239. Hours: 8:30AM-5PM (PST). *Felony, Civil, Probate.*

Civil Records: Access: Mail, in person. Both court and visitors may perform in person searches. Search fee: $5.00 per name. Required to search: name, years to search. Civil cases indexed by defendant, plaintiff. Civil records in index files from 1873.

Criminal Records: Access: Mail, in person. Both court and visitors may perform in person searches. Search fee: $5.00 per name. Required to search: name, years to search. Criminal records in index files from 1873.

General Information: No adoptions, juvenile, medical, probation or sealed records released. SASE required. Turnaround time 1-3 weeks. Copy fee: $.50 per page. Certification fee: $6.00 first page and $1.00 each additional. Fee payee: Mono County Superior Court. Personal checks accepted. Prepayment is required.

Mammoth Lakes Division - Superior Court PO Box 1037, Mammoth Lakes, CA 93546; 760-924-5444; Fax: 760-924-5419. Hours: 9AM-5PM (PST). *Felony, Misdemeanor, Civil, Eviction, Small Claims.*

Civil Records: Access: Mail, in person. Only the court performs in person searches; visitors may not. Search fee: $5.00 per name. Required to search: name, years to search. Civil cases indexed by defendant, plaintiff. Civil records on index cards. Will only search back 10 years.

Criminal Records: Access: Mail, in person. Only the court performs in person searches; visitors may not. Search fee: $5.00 per name. Required to search: name, years to search. Criminal records on computer from 1989, index cards prior. Will only search back 7 years.

General Information: No juvenile or probation records released. SASE required. Turnaround time 1 week. Copy fee: $.50 per page. Certification fee: $6.00 plus $1.00 per page. Fee payee: Mono Superior Court. Personal checks accepted. Prepayment is required.

Monterey County

Superior Court - Monterey Branch 1200 Aguajito Rd, First Floor, Monterey, CA 93940; 831-647-7730. Hours: 8AM-4PM (PST). *Civil, Probate.*

www.co.monterey.ca.us/court

Note: This court holds the civil records from the city of Salinas. Criminal records for Monterey are held in Salinas.

Civil Records: Access: Mail, in person, online. Both court and visitors may perform in person searches. Search fee: $5.00 per name per year. Required to search: name, years to search. Civil cases indexed by defendant, plaintiff. Civil records computerized since 09/90, on microfiche from 1973, index books prior. Online access to calendars and current cases is available for free online at www.co.monterey.ca.us/court/calendar.asp.

General Information: No juvenile or probation records released. SASE required. Turnaround time 1 week. Copy fee: $.75 per page. Certification fee: $6.00 general; $10.00 if for final re dissolution. Fee payee: Superior Court. Personal checks accepted. Prepayment is required.

Superior Court - Salinas Division 240 Church St Rm 318 PO Box 1819, Salinas, CA 93902; 831-755-5052. Hours: 8AM-4PM (PST). *Felony, Misdemeanor.*

www.co.monterey.ca.us/court

Note: All criminal records are filed at the Salinas courthouse. A; civil, probate, and family law cases are files at the Monterey courthouse.

Criminal Records: Access: Mail, in person, online. Both court and visitors may perform in person searches. Search fee: $5.00 per name. Required to search: name, years to search; also helpful: DOB. Felony records computerized since 1998, on microfiche to 1940s. Misdemeanor records computerized since 1992, on microfiche since 1986. Online access to calendars and current cases is available free online at www.co.monterey.ca.us/court/calendar.asp.

General Information: No adoptions, juvenile, medical, probation or sealed records released. SASE required. Turnaround time 1 week. Copy fee: $.75 per page. Certification fee: $6.00. Fee payee: Clerk of Court. Personal checks accepted. Prepayment is required.

King City Division - Consolidated Trial Court 250 Franciscan Way (PO Box 647), King City, CA 93930; Civil phone: 831-385-8339; Criminal phone: 831-385-8338. Hours: 8AM-5PM; Public Hours: 8AM-4PM (PST). *Felony, Misdemeanor, Civil Actions Under $25,000, Eviction, Small Claims.*

www.co.monterey.ca.us/court

Note: Encompasses the cities of King City, Greenfield, Soledad, areas south of King City to the San Luis Obispo County line.

Civil Records: Access: Mail, in person, online. Both court and visitors may perform in person searches. Search fee: $5.00 per name. Required to search: name, years to search. Civil cases indexed by defendant, plaintiff. Civil records on computer from 1992, index files from 1983. Records destroyed after 10 years. Online access to calendars and current cases is available for free online at www.co.monterey.ca.us/court/calendar.asp.

Criminal Records: Access: Mail, in person, online. Both court and visitors may perform in person searches. Search fee: $5.00 per name. Required to search: name, years to search; also helpful: DOB. Criminal records on computer from 1992, index files from 1983. Records destroyed after 10 years. Online access to criminal records is the same as civil.

General Information: No probation reports released. SASE required. Turnaround time 1 week. Copy fee:

$.75 per page. Certification fee: $6.00. Fee payee: Monterey County Courts. Personal checks accepted. Credit cards accepted: Visa, AmEx. Additional fee charged. Prepayment is required.

Marina Division 3180 Del Monte Blvd, Marina, CA 93933; 831-884-1953 Traffic; Fax: 831-884-0106. Hours: 8AM-4PM (PST). *Small Claims, Traffic.*

www.co.monterey.ca.us/court

Note: Small claims phone is 831-884-1951.

Napa County

Superior Court 825 Brown St, PO Box 880, Napa, CA 94559; Civil phone: 627-253-4481; Criminal phone: 627-253-4573; Fax: 627-253-4229, 707-253-4673 (Criminal). Hours: 8AM-5PM (PST). *Felony, Misdemeanor, Civil, Eviction, Small Claims, Probate.*

www.napa.courts.ca.gov

Civil Records: Access: Mail, in person. Both court and visitors may perform in person searches. Search fee: $5.00 per name per year. Required to search: name, years to search. Civil cases indexed by defendant, plaintiff. Civil records on computer since 1989; prior records on index books or microfilm back to 1800s.
Criminal Records: Access: Mail, in person. Both court and visitors may perform in person searches. Search fee: $5.00 per name per year. Required to search: name, years to search, DOB; also helpful: address, SSN. Misdemeanor records on computer since 1986 and felonies since 1989.
General Information: Public access terminal is available. No adoptions, juvenile, medical, probation or sealed records released. SASE required. Turnaround time 2-3 weeks. Copy fee: $1.00 per page. Certification fee: $6.00. Fee payee: Napa Superior Court. Personal checks accepted. Prepayment is required.

Nevada County

Superior Court 201 Church St #7, Nevada City, CA 95959; 530-265-1311; Fax: 530-478-1938. Hours: 8AM-5PM (PST). *Felony, Misdemeanor, Small Claims, Eviction, Probate.*

www.courts.co.nevada.ca.us

Criminal Records: Access: Phone, mail, in person. Only the court performs in person searches; visitors may not. Search fee: No fee unless extensive research required. Required to search: name, years to search; also helpful: DOB. Criminal Records on computer from 1977, prior in books back to 1800s.
General Information: No adoptions, paternity, juvenile, medical, probation or sealed records released. SASE required. Turnaround time 2 weeks. Copy fee: $.50 per page. Certification fee: $6.00. Fee payee: Nevada County Superior Courts. Personal checks accepted. Prepayment is required.

Superior Court - Civil Division 201 Church St, #5, Nevada City, CA 95959; 530-265-1294; Fax: 530-478-5627. Hours: 8AM-5PM (PST). *Civil, Eviction, Small Claims.*

www.courts.co.nevada.ca.us

Note: The phone number for Family Law, Probate and Juvenile is 530-265-1293. The phone number for Evictions and Small Claims is 530-265-1294.
Civil Records: Access: Phone, mail, in person. Both court and visitors may perform in person searches. Search fee: $5.00 per name. Required to search: name, years to search. Civil cases indexed by defendant, plaintiff. Civil records on computer back to 1983. Cases with previous disposition are available on microfilm in most cases. Some of the Limited Civil, Small Claims and Unlawful Detainer cases have been destroyed.
General Information: Public access terminal is available. No probation reports released. SASE required. Turnaround time 2 days. Fax notes: Will not fax results. Copy fee: $.50 per page. Certification fee:

$6.00. Plus copy fees. Fee payee: Superior Court. Personal checks accepted. Prepayment is required.

Truckee Branch - Superior Court 10075 Levon Ave #301, Truckee, CA 96161; Civil phone: 530-582-7837; Criminal phone: 530-582-7836; Fax: 530-582-7875. Hours: 8AM-5PM (PST). *Misdemeanor, Civil, Eviction, Small Claims.*

http://courts.co.nevada.ca.us/truckee_contact.htm

Civil Records: Access: Mail, in person. Both court and visitors may perform in person searches. Search fee: $5.00 per name. Required to search: name, years to search. Civil cases indexed by defendant, plaintiff. Civil records on computer from 1991, index files from 1983. Records destroyed after 10 years.
Criminal Records: Access: Mail, in person. Both court and visitors may perform in person searches. Search fee: $5.00 per name. Required to search: name, years to search. Criminal records on computer from 1991, index files from 1983. Records destroyed after 10 years.
General Information: Public access terminal is available. No probation reports released. SASE required. Turnaround time 1 week. Copy fee: $1.00 per page. Certification fee: $6.00. Fee payee: Superior Court. Personal checks accepted. Prepayment is required.

Orange County

Superior Court - Civil 700 Civic Center Dr W, Santa Ana, CA 92701; 714-834-2208. Hours: 8AM-5PM (PST). *Civil Actions, Small Claims.*

www.occourts.org

Note: This court handles civil actions over $25,000 countywide, but the lower civil and small claims cases are for this central jurisdiction venue (Santa Ana area) only.
Civil Records: Access: Mail, in person, online. Both court and visitors may perform in person searches. Search fee: $5.00 per name per index. Required to search: name, years to search. Civil cases indexed by defendant, plaintiff. Civil records on computer from mid 1980s, partial prior to 1986, microfiche and index file from 1900s. Online access is to be available in late 2002 at www.occourts.org/caseinfo.asp.
General Information: Public access terminal is available. No adoptions, juvenile, medical, probation or sealed records released. SASE required. Turnaround time 1-2 weeks. Copy fee: $.80 per page. Certification fee: $6.00. Fee payee: Clerk of the Court. Personal checks accepted. Prepayment is required.

Superior Court - Criminal Operations 700 Civic Center Dr W, Santa Ana, CA 92701; 714-834-2266. Hours: 8AM-5PM (PST). *Felony.*

www.occourts.org

Criminal Records: Access: Mail, in person, online. Both court and visitors may perform in person searches. Search fee: $5.00 per index. Required to search: name, years to search, DOB. Criminal records on computer from 1988, on microfiche and archived from 1966, index files from 1918. Online access is to be available in late 2002 at www.occourts.org/caseinfo.asp.
General Information: No adoptions, juvenile, medical, probation or sealed records released. SASE required. Turnaround time 1-2 weeks. Copy fee: $.80 per page. Certification fee: $6.00. Fee payee: Clerk of the Court. Personal checks accepted. Prepayment is required.

Central Orange County Superior Court - Limited Jurisdiction 700 Civic Ctr Dr W (PO Box 1138, 92702), Santa Ana, CA 92701; Civil phone: 714-834-3580; Criminal phone: 714-834-3575; Fax: 714-953-9032. Hours: 7:30AM-5PM (PST). *Misdemeanor, Civil Actions Under $25,000, Eviction, Small Claims.*

www.occourts.org/

Note: Includes cities of Santa Ana, Orange, Tustin and surrounding unincorporated territories including Cowan Heights, El Modena, Tustin Marine Air Base, Lemon Heights, Modjeska, Orange Park Acres, Silverado Canyon and Villa Park.
Civil Records: Access: Mail, in person, online. Both the court and visitors may perform in person searches. Search fee: $5.00 per name per year. Required to search: name, years to search. Civil cases indexed by defendant, plaintiff. Civil records on index files from 1985, also on microfiche. Records destroyed after 10 years. Online access is to be available in late 2002 at www.occourts.org/caseinfo.asp.
Criminal Records: Access: Mail, in person, online. Both the court and visitors may perform in person searches. Search fee: $5.00 per name per year. Required to search: name, years to search, DOB. Criminal records on index files from 1986; on computer since 1995. Records destroyed after 7 years, no phyisical file availble then. Online access is to be available in 2002 at www.occourts.org/caseinfo.asp.
General Information: Public access terminal is available. No probation reports released. SASE required. Turnaround time 2-4 days. Copy fee: $.80 per page. Certification fee: $6.00. Fee payee: Clerk of Court. Personal checks accepted. Credit cards accepted: Visa, MasterCard. Prepayment is required.

Harbor - Laguna Hills Superior Court - Civil Division 23141 Moulton Pkwy, Laguna Hills, CA 92653; 949-472-6964. Hours: 8AM-5PM (PST). *Civil Actions Under $25,000, Eviction, Small Claims.*

www.occourts.org

Note: Formerly known as South Orange, this includes Aliso Viejo, Capistrano Bch, Coto De Caza, Dana Pt, Laguna (various), Lake Forest, Mission Viejo, Rancho St. Margarita, San Clemente, San Juan Capistrano, Trabuco Canyon.
Civil Records: Access: Mail, in person, online. Both court and visitors may perform in person searches. Search fee: $5.00 per name per year. Fee only applies if court does search and case number is required. Required to search: name, years to search. Civil cases indexed by defendant, plaintiff. Civil records in index files and on microfiche back to 1987; on computer back to 2000. Online access is to be available in late 2002 at www.occourts.org/caseinfo.asp.
General Information: Public access terminal is available. No unlawful detainer records released for 60 days. SASE required. Turnaround time 2-3 days. Copy fee: $.80 per page. Certification fee: $6.00. Fee payee: Clerk of Courtnex. Personal checks accepted. Credit cards accepted: Visa, MasterCard, Discover. Prepayment is required.

Harbor - Laguna Niguel Superior Court - Criminal Division 30143 Crown Valley Parkway, Justice Center, Laguna Niguel, CA 92677; 949-249-5113. Hours: 8AM-5PM (PST). *Misdemeanor.*

www.occourts.org/

Note: Also known as South Orange County Superior Court. Includes Capistrano Bch, Coto De Caza, Dana Pt, Laguna Hills, Laguna Niguel, Mission Viejo, Rancho St. Margarita, San Clemente, San Juan Capistrano, Trabuco Canyon.
Criminal Records: Access: Mail, in person, online. Both court and visitors may perform in person searches. Search fee: $5.00 per name per year. $1.75 to pull a case file. Required to search: name, years to search, DOB; also helpful: SSN. Criminal records on computer since 1987; prior records on books. Online access to be available late 2002 at www.occourts.org/caseinfo.asp.
General Information: No probation report, unlawful detainer records released. SASE required. Turnaround time 2-3 days. Copy fee: $.80 per page. Certification fee: $6.00. Fee payee: Clerk of Court. Personal checks

accepted. Credit cards accepted: Visa, MasterCard, Discover. Prepayment is required.

Harbor - Newport Beach Superior Court
4601 Jamboree Road #104, Newport Beach, CA 92660-2595; 949-476-4699. Hours: 8AM-5PM (PST). *Misdemeanor, Civil Actions Under $25,000, Eviction, Small Claims.*

www.occourts.org/

Note: Includes Balboa Island, Corona Del Mar, Costa Mesa, Newport Beach, Irvine, Santa Ana Heights, John Wayne/Orange Co Airport, Lido Isle and surrounding unincorporated areas.
Civil Records: Access: Mail, in person, online. Both court and visitors may perform in person searches. Search fee: $5.00 per name. Required to search: name, years to search. Civil cases indexed by defendant, plaintiff. Civil records go back 10 years; computerized records go back 10 years, civil records are indexed on microfiche. Online access is to be available in 2002 at www.occourts.org/caseinfo.asp.
Criminal Records: Access: Mail, in person, online. Only the court performs in person searches; visitors may not. Search fee: $5.00 per name. Required to search: name, years to search; also helpful: DOB. Criminal records on computer go back 10 years; on microfiche -- felonies kept 75 years, misdemeanors 5 years. Online access is to be available in late 2002 at www.occourts.org/caseinfo.asp.
General Information: No probation reports nor police reports released. SASE required. Turnaround time 2-5 days. Copy fee: $1.00 for 1st page; $.80 each add'l. Certification fee: $6.00. Fee payee: Clerk of Court. Personal checks accepted. Checks accepted (must be in-state and be imprinted with name and address). Credit cards accepted: Visa, MasterCard, Discover. Prepayment is required.

North Orange County Superior Court
1275 N Berkeley Ave, PO Box 5000, Fullerton, CA 92838-0500; 714-773-4555; 773-4667 (Small Claims); Civil phone: 714-773-4664; Criminal phone: 714-773-4668. Hours: 7:30AM-5:00PM (PST). *Felony, Misdemeanor, Civil Actions Under $25,000, Eviction, Small Claims.*

www.occourts.org

Note: Includes the cities of Anaheim, Brea, Buena Park, Fullerton, La Habra, La Palma, Placentia, Yorba Linda and surrounding unincorporated area including Anaheim Hills.
Civil Records: Access: Mail, in person, online. Both court and visitors may perform in person searches. Search fee: $5.00 per name, per year, per index. Fee also applies to requests by case number. Required to search: name, years to search. Civil cases indexed by defendant, plaintiff. Civil records on computer from 1991, index files from 1983. Records destroyed after 10 years. Online access is to be available in late 2002 at www.occourts.org/caseinfo.asp.
Criminal Records: Access: Mail, in person, online. The court will perform in person searches. Search fee: $5.00 per name per year. Required to search: name, years to search. All Criminal records are on computer. Records destroyed after 5-7 years from date of conviction. Online access is to be available in late 2002 at www.occourts.org/caseinfo.asp.
General Information: No probation reports or UD's for 60 days released. SASE required. Turnaround time 5 days. Copy fee: $1.00 per page. Certification fee: $6.00. Fee payee: Clerk of Court. Personal checks accepted. Personal checks accepted with proper ID. Credit cards accepted: Visa, MasterCard, Discover. Prepayment is required.

West Orange County Superior Court
8141 13th St, Westminster, CA 92683; 714-896-7181; Civil phone: 714-896-7191; Criminal phone: 714-896-7204; Fax: 714-896-7404 (civ); 896-7219 (criminal). Hours: 8AM-4:30PM (PST). *Misdemeanor, Civil Actions Under $25,000, Eviction, Small Claims.*

www.occourts.org

Note: Includes the cities of Cypress, Fountain Valley, Garden Grove, Huntington Beach, Los Alamitos, Rossmore, Seal Beach, Stanton, Sunset Beach, Surfside, Westminster and adjoining and unincorporated territory.
Civil Records: Access: Mail, in person, online. Both court and visitors may perform in person searches. Search fee: $5.00 per name per year per index. Required to search: name, years to search. Civil cases indexed by defendant, plaintiff. Civil records on computer back to 1992, microfiche from 1983. Records destroyed after 10 years. Online access is to be available in late 2002 at www.occourts.org/caseinfo.asp.
Criminal Records: Access: Mail, in person, online. Both court and visitors may perform in person searches. Search fee: $5.00 per name per year per index. Required to search: name, years to search, DOB. Criminal records on computer back to 1996, microfiche from 1983. Records destroyed after 10 years. Online access is to be available late 2002 at www.occourts.org/caseinfo.asp.
General Information: No probation reports, unlawful detainer (under 60 days old) records released. SASE required. Turnaround time 2 days. Copy fee: $.80 per page. Certification fee: $6.00 per document. Fee payee: Clerk of Court. Personal checks accepted. Credit cards accepted: Visa, MasterCard, Discover. Prepayment is required.

Orange County Probate Court
341 The City Dr, Orange, CA 92868; 714-935-8043. Hours: 8AM-5PM (PST). *Probate.*

www.occourts.org

Note: Jurisdiction includes juvenile, family law, and mental health filings.

Placer County

Superior Court
101 Maple St, Auburn, CA 95603; Civil phone: 530-889-6550; Criminal phone: 530-886-1200. Hours: 8AM-3PM (PST). *Felony, Civil, Eviction, Probate.*

www.placer.ca.gov/courts

Civil Records: Access: Phone, mail, in person. Both court and visitors may perform in person searches. Search fee: $5.00 per year for records prior to 1974; 1975 and forward are $5.00 per name. Required to search: name, years to search. Civil cases indexed by defendant, plaintiff. Civil records on computer from 1992, on microfiche from 1974, archived and index file from 1800s.
Criminal Records: Access: Phone, mail, in person. Both court and visitors may perform in person searches. Search fee: Same fees as civil. Required to search: name, years to search. Criminal records on computer from 1992, on microfiche from 1974, archived and index file from 1800s.
General Information: Public access terminal is available. No adoptions, juvenile, medical, paternity, probation or sealed records released. SASE required. Turnaround time 2 weeks. Copy fee: $.50 for first page, $.25 each add'l. Certification fee: $6.00. Fee payee: Clerk of the Court. Personal checks accepted. Prepayment is required.

Auburn Branch - Superior Court
11532 "B" Ave, Auburn, CA 95603; 530-886-1200; Fax: 530-886-1209. Hours: 8AM-4PM Office (8AM-3PM phone hours) (PST). *Felony, Misdemeanor.*

www.placer.ca.gov/courts

Note: Includes Auburn, Penryn, Newcastle, Bowman, Colfax, Weimar, Alta, Dutch Flat, Loomis. Also

includes criminal for Roseville, Rocklin, Lincoln criminal as of 12/8/97
Criminal Records: Access: Mail, in person. Both court and visitors may perform in person searches. Search fee: $5.00 per name per year. Required to search: name, years to search, DOB. Criminal Records indexed on computer back to 1992; records go back 10 years.
General Information: Public access terminal is available. No probation reports or copies of warrants released. SASE required. Turnaround time 2 weeks. Copy fee: $.50 per page. Certification fee: $6.00. Fee payee: Superior Court. Personal checks accepted. Prepayment is required.

Tahoe Division - Superior Court
PO Box 5669, Tahoe City, CA 96145; 530-581-6340; Fax: 530-581-6344. Hours: 8AM-4PM (PST). *Misdemeanor, Civil Actions Under $25,000, Eviction, Small Claims.*

www.placer.ca.gov/courts

Civil Records: Access: Mail, in person. Only the court may perform in person searches. Search fee: $5.00 per name. Required to search: name, years to search. Civil cases indexed by defendant, plaintiff. Civil records computerized fsince 1999, previous on index cards.
Criminal Records: Access: Mail, in person. Only the court may perform in person searches. Search fee: $5.00 per name. Required to search: name, years to search. Criminal records on index cards. Will only search back 7 years; computerized records since 1999.
General Information: No probation reports released. SASE required. Turnaround time 1 week. Copy fee: $.50 per page. Certification fee: $6.00. Fee payee: Clerk of Court. Personal checks accepted. Write "not to exceed $x.xx" on check. Prepayment is required.

Lincoln Division - Superior Court
c/o Roseville Court, 300 Taylor St, Roseville, CA 95678-2628; 916-783-1600; Fax: 916-783-1690 *Small Claims.*

www.placer.ca.gov/courts

Note: This court and its records have been consolidated with the Roseville Division, address given here.

Roseville Division - Superior Court
300 Taylor St, Roseville, CA 95678; 916-783-1600; Fax: 916-783-1690. Hours: 8AM-4PM (PST). *Small Claims, Traffic.*

www.placer.ca.gov/courts

Note: This court holds the records for the Foresthill Division and Roseville Divison Courts which have closed.

Plumas County

Superior Court - Civil Division
520 Main St, Rm 104, Quincy, CA 95971; 530-283-6305; Fax: 530-283-6415. Hours: 8AM-5PM (PST). *Civil, Small Claims, Probate.*

Civil Records: Access: Phone, fax, mail, in person. Both court and visitors may perform in person searches. Search fee: $5.00 per name per year. Required to search: name, years to search. Civil cases indexed by defendant, plaintiff. Civil records on computer from 1993, archived from 1980, index file from 1850.
General Information: No adoptions, juvenile, confidential, medical, probation or sealed records released. SASE required. Turnaround time 1 week. Fax notes: $5.00 per document. Copy fee: $1.00 per page. Certification fee: $6.00. Fee payee: Plumas County Courts. Personal checks accepted. Prepayment is required.

Superior Court - Criminal Division
520 Main St, Rm 104, Quincy, CA 95971; 530-283-6232; Fax: 530-283-6293. Hours: 8AM-5PM (PST). *Felony, Misdemeanor.*

Criminal Records: Access: Mail, in person. Only the court performs in person searches; visitors may not.

Search fee: $5.00 per name. Required to search: name, years to search, DOB; also, signed release if juvenile. Criminal records indexed on computer back to 1989.

General Information: No probation reports, financial statements or juvenile released. SASE required. Turnaround time 1-2 days. Copy fee: $1.00 per page. Certification fee: $6.00. Fee payee: Superior Court. Personal checks accepted. Prepayment is required.

Chester Branch - Superior Court 1st & Willow Way (PO Box 722), Chester, CA 96020; 530-258-2646; Fax: 530-258-2652. Hours: 8AM-3PM (PST). *Civil Actions Under $25,000, Eviction, Small Claims.*

www.psln.com/pccourt

Civil Records: Access: Phone, mail, in person. Only the court performs in person searches; visitors may not. Search fee: $5.00 per name per year. Required to search: name, years to search. Civil cases indexed by defendant, plaintiff. Traffic on computer, index cards for civil records. Will only search back 7 years. Records on computer go back 13 years.

General Information: No probation reports released. SASE required. Turnaround time 1-2 days. Fax notes: Fee to fax results is $6.00 per document. Copy fee: $1.00 per page. Certification fee: $6.00 to $10.00. Fee payee: Superior Court. Personal checks accepted. Prepayment is required.

Portola Branch - Superior Court 161 Nevada St (PO Box 1054), Portola, CA 96122; 530-832-4286; Fax: 530-832-4286. Hours: 8AM-4PM (PST). *Civil Actions Under $25,000, Eviction, Small Claims.*

Civil Records: Access: Phone, fax, mail, in person. Only the court performs in person searches; visitors may not. Search fee: $5.00 per name. Required to search: name, years to search. Civil cases indexed by defendant, plaintiff. Traffic on computer, computer for civil records. Will only search back 7 years.

Criminal Records: Access: Phone, mail, in person. Only the court performs in person searches; visitors may not. Search fee: $5.00 per name. Required to search: name, years to search. Traffic on computer, computer for criminal records. Will only search back 7 years.

General Information: No probation reports released. SASE required. Turnaround time as soon as possible. Copy fee: $1.00 per page. Certification fee: $6.00. Fee payee: Superior Court. Personal checks accepted. Prepayment is required.

Greenville Branch - Superior Court 115 Hwy 89 (PO Box 706), Greenville, CA 95947; 530-284-7213. Hours: 8AM-5PM (PST). *Small Claims.*

Riverside County

Superior Court - Civil Division 4050 Main St, Riverside, CA 92501; 909-955-1960; Fax: 909-955-1751. Hours: 8AM-5PM (PST). *Civil Actions Over $25,000, Probate.*

www.co.riverside.ca.us/depts/courts

Civil Records: Access: Phone, fax, mail, online, in person. Both court and visitors may perform in person searches. Search fee: $5.00 per name. Required to search: name, years to search. Civil cases indexed by defendant, plaintiff. Civil records on computer and microfiche from 1970, index file from 1956, archived from 1900s. The Automated Case Management System is the pay system for Riverside County Superior Courts for Internet access, but the intent is to make record searching free on the Internet eventually. Records date back to 1984 and include civil, criminal, family law, probate & traffic case information for all Riverside/Indio Courts. For further information, call 909-955-5945.

General Information: Public access terminal is available. No adoptions, juvenile, medical, probation,

unlawful detainers for 60 days or sealed records released. SASE required. Turnaround time 3 days. Fax notes: $1.00 per page. Copy fee: $.50 per page. Certification fee: $6.00. Fee payee: Riverside County Superior Court. Personal checks accepted. Credit cards accepted: Visa, MasterCard, Discover. Prepayment is required.

Superior Court - Criminal Division 4100 Main St, Riverside, CA 92501; 909-955-2300; Fax: 909-955-4007. Hours: 7:30AM-5PM (PST). *Felony, Misdemeanor.*

www.co.riverside.ca.us/depts/courts

Criminal Records: Access: Phone, fax, mail, online, in person. Both court and visitors may perform in person searches. Search fee: No search fee. Required to search: name, years to search, DOB; also helpful: SSN. Criminal Records on microfiche and computer since 1970, index file from 1956. The Automated Case Management System is the pay system for Riverside County Superior Courts for Internet access, but the intent is to make record searching free on the Internet eventually. Records date back to 1984 and include civil, criminal, family law, probate & traffic case information for all Riverside/Indio Courts. For further information, call 909-955-5945.

General Information: Public access terminal is available. No adoptions, juvenile, medical, probation, unlawful detainers for 60 days or sealed records released. SASE required. Turnaround time 1 day to 1 week. Fax notes: $1.00 for 1st page, $.50 each add'l. Must pay fax fee by credit card. Copy fee: $.50 per page. Certification fee: $6.00. Fee payee: Clerk of the Court. Personal checks accepted. Credit cards accepted: Visa, MasterCard, Discover. Prepayment is required.

Banning Division - Superior Court 155 E Hays St, Banning, CA 92220; Civil phone: 909-922-7155; Criminal phone: 909-922-7145; Fax: 909-922-7150; Fax: 909-922-7160. Hours: 7:30AM-5PM (PST). *Misdemeanor, Civil Actions Under $25,000, Eviction, Small Claims.*

www.co.riverside.ca.us/depts/courts

Note: Includes Banning, Cabazon, Highland Springs, Poppet Flatt, Silent Valley, Beaumont, Calimesa, Cherry Valley and Whitewater.

Civil Records: Access: Phone, fax, mail, online, in person. Only the court performs in person searches; visitors may not. No search fee. Required to search: name, years to search; also helpful-case number. Civil cases indexed by defendant, plaintiff. Civil records on computer from 1991, index files from 1983. Records destroyed after 10 years. See Riverside Division location for online information. Phone and fax access limited to short searches.

Criminal Records: Access: Phone, fax, mail, online, in person. Only the court performs in person searches; visitors may not. No search fee. Required to search: name, years to search; also helpful-case number. Criminal records on computer back to 1992, index files from 1983. Records destroyed after 10 years. See Riverside Division for online information.

General Information: Public access terminal available for civil records only. No probation reports released. SASE required. Turnaround time 2 days. Fax notes: Fee to fax results is $.50 per page. Copy fee: $.50 per page. Certification fee: $6.00. Fee payee: Clerk of the Court. Personal checks accepted. Credit cards accepted: Visa, MasterCard, Discover. Prepayment is required.

Blythe Division - Superior Court 265 N Broadway, Blythe, CA 92225; 760-921-7981; Fax: 760-921-7941. Hours: 7:30AM-5PM (PST). *Felony, Misdemeanor, Civil Actions, Eviction, Small Claims.*

www.co.riverside.ca.us/depts/courts

Note: Includes Blythe, Ripley. Phone for Family Law is 760-921-7982.

Civil Records: Access: Phone, fax, mail, online, in person. Both court and visitors may perform in person searches. Search fee: $5.00 per name per year. Required to search: name, years to search. Civil records indexed by defendant, plaintiff. Civil records on computer from 1991, index files from 1983. Records destroyed after 10 years. See the Riverside Division location for online information.

Criminal Records: Access: Phone, fax, mail, online, in person. Both court and visitors may perform in person searches. Search fee: $5.00 per name per year. Required to search: name, years to search; also helpful: DOB, sex. Criminal records on computer from 1991, index files from 1983. Records destroyed after 10 years. See Riverside Division for online information.

General Information: Public access terminal is available. No probation reports released. SASE required. Turnaround time 2 days. Fax notes: $1.00 per page. Copy fee: $.50 per page. Certification fee: $6.00. Fee payee: Clerk of the Court. Personal checks accepted. Credit cards accepted: Visa, MasterCard, Discover. Prepayment is required.

Corona Branch - Superior Court 505 S Buena Vista Rm 206, Corona, CA 91720; Civil phone: 909-272-5620; Criminal phone: 909-272-5630; Fax: 909-272-5651 (Civil) 272-5691 (Criminal). Hours: 7:30AM-5PM (PST). *Misdemeanor, Civil Actions Under $25,000, Eviction, Small Claims.*

www.co.riverside.ca.us/depts/courts

Note: Includes Corona, El Cerrito, Home Gardens, Norco, Santa Ana Canyon.

Civil Records: Access: Fax, mail, online, in person. Both court and visitors may perform in person searches. Search fee: $5.00 per name per year. Required to search: name, years to search. Civil cases indexed by defendant, plaintiff. Civil records on computer from 1991, index files from 1983, microfiche since 1978. Records destroyed after 10 years. Judicial council fax cover required. See Riverside Branch location for online information.

Criminal Records: Access: Fax, mail, online, in person. Both court and visitors may perform in person searches. Search fee: $5.00 per name per year. Required to search: name, years to search, DOB. Criminal records on computer from 1991, index files from 1983, microfiche since 1978. Records destroyed after 10 years. See Riverside Division for online information.

General Information: No probation reports released. SASE required. Turnaround time 2 days. Fax notes: $1.00 per page. Copy fee: $.50 per page. Certification fee: $6.00. Fee payee: Clerk of Court. Personal checks accepted. Credit cards accepted: Visa, MasterCard, Discover. Prepayment is required.

Hemet Division - Superior Court 880 N State St, Hemet, CA 92543; 909-766-2321; Criminal phone: 909-766-2310; Fax: 909-766-2317. Hours: 7:30AM-4:30PM; Criminal, Civil/SC 8AM-Noon; (PST). *Misdemeanor, Civil Actions Under $25,000, Eviction, Small Claims.*

www.co.riverside.ca.us/depts/courts

Note: Includes Aguanga, Anza, Gilman Hot Springs, Hemet, Idylwild, Mountain Center, Pine Cove, Redec, Sage, San Jacinto, Sobba Hot Spring, Valle Vista and Winchester.

Civil Records: Access: Fax, mail, online, in person. Both court and visitors may perform in person searches. Search fee: $5.00 per name. If not on computer, is $5.00 per year. Required to search: name, years to search. Civil cases indexed by defendant, plaintiff. Civil records on computer from 1996, index files from 1983. Records destroyed after 10 years. See Riverside Division location for online information.

Criminal Records: Access: Mail, online, in person. Only the court performs in person searches; visitors may not. Search fee: $5.00 per name. If not on

computer, is $5.00 per year. Required to search: name, years to search. Criminal records on computer from 1996, index files from 1983. Records destroyed after 10 years. See Riverside Division for online information.
General Information: No probation reports released. SASE required. Fax notes: No fee to fax results. Copy fee: $.50 per page. Certification fee: $6.00. Fee payee: Clerk of the Court. Personal checks accepted. Credit cards accepted: Visa, MasterCard, Discover. Prepayment is required.

Indio Division - Superior Court 46200 Oasis St, Indio, CA 92201; Civil phone: 760-863-8208; Criminal phone: 760-863-8206; Fax: 760-863-8707. Hours: 7:30AM-5PM (PST). *Misdemeanor, Civil Actions Under $25,000, Eviction, Small Claims.*
www.co.riverside.ca.us/depts/courts
Note: Includes Desert Center, Eagle Mountain, Indio, La Quinta, Coachella, Bermuda Dunes, Mecca, North Shore, Pinyon Pines, Palm Springs, Salton Sea, Oasis, Thermal. Most Palm Springs records are here.
Civil Records: Access: Phone, fax, mail, online, in person. Visitors must perform in person searches No search fee. Required to search: name, years to search. Civil cases indexed by defendant, plaintiff. Civil records on computer from 1993, index files from 1983. Records destroyed after 10 years. Phone & fax access limited to short searches. See Riverside Division for online information.
Criminal Records: Access: Phone, fax, mail, online, in person. Visitors must perform in person searches No search fee. Required to search: name, years to search, signed release. Criminal records on computer from 1993, index files from 1983. Records destroyed after 10 years. See Riverside Division for online information.
General Information: Public access terminal is available. No probation reports released. SASE required. Turnaround time 2 days. Fax notes: $1.00 per page. Copy fee: $.50 per page. Certification fee: $6.00. Fee payee: Clerk of the Court. Personal checks accepted. Credit cards accepted: Visa, MasterCard, Discover. Prepayment is required.

Lake Elsinore Division - Superior Court c/o Temecula Division Superior Court, 41002 County Center Dr #100, Temecula, CA 92591; 909-245-3370; Fax: 909-245-3366. Hours: 7:30AM-5PM Th, F (PST). *Civil Actions Under $25,000, Eviction, Small Claims.*
www.co.riverside.ca.us/depts/courts
Note: Physical location of Lk Elsinore Ct is 117 S Langstaff in Lk Elsinore and is open Thursday and Friday only. It is best to search records at the Temecula Branch.
Civil Records: Access: Phone, fax, mail, online, in person. Both court and visitors may perform in person searches. No search fee. Required to search: name, years to search; also helpful: case number. Civil cases indexed by defendant, plaintiff. Civil records on computer since 1991, on index books until 08/91. Holds civil records from 3/1/95-3/1/97. See Riverside Branch Location for online information.
General Information: No confidential records released. SASE required. Turnaround time 2 days. Fax notes: Fee to fax results is $1.00 per page. Copy fee: $.50 per page. Certification fee: $6.00. Fee payee: Superior Court. Personal checks accepted. Credit cards accepted: Visa, MasterCard, Discover. Prepayment is required.

Palm Springs Division - Superior Court 3255 East Tahkuits Canyon Way, Palm Springs, CA 92262; 760-320-9764; Fax: 760-778-2269. Hours: 7:30AM-5PM (PST). *Misdemeanor, Traffic.*
www.co.riverside.ca.us/depts/courts
Note: Includes Cathedral City, Palm Springs, Rancho Mirage, Thousand Palms, Indian Wells, Palm Desert,

Desert Hot Springs. See also Indio Court. Call to determine which court to search
Criminal Records: Access: Fax, mail, online, in person. Both court and visitors may perform in person searches. Search fee: $5.00 per name. Required to search: name, years to search. Criminal records on computer from 1991, index files from 1983. Records destroyed after 10 years. See Riverside Division for online information.
General Information: No probation reports released. SASE required. Turnaround time 2-4 days. Fax notes: $1.00 per page. Copy fee: $.50 per page. Certification fee: $6.00. Fee payee: Clerk of the Court. Personal checks accepted. Credit cards accepted: Visa, MasterCard, Discover. Prepayment is required.

Perris Branch - Superior Court 227 N "D" St., Perris, CA 92370; 909-940-6820; 940-6830 (Traffic); Civil phone: 909-940-6840; Criminal phone: 909-940-6840; Fax: 909-940-6810. Hours: 7:30AM-5PM (PST). *Felony, Misdemeanor, Small Claims.*
www.co.riverside.ca.us/depts/courts
Note: Holds all criminal records for the former Three Lakes District including Lake Elsinore and Temecula. Records are for past 10 years.
Civil Records: Access: Phone, mail, fax, online, in person. Both court and visitors may perform in person searches. No search fee. Required to search: name, years to search. Civil cases indexed by defendant, plaintiff. Civil records on computer since 1997, on index books from 1997. See Riverside Division location for online information.
Criminal Records: Access: Mail, online, in person. Both court and visitors may perform in person searches. No search fee. Required to search: name, years to search, DOB. Criminal records on computer since 1990, on index books from 1990. See Riverside Division for online information.
General Information: Mental health, police reports, items marked confidential not released. SASE required. Turnaround time 2 days. Copy fee: $.50 per page. Certification fee: $6.00. Fee payee: Clerk of the Court. Personal checks accepted. Credit cards accepted: Visa, MasterCard, Discover. Prepayment is required.

Temecula Branch - Superior Court 41002 County Center Dr, Temecula, CA 92591; 909-600-6400; Fax: 909-600-6423. Hours: 7:30AM-5PM (PST). *Civil Actions Under $25,000, Eviction, Small Claims.*
www.co.riverside.ca.us/depts/courts
Note: Records for the Lake Elsinore Branch can also be searched here.
Civil Records: Access: Phone, mail, online, in person. Both court and visitors may perform in person searches. Visitors may search on computer only. No search fee. Required to search: name, years to search, DOB. Civil cases indexed by defendant, plaintiff. Civil records on computer go back 10-12 years; records held for 10 years. See Riverside Division location for online information.
General Information: Public access terminal is available. No confidential, adoption or sealed records released. Unlawful detainers not released for 60 days. SASE required. Turnaround time 3days. Copy fee: $.50 per page. Certification fee: $6.00 per document. Fee payee: Clerk of the Court. Personal checks accepted. Credit cards accepted: Visa, MasterCard, Discover. Prepayment is required.

Moreno Valley Branch - Superior Court 13800 Heacock Ave Ste D201, Moreno Valley, CA 92553-3338; 909-955-1960; Fax: 909-341-8876. Hours: 7:30AM-5PM (PST). *Small Claims, Traffic.*
www.co.riverside.ca.us/depts/courts
Civil Records: Access: Phone, fax, mail, online, in person. Both court and visitors may perform in person searches. No search fee. Required to search: name,

years to search. Civil cases indexed by defendant, plaintiff. Civil records on computer. See Riverside Division location for online information.
General Information: No adoptions, juvenile, medical, probation or sealed records released. SASE required. Turnaround time 1 week. Fax notes: $1.00 per page. Copy fee: $.50 per page. Certification fee: $6.00. Fee payee: Clerk of the Court. Personal checks accepted. Credit cards accepted: Visa, MasterCard, Discover. Prepayment is required.

Sacramento County

Superior Court 720 9th St Rm 102, Sacramento, CA 95814; 916-874-5522; Criminal phone: 916-874-6936; Probate phone: 916-874-5621; Fax: 916-874-5620. Hours: 8:30AM-4:30PM (PST). *Felony, Misdemeanor, Civil, Eviction, Small Claims, Probate.*
www.saccourt.com
Note: Probate is located at 3342 Power Inn Rd, Sacramento 95826.
Civil Records: Access: Phone, fax, mail, online, in person. Both court and visitors may perform in person searches. Search fee: $5.00 per name per year. Also charge $9.00 per hour for court. Required to search: name, years to search; also helpful: address. Civil cases indexed by defendant, plaintiff. Civil records on microfiche and archived from 1937, index books from 1800s. All civil records for Sacramento County are available free on the Internet at www.saccourt.com.
Criminal Records: Access: Phone, mail, online, in person. Both court and visitors may perform in person searches. Search fee: $5.00 per name per year. Required to search: name, years to search; also helpful: address, DOB, SSN. Criminal records on computer since 1993 (Superior) 1995 (Municipal), on microfiche and archived from 1962. All criminal records for Sacramento County are available free on the Internet at www.saccourt.com.
General Information: No adoptions, juvenile, medical, probation or sealed records released. SASE required. Turnaround time 1-3 weeks. Copy fee: $.50 per page. Certification fee: $6.00. Fee payee: Superior Court. Personal checks accepted. Prepayment is required.

Galt Division - Superior Court 380 Civic Dr, Galt, CA 95632; 209-745-1577; Fax: 209-745-6176. Hours: 8:30AM-4:30PM (PST). *Misdemeanor, Small Claims.*
www.saccourt.com
Civil Records: Access: Mail, online, in person. Only the court performs in person searches; visitors may not. Search fee: $5.00. is per case. Required to search: name, years to search. Civil cases indexed by defendant, plaintiff. Civil records in index files from 1984. Records destroyed after 10 years. All civil records for Sacramento County are available free on the Internet at www.saccourt.com.
Criminal Records: Access: Mail, online, in person. Only the court performs in person searches; visitors may not. Search fee: $5.00 per case. Required to search: name, years to search, DOB, signed release. Criminal records in index files from 1984. Records destroyed after 10 years. All criminal records for Sacramento County are available free on the Internet at www.saccourt.com.
General Information: No adoptions, juvenile, medical, probation or sealed records released. SASE required. Turnaround time 2-4 weeks. Copy fee: $1.00 per page. Certification fee: $6.00. Final Judgment certificate $7.00. Fee payee: Superior Court. Personal checks accepted. Prepayment is required.

South Sacramento Superior Court - Elk Grove Branch 8978 Elk Grove Blvd, Elk Grove, CA 95624-1994; 916-685-9825; Fax: 916-685-4689. Hours: 8:30AM-4:30PM (PST). *Misdemeanor, Civil Actions Under $25,000, Eviction, Small Claims.*

www.saccourt.com

Note: Includes southern portion of county with two other branches. This court holds all case records for South Sacramento branches.

Civil Records: Access: Mail, online, in person. Both court and visitors may perform in person searches. Search fee: $5.00 per name per year. Required to search: name, years to search. Civil cases indexed by defendant, plaintiff. Civil records in index files from 1984. Records destroyed after 10 years. All civil records for Sacramento County are available free on the Internet at www.saccourt.com.

Criminal Records: Access: Mail, online, in person. Both court and visitors may perform in person searches. Search fee: $5.00 per name per year. Required to search: name, years to search, DOB. Criminal records in index files from 1984. Records destroyed after 10 years. Online access for criminal records is the same as civil.

General Information: No adoptions, juvenile, medical, probation or sealed records released. SASE required. Turnaround time 2-4 days. Copy fee: $.50 per page. Certification fee: $6.00. Final Judgment certificate $7.00. Fee payee: South Sacramento Superior Court. Personal checks accepted. Prepayment is required.

Walnut Grove Branch - Superior Court

14177 Market St, PO Box 371, Walnut Grove, CA 95690; 916-776-1416; Fax: 916-776-1624. Hours: 8AM-Noon, 1-4:30PM (PST). *Misdemeanor, Eviction, Small Claims.*

www.saccourt.com

Civil Records: Access: Fax, mail, online, person. Both court and visitors may perform in person searches. Search fee: $5.00 per name per year. Required to search: name, years to search. Civil cases indexed by defendant, plaintiff. Civil records in index files from 1984. Records destroyed after 10 years. All civil records for Sacramento County are available free on the Internet at www.saccourt.com.

Criminal Records: Access: Fax, mail, online, in person. Both court and visitors may perform in person searches. Search fee: $5.00 per name per year. Required to search: name, years to search, DOB. Criminal records in index files from 1984. Records destroyed after 10 years. All criminal records for Sacramento County are available free on the Internet at www.saccourt.com.

General Information: No adoptions, juvenile, medical, probation or sealed records released. SASE required. Turnaround time 3-4 days. Copy fee: $.50 per page. $5.00 maximum. Certification fee: $6.00. Final Judgment certificate $7.00. Fee payee: Superior Court. Personal checks accepted. Prepayment is required.

San Benito County

Superior Court Courthouse, 440 5th St-Rm 205, Hollister, CA 95023; 831-636-4057; Fax: 831-636-2046. Hours: 8AM-4PM (PST). *Felony, Misdemeanor, Civil, Small Claims, Eviction, Probate.*

www.superior-court.co.san-benito.ca.us

Note: As of 11/2000, Small Claims, Family Law, and Eviction records are located at the Limited Jurisdiction Court, 390 5th St, Hollister. Phone: 831-630-5115. Fax: 831-636-4117. Same search requirements as stated below.

Civil Records: Access: Mail, in person. Only the court performs in person searches; visitors may not. Search fee: $5.00 per name. Required to search: name, years to search. Civil cases indexed by defendant, plaintiff. Civil records on computer since 1990, index books and archived from 1873.

Criminal Records: Access: Mail, in person. Only the court performs in person searches; visitors may not. Search fee: $5.00 per name. Required to search: name, years to search. Criminal records on computer since 1989, index books and archived from 1900.

General Information: No adoptions, juvenile, medical, probation or sealed records released. SASE required. Turnaround time 1-2 weeks. Copy fee: $.50 per page. Certification fee: $7.00. Fee payee: Superior Court. Personal checks accepted. Prepayment is required.

San Bernardino County

Barstow District - Superior Court

235 E Mountain View, Barstow, CA 92311; Civil phone: 760-256-4907; Criminal phone: 760-256-4785. Hours: 8AM-4PM (PST). *Felony, Misdemeanor, Civil, Eviction, Small Claims.*

www.sbcounty.gov/courts/

Note: Includes the City of Barstow and the unincorporated areas of Yermo, Lenwood, Daggett, Hinkley and Baker.

Civil Records: Access: Mail, in person. Both court and visitors may perform in person searches. Search fee: $5.00 per name. Required to search: name, years to search. Civil cases indexed by defendant, plaintiff. Civil records on computer from 1991, index books and microfilm. Microfilm is 3 to 4 weeks current. Records destroyed after 10 years.

Criminal Records: Access: Mail, in person. Both court and visitors may perform in person searches. Search fee: $5.00 per name. Required to search: name, years to search. Criminal records on computer from 1991, index books and microfilm. Microfilm is 3 to 4 weeks current. Records destroyed after 10 years. Only the daily criminal docket is available online free.

General Information: No probation or confidential reports released. SASE required. Turnaround time 2-5 days. Copy fee: $.50 per page. Certification fee: $6.00. Fee payee: Clerk of the Court. Only cashiers checks and money orders accepted. Credit cards accepted: Visa, MasterCard. Accepted for filings only. Prepayment is required.

Central District - Superior Court

351 N Arrowhead Ave, San Bernardino, CA 92415; Civil phone: 909-387-3922; Criminal phone: 909-384-1888; Fax: 909-387-4428 (387-4993 criminal). Hours: 8AM-4PM (PST). *Felony, Misdemeanor, Civil, Eviction, Small Claims, Probate.*

www.sbcounty.gov/courts

Civil Records: Access: Mail, fax, in person, online. Only the court performs in person searches; visitors may not. Search fee: $5.00 per name. Required to search: name, years to search. Civil cases indexed by defendant, plaintiff. Civil records on computer from 1992, microfiche from 1972, archived and index file from 1856. Online access to weekly "Probate Notes" is available free at www.co.san-bernardino.ca.us/courts/probate/default.htm. Address mail search access requests to Research Dept.

Criminal Records: Access: Mail, in person. Only the court performs in person searches; visitors may not. Search fee: $5.00 per name. Required to search: name, years to search, DOB, SSN. Criminal records on computer from 1996, microfiche from 1972, archived and index file from 1856. Only the daily criminal docket is available online free.

General Information: No adoptions, juvenile, medical, probation or sealed records released. SASE required. Turnaround time 1-2 weeks. Copy fee: $.50 per page. Certification fee: $6.00. Fee payee: Clerk of the Court. Business checks accepted. Credit cards accepted: Visa, Discover. Prepayment is required.

Joshua Tree Division - Superior Court

6527 White Feather Rd (PO Box 6602), Joshua Tree, CA 92252; 760-366-5770; Fax: 760-366-4156. Hours: 8AM-4PM (PST). *Felony, Misdemeanor, Civil, Eviction, Small Claims.*

www.sbcounty.gov/courts/

Note: Includes the incorporated area of City of Twenty-Nine Palms, Town of Yucca Valley and Morongo Valley.

Civil Records: Access: Mail, in person. Only the court performs in person searches; visitors may not. Search fee: $5.00 per name per year. Required to search: name, years to search. Civil cases indexed by defendant, plaintiff. Civil records on computer from 1991, index books from 1983. Records destroyed after 10 years.

Criminal Records: Access: Mail, in person. Only the court performs in person searches; visitors may not. Search fee: $5.00 per name per year. Required to search: name, years to search, DOB. Criminal records on computer from 1991, index books from 1983. Records destroyed after 10 years. Only the daily criminal docket is available online free.

General Information: No probation reports, confidential records released. SASE required. Turnaround time 1 week. Copy fee: $.50 per page. Certification fee: $6.00. Fee payee: Joshua Tree Superior Court. Personal checks accepted. Prepayment is required.

Rancho Cucamonga District - Superior Court

8303 N. Haven Ave, Rancho Cucamonga, CA 91730; Civil phone: 909-945-4131; Criminal phone: 909-350-9764; Fax: 909-945-4154. Hours: 8AM-4PM (PST). *Felony, Misdemeanor, Civil, Eviction, Small Claims, Probate.*

www.co.san-bernardino.ca.us/courts/

Note: Formerly West District Superior Ct. Includes cities of Montclair, Ontario, Upland, Rancho Cucamonga, Alta Loma, Etiwanda, Guasti and surrounding unincorporated area of Mt Baldy.

Civil Records: Access: Phone, fax, mail, in person, online. Both court and visitors may perform in person searches. Search fee: $5.00 per name. Required to search: name, years to search. Civil cases indexed by defendant, plaintiff. Civil records on computer since April 1994, index cards prior. Records destroyed after 10 years. Online access to weekly "Probate Notes" is available free at www.co.san-bernardino.ca.us/courts/probate/default.htm.

Criminal Records: Access: Phone, fax, mail, in person. Only the court performs in person searches; visitors may not. Search fee: $5.00 per name. Required to search: name, years to search; also helpful: DOB. Criminal records computerized since 1994, also on index cards and microfiche. Only the daily criminal docket is available online free.

General Information: No probation reports released. SASE required. Turnaround time 2-4 days. Copy fee: $.50 per page. Certification fee: $6.00. Fee payee: Superior Court. Personal checks accepted. Checks over $10.00 accepted. Credit cards accepted: Visa, AmEx. Prepayment is required.

Victorville District - Superior Court

14455 Civic Dr, Victorville, CA 92392; Civil phone: 760-245-6215; Criminal phone: 760-245-6215; Fax: 760-243-8790 (civil); 8794 (criminal). Hours: 8AM-4PM (PST). *Felony, Misdemeanor, Civil, Eviction, Small Claims.*

www.sbcounty.gov/courts/

Note: Includes the Cities of Victorville, Adelanto Hesperia and the unincorporated area of Apple Valley, El Mirage, Helendale, Lucerne Valley, Oro Grande, Phelan, Pinon Hill and Wrightwood.

Civil Records: Access: Mail, in person. Both court and visitors may perform in person searches. Search fee: $5.00 per name. Required to search: name, years to search. Civil cases indexed by defendant, plaintiff. Civil records on microfiche from 1982 to July 1999, on computer from 1989 to present, index books prior. Records destroyed after 10 years.

Criminal Records: Access: Mail, in person. Only the court performs in person searches; visitors may not. Search fee: $5.00 per name. Required to search: name, years to search; also helpful: DOB, date of offense. Criminal index books by defendant 1986 - present. Only the daily criminal docket is available online free. Only court allowed to search computer index.

General Information: No probation reports released. SASE required. Turnaround time within 1 week. Copy fee: $.50 per page. Certification fee: $6.00. Fee payee: Superior Court. Personal checks accepted. $5.00 minimum. Prepayment is required.

Big Bear Lake District - Superior Court

PO Box 2806 (477 summit Blvd.), Big Bear Lake, CA 92315; 909-866-0150; Fax: 909-866-0160. Hours: 8AM-4PM (PST). *Misdemeanor, Civil Actions Under $25,000, Eviction, Small Claims.*

www.sbcounty.gov/courts

Civil Records: Access: Mail, in person. Both court and visitors may perform in person searches. Search fee: $5.00 per name per year. Required to search: name, years to search. Civil cases indexed by defendant, plaintiff. Civil records on computer since 9/1/96; prior on index books. Will only search back 7 years.

Criminal Records: Access: Mail, in person. Both court and visitors may perform in person searches. Search fee: $5.00 per name per year. Required to search: name, years to search, DOB; also helpful: SSN. Criminal records on index books. Will only search back 7 years. Only the daily criminal docket is available online free.

General Information: No probation reports released. SASE required. Turnaround time 1 week. Copy fee: $.50 per page. Certification fee: $6.00. Fee payee: Superior Court. Personal checks accepted. Prepayment is required.

Central Division Branch - Superior Court

351 N Arrowhead, San Bernardino, CA 92415-0220; Civil phone: 909-885-0139; Criminal phone: 909-384-1888; Probate phone: 909-387-3952; Fax: 909-387-4428. Hours: 8AM-4PM (PST). *Misdemeanor, Civil Actions, Eviction, Small Claims, Probate.*

www.sbcounty.gov/courts/

Note: Includes the City of Bernardino, cities of Grand Terrace, Loma Linda, Colton and Highland and the unincorporated area of Del Rosa, Devore, Miscoy, Patton, Verdemont. Specify which city you are searching in.

Civil Records: Access: Phone, mail, fax, in person, online. Both court and visitors may perform in person searches. Search fee: $5.00 per name. Required to search: name, years to search. Civil cases indexed by defendant, plaintiff. Civil records on computer from 1991, index files from 1983, microfiche from 1972. Online access to weekly "Probate Notes" is available free at www.co.san-bernardino.ca.us/courts/probate/default.htm.

Criminal Records: Access: Mail, in person. Both court and visitors may perform in person searches. Search fee: $5.00 per name. Required to search: name, years to search; also helpful: DOB. Criminal records on computer from 1991, index files from 1983, microfiche from 1972. Only the daily criminal docket is available online free.

General Information: No probation reports released. SASE required. Turnaround time 2 days. Fax notes: Fee to fax results is $1.00 per page. Copy fee: $.50 per page. Certification fee: $6.00. Fee payee: San Bernardino Superior Court. Personal checks accepted. Prepayment is required.

Chino Division - Superior Court

13260 Central Ave, Chino, CA 91710; Civil phone: 909-465-5266; Criminal phone: 909-465-5260; Fax: 909-465-5221. Hours: 8AM-4PM (PST). *Misdemeanor, Eviction, Small Claims.*

www.sbcounty.gov/courts/

Note: Includes City of Chino and surrounding unincorporated area. Rancho Cucamonga Courts handles all civil cases since 01/01/99.

Civil Records: Access: Fax, mail, in person. Only the court performs in person searches; visitors may not. Search fee: $5.00 per name. Required to search: name, years to search; also helpful: address. Civil cases indexed by defendant, plaintiff. Civil records on computer from 1991, index books from 1983. Records destroyed after 10 years.

Criminal Records: Access: Mail, in person. Only the court performs in person searches; visitors may not. Search fee: $5.00 per name. Required to search: name, years to search, DOB; also helpful: address. Criminal records on computer from 1991, index books from 1983. Records destroyed after 10 years. Only the daily criminal docket is available online free.

General Information: No probation reports released. SASE required. Turnaround time 2 days. Copy fee: $.50 per page. Certification fee: $6.00. Fee payee: Chino Superior Court. Personal checks accepted. Prepayment is required.

Fontana Division - Superior Court

17780 Arrow Blvd, Fontana, CA 92335; 909-350-9322. Hours: 8AM-4PM (PST). *Felony, Misdemeanor, Civil Actions Under $25,000, Traffic.*

www.sbcounty.gov/courts/

Note: Includes the Cities of Fontana, Rialto, Crestmore and the unincorporated areas of Lytle Creek Canyon and Bloomington.

Civil Records: Access: Mail, in person. Only the court performs in person searches; visitors may not. Search fee: $5.00 per name. Required to search: name, years to search; also helpful: address. Civil cases indexed by defendant, plaintiff. Civil records on computer from 1987, microfilm prior. Records destroyed after 10 years.

Criminal Records: Access: Mail, in person. Both court and visitors may perform in person searches. Search fee: $5.00 per name. Required to search: name, years to search; also helpful: DOB. Criminal records on computer from 1987, microfilm prior. Records destroyed after 10 years. Only the daily criminal docket is available online free.

General Information: No probation reports or police records released. SASE required. Turnaround time 2-5 days. Copy fee: $.50 per page. Certification fee: $6.00. Fee payee: Fontana Courts. Personal checks accepted. Prepayment is required.

Needles District - Superior Court

1111 Bailey Ave, Needles, CA 92363; 760-326-9245; Fax: 760-326-9254. Hours: 8AM-4PM (PST). *Felony, Misdemeanor, Civil Actions Under $25,000, Eviction, Small Claims.*

www.sbcounty.gov/courts

Civil Records: Access: Mail, in person. Only the court performs in person searches; visitors may not. Search fee: $5.00 per name. Required to search: name, years to search. Civil cases indexed by plaintiff. Civil records in index books. Will only search back 7 years.

Criminal Records: Access: Mail, in person. Only the court performs in person searches; visitors may not. Search fee: $5.00 per name. Required to search: name, years to search. Criminal records on computer from 1990, index books prior. Will only search back 7 years. Only the daily criminal docket is available online free.

General Information: No probation reports released. SASE required. Turnaround time 1-2 weeks. Copy fee: $.50 per page. Certification fee: $6.00. Fee payee: Superior Court. Personal checks accepted. Prepayment is required.

Redlands District - Superior Court

216 Brookside Ave, Redlands, CA 92373; Civil phone: 909-888-4260; Criminal phone: 909-885-1269; Fax:

909-798-8588. Hours: 8AM-4PM (PST). *Felony, Misdemeanor, Eviction, Small Claims.*

www.sbcounty.gov/courts/

Note: Includes Cities of Redlands, Yucaipa and the unincorporated areas of Angeles Oaks, Barton Flats, Forest Home and Mentone.

Civil Records: Access: Mail, in person. Only the court performs in person searches; visitors may not. Search fee: $5.00 per name. Required to search: name, years to search. Civil cases indexed by defendant, plaintiff. Civil records on computer from 1991, index books prior. Records destroyed after 10 years.

Criminal Records: Access: Mail, in person. Only the court performs in person searches; visitors may not. Search fee: $5.00 per name. Required to search: name, years to search, DOB. Criminal records on computer from 1998, index books prior. Records destroyed after 10 years. Only the daily criminal docket is available online free.

General Information: No probation reports released. SASE required. Turnaround time 2 days. Copy fee: $.50 per page. Certification fee: $6.00. Fee payee: Superior Court. Prepayment is required.

Twin Peaks District - Superior Court

26010 State Hwy 189 (PO Box 394), Twin Peaks, CA 92391; 909-336-0620; Fax: 909-336-0683. Hours: 8AM-4PM (PST). *Felony, Misdemeanor, Civil under $25,000, Eviction, Small Claims.*

www.sbcounty.gov/courts

Civil Records: Access: Mail, in person. Only the court performs in person searches; visitors may not. Search fee: $5.00 per name per year. Required to search: name, years to search. Civil cases indexed by defendant, plaintiff. Civil records on index cards. Will only search back 7 years.

Criminal Records: Access: Mail, in person. Only the court performs in person searches; visitors may not. Search fee: $5.00 per name per year. Required to search: name, years to search, DOB. Criminal records on computer from 1990, index cards prior. Will only search back 7 years. Only the daily criminal docket is available online free.

General Information: No probation or arrest reports released. SASE required. Turnaround time 1 week. Copy fee: $.50 per page. Certification fee: $6.00. Fee payee: Superior Court. No checks accepted.

San Diego County

Superior Court - Civil

Hall of Justice, PO Box 120128 (330 W Broadway), San Diego, CA 92112-0128; Civil phone: 619-531-3141; Probate phone: 619-687-2292. Hours: 8:30AM-4:30PM (PST). *Civil, Probate, Eviction, Small Claims, Probate.*

www.sandiego.courts.ca.gov/superior

Note: Now has Central Division Limited Jurisdiction civil cases. For any San Diego County requests, always specify which division - Central, East, North or South. Central Div. Probate is located at the Madge Bradley Bldg, 1409 Fourth Avenue, 92101.

Civil Records: Access: Mail, in person. Both court and visitors may perform in person searches. Search fee: $5.00 per name. Required to search: name, years to search. Civil cases indexed by defendant, plaintiff. Civil records index on computer from 06/74. The county-wide system sells a CD-ROM of civil, domestic, mental health, and probate indices. Also, the court's five day calendar is available free at www.sandiego.courts.ca.gov/superior/online/searchcal.html. New case searching is also available.

General Information: Public access terminal is available. No probation reports released. SASE required. Turnaround time 1 day. Copy fee: $.50 per page. Certification fee: $6.00. Fee payee: Clerk of Superior Court. Personal checks accepted. Prepayment is required.

Superior Court - Criminal

PO Box 120128 (220 W Broadway), San Diego, CA 92112-0128; 619-531-3040 Misdemeanor; Criminal phone: 619-685-6220. Hours: 8:30AM-4:30PM (PST). *Felony, Misdemeanor.*

www.sandiego.courts.ca.gov/superior/

Note: Both General and Limited Criminal records are located here.

Criminal Records: Access: Mail, in person. Both court and visitors may perform in person searches. Search fee: $5.00 per name. Fee is per index. Required to search: name, years to search, DOB. Criminal records on computer from 1974 to present, paper ledgers from 1860s. The county system sells a CD-ROM of criminal records; felonies from 6/1974 to 1999; misdemeanors back 10 years. Also, the court's five day calendar is available free at www.sandiego.courts.ca.gov/superior/online/searchcal.html. Online searching of new cases is also available.

General Information: Public access terminal is available. No adoptions, juvenile, medical, probation or sealed records released. SASE required. Turnaround time 1 week. Copy fee: $.50 per page. Certification fee: $6.00. Fee payee: San Diego Superior Court. Personal checks accepted. No out of state personal checks. Prepayment is required.

East County Division - Superior Court

250 E Main St, El Cajon, CA 92020; 619-441-4622. Hours: 8AM-4:30PM (PST). *Felony, Misdemeanor, Civil, Small Claims, Eviction.*

www.sandiego.courts.ca.gov

Note: This court now houses the former municipal court records.

Civil Records: Access: Mail, in person. Both court and visitors may perform in person searches. Search fee: $5.00 per name. Required to search: name, years to search. Civil cases indexed by defendant, plaintiff. Civil records on computer since 1974; microfilm prior. Online searching of 5-day calendars is available free at www.sandiego.courts.ca.gov/superior/online/searchcal.html. New case searching is also available.

Criminal Records: Access: Mail, in person. Both court and visitors may perform in person searches. Search fee: $5.00 per name. Required to search: name, years to search; also helpful: DOB. Criminal records on computer since 1974; microfilm prior. The county system sells a CD-ROM of criminal records; felonies from 6/1974 to 1999; misdemeanors back 10 years. Also, the court's five day calendar is available free at www.sandiego.courts.ca.gov/superior/online/searchcal.html. Online searching of new cases is also available.

General Information: Public access terminal is available. No confidential or sealed records released. SASE required. Turnaround time 3-5 days. Copy fee: $.50 per page. Certification fee: $6.00. Fee payee: Clerk of Superior Court. Personal checks accepted. California checks with preprinted name and address only. Law firm business checks accepted. Prepayment is required.

North County Branch - Superior Court

325 S Melrose Dr, #120, Vista, CA 92083-6627; 760-726-9595; Probate phone: 760-806-6150. Hours: 8:30AM-4:30PM (PST). *Felony, Misdemeanor, Civil Actions, Eviction, Small Claims, Probate.*

www.sandiego.courts.ca.gov

Note: Includes Cities of Oceanside, Del Mar, Carlsbad, Solana Beach, Encinitas, Escondido, San Marcos, Vista and unincorporated towns of Del Dios, Olivehain, San Luis Rey, San Pasqual, Rancho Santa Fe, Valley Center, Bonsall, Palomar Mountain, etc.

Civil Records: Access: Mail, in person. Both court and visitors may perform in person searches. Search fee: $5.00 per name. Required to search: name, years to search. Civil cases indexed by defendant, plaintiff. Civil records on computer back to 1993; prior on microfiche

and index books. Online searching of 5-day calendars is available free at www.sandiego.courts.ca.gov/superior/online/searchcal.html. New case searching is also available.

Criminal Records: Access: Mail, in person. Both court and visitors may perform in person searches. Search fee: $5.00 per name. Required to search: name, years to search. Criminal records on computer back to 1993; prior on microfiche and index books. The county system sells a CD-ROM of criminal records; felonies from 6/1974 to 1999; misdemeanors back 10 years. Also, the court's five day calendar is available free at www.sandiego.courts.ca.gov/superior/online/searchcal.html. Online searching of new cases is also available.

General Information: Public access terminal is available. No sealed or confidential documents released. SASE required. Turnaround time 2-3 days. Copy fee: $.50 per page. Certification fee: $6.00. Fee payee: Clerk of the Superior Court. Personal checks accepted. Out of state checks not accepted. Prepayment is required.

South County Branch - Superior Court

500-C 3rd Ave, Chula Vista, CA 91910; Civil phone: 619-691-4439; Criminal phone: 619-691-4728; Fax: 619-691-4969 (Civil) 4864 is Criminal. Hours: 8:30AM-4:30PM (PST). *Felony, Misdemeanor, Civil Actions, Probate, Eviction, Small Claims.*

www.sandiego.courts.ca.gov

Note: Includes National City, Chula Vista, Coronado, Imperial Beach and that portion of the City of San Diego lying south of the City of Chula Vista and contiguous unincorporated areas.

Civil Records: Access: Fax, mail, in person. Both court and visitors may perform in person searches. Search fee: $5.00 per name per year. Required to search: name, years to search. Civil cases indexed by defendant, plaintiff. Civil records on computer; for case files prior to 1991, contact Superior Court's Main Records Division, Downtown. Online searching of 5-day calendars is available free at www.sandiego.courts.ca.gov/superior/online/searchcal.html. New case searching is also available.

Criminal Records: Access: Phone, fax, mail, in person. Both court and visitors may perform in person searches. Search fee: $5.00 per name. Required to search: name, years to search, DOB. Criminal records on computer, cases files in or before 1986 on microfiche. The county system sells a CD-ROM of criminal records; felonies from 6/1974 to 1999; misdemeanors back 10 years. Also, the court's five day calendar is available for free at www.sandiego.courts.ca.gov/superior/online/searchcal.html. Online searching of new cases is also available.

General Information: Public access terminal is available. No juvenile, medical, probation reports or pronouncement of judgment records released. SASE required. Turnaround time up to 1 week (civil)- Turnaround time depends on availability of clerk (criminal). Copy fee: $.60 per page. Certification fee: $6.00. Fee payee: Superior Court (Civil)-Clerk of the Court (Criminal). Personal checks accepted. Prepayment is required.

Kearny Mesa Branch - Central Division

8950 Clairemont Mesa Blvd, San Diego, CA 92123; 858-694-2066 Small Claims. Hours: 8AM-4PM (PST). *Small Claims, Traffic.*

www.sandiego.courts.ca.gov/superior/index.html

Ramona Branch - East Division

1428 Montecito Rd, Ramona, CA 92065; 760-738-2435. Hours: 8AM-4:30PM (PST). *Misdemeanor, Civil Actions Under $25,000, Eviction, Small Claims.*

www.sandiego.courts.ca.gov

Note: Jurisdiction over the northeast area of the county.

Civil Records: Access: Fax, mail, in person. Both court and visitors may perform in person searches. Search

fee: $5.00 per name. Required to search: name, years to search. Civil cases indexed by defendant, plaintiff. Civil records on computer from 1991, index files since 1983. Files destroyed after 10 years. Online searching of 5-day calendars is available for free at www.sandiego.courts.ca.gov/superior/online/searchcal.html. New case searching is also available.

Criminal Records: Access: Fax, mail, in person. Both court and visitors may perform in person searches. Search fee: $5.00 per name. Required to search: name, years to search, SSN; also helpful: DOB. Criminal records on computer from 1991, index files since 1983. Files destroyed after 10 years. The county system sells a CD-ROM of criminal records; felonies from 6/1974 to 1999; misdemeanors back 10 years. Also, the court's five day calendar is available free at www.sandiego.courts.ca.gov/superior/online/searchcal.html. Online searching of new cases is also available.

General Information: No probation reports or DMV records released. SASE required. Turnaround time 2-3 days. Fax notes: No fee to fax results. Copy fee: $.50 per page. Certification fee: $6.00. Fee payee: Clerk of the Court. Personal checks accepted. Credit cards accepted: Visa, MasterCard. Prepayment is required.

San Marcos Branch - North Divison

338 Via Vera Cruz, San Marcos, CA 92069-2693; 760-940-2888; Fax: 760-940-2802. Hours: 8:30AM-4:30PM (PST). *Misdemeanor, Traffic.*

www.sandiego.courts.ca.gov

Civil Records: Access: Mail, in person. Both court and visitors may perform in person searches. Search fee: $5.00 per name. Required to search: name, years to search; also helpful: address. Civil records on computer since 1994. Online searching of 5-day calendars is available free at www.sandiego.courts.ca.gov/superior/online/searchcal.html. New case searching is also available.

Criminal Records: Access: Mail, in person. Both court and visitors may perform in person searches. Search fee: $5.00 per name. Required to search: name, years to search; also helpful: address. Criminal records on computer since 1994. The county system sells a CD-ROM of criminal records; felonies from 6/1974 to 1999; misdemeanors back 10 years. Also, the court's five day calendar is available free at www.sandiego.courts.ca.gov/superior/online/searchcal.html. Online searching of new cases is also available.

General Information: Juvenile and adoption records are not released. Turnaround time 3 days. Copy fee: $.50 per page. Certification fee: $6.00. Fee payee: Clerk of the Court. Personal checks accepted. Prepayment is required.

San Francisco County

Superior Court - Criminal Division

850 Bryant St #306, San Francisco, CA 94107/94103; 415-553-1159. Hours: 8AM-4:30PM (PST). *Felony.*

www.ci.sf.ca.us/courts

Criminal Records: Access: Fax, mail, in person. Both court and visitors may perform in person searches. Search fee: $5.00 per name per year. Add warehouse retrieval fee of $5.00. Required to search: name, years to search, DOB. If searching by mail, direct your letter to Katherine Hill, Prior Convictions.

General Information: No medical, probation or sealed records released. SASE required. Turnaround time 1 week. Fax notes: No fee to fax results. Copy fee: $1.00 per page. Certification fee: $6.00. Fee payee: Clerk of the Superior Court. Personal checks accepted with ID only. Cashier checks and money orders accepted. Prepayment is required.

Superior Court - Civil Division

400 McAllister St, Rm 103, San Francisco, CA 94102; 415-551-3802; Probate phone: 415-551-3892. Hours: 10AM-4PM *Civil, Small Claims, Eviction, Probate.*

www.ci.sf.ca.us/courts

Civil Records: Access: Mail, in person. Both court and visitors may perform in person searches. Search fee: $5.00 per name per year. Required to search: name, years to search. Civil cases indexed by defendant, plaintiff. Civil cases on computer since 1987; prior records on microfilm and microfiche.

General Information: Public access terminal is available. No medical, probation or sealed records released. SASE required. Turnaround time 2 weeks. Copy fee: $1.00 per page. Certification fee: $6.00 plus $1.00 per page. Fee payee: Clerk of the Superior Court. Personal checks accepted. Credit cards accepted: Visa, MasterCard. Prepayment is required.

Limited Superior - Civil Division 400 McAllister St, Rm 103, San Francisco, CA 94107; 415-551-4032 (Records Section); Civil phone: 415-551-4000; Fax: 415-551-4041. Hours: 8AM-4:30PM (PST). *Civil Actions Under $25,000, Eviction, Small Claims.*

www.ci.sf.ca.us/courts

Note: Includes all of San Francisco County, including former municipal court on Folsom St

Civil Records: Access: Mail, in person. Both court and visitors may perform in person searches. Search fee: $5.00 per name per year. No charge if easily pulled from computer. Required to search: name, years to search. Civil cases indexed by defendant, plaintiff. Civil records on computer from 1991, index files from 1983. Records destroyed after 10 years.

General Information: Public access terminal is available. No sealed records released. SASE required. Turnaround time 2 days. Copy fee: $.75 per page. Certification fee: $6.00 plus $1.00 per page & copy fee. Fee payee: Superior Court. Personal checks accepted. Prepayment is required.

Superior Court - Misdemeanor Division 850 Bryant St Rm 201, San Francisco, CA 94103; 415-553-1665 (Records Dept); Criminal phone: 415-553-9395. Hours: 8AM-4:30PM (PST). *Misdemeanor.*

www.ci.sf.ca.us/courts

Note: Includes all of San Francisco County

Criminal Records: Access: Mail, in person. Both court and visitors may perform in person searches. Search fee: $5.00 per name per year. Required to search: name, years to search; also helpful: DOB. Criminal records (pending) on computer from 1991, index files from 1983. Records are destroyed after 10 years.

General Information: No probation reports released. SASE required. Turnaround time 3-4 weeks. Copy fee: $1.00 per page. Microfilm copies $1.50 per page. Certification fee: $1.75. Fee payee: Superior Court. Personal checks accepted. Prepayment is required.

San Joaquin County

Superior Court - Civil 222 E Weber Ave, Rm 303, Stockton, CA 95202-2709; 209-468-2355; Fax: 209-468-0539. Hours: 7:30AM-5 M-F (office); 8AM-5PM M-F (phones) (PST). *Civil Actions, Eviction, Small Claims, Probate.*

www.stocktoncourt.org/courts

Note: Includes City of Stockton and suburban area, Farmington and Linden, Delta area and surrounding unincorporated areas

Civil Records: Access: Mail, in person. Both court and visitors may perform in person searches. Search fee: $5.00 per name. No fee if search is done by customer. Required to search: name, years to search. Civil cases indexed by defendant, plaintiff. Civil records on computer from 1996; indices/books from 1850-1973; Microfiche 1973-1996. Records destroyed after 10 years.

General Information: Public access terminal is available. No probation, confidential records released. SASE required. Turnaround time 5-7 days. Copy fee:

$.50 per page. Certification fee: $6.00. Fee payee: Superior Court. Personal checks accepted. Prepayment is required.

Superior Court - Criminal Division 222 E Weber Ave Rm 101, Stockton, CA 95202; 209-468-2935. Hours: 7:30AM-5PM (PST). *Felony, Misdemeanor.*

www.stocktoncourt.org/courts

Criminal Records: Access: Mail, in person. Both court and visitors may perform in person searches. Search fee: $5.00 per name. Required to search: name, years to search, signed release; also helpful: DOB, SSN. Criminal Records on computer since 1992, on microfiche since 1972, older records archived to 1800s. Mail access only available to authorized agencies.

General Information: Public access terminal is available. No juvenile, medical, probation, sealed records released. SASE required. Turnaround time 1 week. Copy fee: $.50 per page. Certification fee: $6.00. Fee payee: San Joaquin Superior Court. Personal checks accepted. Cash only for forms and kits. Prepayment is required.

Lodi Division - Superior Court 315 W Elm St (Civil), 230 W Elm St (Criminal), Lodi, CA 95240; Civil phone: 209-331-2101; Criminal phone: 209-331-2121; Fax: 209-331-2135. Hours: 8AM-5PM (PST). *Misdemeanor, Civil Actions Under $25,000, Eviction, Small Claims.*

www.stocktoncourt.org/courts/

Note: Includes eight mile road to Sacramento County line, towns of Acampo, Clements, Lockeford, Terminous, Thornton, Woodbridge.

Civil Records: Access: Phone, mail, fax, in person. Both court and visitors may perform in person searches. Search fee: $6.00 per name. Required to search: name, years to search. Civil cases indexed by defendant, plaintiff. Civil records on computer from 1994, index files from 1989. Records destroyed after 10 years.

Criminal Records: Access: Phone, mail, fax, in person. Both court and visitors may perform in person searches. Search fee: $6.00 per name. Required to search: name, years to search, DOB; also helpful: address, SSN, sex. Criminal records on computer from 1991, index files from 1983. Records destroyed after 10 years.

General Information: Public access terminal is available. (Criminal records only available.) No probation reports released. SASE required. Turnaround time 5 days. Copy fee: $.50 per page. Certification fee: $6.00. Fee payee: Superior Court. Personal checks accepted. Prepayment is required.

Manteca Branch - Superior Court 315 E Center St, Manteca, CA 95336; Civil phone: 209-239-9188; Criminal phone: 209-239-1316. Hours: 8AM-4PM (PST). *Felony, Misdemeanor, Civil Actions Under $25,000, Eviction, Small Claims.*

www.stocktoncourt.org/courts

Note: Includes Cities of Manteca, Ripon, Escalon, French Camp, Lathrop and surrounding unincorporated areas.

Civil Records: Access: Mail, in person. Only the court performs in person searches; visitors may not. Search fee: $5.00 per name. Fee is for cases more than 3 years old. Required to search: name, years to search. Civil cases indexed by defendant, plaintiff. Civil records on computer from 1991, microfiche since 1986, index files from 1983. Records destroyed after 10 years.

Criminal Records: Access: Mail, in person. Only the court performs in person searches; visitors may not. Search fee: $5.00 per name. Fee is for cases prior to 1990. Required to search: name, years to search; also helpful: DOB. Criminal records on computer since 1990, microfiche since 1986, index files from 1983.

Records destroyed after 10 years. Special request form required to view files.

General Information: No judge's notes, probation or police reports released. SASE required. Turnaround time 1-2 days. Copy fee: $.50 per page. Certification fee: $6.00. Fee payee: Superior Court. Personal checks accepted. Prepayment is required.

Tracy Branch - Superior Court 475 E 10th St, Tracy, CA 95376; Civil phone: 209-831-5902; Criminal phone: 209-831-5900; Fax: 209-831-5919. Hours: 8AM-5PM (PST). *Felony, Misdemeanor, Civil Actions Under $25,000, Eviction, Small Claims.*

www.stocktoncourt.org/courts

Note: Includes Cities of Tracy, Banta, portion of Vernalis and surrounding unincorporated area.

Civil Records: Access: Phone, mail, in person. Only the court performs in person searches; visitors may not. Search fee: $5.00 per name. If on computer, no charge. Required to search: name, years to search. Civil cases indexed by defendant, plaintiff. Civil records on computer since 03/95; on index files from 1983. Records destroyed after 10 years.

Criminal Records: Access: Mail, in person. Only the court performs in person searches; visitors may not. Search fee: $5.00 per name. Required to search: name, years to search, DOB. Criminal records on computer from 1991; on index files from 1983. Records destroyed after 10 years.

General Information: No probation reports, DMV history and criminal history records released. SASE required. Turnaround time 5-10 days. Copy fee: $.50 per page. Certification fee: $6.00. Fee payee: Tracy Superior Court. Personal checks accepted. Prepayment is required.

San Luis Obispo County

Superior Court - Civil Division 1035 Palm Street, Room 385, Government Center, San Luis Obispo, CA 93408; 805-781-5677. Hours: 8:30AM-4PM (PST). *Civil Actions, Small Claims, Eviction, Probate.*

www.slocourts.net

Note: This Court has jurisdiction over all of San Luis Obispo County, San Luis Obispo, Morro Bay, Avila Beach areas for Civil actions over $25,000, and also the current and former "limited jurisdiction" (under $25,000) civil cases in the immediate area.

Civil Records: Access: Mail, in person. Both court and visitors may perform in person searches. No search fee. Required to search: name, years to search. Civil cases indexed by defendant, plaintiff. Civil records on computer from 1991, index files from 1983. Records destroyed after 10 years.

General Information: Public access terminal is available. No probation reports released. SASE required. Turnaround time 2-5 days. Copy fee: $.50 per page. Certification fee: $6.00. Fee payee: Superior Court. Personal checks accepted. Prepayment required.

Superior Court - Criminal Division Government Center, Rm 220, 1035 Palm Street, San Luis Obispo, CA 93408; Criminal phone: 805-781-5670. 8:30AM-4PM (PST). *Felony, Misdemeanor.*

www.slocourts.net

Note: Due to re-organization of the courts in this city, this court now handles misdemeanor cases which were formerly handled by the limited jurisdiction court. The civil cases are now located at the new Superior Court - Civil Division.

Criminal Records: Access: Mail, in person. Both court and visitors may perform in person searches. Search fee: $5.00 per name. Required to search: name, years to search. Criminal records on computer and microfiche from 1975, archived and index file from late 1800s.

General Information: Public access terminal is available. No adoptions, juvenile, medical, probation or sealed records released. SASE required. Turnaround time 2-5 days. Copy fee: $.50 per page. Certification fee: $6.00. Fee payee: Superior Court Criminal Court Operations. Personal checks accepted. Prepayment is required.

Grover Beach Branch - Superior Court
214 S 16th St, Grover Beach, CA 93433-2299; Civil phone: 805-473-7077; Criminal phone: 805-473-7072. Hours: 8:30AM-4PM (PST). *Misdemeanor, Civil Actions Under $25,000, Eviction, Small Claims.*

www.slocourts.net

Note: Includes Nipomo, Grover Beach, Arroyo Grande, Pismo Beach, Ociano, South Coast unincorporated areas.
Civil Records: Access: Phone, mail, in person. Only the court performs in person searches; visitors may not. Search fee: First name is free, then $5.00 per name. Required to search: name, years to search. Civil cases indexed by defendant, plaintiff. Civil records on index cards to 1976; on computer back to 1986. Records destroyed after 10 years.
Criminal Records: Access: Phone, mail, in person. Only the court performs in person searches; visitors may not. Search fee: First name is free, then $5.00 per name. Required to search: name, years to search. Criminal records on index cards to 1976; on computer back to 1986. Records destroyed after 10 years.
General Information: No probation reports released. SASE required. Turnaround 2-3 weeks civil; 1 week criminal. Copy fee: $.50 per page. Certification fee: $6.00. Fee payee: Superior Court. Personal checks accepted. Prepayment is required.

Paso Robles Branch - Superior Court
549 10th St, Paso Robles, CA 93446-2593; Civil phone: 805-237-3080; Criminal phone: 805-237-3080. Hours: 8:30AM-4PM (PST). *Misdemeanor, Civil Actions Under $25,000, Eviction, Small Claims.*

www.slocourts.net

Note: Includes Atascadero, Templeton, Paso Robles, San Miguel, Shandon, Cholame, areas north and east of the Cuesta Grade.
Civil Records: Access: Phone, mail, in person. Both the court and visitors may perform in person searches. Search fee: $5.00 per name. Search is free if only one name. Required to search: name, years to search. Civil cases indexed by defendant, plaintiff. Civil records on computer from 1975, index files from 1983. Records destroyed after 10 years. Mail requests limited to 5 at a time.
Criminal Records: Access: Phone, mail, in person. Both the court and visitors may perform in person searches. Search fee: $5.00. Search is free for only one name. Required to search: name, years to search; also helpful: DOB. Criminal records on computer from 1975, index files from 1983. Records destroyed after 10 years. Mail requests limited to 5 at a time.
General Information: Public access terminal is available. No driving histories, rap sheets, sealed or probation reports released. SASE required. Turnaround time 1-2 days. Copy fee: $.50 per page. Certification fee: $6.00. Fee payee: Superior Court. Personal checks accepted. Prepayment is required.

San Mateo County

Superior Court 400 County Center, Redwood City, CA 94063; Civil phone: 650-363-4711; Criminal phone: 650-363-4302; Fax: 650-363-4914. Hours: 8AM-4PM (PST). *Felony, Civil Actions Over $25,000, Probate.*

www.sanmateocourt.org

Civil Records: Access: Mail, in person. Both court and visitors may perform in person searches. Search fee:

$5.00 per name. Required to search: name, years to search. Civil cases indexed by defendant, plaintiff. Civil records on computer from 1978; index books prior.
Criminal Records: Access: Mail, in person. Both court and visitors may perform in person searches. Search fee: $5.00 per name. Required to search: name, years to search; also helpful: address, DOB, SSN. Criminal records on computer since 1964; prior on books.
General Information: Public access terminal is available. No confidential jackets on conservatorships & guardianships, adoptions, juvenile, medical, probation or sealed records released. SASE required. Turnaround time 1 week. Copy fee: $.75 per page. Certification fee: $6.00. Fee payee: Superior Court. Personal checks accepted. Prepayment is required.

Northern Branch - Superior Court
1050 Mission Rd, South San Francisco, CA 94080; 650-877-5773; Civil phone: 877-5778 (Sm Claims). Hours: 8AM-4PM (PST). *Misdemeanor, Small Claims, Traffic.*

www.sanmateocourt.org/locnor.htm

Note: Includes Brisbane, Daly City (including Westlake), Pacifica, San Bruno, South San Francisco, the northern coastal towns and all unincorporated areas in the north end of the county including Colma and Broadmoor.
Criminal Records: Access: Mail, in person. Both court and visitors may perform in person searches. Search fee: $5.00 per name. Required to search: name, years to search; also helpful: DOB. Criminal records on computer back to 1991, index files from 1983. Records destroyed after 10 years.
General Information: Public access terminal is available. No probation reports or confidential information records released. SASE required. Turnaround time 2 days-2 weeks. Copy fee: $.75 per page. Certification fee: $6.00. Fee payee: Superior Court. Personal checks accepted. Prepayment is required.

San Mateo Combined Superior Court
400 County Center, Redwood City, CA 94063; 650-363-4302. Hours: 8AM-4PM (PST). *Misdemeanor, Civil, Eviction, Small Claims.*

www.co.sanmateo.ca.us/sanmateocourts/dome.htm

Note: Includes Atherton, Menlo Park, Portola Valley, Redwood City, San Carlos, Woodside, East Palo Alto and all unincorporated areas including La Honda and the southern coastal area south of Tunitas Creek Road which includes Pescadara and San Gregorio.
Civil Records: Access: Mail, in person. Both court and visitors may perform in person searches. Search fee: $5.00 per name. Required to search: name, years to search. Civil cases indexed by defendant, plaintiff. Civil Records on computer since 1991.
Criminal Records: Access: Mail, in person. Both court and visitors may perform in person searches. Search fee: $5.00 per name. Required to search: name, years to search. Criminal records on computer from 1991, index files from 1983. Records destroyed after 10 years.
General Information: Public access terminal is available. No probation reports or confidential information records released. SASE required. Turnaround time 2 weeks. Copy fee: $.75 per page. Certification fee: $6.00. Fee payee: Superior Court. Personal checks accepted. Write "not to exceed $x.xx" on check. Credit cards accepted: Visa, MasterCard. Credit card accepted in person only. Prepayment is required.

Santa Barbara County

Superior Court - Civil - Anacapa Division
Box 21107 (1100 Anacapa St), Santa Barbara, CA 93121; 805-568-2220; Civil phone: 805-568-2238; Criminal phone: 805-568-2753; Fax: 805-568-2219. Hours: 8AM-4:45PM (PST). *Civil Actions, Eviction, Small Claims, Probate.*

www.sbcourts.org/index.htm

Note: Also known as the Anacapa Division.
Civil Records: Access: Phone, fax, mail, in person. Both court and visitors may perform in person searches. Search fee: $5.00 per name. Required to search: name, years to search. Civil cases indexed by defendant, plaintiff. Civil records on computer and microfiche from 1975, archived and index file from 1920. A CD-rom of monthy court indices from all divisions is available for $40.00.
General Information: Public access terminal is available. No adoptions, juvenile, medical, probation or sealed records released. SASE required. Turnaround time 1 week. Copy fee: $.75 per page. Certification fee: $6.00; if marriage dissolution, is $10.00. Fee payee: Superior Court. Personal checks accepted. Credit cards accepted: Visa, MasterCard. Prepayment is required.

Superior Court - Criminal - Figueroa Division
118 E Figueroa St, Santa Barbara, CA 93101; 805-568-2735; Civil phone: 805-568-2238; Criminal phone: 805-568-2752/2753; Fax: 805-568-3208. 7:45AM-4PM (PST). *Felony, Misdemeanor.*

www.sbcourts.org/index.htm

Note: Includes the City of Santa Barbara, Goleta and adjacent unincorporated areas, Carpenteria, Montecito. For civil cases heard here prior to 09/01/98, call Anacapa Division at 805-568-2200.
Criminal Records: Access: Mail, in person. Both court and visitors may perform in person searches. Search fee: $5.00 per name. Required to search: name, years to search; also helpful: DOB. Criminal records on computer from 1991, index files from 1983, microfiche from 1975. Records destroyed after 10 years. A CD-rom of monthy court indices from all divisions is available for $40.00. Will accept fax requests from gov't agencies only.
General Information: No probation reports released. SASE required. Turnaround time 2 days. Copy fee: $.75 per page. Certification fee: $6.00. Fee payee: Clerk of the Court. Personal checks accepted. Prepayment is required.

Santa Maria Cook Division - Superior Court
312-C East Cook St (PO Box 5369), Santa Maria, CA 93454-5369; 805-346-7414; Civil phone: 805-346-7405; Fax: 805-346-7616. Hours: 7:30AM-4:30PM (PST). *Civil Actions Under $25,000, Probate, Eviction, Small Claims.*

www.sbcourts.org/general_info/index.htm

Note: This Cook Division handles Civil; its sister court (Miller Division) handles Criminal. Includes Betteravia, Casmalia, Cuyama, Guadalupe, Gary, Los Alamos, New Cuyama, Orcutt, Santa Maria, Sisquoc, Tepusquet and sections of the Vandenburg Air Force Base
Civil Records: Access: Mail, in person. Both court and visitors may perform in person searches. Search fee: $5.00 per name. Required to search: name, years to search. Civil cases indexed by defendant, plaintiff. Civil records in index files from 1983. Records destroyed after 10 years.
General Information: Public access terminal is available. No probation reports, financial, judges notes, confidential or sealed records released. SASE required. Turnaround time 5 days. Fax notes: Will fax results. Copy fee: $.75 per page. Certification fee: $6.00. Fee payee: Clerk of Court. Personal checks accepted. Credit

cards accepted: Visa, MasterCard. Prepayment is required.

Santa Maria Miller Division - Superior Court
312-M East Cook St, Bldg E, Santa Maria, CA 93454-5165; 805-346-7590; Criminal phone: 805-346-7565; Fax: 805-346-7591. Hours: 7:30AM-4:30PM (PST). *Felony, Misdemeanor, Traffic.*

www.sbcourts.org/general_info/index.htm

Note: Miller Division is in the same building complex as the Cook Division, which handles civil, small claims, family cases. Miller includes the same jurisdictional area as Cook Division.
Criminal Records: Access: Mail, fax, in person. Both court and visitors may perform in person searches. Search fee: $5.00 per name. Required to search: name, years to search, DOB. Criminal records in index files from 7/1963. A CD-Rom of weekly court indices from all divisions is available for $48.00.
General Information: Public access terminal is available. No probation reports, financial, judges notes, confidential or sealed records released. SASE required. Turnaround time 2 days. Copy fee: $.75 per page. Certification fee: $6.00. Fee payee: Clerk of Court. Personal checks accepted. Credit cards accepted: Visa, MasterCard. Prepayment is required.

Lompoc Division - Superior Court
115 Civic Center Plz, Lompoc, CA 93436; Civil phone: 805-737-7796; Criminal phone: 805-737-7790; Fax: 805-737-7786. Hours: 8:30AM-4:55PM (PST). *Felony. Misdemeanor, Civil Actions Under $25,000, Eviction, Small Claims.*

www.sbcourts.org/index.htm

Note: Includes Lompoc and adjacent unincorporated areas, including sections of Vandenburg Air Force Base.
Civil Records: Access: Phone, mail, in person. Both court and visitors may perform in person searches. No search fee. Required to search: name, years to search. Civil cases indexed by defendant, plaintiff. Civil records on computer from 1991, index files from 1983. Records destroyed after 10 years. Phone searches only for computerized records.
Criminal Records: Access: Phone, mail, in person. Both court and visitors may perform in person searches. No search fee. Required to search: name, years to search, DOB; also helpful: address. Criminal records on computer from 1991, index files from 1983. Records destroyed after 10 years. Phone searches only for computerized records. Includes Solvang jurisdiction filings from 1997 to present. A CD-Rom of weekly court indices from all divisions is available for $48.00.
General Information: Public access terminal is available. No probation reports released. SASE required. Turnaround time 2 days. Copy fee: $.75 per page. Certification fee: $6.00. Fee payee: Clerk of the Superior Court. Personal checks accepted. Prepayment is required.

Solvang Division - Superior Court
1745 Mission Dr, #C, Solvang, CA 93463; 805-686-5040; Fax: 805-686-5079. Hours: 8AM-4PM (PST). *Misdemeanor, Small Claims, Traffic.*

www.sbcourts.org/general_info/index.htm

Civil Records: Access: Phone, mail, in person. Both court and visitors may perform in person searches. No search fee. Required to search: name, years to search. Civil cases indexed by defendant, plaintiff. Civil records on computer from 1991, index lists prior. Will only search back 7 years.
Criminal Records: Access: Mail, in person. Both court and visitors may perform in person searches. No search fee. Required to search: name, years to search, DOB. Criminal records on computer from 1988, index list prior. A CD-Rom of weekly court indices from all divisions is available for $48.00.

General Information: Public access terminal is available. No sealed or confidential records released. SASE required. Turnaround time 1 week. Copy fee: $.75 per page. Certification fee: $6.75. Fee payee: Superior Court. Personal checks accepted. Credit cards accepted: Visa, MasterCard. Credit cards are only accepted at the counter, not by mail. Prepayment is required.

Santa Clara County

Superior Court - Civil
191 N 1st Street, San Jose, CA 95113; 408-299-2966; Civil phone: 408-299-2964. Hours: 8:30AM-4PM (PST). *Civil, Eviction, Probate.*

www.sccsuperiorcourt.org

Note: Handles cases for San Jose, Milpitas, Santa Clara, Los Gatos and Campbell areas
Civil Records: Access: Mail, in person. Both court and visitors may perform in person searches. Search fee: $5.00 per name per year. Required to search: name, years to search. Civil records on computer 1993 to present; prior on books to 1800s.
General Information: Public access terminal is available. No probation reports or confidential records released. SASE required. Turnaround time 2 weeks. Copy fee: $1.00 per page. Certification fee: $6.00. Fee payee: Superior Court. Personal checks accepted. Prepayment is required.

Superior Court - Criminal
190 W Hedding St, San Jose, CA 95110-1774; 408-299-2230; Criminal phone: 408-299-2281. Hours: 8:30AM-4PM (PST). *Felony, Misdemeanor.*

www.sccsuperiorcourt.org

Criminal Records: Access: Mail, in person. Both court and visitors may perform in person searches. Search fee: $5.00 per name per year. Required to search: name, years to search, DOB. Criminal records on microfiche from 1975-2000. Old files are kept in archives or on microfilm.
General Information: No probation, confidential or sealed records released. SASE required. Turnaround time 3-7 days. Copy fee: $1.00 per page. Postage also charged based on number of pages copied. Certification fee: $6.00. Fee payee: Santa Clara Superior Court. Personal checks accepted. Prepayment is required.

South County Facility - Superior Court
12425 Monterey Rd, San Martin, CA 95046-9590; Civil phone: 408-695-5012; Criminal phone: 408-695-5014. Hours: 8:30AM-4PM (PST). *Felony, Misdemeanor, Civil Actions Under $25,000, Eviction, Small Claims.*

http://sccsuperiorcourt.org

Note: Small Claims phone is 408-695-5012. Jurisdiction includes the Cities of Gilroy, Morgan Hill, San Martin and surrounding unincorporated areas.
Civil Records: Access: Mail, in person. Both court and visitors may perform in person searches. Search fee: $5.00 per name per year. Required to search: name, years to search. Civil records on microfiche.
Criminal Records: Access: Mail, in person. Both court and visitors may perform in person searches. Search fee: $5.00 per name per year. Required to search: name, years to search; also helpful: DOB. Same record keeping as civil.
General Information: No adoptions, juvenile, medical, probation or sealed records released. SASE required. Turnaround time 1 week. Copy fee: $1.00 per page. Certification fee: $6.00. Fee payee: Superior Court. Personal checks accepted. Prepayment is required.

Palo Alto Facility - Superior Court
270 Grant Ave, Palo Alto, CA 94306; 650-324-0373. Hours: 8:30AM-4PM (PST). *Felony, Misdemeanor, Small Claims.*

www.sccsuperiorcourt.org

Note: Includes Palo Alto, Mountain View, Los Altos, Los Altos Hills, Stanford University and the surrounding unincorporated areas.
Civil Records: Access: Mail, in person. Both court and visitors may perform in person searches. Search fee: $5.00 per name per year. Required to search: name, years to search.
Criminal Records: Access: Mail, in person. Both court and visitors may perform in person searches. Search fee: $5.00 per name per year. Required to search: name, years to search; also helpful: DOB. Criminal Records on microfiche.
General Information: No probation, doctor report, pretrial report records released. SASE required. Turnaround time 1 week. Copy fee: $1.00 per page. Certification fee: $6.00. Fee payee: Superior Court. Personal checks accepted. Prepayment is required.

Sunnyvale Facility - Superior Court
605 W El Camino Real, Sunnyvale, CA 94087; 408-739-1503. Hours: 8:30AM-4PM (PST). *Felony, Misdemeanor.*

www.sccsuperiorcourt.org

Note: Includes the cities of Sunnyvale and Cupertino. All traffic and small claims are filed at the Palo Alto Facility.
Criminal Records: Access: Mail, in person. Both court and visitors may perform in person searches. Search fee: $5.00 per name per year. Required to search: name, years to search, DOB.
General Information: No probation reports, confidential or sealed records released. SASE required. Turnaround time 2-4 days. Copy fee: $1.00 per page. Certification fee: $6.00. Fee payee: Clerk of Court. Personal checks accepted. Prepayment is required.

Los Gatos Facility - Superior Court
14205 Capri Dr, Los Gatos, CA 95032; 408-866-8331. Hours: 8:30AM-4PM (PST). *Small Claims.*

http://sccsuperiorcourt.org

Note: Includes the towns of Los Gatos and Monte Sereno and the cities of Campbell, Saratoga, and surrounding unincorporated areas as well as San Jose, Milpitas and Santa Clara
Civil Records: Access: Phone, mail, in person. Both court and visitors may perform in person searches. Search fee: $5.00 per name per year. Required to search: name, years to search. Civil cases indexed by defendant, plaintiff. Civil record index on microfiche.
General Information: Copy fee: $1.00 per page. Certification fee: $6.00. Fee payee: Superior Court. Personal checks accepted. Prepayment is required.

Santa Cruz County

Superior Court - Civil
701 Ocean St Rm 110, Santa Cruz, CA 95060; 831-454-2020; Fax: 831-454-2215. Hours: 8AM-4PM (PST). *Civil, Probate.*

www.co.santa-cruz.ca.us/crt/courts.htm

Civil Records: Access: Phone, mail, in person. Both court and visitors may perform in person searches. No search fee. Required to search: name, years to search. Civil cases indexed by defendant, plaintiff. Civil records on computer back to 6/1985; microfiche, archived and index books from 1820.
General Information: Public access terminal is available. No adoptions, juvenile, medical, probation or sealed records released. SASE required. Turnaround time 5-10 days. Copy fee: $.50 per page. Certification fee: $6.00 plus $1.00 per page. Fee payee: Clerk of Court. Personal checks accepted. Prepayment is required.

Superior Court - Criminal
701 Ocean St Rm 120, Santa Cruz, CA 95060; 831-454-2230; Fax: 831-454-2215. Hours: 8AM-4PM (PST). *Felony, Misdemeanor.*

www.co.santa-cruz.ca.us/crt/courts.htm

Criminal Records: Access: Fax, mail, in person. Both court and visitors may perform in person searches. Search fee: $5.00 per name. Required to search: name; also helpful: years to search, DOB. Criminal records on computer since 1985; also on microfiche index by party name back; other records go back to 1880's.

General Information: Public access terminal is available. No juvenile, probation or sealed records released. SASE required. Turnaround time 1-2 weeks. Copy fee: $.50 per page. Certification fee: $6.00 plus $1.00 per page. Fee payee: Clerk of Court. Personal checks accepted. Prepayment is required.

Watsonville Division - Superior Court

1430 Freedom Blvd, Watsonville, CA 95076; 831-763-8060. Hours: 8AM-4PM (PST). *Misdemeanor, Civil Actions Under $25,000, Eviction, Small Claims.*

www.co.santa-cruz.ca.us/crt/courts.htm

Note: Includes all of Santa Cruz County.

Civil Records: Access: Mail, in person. Search fee: $5.00 per name. Required to search: name, years to search. Civil cases indexed by defendant, plaintiff. Civil records on computer from 1992, index books prior. Records destroyed after 10 years.

Criminal Records: Access: Mail, in person. Both court and visitors may perform in person searches. Search fee: $5.00 per name. Required to search: name, years to search; also helpful: DOB. Criminal records on computer from 1992, index books prior. Records destroyed after 10 years.

General Information: No probation or juvenile records released. SASE required. Turnaround time 2-5 days. Copy fee: $.50 per page. Certification fee: $6.00. Fee payee: Superior Court. Personal checks accepted. Prepayment is required.

Shasta County

Superior Court 1500 Court St, Redding, CA 96001; 530-245-6789; Fax: 530-225-5564 Civil; 245-6483 Criminal. Hours: 8:30AM-4:30PM (PST). *Felony, Misdemeanor, Civil, Small Claims, Eviction, Probate.*

www.shastacourts.com

Note: Address Room 319 for civil division and Room 219 for criminal division.

Civil Records: Access: Phone, mail, in person. Both court and visitors may perform in person searches. Search fee: $5.00 per name per year. Required to search: name, years to search. Civil cases indexed by defendant, plaintiff. Civil records on computer from 1992, index books prior.

Criminal Records: Access: Mail, in person, online. Both court and visitors may perform in person searches. Search fee: $5.00 per name per year. Required to search: name, years to search. Criminal records on computer from 1992, index books prior. Online access to the criminal division index is available free at www.shastacourts.com/criminal.shtml. Also, the Integrated Justice System Access at www.shastacourts.com/access.shtml is limited to attorneys involved on county cases.

General Information: No probation or confidential records released. SASE required. Turnaround time 2-7 days. Copy fee: $.50 per page. Certification fee: $6.00. Fee payee: Superior Court. Personal checks accepted. Prepayment is required.

Burney Branch - Superior Court

20509 Shasta St, Burney, CA 96013; 530-335-3571; Fax: 530-225-5684. Hours: 8AM-Noon, 1-4:30PM (PST). *Misdemeanor, Civil, Eviction, Small Claims.*

www.shastacourts.com/burney.shtml

Note: Civil actions handled by Redding Branch since 1992. Prior civil limited jurisdiction records maintained here.

Civil Records: Access: Mail, in person. Only the court performs in person searches; visitors may not. Search fee: $5.00 per name per year. Required to search: name, years to search. Civil cases indexed by defendant, plaintiff. Civil records on computer from 1993, index books prior.

Criminal Records: Access: Mail, in person, online. Only the court performs in person searches; visitors may not. Search fee: $5.00 per name. Required to search: name, years to search, DOB. Criminal records on computer from 1993, index books prior. Online access to the criminal division index is available free at www.shastacourts.com/criminal.shtml. Also, the Integrated Justice System Access at www.shastacourts.com/access.shtml is limited to attorneys involved on county cases.

General Information: No probation, juvenile, or DMV reports released. SASE required. Turnaround time 2-14 days. Copy fee: $1.00 1st page; $.50 each add'l. Certification fee: $6.00. Fee payee: Superior Court. Personal checks accepted. Prepayment is required.

Sierra County

Superior Court PO Box 476 Courthouse Square, Downieville, CA 95936; 530-289-3698; Fax: 530-289-0205. Hours: 8AM-Noon, 1-5PM (PST). *Felony, Misdemeanor, Civil, Eviction, Small Claims, Probate.*

Civil Records: Access: Phone, fax, mail, in person. Only the court performs in person searches; visitors may not. Search fee: $1.75 per name per year. Required to search: name, years to search. Civil cases indexed by defendant, plaintiff. Civil records on computer from 1985, index books from 1852.

Criminal Records: Access: Phone, fax, mail, in person. Both court and visitors may perform in person searches. Search fee: $1.75 per name per year. Required to search: name, years to search. Criminal records on computer from 1985, index books from 1852.

General Information: No adoptions, juvenile, medical, probation or sealed records released. SASE required. Turnaround time 2-4 days. Fax notes: $1.00 per page. Copy fee: $1.00 per page. Certification fee: $6.00 per document. Fee payee: Superior Court. Personal checks accepted. Prepayment is required.

Siskiyou County

Superior Court 311 4th St PO Box 1026, Yreka, CA 96097; Civil phone: 530-842-8196; Criminal phone: 530-842-8195; Fax: 530-842-0164(Civ); 530-842-8178(Crim). Hours: 8AM-5PM; 8AM-3PM (phone hours) (PST). *Felony, Misdemeanor, Civil, Probate.*

Civil Records: Access: Phone, mail, in person. Both court and visitors may perform in person searches. Search fee: $5.00 per name. Fee is per 10 years searched. Required to search: name, years to search. Civil cases indexed by defendant, plaintiff. Civil records on computer since 1991, archived and index book from 1900.

Criminal Records: Access: Phone, mail, in person. Both court and visitors may perform in person searches. Search fee: $5.00 per name. Fee is per 10 years searched. Required to search: name, years to search. Criminal records on computer since 1991, archived and index book from 1900.

General Information: No adoptions, juvenile, medical, probation or sealed records released. SASE required. Turnaround time 1 week. Copy fee: $.50 per page. Certification fee: $6.00. Fee payee: Siskiyou Superior Court. Personal checks accepted. Prepayment is required.

Superior Court 550 Main St, Weed, CA 96094; 530-938-2483; Civil phone: 530-938-3897; Fax: 530-842-0109. Hours: 8AM-5PM (PST). *Misdemeanor, Civil Actions Under $25,000, Eviction, Small Claims.*

Note: This court holds misdemeanor records for Dorris/Tulelake branch.

Civil Records: Access: Mail, fax, in person. Only the court performs in person searches; visitors may not. Search fee: $5.00 per name per 10 years. Required to search: full name, years to search. Civil cases indexed by defendant, plaintiff. Civil records go back to 1980; on computer since 1995. Will only search back 7 years.

Criminal Records: Access: Mail, fax, in person. Only the court performs in person searches; visitors may not. Search fee: $5.00 per name per 10 years. Required to search: full name, years to search, DOB, SSN. Criminal records go back to 1994; computerized records back to 1998.

General Information: Public access terminal is available. SASE required. Turnaround time 10 days. Fax notes: Fee to fax results is $1.00 per page. Copy fee: $.50 per page. Certification fee: $6.00 or $10 for a judgment. Fee payee: Siskiyou Superior Court. Personal checks accepted only from party to the case. Prepayment is required.

Dorris Branch - Superior Court

PO Box 828, Dorris, CA 96023; 530-397-3161; Fax: 530-397-3169. Hours: 8AM-Noon, 1-4PM (PST). *Civil Actions Under $25,000, Eviction, Small Claims.*

Note: All new misdemeanor cases are referred to Southeastern branch in Weed, CA. Only maintains a few criminal records for a year

Civil Records: Access: Mail, in person. Only the court performs in person searches; visitors may not. Search fee: $5.00 per name. Required to search: name, years to search. Civil records on computer back to 1998; prior on books back to 1992.

General Information: Public access terminal is available. (Available at the Yreka Main court only.) No probation reports released. SASE required. Turnaround time 1 week. Copy fee: $.50 per page. Certification fee: $6.00. Fee payee: Siskiyou Superior Court. Personal checks accepted. Prepayment is required.

Solano County

Superior Court - Civil 600 Union Ave, Fairfield, CA 94533; 707-421-6053; Probate phone: 707-421-6471; Fax: 707-435-2950. Hours: 8AM-4PM (PST). *Civil, Eviction, Probate.*

www.solanocourts.com

Note: The Northern Solano Municipal Court has been combined with the Superior Court. Probate is a separate office at the same address. Probate fax is 707-421-6961. Small claims phone is 707-421-7435.

Civil Records: Access: Phone, mail, online, in person. Both court and visitors may perform in person searches. Search fee: $5.00 per name. Required to search: name, years to search. Civil cases indexed by defendant, plaintiff. Civil records on computer since 1992, microfiche since 1971, archived and index files since 1800s. Online access to civil records is available free at the web site; click on "Court Connect.". Phone access limited to short searches.

General Information: Public access terminal is available. No sealed records released. SASE required. Turnaround time 2-3 days. Copy fee: $1.00 per page. Certification fee: $6.00. Fee payee: Solano County Courts. Personal checks accepted. Prepayment is required.

Superior Court - Criminal 530 Union Ave #200, Fairfield, CA 94533; 707-421-7440; 421-7834 Sup Court Records; Fax: 707-421-7439. Hours: 8AM-4PM (PST). *Felony, Misdemeanor.*

www.solanocourts.com

Note: The Northern Solano Municipal Court has been combined with the Superior Court

Criminal Records: Access: Mail, in person, online. Visitors may perform in person searches. Search fee: $5.00 per name. Required to search: name, years to search; also helpful: DOB, SSN. Superior Court records on computer since 1992, microfiche since 1971; Municipal Court records on computer for past 10 years. Online access to criminal records is available free at the web site; click on "Court Connect.".

General Information: No probation reports released. SASE required. Turnaround time 1-3 weeks. Copy fee: $1.00 for first page. Certification fee: $6.00. Fee payee: Solano Superior Court. Personal checks accepted. Prepayment is required.

Vallejo Branch - Superior Court 321
Tuolumne St, Vallejo, CA 94590; Civil phone: 707-553-5346; Criminal phone: 707-553-5341; Fax: 707-553-5661. Hours: 8AM-4PM (PST). *Misdemeanor, Civil, Eviction, Small Claims.*

www.co.solano.ca.us/courts

Note: Includes Cities of Vallejo and Benicia and the unincorporated area adjacent thereto.

Civil Records: Access: Mail, in person, online. Both court and visitors may perform in person searches. Search fee: $5.00 per name. Required to search: name, years to search. Civil cases indexed by defendant, plaintiff. Civil records on computer from 1991, index files from 1983. Records destroyed after 10 years. Online access to civil records is available free at the web site; click on "Court Connect.".

Criminal Records: Access: Mail, in person, online. Only the court performs in person searches; visitors may not. Search fee: $5.00 per name. Required to search: name, years to search. Criminal records on computer from 1991, index files from 1983. Records destroyed after 10 years. Online access to criminal records is available free at the web site; click on "Court Connect.".

General Information: No probation reports released. SASE required. Turnaround time 2 days. Copy fee: $1.00 per page. Certification fee: $6.00. Fee payee: Superior Court. Personal checks accepted. Credit cards accepted: Visa, AmEx. Prepayment is required.

Sonoma County

Superior Court - Criminal 600 Administration
Dr, Room 105J, Santa Rosa, CA 95403-0281; 707-565-1100. Hours: 8AM-4PM (PST). *Felony, Misdemeanor, Probate.*

www.sonomasuperiorcourt.com

Civil Records: Access: Phone, mail, in person. Both court and visitors may perform in person searches. Search fee: $15.00 per hour. Required to search: name, years to search. Civil cases indexed by defendant, plaintiff. Civil records on computer from 1985, microfiche and index books from 1850 to 1984. Phone access limited to 2 names or cases per call.

Criminal Records: Access: Phone, mail, in person. Both court and visitors may perform in person searches. Search fee: $15.00 per hour. Required to search: name, years to search, DOB. Criminal Records on computer back to 1985, microfiche and index books 1850 to 1984. Misdemeanor records destroyed after 10 years.

General Information: Public access terminal is available. No adoptions, juvenile, medical, probation or sealed records released. SASE required. Turnaround time 2-3 weeks. Copy fee: $1.00 per page. 10 page limit. If more than 10 pages must wait 3-5 days. Certification fee: $6.00 plus $1.00 per page. Fee payee: Superior Court. Personal checks accepted. No out of state personal checks accepted. Prepayment is required.

Superior Court - Civil Division 600
Administration Dr, Rm 107J, Santa Rosa, CA 95403; 707-565-1100. Hours: 8AM-4PM (PST). *Civil, Eviction, Small Claims.*

www.sonomasuperiorcourt.com

Civil Records: Access: Mail, in person. Both court and visitors may perform in person searches. No search fee. Required to search: name, years to search. Civil cases indexed by defendant, plaintiff. Civil records on computer to 10/84, index files prior. Records destroyed after 10 years.

General Information: Public access terminal is available. No probation reports or sealed records released. SASE required. Turnaround time 2 days - 2 weeks. Copy fee: $1.00 per page. Certification fee: $6.00. Fee payee: Superior Court. Personal checks accepted. Prepayment is required.

Stanislaus County

Superior Court - Criminal 800 11 Street, Rm
140, PO Box 1098, Modesto, CA 95353; 209-558-6000. Hours: 8AM-Noon, 1-4PM (PST). *Felony, Misdemeanor.*

www.co.stanislaus.ca.us/courts

Note: Physical address Zip Code is 95354

Criminal Records: Access: Mail, in person. Both court and visitors may perform in person searches. Search fee: $5.00 per name per year. Required to search: name, years to search. Criminal Records on microfiche since 1974, archived back to 1800s.

General Information: No adoptions, juvenile, medical, probation or sealed records released. SASE required. Turnaround time 1-2 weeks. Copy fee: $.50 per page. Certification fee: $6.00. Fee payee: Superior Court Clerk. Personal checks accepted. Prepayment required.

Superior Court - Civil 1100 "I" St PO Box 828,
Modesto, CA 95353; 209-558-6000; Fax: 209-525-4348 (civil). Hours: 8AM-4PM (PST). *Civil, Eviction, Small Claims, Probate.*

www.co.stanislaus.ca.us/courts

Note: Ceres Branch has been closed and records transferred here

Civil Records: Access: Mail, fax, in person. Both court and visitors may perform in person searches. Search fee: $5.00 per name. Required to search: name, years to search. Civil cases indexed by defendant, plaintiff. Civil records on computer from 1991, in index files from 1983. Records destroyed after 10 years.

General Information: Public access terminal is available. No probation or juvenile records released. SASE required. Turnaround time 2-5 days. Copy fee: $.50 per page. Certification fee: $6.00. Fee payee: Superior Court. Personal checks accepted. Prepayment is required.

Turlock Division - Superior Court 300 Starr
Ave, Turlock, CA 95380; 209-558-6000; Fax: 209-664-8009. 8AM-Noon, 12:30-4PM (PST). *Small Claims.*

www.co.stanislaus.ca.us/courts

Sutter County

Superior Court - Civil Division 463 2nd St,
Rm 211, Courthouse East, 2nd Floor, Yuba City, CA 95991; 530-822-7352; Fax: 530-822-7192. Hours: 8AM-5PM *Civil, Eviction, Small Claims, Probate.*

www.suttercourts.com

Civil Records: Access: Mail, in person. Both court and visitors may perform in person searches. Search fee: $5.00 per name. Required to search: name, years to search. Civil cases indexed by defendant, plaintiff. Civil records in index books and archived from 1800s, on computer back to 1/95.

General Information: Public access terminal is available. No adoptions, juvenile, medical, probation or

sealed records released. SASE required. Turnaround time 2 days if records on site. Fax notes: Will not fax results. Copy fee: $.50 per page. Certification fee: $6.00. Fee payee: Superior Court. Personal checks accepted. Prepayment is required.

Superior Court - Criminal Division 446 2nd
St, Yuba City, CA 95991; 530-822-7360; Fax: 530-822-7159. Hours: 8AM-5PM (PST). *Felony, Misdemeanor.*

Criminal Records: Access: Fax, mail, in person. Both court and visitors may perform in person searches. Search fee: $5.00 per name. Required to search: name, years to search. Criminal records in index books and archived from 1800s, computerized since 1995.

General Information: Public access terminal is available. No police reports or probation records released. Turnaround time 1 week. Copy fee: $.50 per page. Certification fee: $6.00. Fee payee: Sutter County Superior Court. Personal checks accepted. Prepayment is required.

Tehama County

Superior Court PO Box 310, Red Bluff, CA
96080; 530-527-6441. Hours: 9AM-4PM (PST). *Civil, Small Claims, Eviction, Probate.*

Civil Records: Access: Mail, in person. Both court and visitors may perform in person searches. Search fee: $2.50 per name. Fee is $5.00 if years before 1991 are requested. Required to search: name, years to search. Civil cases indexed by defendant, plaintiff. Civil records on computer back to 1992, archived and index books from 1900s.

General Information: No adoptions, juvenile, mental, probation or sealed records released. SASE required. Turnaround time same day. Copy fee: $.50 per page. Certification fee: $6.00. Fee payee: Tehama County Superior Court Clerk. Personal checks accepted. Prepayment is required.

Superior Court - Criminal Division 445 Pine
St PO Box 1170, Red Bluff, CA 96080; 530-527-3563; Criminal phone: 530-527-7314; Fax: 530-527-0956. Hours: 8AM-5PM (PST). *Felony, Misdemeanor.*

Criminal Records: Access: Mail, in person. Both court and visitors may perform in person searches. Search fee: $5.00 per name. Required to search: name, years to search; also helpful: DOB. Criminal records on computer from 1991, index cards prior. Will only search back 7 years.

General Information: No probation reports released. SASE required. Turnaround time within 1 week. Copy fee: $.50 per page. Certification fee: $6.00. Fee payee: Superior Court. Personal checks accepted. Prepayment is required.

Corning Branch - Superior Court 720 Hoag
St, Corning, CA 96021; 530-824-4601; Fax: 530-824-6457. Hours: 8AM-4PM (PST). *Misdemeanor, Civil Actions Under $25,000, Eviction, Small Claims.*

Civil Records: Access: Mail, in person. Search fee: $5.00 per name. Required to search: name, years to search. Civil cases indexed by defendant, plaintiff. Civil records on index cards. Will only search back 7 years; records on computer since 1990.

Criminal Records: Access: Mail, in person. Only the court may perform in person searches. No search fee. Required to search: name, years to search; also helpful: DOB. Criminal records on computer from 1990, index cards prior. Will only search back 7 years.

General Information: No probation reports released. SASE required. Turnaround time 1 week. Copy fee: $.50 per page. Certification fee: $6.00. Fee payee: Tehama Superior Court. Personal checks accepted. Prepayment is required.

Trinity County

Superior Court 101 Court St PO Box 1258, Weaverville, CA 96093; 530-623-1208; Fax: 530-623-3762. Hours: 9AM-4PM (PST). *Felony, Misdemeanor, Civil, Eviction, Small Claims, Probate.*

Civil Records: Access: Mail, in person. Both court and visitors may perform in person searches. Search fee: $5.00 per name per year. Required to search: name, years to search. Civil cases indexed by defendant, plaintiff. Civil records on microfiche, archived and index files from 1900s.

Criminal Records: Access: Mail, in person. Both court and visitors may perform in person searches. Search fee: $5.00 per name per year. Required to search: name, years to search. Criminal records on microfiche, archived and index files from 1900s.

General Information: No adoptions, juvenile, medical, probation or sealed records released. SASE required. Turnaround time 1 week. Copy fee: $.50 per page. Certification fee: $6.00. Fee payee: Superior Court. Personal checks accepted. Prepayment required.

Tulare County

Superior Court Courthouse, 221 S Mooney, Visalia, CA 93291; Civil phone: 559-733-6454; Criminal phone: 559-733-6830; Fax: 559-737-4547. Hours: 8AM-4PM (PST). *Felony, Civil, Eviction, Small Claims, Probate.*

www.tularesuperiorcourt.ca.gov

Note: This court has records from Exeter, Woodlake, Farmersville, Goshen and Three Rivers. Address criminal record requests to Room 124 and civil to Room 201.

Civil Records: Access: Mail, in person. Both court and visitors may perform in person searches. Search fee: $5.00 per name. Required to search: name, years to search. Civil cases indexed by defendant, plaintiff. Civil records on computer back to 2/1986; microfiche and index books from 1800s.

Criminal Records: Access: Mail, in person. Both court and visitors may perform in person searches. Search fee: $5.00 per name. Required to search: name, years to search, DOB or SSN. Criminal records on computer back to 2/1986; microfiche and index books from 1800s.

General Information: Public access terminal is available. No adoptions, juvenile, mental, probation reports or sealed records released. SASE required. Turnaround time 1 week. Copy fee: $.50 per page. Certification fee: $6.00. Fee payee: Tulare County Superior Court. Personal checks accepted. Prepayment is required.

Dinuba Division - Superior Court 640 S Alta Dinuba, Dinuba, CA 93618; 559-591-5815. Hours: 8AM-4PM (PST). *Felony, Misdemeanor, Civil Actions Under $25,000, Eviction, Small Claims.*

Note: Includes Dinuba, Cutler, Orosi, Seville, Traver, London, Delf, Orange Cove.

Civil Records: Access: Mail, in person. Only the court performs in person searches; visitors may not. Search fee: $5.00 per name. Required to search: name, years to search. Civil cases indexed by defendant, plaintiff. Civil records on computer from 1993, index files from 1983. Records destroyed after 10 years.

Criminal Records: Access: Mail, in person. Only the court performs in person searches; visitors may not. Search fee: $5.00 per name. Required to search: name, years to search, DOB. Criminal records on computer from 1993, index files from 1983. Records destroyed after 10 years.

General Information: No probation reports released. SASE required. Turnaround time 2-3 days. Copy fee: $.50 per page. Certification fee: $6.00. Fee payee:

Dinuba Superior Court. In-state checks accepted. Prepayment is required.

Porterville Division - Superior Court 87 E Morton Ave, Porterville, CA 93257; 559-782-4710; Fax: 559-782-4805. Hours: 8AM-4PM (PST). *Misdemeanor, Civil Actions Under $25,000, Eviction, Small Claims.*

Note: Includes Porterville, Springville, Camp Nelson, Johnsondale, Terra Bella, Ducor, Richgrove, Poplar, Lindsey, Strathmore and surrounding areas.

Civil Records: Access: Mail, in person. Both court and visitors may perform in person searches. Search fee: $5.00 per name. also is per case. Required to search: name, years to search, DOB, SSN, case #. Civil cases indexed by defendant, plaintiff. Civil records on computer from February, 1992, index book prior. Records destroyed after 10 years.

Criminal Records: Access: Mail, in person. Both court and visitors may perform in person searches. Search fee: $5.00 per name. Also is per case. Required to search: name, years to search; also helpful: DOB, SSN, case #. Criminal records on computer from February, 1992, index book prior. Records destroyed after 10 years.

General Information: Public access terminal is available. No probation reports released. SASE required. Turnaround time 2 days. Copy fee: $.50 per page. Certification fee: $6.00. Fee payee: Porterville Superior Court. Personal checks accepted. Prepayment is required.

Tulare/Pixley Division - Superior Court 425 E Kern St (PO Box 1136), Tulare, CA 93275; 559-685-2556; Fax: 559-685-2663. Hours: 8AM-4PM (PST). *Misdemeanor, Civil Actions Under $25,000, Eviction, Small Claims.*

Note: Includes Tulare, Pixley, Tipton, Earlimart, Alpaugh, Allensworth, Woodville, Waukena and surrounding areas.

Civil Records: Access: Mail, fax, in person. Both court and visitors may perform in person searches. Search fee: $5.00 per name. Required to search: name, years to search. Civil cases indexed by defendant, plaintiff. Civil records in index books. Records destroyed after 10 years; on computer back to 1992.

Criminal Records: Access: Mail, fax, in person. Both court and visitors may perform in person searches. Search fee: $5.00 per name. Required to search: name, years to search, DOB; also helpful: address, SSN. Criminal records in index books. Records destroyed after 10 years; on computer back to 1992.

General Information: Public access terminal is available. No probation reports released. SASE required. Turnaround time 2 days. Copy fee: $.50 per page. Certification fee: $6.00. Fee payee: Superior Court. Personal checks accepted. Prepayment is required.

Tuolumne County

Superior Court - Civil 41 W Yaney, Sonora, CA 95370; 209-533-5555; Fax: 209-533-6944. Hours: 8AM-5PM (PST). *Civil, Eviction, Small Claims, Probate.*

www.courtinfo.ca.gov/courts/trial/tuolumne

Civil Records: Access: Mail, in person. Both court and visitors may perform in person searches. Search fee: $5.00 per name. Fee is per record. Required to search: name, years to search. Civil cases indexed by defendant, plaintiff. Civil records on computer back to 1994, microfiche and archived from 1900s, index files from 1800s.

General Information: Public access terminal is available. No adoptions, juvenile, medical, probation or sealed records released. SASE required. Turnaround time 1 week. Copy fee: $.50 per page. Certification fee: $6.00. Fee payee: Superior Court. Personal checks

accepted. Out of state checks not accepted. Prepayment is required.

Superior Court - Criminal 60 N Washington St, Sonora, CA 95370; 209-533-5671; Fax: 209-533-5581. Hours: 8AM-4PM (PST). *Felony, Misdemeanor, Traffic.*

www.courtinfo.ca.gov/courts/trial/tuolumne

Criminal Records: Access: Mail, in person. Both court and visitors may perform in person searches. Search fee: $5.00 per name. Required to search: name, years to search, DOB. Felony records on computer from 1993; misdemeanors from 1999; index files prior. Will only search back 7 years.

General Information: Public access terminal is available. No sealed records released. Most records are public. SASE required. Turnaround time 1 week. Fax notes: Will only fax to public agencies. Copy fee: $.50 per page. Certification fee: $6.00. Fee payee: Tuolomne County Superior Court. Personal checks accepted. Prepayment is required.

Ventura County

Ventura Superior Court 800 S Victoria Ave PO Box 6489, Ventura, CA 93006-6489; Civil phone: 805-654-2611; Criminal phone: 805-654-2611; Fax: 805-650-4032. Hours: 8AM-5PM (PST). *Felony, Misdemeanor, Civil, Eviction, Small Claims, Probate.*

http://courts.countyofventura.org

Civil Records: Access: Phone, mail, online, in person. Both court and visitors may perform in person searches. Search fee: $5.00 per name. Required to search: name, years to search. Civil cases indexed by defendant, plaintiff. Civil records prior to 10/93 are on microfiche, after are on computer. Access to civil court records 10/93-present is available free online at http://courts.countyofventura.org/case_home.asp. Search by defendant or plaintiff name, case number, or date.

Criminal Records: Access: Phone, mail, online, in person. Both court and visitors may perform in person searches. Search fee: $5.00 per name. Required to search: name, years to search, DOB. Criminal records go back to 1893; criminal records on computer back to 1989. Access to criminal records available free online at from the web site. There are several indices to search.

General Information: Public access terminal is available. No adoptions, mental health, paternity actions, juvenile, medical, probation or sealed records released. SASE required. Turnaround time 5-10 days. Copy fee: $.50 per page. Certification fee: $6.00 per document. Fee payee: Superior Court. Personal checks accepted. Credit cards accepted: Visa, AmEx. Additional fee charged. Prepayment is required.

East County Superior Court PO Box 1200, Simi Valley, CA 93062-1200; 805-582-8080. Hours: 8AM-5PM (PST). *Misdemeanor, Civil, Eviction, Small Claims, Probate, Family Law.*

http://courts.countyofventura.org

Civil Records: Access: Phone, mail, online, in person. Both court and visitors may perform in person searches. Search fee: $5.00 per name. Fee is per court. Required to search: name, years to search. Access to civil court records 10/93-present is available free online at https://public.courts.ventura.org/civcase/case_home.asp. Search by defendant or plaintiff, case number, or date.

Criminal Records: Access: Phone, mail, in person, online. Both court and visitors may perform in person searches. Search fee: $5.00 per name. Fee is per court. Required to search: name, years to search, DOB. Same record keeping as civil. Access to criminal court records at the web site. There are several indices to search.

General Information: Public access terminal is available. No adoptions, mental health, paternity actions, juvenile, medical, probation or sealed records released. SASE required. Turnaround time 5 days. Copy fee: $.50 per page. Certification fee: $6.00. Fee payee: Ventura County Superior Courts. Personal checks accepted. Credit cards accepted: Visa, MasterCard, Discover, AmEx. Additional fee charged. Prepayment is required.

Yolo County

Superior Court 725 Court St, Rm 308, Woodland, CA 95695; 530-666-8598; Civil phone: 530-666-8170; Criminal phone: 530-666-8050; Fax: 530-666-8576. Hours: 8AM-4PM (PST). *Felony, Misdemeanor, Civil, Eviction, Small Claims, Probate.*

www.yolocourts.com

Note: Address civil requests to Room 103 and criminal to Room 111. Small claims phone is 530-666-8060.
Civil Records: Access: Phone, mail, in person. Both court and visitors may perform in person searches. Search fee: $5.00 per name. Required to search: name, years to search. Civil cases indexed by defendant, plaintiff. Civil records on computer from 1995, microfiche, archived and index files from 1800s. Calendars are available online free at www.yolocourts.com/calendar_daily.html.   Probate notes at www.yolocourts.com/probate_notes.html.
Criminal Records: Access: Phone, mail, in person. Both court and visitors may perform in person searches.

Search fee: $5.00 per name. Required to search: name, years to search; also helpful: DOB. Criminal records on computer from 1995, microfiche, archived and index files from 1800s. Calendars are available online free at www.yolocourts.com/calendar_daily.html
General Information: No adoptions, juvenile, medical, probation or sealed records released. SASE required. Turnaround time 2 weeks. Copy fee: $1.00 per page. Certification fee: $6.00. Fee payee: Yolo Superior Court. Personal checks accepted. Prepayment required.

Yuba County

Superior Court 215 5th St, Marysville, CA 95901; 530-749-7600; Fax: 530-749-7351. Hours: 8:30AM-4:30PM (PST). *Felony, Misdemeanor, Civil, Small Claims, Probate.*

Civil Records: Access: Mail, in person. Both court and visitors may perform in person searches. Search fee: $5.00 per name. Required to search: name, years to search. Civil cases indexed by defendant, plaintiff. Civil records on computer from 1992, index books through 1962, archives and index files from 1854.
Criminal Records: Access: Mail, in person. Both court and visitors may perform in person searches. Search fee: $5.00 per name. Required to search: name, years to search. Criminal records on computer from 1992, index

books through 1962, archives and index files from 1854.
General Information: Public access terminal is available. No adoptions, paternity, juvenile, medical, probation or sealed records released. SASE required. Turnaround time 1-4 weeks. Copy fee: $1.00 per page. Certification fee: $6.00. Fee payee: Yuba County Superior Court. Personal checks accepted. Prepayment is required.

Marysville Civil Limited Superior Court
215 5th St, Marysville, CA 95901; 530-749-7600; Fax: 530-749-7354. Hours: 8:30AM-4:30PM (PST). *Civil Actions Under $25,000, Eviction, Small Claims.*

Civil Records: Access: Mail, in person. Both court and visitors may perform in person searches. Search fee: $5.00 per name. Required to search: name, years to search, DOB. Civil cases indexed by defendant, plaintiff. Civil records on computer through 1993, index books prior back to 1850's.
General Information: Public access terminal is available. No labor commissioner judgment, juvenile, or judge's records released. SASE required. Turnaround time 2 days. Fax notes: $20.00 per document and $1.00 per page. Copy fee: $1.00 per page. Certification fee: $6.00. Fee payee: Yuba County Superior Court. Personal checks accepted. Prepayment is required.

California Recording Offices

ORGANIZATION:	58 counties, 58 recording offices. The recording officer is County Recorder. Recordings are usually located in a Grantor/Grantee or General index. The entire state is in the Pacific Time Zone (PST).
REAL ESTATE RECORDS:	Most counties do not perform real estate name searches. Copy fees and certification fees vary.
UCC RECORDS:	Financing statements are filed at the state level, except for real estate related collateral, which are filed with the County Recorder. However, prior to 07/2001, consumer goods and farm collateral were also filed at the County Recorder and these older records can be searched there. All counties will perform UCC searches. Use search request form UCC-11. Search fees are usually $15.00 per debtor name. Copy costs vary.
TAX LIEN RECORDS:	Federal and state tax liens on personal property of businesses are filed with the Secretary of State. Other federal and state tax liens are filed with the County Recorder. Some counties will perform separate tax lien searches. Fees vary for this type of search.
OTHER LIENS:	Judgment (Note - Many judgments are also filed with the Secretary of State), child support, mechanics.
ONLINE ACCESS:	A number of counties offer online access to assessor and real estate information. The system in Los Angeles is a commercial subscription system.

Alameda County

County Recorder, 1106 Madison St, 1st Fl, Oakland, CA 94607. 510-272-6363; Fax 510-272-6382. www.co.alameda.ca.us
Will search UCC records. Tax liens not included in UCC search. Will not search real estate records. **Online Access:** Assessor Records. Access to the Property Value and Tax Information database is available free online at www.co.alameda.ca.us/aswpinq. **Other Phone Numbers:** Assessor 510-272-3755; Treasurer 510-272-6800.

Alpine County

County Recorder, PO Box 217, Markleeville, CA 96120. County Recorder, R/E and UCC Recording 530-694-2286; Fax 530-694-2491.
Will search UCC records. This agency will not do a tax lien search. Will not search real estate records. **Other Phone Numbers:** Assessor 530-694-2283; Treasurer 530-694-2286.

Amador County

County Recorder, 500 Argonaut Lane, Jackson, CA 95642. County Recorder, R/E and UCC Recording 209-223-6468; Fax 209-223-6204.
Will search UCC records. This agency will not do a tax lien search. Will not search real estate records. **Online Access:** Recording, Fictitious Name, Birth, Death, Marriage Records. Access to the county clerk database is available free at www.criis.com/amador/official.htm. There is a free "test" recorder grantor/grantee "images" search page at www.criis.com/amador_test.html. **Other Phone Numbers:** Assessor 209-223-6351 x209; Treasurer 209-223-6364; Appraiser/Auditor 209-223-6351; Elections 209-223-6465; Vital Records 209-223-6468.

Butte County

County Recorder, 25 County Center Dr, Oroville, CA 95965-3375. County Recorder, R/E and UCC Recording 530-538-7691; Fax 530-538-7975. www.buttecounty.net
Will search UCC records. Will not search real estate records. **Online Access:** Real Estate, Fictitious Name, Marriage, Birth, Death, Recording Records. Access to the County Recorder's database of official documents is free at http://clerk-recorder.buttecounty.net/election/index.html. Records go back to 1988. **Other Phone Numbers:** Assessor 530-538-7721; Treasurer 530-538-7576; Appraiser/Auditor 530-538-7721; Elections 530-538-7761; Vital Records 530-538-7690.

Calaveras County

County Recorder, Government Center, 891 Mountain Ranch Rd, San Andreas, CA 95249. 209-754-6372; Fax 209-754-6733.
Will search UCC records. This agency will not do a tax lien search. Will not search real estate records. **Online Access:** Property Records. Access to the GIS Project of property information is available free at www.co.calaveras.ca.us/departments/gisproj.html. Click on "The Parcel Information System.". **Other Phone Numbers:** Assessor 209-754-6356; Treasurer 209-754-6350; Appraiser/Auditor 209-754-6356; Elections 209-754-6376; Vital Records 209-754-6372.

Colusa County

County Recorder, 546 Jay St, Colusa, CA 95932. County Recorder, R/E and UCC Recording 530-458-0500; Fax 530-458-0512. www.colusacountyclerk.com
Will search UCC records. This agency will not do a tax lien search. Will search for a specific deed. **Other Phone Numbers:** Assessor 530-458-0450; Treasurer 530-458-0440; Elections 530-458-0500; Vital Records 530-458-0500.

Contra Costa County

County Recorder, PO Box 350, Martinez, CA 94553. 925-646-2360; Fax 925-646-2135. www.co.contra-costa.ca.us/depart/elect/Rindex.html
The County Clerk is located at 822 Main St, Martinez, CA 94553, 925-646-2955. This agency will not perform searches. **Online Access:** Recording, Fictitious Business Name, Marriage, Death, Birth Records. Recorder office records back to 1996 are available free at www.criis.com/contracosta/srecord_current.shtml. County Birth records are at www.criis.com/contracosta/sbirth.shtml. County Death records are at www.criis.com/contracosta/sdeath.shtml. Fictitious Business names are at www.criis.com/contracosta/sfictitious.shtml. Marriage records are at www.criis.com/contracosta/smarriage.shtml. **Other Phones:** Assessor 925-313-7400 (res); 313-7500 (busi).

Del Norte County

County Recorder, 981 H St #160, Crescent City, CA 95531. 707-464-7216; Fax 707-464-0321.
Will search UCC records. This agency will not do a tax lien search. Will not search real estate records. **Other Phone Numbers:** Assessor 707-464-7200; Treasurer 707-464-7283.

El Dorado County

County Recorder, 360 Fair Lane, Placerville, CA 95667-4197. County Recorder, R/E and UCC Recording 530-621-5490; Fax 530-621-2147. www.co.el-dorado.ca.us/countyclerk/
Will search UCC records. UCC search includes tax liens if requested. Will not search real estate records. **Online Access:** Real Estate, Personal Property, Vital Statistic, Fictitious Name Records. Access to the Recorder's index is available free on the Internet at http://main.co.el-dorado.ca.us/CGI/WWB012/WWM 501/R. Records go back to 1949. Official records on the County Recorder database are available free at http://main.co.el-dorado.ca.us/CGI/WWB012/WWM 501/C. Search by date range and name or document number. County vital statistics - births, deaths, non-confidential marriages, and fictitious names - are available free on the Internet at http://main.co.el-dorado.ca.us/CGI/WWB012/WWM500/C. **Other Phone Numbers:** Assessor 530-621-5719; Treasurer 530-621-5800; Vital Records 530-621-5490.

Fresno County

County Recorder, PO Box 766, Fresno, CA 93712. County Recorder, R/E and UCC Recording 559-488-3471; Fax 559-488-6774. www.fresno.ca.gov/0420/recorders_web/index.htm
Husband and wife count as one search, if so indicated. Will not search UCC records. Will not search real estate records. **Online Access:** Assessor, Birth, Death, Marriage Records. Recording office records on the county recorder database are available free at http://assessor.fresno.ca.gov/fresno/srecord_oracle.shtml. County Birth Records are at http://assessor.fresno.ca.gov/fresno/sbirth_oracle.shtml. County death records are at http://assessor.fresno.ca.gov/fresno/sdeath_oracle.shtml. Marriage records are at http://assessor.fresno.ca.gov/fresno/smarriage_oracle.shtml. **Other Phone Numbers:** Assessor 559-488-3514; Treasurer 559-488-3486; Vital Records 559-488-3476.

Glenn County

County Recorder, 526 W. Sycamore St, Willows, CA 95988. County Recorder, R/E and UCC Recording 530-934-6412; Fax 530-934-6305.
Will not search UCC records. Will not search real estate records. **Other Phone Numbers:** Assessor 530-934-6402; Treasurer 530-934-6410; Elections 530-934-6414; Vital Records 530-934-6412.

Humboldt County

County Recorder, 825 Fifth St, 5th Floor, Eureka, CA 95501. County Recorder, R/E and UCC Recording 707-445-7593; Fax 707-445-7324.

Will search UCC records. This agency will not do a tax lien search. Will not search real estate records. **Other Phone Numbers:** Assessor 707-445-7276; Treasurer 707-445-7331; Vital Records 707-445-7382.

Imperial County

County Recorder, 940 Main St, Room 202, El Centro, CA 92243-2865. 760-339-4272 R/E Recording: 760-482-4275 UCC Recording: 760-482-4275.

Will search UCC records. Tax liens not included in UCC search. Will not search real estate records. **Other Phone Numbers:** Assessor 760-482-4244; Treasurer 760-482-6281; Vital Records 760-482-4272.

Inyo County

County Recorder, PO Box F, Independence, CA 93526. County Recorder, R/E and UCC Recording 760-878-0222; Fax 760-878-1805.

Will search UCC records. This agency will not do a tax lien search. Will not search real estate records. **Online Access:** Recording, Fictitious Name, Birth, Death, Marriage Records. Access to the county clerk database may be available free at www.criis.com/inyo/official.shtml. **Other Phones:** Assessor 760-878-0302; Treasurer 760-878-0333; Appraiser/Auditor 760-878-0302; Elections 760-878-0223; Vital Records 760-878-0410.

Kern County

County Recorder, 1655 Chester Ave, Hall of Records, Bakersfield, CA 93301. County Recorder, R/E and UCC Recording 661-868-6400; Fax 661-868-6401. www.co.kern.ca.us/recorder

Will not search UCC records. Mortgage searches available. **Online Access:** Assessor, Property Tax, Fictitious Business Name, Vital Statistic, Recording, Real Estate Records. Records on the County of Kern Online Assessor database are available free online at http://assessor.co.kern.ca.us/kips/property_search.asp. Birth, Death, Marriage records may be purchased through vitalchek at www.vitalchek.com. Also, search county clerk's fictitious business name database for free at www.co.kern.ca.us/ctyclerk/dba/default.asp. The recorders database of deeds is available free at http://recorder.co.kern.ca.us/kips/property_search.asp. Also, search the treasurer database for fictious business names and property tax assessment information free at http://kerndata.com. Online maps also available. **Other Phone Numbers:** Assessor 661-868-3485; Treasurer 661-868-3490; Appraiser/Auditor 661-868-3485; Elections 661-868-3590; Vital Records 661-868-6449.

Kings County

County Recorder, 1400 W. Lacey Blvd., Hanford, CA 93230. 559-582-3211 x2475 R/E Recording: 559-582-3211 x2470 UCC Recording: 559-582-3211 x2470; Fax 559-582-6639. www.countyofkings.com

Will search UCC records. This agency will not do a tax lien search. Will not search real estate records. **Other Phone Numbers:** Assessor 559-582-3211 x2486; Treasurer 559-582-3211 x2477; Elections 559-582-3211 x2439; Vital Records 559-582-3211 x2470.

Lake County

County Recorder, 255 N. Forbes, Room 223, Lakeport, CA 95453. County Recorder, R/E and UCC Recording 707-263-2293; Fax 707-263-3703.

Will search UCC records. This agency will not do a tax lien search. Will not search real estate records. **Other Phone Numbers:** Assessor 707-263-2302; Treasurer 707-263-2236; Elections 707-263-2372; Vital Records 707-263-2293.

Lassen County

County Recorder, 220 S. Lassen St, Suite 5, Susanville, CA 96130. County Recorder, R/E and UCC Recording 530-251-8234; Fax 530-257-3480. http://clerk.lassencounty.org

Will search UCC records. This agency will not do a tax lien search. Will not search real estate records. **Online Access:** Real Estate, Recording Records. Access to the county recorder database is available free at http://icris.lassencounty.org. Registration is required. Recorded documents go back to 7/1985. Vital statistics back to 7/12/1999. **Other Phone Numbers:** Assessor 530-251-8241; 251-8242; Treasurer 530-251-8220; Elections 530-251-8217; Vital Records 530-251-8234.

Los Angeles County

County Recorder, PO Box 53195, Real Estate Records Section, Los Angeles, CA 90053-0115. 562-462-2125, 800-815-2666; http://regrec.co.la.ca.us

Will search UCC records. Tax liens not included in UCC search. Will not search real estate records. **Online Access:** Assessor, Fictitious Business Name, Inmates Records. Search county inmates list at http://pajis.lasd.org/ajis_search.cfm. For assessments use the PDB Inquiry System dial-up service; $100.00 monthly plus $1.00 per inquiry, also $75 sign-up fee for 3-year dial-up. Usage fee is $6.50 per hour or $.11 per minute. Send registration request with request reason to Data Systems Spvr2 Tech Admin, LA County Assessor's, 500 W Temple St Rm 293, LA, CA 90012. For further info call 213-974-3237 or visit http://assessor.co.la.ca.us/outsidesales/online.asp. Tax info line: 213-974-3838. Also, property and assessor information (no name searching) is available free online at http://assessor.co.la.ca.us/DataMaps/pais.asp. Search the map or by address. Search county Fictitious Names free online at http://regrec.co.la.ca.us/fbn/FBN.cfm. **Other Phone Numbers:** Assessor 562-974-3211; Treasurer 562-974-2101.

Madera County

County Recorder, 209 W. Yosemite, Madera, CA 93637. County Recorder, R/E and UCC Recording 559-675-7724; Fax 559-675-7870.

Will search UCC records. Will not search real estate records. **Other Phone Numbers:** Assessor 559-675-7710; Treasurer 559-675-7713; Elections 559-675-7720; Vital Records 559-675-7724.

Marin County

County Recorder, PO Box C, San Rafael, CA 94913. 415-499-6092; Fax 415-499-7893. www.co.marin.ca.us/depts/AR/main/index.cfm

Will not search UCC records. Will not search real estate records. **Online Access:** Real Estate, Property Tax, Grantor/Grantee, Recording, Vital Statistic Records. Search the county Grantor/Grantee index free at www.co.marin.ca.us/depts/AR/RiiMs/index.asp. Also, search the property tax database at www.co.marin.ca.us/depts/AR/COMPASS/index.asp but there is no name searching. Also, search the real estate sales lists by month and year by selecting the year. Also, search the vital records for document index number at www.co.marin.ca.us/depts/AR/VitalStatistics/index.asp. Birth records go back to 1967; deaths to 1979. Marriage records go back to 1948. **Other Phone Numbers:** Assessor 415-499-7215; Treasurer 415-499-6145.

Mariposa County

County Recorder, PO Box 35, Mariposa, CA 95338. 209-966-5719.

This agency will not perform searches. **Other Phone Numbers:** Assessor 209-966-2332; Treasurer 209-966-2621.

Mendocino County

County Recorder, 501 Low Gap Rd, Room 1020, Ukiah, CA 95482. County Recorder, R/E and UCC Recording 707-463-4376; Fax 707-463-4257. www.co.mendocino.ca.us

Will search UCC records. This agency will not do a tax lien search. Real estate record owner searches available. **Other Phones:** Assessor 707-463-4311; Treasurer 707-463-4388; Appraiser/Auditor 707-463-4311; Elections 707-463-4374; Vital Records 707-463-4371.

Merced County

County Recorder, 2222 M St, Merced, CA 95340. 209-385-7627; Fax 209-725-3900.

Will not search UCC records. Will not search real estate records. **Other Phone Numbers:** Assessor 209-385-7631; Treasurer 209-385-7307.

Modoc County

County Recorder, 204 Court St, Alturas, CA 96101. County Recorder, R/E and UCC Recording 530-233-6205; Fax 530-233-6666.

Will search UCC records. This agency will not do a tax lien search. Will not search real estate records. **Online Access:** Recording, Fictitious Name, Birth, Death, Marriage Records. Access to the county clerk database may be available free at www.criis.com/modoc/official.shtml. **Other Phone Numbers:** Assessor 530-233-6217; 233-6218; Treasurer 530-233-6223; Appraiser/Auditor 530-233-6221; Elections 530-233-6201; Vital Records 530-233-6205.

Mono County

County Recorder, PO Box 237, Bridgeport, CA 93517. County Recorder, R/E and UCC Recording 760-932-5240; Fax 760-932-7145.

Will search UCC records. UCC search does not include tax liens Real estate record owner searches available. **Other Phone Numbers:** Assessor 760-932-5204; Treasurer 760-932-5265; Elections 760-932-5240; Vital Records 760-932-5240.

Monterey County

County Recorder, PO Box 29, Salinas, CA 93902. County Recorder, R/E and UCC Recording 831-755-5041; Fax 831-755-5064. www.co.monterey.ca.us/recorder/

This agency will not perform searches. **Other Phone Numbers:** Assessor 831-755-5035; Treasurer 831-755-5015; Vital Records 813-755-5041.

Napa County

County Recorder, PO Box 298, Napa, CA 94559-0298. 707-253-4246; Fax 707-259-8149. www.co.napa.ca.us/departments/recorder/

Will search UCC records. Real estate record owner searches available. **Other Phone Numbers:** Assessor 707-253-4466; Treasurer 707-253-4311; Elections 707-253-4321.

Nevada County

County Recorder, 950 Maidu Ave, Nevada City, CA 95959. 530-265-1221; Fax 530-265-1497. http://recorder.co.nevada.ca.us

This agency will not perform searches. **Online Access:** Recording, Fictious Name, Birth, Death, Marriage Records. Access to the county clerk database is available free at www.criis.com/nevada/official.shtml. **Other Phone Numbers:** Assessor 530-265-1232; Treasurer 530-265-1285; Elections 530-265-1298.

Orange County

County Recorder, PO Box 238, Santa Ana, CA 92702-0238. 714-834-2500 R/E Recording: 714-834-2887 (questions); Fax 714-834-2675.
Will search UCC records. UCC search includes tax liens if requested. Will not search real estate records. **Online Access:** Grantor/Grantee, Deed, Lien, Judgment Records. Orange County Grantor/Grantee records are available free online at http://cr.ocgov.com/grantorgrantee. **Other Phone Numbers:** Assessor 714-834-2727; Treasurer 714-834-2682.

Placer County

County Recorder, 2954 Richardson Dr., Auburn, CA 95603. 530-886-5600; Fax 530-886-5687. www.placer.ca.gov/clerk/clerk.htm
Will search UCC records. This agency will not do a tax lien search. Will not search real estate records. **Online Access:** Recording, Fictitious Name, Birth, Death, Marriage Records. Recorder office records are available free at the web site. County Birth records are at www.criis.com/placer/sbirth.shtml. County Death records are at www.criis.com/placer/sdeath.shtml. County Marriage records are at www.criis.com/placer/smarriage.shtm. County Fictitious Business Names are at www.criis.com/placer/sfictitious.shtml. **Other Phone Numbers:** Assessor 530-889-4300.

Plumas County

County Recorder, 520 Main St, Room 102, Quincy, CA 95971. 530-283-6218; Fax 530-283-6155.
Will search UCC records. UCC search includes tax liens if requested. Will not search real estate records. **Other Phone Numbers:** Assessor 530-283-6380; Treasurer 530-283-6260.

Riverside County

County Recorder, PO Box 751, Attn: County Recorder/Clerk, Riverside, CA 92502-0751. 909-486-7000; Fax 909-486-7007. http://riverside.asrclkrec.com
Will search UCC records. UCC search includes tax liens if requested. Will not search real estate records. **Online Access:** Assessor, Property Tax, Fictitious Name, Grantor/Grantee Records. Property tax information from the County Treasurer database is available free from EZproperty.com on the internet at https://riverside.ca.ezgov.com/ezproperty/review_search.jsp. Also, access to the county fictitious name database and Grantor/Grantee index is available at http://riverside.asrclkrec.com/OS.asp. The FBN search is free; a fee is charged for documents from the Grantor/Grantee index. **Other Phone Numbers:** Assessor 909-275-6250; Treasurer 909-275-3900.

Sacramento County

County Clerk & Recorder, PO Box 839, Sacramento, CA 95812-0839. 916-874-6334; 800-313-7133 R/E Recording: 916-874-6334 UCC Recording: 916-874-6334; www.co.sacramento.ca.us
Assessor office is at 3701 Power Inn Rd. Will search UCC records. Phone and mail requests accepted. UCC search includes tax liens if requested. Will not search real estate records. **Online Access:** Assessor, Recording, Grantor/Grantee, Deed, Business License Records. Access to the Dept. of Finance Clerk-recorder assessment database is available free at www.erosi.saccounty.net/Inputs.asp. Online records go back to 1965. Also, clerk recorder data is soon to be online at www.criis.com/sacramento/official.shtml and may include Fictitious Names, Birth, Death, Marriages. Also, search City of West Sacramento business licenses at www.ci.west-sacramento.ca.us/cityhall/departments/finance/buslic/blfind.cfm. **Other Phone Numbers:** Assessor 916-874-5231; Treasurer 916-874-6725; Appraiser/Auditor 916-874-5231; Elections 916-874-6451; Vital Records 916-874-6334.

San Benito County

County Recorder, 440 Fifth St, Room 206, Hollister, CA 95023. County Recorder, R/E and UCC Recording 831-636-4046 UCC Recording: 831-636-4029; Fax 831-636-2939.
Will search UCC records. This agency will not do a tax lien search. Will not search real estate records. **Other Phone Numbers:** Assessor 831-636-4030; Elections 831-636-4016; Vital Records 831-636-4029.

San Bernardino County

County Recorder, 222 W. Hospitality Ln., 1st Floor, San Bernardino, CA 92415-0022. County Recorder, R/E and UCC Recording 909-387-8306; Fax 909-386-9050. www.co.san-bernardino.ca.us
This agency will not perform searches. **Online Access:** Recorder, Assessor, Fictitious Name Records. Records on the County Assessor database are available free on the Internet at www.co.san-bernardino.ca.us/tax/trsearch.asp. For automated call distribution, call 909-387-8306; for fictitious names information, call 909-386-8970. Fictitious business names are also available online at www.co.san-bernardino.ca.us/ACR/RecSearch.htm. Also, the Auditor/Controller Grantor/Grantee recording index is avaialble free at www.co.san-bernardino.ca.us/ACR/or/recsearch.asp. **Other Phone Numbers:** Assessor 909-387-6730; Treasurer 909-387-8308; Elections 909-387-8300; Vital Records 909-387-8314; Admin. 909-387-8924.

San Diego County

County Recorder, PO Box 121750, San Diego, CA 92112. 619-238-8158; 619-237-0502 R/E Recording: 619-238-8158 UCC Recording: 619-238-8158; Fax 619-557-4155. www.co.san-diego.ca.us
Will search UCC records. Tax liens not included in UCC search. Real estate owner, mortgage, and property transfer searches available. **Online Access:** Assessor, Fictitious Name, Real Estate, Grantor/Grantee, Inmates, Most Wanted, Warrant, Sex Offender, Pets, Missing Children, Tax Sale Records. Records on the County Assessor/Recorder/County Clerk Online Services site are available free online at www.co.san-diego.ca.us/cnty/cntydepts/general/assessor/online.html including fictitious business names, indexes, maps, property information. Grantee/grantor index search by name for individual record data at http://arcc.co.san-diego.ca.us/services/grantorgrantee. Also, online search inmates at http://199.106.18.5/waar/waar.html. Also, search www.sdcounty.ca.gov/general/online.html for most wanted, warrants, sex offenders, found pet, missing children, tax sales, real estate. **Other Phone Numbers:** Assessor 619-236-3771; Treasurer 619-236-3121; Vital Records 619-237-0502.

San Francisco County

County Recorder, City Hall, Room 190, 1 Dr. Carlton E. Goodlet Pl., San Francisco, CA 94102. 415-554-4176; Fax 415-554-4179.
This agency will not perform searches. **Online Access:** Property Tax, Recording, Fictitious Name, Birth, Death, Marriage Records. Access to the City Property Tax database is available free at https://cityservices.sfgov.org/serv/ttx_pt. No name searching; and address or Block/lot # is required. Also, online access to recording, birth, death, marriage and fictitious name records on the county clerk database may be available free at www.criis.com/sanfrancisco/official.htm. Fictitious business names are also searchable at http://cityservices.sfgov.org/serv/clerk_fbn. **Other Phone Numbers:** Assessor 415-554-5507; 554-5500.

San Joaquin County

County Recorder, PO Box 1968, Stockton, CA 95201. 209-468-3939; Fax 209-468-8040.
This agency will not perform searches. **Other Phone Numbers:** Assessor 209-468-2630; Treasurer 209-468-2133; Vital Records 803-245-8075.

San Luis Obispo County

County Recorder, 1144 Monterey St., Suite C, San Luis Obispo, CA 93408. County Recorder, R/E and UCC Recording 805-781-5080; Fax 805-781-1111. www.co.slo.ca.us
There is also a North County office at 5955 Capistrano, #B, Atascadero CA 93422, 805-461-6041. Will search UCC records. Mail requests only; use their UUC-3 form for search requests. This agency will not do a tax lien search. Will not search real estate records. **Other Phone Numbers:** Assessor 805-781-5643; Treasurer 805-781-5842; Elections 805-781-5228; Vital Records 805-781-5080.

San Mateo County

County Recorder, 555 County Center, 1st Fl, Redwood City, CA 94063. County Recorder, R/E and UCC Recording 650-363-4713; Fax 650-363-4843. www.care.co.sanmateo.ca.us
Will search UCC records. This agency will not do a tax lien search. Will not search real estate records. **Online Access:** Property Tax, Fictitious Name, Voter Registration Records. Records on the county property taxes and fictitious names databases are available free at www.care.co.sanmateo.ca.us/frames/our_office/ceo_d.htm. Search by address, city or parcel ID#. Also, a voter registration confirmation site is available free; birthdate and address required. There is also a secured property search, but no name searching. **Other Phone Numbers:** Assessor 650-363-4500; Treasurer 650-363-4840; Appraiser/Auditor 650-363-4500; Elections 650-312-5222; Vital Records 650-363-4500.

Santa Barbara County

County Recorder, PO Box 159, Santa Barbara, CA 93102-0159. County Recorder, R/E and UCC Recording 805-568-2250; Fax 805-568-2266. www.sb-democracy.com
County also has a branch office in Santa Maria at 511 E Lakeside Pkwy, #115, 93455, 805-346-8370; thisoffice does not handle recordings. Will not search UCC records. Will not search real estate records. **Online Access:** Assessor Records. Access to assessor online property info system (OPIS) in available free at the web site with parcel #. Records go back 10 years. Database is free to view but only subscribers will be able to download. Full access requires registration. Contact Larry Herrera for an account. herrera@co.santa-barbara.ca.us. **Other Phone Numbers:** Assessor 805-568-2550; Treasurer 805-568-2490; Appraiser/Auditor 805-568-2550; Elections 805-568-2200; Vital Records 805-568-2257.

Santa Clara County

County Clerk/Recorder, County Government Center, 70 W. Hedding St., 1st Floor, East Wing, San Jose, CA 95110. 408-299-2481 R/E Recording: 408-299-5667; Fax 408-280-1768. www.clerkrecordersearch.org
Will not search UCC records. Will search by real estate document type in index. **Online Access:** Recording, Grantor/Grantee, Marriage, Death Records. Access to the County Clerk-Recorder database is available free at the web site. **Other Phone Numbers:** Assessor 408-299-5500; Vital Records 408-299-5669; Official Record Copies 408-299-5670.

Santa Cruz County

County Recorder, 701 Ocean St, Rm 230, Room 230, Santa Cruz, CA 95060. 831-454-2800; Fax 831-454-3169. www.co.santa-cruz.ca.us/rcd/
Will search UCC records. This agency will not do a tax lien search. Will not search real estate records. **Online Access:** Assessor, Property Tax, Fictitious Business Name, Recording, Deed, Judgment, Vital Statistic Records. Access to the assessor's parcel information data is available free at http://sccounty01.co.santa-cruz.ca.us/ASR. No name searching. Also, search for property information using the GIS map at http://gis.co.santa-cruz.ca.us. Also, search the recorder's fictitious business names free at http://sccounty01.co.santa-cruz.ca.us/clerkrecorder/Asp/FBNInquiry.asp. Also, access to the recorder's official records is avaialble free at http://sccounty01.co.santa-cruz.ca.us/clerkrecorder/Asp/ORInquiry.asp. Online indexes go back to 1978. Births, Deaths, and Marriages are also searchable back to 1984. **Other Phone Numbers:** Assessor 831-454-2002; Elections 831-454-2060.

Shasta County

County Recorder, 1500 Court St., Room 102, Redding, CA 96001. 530-225-5671; Fax 530-225-5673. www.co.shasta.ca.us
Will search UCC records. This agency will not do a tax lien search. Will not search real estate records. **Online Access:** Assessor Records. Records on the City of Redding Parcel Search By Parcel Number Server are available free at http://cor400.ci.redding.ca.us/nd/gow3lkap.ndm/input. CA state law has removed owner names. **Other Phones:** Assessor 530-225-3600.

Sierra County

County Recorder, PO Drawer D, Downieville, CA 95936. County Recorder, R/E and UCC Recording 530-289-3295; Fax 530-289-3300.
Will search UCC records. This agency will not do a tax lien search. Real estate record owner searches available. **Other Phones:** Assessor 530-289-3283; Treasurer 530-289-3286; Appraiser/Auditor 530-289-3283; Elections 530-289-3295; Vital Records 530-289-3295.

Siskiyou County

County Recorder, PO Box 8, Yreka, CA 96097. 530-842-8065; Fax 530-842-8077.
Will search UCC records. This agency will not do a tax lien search. Will not search real estate records. **Other Phone Numbers:** Assessor 530-842-8036.

Solano County

County Recorder, 701 Texas St, Fairfield, CA 94533. County Recorder, R/E and UCC Recording 707-421-6290; Fax 707-421-6911. www.solanocounty.com
Will not search UCC records. This agency will not do a tax lien search. Real estate owner, mortgage, and property transfer searches available. Searches only performed to 1974 and only if searcher is purchasing copies. **Online Access:** Property Tax, Recording, Deed, Judgment, Lien Records. Search the treasurer/tax collector/county clerk property database ifree at www.solanocounty.com/treasurer/propquery.asp. Also,

the recorder's index is to be online in late 2002; see www.solanocounty.com/assessrecord. **Other Phone Numbers:** Assessor 707-421-6200; Appraiser/Auditor 707-421-6210; Vital Records 707-421-6294.

Sonoma County

County Recorder, PO Box 1709, Santa Rosa, CA 95406-1709. 707-565-2651; Fax 707-565-3905.
Will search UCC records. Tax liens not included in UCC search. Will not search real estate records. **Other Phone Numbers:** Assessor 707-565-1888.

Stanislaus County

County Recorder, PO Box 1008, Modesto, CA 95353. County Recorder, R/E and UCC Recording 209-525-5260; Fax 209-525-5207. www.co.stanislaus.ca.us
Assessor is located at 1010 10th St. #2400. Will search UCC records. This agency will not do a tax lien search. Will not search real estate records. **Online Access:** Recording, Fictitious Name, Birth, Death, Marriage Records. Recorder office records are available free at www.criis.com/stanislaus/srecord_current.shtml. County Birth records are at www.criis.com/stanislaus/sbirth.shtml. Death records are at www.criis.com/stanislaus/sdeath.shtml. Marriage records are at www.criis.com/stanislaus/smarriage.shtml. County Fictitious Business Name records are at www.criis.com/stanislaus/sfictitious.shtml. **Other Phone Numbers:** Assessor 209-525-6461; Elections 209-525-5200; Vital Records 209-525-5291.

Sutter County

County Recorder, PO Box 1555, Yuba City, CA 95992-1555. County Recorder, R/E and UCC Recording 530-822-7134; Fax 530-822-7214.
Will search UCC records. This agency will not do a tax lien search. Will not search real estate records. **Other Phone Numbers:** Assessor 530-822-7160; Treasurer 530-822-7117; Appraiser/Auditor 530-822-7160; Elections 530-822-7120; Vital Records 530-822-7134.

Tehama County

County Recorder, PO Box 250, Red Bluff, CA 96080. County Recorder, R/E and UCC Recording 530-527-3350; Fax 530-527-1140.
Will search UCC records. This agency will not do a tax lien search. Will not search real estate records. **Other Phone Numbers:** Assessor 530-527-5931; Treasurer 530-527-4535; Appraiser/Auditor 530-527-5931; Elections 530-527-8190; Vital Records 530-527-3350.

Trinity County

County Recorder, PO Box 1215, Weaverville, CA 96093-1258. 530-623-1215; Fax 530-623-8398. www.trinitycounty.org/Departments/assessor-clerk-elect/clerkrecorder.htm
Will not search UCC records. Will not search real estate records. **Online Access:** Vital Statistic Records. Access to the Recorder's vital statistics database is available free at http://halfile.trinitycounty.org. For user name, enter "vital"; leave password field empty. **Other Phone Numbers:** Assessor 530-623-1257; Treasurer 530-623-1251; Elections 530-623-1220; Vital Records 530-623-1215.

Tulare County

County Recorder, County Civic Center, Room 103, 221 S. Mooney Blvd., Visalia, CA 93291-4593. 559-733-6377; Fax 559-740-4329. www.co.tulare.ca.us
Will search UCC records. This agency will not do a tax lien search. Will not search real estate records. **Online Access:** Recording, Deed, Judgment, Lien, Vital Statistic, Fictitious Name Records. Search the recorders database including births, marriages, deaths free at http://209.78.90.65/riimsweb/orinquiry.asp. **Other Phone Numbers:** Assessor 559-733-6361; Elections 559-733-6377.

Tuolumne County

County Recorder, 2 S. Green St, County Administration Center, Sonora, CA 95370. 209-533-5531; Fax 209-533-6543.
Will search UCC records. This agency will not do a tax lien search. Will not search real estate records. **Other Phone Numbers:** Assessor 209-533-5535; Treasurer 209-533-5544; Appraiser/Auditor 209-533-5551; Elections 209-533-5570.

Ventura County

County Recorder, 800 S. Victoria Ave, Government Center, Ventura, CA 93009. 805-654-2292; Fax 805-654-2392. www.ventura.org/assessor/index.html
This agency will not perform searches. **Online Access:** Recording, Fictitious Name, Birth, Death, Marriage Records. Access to the county clerks database is available free at www.criis.com/ventura/official.htm. **Other Phone Numbers:** Assessor 805-654-2181; Treasurer 805-654-3735.

Yolo County

County Recorder, PO Box 1130, Woodland, CA 95776-1130. 530-666-8130; Fax 530-666-8109. www.yolocounty.org/org/Recorder
Will not search UCC records. Will not search real estate records. **Online Access:** Assessor, Birth, Death, Marriage, Fictitious Business Name Records. Access to recordings on the county clerk database are available free at www.criis.com/yolo/srecord_current.shtml. County Birth records are at www.criis.com/yolo/sbirth.shtml. County Death records are at www.criis.com/yolo/sdeath.shtml. Marriage records are at www.criis.com/yolo/smarriage.shtml. County Fictitious Business Name records are at www.criis.com/yolo/sfictitious.shtml. Also, City of Davis business licenses are free at www.city.davis.ca.us/ed/business. **Other Phones:** Assessor 530-666-8135; Treasurer 530-666-8625.

Yuba County

County Recorder, 935 14th St, Marysville, CA 95901. County Recorder, R/E and UCC Recording 530-741-6547; Fax 530-741-6285.
Will search UCC records. This agency will not do a tax lien search. Will not search real estate records. **Other Phone Numbers:** Assessor 530-741-6222; 741-6221; Treasurer 530-741-6236; Elections 530-741-6545; Vital Records 530-741-6547; Clerk 530-741-6341.

California County Locator

You will usually be able to find the city name in the City/County Cross Reference below. In that case, it is a simple matter to determine the county from the cross reference. However, only the official US Postal Service city names are included in this index. There are an additional 40,000 place names that people use in their addresses. Therefore, we have also included a ZIP/City Cross Reference immediately following the City/County Cross Reference.

If you know the ZIP Code but the city name does not appear in the City/County Cross Reference index, look up the ZIP Code in the ZIP/City Cross Reference, find the city name, then look up the city name in the City/County Cross Reference. For example, you want to know the county for an address of Menands, NY 12204. There is no "Menands" in the City/County Cross Reference. The ZIP/City Cross Reference shows that ZIP Codes 12201-12288 are for the city of Albany. Looking back in the City/County Cross Reference, Albany is in Albany County.

City/County Cross Reference

ACAMPO San Joaquin
ACTON Los Angeles
ADELANTO San Bernardino
ADIN (96006) Modoc(66), Lassen(33)
AGOURA HILLS Los Angeles
AGUANGA Riverside
AHWAHNEE (93601) Madera(95), Mariposa(4)
ALAMEDA Alameda
ALAMO Contra Costa
ALBANY Alameda
ALBION Mendocino
ALDERPOINT Humboldt
ALHAMBRA Los Angeles
ALISO VIEJO Orange
ALLEGHANY Sierra
ALPAUGH Tulare
ALPINE San Diego
ALTA Placer
ALTA LOMA San Bernardino
ALTADENA Los Angeles
ALTAVILLE Calaveras
ALTURAS Modoc
ALVISO Santa Clara
AMADOR CITY Amador
AMBOY San Bernardino
AMERICAN CANYON Napa
ANAHEIM Orange
ANDERSON Shasta
ANGELS CAMP Calaveras
ANGELUS OAKS San Bernardino
ANGWIN Napa
ANNAPOLIS Sonoma
ANTELOPE Sacramento
ANTIOCH Contra Costa
ANZA Riverside
APPLE VALLEY San Bernardino
APPLEGATE Placer
APTOS Santa Cruz
ARBUCKLE (95912) Colusa(98), Yolo(1)
ARCADIA Los Angeles
ARCATA Humboldt
ARMONA Kings
ARNOLD Calaveras
AROMAS (95004) Monterey(52), San Benito(47)
ARROYO GRANDE San Luis Obispo
ARTESIA Los Angeles
ARTOIS Glenn
ARVIN Kern
ATASCADERO San Luis Obispo
ATHERTON San Mateo
ATWATER Merced
ATWOOD Orange
AUBERRY Fresno
AUBURN Placer
AVALON Los Angeles
AVENAL Kings
AVERY Calaveras
AVILA BEACH San Luis Obispo
AZUSA Los Angeles
BADGER Tulare
BAKER San Bernardino

BAKERSFIELD Kern
BALDWIN PARK Los Angeles
BALLICO Merced
BANGOR (95914) Butte(91), Yuba(8)
BANNING Riverside
BANTA (95304) San Joaquin(98), Alameda(1)
BARD Imperial
BARSTOW San Bernardino
BASS LAKE Madera
BAYSIDE Humboldt
BEALE AFB Yuba
BEAUMONT Riverside
BECKWOURTH Plumas
BELDEN Plumas
BELL Los Angeles
BELL GARDENS Los Angeles
BELLA VISTA Shasta
BELLFLOWER Los Angeles
BELMONT San Mateo
BELVEDERE TIBURON Marin
BEN LOMOND Santa Cruz
BENICIA Solano
BENTON Mono
BERKELEY Alameda
BERRY CREEK Butte
BETHEL ISLAND Contra Costa
BEVERLY HILLS Los Angeles
BIEBER Lassen
BIG BAR Trinity
BIG BEAR CITY San Bernardino
BIG BEAR LAKE San Bernardino
BIG BEND Shasta
BIG CREEK Fresno
BIG OAK FLAT Tuolumne
BIG PINE Inyo
BIG SUR Monterey
BIGGS Butte
BIOLA Fresno
BIRDS LANDING Solano
BISHOP Inyo
BLAIRSDEN-GRAEAGLE Plumas
BLOCKSBURG Humboldt
BLOOMINGTON San Bernardino
BLUE JAY San Bernardino
BLUE LAKE Humboldt
BLYTHE Riverside
BODEGA Sonoma
BODEGA BAY Sonoma
BODFISH Kern
BOLINAS Marin
BONITA San Diego
BONSALL San Diego
BOONVILLE Mendocino
BORON Kern
BORREGO SPRINGS (92004) San Diego(95), Imperial(4)
BOULDER CREEK Santa Cruz
BOULEVARD San Diego
BOYES HOT SPRINGS Sonoma
BRADLEY (93426) Monterey(57), San Luis Obispo(42)
BRANDEIS Ventura

BRANSCOMB Mendocino
BRAWLEY Imperial
BREA Orange
BRENTWOOD Contra Costa
BRIDGEPORT Mono
BRIDGEVILLE (95526) Humboldt(90), Trinity(9)
BRISBANE San Mateo
BROOKDALE Santa Cruz
BROOKS Yolo
BROWNS VALLEY Yuba
BROWNSVILLE (95919) Yuba(88), Butte(11)
BRYN MAWR San Bernardino
BUELLTON Santa Barbara
BUENA PARK Orange
BURBANK Los Angeles
BURLINGAME San Mateo
BURNEY Shasta
BURNT RANCH Trinity
BURREL Fresno
BURSON Calaveras
BUTTE CITY Glenn
BUTTONWILLOW Kern
BYRON (94514) Contra Costa(88), Alameda(10)
CABAZON Riverside
CADIZ San Bernardino
CALABASAS Los Angeles
CALEXICO Imperial
CALIENTE Kern
CALIFORNIA CITY Kern
CALIFORNIA HOT SPRINGS Tulare
CALIMESA Riverside
CALIPATRIA Imperial
CALISTOGA (94515) Napa(89), Sonoma(10)
CALLAHAN Siskiyou
CALPELLA Mendocino
CALPINE Sierra
CAMARILLO Ventura
CAMBRIA San Luis Obispo
CAMINO El Dorado
CAMP MEEKER Sonoma
CAMP NELSON Tulare
CAMP PENDLETON San Diego
CAMPBELL Santa Clara
CAMPO San Diego
CAMPO SECO Calaveras
CAMPTONVILLE (95922) Yuba(95), Sierra(4)
CANBY Modoc
CANOGA PARK Los Angeles
CANTIL Kern
CANTUA CREEK Fresno
CANYON Contra Costa
CANYON COUNTRY Los Angeles
CANYONDAM Plumas
CAPAY Yolo
CAPISTRANO BEACH Orange
CAPITOLA Santa Cruz
CARDIFF BY THE SEA San Diego
CARLOTTA Humboldt

CARLSBAD San Diego
CARMEL Monterey
CARMEL VALLEY Monterey
CARMICHAEL Sacramento
CARNELIAN BAY Placer
CARPINTERIA Santa Barbara
CARSON Los Angeles
CARUTHERS Fresno
CASMALIA Santa Barbara
CASPAR Mendocino
CASSEL Shasta
CASTAIC Los Angeles
CASTELLA Shasta
CASTRO VALLEY Alameda
CASTROVILLE Monterey
CATHEDRAL CITY Riverside
CATHEYS VALLEY Mariposa
CAYUCOS San Luis Obispo
CAZADERO Sonoma
CEDAR GLEN San Bernardino
CEDAR RIDGE Nevada
CEDARPINES PARK San Bernardino
CEDARVILLE Modoc
CERES Stanislaus
CERRITOS Los Angeles
CHALLENGE (95925) Butte(50), Yuba(50)
CHATSWORTH Los Angeles
CHESTER Plumas
CHICAGO PARK Nevada
CHICO Butte
CHILCOOT Plumas
CHINESE CAMP Tuolumne
CHINO San Bernardino
CHINO HILLS San Bernardino
CHOLAME San Luis Obispo
CHOWCHILLA (93610) Madera(97), Merced(2)
CHUALAR Monterey
CHULA VISTA San Diego
CIMA San Bernardino
CITRUS HEIGHTS Sacramento
CITY OF INDUSTRY Los Angeles
CLAREMONT Los Angeles
CLARKSBURG Yolo
CLAYTON Contra Costa
CLEARLAKE Lake
CLEARLAKE OAKS Lake
CLEARLAKE PARK Lake
CLEMENTS San Joaquin
CLIO Plumas
CLIPPER MILLS Butte
CLOVERDALE Sonoma
CLOVIS Fresno
COACHELLA Riverside
COALINGA Fresno
COARSEGOLD Madera
COBB Lake
COLEVILLE Mono
COLFAX Placer
COLLEGE CITY Colusa
COLOMA El Dorado
COLTON (92324) San Bernardino(96), Riverside(3)

COLUMBIA Tuolumne
COLUSA Colusa
COMPTCHE Mendocino
COMPTON Los Angeles
CONCORD Contra Costa
COOL El Dorado
COPPEROPOLIS Calaveras
CORCORAN (93212) Kings(97), Tulare(2)
CORNING Tehama
CORONA Riverside
CORONA DEL MAR Orange
CORONADO San Diego
CORTE MADERA Marin
COSTA MESA Orange
COTATI Sonoma
COTTONWOOD (96022) Tehama(51), Shasta(48)
COULTERVILLE (95311) Mariposa(93), Tuolumne(6)
COURTLAND Sacramento
COVELO Mendocino
COVINA Los Angeles
COYOTE Santa Clara
CRESCENT CITY Del Norte
CRESCENT MILLS Plumas
CRESSEY Merced
CREST PARK San Bernardino
CRESTLINE San Bernardino
CRESTON San Luis Obispo
CROCKER NAT BANK San Francisco
CROCKETT Contra Costa
CROWS LANDING Stanislaus
CULVER CITY Los Angeles
CUPERTINO Santa Clara
CUTLER Tulare
CUTTEN Humboldt
CUYAMA Santa Barbara
CYPRESS Orange
DAGGETT San Bernardino
DALY CITY San Mateo
DANA POINT Orange
DANVILLE Contra Costa
DARDANELLE Tuolumne
DARWIN Inyo
DAVENPORT Santa Cruz
DAVIS Yolo
DAVIS CREEK Modoc
DEATH VALLEY Inyo
DEER PARK Napa
DEL MAR San Diego
DEL REY Fresno
DELANO Kern
DELHI Merced
DENAIR Stanislaus
DESCANSO San Diego
DESERT CENTER Riverside
DESERT HOT SPRINGS Riverside
DI GIORGIO Kern
DIABLO Contra Costa
DIAMOND BAR Los Angeles
DIAMOND SPRINGS El Dorado
DILLON BEACH Marin
DINUBA (93618) Tulare(98), Fresno(1)
DIXON Solano
DOBBINS Yuba
DORRIS Siskiyou
DOS PALOS (93620) Merced(87), Fresno(12)
DOS RIOS Mendocino
DOUGLAS CITY Trinity
DOUGLAS FLAT Calaveras
DOWNEY Los Angeles
DOWNIEVILLE Sierra
DOYLE Lassen
DRYTOWN Amador
DUARTE Los Angeles
DUBLIN Alameda
DUCOR Tulare
DULZURA San Diego
DUNCANS MILLS Sonoma
DUNLAP Fresno
DUNNIGAN Yolo

DUNSMUIR (96025) Siskiyou(93), Shasta(6)
DURHAM Butte
DUTCH FLAT Placer
EAGLEVILLE Modoc
EARLIMART Tulare
EARP San Bernardino
EAST IRVINE Orange
ECHO LAKE El Dorado
EDISON Kern
EDWARDS Kern
EL CAJON San Diego
EL CENTRO Imperial
EL CERRITO Contra Costa
EL DORADO El Dorado
EL DORADO HILLS El Dorado
EL GRANADA San Mateo
EL MACERO Yolo
EL MONTE Los Angeles
EL NIDO Merced
EL PORTAL Mariposa
EL SEGUNDO Los Angeles
EL SOBRANTE Contra Costa
EL TORO Orange
EL VERANO Sonoma
ELDRIDGE Sonoma
ELK Mendocino
ELK CREEK (95939) Glenn(94), Colusa(5)
ELK GROVE Sacramento
ELMIRA Solano
ELVERTA (95626) Sacramento(86), Placer(10), Sutter(3)
EMERYVILLE Alameda
EMIGRANT GAP Placer
EMPIRE Stanislaus
ENCINITAS San Diego
ENCINO Los Angeles
ESCALON San Joaquin
ESCONDIDO San Diego
ESPARTO Yolo
ESSEX San Bernardino
ETNA Siskiyou
EUREKA Humboldt
EXETER Tulare
FAIR OAKS Sacramento
FAIRFAX Marin
FAIRFIELD Solano
FALL RIVER MILLS Shasta
FALLBROOK San Diego
FARMERSVILLE Tulare
FARMINGTON (95230) San Joaquin(35), Stanislaus(35), Calaveras(27), Tuolumne(3)
FAWNSKIN San Bernardino
FEATHER FALLS Butte
FELLOWS Kern
FELTON Santa Cruz
FERNDALE Humboldt
FIDDLETOWN (95629) El Dorado(74), Amador(25)
FIELDS LANDING Humboldt
FILLMORE Ventura
FINLEY Lake
FIREBAUGH (93622) Fresno(89), Madera(8), Merced(2)
FISH CAMP (93623) Mariposa(81), Madera(18)
FIVE POINTS Fresno
FLORISTON Nevada
FLOURNOY Tehama
FOLSOM Sacramento
FONTANA San Bernardino
FOOTHILL RANCH Orange
FORBESTOWN (95941) Butte(84), Yuba(15)
FOREST FALLS San Bernardino
FOREST KNOLLS Marin
FOREST RANCH Butte
FORESTHILL Placer
FORESTVILLE Sonoma
FORKS OF SALMON Siskiyou
FORT BIDWELL Modoc

FORT BRAGG Mendocino
FORT DICK Del Norte
FORT IRWIN San Bernardino
FORT JONES Siskiyou
FORT ORD Monterey
FORTUNA Humboldt
FOUNTAIN VALLEY Orange
FOWLER Fresno
FRAZIER PARK Kern
FREEDOM Santa Cruz
FREMONT Alameda
FRENCH CAMP San Joaquin
FRENCH GULCH Shasta
FRESNO Fresno
FRIANT (93626) Fresno(60), Madera(40)
FT ORD Monterey
FULLERTON Orange
FULTON Sonoma
GALT (95632) Sacramento(95), San Joaquin(4)
GARBERVILLE Humboldt
GARDEN GROVE Orange
GARDEN VALLEY El Dorado
GARDENA Los Angeles
GASQUET (95543) Del Norte(97), Trinity(2)
GAZELLE Siskiyou
GEORGETOWN El Dorado
GERBER Tehama
GEYSERVILLE Sonoma
GILROY Santa Clara
GLEN ELLEN Sonoma
GLENCOE Calaveras
GLENDALE Los Angeles
GLENDORA Los Angeles
GLENHAVEN Lake
GLENN Glenn
GLENNVILLE Kern
GOLD RUN Placer
GOLETA Santa Barbara
GONZALES Monterey
GOODYEARS BAR Sierra
GOSHEN Tulare
GRANADA HILLS Los Angeles
GRAND TERRACE San Bernardino
GRANITE BAY Placer
GRASS VALLEY Nevada
GRATON Sonoma
GREEN VALLEY LAKE San Bernardino
GREENBRAE Marin
GREENFIELD Monterey
GREENVIEW Siskiyou
GREENVILLE Plumas
GREENWOOD El Dorado
GRENADA Siskiyou
GRIDLEY Butte
GRIMES Colusa
GRIZZLY FLATS El Dorado
GROVELAND (95321) Tuolumne(97), Mariposa(2)
GROVER BEACH San Luis Obispo
GUADALUPE Santa Barbara
GUALALA Mendocino
GUASTI San Bernardino
GUATAY San Diego
GUERNEVILLE Sonoma
GUINDA Yolo
GUSTINE Merced
HACIENDA HEIGHTS Los Angeles
HALF MOON BAY San Mateo
HAMILTON CITY Glenn
HANFORD Kings
HAPPY CAMP Siskiyou
HARBOR CITY Los Angeles
HARMONY San Luis Obispo
HAT CREEK Shasta
HATHAWAY PINES Calaveras
HAWAIIAN GARDENS Los Angeles
HAWTHORNE Los Angeles
HAYFORK Trinity
HAYWARD Alameda
HEALDSBURG Sonoma
HEBER Imperial

HELENDALE San Bernardino
HELM Fresno
HEMET Riverside
HERALD Sacramento
HERCULES Contra Costa
HERLONG Lassen
HERMOSA BEACH Los Angeles
HESPERIA San Bernardino
HICKMAN Stanislaus
HIGHLAND San Bernardino
HILMAR Merced
HINKLEY San Bernardino
HOLLISTER San Benito
HOLT San Joaquin
HOLTVILLE Imperial
HOLY CITY Santa Clara
HOMELAND Riverside
HOMEWOOD Placer
HONEYDEW Humboldt
HOOD Sacramento
HOOPA Humboldt
HOPLAND Mendocino
HORNBROOK Siskiyou
HORNITOS Mariposa
HORSE CREEK Siskiyou
HUGHSON Stanislaus
HUME Fresno
HUNTINGTON BEACH Orange
HUNTINGTON LAKE Fresno
HUNTINGTON PARK Los Angeles
HURON Fresno
HYAMPOM Trinity
HYDESVILLE Humboldt
IDYLLWILD Riverside
IGO Shasta
IMPERIAL Imperial
IMPERIAL BEACH San Diego
INDEPENDENCE Inyo
INDIAN WELLS Riverside
INDIO Riverside
INGLEWOOD Los Angeles
INVERNESS Marin
INYOKERN (93527) Kern(93), Inyo(3), Tulare(2)
IONE Amador
IRVINE Orange
ISLETON Sacramento
IVANHOE Tulare
JACKSON Amador
JACUMBA San Diego
JAMESTOWN Tuolumne
JAMUL San Diego
JANESVILLE Lassen
JENNER Sonoma
JOHANNESBURG Kern
JOLON Monterey
JOSHUA TREE San Bernardino
JULIAN San Diego
JUNCTION CITY Trinity
JUNE LAKE Mono
KAWEAH Tulare
KEELER Inyo
KEENE Kern
KELSEYVILLE Lake
KENTFIELD Marin
KENWOOD Sonoma
KERMAN Fresno
KERNVILLE (93238) Kern(88), Tulare(11)
KETTLEMAN CITY Kings
KEYES Stanislaus
KING CITY Monterey
KINGS BEACH Placer
KINGS CANYON NATIONAL PK Tulare
KINGSBURG (93631) Fresno(82), Tulare(12), Kings(5)
KIRKWOOD Alpine
KIT CARSON Amador
KLAMATH Del Norte
KLAMATH RIVER Siskiyou
KNEELAND Humboldt
KNIGHTS LANDING (95645) Sutter(83), Yolo(16)

KNIGHTSEN Contra Costa
KORBEL Humboldt
KYBURZ El Dorado
LA CANADA FLINTRIDGE Los Angeles
LA COUNTY TAX COLLECTOR Los Angeles
LA CRESCENTA Los Angeles
LA GRANGE (95329) Tuolumne(56), Mariposa(35), Stanislaus(8)
LA HABRA Orange
LA HONDA San Mateo
LA JOLLA San Diego
LA MESA San Diego
LA MIRADA Los Angeles
LA PALMA Orange
LA PUENTE Los Angeles
LA QUINTA Riverside
LA VERNE Los Angeles
LADERA RANCH Orange
LAFAYETTE Contra Costa
LAGUNA BEACH Orange
LAGUNA HILLS Orange
LAGUNA NIGUEL Orange
LAGUNITAS Marin
LAKE ARROWHEAD San Bernardino
LAKE CITY Modoc
LAKE ELSINORE Riverside
LAKE FOREST Orange
LAKE HUGHES Los Angeles
LAKE ISABELLA Kern
LAKEHEAD Shasta
LAKEPORT Lake
LAKESHORE Fresno
LAKESIDE San Diego
LAKEVIEW Riverside
LAKEWOOD Los Angeles
LAMONT Kern
LANCASTER Los Angeles
LANDERS San Bernardino
LARKSPUR Marin
LATHROP San Joaquin
LATON (93242) Fresno(87), Kings(12)
LAWNDALE Los Angeles
LAYTONVILLE Mendocino
LE GRAND Merced
LEBEC (93243) Kern(70), Los Angeles(29)
LEE VINING Mono
LEGGETT Mendocino
LEMON COVE Tulare
LEMON GROVE San Diego
LEMOORE Kings
LEWISTON Trinity
LIKELY Modoc
LINCOLN Placer
LINCOLN ACRES San Diego
LINDEN (95236) San Joaquin(94), Calaveras(5)
LINDSAY Tulare
LITCHFIELD Lassen
LITTLE LAKE Inyo
LITTLERIVER Mendocino
LITTLEROCK Los Angeles
LIVE OAK Sutter
LIVERMORE Alameda
LIVINGSTON Merced
LLANO Los Angeles
LOCKEFORD San Joaquin
LOCKWOOD Monterey
LODI San Joaquin
LOLETA Humboldt
LOMA LINDA San Bernardino
LOMA MAR San Mateo
LOMITA Los Angeles
LOMPOC Santa Barbara
LONE PINE Inyo
LONG BARN Tuolumne
LONG BEACH Los Angeles
LOOKOUT Modoc
LOOMIS Placer
LOS ALAMITOS Orange
LOS ALAMOS Santa Barbara
LOS ALTOS Santa Clara

LOS ANGELES Los Angeles
LOS BANOS Merced
LOS GATOS (95033) Santa Cruz(66), Santa Clara(33)
LOS MOLINOS Tehama
LOS OLIVOS Santa Barbara
LOS OSOS San Luis Obispo
LOST HILLS Kern
LOTUS El Dorado
LOWER LAKE Lake
LOYALTON Sierra
LUCERNE Lake
LUCERNE VALLEY San Bernardino
LUDLOW San Bernardino
LYNWOOD Los Angeles
LYOTH San Joaquin
LYTLE CREEK San Bernardino
MACDOEL Siskiyou
MAD RIVER Trinity
MADELINE Lassen
MADERA Madera
MADISON Yolo
MAGALIA Butte
MALIBU (90265) Los Angeles(94), Ventura(5)
MAMMOTH LAKES Mono
MANCHESTER Mendocino
MANHATTAN BEACH Los Angeles
MANTECA San Joaquin
MANTON (96059) Tehama(70), Shasta(29)
MARCH AIR FORCE BASE Riverside
MARICOPA (93252) Kern(59), Santa Barbara(24), Ventura(12), San Luis Obispo(2)
MARINA Monterey
MARINA DEL REY Los Angeles
MARIPOSA Mariposa
MARKLEEVILLE Alpine
MARSHALL Marin
MARTELL Amador
MARTINEZ Contra Costa
MARYSVILLE Yuba
MATHER Sacramento
MAXWELL Colusa
MAYWOOD Los Angeles
MC FARLAND Kern
MC KITTRICK Kern
MCARTHUR (96056) Lassen(48), Shasta(36), Modoc(15)
MCCLELLAN Sacramento
MCCLELLAN AFB Sacramento
MCCLOUD Siskiyou
MCKINLEYVILLE Humboldt
MEADOW VALLEY Plumas
MEADOW VISTA Placer
MECCA Riverside
MENDOCINO Mendocino
MENDOTA Fresno
MENIFEE Riverside
MENLO PARK San Mateo
MENTONE San Bernardino
MERCED Merced
MERIDIAN Sutter
MI WUK VILLAGE Tuolumne
MIDDLETOWN Lake
MIDPINES Mariposa
MIDWAY CITY Orange
MILFORD Lassen
MILL CREEK Tehama
MILL VALLEY Marin
MILLBRAE San Mateo
MILLVILLE Shasta
MILPITAS Santa Clara
MINERAL Tehama
MIRA LOMA Riverside
MIRAMONTE (93641) Fresno(83), Tulare(16)
MIRANDA Humboldt
MISSION HILLS Los Angeles
MISSION VIEJO Orange
MOBIL OIL CREDIT CORPORATION Contra Costa

MOCCASIN Tuolumne
MODESTO Stanislaus
MOJAVE Kern
MOKELUMNE HILL Calaveras
MONO HOT SPRINGS Fresno
MONROVIA Los Angeles
MONTAGUE Siskiyou
MONTARA San Mateo
MONTCLAIR San Bernardino
MONTE RIO Sonoma
MONTEBELLO Los Angeles
MONTEREY Monterey
MONTEREY PARK Los Angeles
MONTGOMERY CREEK Shasta
MONTGOMERY WARD Contra Costa
MONTROSE Los Angeles
MOORPARK Ventura
MORAGA Contra Costa
MORENO VALLEY Riverside
MORGAN HILL Santa Clara
MORONGO VALLEY San Bernardino
MORRO BAY San Luis Obispo
MOSS BEACH San Mateo
MOSS LANDING Monterey
MOUNT AUKUM El Dorado
MOUNT HAMILTON Santa Clara
MOUNT HERMON Santa Cruz
MOUNT LAGUNA San Diego
MOUNT SHASTA Siskiyou
MOUNT WILSON Los Angeles
MOUNTAIN CENTER Riverside
MOUNTAIN PASS San Bernardino
MOUNTAIN RANCH Calaveras
MOUNTAIN VIEW Santa Clara
MT BALDY Los Angeles
MURPHYS Calaveras
MURRIETA Riverside
MYERS FLAT Humboldt
NAPA Napa
NATIONAL CITY San Diego
NAVARRO Mendocino
NEEDLES San Bernardino
NELSON Butte
NESTOR San Diego
NEVADA CITY Nevada
NEW ALMADEN Santa Clara
NEW CUYAMA Santa Barbara
NEWARK Alameda
NEWBERRY SPRINGS San Bernardino
NEWBURY PARK Ventura
NEWCASTLE Placer
NEWHALL Los Angeles
NEWMAN Stanislaus
NEWPORT BEACH Orange
NEWPORT COAST Orange
NICASIO Marin
NICE Lake
NICOLAUS Sutter
NILAND Imperial
NIPOMO San Luis Obispo
NIPTON San Bernardino
NORCO Riverside
NORDEN Nevada
NORTH FORK Madera
NORTH HIGHLANDS Sacramento
NORTH HILLS Los Angeles
NORTH HOLLYWOOD Los Angeles
NORTH PALM SPRINGS Riverside
NORTH SAN JUAN (95960) Nevada(55), Sierra(36), Yuba(7)
NORTHRIDGE Los Angeles
NORWALK Los Angeles
NOVATO Marin
NUBIEBER Lassen
NUEVO Riverside
O NEALS Madera
OAK PARK Ventura
OAK RUN Shasta
OAK VIEW Ventura
OAKDALE Stanislaus
OAKHURST Madera
OAKLAND Alameda

OAKLEY Contra Costa
OAKVILLE Napa
OBRIEN Shasta
OCCIDENTAL Sonoma
OCEANO San Luis Obispo
OCEANSIDE San Diego
OCOTILLO Imperial
OJAI Ventura
OLANCHA Inyo
OLD STATION Shasta
OLEMA Marin
OLIVEHURST Yuba
OLYMPIC VALLEY Placer
ONTARIO San Bernardino
ONYX Kern
ORANGE Orange
ORANGE COVE (93646) Fresno(89), Tulare(10)
ORANGEVALE Sacramento
OREGON HOUSE Yuba
ORICK Humboldt
ORINDA Contra Costa
ORLAND Glenn
ORLEANS Humboldt
ORO GRANDE San Bernardino
OROSI Tulare
OROVILLE Butte
OXNARD Ventura
PACIFIC GROVE Monterey
PACIFIC PALISADES Los Angeles
PACIFICA San Mateo
PACOIMA Los Angeles
PAICINES San Benito
PALA San Diego
PALERMO Butte
PALM DESERT Riverside
PALM SPRINGS Riverside
PALMDALE Los Angeles
PALO ALTO Santa Clara
PALO CEDRO Shasta
PALO VERDE Imperial
PALOMAR MOUNTAIN San Diego
PALOS VERDES PENINSULA Los Angeles
PANORAMA CITY Los Angeles
PARADISE Butte
PARAMOUNT Los Angeles
PARKER DAM San Bernardino
PARLIER Fresno
PASADENA Los Angeles
PASKENTA Tehama
PASO ROBLES San Luis Obispo
PATTERSON Stanislaus
PATTON San Bernardino
PAUMA VALLEY San Diego
PAYNES CREEK Tehama
PEARBLOSSOM Los Angeles
PEBBLE BEACH Monterey
PENN VALLEY Nevada
PENNGROVE Sonoma
PENRYN Placer
PERRIS Riverside
PESCADERO San Mateo
PETALUMA Sonoma
PETROLIA Humboldt
PHELAN San Bernardino
PHILLIPSVILLE Humboldt
PHILO Mendocino
PICO RIVERA Los Angeles
PIEDMONT Alameda
PIEDRA Fresno
PIERCY Mendocino
PILOT HILL El Dorado
PINE GROVE Amador
PINE VALLEY San Diego
PINECREST Tuolumne
PINOLE Contra Costa
PINON HILLS San Bernardino
PIONEER Amador
PIONEERTOWN San Bernardino
PIRU Ventura
PISMO BEACH San Luis Obispo

PITTSBURG Contra Costa
PIXLEY Tulare
PLACENTIA Orange
PLACERVILLE El Dorado
PLANADA Merced
PLATINA (96076) Tehama(46), Shasta(28), Trinity(25)
PLAYA DEL REY Los Angeles
PLEASANT GROVE (95668) Sutter(71), Placer(28)
PLEASANT HILL Contra Costa
PLEASANTON Alameda
PLYMOUTH Amador
POINT ARENA Mendocino
POINT MUGU NAWC Ventura
POINT REYES STATION Marin
POLLOCK PINES El Dorado
POMONA Los Angeles
POPE VALLEY Napa
PORT COSTA Contra Costa
PORT HUENEME Ventura
PORT HUENEME CBC BASE Ventura
PORTERVILLE Tulare
PORTOLA Plumas
PORTOLA VALLEY San Mateo
POSEY Tulare
POTRERO San Diego
POTTER VALLEY Mendocino
POWAY San Diego
PRATHER Fresno
PRINCETON (95970) Glenn(79), Colusa(20)
PROBERTA Tehama
QUINCY Plumas
RACKERBY Yuba
RAIL ROAD FLAT Calaveras
RAISIN Fresno
RAMONA San Diego
RANCHITA San Diego
RANCHO CORDOVA Sacramento
RANCHO CUCAMONGA San Bernardino
RANCHO MIRAGE Riverside
RANCHO PALOS VERDES Los Angeles
RANCHO SANTA FE San Diego
RANCHO SANTA MARGARITA Orange
RANDSBURG Kern
RAVENDALE Lassen
RAYMOND (93653) Madera(85), Mariposa(14)
RED BLUFF Tehama
RED MOUNTAIN Kern
REDCREST Humboldt
REDDING Shasta
REDLANDS San Bernardino
REDONDO BEACH Los Angeles
REDWAY Humboldt
REDWOOD CITY San Mateo
REDWOOD ESTATES Santa Clara
REDWOOD VALLEY Mendocino
REEDLEY (93654) Fresno(97), Tulare(2)
REPRESA Sacramento
RESCUE El Dorado
RESEDA Los Angeles
RIALTO San Bernardino
RICHGROVE Tulare
RICHMOND Contra Costa
RICHVALE Butte
RIDGECREST Kern
RIMFOREST San Bernardino
RIO DELL Humboldt
RIO LINDA Sacramento
RIO NIDO Sonoma
RIO OSO Sutter
RIO VISTA (94571) Solano(94), Sacramento(5)
RIPLEY (92272) Riverside(98), San Diego(1)
RIPON San Joaquin
RIVER PINES Amador
RIVERBANK Stanislaus
RIVERDALE (93656) Fresno(88), Kings(11)
RIVERSIDE Riverside

ROBBINS Sutter
ROCKLIN Placer
RODEO Contra Costa
ROHNERT PARK Sonoma
ROSAMOND (93560) Kern(98), Los Angeles(1)
ROSEMEAD Los Angeles
ROSEVILLE Placer
ROSS Marin
ROUGH AND READY Nevada
ROUND MOUNTAIN Shasta
ROWLAND HEIGHTS Los Angeles
RUMSEY Yolo
RUNNING SPRINGS San Bernardino
RUTHERFORD Napa
RYDE Sacramento
SACRAMENTO Sacramento
SAINT HELENA Napa
SALIDA Stanislaus
SALINAS Monterey
SALTON CITY Imperial
SALYER Trinity
SAMOA Humboldt
SAN ANDREAS Calaveras
SAN ANSELMO Marin
SAN ARDO Monterey
SAN BERNARDINO San Bernardino
SAN BRUNO San Mateo
SAN CARLOS San Mateo
SAN CLEMENTE Orange
SAN DIEGO San Diego
SAN DIMAS Los Angeles
SAN FERNANDO Los Angeles
SAN FRANCISCO San Francisco
SAN GABRIEL Los Angeles
SAN GERONIMO Marin
SAN GREGORIO San Mateo
SAN JACINTO Riverside
SAN JOAQUIN Fresno
SAN JOSE Santa Clara
SAN JUAN BAUTISTA San Benito
SAN JUAN CAPISTRANO Orange
SAN LEANDRO Alameda
SAN LORENZO Alameda
SAN LUCAS Monterey
SAN LUIS OBISPO San Luis Obispo
SAN LUIS REY San Diego
SAN MARCOS San Diego
SAN MARINO Los Angeles
SAN MARTIN Santa Clara
SAN MATEO San Mateo
SAN MIGUEL (93451) San Luis Obispo(57), Monterey(42)
SAN PABLO Contra Costa
SAN PEDRO Los Angeles
SAN QUENTIN Marin
SAN RAFAEL Marin
SAN RAMON Contra Costa
SAN SIMEON San Luis Obispo
SAN YSIDRO San Diego
SANGER Fresno
SANTA ANA Orange
SANTA BARBARA Santa Barbara
SANTA CLARA Santa Clara
SANTA CLARITA Los Angeles
SANTA CRUZ Santa Cruz
SANTA FE SPRINGS Los Angeles
SANTA MARGARITA San Luis Obispo
SANTA MARIA Santa Barbara
SANTA MONICA Los Angeles
SANTA PAULA Ventura
SANTA RITA PARK Merced
SANTA ROSA Sonoma
SANTA YNEZ Santa Barbara
SANTA YSABEL San Diego
SANTEE San Diego
SARATOGA Santa Clara
SAUSALITO Marin
SCOTIA Humboldt
SCOTT BAR Siskiyou
SCOTTS VALLEY Santa Cruz
SEAL BEACH Orange

SEASIDE Monterey
SEBASTOPOL Sonoma
SEELEY Imperial
SEIAD VALLEY Siskiyou
SELMA Fresno
SEQUOIA NATIONAL PARK Tulare
SHAFTER Kern
SHANDON San Luis Obispo
SHASTA Shasta
SHASTA LAKE Shasta
SHAVER LAKE Fresno
SHEEP RANCH Calaveras
SHERIDAN Placer
SHERMAN OAKS Los Angeles
SHINGLE SPRINGS El Dorado
SHINGLETOWN Shasta
SHOSHONE Inyo
SIERRA CITY Sierra
SIERRA MADRE Los Angeles
SIERRAVILLE Sierra
SILVERADO Orange
SIMI VALLEY Ventura
SKYFOREST San Bernardino
SLOUGHHOUSE Sacramento
SMARTVILLE (95977) Nevada(62), Yuba(37)
SMITH RIVER Del Norte
SNELLING Merced
SODA SPRINGS Nevada
SOLANA BEACH San Diego
SOLEDAD Monterey
SOLVANG Santa Barbara
SOMERSET El Dorado
SOMES BAR Siskiyou
SOMIS Ventura
SONOMA Sonoma
SONORA Tuolumne
SOQUEL Santa Cruz
SOULSBYVILLE Tuolumne
SOUTH DOS PALOS Merced
SOUTH EL MONTE Los Angeles
SOUTH GATE Los Angeles
SOUTH LAKE TAHOE El Dorado
SOUTH PASADENA Los Angeles
SOUTH SAN FRANCISCO San Mateo
SPRECKELS Monterey
SPRING VALLEY San Diego
SPRINGVILLE Tulare
SQUAW VALLEY Fresno
STANDARD Tuolumne
STANDISH Lassen
STANTON Orange
STEVENSON RANCH Los Angeles
STEVINSON Merced
STEWARTS POINT Sonoma
STINSON BEACH Marin
STIRLING CITY Butte
STOCKTON San Joaquin
STONYFORD Colusa
STORRIE Plumas
STRATFORD Kings
STRATHMORE Tulare
STRAWBERRY Tuolumne
STRAWBERRY VALLEY (95981) Yuba(66), Plumas(33)
STUDIO CITY Los Angeles
SUGARLOAF San Bernardino
SUISUN CITY Solano
SULTANA Tulare
SUMMERLAND Santa Barbara
SUN CITY Riverside
SUN VALLEY Los Angeles
SUNLAND Los Angeles
SUNNYVALE Santa Clara
SUNOL Alameda
SUNSET BEACH Orange
SURFSIDE Orange
SUSANVILLE Lassen
SUTTER Sutter
SUTTER CREEK Amador
SYLMAR Los Angeles
TAFT Kern

TAHOE CITY Placer
TAHOE VISTA Placer
TAHOMA El Dorado
TALMAGE Mendocino
TARZANA Los Angeles
TAYLORSVILLE Plumas
TECATE San Diego
TECOPA Inyo
TEHACHAPI Kern
TEHAMA Tehama
TEMECULA Riverside
TEMPLE CITY Los Angeles
TEMPLETON San Luis Obispo
TERMO Lassen
TERRA BELLA Tulare
THE SEA RANCH Sonoma
THERMAL (92274) Riverside(64), Imperial(35)
THORNTON San Joaquin
THOUSAND OAKS (91362) Ventura(83), Los Angeles(16)
THOUSAND PALMS Riverside
THREE RIVERS Tulare
TIPTON Tulare
TOLLHOUSE Fresno
TOLUCA LAKE Los Angeles
TOMALES Marin
TOPANGA Los Angeles
TOPAZ Mono
TORRANCE Los Angeles
TRABUCO CANYON Orange
TRACY (95391) San Joaquin(54), Alameda(45)
TRANQUILLITY Fresno
TRAVER Tulare
TRAVIS AFB Solano
TRES PINOS San Benito
TRINIDAD Humboldt
TRINITY CENTER (96091) Siskiyou(66), Trinity(33)
TRONA San Bernardino
TRUCKEE Nevada
TUJUNGA Los Angeles
TULARE Tulare
TULELAKE (96134) Modoc(70), Siskiyou(29)
TUOLUMNE Tuolumne
TUPMAN Kern
TURLOCK Stanislaus
TUSTIN Orange
TWAIN Plumas
TWAIN HARTE Tuolumne
TWENTYNINE PALMS San Bernardino
TWIN BRIDGES El Dorado
TWIN PEAKS San Bernardino
UKIAH Mendocino
UNION CITY Alameda
UNIVERSAL CITY Los Angeles
UPLAND San Bernardino
UPPER LAKE Lake
VACAVILLE Solano
VALENCIA Los Angeles
VALLECITO Calaveras
VALLEJO Solano
VALLEY CENTER San Diego
VALLEY FORD Sonoma
VALLEY HOME Stanislaus
VALLEY SPRINGS Calaveras
VALLEY VILLAGE Los Angeles
VALYERMO Los Angeles
VAN NUYS Los Angeles
VENICE Los Angeles
VENTURA Ventura
VERDUGO CITY Los Angeles
VERNALIS (95385) Stanislaus(71), San Joaquin(28)
VICTOR San Joaquin
VICTORVILLE San Bernardino
VIDAL San Bernardino
VILLA GRANDE Sonoma
VILLA PARK Orange
VINA Tehama

VINEBURG Sonoma
VINTON Plumas
VISALIA Tulare
VISTA San Diego
VOLCANO Amador
WALLACE Calaveras
WALNUT Los Angeles
WALNUT CREEK Contra Costa
WALNUT GROVE (95690)
    Sacramento(73), Solano(17), San
    Joaquin(9)
WARNER SPRINGS San Diego
WASCO Kern
WASHINGTON Nevada
WATERFORD Stanislaus
WATSONVILLE Santa Cruz
WAUKENA Tulare
WEAVERVILLE Trinity
WEED Siskiyou
WEIMAR Placer

WELDON Kern
WENDEL Lassen
WEOTT Humboldt
WEST COVINA Los Angeles
WEST HILLS Los Angeles
WEST HOLLYWOOD Los Angeles
WEST POINT Calaveras
WEST SACRAMENTO Yolo
WESTLAKE VILLAGE Los Angeles
WESTLEY Stanislaus
WESTMINSTER Orange
WESTMORLAND Imperial
WESTPORT Mendocino
WESTWOOD (96137) Plumas(64),
    Lassen(35)
WHEATLAND Yuba
WHISKEYTOWN Shasta
WHITE WATER Riverside
WHITETHORN (95589) Humboldt(97),
    Mendocino(2)

WHITMORE Shasta
WHITTIER Los Angeles
WILDOMAR Riverside
WILLIAMS Colusa
WILLITS Mendocino
WILLOW CREEK Humboldt
WILLOWS Glenn
WILMINGTON Los Angeles
WILSEYVILLE Calaveras
WILTON Sacramento
WINCHESTER Riverside
WINDSOR Sonoma
WINNETKA Los Angeles
WINTERHAVEN Imperial
WINTERS Yolo
WINTON Merced
WISHON Madera
WITTER SPRINGS Lake
WOFFORD HEIGHTS Kern
WOODACRE Marin

WOODBRIDGE San Joaquin
WOODLAKE Tulare
WOODLAND Yolo
WOODLAND HILLS Los Angeles
WOODY Kern
WRIGHTWOOD San Bernardino
YERMO San Bernardino
YETTEM Tulare
YOLO Yolo
YORBA LINDA Orange
YORKVILLE Mendocino
YOSEMITE NATIONAL PARK Mariposa
YOUNTVILLE Napa
YREKA Siskiyou
YUBA CITY Sutter
YUCAIPA (92399) San Bernardino(98),
    Riverside(1)
YUCCA VALLEY San Bernardino
ZAMORA Yolo
ZENIA Trinity

ZIP/City Cross Reference

90000-90068 LOS ANGELES	90740-90740 SEAL BEACH	91358-91358 THOUSAND OAKS	91718-91720 CORONA
90069-90069 WEST HOLLYWOOD	90742-90742 SUNSET BEACH	91359-91359 WESTLAKE VILLAGE	91722-91724 COVINA
90070-90189 LOS ANGELES	90743-90743 SURFSIDE	91360-91360 THOUSAND OAKS	91729-91730 RANCHO CUCAMONGA
90201-90201 BELL	90744-90744 WILMINGTON	91361-91361 WESTLAKE VILLAGE	91731-91732 EL MONTE
90202-90202 BELL GARDENS	90745-90747 CARSON	91362-91362 THOUSAND OAKS	91733-91733 SOUTH EL MONTE
90209-90213 BEVERLY HILLS	90748-90748 WILMINGTON	91363-91363 WESTLAKE VILLAGE	91734-91735 EL MONTE
90220-90224 COMPTON	90749-90749 CARSON	91364-91371 WOODLAND HILLS	91737-91737 ALTA LOMA
90230-90233 CULVER CITY	90800-90899 LONG BEACH	91372-91372 CALABASAS	91739-91739 RANCHO CUCAMONGA
90239-90242 DOWNEY	91001-91003 ALTADENA	91375-91376 AGOURA HILLS	91740-91741 GLENDORA
90245-90245 EL SEGUNDO	91006-91007 ARCADIA	91377-91377 OAK PARK	91743-91743 GUASTI
90247-90249 GARDENA	91009-91010 DUARTE	91380-91380 SANTA CLARITA	91744-91744 LA PUENTE
90250-90251 HAWTHORNE	91011-91012 LA CANADA FLINTRIDGE	91381-91381 STEVENSON RANCH	91745-91745 HACIENDA HEIGHTS
90254-90254 HERMOSA BEACH	91016-91017 MONROVIA	91382-91383 SANTA CLARITA	91746-91747 LA PUENTE
90255-90255 HUNTINGTON PARK	91020-91021 MONTROSE	91384-91384 CASTAIC	91748-91748 ROWLAND HEIGHTS
90260-90261 LAWNDALE	91023-91023 MOUNT WILSON	91385-91385 VALENCIA	91749-91749 LA PUENTE
90262-90262 LYNWOOD	91024-91025 SIERRA MADRE	91386-91387 CANYON COUNTRY	91750-91750 LA VERNE
90263-90265 MALIBU	91030-91031 SOUTH PASADENA	91388-91388 VAN NUYS	91752-91752 MIRA LOMA
90266-90267 MANHATTAN BEACH	91040-91041 SUNLAND	91390-91390 SANTA CLARITA	91754-91756 MONTEREY PARK
90270-90270 MAYWOOD	91042-91043 TUJUNGA	91392-91392 SYLMAR	91758-91758 ONTARIO
90272-90272 PACIFIC PALISADES	91046-91046 VERDUGO CITY	91393-91393 NORTH HILLS	91759-91759 MT BALDY
90274-90274 PALOS VERDES	91050-91051 PASADENA	91394-91394 GRANADA HILLS	91760-91760 NORCO
PENINSULA	91052-91052 LA COUNTY TAX	91395-91395 MISSION HILLS	91761-91762 ONTARIO
90275-90275 RANCHO PALOS VERDES	COLLECTOR	91396-91396 WINNETKA	91763-91763 MONTCLAIR
90277-90278 REDONDO BEACH	91066-91077 ARCADIA	91399-91399 WOODLAND HILLS	91764-91764 ONTARIO
90280-90280 SOUTH GATE	91100-91107 PASADENA	91400-91401 VAN NUYS	91765-91765 DIAMOND BAR
90290-90290 TOPANGA	91108-91108 SAN MARINO	91402-91402 PANORAMA CITY	91766-91769 POMONA
90291-90291 VENICE	91109-91117 PASADENA	91403-91403 SHERMAN OAKS	91770-91772 ROSEMEAD
90292-90292 MARINA DEL REY	91118-91118 SAN MARINO	91404-91411 VAN NUYS	91773-91773 SAN DIMAS
90293-90293 PLAYA DEL REY	91121-91191 PASADENA	91412-91412 PANORAMA CITY	91775-91778 SAN GABRIEL
90294-90294 VENICE	91200-91210 GLENDALE	91413-91413 SHERMAN OAKS	91780-91780 TEMPLE CITY
90295-90295 MARINA DEL REY	91214-91214 LA CRESCENTA	91416-91416 ENCINO	91784-91786 UPLAND
90296-90296 PLAYA DEL REY	91221-91222 GLENDALE	91423-91423 SHERMAN OAKS	91788-91789 WALNUT
90300-90398 INGLEWOOD	91224-91224 LA CRESCENTA	91426-91426 ENCINO	91790-91793 WEST COVINA
90400-90411 SANTA MONICA	91225-91226 GLENDALE	91461-91494 VAN NUYS	91795-91795 WALNUT
90500-90510 TORRANCE	91301-91301 AGOURA HILLS	91495-91495 SHERMAN OAKS	91797-91797 BALDWIN PARK
90601-90612 WHITTIER	91302-91302 CALABASAS	91496-91499 VAN NUYS	91797-91797 POMONA
90620-90622 BUENA PARK	91303-91305 CANOGA PARK	91500-91526 BURBANK	91798-91798 ONTARIO
90623-90623 LA PALMA	91306-91306 WINNETKA	91600-91603 NORTH HOLLYWOOD	91799-91799 POMONA
90624-90624 BUENA PARK	91307-91308 WEST HILLS	91604-91604 STUDIO CITY	91800-91899 ALHAMBRA
90630-90630 CYPRESS	91309-91309 CANOGA PARK	91605-91606 NORTH HOLLYWOOD	91901-91901 ALPINE
90631-90633 LA HABRA	91310-91310 CASTAIC	91607-91607 VALLEY VILLAGE	91902-91902 BONITA
90637-90639 LA MIRADA	91311-91313 CHATSWORTH	91608-91608 UNIVERSAL CITY	91903-91903 ALPINE
90640-90640 MONTEBELLO	91316-91316 ENCINO	91609-91609 NORTH HOLLYWOOD	91905-91905 BOULEVARD
90650-90659 NORWALK	91319-91320 NEWBURY PARK	91610-91610 TOLUCA LAKE	91906-91906 CAMPO
90660-90665 PICO RIVERA	91321-91322 NEWHALL	91611-91612 NORTH HOLLYWOOD	91908-91908 BONITA
90670-90671 SANTA FE SPRINGS	91324-91330 NORTHRIDGE	91614-91614 STUDIO CITY	91909-91915 CHULA VISTA
90680-90680 STANTON	91331-91334 PACOIMA	91615-91616 NORTH HOLLYWOOD	91916-91916 DESCANSO
90701-90702 ARTESIA	91335-91337 RESEDA	91617-91617 VALLEY VILLAGE	91917-91917 DULZURA
90703-90703 CERRITOS	91340-91341 SAN FERNANDO	91618-91618 UNIVERSAL CITY	91921-91921 CHULA VISTA
90704-90704 AVALON	91342-91343 SYLMAR	91618-91618 NORTH HOLLYWOOD	91931-91931 GUATAY
90706-90707 BELLFLOWER	91343-91343 NORTH HILLS	91701-91701 ALTA LOMA	91932-91933 IMPERIAL BEACH
90710-90710 HARBOR CITY	91344-91344 GRANADA HILLS	91702-91702 AZUSA	91934-91934 JACUMBA
90711-90715 LAKEWOOD	91345-91346 MISSION HILLS	91706-91706 BALDWIN PARK	91935-91935 JAMUL
90716-90716 HAWAIIAN GARDENS	91350-91350 SANTA CLARITA	91708-91708 CHINO	91941-91944 LA MESA
90717-90717 LOMITA	91351-91351 CANYON COUNTRY	91709-91709 CHINO HILLS	91945-91946 LEMON GROVE
90720-90721 LOS ALAMITOS	91352-91353 SUN VALLEY	91710-91710 CHINO	91947-91947 LINCOLN ACRES
90723-90723 PARAMOUNT	91354-91355 VALENCIA	91711-91711 CLAREMONT	91948-91948 MOUNT LAGUNA
90731-90734 SAN PEDRO	91356-91357 TARZANA	91714-91716 CITY OF INDUSTRY	91950-91951 NATIONAL CITY

ZIP Range	City
91962-91962	PINE VALLEY
91963-91963	POTRERO
91976-91979	SPRING VALLEY
91980-91987	TECATE
91990-91995	POTRERO
92003-92003	BONSALL
92004-92004	BORREGO SPRINGS
92007-92007	CARDIFF BY THE SEA
92008-92013	CARLSBAD
92014-92014	DEL MAR
92018-92018	CARLSBAD
92019-92022	EL CAJON
92023-92024	ENCINITAS
92025-92027	ESCONDIDO
92028-92028	FALLBROOK
92029-92033	ESCONDIDO
92036-92036	JULIAN
92037-92039	LA JOLLA
92040-92040	LAKESIDE
92046-92046	ESCONDIDO
92049-92052	OCEANSIDE
92053-92053	NESTOR
92054-92054	OCEANSIDE
92055-92055	CAMP PENDLETON
92056-92058	OCEANSIDE
92059-92059	PALA
92060-92060	PALOMAR MOUNTAIN
92061-92061	PAUMA VALLEY
92064-92064	POWAY
92065-92065	RAMONA
92066-92066	RANCHITA
92067-92067	RANCHO SANTA FE
92068-92068	SAN LUIS REY
92069-92069	SAN MARCOS
92070-92070	SANTA YSABEL
92071-92072	SANTEE
92073-92073	SAN DIEGO
92074-92074	POWAY
92075-92075	SOLANA BEACH
92078-92079	SAN MARCOS
92082-92082	VALLEY CENTER
92083-92085	VISTA
92086-92086	WARNER SPRINGS
92088-92088	FALLBROOK
92090-92090	EL CAJON
92091-92091	RANCHO SANTA FE
92092-92093	LA JOLLA
92096-92096	SAN MARCOS
92100-92117	SAN DIEGO
92118-92118	CORONADO
92119-92142	SAN DIEGO
92143-92143	SAN YSIDRO
92145-92172	SAN DIEGO
92173-92173	SAN YSIDRO
92174-92177	SAN DIEGO
92178-92178	CORONADO
92179-92199	SAN DIEGO
92201-92203	INDIO
92210-92210	INDIAN WELLS
92211-92211	PALM DESERT
92220-92220	BANNING
92222-92222	BARD
92223-92223	BEAUMONT
92225-92226	BLYTHE
92227-92227	BRAWLEY
92230-92230	CABAZON
92231-92232	CALEXICO
92233-92233	CALIPATRIA
92234-92235	CATHEDRAL CITY
92236-92236	COACHELLA
92239-92239	DESERT CENTER
92240-92241	DESERT HOT SPRINGS
92242-92242	EARP
92243-92244	EL CENTRO
92249-92249	HEBER
92250-92250	HOLTVILLE
92251-92251	IMPERIAL
92252-92252	JOSHUA TREE
92253-92253	LA QUINTA
92254-92254	MECCA
92255-92255	PALM DESERT
92256-92256	MORONGO VALLEY
92257-92257	NILAND
92258-92258	NORTH PALM SPRINGS
92259-92259	OCOTILLO
92260-92261	PALM DESERT
92262-92264	PALM SPRINGS
92266-92266	PALO VERDE
92267-92267	PARKER DAM
92268-92268	PIONEERTOWN
92270-92270	RANCHO MIRAGE
92272-92272	RIPLEY
92273-92273	SEELEY
92274-92274	THERMAL
92275-92275	SALTON CITY
92276-92276	THOUSAND PALMS
92277-92278	TWENTYNINE PALMS
92280-92280	VIDAL
92281-92281	WESTMORLAND
92282-92282	WHITE WATER
92283-92283	WINTERHAVEN
92284-92284	YUCCA VALLEY
92285-92285	LANDERS
92286-92286	YUCCA VALLEY
92292-92292	PALM SPRINGS
92301-92301	ADELANTO
92304-92304	AMBOY
92305-92305	ANGELUS OAKS
92307-92308	APPLE VALLEY
92309-92309	BAKER
92310-92310	FORT IRWIN
92311-92312	BARSTOW
92313-92313	GRAND TERRACE
92314-92314	BIG BEAR CITY
92315-92315	BIG BEAR LAKE
92316-92316	BLOOMINGTON
92317-92317	BLUE JAY
92318-92318	BRYN MAWR
92319-92319	CADIZ
92320-92320	CALIMESA
92321-92321	CEDAR GLEN
92322-92322	CEDARPINES PARK
92323-92323	CIMA
92324-92324	COLTON
92325-92325	CRESTLINE
92326-92326	CREST PARK
92327-92327	DAGGETT
92328-92328	DEATH VALLEY
92329-92329	PHELAN
92332-92332	ESSEX
92333-92333	FAWNSKIN
92334-92337	FONTANA
92338-92338	LUDLOW
92339-92339	FOREST FALLS
92340-92340	HESPERIA
92341-92341	GREEN VALLEY LAKE
92342-92342	HELENDALE
92345-92345	HESPERIA
92346-92346	HIGHLAND
92347-92347	HINKLEY
92350-92350	LOMA LINDA
92351-92351	BAKER
92352-92352	LAKE ARROWHEAD
92353-92353	LAKEVIEW
92354-92354	LOMA LINDA
92356-92356	LUCERNE VALLEY
92357-92357	LOMA LINDA
92358-92358	LYTLE CREEK
92359-92359	MENTONE
92363-92363	NEEDLES
92364-92364	NIPTON
92365-92365	NEWBERRY SPRINGS
92366-92366	MOUNTAIN PASS
92368-92368	ORO GRANDE
92369-92369	PATTON
92371-92371	PHELAN
92372-92372	PINON HILLS
92373-92375	REDLANDS
92376-92377	RIALTO
92378-92378	RIMFOREST
92382-92382	RUNNING SPRINGS
92384-92384	SHOSHONE
92385-92385	SKYFOREST
92386-92386	SUGARLOAF
92389-92389	TECOPA
92391-92391	TWIN PEAKS
92392-92394	VICTORVILLE
92397-92397	WRIGHTWOOD
92398-92398	YERMO
92399-92399	YUCAIPA
92400-92427	SAN BERNARDINO
92500-92517	RIVERSIDE
92518-92518	MARCH AIR FORCE BASE
92519-92522	RIVERSIDE
92530-92532	LAKE ELSINORE
92536-92536	AGUANGA
92539-92539	ANZA
92543-92546	HEMET
92548-92548	HOMELAND
92549-92549	IDYLLWILD
92551-92557	MORENO VALLEY
92561-92561	MOUNTAIN CENTER
92562-92564	MURRIETA
92567-92567	NUEVO
92570-92572	PERRIS
92581-92583	SAN JACINTO
92584-92584	MENIFEE
92585-92587	SUN CITY
92589-92593	TEMECULA
92595-92595	WILDOMAR
92596-92596	WINCHESTER
92599-92599	PERRIS
92601-92601	ATWOOD
92602-92604	IRVINE
92605-92605	HUNTINGTON BEACH
92606-92606	IRVINE
92607-92607	LAGUNA NIGUEL
92609-92609	EL TORO
92610-92610	FOOTHILL RANCH
92612-92612	IRVINE
92613-92613	ORANGE
92614-92614	IRVINE
92615-92615	HUNTINGTON BEACH
92616-92620	IRVINE
92621-92622	BREA
92623-92623	IRVINE
92624-92624	CAPISTRANO BEACH
92625-92625	CORONA DEL MAR
92626-92628	COSTA MESA
92629-92629	DANA POINT
92630-92630	LAKE FOREST
92631-92631	BREA
92632-92635	FULLERTON
92637-92637	LAGUNA HILLS
92640-92640	FULLERTON
92641-92645	GARDEN GROVE
92646-92649	HUNTINGTON BEACH
92650-92650	EAST IRVINE
92651-92652	LAGUNA BEACH
92653-92654	LAGUNA HILLS
92655-92655	MIDWAY CITY
92656-92656	ALISO VIEJO
92657-92657	NEWPORT COAST
92658-92663	NEWPORT BEACH
92664-92669	ORANGE
92670-92670	PLACENTIA
92672-92674	SAN CLEMENTE
92675-92675	SAN JUAN CAPISTRANO
92676-92676	SILVERADO
92677-92677	LAGUNA NIGUEL
92678-92679	TRABUCO CANYON
92680-92681	TUSTIN
92683-92685	WESTMINSTER
92686-92687	YORBA LINDA
92688-92688	RANCHO SANTA MARGARITA
92690-92692	MISSION VIEJO
92693-92693	SAN JUAN CAPISTRANO
92694-92694	MISSION VIEJO
92694-92694	LADERA RANCH
92697-92698	IRVINE
92698-92698	ALISO VIEJO
92701-92707	SANTA ANA
92708-92708	FOUNTAIN VALLEY
92709-92710	IRVINE
92711-92712	SANTA ANA
92713-92720	IRVINE
92725-92725	SANTA ANA
92728-92728	FOUNTAIN VALLEY
92730-92730	IRVINE
92735-92735	SANTA ANA
92780-92782	TUSTIN
92799-92799	SANTA ANA
92800-92809	ANAHEIM
92811-92811	ATWOOD
92812-92817	ANAHEIM
92821-92823	BREA
92825-92825	ANAHEIM
92831-92838	FULLERTON
92840-92846	GARDEN GROVE
92850-92850	ANAHEIM
92856-92859	ORANGE
92860-92860	NORCO
92861-92861	VILLA PARK
92862-92869	ORANGE
92870-92871	PLACENTIA
92877-92883	CORONA
92885-92887	YORBA LINDA
92899-92899	ANAHEIM
93001-93009	VENTURA
93010-93012	CAMARILLO
93013-93014	CARPINTERIA
93015-93016	FILLMORE
93020-93021	MOORPARK
93022-93022	OAK VIEW
93023-93024	OJAI
93030-93035	OXNARD
93040-93040	PIRU
93041-93041	PORT HUENEME
93042-93042	POINT MUGU NAWC
93043-93043	PORT HUENEME CBC BASE
93044-93044	PORT HUENEME
93060-93061	SANTA PAULA
93062-93063	SIMI VALLEY
93064-93064	BRANDEIS
93065-93065	SIMI VALLEY
93066-93066	SOMIS
93067-93067	SUMMERLAND
93093-93099	SIMI VALLEY
93101-93111	SANTA BARBARA
93116-93118	GOLETA
93120-93190	SANTA BARBARA
93199-93199	GOLETA
93201-93201	ALPAUGH
93202-93202	ARMONA
93203-93203	ARVIN
93204-93204	AVENAL
93205-93205	BODFISH
93206-93206	BUTTONWILLOW
93207-93207	CALIFORNIA HOT SPRINGS
93208-93208	CAMP NELSON
93210-93210	COALINGA
93212-93212	CORCORAN
93214-93214	CUYAMA
93215-93216	DELANO
93217-93217	DI GIORGIO
93218-93218	DUCOR
93219-93219	EARLIMART
93220-93220	EDISON
93221-93221	EXETER
93222-93222	FRAZIER PARK
93223-93223	FARMERSVILLE
93224-93224	FELLOWS
93225-93225	FRAZIER PARK
93226-93226	GLENNVILLE
93227-93227	GOSHEN
93230-93232	HANFORD
93234-93234	HURON
93235-93235	IVANHOE
93237-93237	KAWEAH
93238-93238	KERNVILLE
93239-93239	KETTLEMAN CITY
93240-93240	LAKE ISABELLA
93241-93241	LAMONT
93242-93242	LATON
93243-93243	LEBEC
93244-93244	LEMON COVE
93245-93246	LEMOORE

93247-93247 LINDSAY	93530-93530 KEELER	93667-93667 TOLLHOUSE	94527-94527 CONCORD
93249-93249 LOST HILLS	93531-93531 KEENE	93668-93668 TRANQUILLITY	94528-94528 DIABLO
93250-93250 MC FARLAND	93532-93532 LAKE HUGHES	93669-93669 WISHON	94529-94529 CONCORD
93251-93251 MC KITTRICK	93534-93539 LANCASTER	93670-93670 YETTEM	94530-94530 EL CERRITO
93252-93252 MARICOPA	93541-93541 LEE VINING	93673-93673 TRAVER	94531-94531 ANTIOCH
93254-93254 NEW CUYAMA	93542-93542 LITTLE LAKE	93675-93675 SQUAW VALLEY	94533-94533 FAIRFIELD
93255-93255 ONYX	93543-93543 LITTLEROCK	93700-93888 FRESNO	94535-94535 TRAVIS AFB
93256-93256 PIXLEY	93544-93544 LLANO	93901-93915 SALINAS	94536-94539 FREMONT
93257-93258 PORTERVILLE	93545-93545 LONE PINE	93920-93920 BIG SUR	94540-94545 HAYWARD
93260-93260 POSEY	93546-93546 MAMMOTH LAKES	93921-93923 CARMEL	94546-94546 CASTRO VALLEY
93261-93261 RICHGROVE	93549-93549 OLANCHA	93924-93924 CARMEL VALLEY	94547-94547 HERCULES
93262-93262 SEQUOIA NATIONAL PARK	93550-93552 PALMDALE	93925-93925 CHUALAR	94548-94548 KNIGHTSEN
93263-93263 SHAFTER	93553-93553 PEARBLOSSOM	93926-93926 GONZALES	94549-94549 LAFAYETTE
93265-93265 SPRINGVILLE	93554-93554 RANDSBURG	93927-93927 GREENFIELD	94550-94551 LIVERMORE
93266-93266 STRATFORD	93555-93556 RIDGECREST	93928-93928 JOLON	94552-94552 CASTRO VALLEY
93267-93267 STRATHMORE	93558-93558 RED MOUNTAIN	93930-93930 KING CITY	94553-94553 MARTINEZ
93268-93268 TAFT	93560-93560 ROSAMOND	93932-93932 LOCKWOOD	94555-94555 FREMONT
93270-93270 TERRA BELLA	93561-93561 TEHACHAPI	93933-93933 MARINA	94556-94556 MORAGA
93271-93271 THREE RIVERS	93562-93562 TRONA	93940-93940 MONTEREY	94557-94557 HAYWARD
93272-93272 TIPTON	93563-93563 VALYERMO	93941-93941 FT ORD	94558-94559 NAPA
93274-93275 TULARE	93570-93570 KEENE	93941-93941 FORT ORD	94560-94560 NEWARK
93276-93276 TUPMAN	93581-93582 TEHACHAPI	93941-93944 MONTEREY	94561-94561 OAKLEY
93277-93279 VISALIA	93584-93586 LANCASTER	93950-93950 PACIFIC GROVE	94562-94562 OAKVILLE
93280-93280 WASCO	93590-93590 PALMDALE	93953-93953 PEBBLE BEACH	94563-94563 ORINDA
93282-93282 WAUKENA	93592-93592 TRONA	93954-93954 SAN LUCAS	94564-94564 PINOLE
93283-93283 WELDON	93596-93596 BORON	93955-93955 SEASIDE	94565-94565 PITTSBURG
93285-93285 WOFFORD HEIGHTS	93599-93599 PALMDALE	93960-93960 SOLEDAD	94566-94566 PLEASANTON
93286-93286 WOODLAKE	93601-93601 AHWAHNEE	93962-93962 SPRECKELS	94567-94567 POPE VALLEY
93287-93287 WOODY	93602-93602 AUBERRY	94002-94003 BELMONT	94568-94568 DUBLIN
93290-93292 VISALIA	93603-93603 BADGER	94005-94005 BRISBANE	94569-94569 PORT COSTA
93300-93399 BAKERSFIELD	93604-93604 BASS LAKE	94010-94012 BURLINGAME	94570-94570 MORAGA
93401-93401 SAN LUIS OBISPO	93605-93605 BIG CREEK	94013-94017 DALY CITY	94571-94571 RIO VISTA
93402-93402 LOS OSOS	93606-93606 BIOLA	94018-94018 EL GRANADA	94572-94572 RODEO
93403-93410 SAN LUIS OBISPO	93607-93607 BURREL	94019-94019 HALF MOON BAY	94573-94573 RUTHERFORD
93412-93412 LOS OSOS	93608-93608 CANTUA CREEK	94020-94020 LA HONDA	94574-94574 SAINT HELENA
93420-93421 ARROYO GRANDE	93609-93609 CARUTHERS	94021-94021 LOMA MAR	94575-94575 MORAGA
93422-93423 ATASCADERO	93610-93610 CHOWCHILLA	94022-94024 LOS ALTOS	94576-94576 DEER PARK
93424-93424 AVILA BEACH	93611-93613 CLOVIS	94025-94026 MENLO PARK	94577-94579 SAN LEANDRO
93426-93426 BRADLEY	93614-93614 COARSEGOLD	94027-94027 ATHERTON	94580-94580 SAN LORENZO
93427-93427 BUELLTON	93615-93615 CUTLER	94028-94028 PORTOLA VALLEY	94581-94581 NAPA
93428-93428 CAMBRIA	93616-93616 DEL REY	94029-94029 MENLO PARK	94582-94582 PLEASANTON
93429-93429 CASMALIA	93618-93618 DINUBA	94030-94031 MILLBRAE	94583-94583 SAN RAMON
93430-93430 CAYUCOS	93620-93620 DOS PALOS	94035-94035 MOUNTAIN VIEW	94585-94585 SUISUN CITY
93431-93431 CHOLAME	93621-93621 DUNLAP	94037-94037 MONTARA	94586-94586 SUNOL
93432-93432 CRESTON	93622-93622 FIREBAUGH	94038-94038 MOSS BEACH	94587-94587 UNION CITY
93433-93433 GROVER BEACH	93623-93623 FISH CAMP	94039-94043 MOUNTAIN VIEW	94588-94588 PLEASANTON
93434-93434 GUADALUPE	93624-93624 FIVE POINTS	94044-94045 PACIFICA	94589-94592 VALLEJO
93435-93435 HARMONY	93625-93625 FOWLER	94059-94059 REDWOOD CITY	94593-94593 CROCKER NAT BANK
93436-93438 LOMPOC	93626-93626 FRIANT	94060-94060 PESCADERO	94594-94594 MONTGOMERY WARD
93440-93440 LOS ALAMOS	93627-93627 HELM	94061-94065 REDWOOD CITY	94595-94598 WALNUT CREEK
93441-93441 LOS OLIVOS	93628-93628 HUME	94066-94067 SAN BRUNO	94599-94599 YOUNTVILLE
93442-93443 MORRO BAY	93629-93629 HUNTINGTON LAKE	94070-94071 SAN CARLOS	94601-94607 OAKLAND
93444-93444 NIPOMO	93630-93630 KERMAN	94074-94074 SAN GREGORIO	94608-94608 EMERYVILLE
93445-93445 OCEANO	93631-93631 KINGSBURG	94080-94083 SOUTH SAN FRANCISCO	94609-94619 OAKLAND
93446-93447 PASO ROBLES	93633-93633 KINGS CANYON NATIONAL	94085-94091 SUNNYVALE	94620-94620 PIEDMONT
93448-93449 PISMO BEACH	PK	94096-94098 SAN BRUNO	94621-94661 OAKLAND
93450-93450 SAN ARDO	93634-93634 LAKESHORE	94099-94099 SOUTH SAN FRANCISCO	94662-94662 EMERYVILLE
93451-93451 SAN MIGUEL	93635-93635 LOS BANOS	94100-94188 SAN FRANCISCO	94666-94666 OAKLAND
93452-93452 SAN SIMEON	93637-93639 MADERA	94203-94299 SACRAMENTO	94701-94705 BERKELEY
93453-93453 SANTA MARGARITA	93640-93640 MENDOTA	94300-94310 PALO ALTO	94706-94706 ALBANY
93454-93458 SANTA MARIA	93641-93641 MIRAMONTE	94400-94497 SAN MATEO	94707-94720 BERKELEY
93460-93460 SANTA YNEZ	93642-93642 MONO HOT SPRINGS	94501-94502 ALAMEDA	94801-94802 RICHMOND
93461-93461 SHANDON	93643-93643 NORTH FORK	94503-94503 AMERICAN CANYON	94803-94803 EL SOBRANTE
93463-93464 SOLVANG	93644-93644 OAKHURST	94504-94504 MOBIL OIL CREDIT	94804-94805 RICHMOND
93465-93465 TEMPLETON	93645-93645 O NEALS	CORPORATION	94806-94806 SAN PABLO
93483-93483 GROVER BEACH	93646-93646 ORANGE COVE	94506-94506 DANVILLE	94807-94808 RICHMOND
93501-93502 MOJAVE	93647-93647 OROSI	94507-94507 ALAMO	94820-94820 EL SOBRANTE
93504-93505 CALIFORNIA CITY	93648-93648 PARLIER	94508-94508 ANGWIN	94850-94850 RICHMOND
93510-93510 ACTON	93649-93649 PIEDRA	94509-94509 ANTIOCH	94901-94903 SAN RAFAEL
93512-93512 BENTON	93650-93650 FRESNO	94510-94510 BENICIA	94904-94904 GREENBRAE
93513-93513 BIG PINE	93651-93651 PRATHER	94511-94511 BETHEL ISLAND	94911-94913 SAN RAFAEL
93514-93515 BISHOP	93652-93652 RAISIN	94512-94512 BIRDS LANDING	94914-94914 KENTFIELD
93516-93516 BORON	93653-93653 RAYMOND	94513-94513 BRENTWOOD	94915-94915 SAN RAFAEL
93517-93517 BRIDGEPORT	93654-93654 REEDLEY	94514-94514 BYRON	94920-94920 BELVEDERE TIBURON
93518-93518 CALIENTE	93656-93656 RIVERDALE	94515-94515 CALISTOGA	94922-94922 BODEGA
93519-93519 CANTIL	93657-93657 SANGER	94516-94516 CANYON	94923-94923 BODEGA BAY
93522-93522 DARWIN	93660-93660 SAN JOAQUIN	94517-94517 CLAYTON	94924-94924 BOLINAS
93523-93524 EDWARDS	93661-93661 SANTA RITA PARK	94518-94522 CONCORD	94925-94925 CORTE MADERA
93526-93526 INDEPENDENCE	93662-93662 SELMA	94523-94523 PLEASANT HILL	94926-94926 COTATI
93527-93527 INYOKERN	93664-93664 SHAVER LAKE	94524-94524 CONCORD	94927-94928 ROHNERT PARK
93528-93528 JOHANNESBURG	93665-93665 SOUTH DOS PALOS	94525-94525 CROCKETT	94929-94929 DILLON BEACH
93529-93529 JUNE LAKE	93666-93666 SULTANA	94526-94526 DANVILLE	94930-94930 FAIRFAX

Zip Range	City
94931-94931	COTATI
94933-94933	FOREST KNOLLS
94937-94937	INVERNESS
94938-94938	LAGUNITAS
94939-94939	LARKSPUR
94940-94940	MARSHALL
94941-94942	MILL VALLEY
94945-94945	NOVATO
94946-94946	NICASIO
94947-94949	NOVATO
94950-94950	OLEMA
94951-94951	PENNGROVE
94952-94955	PETALUMA
94956-94956	POINT REYES STATION
94957-94957	ROSS
94960-94960	SAN ANSELMO
94963-94963	SAN GERONIMO
94964-94964	SAN QUENTIN
94965-94966	SAUSALITO
94970-94970	STINSON BEACH
94971-94971	TOMALES
94972-94972	VALLEY FORD
94973-94973	WOODACRE
94974-94974	SAN QUENTIN
94975-94975	PETALUMA
94976-94976	CORTE MADERA
94977-94977	LARKSPUR
94978-94978	FAIRFAX
94979-94979	SAN ANSELMO
94998-94998	NOVATO
94999-94999	PETALUMA
95001-95001	APTOS
95002-95002	ALVISO
95003-95003	APTOS
95004-95004	AROMAS
95005-95005	BEN LOMOND
95006-95006	BOULDER CREEK
95007-95007	BROOKDALE
95008-95009	CAMPBELL
95010-95010	CAPITOLA
95011-95011	CAMPBELL
95012-95012	CASTROVILLE
95013-95013	COYOTE
95014-95016	CUPERTINO
95017-95017	DAVENPORT
95018-95018	FELTON
95019-95019	FREEDOM
95020-95021	GILROY
95023-95024	HOLLISTER
95026-95026	HOLY CITY
95030-95033	LOS GATOS
95035-95036	MILPITAS
95037-95038	MORGAN HILL
95039-95039	MOSS LANDING
95041-95041	MOUNT HERMON
95042-95042	NEW ALMADEN
95043-95043	PAICINES
95044-95044	REDWOOD ESTATES
95045-95045	SAN JUAN BAUTISTA
95046-95046	SAN MARTIN
95050-95056	SANTA CLARA
95060-95065	SANTA CRUZ
95066-95067	SCOTTS VALLEY
95070-95071	SARATOGA
95073-95073	SOQUEL
95075-95075	TRES PINOS
95076-95077	WATSONVILLE
95100-95139	SAN JOSE
95140-95140	MOUNT HAMILTON
95141-95196	SAN JOSE
95201-95219	STOCKTON
95220-95220	ACAMPO
95221-95221	ALTAVILLE
95222-95222	ANGELS CAMP
95223-95223	ARNOLD
95224-95224	AVERY
95225-95225	BURSON
95226-95226	CAMPO SECO
95227-95227	CLEMENTS
95228-95228	COPPEROPOLIS
95229-95229	DOUGLAS FLAT
95230-95230	FARMINGTON
95231-95231	FRENCH CAMP
95232-95232	GLENCOE
95233-95233	HATHAWAY PINES
95234-95234	HOLT
95236-95236	LINDEN
95237-95237	LOCKEFORD
95240-95242	LODI
95245-95245	MOKELUMNE HILL
95246-95246	MOUNTAIN RANCH
95247-95247	MURPHYS
95248-95248	RAIL ROAD FLAT
95249-95249	SAN ANDREAS
95250-95250	SHEEP RANCH
95251-95251	VALLECITO
95252-95252	VALLEY SPRINGS
95253-95253	VICTOR
95254-95254	WALLACE
95255-95255	WEST POINT
95257-95257	WILSEYVILLE
95258-95258	WOODBRIDGE
95267-95296	STOCKTON
95296-95296	LYOTH
95297-95298	STOCKTON
95301-95301	ATWATER
95303-95303	BALLICO
95304-95304	BANTA
95305-95305	BIG OAK FLAT
95306-95306	CATHEYS VALLEY
95307-95307	CERES
95309-95309	CHINESE CAMP
95310-95310	COLUMBIA
95311-95311	COULTERVILLE
95312-95312	CRESSEY
95313-95313	CROWS LANDING
95314-95314	DARDANELLE
95315-95315	DELHI
95316-95316	DENAIR
95317-95317	EL NIDO
95318-95318	EL PORTAL
95319-95319	EMPIRE
95320-95320	ESCALON
95321-95321	GROVELAND
95322-95322	GUSTINE
95323-95323	HICKMAN
95324-95324	HILMAR
95325-95325	HORNITOS
95326-95326	HUGHSON
95327-95327	JAMESTOWN
95328-95328	KEYES
95329-95329	LA GRANGE
95330-95330	LATHROP
95333-95333	LE GRAND
95334-95334	LIVINGSTON
95335-95335	LONG BARN
95336-95337	MANTECA
95338-95338	MARIPOSA
95340-95341	MERCED
95342-95342	ATWATER
95343-95344	MERCED
95345-95345	MIDPINES
95346-95346	MI WUK VILLAGE
95347-95347	MOCCASIN
95348-95348	MERCED
95350-95358	MODESTO
95360-95360	NEWMAN
95361-95361	OAKDALE
95363-95363	PATTERSON
95364-95364	PINECREST
95365-95365	PLANADA
95366-95366	RIPON
95367-95367	RIVERBANK
95368-95368	SALIDA
95369-95369	SNELLING
95370-95370	SONORA
95372-95372	SOULSBYVILLE
95373-95373	STANDARD
95374-95374	STEVINSON
95375-95375	STRAWBERRY
95376-95378	TRACY
95379-95379	TUOLUMNE
95380-95382	TURLOCK
95383-95383	TWAIN HARTE
95384-95384	VALLEY HOME
95385-95385	VERNALIS
95386-95386	WATERFORD
95387-95387	WESTLEY
95388-95388	WINTON
95389-95389	YOSEMITE NATIONAL PARK
95390-95390	RIVERBANK
95391-95391	TRACY
95397-95397	MODESTO
95401-95409	SANTA ROSA
95410-95410	ALBION
95412-95412	ANNAPOLIS
95415-95415	BOONVILLE
95416-95416	BOYES HOT SPRINGS
95417-95417	BRANSCOMB
95418-95418	CALPELLA
95419-95419	CAMP MEEKER
95420-95420	CASPAR
95421-95421	CAZADERO
95422-95422	CLEARLAKE
95423-95423	CLEARLAKE OAKS
95424-95424	CLEARLAKE PARK
95425-95425	CLOVERDALE
95426-95426	COBB
95427-95427	COMPTCHE
95428-95428	COVELO
95429-95429	DOS RIOS
95430-95430	DUNCANS MILLS
95431-95431	ELDRIDGE
95432-95432	ELK
95433-95433	EL VERANO
95435-95435	FINLEY
95436-95436	FORESTVILLE
95437-95437	FORT BRAGG
95439-95439	FULTON
95441-95441	GEYSERVILLE
95442-95442	GLEN ELLEN
95443-95443	GLENHAVEN
95444-95444	GRATON
95445-95445	GUALALA
95446-95446	GUERNEVILLE
95448-95448	HEALDSBURG
95449-95449	HOPLAND
95450-95450	JENNER
95451-95451	KELSEYVILLE
95452-95452	KENWOOD
95453-95453	LAKEPORT
95454-95454	LAYTONVILLE
95456-95456	LITTLERIVER
95457-95457	LOWER LAKE
95458-95458	LUCERNE
95459-95459	MANCHESTER
95460-95460	MENDOCINO
95461-95461	MIDDLETOWN
95462-95462	MONTE RIO
95463-95463	NAVARRO
95464-95464	NICE
95465-95465	OCCIDENTAL
95466-95466	PHILO
95468-95468	POINT ARENA
95469-95469	POTTER VALLEY
95470-95470	REDWOOD VALLEY
95471-95471	RIO NIDO
95472-95473	SEBASTOPOL
95476-95476	SONOMA
95480-95480	STEWARTS POINT
95481-95481	TALMAGE
95482-95482	UKIAH
95485-95485	UPPER LAKE
95486-95486	VILLA GRANDE
95487-95487	VINEBURG
95488-95488	WESTPORT
95490-95490	WILLITS
95492-95492	WINDSOR
95493-95493	WITTER SPRINGS
95494-95494	YORKVILLE
95497-95497	THE SEA RANCH
95501-95503	EUREKA
95511-95511	ALDERPOINT
95514-95514	BLOCKSBURG
95518-95518	ARCATA
95519-95519	MCKINLEYVILLE
95521-95521	ARCATA
95524-95524	BAYSIDE
95525-95525	BLUE LAKE
95526-95526	BRIDGEVILLE
95527-95527	BURNT RANCH
95528-95528	CARLOTTA
95531-95532	CRESCENT CITY
95534-95534	CUTTEN
95536-95536	FERNDALE
95537-95537	FIELDS LANDING
95538-95538	FORT DICK
95540-95540	FORTUNA
95542-95542	GARBERVILLE
95543-95543	GASQUET
95545-95545	HONEYDEW
95546-95546	HOOPA
95547-95547	HYDESVILLE
95548-95548	KLAMATH
95549-95549	KNEELAND
95550-95550	KORBEL
95551-95551	LOLETA
95552-95552	MAD RIVER
95553-95553	MIRANDA
95554-95554	MYERS FLAT
95555-95555	ORICK
95556-95556	ORLEANS
95558-95558	PETROLIA
95559-95559	PHILLIPSVILLE
95560-95560	REDWAY
95562-95562	RIO DELL
95563-95563	SALYER
95564-95564	SAMOA
95565-95565	SCOTIA
95567-95567	SMITH RIVER
95568-95568	SOMES BAR
95569-95569	REDCREST
95570-95570	TRINIDAD
95571-95571	WEOTT
95573-95573	WILLOW CREEK
95585-95585	LEGGETT
95587-95587	PIERCY
95589-95589	WHITETHORN
95595-95595	ZENIA
95601-95601	AMADOR CITY
95602-95604	AUBURN
95605-95605	WEST SACRAMENTO
95606-95606	BROOKS
95607-95607	CAPAY
95608-95609	CARMICHAEL
95610-95611	CITRUS HEIGHTS
95612-95612	CLARKSBURG
95613-95613	COLOMA
95614-95614	COOL
95615-95615	COURTLAND
95616-95617	DAVIS
95618-95618	EL MACERO
95619-95619	DIAMOND SPRINGS
95620-95620	DIXON
95621-95621	CITRUS HEIGHTS
95622-95622	NICOLAUS
95623-95623	EL DORADO
95624-95624	ELK GROVE
95625-95625	ELMIRA
95626-95626	ELVERTA
95627-95627	ESPARTO
95628-95628	FAIR OAKS
95629-95629	FIDDLETOWN
95630-95630	FOLSOM
95631-95631	FORESTHILL
95632-95632	GALT
95633-95633	GARDEN VALLEY
95634-95634	GEORGETOWN
95635-95635	GREENWOOD
95636-95636	GRIZZLY FLATS
95637-95637	GUINDA
95638-95638	HERALD
95639-95639	HOOD
95640-95640	IONE
95641-95641	ISLETON
95642-95642	JACKSON
95643-95643	PLACERVILLE
95644-95644	KIT CARSON

ZIP Range	City	ZIP Range	City	ZIP Range	City	ZIP Range	City
95645-95645	KNIGHTS LANDING	95758-95759	ELK GROVE	95979-95979	STONYFORD	96076-96076	PLATINA
95646-95646	KIRKWOOD	95762-95762	EL DORADO HILLS	95980-95980	STORRIE	96078-96078	PROBERTA
95648-95648	LINCOLN	95763-95763	FOLSOM	95981-95981	STRAWBERRY VALLEY	96079-96079	SHASTA LAKE
95650-95650	LOOMIS	95765-95765	ROCKLIN	95982-95982	SUTTER	96080-96080	RED BLUFF
95651-95651	LOTUS	95776-95776	WOODLAND	95983-95983	TAYLORSVILLE	96084-96084	ROUND MOUNTAIN
95652-95652	MCCLELLAN AFB	95798-95799	WEST SACRAMENTO	95984-95984	TWAIN	96085-96085	SCOTT BAR
95652-95652	MCCLELLAN	95800-95842	SACRAMENTO	95986-95986	WASHINGTON	96086-96086	SEIAD VALLEY
95653-95653	MADISON	95843-95843	ANTELOPE	95987-95987	WILLIAMS	96087-96087	SHASTA
95654-95654	MARTELL	95851-95899	SACRAMENTO	95988-95988	WILLOWS	96088-96088	SHINGLETOWN
95655-95655	MATHER	95901-95901	MARYSVILLE	95991-95993	YUBA CITY	96089-96089	SHASTA LAKE
95656-95656	MOUNT AUKUM	95903-95903	BEALE AFB	96001-96003	REDDING	96090-96090	TEHAMA
95658-95658	NEWCASTLE	95910-95910	ALLEGHANY	96006-96006	ADIN	96091-96091	TRINITY CENTER
95659-95659	NICOLAUS	95912-95912	ARBUCKLE	96007-96007	ANDERSON	96092-96092	VINA
95660-95660	NORTH HIGHLANDS	95913-95913	ARTOIS	96008-96008	BELLA VISTA	96093-96093	WEAVERVILLE
95661-95661	ROSEVILLE	95914-95914	BANGOR	96009-96009	BIEBER	96094-96094	WEED
95662-95662	ORANGEVALE	95915-95915	BELDEN	96010-96010	BIG BAR	96095-96095	WHISKEYTOWN
95663-95663	PENRYN	95916-95916	BERRY CREEK	96011-96011	BIG BEND	96096-96096	WHITMORE
95664-95664	PILOT HILL	95917-95917	BIGGS	96013-96013	BURNEY	96097-96097	YREKA
95665-95665	PINE GROVE	95918-95918	BROWNS VALLEY	96014-96014	CALLAHAN	96099-96099	REDDING
95666-95666	PIONEER	95919-95919	BROWNSVILLE	96015-96015	CANBY	96101-96101	ALTURAS
95667-95667	PLACERVILLE	95920-95920	BUTTE CITY	96016-96016	CASSEL	96103-96103	BLAIRSDEN-GRAEAGLE
95668-95668	PLEASANT GROVE	95922-95922	CAMPTONVILLE	96017-96017	CASTELLA	96104-96104	CEDARVILLE
95669-95669	PLYMOUTH	95923-95923	CANYONDAM	96019-96019	SHASTA LAKE	96105-96105	CHILCOOT
95670-95670	RANCHO CORDOVA	95924-95924	CEDAR RIDGE	96020-96020	CHESTER	96106-96106	CLIO
95671-95671	REPRESA	95925-95925	CHALLENGE	96021-96021	CORNING	96107-96107	COLEVILLE
95672-95672	RESCUE	95926-95929	CHICO	96022-96022	COTTONWOOD	96108-96108	DAVIS CREEK
95673-95673	RIO LINDA	95930-95930	CLIPPER MILLS	96023-96023	DORRIS	96109-96109	DOYLE
95674-95674	RIO OSO	95931-95931	COLLEGE CITY	96024-96024	DOUGLAS CITY	96110-96110	EAGLEVILLE
95675-95675	RIVER PINES	95932-95932	COLUSA	96025-96025	DUNSMUIR	96111-96111	FLORISTON
95676-95676	ROBBINS	95934-95934	CRESCENT MILLS	96027-96027	ETNA	96112-96112	FORT BIDWELL
95677-95677	ROCKLIN	95935-95935	DOBBINS	96028-96028	FALL RIVER MILLS	96113-96113	HERLONG
95678-95678	ROSEVILLE	95936-95936	DOWNIEVILLE	96029-96029	FLOURNOY	96114-96114	JANESVILLE
95679-95679	RUMSEY	95937-95937	DUNNIGAN	96031-96031	FORKS OF SALMON	96115-96115	LAKE CITY
95680-95680	RYDE	95938-95938	DURHAM	96032-96032	FORT JONES	96116-96116	LIKELY
95681-95681	SHERIDAN	95939-95939	ELK CREEK	96033-96033	FRENCH GULCH	96117-96117	LITCHFIELD
95682-95682	SHINGLE SPRINGS	95940-95940	FEATHER FALLS	96034-96034	GAZELLE	96118-96118	LOYALTON
95683-95683	SLOUGHHOUSE	95941-95941	FORBESTOWN	96035-96035	GERBER	96119-96119	MADELINE
95684-95684	SOMERSET	95942-95942	FOREST RANCH	96037-96037	GREENVIEW	96120-96120	MARKLEEVILLE
95685-95685	SUTTER CREEK	95943-95943	GLENN	96038-96038	GRENADA	96121-96121	MILFORD
95686-95686	THORNTON	95944-95944	GOODYEARS BAR	96039-96039	HAPPY CAMP	96122-96122	PORTOLA
95687-95688	VACAVILLE	95945-95945	GRASS VALLEY	96040-96040	HAT CREEK	96123-96123	RAVENDALE
95689-95689	VOLCANO	95946-95946	PENN VALLEY	96041-96041	HAYFORK	96124-96124	CALPINE
95690-95690	WALNUT GROVE	95947-95947	GREENVILLE	96044-96044	HORNBROOK	96125-96125	SIERRA CITY
95691-95691	WEST SACRAMENTO	95948-95948	GRIDLEY	96045-96045	HORSE CREEK	96126-96126	SIERRAVILLE
95692-95692	WHEATLAND	95949-95949	GRASS VALLEY	96046-96046	HYAMPOM	96127-96127	SUSANVILLE
95693-95693	WILTON	95950-95950	GRIMES	96047-96047	IGO	96128-96128	STANDISH
95694-95694	WINTERS	95951-95951	HAMILTON CITY	96048-96048	JUNCTION CITY	96129-96129	BECKWOURTH
95695-95695	WOODLAND	95953-95953	LIVE OAK	96049-96049	REDDING	96130-96130	SUSANVILLE
95696-95696	VACAVILLE	95954-95954	MAGALIA	96050-96050	KLAMATH RIVER	96132-96132	TERMO
95697-95697	YOLO	95955-95955	MAXWELL	96051-96051	LAKEHEAD	96133-96133	TOPAZ
95698-95698	ZAMORA	95956-95956	MEADOW VALLEY	96052-96052	LEWISTON	96134-96134	TULELAKE
95699-95699	DRYTOWN	95957-95957	MERIDIAN	96053-96053	MCARTHUR	96135-96135	VINTON
95701-95701	ALTA	95958-95958	NELSON	96054-96054	LOOKOUT	96136-96136	WENDEL
95703-95703	APPLEGATE	95959-95959	NEVADA CITY	96055-96055	LOS MOLINOS	96137-96137	WESTWOOD
95709-95709	CAMINO	95960-95960	NORTH SAN JUAN	96056-96056	MCARTHUR	96140-96140	CARNELIAN BAY
95712-95712	CHICAGO PARK	95961-95961	OLIVEHURST	96057-96057	MCCLOUD	96141-96141	HOMEWOOD
95713-95713	COLFAX	95962-95962	OREGON HOUSE	96058-96058	MACDOEL	96142-96142	TAHOMA
95714-95714	DUTCH FLAT	95963-95963	ORLAND	96059-96059	MANTON	96143-96143	KINGS BEACH
95715-95715	EMIGRANT GAP	95965-95966	OROVILLE	96061-96061	MILL CREEK	96145-96145	TAHOE CITY
95717-95717	GOLD RUN	95967-95967	PARADISE	96062-96062	MILLVILLE	96146-96146	OLYMPIC VALLEY
95720-95720	KYBURZ	95968-95968	PALERMO	96063-96063	MINERAL	96148-96148	TAHOE VISTA
95721-95721	ECHO LAKE	95969-95969	PARADISE	96064-96064	MONTAGUE	96150-96158	SOUTH LAKE TAHOE
95722-95722	MEADOW VISTA	95970-95970	PRINCETON	96065-96065	MONTGOMERY CREEK	96160-96162	TRUCKEE
95724-95724	NORDEN	95971-95971	QUINCY	96067-96067	MOUNT SHASTA	96635-96688	FPO
95726-95726	POLLOCK PINES	95972-95972	RACKERBY	96068-96068	NUBIEBER		
95728-95728	SODA SPRINGS	95973-95973	CHICO	96069-96069	OAK RUN		
95735-95735	TWIN BRIDGES	95974-95974	RICHVALE	96070-96070	OBRIEN		
95736-95736	WEIMAR	95975-95975	ROUGH AND READY	96071-96071	OLD STATION		
95741-95743	RANCHO CORDOVA	95976-95976	CHICO	96073-96073	PALO CEDRO		
95746-95746	GRANITE BAY	95977-95977	SMARTVILLE	96074-96074	PASKENTA		
95747-95747	ROSEVILLE	95978-95978	STIRLING CITY	96075-96075	PAYNES CREEK		

Colorado

General Help Numbers:

Governor's Office

136 State Capitol Bldg
Denver, CO 80203-1792
www.state.co.us/gov_dir/
governor_office.html

303-866-2471
Fax 303-866-2003
8AM-5PM

Attorney General's Office

Department of Law
1525 Sherman St, 5th Floor
Denver, CO 80203
www.ago.state.co.us

303-866-4500
Fax 303-866-5691
8AM-5PM

State Court Administrator

1301 Pennsylvania St, Suite 300
Denver, CO 80203-2416303-837-2340
www.courts.state.co.us

303-861-1111

8AM-5PM

State Archives

Archives & Public Records
1313 Sherman St, Room 1B-20
Denver, CO 80203
www.archives.state.co.us

303-866-2055
Fax 303-866-2257
8AM-4:30PM

State Specifics:

Capital:

Denver
Denver County

Time Zone:

MST

Number of Counties:

64

Population:

4,417,714

Web Site:

www.state.co.us

State Agencies

Criminal Records

Bureau of Investigation, State Repository, Identification Unit, 690 Kipling St, Suite 3000, Denver, CO 80215; 303-239-4208, 303-239-5858 (Fax), 8AM-4:30PM.

http://cbi.state.co.us

Note: A sex offender registry is not available electronically; access is through local law-enforcement.

Indexing & Storage: Records are available from 1967 on. Records prior to 1967 are in on-site computer archives. It takes less than 72 hours before new records are available for inquiry. Records are indexed on inhouse computer,

fingerprint cards. 12% of all arrests in database have final dispositions recorded, over 12% for those arrests within last 5 years.

Searching: The requester must sign a disclaimer stating "This record shall not be used for the direct solicitation of business for pecuniary gain." Include the following in your request: full name, date of birth, sex, race, and disclaimer. The SSN is optional, but suggested. Fingerprints are optional unless statutorily-required. Records are 100% fingerprint supported. If charged after fingerprinted, the practice of notifying the state is becoming more common, though this not yet statewide. The following data is not released: sealed records, juvenile records and pending mental comps. All records or arrests are released, including those without dispositions.

Access by: mail, in person, online.

Fee & Payment: Name check-$10.00 per name; fingerprint search-$13.00 per fingerprint. A state mandated fingerprint search plus notification of subsequent arrest in CO-$14.00; or nationwide fingerprint search-$22.00. Possible fee changes take place in July each year. Fee payee: Colorado Bureau of Investigations (CBI). Prepayment required. No personal checks accepted. Credit cards accepted: MasterCard, Visa.

Mail search: Turnaround time: 3 days. No self addressed stamped envelope is required.

In person search: You may request information in person.

Online search: There is a remote access system available called the Electronic Clearance System (ECS). This is an overnight batch system, open M-F from 7AM to 4PM. The fee is $5.50 per record. There is no set-up fee, but requesters must register and meet quotas. Billing is monthly. For more information, call 303-239-4233.

Corporation Records
Trademarks/Servicemarks
Fictitious Name
Limited Liability Company
Records
Assumed Name

Secretary of State, Business Division, 1560 Broadway, Suite 200, Denver, CO 80202; 303-894-2200 x2 (Business Entities), 900-555-1717 (Status-Name), 303-894-2242 (Fax), 7:30AM-5PM.

www.sos.state.co.us

Indexing & Storage: Records are available for all active companies. Inactive company records are archived. New records are available for inquiry immediately. Records are indexed on microfilm, inhouse computer.

Searching: Include the following in your request: full name of business.

Access by: mail, phone, fax, in person, online.

Fee & Payment: There is no fee for searching active companies; there is a $5.00 per business name searched fee for archived records. The copy fee is $.50 per page. Fee payee: Secretary of State. Personal checks accepted. No credit cards accepted.

Mail search: Turnaround time: 2 to 3 days.

Phone search: The 900 number service is available for $1.50 per minute.

Fax search: Orders requested by fax are $3.00 and are processed the same as other searches.

In person search: A public access terminal offers free searching.

Online search: The Sec. of State's Business Record Search page offers free searching of

corporate names and associate information at www.sos.state.co.us/pubs/business/main.htm.

Expedited service: Expedited service is available for mail, phone and fax searches. Turnaround time: 1 day. Add $50.00 per business name.

Uniform Commercial Code
Federal Tax Liens
State Tax Liens

Secretary of State, UCC Division, 1560 Broadway, Suite 200, Denver, CO 80202; 303-894-2200, 303-869-4864 (Fax), 7:30AM-5PM.

www.sos.state.co.us

Note: State tax liens are handled by the Department of Revenue. These liens can be filed at any one of the state's county recording offices, and so should be searched as such.

Indexing & Storage: Records are available from 1966. Records are indexed on computer from 1979, and on microfiche from 1987 to 1997. It takes 5 days before new records are available for inquiry.

Searching: Use search request form UCC-11. The search includes all tax liens recorded at the state level. This includes all IRS liens. Include the following in your request: debtor name.

Access by: mail, phone, fax, in person, online.

Fee & Payment: The search fee is $13.00 per name searched. Copies are $1.25 per page. Fee payee: Secretary of State. Personal checks accepted. No credit cards accepted.

Mail search: Turnaround time: 10 days. A self addressed stamped envelope is requested.

Phone search: The latest 4 liens are available by telephone, press 2 when connected using number listed above.

Fax search: Fax searching available.

In person search: Searching is available in person.

Online search: There is free record searching at this agency's web site.

Expedited service: Expedited service is available for mail, phone and in person searches. Turnaround time: 1 day. There is a $50.00 fee per debtor name.

Sales Tax Registrations
Trade Names

Revenue Department, Taxpayers Services Office, 1375 Sherman St, Denver, CO 80261 (Courier: 1625 Broadway, Ste 805, Denver, CO 80261); 303-232-2416, 303-866-3211 (Fax), 8AM-4:30PM.

www.revenue.state.co.us

Indexing & Storage: Records are available from 1988 and are computerized. Records are indexed on computer.

Searching: This agency will confirm that a business is registered and, if the business is in the Trade Name Information file, they will, also, provide the business name, status, if liens, filing date, and address. Include the following in your request: business name. They will also search by tax permit number.

Access by: mail, phone, in person, online.

Fee & Payment: There is no search fee.

Mail search: A self addressed stamped envelope is requested.

Phone search: No fee for telephone request. They will only search by trade name.

In person search: They will release the owner's name if petitioned in writing.

Online search: You can search trade names at www.businesstax.state.co.us/pgBusTax.htm. You can verfiy a sales tax license or exemption number at www.taxview.state.co.us.

Other access: Tradename lists are available on diskette, tape or paper.

Birth Certificates

Department of Public Health & Environment, Vital Records Section HSVR-A1, 4300 Cherry Creek Dr S, Denver, CO 80246-1530; 303-756-4464 (Recorded Message), 303-692-2224 (Credit Card Ordering), 303-692-2234, 800-423-1108 (Fax), 8:30AM-4:30PM.

www.cdphe.state.co.us/hs/certs.asp

Note: Certified copies for birth years 1912 to present can also be ordered at most county health departments.

Indexing & Storage: Records are available from 1910 to present. New records are available for inquiry immediately. Records are indexed on microfiche, inhouse computer.

Searching: The person named on the record, members of the immediate family, legal representatives of those named above, and others demonstrating a direct and tangible interest in the record may request a copy. Include the following in your request: full name, names of parents, mother's maiden name, date of birth, place of birth, relationship to person of record, reason for information request. Birth Certificates are filed under person of record's last name.

Access by: mail, phone, fax, in person, online.

Fee & Payment: Search fee is $15.00 per name. Add $5.00 if you use a credit card. Add $6.00 per name requested for additional copies. You can order by fax using a credit card. Fee payee: Vital Records. Prepayment required. Personal checks accepted. Credit cards accepted: MasterCard, Visa, AmEx, Discover.

Mail search: Turnaround time: 2 weeks. Include a daytime telephone number. No self addressed stamped envelope is required.

Phone search: You must use a credit card for an additional $5.00 fee. Turnaround time is 5 working days.

Fax search: Turnaround time 1 day, credit card required.

In person search: Turnaround time is 30-45 minutes.

Online search: Records can be ordered online from a state designated vendor - VitalChek. Go to www.vitalchek.com/default.asp

Expedited service: Expedited service is available for fax searches. Turnaround time: next day. Add credit card fee ($5.00) and express delivery fee.

Death Records

Department of Public Health & Environment, Vital Records Section HSVR-A1, 4300 Cherry Creek Dr S, Denver, CO 80246-1530; 303-756-4464 (Recorded Message), 303-692-2224 (Credit

Card Ordering), 303-692-2234, 800-423-1108 (Fax), 8:30AM-4:30PM.

www.cdphe.state.co.us/hs/certs.asp

Indexing & Storage: Records are available from 1900 to present. It takes within 4 weeks before new records are available for inquiry. Records are indexed on microfiche, inhouse computer.

Searching: Certified copies may be issued to: parents; grandparents; stepparents; siblings; spouse; adult children, stepchildren or grandchildren of the deceased; legal representatives of above; genealogists, probate researchers or those with a tangible interest. Include the following in your request: full name, date of death, place of death, names of parents, relationship to person of record, reason for information request. Death certificates are indexed by decedent's last name and the year of death. Include date of birth or age at death.

Access by: mail, phone, fax, in person, online.

Fee & Payment: Search fee is $15.00 per name. Add $5.00 if you use a credit card. Add $6.00 per name requested for an additional copy. Fee payee: Vital Records. Prepayment required. Personal checks accepted. Credit cards accepted: MasterCard, Visa, AmEx, Discover.

Mail search: Turnaround time: 3 weeks. Also include a day time phone number.

Phone search: You must use a credit card. Turnaround time is 5 working days.

Fax search: Same criteria as phone searching, but turnaround time is next day.

In person search: You may request records in person for same day service. Turnaround time 30-45 minutes.

Online search: Records can be ordered online from a state designated vendor - VitalChek. Go to www.vitalchek.com/default.asp

Expedited service: Expedited service is available for fax searches. Turnaround time: next day. Add use of credit card fee ($5.00) and express delivery fee.

Marriage Certificates

Department of Public Health & Environment, Vital Records Section, 4300 Cherry Creek Dr S, Denver, CO 80246-1530; 303-756-4464 (Recorded Message), 303-692-2224 (Credit Card Ordering), 303-692-2234, 800-423-1108 (Fax), 8:30AM-4:30PM.

www.cdphe.state.co.us/hs/certs.asp

Note: Records available include 1900 to 1939, and 1975 to present. Verifications for the years 1940 to 1974 are not available from this office and must be obtained from the county where the license was obtained.

Indexing & Storage: It takes 6 months before new records are available for inquiry.

Searching: Records are open to the public. The state refers to the records as "verifications." Include the following in your request: date of marriage, county of license issue. The index for records from 1900 to 1939 is by groom only.

Access by: mail, phone, fax, in person, online.

Fee & Payment: The state fee for a marriage verification is $15.00. If the year is not known and the entire index is searched, there is an additional $5.00. Fee payee: Vital Records. Prepayment required. Credit card use is only for fax, phone, and Internet searches. Personal checks accepted.

Credit cards accepted: MasterCard, Visa, AmEx, Discover.

Mail search: Turnaround time: 2 weeks.

Phone search: Turnaround time is 5 days. There is an additional $5.00 fee for use of a credit card.

Fax search: Use of credit card (extra $5.00) required, turnaround time 1 day.

In person search: Turnaround time is 30 to 45 minutes. These indexes can also be searched, for no fee, at many public libraries throughout the state.

Online search: Records can be ordered online from a state designated vendor - VitalChek. Go to www.vitalchek.com/default.asp

Expedited service: Expedited service is available. Use of credit card is required (extra $5.00 fee). Total fee depends on delivery service requested.

Divorce Records

Department of Public Health & Environment, Vital Records Section, 4300 Cherry Creek Dr S, Denver, CO 80246-1530; 303-756-4464 (Recorded Message), 303-692-2224 (Credit Card Ordering), 303-692-2234, 800-423-1108 (Fax), 8:30AM-4:30PM.

www.cdphe.state.co.us/hs/certs.asp

Note: This office holds records from 1900 to 1939, and 1968 to present. Searches must be performed at the county level for all other years.

Indexing & Storage: Records are available 1968 to current within this office. Records are available 1900-1939 at State Office. It takes 6 months before new records are available for inquiry.

Searching: Records are open to the public. Include the following in your request: date of action, county. The state only has an INDEX of the records and will provide a certified verification. Actual copies of the dissolution must be obtained from the county where the event was finalized.

Access by: mail, phone, fax, in person, online.

Fee & Payment: The state fee for a divorce verification is $15.00. If the year is not known and the entire index is searched, there is an additional $5.00. Fee payee: Vital Records. Prepayment required. Personal checks accepted. Credit cards accepted: MasterCard, Visa, AmEx, Discover.

Mail search: Turnaround time: 2 weeks. A self addressed stamped envelope is requested.

Phone search: A credit card is required with an additional fee of $5.00. Turnaround time is 5 business days.

Fax search: Same criteria as phone searching, but turnaround time is next business day.

In person search: Records can be obtained across the counter within 30 to 45 minutes.

Online search: Divorces from 1968-to present can be searched at no charge on the web at www.quickinfo.net/madi/comadi.html. Only index information (names and dates) is available. You may order a certified verification for $15.00 at www.cdphe.state.co.us/hs/certs.asp.

Expedited service: Expedited service is available for fax searches. Turnaround time: 1 day. Use of credit card is required (extra $5.00 fee). Total fee depends on delivery service requested.

Workers' Compensation Records

Division of Workers' Compensation, Customer Service, 1515 Arapahoe St, Tower 2, Ste 500, Denver, CO 80202-2117; 303-318-8700, 303-818-8710 (Fax), 8AM-5PM.

www.coworkforce.com/DWC

Indexing & Storage: Records are available as far back 1979, many records have been scanned and are stored electonically. If the physical records have been destroyed, the wage information is still on computer. New records are available for inquiry immediately. Records are indexed on inhouse computer.

Searching: If you are not a party to the claim, you must have a notarized release from claimant not older than 90 days. Judges notes, transcripts and depositions are not released. Older purged files will get a screen print only. Include the following in your request: claimant name, Social Security Number.

Access by: mail, phone, fax, in person.

Fee & Payment: There is no search fee, copies are $.25 per page, rush copies are $.50 per page, the fee to return via fax is $1.00 per page. Fee payee: Division of Workers' Compensation. Prepayment required. Approved accounts are billed monthly. Personal checks accepted. No credit cards accepted.

Mail search: Turnaround time: 1 to 2 days. A self addressed stamped envelope is requested.

Phone search: Limited information is given over the phone only if caller is a party to the case.

Fax search: Turnaround time is 1-2 days, unless otherwise requested.

In person search: You should call first so that they can locate records. Bring ID and notarized statement.

Other access: Lists and/or labels of carriers, adjusting companies, and attorneys are available upon request. Fees range from $3.00 to $7.00 (for list, not per name) plus postage.

Driver Records

Motor Vehicle Business Group, Driver Control, Denver, CO 80261-0016 (Courier: 1881 Pierce Street, Lakewood, CO 80214); 303-205-5613, 303-205-5990 (Fax), 8AM-5PM.

www.mv.state.co.us

Note: Copies of tickets may be obtained this address for a fee of $2.20 per record. All requests must be submitted in writing and include the driver's name, DOB, and the specific ticket number.

Indexing & Storage: Records are available for up to 7 years. The "worse" the record, the farther back the record will be kept. It takes 3 to 12 days before new records are available for inquiry.

Searching: Address and personal data is given to certain pre-approved, permissible requesters. Otherwise the "Requester Release and Information Request/Notice of Intended Use" form must be signed by requester. Include the following in your request: name, date of birth, driver's license number.

Access by: mail, in person.

Fee & Payment: The fee is $2.20 per record, $2.70 if certified. Fee payee: Department of

Revenue. Prepayment required. Personal checks accepted. No credit cards accepted.

Mail search: Turnaround time: 24 hours. No self addressed stamped envelope is required.

In person search: Turnaround time is immediate. Up to 50 records will be processed while you wait.

Other access: Colorado offers magnetic tape retrieval for high volume users, call 303-205-5762. Records are restricted to a one time use and cannot be stored and resold.

Accident Reports

Motor Vehicle Business Group, Driver Control, Denver, CO 80261-0016 (Courier: 1881 Pierce Street, Lakewood, CO 80261); 303-205-5613, 8AM-5PM.

www.mv.state.co.us

Indexing & Storage: Records are available for 6 years plus current year from date of the accident. It takes 30 to 60 days before new records are available for inquiry.

Searching: Use of "Requestor Release and Information Request" form is required. Include the following in your request: full name, date of accident, location of accident.

Access by: mail, in person.

Fee & Payment: The fee is $2.20 per record for walk-in or mail-in searches. Fee payee: Department of Revenue. Prepayment required. Personal checks accepted. No credit cards accepted.

Mail search: Turnaround time: variable. No self addressed stamped envelope is required.

In person search: Turnaround time depends on availability of report.

Vehicle Ownership
Vehicle Identification

Motor Vehicle Business Group, Driver Control, Denver, CO 80261-0016 (Courier: 1881 Pierce Street, Lakewood, CO 80214); 303-205-5608 (Titles), 303-205-5607 (Registration), 303-205-5990 (Fax), 8AM-5PM.

www.mv.state.co.us/mv.html

Indexing & Storage: Records are available 10 years back plus the current year.

Searching: Handicap and disabled vet plate data are not released. To obtain vehicle or ownership information, or for title and lien records, the requester's driver license number, and the Requestor Release and Information Request Form (DR 2489) are required.

Access by: mail, in person.

Fee & Payment: The fee for searches is $2.20 per record. Fee payee: Department of Revenue. Prepayment required. Personal checks accepted. No credit cards accepted.

Mail search: Turnaround time: 24 hours. A self addressed stamped envelope is requested.

In person search: Turnaround time is while you wait.

Other access: Bulk requests of vehicle information on magnetic tape, computer paper, and on microfiche are available. Direct inquires to the

Data Services Section, Motor Vehicle Extractions, at the address listed above.

Vessel Ownership
Vessel Registration

Colorado State Parks, Registration, 13787 S Highway 85, Littleton, CO 80125; 303-791-1920, 303-470-0782 (Fax), 8AM-5PM.

http://parks.state.co.us/boating

Note: Liens must be searched at the Secretary of State.

Indexing & Storage: Records are available for the past 5 years. Older records are available on microfiche. All sail and motorized vessels must be registered.

Searching: To search, submit the registration # or serial #, DOB and a Release of Registration Records Form must be completed and signed. The following data is not released: residence addresses.

Access by: mail, fax, in person.

Fee & Payment: There is a $2.00 search fee plus a $1.00 charge per page for copies. Fee payee: Colorado State Parks. Prepayment required. Personal checks accepted. No credit cards accepted.

Mail search: Turnaround time: 1-3 weeks. No self addressed stamped envelope is required.

Fax search: Turnaround time varies. Results are faxed or mailed back.

In person search: Searching is available in person.

Legislation Records

Colorado General Assembly, State Capitol, 200 E Colfax Ave, Denver, CO 80203-1776; 303-866-2316 (Senate), 303-866-3055 (Bill Data (if in session)), 303-866-2390 (Archives), 303-866-2904 (House), 8AM-5PM.

www.state.co.us/gov_dir/stateleg.html

Note: The House is room 271, the Senate room 274. The legislative Council Library can be reached at 303-866-4011.

Indexing & Storage: Records are available from 1998 to present on computer, older records are on microfiche and CD-Rom. Records are indexed on inhouse computer, microfiche, CD.

Searching: Include the following in your request: bill number, year.

Access by: mail, phone, in person, online.

Fee & Payment: There is no fee for searching the current year. Prior years or voluminous requests will require a fee determined on extent of request. Fee payee: State of Colorado. Personal checks accepted. No credit cards accepted.

Mail search: Turnaround time: same day if possible. Mail searches are done only if in-depth research is not required. No self addressed stamped envelope is required. No fee for mail request.

Phone search: No fee for telephone request. Only general information is provided over the phone.

In person search: No fee for request.

Online search: The web site gives access to bills, status, journals from the last two sessions, and much more.

Voter Registration

Department of State, Elections Department, 1560 Broadway #200, Denver, CO 80202; 303-894-2680, 303-894-7732 (Fax), 8:30AM-5PM.

www.state.co.us/gov_dir/sos

Indexing & Storage: Records are available for the current year only.

Searching: Voters may request not to have their information released. Provide name and address or DOB to search. The following data is not released: Social Security Numbers.

Access by: mail, fax, in person.

Fee & Payment: The fee is $.50 per name. Fee payee: Department of State. Prepayment required. No credit cards accepted.

Mail search: Turnaround time: 2 to 3 days. A self addressed stamped envelope is requested.

Fax search: Same criteria as mail searching.

In person search: Searching is available in person.

Other access: The entire database is available on tape or CD-ROM. The cost is $500. No customization is available.

GED Certificates

Colorado Dept of Education, GED Testing, 201 E Colfax Ave Rm 100, Denver, CO 80203; 303-866-6613.

www.cde.state.co.us/index_adult.htm

Searching: All written requests must have a yes or no answer to the following question in the upper right hand corner of the request: Did the person who received the GED ever attend a Colorado public school (as in elementary or high school)? All of the following are required to search: a signed release, name, date/year of test, date of birth, Social Security Number, and location of testing.

Access by: mail, in person.

Fee & Payment: The search fee $4.00 per transcript. Fee payee: GED Testing. Prepayment required. Money orders & personal checks accepted. No credit cards accepted.

Mail search: Turnaround time: 7 days. The agency requests use of their request form, which can be downloaded from the web site. No self addressed stamped envelope is required.

In person search: Turnaround time is up to 15 working days.

Hunting License Information
Fishing License Information
Access to Records is Restricted

Department of Natural Resources, Wildlife Division, 6060 Broadway, Denver, CO 80216; 303-297-1192, 303-294-0874 (Fax), 8AM-5PM.

www.wildlife.state.co.us

Note: The state attorney general has decided that no information on holders of individual hunting and fishing licenses can be given to the public. It is only available to law enforcement officials or to the licensed individual.

Colorado State Licensing Agencies

Licenses Searchable Online

Acupuncturist #14	www.dora.state.co.us/pls/real/ARMS_Search.Set_Up
Architect #15	www.dora.state.co.us/pls/real/ARMS_Search.Set_Up
Architectural Firm #15	www.dora.state.co.us/pls/real/ARMS_Search.Set_Up
Audiologist #14	www.dora.state.co.us/pls/real/ARMS_Search.Set_Up
Barber #16	www.dora.state.co.us/pls/real/ARMS_Search.Disclaimer_Page
Chiropractor #17	www.dora.state.co.us/pls/real/ARMS_Search.Disclaimer_Page
Cosmetician #16	www.dora.state.co.us/pls/real/ARMS_Search.Disclaimer_Page
Cosmetologist #16	www.dora.state.co.us/pls/real/ARMS_Search.Disclaimer_Page
Counselor, Professional #20	www.dora.state.co.us/pls/real/ARMS_Search.Disclaimer_Page
Credit Union #9	www.dora.state.co.us/Financial-Services/homeregu.html#credit
Dental Hygienist #18	www.dora.state.co.us/pls/real/ARMS_Search.Disclaimer_Page
Dentist #18	www.dora.state.co.us/pls/real/ARMS_Search.Disclaimer_Page
Electrical Contractor #41	www.dora.state.co.us/pls/real/ARMS_Search.Disclaimer_Page
Electrician Journeyman/Master #41	www.dora.state.co.us/pls/real/ARMS_Search.Disclaimer_Page
Engineer/Engineer in Training #19	www.dora.state.co.us/pls/real/ARMS_Search.Disclaimer_Page
Family Therapist #20	www.dora.state.co.us/pls/real/ARMS_Search.Disclaimer_Page
Hearing Aid Dealer #14	www.dora.state.co.us/pls/real/ARMS_Search.Set_Up
Insurance Agency #10	www.dora.state.co.us/pls/real/INS_Agent.Search_Form
Insurance Company #10	www.dora.state.co.us/pls/real/INS_Company.Search_Form
Insurance Producer #10	www.dora.state.co.us/pls/real/INS_Agent.Search_Form
Land Surveyor #19	www.dora.state.co.us/pls/real/ARMS_Search.Disclaimer_Page
Land Surveyor Intern #19	www.dora.state.co.us/pls/real/ARMS_Search.Disclaimer_Page
Lobbyist #37	www.sos.state.co.us/pubs/bingo_raffles/new2001lobbyist_dir.htm
Manicurist #16	www.dora.state.co.us/pls/real/ARMS_Search.Disclaimer_Page
Manufactured Housing Dealer #22	www.dola.state.co.us/doh/Documents/dealers.htm
Manufactured Housing Mfg. #22	www.dola.state.co.us/doh/Documents/parkt.htm
Marriage Therapist #20	www.dora.state.co.us/pls/real/ARMS_Search.Disclaimer_Page
Medical Doctor #21	www.dora.state.co.us/pls/real/ARMS_Search.Disclaimer_Page
Midwife #28	www.dora.state.co.us/pls/real/ARMS_Search.Disclaimer_Page
Nurse #1	www.dora.state.co.us/pls/real/ARMS_Search.Disclaimer_Page
Nurses' Aide #1	www.dora.state.co.us/pls/real/ARMS_Search.Disclaimer_Page
Nursing Care Facility #23	www.dora.state.co.us/pls/real/ARMS_Search.Set_Up
Nursing Home Administrator #23	www.dora.state.co.us/pls/real/ARMS_Search.Set_Up
Optometrist #33	www.dora.state.co.us/pls/real/ARMS_Search.Disclaimer_Page
Outfitter #24	www.dora.state.co.us/pls/real/ARMS_Search.Disclaimer_Page
Pharmacist/Pharmacist /Intern #26	www.dora.state.co.us/pls/real/ARMS_Search.Disclaimer_Page
Pharmacy #26	www.dora.state.co.us/pls/real/ARMS_Search.Disclaimer_Page
Physical Therapist #32	www.dora.state.co.us/pls/real/ARMS_Search.Disclaimer_Page
Physician Assistant #21	www.dora.state.co.us/pls/real/ARMS_Search.Disclaimer_Page
Plumber Journeyman/Master/Residential #35	www.dora.state.co.us/pls/real/ARMS_Search.Disclaimer_Page
Podiatrist #27	www.dora.state.co.us/pls/real/ARMS_Search.Disclaimer_Page
Psychologist #20	www.dora.state.co.us/pls/real/ARMS_Search.Disclaimer_Page
Public Accountant-CPA #13	www.dora.state.co.us/pls/real/ARMS_Search.Disclaimer_Page
Real Estate Appraiser #12	www.dora.state.co.us/pls/real/re_estate_home
Real Estate Broker/Salesperson #12	www.dora.state.co.us/pls/real/re_estate_home
River Outfitter #38	www.dora.state.co.us/pls/real/ARMS_Search.Disclaimer_Page
Savings & Loan Association #9	www.dora.state.co.us/Financial-Services/homeregu.html#savings
Securities Broker #34	http://pdpi.nasdr.com/pdpi/disclaimer_frame.htm
Securities Dealer #34	http://pdpi.nasdr.com/pdpi/disclaimer_frame.htm
Social Worker #20	www.dora.state.co.us/pls/real/ARMS_Search.Disclaimer_Page
Stock Broker #34	http://pdpi.nasdr.com/pdpi/disclaimer_frame.htm
Veterinarian #31	www.dora.state.co.us/pls/real/ARMS_Search.Disclaimer_Page
Veterinary Student #31	www.dora.state.co.us/pls/real/ARMS_Search.Disclaimer_Page

Licensing Quick Finder

Acupuncturist #14 303-894-2464	Horse Racing #11 303-205-2990	Pet Animal/Bird Dealer #2 303-239-4166
Architect #15 303-894-7441	Insurance Agency #10 303-894-2419	Pharmacist/Pharmacist /Intern #26 303-894-7750
Architectural Firm #15 303-894-7441	Insurance Company #10 303-894-2419	Pharmacy #26 303-894-7750
Artificial Inseminator #31 303-894-7755	Insurance Producer #10 303-894-2419	Physical Therapist #32 303-894-2440
Asbestos Building Inspector #5 303-692-3158	Investment Advisors #34 303-894-2320	Physician Assistant #21 303-894-7690
Asbestos Inspector/Management Planner #5	Kennel #2 303-239-4166	Physiotherapist #32 303-894-2440
.... 303-692-3158	Land Surveyor #19 303-894-7788	Plumber Journeyman/Master/Residential #35
Asbestos Project Designer #5 303-692-3158	Land Surveyor Intern #19 303-894-7788	.... 303-894-2300 x110
Asbestos Worker/Supervisor #5 303-692-3158	Lead Abatement Firm #5 303-692-3158	Podiatrist #27 303-894-2464
Attorney #4 303-893-8096	Lead Abatement Inspector/Risk Assessor #5	Psychiatric Technician #1 303-894-2430
Audiologist #14 303-894-2464	 303-692-3158	Psychologist #20 303-894-7766
Bail Bond Agent #10 303-894-7583	Lead Abatement Worker/Supvr #5 303-692-3158	Public Accountant-CPA #13 303-894-7441
Bank, Commercial/Industrial #8 303-894-7575	Life Care Institution #9 303-894-2336	Public Adjuster #10 303-894-7499
Barber #16 303-894-7772	Liquor Control #39 303-205-2300	Real Estate Appraiser #12 303-894-2166
Bulk Milk Hauler #6 303-692-3643	Lobbyist #37 303-894-2200	Real Estate Broker/Salesperson #12 ... 303-894-2166
Child Care Facility #29 800-799-5876	Manicurist #16 303-894-7772	River Outfitter #38 303-894-7772
Chiropractor #17 303-894-7762	Manufactured Housing Dealer #22 303-866-4616	Savings & Loan Association #9 303-894-2336
Collection Agency #3 303-866-5706	Manufactured Housing Mfg. #22 303-866-4616	School Administrator/Principal #40 303-866-6628
Commercial Driving School #7 303-205-5841	Manufacturer Housing Installer #22 303-866-4616	School Special Service Associate #40.. 303-866-6628
Cosmetician #16 303-894-7772	Marriage Therapist #20 303-894-7766	Securities Broker #34 303-894-2320
Cosmetologist #16 303-894-7772	Medical Doctor #21 303-894-7690	Securities Dealer #34 303-894-2320
Counselor, Professional #20 303-894-7766	Midwife #28 303-894-2464	Securities Sales Promoter #34 303-894-2320
Court Reporter #36 303-837-3695	Milk/Cream Sampler/Tester #6 303-692-3643	Ski Lift #25 303-894-7785
Credit Union #9 303-894-2336	Money Order Company #8 303-894-7575	Small Business Development Credit Corp. #9
Dairy Farm #6 303-692-3643	Motor Vehicle Buyer/Wholesaler #42... 303-205-5604	 303-894-2336
Dairy Plant #6 303-692-3643	Motor Vehicle Dealer, Franchised #42.. 303-205-5604	Social Worker #20 303-894-7766
Debt Management Company #8 303-894-7575	Motor Vehicle Dealer, Used #42 303-205-5604	Solicitor/Telemarketer #3 303-866-5079
Dental Hygienist #18 303-894-7758	Motor Vehicle Manufacturer Rep. #42 . 303-205-5604	Stock Broker #34 303-894-2320
Dentist #18 303-894-7758	Motor Vehicle Salesperson #42 303-205-5604	Substitute Teacher #40 303-866-6968
Egg Seller #2 303-239-4140	Notary Public #37 303-894-2680	Teacher #40 303-866-6628
Electrical Contractor #41 303-894-2300	Nurse #1 303-894-2430	Tramway #25 303-894-7785
Electrician Journeyman/Master #41 303-894-2300	Nursery #2 303-239-4140	Trust Company #8 303-894-7575
Engineer/Engineer in Training #19 303-894-7788	Nurses' Aide #1 303-894-2816	Veterinarian #31 303-894-7755
Family Care Home #29 303-866-5958	Nursing Care Facility #23 303-894-7800	Veterinary Student #31 303-894-7755
Family Therapist #20 303-894-7766	Nursing Home Administrator #23 303-894-7760	Vocational Education Teacher #40 303-866-6628
Food Plant Operator #2 303-239-4140	Optometrist #33 303-894-7750	Wireman, Residential #41 303-894-2300
Greyhound Racing #11 303-205-2990	Outfitter #24 303-894-7778	
Hearing Aid Dealer #14 303-894-2464	Pesticide Applicator #2 303-239-4140	

Licensing Agency Information

#1 Board of Nursing, 1560 Broadway, #880, Denver, CO 80202; 303-894-2430, Fax: 303-894-2821.
www.dora.state.co.us/Nursing
Search database at www.dora.state.co.us/pls/real/ARMS_Search.Disclaimer_Page

#2 Agriculture Department, 700 Kipling St, #4000, Lakewood, CO 80215-5894; 303-239-4100, Fax: 303-239-4125.
www.ag.state.co.us
Agency email: jim.thurman@ag.state.co.us.

#3 Attorney General's Office, 1525 Sherman St, 5th Fl, Denver, CO 80203; 303-866-4500, Fax: 303-866-5691.
www.ago.state.co.us
Agency email: attorney.general@state.co.us.

#4 Board of Law Examiners, 600 17th St, Dominion Plaza Bldg, #910S, Denver, CO 80202; 303-893-8096, Fax: 303-534-3643.
www.courts.state.co.us/ble/ble.htm. Agency email: kuenhold@amigo.net.

#5 Department of Public Health & Environment, Air Pollution Control Division, 4300 Cherry Creek Dr S, Denver, CO 80246; 303-692-3150, Fax: 303-782-0278.
www.cdphe.state.co.us/ap/asbeshom.asp
Agency email: larry.dover@state.co.us.

#6 Consumer Protection Division, Department of Public Health and Environment, 4300 Cherry Creek, Denver, CO 80246-1530; 303-692-3620, Fax: 303-753-6809.
www.cdphe.state.co.us/cp/Dairy/dairy.asp

#7 Department of Revenue, 1375 Sherman St, Denver, CO 80261; 303-866-3091, Fax: 303-205-5634.

#8 Division of Banking, 1560 Broadway, #1175, Denver, CO 80202; 303-894-7575, Fax: 303-894-7570.
www.dora.state.co.us/Banking
Agency email: Banking@dora.state.co.us.

#9 Division of Financial Services, 1560 Broadway, #1520, Denver, CO 80202; 303-894-2336, Fax: 303-894-7886.
www.dora.state.co.us/Financial-Services

#10 Division of Insurance, 1560 Broadway, #850, Denver, CO 80202; 303-894-7499, Fax: 303-894-7455.
www.dora.state.co.us/Insurance
Agency email: nancy.ryan@dora.state.co.us.
Search database at www.dora.state.co.us/pls/real/INS_Search.Disclaimer_Page

#11 Division of Racing Events, 1881 Pierce St, #108, Lakewood, CO 80214; 303-205-2990, Fax: 303-205-2950.
www.state.co.us/gov_dir/revenue_dir/racing_dir/coracing.html
Agency email: Racing@spike.dor.state.co.us.

#12 Division of Real Estate, 1900 Grant St, #600, Denver, CO 80203; 303-894-2166, Fax: 303-894-2683.
www.dora.state.co.us/Real-Estate
Search database at www.dora.state.co.us/pls/real/re_estate_home

#13 Division of Registrations, 1560 Broadway, #1340, Denver, CO 80202; 303-894-7800, Fax: 303-894-7802.
www.dora.state.co.us/Accountants. Agency email: robert.longway@state.co.us.
Search database at www.dora.state.co.us/pls/real/ARMS_Search.Disclaimer_Page

#14 Division of Registrations, 1560 Broadway, #1550, Denver, CO 80202; 303-894-7855, Fax: 303-894-7885.
www.dora.state.co.us
Agency email: acupuncture@dora.state.co.us.
Search database at www.dora.state.co.us/pls/real/ARMS_Search.Set_Up

#15 Division of Registrations, 1560 Broadway, #1340, Denver, CO 80202; 303-894-7801, Fax: 303-894-7802.
www.dora.state.co.us/Architects
Agency email: robert.longway@dora.state.co.us.
Search database at www.dora.state.co.us/pls/real/ARMS_Search.Disclaimer_Page

#16 Division of Registrations, 1560 Broadway, #1340, Denver, CO 80202; 303-894-7772, Fax: 303-894-7802.
www.dora.state.co.us/Barbers_Cosmetologists.
Agency email: barber-cosmetology@dora.state.co.us.
Search database at www.dora.state.co.us/pls/real/ARMS_Search.Disclaimer_Page

#17 Division of Registrations, Board of Chiropractors, 1560 Broadway, #1310, Denver, CO 80202; 303-894-7800.
www.dora.state.co.us/chiropratic
Search database at www.dora.state.co.us/pls/real/ARMS_Search.Disclaimer_Page

#18 Division of Registrations, Board of Dental Examiners, 1560 Broadway, #1310, Denver, CO 80202; 303-894-7758, Fax: 303-894-7764.
www.dora.state.co.us/Dental
Agency email: Dental@dora.state.co.us.
Search database at www.dora.state.co.us/pls/real/ARMS_Search.Disclaimer_Page

#19 Division of Registrations, 1560 Broadway, #1370, Denver, CO 80202; 303-894-7788, Fax: 303-894-7790.
www.dora.state.co.us/Engineers_Surveyors/
Search database at www.dora.state.co.us/pls/real/ARMS_Search.Disclaimer_Page

#20 Division of Registrations, 1560 Broadway, #1370, Denver, CO 80202; 303-894-7766, Fax: 303-894-7747.
www.dora.state.co.us/Mental-Health. Agency email: MentalHealth@dora.state.co.us.
Search database at www.dora.state.co.us/pls/real/ARMS_Search.Disclaimer_Page

#21 Div of Registrations, Dept of Regulatory Agencies, Board of Medical Examiners, 1560 Broadway, #1300, Denver, CO 80202-5140; 303-894-7690, Fax: 303-894-7692.
www.dora.state.co.us/Medical. Agency email: medical@dora.state.co.us.
Search database at www.dora.state.co.us/pls/real/ARMS_Search.Disclaimer_Page

#22 Division of Housing, 1313 Sherman St, Denver, CO 80203; 303-866-4656, Fax: 303-866-4077.
www.dola.state.co.us/doh/doh.htm
Agency email: diana.jones@state.co.us.

#23 Division of Registrations, 1560 Broadway, #1310, Denver, CO 80202; 303-894-7800, Fax: 303-894-7764.
Search database at www.dora.state.co.us/pls/real/ARMS_Search.Set_Up

#24 Division of Registrations, 1560 Broadway, #1340, Denver, CO 80202; 303-894-7778, Fax: 303-894-7802.
www.dora.state.co.us/Outfitters. Agency email: Outfitters@dora.state.co.us.
Search database at www.dora.state.co.us/pls/real/ARMS_Search.Disclaimer_Page

#25 Division of Registrations, 1560 Broadway, #1370, Denver, CO 80202; 303-894-7785, Fax: 303-894-7790.
www.dora.state.co.us/Tramway
Agency email: webmaster@dora.state.co.us.

#26 Division of Registrations, 1560 Broadway, #1310, Denver, CO 80202-5146; 303-894-7750, Fax: 303-894-7764.
www.dora.state.co.us/Pharmacy
Agency email: pharmacy@dora.state.co.us.
Search database at www.dora.state.co.us/pls/real/ARMS_Search.Disclaimer_Page

#27 Division of Registrations, 1560 Broadway, #1545, Denver, CO 80202; 303-894-2464, Fax: 303-894-7885.
www.dora.state.co.us/Podiatrists
Agency email: podiatrists@dora.state.co.us.
Search database at www.dora.state.co.us/pls/real/ARMS_Search.Disclaimer_Page

#28 Division of Registrations, Midwives Registration, 1560 Broadway, #1545, Denver, CO 80202; 303-894-2464, Fax: 303-894-7885.
www.dora.state.co.us/Midwives
Agency email: midwives@dora.state.co.us.
Search database at www.dora.state.co.us/pls/real/ARMS_Search.Disclaimer_Page

#29 Department of Human Services, Division of Child Care, 1575 Sherman St, Denver, CO 80202; 800-799-5958, Fax: 303-866-4453.
www.cdhs.state.co.us/cyf/ccare/index.html

#31 Division of Registrations, 1560 Broadway, #1310, Denver, CO 80202-5146; 303-894-7755, Fax: 303-894-7764.
www.dora.state.co.us/Veterinarians
Search database at www.dora.state.co.us/pls/real/ARMS_Search.Disclaimer_Page

#32 Division of Registrations, Physical Therapy Registration, 1560 Broadway, #1545, Denver, CO 80202; 303-894-2440, Fax: 303-894-7885.
www.dora.state.co.us/Physical-Therapy. Agency email: pt@dora.state.co.us.
Search database at www.dora.state.co.us/pls/real/ARMS_Search.Disclaimer_Page

#33 Division of Registrations, Board of Optometry Examiners, 1560 Broadway, #1310, Denver, CO 80202-5146; 303-894-7751, Fax: 303-894-7764.
www.dora.state.co.us/Optometry. Agency email: optometry@dora.state.co.us.
Search database at www.dora.state.co.us/pls/real/ARMS_Search.Disclaimer_Page

#34 Department of Regulatory Agencies, Division of Securities, 1580 Lincoln, #420, Denver, CO 80203-1506; 303-881-2126, Fax: 303-861-2126.
www.dora.state.co.us/Securities/brokers.htm.
Agency email: Securities@DORA.state.co.us.
Search database at http://pdpi.nasdr.com/pdpi/disclaimer_frame.htm

#35 Examining Board of Plumbers, 1580 Logan St, #550, Denver, CO 80203-1941; 303-894-2300, Fax: 303-894-2310.
www.dora.state.co.us/Plumbing
Agency email: Plumbing@dora.state.co.us.
Search database at www.dora.state.co.us/pls/real/ARMS_Search.Disclaimer_Page

#36 Judicial Department, Human Resources Office, 1301 Pennsylvania St, #300, Denver, CO 80203; 303-837-3695, Fax: 303-837-2340.
www.courts.state.co.us

#37 Office of Secretary of State, 1560 Broadway, #200, Denver, CO 80202; 303-894-2200, Fax: 303-894-2242.
www.sos.state.co.us/pubs/business/main.htm
Search database at www.sos.state.co.us/pubs/bingo_raffles/main.htm

#38 Division of Registrations, Outfitters Registration, 1560 Broadway, #1340, Denver, CO 80202; 303-894-7778, Fax: 303-470-0782.
www.dora.state.co.us/Outfitters
Agency email: outfitters@dora.state.co.us.
Search database at www.dora.state.co.us/pls/real/ARMS_Search.Disclaimer_Page

#39 Revenue Department, Alcohol Control Division, 1881 Pierce, #108A, Lakewood, CO 80214; 303-205-2300, Fax: 303-205-2341.
www.state.co.us/gov_dir/revenue_dir/liquor_dir/lic&permit.htm
Agency email: nhamby@spike.dor.state.co.us.

#40 Department of Education, 201 E Colifax, Denver, CO 80203; 303-866-6600, Fax: 303-830-0793.
www.cde.state.co.us/index_license.htm
Agency email: webmaster@cde.state.co.us.

#41 Electrical Board, 1580 Logan St, #550, Denver, CO 80203-1939; 303-894-2300, Fax: 303-894-2310.
www.dora.state.co.us/Electrical. Agency email: ella.peltier@dora.state.co.us.
Search database at www.dora.state.co.us/pls/real/ARMS_Search.Disclaimer_Page

#42 Motor Vehicle Dealer Board, 1881 Pierce St Rm 142, Lakewood, CO 80215; 303-205-5604, Fax: 303-205-5977.
www.mv.state.co.us
Agency email: dealers@spike.dor.state.co.us.

Colorado Federal Courts

The following list indicates the district and division name for each county in the state.

County/Court Cross Reference

Adams.....................................Denver	Fremont...Denver	Montrose.......................................Denver
Alamosa................................Denver	Garfield..Denver	Morgan..Denver
Arapahoe..............................Denver	Gilpin...Denver	Otero..Denver
Archuleta..............................Denver	Grand...Denver	Ouray...Denver
Baca......................................Denver	Gunnison.......................................Denver	Park..Denver
Bent......................................Denver	Hinsdale..Denver	Phillips...Denver
Boulder.................................Denver	Huerfano..Denver	Pitkin..Denver
Chaffee.................................Denver	Jackson..Denver	Prowers..Denver
Cheyenne..............................Denver	Jefferson..Denver	Pueblo..Denver
Clear Creek..........................Denver	Kiowa...Denver	Rio Blanco.....................................Denver
Conejos................................Denver	Kit Carson.....................................Denver	Rio Grande.....................................Denver
Costilla.................................Denver	La Plata...Denver	Routt...Denver
Crowley................................Denver	Lake...Denver	Saguache..Denver
Custer...................................Denver	Larimer..Denver	San Juan...Denver
Delta.....................................Denver	Las Animas....................................Denver	San Miguel.....................................Denver
Denver...................................Denver	Lincoln..Denver	Sedgwick.......................................Denver
Dolores.................................Denver	Logan...Denver	Summit...Denver
Douglas.................................Denver	Mesa..Denver	Teller..Denver
Eagle.....................................Denver	Mineral..Denver	Washington....................................Denver
El Paso..................................Denver	Moffat..Denver	Weld...Denver
Elbert....................................Denver	Montezuma....................................Denver	Yuma..Denver

US District Court

District of Colorado

Denver Division US Courthouse, Room C-145, 1929 Stout St, Denver, CO 80294-3589 (Courier Address: Use mail address for courier delivery), 303-844-3433.

www.co.uscourts.gov

Counties: All counties in Colorado.

Indexing & Storage: Cases are indexed by defendant, plaintiff, and case number. New cases are available in the index immediately after filing date. Open records are located at this court.

Fee & Payment Notes: Payment may be made by money order, cashier check, personal check, Visa, Mastercard. There is no prepayment required for any copies unless the bill is over $100.00. Payee: Clerk, US District Court.

Phone Search: Over the phone, the court will release anything of public record, although they will not read long excerpts over the phone.

In Person Search: In person searching available.

PACER: Toll-free dial-up access: 888-481-7027. Local dial-up access: 303-335-2335. Case records are available back to 1990. Records are purged on a varying schedule. New records are available online after 1 day. PACER is available online at http://pacer.cod.uscourts.gov.

US Bankruptcy Court

District of Colorado

Denver Division US Custom House, Room 114, 721 19th St, Denver, CO 80202-2508 (Courier Address: Use mail address for courier delivery), 303-844-4045.

www.co.uscourts.gov

Counties: All counties in Colorado.

Indexing & Storage: Cases are indexed by debtor as well as by case number. New cases are available in the index 24-48 hours after filing date. Records are also on microfilm of all cases prior to June 1990. Open records are located at this court.

Fee & Payment Notes: Payment may be made by money order, cashier check, personal check. Personal checks are not accepted from debtors. Payee: Clerk, US Bankruptcy Court. You are allowed to make your own copies. These copies cost $.10 per page. Records are available for viewing from 8:00 a.m. to 4:45 p.m., Monday through Friday in Room 114.

Phone Search: An automated voice case information service (VCIS) is available. Call VCIS at 303-844-0267.

Mail Search: A stamped self addressed envelope is not required.

In Person Search: In person searching available.

PACER:. Case records are available back to July 1981. New civil records are available online after 1 day. PACER is available online at http://pacer.cob.uscourts.gov.

Electronic Filing: Information is available online at https://ecf.cob.uscourts.gov

Standards for Federal Courts: The search fee is $20.00 per item (one party name or case number). Certification fee is $7.00 per document. Copy fee is $.50 per page. All fees standard unless noted in profile. Mail Search: always enclose a stamped self addressed envelope unless otherwise noted. Before releasing records, all courts require prepayment unless noted in profile.

Open records are located at the court unless otherwise noted. District courts index by defendant and plaintiff as well as by case number. Bankruptcy courts usually index by debtor and case number. While most courts now have their indexes on computer, many still maintain index card files as well.

The universal PACER sign-up number is 800-676-6856. Find PACER and the Party/Case Index on the Web at http://pacer.psc.uscourts.gov. PACER dial-up access is $.60 per minute. Also, courts offering internet access via RACER, PACER, Web-PACER or the new CM-ECF charge $.07 per page fee unless noted as free.

Colorado County Courts

Court	Jurisdiction	No. of Courts	How Organized
District Courts*	General	14	22 Districts
County Courts*	Limited	17	63 Counties
Combined Courts*		49	
Denver Probate Courts*	Probate	1	
Municipal Courts	Municipal	206	
Denver Juvenile Courts	Special	1	
Water Courts	Special	7	7 Districts

* Profiled in this Sourcebook.

	CIVIL								
Court	Tort	Contract	Real Estate	Min. Claim	Max. Claim	Small Claims	Estate	Eviction	Domestic Relations
District Courts*	X	X	X	$0	No Max		X		X
County Courts*	X	X	X	$0	$15,000	$7500		X	
Denver Probate Courts*							X		
Denver Juvenile Courts									
Water Courts			X	$0	No Max				

	CRIMINAL				
Court	Felony	Misdemeanor	DWI/DUI	Preliminary Hearing	Juvenile
District Courts*	X				X
County Courts*		X	X	X	
Denver Probate Courts*					
Denver Juvenile Courts					X
Water Courts					

ADMINISTRATION   State Court Administrator, 1301 Pennsylvania St, Suite 300, Denver, CO, 80203; 303-861-1111, Fax: 303-837-2340. www.courts.state.co.us

COURT STRUCTURE   As of 9/1/2001, the maximum civil claim in County Courts was increased to $15,000. The District and County Courts have overlapping jurisdiction over civil cases involving less than $15,000 ($10,000 prior to 9/1/2001). Fortunately, District and County Courts are combined in most counties. Combined courts usually search both civil or criminal indexes for a single fee, except as indicated in the profiles.

Municipal courts only have jurisdiction over traffic, parking, and ordinance violations.

ONLINE ACCESS   There is no official government system, but we can mention a unique commercial system. As a result of an initiative of the Colorado Judicial Branch, all district courts and all county courts except Denver County Court are available on the Internet at www.cocourts.com. Real-time records include civil, civil water, small claims, domestic, felony, misdemeanor, and traffic cases and can be accessed by name or case number. Court records go as far back as 1995. There is a fee for this subscription Internet access, generally $5.00 per search and there are discounts for volume users. Contact Jeff Mueller, Major Accounts, by telephone at 866-COCOURT, or by email at Jeffm@cocourts.com. Note: Denver County Court civil records are available free online.

ADDITIONAL INFORMATION

November 15, 2001, Broomfield City & County came into existence, derived from the counties of Adams, Boulder, Jefferson and Weld. A District and County Court (presumed to be 17th Judicial District) was established.

All state agencies require a self-addressed, stamped envelope (SASE) for return of information.

Co-located with seven district courts are divisions known as Water Courts. The Water Courts are located in Weld, Pueblo, Alamosa, Montrose, Garfield, Routt, and La Platta counties; see the District Court discussion for those counties to determine the jurisdictional area for the Water Court. Water Court records are maintained by the Water Clerk and fees are similar to those for other court records. To retrieve a Water Court record, one must furnish the Case Number or the Legal Description (section, township, and range) or the Full Name of the respondent (note that the case number or legal description are preferred).

PROBATE COURTS

Denver is the only county where Probate Court is separate from the District Court.

Adams County

17th District Court 1100 Judicial Center Drive, Brighton, CO 80601; 303-659-1161; Fax: 303-654-3216. Hours: 8AM-5PM (MST). *Felony, Civil Actions Over $10,000, Probate.*

www.17thjudicialdistrict.com

Note: The District and County courts have combined, but records are searched separately unless requester asks to search both courts (at no extra fee).

Civil Records: Access: Mail, in person, online. Both court and visitors may perform in person searches. Search fee: $5.00 per name. Fee is $10.00 for cases before 1976. There is no fee if search done by visitor. Required to search: name, years to search. Civil cases indexed by defendant, plaintiff. Civil records on computer from Jan 1976, index books back to early 1900s. Online access to civil records is available at www.cocourts.com.

Criminal Records: Access: Mail, in person, online. Both court and visitors may perform in person searches. Search fee: $5.00 per name. Fee is $8.00 for cases before 1976. Required to search: name, years to search, DOB. Criminal records on computer from Jan 1976, index books back to early 1900s. Online access to criminal records is available at www.cocourts.com.

General Information: No adoptions, sealed, juvenile, mental health or expunged cases released. SASE required. Turnaround time 2 days. Copy fee: $.75 per page. Certification fee: $5.00. Fee payee: Clerk of the District Court. Personal checks accepted. Credit cards accepted. Accepted in person only. Prepayment is required.

County Court 1100 Judicial Center Drive, Brighton, CO 80601; 303-659-1161. Hours: 8AM-5PM (MST). *Misdemeanor, Civil Actions Under $15,000, Eviction, Small Claims.*

Note: The District and County courts have combined, but records are searched separately unless specifically asked to search both courts for no additional fee.

Civil Records: Access: Mail, in person, online. Both court and visitors may perform in person searches. Search fee: $5.00 per name. $8.00 per name for pre-computer records. Required to search: name, years to search. Civil cases indexed by defendant, plaintiff. Civil records on computer from Jan 1990, index books back to 1965. Online access to civil records is available at www.cocourts.com.

Criminal Records: Access: Mail, in person, online. Both court and visitors may perform in person searches. Search fee: $5.00 per name. $8.00 per name for pre-computer records. Required to search: name, years to search, DOB. Criminal records on computer from Jan 1990, index books back to 1965. Online access to criminal records is available at www.cocourts.com.

General Information: No adoptions, sealed, juvenile, mental health or expunged cases released. SASE

required. Turnaround time 2 working days. Copy fee: $.75 per page. Certification fee: $5.00. Fee payee: Adams County Combined Court. Personal checks accepted. Credit cards accepted: Visa, MasterCard. In person only. Prepayment is required.

Alamosa County

Alamosa Combined Court 702 4th St, Alamosa, CO 81101; 719-589-4996; Fax: 719-589-4998. Hours: 8AM-noon, 1-4:30PM (MST). *Felony, Civil, Eviction, Small Claims, Probate.*

Civil Records: Access: Mail, in person, online. Both the court and visitors may perform in person searches. Search fee: $5.00 per name. Required to search: name, years to search. Civil cases indexed by defendant. Civil records on computer from May 1978, index books back to 1913. Online access to civil records is available at www.cocourts.com.

Criminal Records: Access: Mail, in person, online. Both the court and visitors may perform in person searches. Search fee: $5.00 per name. Required to search: name, years to search, DOB. Criminal records on computer from May 1978, index books back to 1913. Online access to criminal records is available at www.cocourts.com.

General Information: Public access terminal is available. No adoptions, sealed, juvenile, mental health or expunged cases released. SASE required. Turnaround time 10 days. Fax notes: Fee to fax results is $10.00 minimum plus $1.00 per page after 1st 10. Copy fee: $.75 per page. Certification fee: $5.00. Fee payee: Clerk, Combined Court. Personal checks accepted. Prepayment is required.

Arapahoe County

18th District Court 7325 S Potomac, Englewood, CO 80112; 303-649-6355. Hours: 8AM-5PM (MST). *Felony, Civil Actions Over $10,000, Probate.*

Civil Records: Access: Phone, mail, in person, online. Both court and visitors may perform in person searches. Search fee: $5.00 per name. Required to search: name, years to search. Civil cases indexed by defendant, plaintiff. Civil records on computer from 1985, microfiche back to 1903. Online access to civil records is available at www.cocourts.com.

Criminal Records: Access: Phone, mail, in person, online. Both court and visitors may perform in person searches. Search fee: $5.00 per name. Required to search: name, years to search, DOB. Criminal records on computer from 1985, microfiche back to 1903. Online access to criminal records is available at www.cocourts.com.

General Information: No adoptions, sealed, juvenile, mental health or expunged cases released. SASE required. Turnaround time 1-2 days. Fax notes: No fee to fax results. Copy fee: $.75 per page. Certification fee:

$5.00. Fee payee: Clerk of District Court. Personal checks accepted. Prepayment is required.

Arapahoe County Court Division B 15400 E 14th Pl, Aurora, CO 80011; 303-363-8004; Fax: 303-363-7155. Hours: 8AM-5PM (MST). *Misdemeanor, Civil Actions Under $15,000, Eviction, Small Claims.*

Civil Records: Access: Phone, mail, in person, online. Both court and visitors may perform in person searches. Search fee: $5.00 per name. Required to search: name, years to search. Civil cases indexed by defendant, plaintiff. Civil records on computer from April 1986, microfiche from 1980-1983, index cards from 1980. Online access to civil records is available at www.cocourts.com.

Criminal Records: Access: Phone, mail, in person, online. Both court and visitors may perform in person searches. Search fee: $5.00 per name. Required to search: name, years to search, DOB. Criminal records on computer from April 1986, microfiche from 1980-1983, index cards from 1980. Online access to criminal records is available at www.cocourts.com.

General Information: No adoptions, sealed, juvenile, mental health or expunged cases released. SASE required. Turnaround time 2 days. Copy fee: $.75 per page. Certification fee: $5.00. Fee payee: Clerk of County Court. Personal checks accepted. Credit cards accepted: Visa, MasterCard. Prepayment is required.

Littleton County Court Division A 1790 W Littleton Blvd, Littleton, CO 80120-2060; 303-798-4591. Hours: 8AM-5PM (MST). *Misdemeanor, Civil Actions Under $15,000, Eviction, Small Claims.*

Civil Records: Access: Phone, mail, fax, in person, online. Both court and visitors may perform in person searches. Search fee: $5.00 per name. Required to search: name, years to search. Civil cases indexed by defendant, plaintiff. Civil records on computer from 1986, index cards from 1965, microfiche from 1861 in District Court. Online access to civil records is available at www.cocourts.com. Registration required; transaction fee. Only court performs searches prior to March 1986.

Criminal Records: Access: Mail, fax, in person, online. Both court and visitors may perform in person searches. Search fee: $5.00 per name. Required to search: name, years to search, DOB. Criminal records on computer from 1986, index cards from 1965, microfiche from 1861 in District Court. Online access to criminal records is available at www.cocourts.com. Only court performs searches prior to March 1986.

General Information: No adoptions, sealed, juvenile, mental health or expunged cases released. SASE required. Turnaround time 2 weeks. Copy fee: $.75 per page. Certification fee: $5.00. Fee payee: Clerk of County Court. Personal checks accepted. Credit cards accepted: Visa, MasterCard, Discover. Prepayment is required.

Archuleta County

6th District & County Courts PO Box 148, Pagosa Springs, CO 81147; 970-264-2400; Fax: 970-264-2407. Hours: 8AM-5PM (MST). *Felony, Misdemeanor, Civil, Eviction, Small Claims, Probate.*

Civil Records: Access: Mail, in person, online. Only the court performs in person searches; visitors may not. Search fee: $5.00 per name. Specific case information is $2.00 per file. Required to search: name, years to search. Civil cases indexed by defendant, plaintiff. Civil records on index cards from 1976, index books back to 1885. Online access to civil records is available at www.cocourts.com.

Criminal Records: Access: Mail, in person, online. Only the court performs in person searches; visitors may not. Search fee: $5.00 per name. Specific case information $2.00 per file. Required to search: name, years to search, DOB. Criminal records on index cards from 1976, index books back to 1885. Online access to criminal records is available at www.cocourts.com.

General Information: No adoptions, sealed, juvenile, mental health or expunged cases released. SASE required. Turnaround time 5 days. Copy fee: $.75 per page. Certification fee: $5.00. Fee payee: Archuleta Combined Court. Personal checks accepted. Prepayment is required.

Baca County

Baca County District & County Courts 741 Main St, Springfield, CO 81073; 719-523-4555. Hours: 8AM-5PM (MST). *Felony, Misdemeanor, Civil, Eviction, Small Claims, Probate.*

Civil Records: Access: Mail, in person, online. Only the court performs in person searches; visitors may not. Search fee: $5.00 per name. Required to search: name, years to search. Civil cases indexed by defendant, plaintiff. Civil records on index cards from 1945, index books back to 1910. Online access to civil records is available at www.cocourts.com.

Criminal Records: Access: Mail, in person, online. Only the court performs in person searches; visitors may not. Search fee: $5.00 per name. Required to search: name, years to search, DOB. Criminal records on index cards from 1945, index books back to 1910. Online access to criminal records is available at www.cocourts.com.

General Information: No adoptions, sealed, juvenile, mental health or expunged cases released. SASE required. Turnaround time 1-2 days. Copy fee: $.75 per page. Certification fee: $5.00. Fee payee: Baca County Courts. Personal checks accepted. Prepayment is required.

Bent County

16th District Court Bent County Courthouse, 725 Bent, Las Animas, CO 81054; 719-456-1353; Fax: 719-456-0040. Hours: 8AM-12, 1-5PM (MST). *Felony, Misdemeanor, Civil, Eviction, Small Claims, Probate.*

www.courts.state.co.us/district/16th/dist-16.htm

Civil Records: Access: Mail, in person, online. Both court and visitors may perform in person searches. Search fee: $5.00 per name. Required to search: name, years to search. Civil cases indexed by defendant, plaintiff. Civil records on index cards from 1975, prior to 1975 some on microfilm, on computer from 11/95 forward- all indexes available at this office. Online access to civil records is available at www.cocourts.com.

Criminal Records: Access: Mail, in person, online. Both court and visitors may perform in person searches. Search fee: $5.00 per name. Required to search: name, years to search, DOB, signed release. Criminal records on index cards from 1975, prior to 1975 some on microfilm, on computer from 11/95 forward- all

indexes available at this office. Online access to criminal records is available at www.cocourts.com.

General Information: No adoptions, sealed, juvenile, mental health or expunged cases released. SASE required. Turnaround time 4-5 days. Copy fee: $.75 per page. Certification fee: $5.00. Fee payee: Clerk of Combined Court. Personal checks accepted. Prepayment is required.

Boulder County

20th District & County Courts 6th & Canyon, 1777 6th St, Boulder, CO 80306; 303-441-3750. Hours: 8AM-5PM (MST). *Felony, Misdemeanor, Civil, Eviction, Small Claims, Probate.*

Civil Records: Access: Mail, in person, online. Only the court performs in person searches; visitors may not. Search fee: $5.00 per name. Required to search: name, years to search. Civil cases indexed by defendant, plaintiff. Civil records on computer from 1983, microfiche prior from 1977, all prior records in books. Online access to civil records is available at www.cocourts.com.

Criminal Records: Access: Mail, in person, online. Only the court performs in person searches; visitors may not. Search fee: $5.00 per name. Required to search: name, years to search, DOB, signed release. Criminal records on computer from 1983, microfiche prior from 1977, all prior records in books. Online access to criminal records is available at www.cocourts.com.

General Information: No adoptions, sealed, juvenile, mental health or expunged cases released. SASE required. Turnaround time 5 days. Copy fee: $.75 per page. Certification fee: $5.00. Fee payee: 20th Judicial District. Business checks accepted. Attorney checks accepted. Credit cards accepted: Visa, MasterCard.

Broomfield County

Broomfield District & County 1 DesCombes Dr, Broomfield, CO 80020; 303-438-6341; Fax: 303-438-6348. Hours: 8AM-5PM (MST). *Felony, Misdemeanor, Civil, Eviction, Small Claims, Probate.*

www.co.broomfield.co.us/

Note: This is a new county created in late 2001, record keeping is limited. Previous felony and upper civil judgments should be searched in Adams, Boulder, Jefferson and Weld counties. This court holds the Municipal court records, prior to county organization.

Civil Records: Access: Mail, in person, online. Both court and visitors may perform searches. Search fee: $5.00 per name. Required to search: name, DOB or other identifier. Civil cases indexed by defendant, plaintiff. Civil records on computer since 11/01. Online access to civil records is available at www.cocourts.com.

Criminal Records: Access: Mail, in person, online. Both court and visitors may perform searches. Search fee: $5.00 per name. Required to search: name, DOB or other identifier. Civil records on computer since 11/01. Online access to criminal records is available at www.cocourts.com.

General Information: Public access terminal is available. No adoptions, sealed, juvenile, mental health or expunged cases released. SASE helpful. Turnaround time 1-2 days. Copy fee: $.75 per page. Certification fee: $5.00. Fee payee: Broomfield County Courts. Personal checks accepted. Prepayment is required.

Chaffee County

11th District & County Courts PO Box 279, Salida, CO 81201; 719-539-2561/6031; Fax: 719-539-6281. Hours: 8AM-5PM (MST). *Felony, Misdemeanor, Civil, Eviction, Small Claims, Probate.*

Note: This court combined in 2002; formerly two courts: one county court, one district court.

Civil Records: Access: Phone, fax, mail, in person, online. Only the court performs in person searches; visitors may not. Search fee: $5.00 per name. Fee applies if 3 or more files involved. Required to search: name, years to search. Civil cases indexed by defendant, plaintiff. Civil records on computer back to 1995; index cards from April 1976, index books back to late 1800s. Online access to civil records is available at www.cocourts.com.

Criminal Records: Access: Phone, fax, mail, in person, online. Only the court performs in person searches; visitors may not. Search fee: $5.00 per name. Fee applies if 3 or more files involved. Required to search: name, years to search, DOB. Criminal records on computer back to 1995; index cards back to April 1976, index books back to late 1800s. Online access to criminal records is available at www.cocourts.com.

General Information: No adoptions, sealed, juvenile, mental health or expunged cases released. SASE required. Turnaround time 2-3 days. Fax notes: Fee to fax results is $.50 per page. Copy fee: $.75 per page. Certification fee: $5.00. Fee payee: Clerk of District Court. Personal checks accepted. Prepayment is required.

Cheyenne County

District & County Courts PO Box 696, Cheyenne Wells, CO 80810; 719-767-5649. Hours: 8AM-4:30PM (MST). *Felony, Misdemeanor, Civil, Eviction, Small Claims, Probate.*

Civil Records: Access: Mail, in person, online. Only the court performs in person searches; visitors may not. Search fee: $5.00 per name. Required to search: name, years to search. Civil cases indexed by defendant, plaintiff. Civil records on computer since 11/1/95, index cards from 1960, index books back to early 1900s. Online access to civil records is available at www.cocourts.com.

Criminal Records: Access: Mail, in person, online. Only the court performs in person searches; visitors may not. Search fee: $5.00 per name. Required to search: name, years to search, DOB, notorized signed release. Criminal records on computer since 11/1/95, index cards from 1960, index books back to early 1900s. Online access to criminal records is available at www.cocourts.com.

General Information: No adoptions, sealed, juvenile, mental health or expunged cases released. SASE required. Turnaround time 5-7 days. Fax notes: Fee to fax results is $1.00 per page. Copy fee: $.75 per page. Certification fee: $5.00 per doc. Fee payee: Cheyenne County Combined Court. Business checks accepted. Will bill attorneys only.

Clear Creek County

5th District & County Courts PO Box 367, Georgetown, CO 80444; 303-569-3273; Fax: 303-569-3274. Hours: 8AM-5PM (MST). *Felony, Misdemeanor, Civil, Eviction, Small Claims, Probate.*

Civil Records: Access: Mail, in person, online. Both court and visitors may perform in person searches. Search fee: $5.00 per name. Required to search: name, years to search. Civil cases indexed by defendant, plaintiff. Civil records on index cards from 1976, ledger books back to late 1800. Online access to civil records is available at www.cocourts.com. No searches done on records prior to 1976.

Criminal Records: Access: Mail, in person, online. Both court and visitors may perform in person searches. Search fee: $5.00 per name. Required to search: name, years to search, DOB. Criminal records on index cards from 1976, ledger books back to late 1800, computerized since 9/95. Online access to criminal records is available at www.cocourts.com.

General Information: No adoptions, sealed, juvenile, mental health or expunged cases released. SASE required. Turnaround time 1 week. Copy fee: $.75 per page. Certification fee: $5.00 per page. Fee payee: Clerk of Combined Court. Personal checks accepted. Prepayment is required.

Conejos County

12th District & County Courts 6683 County Road 13, Conejos, CO 81129; 719-376-5466; Fax: 719-376-5939. Hours: 8AM-4PM (MST). *Felony, Misdemeanor, Civil, Eviction, Small Claims, Probate.*

Civil Records: Access: Mail, in person, online. Only the court performs in person searches; visitors may not. Search fee: $5.00 per name. Required to search: name, years to search. Civil cases indexed by defendant, plaintiff. Civil records on computer since 6/94, on index cards from 1980. Online access to civil records is available at www.cocourts.com.
Criminal Records: Access: Mail, in person, online. Only the court performs in person searches; visitors may not. Search fee: $5.00 per name. Required to search: name, years to search, DOB. Criminal records on computer since 6/94, on index cards from 1980. Online access to criminal records is available at www.cocourts.com.
General Information: No adoptions, sealed, juvenile, mental health or expunged cases released. SASE required. Turnaround time 2 weeks. Copy fee: $.75 per page. Certification fee: $5.00. Fee payee: Conejos Combined Court. Personal checks accepted. Prepayment is required.

Costilla County

12th District & County Courts PO Box 301, San Luis, CO 81152; 719-672-3681; Fax: 719-672-3681. Hours: 8AM-Noon, 1-4PM (MST). *Felony, Misdemeanor, Civil, Eviction, Small Claims, Probate.*
www.courts.state.co.us/district/12th/dist-12.shtml
Civil Records: Access: Mail, in person, online. Both court and visitors may perform in person searches. Search fee: $5.00 per name. There is no fee if the visitor performs the search. Required to search: name, years to search; also helpful: address. Civil cases indexed by defendant, plaintiff. Civil records on index cards from 1970, index books back to 1865, indexed on computer since 1994. In CO state archives prior to 1970. Online access to civil records is available at www.cocourts.com.
Criminal Records: Access: Fax, mail, in person, online. Only the court performs in person searches; visitors may not. Search fee: $5.00 per name. Required to search: name, years to search, DOB; also helpful: address, SSN. Criminal records on index cards from 1970, index books back to 1865, indexed on computer since 1994. In CO state archived prior to 1970. Online access to criminal records is available at www.cocourts.com.
General Information: No adoptions, sealed, juvenile, mental health, certain criminal cases or expunged cases released. SASE required. Turnaround time 1-2 weeks. Fax notes: Fee to fax results is $10.00 per document. Copy fee: $.75 per page. Certification fee: $5.00 per document. Fee payee: Costilla Combined Courts. Personal checks accepted. Prepayment is required.

Crowley County

16th District & County Courts 110 E 6th St, #303, Ordway, CO 81063; 719-267-4468; Fax: 719-267-3753. Hours: 8AM-4:30PM (MST). *Felony, Misdemeanor, Civil, Eviction, Small Claims, Probate.*
www.courts.state.co.us/district/16th/dist-16.htm
Civil Records: Access: Phone, mail, fax, in person, online. Only the court performs in person searches; visitors may not. Search fee: $5.00 per name. Required to search: name, years to search. Civil cases indexed by defendant, plaintiff. Civil records on computer back to

1995, fiche since 1980'2, index books back to 1925. Online access to civil records is available at www.cocourts.com.
Criminal Records: Access: Mail, fax, in person, online. Only the court performs in person searches; visitors may not. Search fee: $5.00 per name. Required to search: name, years to search, DOB, SSN. Criminal records on computer back to 1995, fiche since 1980's, index books back to 1925. Online access to criminal records is available at www.cocourts.com.
General Information: No adoptions, sealed, juvenile, mental health or expunged cases released. SASE required. Turnaround time 3-5 days. Fax notes: Fee to fax results is $1.00 per page. Copy fee: $.75 per page. Certification fee: $5.00. Fee payee: Crowley Combined Court. Personal checks accepted. Prepayment is required.

Custer County

11th District & County Courts PO Box 60, Westcliffe, CO 81252; 719-783-2274; Fax: 719-783-2995. Hours: 8AM-2PM (MST). *Felony, Misdemeanor, Civil, Eviction, Small Claims, Probate.*
Civil Records: Access: Mail, in person, online. Only the court may perform in person searches. Search fee: $5.00 per name. Required to search: name, years to search. Civil cases indexed by defendant, plaintiff. Civil records on index cards from 1973, ledger books back to 1965, on computer since 1993, archived from 1879-1965. Online access to civil records is available at www.cocourts.com.
Criminal Records: Access: Mail, in person, online. Both court and visitors may perform in person searches. Search fee: $5.00 per name. Required to search: name, years to search, DOB. Criminal records on index cards from 1973, ledger books back to 1965, on computer since 1993, archived from 1879-1965. Online access to criminal records is available at www.cocourts.com.
General Information: No adoptions, sealed, juvenile, mental health or expunged cases released. SASE required. Turnaround time 1-2 weeks. Copy fee: $.75 per page. Certification fee: $5.00. Fee payee: Custer Combined Court. Personal checks accepted. Prepayment is required.

Delta County

District & County Courts 501 Palmer St Rm 338, Delta, CO 81416; 970-874-6280. Hours: 8:30AM-4:30PM (MST). *Felony, Misdemeanor, Civil, Eviction, Small Claims, Probate.*
www.7thjudicialdistrictco.org/delta.html
Civil Records: Access: Mail, in person, online. Only the court performs in person searches; visitors may not. Search fee: $5.00 per name. Required to search: name, years to search. Civil cases indexed by defendant, plaintiff. Civil records on computer back to 10/1994, index cards from 1972, index books back to 1900. Online access to civil records is available at www.cocourts.com.
Criminal Records: Access: Mail, in person, online. Only the court performs in person searches; visitors may not. Search fee: $5.00 per name. Required to search: name, years to search, DOB, signed release. Criminal records on computer back to 10/1994, index cards from 1972, index books back to 1900. Online access to criminal records is available at www.cocourts.com.
General Information: No adoptions, sealed, juvenile, mental health or expunged cases released. SASE required. Turnaround time 3 days. Copy fee: $.75 per page. Certification fee: $5.00. Fee payee: Clerk of Court. Only cashiers checks and money orders accepted. Prepayment is required.

Denver County

2nd District Court 1437 Bannock, Office of the Court Clerk, Denver, CO 80202; Civil phone: 720-865-8301; Criminal phone: 720-865-9060. Hours: 8AM-5PM (MST). *Felony, Civil Actions Over $10,000.*
www.courts.state.co.us/district/02nd/dcadmn02.htm
Civil Records: Access: Mail, in person. Both court and visitors may perform in person searches. No search fee. Required to search: name, years to search. Civil cases indexed by defendant, plaintiff. Civil records on computer from 1974, index books back to the late 1800s if convicted of criminal charges.
Criminal Records: Access: Mail, in person. Both court and visitors may perform in person searches. No search fee. Required to search: name, years to search, DOB. Criminal records on computer from 1974, index books back to the late 1800s if convicted of criminal charges.
General Information: No adoptions, sealed, juvenile, mental health or expunged cases released. SASE required. Turnaround time 1 week. Copy fee: $.75 per page. Certification fee: $5.00. Fee payee: Denver District Court. Personal checks accepted. Prepayment is required.

County Court - Civil Division 1515 Cleveland Pl 4th Floor, Denver, CO 80202; 303-640-5161; Fax: 303-640-4730. Hours: 8AM-5PM (MST). *Civil Actions Under $15,000, Eviction, Small Claims.*
www.courts.state.co.us/district/02nd/dcadmn02.htm
Civil Records: Access: Mail, in person, online. Only the court may perform in person searches. No search fee. Required to search: name, years to search. Civil cases indexed by defendant, plaintiff. Civil records on computer from 1987, microfiche since 1965. Online searching of Denver County Civil Division court cases is available at www.denvergov.org/civilcourts.asp. Search by name, business name, or case number.
General Information: No adoptions, sealed, juvenile, mental health or expunged cases released. SASE required. Turnaround time 1 week. Copy fee: $1.00 per page. Certification fee: $5.00. Fee payee: Denver County Court. Personal checks accepted. Prepayment is required.

County Court - Criminal Division 1437 Bannock St Room 111A, Denver, CO 80202; 720-865-7820. Hours: 8AM-5PM (MST). *Misdemeanor.*
www.courts.state.co.us/district/02nd/dcadmn02.htm
Criminal Records: Access: Mail, in person. Only the court may perform in person searches No search fee. Required to search: name, years to search, DOB; also helpful: address. Criminal records computerized since 1978.
General Information: No adoptions, sealed, juvenile, mental health or expunged cases released. SASE required. Turnaround time 1 week. Copy fee: $.75 per page. Certification fee: $5.00. Fee payee: Denver County Court. Personal checks accepted. Prepayment is required.

Probate Court 1437 Bannock, Rm 230, Denver, CO 80202; 720-865-8310; Fax: 720-865-8576. Hours: 8AM-5PM (MST). *Probate.*
www.cobar.org/probate.ct/index.htm

Dolores County

22nd District & County Courts PO Box 511, Dove Creek, CO 81324; 970-677-2258. Hours: 8AM-5PM M & T; 8AM-Noon W, F (MST). *Felony, Misdemeanor, Civil, Eviction, Small Claims, Probate.*
Civil Records: Access: Phone, mail, in person. Only the court performs in person searches; visitors may not. No search fee. Required to search: name, years to search. Civil cases indexed by defendant, plaintiff. Civil records on index cards from 1972, index books back to

1895, on computer from 06/95 to present. Online access to civil records is available at www.cocourts.com.

Criminal Records: Access: Phone, mail, in person, online. Only the court performs in person searches; visitors may not. No search fee. Required to search: name, years to search, DOB. Criminal records on index cards from 1972, index books back to 1895, on computer from 06/95 to present. Online access to criminal records is available at www.cocourts.com.

General Information: No adoptions, sealed, juvenile, mental health or expunged cases released. SASE required. Turnaround time 1 week. Copy fee: $.75 per page. Certification fee: $.75 per page. Fee payee: Dolores County Combined. Only cashiers checks and money orders accepted. Prepayment is required.

Douglas County

Douglas County Combined Court 4000 Justice Way #2009, Castle Rock, CO 80104; 303-663-7200. Hours: 8AM-5PM (MST). *Felony, Misdemeanor, Civil, Eviction, Small Claims, Probate.*

Civil Records: Access: Mail, in person, online. Both court and visitors may perform in person searches. Search fee: $5.00 per name. $20.00 per hour for extensive search. Required to search: name, years to search. Civil cases indexed by defendant, plaintiff. Civil records on computer back to 1/1988, index cards from 1975, index books to 1880s. Online access to civil records is available at www.cocourts.com.

Criminal Records: Access: Mail, in person, online. Only the court may perform inperson searches; visitors may not. Search fee: $5.00 per name. $20.00 per hour for extensive search. Required to search: name, years to search. Criminal records on computer back to 1/1988, index cards from 1975, index books to 1880s. Online access to criminal records is available at www.cocourts.com.

General Information: No adoptions, sealed, juvenile, mental health or expunged cases released. SASE required. Turnaround time 1 week. Copy fee: $.75 per page. Certification fee: $5.00. Fee payee: Clerk of Combined Courts. Only cashiers checks and money orders accepted. Prepayment is required.

Eagle County

Eagle Combined Court PO Box 597, Eagle, CO 81631; 970-328-6373; Fax: 970-328-6328. Hours: 8AM-5PM (MST). *Felony, Misdemeanor, Civil, Eviction, Small Claims, Probate.*

Civil Records: Access: Fax, mail, in person, online. Visitors must perform in person searches for themselves. Search fee: $5.00 per name. Required to search: name, years to search. Civil cases indexed by defendant, plaintiff. Civil records on computer since 09/95; prior on fiche to 1970, books to 1930. Online access to civil records is available at www.cocourts.com.

Criminal Records: Access: Fax, mail, in person, online. Visitors must perform in person searches for themselves. Search fee: $5.00 per name. Required to search: name, years to search, DOB. Criminal records on computer since 09/95; prior on fiche to 1970, books to 1930. Online access to criminal records is available at www.cocourts.com.

General Information: No adoptions, sealed, juvenile, mental health or expunged cases released. SASE required. Turnaround time 5-7 days. Fax notes: $1.00 per page. Fax fee must be paid with credit card. Copy fee: $.75 per page. Certification fee: $5.00. Fee payee: Eagle Combined Courts. Personal checks accepted. Credit cards accepted: Visa, MasterCard. Prepayment is required.

El Paso County

El Paso Combined Court 20 E Vermijo Rm 105, Colorado Springs, CO 80903; 719-448-7650; Fax: 719-448-7685. Hours: 8AM-5PM (MST). *Felony, Misdemeanor, Civil Actions, Probate.*

www.gofourth.org

Note: Records for the County and District Courts are combined.

Civil Records: Access: Fax, mail, in person, online. Both court and visitors may perform in person searches. Search fee: $5.00 per name. Required to search: name, years to search. Civil cases indexed by defendant, plaintiff. Civil records on computer from Jan, 1975, index cards to 1975, index books to 1861. Online access to civil records is available at www.cocourts.com.

Criminal Records: Access: Fax, mail, in person, online. Both court and visitors may perform in person searches. Search fee: $5.00 per name; if pre-1975, fee is $20.00 per hour. Required to search: name, years to search, DOB; also helpful: SSN. Criminal records on computer from Jan, 1975, index cards to 1975, index books to 1861. Online access to criminal records is available at www.cocourts.com.

General Information: No adoptions, sealed, juvenile, mental health, expunged cases or other access restricted cases released. SASE required. Turnaround time 5-7 days. Fax notes: Fee is $.75 per page plus $1.50 if long distance. Copy fee: $.75 per page. Certification fee: $5.00. Fee payee: Clerk of District Court. Personal checks accepted. Credit cards accepted: Visa, MasterCard, Discover. Prepayment is required.

Elbert County

Elbert District & County Courts PO Box 232, Kiowa, CO 80117; 303-621-2131. Hours: 8AM-5PM (MST). *Felony, Misdemeanor, Civil, Eviction, Small Claims, Probate.*

Civil Records: Access: Mail, in person, online. Only the court performs in person searches; visitors may not. Search fee: $5.00 per name. Required to search: full name, years to search. Civil cases indexed by defendant, plaintiff. Civil records on computer back to 1995, index cards from 1978-1994, index books from 1920s, archived prior to 1920. Online access to civil records is available at www.cocourts.com.

Criminal Records: Access: Mail, in person, online. Only the court performs in person searches; visitors may not. Search fee: $5.00 per name. Required to search: full name, years to search, DOB, signed release. Criminal records on computer back to 1995, index cards from 1978, index books from 1920s. Online access to criminal records is available at www.cocourts.com.

General Information: No adoptions, sealed, juvenile, mental health or expunged cases released. SASE required. Turnaround time 1-2 weeks. Copy fee: $.75 per page. Certification fee: $5.00. Fee payee: Elbert Combined Courts. Business checks accepted. Prepayment is required.

Fremont County

District & County Courts 136 Justice Center Rd, Rm 103, Canon City, CO 81212; 719-269-0100; Fax: 719-269-0134. Hours: 8AM-5PM (MST). *Felony, Misdemeanor, Civil, Eviction, Small Claims, Probate.*

www.courts.state.co.us

Civil Records: Access: Mail, fax, in person, online. Only the court performs in person searches; visitors may not. Search fee: $5.00 per name. Required to search: name, years to search; also helpful: address. Civil cases indexed by defendant, plaintiff. Civil records on index cards from 1978, index books in Denver (except criminal) back to 1861. Online access to civil records is available at www.cocourts.com.

Criminal Records: Access: Mail, fax, in person, online. Only the court performs in person searches;

visitors may not. Search fee: $5.00 per name. Required to search: name, years to search; also helpful: address, DOB. Criminal records on index cards from 1978, index books in Denver (except criminal) back to 1861. Online access to criminal records is available at www.cocourts.com.

General Information: No adoptions, sealed, juvenile, mental health or expunged cases released. SASE required. Turnaround time 10 working days. Copy fee: $.75 per page. Certification fee: $5.00. Fee payee: Clerk of the Combined Courts. Personal checks accepted. Prepayment is required.

Garfield County

9th District & County Courts 109 8th St #104, Glenwood Springs, CO 81601; 970-945-5075; Fax: 970-945-8756. Hours: 8AM-5PM (MST). *Felony, Misdemeanor, Civil, Eviction, Small Claims, Probate.*

Note: This court handles cases in the county for the area east of New Castle.

Civil Records: Access: Mail, in person, online. Only the court performs in person searches; visitors may not. Search fee: $5.00 per name. Required to search: name, years to search. Civil cases indexed by defendant, plaintiff. Civil records on computer from 1992, on fiche from 1970, index books back to late 1800s. Online access to civil records is available at www.cocourts.com.

Criminal Records: Access: Mail, in person, online. Only the court performs in person searches; visitors may not. Search fee: $5.00 per name. Required to search: name, years to search. Criminal records on computer from 1992, on fiche from 1970, index books back to late 1800s. Online access to criminal records is available at www.cocourts.com.

General Information: No adoptions, sealed, juvenile, mental health or expunged cases released. SASE required. Turnaround time 1-2 weeks. Copy fee: $.75 per page. Certification fee: $5.00. Fee payee: Garfield Combined Courts. Personal checks accepted. Credit cards accepted: Visa, MasterCard. Prepayment is required.

County Court - Rifle 110 E 18th St, Rifle, CO 81650; 970-625-5100; Fax: 970-625-1125. Hours: 8AM-5PM (MST). *Misdemeanor, Civil Actions Under $15,000, Eviction, Small Claims.*

Note: This court handles cases in the county for the area from New Castle to the west.

Civil Records: Access: Phone, fax, mail, in person, online. Only the court performs in person searches; visitors may not. No search fee. Required to search: name, years to search. Civil cases indexed by defendant, plaintiff. Civil records on index cards from 1965, computerized since 1994. Online access to civil records is available at www.cocourts.com.

Criminal Records: Access: Phone, fax, mail, in person, online. Only the court performs in person searches; visitors may not. No search fee. Required to search: name, years to search, DOB. Criminal records on index cards from 1965, computerized since 1994. Online access to criminal records is available at www.cocourts.com.

General Information: No adoptions, sealed, juvenile, mental health or expunged cases released. SASE required. Turnaround time 1 week. Fax notes: $1.00 per page to send or receive a fax. Copy fee: $.75 per page. Certification fee: $5.00 per page. Fee payee: Associate County Court. Personal checks accepted. Credit cards accepted: MasterCard, Visa. Prepayment is required.

Gilpin County

1st District & County Courts 2960 Dory Hill Rd #200, Golden, CO 80403-8768; 303-582-5323; Fax: 303-582-3112. Hours: 8AM-5PM (MST). *Felony, Misdemeanor, Civil, Eviction, Small Claims, Probate.*

Civil Records: Access: Mail, in person, online. Only the court performs in person searches; visitors may not. Search fee: $5.00 per name. Fee is for past 7 years. Required to search: name, years to search. Civil cases indexed by defendant, plaintiff. Civil records on computer (County-1993, District-1994), on index cards from 1970s, index books from 1950s. Online access to civil records is available at www.cocourts.com. **Criminal Records:** Access: Mail, in person, online. Only the court performs in person searches; visitors may not. Search fee: $10.00 per name. Fee is for past 7 years. Required to search: name, years to search, DOB. Criminal records on computer (County-1993, District-1994), on index cards from 1970s, index books from 1950s. Online access to criminal records is available at www.cocourts.com.

General Information: No adoptions, sealed, juvenile, mental health or expunged cases released. SASE required. Turnaround time 5 days. Copy fee: $.75 per page. Certification fee: $5.00. Fee payee: Clerk of the Combined Courts. Personal checks accepted. Prepayment is required.

Grand County

14th District & County Courts PO Box 192, Hot Sulphur Springs, CO 80451; 970-725-3357. Hours: 8AM-5PM (MST). *Felony, Misdemeanor, Civil, Eviction, Small Claims, Probate.*

Civil Records: Access: Phone, mail, in person, online. Only the court performs in person searches; visitors may not. Search fee: $5.00 per name if 1976-1991. $20.00 if pre-1976. No fee 1992-present. Required to search: name, years to search. Civil cases indexed by defendant, plaintiff. Civil records on computer from July, 1991, fiche from 1970, index books from 1900. Online access to civil records is available at www.cocourts.com. Phone requests accepted only if no fees involved. **Criminal Records:** Access: Phone, mail, in person, online. Only the court performs in person searches; visitors may not. Search fee: $5.00 per name if 1976-1991. $20.00 if pre-1976. No fee 1992-present. Required to search: name, years to search, DOB. Criminal records on computer from July, 1991, fiche from 1970, index books from 1900. Online access to criminal records is available at www.cocourts.com. Phone requests accepted only if no fees involved.

General Information: No adoptions, sealed, juvenile, mental health or expunged cases released. SASE required. Turnaround time 1 week. Copy fee: $.75 per page. Certification fee: $5.00. Fee payee: Grand County Combined Court. Personal checks accepted. Prepayment is required.

Gunnison County

7th District & County Courts 200 E Virginia Ave, Gunnison, CO 81230; 970-641-3500; Fax: 970-641-6876. Hours: 8:30AM-4:30PM (MST). *Felony, Misdemeanor, Civil, Eviction, Small Claims, Probate.*

Civil Records: Access: Mail, in person, online. Only the court performs in person searches; visitors may not. Search fee: $5.00 per name. Required to search: name, years to search. Civil cases indexed by defendant. Civil records on computer from 1994, index cards from 1977, index books back to 1877. Online access to civil records is available at www.cocourts.com. **Criminal Records:** Access: Mail, in person, online. Only the court performs in person searches; visitors may not. Search fee: $5.00 per name. Required to search: name, years to search, DOB. Criminal records on computer from 1994, index cards from 1977, index books back to 1877. Online access to criminal records is available at www.cocourts.com.

General Information: No adoptions, sealed, juvenile, mental health or expunged cases released. SASE required. Turnaround time 1-2 days. Copy fee: $.75 per page. Certification fee: $5.00. Fee payee: Gunnison Combined Courts. Personal checks accepted. Prepayment is required.

Hinsdale County

7th District & County Courts PO Box 245, Lake City, CO 81235; 970-944-2227; Fax: 970-944-2289. Hours: 8:30-Noon MWF (Jun-Aug) 8:30-12:00 TF (Sept-May) (MST). *Felony, Misdemeanor, Civil, Eviction, Small Claims, Probate.*

Civil Records: Access: Phone, fax, mail, in person, online. Only the court performs in person searches; visitors may not. No search fee. Required to search: name, years to search. Civil cases indexed by defendant, plaintiff. Civil records on index cards from 1975, index books back to 1900. Online access to civil records is available at www.cocourts.com. **Criminal Records:** Access: Phone, fax, mail, in person, online. Only the court performs in person searches; visitors may not. Search fee: Fee depends on time required for search. Required to search: name, years to search, DOB. Criminal records on index cards from 1975, index books back to 1900. Online access to criminal records is available at www.cocourts.com.

General Information: No adoptions, sealed, juvenile, mental health or expunged cases released. SASE required. Turnaround time 2-4 weeks. Fax notes: $.75 per page. 1-10 pgs $2.00, 11-20 pgs $5.00, 21-30 pgs $10.00. Copy fee: $.75 per page. Certification fee: $5.00. Fee payee: Clerk of the Combined Courts. Personal checks accepted. Prepayment is required.

Huerfano County

3rd District & County Courts 401 Main St, #304, Walsenburg, CO 81089; 719-738-1040; Fax: 719-738-1267. Hours: 8AM-4PM (MST). *Felony, Misdemeanor, Civil, Eviction, Small Claims, Probate.*

Civil Records: Access: Mail, in person, online. Only the court performs in person searches; visitors may not. Search fee: $5.00 per name. Required to search: name, years to search. Civil cases indexed by defendant, plaintiff. Civil records on computer from 1995 (county court only), index cards from 1978, index books from 1861. Online access to civil records is available at www.cocourts.com. **Criminal Records:** Access: Mail, in person, online. Only the court performs in person searches; visitors may not. Search fee: $5.00 per name. Required to search: name, years to search, DOB. Criminal records on computer from 1995 (county court only), index cards from 1978, index books from 1861. Online access to criminal records is available at www.cocourts.com.

General Information: No adoptions, sealed, juvenile, mental health or expunged cases released. SASE required. Turnaround time 2 weeks. Copy fee: $.75 per page. Certification fee: $5.00. Fee payee: Huerfano County Combined Courts. Personal checks accepted. Prepayment is required.

Jackson County

8th District & County Courts PO Box 308, Walden, CO 80480; 970-723-4363. Hours: 9AM-1PM (MST). *Felony, Misdemeanor, Civil, Eviction, Small Claims, Probate.*

Civil Records: Access: Mail, in person, online. Only the court performs in person searches; visitors may not. No search fee. Required to search: name, years to search. Civil cases indexed by defendant, plaintiff. Civil records on computer since 1994; prior on index cards from 1974, index books from the 1900s. Online access to civil records is available at www.cocourts.com. **Criminal Records:** Access: Mail, in person, online. Only the court performs in person searches; visitors may not. No search fee. Required to search: name, years to search, DOB. Criminal records on computer since 1994; prior on index cards from 1974, index books from the 1900s. Online access to criminal records is available at www.cocourts.com.

General Information: No adoptions, sealed, juvenile, mental health or expunged cases released. SASE required. Turnaround time 1 week. Copy fee: $.75 per page. Will bill in excess of 10 pages. Certification fee: $5.00. Fee payee: Clerk of the Combined Courts. Personal checks accepted. If a file has been pulled, information found and it is in excess of 10 pages, will bill the requesting party providing the request is honorable.

Jefferson County

1st District & County Courts 100 Jefferson County Parkway, Golden, CO 80401-6002; 303-271-6267; Fax: 303-271-6188. Hours: 8AM-5PM (MST). *Felony, Misdemeanor, Civil, Eviction, Small Claims, Probate.*

Civil Records: Access: Mail, in person, online. Both court and visitors may perform in person searches. Search fee: $5.00 per name. Fee is per case. Required to search: name, years to search; also helpful: address. Civil cases indexed by defendant, plaintiff. Civil records on computer from 1985, microfiche from 1975, index books from 1963-1974, archived prior to 1963. Online access to civil records is available at www.cocourts.com. **Criminal Records:** Access: Mail, in person, online. Both court and visitors may perform in person searches. Search fee: $5.00 per name. Fee varies depending on # of years searched. Required to search: name, years to search, DOB; also helpful: address. Criminal records on computer from 1985, microfiche from 1975, index books from 1963-1974, archived prior to 1963. Online access to criminal records is available at www.cocourts.com.

General Information: No adoptions, sealed, juvenile, mental health or expunged cases released. SASE required. Turnaround time 1 week. Copy fee: $.75 per page. Certification fee: $5.00. Fee payee: Clerk of Combined Courts. Personal checks accepted. Prepayment is required.

Kiowa County

15th District & County Courts PO Box 353, Eads, CO 81036; 719-438-5558; Fax: 719-438-5300. Hours: 8AM-5PM (MST). *Felony, Misdemeanor, Civil, Eviction, Small Claims, Probate.*

www.courts.state.co.us/district/15th/dist-15.shtml

Civil Records: Access: Phone, fax, mail, in person, online. Only the court performs in person searches; visitors may not. Search fee: $5.00 per name. Required to search: name, years to search. Civil cases indexed by defendant, plaintiff. Civil records on index cards from the 1960s, index books from 1889. Recent records are computerized. Online access to civil records is available at www.cocourts.com. **Criminal Records:** Access: Phone, fax, mail, in person, online. Only the court performs in person searches; visitors may not. Search fee: $5.00 per name. Required to search: name, years to search, DOB. Criminal records on index cards from the 1960s, index books from 1889. Recent records are computerized. Online access to criminal records is available at www.cocourts.com.

General Information: No adoptions, sealed, juvenile, mental health or expunged cases released. SASE required. Turnaround time 1 week. Fax notes: $1.00 per document. Copy fee: $.75 per page. Certification fee:

$5.00. Fee payee: Kiowa County Court. Business checks accepted.

Kit Carson County

13th District & County Courts 251 16th Street, #301, Burlington, CO 80807; 719-346-5524. Hours: 8AM-4PM (MST). *Felony, Misdemeanor, Civil, Eviction, Small Claims, Probate.*

Civil Records: Access: Mail, in person, online. Only the court performs in person searches; visitors may not. Search fee: $5.00 per name. Required to search: name, years to search. Civil cases indexed by defendant, plaintiff. Civil records on index cards from 1910, index books from 1889. Online access to civil records is available at www.cocourts.com.
Criminal Records: Access: Mail, in person, online. Only the court performs in person searches; visitors may not. No search fee. Required to search: name, years to search, DOB. Criminal records on index cards from 1910, index books from 1889. Online access to criminal records is available at www.cocourts.com.
General Information: No adoptions, sealed, juvenile, mental health or expunged cases released. SASE required. Turnaround time 1 week. Fax notes: $5.00 fee per document to fax. Copy fee: $.75 per page. Certification fee: $5.00. Fee payee: Combined Courts. No personal checks accepted. Prepayment is required.

La Plata County

6th District Court PO Box 3340, Durango, CO 81302-3340; 970-247-2304; Fax: 970-247-4348. Hours: 8AM-5PM (MST). *Felony, Civil Actions Over $10,000, Probate.*

Civil Records: Access: Mail, in person, online. Only the court performs in person searches; visitors may not. Search fee: $5.00 per name. Fee is per case. Required to search: name, years to search. Civil cases indexed by defendant, plaintiff. Civil records on computer from 1990, index cards from 1976, index books from 1874. Online access to civil records is available at www.cocourts.com.
Criminal Records: Access: Mail, in person, online. Only the court performs in person searches; visitors may not. Search fee: $5.00 per name. Required to search: name, years to search, DOB. Criminal records on computer from 1990, index cards from 1976, index books from 1874. Online access to criminal records is available at www.cocourts.com.
General Information: No adoptions, sealed, juvenile, mental health or expunged cases released. SASE required. Turnaround time 3-7 days. Fax notes: Fee to fax results is $3.00 per document. Copy fee: $.75 per page. Certification fee: $5.00. Fee payee: Clerk of the Combined Courts. Personal checks accepted. Prepayment is required.

County Court PO Box 759, Durango, CO 81302; 970-247-2004; Fax: 970-247-4348. Hours: 8AM-5PM (MST). *Misdemeanor, Civil Actions Under $15,000, Eviction, Small Claims.*

www.courts.state.co.us/counties.htm

Civil Records: Access: Mail, in person, online. Only the court performs in person searches; visitors may not. Search fee: $5.00 per name. Fee is per case. Required to search: name, years to search. Civil cases indexed by defendant, plaintiff. Civil records on computer from February, 1990, index cards from 1965, index books in Denver prior to 1965. Online access to civil records is available at www.cocourts.com.
Criminal Records: Access: Mail, in person, online. Only the court performs in person searches; visitors may not. Search fee: $5.00 per name. Required to search: name, years to search, DOB. Criminal records on computer from February, 1990, index cards from 1965, index books in Denver prior to 1965. Online

access to criminal records is available at www.cocourts.com.
General Information: No adoptions, sealed, juvenile, mental health or expunged cases released. SASE required. Turnaround time 7-10 days. Copy fee: $.75 per page. Certification fee: $5.00. Fee payee: Clerk of the Combined Courts. Personal checks accepted. Prepayment is required.

Lake County

Lake County Combined Courts PO Box 55, Leadville, CO 80461; 719-486-0535. Hours: 8AM-Noon, 1-5PM (MST). *Felony, Misdemeanor, Civil, Eviction, Small Claims, Probate.*

Civil Records: Access: Mail, in person, online. Only the court performs in person searches; visitors may not. Search fee: $20.00 per name. Required to search: name, years to search. Civil cases indexed by defendant, plaintiff. Civil records on index cards from 1988 (District), 1970 (County), index books from 1865. Online access to civil records is available at www.cocourts.com.
Criminal Records: Access: Mail, in person, online. Only the court performs in person searches; visitors may not. Search fee: $20.00 per name. Required to search: name, years to search, DOB. Criminal records on index cards from 1988 (District), 1970 (County), index books from 1865. Online access to criminal records is available at www.cocourts.com.
General Information: No adoptions, sealed, juvenile, mental health or expunged cases released. SASE required. Turnaround time 30 days. Copy fee: $.75 per page. Certification fee: $5.00. Fee payee: Lake County Court. Business checks accepted. Prepayment is required.

Larimer County

8th District Court 201 La Porte Ave #100, Ft Collins, CO 80521; 970-498-6100; Fax: 970-498-6110. Hours: 8AM-5PM (MST). *Felony, Civil Actions Over $10,000, Probate.*

Civil Records: Access: Phone, mail, in person, online. Both court and visitors may perform in person searches. Search fee: $5.00 per name. Required to search: name; also helpful: years to search. Civil cases indexed by defendant, plaintiff. Civil records on computer from 1976, index books back to 1861. Online access to civil records is available at www.cocourts.com.
Criminal Records: Access: Mail, in person, online. Only the court performs in person searches; visitors may not. Search fee: $5.00 per name. Required to search: name; also helpful: years to search, DOB, SSN. Criminal records on computer from 1976, index books back to 1861. Online access to criminal records is available at www.cocourts.com.
General Information: No adoptions, sealed, juvenile, mental health or expunged cases released. SASE required. Turnaround time 7-10 days. Copy fee: $.75 per page. Certification fee: $5.00. Fee payee: Clerk of District Court. Personal checks accepted. Prepayment is required.

County Court 201 La Porte Ave #100, Ft Collins, CO 80521; 970-498-6100; Fax: 970-498-6110. Hours: 8AM-5PM (MST). *Misdemeanor, Civil Actions Under $15,000, Eviction, Small Claims.*

Civil Records: Access: Mail, in person, online. Both the court and visitors may perform in person searches. Search fee: $5.00 per name. Required to search: name, years to search; also helpful: address. Civil cases indexed by defendant, plaintiff. Some records on computer from 1986, index cards from 1965. Online access to civil records is available at www.cocourts.com.
Criminal Records: Access: Mail, in person, online. Both the court and visitors may perform in person

searches. Search fee: $5.00 per name. Required to search: name, years to search, DOB, signed release, offense; also helpful: address. Some records on computer from 1986, index cards from 1965. Online access to criminal records is available at www.cocourts.com.
General Information: No sealed cases released. SASE required. Turnaround time 3-5 days. Copy fee: $.75 per page. Certification fee: $5.00. Fee payee: Larimer County Combined Court. Personal checks accepted. Prepayment is required.

Las Animas County

3rd District Court 200 E 1st St Rm 304, Trinidad, CO 81082; 719-846-3316/2221; Fax: 719-846-9367. Hours: 8AM-5PM (MST). *Felony, Misdemeanor, Civil, Eviction, Small Claims, Probate.*

Civil Records: Access: Mail, in person, online. Only the court performs in person searches; visitors may not. Search fee: $5.00 per name. Required to search: name, years to search. Civil cases indexed by defendant, plaintiff. Civil records on index cards from 1976, index books to 1950. Online access to civil records is available at www.cocourts.com.
Criminal Records: Access: Mail, in person, online. Only the court performs in person searches; visitors may not. Search fee: $5.00 per name. Required to search: name, years to search, DOB; also helpful: SSN. Criminal records on index cards from 1976, index books to 1950. Online access to criminal records is available at www.cocourts.com.
General Information: No adoptions, sealed, juvenile, mental health or expunged cases released. SASE required. Turnaround time 1 week. Fax notes: Fee to fax results is $2.00 per page. Copy fee: $.75 per page. Certification fee: $5.00. Fee payee: Combined courts. Only cashiers checks and money orders accepted. Prepayment is required.

Lincoln County

18th District & County Courts PO Box 128, Hugo, CO 80821; 719-743-2455. Hours: 8AM-5PM (MST). *Felony, Misdemeanor, Civil, Eviction, Small Claims, Probate.*

Civil Records: Access: Phone, mail, in person, online. Only the court performs in person searches; visitors may not. Search fee: $5.00. Required to search: name, years to search. Civil cases indexed by defendant, plaintiff. Civil records on computer since 12/94, index cards from 1977, index books back to 1889, archived 10 years back. Online access to civil records is available at www.cocourts.com.
Criminal Records: Access: Phone, mail, in person, online. Only the court performs in person searches; visitors may not. Search fee: $5.00. Required to search: name, years to search, DOB. Criminal records on computer since 12/94, index cards from 1977, index books back to 1889, archived 10 years back. Online access to criminal records is available at www.cocourts.com.
General Information: No adoptions, sealed, juvenile, mental health or expunged cases released. SASE required. Turnaround time within 10 days. Copy fee: $.75 per page. Certification fee: $5.00. Fee payee: Lincoln County Combined Courts. Personal checks accepted. Prepayment is required.

Logan County

13th District Court PO Box 71, Sterling, CO 80751; 970-522-6565; Fax: 970-522-6566. Hours: 8AM-4PM (MST). *Felony, Civil Actions Over $10,000, Probate.*

Civil Records: Access: Mail, in person, online. Only the court performs in person searches; visitors may not. Search fee: $5.00 per name. Required to search: name, years to search. Civil cases indexed by defendant, plaintiff. Civil records computerized since 08/95, on index cards from 1973, index books back to 1887. Online access to civil records is available at www.cocourts.com.

Criminal Records: Access: Mail, in person, online. Only the court performs in person searches; visitors may not. Search fee: $5.00 per name. Required to search: name, years to search, DOB. Criminal records computerized since 08/95, on index cards from 1973, index books back to 1887. Online access to criminal records is available at www.cocourts.com.

General Information: No adoptions, sealed, juvenile, mental health or expunged cases released. SASE required. Turnaround time 1-2 weeks. Fax notes: Fee to fax results is $1.00 per page local; $2.00 per page long distance. Copy fee: $.75 per page. Certification fee: $5.00. Fee payee: Logan District Court. Personal checks accepted. Prepayment is required.

County Court PO Box 1907, Sterling, CO 80751; 970-522-1572; Fax: 970-522-2875. Hours: 8AM-4PM (MST). *Misdemeanor, Civil Actions Under $15,000, Eviction, Small Claims.*

Civil Records: Access: Phone, mail, in person, online. Both court and visitors may perform in person searches. Search fee: $5.00 per name. Required to search: name, years to search. Civil cases indexed by defendant, plaintiff. Civil records on computer since 08/95; prior on index cards from 1972 and index books from 1965. Online access to civil records is available at www.cocourts.com.

Criminal Records: Access: Phone, mail, in person, online. Both court and visitors may perform in person searches. Search fee: $5.00 per name. Required to search: name, years to search, DOB. Criminal records on computer since 08/95; prior on index cards from 1972 and index books from 1965. Online access to criminal records is available at www.cocourts.com.

General Information: No adoptions, sealed, juvenile, mental health or expunged cases released. SASE required. Turnaround time 1-2 weeks. Fax notes: Fee to fax results is $2.00 per document. Copy fee: $.75 per page. Certification fee: $5.00. Fee payee: Logan County Court. Business checks accepted.

Mesa County

21st District Court Mesa County District Court, PO Box 20000-5030, Grand Junction, CO 81502; 970-257-3625. Hours: 8AM-5PM (MST). *Felony, Civil Actions Over $10,000, Probate.*

Civil Records: Access: Phone, mail, in person, online. Both court and visitors may perform in person searches. Search fee: $5.00 per name. Required to search: name, years to search. Civil cases indexed by defendant, plaintiff. Civil records on computer since 1994, on microfiche to 1985, books from late 1800s. Online access to civil records is available at www.cocourts.com.

Criminal Records: Access: Mail, in person, online. Only the court performs in person searches; visitors may not. Search fee: $5.00 per name. Required to search: name, years to search, DOB. Criminal records on computer since 1994, on microfiche to 1985, books from late 1800s. Online access to criminal records is available at www.cocourts.com.

General Information: No adoptions, sealed, juvenile, mental health or expunged cases released. SASE required. Turnaround time 5-7 days. Copy fee: $.75 per page. Certification fee: $5.00. Fee payee: Mesa County Combined Court. Business checks accepted. Credit cards accepted: Visa, MasterCard. Prepayment is required.

County Court PO Box 20000, Grand Junction, CO 81502-5032; 970-257-3640. Hours: 8AM-5PM (MST). *Misdemeanor, Civil Actions Under $15,000, Eviction, Small Claims.*

Civil Records: Access: Mail, in person, online. Only the court performs in person searches; visitors may not. Will lookup up to 5 records for free for in-person requestors. Search fee: $5.00 per name; $10 per hour for research lists. Required to search: name, years to search. Civil cases indexed by defendant, plaintiff. Civil records on computer from 10/89. Online access to civil records is available at www.cocourts.com.

Criminal Records: Access: Mail, in person, online. Only the court performs in person searches; visitors may not. Will lookup up to 5 records for free for in-person requestors. Search fee: $5.00 per name; $10 per hour for research lists. Required to search: name, years to search, DOB. Criminal records on computer from 10/89. Online access to criminal records is available at www.cocourts.com.

General Information: Public access terminal is available. No adoptions, sealed, juvenile, mental health or expunged cases released. SASE required. Turnaround time immediate if case is on computer. Copy fee: $.75 per page. Certification fee: $5.00. Fee payee: Mesa County Court. Personal checks accepted. Credit cards accepted: Visa, MasterCard. Accepted in person only. Prepayment is required.

Mineral County

12th District & County Courts PO Box 427, Creede, CO 81130; 719-658-2575; Fax: 719-658-2575. Hours: 10AM-3PM (MST). *Felony, Misdemeanor, Civil, Eviction, Small Claims, Probate.*

Civil Records: Access: Mail, in person, online. Only the court performs in person searches; visitors may not. Search fee: $5.00 per name. Required to search: name, years to search. Civil cases indexed by defendant, plaintiff. Civil records on computer since July 1993, on index cards from 1977, index books back to 1893. Online access to civil records is available at www.cocourts.com.

Criminal Records: Access: Mail, in person, online. Only the court performs in person searches; visitors may not. Search fee: $5.00 per name. Required to search: name, years to search, DOB. Criminal records on computer since July 1993, on index cards from 1977, index books back to 1893. Online access to criminal records is available at www.cocourts.com.

General Information: No adoptions, sealed, juvenile, mental health or expunged cases released. SASE required. Turnaround time 2-3 days. Copy fee: $.75 per page. Certification fee: $5.00. Fee payee: Mineral Combined Courts. Personal checks accepted. Prepayment is required.

Moffat County

Moffat County Combined Court 221 W Victory Wy, Craig, CO 81625; 970-824-8254. Hours: 8AM-5PM (MST). *Felony, Misdemeanor, Civil, Eviction, Small Claims, Probate.*

Civil Records: Access: Phone, mail, in person, online. Only the court performs in person searches; visitors may not. Search fee: $5.00 for records 1976-91; $20.00 prior to 1976. Required to search: name, years to search. Civil cases indexed by defendant, plaintiff. Civil records on computer from 1992, index cards from 1976, either microfilmed or archived back to 1911. Online access to civil records is available at www.cocourts.com.

Criminal Records: Access: Mail, in person, online. Only the court performs in person searches; visitors may not. Search fee: $5.00 1976-1991; $20.00 prior to 1976. Required to search: name, years to search, DOB. Criminal records on computer from 1992, index cards from 1976, either microfilmed or archived back to

1911. Online access to criminal records is available at www.cocourts.com.

General Information: No adoptions, sealed, juvenile, mental health or expunged cases released. SASE required. Turnaround time 1-2 weeks. Copy fee: $.75 per page. Certification fee: $5.00. Fee payee: Moffat County Combined Courts. Personal checks accepted. Prepayment is required.

Montezuma County

22nd District Court 109 W Main St, #210, Cortez, CO 81321; 970-565-1111. Hours: 8AM-4:30PM (MST). *Felony, Civil Actions Over $10,000, Probate.*

Civil Records: Access: Phone, mail, in person, online. Only the court performs in person searches; visitors may not. Search fee: $5.00 per name or case number, or $20.00 per hour to search. Required to search: name, years to search. Civil cases indexed by defendant, plaintiff. Civil records on computer back to 6/95, microfiche up to 1988, index cards from 1975, index books back to late 1890s. Online access to civil records is available at www.cocourts.com.

Criminal Records: Access: Mail, in person, online. Only the court performs in person searches; visitors may not. Search fee: $5.00 per name or case number, or $20.00 per hour to search. Required to search: name, years to search, DOB. Criminal records on computer back to 6/95, microfiche up to 1988, index cards from 1975, index books back to late 1890s. Online access to criminal records is available at www.cocourts.com.

General Information: No adoptions, sealed, juvenile, mental health or expunged cases released. SASE required. Turnaround time 1-2 weeks. Copy fee: $.75 per page. Certification fee: $5.00. Fee payee: Montezuma District Court. Personal checks accepted. Will bill mailing and copy costs.

County Court 601 N Mildred Rd, Cortez, CO 81321; 970-565-7580; Fax: 970-565-8798. Hours: 8AM-4:30PM (MST). *Misdemeanor, Civil Actions Under $15,000, Eviction, Small Claims.*

Civil Records: Access: Mail, in person, online. Only the court performs in person searches; visitors may not. Search fee: $5.00. Required to search: name, years to search. Civil cases indexed by defendant, plaintiff. Civil records on computer since 1993. Online access to civil records is available at www.cocourts.com.

Criminal Records: Access: Mail, in person, online. Only the court performs in person searches; visitors may not. Search fee: $5.00. Required to search: name, years to search, DOB. Criminal records on index cards from 1975, index books prior. Online access to criminal records is available at www.cocourts.com.

General Information: No adoptions, sealed, juvenile, mental health or expunged cases released. SASE required. Turnaround time 5-7 days. Copy fee: $.75 per page. Certification fee: $5.00. Fee payee: Montezuma County Court. Personal checks accepted. Prepayment is required.

Montrose County

7th District & County Courts 1200 N Grand Ave #A, Montrose, CO 81401-3164; 970-252-4300; 242-4309; Fax: 970-252-4345. Hours: 8:30AM-4:30PM (MST). *Felony, Misdemeanor, Civil, Eviction, Small Claims, Probate.*

www.courts.state.co.us

Civil Records: Access: Mail, in person, online. Search fee: $5.00 per name. Required to search: name, years to search. Civil cases indexed by defendant, plaintiff. Civil records on index cards from 1975, index books back to 1890. Online access to civil records is available at www.cocourts.com.

Criminal Records: Access: Mail, in person, online. Only the court performs in person searches; visitors may not. Search fee: $5.00 per name. Required to search: name, years to search, DOB. Criminal records on index cards from 1975, index books back to 1890. Online access to criminal records is available at www.cocourts.com.

General Information: No adoptions, sealed, juvenile, mental health or expunged cases released. SASE required. Turnaround time 1 week. Copy fee: $.75 per page. Certification fee: $5.00. Fee payee: Montrose Combined Courts. Personal checks accepted. Prepayment is required.

Morgan County

13th District Court PO Box 130, Ft Morgan, CO 80701; 970-542-3435; Fax: 970-542-3436. Hours: 8AM-4PM (MST). *Felony, Civil Actions Over $10,000, Probate.*

Civil Records: Access: Fax, mail, in person, online. Only the court performs in person searches; visitors may not. No search fee. Required to search: name, years to search. Civil cases indexed by defendant, plaintiff. Civil records on index cards from 1967, index books back to 1906; computerized since 08/95. Online access to civil records is available at www.cocourts.com.

Criminal Records: Access: Fax, mail, in person, online. Only the court performs in person searches; visitors may not. No search fee. Required to search: name, years to search, DOB, SSN; also helpful: signed release, sex. Criminal records on index cards from 1967, index books back to 1906, computerized since 08/95. Online access to criminal records is available at www.cocourts.com.

General Information: No adoptions, sealed, juvenile, mental health or expunged cases released. SASE required. Turnaround time 2-3 days. Copy fee: $.75 per page. Certification fee: $5.00. Fee payee: Morgan District Court. Personal checks accepted. Will bill copy fees to attorneys.

County Court PO Box 695, Ft Morgan, CO 80701; 970-542-3414; Fax: 970-542-3416. Hours: 8AM-4PM (MST). *Misdemeanor, Civil Actions Under $15,000, Eviction, Small Claims.*

Civil Records: Access: Mail, in person, online. Only the court performs in person searches; visitors may not. Search fee: $5.00 per name. Required to search: name, years to search. Civil cases indexed by defendant, plaintiff. Civil records on computer since 08/95; prior on index cards from 1980. Online access to civil records is available at www.cocourts.com.

Criminal Records: Access: Mail, in person, online. Only the court performs in person searches; visitors may not. Search fee: $5.00 per name. Required to search: name, years to search, DOB. Criminal records on computer since 08/95; prior on index cards from 1980. Online access to criminal records is available at www.cocourts.com.

General Information: No adoptions, sealed, juvenile, mental health or expunged cases released. Copy fee: $.75 per page. Certification fee: $5.00. Fee payee: Morgan County Court. Personal checks accepted. Prepayment is required.

Otero County

16th District Court Courthouse Rm 207, 13 W 3rd St, La Junta, CO 81050; 719-384-4951; Fax: 719-384-4991. Hours: 8AM-5PM (MST). *Felony, Civil, Probate.*

www.courts.state.co.us/district/16th/dist-16.htm

Note: This court is in the process of combining with the County Court at the same address. Records remain separate as of Summer, 2002.

Civil Records: Access: Mail, in person, online. Both the court and visitors may perform in person searches. Search fee: $5.00 per name. Required to search: name, years to search. Civil cases indexed by defendant,

plaintiff. Civil records on index cards from 1978, index books back to 1889, microfiche from 1889-1992. Online access to civil records is available at www.cocourts.com.

Criminal Records: Access: Mail, in person, online. Both the court and visitors may perform in person searches. Search fee: $5.00 per name. Required to search: name, years to search, DOB. Criminal records on index cards from 1978, index books back to 1889, microfiche from 1889-1992. Online access to criminal records is available at www.cocourts.com.

General Information: Public access terminal is available. No adoptions, sealed, juvenile, mental health or expunged cases released. SASE required. Turnaround time 1 week. Copy fee: $.75 per page. Certification fee: $5.00. Fee payee: Otero County Combined Courts. Personal checks accepted. Prepayment is required.

County Court Courthouse Rm 105, 13 W 3rd St, La Junta, CO 81050; 719-384-4721; Fax: 384-4772. Hours: 8AM-Noon, 1-5PM (MST). *Misdemeanor, Civil Actions Under $15,000, Eviction, Small Claims.*

Civil Records: Access: Mail, fax, in person, online. Only the court performs in person searches; visitors may not. Search fee: $5.00 per name. Required to search: name, years to search. Civil cases indexed by defendant, plaintiff. Civil records on microfilm prior to 1991, index cards back to 1950s; on computer back 6 years. Online access to civil records is available at www.cocourts.com.

Criminal Records: Access: Mail, fax, in person, online. Only the court performs in person searches; visitors may not. Search fee: $5.00 per name. Required to search: name; also helpful: years to search. Criminal records on microfilm prior to 1991, index cards back to 1950s; on computer back 6 years. Online access to criminal records is available at www.cocourts.com.

General Information: Public access terminal is available. No adoptions, sealed, juvenile, sexual abuse, assault, mental health or expunged cases released. SASE required. Turnaround time 5 days. Fax notes: Fee to fax results is $1.00 per page. Copy fee: $.75 per page. Certification fee: $5.00. Fee payee: Otero County Courts. Personal checks accepted. Prepayment is required.

Ouray County

7th District & County Courts PO Box 643, Ouray, CO 81427; 970-325-4405; Fax: 970-325-7364. Hours: 8:30AM-Noon, 1-4PM (MST). *Felony, Misdemeanor, Civil, Eviction, Small Claims, Probate.*

Civil Records: Access: Mail, in person, online. Only the court performs in person searches; visitors may not. Search fee: $5.00 per name. Required to search: name, years to search. Civil cases indexed by defendant, plaintiff. Civil records on computer since 1994, index cards from 1976, index books back to 1886, archived prior to 1925. Online access to civil records is available at www.cocourts.com.

Criminal Records: Access: Mail, in person, online. Only the court performs in person searches; visitors may not. Search fee: $5.00 per name. Required to search: name, years to search, DOB. Criminal records on computer since 1994, index cards from 1976, index books back to 1886, archived prior to 1925. Online access to criminal records is available at www.cocourts.com.

General Information: No adoptions, sealed, juvenile, financial, drug/alcohol evaluations, mental health or expunged cases released. SASE requested. Turnaround time 1 week. Fax notes: Fee to fax results is $.75 per page. Copy fee: $.75 per page. Certification fee: $5.00. Fee payee: Ouray Combined Courts. Personal checks accepted. Prepayment is required.

Park County

Park County Combined Courts PO Box 190, Fairplay, CO 80440; 719-836-2940 x226; Fax: 719-836-2892. Hours: 8AM-5PM (MST). *Felony, Misdemeanor, Civil, Eviction, Small Claims, Probate.*

Civil Records: Access: Mail, in person, online. Only the court performs in person searches; visitors may not. Search fee: $5.00 per name. Required to search: name, years to search. Civil cases indexed by defendant, plaintiff. Civil records computerized since 1995, on index cards from 1978, index books back to 1950, archived prior to 1950. Online access to civil records is available at www.cocourts.com.

Criminal Records: Access: Mail, in person, online. Only the court performs in person searches; visitors may not. Search fee: $5.00 per name. Required to search: name, years to search, DOB, signed release. Criminal records computerized since 1995, on index cards from 1978, index books back to 1950, archived prior to 1950. Online access to criminal records is available at www.cocourts.com.

General Information: No adoptions, sealed, juvenile, mental health or expunged cases released. SASE required. Turnaround time within 1 week. Fax notes: Fee to fax results is $1.00 per page. Copy fee: $.50 per page. Certification fee: $5.00. Fee payee: Park County Combined Court. Personal checks accepted. Prepayment is required.

Phillips County

13th District & County Courts 221 S Interocean, Holyoke, CO 80734; 970-854-3279; Fax: 970-854-3179. Hours: 8AM-Noon, 1-4PM (MST). *Felony, Misdemeanor, Civil, Eviction, Small Claims, Probate.*

Civil Records: Access: Phone, fax, mail, in person. Only the court performs in person searches; visitors may not. No search fee. Required to search: name, years to search. Civil cases indexed by defendant, plaintiff. Civil records on computer since 1995; records go back to 1880. Online access to civil records is available at www.cocourts.com.

Criminal Records: Access: Phone, fax, mail, in person. Only the court performs in person searches; visitors may not. No search fee. Required to search: name, years to search, DOB. Criminal records on computer since 1995; records go back to 1880. Online access to criminal records is available at www.cocourts.com.

General Information: No adoptions, sealed, juvenile, mental health or expunged cases released. SASE required. Turnaround time 1-3 days. Copy fee: $.75 per page. Certification fee: $5.00. Fee payee: Phillips County Combined Court. Personal checks accepted. Prepayment is required.

Pitkin County

9th District & County Courts 506 E Main St, Ste 300, Aspen, CO 81611; 970-925-7635; Fax: 970-925-6349. Hours: 8AM-Noon, 1-5PM (MST). *Felony, Misdemeanor, Civil, Eviction, Small Claims, Probate.*

Civil Records: Access: Phone, mail, fax, in person, online, e-mail. Both court and visitors may perform in person searches. Search fee: No fee for computer search. Required to search: name, years to search. Civil cases indexed by defendant. Civil records on computer back to 1990, microfiche from 1940-1970, index cards from 1975. Online access to civil records is available at www.cocourts.com.

Criminal Records: Access: Mail, fax, in person, online. Both court and visitors may perform in person searches. Search fee: There is no fee for searching computer, otherwise rate determined by time and volume. Required to search: name, years to search, DOB, SSN. Criminal records on computer back to

1990, microfiche from 1940-1970, index cards from 1975. Online access to criminal records is available at www.cocourts.com.

General Information: No adoptions, sealed, juvenile, mental health or expunged cases released. Turnaround time 1 week. Fax notes: Fee to fax results is $1.00 per page. Copy fee: $.75 per page. Certification fee: $5.00. Fee payee: Pitkin County Combined Court. Only cashiers checks and money orders accepted. Credit cards accepted: Visa, MasterCard. Prepayment is required.

Prowers County

15th District Court 301 S Main St #300, Lamar, CO 81052-2834; 719-336-7424; Fax: 719-336-9757. Hours: 8AM-5PM (MST). *Felony, Civil Actions Over $10,000, Probate.*

Civil Records: Access: Fax, mail, in person, online. Only the court performs in person searches; visitors may not. No search fee. Required to search: name, years to search. Civil cases indexed by defendant, plaintiff. Civil records computerized since 1995, on microfiche from 1920, index books from the late 1800s. Online access to civil records is available at www.cocourts.com.

Criminal Records: Access: Fax, mail, in person, online. Only the court performs in person searches; visitors may not. No search fee. Required to search: name, years to search, DOB. Criminal records computerized since 1995, on microfiche from 1920, index books from the late 1800s. Online access to criminal records is available at www.cocourts.com.

General Information: No adoptions, sealed, juvenile, mental health or expunged cases released. SASE required. Turnaround time 1 week. Fax notes: $1.00 per page. Copy fee: $.75 per page. Certification fee: $5.00. Fee payee: Clerk of District Court. Only cashiers checks and money orders accepted. Prepayment is required.

County Court 301 S Main St #100, Lamar, CO 81052-2634; 719-336-7416; Fax: 719-336-4145. Hours: 8AM-5PM (MST). *Misdemeanor, Civil Actions Under $15,000, Eviction, Small Claims.*

Civil Records: Access: Mail, phone, in person, online. Both court and visitors may perform in person searches. No search fee. Required to search: name, years to search. Civil cases indexed by defendant, plaintiff. Civil records on computer since 10/95, prior on books to 1965. Online access to civil records is available at www.cocourts.com.

Criminal Records: Access: Mail, phone, in person, online. Both court and visitors may perform in person searches. No search fee. Required to search: name, years to search; also helpful: DOB. Criminal records on computer since 10/95, prior on books to 1965. Online access to criminal records is available at www.cocourts.com.

General Information: No adoptions, sealed, juvenile, mental health or expunged cases released. SASE required. Turnaround time 2-3 days. Copy fee: $.75 per page. Certification fee: $5.00. Fee payee: Prowers County Court. Personal checks accepted. Prepayment is required.

Pueblo County

Combined Courts 320 West 10th St, Pueblo, CO 81003; 719-583-7125; Fax: 719-583-7126. Hours: 8AM-5PM (MST). *Felony, Misdemeanor, Civil, Eviction, Small Claims, Probate.*

Civil Records: Access: Mail, in person, online. Only the court performs in person searches; visitors may not. Search fee: $5.00 per name. Required to search: name, years to search; also helpful: address. Civil cases indexed by defendant, plaintiff. Civil records on computer from 1976, index books back to the 1890s.

Online access to civil records is available at www.cocourts.com.

Criminal Records: Access: Mail, in person, online. Only the court performs in person searches; visitors may not. Search fee: $5.00 per name. Required to search: name, years to search, DOB; also helpful: address, SSN. Criminal records on computer from 1976, index books back to the 1890s. Online access to criminal records is available at www.cocourts.com.

General Information: No adoptions, sealed, juvenile, mental health or expunged cases released. SASE required. Turnaround time 3-5 days. Copy fee: $.75 per page. Certification fee: $5.00. Fee payee: Clerk of Court. Personal checks accepted. Prepayment is required.

Rio Blanco County

9th District & County Courts 555 Main St Rm 303, PO Box 1150, Meeker, CO 81641; 970-878-5622; Fax: 970-878-4295. Hours: 8AM-Noon, 1-5PM (MST). *Felony, Misdemeanor, Civil, Eviction, Small Claims, Probate.*

Civil Records: Access: Phone, fax, mail, in person. Only the court performs in person searches; visitors may not. Search fee: $5.00 per name. May charge for lengthy in-person search request. Required to search: name; also helpful: years to search. Civil cases indexed by defendant, plaintiff. Civil records on computer since 8/1984, on index cards from April 1976, index books back to 1889. Online access to civil records is available at www.cocourts.com.

Criminal Records: Access: Phone, fax, mail, in person, online. Only the court performs in person searches; visitors may not. Search fee: $5.00 per name. May charge for lengthy in-person search request. Required to search: name, years to search; also helpful: DOB. Criminal records on computer since 8/1984, on index cards from April 1976, index books back to 1889. Online access to criminal records is available at www.cocourts.com.

General Information: No adoptions, sealed, juvenile, mental health or expunged cases released. SASE required. Turnaround time 2 days. Fax notes: Fee to fax results is $1.00 per page. Copy fee: $.75 per page. Certification fee: $5.00. Fee payee: Clerk of the Combined Courts. Business checks accepted. Prepayment is required.

Rio Grande County

12th District & County Courts 6th & Cherry, PO Box 427, Del Norte, CO 81132; 719-657-3394. Hours: 8AM-Noon, 1-4PM (MST). *Felony, Misdemeanor, Civil, Eviction, Small Claims, Probate.*

Civil Records: Access: Mail, in person, online. Only the court performs in person searches; visitors may not. Search fee: $5.00 per name. Required to search: name, years to search. Civil cases indexed by defendant, plaintiff. Civil records on computer from 5/95, County on index cards from 1950s, District from 1977. All on index books from the 1800s. Online access to civil records 1995 to present is available at www.cocourts.com.

Criminal Records: Access: Mail, in person, online. Only the court performs in person searches; visitors may not. Search fee: $5.00 per name. Required to search: name, DOB; also helpful: years to search. Criminal records on computer from 5/95, County on index cards from 1950s, District from 1977. All on index books from the 1800s. Online access to criminal records is available at www.cocourts.com.

General Information: No adoptions, sealed, juvenile, mental health or expunged cases released. SASE required. Turnaround time 2-4 days. Fax notes: Fee to fax results is $10.00 for 10 pg document. Copy fee: $.75 per page. Certification fee: $5.00. Fee payee: Rio Grande Combined Court. Personal checks accepted. In-

state personal & business checks accepted. Prepayment is required.

Routt County

Routt Combined Courts PO Box 773117, Steamboat Springs, CO 80477; 970-879-5020; Fax: 970-879-3531. Hours: 8AM-5PM (MST). *Felony, Misdemeanor, Civil, Eviction, Small Claims, Probate.*

Civil Records: Access: Mail, in person, online. Both court and visitors may perform in person searches. Search fee: $5.00 for 1976-1991; prior to 1976 $20.00. There is no fee to search computer records. Required to search: name, years to search. Civil cases indexed by defendant. Civil records on computer back to 1994, on index cards from 1977, microfiche from 1/1977 to 12/1990, archived from 1877. Online access to civil records is available at www.cocourts.com.

Criminal Records: Access: Mail, in person, online. Both court and visitors may perform in person searches. Search fee: Same fees as civil. Required to search: name, years to search, DOB, maiden name, aliases. Criminal records on computer back to 1994, on index cards from 1977, microfiche from 1/1977 to 12/1990, archived from 1877. Online access to criminal records is available at www.cocourts.com.

General Information: No adoptions, sealed, juvenile, mental health or expunged cases released. SASE required. Turnaround time 7-10 days. Copy fee: $.75 per page. Certification fee: $5.00 per document. Fee payee: Routt Combined Court. Personal checks accepted. Visa/MC accepted. Prepayment is required.

Saguache County

12th District & County Courts PO Box 164, Saguache, CO 81149; 719-655-2522; Fax: 719-655-2522. Hours: 8AM-Noon, 1-5PM (MST). *Felony, Misdemeanor, Civil, Eviction, Small Claims, Probate.*

Civil Records: Access: Mail, in person, online. Only the court performs in person searches; visitors may not. No search fee. Required to search: name, years to search. Civil cases indexed by defendant, plaintiff. Civil records on computer since 06/94, on index cards from 1980s, index books back to 1866. Online access to civil records is available at www.cocourts.com.

Criminal Records: Access: Mail, in person, online. Only the court performs in person searches; visitors may not. No search fee. Required to search: name, years to search, DOB. Criminal records on computer since 06/94, on index cards from 1980s, index books back to 1866. Online access to criminal records is available at www.cocourts.com.

General Information: No adoptions, sealed, juvenile, mental health or expunged cases released. SASE required. Turnaround time within 10-12 days. Copy fee: $.75 per page. Certification fee: $5.00. Fee payee: Saguache Combined Courts. Personal checks accepted. Prepayment is required.

San Juan County

6th District & County Courts PO Box 900, Silverton, CO 81433; 970-387-5790. Hours: 8AM-4PM T & TH, 8AM-Noon W (MST). *Felony, Misdemeanor, Civil, Eviction, Small Claims, Probate.*

Civil Records: Access: Phone, mail, in person, online. Only the court may perform in person searches. Search fee: $20.00 per hour. Fee is for lengthy search. Required to search: name, years to search. Civil cases indexed by defendant, plaintiff. Civil records on computer since 1995; prior on index cards from 1975, index books back to 1876. Online access to civil records is available at www.cocourts.com.

Criminal Records: Access: Mail, in person, online. Only the court may perform in person searches. Search fee: $8.00 per name. Required to search: name, years to search, DOB, signed release. Criminal records on computer since 1995; prior on index cards from 1975, index books back to 1876. Online access to criminal records is available at www.cocourts.com.

General Information: No adoptions, sealed, juvenile, mental health, open domestic, probate or expunged cases released. SASE required. Turnaround time 1 week. Copy fee: $.75 per page. Certification fee: $5.00. Fee payee: San Juan County Court. Business checks accepted. Prepayment is required.

San Miguel County

7th District & County Courts PO Box 919, Telluride, CO 81435; 970-728-3891; Fax: 970-728-6216. Hours: 9AM-Noon, 1PM-4:30PM (MST). *Felony, Misdemeanor, Civil, Eviction, Small Claims, Probate.*

Civil Records: Access: Phone, mail, in person, online. Only the court performs in person searches; visitors may not. Search fee: $5.00 per name if after 1994. Required to search: name, years to search. Civil cases indexed by defendant, plaintiff. Civil records on index cards from 1970, index books back to 1861, archived back to 1880; on computer back to 1994. Online access to civil records is available at www.cocourts.com. Will do very limited phone searches back to 1994.

Criminal Records: Access: Phone, mail, in person, online. Only the court performs in person searches; visitors may not. Search fee: $5.00 per name if after 1994. Required to search: name, years to search, DOB. Criminal records on index cards from 1970, index books back to 1861, archived back to 1880; on computer back to 1994. Online access to criminal records is available at www.cocourts.com. Will do very limited phone searches back to 1994.

General Information: No adoptions, sealed, juvenile, mental health or expunged cases released. SASE required. Turnaround time 30 days. Copy fee: $.75 per page. Certification fee: $5.00. Fee payee: Combined Courts. Personal checks accepted. Prepayment is required.

Sedgwick County

13th District & County Courts Third & Pine, Julesburg, CO 80737; 970-474-3627; Fax: 970-474-2026. Hours: 8AM-1PM (MST). *Felony, Misdemeanor, Civil, Eviction, Small Claims, Probate.*

www.courts.state.co.us

Civil Records: Access: Fax, mail, in person, online. Both court and visitors may perform in person searches. No search fee. Required to search: name; also helpful: years to search. Civil cases indexed by defendant, plaintiff. Civil records on index cards from early 1970s, index books back to 1889; on computer back to 8/1995. Online access to civil records is available at www.cocourts.com.

Criminal Records: Access: Fax, mail, in person, online. Both court and visitors may perform in person searches. Search fee: The court reserves the right to charge if an extensive search is required. Required to search: name, DOB; also helpful: years to search. Criminal records on index cards from early 1970s, index books back to 1889; on computer back to 8/1995. Online access to criminal records is available at www.cocourts.com.

General Information: No adoptions, sealed, juvenile, mental health or expunged cases released. SASE required. Turnaround time 1-2 days. Fax notes: Fee to fax results is $5.00 per document. Copy fee: $.75 per page. Certification fee: $5.00. Fee payee: Sedgwick County Combined Court. Personal checks accepted. Prepayment is required.

Summit County

5th District & County Courts PO Box 185, Breckenridge, CO 80424; 970-453-2241. Hours: 8AM-5PM (MST). *Felony, Misdemeanor, Civil, Eviction, Small Claims, Probate.*

www.courts.state.co.us

Note: District Court uses PO Box 269.

Civil Records: Access: In person, online. Visitors must perform in person searches for themselves. No search fee. Required to search: name. Civil cases indexed by defendant, plaintiff. Civil records on index cards from the early 1970s, index books back to 1861, archived from 1980 and prior. Online access to civil records is available at www.cocourts.com.

Criminal Records: Access: In person, online. Visitors must perform in person searches for themselves. No search fee. Required to search: name, DOB, signed release. Criminal records name index on computer as of 09/95. Online access to criminal records is available at www.cocourts.com.

General Information: No adoptions, sealed, juvenile, mental health or expunged cases released. Copy fee: $.75 per page. Certification fee: $5.00. Only cashiers checks and money orders accepted. Cash accepted in person. Prepayment is required.

Teller County

4th District & County Courts PO Box 997, Cripple Creek, CO 80813; 719-689-2543. Hours: 8AM-5PM (MST). *Felony, Misdemeanor, Civil, Eviction, Small Claims, Probate.*

www.tellercountycourts.com

Civil Records: Access: Mail, in person, online. Only the court performs in person searches; visitors may not. Search fee: $5.00 per name. If not on computer, fee is $20.00 per hour. Required to search: name, years to search. Civil cases indexed by defendant, plaintiff. Civil records computerized back to 1988, on index cards from 1960, index books back to 1899. Online access to civil records is available at www.cocourts.com. Also, a record request form is available to download at https://33.securedata.net/gofourth/pub_data_req_form.htm.

Criminal Records: Access: Mail, in person, online. Only the court performs in person searches; visitors may not. Search fee: $5.00 per name. If records not on computer, fee is $20.00 per hour. Required to search: name, years to search, DOB; also helpful: address, SSN. Criminal records computerized back to 1988, on index cards from 1960, index books back to 1899. Online access to criminal records is available at www.cocourts.com.

General Information: No adoptions, sealed, juvenile, mental health or expunged cases released. SASE required. Turnaround time 3-5 days, 4-6 weeks if not computerized. Copy fee: $.75 per page. Certification fee: $5.00. Fee payee: Teller County Combined Courts. Any form of payment is acceptable, including Visa/MC. Prepayment is required.

Washington County

Washington County Combined Court PO Box 455, Akron, CO 80720; 970-345-2756; Fax: 970-345-2829. Hours: 8AM-Noon, 1-5PM (MST). *Felony, Misdemeanor, Civil, Eviction, Small Claims, Probate.*

Civil Records: Access: Phone, mail, in person, online. Only the court may perform in person searches. No search fee. Required to search: name, years to search. Civil cases indexed by defendant. Civil records on index cards from 1970, index books back to 1887;

computerized since 1995. Online access to civil records is available at www.cocourts.com.

Criminal Records: Access: Phone, mail, in person, online. Only the court performs in person searches; visitors may not. No search fee. Required to search: name, years to search, DOB. Criminal records on index cards from 1970, index books back to 1887; computerized since 1995. Online access to criminal records is available at www.cocourts.com.

General Information: No adoptions, sealed, juvenile, mental health or expunged cases released. SASE required. Turnaround time 2-3 days. Copy fee: $.75 per page. Certification fee: $5.00. Fee payee: Washington County Combined Court. Personal checks accepted. Prepayment is required.

Weld County

19th District & County Courts PO Box 2038, Greeley, CO 80632; 970-351-7300; Fax: 970-356-4356. Hours: 8AM-5PM (MST). *Felony, Misdemeanor, Civil, Eviction, Small Claims, Probate.*

Civil Records: Access: Mail, in person, online. Only the court performs in person searches; visitors may not. Search fee: $5.00 per name. Required to search: name, years to search. Civil cases indexed by defendant, plaintiff. Civil records on computer from 1975 (District), 1990 (County), index cards from 1958, index books back to 1876. Online access to civil records is available at www.cocourts.com.

Criminal Records: Access: Mail, in person, online. Only the court performs in person searches; visitors may not. Search fee: $5.00 per name. Required to search: name, years to search; also helpful: DOB. Criminal records on computer from 1975 (District), 1990 (County), index cards from 1958, index books back to 1876. Online access to criminal records is available at www.cocourts.com.

General Information: No adoptions, sealed, juvenile, mental health or expunged cases released. SASE required. Turnaround time 3 days. Copy fee: $.75 per page. Certification fee: $5.00. Fee payee: Clerk of Court. Personal checks accepted. Prepayment is required.

Yuma County

13th District & County Courts PO Box 347, Wray, CO 80758; 970-332-4118; Fax: 970-332-4119. Hours: 8AM-4PM (MST). *Felony, Misdemeanor, Civil, Eviction, Small Claims, Probate.*

Civil Records: Access: Mail, in person, online. Only the court performs in person searches; visitors may not. Search fee: $5.00 per name. Required to search: name, years to search. Civil cases indexed by defendant. Civil records on index cards from 1982, index books back to 1889. Online access to civil records is available at www.cocourts.com.

Criminal Records: Access: Mail, in person, online. Only the court performs in person searches; visitors may not. Search fee: $5.00 per name. Required to search: name. Criminal records on index cards from 1982, index books back to 1889. Online access to criminal records is available at www.cocourts.com.

General Information: No adoptions, sealed, juvenile, mental health or expunged cases released. SASE required. Turnaround time 2-5 days. Copy fee: $.75 per page. Certification fee: $5.00. Fee payee: Yuma County Combined Court. Personal checks accepted. Prepayment is required.

Colorado Recording Offices

ORGANIZATION: 63 counties, 63 recording offices. The recording officer is County Clerk and Recorder. The entire state is in the Mountain Time Zone (MST).

November 15, 2001, Broomfield City and County comes into existence, derived from portions of Adams, Boulder, Jefferson and Weld counties. County offices are located at 1 Descombes Dr, Broomfield, CO 80020; 303-469-3301; hours 8AM-5PM. To determine if an address is in Broomfield, parcel search by address at www.co.broomfield.co.us/centralrecords/assessor.shtml

REAL ESTATE RECORDS: Counties do not perform real estate searches. Copy fees are usually $1.25 per page and certification fees are usually $1.00 per document. Tax records are located in the Assessor's Office.

UCC RECORDS: Financing statements are filed at the state level, except for real estate related collateral, which are filed with the County Clerk & Recorder. However, prior to 07/2001, consumer goods and farm collateral were also filed at the County Clerk & Recorder and these older records can be searched there. Nearly all counties perform UCC searches. Use search request form UCC-11. Search fees are usually $5.00 per debtor name for the first year and $2.00 for each additional year searched (or $13.00 for a five year search). Copies usually cost $1.25 per page.

TAX LIEN RECORDS: Federal and some state tax liens on personal property are filed with the Secretary of State. Other federal and state tax liens are filed with the County Clerk and Recorder. Many counties will perform tax lien searches, usually at the same fees as UCC searches. Copies usually cost $1.25 per page

OTHER LIENS: Judgments, motor vehicle, mechanics.

ONLINE ACCESS: To date, over 20 Colorado Counties offer free access to property assessor records.

At the state level, the Secretary of State offers web access to UCCs, and the Department of Revenue offers trade name searches. See the State Agencies section for details.

Adams County

County Clerk & Recorder, 450 S. 4th Ave, Administrative Building, Brighton, CO 80601-3197. County Clerk & Recorder, R/E and UCC Recording 303-654-6020; Fax 303-654-6009.
Will search UCC records. UCC search includes tax liens. Will not search real estate records. **Online Access:** Assessor, Property Records. Records from the Adams County Assessor database are available free at www.co.adams.co.us/gis/html/QuickSearchFSIE.htm. Also, search property information on the GIS mapping page for free at www.co.adams.co.us/gis. **Other Phone Numbers:** Assessor 303-654-6038; Treasurer 303-654-6160; Elections 303-654-6030.

Alamosa County

County Clerk & Recorder, PO Box 630, Alamosa, CO 81101. 719-589-6681; Fax 719-589-6118.
Will search UCC records. Tax liens not included in UCC search. Separate tax lien search aviable. Will not search real estate records. **Other Phone Numbers:** Assessor 719-589-6365; Treasurer 719-589-3626.

Arapahoe County

County Clerk & Recorder, 5334 S. Prince St, Littleton, CO 80166-0060. County Clerk & Recorder, R/E and UCC Recording 303-795-4520; Fax 303-794-4625. www.co.arapahoe.co.us
Will search UCC records. Tax Lien search fee-$5.00 1st year; $2.00 thereafter. Will not search real estate records. **Online Access:** Assessor Records. Records on the Arapahoe County Assessor database are available free online at www.co.arapahoe.co.us/as/ResForm.htm. **Other Phone Numbers:** Assessor 303-795-4600; Treasurer 303-795-4550; Appraiser/Auditor 303-795-4611; Elections 303-795-4511; Vital Records 303-756-4464.

Archuleta County

County Clerk & Recorder, PO Box 2589, Pagosa Springs, CO 81147-2589. County Clerk & Recorder, R/E and UCC Recording 970-264-5633; Fax 970-264-6423.
Will search UCC records. This agency will not do a tax lien search. Will not search real estate records. **Other Phone Numbers:** Assessor 970-264-4896; Treasurer 970-264-2152; Elections 970-264-5633.

Baca County

County Clerk & Recorder, 741 Main St, Courthouse, Springfield, CO 81073. County Clerk & Recorder, R/E and UCC Recording 719-523-4372; Fax 719-523-4881.
Will search UCC records. UCC search includes tax liens. Separate search costs same as UCC search Will not search real estate records. **Other Phone Numbers:** Assessor 719-523-4332; Treasurer 719-523-4262; Appraiser/Auditor 719-523-4332; Elections 719-523-4372; Vital Records 719-523-6665.

Bent County

County Clerk & Recorder, PO Box 350, Las Animas, CO 81054. 719-456-2009; Fax 719-456-0375.
Will search UCC records. This agency will not do a tax lien search. Will not search real estate records. **Other Phone Numbers:** Assessor 719-456-2010; Treasurer 719-456-2211.

Broomfield County

County Clerk & Recorder, One DesCombes Dr, Broomfield, CO 80020. 303-469-3301; Fax 303-438-6252 www.co.broomfield.co.us
Note: Became a county in 2001; further information is available at web site. Includes Zip Codes 80005, 80020, 80021, 80038, 80234. Will not search UCC records. Will not search real estate records. **Online Access:** Assessor, Real Estate records. Access to the assessor property database is available free at http://ims.ci.broomfield.co.us/website/htmlviewer/Parcelsearch/. Search by address or parcel ID only. No name searching. **Other Phone Numbers:** Central Records, all departments 303-464-5819.

Boulder County

County Clerk & Recorder, 1750 33rd St #201, Boulder, CO 80301. 303-413-7770; www.co.boulder.co.us
Will search UCC records. UCC search includes tax liens. Separate tax lien search costs same as UCC search Will not search real estate records. **Online Access:** Assessor, Property Tax, Voter Registration Records. Search the assessor's property database for free at www.co.boulder.co.us/assessor/disclaimer.htm. No name searching. Also, the county treasurer has data available electronically and on microfiche; Alpha index by owner name is $25.00 per set. Also, search property tax records at www.co.boulder.co.us/treas/disclaim.htm. No name searching. Also, search voter registration at www.co.boulder.co.us. Click on "Check your Voter Registration." Name and DOB required. **Other Phone Numbers:** Assessor 303-441-3530; Treasurer 303-441-3520; Elections 303-413-7740.

Chaffee County

County Clerk & Recorder, PO Box 699, Salida, CO 81201. 719-539-6913 R/E Recording: 719-539-4004; Fax 719-539-8588.
Will not search UCC records. UCC search includes tax liens. Real estate owner, mortgage, and property transfer searches available. **Other Phone Numbers:** Assessor 719-539-4016; Treasurer 719-539-6808; Elections 719-539-6913.

Cheyenne County

County Clerk & Recorder, PO Box 567, Cheyenne Wells, CO 80810. County Clerk & Recorder, R/E and UCC Recording 719-767-5685; Fax 719-767-5540.
Will search UCC records. This agency will not do a tax lien search. Will not search real estate records. **Other Phone Numbers:** Assessor 719-767-5664; Treasurer 719-767-5657; Elections 719-767-5685; Vital Records 719-767-5661.

Clear Creek County

County Clerk & Recorder, PO Box 2000, Georgetown, CO 80444-2000. County Clerk & Recorder, R/E and UCC Recording 303-679-2339; Fax 303-679-2441. www.co.clear-creek.co.us/Depts/depts.htm
Will not search UCC records. Will not search real estate records. **Other Phones:** Assessor 303-679-2322; Treasurer 303-679-2353; Appraiser/Auditor 303-679-2322; Elections 679-2339; Vital Records 679-2357.

Conejos County

County Clerk & Recorder, PO Box 127, Conejos, CO 81129-0127. 719-376-5422; Fax 719-376-5661.
Will search UCC records. UCC search includes tax liens if requested. Separate tax liens search costs the same as UCC search Real estate owner, mortgage, and property transfer searches available. **Other Phone Numbers:** Assessor 719-376-5585; 303-894-2202.

Costilla County

County Clerk & Recorder, PO Box 308, San Luis, CO 81152. 719-672-3301; Fax 719-672-3962.
This agency will not perform searches. **Other Phone Numbers:** Assessor 719-672-3642.

Crowley County

County Clerk & Recorder, 110 W. 6th St., Ordway, CO 81063-1092. 719-267-4643 x3; Fax 719-267-4608.
Will not search UCC records. Will not search real estate records. **Other Phone Numbers:** Assessor 719-267-4421 x5; Treasurer 719-267-4624 x4.

Custer County

County Clerk & Recorder, PO Box 150, Westcliffe, CO 81252. County Clerk & Recorder, R/E and UCC Recording 719-783-2441; Fax 719-783-2885.
Will search UCC records. UCC search includes tax liens if requested. Will not search real estate records. **Other Phones:** Assessor 719-783-2218; Treasurer 719-783-2341; Appraiser/Auditor 719-783-2218; Elections 719-783-2441; Vital Records 719-783-2441.

Delta County

County Clerk & Recorder, 501 Palmer St, Suite 211, Delta, CO 81416. County Clerk & Recorder, R/E and UCC Recording 970-874-2150; Fax 970-874-2161.
Will search UCC records. This agency will not do a tax lien search. Will not search real estate records. **Other Phone Numbers:** Assessor 970-874-2120; Treasurer 970-874-2135; Appraiser/Auditor 970-874-2120; Elections 970-874-2150; Vital Records 970-874-2150.

Denver County

County Clerk & Recorder, 1437 Bannock St #200, Denver, CO 80202. 303-640-7290; Fax 303-640-3628. www.denvergov.org
Will search UCC records. Tax liens not included in UCC search. Separate tax lien searches performed at same cost as UCC searches Will not search real estate records. **Online Access:** Assessor Records. Records on the Denver City and Denver County Assessor database are available at www.denvergov.org/realproperty.asp. **Other Phone Numbers:** Assessor 303-640-5555; Treasurer 303-640-5555.

Dolores County

County Clerk & Recorder, PO Box 58, Dove Creek, CO 81324-0058. County Clerk & Recorder, R/E and UCC Recording 970-677-2381; Fax 970-677-2815.
Will search UCC records. UCC search includes tax liens if requested. Separate tax lien search costs the same as a UCC search Will not search real estate records. **Other Phone Numbers:** Assessor 970-677-2385; Treasurer 970-677-2386; Appraiser/Auditor 970-677-2385; Elections 970-677-2381; Vital Records 970-677-2381.

Douglas County

County Clerk & Recorder, PO Box 1360, Castle Rock, CO 80104. 303-660-7446; Fax 303-688-3060. www.douglas.co.us/assessor
Will search UCC records. This agency will not do a tax lien search. Will not search real estate records. **Online Access:** Assessor, Property Records. Records on the county assessor database are available free at www.douglas.co.us/assessor. **Other Phone Numbers:** Assessor 303-660-7450.

Eagle County

County Clerk & Recorder, PO Box 537, Eagle, CO 81631. 970-328-8710 R/E Recording: 970-328-8723 UCC Recording: 970-328-8723; Fax 970-328-8716. www.eagle-county.com/dept.htm
Will search UCC records. UCC search includes tax liens. Will not search real estate records. **Online Access:** Assessor, Property, Sales Grantor/Grantee Records. Records on the County Assessor-Treasurer databases are available free online at www.eagle-county.com/Goodturns/assessor/search.asp?. **Other Phone Numbers:** Assessor 970-328-8640; Treasurer 970-328-8860; Elections 970-328-8715.

El Paso County

County Clerk & Recorder, PO Box 2007, Colorado Springs, CO 80901-2007. 719-520-6200; Fax 719-520-6230. www.co.el-paso.co.us or www.elpasoco.com
Will not search UCC records. UCC search includes federal tax liens Will not search real estate records. **Online Access:** Assessor Records. Records on the county Assessor database are available free online at http://land.elpasoco.com/default.htm. **Other Phone Numbers:** Assessor 719-520-6600; Treasurer 719-520-6666; Elections 719-520-8683; Vital Records 719-520-7475.

Elbert County

County Clerk & Recorder, PO Box 37, Kiowa, CO 80117. 303-621-3129, 303-621-3116; Fax 303-621-3168.
Will search UCC records. This agency will not do a tax lien search. Will not search real estate records. **Other Phone Numbers:** Assessor 303-621-3101; Treasurer 303-621-2341.

Fremont County

County Clerk & Recorder, 615 Macon Ave, Room 100, Canon City, CO 81212-3311. 719-276-7330; Fax 719-276-5342.
Will search UCC records. This agency will not do a tax lien search. Will not search real estate records. **Other Phone Numbers:** Assessor 719-276-7310.

Garfield County

County Clerk & Recorder, 109 8th St, Suite 200, Glenwood Springs, CO 81601. 970-945-2377; Fax 970-947-1078.
Will search UCC records. Tax liens not included in UCC search. Separate Federal tax lien searches performed at same cost as UCC searches. Will not search real estate records. **Other Phone Numbers:** Assessor 970-945-1377; Elections 970-945-2377.

Gilpin County

County Clerk & Recorder, PO Box 429, Central City, CO 80427. 303-582-5321; Fax 303-582-3086.
Will search UCC records. This agency will not do a tax lien search. Will not search real estate records. **Other Phone Numbers:** Assessor 303-582-5451; Treasurer 303-582-5322; Appraiser/Auditor 303-582-5451; Elections 303-582-5321.

Grand County

County Clerk & Recorder, PO Box 120, Hot Sulphur Springs, CO 80451. 970-725-3347 x273; Fax 970-725-0100. www.gcgovernment.com
Will search UCC records. This agency will not do a tax lien search. Will not search real estate records. **Online Access:** Property, Assessor, Grantor/Grantee, Recording Records. Access to the Clerk&Recorder database is available free at www.gcpermit.com/clerks. Also, the accessor database is available free at www.gcpermit.com/assessor. Also, property ownership information is available free at www.co.grand.co.us/Assessor/Download_Page.html. **Other Phone Numbers:** Assessor 970-725-3347 x219; Treasurer 970-725-3347 x269; Elections 970-725-3347 x224; Vital Records 970-725-3347 x213.

Gunnison County

County Clerk & Recorder, 200 E. Virginia Ave, Courthouse, Gunnison, CO 81230. 970-641-1516 R/E Recording: 970-641-7937; Fax 970-641-7690.
Will not search UCC records. Will not search real estate records.

Hinsdale County

County Clerk & Recorder, PO Box 9, Lake City, CO 81235. 970-944-2228; Fax 970-944-2202.
Will not search UCC records. Tax lien searches available. Will not search real estate records. **Other Phone Numbers:** Assessor 970-944-2224; Treasurer 970-944-2223.

Huerfano County

County Clerk & Recorder, Courthouse, Suite 204, 410 Main St., Walsenburg, CO 81089. 719-738-2380; Fax 719-738-2364.
Will not search UCC records. UCC search includes tax liens. Separate tax lien search costs same as UCC search Will not search real estate records. **Other Phone Numbers:** Assessor 719-738-1280; Treasurer 719-782-1191.

Jackson County

County Clerk & Recorder, PO Box 337, Walden, CO 80480-0337. 970-723-4334.
Will search UCC records. UCC search includes tax liens. Separate tax lien search costs same as UCC search. Will not search real estate records. **Other Phone Numbers:** Assessor 970-723-4751; Treasurer 970-723-4220.

Jefferson County

County Clerk & Recorder, 100 Jefferson County Parkway, #2530, Golden, CO 80419-2530. 303-271-8188 R/E Recording: 303-271-8121; Fax 303-271-8180.
http://206.247.49.21/ext/dpt/officials/clkrec/index.htm
Will search UCC records. This agency will not do a tax lien search. Real estate record owner and mortgage searches available. **Online Access:** Assessor, Property, Grantor/Grantee, Deed, Judgment, Recording Records. Records on the county Assessor database are available free online at http://206.247.49.21/ext/dpt/officials/assessor/index.htm. Also, search the recorder's Grantor/Grantee index for free at http://ww4.co.jefferson.co.us/crint/disclaimer.htm. **Other Phone Numbers:** Assessor 303-271-8666.

Kiowa County

County Clerk & Recorder, PO Box 37, Eads, CO 81036-0037. 719-438-5421; Fax 719-438-5327.
This agency will not perform searches. **Other Phone Numbers:** Assessor 719-438-5521.

Kit Carson County

County Clerk & Recorder, PO Box 249, Burlington, CO 80807-0249. 719-346-8638; Fax 719-346-7242. Will search UCC records. Tax liens not included in UCC search. Separate tax lien searches performed. Will not search real estate records. **Other Phone Numbers:** Assessor 719-346-8946; Treasurer 719-346-8434; Elections 719-346-8638; Vital Records 719-346-8133.

La Plata County

County Clerk & Recorder, PO Box 519, Durango, CO 81302-0519. 970-382-6281; Fax 970-382-6299. www.laplatainfo.com
This agency will not perform searches. **Online Access:** Assessor Records. Records on the county Assessor database are available free online at www.laplatainfo.com/search2.html. **Other Phones:** Assessor 970-382-6226; Treasurer 970-382-6245.

Lake County

County Clerk & Recorder, PO Box 917, Leadville, CO 80461. County Clerk & Recorder, R/E and UCC Recording 719-486-4131 UCC Recording: 719-894-2200; Fax 719-486-3972.
This agency will not perform searches. **Other Phones:** Assessor 719-486-0413; Treasurer 719-486-0530; Elections 719-486-1410; Vital Records 719-486-0708.

Larimer County

County Clerk & Recorder, PO Box 1280, Fort Collins, CO 80522-1280. County Clerk & Recorder, R/E and UCC Recording 970-498-7860; Fax 970-498-7830. www.larimer.org
Will search UCC records. UCC search includes tax liens. Separate tax lien search costs the same as UCC search Will not search real estate records. **Online Access:** Property Tax, Assessor, Treasurer, Voter Registration Records. Assessor records on the Larimer County Property Records database are available free at the web site. Search for County Treasurer Property Tax Records at www.co.larimer.co.us/depts/treasu/query/search.cfm. No name searching Also, search the County Clerk Recorder records for years 1971 to 1989 at www.co.larimer.co.us/depts/clerkr/query/arch_search.htm. Search the County Clerk Recorder records for years 1990 to present at www.co.larimer.co.us/depts/clerkr/query/search.htm. Search for County Voter records at www.co.larimer.co.us/depts/clerkr/elections/voter_inquiry.cfm. **Other Phone Numbers:** Assessor 970-498-7050; Treasurer 970-498-7020; Elections 970-498-7820; Vital Records 970-498-5710.

Las Animas County

County Clerk & Recorder, PO Box 115, Trinidad, CO 81082. 719-846-3314; Fax 719-845-2573.
This agency will not perform searches. **Other Phones:** Assessor 719-846-2295; Treasurer 719-846-2295.

Lincoln County

County Clerk & Recorder, PO Box 67, Hugo, CO 80821-0067. 719-743-2444; Fax 719-743-2838. Will search UCC records. Tax liens not included in UCC search. Separate tax lien searches performed at same fees as UCC searches. Will not search real estate records. **Other Phones:** Assessor 719-742-2358; Treasurer 719-742-2633; Vital Records 719-743-2796.

Logan County

County Clerk & Recorder, 315 Main St, Logan County Courthouse, Sterling, CO 80751. County Clerk & Recorder, R/E and UCC Recording 970-522-1544; Fax 970-522-2063. www.loganco.gov/departments.htm
Will search UCC records prior to 1/2001. UCC search includes tax liens if requested. Separate tax lien search costs same as UCC search Will not search real estate records. **Online Access:** Assessor, Real Estate Records.

Access to the Assessor's Property Search database is available free at www.loganco-assessor.org/search.asp?. **Other Phone Numbers:** Assessor 970-522-2797; Treasurer 970-522-2462; Elections 970-522-1544.

Mesa County

County Clerk & Recorder, PO Box 20000-5007, Grand Junction, CO 81502-5007. County Clerk & Recorder, R/E and UCC Recording 970-244-1679; Fax 970-256-1588. www.co.mesa.co.us
Will search UCC records. UCC search includes federal tax liens only Will not search real estate records. **Online Access:** Assessor, Real Estate, Property Tax Records. Records on the county Assessor database are available free at http://205.169.141.11/Assessor/Database/netsearch.html. Any search is by address or parcel #. You may also do parcel searches at http://mcweb.co.mesa.co.us/imd/gis/autoFrame.htm. There is also a GIS-mapping search page for property information at http://198.204.117.70/maps/index.htm. Also, an interactive Voice Response System lets callers access real property information at 970-256-1563. Fax back service is available. Also, search the Treasurer's Tax Status Information database for free at http://205.169.141.11/Treasurer/Database/NETSearch.HTML#Top. **Other Phone Numbers:** Assessor 970-244-1610; Treasurer 970-244-1824; Elections 970-244-1662; Vital Records 970-248-6900 (birth/death); Marriage Records 970-244-1679.

Mineral County

County Clerk & Recorder, PO Box 70, Creede, CO 81130. County Clerk & Recorder, R/E and UCC Recording 719-658-2440; Fax 719-658-2931.
Will search UCC records. UCC search includes tax liens if requested. Separate tax lien search costs $5.00 for first year, then $2.00 per year. Will not search real estate records. **Other Phone Numbers:** Assessor 719-658-2669; Treasurer 719-658-2325; Elections 719-658-2440; Vital Records 719-658-2497.

Moffat County

County Clerk & Recorder, 221 W. Victory Way, Craig, CO 81625-2716. County Clerk & Recorder, R/E and UCC Recording 970-824-9104; Fax 970-824-4975.
Will search UCC records. UCC search includes tax liens if requested. Will not search real estate records. **Other Phone Numbers:** Assessor 970-824-9102; Treasurer 970-824-9111; Elections 970-824-9104; Vital Records 970-824-9233.

Montezuma County

County Clerk & Recorder, 109 W. Main St, Room 108, Cortez, CO 81321. 970-565-3728 R/E Recording: 970-565-3728 x3 UCC Recording: 303-894-2200; Fax 970-564-0215. www.montezumainfo.com
Will not search real estate records. **Other Phone Numbers:** Assessor 970-565-3428; Treasurer 970-565-7550; Elections 970-565-3728 x4; Vital Records 970-565-3728 x3.

Montrose County

County Clerk & Recorder, PO Box 1289, Montrose, CO 81402. 970-249-3362; Fax 970-249-0757.
This agency will not perform searches. **Other Phone Numbers:** Assessor 970-249-3753; Treasurer 970-249-3565.

Morgan County

County Clerk & Recorder, PO Box 1399, Fort Morgan, CO 80701. County Clerk & Recorder, R/E and UCC Recording 970-542-3521; Fax 970-542-3520.
Will search UCC records. This agency will not do a tax lien search. Will not search real estate records. **Other Phone Numbers:** Assessor 970-542-3512; Treasurer 970-542-3518; Appraiser/Auditor 970-542-3512; Elections 970-542-3521; Vital Records 970-867-4918.

Otero County

County Clerk & Recorder, PO Box 511, La Junta, CO 81050-0511. 719-383-3020; Fax 719-383-3090. Will not search UCC records. Will not search real estate records. **Other Phone Numbers:** Assessor 719-383-3010; Treasurer 719-383-3030; Elections 719-383-3024; Vital Records 719-383-3040.

Ouray County

County Clerk & Recorder, PO Bin C, Ouray, CO 81427. County Clerk & Recorder, R/E and UCC Recording 970-325-4961 UCC Recording: 970-894-2200; Fax 970-325-0452. http://co.ouray.co.us
Will search UCC records. This agency will not do a tax lien search. Will not search real estate records. **Other Phone Numbers:** Assessor 970-325-4371; Treasurer 970-325-4487; Elections 970-325-4961; Vital Records 970-325-4487.

Park County

County Clerk & Recorder, PO Box 220, Fairplay, CO 80440. County Clerk & Recorder, R/E and UCC Recording 719-836-4333; Fax 719-836-4348. www.parkco.org
Will search UCC records. Separate tax lien search costs same as UCC search. Will not search real estate records. **Online Access:** Assessor Records. Records on the county Assessor database are available free online at www.parkco.org/Search2.asp? including tax information, owner, address, building characteristics, legal and deed information. **Other Phones:** Assessor 719-836-2771 x186; Treasurer 719-836-2771 x242; Elections 719-836-4223; Vital Records 719-836-4227.

Phillips County

County Clerk & Recorder, 221 S. Interocean, Holyoke, CO 80734. 970-854-3131; Fax 970-854-4745.
This agency will not perform searches. **Other Phones:** Assessor 970-854-3151; Treasurer 970-852-2822.

Pitkin County

County Clerk & Recorder, 530 E. Main St., #101, Aspen, CO 81611. 970-920-5180; Fax 970-920-5196. www.pitkingov.com
This agency will not perform searches. **Online Access:** Assessor, Inmates Records. Records on the county Assessor database are available free online at www.mitchandco.com/realestate/pitkin/index.cfm. Also, the sheriff's current inmate list is available free at www.pitkin-sheriff.com/inmate/jailcip.html. **Other Phone Numbers:** Assessor 970-920-5160.

Prowers County

County Clerk & Recorder, 301 S. Main St #210, Lamar, CO 81052. County Clerk & Recorder, R/E and UCC Recording 719-336-8011; Fax 719-336-5306.
Will search UCC records. This agency will not do a tax lien search. Will not search real estate records. **Other Phone Numbers:** Assessor 719-336-8000; Treasurer 719-336-8081; Appraiser/Auditor 719-336-8000; Elections 719-336-8011; Vital Records 719-336-2606.

Pueblo County

County Clerk & Recorder, PO Box 878, Pueblo, CO 81002-0878. 719-583-6625 R/E Recording: 719-583-6629; Fax 719-583-6549. www.co.pueblo.co.us/index2.htm
Will search UCC records. This agency will not do a tax lien search. Will not search real estate records. **Online Access:** Assessor, Real Estate Records. Access to the county assessor database is available free at http://pueblocountyassessor.org/FrontPage.html. **Other Phone Numbers:** Assessor 719-583-6564; Treasurer 719-583-6015; Appraiser/Auditor 719-583-6596; Elections 719-583-6620; Vital Records 719-583-4555; Main switchboard 719-583-6000.

Rio Blanco County

County Clerk & Recorder, PO Box 1067, Meeker, CO 81641. 970-878-5068.
Will not search UCC records, requesters sent to state level. Tax lien records filed with real property records. Will not search real estate records. **Other Phone Numbers:** Assessor 970-878-5686; Treasurer 970-878-3614.

Rio Grande County

County Clerk & Recorder, PO Box 160, Del Norte, CO 81132. 719-657-3334; Fax 719-657-2621.
Will search UCC records. This agency will not do a tax lien search. Will not search real estate records. **Other Phone Numbers:** Assessor 719-657-3326.

Routt County

County Clerk & Recorder, PO Box 773598, Steamboat Springs, CO 80477. County Clerk & Recorder, R/E and UCC Recording 970-870-5556; Fax 970-870-1329. www.co.routt.co.us/clerk
Will search UCC records. UCC search includes tax liens. Will not search real estate records. **Online Access:** Real Estate, Assessor, Treasurer Records. Records on the county Assessor/Treasurer Property Search database are available free online at http://pioneer.yampa.com/asp/assessor/search.asp?. Records on the Routt County Clerk and Recorder Reception Search database are available free online at http://pioneer.yampa.com/asp/clerk/search.asp?. **Other Phone Numbers:** Assessor 970-879-2756; Treasurer 970-870-5555; Appraiser/Auditor 970-870-5554; Elections 970-870-5556; Vital Records 970-879-1632.

Saguache County

County Clerk & Recorder, PO Box 176, Saguache, CO 81149-0176. 719-655-2512; Fax 719-655-2635.
This agency will not perform searches. **Other Phone Numbers:** Assessor 719-655-2521; Treasurer 719-655-2656.

San Juan County

County Clerk & Recorder, PO Box 466, Silverton, CO 81433-0466. County Clerk & Recorder, R/E and UCC Recording 970-387-5671; Fax 970-387-5671.
Will search UCC records. UCC search includes tax liens if requested. Will not search real estate records. **Other Phone Numbers:** Assessor 970-387-5632; Treasurer 970-389-5488; Elections 970-387-5671; Vital Records 970-387-5488.

San Miguel County

County Clerk & Recorder, PO Box 548, Telluride, CO 81435-0548. 970-728-3954; Fax 970-728-4808.
Will search UCC records. This agency will not do a tax lien search. Will not search real estate records. **Other Phone Numbers:** Assessor 970-728-3174; Treasurer 970-728-4451.

Sedgwick County

County Clerk & Recorder, PO Box 50, Julesburg, CO 80737. County Clerk & Recorder, R/E and UCC Recording 970-474-3346; Fax 970-474-0954.
Will not search or retrieve UCC records unless provided the book and page number. Will not search real estate records. **Other Phone Numbers:** Assessor 970-474-2531; Treasurer 970-474-3473; Elections 970-474-3346; Vital Records 970-474-3473.

Summit County

County Clerk & Recorder, PO Box 1538, Breckenridge, CO 80424. County Clerk & Recorder, R/E and UCC Recording 970-453-3475; Fax 970-453-3540. www.co.summit.co.us
Will search UCC records. UCC search includes tax liens. Will not search real estate records. **Other Phone Numbers:** Assessor 970-453-3480; Treasurer 970-453-3440; Appraiser/Auditor 970-453-3480; Elections 970-453-3479; Vital Records 970-453-3472.

Teller County

County Clerk & Recorder, PO Box 1010, Cripple Creek, CO 80813-1010. 719-689-2951 R/E Recording: 719-689-2951 extension 4; Fax 719-689-3524. www.co.teller.co.us
Will search UCC records. Separate tax lien search costs same as UCC search. Will not search real estate records. **Other Phone Numbers:** Assessor 719-689-2941; Treasurer 719-689-2985; Elections 719-689-2951 x5 or 6; Vital Records 719-689-2951 x4.

Washington County

County Clerk & Recorder, PO Box L, Akron, CO 80720-0380. County Clerk & Recorder, R/E and UCC Recording 970-345-6565 UCC Recording: 303-894-2200; Fax 970-345-6607.
This agency will not perform searches. **Other Phone Numbers:** Assessor 970-345-6662; Treasurer 970-345-6601; Appraiser/Auditor 970-345-6662; Elections 970-345-6565; Vital Records 970-345-6627.

Weld County

County Clerk & Recorder, PO Box 459, Greeley, CO 80632-0459. 970-353-3065 x3065 R/E Recording: 970-304-6530 x3065 UCC Recording: 970-304-6530 x3065; Fax 970-353-1964. www.co.weld.co.us
Will not search UCC records. Separate tax lien search available. Will not search real estate records. **Online Access:** Real Estate Records. Search property information on the map server database available at the web site. Click on the "Property Information and mapping" button then search by name. **Other Phone Numbers:** Assessor 970-304-3845 x3650; Treasurer 970-304-3845 x3290; Elections 970-304-6525 x3070.

Yuma County

County Clerk & Recorder, PO Box 426, Wray, CO 80758-0426. County Clerk & Recorder, R/E and UCC Recording 970-332-5809.
Will search UCC records. UCC search includes tax liens. Will not search real estate records. **Other Phone Numbers:** Assessor 970-332-5032; Treasurer 970-332-4965; Appraiser/Auditor 970-332-5032; Elections 970-332-5809; Vital Records 970-332-5809.

Colorado County Locator

You will usually be able to find the city name in the City/County Cross Reference below. In that case, it is a simple matter to determine the county from the cross reference. However, only the official US Postal Service city names are included in this index. There are an additional 40,000 place names that people use in their addresses. Therefore, we have also included a ZIP/City Cross Reference immediately following the City/County Cross Reference.

If you know the ZIP Code but the city name does not appear in the City/County Cross Reference index, look up the ZIP Code in the ZIP/City Cross Reference, find the city name, then look up the city name in the City/County Cross Reference. For example, you want to know the county for an address of Menands, NY 12204. There is no "Menands" in the City/County Cross Reference. The ZIP/City Cross Reference shows that ZIP Codes 12201-12288 are for the city of Albany. Looking back in the City/County Cross Reference, Albany is in Albany County.

City/County Cross Reference

AGATE Elbert
AGUILAR Las Animas
AKRON Washington
ALAMOSA Alamosa
ALLENSPARK (80510) Boulder(98), Larimer(1)
ALMA Park
ALMONT Gunnison
AMHERST Phillips
ANTON Washington
ANTONITO Conejos
ARAPAHOE Cheyenne
ARBOLES Archuleta
ARLINGTON (81021) Kiowa(78), Lincoln(21)
ARRIBA Lincoln
ARVADA Jefferson
ASPEN Pitkin
ATWOOD Logan
AULT Weld
AURORA Arapahoe
AUSTIN Delta
AVON Eagle
AVONDALE Pueblo
BAILEY Park
BASALT (81621) Eagle(65), Pitkin(34)
BATTLEMENT MESA Garfield
BAYFIELD La Plata
BEDROCK Montrose
BELLVUE Larimer
BENNETT (80102) Adams(52), Arapahoe(41), Elbert(5)
BERTHOUD (80513) Larimer(91), Weld(8)
BETHUNE Kit Carson
BEULAH Pueblo
BLACK HAWK Gilpin
BLANCA Costilla
BONCARBO Las Animas
BOND Eagle
BOONE Pueblo
BOULDER Boulder
BOYERO Lincoln
BRANSON Las Animas
BRECKENRIDGE Summit
BRIGGSDALE Weld
BRIGHTON (80603) Adams(56), Weld(43)
BRISTOL Prowers
BROOMFIELD Broomfield
BRUSH (80723) Morgan(98), Washington(1)
BUENA VISTA Chaffee
BUFFALO CREEK Jefferson
BURLINGTON (80807) Kit Carson(98), Yuma(1)
BURNS Eagle
BYERS (80103) Arapahoe(88), Adams(11)
CAHONE Dolores
CALHAN (80808) El Paso(93), Elbert(6)
CAMPO Baca
CANON CITY Fremont
CAPULIN Conejos
CARBONDALE (81623) Garfield(64), Eagle(13), Pitkin(12), Gunnison(9)
CARR Weld
CASCADE El Paso
CASTLE ROCK Douglas
CEDAREDGE Delta
CENTER (81125) Saguache(67), Rio Grande(29), Alamosa(3)
CENTRAL CITY Gilpin

CHAMA Costilla
CHERAW Otero
CHEYENNE WELLS Cheyenne
CHIMNEY ROCK Archuleta
CHROMO Archuleta
CIMARRON (81220) Gunnison(81), Montrose(18)
CLARK Routt
CLIFTON Mesa
CLIMAX Lake
COAL CREEK Fremont
COALDALE Fremont
COALMONT Jackson
COKEDALE Las Animas
COLLBRAN Mesa
COLORADO CITY Pueblo
COLORADO SPRINGS El Paso
COMMERCE CITY Adams
COMO Park
CONEJOS Conejos
CONIFER Jefferson
COPE (80812) Washington(96), Yuma(3)
CORTEZ Montezuma
CORY Delta
COTOPAXI Fremont
COWDREY Jackson
CRAIG Moffat
CRAWFORD (81415) Delta(78), Montrose(21)
CREEDE Mineral
CRESTED BUTTE Gunnison
CRESTONE Saguache
CRIPPLE CREEK Teller
CROOK Logan
CROWLEY Crowley
DACONO Weld
DE BEQUE (81630) Mesa(68), Garfield(31)
DEER TRAIL (80105) Arapahoe(50), Elbert(27), Adams(22)
DEL NORTE (81132) Rio Grande(88), Saguache(11)
DELTA (81416) Delta(95), Montrose(4)
DENVER Denver
DILLON Summit
DINOSAUR Moffat
DIVIDE Teller
DOLORES Montezuma
DOVE CREEK (81324) Dolores(98), San Miguel(1)
DRAKE Larimer
DUMONT Clear Creek
DUPONT Adams
DURANGO La Plata
EADS Kiowa
EAGLE Eagle
EASTLAKE Adams
EATON Weld
ECKERT Delta
ECKLEY Yuma
EDWARDS Eagle
EGNAR (81325) Dolores(84), San Miguel(15)
EL JEBEL Eagle
ELBERT (80106) El Paso(58), Elbert(39), Douglas(1)
ELDORADO SPRINGS Boulder
ELIZABETH Elbert
EMPIRE Clear Creek
ENGLEWOOD Arapahoe
ERIE (80516) Weld(57), Boulder(42)

ESTES PARK Larimer
EVANS Weld
EVERGREEN (80439) Jefferson(85), Clear Creek(14)
FAIRPLAY (80440) Park(64), Adams(35)
FIRESTONE Weld
FLAGLER (80815) Kit Carson(85), Washington(14)
FLEMING Logan
FLORENCE Fremont
FLORISSANT (80816) Teller(76), Park(23)
FORT COLLINS Larimer
FORT GARLAND Costilla
FORT LUPTON Weld
FORT LYON Bent
FORT MORGAN (80701) Morgan(92), Adams(7)
FOUNTAIN El Paso
FOWLER (81039) Otero(91), Pueblo(6), Crowley(1)
FOXTON Jefferson
FRANKTOWN Douglas
FRASER Grand
FREDERICK Weld
FRISCO Summit
FRUITA Mesa
GALETON Weld
GARCIA Costilla
GARDNER Huerfano
GATEWAY Mesa
GENOA (80818) Lincoln(82), Washington(17)
GEORGETOWN Clear Creek
GILCREST Weld
GILL Weld
GLADE PARK Mesa
GLEN HAVEN Larimer
GLENWOOD SPRINGS Garfield
GOLDEN Jefferson
GRANADA (81041) Prowers(92), Baca(7)
GRANBY Grand
GRAND JUNCTION Mesa
GRAND LAKE Grand
GRANITE (81228) Lake(66), Chaffee(33)
GRANT Park
GREELEY Weld
GREEN MOUNTAIN FALLS El Paso
GROVER Weld
GUFFEY Park
GULNARE Las Animas
GUNNISON Gunnison
GYPSUM (81637) Eagle(91), Garfield(8)
HAMILTON (81638) Moffat(58), Routt(32), Rio Blanco(8)
HARTMAN Prowers
HARTSEL Park
HASTY Bent
HASWELL (81045) Kiowa(66), Cheyenne(18), Lincoln(14)
HAXTUN (80731) Phillips(54), Logan(24), Yuma(21)
HAYDEN Routt
HENDERSON Adams
HEREFORD Weld
HESPERUS La Plata
HILLROSE Morgan
HILLSIDE Fremont
HOEHNE Las Animas
HOLLY (81047) Prowers(93), Kiowa(4), Baca(2)

HOLYOKE (80734) Phillips(95), Yuma(4)
HOMELAKE Rio Grande
HOOPER (81136) Alamosa(95), Saguache(4)
HOT SULPHUR SPRINGS Grand
HOTCHKISS Delta
HOWARD Fremont
HUDSON Weld
HUGO Lincoln
HYGIENE Boulder
IDAHO SPRINGS Clear Creek
IDALIA Yuma
IDLEDALE Jefferson
IGNACIO La Plata
ILIFF Logan
INDIAN HILLS Jefferson
JAMESTOWN Boulder
JAROSO Costilla
JEFFERSON Park
JOES Yuma
JOHNSTOWN (80534) Weld(98), Larimer(1)
JULESBURG Sedgwick
KARVAL Lincoln
KEENESBURG Weld
KERSEY Weld
KIM Las Animas
KIOWA Elbert
KIRK (80824) Yuma(98), Kit Carson(1)
KIT CARSON Cheyenne
KITTREDGE Jefferson
KREMMLING Grand
LA JARA Conejos
LA JUNTA Otero
LA SALLE Weld
LA VETA Huerfano
LAFAYETTE Boulder
LAKE CITY Hinsdale
LAKE GEORGE (80827) Teller(72), Park(27)
LAKEWOOD Jefferson
LAMAR (81052) Prowers(98), Bent(1)
LAPORTE Larimer
LARKSPUR Douglas
LAS ANIMAS Bent
LAZEAR Delta
LEADVILLE Lake
LEWIS Montezuma
LIMON (80828) Lincoln(69), Elbert(30)
LINDON Washington
LITTLETON Arapahoe
LIVERMORE Larimer
LOG LANE VILLAGE Morgan
LOMA Mesa
LONGMONT (80504) Weld(66), Boulder(31), Larimer(2)
LOUISVILLE Boulder
LOUVIERS Douglas
LOVELAND Larimer
LUCERNE Weld
LYONS (80540) Larimer(51), Boulder(48)
MACK Mesa
MAHER Delta
MANASSA Conejos
MANCOS (81328) Montezuma(95), La Plata(4)
MANITOU SPRINGS El Paso
MANZANOLA (81058) Otero(77), Crowley(22)
MARVEL La Plata

MASONVILLE Larimer
MATHESON Elbert
MAYBELL Moffat
MC CLAVE Bent
MC COY (80463) Eagle(76), Routt(23)
MEAD (80542) Weld(91), Boulder(8)
MEEKER (81641) Rio Blanco(93), Moffat(4), Garfield(1)
MEREDITH Pitkin
MERINO (80741) Logan(90), Washington(7), Morgan(1)
MESA Mesa
MESA VERDE NATIONAL PARK Montezuma
MILLIKEN Weld
MINTURN Eagle
MODEL (81059) Las Animas(76), Otero(23)
MOFFAT Saguache
MOLINA Mesa
MONARCH Chaffee
MONTE VISTA (81144) Rio Grande(96), Alamosa(3)
MONTROSE Montrose
MONUMENT El Paso
MORRISON Jefferson
MOSCA Alamosa
NATHROP Chaffee
NATURITA Montrose
NEDERLAND Boulder
NEW CASTLE Garfield
NEW RAYMER (80742) Weld(63), Morgan(36)
NIWOT Boulder
NORWOOD San Miguel
NUCLA Montrose
NUNN Weld
OAK CREEK Routt
OHIO CITY Gunnison
OLATHE Montrose
OLNEY SPRINGS (81062) Crowley(94), Pueblo(5)
OPHIR San Miguel
ORCHARD (80649) Morgan(56), Weld(43)
ORDWAY (81063) Crowley(95), Lincoln(4)
OTIS (80743) Washington(97), Logan(2)
OURAY Ouray
OVID Sedgwick

PADRONI Logan
PAGOSA SPRINGS Archuleta
PALISADE Mesa
PALMER LAKE (80133) El Paso(90), Douglas(9)
PAOLI Phillips
PAONIA Delta
PARACHUTE Garfield
PARADOX Montrose
PARKER (80138) Douglas(78), Elbert(21)
PARLIN Gunnison
PARSHALL Grand
PEETZ Logan
PENROSE Fremont
PEYTON El Paso
PHIPPSBURG Routt
PIERCE Weld
PINE (80470) Jefferson(66), Park(33)
PINECLIFFE Boulder
PITKIN Gunnison
PLACERVILLE San Miguel
PLATTEVILLE Weld
PLEASANT VIEW Montezuma
PONCHA SPRINGS Chaffee
POWDERHORN Gunnison
PRITCHETT (81064) Baca(76), Las Animas(23)
PRYOR Huerfano
PUEBLO Pueblo
RAMAH (80832) El Paso(52), Elbert(38), Lincoln(8)
RAND Jackson
RANGELY Rio Blanco
RED CLIFF Eagle
RED FEATHER LAKES Larimer
RED WING Huerfano
REDVALE Montrose
RICO Dolores
RIDGWAY Ouray
RIFLE (81650) Garfield(95), Rio Blanco(4)
ROCKVALE Fremont
ROCKY FORD Otero
ROGGEN Weld
ROLLINSVILLE Gilpin
ROMEO Conejos
RUSH (80833) El Paso(48), Lincoln(39), Elbert(11)

RYE Pueblo
SAGUACHE Saguache
SALIDA Chaffee
SAN ACACIO Costilla
SAN LUIS Costilla
SAN PABLO Costilla
SANFORD (81151) Conejos(90), Costilla(8), Rio Grande(1)
SARGENTS Saguache
SEDALIA Douglas
SEDGWICK Sedgwick
SEGUNDO Las Animas
SEIBERT (80834) Kit Carson(90), Washington(9)
SEVERANCE Weld
SHAWNEE Park
SHERIDAN LAKE Kiowa
SILT Garfield
SILVER CLIFF Custer
SILVER PLUME Clear Creek
SILVERTHORNE Summit
SILVERTON San Juan
SIMLA (80835) Elbert(88), El Paso(11)
SLATER Moffat
SLICK ROCK San Miguel
SNOWMASS Pitkin
SNOWMASS VILLAGE Pitkin
SNYDER Morgan
SOMERSET (81434) Gunnison(90), Delta(9)
SOUTH FORK Rio Grande
SPRINGFIELD Baca
STARKVILLE Las Animas
STEAMBOAT SPRINGS Routt
STERLING Logan
STONEHAM Weld
STONINGTON Baca
STRASBURG (80136) Adams(70), Arapahoe(29)
STRATTON Kit Carson
SUGAR CITY (81076) Crowley(94), Lincoln(3), Kiowa(1)
SWINK Otero
TABERNASH Grand
TELLURIDE San Miguel
TIMNATH Larimer
TOPONAS Routt

TOWAOC Montezuma
TRINCHERA Las Animas
TRINIDAD Las Animas
TWIN LAKES Lake
TWO BUTTES (81084) Baca(89), Prowers(10)
U S A F ACADEMY El Paso
VAIL Eagle
VERNON Yuma
VICTOR Teller
VILAS Baca
VILLA GROVE Saguache
VIRGINIA DALE Larimer
VONA (80861) Kit Carson(99), Yuma(1)
WALDEN Jackson
WALSENBURG Huerfano
WALSH Baca
WARD Boulder
WATKINS (80137) Arapahoe(54), Adams(45)
WELDONA Morgan
WELLINGTON (80549) Larimer(95), Weld(4)
WESTCLIFFE Custer
WESTMINSTER Adams
WESTON Las Animas
WETMORE (81253) Custer(65), Fremont(29), Pueblo(5)
WHEAT RIDGE Jefferson
WHITEWATER Mesa
WIGGINS (80654) Morgan(97), Adams(2)
WILD HORSE Cheyenne
WILEY (81092) Prowers(59), Bent(37), Kiowa(3)
WINDSOR Weld
WINTER PARK Grand
WOLCOTT Eagle
WOODLAND PARK Teller
WOODROW Washington
WOODY CREEK Pitkin
WRAY Yuma
YAMPA Routt
YELLOW JACKET Montezuma
YODER El Paso
YUMA Yuma

ZIP/City Cross Reference

ZIP	City
80001-80007	ARVADA
80010-80019	AURORA
80020-80021	BROOMFIELD
80022-80022	COMMERCE CITY
80024-80024	DUPONT
80025-80025	ELDORADO SPRINGS
80026-80026	LAFAYETTE
80027-80028	LOUISVILLE
80030-80031	WESTMINSTER
80033-80034	WHEAT RIDGE
80035-80036	WESTMINSTER
80037-80037	COMMERCE CITY
80038-80038	BROOMFIELD
80040-80047	AURORA
80101-80101	AGATE
80102-80102	BENNETT
80103-80103	BYERS
80104-80104	CASTLE ROCK
80105-80105	DEER TRAIL
80106-80106	ELBERT
80107-80107	ELIZABETH
80110-80112	ENGLEWOOD
80116-80116	FRANKTOWN
80117-80117	KIOWA
80118-80118	LARKSPUR
80120-80130	LITTLETON
80131-80131	LOUVIERS
80132-80132	MONUMENT
80133-80133	PALMER LAKE
80134-80134	PARKER
80135-80135	SEDALIA
80136-80136	STRASBURG
80137-80137	WATKINS
80138-80138	PARKER
80150-80155	ENGLEWOOD

ZIP	City
80160-80166	LITTLETON
80201-80214	DENVER
80215-80215	LAKEWOOD
80216-80225	DENVER
80226-80226	LAKEWOOD
80227-80227	DENVER
80228-80228	LAKEWOOD
80229-80231	DENVER
80232-80232	LAKEWOOD
80233-80299	DENVER
80301-80329	BOULDER
80401-80419	GOLDEN
80420-80420	ALMA
80421-80421	BAILEY
80422-80422	BLACK HAWK
80423-80423	BOND
80424-80424	BRECKENRIDGE
80425-80425	BUFFALO CREEK
80426-80426	BURNS
80427-80427	CENTRAL CITY
80428-80428	CLARK
80429-80429	CLIMAX
80430-80430	COALMONT
80432-80432	COMO
80433-80433	CONIFER
80434-80434	COWDREY
80435-80435	DILLON
80436-80436	DUMONT
80437-80437	EVERGREEN
80438-80438	EMPIRE
80439-80439	EVERGREEN
80440-80440	FAIRPLAY
80441-80441	FOXTON
80442-80442	FRASER
80443-80443	FRISCO

ZIP	City
80444-80444	GEORGETOWN
80446-80446	GRANBY
80447-80447	GRAND LAKE
80448-80448	GRANT
80449-80449	HARTSEL
80451-80451	HOT SULPHUR SPRINGS
80452-80452	IDAHO SPRINGS
80453-80453	IDLEDALE
80454-80454	INDIAN HILLS
80455-80455	JAMESTOWN
80456-80456	JEFFERSON
80457-80457	KITTREDGE
80459-80459	KREMMLING
80461-80461	LEADVILLE
80463-80463	MC COY
80465-80465	MORRISON
80466-80466	NEDERLAND
80467-80467	OAK CREEK
80468-80468	PARSHALL
80469-80469	PHIPPSBURG
80470-80470	PINE
80471-80471	PINECLIFFE
80473-80473	RAND
80474-80474	ROLLINSVILLE
80475-80475	SHAWNEE
80476-80476	SILVER PLUME
80477-80477	STEAMBOAT SPRINGS
80478-80478	TABERNASH
80479-80479	TOPONAS
80480-80480	WALDEN
80481-80481	WARD
80482-80482	WINTER PARK
80483-80483	YAMPA
80487-80488	STEAMBOAT SPRINGS
80497-80498	SILVERTHORNE

ZIP	City
80501-80504	LONGMONT
80510-80510	ALLENSPARK
80511-80511	ESTES PARK
80512-80512	BELLVUE
80513-80513	BERTHOUD
80514-80514	DACONO
80515-80515	DRAKE
80516-80516	ERIE
80517-80517	ESTES PARK
80520-80520	FIRESTONE
80521-80528	FORT COLLINS
80530-80530	FREDERICK
80532-80532	GLEN HAVEN
80533-80533	HYGIENE
80534-80534	JOHNSTOWN
80535-80535	LAPORTE
80536-80536	LIVERMORE
80537-80539	LOVELAND
80540-80540	LYONS
80541-80541	MASONVILLE
80542-80542	MEAD
80543-80543	MILLIKEN
80544-80544	NIWOT
80545-80545	RED FEATHER LAKES
80546-80546	SEVERANCE
80547-80547	TIMNATH
80548-80548	LAPORTE
80548-80548	VIRGINIA DALE
80549-80549	WELLINGTON
80550-80551	WINDSOR
80553-80553	FORT COLLINS
80601-80603	BRIGHTON
80610-80610	AULT
80611-80611	BRIGGSDALE
80612-80612	CARR

80614-80614 EASTLAKE	80826-80826 LIMON	81121-81121 ARBOLES	81330-81330 MESA VERDE NATIONAL PARK
80615-80615 EATON	80827-80827 LAKE GEORGE	81122-81122 BAYFIELD	81331-81331 PLEASANT VIEW
80620-80620 EVANS	80828-80828 LIMON	81123-81123 BLANCA	81332-81332 RICO
80621-80621 FORT LUPTON	80829-80829 MANITOU SPRINGS	81124-81124 CAPULIN	81333-81333 SLICK ROCK
80622-80622 GALETON	80830-80830 MATHESON	81125-81125 CENTER	81334-81334 TOWAOC
80623-80623 GILCREST	80831-80831 PEYTON	81126-81126 CHAMA	81335-81335 YELLOW JACKET
80624-80624 GILL	80832-80832 RAMAH	81127-81127 CHIMNEY ROCK	81401-81402 MONTROSE
80631-80639 GREELEY	80833-80833 RUSH	81128-81128 CHROMO	81410-81410 AUSTIN
80640-80640 HENDERSON	80834-80834 SEIBERT	81129-81129 CONEJOS	81411-81411 BEDROCK
80642-80642 HUDSON	80835-80835 SIMLA	81130-81130 CREEDE	81413-81413 CEDAREDGE
80643-80643 KEENESBURG	80836-80836 STRATTON	81131-81131 CRESTONE	81414-81414 CORY
80644-80644 KERSEY	80840-80841 U S A F ACADEMY	81132-81132 DEL NORTE	81415-81415 CRAWFORD
80645-80645 LA SALLE	80860-80860 VICTOR	81133-81133 FORT GARLAND	81416-81416 DELTA
80646-80646 LUCERNE	80861-80861 VONA	81134-81134 GARCIA	81418-81418 ECKERT
80648-80648 NUNN	80862-80862 WILD HORSE	81135-81135 HOMELAKE	81419-81419 HOTCHKISS
80649-80649 ORCHARD	80863-80863 WOODLAND PARK	81136-81136 HOOPER	81420-81420 LAZEAR
80650-80650 PIERCE	80864-80864 YODER	81137-81137 IGNACIO	81421-81421 MAHER
80651-80651 PLATTEVILLE	80866-80866 WOODLAND PARK	81138-81138 JAROSO	81422-81422 NATURITA
80652-80652 ROGGEN	80900-80997 COLORADO SPRINGS	81140-81140 LA JARA	81423-81423 NORWOOD
80653-80653 WELDONA	81001-81005 PUEBLO	81141-81141 MANASSA	81424-81424 NUCLA
80654-80654 WIGGINS	81019-81019 COLORADO CITY	81143-81143 MOFFAT	81425-81425 OLATHE
80701-80701 FORT MORGAN	81020-81020 AGUILAR	81144-81144 MONTE VISTA	81426-81426 OPHIR
80705-80705 LOG LANE VILLAGE	81021-81021 ARLINGTON	81146-81146 MOSCA	81427-81427 OURAY
80720-80720 AKRON	81022-81022 AVONDALE	81147-81147 PAGOSA SPRINGS	81428-81428 PAONIA
80721-80721 AMHERST	81023-81023 BEULAH	81148-81148 ROMEO	81429-81429 PARADOX
80722-80722 ATWOOD	81024-81024 BONCARBO	81149-81149 SAGUACHE	81430-81430 PLACERVILLE
80723-80723 BRUSH	81025-81025 BOONE	81150-81150 SAN ACACIO	81431-81431 REDVALE
80726-80726 CROOK	81026-81026 EADS	81151-81151 SANFORD	81432-81432 RIDGWAY
80727-80727 ECKLEY	81027-81027 BRANSON	81152-81152 SAN LUIS	81433-81433 SILVERTON
80728-80728 FLEMING	81028-81028 BRISTOL	81153-81153 SAN PABLO	81434-81434 SOMERSET
80729-80729 GROVER	81029-81029 CAMPO	81154-81154 SOUTH FORK	81435-81435 TELLURIDE
80731-80731 HAXTUN	81030-81030 CHERAW	81155-81155 VILLA GROVE	81501-81506 GRAND JUNCTION
80732-80732 HEREFORD	81032-81032 COKEDALE	81157-81157 PAGOSA SPRINGS	81520-81520 CLIFTON
80733-80733 HILLROSE	81033-81034 CROWLEY	81201-81201 SALIDA	81521-81521 FRUITA
80734-80734 HOLYOKE	81036-81036 EADS	81210-81210 ALMONT	81522-81522 GATEWAY
80735-80735 IDALIA	81038-81038 FORT LYON	81211-81211 BUENA VISTA	81523-81523 GLADE PARK
80736-80736 ILIFF	81039-81039 FOWLER	81212-81215 CANON CITY	81524-81524 LOMA
80737-80737 JULESBURG	81040-81040 GARDNER	81220-81220 CIMARRON	81525-81525 MACK
80740-80740 LINDON	81041-81041 GRANADA	81221-81221 COAL CREEK	81526-81526 PALISADE
80741-80741 MERINO	81042-81042 GULNARE	81222-81222 COALDALE	81527-81527 WHITEWATER
80742-80742 NEW RAYMER	81043-81043 HARTMAN	81223-81223 COTOPAXI	81601-81602 GLENWOOD SPRINGS
80743-80743 OTIS	81044-81044 HASTY	81224-81225 CRESTED BUTTE	81610-81610 DINOSAUR
80744-80744 OVID	81045-81045 HASWELL	81226-81226 FLORENCE	81611-81612 ASPEN
80745-80745 PADRONI	81046-81046 HOEHNE	81227-81227 MONARCH	81615-81615 SNOWMASS VILLAGE
80746-80746 PAOLI	81047-81047 HOLLY	81228-81228 GRANITE	81620-81620 AVON
80747-80747 PEETZ	81049-81049 KIM	81230-81231 GUNNISON	81621-81621 BASALT
80749-80749 SEDGWICK	81050-81050 LA JUNTA	81232-81232 HILLSIDE	81623-81623 CARBONDALE
80750-80750 SNYDER	81052-81052 LAMAR	81233-81233 HOWARD	81624-81624 COLLBRAN
80751-80751 STERLING	81054-81054 LAS ANIMAS	81235-81235 LAKE CITY	81625-81626 CRAIG
80754-80754 STONEHAM	81055-81055 LA VETA	81236-81236 NATHROP	81628-81628 EL JEBEL
80755-80755 VERNON	81057-81057 MC CLAVE	81237-81237 OHIO CITY	81630-81630 DE BEQUE
80757-80757 WOODROW	81058-81058 MANZANOLA	81239-81239 PARLIN	81631-81631 EAGLE
80758-80758 WRAY	81059-81059 MODEL	81240-81240 PENROSE	81632-81632 EDWARDS
80759-80759 YUMA	81062-81062 OLNEY SPRINGS	81241-81241 PITKIN	81633-81633 DINOSAUR
80801-80801 ANTON	81063-81063 ORDWAY	81242-81242 PONCHA SPRINGS	81635-81635 PARACHUTE
80802-80802 ARAPAHOE	81064-81064 PRITCHETT	81243-81243 POWDERHORN	81636-81636 BATTLEMENT MESA
80804-80804 ARRIBA	81065-81065 PRYOR	81244-81244 ROCKVALE	81637-81637 GYPSUM
80805-80805 BETHUNE	81066-81066 RED WING	81246-81246 CANON CITY	81638-81638 HAMILTON
80806-80806 BOYERO	81067-81067 ROCKY FORD	81247-81247 GUNNISON	81639-81639 HAYDEN
80807-80807 BURLINGTON	81069-81069 RYE	81248-81248 SARGENTS	81640-81640 MAYBELL
80808-80808 CALHAN	81070-81070 SEGUNDO	81249-81249 SILVER CLIFF	81641-81641 MEEKER
80809-80809 CASCADE	81071-81071 SHERIDAN LAKE	81250-81250 COTOPAXI	81642-81642 MEREDITH
80810-80810 CHEYENNE WELLS	81073-81073 SPRINGFIELD	81251-81251 TWIN LAKES	81643-81643 MESA
80812-80812 COPE	81074-81074 STARKVILLE	81252-81252 WESTCLIFFE	81645-81645 MINTURN
80813-80813 CRIPPLE CREEK	81075-81075 STONINGTON	81253-81253 WETMORE	81646-81646 MOLINA
80814-80814 DIVIDE	81076-81076 SUGAR CITY	81290-81290 FLORENCE	81647-81647 NEW CASTLE
80815-80815 FLAGLER	81077-81077 SWINK	81301-81303 DURANGO	81648-81648 RANGELY
80816-80816 FLORISSANT	81081-81081 TRINCHERA	81320-81320 CAHONE	81649-81649 RED CLIFF
80817-80817 FOUNTAIN	81082-81082 TRINIDAD	81321-81321 CORTEZ	81650-81650 RIFLE
80818-80818 GENOA	81084-81084 TWO BUTTES	81323-81323 DOLORES	81652-81652 SILT
80819-80819 GREEN MOUNTAIN FALLS	81087-81087 VILAS	81324-81324 DOVE CREEK	81653-81653 SLATER
80820-80820 GUFFEY	81089-81089 WALSENBURG	81325-81325 EGNAR	81654-81654 SNOWMASS
80821-80821 HUGO	81090-81090 WALSH	81326-81326 HESPERUS	81655-81655 WOLCOTT
80822-80822 JOES	81091-81091 WESTON	81327-81327 LEWIS	81656-81656 WOODY CREEK
80823-80823 KARVAL	81092-81092 WILEY	81328-81328 MANCOS	81657-81658 VAIL
80824-80824 KIRK	81101-81102 ALAMOSA	81329-81329 MARVEL	
80825-80825 KIT CARSON	81120-81120 ANTONITO		

Connecticut

General Help Numbers:

Governor's Office

State Capitol, 210 Capitol Ave   860-566-4840
Hartford, CT 06106   Fax 860-566-4677
www.state.ct.us/governor   8AM-5PM

Attorney General's Office

PO Box 120   860-808-5318
Hartford, CT 06141-0120   Fax 860-808-5387
www.cslib.org/attygenl   8:30AM-4:30PM

State Court Administrator

231 Capitol Ave   860-757-2100
Hartford, CT 06106   Fax 860-757-2130
www.jud.state.ct.us   8AM-5PM

State Archives

History & Genealogy Unit   860-757-6580
231 Capitol Ave   Fax 860-757-6503
Hartford, CT 06106   9AM-5PM M-F
www.cslib.org/archives.htm

State Specifics:

Capital: Hartford
                                       Hartford County

Time Zone: EST

Number of Counties: 8

Population: 3,425,074

Web Site: www.state.ct.us

State Agencies

Criminal Records

Department of Public Safety, Bureau of Identification, PO Box 2794, Middletown, CT 06757-9294 (Courier: 1111 Country Club Rd, Middleton, CT 06457); 860-685-8480, 860-685-8361 (Fax), 8:30AM-4:30PM.

www.state.ct.us/dps

Note: A State Record Center also receives criminal records from the courts 3 months to 5 years after disposition, but this Center will not do public criminal record searches. The Center phone number is 860-741-3714.

Indexing & Storage: Records are available from the 1950's on. Records were first computerized in 1983. It takes about 30 days before new records are available for inquiry. 90% of all arrests in database have final dispositions recorded, 90% for those arrests within last 5 years.

Searching: Records are open to the public using a name search. Fingerprint searches are not available to the public. A sex offender data is not available to the public due to current court order. Include the following in your request: date of birth. Request forms may be downloaded from the web site. Approximately 90% of the records on file are fingerprint supported. The following data is not released: pending cases, dismissals or juvenile records. The records released to the public only contain convictions. Nolles are usually released if in conjunction with a conviction.

Access by: mail, in person.

Fee & Payment: The fee is $25.00 per request. The copy fee is $.25 per page. Fee payee: Commissioner of Public Safety. Prepayment required. Personal checks accepted. No credit cards accepted.

Mail search: Turnaround time: 7 to 10 days. Records requests must be in writing.

In person search: Request must be on agency form; results are mailed only. If you come in-person, the results are still mailed.

Corporation Records
Limited Partnership Records
Trademarks/Servicemarks
Limited Liability Company Records

Secretary of State, Commercial Recording Division, 30 Trinity St, Hartford, CT 06106; 860-509-6001, 860-509-6069 (Fax), 8:30AM-4:30PM.

www.sots.state.ct.us

Note: Assumed names are found at the town level.

Indexing & Storage: New records are available for inquiry immediately. Records are indexed on microfilm, inhouse computer.

Searching: Include the following in your request: full name of business, specific records that you need copies of. In addition to the articles of incorporation, corporation records include the following information: Annual Reports, Officers, Directors, Prior (merged) names, Inactive and Reserved names.

Access by: mail, phone, in person, online.

Fee & Payment: The search fee is $25.00 per business name for UCC searches performed by the office personnel. Fee payee: Secretary of State. Prepayment required. Personal checks accepted. Credit cards accepted: MasterCard, Visa.

Mail search: Turnaround time: 2 to 3 days. No self addressed stamped envelope is required.

Phone search: Only limited, basic information is available by phone.

In person search: Certain, limited information is available at no charge.

Online search: Click on the CONCORD option at the web site for free access to corporation and UCC records. The system is open from 7AM to 11PM. You can search by business name only.

Expedited service: Expedited service is available on limited filings for an add'l $25.00. Turnaround time: 24 hours. Add $25.00 per business name. The fee is per transaction requested; review is one transaction, copy is another, etc.

Uniform Commercial Code
Federal Tax Liens
State Tax Liens

UCC Division, Secretary of State, PO Box 150470, Hartford, CT 06115-0470 (Courier: 30 Trinity St, Hartford, CT 06106); 860-509-6004, 860-509-6069 (Fax), 8:30AM-4PM.

www.sots.state.ct.us

Indexing & Storage: Records are available from 8/94 on computer, earlier records are on microfilm from 10/80. It takes one month or less before new records are available for inquiry.

Searching: Use search request form UCC-11. The search includes tax liens. Include the following in your request: debtor name or original.

Access by: mail, in person, online.

Fee & Payment: UCC searches include tax liens and are free if requested in person, $25.00 per name by mail. Financing statements copies are $20.00 for a plain copy or $25.00 for a certified copy. Fee payee: Secretary of State. Prepayment required. Credit cards are accepted for in-person searching only. Personal checks accepted. Credit cards accepted: MasterCard, Visa.

Mail search: Turnaround time: 3 to 5 days. A self addressed stamped envelope is requested.

In person: Searching is available in person.

Online search: Records may be accessed at no charge on the Internet. Click on the CONCORD option. The system is open 7AM to 11PM.

Sales Tax Registrations

Department of Revenue Services, Taxpayer Services Division, 25 Sigourney St, Hartford, CT 06106; 860-297-4885, 860-297-5714 (Fax), 8AM-5PM.

www.drs.state.ct.us

Searching: This agency will only confirm that the business is registered and active. They will provide no other information. Include the following in your request: business name. They will also search by tax permit number.

Access by: mail, phone, fax, in person.

Fee & Payment: There is no search fee

Mail search: Turnaround time: 1 day.

Phone search: Records are available by phone.

Fax search: Same criteria as mail searches.

In person: Searching is available in person.

Birth Certificates
Death Records
Marriage Certificates
Divorce Records
Access to Records is Restricted

Department of Public Health, Vital Records Section MS# 11VRS, PO Box 340308, Hartford, CT 06134-0308 (Courier: 410 Capitol Ave, Hartford, CT 06134); 860-509-7897, 860-509-7964 (Fax), 8:30AM-4:30PM M-F.

www.dph.state.ct.us/OPPE/hpvital.htm

Note: The state is in the process of microfilming all records. You must contact the town/city clerk of occurrence to obtain copies of records. The web site has a great list of towns and phone numbers. Records are $5.00 each.

Workers' Compensation Records

Workers Compensation Commission, 21 Oak Street, Hartford, CT 06106; 860-493-1500, 860-247-1361 (Fax), 7:45AM-4:30PM.

http://wcc.state.ct.us

Note: All files are kept at one of the eight district offices. This agency will forward the request to the proper district office. Requester with authorization may e-mail requests to peter.miecznikowski@state.ct.us.

Indexing & Storage: Records are available on microfilm from 1914 thru 1985 and computerized from 1985 forward, for insurance coverage files. The case files since 1995 are indexed on computer. It takes 1 month before new records are available for inquiry.

Searching: Claims information is not released without a signed release from the employee. Include the following in your request: claimant name, Social Security Number (if available), date of injury, name and address of employer. Include as much information as possible. The following data is not released: medical records.

Access by: mail, phone, fax, in person.

Fee & Payment: Fees vary depending upon the nature of the request and are determined at that time. Fee payee: Workers Compensation Commission. Personal checks accepted. No credit cards accepted.

Mail search: Turnaround time: variable. A self addressed stamped envelope is requested.

Phone search: You may call for information.

Fax search: A mail request must follow.

In person search: You may request information in person.

Other access: The agency will sell self-insured lists for $5.00.

Driver Records

Department of Motor Vehicles, Copy Records Unit, 60 State St., Wethersfield, CT 06161-0503; 860-263-5154, 8:30AM-4:30PM T-F.

www.ct.gov/dmv/site/default.asp

Note: Copies of tickets may be obtained from the Superior Court Records Center, 860-741-3714 for a fee of $3.00, or $5.00 for certified copy. For ticket paid by mail, call the Centralized Infraction Bureau at 860-529-0501, $1.00 or $2.00 if certified.

Indexing & Storage: Records are available for 3/5/10 years to present, dependent upon the type of violation. It takes 5 to 7 days before new records are available for inquiry. Records are normally destroyed after 5 years at the discretion of the commissioner. The state does not report accidents on the driving record.

Searching: Mail and in person requesters must complete From J-23 and state permissible use. Casual requests must include evidence of the individual's consent. The form can be ordered from the web at http://dmvct.org/formsrec.htm or by calling 860-263-5700. Include the following in your request: two forms of ID (one with photo), signed Form J-23. The driver's license number, name and address are needed when searching, the DOB is optional. A DWI first offense violation will not appear if the offender attends an "Accelerated Alcohol Class."

Access by: mail, in person, online.

Fee & Payment: The fee for walk-in or mail-in driving records is $10.00 per record. The fee for ordering online or on a tape-to-tape system is $5.00. The fee for a license status check is $5.50. Fee payee: Department of Motor Vehicles. Prepayment required. Personal checks accepted. No credit cards accepted.

Mail search: Turnaround time: 2 weeks. A self addressed stamped envelope is requested.

In person search: The state will process up to 3 requests (at one time) for walk-in requesters who have a permissible use as stipulated in C.G.S.#14-10. Please note the office is closed on Mondays.

Online search: Online access is provided to approved businesses that enter into written contract. The contract requires a prepayment with minimum hits annually and a surety bond. Fee is $5.00 per record. The address is part of the record. For more information, call 203-805-6093.

Other access: Magnetic tape ordering is available for approved users, call 203-805-6093 for details.

Vehicle Ownership
Vehicle Identification

Department of Motor Vehicles, Copy Record Unit, 60 State St, Wethersfield, CT 06161-1896; 860-263-5154, 8:AM-4:30PM T- F.

www.ct.gov/dmv/site/default.asp

Note: Section 14-10 of the Connecticut General Statutes regulates the release of record information in accordance with federal DPPA guidelines.

Indexing & Storage: Records are available for 3 years to present. Any records prior to this period may be destroyed at the discretion of the commissioner. It takes six weeks before new records are available for inquiry. Records are normally destroyed after http://dmvct.org/formsrec.htm

Searching: Permissible users of the information are listed on back of Form J-23. Otherwise, requester must include evidence of subject's written consent. Form J-23 can be downloaded from the web site by obtained calling 860-263-5700. Include the following in your request: two forms of ID and one must contain a photo of the person signing the Form. Name searches and license plate searches are available to J-23 approved requesters. Businesses requesting for permissible purposes may only confirm the accuracy of personal information submitted by an individual to them.

Access by: mail, in person, online.

Fee & Payment: Title searches-$17.50 per search; current owner searches-$4.50 to $7.00 per search; insurance information-$7.00. There is a full charge for a "no record found." Fee payee: Department of Motor Vehicles. Prepayment required. Personal checks accepted. No credit cards accepted.

Mail search: Turnaround time: 3 to 4 working days. The agency requests that you use their Form J-23. A self addressed stamped envelope is requested.

In person search: The state will process up to 3 requests (file information only) for walk-in customers. Drop off requests accepted. Please note the office is closed on Mondays.

Online search: Vehicle record information is available on a volume basis to approved businesses that enter into a written agreement. The contract requires an annual fee and a surety bond. For more information, call 203-805-6093.

Accident Reports

Department of Public Safety, Reports and Records Unit, PO Box 2794, Middletown, CT 06457-9294; 860-685-8250, 8:30AM-4:30PM.

Indexing & Storage: Records are available from 10 years to present. Searching by name only goes back 5 years.

Searching: The request should include data and location of incident, names of operators, and the 9 digit case number (if known). The following data is not released: pending cases or sealed records.

Access by: mail.

Fee & Payment: Prepayment of the $8.00 fee per record is required. Fee payee: Commissioner of Public Safety. Personal checks accepted. No credit cards accepted.

Mail search: Turnaround time: 2 to 4 weeks. A self addressed stamped envelope is requested.

Vessel Ownership
Vessel Registration

Department of Motor Vehicles, Marine Vessel Section, 60 State Street, Wethersfield, CT 06161-3032; 860-263-5151, 860-263-5555 (Fax), 8AM-5PM T-F; til 12:30 PM Sat.

http://dmvct.org

Note: Lien information is found at the Secretary of State.

Indexing & Storage: Records are available from 1981, records are maintained on computer for 4 years then placed on microfiche. All motorized boats any length, and all vessels over 19.5 ft without motor must be registered.

Searching: All requests must be in writing. Requests follow requirements of DPPA. Either the name, CT registration number or hull number is needed to do a search.

Access by: mail, in person.

Fee & Payment: The fee is $4.50 for a current owner search, $7.00 for a copy of the registration and $17.50 for a complete boat history. Fee payee: Department of Motor Vehicles. Prepayment required. No credit cards accepted.

Mail search: Turnaround time: 1 to 2 weeks. No self addressed stamped envelope is required.

In person search: Results are returned by mail. The agency is closed to the public on Mondays.

Other access: Bulk list information is available by contract. The fee depends on data requested. Call 860-263-5241 for ordering procedures.

Legislation Records

Connecticut General Assembly, State Library, Bill Room at State Library, 231 Capitol Ave, Bill Room, Hartford, CT 06106; 860-757-6550, 860-757-6594 (Fax), 9AM-5PM.

www.cga.state.ct.us/default.asp

Indexing & Storage: Records are available for the current session only. Records are indexed on inhouse computer.

Searching: Include the following in your request: bill number. You may also ask for bills by subject or statute number. Past bills are located in another office (call 860-757-6590).

Access by: mail, phone, fax, in person, online.

Fee & Payment: Fees: No charge for current bills; $.25 per page if you request a large document or a bill that has not been printed. They will compute the charge. Fee payee: Connecticut State Library. Personal checks accepted. No credit cards accepted.

Mail search: Turnaround time: 4 to 7 days. No self addressed stamped envelope is required.

Phone search: You may call for information.

Fax search: Copies of bills totaling 30 pages or less can be returned by fax if local or toll free.

In person search: You may request information in person.

Online search: From the web site you can track bills, find update or status, and print copies of bills. Also, you can request via e-mail at billroom@cslib.org.

Voter Registration

Records not maintained by a state level agency.

Note: Records are open at the town level. There are 169 towns.

GED Certificates

Department of Education, GED Records, 25 Industrial Park Rd, Middletown, CT 06457; 860-807-2110, 860-807-2112 (Fax), 8AM-5PM.

www.state.ct.us/sde

Searching: Include the following in your request: signed release, Social Security Number, date of birth. The year of the test is helpful. For records prior to 1982, the location of the test is needed.

Access by: mail, fax, in person.

Fee & Payment: There is no search fee.

Mail search: Turnaround time: 2 to 3 days. No self addressed stamped envelope is required.

Fax search: There is no fee to fax back to a local phone number.

In person search: Photo ID is required.

Hunting License Information
Fishing License Information

Department of Environmental Protection, License Division, 79 Elm St, Hartford, CT 06106; 860-424-3105, 860-424-4072 (Fax), 9AM-4PM.

www.dep.state.ct.us

Indexing & Storage: Records are available from 1995 to present. It takes 1 day before new records are available for inquiry. Records are indexed on inhouse computer.

Searching: Only deer tag information is released. Include the following in your request: full name, Social Security Number. Records are indexed by Social Security Number. All requests must be in writing.

Access by: mail, in person.

Fee & Payment: There is no search fee. Copies are $.50 per page. Fee payee: Department of Environmental Protection. Prepayment required. Personal checks accepted. No credit cards accepted.

Mail search: Turnaround time: 1 to 3 days. No self addressed stamped envelope is required.

In person search: Must have the request in writing.

Connecticut State Licensing Agencies

Licenses Searchable Online

Acupuncturist #11 .... www.state.ct.us/dph/scripts/hlthprof.asp
Alcohol/Drug Counselor #11 .... www.state.ct.us/dph/scripts/hlthprof.asp
Antenna Service Dealer/Technician #5 .... www.dcpaccess.state.ct.us/DCPPublic/LicenseLookup.asp
Appraiser, MVR #2 .... www.state.ct.us/cid/license/licweb1.asp
Appraiser, MVPD #2 .... www.state.ct.us/cid/license/licweb1.asp
Architect #3 .... www.dcpaccess.state.ct.us/DCPPublic/LicenseLookup.asp
Architectural Firm #3 .... www.dcpaccess.state.ct.us/DCPPublic/LicenseLookup.asp
Asbestos Professional #11 .... www.state.ct.us/dph/scripts/hlthprof.asp
Athletic Promoter #7 .... www.dcpaccess.state.ct.us/DCPPublic/LicenseLookup.asp
Audiologist #11 .... www.state.ct.us/dph/scripts/hlthprof.asp
Automobile Insurance Adjuster #2 .... www.state.ct.us/cid/license/licweb1.asp
Bail Bond Agent #2 .... www.state.ct.us/cid/license/licweb1.asp
Bank #6 .... www.state.ct.us/dob/pages/banklist.htm
Bank & Trust Company #6 .... www.state.ct.us/dob/pages/bcharter.htm
Bank Branch #6 .... www.state.ct.us/dob/pages/branch1.htm
Barber #11 .... www.state.ct.us/dph/scripts/hlthprof.asp
Bedding Mfg/Renovation #4 .... www.dcpaccess.state.ct.us/DCPPublic/LicenseLookup.asp
Boxer #7 .... www.dcpaccess.state.ct.us/DCPPublic/LicenseLookup.asp
Building Contractor #7 .... www.dcpaccess.state.ct.us/DCPPublic/LicenseLookup.asp
Casualty Adjuster #2 .... www.state.ct.us/cid/license/licweb1.asp
Check Cashing Service #6 .... www.state.ct.us/dob/pages/chckcash.htm
Chiropractor #11 .... www.state.ct.us/dph/scripts/hlthprof.asp
Collection Agency #6 .... www.state.ct.us/dob/pages/collect.htm
Collection Agency, Consumer #6 .... www.state.ct.us/dob/pages/collect.htm
Cosmetologist #11 .... www.state.ct.us/dph/scripts/hlthprof.asp
Counselor, Professional #11 .... www.state.ct.us/dph/scripts/hlthprof.asp
Credit Union #6 .... www.state.ct.us/dob/pages/culist.htm
Debt Adjuster #6 .... www.state.ct.us/dob/pages/debtadj.htm
Dental Anes/Conscious Sedation Permittee #11 ..... www.state.ct.us/dph/scripts/hlthprof.asp
Dentist/Dental Hygienist #11 .... www.state.ct.us/dph/scripts/hlthprof.asp
Dietician/Nutritionist #11 .... www.state.ct.us/dph/scripts/hlthprof.asp
Electrical Contractor/Inspector #7 .... www.dcpaccess.state.ct.us/DCPPublic/LicenseLookup.asp
Electrical Journeyman/Apprentice #4 .... www.dcpaccess.state.ct.us/DCPPublic/LicenseLookup.asp
Electrical Sign Installer #7 .... www.dcpaccess.state.ct.us/DCPPublic/LicenseLookup.asp
Electrician #7 .... www.dcpaccess.state.ct.us/DCPPublic/LicenseLookup.asp
Electrologist/Hypertricologist #11 .... www.state.ct.us/dph/scripts/hlthprof.asp
Electronics Service Dealer/Technician #5 .... www.dcpaccess.state.ct.us/DCPPublic/LicenseLookup.asp
Elevator Inspector/Mechanic #4 .... www.dcpaccess.state.ct.us/DCPPublic/LicenseLookup.asp
Embalmer #11 .... www.state.ct.us/dph/scripts/hlthprof.asp
Emergency Medical Service Professional #11 .... www.state.ct.us/dph/scripts/hlthprof.asp
Emergency Medical Technician #11 .... www.state.ct.us/dph/scripts/hlthprof.asp
Engineer #4 .... www.dcpaccess.state.ct.us/DCPPublic/LicenseLookup.asp
Fire Protection Inspector/Contractor #4 .... www.dcpaccess.state.ct.us/DCPPublic/LicenseLookup.asp
Funeral Director #11 .... www.state.ct.us/dph/scripts/hlthprof.asp
Funeral Home #11 .... www.state.ct.us/dph/scripts/hlthprof.asp
Glazier #4 .... www.dcpaccess.state.ct.us/DCPPublic/LicenseLookup.asp
Hairdresser #11 .... www.state.ct.us/dph/scripts/hlthprof.asp
Hearing Instrument Specialist #11 .... www.state.ct.us/dph/scripts/hlthprof.asp
Heating, Piping, Cooling Contr./Journeyman #4 ..... www.dcpaccess.state.ct.us/DCPPublic/LicenseLookup.asp
Homeopathic Physician #11 .... www.state.ct.us/dph/scripts/hlthprof.asp
Hypertrichologist #11 .... www.state.ct.us/dph/scripts/hlthprof.asp
Insurance Adjuster/Public Adjuster #2 .... www.state.ct.us/cid/license/licweb1.asp
Insurance Agent, Fraternal #2 .... www.state.ct.us/cid/license/licweb1.asp
Insurance Agent/Broker/Consultant #2 .... www.state.ct.us/cid/license/licweb1.asp
Insurance Appraiser #2 .... www.state.ct.us/cid/license/licweb1.asp
Insurance Company/Producer #2 .... www.state.ct.us/cid/license/licweb1.asp
Interior Designer #7 .... www.dcpaccess.state.ct.us/DCPPublic/LicenseLookup.asp
Land Surveyor Firm #3 .... www.dcpaccess.state.ct.us/DCPPublic/LicenseLookup.asp
Lead Planner/Project Designer #11 .... www.state.ct.us/dph/scripts/hlthprof.asp
Lead Professional #11 .... www.state.ct.us/dph/scripts/hlthprof.asp
Liquor License #15 .... www.dcpaccess.state.ct.us/DCPPublic/LicenseLookup.asp

Loan Company, Small #6.........................www.state.ct.us/dob/pages/smallloan.htm
Lobbyist #18 ....www.ethics.state.ct.us/publicinfo.htm
Marriage & Family Therapist #11..............www.state.ct.us/dph/scripts/hlthprof.asp
Massage Therapist #11............................www.state.ct.us/dph/scripts/hlthprof.asp
Medical Doctor #11..................................www.state.ct.us/dph/scripts/hlthprof.asp
Medical Response Technician #11..............www.state.ct.us/dph/scripts/hlthprof.asp
Midwife #11...www.state.ct.us/dph/scripts/hlthprof.asp
Mobile Home Park/Seller #17 ....www.dcpaccess.state.ct.us/DCPPublic/LicenseLookup.asp
Money Forwarder #6.................................www.state.ct.us/dob/pages/$forward.htm
Mortgage (1st) Broker/Lender #6..............www.state.ct.us/dob/pages/1stmtg.htm
Mortgage (2nd) Broker/Lender #6.............www.state.ct.us/dob/pages/2ndmtg.htm
Naturopathic Physician #11.......................www.state.ct.us/dph/scripts/hlthprof.asp
Nurse #11..www.state.ct.us/dph/scripts/hlthprof.asp
Nurse, Advance Registered Practice #11 ...www.state.ct.us/dph/scripts/hlthprof.asp
Nurse-LPN #11..www.state.ct.us/dph/scripts/hlthprof.asp
Nursing Home Administrator #11................www.state.ct.us/dph/scripts/hlthprof.asp
Occupational Therapist/Assistant #11 ....www.state.ct.us/dph/scripts/hlthprof.asp
Optical Shop #11 ....www.state.ct.us/dph/scripts/hlthprof.asp
Optician #11..www.state.ct.us/dph/scripts/hlthprof.asp
Optometrist #11.......................................www.state.ct.us/dph/scripts/hlthprof.asp
Osteopathic Physician #11........................www.state.ct.us/dph/scripts/hlthprof.asp
Paramedic #11...www.state.ct.us/dph/scripts/hlthprof.asp
Pharmacist/Pharmacist Intern #4..............www.dcpaccess.state.ct.us/DCPPublic/LicenseLookup.asp
Pharmacy #4..www.dcpaccess.state.ct.us/DCPPublic/LicenseLookup.asp
Physical Therapist/Assistant #11...............www.state.ct.us/dph/scripts/hlthprof.asp
Physician Assistant #11............................www.state.ct.us/dph/scripts/hlthprof.asp
Pipefitter #7 ....www.dcpaccess.state.ct.us/DCPPublic/LicenseLookup.asp
Plumber #4..www.dcpaccess.state.ct.us/DCPPublic/LicenseLookup.asp
Podiatrist #11...www.state.ct.us/dph/scripts/hlthprof.asp
Psychologist #11......................................www.state.ct.us/dph/scripts/hlthprof.asp
Public Service Technician #4.....................www.dcpaccess.state.ct.us/DCPPublic/LicenseLookup.asp
Radiographer #11.....................................www.state.ct.us/dph/scripts/hlthprof.asp
Real Estate Appraiser #17 ....www.dcpaccess.state.ct.us/DCPPublic/LicenseLookup.asp
Real Estate Broker/Salesperson #17.........www.dcpaccess.state.ct.us/DCPPublic/LicenseLookup.asp
Reinsurance Intermediary #2.....................www.state.ct.us/cid/license/licweb1.asp
Respiratory Care Practitioner #11..............www.state.ct.us/dph/scripts/hlthprof.asp
Sales Finance Company #6.......................www.state.ct.us/dob/pages/salefinc.htm
Sanitarian #11..www.state.ct.us/dph/scripts/hlthprof.asp
Savings & Loan Association Bank #6 ....www.state.ct.us/dob/pages/bcharter.htm
Savings Bank #6......................................www.state.ct.us/dob/pages/bcharter.htm
Sheet Metal #4...www.dcpaccess.state.ct.us/DCPPublic/LicenseLookup.asp
Social Worker #11....................................www.state.ct.us/dph/scripts/hlthprof.asp
Solar Energy Contractor/Journeyman #4....www.dcpaccess.state.ct.us/DCPPublic/LicenseLookup.asp
Speech Pathologist #11............................www.state.ct.us/dph/scripts/hlthprof.asp
Sprinkler Layout Technician #4..................www.dcpaccess.state.ct.us/DCPPublic/LicenseLookup.asp
Subsurface Sewage Cleaner/Installer #11...www.state.ct.us/dph/scripts/hlthprof.asp
Surplus Line Broker #2 ....www.state.ct.us/cid/license/licweb1.asp
Surveyor, Land #3 ....www.dcpaccess.state.ct.us/DCPPublic/LicenseLookup.asp
Veterinarian #11.......................................www.state.ct.us/dph/scripts/hlthprof.asp
Weigher #8 ....www.dcpaccess.state.ct.us/DCPPublic/LicenseLookup.asp
Weights & Measures Dealer/Repairer/Reg. #8.......www.dcpaccess.state.ct.us/DCPPublic/LicenseLookup.asp
Well Driller #7 ....www.dcpaccess.state.ct.us/DCPPublic/LicenseLookup.asp
Wrestler/Wrestling Manager #7 ....www.dcpaccess.state.ct.us/DCPPublic/LicenseLookup.asp

Licensing Quick Finder

Acupuncturist #11 ... 860-509-7603	Audiologist #11 ... 860-509-7603	Boxer #7 ... 860-566-6980
Alcohol/Drug Counselor #11 ... 860-509-7603	Automobile Insurance Adjuster #2 ... 860-297-3845	Broker/Dealer Agent #6 ... 860-240-8299
Amusement Park #25 ... 860-685-8470	Bail Bond Agent #2 ... 860-297-3845	Building Contractor #7 ... 860-566-2825
Antenna Service Dealer/Technician #5 . 860-566-3275	Bail Enforcement Agent #13 ... 860-685-8046	Bus Driver #23 ... 860-263-5720
Appraiser (MVR) #2 ... 860-297-3845	Bailbondsman #13 ... 860-685-8046	Business Opportunity Offering #6 ... 860-240-8299
Appraiser, MVPD #2 ... 860-297-3845	Bait Seller (Live Bait) #10 ... 860-424-3474	Carnival Operator #25 ... 860-685-8470
Aquaculture Operation #20 ... 203-874-0696	Bank #6 ... 860-240-8299	Casino #12 ... 860-594-0567
Arborist #7 ... 860-566-3290	Bank & Trust Company #6 ... 860-240-8299	Casualty Adjuster #2 ... 860-297-3845
Architect #3 ... 860-566-2093	Bank Branch #6 ... 860-240-8299	Cattle/Swine Dealer #22 ... 860-713-2512
Architectural Firm #3 ... 860-566-2093	Banking Office, Non-depository #6 ... 860-240-8299	Chauffeur/Livery Company #24 ... 860-594-2865
Asbestos Professional #11 ... 860-509-7603	Barber #11 ... 860-509-7603	Check Cashing Service #6 ... 860-240-8299
Athletic Promoter #7 ... 860-566-6980	Bedding Mfg/Renovation #4 ... 860-713-6000	Cheese Dealer #22 ... 860-713-2512
Attorney #1 ... 860-568-5157	Bird/Poultry Permit #22 ... 860-713-2512	Chiropractor #11 ... 860-509-7603

Collection Agency #6 860-240-8299
Collection Agency, Consumer #6 860-240-8299
Conch/Depuration/Oyster License #20 . 203-874-0696
Cosmetologist #11 860-509-7603
Counselor, Professional #11 860-509-7603
Cranes/Hoisting Equipment #25 860-685-8470
Credit Union #6 860-240-8299
Dairy Laboratory Analyst #22 860-713-2512
Dairy Sample Collector #22 860-713-2512
Dairy Transporter #22 860-713-2512
Day Care Provider #11 860-509-8000
Debt Adjuster #6 860-240-8299
Demolition Operator #25 860-685-8470
Dental Anes/Conscious Sedation Permittee #11
.... 860-509-7603
Dentist/Dental Hygienist #11 860-509-7603
Dietician/Nutritionist #11 860-509-7603
Digger of Shellfish #20 203-874-0696
Dog Racing #12 860-594-0567
Dog Training Facility/Kennel #22 860-713-2512
Driving Instructor #23 860-263-5720
Electrical Contractor/Inspector #7 860-566-2825
Electrical Journeyman/Apprentice #4 ... 860-713-6000
Electrical Sign Installer #7 860-566-2825
Electrician #7 860-566-2825
Electrologist/Hypertricologist #11 860-509-7603
Electronics Service Dealer/Tech. #5 860-566-3275
Elevator Inspector/Mechanic #4 860-713-6000
Embalmer #11 860-509-7603
Emergency Medical Service Professional #11
.... 860-509-7603
Emergency Medical Technician #11 860-509-7603
Engineer #4 860-713-6000
Explosive Handler #25 860-685-8470
Explosive Hauler #25 860-685-8470
Fire Protection Inspector/Contractor #4 860-713-6000
Firearms Registration #19 860-685-8290
Fireworks Display Operator #25 860-685-8470
Fisher #10 860-424-3105
Funeral Director #11 860-509-7603
Funeral Home #11 860-509-7603
Fur Breeder #22 860-713-2512
Game Breeder #10 860-424-3011
Glazier #4 860-713-6000
Gun Dealer #19 860-685-8290
Hairdresser #11 860-509-7603
Hearing Instrument Specialist #11 860-509-7603
Heating, Piping & Cooling Contractor/Journeyman #4
.... 860-713-6000
Homeopathic Physician #11 860-509-7603
Hypertrichologist #11 860-509-7603
Insurance Adjuster/Public Adjuster #2 . 860-297-3845
Insurance Agent, Fraternal #2 860-297-3845
Insurance Agent/Broker/Consultant #2 . 860-297-3845
Insurance Appraiser #2 860-297-3845
Insurance Company/Producer #2 860-297-3817
Interior Designer #7 860-566-2825

Investment Advisor/Agent #6 860-240-8299
Issuer Agent (Financial) #6 860-240-8299
Jai Alai #12 860-594-0567
Junkyard Operator #27 860-263-5447
Land Surveyor Firm #3 860-566-3290
Lead Planner/Project Designer #11 860-509-7603
Lead Professional #11 860-509-7603
Liquor License #15 860-713-6200
Livestock Dealer #22 860-713-2512
Loan Company, Small #6 860-240-8299
Lobbyist #18 860-566-4472
Lobster Seller #10 860-424-6043
Lottery #12 860-594-0567
Marriage & Family Therapist #11 860-609-7603
Massage Therapist #11 860-509-7603
Medical Doctor #11 860-509-7603
Medical Response Technician #11 860-509-7603
Midwife #11 860-509-7603
Milk Dealer/Producer #22 860-713-2512
Mobile Home Park/Seller #17 860-713-6150
Money Forwarder #6 860-240-8299
Mortgage (1st) Broker/Lender #6 860-240-8299
Mortgage (2nd) Broker/Lender #6 860-240-8299
Motion Picture Theater #25 860-685-8470
Motion Picture Theater Mgr #25 860-685-8470
Motor Bus Company #24 860-594-2865
Mover, Household Goods #24 860-594-2865
Naturopathic Physician #11 860-509-7603
Notary Public #16 860-509-6200
Nurse #11 860-509-7603
Nurse, Advance Registered Practice #11
.... 860-509-7603
Nurse-LPN #11 860-509-7603
Nurses' Aide #11 860-509-7603
Nursing Home Administrator #11 860-509-7603
Occupational Therapist/Assistant #11 .. 860-509-7603
Off-Track Betting #12 860-594-0567
Optical Shop #11 860-509-7603
Optician #11 860-509-7603
Optometrist #11 860-509-7603
Osteopathic Physician #11 860-509-7603
Paramedic #11 860-509-7603
Pawnbroker #21 860-297-4874
Pesticide Dealer/Applicator #14 860-424-3369
Pet Groomer #22 860-713-2512
Pet Store Operator #22 860-713-2512
Pharmacist/Pharmacist Intern #4 860-713-6000
Pharmacy #4 860-713-6000
Physical Therapist/Assistant #11 860-509-7603
Physician Assistant #11 860-509-7603
Pipefitter #7 860-566-2825
Plumber #4 860-713-6000
Podiatrist #11 860-509-7603
Premium Finance Company #2 860-297-3845
Private Investigator #13 860-685-8046
Psychologist #11 860-509-7603
Public Accountant-CPA #16 860-509-6179

Public Service Technician #4 860-713-6000
Radiographer #11 860-509-7603
Real Estate Appraiser #17 860-713-6150
Real Estate Broker/Salesperson #17 ... 860-713-6150
Reinsurance Intermediary #2 860-297-3845
Rental Car Company #2 860-297-3953
Respiratory Care Practitioner #11 860-509-7603
Sales Finance Company #6 860-240-8299
Sanitarian #11 860-509-7603
Savings & Loan Association Bank #6 . 860-240-8299
Savings Bank #6 860-240-8299
School Administrator/Supervisor #9 860-566-5201
School Bus Driver #23 860-263-5720
School Guidance Counselor #9 860-566-5201
School Library Media Associate #9 860-566-5201
School Principal/Superintendent #9 860-566-5201
Securities Agent #6 860-240-8299
Securities Broker/Dealer #6 860-240-8299
Security Guard #13 860-685-8046
Septic Tank Cleaner #11 860-509-8000
Sewage Disposal System Installer #11 . 860-509-8000
Sex Offender #26 860-685-8060
Sheet Metal #4 860-713-6000
Social Worker #11 860-509-7603
Solar Energy Contr./Journeyman #4 860-713-6000
Solid Waste Facility Operator #10 860-424-4051
Speech Pathologist #11 860-509-7603
Sprinkler Layout Technician #4 860-713-6000
Subsurface Sewage Cleaner/Installer #11
.... 860-509-7603
Surplus Line Broker #2 860-297-3845
Surveyor, Land #3 860-566-3290
Tattoo Artist #11 860-509-8000
Taxable Entity #21 860-297-4874
Taxi Company #24 860-594-2865
Taxidermist #10 860-424-3105
Teacher #9 860-566-5201
Ticket Broker #12 860-667-5073
Towing Operator #27 860-263-5447
Trapper #10 860-424-3105
Tree Surgeon #7 860-566-2825
Truck Driver #23 860-263-5720
Utilization Review Company #2 860-297-3862
Vehicle Dealer #27 860-263-5447
Vehicle Repairer #27 860-263-5447
Veterinarian #11 860-509-7603
Viatical Settlement Broker/Provider #2 . 860-297-3845
Water Distribution System Operator #11
.... 860-509-8000
Water Treatment Plant Operator #11 ... 860-509-8000
Weigher #8 860-713-6160
Weights & Measures Dealer/Repairer/Regulator #8
.... 860-713-6160
Well Driller #7 860-566-2825
Wildlife Control Operator #10 860-424-3011
Wildlife Rehabilitator #10 860-424-3011
Wrestler/Wrestling Manager #7 860-566-2825

Licensing Agency Information

#1 Bar Examining Committee, 80 Washington St, Hartford, CT 06106-4424; 860-568-5157. www.jud.state.ct.us/colp/Barexam.html.

#2 Department of Insurance, Licensing Division, 153 Market St, Hartford, CT 06142-0816; 860-297-3845, Fax: 860-297-3872. www.state.ct.us/cid
Agency email: moira.herbert@po.state.ct.us.
Search database at www.state.ct.us/cid/license/licweb1.asp

#3 Consumer Protection Department, Board of Architects, 165 Capitol Ave, #110, Hartford, CT 06106; 860-713-6135, Fax: 860-713-7239. Search database at www.dcpaccess.state.ct.us/DCPPublic/LicenseLookup.asp. Lists can be downloaded at www.dcpaccess.state.ct.us/DCPRosterDownload/pRosterDownload.asp.

#4 Consumer Protection Department, Board of Trades Division, 165 Capitol Ave, Hartford, CT 06106; 860-713-6000, Fax: 860-713-7239. Agency email: License.services@po.state.ct.us. Search database at www.dcpaccess.state.ct.us/DCPPublic/LicenseLookup.asp. Lists can be downloaded at www.dcpaccess.state.ct.us/DCPRosterDownload/pRosterDownload.asp.

#5 Consumer Protection Dept/Occupational Licensing, Board of Television & Radio Service Examiners, 165 Capitol Ave, Hartford, CT 06106; 860-713-6135, Fax: 860-713-7239. www.state.ct.us/dcp/
Search database at www.dcpaccess.state.ct.us/DCPPublic/LicenseLookup.asp

#6 Department of Banking, 260 Constitution Plaza, Hartford, CT 06106-1800; 860-240-8299, Fax: 860-240-8178. www.state.ct.us/dob
Agency email: john.burke@po.state.ct.us.
Search database at www.state.ct.us/dob

#7 Department of Consumer Protection, Occupational Licensing Division, 165 Capitol Ave, Hartford, CT 06106; 860-713-6300, Fax: 860-713-7239. www.state.ct.us/dcp
Agency email: license.services@po.state.ct.us.
Search database at www.dcpaccess.state.ct.us/DCPPublic/LicenseLookup.asp. Lists can be downloaded at www.dcpaccess.state.ct.us/DCPRosterDownload/pRosterDownload.asp.

#8 Department of Consumer Protection, Food Standards Division, 165 Capitol Ave, State Office Bldg, Hartford, CT 06106-1630; 860-713-6160, Fax: 860-713-7244.
www.state.ct.us/dcp/
Search database at www.dcpaccess.state.ct.us/DCPPublic/LicenseLookup.asp. Lists can be downloaded at www.dcpaccess.state.ct.us/DCPRosterDownload/pRosterDownload.asp

#9 Department of Education, Bureau of Certification & Professional Development, PO Box 150471, Rm 243, Hartford, CT 06115-0471; 860-566-5201, Fax: 860-566-8929. www.state.ct.us/sde
Agency email: teacher.cert@po.state.ct.us.

#10 Department of Environmental Protection, Bureau of Natural Resources, 79 Elm St, Hartford, CT 06106; 860-424-3372, Fax: 860-424-4051. http://dep.state.ct.us/pao/index.htm.

#11 Department of Public Health & Addiction Services, 410 Capital Ave, Mail Stop 12MQA, Hartford, CT 06134-0308; 860-509-7603, Fax: 860-509-7607.
www.state.ct.us/dph
Search database at www.state.ct.us/dph/scripts/hlthprof.asp

#12 Division of Special Revenue, PO Box 11424 (555 Russell Rd), Newington, CT 06111; 860-594-0656, Fax: 860-594-0649
Agency email: dosr@po.state.ct.us.

#13 Division of State Police, Special Licensing Division, 1111 Country Club Rd, Middletown, CT 06457; 860-685-8046, Fax: 860-685-8496. www.state.ct.us/dps

#14 Environmental Protection Department, 79 Elm St, Hartford, CT 06134; 860-424-3372, Fax: 860-509-8457.

#15 Liquor Control Department, 165 Capitol Ave, Hartford, CT 06106; 860-713-6200, Fax: 860-713-7235. www.dosr.state.ct.us
Agency email: dosr@po.state.ct.us.
Search database at www.dcpaccess.state.ct.us/DCPPublic/LicenseLookup.asp. Lists can be downloaded at www.dcpaccess.state.ct.us/DCPRosterDownload/pRosterDownload.asp

#16 Office of the Secretary of the State, Records Division, PO Box 150470 (30 Trinity St), Hartford, CT 06115; 860-509-6200, Fax: 860-509-6230.
www.sots.state.ct.us.

#17 Consumer Protection Department, Real Estate Division, 165 Capitol Ave, Rm 110, Hartford, CT 06106; 860-713-6150, Fax: 860-713-7239. www.dcp.state.ct.us/licensing
Search database at www.dcpaccess.state.ct.us/DCPPublic/LicenseLookup.asp. Lists can be downloaded at www.dcpaccess.state.ct.us/DCPRosterDownload/pRosterDownload.asp

#18 Ethics Commission, 20 Trinity St, Hartford, CT 06106; 860-566-4472, Fax: 860-566-3806. www.ethics.state.ct.us
Search database at www.ethics.state.ct.us/publicinfo.htm. May not have full lobbyist rosters. Also search reports and enforcement actions.

#19 Department of Public Safety, Division of State Police, Licensing/Registration, 1111 Country Club Rd, Middletown, CT 06457-9294; 860-685-8290.

#20 Department of Agriculture, Bureau of Aquaculture, PO Box 97 (190 Rogers Ave), Milford, CT 06460; 203-874-0696. www.state.ct.us/doag/

#21 Department of Revenue Svcs, Audit Unit (Licensing), PO Box 2937 (25 Sigourney St, 06106), Hartford, CT 06104; 860-297-5962, Fax: 860-297-4797. www.drs.state.ct.us

#22 Department of Agriculture, Bureau of Regulation & Inspection, 765 Asylum Av, Hartford, CT 06105; 860-713-2512, Fax: 860-713-2585. www.state.ct.us/doag
Agency email: ctdeptag@po.state.ct.us.

#23 Department of Motor Vehicles, Specialized Licenses & Permits, 60 State St, Wethersfield, CT 06109; 860-263-5720. www.ct.gov/dmv/site/default.asp

#24 Department of Transportation, Motor Transport Svcs, PO Box 317546 (2800 Berlin Turnpike,), Newington, CT 06131-7546; 860-594-2865, Fax: 860-594-2859.

#25 Department of Public Safety, Division of Fire, Emergency & Building Svcs, 1111 Country Club Rd, Middletown, CT 06457-9294; 860-685-8470. www.state.ct.us/dps/dfebs/dfebs.htm

#26 Department of Public Safety, Division of State Police, Sex Offender Registry, PO Box 2794, Middletown, CT 06457; 860-685-8060. www.state.ct.us/dps/SexOffenderRegistryNOTICE.htm

#27 Department of Motor Vehicles, Dealer and Repairer Division, 60 State St, Wethersfield, CT 06109; 860-263-5447. www.ct.gov/dmv/site/default.asp

Connecticut Federal Courts

The following list indicates the district and division name for each county in the state. If the bankruptcy court location is different from the district court, then the location of the bankruptcy court appears in parentheses.

County/Court Cross Reference

Fairfield	Bridgeport	New Haven	New Haven
Hartford	Hartford	New London	New Haven
Litchfield	New Haven (Hartford)	Tolland	Hartford
Middlesex	New Haven (Hartford)	Windham	Hartford

Standards for Federal Courts: The search fee is $20.00 per item (one party name or case number). Certification fee is $7.00 per document. Copy fee is $.50 per page. All fees standard unless noted in profile. Mail Search: always enclose a stamped self addressed envelope unless otherwise noted. Before releasing records, all courts require prepayment unless noted in profile.
Open records are located at the court unless otherwise noted. District courts index by defendant and plaintiff as well as by case number. Bankruptcy courts usually index by debtor and case number. While most courts now have their indexes on computer, many still maintain index card files as well.
The universal PACER sign-up number is 800-676-6856. Find PACER and the Party/Case Index on the Web at http://pacer.psc.uscourts.gov. PACER dial-up access is $.60 per minute. Also, courts offering internet access via RACER, PACER, Web-PACER or the new CM-ECF charge $.07 per page fee unless noted as free.

US District Court

District of Connecticut

Bridgeport Division Office of the clerk, Room 400, 915 Lafayette Blvd, Bridgeport, CT 06604 (Courier Address: Use mail address for courier delivery), 203-579-5861.
www.ctd.uscourts.gov
Counties: Fairfield (prior to 1993). Since January 1993, cases from any county may be assigned to any of the divisions in the district.
Indexing & Storage: Cases are indexed by defendant, plaintiff, and case number. New cases are available in the index immediately after filing date. Records are stored by docket number, accession number and box number. Open records are located at this court.
Fee & Payment Notes: Payment may be made by money order, cashier check. Business checks are not accepted. Personal checks are not accepted. Payee: Clerk, US District Court. You are allowed to make your own copies. These copies cost $.25 per page.
Phone Search: Only docket information is available by phone.
Mail Search: A stamped self addressed envelope is not required.
In Person Search: In person searching available.

PACER: Toll-free dial-up access: 800-292-0658. Local dial-up access: 203-773-2451. Case records are available back to November 1, 1991. New records are available online after 1 day. PACER is available online at http://pacer.ctd.uscourts.gov.

Hartford Division 450 Main St, Hartford, CT 06103 (Courier Address: Use mail address for courier delivery), 860-240-3200.
www.ctd.uscourts.gov
Counties: Hartford, Tolland, Windham (prior to 1993). Since 1993, cases from any county may be assigned to any of the divisions in the district.
Indexing & Storage: Cases are indexed by defendant, plaintiff, and case number. New cases are available in the index immediately after filing date. Records are kept where the assigned judge sits, and are stored by a federal record number system. Open records are located at this court.
Fee & Payment Notes: Payment may be made by money order, cashier check, personal check. Payee: Clerk, US District Court. You are allowed to make your own copies. These copies cost $.25 per page.
Phone Search: Only docket information is available by phone.
In Person Search: In person searching available.
PACER: Toll-free dial-up access: 800-292-0658. Local dial-up access: 203-773-2451. Case records are available back to November 1, 1991. New records are available online after 1 day. PACER is available online at http://pacer.ctd.uscourts.gov.

New Haven Division 141 Church St, New Haven, CT 06510 (Courier Address: Use mail address for courier delivery), 203-773-2140.
www.ctd.uscourts.gov
Counties: Litchfield, Middlesex, New Haven, New London (prior to 1993). Since 1993, cases from any county may be assigned to any of the divisions in the district.
Indexing & Storage: Cases are indexed by defendant, plaintiff, and case number. New cases are available in the index immediately after filing date. Older records are indexed on microfiche. District wide searches are available for information from 1982 to the present from this court.
Fee & Payment Notes: Payment may be made by money order, cashier check, business check. Personal checks are not accepted. There is a

$15.00 search fee charged for each additional name after the first. Payee: District Court Clerk. You are allowed to make your own copies. These copies cost $.25 per page.
Phone Search: Only docket information is available by phone.
In Person Search: In person searching available.
PACER: Toll-free dial-up access: 800-292-0658. Local dial-up access: 203-773-2451. Case records are available back to November 1, 1991. New records are available online after 1 day. PACER is available online at http://pacer.ctd.uscourts.gov.

US Bankruptcy Court

District of Connecticut

Bridgeport Division 915 Lafayette Blvd, Bridgeport, CT 06604 (Courier Address: Use mail address for courier delivery), 203-579-5808.
www.ctb.uscourts.gov
Counties: Fairfield.
Indexing & Storage: Cases are indexed by debtor as well as by case number. New cases are available in the index immediately after filing date. District wide searches are available from this division.
Fee & Payment Notes: Payment may be made by money order, cashier check, business check. Personal checks are not accepted. Payee: Clerk, US Bankruptcy Court. You are allowed to make your own copies. These copies cost $.25 per page.
Phone Search: An automated voice case information service (VCIS) is available. Call VCIS at 800-800-5113 or 860-240-3345.
In Person Search: In person searching available.
PACER: Local dial-up access: 860-240-3570, 860-240-3571, 860-240-3572. Case records are available back to 1979. Records are purged every 6 months. New civil records are available online after 1 day. PACER is available online at http://pacer.ctb.uscourts.gov. Document images available.
Electronic Filing: (Currently in the process of implementing CM/ECF.)

Hartford Division 450 Main St, Hartford, CT 06103 (Courier Address: Use mail address for courier delivery), 860-240-3675.
www.ctb.uscourts.gov

Counties: Hartford, Litchfield, Middlesex, Tolland, Windham.

Indexing & Storage: Cases are indexed by debtor as well as by case number. New cases are available in the index 1 week after filing date. Open records are located at this court.

Fee & Payment Notes: Payment may be made by money order, cashier check, personal check. Payee: Clerk, US Bankruptcy Court. You are allowed to make your own copies. These copies cost $.25 per page.

Phone Search: Only docket information is available by phone. An automated voice case information service (VCIS) is available. Call VCIS at 800-800-5113 or 860-240-3345.

In Person Search: In person searching available.

PACER: Local dial-up access: 860-240-3570, 860-240-3571, 860-240-3572. Case records are available back to 1979. Records are purged every 6 months. New civil records are available online after 1 day. PACER is available online at http://pacer.ctb.uscourts.gov. Document images available.

Electronic Filing: (Currently in the process of implementing CM/ECF.)

New Haven Division The Connecticut Financial Center, 157 Church St, 18th Floor, New Haven, CT 06510 (Courier Address: Use mail address for courier delivery), 203-773-2009. www.ctb.uscourts.gov

Counties: New Haven, New London.

Indexing & Storage: Cases are indexed by debtor as well as by case number. New cases are available in the index 1 week after filing date. Open records are located at this court.

Fee & Payment Notes: Payment may be made by money order, cashier check, personal check. Payee: Clerk, US Bankruptcy Court. You are allowed to make your own copies. These copies cost $.25 per page.

Phone Search: Only docket information is available by phone. An automated voice case information service (VCIS) is available. Call VCIS at 800-800-5113 or 860-240-3345.

In Person Search: In person searching available.

PACER: Local dial-up access: 860-240-3570, 860-240-3571, 860-240-3572. Case records are available back to 1979. Records are purged every 6 months. New civil records are available online after 1 day. PACER is available online at http://pacer.ctb.uscourts.gov. Document images available.

Electronic Filing: (Currently in the process of implementing CM/ECF.)

Connecticut County Courts

Court	Jurisdiction	No. of Courts	How Organized
Judicial District Courts*	General	13	13 Geographic Areas
Geographic Area Courts*	Limited	20	20 Geographic Areas
Probate Courts*	Probate	129	

* Profiled in this Sourcebook.

	CIVIL								
Court	Tort	Contract	Real Estate	Min. Claim	Max. Claim	Small Claims	Estate	Eviction	Domestic Relations
Judicial District Courts*	X	X	X	No Min	No Max				X
Geographic Area Courts*						$3500		X	
Probate Courts*							X		

	CRIMINAL				
Court	Felony	Misdemeanor	DWI/DUI	Preliminary Hearing	Juvenile
Judicial District Courts*	X				X
Geographic Area Courts*		X	X	X	
Probate Courts*					

ADMINISTRATION   Chief Court Administrator, 231 Capitol Av, Hartford, CT, 06106; 860-757-2100, Fax: 860-757-2130. www.jud.state.ct.us

COURT STRUCTURE   The Superior Court is the sole court of original jurisdiction for all causes of action, except for matters over which the probate courts have jurisdiction as provided by statute. The state is divided into 13 Judicial Districts, 20 Geographic Area Courts, and 14 Juvenile Districts. The Superior Court - comprised primarily of the Judicial District Courts and the Geographical Area Courts - has five divisions: Criminal, Civil, Family, Juvenile, and Administrative Appeals. When not combined, the Judicial District Courts handle felony and civil cases while the Geographic Area Courts handle misdemeanors, and most handle small claims

ONLINE ACCESS   The Judicial Branch provides access to civil and family records via the Internet, located online at www.jud2.state.ct.us. Click on "Party Name Inquiry." The site contains party name search, assignment lists and calendars. Also, questions about the fuller commercial system available through Judicial Information Systems should be directed to the CT JIS Office at 860-282-6500. There is currently no online access to criminal records; however, criminal and motor vehicle data is available for purchase in database format.

PROBATE   Probate is handled by city Probate Courts, which we have listed, and are not part of the state court system. Information request requirements are consistent across the state; requesters must provide full name of decedent, year and place of death, and SASE. There is no search fee; the certification fee is $5.00 for 1st 2 pages and $2.00 for each additional page; and, the copy fee is $1.00 per page.

Fairfield County

Bridgeport Judicial District Court
1061 Main St Attn: criminal or civil, Bridgeport, CT 06604; 203-579-6527. Hours: 9AM-5PM (EST). *Felony, Civil Actions.*

Civil Records: Access: Mail, online, in person. Only the court performs in person searches; visitors may not. No search fee. Required to search: name, years to search; also helpful: address. Civil cases indexed by defendant, plaintiff. Civil records on computer for 2 years, on microfiche from 1975 to 1990, prior on index cards. After 5 years sent to Records Center at Enfield, CT. Access to civil case records is available free on the Internet at www.jud2.state.ct.us.

Criminal Records: Access: Mail, in person. Only the court performs in person searches; visitors may not. No search fee. Required to search: name, years to search, DOB. Criminal records on computer since 1997, on microfiche from 1975 to 1996.

General Information: No sealed, adoption records released. SASE required. Turnaround time 2-3 weeks for civil, 4 weeks for criminal. Copy fee: $1.00 per page. Certification fee: $2.00. Fee payee: Chief Clerk Superior Court. Personal checks accepted. Prepayment is required.

Danbury Judicial District Court
146 White St, Danbury, CT 06810; 203-207-8600. Hours: 9AM-5PM (EST). *Felony, Civil Actions.*

Civil Records: Access: Mail, online, in person. Only the court performs in person searches; visitors may not. No search fee. Required to search: name, years to search. Civil cases indexed by plaintiff and defendant. Civil records on microfilm from 11-87, prior on index cards. Free access to civil case records is available on Internet at www.jud2.state.ct.us.

Criminal Records: Access: Mail, in person. Only the court performs in person searches; visitors may not. No search fee. Required to search: name, years to search, DOB. Criminal records on microfilm from 11-87, prior on index cards but only list docket number and disposal date.

General Information: No sealed records released. Turnaround time 2-4 days for civil and family, 3-4 days for motor vehicle and criminal. Fax notes: Will not fax results. Copy fee: $1.00 per page. Certification fee: $2.00 and $1.00 per page. Fee payee: Clerk of Superior Court. Personal checks accepted. Require ID with personal check. Prepayment is required.

Stamford-Norwalk Judicial District Court
123 Hoyt St, Stamford, CT 06905; Civil phone: 203-965-5307; Criminal phone: 203-965-5208. Hours: 9AM-Noon, 1:30PM-4PM (EST). *Felony, Civil Actions.*

Civil Records: Access: Mail, online, in person. Both court and visitors may perform in person searches. No search fee. Required to search: name, years to search. Civil cases indexed by defendant, plaintiff. Only pending civil cases on computer, on microfiche from 1970s, on index cards from 1958. Access to civil case records is available free on the Internet at www.jud2.state.ct.us.

Criminal Records: Access: Phone, mail, in person. Only the court performs in person searches; visitors may not. No search fee. Required to search: name, years to search. Only pending cases on computer, on microfiche from 1970s, on index cards from 1958.

General Information: No sealed records released. Copy fee: $1.00 per page. Certification fee: $2.00. Fee payee: Clerk of Superior Court. Personal checks accepted.

Geographical Area Court #2
172 Golden Hill St, Bridgeport, CT 06604; Civil phone: 203-579-6527; Criminal phone: 203-579-6560. Hours: 9AM-4PM (EST). *Misdemeanor, Eviction, Small Claims.*

Civil Records: Access: Phone, mail, online, in person. Both court and visitors may perform in person searches. No search fee. Required to search: name, years to search. Civil cases indexed by defendant. Civil records pending and from 1990 on computer, on microfiche from 1982 to 1990, prior on index cards. After microfilmed and entered on index cards, sent to Records Center at Enfield, CT. Access to civil case records is available free on the Internet at www.jud2.state.ct.us.

Criminal Records: Access: In person only. Visitors must perform in person searches for themselves. No search fee. Required to search: name, years to search. Criminal records pending and from 1990 on computer, on microfiche from 1982. Refer mail requests to the state criminal records agency, PO Box 2794, Middletown CT 06457, www.state.ct.us/dps/SPBI.htm.

General Information: No sealed records released. Turnaround time up to 4 weeks. Copy fee: $1.00 per page. Certification fee: $3.00. Fee payee: Clerk of Superior Court. Personal checks accepted. Prepayment is required.

Geographical Area Court #20
17 Belden Ave, Norwalk, CT 06850; 203-846-3237; Civil phone: 203-965-5307; Criminal phone: 203-846-3237. Hours: 9AM-5PM (EST). *Misdemeanor, Eviction, Small Claims.*

Civil Records: Access: Online, in person. Visitors must perform in person searches for themselves. No search fee. Required to search: name, years to search. Civil cases indexed by defendant, plaintiff. Civil records on computer from 1986. Access to civil case records is available free on the Internet at www.jud2.state.ct.us.

Criminal Records: Access: In person only. Visitors must perform in person searches for themselves. No search fee. Required to search: name, years to search; also helpful: DOB. Criminal records on computer from 1986, prior records on index cards.

General Information: Copy fee: $1.00 per page. Certification fee: $2.00. Fee payee: Superior Court GA #20. Only cashiers checks and money orders accepted. Prepayment is required.

Geographical Area Court #3
146 White St, Danbury, CT 06810; 203-207-8600. Hours: 9AM-5PM (EST). *Misdemeanor, Eviction, Small Claims.*

Civil Records: Access: Mail, online, in person. Only the court performs in person searches; visitors may not. No search fee. Required to search: name, years to search. Civil cases indexed by defendant. Civil records on microfilm from 11-87, prior on index cards, but only list docket number and disposal date, then referred to Records Center at Enfield, CT. In person searches returned by mail. Access to civil case records is available free on the Internet at www.jud2.state.ct.us.

Criminal Records: Access: Phone, mail, in person. Visitors must perform in person searches for themselves. No search fee. Required to search: name, years to search; also helpful: DOB. Criminal records on computer from 11/9/87. The court refers all requests to one of the 2 statewide agencies.

General Information: No youthful offender or dispositions by dismissal after 20 days from date of judgment records released. SASE required. Turnaround time up to 1 week. Copy fee: $1.00 per page. Certification fee: $2.00. Fee payee: Clerk of Superior Court. Personal checks accepted. Prepayment is required.

Bethel Probate Court
1 School St, PO Box 144, Bethel, CT 06801; 203-794-8508; Fax: 203-794-8564. Hours: 9AM-1:00PM (EST). *Probate.*

Bridgeport Probate District
202 State St, McLevy Hall, 3rd Floor, Bridgeport, CT 06604; 203-576-3945; Fax: 203-576-7898. Hours: 9AM-5PM M-Th; 9AM-4PM F (EST). *Probate.*

Brookfield Probate Court
100 Pocono Rd, PO Box 5192, Brookfield, CT 06804; 203-775-3700; Fax: 203-775-5316. Hours: 9AM-3:30PM (EST). *Probate.*

Danbury Probate Court
155 Deer Hill Ave, Danbury, CT 06810; 203-797-4521; Fax: 203-796-1526. Hours: 8:30AM-4:30PM (EST). *Probate.*

Darien Probate Court
Town Hall, 2 Renshaw Rd, Darien, CT 06820; 203-656-7342; Fax: 203-656-0774. Hours: 9AM-12:30PM, 1:30-4:30PM; 9AM-12:30PM Fri July-Labor Day (EST). *Probate.*

Fairfield Probate Court
Independence Hall, 725 Old Post Rd, Fairfield, CT 06430; 203-256-3041; Fax: 203-256-3044. Hours: 9AM-5PM, 9AM-4:30PM (July-Aug) (EST). *Probate.*

Greenwich Probate Court
101 Field Point Rd, PO Box 2540, Greenwich, CT 06836; 203-622-3766; Fax: 203-622-6451. Hours: 8AM-4PM, 8AM-Noon Fri July-Aug (EST). *Probate.*

New Canaan Probate Court
77 Main St, New Canaan, CT 06840; 203-972-7500; Fax: 203-966-5555. Hours: 8:30AM-4:30PM; (8:30AM-1PM Fri July-Aug) (EST). *Probate.*

New Fairfield Probate Court
4 Brush Hill Rd, New Fairfield, CT 06812; 203-312-5627; Fax: 203-312-5612. Hours: 9AM-Noon W-Th (and by app't) (EST). *Probate.*

Newtown Probate Court
Edmond Town Hall, 45 Main St, Newtown, CT 06470; 203-270-4280; Fax: 203-270-4283. Hours: 8:30AM-Noon,1-4:30PM (EST). *Probate.*

Norwalk Probate Court
125 East Ave, PO Box 2009, Norwalk, CT 06852-2009; 203-854-7737; Fax: 203-854-7825. Hours: 9AM-4:30PM (EST). *Probate.*

Note: District includes Town of Wilton

Redding Probate Court
Town Hall, Lonetown Rd, PO Box 1125, Redding, CT 06875-1125; 203-938-2326; Fax: 203-938-8816. Hours: 9AM-1PM (EST). *Probate.*

Ridgefield Probate Court
Town Hall, 400 Main St, Ridgefield, CT 06877; 203-431-2776; Fax: 203-431-2772. Hours: 8:30AM-4:30PM (EST). *Probate.*

Shelton Probate Court
40 White St, PO Box 127, Shelton, CT 06484; 203-924-8462; Fax: 203-924-8943. Hours: 9AM-5PM; 9AM-6:30PM 1st & 3rd Tues. of month (EST). *Probate.*

Sherman Probate Court
Mallory Town Hall, Rt. 39 Center, PO Box 39, Sherman, CT 06784; 860-355-1821; Fax: 860-350-5041. Hours: 9AM-Noon Tu (and by app't) (EST). *Probate.*

Stamford Probate Court
888 Washington Blvd, 8th Floor, PO Box 10152, Stamford, CT 06904-2152; 203-323-2149; Fax: 203-964-1830. Hours: 9AM-4PM (EST). *Probate.*

Stratford Probate Court 2725 Main St, Town Hall, Stratford, CT 06615; 203-385-4023; Fax: 203-375-6253. Hours: 9:30AM-4:30PM (EST). *Probate.*

Trumbull Probate Court Town Hall, 5866 Main St, Trumbull, CT 06611-5416; 203-452-5068; Fax: 203-452-5092. Hours: 9AM-4:30PM (EST). *Probate.*

Note: District includes Town of Easton

Westport Probate Court Town Hall, 110 Myrtle Ave, Westport, CT 06880; 203-341-1100; Fax: 203-341-1153. Hours: 9AM-4:30PM (EST). *Probate.*

Note: District includes Town of Weston

Hartford County

Hartford Judicial District Court - Civil 95 Washington St, Hartford, CT 06106; 860-548-2700; Fax: 860-548-2711. Hours: 9AM-5PM (EST). *Civil Actions.*

www.jud.state.ct.us

Civil Records: Access: Mail, online, in person. Both court and visitors may perform in person searches. No search fee. Required to search: name, years to search. Civil cases indexed by defendant, plaintiff. Civil records on computer if active, otherwise on microfiche, older records at Enfield Records Center. Access to active civil case records is available free on the Internet at www.jud2.state.ct.us.

General Information: Public access terminal is available. No paternity, support agreement, sealed files, acknowledgments (filed before 10/01/95) records released. SASE required. Turnaround time 7-10 days. Copy fee: $1.00 per page. Certification fee: $2.00. Fee payee: Clerk of Superior Court. Personal checks accepted. Credit cards accepted: Visa, MasterCard. Accepted in person only. $10.00 minimum. Prepayment is required.

Hartford Judicial District Court - Criminal 101 LaFayette St, Hartford, CT 06106; 860-566-1634. Hours: 9AM-5PM (EST). *Felony.*

Criminal Records: Access: Mail, in person. Only the court performs in person searches; visitors may not. No search fee. Required to search: name, years to search; also helpful: DOB. Criminal records on computer from 1989.

General Information: No youthful offender records or dismissals released. SASE required. Turnaround time 7-10 days. Copy fee: $1.00 per page. Certification fee: $2.00. Fee payee: Clerk of Superior Court. Personal checks accepted. Prepayment is required.

New Britain Judicial District Court 20 Franklin Square, New Britain, CT 06051; Civil phone: 860-515-5180; Criminal phone: 860-515-5080. Hours: 9AM-5PM (EST). *Felony, Civil Actions, Small Claims.*

Civil Records: Access: Phone, mail, online, in person. Both court and visitors may perform in person searches. No search fee. Required to search: name, years to search. Civil cases indexed by plaintiff. Civil records on computer up to one year after closing, index cards back to 1989, prior in Hartford. Access to civil case records is available free on the Internet at www.jud2.state.ct.us.

Criminal Records: Access: Phone, mail, in person. Both court and visitors may perform in person searches. No search fee. Required to search: name, years to search. Criminal records on computer for 2 years, then purged when cases sent to State Record Center.

General Information: Public access terminal is available. Certain paternity, family case studies and sealed records not released. SASE required. Turnaround time 3 days. Copy fee: $1.00 per page. Certification fee: $2.00. Fee payee: Clerk of Superior Court. Prepayment is required.

Geographical Area Court #12 410 Center St, Manchester, CT 06040; 860-647-1091. Hours: 9AM-5PM; Phone Hours: 9AM-4PM (EST). *Misdemeanor, Eviction, Small Claims.*

Note: Evictions are handled by a special Housing Court, 18 Trinity, Hartford, CT; 860-566-8550.

Civil Records: Access: Mail, online, in person. Both court and visitors may perform in person searches. No search fee. Required to search: name, years to search. Civil cases indexed by defendant. Civil records on computer for 3 years. Access to civil case records is available free on the Internet at www.jud2.state.ct.us.

Criminal Records: Access: Mail, in person. Only the court performs in person searches; visitors may not. No search fee. Required to search: name, years to search, DOB. Criminal records on computer since 1999, available since 1979. In person search results returned by mail only.

General Information: No non disclosable records released. SASE required. Turnaround time 1-2 weeks. Copy fee: $1.00 per page. Certification fee: $2.00. Fee payee: Clerk of Superior Court.

Geographical Area Court #13 111 Phoenix, Enfield, CT 06082; 860-741-3727. Hours: 9AM-1PM, 2:30-4PM (EST). *Misdemeanor.*

Note: Eviction cases are handled by Hartford Housing, 860-756-7920.

Civil Records: Access: Online, in person. Visitors must perform in person searches for themselves. No search fee. Required to search: name, years to search. Civil cases indexed by defendant. Civil records on computer for 1 year, microfiche by year, archived at Record Center at Enfield, CT. Access to civil case records is available free on the Internet at www.jud2.state.ct.us.

Criminal Records: Access: In person, mail. Visitors must perform in person searches for themselves. No search fee. Required to search: name, years to search, DOB. Criminal records on computer for 3 years, microfiche by year, archived at Record Center at Enfield, CT.

General Information: No copy fee. Certification fee: None; Certification available from State Record Center. Fee payee: Clerk of Superior Court. Personal checks accepted. Prepayment is required.

Geographical Area Court #15 20 Franklin Square, New Britain, CT 06051; Civil phone: 860-515-5180; Criminal phone: 860-515-5080. Hours: 8:15AM-5PM (EST). *Misdemeanor, Eviction, Small Claims.*

Civil Records: Access: Mail, online, in person. Only the court performs in person searches; visitors may not. No search fee. Required to search: name, years to search. Civil cases indexed by defendant, plaintiff. Civil records on computer for 3 years, then on microfiche. All info in archives at Record Center at Enfield, CT. Access to civil case records is available free on the Internet at www.jud2.state.ct.us.

Criminal Records: Access: Mail, in person. Only the court performs in person searches; visitors may not. No search fee. Required to search: name, years to search, DOB. Criminal records on computer from 1985, then on microfiche. All info in archives at Record Center @ Enfield, CT. Data is purged every two years.

General Information: No sealed records released. SASE required. Turnaround time 1 month. Copy fee: $1.00 per page. Certification fee: $2.00. Certification fee is for criminal division. Civil fee varies. Fee payee: Clerk of Superior Court. Business checks accepted. Prepayment is required.

Geographical Area Court #17 131 N Main St, Bristol, CT 06010; 860-582-8111. Hours: 9AM-5PM (EST). *Misdemeanor, Eviction, Small Claims.*

www.jud2.state.ct.us

Criminal Records: Access: Phone, mail, in person. Only the court performs in person searches; visitors

may not. No search fee. Required to search: name, years to search, DOB. Criminal records on computer from 1986, on microfiche from 1982, prior on index cards from 1979-1992, microfiche 1988-1996 and docket books; records on computer for 5 years, then put on microfiche.

General Information: No dismissals, not guilty, youthful offender or NOLLE records released. SASE required. Turnaround time 1-2 days. Copy fee: $1.00 per page. Fee payee: Clerk of Superior Court. Personal checks accepted. Prepayment is required.

Geographical Area Court #14 101 LaFayette St, Hartford, CT 06106; 860-566-1630. Hours: 9AM-5PM (EST). *Misdemeanor.*

Criminal Records: Access: Mail, in person. Only the court performs in person searches; visitors may not. No search fee. Required to search: name, years to search, DOB. Computerized records for past 3 years.

General Information: SASE required. Turnaround time 1 week. Copy fee: $1.00 per page. Certification fee: $2.00. Fee payee: Clerk of Superior Court. Personal checks accepted. Prepayment is required.

Geographical Area Court #16 105 Raymond Rd, West Hartford, CT 06107; 860-236-4551; Fax: 860-236-9311. Hours: 9AM-5PM (EST). *Misdemeanor.*

Criminal Records: Access: Mail, in person. Only the court performs in person searches; visitors may not. No search fee. Required to search: name, years to search, DOB, signed release.

General Information: No dismissal, Nolles, YO records released. SASE required. Turnaround time 3-5 days. Copy fee: $1.00 per page. Certification fee: $3.00. Fee payee: Clerk of Superior Court. Personal checks accepted. Credit cards accepted: Visa, MasterCard. Accepted in person only. Prepayment is required.

Avon Probate Court 60 W Main St, Avon, CT 06001-0578; 860-409-4348; Fax: 860-409-4368. Hours: 9AM-Noon (EST). *Probate.*

Berlin Probate Court 177 Columbus Blvd, PO Box 400, New Britain, CT 06050-0400; 860-826-2696; Fax: 860-826-2695. Hours: 9AM-4PM (EST). *Probate.*

Note: District includes Town of New Britain

Bloomfield Probate Court Town Hall, 800 Bloomfield Ave, Bloomfield, CT 06002; 860-769-3548; Fax: 860-769-3598. Hours: 9AM-1PM, 2AM-4:30PM (EST). *Probate.*

Bristol Probate Court 111 N Main St, City Hall, 3rd Fl, Bristol, CT 06010; 860-584-6230; Fax: 860-584-3818. Hours: 9AM-5PM (EST). *Probate.*

Burlington Probate Court 200 Spielman Highway, Burlington, CT 06013; 860-673-2108; Fax: 860-675-9312. Hours: 1PM-6PM M-Th (and by app't) (EST). *Probate.*

Canton Probate Court Canton Town Hall, 4 Market St, PO Box 175, Collinsville, CT 06022-0175; 860-693-7851; Fax: 860-693-7889. Hours: 8:30AM-1PM Tu-Th (and by app't) (EST). *Probate.*

East Granby Probate Court PO Box 542, 9 Center St, East Granby, CT 06026-0542; 860-653-3434; Fax: 860-653-7085. Hours: 10AM-1PM Tu; 9AM-Noon W-Th (and by app't) (EST). *Probate.*

East Hartford Probate Court Town Hall, 740 Main St, East Hartford, CT 06108; 860-291-7278; Fax: 860-289-0831. Hours: 9AM-4PM (EST). *Probate.*

East Windsor Probate Court Town Hall, 1540 Sullivan Ave, South Windsor, CT 06074; 860-644-2511 X271; Fax: 860-648-5047. Hours: 8AM-2PM (EST). *Probate.*

Note: District includes Town of South Windsor

Enfield Probate Court 820 Enfield St, Enfield, CT 06082; 860-253-6305; Fax: 860-253-6388. Hours: 9AM-4:30PM (till 6:30PM 1st Monday) (EST). *Probate.*

Farmington Probate Court One Monteith Dr, Farmington, CT 06032; 860-675-2360; Fax: 860-673-8262. Hours: 9AM-4PM (EST). *Probate.*

Glastonbury Probate Court PO Box 6523, 2155 Main St, Glastonbury, CT 06033-6523; 860-652-7629; Fax: 860-368-2520. Hours: 9:30AM-4:30PM (EST). *Probate.*

Granby Probate Court 15 N Granby Rd, Town Hall, PO Box 240, Granby, CT 06035-0240; 860-653-8944; Fax: 860-653-4769. Hours: 9AM-Noon T,W,F (EST). *Probate.*

Hartford Probate Court 10 Prospect St, 4th Fl, Hartford, CT 06103; 860-522-1813; Fax: 860-724-1503. Hours: 9AM-4PM (4-6:30PM Mon. by app't) (EST). *Probate.*

Note: In 2003, court will merge with Hartland Probate to form the New District of Hartford Probate Court.

Hartland Probate Court PO Box 457, Riverton, CT 06065; 860-653-0287; Fax: 860-738-1003. Hours: 10AM-1PM M-Tu (EST). *Probate.*

Note: In 2003, court will merge with Hartland Probate to form the New District of Hartford Probate Court.

Manchester Probate Court 66 Center St, Manchester, CT 06040; 860-647-3227; Fax: 860-647-3236. Hours: 8:30AM-Noon, 1-4:30PM (EST). *Probate.*

Marlborough Probate Court 26 N Main St, PO Box 29, Marlborough, CT 06447; 860-295-6239; Fax: 860-295-0317. Hours: 9AM-4:30PM M; 2:30-7PM T; 2:30PM-4:30 Th (and by app't) (EST). *Probate.*

Note: Hours are 9AM-4:30PM on Mon, 2:30PM-7PM on Tues, and 2:30PM-4:30PM on Thurs

Newington Probate Court 66 Cedar Street, Rear, Newington, CT 06111; 860-665-1285; Fax: 860-665-1331. Hours: 9AM-4PM M-W, F; 9AM-7PM Th (EST). *Probate.*

Note: District includes towns of Rocky Hill, Wethersfield

Plainville Probate Court 1 Central Square, Plainville, CT 06062; 860-793-0221 x250; Fax: 860-793-2424. Hours: 9AM-3PM M-Th; 9AM-1PM F (EST). *Probate.*

Simsbury Probate Court 933 Hopmeadow St, PO Box 495, Simsbury, CT 06070; 860-658-3277; Fax: 860-658-3206. Hours: 8:30AM-!PM, 2-4:30PM (and by app't) (EST). *Probate.*

Southington Probate Court Town Hall, 75 Main St, PO Box 165, Southington, CT 06489; 860-276-6253; Fax: 860-276-6255. Hours: 8:30AM-4:30PM M-W, F; 8:30AM-7PM Th (EST). *Probate.*

Suffield Probate Court 83 Mountain Rd, Town Hall, PO Box 234, Suffield, CT 06078; 860-668-3835; Fax: 860-668-3029. Hours: 9AM-1PM (and by app't) (EST). *Probate.*

West Hartford Probate Court 50 S Main St, West Hartford, CT 06107; 860-523-3174; Fax: 860-236-8352. Hours: 8:30AM-4:30PM (EST). *Probate.*

Windsor Locks Probate Court Town Office Bldg, 50 Church St, Windsor Locks, CT 06096; 860-627-1450; Fax: 860-627-1451. Hours: 9AM-2PM M-Th (EST). *Probate.*

Windsor Probate Court 275 Broad St, PO Box 342, Windsor, CT 06095; 860-285-1976; Fax: 860-285-1909. Hours: 8:30AM-4:30PM M-Th; 8:30AM-Noon Fri (EST). *Probate.*

Litchfield County

Litchfield Judicial District Court PO Box 247, Litchfield, CT 06759; 860-567-0885; Fax: 860-567-4779. Hours: 9AM-5PM (EST). *Felony, Civil Actions.*

Civil Records: Access: Fax, mail, online, in person. Only the court performs in person searches; visitors may not. No search fee. Required to search: name, years to search. Civil cases indexed by defendant, plaintiff. Pending cases only on computer, on index cards from 1972. Access to civil case records is available free on the Internet at www.jud2.state.ct.us.
Criminal Records: Access: Fax, mail, in person. Only the court performs in person searches; visitors may not. No search fee. Required to search: name, years to search; also helpful: DOB. Pending cases only on computer, on index cards from 1972.
General Information: No sealed files released. SASE required. Turnaround time 3-4 weeks. Fax notes: No fee to fax results. Copy fee: $1.00 per page. Certification fee: $2.00. Fee payee: Clerk of Superior Court. Personal checks accepted. Prepayment is required.

Geographical Area Court #18 80 Doyle Rd (PO Box 667), Bantam, CT 06750; 860-567-3942. Hours: 9AM-5PM (EST). *Misdemeanor, Eviction, Small Claims.*

Civil Records: Access: Mail, online, in person. Both court and visitors may perform in person searches. No search fee. Required to search: name, years to search. Civil cases indexed by defendant. Civil records on computer for 2 years, on microfiche from 1986. Access to civil case records is available free on the Internet at www.jud2.state.ct.us.
Criminal Records: Access: Mail, in person. Only the court performs in person searches; visitors may not. No search fee. Required to search: name, years to search, DOB; also helpful: address. Criminal records on computer for 1 year, microfiche from 1986, on index cards for 40 years. Archived at Records Center at Enfield, CT.
General Information: No youthful offender or non-discloseable records released. SASE required. Turnaround time 1 week. Copy fee: $1.00 per page. Certification fee: $2.00. Fee payee: Clerk of Superior Court. Personal checks accepted.

Barkhamsted Probate Court 67 Ripley Rd, PO Box 185, Pleasant Valley, CT 06063-0185; 860-379-8665; Fax: 860-379-9284. Hours: 10AM-1PM M-W (and by app't) (EST). *Probate.*

Canaan Probate Court Town Hall, 100 Pease St, PO Box 905, Canaan, CT 06018-0905; 860-824-7114; Fax: 860-824-3139. Hours: 9AM-1PM (and by app't) (EST). *Probate.*

Cornwall Probate Court PO Box 157, Town Office Bldg, Cornwall, CT 06753-0157; 860-672-2677; Fax: 860-672-2677. Hours: 9AM-12PM T & Th (EST). *Probate.*

Harwinton Probate Court Town Hall, 100 Bentley Dr, Harwinton, CT 06791; 860-485-1403; Fax: 860-485-0051. Hours: 1-6PM Tu-W (and by app't) (EST). *Probate.*

Kent Probate Court Town Hall, 41 Kent Green Blvd, PO Box 185, Kent, CT 06757-0185; 860-927-3729; Fax: 860-927-1313. Hours: 9AM-Noon Tu & Th (and by app't) (EST). *Probate.*

Litchfield Probate Court 74 West St, PO Box 505, Litchfield, CT 06759; 860-567-8065; Fax: 860-567-2538. Hours: 9AM-1PM (and by app't) (EST). *Probate.*

Note: District includes towns of Morris, Warren, and Litchfield

New Hartford Probate Court Town Hall, 530 Main St, PO Box 308, New Hartford, CT 06057; 860-379-3254; Fax: 860-379-8560. Hours: 9AM-Noon M,W (and by app't) (EST). *Probate.*

New Milford Probate Court 10 Main St, New Milford, CT 06776; 860-355-6029; Fax: 860-355-6002. Hours: 9AM-Noon, 1-5PM M-Th, closed Friday (EST). *Probate.*

Note: District includes Town of Bridgewater

Norfolk Probate Court 19 Maple Ave, PO Box 648, Norfolk, CT 06058; 860-542-5134; Fax: 860-542-5876. Hours: 9AM-Noon Tu & Th (and by app't) (EST). *Probate.*

Plymouth Probate Court 80 Main St, Terryville, CT 06786; 860-585-4014. Hours: 9AM-2PM Tu & Th (and by app't) (EST). *Probate.*

Roxbury Probate Court Town Hall, 29 North St, PO Box 203, Roxbury, CT 06783; 860-354-1184; Fax: 860-355-3091. Hours: 9AM-3PM Tu-Th (and by app't) (EST). *Probate.*

Salisbury Probate Court Town Hall, 27 Main St, PO Box 525, Salisbury, CT 06068; 860-435-5183; Fax: 860-435-5172. Hours: 9AM-Noon (and by app't) (EST). *Probate.*

Sharon Probate Court 63 Main St, PO Box 1177, Sharon, CT 06069; 860-364-5514; Fax: 860-364-5789. Hours: 2-4PM M-W & F (and by app't) (EST). *Probate.*

Thomaston Probate Court 158 Main St, Town Hall Bldg, PO Box 136, Thomaston, CT 06787; 860-283-4874; Fax: 860-283-1013 (police dept). Hours: 3-6PM M-W (and by app't) (EST). *Probate.*

Torrington Probate Court Municipal Bldg, 140 Main St, Torrington, CT 06790; 860-489-2215; Fax: 860-496-5910. Hours: 8:30AM-4:30PM (EST). *Probate.*

Note: District includes Town of Goshen

Washington Probate Court Town Hall, 2 Bryan Mem. Plaza, PO Box 295, Washington Depot, CT 06794; 860-868-7974; Fax: 860-868-0512. Hours: 9AM-Noon, 1-3PM M,W,F (and by app't) (EST). *Probate.*

Watertown Probate Court 37 DeForest St, Town Hall, Watertown, CT 06795; 860-945-5237; Fax: 860-945-4741. Hours: 9AM-Noon, 1-3PM (EST). *Probate.*

Winchester Probate Court 338 Main St, PO Box 625, Winsted, CT 06098; 860-379-5576; Fax: 860-738-7053. Hours: 9AM-12,1-4PM M-W, 9Am-2PM, 3-7PM Th, til noon Fri (EST). *Probate.*

Note: District includes towns of Colebrook, Winsted

Woodbury Probate Court 281 Main St, South, PO Box 84, Woodbury, CT 06798; 203-263-2417; Fax: 203-263-2748. Hours: 9AM-4PM Tu,Th (and by app't) (EST). *Probate.*

Note: District includes Town of Bethlehem

Middlesex County

Middlesex District Court - Criminal & GA Court #9 1 Court St, 1st Flr, Middletown, CT 06457-3348; 860-343-6445. Hours: 9AM-5PM (EST). *Felony, Misdemeanor.*

Criminal Records: Access: Mail, in person. Only the court performs in person searches; visitors may not. No search fee. Required to search: name, years to search, DOB, signed release; also helpful: address, SSN. Criminal records on computer for 1 year from disposition or sentence, on microfiche prior to 1984, prior on index cards to 1961.

General Information: No youthful offender records or dismissals released. Turnaround time 3-4 days. Copy fee: $1.00 per page. Certification fee: $2.50. Fee payee: Clerk, Superior Court. Personal checks accepted. Prepayment is required.

Middlesex Judicial District Court - Civil 1 Court St, 2nd Floor, Middletown, CT 06457-3374; 860-343-6400; Fax: 860-343-6423. Hours: 9AM-5PM (EST). *Civil Actions.*

Civil Records: Access: Mail, online, in person. Both the court and visitors may perform in person searches. No search fee. Required to search: name, years to search; also helpful: type of case. Civil cases indexed by defendant, plaintiff. Civil records on computer 1 year post-judgment; on index card back 15 years, prior on docket books, microfiche. Access to civil case records is available free on the Internet at www.jud2.state.ct.us.

General Information: No sealed records released. SASE required. Turnaround time 1 week. Copy fee: $1.00 per page. Certification fee: $2.00; judgment file copy-$15.00; judgment in foreclosure action-$20.00; Exemplification copies-$20.00. Fee payee: Clerk, Superior Court. Personal checks accepted. Name and address must be on pre-printed check. Prepayment is required.

Clinton Probate Court 50 E Main St, PO Box 130, Clinton, CT 06413-0130; 860-669-6447; Fax: 860-669-6447 (call first). Hours: 10AM-3PM M-Th (Fri. by app't) (EST). *Probate.*

Deep River Probate Court Town Hall, 174 Main St, PO Box 391, Deep River, CT 06417; 860-526-6026; Fax: 860-526-6094 (call first). Hours: 9AM-Noon, 1PM-4PM Tu,Th (and by app't) (EST). *Probate.*

East Haddam Probate Court PO Box 217, 7 Main St, East Haddam, CT 06423; 860-873-5028; Fax: 860-873-5025. Hours: 10AM-2PM (and by app't) (EST). *Probate.*

East Hampton Probate Court 20 East High St, Annex, East Hampton, CT 06424; 860-267-9262; Fax: 860-267-6453. Hours: 9AM-2PM T-Th (EST). *Probate.*

Essex Probate Court Town Hall, 29 West Ave, Essex, CT 06426; 860-767-4340 X125; Fax: 860-767-8509. Hours: 9AM-1PM (and by app't) (EST). *Probate.*

Haddam Probate Court 30 Field Park Dr, Haddam, CT 06438; 860-345-8531; Fax: 860-345-3730. Hours: 10AM-2PM T-Th (and by app't) (EST). *Probate.*

Killingworth Probate Court 323 Route 81, Killingworth, CT 06419; 860-663-2304; Fax: 860-663-3305. Hours: 9AM-Noon M,W,F (and by app't) (EST). *Probate.*

Middletown Probate Court 94 Court St, Middletown, CT 06457; 860-347-7424; Fax: 860-346-1520. Hours: 8:30AM-4:30PM (EST). *Probate.*

Note: District includes towns of Cornwall, Durham, Middlefield

Old Saybrook Probate Court 251 Main St, Old Saybrook, CT 06475; 860-395-3128; Fax: 860-395-3125. Hours: 9AM-1PM M,T,TH,F (Wed. eves by app't) (EST). *Probate.*

Note: Court is open on Wed. evenings, also

Portland Probate Court 33 E Main St, PO Box 71, Portland, CT 06480; 860-342-6739; Fax: 860-342-0001. Hours: 9AM-2PM (EST). *Probate.*

Saybrook Probate Court 65 Main St, PO Box 628, Chester, CT 06412; 860-526-0007; Fax: 860-526-0004. Hours: 9:30AM-12:30PM T-Th (and by app't) (EST). *Probate.*

Note: District includes Town of Chester

Westbrook Probate Court 1163 Boston Post Rd, PO Box 676, Westbrook, CT 06498; 860-399-5661; Fax: 860-399-9832. Hours: 1-4:30PM (EST). *Probate.*

New Haven County

Ansonia-Milford Judicial District Court 14 W River St (PO Box 210), Milford, CT 06460; 203-877-4293. Hours: 9AM-4PM (EST). *Felony, Civil Actions.*

Civil Records: Access: Mail, fax, online, in person. Only the court performs in person searches; visitors may not. No search fee. Required to search: name, years to search. Civil cases indexed by defendant, plaintiff. Civil records on computer back to 1993, on index cards from 1978. Purged computer records are on microfilm. Maintain 75 years at Records Center at Enfield, CT. Access to civil case records is available free on the Internet at www.jud2.state.ct.us.

Criminal Records: Access: Mail, in person. Only the court performs in person searches; visitors may not. No search fee. Required to search: name, years to search, DOB; also helpful-SSN. Criminal records on computer back to 1993, on index cards from 1978. Purged computer records are on microfilm. Maintain 75 years at Records Center at Enfield, CT.

General Information: SASE required. Turnaround time 1-2 weeks. Fax notes: Will fax back results only to toll-free or local numbers. Copy fee: $1.00 per page. Fee payee: Clerk of Superior Court. Personal checks accepted. Prepayment is required.

Meriden Judicial District Court 54 W Main St, Meriden, CT 06451; 203-238-6666. Hours: 9AM-4PM (EST). *Civil Actions.*

Civil Records: Access: Mail, online, in person. Only the court performs in person searches; visitors may not. No search fee. Required to search: name, years to search. Civil cases indexed by defendant, plaintiff. Pending and 1 yr after disposed cases on computer, on microfiche from 1984, prior on index cards. Access to civil case records is available free on the Internet at www.jud2.state.ct.us.

General Information: No acknowledgments of paternity, agreements to support prior to 10/01/95 records released. SASE required. Turnaround time 1-2 days. Copy fee: $1.00 per page. Certification fee: $2.00. Fee payee: Clerk of Superior Court. Personal checks accepted. In state personal checks accepted. Prepayment is required.

New Haven Judicial District Court 235 Church St, New Haven, CT 06510; 203-503-6800; Fax: 203-789-6424. Hours: 9AM-5PM (EST). *Felony, Civil Actions family.*

www.jud.state.ct.us/directory/directory/location/newhaven.htm

Civil Records: Access: Phone, mail, online, in person. Only the court performs in person searches; visitors may not. No search fee. Required to search: name, years to search. Civil cases indexed by defendant, plaintiff.

Pending cases on computer, disposed cases deleted after 1 year, on microfiche from 1972, prior on index cards. Access to civil case records is available free on the Internet at www.jud2.state.ct.us.

Criminal Records: Access: Mail, in person. Only the court performs in person searches; visitors may not. No search fee. Required to search: name, years to search, DOB. Pending criminal cases on computer, disposed deleted after 1 year, prior on index cards.

General Information: Public access terminal is available. (Live civil cases only.) No sealed records released. SASE required. Turnaround time 2-5 weeks. Copy fee: $1.00 per page. Certification fee: $2.00. Fee payee: Clerk of Superior Court. Personal checks accepted. CT personal checks accepted if address on check matches address on drivers license. Prepayment is required.

Waterbury Judicial District Court 300 Grand St, Waterbury, CT 06702; 203-596-4023; Civil phone: Small claims: 203-596-4050; Fax: 203-596-4032. Hours: 9AM-5PM (EST). *Civil Actions, Small Claims.*

Note: Address mail requests for Misdemeanor criminal searches to 400 Grand St. (Geographical Area Court #4)

Civil Records: Access: Fax, mail, online, in person. Only the court performs in person searches; visitors may not. No search fee. Required to search: name, years to search. Civil cases indexed by defendant. Civil records on computer back to 1990; none-computer records go back to 1900. Phone access limited to one search. Access to civil case records is available free on the Internet at www.jud2.state.ct.us.

General Information: SASE required. Turnaround time 1-2 weeks. Copy fee: $1.00 per page. Certification fee: $2.00. Fee payee: Clerk of Superior Court. Personal checks accepted. Prepayment is required.

Geographical Area Court #22 14 W River St, Milford, CT 06460; 203-874-0674 (Small Claims); Civil phone: 203-877-4293; Criminal phone: 203-874-1116. Hours: 1-2:30PM, 4-5PM (EST). *Misdemeanor, Eviction, Small Claims.*

Civil Records: Access: Mail, online, in person. Only the court performs in person searches; visitors may not. No search fee. Required to search: name, years to search. Civil cases indexed by defendant, plaintiff. Civil records on computer for 6 months, after disposal, on microfiche from 1986, prior on index cards and docket books. Access to civil case records is available free on the Internet at www.jud2.state.ct.us.

Criminal Records: Access: Mail, in person. Only the court performs in person searches; visitors may not. No search fee. Required to search: name, years to search; also helpful: DOB. Criminal records on computer for 6 months, after disposal, on microfiche from 1986, prior on index cards and docket books.

General Information: SASE required. Turnaround time 1 week. Copy fee: $1.00 per page. Certification fee: $2.00. Fee payee: Clerk of Superior Court. Personal checks accepted. Prepayment is required.

Geographical Area Court #4 400 Grand St, Waterbury, CT 06702; 203-236-8100; Fax: 203-236-8099. Hours: 9AM-5PM (EST). *Felony, Misdemeanor, Traffic.*

www.jud.state.ct.us

Criminal Records: Access: Phone, mail, in person. Only the court performs in person searches; visitors may not. No search fee. Required to search: name, years to search; also helpful: DOB. Criminal records on computer since 1985.

General Information: No youthful offenders records or dismissals released. SASE required. Turnaround time 1-2 weeks. Copy fee: $1.00 per page. Certification fee: $2.00. Fee payee: Clerk of Superior Court. Personal checks accepted. Prepayment is required.

Geographical Area Court #5 106 Elizabeth St, Derby, CT 06418; 203-735-7438. Hours: 9AM-4PM (EST). *Misdemeanor, Eviction, Small Claims.*

Civil Records: Access: Mail, online, in person. Only the court performs in person searches; visitors may not. No search fee. Required to search: name, years to search. Civil cases indexed by defendant, plaintiff. Pending and records for 1 yr after disposal on computer, on microfiche from 1986, prior on index cards. In person search results are mailed back. Access to civil case records is available free on the Internet at www.jud2.state.ct.us.

Criminal Records: Access: Mail, in person. Only the court performs in person searches; visitors may not. No search fee. Required to search: name, years to search, DOB. Pending and records for 1 yr after disposal on computer, on microfiche from 1986, prior on index cards. In person search results returned by mail only.

General Information: No sealed records released. SASE required. Turnaround time 1-2 weeks. Copy fee: $1.00 per page. Certification fee: $2.00. Fee payee: Clerk of Superior Court. Personal checks accepted. Prepayment is required.

Geographical Area Court #6 121 Elm St, New Haven, CT 06510; 203-789-7461; Civil phone: 203-503-6800; Fax: 203-789-6455. Hours: 9AM-5PM (EST). *Misdemeanor, Eviction, Small Claims.*

Civil Records: Access: Mail, online, in person. Only the court performs in person searches; visitors may not. No search fee. Required to search: name, years to search. Civil records on log book for small claims. Records go back to 1800's. Access to civil case records is available free on the Internet at www.jud2.state.ct.us.

Criminal Records: Access: Mail, in person. Only the court performs in person searches; visitors may not. No search fee. Required to search: name, years to search, DOB. Criminal records on computer back 13 months, microfiche from 1986, prior archived for criminal and motor vehicle. In person search results mailed back.

General Information: No dismissals, juvenile records released. SASE required. Turnaround time 2-3 weeks. Copy fee: $1.00 per page. Certification fee: $2.00. Fee payee: Superior Court. Personal checks accepted. Prepayment is required.

Geographical Area Court #7 54 W Main St, Meriden, CT 06451; Criminal phone: 203-238-6130; Fax: 203-238-6322. Hours: 9AM-5PM (EST). *Misdemeanor, Small Claims.*

Civil Records: Access: Mail, online, in person. Only the court performs in person searches; visitors may not. No search fee. Required to search: name, years to search. Civil cases indexed by defendant, plaintiff. Pending and 1 yr after disposed cases on computer, on microfiche from 1985, prior on index cards. All manual records by docket number. Access to civil case records is available free on the Internet at www.jud2.state.ct.us.

Criminal Records: Access: Phone, mail, in person. Only the court performs in person searches; visitors may not. No search fee. Required to search: name, years to search, DOB. Criminal records on computer since 1986, purged every 6 months and maintained in Enfield, CT.

General Information: No sealed records released. SASE required. Turnaround time 1-2 days. Copy fee: $1.00 per page. Certification fee: $10.00. Fee payee: Clerk of Superior Court. Personal checks accepted. Prepayment is required.

Bethany Probate Court Town Hall, 40 Peck Rd, Bethany, CT 06524; 203-393-3744; Fax: 203-393-0821. Hours: 9AM-Noon T,TH (EST). *Probate.*

Branford Probate Court PO Box 638, 1019 Main St, Branford, CT 06405-0638; 203-488-0318; Fax: 203-315-4715. Hours: 9AM-Noon, 1-4:30PM (till Noon, Fridays in Summer) (EST). *Probate.*

Cheshire Probate Court 84 S Main St, Cheshire, CT 06410; 203-271-6608; Fax: 203-271-6628. Hours: 8:30AM-1PM, 1:30PM-4PM M-Th (EST). *Probate.*

Note: District includes town of Prospect. On Fridays, they close at 12:30

Derby Probate Court 253 Main St, 2nd Fl, Ansonia, CT 06401; 203-734-1277; Fax: 203-736-1434. Hours: 8AM-5PM M-Th; 8-4 F (EST). *Probate.*

Note: District includes towns of Ansonia, Seymour

East Haven Probate Court 250 Main St, Town Hall, East Haven, CT 06512; 203-468-3895. Hours: 9AM-3:30PM, except 1PM on Fri (EST). *Probate.*

Guilford Probate Court Town Hall, 31 Park St, Guilford, CT 06437; 203-453-8006; Fax: 203-453-8017. Hours: 9AM-Noon,1-4PM M,T,Th,F; 9AM-Noon W (EST). *Probate.*

Hamden Probate Court 2372 Whitney Ave, Memorial Town Hall, Hamden, CT 06518; 203-287-2570; Fax: 203-287-2571. Hours: 8:30AM-4:30PM (EST). *Probate.*

Madison Probate Court 8 Campus Dr, PO Box 205, Madison, CT 06443; 203-245-5661; Fax: 203-245-5653. Hours: 9AM-3PM (and by app't) (EST). *Probate.*

Meriden Probate Court City Hall, E Main St, Rm 113, Meriden, CT 06450; 203-630-4150; Fax: 203-630-4043. Hours: 8:30AM-7PM M; 8:30-4:30 T-F (EST). *Probate.*

Milford Probate Court Parsons Office Complex, 70 W River St, PO Box 414, Milford, CT 06460; 203-783-3205; Fax: 203-783-3364. Hours: 9AM-5PM (EST). *Probate.*

Naugatuck Probate Court Town Hall, 229 Church St, Naugatuck, CT 06770; 203-720-7046; Fax: 203-729-9452. Hours: 9AM-4PM M-Th; 9AM-3PM F (EST). *Probate.*

Note: District includes Town of Beacon Falls

New Haven Probate Court 200 Orange St, 1st Floor, PO Box 905, New Haven, CT 06504; 203-946-4880; Fax: 203-946-5962. Hours: 9AM-4PM (EST). *Probate.*

North Branford Probate Court 1599 Foxon Rd, PO Box 214, North Branford, CT 06471; 203-315-6007; Fax: 203-315-6025. Hours: 8:45AM-12:45PM (EST). *Probate.*

North Haven Probate Court 18 Church St, PO Box 175, North Haven, CT 06473-0175; 203-239-5321 X775; Fax: 203-239-1874. Hours: 8:30AM-4:30PM M-Th (and by app't) (EST). *Probate.*

Orange Probate Court 525 Orange Center Rd, Orange, CT 06477; 203-891-2160; Fax: 203-891-2161. Hours: 9AM-Noon (EST). *Probate.*

Oxford Probate Court Town Hall, Rt. 67, Oxford, CT 06478; 203-888-2543 x3014; Fax: 203-888-2136. Hours: 7-9PM Mon, 7-9PM Tu-W, 1-5PM, 7-9PM Th (EST). *Probate.*

Southbury Probate Court Townhall Annex, 421 Main St South, PO Box 674, Southbury, CT 06488; 203-262-0641; Fax: 203-264-9310. Hours: 9AM-4:30PM (and by app't) (EST). *Probate.*

Wallingford Probate Court Town Hall, 45 S Main St, Rm 114, Wallingford, CT 06492; 203-294-2100; Fax: 203-294-2109. Hours: 9AM-5PM (EST). *Probate.*

Waterbury Probate Court 236 Grand St, Waterbury, CT 06702; 203-755-1127; Fax: 203-597-0824. Hours: 9AM-4:45PM MTWF; 9AM-6PM Th; 9AM-Noon Sat (EST). *Probate.*

Note: District includes towns of Middlebury, Wolcott

West Haven Probate Court 355 Main St, PO Box 127, West Haven, CT 06516; 203-937-3552/3/4/5; Fax: 203-937-3556. Hours: 9AM-4PM (EST). *Probate.*

Woodbridge Probate Court Town Hall, 11 Meetinghouse Ln, Woodbridge, CT 06525; 203-389-3410; Fax: 203-389-3480. Hours: 3-7PM M, 9AM-1PM W (EST). *Probate.*

New London County

New London Judicial District Court 70 Huntington St, New London, CT 06320; 860-443-5363. Hours: 9AM-5PM (EST). *Felony, Civil Actions.*

Civil Records: Access: Mail, online, in person. No search fee. Required to search: exact name, years to search. Civil cases indexed by defendant, plaintiff. Civil records pending and 1 yr after disposed on computer, on microfiche from mid-70s. In person access limited to five names. Access to civil case records is available free on the Internet at www.jud2.state.ct.us.

Criminal Records: Access: Mail, in person. Only the court performs in person searches; visitors may not. No search fee. Required to search: name, years to search; also helpful: DOB. Criminal records on computer from 1991, prior on index cards.

General Information: No sealed or youthful offender records released. SASE required. Turnaround time 2 weeks. Copy fee: $1.00 per page. Certification fee: $2.00. Fee payee: Clerk of Superior Court. Personal checks accepted. Prepayment is required.

Norwich Judicial District Court 1 Courthouse Square, Norwich, CT 06360; 860-887-3515; Fax: 860-887-8643. Hours: 9AM-5PM (EST). *Civil Actions.*

www.jud.state.ct.us

Civil Records: Access: Phone, mail, fax, online, in person. Only the court performs in person searches; visitors may not. No search fee. Required to search: name, years to search. Civil cases indexed by defendant, plaintiff. Pending and disposed cases on computer from 1992, on microfiche from 1975, prior on index cards. Access to civil case records is available free at the web site.

General Information: No criminal search warrant, acknowledgment of paternity prior to 1995, sealed records released. SASE required. Turnaround time up to a month. Copy fee: $1.00 per page. Judgment copies $10.00. Certification fee: $2.00. Certified copy of Judgment $15.00. Fee payee: Clerk of Superior Court. Personal checks accepted. Checks must have imprinted name and address and match valid CT driver license. Prepayment is required.

Geographical Area Court #10 112 Broad St, New London, CT 06320; 860-443-8343. Hours: 9AM-5PM (EST). *Misdemeanor, Eviction, Small Claims.*

www.jud.state.ct.us

Civil Records: Access: Mail, online, in person. Both court and visitors may perform in person searches. No search fee. Required to search: name, years to search. Civil cases indexed by defendant. Civil records on microfiche from early '85, prior on index cards and docket books. Access to civil case records is available free on the Internet at www.jud2.state.ct.us.

Criminal Records: Access: Mail, in person. Only the court performs in person searches; visitors may not. No search fee. Required to search: name, years to search, DOB; also helpful: SSN. Criminal records on computer for 2 years; on microfiche back to 1962.

General Information: No sealed, dismissed, youth or program records released. SASE required. Turnaround time up to 1 month. Fax notes: Will not fax results. Copy fee: $1.00 per page. Certification fee: None; Certification available from State Record Center. Fee payee: Clerk, Superior Court. Personal checks accepted.

Geographical Area Court #21 1 Courthouse
Sq, Norwich, CT 06360; Civil phone: 860-887-3515; Criminal phone: 860-889-7338. Hours: 1-2:30PM, 4-5PM (EST). *Misdemeanor, Eviction, Small Claims.*

www.jud.state.ct.us

Civil Records: Access: Mail, online, in person. No search fee. Required to search: name, years to search. Civil cases indexed by defendant. Pending and 2-4 years history of disposed on computer, on microfiche from 1986, prior on index cards and docket books. Small claims, evictions not on computer. Access to civil case records is available free on the Internet at www.jud2.state.ct.us.

Criminal Records: Access: In person only. Visitors must perform in person searches for themselves. No search fee. Required to search: name, years to search, DOB. Pending and 2-4 years history of disposed on computer, on microfiche from 1986, prior on index cards and docket books. Mail requests are referred to the Judicial Records Center in Enfield.

General Information: No youthful offender or dismissed/erased records released. SASE required. Turnaround time 1-2 weeks. Copy fee: $1.00 per page. Certification fee: $2.00. Certified copy of Judgment $15.00. Fee payee: Superior Court GA #21. Personal checks accepted. Prepayment is required.

Bozrah Probate Court Town Hall, 2nd FL, One
River Rd, Bozrah, CT 06334; 860-889-2958; Fax: 860-887-7571. Hours: 10AM-1PM M,W (and by app't) (EST). *Probate.*

Colchester Probate Court Town Hall, 127
Norwich Ave, Colchester, CT 06415; 860-537-7290; Fax: 860-537-0547. Hours: 12:30PM-4:30PM M,F; 9AM-12:30PM 1:00-4:30PM T,TH (EST). *Probate.*

East Lyme Probate Court PO Box 519, 108
Pennsylvania Ave, Niantic, CT 06357; 860-739-6931; Fax: 860-739-6930. Hours: 8:30AM-12:30PM (EST). *Probate.*

Griswold Probate Court Town Hall, 32 School
St, PO Box 369, Jewett City, CT 06351; 860-376-0216; Fax: 860-376-0216. Hours: 5PM-8PM M; 1PM-5PM T-F (EST). *Probate.*

Lebanon Probate Court Town Hall, 579 Exeter
Rd, Lebanon, CT 06249; 860-642-7429; Fax: 860-642-7716. Hours: 10AM-Noon, 1:30-4PM T; 4-6PM Th; 10AM-Noon F (and by appt.) (EST). *Probate.*

Ledyard Probate Court 741 Colonel Ledyard
Hwy, Route 17, Ledyard, CT 06339; 860-464-3219; Fax: 860-464-8531. Hours: 8:30AM-1:30PM M; 8:30AM-12:30PM Tu & Th; 8:30AM-3:30PM W; closed Fri (app't only) (EST). *Probate.*

Lyme Probate Court Town Hall, 480 Hamburg
Rd, Lyme, CT 06371; 860-434-7733; Fax: 860-434-2989. Hours: 2-4PM (and by app't) (EST). *Probate.*

Montville Probate Court 310 Norwich-New
London Turnpike, Uncasville, CT 06382; 860-848-9847 X319; Fax: 860-848-2116. Hours: 9AM-1PM M,T,Th,F; 9AM-4:30PM W (EST). *Probate.*

New London Probate Court 181 Captain's
Walk, Municipal Bldg, PO Box 148, New London, CT 06320; 860-443-7121; Fax: 860-437-8155. Hours: 9AM-4PM (EST). *Probate.*

Note: District includes Town of Waterford

North Stonington Probate Court 391
Norwich Westerly Rd, Route #2, PO Box 204, North Stonington, CT 06359; 860-535-8441; Fax: 860-535-8441 (call first). Hours: 9AM-Noon M & W; 1-4PM T, F; 4-7PM Th (EST). *Probate.*

Norwich Probate Court 100 Broadway, Rm
122, PO Box 38, Norwich, CT 06360; 860-887-2160; Fax: 860-887-2401. Hours: 9AM-4:30PM (EST). *Probate.*

Note: District includes Towns of Franklin, Lisbon, Preston, Sprague, Voluntown

Old Lyme Probate Court 52 Lyme St,
Memorial Town Hall, Old Lyme, CT 06371; 860-434-1406 X222; Fax: 860-434-9283. Hours: 9AM-Noon, 1-4PM (EST). *Probate.*

Salem Probate Court 270 Hartford Rd, Salem,
CT 06420; 860-859-3873, 203-859-3036 (After hours); Fax: 860-537-0547. Hours: 10:00-Noon Fridays and app't (EST). *Probate.*

Stonington Probate Court 152 Elm St, PO
Box 312, Stonington, CT 06378; 860-535-5090; Fax: 860-535-0520. Hours: 9AM-Noon, 1-4PM (EST). *Probate.*

Note: District includes Town of Mystic

Tolland County

Tolland Judicial District Court - Civil 69
Brooklyn St, Rockville, CT 06066; 860-96-4920. Hours: 9AM-5PM (EST). *Civil Actions.*

Civil Records: Access: Mail, online, in person. Only the court performs in person searches; visitors may not. No search fee. Required to search: name, years to search. Civil cases indexed by defendant, plaintiff. Civil records on computer from 2000, on microfiche from 1980, all prior on index cards. Access to civil case records is available free on the Internet at www.jud2.state.ct.us.

General Information: No youthful offender, dismissed or not guilty verdict records released. SASE required. Turnaround time 1-2 weeks. Copy fee: $1.00 per page. Certification fee: $2.00. Fee payee: Clerk of Superior Court. Personal checks accepted. Prepayment is required.

Tolland Judicial District Court - Criminal
20 Park St, Vernon, CT 06066; 860-870-3200. Hours: 9AM-5PM (EST). *Felony.*

Note: The address can use either Rockville or Vernon, but the US Postal Service will sometimes return mail addressed to Rockville.

Criminal Records: Access: Mail, in person. Only the court performs in person searches; visitors may not. No search fee. Required to search: name, years to search; also helpful: DOB. Criminal records are for active cases only. Completed cases must be searched in Enfield through DPS.

General Information: No youthful offender, dismissed or not guilty verdict records released. SASE required. Turnaround time 1 week. Copy fee: $1.00 per page. Certification fee: $2.00. Fee payee: Clerk of Superior Court. Personal checks accepted. Prepayment is required.

Geographical Area Court #19 20 Park St, PO
Box 980, Rockville, CT 06066-0980; 860-870-3200. Hours: 9AM-4PM (EST). *Misdemeanor.*

www.jud.state.ct.us

Criminal Records: Access: Mail, in person. Only the court performs in person searches; visitors may not. No search fee. Required to search: name, years to search, DOB. Criminal records on computer approx. 2 yrs from disposition, on microfiche from 1985, prior on index cards.

General Information: No youthful offender records released. SASE required. Turnaround time 1-7 days. Copy fee: $1.00 per page. Certification fee: $2.00. Fee payee: Clerk of Superior Court. Personal checks accepted. Prepayment is required.

Andover Probate Court 222 Bolton Center Rd,
Bolton, CT 06043; 860-647-7979; Fax: 860-649-3187. Hours: 8:30-4:30PM M,T,W; 10:00-4:30PM TH; 8:30-1:00PM F (EST). *Probate.*

Note: District includes towns of Andover, Bolton and Columbia

Ellington Probate Court PO Box 268, 14 Park
Place, Rockville, CT 06066; 860-872-0519; Fax: 860-870-5140. Hours: 8:30-4:30 M-W; 8:30-7PM TH; 8:30-1PM F (EST). *Probate.*

Note: District includes Towns of Vernon, Ellington.

Hebron Probate Court 15 Gilead St, Hebron,
CT 06248; 860-228-5971; Fax: 860-228-4859. Hours: 8AM-4PM Tu; 4-6PM Th (and by app't) (EST). *Probate.*

Mansfield Probate Court 4 South Eagleville
Rd, Storrs, CT 06268; 860-429-3313; Fax: 860-429-4088. Hours: 9AM-12PM 2-5PM T (EST). *Probate.*

Stafford Probate Court Town Hall, 1 Main St,
PO Box 63, Stafford Springs, CT 06076; 860-684-3423; Fax: 860-684-7173. Hours: 9AM-Noon, 1-4:30PM M; 9AM-Noon Tu-F (and by app't) (EST). *Probate.*

Note: District includes towns of Union and Somers. Somers Probate Court was merged in withy this court in Jan. 1999.

Tolland Probate Court 21 Tolland Green,
Tolland, CT 06084; 860-871-3640; Fax: 860-871-3641. Hours: 9AM-1:30 M-W; 5:30-8:30PM Th (and by app't) (EST). *Probate.*

Note: District includes Town of Willington

Windham County

Windham Judicial District Court 155 Church
St, Putnam, CT 06260; 860-928-7749; Fax: 860-928-7076. Hours: 9AM-5PM (EST). *Civil Actions.*

Civil Records: Access: Phone, mail, online, in person. Only the court performs in person searches; visitors may not. No search fee. Required to search: name, years to search. Civil cases indexed by defendant, plaintiff. Civil records on computer for 1 year, prior on index cards, prior to 70s archived. Access to civil case records is available free on the Internet at www.jud2.state.ct.us.

General Information: No sealed, dismissed criminal, not guilty verdict records released. SASE required. Turnaround time 1-2 days. Copy fee: $1.00 per page. Certification fee: $2.00. Fee payee: Clerk of Superior Court. Personal checks accepted. Prepayment is required.

Geographical Area Court #11 120 School St
#110, Danielson, CT 06239-3024; 860-779-8480; Fax: 860-779-8488. Hours: 9AM-5PM (EST). *Felony, Misdemeanor, Eviction, Small Claims.*

Civil Records: Access: Phone, mail, online, in person. Both the court and visitors may perform in person searches. No search fee. Required to search: name, years to search. Civil cases indexed by defendant. Small claims records on computer since 08/96; all other records on index cards. Access to civil case records is available free on the Internet at www.jud2.state.ct.us.

Criminal Records: Access: Phone, mail, in person. Only the court performs in person searches; visitors may not. No search fee. Required to search: name, years to search, DOB. Pending criminal and 1 year after disposed on computer, on microfiche from 1986, prior on index cards.

General Information: Public access terminal is available for civil searches only. No sealed records released. SASE required. Turnaround time 1-2 weeks. Copy fee: $1.00 per page. Certification fee: $2.00. Fee payee: Clerk of Superior Court. Personal checks accepted.

Ashford Probate Court 20 Pompey Hollow Rd, PO Box 61, Ashford, CT 06278; 860-429-4986. Hours: 1AM-3:30PM Th (and by app't) (EST). *Probate.*

Brooklyn Probate Court Town Hall, 4 Wolf Den Rd, PO Box 356, Brooklyn, CT 06234-0356; 860-774-5973; Fax: 860-779-3744. Hours: 10AM-4:30PM T (and by app't) (EST). *Probate.*

Canterbury Probate Court 43 Maple Lane, Canterbury, CT 06331; 860-546-9605; Fax: 860-546-7805. Hours: 9AM-4:00PM Wed (and by app't) (EST). *Probate.*

Chaplin Probate Court c/o Eastford Probate District, PO Box 61, Ashford, CT 06278-0061; 860-974-1885; Fax: 860-974-0624. *Probate.*

Eastford Probate Court PO Box 207, 16 Westford Rd, Eastford, CT 06242-0207; 860-974-3024; Fax: 860-974-0624. Hours: 2-4PM Tu (and by app't) (EST). *Probate.*

Hampton Probate Court Town Hall, 164 Main St, PO Box 143, Hampton, CT 06247; 860-455-9132 x8; Fax: 860-455-0517. Hours: 1-4PM Th (and by app't) (EST). *Probate.*

Killingly Probate Court 172 Main St, Danielson, CT 06239; 860-779-5319; Fax: 860-779-5394. Hours: 8:30AM-Noon, 1-4:30PM (EST). *Probate.*

Plainfield Probate Court Town Hall, 8 Community Ave, Plainfield, CT 06374; 860-230-3031; Fax: 860-230-3033. Hours: 8:30-3:30PM M-Th; 8:30AM-Noon Fri (EST). *Probate.*

Note: Will combine with Sterling Probate Court at this address in Jan. 2003.

Pomfret Probate Court 5 Haven Rd, Rt. 44, Pomfret Center, CT 06259; 860-974-0186; Fax: 860-974-3950. Hours: 10AM-4PM Tu-Th (and by app't) (EST). *Probate.*

Putnam Probate Court Town Hall, 126 Church St, Putnam, CT 06260; 860-963-6868; Fax: 860-963-6814. Hours: 9AM-Noon M-F. (EST). *Probate.*

Sterling Probate Court 1114 Plainfield Pike, PO Box 157, Oneco, CT 06373; 860-564-8488; Fax: 860-564-1660. Hours: 8:30AM-Noon M,W (and by app't) (EST). *Probate.*

Note: Jan. 2003 will combine with, and move to, the Plainfield Probate Court (Town Hall, 8 Community Av, Plainfield, 06374, 860-230-3031, Fax 230-3033.

Thompson Probate Court 815 Riverside Dr, Town Hall, PO Box 74, North Grosvenordale, CT 06255; 860-923-2203; Fax: 860-923-3836. Hours: 9AM-Noon (and by app't) (EST). *Probate.*

Windham Probate Court 979 Main St, PO Box 34, Willimantic, CT 06226; 860-465-3049; Fax: 860-465-3012. Hours: 9AM-1PM M,Tu,Th; 9AM-1PM Fri (EST). *Probate.*

Note: District includes Town of Scottland

Woodstock Probate Court 415 Route 169, Woodstock, CT 06281; 860-928-2223; Fax: 860-963-7557. Hours: 3PM-6PM W, 1:30PM-4:30PM Th (and by app't) (EST). *Probate.*

Connecticut Recording Offices

ORGANIZATION: 8 counties and 170 towns/cities. There is no county recording in this state. The recording officer is Town/City Clerk. Be careful not to confuse searching in the following towns/cities as equivalent to a county-wide search: Fairfield, Hartford, Litchfield, New Haven, New London, Tolland, and Windham. The entire state is in the Eastern Time Zone (EST).

REAL ESTATE RECORDS: Many towns do not perform real estate searches. Copy fees are usually $1.00 per page. Certification fees are usually $1.00 per document or per page.

UCC RECORDS: Connecticut adopted Revised Article 9 on October 1, 2001. Financing statements are filed at the state level, except for real estate related collateral, which are filed only with the Town/City Clerk. Some towns will perform UCC searches. Copies usually cost $1.00 per page.

TAX LIEN RECORDS: All federal and state tax liens on personal property are filed with the Secretary of State. Federal and state tax liens on real property are filed with the Town/City Clerk. Towns will not perform tax lien searches.

OTHER LIENS: Mechanics, judgments, lis pendens, municipal, welfare, carpenter, sewer & water, city/town.

ONLINE ACCESS: A number of towns offer free access to assessor information. The State's Municipal Public Access Initiative has produced a website of Town and Municipality general information at http://www.munic.state.ct.us/. Also, a private vendor has placed assessor records from a number of towns on the Internet. Visit http://data.visionappraisal.com

Andover Town

Town Clerk, PO Box 328, Andover, CT 06232-0328. Town Clerk, R/E and UCC Recording 860-742-0188; Fax 860-742-7535.
Will search UCC records. This agency will not do a tax lien search. Will not search real estate records. **Other Phone Numbers:** Assessor 860-742-7305; Tax Collector 860-742-4035.

Ansonia City

City Clerk, 253 Main St, City Hall, Ansonia, CT 06401. 203-736-5980.
Will search UCC records. This agency will not do a tax lien search. Will not search real estate records. **Other Phone Numbers:** Assessor 203-734-5950; Treasurer 203-734-5920; Elections 203-736-5970; Vital Records 203-736-5980.

Ashford Town

Town Clerk, 25 Pompey Hollow Road, Ashford, CT 06278. 860-429-7044 R/E Recording: 860-429-7044; Fax 860-487-2025.
This agency will not perform searches. **Other Phone Numbers:** Assessor 860-429-8583.

Avon Town

Town Clerk, 60 W. Main St, Avon, CT 06001. 860-409-4310; Fax 860-677-8428.
This agency will not perform searches. **Other Phone Numbers:** Assessor 860-409-4335; Elections 860-409-4350; Vital Records 860-409-4310.

Barkhamsted Town

Town Clerk, 67 Ripley Hill Rd., Pleasant Valley, CT 06063. Town Clerk, R/E and UCC Recording 860-379-8665; Fax 860-379-9284.
This agency will not perform searches. **Other Phones:** Assessor 860-379-3600; Treasurer 860-379-8665; Elections 860-379-8665; Vital Records 860-379-8665.

Beacon Falls Town

Town Clerk, 10 Maple Ave, Beacon Falls, CT 06403. Town Clerk, R/E and UCC Recording 203-729-8254; Fax 203-720-1078.
This agency will not perform searches. **Other Phone Numbers:** Assessor 203-723-5253; Vital Records 203-729-8254.

Berlin Town

Town Clerk, PO Box 1, Kensington, CT 06037. Town Clerk, R/E and UCC Recording 860-828-7075; Fax 860-828-7180. www.town.berlin.ct.us
Will search UCC records. This agency will not do a tax lien search. Will not search real estate records. **Other Phone Numbers:** Assessor 860-828-7039; Treasurer 860-828-7023; Elections 860-828-7075; Vital Records 860-828-7075.

Bethany Town

Town Clerk, 40 Peck Road, Bethany, CT 06524-3338. 203-393-2100 x104, x105 R/E Recording: 203-393-0820; Fax 203-393-0821.
This agency will not perform searches. **Other Phone Numbers:** Assessor 203-393-1977; Treasurer 203-393-2100 x100.

Bethel Town

Town Clerk, 1 School St., Bethel, CT 06801. Town Clerk, R/E and UCC Recording 203-794-8505; Fax 203-794-8588.
This agency will not perform searches. **Other Phone Numbers:** Assessor 203-794-8507.

Bethlehem Town

Town Clerk, PO Box 160, Bethlehem, CT 06751. Town Clerk, R/E and UCC Recording 203-266-7510; Fax 203-266-7670. www.ci.bethlehem.ct.us
Will search UCC records. This agency will not do a tax lien search. Will not search real estate records. **Other Phone Numbers:** Assessor 203-266-5479; Treasurer 203-266-7677; Elections 203-266-7961; Vital Records 203-266-7510.

Bloomfield Town

Town Clerk, PO Box 337, Bloomfield, CT 06002. 860-769-3506 R/E Recording: 860-769-3507; Fax 860-769-3597.
Will search UCC records. This agency will not do a tax lien search. Will not search real estate records. **Other Phone Numbers:** Assessor 860-769-3530; Elections 860-769-3507; Vital Records 860-769-3507.

Bolton Town

Town Clerk, 222 Bolton Center Road, Bolton, CT 06043-7698. 860-649-8066 R/E Recording: 860-649-8066 x106 UCC Recording: 860-649-8066 x107; Fax 860-643-0021.
This agency will not perform searches. **Other Phone Numbers:** Assessor 860-649-8066 x100; Treasurer 860-649-7780; Elections 860-649-8066 x116; Vital Records 860-649-8066 x106.

Bozrah Town

Town Clerk, PO Box 158, Bozrah, CT 06334. 860-889-2689 R/E Recording: 860-889-2689; Fax 860-887-5449.
Will search UCC records. This agency will not do a tax lien search. Will not search real estate records. **Other Phone Numbers:** Assessor 860-889-2689.

Branford Town

Town Clerk, PO Box 150, Branford, CT 06405. 203-488-6305; Fax 203-481-5561.
This agency will not perform searches. **Other Phone Numbers:** Assessor 203-488-2039 x144.

Bridgeport Town

Town Clerk, 45 Lyon Terrace, City Hall, Room 124, Bridgeport, CT 06604. 203-576-7207.
This agency will not perform searches. **Other Phone Numbers:** Assessor 203-576-7077; Treasurer 203-576-7286; Appraiser/Auditor 203-576-7241; Elections 203-576-7281; Vital Records 203-576-7477; City Hall Information 203-576-7200.

Bridgewater Town

Town Clerk, PO Box 216, Bridgewater, CT 06752-0216. Town Clerk, R/E and UCC Recording 860-354-5102; Fax 860-350-5944.
Will search UCC records. This agency will not do a tax lien search. Will not search real estate records. **Other Phone Numbers:** Assessor 860-355-9379; Treasurer 860-354-2683; Elections 860-354-5102; Vital Records 860-354-5102.

Bristol City

City Clerk, PO Box 114, Bristol, CT 06010-0114. City Clerk, R/E and UCC Recording 860-584-7656.
Will search UCC records. This agency will not do a tax lien search. Will not search real estate records. **Other**

Phone Numbers: Assessor 860-584-7651; Treasurer 860-584-7618; Elections 860-584-7656; Vital Records 860-584-7656.

Brookfield Town

Town Clerk, PO Box 5106, Brookfield, CT 06804-5106. 203-775-7313; Fax 203-775-5231.
This agency will not perform searches. **Online Access:** Assessor Records. Search the town assessor database at http://data.visionappraisal.com/BrookfieldCT. Free registration for full data. **Other Phone Numbers:** Assessor 203-775-7302; Treasurer 203-775-7308; Elections 203-775-7313; Vital Records 203-775-7313.

Brooklyn Town

Town Clerk, PO Box 356, Brooklyn, CT 06234. Town Clerk, R/E and UCC Recording 860-774-9543; Fax 860-779-3744.
Will search UCC records. This agency will not do a tax lien search. Will not search real estate records. **Other Phone Numbers:** Assessor 860-774-5611; Treasurer 860-774-9543; Elections 860-774-9543; Vital Records 860-774-9543.

Burlington Town

Town Clerk, 200 Spielman Highway, Burlington, CT 06013. 860-673-2108 R/E Recording: 860-673-2108; Fax 860-675-9312.
Will search UCC records. This agency will not do a tax lien search. Will not search real estate records. **Other Phone Numbers:** Assessor 860-673-3901.

Canaan Town

Town Clerk, PO Box 47, Falls Village, CT 06031. 860-824-0707; Fax 860-824-4506.
Will search UCC records. This agency will not do a tax lien search. Will not search real estate records. **Other Phone Numbers:** Assessor 860-824-0707.

Canterbury Town

Town Clerk, PO Box 27, Canterbury, CT 06331-0027. 860-546-9377 R/E Recording: 860-546-9377 UCC Recording: 860-546-9377; Fax 860-546-7805.
This agency will not perform searches. **Other Phones:** Assessor 860-546-6035; Treasurer 860-546-2089; Elections 860-546-9377; Vital Records 860-546-9377.

Canton Town

Town Clerk, PO Box 168, Collinsville, CT 06022. Town Clerk, R/E and UCC Recording 860-693-7870; Fax 860-693-7840.
This agency will not perform searches. **Other Phone Numbers:** Assessor 860-693-7842; Treasurer 860-693-7852; Elections 860-693-7870; Vital Records 860-693-7870.

Chaplin Town

Town Clerk, PO Box 286, Chaplin, CT 06235. Town Clerk, R/E and UCC Recording 860-455-9455; Fax 860-455-0027.
This agency will not perform searches. **Other Phones:** Assessor 860-455-9333; Treasurer 860-455-9455; Elections 860-455-9455; Vital Records 860-455-9455.

Cheshire Town

Town Clerk, 84 S. Main St, Town Hall, Cheshire, CT 06410. 203-271-6601.
Will search UCC records. This agency will not do a tax lien search. Will not search real estate records. **Other Phone Numbers:** Assessor 203-271-6620.

Chester Town

Town Clerk, PO Box 328, Chester, CT 06412-0328. Town Clerk, R/E and UCC Recording 860-526-0006; Fax 860-526-0004.
Will search UCC records. This agency will not do a tax lien search. Will not search real estate records. **Online**

Access: Assessor Records. Search the Assessor's Taxpayer Information System database at http://data.visionappraisal.com/ChesterCT. Free registration for full data. **Other Phone Numbers:** Assessor 860-526-0012; Treasurer 860-526-0010; Elections 860-526-0005; Vital Records 860-526-0006.

Clinton Town

Town Clerk, 54 E. Main St, Clinton, CT 06413. Town Clerk, R/E and UCC Recording 860-669-9101.
Will search UCC records. This agency will not do a tax lien search. Will not search real estate records. **Other Phone Numbers:** Assessor 860-669-9269; Treasurer 860-669-9465; Elections 860-669-9101; Vital Records 860-669-9101.

Colchester Town

Town Clerk, 127 Norwich Ave, Colchester, CT 06415. Town Clerk, R/E and UCC Recording 860-537-7215; Fax 860-537-0547.
This agency will not perform searches. **Online Access:** Assessor Records. Search the town assessor database at http://data.visionappraisal.com/ColchesterCT. Free registration for full data. **Other Phone Numbers:** Assessor 860-537-7205; Treasurer 860-537-7225; Elections 860-537-7204; Vital Records 860-537-7215.

Colebrook Town

Town Clerk, PO Box 5, Colebrook, CT 06021. 860-379-3359 R/E Recording: 203-379-3359; Fax 860-379-7215.
This agency will not perform searches. **Other Phone Numbers:** Assessor 203-379-3738.

Columbia Town

Town Clerk, 323 Jonathan Trumbull Hwy, Columbia, CT 06237. 860-228-3284; Fax 860-228-1952.
Will search UCC records. This agency will not do a tax lien search. Will not search real estate records. **Online Access:** Assessor Records. Search the town assessor data at http://data.visionappraisal.com/ColumbiaCT. Free registration for full data. **Other Phone Numbers:** Assessor 860-228-9555.

Cornwall Town

Town Clerk, PO Box 97, Cornwall, CT 06753-0097. Town Clerk, R/E and UCC Recording 860-672-2709.
Will search UCC records. This agency will not do a tax lien search. Will not search real estate records. **Other Phone Numbers:** Assessor 860-672-2703; Treasurer 860-672-2707; Vital Records 860-672-2709.

Coventry Town

Town Clerk, 1712 Main St, Coventry, CT 06238. Town Clerk, R/E and UCC Recording 860-742-7966; Fax 860-742-8911.
This agency will not perform searches. **Other Phones:** Assessor 860-742-4067; Treasurer 860-742-7966; Elections 860-742-4061; Vital Records 860-742-7966.

Cromwell Town

Town Clerk, 41 West St, Cromwell, CT 06416-2100. 860-632-3440; Fax 860-632-7048. www.cromwellct.com
This agency will not perform searches. **Other Phone Numbers:** Assessor 860-632-3442.

Danbury City

Town Clerk, 155 Deer Hill Ave, City Hall, Danbury, CT 06810. 203-797-4531.
Will search UCC records. This agency will not do a tax lien search. Will not search real estate records. **Online Access:** Assessor Records. Search the city assessor database at http://data.visionappraisal.com/DanburyCT. Free registration for full data. **Other Phone Numbers:** Assessor 203-797-4554; Treasurer 203-797-4650.

Darien Town

Town Clerk, 2 Renshaw Road, Darien, CT 06820-5397. 203-656-7307.
This agency will not perform searches. **Other Phones:** Assessor 203-656-7310; Treasurer 203-656-7334.

Deep River Town

Town Clerk, 174 Main St, Town Hall, Deep River, CT 06417. Town Clerk, R/E and UCC Recording 860-526-6024; Fax 860-526-6023.
Will search UCC records. This agency will not do a tax lien search. Will not search real estate records. **Other Phone Numbers:** Assessor 860-526-6029; Elections 860-526-6024; Vital Records 860-526-6024.

Derby City

City Clerk, 35 Fifth St, Derby, CT 06418-1897. City Clerk, R/E and UCC Recording 203-736-1462; Fax 203-736-1458.
Will search UCC records. This agency will not do a tax lien search. Will not search real estate records. **Other Phone Numbers:** Assessor 203-736-1455; Treasurer 203-736-1452; Appraiser/Auditor 203-736-1452; Elections 203-736-1462; Vital Records 203-736-1462.

Durham Town

Town Clerk, PO Box 428, Durham, CT 06422. Town Clerk, R/E and UCC Recording 860-349-3452; Fax 860-349-0547.
Will search UCC records. This agency will not do a tax lien search. Will not search real estate records. **Other Phone Numbers:** Assessor 860-349-3453; Treasurer 860-349-3625; Elections 860-349-3452; Vital Records 860-349-3452.

East Granby Town

Town Clerk, PO Box TC, East Granby, CT 06026-0459. Town Clerk, R/E and UCC Recording 860-653-6528; Fax 860-653-4017.
This agency will not perform searches. **Other Phone Numbers:** Assessor 860-653-2852; Treasurer 860-653-0096; Elections 860-653-0097; Vital Records 860-653-6528; Selectmen 860-653-2576.

East Haddam Town

Town Clerk, PO Box K, Town Office Bldg, Town Office Building. PO Box K, East Haddam, CT 06423. 860-873-5027 R/E Recording: 203-873-8279.
Will search UCC records. This agency will not do a tax lien search. Will not search real estate records. **Other Phone Numbers:** Assessor 203-873-5026.

East Hampton Town

Town Clerk, 20 E. High St, Town Hall, East Hampton, CT 06424. 860-267-2519 R/E Recording: 203-267-2519; Fax 860-267-1027.
This agency will not perform searches. **Other Phone Numbers:** Assessor 203-267-2510.

East Hartford Town

Town Clerk, 740 Main St, East Hartford, CT 06108-3126. 860-291-7230; Fax 860-289-0831. www.ci.east-hartford.ct.us
Will search UCC records. This agency will not do a tax lien search. Will not search real estate records. **Other Phone Numbers:** Assessor 860-291-7260 x268; Vital Records 860-291-7230.

East Haven Town

Town Clerk, 250 Main St, East Haven, CT 06512-3034. 203-468-3201; Fax 203-468-3372.
This agency will not perform searches. **Other Phone Numbers:** Assessor 203-468-3233; Vital Records 203-468-3201.

East Lyme Town

Town Clerk, PO Box 519, Niantic, CT 06357. Town Clerk, R/E and UCC Recording 860-739-6931; Fax 860-739-6930.
Will search UCC records. This agency will not do a tax lien search. Will not search real estate records. **Online Access:** Assessor Records. Search the town assessor data at http://data.visionappraisal.com/EastLymeCT. Free registration for full data. **Other Phone Numbers:** Assessor 860-739-6931; Treasurer 860-739-6931; Vital Records 860-739-6931.

East Windsor Town

Town Clerk, PO Box 213, Broad Brook, CT 06016-0213. 860-623-9467 R/E Recording: 860-292-8255; Fax 860-623-4798.
Will search UCC records. This agency will not do a tax lien search. Will not search real estate records. **Other Phone Numbers:** Assessor 860-623-8878; Treasurer 860-292-5909; Elections 860-292-5915; Vital Records 860-292-8255.

Eastford

Town Clerk, PO Box 273, Eastford, CT 06242. 860-974-1885 R/E Recording: 860-974-1885; Fax 860-974-0624.
This agency will not perform searches. **Other Phone Numbers:** Assessor 860-974-1291.

Easton Town

Town Clerk, 225 Center Road, Easton, CT 06612. 203-268-6291; Fax 203-261-6080.
Will search UCC records. This agency will not do a tax lien search. Will not search real estate records. **Other Phone Numbers:** Assessor 203-268-6291; Treasurer 203-268-6291; Appraiser/Auditor 203-268-6291; Elections 203-268-6291; Vital Records 203-268-6291.

Ellington Town

Town Clerk, PO Box 187, Ellington, CT 06029-0187. 860-875-3190 R/E Recording: 860-875-3105 UCC Recording: 860-875-3105; Fax 860-875-0788.
Will search UCC records. This agency will not do a tax lien search. Will not search real estate records. **Other Phone Numbers:** Assessor 860-870-3109; Treasurer 860-875-3115; Elections 860-875-3107; Vital Records 860-875-3105.

Enfield Town

Town Clerk, 820 Enfield St, Enfield, CT 06082-2997. 860-253-6440 R/E Recording: 860-253-6435 UCC Recording: 860-253-6435; Fax 860-253-6310.
This agency will not perform searches. **Online Access:** Tax Sales Records. Search the town's tax sale list free at www.enfield.org/Link_Tax.htm. Use Control+F and search for name. **Other Phone Numbers:** Assessor 860-253-6339; Treasurer 860-253-6330; Elections 860-253-6320; Vital Records 860-253-6440.

Essex Town

Town Clerk, PO Box 98, Essex, CT 06426. 860-767-4344 R/E Recording: 860-767-4344 x129 UCC Recording: 860-767-4344 x129.
Will search UCC records. This agency will not do a tax lien search. Will not search real estate records. **Other Phone Numbers:** Assessor 860-767-4340 x124; Treasurer 860-767-4340 x122; Elections 860-767-4344 x129; Vital Records 860-767-4344 x129.

Fairfield Town

Town Clerk, 611 Old Post Road, Fairfield, CT 06430-6690. Town Clerk, R/E and UCC Recording 203-256-3090.
Will search UCC records. This agency will not do a tax lien search. Will not search real estate records. **Online Access:** Assessor Records. Search the town assessor database at http://data.visionappraisal.com/FairfieldCT. Free registration for full data. **Other Phone Numbers:** Assessor 203-256-3110; Elections 203-256-3090; Vital Records 203-256-3090.

Farmington Town

Town Clerk, 1 Monteith Drive, Farmington, CT 06032-1053. 860-673-8247 R/E Recording: 860-673-8247; Fax 860-675-7140.
Will search UCC records. This agency will not do a tax lien search. Will provide information on a simple real estate search. **Other Phone Numbers:** Assessor 860-673-8245.

Franklin Town

Town Clerk, 7 Meeting House Hill Road, Town Hall, Franklin, CT 06254. 860-642-7352 R/E Recording: 203-642-7352; Fax 860-642-6606.
This agency will not perform searches. **Other Phone Numbers:** Assessor 203-642-6475; Treasurer 860-642-7352.

Glastonbury Town

Town Clerk, 2155 Main St, Glastonbury, CT 06033. Town Clerk, R/E and UCC Recording 860-652-7616; Fax 860-652-7639. www.glasct.org
This agency will not perform searches. **Online Access:** Property Records. Search town property information free on the GIS Interactive Mapping site at www.glasct.org/isa/intermaps.html. Click on "Property Information (Parcels).". **Other Phone Numbers:** Assessor 860-652-7604; Elections 860-652-7616; Vital Records 860-652-7616.

Goshen Town

Town Clerk, PO Box 54, Goshen, CT 06756-0054. Town Clerk, R/E and UCC Recording 860-491-3647.
This agency will not perform searches. **Other Phone Numbers:** Assessor 860-491-2115; Elections 860-491-2398 x236; Vital Records 860-491-3275.

Granby Town

Town Clerk, 15 N. Granby Road, Granby, CT 06035. 860-844-5308.
This agency will not perform searches. **Online Access:** Assessor Records. Search the town assessor's database at http://data.visionappraisal.com/GranbyCT. Free registration required for full data. **Other Phone Numbers:** Assessor 203-844-5311.

Greenwich Town

Town Clerk, PO Box 2540, Greenwich, CT 06836. 203-622-7897.
This agency will not perform searches. **Other Phone Numbers:** Assessor 203-622-7885.

Griswold Town

Town Clerk, PO Box 369, Jewett City, CT 06351. Town Clerk, R/E and UCC Recording 860-376-7064; Fax 860-376-7070.
Will search UCC records. This agency will not do a tax lien search. Will not search real estate records. **Other Phone Numbers:** Assessor 860-376-7072; Treasurer 860-376-7075; Appraiser/Auditor 860-376-7072; Elections 860-376-7062; Vital Records 860-376-7063.

Groton Town

Town Clerk, 45 Fort Hill Road, Groton, CT 06340. Town Clerk, R/E and UCC Recording 860-441-6642.
This agency will not perform searches. **Other Phone Numbers:** Assessor 860-441-6660; Treasurer 860-441-6609; Elections 860-441-6640; Vital Records 860-441-6640.

Guilford Town

Town Clerk, 31 Park St, Town Hall, Guilford, CT 06437. 203-453-8001; www.ci.guilford.ct.us
This agency will not perform searches. **Other Phone Numbers:** Assessor 203-453-8010; Treasurer 203-453-8022.

Haddam Town

Town Clerk, PO Box 87, Haddam, CT 06438. 860-345-8531 R/E Recording: 860-345-8531; Fax 860-345-3730.
Will search UCC records. This agency will not do a tax lien search. Will not search real estate records. **Other Phone Numbers:** Assessor 860-345-8531 x213.

Hamden Town

Town Clerk, 2372 Whitney Ave, Memorial Town Hall, Hamden, CT 06518. 203-287-2510 R/E Recording: 203-287-2500; Fax 203-287-2518.
Will search UCC records. Will search real estate records. **Online Access:** Assessor Records. Search the town assessor's database at http://data.visionappraisal.com/hamdenct. Free registration required for full access. **Other Phones:** Assessor 203-287-2529; Treasurer 203-387-2530.

Hampton Town

Town Clerk, PO Box 143, Hampton, CT 06247-0143. 860-455-9132 R/E Recording: 860-455-9132 x1 UCC Recording: 860-455-9132 x1; Fax 860-455-0517.
Will search UCC records. This agency will not do a tax lien search. Will not search real estate records. **Other Phone Numbers:** Assessor 860-455-9132 x5; Treasurer 860-455-9132 x4; Elections 860-455-9132 x1; Vital Records 860-455-9132 x1.

Hartford City

City Clerk, 550 Main St, Hartford, CT 06103-2992. 860-543-8580 R/E Recording: 860-722-8040; Fax 860-722-8041.
This agency will not perform searches. **Other Phones:** Assessor 860-543-8540; Treasurer 860-543-8530.

Hartland Town

Town Clerk, Town Office Building, 22 South Road, East Hartland, CT 06027. 860-653-3542; Fax 860-653-7919.
Will search UCC records. This agency will not do a tax lien search. Will not search real estate records. **Other Phone Numbers:** Assessor 860-653-9687; Selectmen 860-653-6800.

Harwinton Town

Town Clerk, 100 Bentley Drive, Town Hall, Harwinton, CT 06791. Town Clerk, R/E and UCC Recording 860-485-9613; Fax 860-485-0051.
This agency will not perform searches. **Other Phones:** Assessor 860-485-0898; Treasurer 860-485-9051; Elections 860-485-9613; Vital Records 860-485-9613.

Hebron Town

Town Clerk, PO Box 156, Hebron, CT 06248. 860-228-5971 x124 R/E Recording: 860-228-5971 UCC Recording: 860-228-5971; Fax 860-228-4859.
This agency will not perform searches. **Other Phone Numbers:** Assessor 860-228-5971; Treasurer 860-228-5971; Appraiser/Auditor 860-228-5971; Elections 860-228-5971; Vital Records 860-228-5971.

Kent Town

Town Clerk, PO Box 678, Kent, CT 06757-0678. 860-927-3433 R/E Recording: 860-927-3433; Fax 860-927-4541.
Will search UCC records. This agency will not do a tax lien search. Will not search real estate records. **Other Phone Numbers:** Assessor 860-927-3160.

Killingly Town

Town Clerk, PO Box 6000, Danielson, CT 06239. 860-779-5307 R/E Recording: 860-774-8601; Fax 860-779-5394.

This agency will not perform searches. **Other Phones:** Assessor 860-779-5323; Treasurer 860-779-5337; Elections 860-779-5302; Vital Records 860-779-5307.

Killingworth Town

Town Clerk, 323 Route 81, Killingworth, CT 06419-1298. 860-663-1616 R/E Recording: 860-663-1765; Fax 860-663-3305.

Will search UCC records. This agency will not do a tax lien search. Will not search real estate records. **Other Phones:** Assessor 860-663-2002; Vital Records 860-663-4048.

Lebanon Town

Town Clerk, 579 Exeter Road, Town Hall, Lebanon, CT 06249. 860-642-7319.

Will search UCC records. This agency will not do a tax lien search. Will not search real estate records. **Other Phone Numbers:** Assessor 860-642-6141; Vital Records 860-642-7319.

Ledyard Town

Town Clerk, 741 Col. Ledyard Highway, Ledyard, CT 06339. 860-464-3259 R/E Recording: 860-464-3259; Fax 860-464-1126. www.town.ledyard.ct.us

This agency will not perform searches. **Other Phone Numbers:** Assessor 860-464-3237; Treasurer 860-464-3228; Vital Records 860-464-3259.

Lisbon Town

Town Clerk, 1 Newent Road, RD 2 Town Hall, Lisbon, CT 06351-9802. 860-376-2708; Fax 860-376-6545.

Will search UCC records. This agency will not do a tax lien search. Will not search real estate records. **Other Phone Numbers:** Assessor 860-376-5115; Treasurer 860-376-3400.

Litchfield Town

Town Clerk, PO Box 488, Litchfield, CT 06759-0488. Town Clerk, R/E and UCC Recording 860-567-7561.

This agency will not perform searches. **Other Phone Numbers:** Assessor 860-567-7559; Treasurer 860-567-7554; Vital Records 860-567-7561; Registrar 860-567-7558.

Lyme Town

Town Clerk, 480 Hamburg Rd., Town Hall, Lyme, CT 06371. Town Clerk, R/E and UCC Recording 860-434-7733; Fax 860-434-2989.

Will search UCC records. This agency will not do a tax lien search. Will not search real estate records. **Other Phone Numbers:** Assessor 860-434-8094; Treasurer 860-434-7733; Appraiser/Auditor 860-434-8094; Elections 860-434-7733; Vital Records 860-434-7733.

Madison Town

Town Clerk, 8 Campus Dr., Madison, CT 06443-2538. Town Clerk, R/E and UCC Recording 203-245-5672; Fax 203-245-5613.

Will search UCC records. This agency will not do a tax lien search. Will not search real estate records. **Online Access:** Assessor Records. Search the Town assessor database at http://data.visionappraisal.com/MadisonCT. Free Registration required for full access. **Other Phone Numbers:** Assessor 203-245-5652; Elections 203-245-5671; Vital Records 203-245-5672.

Manchester Town

Town Clerk, PO Box 191, Manchester, CT 06045-0191. 860-647-3037 R/E Recording: 860-647-3037 UCC Recording: 860-647-3037; Fax 860-647-3029. www.ci.manchester.ct.us/Town_Clerk/index.htm

Will search UCC records. This agency will not do a tax lien search. Will not search real estate records. **Online Access:** Assessor Records. Search the Town assessor data at http://data.visionappraisal.com/ManchesterCT. Free registration required for full access. **Other Phone Numbers:** Assessor 860-647-3016; Treasurer 860-647-3023; Elections 860-647-3037; Vital Records 860-647-3037.

Mansfield Town

Town Clerk, 4 S. Eagleville Road, Mansfield, CT 06268. 860-429-3302 R/E Recording: 860-429-3302. This agency will not perform searches. **Other Phones:** Assessor 860-429-3327; Elections 860-429-3369.

Marlborough Town

Town Clerk, PO Box 29, Marlborough, CT 06447. 860-295-6206 R/E Recording: 860-295-0713; Fax 860-295-0317.

Will search UCC records. This agency will not do a tax lien search. Will not search real estate records. **Other Phone Numbers:** Assessor 860-295-6201.

Meriden City

City Clerk, 142 E. Main St, Meriden, CT 06450-8022. City Clerk, R/E and UCC Recording 203-630-4030; Fax 203-630-4059. www.cityofmeriden.org/government/

Will search UCC records. This agency will not do a tax lien search. Will not search real estate records. **Other Phone Numbers:** Assessor 203-630-4071; Elections 203-630-4075; Vital Records 203-630-4030.

Middlebury Town

Town Clerk, PO Box 392, Middlebury, CT 06762-0392. Town Clerk, R/E and UCC Recording 203-758-2557.

Will search UCC records. This agency will not do a tax lien search. Will not search real estate records. **Other Phone Numbers:** Assessor 203-758-1447; Elections 203-758-2557; Vital Records 203-758-2557.

Middlefield Town

Town Clerk, PO Box 179, Middlefield, CT 06455. Town Clerk, R/E and UCC Recording 860-349-7116; Fax 860-349-7115. www.munic.state.ct.us/MIDDLEFIELD/contents.htm

Will search UCC records. This agency will not do a tax lien search. Will not search real estate records. **Online Access:** Assessor Records. Search the town assessor data at http://data.visionappraisal.com/MiddlefieldCT. Free registration required for full data. **Other Phones:** Assessor 860-349-7111; Treasurer 860-349-7114; Elections 860-349-7119; Vital Records 860-349-7116.

Middletown City

City Clerk, PO Box 1300, Middletown, CT 06457. City Clerk, R/E and UCC Recording 860-344-3459; Fax 860-344-3591. www.cityofmiddletown.com/Departments.htm

Will search UCC records. This agency will not do a tax lien search. Will not search real estate records. **Other Phone Numbers:** Assessor 860-344-3454; Treasurer 860-344-3438; Elections 860-344-3459; Vital Records 860-344-3474.

Milford City

City Clerk, 70 West River St, Milford, CT 06460-3364. 203-783-3210.

Will search UCC records. This agency will not do a tax lien search. Will not search real estate records. **Online Access:** Assessor Records. Search the city assessor's database at http://data.visionappraisal.com/milfordct. Free registration required for full data. **Other Phone Numbers:** Assessor 203-788-3215; Vital Records 203-783-3210.

Monroe Town

Town Clerk, 7 Fan Hill Road, Monroe, CT 06468-1800. 203-452-5417 R/E Recording: 203-452-5427 UCC Recording: 203-452-5427; Fax 203-261-6197.

Will search UCC records. This agency will not do a tax lien search. Will not search real estate records. **Other Phone Numbers:** Assessor 203-452-5469; Treasurer 203-452-5433; Elections 203-452-5417; Vital Records 203-452-5427.

Montville Town

Town Clerk, 310 Norwich-New London Tpke., Town Hall, Uncasville, CT 06382. 860-848-1349 R/E Recording: 860-848-1349; Fax 860-848-1521.

This agency will not perform searches. **Other Phone Numbers:** Assessor 860-848-8221 #5; Treasurer 860-848-0139.

Morris Town

Town Clerk, PO Box 66, Morris, CT 06763-0066. 860-567-7433; Fax 860-567-7432.

This agency will not perform searches. **Other Phones:** Assessor 860-567-7435; Treasurer 860-567-7435; Elections 860-567-7433; Vital Records 860-567-7433.

Naugatuck Town

Town Clerk, Town Hall, 229 Church St, Naugatuck, CT 06770. 203-720-7000 R/E Recording: 203-720-7055; Fax 203-720-7099.

This agency will not perform searches. **Online Access:** Assessor Records. Search the town assessor database at http://data.visionappraisal.com/NaugatuckCT. Free registration required for full data. **Other Phones:** Assessor 203-720-7016; Treasurer 203-729-4571; Elections 203-720-7047; Vital Records 203-720-7055.

New Britain Town

Town Clerk, 27 W. Main St, New Britain, CT 06051. 860-826-3344 R/E Recording: 860-826-3344; Fax 860-826-3348.

This agency will not perform searches. **Other Phone Numbers:** Assessor 860-826-3323.

New Canaan Town

Town Clerk, 77 Main St, Town Hall, New Canaan, CT 06840. 203-972-2323; Fax 203-966-2387.

This agency will not perform searches. **Other Phones:** Assessor 203-927-2335; Treasurer 203-927-2340; Elections 203-972-8877; Vital Records 203-972-2323.

New Fairfield Town

Town Clerk, Route 39, Town Hall, New Fairfield, CT 06812. 203-312-5616 R/E Recording: 203-746-8110.

Will search UCC records. This agency will not do a tax lien search. Will not search real estate records. **Other Phone Numbers:** Assessor 203-312-5624.

New Hartford Town

Town Clerk, PO Box 426, New Hartford, CT 06057. Town Clerk, R/E and UCC Recording 860-379-5037; Fax 860-379-0940.

This agency will not perform searches. **Other Phones:** Assessor 860-379-5235; Treasurer 860-379-3389; Elections 860-738-9721; Vital Records 860-379-5037.

New Haven City

City Clerk, 200 Orange St, Room 202, New Haven, CT 06510. 203-946-8339 R/E Recording: 203-946-8344 UCC Recording: 203-946-8344; Fax 203-946-6974.

Will search UCC records. This agency will not do a tax lien search. Will not search real estate records. **Online Access:** Assessor Records. Search the city assessor data at http://data.visionappraisal.com/NewhavenCT. Free registration required for full data. **Other Phones:** Assessor 203-787-8066; Treasurer 203-946-8300; Elections 203-946-8346; Vital Records 203-946-8084.

New London City

City Clerk, 181 State St, New London, CT 06320. City Clerk, R/E and UCC Recording 860-447-5205; Fax 860-447-1644.

File here only for the city of New London, not for the county. There is no county filing in Connecticut. Will search UCC records. This agency will not do a tax lien search. Will not search real estate records. **Online Access:** Assessor Records. Search the city assessor's data at http://data.visionappraisal.com//NewLondonCT. Free registration required for full access. **Other Phone Numbers:** Assessor 860-447-5216; Treasurer 860-447-5209; Appraiser/Auditor 860-447-5216; Elections 860-447-5206; Vital Records 860-447-5205.

New Milford Town

Town Clerk, PO Box 360, New Milford, CT 06776. 860-355-6020; Fax 860-355-6002. www.newmilford.org/agencies/home.htm
Will search UCC records. This agency will not do a tax lien search. Will not search real estate records. **Online Access:** Assessor Records. Search the town assessor data at http://data.visionappraisal.com/NewMilfordCT. Free registration required for full access. **Other Phone Numbers:** Assessor 860-355-6070; Vital Records 860-355-6020.

Newington Town

Town Clerk, 131 Cedar St, Newington, CT 06111-2696. Town Clerk, R/E and UCC Recording 860-665-8545; www.ci.newington.ct.us
This agency will not perform searches. **Other Phone Numbers:** Assessor 860-665-8530; Elections 860-665-8516; Vital Records 860-665-8545.

Newtown Town

Town Clerk, 45 Main St, Newtown, CT 06470. 203-270-4210.
This agency will not perform searches. **Other Phones:** Assessor 203-270-4240; Treasurer 203-270-4221; Elections 203-270-4250; Vital Records 203-270-4210.

Norfolk Town

Town Clerk, PO Box 552, Norfolk, CT 06058-0552. 860-542-5679.
This agency will not perform searches. **Other Phones:** Assessor 860-542-5287; Treasurer 860-542-5679; Elections 860-542-5679; Vital Records 860-542-5679.

North Branford Town

Town Clerk, PO Box 287, North Branford, CT 06471-0287. 203-315-6015.
This agency will not perform searches. **Other Phone Numbers:** Assessor 203-315-6013; Treasurer 203-315-6002; Vital Records 203-315-6015.

North Canaan Town

Town Clerk, PO Box 338, North Canaan, CT 06018. 860-824-3138 R/E Recording: 860-824-7246; Fax 860-824-3139.
Will search UCC records. This agency will not do a tax lien search. Will not search real estate records. **Other Phone Numbers:** Assessor 860-824-3137.

North Haven Town

Town Clerk, 18 Church St, Town Hall, North Haven, CT 06473. 203-239-5321 x541 R/E Recording: 203-239-5321.
This agency will not perform searches. **Other Phone Numbers:** Assessor 203-239-5321 x700.

North Stonington Town

Town Clerk, 40 Main St, North Stonington, CT 06359. 860-535-2877 x21; Fax 860-535-4554.
Will search UCC records. This agency will not do a tax lien search. Will not search real estate records. **Other**

Phone Numbers: Assessor 860-535-2877 x23; Treasurer 860-535-2877 x10.

Norwalk City

Town Clerk, PO Box 5125, Norwalk, CT 06856-5125. 203-854-7746.
Will search UCC records. This agency will not do a tax lien search. Will not search real estate records. **Other Phone Numbers:** Assessor 203-854-7887.

Norwich City

City Clerk, 100 Broadway, City Hall, Room 214, Norwich, CT 06360. 860-823-3732 R/E Recording: 860-886-2381; Fax 860-823-3790.
This agency will not perform searches. **Online Access:** Assessor Records. Search the city assessor's database at http://data.visionappraisal.com/NorwichCT. Free registration required for full data. **Other Phone Numbers:** Assessor 860-886-2381 x222.

Old Lyme Town

Town Clerk, 52 Lyme St, Old Lyme, CT 06371. 860-434-1605 x221 R/E Recording: 860-434-1605 x221; Fax 860-434-9283.
Will search UCC records. This agency will not do a tax lien search. Will not search real estate records. **Online Access:** Assessor Records. Search the town Assessor's data at http://data.visionappraisal.com/OLDLYMECT. Free registration required for full access. **Other Phone Numbers:** Assessor 860-434-1605 x218; Treasurer 860-434-1605 x232; Appraiser/Auditor 860-434-1605 x218; Elections 860-434-1605 x230; Vital Records 860-434-1605 x221.

Old Saybrook Town

Town Clerk, 302 Main St, Old Saybrook, CT 06475. Town Clerk, R/E and UCC Recording 860-395-3135 UCC Recording: 860-395-3137; Fax 860-395-5014. www.oldsaybrookct.com
Will not search real estate records. **Online Access:** Real Estate Records. Real Estate records on the Assessor's database are available free online at http://209.150.7.14/assessor/index.cfm. **Other Phones:** Assessor 860-395-3137; Treasurer 860-395-3132; Elections 860-395-3135; Vital Records 860-395-3135.

Orange Town

Town Clerk, Town Hall, 617 Orange Center Rd., Orange, CT 06477. 203-891-2122 R/E Recording: 203-795-0751; Fax 203-891-2185.
Will search UCC records. This agency will not do a tax lien search. Will not search real estate records. **Other Phone Numbers:** Assessor 203-891-2122 x722.

Oxford Town

Town Clerk, 486 Oxford Road, Oxford, CT 06478. 203-888-2543.
This agency will not perform searches. **Other Phones:** Assessor 203-888-2543; Treasurer 203-888-2543; Elections 203-888-2543; Vital Records 203-888-2543.

Plainfield Town

Town Clerk, 8 Community Ave, Town Hall, Plainfield, CT 06374. 860-564-4075 R/E Recording: 860-230-3009 UCC Recording: 860-230-3009.
This agency will not perform searches. **Other Phone Numbers:** Assessor 860-230-3006; Treasurer 860-230-3003; Elections 860-230-3024; Vital Records 860-230-3009.

Plainville Town

Town Clerk, 1 Central Square, Municipal Center, Plainville, CT 06062. 860-793-0221 R/E Recording: 860-793-0221.
This agency will not perform searches. **Other Phone Numbers:** Assessor 860-793-0221 x242.

Plymouth Town

Town Clerk, 80 Main St, Town Hall, Terryville, CT 06786. 860-585-4039; Fax 860-585-4015.
Will search UCC records. This agency will not do a tax lien search. Will not search real estate records. **Other Phone Numbers:** Assessor 860-585-4006; Treasurer 860-585-4009; Elections 860-585-4033; Vital Records 860-585-4039.

Pomfret Town

Town Clerk, 5 Haven Road, Pomfret Center, CT 06259. Town Clerk, R/E and UCC Recording 860-974-0343; Fax 860-974-3950.
Will search UCC records. This agency will not do a tax lien search. Will not search real estate records. **Other Phone Numbers:** Assessor 860-974-1674; Vital Records 860-974-0343.

Portland Town

Town Clerk, PO Box 71, Portland, CT 06480. Town Clerk, R/E and UCC Recording 860-342-6743; Fax 860-342-0001.
Will search UCC records. This agency will not do a tax lien search. Will not search real estate records. **Other Phone Numbers:** Assessor 860-342-6744; Treasurer 860-342-6726; Elections 860-342-6743; Vital Records 860-342-6743.

Preston Town

Town Clerk, 389 Route 2, Town Hall, Preston, CT 06365-8830. 860-887-9821 R/E Recording: 860-887-9821; Fax 860-885-1905.
This agency will not perform searches. **Other Phone Numbers:** Assessor 860-889-2529.

Prospect Town

Town Clerk, 36 Center St, Prospect, CT 06712-1699. 203-758-4461; Fax 203-758-4466.
Will search UCC records. This agency will not do a tax lien search. Will not search real estate records. **Other Phone Numbers:** Assessor 203-758-4461; Vital Records 203-758-4461.

Putnam Town

Town Clerk, 126 Church St, Putnam, CT 06260. Town Clerk, R/E and UCC Recording 860-963-6807; Fax 860-963-2001.
Will search UCC records. This agency will not do a tax lien search. Will not search real estate records. **Other Phone Numbers:** Assessor 860-963-6802; Treasurer 860-963-6809.

Redding Town

Town Clerk, PO Box 1028, Redding, CT 06875-1028. Town Clerk, R/E and UCC Recording 203-938-2377; Fax 203-938-8816.
This agency will not perform searches. **Other Phone Numbers:** Assessor 203-938-2626.

Ridgefield Town

Town Clerk, 400 Main St, Ridgefield, CT 06877. 203-431-2783 R/E Recording: 203-438-7301; Fax 203-431-2722. www.ridgefieldct.org/government/townclerk/townclerk.htm
Will not earch UCC records. This agency will not do a tax lien search. Will not search real estate records. **Other Phone Numbers:** Assessor 203-431-2706; Treasurer 203-431-2763; Elections 203-431-2771/2772; Vital Records 203-431-2783.

Rocky Hill Town

Town Clerk, PO Box 657, Rocky Hill, CT 06067. 860-258-2705.
This agency will not perform searches. **Other Phone Numbers:** Assessor 860-258-2774.

Roxbury Town

Town Clerk, 29 North St., Roxbury, CT 06783-1405. 860-354-3328 R/E Recording: 860-354-3328 UCC Recording: 860-354-3328; Fax 860-354-0560. Will search UCC records. This agency will not do a tax lien search. Will not search real estate records. **Other Phone Numbers:** Assessor 860-354-2634; Treasurer 860-354-9938; Vital Records 860-354-3328.

Salem Town

Town Clerk, Town Office Building, 270 Hartford Road, Salem, CT 06420. 860-859-3873 x170 R/E Recording: 860-859-3873; Fax 860-859-1184. Will search UCC records. This agency will not do a tax lien search. Will not search real estate records. **Other Phone Numbers:** Assessor 860-859-3873.

Salisbury Town

Town Clerk, PO Box 548, Salisbury, CT 06068. 860-435-5182; Fax 860-435-5172. Will search UCC records. This agency will not do a tax lien search. Will not search real estate records. **Other Phone Numbers:** Assessor 860-435-5176; Treasurer 860-435-5174.

Scotland Town

Town Clerk, PO Box 122, Scotland, CT 06264. 860-423-9634 R/E Recording: 860-423-9634; Fax 860-423-3666. Will search UCC records. This agency will not do a tax lien search. Will not search real estate records. **Other Phone Numbers:** Assessor 860-423-9634; Treasurer 860-423-9634.

Seymour Town

Town Clerk, 1 First St, Town Hall, Seymour, CT 06483-2817. 203-888-0519. This agency will not perform searches. **Other Phones:** Assessor 203-881-5013; Treasurer 203-888-0581.

Sharon Town

Town Clerk, PO Box 224, Sharon, CT 06069-0224. 860-364-5224 R/E Recording: 860-364-5224; Fax 860-364-5224. This agency will not perform searches. **Other Phone Numbers:** Assessor 860-364-0205.

Shelton City

City Clerk, PO Box 364, Shelton, CT 06484-0364. 203-924-1555 R/E Recording: 203-924-1562; Fax 203-924-1721. Will search UCC records. This agency will not do a tax lien search. Will not search real estate records. **Other Phone Numbers:** Assessor 203-924-1555 x335.

Sherman Town

Town Clerk, PO Box 39, Sherman, CT 06784-0039. Town Clerk, R/E and UCC Recording 860-354-5281; Fax 860-350-5041. This agency will not perform searches. **Other Phone Numbers:** Assessor 860-355-0376; Treasurer 860-354-5281; Vital Records 860-354-5281.

Simsbury Town

Town Clerk, PO Box 495, Simsbury, CT 06070. 860-658-3243; Fax 860-658-3206. Will search UCC records. This agency will not do a tax lien search. Will not search real estate records. **Other Phone Numbers:** Assessor 860-658-3243.

Somers Town

Town Clerk, PO Box 308, Somers, CT 06071. 860-763-8206; Fax 860-763-8228. This agency will not perform searches. **Other Phone Numbers:** Assessor 860-763-8203; Treasurer 860-763-8204; Vital Records 860-763-8206.

South Windsor Town

Town Clerk, 1540 Sullivan Ave, South Windsor, CT 06074. 860-644-2511 x225 R/E Recording: 860-644-2511; Fax 860-644-3781. www.southwindsor.org This agency will not perform searches. **Other Phone Numbers:** Assessor 860-644-2511 x213; Treasurer 860-644-2511 x261.

Southbury Town

Town Clerk, 501 Main St South, Southbury, CT 06488-2295. Town Clerk, R/E and UCC Recording 203-262-0657; Fax 203-264-9762. This agency will not perform searches. **Other Phones:** Assessor 203-262-0647; Treasurer 203-262-0663; Elections 203-262-0657; Vital Records 203-262-0657.

Southington Town

Town Clerk, PO Box 152, Southington, CT 06489. 860-276-6211 R/E Recording: 860-276-6211; Fax 860-276-6229. Will search UCC records. This agency will not do a tax lien search. Will not search real estate records. **Other Phone Numbers:** Assessor 860-276-6205.

Sprague Town

Town Clerk, PO Box 162, Baltic, CT 06330. 860-822-3001 R/E Recording: 860-822-6223; Fax 860-822-3013. This agency will not perform searches. **Other Phones:** Assessor 860-822-3002; Treasurer 860-822-3004.

Stafford Town

Town Clerk, PO Box 11, Stafford Springs, CT 06076. 860-684-1765 R/E Recording: 860-684-2532; Fax 860-684-1765. This agency will not perform searches. **Other Phone Numbers:** Assessor 860-684-1786.

Stamford City

City Clerk, PO Box 10152, Stamford, CT 06904. City Clerk, R/E and UCC Recording 203-977-4054 UCC Recording: 203-977-4707; Fax 203-977-4943. www.cityofstamford.org/Welcome.htm Will search UCC records. This agency will not do a tax lien search. Will not search real estate records. **Online Access:** Assessor, Real Estate, Personal Property Records. Access to the city tax assessor database is available at www.cityofstamford.org/Tax/main.htm. A land records index should be online in Fall, 2001. **Other Phone Numbers:** Assessor 203-977-4019; Treasurer 203-977-4185; Elections 203-977-4011; Vital Records 203-977-4055.

Sterling Town

Town Clerk, PO Box 157, Oneco, CT 06373-0157. Town Clerk, R/E and UCC Recording 860-564-2657; Fax 860-564-1660. Will search UCC records. This agency will not do a tax lien search. Will not search real estate records. **Other Phone Numbers:** Assessor 860-564-3030; Treasurer 860-564-2904; Elections 860-564-2657; Vital Records 860-564-2657.

Stonington Town

Town Clerk, PO Box 352, Stonington, CT 06378. 860-535-5060 R/E Recording: 860-535-4721; Fax 860-535-5062. This agency will not perform searches. **Other Phones:** Assessor 860-535-5098; Elections 860-535-5047.

Stratford Town

Town Clerk, 2725 Main St, Room 101, Stratford, CT 06615. 203-385-4020; Fax 203-385-4108. Will search UCC records. This agency will not do a tax lien search. Will not search real estate records. **Other** Phone Numbers: Assessor 203-385-4025; Elections 203-385-4028.

Suffield Town

Town Clerk, 83 Mountain Road, Town Hall, Suffield, CT 06078. 860-668-3880; Fax 860-668-3898. Will search UCC records. This agency will not do a tax lien search. Will not search real estate records. **Online Access:** Assessor Records. Search the town assessor's database at http://data.visionappraisal.com/SuffieldCT. Free registration required for full access. **Other Phone Numbers:** Assessor 860-668-3866; Treasurer 860-668-3851; Appraiser/Auditor 860-668-3850; Elections 860-668-3880.

Thomaston Town

Town Clerk, 158 Main St, Thomaston, CT 06787. 860-283-4141 R/E Recording: 860-283-4141; Fax 860-283-1013. This agency will not perform searches. **Other Phones:** Assessor 860-283-0305; Treasurer 860-283-9678.

Thompson Town

Town Clerk, PO Box 899, No. Grosvenor Dale, CT 06255. 860-923-9900 R/E Recording: 860-923-9900; Fax 860-923-3836. Will search UCC records. This agency will not do a tax lien search. Will not search real estate records. **Online Access:** Assessor Records. Search the town assessor data at http://data.visionappraisal.com/ThompsonCT. Free registration for full data. **Other Phone Numbers:** Assessor 860-923-2259.

Tolland Town

Town Clerk, Hicks Memorial Municipal Center, 21 Tolland Green, Tolland, CT 06084. 860-871-3630 R/E Recording: 860-871-3630; Fax 860-871-3663. Do not confuse this town with the County of Tolland. Only Town of Tolland filings go here. This agency will not perform searches. **Other Phone Numbers:** Assessor 860-871-3650; Treasurer 860-871-3658; Elections 860-871-3634; Vital Records 860-871-3630.

Torrington City

Town Clerk, 140 Main St, City Hall, Torrington, CT 06790. 860-489-2236 R/E Recording: 860-489-2241; Fax 860-489-2548. www.torrington-ct.org Will search UCC records. This agency will not do a tax lien search. Will not search real estate records. **Other Phone Numbers:** Assessor 860-489-2222; Treasurer 860-489-2334; Elections 860-489-2236; Vital Records 860-489-2236.

Trumbull Town

Town Clerk, 5866 Main St, Trumbull, CT 06611. 203-452-5035; Fax 203-452-5094. Will search UCC records. This agency will not do a tax lien search. Will not search real estate records. **Other Phone Numbers:** Assessor 203-452-5016; Treasurer 203-452-5014; Elections 203-452-5058; Vital Records 203-452-5035.

Union Town

Town Clerk, 1043 Buckley Highway, Route 171, Union, CT 06076-9520. 860-684-3770 R/E Recording: 860-684-3770; Fax 860-684-8830. Will search UCC records. This agency will not do a tax lien search. Will not search real estate records. **Other Phone Numbers:** Assessor 860-684-5705.

Vernon Town

Town Clerk, 14 Park Place, Rockville, CT 06066. Town Clerk, R/E and UCC Recording 860-870-3662; Fax 860-870-3683. www.munic.state.ct.us/vernon/vernon.htm This agency will not perform searches. **Other Phones:** Assessor 860-870-3625; Treasurer 860-870-3660.

Voluntown Town

Town Clerk, PO Box 96, Voluntown, CT 06384-0096. Town Clerk, R/E and UCC Recording 860-376-4089; Fax 860-376-3295. www.voluntown.gov
Will search UCC records. This agency will not do a tax lien search. Will not search real estate records. **Other Phone Numbers:** Assessor 860-376-3927; Treasurer 860-376-3927.

Wallingford Town

Town Clerk, PO Box 427, Wallingford, CT 06492. Town Clerk, R/E and UCC Recording 203-294-2145; Fax 203-294-2150.
This agency will not perform searches. **Other Phone Numbers:** Assessor 203-294-2001; Treasurer 203-294-2042; Appraiser/Auditor 203-294-2001; Elections 203-294-2125; Vital Records 203-294-2145.

Warren Town

Town Clerk, 7 Sackett Hill Road, Town Hall, Warren, CT 06754. 860-868-0090 R/E Recording: 860-868-0090; Fax 860-868-7746.
Will search UCC records. This agency will not do a tax lien search. Will not search real estate records. **Other Phone Numbers:** Assessor 860-868-7881.

Washington Town

Town Clerk, PO Box 383, Washington Depot, CT 06794. 860-868-2786 R/E Recording: 860-868-2786; Fax 860-868-3103.
Will search UCC records. This agency will not do a tax lien search. Will not search real estate records. **Other Phone Numbers:** Assessor 860-868-0398.

Waterbury City

Town Clerk, 235 Grand St, City Hall, Waterbury, CT 06702. Town Clerk, R/E and UCC Recording 203-574-6806; Fax 203-574-6887.
Will search UCC records. This agency will not do a tax lien search. Will not search real estate records. **Other Phone Numbers:** Assessor 203-574-6821; Elections 203-574-6751; Vital Records 203-574-6801.

Waterford Town

Town Clerk, 15 Rope Ferry Road, Waterford, CT 06385. Town Clerk, R/E and UCC Recording 860-444-5831; Fax 860-437-0352.
Will search UCC records. This agency will not do a tax lien search. Will not search real estate records. **Other Phone Numbers:** Assessor 860-444-5820; Vital Records 860-444-5831.

Watertown Town

Town Clerk, 37 DeForest St, Watertown, CT 06795. Town Clerk, R/E and UCC Recording 860-945-5230.
This agency will not perform searches. **Other Phones:** Assessor 860-945-5235; Treasurer 860-945-5261; Elections 860-945-5230; Vital Records 860-945-5230.

West Hartford Town

Town Clerk, 50 S. Main St, Room 313 Town Hall Common, West Hartford, CT 06107-2431. 860-523-3148 R/E Recording: 860-523-3100; Fax 860-523-3522.
This agency will not perform searches. **Other Phone Numbers:** Assessor 860-523-3119; Treasurer 860-523-3188; Appraiser/Auditor 860-523-3119; Elections 860-523-3181; Vital Records 860-523-3151.

West Haven City

City Clerk, PO Box 526, West Haven, CT 06516. 203-937-3534 R/E Recording: 203-937-3535; Fax 203-937-3706.
Will search UCC records. This agency will not do a tax lien search. Will not search real estate records. **Online**

Access: Assessor Records. Search the town assessor's data at http://data.visionappraisal.com/Westhavenct. Free registration required for full access. **Other Phone Numbers:** Assessor 203-937-3517.

Westbrook Town

Town Clerk, PO Box 676, Westbrook, CT 06498-0676. 860-399-3044 R/E Recording: 860-399-9723; Fax 860-399-9832.
This agency will not perform searches. **Other Phone Numbers:** Assessor 860-399-3045.

Weston Town

Town Clerk, PO Box 1007, Weston, CT 06883. 203-222-2616 R/E Recording: 203-222-2682; Fax 203-222-8871. www.weston-ct.com
Will search UCC records. This agency will not do a tax lien search. Will not search real estate records. **Other Phone Numbers:** Assessor 203-222-2606.

Westport Town

Town Clerk, PO Box 549, Westport, CT 06881. 203-341-1110 R/E Recording: 203-226-8311; Fax 203-341-1112. www.ci.westport.ct.us/govt/services
Will search UCC records. This agency will not do a tax lien search. Will not search real estate records. **Online Access:** Assessor Records. Access to the 2000 assessments database is available free at www.ci.westport.ct.us/govt/services/finance/assessor/default.asp. **Other Phone Numbers:** Assessor 203-226-8311 x103.

Wethersfield Town

Town Clerk, 505 Silas Deane Highway, Wethersfield, CT 06109. Town Clerk, R/E and UCC Recording 860-721-2880; Fax 860-721-2994. www.wethersfieldct.com/govt.htm
Will search UCC records. This agency will not do a tax lien search. Will not search real estate records. **Online Access:** Assessor Records. Search the town assessor's grand list free at www.wethersfieldct.com/assess/service.htm. No name searching; download as ascii or Excel file format. **Other Phone Numbers:** Assessor 860-721-2810; Treasurer 860-721-2861; Elections 860-721-2819; Vital Records 860-721-2880.

Willington Town

Town Clerk, 40 Old Farms Road, Willington, CT 06279. Town Clerk, R/E and UCC Recording 860-487-3121; Fax 860-429-8415. www.willingtonct.org
This agency will not perform searches. **Other Phones:** Assessor 860-487-3122; Treasurer 860-487-3133; Elections 860-487-3121; Vital Records 860-487-3121.

Wilton Town

Town Clerk, 238 Danbury Road, Wilton, CT 06897. Town Clerk, R/E and UCC Recording 203-563-0106; Fax 203-563-0299. www.munic.state.ct.us/WILTON/wilton.htm
Will search UCC records. This agency will not do a tax lien search. Will not search real estate records. **Other Phone Numbers:** Assessor 203-563-0121; Treasurer 203-563-0114; Elections 203-563-0112; Vital Records 203-563-0106.

Winchester Town

Town Clerk, 338 Main St, Town Hall, Winsted, CT 06098-1697. Town Clerk, R/E and UCC Recording 860-738-6963; Fax 860-738-6595. http://townofwinchester.org
Will search UCC records. This agency will not do a tax lien search. Will not search real estate records. **Other Phone Numbers:** Assessor 860-379-5461; Treasurer 860-738-6961; Appraiser/Auditor 860-379-5461;

Elections 860-738-6963 x355; Vital Records 860-738-6963.

Windham Town

Town Clerk, PO Box 94, Willimantic, CT 06226. 860-465-3013 R/E Recording: 860-456-3593; Fax 860-465-3012. www.windhamct.com
This agency will not perform searches. **Other Phone Numbers:** Assessor 860-465-3025; Treasurer 860-465-3060.

Windsor Locks Town

Town Clerk, 50 Church St, Town Office Building, Windsor Locks, CT 06096. Town Clerk, R/E and UCC Recording 860-627-1441.
This agency will not perform searches. **Online Access:** Assessor Records. Search the town assessor database at http://data.visionappraisal.com/WINDSORLOCKSCT. Free registration for full data. **Other Phone Numbers:** Assessor 860-627-1448; Treasurer 860-627-1449; Elections 860-654-1619; Vital Records 860-627-1441.

Windsor Town

Town Clerk, PO Box 472, Windsor, CT 06095-0472. Town Clerk, R/E and UCC Recording 860-285-1902; Fax 860-285-1909. www.townofwindsorct.com
This agency will not perform searches. **Online Access:** Assessor, Real Estate Records. Search the town clerk's Recording database free at www.townofwindsorct.com/records.htm. Records go back to 1991; plan is to go back to 1970. Also, search the town assessor's Taxpayer Information System at http://data.visionappraisal.com/WINDSORCT. Free egistration required for full access. **Other Phones:** Assessor 860-285-1817; Treasurer 860-285-1890; Elections 860-285-1902; Vital Records 860-285-1902.

Wolcott Town

Town Clerk, 10 Kenea Ave, Town Hall, Wolcott, CT 06716. 203-879-8100 R/E Recording: 203-879-4666; Fax 203-879-8105.
Will search UCC records. This agency will not do a tax lien search. Will not search real estate records. **Other Phone Numbers:** Assessor 203-879-8100; Treasurer 203-879-8100; Elections 203-879-8100; Vital Records 203-879-8100.

Woodbridge Town

Town Clerk, 11 Meetinghouse Lane, Woodbridge, CT 06525. Town Clerk, R/E and UCC Recording 203-389-3422; Fax 203-389-3473. www.munic.state.ct.us/woodbridge/townclerk.html
Will search UCC records. This agency will not do a tax lien search. Will not search real estate records. **Online Access:** Assessor Records. Search the town assessor's data at http://data.visionappraisal.com/woodbridgeCT. Free registration required for full data. **Other Phone Numbers:** Assessor 203-389-3416; Treasurer 203-389-3414; Appraiser/Auditor 203-389-3414; Elections 203-389-3408; Vital Records 203-389-3424.

Woodbury Town

Town Clerk, PO Box 369, Woodbury, CT 06798-3407. 203-263-2144; Fax 203-263-4755.
This agency will not perform searches. **Other Phone Numbers:** Assessor 203-263-2435.

Woodstock Town

Town Clerk, Town Office Building, 415 Route 169, Woodstock, CT 06281. 860-928-6595 R/E Recording: 860-928-6595; Fax 860-963-7557. www.townofwoodstock.com
This agency will not perform searches. **Other Phone Numbers:** Assessor 860-928-6929.

Connecticut County Locator

You will usually be able to find the city name in the City/County Cross Reference below. In that case, it is a simple matter to determine the county from the cross reference. However, only the official US Postal Service city names are included in this index. There are an additional 40,000 place names that people use in their addresses. Therefore, we have also included a ZIP/City Cross Reference immediately following the City/County Cross Reference.

If you know the ZIP Code but the city name does not appear in the City/County Cross Reference index, look up the ZIP Code in the ZIP/City Cross Reference, find the city name, then look up the city name in the City/County Cross Reference. For example, you want to know the county for an address of Menands, NY 12204. There is no "Menands" in the City/County Cross Reference. The ZIP/City Cross Reference shows that ZIP Codes 12201-12288 are for the city of Albany. Looking back in the City/County Cross Reference, Albany is in Albany County.

City/County Cross Reference

ABINGTON Windham
AMSTON Tolland
ANDOVER Tolland
ANSONIA New Haven
ASHFORD Windham
AVON Hartford
BALLOUVILLE Windham
BALTIC (06330) New London(93), Windham(6)
BANTAM Litchfield
BARKHAMSTED Litchfield
BEACON FALLS New Haven
BETHANY New Haven
BETHEL Fairfield
BETHLEHEM Litchfield
BLOOMFIELD Hartford
BOLTON Tolland
BOTSFORD Fairfield
BOZRAH New London
BRANFORD New Haven
BRIDGEPORT Fairfield
BRIDGEWATER Litchfield
BRISTOL Hartford
BROAD BROOK Hartford
BROOKFIELD Fairfield
BROOKLYN Windham
BURLINGTON Hartford
CANAAN Litchfield
CANTERBURY (06331) Windham(97), New London(2)
CANTON Hartford
CANTON CENTER Hartford
CENTERBROOK Middlesex
CENTRAL VILLAGE Windham
CHAPLIN Windham
CHESHIRE New Haven
CHESTER Middlesex
CLINTON Middlesex
COBALT Middlesex
COLCHESTER (06415) New London(90), Middlesex(9)
COLEBROOK Litchfield
COLLINSVILLE Hartford
COLUMBIA Tolland
CORNWALL Litchfield
CORNWALL BRIDGE Litchfield
COS COB Fairfield
COVENTRY Tolland
CROMWELL Middlesex
DANBURY Fairfield
DANIELSON Windham
DARIEN Fairfield
DAYVILLE Windham
DEEP RIVER Middlesex
DERBY New Haven
DURHAM Middlesex
EAST BERLIN Hartford
EAST CANAAN Litchfield
EAST GLASTONBURY Hartford
EAST GRANBY Hartford
EAST HADDAM Middlesex
EAST HAMPTON Middlesex
EAST HARTFORD Hartford
EAST HARTLAND Hartford
EAST HAVEN New Haven
EAST KILLINGLY Windham
EAST LYME New London
EAST WINDSOR Hartford
EAST WINDSOR HILL Hartford
EAST WOODSTOCK Windham

EASTFORD (06242) Windham(96), Tolland(3)
EASTON Fairfield
ELLINGTON Tolland
ENFIELD Hartford
ESSEX Middlesex
FABYAN Windham
FAIRFIELD Fairfield
FALLS VILLAGE Litchfield
FARMINGTON Hartford
GALES FERRY New London
GAYLORDSVILLE Litchfield
GEORGETOWN Fairfield
GILMAN New London
GLASGO New London
GLASTONBURY Hartford
GOSHEN Litchfield
GRANBY Hartford
GREENS FARMS Fairfield
GREENWICH Fairfield
GROSVENOR DALE Windham
GROTON New London
GUILFORD New Haven
HADDAM Middlesex
HADLYME New London
HAMDEN New Haven
HAMPTON Windham
HANOVER New London
HARTFORD Hartford
HARWINTON Litchfield
HAWLEYVILLE Fairfield
HEBRON Tolland
HIGGANUM Middlesex
IVORYTON Middlesex
JEWETT CITY New London
KENSINGTON Hartford
KENT Litchfield
KILLINGWORTH Middlesex
LAKESIDE Litchfield
LAKEVILLE Litchfield
LEBANON New London
LEDYARD New London
LITCHFIELD Litchfield
MADISON New Haven
MANCHESTER Hartford
MANSFIELD CENTER (06250) Tolland(97), Windham(2)
MANSFIELD DEPOT Tolland
MARION Hartford
MARLBOROUGH Hartford
MELROSE Hartford
MERIDEN New Haven
MIDDLE HADDAM Middlesex
MIDDLEBURY New Haven
MIDDLEFIELD Middlesex
MIDDLETOWN Middlesex
MILFORD New Haven
MILLDALE Hartford
MONROE Fairfield
MONTVILLE New London
MOODUS Middlesex
MOOSUP Windham
MORRIS Litchfield
MYSTIC New London
NAUGATUCK New Haven
NEW BRITAIN Hartford
NEW CANAAN Fairfield
NEW FAIRFIELD Fairfield
NEW HARTFORD Litchfield
NEW HAVEN New Haven

NEW LONDON New London
NEW MILFORD Litchfield
NEW PRESTON MARBLE DALE Litchfield
NEWINGTON Hartford
NEWTOWN Fairfield
NIANTIC New London
NORFOLK Litchfield
NORTH BRANFORD New Haven
NORTH CANTON Hartford
NORTH FRANKLIN New London
NORTH GRANBY Hartford
NORTH GROSVENORDALE Windham
NORTH HAVEN New Haven
NORTH STONINGTON New London
NORTH WESTCHESTER New London
NORTH WINDHAM Windham
NORTHFIELD Litchfield
NORTHFORD New Haven
NORWALK Fairfield
NORWICH New London
OAKDALE New London
OAKVILLE Litchfield
OLD GREENWICH Fairfield
OLD LYME New London
OLD MYSTIC New London
OLD SAYBROOK Middlesex
ONECO Windham
ORANGE New Haven
OXFORD New Haven
PAWCATUCK New London
PEQUABUCK Litchfield
PINE MEADOW Litchfield
PLAINFIELD Windham
PLAINVILLE Hartford
PLANTSVILLE Hartford
PLEASANT VALLEY Litchfield
PLYMOUTH Litchfield
POMFRET Windham
POMFRET CENTER Windham
POQUONOCK Hartford
PORTLAND Middlesex
PRESTON New London
PROSPECT New Haven
PUTNAM Windham
QUAKER HILL New London
QUINEBAUG Windham
REDDING Fairfield
REDDING CENTER Fairfield
REDDING RIDGE Fairfield
RIDGEFIELD Fairfield
RIVERSIDE Fairfield
RIVERTON Litchfield
ROCKFALL Middlesex
ROCKY HILL Hartford
ROGERS Windham
ROXBURY Litchfield
SALEM New London
SALISBURY Litchfield
SANDY HOOK Fairfield
SCOTLAND Windham
SEYMOUR New Haven
SHARON Litchfield
SHELTON Fairfield
SHERMAN (06784) Fairfield(98), Litchfield(1)
SIMSBURY Hartford
SOMERS Tolland
SOMERSVILLE Tolland
SOUTH BRITAIN New Haven
SOUTH GLASTONBURY Hartford

SOUTH KENT Litchfield
SOUTH LYME New London
SOUTH WILLINGTON Tolland
SOUTH WINDHAM Windham
SOUTH WINDSOR Hartford
SOUTH WOODSTOCK Windham
SOUTHBURY New Haven
SOUTHINGTON Hartford
SOUTHPORT Fairfield
STAFFORD Tolland
STAFFORD SPRINGS (06076) Tolland(94), Windham(5)
STAFFORDVILLE Tolland
STAMFORD Fairfield
STERLING Windham
STEVENSON Fairfield
STONINGTON New London
STORRS MANSFIELD Tolland
STRATFORD Fairfield
SUFFIELD Hartford
TACONIC Litchfield
TAFTVILLE New London
TARIFFVILLE Hartford
TERRYVILLE Litchfield
THOMASTON Litchfield
THOMPSON Windham
TOLLAND Tolland
TORRINGTON Litchfield
TRUMBULL Fairfield
UNCASVILLE New London
UNIONVILLE Hartford
VERNON ROCKVILLE Tolland
VERSAILLES New London
VOLUNTOWN (06384) New London(97), Windham(2)
W HARTFORD Hartford
WALLINGFORD New Haven
WASHINGTON DEPOT Litchfield
WATERBURY New Haven
WATERFORD New London
WATERTOWN Litchfield
WAUREGAN Windham
WEATOGUE Hartford
WEST CORNWALL Litchfield
WEST GRANBY Hartford
WEST HARTFORD Hartford
WEST HARTLAND Hartford
WEST HAVEN New Haven
WEST MYSTIC New London
WEST SIMSBURY Hartford
WEST SUFFIELD Hartford
WESTBROOK Middlesex
WESTON Fairfield
WESTPORT Fairfield
WETHERSFIELD Hartford
WILLIMANTIC Windham
WILLINGTON Tolland
WILTON Fairfield
WINCHESTER CENTER Litchfield
WINDHAM Windham
WINDSOR Hartford
WINDSOR LOCKS Hartford
WINSTED Litchfield
WOLCOTT New Haven
WOODBRIDGE New Haven
WOODBURY Litchfield
WOODSTOCK Windham
WOODSTOCK VALLEY Windham
YANTIC New London

ZIP/City Cross Reference

06001-06001	AVON	
06002-06002	BLOOMFIELD	
06006-06006	WINDSOR	
06010-06011	BRISTOL	
06013-06013	BURLINGTON	
06016-06016	BROAD BROOK	
06018-06018	CANAAN	
06019-06019	CANTON	
06020-06020	CANTON CENTER	
06021-06021	COLEBROOK	
06022-06022	COLLINSVILLE	
06023-06023	EAST BERLIN	
06024-06024	EAST CANAAN	
06025-06025	EAST GLASTONBURY	
06026-06026	EAST GRANBY	
06027-06027	EAST HARTLAND	
06028-06028	EAST WINDSOR HILL	
06029-06029	ELLINGTON	
06030-06030	FARMINGTON	
06031-06031	FALLS VILLAGE	
06032-06032	FARMINGTON	
06033-06033	GLASTONBURY	
06034-06034	FARMINGTON	
06035-06035	GRANBY	
06037-06037	KENSINGTON	
06039-06039	LAKEVILLE	
06040-06041	MANCHESTER	
06043-06043	BOLTON	
06045-06045	MANCHESTER	
06049-06049	MELROSE	
06050-06053	NEW BRITAIN	
06057-06057	NEW HARTFORD	
06058-06058	NORFOLK	
06059-06059	NORTH CANTON	
06060-06060	NORTH GRANBY	
06061-06061	PINE MEADOW	
06062-06062	PLAINVILLE	
06063-06063	PLEASANT VALLEY	
06063-06063	BARKHAMSTED	
06064-06064	POQUONOCK	
06065-06065	RIVERTON	
06066-06066	VERNON ROCKVILLE	
06067-06067	ROCKY HILL	
06068-06068	SALISBURY	
06069-06069	SHARON	
06070-06070	SIMSBURY	
06071-06071	SOMERS	
06072-06072	SOMERSVILLE	
06073-06073	SOUTH GLASTONBURY	
06074-06074	SOUTH WINDSOR	
06075-06075	STAFFORD	
06076-06076	STAFFORD SPRINGS	
06077-06077	STAFFORDVILLE	
06078-06078	SUFFIELD	
06079-06079	TACONIC	
06080-06080	SUFFIELD	
06081-06081	TARIFFVILLE	
06082-06083	ENFIELD	
06084-06084	TOLLAND	
06085-06087	UNIONVILLE	
06088-06088	EAST WINDSOR	
06089-06089	WEATOGUE	
06090-06090	WEST GRANBY	
06091-06091	WEST HARTLAND	
06092-06092	WEST SIMSBURY	
06093-06093	WEST SUFFIELD	
06094-06094	WINCHESTER CENTER	
06095-06095	WINDSOR	
06096-06096	WINDSOR LOCKS	
06098-06098	WINSTED	
06100-06106	HARTFORD	
06107-06107	W HARTFORD	
06107-06107	WEST HARTFORD	
06108-06108	EAST HARTFORD	
06109-06109	WETHERSFIELD	
06110-06110	W HARTFORD	
06110-06110	WEST HARTFORD	
06111-06111	NEWINGTON	
06112-06115	HARTFORD	
06117-06117	W HARTFORD	
06117-06117	WEST HARTFORD	
06118-06118	EAST HARTFORD	
06119-06119	W HARTFORD	
06119-06119	WEST HARTFORD	
06120-06126	HARTFORD	
06127-06127	W HARTFORD	
06127-06127	WEST HARTFORD	
06128-06128	EAST HARTFORD	
06129-06129	WETHERSFIELD	
06131-06131	NEWINGTON	
06132-06132	HARTFORD	
06133-06133	W HARTFORD	
06133-06133	WEST HARTFORD	
06134-06134	HARTFORD	
06137-06137	W HARTFORD	
06137-06137	WEST HARTFORD	
06138-06138	EAST HARTFORD	
06140-06199	HARTFORD	
06226-06226	WILLIMANTIC	
06230-06230	ABINGTON	
06231-06231	AMSTON	
06232-06232	ANDOVER	
06233-06233	BALLOUVILLE	
06234-06234	BROOKLYN	
06235-06235	CHAPLIN	
06237-06237	COLUMBIA	
06238-06238	COVENTRY	
06239-06239	DANIELSON	
06241-06241	DAYVILLE	
06242-06242	EASTFORD	
06243-06243	EAST KILLINGLY	
06244-06244	EAST WOODSTOCK	
06245-06245	FABYAN	
06246-06246	GROSVENOR DALE	
06247-06247	HAMPTON	
06248-06248	HEBRON	
06249-06249	LEBANON	
06250-06250	MANSFIELD CENTER	
06251-06251	MANSFIELD DEPOT	
06254-06254	NORTH FRANKLIN	
06255-06255	NORTH GROSVENORDALE	
06256-06256	NORTH WINDHAM	
06258-06258	POMFRET	
06259-06259	POMFRET CENTER	
06260-06260	PUTNAM	
06262-06262	QUINEBAUG	
06263-06263	ROGERS	
06264-06264	SCOTLAND	
06265-06265	SOUTH WILLINGTON	
06266-06266	SOUTH WINDHAM	
06267-06267	SOUTH WOODSTOCK	
06268-06269	STORRS MANSFIELD	
06277-06277	THOMPSON	
06278-06278	ASHFORD	
06279-06279	WILLINGTON	
06280-06280	WINDHAM	
06281-06281	WOODSTOCK	
06282-06282	WOODSTOCK VALLEY	
06320-06320	NEW LONDON	
06330-06330	BALTIC	
06331-06331	CANTERBURY	
06332-06332	CENTRAL VILLAGE	
06333-06333	EAST LYME	
06334-06334	BOZRAH	
06335-06335	GALES FERRY	
06336-06336	GILMAN	
06337-06337	GLASGO	
06339-06339	LEDYARD	
06340-06349	GROTON	
06350-06350	HANOVER	
06351-06351	JEWETT CITY	
06353-06353	MONTVILLE	
06354-06354	MOOSUP	
06355-06355	MYSTIC	
06357-06357	NIANTIC	
06359-06359	NORTH STONINGTON	
06360-06360	NORWICH	
06365-06365	PRESTON	
06370-06370	OAKDALE	
06371-06371	OLD LYME	
06372-06372	OLD MYSTIC	
06373-06373	ONECO	
06374-06374	PLAINFIELD	
06375-06375	QUAKER HILL	
06376-06376	SOUTH LYME	
06377-06377	STERLING	
06378-06378	STONINGTON	
06379-06379	PAWCATUCK	
06380-06380	TAFTVILLE	
06382-06382	UNCASVILLE	
06383-06383	VERSAILLES	
06384-06384	VOLUNTOWN	
06385-06386	WATERFORD	
06387-06387	WAUREGAN	
06388-06388	WEST MYSTIC	
06389-06389	YANTIC	
06401-06401	ANSONIA	
06403-06403	BEACON FALLS	
06404-06404	BOTSFORD	
06405-06405	BRANFORD	
06408-06408	CHESHIRE	
06409-06409	CENTERBROOK	
06410-06411	CHESHIRE	
06412-06412	CHESTER	
06413-06413	CLINTON	
06414-06414	COBALT	
06415-06415	COLCHESTER	
06416-06416	CROMWELL	
06417-06417	DEEP RIVER	
06418-06418	DERBY	
06419-06419	KILLINGWORTH	
06420-06420	SALEM	
06422-06422	DURHAM	
06423-06423	EAST HADDAM	
06424-06424	EAST HAMPTON	
06426-06426	ESSEX	
06430-06432	FAIRFIELD	
06436-06436	GREENS FARMS	
06437-06437	GUILFORD	
06438-06438	HADDAM	
06439-06439	HADLYME	
06440-06440	HAWLEYVILLE	
06441-06441	HIGGANUM	
06442-06442	IVORYTON	
06443-06443	MADISON	
06444-06444	MARION	
06447-06447	MARLBOROUGH	
06450-06454	MERIDEN	
06455-06455	MIDDLEFIELD	
06456-06456	MIDDLE HADDAM	
06457-06459	MIDDLETOWN	
06460-06460	MILFORD	
06461-06461	BRIDGEPORT	
06466-06466	MILFORD	
06467-06467	MILLDALE	
06468-06468	MONROE	
06469-06469	MOODUS	
06470-06470	NEWTOWN	
06471-06471	NORTH BRANFORD	
06472-06472	NORTHFORD	
06473-06473	NORTH HAVEN	
06474-06474	NORTH WESTCHESTER	
06475-06475	OLD SAYBROOK	
06477-06477	ORANGE	
06478-06478	OXFORD	
06479-06479	PLANTSVILLE	
06480-06480	PORTLAND	
06481-06481	ROCKFALL	
06482-06482	SANDY HOOK	
06483-06483	SEYMOUR	
06484-06484	SHELTON	
06487-06487	SOUTH BRITAIN	
06488-06488	SOUTHBURY	
06489-06489	SOUTHINGTON	
06490-06490	SOUTHPORT	
06491-06491	STEVENSON	
06492-06495	WALLINGFORD	
06497-06497	STRATFORD	
06498-06498	WESTBROOK	
06500-06511	NEW HAVEN	
06512-06512	EAST HAVEN	
06513-06513	NEW HAVEN	
06514-06514	HAMDEN	
06515-06515	NEW HAVEN	
06516-06516	WEST HAVEN	
06517-06518	HAMDEN	
06519-06521	NEW HAVEN	
06524-06524	BETHANY	
06525-06525	WOODBRIDGE	
06530-06540	NEW HAVEN	
06600-06610	BRIDGEPORT	
06611-06611	TRUMBULL	
06612-06612	EASTON	
06614-06615	STRATFORD	
06650-06699	BRIDGEPORT	
06701-06710	WATERBURY	
06712-06712	PROSPECT	
06716-06716	WOLCOTT	
06720-06749	WATERBURY	
06750-06750	BANTAM	
06751-06751	BETHLEHEM	
06752-06752	BRIDGEWATER	
06753-06753	CORNWALL	
06754-06754	CORNWALL BRIDGE	
06755-06755	GAYLORDSVILLE	
06756-06756	GOSHEN	
06757-06757	KENT	
06758-06758	LAKESIDE	
06759-06759	LITCHFIELD	
06762-06762	MIDDLEBURY	
06763-06763	MORRIS	
06770-06770	NAUGATUCK	
06776-06776	NEW MILFORD	
06777-06777	NEW PRESTON MARBLE DALE	
06778-06778	NORTHFIELD	
06779-06779	OAKVILLE	
06781-06781	PEQUABUCK	
06782-06782	PLYMOUTH	
06783-06783	ROXBURY	
06784-06784	SHERMAN	
06785-06785	SOUTH KENT	
06786-06786	TERRYVILLE	
06787-06787	THOMASTON	
06790-06790	TORRINGTON	
06791-06791	HARWINTON	
06793-06794	WASHINGTON DEPOT	
06795-06795	WATERTOWN	
06796-06796	WEST CORNWALL	
06798-06798	WOODBURY	
06801-06801	BETHEL	
06804-06804	BROOKFIELD	
06807-06807	COS COB	
06810-06811	DANBURY	
06812-06812	NEW FAIRFIELD	
06813-06817	DANBURY	
06820-06820	DARIEN	
06829-06829	GEORGETOWN	
06830-06836	GREENWICH	
06840-06842	NEW CANAAN	
06850-06860	NORWALK	
06870-06870	OLD GREENWICH	
06875-06875	REDDING CENTER	
06876-06876	REDDING RIDGE	
06877-06877	RIDGEFIELD	
06878-06878	RIVERSIDE	
06879-06879	RIDGEFIELD	
06880-06881	WESTPORT	
06883-06883	WESTON	
06888-06889	WESTPORT	
06896-06896	REDDING	
06897-06897	WILTON	
06900-06928	STAMFORD	

Delaware

General Help Numbers:

Governor's Office

820 N. French St
Wilmington, DE 19801
www.state.de.us/governor/index.htm

302-577-3210
Fax 302-577-3118
8AM-5:30PM

Attorney General's Office

Carvel State Office Bldg
820 N French St
Wilmington, DE 19801
www.state.de.us/attgen

302-577-8400
Fax 302-577-6630
8:30AM-5PM

State Court Administrator

Supreme Court of Delaware
820 N French, 11th Fl
Wilmington, DE 19801
http://courts.state.de.us/supreme/index.htm

302-577-2480
Fax 302-577-3139
8:30AM-5PM

State Archives

121 Duke of York St
Dover, DE 19901
www.archives.lib.de.us

302-744-5000
Fax 302-739-6710
8:30AM-4:15PM M-F
(till 8PM on E & TH)

State Specifics:

Capital:	Dover
	Kent County
Time Zone:	EST
Number of Counties:	3
Population:	796,165
Web Site:	http://delaware.gov

State Agencies

Criminal Records

Delaware State Police, State Bureau of Identification, PO Box 430, Dover, DE 19903-0430 (Courier: 1407 N Dupont Highway, Dover, DE 19930); 302-739-5880, 302-739-4794 (Fingerprinting/Crim. Background), 302-739-5888 (Fax), 8AM-4PM.

www.state.de.us/dsp

Note: Sex offender data is available online at www.state.de.us/dsp/sexoff/search.htm.

Indexing & Storage: Records are available from 1935. It takes up to 3 days before new records are available for inquiry. 81% of all arrests in database have final dispositions recorded, 92% for those arrests within last 5 years.

Searching: You do not need to use the state's forms. Must have a signed release form for the

fingerprint search and release of information. Include the following in your request: fingerprints, full name, signed release. The agency does not destroy records. The following data is not released: traffic ticket information. If the disposition is not known by this agency, the record will say "disposition not known." Will only release records with dispositions to pre-employment screeners.

Access by: mail, in person.

Fee & Payment: The search fee is $30.00 per request. Fee payee: Delaware State Police. Prepayment required. Funds must be certified or money order. No credit cards accepted.

Mail search: Turnaround time: 14 days. Must have a signed release and full set of fingerprints. A self addressed stamped envelope is requested.

In person search: It can take up to 14 days before records are ready for pickup.

Corporation Records
Partnerships
Limited Partnership Records
Trademarks/Servicemarks
Limited Liability Company
   Records
Limited Liability
   Partnerships

Secretary of State, Division of Corporations, PO Box 898, Dover, DE 19903 (Courier: John G Townsend Bldg, 401 Federal Street #4, Dover, DE 19901); 302-739-3073, 302-739-3812 (Fax), 8AM-4:30PM.

www.state.de.us/corp

Note: There is no online access to the public; however, there is a system available to only registered agents.

Indexing & Storage: Records are available from the formation of the Division. Indexes are maintained on imaging system and in-house computer. Delaware Registered Agents have online access. New records are available for inquiry immediately.

Searching: Include the following in your request: full name of business. In addition to the articles of incorporation, corporation records include the following information: Annual Reports, Officers, Directors, Prior (merged) names, Inactive and Reserved names.

Access by: mail, phone, fax, in person.

Fee & Payment: Fees are $20.00 for a status of an entity; $20.00 for certified plus $1.00 per page; plain copies are $5.00 for the first page and $1.00 each additional. Fee payee: Delaware Secretary of State. Prepayment required. Personal checks accepted. Credit cards accepted: MasterCard, Visa, Discover.

Mail search: Turnaround time: 3 days. No self addressed stamped envelope is required.

Phone search: There is no fee for general information given over the phone.

Fax search: Fax requests can be received by fax, but are not returned by fax.

In person search: Requests are returned by regular mail unless expedite fee is paid.

Expedited service: Expedited service available for mail, fax, phone, and in person. Fees are up to $100.00 for 24 hour; up to $200.00 for same day; $500.00 for 2 hour.

Uniform Commercial Code
Federal Tax Liens

UCC Division, Secretary of State, PO Box 793, Dover, DE 19903 (Courier: Townsend Bldg, 401 Federal Street, Dover, DE 19901); 302-739-3077, 302-739-3813 (Fax), 8:30AM-4:30PM.

www.state.de.us/corp/ucc.htm

Note: Effective December 1, 2001, all non "Search to Reflect" UCC Searches are referred to a Delaware Authorized Searcher, who performs the search. The web site maintains a list of these private vendors.

Indexing & Storage: Records are available from 1967. Records are computerized since 1992. Records are indexed on inhouse computer.

Searching: Use search request form UCC-11, downloadable from web. The search includes federal tax liens on businesses since 1976. Federal tax liens on individuals may show here, also. All state tax liens are filed at the county level. Include the following in your request: debtor name.

Access by: mail, fax, in person.

Fee & Payment: Copies are $2.00 a page, $5.00 minimum. Add $25.00 for certification. Fee payee: Secretary of State. Prepayment required. Volume users may establish an account. Personal checks accepted. Credit cards accepted: MasterCard, Visa, Discover.

Mail search: Turnaround time: 5 to 7 days. You may request information by mail. No self addressed stamped envelope is required.

Fax search: Same criteria as searching by mail.

In person search: Unless expedited fees are paid, results are mailed or you must come back in 5 days.

Other access: Bulk purchase of paper copies is $2.00 per page.

Expedited service: Expedited service is available for mail and phone searches. Three levels of expedited service are available at extra fees as follows: 24 hrs-$25.00; same day-$50.00; 2 hrs-$75.00.

State Tax Liens
Records not maintained by a state
    level agency.

Note: Records are at the county level.

Sales Tax Registrations

Finance Department, Division of Revenue, PO Box 8750, Wilmington, DE 19899-8750 (Courier: Carvel State Office Bldg, 820 N French St, 9th Fl, Wilmington, DE 19801); 302-577-8250, 302-577-8203 (Fax), 8AM-4:30PM.

www.state.de.us/revenue

Note: This state has a gross receipts tax, not a sales tax per se. They will release the information found on the face of the business licensee issued to the business.

Indexing & Storage: Records are available back to 1998 on computer and from 1992-2001 on optical readers.

Searching: This state will do an alpha search for a business name and will provide the business name, address and business license number, type of business, and amount of license fee paid. They will not release business owner or officer names.

Include the following in your request: business name. The federal tax ID can also be used.

Access by: mail, phone, fax, in person.

Mail search: Turnaround time: 1 week. A self addressed stamped envelope is requested. No fee for mail request.

Phone search: No fee for telephone request. There is a limit of 3 searches per phone call.

Fax search: There is no fee for fax searches. Turnaround time is 2 days.

In person search: No fee for request.

Birth Certificates

Department of Health, Office of Vital Statistics, PO Box 637, Dover, DE 19903 (Courier: William Penn & Federal Sts, Jesse Cooper Bldg, Dover, DE 19901); 302-739-4721, 302-736-1862 (Fax), 8AM-4:30PM (Counter closes at 4:20 PM).

www.deph.org/vs.htm

Indexing & Storage: Records are available from 72 years. Prior records are at the State Archives. Records are indexed on microfilm, microfiche, and index cards.

Searching: Must have a signed release from person of record or immediate family member. Others may only obtain records if they demonstrate the record is needed for the determination or protection of their personal property rights or for genealogical uses. Include the following in your request: full name, names of parents, mother's maiden name, date of birth, place of birth, reason for information request, relationship to person of record.

Access by: mail, fax, in person, online.

Fee & Payment: Search fee is $8.00 per name for every 5 years searched. Add $6.00 if you use a credit card. Fee payee: Office of Vital Statistics. Prepayment required. Personal checks accepted. Credit cards accepted: MasterCard, Visa, AmEx, Discover.

Mail search: Turnaround time: 1 day to 1 week. No self addressed stamped envelope is required.

Fax search: Available from VitalChek. Use of credit card and photo ID required.

In person search: Turnaround time is generally 10 minutes or less.

Online search: Access available at vitalchek.com, a state designated vendor.

Expedited service: Expedited service is available for mail, fax and in person searches. Turnaround time: overnight delivery. Add $15.00 per package.

Death Records

Department of Health, Office of Vital Statistics, PO Box 637, Dover, DE 19903 (Courier: William Penn & Federal Sts, Jesse Cooper Bldg, Dover, DE 19901); 302-739-4721, 302-736-1862 (Fax), 8AM-4:30PM.

www.deph.org/vs.htm

Indexing & Storage: Records are available for the past 40 years. Prior records are at the State Archives. It takes 3 days before new records are available for inquiry. Records are indexed on microfilm, microfiche, and index cards.

Searching: Must have a signed release from immediate family member. Include the following in your request: full name, date of death, place of death, names of parents, reason for information request, relationship to person of record.

Access by: mail, fax, in person, online.

Fee & Payment: The search fee is $8.00 per name for every 5 years searched. Add $6.00 if you use a credit card. Fee payee: Office of Vital Statistics. Prepayment required. Personal checks accepted. Credit cards accepted: MasterCard, Visa, AmEx, Discover.

Mail search: Turnaround time: 1 day. No self addressed stamped envelope is required.

Fax search: Records are available form VitalChek. Use of credit card and photo ID required.

In person search: Turnaround time is 10 to 15 minutes.

Online search: Access available at vitalchek.com, a state designated vendor.

Expedited service: Expedited service is available for mail, fax and in person searches. Turnaround time: overnight delivery. Add $15.00 per package.

Marriage Certificates

Department of Health, Office of Vital Statistics, PO Box 637, Dover, DE 19903 (Courier: William Penn & Federal Sts, Jesse Cooper Bldg, Dover, DE 19901); 302-739-4721, 302-739-1862 (Fax), 8AM-4:30PM.

Indexing & Storage: Records are available for 40 years. Prior records are in the State Public Archives. It takes 5 days before new records are available for inquiry. Records are indexed on microfilm, microfiche, and index cards.

Searching: Must have a signed release from person or persons of record or immediate family member. Include the following in your request: names of husband and wife, date of marriage, place or county of marriage, relationship to person of record, reason for information request, wife's maiden name.

Access by: mail, fax, in person, online.

Fee & Payment: The search fee is $8.00 per name for every 5 years searched. Add $6.00 if you use a credit card. Fee payee: Office of Vital Statistics. Prepayment required. Personal checks accepted. Credit cards accepted: MasterCard, Visa, AmEx, Discover.

Mail search: Turnaround time: 1 day. No self addressed stamped envelope is required.

Fax search: This is available through VitalChek. Credit card and photo ID are required.

In person search: Turnaround time is 10 to 15 minutes.

Online search: Access is available via VitalChek.com, a state designated vendor.

Expedited service: Expedited service is available for mail, fax and in person searches. Turnaround time: overnight delivery. Add $15.00 per package.

Divorce Records

Records not maintained by a state level agency.

Note: This agency will verify whether a divorce occurred after 1935 but will issue no copies of the record. For records 1976 to present go to the Family Court at the county; prior to 1976 go to the Prothonotary at the county level.

Workers' Compensation Records

Labor Department, Industrial Accident Board, 4425 N Market Street, Wilmington, DE 19802; 302-761-8200, 302-761-6601 (Fax), 8AM-4:30PM.

www.delawareworks.com

Note: Case records must have been adjudicated to be considered public. First reports of injury only (non-adjudicated) are not covered under FOIA.

Indexing & Storage: Records are available from 1985. New records are available for inquiry immediately.

Searching: Must have signed authorization from injured party in letter form or a court subpoena. They will not honor out-of-state requests. Information required includes claimant name, SSN, and date of accident.

Access by: mail.

Fee & Payment: There is no fee. Copies are $.25 each. Fee payee: DOL/IA. Prepayment required. Payment is for copies only. Personal checks accepted. No credit cards accepted.

Mail search: Turnaround time: 2 to 5 days. A self addressed stamped envelope is requested.

Driver Records

Division of Motor Vehicles, Driver Services, PO Box 698, Dover, DE 19903 (Courier: 303 Transportation Circle, Dover, DE 19901); 302-744-2506, 302-739-2602 (Fax), 8AM-4:30PM M-T-TH-F; 12:00PM-8PM W.

www.delaware.gov/yahoo/DMV

Note: For tickets: Delaware does not keep copies of tickets in a central repository for request purposes and suggests you go to the appropriate local jurisdiction.

Indexing & Storage: Records are available for 3 years to present for public record purposes. It takes 2 to 3 weeks before new records are available for inquiry.

Searching: Records cannot be sold from one vendor to another. Vendors can only sell to the end users. Casual requesters can obtain records only with MV703 Form requiring notarized signature of subject. Include the following in your request: full name, driver's license number, date of birth. Authorized account holders must have an application and contract on file. The following data is not released: Social Security Numbers or medical information.

Access by: mail, in person, online.

Fee & Payment: The fee for all search modes is $4.00 per request. Fee payee: Division of Motor Vehicles. Prepayment required. Personal checks accepted. No credit cards accepted.

Mail search: Turnaround time: 3 to 5 days. A self addressed stamped envelope is requested.

In person search: Walk-in requesters may obtain records from centers in Wilmington, New Castle, Dover, and Georgetown.

Online search: Online searching is single inquiry only, no batch request mode is offered. Searching is done by driver's license number or name and DOB. A signed contract application and valid "business license" is required. Access is provided 24 hours daily through a 900 number at a fee of $1.00 per minute, plus the $4.00 per record fee. For more information, call 302-744-2606.

Other access: Tape-to-tape is offered for high volume, batch requesters. Also, the state will release data from the driver license file on tapes or cartridges, but this cannot be resold.

Vehicle Ownership
Vehicle Identification

Division of Motor Vehicles, Correspondence Section, PO Box 698, Dover, DE 19903 (Courier: 303 Transportation Circle, Dover, DE 19901); 302-744-2511, 302-739-2042 (Fax), 8:30AM-4:30PM M-T-TH-F; 12-8PM W.

www.delaware.gov/yahoo/DMV

Indexing & Storage: Records are available for 3 years to present. It takes 2 to 3 weeks before new records are available for inquiry.

Searching: Casual requesters can only obtain records with notarized consent. Those routinely seeking information must complete an Application and Contract for Direct Access to become an account holder. Casual requesters must use Form MV703 which requires notarized signature of subject.

Access by: mail, in person, online.

Fee & Payment: The fee for ownership, plate, and registration searches is $4.00 per record, $8.00 if certified. Fee payee: Division of Motor Vehicles. Prepayment required. Personal checks accepted. No credit cards accepted.

Mail search: Turnaround time: 3 to 5 days. A self addressed stamped envelope is requested.

In person search: Turnaround time is while you wait.

Online search: There is an additional $1.00 per minute fee for using the on-line "900 number" system. Records are $4.00 each. The system is single inquiry mode and open from 8 AM to 4:30 PM, except on Wed. from noon to 8PM. For more information, call 302-744-2606. This program is strictly monitored and not available for non-permissible uses.

Other access: Bulk information can be obtained on a customized basis in tape, cartridge or paper format. However, the purpose of the request is carefully screened and information cannot be resold.

Accident Reports

Delaware State Police, Traffic Records, PO Box 430, Dover, DE 19903 (Courier: 1441 N Dupont Hwy, Dover, DE 19901); 302-739-5931, 302-739-5982 (Fax), 8AM-4PM.

Indexing & Storage: It takes 2 to 3 weeks before new records are available for inquiry.

Searching: Include the following in your request: full name, date of accident, location of accident.

Access by: mail, phone.

Fee & Payment: The fee is $18.50 per report, $60.00 if fatal accident report. Fee payee: Delaware State Police. Prepayment required. Personal checks accepted. No credit cards accepted.

Mail search: Turnaround time: 3 to 5 days. A self addressed stamped envelope is requested.

Phone search: You cannot search by phone, but you can verify by phone if a report exists.

Vessel Ownership
Vessel Registration

Dept of Natural Resources & Environmental Control, Delaware Boat Registration Office, 89 Kings Highway, Dover, DE 19901; 302-739-3498, 302-739-6157 (Fax), 8AM-4:30PM.

www.dnrec.state.de.us/dnrec2000/Boating.asp

Note: Liens are filed with UCC filings, not at this location.

Indexing & Storage: Records are available from 1978 to present. Records are registration only, no titles, and are indexed on microfiche from 1978 to 1989. Records are computer indexed from 1990 to the present. All motorized craft are registered. It takes one month or less before new records are available for inquiry.

Searching: No searching of records is allowed. However, they will verify information over the phone using "yes" and "no" only. Liens are not filed here, they are filed with UCCs. Either the owner's name, hull ID# or registration number must be submitted for a verification.

Access by: mail, phone, fax, in person.

Fee & Payment: There is no fee.

Mail search: Records are available by mail.

Phone search: They will verify information over the phone using "yes" and "no" only.

Fax search: If DPPA approved.

In person search: Verification only.

Legislation Records

Legislative Hall, Division of Research, PO Box 1401, Dover, DE 19903; 302-744-4114, 302-739-5318 (Archives for old bills), 800-282-8545 (In-state), 8AM-4:30PM.

www.legis.state.de.us

Indexing & Storage: Records are available for current and 1 prior session only. Records are indexed on microfiche.

Searching: Include the following in your request: bill number.

Access by: mail, phone, in person, online.

Fee & Payment: There is no charge unless you want many copies or a copy of a large document. They will compute the charges. Fee payee: State of Delaware. Personal checks accepted. No credit cards accepted.

Mail search: Turnaround time: variable. No self addressed stamped envelope is required.

Phone search: You may call for copies.

In person search: You may request copies in person.

Online search: Access information at the Internet site, no fee.

Voter Registration

Commissioner of Elections, 32 W Lockerman, M-101, Dover, DE 19904; 302-739-4277, 8AM-4:30PM.

www.state.de.us/election

Indexing & Storage: Records are available for both active and inactive records.

Searching: There is no individual record searching permitted, except in person. The following data is not released: Social Security Numbers or telephone numbers.

Access by: in person.

Fee & Payment: There is no search fee, the copy fee is $.25 per copy. Fee payee: State of Delaware. Prepayment required. No credit cards accepted. Records are available by mail.

In person search: Searching is available in person.

Other access: The entire state database is available on tape for $250. Individual districts (378) are available on disk for $2.00 per district or $.025 per name on labels. Also, there are several different types of printed lists available.

GED Certificates

Department of Education, Adult Education - GED Testing, PO Box 1402, Dover, DE 19903; 302-739-3743, 302-739-2770 (Fax).

www.doe.state.de.us

Searching: Include the following in your request: signed release, date of birth, Social Security Number, location of test center. The year of the test is very helpful.

Access by: mail, fax, in person.

Fee & Payment: There is no fee for a verification. A duplicate certificate is available for $4.00. Fee payee: Department of Education Suggest using a money order.

Mail search: Turnaround time: 1 to 2 days. No self addressed stamped envelope is required.

Fax search: Same criteria as mail searching.

In person search: Requester must present a photo ID.

Hunting License Information
Fishing License Information
Access to Records is Restricted

Natural Resources & Environmental Control Dept, Division of Fish & Wildlife, 89 Kings Hwy, Dover, DE 19901; 302-739-5296, 302-739-6157 (Fax), 8AM-4:30PM.

www.dnrec.state.de.us/fw/fwwel.htm

Note: Records are not on a computerized database, but kept in paper and filed alphabetically. They will release name, address, driver license number, and physical characteristics.

Delaware State Licensing Agencies

Licenses Searchable Online

Engineer #12 ....www.dape.org
Engineering Firm #12 ....www.dape.org
Optometrist #11 ....www.odfinder.org/LicSearch.asp
Real Estate Appraiser #11...........................www.asc.gov/content/category1/appr_by_state.asp
School Admin. Supervisor/Asst. #4.............www.doe.state.de.us/EduDir/EduDirStart.asp
School Counselor #4 ....www.doe.state.de.us/EduDir/EduDirStart.asp
School Principal/Superintendent #4 ....www.doe.state.de.us/EduDir/EduDirStart.asp
Teacher #4 ....www.doe.state.de.us/EduDir/EduDirStart.asp

Licensing Quick Finder

Adult Entertainment #11 302-744-4507
Aesthetician #11 302-744-4518
Alarm Company/Employee #3 302-739-5991
Alcoholic Beverage Establishment #1.. 302-577-5222
Ambulance Attendant #18 302-739-4773
Architect #11 302-744-4518
Armored Car Agency/Employee #3 302-739-5991
Asbestos Abatement Worker #15......... 302-739-4611
Athletic Trainer #11.............................. 302-744-4506
Attorney #2 302-651-3113
Audiologist #11 302-744-4522
Barber #11 302-744-4518
Boiler Inspector #14............................. 302-744-2735
Boxer #11 302-787-5720
Chiropractor #11 302-744-4504
Constable #3... 302-739-5991
Contractor Class A #15........................ 302-739-4611
Contractor, General #5......................... 302-577-8778
Cosmetologist #11 302-744-4518
Counselor, Professional #11 302-744-4520
Deadly Weapons Dealer #11 302-744-4509
Dental Hygienist #11 302-744-4520
Dental Radiographer #16 302-744-4546
Dentist #11 302-744-4520
Dietician/Nutritionist #11 302-744-4512
Electrician #11 302-744-4505
Electrologist #11 302-744-4504
Emergency Medical Technician-Paramedic #7
.... 302-739-6637

Engineer #12 302-577-6500
Engineering Firm #12 302-577-6500
Funeral Director #11............................ 302-744-4506
Gaming Control #11 302-744-4530
Geologist #11 302-744-4507
Harness Racing #6............................... 302-739-4811
Hearing Aid Dealer/Fitter #11............. 302-744-4504
Horse Racing (Thorobred) #6 302-739-4811
Human Relations Specialist (Education) #13
.... 888-759-9133
Insurance Adjuster/Advisor #8 302-739-4254
Insurance Agent/Consultant #8........... 302-739-4254
Insurance Broker/Dealer #8 302-739-4254
Land Surveyor #11............................... 302-744-4518
Landscape Architect #11...................... 302-744-4518
Library Media Specialist #13 888-759-9133
Lobbyist #9 302-739-2397
Massage #11... 302-744-4506
Medical Doctor/Surgeon #11............... 302-744-4529
Medical Practice #11 302-744-4529
Mental Health Counselor #11 302-744-4507
Midwife Nurse #11.............................. 302-744-4517
Nail Technician #11 302-744-4518
Notary Public #9.................................. 302-739-3073
Nuclear Medicine Technologist #16 302-744-4546
Nurse #11 302-744-4517
Nursing Home Administrator #11 302-744-4505
Occupational Therapist/Assistant #11.. 302-744-4507
Optometrist #11 302-744-4512

Osteopathic Physician #11.................. 302-744-4529
Pesticide Applicator #10..................... 302-739-4811
Pharmacist #7 302-739-4798
Physical Therapist/Assistant #11 302-744-4506
Pilot, River #11 302-744-4504
Plumber #11 302-744-4504
Podiatrist #11 302-744-4507
Private Investigative Agency/Employee #3
.... 302-739-5991
Private Security Agency/Employee #3.. 302-739-5991
Professional Svc. Firm #15 302-739-4611
Project Monitor (Const.) #15 302-739-4611
Psychological Assistant #11................ 302-744-4520
Psychologist #11 302-744-4507
Public Accountant-CPA #11 302-744-4505
Radiation Therapist #16...................... 302-744-4546
Real Estate Appraiser #11................... 302-744-4505
Real Estate Broker/Agent #11 302-744-4519
School Admin. Supervisor/Asst. #4...... 302-739-4601
School Counselor #4............................ 302-739-4601
School Principal/Superintendent #4.... 302-739-4601
Securities Agent #8 302-739-4254
Social Worker #11 302-744-4507
Speech Pathologist/Audiologist #11 ... 302-744-4504
Teacher #4 302-739-4601
Veterinarian #11.................................. 302-744-4506
Waste Water Operator #17 302-739-5731
Water Supply Operator #7 302-739-5410
X-ray Technician #7 302-739-3787

Licensing Agency Information

#1 Alcoholic Beverage Control Division, 820 N French St, Carvel State Office Bldg, Wilmington, DE 19801; 302-577-5222, Fax: 302-577-3204.

#2 Board of Bar Examiners, 200 W 9th St, #300B, Wilmington, DE 19801; 302-577-7038, Fax: 302-658-4605. http://courts.state.de.us/bbe

#3 State Police, State Bureau of Identification, Detective Licensing, U.C.R./N.I.B.R.S., PO Box 430, Dover, DE 19903; 302-739-5991, Fax: 302-739-5888. www.state.de.us/dsp/sbi.htm
Agency email: panderson@state.de.us.

#4 Department of Education, PO Box 1402 (401 Federal St), Dover, DE 19903; 302-739-4601, Fax: 302-739-3092. www.doe.state.de.us
Search database at www.doe.state.de.us/EduDir/EduDirStart.asp

#5 Division of Revenue, 820 N French St, Carvel State Office Bldg, Wilmington, DE 19801; 302-577-3363, Fax: 302-577-8203.
www.state.de.us/revenue/index.htm
Agency email: wremington@state.de.us.

#6 Harness Racing Commission, 2320 S DuPont Hwy, Dover, DE 19901; 302-739-4811, Fax: 302-697-4748. www.state.de.us/deptagri
Agency email: johnwayne@dda.state.de.us.

#7 Health & Social Services Department, Division of Public Health, PO Box 637, Dover, DE 19903.

#8 Insurance Department, 841 Silver Lake Blvd, Dover, DE 19904; 302-739-4254, Fax: 302-739-5280. www.state.de.us/inscom.
Agency email: licensing@deins.state.de.us.

#9 Notary Division, Office of Secretary of State, PO Box 898, Dover, DE 19903; 302-739-3073, Fax: 302-739-3812.

#10 Department of Agriculture, Pesticide Section, 2320 S DuPont Hwy, Dover, DE 19901; 302-739-4811, Fax: 302-697-6287.
www.state.de.us/deptagri/index.htm
Agency email: grier@smtp.dda.state.de.us.

#11 Division of Professional Regulations, Department of Admin. Svcs., 861 Silver Lake Blvd, Cannon Bldg #203, Dover, DE 19904; 302-739-4522, Fax: 302-739-2711.
www.professionallicensing.state.de.us

#12 Assoc. of Professional Engineers, Engineering Licensing Board, 56 W Main St #208 Plza 273, Christiana, DE 19702-1500; 302-368-6708, Fax: 302-368-6710. www.dape.org
Agency email: office@dape.org.

#13 Department of Public Instruction, Office of Certification, PO Box 1402, Townsend Bldg, Dover, DE 19903; 888-759-9133.
www.doe.state.de.us

#14 Department of Public Safety, Division of Boiler Safety, PO Box 674, Dover, DE 19903-0674; 302-744-2735, Fax: 302-739-2526.
www.delawareboilersafety.com

#15 Division of Facilities Mgmt, 149 Transportation Circle, Dover, DE 19901; 302-739-3930, Fax: 302-739-3127.

#16 Division of Public Health, Office of Radiation Control, PO Box 637, Dover, DE 19903; 302-744-4546, Fax: 302-739-3839.

#17 Department of Natural Resources & Environmental Control, Division of Water Resources, 89 Kings Hwy, Dover, DE 19901; 302-739-4860, Fax: 302-739-8369.

#18 Fire Prevention Commission, 1463 Chestnut Grove Rd, Dover, DE 19904; 302-739-3160, Fax: 302-739-4436.
www.delawarestatefirecommission.com. Agency email: firecommission@state.de.us.

Delaware Federal Courts

The following list indicates the district and division name for each county in the state.

County/Court Cross Reference

Kent..Wilmington
New Castle...Wilmington
Sussex...Wilmington

US District Court

District of Delaware

Wilmington Division US Courthouse, Lock Box 18, 844 N King St, Wilmington, DE 19801 (Courier Address: US Courthouse, 844 N King St, Clerk's Office, 4th Floor, Room 4209, Wilmington, DE 19801), 302-573-6170.

www.ded.uscourts.gov

Counties: All counties in Delaware.

Indexing & Storage: Cases are indexed by defendant, plaintiff, and case number. New cases are available in the index 1 day after filing date. Open records are located at this court.

Fee & Payment Notes: Payment may be made by money order, cashier check, personal check. A copy vendor is used for civil court documents. Parcels Inc, 800-343-1742 -- orders may be placed with them directly. Payee: Clerk, US District Court.

Phone Search: They will search civil and criminal cases from 1982 to the present over the phone. The only information released over the phone is whether a case was found and, if so, its case number.

Mail Search: Search can include all computer, microfiche and judgment indexes. A stamped self addressed envelope is not required.

In Person Search: In person searching available.

PACER: Toll-free dial-up access: 888-793-9488. Local dial-up access: 302-573-6651. Case records are available back to January 1991. Records are purged every few years (not since 1/91). New records are available online after 2 days. PACER is available online at http://pacer.ded.uscourts.gov.

Opinions Online: Court opinions are available online at www.lawlib.widener.edu/pages/deopind.htm

US Bankruptcy Court

District of Delaware

Wilmington Division 824 Market St, 5th Floor, Marine Midland Plaza, Wilmington, DE 19801 (Courier Address: Use mail address for courier delivery), 302-573-6174.

www.deb.uscourts.gov

Counties: All counties in Delaware.

Indexing & Storage: Cases are indexed by debtor as well as by case number. New cases are available in the index 1 day after filing date. Open records are located at this court.

Fee & Payment Notes: Payment may be made by money order, cashier check, personal check. Payee: Clerk, US Bankruptcy Court. You are allowed to make your own copies. These copies cost $.50 per page. There is an in-house private copy service that you must use.

Phone Search: The only information that is released over the telephone is whether the search is positive or negative. If positive they will release the case number. An automated voice case information service (VCIS) is available. Call VCIS at 888-667-5530 or 302-573-6233.

In Person Search: In person searching available.

PACER:. Case records are available back to 1991. Records are purged every four years. New civil records are available online after 1 day.

Electronic Filing: Information is available online at https://ecf.deb.uscourts.gov/

Other Online Access: Online access to WebPacer is available free at www.deb.uscourts.gov/wconnect/wc.dll?usbcn_racer~main.

Standards for Federal Courts: The search fee is $20.00 per item (one party name or case number). Certification fee is $7.00 per document. Copy fee is $.50 per page. All fees standard unless noted in profile. Mail Search: always enclose a stamped self addressed envelope unless otherwise noted. Before releasing records, all courts require prepayment unless noted in profile.

Open records are located at the court unless otherwise noted. District courts index by defendant and plaintiff as well as by case number. Bankruptcy courts usually index by debtor and case number. While most courts now have their indexes on computer, many still maintain index card files as well.

The universal PACER sign-up number is 800-676-6856. Find PACER and the Party/Case Index on the Web at http://pacer.psc.uscourts.gov. PACER dial-up access is $.60 per minute. Also, courts offering internet access via RACER, PACER, Web-PACER or the new CM-ECF charge $.07 per page fee unless noted as free.

Delaware County Courts

Court	Jurisdiction	No. of Courts	How Organized
Superior Courts*	General	3	
Chancery Courts*	General	3	
Court of Common Pleas*	Limited	3	
Justice of the Peace Courts*	Municipal	19	
Alderman's Courts	Municipal	9	
Family Courts	Special	3	

* Profiled in this Sourcebook.

Court	CIVIL								
	Tort	Contract	Real Estate	Min. Claim	Max. Claim	Small Claims	Estate	Eviction	Domestic Relations
Superior Courts*	X	X	X	$50000	No Max				
Chancery Courts*	X	X	X	$0	No Max		X		
Court of Common Pleas*	X	X	X	$0	$50000				
Justice of the Peace Courts*			X	$0	$15000	$5000		X	
Alderman's Courts						$2500			
Family Courts									X

Court	CRIMINAL				
	Felony	Misdemeanor	DWI/DUI	Preliminary Hearing	Juvenile
Superior Courts*	X	X			
Chancery Courts*					
Court of Common Pleas*		X		X	
Justice of the Peace Courts*		X	X		
Alderman's Courts		X	X		
Family Courts		X			X

ADMINISTRATION Administrative Office of the Courts, PO Box 8911, Wilmington, DE, 19899; 302-577-2480, Fax: 302-577-3139. http://courts.state.de.us/supreme/index.htm

COURT STRUCTURE Superior Courts have jurisdiction over felonies and all drug offenses, the Court of Common Pleas has jurisdiction over all misdemeanors. Court of Chancery handles corporation and equity matters, as well as probate and estates. Guardianships are handled by the Register of Wills, corporate matters such as equity disputes and injunctions are handled by the Clerk of Chancery. The Municipal Court of Wilmington merged with the Court of Common Pleas in New Castle in May 1998.

ONLINE ACCESS Only Supreme Court Final Orders and Opinions are available at http://courts.state.de.us/supreme/opinions.htm

An online system called CLAD, developed by Mead Data Central and the New Castle Superior Court, is currently available in Delaware. CLAD contains only toxic waste, asbestos, and class action cases; however, based on CLAD's success, Delaware may pursue development of online availability of other public records by working in conjunction with private information resource enterprises.

ADDITIONAL INFORMATION Effective 1/15/95, the civil case limit of the Justice of the Peace Courts increased from $5,000 to $15,000; the Courts of Common Pleas' limit went from $15,000 to $50,000.

Criminal histories are available with a signed release from the offender at the Delaware State Police Headquarters, Criminal Records Section in Dover DE. For information on criminal history retrieval requirements, call 302-739-5880.

Kent County

Superior Court Office of Prothonotary, 38 The Green, Dover, DE 19901; 302-739-3184; Fax: 302-739-6717. Hours: 8AM-5PM (EST). *Felony, Misdemeanor, Civil Actions Over $50,000.*

http://courts.state.de.us/superior

Civil Records: Access: Mail, in person. Only the court performs in person searches; visitors may not. No search fee. Required to search: name, years to search. Civil cases indexed by defendant, plaintiff. Judgments on computer from 1996, on microfiche from 1918.
Criminal Records: Access: In person only. Visitors must perform in person searches for themselves. No search fee. Required to search: name, years to search, DOB; also helpful: race. Judgments on computer from 1996, on microfiche from 1918. Contact Dept of Records for search assistance.
General Information: No sealed or psychological evaluation records released. SASE required. Copy fee: $1.00 per page. Certification fee: $6.00 fee for 3 pages and $1.00 each add'l page. Fee payee: Prothonotary. Personal checks accepted. Prepayment is required.

Chancery Court 38 The Green, Dover, DE 19901; 302-736-2242; Probate phone: 302-744-2330; Fax: 302-736-2240. 8:30AM-4:30PM (EST). *Civil, Probate.*

http://courts.state.de.us/chancery

Civil Records: Access: In person only. Visitors must perform in person searches for themselves. No search fee. Required to search: name, years to search. Civil cases indexed by defendant, plaintiff. Civil records on index books. The Court of Chancery oversees corporate and equity matters and guardianship. The Register of Wills oversees estate, and probate matters.
General Information: No juvenile, sealed or mental health records released. Turnaround time 24 hrs. Fax notes: Fee to fax results is $1.00 per document. Copy fee: $1.00 per page. Certification fee: $10.00 plus $1.00 per page. Fee payee: Register in Chancery (Register of Wills for Probate). Personal checks accepted. May bill law firms and businesses.

Court of Common Pleas 38 The Green, Dover, DE 19901; 302-739-4618; Fax: 302-739-4501. Hours: 8:30AM-4:30PM (EST). *Misdemeanor, Civil Actions Under $50,000.*

http://courts.state.de.us/commonpleas

Civil Records: Access: Mail, in person. Both court and visitors may perform in person searches. No search fee. Required to search: name, years to search. Civil cases indexed by defendant, plaintiff. Civil records on computer from 1992, on microfiche from 10/85, archived prior.
Criminal Records: Access: Mail, in person. Visitors must perform in person searches for themselves. No search fee. Required to search: name, years to search, DOB, offense, date of offense. Criminal records on computer from 1/94, on microfiche from 10/85, archived prior.
General Information: No sealed records released. SASE required. Turnaround time 1-3 days. Copy fee: $1.00 per page. Certification fee: $5.00. Fee payee: Court of Common Pleas. Personal checks accepted. Prepayment is required.

Dover Justice of the Peace #16 480 Bank Lane, Dover, DE 19904; 302-739-4316; Fax: 302-739-6797. Hours: 8AM-4PM (EST). *Civil Actions Under $15,000, Eviction, Small Claims.*

http://courts.state.de.us/jpcourt

Civil Records: Access: Mail, in person. Both court and visitors may perform in person searches. No search fee. Required to search: name, years to search. Civil cases indexed by defendant, plaintiff. Civil records computerized since 10/98.

General Information: Copy fee: $.25 per page. Certification fee: $10.00. Fee payee: JCP Court 16. Personal checks accepted. Prepayment is required.

Dover Justice of the Peace #7 480 Bank Lane, Dover, DE 19903; 302-739-4554; Fax: 302-739-6797. Hours: Open 24 hours (EST). *Misdemeanor.*

http://courts.state.de.us/jpcourt

Criminal Records: Only the court performs in person searches; visitors may not. Search fee: $7.00 per name. Fee is per charge. Required to search: name, years to search, DOB, signed release; also helpful: address, offense, date of offense.
General Information: Fee payee: State of Delaware. Prepayment is required.

Harrington Justice of the Peace #6 17111 South DuPont Hwy, Harrington, DE 19952; 302-398-8247; Fax: 302-397-4237. Hours: 8AM-4PM (EST). *Misdemeanor.*

http://courts.state.de.us/jpcourt

Criminal Records: Access: In person, mail. Only the court performs in person searches; visitors may not. No search fee. Required to search: name, years to search, DOB. Court form required for all searches.
General Information: Turnaround time 2-3 days. Fee payee: State of Delaware. Prepayment is required.

Smyrna Justice of the Peace #8 100 Monrovia Ave, Smyrna, DE 19977; 302-653-7083; Fax: 302-653-2888. 8AM-4PM (EST). *Misdemeanor.*

http://courts.state.de.us/jpcourt

Criminal Records: Only the court performs in person searches; visitors may not. No search fee. Required to search: name, years to search; also helpful: DOB.
General Information: Fee payee: State of Delaware. Prepayment is required.

New Castle County

Superior Court Office of the Prothonotary, 1020 N King Street, Wilmington, DE 19801; 302-577-2400; Fax: 302-577-6487/577-6212. Hours: 8:30AM-5PM *Felony, Misdemeanor, Civil Actions Over $50,000.*

http://courts.state.de.us/superior

Civil Records: Access: In person only. Visitors must perform in person searches for themselves. No search fee. Required to search: name, years to search. Civil cases indexed by defendant, plaintiff. Civil records on computer from 4/80, prior on microfiche.
Criminal Records: Access: In person only. Visitors must perform in person searches for themselves. No search fee. Required to search: name, DOB; also helpful: years to search. Criminal records on computer from 4/80, prior on microfiche.
General Information: Public access terminal is available. (Civil only.) No psychological evaluation, sealed records released. Copy fee: $1.00 per page. Certification fee: $6.00. Fee payee: Prothonotary's Office. Personal checks accepted. Prepayment is required.

Chancery Court 1020 N King St, Wilmington, DE 19801; 302-571-7540; Probate phone: 302-571-7545; Fax: 302-571-7751. Hours: 8:30AM-5PM (EST). *Civil, Probate.*

http://courts.state.de.us/chancery

Civil Records: Access: Phone, fax, mail, in person. Both court and visitors may perform in person searches. No search fee. Required to search: name; also helpful: years to search. Civil cases indexed by defendant, plaintiff. Civil records indexed on computer since 1963, in books prior to 1963. The civil records for the Court of Chancery deal with corporate and equity matters, there is no money jurisdiction. The Register of Wills oversees estates, guardianships and probate.

General Information: Public access terminal is available. No guardianship records released. SASE requested. Turnaround time 2 days. Fax notes: $5.00 for first page, $2.00 each add'l. Copy fee: $1.00 per page. $2.00 if from microfilm. Certification fee: $5.00. Fee payee: Register in Chancery (Register of Wills for Probate). Personal checks accepted. Will bill fax requests.

Court of Common Pleas 1000 N King St, Wilmington, DE 19801-3348; 302-577-2430; Fax: 302-577-2193. Hours: 8:30AM-4:30PM (EST). *Misdemeanor, Civil Actions Under $50,000.*

http://courts.state.de.us/commonpleas

Note: Fax for civil is 302-577-2431.
Civil Records: Access: Phone, fax, mail, in person. Both court and visitors may perform in person searches. No search fee. Required to search: name, years to search. Civil cases indexed by defendant, plaintiff. Civil records on computer from 1993; prior records on docket books.
Criminal Records: Access: Phone, fax, mail, in person. Both court and visitors may perform in person searches. No search fee. Required to search: name, years to search; also helpful: DOB. Criminal records on computer from 1993; prior records on docket books.
General Information: No closed records released. SASE required. Turnaround time up to a week. Fax notes: $1.00 per page. Copy fee: $1.00 per page. Certification fee: $5.00. Fee payee: Court of Common Pleas. Personal checks accepted. Prepayment required.

Middletown Justice of the Peace #9 757 N Broad St, Middletown, DE 19709; 302-378-5221. Hours: 8AM-4PM (EST). *Civil Under$15,000, Misdemeanor, Eviction, Small Claims.*

http://courts.state.de.us/jpcourt

Note: Due to a court fire, criminal cases 7/24/2000 to 5/1/2001 are heard at New Castle JP Court 11, 323-4450. Civil cases are heard at Prices Corner (Wilmington) JP Court 12, 995-8646.
Civil Records: Access: In person only. Both court and visitors may perform in person searches. No search fee. Required to search: name, years to search. Civil cases indexed by defendant. Due to fire, records on computer only back to mid-1990s. The court will not do name searches, but will search if a civil action # is presented.
Criminal Records: Access: In person only. Visitors must perform in person searches for themselves. No search fee. Required to search: name, years to search, DOB. Due to fire, records on computer only back to mid-1990s.
General Information: Copy fee: $.25 per page. Certification fee: Civil record certification is $7.00, criminal is $10.00.

Prices Corner Justice of the Peace #12 212 Greenbank Rd, Wilmington, DE 19808; 302-995-8646; Fax: 302-995-8642. 8:30AM-4:30PM (EST). *Civil Actions Under $15,000, Eviction, Small Claims.*

http://courts.state.de.us/jpcourt

Civil Records: Access: In person only. Visitors must perform in person searches for themselves. No search fee. Required to search: name, years to search.
General Information: No sealed, juvenile, adoption or mental health records released. Certification fee: $10.00. Fee payee: Justice of the Peace Court 12. Personal checks accepted. Prepayment is required.

Wilmington Justice of the Peace #13 1010 Concord Ave, Concord Professional Center, Wilmington, DE 19802; 302-577-2550; Fax: 302-577-2526. Hours: 8AM-4PM (EST). *Civil Actions Under $15,000, Eviction, Small Claims.*

http://courts.state.de.us/jpcourt

Civil Records: Access: In person only. Visitors must perform in person searches for themselves. No search fee. Required to search: name, years to search. Civil cases indexed by defendant, plaintiff. Civil records are computerized since 09/01/99. The court will pull specific case data if CA# given, if and when time permitting.

General Information: No sealed, juvenile, adoption or mental health records released. Copy fee: $.25 per page. Certification fee: $10.00. Fee payee: Justice of the Peace Court #13. Personal checks accepted. Prepayment is required.

New Castle Justice of the Peace #11 61
Christiana Rd, New Castle, DE 19720; 302-323-4450; Fax: 302-323-4452. Open 24 hours. *Misdemeanor.*

http://courts.state.de.us/jpcourt

Criminal Records: Access: In person, mail. Visitors must perform in person searches for themselves. No search fee. Required to search: name, years to search.

General Information: Turnaround time 2-3 days. Fee payee: State of Delaware. Prepayment is required.

Prices Corner Justice of the Peace #10
210 Greenbank Rd, Wilmington, DE 19808; 302-995-8640; Fax: 302-995-8642. Hours: 8AM-11PM (EST). *Misdemeanor.*

http://courts.state.de.us/jpcourt

Criminal Records: Access: In person, mail. Only the court performs in person searches; visitors may not. Search fee: $7.00 per name. Required to search: name, years to search, DOB.

General Information: Turnaround time 2 weeks. Fee payee: Justice of the Peace Court 10. Prepayment is required.

Wilmington Justice of the Peace #15 130
Hickman Rd #13, Claymont, DE 19703; 302-798-5327; Fax: 302-798-4508. Hours: 8AM-4PM M; 8AM-Midnight T-F; 8AM-4PM Sat (EST). *Misdemeanor.*

http://courts.state.de.us/jpcourt

Note: Effective 06/01/99, the court assumed DUI and truancy cases. This court was formally located at 716 Philadelphia Pike in Wilmington

Criminal Records: Access: In person, mail. Only the court performs in person searches; visitors may not. Search fee: $7.00 per name. Fee is per case & includes certification & copy fees. Required to search: name, years to search, DOB; also helpful: offense.

General Information: Turnaround time 2-4 weeks. Fee payee: State of Delaware. Prepayment is required.

Wilmington Justice of the Peace #18 1301
E 12th St, PO Box 9279, Wilmington, DE 19809; 302-429-7740; Fax: 302-577-6140. Hours: 8:30AM-Midnight (EST). *Misdemeanor.*

http://courts.state.de.us/jpcourt

Criminal Records: Access: In person, mail. Only the court performs in person searches; visitors may not. Search fee: $7.50 per name. Required to search: name, years to search, DOB.

General Information: Turnaround time varies.

Wilmington Justice of the Peace #20
Public Safety Building, 300 N Walnut Street, Wilmington, DE 19801; 302-577-7234; Fax: 302-577-7237. Hours: 8AM-midnight (EST). *Misdemeanor.*

http://courts.state.de.us/jpcourt

Criminal Records: Visitors must perform in person searches for themselves. No search fee. Required to search: name, years to search.

General Information: Fee payee: Justice of the Peace Court #13.

Sussex County

Superior Court PO Box 756 (The Circle), Georgetown, DE 19947; 302-856-5740; Fax: 302-856-5739. Hours: 8AM-4:30PM (EST). *Felony, Misdemeanor, Civil Actions.*

http://courts.state.de.us/superior

Civil Records: Access: In person only. Visitors must perform in person searches for themselves. No search fee. Required to search: name, years to search. Civil cases indexed by defendant, plaintiff. Civil records on computer from 6/91 or as far back as 1980 if case was pending in 1991; microfiche prior.

Criminal Records: Access: In person only. Visitors must perform in person searches for themselves. No search fee. Required to search: name, years to search, DOB. Criminal records on manual index; computerized records since 1983.

General Information: Public access terminal is available. No divorce, victim info, sealed records, expungments, or CCDW permit records released. Copy fee: $.30 per page. Certification fee: $6.00 plus $1.00 per page after the first three. Fee payee: Prothonotary. Personal checks accepted. Prepayment is required.

Chancery Court PO Box 424 (The Circle), Georgetown, DE 19947; 302-855-7842; Probate phone: 302-855-7875. 8:30AM-4:30PM (EST). *Civil, Probate.*

http://courts.state.de.us/chancery

Civil Records: Access: Phone, mail, in person. Both court and visitors may perform in person searches. No search fee. Required to search: name, years to search. Civil cases indexed by defendant, plaintiff. Civil records on index books.

General Information: All records public. Turnaround time 1-3 days. Copy fee: $1.00 per page. Certification fee: $10.00 plus $1.00 per page. Fees charged by Register of Wills for Probate are separate. Fee payee: Register in Chancery (or Register of Wills for Probate). Personal checks accepted. Prepayment is required.

Court of Common Pleas PO Box 426, Georgetown, DE 19947; 302-856-5333; Fax: 302-856-5056. Hours: 8:30AM-4:30PM (EST). *Misdemeanor, Civil Actions Under $50,000.*

http://courts.state.de.us/commonpleas

Civil Records: Access: Phone, fax, mail, in person. Both the court and visitors may perform in person searches. Search fee: $10.00 per name. Required to search: name, years to search. Civil cases indexed by defendant. Civil records on computer from 1993, on microfiche from 10/85, archives prior.

Criminal Records: Access: Phone, fax, mail, in person. Both the court and visitors may perform in person searches. Search fee: $10.00 per name. Required to search: name, years to search, DOB, offense, date of offense. Criminal records on computer from 1994, on microfiche from 10/85, archives prior.

General Information: Public access terminal is available. No closed case records released. SASE required. Turnaround time 1-2 weeks. Fax notes: No fee to fax results. Copy fee: $1.00 per page. Certification fee: $5.00. Fee payee: Court of Common Pleas. Personal checks accepted. Prepayment is required.

Georgetown Justice of the Peace #17
23730 Shortly Rd, Georgetown, DE 19947; 302-856-1447; Fax: 302-856-5923. Hours: 8AM-4PM (EST). *Civil Actions Under $15,000, Eviction, Small Claims.*

http://courts.state.de.us/jpcourt

Civil Records: Access: Mail, in person. Both court and visitors may perform in person searches. No search fee. Required to search: name, years to search. Civil cases indexed by defendant, plaintiff. Civil records on index books from 1966 to present.

General Information: SASE requested. Turnaround time 1-2 days. Copy fee: $10.00 per page. Certification fee: $10.00. Fee payee: State of Delaware. Personal checks accepted. Prepayment is required.

Seaford Justice of the Peace #19 408 Stein
Highway, Seaford, DE 19973; 302-629-5433; Fax: 302-628-2049. Hours: 8AM-4PM (EST). *Civil Actions Under $15,000, Eviction, Small Claims.*

http://courts.state.de.us/jpcourt

Civil Records: Access: In person mail. Visitors must perform in person searches for themselves. No search fee. Required to search: name, years to search. Civil cases indexed by defendant, plaintiff. Civil records in docket books since 1985; computerized records since 9/98. In person access requires identification.

General Information: Copy fee: $1.00 per page. Certification fee: $10.00. Fee payee: State of Delaware. Personal checks accepted. Prepayment is required.

Milford Justice of the Peace #5 715 S
DuPont Highway, Milford, DE 19963; 302-422-5922. Hours: 8AM-4PM (EST). *Misdemeanor.*

http://courts.state.de.us/jpcourt

Note: Some old civil cases also located here.

Criminal Records: Access: In person only. Visitors must perform in person searches for themselves. No search fee. Required to search: name, years to search, DOB. Court refers written requests to State Bureau of Investigation in Dover at 302-739-5882.

General Information: No juvenile records released. Copy fee: $1.00 per page. Certification fee: $7.00. Fee payee: State of Delaware. Personal checks accepted. Credit cards accepted: Visa, MasterCard, Discover. Prepayment is required.

Georgetown Justice of the Peace #3 17
Shortly Rd, Georgetown, DE 19947; 302-856-1445; Fax: 302-856-5844. Hours: 24 hours. *Misdemeanor.*

http://courts.state.de.us/jpcourt

Criminal Records: Only the court performs in person searches; visitors may not. Search fee: $7.00 per name. Search fee includes certification. Also must be recent case. Required to search: name, years to search, DOB.

General Information: Fee payee: State of Delaware. Prepayment is required.

Millsboro Justice of the Peace #1 553 E
DuPont Hwy, Millsboro, DE 19966; 302-934-7268; Fax: 302-934-1414. 8AM-4PM (EST). *Misdemeanor.*

http://courts.state.de.us/jpcourt

Criminal Records: Access: In person, mail. Only the court performs in person searches. No search fee. Required to search: name, years to search, DOB.

General Information: Turnaround time same day. Prepayment is required.

Rehoboth Beach Justice of the Peace #2
31 Route 24, Rehoboth Beach, DE 19971-9738; 302-645-6163; Fax: 302-645-8842. Hours: 8AM-4PM M & Sat; 8AM-Noon T-F (EST). *Misdemeanor.*

http://courts.state.de.us/jpcourt

Criminal Records: Both court and visitors may perform in person searches. No search fee. Required to search: name, years to search, DOB.

General Information: Fee payee: State of Delaware. Prepayment is required.

Seaford Justice of the Peace #4 408 Stein
Highway, Seaford, DE 19973; 302-628-2036; Fax: 302-528-2049. Hours: 8AM-4PM M & Sat; 8AM-Noon T-F (EST). *Misdemeanor.*

http://courts.state.de.us/jpcourt

Criminal Records: Visitors must perform in person searches for themselves. No search fee. Required to search: name, years to search.

Delaware Recording Offices

ORGANIZATION: Delaware has 3 counties and 3 recording offices. The recording officer is County Recorder in both jurisdictions. Delaware is in the Eastern Time Zone (EST).

REAL ESTATE RECORDS: Counties do not perform real estate searches, but will provide copies.

UCC RECORDS: Financing statements are filed at the state level, except for real estate related collateral, which are filed only with the County Recorder. All counties perform UCC searches. Copy and certification fees vary.

TAX LIEN RECORDS: Federal tax liens on personal property of businesses are filed with the Secretary of State. Other federal and all state tax liens on personal property are filed with the County Recorder. Copy and certification fees vary.

ONLINE ACCESS: There is no statewide online system for county recorded documents.

Kent County

County Recorder of Deeds, County Administration Bldg., Room 218, 414 Federal St., Dover, DE 19901. 302-744-2314; Fax 302-736-2035.
Will search UCC records. Will not search real estate records. **Other Phone Numbers:** Assessor 302-744-2401; Treasurer 302-744-2341.

New Castle County

County Recorder of Deeds, 800 French St, 4th Floor, Wilmington, DE 19801. County Recorder of Deeds, R/E and UCC Recording 302-571-7550; Fax 302-571-7708. www.co.new-castle.de.us
Will search UCC records. This agency will not do a tax lien search. Will not search real estate records. **Online Access:** Real Estate, Property Assessor Records. Records on the City of New Castle Geographic Information System database are available free online at www.2isystems.com/newcastle/Search2.cfm. Property information can also be found at www.co.new-castle.de.us/LandUse/LandUse1.htm. No name searching. **Other Phone Numbers:** Assessor 302-395-5400; Treasurer 302-395-5177; Appraiser/Auditor 302-395-5400; Elections 302-577-3464.

Sussex County

County Recorder of Deeds, PO Box 827, Georgetown, DE 19947-0827. 302-855-7785; Fax 302-855-7787.
Will search UCC records. This agency will not do a tax lien search. Will not search real estate records. **Other Phone Numbers:** Assessor 302-855-7824; Treasurer 302-855-7763.

Delaware County Locator

You will usually be able to find the city name in the City/County Cross Reference below. In that case, it is a simple matter to determine the county from the cross reference. However, only the official US Postal Service city names are included in this index. There are an additional 40,000 place names that people use in their addresses. Therefore, we have also included a ZIP/City Cross Reference immediately following the City/County Cross Reference.

If you know the ZIP Code but the city name does not appear in the City/County Cross Reference index, look up the ZIP Code in the ZIP/City Cross Reference, find the city name, then look up the city name in the City/County Cross Reference. For example, you want to know the county for an address of Menands, NY 12204. There is no "Menands" in the City/County Cross Reference. The ZIP/City Cross Reference shows that ZIP Codes 12201-12288 are for the city of Albany. Looking back in the City/County Cross Reference, Albany is in Albany County.

City/County Cross Reference

BEAR New Castle
BETHANY BEACH Sussex
BETHEL Sussex
BRIDGEVILLE Sussex
CAMDEN WYOMING Kent
CHESWOLD Kent
CLAYMONT New Castle
CLAYTON (19938) Kent(89), New
   Castle(10)
DAGSBORO Sussex
DELAWARE CITY New Castle
DELMAR Sussex
DOVER Kent
DOVER AFB Kent
ELLENDALE Sussex
FARMINGTON Kent

FELTON Kent
FENWICK ISLAND Sussex
FRANKFORD Sussex
FREDERICA Kent
GEORGETOWN Sussex
GREENWOOD (19950) Sussex(56),
   Kent(43)
HARBESON Sussex
HARRINGTON Kent
HARTLY Kent
HOCKESSIN New Castle
HOUSTON Kent
KENTON Kent
KIRKWOOD New Castle
LAUREL Sussex
LEWES Sussex

LINCOLN Sussex
LITTLE CREEK Kent
MAGNOLIA Kent
MARYDEL Kent
MIDDLETOWN New Castle
MILFORD (19963) Sussex(60), Kent(39)
MILLSBORO Sussex
MILLVILLE Sussex
MILTON Sussex
MONTCHANIN New Castle
NASSAU Sussex
NEW CASTLE New Castle
NEWARK New Castle
OCEAN VIEW Sussex
ODESSA New Castle
PORT PENN New Castle

REHOBOTH BEACH Sussex
ROCKLAND New Castle
SAINT GEORGES New Castle
SEAFORD Sussex
SELBYVILLE Sussex
SMYRNA (19977) Kent(87), New
   Castle(12)
TOWNSEND New Castle
VIOLA Kent
WILMINGTON New Castle
WINTERTHUR New Castle
WOODSIDE Kent
YORKLYN New Castle

ZIP/City Cross Reference

19701-19701 BEAR
19702-19702 NEWARK
19703-19703 CLAYMONT
19706-19706 DELAWARE CITY
19707-19707 HOCKESSIN
19708-19708 KIRKWOOD
19709-19709 MIDDLETOWN
19710-19710 MONTCHANIN
19711-19718 NEWARK
19720-19721 NEW CASTLE
19725-19726 NEWARK
19730-19730 ODESSA
19731-19731 PORT PENN
19732-19732 ROCKLAND
19733-19733 SAINT GEORGES
19734-19734 TOWNSEND

19735-19735 WINTERTHUR
19736-19736 YORKLYN
19800-19899 WILMINGTON
19901-19901 DOVER
19902-19902 DOVER AFB
19903-19906 DOVER
19930-19930 BETHANY BEACH
19931-19931 BETHEL
19933-19933 BRIDGEVILLE
19934-19934 CAMDEN WYOMING
19936-19936 CHESWOLD
19938-19938 CLAYTON
19939-19939 DAGSBORO
19940-19940 DELMAR
19941-19941 ELLENDALE
19942-19942 FARMINGTON

19943-19943 FELTON
19944-19944 FENWICK ISLAND
19945-19945 FRANKFORD
19946-19946 FREDERICA
19947-19947 GEORGETOWN
19950-19950 GREENWOOD
19951-19951 HARBESON
19952-19952 HARRINGTON
19953-19953 HARTLY
19954-19954 HOUSTON
19955-19955 KENTON
19956-19956 LAUREL
19958-19958 LEWES
19960-19960 LINCOLN
19961-19961 LITTLE CREEK
19962-19962 MAGNOLIA

19963-19963 MILFORD
19964-19964 MARYDEL
19966-19966 MILLSBORO
19967-19967 MILLVILLE
19968-19968 MILTON
19969-19969 NASSAU
19970-19970 OCEAN VIEW
19971-19971 REHOBOTH BEACH
19973-19973 SEAFORD
19975-19975 SELBYVILLE
19977-19977 SMYRNA
19979-19979 VIOLA
19980-19980 WOODSIDE

District of Columbia

General Help Numbers:

Mayor's Office

1350 pennsylvania Ave NW   202-727-2980
Washington, DC 20004   Fax 202-727-0505
http://dc.gov/mayor/index.htm   8:30AM-5:30PM

District Court Administrator

500 Indiana Ave NW, Room 1500   202-879-1700
Washington, DC 20001   Fax 202-879-4829
www.dcsc.gov   8:30AM-5PM

District Archives

Office of Archives/Public Records   202-671-1105
1300 Naylor Ct NW   Fax 202-727-6076
Washington, DC 20001-42259AM-3:30PM research hours

District Specifics:

Time Zone: EST

Population: 571,822

Web Site: www.washingtondc.gov

District Agencies

Criminal Records

Metropolitan Police Department, Identification and Records Section, 300 Indiana Ave NW, Rm 3055, Washington, DC 20001; 202-727-4245 (Police), 202-879-1373 (Superior Court), 202-638-5352 (Fax), 8AM-5PM.

www.mpdc.dc.gov/main.shtm

Note: The Superior Court, Criminal Division, is located at 500 Indiana NW, same zip (fax # given above). They do not charge a fee for a search and they will indicate over the phone if there is an existing record. Details of both locations are given below.

Indexing & Storage: Records are available for 10 years. Records at the Superior Court are indexed in microfilm from 1974 on, index cards from 1970 on, in house computer from 1978 on and District

Archives from 1962 on. Police Dept. keeps felony records back to '92, misdemeanors to '97. It takes 1 day before new records are available for inquiry. 46% of all arrests in database have final dispositions recorded, 84% for those arrests within last 5 years.

Searching: Include the following in your request: signed, notorized release from subject, full name (middle initial), date and place of birth, year. The SSN, race, curent address and case number, if known, are helpful. Fingerprints searches are not available. The following data is not released: pending cases. Neither records location will supply records without dispositions.

Access by: mail, in person.

Fee & Payment: The fee is $5.00 per name from the Police Dept.; Search fee at Superior Court is $10.00. Fee payee: Metropolitan Police/Superior

Court, Criminal Division Personal checks accepted. No credit cards accepted.

Mail search: Turnaround time: 2 to 4 weeks. A self addressed stamped envelope is required.

In person search: Records are returned by mail.

Online search: The Sex Offender Registry can be searched at www.mpdc.org/serv/sor/impreminder.shtm

Corporation Records
Limited Partnership Records
Limited Liability Company Records

Department of Consumer & Regulatory Affairs, 941 N Capitol St NE, Washington, DC 20002-4259; 202-442-4434, 8:30AM-4:15PM.

www.dcra.org

Indexing & Storage: Records are available from the 1850s. There is no trademark or servicemark statute. Records are indexed on inhouse computer.

Searching: Include the following in your request: full name of business. The web site provides download capability of forms.

Access by: mail, phone, in person.

Fee & Payment: Fees: $25.00 per legal document in folder. A document can be 1-100 pages. A Good Standing is $10.00, $20.00 if a not-for-profit. Fee payee: DC Treasury. Prepayment required. Personal checks accepted. Credit cards accepted for in person searches only.

Mail search: Turnaround time: 5 to 10 days.

Phone search: They will release agent's name and address, date of incorporation, and status over the phone at no fee. Names and addresses of Officers and Directors will not be released over the phone.

In person search: You may request information in person. There is no fee unless copies of documents are needed. You may use a credit card.

Other access: For information concerning lists and bulk file purchases, contact the Office of Information Services.

Uniform Commercial Code
Federal Tax Liens
State Tax Liens

UCC Recorder, District of Columbia Recorder of Deeds, 515 D Street NW, Washington, DC 20001; 202-727-0400, 202-727-7114, 8:15AM-4:45PM.

http://countyrecords.landata.com/WashDC

Note: Records from 1983 forward are located in Room 101, prior records are in Room 304. This agency will not perform name searches (you must do yourself or hire someone).

Indexing & Storage: Records are available from the 1900's. Records are indexed on microfiche.

Searching: Local tax liens are called district tax liens. Include the following in your request: debtor name. Searches from 1973 forward are not performed by state personnel. Use the inhouse terminal or the web site. Searches prior to 1973 need a book and page number.

Access by: mail, in person, online.

Fee & Payment: Copies cost $2.25 per page. Fee payee: DC Treasurer. Prepayment required. Personal checks accepted. No credit cards accepted.

Mail search: Turnaround time: 2 weeks. No name searches.

In person search: There is a public access terminal available to look up names to find instrument numbers.

Online search: Search by name or document number at the web site. Registration is required, but there is no fee. It is the intent of the Washington DC Recorder of Deeds to sell

document images through this site in the near future.

Sales Tax Registrations

Office of Tax and Revenue, Audit Division, 941 N. Capitol Street NE, Washington, DC 20002; 202-727-4829, 202-442-6550 (Fax), 8:15AM-4:30PM.

http://cfo.dc.gov/etsc/main.shtm

Indexing & Storage: Records are available from the 1980's. Records are computerized since 1990, otherwise are hard copies.

Searching: This agency will only confirm that the business is registered. They will provide no other information. Include the following in your request: business name, federal employer identification number, address. They will also search by tax permit number.

Access by: mail, phone, fax.

Mail search: Turnaround time: 3 to 5 days. A self addressed stamped envelope is requested. No fee for mail request.

Phone search: No fee for telephone request.

Fax search: Same criteria as mail searches.

Birth Certificates

Department of Health, Vital Records Division, 825 North Capitol St NE, 2st Fl, Washington, DC 20002; 202-442-9009, 800-255-2414, 8:30AM-3:30PM.

www.dchealth.com

Indexing & Storage: Records are available from 1874 to present. New records are available for inquiry immediately. Records are indexed on microfiche, inhouse computer.

Searching: Records less than 100 years old are only released to person of record or immediate family members or to legal representative of family. Requester should include a copy of photo ID and daytime phone number. Include the following in your request: full name, date of birth, place of birth, names of parents, name of the hospital.

Access by: mail, phone, fax, in person.

Fee & Payment: The $12.00 fee is for the short form of birth certificate for every consecutive 3 years searched. The archival long form costs $18.00. All copies are certified. Fee payee: DC Treasurer. Prepayment required. Credit cards are only accepted for expedited services. Personal checks accepted. Credit cards accepted: MasterCard, Visa, AmEx, Discover.

Mail search: Turnaround time: 2 weeks. All genealogical searches must be done by mail and cannot be expedited. No self addressed stamped envelope is required.

Phone search: Phone requests are considered expedited and extra fees are involved.

Fax search: See expedited services.

In person search: Searching is available in person.

Expedited service: Expedited service is available for fax searches. Expedited service is available from VitalChek and requires a credit card and additional $8.95 fee for regular mail or $23.95 for overnight delivery after processing.

Death Records

Department of Health, Vital Records Division, 825 North Capitol St NE, 1st Fl, Washington, DC 20002; 202-442-9009, 800-255-2414 (Vital Chek), 8:30AM-3:30PM.

www.dchealth.com

Indexing & Storage: Records are available from August 1874 on. New records are available for inquiry immediately. Records are indexed on microfiche, inhouse computer.

Searching: Records up to 50 years old are only released to immediate family members of person of record or to legal representative of family. Requester should include copy of a photo ID and daytime phone number. Include the following in your request: full name, date of death, Social Security Number.

Access by: mail, phone, fax, in person.

Fee & Payment: All copies are certified. Fee payee: DC Treasurer. Prepayment required. Credit cards are only accepted for expedited services. Personal checks accepted. Credit cards accepted: MasterCard, Visa, AmEx, Discover.

Mail search: Turnaround time: 2 weeks. Genealogical searches must be in writing and cannot be expedited. No self addressed stamped envelope is required. Search costs $12.00 for each name in request.

Phone search: See expedited services.

Fax search: See expedited services.

In person search: Search costs $12.00 for each name in request. Turnaround time is 1/2 hour unless extensive search required.

Expedited service: Expedited service is available for fax searches. Expedited service is available from VitalChek, credit card required. Fee is an additional $8.95 or $23.95 if overnight delivery is required.

Marriage Certificates

Superior Court House, Marriage Bureau, 500 Indiana Ave, NW, Room 4485, Washington, DC 20001; 202-879-4840, 202-879-1280 (Fax), 9AM-4PM.

www.dcbar.org/dcsc/fam.html

Indexing & Storage: Records are available from 1811 on. New records are available for inquiry immediately. Records are indexed on microfilm, books (volumes).

Searching: Include the following in your request: both names, wife's maiden name, date of marriage.

Access by: mail, in person.

Fee & Payment: Search fee is $10.00. Extra copies are $.50 per page. Fee payee: Clerk of the Superior Court. Prepayment required. Only money orders are accepted unless requester is an attorney or a minister/priest/rabbi. No credit cards accepted.

Mail search: Turnaround time: 1 to 2 weeks. A self addressed stamped envelope is requested.

In person search: Search costs $10.00 per request. Turnaround time is within the same day.

Divorce Records

Superior Court House, Divorce Records, 500 Indiana Ave, NW, Room 4230, Washington, DC 20001; 202-879-1261, 202-879-1572 (Fax), 9AM-4PM.

www.dcbar.org/dcsc/fam.html

Indexing & Storage: Records are available from 1956 on. Records prior to 1956 are located at the US District Court at 202-273-0520. New records are available for inquiry immediately. Records are indexed on microfilm, books (volumes).

Searching: Include the following in your request: names of husband and wife, date of divorce, year divorce case began, case number (if known). The following data is not released: sealed records.

Access by: mail, fax, in person.

Fee & Payment: Search fee is $10.00. Certification is $6.50. Copy fee is $.50 per page. Fee payee: Clerk of the Superior Court. Prepayment required. Use either a money order or a cashier's check if ordering by mail. No credit cards accepted.

Mail search: Turnaround time: 3 weeks. Written requests must include requester's phone number so the court can call back with the charge. A self addressed stamped envelope is requested.

Fax search: Requesters must prepay before records are returned.

In person search: Turnaround time is same day for record after 1988. Prior records are kept off site and will take longer to retrieve.

Workers' Compensation Records

Office of Workers' Compensation, PO Box 56098 3rd Floor, Washington, DC 20011 (Courier: 77 P St, NE 2nd Fl, Washington, DC 20011); 202-671-1000, 202-671-1929 (Fax), 8:30AM-5PM.

www.does.dc.gov/main.shtm

Indexing & Storage: Records are available from June 1982 on. Records are archived after a year and will take longer to locate. Records are only from private employers. New records are available for inquiry immediately. Records are indexed on inhouse computer.

Searching: Only claimant or parties to claim can access records. All others must have signed release from claimant. Include the following in your request: claimant name, Social Security Number, date of accident, employer.

Access by: mail, fax, in person.

Fee & Payment: There is no search fee, copies are $.25 per page. Fee payee: DC Treasurer. Prepayment required. Personal checks accepted. No credit cards accepted.

Mail search: Turnaround time: 2 to 3 days. A self addressed stamped envelope is requested.

Fax search: Limit 2 pages, turnaround time is 2-3 days.

In person search: Limited to interested parties or with signed release from claimant.

Driver Records

Department of Motor Vehicles, Driver Records Division, 301 "C" St, NW, Rm 1000, Washington, DC 20001; 202-727-6761, 202-727-5000 (General), 8:15AM-4PM M-T-TH-F; 8:15AM-7:00PM W.

www.dmv.washingtondc.gov/main.shtm

Note: Copies of tickets are available from the Bureau of Traffic Adjudication, Correspondence Unit, 65 "K" Street, NE, Washington 20002. The fee is $1.00 per ticket.

Indexing & Storage: Records are available for 3 years for moving violations, suspensions/revocations for 5 years, and DWIs for an indefinite period. Accidents are listed on the record if there is a conviction, but fault is not indicated.

Searching: The agency' policy is stricter than DPPA. Personal information is suppressed unless authority is granted by subject. Mail requesters must submit name and DL number; DOB is optional. Online requesters must submit DL, name and DOB; the sex and middle initial is optional.

Access by: mail, in person, online.

Fee & Payment: The cost for a driving record by any method is $5.00. Fee payee: DC Treasurer. Prepayment required. Personal checks accepted. No credit cards accepted.

Mail search: Turnaround time: 3 days. No self addressed stamped envelope is required.

In person search: Walk-in requesters may obtain up to 5 records at once. The rest are available overnight.

Online search: Online requests are taken throughout the day and are available in batch the next morning after 8:15 am. There is no minimum order requirement. Fee is $5.00 per record. Billing is a "bank" system which draws from pre-paid account. Requesters are restricted to high volume, ongoing users. Each requester must be approved and sign a contract. For more information, call 202- 727-5692.

Vehicle Ownership
Vehicle Identification

Department of Motor Vehicles, Vehicle Control Division, 301 "C" St, NW, Room 1063, Washington, DC 20001; 202-727-4768, 8:15AM-4PM M-T-TH-F; 8:15AM-7PM W.

www.dmv.washingtondc.gov/main.shtm

Searching: Records are classified as either "Authorized" or "General." Authorized is for law enforcment. General records (DPPA permissible use purposes) suppress personal information. Casual requesters must have permission of the subject. The following data is not released: Social Security Numbers or financial information.

Access by: mail, in person.

Fee & Payment: The current fee is $5.00 per request for VIN, registration or lien information. Fee payee: DC Treasurer. Prepayment required. Cash is accepted for in person transactions. Personal checks accepted. No credit cards accepted.

Mail search: Turnaround time: 10 days. No self addressed stamped envelope is required.

In person search: You may request information in person.

Other access: Bulk requests can be obtained for commercial purposes upon approval by the Chief of the Bureau of Motor Vehicles if it is determined that the requested use "is for the public interest." Commercial purposes are not permitted.

Accident Reports

Criminal Justice Information Div, Accident Report Section, 300 Indiana Ave NW, Room 3055, Washington, DC 20001; 202-727-4245, 202-727-4357, 7AM-4PM (8PM on Wed).

www.dmv.washingtondc.gov

Note: This office holds the officer investigated accident reports known as PD-10s "Citizen reports" can be secured for $2.00 each at the Insurance Operations Branch at 202-727-4601.

Searching: Include the following in your request: date of accident, location of accident, full name. The six-digit identifying number is helpful if known.

Access by: mail, in person.

Fee & Payment: The fee is $2.00 per report for walk-in or mail-in requests. Fee payee: DC Treasurer. Prepayment required. Personal checks accepted. No credit cards accepted.

Mail search: Turnaround time: 3 days. A self addressed stamped envelope is requested.

In person search: You may request information in person.

Vessel Ownership
Vessel Registration
Access to Records is Restricted

Metropolitan Police Dept, Harbor Patrol, 550 Water St SW, Washington, DC 20024; 202-727-4582, 202-727-3663 (Fax).

http://mpdc.dc.gov/main.shtm

Note: All vessels regardless of size must be titled and registered. Information is not open to the public. Any emergency requests must be in writing and the agency will use some discretion in release of data for lawful purposes.

Legislation Records

Council of the District of Columbia, 441 4th Street, Rm 714, Washington, DC 20004; 202-724-8050, 202-347-3070 (Fax), 9AM-5:30PM.

www.dccouncil.washington.dc.us

Indexing & Storage: Records are available from 1975 to present. Records are indexed on microfilm.

Searching: Include the following in your request: bill number.

Access by: mail, phone, fax, in person, online.

Fee & Payment: 1993-2000 bills are considered current and are on paper. 1975 through 1988 are on microfilm, and you must do your own copying at $.10 per page. 1989-1992 are stored offsite at archives. Fee payee: DC Treasurer. Prepayment required. Personal checks accepted. No credit cards accepted.

Mail search: Turnaround time: 1 to 4 days. No self addressed stamped envelope is required.

Phone search: No fee for telephone request. Bill status is given over the phone.

Fax search: Same criteria as phone searching.

In person search: You may request copies in person.

Online search: Bill text and status may be reviewed at the Internet site.

Voter Registration

DC Board of Elections and Ethics, 441 4th St NW, #250 North, Washington, DC 20001; 202-727-2525, 8:30AM-4:45PM.

www.dcboee.org

Indexing & Storage: Records are available for active records. The database is updated every four months.

Searching: Records are open to the public. The following data is not released: Social Security Numbers or date of birth.

Access by: mail, phone, fax, in person.

Fee & Payment: There is no fee for a search, but there is a $.10 copy fee. Fee payee: DC Treasurer. Prepayment required. If purchasing the database, certified funds are required. No credit cards accepted.

Mail search: Turnaround time: 7 to 10 days.

Phone search: For verification purposes only.

Fax search: Fax searching available.

In person search: Information is available immediately.

Other access: Records can be purchased on tape, labels, and printed lists from the SHARE Program. A variety of data is available from party registration to voter history. Minimum fee is $50 plus supplies. Call Karen Jordan at 202-727-6783 for details.

GED Certificates

GED Testing Center, State Education Agency, 4200 Connecticut Ave. NW, MB1005, Washington, DC 20008; 202-274-7173, 202-274-6507 (Fax), 9AM-1PM.

Searching: Include the following in your request: a signed release, name at time of test, DOB, date/year test, SSN, and city of test.

Access by: mail, in person.

Fee & Payment: There is no fee for verification. Copies of transcripts are $5.00 per copy. Fee payee: UDC - GED Testing Center Money orders are accepted. No credit cards accepted.

Mail search: Turnaround time: 10-14 days. No self addressed stamped envelope is required.

In person search: Results are still mailed within two weeks.

Fishing License Information

Access to Records is Restricted

Environmental Health Regulation, Fisheries & Wildlife Division, 51 N Street NE - 5th Fl, Washington, DC 20002-3323; 202-535-2266, 202-535-1359 (Fax), 8AM-5PM.

Note: Hunting of any kind is prohibited within the District of Columbia. Records are not available to the public, they are only released as a Freedom of Information Act request. Certain data may be released to attorneys for pending litigation or statistical use with a written request.

District of Columbia State Licensing Agencies

Licenses Searchable Online

Acupuncturist #2 .... http://dchealth.dc.gov/prof_license/services/search_licensing.asp

Addiction Counselor #2 .... http://dchealth.dc.gov/prof_license/services/search_licensing.asp

Attorney #3 .... www.dcbar.org/memberlookup/searchform.cfm

Chiropractor #2 .... http://dchealth.dc.gov/prof_license/services/search_licensing.asp

Counselor, Professional #2 .... http://dchealth.dc.gov/prof_license/services/search_licensing.asp

Dance Therapist #2 .... http://dchealth.dc.gov/prof_license/services/search_licensing.asp

Dental Hygienist #2 .... http://dchealth.dc.gov/prof_license/services/search_licensing.asp

Dentist #2 .... http://dchealth.dc.gov/prof_license/services/search_licensing.asp

Dietitian/Nutritionist #2 .... http://dchealth.dc.gov/prof_license/services/search_licensing.asp

Investment Advisor #7 .... http://disr.washingtondc.gov/services/licenseing_security_prof/index.shtm

Investment Advisor Representative #7 .... http://disr.washingtondc.gov/services/licenseing_security_prof/index.shtm

Massage Therapist #2 .... http://dchealth.dc.gov/prof_license/services/search_licensing.asp

Medical Doctor #2 .... http://dchealth.dc.gov/prof_license/services/search_licensing.asp

Midwife Nurse #2 .... http://dchealth.dc.gov/prof_license/services/search_licensing.asp

Naturopath #2 .... http://dchealth.dc.gov/prof_license/services/search_licensing.asp

Nurse Anesthetist #2 .... http://dchealth.dc.gov/prof_license/services/search_licensing.asp

Nurse, Clinical #2 .... http://dchealth.dc.gov/prof_license/services/search_licensing.asp

Nurse, Licensed Practical #2 .... http://dchealth.dc.gov/prof_license/services/search_licensing.asp

Nurse-LPN #2 .... http://dchealth.dc.gov/prof_license/services/search_licensing.asp

Nursing Home Administrator #2 .... http://dchealth.dc.gov/prof_license/services/search_licensing.asp

Occupational Therapist #2 .... http://dchealth.dc.gov/prof_license/services/search_licensing.asp

Optometrist #2 .... www.odfinder.org/LicSearch.asp

Osteopath #2 .... http://dchealth.dc.gov/prof_license/services/search_licensing.asp

Pharmacist #2 .... http://dchealth.dc.gov/prof_license/services/search_licensing.asp

Physical Therapist #2 .... http://dchealth.dc.gov/prof_license/services/search_licensing.asp

Physician Assistant #2 .... http://dchealth.dc.gov/prof_license/services/search_licensing.asp

Podiatrist #2 .... http://dchealth.dc.gov/prof_license/services/search_licensing.asp

Psychologist #2 .... http://dchealth.dc.gov/prof_license/services/search_licensing.asp

Real Estate Appraiser #5 .... www.asc.gov/content/category1/appr_by_state.asp

Recreational Therapist #2 .... http://dchealth.dc.gov/prof_license/services/search_licensing.asp

Respiratory Care #2 .... http://dchealth.dc.gov/prof_license/services/search_licensing.asp

Securities Agent #7 .... http://disr.washingtondc.gov/services/licenseing_security_prof/index.shtm

Securities Broker/Dealer #7 .... http://disr.washingtondc.gov/services/licenseing_security_prof/index.shtm

Social Worker #2 .... http://dchealth.dc.gov/prof_license/services/search_licensing.asp

Licensing Quick Finder

Acupuncturist #2	202-442-9200
Addiction Counselor #2	202-442-9200
Air Conditioning/Refrigeration #5	202-442-4459
Alcohol Mfg./Vendor/Dist. #1	202-442-4423
Architect #5	202-442-4461
Asbestos Abatement Worker/Contr. #5	202-442-4459
Athletic Trainer/Coach #8	202-442-5377
Attorney #3	202-626-3475
Auctioneer #5	202-442-9200
Automobile Repossessor #5	202-442-9200
Bank #10	202-727-1563
Barber #5	202-442-4459
Bingo Operation #13	202-645-8041
Boxing/Wrestling Event/Professional #5	202-442-4472
Chiropractor #2	202-442-9200
Contractor #5	202-442-4459
Cosmetologist #5	202-442-4459
Counselor, Professional #2	202-442-9200
Credit Union #10	202-727-1563
Dance Therapist #2	202-442-9200
Dental Hygienist #2	202-442-9200
Dentist #2	202-442-9200
Dietitian/Nutritionist #2	202-442-9200
Electrician #5	202-442-4459
Emergency Medical Technician #11	202-442-9111
Engineer #5	202-442-4459
Firearms Instructor #14	410-799-0191
Firearms Permit #14	410-799-0191
Funeral Director #5	202-442-4461
Gas Fitter #5	202-442-4459
Hearing Aid Dispenser #2	202-442-9200

Insurance Broker/Agent #12	202-727-7425
Interior Designer #5	202-442-4461
Investment Advisor #7	202-442-7853
Investment Advisor Representative #7	202-442-7853
K-9 Units #14	410-799-0191
Lobbyist #9	202-939-8717
Lottery Retailer #13	202-645-8042
Massage Therapist #2	202-442-9200
Mechanic, Master #5	202-442-9200
Medical Doctor #2	202-442-9200
Midwife Nurse #2	202-442-9200
Mortgage Broker/Lender #10	202-727-1563
Motor Vehicle Dealer/Salesperson #5	202-442-9200
Naturopath #2	202-442-9200
Notary Public #15	202-727-3117
Nurse Anesthetist #2	202-442-9200
Nurse, Clinical #2	202-442-9200
Nurse, Licensed Practical #2	202-442-9200
Nurse-LPN #2	202-442-9200
Nursing Home Administrator #2	202-442-9200
Occupational Therapist #2	202-442-9200
Optometrist #2	202-442-9200
Osteopath #2	202-442-9200
Parking Lot Attendant #5	202-442-9200
Pesticide Applicator #4	202-442-4307
Pesticide Dealer #4	202-442-4307
Pesticide Employee/Operator #4	202-442-4307
Pharmacist #2	202-442-9200
Physical Therapist #2	202-442-9200
Physician Assistant #2	202-442-9200
Plumber #5	202-727-7170

Podiatrist #2	202-442-9200
Private Investigator #14	410-799-0191
Property Manager #5	202-442-9200
Psychologist #2	202-442-9200
Psychometrist/School Psychologist #8	202-442-5377
Public Accountant #5	202-442-4461
Real Estate Appraiser #5	202-442-4472
Real Estate Broker/Salesperson #5	202-442-4400
Recreational Therapist #2	202-442-9200
Respiratory Care #2	202-442-9200
Savings & Loan Company #10	202-727-1563
School Attendance Officer/Worker #8	202-442-5377
School Counselor #8	202-442-5377
School Librarian/Media Specialist #8	202-442-5377
School Social Worker #8	202-442-5377
Securities Agent #7	202-442-7826
Securities Broker/Dealer #7	202-442-7826
Security Agency #14	410-799-0191
Security Alarm Dealer/Agent #5	202-442-9200
Security Guard #14	410-799-0191
Social Worker #2	202-442-9200
Solicitor #5	202-442-9200
Solid Waste Collector #5	202-442-9200
Speech Language Pathologist/Audiologist #8	202-442-5377
Steam Fitter #5	202-442-4459
Surveyor, Land #5	202-442-4459
Teacher/Teacher Trainer #8	202-442-5377
Tour Guide #5	202-442-9200
Veterinarian #5	202-442-9200

Licensing Agency Information

#1 Dept. of Consumer Regulatory Affairs, Alcohol & Beverage Control Division, 941 N Capitol St NE, Washington, DC 20002-4259; 202-442-4445.
http://dcra.dc.gov/services/abra/index.shtm

#2 Department of Consumer & Regulatory Affairs, Health Care Licensing, 825 N Capitol St NE, 2nd Fl, Washington, DC 20002-4210; 202-442-9200, Fax: 202-442-9431.
www.dchealth.com
Search database at http://dchealth.dc.gov/prof_license/services/search_licensing.asp

#3 District of Columbia Bar Association, 1250 H St NW, 6th Fl, Washington, DC 20005; 202-737-4700, Fax: 202-626-3471.
www.dcbar.org
Search database at www.dcbar.org/memberlookup/searchform.cfm

#4 Department of Consumer & Regulatory Affairs, Pesticides - Business Services Division, 941 N Capitol St NE, Room 100, Washington, DC 20002; 202-535-2299.

#5 Department of Consumer & Regulatory Affairs, License & Certification Division - Central Verifications, 941 N Capitol St NE, Washington, DC 20002-4259; 202-442-9200.
http://dcra.dc.gov/about/index_bandc.shtm

#7 Department of Insurance & Securities Regulation, Securities Bureau, 810 1st St NE #602, Washington, DC 20002-4227; 202-727-8000, Fax: 202-535-1199.
http://disr.washingtondc.gov/main.shtm
Search database at http://disr.washingtondc.gov/services/licenseing_security_prof/index.shtm

#8 Public Schools, Licensure & Credentials, 825 N Capitol St NE #9026, Washington, DC 20002; 202-442-5377, Fax: 202-442-5311.
www.k12.dc.us/dcps/home.html

#9 Director of Campaign Finance, Office of Campaign Finance, 2000 14th St NW, #420, Washington, DC 20009; 202-671-0550, Fax: 202-671-0658.
www.dcocf.org
Search database at www.dcocf.org/ocfpdf/registrantsfilers2001JanPUB.PDF

#10 Economic Development, Banking & Financial Institutions Office, 1400 L St NW #400, Washington, DC 20005; 202-727-1563, Fax: 202-727-1588.
www.dbfi.dc.gov

#11 Emergency, Health & Medical Svcs. Office, 825 N Capitol NE, Washington, DC 20002; 202-442-9111, Fax: 202-442-4812.
www.dchealth.com
Agency email: sadams@dchealth.com.

#12 Dept of Insurance & Securities Regulation, 810 1st St NE #701, Washington, DC 20002; 202-727-8000.
www.disr.washingtondc.gov
Agency email: disr@dcgov.org.

#13 Lottery & Charitable Games Control Board, 2101 Martin Luther King Jr Ave SE, Washington, DC 20020; 202-645-8041, Fax: 202-645-0006.

#14 Metropolitian Police Department, Licensing Division, 7751 Washington Blvd, Jessup, MD 20794; 410-799-0191, Fax: 410-799-5934.

#15 Notary Commissions & Authentications Section, Office of the Secretary, 441 4th St NW #810A South, Washington, DC 20001; 202-727-3117, Fax: 202-727-8457.

District of Columbia Federal Courts

US District Court

District of Columbia

Washington DC Division US Courthouse, Clerk's Office, Room 1225, 333 Constitution Ave NW, Washington, DC 20001 (Courier Address: Use mail address for courier delivery), 202-727-2947, Fax: 202-354-3524.

www.dcd.uscourts.gov

Indexing & Storage: Cases are indexed by defendant, plaintiff, and case number. New cases are available in the index 48 hours after filing date. Civil records are indexed on computer since 1987 with an archive program available of some older cases, microfiche from 1932 to mid-1991. Criminal records are indexed on computer since mid-1991, microfiche from 1932 to mid-1991. District wide searches are available from this court. Archived records are not available over the phone; the court must be contacted in writing and will be made available through a copy service. Turnaround time: 3-5 days.

Fee & Payment Notes: Payment may be made by. Payee: Clerk, US District Court.

Phone Search: Searchers calling locally will not be given information over the phone. Out of state calls will be given the 3 most current docket entries only.

In Person Search: In person searching available.

PACER: Access fee is. Toll-free dial-up access: 888-253-6878. Local dial-up access: 202-273-

0606. PACER is available online at http://pacer.dcd.uscourts.gov.

Electronic Filing: Information is available online at https://ecf.dcd.uscourts.gov

Opinions Online: Court opinions are available online at www.dcd.uscourts.gov

US Bankruptcy Court

District of Columbia

Washington DC Division E Barrett Prettyman Courthouse, Room 4400, 333 Constitution Ave NW, Washington, DC 20001 (Courier Address: Use mail address for courier delivery), 202-273-0042.

www.dcb.uscourts.gov

Indexing & Storage: Cases are indexed by debtor and creditors as well as by case number. New cases are available in the index 24 hours after filing date. Records are indexed on computer from 1990 to present. For records prior to 1990, Open records are located at this court.

Fee & Payment Notes: Payment may be made by money order, cashier check, business check. Personal checks are not accepted. Cash accepted in person. Payee: Clerk, US Bankruptcy Court.

Phone Search: An automated voice case information service (VCIS) is available. Call VCIS at 202-273-0048.

In Person Search: In person searching available.

PACER: Toll-free dial-up access: 888-289-2414. Local dial-up access: 202-273-0630. Case records are available back to 1991. Records are purged every six months. New civil records are available online after 2 days. PACER is available online at http://pacer.dcb.uscourts.gov.

Electronic Filing: (Currently in the process of implementing CM/ECF.)

Standards for Federal Courts: The search fee is $20.00 per item (one party name or case number). Certification fee is $7.00 per document. Copy fee is $.50 per page. All fees standard unless noted in profile. Mail Search: always enclose a stamped self addressed envelope unless otherwise noted. Before releasing records, all courts require prepayment unless noted in profile.

Open records are located at the court unless otherwise noted. District courts index by defendant and plaintiff as well as by case number. Bankruptcy courts usually index by debtor and case number. While most courts now have their indexes on computer, many still maintain index card files as well.

The universal PACER sign-up number is 800-676-6856. Find PACER on the Web and the Party/Case Index at http://pacer.psc.uscourts.gov. PACER dial-up access is $.60 per minute. Also, courts offering internet access via RACER, PACER, Web-PACER or the new CM-ECF charge $.07 per page fee unless noted as free.

District of Columbia Courts

Court	Jurisdiction	No. of Courts	How Organized
Superior Courts*	General	3	
Probate/Tax Court*	Special	1	

* Profiled in this Sourcebook.

CIVIL									
Court	Tort	Contract	Real Estate	Min. Claim	Max. Claim	Small Claims	Estate	Eviction	Domestic Relations
Superior Courts*	X	X	X	$5000	No Max	$5000		X	X
Probate/Tax Courts*							X		

CRIMINAL					
Court	Felony	Misdemeanor	DWI/DUI	Preliminary Hearing	Juvenile
Superior Courts*	X	X	X	X	X
Probate/Tax Courts*					

ADMINISTRATION   Executive Office, 500 Indiana Av NW, Room 1500, Washington, DC, 20001; 202-879-1700, Fax: 202-879-4829. www.dcsc.gov

COURT STRUCTURE   The Superior Court in DC is divided into 17 divisions, 4 of which are shown in this book: Criminal, Civil, Family, and Tax-Probate. The Tax-Probate Division of the Superior Court handles probate. Eviction is part of the court's Landlord and Tenant Branch (202-879-4879).

ONLINE ACCESS   The Superior Court and Court of Appeals offer access to opinions at www.dcbar.org Limited cases (those filed electronically) are available at www.dcbar.org/dcsc/efiling.html

Superior Court - Criminal Division 500 Indiana Ave NW Room 4001, Washington, DC 20001; 202-879-1373; Fax: 202-638-5352. Hours: 8:30AM-4PM (EST). *Felony, Misdemeanor.*

www.dcsc.gov

Criminal Records: Access: Phone, mail, in person. Both court and visitors may perform in person searches. No search fee. Required to search: name, years to search, DOB. Criminal records on computer from 1978, on microfiche from 1974, on index from 1970, archived from 1962.

General Information: No sealed records released. Turnaround time depends on case involved. No copy fee.

Superior Court - Civil Division 500 Indiana Ave NW JM 170, Washington, DC 20001; 202-879-1133; Fax: 202-737-0827. Hours: 8:30AM-4PM M-F; 9AM-Noon Sat (EST). *Civil Actions, Small Claims.*

www.dcbar.org/dcsc

Civil Records: Access: Phone, mail, in person, online. Both court and visitors may perform in person searches. Search fee: $10.00 per name. Required to search: name. Civil cases indexed by defendant, plaintiff. Civil records on computer from 1983, on microfiche, archived and on index from 1976. Limited cases are available free via the e-Filing Project. Attorneys and legal professionals participating in the project must register for the CourtLink eFile service either by logging onto www.courtlink.com or calling 1-888-529-7587. Also, see www.dcbar.org/dcsc/efiling.html. Only out-of-District inquires are taken by phone.

General Information: Public access terminal is available. No sealed records released. SASE required. Turnaround time depends on case involved. Copy fee: $.50 per page. Certification fee: $5.00. Fee payee: Clerk-Superior Court of DC. Only cashiers checks and money orders accepted. Prepayment is required.

Superior Court - Landlord & Tenant Branch 500 Indiana Ave NW Room JM 255, Washington, DC 20001; 202-879-4879. Hours: 8:30AM-4PM M-F; 9AM-Noon Sat (EST). *Eviction.*

www.dcsc.gov

Civil Records: Access: In person, mail. Both court and visitors may perform in person searches. Search fee: $10.00. Civil records go back to 1993; computerized records go back to 1985. Only out-of-District inquires are taken by phone.

General Information: Public access terminal is available. Turnaround time depends on case involved. Copy fee: $.50 each. Fee payee: Clerk-Superior Court of DC. Prepayment is required.

Superior Court - Probate Division 500 Indiana Ave NW, Washington, DC 20001; 202-879-4800; Fax: 202-393-5849/879-1452(auditing). Hours: 9AM-4PM (EST). *Probate.*

District of Columbia Recording Offices

ORGANIZATION: District of Columbia is in the Eastern Time Zone (EST).

REAL ESTATE RECORDS: The District does not perform real estate searches.

UCC RECORDS: Financing statements are filed with the Recorder, including real estate related collateral. UCC searches performed for $30.00 per debtor name. Copies cost $2.25 per page.

TAX LIEN RECORDS: Federal tax liens on personal property of businesses are filed with the Secretary of State. Other federal and all state tax liens on personal property are filed with the Recorder.

ONLINE ACCESS: Search the recorders database at http://countyrecords.landata.com/WashDC. Registration is required; images are available for free, temporarily. Also, search the real property tax database for free at http://cfo.washingtondc.gov/services/tax/property/database.shtm

District of Columbia

Recorder of Deeds, 515 D Street NW, Room 203, Washington, DC 20001. 202-727-7110.
Will search UCC records. UCC search includes tax liens if requested. Will not search real estate records. **Online Access:** Real Estate, Assessor, Recording, Deed, Judgment, Lien, UCC Records. Search the recorders database at http://countyrecords.landata.com/WashDC. Registration is required; images are available for free, temporarily. Also, search the District real property tax database for free at http://cfo.washingtondc.gov/services/tax/property/database.shtm. **Other Phone Numbers:** Assessor 202-727-6447; Treasurer 202-727-6055.

District of Columbia County Locator

You will usually be able to find the city name in the City/County Cross Reference below. In that case, it is a simple matter to determine the county from the cross reference. However, only the official US Postal Service city names are included in this index. There are an additional 40,000 place names that people use in their addresses. Therefore, we have also included a ZIP/City Cross Reference immediately following the City/County Cross Reference.

If you know the ZIP Code but the city name does not appear in the City/County Cross Reference index, look up the ZIP Code in the ZIP/City Cross Reference, find the city name, then look up the city name in the City/County Cross Reference. For example, you want to know the county for an address of Menands, NY 12204. There is no "Menands" in the City/County Cross Reference. The ZIP/City Cross Reference shows that ZIP Codes 12201-12288 are for the city of Albany. Looking back in the City/County Cross Reference, Albany is in Albany County.

City/County Cross Reference

ANACOSTIA ANNEX District of Columbia
WASHINGTON District of Columbia
WASHINGTON NAVY YARD District of Columbia

ZIP/City Cross Reference

20000-20373 WASHINGTON
20373-20373 ANACOSTIA ANNEX
20374-20374 WASHINGTON
20374-20374 WASHINGTON NAVY YARD
20375-20376 WASHINGTON
20376-20376 WASHINGTON NAVY YARD
20380-20388 WASHINGTON
20388-20388 WASHINGTON NAVY YARD
20389-20391 WASHINGTON
20391-20391 WASHINGTON NAVY YARD
20392-20398 WASHINGTON
20398-20398 WASHINGTON NAVY YARD
20401-20599 WASHINGTON

Florida

General Help Numbers:

Governor's Office

The Capitol – 400 S Monroe St   850-488-4441
Tallahassee, FL 32399-0001   Fax 850-487-0801
www.myflorida.com/b_eog/owa/b_eog_www.html.main_p
age   8AM-5PM

Attorney General's Office

Legal Affairs Department   850-414-3300
The Capitol, PL-01   Fax 850-488-4872
Tallahassee, FL 32399-1050   8AM-5PM
http://legal.firn.edu

State Court Administrator

Supreme Court Bldg, 500 S Duval St   850-922-5082
Tallahassee, FL 32399-1900   Fax 850-488-0156
www.flcourts.org   8AM-5PM

State Archives

Archives & Records   850-245-6700
R A Gray Bldg, 500 S Bronough   Fax 850-488-4894
Tallahassee, FL 32399-0250   8AM-5PM M-F;
http://dlis.dos.state.fl.us/barm/   9AM-3PM SA

State Specifics:

Capital: Tallahassee
          Leon County

Time Zone: EST*

* Florida's ten western-most counties are CST:
They are: Bay, Calhoun, Escambia, Gulf, Holmes,
Jackson, Okaloosa, Santa Rosa, Walton, Washington.

Number of Counties: 67

Population: 16,396,515

Web Site: www.myflorida.com/

State Agencies

Criminal Records

Florida Department of Law Enforcement, User Services Bureau, PO Box 1489, Tallahassee, FL 32302 (Courier: 2331 Phillip Rd, Tallahassee, FL 32308); 850-410-8109, 850-410-8107, 850-410-8201 (Fax), 8AM-5PM.

www.fdle.state.fl.us/index.asp

Note: Sex offender data is available online at www.fdle.state.fl.us/sexual_predators.

Indexing & Storage: Records are available from the early 1930's. It takes 1 day before new records are available for inquiry. Records are indexed on microfilm, NIST Archive inhouse computer. 70% of all felony arrests in database have final dispositions recorded; 63% of misdemeanors. 68% of all records within last 5 years include dispositions.

Searching: Include the following in your request: date of birth, race, sex, name. You can submit

fingerprints, for the same fee, but it is not required. 100% of the arrest records are fingerprint-supported. The following data is not released: sealed or expunged records, juvenile records prior to 10/94. All records are released, including those without dispositions.

Access by: mail, in person, online.

Fee & Payment: The fee is $15.00 per individual. Pre-paid accounts receive turnaround time of two working days. Fee payee: Department of Law

Enforcement. Prepayment required. Personal checks accepted. Credit cards accepted only for online requests.

Mail search: Turnaround time: 5 working days. No self addressed stamped envelope is required.

In person search: In person requests are treated the same as mail requests; processing takes 5 working days.

Online search: Criminal history information from 1967 forward may be ordered over the Department Program Internet site at www2.fdle.state.fl.us. A $15.00 fee applies. Juvenile records from 10/1994 forward are also available. Credit card ordering will return records to your screen or via e-mail.

Expedited service: Expedited service is available for mail and phone searches. Turnaround time: overnight delivery.

Corporation Records
Limited Partnership Records
Limited Liability Company Records
Trademarks/Servicemarks
Fictitious Names
Federal Tax Liens

Division of Corporations, Department of State, PO Box 6327, Tallahassee, FL 32314 (Courier: 409 E Gaines St, Tallahassee, FL 32399); 850-488-9000 (Telephone Inquires), 850-245-6053 (Copy Requests), 850-245-6056 (Annual Reports), 8AM-5PM.

www.sunbiz.org

Note: This agency recommends accessing the Internet site. Send requests for Judgment Lien Filings to PO Box 6250.

Indexing & Storage: Records are available from the late 1800's. New records are available for inquiry immediately. Records are indexed on inhouse computer, on-line.

Searching: Addresses of judges and police are not released. Include the following in your request: full name of business. In addition to the articles of incorporation, corporation records include the following information: Annual Reports (date of filing and updates), Officers, Directors, Prior (merged) names, Inactive names, and US Tax ID number.

Access by: mail, phone, in person, online.

Fee & Payment: Copies of documents on microfilm or by image are $1.00 per page. Certification for corporate documents is $8.75, $52.50 for limited partnership records, and $30.00 for Limited Liability Company records. $10.00 for copy of Articles of Incorporation. Fee payee: Secretary of State. Prepayment required. Personal checks accepted. Accepts credit cards for online filing of annuals, only.

Mail search: Turnaround time: 2 to 3 days.

Phone search: The agency will not release name availability over the phone.

In person search: Copies (non-certified) are $1.00 per page.

Online search: The state's excellent Internet site gives detailed information on all corporate, trademark, limited liability company and limited partnerships (from 01/96): fictitious names (from 01/97); and lien records (from 01/97).

Other access: The state offers record purchases on microfiche sets and on CD disks.

Uniform Commercial Code

UCC Filings, C/O Image API, PO Box 5588, Tallahassee, FL 32314 (Courier: 2670 Executive Center Circle W, #100, Tallahassee, FL 32301); 850-222-8526, 850-487-6013 (Fax), 8AM-5PM.

www.floridaucc.com

Note: The Secretary of State privatized the filing and searching of UCC. The vendor, Image API, Inc., is responsible for all filings, photocopy and certification requests, forms, and database availability for searches.

Indexing & Storage: Records are available from 1966, if active, 1997 forward on the web. Records are on computer and microfiche. Records filed by electronic process are available in image format. New records are available for inquiry immediately.

Searching: Information on Tax Liens is maintained at the Department of State, Division of Corporations.

Federal tax liens on businesses are filed here; state tax liens are not. It is suggested to search state tax liens at the county level. Include the following in your request: debtor name. The state will not do a search. You must hire an outside firm, the web page, or use the state designated vendor.

Access by: mail, in person, online.

Fee & Payment: Fees are $1.00 per page for mail searching. Fee payee: Secretary of State. Prepayment required. Personal checks accepted. No credit cards accepted.

Mail search: Turnaround time: 3 to 5 days. No self addressed stamped envelope is required.

In person search: Searching is available in person.

Online search: The state Internet site allows access for no charge. Search by name or document number, for records 1997 to present.

Other access: Microfilm reels and CD's of images are available for bulk purchase requesters. Call for more information.

State Tax Liens
Records not maintained by a state level agency.

Note: These records are filed and found at the county level.

Sales Tax Registrations

Florida Department of Revenue, 168 Blountstown Highway #C, Tallahassee, FL 32304-3702; 850-488-9925, 850-922-5936 (Fax), 8AM-5PM.

www.state.fl.us/dor

Indexing & Storage: Records are available for 5 years, then they are purged.

Searching: This agency will confirm that a business is registered and has filed returns with the department. The following are required to search; business name, tax ID number, and business location. Federal ID is helpful. They can also search by the owner's name.

Access by: mail, fax, in person.

Fee & Payment: There is no fee.

Mail search: The turnaround time is 7-10 days.

Fax search: Same criteria as mail searching.

In person search: Records are still returned by mail.

Birth Certificates

Department of Health, Office of Vital Statistics, PO Box 210, Jacksonville, FL 32231-0042 (Courier: 1217 Pearl St, Jacksonville, FL 32202); 904-359-6900, 904-359-6993 (Fax), 8AM-5PM.

www.doh.state.fl.us

Note: The web site includes general information and ordering instructions.

Indexing & Storage: Records are available from 1865 to present, however few records were filed prior to 1917. It takes 4 weeks after birth before new records are available for inquiry. Records are indexed on microfiche, inhouse computer.

Searching: Records released only to individual named, if of legal age, or to parents or legal guardians. If deceased, proof of death required for same if a certification of birth needed. Include the following in your request: full name, names of parents, mother's maiden name, date of birth, county.

Access by: mail, phone, fax, in person.

Fee & Payment: Fee is $9.00 plus $5.00 if ordered by credit card. $4.00 per copy when ordering additional same name at the same time. If the specific year is not known, additional years may be searched for a fee of $2.00 per year with a maximum fee of $55.00. Fee payee: Office of Vital Statistics. Prepayment required. Credit cards accepted through VitalChek Corporation (800-255-2414). A $5.00 fee is added for all credit card transactions. Personal checks accepted. Credit cards accepted: MasterCard, Visa, AmEx, Discover.

Mail search: Turnaround time: 15 to 20 days. No self addressed stamped envelope is required.

Phone search: See expedited services.

Fax search: See expedited services.

In person search: Turnaround time is same day.

Other access: Commemorative birth certificates in large size, signed by the governor, and suitable for framing are available. The fee is $34.00 or $25.00 when ordered in conjunction with other certified copies of the same record. Allow 4 to 6 weeks for delivery.

Expedited service: Expedited service is available for mail, phone and fax searches. Cost is $24.00 and if you wish to use Federal Express, an additional fee of $13.00 is charged. Turnaround time is 2 days plus delivery time.

Death Records

Department of Health, Office of Vital Statistics, PO Box 210, Jacksonville, FL 32231-0042 (Courier: 1217 Pearl St, Jacksonville, FL 32202); 904-359-6900, 904-359-6993 (Fax), 8AM-5PM.

www.doh.state.fl.us

Note: The web site contains general information, ordering instructions, and forms.

Indexing & Storage: Records are available from 1877 to present. It takes 4 weeks after death before new records are available for inquiry. Records are indexed on microfiche, inhouse computer.

Searching: The death certificate minus cause of death is public information. Cause is released 50 years after death to public. Otherwise, requester must be family member or demonstrate legal interest in the estate. Include the following in your request: full name, date of death, county. The following data is not released: cause of death.

Access by: mail, phone, fax, in person.

Fee & Payment: Fee is $5.00 for the first year searched. If the specific year is not known, additional years may be searched for $2.00 per year with a maximum fee of $55.00. Add $4.00 per copy when ordering additional copies at the same time. Fee payee: Office of Vital Statistics. Prepayment required. Credit cards are accepted through VitalChek Corporation (800-255-2414). Personal checks accepted. Credit cards accepted: MasterCard, Visa, AmEx, Discover.

Mail search: Turnaround time: 15 to 20 days. No self addressed stamped envelope is required.

Phone search: See expedited service.

Fax search: See expedited service.

In person search: Turnaround time is same day.

Expedited service: Expedited service is available for mail, phone and fax searches. Include $5.00 credit card fee. Cost is $20.00 and if you wish to use Federal Express, an additional fee of $13.00 is charged. Turnaround time is 2 days plus delivery time.

Marriage Certificates

Department of Health, Office of Vital Statistics, PO Box 210, Jacksonville, FL 32231-0042 (Courier: 1217 Pearl St, Jacksonville, FL 32202); 904-359-6900, 904-359-6993 (Fax), 8AM-5PM.

www.doh.state.fl.us

Note: The web site contains general information, ordering instructions and order forms to download.

Indexing & Storage: Records are available from 1927 to present on microfiche, from 1970 to present on computer.

Searching: Records are indexed by husband's name and/or by wife's maiden name. Include date of marriage and county of marriage in request. The following data is not released: Social Security Numbers.

Access by: mail, phone, fax, in person.

Fee & Payment: The fee is $5.00 per name for the first year searched. Additional years may be searched for $2.00 per year with a maximum fee of $55.00. Add $4.00 per copy when ordering additional copies at the same time. Credit card fee is $4.50. Fee payee: Office of Vital Statistics. Prepayment required. Credit cards are accepted through VitalChek Corporation (800 255-2414). Personal checks accepted. Credit cards accepted: MasterCard, Visa, AmEx, Discover.

Mail search: Turnaround time: 15 to 20 days. No self addressed stamped envelope is required.

Phone search: See expedited service.

Fax search: See expedited service.

In person search: Turnaround time is same day.

Other access: A large size, commemorative marriage certificate signed by the governor is available for $30.00 or $25.00 when ordered in conjunction with other certified copies of the same record. Allow 4 to 6 weeks for delivery.

Expedited service: Expedited service is available for mail, phone and fax searches. Include use of credit card. Total cost is $20.00 and if you wish to use Federal Express, an additional fee of $13.00 is charged. Turnaround time is 2 days plus delivery time.

Divorce Records

Department of Health, Office of Vital Statistics, PO Box 210, Jacksonville, FL 32231-0042 (Courier: 1217 Pearl St, Jacksonville, FL 32202); 904-359-6900, 904-359-6993 (Fax), 8AM-5PM.

www.doh.state.fl.us

Note: The web site provides general information and ordering instructions.

Indexing & Storage: Records are available from 1927 to present. It takes 6-8 weeks after divorce before new records are available for inquiry.

Searching: Records are indexed by husband's name only. Include county of divorce in request. In each of the last 5 years in Florida, there have been 140,000 marriages and 80,000 divorces per year. (This is over 1025 per court day.)

Access by: mail, phone, fax, in person.

Fee & Payment: Fees are $5.00 per request for the first year and $2.00 per year for each additional search year, with a maximum search fee of $55.00. Add $4.00 per copy per name when ordering additional copies at the same time. Fee payee: Office of Vital Statistics. Prepayment required. Credit cards are accepted through VitalChek Corporation (800-255-2414). A $5.00 fee is added for credit cards. Personal checks accepted. Credit cards accepted: MasterCard, Visa, AmEx, Discover.

Mail search: Turnaround time: 15 to 20 days. No self addressed stamped envelope is required.

Phone search: See expedited service.

Fax search: See expedited service.

In person search: The fee is nonrefundable. Turnaround time is same day.

Expedited service: Expedited service is available for mail, phone and fax searches. Turnaround time: 2 days. The fee of $20.00 includes the credit card surcharge. If you wish to use Federal Express, an additional fee of $13.00 is charged.

Workers' Compensation Records

Workers Compensation Division, Information Management Unit, 200 E Gaines St, Tallahassee, FL 32399-4226; 850-488-3030, 850-414-7341 (Fax), 7:30AM-5PM.

http://www2.myflorida.com/les

Indexing & Storage: Records are available from 1985 on microfilm. Indexes are also on microfiche (older) and on an image process (recent). It takes 3 days (imaged) before new records are available for inquiry. Records are indexed on microfilm, microfiche.

Searching: To get medical records you must have a signed release of subject, except for legal representatives or an involved insurance company. Include the following in your request: claimant name, Social Security Number, date of accident.

Access by: mail, fax, in person.

Fee & Payment: There is no search fee, but copies are $.15 per page after 14 pages. Fee payee: Workers Compensation Trust Fund. Prepayment required. Personal checks accepted. No credit cards accepted.

Mail search: Turnaround time: 2 weeks. They will send an invoice, and will send you the copies after they receive the check. No self addressed stamped envelope is required.

Fax search: Same criteria as mail searching.

In person search: Requests are still returned by mail, unless you have a subpoena.

Driver Records

Division of Drivers Licenses, Bureau of Records, PO Box 5775, Tallahassee, FL 32314-5775 (Courier: 2900 Apalachee Pky, MS90, Neil Kirkman Bldg, Tallahassee, FL 32399); 850-488-0250, 850-487-7080 (Fax), 8AM-5PM.

www.hsmv.state.fl.us

Note: Copies of tickets may be obtained from the same address listed above. The fee is $.50 each or $1.00 for certified copies.

Indexing & Storage: Records are available for a 3 year record or for a 7 year record. Accidents will appear only if a citation is issued, but the record will not show fault.

Searching: Driving records are deemed public information and no restrictions to requests or usage are maintained, as long as the usage is of a legal nature. Casual requesters cannot obtain personal information without consent. Either the driver license number or the name, DOB and sex are required for ordering.

Access by: mail, in person, online.

Fee & Payment: The fee is $3.10 for a certified three or seven year record. Online is $2.10, and these records not considered certified. There is a full charge for a "no record found." Fee payee: Division of Drivers Licenses. Prepayment required. Personal checks accepted. No credit cards accepted.

Mail search: Turnaround time: 10 days. No self addressed stamped envelope is required.

In person search: Normally, up to 50 requests can be processed for walk-in requests, while you wait. Some Clerks of Courts will also process driving records.

Online search: Online requests an on interactive basis. The state differentiates between high and low volume users. Requesters with 5,000 or more records per month are considered Network Providers. Call 850-488-6264 to become a Provider. Requesters with less than 5,000 requests per month (called Individual Users) are directed to a Provider. A list of providers is found at the web site. Check the status of any Florida Driver License free at http://www2.hsmv.state.fl.us/dlstatus.html. Simple enter the driver license number.

Other access: The state will process magnetic tape requests. Also, they will provide customized database searches of the license information. Call 850-487-4467 for more details.

Vehicle Ownership
Vehicle Identification

Division of Motor Vehicles, Information Research Section, Neil Kirkman Bldg, A-126, Tallahassee, FL 32399; 850-488-5665, 850-921-6122, 850-488-8983 (Fax), 8AM-4:30PM.

www.hsmv.state.fl.us

Note: The state has not converted from an "opt-out" to an opt-in" policy, but other wise is in compliiance with the DPPA.

Indexing & Storage: Records are available for 12 years.

Searching: FL imposes no access restrictions as long as the request is of a legal nature. However, casual requesters cannot obtain personal information without consent of subject. Please submit the city (residence) and DOB if doing a name search.

Access by: mail, in person, online.

Fee & Payment: The fee for a computer printout of information is $.50, $1.00 per page copy fee, and $3.00 if certification is needed. The current license plate registration is $2.00. A complete microfilm title history can be $15.00 or more. Fee payee: Division of Motor Vehicles. Prepayment required. Personal checks accepted. No credit cards accepted.

Mail search: Turnaround time: 2 to 3 weeks. If records are on microfiche, the wait may be as long as 4 weeks. No self addressed stamped envelope is required.

In person search: In cases when the information is not readily available the wait is 2 to 3 days.

Online search: Florida has contracted to release vehicle information through approved Network Providers. Accounts must first be approved by the state. For each record accessed, the charge is $.50 plus a transactional fee, and the subscriber fee. Users must work from an estimated 2 1/2 month pre-paid bank. New subscribers must complete an application with the Department 850-488-6710.

Other access: A user may obtain ownership information by county or statewide vehicle class code basis. For more information, call the Motor Vehicle Data Listing Information Services at 850-488-46710.

Accident Reports

DHSMV- MS-28, Crash Records-Room A325, Neil Kirkman Bldg, 2900 Apalachee Prky, Tallahassee, FL 32399-0538; 850-488-5017, 850-922-0488 (Fax), 8AM-4:45PM.

www.hsmv.state.fl.us

Note: They will not provide homicide reports, which must come from the investigating agency.

Indexing & Storage: Records are available from 1941 to the present. Records are stored on microfilm from 1983 forward. It takes 12 weeks before new records are available for inquiry. Records are indexed on microfilm and computer.

Searching: Records sealed by court order and juvenile information cannot be accessed. Homicide reports less than 5 years old should be requested from the local law enforcement agency that wrote the report, if over 5 years call 850-188-1009. Include the following in your request: the full name of driver, exact date of crash (after 1983), county and city, local agency that investigated. For reports prior to 1983 the exact date, county, location and if crash involved a fatality must be supplied with request.

Access by: mail, in person.

Fee & Payment: The cost is $2.00 per report. You cannot search by phone; however, you can call to determine if report is available. Fee payee: Department of Highway Safety and Motor Vehicles. Prepayment required. Personal checks accepted. No credit cards accepted.

Mail search: Turnaround time: 2 to 4 weeks. A self addressed stamped envelope is requested.

In person search: You may request information in person at the customer service counter on 1st floor (Room B-133).

Other access: List or bulk purchase is available by special request.

Vessel Ownership
Vessel Registration

Dept of Highway Safety, Vessel Records, Bureau of Titles & Registrations, 2900 Apalachee Parkway, MS 68, Tallahassee, FL 32399; 850-922-9000, 850-921-1935 (Fax).

www.hsmv.state.fl.us

Indexing & Storage: Records are available for 12 years to present. Records are indexed on computer. Motorized vessels must be titled and registered. Non-powered vessels are not required to be registered; however, non-powered vessels 16 ft and over must be titled. Liens show on records. It takes 6 weeks before new records are available for inquiry.

Searching: A written request is required for all searches. To search one of the following is required: Florida registration #, title #, hull id #, or the exact name.

Access by: mail, in person.

Fee & Payment: $.50 per page for computer print-out. $1.00 per photocopy of record. Additional $3.00 for each item to be certified. Fee payee: Dept of Highway Safety. Personal checks accepted. No credit cards accepted.

Mail search: Turnaround time: 1 week. No self addressed stamped envelope is required.

In person search: Searching is available in person.

Other access: A bulk purchase program is available for magnetic tape, labels or printed list. There is a $50.00 deposit required and a fee of $.01 per record.

Legislation Records

Office of Legislative Services, Legislative Information Services Division, 111 W Madison St, Pepper Bldg, Rm 704, Tallahassee, FL 32399-1400; 850-488-4371, 850-487-5915 (Senate Bills), 850-488-7475 (House Bills), 850-488-8427 (Session Laws), 850-921-5334 (Fax), 8AM-5PM.

www.leg.state.fl.us/Welcome/index.cfm

Indexing & Storage: Records are available from 1965 to present in book format, from 1972 to present on microfiche, and current and prior year on computer.

Searching: Include the following in your request: bill number. You may search by subject also.

Access by: mail, phone, in person, online.

Mail search: Turnaround time: 3 days. No self addressed stamped envelope is required.

Phone search: You may call for copies. There is an in-state toll-free line, 800-342-1827, for bill information.

In person search: You may request copies in person.

Online search: Their Internet site contains full text of bills and a bill history session outlining actions taken on bills. The site is updated every day at 11 PM. Records go back to 1998. There is a more extensive online information service available. This system also includes information on lobbyists. Fees are involved.

Voter Registration
Access to Records is Restricted

Department of State, Division of Elections, Collins Building, Room 100, Tallahassee, FL 32399-0250; 850-245-6200, 850-245-6217 (Fax), 8AM-5PM.

http://election.dos.state.fl.us

Note: All individual searching must be done at the county level. However, the state maintains a central voter file for data and statistical purposes.

GED Certificates

GED Testing Office, 325 W Gaines St Rm 634, Tallahassee, FL 32399; 850-488-6622, 8AM-5PM.

www.firn.edu/doe

Searching: To verify, the following is required: name, date of birth, year of test, Social Security Number, and county/city of test. If known, the GED Diploma number is helpful. A signed release is needed to get a copy of a transcript or diploma.

Access by: mail, phone, in person.

Fee & Payment: The fee is $4.00 per copy of transcript or diploma. There is no fee for verification. Money orders and cashiers' checks are required. Personal checks are not accepted. No credit cards accepted.

Mail search: Turnaround time 7-10 working days. A self addressed stamped envelope is requested.

Phone search: Depending on workload, personnel may be able to verify over the telephone.

In person search: Searching is available in person.

Hunting License Information
Fishing License Information

Fish & Wildlife Cons. Comm, Licensing & Permit Board, 2590 Executive Center Circle, #200, Tallahassee, FL 32301; 850-488-3641, 850-414-8212 (Fax), 8AM-5PM.

www.floridaconservation.org

Indexing & Storage: Records are available from 2/97 forward.

Searching: Requests must be in writing. The agency will release address, telephone number, and type of license. Include the following in your request: date of birth, address.

Access by: mail, in person.

Fee & Payment: There is no search fee.

Mail search: Turnaround time: 2 to 4 days.

In person search: Searching is available in person.

Florida State Licensing Agencies

Licenses Searchable Online

Acupuncturist #1 .... www.doh.state.fl.us/irm00praes/praslist.asp
Air Ambulance #20 .... www.doh.state.fl.us/ems/emslookup.html
Air Conditioning Contractor #16 .... www.state.fl.us/oraweb/owa/www_dbpr2.qry_lic_menu
Alarm System Contractor #6 .... https://www.myfloridalicense.com/licensing/wl11.jsp?SID=
Alcoholic Beverage Permit #6 .... https://www.myfloridalicense.com/licensing/wl11.jsp?SID=
Ambulance Service #20 .... www.doh.state.fl.us/ems/emslookup.html
Asbestos Remover/Contractor #16 .... www.state.fl.us/oraweb/owa/www_dbpr2.qry_lic_menu
Asbestos Surveyor Consultant #16 .... www.state.fl.us/oraweb/owa/www_dbpr2.qry_lic_menu
Assisted Living Facility #26 .... www.floridahealthstat.com/qs/owa/facilitylocator.facllocator
Athletic Agent #6 .... https://www.myfloridalicense.com/licensing/wl11.jsp?SID=
Athletic Trainer #1 .... www.doh.state.fl.us/irm00praes/praslist.asp
Attorney #23 .... www.flabar.org/newflabar/findlawyer.html
Auction Company #22 .... www.state.fl.us/oraweb/owa/www_dbpr2.qry_lic_menu
Auctioneer #22 .... www.state.fl.us/oraweb/owa/www_dbpr2.qry_lic_menu
Bank #5 .... www.dbf.state.fl.us/cf/dogi/Inst_search.cfm
Barber/Barber Assistant/Barber Shop #6 .... https://www.myfloridalicense.com/licensing/wl11.jsp?SID=
Boxer #6 .... https://www.myfloridalicense.com/licensing/wl11.jsp?SID=
Building Code Administrator #6 .... https://www.myfloridalicense.com/licensing/wl11.jsp?SID=
Building Contractor #16 .... www.state.fl.us/oraweb/owa/www_dbpr2.qry_lic_menu
Building Inspector #6 .... https://www.myfloridalicense.com/licensing/wl11.jsp?SID=
Chiropractor #1 .... www.doh.state.fl.us/irm00praes/praslist.asp
Clinical Lab Personnel #1 .... www.doh.state.fl.us/irm00praes/praslist.asp
Collection Agency #5 .... https://ssl.dbf.state.fl.us/cf/lic/pubinqry/pub2/index.cfm
Community Association Manager #6 .... https://www.myfloridalicense.com/licensing/wl11.jsp?SID=
Company in Receivership #14 .... www.doi.state.fl.us/Receiver/indextest.html
Construction Business #16 .... www.state.fl.us/oraweb/owa/www_dbpr2.qry_lic_menu
Contractor, General #16 .... www.state.fl.us/oraweb/owa/www_dbpr2.qry_lic_menu
Cosmetologist, Hair Braider, Nails/Salon #6 .... https://www.myfloridalicense.com/licensing/wl11.jsp?SID=
Credit Union #5 .... www.dbf.state.fl.us/cf/dogi/Inst_search.cfm
Crematory #6 .... https://www.myfloridalicense.com/licensing/wl11.jsp?SID=
Dentist/Dental Assistant #1 .... www.doh.state.fl.us/irm00praes/praslist.asp
Dietician/Nutritionist #1 .... www.doh.state.fl.us/irm00praes/praslist.asp
Doctor, Limited License #1 .... www.doh.state.fl.us/irm00praes/praslist.asp
Electrical Contractor #16 .... www.state.fl.us/oraweb/owa/www_dbpr2.qry_lic_menu
Electrologist/Electrologist Facility #1 .... www.doh.state.fl.us/irm00praes/praslist.asp
Elevator Certificates of Operation #6 .... https://www.myfloridalicense.com/licensing/wl11.jsp?SID=
Embalmer #6 .... https://www.myfloridalicense.com/licensing/wl11.jsp?SID=
Emerg. Insect Sting Treatment #20 .... www.doh.state.fl.us/ems/emslookup.html
Emergency Medical Technician #20 .... www.doh.state.fl.us/ems/emslookup.html
Finance Company, Consumer #5 .... https://ssl.dbf.state.fl.us/cf/lic/pubinqry/pub3/index.cfm
Financial Institution #5 .... www.dbf.state.fl.us/cf/dogi/Inst_search.cfm
Firearms Instructor #18 .... http://licgweb.dos.state.fl.us/access/individual.html
Firearms License, Statewide #18 .... http://licgweb.dos.state.fl.us/access/individual.html
Food Services Establishment #6 .... https://www.myfloridalicense.com/licensing/wl11.jsp?SID=
Funeral Director, Funeral Home #6 .... https://www.myfloridalicense.com/licensing/wl11.jsp?SID=
Geologist/Geology Firm #6 .... https://www.myfloridalicense.com/licensing/wl11.jsp?SID=
Health Facility #26 .... www.floridahealthstat.com/qs/owa/facilitylocator.facllocator
Hearing Aid Specialist #1 .... www.doh.state.fl.us/irm00praes/praslist.asp
Home Health Care Agency #26 .... www.floridahealthstat.com/qs/owa/facilitylocator.facllocator
Hospital #26 .... www.floridahealthstat.com/qs/owa/facilitylocator.facllocator
Hotel/Restaurant #6 .... https://www.myfloridalicense.com/licensing/wl11.jsp?SID=
Installment Seller, Retail #5 .... www.dbf.state.fl.us/licensing/
Insurance Adjuster/Agent/Title Agent #14 .... www.doi.state.fl.us/Data/AAR/index.htm
Insurance-related Company #14 .... www.doi.state.fl.us/Consumers/indextest.html
International Bank Office #5 .... www.dbf.state.fl.us/cf/dogi/Inst_search.cfm
Kickboxer #6 .... https://www.myfloridalicense.com/licensing/wl11.jsp?SID=
Lab License #26 .... www.floridahealthstat.com/qs/owa/facilitylocator.facllocator
Liquor Store #6 .... https://www.myfloridalicense.com/licensing/wl11.jsp?SID=
Lobbyist/Principal #28 .... www.leg.state.fl.us/lobbyist/index.cfm
Lodging Establishment #6 .... https://www.myfloridalicense.com/licensing/wl11.jsp?SID=
Marriage & Family Therapist #1 .... www.doh.state.fl.us/irm00praes/praslist.asp
Massage Therapist/School/Facility #1 .... www.doh.state.fl.us/irm00praes/praslist.asp

Mechanical Contractor #16 .... www.state.fl.us/oraweb/owa/www_dbpr2.qry_lic_menu
Medical Doctor #1 .... www.doh.state.fl.us/irm00praes/praslist.asp
Medical Faculty Certificate #1 .... www.doh.state.fl.us/irm00praes/praslist.asp
Mental Health Counselor #1 .... www.doh.state.fl.us/irm00praes/praslist.asp
Midwife #1 .... www.doh.state.fl.us/irm00praes/praslist.asp
Mortgage Broker School #5 .... https://ssl.dbf.state.fl.us/cf/lic/mbschools/index.cfm
Mortgage Broker/Firm #5 .... https://ssl.dbf.state.fl.us/cf/lic/pubinqry/pub1/index.cfm
Motel/Restaurant #6 .... https://www.myfloridalicense.com/licensing/wl11.jsp?SID=
Nail Specialist #6 .... https://www.myfloridalicense.com/licensing/wl11.jsp?SID=
Naturopath #1 .... www.doh.state.fl.us/irm00praes/praslist.asp
Notary Public #19 .... http://notaries.dos.state.fl.us/not001.html
Nuclear Radiology Physicist #1 .... www.doh.state.fl.us/irm00praes/praslist.asp
Nurse #1 .... www.doh.state.fl.us/irm00praes/praslist.asp
Nurse, Practical #1 .... www.doh.state.fl.us/irm00praes/praslist.asp
Nursing Assistant #1 .... www.doh.state.fl.us/irm00praes/praslist.asp
Nursing Home Administrator #1 .... www.doh.state.fl.us/irm00praes/praslist.asp
Nutrition Counselor #1 .... www.doh.state.fl.us/irm00praes/praslist.asp
Occupational Therapist #1 .... www.doh.state.fl.us/irm00praes/praslist.asp
Optician/Optician Apprentice #1 .... www.doh.state.fl.us/irm00praes/praslist.asp
Optometrist #1 .... www.doh.state.fl.us/irm00praes/praslist.asp
Orthotist/Prosthetist #1 .... www.doh.state.fl.us/irm00praes/praslist.asp
Osteopathic Physician/Limited Osteopath #1 .... www.doh.state.fl.us/irm00praes/praslist.asp
Paramedic #20 .... www.doh.state.fl.us/ems/emslookup.html
Pari-Mutuel Wagering #6 .... https://www.myfloridalicense.com/licensing/wl11.jsp?SID=
Pedorthist #1 .... www.doh.state.fl.us/irm00praes/praslist.asp
Pest Control Operator #4 .... www.safepesticideuse.com/safety/Search/CompanySearch.asp
Pesticide Applicator #4 .... www.safepesticideuse.com/safety/Search/PersonSearch.asp
Pesticide Applicator (Com., Private, Public) #32 ...... http://safepesticideuse.com/safety/default.htm
Pesticide Dealer #32 .... http://safepesticideuse.com/safety/default.htm
Pharmacist, Consulting #1 .... www.doh.state.fl.us/irm00praes/praslist.asp
Pharmacist/Pharmacist Intern #1 .... www.doh.state.fl.us/irm00praes/praslist.asp
Physical Therapist/Assistant #1 .... www.doh.state.fl.us/irm00praes/praslist.asp
Physician Assistant #1 .... www.doh.state.fl.us/irm00praes/praslist.asp
Physicist, Medical #1 .... www.doh.state.fl.us/irm00praes/praslist.asp
Pilot, State/Deputy #6 .... https://www.myfloridalicense.com/licensing/wl11.jsp?SID=
Plumbing Contractor #16 .... www.state.fl.us/oraweb/owa/www_dbpr2.qry_lic_menu
Polygraph Examiner #34 .... www.floridapolygraph.org/members.html
Private Investigator/Agency #18 .... http://licgweb.dos.state.fl.us/access/individual.html
Psychologist/Limited License Psychologist #1 .... www.doh.state.fl.us/irm00praes/praslist.asp
Public Accountant-CPA #21 .... https://www.myfloridalicense.com/licensing/wl11.jsp?SID=
Racing, Dog/Horse #6 .... https://www.myfloridalicense.com/licensing/wl11.jsp?SID=
Real Estate Appraiser #24 .... www.state.fl.us/oraweb/owa/www_dbpr2.qry_lic_menu
Real Estate Broker/Salesperson #24 .... www.state.fl.us/oraweb/owa/www_dbpr2.qry_lic_menu
Recovery Agent School/Instructor/Mgr. #18 .... http://licgweb.dos.state.fl.us/access/agency.html
Recovery Agent/Agency/Intern #18 .... http://licgweb.dos.state.fl.us/access/agency.html
Respiratory Care Therapist/Provider #1 .... www.doh.state.fl.us/irm00praes/praslist.asp
Roofing Contractor #16 .... www.state.fl.us/oraweb/owa/www_dbpr2.qry_lic_menu
Sales Finance Company #5 .... www.dbf.state.fl.us/licensing/
Savings & Loan Association, Charter #5 .... www.dbf.state.fl.us/cf/dogi/Inst_search.cfm
School Psychologist #1 .... www.doh.state.fl.us/irm00praes/praslist.asp
Security Officer School #18 .... http://licgweb.dos.state.fl.us/access/agency.html
Security Officer/Instructor #18 .... http://licgweb.dos.state.fl.us/access/individual.html
Social Worker, Clinical #1 .... www.doh.state.fl.us/irm00praes/praslist.asp
Solar Energy Contractor #16 .... www.state.fl.us/oraweb/owa/www_dbpr2.qry_lic_menu
Speech-Language Pathologist/Audiologist #1 .... www.doh.state.fl.us/irm00praes/praslist.asp
Surveyor, Mapping #6 .... https://www.myfloridalicense.com/licensing/wl11.jsp?SID=
Swimming Pool/Spa Contractor #16 .... www.state.fl.us/oraweb/owa/www_dbpr2.qry_lic_menu
Talent Agency #6 .... https://www.myfloridalicense.com/licensing/wl11.jsp?SID=
Therapeutic Radiologic Physician #1 .... www.doh.state.fl.us/irm00praes/praslist.asp
Tobacco Wholesale #6 .... https://www.myfloridalicense.com/licensing/wl11.jsp?SID=
Trust Company #5 .... www.dbf.state.fl.us/cf/dogi/Inst_search.cfm
Underground Utility Contractor #16 .... www.state.fl.us/oraweb/owa/www_dbpr2.qry_lic_menu
Veterinarian/Veterinary Establishment #6 .... https://www.myfloridalicense.com/licensing/wl11.jsp?SID=
Yacht & Ship Broker/Salesman #6 .... https://www.myfloridalicense.com/licensing/wl11.jsp?SID=

Licensing Quick Finder

Acupuncturist #1 850-488-0595
Adoption Service #9 850-921-2594
Adult & Foster Care #9 850-921-2594
Air Ambulance #20 850-245-4440
Air Conditioning Contractor #16 904-727-6530
Alarm System Contractor #6 850-455-6685
Alcoholic Beverage Permit #6 850-487-6793
Ambulance Service #20.......................850-245-4440
Animal Registration (Livestock Marks/Brands) #3
....850-922-0187
Architectural Firm #30 850-487-1395
Asbestos Remover/Contractor #16 850-921-6347
Asbestos Surveyor Consultant #16 850-921-6347
Assisted Living Facility #26 850-487-2515
Athletic Agent #6................................850-488-8500
Athletic Trainer #1.............................850-488-0595
Attorney #23 850-487-1292
Auction Company #22 850-488-5189
Auctioneer #22.....................................850-488-5189
Automobile Dealer, New #13................850-488-4958
Automobile Dealer/Sales #13...............850-488-4958
Automobile Repossessor #18 850-488-5381
Bail Bondsman #14 850-922-3137
Bank #5..850-410-9805
Barber/Barber Assist./Barber Shop #6 ..850-488-6888
Boxer #6..850-488-8500
Broker Dealer/Branch Office #5 850-410-9805
Broker/Dealer/Associated Person #5...850-410-9805
Building Code Administrator #6............850-922-5335
Building Contractor #16 904-727-6530
Building Inspector #6...........................850-922-5335
Cemetery Lot Salesperson #5..............850-410-9898
Child Care Center #10..........................850-487-3166
Child Care/Child Placing Facility #9 850-921-2594
Chiropractor #1 850-488-0595
Clinical Lab Personnel #1.....................850-488-0595
Clinical Laboratory #26.........................850-487-3063
Collection Agency #5...........................850-410-9805
Community Association Manager #6....850-922-5335
Company in Receivership #14 800-882-3054
Concealed Weapon License #18 850-488-5381
Construction Business #16...................904-727-6530
Contractor, General #16 904-727-6530
Cosmetologist, Hair Braider, Nails/Salon #6
....850-488-5702
Credit Union #5...................................850-410-9805
Crematory #6 850-488-8690
Day Care Center/Child Care Center/Nursery School
#10..850-487-3166
Dentist/Dental Assistant #1 850-488-0595
Dietician/Nutritionist #1 850-488-0595
Doctor, Limited License #1 850-488-0595
Electrical Contractor #16 850-488-3109
Electrologist/Electrologist Facility #1 850-488-0595
Elevator Certificates of Operation #6 ...904-488-9097
Embalmer #6 850-488-8690
Emerg. Insect Sting Treatment #20......850-245-4440
Emergency Medical Technician #20 850-245-4440
Engineer
Engineers #33.....................................850-521-0500
Engineering Firm #33 850-521-0500
Feed Distributor #32............................850-488-7626
Fertilizer Distributor #32......................850-487-2085
Finance Company, Consumer #5.........850-410-9805
Financial Institution #5.........................850-410-9805

Fire Equipment Dealer/Installer #14.....850-922-3172
Firearms Instructor #18 850-488-5381
Firearms License, Statewide #18........850-488-5381
Fishing, Commercial Fresh Water #25..904-488-4066
Food Services Establishment #6..........850-922-5335
Foster Family Home #9 850-921-2594
Fumigation Performance Special ID #4 850-921-4177
Funeral Director, Funeral Home #6......850-488-8690
Geologist/Geology Firm #6..................850-488-1105
Guidance Counselor #2.......................850-488-2317
Health Facility #26 850-487-2527
Hearing Aid Specialist #1 850-488-0595
Home Health Care Agency #26 850-414-6010
Hospital #26 850-487-2717
Hotel/Restaurant #6 850-488-7891
In Home Family Day Care Center #10..850-487-3166
Installment Seller, Retail #5.................850-410-9805
Insurance Adjuster/Agent/Title Agent #14
....904-922-3137
Insurance-related Company #14..........904-922-3137
Interior Design Business/Individual #30 850-487-1395
International Bank Office #5..................850-410-9805
Investment Advisor (Credit Unions) #5 .850-410-9805
Investment/Securities Dealer #5 850-410-9805
Kickboxer #6..850-488-8500
Lab License #26 850-487-3109
Landscape Architecture, Business/Individual #30
....850-487-1395
Landscape Maint. & Pest Control Mgmt. Co. #4
....850-921-4177
Liquor Store #6....................................850-488-8288
Livestock Hauler #3.............................850-922-0187
Lobbyist/Principal #28 850-922-4990
Lodging Establishment #6 850-922-5335
LPG-Liquefied Petroleum Gas Licensing #32
....850-488-0645
Marriage & Family Therapist #1...........850-488-0595
Massage Therapist/School/Facility #1 ..850-488-0595
Mechanical Contractor #16 904-727-6530
Medical Doctor #1................................850-488-0595
Medical Faculty Certificate #1 850-488-0595
Mental Health Counselor #1.................850-488-0595
Midwife #1 850-488-0595
Milk Hauler/Tester #31 850-487-1450
Mobile Home Dealer/Broker/Mfg #13...850-488-4958
Money Transmitter #5 850-410-9805
Mortgage Broker School #5..................850-410-9805
Mortgage Broker/Firm #5 850-410-9805
Motel/Restaurant #7............................904-488-1133
Motel/Restaurant #6............................904-488-1133
Nail Specialist #6.................................850-922-5335
Naturopath #1......................................850-488-0595
Notary Public #19 850-488-7521
Nuclear Radiology Physicist #1............850-488-0595
Nurse #1 850-488-0595
Nurse, Practical #1 850-488-0595
Nursing Assistant #1 850-488-0595
Nursing Home Administrator #1 850-488-0595
Nutrition Counselor #1.........................850-488-0595
Occupational Therapist #1 850-488-0595
Optician/Optician Apprentice #1...........850-488-0595
Optometrist #1 850-488-0595
Organic Certifying Agent #32 850-488-3863
Orphanage #9.......................................850-921-2594
Orthotist/Prosthetist #1 850-488-0595

Osteopathic Physician/Limited Osteopathic Physician
#1...850-488-0595
Paramedic #20 850-245-4440
Pari-Mutuel Wagering #6 850-488-9161
Pedorthist #1 850-488-0595
Pest Control Operator #4 850-921-4177
Pest Control, Structural #4...................850-921-4177
Pesticide Applicator #4........................850-921-4177
Pesticide Applicator (Commercial, Private, Public) #32
....850-487-0532
Pesticide Dealer #32 850-487-0532
Pet Shop #25..904-488-6253
Pharmacist, Consulting #1 850-488-0595
Pharmacist/Pharmacist Intern #1.........850-488-0595
PHPC Public Health Pest Control #4 ...850-921-4177
Physical Therapist/Assistant #1 850-488-0595
Physician Assistant #1 850-488-0595
Physicist, Medical #1...........................850-488-0595
Pilot, State/Deputy #6 850-488-0698
Plumbing Contractor #16 904-727-6530
Polygraph Examiner #34......................954-321-4264
Private Investigator/Agency #18 850-488-5381
Psychologist/Limited License Psychologist #1
....850-488-0595
Public Accountant-CPA #21.................850-487-1395
Racing, Dog/Horse #6..........................850-488-9130
Real Estate Appraiser #24 407-245-0800
Real Estate Broker/Salesperson #24...407-245-0800
Recovery Agent School/Instructor/Mgr. #18
....850-488-5381
Recovery Agent/Agency/Intern #18 850-488-5381
Recreational Vehicle Dealer #13 850-488-4958
Respiratory Care Therapist/Provider #1
....850-488-0595
Roofing Contractor #16 904-727-6530
Sales Finance Company #5 850-410-9805
Savings & Loan Association, Charter #5
....850-410-9805
School Admin./Supervisor #2...............850-488-2317
School Educ. Media Specialist #2........850-487-4822
School Principal #2...............................850-488-2317
School Psychologist #1 850-488-0595
Securities Registration #5....................850-410-9805
Security Officer School #18..................850-488-5381
Security Officer/Instructor #18 850-488-5381
Seed Dealer #32..................................850-488-3863
Social Worker, Clinical #1 850-488-0595
Solar Energy Contractor #16 904-727-6530
Solid Waste Facility Operator #8 850-922-6104
Speech-Language Pathologist/Audiologist #1
....850-488-0595
Surveyor, Mapping #6..........................850-413-7480
Sweepstakes Operator (Game Promotions) #18
....850-488-5381
Swimming Pool/Spa Contractor #16 904-727-6530
Talent Agency #6 850-922-5335
Teacher #2 850-487-4822
Therapeutic Radiologic Physician #1...850-488-0595
Timeshare Agent #5.............................850-410-9805
Tobacco Wholesale #6.........................850-487-6793
Trust Company #5................................850-410-9805
Underground Utility Contractor #16 904-727-6530
Veterinarian/Veterinary Estbl. #6 850-487-1820
Yacht & Ship Broker/Salesman #6.......850-488-1636
Zoo #25..904-488-6253

Licensing Agency Information

#1 Department of Health, Division of Medical Quality Assurance, 4052 Bald Cypress Way, Tallahassee, FL 32399; 850-488-0595. www.doh.state.flus/mqa Search database at http://www9.myflorida.com/Mqa/PRAES/index.html

#2 Education Center, Bureau of Teacher Certification, 325 W Gaines, #701, Tallahassee, FL 32399; 850-201-7400.

#3 Department of Agriculture & Consumer Services, Division of Animal Industry, 407 S Calhoun, Mayo Bldg, Rm 335, Tallahassee, FL 32399-0800; 850-410-0900, Fax: 850-487-3641. http://doacs.state.fl.us/ai/ai.html Agency email: brown@doacs.state.fl.us.

#4 Department of Agriculture & Consumer Services, Bureau of Entomology & Pest Control, 1203 Government Square Blvd #300, Tallahassee, FL 32301; 850-921-4177, Fax: 850-410-7024. www.floridatermitehelp.org. Agency email: galet@doacs.state.fl.us. Search database at www.safepesticideuse.com/safety/Search/PersonSearch.asp

#5 Department of Banking & Finance, 101 E Gaines St, Fletcher Bldg #636, Tallahassee, FL 32399-0350; 850-410-9805, Fax: 850-410-9914. www.dbf.state.fl.us Search database at www.dbf.state.fl.us/cf/dogi/Inst_search.cfm

#6 Department of Business & Professional Regulation, 1940 N Monroe St #300, Tallahassee, FL 32399; 850-922-5335, Fax: 850-488-1514. www.state.fl.us/dbpr Search database at https://www.myfloridalicense.com/licensing/wl11.jsp?SID=

#8 Department of Environmental Regulation, Division of Waste Management, 2600 Blair Stone Rd, Tallahassee, FL 32399-2400; 850-922-6104. www.dep.state.fl.us

#9 Department of Children & Families, Interstate Corporate Office, 1317 Winewood Blvd, Bldg 7, #220, Tallahassee, FL 32399-0700; 850-921-2594, Fax: 850-488-0751. www.state.fl.us/cf_web/ Search database at www.state.fl.us/cf_web. This agency provides an informative searchable online list of children available for adoption through them.

#10 Department of Health, 3401 W Tharp, Tallahassee, FL 32303; 850-487-3166, Fax: 850-487-3168.

#13 Department of Highway Safety & Motor Vehicles, Bureau of Field Operations, 2900 Apalachee Pkwy MS65, Tallahassee, FL 32399-0500; 850-488-4958, Fax: 850-922-9840. www.hsmv.state.fl.us Agency email: Reynolds.Ron@hsmv.state.fl.us.

#14 Department of Insurance, Bureau of Agents & Agency Licensing, 200 E Gaines St, Larsen Bldg, Tallahassee, FL 32399; 850-922-3100. www.doi.state.fl.us Search database at www.doi.state.fl.us

#16 Department of Professional Regulation, Construction Industry Licensing Board, 7960 Arlington Expwy #300, Jacksonville, FL 32211-7467; 904-727-3689, Fax: 904-727-3677. www.state.fl.us/dbpr. Agency email: cathleen.o'dowd@mail.dbpr.state.fl.us. Search database at www.state.fl.us/oraweb/owa/www_dbpr2.qry_lic_menu

#18 Department of State, Division of Licensing, 2520 N Monroe St, Tallahassee, FL 32303; 850-488-5381, Fax: 850-487-7950. http://licgweb.dos.state.fl.us Agency email: eshores@mail.dos.state.fl.us.

#19 Department of State, Bureau of Notaries Public, The Capitol Bldg, Rm 1801, Tallahassee, FL 32399-0250; 850-488-7521, Fax: 850-488-1768. http://notaries.dos.state.fl.us/index.html Search database at http://notaries.dos.state.fl.us/not001.html

#20 Emergency Medical Services, 4025 Esplanade Way Bin C-18, Tallahassee, FL 32399; 850-245-4440, Fax: 850-487-2911. www.doh.state.fl.us/ems. Agency email: lisa_vanderwerf-hourigan@doh.state.fl.us. Search database at www.doh.state.fl.us/ems/emslookup.html

#21 Department of Business & Professional Regulation, Board of Accounting, 240 NW 76th Drive, Ste. A, Gainesville, FL 32607; 850-487-1395, Fax: 352-333-2508. www.state.fl.us/dbpr/cpa/index.shtml Agency email: CallCenter@dbpr.state.fl.us. Search database at https://www.myfloridalicense.com/licensing/wl11.jsp?SID=

#22 Department of Business & Professional Regulation, Board of Auctioneers, 1940 N Monroe St, Tallahassee, FL 32399; 850-488-5189, Fax: 850-922-6959. www.state.fl.us/dbpr/pro/auct/auc_index.shtml. Agency email: Julie.Baker@dbpr.state.fl.us. Search database at www.state.fl.us/oraweb/owa/www_dbpr2.qry_lic_menu

#23 Board of Bar Examiners, 1891 Elder Ct, Tallahassee, FL 32399-1750; 850-487-1292. www.barexam.org/florida Search database at www.flabar.org/newflabar/findlawyer.html

#24 Department of Business & Professional Regulation, Real Estate Commission, 1940 N Monroe St, Tallahassee, FL 32399; 407-245-0800. www.state.fl.us/dbpr/re/frec_welcome.shtml Search database at www.state.fl.us/oraweb/owa/www_dbpr2.qry_lic_menu

#25 Game & Fresh Water Fish Commission, 2590 Executive Center Cir, Tallahassee, FL 32301; 850-488-3641, Fax: 850-414-2628. www.marinefisheries.or

#26 Facilities Licensing, Agency for Health Care Administration (AHCA), 2727 Mahan Dr, Tallahassee, FL 32308-5401; 850-487-2528, Fax: 850-410-1512. www.floridahealthstat.com Search database at www.floridahealthstat.com/qs/owa/facilitylocator.facllocator

#28 Lobbyist Registration, 111 W Madison St Rm G-68, Tallahassee, FL 32399-1425; 850-922-4990. www.leg.state.fl.us/lobbyist/index.cfm Search database at www.leg.state.fl.us/lobbyist/index.cfm

#30 Department of Professional Regulation, Bureau of Architects, Interior Desigers & Landscape Architects, 1940 N Monroe St, Tallahassee, FL 32399-0751; 850-487-1395. www.state.fl.us/dbpr/pro/arch/arc_index.shtml

#31 Department of Agriculture & Consumer Services, Division of Dairy Industry, 3125 Conner Blvd, Mail Stop C-27, Tallahassee, FL 32399-1650; 850-487-1450, Fax: 850-922-9444. http://doacs.state.fl.us/~dairy/index.html

#32 Agricultural and Environmental Division, Bureau of Compliance Monitoring, 3125 Conner Blvd, Bldg 8, Tallahassee, FL 32399-1650; 850-488-8731. http://doacs.state.fl.us/onestop/index.html

#33 Board of Professional Engineers, 1208 Hays Street, Tallahassee, FL 32301; 850-521-0500, Fax: 850-521-0521. www.fbpe.org Search database at www.fbpe.org/pesearch/Pesearch.htm

#34 Florida Polygraph Association, Lt. Scott A. Gooding, BCSO, 2601 West Broward Boulevard, Ft. Lauderdale, FL 33311; 954-321-4264, Fax: 954-321-4566. www.floridapolygraph.org/index.shtml Search database at www.floridapolygraph.org/members.html

Florida Federal Courts

The following list indicates the district and division name for each county in the state. If the bankruptcy court location is different from the district court, then the location of the bankruptcy court appears in parentheses.

County/Court Cross Reference

County	District	Division
Alachua	Northern	Gainesville (Tallahassee)
Baker	Middle	Jacksonville
Bay	Northern	Panama City (Tallahassee)
Bradford	Middle	Jacksonville
Brevard	Middle	Orlando
Broward	Southern	Fort Lauderdale (Miami)
Calhoun	Northern	Panama City (Tallahassee)
Charlotte	Middle	Fort Myers (Tampa)
Citrus	Middle	Ocala (Jacksonville)
Clay	Middle	Jacksonville
Collier	Middle	Fort Myers (Tampa)
Columbia	Middle	Jacksonville
Dade	Southern	Miami
De Soto	Middle	Fort Myers (Tampa)
Dixie	Northern	Gainesville (Tallahassee)
Duval	Middle	Jacksonville
Escambia	Northern	Pensacola
Flagler	Middle	Jacksonville
Franklin	Northern	Tallahassee
Gadsden	Northern	Tallahassee
Gilchrist	Northern	Gainesville (Tallahassee)
Glades	Middle	Fort Myers (Tampa)
Gulf	Northern	Panama City (Tallahassee)
Hamilton	Middle	Jacksonville
Hardee	Middle	Tampa
Hendry	Middle	Fort Myers (Tampa)
Hernando	Middle	Tampa
Highlands	Southern	Fort Pierce (Miami)
Hillsborough	Middle	Tampa
Holmes	Northern	Panama City (Tallahassee)
Indian River	Southern	Fort Pierce (Miami)
Jackson	Northern	Panama City (Tallahassee)
Jefferson	Northern	Tallahassee
Lafayette	Northern	Gainesville (Tallahassee)
Lake	Middle	Ocala (Orlando)
Lee	Middle	Fort Myers (Tampa)
Leon	Northern	Tallahassee
Levy	Northern	Gainesville (Tallahassee)
Liberty	Northern	Tallahassee
Madison	Northern	Tallahassee
Manatee	Middle	Tampa
Marion	Middle	Ocala (Jacksonville)
Martin	Southern	Fort Pierce (Miami)
Monroe	Southern	Key West (Miami)
Nassau	Middle	Jacksonville
Okaloosa	Northern	Pensacola
Okeechobee	Southern	Fort Pierce (Miami)
Orange	Middle	Orlando
Osceola	Middle	Orlando
Palm Beach	Southern	W. Palm Beach (Miami)
Pasco	Middle	Tampa
Pinellas	Middle	Tampa
Polk	Middle	Tampa
Putnam	Middle	Jacksonville
Santa Rosa	Northern	Pensacola
Sarasota	Middle	Tampa
Seminole	Middle	Orlando
St. Johns	Middle	Jacksonville
St. Lucie	Southern	Fort Pierce (Miami)
Sumter	Middle	Ocala (Jacksonville)
Suwannee	Middle	Jacksonville
Taylor	Northern	Tallahassee
Union	Middle	Jacksonville
Volusia	Middle	Orlando (Jacksonville)
Wakulla	Northern	Tallahassee
Walton	Northern	Pensacola
Washington	Northern	Panama City (Tallahassee)

Standards for Federal Courts: The search fee is $20.00 per item (one party name or case number). Certification fee is $7.00 per document. Copy fee is $.50 per page. All fees standard unless noted in profile. Mail Search: always enclose a stamped self addressed envelope unless otherwise noted. Before releasing records, all courts require prepayment unless noted in profile.

Open records are located at the court unless otherwise noted. District courts index by defendant and plaintiff as well as by case number. Bankruptcy courts usually index by debtor and case number. While most courts now have their indexes on computer, many still maintain index card files as well.

The universal PACER sign-up number is 800-676-6856. Find PACER and the Party/Case Index on the Web at http://pacer.psc.uscourts.gov. PACER dial-up access is $.60 per minute. Also, courts offering internet access via RACER, PACER, Web-PACER or the new CM-ECF charge $.07 per page fee unless noted as free.

US District Court

Middle District of Florida

Fort Myers Division 2110 First St, Room 2-194, Fort Myers, FL 33901 (Courier Address: Use mail address for courier delivery), 239-461-2000.

www.flmd.uscourts.gov

Counties: Charlotte, Collier, De Soto, Glades, Hendry, Lee.

Indexing & Storage: Cases are indexed by defendant, plaintiff, and case number. New cases are available in the index immediately after filing date. The civil case index is computerized, but the criminal index is not. Records are also indexed on microfiche. Open records are located at this court.

Fee & Payment Notes: Payment may be made by money order, cashier check, personal check. Payee: Clerk, US District Court. You are allowed

to make your own copies. These copies cost - current fee is not known - per page.

Phone Search: Docket information is available by phone.

In Person Search: In person searching available.

PACER: Toll-free dial-up access: 888-815-8701. Local dial-up access: 813-301-5820. Case records are available back to 1989-90. Records are purged three years after case closed. New records are available online after 1 day. PACER is available online at http://pacer.flmd.uscourts.gov.

Jacksonville Division PO Box 53558, Jacksonville, FL 32201 (Courier Address: Suite 110, 311 W Monroe St, Jacksonville, FL 32202), 904-549-1900.

www.flmd.uscourts.gov

Counties: Baker, Bradford, Clay, Columbia, Duval, Flagler, Hamilton, Nassau, Putnam, St. Johns, Suwannee, Union.

Indexing & Storage: Cases are indexed by defendant, plaintiff, and case number. New cases are available in the index 1 day after filing date. Open records are located at this court.

Fee & Payment Notes: Payment may be made by money order, cashier check, personal check. Payee: Clerk, US District Court. You are allowed to make your own copies. These copies cost $.50 per page.

Phone Search: Searching not available by phone.

In Person Search: In person searching available.

PACER: Toll-free dial-up access: 888-815-8701. Local dial-up access: 813-301-5820. Case records are available back to 1989-90. Records are purged three years after case closed. New records are available online after 1 day. PACER is available online at http://pacer.flmd.uscourts.gov.

Ocala Division c/o Jacksonville Division, PO Box 53558, Jacksonville, FL 32201 (Courier Address: 311 W Monroe St, Suite 110, Jacksonville, FL 32202), 904-232-2854.

www.flmd.uscourts.gov

Counties: Citrus, Lake, Marion, Sumter.

Indexing & Storage: New cases are available in the index after filing date. Open records are located at the Jacksonville Division.

Fee & Payment Notes: Payment may be made by money order, cashier check. Business checks are not accepted. Personal checks are not accepted.

Phone Search: Searching not available by phone.

In Person Search: In person searching available.

PACER: Toll-free dial-up access: 888-815-8701. Local dial-up access: 813-301-5820. Case records are available back to 1989-90. Records are purged three years after case closed. New records are available online after 1 day. PACER is available online at http://pacer.flmd.uscourts.gov.

Orlando Division Room 218, 80 North Hughey Ave, Orlando, FL 32801 (Courier Address: Use mail address for courier delivery), 407-835-4200.

www.flmd.uscourts.gov

Counties: Brevard, Orange, Osceola, Seminole, Volusia.

Indexing & Storage: Cases are indexed by defendant, plaintiff, and case number. New cases are available in the index immediately after filing date. Records are stored by case number according to year closed. Open records are located at this court.

Fee & Payment Notes: Payment may be made by money order, cashier check, personal check. All checks, except foreign, are accepted. Payee: Clerk, US District Court. You are allowed to make your own copies. These copies cost $.50 per page.

Phone Search: Docket information is available by phone.

In Person Search: In person searching available.

PACER: Toll-free dial-up access: 888-815-8701. Local dial-up access: 813-301-5820. Case records are available back to 1989-90. Records are purged three years after case closed. New records are available online after 1 day. PACER is available online at http://pacer.flmd.uscourts.gov.

Tampa Division Office of the clerk, 801 N Florida Ave #223, Tampa, FL 33602-4500 (Courier Address: Use mail address for courier delivery), 813-301-5400.

www.flmd.uscourts.gov

Counties: Hardee, Hernando, Hillsborough, Manatee, Pasco, Pinellas, Polk, Sarasota.

Indexing & Storage: Cases are indexed by defendant, plaintiff, and case number. New cases are available in the index 1 day after filing date. Open records are located at this court.

Fee & Payment Notes: Payment may be made by money order, cashier check, personal check. Payee: Clerk, US District Court. You are allowed to make your own copies. These copies cost $.25 per page.

Phone Search: Only docket information is available by phone.

In Person Search: In person searching available.

PACER: Toll-free dial-up access: 888-815-8701. Local dial-up access: 813-301-5820. Case records are available back to 1989-90. Records are purged three years after case closed. New records are available online after 1 day. PACER is available online at http://pacer.flmd.uscourts.gov.

US Bankruptcy Court

Middle District of Florida

Jacksonville Division PO Box 559, Jacksonville, FL 32201 (Courier Address: Room 206, 311 W Monroe, Jacksonville, FL 32202), 904-232-2852.

www.flmb.uscourts.gov

Counties: Baker, Bradford, Citrus, Clay, Columbia, Duval, Flagler, Hamilton, Marion, Nassau, Putnam, St. Johns, Sumter, Suwannee, Union, Volusia.

Indexing & Storage: Cases are indexed by debtor as well as by case number. New cases are available in the index immediately after filing date. This court has no specific time that they send closed records to the Atlanta Federal Records Center.

Fee & Payment Notes: Payment may be made by money order, cashier check, business check. Personal checks are not accepted. Pacific Photo is the contracted search and copy center for this district; 904-355-1062. Payee: Clerk, US Bankruptcy Court.

Phone Search: An automated voice case information service (VCIS) is available. Call VCIS at 904-232-1313.

Mail Search: A stamped self addressed envelope is not required.

In Person Search: In person searching available.

PACER: Local dial-up access: 904-232-1311. Case records are available back to 1981. Records are purged every year. New civil records are available online after 1 week.

Electronic Filing: (Currently in the process of implementing CM/ECF.)

Other Online Access: Court does not participate in the U.S. party case index.

Orlando Division Suite 950, 135 W Central Blvd, Orlando, FL 32801 (Courier Address: Use mail address for courier delivery), 407-648-6365.

www.flmb.uscourts.gov

Counties: Brevard, Lake, Orange, Osceola, Seminole.

Indexing & Storage: Cases are indexed by debtor and creditors as well as by case number. New cases are available in the index 1-2 days after filing date. This court has no specific time that they send closed records to the Atlanta Federal Records Center.

Fee & Payment Notes: Payment may be made by money order, cashier check, business check. Personal checks are not accepted. Pacific Photo is the contracted search and copy center for this district; 904-355-1062. Payee: Clerk, US Bankruptcy Court.

Phone Search: An automated voice case information service (VCIS) is available. Call VCIS at 407-648-6800.

In Person Search: In person searching available.

PACER: Local dial-up access: 407-648-6212. Case records are available back to 1986. Records are never purged. New civil records are available online after 1 day.

Electronic Filing: (Currently in the process of implementing CM/ECF.)

Other Online Access: Court does not participate in the U.S. party case index.

Tampa Division 801 N Florida Ave #727, Tampa, FL 33602 (Courier Address: Use mail address for courier delivery), 813-301-5065.

www.flmb.uscourts.gov

Counties: Charlotte, Collier, De Soto, Glades, Hardee, Hendry, Hernando, Hillsborough, Lee, Manatee, Pasco, Pinellas, Polk, Sarasota.

Indexing & Storage: Cases are indexed by debtor as well as by case number. New cases are available in the index immediately after filing date. This court has no specific time that they send closed records to the Atlanta Federal Records Center.

Fee & Payment Notes: Payment may be made by money order, cashier check, business check. Personal checks are not accepted. Pacific Photo is the contracted search and copy center for this district; 904-355-1062. Payee: Clerk, US Bankruptcy Court.

Phone Search: An automated voice case information service (VCIS) is available. Call VCIS at 813-301-5210.

In Person Search: In person searching available.

PACER: Local dial-up access: 813-301-5206. Case records are available back to 1992. Records are purged every six months. New civil records are available online after 1 day.

Electronic Filing: (Currently in the process of implementing CM/ECF.)

Other Online Access: Court does not participate in the U.S. party case index.

US District Court

Northern District of Florida

Gainesville Division 401 SE First Ave, Room 243, Gainesville, FL 32601 (Courier Address: Use mail address for courier delivery), 352-380-2400, Fax: 352-380-2424.

www.flnd.uscourts.gov

Counties: Alachua, Dixie, Gilchrist, Lafayette, Levy. Records for cases prior to July 1996 are maintained at the Tallahassee Division.

Indexing & Storage: Cases are indexed by defendant, plaintiff, and case number. New cases are available in the index 3 days after filing date. Open records are located at this court.

Fee & Payment Notes: Payment may be made by money order, cashier check, personal check. Payee: Clerk, US District Court.

Phone Search: Only 1-3 names may be searched over the phone, and only docket information will be released.

In Person Search: In person searching available.

PACER: Toll-free dial-up access: 800-844-0479. Local dial-up access: 850-942-8897. Case records are available back to 1992. Records are purged three years after case closed. New records are available online after 2 days. PACER is available online at http://pacer.flnd.uscourts.gov.

Panama City Division 30 W. Government St., Panama City, FL 32401 (Courier Address: Use mail address for courier delivery), 850-769-4556, Fax: 850-769-7528.

www.flnd.uscourts.gov

Counties: Bay, Calhoun, Gulf, Holmes, Jackson, Washington.

Indexing & Storage: New cases are available in the index after filing date. Open records are located at this court.

Fee & Payment Notes: Payment may be made by money order, cashier check. Business checks are not accepted. Personal checks are not accepted.

Phone Search: Searching not available by phone.

In Person Search: In person searching available.

PACER: Toll-free dial-up access: 800-844-0479. Local dial-up access: 850-942-8897. Case records are available back to 1992. Records are purged three years after case closed. New records are available online after 2 days. PACER is available online at http://pacer.flnd.uscourts.gov.

Pensacola Division US Courthouse, 1 N Palafox St, #226, Pensacola, FL 32501 (Courier Address: Use mail address for courier delivery), 850-435-8440, Fax: 850-433-5972.

www.flnd.uscourts.gov

Counties: Escambia, Okaloosa, Santa Rosa, Walton.

Indexing & Storage: Cases are indexed by defendant, plaintiff, and case number. New cases are available in the index 2-3 days after filing date. Records are indexed on computer as of August 1992. District wide searches are available for information from August 1992 from this division. This division maintains records for the Panama City office.

Fee & Payment Notes: Payment may be made by money order, cashier check, personal check. Payee: Clerk, US District Court.

Phone Search: Only basic information is released over the phone. They will not release all docket information over the phone.

In Person Search: In person searching available.

PACER: Toll-free dial-up access: 800-844-0479. Local dial-up access: 850-942-8897. Case records are available back to 1992. Records are purged three years after case closed. New records are available online after 2 days. PACER is available online at http://pacer.flnd.uscourts.gov.

Tallahassee Division Suite 122, 110 E Park Ave, Tallahassee, FL 32301 (Courier Address: Use mail address for courier delivery), 850-942-8826, Fax: 850-942-8830.

www.flnd.uscourts.gov

Counties: Franklin, Gadsden, Jefferson, Leon, Liberty, Madison, Taylor, Wakulla.

Indexing & Storage: Cases are indexed by defendant, plaintiff, and case number. New cases are available in the index immediately after filing date. Records are also indexed by year closed. Open records are located at this court.

Fee & Payment Notes: Payment may be made by money order, cashier check, personal check. Payee: Clerk, US District Court.

Phone Search: Basic information about a case requested by name (case number) or by case number (names of parties or their attorneys, date of complaint, or general status) is available by telephone at no charge.

Mail Search: A stamped self addressed envelope is not required.

In Person Search: In person searching available.

PACER: Toll-free dial-up access: 800-844-0479. Local dial-up access: 850-942-8897. Case records are available back to 1992. Records are purged three years after case closed. New records are available online after 2 days. PACER is available online at http://pacer.flnd.uscourts.gov.

US Bankruptcy Court

Northern District of Florida

Pensacola Division Suite 700, 220 W Garden St, Pensacola, FL 32501 (Courier: Use mail address for courier delivery), 850-435-8475.

www.flnb.uscourts.gov/

Counties: Escambia, Okaloosa, Santa Rosa, Walton.

Indexing & Storage: Cases are indexed by debtor as well as by case number. New cases are available in the index 5-7 days after filing date. Open records are located at this court.

Fee & Payment Notes: Payment may be made by money order, cashier check, business check. Personal checks are not accepted. Payee: Clerk, US Bankruptcy Court.

Phone Search: An automated voice case information service (VCIS) is available. Call VCIS at 850-942-8358.

Mail Search: A stamped self addressed envelope is not required.

In Person Search: In person searching available.

PACER: Sign-up number is 904-435-8475. Toll-free dial-up access: 888-765-1751. Local dial-up access: 850-444-0189. Use of PC Anywhere V4.0 recommended. Password is bkc for version 7.5; password is bkcpc for version 8.0. Case records are available back to September 1985. Records are purged when cases are closed. New civil records are available online after 2 days. PACER is available online at http://pacer.flnb.uscourts.gov.

Tallahassee Division Room 3120, 227 N Bronough St, Tallahassee, FL 32301-1378 (Courier Address: Use mail address for courier delivery), 850-942-8933.

www.flnb.uscourts.gov/

Counties: Alachua, Bay, Calhoun, Dixie, Franklin, Gadsden, Gilchrist, Gulf, Holmes, Jackson, Jefferson, Lafayette, Leon, Levy, Liberty, Madison, Taylor, Wakulla, Washington.

Indexing & Storage: Cases are indexed by debtor as well as by case number. New cases are available

in the index 2-3 days after filing date. Open records are located at this court.

Fee & Payment Notes: Payment may be made by money order, cashier check, business check. Personal checks are not accepted. Payee: Clerk, US Bankruptcy Court.

Phone Search: Only docket information is available by phone. An automated voice case information service (VCIS) is available. Call VCIS at 850-942-8358.

In Person Search: In person searching available.

PACER: Toll-free dial-up access: 888-765-1752. Local dial-up access: 850-942-8815. Use of PC Anywhere V4.0 recommended. Password is bkc for version 7.5; password is bkcpc for version 8.0. Case records are available back to September 23, 1985. Records are purged every six months. New civil records are available online after 1 day. PACER is available online at http://pacer.flnb.uscourts.gov.

US District Court

Southern District of Florida

Fort Lauderdale Division 299 E Broward Blvd, Fort Lauderdale, FL 33301 (Courier Address: Use mail address for courier delivery), 954-769-5400.

www.flsd.uscourts.gov

Counties: Broward.

Indexing & Storage: Cases are indexed by defendant, plaintiff, and case number. New cases are available in the index immediately after filing date. The full name of any party of the case, case number or case type is required to search for records. Civil cases are in the computer from August 1990 to present. Criminal cases are in the computer from January 1992. Cases from 1983 are on microfiche. Cases prior to 1983 are on microfilm. Records that are more than 5 years old are, at the discretion of the clerk, sent to the Atlanta Federal Records Center. Call records department to get location of records.

Fee & Payment Notes: Payment may be made by money order, cashier check, business check, Visa, Mastercard. Personal checks are not accepted. Payee: U.S. Courts. You are allowed to make your own copies. These copies cost $.25 per page. The copy service (954-832-0111) will pull records and make copies for $.25 per copy. Copy machines are also available in the lobby.

Phone Search: Searching not available by phone. Only docket information is available by phone.

In Person Search: In person searching available.

PACER: Toll-free dial-up access: 800-372-8846. Local dial-up access: 305-536-7265. Case records are available back to August 1990. Records are purged three years after case closed. New records are available online after 1 day. PACER is available online at http://pacer.flsd.uscourts.gov. Document images available.

Fort Pierce Division c/o Miami Division, Room 150, 301 N Miami Ave, Miami, FL 33128 (Courier Address: Use mail address for courier delivery), 305-523-5210.

www.flsd.uscourts.gov

Counties: Highlands, Indian River, Martin, Okeechobee, St. Lucie.

Indexing & Storage: Cases are indexed by defendant, plaintiff, and case number. New cases are available in the index immediately after filing date. Open records are located at the Miami Division. Records are transferred to the Federal Records Center any time after 5 years at the discretion of the clerk.

Fee & Payment Notes: Payment may be made by money order, cashier check, personal check. Payee: US Court.

Phone Search: Docket information is available by phone.

In Person Search: In person searching available.

PACER: Toll-free dial-up access: 800-372-8846. Local dial-up access: 305-536-7265. Case records are available back to August 1990. Records are purged three years after case closed. New records are available online after 1 day. PACER is available online at http://pacer.flsd.uscourts.gov. Document images available.

Key West Division 301 Simonton St., Key West, FL 33040 (Courier Address: Use mail address for courier delivery), 305-295-8100.

www.flsd.uscourts.gov

Counties: Monroe.

Indexing & Storage: Cases are indexed by defendant, plaintiff, and case number. New cases are available in the index immediately after filing date. The full name of either party in the case, case number or case type is required to search for records. Open records are located at the Division. Records that are more than 5 years old are, at the discretion of the clerk, are sent to the Atlanta Federal Records Center. Call records department to get location of records.

Fee & Payment Notes: Payment may be made by money order, cashier check, personal check. Payee: U.S. Courts. You are allowed to make your own copies. These copies cost $.50 per page. The copy service will pull records and make copies for $.04 per copy. Copy machines are also available in the lobby.

Phone Search: Searching not available by phone.

In Person Search: In person searching available.

PACER: Toll-free dial-up access: 800-372-8846. Local dial-up access: 305-536-7265. Case records are available back to August 1990. Records are purged three years after case closed. New records are available online after 1 day. PACER is available online at http://pacer.flsd.uscourts.gov. Document images available.

Miami Division Room 150, 301 N Miami Ave, Miami, FL 33128-7788 (Courier Address: Use mail address for courier delivery), 305-523-5700.

www.flsd.uscourts.gov

Counties: Dade.

Indexing & Storage: Cases are indexed by defendant, plaintiff, and case number. New cases are available in the index 1 day after filing date. The full name of either party in the case, case number or case type is required to search for records. Records that are more than 5 years old are, at the discretion of the clerk, sent to the Atlanta Federal Records Center. Call records department to get location of records.

Fee & Payment Notes: Payment may be made by money order, cashier check, personal check, Visa, Mastercard. Payee: U.S. Courts. You are allowed to make your own copies. These copies cost $.25 per page. Copy machines are also available in the lobby area of the Records and Docketing Section. There is also an on-site copy service that can pull records and make copies. Call for more information.

Phone Search: Only docket information is available by phone.

In Person Search: In person searching available.

PACER: Toll-free dial-up access: 800-372-8846. Local dial-up access: 305-536-7265. Case records are available back to August 1990. Records are purged three years after case closed. New records are available online after 1 day. PACER is available online at http://pacer.flsd.uscourts.gov. Document images available.

West Palm Beach Division Room 402, 701 Clematis St, West Palm Beach, FL 33401 (Courier Address: Use mail address for courier delivery), 561-803-3400.

www.flsd.uscourts.gov

Counties: Palm Beach.

Indexing & Storage: Cases are indexed by defendant, plaintiff, and case number. New cases are available in the index immediately after filing date. The full name of either party in the case, case number or case type is required to search for records. Open records are located at this court.

Fee & Payment Notes: Payment may be made by money order, cashier check, business check, Visa, Mastercard. Personal checks are not accepted. Payee: U.S. Courts. You are allowed to make your own copies. These copies cost $.50 per page. A copy service is available to pull records and make

copies. Copy machines are also available in the lobby.

Phone Search: Docket information is available by phone.

In Person Search: In person searching available.

PACER: Toll-free dial-up access: 800-372-8846. Local dial-up access: 305-536-7265. Case records are available back to August 1990. Records are purged three years after case closed. New records are available online after 1 day. PACER is available online at http://pacer.flsd.uscourts.gov. Document images available.

US Bankruptcy Court
Southern District of Florida

Miami Division Room 1517, 51 SW 1st Ave, Miami, FL 33130 (Courier Address: Use mail address for courier delivery), 305-536-5216.

www.flsb.uscourts.gov

Counties: Broward, Dade, Highlands, Indian River, Martin, Monroe, Okeechobee, Palm Beach, St. Lucie. Cases may also be assigned to Fort Lauderdale or to West Palm Beach.

Indexing & Storage: Cases are indexed by debtor and creditors as well as by case number. New cases are available in the index 48 hours after filing date. Open. Case records may be held in the Fort Lauderdale or West Palm Beach office, depending on the judge assigned.

Fee & Payment Notes: Payment may be made by money order, cashier check. Business checks are not accepted. Personal checks are not accepted. Checks from law firms are accepted. Payee: US Courts.

Phone Search: An automated voice case information service (VCIS) is available. Call VCIS at 800-473-0226 or 305-536-5979.

In Person Search: In person searching available.

PACER: Toll-free dial-up access: 888-443-0081. Local dial-up access: 305-536-7492. Case records are available back to 1986. Records are purged every six months. New civil records are available online after 1 day. PACER is available online at http://pacer.flsb.uscourts.gov/login.html.

Florida County Courts

Court	Jurisdiction	No. of Courts	How Organized
Circuit Courts*	General	10	20 Circuits
County Courts*	Limited	13	
Combined Courts*		81	

* Profiled in this Sourcebook.

					CIVIL				
Court	Tort	Contract	Real Estate	Min. Claim	Max. Claim	Small Claims	Estate	Eviction	Domestic Relations
Circuit Courts*	X	X	X	$15,000	No Max		X		X
County Courts*	X	X	X	$0	$15,000	$2500		X	

			CRIMINAL		
Court	Felony	Misdemeanor	DWI/DUI	Preliminary Hearing	Juvenile
Circuit Courts*	X				X
County Courts*		X	X	X	

ADMINISTRATION

Office of State Courts Administrator, Supreme Court Bldg, 500 S Duval, Tallahassee, FL, 32399-1900; 850-922-5082, Fax: 850-488-0156. www.flcourts.org

COURT STRUCTURE

All counties have combined Circuit and County Courts. The Circuit Court is the court of general jurisdiction.

ONLINE ACCESS

There is a statewide, online computer system for internal use only; there is no statewide external access available nor planned currently. A number of courts do offer online access to the public, usually, this is through the Clerk of the Circuit Court. However, the Florida Legislature mandated that court documents must be imaged and available for inspection over a publicly available website. In response to concerns of indentity theft and fraud, the Florida Legislature recently passed new laws concerning privacy of public documents on public websites. These laws now make it possible for certain of these documents viewed on the Clerk websites to be either redacted of sensitive information or in some cases removed completely. The Clerk of the Circuit Court cannot place an image or copy of the following documents on a publicly available Internet website for general public display: Military discharges; Death certificates; Court files, records or papers relating to Family Law, Juvenile Law or Probate Law cases.

ADDITIONAL INFORMATION

All courts have one address and switchboard; however, the divisions within a court are completely separate. Requesters should specify which court and which division, e.g., Circuit Civil, County Civil, etc., the request is directed to, even though some counties will automatically check both with one request.

Fees are set by statute and are as follows: Search Fee - $1.00 per name per year; Certification Fee - $1.00 per document plus copy fee; Copy Fee - $1.00 per certified page; $.15 per non-certified page.

Most courts have very lengthy phone recording systems.

📖 📖 📖 📖 📖 📖

Alachua County

Circuit & County Courts PO Box 600, Gainesville, FL 32602; Civil phone: 352-374-3636; Criminal phone: 352-374-3636; Fax: 352-338-3201. Hours: 8:30AM-5PM (EST). *Felony, Misdemeanor, Civil, Eviction, Small Claims, Probate.*

www.alachuaclerk.org

Civil Records: Access: Phone, fax, mail, online, in person. Both court and visitors may perform in person searches. Search fee: $1.00 per name per year. Required to search: name, years to search; also helpful: address. Civil cases indexed by defendant, plaintiff. Civil records on computer from 1979, some records on docket books. Search Circuit's Civil open cases free at http://circuit8.org/case/index.html by division; password

required. Contact court for information, 352-374-3636. County Clerk online access is available free at www.clerk-alachua-fl.org/clerk/pubrec.html. Civil records can be searched by name or case number.

Criminal Records: Access: Fax, mail, online, in person. Both court and visitors may perform in person searches. Search fee: $1.00 per name per year. Required to search: name, years to search, DOB; also helpful: address, SSN, race, sex. Criminal records on computer since 1974. Search the Circuit's criminal open cases free on the web at http://circuit8.org/case/index.html by division; password required. Contact court for information, 352-374-3636.

General Information: Public access terminal is available. No juvenile, child abuse or sexual battery records released. SASE required. Turnaround time 5

working days. Fax notes: Fax back fee $1.00. Copy fee: $1.00 per page. Records can be searched by name or case number Certification fee: $1.00. Fee payee: Clerk of Circuit Court. Personal checks accepted. Credit cards accepted: Visa, MasterCard. Visa, MC. Prepayment is required.

Baker County

Circuit & County Courts - Civil 339 E Macclenny Ave, Macclenny, FL 32063; 904-259-0202, 904-259-0209 (Circuit civ); Civil phone: 904-259-0208 (Cty); Probate phone: 904-259-0209; Fax: 904-259-4176. Hours: 8:30AM-5PM (EST). *Civil, Eviction, Small Claims, Probate.*

http://circuit8.org

Civil Records: Access: Mail, in person. Both the court and visitors may perform in person searches. Search fee: $1.00 per name per year. Required to search: name, years to search; also helpful: address. Civil cases indexed by defendant, plaintiff. Civil records on computer back to 1996; prior on index cards and docket books.

General Information: Public access terminal is available. No juvenile, child abuse or sexual battery records released. SASE preferred. Turnaround time 2 days. Copy fee: $1.00 per page. Certification fee: $2.00. Fee payee: Clerk of Circuit Court. Business checks accepted. Prepayment is required.

Circuit & County Courts - Criminal 339 E Macclenny Ave, Macclenny, FL 32063; 904-259-0203; Fax: 904-259-4176. Hours: 8:30AM-5PM (EST). *Felony, Misdemeanor.*

http://circuit8.org

Criminal Records: Access: Mail, in person, online. Only the court performs in person searches; visitors may not. Search fee: $1.00 per name per year. Required to search: name, years to search, DOB. Criminal records on computer since 1989. Some records on docket books. Access to the circuit-wide criminal quick lookup available at http://circuit8.org/golem/gencrim.html. Account and password is required; restricted usage.

General Information: No juvenile or guardianship records released. SASE required. Turnaround time 1-2 days. Copy fee: $1.00 per page. Certification fee: $1.00. Fee payee: Clerk of Circuit Court. Business checks accepted. Prepayment is required.

Bay County

Circuit Court - Civil PO Box 2269, Panama City, FL 32402; 850-747-5715; Fax: 850-747-5188. Hours: 8AM-5PM (CST). *Civil Actions Over $15,000, Probate.*

www.baycoclerk.com

Civil Records: Access: Phone, fax, mail, in person. Both court and visitors may perform in person searches. Search fee: $1.00 per name per year. Required to search: name, years to search. Civil cases indexed by defendant, plaintiff. Civil records on computer from 1984, on microfiche from 1950 to 1980, archived from 1913 to 1979. Some records on dockets. Online database access with images should be available in late 2002 at the web site.

General Information: No juvenile, adoption, child abuse or sexual battery records released. Turnaround time 2 days. Fax notes: $2.00 per page. Copy fee: $1.00 per page. Certification fee: $1.00. Fee payee: Clerk of Circuit Court. Personal checks accepted. Prepayment is required.

Circuit Court - Criminal PO Box 2269, Panama City, FL 32402; 850-747-5123; Fax: 850-747-5188. Hours: 8AM-4:30PM (CST). *Felony.*

www.baycoclerk.com

Criminal Records: Access: Fax, mail, in person. Both court and visitors may perform in person searches. Search fee: $1.00 per name per year. Required to search: name, years to search, DOB; also helpful: SSN, signed release. Criminal records on computer back to 1986, on microfilm from 1938 to 1982, prior archived. Online database access with images should be available in late 2002 at the web site.

General Information: No sealed, juvenile or expunged records released. SASE requested. Turnaround time 3-5 days. Fax notes: $2.00 per document. Copy fee: $1.00 per page. Certification fee: $1.00 per page. Fee payee: Clerk of Circuit Court. Personal checks accepted. Prepayment is required.

County Court - Civil PO Box 2269, Panama City, FL 32402; 850-747-5141; Fax: 850-747-5188. Hours: 8AM-4:30PM (CST). *Civil Actions Under $15,000, Eviction, Small Claims.*

www.baycoclerk.com

Civil Records: Access: Phone, fax, mail, in person. Both court and visitors may perform in person searches. Search fee: $1.00 per name per year. Required to search: name, years to search. Civil cases indexed by defendant, plaintiff. Civil records on computer from 1986, on microfiche from 1950 to 1980, archived from 1913 to 1979. Some records on docket books. Online database access with images should be available late 2002 at the web site.

General Information: Public access terminal is available. No juvenile, child abuse or sexual battery records released. SASE requested. Turnaround time 2 days. Fax notes: $2.00 per page. Copy fee: $1.00 per page. Certification fee: $1.00 per page. Fee payee: Clerk of Circuit Court. Personal checks accepted. Prepayment is required.

County Court - Misdemeanor PO Box 2269, Panama City, FL 32402; 850-747-5144; Fax: 850-747-5188. Hours: 8AM-4:30PM (CST). *Misdemeanor.*

www.baycoclerk.com

Criminal Records: Access: Phone, fax, mail, in person. Both court and visitors may perform in person searches. Search fee: $1.00 per name per year. Required to search: name, years to search; also helpful: DOB, SSN. Criminal records on computer from 1984, felonies on microfilm from 1950 to 1987, archived from 1913. Misdemeanors from 1996-present; pending cases back to 1980. Online database access with images should be available in late 2002 at the web site.

General Information: Public access terminal is available. No sealed or expunged records released. SASE requested. Turnaround time 7-10 days. Fax notes: $2.00 per document. Copy fee: $1.00 per page. Certification fee: $1.00. Fee payee: Clerk of Circuit Court. Personal checks accepted. Prepayment is required.

Bradford County

Circuit Court PO Drawer B, Starke, FL 32091; 904-964-6280; Fax: 904-964-4454. Hours: 8AM-5PM (EST). *Felony, Civil Actions Over $15,000, Probate.*

http://circuit8.org

Civil Records: Access: Phone, mail, in person. Both court and visitors may perform in person searches. Search fee: $1.00 per name per year. Required to search: name, years to search. Civil cases indexed by defendant, plaintiff. Civil records on computer since late 1987, others on index books.

Criminal Records: Access: Phone, mail, in person, online. Both court and visitors may perform in person searches. Search fee: $1.00 per name per year. Required to search: name, years to search, DOB, SSN. Criminal records on computer since 1989, others on index books. Access to the circuit-wide criminal quick lookup available at http://circuit8.org/golem/gencrim.html. Account and password is required; restricted usage.

General Information: No juvenile, child abuse or sexual battery records released. SASE required. Turnaround time 1 week. Copy fee: $1.00 per page. Certification fee: $1.00 per document. Fee payee: Clerk at Circuit Court. Business checks accepted. Prepayment is required.

County Court PO Drawer B, Starke, FL 32091; 904-964-6280; Fax: 904-964-4454. Hours: 8AM-5PM (EST). *Misdemeanor, Civil Actions Under $15,000, Eviction, Small Claims.*

www.bradford-co-fla.org

Civil Records: Access: Mail, fax, in person, online. Both court and visitors may perform in person searches.

Search fee: $1.00 per name per year. Required to search: name, years to search. Civil cases indexed by defendant, plaintiff. Civil records on computer back to 1988. Some records on docket books, some microfiche. Access to court records from the County Clerk is available free at www.myfloridacounty.com/services/officialrecords_intro.shtml.

Criminal Records: Access: Mail, fax, in person. Both court and visitors may perform in person searches. Search fee: $1.00 per name per year. Required to search: name, years to search, DOB, SSN. Criminal records on computer back to 1988. Some records on docket books.

General Information: No juvenile records released. SASE required. Turnaround time 2 days. Copy fee: $1.00 per page. Certification fee: $1.00 per document. Fee payee: Clerk of Court. Business checks accepted. Prepayment is required.

Brevard County

Circuit Court - Civil PO Box 2767, Offical Records Copy Desk, Titusville, FL 32781-2767; 321-264-5245; Fax: 321-264-5246. Hours: 8AM-5PM (EST). *Civil, Eviction, Small Claims, Probate.*

www.clerk.co.brevard.fl.us

Civil Records: Access: Phone, fax, mail, online, in person. Both court and visitors may perform in person searches. Search fee: $1.00 per name per year. Required to search: name, years to search. Civil cases indexed by defendant, plaintiff. Civil records on computer since 1987, on microfiche since early 1900s. Some records on docket books. Access County Court records free from FACTSweb at www.clerk.co.brevard.fl.us/pages/facts1.htm. Online records back to 1988 can be searched by name, case number or citation number.

General Information: Public access terminal is available. No juvenile, child abuse or sexual battery victim records released. SASE not required. Turnaround time 1 week. Fax notes: $2.00 for first page, $1.00 each add'l. Fax fee for long distance $3.00 1st page, $1.00 each additional page. Copy fee: $1.00 per page. Certification fee: $1.00. Fee payee: Circuit Clerk. Personal checks accepted. Check by fax or phone accepted. Credit cards accepted: Visa, MasterCard, Discover. Prepayment is required.

Circuit Court - Felony PO Box 999, 700 S Park Ave, Titusville, FL 32781; 321-264-5350; Fax: 321-264-5395. Hours: 8AM-5PM (EST). *Felony.*

www.clerk.co.brevard.fl.us

Criminal Records: Access: Phone, fax, mail, online, in person. Both court and visitors may perform in person searches. Search fee: $1.00 per name per year. Required to search: name, DOB, SSN. Criminal records on computer since 1988, on microfiche from early 1900s. Some records on docket books. Online access to county criminal court records available free through FACTSweb at www.clerk.co.brevard.fl.us/pages/facts1.htm. Search by name, case number or citation number.

General Information: Public access terminal is available. No juvenile, child abuse, sexual battery or adoption records released. SASE not required. Turnaround time 1 week, phone turnaround time same day. Fax notes: $1.00 per page. Fax fee for long distance $2.00. Copy fee: $1.00 per page. Certification fee: $1.00. Fee payee: Circuit Clerk. Personal checks accepted. Credit cards accepted: Visa, MasterCard. Prepayment is required.

County Court - Misdemeanor PO Box 2767 (700 S Park Ave, Bldg B), Titusville, FL 32781; 321-637-5413; Fax: 321-264-5246. Hours: 8AM-4:30PM (EST). *Misdemeanor.*

www.clerk.co.brevard.fl.us

Criminal Records: Access: Phone, fax, mail, online, in person. Both court and visitors may perform in person searches. Search fee: $1.00 per name per year. Required to search: name, years to search, DOB; also helpful: SSN, race, sex, signed release. Criminal records on computer since 1990, on microfiche from early 1900s. Some records on docket books and index cards. Access to County criminal records available free from FACTSweb at www.clerk.co.brevard.fl.us/pages/facts1.htm. Online records back to 1988 can be searched by name, case number or citation number.

General Information: Public access terminal is available. No juvenile, child abuse, sexual battery or adoption records released. SASE not required. Turnaround time 1 week, phone turnaround time 2 days. Fax notes: $1.00 per page. Fax fee for long distance $2.00 for 1st page. Copy fee: $1.00 per page. Certification fee: $1.00. Fee payee: Circuit Clerk. Personal checks accepted. Credit cards accepted: Visa, MasterCard, AmEx, Discover. Prepayment is required.

Broward County

Circuit & County Courts 201 SE 6th St, Ft Lauderdale, FL 33301; 954-765-6565; Probate phone: 954-831-7154; Fax: 954-831-7166. Hours: 9AM-4PM (EST). *Felony, Misdemeanor, Civil, Eviction, Small Claims, Probate.*

www.17th.flcourts.org

Civil Records: Access: Phone, fax, mail, online, in person, email. Both court and visitors may perform in person searches. Search fee: $1.00 per name per year. Add $4.00 for written response (affidavit). Required to search: name, years to search. Civil cases indexed by defendant, plaintiff. Civil records on computer from 1986. Some records on dockets. Will search back 10 years. The county clerk online fee system is being replaced by a web system. The web allows basic information free at www.browardclerk.org/bccoc2/default.asp. Search by name or case number or case type. The "Premium Access" for detailed case information requires a fee, registration and password. Call 954-831-5654 for information or visit the web site.

Criminal Records: Access: Phone, fax, mail, online, in person, email. Both court and visitors may perform in person searches. Search fee: $1.00 per name per year. Add $4.00 for written response (affidavit). Required to search: name, years to search, DOB; also helpful: SSN. Criminal records on computer since 1980. The clerk allows basic information free at www.browardclerk.org/bccoc2/default.asp. Search by name or case number or case type. The "Premium Access" for detailed case information requires a fee, registration and password.

General Information: Public access terminal is available. Turnaround time 1-14 days. Copy fee: $1.00 per page. Certification fee: $1.00. Fee payee: Clerk of the Court. Only cashiers checks and money orders accepted.

Calhoun County

Circuit & County Court 20859 E Central Ave #130 (425 E Central), Blountstown, FL 32424; 850-674-4545; Fax: 850-674-5553. Hours: 8AM-4PM (CST). *Felony, Misdemeanor, Civil, Eviction, Small Claims, Probate.*

Civil Records: Access: Phone, mail, in person. Both court and visitors may perform in person searches. Search fee: $7.00 per name. Required to search: name, years to search. Civil cases indexed by defendant, plaintiff. Civil records on computer back to 1986, books from 1970s.

Criminal Records: Access: Phone, mail, in person. Both court and visitors may perform in person searches. Search fee: $7.00 per name. Required to search: name, years to search. Criminal records on computer back to 1986, on docket books from 1970s.

General Information: No juvenile, child abuse or sexual battery records released. SASE required. Turnaround time 2 days. Fax notes: No fee to fax results. Copy fee: $1.00 per page. Certification fee: $1.00. Fee payee: Clerk of Court. Personal checks accepted. Prepayment is required.

Charlotte County

Circuit & County Courts - Civil Division PO Box 511687, Punta Gorda, FL 33951-1687; 941-637-2279; Fax: 941-637-2116. Hours: 8AM-5PM (EST). *Civil, Eviction, Small Claims, Probate.*

http://co.charlotte.fl.us/clrkinfo/clerk_default.htm

Civil Records: Access: Mail, in person, online. Both court and visitors may perform in person searches. Search fee: $1.00 per name per year. Required to search: name, years to search. Civil cases indexed by defendant, plaintiff. Civil records on computer back to 1982, on microfiche since 1987. Online access to civil & probate records is available by subscription, see the web site. Original payment is $186.00 ($150 refundable) plus a usage fee based on number of transactions. Allows printing of copies. For more information, call 941-637-4848.

General Information: Public access terminal is available. No juvenile, child abuse, sexual battery, adoption records released. SASE requested. Turnaround time 1-2 days. Fax notes: Fee to fax results is $2.00 per page. Copy fee: $1.00 per page. Certification fee: $1.00 per document. Fee payee: Clerk of Circuit Court. Personal checks accepted. Prepayment is required.

Circuit & County Courts - Criminal Division PO Box 511687, Punta Gorda, FL 33951-1687; 941-637-2269; Fax: 941-637-2159. Hours: 8AM-5PM (EST). *Felony, Misdemeanor.*

http://co.charlotte.fl.us/clrkinfo/clerk_default.htm

Criminal Records: Access: Phone, mail, in person, online. Both court and visitors may perform in person searches. Search fee: $1.00 per name per year. Required to search: name, years to search, DOB; also helpful: address, SSN, race, sex. Criminal records on computer since 1985, misdemeanors on index cards, felonies on judgment books, imaging on disc from 1993. Online access to criminal records available by subscription or free; see the web site. The full subscription requires an original payment of $186.00 ($150 refundable) plus a usage fee based on number of transactions. Allows printing of copies. For more information, call 941-637-2199. The free access at http://co.charlotte.fl.us/public/public_access.htm requires that you provide a name and birthdate.

General Information: Public access terminal is available. No juvenile, child abuse or sexual battery records released. SASE requested. Turnaround time 1 week. Fax notes: Fee to fax results is $2.00 per page. Copy fee: $1.00 per page. Certification fee: $1.00. Fee payee: Clerk of Circuit Court. Personal checks accepted. Prepayment is required.

Citrus County

Circuit Court 110 N Apopka Rm 101, Inverness, FL 34450; 352-341-6400; Fax: 352-341-6413. Hours: 8AM-5PM (EST). *Felony, Civil Actions Over $15,000, Probate.*

www.clerk.citrus.fl.us

Civil Records: Access: Phone, fax, mail, in person, online. Both court and visitors may perform in person searches. Search fee: $1.00 per name per year. Required to search: name, years to search; also helpful: address. Civil cases indexed by defendant, plaintiff. Civil records on computer from 1989, archived from 1940 to 1991. Some records on docket books. By phone only back to 1989. Indicate on search request the type(s) of cases.

Criminal Records: Access: Phone, fax, mail, in person. Both court and visitors may perform in person

searches. Search fee: $1.00 per name per year. Required to search: name, years to search, DOB; also helpful: address, SSN, race, sex. Criminal records on computer from 1989, on microfiche from 1948 to 1987, archived from 1940-1991. By phone only back to 1989.

General Information: Public access terminal is available. No juvenile, adoption, child abuse or sexual battery records released. SASE required. Turnaround time 1-2 days. Fax notes: $1.00 per page for local; $2.00 per page for long distance. Copy fee: $1.00 per page. Certification fee: $1.00. Fee payee: Clerk of Circuit Court. Personal checks accepted. Prepayment is required.

County Court 110 N Apopka, Rm 101, Inverness, FL 34450; 352-341-6400; Fax: 352-341-6413. Hours: 8AM-5PM (EST). *Misdemeanor, Civil Actions Under $15,000, Eviction, Small Claims.*

www.clerk.citrus.fl.us

Note: Marriage license information available online.

Civil Records: Access: Phone, fax, mail, in person. Both court and visitors may perform in person searches. Search fee: $1.00 per name per year. Required to search: name, years to search; also helpful: address. Civil cases indexed by defendant, plaintiff. Civil records on computer from 1990, prior records on docket books. Indicate type of case(s) you are looking for on your search request.

Criminal Records: Access: Mail, in person. Both court and visitors may perform in person searches. Search fee: $1.00 per name per year. Required to search: name, years to search, DOB; also helpful: address, SSN, race, sex. Criminal records on computer from 1990, prior records on docket books.

General Information: Public access terminal is available. (Criminal only.) No juvenile, child abuse or sexual battery records released. SASE required. Turnaround time 1-3 days. Fax notes: $1.00 per page. Fax fee for long distance $2.00 per page. Copy fee: $1.00 per page. Certification fee: $1.00. Fee payee: Clerk of Circuit Court. Personal checks accepted. Prepayment is required.

Clay County

Circuit Court PO Box 698, Green Cove Springs, FL 32043; 904-284-6302; Fax: 904-284-6390. Hours: 8:30AM-4:30PM (EST). *Felony, Civil Actions Over $15,000, Probate.*

http://clerk.co.clay.fl.us

Civil Records: Access: Mail, online, in person. Both court and visitors may perform in person searches. Search fee: $1.00 per name per year. Required to search: name, years to search; also helpful: address. Civil cases indexed by defendant, plaintiff. Civil records on computer from 1985, prior records on docket books. Clerk of the circuit court provides free access to records from the web site. This has taken the place of the commercial system.

Criminal Records: Access: Mail, in person. Both court and visitors may perform in person searches. Search fee: $1.00 per name per year. Required to search: name, years to search, DOB; also helpful: address, SSN, race, sex. Criminal records (Felony) on computer from 1967, prior records on docket books. Clerk of the circuit court provides free access to records from http://clerk.co.clay.fl.us.

General Information: Public access terminal is available. No juvenile, child abuse or sexual battery records released. Turnaround time 1-3 days. Copy fee: $1.00 per page. Certification fee: $1.00. Fee payee: Clerk of Circuit Court. Only cashiers checks and money orders accepted. Prepayment is required.

County Court PO Box 698, Green Cove Springs, FL 32043; 904-284-6316; Fax: 904-284-6390. Hours: 8:30AM-4:30PM (EST). *Misdemeanor, Civil Actions Under $15,000, Eviction, Small Claims.*

http://clerk.co.clay.fl.us

Civil Records: Access: Mail, online, in person. Both court and visitors may perform in person searches. Search fee: $1.00 per name per year. Required to search: name, years to search; also helpful: address. Civil cases indexed by defendant, plaintiff. Civil records on computer back to 1992, prior records on docket books. Online access to records is available at no fee from web site. Click on "Online Information." Online records go back to 1992.

Criminal Records: Access: Mail, in person, online. Both court and visitors may perform in person searches. Search fee: $1.00 per name per year. Required to search: name, years to search, DOB, SSN; also helpful: address, race, sex. Criminal records on computer back to 1992, prior records on docket books. Online access to criminal records is the same as civil.

General Information: Public access terminal is available. No juvenile, child abuse or sexual battery records released. Turnaround time 1-2 days. Fax notes: Fee to fax results is $2.00 1st page; $1.00 each add'l. Copy fee: $1.00 per page. Certification fee: $1.00. Fee payee: Clerk of Circuit Court. Personal checks accepted. Prepayment is required.

Collier County

Circuit Court PO Box 413044, Naples, FL 34101-3044; 239-732-2646. Hours: 8AM-5PM (EST). *Felony, Civil Actions Over $15,000, Probate.*

www.clerk.collier.fl.us

Civil Records: Access: Mail, online, in person. Both court and visitors may perform in person searches. Search fee: $1.00 per name per year. Required to search: name, years to search. Civil cases indexed by defendant, plaintiff. Civil records on computer from 1990, on microfiche from 1922 to 1994, archived from 1922. Online access is now available free at www.clerk.collier.fl.us/clerkspublicac/Default.htm. Records include probate, traffic and domestic.

Criminal Records: Access: Mail, online, in person. Both court and visitors may perform in person searches. Search fee: $1.00 per name per year. Required to search: name, years to search, DOB; also helpful: SSN. Criminal records on computer from 1990, on microfiche from 1922 to 1994, archived from 1922. Online access is now available free at www.clerk.collier.fl.us/clerkspublicac/Default.htm.

General Information: Public access terminal is available. No sealed by court or statute records released. Turnaround time within 1 week. Copy fee: $1.00 per page. Certification fee: $1.00. Fee payee: Clerk of Circuit Court. Personal checks accepted. Prepayment is required.

County Court PO Box 413044, Naples, FL 34101-3044; 239-732-2646; Fax: 239-774-8020. Hours: 8AM-5PM (EST). *Misdemeanor, Civil Actions Under $15,000, Eviction, Small Claims.*

www.clerk.collier.fl.us

Civil Records: Access: Mail, online, in person. Both court and visitors may perform in person searches. Search fee: $1.00 per name per year. Required to search: name, years to search; also helpful: address. Civil cases indexed by defendant, plaintiff. Civil records on computer from 1990, on microfiche from 1922 to 1995. Online access is now available free at www.clerk.collier.fl.us/clerkspublicac/Default.htm. Records include probate, traffic and domestic.

Criminal Records: Access: Mail, online, in person. Both court and visitors may perform in person searches. Search fee: $1.00 per name per year. Required to search: name, years to search, DOB; also helpful:

address, SSN, race, sex. Criminal records on computer from 1990, on microfiche from 1922 to 1995. Online access is now available free at www.clerk.collier.fl.us/clerkspublicac/Default.htm.

General Information: Public access terminal is available. No juvenile, child abuse or sexual battery records released. SASE required. Turnaround time 1 week. Copy fee: $1.00 per page. Certification fee: $1.00. Fee payee: Clerk of County Court. Personal checks accepted. Prepayment is required.

Columbia County

Circuit & County Courts PO Drawer 2069, Lake City, FL 32056; 386-719-7403. Hours: 8AM-5PM (EST). *Felony, Misdemeanor, Civil, Eviction, Small Claims, Probate.*

Civil Records: Access: Mail, in person, online. Both court and visitors may perform in person searches. Search fee: $1.00 per name per year. Fee is per department. Required to search: name, years to search. Civil cases indexed by defendant, plaintiff. Civil records on computer from 1987, archived from 1800s. DOB and SSN also helpful for searching. Limited online access to Clerk of Circuit Court's database is available free at www.columbiaclerk.com/Public_Records/public_records.html. Search by name, file number or document type.

Criminal Records: Access: In person only. Both court and visitors may perform in person searches. Search fee: $1.00 per name per year. Fee is per department. Required to search: name, years to search, DOB; also helpful: SSN. Criminal records on computer from 1987, archived from 1800s.

General Information: No names of victims of sex related offenses, juveniles, incompetence or mental health records released. SASE required. Turnaround time 1 day. Fax notes: Fee to fax results is $1.00 per page. Copy fee: $1.00 per page. Certification fee: $1.00. Fee payee: Clerk of Circuit Court. Cashier's check or money orders only. Prepayment is required.

Dade County

Note: also known s Miami-Dade.

Circuit & County Courts - Civil 73 W Flagler St, Miami, FL 33130; 305-275-1155; Fax: 305-375-5819. Hours: 9AM-4PM (EST). *Civil, Eviction, Small Claims, Probate.*

http://jud11.flcourts.org

Civil Records: Access: Phone, fax, mail, online, in person. Both court and visitors may perform in person searches. Search fee: $1.00 per name per year. Required to search: name, years to search. Civil cases indexed by defendant, plaintiff. Civil records on computer from 1984, archived from 1836. Microfilm in county recorder's office. Two sources exist. Subscription online access requires $125.00 setup fee, $52.00 monthly and $.25 per minute after the first 208 minutes each month. Docket information can be searched by case number or name. Call 305-596-8148 for more information. Also, online access to civil court records on the county clerk database are available free at www.co.miami-dade.fl.us/public-records/default.asp.

General Information: Public access terminal is available. No juvenile, child abuse or sexual battery records released. SASE requested. Turnaround time 1 week. Copy fee: $1.00 per page. Certification fee: $1.00. Fee payee: Clerk of Circuit & County Courts. Personal checks accepted. Credit cards accepted: Visa, MasterCard. Visa, MC +$15.00 add'l charge. Prepayment is required.

Circuit & County Courts - Criminal 1351 NW 12th St, #9000, Miami, FL 33125; 305-275-1155; Fax: 305-548-5526. Hours: 9AM-4PM (EST). *Felony, Misdemeanor.*

http://jud11.flcourts.org

Criminal Records: Access: Phone, fax, mail, online, in person. Both court and visitors may perform in person searches. Search fee: $1.00 per year. Required to search: name, years to search, DOB; also helpful: address, SSN, race, sex. Criminal records on computer back to 1971, on microfiche from 1975, archived from 1836. Fees for criminal online access requires $125.00 setup, $52.00 per month for the first 208 minutes and a $.25 per minute charge thereafter. Searching is by name or case number. Call 305-596-8148 for more information.

General Information: Public access terminal is available. No juvenile, child abuse or sexual battery records released. SASE required. Turnaround time 10-15 days. Copy fee: $1.00 per page. Certification fee: $1.00. Fee payee: Clerk of Circuit and County Court. Personal checks accepted. Credit cards accepted: Visa, MasterCard. Credit cards accepted in person only. Prepayment is required.

De Soto County

Circuit & County Courts 115 E Oak Street, Arcadia, FL 34266; 863-993-4876; Civil phone: 863-993-4880; Probate phone: 863-993-4880; Fax: 863-993-4669. Hours: 8AM-5PM (EST). *Felony, Misdemeanor, Civil, Eviction, Small Claims, Probate.*

http://12circuit.state.fl.us

Note: County Court & Evictions 863-993-4880.

Civil Records: Access: Phone, fax, mail, in person. Both court and visitors may perform in person searches. Search fee: $1.00 per name per year. Required to search: name, years to search. Civil cases indexed by defendant, plaintiff. Civil records on computer from 1986, on microfiche from 1974, archived from 1887.

Criminal Records: Access: Phone, fax, mail, in person. Both court and visitors may perform in person searches. Search fee: $1.00 per name per year. Required to search: name, years to search, DOB; also helpful: SSN, aliases. Criminal records on computer since 1986, archived since 1887.

General Information: Public access terminal is available. No juvenile or sex related records released. SASE requested. Turnaround time 2 days. Fax notes: $1.00 per page. Copy fee: $1.00 per page. Certification fee: $1.00. Fee payee: Clerk of the Court. Personal checks accepted. Prepayment is required.

Dixie County

Circuit & County Courts PO Drawer 1206, Cross City, FL 32628-1206; 352-498-1200; Fax: 352-498-1201. Hours: 9AM-5PM (EST). *Felony, Misdemeanor, Civil, Eviction, Small Claims, Probate.*

Civil Records: Access: Mail, in person. Both the court and visitors may perform in person searches. Search fee: $1.00 per name per year. Required to search: name, years to search; also helpful: address. Civil cases indexed by defendant, plaintiff. Civil records on computer since 1987.

Criminal Records: Access: Mail, in person. Both the court and visitors may perform in person searches. Search fee: $1.00 per name per year. Required to search: name, years to search, DOB; also helpful: address, SSN, race, sex. Criminal records on computer since 1989.

General Information: Public access terminal is available. No juvenile, child abuse or sexual battery records released. SASE required. Turnaround time 1 week. Fax notes: Fee to fax results is $1.00 per page. Copy fee: $1.00 per page. Certification fee: $1.00 per page. Fee payee: Clerk of Circuit Court. Personal checks accepted. Prepayment is required.

Duval County

Circuit & County Courts - Civil Division
330 E Bay St, Jacksonville, FL 32202; 904-630-2039; Fax: 904-630-7506. Hours: 8:30AM-4:30PM (EST). *Civil, Eviction, Small Claims, Probate.*

www.coj.net/pub/clerk/default.htm

Civil Records: Access: Fax, mail, online, in person. Both court and visitors may perform in person searches. Search fee: $1.00 per name per year. Required to search: name, years to search; also helpful: address. Civil cases indexed by defendant, plaintiff. Civil records (Circuit) on computer from 1968, county from 1984. County civil on index books from 1975 to 1986, prior on docket books. Circuit civil on index books from 1900s to 1968. Two sources are available. Online access requires $100.00 setup fee, but no access charges. For more information, call Leslie Peterson at 904-630-1212 x5115. Also, court records and more are available free at the Clerk of Circuit Court search site at www.coj.net/legal/officialrecords.
General Information: Public access terminal is available. No juvenile, child abuse or sexual battery records released. Turnaround time for county records 5-7 days, circuit 2-4 days. Fax notes: $1.00 per page. Copy fee: $1.00 per page. Certification fee: $1.00. Fee payee: Clerk of Circuit Court. Business checks accepted. Prepayment is required.

Circuit & County Courts - Criminal Division
330 E Bay St, Rm M106, Jacksonville, FL 32202; 904-630-2070; Fax: 904-630-7505. Hours: 8AM-5PM (EST). *Felony, Misdemeanor.*

www.coj.net/pub/clerk/default.htm

Criminal Records: Access: Mail, online, in person. Visitors must perform in person searches for themselves. No search fee. Required to search: name, years to search, DOB; also helpful: address, SSN, race, sex. Criminal records (Circuit) on computer from 1968, county from 1986. County civil on index books from 1975 to 1986, prior on docket books. Circuit civil on index books from 1900s to 1968. Online access to criminal records requires $100.00 setup fee, but no access charges. Records go back to 1992. For more information, call Leslie Peterson at 904-630-1212 x5115. Also, court records and more are available free at the Clerk of Circuit Court search site at www.coj.net/legal/officialrecords.
General Information: Public access terminal is available. No juvenile, child abuse or sexual battery records released. SASE helpful. Turnaround time 2-3 days. Copy fee: $1.00 per page. Certification fee: $1.00. Fee payee: Clerk of the Court. Business checks accepted. Prepayment is required.

Escambia County

Circuit & County Courts - Civil Division
190 Governmental Center, Pensacola, FL 32501; 850-595-4170; Civil phone: 850-595-4130 (Circ Ct. Civil); Probate phone: 850-595-4300. Hours: 8AM-5PM (CST). *Civil, Eviction, Small Claims, Probate.*

www.clerk.co.escambia.fl.us

Civil Records: Access: Phone, fax, mail, in person, online. Both court and visitors may perform in person searches. Search fee: $1.00 per year per name. Required to search: name, years to search; also helpful: address. Civil cases indexed by defendant, plaintiff. Civil records on computer from mid 1986, prior on index books. Judgments and small claims on microfiche from 1952, evictions from 1973. Online access to county clerk records available free at www.clerk.co.escambia.fl.us/public_records.html. Search by name, citation, or case number. Small claims, traffic, and marriage data also available.
General Information: Public access terminal is available. No juvenile, child abuse, adoption, mental

health or sexual battery records released. SASE requested. Turnaround time 1-5 days. Copy fee: $1.00 per page. Certification fee: $1.00. Fee payee: Clerk of Circuit Court. Personal checks accepted. Prepayment is required.

Circuit & County Courts - Criminal Division
190 Governmental Center, Pensacola, FL 32501; 850-595-4150; Fax: 850-595-4198. Hours: 8AM-5PM (CST). *Felony, Misdemeanor.*

www.clerk.co.escambia.fl.us

Note: Misdemeanor records phone is 850-595-4185.
Criminal Records: Access: Fax, mail, in person, online. Both the court and visitors may perform in person searches. Search fee: $1.00 per name per year. Required to search: name, years to search, DOB; also helpful: address, SSN, race, sex. Criminal records on computer and microfiche from 1973, archived from 1940 to 1972. Online access to county criminal records available free at www.clerk.co.escambia.fl.us/public_records.html. Search by name, citation, or case number.
General Information: Public access terminal is available. No juvenile, child abuse, mental health, adoption or sexual battery records released. SASE requested. Turnaround time within 1 week. Fax notes: $1.00 per page. If more than 5 pages $2.00, each additional group of 5 pages charge increases by $1.00, plus phone charge. Copy fee: $1.00 per page. Certification fee: $1.00. Fee payee: Clerk of Circuit Court. Personal checks accepted. Prepayment is required.

Flagler County

Circuit & County Courts
PO Box 787, Bunnell, FL 32110; 386-437-7430; Civil phone: 386-437-7431; Criminal phone: 386-437-7419; Fax: 386-437-7454 crim; 586-2116 civil. Hours: 8AM-4:30PM (EST). *Felony, Misdemeanor, Civil, Eviction, Small Claims, Probate.*

http://clerk.co.flagler.fl.us

Civil Records: Access: Phone, fax, mail, in person, email, online. Both court and visitors may perform in person searches. Search fee: $1.00 per name per year. Required to search: name, years to search; also helpful: address. Civil cases indexed by defendant, plaintiff. Civil records on computer from 1990. All archived from 1917, some on index books. Online access to the Clerk of Circuit Court index is available at www.myfloridacounty.com. Search free; documents are $1 per page.
Criminal Records: Access: Phone, fax, mail, in person, email. Both court and visitors may perform in person searches. Search fee: $1.00 per name per year. Required to search: name, years to search, DOB; also helpful: address, SSN, race, sex. Felony records on computer back to 1999; misdemeanors back to 1988. All archived from 1917, some on index books.
General Information: Public access terminal is available. No juvenile, child abuse or sexual battery records released. Turnaround time 3-5 days. Fax notes: $1.00 per page. Copy fee: $1.00 per page. Certification fee: $1.00. Fee payee: Clerk of Circuit Court. Business checks accepted. Prepayment is required.

Franklin County

Circuit & County Courts
33 Market St, #203, Apalachicola, FL 32321; 850-653-8862; Fax: 850-653-2261. Hours: 8:30AM-4:30PM (EST). *Felony, Misdemeanor, Civil, Eviction, Small Claims, Probate.*

www.co.leon.fl.us/court/court.htm

Civil Records: Access: Mail, in person. Both court and visitors may perform in person searches. Search fee: $1.00 per name per year. Required to search: name, years to search; also helpful: address. Civil cases

indexed by defendant, plaintiff. Civil records on computer from 3/92.
Criminal Records: Access: Mail, in person. Both court and visitors may perform in person searches. Search fee: $1.00 per name per year. Required to search: name, years to search, DOB; also helpful: address, SSN, race, sex. Criminal records on computer since 1989.
General Information: Public access terminal is available. No juvenile, child abuse or sexual battery records released. SASE requested. Turnaround time 2-5 days. Copy fee: $1.00 per page. Certification fee: $1.00. Fee payee: Clerk of Circuit Court. In-county personal checks accepted. Prepayment is required.

Gadsden County

Circuit & County Courts - Criminal Division
24 N Adams, Quincy, FL 32351; 850-875-8609; Fax: 850-875-7625. Hours: 8:30AM-5PM (EST). *Felony, Misdemeanor.*

www.co.leon.fl.us/court/court.htm

Note: Requests may be sent to PO Box 1649, ZIP is 32353
Criminal Records: Access: Fax, mail, in person, online. Both court and visitors may perform in person searches. Search fee: $1.00 per name per year. Required to search: name, years to search, DOB; also helpful: SSN. Criminal records on computer from 1984, some on index books and cards. Online access to criminal court records are available free from the County Clerk at www.clerk.co.gadsden.fl.us.
General Information: No juvenile or sex offender records released. Turnaround time 3-5 days. Fax notes: $1.00 per page. Copy fee: $.15 per page. Certification fee: $1.15 per page. Fee payee: Clerk of Circuit Court. Personal checks accepted. Prepayment is required.

Circuit & County Courts - Civil Division
PO Box 1649, Quincy, FL 32353; 850-875-8621; Fax: 850-875-8612. Hours: 8:30AM-5PM (EST). *Civil, Eviction, Small Claims, Probate.*

www.clerk.co.gadsden.fl.us

Civil Records: Access: Phone, fax, mail, online, email, in person. Both court and visitors may perform in person searches. Search fee: $1.00 per name. Required to search: name, years to search. Civil cases indexed by defendant, plaintiff. Civil records on computer since 1984. Online access to civil court records are available free from the County Clerk at www.clerk.co.gadsden.fl.us.
General Information: Public access terminal is available. No juvenile, child abuse or sexual battery records released. Turnaround time 1 week. Fax notes: $1.00 per page. Copy fee: $.15 per page. Certification fee: $1.00. Fee payee: Clerk of Circuit Court. Only cashiers checks and money orders accepted. Prepayment is required.

Gilchrist County

Circuit & County Courts
PO Box 37, Trenton, FL 32693; 352-463-3170; Fax: 352-463-3166. Hours: 8AM-5PM (EST). *Felony, Misdemeanor, Civil, Eviction, Small Claims, Probate.*

http://circuit8.org

Civil Records: Access: Mail, in person. Both court and visitors may perform in person searches. Search fee: $1.00 per name per year. Add $4.00 for written response (affidavit). Required to search: name, years to search; also helpful: address. Civil cases indexed by defendant, plaintiff. Civil records on computer from 1987, prior on index books.
Criminal Records: Access: Mail, in person. Only the court performs in person searches; visitors may not. Search fee: $1.00 per name per year. Add $4.00 for written response (affidavit). Required to search: name, years to search, DOB; also helpful: address, SSN, race,

sex. Criminal records on computer since 1989, prior on index books.

General Information: No juvenile, child abuse or sexual battery records released. Turnaround time 2-3 days. Fax notes: $1.00 per page. Available for civil only. Copy fee: $1.00 per page. Certification fee: $1.00. Fee payee: Clerk of Circuit Court. Personal checks accepted. Prepayment is required.

Glades County

Circuit & County Courts PO Box 10, Moore Haven, FL 33471; 863-946-0113; Fax: 863-946-0560. Hours: 8AM-5PM (EST). *Felony, Misdemeanor, Civil, Eviction, Small Claims, Probate.*

Civil Records: Access: Phone, fax, mail, in person. Only the court performs in person searches; visitors may not. Search fee: $1.00 per name per year. Add $4.00 for written response (affidavit). Required to search: name, years to search; also helpful: address. Civil cases indexed by defendant, plaintiff. Civil records on computer from 1991.

Criminal Records: Access: Phone, mail, fax, in person. Only the court performs in person searches; visitors may not. Search fee: $1.00 per name per year. Add $4.00 for written response (affidavit). Required to search: name, years to search, DOB; also helpful: address, SSN, race, sex. Criminal records on computer from 1991.

General Information: No juvenile, child abuse or sexual battery records released. SASE not required. Turnaround time 2-3 days. Copy fee: $1.00 per page. Certification fee: $1.00. Fee payee: Clerk of Circuit Court. Personal checks accepted. Prepayment is required.

Gulf County

Circuit & County Courts 1000 Cecil Costin Blvd, Port St Joe, FL 32456; 850-229-6112; Fax: 850-229-6174. Hours: 9AM-5PM (EST). *Felony, Misdemeanor, Civil, Eviction, Small Claims, Probate.*

Civil Records: Access: Fax, mail, in person. Both court and visitors may perform in person searches. Search fee: $1.00 per name per year. Required to search: name, years to search. Civil cases indexed by defendant, plaintiff. Civil records on computer from 1990; archived to 1925.

Criminal Records: Access: Fax, mail, in person. Both court and visitors may perform in person searches. Search fee: $1.00 per name per year. Required to search: name, years to search, DOB; also helpful: SSN. Criminal records on computer from 1990; archived to 1925.

General Information: No juvenile, adoption, child abuse or sexual battery records released. SASE required. Turnaround time 1-3 days. Fax notes: $1.50 per page. Copy fee: $.15 per page. Certification fee: $1.00. Fee payee: Clerk of Circuit Court. Personal checks accepted. Prepayment is required.

Hamilton County

Circuit & County Courts 207 NE 1st St #106, Jasper, FL 32052; 386-792-1288; Fax: 386-792-3524. Hours: 8:30AM-4:30PM (EST). *Felony, Misdemeanor, Civil, Eviction, Small Claims, Probate.*

Civil Records: Access: Mail, in person. Both court and visitors may perform in person searches. Search fee: $1.00 per name per year. Required to search: name, years to search; also helpful: address. Civil records on computer from 1/91, county civil from 3/91.

Criminal Records: Access: Mail, in person. Both court and visitors may perform in person searches. Search fee: $1.00 per name per year. Required to search: name, years to search, DOB; also helpful: address, SSN, race, sex. Criminal records on computer-Felony since 3/90, Misdemeanor since 1/89.

General Information: No juvenile, child abuse or sexual battery records released. SASE requested. Turnaround time 2-3 days. Copy fee: $1.00 per page. Certification fee: $1.00. Fee payee: Clerk of Circuit Court. Personal checks accepted. Prepayment required.

Hardee County

Circuit & County Courts PO Drawer 1749, Wauchula, FL 33873-1749; 863-773-4174; Fax: 863-773-4422. Hours: 8AM-5PM (EST). *Felony, Misdemeanor, Civil, Eviction, Small Claims, Probate.*

www.jud10.org

Civil Records: Access: Mail, in person. Both court and visitors may perform in person searches. Search fee: $1.00 per name per year. Required to search: name, years to search; also helpful: address. Civil records on computer from 1984.

Criminal Records: Access: Mail, in person. Both court and visitors may perform in person searches. Search fee: $1.00 per name per year. Required to search: name, years to search, DOB; also helpful: address, race, sex. Criminal records on computer from 1984.

General Information: Public access terminal is available. No juvenile, child abuse or sexual battery records released. SASE requested. Turnaround time 3 days. Fax notes: Fee to fax results is $1.00 per page. Copy fee: $1.00 per page. Certification fee: $1.00. Fee payee: Clerk of Circuit Court. Business checks accepted. Prepayment is required.

Hendry County

Circuit & County Courts PO Box 1760, LaBelle, FL 33975-1760; 863-675-5217; Fax: 863-675-5238. Hours: 8:30AM-5PM (EST). *Felony, Misdemeanor, Civil, Eviction, Small Claims, Probate.*

Civil Records: Access: Mail, in person. Both court and visitors may perform in person searches. Search fee: $1.00 per name per year. Required to search: name, years to search; also helpful: address. Civil cases indexed by defendant, plaintiff. Civil records on computer since 5/92, archived from 1923, on microfiche prior to 1989 if filed.

Criminal Records: Access: Mail, in person. Both court and visitors may perform in person searches. Search fee: $1.00 per name per year. Required to search: name, years to search, DOB; also helpful: address, SSN, race, sex. Criminal records on computer since 1989, prior on microfiche, archived since 1923.

General Information: No juvenile, child abuse or sexual battery records released. SASE helpful. Turnaround time varies. Copy fee: $1.00 per page. Certification fee: $1.00. Fee payee: Clerk of Circuit Court. Personal checks accepted. Prepayment required.

Hernando County

Circuit & County Courts 20 N Main St, Brooksville, FL 34601; 352-754-4201; Fax: 352-754-4247. Hours: 8AM-5PM (EST). *Felony, Misdemeanor, Civil, Eviction, Small Claims, Probate.*

www.clerk.co.hernando.fl.us

Civil Records: Access: Mail, online, in person. Both court and visitors may perform in person searches. Search fee: $1.00 per name per year. Required to search: name, years to search. Civil cases indexed by defendant, plaintiff. Civil records on computer from 1982, archived from late 1800s. Online access to court records is now available free at www.clerk.co.hernando.fl.us/disclaimer.asp. Online records may go as far back as 1/1983. Your browser must be Javascript enables (MS Explorer 4.0 or above).

Criminal Records: Access: Mail, online, in person. Both court and visitors may perform in person searches. Search fee: $1.00 per name per year. Required to search: name, years to search, DOB; also helpful: SSN. Criminal records on computer from 1982, archived

from late 1800s. Index and docket information is available for felony and misdemeanor records. Online access to criminal records is the same as civil.

General Information: Public access terminal is available. No juvenile, child abuse or sexual battery records released. Turnaround time approx 5 days. Copy fee: $1.00 per page. Certification fee: $1.00. Fee payee: Clerk of Circuit Court. Personal checks accepted. Prepayment is required.

Highlands County

Circuit & County Courts 590 S Commerce Ave, Sebring, FL 33870-3867; Civil phone: 863-386-6591; Criminal phone: 863-386-6597; Fax: 863-386-6575. Hours: 8AM-4:30PM (EST). *Felony, Misdemeanor, Civil, Eviction, Small Claims, Probate.*

www.jud10.org

Civil Records: Access: Mail, in person, online. Both court and visitors may perform in person searches. Search fee: $1.00 per name per year. Required to search: name, years to search. Civil cases indexed by defendant, plaintiff. Civil records on computer since 1992, prior on microfiche and film. Online access to county clerk records available free at www.clerk.co.highlands.fl.us/highlands.fl/civil-records-search.jsp. Also includes small claims, probate, and tax deeds.

Criminal Records: Access: Mail, in person. Both court and visitors may perform in person searches. Search fee: $1.00 per name per year. Required to search: name, years to search; also helpful: SSN. Criminal records on computer since 1991, prior on microfiche and film.

General Information: Public access terminal is available. No juvenile, child abuse or sexual battery records released. Turnaround time 1 week. Copy fee: $1.00 per page. Certification fee: $2.00. Fee payee: Clerk of Courts. Personal checks accepted. Prepayment is required.

HillsBorough

Circuit & County Courts 419 Pierce St, Tampa, FL 33602; 813-276-8100; Fax: 813-272-7707. Hours: 8AM-5PM (EST). *Felony, Misdemeanor, Civil, Eviction, Small Claims, Probate.*

www.hillsclerk.com

Note: Telephone extension for civil is 7803, for criminal is 7802.

Civil Records: Access: Fax, mail, online, in person. Both court and visitors may perform in person searches. Search fee: $1.00 per name per year. Required to search: name, years to search; also helpful: address. Civil cases indexed by defendant, plaintiff. Civil records on computer since 5/85, prior on microfiche since early 1900s. Online access requires $50.00 set-up/software fee plus initial $50.00 towards access charges of $.20 per minute. Probate, traffic and domestic records are included. Call the help desk at 813-276-8100, Ext. 7000 for more information.

Criminal Records: Access: Fax, mail, online, in person. Both court and visitors may perform in person searches. Search fee: $1.00 per name per year. Required to search: name, years to search, DOB; also helpful: address, SSN, race, sex. Criminal records on computer since 1989, prior on microfiche since 1975, archived from 1953 to 1974. Some felonies on docket books. Online access to criminal records is the same as civil.

General Information: Public access terminal is available. No juvenile, child abuse or sexual battery records released. Turnaround time 1-2 days. Fax notes: No fee to fax results. Fax account required. Copy fee: $1.00 per page. Certification fee: $1.00. Fee payee: Clerk of Circuit Court. Personal checks accepted. Local personal checks accepted. Prepayment is required.

Holmes County

Circuit & County Courts PO Box 397, Bonifay, FL 32425; 850-547-1100; Fax: 850-547-6630. Hours: 8AM-4PM (CST). *Felony, Misdemeanor, Civil, Eviction, Small Claims, Probate.*

Civil Records: Access: Mail, in person. Both court and visitors may perform in person searches. Search fee: $1.00 per name per year. Required to search: name, years to search; also helpful: address. Civil cases indexed by defendant, plaintiff. Civil records on computer from 10/91, archived from early 1900s.

Criminal Records: Access: Mail, in person. Both court and visitors may perform in person searches. Search fee: $1.00 per name per year. Required to search: name, years to search, DOB; also helpful: address, SSN, race, sex. Criminal records on computer since 1989, prior archived since early 1900s.

General Information: Public access terminal is available. No juvenile, child abuse or sexual battery records released. SASE required. Turnaround time 1 week. Copy fee: $1.00 per page. Certification fee: $1.00. Fee payee: Holmes County Clerk of Court. Personal checks accepted. Prepayment is required.

Indian River County

Circuit & County Courts PO Box 1028, Vero Beach, FL 32961; 772-770-5185; Fax: 772-770-5008. Hours: 8:30AM-5PM (EST). *Felony, Misdemeanor, Civil, Eviction, Small Claims, Probate.*

Civil Records: Access: Mail, in person, online. Both court and visitors may perform in person searches. Search fee: $1.00 per name per year. Required to search: name, years to search; also helpful: address. Civil cases indexed by defendant, plaintiff. Civil records on computer since 1984, prior on microfiche. Online access to county recordings index is available free at http://bdc.co.indian-river.fl.us. Records go back to 1983. Full access to court records is available via the clerk's subscription service. Fee is $200.00 per month. For information about free and fee access, call Gary at 772-567-8000 x216.

Criminal Records: Access: Mail, in person, online. Both court and visitors may perform in person searches. Search fee: $1.00 per name per year. Required to search: name, years to search, DOB; also helpful: address, SSN, race, sex. Criminal records on computer (Felony since 1986, Misdemeanor since 1983), both archived since 1925. Online access to criminal records is the same as civil.

General Information: Public access terminal is available. No juvenile, child abuse or sexual battery records released. SASE helpful. Turnaround time 2 days. Copy fee: $1.00 per page. Certification fee: $1.00. Fee payee: Clerk of Circuit Court. Personal checks accepted. Prepayment is required.

Jackson County

Circuit & County Courts PO Box 510, Marianna, FL 32447; 850-482-9552; Fax: 850-482-7849. Hours: 8AM-4:30PM (CST). *Felony, Misdemeanor, Civil, Eviction, Small Claims, Probate.*

www.jacksonclerk.com

Civil Records: Access: Fax, mail, in person, online. Both court and visitors may perform in person searches. Search fee: $1.00 per name per year. Required to search: name, years to search; also helpful: address. Civil cases indexed by defendant, plaintiff. Civil records go back to 1900; computerized records go back to 1989. Online access to civil record indices is available free from myfloridacounty.com at www.jacksonclerk.com.

Criminal Records: Access: Fax, mail, in person. Both court and visitors may perform in person searches. Search fee: $1.00 per name per year. Required to search: name, years to search, DOB; also helpful:

address, SSN, race, sex. Criminal records go back to 1900; computerized records since 1989.

General Information: Public access terminal is available. No juvenile, child abuse or sexual battery records released. SASE helpful. Turnaround time 1-5 days. Fax notes: $3.00 for first page, $1.00 each add'l. Copy fee: $1.00 per page. Certification fee: $1.00. Fee payee: Clerk of Circuit Court. Personal checks accepted. Credit cards accepted: Visa, MasterCard, AmEx. Prepayment is required.

Jefferson County

Circuit & County Courts Jefferson County Courthouse, Rm 10, Monticello, FL 32344; 850-342-0218; Fax: 850-342-0222. Hours: 8AM-5PM (EST). *Felony, Misdemeanor, Civil, Eviction, Small Claims, Probate.*

Civil Records: Access: Mail, in person. Only the court may perform in person searches. Search fee: $1.00 per name per year. Required to search: name, years to search; also helpful: address. Civil cases indexed by defendant, plaintiff. Civil records on computer since 7/90, prior on dockets.

Criminal Records: Access: Fax, mail, in person. Only the court may perform in person searches. Search fee: $1.00 per name per year. Required to search: name, years to search, DOB; also helpful: address, SSN, race, sex. Criminal records on computer since 1989, prior on microfiche from 1969 to 1980, archived since 1950s, prior to 1950 on dockets.

General Information: No juvenile, child abuse or sexual battery records released. Turnaround time 1 week. Fax notes: Fee to fax results is $2.00 per page. Copy fee: $1.00 per page. Certification fee: $1.00. Fee payee: Clerk of Circuit Court. Personal checks accepted. Prepayment is required.

Lafayette County

Circuit & County Courts PO Box 88, Mayo, FL 32066; 386-294-1600; Fax: 386-294-4231. Hours: 8AM-5PM (EST). *Felony, Misdemeanor, Civil, Eviction, Small Claims, Probate.*

Civil Records: Access: Phone, mail, fax, in person. Both court and visitors may perform in person searches. No search fee. Required to search: name, years to search; also helpful: address. Civil cases indexed by defendant, plaintiff. Civil records on computer since 1997, on books back to early 1900s.

Criminal Records: Access: Phone, mail, fax, in person. Both court and visitors may perform in person searches. No search fee. Required to search: name, years to search, DOB; also helpful: address, SSN, race, sex. Criminal records computerized since 1989.

General Information: Public access terminal is available. No juvenile, child abuse or sexual battery records released. SASE required. Turnaround time 5-7 days. Copy fee: $1.00 per page. Certification fee: $1.00. Fee payee: Clerk of Circuit Court. Personal checks accepted. Prepayment is required.

Lake County

Circuit & County Courts 550 W Main St or PO Box 7800, Tavares, FL 32778; 352-742-4100; Fax: 352-742-4166. Hours: 8:30AM-5PM (EST). *Felony, Misdemeanor, Civil, Eviction, Small Claims, Probate.*

www.lakecountyclerk.org/default1.asp

Civil Records: Access: Fax, mail, in person, online. Both court and visitors may perform in person searches. Search fee: $1.00 per name per year. Required to search: name, years to search; also helpful: address. Civil cases indexed by defendant, plaintiff. Civil records on computer since 1984, county civil on index books since 11/51, circuit civil since 1888. Online access to Clerk of Court records available free at www.lakecountyclerk.org/services.asp?subject=Online _Court_Records. County civil records go back to 1985;

circuit records go back to 9/1984. Also, marriage licenses back to 2000 available at the main website. Also, recordings, liens, and judgments on the Circuit Clerk website are available free at www.lakecountyclerk.org/services.asp?subject=Online _Official_Records.

Criminal Records: Access: Fax, mail, in person. Both court and visitors may perform in person searches. Search fee: $1.00 per name per year. Required to search: name, years to search, DOB; also helpful: address, SSN, race, sex. Criminal records on computer since 1983, on microfiche since 1970s, archived since 1920s. Some on index books.

General Information: Public access terminal is available. No juvenile, child abuse or sexual battery records released. SASE helpful. Turnaround time 7-10 days. Fax notes: $1.00 per page. Copy fee: $1.00 per page. Certification fee: $1.00. Fee payee: Clerk of Circuit Court. Personal checks accepted. Prepayment is required.

Lee County

Circuit & County Courts PO Box 2469, Ft Myers, FL 33902; 239-335-2283. Hours: 7:45AM-5PM (EST). *Felony, Misdemeanor, Civil, Eviction, Small Claims, Probate.*

www.leeclerk.org

Civil Records: Access: Mail, online, in person, phone, fax, online. Both court and visitors may perform in person searches. Search fee: $1.00 per name per year. Required to search: name, years to search. Civil cases indexed by defendant, plaintiff. Civil records on computer since 1988, prior on microfilm and dockets. The fee system has been replaced by free Internet access at the web site. Registration required. Online records go back to 1988. Call 239-335-2975 for more information. Includes traffic, felony, misdemeanor, civil, small claims and probate.

Criminal Records: Access: Mail, online, in person. Both court and visitors may perform in person searches. Search fee: $1.00 per name per year. Required to search: name, years to search, DOB; also helpful: address, SSN, race, sex. Criminal records on computer- (Felony since 1978, Misdemeanor since 1986), prior on microfilm. Online access to criminal records is the same as civil.

General Information: Public access terminal is available. No juvenile, child abuse or sexual offense records released. SASE required. Turnaround time 5 days. Copy fee: $1.00 per page. Certification fee: $1.00 per document. Fee payee: Clerk of Circuit Court. Personal checks accepted. Prepayment is required.

Leon County

Circuit & County Courts PO Box 726, Tallahassee, FL 32302; 850-577-4000; Civil phone: 850-577-4170; Criminal phone: 850-577-4070; Probate phone: 850-577-4180. Hours: 8:30AM-5PM (EST). *Felony, Misdemeanor, Civil, Eviction, Small Claims, Probate.*

www.clerk.leon.fl.us

Civil Records: Access: Mail, online, in person. Both court and visitors may perform in person searches. Search fee: $1.00 per name per year. Required to search: name, years to search; also helpful: address. Civil cases indexed by defendant, plaintiff. Civil records on computer since 8/86, prior on docket books. There is a commercial search for case information at the web site. Certain images are not released, nor are SSNs. There is a $100 per month user fee and registration. is required.

Criminal Records: Access: Mail, online, in person. Both court and visitors may perform in person searches. Search fee: $1.00 per name per year. Required to search: name, years to search, DOB; also helpful: address, SSN, race, sex. Criminal records on computer since 1976, on microfiche since 1937, archived since late 1800s/early 1900s. Online access to criminal records is the same as civil.

General Information: Public access terminal is available. No juvenile, child abuse or sexual battery records released. SASE helpful. Turnaround time 1-5 days. Copy fee: $1.00 per page. Certification fee: $1.00. Fee payee: Clerk of Circuit Court. Personal checks accepted. Credit cards accepted: Visa, MasterCard. Prepayment is required.

Levy County

Circuit & County Courts PO Box 610, Bronson, FL 32621; 352-486-5100. 8AM-5PM (EST). *Felony, Misdemeanor, Civil, Eviction, Small Claims, Probate.*

http://circuit8.org

Civil Records: Access: Mail, in person, online. Both court and visitors may perform in person searches. Search fee: $1.00 per name per year. Required to search: name, years to search; also helpful: address. Civil cases indexed by defendant, plaintiff. Civil records on computer from 1986, microfiche to 1981 (in process), prior on docket books. Online access to the Clerk of Circuit Court recording records available free www.levyclerk.com/Public_Records/Public_Records.html.

Criminal Records: Access: Mail, in person, online. Both court and visitors may perform in person searches. Search fee: $1.00 per name per year. Required to search: name, years to search, DOB, signed release; also helpful: address, SSN, race, sex. Criminal records on computer from 1986 to present, prior on docket books. Access to the circuit-wide criminal quick lookup available at http://circuit8.org/golem/gencrim.html. Account and password is required; restricted usage.

General Information: Public access terminal is available. No juvenile, child abuse or sexual battery records released. SASE required. Turnaround time 2-3 days. Copy fee: $1.00 per page. Certification fee: $1.00. Fee payee: Clerk of Circuit Court. Business checks accepted. Prepayment is required.

Liberty County

Circuit & County Courts PO Box 399, Bristol, FL 32321; 850-643-2215; Fax: 850-643-2866. Hours: 8AM-5PM (EST). *Felony, Misdemeanor, Civil, Eviction, Small Claims, Probate.*

www.libertyclerk.com

Civil Records: Access: Mail, in person. Both court and visitors may perform in person searches. Search fee: $1.00 per name per year. Required to search: name, years to search; also helpful: address. Civil cases indexed by defendant, plaintiff. Civil records on docket books.

Criminal Records: Access: Mail, in person. Both court and visitors may perform in person searches. Search fee: $1.00 per name per year. Required to search: name, years to search, DOB; also helpful: address, SSN, race, sex. Criminal records on docket books.

General Information: No juvenile, child abuse or sexual battery records released. SASE required. Turnaround time 1 week. Copy fee: $1.00 per page. Certification fee: $1.00. Fee payee: Clerk of Circuit Court. Business checks accepted. Prepayment required.

Madison County

Circuit & County Courts PO Box 237, Madison, FL 32341; 850-973-1500; Fax: 850-973-2059. Hours: 8AM-5PM (EST). *Felony, Misdemeanor, Civil, Eviction, Small Claims, Probate.*

Civil Records: Access: Phone, mail, in person. Both court and visitors may perform in person searches. Search fee: $1.00 per name per year. Required to search: name, years to search; also helpful: address. Civil cases indexed by defendant, plaintiff. Civil records on computer since 1988, prior on docket books.

Criminal Records: Access: Phone, mail, in person. Both court and visitors may perform in person searches. Search fee: $1.00 per name per year. Required to search: name, years to search, DOB; also helpful: address, SSN, race, sex. Criminal records on computer since 1988, prior on docket books.

General Information: No juvenile, child abuse or sexual battery records released. SASE requested. Turnaround time 1-3 days. Copy fee: $1.00 per page. Certification fee: $1.00. Fee payee: Clerk of Circuit Court. Personal checks accepted. Prepayment required.

Manatee County

Circuit & County Courts PO Box 25400, Bradenton, FL 34206; 941-749-1800; Fax: 941-741-4082. Hours: 8:30AM-5PM (EST). *Felony, Misdemeanor, Civil, Eviction, Small Claims, Probate.*

www.manateeclerk.com

Civil Records: Access: Phone, fax, mail, online, in person, email. Both court and visitors may perform in person searches. Search fee: $1.00 per name per year. Required to search: name, years to search; also helpful: address. Civil cases indexed by defendant, plaintiff. Civil records on computer since 9/80, prior on microfilm back to 1972. A subscription online service is available for $50 plus $60 per user fee advance; for sign-up information visit the web site. Also, court records the Circuit clerk's office are available free at www.manateeclerk.com/mpa/cvweb.asp.

Criminal Records: Access: Phone, fax, mail, online, in person, email. Both court and visitors may perform in person searches. Search fee: $1.00 per name per year. Required to search: name, years to search, DOB; also helpful: address, charge, race, sex. Criminal records on computer since 1981, prior on docket books back to 1972. Online access to criminal online records is the same as civil.

General Information: Public access terminal is available. No juvenile, adoption, child abuse or sexual battery victim records released. SASE helpful. Turnaround time 2 days. Fax notes: Will not fax results. Copy fee: $1.00 per page. Certification fee: $1.00. Fee payee: Clerk of Circuit Court. Personal checks accepted. Credit cards accepted: Visa, MasterCard. Prepayment is required.

Marion County

Circuit & County Courts PO Box 1030, Ocala, FL 34478; 352-620-3892 (cty civ); Civil phone: 352-620-3891 (Circ); Criminal phone: 352-620-3861; Probate phone: 352-620-3874; Fax: 352-620-3300 (civ); 840-5668 (crim). 8AM-5PM (EST). *Felony, Misdemeanor, Civil, Eviction, Small Claims, Probate.*

www.marioncountyclerk.org

Civil Records: Access: Fax, mail, in person, online. Both court and visitors may perform in person searches. Search fee: $1.00 per name per year. Required to search: name, years to search; also helpful: address. Civil cases indexed by defendant, plaintiff. Civil records on computer since 1983, on microfiche since 1958. Online access to county clerk civil records available free online at www.marioncountyclerk.org/Courts/factsweb.htm. Search by name or case number. The site's time default field must be used.

Criminal Records: Access: Fax, mail, in person. Both court and visitors may perform in person searches. Search fee: $1.00 per name per year. Required to search: name, years to search, DOB; also helpful: address, SSN, race, sex. Criminal records on computer. Felonies since 1984, on microfiche from 1950 to 1979, prior on index cards. Misdemeanors since 1983, on microfiche from 1900 to 1982, archived since 1900s, prior on index cards.

General Information: Public access terminal is available. No juvenile records released. SASE requested. Turnaround time 1-2 weeks. Copy fee: $1.00 per page. Certification fee: $1.00. Fee payee: Clerk of Court. Personal checks accepted. Prepayment required.

Martin County

Circuit & County Courts PO Box 9016, Stuart, FL 34995; 772-288-5576; Fax: 772-288-5724; 288-5991 (civil). Hours: 8AM-5PM (EST). *Felony, Misdemeanor, Civil, Eviction, Small Claims, Probate.*

www.martin.fl.us/GOVT/co/clerk

Civil Records: Access: Phone, fax, mail, online, in person. Both court and visitors may perform in person searches. Search fee: $1.00 per name per year. Required to search: name, years to search; also helpful: address. Civil cases indexed by defendant, plaintiff. Civil records on computer since 10/86, prior on microfiche and archived. Online access to civil case information on the records division database available free at http://clerk-web.martin.fl.us/wb_or1. Also includes small claims, recordings, other document types.

Criminal Records: Access: Phone, fax, mail, online, in person. Both court and visitors may perform in person searches. Search fee: $1.00 per name per year prior to 1990. Required to search: name, years to search, DOB; also helpful: address, SSN. Criminal records on computer. Felonies since 1986, on microfiche since 1956, prior on index cards and docket books. Misdemeanors since 1985, on microfiche since 1973, prior on index cards and docket books. Online access to criminal records is the same as civil. Records indexed form 01/01/86, and images from 11/01/93.

General Information: Public access terminal is available. No juvenile, child abuse or sexual battery records released. Turnaround time 1 week. Fax notes: $1.25 per page. Copy fee: $1.00 per page. Certification fee: $1.00. Fee payee: Clerk of Circuit Court. Personal checks accepted. Prepayment is required.

Miami-Dade County

See Dade County

Monroe County

Circuit & County Courts 500 Whitehead St, Key West, FL 33040; 305-294-4641; Civil phone: 305-292-3310; Criminal phone: 305-292-3390; Fax: 305-295-3623. Hours: 8:30AM-5PM (EST). *Felony, Misdemeanor, Civil, Eviction, Small Claims, Probate.*

www.co.monroe.fl.us

Civil Records: Access: Mail, fax, in person, online. Both court and visitors may perform in person searches. Search fee: $1.00 per name per year. Required to search: name, years to search; also helpful: address. Civil cases indexed by defendant, plaintiff. Civil records on computer since 1983, on microfiche since 1972, prior on docket books. Some records purged after 2 years. Probate from 1972. Online access to civil cases if available free at www.clerk-of-the-court.com/searchCivilCases.asp.

Criminal Records: Access: Mail, fax, in person, online. Both court and visitors may perform in person searches. Search fee: $1.00 per name per year. Required to search: name, years to search, DOB; also helpful: address, SSN, race, sex. Criminal records (pending felony and misdemeanors) on computer, others since 1992, non-pending on microfiche since 1945. Online access to criminal records is available free at www.clerk-of-the-court.com/searchCriminalCases.asp. Includes traffic cases online.

General Information: Public access terminal is available. No juvenile, child abuse or sexual battery records released. SASE helpful. Turnaround time 1-2 weeks. Fax notes: Fee to fax results is $1.00 per page. Copy fee: $1.00 per page. Certification fee: $1.00. Fee payee: Clerk of Circuit Court. Personal checks accepted. Prepayment is required.

Criminal Records: Access: Phone, mail, in person. Both court and visitors may perform in person searches. Search fee: $1.00 per name per year. Required to search: name, years to search, DOB; also helpful: address, SSN, race, sex. Criminal records on computer since 1988, prior on docket books.

General Information: No juvenile, child abuse or sexual battery records released. SASE requested. Turnaround time 1-3 days. Copy fee: $1.00 per page. Certification fee: $1.00. Fee payee: Clerk of Circuit Court. Personal checks accepted. Prepayment required.

per page. Certification fee: $1.00. Fee payee: Clerk of Court. Personal checks accepted. Prepayment required.

Nassau County

Circuit & County Courts PO Box 456, Fernandina Beach, FL 32035; 904-321-5795; Fax: 904-321-5723. Hours: 9AM-5PM (EST). *Felony, Misdemeanor, Civil, Eviction, Small Claims, Probate.*

www.nassauclerk.com

Civil Records: Access: Phone, fax, mail, in person. Only the court performs in person searches; visitors may not. Search fee: $1.00 per name per year. Required to search: name, years to search; also helpful: address. Civil cases indexed by defendant, plaintiff. Civil records on computer since 1993, on microfiche since 1982, prior on docket books.

Criminal Records: Access: Phone, fax, mail, in person. Only the court performs in person searches; visitors may not. Search fee: $1.00 per name per year. Required to search: name, years to search, DOB; also helpful: address, SSN, race, sex. Criminal records on computer since 1985, on microfiche to 1982, prior on docket books. Past 5 years only can be done on phone.

General Information: No juvenile, child abuse or sexual battery records released. SASE required. Turnaround time 1 week. Fax notes: $1.00 per page. Copy fee: $1.00 per page. Certification fee: $1.00. Fee payee: Clerk of Circuit Court. Personal checks accepted. Prepayment is required.

Okaloosa County

Circuit & County Courts 1250 Eglin Pkwy, Shalimar, FL 32579; 850-651-7200; Fax: 850-651-7230. Hours: 8AM-5PM (CST). *Felony, Misdemeanor, Civil, Eviction, Small Claims, Probate.*

www.clerkofcourts.cc

Civil Records: Access: Mail, online, in person. Both court and visitors may perform in person searches. Search fee: $6.00 per name. Add $1.00 for each year searched prior to 6/86. Required to search: name, years to search; also helpful: address. Civil cases indexed by defendant, plaintiff. Civil records on computer from 6/86, archived from 1915, prior on index cards. Access to the full online system requires monthly fee of $100.00. Searching is by name or case number. Records also include probate, traffic and domestic records. For more information, call 850-689-5821. Also, civil records available free on at www.clerkofcourts.cc/orsearch/contract.htm. Records go back to 1/86. Search civil index by defendant or plaintiff, date, or file type.

Criminal Records: Access: Mail, online, in person. Both court and visitors may perform in person searches. Search fee: $6.00 per name. Add $1.00 for each year searched prior to 6/89. Required to search: name, years to search, DOB; also helpful: address, SSN, race, sex. Criminal records on computer from 6/86, archived from 1915, prior on index cards. Online access is available through the fee online system, same as civil. Both felony and misdemeanor indexes can be searched. Also, the county clerk is planning to place criminal records free on the Internet at www.clerkofcourts.cc/orsearch/contract.htm.

General Information: Public access terminal is available. No juvenile, child abuse or sexual battery records released. SASE required. Turnaround time 1 week. Copy fee: $1.00 per page. Certification fee: $2.00. Fee payee: Clerk of Circuit Court. Personal checks accepted. Prepayment is required.

Okeechobee County

Circuit & County Courts 304 NW 2nd St Rm 101, Okeechobee, FL 34972; 863-763-2131. Hours: 8:30AM-5PM (EST). *Felony, Misdemeanor, Civil, Eviction, Small Claims, Probate.*

Civil Records: Access: Mail, in person. Both court and visitors may perform in person searches. Search fee: $1.00 per name per year. Required to search: name,

years to search; also helpful: address. Civil cases indexed by defendant, plaintiff. Civil records on computer since 1990, on index cards from 1983 to 1988.

Criminal Records: Access: Mail, in person. Both court and visitors may perform in person searches. Search fee: $1.00 per name per year. Required to search: name, years to search, DOB; also helpful: address, SSN, race, sex. Criminal records on computer since 1989, on index cards from 1932 to 1988. Online access to the sheriff's Sex Offender list is available free at www.sheriff.co.okeechobee.fl.us.

General Information: No juvenile, child abuse or sexual battery records released. SASE required. Turnaround time for criminal 2 weeks, civil 1-2 weeks. Copy fee: $1.00 per page. Certification fee: $1.00. Fee payee: Clerk of Circuit Court. Personal checks accepted. Prepayment is required.

Orange County

Circuit & County Courts 425 N Orange Ave, Orlando, FL 32801-1544; 407-836-2060. Hours: 8AM-5PM (EST). *Felony, Misdemeanor, Civil, Eviction, Small Claims, Probate.*

http://orangeclerk.onetgov.net

Note: Mail requests should use room numbers: civil circuit-310; civil county-350; crim circuit-210; crim county-250.

Civil Records: Access: Mail, online, in person. Both court and visitors may perform in person searches. Search fee: $1.00 per name per year. Required to search: name, years to search. Civil cases indexed by defendant, plaintiff. Civil records are on computer as follows: Circuit civil-1992; Domestic civil-1992; probate-1993; traffic-1980. The Teleclerk countywide remote online system has been replaced by the free iclerk system at http://orangeclerk1.onetgov.net/restricted/iclerk/index.htm. Set your browser "privacy" to "low. Use "public" as username and password. For more information, call 407-836-2060.

Criminal Records: Access: Mail, online, in person. Both court and visitors may perform in person searches. Search fee: $1.00 per name per year. Required to search: name, years to search, DOB. Criminal records on computer from 1988. Online access to criminal records is the same as civil.

General Information: Public access terminal is available. (Available in Records Management Division.) No sex related or adoption records released. SASE helpful. Turnaround time 2 days. Copy fee: $1.00 per page. For more information call 407-836-2064 Certification fee: $1.00. Fee payee: Orange County Clerk of Courts. Personal checks accepted from Orange County only. Prepayment is required.

County Court - Apopka Branch 1111 N Rock Springs Rd, Apopka, FL 32712; 407-654-1030. Hours: 8AM-5PM (EST). *Misdemeanor, Civil Actions Under $15,000, Eviction, Small Claims.*

http://orangeclerk.ocfl.net

Note: Records maintained at Orlando office.

Civil Records: Access: Mail, online, in person. Both court and visitors may perform in person searches. Search fee: $1.00 per name per year. Required to search: name, years to search. Civil cases indexed by defendant, plaintiff. Civil records (Pending) on computer. All dockets on microfilm or microfiche. Some records on index cards. The Teleclerk countywide remote online system has been replaced by the free Iclerk system at http://orange clerk1.onetgov.net/restricted/iclerk/index.htm. Set your browser "privacy" to low. Use "public" as username and password. Probate records available.

Criminal Records: Access: Mail, online, in person. Both court and visitors may perform in person searches. Search fee: $5.00 per name. Required to search: name,

years to search, DOB; also helpful: SSN. Criminal records (Pending) on computer. All dockets on microfilm or microfiche. Some records on index cards. Online access to criminal records is the same as civil.

General Information: Public access terminal is available. No sex related or adoption records released. SASE helpful. Turnaround time 2 days. Copy fee: $1.00 per page. Certification fee: $2.00. Fee payee: Clerk of County Court. Personal checks accepted. Prepayment is required.

County Court - NE Orange Division 450 N Lakemont Ave, Winter Park, FL 32792; 407-671-1116. Hours: 8AM-5PM (EST). *Misdemeanor, Civil Actions Under $15,000, Eviction, Small Claims.*

http://orangeclerk.ocfl.net

Civil Records: Access: Phone, mail, online, in person. Only the court performs in person searches; visitors may not. Search fee: $1.00 per name per year. Required to search: name, years to search. Civil cases indexed by defendant, plaintiff. Civil records (Pending) on computer. All dockets on microfilm or microfiche. The Teleclerk countywide remote online system has been replaced by the free Iclerk system at http://orangeclerk1.onetgov.net/restricted/iclerk/index.htm. Set your browser "privacy" to "low." Use "public" as username and password.

Criminal Records: Access: Phone, mail, online, in person. Only the court performs in person searches; visitors may not. Search fee: $1.00 per name per year. Required to search: name, years to search, DOB; also helpful: SSN. Criminal records (Pending) on computer. All dockets on microfilm or microfiche. Online access to criminal records is the same as civil.

General Information: No sex related or adoption records released. SASE helpful. Turnaround time 2 days. Copy fee: $1.00 per page. Certification fee: $1.00. Fee payee: Clerk of County Court. Only cashiers checks and money orders accepted. Prepayment is required.

County Court #3 475 W Story Rd, Ocoee, FL 34761; 407-656-3229. Hours: 8AM-5PM (EST). *Misdemeanor, Civil Actions Under $15,000, Eviction, Small Claims.*

http://orangeclerk.ocfl.net

Civil Records: Access: Mail, online, in person. Both court and visitors may perform in person searches. Search fee: $1.00 per name per year. Required to search: name, years to search. Civil cases indexed by defendant, plaintiff. Civil records go back to 1890; on computer back to 1990. All dockets are on microfilm or microfiche. The Teleclerk countywide remote online system has been replaced by the free iclerk system at http://orangeclerk1.onetgov.net/restricted/iclerk/index.htm. Set your browser "privacy" to "low. Use "public" as username and password. For more information, call 407-836-2060.

Criminal Records: Access: Mail, online, in person. Both court and visitors may perform in person searches. Search fee: $1.00 per name per year. Required to search: name, years to search, DOB; also helpful: SSN. Criminal records go back to 1890; on computer back to 1990. All dockets are on microfilm or microfiche. Online access to criminal records is the same as civil.

General Information: Public access terminal is available. No sex related or adoption records released. SASE helpful. Turnaround time 2 days (depending on file). Copy fee: $1.00 per page. Certification fee: $2.00 per page. Fee payee: Clerk of County Court. Personal checks accepted. Credit cards accepted: Visa, MasterCard. Accepted for civil payments only. Prepayment is required.

Osceola County

Circuit Court - Civil 2 Courthouse Sq, Kissimmee, FL 34741; 407-847-1300 #3 X1448. Hours: 8:30AM-5PM (EST). *Civil Actions Over $5,000.*

www.ninja9.net

Civil Records: Access: Mail, in person, online. Both court and visitors may perform in person searches. Search fee: $1.00 per name per year. Required to search: name, years to search. Civil cases indexed by defendant, plaintiff. Civil records on computer from 1990, on docket books from 1800s to 1990. Online access to court records on the Clerk of Circuit Court database are available free at www.osceolaclerk.org.

General Information: Public access terminal is available. (Only civil available) No appeal records released. SASE required. Turnaround time 1-2 days. Copy fee: $1.00 per page. Certification fee: $1.00. Fee payee: Clerk of Court. Business checks accepted. Prepayment is required.

Circuit & County Courts - Criminal Division 2 Courthouse Square, Kissimmee, FL 34741; 407-343-3543/3556. Hours: 8:30AM-5PM (EST). *Felony, Misdemeanor.*

www.osceolaclerk.com

Criminal Records: Access: Mail, in person, online. Both the court and visitor may perform in person searches as long as the case occurred 1990 or after. Search fee: $1.00 per name per year. Required to search: name, years to search, DOB, SSN. Criminal records on computer back to 1990, on index since 1978, prior on docket books from 1800s to 1978. Online access to criminal records available frcc at www.osceolaclerkcourt.org/search.htm. Includes party index and case summary searching.

General Information: Public access terminal is available. No juvenile or sealed records released. SASE requested. Turnaround time 1 week. Copy fee: $1.00 per page. Certification fee: $1.00. Fee payee: Money orders payable to Clerk of the Court. Business checks accepted. Credit cards accepted, but a surcharge is added. Prepayment is required.

County Court - Civil 2 Courthouse Sq, Kissimmee, FL 34741; 407-847-1300. Hours: 8:30AM-5PM (EST). *Eviction, Small Claims.*

www.osceolaclerk.com

Civil Records: Access: Mail, in person, online. Both court and visitors may perform in person searches. Search fee: $1.00 per name per year. Required to search: name, years to search. Civil cases indexed by defendant, plaintiff. Civil records on computer from 1991, on index cards from 1972 to 1991, on docket books from 1800s to 1972. Online access to court records on the Clerk of Circuit Court database are available free at www.osceolaclerkcourt.org.

General Information: Public access terminal is available. (Only civil available) No juvenile records released. SASE helpful. Turnaround time 1 week. Copy fee: $1.00 per page. Certification fee: $1.00. Fee payee: Clerk of Court. Business checks accepted. Prepayment is required.

Palm Beach County

Circuit Court - Civil Division PO Box 4667, West Palm Beach, FL 33402; 561-355-2986; Fax: 561-355-4643. Hours: 8AM-5PM (EST). *Civil.*

www.pbcountyclerk.com

Civil Records: Access: Phone, mail, online, in person. Both court and visitors may perform in person searches. Search fee: $1.00 per name per year. Required to search: name, years to search; also helpful: address. Civil cases indexed by defendant, plaintiff. Civil records (Circuit) on computer from 1982, prior records on microfiche and dockets. County on computer from 1987, prior on microfilm. Access to the countywide remote online system requires $145 setup and $65 per month fees. Civil index goes back to '88. Records also include probate, traffic and domestic. Contact Betty Jones at 561-355-6783 for information. Also, online access to the 15th judicial circuit records available at http://web3172.co.palm-beach.fl.us/aemasp/default.asp. Registration and password is required.

General Information: Public access terminal is available. No juvenile, child abuse or sexual battery records released. SASE required. Turnaround time 1 week. Copy fee: $1.00 per page. Certification fee: $1.00. Fee payee: Clerk of Circuit Court. Personal checks accepted. Prepayment is required.

Circuit & County Courts - Criminal Division 205 North Dixie Hwy, West Palm Beach, FL 33401; 561-355-2519; Fax: 561-355-3802. Hours: 8AM-5PM (EST). *Felony, Misdemeanor.*

www.pbcountyclerk.com

Criminal Records: Access: Phone, fax, mail, online, in person. Both court and visitors may perform in person searches. Search fee: $1.00 per name per year. Required to search: name, years to search, DOB, aliases. Criminal records on computer & microfiche (some files) from 1970s, archived from 1920s. Access to the countywide criminal online system requires $145 setup and $65 per month fee. Records also include probate, traffic and domestic. Contact Mr. McArthur for information. Also, online access to 15th judicial circuit records is available on the web http://web3172.co.palm-beach.fl.us/aemasp/default.asp. Registration and password is required.

General Information: Public access terminal is available. No juvenile, child abuse or sexual battery records released. SASE not required. Turnaround time 1 day. Copy fee: $1.00 per page. Certification fee: $1.00. Fee payee: Clerk of Circuit Court. Personal checks accepted. Prepayment is required.

County Court - Civil Division 205 N Dixie HWY, West Palm Beach, FL 33402; 561-355-2986; Fax: 561-355-4643. Hours: 8AM-5PM (EST). *Eviction, Small Claims.*

www.pbcountyclerk.com

Civil Records: Access: Phone, mail, online, in person. Both court and visitors may perform in person searches. Search fee: $1.00 per name per year. Required to search: name, years to search; also helpful: address. Civil cases indexed by defendant, plaintiff. Civil records (Circuit) on computer from 1982, prior records on microfiche and dockets. County on computer from 1987, prior on microfilm. Access to the countywide remote online system requires $145 setup and $65 per month fees. Civil index goes back to '88. Records also include probate, traffic and domestic. Contact M. McArthur at 561-355-6846 for information. Also, online access to the 15th judicial circuit records available at http://web3172.co.palm-beach.fl.us/aemasp/default.asp. Registration and password are required.

General Information: Public access terminal is available. No juvenile, child abuse or sexual battery records released. SASE required. Turnaround time 1 week. Copy fee: $1.00 per page. Certification fee: $1.00. Fee payee: Clerk of Circuit Court. Personal checks accepted. Prepayment is required.

Circuit Court - Probate Division PO Box 4238, West Palm Beach, FL 33402; 561-355-2900. Hours: 8AM-5PM (EST). *Probate.*

www.pbcountyclerk.com

Note: Online access to 15th judicial circuit records is available at http://web3172.co.palm-beach.fl.us/aemasp/default.asp. Registration and password are required.

Pasco County

Circuit & County Courts - Civil Division 38053 Live Oak Ave, Dade City, FL 33523; 352-521-4482. Hours: 8:30AM-5PM (EST). *Civil, Eviction, Small Claims, Probate.*

www.jud6.org

Civil Records: Access: Mail, online, in person. Both court and visitors may perform in person searches. Search fee: $1.00 per name per year. Required to search: name, years to search. Civil cases indexed by defendant, plaintiff. Civil records on computer from 1985, on docket cards and docket books from 1900s. Online access to Clerk of Court records via the Internet is to be available in late 2001. Current access to the countywide remote online system requires a $100 deposit, $50 annual fee and $10 monthly minimum. There is a $.10 per screen charge. Probate records also available. Call 352-521-4201 for more information.

General Information: Public access terminal is available. No adoption records released. Turnaround time 2-4 days. Copy fee: $1.00 per page. Certification fee: $1.00. Fee payee: Clerk of Court. Personal checks accepted. Prepayment is required.

Circuit & County Courts - Criminal Division 38053 Live Oak Ave, Dade City, FL 33523-3894; 352-521-4504. Hours: 8:30AM-5PM (EST). *Felony, Misdemeanor.*

www.jud6.org

Criminal Records: Access: Mail, online, in person. Both court and visitors may perform in person searches. Search fee: $1.00 per name per year. Required to search: name, years to search, address, DOB; also helpful: SSN. Criminal records on computer since 1978. Access to the countywide criminal online system requires $100 deposit, $50 annual fee and $10 monthly minimum. There is a $.10 per screen charge. The system is open 24 hours daily. Search by name or case number. Call 352-521-4201 for more information.

General Information: Public access terminal is available. No confidential, sealed or juvenile records released. Turnaround time 2-4 days. Copy fee: $1.00 per page. Certification fee: $1.00. Fee payee: Clerk of Courts. Personal checks accepted. Out of state personal checks not accepted. Prepayment is required.

Pinellas County

Circuit & County Courts - Civil Division 315 Court St RM170, Clearwater, FL 33756; 727-464-3267; Fax: 727-464-4070. Hours: 8AM-5PM (EST). *Civil, Eviction, Small Claims, Probate.*

www.jud6.org

Civil Records: Access: Fax, mail, online, in person. Both court and visitors may perform in person searches. Search fee: $1.00 per name per year. Required to search: name, years to search. Civil cases indexed by defendant, plaintiff. Civil records on computer from 1980, on microfiche from 1900s to 1982, older data in warehouse. Access to the countywide remote online system requires $60 fee plus $5.00 per month and $.05 per screen. Civil index goes back to 1972. Contact Sue Maskeny at 727-464-3779 for information. Includes probate and traffic records.

General Information: Public access terminal is available. No adoption or juvenile records released. SASE helpful. Turnaround time 1 week. Fax notes: $1.00 per page. Copy fee: $1.00 per page. Certification fee: $1.00. Fee payee: Clerk of the Court. Personal checks accepted. Prepayment is required.

Criminal Justice Center Circuit Criminal Court Records, 14250 49th St N, Clearwater, FL 34622; 727-464-6793; Fax: 727-464-6233. 8AM-5PM (EST). *Felony.*

www.jud6.org

Criminal Records: Access: Fax, mail, online, in person. Both court and visitors may perform in person searches. Search fee: $1.00 per name per year. Required to search: name, years to search, DOB. Criminal records on computer from 1977, on microfilm from 1912 to 1976, on docket books from 1912. Access to the countywide criminal online system requires $60 fee plus $5.00 per month plus $.05 per screen. Criminal index goes back to 1972. Contact Sue Maskeny at 727-464-3779 for information.

General Information: Public access terminal is available. Turnaround time 1 week. Fax notes: $1.00 per page. Copy fee: $1.00 per page. Certification fee: $1.00. Fee payee: Clerk of Circuit Court. Personal checks accepted. Prepayment is required.

County Court - Criminal Division 14250 49th St N, Clearwater, FL 34622-2831; 727-464-7000; Fax: 727-464-7040. 8AM-5PM (EST). *Misdemeanor.*

www.jud6.org

Criminal Records: Access: Mail, online, in person. Both court and visitors may perform in person searches. Search fee: $1.00 per name per year. Required to search: name, years to search; also helpful: address, DOB, SSN. Criminal records on computer since 10/77, prior on index books. Prior to 1993 on microfilm. Access to the countywide criminal online system requires $60 fee plus $5.00 a month and $.05 per screen. Criminal index goes back to 1972. Contact Sue Maskeny at 727-464-3779 for information.

General Information: Public access terminal is available. No sealed or non-arrested case records released. Turnaround time 3-5 days. Copy fee: $1.00 per page. Certification fee: $1.00. Fee payee: Clerk of Courts. Personal checks accepted. Prepayment is required.

Polk County

Circuit Court - Civil Division PO Box 9000, Drawer CC2, Bartow, FL 33831-9000; 863-534-4488; Probate phone: 863-534-4478; Fax: 863-534-7707. 8AM-5PM (EST). *Civil Actions Over $15,000, Probate.*

www.polk-county.net/clerk/clerk.html

Civil Records: Access: Phone, mail, online, in person. Both court and visitors may perform in person searches. Search fee: $1.00 per name per year. Required to search: name. Civil cases indexed by defendant, plaintiff. Civil Records on computer since 1978; on microfiche from 1800s to 1978. Case index information back to 1990 available free from the County Clerk's web site at www.polk-county.net/clerk/Public_Records/Public_index.html. Includes land and lien searching.

General Information: No sex related cases, adoption, confidential, victims or child abuse records released. SASE required. Turnaround time 2-3 days. Copy fee: $1.00 per page. Certification fee: $1.00. Fee payee: Clerk of Court. Personal checks accepted. Prepayment is required.

Circuit & County Courts - Felony Division PO Box 9000 Drawer CC9, Bartow, FL 33830; 863-534-4000; Fax: 863-534-4137. Hours: 8AM-5PM (EST). *Felony.*

www.polk-county.net/clerk/clerk.html

Criminal Records: Access: Phone, mail, online, in person. Both court and visitors may perform in person searches. Search fee: $1.00 per name per year. Required to search: name, years to search, DOB; also helpful: SSN. Criminal records on computer-felonies since 1977, misdemeanors purged periodically. Both on microfiche and archived since 1800s. Case index information back to 1990 available free from the County Clerk's web site at www.polk-county.net/clerk/Public_Records/Public_index.html.

General Information: Public access terminal is available. No sex related cases, victims or child abuse released. Turnaround time varies. Indicate on request when record is needed. Copy fee: $1.00 per page. Certification fee: $1.00 per page. Fee payee: Clerk of Circuit Court. Personal checks accepted. Prepayment is required.

Circuit & County Courts - Misdemeanor Division PO Box 9000 Drawer CC10, Bartow, FL 33831-9000; 863-534-4446; Fax: 863-534-4137. Hours: 8AM-5PM (EST). *Misdemeanor.*

www.polk-county.net/clerk/clerk.html

Criminal Records: Access: Phone, mail, online, in person. Both court and visitors may perform in person searches. Search fee: 3 year search: $4.10; lifetime: $5.10. Required to search: name, years to search, DOB; also helpful: SSN. Criminal records on computer; felonies since 1977, misdemeanors purged periodically. Both on microfiche and archived since 1800s. Two options are available. Online access to the complete database requires $150 setup fee. Call 863-534-7575 for more information. Second, case index information back to 1990 available free from the County Clerk's web site at www.polk-county.net/clerk/Public_Records/Public_index.html.

General Information: Public access terminal is available. No sex related cases, victims or child abuse released. Turnaround time varies. Indicate on request when record is needed. Copy fee: $1.00 per page. Certification fee: $1.00. Fee payee: Clerk of Circuit Court. Personal checks accepted. Prepayment is required.

County Court - Civil Division PO Box 9000 Drawer CC12, Bartow, FL 33830-9000; 863-534-4556; Fax: 863-534-4045. Hours: 8AM-5PM (EST). *Civil Actions Under $15,000, Eviction, Small Claims.*

www.polk-county.net/clerk/clerk.html

Civil Records: Access: Phone, mail, online, in person. Both court and visitors may perform in person searches. No search fee. Required to search: name, years to search. Civil cases indexed by defendant, plaintiff. Civil records on computer from 1983, on microfiche from 1961 to 1995. Two options are available. Online access to the complete database requires $150 setup fee and $.15 per minute charge with a $50 minimum per quarter. Call 863-534-7575 for more information. Second, case index information back to 1990 available free from the County Clerk's web site at www.polk-county.net/clerk/Public_Records/Public_index.html. Includes land and lien searching.

General Information: Public access terminal is available. Turnaround time 1-5 days. Copy fee: $1.00 per page. Certification fee: $1.00. Fee payee: Clerk of Court. Only cashiers checks and money orders accepted. Prepayment is required.

Putnam County

Circuit & County Courts - Civil Division PO Box 758, Palatka, FL 32178; 386-329-0361; Fax: 386-329-0888. Hours: 8:30AM-5PM (EST). *Civil, Eviction, Small Claims, Probate.*

Civil Records: Both court and visitors may perform in person searches. Search fee: $1.00 per name per year. Required to search: name, years to search. Civil cases indexed by defendant, plaintiff. Civil records on computer from 1984, on microfiche from 1973 to 1984, on index cards and docket books from 1900s to 1973. Access to the countywide remote online system requires $400 setup fee and $40. monthly charge plus $.05 per minute over 20 hours. Civil records go back to 1984. System includes criminal and real property records. Contact Ryel Christiansen to register.

General Information: Public access terminal is available. No juvenile or incompetency records

released. SASE requested. Turnaround time 2-3 days. Fax notes: Fee to fax results is $2.25 per page. Copy fee: $1.00 per page. Certification fee: $1.00. Fee payee: Clerk of Court. Personal checks accepted. Prepayment is required.

Circuit & County Courts - Criminal Division PO Box 758, Palatka, FL 32178; 386-329-0249; Fax: 386-329-0888. Hours: 8:30AM-5PM (EST). *Felony, Misdemeanor.*

Criminal Records: Access: Mail, fax, in person, e-mail. Both court and visitors may perform in person searches. Search fee: $1.00 per name per year. Required to search: name, years to search; also helpful: DOB. Criminal records on computer from 1988, in files from 1930s to 1988. Access to the countywide criminal online system requires $400 setup fee and $40. monthly charge plus $.05 per minute over 20 hours. Criminal records go back to 1972. System includes civil and real property records. Contact Ryel Christiansen to register.

General Information: Public access terminal is available. No juvenile records released. Turnaround time 2-3 days. Fax notes: Fee to fax results is $2.25 per page. Copy fee: $1.00 per page. Certification fee: $1.00. Fee payee: Clerk of Circuit Court. Personal checks accepted. Prepayment is required.

Santa Rosa County

Circuit & County Courts - Civil Division PO Box 472, Milton, FL 32572; 850-623-0135; Fax: 850-626-7248. Hours: 8AM-4:30PM (CST). *Civil, Eviction, Small Claims, Probate.*

http://clerk.co.santa-rosa.fl.us

Civil Records: Access: Fax, mail, in person. Both court and visitors may perform in person searches. Search fee: $1.00 per name per year. Required to search: name, years to search. Civil cases indexed by defendant, plaintiff. Civil records (Circuit) on computer from 1990, archived and on docket books from 1900s. County on computer from 11/92, on microfiche from 1900s, on docket books from early 1900s.

General Information: Public access terminal is available. No adoption records released. SASE required. Turnaround time ASAP. Fax notes: $2.00 per page. Copy fee: $1.00 per page. Certification fee: $1.00. Fee payee: Clerk of Courts. Personal checks accepted. Prepayment is required.

Circuit & County Courts - Criminal Division PO Box 472, Milton, FL 32572; 850-983-1011; Criminal phone: 850-623-0135 x1007 fel.; Fax: 850-626-5705. Hours: 8AM-4:30PM (CST). *Felony, Misdemeanor.*

http://clerk.co.santa-rosa.fl.us

Note: Misdemeanor phone number is 850-623-0135 x1007 or x2140; fax 850-626-0346.

Criminal Records: Access: Mail, in person. Both court and visitors may perform in person searches. Search fee: $1.00 per name per year. Required to search: name, years to search, DOB; also helpful: SSN. Criminal records on computer back to 1989; felonies on index cards from 1925, misdemeanors on docket books from 1900s.

General Information: Public access terminal is available. No records released before sentencing. SASE required. Turnaround time 1-5 days. Fax notes: Fee to fax results is $2.00 per page. Copy fee: $1.00 per page. Certification fee: $1.00 per page. Fee payee: Clerk's Office (include Division/Department name). Personal checks accepted. Prepayment is required.

Sarasota County

Circuit & County Courts - Civil PO Box 3079, Sarasota, FL 34230; 941-951-5206. Hours: 8:30AM-5PM (EST). *Civil, Eviction, Small Claims, Probate.*

www.clerk.co.sarasota.fl.us

Civil Records: Access: Mail, online, in person. Both court and visitors may perform in person searches. Search fee: $1.00 per name per year. Required to search: name, years to search. Civil cases indexed by defendant, plaintiff. Civil records on computer from 1983, circuit & county on docket books from 1900s to 1983. Civil and DV case records from the Clerk of Circuit Court database are available free online at www.clerk.co.sarasota.fl.us/civilapp/civilinq.asp. Criminal, probate and domestic records are also available. Probate court records are available at www.clerk.co.sarasota.fl.us/probapp/probinq.asp

General Information: Public access terminal is available. No adoption, mental health, or sealed records released. SASE helpful. Turnaround time 1 week. Copy fee: $1.00 per page. Certification fee: $1.00. Fee payee: Clerk of Circuit Court. Personal checks accepted. Credit cards will be accepted as of 07/97. Prepayment is required.

Circuit & County Courts - Criminal
PO Box 3079, Sarasota, FL 34230; 941-362-4066. Hours: 8:30AM-5PM (EST). *Felony, Misdemeanor.*

www.clerk.co.sarasota.fl.us

Criminal Records: Access: Mail, online, in person. Both court and visitors may perform in person searches. Search fee: $1.00 per name per year. Required to search: name, years to search, DOB, SSN. Criminal records on computer since 1983, (circuit) on docket books from 1900s to 1983, (county) on docket books from 1960s to 1983. Criminal case records from the Clerk of the Circuit Court database available free online at www.clerk.co.sarasota.fl.us/crimdisclaim.htm. Civil, probate and domestic records are also available.

General Information: Public access terminal is available. No juvenile records released. SASE helpful. Turnaround time 1 week. Copy fee: $1.00 per page. Certification fee: $1.00. Fee payee: Clerk of Circuit Court. Personal checks accepted. Prepayment is required.

Seminole County

Circuit & County Courts - Civil Division
PO Box 8099, Sanford, FL 32772; 407-665-4330; Fax: 407-330-7193. Hours: 8AM-4:30PM (EST). *Civil, Eviction, Small Claims, Probate.*

www.18thcircuit.state.fl.us

Civil Records: Access: Mail, in person, online. Both court and visitors may perform in person searches. Search fee: $1.00 per name per year. Required to search: name, years to search. Civil cases indexed by defendant, plaintiff. Civil records on computer since 1986, on microfiche since 1913. Access to the County Clerk's online records available free at www.seminoleclerk.org/OfficialRecords. Search by name, clerk's file number, or book & page.

General Information: Public access terminal is available. No confidential files pursuant to law or sealed records released. SASE required. Turnaround time 1 week. Copy fee: $1.00 per page. Certification fee: $1.00 per page. Fee payee: Clerk of the Circuit Court. Personal checks accepted. Prepayment is required.

Circuit & County Courts - Criminal Division
301 N Park Ave, Sanford, FL 32771; 407-665-4356 (Felony) 4377 (Misd). Hours: 8AM-4:30PM (EST). *Felony, Misdemeanor.*

www.seminoleclerk.org

Criminal Records: Access: Mail, in person. Both court and visitors may perform in person searches. Search fee: $1.00 per name per year. Required to search: name, years to search, DOB; also helpful: race, sex. Criminal records on computer from 1986; prior on microfiche.

General Information: Public access terminal is available. No records of investigations which have not resulted in an arrest released. SASE not required.

Turnaround time 2 days for felonies, no set time for misdemeanors. Copy fee: $1.00 per page. Certification fee: $4.00. Fee payee: Clerk of Courts. Business checks accepted. Local personal and company checks allowed. Prepayment is required.

St. Johns County

Circuit & County Courts - Civil Division
PO Drawer 300, St Augustine, FL 32085-0300; 904-823-2333; Fax: 904-823-2294. Hours: 8AM-5PM (EST). *Civil, Eviction, Small Claims, Probate.*

www.co.st-johns.fl.us

Civil Records: Access: Fax, mail, online, in person. Both court and visitors may perform in person searches. Search fee: $1.00 per name per year. Required to search: name, years to search. Civil cases indexed by defendant, plaintiff. Civil records on computer from 1984, on microfiche from 1976 to 1986, on docket books from 1820 to 1983. County on computer from 1991, microfiche from 1983 to 1991, docket books from 1820 to 1983. Access to the countywide remote online system requires $200 setup fee plus a monthly fee of $50. Searching is by name or case number. Call Mark Dearing at 904-823-2333 x361 for more information. Also, online access to the county Clerk of Circuit Court recording database available free at www.co.st-johns.fl.us/Const-Officers/Clerk-of-Court/doris/searchdocs.asp. Includes civil and probate records.

General Information: Public access terminal is available. No confidential or sealed records released. SASE required. Turnaround time 4-5 days. Fax notes: Fee to fax results: Long distance: $2.25 for 1st page, $1.00 each add'l; Local: $1.25 1st page, $1.00 each add'l. Copy fee: $1.00 per page. Certification fee: $1.00. Fee payee: Clerk of Circuit Court. Personal checks accepted. Credit cards accepted: Visa, MasterCard. Prepayment is required.

Circuit & County Courts - Criminal Division
PO Drawer 300, St Augustine, FL 32085-0300; 904-823-2333; Fax: 904-823-2294. Hours: 8AM-5PM (EST). *Felony, Misdemeanor.*

www.co.st-johns.fl.us

Criminal Records: Access: Fax, mail, online, in person. Both court and visitors may perform in person searches. Search fee: $1.00 per name per year. Required to search: name, years to search, DOB; also helpful: address, SSN. Criminal Records on computer. Felony since 1986, Misdemeanor since 1984. Felony on log books from 1950 to 1984. Access to the countywide criminal online system requires $200 setup fee plus a monthly fee of $50. Searching is by name or case number. Call Mark Dearing at 904-823-2333 x361 for more information.

General Information: Public access terminal is available. No juvenile or sexual offense records released. SASE required. Turnaround time 4-5 days. Fax notes: Fee to fax results is $1.00 per page. Copy fee: $1.00 per page. Certification fee: $1.00. Fee payee: Clerk of Circuit Court. Personal checks accepted. Credit cards accepted: Visa, MasterCard. Escrow & billing accounts available to government agencies.

St. Lucie County

Circuit & County Courts - Civil Division
PO Drawer 700, Ft Pierce, FL 34954; 772-462-2758 (Circuit); Civil phone: 772-785-5880 (County); Fax: 772-462-1998 (Circ.) 772-871-5387 (Cty). Hours: 8AM-5PM (EST). *Civil, Eviction, Small Claims, Probate.*

Note: Small claims phone is 772-785-5884.

Civil Records: Access: Mail, in person, online. Both court sand visitors may perform in person searches. Search fee: $1.00 per name per year. Required to search: name, years to search. Civil cases indexed by defendant, plaintiff. Circuit records on computer back to

1992. Circuit on microfiche from 1981 to 1992, County from 1981 to 1992. Circuit on docket books from 1900s to 1981, County from 1900s to 1981. Online access to civil records is to be online by 2003 at http://public.slcclerkofcourt.com. Case tracking should also be available. Bond record tracking is available. Small Claims and County Civil files and microfiche located at the Courthouse Annex, 250 NW County Club Dr, Pt St. Lucie, FL 34986.

General Information: Public access terminal is available. No sealed cases or adoption records released. Turnaround time 1 day. Copy fee: $1.00 per page. Certification fee: $1.00 per document. Fee payee: Clerk of Court. Personal checks accepted. Drivers license & photo ID required. Prepayment is required.

Circuit & County Courts - Criminal Division
PO Drawer 700, Ft Pierce, FL 34954; 772-462-6900; Fax: 772-462-2833. Hours: 8AM-5PM (EST). *Felony, Misdemeanor.*

www.martin.fl.us/GOVT/co/schack

Criminal Records: Access: Fax, mail, in person, online. Both court and visitors may perform in person searches. Search fee: $1.00 per name per year. Required to search: name, years to search, DOB, signed release; also helpful: address, SSN, race, sex. Criminal records on computer back to 1982, on microfiche to 1960, on books prior to 1900s. Online access to bonds, traffic and misdemeanor records is available free at http://public.slcclerkofcourt.com. Online records go back to 7/6/1992. Felony records are to be online in 2002. Case tracking should also be available.

General Information: Public access terminal is available. No sealed or expunged records released. Turnaround time 1-2 weeks, FAX turnaround time 1-5 days. Fax notes: Fee to fax results is $2.00 per page. Copy fee: $1.00 per page. Certification fee: $2.00. Fee payee: Clerk of Court. Personal checks accepted. Prepayment is required.

Sumter County

Circuit & County Courts - Civil Division
209 N Florida St, Bushnell, FL 33513; 352-793-0215; Fax: 352-568-6608. Hours: 8:30AM-5PM (EST). *Civil, Eviction, Small Claims, Probate.*

Civil Records: Access: Fax, mail, in person. Both court and visitors may perform in person searches. Search fee: $1.00 per name per year. Required to search: name, years to search. Civil cases indexed by defendant, plaintiff. Civil records go back to 1800s; on computer go back to 12/1999; in docket books from 1986 to 11/30/99 (circuit only).

General Information: No juvenile or adoption records released. SASE requested. Turnaround time 1 week, phone turnaround 30 min. to 1 hour. Fax notes: $1.00 per page. Copy fee: $1.00 per page. Certification fee: $1.00 per document. Fee payee: Clerk of Circuit Court. Personal checks accepted. Prepayment is required.

Circuit & County Courts - Criminal Division
209 N Florida St, Bushnell, FL 33513; 352-793-0211; Fax: 352-568-6608. Hours: 8:30AM-5PM (EST). *Felony, Misdemeanor.*

Criminal Records: Access: Mail, in person. Only the court performs in person searches; visitors may not. Search fee: $1.00 per name per year. Required to search: name, years to search, DOB. Criminal records (circuit) on computer since 2000, on index books from 1965 to 1999, prior in vaults. County on computer since 1982, on microfiche from 1960 to 1982, on docket books since early 1900s.

General Information: No juvenile records released. SASE requested. Turnaround time 1 week. Fax notes: Fee to fax results is $1.00 per page. Copy fee: $1.00 per page. Certification fee: $1.00. Fee payee: Clerk of Court. Only cashiers checks and money orders accepted. Prepayment is required.

Suwannee County

Circuit & County Courts 200 S Ohio Ave, Live Oak, FL 32060; 386-362-0500; Fax: 386-362-0548. Hours: 8AM-5PM (EST). *Felony, Misdemeanor, Civil, Eviction, Small Claims, Probate.*

www.suwanneeclerkofcourt.com

Civil Records: Access: Mail, in person, online. Both court and visitors may perform in person searches. Search fee: $1.00 per name per year. Fee is per index. Required to search: name, years to search; also helpful: address. Civil cases indexed by defendant, plaintiff. Civil records on computer from 1983, archived from 1859 to 1983. Online access to County Clerk of Circuit Court records is available at the web site. Written requests require prepayment.

Criminal Records: Access: Mail, in person, online. Both court and visitors may perform in person searches. Search fee: $1.00 per name per year. Fee is per index. Required to search: name, years to search, DOB, signed release; also helpful: address, SSN. Criminal records on computer from 1983, archived from 1859 to 1983. Online access to criminal records is the same as civil. Written requests require prepayment.

General Information: Public access terminal is available. No juvenile or adoption records released. SASE required. Turnaround time 1 week. Copy fee: $1.00 per page. Certification fee: $1.00. Fee payee: Suwannee Court Clerk. Personal checks accepted. Prepayment is required.

Taylor County

Circuit & County Courts PO Box 620, Perry, FL 32348; 850-838-3506; Fax: 850-838-3549. Hours: 8AM-5PM (EST). *Felony, Misdemeanor, Civil, Eviction, Small Claims, Probate.*

Civil Records: Access: Phone, fax, mail, in person. Only the court performs in person searches; visitors may not. Search fee: $1.00 per name per year. Required to search: name, years to search. Civil cases indexed by defendant, plaintiff. Civil records on computer back to 1982; on index from 1973 to 1991, prior on index books to 1856.

Criminal Records: Access: Phone, fax, mail, in person. Only the court performs in person searches; visitors may not. Search fee: $1.00 per name per year. Required to search: name, years to search, DOB; also helpful: SSN, race, sex. Criminal records on computer back to 1982; on index from 1973 to 1991, prior on index books to 1950.

General Information: No juvenile records released. SASE helpful. Turnaround time 1 week. Copy fee: $1.00 per page. Certification fee: $1.00. Fee payee: Taylor County Clerk of Court. Business checks accepted. Prepayment is required.

Union County

Circuit & County Courts Courthouse Rm 103, Lake Butler, FL 32054; 386-496-3711; Fax: 386-496-1718. Hours: 8AM-5PM (EST). *Felony, Misdemeanor, Civil, Eviction, Small Claims, Probate.*

http://circuit8.org

Civil Records: Access: Fax, mail, in person. Only the court may perform in person searches. Search fee: $1.00 per name per year. Required to search: name, years to search. Civil cases indexed by defendant, plaintiff. Civil records on docket books from 1921.

Criminal Records: Access: Fax, mail, in person, online. Only the court may perform in person searches. Search fee: $1.00 per name per year. Required to search: name, years to search, DOB; also helpful: SSN. Criminal records on docket books from 1921. Access to the circuit-wide criminal quick lookup available at

http://circuit8.org/golem/gencrim.html. Account and password is required; restricted usage.

General Information: No juvenile records released. SASE preferred. Turnaround time 2-3 days. Fax notes: $1.00 per page. Copy fee: $1.00 per page. Certification fee: $1.00. Fee payee: Clerk of Court. Personal checks accepted. Prepayment is required.

Volusia County

Circuit & County Courts - Civil Division PO Box 6043, De Land, FL 32721; 386-736-5915; Fax: 386-822-5711. Hours: 8AM-4:30PM (EST). *Civil, Eviction, Small Claims, Probate.*

www.clerk.org

Civil Records: Access: Fax, mail, online, in person. Both court and visitors may perform in person searches. Search fee: $1.00 per name per year. Required to search: name, years to search. Civil cases indexed by defendant, plaintiff. Civil records on computer from 1986, on docket books from 1863 to 1986. Access to the countywide remote online system requires $125 setup fee plus a $25 monthly fee. Windows required. Search by name or case number. Call Tom White 904-736-5915 for more information. Criminal, probate and traffic records are also available.

General Information: Public access terminal is available. No sealed records released. SASE requested. Turnaround time 1-2 weeks. Fax notes: Fee to fax results is $1.00 per page. Copy fee: $1.00 per page. Certification fee: $1.00. Fee payee: Clerk of Circuit Court. Personal checks accepted. Prepayment required.

Circuit & County Courts - Criminal Division PO Box 6043, De Land, FL 32721-6043; 386-736-5909; Fax: 386-740-5175. Hours: 8AM-4:30PM (EST). *Felony, Misdemeanor.*

www.clerk.org

Criminal Records: Access: Mail, online, in person. Both court and visitors may perform in person searches. Search fee: $1.00 per name per year. Required to search: name, years to search, DOB; also helpful: SSN, race, sex. Criminal records 1982 to present on computer, on microfiche from 1856 to 1988, on docket books prior to 1983. Two access methods are available. Access to the Clerk of Circuit Courts database of Citation Violations and 24-hour Arrest Reports is available free at www.clerk.org/publicrecords/or.tshtml. Access to the countywide criminal online system requires $125 setup fee plus a $25 monthly. Windows required. Search by name or case number back to 1988. Call 904-822-5710 for more information. Civil, probate and traffic records are also available.

General Information: No confidential, sexual battery and juvenile records released. SASE required. Turnaround time up to 1 week. Fax notes: $1.50 per page. Copy fee: $1.00 per page. Certification fee: $1.00. Fee payee: Clerk of Court. Personal checks accepted. Personal and out of state checks accepted with proper ID. Prepayment is required.

Wakulla County

Circuit & County Courts 3056 Crawfordville Hwy, Crawfordville, FL 32327; 850-926-0905; Fax: 850-926-0938 (Civil); 926-0936 (Crim). Hours: 8AM-5PM (EST). *Felony, Misdemeanor, Civil, Eviction, Small Claims, Probate.*

www.co.leon.fl.us/court/court.htm

Civil Records: Access: Phone, fax, mail, in person. Both court and visitors may perform in person searches. Search fee: $1.00 per name per year. Required to search: name, years to search. Civil cases indexed by defendant, plaintiff. Civil records on computer since 1990, on docket books from 1800s.

Criminal Records: Access: Fax, mail, in person. Both court and visitors may perform in person searches. Search fee: $1.00 per name per year. Required to search: name, years to search, DOB; also helpful: SSN. Criminal records on computer since 1990, on docket books from 1800s. Visitors may review docket books, only court performs name searches.

General Information: No juvenile, adoption records released. SASE helpful. Turnaround time 3-4 days. Fax notes: Fee to fax results is $1.00 per page. Copy fee: $1.00 per page. Certification fee: $1.00. Fee payee: Clerk of Court. Personal checks accepted. Prepayment is required.

Walton County

Circuit & County Courts PO Box 1260, De Funiak Springs, FL 32435; 850-892-8115; Fax: 850-892-7551. Hours: 8AM-4:30PM (CST). *Felony, Misdemeanor, Civil, Eviction, Small Claims, Probate.*

www.co.walton.fl.us/clerk

Civil Records: Access: Fax, mail, online, in person. Only the court may perform in person searches. Search fee: $1.00 per name per year. Required to search: name, years to search. Civil cases indexed by defendant, plaintiff. Civil records on computer from 1988, on dockets from 1900s. Access to the county online system requires a setup fee of at least $30 plus $100 monthly. System includes probate, traffic, domestic and criminal data. Search by name or case number. Call David Langford for more information, 850-892-8115. Also, the web site offers access to civil record indices.

Criminal Records: Access: Fax, mail, online, in person. Only the court may perform in person searches. Search fee: $1.00 per name per year. Required to search: name, years to search, DOB. Criminal records on computer from 1988, on dockets from 1900s. Online access to criminal records is the same as civil.

General Information: No sealed, expunged, or pre-sentence investigation records released. SASE helpful. Turnaround time 24 hours. Fax notes: $1.00 per page. Copy fee: $1.00 per page. Certification fee: $1.00. Fee payee: Clerk of Courts. Personal checks accepted. Prepayment is required.

Washington County

Circuit & County Courts PO Box 647, Chipley, FL 32428-0647; 850-638-6285; Fax: 850-638-6297. Hours: 8AM-4PM (CST). *Felony, Misdemeanor, Civil, Eviction, Small Claims, Probate.*

Civil Records: Access: Phone, fax, mail, in person, online. Both court and visitors may perform in person searches. Search fee: $1.00 per name per year. Required to search: name, years to search. Civil cases indexed by defendant, plaintiff. Civil records on computer from 1985; on docket books from 1940. Online access to the Clerk of Circuit Court index is available at www.myfloridacounty.com. Search free; documents are $1 per page.

Criminal Records: Access: Phone, fax, mail, in person. Only the court performs in person searches; visitors may not. Search fee: $1.00 per name per year. Required to search: name, years to search. Criminal records on computer back to 1981, on docket books from 1900.

General Information: Public access terminal is available. (Only civil records available.) No adoption or juvenile records released. SASE requested. Turnaround time 1 day. Copy fee: $1.00 per page. Certification fee: $1.00. Fee payee: Clerk of Court. Business checks accepted. Local personal checks accepted. Prepayment is required.

Florida Recording Offices

ORGANIZATION: 67 counties, 67 recording offices. The recording officer is Clerk of the Circuit Court. All transactions are recorded in the "Official Record," a grantor/grantee index. Some counties will search by type of transaction while others will return everything on the index. 57 counties are in the Eastern Time Zone (EST) and 10 are in the Central Time Zone (CST).

REAL ESTATE RECORDS: Any name searched in the "Official Records" will usually include all types of liens and property transfers for that name. Most counties will perform searches. In addition to the usual $1.00 per page copy fee, certification of documents usually cost $1.00 per document. Tax records are located at the Property Appraiser Office.

Note that a number of counties make their real estate records available online.

UCC RECORDS: Financing statements are filed at the state level, and real estate related collateral at the Clerk of the Circuit Court. Until 1/2002, farm related financing was also filed at the clerk's office. All but a few counties will perform UCC searches. Use search request form UCC-11. Search fees are usually $1.00 per debtor name per year searched and include all lien and real estate transactions on record. Copies usually cost $1.00 per page.

TAX LIEN RECORDS: Federal tax liens on personal property of businesses are filed with the Secretary of State. All other federal and state tax liens on personal property are filed with the county Clerk of Circuit Court. Usually tax liens on personal property are filed in the same index with UCC financing statements and real estate transactions. Most counties will perform a tax lien as part of a UCC search. Copies usually cost $1.00 per page.

OTHER LIENS: Judgments, hospital, mechanics, sewer, ambulance.

ONLINE ACCESS: There are numerous county agencies that provide ONLINE ACCESS: to records. ONLINE ACCESS: to the over 51 county's Circuit Clerks of Courts is available free at www.myfloridacounty.com/services/officialrecords_intro.shtml

On or after October 1, 2002, any person preparing or filing a document for recording in the Official Record may not include a social security number in such document unless required by law. The Clerk of the Circuit Court cannot place an image or copy of the following documents on a publicly available Internet website for general public display: Military discharges; Death certificates; Court files, records or papers relating to Family Law, Juvenile Law or Probate Law cases.

Any person has the right to request the Clerk/County Recorder to redact/remove his social security number from an image or copy of an Official Record that has been placed on such Clerk/County Recorder's publicly available Internet website.

Alachua County

County Clerk of the Circuit Court, PO Box 600, Gainesville, FL 32602. 352-374-3625; Fax 352-491-4649. www.clerk-alachua-fl.org
Will search UCC records. Tax liens not included in UCC search. Real estate owner, mortgage, and property transfer searches available. **Online Access:** Property Appraiser, Real Estate, Lien, Vital Statistic, Recording Records. Access to the Clerk of Courts recording database are available free at www.clerk-alachua-fl.org/clerk/pubrec.html. Records go back to 1/1993. Also, search the County Property Search page free online at www.acpafl.org/services/search/search.asp. There is also a sales search here. Also, online access to the state recorders' meta-search site is available free at www.myfloridacounty.com. Click on Official Records. **Other Phones:** Treasurer 352-374-3605; Appraiser 352-374-5230; Finance Director 352-374-3605.

Baker County

County Clerk of the Circuit Court, 339 E. MacClenny Ave, MacClenny, FL 32063. 904-259-0208; Fax 904-259-4176. Will search UCC records. Tax liens not included in UCC search. Separate tax lien searches performed at $1.00 per year. Real estate owner, mortgage, and property transfer searches available. **Online Access:** Real Estate, Lien, Recording Records. Search the state recorders' meta-search site for free at www.myfloridacounty.com. Click on Official records. **Other Phones:** Treasurer 904-259-6880; Appraiser/Auditor 904-259-3191; Elections 904-259-6339.

Bay County

County Clerk of the Circuit Court, PO Box 2269, Panama City, FL 32402. 850-747-5104; Fax 850-747-5199. www.baycoclerk.com

Will search UCC records. This agency will not do a tax lien search. Real estate record owner searches available 1987 to present. **Online Access:** Property Tax, Real Estate, Tax Lien, Recording Records. Access to the Clerk of the Circuit Court Recordings database is available free at www.clerk.co.bay.fl.us/orsearch. Records go back to 1/1987. Also, search the property appraiser database at http://bcpa.elementaldata.com/search.asp; search the tax collector data at http://bctc.elementaldata.com/disclaimer.asp. Property information from the Assessor database is free online at http://bcpa.co.bay.fl.us/database.htm. Also, online access to the state recorders' meta-search site is available free at www.myfloridacounty.com. Click on Official Records. **Other Phone Numbers:** Assessor 850-784-4095; Appraiser/Auditor 850-784-4095.

Bradford County

County Clerk of the Circuit Court, PO Drawer B, Starke, FL 32091. 904-966-6280; Fax 904-964-4454. Will not search UCC records. Will not search tax lien records. Will not search real estate records. **Online Access:** Real Estate, Appraisal, Deed, Judgment, Marriage, Lien, Court Records. Access to the recorders database is available at www.mybradfordcounty.com. Click on "Official Records." Also, search the property appraiser database at www.bradfordappraiser.com/Search_F.asp. Also, online access to the state recorders' meta-search site is available free at www.myfloridacounty.com. Click on Official Records. **Other Phones:** Appraiser/Auditor 904-964-6280.

Brevard County

County Clerk of the Circuit Court, PO Box 2767, Titusville, FL 32781. 321-264-5244, 264-5350; Fax 321-264-5246. www.clerk.co.brevard.fl.us

Will search UCC records. UCC search includes tax liens if requested. Real estate record searches are available. **Online Access:** Property Appraiser, Real Estate, Lien, Marriage, Recording, Tax Sale Records. Access to the Circuit Clerk's tax lien (1981-95), land records (1995 to present) and marriage records is free at www.clerk.co.brevard.fl.us/pages/pubrec9.htm. Indexed records from 1/1981 to 9/30/1995 are at http://crystalweb1.clerk.co.brevard.fl.us/Indexing/f_indexing.cfm. Also, property tax records are available free at www.brevardpropertyappraiser.com/asp/disclaimer.asp. Search by name or map. Also, tax deed sales are listed free at www.clerk.co.brevard.fl.us/taxdeed/taxdeed.htm. **Other Phone Numbers:** Assessor 321-264-6700; Appraiser/Auditor 321-264-6700.

Broward County

Director of County Records, 115 S Andrews Ave, Rm 114, Fort Lauderdale, FL 33301. Director of County Records, R/E and UCC Recording 954-357-7281; Fax 954-357-7267. www.broward.org/records
Will search UCC records. Tax liens not included in UCC search. Real estate record owner and property searches available. **Online Access:** Property Appraiser, Real Estate, Lien, Recording, Occupational License Records. Access to the county Public Search database 1978-present is available at http://205.166.161.12/oncoreweb/start/disclaim.asp. Additionally, professional users may register and receive a password for additional access options. Also, Property Appraiser records are available free online at www.bcpa.net/search.htm. Also, search occupational licenses at www.co.broward.fl.us/rise.htm. **Other Phones:** Assessor 954-357-6904; Treasurer 954-357-7235; Appraiser/Auditor 954-357-6908; Elections 954-357-7050; Vital Records Birth 954-467-4413/Death records 954-467-4424.

Calhoun County

County Clerk of the Circuit Court, 20859 SE Central Ave, Rm 130, Blountstown, FL 32424. 850-674-4545; Fax 850-674-5553. www.calhounclerk.com

Will search UCC records. This agency will not do a tax lien search. Real estate owner, mortgage, and property transfer searches available. **Online Access:** Real Estate, Lien, Deed, Judgment, Recording Records. Search the state recorders' meta-search site for free at www.myfloridacounty.com. Click on Official Records. **Other Phone Numbers:** Assessor 850-674-8242; Appraiser/Auditor 850-674-8242.

Charlotte County

County Clerk of the Circuit Court, PO Box 510156, Punta Gorda, FL 33951-0156. 941-637-2245; Fax 941-637-2172. www.co.charlotte.fl.us

Will search UCC records. Tax liens not included in UCC search. Real estate record owner and mortgage searches available. **Online Access:** Property Appraiser, Real Estate, Lien, Recording Records. Property records are available free at www.ccappraiser.com/record.asp. Sales records are also available here and at the tax collector database, which is free at www.cctaxcol.com/record.asp?. Also, recordings from the county clerk database are available free online at http://208.47.160.70. Search by book/page or grantor/grantee. A subscription service (CASWEB) is also available, which includes images, court records, recordings, etc. Bulk database record purchases, by year, are also available. Also, online access to the state recorders' meta-search site is available free at www.myfloridacounty.com. Click on Official Records. **Other Phones:** Appraiser/Auditor 941-743-1488.

Citrus County

County Clerk of the Circuit Court, 110 N. Apopka Ave. Room 101, Inverness, FL 34450-4299. 352-341-6468; Fax 352-341-6477. www.clerk.citrus.fl.us

Will search UCC records. UCC search includes tax liens if requested. Will search for any real estate records in the official records index. **Online Access:** Property Appraiser, Real Estate, Lien, Recording, Marriage Records. Access to the Clerk of Circuit Court records is available free at www.clerk.citrus.fl.us/hart_wwwroot. Search Marriage License records free online at www.clerk.citrus.fl.us/marrsearch.asp. Search by first and last name. Also, Property records are available free online at www.pa.citrus.fl.us/ccpaask.html. Also, online access to state recorders' meta-search site is available at www.myfloridacounty.com. Click on Official Records. **Other Phones:** Appraiser 352-637-9820.

Clay County

County Clerk of the Circuit Court, PO Box 698, Green Cove Springs, FL 32043-0698. 904-284-6300 R/E Recording: 904-284-6362 UCC Recording: 904-284-6362; Fax 904-284-6390. http://clerk.co.clay.fl.us

Will search UCC records. UCC search includes tax liens if requested. Will search for any real estate records in official records, except title searches. **Online Access:** Appraiser, Real Estate, Lien, Recording Records. The county clerk of circuit court allows free online access to recording records at http://clerk.co.clay.fl.us/Disclaimer_page.htm. This replaces the commercial system. Records go back to 1990 Also, the Clay County Property Appraiser's office records are available free at www.ccpao.com/ccpao/ccpao.asp?page=Disclaimer. Search by name, street name and number, or real estate number. Also, search tangible personal property free on the tax collector database at www.ccpao.com/tpp. Online access to the state recorders' meta-search site is available free at www.myfloridacounty.com. Click on Official Records. **Other Phones:** Appraiser/Auditor 904-284-6320.

Collier County

County Clerk of the Circuit Court, PO Box 413044, Naples, FL 34101-3044. 239-732-2606; Fax 239-774-8003. www.clerk.collier.fl.us

Will search UCC records. UCC search includes tax liens if requested. Real estate owner, mortgage, and property transfer searches available. **Online Access:** Property Appraiser, Real Estate, Lien, UCC, Vital Statistic, Recording, Tax Sales, Wanted/Missing Person Records. Access to records on the Property Appraiser database are available free online at www.collierappraiser.com/Disclaimer.asp. The sheriff's wanted and missing persons lists are at www.colliersheriff.org. Online access to clerk of courts court records, lien, real estate, UCCs and vital records is available free at www.clerk.collier.fl.us/clerkspublicac/Default.htm. Records include probate, traffic and domestic. Lending agency information is available. Also, Online access to the state recorders' meta-search site is available free at www.myfloridacounty.com. Click on Official Records. Tax deeds sales data is free at www.clerk.collier.fl.us/OfficialRecords/Tax_Deeds/Tax%20Deeds.htm. **Other Phones:** Appraiser/Auditor 239-774-8175.

Columbia County

County Clerk of the Circuit Court, PO Box 2069, Lake City, FL 32056-2069. 386-758-1342 R/E Recording: 386-758-1031 UCC Recording: 386-758-1031; Fax 386-758-1337. www.columbiaclerk.com

Will search UCC records. UCC search includes tax liens if requested. Real estate owner, mortgage, and property transfer searches available. **Online Access:** Real Estate, Lien, Recording, Probate, Property Tax Records. Access to the Clerk of Circuit Courts recording data is at www.mycolumbiacounty.com. Search by name, book/page, file number of document type. Also, online access to the state recorders' meta-search site is available at www.myfloridacounty.com. Click on Official Records. Also, search the tax rolls for free at www.columbiataxcollector.com/collectmax/collect30.asp. **Other Phone Numbers:** Treasurer 386-758-1042; Appraiser/Auditor 386-758-1087; Elections 386-758-1028; Vital Records 386-758-1150.

Dade County

County Clerk of the Circuit Court, 22 N.W. 1st St, Miami, FL 33128. 305-275-1155; Fax 305-372-7775. www.metro-dade.com/clerk

Will search UCC records. UCC search includes tax liens if requested. Real estate owner, mortgage, and property transfer searches available. **Online Access:** Property Appraiser, Real Estate, Lien, Recording, Marriage, Tax Deed Sale Records. Three sources available. Record access to 11 databases requires an initial setup fee is $125 and a minimum monthly fee of $52 for 208 minutes of use, $.25 ea. add'l minute. Records date back to 1975. Includes property appraisal, building permits, tax collection and other data. Contact 305-596-8148 for information. There's a 2nd subscription service for county recorder only for $50 per month at www.co.miami-dade.fl.us/public-records/features.asp. Third, recorder records are available free at www.co.miami-dade.fl.us/public-records/default.asp. Appraiser records are available free online at www.co.miami-dade.fl.us/pa/record.htm. Tax deed sales: www.co.miami-dade.fl.us/clerk/Tax-Deeds/home.htm. **Other Phone Numbers:** Assessor 305-375-4099; Appraiser/Auditor 305-375-5447.

De Soto County

County Clerk of the Circuit Court, 115 E. Oak St, Arcadia, FL 34266. 863-993-4876; Fax 863-993-4669.

Will search UCC records. UCC search includes tax liens if requested. Will not search real estate records. **Online Access:** Real Estate, Lien, Recording, Property Tax Records. Search the state recorders' meta-search site for free at www.myfloridacounty.com. Click on Official Records. Also, access to the property appraiser data is available free at http://qpublic.net/desoto/search.html. **Other Phone Numbers:** Assessor 863-993-4866; Appraiser/Auditor 863-993-4866.

Dixie County

County Clerk of the Circuit Court, PO Box 1206, Cross City, FL 32628. County Clerk of the Circuit Court, R/E and UCC Recording 352-498-1200; Fax 352-498-1201. Will search UCC records. This agency will not do a tax lien search. Will not search real estate records. **Online Access:** Real Estate, Lien, Recording Records. Search the state recorders' meta-search site for free at www.myfloridacounty.com. Click on Official Records. **Other Phone Numbers:** Appraiser/Auditor 352-498-1212; Elections 352-498-1216.

Duval County

County Clerk of the Circuit Court, 330 E. Bay St #103, Courthouse, Jacksonville, FL 32202. 904-630-2043; Fax 904-630-2959. www.ci.jax.fl.us

Online access to the state recorders' meta-search site is available free at www.myfloridacounty.com. Click on Official Records. Will search UCC records. Real estate record owner and mortgage searches available. **Online Access:** Property Appraiser, Real Estate, Lien, Recording, Grantor/Grantee, Vital Statistic Records. Access to the Clerk of Circuit Court and City of Jacksonville Official Records (a grantor/grantee index) is available free at http://apps1.coj.net/legal/officialrecords. Also, Appraiser property records for Duval County and City of Jacksonville are at http://pawww.coj.net/pub/property/lookup.htm. Search the state recorders' meta-search site for free at www.myfloridacounty.com **Other Phones:** Treasurer 904-630-2068; Appraiser/Auditor 904-630-2020.

Escambia County

County Clerk of the Circuit Court, 223 Palafox Place, Old Courthouse, Pensacola, FL 32501. 850-595-3930; Fax 850-595-4827. www.clerk.co.escambia.fl.us

Will search UCC records. UCC search includes tax liens if requested. Real estate owner, mortgage, and property transfer searches available. **Online Access:** Property Appraiser, Real Estate, Lien, Recording, Marriage, Property Tax, Tax Sale Records. Access to Clerk of Court Public Records is available free at www.clerk.co.escambia.fl.us/public_records.html. This includes grantor/grantee index and marriage, traffic and court records. Also, online access to the tax collector's Property Tax Inquiry database is available free online at http://ectc.co.escambia.fl.us/ectc/index2.html. Click on ECTC Online then on "Cyber-Tax." Tax sale information is also available. Also, search property appraiser records at www.escpa.org/searchform.asp. **Other Phones:** Assessor 850-434-2735; Treasurer 850-436-5200; Appraiser/Auditor 850-434-2735.

Flagler County

County Clerk of the Circuit Court, PO Box 787, Recording Division, Bunnell, FL 32010. 386-437-7433; Fax 386-437-7406. http://clerk.co.flagler.fl.us

Will search UCC records. Will search for any real estate records in general index. **Online Access:** Property Appraiser, Recording, Real Estate, Lien Records. Official records from the clerk's index are to be online in 2002. The index is now available on CD-rom for $31.39. For information, contact Judy Daughtry at 386-437-7434. Also, online access to the state recorders' meta-search site is available free at www.myflaglercounty.com. Click on Official Records. Also, property information from the tax appraiser is available free at www.qpublic.net/flagler/search.html. **Other Phones:** Assessor 386-437-7450; Treasurer 386-437-7414; Appraiser/Auditor 386-437-7450.

Franklin County

County Clerk of the Circuit Court, 33 Market St #203, Apalachicola, FL 32320. 850-653-8861 x108 or x109; Fax 850-653-2261. www.franklinclerk.com
Toll-free phone is 850-697-2112. There is also an office at Carrabelle Annex, 203 5th St #5, Carrabelle, FL 32322; 850-697- 3263. Will search UCC records. This agency will not do a tax lien search. Will not search real estate records. **Online Access:** Real Estate, Lien, Recording Records. Search the state recorders' meta-search site for free at www.myfloridacounty.com. Click on Official Records. **Other Phones:** Treasurer 850-653-8861; Appraiser/Auditor 850-653-9236.

Gadsden County

County Clerk of the Circuit Court, PO Box 1649, Quincy, FL 32353-1649. 850-875-8603; Fax 850-875-8612. www.clerk.co.gadsden.fl.us
Will search UCC records. UCC search includes tax liens. Will search real estate records. **Online Access:** Real Estate, Recording, Judgment, Deed, Lien, Vital Statistic, Property Appraiser Records. Access to the official records index is available free at www.clerk.co.gadsden.fl.us/OfficialRecords. Index records go back to 1985. Provides index numbers only. Also, access to the property appraiser database is available free at www.qpublic.net/gadsden/search.html. **Other Phone Numbers:** Assessor 850-627-7168; Appraiser/Auditor 850-627-7168.

Gilchrist County

County Clerk of the Circuit Court, PO Box 37, Trenton, FL 32693. County Clerk of the Circuit Court, R/E and UCC Recording 352-463-3170; Fax 352-463-3166. www.co.gilchrist.fl.us/cophone
Will search UCC records. Tax liens not included in UCC search. Will not search real estate records. **Online Access:** Real Estate, Property Appraiser, Lien, Recording Records. Access to the property appraiser database is available free at www.qpublic.net/gilchrist/search.html. Sales searches are also available. Also, Online access to the state recorders' meta-search site is available free at www.myfloridacounty.com. Click on Official Records. **Other Phone Numbers:** Assessor 352-463-3190; Appraiser/Auditor 352-463-3190; Elections 352-463-3194.

Glades County

County Clerk of the Circuit Court, PO Box 10, Moore Haven, FL 33471. County Clerk of the Circuit Court, R/E and UCC Recording 863-946-0113; Fax 863-946-0560.
Will search UCC records. Will search for any real estate records on general index. **Online Access:** Real Estate, Lien, Recording Records. Search the state recorders' meta-search site for free at www.myfloridacounty.com. Click on Official Records. **Other Phone Numbers:** Appraiser/Auditor 863-946-0818.

Gulf County

County Clerk of the Circuit Court, 1000 5th St, Port St. Joe, FL 32456-1699. County Clerk of the Circuit Court, R/E and UCC Recording 850-229-6113; Fax 850-229-6174. www.gulfclerk.com
Will search UCC records. Will search for any real estate records in general index. **Online Access:** Real Estate, Lien, Deed, Judgment, Marriage, Death, Recording Records. Search the state recorders' meta-search site for free at www.myfloridacounty.com. Click on Official Records. **Other Phone Numbers:** Assessor 850-229-6115; Treasurer 850-229-6116; Appraiser/Auditor 850-229-6115; Elections 850-229-6117; Vital Records 850-227-1276.

Hamilton County

County Clerk of the Circuit Court, 207 NE 1st St, Room 106, Jasper, FL 32052. 386-792-1288; Fax 386-792-3524.
Will search UCC records. UCC search includes tax liens if requested. Will search for any real estate records in general index. **Online Access:** Real Estate, Lien, Recording Records. Search the state recorders' meta-search site for free at www.myfloridacounty.com. Click on Official Records. **Other Phone Numbers:** Treasurer 386-792-1288; Appraiser/Auditor 386-792-1284; Elections 386-792-1426; Vital Records 386-792-1288.

Hardee County

County Clerk of the Circuit Court, PO Drawer 1749, Wauchula, FL 33873. 863-773-4174; Fax 863-773-4422.
Will search UCC records. This agency will not do a tax lien search. Will not search real estate records. **Online Access:** Real Estate, Recording, Lien, Property Appraiser Records. Search the state recorders' meta-search site for free at www.myfloridacounty.com. Click on Official Records. Also, online assess to the property appraiser data is available free at www.hardeecounty.net/cfaps/appraiser/propform.cfm. **Other Phone Numbers:** Assessor 863-773-2196; Appraiser/Auditor 863-773-2196.

Hendry County

County Clerk of the Circuit Court, PO Box 1760, La Belle, FL 33975-1760. County Clerk of the Circuit Court, R/E and UCC Recording 863-675-5217 UCC Recording: 863-675-5202; Fax 863-675-5238.
Will search UCC records. UCC search includes tax liens. Real estate owner, mortgage, and property transfer searches available. **Online Access:** Real Estate, Lien, Recording Records. Search the state recorders' meta-search site for free at www.myfloridacounty.com. Click on Official Records. Also, access the property appraiser database at http://dev.hendryprop.com/GIS/Search_F.asp. **Other Phone Numbers:** Treasurer 863-675-5280; Appraiser/Auditor 863-675-5270; Elections 863-675-5231; Vital Records 863-675-5217.

Hernando County

County Clerk of the Circuit Court, 20 N. Main, Room 215, Brooksville, FL 34601. 352-754-4201 x214/5 R/E Recording: 352-754-4201 x214 or 215; Fax 352-754-4243. www.co.hernando.fl.us
Will search UCC records. Tax liens not included in UCC search. Real estate record owner and property searches available. **Online Access:** Property Appraiser, Real Estate, Lien, Marriage, Recording Records. Access to the clerk; Official Records database is now available free at www.clerk.co.hernando.fl.us/disclaimer.asp. Your browser must be Javascript enabled. Includes recordings, marriages, and court records. Also, the county now offers 2 levels of the Public Inquiry System Property Appraiser Real Estate database - Easy Search & Real Time Search - free online at www.co.hernando.fl.us/pa/propsearch.htm. Search by owner, address, or parcel key. Also, Online access to the state recorders' meta-search site is available free at www.myfloridacounty.com. Click on Official Records. **Other Phone Numbers:** Treasurer 352-754-4190; Appraiser/Auditor 352-754-4190.

Highlands County

County Clerk of the Circuit Court, 590 S. Commerce Ave, Sebring, FL 33870. County Clerk of the Circuit Court, R/E and UCC Recording 863-402-6590 UCC recording: 800-822-5436; www.clerk.co.highlands.fl.us
Online access to the state recorders' meta-search site is available free at www.myfloridacounty.com. Click on Official Records. This agency will not perform searches. **Online Access:** Property Appraiser, Personal Property, Real Estate, Lien, Recording Records. Property appraiser records are available free online at www.appraiser.co.highlands.fl.us/search.html; tangible personal property records are available. Also, online access to the recorders' meta-search site is available at www.myflorida.com. Click on Official Records. Also, online access to deeds, mortgages, judgments from the county recording database are available free at www.clerk.co.highlands.fl.us/highlands.fl/official-records-search.jsp. Records go back to 1983. Also, online access to the county tax collector database is available free at www.collector.co.highlands.fl.us/search/index.html. **Other Phone Numbers:** Assessor 863-402-6659; Treasurer 863-402-6685; Appraiser/Auditor 863-402-6661; Elections 863-402-6654; Vital Records 863-402-6040.

Hillsborough County

County Clerk of the Circuit Court, PO Box 1110-Recording #313, Tampa, FL 33601-1110. 813-276-8100 x7507 R/E Recording: 813-276-8100 UCC Recording: 813-276-8100; Fax 813-276-2114. www.hillsclerk.com
Will search UCC records. UCC search includes tax liens. Real estate owner, mortgage, and property transfer searches available. **Online Access:** Property Appraiser, Personal Property, Real Estate, Lien, Deed, Recording Records. Property appraiser records are available free at www.hcpafl.org/disclaimer.html. Receive owner data, legal, sales, value summaries. Also, access to state recorders' search site is available at www.myfloridacounty.com. Click on official records. Also, the clerk's recordings can be searched free at http://publicrecord.hillsclerk.com. The County also offers access to county court, real estate, and lien records through a fee online service. Courts, traffic and domestic records included. Access is $.25 per minute or $5.00 per month, whichever is greater, plus a $50.00 one-time set-up fee with software. Contact the help desk at 813-276-8100 x7000 for more information. **Other Phone Numbers:** Appraiser/Auditor 813-272-6100.

Holmes County

County Clerk of the Circuit Court, PO Box 397, Bonifay, FL 32425. 850-547-1102; Fax 850-547-6630.
Will search UCC records. Will not search real estate records. **Online Access:** Real Estate, Lien, Recording Records. Search the state recorders' meta-search site for free at www.myfloridacounty.com. Click on Official Records. **Other Phone Numbers:** Treasurer 850-547-1115; Appraiser/Auditor 850-547-1113; Elections 850-547-1107.

Indian River County

County Clerk of the Circuit Court, PO Box 1028, Vero Beach, FL 32961-1028. 772-770-5185 x184; http://indian-river.fl.us
Will search UCC records. Tax liens not included in UCC search. Will not search real estate records. **Online Access:** Property Appraiser, Real Estate, Lien, Vital Statistic Records. Appraiser information is free, but only some of the recording office information is. Appraiser records are available free online at http://ircpa.irene.net/search.html. Online access to recording indexes on the Clerk of the Circuit Court database are available free at http://bdc.co.indian-river.fl.us. Records go back to 1983. Full real estate, lien and court and vital records are available from the Clerk of the Circuit Court at the fee site, subscription is $200 per month. For information about free and fee access, call Gary at 772-567-8000 x216. **Other Phone Numbers:** Appraiser/Auditor 772-567-8188.

Jackson County

County Clerk of the Circuit Court, PO Drawer 510, Marianna, FL 32447. 850-482-9552; Fax 850-482-7849. www.jacksoncountyclerk.com
This agency will not perform searches. **Online Access:** Real Estate, Lien, Recording, Marriage, Death, Probate Records. Access to the Clerk of Circuit Court Official Records database is available free at www.jacksoncountyclerk.com/records.html. Images will go back to 5/1996 Also, online access to the state recorders' meta-search site is available free at www.myfloridacounty.com. Click on Official Records. **Other Phone Numbers:** Treasurer 850-482-9653; Appraiser/Auditor 850-482-9646.

Jefferson County

County Clerk of the Circuit Court, Courthouse, Room 10, Monticello, FL 32344. 850-342-0218 x27 R/E Recording: 850-342-0218 x 227 UCC Recording: 850-342-0218 extension 227; Fax 850-342-0222. http://co.jefferson.fl.us
Will search UCC records. Will search state tax liens for $1.00 per year per name. Will search real estate records. **Online Access:** Property, Real Estate, Lien, Recording Records. Access to the Property Appraiser database is available free at http://qpublic.net/jefferson/search.html. Sales searches are also available. Also, online access to the Clerk of Circuit Court recordings database is available free at www.myjeffersoncounty.com. Also, online access to the state recorders' meta-search site is available free at www.myfloridacounty.com. Click on Official Records. **Other Phone Numbers:** Assessor 850-997-3356; Treasurer 850-342-0218 x 232; Appraiser/Auditor 850-997-3356; Elections 850-997-3348.

Lafayette County

County Clerk of the Circuit Court, PO Box 88, Mayo, FL 32066. 386-294-1600; Fax 386-294-4231. www.lafayetteclerk.com
This agency will not perform searches. **Online Access:** Real Estate, Lien, Recording Records. Search the state recorders' meta-search site for free at www.myfloridacounty.com. Click on Official Records. **Other Phones:** Assessor 386-294-1991; Treasurer 386-294-1961; Appraiser/Auditor 386-294-1991.

Lake County

County Clerk of the Circuit Court, PO Box 7800, Tavares, FL 32778-7800. 352-742-4114; Fax 352-742-4191. www.lakecountyclerk.org
Will search UCC records. UCC search includes tax liens if requested. Will search real estate records. **Online Access:** Property Appraiser, Real Estate, Lien, Marriage, Recording Records. The new county clerk official records database is available free online at www.lakecountyclerk.org/services.asp?subject=Online_Official_Records. Records go as far back as 1974. Includes court records. Also, records on the County Property Assessor database are available free online at www.lakecopropappr.com/search.asp. Also, marriage records back to 11/2000 are available at www.lakecountyclerk.org/departments.asp?subject=Marriage_Licenses. Also, online access to the state recorders' meta-search site is available free at www.myfloridacounty.com. Click on Official records. **Other Phone Numbers:** Assessor 352-343-9748; Treasurer 352-742-9808; Appraiser/Auditor 352-343-9748; Elections 352-343-9734; Vital Records 352-742-6320; Tax Collector 352-343-9622.

Lee County

County Clerk of the Circuit Court, PO Box 2278, Fort Myers, FL 33902-2278. 239-335-2283; http://leeclerk.org/index.asp

There is also a Cape Coral Branch Office - Lee County Government Center, 1039 SE 9th Place, Cape Coral, FL 33990. Will search UCC records. UCC search includes tax liens if requested. Real estate owner, mortgage, and property transfer searches available. **Online Access:** Property Appraiser, Real Estate, Occupational License, Lien, Recording Records. Access to the appraiser database is available free at www.property-appraiser.lee.fl.us/Queries/FindParcel.htm, or the tax roll database at www.leetc.com/Taxes/default.asp. Also, access to the county "license" database is available at www.leetc.com/OccupationalLicense/default.asp. Also, search the clerk of circuit court data at http://leeclerk.org/SearchOfficialRecords.htm. Records go back to 1988. Also, a subscription service ($50 set-up, $25 per month) allows full access to clerk's records. Also, online access to the state recorders' meta-search site is available free at www.myfloridacounty.com. Click on Official Records. **Other Phone Numbers:** Assessor 239-339-6100; Appraiser/Auditor 239-335-2283.

Leon County

County Clerk of the Circuit Court, PO Box 726, Tallahassee, FL 32302. 850-577-4030 R/E Recording: 850-577-4050; Fax 850-921-1310. www.clerk.leon.fl.us
Will search UCC records. Tax liens not included in UCC search. Will search for any real estate records in general index. **Online Access:** Property Appraiser, Real Estate, Lien, Marriage, Recording, Permit, Foreclosure Records. Real Estate, lien, and foreclosure records from the County Clerk are available free online at www.clerk.leon.fl.us. Lending agency information is also available. Also, access to full document images requires user name and password, plus $100 per month. Property Appraiser database records are available free at www.co.leon.fl.us/propappr/search.cfm. Also, online access to the state recorders' meta-search site is available free at www.myfloridacounty.com. Click on Official Records. Also, search the county tax collector tax rolls database for free at http://dta.co.leon.fl.us/tax/default.asp. Also, search the county "permits" data at www.tlcgis.org/tallahassee. Search marriages at http://cvweb.clerk.leon.fl.us/index_marriage.html. **Other Phones:** Assessor 850-488-6102; Appraiser/Auditor 850-488-6102.

Levy County

County Clerk of the Circuit Court, PO Drawer 610, Bronson, FL 32621. County Clerk of the Circuit Court, R/E and UCC Recording 352-486-5229; Fax 352-986-5166. www.levyclerk.com
Will provide UCC records if given book and page number. This agency will not do a tax lien search. Real estate owner, mortgage, and property transfer records available if you provide book and page number. **Online Access:** Real Estate, Lien, Recording Records. Access to the Clerk of Circuit Court recording database are available free at http://63.144.218.154/scripts/LevyClerk.exe?K. Search by name, book/page, file number or document type. Also, online access to the state recorders' meta-search site is available free at www.myfloridacounty.com. Click on Official Records. Also, access to the property appraiser data is available free at www.qpublic.net/levy/search.html. **Other Phone Numbers:** Assessor 352-486-5175; Treasurer 352-486-5275; Appraiser/Auditor 352-486-4311; Elections 352-486-5163; Vital Records 352-486-5274.

Liberty County

County Clerk of the Circuit Court, PO Box 399, Bristol, FL 32321. 850-643-2215; Fax 850-643-2866. www.libertyclerk.com
Will search UCC records. This agency will not do a tax lien search. Will search real estate records. **Online Access:** Real Estate, Lien, Recording Records. Search

the state recorders' meta-search site for free at www.myfloridacounty.com. Click on Official Records. **Other Phones:** Assessor 850-643-2279; Treasurer 850-643-2442; Appraiser/Auditor 850-643-2279.

Madison County

County Clerk of the Circuit Court, PO Box 237, Madison, FL 32341-0237. 850-973-1500 R/E Recording: 850-973-1500 x27 UCC Recording: 850-973-1500 x27; Fax 850-973-2059.
Will search UCC records. UCC search includes tax liens if requested. Real estate owner, mortgage, and property transfer searches available. **Online Access:** Real Estate, Lien, Recording, Property Appraiser Records. Search the state recorders' meta-search site for free at www.myfloridacounty.com. Click on Official records. Also, access to the property appraiser's rproperty cards and sale databases is available free at www.madpa.org/db/disclaimer.asp. **Other Phone Numbers:** Assessor 850-973-6133; Appraiser/Auditor 850-973-6133.

Manatee County

County Clerk of the Circuit Court, PO Box 25400, Bradenton, FL 34206. 941-741-4041 R/E Recording: 941-741-4040 or 4041; Fax 941-741-4082. www.clerkofcourts.com
Will search UCC records. UCC search includes tax liens. Real estate owner, mortgage, and property transfer searches available. **Online Access:** Appraiser, Real Estate, Lien, Vital Statistic, Recording Records. Several sources exist. Real estate and recordings records are available free from the Clerk of Circuit Court and Comptroller's database at www.clerkofcourts.com/PubRec/RecordedDocs/ormain.htm. Also, Online access to the state recorders' meta-search site is available free at www.myfloridacounty.com. Click on Official Records. Also, Property Appraiser records are available free online at www.manateepao.com. On the 4th county online system, real estate and vital records are available at no fee to view, but you are limited to 2 hours access. Lending agency information is available. Call Martha Pope at 941-741-4051 for information. **Other Phone Numbers:** Assessor 941-748-8208; Treasurer 941-748-4800; Appraiser/Auditor 941-748-8208.

Marion County

County Clerk of the Circuit Court, PO Box 1030, Ocala, FL 34478-1030. County Clerk of the Circuit Court, R/E and UCC Recording 352-620-3925; Fax 352-620-3930. www.marioncountyclerk.org
Will search UCC records. Tax liens not included in UCC search. Real estate owner, mortgage, and property transfer searches available. **Online Access:** Property Appraiser, Real Estate, Lien, Marriage, Recording Records. Records on the County Clerk of Court records database are available free online at www.marioncountyclerk.org. Also, records on the Marion County Property Appraiser database are available online free at www.propappr.marion.fl.us. Also, online access to the state recorders' meta-search site is available free at www.myfloridacounty.com. Click on Official Records. **Other Phone Numbers:** Appraiser/Auditor 352-368-8300.

Martin County

County Clerk of the Circuit Court, PO Box 9016, Stuart, FL 34995. County Clerk of the Circuit Court, R/E and UCC Recording 772-288-5554; Fax 772-223-7920. www.martin.fl.us/GOVT
Will search UCC records. Tax liens not included in UCC search. Real estate record owner and mortgage searches available. **Online Access:** Property Appraiser, Real Estate, Lien, Recording, Personal Property Records. Access to the clerk of the circuit court recordings database are available free online at http://clerk-web.martin.fl.us/wb_or1. Also, records on

the county property appraiser database are available free online at http://paoweb.martin.fl.us. Choose from "Online Property Searches." Personal property searches are also available. The county tax collector data files are available free online at www.martin.fl.us/GOVT/co/tax/search. Also, online access to the state recorders' meta-search site is available free at www.myfloridacounty.com. **Other Phone Numbers:** Assessor 772-288-5608; Appraiser/Auditor 772-288-5608; Elections 772-288-5637.

Monroe County

County Clerk of the Circuit Court, PO Box 1980, Key West, FL 33041-1980. 305-292-3540; Fax 305-295-3623. www.co.monroe.fl.us
Will search UCC records. UCC search includes tax liens. Real estate owner, mortgage, and property transfer searches available. **Online Access:** Recording, Real Estate, Deed, Lien Records. Access to the clerk of circuit courts database is available free at www.clerk-of-the-court.com/searchOfficialRecords.asp. **Other Phone Numbers:** Treasurer 305-292-3550; Appraiser/Auditor 305-292-3378; Vital Records 305-292-3507.

Nassau County

County Clerk of the Circuit Court, PO Box 456, Fernandina, FL 32035. 904-321-5714; Fax 904-321-5723. www.nassauclerk.com
Will search UCC records. UCC search includes tax liens if requested. Will not search real estate records. **Online Access:** Real Estate, Lien, Recording Records. Search the state recorders' meta-search site for free at www.myfloridacounty.com. Click on Official Records. Also, the recorders database is available free at www.nassauclerk.com/county/official_records_login.htm. **Other Phone Numbers:** Assessor 904-491-7300; Appraiser/Auditor 904-491-7300.

Okaloosa County

County Clerk of the Circuit Court, PO Drawer 1359, Crestview, FL 32536. County Clerk of the Circuit Court, R/E and UCC Recording 850-689-5847; Fax 850-689-5886.
Online access to the state recorders' meta-search site is available free at www.myfloridacounty.com. Click on Official Records. Will search UCC records. Tax liens not included in UCC search. Real estate owner, mortgage, and property transfer searches available. **Online Access:** Property Appraiser, Real Estate, Lien, Recording, Vital Statistic Records. Several databases are available. Access to Okaloosa County online system requires a monthly usage fee of $100. No addresses listed. Lending agency information, traffic and domestic records are. For information, contact Don Howard at 850-689-5821. Online access to land records is available free at www.clerkofcourts.cc/orsearch/contract.htm. Access to marriage records is available free at www.clerkofcourts.cc/marsearch/marriage.asp. Property Appraiser records are available free online at www.okaloosapa.com/search.html. Also, online access to the state recorders' meta-search site is available free at www.myfloridacounty.com **Other Phone Numbers:** Treasurer 850-689-5801; Appraiser/Auditor 850-689-5900; Elections 850-651-7272.

Okeechobee County

County Clerk of the Circuit Court, 304 N.W. 2nd St, Room 101, Okeechobee, FL 34972. 863-763-2131 R/E Recording: 863-763-0239 UCC Recording: 863-763-0239.
Will search UCC records. This agency will not do a tax lien search. Will search real estate records. **Online Access:** Property Appraiser Records. Search the statewide recording database at www.myfloridacounty.com. Documents are free to view, but there is a fee to order. Access to the property appraiser database is available free at http://www2.okeechobeepa.com/GIS/Search_F.asp.
Other Phones: Assessor 863-763-4422; Treasurer 863-763-3421; Appraiser/Auditor 863-763-4422; Elections 863-763-4014; Vital Records 863-462-5819.

Orange County

County Comptroller, PO Box 38, Orlando, FL 32802-0038. County Comptroller, R/E and UCC Recording 407-836-5115; Fax 407-836-5120. www.occompt.com
Will search UCC records. UCC search includes tax liens. Real estate record owner and mortgage searches available. **Online Access:** Property Appraiser, Recording, Real Estate, Lien, Vital Statistic, Land Sales, Personal Property Records. Real Estate, Lien, and Marriage records on the county Comptroller database are available free at www.occompt.com/2002/records.html. Lending Agency information is available. Also, property records on the Property Appraiser database are available for free at www.ocpafl.org/docs/disclaimer.html. At this main site, click on "Record Searches." Also search Tangible Personal Property records and residential sales. **Other Phone Numbers:** Assessor 407-836-5044; Treasurer 407-836-5715; Appraiser/Auditor 407-836-5000; Elections 407-836-2070; Vital Records 407-623-1182.

Osceola County

County Clerk of the Circuit Court, 2 Courthouse Square, Suite 2000, 17 S. Vernon Ave., Kissimmee, FL 34741-5491. 407-343-3500 x3517 R/E Recording: 407-343-3517 UCC Recording: 407-343-3517; Fax 407-343-3534. www.osceolaclerk.com
Will search UCC records. UCC search includes tax liens if requested. Real estate owner, mortgage, and property transfer searches available. **Online Access:** Real Estate, Property Appraiser Records. Access to the county Clerk of Circuit Court database features court records only at this time; see www.osceolaclerkcourt.org. Search by party name. While property appraiser records are soon to be available free online at www.property-appraiser.com/records.htm, you may currently purchase property data from the county information system database. For information, call 407-343-3700. Data is delivered in either 8mm data cartridges, CD-ROM, or 3.5" diskettes. Fees vary; tax roll data is available for $75.00. Also, land records may be available online at www.osceolaclerkrecording.org. **Other Phone Numbers:** Appraiser/Auditor 407-343-3700; Elections 407-343-3900.

Palm Beach County

County Clerk of the Circuit Court, PO Box 4177, West Palm Beach, FL 33402. County Clerk of the Circuit Court, R/E and UCC Recording 561-355-2991; Fax 561-355-2633. www.co.palm-beach.fl.us
Will search UCC records. Tax liens not included in UCC search. Search includes all real estate records on general index. **Online Access:** Property Appraiser, Real Estate, Lien, Recording, Vital Statistic Records. Access to the clerk of circuit court recording database are available for free at www.pbcountyclerk.com/records_home.html. Records go back to 1968; includes marriage records 1979 to present. Images go back to 1993. They are planning a subscription full-index system and also CD-Roms of indexes as far back as 1968. Also, records on the county Property Appraiser database are available free online at www.co.palm-beach.fl.us/papa. **Other Phone Numbers:** Assessor 561-355-2866; Appraiser/Auditor 561-355-2866; Elections 561-355-2650; Vital Records 561-653-2350.

Pasco County

County Clerk of the Circuit Court, 38053 Live Oak Ave., Room 205, Dade City, FL 33523-3894. 352-521-4469; http://pascogov.com
Will search UCC records. Real estate owner, mortgage, and property transfer searches available. **Online Access:** Property Appraiser, Real Estate, Lien, Vital Statistic, Recording, Occ License Records. Several sources available. Access to real estate, liens, marriage records requires $25 annual fee plus a $50 deposit. Billing rate is $.05 per minute, $.03 evenings. For information, call 352-521-4529. There is a fax back service. Also, free internet access to indexes is at www.pascoclerk.com. Click on "records." Also, online access to the state recorders' meta-search site is available at www.myfloridacounty.com. Click on Official records. Also, property records on the Property Appraiser database are available free at http://appraiser.pascogov.com. Sales data and maps are available. Search tax records and occupational licences free at http://taxcollector.pascogov.com. **Other Phone Numbers:** Assessor 352-521-4433; Appraiser/Auditor 352-521-4433.

Pinellas County

County Clerk of the Circuit Court, 315 Court St, Room 150, Clearwater, FL 33756. 727-464-4876; Fax 727-464-4383. http://clerk.co.pinellas.fl.us/recsonl.htm
Will search UCC records. Tax liens not included in UCC search. Real estate owner, mortgage, and property transfer searches available. **Online Access:** Property Appraiser, Real Estate, Lien, Judgment, Recording, Tax Deed Sale, Traffic/Boating Fine Records. Assessor/property records are available free online at www.pao.co.pinellas.fl.us/search2.html. Also, tax deed sales indexes are avaialble free at http://clerk.co.pinellas.fl.us/recsonl.htm. Also, the county clerk of circuit court's recordings are available free online at http://clerk.co.pinellas.fl.us. Click on official records or probate under "E-business." Also, online access to the state recorders' meta-search site is available free at www.myfloridacounty.com. Click on Official Records. Search traffic and boating fines at https://pubtitleu.co.pinellas.fl.us/credit/accountspayable/CourtChargeIntro.jsp. **Other Phone Numbers:** Assessor 727-464-3207; Appraiser/Auditor 727-464-3207.

Polk County

County Clerk of the Circuit Court, PO Box 9000 Drawer CC-8, Bartow, FL 33831-9000. County Clerk of the Circuit Court, R/E and UCC Recording 863-534-4516; Fax 863-534-4008. www.polk-county.net
Will search UCC records. UCC search includes tax liens. Search includes all real estate records on general index. **Online Access:** Property Appraiser, Real Estate, Lien, Vital Statistic, Recording, Personal Property Records. Search the county clerk database at www.polk-county.net/clerk/clerk.html for free court records, deeds, mortgages, plats, marriages, resolutions. For copies of documents, call 863-534-4524. Fee is $1.00 per page. Also, property and personal property records from the County Property Appraiser database are available free at www.polkpa.org. **Other Phone Numbers:** Assessor 863-534-4777; Appraiser/Auditor 863-534-4777.

Putnam County

County Clerk of the Circuit Court, PO Box 758, Palatka, FL 32178-0758. County Clerk of the Circuit Court, R/E and UCC Recording 386-329-0256; Fax 386-329-0889. www.putnam-fl.com/clk
Will search UCC records. Real estate owner, mortgage, and property transfer searches available. **Online Access:** Real Estate, Lien, Recording, Tax Assessor, Occ License, Warrant Records. Access to the county clerk database requires a $400 setup fee and monthly charge of $40 plus $.05 per minute over 20 hours. Includes civil court records and real property records back to 10/1983. For information, call 904-329-0353. Also, online access to the state recorders' meta-search

site is available free at www.myfloridacounty.com. Click on Official Records. Also, the sheriff;s warrant list is at www.putnamsheriff.org/warrant.htm. Also, search the online tax rolls at www.putnam-fl.com/app/disclaimer.htm. No name searching. Also, searchthe treasurer's tax rolls and occupational licensing at www.putnam-fl.com/txc/onlineinquiry.htm. **Other Phone Numbers:** Appraiser/Auditor 386-329-0286; Elections 386-329-0455; Vital Records 386-329-0420.

Santa Rosa County

County Clerk of the Circuit Court, PO Box 472, Milton, FL 32572. County Clerk of the Circuit Court, R/E and UCC Recording 850-983-1966; Fax 850-983-1991. www.srcpa.org
Will search UCC records. UCC search includes tax liens if requested. Will not search real estate records. **Online Access:** Property Appraiser, Real Estate, Lien, Recording Records. Property records are available free at www.srcpa.org/property.php or at the main Property Appraiser page click on "Record Search." Also, online access to the state recorders' meta-search site is available free at www.myfloridacounty.com. Click on Official Records. **Other Phones:** Assessor 850-983-1880; Treasurer 850-983-1950; Appraiser/Auditor 850-983-1880; Elections 850-983-1900; Clerk of Courts-Research Dept 850-983-1970.

Sarasota County

County Clerk of the Circuit Court, PO Box 3079, Sarasota, FL 34230. 941-362-4066; www.clerk.co.sarasota.fl.us
Will search UCC records. UCC search includes tax liens if requested. Real estate record owner and mortgage searches available. **Online Access:** Property Appraiser, Real Estate, Lien, Vital Statistic, Recording Records. Access to the Clerk of Circuit Court recordings database are available free at www.clerk.co.sarasota.fl.us/online.htm. Includes civil, criminal, and traffic court indexes. Also search indexes at www.clerk.co.sarasota.fl.us/isol. Marriage licenses may be searched free by groom/bride name, license #, or date. Probate records are also available. Online access to the state recorders' meta-search site is available free at www.myfloridacounty.com. Click on Official Records. Also, records on the Property Appraiser database are available free online at www.sarasotaproperty.net/scpa_recs.htm; includes subdivision/condominium sales. **Other Phone Numbers:** Appraiser/Auditor 941-951-5650.

Seminole County

Clerk of the Circuit Court, PO Box 8099-Attn Recording Dept, Sanford, FL 32772-8099. 407-665-4336 R/E Recording: 407-665-4409 UCC Recording: 407-65-44409; www.seminoleclerk.org
Will search UCC records. This agency will not do a tax lien search. Will not search real estate records. **Online Access:** Property Appraiser, Real Estate, Lien, Recording Records. The county clerk of circuit court's recordings database is available free at http://officialrecords.seminoleclerk.org/NV_Records. Also, property appraisal records are available free at www.scpafl.org/pls/web/web.seminole_county_disclaimer. There is also a map search. **Other Phone Numbers:** Appraiser/Auditor 407-665-7502.

St. Johns County

County Clerk of the Circuit Court, PO Drawer 300, St. Augustine, FL 32085-0300. County Clerk of the Circuit Court, R/E and UCC Recording 904-823-2333 x330; Fax 904-823-2294. www.co.st-johns.fl.us
Will search UCC records. Tax liens included in UCC search if requested. Real estate record owner and property searches available. **Online Access:** Property Appraiser, Real Estate, Lien, Recording, Civil Records. Access to the county Clerk of Circuit Court recording

database is available free at www.co.st-johns.fl.us/Const-Officers/Clerk-of-Court/doris/searchdocs.asp. Search by name, parcel ID, instrument type. Includes civil and probate records, UCCs. Also, online access to the state recorders' meta-search site is at www.myfloridacounty.com. Click on Official Records. **Other Phones:** Appraiser/Auditor 904-823-2200; Elections 904-823-2238.

St. Lucie County

County Clerk of the Circuit Court, PO Box 700, Fort Pierce, FL 34954. County Clerk of the Circuit Court, R/E and UCC Recording 772-462-6928 UCC Recording: 772-462-6927; Fax 772-462-1283. www.stlucieco.gov
Will search UCC records. Tax lien search is included in UCC search. Will search real estate records. **Online Access:** Property Appraiser, Real Estate, Lien, Recording, Marriage, Fictitious Name Records. Access to the clerk of circuit courts database of recordings, deeds, liens, mortgages, marriages, fictitious names is available free at http://public.slcclerkofcourt.com. Business searching is also available for a small fee. Also, online access to the state recorders' meta-search site is available free at www.myfloridacounty.com. Click on Official Records. Also, property appraiser records are available free online at www.paslc.org. Click on the "real property database" or "interactive map.". **Other Phone Numbers:** Assessor 772-462-1650; Treasurer 772-462-1476; Appraiser/Auditor 772-489-1600; Vital Records 772-462-3800.

Sumter County

County Clerk of the Circuit Court, 209 N. Florida St, Room 106, Bushnell, FL 33513. 352-793-0215; Fax 352-793-0218.
Will search UCC records. UCC search includes tax liens if requested. Real estate record owner and mortgage searches available. **Online Access:** Real Estate, Lien, Recording Records. Search the state recorders' search site at www.myfloridacounty.com. Click on Official records. **Other Phones:** Appraiser/Auditor 352-793-0210.

Suwannee County

County Clerk of the Circuit Court, 200 S. Ohio Ave, Live Oak, FL 32060. County Clerk of the Circuit Court, R/E and UCC Recording 386-362-0554; Fax 386-362-0548. www.suwanneeclerkofcourt.com
Will search UCC records. Tax liens not included in UCC search. Will not search real estate records. **Online Access:** Real Estate, Lien, Recording, Property Tax Records. Access of the county clerk of circuit database is available free at www.suwanneeclerkofcourt.com/court/kiosk.html. Also, search the tax collector database free at www.suwanneecountytax.com/collectmax/collect30.asp. **Other Phone Numbers:** Treasurer 386-364-3414; Appraiser/Auditor 386-362-1385; Elections 386-362-2616; Vital Records 386-362-0554.

Taylor County

County Clerk of the Circuit Court, PO Box 620, Perry, FL 32348. County Clerk of the Circuit Court, R/E and UCC Recording 850-838-3506; Fax 850-838-3549. http://taco.perryfl.com
This agency will not perform searches. **Online Access:** County Commissioner Records. Access to county commission records is available free at http://taco.perryfl.com/search.htm. Online records go back to 1988. **Other Phone Numbers:** Treasurer 850-838-3517; Appraiser/Auditor 850-838-3511; Elections 850-838-3515; Vital Records 850-838-3506.

Union County

County Clerk of the Circuit Court, State Road 100, Courthouse Room 103, Lake Butler, FL 32054. 386-496-3711; Fax 386-496-1718.

Will search UCC records. UCC search includes tax liens. Real estate owner, mortgage, and property transfer searches available. **Online Access:** Real Estate, Lien, Recording Records. Search the state recorders' meta-search site for free at www.myfloridacounty.com. Click on Official records. **Other Phones:** Treasurer 496-1026; Appraiser 496-3431; Elections 496-2236.

Volusia County

County Clerk of the Circuit Court, PO Box 6043, De Land, FL 32721. 386-736-5912; Fax 386-740-5104. www.clerk.org
Will search UCC records. Tax liens not included in UCC search. Real estate record owner searches available. **Online Access:** Property Appraiser, Real Estate, Lien, Vital Statistic, Recording, Citation Violation, Arrest Records. Property records are available free at www.clerk.org/publicrecords/or.tshtml. Indexes go back to 3/1996; will soon have documents back to 1990. Volusia County also offers full Real Estate, Lien, and vital records on a commercial Internet site. The initial set up fee is $125 with a flat monthly fee of $25. For information, contact the clerk. Also, search the 24-arrest ledger and citations back to 1990 at www.clerk.org/publicrecords/cv.tshtml. Enter your name to access. Also, online access to the state recorders' meta-search site is available free at www.myfloridacounty.com. Click on Official records. Also, search the property appraiser database free at http://webserver.vcgov.org/vc_search.html. **Other Phone Numbers:** Appraiser/Auditor 386-736-5902.

Wakulla County

County Clerk of the Circuit Court, Wakulla County Court House, 3056 Crawfordville Hwy, Crawfordville, FL 32327. 850-926-0905 R/E Recording: 850-926-0905 x226 UCC Recording: 850-926-0905 x226; Fax 850-926-0938.
Will search UCC records. Will not search real estate records. **Online Access:** Real Estate, Lien, Recording, Property Appraiser Records. The state recorders' meta-search site is available for free at www.myfloridacounty.com. Click on Official records. Also, search the property appraiser database free at http://wakulla.acsgrm.com/Property_Search.php. **Other Phone Numbers:** Treasurer 850-926-3371; Appraiser/Auditor 850-926-3271.

Walton County

County Clerk of the Circuit Court, P.O.Box 1260, De Funiak Springs, FL 32433. 850-892-8115; Fax 850-892-7551. www.co.walton.fl.us/clerk
Will search UCC records. UCC search includes tax liens if requested. Real estate owner, mortgage, and property transfer searches available. **Online Access:** Real Estate, Lien, Vital Statistic, Grantor/Grantee Records. Records back to 1/1976 on the County Clerk database are available free online at www.co.walton.fl.us/clerk/or/ordisclm.htm. This has taken the place of the commercial system. Also, property appraiser records are available free at www.co.walton.fl.us/propertyappraiser/taxsearch. **Other Phone Numbers:** Treasurer 850-892-8121; Appraiser/Auditor 850-892-8123.

Washington County

County Clerk of the Circuit Court, PO Box 647, Chipley, FL 32428. County Clerk of the Circuit Court, R/E and UCC Recording 850-638-6285; Fax 850-638-6297. www.myflorida.com
This agency will not perform searches. **Online Access:** Recording, Deed, Judgment, Lien Records. Search the state recorders' meta-search site for free at www.myfloridacounty.com. Click on Official Records. **Other Phone Numbers:** Assessor 850-638-6275; Treasurer 850-638-6205; Appraiser/Auditor 850-638-6205; Elections 638-6230; Vital Records 638-6230.

Florida County Locator

You will usually be able to find the city name in the City/County Cross Reference below. In that case, it is a simple matter to determine the county from the cross reference. However, only the official US Postal Service city names are included in this index. There are an additional 40,000 place names that people use in their addresses. Included is a ZIP/City Cross Reference following the City/County Cross Reference.

City/County Cross Reference

ABMPS Dade
ALACHUA Alachua
ALFORD Jackson
ALTAMONTE SPRINGS Seminole
ALTHA Calhoun
ALTOONA (32702) Lake(82), Marion(17)
ALTURAS Polk
ALVA (33920) Lee(86), Hendry(13)
ANNA MARIA Manatee
ANTHONY Marion
APALACHICOLA Franklin
APOLLO BEACH Hillsborough
APOPKA Orange
ARCADIA De Soto
ARCHER (32618) Alachua(74), Levy(25)
ARGYLE Walton
ARIPEKA Pasco
ASTATULA Lake
ASTOR (32102) Lake(84), Volusia(15)
ATLANTIC BEACH Duval
AUBURNDALE Polk
AVON PARK Highlands
BABSON PARK Polk
BAGDAD Santa Rosa
BAKER Okaloosa
BALM Hillsborough
BARBERVILLE Volusia
BARTOW Polk
BASCOM Jackson
BAY PINES Pinellas
BELL Gilchrist
BELLE GLADE Palm Beach
BELLEAIR BEACH Pinellas
BELLEAIR SHORES Pinellas
BELLEVIEW Marion
BEVERLY HILLS Citrus
BIG PINE KEY Monroe
BLOUNTSTOWN Calhoun
BOCA GRANDE Lee
BOCA RATON Palm Beach
BOKEELIA Lee
BONIFAY (32425) Holmes(90), Washington(9)
BONITA SPRINGS Lee
BOSTWICK Putnam
BOWLING GREEN (33834) Hardee(72), Manatee(17), Polk(6), Hillsborough(2)
BOYNTON BEACH Palm Beach
BRADENTON Manatee
BRADENTON BEACH Manatee
BRADLEY Polk
BRANDON Hillsborough
BRANFORD (32008) Suwannee(54), Gilchrist(36), Lafayette(8), Dixie(1)
BRISTOL Liberty
BRONSON Levy
BROOKER (32622) Bradford(82), Alachua(17)
BROOKSVILLE Hernando
BRYANT Palm Beach
BRYCEVILLE (32009) Nassau(98), Duval(1)
BUNNELL Flagler
BUSHNELL Sumter
CALLAHAN Nassau
CAMPBELLTON Jackson
CANAL POINT Palm Beach
CANDLER Marion
CANTONMENT Escambia
CAPE CANAVERAL Brevard
CAPE CORAL Lee
CAPTIVA Lee
CARRABELLE Franklin

CARYVILLE (32427) Washington(93), Holmes(6)
CASSADAGA Volusia
CASSELBERRY Seminole
CEDAR KEY Levy
CENTER HILL Sumter
CENTURY Escambia
CHATTAHOOCHEE Gadsden
CHIEFLAND Levy
CHIPLEY Washington
CHOKOLOSKEE Collier
CHRISTMAS Orange
CITRA Marion
CLARCONA Orange
CLARKSVILLE Calhoun
CLEARWATER Pinellas
CLEARWATER BEACH Pinellas
CLERMONT Lake
CLEWISTON (33440) Hendry(97), Palm Beach(2)
COCOA Brevard
COCOA BEACH Brevard
COLEMAN Sumter
COPELAND Collier
CORTEZ Manatee
COTTONDALE (32431) Jackson(78), Washington(21)
CRAWFORDVILLE Wakulla
CRESCENT CITY Putnam
CRESTVIEW (32539) Okaloosa(91), Walton(8)
CROSS CITY Dixie
CRYSTAL BEACH Pinellas
CRYSTAL RIVER Citrus
CRYSTAL SPRINGS Pasco
CYPRESS Jackson
DADE CITY Pasco
DANIA Broward
DAVENPORT Polk
DAY Lafayette
DAYTONA BEACH Volusia
DE LEON SPRINGS Volusia
DEBARY Volusia
DEERFIELD BEACH Broward
DEFUNIAK SPRINGS Walton
DELAND Volusia
DELRAY BEACH Palm Beach
DELTONA Volusia
DESTIN (32541) Okaloosa(92), Walton(7)
DOCTORS INLET Clay
DOVER Hillsborough
DUNDEE Polk
DUNEDIN Pinellas
DUNNELLON Citrus
DURANT Hillsborough
EAGLE LAKE Polk
EARLETON Alachua
EAST PALATKA Putnam
EASTLAKE WEIR Marion
EASTPOINT Franklin
EATON PARK Polk
EBRO (32437) Washington(89), Bay(10)
EDGEWATER Volusia
EGLIN AFB Okaloosa
ELFERS Pasco
ELKTON St. Johns
ELLENTON Manatee
ENGLEWOOD Sarasota
ESTERO Lee
EUSTIS Lake
EVERGLADES CITY Collier
EVINSTON Alachua
FAIRFIELD Marion
FEDHAVEN Polk

FELDA Hendry
FELLSMERE Indian River
FERNANDINA BEACH Nassau
FERNDALE Lake
FLAGLER BEACH Flagler
FLORAHOME Putnam
FLORAL CITY Citrus
FORT LAUDERDALE Broward
FORT MC COY Marion
FORT MEADE Polk
FORT MYERS Lee
FORT MYERS BEACH Lee
FORT OGDEN De Soto
FORT PIERCE St. Lucie
FORT WALTON BEACH Okaloosa
FORT WHITE Columbia
FOUNTAIN Bay
FREEPORT Walton
FROSTPROOF Polk
FRUITLAND PARK Lake
GAINESVILLE Alachua
GENEVA Seminole
GEORGETOWN Putnam
GIBSONTON Hillsborough
GLEN SAINT MARY Baker
GLENWOOD Volusia
GOLDENROD Seminole
GONZALEZ Escambia
GOODLAND Collier
GOTHA Orange
GRACEVILLE (32440) Jackson(86), Holmes(13)
GRAHAM Bradford
GRAND ISLAND Lake
GRAND RIDGE (32442) Jackson(91), Calhoun(8)
GRANDIN Putnam
GRANT Brevard
GREEN COVE SPRINGS (32043) Clay(98), Putnam(1)
GREENSBORO Gadsden
GREENVILLE (32331) Taylor(38), Madison(32), Jefferson(28)
GREENWOOD Jackson
GRETNA Gadsden
GROVELAND Lake
GULF BREEZE Santa Rosa
GULF HAMMOCK Levy
HAINES CITY Polk
HALLANDALE Broward
HAMPTON (32044) Bradford(94), Alachua(6)
HAROLD Santa Rosa
HASTINGS St. Johns
HAVANA Gadsden
HAWTHORNE (32640) Alachua(61), Putnam(38)
HERNANDO Citrus
HIALEAH Dade
HIGH SPRINGS Alachua
HIGHLAND CITY Polk
HILLIARD Nassau
HOBE SOUND Martin
HOLDER Citrus
HOLIDAY Pasco
HOLLISTER Putnam
HOLLYWOOD Broward
HOLMES BEACH Manatee
HOLT (32564) Santa Rosa(89), Okaloosa(10)
HOMELAND Polk
HOMESTEAD Dade
HOMOSASSA Citrus
HOMOSASSA SPRINGS Citrus

HORSESHOE BEACH Dixie
HOSFORD Liberty
HOWEY IN THE HILLS Lake
HUDSON Pasco
HURLBURT FIELD Okaloosa
IMMOKALEE Collier
INDIALANTIC Brevard
INDIAN LAKE ESTATES Polk
INDIAN ROCKS BEACH Pinellas
INDIANTOWN Martin
INGLIS (34449) Levy(89), Citrus(10)
INTERCESSION CITY Osceola
INTERLACHEN Putnam
INVERNESS Citrus
ISLAMORADA Monroe
ISLAND GROVE Alachua
ISTACHATTA Hernando
JACKSONVILLE Duval
JACKSONVILLE BEACH Duval
JASPER Hamilton
JAY Santa Rosa
JENNINGS Hamilton
JENSEN BEACH Martin
JUPITER (33478) Palm Beach(93), Martin(6)
KATHLEEN Polk
KENANSVILLE Osceola
KEY BISCAYNE Dade
KEY COLONY BEACH Monroe
KEY LARGO Monroe
KEY WEST Monroe
KEYSTONE HEIGHTS (32656) Clay(83), Bradford(16)
KILLARNEY Orange
KINARD Calhoun
KISSIMMEE (34759) Polk(72), Osceola(27)
LA CROSSE Alachua
LABELLE Hendry
LACOOCHEE Pasco
LADY LAKE (32162) Sumter(66), Marion(33)
LAKE ALFRED Polk
LAKE BUTLER (32054) Union(88), Bradford(11)
LAKE CITY Columbia
LAKE COMO Putnam
LAKE GENEVA Clay
LAKE HAMILTON Polk
LAKE HARBOR Palm Beach
LAKE HELEN Volusia
LAKE MARY Seminole
LAKE MONROE Seminole
LAKE PANASOFFKEE Sumter
LAKE PLACID Highlands
LAKE WALES Polk
LAKE WORTH Palm Beach
LAKELAND Polk
LAMONT (32336) Jefferson(71), Taylor(28)
LANARK VILLAGE Franklin
LAND O LAKES Pasco
LARGO Pinellas
LAUREL Sarasota
LAUREL HILL (32567) Walton(66), Okaloosa(33)
LAWTEY (32058) Bradford(96), Union(3)
LECANTO (34461) Citrus(97), Levy(2)
LEE Madison
LEESBURG Lake
LEHIGH ACRES Lee
LITHIA (33547) Hillsborough(98), Polk(1)
LIVE OAK Suwannee
LLOYD Jefferson
LOCHLOOSA Alachua
LONG KEY Monroe

LONGBOAT KEY (34228) Sarasota(62), Manatee(37)
LONGWOOD Seminole
LORIDA Highlands
LOUGHMAN Polk
LOWELL Marion
LOXAHATCHEE Palm Beach
LULU Columbia
LUTZ (33559) Hillsborough(60), Pasco(39)
LYNN HAVEN Bay
MACCLENNY Baker
MADISON Madison
MAITLAND Orange
MALABAR Brevard
MALONE Jackson
MANASOTA Manatee
MANGO Hillsborough
MARATHON Monroe
MARATHON SHORES Monroe
MARCO ISLAND Collier
MARIANNA Jackson
MARY ESTHER Okaloosa
MASCOTTE Lake
MAYO Lafayette
MC ALPIN Suwannee
MC DAVID Escambia
MC INTOSH Marion
MELBOURNE Brevard
MELBOURNE BEACH Brevard
MELROSE (32666) Putnam(52), Alachua(19), Bradford(16), Clay(11)
MERRITT ISLAND Brevard
MEXICO BEACH Bay
MIAMI Dade
MICANOPY (32667) Marion(97), Alachua(2)
MICCOSUKEE CPO Leon
MID FLORIDA Seminole
MIDDLEBURG Clay
MIDWAY Gadsden
MILLIGAN Okaloosa
MILTON Santa Rosa
MIMS (32754) Brevard(92), Volusia(7)
MINNEOLA Lake
MIRAMAR BEACH Walton
MOLINO Escambia
MONTICELLO Jefferson
MONTVERDE Lake
MOORE HAVEN Glades
MORRISTON (32668) Levy(81), Marion(18)
MOSSY HEAD Walton
MT DORA (32757) Lake(93), Orange(6)
MOUNT PLEASANT Gadsden
MULBERRY Polk
MURDOCK Charlotte
MYAKKA CITY Manatee
NALCREST Polk
NAPLES Collier
NEPTUNE BEACH Duval
NEW PORT RICHEY Pasco
NEW SMYRNA BEACH Volusia
NEWBERRY (32669) Alachua(74), Gilchrist(22), Levy(3)
NICEVILLE Okaloosa
NICHOLS Polk
NOBLETON Hernando
NOCATEE De Soto

NOKOMIS Sarasota
NOMA Holmes
NORTH FORT MYERS Lee
NORTH PALM BEACH Palm Beach
NORTH PORT Sarasota
O BRIEN Suwannee
OAK HILL Volusia
OAKLAND Orange
OCALA Marion
OCHOPEE (34141) Collier(67), Dade(26), Monroe(5)
OCKLAWAHA Marion
OCOEE Orange
ODESSA (33556) Hillsborough(78), Pasco(21)
OKAHUMPKA Lake
OKEECHOBEE (34974) Okeechobee(89), Glades(3), Martin(3), Highlands(3)
OLD TOWN Dixie
OLDSMAR Pinellas
OLUSTEE Baker
ONA (33865) Hardee(85), Manatee(12), De Soto(1)
ONECO Manatee
OPA LOCKA Dade
ORANGE CITY Volusia
ORANGE LAKE Marion
ORANGE PK (32073) Clay(95), Duval(4)
ORANGE SPRINGS Marion
ORLANDO Brevard
ORMOND BEACH Volusia
OSPREY Sarasota
OSTEEN Volusia
OTTER CREEK Levy
OVERSTREET Gulf
OVIEDO Seminole
OXFORD (34484) Sumter(98), Marion(1)
OZONA Pinellas
PAHOKEE Palm Beach
PAISLEY Lake
PALATKA Putnam
PALM BAY Brevard
PALM BEACH Palm Beach
PALM CITY Martin
PALM COAST Flagler
PALM HARBOR Pinellas
PALMDALE Glades
PALMETTO Manatee
PANACEA (32346) Wakulla(88), Franklin(11)
PANAMA CITY Bay
PANAMA CITY BEACH (32413) Bay(88), Walton(11)
PARRISH Manatee
PATRICK A F B Brevard
PAXTON Walton
PENNEY FARMS Clay
PENSACOLA Escambia
PERRY Taylor
PIERSON Volusia
PINELAND Lee
PINELLAS PARK Pinellas
PINETTA Madison
PLACIDA Charlotte
PLANT CITY Hillsborough
PLYMOUTH Orange
POINT WASHINGTON Walton

POLK CITY Polk
POMONA PARK Putnam
POMPANO BEACH Broward
PONCE DE LEON (32455) Holmes(83), Walton(16)
PONTE VEDRA BEACH St. Johns
PORT CHARLOTTE Charlotte
PORT ORANGE Volusia
PORT RICHEY Pasco
PORT SAINT JOE Gulf
PORT SAINT LUCIE St. Lucie
PORT SALERNO Martin
PUNTA GORDA Charlotte
PUTNAM HALL Putnam
QUINCY Gadsden
RAIFORD (32083) Union(94), Bradford(5)
REDDICK Marion
RIVER RANCH Polk
RIVERVIEW Hillsborough
ROCKLEDGE Brevard
ROSELAND Indian River
ROSEMARY BEACH Bay
ROTONDA WEST Charlotte
RUSKIN Hillsborough
SAFETY HARBOR Pinellas
SAINT AUGUSTINE St. Johns
SAINT CLOUD Osceola
SAINT JAMES CITY Lee
SAINT LEO Pasco
SAINT MARKS Wakulla
SAINT PETERSBURG Pinellas
SALEM Taylor
SAN ANTONIO Pasco
SAN MATEO Putnam
SANDERSON Baker
SANFORD Seminole
SANIBEL Lee
SANTA ROSA BEACH Walton
SARASOTA Sarasota
SATELLITE BEACH Brevard
SATSUMA Putnam
SCOTTSMOOR Brevard
SEBASTIAN Indian River
SEBRING Highlands
SEFFNER Hillsborough
SEMINOLE Pinellas
SEVILLE (32190) Volusia(98), Putnam(1)
SHADY GROVE Taylor
SHALIMAR Okaloosa
SHARPES Brevard
SILVER SPRINGS Marion
SNEADS Jackson
SOPCHOPPY Wakulla
SORRENTO Lake
SOUTH BAY Palm Beach
SOUTH FLORIDA Broward
SPARR Marion
SPRING HILL Hernando
STARKE (32091) Bradford(81), Clay(18)
STEINHATCHEE (32359) Taylor(72), Dixie(27)
STUART Martin
SUGARLOAF SHORES Monroe
SUMATRA Liberty
SUMMERFIELD Marion
SUMMERLAND KEY Monroe
SUMTERVILLE Sumter

SUN CITY Hillsborough
SUN CITY CENTER Hillsborough
SUNNYSIDE Bay
SUWANNEE Dixie
SYDNEY Hillsborough
TALLAHASSEE Leon
TALLEVAST Manatee
TAMPA Hillsborough
TANGERINE Orange
TARPON SPRINGS Pinellas
TAVARES Lake
TAVERNIER Monroe
TELOGIA Liberty
TERRA CEIA Manatee
THONOTOSASSA Hillsborough
TITUSVILLE Brevard
TRENTON (32693) Gilchrist(64), Levy(35)
TRILBY Pasco
UMATILLA (32784) Lake(69), Marion(30)
VALPARAISO Okaloosa
VALRICO Hillsborough
VENICE Sarasota
VENUS (33960) Highlands(86), Glades(13)
VERNON (32462) Washington(70), Walton(22), Bay(6)
VERO BEACH Indian River
WABASSO Indian River
WACISSA Jefferson
WAKULLA SPRINGS Leon
WALDO (32694) Alachua(97), Bradford(2)
WAUCHULA Hardee
WAUSAU Washington
WAVERLY Polk
WEBSTER (33597) Sumter(84), Hernando(15)
WEIRSDALE (32195) Marion(83), Lake(16)
WELAKA Putnam
WELLBORN Suwannee
WEST PALM BEACH Palm Beach
WESTON Broward
WESTVILLE (32464) Holmes(98), Walton(1)
WEWAHITCHKA Gulf
WHITE SPRINGS (32096) Hamilton(80), Suwannee(11), Columbia(8)
WILDWOOD Sumter
WILLISTON (32696) Levy(91), Marion(8)
WIMAUMA (33598) Hillsborough(94), Manatee(5)
WINDERMERE Orange
WINTER BEACH Indian River
WINTER GARDEN (34787) Orange(96), Lake(3)
WINTER HAVEN Polk
WINTER PARK Orange
WINTER SPRINGS Seminole
WOODVILLE Leon
WORTHINGTON SPRINGS Union
YALAHA Lake
YANKEETOWN Levy
YOUNGSTOWN (32466) Bay(97), Washington(2)
YULEE Nassau
ZELLWOOD Orange
ZEPHYRHILLS Pasco
ZOLFO SPR (33890) Hardee(98), De Soto(1)

ZIP/City Cross Reference

32003-32003 ORANGE PARK
32004-32004 PONTE VEDRA BEACH
32007-32007 BOSTWICK
32008-32008 BRANFORD
32009-32009 BRYCEVILLE
32011-32011 CALLAHAN
32013-32013 DAY
32024-32025 LAKE CITY
32026-32026 RAIFORD
32030-32030 DOCTORS INLET
32033-32033 ELKTON
32034-32035 FERNANDINA BEACH
32038-32038 FORT WHITE

32040-32040 GLEN SAINT MARY
32041-32041 YULEE
32042-32042 GRAHAM
32043-32043 GREEN COVE SPRINGS
32044-32044 HAMPTON
32046-32046 HILLIARD
32050-32050 MIDDLEBURG
32052-32052 JASPER
32053-32053 JENNINGS
32054-32054 LAKE BUTLER
32055-32056 LAKE CITY
32058-32058 LAWTEY
32059-32059 LEE

32060-32060 LIVE OAK
32061-32061 LULU
32062-32062 MC ALPIN
32063-32063 MACCLENNY
32064-32064 LIVE OAK
32065-32065 ORANGE PARK
32066-32066 MAYO
32067-32067 ORANGE PARK
32068-32068 MIDDLEBURG
32071-32071 O BRIEN
32072-32072 OLUSTEE
32073-32073 ORANGE PARK
32079-32079 PENNEY FARMS

32080-32080 SAINT AUGUSTINE
32082-32082 PONTE VEDRA BEACH
32083-32083 RAIFORD
32084-32086 SAINT AUGUSTINE
32087-32087 SANDERSON
32091-32091 STARKE
32092-32092 SAINT AUGUSTINE
32094-32094 WELLBORN
32095-32095 SAINT AUGUSTINE
32096-32096 WHITE SPRINGS
32097-32097 YULEE
32099-32099 JACKSONVILLE
32100-32100 DAYTONA BEACH

ZIP Range	City
32102-32102	ASTOR
32105-32105	BARBERVILLE
32110-32110	BUNNELL
32111-32111	CANDLER
32112-32112	CRESCENT CITY
32113-32113	CITRA
32114-32128	DAYTONA BEACH
32129-32129	PORT ORANGE
32130-32130	DE LEON SPRINGS
32131-32131	EAST PALATKA
32132-32132	EDGEWATER
32133-32133	EASTLAKE WEIR
32134-32134	FORT MC COY
32135-32135	PALM COAST
32136-32136	FLAGLER BEACH
32137-32137	PALM COAST
32138-32138	GRANDIN
32139-32139	GEORGETOWN
32140-32140	FLORAHOME
32141-32141	EDGEWATER
32142-32142	PALM COAST
32145-32145	HASTINGS
32147-32147	HOLLISTER
32148-32149	INTERLACHEN
32151-32151	FLAGLER BEACH
32157-32157	LAKE COMO
32158-32159	LADY LAKE
32160-32160	LAKE GENEVA
32162-32162	LADY LAKE
32164-32164	PALM COAST
32168-32170	NEW SMYRNA BEACH
32173-32176	ORMOND BEACH
32177-32178	PALATKA
32179-32179	OCKLAWAHA
32180-32180	PIERSON
32181-32181	POMONA PARK
32182-32182	ORANGE SPRINGS
32183-32183	OCKLAWAHA
32185-32185	PUTNAM HALL
32187-32187	SAN MATEO
32189-32189	SATSUMA
32190-32190	SEVILLE
32192-32192	SPARR
32193-32193	WELAKA
32195-32195	WEIRSDALE
32198-32198	DAYTONA BEACH
32200-32232	JACKSONVILLE
32233-32233	ATLANTIC BEACH
32234-32239	JACKSONVILLE
32240-32240	JACKSONVILLE BEACH
32241-32247	JACKSONVILLE
32250-32250	JACKSONVILLE BEACH
32254-32260	JACKSONVILLE
32266-32266	NEPTUNE BEACH
32267-32297	JACKSONVILLE
32301-32304	TALLAHASSEE
32305-32305	WAKULLA SPRINGS
32305-32308	TALLAHASSEE
32309-32309	MICCOSUKEE CPO
32309-32318	TALLAHASSEE
32320-32320	APALACHICOLA
32321-32321	BRISTOL
32322-32322	CARRABELLE
32323-32323	LANARK VILLAGE
32324-32324	CHATTAHOOCHEE
32326-32327	CRAWFORDVILLE
32328-32328	EASTPOINT
32329-32329	APALACHICOLA
32330-32330	GREENSBORO
32331-32331	GREENVILLE
32332-32332	GRETNA
32333-32333	HAVANA
32334-32334	HOSFORD
32335-32335	SUMATRA
32336-32336	LAMONT
32337-32337	LLOYD
32340-32341	MADISON
32343-32343	MIDWAY
32344-32345	MONTICELLO
32346-32346	PANACEA
32347-32348	PERRY
32350-32350	PINETTA
32351-32351	QUINCY
32352-32352	MOUNT PLEASANT
32352-32353	QUINCY
32355-32355	SAINT MARKS
32356-32356	SALEM
32357-32357	SHADY GROVE
32358-32358	SOPCHOPPY
32359-32359	STEINHATCHEE
32360-32360	TELOGIA
32361-32361	WACISSA
32362-32362	WOODVILLE
32395-32399	TALLAHASSEE
32400-32406	PANAMA CITY
32407-32407	PANAMA CITY BEACH
32408-32409	PANAMA CITY
32410-32410	MEXICO BEACH
32411-32413	PANAMA CITY
32413-32413	PANAMA CITY BEACH
32417-32417	PANAMA CITY
32420-32420	ALFORD
32421-32421	ALTHA
32422-32422	ARGYLE
32423-32423	BASCOM
32424-32424	BLOUNTSTOWN
32425-32425	BONIFAY
32426-32426	CAMPBELLTON
32427-32427	CARYVILLE
32428-32428	CHIPLEY
32430-32430	CLARKSVILLE
32431-32431	COTTONDALE
32432-32432	CYPRESS
32433-32433	DEFUNIAK SPRINGS
32434-32434	MOSSY HEAD
32435-32435	DEFUNIAK SPRINGS
32437-32437	EBRO
32438-32438	FOUNTAIN
32439-32439	FREEPORT
32440-32440	GRACEVILLE
32442-32442	GRAND RIDGE
32443-32443	GREENWOOD
32444-32444	LYNN HAVEN
32445-32445	MALONE
32446-32448	MARIANNA
32449-32449	KINARD
32452-32452	NOMA
32453-32453	OVERSTREET
32454-32454	POINT WASHINGTON
32455-32455	PONCE DE LEON
32456-32457	PORT SAINT JOE
32459-32459	SANTA ROSA BEACH
32460-32460	SNEADS
32461-32461	SUNNYSIDE
32461-32461	ROSEMARY BEACH
32462-32462	VERNON
32463-32463	WAUSAU
32464-32464	WESTVILLE
32465-32465	WEWAHITCHKA
32466-32466	YOUNGSTOWN
32500-32526	PENSACOLA
32530-32530	BAGDAD
32531-32531	BAKER
32533-32533	CANTONMENT
32534-32534	PENSACOLA
32535-32535	CENTURY
32536-32536	CRESTVIEW
32537-32537	MILLIGAN
32538-32538	PAXTON
32539-32539	CRESTVIEW
32540-32541	DESTIN
32542-32542	EGLIN AFB
32544-32544	HURLBURT FIELD
32547-32549	FORT WALTON BEACH
32550-32550	MIRAMAR BEACH
32559-32559	PENSACOLA
32560-32560	GONZALEZ
32561-32562	GULF BREEZE
32563-32563	HAROLD
32563-32563	GULF BREEZE
32564-32564	HOLT
32565-32565	JAY
32566-32566	GULF BREEZE
32567-32567	LAUREL HILL
32568-32568	MC DAVID
32569-32569	MARY ESTHER
32570-32572	MILTON
32573-32576	PENSACOLA
32577-32577	MOLINO
32578-32578	NICEVILLE
32579-32579	SHALIMAR
32580-32580	VALPARAISO
32581-32582	PENSACOLA
32583-32583	MILTON
32588-32588	NICEVILLE
32589-32598	PENSACOLA
32600-32614	GAINESVILLE
32615-32616	ALACHUA
32617-32617	ANTHONY
32618-32618	ARCHER
32619-32619	BELL
32621-32621	BRONSON
32622-32622	BROOKER
32625-32625	CEDAR KEY
32626-32626	CHIEFLAND
32627-32627	GAINESVILLE
32628-32628	CROSS CITY
32631-32631	EARLETON
32633-32633	EVINSTON
32634-32634	FAIRFIELD
32635-32635	GAINESVILLE
32639-32639	GULF HAMMOCK
32640-32640	HAWTHORNE
32641-32641	GAINESVILLE
32643-32643	HIGH SPRINGS
32644-32644	CHIEFLAND
32648-32648	HORSESHOE BEACH
32653-32653	GAINESVILLE
32654-32654	ISLAND GROVE
32655-32655	HIGH SPRINGS
32656-32656	KEYSTONE HEIGHTS
32658-32658	LA CROSSE
32662-32662	LOCHLOOSA
32663-32663	LOWELL
32664-32664	MC INTOSH
32666-32666	MELROSE
32667-32667	MICANOPY
32668-32668	MORRISTON
32669-32669	NEWBERRY
32680-32680	OLD TOWN
32681-32681	ORANGE LAKE
32683-32683	OTTER CREEK
32686-32686	REDDICK
32692-32692	SUWANNEE
32693-32693	TRENTON
32694-32694	WALDO
32696-32696	WILLISTON
32697-32697	WORTHINGTON SPRINGS
32701-32701	ALTAMONTE SPRINGS
32702-32702	ALTOONA
32703-32704	APOPKA
32706-32706	CASSADAGA
32707-32707	CASSELBERRY
32708-32708	WINTER SPRINGS
32709-32709	CHRISTMAS
32710-32710	CLARCONA
32712-32712	APOPKA
32713-32713	DEBARY
32714-32717	ALTAMONTE SPRINGS
32718-32718	CASSELBERRY
32719-32719	WINTER SPRINGS
32720-32721	DELAND
32722-32722	GLENWOOD
32723-32723	DELAND
32725-32725	DELTONA
32726-32727	EUSTIS
32728-32728	DELTONA
32730-32730	CASSELBERRY
32732-32732	GENEVA
32733-32733	GOLDENROD
32735-32735	GRAND ISLAND
32736-32736	EUSTIS
32738-32739	DELTONA
32744-32744	LAKE HELEN
32745-32745	MOUNT DORA
32746-32746	LAKE MARY
32747-32747	LAKE MONROE
32750-32750	LONGWOOD
32751-32751	MAITLAND
32752-32752	LONGWOOD
32753-32753	DEBARY
32754-32754	MIMS
32756-32757	MOUNT DORA
32759-32759	OAK HILL
32762-32762	OVIEDO
32763-32763	ORANGE CITY
32764-32764	OSTEEN
32765-32766	OVIEDO
32767-32767	PAISLEY
32768-32768	PLYMOUTH
32771-32773	SANFORD
32774-32774	ORANGE CITY
32775-32775	SCOTTSMOOR
32776-32776	SORRENTO
32777-32777	TANGERINE
32778-32778	TAVARES
32779-32779	LONGWOOD
32780-32783	TITUSVILLE
32784-32784	UMATILLA
32789-32790	WINTER PARK
32791-32791	LONGWOOD
32792-32793	WINTER PARK
32794-32794	MAITLAND
32795-32795	LAKE MARY
32796-32796	TITUSVILLE
32798-32798	ZELLWOOD
32799-32799	MID FLORIDA
32800-32899	ORLANDO
32901-32902	MELBOURNE
32903-32903	INDIALANTIC
32904-32904	MELBOURNE
32905-32911	PALM BAY
32912-32919	MELBOURNE
32920-32920	CAPE CANAVERAL
32922-32924	COCOA
32925-32925	PATRICK A F B
32926-32927	COCOA
32931-32932	COCOA BEACH
32934-32936	MELBOURNE
32937-32937	SATELLITE BEACH
32940-32941	MELBOURNE
32948-32948	FELLSMERE
32949-32949	GRANT
32950-32950	MALABAR
32951-32951	MELBOURNE BEACH
32952-32954	MERRITT ISLAND
32955-32956	ROCKLEDGE
32957-32957	ROSELAND
32958-32958	SEBASTIAN
32959-32959	SHARPES
32960-32969	VERO BEACH
32970-32970	WABASSO
32971-32971	WINTER BEACH
32976-32978	SEBASTIAN
33001-33001	LONG KEY
33002-33003	HIALEAH
33004-33004	DANIA
33008-33009	HALLANDALE
33010-33018	HIALEAH
33019-33029	HOLLYWOOD
33030-33035	HOMESTEAD
33036-33036	ISLAMORADA
33037-33037	KEY LARGO
33039-33039	HOMESTEAD
33040-33041	KEY WEST
33042-33042	SUMMERLAND KEY
33043-33043	BIG PINE KEY
33044-33044	SUGARLOAF SHORES
33045-33045	KEY WEST
33050-33050	MARATHON
33051-33051	KEY COLONY BEACH
33052-33052	MARATHON SHORES
33054-33056	OPA LOCKA
33060-33069	POMPANO BEACH
33070-33070	TAVERNIER
33071-33077	POMPANO BEACH
33081-33081	HOLLYWOOD
33082-33082	SOUTH FLORIDA

ZIP Range	City
33083-33084	HOLLYWOOD
33090-33092	HOMESTEAD
33093-33097	POMPANO BEACH
33100-33102	MIAMI
33103-33104	ABMPS
33107-33148	MIAMI
33149-33149	KEY BISCAYNE
33150-33299	MIAMI
33300-33326	FORT LAUDERDALE
33327-33327	WESTON
33328-33394	FORT LAUDERDALE
33401-33407	WEST PALM BEACH
33408-33408	NORTH PALM BEACH
33409-33422	WEST PALM BEACH
33424-33426	BOYNTON BEACH
33427-33429	BOCA RATON
33430-33430	BELLE GLADE
33431-33434	BOCA RATON
33435-33437	BOYNTON BEACH
33438-33438	CANAL POINT
33439-33439	BRYANT
33440-33440	CLEWISTON
33441-33443	DEERFIELD BEACH
33444-33448	DELRAY BEACH
33454-33454	LAKE WORTH
33455-33455	HOBE SOUND
33458-33458	JUPITER
33459-33459	LAKE HARBOR
33460-33464	LAKE WORTH
33464-33464	BOCA RATON
33465-33467	LAKE WORTH
33468-33469	JUPITER
33470-33470	LOXAHATCHEE
33471-33471	MOORE HAVEN
33474-33474	BOYNTON BEACH
33475-33475	HOBE SOUND
33476-33476	PAHOKEE
33477-33478	JUPITER
33480-33480	PALM BEACH
33481-33481	BOCA RATON
33482-33484	DELRAY BEACH
33486-33488	BOCA RATON
33491-33491	CANAL POINT
33493-33493	SOUTH BAY
33496-33499	BOCA RATON
33503-33503	BALM
33504-33504	BAY PINES
33508-33511	BRANDON
33513-33513	BUSHNELL
33514-33514	CENTER HILL
33521-33521	COLEMAN
33523-33523	DADE CITY
33524-33524	CRYSTAL SPRINGS
33525-33526	DADE CITY
33527-33527	DOVER
33530-33530	DURANT
33534-33534	GIBSONTON
33537-33537	LACOOCHEE
33538-33538	LAKE PANASOFFKEE
33539-33544	ZEPHYRHILLS
33547-33547	LITHIA
33548-33549	LUTZ
33550-33550	MANGO
33556-33556	ODESSA
33558-33559	LUTZ
33564-33567	PLANT CITY
33568-33569	RIVERVIEW
33570-33570	RUSKIN
33571-33571	SUN CITY CENTER
33572-33572	APOLLO BEACH
33573-33573	SUN CITY CENTER
33574-33574	SAINT LEO
33576-33576	SAN ANTONIO
33583-33584	SEFFNER
33585-33585	SUMTERVILLE
33586-33586	SUN CITY
33587-33587	SYDNEY
33592-33592	THONOTOSASSA
33593-33593	TRILBY
33594-33595	VALRICO
33597-33597	WEBSTER
33598-33598	WIMAUMA
33600-33697	TAMPA
33700-33743	SAINT PETERSBURG
33744-33744	BAY PINES
33747-33747	SAINT PETERSBURG
33755-33767	CLEARWATER
33767-33767	CLEARWATER BEACH
33769-33769	CLEARWATER
33770-33771	LARGO
33772-33772	SEMINOLE
33773-33774	LARGO
33775-33776	SEMINOLE
33777-33777	LARGO
33777-33777	SEMINOLE
33778-33779	LARGO
33780-33782	PINELLAS PARK
33784-33784	SAINT PETERSBURG
33785-33785	INDIAN ROCKS BEACH
33786-33786	BELLEAIR BEACH
33801-33815	LAKELAND
33820-33820	ALTURAS
33821-33821	ARCADIA
33823-33823	AUBURNDALE
33825-33826	AVON PARK
33827-33827	BABSON PARK
33830-33831	BARTOW
33834-33834	BOWLING GREEN
33835-33835	BRADLEY
33836-33837	DAVENPORT
33838-33838	DUNDEE
33839-33839	EAGLE LAKE
33840-33840	EATON PARK
33841-33841	FORT MEADE
33842-33842	FORT OGDEN
33843-33843	FROSTPROOF
33844-33845	HAINES CITY
33846-33846	HIGHLAND CITY
33847-33847	HOMELAND
33848-33848	INTERCESSION CITY
33849-33849	KATHLEEN
33850-33850	LAKE ALFRED
33851-33851	LAKE HAMILTON
33852-33852	LAKE PLACID
33853-33853	LAKE WALES
33854-33854	FEDHAVEN
33855-33855	INDIAN LAKE ESTATES
33856-33856	NALCREST
33857-33857	LORIDA
33858-33858	LOUGHMAN
33859-33859	LAKE WALES
33860-33860	MULBERRY
33862-33862	LAKE PLACID
33863-33863	NICHOLS
33864-33864	NOCATEE
33865-33865	ONA
33867-33867	RIVER RANCH
33868-33868	POLK CITY
33870-33872	SEBRING
33873-33873	WAUCHULA
33875-33876	SEBRING
33877-33877	WAVERLY
33880-33888	WINTER HAVEN
33890-33890	ZOLFO SPRINGS
33896-33897	DAVENPORT
33898-33898	LAKE WALES
33900-33903	FORT MYERS
33903-33903	NORTH FORT MYERS
33904-33904	CAPE CORAL
33905-33908	FORT MYERS
33909-33910	CAPE CORAL
33911-33913	FORT MYERS
33914-33915	CAPE CORAL
33916-33917	FORT MYERS
33917-33917	NORTH FORT MYERS
33918-33918	FORT MYERS
33918-33918	NORTH FORT MYERS
33919-33919	FORT MYERS
33920-33920	ALVA
33921-33921	BOCA GRANDE
33922-33922	BOKEELIA
33923-33923	BONITA SPRINGS
33924-33924	CAPTIVA
33925-33925	CHOKOLOSKEE
33926-33926	COPELAND
33927-33927	PUNTA GORDA
33928-33928	ESTERO
33929-33929	EVERGLADES CITY
33930-33930	FELDA
33931-33932	FORT MYERS BEACH
33933-33933	GOODLAND
33934-33934	IMMOKALEE
33935-33935	LABELLE
33936-33936	LEHIGH ACRES
33937-33937	MARCO ISLAND
33938-33938	MURDOCK
33939-33942	NAPLES
33943-33943	OCHOPEE
33944-33944	PALMDALE
33945-33945	PINELAND
33946-33946	PLACIDA
33947-33947	ROTONDA WEST
33948-33949	PORT CHARLOTTE
33950-33951	PUNTA GORDA
33952-33954	PORT CHARLOTTE
33955-33955	PUNTA GORDA
33956-33956	SAINT JAMES CITY
33957-33957	SANIBEL
33959-33959	BONITA SPRINGS
33960-33960	VENUS
33961-33964	NAPLES
33965-33965	FORT MYERS
33969-33969	MARCO ISLAND
33970-33972	LEHIGH ACRES
33975-33975	LABELLE
33980-33981	PORT CHARLOTTE
33982-33983	PUNTA GORDA
33990-33993	CAPE CORAL
33994-33994	FORT MYERS
33999-33999	NAPLES
34001-34042	APO
34050-34099	FPO
34101-34120	NAPLES
34133-34136	BONITA SPRINGS
34137-34137	COPELAND
34138-34138	CHOKOLOSKEE
34139-34139	EVERGLADES CITY
34140-34140	GOODLAND
34141-34141	OCHOPEE
34142-34143	IMMOKALEE
34145-34146	MARCO ISLAND
34201-34212	BRADENTON
34215-34215	CORTEZ
34216-34216	ANNA MARIA
34217-34217	BRADENTON BEACH
34218-34218	HOLMES BEACH
34219-34219	PARRISH
34220-34221	PALMETTO
34222-34222	ELLENTON
34223-34224	ENGLEWOOD
34228-34228	LONGBOAT KEY
34229-34229	OSPREY
34230-34243	SARASOTA
34250-34250	TERRA CEIA
34251-34251	MYAKKA CITY
34260-34260	MANASOTA
34264-34264	ONECO
34265-34266	ARCADIA
34267-34267	FORT OGDEN
34268-34268	NOCATEE
34269-34269	ARCADIA
34270-34270	TALLEVAST
34272-34272	LAUREL
34274-34275	NOKOMIS
34276-34278	SARASOTA
34280-34282	BRADENTON
34284-34285	VENICE
34286-34289	NORTH PORT
34292-34293	VENICE
34295-34295	ENGLEWOOD
34420-34421	BELLEVIEW
34423-34429	CRYSTAL RIVER
34430-34434	DUNNELLON
34436-34436	FLORAL CITY
34442-34442	HERNANDO
34445-34445	HOLDER
34446-34446	HOMOSASSA
34447-34447	HOMOSASSA SPRINGS
34448-34448	HOMOSASSA
34449-34449	INGLIS
34450-34453	INVERNESS
34460-34461	LECANTO
34464-34465	BEVERLY HILLS
34470-34483	OCALA
34484-34484	OXFORD
34487-34487	HOMOSASSA
34488-34489	SILVER SPRINGS
34491-34492	SUMMERFIELD
34498-34498	YANKEETOWN
34601-34605	BROOKSVILLE
34606-34608	SPRING HILL
34609-34610	BROOKSVILLE
34611-34611	SPRING HILL
34613-34614	BROOKSVILLE
34615-34630	CLEARWATER
34634-34635	BELLEAIR SHORES
34635-34635	INDIAN ROCKS BEACH
34636-34636	ISTACHATTA
34639-34639	LAND O LAKES
34640-34649	LARGO
34652-34656	NEW PORT RICHEY
34660-34660	OZONA
34661-34661	NOBLETON
34664-34666	PINELLAS PARK
34667-34667	HUDSON
34668-34668	PORT RICHEY
34669-34669	HUDSON
34673-34673	PORT RICHEY
34674-34674	HUDSON
34677-34677	OLDSMAR
34679-34679	ARIPEKA
34680-34680	ELFERS
34681-34681	CRYSTAL BEACH
34682-34685	PALM HARBOR
34688-34689	TARPON SPRINGS
34690-34691	HOLIDAY
34695-34695	SAFETY HARBOR
34697-34698	DUNEDIN
34705-34705	ASTATULA
34711-34713	CLERMONT
34729-34729	FERNDALE
34731-34731	FRUITLAND PARK
34734-34734	GOTHA
34736-34736	GROVELAND
34737-34737	HOWEY IN THE HILLS
34739-34739	KENANSVILLE
34740-34740	KILLARNEY
34741-34747	KISSIMMEE
34748-34749	LEESBURG
34753-34753	MASCOTTE
34755-34755	MINNEOLA
34756-34757	MONTVERDE
34758-34759	KISSIMMEE
34760-34760	OAKLAND
34761-34761	OCOEE
34762-34762	OKAHUMPKA
34769-34773	SAINT CLOUD
34777-34778	WINTER GARDEN
34785-34785	WILDWOOD
34786-34786	WINDERMERE
34787-34787	WINTER GARDEN
34788-34789	LEESBURG
34797-34797	YALAHA
34945-34951	FORT PIERCE
34952-34953	PORT SAINT LUCIE
34954-34954	FORT PIERCE
34956-34956	INDIANTOWN
34957-34958	JENSEN BEACH
34972-34974	OKEECHOBEE
34979-34982	FORT PIERCE
34983-34988	PORT SAINT LUCIE
34990-34991	PALM CITY
34992-34992	PORT SALERNO
34994-34997	STUART

Georgia

General Help Numbers:

Governor's Office
203 State Capitol
Atlanta, GA 30334
www.ganet.org/governor/
index_flash.html

404-656-1776
Fax 404-657-7332
8AM-4:30PM

Attorney General's Office
40 Capitol Square SW
Atlanta, GA 30334-1300
www.law.state.ga.us

404-656-3300
Fax 404-651-9148
8AM-5PM

State Court Administrator
244 Washington St SW, Suite 300
Atlanta, GA 30334
www.georgiacourts.org/

404-656-5171
Fax 404-651-6449
8:30AM-5PM

State Archives
Archives & History Department
330 Capitol Ave SE
Atlanta, GA 30334
www.sos.state.ga.us/archives/

404-656-2393
Fax 404-657-8427
8 AM - 4:45 PM

State Specifics:

Capital: Atlanta
                              Fulton County

Time Zone: EST

Number of Counties: 159

Population: 8,383,915

Web Site: www.georgia.gov

State Agencies

Criminal Records

Georgia Bureau of Investigations, Attn: GCIC, PO Box 370748, Decatur, GA 30037-0748 (Courier: 3121 Panthersville Rd, Decatur, GA 30034); 404-244-2590, 404-244-2878 (Fax), 8AM-4PM.

www.ganet.org/gbi

Note: GCIC is the central repository of criminal records for the State. Sex offender data is at www.state.ga.us/gbi/disclaim.html.

Indexing & Storage: Records are available from 1972 forward. It takes 1-3 days before new records are available for inquiry. Records are indexed on fingerprint cards. 70% of all arrests in database have final dispositions recorded, 81% for those arrests within last 5 years.

Searching: Records are available to employers, government agencies including licensing agencies, and adoption and foster care providers. Include the following in your request: name, set of fingerprints, date of birth, sex, race, Social Security Number. Certain law enforcement agencies, who are online, and local agencies may access and retrieve records for investigative/background purposes. These agencies have the option of requesting a signed release from subject or including a set of fingerprints. The following data is not released: juvenile records, traffic ticket information or out-of-state or federal charges. Information released includes arrest, disposition, and custodial information for offenses designated as fingerprintable by the State AG. Records without dispositions are released.

Access by: mail, in person.

Fee & Payment: The fee is $15.00 per name. If statutues require a FBI check, submit 2 sets of fingerprints and a total search fee of $24.00 per name. A $3.00 fee is charged for an "Inspection Challenge" of your own personal record. Agencies may establish an account. Fee payee: Georgia Bureau of Investigations. Prepayment required. Money orders are accepted. No credit cards accepted.

Mail search: Turnaround time: 7 to 10 days. No self addressed stamped envelope is required.

In person search: In-person requests are returned by mail in about 14 days.

Corporation Records
Limited Partnership Records
Limited Liability Partnerships
Limited Liability Company Records

Secretary of State, Corporation Division, 315 W Tower, #2 ML King Drive, Atlanta, GA 30334-1530; 404-656-2817, 404-651-9059 (Fax), 8AM-5PM.

www.sos.state.ga.us/corporations

Note: Trade Names, Fictitious Names, assumed names and DBAs are found at the county level.

Indexing & Storage: Records are available from the 1960s, and earlier if the filer has moved records from the county level to the state level. Indexes are maintained on microfilm and document imaging systems. New records are available for inquiry immediately.

Searching: Date of incorporation, current status and registered name and address available at web site or by phone. Officer names available at web site only. Copies and/or certificates can be ordered by mail or from the web.

Access by: mail, phone, in person, online.

Fee & Payment: There is no fee for a web site search; there is a $10.00 fee for a Certificate of Existence (good standing) or certified copies. Fee payee: Secretary of State. Prepayment required. Web requests must be paid by credit card. Personal checks accepted. Credit cards accepted: MasterCard, Visa, AmEx.

Mail search: Turnaround time: 1 day. No self addressed stamped envelope is required.

Phone search: Same information shown at web site is available over the phone.

In person search: Immediate records only if expedited service fees paid.

Online search: Records are available from the corporation database on the Internet site above or The corporate database can be searched by entity name or registered agent for no fee. Document Image and certificates are available for a $10.00 fee at www.ganet.org/services/corp/corpsearch.shtml. Major credit cards accepted. Other services include name reservation, filing procedures, downloading of forms/applications.

Expedited service: Expedited service is available for mail and in person searches. Turnaround time: 24 hours. Add $50.00 per business name.

Trademarks/Servicemarks

Secretary of State, Trademark Division, 2 Martin Luther King, Room 315, W Tower, Atlanta, GA 30334; 404-656-2861, 404-657-6380 (Fax), 8AM-5PM.

www.sos.state.ga.us/corporations/trademarks.htm

Note: Applications and filing instructions can be obtained at the web site.

Indexing & Storage: Records are available from the beginning of the Division and are maintained on computer. It takes 24 hours before new records are available for inquiry.

Searching: Search by mark name or description or by owner name or by goods and services.

Access by: mail, phone, in person, online.

Fee & Payment: There is no fee. No credit cards accepted.

Mail search: Turnaround time: 2 to 3 days. No self addressed stamped envelope is required.

Phone search: Records are available by phone.

In person search: They will take your request in person, but they will mail back the records.

Online search: A record database is searchable from the web site.

Uniform Commercial Code

Superior Court Clerks' Cooperative Authority, 1875 Century Blvd, #100, Atlanta, GA 30345; 404-327-9058, 404-327-7877 (Fax), 9AM-5PM.

http://www2.gsccca.org

Note: High volume, ongoing requesters can open a "search account" and receive expedited service.

Indexing & Storage: Records are available from 1-1-95, indexed on computer.

Searching: All uniform commercial code filings are filed at the county level. As of January 1, 1995, new UCC filings are indexed statewide (older filings are only available at the county). Submit a UCC-11 to the address above to search new filings. Include the following in your request: debtor name, Social Security or federal employer number. All tax liens are filed at the county level only.

Access by: mail, phone, fax, in person, online.

Fee & Payment: Uncertified copies made by searcher are $.25 each, if copies by this office the fee is $1.00 per page. Certified copies are only available at the county level. A search is $10.00. Fee payee: GSCCCA. Prepayment required. Personal checks accepted. No credit cards accepted.

Mail search: Turnaround time: 1 day. No self addressed stamped envelope is required.

Phone search: This is only for expedited service or for accounts.

Fax search: However, this is only available to established accounts.

In person search: Searching is available in person.

Online search: Online access is available for regular, ongoing requesters. There is a monthly charge of $9.95 and a $.25 fee per image. Billing is monthly. The system is open 24 hours daily. The online service also includes real estate indexes and images. Minimum baud rate is 9600; 28.8 is supported. Information from 01/01/95 forward is available. Call 800-304-5175 or 404-327-9058 for a subscription package.

Other access: The entire UCC Central Index System can be purchased on a daily, weekly, biweekly basis. For more information, contact the Director's office.

Expedited service: Expedited service is available for mail and phone searches. Turnaround time: a few hours. Add $25.00 per search.

Federal Tax Liens
State Tax Liens

Records not maintained by a state level agency.

Note: All tax liens are filed at the county level.

Sales Tax Registrations

Sales & Use Tax Division, Taxpayer Services Unit, 270 Washington St SW, Atlanta, GA 30334; 404-651-8651, 404-651-9490 (Fax), 8AM-4:30PM.

http://www2.state.ga.us/departments/dor

Indexing & Storage: Records are available for all active accounts, which are kept on computer. Inactive accounts are on microfilm.

Searching: This agency will only confirm that a business is registered and active, if a tax permit number is provided. A tax number is required to search.

Access by: phone, in person. No searching by mail.

Phone search: No fee for telephone request.

In person search: No fee for request. Generally, the information is returned by mail in two weeks.

Birth Certificates

Department of Human Resources, Vital Records Unit, 2600 Skyland Dr NE, Atlanta, GA 30319; 404-679-4701, 877-572-6343 (Credit Card Line), 404-679-4730 (Fax), 8AM-4PM.

www.ph.dhr.state.ga.us/programs/vitalrecords

Indexing & Storage: Records are available from 1919 to present. It takes 1 month before new records are available for inquiry. Records are indexed on inhouse computer.

Searching: For investigative purposes or distant relatives, a notarized, signed release form from person of record is required. Include the following in your request: full name, names of parents, mother's maiden name, date of birth, place of birth.

Access by: mail, phone, fax, in person.

Fee & Payment: The fee is $10.00 per record. Add $5.00 per name requested for second copies. Multi year searches are $10.00 per ten years or portions thereof. Fee payee: Georgia Department of Human Resources. Prepayment required. Credit cards accepted: MasterCard, Visa, AmEx, Discover.

Mail search: Turnaround time: 2 to 3 weeks. No self addressed stamped envelope is required.

Phone search: You may make requests using a credit card for an additional $9.95 fee. Turnaround time 2 days.

Fax search: Same criteria as phone searching.

In person search: Turnaround time is usually 30 minutes.

Expedited service: Expedited service is available for mail, phone and fax searches. Turnaround time: overnight delivery. Add $16.81 for overnight service plus use of credit card/fee required.

Death Records

Department of Human Resources, Vital Records Unit, 2600 Skyland Dr NE, Atlanta, GA 30319; 404-679-4701, 877-572-6343 (Credit Card Line), 404-679-4730 (Fax), 8AM-4PM.

www.ph.dhr.state.ga.us/programs/vitalrecords/

Indexing & Storage: Records are available from 1919 to present. It takes 1 month before new records are available for inquiry. Records are indexed on inhouse computer.

Searching: Death certificates are available to the general public. Cause of death is released to next of kin only. Include the following in your request: full name, date of death, place of death. Age at death, sex and race are helpful.

Access by: mail, phone, fax, in person.

Fee & Payment: The fee is $10.00 per name. Add $5.00 per name for second copies. Multi year searches are $10.00 per 10 years or portions thereof. Fee payee: Georgia Department of Human Resources. Prepayment required. Credit cards accepted: MasterCard, Visa, AmEx, Discover.

Mail search: Turnaround time: 2 to 3 weeks. No self addressed stamped envelope is required.

Phone search: You can make requests using a credit card for an additional $9.95 service fee. Turnaround time 2 days.

Fax search: Same criteria as phone searching.

In person search: Turnaround time 30 minutes.

Other access: The death index is available for the years 1919-1998 on microfiche for $50.00.

Expedited service: Expedited service is available for mail, phone and fax searches. Turnaround time: overnight delivery. Add $16.81 for overnight delivery, plus include credit card fee.

Marriage Certificates

Department of Human Resources, Vital Records Unit, 2600 Skyland Dr NE, Atlanta, GA 30319; 404-679-4701, 877-572-6343 (Credit Card Line), 404-679-4730 (Fax), 8AM-4PM.

www.ph.dhr.state.ga.us/programs/vitalrecords/

Indexing & Storage: Records are available from 1952 on. Prior to 1952, records must be obtained from the county probate office. It takes 1 month. before new records are available for inquiry. Records are indexed on inhouse computer.

Searching: Certified copies of marriage licenses are available to the general public; but copies of the marriage application are only issued to bride and groom. Records may not be ordered via e-mail. Include the following in your request: full names of husband and wife, date of marriage, place or county of marriage.

Access by: mail, phone, fax, in person.

Fee & Payment: The search fee is $10.00 per name. Add $5.00 per name requested for second copies. Multi-year search are $10.00 per ten years or portions thereof. Fee payee: Georgia Department of Human Resources. Prepayment required. Credit cards accepted: MasterCard, Visa, AmEx, Discover.

Mail search: Turnaround time: 2 to 3 weeks. No self addressed stamped envelope is required.

Phone search: You can make requests using a credit card for an additional $9.95 fee. Turnaround time 2 days.

Fax search: Same criteria as phone searches.

In person search: Turnaround time 30 minutes.

Other access: The marriage index is available on microfiche for $50.00, the set includes the years 1964-1998.

Expedited service: Expedited service is available for mail, phone and fax searches. Turnaround time: overnight delivery. Add $16.81 for express delivery plus the credit card surcharge.

Divorce Records

Department of Human Resources, Vital Records Unit, 2600 Skyland Dr NE, Atlanta, GA 30319; 404-679-4701, 877-572-6343 (Credit Card Line), 404-679-4730 (Fax), 8AM-4PM.

www.ph.dhr.state.ga.us/programs/vitalrecords/

Note: Divorce records are found at the county of issue. However, this agency will do search to identify the county of record, but cannot issue a record. Certified copies are only available at the county level.

Indexing & Storage: Records are available from the counties.

Access by: mail, phone, fax, in person.

Fee & Payment: The fee is $10.00, $5.00 for a second copy. Fee payee: GA Department of Human Resources. Personal checks accepted. Credit cards accepted: MasterCard, Visa, AmEx, Discover.

Mail search: Records are available by mail.

Phone search: Requires use of credit card for additional $9.95.

Fax search: Same criteria as phone searches.

In person search: Searching is available in person.

Other access: Divorce microfiche indexes are available to the public, sold in complete set for the years 1919-1998 for $50.00.

Expedited service: Expedited service is available for fax searches. Add $16.81 for express delivery plus the credit card use fee.

Workers' Compensation Records

State Board of Workers Compensation, 270 Peachtree St, NW, Atlanta, GA 30303-1299; 404-656-3875, 8AM-4:30PM.

www.ganet.org/sbwc

Indexing & Storage: Records are available from 1989. Records are maintained for 10 years. Records are indexed on inhouse computer.

Searching: Must have a court order signed by a judge to obtain records from this agency unless you are a party to the case. Include the following in your request: claimant name, Social Security Number.

Access by: mail.

Fee & Payment: The agency will bill for required fees. Fee payee: State Board of Workers Compensation. Personal checks accepted. No credit cards accepted.

Mail search: Turnaround time: 2 to 3 weeks. The fee is $7.00 for the first 10 pages plus $.50 per page for over 10 pages. Certification for a document is $7.00. No self addressed stamped envelope is required. No fee for mail request.

Driver Records

Department of Motor Vehicle Safety, Driver's Services Section, MVR Unit, PO Box 80447, Conyers, GA 30013 (Courier: 2206 East View Parkway, Conyers, GA 30013); 678-413-8441, 8AM-3:30PM.

www.dmvs.ga.gov

Note: Copies of tickets are not available from a central depository. It is recommended you go directly to the issuing court.

Indexing & Storage: Records are available for either a 3 year record or a 7 year record. Accident involvement is shown if the driver was cited. The driver's address is part of the record. It takes ten days or more before new records are available for inquiry.

Searching: Georgia has strict rules concerning driver record access. If an individual requests a driving record on another, the driver's notarized signature is needed (except for court subpoena). Large requesters must have "bulk-user certificates" on file. The driver's full name and DOB are needed to request a record. The license number is optional.

Access by: mail, in person.

Fee & Payment: $5.00 for a 3 year period; $7.00 for a 7 year period. Fee payee: Department of Motor Vehicle Safety Prepayment required. No credit cards accepted.

Mail search: Turnaround time: 2 weeks. No self addressed stamped envelope is required.

In person search: Walk-in requesters may receive up to three records while waiting, additional requests are processed overnight. Walk-in requests are also available from the State Patrol Posts.

Other access: Georgia offers magnetic tape processing for high volume users.

Vehicle Ownership
Vehicle Identification

Department of Motor Vehicle Safety, Motor Vehicle Services - Research, PO Box 740381, Atlanta, GA 30374-0381; 404-362-6500, 8AM-4:30PM.

www.dmvs.ga.gov

Indexing & Storage: Records are available from 1997 forward.

Searching: Records are not open to the general public and are restricted to authorized (notarized) agents or individuals, judgment creditor, tax collector, law enforcement officials, license dealers, etc. There is an online access mode for only GA licensed dealers. Records are only released to casual requesters with notarized consent of the subject

Access by: mail, in person.

Fee & Payment: Fees: $1.00 per record for VIN and title histories; $.50 for a tag search with computer print-out; $1.00 for a tag search with copy of file. Lien information is considered part of the title history. There is a full charge for a "no record found." Fee payee: Department of Motor Vehicle Safety. Prepayment required. No credit cards accepted.

Mail search: Turnaround time: 2 weeks. A self addressed stamped envelope is requested.

In person search: Turnaround time is while you wait.

Accident Reports

Department of Motor Vehicle Safety, Accident Reporting Section, PO Box 80447, Conyers, GA 30013; 678-413-8580, 8AM-4:30PM.

Indexing & Storage: Records are available for 10 years to present. It takes 30 days before new records are available for inquiry.

Searching: Only persons involved in the accident or their legal representative may obtain a copy, unless the subject has given written permission. Include the following in your request: full name, date of accident, location of accident.

Access by: mail, in person.

Fee & Payment: The fee for a report is $5.00. There is no charge for a "no record found." Fee payee: Department of Motor Vehicle Safety. Prepayment required. Cash, money orders, certified checks, and cashier's checks are all accepted. No credit cards accepted.

Mail search: Turnaround time: 1 week to 10 days. No self addressed stamped envelope is required.

In person search: Request must be in writing. Turnaround time is within the hour.

Vessel Ownership
Vessel Registration

Georgia Dept of Natural Resources, 2189 Northlake Parkway Bldg 10 #108, Tucker, GA 30084; 770-414-3338, 770-414-3344 (Fax), 8AM-4:30PM.

www.ganet.org/dnr

Note: Liens are at the county level and will not show on records at this location.

Indexing & Storage: Records are available from 1986 to present. Records are indexed on microfiche from 1986 to 1993 and on computer from 1994 to present. All motorized boats must be registered. All sailboats 12 ft or longer must be registered.

Searching: Either the name, registration # or hull # must be submitted.

Access by: mail, phone, fax, in person.

Fee & Payment: There is no search fee.

Mail search: Turnaround time: 1 to 2 weeks. No self addressed stamped envelope is required.

Phone search: Verification only.

Fax search: Same criteria as mail searching.

In person search: Searching is available in person.

Legislation Records

General Assembly of Georgia, State Capitol, Atlanta, GA 30334; 404-656-5040 (Senate), 404-656-5015 (House), 404-656-2370 (Archives), 404-656-5043 (Fax), 8:30AM-4:30PM.

www.legis.state.ga.us

Indexing & Storage: Records are available from 1967 to present. Records are computerized since 1995, on hard copy 95-2000, and on microfilm 67-94. The older the document, the longer the turnaround time.

Searching: Include the following in your request: bill number, year. Either Senate or House Clerk can look up bills, but to receive copies of documents before 1967, go to respective area. Also, the State Archives has copies of all bills.

Access by: mail, phone, in person, online.

Fee & Payment: The fee is $.10 per printed page. Fee payee: General Assembly of Georgia. Personal checks accepted. No credit cards accepted.

Mail search: Turnaround time: variable. Address questions to Senate to Room 353, House questions to Room 307. No self addressed stamped envelope is required.

Phone search: You may request bills by phone.

In person search: You may request bills in person.

Online search: The Internet site listed above has bill information. Also, you can search at www.ganet.org/services/leg.

Voter Registration

Secretary of State, Elections Division, 2 Martin Luther King Dr SE, Suite 1104, Atlanta, GA 30334; 404-656-2871, 404-651-9531 (Fax), 8AM-5PM.

www.sos.state.ga.us/elections

Indexing & Storage: Records are available from 1995, on computer. Data is keyed in by county personnel onto the state computer.

Searching: Records may be ordered in a database format directly from the web site. Include the following in your request: full name, Social Security Number if available, date of birth. All requests must be in writing. Records may be requested at county level, also. The following data is not released: Social Security Numbers or bulk information or lists for commercial purposes.

Access by: mail, fax, online.

Fee & Payment: There is no fee for individual requests. Copies are $.25 per page. There are fees to purchase the database, and these fees can be found at the web site.

Mail search: Turnaround time: 2 to 3 days. No self addressed stamped envelope is required.

Fax search: Fax searching of statutus is available.

Online search: Name and DOB needed to search registration information at the web site. Go to "Poll Locator." The results will provide address and district-precinct information, no SSNs released.

Other access: CDs, Internet files, disks, and paper lists are available for purchase for non-commercial purposes. Look at the web site for pricing.

GED Certificates

GED Testing Services, 1800 Century Pl #555, Atlanta, GA 30345; 404-679-1644, 8:30AM-4:30PM M-F.

www.dtae.org

Searching: To search, all are required: a signed release, name, year of test, date of birth, and Social Security Number.

Access by: mail.

Fee & Payment: The fee for a verification or for a copy of a transcript is $5.00 per record. A duplicate diploma is $5.00. Fee payee: GED Testing Services. Prepayment required. Money orders are accepted. No credit cards accepted.

Mail search: Turnaround time: 2 weeks. No self addressed stamped envelope is required.

Hunting License Information
Fishing License Information

Department of Natural Resources, Hunting & Fishing Licenses, 21889 North Lake Pkwy, Bldg 610, #108, Tucker, GA 30084; 770-918-6400, 770-414-3344 (Fax), 8AM-4:30PM.

www.georgiawildlife.com

Note: The request must be in writing and cite that under the Georgia Open Records Act you request that a search be done.

Searching: Include name. The SSN, DOB and address are helpful. The database may not be current for non-resident licenses and license purchases made via the web site.

Access by: mail, phone, in person.

Fee & Payment: There is no fee unless the search is extensive.

Mail search: Turnaround time: variable. No self addressed stamped envelope is required.

Phone search: They will only confirm.

In person search: Searching is available in person.

Georgia State Licensing Agencies

Licenses Searchable Online

Acupuncturist #41	www.medicalboard.state.ga.us/bdsearch/index.html
Air Conditioning Contractor #9	https://secure.sos.state.ga.us/myverification/
Architect #15	https://secure.sos.state.ga.us/myverification/
Athletic Agent #12	https://secure.sos.state.ga.us/myverification/
Athletic Trainer #16	https://secure.sos.state.ga.us/myverification/
Auctioneer/Auction Dealer #12	https://secure.sos.state.ga.us/myverification/
Audiologist #16	https://secure.sos.state.ga.us/myverification/
Bank #17	www.ganet.org/dbf/other_institutions.html
Barber/Barber Shop #19	https://secure.sos.state.ga.us/myverification/
Cardiac Technician #41	www.medicalboard.state.ga.us/bdsearch/index.html
Charity #45	www.sos.state.ga.us/securities/charitysearch.htm
Check Casher/Seller #17	www.ganet.org/dbf/other_institutions.html
Chiropractor #18	https://secure.sos.state.ga.us/myverification/
Contractor, General #9	https://secure.sos.state.ga.us/myverification/
Cosmetologist/Cosmetology Shop #19	https://secure.sos.state.ga.us/myverification/
Counselor #10	https://secure.sos.state.ga.us/myverification/
Credit Union #17	www.ganet.org/dbf/other_institutions.html
Dental Hygienist #20	https://secure.sos.state.ga.us/myverification/
Dentist #20	https://secure.sos.state.ga.us/myverification/
Detox Specialist #41	www.medicalboard.state.ga.us/bdsearch/index.html
Dietitian #2	https://secure.sos.state.ga.us/myverification/
Drug Wholesale/Retail/Mfg (Hospital) #31	https://secure.sos.state.ga.us/myverification/
EDP - Electronic Data Processor #17	www.ganet.org/dbf/other_institutions.html
Electrical Contractor #9	https://secure.sos.state.ga.us/myverification/
Embalmer #12	https://secure.sos.state.ga.us/myverification/
Engineer #11	https://secure.sos.state.ga.us/myverification/
Esthetician #19	https://secure.sos.state.ga.us/myverification/
Family Therapist #10	https://secure.sos.state.ga.us/myverification/
Forester #36	https://secure.sos.state.ga.us/myverification/
Funeral Director/Apprentice #12	https://secure.sos.state.ga.us/myverification/
Funeral Establishment #12	https://secure.sos.state.ga.us/myverification/
Geologist #44	https://secure.sos.state.ga.us/myverification/
Hearing Aid Dealer/Dispenser #21	https://secure.sos.state.ga.us/myverification/
Holding Company/Representative Office #17	www.ganet.org/dbf/other_institutions.html
Insurance Agent #8	www.inscomm.state.ga.us/AGENTS/AgentStatus.asp
Interior Designer #15	https://secure.sos.state.ga.us/myverification/
Landscape Architect #27	https://secure.sos.state.ga.us/myverification/
Low Voltage Contractor #9	https://secure.sos.state.ga.us/myverification/
Manicurist #19	https://secure.sos.state.ga.us/myverification/
Marriage Counselor #10	https://secure.sos.state.ga.us/myverification/
Medical Doctor #41	www.medicalboard.state.ga.us/bdsearch/index.html
Mortgage Institution #17	www.ganet.org/dbf/mortgage.html
Nail Care #19	https://secure.sos.state.ga.us/myverification/
Nuclear Pharmacist #31	https://secure.sos.state.ga.us/myverification/
Nurse-LPN #2	https://secure.sos.state.ga.us/myverification/
Nurse-RN #28	https://secure.sos.state.ga.us/myverification/
Nursing Home Administrator #16	https://secure.sos.state.ga.us/myverification/
Occupational Therapist/Assistant #2	https://secure.sos.state.ga.us/myverification/
Optician, Dispensing #21	https://secure.sos.state.ga.us/myverification/
Optometrist #21	https://secure.sos.state.ga.us/myverification/
Osteopathic Physician #41	www.medicalboard.state.ga.us/bdsearch/index.html
Paramedic #41	www.medicalboard.state.ga.us/bdsearch/index.html
Pesticide Applicator #4	www.kellysolutions.com/ga/Applicators/index.htm
Pesticide Contractor/Employee #4	www.kellysolutions.com/ga/Applicators/index.htm
Pharmacist #31	https://secure.sos.state.ga.us/myverification/
Pharmacy School, Clinic Researcher #31	https://secure.sos.state.ga.us/myverification/
Physical Therapist/Therapist Asst #2	https://secure.sos.state.ga.us/myverification/
Physician Assistant #41	www.medicalboard.state.ga.us/bdsearch/index.html
Plumber Journeyman/Contractor #9	https://secure.sos.state.ga.us/myverification/
Podiatrist #33	https://secure.sos.state.ga.us/myverification/
Poison Pharmacist #31	https://secure.sos.state.ga.us/myverification/
Private Detective #12	https://secure.sos.state.ga.us/myverification/
Psychologist #16	https://secure.sos.state.ga.us/myverification/

Public Accountant-CPA #14..................................https://secure.sos.state.ga.us/myverification/
Real Estate Appraiser #46.....................................www.asc.gov/content/category1/appr_by_state.asp
Rebuilder #12 ....https://secure.sos.state.ga.us/myverification/
Respiratory Care Practitioner #41........................www.medicalboard.state.ga.us/bdsearch/index.html
Salvage Pool Operator #12....................................https://secure.sos.state.ga.us/myverification/
Salvage Yard Dealer #12.......................................https://secure.sos.state.ga.us/myverification/
School Librarian #40...https://secure.sos.state.ga.us/myverification/
Security Agency #12...https://secure.sos.state.ga.us/myverification/
Security Guard #12...https://secure.sos.state.ga.us/myverification/
Social Worker #10 ....https://secure.sos.state.ga.us/myverification/
Speech-Language Pathologist #16.........................https://secure.sos.state.ga.us/myverification/
Surveyor, Land #11 ....https://secure.sos.state.ga.us/myverification/
Used Car Dealer #12...https://secure.sos.state.ga.us/myverification/
Used Car Parts Dist. #12......................................https://secure.sos.state.ga.us/myverification/
Utility Contractor #9 ....https://secure.sos.state.ga.us/myverification/
Veterinarian/Veterinary Technician #39.................https://secure.sos.state.ga.us/myverification/
Waste Water Collection System Operator #43 ....https://secure.sos.state.ga.us/myverification/
Waste Water Industrial #43 ....https://secure.sos.state.ga.us/myverification/
Waste Water Laboratory Analyst #43 ....https://secure.sos.state.ga.us/myverification/
Waste Water Treatment/Dist System Oper. #43.....https://secure.sos.state.ga.us/myverification/
Water Operator Class 1-3 #43...............................https://secure.sos.state.ga.us/myverification/

Licensing Quick Finder

Acupuncturist #41 — 404-657-6490
Air Conditioning Contractor #9 — 478-207-1416
Amusement Ride Inspector #48 — 404-679-0687
Animal Technician #39 — 478-207-1686
Architect #15 — 478-207-1400
Athletic Agent #12 — 478-207-1460
Athletic Trainer #16 — 478-207-1670
Attorney #47 — 404-527-8700
Auctioneer/Auction Dealer #12 — 478-207-1460
Audiologist #16 — 478-207-1670
Bank #17 — 770-986-1633
Barber/Barber Shop #19 — 478-207-1430
Cardiac Technician #41 — 404-656-3923
Cemetery #45 — 404-656-3920
Charity #45 — 404-656-3920
Check Casher/Seller #17 — 770-986-1633
Chiropractor #18 — 478-207-1686
Contractor, General #9 — 478-207-1416
Cosmetologist/Cosmetology Shop #19 — 478-207-1430
Counselor #10 — 478-207-1670
Court Reporter #1 — 404-656-6422
Credit Union #17 — 770-986-1637
Dental Hygienist #20 — 912-207-1680
Dentist #20 — 912-207-1680
Detox Specialist #41 — 404-656-3913
Dietitian #2 — 478-207-1620
Drug Whlse/Retail/Mfg (Hospital) #31 — 478-207-1686
EDP - Electronic Data Processor #17 — 770-986-1633
Electrical Contractor #9 — 478-207-1416
Embalmer #12 — 478-207-1460
Emergency Medical Technician #49 — 404-679-0547
Engineer #11 — 478-207-1450
Esthetician #19 — 478-207-1430
Family Therapist #10 — 478-207-1670
Forester #36 — 478-207-1400
Funeral Director/Apprentice #12 — 478-207-1460
Funeral Establishment #12 — 478-207-1460
Geologist #44 — 478-207-1400
Hearing Aid Dealer/Dispenser #21 — 912-207-1686

Holding Company/Representative Office #17 — 770-986-1633
Insurance Adjuster #8 — 404-656-2101
Insurance Agent #8 — 404-656-2101
Insurance Counselor #8 — 404-656-2101
Interior Designer #15 — 478-207-1400
Investment Advisor (Firm) #45 — 404-656-3920
Landfill Inspector/Operator #5 — 404-362-2696
Landscape Architect #27 — 478-207-1400
Liquor Control #6 — 404-651-9516
Low Voltage Contractor #9 — 478-207-1416
Manicurist #19 — 478-207-1430
Marriage Counselor #10 — 478-207-1670
Medical Doctor #41 — 404-657-6489
Mortgage Institution #17 — 770-986-1269
Nail Care #19 — 478-207-1430
Notary Public #3 — 404-327-6023
Nuclear Pharmacist #31 — 478-207-1686
Nurse-LPN #2 — 478-207-1620
Nurse-RN #28 — 404-657-0775
Nursing Home Administrator #16 — 478-207-1670
Occupational Therapist/Assistant #2 — 478-207-1620
Optician, Dispensing #21 — 912-207-1686
Optometrist #21 — 912-207-1686
Osteopathic Physician #41 — 404-657-6489
Paramedic #41 — 404-656-3923
Pesticide Applicator #4 — 404-656-4958
Pesticide Contractor/Employee #4 — 404-656-4958
Pharmacist #31 — 478-207-1686
Pharmacy School, Clinic Researcher #31 — 478-207-1686
Physical Therapist/Therapist Asst #2 — 478-207-1620
Physician Assistant #41 — 404-657-4688
Plumber Journeyman/Contractor #9 — 478-207-1416
Podiatrist #33 — 478-207-1686
Poison Pharmacist #31 — 478-207-1686
Private Detective #12 — 478-207-1460
Psychologist #16 — 478-207-1670
Public Accountant-CPA #14 — 478-207-1400

Public Adjuster #8 — 404-656-2101
Real Estate Appraiser #46 — 404-656-3916
Real Estate Broker #46 — 404-656-3916
Real Estate Community Assn. Mgr. #46 — 404-656-3916
Real Estate Sales Agent #46 — 404-656-3916
Rebuilder (Motor Vehicle) #12 — 478-207-1460
Respiratory Care Practitioner #41 — 404-656-3914
Salvage Pool Operator #12 — 478-207-1460
Salvage Yard Dealer #12 — 478-207-1460
School Administrator/Supervisor #7 — 404-657-9000
School Bus Driver #51 — 404-624-7467
School Counselor #7 — 404-657-9000
School Librarian #40 — 478-207-1400
School Media Specialist #7 — 404-657-9000
School Social Worker #7 — 404-657-9000
Securities Dealer/Salesperson #45 — 404-656-3920
Security Agency #12 — 478-207-1460
Security Guard #12 — 478-207-1460
Shorthand Court Reporter/Stenomask #1 — 404-656-6422
Social Worker #10 — 478-207-1670
Speech-Language Pathologist #16 — 478-207-1670
Surplus Line Broker #8 — 404-656-2101
Surveyor, Land #11 — 478-207-1450
Teacher #7 — 404-657-9000
Timber Dealer/Processor #4 — 404-656-4958
Truck Driver #51 — 404-624-7467
Used Car Dealer #12 — 478-207-1460
Used Car Parts Dist. #12 — 478-207-1460
Utility Contractor #9 — 478-207-1416
Veterinarian/Veterinary Technician #39 — 478-207-1686
Veterinary Faculty #39 — 478-207-1686
Waste Water Collection System Operator #43 — 912-207-1400
Waste Water Industrial #43 — 912-207-1400
Waste Water Laboratory Analyst #43 — 912-207-1400
Waste Water Treatment/Distribution System Operator #43 — 912-207-1400
Water Operator Class 1-3 #43 — 912-207-1400

Licensing Agency Information

#1 Clerk of the Board, Board of Court Reporting, 244 Washington St SW, #300, Atlanta, GA 30334; 404-656-6422, Fax: 404-651-6449. Agency email: johnsole@aoc.courts.state.ga.us.

#2 Examining Boards Division, Board of Examiners of Licensed Practical Nurses, 237 Coliseum Dr, Macon, GA 31217; 478-207-1620, Fax: 478-207-1633. www.sos.state.ga.us/plb/lpn
Search database at
https://secure.sos.state.ga.us/myverification

#3 Clerks Authority, Notary Public Division, 1875 Century Blvd #100, Atlanta, GA 30345; 404-327-6023, Fax: 404-327-7887.
www2.gsccca.org/Projects/aboutnp.html. Agency email: mike.smith@gsccca.org.

#4 Department of Agriculture, Pesticide Division, Capitol Sq, Rm 550, Atlanta, GA 30334; 404-656-4958, Fax: 404-657-8378. www.agr.state.ga.us
Search database at
www.kellysolutions.com/ga/Applicators/index.htm

#5 Department of Natural Resources, Environmental Protection Division, 4244 International Pky, #104, Atlanta, GA 30354; 404-362-2696, Fax: 404-362-2693.
www.state.ga.us/dnr/environ/

#6 Department of Revenue, Centralized Tax Payer Registration, 270 Washington Rm 203, Atlanta, GA 30334-0390; 404-651-9516.
www2.state.ga.us/Departments/DOR

#7 Education Department, Teacher Certification, 1452 Twin Towers East, Atlanta, GA 30334; 404-657-9000. www.gapsc.com

#8 Licensing Division, Insurance Commissioner's Office, 2 Martin Luther King Jr Dr, West Tower, #802, Atlanta, GA 30334; 404-656-2101, Fax: 404-656-0874.

#9 State Construction Industry Licensing Board, 237 Coliseum Dr, Macon, GA 31217; 478-207-1416, Fax: 478-207-1425.
www.sos.state.ga.us/plb/construct
Search database at
https://secure.sos.state.ga.us/myverification

#10 Examining Boards Division, Board of Prof. Counselors, Social Workers, & Marriage/Family Therapists, 237 Coliseum Dr, Macon, GA 31217; 478-207-1670, Fax: 478-207-1676.
www.sos.state.ga.us/plb/counselors
Search database at
https://secure.sos.state.ga.us/myverification

#11 Examining Boards Division, Professional Engineers & Land Surveyors Board, 237 Coliseum Dr, Macon, GA 31217-3858; 478-207-1450, Fax: 478-207-1456. www.sos.state.ga.us/plb/geologists
Agency email: pels@sos.state.ga.us.
Search database at
https://secure.sos.state.ga.us/myverification

#12 Professional Licensing, Licensing Boards, 237 Coliseum Dr, Macon, GA 31217; 478-207-1460, Fax: 478-207-1468.
www.sos.state.ga.us/plb
Search database at
https://secure.sos.state.ga.us/myverification

#14 Examining Boards Division, Board of Accountancy, 237 Coliseum Dr, Macon, GA 31217; 478-207-1400, Fax: 478-207-1410.
www.sos.state.ga.us

#15 Examining Boards Division, Board of Architects and Interior Designers, 237 Coliseum Dr, Macon, GA 31217; 478-207-1400, Fax: 478-207-1410. www.sos.state.ga.us/plb/architects
Search database at
https://secure.sos.state.ga.us/myverification

#16 Examining Boards Division, State Examining Board-Medical, 237 Coliseum, Macon, GA 31217; 478-207-1670, Fax: 478-207-1676.
www.sos.state.ga.us/plb/
Search database at
https://secure.sos.state.ga.us/myverification

#17 Department of Banking and Finance, Regulated Institutions, 2990 Brandywine Rd #200, Atlanta, GA 30341; 770-986-1633, Fax: 770-986-1654. www.ganet.org/dbf/index.html
Search database at
www.ganet.org/dbf/regulated_institutions.html

#18 Examining Boards Division, Board of Chiropractic Examiners, 237 Coliseum Dr, Macon, GA 31217; 478-207-1686, Fax: 478-207-1699.
www.sos.state.ga.us/plb/chiro
Search database at
https://secure.sos.state.ga.us/myverification

#19 Examining Boards Division, Board of Cosmetology, 237 Coliseum Drive, Macon, GA 31217; 478-207-1430, Fax: 478-207-1442.
www.sos.state.ga.us/plb/barber_cosmet
Search database at
https://secure.sos.state.ga.us/myverification

#20 Examining Boards Division, Board of Dentistry, 237 Coliseum Drive, Macon, GA 31217-3858; 912-207-1680, Fax: 912-207-1685.
www.sos.state.ga.us/plb/dentistry
Search database at
https://secure.sos.state.ga.us/myverification

#21 Examining Boards Division, Board of Hearing Aid Disp., Board of Dispensing Opticians, Examiners in Optometry, 237 Coliseum Dr, Macon, GA 31217; 912-207-1686, Fax: 912-207-1699. www.sos.state.ga.us/plb/opticians
Search database at
https://secure.sos.state.ga.us/myverification

#27 Examining Boards Division, Board of Landscape Architects, 237 Colissum Dr, Macon, GA 31217-3858; 478-207-1400, Fax: 478-207-1410. www.sos.state.ga.us/plb/landscape
Search database at
https://secure.sos.state.ga.us/myverification

#28 Examining Boards Division, Board of Nursing, 237 Coliseum Dr, Macon, GA 30217-3858; 478-207-1640, Fax: 478-207-1660.
www.sos.state.ga.us/plb/rn
Search database at
https://secure.sos.state.ga.us/myverification

#31 Examining Boards Division, Board of Pharmacy, 237 Coliseum Dr, Macon, GA 31217; 478-207-1686, Fax: 478-207-1699.
www.sos.state.ga.us/plb/pharmacy
Search database at
https://secure.sos.state.ga.us/myverification

#33 Examining Boards Division, Board of Podiatry Examiners, 237 Coliseum Dr, Macon, GA 31217; 478-207-1686, Fax: 478-207-1699.

www.sos.state.ga.us/plb/podiatry
Search database at
https://secure.sos.state.ga.us/myverification

#36 Examining Boards Division, Board of Registration for Foresters, 237 Coliseum Dr, Macon, GA 31217; 478-207-1400, Fax: 478-207-1410. www.sos.state.ga.us/plb/foresters
Search database at
https://secure.sos.state.ga.us/myverification

#39 Examining Boards Division, Board of Veterinary Medicine, 237 Coliseum Dr, Macon, GA 31217; 478-207-1686, Fax: 478-207-1699.
www.sos.state.ga.us/plb/veterinary
Search database at
https://secure.sos.state.ga.us/myverification

#40 Examining Boards Division, Board for the Certification of Librarians, 237 Coliseum Dr, Macon, GA 31217; 478-207-1400, Fax: 478-207-1410. www.sos.state.ga.us/plb/librarians
Search database at
https://secure.sos.state.ga.us/myverification

#41 Examining Boards Division, Composite Board of Medical Examiners, 2 Peachtree St, 10th Fl, Atlanta, GA 30303; 404-656-3913, Fax: 404-656-9723. www.medicalboard.state.ga.us
Search database at www.medicalboard.state.ga.us/bdsearch/index.html

#43 Examining Boards Division, 237 Coliseum Dr, Macon, GA 31217; 404-207-1400, Fax: 404-207-1410. www.sos.state.ga.us/plb/water
Agency email: tacarter@sos.state.ga.us.
Search database at
https://secure.sos.state.ga.us/myverification

#44 Examining Boards Division, Board of Registration for Professional Geologists, 237 Coliseum Dr, Macon, GA 31217; 478-207-1400, Fax: 478-207-1410.
www.sos.state.ga.us/ebd-geologists
Search database at
https://secure.sos.state.ga.us/myverification

#45 Securities & Business Regulation, Office of Secretary of State, 2 Martin Luther King Jr Dr, West Tower, #802, Atlanta, GA 30334-1530; 404-656-3920, Fax: 404-657-8410.
www.sos.state.ga.us/securities
Search database at www.sos.state.ga.us/securities

#46 Real Estate Commission/Appraiser Board, 229 Peachtree St NE, International Tower, #1000, Atlanta, GA 30303-1605; 404-656-3916, Fax: 404-656-6650. www.grec.state.ga.us
Agency email: grecmail@grec.state.ga.us.
#47 State Bar of Georgia, 104 Marietta St NW #100, Atlanta, GA 30303; 404-527-8700, Fax: 404-527-8717. www.gabar.org

#48 Department of Labor, Safety Engineering Division, 1700 Century Circle NE, Atlanta, GA 30345; 404-679-0687, Fax: 404-679-5818.

#49 Emergency Medical Svcs, 2600 Skyland Dr, Atlanta, GA 30319; 404-679-0547, Fax: 404-679-0526.
www.ph.dhr.state.ga.us/programs/ems/index.shtml

#51 Department of Public Safety, Commercial Driver's License Unit, PO Box 1456, Atlanta, GA 30371; 404-624-7467, Fax: 404-624-7707.
www.ganet.org/dps

Georgia Federal Courts

The following list indicates the district and division name for each county in the state. If the bankruptcy court location is different from the district court, then the location of the bankruptcy court appears in parentheses.

County/Court Cross Reference

County	District	Division
Appling	Southern	Brunswick (Savannah)
Atkinson	Southern	Waycross (Savannah)
Bacon	Southern	Waycross (Savannah)
Baker	Middle	Albany/Americus (Macon)
Baldwin	Middle	Macon
Banks	Northern	Gainesville
Barrow	Northern	Gainesville
Bartow	Northern	Rome
Ben Hill	Middle	Albany/Americus (Macon)
Berrien	Middle	Valdosta (Columbus)
Bibb	Middle	Macon
Bleckley	Middle	Macon
Brantley	Southern	Waycross (Savannah)
Brooks	Middle	Thomasville (Columbus)
Bryan	Southern	Savannah
Bulloch	Southern	Statesboro (Augusta)
Burke	Southern	Augusta
Butts	Middle	Macon
Calhoun	Middle	Albany/Americus (Macon)
Camden	Southern	Brunswick (Savannah)
Candler	Southern	Statesboro (Augusta)
Carroll	Northern	Newnan
Catoosa	Northern	Rome
Charlton	Southern	Waycross (Savannah)
Chatham	Southern	Savannah
Chattahoochee	Middle	Columbus
Chattooga	Northern	Rome
Cherokee	Northern	Atlanta
Clarke	Middle	Athens (Macon)
Clay	Middle	Columbus
Clayton	Northern	Atlanta
Clinch	Middle	Valdosta (Columbus)
Cobb	Northern	Atlanta
Coffee	Southern	Waycross (Savannah)
Colquitt	Middle	Thomasville (Columbus)
Columbia	Southern	Augusta
Cook	Middle	Valdosta (Columbus)
Coweta	Northern	Newnan
Crawford	Middle	Macon
Crisp	Middle	Albany/Americus (Macon)
Dade	Northern	Rome
Dawson	Northern	Gainesville
De Kalb	Northern	Atlanta
Decatur	Middle	Thomasville (Columbus)
Dodge	Southern	Dublin (Augusta)
Dooly	Middle	Macon
Dougherty	Middle	Albany/Americus (Macon)
Douglas	Northern	Atlanta
Early	Middle	Albany/Americus (Macon)
Echols	Middle	Valdosta (Columbus)
Effingham	Southern	Savannah
Elbert	Middle	Athens (Macon)
Emanuel	Southern	Statesboro (Augusta)
Evans	Southern	Statesboro (Augusta)
Fannin	Northern	Gainesville
Fayette	Northern	Newnan
Floyd	Northern	Rome
Forsyth	Northern	Gainesville
Franklin	Middle	Athens (Macon)
Fulton	Northern	Atlanta
Gilmer	Northern	Gainesville
Glascock	Southern	Augusta
Glynn	Southern	Brunswick (Savannah)
Gordon	Northern	Rome
Grady	Middle	Thomasville (Columbus)
Greene	Middle	Athens (Macon)
Gwinnett	Northern	Atlanta
Habersham	Northern	Gainesville
Hall	Northern	Gainesville
Hancock	Middle	Macon
Haralson	Northern	Newnan
Harris	Middle	Columbus
Hart	Middle	Athens (Macon)
Heard	Northern	Newnan
Henry	Northern	Atlanta
Houston	Middle	Macon
Irwin	Middle	Valdosta (Columbus)
Jackson	Northern	Gainesville
Jasper	Middle	Macon
Jeff Davis	Southern	Brunswick (Savannah)
Jefferson	Southern	Augusta
Jenkins	Southern	Statesboro (Augusta)
Johnson	Southern	Dublin (Augusta)
Jones	Middle	Macon
Lamar	Middle	Macon
Lanier	Middle	Valdosta (Columbus)
Laurens	Southern	Dublin (Augusta)
Lee	Middle	Albany/Americus (Macon)
Liberty	Southern	Savannah
Lincoln	Southern	Augusta
Long	Southern	Brunswick (Savannah)
Lowndes	Middle	Valdosta (Columbus)
Lumpkin	Northern	Gainesville
Macon	Middle	Macon
Madison	Middle	Athens (Macon)
Marion	Middle	Columbus
McDuffie	Southern	Augusta
McIntosh	Southern	Brunswick (Savannah)
Meriwether	Northern	Newnan
Miller	Middle	Albany/Americus (Macon)
Mitchell	Middle	Albany/Americus (Macon)
Monroe	Middle	Macon
Montgomery	Southern	Dublin (Augusta)
Morgan	Middle	Athens (Macon)
Murray	Northern	Rome
Muscogee	Middle	Columbus
Newton	Northern	Atlanta
Oconee	Middle	Athens (Macon)
Oglethorpe	Middle	Athens (Macon)
Paulding	Northern	Rome

Peach	Middle	Macon
Pickens	Northern	Gainesville
Pierce	Southern	Waycross (Savannah)
Pike	Northern	Newnan
Polk	Northern	Rome
Pulaski	Middle	Macon
Putnam	Middle	Macon
Quitman	Middle	Columbus
Rabun	Northern	Gainesville
Randolph	Middle	Columbus
Richmond	Southern	Augusta
Rockdale	Northern	Atlanta
Schley	Middle	Albany/Americus (Macon)
Screven	Southern	Statesboro (Augusta)
Seminole	Middle	Thomasville (Columbus)
Spalding	Northern	Newnan
Stephens	Northern	Gainesville
Stewart	Middle	Columbus
Sumter	Middle	Albany/Americus (Macon)
Talbot	Middle	Columbus
Taliaferro	Southern	Augusta
Tattnall	Southern	Statesboro (Augusta)
Taylor	Middle	Columbus
Telfair	Southern	Dublin (Augusta)
Terrell	Middle	Albany/Americus (Macon)
Thomas	Middle	Thomasville (Columbus)
Tift	Middle	Valdosta (Columbus)
Toombs	Southern	Statesboro (Augusta)
Towns	Northern	Gainesville
Treutlen	Southern	Dublin (Augusta)
Troup	Northern	Newnan
Turner	Middle	Albany/Americus (Macon)
Twiggs	Middle	Macon
Union	Northern	Gainesville
Upson	Middle	Macon
Walker	Northern	Rome
Walton	Middle	Athens (Macon)
Ware	Southern	Waycross (Savannah)
Warren	Southern	Augusta
Washington	Middle	Macon
Wayne	Southern	Brunswick (Savannah)
Webster	Middle	Albany/Americus (Macon)
Wheeler	Southern	Dublin (Augusta)
White	Northern	Gainesville
Whitfield	Northern	Rome
Wilcox	Middle	Macon
Wilkes	Southern	Augusta
Wilkinson	Middle	Macon
Worth	Middle	Albany/Americus (Macon)

Standards for Federal Courts: The search fee is $20.00 per item (one party name or case number). Certification fee is $7.00 per document. Copy fee is $.50 per page. All fees standard unless noted in profile. Mail Search: always enclose a stamped self addressed envelope unless otherwise noted. Before releasing records, all courts require prepayment unless noted in profile.

Open records are located at the court unless otherwise noted. District courts index by defendant and plaintiff as well as by case number. Bankruptcy courts usually index by debtor and case number. While most courts now have their indexes on computer, many still maintain index card files as well.

The universal PACER sign-up number is 800-676-6856. Find PACER and the Party/Case Index on the Web at http://pacer.psc.uscourts.gov. PACER dial-up access is $.60 per minute. Also, courts offering internet access via RACER, PACER, Web-PACER or the new CM-ECF charge $.07 per page fee unless noted as free.

US District Court

Middle District of Georgia

Albany/Americus Division PO Box 1906, Albany, GA 31702 (Courier Address: Room 106, 345 Broad Ave, Albany, GA 31701), 229-430-8432, Fax: 229-430-8538.

www.gamd.uscourts.gov

Counties: Baker, Ben Hill, Calhoun, Crisp, Dougherty, Early, Lee, Miller, Mitchell, Schley, Sumter, Terrell, Turner, Webster, Worth. Ben Hill and Crisp were transferred from the Macon Division as of October 1, 1997.

Indexing & Storage: Cases are indexed by defendant, plaintiff, and case number. New cases are available in the index immediately after filing date. Records are on the computer from 1991.

Prior records are indexed on index cards. District wide searches are available from any division in this district for files after 1/91. Open records are located at this court.

Fee & Payment Notes: Payment may be made by money order, cashier check, in-state business check. Personal checks are not accepted. Payee: Clerk, USDC.

Phone Search: Only docket information is available by phone.

In Person Search: In person searching available.

PACER: Toll-free dial-up access: 888-234-3839. Local dial-up access: 912-752-8170. Case records are available back to January 1991. Records are never purged. New records are available online after 1-2 days. PACER is available online at http://pacer.gamd.uscourts.gov.

Athens Division PO Box 1106, Athens, GA 30603 (Courier: 115 E Hancock Ave, Athens, GA 30601), 706-227-1094, Fax: 706-546-2190.

www.gamd.uscourts.gov

Counties: Clarke, Elbert, Franklin, Greene, Hart, Madison, Morgan, Oconee, Oglethorpe, Walton. Closed cases before April 1997 are located in the Macon Division.

Indexing & Storage: Cases are indexed by defendant, plaintiff, and case number. New cases are available in the index 2 days after filing date. Open records are located at this court.

Fee & Payment Notes: Payment may be made by money order, cashier check, business check. Personal checks are not accepted. Payee: US District Court.

Phone Search: Searching not available by phone.

In Person Search: In person searching available.

PACER: Toll-free dial-up access: 888-234-3839. Local dial-up access: 912-752-8170. Case records are available back to January 1991. Records are never purged. New records are available online

after 1-2 days. PACER is available online at http://pacer.gamd.uscourts.gov.

Columbus Division PO Box 124, Columbus, GA 31902 (Courier Address: Room 216, 120 12th St, Columbus, GA 31901), 706-649-7816.

www.gamd.uscourts.gov

Counties: Chattahoochee, Clay, Harris, Marion, Muscogee, Quitman, Randolph, Stewart, Talbot, Taylor.

Indexing & Storage: Cases are indexed by defendant, plaintiff, and case number. New cases are available in the index immediately after filing date. Open records are located at this court.

Fee & Payment Notes: Payment may be made by money order, cashier check, business check. Personal checks are not accepted. Payee: Clerk, US Courts.

Phone Search: Searching not available by phone. Only docket information is available by phone.

In Person Search: In person searching available.

PACER: Toll-free dial-up access: 888-234-3839. Local dial-up access: 912-752-8170. Case records are available back to January 1991. Records are never purged. New records are available online after 1-2 days. PACER is available online at http://pacer.gamd.uscourts.gov.

Macon Division PO Box 128, Macon, GA 31202-0128 (Courier Address: 475 Mulberry, Suite 216, Macon, GA 31201), 912-752-3497, Fax: 912-752-3496.

www.gamd.uscourts.gov

Counties: Baldwin, Ben Hill, Bibb, Bleckley, Butts, Crawford, Crisp, Dooly, Hancock, Houston, Jasper, Jones, Lamar, Macon, Monroe, Peach, Pulaski, Putnam, Twiggs, Upson, Washington, Wilcox, Wilkinson. Athens Division cases closed before April 1997 are also located here.

Indexing & Storage: Cases are indexed by defendant, plaintiff, and case number. New cases are available in the index immediately after filing date. Records after 1/91 can be searched from any court in this district. Open records are located at this court.

Fee & Payment Notes: Payment may be made by money order, cashier check, business check. Personal checks are not accepted. Payee: US Courts.

Phone Search: Only docket information is available by phone.

Fax Search: Handled same as mail search. Will fax results at $3.00 per page.

In Person Search: In person searching available.

PACER: Toll-free dial-up access: 888-234-3839. Local dial-up access: 912-752-8170. Case records are available back to January 1991. Records are never purged. New records are available online after 1-2 days. PACER is available online at http://pacer.gamd.uscourts.gov.

Thomasville Division c/o Valdosta Division, PO Box 68, Valdosta, GA 31601 (Courier Address: Room 212, 401 N Patterson, Valdosta, GA 31603), 912-226-3651.

www.gamd.uscourts.gov

Counties: Brooks, Colquitt, Decatur, Grady, Seminole, Thomas.

Indexing & Storage: New cases are available in the index after filing date. Open records are located at the Valdosta Division.

Fee & Payment Notes: Payment may be made by money order, cashier check. Business checks are not accepted. Personal checks are not accepted.

Phone Search: Searching not available by phone.

In Person Search: In person searching available.

PACER: Toll-free dial-up access: 888-234-3839. Local dial-up access: 912-752-8170. Case records are available back to January 1991. Records are never purged. New records are available online after 1-2 days. PACER is available online at http://pacer.gamd.uscourts.gov.

Valdosta Division PO Box 68, Valdosta, GA 31603 (Courier Address: Room 212, 401 N Patterson, Valdosta, GA 31601), 912-242-3616, Fax: 912-244-9547.

www.gamd.uscourts.gov

Counties: Berrien, Clinch, Cook, Echols, Irwin, Lanier, Lowndes, Tift.

Indexing & Storage: Cases are indexed by defendant, plaintiff, and case number. New cases are available in the index immediately after filing date. Open records are located at this court.

Fee & Payment Notes: Payment may be made by money order, cashier check, business check. Personal checks are not accepted. Payee: US Courts. You are allowed to make your own copies. These copies cost - current fee is not known - per page.

Phone Search: Docket information available by phone.

Mail Search: A stamped self addressed envelope is not required.

In Person Search: In person searching available.

PACER: Toll-free dial-up access: 888-234-3839. Local dial-up access: 912-752-8170. Case records are available back to January 1991. Records are never purged. New records are available online after 1-2 days. PACER is available online at http://pacer.gamd.uscourts.gov.

US Bankruptcy Court

Middle District of Georgia

Columbus Division PO Box 2147, Columbus, GA 31902 (Courier: 901 Front Ave, 1 Arsenal Pl, Columbus, GA 31902), 706-649-7837.

www.gamb.uscourts.gov

Counties: Berrien, Brooks, Chattahoochee, Clay, Clinch, Colquitt, Cook, Decatur, Echols, Grady, Harris, Irwin, Lanier, Lowndes, Marion, Muscogee, Quitman, Randolph, Seminole, Stewart,Talbot, Taylor, Thomas, Tift.

Indexing & Storage: Cases are indexed by debtor as well as by case number. New cases are available in the index immediately after filing date. An alias name of the debtor may be required to search for records. Open records are located at this court.

Fee & Payment Notes: Payment may be made by money order, cashier check, business check. Personal checks are not accepted. Payee: Clerk, US Bankruptcy Court.

Phone Search: Docket information is available by phone. An automated voice case information service (VCIS) is available. Call VCIS at 800-211-3015 or 912-752-8183.

In Person Search: In person searching available.

PACER: Toll-free dial-up access: 800-546-7343. Local dial-up access: 912-752-3551. Case records are available back to March 1990 (some back to 1985). Records are purged except last 12 months. New civil records are available online after 1 day. PACER is available online at http://pacer.gamb.uscourts.gov.

Electronic Filing: (Currently in the process of implementing CM/ECF.)

Macon Division PO Box 1957, Macon, GA 31201 (Courier Address: 433 Cherry St, Macon, GA 31202), 912-752-3506, Fax: 912-752-8157.

www.gamb.uscourts.gov

Counties: Baldwin, Baker, Ben Hill, Bibb, Bleckley, Butts, Calhoun, Clarke, Crawford, Crisp, Dooly, Dougherty, Early, Elbert, Franklin, Greene, Hancock, Hart, Houston, Jasper, Jones, Lamar, Lee, Macon, Madison, Miller, Mitchell, Monroe, Morgan, Oconee, Oglethorpe,Peach, Pulaski, Putnam, Schley, Sumter, Terrell, Turner, Twiggs, Upson, Walton, Washington, Webster, Wilcox, Wilkinson, Worth.

Indexing & Storage: Cases are indexed by debtor and creditors as well as by case number. New cases are available in the index 1-2 days after filing date. Any alias name of the debtor may be required to search for records. Open records are located at this court.

Fee & Payment Notes: Payment may be made by money order, cashier check, business check. Personal checks are not accepted. Payee: Clerk, US Bankruptcy Court.

Phone Search: This court will only search for basic information by phone and limits the number of searches to 3 per phone call. An automated voice case information service (VCIS) is available. Call VCIS at 800-211-3015 or 478-752-8183.

In Person Search: In person searching available.

PACER: Toll-free dial-up access: 800-546-7343. Local dial-up access: 912-752-3551. Case records are available back to March 1990 (some back to 1985). Records are purged except last 12 months. New civil records are available online after 1 day.

PACER is available online at http://pacer.gamb.uscourts.gov.

Electronic Filing: (Currently in the process of implementing CM/ECF.)

US District Court

Northern District of Georgia

Atlanta Division 2211 US Courthouse, 75 Spring St SW, Atlanta, GA 30303-3361 (Courier Address: Use mail address for courier delivery), 404-215-1660.

www.gand.uscourts.gov

Counties: Cherokee, Clayton, Cobb, De Kalb, Douglas, Fulton, Gwinnett, Henry, Newton, Rockdale.

Indexing & Storage: Cases are indexed by defendant, plaintiff, and case number. New cases are available in the index 1 day after filing date. Open records are located at this court.

Fee & Payment Notes: Payment may be made by money order, cashier check. Business checks are not accepted. Personal checks are not accepted. Payee: Clerk, US District Court.

Phone Search: Only docket information is available by phone.

Mail Search: A stamped self addressed envelope is not required.

In Person Search: In person searching available.

PACER: Toll-free dial-up access: 800-801-6932. Local dial-up access: 404-730-9668. Case records are available back to August 1992. Records are purged on a varied schedule. New records are available online after 1 day. PACER is available online at http://pacer.gand.uscourts.gov.

Gainesville Division Federal Bldg, Room 201, 121 Spring St SE, Gainesville, GA 30501 (Courier Address: Use mail address for courier delivery), 678-450-2760.

www.gand.uscourts.gov

Counties: Banks, Barrow, Dawson, Fannin, Forsyth, Gilmer, Habersham, Hall, Jackson, Lumpkin, Pickens, Rabun, Stephens, Towns, Union, White.

Indexing & Storage: Cases are indexed by defendant, plaintiff, and case number. New cases are available in the index 24 hours after filing date. Open records are located at this court.

Fee & Payment Notes: Payment may be made by money order. Business checks are not accepted. Personal checks are not accepted. The court will only accept US Postal money orders, law firm checks and cashier's checks. Payee: Clerk, US District Court.

Phone Search: Searching not available by phone.

In Person Search: In person searching available.

PACER: Toll-free dial-up access: 800-801-6932. Local dial-up access: 404-730-9668. Case records are available back to August 1992. Records are purged on a varied schedule. New records are available online after 1 day. PACER is available online at http://pacer.gand.uscourts.gov.

Newnan Division PO Box 939, Newnan, GA 30264 (Courier Address: 18 Greenville St, #352, Newnan, GA 30263), 678-423-3060.

www.gand.uscourts.gov

Counties: Carroll, Coweta, Fayette, Haralson, Heard, Meriwether, Pike, Spalding, Troup.

Indexing & Storage: Cases are indexed by defendant, plaintiff, and case number. New cases are available in the index immediately after filing date. Open records are located at this court.

Fee & Payment Notes: Payment may be made by money order, cashier check. Business checks are not accepted. Personal checks are not accepted. Only attorney firm checks will be accepted. Payee: Clerk, US District Court.

Phone Search: Only docket information is available by phone.

Mail Search: A stamped self addressed envelope is not required.

In Person Search: In person searching available.

PACER: Toll-free dial-up access: 800-801-6932. Local dial-up access: 404-730-9668. Case records are available back to August 1992. Records are purged on a varied schedule. New records are available online after 1 day. PACER is available online at http://pacer.gand.uscourts.gov.

Rome Division PO Box 1186, Rome, GA 30162-1186 (Courier Address: 600 E 1st St, Room 304, Rome, GA 30161), 706-291-5629.

www.gand.uscourts.gov

Counties: Bartow, Catoosa, Chattooga, Dade, Floyd, Gordon, Murray, Paulding, Polk, Walker, Whitfield.

Indexing & Storage: Cases are indexed by defendant, plaintiff, and case number. New cases are available in the index immediately after filing date. Records are also indexed on microfiche. Only records prior to 1978 are on index cards. Open records are located at this court.

Fee & Payment Notes: Payment may be made by money order, cashier check. Business checks are not accepted. Personal checks are not accepted. Attorney checks also accepted. Payee: Clerk, US District Court.

Phone Search: Only docket information showing if a suit has been filed, date of filing, and if case is pending or closed will be released over the phone.

In Person Search: In person searching available.

PACER: Toll-free dial-up access: 800-801-6932. Local dial-up access: 404-730-9668. Case records are available back to August 1992. Records are purged on a varied schedule. New records are available online after 1 day. PACER is available online at http://pacer.gand.uscourts.gov.

US Bankruptcy Court

Northern District of Georgia

Atlanta Division 1340 US Courthouse, 75 Spring St SW, Atlanta, GA 30303-3361 (Courier Address: Use mail address for courier delivery), 404-215-1000.

www.ganb.uscourts.gov

Counties: Cherokee, Clayton, Cobb, DeKalb, Douglas, Fulton, Gwinnett, Henry, Newton, Rockdale.

Indexing & Storage: Cases are indexed by debtor as well as by case number. New cases are available in the index 1-2 days after filing date. Records are also indexed on microfiche. Open records are located at this court.

Fee & Payment Notes: Payment may be made by money order, cashier check, business check. Personal checks are not accepted. Debtor's checks are not accepted. Payee: Clerk, US Bankruptcy Court.

Phone Search: Docket information is available by phone. An automated voice case information service (VCIS) is available. Call VCIS at 800-510-8284 or 404-730-2866.

Fax Search: Fax requests are handled by a copy service. To set-up a fax request, call the service at 404-681-9125.

In Person Search: In person searching available.

PACER: Toll-free dial-up access: 800-436-8395. Local dial-up access: 404-730-3264. Case records are available back to August 1986. Records are never purged. New civil records are available online after 2 days.

Electronic Filing: Information is available online at http://ecf.ganb.uscourts.gov

Gainesville Division 121 Spring St SE, Room 120, Gainesville, GA 30501 (Courier Address: Use mail address for courier delivery), 678-450-2700.

www.ganb.uscourts.gov

Counties: Banks, Barrow, Dawson, Fannin, Forsyth, Gilmer, Habersham, Hall, Jackson, Lumpkin, Pickens, Rabun, Stephens, Towns, Union, White.

Indexing & Storage: Cases are indexed by debtor as well as by case number. New cases are available in the index 1-2 days after filing date. This court maintains index cards on older cases. Open records are located at this court.

Fee & Payment Notes: Payment may be made by money order, cashier check, personal check. Debtors checks not accepted. Payee: Clerk, US Bankruptcy Court.

Phone Search: Docket information available by phone. An automated voice case information service (VCIS) is available. Call VCIS at 800-510-8284 or 404-730-2866.

In Person Search: In person searching available.

PACER: Toll-free dial-up access: 800-436-8395. Local dial-up access: 404-730-3264. Case records are available back to August 1986. Records are never purged. New civil records are available online after 2 days.

Electronic Filing: Information is available online at http://ecf.ganb.uscourts.gov

Newnan Division Clerk, PO Box 2328, Newnan, GA 30264 (Courier: Room 220, 18 Greenville, Newnan, GA 30263), 678-423-3000.

www.ganb.uscourts.gov

Counties: Carroll, Coweta, Fayette, Haralson, Heard, Meriwether, Pike, Spalding, Troup.

Indexing & Storage: Cases are indexed by debtor as well as by case number. New cases are available in the index 1 day after filing date. Records are also indexed on microfiche. Open records are located at this court.

Fee & Payment Notes: Payment may be made by money order, cashier check, personal check. Debtor's checks are not accepted. Payee: Clerk, US Bankruptcy Court.

Phone Search: Only docket information is available by phone. The debtor's address and social security number will not be released. There is no charge if a case number is provided. An

automated voice case information service (VCIS) is available. Call VCIS at 800-510-8284 or 404-730-2866.

Mail Search: A stamped self addressed envelope is not required.

In Person Search: In person searching available.

PACER: Toll-free dial-up access: 800-436-8395. Local dial-up access: 404-730-3264. Case records are available back to August 1986. Records are never purged. New civil records are available online after 2 days.

Electronic Filing: Information is available online at http://ecf.ganb.uscourts.gov

Rome Division Clerk, 600 E 1st St, Room 339, Rome, GA 30161-3187 (Courier: Use mail address for courier delivery), 706-291-5639.

www.ganb.uscourts.gov

Counties: Bartow, Catoosa, Chattooga, Dade, Floyd, Gordon, Murray, Paulding, Polk, Walker, Whitfield.

Indexing & Storage: Cases are indexed by debtor as well as by case number. New cases are available in the index 24 hours after filing date. Open records are located at this court.

Fee & Payment Notes: Payment may be made by money order, cashier check, personal check. Payee: Clerk, US Bankruptcy Court.

Phone Search: Docket information is available by phone. An automated voice case information service (VCIS) is available. Call VCIS at 800-510-8284 or 404-730-2866.

In Person Search: In person searching available.

PACER: Toll-free dial-up access: 800-436-8395. Local dial-up access: 404-730-3264. Case records are available back to August 1986. Records are never purged. New civil records are available online after 2 days.

Electronic Filing: Information is available online at http://ecf.ganb.uscourts.gov

US District Court

Southern District of Georgia

Augusta Division PO Box 1130, Augusta, GA 30903 (Courier Address: Use mail address for courier delivery., 500 E Ford St, First Floor,), 706-849-4400.

www.gasd.uscourts.gov

Counties: Burke, Columbia, Glascock, Jefferson, Lincoln, McDuffie, Richmond, Taliaferro, Warren, Wilkes.

Indexing & Storage: Cases are indexed by defendant, plaintiff, and case number. New cases are available in the index immediately after filing date. Records are alphabetically indexed and stored by chronological case number order. Open records are located at this court.

Fee & Payment Notes: Payment may be made by money order, cashier check, personal check. Payee: US Courts.

Phone Search: Docket information available by phone.

In Person Search: In person searching available.

PACER: Toll-free dial-up access: 800-801-6934. Local dial-up access: 912-650-4046. Document images available. Case records are available back to June 1995. New records are available online after 1 day. PACER is available online at http://pacer.gasd.uscourts.gov. Document images available.

Brunswick Division
PO Box 1636, Brunswick, GA 31521 (Courier Address: Room 222, 801 Glouchester, Brunswick, GA 31520), 912-280-1330.

www.gasd.uscourts.gov

Counties: Appling, Camden, Glynn, Jeff Davis, Long, McIntosh, Wayne.

Indexing & Storage: Cases are indexed by defendant, plaintiff, and case number. New cases are available in the index immediately after filing date. The records from the last 1 1/2 years are indexed on computer. Prior records are indexed on microfiche. Open records are located at this court.

Fee & Payment Notes: Payment may be made by money order, cashier check, personal check. Payee: Clerk, US District Court.

Phone Search: Only docket information is available by phone.

In Person Search: In person searching available.

PACER: Toll-free dial-up access: 800-801-6934. Local dial-up access: 912-650-4046. Case records are available back to June 1995. New records are available online after 1 day. PACER is available online at http://pacer.gasd.uscourts.gov. Document images available.

Dublin Division
c/o Augusta Division, PO Box 1130, Augusta, GA 30903 (Courier: 500 E Ford St, Augusta, GA 30901), 706-849-4400.

www.gasd.uscourts.gov

Counties: Dodge, Johnson, Laurens, Montgomery, Telfair, Treutlen, Wheeler.

Indexing & Storage: New cases are available in the index after filing date. Open records are located at the Augusta Division.

Fee & Payment Notes: Payment may be made by money order, cashier check. Business checks are not accepted. Personal checks are not accepted.

Phone Search: Searching not available by phone.

Mail Search: A stamped self addressed envelope is not required.

In Person Search: In person searching available.

PACER: Toll-free dial-up access: 800-801-6934. Local dial-up access: 912-650-4046. Case records are available back to June 1995. New records are available online after 1 day. PACER is available online at http://pacer.gasd.uscourts.gov. Document images available.

Savannah Division
PO Box 8286, Savannah, GA 31412 (Courier Address: Room 306, 125 Bull St, Savannah, GA 31401), 912-650-4020, Fax: 912-650-4030.

www.gasd.uscourts.gov

Counties: Bryan, Chatham, Effingham, Liberty.

Indexing & Storage: Cases are indexed by defendant, plaintiff, and case number. New cases are available in the index immediately after filing date. Records have been indexed on computer from 1992. Prior records are indexed on microfiche. Open records are located at this court.

Fee & Payment Notes: Payment may be made by money order, cashier check, personal check. Payee: Clerk, US District Court.

Phone Search: Searching not available by phone. Only docket information is available by phone.

Mail Search: A stamped self addressed envelope is not required.

In Person Search: In person searching available.

PACER: Toll-free dial-up access: 800-801-6934. Local dial-up access: 912-650-4046. Case records are available back to June 1995. New records are available online after 1 day. PACER is available online at http://pacer.gasd.uscourts.gov. Document images available.

Statesboro Division
c/o Savannah Division, PO Box 8286, Savannah, GA 31412 (Courier Address: Use mail address for courier delivery), 912-650-4020.

www.gasd.uscourts.gov

Counties: Bulloch, Candler, Emanuel, Evans, Jenkins, Screven, Tattnall, Toombs.

Indexing & Storage: New cases are available in the index after filing date. Open records are located at the Savannah Division.

Fee & Payment Notes: Payment may be made by money order, cashier check. Business checks are not accepted. Personal checks are not accepted.

Phone Search: Searching not available by phone.

Mail Search: A stamped self addressed envelope is not required.

In Person Search: In person searching available.

PACER: Toll-free dial-up access: 800-801-6934. Local dial-up access: 912-650-4046. Case records are available back to June 1995. New records are available online after 1 day. PACER is available online at http://pacer.gasd.uscourts.gov. Document images available.

Waycross Division
c/o Savannah Division, PO Box 8286, Savannah, GA 31412 (Courier Address: Room 306, 125 Bull St, Savannah, GA 31401), 912-650-4020.

www.gasd.uscourts.gov

Counties: Atkinson, Bacon, Brantley, Charlton, Coffee, Pierce, Ware.

Indexing & Storage: New cases are available in the index after filing date. Open records are located at the SavannahDivision.

Fee & Payment Notes: Payment may be made by money order, cashier check. Business checks are not accepted. Personal checks are not accepted.

Phone Search: Searching not available by phone.

Mail Search: A stamped self addressed envelope is not required.

In Person Search: In person searching available.

PACER: Toll-free dial-up access: 800-801-6934. Local dial-up access: 912-650-4046. Case records are available back to June 1995. New records are available online after 1 day. PACER is available online at http://pacer.gasd.uscourts.gov. Document images available.

US Bankruptcy Court
Southern District of Georgia

Augusta Division
PO Box 1487, Augusta, GA 30903 (Courier Address: 933 Broad St - 3rd Fl, Augusta, GA 30901), 706-724-2421.

www.gas.uscourts.gov

Counties: Bulloch, Burke, Candler, Columbia, Dodge, Emanuel, Evans, Glascock, Jefferson, Jenkins, Johnson, Laurens, Lincoln, McDuffie,

Montgomery, Richmond, Screven, Taliaferro, Tattnall, Telfair, Toombs, Treutlen, Warren, Wheeler, Wilkes.

Indexing & Storage: Cases are indexed by debtor as well as by case number. New cases are available in the index 24 hours after filing date. District wide searches are available for information from August 1986 from this court. This court handles files for the Statesboro and Dublin divisions as well as the Augusta files.

Fee & Payment Notes: Payment may be made by money order, cashier check, business check. Personal checks are not accepted. Payee: Clerk, US Bankruptcy Court.

Phone Search: If case number is provided over the phone, all docket information will be released.

In Person Search: In person searching available.

PACER: Toll-free dial-up access: 800-295-8679. Local dial-up access: 912-650-4190. Document images available on Pacer. Case records are available back to August 1986. Records are purged annually. PACER is available online at http://pacer.gasb.uscourts.gov. This appears to be a homogenization of RACER and PACER; the fee is $.07 per page.

Other Online Access: Court does not participate in the U.S. party case index.

Savannah Division
PO Box 8347, Savannah, GA 31412 (Courier Address: Room 213, 125 Bull St, Savannah, GA 31412), 912-650-4100.

www.gas.uscourts.gov

Counties: Appling, Atkinson, Bacon, Brantley, Bryan, Camden, Charlton, Chatham, Coffee, Effingham, Glynn, Jeff Davis, Liberty, Long, McIntosh, Pierce, Ware, Wayne.

Indexing & Storage: Cases are indexed by debtor as well as by case number. New cases are available in the index immediately after filing date. Cases are also indexed by Social Security number. District wide searches are available for information from August 1, 1985 at this court. This court handles files for the Waycross and Brunswick divisions as well as the Savannah files.

Fee & Payment Notes: Payment may be made by money order, cashier check, business check. Personal checks are not accepted. Payee: Clerk, US Bankruptcy Court.

Phone Search: Phone search is limited to information on computer.

Mail Search: A stamped self addressed envelope is not required.

In Person Search: In person searching available.

PACER: Toll-free dial-up access: 800-891-9583. Local dial-up access: 912-650-4190. Case records are available back to 1988. Records are purged every six months. New civil records are available online after 1 day. PACER is available online at http://pacer.gasb.uscourts.gov. This appears to be a homogenization of RACER and PACER; the fee is $.07 per page. Document images available.

Other Online Access: Court does not participate in the U.S. party case index.

Georgia County Courts

Court	Jurisdiction	No. of Courts	How Organized
Superior Courts*	General	100	49 Circuits
State Courts*	Limited	69	69 Counties
Combined Courts*		43	
Magistrate Courts*	Limited	159	By County
Combined Superior/ Magistrate Court*		17	
Civil Courts*	Limited	2	Bibb, Richmond
County Recorder's Courts	Limited	4	Chatham, DeKalb, Gwinnett, Muscogee
Municipal Courts	Municipal	2	Columbus, Moscogee
Municipal Courts	Municipal	474	Includes City Court of Atlanta
Probate Courts*	Probate	159	By County
Juvenile Courts	Special	159	By County

* Profiled in this Sourcebook.

Court	CIVIL								
	Tort	Contract	Real Estate	Min. Claim	Max. Claim	Small Claims	Estate	Eviction	Domestic Relations
Superior Courts*	X	X	X	$0	No Max	X		X	X
State Courts*	X	X		$0	No Max	X		X	
Combined Courts*	X	X		$0	No Max	$0		X	
Magistrate Courts*	X	X		$0	$15,000	$15,000		X	
Combined Superior/ Magistrate Court*									
Civil Courts*	X	X		$0	$7500	$7500			
Recorder's Courts									
Municipal Courts									
Probate Courts*							X		
Juvenile Courts									

Court	CRIMINAL				
	Felony	Misdemeanor	DWI/DUI	Preliminary Hearing	Juvenile
Superior Courts*	X	X	X	X	
State Courts*		X	X	X	
Combined Courts*				X	
Magistrate Courts*		X		X	
Combined Superior/ Magistrate Court*			X	X	
Civil Courts*				X	
Recorder's Courts		X	X	X	
Municipal Courts		X	X	X	
Probate Courts*		X	X	X	
Juvenile Courts					X

ADMINISTRATION	Court Administrator, 244 Washington St SW, Suite 550, Atlanta, GA, 30334; 404-656-5171, Fax: 404-651-6449. www.georgiacourts.org/aoc/index.html
COURT STRUCTURE	Georgia's Superior Courts are arranged in 49 circuits of general jurisdiction, and these assume the role of a State Court if the county does not have one. The 69 State Courts, like Superior Courts, can conduct jury trials, but are limited jurisidiction. Each county has a Probate, a Juvenile, and a Magistrate Court; the latter has jurisdiction over civil actions under $15,000, also one type of misdemeanor related to passing bad checks. Magistrate Courts also issue arrest warrants and set bond on all felonies. Probate courts can, in certain cases, issue search and arrest warrants, and hear miscellaneous misdemeanors.
ONLINE ACCESS	Cobb, Dougherty, and Gwinnett Counties offer Internet access to court records as does Cherokee County Magistrate Court, but there is no online access available statewide, although statewide access is being planned.
ADDITIONAL INFORMATION	In most Georgia counties the courts will not perform criminal record searches, and, in many cases, will not do civil record searches. An in-person search or the use of a record retriever is required. The Georgia Crime Information Center is the felony criminal history state repository.

Appling County

Superior & State Court PO Box 269, Baxley, GA 31513; 912-367-8126. Hours: 8AM-5PM (EST). *Felony, Misdemeanor, Civil.*

Civil Records: Access: In person only. Visitors must perform in person searches for themselves. No search fee. Required to search: name, years to search. Civil cases indexed by defendant, plaintiff. Civil records on docket books back to 1800s.
Criminal Records: Access: In person only. Visitors must perform in person searches for themselves. No search fee. Required to search: name, years to search, DOB; also helpful: SSN, race, sex. Criminal records on docket books back to 1800s.
General Information: No juvenile, adoption, sealed, sexual, mental health or expunged records released. Copy fee: $.25 for first page, $.10 each add'l. Certification fee: $2.50 plus $.50 per page after first. Fee payee: Court Clerk. Personal checks accepted.

Magistrate Court Box 366, Baxley, GA 31515; 912-367-8116, 367-8117; Fax: 912-367-8182. Hours: 8:30AM-5PM (EST). *Civil Actions Under $15,000, Eviction, Small Claims.*

Probate Court 36 S Main St #B, Baxley, GA 31513; 912-367-8114; Fax: 912-367-8166. Hours: 8:30AM-5PM (EST). *Probate.*

Atkinson County

Superior Court PO Box 6, South Main, Courthouse Square, Pearson, GA 31642; 912-422-3343; Fax: 912-422-7025. Hours: 8AM-5PM (EST). *Felony, Misdemeanor, Civil.*

Civil Records: Access: In person only. Visitors must perform in person searches for themselves. No search fee. Required to search: name, years to search. Civil cases indexed by defendant. Civil records in docket books back to 1919.
Criminal Records: Access: In person only. Visitors must perform in person searches for themselves. No search fee. Required to search: name, years to search. Criminal records in docket books back to 1919.
General Information: No juvenile, adoption, sealed, sexual, mental health or expunged records released. Copy fee: $.25 per page. Certification fee: $2.50 plus $.50 per page after first. Fee payee: Clerk of Superior Court. Personal checks accepted. Prepayment is required.

Magistrate Court PO Box 674, Pearson, GA 31642; 912-422-7158; Fax: 912-422-7989. Hours: 8AM-5PM (EST). *Civil Actions Under $15,000, Eviction, Small Claims.*

Probate Court PO Box 855, Pearson, GA 31642; 912-422-3552; Fax: 912-422-7842. Hours: 8AM-5PM (EST). *Probate.*

Bacon County

Superior Court PO Box 376, Alma, GA 31510; 912-632-4915. Hours: 9AM-5PM (EST). *Felony, Misdemeanor, Civil.*

Civil Records: Access: Mail, in person. Both court and visitors may perform in person searches. No search fee. Required to search: name, years to search. Civil cases indexed by defendant, plaintiff. Civil records on index from 1970, archived to 1918, computerized since 2000.
Criminal Records: Access: Mail, in person. Both court and visitors may perform in person searches. No search fee. Required to search: name, years to search, DOB; also helpful: SSN, race, sex. Criminal records on index from 1970, archived to 1918, computerized since 2000.
General Information: No juvenile, adoption, sealed, sexual, mental health, expunged or first offender records released. SASE required. Turnaround time 1 week. Copy fee: $.25 per page. Certification fee: $2.50 plus $.50 per page after first. Fee payee: Clerk of Superior Court. Personal checks accepted. Prepayment required.

Magistrate Court Box 389, Alma, GA 31510; 912-632-5961. Hours: 9AM-5PM (EST). *Civil Actions Under $15,000, Eviction, Small Claims, Probate.*

Probate Court PO Box 389, Alma, GA 31510; 912-632-7661; Fax: 912-632-7662. Hours: 9AM-5PM (EST). *Probate.*

Baker County

Superior Court PO Box 10, Governmental Bldg, Newton, GA 31770; 229-734-3004; Fax: 229-734-8822. Hours: 9AM-5PM (EST). *Felony, Misdemeanor, Civil.*

Civil Records: Access: In person only. Visitors must perform in person searches for themselves. No search fee. Required to search: name, years to search. Civil cases indexed by defendant. Civil records on index from 1850.
Criminal Records: Access: In person only. Visitors must perform in person searches for themselves. No search fee. Required to search: name, years to search, DOB; also helpful: SSN, race, sex. Criminal records on index from 1850.
General Information: No juvenile, adoption, sealed, sexual or expunged records released. Copy fee: $.25 per page. Certification fee: $2.50 plus $.50 per page after first. Fee payee: Court Clerk. Personal checks accepted. Prepayment is required.

Magistrate Court Box 548, Newton, GA 31770; 229-734-3009; Fax: 229-734-8822. Hours: 9AM-5PM (EST). *Civil Actions Under $15,000, Eviction, Small Claims.*

Probate Court PO Box 548, Newton, GA 31770; 229-734-3007; Fax: 229-734-8822. Hours: 9AM-5PM M-W & F; 9AM-Noon Th (EST). *Probate.*

Baldwin County

Superior & State Court PO Drawer 987, Milledgeville, GA 31061; 478-445-4007; Fax: 478-445-1404. Hours: 8:30AM-5PM (EST). *Felony, Misdemeanor, Civil.*

Civil Records: Access: In person only. Visitors must perform in person searches for themselves. No search fee. Required to search: name, years to search. Civil cases indexed by defendant, plaintiff. Civil records on docket from 1861; on computer back to 1996.
Criminal Records: Access: In person only. Visitors must perform in person searches for themselves. No search fee. Required to search: name, years to search. Criminal records on docket from 1861; on computer back to 1996.
General Information: Public access terminal is available. No juvenile, adoption, sealed, sexual, mental health or expunged records released. Copy fee: $.25 per page. Certification fee: $2.50 plus $.50 per page after first. Personal checks accepted. Prepayment is required.

Magistrate Court 121 N Wilkenson #107, Milledgeville, GA 31061; 478-445-4446; Fax: 478-445-5918. Hours: 8:30AM-5PM (EST). *Civil Actions Under $15,000, Eviction, Small Claims.*

Probate Court 121 N Wilkinson St #109, Milledgeville, GA 31061; 478-445-4807; Fax: 478-445-5178. Hours: 8:30AM-5PM (EST). *Probate.*

Banks County

Superior Court PO Box 337, 144 Yorah Homer Road, Homer, GA 30547; 706-677-6240; Fax: 706-677-2337. Hours: 8:00AM-5PM (EST). *Felony, Misdemeanor, Civil.*

Civil Records: Access: In person only. Visitors must perform in person searches for themselves. No search fee. Required to search: name, years to search. Civil cases indexed by defendant, plaintiff. Civil records on docket from 1960.
Criminal Records: Access: In person only. Visitors must perform in person searches for themselves. No search fee. Required to search: name, years to search, DOB, signed release; also helpful: SSN, race, sex. Criminal records on docket from 1960.

General Information: No juvenile, adoption, sealed, sexual, mental health or expunged records released. Copy fee: $.25 per page. Certification fee: $3.75. Fee payee: Clerk of Superior Court. Personal checks accepted.

Magistrate Court Box 364, Homer, GA 30547; 706-677-6270; Fax: 706-677-6215. Hours: 8:30AM-5PM (EST). *Civil Actions Under $15,000, Eviction, Small Claims.*

Probate Court PO Box 7, Homer, GA 30547; 706-677-6250; Fax: 706-677-2337. Hours: 80AM-5PM (EST). *Probate.*

Barrow County

Superior Court PO Box 1280, Winder, GA 30680; 770-307-3035; Fax: 770-867-4800. Hours: 8AM-5PM (EST). *Felony, Misdemeanor, Civil.*

Civil Records: Access: In person only. Visitors must perform in person searches for themselves. No search fee. Required to search: name, years to search. Civil cases indexed by defendant, plaintiff. Civil records on computer from 1990, docket from 1915.

Criminal Records: Access: In person only. Visitors must perform in person searches for themselves. No search fee. Required to search: name, years to search, DOB; also helpful: SSN, race, sex. Criminal records on computer from 1990, docket from 1915.

General Information: Public access terminal is available. No juvenile, adoption, sealed, sexual, mental health or expunged records released. Copy fee: $.25 per page. Certification fee: $2.50 plus $.50 per page after first. Fee payee: Clerk of Superior Court. Business checks accepted. Prepayment is required.

Magistrate Court 30 N Broad St, Ste 321, Winder, GA 30680; 770-307-3050; Fax: 770-868-1440. Hours: 8AM-5PM (EST). *Civil Actions Under $15,000, Eviction, Small Claims.*

Probate Court Barrow County Courthouse, 30 N Broad St, Winder, GA 30680; 770-307-3045; Fax: 770-867-8041. Hours: 8AM-5PM (EST). *Probate.*

Bartow County

Superior Court 135 W Cherokee #233, Cartersville, GA 30120; 770-387-5025; Fax: 770-387-5611. Hours: 8AM-5PM (EST). *Felony, Misdemeanor, Civil.*

Civil Records: Access: In person only. Visitors must perform in person searches for themselves. No search fee. Required to search: name, years to search. Civil cases indexed by defendant, plaintiff. Civil records on computer from 9/92, on books from 1900s.

Criminal Records: Access: In person only. Visitors must perform in person searches for themselves. No search fee. Required to search: name, years to search, address, DOB, SSN, signed release. Criminal records on computer for 10 years, prior on books.

General Information: No juvenile, adoptions or sealed records released. Copy fee: $.25 per page. Certification fee: $2.50 plus $.25 each add'l page. Fee payee: Clerk of Superior Court. Personal checks accepted. Prepayment is required.

Magistrate Court 135 W Cherokee Ave #225, Cartersville, GA 30120; 770-387-5070; Fax: 770-387-5073. 7AM-5:30PM (EST). *Civil Actions Under $15,000, Eviction, Small Claims, Misdemeanors.*

Probate Court 135 W Cherokee #243A, Cartersville, GA 30120; 770-387-5075; Fax: 770-387-5074. Hours: 8AM-5PM (EST). *Probate.*

Ben Hill County

Superior Court PO Box 1104, 401 Central, Fitzgerald, GA 31750; 229-426-5135; Fax: 229-426-5487. Hours: 8:30AM-4:30PM (EST). *Felony, Misdemeanor, Civil.*

Civil Records: Access: In person only. Visitors must perform in person searches for themselves. No search fee. Required to search: name, years to search. Civil cases indexed by defendant. Civil records on computer from 1994, archived from 1907, docket 1907.

Criminal Records: Access: In person only. Visitors must perform in person searches for themselves. No search fee. Required to search: name, years to search, signed release; also helpful: DOB, SSN. Criminal records on computer from 1994, archived from 1907, docket 1907.

General Information: No juvenile, adoption, sealed, sexual, mental health or expunged records released. Copy fee: $.25 per page; $1.00 per page if mailed. Certification fee: $2.00 plus $.50 per page. Fee payee: Clerk. Personal checks accepted. Prepayment required.

Magistrate Court Box 1163, Fitzgerald, GA 31750; 229-426-5140; Fax: 229-426-5123. Hours: 8:30AM-5:30PM (EST). *Civil Actions Under $15,000, Eviction, Small Claims.*

Probate Court 111 S Sheridan St, Fitzgerald, GA 31750; 229-426-5137; Fax: 229-426-5486. Hours: 8:30AM-4:30PM (EST). *Probate.*

Berrien County

Superior Court 101 E Marion Ave, Ste 3, Nashville, GA 31639; 229-686-5506. Hours: 8AM-5PM (EST). *Felony, Misdemeanor, Civil.*

Civil Records: Access: Mail, in person. Both court and visitors may perform in person searches. No search fee. Required to search: name, years to search. Civil cases indexed by defendant, plaintiff. Civil records on docket back to 1800.

Criminal Records: Access: Mail, in person. Both court and visitors may perform in person searches. No search fee. Required to search: name, years to search, DOB; also helpful: SSN, race, sex. Criminal records on docket back to 1800.

General Information: No juvenile, adoption, sealed, sexual, mental health or expunged records released. Turnaround time same day. Copy fee: $.25 per page. Certification fee: $2.50 plus $.50 per page after first. Fee payee: Court Clerk. Personal checks accepted. Prepayment is required.

Magistrate Court PO Box 267, Nashville, GA 31639; 229-686-7019; Fax: 229-686-6328. Hours: 8:30AM-4:30PM (EST). *Civil Actions Under $15,000, Eviction, Small Claims.*

Probate Court 101 E Marion Ave, Ste 2, Nashville, GA 31639; 229-686-5213; Fax: 229-686-9495. Hours: 7AM-5PM Sun-Sat (EST). *Probate.*

Bibb County

Superior Court PO Box 1015, 601 Mulberry St Rm 216, Macon, GA 31202; 478-749-6527. Hours: 8:30AM-5PM (EST). *Felony, Civil.*

Civil Records: Access: Mail, in person. Both court and visitors may perform in person searches. Search fee: $10.00 per name. Required to search: name, years to search. Civil cases indexed by defendant, plaintiff. Civil records on computer from 1993, on books from 1823.

Criminal Records: Access: Mail, in person. Both court and visitors may perform in person searches. Search fee: $10.00 per name. Required to search: name, years to search, DOB, signed release; also helpful: SSN. Criminal records on computer since 1989.

General Information: No adoption or sealed records released. Turnaround time same day. Copy fee: $.25 per page. Fee is $1.00 if court makes copy. Certification fee: $2.50 plus $.50 per page after first. Fee payee: Superior Court Clerk. Only cashiers checks and money orders accepted. Prepayment is required.

State Court PO Box 5086, Macon, GA 31213-7199; 478-749-6676; Fax: 478-749-6326. Hours: 8AM-5PM (EST). *Misdemeanor, Civil.*

Civil Records: Access: Mail, in person. Both court and visitors may perform in person searches. Search fee: $10.00 per name. Required to search: name, years to search. Civil cases indexed by defendant, plaintiff. Civil records on computer from 1989, docket from 1952.

Criminal Records: Access: Mail, in person. Both court and visitors may perform in person searches. Search fee: $10.00 per name. Required to search: name, years to search, DOB; also helpful: SSN, race, sex. Criminal records on computer from 1989, docket from 1945.

General Information: Public access terminal is available. No juvenile, adoption, sealed, sexual, mental health or expunged records released. SASE required. Turnaround time 1 day. Copy fee: $.30 per page. Certification fee: $2.50 plus $.30 per page. Fee payee: Court Clerk. Business checks accepted. Prepayment is required.

Civil & Magistrate Court 601 Mulberry #110, Bibb County Courthouse, Macon, GA 31201; 478-749-6495; Fax: 478-722-5861. Hours: 8AM-5PM (EST). *Civil Actions Under $25,000, Eviction, Small Claims.*

Probate Court 207 Bibb County Courthouse, PO Box 6518, Macon, GA 31208-6518; 478-749-6494; Fax: 478-749-6686. Hours: 8AM-5PM (EST). *Probate.* www.co.bibb.ga.us/probate

Bleckley County

Superior Court 306 SE 2nd St, Cochran, GA 31014; 478-934-3210; Fax: 478-934-3205. Hours: 8:30AM-5PM (EST). *Felony, Misdemeanor, Civil.*

Civil Records: Access: In person only. Visitors must perform in person searches for themselves. No search fee. Required to search: name, years to search. Civil cases indexed by defendant, plaintiff. Civil records archived from 1913, docket from 1913.

Criminal Records: Access: In person only. Visitors must perform in person searches for themselves. No search fee. Required to search: name, years to search, DOB; also helpful: SSN, race, sex. Criminal records archived from 1913, docket from 1913.

General Information: No juvenile, adoption, sealed, sexual, mental health or expunged records released. Copy fee: $.25 per page. Certification fee: $2.50 plus $.50 per page after first. Fee payee: Clerk of the Superior Court. Personal checks not accepted. Prepayment is required.

Magistrate Court 306 2nd St SE, Cochran, GA 31014; 478-934-3202; Fax: 478-934-37826. Hours: 8:30AM-5PM (EST). *Civil Actions Under $15,000, Eviction, Small Claims.*

Probate Court 306 SE Second St, Cochran, GA 31014; 478-934-3204; Fax: 478-934-3205. Hours: 8:30AM-5PM (EST). *Probate.*

Brantley County

Superior Court PO Box 1067, 117 Brantley St, Nahunta, GA 31553; 912-462-5635; Fax: 912-462-6247. Hours: 8AM-5PM (EST). *Felony, Misdemeanor, Civil.*

Civil Records: Access: In person only. Visitors must perform in person searches for themselves. No search fee. Required to search: name, years to search. Civil cases indexed by defendant, plaintiff. Civil records on dockets from 1920; computerized records go back 1998.

Criminal Records: Access: In person only. Visitors must perform in person searches for themselves. No search fee. Required to search: name, years to search, DOB, SSN, signed release; also helpful: race, sex. Criminal records on dockets from 1920.

General Information: No juvenile, adoption, sealed, 1st offenders, expunged or confidential records released. Copy fee: $.25 per page. Certification fee: $2.50 plus $.50 per page after first. Fee payee: Superior Court Clerk. Personal checks accepted. Prepayment is required.

Magistrate Court PO Box 998, Nahunta, GA 31553; 912-462-6780; Fax: 912-462-5538. Hours: 8AM-4:30PM (EST). *Civil Actions Under $15,000, Eviction, Small Claims.*

Probate Court PO Box 207, Nahunta, GA 31553; 912-462-5192; Fax: 912-462-8360. Hours: 8AM-5PM (EST). *Probate.*

Brooks County

Superior Court PO Box 630, Quitman, GA 31643; 229-263-4747/5150; Fax: 229-263-5050. Hours: 8AM-5PM (EST). *Felony, Misdemeanor, Civil.*

http://www2.state.ga.us/courts/superior/dca/dca2sohp.htm

Civil Records: Access: In person, phone if specific date is known. Visitors must perform in person searches for themselves. No search fee. Required to search: name, years to search. Civil cases indexed by defendant, plaintiff. Civil records in books back to 1857.

Criminal Records: Access: In person only. Visitors must perform in person searches for themselves. No search fee. Required to search: name, years to search, DOB; also helpful: SSN, race, sex. Criminal records in books back to 1857.

General Information: No juvenile, adoption, sealed, sexual, mental health or expunged records released. Copy fee: $.25 per page. Certification fee: $2.50 plus $.50 per page after first. Fee payee: Clerk Superior Court. Business checks accepted.

Magistrate Court PO Box 387, Quitman, GA 31643; 229-263-9989; Fax: 229-263-7847. Hours: 8AM-5PM (EST). *Civil Actions Under $15,000, Eviction, Small Claims.*

Probate Court PO Box 665, Quitman, GA 31643; 229-263-5567; Fax: 229-263-7559. Hours: 8:30AM-5PM (EST). *Probate.*

Bryan County

Superior & State Court PO Box 670, Pembroke, GA 31321; 912-653-3872; Fax: 912-653-3870. Hours: 8AM-5PM (EST). *Felony, Misdemeanor, Civil.*

Civil Records: Access: Mail, in person. Visitors must perform in person searches for themselves. No search fee. Required to search: name, years to search. Civil cases indexed by defendant, plaintiff. Civil records on dockets from 1960, recent records are computerized since 9/93.

Criminal Records: Access: Mail, in person. Visitors must perform in person searches for themselves. No search fee. Required to search: name, years to search, DOB; also helpful: SSN, race, sex. Criminal records on dockets from 1960, recent records are computerized since 9/93.

General Information: Public access terminal is available. No juvenile, adoption, sealed, sexual, mental health or expunged records released. SASE requested. Turnaround time 1-2 days. Copy fee: $.25 per page. Certification fee: $2.50 plus $.25 per page after first. Fee payee: Clerk of Superior & State Court. Personal checks accepted. Prepayment is required.

Magistrate Court Box 670, Pembroke, GA 31321; 912-653-3861; Fax: 912-653-5254. Hours: 8AM-5PM (EST). *Civil Actions Under $15,000, Eviction, Small Claims.*

Probate Court PO Box 418, Pembroke, GA 31321; 912-653-3856; Fax: 912-653-3845. Hours: 8AM-12, 1-5PM (EST). *Probate.*

www.georgiacourts.org/probate/bryan

Bulloch County

Superior & State Court Judicial Annex Bldg, 20 Siebald St, Statesboro, GA 30458; 912-764-9009. Hours: 8:30AM-5PM (EST). *Felony, Misdemeanor, Civil.*

Civil Records: Access: In person only. Visitors must perform in person searches for themselves. No search fee. Required to search: name, years to search. Civil cases indexed by defendant. Civil records on computer from 1991, dockets back to 1796.

Criminal Records: Access: In person only. Visitors must perform in person searches for themselves. No search fee. Required to search: name, years to search. Criminal records on computer from 1991, dockets back to 1796.

General Information: Public access terminal is available. No juvenile, adoption, sexual, mental health or expunged records released. Copy fee: $.25 per page. Certification fee: $2.50 plus $.50 per page after first. Fee payee: Court Clerk. Personal checks accepted. Prepayment is required.

Magistrate Court Box 1004, Statesboro, GA 30459-1004; 912-764-6458, 912-764-5050; Fax: 912-489-6731. Hours: 8:30AM-5PM (EST). *Civil Actions Under $15,000, Eviction, Small Claims.*

Probate Court PO Box 1005, Statesboro, GA 30459; 912-489-8749; Fax: 912-764-8740. Hours: 8:30AM-5PM (EST). *Probate.*

Burke County

Superior & State Court PO Box 803, 111 E 6th St, Rm 107, Waynesboro, GA 30830; 706-554-2279; Fax: 706-554-7887. Hours: 9AM-5PM (EST). *Felony, Misdemeanor, Civil.*

Civil Records: Access: In person only. Visitors must perform in person searches for themselves. No search fee. Required to search: name, years to search. Civil cases indexed by defendant. Civil records on minute books back to 1856, indexed on computer since 1996.

Criminal Records: Access: In person only. Visitors must perform in person searches for themselves. No search fee. Required to search: name, years to search, DOB; also helpful: SSN, race, sex. Criminal records on minute books back to 1856, indexed on computer since 1996.

General Information: No juvenile, adoption, sexual, mental health or expunged records released. Fax notes: Fee to fax results is $1.00 1st page; $.25 each add'l. Copy fee: $.25 per page. Certification fee: $2.50 plus $.50 per page after first. Fee payee: Clerk of Superior Court. Personal checks accepted. Prepayment is required.

Magistrate Court Box 401, Waynesboro, GA 30830; 706-554-4281; Fax: 706-554-8772. Hours: 9AM-5PM (EST). *Civil Actions Under $15,000, Eviction, Small Claims.*

Probate Court PO Box 322, Waynesboro, GA 30830; 706-554-3000; Fax: 706-554-6693. Hours: 9AM-5PM (EST). *Probate.*

Butts County

Superior Court PO Box 320, 26 3rd St, Jackson, GA 30233; 770-775-8215. Hours: 8AM-5PM (EST). *Felony, Misdemeanor, Civil.*

Civil Records: Access: In person only. Visitors must perform in person searches for themselves. No search fee. Required to search: name, years to search. Civil cases indexed by defendant, plaintiff. Civil records on dockets from 1966.

Criminal Records: Access: In person only. Visitors must perform in person searches for themselves. No search fee. Required to search: name, years to search, signed release; also helpful: DOB, SSN, race, sex. Criminal records on dockets from 1966.

General Information: No juvenile, adoption, sexual, mental health or expunged records released. Copy fee: $.25 per page. Certification fee: $2.50 plus $.50 per page. Fee payee: Clerk of Superior Court. Personal checks accepted. Prepayment is required.

Magistrate Court Box 457, Jackson, GA 30233; 770-775-8220; Fax: 770-775-1954. Hours: 8AM-5PM (EST). *Civil Actions Under $15,000, Eviction, Small Claims.*

Probate Court 25 Third Street, #7, Jackson, GA 30233; 770-775-8204; Fax: 770-775-8211. Hours: 8AM-5PM (EST). *Probate.*

Calhoun County

Superior Court PO Box 69, Morgan, GA 31766; 229-849-2715; Fax: 229-849-0072. Hours: 8AM-5PM (EST). *Felony, Misdemeanor, Civil.*

Civil Records: Access: Mail, in person. Both court and visitors may perform in person searches. No search fee. Required to search: name, years to search. Civil cases indexed by defendant, plaintiff. Civil records on dockets back to 1854.

Criminal Records: Access: Mail, in person. Both court and visitors may perform in person searches. No search fee. Required to search: name, years to search, DOB, SSN. Criminal records on dockets back to 1854.

General Information: Public access terminal is available. No juvenile, adoption, sexual, mental health or expunged records released. SASE required. Turnaround time 1-2 days. Fax notes: $1.50 per fax; no charge to toll-free numbers. Copy fee: $.25 per page. Certification fee: $3.00. Fee payee: Superior Court Clerk. Personal checks accepted. Prepayment is required.

Magistrate & Probate Court PO Box 87, Morgan, GA 31766; 229-849-2115, 849-2116; Fax: 229-849-2117. Hours: 8AM-5PM (EST). *Civil Actions Under $15,000, Eviction, Small Claims, Probate.*

Camden County

Superior Court PO Box 550, 202 E 4th Street, Woodbine, GA 31569; 912-576-5624. Hours: 9AM-5PM (EST). *Felony, Misdemeanor, Civil.*

Civil Records: Access: In person only. Visitors must perform in person searches for themselves. No search fee. Required to search: name, years to search. Civil cases indexed by defendant, plaintiff. Civil records on computer from 1989, on dockets from 1776.

Criminal Records: Access: In person only. Visitors must perform in person searches for themselves. No search fee. Required to search: name, years to search, signed release; also helpful: DOB, SSN. Criminal records on computer from 1989, on dockets from 1776.

General Information: Public access terminal is available. No juvenile, adoption, sexual or expunged records released. Copy fee: $.25 per page. Certification fee: $2.00 plus $.50 per page after first. Fee payee: Clerk of Superior Court. Personal checks accepted. Prepayment is required.

Magistrate Court Box 386, Woodbine, GA 31569; 912-576-5658. Hours: 9AM-5PM (EST). *Civil Actions Under $15,000, Eviction, Small Claims.*

Probate Court PO Box 818, Woodbine, GA 31569; 912-576-3785; Fax: 912-576-5484. Hours: 9AM-Noon, 1-5PM (EST). *Probate, Misdemeanor Drug.*

Candler County

Superior & State Court PO Drawer 830, Metter, GA 30439; 912-685-5257; Fax: 912-685-2946. Hours: 8:30AM-5PM (EST). *Felony, Misdemeanor, Civil.*

Civil Records: Access: In person only. Visitors must perform in person searches for themselves. No search fee. Required to search: name, years to search. Civil cases indexed by defendant, plaintiff. Civil records on dockets from 1914.
Criminal Records: Access: In person only. Visitors must perform in person searches for themselves. No search fee. Required to search: name, years to search. Criminal records on dockets from 1914.
General Information: Public access terminal is available. No juvenile, adoption, mental health, expunged or sealed records released. Copy fee: $.25 per page. Certification fee: $2.00 plus $.50 per page. Fee payee: Clerk of Superior & State Court. Personal checks accepted. Prepayment is required.

Magistrate Court 1 Courthouse Square, Metter, GA 30439; 912-685-2888; Fax: 912-685-6426. Hours: 9AM-5PM (EST). *Civil Actions Under $15,000, Eviction, Small Claims.*

Probate Court Courthouse Square, Metter, GA 30439; 912-685-2357; Fax: 912-685-5130. Hours: 8AM-5PM (EST). *Probate.*

Carroll County

Superior & State Court PO Box 1620, Carrollton, GA 30117; 770-830-5830; Fax: 770-830-5988. Hours: 8AM-5PM (EST). *Felony, Misdemeanor, Civil.*

Civil Records: Access: Mail, in person. Both court and visitors may perform in person searches. Search fee: $5.00 per name. Required to search: name, years to search. Civil cases indexed by defendant, plaintiff. Civil records on computer from 1986, docket.
Criminal Records: Access: Mail, in person. Both court and visitors may perform in person searches. Search fee: $5.00 per name. Required to search: name, years to search, DOB; also helpful: SSN, race, sex. Criminal records on computer from 1986, docket.
General Information: No juvenile, adoption, sexual, mental health or expunged records released. SASE required. Turnaround time 1 week. Copy fee: $1.00 per page. Certification fee: $2.50 plus $.50 per page after first. Fee payee: Clerk of Superior & State Court. Personal checks accepted. Prepayment is required.

Magistrate Court 307 Courtyard Sq, Carrollton, GA 30117; 770-830-0116. Hours: 9AM-5PM (EST). *Civil Actions Under $15,000, Eviction, Small Claims.*

Probate Court Carroll County Courthouse, 311 newnan Street, Rm 204, Carrollton, GA 30117; 770-830-5840; Fax: 770-830-5995. Hours: 8AM-5PM (EST). *Probate.*

Catoosa County

Superior & Magistrate Court 875 Lafayette St, Ringgold, GA 30736; 706-935-4231. Hours: 8:30AM-5PM (EST). *Felony, Misdemeanor, Civil, Eviction, Small Claims.*

Civil Records: Access: In person only. Both the court and visitors may perform in person searches. No search fee. Required to search: name, years to search. Civil

cases indexed by defendant, plaintiff. Civil records on dockets from 1800.
Criminal Records: Access: In person only. Visitors must perform in person searches for themselves. No search fee. Required to search: name, years to search, DOB; also helpful: SSN, race, sex. Criminal records on dockets from 1800.
General Information: No juvenile, adoption, sexual, mental health or expunged records released. Copy fee: $1.00 per page. Certification fee: $2.50 plus $.50 per page after first. Fee payee: Superior Court - Court Clerk. Personal checks accepted. Prepayment is required.

Probate Court 875 LaFayette St, Justice Bldg, Ringgold, GA 30736; 706-935-3511; Fax: 706-935-3515. Hours: 9AM-5PM (EST). *Probate.*

Charlton County

Superior Court Courthouse, PO Box 760, Folkston, GA 31537; 912-496-2354. Hours: 8:30AM-5PM (EST). *Felony, Misdemeanor, Civil.*

Civil Records: Access: In person. Visitors must perform in person searches. No search fee. Required to search: name, years to search. Civil cases indexed by defendant. Civil records on index from 1954.
Criminal Records: Access: In person. Visitors must perform in person searches. No search fee. Required to search: name, years to search, DOB, SSN. Criminal records on index from 1954.
General Information: No juvenile, adoption, sexual, mental health or expunged records released. Copy fee: $.25 per page. Certification fee: $2.50 plus $.50 per page after first. Fee payee: Court Clerk. Personal checks accepted.

Magistrate Court 100 S 3rd Street, Folkston, GA 31537; 912-496-2617. Hours: 8AM-5PM (EST). *Civil Actions Under $15,000, Eviction, Small Claims.*

Probate Court 100 S 3rd St, Folkston, GA 31537; 912-496-2230; Fax: 912-496-1156. Hours: 8AM-5PM (EST). *Probate.*

Chatham County

Superior Court PO Box 10227, 133 Montgomery St, Savannah, GA 31412; 912-652-7197; Fax: 912-652-7380. Hours: 8AM-5PM (EST). *Felony, Misdemeanor, Civil.*

www.chathamcourts.org

Civil Records: Access: Mail, in person. Both court and visitors may perform in person searches. No search fee. Required to search: name, years to search. Civil cases indexed by defendant, plaintiff. Civil records on computer from 1984, archived back to 1900, dockets back to 1900s.
Criminal Records: Access: Mail, in person. Both court and visitors may perform in person searches. No search fee. Required to search: name, years to search, signed release; also helpful: DOB, SSN. Criminal records on computer from 1984, archived back to 1900, dockets back to 1900s.
General Information: Public access terminal is available. No juvenile, adoption or 1st offender records released. SASE requested. Turnaround time 1 week. Copy fee: $.25 per page. Certification fee: $2.00 plus $.50 per page. Fee payee: Court Clerk. Personal checks accepted. Prepayment is required.

State Court County Courthouse 133 Montgomery St, Savannah, GA 31401; 912-652-7224; Fax: 912-652-7229. Hours: 8AM-5PM (EST). *Misdemeanor, Civil.*

www.chathamcourts.org

Civil Records: Access: Mail, fax, in person. Both court and visitors may perform in person searches. No search fee. Required to search: name, years to search, address. Civil cases indexed by defendant, plaintiff. Civil records on computer from 1983, prior on books. Current state

court cases only are available free online at www.chathamcourts.org. Search by name or case number.

Criminal Records: Access: Mail, fax, in person. Both court and visitors may perform in person searches. No search fee. Required to search: name, years to search. Criminal records on computer from 1983, prior on books.
General Information: Public access terminal is available. No first time criminal offender or sealed civil records released. SASE required. Turnaround time 2 days. Copy fee: $1.00 per page. Certification fee: $2.50 plus $.50 per page. Fee payee: Clerk of State Court. Only cashiers checks and money orders accepted. Prepayment is required.

Magistrate Court 133 Montgomery St Room 303, Savannah, GA 31401; 912-652-7181; Fax: 912-652-7550. Hours: 8AM-5PM (EST). *Civil Actions Under $15,000, Eviction, Small Claims.*

www.chathamcourts.org

Probate Court 133 Montgomery St, Rm 509, PO Box 509, Savannah, GA 31401; 912-652-7264; Fax: 912-652-7262. Hours: 8AM-5PM (EST). *Probate.*

www.chathamcourts.org

Chattahoochee County

Superior & Magistrate Court PO Box 120, Cusseta, GA 31805; 706-989-3424; Fax: 706-989-0396. Hours: 8AM-5PM (EST). *Felony, Misdemeanor, Civil, Eviction, Small Claims.*

Note: Magistrate Court is 706-989-3643.
Civil Records: Access: In person only. Visitors must perform in person searches for themselves. No search fee. Required to search: name, years to search. Civil cases indexed by defendant, plaintiff. Civil records on dockets from 1854.
Criminal Records: Access: In person only. Visitors must perform in person searches for themselves. No search fee. Required to search: name, years to search, DOB; also helpful: SSN, race, sex. Criminal records on dockets from 1854.
General Information: Public access terminal is available. No juvenile, adoption, sexual, mental health or expunged records released. Copy fee: $.25 per page. Certification fee: $2.50 plus $.50 per page after first. Fee payee: Court Clerk. Business checks accepted. Prepayment is required.

Probate Court PO Box 119, Cusseta, GA 31805; 706-989-3603; Fax: 706-989-2005. Hours: 8AM-Noon, 1-5PM (EST). *Probate.*

Chattooga County

Superior & State Court PO Box 159, Summerville, GA 30747; 706-857-0706. Hours: 8:30AM-5PM (EST). *Felony, Misdemeanor, Civil, Eviction, Small Claims.*

Civil Records: Access: In person only. Visitors must perform in person searches for themselves. No search fee. Required to search: name, years to search. Civil cases indexed by defendant, plaintiff. Civil records on dockets from 1960.
Criminal Records: Access: In person only. Visitors must perform in person searches for themselves. No search fee. Required to search: name, years to search, DOB; also helpful: SSN, race, sex. Criminal records on dockets from 1960.
General Information: No juvenile, adoption, sexual, mental health or expunged records released. Copy fee: $.25 per page. Certification fee: $2.50 plus $.50 per page after first. Fee payee: Clerk of Court. Personal checks accepted. Prepayment is required.

Magistrate Court 10017 Commerce St, Summerville, GA 30747; 706-857-0711; Fax: 706-857-

0675. Hours: 9AM-5PM (EST). *Civil Actions Under $15,000, Eviction, Small Claims.*

Probate Court PO Box 467, Summerville, GA 30747; 706-857-0709; Fax: 706-857-0709. Hours: 8:30AM-Noon, 1-5PM (EST). *Probate.*

Cherokee County

Superior & State Court 90 North St, Ste G170, Canton, GA 30114; 770-479-0538. Hours: 8:30AM-5PM (EST). *Felony, Misdemeanor, Civil.*

Note: This court location also handles juvenile records.
Civil Records: Access: In person only. Visitors must perform in person searches for themselves. No search fee. Required to search: name. Civil cases indexed by defendant, plaintiff. Civil records on computer from 1990, archived 1900-1991, on dockets back to 1900.
Criminal Records: Access: In person only. Both court and visitors may perform in person searches. No search fee. Required to search: name, years to search, DOB; also helpful: SSN, race, sex. Criminal records on computer from 1990, archived 1900-1990, on dockets back to 1900.
General Information: Public access terminal is available. No juvenile, adoption, sexual, mental health, expunged or confidential records released. Copy fee: $.25 per page. Certification fee: $2.00 plus $.50 per add'l page. Fee payee: Clerk of Court. Only cashiers checks and money orders accepted. Prepayment is required.

Magistrate Court 90 North St #150, Canton, GA 30114; 770-479-8516; Fax: 770-720-6323. Hours: 8:30AM-5PM (EST). *Civil Actions Under $15,000, Eviction, Small Claims.*

www.cccourt.com

Note: Search the magistrate court database online at www.ncourt.com/search.html#database.

Probate Court 90 North St, Rm 340, Canton, GA 30114; 770-479-0541; Fax: 770-479-0567. *Probate.*

Clarke County

Superior & State Court PO Box 1805, Athens, GA 30603; 706-613-3190. Hours: 8AM-5PM (EST). *Felony, Misdemeanor, Civil.*

Note: Located at 325 E Washington, Room 450, 30601. This court will perform no searches for the public.
Civil Records: Access: In person only. Visitors must perform in person searches for themselves. No search fee. Required to search: name, years to search. Civil cases indexed by defendant, plaintiff. Civil records on computer from 1993, docket books from 1801.
Criminal Records: Access: In person only. Visitors must perform in person searches for themselves. No search fee. Required to search: name, years to search, DOB. Criminal records on computer from 1993, docket books from 1801.
General Information: Public access terminal is available. No juvenile, adoptions, sealed, sexual, mental health or expunged records released. Copy fee: In-house copies are $.25 each; by mail is $1.00 per page. Certification fee: $2.50 plus $.50 per page after first. Fee payee: County Clerk. Personal checks accepted. Prepayment is required.

Magistrate Court PO Box 1868, 325 E Washington St, Athens, GA 30601; 706-613-3310; Fax: 706-613-3314. Hours: 8AM-5PM (EST). *Civil Actions Under $15,000, Eviction, Small Claims.*

Probate Court 325 E Washington St, Athens, GA 30601; 706-613-3320; Fax: 706-613-3323. Hours: 8AM-5PM (EST). *Probate.*

Clay County

Superior Court PO Box 550, Ft Gaines, GA 39851; 229-768-2631; Fax: 229-768-3047. Hours: 8AM-4:30PM (EST). *Felony, Misdemeanor, Civil, Eviction.*

Civil Records: Access: In person only. Visitors must perform in person searches for themselves. No search fee. Required to search: name, years to search. Civil cases indexed by defendant, plaintiff. Civil records on computer from 1990, on dockets from 1854.
Criminal Records: Access: In person only. Visitors must perform in person searches for themselves. No search fee. Required to search: name, years to search. Criminal records on computer from 1990, on dockets from 1854.
General Information: Public access terminal is available. No juvenile, adoption, sexual, mental health or expunged records released. Copy fee: $1.00 per page. Certification fee: $3.00. Fee payee: Superior Court Clerk. Personal checks accepted. Prepayment is required.

Magistrate Court PO Box 73, Ft Gaines, GA 31751; 229-768-2841; Fax: 229-768-3443. Hours: 8AM-4:30PM (EST). *Civil Actions Under $15,000, Eviction, Small Claims.*

Probate Court 210 S Washington, Ft. Gaines, GA 31751; 229-768-2445; Fax: 229-768-2710. Hours: 8AM-4:30PM (EST). *Probate.*

Clayton County

Superior Court 9151 Tara Blvd, Suite ICL19, Jonesboro, GA 30236-4912; 770-477-3405. Hours: 8AM-5PM (EST). *Felony, Civil.*

www.co.clayton.ga.us/superior_court/clerk_of_courts
Civil Records: Access: In person only. Visitors must perform in person searches for themselves. No search fee. Required to search: name, years to search. Civil cases indexed by defendant. Civil records on docket books for all records, on computer from 1996, on microfilm from 1990, archived from 1800-1982, dockets to 1800.
Criminal Records: Access: In person only. Visitors must perform in person searches for themselves. No search fee. Required to search: name, years to search, DOB; also helpful: SSN, race, sex. Criminal record keeping as civil.
General Information: Public access terminal is available. (For civil records only.) No adoption, sexual, mental health or expunged records released. Copy fee: $.25 per page. Certification fee: $2.50 plus $.50 per page after first. Fee payee: Clerk of Superior Court. Only cashiers checks and money orders accepted. Attorney checks accepted. Prepayment is required.

State Court 9151 Tara Blvd #1CL181, Jonesboro, GA 30236; 770-477-4522; Criminal phone: 770-477-4522. Hours: 8AM-5PM (EST). *Misdemeanor.*

www.co.clayton.ga.us/state_court/clerk_of_courts
Criminal Records: Access: In person only. Visitors must perform in person searches for themselves. No search fee. Required to search: name, years to search. Criminal records on computer from 1985.
General Information: No juvenile, adoption, sexual, mental health or expunged records released. Copy fee: $.25 per page. Certification fee: $2.50 plus $.50 per page after first. Fee payee: Court Clerk. Business checks accepted.

Magistrate Court 9151 Tara Blvd, #2TC08, Jonesboro, GA 30236-4912; 770-477-3444; Fax: 770-473-5750. Hours: 8AM-5PM (EST). *Civil Actions Under $15,000, Eviction, Small Claims.*

www.co.clayton.ga.us/courts.htm

Clinch County

Superior & State Court PO Box 433, Homerville, GA 31634; 912-487-5854; Fax: 912-489-3083. Hours: 8AM-5PM (EST). *Felony, Misdemeanor, Civil.*

Civil Records: Access: Mail, in person. Both court and visitors may perform in person searches. No search fee. Required to search: name, years to search. Civil cases indexed by defendant, plaintiff. Civil records on dockets from 1900.
Criminal Records: Access: Mail, in person. Both court and visitors may perform in person searches. No search fee. Required to search: name, years to search, DOB; also helpful: SSN, race, sex. Criminal records on dockets from 1900.
General Information: No juvenile, adoption, sexual, mental health or expunged records released. SASE requested. Turnaround time 1-2 days. Copy fee: $.25 per page. Certification fee: $3.00. Fee payee: Court Clerk. Personal checks accepted.

Magistrate Court 100 Court Square, Homerville, GA 31634; 912-487-2514; Fax: 912-487-3658. Hours: 9AM-5PM (EST). *Civil Actions Under $15,000, Eviction, Small Claims.*

Probate Court PO Box 364, Homerville, GA 31634; 912-487-5523; Fax: 912-487-3083. Hours: 9AM-5PM (EST). *Probate.*

Cobb County

Superior Court PO Box 3370, Marietta, GA 30061; 770-528-1300; Fax: 770-528-1382. Hours: 8AM-5PM (EST). *Felony, Misdemeanor, Civil.*

www.cobbgasupctclk.com/index.htm
Civil Records: Access: Online, in person. Visitors must perform in person searches for themselves. No search fee. Required to search: name, years to search. Civil cases indexed by defendant, plaintiff. Civil records on computer from 1982, records on dockets from 1958. Civil or criminal indexes of Clerk of Superior Court are available free online at the web site. Search by name, type or case number. The data is updated every Friday.
Criminal Records: Access: Mail, online, in person. Visitors must perform in person searches for themselves. No search fee. Required to search: name, years to search, signed release. Criminal records on computer from 1982, Records on dockets from 1958. Online access to criminal records is the same as civil.
General Information: Public access terminal is available. No juvenile, adoption, sexual, mental health or expunged records released. Fax notes: Will not fax results. Copy fee: $.25 per page. Certification fee: $2.00 plus $.50 per page. Fee payee: Clerk of Superior Court. Personal checks accepted. Prepayment is required.

State Court - Civil & Criminal Divisions 12 East Park Square, Marietta, GA 30090-9630; Civil phone: 770-528-1219; Criminal phone: 770-528-1255. Hours: 8AM-5PM (EST). *Misdemeanor, Civil, Eviction.*

www.cobbstatecourtclerk.com
Civil Records: Access: In person only. Visitors must perform in person searches for themselves. Search fee: No search fee unless offsite (pre-1995), then $7.00. Required to search: name, years to search. Civil cases indexed by defendant, plaintiff. Civil records on computer since 03/10/97, docket books from 1965.
Criminal Records: Access: In person only. Both court and visitors may perform in person searches. Search fee: None unless offsite (pre-1996), then $7.00.

Clayton County

Probate Court 121 S McDonough St, Annex 3, Jonesboro, GA 30236-3694; 770-477-3299; Fax: 770-477-3306. Hours: 8AM-5PM (EST). *Probate.*

www.co.clayton.ga.us/probate_court

Required to search: name, years to search, offense; also helpful: DOB. Criminal records on computer since 05/99, on microfiche 01/81 - 04/99.

General Information: Public access terminal is available. No juvenile, adoption, sexual, mental health, expunged or sealed records released. Copy fee: $.25 per page. Certification fee: $3.00. Fee payee: State Court Clerk. Prepayment is required.

Magistrate Court 32 Waddell St, 3rd Fl, Marietta, GA 30090-9656; 770-528-8900; Fax: 770-528-8947. Hours: 8AM-5PM (EST). *Civil Actions Under $15,000, Small Claims.*

www.cobbcounty.org/judicial/magistrate/index.htm

Probate Court 32 Waddell St, Marietta, GA 30060; 770-528-1990; Fax: 770-528-1996. Hours: 8AM-4:30PM (EST). *Probate.*

Coffee County

Superior & State Court 101 S Peterson Ave, Douglas, GA 31533; 912-384-2865. Hours: 8:30AM-5PM (EST). *Felony, Misdemeanor, Civil.*

Civil Records: Access: In person only. Visitors must perform in person searches for themselves. No search fee. Required to search: name. Civil cases indexed by defendant, plaintiff. Civil records on dockets.

Criminal Records: Access: In person only. Visitors must perform in person searches for themselves. No search fee. Required to search: name, years to search. Criminal records on dockets.

General Information: No juvenile, adoption, sexual, mental health or expunged records released. Copy fee: $.25 per page. Certification fee: $3.00. Fee payee: Clerk Superior Court. Business checks accepted.

Magistrate Court 101 S Peterson Ave, Douglas, GA 31533; 912-384-2983; Fax: 912-384-0291. Hours: 8:30AM-5PM (EST). *Civil Actions Under $15,000, Eviction, Small Claims.*

Probate Court 109 S Peterson Ave, Douglas, GA 31533; 912-384-5213; Fax: 912-384-0291. Hours: 9AM-5PM (EST). *Probate, Civil.*

Colquitt County

Superior & State Court PO Box 2827, Moultrie, GA 31776; 229-616-7420. Hours: 8AM-5PM (EST). *Felony, Misdemeanor, Civil.*

http://www2.state.ga.us/courts/superior/dca/dca2sohp.htm

Civil Records: Access: In person only. Visitors must perform in person searches for themselves. No search fee. Required to search: name, years to search. Civil cases indexed by defendant, plaintiff. Civil records go back to 1800's, civil records on dockets books, computerized records go back to 1999.

Criminal Records: Access: In person only. Visitors must perform in person searches for themselves. No search fee. Required to search: name, years to search. Criminal records on dockets books; computerized records go back to 1999.

General Information: No juvenile, adoption, sexual, mental health or expunged records released. Fax notes: Will not fax results. Copy fee: $.25 per page w/out assistance, $1.00 per page w/assistance. Certification fee: $2.00. Fee payee: Court Clerk. Personal checks accepted. Prepayment is required.

Magistrate Court PO Box 70, Moultrie, GA 31776; 229-616-7450; Fax: 229-616-7494. Hours: 8AM-5PM (EST). *Civil Actions Under $15,000, Eviction, Small Claims.*

Probate Court PO Box 264, Moultrie, GA 31776-0264; 229-616-7415; Fax: 229-616-7489. Hours: 8AM-5PM (EST). *Probate.*

Columbia County

Superior Court PO Box 2930, Evans, GA 30809; 706-541-1139; Fax: 706-541-4013. Hours: 8AM-5PM (EST). *Felony, Misdemeanor, Civil.*

Note: This court is moving from 1954 Appling-Harlem Highway in Appling to 640 Ronald Reagan Dr in Evans, GA 30809 sometime in Fall, 2002. Mail: use PO Box 2930. Phone numbers will remain the same.

Civil Records: Access: In person only. Visitors must perform in person searches for themselves. No search fee. Required to search: name, years to search. Civil cases indexed by plaintiff. Civil records on computer from 1987, prior on docket books.

Criminal Records: Access: In person only. Visitors must perform in person searches for themselves. No search fee. Required to search: name, years to search, DOB; also helpful: SSN, race, sex. Criminal records on computer from 1987, prior on docket books.

General Information: Public access terminal is available. No juvenile, adoption, sexual, mental health or expunged records released. Copy fee: $.25 per page. Certification fee: $2.00 plus $.50 per page. Fee payee: Clerk of Superior Court. Personal checks accepted.

Magistrate Court PO Box 777, Evans, GA 30809; 706-868-3316. Hours: 8AM-5PM (EST). *Civil Actions Under $15,000, Eviction, Small Claims.*

Probate Court PO Box 525, Appling, GA 30802; 706-541-1254; Fax: 706-541-4001. Hours: 8AM-5PM (EST). *Probate.*

Cook County

Superior Court 212 N Hutchinson Ave, Adel, GA 31620; 229-896-7717. Hours: 8:30AM-4:30PM (EST). *Felony, Misdemeanor, Civil.*

Civil Records: Access: Phone, mail, in person. Both court and visitors may perform in person searches. Search fee: $10.00 per name, per five year period. Required to search: name, years to search. Civil cases indexed by defendant. Civil records on dockets books, microfilm.

Criminal Records: Access: Mail, in person. Both court and visitors may perform in person searches. Search fee: $10.00 per name per 5 year period. Required to search: name, years to search, DOB, signed release; also helpful: SSN, race, sex. Criminal records on dockets books, microfilm.

General Information: No juvenile, adoption, sexual, 1st offenders, mental health or expunged records released. SASE not required. Turnaround time same day. Fax notes: Will not fax results. Copy fee: $1.00 per page. Certification fee: $2.50 plus $.50 per page after first. Fee payee: Court Clerk. Business checks accepted. Prepayment is required.

Magistrate Court 1000 County Farm Road, Adel, GA 31620; 229-896-3151. Hours: 8AM-4:30PM (EST). *Civil Actions Under $15,000, Eviction, Small Claims.*

Probate Court 212 N Hutchinson Ave, Adel, GA 31620; 229-896-3941; Fax: 229-896-8063. Hours: 8:30AM-5PM (EST). *Probate, Misdemeanor Traffic.*

Coweta County

Superior Court PO Box 943, 200 Court Square, Newnan, GA 30264; 770-254-2693/2695; Fax: 770-254-3700. Hours: 8AM-5PM (EST). *Felony, Civil.*

Civil Records: Access: Phone, mail, in person. Both court and visitors may perform in person searches. No search fee. Required to search: name, years to search. Civil cases indexed by defendant, plaintiff. Civil records on computer from 1990, dockets books to 1970.

Criminal Records: Access: Phone, mail, in person. Both court and visitors may perform in person searches.

No search fee. Required to search: name, years to search, DOB; also helpful: SSN, race, sex. Criminal records on computer back to 1919. Can only conduct felony searches from 1990 to present.

General Information: Public access terminal is available. No juvenile, adoption, sexual, mental health or expunged records released. Turnaround time 2 days. Copy fee: $.25 per page. Certification fee: $2.50 plus $.50 per page after first. Fee payee: Clerk of Superior & State Court. Business checks accepted. Prepayment is required.

State Court 9A E Broad St, Newnan, GA 30263; 770-254-2699. Hours: 8AM-5PM (EST). *Misdemeanor, Civil.*

Note: This is a new court in new location as of 5/2001.

Civil Records: Access: Phone, in person. Both court and visitors may perform in person searches. Search fee: None, unless records are off-site (pre-1990), fee is $5.00. Required to search: name, years to search. Civil cases indexed by defendant, plaintiff. Civil records on computer from 1990, dockets books to 1970. No real estate; this court handles general civil.

Criminal Records: Access: In person only. Both court and visitors may perform in person searches. Search fee: None, but if records are off-site (pre-1990), fee is $5.00. Required to search: name, years to search, DOB. Criminal records on docket books back to 1919; on computer from 1990. Can only conduct felony searches from 1990 to present.

General Information: Public access terminal is available. No juvenile, adoption, sexual, mental health or expunged records released. Copy fee: $.25 per page. Certification fee: $2.50 plus $.50 per page after first. Fee payee: Clerk of Superior & State Court. Prepayment is required.

Magistrate Court 34 E Broad St, Newnan, GA 30263; 770-254-2610; Fax: 770-254-2606. Hours: 8AM-5PM (EST). *Civil Actions Under $15,000, Eviction, Small Claims.*

Probate Court 22 E Broad St, Newnan, GA 30263; 770-254-2640; Fax: 770-254-2648. Hours: 8AM-5PM (EST). *Probate.*

Crawford County

Superior Court PO Box 1037, Roberta, GA 31058; 478-836-3328. Hours: 9AM-5PM (EST). *Felony, Misdemeanor, Civil.*

Civil Records: Access: In person only. Visitors must perform in person searches for themselves. No search fee. Required to search: name, years to search. Civil cases indexed by defendant, plaintiff. Civil records on dockets books to 1830, records computerized since 1998.

Criminal Records: Access: In person only. Visitors must perform in person searches for themselves. No search fee. Required to search: name, years to search, DOB; also helpful: SSN, race, sex. Criminal records on dockets books to 1830, records computerized since 1998.

General Information: Public access terminal is available. (Access limited to deeds from 01/99 to present.) No juvenile, adoption, sexual, mental health or expunged records released. Copy fee: $.25 per page. Certification fee: $2.50 plus $.50 per page after first. Fee payee: Clerk of Superior Court. Personal checks accepted. Prepayment is required.

Magistrate Court PO Box 568, Roberta, GA 31078; 478-836-5804; Probate phone: 478-836-4439; Fax: 478-836-4340. Hours: 9AM-5PM (EST). *Civil Actions Under $15,000, Eviction, Small Claims.*

Probate Court PO Box 1028, Roberta, GA 31078; 478-836-3313. Hours: 8:30AM-4:30PM (EST). *Probate.* Note: The record search fee is $4.00.

Crisp County

Superior & Juvenile Court PO Box 747, Cordele, GA 31010-0747; 229-276-2616. Hours: 8:30AM-5PM (EST). *Felony, Misdemeanor, Civil Actions Over $15,000.*

Civil Records: Access: Mail, in person. Visitors must perform in person searches for themselves. No search fee. Required to search: name, years to search. Civil cases indexed by defendant. Civil records on docket books to 1905, computerized since 1994.

Criminal Records: Access: Mail, in person. Visitors must perform in person searches for themselves. No search fee. Required to search: name, years to search; also helpful: SSN. Criminal records on docket books to 1905, computerized since 1994.

General Information: Public access terminal is available. No juvenile, adoption, sexual, mental health or expunged records released. SASE required. Turnaround time 1-2 days. Fax notes: Fee to fax results is $2.50 first page, $1.00 each add'l. Copy fee: $.25 per page. Certification fee: $2.00 plus $.50 per page. Fee payee: Clerk of Superior Court. Personal checks accepted. Prepayment is required.

Magistrate Court 210 S 7th St Room 102, Cordese, GA 31015; 229-276-2618. Hours: 8:30AM-5PM (EST). *Civil Actions Under $15,000, Eviction, Small Claims.*

Probate Court 210 S. 7th St, Rm 103, Cordele, GA 31015; 229-276-2621; Fax: 229-273-9184. Hours: 9AM-5PM (EST). *Probate.*

Dade County

Superior Court PO Box 417, Trenton, GA 30752; 706-657-4778; Sm Claims 706-657-4113. Hours: 8:30AM-5PM (EST). *Felony, Misdemeanor, Civil, Eviction, Small Claims.*

www.gsccca.org/clerks

Civil Records: Access: Phone, fax, mail, in person. Both court and visitors may perform in person searches. No search fee. Required to search: name, years to search. Civil cases indexed by defendant, plaintiff. Civil records on computer back to 1/1999; prior on docket books.

Criminal Records: Access: Mail, fax, in person. Both court and visitors may perform in person searches. Search fee: $5.00 per name. Required to search: name, years to search, DOB, signed release. Criminal records on computer back to 1/1999; prior on docket books to 1900's.

General Information: Public access terminal is available. No juvenile, adoption, sexual, mental health or expunged records released. SASE requested. Turnaround time 1 day. Fax notes: Fee to fax results is $1.00 per page. Copy fee: $1.32 per page. Certification fee: $2.00 plus $.50 per page after first. Fee payee: Superior Court. Personal checks accepted. Prepayment is required.

Magistrate Court PO Box 1263, Trenton, GA 30752; 706-657-4113; Fax: 706-657-9618. Hours: 8AM-5PM (EST). *Civil Actions Under $15,000, Eviction, Small Claims.*

Probate Court PO Box 605, Trenton, GA 30752; 706-657-4414; Fax: 706-657-4305. Hours: 8:30AM-5PM (EST). *Probate.*

Dawson County

Superior Court 25 Tucker Ave, #106, Dawsonville, GA 30534; 706-344-3510 X227; Fax: 706-344-3511. Hours: 8AM-5PM (EST). *Felony, Misdemeanor, Civil.*

Civil Records: Access: Phone, mail, fax, in person. Visitors must perform in person searches for

themselves. No search fee. Required to search: name, years to search. Civil cases indexed by plaintiff. Civil records on computer back to 1994, prior in dockets books.

Criminal Records: Access: mail, fax, in person. Visitors must perform in person searches for themselves. No search fee. Required to search: name, years to search, DOB; also helpful: SSN, race, sex. Criminal records on computer back to 1994, prior in dockets books.

General Information: Public access terminal is available. No juvenile, adoption, sexual, mental health or expunged records released. Copy fee: $.25 per page. Certification fee: $2.50. Fee payee: Superior Court. Prepayment is required.

Magistrate Court PO Box 254, Dawsonville, GA 30534; 706-344-3730; Fax: 706-344-3537. Hours: 10AM-8PM M,T; 10AM-2PM W; 8:30AM-5PM F (EST). *Civil Actions Under $15,000, Eviction, Small Claims.*

Probate Court 25 Tucker Ave #211, Dawsonville, GA 30534; 706-344-3580; Fax: 706-265-6155. Hours: 8AM-5PM (EST). *Probate.*

De Kalb County

Superior Court 556 N McDonough St, Decatur, GA 30030; 404-371-2836; Fax: 404-371-2635. Hours: 8:30AM-5PM (EST). *Felony, Misdemeanor, Civil.*

Civil Records: Access: In person only. Visitors must perform in person searches for themselves. No search fee. Required to search: name, years to search. Civil cases indexed by defendant, plaintiff. Civil records on computer from 1988, prior archived.

Criminal Records: Access: In person only. Visitors must perform in person searches for themselves. No search fee. Required to search: name, years to search, DOB; also helpful: SSN, race, sex. Criminal records on computer from 1980, on microfilm from 1947.

General Information: Public access terminal is available. No juvenile, adoption, sexual, mental health or expunged records released. Copy fee: Copies made by the court are $1.00 per page, do it yourself is $.25 per page. Certification fee: $2.50 plus $.50 per page after first. Fee payee: Clerk of Superior Court. Personal checks accepted. Prepayment is required.

State Court 556 N McDonough St, Decatur, GA 30030; 404-371-2261; Fax: 404-371-3064. Hours: 8:30AM-5PM (EST). *Misdemeanor, Civil.*

www.dekalbstatecourt.net

Civil Records: Access: Mail, in person. Visitors must perform in person searches for themselves. No search fee. Required to search: name, years to search. Civil cases indexed by defendant, plaintiff. Civil records on docket books. The court will perform limited searches.

Criminal Records: Access: In person only. Visitors must perform in person searches for themselves. No search fee. Required to search: name. Criminal records on docket books.

General Information: Public access terminal is available. Turnaround time 7 days. Copy fee: $.25 per page. Certification fee: $5.00. Fee payee: Court Clerk. Personal checks accepted. Prepayment is required.

Magistrate Court 807 DeKalb County Courthouse, Decatur, GA 30030; 404-371-4766; Fax: 404-371-2986. Hours: 8:30AM-5PM (EST). *Civil Actions Under $15,000, Eviction, Small Claims.*

Probate Court 103 County Courthouse, 556 N McDonough St, Rm 103, Decatur, GA 30030; 404-371-2718; Fax: 404-371-7055. Hours: 8:30AM-4PM (EST). *Probate.*

www.co.dekalb.ga.us/probate

Decatur County

Superior & State Court PO Box 336, Bainbridge, GA 31718; 229-248-3025. Hours: 9AM-5PM (EST). *Felony, Misdemeanor, Civil.*

Civil Records: Access: In person only. Visitors must perform in person searches for themselves. No search fee. Required to search: name, years to search. Civil cases indexed by defendant, plaintiff. Civil records on docket books from 1823; computerized from 1996.

Criminal Records: Access: In person only. Visitors must perform in person searches for themselves. No search fee. Required to search: name, years to search, DOB; also helpful: SSN, race, sex. Criminal records on docket books from 1823; computerized from 1996.

General Information: Public access terminal is available. No juvenile, adoption, sexual, mental health or expunged records released. Copy fee: $.25 per page. Certification fee: $2.00 plus $.50 per page. Fee payee: Court Clerk. No personal checks accepted.

Magistrate Court 912 Spring Creek Rd Box #3, Bainbridge, GA 31717; 229-248-3014; Fax: 229-248-3862. Hours: 9AM-5PM (EST). *Civil Actions Under $15,000, Eviction, Small Claims.*

Probate Court PO Box 234, Bainbridge, GA 39818; 229-248-3016; Fax: 229-248-3858. Hours: 9AM-5PM (EST). *Probate.*

Note: The ZIP Code changed 7/1/2002.

Dodge County

Superior Court PO Drawer 4276, 5401 Anson Av, Eastman, GA 31023; 478-374-2871. Hours: 9AM-5PM (EST). *Felony, Misdemeanor, Civil.*

Civil Records: Access: In person only. Visitors must perform in person searches for themselves. No search fee. Required to search: name, years to search. Civil cases indexed by defendant. Civil records on docket books.

Criminal Records: Access: In person only. Visitors must perform in person searches for themselves. No search fee. Required to search: name, years to search, DOB, signed release; also helpful: SSN, race, sex. Criminal records on docket books and computer.

General Information: No juvenile, adoption, sexual, mental health or expunged records released. Copy fee: $.25 per page. Certification fee: $2.00 plus $.50 per page after first. Fee payee: Court Clerk. Personal checks accepted. Prepayment is required.

Magistrate Court 5018 Courthouse Circle #202, Eastman, GA 31023; 478-374-7243/8144; Fax: 478-374-5716. Hours: 8:30AM-Noon; 1PM-4:30PM (EST). *Civil Actions Under $15,000, Eviction, Small Claims.*

Probate Court PO Box 514, Eastman, GA 31023; 478-374-3775; Fax: 478-374-9197. Hours: 9AM-Noon, 1-5PM (EST). *Probate.*

Dooly County

Superior Court PO Box 326, Vienna, GA 31092-0326; 229-268-4234; Fax: 229-268-1427. Hours: 8:30AM-5PM (EST). *Felony, Misdemeanor, Civil.*

Civil Records: Access: Fax, mail, in person. Visitors must perform in person searches for themselves. No search fee. Required to search: name, years to search. Civil cases indexed by defendant, plaintiff. Civil records on computer since 1995. Prefer to have public perform searches.

Criminal Records: Access: Fax, mail, in person. Visitors must perform in person searches for themselves. No search fee. Required to search: name, years to search, DOB, signed release; also helpful: SSN, race, sex. Criminal records on computer since 1995, docket books prior to 1857. Prefer to have public to perform searches.

General Information: Public access terminal is available. No juvenile, adoption, sexual, mental health or expunged records released. SASE required. Turnaround time varies. Copy fee: $1.00 per page. Certification fee: $2.50. Fee payee: Dooly County Superior Court Clerk. Personal checks accepted. Prepayment is required.

Magistrate Court PO Box 336, Vienna, GA 31092; 229-268-4324; Fax: 229-268-3585. Hours: 8AM-Noon, 1-5PM (EST). *Civil Actions Under $15,000, Eviction, Small Claims.*

Probate Court PO Box 304, Vienna, GA 31092; 229-268-4217; Fax: 229-268-6142. Hours: 8AM-5PM M,T,Th,F; 8:30AM-Noon W & Sat or by appointment (EST). *Probate.*

Dougherty County

Superior & State Court PO Box 1827, Albany, GA 31702; 229-431-2198. Hours: 8:30AM-5PM (EST). *Felony, Misdemeanor, Civil.*

www.dougherty.ga.us

Civil Records: Access: Online, in person. Visitors must perform in person searches for themselves. No search fee. Required to search: name, years to search. Civil cases indexed by defendant, plaintiff. Civil records on computer from 1992, overall records go back to 1854. Access to civil and criminal court docket data available free at the web site. The same system permits access to probate, tax, deeds, and death certificate records.
Criminal Records: Access: Online, in person. Visitors must perform in person searches for themselves. No search fee. Required to search: name, years to search SSN. Criminal records on computer from 1992, overall records go back to 1854. Online access to criminal records is the same as civil.
General Information: Public access terminal is available. No juvenile, adoption, sexual, mental health or expunged records released. Copy fee: If court makes copy then $1.00, if yourself then $.25. Certification fee: $3.00 first page then $1.00 each additional. Fee payee: Court Clerk. Personal checks accepted. Prepayment is required.

Magistrate Court 225 Pine Ave, Room 308, Albany, GA 31701; 229-431-3216; Fax: 229-434-2692. Hours: 8:30AM-5PM (EST). *Civil Actions Under $15,000, Eviction, Small Claims.*
Note: Online access to court records is available through the county clerk's system at www.dougherty.ga.us.

Probate Court PO Box 1827, Albany, GA 31702; 229-431-2102; Fax: 229-434-2694. Hours: 8:30AM-5PM (EST). *Probate.*

www.albany.ga.us/exec/site/?mid=231&fid=2092

Note: Search the probate court index at www.dougherty.ga.us.

Douglas County

Superior Court Douglas County Courthouse, 8700 Hospital Dr, Douglasville, GA 30134; 770-920-7252. Hours: 8AM-5PM (EST). *Felony, Misdemeanor, Civil.*

Civil Records: Access: In person only. Visitors must perform in person searches for themselves. No search fee. Required to search: name, years to search. Civil cases indexed by defendant, plaintiff. Civil records on computer from 1994, prior on docket books to 1871.
Criminal Records: Access: In person only. Visitors must perform in person searches for themselves. No search fee. Required to search: name, years to search, DOB, signed release; also helpful: address, SSN. Criminal records on computer from 1994, prior on docket books to 1871.
General Information: Public access terminal is available. No juvenile, adoption, sexual, mental health

or expunged records released. Copy fee: $.25 per page. Certification fee: $2.50 plus $.50 per page. Fee payee: Clerk of Superior Court. Personal checks accepted. Prepayment is required.

Magistrate Court 8700 Hospital Dr, Douglasville, GA 30134; 770-920-7215. Hours: 8AM-5PM (EST). *Civil Actions Under $15,000, Eviction, Small Claims.*

Probate Court 8700 Hospital Dr, Douglasville, GA 30134; 770-920-7249; Fax: 770-920-7381. Hours: 8AM-5PM (EST). *Probate.*

Early County

Superior & State Court PO Box 849, Blakely, GA 31723; 229-723-3033; Fax: 229-723-4411. Hours: 8AM-5PM (EST). *Felony, Misdemeanor, Civil.*

Civil Records: Access: In person only. Visitors must perform in person searches for themselves. No search fee. Required to search: name, years to search. Civil cases indexed by defendant, plaintiff. Civil records on dockets.
Criminal Records: Access: In person only. Visitors must perform in person searches for themselves. No search fee. Required to search: name, years to search, DOB; also helpful: SSN, race, sex. Criminal records on dockets.
General Information: No juvenile, adoption, sexual, mental health or expunged records released. Copy fee: $.50 per page. Certification fee: $2.50 plus $.50 per page after first. Fee payee: Court Clerk. Personal checks accepted. Prepayment is required.

Magistrate Court Early County Courthouse, Rm 8, Blakely, GA 31723; 229-723-3454 and 229-723-5492; Fax: 229-723-5246. Hours: 8AM-5PM (EST). *Civil Actions Under $15,000, Eviction, Small Claims.*

Echols County

Superior Court PO Box 213, Statenville, GA 31648; 229-559-5642; Fax: 229-559-5792. Hours: 8AM-Noon, 1-4:30PM. *Felony, Misdemeanor, Civil.*

http://www2.state.ga.us/courts/superior/dca/dca2sohp.htm

Civil Records: Access: In person only. Visitors must perform in person searches for themselves. No search fee. Required to search: name, years to search. Civil cases indexed by defendant, plaintiff. Civil records on dockets books, computerized since 1995.
Criminal Records: Access: In person only. Visitors must perform in person searches for themselves. No search fee. Required to search: name, years to search. Criminal records on dockets books, computerized since 1995.
General Information: No juvenile, adoption, sexual, mental health or expunged records released. Copy fee: $1.00 per page. Certification fee: Certification $2.00 1st page, $.50 each additional page. Fee payee: Court Clerk. Personal checks accepted. Prepayment required.

Magistrate & Probate Court PO Box 118, Statenville, GA 31648; 229-559-7526; Fax: 229-559-5792. Hours: 8:30AM-4:30PM (EST). *Civil Actions Under $15,000, Eviction, Small Claims, Probate.*

Effingham County

Superior & State Court PO Box 387, Springfield, GA 31329; 912-754-2118. Hours: 8:30AM-5PM (EST). *Felony, Misdemeanor, Civil.*

Civil Records: Access: Mail, in person. Both court and visitors may perform in person searches. Search fee: $20.00 per name. Required to search: name, years to search. Civil cases indexed by defendant, plaintiff. Civil records on computer from 1991, dockets books.
Criminal Records: Access: Mail, in person. Both court and visitors may perform in person searches. Search fee: $20.00 per name. Required to search: name, years

to search, DOB; also helpful: SSN, race, sex. Criminal records on computer from 1991, dockets books.
General Information: Public access terminal is available. No juvenile, adoption, sexual, mental health or expunged records released. SASE required. Turnaround time 3-5 days. Copy fee: $.25 per page. Certification fee: $2.50 plus $.50 per page each add'l. Fee payee: Court Clerk. Business checks accepted. Prepayment is required.

Magistrate Court PO Box 819, Springfield, GA 31329; 912-754-2124/29/50; Fax: 912-754-4893. Hours: 8AM-5PM (EST). *Civil Actions Under $15,000, Eviction, Small Claims.*

http://georgiacourts.org/counties/effingham/index.html

Probate Court 901 Pine St, PO Box 387, Springfield, GA 31329; 912-754-2112; Fax: 912-754-3894. Hours: 8:30AM-5PM (EST). *Probate.*

Elbert County

Superior & State Court PO Box 619, Elberton, GA 30635; 706-283-2005; Fax: 706-213-7286. Hours: 8AM-5PM (EST). *Felony, Misdemeanor, Civil.*

Civil Records: Access: In person only. Visitors must perform in person searches for themselves. No search fee. Required to search: name, years to search. Civil cases indexed by defendant, plaintiff. Civil records on computer from 1986 (excluding felonies), dockets books prior.
Criminal Records: Access: In person only. Visitors must perform in person searches for themselves. No search fee. Required to search: name, years to search. Criminal records on computer from 1986 (excluding felonies), dockets books prior.
General Information: Public access terminal is available. No juvenile, adoption, sexual, mental health or expunged records released. Copy fee: $.25 per page. Certification fee: $2.00 plus $.50 per page. Fee payee: Clerk of Court. Personal checks accepted. Prepayment is required.

Magistrate Court PO Box 763, Elberton, GA 30635; 706-283-2027; Fax: 706-283-2004. Hours: 8AM-5PM (EST). *Civil Actions Under $15,000, Eviction, Small Claims.*

Probate Court Elbert County Courthouse, Elberton, GA 30635; 706-283-2016; Fax: 706-283-9668. Hours: 8AM-5PM (EST). *Probate.*

Emanuel County

Superior & State Court PO Box 627, Swainsboro, GA 30401; 478-237-8911; Fax: 478-237-2173. Hours: 8AM-5PM (EST). *Felony, Misdemeanor, Civil.*

Civil Records: Access: In person only. Visitors must perform in person searches for themselves. No search fee. Required to search: name, years to search. Civil cases indexed by defendant, plaintiff. Civil records computerized since 1999, earlier on dockets books.
Criminal Records: Access: In person only. Visitors must perform in person searches for themselves. No search fee. Required to search: name, years to search, DOB; also helpful: SSN, race, sex. Criminal records computerized since 1999, earlier on dockets books.
General Information: No juvenile, adoption, sexual, mental health or expunged records released. Copy fee: $.25 per page. Certification fee: $2.50 plus $.50 per page. Fee payee: Court Clerk. Personal checks accepted. Prepayment is required.

Magistrate Court 107 N Main St, Swainsboro, GA 30401; 478-237-7278; Fax: 478-237-2593. Hours: 8AM-5PM (EST). *Civil Actions Under $15,000, Eviction, Small Claims.*

Probate Court PO Drawer 70, Swainsboro, GA 30401; 478-237-7091; Fax: 478-237-2633. Hours: 8AM-5PM (EST). *Probate.*

Evans County

Superior & State Court PO Box 845, Claxton, GA 30417; 912-739-3868; Fax: 912-739-2504. Hours: 8AM-5PM (EST). *Felony, Misdemeanor, Civil.*

Civil Records: Access: In person only. Visitors must perform in person searches for themselves. No search fee. Required to search: name, years to search. Civil cases indexed by defendant, plaintiff. Civil records on computer from 1989, dockets bookstore 1915.

Criminal Records: Access: In person only. Visitors must perform in person searches for themselves. No search fee. Required to search: name, years to search, DOB; also helpful: SSN, race, sex. Criminal records on computer from 1989, dockets books to 1915.

General Information: Public access terminal is available. No juvenile, adoption, sexual, mental health or expunged records released. Copy fee: $1.00 per page. Certification fee: $2.50 plus $.50 per page after first. Fee payee: Court Clerk. Personal checks accepted. Prepayment is required.

Magistrate Court Courthouse Annex, 7 Freeman St, Claxton, GA 30417; 912-739-3745; Fax: 912-739-8856. Hours: 8AM-5PM (EST). *Civil Actions Under $15,000, Eviction, Small Claims.*

Probate Court 123 W Main St, PO Box 852, Claxton, GA 30417; 912-739-4080; Fax: 912-739-4077. Hours: 8AM-5PM (EST). *Probate.*

Fannin County

Superior Court PO Box 1300, 420 W Main St, Blue Ridge, GA 30513; 706-632-2039. Hours: 9AM-5PM (EST). *Felony, Misdemeanor, Civil.*

http://9thjudicialdistrict-ga.org/dca9apphp.shtml

Civil Records: Access: In person only. Visitors must perform in person searches for themselves. Search fee: No search fee. Required to search: name, years to search. Civil cases indexed by defendant, plaintiff. Civil records on docket books back to the early 1900's.

Criminal Records: Access: In person only. Visitors must perform in person searches for themselves. Search fee: No search fee. Required to search: name, years to search, DOB, signed release; also helpful: SSN, race, sex. Criminal records on docket books back to the early 1900's.

General Information: No juvenile, adoption, sexual, mental health or expunged records released. Copy fee: $.25 per page. $1.00 per page if the court make copies. Certification fee: $2.50 plus $.50 per page after first. Fee payee: Court Clerk. Personal checks accepted. Prepayment is required.

Magistrate Court 420 W Main St, #7, Blue Ridge, GA 30513; 706-632-5558; Fax: 706-632-8236. Hours: 9AM-5PM (EST). *Civil Actions Under $15,000, Eviction, Small Claims, Misdemeanors.*

Probate Court 420 W Main St #2, Blue Ridge, GA 30513; 706-632-3011; Fax: 706-632-7167. Hours: 8AM-5PM (EST). *Probate.*

Fayette County

Superior Court PO Box 130, Fayetteville, GA 30214; 770-461-4703. Hours: 8AM-5PM (EST). *Felony, Misdemeanor, Civil.*

Civil Records: Access: In person only. Visitors must perform in person searches for themselves. No search fee. Required to search: name, years to search. Civil cases indexed by defendant, plaintiff. Civil records on computer since 1989; prior records on dockets books.

Criminal Records: Access: In person only. Visitors must perform in person searches for themselves. No search fee. Required to search: name, years to search, DOB; also helpful: SSN, race, sex. Criminal records on computer since 1989; prior records on dockets books.

General Information: Public access terminal is available. No juvenile, adoption, sexual, mental health or expunged records released. Copy fee: $.25 per page. Certification fee: $2.00 plus $.50 per page after first. Fee payee: Court Clerk. Only cashiers checks and money orders accepted.

Magistrate Court PO Box 1076, Fayetteville, GA 30214; 770-461-4703. Hours: 8AM-5PM (EST). *Civil Actions Under $15,000, Eviction, Small Claims.*

Probate Court 145 Johnson Ave, Fayetteville, GA 30214; 770-461-9555 x2430; Fax: 770-460-8685. Hours: 8AM-5PM (EST). *Probate.*

Floyd County

Superior Court PO Box 1110, #3 Government Plaza #101, Rome, GA 30163; 706-291-5190; Fax: 706-233-0035. Hours: 8AM-5PM (EST). *Felony, Misdemeanor, Civil.*

www.floydsuperiorcourt.org

Civil Records: Access: Phone, in person. Visitors must perform in person searches for themselves. No search fee. Required to search: name, years to search. Civil cases indexed by defendant, plaintiff. Civil records on computer since 11/95; prior on docket books to 1833. The court will only do a name search to determine if a case exists, then provides a case number.

Criminal Records: Access: Fax, mail, in person. Both court and visitors may perform in person searches. No search fee. Required to search: name, years to search, signed release. Criminal records on computer since 11/95; prior on docket books back to 1833. The court will only do a name search to determine if a case exists, then provides a case number.

General Information: Public access terminal is available. No juvenile, adoption, sexual, mental health or expunged records released. Fax notes: $.50 per page. Copy fee: $.50 per page. Certification fee: $2.00 plus copy fee. Fee payee: Court Clerk. Personal checks accepted. Prepayment is required.

Magistrate Court 3 Government Plaza, Rm 227, 410 Tribute St, Rm 227, Rome, GA 30161; 706-291-5250; Fax: 706-291-5269. Hours: 8:45AM-4:45PM (EST). *Civil Actions Under $15,000, Eviction, Small Claims.*

Probate Court 3 Government Plaza #201, County Administrative Offices, Rome, GA 30162; 706-291-5138; Fax: 706-291-5189. Hours: 8AM-4:30PM (EST). *Probate.*

Forsyth County

Superior & State Court 100 Courthouse Square, Rm 010, Cumming, GA 30040; 770-781-2120. Hours: 8:30AM-5PM (EST). *Felony, Misdemeanor, Civil, Eviction, Small Claims.*

Civil Records: Access: In person only. Visitors must perform in person searches for themselves. No search fee. Required to search: name, years to search. Civil cases indexed by defendant. Civil records on computer since 1996; prior records on docket books back to 1832.

Criminal Records: Access: In person only. Visitors must perform in person searches for themselves. No search fee. Required to search: name, years to search; also helpful: SSN. Criminal records on computer since late 1989.

General Information: Public access terminal is available. No juvenile, adoption, sexual, mental health or expunged records released. Copy fee: $.25 per page. Certification fee: $2.50 plus $.50 per page after first.

Fee payee: Court Clerk. Personal checks accepted. Prepayment is required.

Magistrate Court 121 Dahlonega St, Cumming, GA 30040; 770-781-2211; Fax: 770-844-7581. Hours: 8AM-5PM (EST). *Civil Actions Under $15,000, Eviction, Small Claims, Probate.*

Probate Court County Courthouse Annex, Rm 101, 112 W Maple St, Cumming, GA 30130; 770-781-2140; Fax: 770-886-2839. Hours: 8:30AM-5PM (EST). *Probate.*

Franklin County

Superior Court PO Box 70, Carnesville, GA 30521; 706-384-2514. Hours: 8AM-5PM (EST). *Felony, Misdemeanor, Civil.*

Civil Records: Access: In person only. Visitors must perform in person searches for themselves. No search fee. Required to search: name, years to search. Civil cases indexed by defendant, plaintiff. Civil records on computer since 1995; prior records on docket books.

Criminal Records: Access: In person only. Visitors must perform in person searches for themselves. No search fee. Required to search: name, years to search, DOB; also helpful: SSN, race, sex. Criminal records on computer since 1995; prior records on docket books.

General Information: Public access terminal is available. No juvenile, adoption, sexual, mental health or expunged records released. Copy fee: $.25 per page. Certification fee: $2.50 and $.50 each add'l page. Fee payee: Court Clerk. Personal checks accepted. Prepayment is required.

Magistrate Court PO Box 467, Carnesville, GA 30521; 706-384-7473; Fax: 706-384-4346. Hours: 8AM-5PM (EST). *Civil Actions Under $15,000, Eviction, Small Claims.*

Probate Court PO Box 207, Carnesville, GA 30521; 706-384-2403; Fax: 706-384-2636. Hours: 8AM-5:00PM (EST). *Probate.*

Fulton County

Superior Court 136 Pryor St SW, Rm C-155, Superior Court Clerk, Atlanta, GA 30303; Civil phone: 404-730-5344; Fax: 404-302-3430. Hours: 8:30AM-5PM (EST). *Civil.*

www.fcclk.org

Civil Records: Access: In person only. Both court and visitors may perform in person searches. No search fee. Required to search: name, years to search. Civil cases indexed by defendant, plaintiff. Civil records on computer since 1972.

General Information: Public access terminal is available. No juvenile, adoption, sexual, mental health, sealed or expunged records released. Copy fee: $.25 per page. Certification fee: $2.50 for 1st page; $.50 each add'l. Fee payee: Court Clerk. Personal checks accepted. Prepayment is required.

Superior Court 136 Pryor St SW, Rm C-515, Superior Court Clerk, Atlanta, GA 30303; Criminal phone: 404-730-5242; Fax: 404-730-7993. Hours: 8:30AM-5PM (EST). *Felony, Misdemeanor, Eviction.*

www.fcclk.org

Criminal Records: Access: In person only. Visitors must perform in person searches for themselves. No search fee. Required to search: name, years to search, DOB, signed release; also helpful: SSN, race, sex. Criminal records on computer from 1973.

General Information: Public access terminal is available. No juvenile, adoption, sexual, mental health, sealed or expunged records released. Copy fee: $.25 per page. Certification fee: $2.50 for 1st page; $.50 each add'l. Fee payee: Court Clerk. Personal checks accepted. Prepayment is required.

State Court TG100 Justice Center Tower, 185 Central Ave SW, Atlanta, GA 30303; 404-730-5000; Fax: 404-730-8141 Civil; 335-3521 Criminal. Hours: 8:30AM-5PM (EST). *Misdemeanor, Civil.*

www.fultonstatecourt.com/

Civil Records: Access: In person only. Both the court and visitors may perform in person searches. Search fee: $15.00 if court performs search. Civil cases indexed by defendant, plaintiff. Civil records on computer from 1984, books back to 1982.

Criminal Records: Access: In person only. Both the court and visitors may perform in person searches. Search fee: $15.00 if court performs search. Required to search: name, years to search, DOB, signed release; also helpful: approximate date of arrest, SSN, race, aliases, sex. Criminal records on computer from 1984, books back to 1982.

General Information: Public access terminal is available. No juvenile, adoption, sexual, mental health or expunged records released. Copy fee: $.25 per page. Certification fee: $2.50 per page. Fee payee: Court Clerk. Business checks accepted. Prepayment is required.

Magistrate Court 185 Central Ave SE, TG-400, Justice Center Tower, Atlanta, GA 30303; 404-730-4552; Civil phone: 404-730-5045; Criminal phone: 404-730-4752; Fax: 404-893-2683. Hours: 8:30AM-5PM (EST). *Civil Actions Under $15,000, Eviction, Small Claims.*

Probate Court 185 Central Ave. SW, T2705 Justice Ctr Tower, Atlanta, GA 30303; 404-730-4690; Fax: 404-730-7998. Hours: 8:30AM-5PM (EST). *Probate.*

Gilmer County

Superior Court #1 Westside Square, Ellijay, GA 30540; 706-635-4462; Fax: 706-635-1462. Hours: 8:30AM-5PM (EST). *Felony, Misdemeanor, Civil.*

http://9thjudicialdistrict-ga.org/dca9apphp.shtml

Civil Records: Access: In person only. Visitors must perform in person searches for themselves. No search fee. Required to search: name, years to search. Civil cases indexed by defendant, plaintiff. Civil records on docket books computerized records since 1994.

Criminal Records: Access: In person only. Visitors must perform in person searches for themselves. No search fee. Required to search: name, years to search, signed release; also helpful: DOB, SSN. Criminal records on docket books; computerized since 1994.

General Information: Public access terminal is available. No juvenile, adoption, sealed, sexual, mental health, expunged or sealed records released. Copy fee: $.25 per page. Certification fee: $2.50 plus $.50 per page after first. Fee payee: Superior Court Clerk. Personal checks accepted. Prepayment is required.

Magistrate Court #1 Westside Square, Ellijay, GA 30540; 706-635-2515; Fax: 706-635-7756. Hours: 8:30AM-5PM (EST). *Civil Actions Under $15,000, Eviction, Small Claims.*

Probate Court One Westside Square, Ellijay, GA 30540; 706-635-4763; Fax: 706-635-4761. Hours: 8:30AM-5PM (EST). *Probate.*

Glascock County

Superior Court PO Box 231, 62 E Main St, Gibson, GA 30810; 706-598-2084; Fax: 706-598-2577. Hours: 8AM-Noon, 1-5PM (EST). *Felony, Misdemeanor, Civil.*

Civil Records: Access: In person only. Visitors must perform in person searches for themselves. No search fee. Required to search: name, years to search. Civil

cases indexed by defendant, plaintiff. Civil records on computer from 1991, records go back to 1990.

Criminal Records: Access: In person only. Visitors must perform in person searches for themselves. No search fee. Required to search: name, years to search, DOB; also helpful: SSN, race, sex. Criminal records on computer from 1991 records go back to 1990.

General Information: Public access terminal is available. (Public Access in county cases only) No juvenile, adoption, sexual, mental health or expunged records released. Copy fee: $.25 per page. Legal size copies $1.00 per page. Certification fee: $2.50 plus $.150 per page after first. Fee payee: Court Clerk. Personal checks accepted. Prepayment is required.

Magistrate Court PO Box 201, Gibson, GA 30810; 706-598-2013. Hours: 4-8PM T; 9AM-1PM W & Sat (EST). *Civil Actions Under $15,000, Eviction, Small Claims.*

Probate Court PO Box 64, Gibson, GA 30810; 706-598-3241. 8AM-Noon, 1-5PM (EST). *Probate.*

Glynn County

Superior Court PO Box 1355, Brunswick, GA 31521; 912-554-7272; Fax: 912-267-5625. Hours: 8AM-5PM (EST). *Felony, Civil.*

Civil Records: Access: Phone, fax, mail, in person. Both court and visitors may perform in person searches. No search fee. Required to search: name, years to search. Civil cases indexed by defendant, plaintiff. Civil records on computer back to 1987, archived and in docket books from 1800's.

Criminal Records: Access: Phone, fax, mail, in person. Both court and visitors may perform in person searches. No search fee. Required to search: name, years to search, DOB, signed release; also helpful: SSN, race, sex. Criminal records on computer back to 1987, index back to 1800's.

General Information: No juvenile, adoption, sexual, mental health or expunged records released. SASE requested. Turnaround time 1-3 days. Fax notes: Fee to fax results is $5.00 per document. Copy fee: $.25 per page. If court does copy, fee is $1.00 per page. Certification fee: $2.50 plus $.50 per page after first. Fee payee: Court Clerk. Personal checks accepted. Will bill copy & certification fees.

State Court 701 "H" St. #104, Brunswick, GA 31520; 912-554-7325; Fax: 912-261-3849. Hours: 9AM-5PM (EST). *Misdemeanor, Civil.*

Civil Records: Access: In person only. Visitors must perform in person searches for themselves. No search fee. Required to search: name, years to search. Civil cases indexed by defendant. Civil records on dockets books to 1980; on computer back to 1994.

Criminal Records: Access: In person only. Visitors must perform in person searches for themselves. No search fee. Required to search: name, years to search. Criminal records on dockets books to 1979; on computer back to 1994.

General Information: Public access terminal is available. No juvenile, adoption, sexual, mental health or expunged records released. Copy fee: $.25 per page. Certification fee: $2.00 plus $.50 per page. Fee payee: Clerk of State Court. Only cashiers checks and money orders accepted. Prepayment is required.

Magistrate Court PO Box 1355, Brunswick, GA 31521; 912-554-7250. Hours: 8:30AM-5PM (EST). *Civil Actions Under $15,000, Eviction, Small Claims.*

Probate Court 701 H St, Box 302, Brunswick, GA 31520; 912-554-7231; Fax: 912-466-8001. Hours: 8:30AM-5PM (EST). *Probate, Civil, Small Claims.*

www.glynncounty.org

Gordon County

Superior Court 100 Wall St #102, Calhoun, GA 30701; 706-629-9533; Fax: 706-629-2139. Hours: 8:30AM-5PM (EST). *Felony, Misdemeanor, Civil.*

Civil Records: Access: Fax, mail, in person. Both court and visitors may perform in person searches. No search fee. Required to search: name, years to search. Civil cases indexed by defendant, plaintiff. Civil records on computer since 03/97; prior records on docket books.

Criminal Records: Access: Fax, mail, in person. Both court and visitors may perform in person searches. No search fee. Required to search: name, years to search. Criminal records on computer since 03/97; prior records on docket books.

General Information: No sealed records released. SASE required. Turnaround time 1-2 days. Copy fee: $1.00 per page. Certification fee: $2.50 plus $.50 per page after first. Fee payee: Superior Court Clerk. Personal checks accepted. Prepayment is required.

Magistrate Court PO Box 1025, 100 Wall St, Calhoun, GA 30703; 706-629-6818 X121/122/143/144; Fax: 706-602-1751. Hours: 8:30AM-5PM (EST). *Civil Actions Under $15,000, Eviction, Small Claims.*

Probate Court PO Box 669, Calhoun, GA 30703; 706-629-7314; Fax: 706-629-4698. Hours: 8:30AM-5PM (EST). *Probate.*

Grady County

Superior Court 250 N Broad St, Box 8, Cairo, GA 31728; 229-377-2912. Hours: 8AM-5PM (EST). *Felony, Misdemeanor, Civil.*

Civil Records: Access: In person only. Court will assist visitors with searches. No search fee. Required to search: name, years to search. Civil cases indexed by defendant, plaintiff. Civil records on computer since 1993; prior records on docket books.

Criminal Records: Access: In person only. Court will assist visitors with searches. No search fee. Required to search: name, years to search. Criminal records on computer since 1993; prior records on docket books.

General Information: Public access terminal is available. No juvenile or adoption records released. Copy fee: $.25 per page. Certification fee: $2.00 plus $.50 per page. Fee payee: Superior Court Clerk. Personal checks accepted. Prepayment is required.

Magistrate Court 250 N Broad St, Box 2, Cairo, GA 31728; 229-377-4132; Fax: 229-377-4127. Hours: 8AM-5PM (EST). *Civil Actions Under $15,000, Eviction, Small Claims.*

Probate Court Courthouse, 250 N Broad St, Box 1, Cairo, GA 31728; 229-377-4621; Fax: 229-377-4127. Hours: 8AM-5PM (EST). *Probate.*

Greene County

Superior & Juvenile Court 113 North Main St, #109, Greensboro, GA 30642; 706-453-3340; Fax: 706-453-9179. Hours: 8AM-5PM (EST). *Felony, Misdemeanor, Civil, Eviction, Small Claims.*

Civil Records: Access: In person only. Visitors must perform in person searches for themselves. No search fee. Required to search: name, years to search. Civil cases indexed by defendant, plaintiff. Overall records go back to 1700. Computerized records go back to 2000.

Criminal Records: Access: In person only. Visitors must perform in person searches for themselves. No search fee. Required to search: name, years to search; also helpful: SSN. Overall records go back to 1700. Computerized records go back to 2000.

General Information: No juvenile or adoption records released. Fax notes: Fax back fee $1.00 per page. Copy fee: $.25 per page. Certification fee: Fee is $2.50 plus

$.25 per page. Fee payee: Superior Court Clerk. Personal checks accepted. Prepayment is required.

Magistrate & Probate Court 113 N Main St #113, Greensboro, GA 30642; 706-453-3346; Fax: 706-453-7649. Hours: 8AM-5PM (EST). *Civil Actions Under $15,000, Eviction, Small Claims, Probate.*

Gwinnett County

Superior & State Court PO Box 880 (75 Langley Dr.), Lawrenceville, GA 30046; 770-822-8100. Hours: 8AM-5PM (EST). *Felony, Misdemeanor, Civil, Eviction, Small Claims.*

www.gwinnettcourts.com/courts/Supcourt.htm

Civil Records: Access: Online, in person. Visitors must perform in person searches for themselves. No search fee. Required to search: name, years to search. Civil cases indexed by defendant, plaintiff. Civil records on computer from 1990, prior records on card index. Online access to court case party index is available free online at www.gwinnettcourts.com/misc/casendx.htm. Search by name or case number.

Criminal Records: Access: Online, in person. Visitors must perform in person searches for themselves. No search fee. Required to search: name, years to search. Criminal records on computer from 1990, prior records on card index. Online access to criminal records is the same as civil.

General Information: Public access terminal is available. No sealed records released. Copy fee: $.25 per page. Certification fee: $2.50 plus $.50 per page. Fee payee: Superior Court Clerk. Personal checks accepted. Prepayment is required.

Magistrate Court 75 Langley Dr, Justice & Admin. Ctr., Lawrenceville, GA 30045-6900; 770-822-8080; Fax: 770-822-8075. Hours: 8AM-5PM (EST). *Civil Actions Under $15,000, Eviction, Small Claims.*

www.gwinnettcourts.com/courts/Magcourt.htm

Probate Court 75 Langley Dr, Justice & Admin. Ctr, Lawrenceville, GA 30045; 770-822-8250; Fax: 770-822-8267. 8:30AM-4:30PM (EST). *Probate.*

www.gwinnettcourts.com/courts/Procourt.htm

Note: Search records by name for free at the web site; click on "Data Search."

Habersham County

Superior & State Court 555 Monroe St, Unit 35, Clarkesville, GA 30523; 706-754-2923. Hours: 8AM-5PM (EST). *Felony, Misdemeanor, Civil.*

Civil Records: Access: In person only. Visitors must perform in person searches for themselves. No search fee. Required to search: name, years to search. Civil cases indexed by defendant, plaintiff. Civil records on index books from 1819.

Criminal Records: Access: In person only. Visitors must perform in person searches for themselves. No search fee. Required to search: name, years to search. Criminal records on index books from 1819.

General Information: Public access terminal is available. No juvenile, adoption, sexual, mental health or expunged records released. Copy fee: $.25 per page. Fee payee: Court Clerk. Personal checks accepted. Prepayment is required.

Magistrate Court PO Box 580, Clarkesville, GA 30523; Civil phone: 706-754-4871; Criminal phone: 706-754-0126. Hours: 8AM-5PM (EST). *Civil Actions Under $15,000, Eviction, Small Claims.*

Probate Court Habersham County Courthouse, PO Box 625, Clarkesville, GA 30523; 706-754-2013; Fax: 706-754-5093. Hours: 8AM-5PM (EST). *Probate.*

Hall County

Superior & State Court PO Box 1336, Gainesville, GA 30503; 770-531-7025; Fax: 770-531-7070; 536-0702 real estate. Hours: 8AM-5PM (EST). *Felony, Misdemeanor, Civil.*

Civil Records: Access: In person only. Visitors must perform in person searches for themselves. No search fee. Required to search: name, years to search. Civil cases indexed by defendant, plaintiff. Civil records on computer back to 1989, dockets books from late 1900s.

Criminal Records: Access: In person only. Visitors must perform in person searches for themselves. No search fee. Required to search: name, years to search. Criminal records on computer back to 1989, dockets books from late 1900s.

General Information: No juvenile, adoption, sexual, mental health or expunged records released. Fax notes: Fee to fax results is $1.00 per page. Copy fee: $1.00 per page. Certification fee: $2.00 plus $.50 per page. Fee payee: Court Clerk. Personal checks accepted. Prepayment is required.

Magistrate Court PO Box 1435, Gainesville, GA 30503; 770-531-6912; Fax: 770-531-6917. Hours: 8AM-5PM (EST). *Civil Actions Under $15,000, Eviction, Small Claims, Misdemeanors.*

www.hallcounty.org/clerk.asp

Probate Court Hall County Courthouse, Rm 123, 116 Spring St, Gainesville, GA 30501; 770-531-6923; Fax: 770-531-4946. Hours: 8AM-5PM (EST). *Probate.*

www.hallcounty.org/clerk.asp

Note: The search fee is $4.00 per record

Hancock County

Superior Court PO Box 451, Courthouse Square, Sparta, GA 31087; 706-444-6644; Fax: 706-444-6221. Hours: 8AM-5PM, 8AM-Noon Th (EST). *Felony, Misdemeanor, Civil.*

Civil Records: Access: Mail, in person. Both court and visitors may perform in person searches. Search fee: $5.00 per name. Required to search: name, years to search. Civil cases indexed by defendant, plaintiff. Civil records on docket books from 1991.

Criminal Records: Access: Mail, in person. Both court and visitors may perform in person searches. Search fee: $5.00 per name. Required to search: name, years to search, DOB, signed release; also helpful: SSN, race, sex. Criminal records on books since 1991.

General Information: Public access terminal is available. (Includes deeds, UCCs and notary publics only.) No juvenile, adoptions, sealed, sexual, mental health or expunged records released. SASE required. Turnaround time 1 week. Copy fee: $.25 per page. Certification fee: First page is $2.50, each add'l is $.50. Fee payee: Clerk of Superior Court. Personal checks accepted. Prepayment is required.

Magistrate Court 601 Courthouse Square, Sparta, GA 31087; 706-444-6234; Fax: 706-444-6221. Hours: 9AM-5PM (EST). *Civil Actions Under $15,000, Eviction, Small Claims.*

Probate Court 601 Court St, Sparta, GA 31087; 706-444-5343; Fax: 706-444-8024. Hours: 8AM-5PM M-W & F; 8AM-Noon Th (EST). *Probate.*

Haralson County

Superior Court Drawer 849, 4485 Georgia Hwy 120, Buchanan, GA 30113; 770-646-2005; Fax: 770-646-2035. Hours: 8:30AM-5PM (EST). *Felony, Misdemeanor, Civil.*

Civil Records: Access: Mail, in person. Both court and visitors may perform in person searches. No search fee. Required to search: name, years to search. Civil cases

indexed by defendant, plaintiff. Civil records on dockets books from the 1800s.

Criminal Records: Access: Mail, in person. Both court and visitors may perform in person searches. No search fee. Required to search: name, years to search, signed release. Criminal records on dockets books from the 1800s.

General Information: No juvenile, adoption, sexual, mental health or expunged records released. SASE required. Turnaround time 1 wk. Copy fee: $.25 per page. Certification fee: $2.50 plus $.50 per page after first. Fee payee: Clerk of Superior Court. Personal checks accepted. Prepayment is required.

Magistrate Court PO Box 1040, Buchanan, GA 30113; 770-646-2015; Fax: 770-646-12017. Hours: 8:30AM-5PM (EST). *Civil Actions Under $15,000, Eviction, Small Claims.*

Probate Court PO Box 620, Buchanan, GA 30113; 770-646-2008; Fax: 770-646-3419. Hours: 8:30AM-5PM (EST). *Probate.*

Harris County

Superior Court PO Box 528, Hamilton, GA 31811; 706-628-4944; Fax: 706-628-7039. Hours: 8AM-5PM (EST). *Felony, Misdemeanor, Civil.*

Civil Records: Access: In person only. Visitors must perform in person searches for themselves. No search fee. Required to search: name, years to search. Civil cases indexed by defendant, plaintiff. Civil records on dockets books from 1900; on computer back to 1999.

Criminal Records: Access: In person only. Visitors must perform in person searches for themselves. No search fee. Required to search: name, years to search, DOB; also helpful: race, sex. Criminal records on dockets books from 1900; on computer back to 1999.

General Information: Juvenile, adoption, sexual, mental health or expunged records are only released with a signed release. Copy fee: $.25 per page. Certification fee: $2.50 plus $.50 per page after first. Fee payee: Court Clerk. No personal checks accepted. Prepayment is required.

Magistrate Court PO Box 347, Hamilton, GA 31811; 706-628-4977; Fax: 706-628-5416. Hours: 8AM-5PM (EST). *Civil Actions Under $15,000, Eviction, Small Claims.*

Probate Court PO Box 569, Hamilton, GA 31811; 706-628-5038; Fax: 706-628-7322. Hours: 8AM-Noon, 1-5PM (EST). *Probate.*

Hart County

Superior Court PO Box 386, Hartwell, GA 30643; 706-376-7189; Fax: 706-376-1277. Hours: 8:30AM-5PM (EST). *Felony, Misdemeanor, Civil.*

Civil Records: Access: In person only. Visitors must perform in person searches for themselves. No search fee. Required to search: name, years to search. Civil cases indexed by defendant, plaintiff. Civil records on computer back to 1991, dockets books from 1853.

Criminal Records: Access: In person only. Visitors must perform in person searches for themselves. No search fee. Required to search: name, years to search, DOB; also helpful: SSN, race, sex. Criminal records on computer back to 1991, dockets books from 1853.

General Information: Public access terminal is available. No juvenile, adoption, sexual, mental health or expunged records released. Copy fee: $.25 per page. Certification fee: $2.50 plus $.50 per page after first. Fee payee: Clerk of Court. Personal checks accepted. Prepayment is required.

Magistrate Court PO Box 698, Hartwell, GA 30643; 706-376-6817; Fax: 706-376-6821. Hours: 8:30AM-5PM (EST). *Civil Actions Under $15,000, Eviction, Small Claims.*

Probate Court PO Box 1159, Hartwell, GA 30643; 706-376-2565; Fax: 706-376-9032. Hours: 8:30AM-5PM (EST). *Probate.*

Heard County

Superior Court PO Box 249, Franklin, GA 30217; 706-675-3301. Hours: 8:30AM-5PM (EST). *Felony, Misdemeanor, Civil.*

Civil Records: Access: In person only. Visitors must perform in person searches for themselves. No search fee. Required to search: name, years to search. Civil cases indexed by defendant, plaintiff. Civil records on docket books from 1800s.
Criminal Records: Access: In person only. Visitors must perform in person searches for themselves. No search fee. Required to search: name, years to search, DOB, signed release; also helpful: SSN, race, sex. Criminal records on docket books from 1800s.
General Information: No juvenile, adoptions, sealed, sexual, mental health or expunged records released. Copy fee: $.25 per page. Certification fee: $2.50 plus $.50 per page after first. Fee payee: Court Clerk. Personal checks accepted. Prepayment is required.

Magistrate Court PO Box 395, Franklin, GA 30217; 706-675-3002; Fax: 706-675-0819. Hours: 8:30AM-5PM (EST). *Civil Actions Under $15,000, Eviction, Small Claims.*

Probate Court PO Box 478, Franklin, GA 30217; 706-675-3353; Fax: 706-675-0819. Hours: 8:30AM-5PM (EST). *Probate.*

Henry County

Superior Court One Courthouse Square, McDonough, GA 30253; 770-954-2121. Hours: 8AM-5PM (EST). *Felony, Misdemeanor, Civil.*

Civil Records: Access: Phone, mail, in person. Visitors must perform in person searches for themselves. No search fee. Required to search: name, years to search. Civil cases indexed by defendant, plaintiff. Civil records on dockets books from 1800s.
Criminal Records: Access: Phone, mail, in person. Visitors must perform in person searches for themselves. No search fee. Required to search: name, years to search, DOB, signed release; also helpful: SSN, race, sex. Criminal records on dockets books from 1800s.
General Information: No juvenile, adoption, sexual, mental health or expunged records released. Fax notes: No fee to fax results. Copy fee: $.25 per page. Certification fee: $2.50 plus $.50 per page thereafter. Fee payee: Clerk of Superior Court. Personal checks accepted. Prepayment is required.

Magistrate Court 30 Atlanta St, McDonough, GA 30253; 770-954-2111; Fax: 770-957-2144. Hours: 8AM-5PM (EST). *Civil Actions Under $15,000, Eviction, Small Claims.*

Probate Court 20 Lawrenceville St, McDonough, GA 30253; 770-954-2303; Fax: 770-954-2308. Hours: 8AM-5PM (EST). *Probate.*

Houston County

Superior Court 800 Carroll St, Perry, GA 31069; 478-987-2170; Fax: 478-987-3252. Hours: 8:30AM-5PM (EST). *Felony, Misdemeanor, Civil.*

Civil Records: Access: Phone, fax, mail, in person. Both court and visitors may perform in person searches. No search fee. Required to search: name, years to search. Civil cases indexed by defendant, plaintiff. Civil records on computer from 1984, dockets books back to 1823.
Criminal Records: Access: Fax, mail, in person. Both court and visitors may perform in person searches. No

search fee. Required to search: name, years to search, DOB; also helpful: SSN, race, sex. Criminal records on computer from 1984, dockets books back to 1823.
General Information: Public access terminal is available. No juvenile, adoption, mental health or expunged records released. Turnaround time 1-2 days. Copy fee: $.25 per page. Certification fee: $2.50 plus $.50 per page after first. Fee payee: Court Clerk. Personal checks accepted. Prepayment is required.

State Court 202 Carl Vinson Pkwy, Warner Robins, GA 31088; 478-542-2105; Fax: 478-542-2077. Hours: 8AM-5PM (EST). *Misdemeanor, Civil.*

Civil Records: Access: Mail, fax, in person. Both court and visitors may perform in person searches. No search fee. Required to search: name, years to search. Civil cases indexed by defendant. Civil records on computer from 1987, dockets books from 1965.
Criminal Records: Access: Mail, fax, in person. Both court and visitors may perform in person searches. No search fee. Required to search: name, years to search, DOB; also helpful: SSN, race, sex. Criminal records on computer from 1987, dockets books from 1965.
General Information: No juvenile, adoption, sexual, mental health or expunged records released. SASE requested. Turnaround time 1 week. Copy fee: $.25 per page. Certification fee: $2.50 plus $.50 per page after first. Fee payee: Court Clerk. Only cashiers checks and money orders accepted. Prepayment is required.

Magistrate Court 89 Cohen Walker Dr, Warner Robins, GA 31088; 478-987-4695; Fax: 478-987-5249. Hours: 8AM-5PM (EST). *Civil Actions Under $15,000, Eviction, Small Claims.*

http://georgiacourts.org/magistrate/houston

Probate Court PO Box 1801, Perry, GA 31069; 478-987-2770; Fax: 478-988-4511. Hours: 8AM-4PM (EST). *Probate.*

www.courts.state.wi.us

Irwin County

Superior Court 113 N Irwin Ave, Ocilla, GA 31774; 229-468-5356. Hours: 8AM-5PM (EST). *Felony, Misdemeanor, Civil.*

Civil Records: Access: Phone, mail, in person. Court does not perform in person searches; visitors must perform searches for themselves. No search fee. Required to search: name, years to search. Civil cases indexed by defendant, plaintiff. Civil records on dockets books from 1870s, records are not computerized. Court will not do general record searches, the specific case file must be given.
Criminal Records: Access: Phone, mail, in person. Court does not perform in person searches; visitors must perform searches for themselves. No search fee. Required to search: name, years to search, DOB, signed release; also helpful: SSN, race, sex. Criminal records on dockets books from 1900, records are not computerized. Court will not do general record searches, the specific case file must be given.
General Information: No juvenile, adoption, sexual, mental health or expunged records released. Turnaround time 2 days. Copy fee: $1.00 for first page, $.25 each add'l. Certification fee: $2.50 plus $.50 per page after first. Fee payee: Court Clerk. Personal checks accepted. Prepayment is required.

Magistrate Court 207 S Irwin Ave # 3, Ocilla, GA 31774; 229-468-7671; Fax: 229-468-9672. Hours: 8AM-5PM (EST). *Civil Actions Under $15,000, Eviction, Small Claims.*

Probate Court 202 S Irwin St, Ocilla, GA 31774; 229-468-5138; Fax: 229-468-5702. Hours: 8AM-5PM (EST). *Probate.*

Jackson County

Superior & State Court PO Box 7, Jefferson, GA 30549; 706-367-6360; Fax: 706-367-2468. Hours: 8AM-5PM (EST). *Felony, Misdemeanor, Civil.*

Civil Records: Access: In person only. Visitors must perform in person searches for themselves. No search fee. Required to search: name, years to search. Civil cases indexed by defendant, plaintiff. Civil records on computer from 1992, on dockets books from 1800s.
Criminal Records: Access: In person only. Visitors must perform in person searches for themselves. No search fee. Required to search: name, years to search, DOB; also helpful: SSN, race, sex. Criminal records on computer from 1992, on dockets books from 1800s.
General Information: Public access terminal is available. No juvenile, adoption, sexual, mental health or expunged records released. Copy fee: $.25 per page. Certification fee: $2.50 plus $.50 per page after first. Fee payee: Court Clerk. Personal checks accepted. Prepayment is required.

Magistrate Court PO Box 751, Commerce, GA 30529; 706-335-6545; Fax: 706-335-5221. Hours: 8AM-5PM (EST). *Civil Actions Under $15,000, Eviction, Small Claims.*

Probate Court 85 Washington St, Jefferson, GA 30549; 706-367-6366; Fax: 706-367-2468. Hours: 8:00AM-5PM (EST). *Probate.*

Jasper County

Superior Court 126 W Green Street, #200, Monticello, GA 31064; 706-468-4901; Fax: 706-468-4946. Hours: 8AM-5PM (EST). *Felony, Misdemeanor, Civil.*

Civil Records: Access: In person only. Visitors must perform in person searches for themselves. No search fee. Required to search: name, years to search. Civil cases indexed by defendant, plaintiff. Civil records on computer from 1990, dockets books from 1807.
Criminal Records: Access: In person only. Visitors must perform in person searches for themselves. No search fee. Required to search: name, years to search, DOB; also helpful: SSN, race, sex. Criminal records on computer from 1990, dockets books from 1807.
General Information: No juvenile, adoption, sexual, mental health or expunged records released. Copy fee: $.25 per page. Certification fee: $2.50 plus $.50 per page after first. Fee payee: Court Clerk. Personal checks accepted.

Magistrate Court 126 W Green St #200, Monticello, GA 31064; 706-468-4909; Fax: 706-468-4946. Hours: 8:30AM-4:30PM (EST). *Civil Actions Under $15,000, Eviction, Small Claims.*

Probate Court Jasper County Courthouse, 126 W Green St #201, Monticello, GA 31064; 706-468-4903; Fax: 706-468-4926. Hours: 8AM-4:30PM (EST). *Probate.*

Jeff Davis County

Superior & State Court PO Box 248, Hazlehurst, GA 31539; 912-375-6615 & 375-0378; Fax: 912-375-6637. Hours: 8AM-5PM (EST). *Felony, Misdemeanor, Civil.*

Civil Records: Access: Fax, mail, in person. Both court and visitors may perform in person searches. No search fee. Required to search: name, years to search. Civil cases indexed by defendant, plaintiff. Civil records on dockets books from 1805, limited records on computer back 3 years.
Criminal Records: Access: Fax, mail, in person. Both court and visitors may perform in person searches. Search fee: $3.00 per name. Required to search: name,

years to search. Criminal records on dockets books from 1805, limited records on computer back 3 years.

General Information: No juvenile, confidential, adoption or sealed records released. Turnaround time 1 week, fax immediately. Fax notes: Fee to fax results is $2.00 1st page, $1.00 each add'l. Copy fee: $.25 per page. Certification fee: $2.50 plus $.50 per page after first. Fee payee: Court Clerk. Personal checks accepted.

Magistrate Court PO Box 568, Hazlehurst, GA 31539; 912-375-6630; Fax: 912-375-6629. Hours: 8AM-5PM (EST). *Civil Actions Under $15,000, Eviction, Small Claims.*

Probate Court PO Box 446, Hazlehurst, GA 31539; 912-375-6626,; Fax: 912-375-0378. Hours: 9AM-5PM (EST). *Probate.*

Jefferson County

Superior & State Court PO Box 151, Louisville, GA 30434; 478-625-7922; Fax: 478-625-4002. Hours: 9AM-5PM (EST). *Felony, Misdemeanor, Civil.*

Civil Records: Access: Mail, in person. Both court and visitors may perform in person searches. No search fee. Required to search: name, years to search. Civil cases indexed by defendant, plaintiff. Civil records on dockets books from 1865; on computer back to 1995.

Criminal Records: Access: Mail, in person. Both court and visitors may perform in person searches. No search fee. Required to search: name, years to search, DOB or SSN. Criminal records on dockets books from 1865; on computer back to 1995.

General Information: Public access terminal is available. No juvenile, adoption, sexual, mental health or expunged records released. SASE required. Turnaround time 1 week. Copy fee: $.25 per page. Certification fee: $2.50 plus $1.00 per add'l page. Fee payee: Court Clerk. Personal checks accepted.

Magistrate Court PO Box 749, Louisville, GA 30434; 478-625-8834; Fax: 478-625-9736. Hours: 8AM-5PM (EST). *Civil Actions Under $15,000, Eviction, Small Claims.*

Probate Court PO Box 307, PO Box 307, Louisville, GA 30434; 478-625-3258; Fax: 478-625-9589. Hours: 9AM-4:30PM (EST). *Probate.*

Jenkins County

Superior & State Court PO Box 659, Millen, GA 30442; 478-982-4683; Fax: 478-982-1274. Hours: 8:30AM-5PM (EST). *Felony, Misdemeanor, Civil.*

Civil Records: Access: In person only. Visitors must perform in person searches for themselves. No search fee. Required to search: name, years to search. Civil cases indexed by defendant. Civil records on dockets books.

Criminal Records: Access: In person only. Visitors must perform in person searches for themselves. No search fee. Required to search: name, years to search, DOB; also helpful: SSN, race, sex. Criminal records on dockets books.

General Information: No juvenile, adoption, sexual, mental health or expunged records released. Copy fee: $.25 per page. Certification fee: $2.50 plus $.50 per page after first. Fee payee: Clerk of Court. Prepayment is required.

Magistrate Court PO Box 892, Millen, GA 30442; 478-982-5580; Fax: 478-982-4911. Hours: 8:30AM-5PM (EST). *Civil Actions Under $15,000, Eviction, Small Claims.*

Probate Court PO Box 904, Millen, GA 30442; 478-982-5581; Fax: 478-982-2829. Hours: 8:30AM-5PM (EST). *Probate.*

Johnson County

Superior & Magistrate Court PO Box 321, Wrightsville, GA 31096; 478-864-3484; Fax: 478-864-1343. Hours: 9AM-5PM (EST). *Felony, Misdemeanor, Civil, Eviction, Small Claims.*

Civil Records: Access: In person only. Visitors must perform in person searches for themselves. No search fee. Required to search: name, years to search. Civil cases indexed by defendant, plaintiff. Civil records on computer from 1991, dockets books from 1859.

Criminal Records: Access: In person only. Visitors must perform in person searches for themselves. No search fee. Required to search: name, years to search, DOB; also helpful: SSN, race, sex. Criminal records on computer from 1991, dockets books from 1859.

General Information: No juvenile, adoption, sexual, mental health or expunged records released. Copy fee: $.25 per page. Certification fee: $3.00. Fee payee: Court Clerk. Personal checks accepted. Prepayment is required.

Probate Court PO Box 264, Wrightsville, GA 31096; 478-864-3316; Fax: 478-864-0528. *Probate.*

Jones County

Superior Court PO Box 39, 110 South Jefferson St, Gray, GA 31032; 478-986-6671/6674. Hours: 8:30AM-4:30PM (EST). *Felony, Misdemeanor, Civil.*

Civil Records: Access: In person only. Visitors must perform in person searches for themselves. No search fee. Required to search: name, years to search. Civil cases indexed by defendant, plaintiff. Civil records on computer since 1989, dockets books from 1800s. The court will fax records not requiring a search, $5.00 minimum.

Criminal Records: Access: In person only. Visitors must perform in person searches for themselves. No search fee. Required to search: name, years to search, signed release. Criminal records on docket books, computerized since 1995.

General Information: No juvenile, adoption, sexual, mental health or expunged records released. Copy fee: $.50 per page. Certification fee: $2.50 plus $.50 per page after first. Fee payee: Superior Court. Personal checks accepted. Prepayment is required.

Magistrate & Probate Court PO Box 1359, Gray, GA 31032; 478-986-6668; Fax: 478-986-1715. Hours: 8:30AM-4:30PM (EST). *Civil Actions Under $15,000, Eviction, Small Claims, Probate.*

Lamar County

Superior Court 326 Thomaston St, Box 7, Barnesville, GA 30204; 770-358-5145; Fax: 770-358-5814. Hours: 8AM-5PM (EST). *Felony, Misdemeanor, Civil.*

Civil Records: Access: In person only. Visitors must perform in person searches for themselves. No search fee. Required to search: name, years to search. Civil cases indexed by defendant. Civil records on dockets books from 1921; on computer back to 9/2000.

Criminal Records: Access: In person only. Visitor must perform in person searches for themselves. No search fee. Required to search: name, years to search, DOB, offense, date of offense; also helpful: SSN, race, sex. Criminal records on dockets books from 1921; on computer back to 9/2000.

General Information: No juvenile, adoption, sexual, mental health or expunged records released. Copy fee: $1.00 for first page, $.25 each add'l. Certification fee: $2.50 the first page and $.50 each additional. Fee payee: Court Clerk. Personal checks accepted. Prepayment is required. Will bill copy fees.

Magistrate Court 121 Roberta Dr, #B, Barnesville, GA 30204; 770-358-5154; Fax: 770-358-

5214. Hours: 8AM-5PM (EST). *Civil Actions Under $15,000, Eviction, Small Claims.*

Probate Court 326 Thomaston St, Barnesville, GA 30204; 770-358-5155; Fax: 770-358-5348. Hours: 8AM-5PM (EST). *Probate.*

Lanier County

Superior Court County Courthouse, 100 Main St, Lakeland, GA 31635; 229-482-3594; Fax: 229-482-8333. Hours: 8AM-Noon, 1-5PM (EST). *Felony, Misdemeanor, Civil.*

Civil Records: Access: In person only. Visitors must perform in person searches for themselves. No search fee. Required to search: name, years to search. Civil cases indexed by defendant, plaintiff. Civil records on dockets books from 1921; on computer back to 1995.

Criminal Records: Access: In person only. Visitors must perform in person searches for themselves. No search fee. Required to search: name, years to search, DOB, signed release. Criminal records on dockets books from 1921; on computer back to 1995.

General Information: Public access terminal is available. No juvenile, adoption, sexual, mental health or expunged records released. Copy fee: $.25 per page. Certification fee: $3.00. Fee payee: Court Clerk. Personal checks accepted. Prepayment is required.

Magistrate Court 100 Main St, County Courthouse, Lakeland, GA 31635; 229-482-2207. Hours: 8AM-Noon; 1PM-5PM (EST). *Civil Actions Under $15,000, Eviction, Small Claims.*

Probate Court County Courthouse, 100 Main St, Lakeland, GA 31635; 229-482-3668; Fax: 229-482-8333. Hours: 8AM-5PM (EST). *Probate.*

Laurens County

Superior & Magistrate Court PO Box 2028, Dublin, GA 31040; 478-272-3210. Hours: 8:30AM-5:30PM (EST). *Felony, Misdemeanor, Civil, Eviction, Small Claims.*

Civil Records: Access: In person only. Visitors must perform in person searches for themselves. No search fee. Required to search: name, years to search. Civil cases indexed by defendant, plaintiff. Civil records on computer from 1992, dockets books from 1800s.

Criminal Records: Access: In person only. Visitors must perform in person searches for themselves. No search fee. Required to search: name, years to search; also helpful: SSN. Criminal records on computer from 1992, dockets books from 1800s.

General Information: No juvenile, adoption, sexual, mental health or expunged records released. Copy fee: $.25 per page. Certification fee: $2.50 plus $.50 per page after first. Fee payee: Court Clerk. Personal checks accepted. Prepayment is required.

Probate Court PO Box 2098, Dublin, GA 31040; 478-272-2566; Fax: 478-277-2932. Hours: 8:30AM-5:30PM (EST). *Probate.*

Lee County

Superior Court PO Box 597, Leesburg, GA 31763; 229-759-6018. Hours: 8AM-5PM (EST). *Felony, Misdemeanor, Civil.*

Civil Records: Access: Mail, in person. Both court and visitors may perform in person searches. No search fee. Required to search: name, years to search. Civil cases indexed by defendant, plaintiff. Civil records on docket books from 1850.

Criminal Records: Access: Mail, in person. Both court and visitors may perform in person searches. Search fee: $5.00. Required to search: name, years to search, DOB; also helpful: SSN, race, sex. Criminal records on docket books from 1850, computerized since 1996.

General Information: No juvenile, adoption, sexual, mental health or expunged records released. SASE required. Turnaround time 1 week. Copy fee: $1.00 per page. Certification fee: $2.00. Fee payee: Court Clerk. Personal checks accepted. Prepayment is required.

Magistrate Court PO Box 522, Leesburg, GA 31763; 229-759-6016; Fax: 229-759-3303. Hours: 8AM-5PM (EST). *Civil Actions Under $15,000, Eviction, Small Claims.*

Probate Court PO Box 592, Leesburg, GA 31763; 229-759-6005; Fax: 229-759-3345. Hours: 8AM-5PM (EST). *Probate, Traffic.*

Liberty County

Superior & State Court PO Box 50, Hinesville, GA 31313-0050; 912-876-3625; Fax: 912-876-7394. Hours: 8AM-5PM (EST). *Felony, Misdemeanor, Civil.* www.libertyco.com

Civil Records: Access: Fax, mail, in person. Both court and visitors may perform in person searches. Search fee: $5.00. Required to search: name, years to search, signed release. Civil cases indexed by defendant, plaintiff. Civil records on computer from 1986, dockets books from 1700s.

Criminal Records: Access: Mail, in person. Both court and visitors may perform in person searches. Search fee: $5.00 per name. Required to search: name, years to search, DOB, signed release; also helpful: SSN, race, sex. Criminal records on computer from 1986, dockets books from 1700s.

General Information: Public access terminal is available. No juvenile, adoption, sexual, mental health or expunged records released. SASE not required. Turnaround time 1-2 days. Fax notes: Fax fee $5.00 1st 5 pages, $1.00 each additional page. Need prepaid account for fax retrieval. Copy fee: $1.00 per page. Certification fee: $2.50 plus $.50 per page after first. Fee payee: Court Clerk. Business checks accepted. Prepayment is required.

Magistrate Court PO Box 912, Hinesville, GA 31310; 912-368-2063; Fax: 912-876-2474. Hours: 8AM-5PM (EST). *Civil Actions Under $15,000, Eviction, Small Claims.* www.libertyco.com

Probate Court PO Box 28, Hinesville, GA 31310; 912-876-3635; Fax: 912-876-3589. Hours: 8AM-5PM (EST). *Probate.*

Lincoln County

Superior Court PO Box 340, Lincolnton, GA 30817; 706-359-5505. Hours: 9AM-5PM (EST). *Felony, Misdemeanor, Civil.*

Civil Records: Access: In person only. Visitors must perform in person searches for themselves. No search fee. Required to search: name, years to search. Civil cases indexed by defendant, plaintiff. Civil records on index books from 1796, computerized since 1992. There is no public terminal, must search in the books.

Criminal Records: Access: In person only. Visitors must perform in person searches for themselves. No search fee. Required to search: name, years to search. Criminal records on index books from 1796, records are not computerized.

General Information: No adoption or juvenile records released. Copy fee: $.25 per page. Certification fee: $2.50. Fee payee: Superior Court Clerk. Personal checks accepted. Prepayment is required.

Magistrate & Probate Court PO Box 205 (210 Humphrey St), Lincolnton, GA 30817; 706-359-5519; Probate phone: 706-359-5528; Fax: 706-359-5520. Hours: 9AM-5PM (EST). *Civil Actions Under*

$15,000, Eviction, Small Claims, Probate. Note: Probate fax is 706-359-4729.

Long County

Superior & State Court PO Box 458, Ludowici, GA 31316; 912-545-2123; Fax: 912-545-2020. Hours: 8:30AM-5PM (EST). *Felony, Misdemeanor, Civil.*

Civil Records: Access: Mail, fax, in person. Only the court performs in person searches; visitors may not. Search fee: $5.00 per name. Required to search: name, years to search. Civil cases indexed by defendant, plaintiff. Civil records on docket books, archived from 1921.

Criminal Records: Access: Mail, fax, in person. Only the court performs in person searches; visitors may not. Search fee: $5.00 per name. Required to search: name, years to search, DOB; also helpful: SSN, race, sex. Criminal records on docket books, archived from 1921.

General Information: No juvenile, adoption, sealed, sexual, mental health, expunged or confidential records released. SASE required. Turnaround time 1 week. Copy fee: $.25 per page. Certification fee: $2.50 1st pg; $.50 each add'l. Fee payee: Court Clerk. Business checks accepted. Prepayment is required.

Magistrate & Probate Court PO Box 426, Ludowici, GA 31316; 912-545-2131; Fax: 912-545-2150. Hours: 8:30AM-4:30PM (EST). *Civil Actions Under $15,000, Eviction, Small Claims, Probate.*

Lowndes County

Superior & State Court PO Box 1349, Valdosta, GA 31603; 229-333-5127. Hours: 8AM-5PM (EST). *Felony, Misdemeanor, Civil.* http://www2.state.ga.us/courts/superior/dca/dca2sohp.htm

Civil Records: Access: Mail, in person. Both court and visitors may perform in person searches. Search fee: $3.00 per name for mail requests. Required to search: name, years to search. Civil cases indexed by defendant, plaintiff. Civil records on computer from 1990, prior on dockets books.

Criminal Records: Access: In person only. Visitors must perform in person searches for themselves. No search fee. Required to search: name, years to search, DOB; also helpful: SSN, race, sex. Criminal records on computer back to 1984; prior records on docket books.

General Information: Public access terminal is available. No juvenile, adoption, sexual, mental health or expunged records released. Turnaround time 1 week. Fax notes: Fee to fax results is $.25 per page. Copy fee: $.25 per page. Certification fee: $2.50 plus $.50 per page after first; $5.00 minimum. Fee payee: Court Clerk. Only cashiers checks and money orders accepted. Prepayment is required.

Magistrate Court PO Box 1349, Valdosta, GA 31603; 229-333-5112; Fax: 229-671-3440. Hours: 9AM-5PM (EST). *Civil Actions Under $15,000, Eviction, Small Claims.*

Probate Court PO Box 72, Valdosta, GA 31603; 229-333-5103; Fax: 229-333-7646. Hours: 8AM-5PM (EST). *Probate.* www.lowndescounty.com

Lumpkin County

Superior, Juvenile & Magistrate Court 99 Courthouse Hill, #D, Dahlonega, GA 30533-0541; 706-864-3736; Fax: 706-864-5298. Hours: 8AM-5PM (EST). *Felony, Misdemeanor, Civil, Eviction, Small Claims.*

Note: For Magistrate Court criminal records info, call 706-864-7760.

Civil Records: Access: In person only. Visitors must perform in person searches for themselves. No search

fee. Required to search: name, years to search; also helpful: address. Civil cases indexed by defendant, plaintiff. Civil records on computer from 1988, prior on dockets books to 1833.

Criminal Records: Access: In person only. Visitors must perform in person searches for themselves. No search fee. Required to search: name, years to search, DOB; also helpful: address, SSN, race, sex. Criminal records on computer from 1988, prior on dockets books to 1833.

General Information: Public access terminal is available. No juvenile, adoption, sealed records released. Fee payee: Court Clerk. Personal checks accepted. Prepayment is required.

Probate Court 99 Courthouse Hill, #C, Dahlonega, GA 30533; 706-864-3847; Fax: 706-864-9271. Hours: 8:30AM-4:30PM (EST). *Probate.*

Macon County

Superior Court PO Box 337, Oglethorpe, GA 31068; 478-472-7661. Hours: 8AM-5PM (EST). *Felony, Misdemeanor, Civil.*

Civil Records: Access: Mail, in person. Both court and visitors may perform in person searches. No search fee. Civil cases indexed by defendant, plaintiff. Civil records on dockets books from 1800s.

Criminal Records: Access: In person only. Both court and visitors may perform in person searches. No search fee. Criminal records on dockets books from 1800s.

General Information: No juvenile, adoption, sexual, mental health or expunged records released. SASE required. Turnaround time 1 week. Fax notes: No fee to fax results. Copy fee: $.25 per page. Certification fee: $2.00. Fee payee: Court Clerk. Business checks accepted. Prepayment is required.

Magistrate Court PO Box 605, Oglethorpe, GA 31068; 478-472-8509. Hours: 8AM-Noon, 1-5PM (EST). *Civil Actions Under $15,000, Eviction, Small Claims.*

Probate Court PO Box 216, Oglethorpe, GA 31068; 478-472-7685. Hours: 8AM-Noon, 1-5PM (EST). *Probate.*

Madison County

Superior Court PO Box 247, Danielsville, GA 30633; 706-795-3352; Fax: 706-795-2209. Hours: 8AM-5PM (EST). *Felony, Misdemeanor, Civil.*

Civil Records: Access: In person only. Visitors must perform in person searches for themselves. No search fee. Required to search: name, years to search. Civil cases indexed by defendant. Civil records on computer since 1976; prior records on dockets books from 1800s.

Criminal Records: Access: In person only. Visitors must perform in person searches for themselves. No search fee. Required to search: name, years to search, DOB; also helpful: SSN, race, sex. Criminal records on computer since 1960.

General Information: Public access terminal is available. No juvenile, adoption, sexual, mental health or expunged records released. Copy fee: $.25 per page. Certification fee: $2.50 plus $.50 per page after first. Fee payee: Court Clerk. No personal checks accepted. Prepayment is required.

Magistrate Court PO Box 6, Danielsville, GA 30633; 706-795-5679; Fax: 706-795-2222. Hours: 8AM-5PM (EST). *Civil Actions Under $15,000, Eviction, Small Claims.*

Probate Court PO Box 207, Danielsville, GA 30633; 706-795-3354; Fax: 706-795-5933. Hours: 8AM-5PM (EST). *Probate.*

Marion County

Superior Court PO Box 41, Buena Vista, GA 31803; 229-649-7321; Fax: 229-649-7931. Hours: 8:30AM-5PM (EST). *Felony, Misdemeanor, Civil.*

Civil Records: Access: In person only. Visitors must perform in person searches for themselves. No search fee. Required to search: name, years to search. Civil cases indexed by defendant, plaintiff. Civil records on books.

Criminal Records: Access: In person only. Visitors must perform in person searches for themselves. No search fee. Required to search: name, years to search; also helpful: SSN. Criminal records on books.

General Information: No juvenile, adoption, sexual, mental health or expunged records released. Copy fee: $.25 per page. Certification fee: $2.50 plus $.50 per page after first. Fee payee: Court Clerk. Personal checks accepted. Prepayment is required.

Magistrate & Probate Court PO Box 207, Buena Vista, GA 31803; 229-649-5542; Fax: 229-649-2059. Hours: 8:30AM-5PM (EST). *Civil Under $15,000, Eviction, Small Claims, Probate.*

McDuffie County

Superior Court PO Box 158, 337 Main St, Thomson, GA 30824; 706-595-2134. Hours: 8AM-5PM (EST). *Felony, Misdemeanor, Civil.*

Civil Records: Access: In person only. Visitors must perform in person searches for themselves. No search fee. Required to search: name, years to search. Civil cases indexed by defendant, plaintiff. Civil records on computer from 1991, dockets books from 1871.

Criminal Records: Access: In person only. Visitors must perform in person searches for themselves. No search fee. Required to search: name, years to search, signed release; also helpful: DOB. Civil records on computer from 1991, dockets books from 1800s.

General Information: Public access terminal is available. No juvenile or adoption records released. Copy fee: $.25 per page self; $1.00 per page assisted. Certification fee: $2.50 plus $.50 per page after first. Fee payee: Clerk Superior Court. Personal checks accepted. Prepayment is required.

Magistrate Court PO Box 252, Thomson, GA 30824; 706-597-2618; Fax: 706-595-2041. Hours: 8AM-5PM (EST). *Civil Actions Under $15,000, Eviction, Small Claims.*

Probate Court PO Box 2028, Thomson, GA 30824; 706-595-2124; Fax: 706-595-4710. Hours: 8AM-5PM (EST). *Probate.*

McIntosh County

Superior & State Court PO Box 1661, Darien, GA 31305; 912-437-6641; Fax: 912-437-6673. Hours: 8AM-4:30PM (EST). *Felony, Misdemeanor, Civil.*

Civil Records: Access: In person only. Visitors must perform in person searches for themselves. No search fee. Required to search: name, years to search. Civil cases indexed by defendant, plaintiff. Civil records on computer from 1991, dockets books from 1872.

Criminal Records: Access: In person only. Visitors must perform in person searches for themselves. No search fee. Required to search: name, years to search, DOB; also helpful: SSN, race, sex. Criminal records on computer from 1991, dockets books from 1872.

General Information: Public access terminal is available. No juvenile, adoption, sexual, or expunged records released. Copy fee: $.25 per pg unassisted; $.50 if helped. Certification fee: $2.00. Fee payee: Court Clerk. Personal checks accepted. Prepayment is required.

Magistrate Court PO Box 459, Darien, GA 31305; 912-437-4888; Fax: 912-437-2768. Hours: 8AM-4:30PM (EST). *Civil Actions Under $15,000, Eviction, Small Claims.*

Probate Court PO Box 453, Darien, GA 31305; 912-437-6636; Fax: 912-437-6635. Hours: 8AM-5PM (EST). *Probate.*

Meriwether County

Superior Court PO Box 160, Greenville, GA 30222; 706-672-4416; Fax: 706-672-1296. Hours: 9AM-5PM (EST). *Felony, Misdemeanor, Civil.*

Civil Records: Access: In person only. Visitors must perform in person searches for themselves. Search fee: No search fee. Required to search: name, years to search. Civil cases indexed by defendant, plaintiff. Civil records on microfilm and computer from 1990, prior on writ and minute books to 1827.

Criminal Records: Access: In person only. Visitors must perform in person searches for themselves. Search fee: No search fee. Required to search: name, years to search, DOB, SSN. Criminal records go back to 1827; on computer back to 1991.

General Information: Public access terminal is available. No juvenile, adoption, sexual, mental health or expunged records released. Fax notes: Fee to fax results is $2.50 first pg; $1.00 each add'l. Copy fee: $.25 per page. Certification fee: $2.50 plus $.50 per page after first. Fee payee: Court Clerk. Business checks accepted.

Magistrate Court PO Box 702, 124 N Court Sq, Greenville, GA 30222; 706-672-1247; Fax: 706-672-1172. Hours: 8:30AM-Noon; 1PM-4:30PM (EST). *Civil Actions Under $15,000, Eviction, Small Claims.*

Probate Court PO Box 608, Greenville, GA 30222; 706-672-4952; Fax: 706-672-9465. Hours: 8:30AM-5PM (EST). *Probate.*

Miller County

Superior & State Court PO Box 66, Colquitt, GA 31737; 229-758-4102. Hours: 8AM-5PM (EST). *Felony, Misdemeanor, Civil.*

Civil Records: Access: In person only. Visitors must perform in person searches for themselves. No search fee. Required to search: name, years to search. Civil cases indexed by defendant, plaintiff. Civil records on dockets books from 1800s, computerized from 1995.

Criminal Records: Access: In person only. Visitors must perform in person searches for themselves. No search fee. Required to search: name, years to search. Criminal records on dockets books from 1800s, computerized from 1995.

General Information: Public access terminal is available. No juvenile or adoption records released. Copy fee: $1.00 per page. Certification fee: $2.50 plus $1.00 per page after first. Fee payee: Court Clerk. Business checks accepted. Prepayment is required.

Magistrate & Probate Court 155 S 1st St, Box 1, Room 110, Colquitt, GA 31737; 229-758-4110; Fax: 229-758-8133. Hours: 9AM-5PM (EST). *Civil Actions Under $15,000, Small Claims, Probate.*

Mitchell County

Superior & State Court PO Box 427, Camilla, GA 31730; 229-336-2022. Hours: 8:30AM-5PM (EST). *Felony, Misdemeanor, Civil.*

Civil Records: Access: In person only. Visitors must perform in person searches for themselves. No search fee. Required to search: name, years to search. Civil cases indexed by defendant. Civil records on dockets books from 1800s.

Criminal Records: Access: In person only. Visitors must perform in person searches for themselves. No search fee. Required to search: name, years to search, DOB; also helpful: SSN, race, sex. Criminal records on dockets books from 1800s.

General Information: No juvenile, adoption, sexual, mental health or expunged records released. Copy fee: $.25 per page. Certification fee: $2.50 plus $.50 per page after first. Fee payee: Court Clerk. Only cashiers checks and money orders accepted. Prepayment is required.

Magistrate Court PO Box 664, Pelham, GA 31779; 229-294-4460; Fax: 229-294-4951. Hours: 8:30AM-Noon; 1PM-5PM (EST). *Civil Actions Under $15,000, Eviction, Small Claims.*

Probate Court PO Box 229, Camilla, GA 31730; 229-336-2016; Fax: 229-336-2004. Hours: 8:30AM-5PM (EST). *Probate.*

Monroe County

Superior Court PO Box 450, 1 Courthouse Square, Forsyth, GA 31029; 478-994-7022; Fax: 478-994-7053. 8:30AM-4:30PM (EST). *Felony, Misdemeanor, Civil.*

Civil Records: Access: In person only. Visitors must perform in person searches for themselves. No search fee. Required to search: name, years to search. Civil cases indexed by defendant, plaintiff. Civil records on computer from 1986, dockets books from 1800s.

Criminal Records: Access: Mail, in person. Both court and visitors may perform in person searches. No search fee. Required to search: name, years to search, signed release. Criminal records on computer from 1989.

General Information: Public access terminal is available. No juvenile, adoption, sexual, mental health or expunged records released. Mail requests not accepted. Turnaround time 1 day. Copy fee: $1.00 per page. Certification fee: $2.50 plus $.50 per page after first. Fee payee: Court Clerk. Personal checks accepted. Prepayment is required.

Magistrate Court PO Box 974, Forsyth, GA 31029; 478-994-7018; Fax: 478-994-7284. Hours: 8:30AM-Noon, 1:30-4:30PM (EST). *Civil Actions Under $15,000, Eviction, Small Claims.*

Probate Court PO Box 187, Forsyth, GA 31029; 478-994-7036; Fax: 478-994-7054. Hours: 8:30AM-4:30PM (EST). *Probate.*

Montgomery County

Superior Court PO Box 311, Mt Vernon, GA 30445; 912-583-4401. Hours: 8AM-5PM (EST). *Felony, Misdemeanor, Civil.*

Civil Records: Access: In person only. Visitors must perform in person searches for themselves. No search fee. Required to search: name, years to search. Civil cases indexed by defendant, plaintiff. Civil records on computer from 1993, on dockets from 1793.

Criminal Records: Access: In person only. Visitors must perform in person searches for themselves. No search fee. Required to search: name, years to search, DOB; also helpful: SSN, race, sex. Criminal records on computer from 1993, on dockets from 1793.

General Information: No juvenile or adoption records released. Fax notes: Fee to fax results is $2.50 per page. Copy fee: $1.00 per page. Certification fee: $2.50 per page. Fee payee: Superior Court Clerk. Personal checks accepted.

Magistrate Court PO Box 174, Mt Vernon, GA 30445; 912-583-2170; Fax: 912-583-4343. Hours: 8AM-5PM (EST). *Civil Actions Under $15,000, Eviction, Small Claims.*

Probate Court PO Box 444, Mt Vernon, GA 30445; 912-583-2681; Fax: 912-583-4343. Hours: 9AM-5PM (EST). *Probate.*

Morgan County

Superior Court PO Box 130, 149 E Jefferson St, Madison, GA 30650; 706-342-3605. Hours: 9AM-5PM (EST). *Felony, Misdemeanor, Civil.*

Civil Records: Access: In person only. Visitors must perform in person searches for themselves. No search fee. Required to search: name, years to search. Civil cases indexed by defendant, plaintiff. Civil records on computer from 1986, on dockets from 1900s.

Criminal Records: Access: In person only. Visitors must perform in person searches for themselves. No search fee. Required to search: name, years to search, signed release. Criminal records on computer from 1986, on dockets from 1900s.

General Information: Public access terminal is available. No juvenile, adoption, sexual, mental health or expunged records released. Copy fee: $.25 per page. Certification fee: $2.50 plus $.50 per page after first. Fee payee: Superior Court Clerk. Personal checks accepted. Prepayment is required.

Magistrate Court 149 E Jefferson St, Rm 110, Madison, GA 30650; 706-342-3088; Fax: 706-343-0000. Hours: 8AM-5PM (EST). *Civil Actions Under $15,000, Eviction, Small Claims.*

www.morganga.org

Probate Court PO Box 857, Madison, GA 30650; 706-342-1373; Fax: 706-342-5085. Hours: 8AM-5PM (EST). *Probate.*

Murray County

Superior Court PO Box 1000, Chatsworth, GA 30705; 706-695-2932. Hours: 8:30AM-5PM (EST). *Felony, Misdemeanor, Civil.*

Civil Records: Access: In person only. Visitors must perform in person searches for themselves. No search fee. Required to search: name, years to search. Civil cases indexed by defendant, plaintiff. Civil records on dockets from 1940, prior to 1940 archived; computerized records since 2000.

Criminal Records: Access: In person only. Visitors must perform in person searches for themselves. No search fee. Required to search: name, years to search, signed release. Criminal records on dockets from 1940, prior to 1940 archived; computerized records since 2000.

General Information: Public access terminal is available. No juvenile, adoption, sexual, mental health or expunged records released. Copy fee: $.25 per page. Certification fee: $2.50 plus $.50 per page after first. Fee payee: Superior Court Clerk. Personal checks accepted. Prepayment is required.

Magistrate Court 121 N 4th Ave, Chatsworth, GA 30705; 706-695-3021; Fax: 706-695-7525. Hours: 8AM-Noon, 1-5PM (EST). *Civil Actions Under $15,000, Eviction, Small Claims.*

Probate Court 115 Fort St, Chatsworth, GA 30705; 706-695-3812; Fax: 706-517-1340. Hours: 8:30AM-5PM (EST). *Probate.*

Muscogee County

Superior & State Court PO Box 2145, Columbus, GA 31902; 706-653-4351; Fax: 706-653-4359. Hours: 8:30AM-5PM (EST). *Felony, Misdemeanor, Civil.*

Civil Records: Access: Mail, in person. Both court and visitors may perform in person searches. Search fee: $30.00 per name. Required to search: name, years to search. Civil cases indexed by defendant, plaintiff. Civil

records on computer from 1989, on dockets from 1919 to 1989.

Criminal Records: Access: Mail, in person. Both court and visitors may perform in person searches. Search fee: $30.00 per name. Required to search: name, years to search, DOB; also helpful: SSN. Criminal records on computer since 1989, on dockets from 1989 to 1957.

General Information: Public access terminal is available. No adoption, sealed or first offender records released. Turnaround time 1 week. Copy fee: $.25 per page. Certification fee: $2.50 plus $.50 per page after first. Fee payee: Superior Court Clerk. Business checks accepted. Prepayment is required.

Magistrate Court Box 1340, Columbus, GA 31902; 706-653-4390; Fax: 706-653-4559. Hours: 8:30AM-5PM (EST). *Civil Actions Under $15,000, Eviction, Small Claims.*

Probate Court PO Box 1340, Columbus, GA 31902; 706-653-4333. 8:30AM-4PM (EST). *Probate.*

Newton County

Superior Court 1132 Usher St, Covington, GA 30014; 770-784-2035. Hours: 8AM-5PM (EST). *Felony, Misdemeanor, Civil.*

Civil Records: Access: In person only. Visitors must perform in person searches for themselves. No search fee. Required to search: name, years to search. Civil cases indexed by defendant, plaintiff. Civil records on computer from 1991, on dockets from 1900s.

Criminal Records: Access: In person only. Visitors must perform in person searches for themselves. No search fee. Required to search: name, years to search, signed release. Criminal records on computer from 1991, on dockets from 1900s.

General Information: Public access terminal is available. No adoption, sexual, mental health or expunged records released. Copy fee: $.25 per page. Certification fee: $2.50 plus $.50 per page after first. Fee payee: Superior Court Clerk. Personal checks accepted. Prepayment is required.

Magistrate & Probate Court 1132 Usher St, Rm 148, Covington, GA 30014; 770-784-2045 or 770-784-2050; Fax: 770-784-2145. Hours: 8AM-5PM (EST). *Civil Actions Under $15,000, Eviction, Small Claims, Probate.*

Oconee County

Superior & Magistrate Courts PO Box 1099, Watkinsville, GA 30677; 706-769-3940; Fax: 706-769-3948. Hours: 8AM-5PM (EST). *Felony, Misdemeanor, Civil, Eviction, Small Claims.*

Civil Records: Access: In person only. Visitors must perform in person searches for themselves. No search fee. Required to search: name, years to search. Civil cases indexed by defendant, plaintiff. Civil records on computer from 1989, on dockets from 1875.

Criminal Records: Access: In person only. Visitors must perform in person searches for themselves. No search fee. Required to search: name, years to search; also helpful: DOB, SSN. Criminal records on computer from 1989, on dockets from 1875.

General Information: No juvenile, adoption, sexual, mental health or expunged records released. Copy fee: $.25 per page. Certification fee: $2.50 plus $.50 per page after first. Fee payee: Superior Court Clerk. Personal checks accepted. Prepayment is required.

Probate Court PO Box 54, Watkinsville, GA 30677; 706-769-3936; Fax: 706-769-3934. Hours: 8AM-5PM (EST). *Probate.*

Oglethorpe County

Superior Court PO Box 68, Lexington, GA 30648; 706-743-5731; Fax: 706-743-5335. Hours: 8AM-5PM (EST). *Felony, Misdemeanor, Civil.*

Civil Records: Access: Mail, in person. Visitors must perform in person searches for themselves. No search fee. Required to search: name, years to search. Civil cases indexed by defendant. Civil records on computer from 1992, on dockets from 1900s.

Criminal Records: Access: In person only. Visitors must perform in person searches for themselves. No search fee. Required to search: name, years to search, DOB; also helpful: SSN, race, sex. Criminal records on computer from 1992, on dockets from 1900s.

General Information: No juvenile or adoption records released. Turnaround time 2-3 days. Copy fee: $.25 per page. Certification fee: $2.50 plus $.50 per page after first. Fee payee: Superior Court Clerk. Personal checks accepted. Prepayment is required.

Magistrate Court Box 356, Lexington, GA 30648; 706-743-8321; Fax: 706-743-3177. Hours: 8AM-5PM (EST). *Civil Actions Under $15,000, Eviction, Small Claims.*

Probate Court PO Box 70, Lexington, GA 30648; 706-743-5350; Fax: 706-743-8219. Hours: 8AM-5PM (EST). *Probate.*

Paulding County

Superior Court 11 Courthouse Square, Rm G2, Dallas, GA 30132; 770-443-7529. Hours: 8AM-5PM (EST). *Felony, Misdemeanor, Civil.*

Civil Records: Access: In person only. Visitors must perform in person searches for themselves. Search fee: No search fee. Required to search: name, years to search. Civil cases indexed by defendant, plaintiff. Civil records on computer from 1990, archived from 1850.

Criminal Records: Access: In person only. Visitors must perform in person searches for themselves. Search fee: No search fee. Required to search: name, years to search, DOB; also helpful: SSN, race, sex. Criminal records on docket books.

General Information: No juvenile, adoption, sexual, mental health or expunged records released. Copy fee: $.25 per page; $1 per page if office assists. Certification fee: $2.50 plus $.50 per page after first. Fee payee: Court Clerk. Personal checks accepted. Prepayment is required.

Magistrate & Probate Court 124 Main St, Dallas, GA 30132; 770-445-2123; Fax: 770-445-1127. Hours: 8AM-5PM (EST). *Civil Actions Under $15,000, Eviction, Small Claims, Probate.*

Probate Court 11 Courthouse Square, Rm 106, Dallas, GA 30132; 770-443-7541; Fax: 770-443-7631. Hours: 8AM-5PM (EST). *Probate.*

Peach County

Superior Court PO Box 389, Ft Valley, GA 31030; 478-825-5331. Hours: 8:30AM-5PM (EST). *Felony, Misdemeanor, Civil.*

Civil Records: Access: Mail, in person. Both court and visitors may perform in person searches. No search fee. Required to search: name, years to search. Civil cases indexed by defendant, plaintiff. Civil records on computer back to 1997; on dockets from 1925.

Criminal Records: Access: Mail, in person. Both court and visitors may perform in person searches. No search fee. Required to search: name, years to search, DOB; also helpful: SSN, race, sex. Criminal records on computer back to 1997; on dockets from 1925.

General Information: No juvenile, adoption, sexual, mental health or expunged records released. SASE required. Turnaround time 1 week. Copy fee: $.25 per page. Certification fee: $3.00. Fee payee: Court Clerk. Personal checks accepted. Prepayment is required.

Magistrate Court 700 Spruce St, Bldg A, Ft Valley, GA 31030; 478-825-2060; Fax: 478-825-1893. Hours: 8AM-5PM (EST). *Civil Actions Under $15,000, Eviction, Small Claims.*

Probate Court PO Box 327, Ft Valley, GA 31030; 478-825-2313; Fax: 478-825-2678. *Probate.*

Pickens County

Superior Court 52 N Main St Ste 102, Jasper, GA 30143; 706-253-8763. Hours: 8AM-5PM (EST). *Felony, Misdemeanor, Civil.*

http://9thjudicialdistrict-ga.org/dca9apphp.shtml

Civil Records: Access: In person only. Visitors must perform in person searches for themselves. No search fee. Required to search: name, years to search. Civil cases indexed by defendant, plaintiff. Civil records on computer from 1988, dockets from 1854.

Criminal Records: Access: In person only. Visitors must perform in person searches for themselves. No search fee. Required to search: name, years to search, DOB, signed release; also helpful: SSN, race, sex. Criminal records on computer from 1988, dockets from 1854.

General Information: Public access terminal is available. No juvenile, adoption, sexual, mental health or expunged records released. Copy fee: $.25 per page. $1.00 per page if the court makes the copies. Certification fee: $2.50 plus $.50 per page after first. Fee payee: Court Clerk. Personal checks accepted. Prepayment is required.

Magistrate Court 50 N Main St #105, Jasper, GA 30143; 706-253-8747; Fax: 706-253-8750. Hours: 8AM-5PM (EST). *Civil Actions Under $15,000, Eviction, Small Claims.*

Probate Court 50 N Main St, #C, Jasper, GA 30143; 706-692-2515. Hours: 8AM-Noon, 1-5PM (EST). *Probate.*

Pierce County

Superior Court PO Box 588, Blackshear, GA 31516; 912-449-2020. Hours: 9AM-5PM (EST). *Felony, Misdemeanor, Civil.*

Civil Records: Access: In person only. Visitors must perform in person searches for themselves. No search fee. Required to search: name, years to search. Civil cases indexed by defendant. Civil records on computer from 1991, on index from 1800s.

Criminal Records: Access: In person only. Visitors must perform in person searches for themselves. No search fee. Required to search: name, years to search. Criminal records on computer from 1991, on index from 1800s.

General Information: Copy fee: $.25 per page. Certification fee: $2.50 first page, $.50 each additional. Fee payee: Superior Court Clerk. Personal checks accepted. Prepayment is required.

State Court PO Box 588, Blackshear, GA 31516; 912-449-2020. Hours: 9AM-5PM (EST). *Misdemeanor, Civil.*

Civil Records: Access: In person only. Visitors must perform in person searches for themselves. No search fee. Required to search: name, years to search. Civil cases indexed by defendant, plaintiff. Civil records on computer from 1991, on docket books from 1800s.

Criminal Records: Access: In person only. Visitors must perform in person searches for themselves. No search fee. Required to search: name, years to search, DOB; also helpful: SSN, race, sex. Criminal records on computer from 1991, on docket books from 1800s.

General Information: No juvenile, adoption, sealed, sexual, mental health or expunged records released. Copy fee: If court does copy $.50, if yourself then $.25. Certification fee: $2.50 plus $.50 per page after first. Fee payee: Clerk of Court. Business checks accepted. Prepayment is required.

Magistrate Court 3550 Highway 84 West, Blackshear, GA 31516; 912-449-2027, 449-2007; Fax: 912-449-2103. Hours: 9AM-5PM (EST). *Civil Actions Under $15,000, Eviction, Small Claims.*

Probate Court PO Box 406, Blackshear, GA 31516; 912-449-2029; Fax: 912-449-2024. Hours: 9AM-5PM (EST). *Probate.*

Pike County

Superior Court PO Box 10, Zebulon, GA 30295; 770-567-2000. Hours: 8AM-5PM (EST). *Felony, Misdemeanor, Civil.*

Civil Records: Access: In person only. Visitors must perform in person searches for themselves. No search fee. Required to search: name, years to search. Civil cases indexed by defendant, plaintiff. Civil records on dockets books from 1823.

Criminal Records: Access: In person only. Visitors must perform in person searches for themselves. No search fee. Required to search: name, years to search. Criminal records on dockets books from 1823.

General Information: No juvenile, adoption, sexual, mental health or expunged records released. Copy fee: $.25 per page. Certification fee: $2.50 plus $.50 per page after first. Fee payee: Court Clerk. Personal checks accepted. Prepayment is required.

Magistrate Court PO Box 466, Zebulon, GA 30295; 770-567-2004; Fax: 770-567-2023. Hours: 8AM-5PM (EST). *Civil Actions Under $15,000, Eviction, Small Claims.*

Probate Court PO Box 324, Zebulon, GA 30295; 770-567-8734; Fax: 770-567-2006. Hours: 9AM-5PM (EST). *Probate.*

Polk County

Superior Court PO Box 948, Cedartown, GA 30125; 770-749-2114; Fax: 770-749-2148. Hours: 9AM-5PM (EST). *Felony, Misdemeanor, Civil.*

Civil Records: Access: In person only. Visitors must perform in person searches for themselves. No search fee. Required to search: name, years to search. Civil cases indexed by defendant, plaintiff. Civil records on computer from 1991, alpha indexes from 1930.

Criminal Records: Access: Mail, in person. Visitors must perform in person searches for themselves. No search fee. Required to search: name, years to search, DOB, signed release; also helpful: SSN, race, sex. Criminal records on computer from 1991, alpha indexes from 1930.

General Information: Public access terminal is available. No juvenile, adoption, sexual, mental health or expunged records released. Fax notes: Fee to fax results is $2.00 per page. Copy fee: $.25 per page. Certification fee: $2.50 plus $.50 per page after first. Fee payee: Court Clerk. Personal checks accepted. Prepayment is required.

Magistrate Court 100 Prior St, Courthouse 2, Cedartown, GA 30125; 770-749-2187; Fax: 770-749-2189. Hours: 9AM-5PM (EST). *Civil Actions Under $15,000, Eviction, Small Claims.*

Probate Court Polk County Courthouse. Rm 102, Cedartown, GA 30125; 770-749-2128; Fax: 770-749-2150. Hours: 9AM-5PM (EST). *Probate.*

Pulaski County

Superior Court PO Box 60, Hawkinsville, GA 31036; 478-783-1911; Fax: 478-892-3308. Hours: 8AM-5PM (EST). *Felony, Misdemeanor, Civil.*

Civil Records: Access: Phone, mail, in person. Both court and visitors may perform in person searches. No search fee. Required to search: name, years to search. Civil cases indexed by defendant, plaintiff. Civil records on computer from 1986, alpha index from early 1800s.

Criminal Records: Access: Mail, in person. Both court and visitors may perform in person searches. No search fee. Required to search: name, years to search, signed release; also helpful: DOB, SSN. Criminal records on computer from 1986, alpha index from early 1800s.

General Information: No juvenile, adoption, sexual, mental health or expunged records released. Turnaround time 1 week. Copy fee: $1.00 per page. Certification fee: $.50 per page. Fee payee: Court Clerk. Personal checks accepted. Prepayment is required.

Magistrate Court PO Box 667, Hawkinsville, GA 31036; 478-783-1357; Fax: 478-892-3308. Hours: 8AM-5PM (EST). *Civil Actions Under $15,000, Eviction, Small Claims.*

Probate Court Pulaski County Courthouse, Hawkinsville, GA 31036; 478-783-2061; Fax: 478-783-9219. Hours: 8AM-5PM (EST). *Probate.*

Putnam County

Superior & State Court County Courthouse, Eatonton, GA 31024; 706-485-4501; Fax: 706-485-2515. Hours: 8AM-5PM (EST). *Felony, Misdemeanor, Civil.*

Civil Records: Access: In person only. Visitors must perform in person searches for themselves. No search fee. Required to search: name, years to search. Civil cases indexed by defendant, plaintiff. Civil records on computer since 1992; prior records on dockets to early 1808.

Criminal Records: Access: In person only. Visitors must perform in person searches for themselves. No search fee. Required to search: name, years to search, DOB; also helpful: SSN, race, sex. Criminal records on computer since 1997; prior records on dockets to early 1930s.

General Information: Public access terminal is available. No juvenile, adoption, sexual, mental health or expunged records released. Copy fee: $1.00 per page. Certification fee: $3.00. Fee payee: Court Clerk. Personal checks accepted. Prepayment is required.

Magistrate Court 108 S Madison Ave, #101, Eatonton, GA 31024; 706-485-4306; Fax: 706-485-2515. Hours: 8AM-5PM (EST). *Civil Actions Under $15,000, Eviction, Small Claims.*

Probate Court County Courthouse, 100 S Jefferson St, Eatonton, GA 31024; 706-485-5476/9761; Fax: 706-485-2515. Hours: 8AM-5PM (EST). *Probate.*

Quitman County

Superior Court PO Box 307, Georgetown, GA 31754; 229-334-2578. Hours: 8AM-Noon, 1-5PM (EST). *Felony, Misdemeanor, Civil.*

Civil Records: Access: In person only. Visitors must perform in person searches for themselves. Required to search: name, years to search. Civil records go back to 1920s.

Criminal Records: Access: In person only. Visitors must perform in person searches for themselves. No search fee. Required to search: name, years to search, DOB; also helpful: SSN, race, sex. The court asks mail requesters to mail the sheriff's office with a $10.00 fee and signed, notarized (subject) request.

General Information: No juvenile, adoption, sexual, mental health or expunged records released. Fax notes: Fee to fax results is $3.00 1st pg, $1.00 each add'l. Copy fee: $.50 per page. Certification fee: $2.50 1st page and $.50 each additional. Fee payee: Clerk of Superior Court. Personal checks accepted. Prepayment is required.

Magistrate & Probate Court PO Box 7, Georgetown, GA 31754; 229-334-2224; Fax: 229-334-6826. Hours: 8:30AM-5PM (EST). *Civil Actions Under $15,000, Eviction, Small Claims, Probate.*

Rabun County

Superior Court 25 Courthouse Sq #105, Clayton, GA 30525; 706-782-3615; Fax: 706-782-1391. Hours: 8:30AM-5PM (EST). *Felony, Misdemeanor, Civil.*

Civil Records: Access: Mail, in person. Visitors must perform in person searches for themselves. No search fee. Required to search: name, years to search. Civil cases indexed by defendant, plaintiff. Civil records on dockets from 1949; on computer since.

Criminal Records: Access: Mail, in person. Visitors must perform in person searches for themselves. No search fee. Required to search: name, years to search, DOB, signed release; also helpful: SSN, race, sex. Criminal records on dockets from 1949; on computer since.

General Information: No juvenile, adoption, sexual, mental health or expunged records released. Fax notes: No fee to fax back results. Copy fee: $.25 per page. Certification fee: $5.00. Fee payee: Court Clerk. Personal checks accepted. Prepayment is required.

Magistrate Court 25 Courthouse Sq #105, Clayton, GA 30525; 706-782-2285; Fax: 706-782-1391. Hours: 8:30AM-5PM (EST). *Civil Actions Under $15,000, Eviction, Small Claims.*

Probate Court 25 Courthouse Square, #215, Clayton, GA 30525; 706-782-3614; Fax: 706-782-9278. Hours: 8:30AM-5:00PM (EST). *Probate.*

Randolph County

Superior Court PO Box 98, Cuthbert, GA 31740; 229-732-2216; Fax: 229-732-5881. Hours: 8AM-5PM (EST). *Felony, Misdemeanor, Civil.*

Civil Records: Access: In person only. Visitors must perform in person searches for themselves. No search fee. Required to search: name, years to search. Civil cases indexed by defendant. Civil records on index from 1835.

Criminal Records: Access: In person only. Visitors must perform in person searches for themselves. No search fee. Required to search: name, years to search, DOB; also helpful: SSN, race, sex. Criminal records on index from 1835.

General Information: No juvenile, adoption, sexual, mental health or expunged records released. Copy fee: $.25 per page. Certification fee: $2.00 plus $.50 per page after first. Fee payee: Court Clerk. Personal checks accepted. Prepayment is required.

Magistrate Court PO Box 6, Cuthbert, GA 31740; 229-732-6182; Fax: 229-732-5781. Hours: 9AM-5PM (EST). *Civil Actions Under $15,000, Eviction, Small Claims.*

Probate Court PO Box 424, Cuthbert, GA 31740; 229-732-2671; Fax: 229-732-5781. Hours: 8AM-5PM (EST). *Probate.*

Richmond County

Superior Court 530 Greene St, Augusta, GA 30911; 706-821-2460; Fax: 706-821-2448. Hours: 8:30AM-5PM (EST). *Felony, Misdemeanor, Civil.*

Civil Records: Access: Mail, in person. Visitors must perform in person searches for themselves. No search fee. Required to search: name, years to search. Civil cases indexed by defendant, plaintiff. Civil records on docket books and microfilm from 1940s, real estate from 1986 on computer.

Criminal Records: Access: Mail, in person. Visitors must perform in person searches for themselves. No search fee. Required to search: name, years to search. Criminal records on docket books and microfilm from 1940s, real estate from 1986 on computer.

General Information: No juvenile, adoption, sexual, mental health or expunged records released. SASE requested. Turnaround time 1 week. Copy fee: $.25 per page. Certification fee: $2.50 plus $.50 per page after first. Fee payee: Superior Court Clerk. Business checks accepted. Local checks accepted. Prepayment is required.

State Court 401 Walton Way, #218A, Augusta, GA 30911; 706-821-1233. Hours: 8:30AM-5PM (EST). *Misdemeanor, Civil.*

Civil Records: Access: In person only. Visitors must perform in person searches for themselves. No search fee. Required to search: name, years to search. Civil cases indexed by defendant, plaintiff. Civil records on docket books and microfilm from 1940s, prior archived; computerized records since 2001.

Criminal Records: Access: In person only. Visitors must perform in person searches for themselves. No search fee. Required to search: name, years to search, DOB; also helpful: SSN, race, sex. Criminal records on docket books and microfilm from 1940s, prior archived; computerized records since 2001.

General Information: Public access terminal is available. No juvenile, adoption, sexual, mental health or expunged records released. Copy fee: $.25 per page. Certification fee: $2.50 plus $.50 per page after first. Fee payee: Court Clerk. Only cashiers checks and money orders accepted. Prepayment is required.

Civil & Magistrate Court 530 Greene St, Rm 705, Augusta, GA 30911; 706-821-2370; Fax: 706-821-2381. Hours: 8:30AM-5PM (EST). *Civil Actions Under $45,000, Eviction, Small Claims.*

Civil Records: Access: Phone, mail, in person. Both court and visitors may perform in person searches. No search fee. Required to search: name, years to search. Civil cases indexed by defendant, plaintiff. Civil records on dockets back to 1970s.

General Information: SASE requested. Turnaround time 1 day. Copy fee: $.25 per page. Certification fee: $5.00. Fee payee: Magistrate Court. Business checks accepted. Prepayment is required.

Probate Court 530 Greene St, Rm 401, Augusta, GA 30911; 706-821-2434; Fax: 706-821-2442. Hours: 8:30AM-5PM (EST). *Probate.*

Rockdale County

Superior Court PO Box 937, 922 Court St, Conyers, GA 30012; 770-929-4021. Hours: 8AM-4:45PM (EST). *Felony, Civil.*

Civil Records: Access: In person only. Visitors must perform in person searches for themselves. No search fee. Required to search: name, years to search. Civil cases indexed by defendant, plaintiff. Civil records on computer back to 1993, in books from 1900.

Criminal Records: Access: In person only. Visitors must perform in person searches for themselves. No search fee. Required to search: name, years to search, signed release. Criminal records on computer back to 1990, in books from 1900.

General Information: Public access terminal is available. No juvenile, adoption, sexual, mental health or expunged records released. Copy fee: $.25 per page. Certification fee: $2.50 plus $.50 per page after first. Fee payee: Clerk Superior Court. Personal checks accepted. Prepayment is required.

State Court PO Box 938, Conyers, GA 30012; 770-929-4019. Hours: 8AM-4:45PM (EST). *Misdemeanor, Civil.*

Civil Records: Access: In person only. Visitors must perform in person searches for themselves. No search fee. Required to search: name, years to search. Civil cases indexed by defendant, plaintiff. Civil records on computer from 1994, on dockets to 1994.

Criminal Records: Access: In person only. Visitors must perform in person searches for themselves. No search fee. Required to search: name, years to search. Criminal records on computer from 1990, on dockets from 1987-1990.

General Information: Public access terminal is available. No juvenile, adoption, sexual, mental health or expunged records released. Copy fee: $.25 per page. Certification fee: $2.50 plus $.50 per page after first. Fee payee: Rockdale State Court. Business checks accepted. Prepayment is required.

Magistrate Court PO Box 289, Conyers, GA 30012; 770-929-4014; Fax: 770-785-2496. Hours: 8:30AM-4:30PM (EST). *Civil Actions Under $15,000, Eviction, Small Claims.*

Note: Court also has jurisdiction for bad checks, arrest warrants, preliminary hearings, and county ordinance violations

Probate Court 922 Court St NE, Rm 107, Conyers, GA 30012; 770-929-4058; Fax: 770-918-6463. Hours: 8:30AM-4:30PM (EST). *Probate.*

Schley County

Superior Court PO Box 7, US Hwy 19-Courthouse Square, Ellaville, GA 31806; 229-937-5581; Fax: 229-937-5588. Hours: 8AM-Noon,1-5PM (EST). *Felony, Misdemeanor, Civil.*

www.gsccca.org/clerks

Civil Records: Access: In person only. Visitors must perform in person searches for themselves. Search fee: No search fee. Required to search: name, years to search. Civil cases indexed by defendant. Civil records in books from 1885.

Criminal Records: Access: In person only. Visitors must perform in person searches for themselves. Search fee: No search fee. Required to search: name, years to search, DOB, signed release; also helpful: SSN, race, sex. Criminal records in books from 1934.

General Information: No adoption records released. Copy fee: $.25 per page. Certification fee: $2.50 plus $.50 per page after first. Fee payee: Clerk Superior Court. Personal checks accepted. Prepayment is required.

Magistrate Court PO Box 43, Ellaville, GA 31806; 229-937-2013; Fax: 229-937-2347. Hours: 8AM-5PM (EST). *Civil Actions Under $15,000, Eviction, Small Claims.*

Probate Court PO Box 385, Ellaville, GA 31806; 229-937-2905; Fax: 229-937-5047. Hours: 8:30AM-Noon, 1-5PM (EST). *Probate.*

Screven County

Superior Court PO Box 156, Sylvania, GA 30467; 912-564-2614; Fax: 912-564-2622. Hours: 8:30AM-5PM (EST). *Felony, Misdemeanor, Civil.*

Civil Records: Access: In person only. Visitors must perform in person searches for themselves. No search fee. Required to search: name, years to search. Civil cases indexed by defendant, plaintiff. Civil records on dockets from 1793.

Criminal Records: Access: In person only. Visitors must perform in person searches for themselves. No search fee. Required to search: name, years to search, DOB; also helpful: SSN, race, sex. Criminal records on dockets from 1793.

General Information: No juvenile or adoption records released. Copy fee: $.25 per page. Certification fee: $3.00. Fee payee: Court Clerk. Personal checks accepted. Prepayment is required.

State Court PO Box 156, Sylvania, GA 30467; 912-564-2614; Fax: 912-564-2622. Hours: 8:00AM-5PM (EST). *Misdemeanor, Civil.*

Civil Records: Access: In person only. Visitors must perform in person searches for themselves. No search fee. Required to search: name, years to search. Civil cases indexed by defendant, plaintiff. Civil records on dockets from 1793; computerized records since 1991.

Criminal Records: Access: In person only. Visitors must perform in person searches for themselves. No search fee. Required to search: name, years to search, DOB; also helpful: SSN, race, sex. Criminal records on dockets from 1793; computerized records since 1991.

General Information: Public access terminal is available. No juvenile, adoption, sexual, mental health or expunged records released. Copy fee: $.25 per page. Certification fee: $3.00. Fee payee: Court Clerk. Personal checks accepted. Prepayment is required.

Magistrate Court PO Box 64, Sylvania, GA 30467; 912-564-7375. Hours: 8AM-5PM (EST). *Civil Actions Under $15,000, Eviction, Small Claims.*

Probate Court 216 Mims Rd #107, Sylvania, GA 30467; 912-564-2783; Fax: 912-564-9139. Hours: 8:30AM-5PM (EST). *Probate.*

Seminole County

Superior Court PO Box 672, Main St, Donalsonville, GA 31745; 229-524-2525; Fax: 229-524-8883. Hours: 8:30AM-5PM (EST). *Felony, Misdemeanor, Civil.*

Civil Records: Access: Fax, in person. Both court and visitors may perform in person searches. Search fee: $1.00 per name per year. Required to search: name, years to search. Civil cases indexed by defendant, plaintiff. Civil records on computer from 1994, on dockets from 1921.

Criminal Records: Access: Fax, mail, in person. Both court and visitors may perform in person searches. Search fee: $1.00 per name per year. Required to search: name, years to search, DOB, signed release; also helpful: SSN, race, sex. Criminal records on computer from 1994, on dockets from 1921.

General Information: No juvenile, adoption, sexual, mental health or expunged records released. SASE required. Turnaround time 1 day. Fax notes: $1.00 per page. Copy fee: $1.00 per page. Copy fees are $.25 per page in person. Certification fee: $2.50. Fee payee: Court Clerk. Personal checks accepted. Prepayment is required.

Magistrate & Probate Court Seminole County Courthouse, 200 S Knox Av, #50, Donalsonville, GA 31745; 229-524-5256; Fax: 229-524-8644. Hours: 8AM-5PM (EST). *Civil Actions Under $15,000, Eviction, Small Claims.*

Spalding County

Superior Court PO Box 1046, Griffin, GA 30224; 770-467-4745. Hours: 8AM-5PM (EST). *Felony, Misdemeanor, Civil.*

Civil Records: Access: Mail, in person. Visitors must perform in person searches for themselves. No search fee. Required to search: name, years to search. Civil cases indexed by defendant, plaintiff. Civil records on computer from 1991, on dockets from 1852. Mail for specific case info only, the court will not do name searches.

Criminal Records: Access: Mail, in person. Visitors must perform in person searches for themselves. No search fee. Required to search: name, years to search; also helpful: DOB, SSN, race, sex. Criminal records on computer from 1991, on dockets from 1852. Court will not do name searches, will only do specific case files.

General Information: Public access terminal is available. No juvenile, adoption, sexual, mental health or expunged records released. SASE required. Turnaround time 2 days. Fax notes: Will not fax results. Copy fee: $.25 per page. Certification fee: $2.00 per page, + $.50 each add'l. Fee payee: Court Clerk. Personal checks accepted. Prepayment is required.

State Court PO Box 1046, Griffin, GA 30224; 770-467-4745. Hours: 8AM-5PM (EST). *Misdemeanor, Civil.*

Civil Records: Access: In person only. Visitors must perform in person searches for themselves. No search fee. Required to search: name, years to search. Civil cases indexed by defendant, plaintiff. Civil records on computer back to 1995; prior records on dockets from 1852. Mail access only for specific case information, no name searching.

Criminal Records: Access: Mail, in person. Visitors must perform in person searches for themselves. No search fee. Required to search: name, years to search, DOB; also helpful: SSN, race, sex. Criminal records on computer back to 1995; prior records on dockets from 1852. Mail access for specific case information only, no name searching by the court.

General Information: Public access terminal is available. No juvenile, adoption, sexual, mental health or expunged records released. SASE required. Turnaround time 2 days. Copy fee: $.25 per page. Certification fee: $2.00. Fee payee: Court Clerk. Business checks accepted. Prepayment is required.

Magistrate Court 132 E Solomon St, Griffin, GA 30223; 770-467-4320; Fax: 770-467-0081. Hours: 8AM-5PM (EST). *Civil Actions Under $15,000, Eviction, Small Claims.*

Probate Court 132 E Solomon St, Griffin, GA 30223; 770-467-4340; Fax: 770-467-4243. Hours: 8AM-5PM (EST). *Probate.*

Stephens County

Superior Court 205 Alexander St N, #202, Toccoa, GA 30577; 706-886-3598; Fax: 706-886-5710. Hours: 8AM-5PM (EST). *Felony, Misdemeanor, Civil.*

Civil Records: Access: Mail, fax, in person. Both court and visitors may perform in person searches. Search fee: $7.50 per name. Required to search: name, years to search. Civil cases indexed by defendant, plaintiff. Civil records on computer back to 1988, on dockets from 1906.

Criminal Records: Access: Mail, fax, in person. Both court and visitors may perform in person searches. Search fee: $7.50 per name. Required to search: name, years to search, DOB, signed release; also helpful: SSN, race, sex. Criminal records on computer back to 1988, on dockets from 1906.

General Information: Public access terminal is available. No juvenile, adoption, sexual, mental health

or expunged records released. Turnaround time 1 day. Fax notes: Fee to fax results pre-paid: $2.00 1st page, $1.00 each add'l. Copy fee: $1.00 per page. Certification fee: $2.50 plus $.50 per page after first. Fee payee: Court Clerk. Personal checks accepted. Prepayment is required.

State Court 205 N Alexander St Rm 202, County Government Building, Toccoa, GA 30577; 706-886-3598/9496. Hours: 8AM-5PM (EST). *Misdemeanor, Civil.*

Civil Records: Access: Mail, in person. Visitors must perform in person searches for themselves. Search fee: $7.50 per name. Required to search: name, years to search. Civil cases indexed by defendant, plaintiff. Civil records on computer back to 1988, on dockets from 1906.

Criminal Records: Access: Mail, in person. Visitors must perform in person searches for themselves. Search fee: $7.50 per name. Required to search: name, years to search, DOB, signed release; also helpful: SSN, race, sex. Criminal records on computer back to 1988, on dockets from 1906.

General Information: Public access terminal is available. No juvenile, adoption, sexual, mental health or expunged records released. Turnaround time 1 day. Copy fee: $1.00 per page. Certification fee: $2.50 plus $.50 per page after first. Fee payee: Court Clerk. Personal checks accepted. Prepayment is required.

Magistrate Court 205 N Alexander St, Rm 107, Toccoa, GA 30577; 706-886-6205; Fax: 706-886-5569. Hours: 8:30AM-5:00Pm (EST). *Civil Actions Under $15,000, Eviction, Small Claims.*

Probate Court 205 N Alexander St #103, Toccoa, GA 30577; 706-886-2828; Fax: 706-886-2631. Hours: 8AM-5PM M-Th; 8AM-4:30 F (closed for lunches) (EST). *Probate.*

Stewart County

Superior Court PO Box 910, Main St, Lumpkin, GA 31815; 229-838-6220. Hours: 8AM-4:30PM (EST). *Felony, Misdemeanor, Civil.*

Civil Records: Access: In person only. Visitors must perform in person searches for themselves. No search fee. Required to search: name, years to search; also helpful: address. Civil cases indexed by defendant. Civil records in index books.

Criminal Records: Access: In person only. Visitors must perform in person searches for themselves. No search fee. Required to search: name, years to search; also helpful: address, DOB, SSN. Criminal records in index books to 1840s.

General Information: Public access terminal is available. No juvenile, adoption, sexual, mental health or sealed records are released. Copy fee: $.25 per page. Certification fee: $2.50 plus $.50 per page after first. Fee payee: Clerk of Superior Court. Personal checks accepted.

Magistrate Court PO Box 712, Lumpkin, GA 31815; 229-838-4261; Fax: 229-838-4394. Hours: 8AM-5PM (EST). *Civil Actions Under $15,000, Eviction, Small Claims.*

Probate Court PO Box 876, Lumpkin, GA 31815; 229-838-4394; Fax: 229-838-9084. Hours: 8AM-Noon, 1-5PM (EST). *Probate.*

Sumter County

State Court PO Box 333, Americus, GA 31709; 229-928-4537. 9AM-5PM (EST). *Misdemeanor, Civil.*

Civil Records: Access: In person only. Visitors must perform in person searches for themselves. No search fee. Required to search: name, years to search. Civil

cases indexed by defendant, plaintiff. Civil records on dockets from late 1800s.

Criminal Records: Access: In person only. Visitors must perform in person searches for themselves. No search fee. Required to search: name, years to search, DOB; also helpful: SSN, race, sex. Criminal records on dockets from late 1800s.

General Information: No juvenile, adoption, sealed, sexual, mental health or expunged records released. Copy fee: $.25 per page. Certification fee: $2.50 plus $.50 per page. Fee payee: Court Clerk. Prepayment is required.

Magistrate Court PO Box 563, Americus, GA 31709; 229-928-4524; Fax: 229-928-4527. Hours: 9AM-5PM (EST). *Civil Actions Under $15,000, Eviction, Small Claims.*

Probate Court PO Box 246, Americus, GA 31709; 229-924-7693; Fax: 229-924-2541. Hours: 9AM-5PM (EST). *Probate.*

Talbot County

Superior Court PO Box 325, Talbotton, GA 31827; 706-665-3239; Fax: 706-665-8199. Hours: 9AM-5PM (EST). *Felony, Misdemeanor, Civil.*

Civil Records: Access: In person only. Visitors must perform in person searches for themselves. No search fee. Required to search: name, years to search. Civil cases indexed by defendant, plaintiff. Civil records on dockets from 1827.

Criminal Records: Access: In person only. Visitors must perform in person searches for themselves. No search fee. Required to search: name, years to search. Criminal records on computer since 1991, prior on docket books.

General Information: No juvenile, adoption, sexual, mental health or expunged records released. Copy fee: $.25 per page. Certification fee: $2.00 plus $.50 per page after first. Fee payee: Superior Court. Business checks accepted. Prepayment is required.

Magistrate & Probate Court PO Box 157, Talbotton, GA 31827; 706-665-8866; Fax: 706-665-8240. Hours: 8AM-5PM (EST). *Civil Actions Under $15,000, Eviction, Small Claims, Probate.*

Taliaferro County

Superior Court PO Box 182, Crawfordville, GA 30631; 706-456-2123. Hours: 9AM-5PM (EST). *Felony, Misdemeanor, Civil.*

Civil Records: Access: In person only. Visitors must perform in person searches for themselves. No search fee. Required to search: name, years to search. Civil cases indexed by defendant, plaintiff. Civil records on dockets from 1825.

Criminal Records: Access: In person only. Visitors must perform in person searches for themselves. No search fee. Required to search: name, years to search, DOB; also helpful: SSN, race, sex. Criminal records on dockets from 1825.

General Information: No juvenile, adoption, sexual, mental health or expunged records released. Copy fee: $.25 per page. Certification fee: $2.00. Fee payee: Court Clerk. Personal checks accepted. Prepayment required.

Magistrate & Probate Court PO Box 264, Crawfordville, GA 30631; 706-456-2253; Fax: 706-456-2904. Hours: 8AM-5PM (EST). *Civil Actions Under $15,000, Eviction, Small Claims, Probate.*

Tattnall County

Superior & State Court PO Box 39, Reidsville, GA 30453; 912-557-6716; Fax: 912-557-4861. Hours: 8AM-5PM (EST). *Felony, Misdemeanor, Civil.*

Civil Records: Access: In person only. Visitors must perform in person searches for themselves. No search

fee. Required to search: name, years to search; also helpful: address. Civil cases indexed by defendant, plaintiff. Civil records on computer back to 1990; on dockets from 1800s.

Criminal Records: Access: In person only. Visitors must perform in person searches for themselves. No search fee. Required to search: name, years to search, DOB; also helpful: address, SSN, race, sex. Criminal records on computer back to 1990; on dockets from 1800s.

General Information: Public access terminal is available. No juvenile, adoption, sexual, mental health or expunged records released. Copy fee: $.25 per page. Certification fee: $3.00 plus $.50 per page after first. Fee payee: Court Clerk. Business checks accepted. Prepayment is required.

Magistrate Court PO Box 513, Reidsville, GA 30453; 912-557-4372; Fax: 912-557-3631. Hours: 8AM-5PM (EST). *Civil Actions Under $15,000, Eviction, Small Claims.*

Probate Court PO Box 699, Reidsville, GA 30453; 912-557-6719; Fax: 912-557-3976. Hours: 8:30AM-4:30PM (EST). *Probate.*

Taylor County

Superior Court PO Box 248, Courthouse Square, Butler, GA 31006; 478-862-5594; Fax: 478-862-5334. Hours: 8AM-5PM (EST). *Felony, Misdemeanor, Civil.*

Civil Records: Access: In person only. Both court and visitors may perform in person searches. Search fee: is copy fee. Required to search: name, years to search. Civil cases indexed by defendant, plaintiff. Civil records on computer from 1991, dockets from 1852.

Criminal Records: Access: In person only. Visitors must perform in person searches for themselves. Search fee: is copy fee. Required to search: name, years to search, DOB; also helpful: SSN, race, sex. Criminal records on computer from 1991, dockets from 1852.

General Information: No juvenile, adoption, sexual, mental health or expunged records released. Copy fee: $.25 per page. $1.00 minimum. Certification fee: $2.00 plus $.50 per page. Fee payee: Court Clerk. Personal checks accepted. Prepayment is required.

Magistrate & Probate Court PO Box 536, Butler, GA 31006; 478-862-3357; Fax: 478-862-5334. Hours: 8AM-5PM (EST). *Civil Actions Under $15,000, Eviction, Small Claims, Probate.*

Telfair County

Superior Court Courthouse, 128 Oak St #2, McRae, GA 31055; 229-868-6525; Fax: 229-868-7956. Hours: 8:30AM-4:30PM (EST). *Felony, Misdemeanor, Civil.*

Civil Records: Access: Phone, mail, in person. Visitors must perform in person searches for themselves. No search fee. Required to search: name, years to search. Civil cases indexed by defendant. Civil records on dockets from early 1900s.

Criminal Records: Access: Phone, in person. Visitors must perform in person searches for themselves. No search fee. Required to search: name, years to search, DOB, signed release; also helpful: SSN, race, sex. Criminal records on dockets from early 1900s.

General Information: No juvenile, adoption, sexual, mental health or expunged records released. SASE requested. Turnaround time 1 week. Copy fee: $.25 per page. Certification fee: $3.00. Fee payee: Court Clerk. Personal checks accepted.

Magistrate Court 128 E Oak St #5, McRae, GA 31055; 229-868-6772; Fax: 229-868-6902. Hours: 8:30AM-4:30PM (EST). *Civil Actions Under $15,000, Eviction, Small Claims.*

Probate Court 128 E Oak St #1, McRae, GA 31055; 229-868-6038; Fax: 229-868-7620. Hours: 8:30AM-Noon, 1-4:30PM (EST). *Probate.*

Terrell County

Superior Court PO Box 189 (, 513 S Main St, Dawson, GA 31742; 229-995-2631. Hours: 8:30AM-5PM (EST). *Felony, Misdemeanor, Civil.*

Civil Records: Access: In person only. Visitors must perform in person searches for themselves. No search fee. Required to search: name, years to search. Civil cases indexed by defendant. Civil records on computer from 1988, dockets books from 1900s.

Criminal Records: Access: In person only. Visitors must perform in person searches for themselves. No search fee. Required to search: name, years to search, DOB, signed release; also helpful: SSN, race, sex. Criminal records on computer from 1988, dockets books from 1900s.

General Information: No juvenile, adoption, sexual, mental health or expunged records released. Copy fee: $.25 per page. Certification fee: $3.00 plus $.50 per page after first. Fee payee: Court Clerk. Business checks accepted. Prepayment is required.

Magistrate Court PO Box 793, Dawson, GA 31742; 229-995-3757; Fax: 229-995-4496. Hours: 8AM-5PM (EST). *Civil Actions Under $15,000, Eviction, Small Claims, Misdemeanors.*

Probate Court PO Box 67, Dawson, GA 31742; 229-995-5515; Fax: 229-995-4301. *Probate.*

Thomas County

Superior & State Court PO Box 1995, Thomasville, GA 31799; 229-225-4108; Fax: 229-225-4110. Hours: 8AM-5PM (EST). *Felony, Misdemeanor, Civil.*

www.thomascoclerkofcourt.org

Civil Records: Access: In person only. Visitors must perform in person searches for themselves. No search fee. Required to search: name, years to search. Civil cases indexed by defendant, plaintiff. Civil records on computer from 1989, archived from 1826.

Criminal Records: Access: In person only. Visitors must perform in person searches for themselves. No search fee. Required to search: name, years to search, DOB; also helpful: SSN, race, sex.

General Information: Public access terminal is available. No juvenile, adoption, sexual, mental health or expunged records released. Copy fee: $1.00 per page. Certification fee: $2.00. Fee payee: Court Clerk. Personal checks accepted. Prepayment is required.

Magistrate Court PO Box 879, Thomasville, GA 31799; 229-225-3334; Fax: 229-225-3342. Hours: 8AM-5PM (EST). *Civil Actions Under $15,000, Eviction, Small Claims.*

Probate Court PO Box 1582, Thomasville, GA 31799; 229-225-4116; Fax: 229-227-1698. Hours: 8AM-5PM (EST). *Probate.*

Tift County

Superior & State Court PO Box 354, Tifton, GA 31793; 229-386-7810. Hours: 8AM-5PM (EST). *Felony, Misdemeanor, Civil.*

Civil Records: Access: In person only. Visitors must perform in person searches for themselves. No search fee. Required to search: name, years to search. Civil cases indexed by defendant. Civil records on dockets books from 1905.

Criminal Records: Access: In person only. Visitors must perform in person searches for themselves. No search fee. Required to search: name, years to search,

DOB; also helpful: SSN, race, sex. Criminal records on dockets books from 1905.

General Information: No juvenile, adoption, sexual, mental health or expunged records released. Copy fee: $.25 per page. Certification fee: $2.50 plus $.50 per page after first. Fee payee: Court Clerk. Personal checks accepted. Prepayment is required.

Magistrate Court PO Box 214, Tifton, GA 31793; 229-386-7907; Fax: 229-386-7978. Hours: 8AM-5PM (EST). *Civil Actions Under $15,000, Eviction, Small Claims.*

Probate Court PO Box 792, Tifton, GA 31793; 229-386-7936, 229-386-7914; Fax: 229-386-7913. Hours: 9AM-5PM (EST). *Probate.*

Toombs County

Superior & State Court PO Drawer 530, Lyons, GA 30436; 912-526-3501; Fax: 912-526-1004. Hours: 8:30AM-5PM (EST). *Felony, Misdemeanor, Civil.*

Civil Records: Access: In person only. Visitors must perform in person searches for themselves. No search fee. Required to search: name, years to search. Civil cases indexed by defendant, plaintiff. Civil records on dockets books from 1908, on computer since 1995.

Criminal Records: Access: In person only. Visitors must perform in person searches for themselves. No search fee. Required to search: name, years to search, DOB; also helpful: SSN, race, sex. Criminal records on dockets books from 1908, on computer since 1995.

General Information: No juvenile, adoption, sexual, mental health or expunged records released. Copy fee: $1.00 per page. Certification fee: $2.50 plus $1.00 per page after first. Fee payee: Court Clerk. No personal checks accepted. Prepayment is required.

Magistrate Court PO Box 1460, Lyons, GA 30436; 912-526-8984; Fax: 912-526-8985. Hours: 8:30AM-5PM (EST). *Civil Actions Under $15,000, Eviction, Small Claims.*

Probate Court Toombs County Courthouse, PO Box 1370, Lyons, GA 30436; 912-526-8696; Fax: 912-526-1008. Hours: 8:30AM-5PM (EST). *Probate.*

Towns County

Superior Court 48 River St #E, Hiawassee, GA 30546; 706-896-2130. Hours: 8:30AM-4:30PM (EST). *Felony, Misdemeanor, Civil.*

Civil Records: Access: Phone, mail, in person. Both court and visitors may perform in person searches. No search fee. Required to search: name, years to search. Civil cases indexed by plaintiff. Civil records on dockets books from 1940.

Criminal Records: Access: Phone, mail, in person. Both court and visitors may perform in person searches. No search fee. Required to search: name, years to search, DOB, signed release; also helpful: SSN, race, sex. Criminal records on docket books, indexed by defendant.

General Information: No juvenile, adoption, sexual, mental health or expunged records released. SASE required. Turnaround time same day. Copy fee: $.25 per page. Certification fee: $2.50 per page. Fee payee: Court Clerk. Personal checks accepted. Prepayment is required.

Magistrate & Probate Court PO Box 549 (48 River St), Hiawassee, GA 30546; 706-896-3467; Fax: 706-896-1772. 8:30AM-4:30PM (EST). *Civil Actions Under $15,000, Eviction, Small Claims, Probate.*

Treutlen County

Superior & State Court PO Box 356, Soperton, GA 30457; 912-529-4215. Hours: 8AM-5PM (EST). *Felony, Misdemeanor, Civil.*

Civil Records: Access: Mail, in person. Both court and visitors may perform in person searches. No search fee. Required to search: name, years to search. Civil cases indexed by defendant, plaintiff. Civil records on computer from 1991, dockets books from 1919.

Criminal Records: Access: Mail, in person. Both court and visitors may perform in person searches. No search fee. Required to search: name, years to search, DOB; also helpful: SSN, race, sex. Criminal records on computer from 1991, dockets books from 1919.

General Information: Public access terminal is available. No juvenile, adoption, sexual, mental health or expunged records released. Turnaround time 1-2 days. Copy fee: $.25 per page. Certification fee: $2.50 plus $.50 per page after first. Fee payee: Court Clerk. Personal checks accepted. Prepayment is required.

Magistrate & Probate Court 114 Second St South, Courthouse Annex, Soperton, GA 30457; 912-529-3342; Fax: 912-529-6838. Hours: 9AM-12; 1-5PM (EST). *Civil Actions Under $15,000, Eviction, Small Claims, Probate.*

Troup County

Superior & State Court 118 Ridley Ave (PO Box 866, 30241), LaGrange, GA 30240; 706-883-1740. Hours: 8AM-5PM (EST). *Felony, Misdemeanor, Civil.*

Civil Records: Access: In person only. Visitors must perform in person searches for themselves. No search fee. Required to search: name, years to search. Civil cases indexed by defendant, plaintiff. Civil records on computer from 1994, on docket books from 1940s.

Criminal Records: Access: In person only. Visitors must perform in person searches for themselves. No search fee. Required to search: name, years to search, DOB; also helpful: SSN, race, sex. Criminal records on computer from 1994, on docket books from 1940s.

General Information: Public access terminal is available. (UCC & Taxes.) No juvenile, adoption, sexual, mental health or expunged records released. Copy fee: $.25 per page. Certification fee: $2.75 plus $.25 per page. Fee payee: Court Clerk. Personal checks accepted. Prepayment is required.

Magistrate Court 119 Ridley Ave #101, LaGrange, GA 30240; 706-883-1695; Fax: 706-883-1632. Hours: 8AM-5PM (EST). *Civil Actions Under $15,000, Eviction, Small Claims.*

Probate Court 900 Dallis St, LaGrange, GA 30240; 706-883-1690; Fax: 706-812-7933. Hours: 8AM-5PM (EST). *Probate.*

Turner County

Superior Court PO Box 106, 219 E College Ave, Ashburn, GA 31714; 229-567-2011; Fax: 229-567-0450. Hours: 8AM-5PM (EST). *Felony, Misdemeanor, Civil.*

Civil Records: Access: In person only. Visitors must perform in person searches for themselves. No search fee. Required to search: name, years to search. Civil cases indexed by defendant, plaintiff. Civil records on docket books, archived from 1905.

Criminal Records: Access: In person only. Visitors must perform in person searches for themselves. No search fee. Required to search: name, years to search, DOB, signed release; also helpful: SSN, race, sex. Criminal records on docket books, archived from 1905.

General Information: No juvenile, adoption, sexual, mental health or expunged records released. Copy fee: $1.00 by court, $.25 if do it yourself. Certification fee:

$2.50 plus $1.00 per page after first. Fee payee: Court Clerk. Personal checks accepted. Prepayment required.

Magistrate Court PO Box 1163, Ashburn, GA 31750; 229-426-5140. Hours: 8:30AM-4:30PM (EST). *Civil Actions Under $15,000, Eviction, Small Claims.*

Probate Court PO Box 2506, Ashburn, GA 31714; 229-567-2151; Fax: 229-567-0358. Hours: 8AM-5PM (EST). *Probate.*

Twiggs County

Superior Court PO Box 228, Jeffersonville, GA 31044; 478-945-3350. Hours: 8AM-5PM (EST). *Felony, Misdemeanor, Civil.*

Civil Records: Access: In person only. Visitors must perform in person searches for themselves. No search fee. Required to search: name, years to search. Civil cases indexed by defendant, plaintiff. Civil records on computer from 1991, dockets books to 1901.

Criminal Records: Access: In person only. Visitors must perform in person searches for themselves. No search fee. Required to search: name, years to search, DOB, signed release; also helpful: SSN, race, sex. Criminal records on computer from 1991, dockets books to 1901.

General Information: No juvenile, adoption, sexual, mental health or expunged records released. Copy fee: $.25 per page. Certification fee: $2.50 plus $.50 per page after first. Fee payee: Court Clerk. Personal checks accepted. Prepayment is required.

Magistrate Court PO Box 146, Jeffersonville, GA 31044; 478-945-3428; Fax: 478-945-2083. Hours: 9AM-5PM (EST). *Civil Actions Under $15,000, Eviction, Small Claims.*

Probate Court PO Box 307, Jeffersonville, GA 31044; 478-945-3390/3252; Fax: 478-945-6070. Hours: 9AM-5PM (EST). *Probate, Misdemeanor Traffic.*

Union County

Superior Court 114 Courthouse St, Box 5, Blairsville, GA 30512; 706-439-6022; Fax: 706-439-6026. Hours: 8AM-5PM (EST). *Felony, Misdemeanor, Civil.*

Civil Records: Access: In person only. Both court and visitors may perform in person searches. No search fee. Required to search: name, years to search. Civil cases indexed by defendant, plaintiff. Civil records on computer from 1993, on dockets from 1936.

Criminal Records: Access: In person only. Both court and visitors may perform in person searches. No search fee. Required to search: name, years to search, DOB, signed release; also helpful: SSN, race, sex. Criminal records on docket books from 1930; computerized records since 1997.

General Information: Public access terminal is available. No juvenile, adoption, sexual, mental health or expunged records released. Copy fee: $.25 per page. Certification fee: $2.50 plus $.25 per page after first. Fee payee: Court Clerk. Personal checks accepted. Prepayment is required.

Magistrate Court 114 Courthouse St, #10, Blairsville, GA 30512; 706-439-6008; Fax: 706-439-6104. Hours: 8AM-4:30PM (EST). *Civil Actions Under $15,000, Eviction, Small Claims.*

Probate Court 114 Courthouse St, #8, Blairsville, GA 30512; 706-439-6005; Fax: 706-439-6009. Hours: 8AM-4:30PM (EST). *Probate.*

Upson County

Superior Court PO Box 469, Thomaston, GA 30286; 706-647-7835; Fax: 706-647-8999. Hours: 8AM-5PM (EST). *Felony, Misdemeanor, Civil.*

Civil Records: Access: In person only. Visitors must perform in person searches for themselves. No search fee. Required to search: name, years to search. Civil cases indexed by defendant, plaintiff. Civil records on dockets books from 1927; on computer back to 1990.

Criminal Records: Access: In person only. Visitors must perform in person searches for themselves. No search fee. Required to search: name, years to search, DOB; also helpful: SSN, race, sex. Criminal records on docket books from 1937; on computer back to 1990.

General Information: Public access terminal is available. No juvenile, adoption, sexual, mental health or expunged records released. Copy fee: $.25 per page. Certification fee: $2.50 plus $.50 per page after first. Fee payee: Court Clerk. Personal checks accepted. Prepayment is required.

Magistrate Court PO Box 890, Thomaston, GA 30286; 706-647-6891; Fax: 706-647-1248. Hours: 8AM-5PM (EST). *Civil Actions Under $15,000, Eviction, Small Claims.*

Probate Court PO Box 906, Thomaston, GA 30286; 706-647-7015; Fax: 706-646-7030. Hours: 8AM-5PM (EST). *Probate.*

Walker County

Superior & State Court PO Box 448, LaFayette, GA 30728; 706-638-1772. Hours: 8AM-5PM (EST). *Felony, Misdemeanor, Civil.*

Civil Records: Access: In person only. Visitors must perform in person searches for themselves. No search fee. Required to search: name, years to search. Civil cases indexed by defendant, plaintiff. Civil records on dockets books from 1883; computerized since 2000.

Criminal Records: Access: In person only. Visitors must perform in person searches for themselves. No search fee. Required to search: name, years to search, DOB; also helpful: SSN, race, sex. Criminal records on dockets books from 1883.

General Information: No juvenile, adoption, sexual, mental health or expunged records released. Copy fee: $.25 per page. Certification fee: $2.00. Fee payee: Court Clerk. Personal checks accepted.

Magistrate Court 102 Napier St, LaFayette, GA 30728; 706-638-1217; Fax: 706-638-1218. Hours: 8AM-5PM (EST). *Civil Actions Under $15,000, Eviction, Small Claims.*

Probate Court PO Box 436, LaFayette, GA 30728; 706-638-2852; Fax: 706-638-2869. Hours: 8AM-5PM (EST). *Probate.*
https://www.gaprobate.org/counties/index.html

Walton County

Superior Court PO Box 745, Monroe, GA 30655; 770-267-1307; Fax: 770-267-1441. Hours: 8:30AM-5PM (EST). *Felony, Misdemeanor, Civil.*

Civil Records: Access: In person only. Visitors must perform in person searches for themselves. No search fee. Required to search: name, years to search. Civil cases indexed by defendant, plaintiff. Civil records on computer from 1990, dockets books from 1900s.

Criminal Records: Access: In person only. Visitors must perform in person searches for themselves. No search fee. Required to search: name, years to search; also helpful: DOB, race, sex. Criminal records on computer from 1990, dockets books from 1900s.

General Information: Public access terminal is available. No juvenile, adoption, sexual, mental health or expunged records released. Copy fee: $.25 per page.

Certification fee: $2.50 plus $.50 per page after first. Fee payee: Court Clerk. Personal checks accepted. Prepayment is required.

Magistrate Court PO Box 1188, Monroe, GA 30655; 770-267-1386; Fax: 770-266-1512. Hours: 8:30AM-5PM (EST). *Civil Actions Under $15,000, Eviction, Small Claims.*

Probate Court PO Box 629, Monroe, GA 30655; 770-267-1345, 267-1387; Fax: 770-267-1417. Hours: 8:30AM-5PM (EST). *Probate.*

Note: This location also has traffic and misdemeanor records

Ware County

Superior & State Court PO Box 776, Waycross, GA 31502; 912-287-4340. Hours: 9AM-5PM (EST). *Felony, Misdemeanor, Civil.*

Civil Records: Access: In person only. Visitors must perform in person searches for themselves. No search fee. Required to search: name, years to search. Civil cases indexed by defendant. Civil records on computer since 1995; prior records on dockets books from 1874.

Criminal Records: Access: In person only. Visitors must perform in person searches for themselves. No search fee. Required to search: name, years to search, DOB; also helpful: SSN, race, sex. Criminal records on computer since 1995; prior records on dockets books from 1874.

General Information: No juvenile, adoption, sexual, mental health or expunged records released. Copy fee: $.25 per page; $1.00 if court assists. Certification fee: $2.50 plus $.50 per page after first. Fee payee: Court Clerk. Personal checks accepted. Prepayment required.

Magistrate Court PO Box 17, 201 State St, Rm 102, Waycross, GA 31501; 912-287-4373; Fax: 912-287-4377. Hours: 9AM-5PM (EST). *Civil Actions Under $15,000, Eviction, Small Claims.*

Probate Court Ware County Courthouse, #123, 800 Church St, Waycross, GA 31501; 912-287-4315/6; Fax: 912-287-4317. Hours: 9AM-5PM (EST). *Probate.*

Warren County

Superior Court PO Box 227, 100 Main St, Warrenton, GA 30828; 706-465-2262; Fax: 706-465-0232. Hours: 8AM-5PM (EST). *Felony, Misdemeanor, Civil.*

Civil Records: Access: In person only. Visitors must perform in person searches for themselves. No search fee. Required to search: name, years to search. Civil cases indexed by defendant, plaintiff. Civil records on dockets books to 1950.

Criminal Records: Access: In person only. Visitors must perform in person searches for themselves. No search fee. Required to search: name, years to search, DOB, signed release; also helpful: SSN, race, sex. Criminal records on dockets books to 1950, computerized since 2000.

General Information: No juvenile, adoption, sexual, mental health or expunged records released. Copy fee: $.25 per page. Certification fee: $2.50 1st page plus $.50 each add'l page. Fee payee: Court Clerk. Only cashiers checks and money orders accepted. Prepayment is required.

Magistrate Court PO Box 203, Warrenton, GA 30828; 706-465-3123; Fax: 706-465-1300. Hours: 8AM-5PM (EST). *Civil Actions Under $15,000, Eviction, Small Claims.*

Probate Court PO Box 364, Warrenton, GA 30828; 706-465-2227. 8AM-5PM (EST). *Probate.*

Washington County

Superior & State Court PO Box 231, Sandersville, GA 31082; 478-552-3186. Hours: 9AM-5PM (EST). *Felony, Misdemeanor, Civil.*

Civil Records: Access: Mail, in person. Visitors must perform in person searches for themselves. No search fee. Required to search: name, years to search. Civil cases indexed by defendant, plaintiff. Civil records on dockets books to 1869.

Criminal Records: Access: Mail, in person. Visitors must perform in person searches for themselves. No search fee. Required to search: name, years to search. Criminal records on dockets books to 1869.

General Information: Public access terminal is available. No juvenile, adoption, sexual, mental health or expunged records released. Copy fee: $.25 per page. Certification fee: $2.00. Fee payee: Court Clerk. Personal checks accepted. Prepayment is required.

Magistrate Court PO Box 1053, Sandersville, GA 31082; 478-552-3591. Hours: 9AM-5PM (EST). *Civil Actions Under $15,000, Eviction, Small Claims.*

Probate Court PO Box 669, Sandersville, GA 31082; 478-552-3304; Fax: 478-552-7424. Hours: 9AM-Noon, 1-5PM (EST). *Probate.*

Wayne County

Superior & State Court PO Box 920, Jesup, GA 31598; 912-427-5930; Fax: 912-427-5939. Hours: 8:30AM-5PM (EST). *Felony, Misdemeanor, Civil.*

Civil Records: Access: In person only. Visitors must perform in person searches for themselves. Required to search: name, years to search. Civil cases indexed by defendant, plaintiff. Civil records on computer, on docket books from 1810.

Criminal Records: Access: In person only. Visitors must perform in person searches for themselves. Required to search: name, years to search, DOB. Criminal records on computer, on docket books from 1810.

General Information: Public access terminal is available. No juvenile, adoption, sexual, mental health or expunged records released. Copy fee: $.25 per page. Certification fee: $2.50 plus $.50 per page after first. Fee payee: Superior Court Clerk. Personal checks accepted. Prepayment is required.

Magistrate Court PO Box 27, Jesup, GA 31598; 912-427-5960; Fax: 912-427-5944. Hours: 8:30AM-Noon; 1PM-5PM (EST). *Civil Actions Under $15,000, Eviction, Small Claims.*

Probate Court 174 N Brunswick St, Jesup, GA 31598; 912-427-5940; Fax: 912-427-5944. Hours: 8AM-5PM (EST). *Probate.*

Webster County

Superior Court PO Box 117, Preston, GA 31824; 229-828-3525. Hours: 8AM-4:30PM (EST). *Felony, Misdemeanor, Civil.*

Civil Records: Access: In person only. Visitors must perform in person searches for themselves. No search fee. Required to search: name, years to search. Civil cases indexed by defendant, plaintiff. Civil records on docket books from 1860; computerized records since 2000.

Criminal Records: Access: In person only. Visitors must perform in person searches for themselves. No search fee. Required to search: name, years to search, signed release. Criminal records on docket books from 1860; computerized records since 2000.

General Information: Public access terminal is available. No juvenile, adoption, sexual, mental health or expunged records released. Copy fee: $.25 per page. Certification fee: $2.50 plus $.50 per page after first page. Fee payee: Clerk Superior Court. Personal checks accepted. Prepayment is required.

Magistrate & Probate Court PO Box 135, Preston, GA 31824; 229-828-3615; Fax: 229-828-3616. Hours: 8:00AM-4:30PM (EST). *Civil Actions Under $15,000, Eviction, Small Claims, Probate.*

Note: This court will not give out SSNs

Wheeler County

Superior Court PO Box 38, Alamo, GA 30411; 912-568-7137. Hours: 8AM-4PM (EST). *Felony, Misdemeanor, Civil.*

Civil Records: Access: In person only. Visitors must perform in person searches for themselves. No search fee. Required to search: name, years to search. Civil cases indexed by defendant. Civil records on docket books from 1913.

Criminal Records: Access: In person only. Visitors must perform in person searches for themselves. No search fee. Required to search: name, years to search. Criminal records on docket books from 1913.

General Information: No juvenile or adoption records released. Copy fee: $.25 per page. Certification fee: $2.50 plus $.50 each additional page. Fee payee: Superior Court Clerk. Personal checks accepted. Prepayment is required.

Magistrate & Probate Court PO Box 477, Alamo, GA 30411; 912-568-7133; Fax: 912-568-1743. Hours: 8AM-4PM (EST). *Civil Actions Under $15,000, Eviction, Small Claims, Probate.*

White County

Superior Court 59 S Main St, Ste B, Cleveland, GA 30528; 706-865-2613; Fax: 706-865-7749. Hours: 8:30AM-5PM (EST). *Felony, Misdemeanor, Civil.*

Civil Records: Access: In person only. Visitors must perform in person searches for themselves. No search fee. Required to search: name, years to search. Civil cases indexed by defendant, plaintiff. Civil records on computer from 1996, on docket books from 1857.

Criminal Records: Access: In person only. Visitors must perform in person searches for themselves. No search fee. Required to search: name, years to search. Criminal records on computer from 1996, on docket books from 1857. Will accept mail requests only if a case number is provided.

General Information: Public access terminal is available. No juvenile, adoption, sexual, mental health or expunged records released. Fax notes: Fee to fax results is $1.00 per page. Copy fee: $.25 per page. Certification fee: $2.50 plus $.50 per page after first. Fee payee: Superior Court Clerk. Business checks accepted. Prepayment is required.

Magistrate Court 59 S Main St, #B, Cleveland, GA 30528; 706-865-6636; Fax: 706-865-7749. Hours: 8:30AM-5PM (EST). *Civil Actions Under $15,000, Misdemeanor, Eviction, Small Claims.*

Probate Court 59 S Main St #H, Cleveland, GA 30528; 706-865-4141; Fax: 706-865-1324. Hours: 8:30AM-5PM (EST). *Probate, Misdemeanors.*

Whitfield County

Superior Court PO Box 868, Dalton, GA 30722; 706-275-7450; Fax: 706-275-7456. Hours: 8AM-5PM (EST). *Felony, Misdemeanor, Civil.*

Civil Records: Access: In person only. Visitors must perform in person searches for themselves. No search

fee. Required to search: name, years to search. Civil cases indexed by defendant, plaintiff. Civil records on computer from 1988, on docket books from 1852.

Criminal Records: Access: In person only. Visitors must perform in person searches for themselves. No search fee. Required to search: name, years to search, offense, date of offense. Criminal records on computer from 1988, on docket books from 1852.

General Information: Public access terminal is available. No juvenile, adoption, sexual, mental health or expunged records released. Copy fee: $.50 per page. Certification fee: $3.00. Fee payee: Superior Court Clerk. Business checks accepted. Prepayment required.

Magistrate Court PO Box 386, Dalton, GA 30722-0386; 706-278-5052; Fax: 706-278-8810. Hours: 8AM-5PM M-W, F; 9AM-5PM Th (EST). *Civil Actions Under $15,000, Eviction, Small Claims.*

Probate Court 301 Crawford St, Dalton, GA 30720; 706-275-7400; Fax: 706-275-7486. Hours: 8AM-5PM (EST). *Probate.*

Wilcox County

Superior & Magistrate Courts 103 N Broad St, Abbeville, GA 31001; 229-467-2442; Fax: 229-467-2886. Hours: 9AM-5PM (EST). *Felony, Misdemeanor, Civil, Eviction, Small Claims.*

Civil Records: Access: Mail, in person. Both court and visitors may perform in person searches. No search fee. Required to search: name, years to search. Civil cases indexed by defendant, plaintiff. Civil records on computer since 1995; prior records on docket books from 1950s.

Criminal Records: Access: Mail, in person. Both court and visitors may perform in person searches. No search fee. Required to search: name, years to search, DOB; also helpful: SSN. Criminal records on computer since 1995; prior records on docket books from 1950s.

General Information: Public access terminal is available. No juvenile, adoption, sexual, mental health or expunged records released. Turnaround time 1 week. Copy fee: $.25 per page. Certification fee: $2.50 per page. Fee payee: Superior Court Clerk. Personal checks accepted. Prepayment is required.

Probate Court 103 N Broad St, Abbeville, GA 31001; 229-467-2220; Fax: 229-467-2000. Hours: 9AM-5PM (EST). *Probate.*

Wilkes County

Superior Court 23 E Court St, Rm 205, Washington, GA 30673; 706-678-2423. Hours: 9AM-5PM (EST). *Felony, Misdemeanor, Civil.*

Civil Records: Access: In person only. Visitors must perform in person searches for themselves. No search fee. Required to search: name, years to search. Civil cases indexed by defendant, plaintiff. Civil records on docket books from 1700s, computerized from 1998.

Criminal Records: Access: In person only. Visitors must perform in person searches for themselves. Required to search: name, years to search. Criminal records on docket books from 1700s, computerized from 1998.

General Information: No juvenile or adoption records released. Copy fee: $.25 per page self-serve. Certification fee: $2.50 plus $.50 per page after first. Fee payee: Superior Court Clerk. Personal checks accepted. Prepayment is required.

Magistrate Court 23 E Court St, Rm 427, Washington, GA 30673; 706-678-1881. Hours: 8:30AM-5PM (EST). *Civil Actions Under $15,000, Eviction, Small Claims.*

Probate Court 23 E Court St, Rm 422, Washington, GA 30673; 706-678-2523; Fax: 706-678-4854. Hours: 8:30AM-5PM (EST). *Probate.*

Wilkinson County

Superior Court PO Box 250, Irwinton, GA 31042; 478-946-2221; Fax: 478-946-1497. Hours: 8AM-5PM (EST). *Felony, Misdemeanor, Civil.*

Civil Records: Access: In person only. Visitors must perform in person searches for themselves. No search fee. Required to search: name, years to search. Civil cases indexed by defendant, plaintiff. Civil records on computer from 1991, on docket books from 1900s.

Criminal Records: Access: In person only. Visitors must perform in person searches for themselves. No search fee. Required to search: name, years to search, DOB. Criminal records on computer from 1991, on docket books from 1900s. The court will not do searches.

General Information: No juvenile, adoption, sexual, mental health or expunged records released. Copy fee: $.25 per page. Certification fee: $2.50 per page. Fee payee: Superior Court Clerk. Personal checks accepted. Prepayment is required.

Magistrate & Probate Court PO Box 201, Irwinton, GA 31042; 478-946-2222/2439; Fax: 478-946-3810. Hours: 8AM-5PM (EST). *Civil Actions Under $15,000, Eviction, Small Claims, Probate.*

Worth County

Superior & State Court 201 N Main St, Rm 13, Sylvester, GA 31791; 229-776-8205; Fax: 229-776-8205. Hours: 8AM-5PM (EST). *Felony, Misdemeanor, Civil, Eviction, Small Claims.*

Civil Records: Access: In person only. Visitors must perform in person searches for themselves. No search fee. Required to search: name, years to search. Civil cases indexed by defendant, plaintiff. Civil records computerized since 1995, on books since 1880, real estate records from 9/93.

Criminal Records: Access: In person only. Visitors must perform in person searches for themselves. No search fee. Required to search: name, years to search; also helpful: SSN. Criminal records computerized since 1995.

General Information: Public access terminal is available. No juvenile, adoption, sexual, mental health or expunged records released. Copy fee: $.25 per page. Certification fee: $2.50 plus $.50 per page after first. Fee payee: Superior Court Clerk. Personal checks accepted. Prepayment is required.

Magistrate Court PO Box 64, 201 N Main St, Sylvester, GA 31791; 229-776-8210. Hours: 9AM-5PM (EST). *Civil Actions Under $15,000, Eviction, Small Claims.*

Note: All records are maintained at the Superior Court, not here

Probate Court 201 N Main St, Rm 12, Sylvester, GA 31791; 229-776-8207; Fax: 229-776-1540. Hours: 8AM-5PM (EST). *Probate.*

www.gaprobate.org

Georgia Recording Offices

ORGANIZATION: 159 counties, 159 recording offices. The recording officer is Clerk of Superior Court. All transactions are recorded in a "General Execution Docket." The entire state is in the Eastern Time Zone (EST).

REAL ESTATE RECORDS: Most counties will not perform real estate searches. Copy fees are the same as for UCC. Certification fees are usually $2.00 per document - $1.00 for seal and $1.00 for stamp - plus $.50 per page.

UCC RECORDS: There is no central state agency office for UCC. Financing statements are filed only with the Clerk of Superior Court and one can file in any county. Their system, as of January 1, 1995, merges all new UCC filings into a central statewide database, and allows statewide searching for new filings only from any county office. However, filings prior to that date will remain at the county offices. Only a few counties will perform local UCC searches. Use search request form UCC-11 for local searches. Search fees vary from $2.50 to $25.00 per debtor name. Copies usually cost $.25 per page if you make it and $1.00 per page if the county makes it.

TAX LIEN RECORDS: All tax liens on personal property are filed with the county Clerk of Superior Court in a "General Execution Docket" (grantor/grantee) or "Lien Index." Most counties will not perform tax lien searches. Copy fees are the same as for UCC.

OTHER LIENS: Judgments, hospital, materialman, county tax, lis pendens, child support, labor, mechanics.

ONLINE ACCESS: The Georgia Superior Court Clerk's Cooperative Authority (GSCCCA) at www.gsccca.org/search offers access on a subscription basis for ongoing users, or a free four hour trial for casual requesters. The system includes a UCC Index with records back to 1/1995; Real Estate Deed Index back to 1/1999; Notary Public Index and Plat Index. Subscription is $9.95 per month, per user, for unlimited use, and $.25 for each page printed. You may submit UCC Certified Search requests on-line. The charge for certified searches is $10 per debtor name.

Appling County

County Superior Court Clerk, PO Box 269, Baxley, GA 31513. 912-367-8126; Fax 912-367-8180.
Will search UCC records. This agency will not do a tax lien search. Will not search real estate records. **Other Phones:** Assessor 912-367-8109; Treasurer 367-8100.

Atkinson County

County Superior Court Clerk, PO Box 6, Pearson, GA 31642. 912-422-3343; Fax 912-422-3429.
This agency will not perform searches. **Other Phone Numbers:** Assessor 912-422-7382.

Bacon County

County Superior Court Clerk, PO Box 376, Alma, GA 31510. County Superior Court Clerk, R/E and UCC Recording 912-632-4915; Fax 912-632-6545.
This agency will not perform searches. **Other Phone Numbers:** Assessor 912-632-5215; Treasurer 912-632-5214.

Baker County

County Superior Court Clerk, PO Box 10, Newton, GA 31770. 229-734-3004; Fax 229-734-7770.
This agency will not perform searches. **Other Phone Numbers:** Assessor 229-734-3012.

Baldwin County

County Superior Court Clerk, PO Drawer 987, Milledgeville, GA 31059. 478-445-6327 R/E Recording: 478-445-4008 UCC Recording: 478-445-4008; Fax 478-445-1404.
This agency will not perform searches. **Other Phone Numbers:** Assessor 478-453-5300; Treasurer 478-434-4791; Appraiser/Auditor 478-445-5300; Elections 478-445-4526; Vital Records 478-445-4807.

Banks County

County Superior Court Clerk, PO Box 337, Homer, GA 30547. 706-677-6243 R/E Recording: 706-677-6240 UCC Recording: 706-677-6240; Fax 706-677-2337.
Will search UCC records. This agency will not do a tax lien search. Will do name searches for property and plats only. **Other Phones:** Assessor 706-677-2320; Treasurer 706-677-6200; Elections 706-677-6250.

Barrow County

County Superior Court Clerk, PO Box 1280, Winder, GA 30680. 770-307-3035.
This agency will not perform searches. **Other Phone Numbers:** Assessor 770-307-3108; Treasurer 770-307-3106.

Bartow County

County Superior Court Clerk, 135 W. Cherokee Ave., Suite 233, Cartersville, GA 30120. 770-387-5025; Fax 770-386-0846.
This agency will not perform searches. **Other Phone Numbers:** Assessor 770-387-5090.

Ben Hill County

County Superior Court Clerk, PO Box 1104, Fitzgerald, GA 31750-1104. 229-426-5135; Fax 229-426-5487.
This agency will not perform searches. **Other Phone Numbers:** Assessor 229-423-7323.

Berrien County

County Superior Court Clerk, 101 E. Marion Ave. #3, Nashville, GA 31639. County Superior Court Clerk, R/E and UCC Recording 229-686-5506.
This agency will not perform searches. **Other Phone Numbers:** Assessor 229-686-2149; Treasurer 229-686-7461 (Tax Commissioner); Appraiser/Auditor 229-686-5213; Elections 229-686-5213.

Bibb County

County Superior Court Clerk, PO Box 1015, Macon, GA 31202-1015. 478-749-6527; Fax 478-722-5823.
Will search UCC records. Will search real estate records. **Other Phone Numbers:** Assessor 478-742-2254; Treasurer 478-749-6310.

Bleckley County

County Superior Court Clerk, 306 SE 2nd St, Cochran, GA 31014. 478-934-3210; Fax 478-934-6671.
This agency will not perform searches. **Other Phones:** Assessor 478-934-3209; Treasurer 478-934-3200.

Brantley County

County Superior Court Clerk, PO Box 1067, Nahunta, GA 31553. 912-462-5635 R/E Recording: 912-462-7682 UCC Recording: 912-462-7682; Fax 912-462-5538.
Will search UCC records. This agency will not do a tax lien search. Will not search real estate records. **Other Phone Numbers:** Assessor 912-462-5251; Treasurer 912-462-5256.

Brooks County

County Superior Court Clerk, PO Box 630, Quitman, GA 31643. County Superior Court Clerk, R/E and UCC Recording 229-263-4747; Fax 229-263-5050.
Will search UCC records. This agency will not do a tax lien search. Will not search real estate records. **Other Phone Numbers:** Assessor 229-263-7920.

Bryan County

County Superior Court Clerk, PO Box 670, Pembroke, GA 31321. 912-653-3872 R/E Recording: 912-653-3872 option #4; Fax 912-653-3805.
Will search UCC records. This agency will not do a tax lien search. Will not search real estate records. **Other Phone Numbers:** Assessor 912-653-3889; Treasurer 912-653-3839; Appraiser/Auditor 912-653-3889; Elections 912-653-3859; Vital Records 912-653-3856.

Bulloch County

County Superior Court Clerk, Judicial Annex, 20 Siebald St., Statesboro, GA 30458. 912-764-9009; Fax 912-764-5953.
This agency will not perform searches. **Other Phones:** Assessor 912-764-2181; Treasurer 912-764-6285.

Burke County

County Superior Court Clerk, PO Box 803, Waynesboro, GA 30830-0803. County Superior Court Clerk, R/E and UCC Recording 706-554-2279; Fax 706-554-7887.
Will search UCC records. This agency will not do a tax lien search. Will not search real estate records. **Other Phone Numbers:** Assessor 706-554-2607; Treasurer 706-554-2324; Appraiser/Auditor 706-554-2607; Elections 706-554-7457; Vital Records 706-554-3000.

379 — The Sourcebook to Public Record Information — Recording Offices - Georgia

Butts County
County Superior Court Clerk, PO Box 320, Jackson, GA 30233. 770-775-8215; Fax 770-504-1359. This agency will not perform searches. **Other Phone Numbers:** Assessor 770-775-8207; Treasurer 770-775-8200.

Calhoun County
County Superior Court Clerk, PO Box 69, Morgan, GA 31766. 229-849-2715; Fax 229-849-0072. Will search UCC records. This agency will not do a tax lien search. Will not search real estate records. **Other Phone Numbers:** Assessor 229-849-4685; Treasurer 229-849-2970.

Camden County
County Superior Court Clerk, PO Box 578, Woodbine, GA 31569-0578. 912-576-5622. This agency will not perform searches. **Other Phone Numbers:** Assessor 912-576-3241; Treasurer 912-576-5601.

Candler County
County Superior Court Clerk, PO Drawer 830, Metter, GA 30439. 912-685-5257; Fax 912-685-2160. Will search UCC records. This agency will not do a tax lien search. Will not search real estate records. **Other Phone Numbers:** Assessor 912-685-6346; Treasurer 912-685-5257.

Carroll County
County Superior Court Clerk, PO Box 1620, Carrollton, GA 30112. 770-830-5830 R/E Recording: 770-830-5835 UCC Recording: 770-830-5835 x2248; Fax 770-214-3584. Will search UCC records. This agency will not do a tax lien search. Will not search real estate records. **Other Phone Numbers:** Assessor 770-830-5812; Treasurer 770-830-5801; Appraiser/Auditor 770-830-5843.

Catoosa County
County Superior Court Clerk, 875 Lafayette St, Courthouse, Ringgold, GA 30736. 706-935-4231; Fax none. This agency will not perform searches. **Other Phones:** Assessor 706-965-3772; Treasurer 706-935-2500.

Charlton County
County Superior Court Clerk, PO Box 760, Folkston, GA 31537. 912-496-2354; Fax 912-496-3882. Will search UCC records. This agency will not do a tax lien search. Will not search real estate records. **Other Phone Numbers:** Assessor 912-496-7437.

Chatham County
County Superior Court Clerk, PO Box 10227, Savannah, GA 31412. 912-652-7219; Fax 912-652-7380. This agency will not perform searches. **Other Phone Numbers:** Assessor 912-652-7127.

Chattahoochee County
County Superior Court Clerk, PO Box 120, Cusseta, GA 31805-0120. 706-989-3424 R/E Recording: 709-989-3424; Fax 706-989-0396. Will search UCC records. This agency will not do a tax lien search. Will not search real estate records. **Other Phone Numbers:** Assessor 706-989-3249; Elections 706-989-3602; Vital Records 706-989-3603.

Chattooga County
County Superior Court Clerk, PO Box 159, Summerville, GA 30747. 706-857-0706. This agency will not perform searches. **Other Phones:** Assessor 706-857-3819; Treasurer 706-857-0703.

Cherokee County
County Superior Court Clerk, 90 North St, Suite G-170, Canton, GA 30114. 770-479-0558 UCC Recording: 770-479-6350. Will search UCC records. This agency will not do a tax lien search. Will not search real estate records. **Other Phone Numbers:** Assessor 770-479-0433; Treasurer 770-479-0425; Elections 770-479-0740; Vital Records 770-479-0541.

Clarke County
County Superior Court Clerk, PO Box 1805, Athens, GA 30603. 706-613-3196; Fax 706-613-3189. This agency will not perform searches. **Other Phones:** Assessor 706-613-3140; Treasurer 706-613-3040.

Clay County
County Superior Court Clerk, PO Box 550, Fort Gaines, GA 31751-0550. 229-768-2631; Fax 229-768-3047. This agency will not perform searches. **Other Phones:** Assessor 229-768-2000; Treasurer 229-768-2915.

Clayton County
County Superior Court Clerk, 9151 Tara Blvd, Room 202, Jonesboro, GA 30236. 770-477-3395; www.co.clayton.ga.us/superior_court/clerk_of_courts/ This agency will not perform searches. **Online Access:** Real Estate, UCC, Notary Records. Search real estate, UCC, and notary records free at www.co.clayton.ga.us/superior_court/clerk_of_courts. Also see www.gsccca.org for online access to Deed and UCC indexes. **Other Phone Numbers:** Assessor 770-447-3285; Tax Commissioner 770-477-3311; Probate Court 770-477-3301;

Clinch County
County Superior Court Clerk, PO Box 433, Homerville, GA 31634. 912-487-5854; Fax 912-487-3083. This agency will not perform searches. **Other Phone Numbers:** Assessor 912-487-2561.

Cobb County
County Superior Court Clerk, PO Box 3490, Marietta, GA 30061. 770-528-1363; Fax 770-528-1325. www.cobbgasupctclk.com This agency will not perform searches. **Online Access:** Real Estate, Grantor/Grantee Records. Property records on the County Superior Court Clerk web site are available free at www.cobbgasupctclk.com/index.htm. Search by name, address, land description, instrument type, or book & page. You may also search court records. Also see www.gsccca.org for online access to Deed and UCC indexes. **Other Phone Numbers:** Assessor 770-528-3100; Treasurer 770-528-8600.

Coffee County
County Superior Court Clerk, Courthouse, 101 S. Peterson Ave., Douglas, GA 31533. 912-384-2865 R/E Recording: 912-384-2865 x239 UCC Recording: 912-384-2865 x239. This agency will not perform searches. **Other Phone Numbers:** Assessor 912-384-2136; Treasurer 912-384-4799; Appraiser/Auditor 912-384-2136; Elections 912-384-5213 or 384-7018; Vital Records 912-389-4458.

Colquitt County
County Superior Court Clerk, PO Box 2827, Moultrie, GA 31776-2827. 229-616-7420 R/E Recording: 229-616-7063. This agency will not perform searches. **Other Phone Numbers:** Assessor 229-616-7425.

Columbia County
County Superior Court Clerk, PO Box 100, Appling, GA 30802. 706-541-1139; Fax 706-541-4013. This agency will not perform searches. **Other Phone Numbers:** Assessor 706-541-0920.

Cook County
County Superior Court Clerk, 212 N. Hutchinson Ave, Adel, GA 31620-2497. County Superior Court Clerk, R/E and UCC Recording 229-896-7717. This agency ony records real estate transactions, not UCC. Will not search real estate records. **Other Phone Numbers:** Assessor 229-896-3665; Elections 229-896-3941.

Coweta County
County Superior Court Clerk, Courthouse, First FLoor, 200 Court Square, Newnan, GA 30263. 770-254-2690; Fax 770-254-3700. Will search UCC records. This agency will not do a tax lien search. Will not search real estate records. **Other Phone Numbers:** Assessor 770-254-2680.

Crawford County
County Superior Court Clerk, PO Box 1037, Roberta, GA 31078-1037. County Superior Court Clerk, R/E and UCC Recording 478-836-3328. This agency will not perform searches. **Other Phone Numbers:** Assessor 478-836-2800; Treasurer 478-836-3575; Appraiser/Auditor 478-836-2800; Elections 478-836-3575; Vital Records 478-836-3313.

Crisp County
County Superior Court Clerk, PO Box 747, Cordele, GA 31010-0747. County Superior Court Clerk, R/E and UCC Recording 229-276-2616; Fax 229-273-5730. This agency will not perform searches. **Other Phone Numbers:** Assessor 229-276-2635; Treasurer 229-276-2672; Appraiser/Auditor 229-276-2635.

Dade County
County Superior Court Clerk, PO Box 417, Trenton, GA 30752. 706-657-4778; Fax 706-657-8284. This agency will not perform searches. **Other Phone Numbers:** Assessor 706-657-6341; Appraiser/Auditor 706-657-6341; Elections 706-657-4414; Vital Records 706-657-4414.

Dawson County
County Superior Court Clerk, 25 Tucker Ave, #106, Dawsonville, GA 30534-0222. 706-344-3510 R/E Recording: 706-344-3510 x229 UCC Recording: 706-344-3510 x227; Fax 706-344-3511. Will search UCC records. This agency will not do a tax lien search. Will not search real estate records.

De Kalb County
County Superior Court Clerk, 556 N. McDonough St, Courthouse, Room 208, Decatur, GA 30030. 404-371-2836 R/E Recording: 404-371-2836 x3741 UCC Recording: 404-371-2836 x3735. Will search UCC records. This agency will not do a tax lien search. Will not search real estate records. **Other Phone Numbers:** Assessor 404-371-4938.

Decatur County
County Superior Court Clerk, PO Box 336, Bainbridge, GA 31718. 229-248-3025; Fax 229-248-3029. Will search UCC records. This agency will not do a tax lien search. Will not search real estate records. **Other Phone Numbers:** Assessor 229-248-3008; Treasurer 229-248-3030.

Dodge County
County Superior Court Clerk, PO Box 4276, Eastman, GA 31023-4276. 478-374-2871; Fax 478-374-3035. This agency will not perform searches. **Other Phones:** Assessor 478-374-8122; Treasurer 478-374-3775.

Dooly County

County Superior Court Clerk, PO Box 326, Vienna, GA 31092-0326. County Superior Court Clerk, R/E and UCC Recording 229-268-4234; Fax 229-268-6142. This agency will not perform searches. **Other Phone Numbers:** Assessor 229-268-4719; Treasurer 229-268-4228.

The Georgia Superior Court Clerk's Cooperative Authority (GSCCCA) offers access to all county real estate Deeds and all UCC filings.
See comments in the beginning of this section.

Dougherty County

County Superior Court Clerk, PO Box 1827, Albany, GA 31701. County Superior Court Clerk, R/E and UCC Recording 229-431-2198; Fax 229-431-2850. www.albany.ga.us
Will search UCC records. This agency will not do a tax lien search. Will not search real estate records. **Online Access:** Real Estate, Personal Property, Tax, Courts, Deed, Mortgage, Tax Assessor, Personal Property, UCC, Death, Divorce, Trade Name Records. Access to the clerk of courts Dept. of Deeds public menu is available at www.albany.ga.us/exec/site/?mid=231. Click on "clerk of courts record system" or "county/city tax records system." The tax records system has personal property, deeds, assessments. Also see www.gsccca.org for online access to Deed and UCC indexes. **Other Phone Numbers:** Assessor 229-431-2130; Treasurer 229-431-2130.

Douglas County

County Superior Court Clerk, Douglas County Courthouse, 8700 Hospital Dr., Douglasville, GA 30134. 770-920-7449 R/E Recording: 770-920-7257. This agency will not perform searches. **Other Phone Numbers:** Assessor 770-920-7228.

Early County

County Superior Court Clerk, PO Box 849, Blakely, GA 31723. 229-723-3033; Fax 229-723-4411. This agency will not perform searches. **Other Phones:** Assessor 229-723-3088; Treasurer 229-723-4024.

Echols County

County Superior Court Clerk, PO Box 213, Statenville, GA 31648. 229-559-5642; Fax 229-559-5792. This agency will not perform searches. **Other Phone Numbers:** Assessor 229-559-7370; Treasurer 229-559-5253; Elections 229-559-7526.

Effingham County

County Superior Court Clerk, PO Box 387, Springfield, GA 31329-0387. County Superior Court Clerk, R/E and UCC Recording 912-754-2118.
Will search UCC records. This agency will not do a tax lien search. Will not search real estate records. **Other Phone Numbers:** Assessor 912-754-2125; Elections 912-754-2115; Vital Records 912-754-2112; Tax Commissioner 912-754-2121; Zoning 912-754-2128;

Elbert County

County Superior Court Clerk, PO Box 619, Elberton, GA 30635. County Superior Court Clerk, R/E and UCC Recording 706-283-2005; Fax 706-213-7286. This agency will not perform searches. **Other Phone Numbers:** Assessor 706-283-2008.

Emanuel County

County Superior Court Clerk, PO Box 627, Swainsboro, GA 30401. County Superior Court Clerk, R/E and UCC Recording 478-237-8911; Fax 478-237-2173.
This agency will not perform searches. **Other Phones:** Assessor 478-237-3424; Treasurer 478-237-3881.

Evans County

County Superior Court Clerk, PO Box 845, Claxton, GA 30417. 912-739-3868; Fax 912-739-2504.
Will search UCC records. This agency will not do a tax lien search. Will not search real estate records. **Other Phone Numbers:** Assessor 912-739-3424; Treasurer 912-739-1147; Elections 912-739-0708.

Fannin County

County Superior Court Clerk, PO Box 1300, Blue Ridge, GA 30513. 706-632-2039.
This agency will not perform searches. **Other Phones:** Assessor 706-632-5954; Treasurer 706-632-2645.

Fayette County

County Superior Court Clerk, PO Box 130, Fayetteville, GA 30214. County Superior Court Clerk, R/E and UCC Recording 770-461-4703; www.admin.co.fayette.ga.us
This agency will not perform searches. **Online Access:** Assessor, Real Estate Records. Records on the County Assessor database are available free on the GIS-mapping site at www.fayettecountymaps.com/disclaimer.htm. Also see www.gsccca.org for online access to Deed and UCC indexes. **Other Phones:** Assessor 770-461-6041; Treasurer 770-461-8611.

Floyd County

County Superior Court Clerk, PO Box 1110, Rome, GA 30162-1110. 706-291-5190 R/E Recording: 706-291-5158 UCC Recording: 706-291-5206; Fax 706-233-0035.
Will search UCC records. This agency will not do a tax lien search. Will not search real estate records. **Other Phone Numbers:** Assessor 706-291-5143; Treasurer 706-291-5148.

Forsyth County

County Superior Court Clerk, 100 Courthouse Square, Room 010, Cumming, GA 30040. County Superior Court Clerk, R/E and UCC Recording 770-781-2120 UCC Recording: 770-781-2120 x 2690 or 2681; Fax 770-886-2858.
Will search UCC records. This agency will not do a tax lien search. Will not search real estate records. **Other Phone Numbers:** Assessor 770-781-2106; Treasurer 770-781-2110; Appraiser/Auditor 770-781-2106; Elections 770-781-2118; Vital Records 770-781-2140.

Franklin County

County Superior Court Clerk, PO Box 70, Carnesville, GA 30521. 706-384-2514; Fax 706-384-2185.
This agency will not perform searches. **Other Phone Numbers:** Assessor 706-384-4896.

Fulton County

County Superior Court Clerk, 136 Pryor St, Atlanta, GA 30303. 404-730-5535 R/E Recording: 404-730-5371 UCC Recording: 404-730-5355; Fax 404-730-7993.
This agency will not perform searches. **Other Phones:** Assessor 404-730-6440; Treasurer 404-730-6100.

Gilmer County

County Superior Court Clerk, 1 West Side Square, Courthouse, Box #30, Ellijay, GA 30540. County Superior Court Clerk, R/E and UCC Recording 706-635-4462; Fax 706-635-1462.

This agency will not perform searches. **Other Phones:** Assessor 706-635-2703; Treasurer 706-635-4361.

Glascock County

County Superior Court Clerk, PO Box 231, Gibson, GA 30810. County Superior Court Clerk, R/E and UCC Recording 706-598-2084; Fax 706-598-2577.
Will search UCC records. This agency will not do a tax lien search. Will not search real estate records. **Other Phone Numbers:** Assessor 706-598-2863; Treasurer 706-598-2671; Elections 706-598-3241.

Glynn County

County Superior Court Clerk, PO Box 1355, Brunswick, GA 31521-1355. County Superior Court Clerk, R/E and UCC Recording 912-554-7313; Fax 912-267-5625.
This agency will not perform searches. **Online Access:** Assessor, Property, Recording, UCC Records. Access to the county assessor property tax records is available free on the GIS mapping web site at http://maps.binarybus.com/glynn/disclaimer.asp. Also see www.gsccca.org for online access to Deed and UCC indexes. **Other Phone Numbers:** Assessor 912-267-7093; Treasurer 912-267-5680.

Gordon County

County Superior Court Clerk, Courthouse, Suite 102, 100 Wall St., Calhoun, GA 30701. County Superior Court Clerk, R/E and UCC Recording 706-629-9533; Fax 706-629-2139.
Will search UCC records. This agency will not do a tax lien search. Will not search real estate records. **Other Phone Numbers:** Assessor 706-629-6812; Treasurer 706-629-9242; Elections 706-629-7781; Vital Records 706-629-7314.

Grady County

Superior Court Clerk, 250 N. Broad St, Box 8, Box 8, Cairo, GA 31728. Superior Court Clerk, R/E and UCC Recording 229-377-2912.
Will not search UCC records. Will not search real estate records. **Other Phone Numbers:** Assessor 229-377-3325; Registrar 229-377-1897.

Greene County

County Superior Court Clerk, Courthouse, Suite 109, 113 N. Main St., Greensboro, GA 30642-1107. 706-453-3340; Fax 706-453-9179.
This agency will not perform searches. **Other Phone Numbers:** Assessor 706-453-3355.

Gwinnett County

County Superior Court Clerk, PO Box 2050, Lawrenceville, GA 30046. County Superior Court Clerk, R/E and UCC Recording 770-822-8100; www.gwinnettcourts.com
Will search UCC records. This agency will not do a tax lien search. Will not search real estate records. **Online Access:** Property, Deed, UCC, Judgment Records. See www.gsccca.org for online access to Deed, Plat and UCC indexes. Deed records go back to 1999; UCCs to1995. Also, search for civil court judgments at www.gwinnettcourts.com/misc/casendx.htm. **Other Phone Numbers:** Assessor 770-822-7233; Treasurer 770-822-8000.

Habersham County

County Superior Court Clerk, 555 Monroe St, Unit 35, Clarkesville, GA 30523. 706-754-2923; Fax 706-754-8779.
Will search UCC records. This agency will not do a tax lien search. Will not search real estate records. **Other Phone Numbers:** Assessor 706-754-2013.

Hall County

County Superior Court Clerk, PO Box 1336, Gainesville, GA 30503-1336. 770-531-7052 R/E Recording: 770-531-7058; Fax 770-536-0702.
This agency will not perform searches. **Other Phone Numbers:** Assessor 770-531-6720; Treasurer 770-531-6950.

Hancock County

County Superior Court Clerk, PO Box 451, Sparta, GA 31087. 706-444-6644; Fax 706-444-5685.
This agency will not perform searches. **Other Phone Numbers:** Assessor 706-444-5721.

Haralson County

County Superior Court Clerk, PO Drawer 849, Buchanan, GA 30113. County Superior Court Clerk, R/E and UCC Recording 770-646-2005; Fax 770-646-2035.
Will search UCC records. This agency will not do a tax lien search. Will not search real estate records. **Other Phone Numbers:** Assessor 770-646-2022; Treasurer 770-646-2022; Appraiser/Auditor 770-646-2022; Vital Records 770-646-2008.

Harris County

County Superior Court Clerk, PO Box 528, Hamilton, GA 31811. County Superior Court Clerk, R/E and UCC Recording 706-628-5570; Fax 706-628-7039.
Will search UCC records. This agency will not do a tax lien search. Will not search real estate records. **Other Phone Numbers:** Assessor 706-628-5171; Treasurer 706-628-4958; Elections 706-628-5210; Tax Commissioner 706-628-4843.

Hart County

County Superior Court Clerk, P.O.Box 386, Hartwell, GA 30643. County Superior Court Clerk, R/E and UCC Recording 706-376-7189; Fax 706-376-1277.
Will search UCC records. This agency will not do a tax lien search. Will not search real estate records. **Other Phone Numbers:** Assessor 706-376-3997; Treasurer 706-376-2024; Appraiser/Auditor 706-376-3997; Elections 706-376-2565; Vital Records 706-376-2565.

Heard County

County Superior Court Clerk, PO Box 249, Franklin, GA 30217. 706-675-3301; Fax 706-675-0819.
Will search UCC records. This agency will not do a tax lien search. Will not search real estate records. **Other Phone Numbers:** Assessor 706-675-3786.

Henry County

County Superior Court Clerk, Courthouse, #1 Courthouse Square, McDonough, GA 30253. County Superior Court Clerk, R/E and UCC Recording 770-954-2121.
This agency will not perform searches. **Other Phones:** Assessor 770-954-2420; Treasurer 770-954-2470; Elections 770-954-2069; Vital Records 770-954-2303.

Houston County

County Superior Court Clerk, 800 Carroll St, Perry, GA 31069. County Superior Court Clerk, R/E and UCC Recording 478-987-2170; Fax 478-987-3252. www.houstoncountyga.com
This agency will not perform searches. **Online Access:** Assessor, Real Estate Records. Access to the assessor's Mapguide database is available free at www.assessor.houstoncountyga.org. The Autodesk MapGuide viewer is available to download. Also see www.gsccca.org for online access to Deed and UCC indexes. **Other Phones:** Assessor 478-987-3060; Elections 478-987-1973; Marriage/Death/Birth Records 478-987-2770; Divorce Records 478-987-2170;

Irwin County

County Superior Court Clerk, 113 N Irwin Ave, 301 S. Irwin Ave, Ocilla, GA 31774. 229-468-5356; Fax 229-468-5356.
Will search UCC records. This agency will not do a tax lien search. Will not search real estate records. **Other Phone Numbers:** Assessor 229-468-5514; Treasurer 229-468-5505.

Jackson County

County Superior Court Clerk, PO Box 7, Jefferson, GA 30549. 706-367-6360 R/E Recording: 706-367-6362; Fax 706-367-2468.
Will search UCC records. This agency will not do a tax lien search. Will not search real estate records. **Other Phone Numbers:** Appraiser/Auditor 706-367-6330; Elections 706-367-6377; Vital Records 706-367-6366.

Jasper County

County Superior Court Clerk, Courthouse, Monticello, GA 31064. 706-468-4901; Fax 706-468-4946.
This agency will not perform searches. **Other Phone Numbers:** Assessor 706-468-4904; Treasurer 706-468-4900.

Jeff Davis County

County Superior Court Clerk, PO Box 248, Hazlehurst, GA 31539. County Superior Court Clerk, R/E and UCC Recording 912-375-6615; Fax 912-375-0378.
Will search UCC records. This agency will not do a tax lien search. Will not search real estate records. **Other Phone Numbers:** Assessor 912-375-6624.

Jefferson County

County Superior Court Clerk, PO Box 151, Louisville, GA 30434. 478-625-7922; Fax 478-625-9589.
Will search UCC records. This agency will not do a tax lien search. Will not search real estate records. **Other Phone Numbers:** Assessor 478-625-8209; Treasurer 478-625-7736.

Jenkins County

County Superior Court Clerk, PO Box 659, Millen, GA 30442. 478-982-4683; Fax 478-982-1274.
This agency will not perform searches. **Other Phones:** Assessor 478-982-4939; Treasurer 478-982-4925.

Johnson County

County Superior Court Clerk, PO Box 321, Wrightsville, GA 31096. 478-864-3484; Fax 478-864-1343.
This agency will not perform searches. **Other Phones:** Assessor 478-864-3325; Treasurer 478-864-2565.

Jones County

County Superior Court Clerk, PO Box 39, Gray, GA 31032. 478-986-6671.
Will search UCC records. This agency will not do a tax lien search. Will not search real estate records. **Other Phone Numbers:** Assessor 478-986-6300; Treasurer 478-986-6538.

Lamar County

County Superior Court Clerk, 326 Thomaston St, Courthouse, Barnesville, GA 30204-1669. 770-358-5145; Fax 770-358-5149.
This agency will not perform searches. **Other Phones:** Assessor 770-358-5161; Treasurer 770-358-5162.

Lanier County

County Superior Court Clerk, 100 Main St, County Courthouse, Lakeland, GA 31635. 229-482-3594; Fax 229-482-8333.
Will search UCC records. This agency will not do a tax lien search. Will not search real estate records. **Other Phone Numbers:** Assessor 229-482-2090; Treasurer 229-482-3795.

Laurens County

County Superior Court Clerk, PO Box 2028, Dublin, GA 31040. County Superior Court Clerk, R/E and UCC Recording 478-272-3210; Fax 478-275-2595.
This agency will not perform searches. **Other Phones:** Assessor 478-272-6443; Treasurer 478-272-6994; Elections 478-272-2566; Vital Records 478-272-2051.

Lee County

County Superior Court Clerk, PO Box 597, Leesburg, GA 31763. 229-759-6018; Fax 229-759-6049.
This agency will not perform searches. **Other Phones:** Assessor 229-759-6010; Treasurer 229-759-6000.

Liberty County

County Superior Court Clerk, PO Box 50, Hinesville, GA 31310. County Superior Court Clerk, R/E and UCC Recording 912-876-3625; Fax 912-369-5463. www.libertyco.com
This agency will not perform searches. **Other Phone Numbers:** Assessor 912-876-2823; Treasurer 912-876-3389; Vital Records 912-876-3625.

Lincoln County

County Superior Court Clerk, PO Box 340, Lincolnton, GA 30817. County Superior Court Clerk, R/E and UCC Recording 706-359-5505.
This agency will not perform searches. **Other Phone Numbers:** Assessor 706-359-5502; Appraiser/Auditor 706-359-5502; Elections 706-359-6126; Vital Records 706-359-5528.

Long County

County Superior Court Clerk, PO Box 458, Ludowici, GA 31316. 912-545-2123; Fax 912-545-2020.
This agency will not perform searches. **Other Phones:** Assessor 912-545-9111; Treasurer 912-545-2127.

Lowndes County

County Superior Court Clerk, PO Box 1349, Valdosta, GA 31601-1349. 229-333-5125; Fax 229-333-7637.
This agency will not perform searches. **Other Phones:** Assessor 229-671-2540; Treasurer 229-671-2570.

Lumpkin County

County Superior Court Clerk, 99 Courthouse Hill, Suite D, Dahlonega, GA 30533-0541. County Superior Court Clerk, R/E and UCC Recording 706-864-3736; Fax 706-864-5298.
This agency will not perform searches. **Other Phone Numbers:** Assessor 706-864-2433; Treasurer 706-864-3742; Appraiser/Auditor 706-864-2433; Elections 706-864-6279; Vital Records 706-864-3847.

Macon County

County Superior Court Clerk, PO Box 337, Oglethorpe, GA 31068. County Superior Court Clerk, R/E and UCC Recording 478-472-7661; Fax 478-472-4775.
Will search UCC records. This agency will not do a tax lien search. Will not search real estate records. **Other Phone Numbers:** Assessor 478-472-6560; Treasurer 478-472-7031; Appraiser/Auditor 478-472-6560; Elections 478-472-7685; Vital Records 478-472-7685.

Madison County

County Superior Court Clerk, PO Box 247, Danielsville, GA 30633. County Superior Court Clerk, R/E and UCC Recording 706-795-3352; Fax 706-795-2209.
This agency will not perform searches.

Marion County

County Superior Court Clerk, PO Box 41, Buena Vista, GA 31803. County Superior Court Clerk, R/E and UCC Recording 229-649-7321; Fax 229-649-2059.
This agency will not perform searches. **Other Phone Numbers:** Assessor 229-649-5504; Treasurer 229-649-2603; Appraiser/Auditor 229-649-5504; Elections 229-649-2603; Vital Records 229-649-5542.

McDuffie County

County Superior Court Clerk, PO Box 158, Thomson, GA 30824-0150. County Superior Court Clerk, R/E and UCC Recording 706-595-2134; Fax 706-595-9150.
This agency will not perform searches. **Other Phone Numbers:** Assessor 706-595-2128; Treasurer 706-595-2100; Appraiser/Auditor 706-595-2128; Elections 706-595-2105; Vital Records 706-595-2124.

McIntosh County

County Superior Court Clerk, PO Box 1661, Darien, GA 31305. County Superior Court Clerk, R/E and UCC Recording 912-437-6641; Fax 912-437-6673.
Will search UCC records. This agency will not do a tax lien search. Will not search real estate records. **Online Access:** Deed (2000-present), UCC, Notary Records. Call 800-304-5175 to subscribe to UCCs and Deed indexes. Also see www.gsccca.org for online access to Deed and UCC indexes. **Other Phone Numbers:** Assessor 912-437-6663; Treasurer 912-437-6641; Appraiser/Auditor 912-437-6663; Vital Records 912-437-6636.

Meriwether County

County Superior Court Clerk, PO Box 160, Greenville, GA 30222-0160. 706-672-4416; Fax 706-672-9465.
Will search UCC records. This agency will not do a tax lien search. Will not search real estate records. **Other Phone Numbers:** Assessor 706-672-4222; Treasurer 706-672-4219.

Miller County

County Superior Court Clerk, PO Box 66, Colquitt, GA 31737. County Superior Court Clerk, R/E and UCC Recording 229-758-4102; Fax 229-758-6585.
This agency will not perform searches. **Other Phone Numbers:** Assessor 229-758-4100; Treasurer 229-758-4101; Appraiser/Auditor 229-758-4100; Elections 229-758-4118; Vital Records 229-758-4110.

Mitchell County

County Superior Court Clerk, PO Box 427, Camilla, GA 31730. 229-336-2022; Fax 229-336-2003.
This agency will not perform searches. **Other Phone Numbers:** Assessor 229-336-2005; Treasurer 229-336-2010.

Monroe County

County Superior Court Clerk, PO Box 450, Forsyth, GA 31029-0450. 478-994-7022; Fax 478-994-7053.
This agency will not perform searches. **Other Phone Numbers:** Assessor 478-994-7038; Elections 478-994-7036; Vital Records 478-994-7036.

Montgomery County

County Superior Court Clerk, PO Box 311, Mount Vernon, GA 30445. 912-583-4401.
This agency will not perform searches. **Other Phone Numbers:** Assessor 912-583-4131; Elections 912-583-2681; Vital Records 912-583-2681.

Morgan County

County Superior Court Clerk, PO Box 130, Madison, GA 30650. 706-342-3605.
Will search UCC records. This agency will not do a tax lien search. Will not search real estate records. **Other Phone Numbers:** Assessor 706-342-0551.

Murray County

County Superior Court Clerk, PO Box 1000, Chatsworth, GA 30705. 706-695-2932; Fax 706-517-9672.
This agency will not perform searches. **Other Phones:** Assessor 706-695-2521; Treasurer 706-695-3423.

Muscogee County

County Superior Court Clerk, PO Box 2145, Columbus, GA 31902-2145. 706-653-4358 R/E Recording: 706-653-4356 UCC Recording: 706-653-4356; Fax 706-653-4359.
Will search UCC records. This agency will not do a tax lien search. Will not search real estate records. **Other Phone Numbers:** Assessor 706-653-4398; Treasurer 706-653-4100.

Newton County

County Superior Court Clerk, Newton County Judicial Center, 1132 Usher St., 3rd Floor, Covington, GA 30014. 770-784-2035 R/E Recording: 770-784-2040 UCC Recording: 770-784-2040.
This agency will not perform searches. **Other Phone Numbers:** Assessor 770-784-2000.

Oconee County

County Superior Court Clerk, PO Box 1099, Watkinsville, GA 30677. 706-769-3940; Fax 706-769-3948.
Will search UCC records. This agency will not do a tax lien search. Will not search real estate records. **Other Phone Numbers:** Assessor 706-769-3921.

Oglethorpe County

County Superior Court Clerk, PO Box 68, Lexington, GA 30648-0068. 706-743-5731; Fax 706-743-5335.
Will search UCC records. This agency will not do a tax lien search. Will not search real estate records. **Online Access:** UCC, Real Estate Records. UCC and real estate records are available online from the Oglethorpe County Clerk for a monthly subscription fee of $9.95 plus $.25 per printed page. Guest accounts are available. For information and to open an account, call 404-327-9058. Also see www.gsccca.org for online access to Deed and UCC indexes. **Other Phone Numbers:** Assessor 706-743-5166.

Paulding County

County Superior Court Clerk, 11 Courthouse Sq., Room G-2, Dallas, GA 30132. 770-443-7527.
Will search UCC records. This agency will not do a tax lien search. Will not search real estate records. **Other Phone Numbers:** Assessor 770-443-7606.

Peach County

County Superior Court Clerk, PO Box 389, Fort Valley, GA 31030. 478-825-5331.
This agency will not perform searches. **Other Phones:** Assessor 478-825-5924; Treasurer 478-825-2535.

Pickens County

County Superior Court Clerk, PO Box 130, Jasper, GA 30143. 706-253-8763.
Will search UCC records. This agency will not do a tax lien search. Will not search real estate records. **Other Phone Numbers:** Assessor 706-253-8700.

Pierce County

County Superior Court Clerk, PO Box 588, Blackshear, GA 31516. 912-449-2020.
Will search UCC records. This agency will not do a tax lien search. Will not search real estate records.

Pike County

County Superior Court Clerk, PO Box 10, Zebulon, GA 30295. 770-567-2000.

Will search UCC records. This agency will not do a tax lien search. Will not search real estate records.

Polk County

County Superior Court Clerk, PO Box 948, Cedartown, GA 30125. 770-749-2114; Fax 770-749-2148.
This agency will not perform searches. **Other Phones:** Assessor 770-749-2125; Treasurer 770-749-2108.

Pulaski County

Superior Court Clerk, PO Box 60, Hawkinsville, GA 31036. Superior Court Clerk, R/E and UCC Recording 478-783-1911; Fax 478-892-3308.
This agency will not perform searches. **Other Phones:** Assessor 478-783-4154; Treasurer 478-783-2811; Elections 478-783-2061; Vital Records 478-783-2061.

Putnam County

County Superior Court Clerk, Courthouse, 100 S. Jefferson St., Eatonton, GA 31024-1087. County Superior Court Clerk, R/E and UCC Recording 706-485-4501; Fax 706-485-2515.
This agency will not perform searches. **Other Phone Numbers:** Assessor 706-485-6376; Treasurer 706-485-5441; Elections 706-485-5476; Vital Records 706-485-4501.

Quitman County

County Superior Court Clerk, PO Box 307, Georgetown, GA 31754. 229-334-2578; Fax 229-334-3991.
Will not search UCC records. UCC search includes tax liens if requested. Will not search real estate records. **Other Phone Numbers:** Treasurer 229-334-0903; Appraiser/Auditor 229-334-2159; Elections 229-334-2224.

The Georgia Superior Court Clerk's Cooperative Authority (GSCCCA) offers access to all county real estate Deeds and all UCC filings.
See comments in the beginning of this section.

Rabun County

County Superior Court Clerk, 25 Courthouse Square #105, Clayton, GA 30525. 706-782-3615; Fax 706-782-7588.
Will not search UCC records. This agency will not do a tax lien search. Real estate owner, mortgage, and property transfer searches available. **Other Phone Numbers:** Assessor 706-782-5068; Treasurer 706-782-3813.

Randolph County

County Superior Court Clerk, PO Box 98, Cuthbert, GA 31740. 229-732-2216; Fax 229-732-5881.
This agency will not perform searches. **Other Phone Numbers:** Assessor 229-732-2522; Treasurer 229-732-6440.

Richmond County

County Superior Court Clerk, PO Box 2046, Augusta, GA 30903. 706-821-2460; Fax 706-821-2448.
This agency will not perform searches. **Other Phones:** Assessor 706-821-2310; Treasurer 706-821-2391.

Rockdale County

County Superior Court Clerk, PO Box 937, Conyers, GA 30012. County Superior Court Clerk, R/E and UCC Recording 770-929-4068 UCC Recording: 770-929-4069; Fax 770-860-0381.

This agency will not perform searches. **Other Phones:** Assessor 770-929-4024; Treasurer 770-929-4009.

Schley County

County Superior Court Clerk, PO Box 7, Ellaville, GA 31806-0007. County Superior Court Clerk, R/E and UCC Recording 229-937-5581; Fax 229-937-5047. This agency will not perform searches. **Other Phone Numbers:** Assessor 229-937-2689; Appraiser/Auditor 229-937-2689; Elections 229-937-2905; Vital Records 229-937-2905.

The Georgia Superior Court Clerk's Cooperative Authority (GSCCCA) offers access to all county real estate Deeds and all UCC filings. See comments in the beginning of this section.

Screven County

County Superior Court Clerk, PO Box 156, Sylvania, GA 30467. 912-564-2614; Fax 912-564-2622. This agency will not perform searches. **Other Phone Numbers:** Assessor 912-564-7918.

Seminole County

County Superior Court Clerk, PO Box 672, Donalsonville, GA 31745. 229-524-2525; Fax 229-524-8883. Will not search UCC records. Will not search real estate records. **Other Phones:** Assessor 229-524-5831.

Spalding County

County Superior Court Clerk, PO Box 1046, Griffin, GA 30224. 770-467-4356. Will search UCC records. This agency will not do a tax lien search. Will not search real estate records. **Other Phone Numbers:** Assessor 770-228-9900 x350.

Stephens County

County Superior Court Clerk, Stephens County Courthouse, 205 N. Alexander St. Room 202, Toccoa, GA 30577-2310. County Superior Court Clerk, R/E and UCC Recording 706-886-9496; Fax 706-886-5710. This agency will not perform searches. **Other Phone Numbers:** Assessor 706-886-4753; Elections 706-886-8954; Vital Records 706-886-2828.

Stewart County

County Superior Court Clerk, PO Box 910, Lumpkin, GA 31815-0910. 229-838-6220. This agency will not perform searches.

Sumter County

County Superior Court Clerk, PO Box 333, Americus, GA 31709. County Superior Court Clerk, R/E and UCC Recording 229-924-5626. This agency will not perform searches. **Other Phone Numbers:** Assessor 229-924-0313; Treasurer 229-924-3090; Appraiser/Auditor 229-924-0313; Elections 229-924-7693; Vital Records 229-924-3637 (Health Dept).

Talbot County

County Superior Court Clerk, PO Box 325, Talbotton, GA 31827-0325. 706-665-3239; Fax 706-665-8637. This agency will not perform searches. **Other Phones:** Assessor 706-665-3377; Treasurer 706-665-3240.

Taliaferro County

County Superior Court Clerk, PO Box 182, Crawfordville, GA 30631. 706-456-2123; Fax 706-456-2749.

This agency will not perform searches. **Other Phone Numbers:** Assessor 706-456-2717; Elections 706-456-2253; Vital Records 706-456-2316.

Tattnall County

County Superior Court Clerk, PO Box 39, Reidsville, GA 30453. County Superior Court Clerk, R/E and UCC Recording 912-557-6716; Fax 912-557-4552. Will search UCC records. This agency will not do a tax lien search. Will not search real estate records. **Other Phones:** Assessor 912-557-4010; Appraiser/Auditor 912-557-4010; Probate Court 912-557-6917.

Taylor County

County Superior Court Clerk, PO Box 248, Butler, GA 31006. 478-862-5594; Fax 478-862-5334. This agency will not perform searches.

Telfair County

County Superior Court Clerk, 128 E Oak St, Ste. 2, Oak St, McRae, GA 31055-1604. County Superior Court Clerk, R/E and UCC Recording 229-868-6525; Fax 229-868-7956. This agency will not perform searches. **Other Phone Numbers:** Assessor 229-868-6772.

Terrell County

County Superior Court Clerk, PO Box 189, Dawson, GA 31742. 229-995-2631. This agency will not perform searches. **Other Phones:** Assessor 229-995-5210; Treasurer 229-995-5151.

Thomas County

County Superior Court Clerk, PO Box 1995, Thomasville, GA 31799. 229-225-4108; Fax 229-225-4110. www.thomascoclerkofcourt.org This agency will not perform searches. **Other Phone Numbers:** Assessor 229-225-4133; Treasurer 229-225-4133; Appraiser/Auditor 229-225-4133; Elections 229-225-4101; Vital Records 229-226-4241.

Tift County

County Superior Court Clerk, PO Box 354, Tifton, GA 31793. 229-386-7810; Fax 229-386-7807. Will search UCC records. This agency will not do a tax lien search. Will not search real estate records. **Other Phone Numbers:** Assessor 229-386-7840.

Toombs County

County Superior Court Clerk, PO Drawer 530, Lyons, GA 30436. County Superior Court Clerk, R/E and UCC Recording 912-526-3501; Fax 912-526-1015. This agency will not perform searches. **Other Phone Numbers:** Assessor 912-526-6291; Treasurer 912-526-8575; Appraiser/Auditor 912-526-6291; Elections 912-526-8696.

Towns County

County Superior Court Clerk, 48 River St., Courthouse, Suite E, Hiawassee, GA 30546. County Superior Court Clerk, R/E and UCC Recording 706-896-2130. Will search UCC records. This agency will not do a tax lien search. Will not search real estate records. **Other Phone Numbers:** Assessor 706-896-3984; Treasurer 706-896-2276; Appraiser/Auditor 706-896-3984; Elections 706-896-4353; Vital Records 706-896-3467.

Treutlen County

County Superior Court Clerk, PO Box 356, Soperton, GA 30457. 912-529-4215; Fax none. This agency will not perform searches. **Other Phone Numbers:** Assessor 912-529-4343.

Troup County

County Superior Court Clerk, PO Box 866, LaGrange, GA 30241-0866. County Superior Court Clerk, R/E and UCC Recording 706-883-1740.

This agency will not perform searches. **Other Phone Numbers:** Assessor 706-883-1625; Treasurer 706-883-1620.

Turner County

County Superior Court Clerk, PO Box 106, Ashburn, GA 31714. 229-567-2011; Fax 229-567-0450. This agency will not perform searches. **Other Phone Numbers:** Assessor 229-567-2334; Treasurer 229-567-4313.

Twiggs County

County Superior Court Clerk, PO Box 228, Jeffersonville, GA 31044-0228. 478-945-3350; Fax 478-945-6751. This agency will not perform searches. **Other Phones:** Assessor 478-945-3663; Treasurer 478-945-3629.

Union County

County Superior Court Clerk, 114 Courthouse St #5, Blairsville, GA 30512. 706-439-6022; Fax 706-439-6026. This agency will not perform searches. **Other Phone Numbers:** Assessor 706-439-6011; Treasurer 706-439-6000.

Upson County

County Superior Court Clerk, PO Box 469, Thomaston, GA 30286. 706-647-7835; Fax 706-647-8999. Will search UCC records. This agency will not do a tax lien search. Will not search real estate records. **Other Phone Numbers:** Assessor 706-647-8176; Elections 706-647-7015.

Walker County

County Superior Court Clerk, PO Box 448, La Fayette, GA 30728. 706-638-1742 R/E Recording: 706-638-1780 UCC Recording: 706-638-1757. Will search UCC records. This agency will not do a tax lien search. Will not search real estate records. **Other Phone Numbers:** Assessor 706-638-2929; Treasurer 706-638-2929.

Walton County

County Superior Court Clerk, PO Box 745, Monroe, GA 30655. County Superior Court Clerk, R/E and UCC Recording 770-267-1304 UCC Recording: 770-267-1305; Fax 770-267-1441. Will search UCC records. This agency will not do a tax lien search. Will not search real estate records. **Other Phone Numbers:** Assessor 770-267-1477.

Ware County

County Superior Court Clerk, PO Box 776, Waycross, GA 31502-0776. 912-287-4340. Will search UCC records. This agency will not do a tax lien search. Will not search real estate records. **Other Phone Numbers:** Assessor 912-287-4383; Treasurer 912-287-4305.

Warren County

County Superior Court Clerk, PO Box 227, Warrenton, GA 30828. County Superior Court Clerk, R/E and UCC Recording 706-465-2262; Fax 706-465-0232. Will search UCC records. This agency will not do a tax lien search. Will not search real estate records. **Other Phone Numbers:** Assessor 706-465-3321; Treasurer 706-465-2177.

Washington County

County Superior Court Clerk, PO Box 231, Sandersville, GA 31082-0231. County Superior Court Clerk, R/E and UCC Recording 478-552-3186. Will search UCC records. This agency will not do a tax lien search. Will not search real estate records. **Other Phone Numbers:** Assessor 478-552-2937.

Wayne County

County Superior Court Clerk, PO Box 920, Jesup, GA 31598-0920. County Superior Court Clerk, R/E and UCC Recording 912-427-5930; Fax 912-427-5939. Will search UCC records. This agency will not do a tax lien search. Will not search real estate records. **Other Phone Numbers:** Assessor 912-427-5920; Treasurer 912-427-5900.

Webster County

County Superior Court Clerk, PO Box 117, Preston, GA 31824. 229-828-3525; Fax 229-828-6961. Will search UCC records. This agency will not do a tax lien search. Will not search real estate records. **Other Phone Numbers:** Assessor 229-828-3690.

Wheeler County

County Superior Court Clerk, PO Box 38, Alamo, GA 30411-0038. County Superior Court Clerk, R/E and UCC Recording 912-568-7137; Fax 912-568-7453. Will search UCC records. This agency will not do a tax lien search. Will not search real estate records. **Other Phone Numbers:** Assessor 912-568-7924; Treasurer 912-568-7131; Elections 912-568-7133; Vital Records 912-568-7161.

White County

County Superior Court Clerk, 59 S. Main St, Courthouse, Suite B, Cleveland, GA 30528. County Superior Court Clerk, R/E and UCC Recording 706-865-2613; Fax 706-865-7749. This agency will not perform searches. **Other Phone Numbers:** Assessor 706-865-5328; Appraiser/Auditor 706-865-5328; Elections 706-865-4141; County Commissioner 706-865-2235.

Whitfield County

County Superior Court Clerk, PO Box 868, Dalton, GA 30722. 706-275-7450; Fax 706-275-7456. This agency will not perform searches. **Other Phone s:** Assessor 706-275-7410; Treasurer 706-275-7510.

Wilcox County

County Superior Court Clerk, Courthouse, 103 N. Broad St., Abbeville, GA 31001-1000. County Superior Court Clerk, R/E and UCC Recording 229-467-2442; Fax 229-467-2000. This agency will not perform searches. **Other Phone Numbers:** Assessor 229-467-2428; Appraiser/Auditor 229-467-2028; Elections 229-467-2300; Vital Records 229-467-2220.

Wilkes County

County Superior Court Clerk, 23 E. Court St, Room 205, Washington, GA 30673. County Superior Court Clerk, R/E and UCC Recording 706-678-2423; Fax 706-678-2115. Will not search UCC records. Real estate owner, mortgage, and property transfer searches available.

Other Phone Numbers: Assessor 706-678-7732; Elections 706-678-2523; Vital Records 706-678-2523.

Wilkinson County

County Superior Court Clerk, PO Box 250, Irwinton, GA 31042-0250. County Superior Court Clerk, R/E and UCC Recording 478-946-2221; Fax 478-946-1497. Will search UCC records. This agency will not do a tax lien search. Will not search real estate records. **Other Phones:** Assessor 478-946-2076; Treasurer 478-946-2236 (County Commissioner); Appraiser/Auditor 478-946-2188; Elections 478-946-2222.

Worth County

County Superior Court Clerk, 201 N. Main St, Courthouse, Room 13, Sylvester, GA 31791. 229-776-8205. This agency will not perform searches. **Other Phones:** Assessor 229-776-8203; Treasurer 229-776-8204; Elections 229-776-8208; Vital Records 229-776-8207.

The Georgia Superior Court Clerk's Cooperative Authority (GSCCCA) offers access to all county real estate Deeds and all UCC filings. See comments in the beginning of this section.

Guam

Guam Department of Revenue & Taxation

Clerk, PO Box 23605, GMF, GU 96921. 671-475-5000 x815; Fax 671-472-2643. Will search UCC records. This agency will not do a tax lien search. Will not search real estate records.

Georgia County Locator

You will usually be able to find the city name in the City/County Cross Reference below. In that case, it is a simple matter to determine the county from the cross reference. However, only the official US Postal Service city names are included in this index. There are an additional 40,000 place names that people use in their addresses. Therefore, we have also included a ZIP/City Cross Reference immediately following the City/County Cross Reference.

If you know the ZIP Code but the city name does not appear in the City/County Cross Reference index, look up the ZIP Code in the ZIP/City Cross Reference, find the city name, then look up the city name in the City/County Cross Reference. For example, you want to know the county for an address of Menands, NY 12204. There is no "Menands" in the City/County Cross Reference. The ZIP/City Cross Reference shows that ZIP Codes 12201-12288 are for the city of Albany. Looking back in the City/County Cross Reference, Albany is in Albany County.

City/County Cross Reference

ABBEVILLE Wilcox
ACWORTH (30102) Cherokee(52), Bartow(25), Cobb(21)
ADAIRSVILLE (30103) Bartow(65), Gordon(26), Floyd(8)
ADEL Cook
ADRIAN (31002) Emanuel(54), Johnson(22), Laurens(16), Treutlen(6)
AILEY Montgomery
ALAMO (30411) Wheeler(60), Laurens(39)
ALAPAHA Berrien
ALBANY Dougherty
ALLENHURST (31301) Liberty(76), Long(23)
ALLENTOWN Wilkinson
ALMA (31510) Bacon(95), Pierce(4)
ALPHARETTA Fulton
ALSTON Montgomery
ALTO Habersham
AMBROSE Coffee
AMERICUS Sumter
ANDERSONVILLE (31711) Macon(82), Sumter(16)
APPLING Columbia
ARABI (31712) Crisp(94), Worth(5)
ARAGON (30104) Polk(69), Floyd(24), Bartow(6)
ARGYLE Clinch
ARLINGTON (31713) Calhoun(65), Early(25), Baker(9)
ARMUCHEE (30105) Floyd(67), Chattooga(32)
ARNOLDSVILLE (30619) Oglethorpe(90), Oconee(9)
ASHBURN (31714) Turner(94), Worth(5)
ATHENS Clarke
ATLANTA De Kalb
ATTAPULGUS Decatur
AUBURN Barrow
AUGUSTA Richmond
AUSTELL (30168) Cobb(90), Douglas(9)
AVERA Jefferson
AVONDALE ESTATES De Kalb
AXSON (31624) Atkinson(69), Ware(29)
BACONTON Mitchell
BAINBRIDGE Decatur
BALDWIN Banks
BALL GROUND (30107) Cherokee(79), Pickens(16), Forsyth(3)
BARNESVILLE (30204) Lamar(95), Upson(3)
BARNEY Brooks
BARTOW (30413) Jefferson(87), Washington(12)
BARWICK Brooks
BAXLEY Appling
BELLVILLE Evans
BERLIN Colquitt
BETHLEHEM (30620) Barrow(74), Gwinnett(18), Walton(7)
BISHOP (30621) Oconee(71), Morgan(28)
BLACKSHEAR Pierce
BLAIRSVILLE Union

BLAKELY (31723) Early(97), Miller(2)
BLOOMINGDALE (31302) Chatham(54), Effingham(45)
BLUE RIDGE (30513) Fannin(88), Gilmer(11)
BLUFFTON (31724) Clay(89), Early(10)
BLYTHE (30805) Burke(55), Richmond(44)
BOGART (30622) Oconee(62), Clarke(29), Jackson(7)
BOLINGBROKE Monroe
BONAIRE Houston
BONEVILLE McDuffie
BOSTON (31626) Thomas(82), Brooks(17)
BOSTWICK Morgan
BOWDON (30108) Carroll(95), Heard(4)
BOWDON JUNCTION Carroll
BOWERSVILLE Hart
BOWMAN (30624) Elbert(75), Hart(13), Madison(11)
BOX SPRINGS (31801) Talbot(90), Muscogee(5), Marion(3)
BRASELTON (30517) Jackson(69), Hall(13), Gwinnett(9), Barrow(7)
BREMEN (30110) Haralson(92), Carroll(7)
BRINSON Decatur
BRISTOL (31518) Appling(54), Pierce(39), Wayne(3), Bacon(2)
BRONWOOD Terrell
BROOKFIELD Tift
BROOKLET Bulloch
BROOKS (30205) Spalding(53), Fayette(46)
BROXTON (31519) Coffee(97), Jeff Davis(2)
BRUNSWICK Glynn
BUCHANAN (30113) Haralson(87), Polk(12)
BUCKHEAD (30625) Morgan(95), Putnam(4)
BUENA VISTA Marion
BUFORD (30519) Gwinnett(93), Hall(6)
BUTLER Taylor
BYROMVILLE Dooly
BYRON (31008) Peach(86), Houston(9), Crawford(3)
CADWELL Laurens
CAIRO Grady
CALHOUN Gordon
CALVARY Grady
CAMAK Warren
CAMILLA Mitchell
CANON (30520) Hart(56), Franklin(43)
CANTON Cherokee
CARLTON (30627) Madison(73), Oglethorpe(26)
CARNESVILLE (30521) Franklin(96), Banks(3)
CARROLLTON Carroll
CARTERSVILLE Bartow
CASSVILLE Bartow
CATAULA Harris
CAVE SPRING Floyd
CECIL Cook

CEDAR SPRINGS Early
CEDARTOWN (30125) Polk(98), Floyd(1)
CENTERVILLE Houston
CHATSWORTH Murray
CHAUNCEY Dodge
CHERRYLOG (30522) Gilmer(58), Fannin(41)
CHESTER (31012) Dodge(91), Bleckley(7)
CHESTNUT MOUNTAIN Hall
CHICKAMAUGA (30707) Walker(97), Catoosa(2)
CHULA (31733) Irwin(77), Tift(22)
CISCO Murray
CLARKDALE Cobb
CLARKESVILLE (30523) Habersham(84), Rabun(15)
CLARKSTON De Kalb
CLAXTON (30417) Evans(97), Tattnall(2)
CLAYTON (30525) Rabun(98), Towns(1)
CLERMONT (30527) Hall(90), White(9)
CLEVELAND (30528) White(97), Lumpkin(2)
CLIMAX Decatur
CLINCHFIELD Houston
CLYO Effingham
COBB Sumter
COBBTOWN (30420) Tattnall(56), Candler(37), Evans(5)
COCHRAN Dodge
COHUTTA Whitfield
COLBERT (30628) Madison(93), Oglethorpe(6)
COLEMAN (31736) Randolph(80), Clay(19)
COLLINS Tattnall
COLQUITT (31737) Miller(96), Baker(2)
COLUMBUS Muscogee
COMER (30629) Madison(92), Oglethorpe(7)
COMMERCE Jackson
CONCORD Pike
CONLEY (30288) De Kalb(50), Clayton(49)
CONYERS Rockdale
COOLIDGE (31738) Colquitt(78), Thomas(21)
COOSA Floyd
CORDELE Crisp
CORNELIA Habersham
COTTON Mitchell
COVINGTON Newton
CRANDALL Murray
CRAWFORD Oglethorpe
CRAWFORDVILLE (30631) Taliaferro(91), Wilkes(7), Greene(1)
CRESCENT McIntosh
CULLODEN (31016) Monroe(45), Upson(44), Lamar(10)
CUMMING Forsyth
CUSSETA (31805) Chattahoochee(98), Stewart(1)
CUTHBERT Randolph
DACULA Gwinnett
DAHLONEGA Lumpkin
DAISY Evans

DALLAS (30157) Paulding(98), Cobb(1)
DALTON Whitfield
DAMASCUS (31741) Early(73), Baker(19), Miller(6)
DANIELSVILLE Madison
DANVILLE (31017) Twiggs(91), Wilkinson(5), Bleckley(2)
DARIEN McIntosh
DAVISBORO Washington
DAWSON Terrell
DAWSONVILLE (30534) Dawson(86), Lumpkin(9), Forsyth(2)
DE SOTO Sumter
DEARING McDuffie
DECATUR De Kalb
DEMOREST Habersham
DENTON (31532) Jeff Davis(97), Coffee(2)
DEWY ROSE (30634) Elbert(55), Hart(44)
DEXTER Laurens
DILLARD Rabun
DIXIE Brooks
DOERUN (31744) Colquitt(76), Worth(23)
DONALSONVILLE Seminole
DOUGLAS Coffee
DOUGLASVILLE Douglas
DOVER Screven
DRY BRANCH (31020) Twiggs(95), Bibb(4)
DU PONT (31630) Clinch(97), Echols(2)
DUBLIN Laurens
DUDLEY (31022) Laurens(96), Dodge(1), Bleckley(1)
DULUTH Gwinnett
EAST ELLIJAY Gilmer
EASTANOLLEE (30538) Stephens(72), Franklin(27)
EASTMAN Dodge
EATONTON Putnam
EDEN Effingham
EDISON (31746) Calhoun(90), Clay(7), Randolph(2)
ELBERTON (30635) Elbert(98), Hart(1)
ELKO Houston
ELLABELL (31308) Bryan(78), Bulloch(21)
ELLAVILLE (31806) Schley(53), Macon(46)
ELLENTON Colquitt
ELLENWOOD (30294) De Kalb(41), Clayton(33), Henry(24)
ELLERSLIE Harris
ELLIJAY Gilmer
EMERSON Bartow
ENIGMA (31749) Berrien(67), Tift(31), Irwin(1)
EPWORTH Fannin
ESOM HILL Polk
ETON Murray
EVANS Columbia
EXPERIMENT Spalding
FAIRBURN (30213) Fulton(87), Fayette(12)
FAIRMOUNT (30139) Gordon(62), Pickens(32), Bartow(5)
FARGO (31631) Clinch(85), Echols(11), Charlton(2)
FARMINGTON Oconee

FAYETTEVILLE (30215) Fayette(92), Clayton(7)
FELTON Haralson
FITZGERALD (31750) Ben Hill(87), Irwin(12)
FLEMING Liberty
FLINTSTONE Walker
FLOVILLA Butts
FLOWERY BRANCH Hall
FOLKSTON (31537) Charlton(93), Camden(6)
FOREST PARK Clayton
FORSYTH Monroe
FORT BENNING Muscogee
FORT GAINES Clay
FORT OGLETHORPE Catoosa
FORT STEWART Liberty
FORT VALLEY (31030) Peach(86), Crawford(11), Macon(2)
FORTSON (31808) Harris(67), Muscogee(32)
FOWLSTOWN Decatur
FRANKLIN Heard
FRANKLIN SPRINGS Franklin
FUNSTON Colquitt
GAINESVILLE Hall
GARFIELD (30425) Bulloch(39), Emanuel(39), Jenkins(20)
GAY Meriwether
GENEVA Talbot
GEORGETOWN (31754) Quitman(89), Clay(11)
GIBSON (30810) Glascock(96), Jefferson(2), Warren(1)
GILLSVILLE (30543) Hall(59), Banks(24), Jackson(15)
GIRARD (30426) Burke(80), Screven(19)
GLENN Heard
GLENNVILLE (30427) Tattnall(94), Long(5)
GLENWOOD (30428) Wheeler(73), Laurens(26)
GOOD HOPE (30641) Walton(82), Morgan(16)
GORDON (31031) Wilkinson(66), Twiggs(21), Baldwin(7), Jones(5)
GOUGH Burke
GRACEWOOD Richmond
GRANTVILLE (30220) Meriwether(56), Coweta(43)
GRAY Jones
GRAYSON Gwinnett
GRAYSVILLE Catoosa
GREENSBORO Greene
GREENVILLE (30222) Meriwether(98), Troup(1)
GRIFFIN (30224) Spalding(92), Pike(4), Lamar(2)
GROVETOWN (30813) Columbia(96), Richmond(3)
GUYTON Effingham
HADDOCK (31033) Jones(78), Baldwin(21)
HAGAN Evans
HAHIRA (31632) Lowndes(94), Cook(5)
HAMILTON Harris
HAMPTON (30228) Henry(66), Clayton(28), Spalding(4)
HARALSON Coweta
HARDWICK Baldwin
HARLEM (30814) Columbia(92), McDuffie(7)
HARRISON Washington
HARTSFIELD Colquitt
HARTWELL Hart
HAWKINSVILLE (31036) Pulaski(85), Houston(14)
HAZLEHURST Jeff Davis
HELEN White
HELENA (31037) Telfair(84), Wheeler(8), Dodge(6)
HEPHZIBAH (30815) Richmond(79), Burke(20)
HIAWASSEE Towns

HIGH SHOALS Morgan
HILLSBORO (31038) Jasper(78), Jones(21)
HINESVILLE Liberty
HIRAM (30141) Paulding(96), Cobb(3)
HOBOKEN Brantley
HOGANSVILLE (30230) Troup(64), Heard(17), Meriwether(17)
HOLLY SPRINGS Cherokee
HOMER Banks
HOMERVILLE Clinch
HORTENSE (31543) Wayne(54), Brantley(40), Glynn(4)
HOSCHTON (30548) Jackson(80), Gwinnett(15), Barrow(3)
HOWARD Taylor
HULL (30646) Madison(97), Jackson(1), Clarke(1)
IDEAL Macon
ILA Madison
INMAN Fayette
IRON CITY (31759) Seminole(96), Miller(3)
IRWINTON Wilkinson
IRWINVILLE Irwin
JACKSON (30233) Butts(82), Monroe(10), Henry(3), Lamar(2)
JACKSONVILLE Telfair
JAKIN (31761) Early(97), Seminole(2)
JASPER (30143) Pickens(98), Cherokee(1)
JEFFERSON Jackson
JEFFERSONVILLE Twiggs
JEKYLL ISLAND Glynn
JENKINSBURG (30234) Butts(89), Henry(10)
JERSEY Walton
JESUP Wayne
JEWELL (31045) Warren(64), Hancock(35)
JONESBORO (30238) Clayton(95), Fayette(4)
JULIETTE (31046) Monroe(88), Jones(11)
JUNCTION CITY (31812) Talbot(84), Taylor(15)
KATHLEEN Houston
KENNESAW Cobb
KEYSVILLE (30816) Burke(73), Jefferson(26)
KINGS BAY Camden
KINGSLAND Camden
KINGSTON (30145) Bartow(56), Floyd(43)
KITE (31049) Johnson(57), Emanuel(42)
KNOXVILLE Crawford
LA FAYETTE Walker
LAGRANGE Troup
LAKE PARK (31636) Lowndes(62), Echols(35), Catoosa(1)
LAKELAND Lanier
LAKEMONT Rabun
LAVONIA (30553) Franklin(63), Hart(36)
LAWRENCEVILLE Gwinnett
LEARY (31762) Baker(50), Calhoun(50)
LEBANON Cherokee
LEESBURG Lee
LENOX (31637) Cook(56), Colquitt(20), Berrien(18), Tift(4)
LESLIE Sumter
LEXINGTON Oglethorpe
LILBURN Gwinnett
LILLY Dooly
LINCOLNTON (30817) Lincoln(96), McDuffie(1), Wilkes(1)
LINDALE (30147) Floyd(95), Polk(4)
LITHIA SPRINGS Douglas
LITHONIA De Kalb
LIZELLA (31052) Bibb(54), Crawford(45)
LOCUST GROVE (30248) Henry(92), Spalding(5), Butts(1)
LOGANVILLE Gwinnett
LOOKOUT MOUNTAIN (30750) Walker(66), Dade(33)
LOUISVILLE (30434) Jefferson(96), Burke(3)
LOUVALE Stewart

LOVEJOY Clayton
LUDOWICI Long
LULA (30554) Hall(67), Banks(32)
LUMBER CITY (31549) Telfair(76), Wheeler(23)
LUMPKIN Stewart
LUTHERSVILLE Meriwether
LYERLY Chattooga
LYONS (30436) Toombs(94), Emanuel(5)
MABLETON Cobb
MACON Bibb
MADISON (30650) Morgan(93), Greene(5), Walton(1)
MANASSAS Tattnall
MANCHESTER Meriwether
MANOR Ware
MANSFIELD Jasper
MARBLE HILL (30148) Pickens(73), Dawson(26)
MARIETTA Cobb
MARSHALLVILLE Macon
MARTIN (30557) Franklin(69), Stephens(30)
MATTHEWS Jefferson
MAUK (31058) Taylor(57), Marion(42)
MAXEYS Oglethorpe
MAYSVILLE (30558) Jackson(54), Banks(45)
MC CAYSVILLE Fannin
MC INTYRE Wilkinson
MC RAE Telfair
MCDONOUGH Henry
MEANSVILLE (30256) Pike(55), Upson(42), Lamar(2)
MEIGS (31765) Mitchell(44), Thomas(38), Colquitt(17)
MELDRIM Effingham
MENLO (30731) Chattooga(60), Walker(25), Dade(14)
MERIDIAN McIntosh
MERSHON (31551) Pierce(60), Bacon(39)
MESENA Warren
METTER Candler
MIDLAND (31820) Muscogee(88), Harris(11)
MIDVILLE (30441) Emanuel(67), Burke(32)
MIDWAY Liberty
MILAN (31060) Dodge(79), Telfair(20)
MILLEDGEVILLE Baldwin
MILLEN (30442) Jenkins(93), Burke(4), Screven(1)
MILLWOOD (31552) Ware(91), Coffee(5), Atkinson(2)
MILNER (30257) Lamar(88), Pike(11)
MINERAL BLUFF Fannin
MITCHELL (30820) Glascock(63), Warren(36)
MOLENA (30258) Pike(60), Upson(39)
MONROE Walton
MONTEZUMA (31063) Dooly(64), Macon(35)
MONTICELLO Jasper
MONTROSE (31065) Laurens(90), Bleckley(9)
MORELAND Coweta
MORGAN (31766) Calhoun(94), Randolph(5)
MORGANTON (30560) Fannin(82), Union(17)
MORRIS (31767) Quitman(60), Clay(29), Randolph(4), Stewart(4)
MORROW Clayton
MORVEN Brooks
MOULTRIE Colquitt
MOUNT AIRY Habersham
MOUNT BERRY Floyd
MOUNT VERNON Montgomery
MOUNT ZION Carroll
MOUNTAIN CITY Rabun
MURRAYVILLE (30564) Lumpkin(60), Hall(34), White(5)

MUSELLA (31066) Crawford(94), Monroe(3), Bibb(1)
MYSTIC Irwin
NAHUNTA (31553) Brantley(97), Charlton(2)
NASHVILLE Berrien
NAYLOR (31641) Lowndes(84), Lanier(15)
NELSON Cherokee
NEWBORN Newton
NEWINGTON (30446) Screven(65), Effingham(34)
NEWNAN Coweta
NEWTON Baker
NICHOLLS (31554) Coffee(67), Bacon(22), Ware(9)
NICHOLSON (30565) Jackson(84), Madison(15)
NORCROSS Gwinnett
NORMAN PARK Colquitt
NORRISTOWN Emanuel
NORTH METRO Gwinnett
NORWOOD Warren
NUNEZ Emanuel
OAKFIELD Worth
OAKMAN Gordon
OAKWOOD Hall
OCHLOCKNEE (31773) Thomas(79), Grady(18), Colquitt(1)
OCILLA Irwin
OCONEE Washington
ODUM (31555) Wayne(85), Appling(14)
OFFERMAN Pierce
OGLETHORPE Macon
OLIVER Screven
OMAHA Stewart
OMEGA (31775) Colquitt(59), Tift(26), Worth(13)
ORCHARD HILL Spalding
OXFORD Newton
PALMETTO (30268) Fulton(80), Coweta(19)
PARROTT (31777) Terrell(81), Webster(18)
PATTERSON Pierce
PAVO (31778) Thomas(94), Brooks(4)
PEACHTREE CITY Fayette
PEARSON (31642) Atkinson(95), Clinch(3), Coffee(1)
PELHAM Mitchell
PEMBROKE (31321) Bryan(52), Bulloch(47)
PENDERGRASS (30567) Jackson(72), Hall(27)
PERKINS Jenkins
PERRY Houston
PINE LAKE De Kalb
PINE MOUNTAIN (31822) Harris(84), Troup(14), Meriwether(1)
PINE MOUNTAIN VALLEY Harris
PINEHURST Dooly
PINEVIEW (31071) Wilcox(94), Pulaski(5)
PITTS (31072) Wilcox(50), Crisp(49)
PLAINFIELD Dodge
PLAINS Sumter
PLAINVILLE (30733) Gordon(93), Floyd(6)
POOLER Chatham
PORTAL (30450) Bulloch(98), Emanuel(1)
PORTERDALE Newton
POULAN Worth
POWDER SPRINGS (30127) Cobb(79), Paulding(20)
PRESTON Webster
PULASKI Candler
PUTNEY Dougherty
QUITMAN Brooks
RABUN GAP Rabun
RANGER (30734) Gordon(76), Pickens(23)
RAY CITY (31645) Lanier(50), Berrien(33), Lowndes(16)
RAYLE (30660) Wilkes(77), Oglethorpe(18), Taliaferro(3)

REBECCA (31783) Turner(54), Irwin(35), Ben Hill(10)
RED OAK Fulton
REDAN De Kalb
REGISTER (30452) Bulloch(98), Evans(1)
REIDSVILLE Tattnall
RENTZ Laurens
RESACA (30735) Gordon(62), Murray(23), Whitfield(14)
REX (30273) Clayton(92), Henry(7)
REYNOLDS (31076) Macon(73), Taylor(26)
RHINE (31077) Dodge(94), Telfair(5)
RICEBORO (31323) Liberty(93), Long(6)
RICHLAND (31825) Stewart(88), Webster(11)
RICHMOND HILL Bryan
RINCON Effingham
RINGGOLD (30736) Catoosa(97), Walker(2)
RISING FAWN (30738) Dade(68), Walker(31)
RIVERDALE (30296) Clayton(83), Fulton(10), Fayette(6)
ROBERTA Crawford
ROCHELLE Wilcox
ROCK SPRING (30739) Walker(82), Catoosa(17)
ROCKLEDGE Laurens
ROCKMART (30153) Polk(67), Paulding(28), Haralson(4)
ROCKY FACE (30740) Whitfield(86), Walker(13)
ROCKY FORD Screven
ROME Floyd
ROOPVILLE (30170) Heard(62), Carroll(37)
ROSSVILLE (30741) Walker(67), Catoosa(32)
ROSWELL Fulton
ROYSTON (30662) Franklin(56), Hart(27), Madison(15), Elbert(1)
RUPERT (31081) Taylor(87), Macon(11), Schley(1)
RUTLEDGE Morgan
RYDAL (30171) Bartow(79), Gordon(20)
SAINT GEORGE Charlton
SAINT MARYS Camden
SAINT SIMONS ISLAND Glynn
SALE CITY (31784) Mitchell(67), Colquitt(32)
SANDERSVILLE Washington
SAPELO ISLAND McIntosh
SARDIS Burke
SARGENT Coweta
SASSER Terrell

SAUTEE NACOOCHEE (30571) White(97), Habersham(2)
SAVANNAH Chatham
SCOTLAND Telfair
SCOTTDALE De Kalb
SCREVEN Wayne
SEA ISLAND Glynn
SENOIA (30276) Coweta(81), Meriwether(12), Fayette(5)
SEVILLE Wilcox
SHADY DALE Jasper
SHANNON Floyd
SHARON Taliaferro
SHARPSBURG Coweta
SHELLMAN (31786) Randolph(95), Terrell(2), Calhoun(1)
SHILOH (31826) Harris(72), Talbot(27)
SILOAM Greene
SILVER CREEK (30173) Floyd(92), Polk(7)
SMARR Monroe
SMITHVILLE (31787) Lee(60), Sumter(39)
SMYRNA Cobb
SNELLVILLE Gwinnett
SOCIAL CIRCLE Walton
SOPERTON (30457) Treutlen(94), Montgomery(3), Emanuel(1)
SPARKS Cook
SPARTA (31087) Hancock(97), Baldwin(2)
SPRINGFIELD Effingham
STAPLETON (30823) Jefferson(85), Warren(11), Glascock(1)
STATENVILLE Echols
STATESBORO Bulloch
STATHAM (30666) Barrow(66), Oconee(25), Jackson(8)
STEPHENS Oglethorpe
STILLMORE Emanuel
STOCKBRIDGE (30281) Henry(88), Rockdale(5), Clayton(5)
STOCKTON Lanier
STONE MOUNTAIN De Kalb
SUCHES (30572) Union(76), Fannin(23)
SUGAR VALLEY (30746) Gordon(96), Walker(3)
SUMMERTOWN Emanuel
SUMMERVILLE (30747) Chattooga(95), Walker(4)
SUMNER Worth
SUNNY SIDE Spalding
SURRENCY Appling
SUWANEE Gwinnett
SWAINSBORO Emanuel
SYCAMORE Turner
SYLVANIA Screven
SYLVESTER (31791) Worth(98), Dougherty(1)

TALBOTTON Talbot
TALKING ROCK (30175) Pickens(62), Gilmer(37)
TALLAPOOSA Haralson
TALLULAH FALLS Rabun
TALMO (30575) Jackson(75), Hall(24)
TARRYTOWN (30470) Montgomery(84), Treutlen(15)
TATE Pickens
TAYLORSVILLE (30178) Bartow(81), Polk(17), Paulding(1)
TEMPLE (30179) Carroll(48), Paulding(31), Haralson(19)
TENNGA Murray
TENNILLE (31089) Washington(98), Johnson(1)
THE ROCK (30285) Upson(60), Pike(21), Lamar(18)
THOMASTON Upson
THOMASVILLE Thomas
THOMSON (30824) McDuffie(98), Columbia(1)
TIFTON Tift
TIGER Rabun
TIGNALL (30668) Wilkes(82), Lincoln(17)
TOCCOA Stephens
TOOMSBORO Wilkinson
TOWNSEND McIntosh
TRENTON Dade
TRION (30753) Chattooga(78), Walker(21)
TUCKER De Kalb
TUNNEL HILL (30755) Whitfield(53), Catoosa(46)
TURIN Coweta
TURNERVILLE Habersham
TWIN CITY (30471) Emanuel(85), Bulloch(13)
TY TY (31795) Tift(74), Worth(25)
TYBEE ISLAND Chatham
TYRONE Fayette
UNADILLA (31091) Dooly(98), Houston(1)
UNION CITY Fulton
UNION POINT (30669) Greene(88), Oglethorpe(10)
UPATOI (31829) Muscogee(93), Harris(6)
UVALDA (30473) Toombs(60), Montgomery(39)
VALDOSTA Lowndes
VALONA McIntosh
VARNELL Whitfield
VIDALIA Toombs
VIENNA (31092) Dooly(98), Crisp(1)
VILLA RICA (30180) Carroll(71), Douglas(19), Paulding(9)
WACO (30182) Carroll(62), Haralson(37)
WADLEY Jefferson

WALESKA Cherokee
WALTHOURVILLE Liberty
WARESBORO Ware
WARM SPRINGS Meriwether
WARNER ROBINS Houston
WARRENTON Warren
WARTHEN Washington
WARWICK Worth
WASHINGTON Wilkes
WATKINSVILLE (30677) Oconee(96), Greene(3)
WAVERLY Camden
WAVERLY HALL (31831) Harris(94), Talbot(5)
WAYCROSS (31503) Ware(94), Brantley(4), Pierce(1)
WAYNESBORO Burke
WAYNESVILLE (31566) Camden(57), Brantley(38), Glynn(3)
WEST GREEN (31567) Jeff Davis(56), Coffee(43)
WEST POINT (31833) Troup(70), Harris(29)
WESTON (31832) Webster(85), Randolph(14)
WHIGHAM Grady
WHITE (30184) Bartow(69), Cherokee(30)
WHITE OAK Camden
WHITE PLAINS (30678) Greene(97), Hancock(1)
WHITESBURG (30185) Carroll(95), Douglas(4)
WILDWOOD Dade
WILEY Rabun
WILLACOOCHEE (31650) Coffee(91), Atkinson(8)
WILLIAMSON (30292) Pike(65), Spalding(34)
WINDER (30680) Barrow(98), Oconee(1)
WINSTON Douglas
WINTERVILLE (30683) Clarke(61), Oglethorpe(36), Madison(1)
WOODBINE Camden
WOODBURY Meriwether
WOODLAND Talbot
WOODSTOCK Cherokee
WRAY (31798) Irwin(87), Ben Hill(6), Coffee(5)
WRENS Jefferson
WRIGHTSVILLE (31096) Johnson(84), Washington(10), Laurens(5)
YATESVILLE (31097) Upson(90), Lamar(6), Monroe(2)
YOUNG HARRIS (30582) Towns(80), Union(19)
ZEBULON (30295) Pike(97), Lamar(2)

ZIP/City Cross Reference

30001-30001 AUSTELL
30002-30002 AVONDALE ESTATES
30003-30003 NORCROSS
30004-30005 ALPHARETTA
30006-30008 MARIETTA
30009-30009 ALPHARETTA
30010-30010 NORCROSS
30011-30011 AUBURN
30012-30013 CONYERS
30014-30016 COVINGTON
30017-30017 GRAYSON
30018-30018 JERSEY
30019-30019 DACULA
30020-30020 CLARKDALE
30021-30021 CLARKSTON
30022-30023 ALPHARETTA
30024-30024 SUWANEE
30025-30025 SOCIAL CIRCLE
30026-30026 DULUTH
30026-30026 NORTH METRO
30027-30027 CONLEY
30028-30028 CUMMING

30029-30029 DULUTH
30029-30029 NORTH METRO
30030-30037 DECATUR
30038-30038 LITHONIA
30039-30039 SNELLVILLE
30040-30041 CUMMING
30042-30046 LAWRENCEVILLE
30047-30048 LILBURN
30049-30049 ELLENWOOD
30049-30049 LAWRENCEVILLE
30050-30051 FOREST PARK
30052-30052 LOGANVILLE
30054-30054 OXFORD
30055-30055 MANSFIELD
30056-30056 NEWBORN
30057-30057 LITHIA SPRINGS
30058-30058 LITHONIA
30059-30059 MABLETON
30060-30069 MARIETTA
30070-30070 PORTERDALE
30071-30071 NORCROSS
30072-30072 PINE LAKE

30073-30073 POWDER SPRINGS
30074-30074 REDAN
30075-30077 ROSWELL
30078-30078 SNELLVILLE
30079-30079 SCOTTDALE
30080-30082 SMYRNA
30083-30083 STONE MOUNTAIN
30084-30085 TUCKER
30086-30088 STONE MOUNTAIN
30089-30089 DECATUR
30090-30090 MARIETTA
30091-30093 NORCROSS
30094-30094 CONYERS
30095-30099 DULUTH
30101-30102 ACWORTH
30103-30103 ADAIRSVILLE
30104-30104 ARAGON
30105-30105 ARMUCHEE
30106-30106 AUSTELL
30107-30107 BALL GROUND
30108-30108 BOWDON
30109-30109 BOWDON JUNCTION

30110-30110 BREMEN
30111-30111 CLARKDALE
30113-30113 BUCHANAN
30114-30115 CANTON
30116-30119 CARROLLTON
30120-30121 CARTERSVILLE
30122-30122 LITHIA SPRINGS
30123-30123 CASSVILLE
30124-30124 CAVE SPRING
30125-30125 CEDARTOWN
30126-30126 MABLETON
30127-30127 POWDER SPRINGS
30128-30128 CUMMING
30129-30129 COOSA
30130-30131 CUMMING
30132-30132 DALLAS
30133-30135 DOUGLASVILLE
30136-30136 DULUTH
30137-30137 EMERSON
30138-30138 ESOM HILL
30139-30139 FAIRMOUNT
30140-30140 FELTON

30141-30141 HIRAM	30259-30259 MORELAND	30502-30502 CHESTNUT MOUNTAIN	30641-30641 GOOD HOPE
30142-30142 HOLLY SPRINGS	30260-30260 MORROW	30503-30507 GAINESVILLE	30642-30642 GREENSBORO
30143-30143 JASPER	30261-30261 LAGRANGE	30510-30510 ALTO	30643-30643 HARTWELL
30144-30144 KENNESAW	30262-30262 NEWBORN	30511-30511 BALDWIN	30645-30645 HIGH SHOALS
30145-30145 KINGSTON	30263-30265 NEWNAN	30512-30512 BLAIRSVILLE	30646-30646 HULL
30146-30146 LEBANON	30266-30266 ORCHARD HILL	30513-30513 BLUE RIDGE	30647-30647 ILA
30147-30147 LINDALE	30267-30267 OXFORD	30514-30514 BLAIRSVILLE	30648-30648 LEXINGTON
30148-30148 MARBLE HILL	30268-30268 PALMETTO	30515-30515 BUFORD	30650-30650 MADISON
30149-30149 MOUNT BERRY	30269-30269 PEACHTREE CITY	30516-30516 BOWERSVILLE	30655-30656 MONROE
30150-30150 MOUNT ZION	30270-30270 PORTERDALE	30517-30517 BRASELTON	30660-30660 RAYLE
30151-30151 NELSON	30271-30271 NEWNAN	30518-30519 BUFORD	30662-30662 ROYSTON
30152-30152 KENNESAW	30272-30272 RED OAK	30520-30520 CANON	30663-30663 RUTLEDGE
30153-30153 ROCKMART	30273-30273 REX	30521-30521 CARNESVILLE	30664-30664 SHARON
30154-30154 DOUGLASVILLE	30274-30274 RIVERDALE	30522-30522 CHERRYLOG	30665-30665 SILOAM
30155-30155 DULUTH	30275-30275 SARGENT	30523-30523 CLARKESVILLE	30666-30666 STATHAM
30156-30156 KENNESAW	30276-30276 SENOIA	30525-30525 CLAYTON	30667-30667 STEPHENS
30157-30157 DALLAS	30277-30277 SHARPSBURG	30527-30527 CLERMONT	30668-30668 TIGNALL
30158-30159 NORTH METRO	30278-30278 SNELLVILLE	30528-30528 CLEVELAND	30669-30669 UNION POINT
30160-30160 KENNESAW	30279-30279 SOCIAL CIRCLE	30529-30530 COMMERCE	30671-30671 MAXEYS
30161-30165 ROME	30281-30281 STOCKBRIDGE	30531-30531 CORNELIA	30673-30673 WASHINGTON
30168-30168 AUSTELL	30284-30284 SUNNY SIDE	30533-30533 DAHLONEGA	30677-30677 WATKINSVILLE
30170-30170 ROOPVILLE	30285-30285 THE ROCK	30534-30534 DAWSONVILLE	30678-30678 WHITE PLAINS
30171-30171 RYDAL	30286-30286 THOMASTON	30535-30535 DEMOREST	30680-30680 WINDER
30172-30172 SHANNON	30287-30287 MORROW	30537-30537 DILLARD	30683-30683 WINTERVILLE
30173-30173 SILVER CREEK	30288-30288 CONLEY	30538-30538 EASTANOLLEE	30701-30703 CALHOUN
30174-30174 SUWANEE	30289-30289 TURIN	30539-30539 EAST ELLIJAY	30705-30705 CHATSWORTH
30175-30175 TALKING ROCK	30290-30290 TYRONE	30540-30540 ELLIJAY	30707-30707 CHICKAMAUGA
30176-30176 TALLAPOOSA	30291-30291 UNION CITY	30541-30541 EPWORTH	30708-30708 CISCO
30177-30177 TATE	30292-30292 WILLIAMSON	30542-30542 FLOWERY BRANCH	30710-30710 COHUTTA
30178-30178 TAYLORSVILLE	30293-30293 WOODBURY	30543-30543 GILLSVILLE	30711-30711 CRANDALL
30179-30179 TEMPLE	30294-30294 ELLENWOOD	30544-30544 DEMOREST	30719-30722 DALTON
30180-30180 VILLA RICA	30295-30295 ZEBULON	30545-30545 HELEN	30724-30724 ETON
30182-30182 WACO	30296-30296 RIVERDALE	30546-30546 HIAWASSEE	30725-30725 FLINTSTONE
30183-30183 WALESKA	30297-30298 FOREST PARK	30547-30547 HOMER	30726-30726 GRAYSVILLE
30184-30184 WHITE	30301-30399 ATLANTA	30548-30548 HOSCHTON	30728-30728 LA FAYETTE
30185-30185 WHITESBURG	30401-30401 SWAINSBORO	30549-30549 JEFFERSON	30730-30730 LYERLY
30187-30187 WINSTON	30410-30410 AILEY	30552-30552 LAKEMONT	30731-30731 MENLO
30188-30189 WOODSTOCK	30411-30411 ALAMO	30553-30553 LAVONIA	30732-30732 OAKMAN
30195-30199 DULUTH	30412-30412 ALSTON	30554-30554 LULA	30733-30733 PLAINVILLE
30201-30202 ALPHARETTA	30413-30413 BARTOW	30555-30555 MC CAYSVILLE	30734-30734 RANGER
30203-30203 AUBURN	30414-30414 BELLVILLE	30557-30557 MARTIN	30735-30735 RESACA
30204-30204 BARNESVILLE	30415-30415 BROOKLET	30558-30558 MAYSVILLE	30736-30736 RINGGOLD
30205-30205 BROOKS	30417-30417 CLAXTON	30559-30559 MINERAL BLUFF	30738-30738 RISING FAWN
30206-30206 CONCORD	30420-30420 COBBTOWN	30560-30560 MORGANTON	30739-30739 ROCK SPRING
30207-30208 CONYERS	30421-30421 COLLINS	30562-30562 MOUNTAIN CITY	30740-30740 ROCKY FACE
30209-30210 COVINGTON	30423-30423 DAISY	30563-30563 MOUNT AIRY	30741-30741 ROSSVILLE
30211-30211 DACULA	30424-30424 DOVER	30564-30564 MURRAYVILLE	30742-30742 FORT OGLETHORPE
30212-30212 EXPERIMENT	30425-30425 GARFIELD	30565-30565 NICHOLSON	30746-30746 SUGAR VALLEY
30213-30213 FAIRBURN	30426-30426 GIRARD	30566-30566 OAKWOOD	30747-30747 SUMMERVILLE
30214-30215 FAYETTEVILLE	30427-30427 GLENNVILLE	30567-30567 PENDERGRASS	30750-30750 LOOKOUT MOUNTAIN
30216-30216 FLOVILLA	30428-30428 GLENWOOD	30568-30568 RABUN GAP	30751-30751 TENNGA
30217-30217 FRANKLIN	30429-30429 HAGAN	30571-30571 SAUTEE NACOOCHEE	30752-30752 TRENTON
30218-30218 GAY	30434-30434 LOUISVILLE	30572-30572 SUCHES	30753-30753 TRION
30219-30219 GLENN	30436-30436 LYONS	30573-30573 TALLULAH FALLS	30755-30755 TUNNEL HILL
30220-30220 GRANTVILLE	30438-30438 MANASSAS	30575-30575 TALMO	30756-30756 VARNELL
30221-30221 GRAYSON	30439-30439 METTER	30576-30576 TIGER	30757-30757 WILDWOOD
30222-30222 GREENVILLE	30441-30441 MIDVILLE	30577-30577 TOCCOA	30802-30802 APPLING
30223-30224 GRIFFIN	30442-30442 MILLEN	30580-30580 TURNERVILLE	30803-30803 AVERA
30226-30226 LILBURN	30445-30445 MOUNT VERNON	30581-30581 WILEY	30805-30805 BLYTHE
30227-30227 LAWRENCEVILLE	30446-30446 NEWINGTON	30582-30582 YOUNG HARRIS	30806-30806 BONEVILLE
30228-30228 HAMPTON	30447-30447 NORRISTOWN	30596-30596 ALTO	30807-30807 CAMAK
30229-30229 HARALSON	30448-30448 NUNEZ	30597-30597 DAHLONEGA	30808-30808 DEARING
30230-30230 HOGANSVILLE	30449-30449 OLIVER	30598-30598 TOCCOA	30809-30809 EVANS
30232-30232 INMAN	30450-30450 PORTAL	30599-30599 COMMERCE	30810-30810 GIBSON
30233-30233 JACKSON	30451-30451 PULASKI	30601-30613 ATHENS	30811-30811 GOUGH
30234-30234 JENKINSBURG	30452-30452 REGISTER	30619-30619 ARNOLDSVILLE	30812-30812 GRACEWOOD
30235-30235 JERSEY	30453-30453 REIDSVILLE	30620-30620 BETHLEHEM	30813-30813 GROVETOWN
30236-30238 JONESBORO	30454-30454 ROCKLEDGE	30621-30621 BISHOP	30814-30814 HARLEM
30239-30239 ALPHARETTA	30455-30455 ROCKY FORD	30622-30622 BOGART	30815-30815 HEPHZIBAH
30240-30241 LAGRANGE	30456-30456 SARDIS	30623-30623 BOSTWICK	30816-30816 KEYSVILLE
30243-30246 LAWRENCEVILLE	30457-30457 SOPERTON	30624-30624 BOWMAN	30817-30817 LINCOLNTON
30247-30247 LILBURN	30458-30461 STATESBORO	30625-30625 BUCKHEAD	30818-30818 MATTHEWS
30248-30248 LOCUST GROVE	30464-30464 STILLMORE	30627-30627 CARLTON	30819-30819 MESENA
30249-30249 LOGANVILLE	30466-30466 SUMMERTOWN	30628-30628 COLBERT	30820-30820 MITCHELL
30250-30250 LOVEJOY	30467-30467 SYLVANIA	30629-30629 COMER	30821-30821 NORWOOD
30251-30251 LUTHERSVILLE	30470-30470 TARRYTOWN	30630-30630 CRAWFORD	30822-30822 PERKINS
30252-30253 MCDONOUGH	30471-30471 TWIN CITY	30631-30631 CRAWFORDVILLE	30823-30823 STAPLETON
30254-30254 NEWNAN	30473-30473 UVALDA	30633-30633 DANIELSVILLE	30824-30824 THOMSON
30255-30255 MANSFIELD	30474-30475 VIDALIA	30634-30634 DEWY ROSE	30828-30828 WARRENTON
30256-30256 MEANSVILLE	30477-30477 WADLEY	30635-30635 ELBERTON	30830-30830 WAYNESBORO
30257-30257 MILNER	30499-30499 REIDSVILLE	30638-30638 FARMINGTON	30833-30833 WRENS
30258-30258 MOLENA	30501-30501 GAINESVILLE	30639-30639 FRANKLIN SPRINGS	30900-30999 AUGUSTA

ZIP Range	City
31001-31001	ABBEVILLE
31002-31002	ADRIAN
31003-31003	ALLENTOWN
31004-31004	BOLINGBROKE
31005-31005	BONAIRE
31006-31006	BUTLER
31007-31007	BYROMVILLE
31008-31008	BYRON
31009-31009	CADWELL
31010-31010	CORDELE
31011-31011	CHAUNCEY
31012-31012	CHESTER
31013-31013	CLINCHFIELD
31014-31014	COCHRAN
31015-31015	CORDELE
31016-31016	CULLODEN
31017-31017	DANVILLE
31018-31018	DAVISBORO
31019-31019	DEXTER
31020-31020	DRY BRANCH
31021-31021	DUBLIN
31022-31022	DUDLEY
31023-31023	EASTMAN
31024-31024	EATONTON
31025-31025	ELKO
31026-31026	COCHRAN
31027-31027	DUBLIN
31028-31028	CENTERVILLE
31029-31029	FORSYTH
31030-31030	FORT VALLEY
31031-31031	GORDON
31032-31032	GRAY
31033-31033	HADDOCK
31034-31034	HARDWICK
31035-31035	HARRISON
31036-31036	HAWKINSVILLE
31037-31037	HELENA
31038-31038	HILLSBORO
31039-31039	HOWARD
31040-31040	DUBLIN
31041-31041	IDEAL
31042-31042	IRWINTON
31044-31044	JEFFERSONVILLE
31045-31045	JEWELL
31046-31046	JULIETTE
31047-31047	KATHLEEN
31049-31049	KITE
31050-31050	KNOXVILLE
31051-31051	LILLY
31052-31052	LIZELLA
31054-31054	MC INTYRE
31055-31055	MC RAE
31057-31057	MARSHALLVILLE
31058-31058	MAUK
31059-31059	MILLEDGEVILLE
31060-31060	MILAN
31061-31062	MILLEDGEVILLE
31063-31063	MONTEZUMA
31064-31064	MONTICELLO
31065-31065	MONTROSE
31066-31066	MUSELLA
31067-31067	OCONEE
31068-31068	OGLETHORPE
31069-31069	PERRY
31070-31070	PINEHURST
31071-31071	PINEVIEW
31072-31072	PITTS
31073-31073	PLAINFIELD
31075-31075	RENTZ
31076-31076	REYNOLDS
31077-31077	RHINE
31078-31078	ROBERTA
31079-31079	ROCHELLE
31081-31081	RUPERT
31082-31082	SANDERSVILLE
31083-31083	SCOTLAND
31084-31084	SEVILLE
31085-31085	SHADY DALE
31086-31086	SMARR
31087-31087	SPARTA
31088-31088	WARNER ROBINS
31089-31089	TENNILLE
31090-31090	TOOMSBORO
31091-31091	UNADILLA
31092-31092	VIENNA
31093-31093	WARNER ROBINS
31094-31094	WARTHEN
31095-31095	WARNER ROBINS
31096-31096	WRIGHTSVILLE
31097-31097	YATESVILLE
31098-31099	WARNER ROBINS
31106-31199	ATLANTA
31200-31299	MACON
31301-31301	ALLENHURST
31302-31302	BLOOMINGDALE
31303-31303	CLYO
31304-31304	CRESCENT
31305-31305	DARIEN
31307-31307	EDEN
31308-31308	ELLABELL
31309-31309	FLEMING
31310-31310	HINESVILLE
31312-31312	GUYTON
31313-31313	HINESVILLE
31314-31315	FORT STEWART
31316-31316	LUDOWICI
31318-31318	MELDRIM
31319-31319	MERIDIAN
31320-31320	MIDWAY
31321-31321	PEMBROKE
31322-31322	POOLER
31323-31323	RICEBORO
31324-31324	RICHMOND HILL
31326-31326	RINCON
31327-31327	SAPELO ISLAND
31328-31328	TYBEE ISLAND
31329-31329	SPRINGFIELD
31331-31331	TOWNSEND
31332-31332	VALONA
31333-31333	WALTHOURVILLE
31400-31499	SAVANNAH
31501-31503	WAYCROSS
31510-31510	ALMA
31512-31512	AMBROSE
31513-31515	BAXLEY
31516-31516	BLACKSHEAR
31518-31518	BRISTOL
31519-31519	BROXTON
31520-31521	BRUNSWICK
31522-31522	SAINT SIMONS ISLAND
31523-31525	BRUNSWICK
31527-31527	JEKYLL ISLAND
31532-31532	DENTON
31533-31535	DOUGLAS
31537-31537	FOLKSTON
31539-31539	HAZLEHURST
31542-31542	HOBOKEN
31543-31543	HORTENSE
31544-31544	JACKSONVILLE
31545-31546	JESUP
31547-31547	KINGS BAY
31548-31548	KINGSLAND
31549-31549	LUMBER CITY
31550-31550	MANOR
31551-31551	MERSHON
31552-31552	MILLWOOD
31553-31553	NAHUNTA
31554-31554	NICHOLLS
31555-31555	ODUM
31556-31556	OFFERMAN
31557-31557	PATTERSON
31558-31558	SAINT MARYS
31560-31560	SCREVEN
31561-31561	SEA ISLAND
31563-31563	SURRENCY
31564-31564	WARESBORO
31565-31565	WAVERLY
31566-31566	WAYNESVILLE
31567-31567	WEST GREEN
31568-31568	WHITE OAK
31569-31569	WOODBINE
31598-31599	JESUP
31601-31606	VALDOSTA
31620-31620	ADEL
31622-31622	ALAPAHA
31623-31623	ARGYLE
31624-31624	AXSON
31625-31625	BARNEY
31626-31626	BOSTON
31627-31627	CECIL
31629-31629	DIXIE
31630-31630	DU PONT
31631-31631	FARGO
31632-31632	HAHIRA
31634-31634	HOMERVILLE
31635-31635	LAKELAND
31636-31636	LAKE PARK
31637-31637	LENOX
31638-31638	MORVEN
31639-31639	NASHVILLE
31641-31641	NAYLOR
31642-31642	PEARSON
31643-31643	QUITMAN
31645-31645	RAY CITY
31646-31646	SAINT GEORGE
31647-31647	SPARKS
31648-31648	STATENVILLE
31649-31649	STOCKTON
31650-31650	WILLACOOCHEE
31698-31699	VALDOSTA
31700-31708	ALBANY
31709-31710	AMERICUS
31711-31711	ANDERSONVILLE
31712-31712	ARABI
31713-31713	ARLINGTON
31714-31714	ASHBURN
31715-31715	ATTAPULGUS
31716-31716	BACONTON
31717-31718	BAINBRIDGE
31720-31720	BARWICK
31722-31722	BERLIN
31723-31723	BLAKELY
31724-31724	BLUFFTON
31725-31725	BRINSON
31726-31726	BRONWOOD
31727-31727	BROOKFIELD
31728-31728	CAIRO
31729-31729	CALVARY
31730-31730	CAMILLA
31732-31732	CEDAR SPRINGS
31733-31733	CHULA
31734-31734	CLIMAX
31735-31735	COBB
31736-31736	COLEMAN
31737-31737	COLQUITT
31738-31738	COOLIDGE
31739-31739	COTTON
31740-31740	CUTHBERT
31741-31741	DAMASCUS
31742-31742	DAWSON
31743-31743	DE SOTO
31744-31744	DOERUN
31745-31745	DONALSONVILLE
31746-31746	EDISON
31747-31747	ELLENTON
31749-31749	ENIGMA
31750-31750	FITZGERALD
31751-31751	FORT GAINES
31752-31752	FOWLSTOWN
31753-31753	FUNSTON
31754-31754	GEORGETOWN
31756-31756	HARTSFIELD
31757-31758	THOMASVILLE
31759-31759	IRON CITY
31760-31760	IRWINVILLE
31761-31761	JAKIN
31762-31762	LEARY
31763-31763	LEESBURG
31764-31764	LESLIE
31765-31765	MEIGS
31766-31766	MORGAN
31767-31767	MORRIS
31768-31768	MOULTRIE
31769-31769	MYSTIC
31770-31770	NEWTON
31771-31771	NORMAN PARK
31772-31772	OAKFIELD
31773-31773	OCHLOCKNEE
31774-31774	OCILLA
31775-31775	OMEGA
31776-31776	MOULTRIE
31777-31777	PARROTT
31778-31778	PAVO
31779-31779	PELHAM
31780-31780	PLAINS
31781-31781	POULAN
31782-31782	PUTNEY
31783-31783	REBECCA
31784-31784	SALE CITY
31785-31785	SASSER
31786-31786	SHELLMAN
31787-31787	SMITHVILLE
31789-31789	SUMNER
31790-31790	SYCAMORE
31791-31791	SYLVESTER
31792-31792	THOMASVILLE
31793-31793	TIFTON
31795-31795	TY TY
31796-31796	WARWICK
31797-31797	WHIGHAM
31798-31798	WRAY
31799-31799	THOMASVILLE
31801-31801	BOX SPRINGS
31803-31803	BUENA VISTA
31804-31804	CATAULA
31805-31805	CUSSETA
31806-31806	ELLAVILLE
31807-31807	ELLERSLIE
31808-31808	FORTSON
31810-31810	GENEVA
31811-31811	HAMILTON
31812-31812	JUNCTION CITY
31814-31814	LOUVALE
31815-31815	LUMPKIN
31816-31816	MANCHESTER
31820-31820	MIDLAND
31821-31821	OMAHA
31822-31822	PINE MOUNTAIN
31823-31823	PINE MOUNTAIN VALLEY
31824-31824	PRESTON
31825-31825	RICHLAND
31826-31826	SHILOH
31827-31827	TALBOTTON
31829-31829	UPATOI
31830-31830	WARM SPRINGS
31831-31831	WAVERLY HALL
31832-31832	WESTON
31833-31833	WEST POINT
31836-31836	WOODLAND
31900-31904	COLUMBUS
31905-31905	FORT BENNING
31906-31994	COLUMBUS
31995-31995	FORT BENNING
31997-31999	COLUMBUS
39901-39901	ATLANTA

Hawaii

General Help Numbers:

Governor's Office
State Capitol   808-586-0034
415 S Beretania St   Fax 808-586-0006
Honolulu, HI 96813   7:45AM-5PM
http://gov.state.hi.us

Attorney General's Office
425 Queen St   808-586-1500
Honolulu, HI 96813   Fax 808-586-1239
www.state.hi.us/ag   7:45AM-4:30PM

State Court Administrator
417 S. King St   808-539-4900
Honolulu, HI 96813   Fax 808-539-4855
www.state.hi.us/jud   7:45AM-4:30PM

State Archives
Iolani Palace Grounds   808-586-0329
Honolulu, HI 96813   Fax 808-586-0330
www.state.hi.us/dags/archives   9AM-4PM

State Specifics:

Capital: Honolulu
                                         Honolulu County

Time Zone: HT (Hawaii Standard Time)

Number of Counties: 4

Population: 1,224,398

Web Site: www.state.hi.us

State Agencies

Criminal Records

Hawaii Criminal Justice Data Center, Liane Moriyama, Administrator, 465 S King St, Room 101, Honolulu, HI 96813; 808-587-3106, 8AM-4PM.

www.state.hi.us/hcjdc

Note: The sexual offender registration is no longer available to the public.

Indexing & Storage: Records are available from the 1930's. It takes 1 to 20 days before new records are available for inquiry. Records are indexed on inhouse computer. 89% of all arrests in

database have final dispositions recorded, 81% for those arrests within last 5 years.

Searching: Include the following in your request: any aliases, date of birth, Social Security Number. Submission of fingerprints is an option. 99% of the records are fingerpirnt-supported. Only records with convictions is released to the public. Records without dispositions are not released.

Access by: mail, in person.

Fee & Payment: The search fee for a name-based criminal record search is $15.00. A fingerprint-based search is $25.00. A public access (convictions only) printout, available only in-

person at this office or at main police stations, is $10.00. Certification fee: $10.00. Fee payee: Director of Finance, State of Hawaii. Prepayment required. Money orders and cashiers' checks are the only acceptable methods of payment. No credit cards accepted.

Mail search: Turnaround time: 7 to 10 days. A self addressed stamped envelope is requested.

In person search: The public may access conviction information by computer on-site. Name, SSN, and gender are required. Date of birth is optional. If SSN is unavailable, the staff will do the search.

Corporation Records
Trade Name
Assumed Name
Limited Partnership Records
Trademarks/Servicemarks
Limited Liability Company Records
Limited Liability Partnerships

Business Registration Division, PO Box 40, Honolulu, HI 96810 (Courier: 1010 Richard St, 1st Floor, Honolulu, HI 96813); 808-586-2727, 808-586-2733 (Fax), 7:45AM-4:30PM.

www.businessregistrations.com

Indexing & Storage: Records are available from 1859 to present for active entities, 1900 to present for inactive entities. New records are available for inquiry immediately.

Searching: There are no access restrictions. Records are open to the public. Include the following in your request: full name of business. In addition to the articles of incorporation, corporation records include the following information: Annual Reports, Officers, Directors, DBAs, Prior (merged) names, Inactive and Reserved names.

Access by: mail, phone, fax, in person, online.

Fee & Payment: The copy fee is $.25 per page. There is no search fee. Fee payee: Business Registration Division. Prepayment required. Personal checks accepted. No credit cards accepted.

Mail search: Turnaround time: 2 weeks. A self addressed stamped envelope is requested. No fee for mail request.

Phone search: No fee for telephone request. They will confirm data over the phone or let you know how many copies to prepay.

Fax search: Same criteria as mail searches.

In person search: No fee for request. Turnaround time is while you wait.

Online search: Online access is available through the Internet or via modem dial-up at 808-587-4800. There are no fees, the system is open 24 hours. For assistance during business hours, call 808-586-1919. Also, business names searching is available free online at www.ehawaiigov.com. Business license searching is available free at www.ehawaiigov.org/serv/taxpayer. Search by name, ID number of DBA name.

Uniform Commercial Code
Federal Tax Liens
State Tax Liens

UCC Division, Bureau of Conveyances, PO Box 2867, Honolulu, HI 96803 (Courier: Dept. of Land & Natural Resources, 1151 Punchbowl St, Honolulu, HI 96813); 808-587-0154, 808-587-0136 (Fax), 7:45AM-4:30PM.

www.state.hi.us/dlnr/bc/bc.html

Indexing & Storage: Records are available from 1845. Records are on microfiche from 1976 forward, It takes 1 day before new records are available for inquiry.

Searching: Use search request form UCC-11. Include the following in your request: debtor name. A UCC record does not include tax liens; a separate search is required.

Access by: mail, in person.

Fee & Payment: Fees are $25.00 per debtor name plus $5.00 for each financing statement and statement of assignment reported. Copies cost $1.00 per page. Fee payee: Bureau of Conveyances. Prepayment required. An initial fee of $25.00 must be paid in advance, additional fees will be invoiced. Personal checks accepted. No credit cards accepted.

Mail search: Turnaround time: 1 week. A self addressed stamped envelope is requested.

In person search: There is self-service in the public reference room.

Sales Tax Registrations
State does not impose sales tax.

Birth Certificates

State Department of Health, Vital Records Section, PO Box 3378, Honolulu, HI 96801 (Courier: 1250 Punchbowl St, Room 103, Honolulu, HI 96813); 808-586-4533, 7:45AM-2:30PM.

www.hawaii.gov/doh

Indexing & Storage: Records are available from mid 1800's to present. It takes 3-5 days before new records are available for inquiry. Records are indexed on inhouse computer.

Searching: Must have a signed release form from person of record or immediate family member. Include the following in your request: full name, names of parents, mother's maiden name, date of birth, place of birth, relationship to person of record, reason for information request. Include a daytime phone number in your request. The Vital Records office will call you collect to verify information, if required. If your record is prior to July, 1909, you must know the island of event.

Access by: mail, in person.

Fee & Payment: Fees are $10.00 for first copy and $4.00 for each subsequent copy of same record. Fee payee: State Department of Health. Prepayment required. Money orders, certified checks, and cashier's checks are accepted. No credit cards accepted.

Mail search: Turnaround time: 4 to 6 weeks. No self addressed stamped envelope is required.

In person search: Turnaround time is 10 days or more.

Expedited service: Expedited service is available for mail searches. You must send a pre-paid envelope going to requester.

Death Records

State Department of Health, Vital Records Section, PO Box 3378, Honolulu, HI 96801 (Courier: 1250 Punchbowl St, Room 103, Honolulu, HI 96813); 808-586-4533, 7:45AM-2:30PM.

www.hawaii.gov/doh

Indexing & Storage: Records are available from mid 1800's on, but early records are not complete. It takes 3-5 days before new records are available for inquiry. Records are indexed on inhouse computer.

Searching: Must have a signed release form from immediate family member. Include the following in your request: full name, date of death, place of death, names of parents, relationship to person of record, reason for information request. Include a daytime phone number in your request. The agency may call you collect to verify information, if required. For records prior to July 1909, you must include the island of the event.

Access by: mail, in person.

Fee & Payment: The fee is $10.00 per record and $4.00 for each subsequent copy of same record. Fee payee: State Department of Health. Prepayment required. Cashier's checks and money orders accepted. No credit cards accepted.

Mail search: Turnaround time: 4 to 6 weeks.

In person search: Turnaround time is 10 days or more.

Marriage Certificates

State Department of Health, Vital Records Section, PO Box 3378, Honolulu, HI 96801 (Courier: 1250 Punchbowl St, Room 103, Honolulu, HI 96813); 808-586-4533, 7:45AM-2:30PM.

www.hawaii.gov/doh

Indexing & Storage: Records are available from mid 1800's to present. It takes 3-5 days before new records are available for inquiry. Records are indexed on inhouse computer.

Searching: Must have a signed release form from person of record or immediate family member. Include the following in your request: names of husband and wife, wife's maiden name, date of marriage, place or county of marriage, names of parents, relationship to person of record, reason for information request. Include a daytime phone number. The office will call you collect to verify information, if required. For records prior to July 1909, include the island of the event.

Access by: mail, in person.

Fee & Payment: Fee is $10.00 per record and $4.00 for subsequent copy of same record. Fee payee: State Department of Health. Prepayment required. Cashier's check and money orders accepted. No credit cards accepted.

Mail search: Turnaround time: 4 to 6 weeks. No self addressed stamped envelope is required.

In person search: Turnaround time is 10 days or less.

Divorce Records

State Department of Health, Vital Records Section, PO Box 3378, Honolulu, HI 96801 (Courier: 1250 Punchbowl St, Room 103, Honolulu, HI 96813); 808-586-4533, 7:45AM-2:30PM.

www.hawaii.gov/health

Indexing & Storage: Records are available from July 1951 to present. Prior records are held by the clerk of the court granting the decree. It takes 3-5 days before new records are available for inquiry. Records are indexed on inhouse computer.

Searching: Must have a signed release form from person of record or immediate family member. Include the following in your request: names of husband and wife, date of divorce, place of divorce, relationship to person of record, reason for information request. Include a daytime phone number in your request. This office will call you collect to verify information, if required.

Access by: mail, in person.

Fee & Payment: The fee is $10.00 per record and $4.00 each additional copy of same record. Fee payee: State Department of Health. Prepayment required. Cashier's check and money orders accepted. No credit cards accepted.

Mail search: Turnaround time: 4 to 6 weeks.

In person search: Results are mailed. Turnaround time is same day only if documented emergency.

Workers' Compensation Records

Labor & Industrial Relations, Disability Compensation Division, 830 Punchbowl St, Room 209, Honolulu, HI 96813; 808-586-9174, 808-586-9219 (Fax), 7:45AM-4:30PM.

Indexing & Storage: Records are available for the past 8 years. Prior records are in the State Archives but still must be requested through the Disability Compensation Division. It takes 2 to 4 days from receipt before new records are available for inquiry. Records are indexed on inhouse computer.

Searching: Must have a signed release from injured party or HI circuit court order signed by a judge. Include the following in your request: claimant name, Social Security Number, claim number.

Access by: mail, fax, in person.

Fee & Payment: There is no search fee, copy fee is $.05 per page. Fee payee: Director of Finance. Prepayment required. Personal checks accepted. No credit cards accepted.

Mail search: Turnaround time: 6 to 12 weeks. A self addressed stamped envelope is requested.

Fax search: Same criteria as mail searches.

In person search: In-person requests only saves mail time; results are mailed.

Driver Records

Traffic Violations Bureau, Abstract Section, 1111 Alakea St, 2nd Fl, Honolulu, HI 96813; 808-538-5530, 808-961-7470 (Hawaii), 808-244-2800 (Maui), 808-246-3330 (Kauai), 7:45AM-9:PM.

www.state.hi.us/jud

Note: The Bureau furnishes the certified record abstracts and is actually part of the District Court. The DMV is a separate government agency managed by the City & County of Honolulu.

Indexing & Storage: Records are available for three years for moving violations, five years for no-faults, and ten years for DUIs. Accidents are only listed if a citation is issued for the accident. The driver's address is screened from the record.

Searching: Casual requesters can obtain records; however, personal information is not released. The driver's full name, DOB and either license number or SSN are needed when ordering.

Access by: mail, in person.

Fee & Payment: The fee is $7.00 per request. There is a full charge even if no record is found. Copies of tickets are only available from the court where ticket was issued. The fees are $1.00 for first copy, $.50 each additional copy. Fee payee:

District Court. Prepayment required. The state requires a money order or cashier's check for mail-in requests; in-person requesters may use cash, credit cards, personal or business checks.

Mail search: Turnaround time: 1 week.

In person search: Walk-in requests can be processed in five to twenty minutes at any county district traffic court or at the Traffic Violations Bureau Office in Honolulu.

Other access: Magnetic tape ordering is available in Hawaii for frequent or large orders. The fee is $7.00 per request. Turnaround time is 48-72 hours.

Accident Reports
Records not maintained by a state level agency.

Note: Accident reports are not available from the state. Records are maintained at the county level at the police departments and are only available to those involved.

Vehicle Ownership
Vehicle Identification
Access to Records is Restricted

Vessel Ownership
Vessel Registration

Land & Natural Resources, Division of Boating & Recreation, 333 Queen St Rm 300, Honolulu, HI 96813; 808-587-1970, 808-587-1977 (Fax), 7:45AM-4:30PM.

www.hawaii.gov/dlnr/dbor/dbor.html

Indexing & Storage: Records are available 1950s, computerized since 1994, and on microfiche from 1987 to 1994.

Searching: Requests must be made in writing and must include a statement revealing the purpose for which the information will be used. Name or hull id number or registration number is required for search. The following data is not released: addresses or phone numbers.

Access by: mail, fax, in person.

Fee & Payment: There is no search fee.

Mail search: Turnaround time: 1 to 2 days. No self addressed stamped envelope is required.

Fax search: Same criteria as mail searching.

In person search: Turnaround time is usually the same day.

Legislation Records

Hawaii Legislature, 415 S Beretania St, Honolulu, HI 96813; 808-587-0700 (Bill # and Location), 808-586-6720 (Clerk's Office-Senate), 808-586-6400 (Clerk's Office-House), 808-586-3500 (State Library), 808-586-3584 (Fax), 9AM-5PM.

www.capitol.hawaii.gov

Indexing & Storage: Records are available from 1983 to present. Records are indexed on inhouse computer.

Searching: Include the following in your request: bill number, year. Call the first phone number to get bill number and location of bill. Older bills are stored at the State Archives, 808-586-0329. Any bills that have become Acts can also be found at the library.

Access by: phone, in person, online.

Fee & Payment: There is no search fee nor a copy fee, unless extensive request is made. Records are available by mail.

Phone search: General information is available over the phone, copies can be requested.

In person search: Searching is available in person.

Online search: To dial online for current year bill information line, call 808-296-4636. Or, access the information through the Internet site. There is no fee, the system is up 24 hours.

Voter Registration
Records not maintained by a state level agency.

Note: Voter information is maintained by the County Clerks.

GED Certificates

Department of Education, GED Records, 634 Pensacola, #222, Honolulu, HI 96814; 808-594-0170, 808-594-0181 (Fax), 8AM-4PM.

Note: GED certificates are not issued by this agency. Instead, high school diplomas are issued to qualified individuals.

Searching: Include the following in your request: signed release, date of birth, Social Security Number. Knowing the approximate date and location of the test is helpful. The requirements are for both verifications and copies of transcripts.

Access by: mail, fax, in person.

Fee & Payment: Fees will vary, depending on the record location site.

Mail search: Turnaround time: 5 to 10 days. A self addressed stamped envelope is required.

Fax search: Same criteria as mail search.

In person search: Same criteria as mail search.

Hunting License Information
Fishing License Information
Access to Records is Restricted

Land & Natural Resources Department, 1151 Punchbowl St, Kalanimokui Bldg, Honolulu, HI 96813; 808-587-0100 (Fishing), 808-587-0166 (Hunting), 808-587-0115 (Fax), 7:45AM-4:30PM.

www.state.hi.us/dlnr

Note: Fishing information is kept by the Aquatic Resources Division; Hunting information by the Division of Forestry & Wildlife. Limited record information is released to the public. Generally, this department's information is only released to law enforcement agencies. There is no "search engine" here.

Hawaii State Licensing Agencies

Licenses Searchable Online

Acupuncturist #4 .... www.ehawaiigov.org/serv/pvl
Architect #19 .... www.ehawaiigov.org/serv/pvl
Auction #42 .... www.ehawaiigov.org/serv/pvl
Bank/Bank Agencies/Offices #28 .... www.state.hi.us/dcca/dfi/regulated.html
Barber Shop #5 .... www.ehawaiigov.org/serv/pvl
Barber/Barber Apprentice #5 .... www.ehawaiigov.org/serv/pvl
Beauty Operator/School/Shop #5 .... www.ehawaiigov.org/serv/pvl
Cemetery #42 .... www.ehawaiigov.org/serv/pvl
Chiropractor #6 .... www.ehawaiigov.org/serv/pvl
Collection Agency #42 .... www.ehawaiigov.org/serv/pvl
Condominium Hotel Operator #34 .... www.ehawaiigov.org/serv/pvl
Condominium Managing Agent #34 .... www.ehawaiigov.org/serv/pvl
Contractor #27 .... www.ehawaiigov.org/serv/pvl
Cosmetologist #5 .... www.ehawaiigov.org/serv/pvl
Credit Union #28 .... www.state.hi.us/dcca/dfi/regulated.html
Dental Hygienist #7 .... www.ehawaiigov.org/serv/pvl
Dentist #7 .... www.ehawaiigov.org/serv/pvl
Drug (Prescription) Dist./Whlse. #16 .... www.ehawaiigov.org/serv/pvl
Elected Officials Financial Disclosure #41 .... www.state.hi.us/ethics/noindex/pubrec.htm
Electrician #29 .... www.ehawaiigov.org/serv/pvl
Electrologist #42 .... www.ehawaiigov.org/serv/pvl
Elevator Mechanic #29 .... www.ehawaiigov.org/serv/pvl
Emergency Medical Personnel #13 .... www.ehawaiigov.org/serv/pvl
Employment Agency #42 .... www.ehawaiigov.org/serv/pvl
Engineer #19 .... www.ehawaiigov.org/serv/pvl
Escrow Company #28 .... www.state.hi.us/dcca/dfi/regulated.html
Financial Services Loan Company #28 .... www.state.hi.us/dcca/dfi/regulated.html
Hearing Aid Dealer/Fitter #30 .... www.ehawaiigov.org/serv/pvl
Insurance Adjuster #31 .... www.ehawaiigov.org/serv/hils
Insurance Agent #31 .... www.ehawaiigov.org/serv/hils
Insurance Solicitor #31 .... www.ehawaiigov.org/serv/hils
Landscape Architect #19 .... www.ehawaiigov.org/serv/pvl
Lobbyist #41 .... www.state.hi.us/ethics/noindex/pubrec.htm
Marriage & Family Therapist #42 .... www.ehawaiigov.org/serv/pvl
Massage Therapist/Establishment #42 .... www.ehawaiigov.org/serv/pvl
Mechanic #42 .... www.ehawaiigov.org/serv/pvl
Medical Doctor #13 .... www.ehawaiigov.org/serv/pvl
Mortgage Broker/Solicitor #42 .... www.ehawaiigov.org/serv/pvl
Motor Vehicle Dealer/Broker/Seller #42 .... www.ehawaiigov.org/serv/pvl
Motor Vehicle Repair Dealer #42 .... www.ehawaiigov.org/serv/pvl
Naturopathic Physician #10 .... www.ehawaiigov.org/serv/pvl
Nurse #14 .... www.ehawaiigov.org/serv/pvl
Nursing Home Administrator #12 .... www.ehawaiigov.org/serv/pvl
Occupational Therapist #17 .... www.ehawaiigov.org/serv/pvl
Optician, Dispensing #8 .... www.ehawaiigov.org/serv/pvl
Optometrist #11 .... www.ehawaiigov.org/serv/pvl
Osteopathic Physician #13 .... www.ehawaiigov.org/serv/pvl
Pest Control Field Rep./Operator #32 .... www.ehawaiigov.org/serv/pvl
Pharmacist #16 .... www.ehawaiigov.org/serv/pvl
Pharmacy #16 .... www.ehawaiigov.org/serv/pvl
Pharmacy, Out-of-State #16 .... www.ehawaiigov.org/serv/pvl
Physical Therapist #17 .... www.ehawaiigov.org/serv/pvl
Physician Assistant #13 .... www.ehawaiigov.org/serv/pvl
Plumber #29 .... www.ehawaiigov.org/serv/pvl
Podiatrist #13 .... www.ehawaiigov.org/serv/pvl
Port Pilot #42 .... www.ehawaiigov.org/serv/pvl
Private Detective #18 .... www.ehawaiigov.org/serv/pvl
Private Detective/Investigation Agency #18 .... www.ehawaiigov.org/serv/pvl
Psychologist #20 .... www.ehawaiigov.org/serv/pvl
Public Accountant-CPA #21 .... www.ehawaiigov.org/serv/pvl
Real Estate Appraiser #9 .... www.ehawaiigov.org/serv/pvl
Real Estate Broker/Seller #34 .... www.ehawaiigov.org/serv/pvl
Savings & Loan Association #28 .... www.state.hi.us/dcca/dfi/regulated.html

Savings Bank #28..www.state.hi.us/dcca/dfi/regulated.html
Security Guard/Agency #18 ....www.ehawaiigov.org/serv/pvl
Social Worker #42 ....www.ehawaiigov.org/serv/pvl
Speech Pathologist/Audiologist #22 ....www.ehawaiigov.org/serv/pvl
Surveyor, Land #19 ....www.ehawaiigov.org/serv/pvl
Timeshare #42..www.ehawaiigov.org/serv/pvl
Travel Agency #42 ....www.ehawaiigov.org/serv/pvl
Trust Company #28 ....www.state.hi.us/dcca/dfi/regulated.html
Veterinarian #23 ....www.ehawaiigov.org/serv/pvl

Licensing Quick Finder

Acupuncturist #4 808-586-3000	Electrologist #42 808-586-2699	Pesticide Dealer #2 808-973-9424
Airport-related Occupation #37 808-836-6533	Elevator Mechanic #29......................808-586-3000	Pesticide Product #2........................808-973-9414
Architect #19.................................808-586-3000	Embalmer #43 808-586-8000	Pharmacist #16 808-586-3000
Attorney #38 808-537-1868	Emergency Medical Personnel #13 808-586-3000	Pharmacy #16 808-586-3000
Auction #42 808-586-2699	Employment Agency #42 808-586-2699	Pharmacy, Out-of-State #16 808-586-3000
Bank/Bank Agencies/Offices #28 808-586-2820	Engineer #19..................................808-586-3000	Physical Therapist #17.....................808-586-3000
Barber Shop #5.............................808-586-3000	Escrow Company #28 808-586-2820	Physician Assistant #13 808-586-3000
Barber/Barber Apprentice #5...............808-586-3000	Financial Services Loan Company #28. 808-586-2820	Plumber #29 808-586-3000
Beauty Operator/School/Shop #5.........808-586-3000	Hearing Aid Dealer/Fitter #30 808-586-3000	Podiatrist #13 808-586-2708
Boxer #24 808-586-2701	Insurance Adjuster #31 808-586-2788	Port Pilot #42 808-586-2699
Boxing Manager #24 808-586-2701	Insurance Agent #31 808-586-2788	Private Detective #18 808-586-3000
Boxing Matchmaker #24.....................808-586-2701	Insurance Solicitor #31 808-586-2788	Private Detective/Investigation Agency #18
Boxing Physician #24 808-586-2701	Investment Advisor/Representative #25.808-586-2730	808-586-3000
Boxing Professional (Promoter) #24 808-586-2701	Landscape Architect #19...................808-586-3000	Psychologist #20 808-586-3000
Boxing Second #24 808-586-2701	Lobbyist #41 808-587-0460	Public Accountant-CPA #21..............808-586-3000
Boxing Timekeeper/Judge/Referee #24 808-586-2701	Marine License, Commercial #36........808-587-0100	Radiation Therapist #44 808-586-4700
Cable Franchise #26 808-586-2620	Marriage & Family Therapist #42........808-586-2693	Radiographer #44 808-586-4700
Cemetery #42 808-586-2699	Massage Therapist/Establishment #42. 808-586-2699	Real Estate Appraiser #9 808-586-3000
Chiropractor #6 808-586-3000	Mechanic #42 808-586-2701	Real Estate Broker/Seller #34...........808-587-3222
Clinical Lab Technician #40.................808-453-6653	Medical Doctor #13..........................808-586-3000	Sanitarian #43 808-586-4576
Clinical Lab Cytotechnologist #40 808-453-6653	Mortgage Broker/Solicitor #42............808-586-3000	Savings & Loan Association #28 808-586-2820
Clinical Lab Director #40 808-453-6653	Motor Vehicle Dealer/Broker/Seller #42 808-586-2699	Savings Bank #28...........................808-586-2820
Clinical Lab Technologist/Spec. #40 808-453-6653	Motor Vehicle Repair Dealer #42........808-586-2699	Securities Salesperson #25 808-586-2730
Collection Agency #42 808-586-2699	Naturopathic Physician #10...............808-586-3000	Security Guard/Agency #18 808-586-3000
Condominium Hotel Operator #34........808-587-3222	Notary Public #3.............................808-586-1216	Shorthand Reporter #1.....................808-539-4226
Condominium Managing Agent #34 808-587-3222	Nuclear Medicine Technologist #44 808-586-4700	Social Worker #42 808-586-2696
Contractor #27 808-586-3000	Nurse #14 808-586-3000	Speech Pathologist/Audiologist #22 808-586-3000
Cosmetologist #5 808-586-3000	Nurses' Aide #14 808-586-3000	Surveyor, Land #19 808-586-3000
Credit Union #28 808-586-2820	Nursing Home Administrator #12 808-586-3000	Tattoo Artist #43 808-586-8000
Dental Hygienist #7.........................808-586-3000	Occupational Therapist #17 808-586-2698	Taxi Driver #39 808-733-2540
Dentist #7.....................................808-586-3000	Optician, Dispensing #8 808-586-3000	Teacher #35 808-586-3392
Drug (Prescription) Dist./Whlse. #16....808-586-3000	Optometrist #11 808-586-3000	Timeshare #42................................808-586-2699
Educational Administrator #35 808-586-3420	Osteopathic Physician #13................808-586-3000	Travel Agency #42 808-586-2699
Elected Officials Financial Disclosure #41	Pest Control Field Rep./Operator #32...808-586-3000	Trust Company #28 808-586-2820
....808-587-0460	Pesticide Applicator #2.....................808-973-9409	Veterinarian #23 808-586-3000
Electrician #29 808-586-3000	Pesticide Applicator, Private #2 808-973-9424	

Licensing Agency Information

#1 Board of Certified Shorthand Reporters, 777 Punchbowl St, Honolulu, HI 96813; 808-539-4226, Fax: 808-539-4149. Agency email: csrhi@maui.net.

#2 Department of Agriculture, PO Box 22159, Honolulu, HI 96823-2159; 808-973-9401, Fax: 808-973-9410. www.hawaiiag.org/hdoa
Agency email: hollyer@hawaii.edu.

#3 Department of Attorney General, 425 Queen St, Honolulu, HI 96813; 808-586-1500, Fax: 808-586-1205. www.state.hi.us/ag/notary/content.htm

#4 Department of Commerce & Consumer Affairs, Board of Acupuncture, PO Box 3469 (1010 Richards St, 96813), Honolulu, HI 96801; 808-586-2698, Fax: 808-586-2689.
www.state.hi.us/dcca/pvl/areas_acupuncture.html.
Agency email: acupuncture@dcca.state.hi.us.
Search database at www.ehawaiigov.org/serv/pvl

#5 Department of Commerce & Consumer Affairs, Board of Barbering & Cosmetology, PO Box 3469 (1010 Richards St, 96813), Honolulu, HI 96801; 808-586-2699.

www.state.hi.us/dcca/pvl/areas_barbering.html.
Agency email: barber_cosm@dcca.state.hi.us.
Search database at www.ehawaiigov.org/serv/pvl

#6 Department of Commerce & Consumer Affairs, Board of Chiropractic Examiners, PO Box 3469 (1010 Richards St, 96813), Honolulu, HI 96801; 808-586-2695.
www.state.hi.us/dcca/pvl/areas_chiropractor.html.
Agency email: chiropractor@dcca.state.hi.us.
Search database at www.ehawaiigov.org/serv/pvl

#7 Department of Commerce & Consumer Affairs, Board of Dental Examiners, PO Box 3469 (1010 Richards St 96813), Honolulu, HI 96801; 808-586-2702. www.state.hi.us/dcca/pvl/areas_dentist.html.
Agency email: dental@dcca.state.hi.us.
Search database at www.ehawaiigov.org/serv/pvl

#8 Department of Commerce & Consumer Affairs, Dispensing Optician Program, PO Box 3469 (1010 Richards St, 96813), Honolulu, HI 96801; 808-586-3000, Fax: 808-586-3031.
www.state.hi.us/dcca/pvl/areas_optometry.html.
Agency email: optician@dcca.state.hi.us

Search database at www.ehawaiigov.org/serv/pvl

#9 Department of Commerce & Consumer Affairs, Professional & Vocational Licensing, Attn:REA, PO Box 3469, Honolulu, HI 96801; 808-586-2704.
www.state.hi.us/dcca/pvl/areas_real_estate_apprai ser.html
Agency email: appraiser@dcca.state.hi.us.
Search database at www.ehawaiigov.org/serv/pvl

#10 Department of Commerce & Consumer Affairs, Board of Examiners in Naturopathy, PO Box 3469 (1010 Richards St, 96813), Honolulu, HI 96801; 808-586-2704, Fax: 808-586-3031.
www.state.hi.us/dcca/pvl/areas_natropathy.html.
Agency email: naturopathy@dcca.state.hi.us.
Search database at www.ehawaiigov.org/serv/pvl

#11 Department of Commerce & Consumer Affairs, Board of Examiners in Optometry, PO Box 3469 (1010 Richards St, 96813), Honolulu, HI 96801; 808-586-2694.
www.state.hi.us/dcca/pvl/areas_optometry.html.
Agency email: optometry@dcca.state.hi.us.
Search database at www.ehawaiigov.org/serv/pvl

#12 Department of Commerce & Consumer Affairs, Nursing Home Administrators Program, PO Box 3469 (1010 Richards St, 96813), Honolulu, HI 96801; 808-586-2695. www.state.hi.us/dcca/pvl/areas_nursing_home.html. Agency email: nursing_home@dcca.state.hi.us. Search database at www.ehawaiigov.org/serv/pvl

#13 Department of Commerce & Consumer Affairs, Board of Medical Examiners, PO Box 3469 (1010 Richards St, 96813), Honolulu, HI 96801; 808-586-2708. www.state.hi.us/dcca/pvl/areas_medical.html. Agency email: medical@dcca.state.hi.us. Search database at www.ehawaiigov.org/serv/pvl

#14 Department of Commerce & Consumer Affairs, Board of Nursing, PO Box 3469 (1010 Richards St, 96813), Honolulu, HI 96801; 808-586-2695. www.state.hi.us/dcca/pvl/areas_nurse.html. Agency email: nursing@dcca.state.hi.us. Search database at www.ehawaiigov.org/serv/pvl

#16 Department of Commerce & Consumer Affairs, Board of Pharmacy, PO Box 3469 (1010 Richards St, 96813), Honolulu, HI 96801; 808-586-2694. www.state.hi.us/dcca/pvl/areas_pharmacy.html. Agency email: pharmacy@dcca.state.hi.us. Search database at www.ehawaiigov.org/serv/pvl

#17 Department of Commerce & Consumer Affairs, Board of Physical Therapy, PO Box 3469 (1010 Richards St, 96813), Honolulu, HI 96801; 808-586-2694. www.state.hi.us/dcca/pvl/areas_physical_therapy.html Agency email: phys_therapy@dcca.state.hi.us. Search database at www.ehawaiigov.org/serv/pvl

#18 Department of Commerce & Consumer Affairs, Board of Private Detectives & Guards, PO Box 3469 (1010 Richards St, 96813), Honolulu, HI 96801; 808-586-2701, Fax: 808-586-2589. www.state.hi.us/dcca/pvl/areas_private_detective.html. Agency email: detective@dcca.state.hi.us. Search database at www.ehawaiigov.org/serv/pvl

#19 Department of Commerce & Consumer Affairs, Architects & Surveyors, Board of Prof. Engineers, PO Box 3469 (1010 Richards St, 96813), Honolulu, HI 96801; 808-586-2701. www.state.hi.us/dcca/pvl/areas_engineer.html. Agency email: easla@dcca.state.hi.us. Search database at www.ehawaiigov.org/serv/pvl

#20 Department of Commerce & Consumer Affairs, Board of Psychology, PO Box 3469 (1010 Richards St, 96813), Honolulu, HI 96801; 808-586-2693. www.state.hi.us/dcca/pvl/areas_psychology.html. Agency email: psychology@dcca.state.hi.us. Search database at www.ehawaiigov.org/serv/pvl

#21 Department of Commerce & Consumer Affairs, Board of Public Accountancy, PO Box 3469 (1010 Richards St, 96813), Honolulu, HI 96801; 808-586-2696, Fax: 808-586-2689. www.state.hi.us/dcca/pvl/areas_accountancy.html. Agency email: accountancy@dcca.state.hi.us. Search database at www.ehawaiigov.org/serv/pvl

#22 Department of Commerce & Consumer Affairs, Board of Speech Pathology & Audiology, PO Box 3469 (1010 Richards St, 96813), Honolulu, HI 96801; 808-586-2698. www.state.hi.us/dcca/pvl/areas_speech_pathology.html. Agency email: speech@dcca.state.hi.us. Search database at www.ehawaiigov.org/serv/pvl

#23 Department of Commerce & Consumer Affairs, Board of Veterinary Examiners, PO Box 3469 (1010 Richards St, 96813), Honolulu, HI 96801; 808-586-2699. www.state.hi.us/dcca/pvl/areas_veterinary.html. Agency email: veterinary@dcca.state.hi.us. Search database at www.ehawaiigov.org/serv/pvl

#24 Department of Commerce & Consumer Affairs, Boxing Commission, PO Box 3469 (1010 Richards St, 96813), Honolulu, HI 96801; 808-586-2701, Fax: 808-586-2689 Agency email: boxing@dcca.state.hi.us.

#25 Department of Commerce & Consumer Affairs, Business Registration Division, Securities Compliance Branch, PO Box 3469 (1010 Richards St, 96813), Honolulu, HI 96801; 808-586-2820, Fax: 808-586-2733.

#26 Department of Commerce & Consumer Affairs, Cable TV Division, PO Box 541, Honolulu, HI 96809; 808-586-2620, Fax: 808-586-2625.

#27 Department of Commerce & Consumer Affairs, Contractors License Board, PO Box 3469 (1010 Richards St, 96813), Honolulu, HI 96801; 808-586-2700, Fax: 808-586-3031. www.state.hi.us/dcca/pvl/areas_contractor.html. Agency email: contractor@dcca.state.hi.us. Search database at www.ehawaiigov.org/serv/pvl

#28 Department of Commerce & Consumer Affairs, Division of Financial Institutions, PO Box 2054 (1010 Richards Street, Room 602-A), Honolulu, HI 96805; 808-586-2820, Fax: 808-586-2818. www.state.hi.us/dcca/dfi Agency email: dfi@dcca.state.hi.us. Search database at www.state.hi.us/dcca/dfi/regulated.html

#29 Department of Commerce & Consumer Affairs, Board of Electricians, Plumbers & Elevator Mechanics Licensing, PO Box 3469 (1010 Richards St, 96813), Honolulu, HI 96801; 808-586-2705. www.state.hi.us/dcca/pvl/areas_electrician.html. Agency email: elect_plumb@dcca.state.hi.us. Search database at www.ehawaiigov.org/serv/pvl. Online searching scheduled for late 2000.

#30 Department of Commerce & Consumer Affairs, Hearing Aid Dealers & Fitters Program, PO Box 3469 (1010 Richards St, 96813), Honolulu, HI 96801; 808-586-2698. www.state.hi.us/dcca/pvl/areas_hearing_aid.html. Agency email: hearingaid@dcca.state.hi.us. Search database at www.ehawaiigov.org/serv/pvl

#31 Department of Commerce & Consumer Affairs, Insurance Division, Licensing Branch, 250 S King St, 5th Fl, Honolulu, HI 96813; 808-586-2790, Fax: 808-586-2806. www.ehawaiigov.org Search database at www.ehawaiigov.org/serv/hils

#32 Department of Commerce & Consumer Affairs, Pest Control Board, PO Box 3469, Honolulu, HI 96801; 808-586-2705. www.state.hi.us/dcca/pvl/areas_pest_control.html. Agency email: pest_control@dcca.state.hi.us.

#34 Department of Commerce & Consumer Affairs, Real Estate Commission, 250 S King St #702, Honolulu, HI 96813; 808-586-2643. www.state.hi.us/hirec Agency email: hirec@dcca.state.hi.us. Search database at www.ehawaiigov.org/serv/pvl

#35 Department of Education, Board of Education, PO Box 2360, Honolulu, HI 96804; 808-586-3420, Fax: 808-586-3433.

#36 Department of Land & Natural Resources, Division of Aquatic Resources, 1151 Punch Bowl St Rm 330, Honolulu, HI 96813; 808-587-0100, Fax: 808-587-0115. www.state.hi.us/dlnr/dar Agency email: dlnr_aquatics@exec.state.hi.us.

#37 Department of Transportation, Airports Division, Airport District Manager, Honolulu Intl Airport, Honolulu, HI 96819-1897; 808-836-6533, Fax: 808-836-6682. www.state.hi.us/dot/airports

#38 Bar Association, 1132 Bishop St #906, Honolulu, HI 96813-2814; 808-537-1868, Fax: 808-521-7936. www.hsba.org

#39 Motor Vehicle Licensing Division, City Square Driver License, 1199 Dillingham St Rm A101, Honolulu, HI 96817; 808-532-7730.

#40 Department of Health, Laboratory Licensing, 2725 Waimano Home Rd, Pearl City, HI 96782; 808-453-6653, Fax: 808-453-6662.

#41 State Ethics Commission, 1001 Bishop St, Pacific Tower #970, Honolulu, HI 96813; 808-587-0460, Fax: 808-587-0470. www.state.hi.us/ethics Agency email: ethics@hawaiiethics.org. Search database at www.state.hi.us/ethics/noindex/pubrec.htm

#42 Department of Commerce & Consumer Affairs, Professional & Vocational Licensing Div-Programs, 1010 Richards St 1st Fl, Honolulu, HI 96813; 808-587-3295. www.ehawaiigov/org/serv/pv/ Search database at www.ehawaiigov.org/serv/pvl

#43 Department of Health, Environmental Health Services Division, 591 Ala Moana Blvd, Honolulu, HI 96813; 808-586-8000, Fax: 808-586-4729. www.hawaii.gov/doh

#44 Department of Health, Radiologic Technology Board, 591 Ala Moana Blvd, Honolulu, HI 96813-4921; 808-586-4700, Fax: 808-586-5838.

Hawaii Federal Courts

The following list indicates the district and division name for each county in the state.

County/Court Cross Reference

Hawaii..Honolulu
Honolulu..Honolulu
Kalawao...Honolulu
Kauai..Honolulu
Maui...Honolulu

US District Court

District of Hawaii

Honolulu Division 300 Ala Moana Blvd, Rm C-338, Honolulu, HI 96850 (Courier Address: Use mail address for courier delivery), 808-541-1300, Fax: 808-541-1303.

www.hid.uscourts.gov

Counties: All counties.

Indexing & Storage: Cases are indexed by defendant, plaintiff, and case number. New cases are available in the index immediately after filing date. A microfiche index is also maintained. Open records are located at this court.

Fee & Payment Notes: Payment may be made by money order, cashier check, personal check. Payee: Clerk, US District Court.

Phone Search: Searching not available by phone.

In Person Search: In person searching available.

PACER: Local dial-up access: 808-541-1179. Case records are available back to October 1991. Records are never purged. New civil records are available online after 1 day. New criminal records are available online after 3 days. PACER is available online at http://pacer.hid.uscourts.gov.

US Bankruptcy Court

District of Hawaii

Honolulu Division 1132 Bishop St, Suite 250-L, Honolulu, HI 96813 (Courier Address: Use mail address for courier delivery), 808-522-8100.

www.hib.uscourts.gov

Counties: All counties.

Indexing & Storage: Cases are indexed by debtor as well as by case number. New cases are available in the index 24 hours after filing date. Open records are located at this court.

Fee & Payment Notes: Payment may be made by money order, cashier check, personal check. Debtor's checks are not accepted. Payee: US Bankruptcy Court. You are allowed to make your own copies. These copies cost $.15 per page.

Phone Search: Only docket information is available by phone. An automated voice case information service (VCIS) is available. Call VCIS at 808-522-8122.

In Person Search: In person searching available.

PACER: Toll-free dial-up access: 888-853-3766. Local dial-up access: 808-522-8118. Use of PC Anywhere v4.0 suggested. Additional password is "pals". Case records are available back to 1987. Records are purged varies. New civil records are available online after 1 day. PACER is available online at http://pacer.hib.uscourts.gov. Document images available.

Electronic Filing: (Currently in the process of implementing CM/ECF.)

Standards for Federal Courts: The search fee is $20.00 per item (one party name or case number). Certification fee is $7.00 per document. Copy fee is $.50 per page. All fees standard unless noted in profile. Mail Search: always enclose a stamped self addressed envelope unless otherwise noted. Before releasing records, all courts require prepayment unless noted in profile.

Open records are located at the court unless otherwise noted. District courts index by defendant and plaintiff as well as by case number. Bankruptcy courts usually index by debtor and case number. While most courts now have their indexes on computer, many still maintain index card files as well.

The universal PACER sign-up number is 800-676-6856. Find PACER and the Party/Case Index on the Web at http://pacer.psc.uscourts.gov. PACER dial-up access is $.60 per minute. Also, courts offering internet access via RACER, PACER, Web-PACER or the new CM-ECF charge $.07 per page fee unless noted as free.

Hawaii County Courts

Court	Jurisdiction	No. of Courts	How Organized
Circuit Courts*	General	4	4 Circuits
District Courts*	Limited	7	4 Circuits

* Profiled in this Sourcebook.

Court	CIVIL								
	Tort	Contract	Real Estate	Min. Claim	Max. Claim	Small Claims	Estate	Eviction	Domestic Relations
Circuit Courts*	X	X	X	$5000/ $10,000	No Max		X		X
District Courts*	X	X	X	$0	$20,000	$3500		X	

Court	CRIMINAL				
	Felony	Misdemeanor	DWI/DUI	Preliminary Hearing	Juvenile
Circuit Courts*	X	X	X		X
District Courts*		X	X	X	

ADMINISTRATION Administrative Director of Courts, Judicial Branch, 417 S King St, Honolulu, HI, 96813; 808-539-4900, Fax: 808-539-4855. www.courts.state.hi.us/index.jsp

COURT STRUCTURE Hawaii's trial level is comprised of Circuit Courts (with Family Courts) and District Courts. These trial courts function in four judicial circuits: First (Oahu), Second (Maui/Molokai/Lanai), Third (Hawaii County), and Fifth (Kauai/Niihau) The Fourth Circuit was merged with the Third in 1943.

Circuit Courts are general jurisdiction and handle all jury trials, felony cases, and civil cases over $20,000, also probate and guardianship. The District Court handles criminal cases punishable by a fine and/or less then 1-yr imprisonment and some civil cases up to $20,000, also landlord/tenant and DUI cases.

ONLINE ACCESS Free online access to Circuit Court and family court records is available at the web site www.courts.state.hi.us (click on "Search Court Records"). Search by name or case number. These records are not considered "official" for FCRA compliant searches.

ADD'L INFORMATION Most Hawaii state courts offer a public access terminal to search records at the courthouse.

Civil cases down to $5000 minimum are found at the Circuit Court if a jury is involved.

Hawaii County

3rd Circuit Court Legal Documents Section PO Box 1007, Hilo, HI 96721-1007; 808-961-7404; Fax: 808-961-7416. Hours: 7:45AM-4:30PM (HT). *Felony, Misdemeanor, Civil Actions Over $5,000, Probate.*
www.courts.state.hi.us
Civil Records: Access: Mail, fax, in person, online. Both court and visitors may perform in person searches. Search fee: $5.00 per name. Required to search: name, years to search. Civil cases indexed by defendant, plaintiff. Civil records on computer from 1988, index card system prior to 1988. Online access to Circuit Court and family court records available free at the web site. Search by name or case number. Records go back to early 1900s.
Criminal Records: Access: Mail, in person, online. Both court and visitors may perform in person searches. Search fee: $5.00 per name. Required to search: name, years to search. Criminal records on computer from 1988, index card system prior to 1988. Online access to criminal records is the same as civil.
General Information: Public access terminal is available. No adoption, juvenile, dependencies,

confidential records released. SASE required. Turnaround time 2 days depending upon staff coverage. Copy fee: $1.00 for first page, $.50 each add'l. Certification fee: $2.00. Fee payee: Clerk, 3rd Circuit Court. Personal checks accepted. Prepayment is required.

District Court PO Box 4879, Hilo, HI 96720; 808-961-7470; Fax: 808-961-7447. Hours: 7:45AM-4:30PM (HT). *Misdemeanor, Civil Actions Under $20,000, Eviction, Small Claims.*
www.courts.state.hi.us/index.jsp
Civil Records: Access: Phone, fax, mail, in person. Only the court performs in person searches; visitors may not. Search fee: $5.00 per name. Required to search: name, years to search, case number; also helpful: address. Civil cases indexed by defendant. Civil records on ledgers from statehood.
Criminal Records: Access: Phone, fax, mail, in person. Only the court performs in person searches; visitors may only for a criminal abstract. Search fee: $5.00 per name. Required to search: name, years to search, case number; also helpful: address, DOB, SSN. Criminal records on computer since March 1996. Public access terminal available for criminal abstracts.

General Information: Public access terminal is available. (Available for criminal abstract record only.) No family court records released. SASE requested. Turnaround time 1 week. Fax notes: $2.00 for first page, $1.00 each add'l. Extra fee for out of state faxing. Call for fee information. Copy fee: $1.00 for first page, $.50 each add'l. Off site storage- usual copy fees plus $5.00. Certification fee: $2.00. Fee payee: Clerk of the District Court. Personal checks accepted. Credit cards accepted: Visa, MasterCard.

Honolulu County

1st Circuit Court Legal Documents Branch, 777 Punchbowl St, Honolulu, HI 96813; 808-539-4300; Fax: 808-539-4314. Hours: 7:45AM-4:30PM (HT). *Felony, Civil Actions Over $5,000, Probate, Family.*
www.courts.state.hi.us
Civil Records: Access: Mail, in person, online. Both court and visitors may perform in person searches. Search fee: $5.00 per name. Required to search: name, years to search. Civil cases indexed by defendant, plaintiff. Civil records on computer from 1983, on microfiche and archived from 1900. Online access to Circuit Court & family court records available free at

the web site. Search by name or case number. Records go back to 1984.

Criminal Records: Access: Mail, in person, online. Both court and visitors may perform in person searches. Search fee: $5.00 per name. Required to search: name, years to search, DOB; also helpful: SSN. Criminal records on computer from 1983, on microfiche and archived from 1900. Online access to criminal records is the same as civil.

General Information: Public access terminal is available. No adoptions, paternity or sealed records released. SASE required. Turnaround time same day. Copy fee: $1.00 for first page, $.50 each add'l. Microfilm service fee $5.00; cost of copies $1.00 per page. Certification fee: $2.00. Fee payee: 1st Circuit Court. Business checks accepted. Prepayment is required.

District Court - Civil Division 1111 Alakea St, 3th Floor, Honolulu, HI 96813; 808-538-5151; Fax: 808-538-5444. Hours: 7:45AM-4:30PM (HT). *Civil Actions Under $20,000, Eviction, Small Claims.*

www.courts.state.hi.us/index.jsp

Civil Records: Access: Phone, mail, in person. Both court and visitors may perform in person searches. Search fee: $5.00 per name. Required to search: name, years to search. Civil cases indexed by defendant. Civil records on computer from 1990; plaintiff index only on computer records.

General Information: Public access terminal is available. No sealed records released. SASE required. Turnaround time 1 week. Fax notes: Call for fax fee. Fee payee: District Court of the 1st Circuit. Personal checks accepted. Credit cards accepted: Visa, MasterCard, Discover. Prepayment is required.

District Court - Criminal Division 1111 Alakea St, 3rd Floor Judicial Services, Honolulu, HI 96813; 808-538-5100; Fax: 808-538-5111. Hours: 7:45AM-4:30PM (HT). *Misdemeanor.*

www.courts.state.hi.us/index.jsp

Criminal Records: Access: Fax, mail, in person. Only the court performs in person searches; visitors may not. Search fee: $5.00 per name. Required to search: name, years to search, SSN, signed release, aliases; also helpful: address, DOB.

General Information: No sealed records released. SASE required. Turnaround time 1 week. No copy fee. Fee payee: District Court of the 1st Judicial Circuit. Business checks accepted. Prepayment is required.

Kauai County

5th Circuit Court 3059 Umi St Rm #101, Lihue, HI 96766; 808-246-3300; Fax: 808-246-3310. Hours: 7:45AM-4:30PM (HT). *Felony, Misdemeanor, Civil Actions Over $10,000, Probate.*

www.courts.state.hi.us

Civil Records: Access: Mail, in person, online. Both court and visitors may perform in person searches. Search fee: $5.00 per name. Required to search: name, years to search. Civil cases indexed by defendant. Civil records on computer from 1987, microfiche from 1960. Online access to Circuit Court and family court records available free at the web site. Search by name or case number. Records go back to 1984.

Criminal Records: Access: Mail, in person, online. Both court and visitors may perform in person searches. Search fee: $5.00 per name. Required to search: name, years to search, DOB; also helpful: SSN. Criminal records on computer from 1987, microfiche from 1960. Online access to criminal records is the same as civil.

General Information: Public access terminal is available. No juvenile, dependencies records released. SASE required. Turnaround time 1 week. Copy fee: $1.00 for first page, $.50 each add'l. Certification fee: $2.00. Fee payee: 5th Circuit Court. Only cashiers checks and money orders accepted. Prepayment is required.

District Court of the 5th Circuit 3059 Umi St, Room 111, Lihue, HI 96766; 808-246-3330; Fax: 808-246-3309. Hours: 7:45AM-4:30PM (HT). *Misdemeanor.*

www.courts.state.hi.us/index.jsp

Criminal Records: Access: Phone, fax, mail, in person. Only the court performs in person searches; visitors may not. Search fee: $15.00. Required to search: name, years to search, DOB; also helpful: SSN.

General Information: Fax notes: $2.00 for first page, $1.00 each add'l. Copy fee: $1.00 for first page, $.50 each add'l. Certification fee: $2.00.

District Court of the 5th Circuit 4357 Rice St, #101, Lihue, HI 96766; 808-246-3301; Fax: 808-241-7103. Hours: 7:45AM-4:30PM (HT). *Civil Actions Under $20,000, Eviction, Small Claims.*

www.courts.state.hi.us/index.jsp

Civil Records: Access: Phone, fax, mail, in person. Both court and visitors may perform in person searches. Search fee: $5.00 per case. Required to search: name, years to search. Civil cases indexed by defendant. Civil records on index books.

General Information: No juvenile records released. SASE requested. Turnaround time 1-7 days. Fax notes: $2.00 for first page, $1.00 each add'l. Copy fee: $1.00 for first page, $.50 each add'l. Fee payee: District Court of the Fifth Circuit. Personal checks accepted. In-state personal check accepted. No third party checks. Credit cards accepted: Visa, MasterCard. Credit cards accepted.

Maui County

2nd Circuit Court 2145 Main St, #106, Wailuku, HI 96793; 808-244-2929; Fax: 808-244-2932. Hours: 7:45AM-4:30PM (HT). *Felony, Misdemeanor, Civil Actions Over $5,000, Probate.*

www.courts.state.hi.us

Note: This court also covers the counties of Lanai and Molokai.

Civil Records: Access: Mail, in person, online. Both court and visitors may perform in person searches. Search fee: $5.00 per name. Required to search: name, years to search. Civil cases indexed by defendant, plaintiff. Civil records on computer from 10/88, some prior on microfiche. Online access to Circuit Court & family court records available free at the web site. Search by name or case number. Records go back to 1984.

Criminal Records: Access: Mail, in person, online. Both court and visitors may perform in person searches. Search fee: $5.00 per name. Required to search: name, years to search; also helpful: DOB, SSN. Criminal records on computer from 10/88, some prior on microfiche. Online access to criminal records is the same as civil.

General Information: Public access terminal is available. No juvenile or paternity records released. SASE required. Turnaround time 1 week. Fax notes: Fee to fax results is $5.00 1st page, $2.00 each add'l in USA; $2.00 for first and $1.00 each add'l in Hawaii. Copy fee: File marked pages are $1.00 per page; non-file marked are $.50. Certification fee: $2.00. Fee payee:

Clerk, 2nd Circuit Court. Personal checks accepted. Prepayment is required.

Lanai District Court PO Box 631376, Lanai City, HI 96763; 808-565-6447. Hours: 7:45AM-4:30PM (HT). *Misdemeanor, Civil Actions Under $20,000, Eviction, Small Claims.*

www.courts.state.hi.us/index.jsp

Civil Records: Access: Mail, in person. Only the court performs in person searches; visitors may not. Search fee: $5.00 per search. Required to search: name, years to search. Civil cases indexed by defendant, plaintiff. Civil records on index and docket books back to statehood.

Criminal Records: Access: Mail, in person. Only the court performs in person searches; visitors may not. Search fee: $5.00 per search. Required to search: name, years to search; also helpful: DOB, SSN. Criminal records on computer since 1980.

General Information: Turnaround time 2-3 weeks. Copy fee: $1.00 for first page, $.50 each add'l. Certification fee: $1.00. Fee payee: Lanai District Court. Personal checks accepted. Credit cards accepted if paid through Wailuka Dist. Court. Prepayment is required.

Molokai District Court PO Box 284, Kaunakakai, HI 96748; 808-553-5451; Fax: 808-553-3374. Hours: 7:45AM-4:30PM (HT). *Misdemeanor, Civil Actions Under $20,000, Eviction, Small Claims.*

www.courts.state.hi.us

Civil Records: Access: In person only. Only the court performs in person searches; visitors may not. Search fee: $5.00 per name. Required to search: name, years to search. Civil cases indexed by defendant, plaintiff. Civil records on index and docket books back to statehood.

Criminal Records: Access: In person only. Only the court performs in person searches; visitors may not. Search fee: $5.00 per name. Required to search: name, years to search, DOB, SSN. Criminal records on computer since 1980.

General Information: No juvenile or paternity records released. Copy fee: $1.00 for first page, $.50 each add'l. Certification fee: $5.00. Fee payee: Molokai District Court. Business checks accepted. Prepayment is required.

Wailuku District Court 2145 Main St, Ste 137, Wailuku, HI 96793; 808-244-2800; Fax: 808-244-2849. Hours: 7:45AM-4:30PM (HT). *Misdemeanor, Civil Actions Under $20,000, Eviction, Small Claims.*

www.courts.state.hi.us

Civil Records: Access: Mail, in person. Only the court performs in person searches; visitors may not. Search fee: $5.00 per name. Required to search: name, years to search; also helpful: address. Civil cases indexed by defendant, plaintiff. Civil records on index and docket books.

Criminal Records: Access: Mail, in person. Only the court performs in person searches; visitors may not. Search fee: $5.00 per name. Required to search: name, years to search, DOB, SSN. Criminal records on computer since 1980.

General Information: SASE required. Turnaround time 2-3 weeks. Fax notes: $5.00 for first page, $2.00 each add'l. Within Hawaii; $2.00 first page, $1.00 each add'l. Copy fee: $1.00 for first page, $.50 each add'l. Fee payee: District Court 2nd Circuit. Personal checks accepted. Credit cards accepted: Visa, MasterCard. Prepayment is required.

Hawaii Recording Offices

ORGANIZATION: All UCC financing statements, tax liens, and real estate documents are filed centrally with the Bureau of Conveyances located in Honolulu. The entire state is in the Hawaii Time Zone (HT).

ONLINE ACCESS: There is no statewide online access. Hawaii and Maui counties offer tax assessor information online.

Bureau of Conveyances

Bureau of Conveyances, PO Box 2867, Honolulu, HI 96803. 808-587-0154; Fax 808-587-0136.
Will search UCC records. Tax liens not included in UCC search. Will not search real estate records. **Online Access:** Property Records. Property records on the Hawaii County property assessor records are available free at www.hawaiipropertytax.com. Maui Assessor Property records are available free at www.mauipropertytax.com. There is also a Maui property lookup at http://gil.co.maui.hi.us/kivanet/2/land/lookup/index.cfm?fa=dslladdr. **Other Phone Numbers:** Assessor 808-527-5541/5511. The Honolulu property assessor is located at 842 Bethel St, Honolulu, Hawaii 96813.

Hawaii County Locator

Find the city name in the City/County cross reference below. In that case, it is a simple matter to determine the county from the cross reference. However, only the official US Postal Service city names are included in this index. There are an additional 40,000 place names that people use in their addresses. Therefore, we have also included a ZIP/City Cross Reference immediately following the City/County Cross Reference.

City/County Cross Reference

AIEA Honolulu	HONOLULU Honolulu	KOLOA Kauai	PAHOA Hawaii
ANAHOLA Kauai	HONOMU Hawaii	KUALAPUU Maui	PAIA Maui
BARBERS POINT Honolulu	HOOLEHUA Maui	KULA Maui	PAPAALOA Hawaii
BARBERS POINT N A S Honolulu	KAAAWA Honolulu	KUNIA Honolulu	PAPAIKOU Hawaii
CAMP H M SMITH Honolulu	KAHUKU Honolulu	KURTISTOWN Hawaii	PEARL CITY Honolulu
CAPTAIN COOK Hawaii	KAHULUI Maui	LAHAINA Maui	PEARL HARBOR Honolulu
ELEELE Kauai	KAILUA Honolulu	LAIE Honolulu	PEPEEKEO Hawaii
EWA BEACH Honolulu	KAILUA KONA Hawaii	LANAI CITY Maui	PRINCEVILLE Kauai
FORT SHAFTER Honolulu	KALAHEO Kauai	LAUPAHOEHOE Hawaii	PUKALANI Maui
HAIKU Maui	KALAUPAPA Maui	LAWAI Kauai	PUUNENE Maui
HAKALAU Hawaii	KAMUELA Hawaii	LIHUE Kauai	SCHOFIELD BARRACKS Honolulu
HALEIWA Honolulu	KANEOHE Honolulu	M C B H KANEOHE BAY Honolulu	TAMC Honolulu
HANA Maui	KAPAA Kauai	MAKAWAO Maui	TRIPLER ARMY MEDICAL CTR Honolulu
HANALEI Kauai	KAPAAU Hawaii	MAKAWELI Maui	VOLCANO Hawaii
HANAMAULU Kauai	KAPOLEI Honolulu	MAUNALOA Maui	WAHIAWA Honolulu
HANAPEPE Kauai	KAUMAKANI Kauai	MILILANI Honolulu	WAIALUA Honolulu
HAUULA Honolulu	KAUNAKAKAI Maui	MOUNTAIN VIEW Hawaii	WAIANAE Honolulu
HAWAII NATIONAL PARK Hawaii	KEAAU Hawaii	NAALEHU Hawaii	WAIKOLOA Hawaii
HAWI Hawaii	KEALAKEKUA Hawaii	NINOLE Hawaii	WAILUKU Maui
HICKAM AFB Honolulu	KEALIA Kauai	OCEAN VIEW Hawaii	WAIMANALO Honolulu
HILO Hawaii	KEAUHOU Hawaii	OOKALA Hawaii	WAIMEA Kauai
HOLUALOA Hawaii	KEKAHA Kauai	PAAUHAU Hawaii	WAIPAHU Honolulu
HONAUNAU Hawaii	KIHEI Maui	PAAUILO Hawaii	WAKE ISLAND Honolulu
HONOKAA Hawaii	KILAUEA Kauai	PAHALA Hawaii	WHEELER ARMY AIRFIELD Honolulu

ZIP/City Cross Reference

96701-96701 AIEA	96731-96731 KAHUKU	96760-96760 KURTISTOWN	96785-96785 VOLCANO
96703-96703 ANAHOLA	96732-96733 KAHULUI	96761-96761 LAHAINA	96786-96786 WAHIAWA
96704-96704 CAPTAIN COOK	96734-96734 KAILUA	96762-96762 LAIE	96788-96788 PUKALANI
96705-96705 ELEELE	96737-96737 OCEAN VIEW	96763-96763 LANAI CITY	96789-96789 MILILANI
96706-96706 EWA BEACH	96738-96738 WAIKOLOA	96764-96764 LAUPAHOEHOE	96790-96790 KULA
96707-96707 KAPOLEI	96739-96739 KEAUHOU	96765-96765 LAWAI	96791-96791 WAIALUA
96708-96708 HAIKU	96740-96740 KAILUA KONA	96766-96766 LIHUE	96792-96792 WAIANAE
96709-96709 KAPOLEI	96741-96741 KALAHEO	96767-96767 LAHAINA	96793-96793 WAILUKU
96710-96710 HAKALAU	96742-96742 KALAUPAPA	96768-96768 MAKAWAO	96795-96795 WAIMANALO
96712-96712 HALEIWA	96743-96743 KAMUELA	96769-96769 MAKAWELI	96796-96796 WAIMEA
96713-96713 HANA	96744-96744 KANEOHE	96770-96770 MAUNALOA	96797-96797 WAIPAHU
96714-96714 HANALEI	96745-96745 KAILUA KONA	96771-96771 MOUNTAIN VIEW	96800-96850 HONOLULU
96715-96715 HANAMAULU	96746-96746 KAPAA	96772-96772 NAALEHU	96853-96853 HICKAM AFB
96716-96716 HANAPEPE	96747-96747 KAUMAKANI	96773-96773 NINOLE	96854-96854 WHEELER ARMY AIRFIELD
96717-96717 HAUULA	96748-96748 KAUNAKAKAI	96774-96774 OOKALA	96857-96857 SCHOFIELD BARRACKS
96718-96718 HAWAII NATIONAL PARK	96749-96749 KEAAU	96775-96775 PAAUHAU	96858-96858 FORT SHAFTER
96719-96719 HAWI	96750-96750 KEALAKEKUA	96776-96776 PAAUILO	96859-96859 TRIPLER ARMY MEDICAL CTR
96720-96721 HILO	96751-96751 KEALIA	96777-96777 PAHALA	
96722-96722 PRINCEVILLE	96752-96752 KEKAHA	96778-96778 PAHOA	96859-96859 TAMC
96725-96725 HOLUALOA	96753-96753 KIHEI	96779-96779 PAIA	96860-96860 PEARL HARBOR
96726-96726 HONAUNAU	96754-96754 KILAUEA	96780-96780 PAPAALOA	96861-96861 CAMP H M SMITH
96727-96727 HONOKAA	96755-96755 KAPAAU	96781-96781 PAPAIKOU	96862-96862 BARBERS POINT NAS
96728-96728 HONOMU	96756-96756 KOLOA	96782-96782 PEARL CITY	96862-96862 BARBERS POINT
96729-96729 HOOLEHUA	96757-96757 KUALAPUU	96783-96783 PEPEEKEO	96863-96863 M C B H KANEOHE BAY
96730-96730 KAAAWA	96759-96759 KUNIA	96784-96784 PUUNENE	96898-96898 WAKE ISLAND

Idaho

General Help Numbers:

Governor's Office
PO Box 83720   208-334-2100
Boise, ID 83720-0034   Fax 208-334-2175
http://www2.state.id.us/gov/index.htm   8AM-6PM

Attorney General's Office
PO Box 83720   208-334-2400
Boise, ID 83720-0010   Fax 208-334-2530
http://www2.state.id.us/ag   8AM-5PM

State Court Administrator
PO Box 83720   208-334-2246
Boise, ID 83720-0101   Fax 208-334-2146
http://www2.state.id.us/judicial   9AM-5PM

State Archives
Historical Library & Archives   208-334-3356
450 N 4th Street   Fax 208-334-3198
Boise, ID 83702-6027   9AM-5PM
http://www2.state.id.us/ishs

State Specifics:

Capital: Boise
Ada County

Time Zone: MST*

* Idaho's ten northwestern-most counties are PST:
They are: Benewah, Bonner, Boundary, Clearwater,
Idaho, Kootenai, Latah, Lewis, Nez Perce, Shoshone.

Number of Counties: 44

Population: 1,321,006

Web Site: www.state.id.us

State Agencies

Criminal Records

State Repository, Bureau of Criminal Identification, PO Box 700, Meridian, ID 83680-0700 (Courier: 700 S Stratford Dr, Meridian, ID 83642); 208-884-7130, 208-884-7193 (Fax), 8AM-5PM.

www.isp.state.id.us

Note: A signed release is not required, but suggested; see below. Access to the online Sex Offender Registry is restricted. Registration and password is required at www.isp.state.id.us/identification/sex_offender/public_access.html.

Indexing & Storage: Records are available from 1960 on. It takes about 3 days before new records are available for inquiry. 61% of all arrests in database have final dispositions recorded, 56% for those arrests within last 5 years.

Searching: For sex offender list access, the public may submit a written request on the appropriate form for a $5.00 fee. This service is provided to those agencies qualifying under Idaho Code 18-8283 (c) for special lists; schools and non-profit organizations. Include the following in your request: name, DOB. SSN and alias will aid in identification. Fingerprints are optional but may be required to establish positive identification. Fingerprint searches take 5-7 days. 100% of records are fingerprint-supported. A record of an arrest without disposition after 12 months from date of arrest will only be given if signed release presented. Requests without the release will receive only records with dispositions.

Access by: mail, in person.

Fee & Payment: The $10.00 fee per person is applicable for either a name search or a fingerprint search. Fee payee: BCI. Prepayment required. Cashier check or money order is preferred form of payment. No credit cards accepted.

Mail search: Turnaround time: 5 to 7 days.

In person search: You may request information in person, but results are still mailed.

Corporation Records
Limited Partnerships
Trademarks/Servicemarks
Limited Liability Companys
Limited Liability
Partnerships
Assumed Names

Secretary of State, Corporation Division, PO Box 83720, Boise, ID 83720-0080 (Courier: 700 W Jefferson, Boise, ID 83720); 208-334-2301, 208-334-2080 (Fax), 8AM-5PM.

www.idsos.state.id.us

Note: Effective 1/1/97, fictitious or assumed names are found at this office. (Previously they had recorded at the county level.)

Indexing & Storage: Records are available for all entities. New records are available for inquiry immediately. Records are indexed on inhouse computer.

Searching: Ongoing requesters should establish a pre-paid account. Include the following in your request: full name of business, specific records that you need copies of. In addition to the articles of incorporation, corporation records include the following information: Annual Reports, Officers, Directors, Prior names, Inactive and Reserved names, and Filing History. Cross reference of owners/officers is not avail.

Access by: mail, phone, fax, in person, online.

Fee & Payment: There is no search fee. The fee for copies is $.25 per page. Certification is $10.00 as is a Certification of Existence. Fee payee: Secretary of State. Prepayment required. Agency will invoice for payment. Personal checks accepted. No credit cards accepted.

Mail search: Turnaround time: 1 to 2 days. No self addressed stamped envelope is required.

Phone search: There is a limit of 3 entities per call.

Fax search: Copies cost an additional $.50 each if returned by fax.

In person search: Call first to make an appointment so that they can pull file.

Online search: Business Entity Searches at www.accessidaho.org/apps/sos/corp/search.html is a free Internet service open 24 hours daily.

Other access: There are a variety of formats and media available for bulk purchase requesters. Requesters can subscribers to a monthly CD update.

Expedited service: Expedited service is available for mail, phone and in person searches. Turnaround time: 1 day. Add $20.00 per document.

Uniform Commercial Code
Federal Tax Liens
State Tax Liens

UCC Division, Secretary of State, PO Box 83720, Boise, ID 83720-0080 (Courier: 700 W Jefferson, Boise, ID 83720); 208-334-3191, 208-334-2847 (Fax), 8AM-5PM.

www.idsos.state.id.us

Indexing & Storage: Records are available from 1967. It takes 1 to 2 days before new records are available for inquiry. Records are indexed on inhouse computer.

Searching: The search includes federal tax liens, farm filings, and seed and labor filings. There is also an agricultural commodity lien search. Federal tax liens on individuals are filed at the county level. Include the following in your request: debtor name. For state tax liens that closed prior to 01/07/98, one must search at the county. On that date, the state took over the filing and database of state tax liens.

Access by: mail, phone, fax, in person, online.

Fee & Payment: Information request only by type of search is $6.00 per name, two or more file types is $10.00. Copies are $6.00. Individual copies are available at $1.00 per page. The Commodity lien search is a $5.00 flat fee. Fee payee: Secretary of State. Prepayment is not required, but preferred. Personal checks accepted. No credit cards accepted.

Mail search: Turnaround time: 3 to 5 days. No self addressed stamped envelope is required.

Phone search: They will tell whether a filing exists.

Fax search: Searches can be invoiced. There is an additional fee of $.50 per page.

In person search: You may request information in person.

Online search: There is a free limited search at https://www.accessidaho.org/secure/sos/liens/search.html. We recommend professional searchers to subscribe to the extensive commercial service at this site. There is a $75 annual fee and possible transaction fees.

Other access: A summary data file on current filing is available on 4mm data tape.

Expedited service: Expedited service is available for mail and phone searches. The 24 hour service is available for an extra $10.00.

Sales Tax Registrations

Revenue Operations Division, Records Management, PO Box 36, Boise, ID 83722 (Courier: 800 Park, Boise, ID 83722); 208-334-7660, 208-334-7792 (Records Management), 208-334-7650 (Fax), 8AM-5:00PM.

http://www2.state.id.us/tax

Indexing & Storage: Records are available from 1983. The agency maintains records on computer since 1998 and on microfiche from 1983 to present.

Searching: This agency will only confirm that a business is registered if a tax permit number is provided. They will provide no other information. The only information released is that within public domain. They will also search if provided with a tax permit number, a DBA or an EIN.

Access by: mail, phone, fax, in person, online.

Fee & Payment: There is no search fee, but there is a fee for postage for mail requests or for faxing. Fee payee: ISTC, PO Box 36, Boise, ID 83732. Prepayment required. Personal checks accepted. No credit cards accepted.

Mail search: Turnaround time: 1 to 3 days. The copy fee is $.10 per page, after 20 pages. No self addressed stamped envelope is required.

Phone search: No fee for telephone request. Only general information is released.

Fax search: The fee is $1.00 per page. Turnaround time 24 hours.

In person search: No fee for request.

Online search: E-mail requests are accepted at rmcmichael@tax.state.id.us.

Birth Certificates

Vital Records, PO Box 83720, Boise, ID 83720-0036 (Courier: 450 W State St, 1st Floor, Boise, ID 83702); 208-334-5988, 208-389-9096 (Fax), 8AM-5PM.

http://www2.state.id.us/dhw

Indexing & Storage: Records are available on computer from July 1911 to present.

Searching: Records are confidential for 100 years. Only immediate family or legal representative may receive records as well as those who have a notarized release from persons of record or an immediate family member. Include the following in your request: full name, names of parents, mother's maiden name, date of birth, place of birth, relationship to person of record, reason for information request. Also include a copy of a photo ID and sign the request. The following data is not released: adoption records or sealed records.

Access by: mail, fax, in person.

Fee & Payment: Requesters must include their signature and a copy of a driver's license or photo ID. Fee is $13.00 per name, add $13.00 per name requested for additional copies. Fee payee: Vital Records. Prepayment required. Credit cards accepted for fax requests only. Personal checks accepted. Credit cards accepted: MasterCard, Visa, AmEx, Discover.

Mail search: Turnaround time: 2 to 3 weeks. No self addressed stamped envelope is required.

Fax search: See Expedited Service.

In person search: Monday through Friday, 8:00 a.m. to 4:30 p.m., except holidays.

Expedited service: Expedited service is available for fax searches. The fee is $20.50 plus cost of return Federal Express, if requested. Requests received by noon (MT) will be processed within 2 days if requesting Federal Express delivery; otherwise 1 week turnaround.

Death Records

Vital Records, PO Box 83720, Boise, ID 83720-0036 (Courier: 450 W State St, 1st Floor, Boise, ID 83702); 208-334-5988, 208-389-9096 (Fax), 8AM-5PM.

http://www2.state.id.us/dhw

Indexing & Storage: Records are available from July 1911 to present. Records are indexed on microfilm, inhouse computer.

Searching: Records are confidential for 50 years and are available only to immediate family members or legal representatives or a person who has a notarized release form from persons of record or an immediate family member. Include the following in your request: full name, date of death, place of death, relationship to person of record, reason for information request.

Access by: mail, fax, in person.

Fee & Payment: Include a copy of your driver's license or photo ID and signature with request. The fee is $13.00 per name or additional copy. Fee payee: Vital Records. Prepayment required. Credit cards are accepted with fax requests only. Personal checks accepted. Credit cards accepted: MasterCard, Visa, AmEx, Discover.

Mail search: Turnaround time: 2 to 3 weeks. No self addressed stamped envelope is required.

Fax search: There is an additional $5.00 special handling fee along with a $5.50 Vital Chek fee.

In person search: Monday through Friday, 8 a.m. to 4:30 p.m., except holidays.

Expedited service: Please add $5.00 for each order requiring 2 day special handling sent by express or priority service. This fee is in addition to the cost of FedEx, Postal Express, or Priority Mail.

Marriage Certificates

Vital Records, PO Box 83720, Boise, ID 83720-0036 (Courier: 450 W State St, 1st Floor, Boise, ID 83702); 208-334-5988, 208-389-9096 (Fax), 8AM-5PM.

http://www2.state.id.us/dhw

Indexing & Storage: Records are available from May 1947 to present. Records are indexed on microfilm, inhouse computer.

Searching: Indexes are not available to the public for 50 years. Only immediate family members and legal representatives may obtain recent records, others may obtain records with a notarized release from a family member or person of record. Include the following in your request: names of husband and wife, date of marriage, place or county of marriage.

Access by: mail, fax, in person.

Fee & Payment: Include a copy of a photo ID or driver's license and a signature with request. The fee is $13.00 per name and per each additional copy. Fee payee: Vital Records. Prepayment required. Credit cards accepted with fax requests only. Personal checks accepted. Credit cards accepted: MasterCard, Visa, AmEx, Discover.

Mail search: Turnaround time: 2 to 3 weeks. No self addressed stamped envelope is required.

Fax search: There is an additional $5.00 special handling fee along with a $5.50 VitalChek fee.

In person search: Monday through Friday, 8 a.m. to 4:30 p.m., except holidays.

Expedited service: Please add $5.00 for each order requiring 2 day special handling and sent bt express or priority. This fee is in addition to the cost of FedEx, Postal Express, or Priority Mail.

Divorce Records

Vital Records, PO Box 83720, Boise, ID 83720-0036 (Courier: 450 W State St, 1st Floor, Boise, ID 83702); 208-334-5988, 208-389-9096 (Fax), 8AM-5PM.

http://www2.state.id.us/dhw

Note: This agency only maintains certificates of divorce; copies of decrees are available through the court system.

Indexing & Storage: Records are available from May 1947 to present. New records are available for inquiry immediately. Records are indexed on microfilm, inhouse computer.

Searching: Records are not available to the public for 50 years and are available only to immediate family members, legal representatives, and a person with a notarized signed release form from persons of record or immediate family. Include the following in your request: names of husband and

wife, date of divorce, place of divorce, relationship.

Access by: mail, fax, in person.

Fee & Payment: Include a copy of a driver's license or photo ID and include a signature with request. The fee is $13.00 per name. Fee payee: Vital Records. Prepayment required. Credit cards are accepted with fax requests only. Personal checks accepted. Credit cards accepted: MasterCard, Visa, AmEx, Discover.

Mail search: Turnaround time: 2 to 3 weeks. No self addressed stamped envelope is required.

Fax search: There is an additional $5.00 special handling fee along with a $5.50 Vital Chek fee.

In person search: Searching is available in person.

Expedited service: Please add $5.00 for each order requiring 2 day special handling and sent bt express or priority. This fee is in addition to the cost of FedEx, Postal Express, or Priority Mail.

Workers' Compensation Records

Industrial Commission of Idaho, Attn: Records Management, PO Box 83720, Boise, ID 83720-0041; 208-334-6000, 208-334-2321 (Fax), 8AM-5PM.

http://www2.state.id.us/iic

Indexing & Storage: Records are available from 1917 on. New records are available for inquiry immediately. Records are indexed on microfilm, index cards, inhouse computer.

Searching: Must have a certified release form if you are not a party to the claim. Pre-employment screening companies must also provide an ADA certification and contingent job offer, and cannot get copies of files, only a work history report. Include the following in your request: claimant name, Social Security Number, date of accident and claim number. It is suggested to use their request form, found on the web site under Benefits Administration'. The following data is not released: psychiatric information.

Access by: mail, fax, in person.

Fee & Payment: Copy costs depend upon file size which are those that exceed 100 copied pages or 50 microfilmed pages. Larger files cost $.05 per page on paper and $.10 per page on microfilm. If file is off site, shipping fees of $2.00 per file apply. Fee payee: Industrial Commission. Charges that total under $5.00 are waived. Personal checks accepted. No credit cards accepted.

Mail search: Turnaround time: 3 days. There is a charge for postage. No self addressed stamped envelope is required.

Fax search: Fax searching available.

In person search: One may request information in person. However, not all files are available the same day because some files are not on site and must be ordered from storage.

Other access: There is no bulk data access as per Idaho law.

Driver Records

Idaho Transportation Department, Driver's Services, PO Box 34, Boise, ID 83731-0034 (Courier: 3311 W State, Boise, ID 83703); 208-334-8736, 208-334-8739 (Fax), 8:30AM-5PM.

http://www2.state.id.us/itd/dmv/ds.htm

Note: Copies of tickets may be available from the address listed above for a $4.00 fee per record.

Indexing & Storage: Records are available for at least 3 years for moving violations, DUIs and suspensions. Accidents are not shown on the record. It takes 1 day from receipt before new records are available for inquiry. Records are normally destroyed after 10 years and archived to tape.

Searching: Personal information is not released to casual requesters unless the requestor claims a valid authorization. The driver's license number and DOB are used for the primary search. If no record is found, a secondary search is performed using the name and DOB, or name and license number. The following data is not released: Social Security Numbers or medical information.

Access by: mail, fax, in person, online.

Fee & Payment: The fee is $4.00 per record. Convenience fees are added for online and batch searches. Fee payee: Idaho Transportation Department. Prepayment required. Ongoing requesters can set up an account. Personal checks accepted. Credit cards accepted: MasterCard, Visa.

Mail search: Turnaround time: 3 to 5 days. Mail-in requesters are asked to use the state form. No sclf addressed stamped envelope is required.

Fax search: Fax requests for records are accepted, if paid by a credit card or by account. Call 208-334-8761 to set up an account.

In person search: Walk-in requesters may receive up to ten records while they wait, the rest are processed overnight.

Online search: Idaho offers online access (CICS) to the driver license files through its portal provider, Access Idaho. Fee is $5.50 per record. For more information, call 208-332-0102 or visit www.accessidaho.org.

Other access: Idaho offers bulk retrieval of basic drivers license information with a signed contract. For information, call 208-334-8601

Vehicle Ownership
Vehicle Identification

Idaho Transportation Department, Vehicle Services, PO Box 34, Boise, ID 83731-0034 (Courier: 3311 W State St, Boise, ID 83707); 208-334-8773, 208-334-8542 (Fax), 8:30AM-5PM.

http://www2.state.id.us/itd/dmv/vs.htm

Indexing & Storage: Records are available from 1981. It takes 1 day before new records are available for inquiry.

Searching: Personal information is not released to casual requesters unless the requestor claims a valid authorization. Submit the name, VIN, license plate number for search, current address is also helpful. The following data is not released: Social Security Numbers or medical records.

Access by: mail, fax, in person, online.

Fee & Payment: The fee is $4.00 for current title with lien information or for a registration search. A complete title history (using the microfilm) is $8.00. Convenience fees are added for online and batch searches. Fee payee: Idaho Transportation Department. Prepayment required. Motor vehicle record accounts may be established by calling 208-334-8761. Personal checks accepted. Credit cards accepted: MasterCard, Visa.

Mail search: Turnaround time: 5 to 10 days. Information request forms are available. No self addressed stamped envelope is required.

Fax search: You may fax a request with a major credit card. Results, except for history records, can returned by fax for no additional fee. Turnaround time is three days.

In person search: You may request information in person here or at any county assessor auto licensing location statewide.

Online search: Idaho offers online and batch access to registration and title files through its portal provider, Access Idaho. Records are $4.00 each plus an additional convenience fee. For more information, call 208-332-0102.

Other access: Idaho offers bulk retrieval of registration, ownership, and vehicle information with a signed contract. For more information, call 208-334-8601.

Accident Reports

Idaho Transportation Department, Office of Highway Safety-Accident Records, PO Box 7129, Boise, ID 83707-1129 (Courier: 3311 W State St, Boise, ID 83707); 208-334-8100, 208-334-4430 (Fax), 8AM-12:00PM; 1PM-5PM.

Indexing & Storage: Records are available from 1970's (on microfilm) to present. It takes 3 months before new records are available for inquiry.

Searching: Include the following in your request: full name, date of accident, location of accident, driver's license number.

Access by: mail, phone, fax, in person.

Fee & Payment: The fee is $4.00 per report plus handling and tax. Fee payee: Idaho Transportation Department, Financial Control. Do not send a check with a request, you will be billed. Personal checks accepted. No credit cards accepted.

Mail search: Turnaround time: 2 weeks. A self addressed stamped envelope is requested.

Phone search: No fee for telephone request. Fee charged if copies sent. Turnaround time: 2 weeks.

Fax search: Turnaround time 2 weeks.

In person search: It is suggested that walk-in requesters call first before going to department should the state have to locate the records on microfilm.

Other access: Computer files may be purchased with prepaid deposit plus computer charges. However, the file will not contain addresses, citation information, or drivers' license numbers. Annual databases may be purchased.

Vessel Ownership
Vessel Registration

Idaho Parks & Recreation, PO Box 83720, Boise, ID 83720-0065 (Courier: 5657 Warm Springs, Boise, ID 83712); 208-334-4197, 208-334-2639 (Fax), 8AM-5PM.

www.idahoparks.org

Note: Liens must be searched at the UCC Division at the Secretary of State office.

Indexing & Storage: Records are available from 1987 to present. Older records are available, but to search them, you must know the registration #. Records are indexed on computer. All boats with motors and/or sails must be registered.

Searching: To search, a signed release is required along with one of the following: owner's name, hull #, or registration #.

Access by: mail, in person.

Fee & Payment: There is no search fee.

Mail search: Turnaround time: 2 to 3 weeks. No self addressed stamped envelope is required.

In person search: This is the preferred method.

Legislation Records

Legislative Services Office, Research and Legislation, PO Box 83720, Boise, ID 83720-0054 (Courier: 700 W Jefferson, Lower Level, East, Boise, ID 83720); 208-334-2475, 208-334-2125 (Fax), 8AM-5PM.

http://www2.state.id.us/legislat/legislat.html

Note: Sessions are from January to the end of March.

Indexing & Storage: Records are available from 1971 to present. The current and previous year are available on the Internet.

Searching: Include the following in your request: bill number and year. During session, current bills are in the mailroom on the lower level, State Capitol Bldg.

Access by: mail, phone, fax, in person, online.

Fee & Payment: There is no charge unless the bill is very long. The first 7 pages are free and the fee for pages in excess of 7 is $.20 per page. They will compute the charge. Fee payee: Legislative Services. Will bill for copy charges. Personal checks accepted. No credit cards accepted.

Mail search: Turnaround time: 3 days. Turnaround time may be longer from December through April. No self addressed stamped envelope is required.

Phone search: You may call for information. Information can be returned using your FedEx account number.

Fax search: Same criteria as phone searches. Up to 15 pages can be returned by fax.

In person search: You may request information in person.

Online search: Statutes, bill information, and subject index are available from the web site. They also will answer questions via e-mail. (kford@lso.state.id.us)

Voter Registration

Records not maintained by a state level agency.

Note: Records are maintained by the County Clerks. The counties will generally release name address and voting precinct on individual request. Lists may be purchased but not for commercial purposes.

GED Certificates

Department of Education, GED Testing, PO Box 83720, Boise, ID 83720-0027; 208-332-6980, 208-334-4664 (Fax), 8AM-5PM.

www.sde.state.id.us

Searching: Include the following in your request: Social Security Number, date of birth. A signed release is necessary for copies of transcripts or for scores.

Access by: mail, phone, fax, in person.

Mail search: Turnaround time: 2 to 3 days. No self addressed stamped envelope is required. No fee for mail request.

Phone search: No fee for telephone request. Verification only over the phone.

Fax search: Turnaround time is 1 day.

In person search: No fee for request. Information is released immediately.

Hunting License Information
Fishing License Information

ID Department of Fish & Game, Licenses Division, PO Box 25, Boise, ID 83707-0025 (Courier: 1075 Park Blvd, Boise, ID 83707); 208-334-3717 (License Department), 208-334-3736 (Enforcement Office), 208-334-2148 (Fax), 8AM-5PM.

http://www2.state.id.us/fishgame/fishgame.html

Note: The license division says that if you want an individual name, you must call the Enforcement Office. This office will not release individual records with addresses, they will only confirm is there is a license issued.

Indexing & Storage: Records are available from January 1992 to present.

Searching: Use of their request form is required. Include signature and copy of valid ID.

Access by: mail, phone, in person.

Fee & Payment: There is no fee unless the search is extensive.

Mail search: Turnaround time: variable. No self addressed stamped envelope is required.

Phone search: They will only confirm.

In person search: Searching is available in person.

Idaho State Licensing Agencies

Licenses Searchable Online

Applicator, Commercial/Private #20........................www.agri.state.id.us/agresource/_agtechlookup/querylic.asp

Attorney #29 ....http://www2.state.id.us/isb/mem/attorney_roster.asp

Bank #21 ....http://finance.state.id.us/industry/bank_info.asp

Boiler Inspector #10...www.accessidaho.org/public/dbs/safety/search.html

Collection Agency/Collector #21 ....http://finance.state.id.us/industry/statutes_confin.asp?Chapter=CAA

Community Action Program #27 ....www.puc.state.id.us/consumer/helplist.pdf

Contractor, Public Works #31 ....www.accessidaho.org/public/dbs/pubworks/search.html

Credit Union #21...http://finance.state.id.us/industry/creditunion_section.asp

Dental Hygienist #13.......................................http://www2.state.id.us/isbd/search.htm

Dentist #13 ....http://www2.state.id.us/isbd/search.htm

Electrical Inspect/Contr./Appren./Journey. #10........www.accessidaho.org/public/dbs/electrical/search.html

Engineer #17 ....http://www2.state.id.us/ipels/pelsnumb.htm

Finance Company #21.....................................http://finance.state.id.us/consumer/concredit_section.asp

Guide #15 ....http://www2.state.id.us/oglb/oglbhome.htm

Investment Advisor #21 ....http://finance.state.id.us/industry/securities_resources.asp?resource=IARR

Lobbyist #28 ....www.idsos.state.id.us/elect/lobbyist/lobinfo.htm

Manufactured Commercial Building #10 ....www.accessidaho.org/public/dbs/building/search.html

Manufactured Homes & Housing #10 ....www.accessidaho.org/public/dbs/building/search.html

Manufactured Housing Dealer/Broker/Mfg. #10.....www.accessidaho.org/public/dbs/building/search.html

Mortgage Broker/Banker #21............................http://finance.state.id.us/industry/mortgage_section.asp

Mortgage Company #21 ....http://finance.state.id.us/industry/mortgage_section.asp

Mortician/Mortician Resident Trainee #3.............http://www2.state.id.us/ibol/ibollicense_Search.cfm

Optometrist #19 ....www.odfinder.org/LicSearch.asp

Oral Surgeon #13 ....http://www2.state.id.us/isbd/search.htm

Orthodontist #13 ....http://www2.state.id.us/isbd/search.htm

Outfitter #15...http://www2.state.id.us/oglb/oglbhome.htm

Pesticide Applicator/Operator/Dealer/Mfg #6.........www.agri.state.id.us/QueryLic.htm

Plumbing Insp./Contr./Appren./Journeyman #10.....www.accessidaho.org/public/dbs/plumbing/search.html

Public Accountant-CPA #12.............................http://www2.state.id.us/boa/HTM/license.htm

Public Accountant-LPA #12 ....http://www2.state.id.us/boa/HTM/license.htm

Real Estate Appraiser #19................................www.asc.gov/content/category1/appr_by_state.asp

Savings & Loan Association #21 ....http://finance.state.id.us/industry/bank_section.asp

Securities Broker/Dealer/Seller/Issuer #21 ....http://finance.state.id.us/industry/securities.asp

Surveyor, Land #17 ....http://www2.state.id.us/ipels/pelsnumb.htm

Trust Company #21 ....http://finance.state.id.us/consumer/bank_info.asp

Utility Pay Stations #27 ....www.puc.state.id.us/consumer/paystations.htm

Licensing Quick Finder

Applicator, Commercial/Private #20 208-332-8500
Aquaculture, Commercial #20 208-332-8500
Architect #19 208-334-3233
Artificial Inseminator #20 208-332-8500
Asbestos Worker #10 208-334-2129
Athletic Trainer #30 208-327-7000
Attorney #29 208-344-4500
Bakery #11 208-327-7499
Bank #21 208-332-8005
Barber School Instructor #19 208-334-3233
Barber/Barber Shop/Barber School #19 208-334-3233
Bed & Breakfast #11 208-327-7499
Beekeeper #20 208-332-8500
Beer & Wine License, Wholesale/Retail #25
.... 208-884-7060
Boiler Inspector #10 208-334-2129
Boiler Safety Code #10 208-334-2129
Bottling Plant #11 208-327-7499
Boxer #32 208-334-3888
Boxing/Wrestling Event #32 208-334-3888
Boxing/Wrestling Professional #32 208-334-3888
Brewery #25 208-884-7060
Brokerage Dealer #12 208-334-2490
Building Inspector #10 208-334-3896
Chemigator #20 208-332-8500
Child Care Institution/Agency #7 208-334-5700
Child Care Licensure #7 208-334-5700
Chiropractor #19 208-334-3233
Clinical Laboratory Registration #2 208-334-2235
Clinical Nurse Specialist #14 .... 208-334-3110 X34
Collection Agency/Collector #21 208-332-8002
Commission Merchant #20 208-332-8500
Commodity Dealer #20 208-332-8500
Communication Disorders School Specialist #5
.... 208-332-6800
Community Action Program #27 208-334-0300
Construction Manager #31 208-334-4057
Consumer Loan Company & Credit Sale #21
.... 208-332-8002
Contractor, Public Works #31 208-334-4057
Controlled Substance Registrant #16 ... 208-334-2356
Cosmetologist/Cosmetology Salon #19 208-334-3233
Cosmetology School/Instructor #19 208-334-3233
Counselor #19 208-334-3233
Counselor, Professional #19 208-334-3233
Credit Union #21 208-332-8003
Crematory #3 208-334-3233
Dairy Farm/Dairy Product Processor #20
.... 208-332-8500
Day Care Center Inspector #11 208-327-7499
Day Care Center/Home #7 208-334-5700
Dental Assistant #13 208-334-2369
Dental Hygienist #13 208-334-2369
Dentist #13 208-334-2369
Denturist #19 208-334-3233
Dietitian #30 208-327-7000
Driller, Rotary #26 208-327-7900
Drug Mfg./Repackager/Whlse. #16 208-334-2356
Drug Outlet (i.e. Nursing Home) #16 ... 208-334-2356
Drug Sales, Non-Pharmacy (i.e. Grocery Store) #16
.... 208-334-2356
Egg Distributor/Grader #20 208-332-8500
Electrical Inspector/Contractor/Apprentice/Journeyman
#10 208-334-2183
Electrolysis #19 208-334-3233
Elevator Installation/Repairmen #10 208-334-2129
Emergency Medical Technician #9 208-334-4000

Engineer #17 208-334-3860
Environmental Health Specialist #19 ... 208-334-3233
Esthetician #19 208-334-3233
Euthanasia Agency #1 208-332-8588
Euthanasia Technician #1 208-332-8588
Exceptional Child School Program Advisor #5208-332-6800
Farm Produce Dealer/Broker #20 208-332-8500
Feed Manufacturer, Commercial #20 ... 208-332-8500
Fertilizer Manufacturer, Commerc. #20. 208-332-8500
Finance Company #21 208-332-8002
Fishing, Commercial #22 208-334-3717
Florist/Nurseryman #20 208-332-8620
Food Processing/Mfg. Plant #11 208-327-7499
Food Warehouse, Cold Storage #11 208-327-7499
Foster Home #7 208-334-5700
Funeral Establishment #3 208-334-3233
Fur Buyer #22 208-334-3717
Game Farm (Commercial Wildlife) #22. 208-334-3717
Geologist #18 208-334-2268
Grocery Store #11 208-327-7499
Guide #15 208-327-7380
Hearing Aid Dealer/Fitter #19 208-334-3233
Horse Racing Event/Occupation #33 ... 208-884-7080
Hospital (Child or Elderly) #8 208-334-5500
Insurance Agent Corp./Partnership #24 208-334-4250
Insurance Agent Licensure Examination #24
.... 208-334-4250
Insurance Agent, Non-resident #24 208-334-4320
Insurance Broker License #24 208-334-4250
Insurer, Domestic & Mutual #24 208-334-4250
Insurer, Foreign & Alien #24 208-334-4250
Intermediate Care Facility for the Mentally Retarded #8
.... 208-334-5500
Investment Advisor #21 208-332-8004
Landscape Architect #19 208-334-3233
Liquor License, Retail #25 208-884-7060
Livestock Auction Market #20 208-332-8500
Livestock Brand #25 208-884-7070
Loan Agent #12 208-334-2490
Loan Collection Officer #12 208-334-2490
Lobbyist #28 208-334-2852
Logging #10 208-334-6000
Mammography #2 208-334-2235
Manufactured Commercial Building #10 208-334-3896
Manufactured Homes & Housing #10 .. 208-334-3896
Manufactured Housing Dealer/Broker/Mfg. #10
.... 208-334-3896
Medical Doctor #30 208-327-7000
Medical Resident #30 208-327-7000
Midwife Nurse #14 .... 208-334-3110 X34
Milk & Dairy Product Storage/Hauling/Handling #20
.... 208-332-8500
Mine Safety Training #10 208-334-2129
Mixer-Loader #20 208-332-8500
Mortgage Broker/Banker #21 208-332-8004
Mortgage Company #21 208-332-8004
Mortician/Mortician Resident Trainee #3208-334-3233
Notary Public #28 208-334-2810
Nurse #14 .... 208-334-3110 X34
Nurse Anesthetist #14 .... 208-334-3110 X25
Nurse-LPN #14 208-334-3110
Nursing Assistant #14 208-334-3110
Nursing Care (Skilled) Facility #8 208-334-5500
Nursing Home Administrator #19 208-334-3233
Occupational Therapist/Assistant #30 .. 208-327-7000
Optometrist #19 208-334-3233

Oral Surgeon #13 208-334-2369
Organic Certification #20 208-332-8620
Orthodontist #13 208-334-2369
Osteopathic Physician #30 208-327-7000
Outfitter #15 208-327-7380
Paramedic (EMT) #9 208-334-4000
Pest Control Consultant #6 208-332-8600
Pesticide Applicator/Operator/Dealer/Mfg #6
.... 208-332-8600
Pharmacist/Phamacist Intern/Preceptor #16
.... 208-334-2356
Pharmacy Mail Svc. #16 208-334-2356
Pharmacy/Drug Store #16 208-334-2356
Physical Therapist/Assistant #30 208-327-7000
Physician Assistant #30 208-327-7000
Plumbing Insp./Contr./Apprentice/Journeyman #10
.... 208-334-3442
Podiatrist #19 208-334-3233
Police (Peace) Officer #25 208-884-7250
Psychologist #19 208-334-3233
Public Accountant-CPA #12 208-334-2490
Public Accountant-LPA #12 208-334-2490
Public Commodity Warehouse #20 208-332-8500
Radiation Equipment #3 208-334-3945
Real Estate Appraiser #19 208-334-3233
Recreational Vehicle Manufacturer #10 208-334-3896
Rehabilitation Facility #8 208-334-5500
Residential Care Administrator #19 208-334-3233
Residential Care Facility #8 208-334-5500
Residential School #7 208-334-5700
Respiratory Therapist #30 208-327-7000
Restaurant Sanitation Standard #11 208-327-7499
Savings & Loan Association #21 208-332-8005
School Counselor #5 208-332-6800
School Nurse #5 208-332-6800
School Principal/Superintendent #5 208-332-6800
Securities Broker/Dealer/Seller/Issuer #21
.... 208-332-8004
Seed Company #20 208-332-8620
Septic Tank Pumper #11 208-327-7499
Shooting Preserve #22 208-334-3717
Shorthand Reporter #4 208-334-2517
Social Worker #19 208-334-3233
Soil & Plant Amendment Mfg. #20 208-332-8620
Solicitor (Financial) #21 208-332-8002
Special Education Director #5 208-332-6800
Substance Abuse Treatment Center #7 208-334-5700
Subsurface Sewage Installer #11 208-327-7499
Surveyor, Land #17 208-334-3860
Swimming Pool Installer #11 208-327-7499
Taxidermist #22 208-334-3717
Teacher #5 208-332-6800
Trapper/Junior Trapper #22 208-334-3736
Trust Company #21 208-332-8005
Utility Pay Stations #27 208-334-0300
Utility Regulation Gas/Water/Power/Phone #27
.... 208-334-0300
Veterinarian/Veterinary Technician #1 .. 208-332-8588
Veterinary Drug Outlet/Technician #16. 208-334-2356
Water Laboratory #2 208-334-2235
Water Rights Examiner #26 208-327-7900
Water Well Driller #26 208-327-7900
Weighmaster #20 208-332-8500
Winery #25 208-884-7060
Wrestler #32 208-334-3888
X-ray Equipment #2 208-334-2235

Licensing Agency Information

#1 Board of Veterinary Medicine, PO Box 7249, Boise, ID 83707; 208-332-8588, Fax: 208-334-4062. Agency email: sjensen@agri.state.id.us.

#2 Bureau of Laboratories, 2220 Old Penitentiary Rd, Boise, ID 83712; 208-334-2235, Fax: 208-334-2382.

#3 Bureau of Occupational Licenses, Mortician Board of Examiners, 1109 Main St, #220, Boise, ID 83702-5642; 208-334-3233, Fax: 208-334-3945.
http://www2.state.id.us/ibol/mor.htm
Agency email: ibol@ibol.state.id.us.
Search database at http://www2.state.id.us/ibol/ibollicense_Search.cfm

#4 Certified Shorthand Reporters Board, 550 W State St, Boise, ID 83720-0017; 208-334-2517.

#5 Department of Education, Teacher Certification, PO Box 83720, Boise, ID 83720-0027; 208-332-6800, Fax: 208-334-2094.
www.sde.state.id.us/certification
Agency email: kpotter@sde.state.id.us.

#6 Department of Agriculture, Pesticides Division - Licensing, 2270 Old Penitentiary Rd, Boise, ID 83712; 208-332-8600.
www.agri.state.id.us

#7 Department of Health & Welfare, Division of Family and Community Services, 450 W State St, 5th Fl, Boise, ID 83720; 208-334-5700, Fax: 208-334-6558.
www2.state.id.us/dhw/hwgd_www/contentlist.html#Family

#8 Department of Health & Welfare, Bureau of Facility Standards, PO Box 83720 (450 W. State St, 10th Fl), Boise, ID 83720; 208-373-0502, Fax: 208-334-6558.
http://www2.state.id.us/dhw/

#9 Department of Health & Welfare, Bureau of Emergency Medical Services, 590 W Washington, Boise, ID 83702; 208-334-4000, Fax: 208-334-4015.

#10 Division of Building Safety, PO Box 83720, Boise, ID 83720-0048; 208-334-3950, Fax: 208-334-2683.
www2.state.id.us/dbs/dbs_index.html
Agency email: swallace@dbs.state.id.us.
Search database at
http://www2.state.id.us/dbs/dbs_index.html

#11 Environmental Health Department, Bakery & Related Licensing, 707 N Armstrong Place, Boise, ID 83704; 208-327-7499, Fax: 208-327-8553.
www.cdhd.org/EnvironmentalHealth/

#12 Board of Accountancy, 1109 Main #470, Boise, ID 83702-0002; 208-334-2490, Fax: 208-334-2615.
www2.state.id.us/boa
Agency email: isba@boa.state.id.us.
Search database at www2.state.id.us/boa

#13 Board of Dentistry, PO Box 83720, Boise, ID 83720-0021; 208-334-2369, Fax: 208-334-3247.
www2.state.id.us/isbd. Agency email: smiller@isbd.state.id.us.
Search database at
http://www2.state.id.us/isbd/search.htm

#14 Board of Nursing, 280 N 8th St #210, Boise, ID 83720; 208-334-3110, Fax: 208-334-3262.
www2.state.id.us/ibn/ibnhome.htm
Agency email: lcoley@ibn.state.id.us.
Search database at
www2.state.id.us/ibn/ibnhome.htm

#15 Board of Outfitters & Guides, 1365 N Orchard St, Rm 172, Boise, ID 83706; 208-327-7380, Fax: 208-327-7382.
http://www2.state.id.us/oglb/oglbhome.htm.
Agency email: dsangrey@oglb.state.id.us.
Search database at
http://www2.state.id.us/oglb/oglbhome.htm. Scroll to the bottom of the page to find the appropriate links for searching.

#16 Board of Pharmacy, 3380 Americana Terr #320, PO Box 83720, Boise, ID 83720-0067; 208-334-2356, Fax: 208-334-3536.
www.state.id.us/bop
Agency email: rmarkuson@bop.state.id.us.

#17 Board of Professional Engineers & Surveyors, 600 S Orchard, #A, Boise, ID 83705; 208-334-3860, Fax: 208-334-2008.
www2.state.id.us/ipels/index.htm
Agency email: dcurtis@ipels.state.id.us.
Search database at
www2.state.id.us/ipels/pelsnumb.htm

#18 Board of Professional Geologists, 550 W State St, Boise, ID 83720-0033; 208-334-2268.

#19 Bureau of Occupational Licenses, 1109 Main St, Owyhee Plaza, #220, Boise, ID 83702; 208-334-3233, Fax: 208-334-3945.
www2.state.id.us/ibol
Agency email: rswanbro@ibol.state.id.us.

#20 Department of Agriculture, Inspections/Registrations, 2270 Old Penitentiary Rd, Boise, ID 83712; 208-332-8500, Fax: 208-334-2170.
www.agri.state.id.us

#21 Department of Finance, Financial Bureau, 700 W State St, 2nd Fl, Boise, ID 83720-0031; 208-332-8000, Fax: 208-332-8098.

http://finance.state.id.us/home.asp
Agency email: finance@fin.state.id.us.
Search database at
http://finance.state.id.us/home.asphttp://finance.state.id.us/industry/financial_bureau.asp

#22 Department of Fish & Game, PO Box 25, Boise, ID 83707; 208-334-3700, Fax: 208-334-2114.
www2.state.id.us/fishgame. Agency email: idfginfo@idfg.state.id.us.

#24 ID Department of Insurance, 700 W State St, Boise, ID 83720-0043; 208-334-4250, Fax: 208-334-4398.
www.doi.state.id.us

#25 State Police, PO Box 700, Meridian, ID 83680-0700; 208-884-7000, Fax: 208-884-7090.
www.isp.state.id.us

#26 Department of Water Resources, 1301 N Orchard St, Boise, ID 83706; 208-327-7900, Fax: 208-327-7866.
www.idwr.state.id.us
Agency email: dlarsen@idwr.state.id.us.

#27 Public Utilities Commission, 472 W Washington St, Boise, ID 83702; 208-334-0300, Fax: 208-334-3762.
www.puc.state.id.us

#28 Secretary of State, Rm 203, Statehouse, PO Box 83720, Boise, ID 83720; 208-334-2300, Fax: 208-334-2282.
www.idsos.state.id.us
Agency email: sosinfo@idsos.state.id.us.
Search database at www.idsos.state.id.us

#29 State Bar, PO Box 895, Boise, ID 83701; 208-334-4500, Fax: 208-334-4515.
www2.state.id.us/isb
Search database at http://www2.state.id.us/isb/mem/attorney_roster.asp

#30 Board of Medicine, PO Box 83720, Boise, ID 83720-0058; 208-327-7000, Fax: 208-327-7005.
www.bom.state.id.us
Agency email: info@bom.state.id.us.

#31 Division of Building Safety, Public Works Contractors Board, PO Box 83720 (1090 Watertower St, Meridian, ID), Boise, ID 83720-0073; 208-334-4057, Fax: 208-855-9666.
www2.state.id.us/dbs/dbs_index.html

#32 State Athletic Department, 10 S Latah, #208, Boise, ID 83705; 208-334-3888, Fax: 208-345-1145.

#33 Horse Racing Commission, 700 Stratford Dr, Meridian, ID 83642; 208-884-7080, Fax: 208-884-7098. Agency email: ardie.noyes@isp.state.id.us.

Idaho Federal Courts

The following list indicates the district and division name for each county in the state. If the bankruptcy court location is different from the district court, then the location of the bankruptcy court appears in parentheses.

County/Court Cross Reference

County	Court	County	Court
Ada	Boise	Gem	Boise
Adams	Boise	Gooding	Boise
Bannock	Pocatello	Idaho	Pocatello (Moscow)
Bear Lake	Pocatello	Jefferson	Pocatello
Benewah	Coeur d' Alene	Jerome	Boise
Bingham	Pocatello	Kootenai	Coeur d' Alene
Blaine	Boise	Latah	Moscow
Boise	Boise	Lemhi	Pocatello
Bonner	Coeur d' Alene	Lewis	Moscow
Bonneville	Pocatello	Lincoln	Boise
Boundary	Coeur d' Alene	Madison	Pocatello
Butte	Pocatello	Minidoka	Boise
Camas	Boise	Nez Perce	Moscow
Canyon	Boise	Oneida	Pocatello
Caribou	Pocatello	Owyhee	Boise
Cassia	Boise	Payette	Boise
Clark	Pocatello	Power	Pocatello
Clearwater	Moscow	Shoshone	Coeur d' Alene
Custer	Pocatello	Teton	Pocatello
Elmore	Boise	Twin Falls	Boise
Franklin	Pocatello	Valley	Boise
Fremont	Pocatello	Washington	Boise

Standards for Federal Courts: The search fee is $20.00 per item (one party name or case number). Certification fee is $7.00 per document. Copy fee is $.50 per page. All fees standard unless noted in profile. Mail Search: always enclose a stamped self addressed envelope unless otherwise noted. Before releasing records, all courts require prepayment unless noted in profile.

Open records are located at the court unless otherwise noted. District courts index by defendant and plaintiff as well as by case number. Bankruptcy courts usually index by debtor and case number. While most courts now have their indexes on computer, many still maintain index card files as well.

The universal PACER sign-up number is 800-676-6856. Find PACER and the Party/Case Index on the Web at http://pacer.psc.uscourts.gov. PACER dial-up access is $.60 per minute. Also, courts offering internet access via RACER, PACER, Web-PACER or the new CM-ECF charge $.07 per page fee unless noted as free.

US District Court

District of Idaho

Boise Division MSC 039, Federal Bldg, 550 W Fort St, Room 400, Boise, ID 83724 (Courier Address: Use mail address for courier delivery), 208-334-1361, Fax: 208-334-9362.

www.id.uscourts.gov

Counties: Ada, Adams, Blaine, Boise, Camas, Canyon, Cassia, Elmore, Gem, Gooding, Jerome, Lincoln, Minidoka, Owyhee, Payette, Twin Falls, Valley, Washington.

Indexing & Storage: Cases are indexed by defendant, plaintiff, and case number. New cases are available in the index immediately after filing date. Open records are located at this court.

Fee & Payment Notes: Payment may be made by money order, cashier check, personal check. Prepayment is only required for large requests. Payee: US District Court Clerk.

Phone Search: All public information will be released over the phone.

Fax Search: Handled same as mail request. Check with Court Copy Service.

Mail Search: A stamped self addressed envelope is not required.

In Person Search: In person searching available.

PACER: There is no PACER access to this court.

Opinions Online: Court opinions are available online at www.id.uscourts.gov

Other Online Access: Search records online using RACER. Currently the system is free; visit www.id.uscourts.gov/doc.htm. Court does not participate in the U.S. party case index.

Coeur d' Alene Division c/o Boise Division, MSD 039, Federal Bldg, 550 W Fort St, Room 400, Boise, ID 83724 (Courier Address: Use mail address for courier delivery), 208-334-1361.

www.id.uscourts.gov

Counties: Benewah, Bonner, Boundary, Kootenai, Shoshone.

Indexing & Storage: New cases are available in the index after filing date. Open records are located at the Boise Division.

Fee & Payment Notes: Payment may be made by money order, cashier check. Business checks are not accepted. Personal checks are not accepted.

Phone Search: Searching not available by phone.

In Person Search: In person searching available.

PACER: There is no PACER access to this court.

Opinions Online: Court opinions are available online at www.id.uscourts.gov

Other Online Access: Search records online using RACER. Currently the system is free; visit www.id.uscourts.gov/doc.htm. Court does not participate in the U.S. party case index.

Moscow Division c/o Boise Division, PO Box 039, Federal Bldg, 550 W Fort St, Boise, ID 83724 (Courier Address: Use mail address for courier delivery), 208-334-1361.

www.id.uscourts.gov

Counties: Clearwater, Latah, Lewis, Nez Perce.

Indexing & Storage: New cases are available in the index after filing date. Open records are located at the Boise Division.

Fee & Payment Notes: Payment may be made by money order, cashier check. Business checks are not accepted. Personal checks are not accepted.

Phone Search: Searching not available by phone.

In Person Search: In person searching available.

PACER: There is no PACER access to this court.

Opinions Online: Court opinions are available online at www.id.uscourts.gov

Other Online Access: Search records online using RACER. Currently the system is free; visit www.id.uscourts.gov/doc.htm. Court does not participate in the U.S. party case index.

Pocatello Division c/o Boise Division, 801 E Sherman, Pocatello, ID 83201 (Courier: Use mail address for courier delivery), 208-478-4123.

www.id.uscourts.gov

Counties: Bannock, Bear Lake, Bingham, Bonneville, Butte, Caribou, Clark, Custer, Franklin, Fremont, Idaho, Jefferson, Lemhi, Madison, Oneida, Power, Teton.

Indexing & Storage: New cases are available in the index after filing date. Open records are located at the Boise Division.

Fee & Payment Notes: Payment may be made by money order, cashier check. Business checks are not accepted. Personal checks are not accepted.

Phone Search: Searching not available by phone.

In Person Search: In person searching available.

PACER: There is no PACER access to this court.

Opinions Online: Court opinions are available online at www.id.uscourts.gov

Other Online Access: Search records online using RACER. Currently the system is free; visit www.id.uscourts.gov/doc.htm. Court does not participate in the U.S. party case index.

US Bankruptcy Court

District of Idaho

Boise Division MSC 042, US Courthouse, 550 W Fort St, Room 400, Boise, ID 83724 (Courier Address: Use mail address for courier delivery), 208-334-1074, Fax: 208-334-9362.

www.id.uscourts.gov

Counties: Ada, Adams, Blaine, Boise, Camas, Canyon, Cassia, Elmore, Gem, Gooding, Jerome, Lincoln, Minidoka, Owyhee, Payette, Twin Falls, Valley, Washington.

Indexing & Storage: Cases are indexed by debtor as well as by case number. New cases are available in the index immediately after filing date. Open records are located at this court.

Fee & Payment Notes: Payment may be made by money order, cashier check. Business checks are not accepted. Personal checks are not accepted. Make all search and copy arrangements with private vendor Court Copy Services, 208-334-9463. Payee: Coourt Copy Services. Copy fee: $.25 per page. The fee for copies made by court personnel is $.50 per page.

Phone Search: Only docket information is available by phone. An automated voice case information service (VCIS) is available. Call VCIS at 208-334-9386.

Fax Search: Fax requests are handled by a copy service. Call 208-334-9463 to arrange a fax request.

Mail Search: A stamped self addressed envelope is not required.

In Person Search: In person searching available.

PACER: Sign-up number is 208-334-9342. Access fee is No charge. Local dial-up access: 208-334-9895. Case records are available back to September 1990. Records are purged immediately when case closed. New civil records are available online after 1 day.

Opinions Online: Court opinions are available online at www.id.uscourts.gov

Other Online Access: Search records online using RACER. Currently the system is free; visit www.id.uscourts.gov/doc.htm. Court does not participate in the U.S. party case index.

Coeur d' Alene Division 205 N 4th St, 2nd Floor, Coeur d'Alene, ID 83814 (Courier Address: Use mail address for courier delivery), 208-664-4925, Fax: 208-765-0270.

www.id.uscourts.gov

Counties: Benewah, Bonner, Boundary, Kootenai, Shoshone.

Indexing & Storage: Cases are indexed by debtor as well as by case number. New cases are available in the index immediately after filing date. Open records are located at this court.

Fee & Payment Notes: Payment may be made by money order, cashier check, business check. Personal checks are not accepted. Payee: US Bankruptcy Court.

Phone Search: Only docket information is available by phone. An automated voice case information service (VCIS) is available. Call VCIS at 208-334-9386.

Fax Search: Fax search handled same as mail.

In Person Search: In person searching available.

PACER: Sign-up number is 208-334-9342. Access fee is No charge. Local dial-up access: 208-334-9895. Case records are available back to September 1990. Records are purged immediately when case closed. New civil records are available online after 1 day.

Opinions Online: Court opinions are available online at www.id.uscourts.gov

Other Online Access: Search records online using RACER. Currently the system is free; visit www.id.uscourts.gov/doc.htm. Court does not participate in the U.S. party case index.

Moscow Division 220 E 5th St, Moscow, ID 83843 (Courier: Use mail address for courier delivery), 208-882-7612, Fax: 208-883-1576.

www.id.uscourts.gov

Counties: Clearwater, Idaho, Latah, Lewis, Nez Perce.

Indexing & Storage: Cases are indexed by debtor as well as by case number. New cases are available in the index immediately after filing date. Open records are located at this court.

Fee & Payment Notes: Payment may be made by money order, cashier check, business check. Personal checks are not accepted. Payee: US Bankruptcy Court.

Phone Search: Only docket information is available by phone. An automated voice case information service (VCIS) is available. Call VCIS at 208-334-9386.

In Person Search: In person searching available.

PACER: Sign-up number is 208-334-9342. Access fee is No charge. Local dial-up access: 208-334-9895. Case records are available back to September 1990. Records are purged immediately when case closed. New civil records are available online after 1 day.

Opinions Online: Court opinions are available online at www.id.uscourts.gov

Other Online Access: Search records online using RACER. Currently the system is free; visit www.id.uscourts.gov/doc.htm. Court does not participate in the U.S. party case index.

Pocatello Division 801 E Sherman, Pocatello, ID 83201 (Courier Address: Use mail address for courier delivery), 208-478-4123, Fax: 208-478-4106.

www.id.uscourts.gov

Counties: Bannock, Bear Lake, Bingham, Bonneville, Butte, Caribou, Clark, Custer, Franklin, Fremont, Jefferson, Lemhi, Madison, Oneida, Power, Teton.

Indexing & Storage: Cases are indexed by debtor as well as by case number. New cases are available in the index immediately after filing date. No cases have been sent to the Federal Records Center yet.

Fee & Payment Notes: Payment may be made by money order, cashier check, business check. Personal checks are not accepted. Copy service will bill after first order. Payee: US Bankruptcy Court.

Phone Search: Only docket information is available by phone. An automated voice case information service (VCIS) is available. Call VCIS at 208-334-9386.

Fax Search: Fax searching available with a deposit account. Call for special procedures. Copy service will fax documents at $.50 per page.

In Person Search: In person searching available.

PACER: Sign-up number is 208-334-9342. Access fee is No charge. Local dial-up access: 208-334-9895. Case records are available back to September 1990. Records are purged immediately when case closed. New civil records are available online after 1 day.

Opinions Online: Court opinions are available online at www.id.uscourts.gov

Other Online Access: Search records online using RACER. Currently the system is free; visit www.id.uscourts.gov/doc.htm. Court does not participate in the U.S. party case index.

Idaho County Courts

Court	Jurisdiction	No. of Courts	How Organized
District Courts*	General	Comb.	7 Districts
Magistrates Division*	Limited	2	7 Districts
Combined Courts*		44	

* Profiled in this Sourcebook.

Court				CIVIL					
	Tort	Contract	Real Estate	Min. Claim	Max. Claim	Small Claims	Estate	Eviction	Domestic Relations
District Courts*	X	X	X	$0	No Max				
Magistrates Division*	X	X	X	$0	$10,000	$3000	X	X	X

Court	CRIMINAL				
	Felony	Misdemeanor	DWI/DUI	Preliminary Hearing	Juvenile
District Courts*	X	X	X	X	
Magistrates. Division*			X	X	X

ADMINISTRATION Administrative Director of Courts, Supreme Court Building, 451 W State St, Boise, ID, 83720; 208-334-2246, Fax: 208-334-2146. www2.state.id.us/judicial/

COURT STRUCTURE The District Court oversees felony and most civil cases. Small claims are handled by the Magistrate Division of the District Court. Probate is handled by the Magistrate Division of the District Court.

ONLINE ACCESS There is no statewide computer system offering external access. ISTARS is a statewide intra-court/intra-agency system run and managed by the State Supreme Court. All counties are on ISTARS, and all courts provide Public access terminals on-site.

ADDITIONAL INFORMATION A statewide court administrative rule states that record custodians do not have a duty to "compile or summarize information contained in a record, nor ... to create new records for the requesting party." Under this rule, some courts will not perform searches.

Many courts require a signed release for employment record searches.

The following fees are mandated statewide: Search Fee - none; Certification Fee - $1.00 per document plus copy fee; Copy Fee - $1.00 per page. Not all jurisdictions currently follow these guidelines.

Ada County

District & Magistrate Courts-I 200 W Front, Rm 1155, Boise, ID 83702-5931; 208-287-6900. Hours: 8:30AM-5PM (MST). *Felony, Civil, Eviction, Small Claims, Probate.*

http://www2.state.id.us/fourthjudicial

Civil Records: Access: Mail, in person. Both court and visitors may perform in person searches. No search fee. Required to search: name, years to search; also helpful: address. Civil cases indexed by defendant, plaintiff. Civil records on computer since 1985, microfiche and docket books from 1860s.
Criminal Records: Access: Mail, in person. Both court and visitors may perform in person searches. No search fee. Required to search: name, years to search; also helpful: address, DOB, SSN. Criminal records on computer since 1985, microfiche and docket books from 1860s.
General Information: Public access terminal is available. No juvenile, adoption, child protection records released. SASE required. Turnaround time 1-7 days. Copy fee: $1.00 per page. Certification fee: $2.50 per page. Fee payee: Ada County. Personal checks accepted.

Ada County Traffic Court 200 W Front St, Boise, ID 83702; 208-327-5352. Hours: 8AM-5PM (MST). *Misdemeanor.*

http://www2.state.id.us/fourthjudicial

Criminal Records: Access: Mail, in person. Both court and visitors may perform in person searches. No search fee. Required to search: name, years to search; also helpful: address, DOB, SSN. Criminal records on computer from 1985, microfiche from 1983, docket books back to statehood.
General Information: Public access terminal is available. No alcohol level or confidential evaluation records released. SASE required. Turnaround time up to 1-2 weeks. Copy fee: $1.00 per page. Certification fee: $1.50. Fee payee: Ada County. Personal checks accepted. Prepayment is required.

Adams County

District & Magistrate Courts PO Box 48, Council, ID 83612; 208-253-4561/4233; Fax: 208-253-4880. Hours: 8AM-5PM (MST). *Felony, Misdemeanor, Civil, Eviction, Small Claims, Probate.*

Civil Records: Access: Fax, mail, in person. Both court and visitors may perform in person searches. No search fee. Required to search: name, years to search. Civil cases indexed by defendant, plaintiff. Civil records on computer back to 1993, microfiche from 1972, docket books from 1911.
Criminal Records: Access: Fax, mail, in person. Both court and visitors may perform in person searches. No search fee. Required to search: name, years to search, signed release, DOB or SSN. Criminal records on computer back to 1993, microfiche from 1972, docket books from 1911. Include DOB and/or SSN.
General Information: Public access terminal is available. No juvenile, sealed cases records released. SASE requested. Turnaround time 2 days. Fax notes:

$4.00 per page. Copy fee: $1.00 per page. Certification fee: $1.00. Fee payee: Adams County. Personal checks accepted. Prepayment is required.

Bannock County

District & Magistrate Courts 624 East Center, Pocatello, ID 83205; 208-236-7351, 7352; Civil phone: 208-236-7350; Criminal phone: 208-236-7272; Probate phone: 208-236-7351; Fax: 208-236-7013. Hours: 8AM-5PM (MST). *Felony, Misdemeanor, Civil, Eviction, Small Claims, Probate.*

www.co.bannock.id.us/clkcrt1.htm

Civil Records: Access: Fax, mail, in person. Both court and visitors may perform in person searches. No search fee. Required to search: name, years to search. Civil cases indexed by defendant, plaintiff. Civil records on computer from 1986, on docket books from 1970s.

Criminal Records: Access: Fax, mail, in person. Both court and visitors may perform in person searches. No search fee. Required to search: name, years to search; also helpful: DOB, SSN. Criminal records on computer from 1986, on docket books from 1970s.

General Information: Public access terminal is available. No adoption, mental, juvenile, termination, domestic violence records released. SASE required. Turnaround time 1 day to 2 weeks. Fax notes: $1.00 per page. Copy fee: $1.00 per page. Certification fee: $.50 per page. Fee payee: Bannock County District Court. Personal checks accepted.

Bear Lake County

District & Magistrate Courts PO Box 190, Paris, ID 83261; 208-945-2208; Fax: 208-945-2780. Hours: 8:30AM-5PM (MST). *Felony, Misdemeanor, Civil, Eviction, Small Claims, Probate.*

Civil Records: Access: Fax, mail, in person. Only the court performs in person searches; visitors may not. No search fee. Required to search: name, years to search. Civil cases indexed by defendant, plaintiff. Civil records on computer back to 1991, docket books from early 1900s.

Criminal Records: Access: Fax, mail, in person. Only the court performs in person searches; visitors may not. No search fee. Required to search: name, years to search, DOB; also helpful: SSN, signed release. Criminal records on computer back to 1991, docket books from early 1900s.

General Information: No juvenile, CPA, divorce records released. SASE required. Turnaround time 2-3 days. Fax notes: $1.00 per page. Copy fee: $1.00 per page. Certification fee: $1.50. Fee payee: Clerk of Court. Business checks accepted. Prepayment is required.

Benewah County

District & Magistrate Courts Courthouse, 701 College Ave, St Maries, ID 83861; 208-245-3241; Fax: 208-245-3046. Hours: 9AM-5PM (PST). *Felony, Misdemeanor, Civil, Eviction, Small Claims, Probate.*

Civil Records: Access: Fax, mail, in person. Only the court performs in person searches; visitors may not. Search fee: $5.00 per name. Required to search: name, years to search. Civil cases indexed by defendant, plaintiff. Civil records on computer from 1991, index cards and docket books from early 1900s. Fax requests must include copy of fees check.

Criminal Records: Access: Mail, fax, in person. Only the court performs in person searches; visitors may not. Search fee: $5.00 per name. If printout required $.15 per page. Required to search: name, years to search. Criminal records on computer from 1991, index cards and docket books from early 1900s. Fax requests must include copy of fees check.

General Information: No juvenile, adoptions, mental commitments or sealed records released. SASE required. Turnaround time 3-5 days. Fax notes: No fee

to fax results, if search fee paid. Copy fee: $1.00 per page. Certification fee: $1.00. Fee payee: Clerk of Court. Personal checks accepted. Prepayment is required.

Bingham County

District & Magistrate Courts 501 N Maple St, #402, Blackfoot, ID 83221-1700; 208-785-5005 X342(Dist) X267(Magis); Fax: 208-785-8057. Hours: 8AM-Noon, 1-5PM (MST). *Felony, Misdemeanor, Civil, Eviction, Small Claims, Probate.*

Civil Records: Access: Phone, fax, mail, in person. Both court and visitors may perform in person searches. No search fee. Required to search: name, years to search; also helpful: address. Civil cases indexed by defendant, plaintiff. Civil records on computer from 1989, from microfiche from 1865.

Criminal Records: Access: Phone, fax, mail, in person. Both court and visitors may perform in person searches. No search fee. Required to search: name, years to search, signed release; also helpful: address, DOB, SSN. Criminal records on computer from 1989, from microfiche from 1865.

General Information: Public access terminal is available. No juvenile, adoption, mental records released. SASE required. Turnaround time 1-2 weeks. Fax notes: $1.25 per page. Copy fee: $1.00 per page. Certification fee: $1.00. Fee payee: Clerk of Court. Personal checks accepted. Prepayment is required.

Blaine County

District & Magistrate Courts 201 2nd Ave S #110, Hailey, ID 83333; 208-788-5548; Fax: 208-788-5512. Hours: 9AM-5PM (MST). *Felony, Misdemeanor, Civil, Eviction, Small Claims, Probate.*

Note: The Magistrate Court (Misdemeanor, Small Claims, Eviction, Probate) is in suite #106; Magistrate Court phone is 208-788-5525; fax 208-788-5527.

Civil Records: Access: Fax, mail, in person. Both court and visitors may perform in person searches. No search fee. Required to search: name, years to search. Civil cases indexed by defendant, plaintiff. Civil records on computer from 1992.

Criminal Records: Access: Fax, mail, in person. Both court and visitors may perform in person searches. No search fee. Required to search: name, years to search, DOB, SSN. Criminal records on computer since 1988.

General Information: No juvenile records released. SASE required. Turnaround time 3 days. Fax notes: $1.00 per page. Copy fee: $1.00 per page. Certification fee: $1.00 per document. Fee payee: Clerk of Court. Personal checks accepted. Prepayment is required.

Boise County

District & Magistrate Courts PO Box 126, Idaho City, ID 83631; 208-392-4452; Fax: 208-392-6712. Hours: 8AM-5PM (MST). *Felony, Misdemeanor, Civil, Eviction, Small Claims, Probate.*

Civil Records: Access: In person only. Visitors must perform in person searches for themselves. No search fee. Required to search: name, years to search. Civil cases indexed by defendant, plaintiff. Civil records on computer from 6/90, on docket books from 1863.

Criminal Records: Access: In person only. Visitors must perform in person searches for themselves. No search fee. Required to search: name, years to search, SSN; also helpful: DOB. Criminal records on computer from 6/90, on docket books from 1863.

General Information: Public access terminal is available. No juvenile, adoption records released. Copy fee: $1.00 per page. Certification fee: $1.50 per page. Fee payee: Boise County. Personal checks accepted. Prepayment is required.

Bonner County

District & Magistrate Courts 215 S. First Ave, Bonner Courthouse, Sandpoint, ID 83864; 208-265-1432; Fax: 208-265-1447. Hours: 9AM-5PM (PST). *Felony, Misdemeanor, Civil, Eviction, Small Claims, Probate.*

Civil Records: Access: Mail, fax, in person. Visitors must perform in person searches for themselves. No search fee. Required to search: name, years to search; also helpful: address. Civil cases indexed by defendant, plaintiff. Civil records on computer from 1990, index and docket books from 1907.

Criminal Records: Access: Mail, fax, in person. Visitors must perform in person searches for themselves. No search fee. Required to search: name, years to search; also helpful: address, DOB, SSN. Criminal records on computer from 1990, index and docket books from 1907.

General Information: Public access terminal is available. No juvenile records released. SASE required. Turnaround time 1 week. Fax notes: Fax fee $3.00 per page. Copy fee: $1.00 per page. Certification fee: $1.00. Fee payee: Bonner County Recorder or Clerk. Personal checks accepted. Prepayment is required.

Bonneville County

District & Magistrate Courts 605 N. Capital, Idaho Falls, ID 83402; 208-529-1350; Fax: 208-529-1300. Hours: 8AM-5PM (MST). *Felony, Misdemeanor, Civil, Eviction, Small Claims, Probate.*

www.co.bonneville.id.us

Civil Records: Access: In person only. Visitors must perform in person searches for themselves. No search fee. Required to search: name, years to search. Civil cases indexed by defendant, plaintiff. Civil records on computer from civil from 1991. Docket books by case number ongoing. Actual case records are archived before 10/91.

Criminal Records: Access: In person only. Visitors must perform in person searches for themselves. No search fee. Required to search: name, years to search, DOB, signed release; also helpful: SSN. Criminal misdemeanor records on computer from 1983, felony on computer from 1991, civil from 1991. Criminal on microfiche from 1977, civil from 1923. Docket books by case number ongoing. Actual case records are archived before 10/91.

General Information: Public access terminal is available. No child protective, protection orders, juvenile, sanity, adoption or termination records released. Copy fee: $1.00 per page. Certification fee: $1.00. Fee payee: Bonneville County. Personal checks accepted. For criminal and traffic records only. Prepayment is required.

Boundary County

District & Magistrate Courts Boundary County Courthouse, PO Box 419, Bonners Ferry, ID 83805; 208-267-5504; Fax: 208-267-7814. Hours: 9AM-5PM (PST). *Felony, Misdemeanor, Civil, Eviction, Small Claims, Probate.*

www.boundary-idaho.com

Civil Records: Access: In person only. Visitors must perform in person searches for themselves. No search fee. Required to search: name, years to search; also helpful: address. Civil cases indexed by defendant, plaintiff. Civil records on computer from 1989; by case number, index books, cards or microfiche by name from early 1900s.

Criminal Records: Access: In person only. Visitors must perform in person searches for themselves. No search fee. Required to search: name, years to search, SSN; also helpful: DOB. Criminal records on computer from 1989; by case number, index books, cards or microfiche by name from early 1900s.

General Information: Public access terminal is available. No sealed records released. Copy fee: $1.00 per page. Certification fee: $1.00 per page. Fee payee: Clerk of Court. Personal checks accepted. Prepayment is required.

Butte County

District & Magistrate Courts PO Box 171, Arco, ID 83213; 208-527-8259; Fax: 208-527-3448. Hours: 9AM-5PM (MST). *Felony, Misdemeanor, Civil, Eviction, Small Claims, Probate.*

Civil Records: Access: Phone, fax, mail, in person. Both court and visitors may perform in person searches. No search fee. Required to search: name, years to search; also helpful: address. Civil cases indexed by defendant, plaintiff. Civil records on computer from 1989, archives prior. Docket books by case number from early 1910s.

Criminal Records: Access: Phone, fax, mail, in person. Both court and visitors may perform in person searches. No search fee. Required to search: name, years to search; also helpful: address, DOB, SSN. Criminal records on computer from 1992 archives prior. Docket books by case number from early 1910s.

General Information: No juvenile records released. SASE required. Turnaround time 1 week. Fax notes: Fee to fax results is $1.00 per page. Copy fee: $1.00 per page. Certification fee: $2.50. Fee payee: Butte County Magistrate Court. Personal checks accepted. Prepayment is required.

Camas County

District & Magistrate Courts PO Box 430, Fairfield, ID 83327; 208-764-2238; Fax: 208-764-2349. Hours: 8:30AM-Noon, 1-5PM (MST). *Felony, Misdemeanor, Civil, Eviction, Small Claims, Probate.*

Civil Records: Access: Mail, in person. Both court and visitors may perform in person searches. No search fee. Required to search: name, years to search; also helpful: address. Civil cases indexed by defendant, plaintiff. Civil records from archives from 1917. Register of actions by case number.

Criminal Records: Access: Mail, in person. Both court and visitors may perform in person searches. No search fee. Required to search: name, years to search; also helpful: address, DOB, SSN. Criminal records from archives from 1917. Register of actions by case number.

General Information: Public access terminal is available. No juvenile or domestic violence records released. SASE required. Turnaround time 1 day. Copy fee: $1.00 per page. Certification fee: $1.00. Fee payee: Camas County Courthouse. Personal checks accepted. Prepayment is required.

Canyon County

District & Magistrate Courts 1115 Albany, Caldwell, ID 83605; Civil phone: 208-454-7570; Criminal phone: 208-454-7571. Hours: 8:30AM-5PM (MST). *Felony, Misdemeanor, Civil, Eviction, Small Claims, Probate.*

www.the3rdjudicialdistrict.com

Note: A daily court calendar is available at the web site.

Civil Records: Access: In person only. Visitors must perform in person searches for themselves. Search fee: No search fee. Required to search: name, years to search. Civil cases indexed by defendant, plaintiff. Civil records on computer from 1989, microfiche from 1800s, and docket books.

Criminal Records: Access: In person only. Visitors must perform in person searches for themselves. Search fee: No search fee. Required to search: name, years to search; also helpful: DOB. Criminal records on computer from 1989, microfiche from 1800s, and docket books.

General Information: Public access terminal is available. No adoption, mental, domestic violence

records not released. Copy fee: $1.00 per page. Certification fee: $1.00. Fee payee: Clerk of Court. Only cashiers checks and money orders accepted.

Caribou County

District & Magistrate Courts 159 S. Main, Soda Springs, ID 83276; 208-547-4342; Fax: 208-547-4759. Hours: 9AM-5PM (MST). *Felony, Misdemeanor, Civil, Eviction, Small Claims, Probate.*

Civil Records: Access: Phone, fax, mail, in person. Only the court performs in person searches; visitors may not. No search fee. Required to search: name, years to search. Civil cases indexed by defendant, plaintiff. Civil records on computer from 1989, from archives from 1919 by case number.

Criminal Records: Access: Phone, fax, mail, in person. Only the court performs in person searches; visitors may not. No search fee. Required to search: name, years to search, DOB, SSN; also helpful: address. Criminal records on computer from 1989, from archives from 1919 by case number.

General Information: No adoption, guardianship records released. SASE required. Turnaround time to 1 week. Fax notes: $2.00 for first page, $1.00 each add'l. Copy fee: $1.00 per page. Certification fee: $1.00. Fee payee: Clerk of Court. Business checks accepted. Out of state checks not accepted. Prepayment is required.

Cassia County

District & Magistrate Courts 1459 Overland, Burley, ID 83318; 208-878-7351 Magistrate; 878-4367 Dist; Fax: 208-878-1003. Hours: 8:30AM-5PM (MST). *Felony, Misdemeanor, Civil, Eviction, Small Claims, Probate.*

www.cassiacounty.org/judicial/default.htm

Civil Records: Access: Phone, fax, mail, in person. Both court and visitors may perform in person searches. No search fee. Required to search: name, years to search; also helpful: address. Civil cases indexed by defendant, plaintiff. Civil records on computer from 1990, archives from 1900s.

Criminal Records: Access: Fax, mail, in person. Both court and visitors may perform in person searches. No search fee. Required to search: name, years to search; also helpful: address, DOB, SSN. Criminal records on computer from 1990, archives from 1900s.

General Information: Public access terminal is available. No juvenile, adoption, mental commitment, child protection records released. SASE required. Turnaround time to 1-2 days. Fax notes: $2.50 per page. Copy fee: $1.00 per page. Certification fee: $1.50. Fee payee: Clerk of Court. Personal checks accepted. Prepayment is required.

Clark County

District & Magistrate Courts PO Box 205, DuBois, ID 83423; 208-374-5402; Fax: 208-374-5609. Hours: 9AM-5PM (MST). *Felony, Misdemeanor, Civil, Eviction, Small Claims, Probate.*

Civil Records: Access: Fax, mail, in person. Both court and visitors may perform in person searches. No search fee. Required to search: name, years to search; also helpful: address. Civil cases indexed by defendant, plaintiff. Civil records on computer from 1985, on microfiche for civil judgments and from archives from 1919.

Criminal Records: Access: Fax, mail, in person. Both court and visitors may perform in person searches. No search fee. Required to search: name, years to search; also helpful: address, DOB, SSN. Criminal records on computer from 1985, on microfiche for civil judgments and from archives from 1919.

General Information: Public access terminal is available. No juvenile, adoption records released. SASE required. Turnaround time 3 days. Fax notes: $.50 per page. Copy fee: $1.00 per page. Certification fee: $2.00.

Fee payee: Clerk of Court. Personal checks accepted. Prepayment is required.

Clearwater County

District & Magistrate Courts PO Box 586, Orofino, ID 83544; 208-476-5596; Fax: 208-476-5159. Hours: 8AM-5PM (PST). *Felony, Misdemeanor, Civil, Eviction, Small Claims, Probate.*

Civil Records: Access: Phone, fax, mail, in person. Only the court performs in person searches; visitors may not. No search fee. Required to search: name, years to search. Civil cases indexed by defendant, plaintiff. Civil records on computer from 8/91, in docket books prior to 1911.

Criminal Records: Access: Phone, fax, mail, in person. Only the court performs in person searches; visitors may not. No search fee. Required to search: name or case number, years to search. Criminal records on computer from 8/91, in docket books prior to 1911.

General Information: No juvenile, domestic violence, adoption, social records released. SASE requested. Turnaround time 7 days. Fax notes: $1.00 per page. Copy fee: $1.00 per page. Certification fee: $1.00. Fee payee: Clerk of Court. Business checks accepted. Prepayment is required.

Custer County

District & Magistrate Courts PO Box 385, Challis, ID 83226; 208-879-2359; Fax: 208-879-5246. Hours: 8AM-5PM (MST). *Felony, Misdemeanor, Civil, Eviction, Small Claims, Probate.*

Civil Records: Access: Phone, mail, in person. Only the court performs in person searches; visitors may not. Search fee: $5.00 per name. Required to search: name, years to search. Civil cases indexed by defendant. Civil records on computer from 1989, archived from early 1900s.

Criminal Records: Access: Phone, mail, in person. Only the court performs in person searches; visitors may not. Search fee: $5.00 per name. Required to search: name, years to search, DOB, signed release; also helpful: SSN. Criminal records on computer from 1989, archived from early 1900s.

General Information: No juvenile, adoption records released. Turnaround time 1 week. Copy fee: $1.00 per page. Certification fee: $1.00 per page. Fee payee: Custer County. Personal checks accepted. Prepayment is required.

Elmore County

District & Magistrate Courts 150 S 4th East, Ste 5, Mountain Home, ID 83647; 208-587-2133 x208; Fax: 208-587-2134. Hours: 9AM-5PM (MST). *Felony, Misdemeanor, Civil, Eviction, Small Claims, Probate.*

Civil Records: Access: In person only. Visitors must perform in person searches for themselves. No search fee. Required to search: name; also helpful: years to search. Civil cases indexed by defendant, plaintiff. Civil records on computer from 1992, on microfiche from 1972, archived from early 1900s.

Criminal Records: Access: In person only. Visitors must perform in person searches for themselves. No search fee. Required to search: name, DOB, signed release; also helpful: years to search, SSN. Criminal records on computer from 1992, on microfiche from 1972, archived from early 1900s.

General Information: Public access terminal is available. No juvenile, adoption, domestic violence, mental commitment records released. Copy fee: $1.00 per page. Certification fee: $1.00 per page. Fee payee: Elmore County. Personal checks accepted. Prepayment is required.

Franklin County

District & Magistrate Courts 39 West Oneida, Preston, ID 83263; 208-852-0877; Fax: 208-852-2926. Hours: 9AM-5PM (MST). *Felony, Misdemeanor, Civil, Eviction, Small Claims, Probate.*

Civil Records: Access: Phone, fax, mail, in person. Only the court may perform in person searches. Search fee: $2.00 per name. Fee is for years prior to 1990. No fee for 1990 to present. Required to search: name, years to search. Civil cases indexed by defendant, plaintiff. Civil records on computer from 1987, on microfiche from 1983, archived from 1920.

Criminal Records: Access: Phone, fax, mail, in person. Only the court may perform in person searches. Search fee: $2.00 per name. Fee is for years prior to 1990. No fee for 1990 to present. Required to search: name, years to search; also helpful: DOB, SSN. Criminal records on computer from 1987, on microfiche from 1977, archived from 1920.

General Information: No adoption records released. SASE required. Turnaround time 2-3 days. Fax notes: No fee to fax results. Local calls only. Copy fee: $1.00 per page. Certification fee: $1.00. Fee payee: Clerk of Court. Personal checks accepted. Prepayment required.

Fremont County

District & Magistrate Courts 151 W 1st North, St Anthony, ID 83445; 208-624-7401; Fax: 208-624-4607. Hours: 9AM-5PM (MST). *Felony, Misdemeanor, Civil, Eviction, Small Claims, Probate.*

Civil Records: Access: Phone, fax, mail, in person. Both court and visitors may perform in person searches. No search fee. Required to search: name, years to search; also helpful: address. Civil cases indexed by defendant, plaintiff. Civil records on computer back to 1990, microfiche for last 20 years, prior archives. Thursday is the best day for in person searches.

Criminal Records: Access: Fax, mail, in person. Both court and visitors may perform in person searches. No search fee. Required to search: name, years to search, DOB; also helpful: SSN. Criminal records on computer back to 1990, microfiche for last 20 years, prior archives. Thursday is the best day for in person searches.

General Information: Public access terminal is available. No adoption or juvenile records released. SASE required. Turnaround time 1 week. Fax notes: Fee to fax results is $2.00 per page. Copy fee: $1.00 per page. Certification fee: $1.00. Fee payee: Clerk of Court. Personal checks accepted. Prepayment required.

Gem County

District & Magistrate Courts 415 East Main St, Emmett, ID 83617; 208-365-4561; Fax: 208-365-6172. Hours: 8AM-5PM (MST). *Felony, Misdemeanor, Civil, Eviction, Small Claims, Probate.*

Civil Records: Access: Mail, in person. Both court and visitors may perform in person searches. Search fee: $5.00 per name. Required to search: name, years to search; also helpful: address. Civil cases indexed by defendant, plaintiff. Civil records on computer from 1990, on microfiche and archived from 1916.

Criminal Records: Access: Mail, in person. Both court and visitors may perform in person searches. Search fee: $5.00 per name per court ($10 for both felony and misdemeanor). Required to search: name, years to search, DOB, SSN; also helpful: address. Criminal records on computer from 1990, on microfiche and archived from 1972.

General Information: Public access terminal is available. No juvenile, adoption records or domestic violence released. SASE required. Turnaround time 10 days. Copy fee: $1.00 per page. Certification fee: $1.00 plus $.50 per page. Fee payee: Gem County. Personal checks accepted. Prepayment is required.

Gooding County

District & Magistrate Courts PO Box 477, Gooding, ID 83330; 208-934-4261; Fax: 208-934-4408. Hours: 8AM-5PM (MST). *Felony, Misdemeanor, Civil, Eviction, Small Claims, Probate.*

Civil Records: Access: Phone, fax, mail, in person. Visitors must perform in person searches for themselves. No search fee. Required to search: name, years to search. Civil cases indexed by defendant, plaintiff. Civil records on computer from 1994, on microfiche, docket books from 1860s.

Criminal Records: Access: In person only. Visitors must perform in person searches for themselves. No search fee. Required to search: name, years to search, DOB, SSN. Criminal records on computer from 1994, on microfiche, docket books from 1860s.

General Information: Public access terminal is available. No juvenile, adoption, domestic violence records released. SASE required. Turnaround time 5-10 days. Fax notes: Fee to fax results is $1.00 per page. Copy fee: $1.00 per page. Certification fee: $1.00. Fee payee: Gooding County Clerk. Personal checks accepted. Prepayment is required.

Idaho County

District & Magistrate Courts 320 West Main, Grangeville, ID 83530; 208-983-2776; Fax: 208-983-2376. Hours: 8:30AM-5PM (PST). *Felony, Misdemeanor, Civil, Eviction, Small Claims, Probate.*

Civil Records: Access: Phone, fax, mail, in person. Only the court performs in person searches; visitors may not. No search fee. Required to search: name, years to search. Civil cases indexed by defendant, plaintiff. Civil records on computer from 1989, on microfiche and archived from late 1800s.

Criminal Records: Access: Phone, fax, mail, in person. Only the court performs in person searches; visitors may not. No search fee. Required to search: name, years to search. Criminal records on computer from 1989, on microfiche and archived from late 1800s.

General Information: No domestic violence, juvenile, hospitalization, adoption, termination records released. SASE not required. Turnaround time same week. Fax notes: $1.00 per page. Copy fee: $1.00 per page. Certification fee: $1.00. Fee payee: Idaho County. Personal checks accepted. Prepayment is required.

Jefferson County

District & Magistrate Courts PO Box 71, Rigby, ID 83442; 208-745-7736; Fax: 208-745-6636. Hours: 9AM-5PM (MST). *Felony, Misdemeanor, Civil, Eviction, Small Claims, Probate.*

Civil Records: Access: In person only. Both court and visitors may perform in person searches. No search fee. Required to search: name, years to search. Civil cases indexed by defendant, plaintiff. Civil records archived from early 1900s; on computer back to 8/1992. Type of case also helpful with request.

Criminal Records: Access: In person only. Both court and visitors may perform in person searches. No search fee. Required to search: name, years to search, DOB. Criminal records archived from early 1900s; on comptuer back to 8/1992. Type of case also helpful with request.

General Information: Public access terminal is available. No juvenile, adoption, some domestic records released. Copy fee: $1.00 per page. Certification fee: $1.00 per page. Fee payee: Clerk of Court. Personal checks accepted. Prepayment is required.

Jerome County

District & Magistrate Courts 300 N Lincoln St, Jerome, ID 83338; 208-324-8811; Fax: 208-324-2719. Hours: 8:30AM-5PM (MST). *Felony, Misdemeanor, Civil, Eviction, Small Claims, Probate.*

Civil Records: Access: Fax, mail, in person. Both court and visitors may perform in person searches. No search fee. Required to search: name, years to search. Civil cases indexed by defendant, plaintiff. Civil records on computer from 1989, prior on microfiche back to 1919.

Criminal Records: Access: Fax, mail, in person. Visitors must perform in person searches for themselves. No search fee. Required to search: name, years to search, address, DOB, SSN. Criminal records on computer from 1989, civil from 1988, prior on microfiche back to 1919. Will not do background searches.

General Information: No juvenile records released. SASE required. Turnaround time 2 days. Fax notes: $3.00 for first page, $2.50 each add'l. Copy fee: $1.00 per page. Certification fee: $1.50 per page. Fee payee: Clerk of Court. Personal checks accepted. Prepayment is required.

Kootenai County

District & Magistrate Court 324 West Garden Ave (PO Box 9000), Coeur d'Alene, ID 83816-9000; Records: 206-446-1180; Civil phone: 208-446-1160; Criminal phone: 208-446-1170; Fax: 208-446-1188. Hours: 9AM-5PM (PST). *Felony, Misdemeanor, Civil, Eviction, Small Claims, Probate.*

www.co.kootenai.id.us/departments/districtcourt

Civil Records: Access: In person. Visitors must perform in person searches for themselves. No search fee. Required to search: name, years to search. Civil cases indexed by defendant, plaintiff. Civil records on computer from 1989, on microfiche from 1881, archived from 1819.

Criminal Records: Access: In person only. Visitors must perform in person searches for themselves. No search fee. Required to search: name, years to search; also helpful: DOB, SSN. Criminal records on computer from 1989, on microfiche from 1881, archived from 1819.

General Information: Public access terminal is available. No sealed, adoption, parental termination, mentally incapacitated records released. Copy fee: $1.00 per page. Certification fee: $1.00. Fee payee: Clerk of Court. Personal checks accepted. Credit cards accepted through official payments 800-530-8189. Prepayment is required.

Latah County

District & Magistrate Courts PO Box 8068, Moscow, ID 83843; 208-883-2255; Fax: 208-883-2259. Hours: 8:30AM-5PM M-W, 8AM-5PM TH,F (PST). *Felony, Misdemeanor, Civil, Eviction, Small Claims, Probate.*

Civil Records: Access: Phone, fax, mail, in person. Both court and visitors may perform in person searches. Search fee: $4.00 per name. Required to search: name, years to search; also helpful: address. Civil cases indexed by defendant, plaintiff. Civil records on computer from 1986, archived from May 1888.

Criminal Records: Access: Phone, fax, mail, in person. Both court and visitors may perform in person searches. Search fee: $4.00 per name. Required to search: name, years to search; also helpful: address, DOB, SSN. Criminal records on computer from 1986, archived from May 1888.

General Information: No adoption, juvenile, hospitalization records released. Turnaround time 1-2 days. Copy fee: $1.00 per page. Certification fee: $1.00. Fee payee: Clerk of Court. Personal checks accepted. Prepayment is required.

Lemhi County

District & Magistrate Courts 206 Courthouse Dr, Salmon, ID 83467; 208-756-2815; Fax: 208-756-8424. Hours: 8AM-5PM (MST). *Felony, Misdemeanor, Civil, Eviction, Small Claims, Probate.*

Civil Records: Access: Phone, fax, mail, in person. Both court and visitors may perform in person searches. Search fee: $5.00 per name. Required to search: name, years to search; also helpful: address. Civil cases indexed by defendant, plaintiff. Civil records on computer from 1991, on microfiche from 1964, archives from 1869.

Criminal Records: Access: Phone, fax, mail, in person. Both court and visitors may perform in person searches. Search fee: $5.00 per name. Required to search: name, years to search; also helpful: address, DOB, SSN. Criminal records on computer from 1991, on microfiche from 1964, archives from 1869.

General Information: Public access terminal is available. No PSI, sealed records released. SASE requested. Turnaround time 1 day. Fax notes: Fee to fax results is $1.00 per page. Copy fee: $1.00 per page. Certification fee: $1.00. Fee payee: Lemhi County Clerk. Personal checks accepted. Credit cards accepted: Visa, MasterCard, Discover, AmEx. This is through a service. Prepayment is required.

Lewis County

District & Magistrate Courts 510 Oak St (PO Box 39), Nezperce, ID 83543; 208-937-2251; Fax: 208-937-9233. Hours: 9AM-5PM (PST). *Felony, Misdemeanor, Civil, Eviction, Small Claims, Probate.*

Civil Records: Access: Phone, fax, mail, in person. Both court and visitors may perform in person searches. No search fee. Required to search: name, years to search. Civil cases indexed by defendant, plaintiff. Civil records on computer from 1991, archived from late 1911.

Criminal Records: Access: Phone, fax, mail, in person. Both court and visitors may perform in person searches. No search fee. Required to search: name, years to search; also helpful: DOB, SSN. Criminal records on computer from 1991, archived from late 1911.

General Information: No juvenile, adoption records released. SASE required. Turnaround time 1 week. Fax notes: $1.00 per page. Copy fee: $1.00 per page. Certification fee: $1.00. Fee payee: Clerk of Court. Only cashiers checks and money orders accepted. Two-party checks not accepted. Prepayment is required.

Lincoln County

District & Magistrate Courts Drawer A, Shoshone, ID 83352; 208-886-2173; Fax: 208-886-2458. Hours: 8:30AM-5PM (MST). *Felony, Misdemeanor, Civil, Eviction, Small Claims, Probate.*

Civil Records: Access: In person only. Both the court and visitors may perform in person searches for themselves. No search fee. Required to search: name, years to search. Civil cases indexed by defendant, plaintiff. Civil records on computer from 1992, archives from 1800s.

Criminal Records: Access: In person only. Both the court and vsitors may perform in person searches. No search fee. Required to search: name, years to search; also helpful: DOB, SSN. Criminal records on computer from 1992, archives from 1800s.

General Information: No juvenile, domestic violence, sealed records released. Copy fee: $1.00 per page. Certification fee: $1.00. Fee payee: Lincoln County Courts. Personal checks accepted.

Madison County

District & Magistrate Courts PO Box 389, Rexburg, ID 83440; 208-356-9383; Fax: 208-356-5425. Hours: 9AM-5PM (MST). *Felony, Misdemeanor, Civil, Eviction, Small Claims, Probate.*

Civil Records: Access: In person only. Both court and visitors may perform in person searches. No search fee. Required to search: name, years to search; also helpful: address. Civil cases indexed by defendant, plaintiff. Civil records on computer from 1991, microfiche and archives from early 1900s.

Criminal Records: Access: In person only. Visitors must perform in person searches for themselves. No search fee. Required to search: name, years to search; also helpful: address, DOB, SSN. Criminal records on computer from 1991, microfiche and archives from early 1900s.

General Information: Public access terminal is available. No juvenile records released. Copy fee: $1.00 per page. Certification fee: $1.00. Fee payee: Clerk of Court. Personal checks accepted. Prepayment is required.

Minidoka County

District & Magistrate Courts PO Box 368, Rupert, ID 83350; 208-436-9041 (Dist) 436-7186 (Magis); Fax: 208-436-5857. Hours: 8:30AM-5PM (MST). *Felony, Misdemeanor, Civil, Eviction, Small Claims, Probate.*

Civil Records: Access: Phone, fax, mail, in person. Both the court and visitors may perform in person searches. No search fee. Required to search: name, years to search. Civil cases indexed by defendant, plaintiff. Civil records on computer from 1989, archives from early 1900s.

Criminal Records: Access: Phone, fax, mail, in person. Both the court and visitors may perform in person searches. No search fee. Required to search: name, years to search, DOB, SSN, signed release. Criminal records on computer from 1989, archives from early 1900s.

General Information: Public access terminal is available. Juvenile records released with a signed relase. Turnaround time 1-3 days. Fax notes: $.50 per page. Copy fee: $1.00 per page. Certification fee: $.50 per page. Fee payee: Clerk of Court. Personal checks accepted.

Nez Perce County

District & Magistrate Court PO Box 896 (1230 Main St), Lewiston, ID 83501; 208-799-3040; Fax: 208-799-3058. Hours: 8AM-5PM (PST). *Felony, Misdemeanor, Civil, Eviction, Small Claims, Probate.*

www.co.nezperce.id.us/clerk/clerk.htm

Civil Records: Access: Phone, fax, mail, in person. Both court and visitors may perform in person searches. No search fee. Required to search: name; also helpful: years to search. Civil cases indexed by defendant, plaintiff. Civil records on computer from 1990, microfiche from 1970 and archives from late 1800s.

Criminal Records: Access: Phone, fax, mail, in person. Both court and visitors may perform in person searches. No search fee. Required to search: name, DOB; also helpful: years to search, aliases, SSN. Criminal records on computer from 1990, microfiche from 1970 and archives from late 1800s.

General Information: Public access terminal is available. SASE not required. Turnaround time 10 day waiting period. Fax notes: $1.00 for first page, plus (if long-distance) $.50 each add'l minute. Copy fee: $1.00 per page. Certification fee: $1.00 per page. Fee payee: Clerk of Court. Personal checks accepted. Prepayment is required.

Oneida County

District & Magistrate Courts 10 Court St, Malad City, ID 83252; 208-766-4285 X111,112,114,105; Fax: 208-766-2990. Hours: 9AM-5PM (MST). *Felony, Misdemeanor, Civil, Eviction, Small Claims, Probate.*

Civil Records: Access: Phone, fax, mail, in person. Both court and visitors may perform in person searches. No search fee. Required to search: name, years to search; also helpful: address. Civil cases indexed by case number, defendant, plaintiff. Civil records on computer from 07/90, archives from 1886.

Criminal Records: Access: Phone, fax, mail, in person. Both court and visitors may perform in person searches. No search fee. Required to search: name, years to search; also helpful: address, DOB, SSN. Criminal records on computer from 07/90, archives from 1886.

General Information: No juvenile, adoption records released. SASE requested. Turnaround time 1-2 days. Fax notes: $1.00 per page. Copy fee: $1.00 per page. Certification fee: $1.00. Fee payee: Clerk of Court. Personal checks accepted. Prepayment is required.

Owyhee County

District & Magistrate Courts-I Courthouse, PO Box 128, Murphy, ID 83650; 208-495-2806; Fax: 208-495-1226. Hours: 8:30AM-5PM (MST). *Felony, Misdemeanor, Civil, Eviction, Small Claims, Probate.*

http://owyheecounty.net/court/index.htm

Civil Records: Access: Mail, in person. Both court and visitors may perform in person searches. Search fee: $6.00 per name found. Required to search: name, years to search. Civil cases indexed by defendant, plaintiff. Civil records on computer from 1992, archives from 1800s.

Criminal Records: Access: Fax, mail, in person. Both court and visitors may perform in person searches. Search fee: $6.00 per name found. Required to search: name, years to search; also helpful: DOB. Criminal records on computer from 1992, archives from 1800s. Signed release required for search of juvenile records.

General Information: No adoption, juvenile (except for some that are open), domestic violence records released. Include $.37 for return postage. Turnaround time 5-7 days. Fax notes: Fee to fax results is $1.00 per page (copies) and $5.00 per document. Copy fee: $1.00 per page. Certification fee: $1.00 per page. Fee payee: Owyhee County. Only cashiers checks and money orders accepted. Prepayment is required.

Homedale Magistrate Court 31 W Wyoming, Homedale, ID 83628-3402; 208-337-4540; Fax: 208-337-3035. Hours: 8:30AM-5PM (MST). *Misdemeanor, Civil Actions Under $10,000, Eviction, Small Claims.*

http://owyheecounty.net/court/index.htm

Civil Records: Access: In person only. Only the court performs in person searches; visitors may not. No search fee. Required to search: name, years to search; also helpful: address. Civil cases indexed by defendant. Civil records on computer from 1992, archives from 1975.

Criminal Records: Access: In person only. Only the court performs in person searches; visitors may not. No search fee. Required to search: name, years to search; also helpful: address, DOB, SSN. Criminal records on computer from 1992, archives from 1975.

General Information: No juvenile or mental records released. Fax notes: $5.00 each 1st 2 pages, $2.00 pages 3-10; $.75 each add'l. Copy fee: $1.00 per page. Certification fee: $1.00 per document. Fee payee: Clerk of Court. Prepayment is required.

Payette County

District & Magistrate Courts 1130 3rd Ave N, Payette, ID 83661; 208-642-6000 (Dist) 642-6010(Magis); Fax: 208-642-6011. Hours: 9AM-5PM (MST). *Felony, Misdemeanor, Civil, Eviction, Small Claims, Probate.*

Civil Records: Access: Fax, mail, in person. Both court and visitors may perform in person searches. Search fee: $5.00 per name. Required to search: name, years to search; also helpful: address. Civil cases indexed by defendant, plaintiff. Civil records on computer back to 1992, prior on microfiche or archived from 1917.

Criminal Records: Access: Fax, mail, in person. Both court and visitors may perform in person searches. Search fee: $5.00 per name. Required to search: name, years to search, signed release; also helpful: address, DOB, SSN. Criminal records on computer back to 1992, prior microfiche or archived from 1917.

General Information: Public access terminal is available. No juvenile, adoption records released. SASE required. Turnaround time 1 day. Fax notes: $3.00 1st page, $.50 each add'l. Copy fee: $1.00 per page. Certification fee: $1.00. Fee payee: Clerk of Court. Personal checks accepted. Prepayment is required.

Power County

District & Magistrate Courts 543 Bannock Ave, American Falls, ID 83211; 208-226-7611 (Dist) 226-7618(Magistrate); Fax: 208-226-7612. Hours: 9AM-5PM (MST). *Felony, Misdemeanor, Civil, Eviction, Small Claims, Probate.*

Civil Records: Access: Phone, fax, mail, in person. Both the court and visitors may perform in person searches. Search fee is $5.00. Required to search: name, years to search. Civil cases indexed by defendant. Civil records on computer from 1986, prior archived from early 1900s.

Criminal Records: Access: Phone, fax, mail, in person. Both the court and visitors may perform in person searches. Search fee is $5.00. Required to search: name, years to search, DOB, SSN, signed release. Criminal records on computer from 1986, prior archived from early 1900s.

General Information: Public access terminal is available. No juvenile, mental commitment records released. SASE required. Turnaround time 10 days. Fax notes: Fee to fax results is $1.00 per page. Copy fee: $1.00 per page. Certification fee: $1.50. Fee payee: Power County Magistrate Court. Personal checks accepted. Prepayment is required.

Shoshone County

District & Magistrate Courts 700 Bank St, Wallace, ID 83873; 208-752-1266; Fax: 208-753-0921. Hours: 9AM-5PM (PST). *Felony, Misdemeanor, Civil, Eviction, Small Claims, Probate.*

Civil Records: Access: Phone, fax, mail, in person. Both court and visitors may perform in person searches. No search fee. Required to search: name, years to search; also helpful: address. Civil cases indexed by defendant, plaintiff. Civil records on computer from 1988, archives from 1971. Juvenile case information not available by fax.

Criminal Records: Access: Phone, mail, in person. Both court and visitors may perform in person searches. No search fee. Required to search: name, years to search; also helpful: address, DOB, SSN. Criminal records on computer from 1988, archives from 1971.

General Information: Public access terminal is available. (For records since 1995.) No special proceeding, juvenile records released. SASE required. Turnaround time 1-2 days. Fax notes: $2.00 for first page, $1.00 each add'l. Add $1.00 1st page if long distance. Copy fee: $1.00 per page. Certification fee: $1.00. Fee payee: Clerk of Court. Personal checks accepted. Prepayment is required.

Teton County

District & Magistrate Courts 89 N Main #5, Driggs, ID 83422; 208-354-2239; Fax: 208-354-8496. Hours: 9AM-5PM (MST). *Felony, Misdemeanor, Civil, Eviction, Small Claims, Probate.*

Note: Address and telephone given above are for District Court. If you wish to access only the Magistrate Court and call 208-354-2239.

Civil Records: Access: Phone, fax, mail, in person. Both court and visitors may perform in person searches. Search fee: $5.00 per name. Required to search: name, years to search; also helpful: address. Civil cases indexed by defendant, plaintiff. Civil records on computer from 1992, archives from 1974, I-Star since 1992.

Criminal Records: Access: Phone, fax, mail, in person. Both court and visitors may perform in person searches. Search fee: $5.00 per name. Required to search: name, years to search; also helpful: address, DOB, SSN. Criminal records on computer from 1992, archives from 1974, I-Star since 1993.

General Information: Public access terminal is available. No juvenile, DV records released. SASE required. Turnaround time 3 days. Fax notes: $2.00 per page. Copy fee: $1.00 per page. Certification fee: $1.00. Fee payee: Clerk of Court. Personal checks accepted. Prepayment is required.

Twin Falls County

District & Magistrate Courts PO Box 126, Twin Falls, ID 83303-0126; 208-736-4013; Fax: 208-736-4155. Hours: 8AM-5PM (MST). *Felony, Misdemeanor, Civil, Eviction, Small Claims, Probate.*

www.co.twin-falls.id.us/5thdistrict

Civil Records: Access: Phone, fax, mail, in person. Both court and visitors may perform in person searches. No search fee. Required to search: name, years to search; also helpful: address. Civil cases indexed by defendant, plaintiff. Civil records on computer from 1989, archives from early 1900s.

Criminal Records: Access: Phone, fax, mail, in person. Both court and visitors may perform in person searches. No search fee. Required to search: name, years to search; also helpful: address, DOB, SSN. Criminal records on computer from 1989, archives from early 1900s.

General Information: Public access terminal is available. No adoption, termination, juvenile records released. Turnaround time 1-10 days. Fax notes: $2.50 per page. Copy fee: $1.00 per page. Certification fee: $1.00 per page. Fee payee: Court Services. Personal checks accepted. Prepayment is required.

Valley County

District & Magistrate Courts-I PO Box 1350, Cascade, ID 83611; 208-382-7178; Fax: 208-382-7184. Hours: 8AM-5PM (MST). *Felony, Misdemeanor, Civil, Eviction, Small Claims, Probate.*

Civil Records: Access: Phone, fax, mail, in person. Both court and visitors may perform in person searches.

Search fee: $5.00. Required to search: name, years to search; also helpful: address. Civil cases indexed by defendant, plaintiff. Civil records on computer from 1990, microfiche and archives from early 1900s.

Criminal Records: Access: Phone, fax, mail, in person. Both court and visitors may perform in person searches. Search fee: $5.00. Required to search: name, years to search; also helpful: address, DOB, SSN. Criminal records on computer from 1990, microfiche and archives from early 1900s.

General Information: Public access terminal is available. No juvenile records released. SASE required. Turnaround time 1-3 days. Fax notes: No fee to fax results. Copy fee: $1.00 per page. Certification fee: $1.50 per page. Fee payee: Valley County. Personal checks accepted. Two-party or out of country (w/o printed-stamped US Funds) not accepted. Prepayment is required.

Magistrate Court II Valley County Courthouse Annex, 550 Deinhard Lane, McCall, ID 83638; 208-634-8102; Fax: 208-634-4040. Hours: 9AM-5PM (MST). *Misdemeanor, Civil Actions Under $10,000, Eviction, Small Claims.*

Civil Records: Access: Phone, fax, mail, in person. Only the court performs in person searches; visitors may not. No search fee. Required to search: name, years to search; also helpful: address. Civil cases indexed by defendant. Civil records on computer from 1990, archives from 1984.

Criminal Records: Access: Phone, fax, mail, in person. Only the court performs in person searches; visitors may not. No search fee. Required to search: name, years to search; also helpful: address, DOB, SSN. Criminal records on computer from 1990, archives from 1984.

General Information: No juvenile records released. SASE required. Turnaround time 1-5 days. Fax notes: $5.00 for first page, $2.00 each add'l. Copy fee: $1.00 per page. Certification fee: $1.00 per page. Fee payee: McCall Court. Personal checks accepted.

Washington County

District & Magistrate Courts PO Box 670, Weiser, ID 83672; 208-414-2092; Fax: 208-414-3925. Hours: 8:30AM-5PM (MST). *Felony, Misdemeanor, Civil, Eviction, Small Claims, Probate.*

www.the3rdjudicialdistrict.com

Civil Records: Access: In person only. Visitors must perform in person searches for themselves. No search fee. Required to search: name. Civil cases indexed by defendant, plaintiff. Civil records on computer from 02/90, archives from late 1800s.

Criminal Records: Access: In person only. Visitors must perform in person searches for themselves. No search fee. Required to search: name, years to search, DOB. Criminal records on computer from 02/90, archives from late 1800s.

General Information: Public access terminal is available. No juvenile, adoption, hospitalization, child protection-termination of parental rights records released. Copy fee: $1.00 per page. Certification fee: $1.00. Fee payee: Washington County. Local business checks only. Prepayment is required.

Idaho Recording Offices

ORGANIZATION: 44 counties, 44 recording offices. The recording officer is County Recorder. Many counties utilize a grantor/grantee index containing all transactions recorded with them. 34 counties are in the Mountain Time Zone (MST), and 10 are in the Pacific Time Zone (PST).

REAL ESTATE RECORDS: Most counties will not perform real estate name searches. Certification of copies usually costs $1.00 per document.

UCC RECORDS: Financing statements are filed at the state level except for real estate related filings. All counties will perform UCC searches. Use search request form UCC-4. Search fees are usually $6.00 per debtor name for a listing of filings and $12.00 per debtor name for a listing plus copies at no additional charge. Separately ordered copies usually cost $1.00 per page.

TAX LIEN RECORDS: Until 07/01/98, state tax liens were filed at the local county recorder. Now they are filed with the Secretary of State who has all active case files. Federal tax liens on personal property of businesses are filed with the Secretary of State. Other federal tax liens are filed with the county recorder. Some counties will perform a combined tax lien search for $5.00 while others will not perform tax lien searches.

OTHER LIENS: Judgments, hospital, labor, mechanics.

ONLINE ACCESS: Two counties have web access to assessor records. The Secretary of State's office offers online access to UCCs.

Ada County

County Clerk & Recorder, 200 W Front St, Boise, ID 83702. 208-364-2223 R/E Recording: 208-364-2222 UCC Recording: 208-364-2225.
Will search UCC records. UCC search includes tax liens if requested. Will not search real estate records. **Online Access:** Assessor, Property Records. Search the property assessor database for free at www.adacountyassessor.org. **Other Phone Numbers:** Assessor 208-364-2400; Treasurer 208-364-2233; Elections 208-364-2323; Vital Records 208-334-5980.

Adams County

County Clerk & Recorder, PO Box 48, Council, ID 83612. 208-253-4561; Fax 208-253-4880.
Will search UCC records. This agency will not do a tax lien search. Will not search real estate records. **Other Phone Numbers:** Assessor 208-253-4271; Treasurer 208-253-4263.

Bannock County

County Clerk & Recorder, 624 E. Center, Courthouse, Room 211, Pocatello, ID 83201. County Clerk & Recorder, R/E and UCC Recording 208-236-7340; Fax 208-236-7345.
Will search UCC records. UCC search includes tax liens if requested. Will not search real estate records. **Other Phone Numbers:** Assessor 208-236-7260.

Bear Lake County

County Clerk & Recorder, PO Box 190, Paris, ID 83261. County Clerk & Recorder, R/E and UCC Recording 208-945-2212; Fax 208-945-2780.
Will search UCC records. Tax liens not included in UCC search. Mortgage searches available. **Other Phone Numbers:** Assessor 208-945-2155; Treasurer 208-945-2130; Elections 208-945-2212; Vital Records 208-945-2212.

Benewah County

County Clerk & Recorder, 701 College, St. Maries, ID 83861. County Clerk & Recorder, R/E and UCC Recording 208-245-3212; Fax 208-245-3046.
Will search UCC records. This agency will not do a tax lien search. Will not search real estate records. **Other Phone Numbers:** Assessor 208-245-2821; Treasurer 208-245-2421.

Bingham County

County Clerk & Recorder, 501 N. Maple #205, Blackfoot, ID 83221. 208-785-5005; Fax 208-785-4131.
Will search UCC records. UCC search includes tax liens if requested. Will not search real estate records. **Other Phone Numbers:** Assessor 208-785-5005 x216; Treasurer 208-785-5005 x259.

Blaine County

County Clerk & Recorder, Courthouse, Suite 200, 206 1st Ave. South, Hailey, ID 83333. County Clerk & Recorder, R/E and UCC Recording 208-788-5505; Fax 208-788-5501. www.co.blaine.id.us
Will search UCC records. UCC search includes tax liens if requested. Mortgage searches available. **Other Phone Numbers:** Assessor 208-788-5535; Treasurer 208-788-5530; Appraiser/Auditor 208-788-5535; Elections 208-788-5510.

Boise County

County Clerk & Recorder, PO Box 1300, Idaho City, ID 83631. County Clerk & Recorder, R/E and UCC Recording 208-392-4431; Fax 208-392-4473.
Will search UCC records. This agency will not do a tax lien search. Real estate owner, mortgage, and property transfer searches available. **Other Phone Numbers:** Assessor 208-392-4415; Treasurer 208-392-4441; Appraiser 208-392-4415; Elections 208-392-4431.

Bonner County

County Clerk & Recorder, 215 S. First, Sandpoint, ID 83864. 208-265-1432; Fax 208-265-1447.
Will search UCC records. This agency will not do a tax lien search. Will not search real estate records. **Other Phone Numbers:** Assessor 208-265-1440; Treasurer 208-265-1433.

Bonneville County

County Clerk & Recorder, 605 N. Capital, Idaho Falls, ID 83402-3582. 208-529-1350 R/E Recording: 208-529-1350 x1350 UCC Recording: 208-529-1350 x1350; Fax 208-529-1353. www.co.bonneville.id.us
Will search UCC records. Tax liens not included in UCC search. Will not search real estate records. **Other Phone Numbers:** Assessor 208-529-1350 x1320; Treasurer 208-529-1350 x1380; Elections 208-529-1350 x1363; Vital Records 208-529-1350 x1350.

Boundary County

County Clerk & Recorder, PO Box 419, Bonners Ferry, ID 83805. 208-267-2242; Fax 208-267-7814. www.boundary-idaho.com
Will search UCC records. This agency will not do a tax lien search. Will not search real estate records. **Other Phone Numbers:** Assessor 208-267-3301; Treasurer 208-267-3291.

Butte County

County Clerk & Recorder, PO Box 737, Arco, ID 83213. 208-527-3021 UCC Recording: 208-527-3012; Fax 208-527-3295.
Will not search UCC records. Real estate owner, mortgage, and property transfer searches available. **Other Phone Numbers:** Assessor 208-527-8288; Treasurer 208-527-3047.

Camas County

County Clerk & Recorder, PO Box 430, Fairfield, ID 83327-0430. County Clerk & Recorder, R/E and UCC Recording 208-764-2242; Fax 208-764-2349.
Will search UCC records. This agency will not do a tax lien search. Will not search real estate records. **Other Phone Numbers:** Assessor 208-764-2370; Treasurer 208-764-2126; Appraiser/Auditor 208-764-2370; Elections 208-764-2242; Vital Records 208-764-2242.

Canyon County

County Recorder, 1115 Albany St, Caldwell, ID 83605. County Recorder, R/E and UCC Recording 208-454-7556; www.canyoncounty.org
Will search UCC records. Tax liens not included in UCC search. Will not search real estate records. **Online Access:** Assessor, Property Records. Access to the Assessor and Treasurer's databases requires $35 registration/setup fee and 150 yearly fee. For subscription info, email clane@canyoncounty.org or call 208-454-7401 or visit the web site. **Other Phones:** Assessor 208-454-7431; Treasurer 208-454-7354; Elections 208-454-7562; Vital Records 208-334-5980.

Caribou County

County Clerk & Recorder, PO Box 775, Soda Springs, ID 83276-0775. County Clerk & Recorder, R/E and UCC Recording 208-547-4324; Fax 208-547-4759.
Will search UCC records. UCC search includes tax liens if requested. Will not search real estate records. **Other Phone Numbers:** Assessor 208-547-4749; Treasurer 208-547-3726.

Cassia County

County Clerk & Recorder, 1459 Overland Ave., Room 105, Burley, ID 83318. County Clerk & Recorder, R/E and UCC Recording 208-878-5240; Fax 208-878-1003. www.cassiacounty.org
Will search UCC records. Tax liens not included in UCC search. Will search real estate records. **Other Phone Numbers:** Assessor 208-878-3540; Treasurer 208-878-7202; Appraiser/Auditor 208-878-3540; Elections 208-878-5240; Vital Records 208-878-5240.

Clark County

County Clerk & Recorder, PO Box 205, Dubois, ID 83423. 208-374-5304; Fax 208-374-5609.
Will search UCC records. UCC search includes tax liens if requested. Will not search real estate records. **Other Phone Numbers:** Assessor 208-374-5404.

Clearwater County

County Clerk & Recorder, PO Box 586, Orofino, ID 83544-0586. 208-476-5615 R/E Recording: 208-476-5616 UCC Recording: 208-476-5616; Fax 208-476-9315.
Will search UCC records. This agency will not do a tax lien search. Property transfer searches available. **Other Phone Numbers:** Assessor 208-476-4912; Treasurer 208-476-5213; Appraiser/Auditor 208-476-4912; Elections 208-476-5615; Vital Records 208-476-5615.

Custer County

County Clerk & Recorder, PO Box 385, Challis, ID 83226. 208-879-2360; Fax 208-879-5246.
Will search UCC records. UCC search includes tax liens if requested. Will not search real estate records. **Other Phone Numbers:** Assessor 208-879-2325; Treasurer 208-879-2330.

Elmore County

County Clerk & Recorder, 150 S. 4th East, Suite #3, Mountain Home, ID 83647-3097. County Clerk & Recorder, R/E and UCC Recording 208-587-2130; Fax 208-587-2159.
Will search UCC records. This agency will not do a tax lien search. Will not search real estate records. **Other Phone Numbers:** Assessor 208-587-2126; Treasurer 208-587-2138; Appraiser/Auditor 208-587-2126; Elections 208-587-2130; Vital Records 208-587-2130.

Franklin County

County Clerk & Recorder, 39 W. Oneida, Preston, ID 83263. County Clerk & Recorder, R/E and UCC Recording 208-852-1090; Fax 208-852-1094.
Will search UCC records. This agency will not do a tax lien search. Will not search real estate records. **Other Phone Numbers:** Assessor 208-852-1091; Treasurer 208-852-1095; Appraiser/Auditor 208-852-1091; Elections 208-852-1090.

Fremont County

County Clerk & Recorder, 151 W. 1st N. Room 12, St. Anthony, ID 83445. County Clerk & Recorder, R/E and UCC Recording 208-624-3148; Fax 208-624-7335. www.co.fremont.id.us/departments/index.htm
Will search UCC records. Tax liens not included in UCC search. Will not search real estate records. **Other Phone Numbers:** Assessor 208-624-7894; Treasurer 208-624-3361; Appraiser/Auditor 208-624-7984; Elections 208-624-7332; Vital Records 208-624-3148; Commissioners 208-624-4271.

Gem County

County Clerk & Recorder, 415 E. Main, Emmett, ID 83617. County Clerk & Recorder, R/E and UCC Recording 208-365-4561; Fax 208-365-6172.
Will search UCC records. Tax liens not included in UCC search. Will not search real estate records. **Other Phone Numbers:** Assessor 208-365-2982; Treasurer 208-365-3272; Appraiser/Auditor 208-365-2982 208-365-4561; Elections 208-365-4561; Vital Records 208-334-5980.

Gooding County

County Clerk & Recorder, PO Box 417, Gooding, ID 83330. 208-934-4841; Fax 208-934-5085.
Will search UCC records. Tax liens not included in UCC search. Will not search real estate records. **Other Phone Numbers:** Assessor 208-934-5666; Treasurer 208-935-5673.

Idaho County

County Clerk & Recorder, 320 W. Main, Room 5, Grangeville, ID 83530. 208-983-2751; Fax 208-983-1428.
Will search UCC records. This agency will not do a tax lien search. Will not search real estate records. **Other Phone Numbers:** Assessor 208-983-2742; Treasurer 208-983-2801.

Jefferson County

County Clerk & Recorder, PO Box 275, Rigby, ID 83442. 208-745-7756; Fax 208-745-6636.
Will search UCC records. This agency will not do a tax lien search. Will not search real estate records. **Other Phone Numbers:** Assessor 208-745-9215; Treasurer 208-745-9219.

Jerome County

County Clerk & Recorder, 300 N. Lincoln, Courthouse, Room 301, Jerome, ID 83338. 208-324-8811 R/E Recording: 208-324-8811 x114 UCC Recording: 208-324-8811 x114; Fax 208-324-2719.
Will search UCC records. State tax liens filed at Secretary of State. Will not search real estate records. **Other Phone Numbers:** Assessor 208-324-8811 x17; Treasurer 208-324-8811 x72.

Kootenai County

County Clerk & Recorder, PO Box 9000, Coeur d'Alene, ID 83816-9000. 208-666-8162; www.co.kootenai.id.us/default.asp
Will search UCC records. This agency will not do a tax lien search. Will not search real estate records. **Online Access:** Property, Recording, Unclaimed Property Records. Access to the county mapping/recording database is available for free at www.co.kootenai.id.us/departments/mapping. No name searching. **Other Phone Numbers:** Assessor 208-769-4400 x459; Treasurer 208-769-4400 x146.

Latah County

County Clerk & Recorder, PO Box 8068, Moscow, ID 83843-0568. 208-882-8580 x379 R/E Recording: 208-882-8580 x3379 UCC Recording: 208-882-8580 x3379; Fax 208-883-7203. www.latah.id.us
Will search UCC records. This agency will not do a tax lien search. Will not search real estate records. **Other Phone Numbers:** Assessor 208-882-8580 x3306; Treasurer 208-882-8580 x3343; Appraiser/Auditor 208-882-8580 x3516; Elections 208-883-2278; Vital Records 208-334-5980 (Boise).

Lemhi County

County Clerk & Recorder, 206 Courthouse Drive, Salmon, ID 83467. County Clerk & Recorder, R/E and UCC Recording 208-756-2815; Fax 208-756-8424.
Will search UCC records. UCC search includes tax liens if requested. Will not search real estate records. **Other Phone Numbers:** Assessor 208-756-3116; Treasurer 208-756-2816; Appraiser/Auditor 208-756-3116; Elections 208-756-2815; Vital Records 208-756-2815.

Lewis County

County Clerk & Recorder, PO Box 39, Nezperce, ID 83543. 208-937-2661; Fax 208-937-9234.
Will search UCC records. Tax liens not included in UCC search. Will not search real estate records. **Other Phone Numbers:** Assessor 208-937-2261; Treasurer 208-937-2341; Elections 208-937-2661.

Lincoln County

County Clerk & Recorder, PO Drawer A, Shoshone, ID 83352-2774. County Clerk & Recorder, R/E and UCC Recording 208-886-7641; Fax 208-886-2707.
Will search UCC records. Tax liens not included in UCC search. Will not search real estate records. **Other Phone Numbers:** Assessor 208-886-2161; Treasurer 208-886-7681; Elections 208-886-7641; Vital Records 208-886-7641.

Madison County

County Clerk & Recorder, PO Box 389, Rexburg, ID 83440. County Clerk & Recorder, R/E and UCC Recording 208-356-3662; Fax 208-356-8396. www.co.madison.id.us
Will search UCC records. UCC search includes tax liens. Will not search real estate records. **Other Phone Numbers:** Assessor 208-356-3071; Treasurer 208-356-6871.

Minidoka County

County Clerk & Recorder, PO Box 368, Rupert, ID 83350-0474. County Clerk & Recorder, R/E and UCC Recording 208-436-9511; Fax 208-436-0737.
Will search UCC records. This agency will not do a tax lien search. Will not search real estate records. **Other Phone Numbers:** Assessor 208-436-7181; Treasurer 208-436-7188; Appraiser/Auditor 208-436-7181; Elections 208-436-9511.

Nez Perce County

County Clerk & Recorder, PO Box 896, Lewiston, ID 83501-0896. 208-799-3020; Fax 208-799-3070. www.co.nezperce.id.us
Will search UCC records. Tax liens not included in UCC search. Will not search real estate records. **Other Phone Numbers:** Assessor 208-799-3010; Treasurer 208-799-3030; Elections 208-799-3020; Vital Records 208-799-3020.

Oneida County

County Clerk & Recorder, 10 Court St, Malad, ID 83252. 208-766-4116 x100 R/E Recording: 208-76-4116 x100 or 102 UCC Recording: 208-76-4116 x100 or 102; Fax 208-766-2448.
Will search UCC records. This agency will not do a tax lien search. Will not search real estate records. **Other Phone Numbers:** Assessor 208-766-2954; Treasurer 208-766-2962; Appraiser/Auditor 208-766-4116 x109, 106 or 116; Elections 208-76-4116 x100 or 102.

Owyhee County

County Clerk & Recorder, PO Box 128, Murphy, ID 83650. County Clerk & Recorder, R/E and UCC Recording 208-495-2421; Fax 208-495-1173.
Will search UCC records. UCC search includes tax liens if requested. Will not search real estate records. **Other Phone Numbers:** Assessor 208-495-2817; Treasurer 208-495-1158; Elections 208-495-2421; Vital Records 208-495-2421.

Payette County

County Clerk & Recorder, PO Drawer D, Payette, ID 83661. County Clerk & Recorder, R/E and UCC Recording 208-642-6000; Fax 208-642-6011. www.payettecounty.com
Will search UCC records. This agency will not do a tax lien search. Will not search real estate records. **Other Phone Numbers:** Assessor 208-642-6012; Treasurer 208-642-6005; Appraiser/Auditor 208-642-6012; Elections 208-642-6000.

Power County

County Clerk & Recorder, 543 Bannock, American Falls, ID 83211. County Clerk & Recorder, R/E and UCC Recording 208-226-7611; Fax 208-226-7612. www.co.power.id.us
Will search UCC records. UCC search includes tax liens if requested. Will not search real estate records. **Other Phone Numbers:** Assessor 208-226-7616; Treasurer 208-226-7614; Elections 208-226-7611; Vital Records 208-226-7611.

Shoshone County

County Clerk & Recorder, Courthouse, Suite 120, 700 Bank St., Wallace, ID 83873-2348. County Clerk & Recorder, R/E and UCC Recording 208-752-1264; Fax 208-753-2711.
Will search UCC records. This agency will not do a tax lien search. Will not search real estate records. **Other Phone Numbers:** Assessor 208-752-1202; Treasurer 208-752-1261; Appraiser/Auditor 208-752-1202; Elections 208-752-1264; Vital Records 208-752-1264.

Teton County

County Clerk & Recorder, 89 N. Main #1, Driggs, ID 83422. County Clerk & Recorder, R/E and UCC Recording 208-354-2905; Fax 208-354-8410.
Will search UCC records. UCC search includes tax liens. Real estate owner, mortgage, and property transfer searches available. **Other Phones:** Assessor 208-354-2938; Treasurer 208-354-2254; Appraiser/Auditor 208-354-3507; Elections 208-354-2905.

Twin Falls County

County Clerk & Recorder, PO Box 126, Twin Falls, ID 83303-0126. 208-736-4004; Fax 208-736-4182.
Will search UCC records. Tax liens not included in UCC search. Will not search real estate records. **Other Phone Numbers:** Assessor 208-736-4010; Treasurer 208-736-4008.

Valley County

County Clerk & Recorder, PO Box 1350, Cascade, ID 83611-1350. 208-382-7100; Fax 208-382-7107.
Will search UCC records. This agency will not do a tax lien search. Will not search real estate records. **Other Phone Numbers:** Assessor 208-382-7126; Treasurer 208-382-7110.

Washington County

County Clerk & Recorder, PO Box 670, Weiser, ID 83672-0670. 208-549-2092 R/E Recording: 208-414-2092 UCC Recording: 208-414-2092; Fax 208-549-3925. www.ruralnetwork.net/~wcassr/clerk.htm
Will search UCC records. This agency will not do a tax lien search. Will not search real estate records. **Other Phone Numbers:** Assessor 208-549-2000; Treasurer 208-549-0324; Appraiser/Auditor 208-414-2000; Elections 208-414-2092; Vital Records 208-414-2092 (1907-1911 only); Vital Statistics (Boise, ID) 288-334-5988.

Idaho County Locator

You will usually be able to find the city name in the City/County Cross Reference below. In that case, it is a simple matter to determine the county from the cross reference. However, only the official US Postal Service city names are included in this index. There are an additional 40,000 place names that people use in their addresses. Therefore, we have also included a ZIP/City Cross Reference immediately following the City/County Cross Reference.

If you know the ZIP Code but the city name does not appear in the City/County Cross Reference index, look up the ZIP Code in the ZIP/City Cross Reference, find the city name, then look up the city name in the City/County Cross Reference. For example, you want to know the county for an address of Menands, NY 12204. There is no "Menands" in the City/County Cross Reference. The ZIP/City Cross Reference shows that ZIP Codes 12201-12288 are for the city of Albany. Looking back in the City/County Cross Reference, Albany is in Albany County.

City/County Cross Reference

ABERDEEN Bingham
AHSAHKA Clearwater
ALBION Cassia
ALMO Cassia
AMERICAN FALLS Power
ARBON Power
ARCO Butte
ARIMO Bannock
ASHTON Fremont
ATHOL (83801) Kootenai(90), Bonner(9)
ATLANTA Elmore
ATOMIC CITY Bingham
AVERY Shoshone
BANCROFT Caribou
BANKS Boise
BASALT Bingham
BAYVIEW (83803) Bonner(64), Kootenai(35)
BELLEVUE Blaine
BERN Bear Lake
BLACKFOOT Bingham
BLANCHARD Bonner
BLISS Gooding
BLOOMINGTON Bear Lake
BOISE Ada
BONNERS FERRY Boundary
BOVILL Latah
BRUNEAU Owyhee
BUHL Twin Falls
BURLEY Cassia
CALDER Shoshone
CALDWELL (83607) Canyon(94), Payette(3), Gem(1)
CAMBRIDGE Washington
CAREY Blaine
CAREYWOOD Bonner
CARMEN Lemhi
CASCADE Valley
CASTLEFORD Twin Falls
CATALDO (83810) Kootenai(98), Shoshone(1)
CHALLIS (83226) Custer(98), Lemhi(1)
CHESTER Fremont
CLARK FORK Bonner
CLARKIA Shoshone
CLAYTON Custer
CLIFTON Franklin
COBALT Lemhi
COCOLALLA Bonner
COEUR D ALENE Kootenai
COLBURN Bonner
CONDA Caribou
COOLIN Bonner
CORRAL Camas
COTTONWOOD Idaho
COUNCIL Adams
CRAIGMONT Lewis
CULDESAC (83524) Nez Perce(96), Lewis(3)
DAYTON Franklin
DEARY Latah
DECLO Cassia
DESMET Benewah
DIETRICH Lincoln
DINGLE Bear Lake
DONNELLY Valley
DOVER Bonner
DOWNEY Bannock
DRIGGS Teton

DUBOIS Clark
EAGLE Ada
EASTPORT Boundary
EDEN Jerome
ELBA Cassia
ELK CITY Idaho
ELK RIVER Clearwater
ELLIS (83235) Custer(81), Lemhi(18)
EMMETT Gem
FAIRFIELD Camas
FELT Teton
FENN Idaho
FERDINAND Idaho
FERNWOOD Benewah
FILER Twin Falls
FIRTH Bingham
FISH HAVEN Bear Lake
FORT HALL Bingham
FRANKLIN Franklin
FRUITLAND Payette
FRUITVALE Adams
GARDEN VALLEY Boise
GENESEE (83832) Latah(58), Nez Perce(41)
GENEVA Bear Lake
GEORGETOWN Bear Lake
GIBBONSVILLE Lemhi
GLENNS FERRY Elmore
GOODING Gooding
GRACE Caribou
GRAND VIEW (83624) Owyhee(95), Elmore(4)
GRANGEVILLE Idaho
GREENCREEK Idaho
GREENLEAF Canyon
HAGERMAN (83332) Gooding(82), Twin Falls(17)
HAILEY Blaine
HAMER Jefferson
HAMMETT (83627) Elmore(98), Owyhee(1)
HANSEN Twin Falls
HARRISON Kootenai
HARVARD Latah
HAYDEN Kootenai
HAZELTON Jerome
HEADQUARTERS Clearwater
HEYBURN (83336) Minidoka(77), Cassia(22)
HILL CITY Camas
HOLBROOK Oneida
HOMEDALE Owyhee
HOPE Bonner
HORSESHOE BEND (83629) Boise(91), Gem(8)
HOWE Butte
HUSTON Canyon
IDAHO CITY Boise
IDAHO FALLS Bonneville
INDIAN VALLEY (83632) Adams(90), Washington(10)
INKOM Bannock
IONA Bonneville
IRWIN Bonneville
ISLAND PARK Fremont
JEROME (83338) Jerome(98), Gooding(1)
JULIAETTA (83535) Latah(91), Nez Perce(8)
KAMIAH (83536) Idaho(76), Lewis(23)
KELLOGG Shoshone

KENDRICK (83537) Nez Perce(72), Latah(23), Clearwater(4)
KETCHUM (83340) Blaine(98), Custer(1)
KIMBERLY Twin Falls
KING HILL Elmore
KINGSTON Shoshone
KOOSKIA Idaho
KOOTENAI Bonner
KUNA (83634) Ada(95), Canyon(4)
LACLEDE Bonner
LAKE FORK Valley
LAPWAI Nez Perce
LAVA HOT SPRINGS Bannock
LEADORE (83464) Lemhi(97), Clark(2)
LEMHI Lemhi
LENORE (83541) Nez Perce(52), Clearwater(47)
LETHA Gem
LEWISTON Nez Perce
LEWISVILLE Jefferson
LOWMAN Boise
LUCILE Idaho
MACKAY Custer
MACKS INN Fremont
MALAD CITY Oneida
MALTA Cassia
MARSING Owyhee
MAY (83253) Lemhi(86), Custer(13)
MC CALL (83638) Valley(96), Adams(2)
MC CAMMON Bannock
MCCALL (83638) Valley(96), Adams(2)
MEDIMONT Kootenai
MELBA (83641) Canyon(73), Owyhee(14), Ada(12)
MENAN (83434) Jefferson(90), Madison(9)
MERIDIAN Ada
MESA Adams
MIDDLETON Canyon
MIDVALE Washington
MINIDOKA Minidoka
MONTEVIEW Jefferson
MONTPELIER Bear Lake
MOORE (83255) Butte(93), Custer(6)
MORELAND Bingham
MOSCOW Latah
MOUNTAIN HOME Elmore
MOUNTAIN HOME A F B Elmore
MOYIE SPRINGS Boundary
MULLAN Shoshone
MURPHY Owyhee
MURRAY Shoshone
MURTAUGH (83344) Twin Falls(78), Cassia(21)
NAMPA (83687) Canyon(98), Ada(1)
NAPLES Boundary
NEW MEADOWS (83654) Adams(98), Idaho(1)
NEW PLYMOUTH Payette
NEWDALE (83436) Madison(60), Teton(27), Fremont(12)
NEZPERCE Lewis
NORDMAN Bonner
NORTH FORK Lemhi
NOTUS Canyon
OAKLEY Cassia
OLA Gem
OLDTOWN Bonner
OROFINO Clearwater
OSBURN Shoshone

OVID Bear Lake
PALISADES Bonneville
PARIS Bear Lake
PARKER Fremont
PARMA (83660) Canyon(89), Payette(10)
PAUL (83347) Lincoln(57), Minidoka(27), Jerome(14)
PAYETTE Payette
PECK Nez Perce
PICABO Blaine
PIERCE Clearwater
PINEHURST Shoshone
PINGREE Bingham
PLACERVILLE Boise
PLUMMER Benewah
POCATELLO Bannock
POLLOCK (83547) Idaho(80), Adams(20)
PONDERAY Bonner
PORTHILL Boundary
POST FALLS Kootenai
POTLATCH Latah
PRESTON Franklin
PRIEST RIVER Bonner
PRINCETON Latah
RATHDRUM Kootenai
REUBENS (83548) Nez Perce(72), Lewis(28)
REXBURG Madison
RICHFIELD Lincoln
RIGBY Jefferson
RIGGINS Idaho
RIRIE (83443) Bonneville(55), Jefferson(44)
ROBERTS Jefferson
ROCKLAND Power
ROGERSON Twin Falls
RUPERT Minidoka
SAGLE Bonner
SAINT ANTHONY Fremont
SAINT CHARLES Bear Lake
SAINT MARIES (83861) Benewah(87), Kootenai(12)
SALMON Lemhi
SAMUELS Bonner
SANDPOINT Bonner
SANTA Benewah
SHELLEY Bingham
SHOSHONE Lincoln
SHOUP Lemhi
SILVERTON Shoshone
SMELTERVILLE Shoshone
SODA SPRINGS (83276) Caribou(91), Bear Lake(8)
SPALDING Nez Perce
SPENCER Clark
SPIRIT LAKE (83869) Kootenai(72), Bonner(27)
SPRINGFIELD Bingham
SQUIRREL Fremont
STANLEY Custer
STAR (83669) Ada(91), Canyon(8)
STITES Idaho
STONE Oneida
SUGAR CITY (83448) Madison(87), Fremont(12)
SUN VALLEY Blaine
SWAN VALLEY Bonneville
SWANLAKE Bannock
SWEET (83670) Gem(91), Boise(8)

TENDOY Lemhi
TENSED Benewah
TERRETON Jefferson
TETON (83451) Fremont(64), Madison(35)
TETONIA Teton
THATCHER Franklin

TROY Latah
TWIN FALLS Twin Falls
UCON Bonneville
VICTOR Teton
VIOLA Latah
WALLACE Shoshone

WARREN Idaho
WAYAN (83285) Caribou(50),
   Bonneville(49)
WEIPPE Clearwater
WEISER Washington
WENDELL Gooding

WESTON Franklin
WHITE BIRD Idaho
WILDER Canyon
WINCHESTER Lewis
WORLEY Kootenai
YELLOW PINE Valley

ZIP/City Cross Reference

83201-83202 POCATELLO	83326-83326 ELBA	83530-83530 GRANGEVILLE	83670-83670 SWEET
83203-83203 FORT HALL	83327-83327 FAIRFIELD	83531-83531 FENN	83671-83671 WARREN
83204-83209 POCATELLO	83328-83328 FILER	83533-83533 GREENCREEK	83672-83672 WEISER
83210-83210 ABERDEEN	83330-83330 GOODING	83534-83534 HEADQUARTERS	83676-83676 WILDER
83211-83211 AMERICAN FALLS	83332-83332 HAGERMAN	83535-83535 JULIAETTA	83677-83677 YELLOW PINE
83212-83212 ARBON	83333-83333 HAILEY	83536-83536 KAMIAH	83680-83680 MERIDIAN
83213-83213 ARCO	83334-83334 HANSEN	83537-83537 KENDRICK	83686-83687 NAMPA
83214-83214 ARIMO	83335-83335 HAZELTON	83538-83538 COTTONWOOD	83700-83799 BOISE
83215-83215 ATOMIC CITY	83336-83336 HEYBURN	83539-83539 KOOSKIA	83801-83801 ATHOL
83217-83217 BANCROFT	83337-83337 HILL CITY	83540-83540 LAPWAI	83802-83802 AVERY
83218-83218 BASALT	83338-83338 JEROME	83541-83541 LENORE	83803-83803 BAYVIEW
83220-83220 BERN	83340-83340 KETCHUM	83542-83542 LUCILE	83804-83804 BLANCHARD
83221-83221 BLACKFOOT	83341-83341 KIMBERLY	83543-83543 NEZPERCE	83805-83805 BONNERS FERRY
83223-83223 BLOOMINGTON	83342-83342 MALTA	83544-83544 OROFINO	83806-83806 BOVILL
83226-83226 CHALLIS	83343-83343 MINIDOKA	83545-83545 PECK	83808-83808 CALDER
83227-83227 CLAYTON	83344-83344 MURTAUGH	83546-83546 PIERCE	83809-83809 CAREYWOOD
83228-83228 CLIFTON	83346-83346 OAKLEY	83547-83547 POLLOCK	83810-83810 CATALDO
83229-83229 COBALT	83347-83347 PAUL	83548-83548 REUBENS	83811-83811 CLARK FORK
83230-83230 CONDA	83348-83348 PICABO	83549-83549 RIGGINS	83812-83812 CLARKIA
83231-83231 MOORE	83349-83349 RICHFIELD	83551-83551 SPALDING	83813-83813 COCOLALLA
83232-83232 DAYTON	83350-83350 RUPERT	83552-83552 STITES	83814-83816 COEUR D ALENE
83233-83233 DINGLE	83352-83352 SHOSHONE	83553-83553 WEIPPE	83821-83821 COOLIN
83234-83234 DOWNEY	83353-83354 SUN VALLEY	83554-83554 WHITE BIRD	83822-83822 OLDTOWN
83235-83235 ELLIS	83355-83355 WENDELL	83555-83555 WINCHESTER	83823-83823 DEARY
83236-83236 FIRTH	83401-83415 IDAHO FALLS	83601-83601 ATLANTA	83824-83824 DESMET
83237-83237 FRANKLIN	83420-83420 ASHTON	83602-83602 BANKS	83825-83825 DOVER
83238-83238 GENEVA	83421-83421 CHESTER	83604-83604 BRUNEAU	83826-83826 EASTPORT
83239-83239 GEORGETOWN	83422-83422 DRIGGS	83605-83607 CALDWELL	83827-83827 ELK RIVER
83241-83241 GRACE	83423-83423 DUBOIS	83610-83610 CAMBRIDGE	83830-83830 FERNWOOD
83243-83243 HOLBROOK	83424-83424 FELT	83611-83611 CASCADE	83832-83832 GENESEE
83244-83244 HOWE	83425-83425 HAMER	83612-83612 COUNCIL	83833-83833 HARRISON
83245-83245 INKOM	83427-83427 IONA	83615-83615 DONNELLY	83834-83834 HARVARD
83246-83246 LAVA HOT SPRINGS	83428-83428 IRWIN	83616-83616 EAGLE	83835-83835 HAYDEN
83250-83250 MC CAMMON	83429-83429 ISLAND PARK	83617-83617 EMMETT	83836-83836 HOPE
83251-83251 MACKAY	83431-83431 LEWISVILLE	83619-83619 FRUITLAND	83837-83837 KELLOGG
83252-83252 MALAD CITY	83433-83433 MACKS INN	83620-83620 FRUITVALE	83839-83839 KINGSTON
83253-83253 MAY	83434-83434 MENAN	83622-83622 GARDEN VALLEY	83840-83840 KOOTENAI
83254-83254 MONTPELIER	83435-83435 MONTEVIEW	83623-83623 GLENNS FERRY	83841-83841 LACLEDE
83255-83255 MOORE	83436-83436 NEWDALE	83624-83624 GRAND VIEW	83842-83842 MEDIMONT
83256-83256 MORELAND	83437-83437 PALISADES	83626-83626 GREENLEAF	83843-83844 MOSCOW
83260-83260 OVID	83438-83438 PARKER	83627-83627 HAMMETT	83845-83845 MOYIE SPRINGS
83261-83261 PARIS	83440-83441 REXBURG	83628-83628 HOMEDALE	83846-83846 MULLAN
83262-83262 PINGREE	83442-83442 RIGBY	83629-83629 HORSESHOE BEND	83847-83847 NAPLES
83263-83263 PRESTON	83443-83443 RIRIE	83630-83630 HUSTON	83848-83848 NORDMAN
83271-83271 ROCKLAND	83444-83444 ROBERTS	83631-83631 IDAHO CITY	83849-83849 OSBURN
83272-83272 SAINT CHARLES	83445-83445 SAINT ANTHONY	83632-83632 INDIAN VALLEY	83850-83850 PINEHURST
83274-83274 SHELLEY	83446-83446 SPENCER	83633-83633 KING HILL	83851-83851 PLUMMER
83276-83276 SODA SPRINGS	83447-83447 SQUIRREL	83634-83634 KUNA	83852-83852 PONDERAY
83277-83277 SPRINGFIELD	83448-83448 SUGAR CITY	83635-83635 LAKE FORK	83853-83853 PORTHILL
83278-83278 STANLEY	83449-83449 SWAN VALLEY	83636-83636 LETHA	83854-83854 POST FALLS
83280-83280 STONE	83450-83450 TERRETON	83637-83637 LOWMAN	83855-83855 POTLATCH
83281-83281 SWANLAKE	83451-83451 TETON	83638-83638 MC CALL	83856-83856 PRIEST RIVER
83283-83283 THATCHER	83452-83452 TETONIA	83638-83638 MCCALL	83857-83857 PRINCETON
83285-83285 WAYAN	83454-83454 UCON	83639-83639 MARSING	83858-83858 RATHDRUM
83286-83286 WESTON	83455-83455 VICTOR	83641-83641 MELBA	83860-83860 SAGLE
83287-83287 FISH HAVEN	83460-83460 REXBURG	83642-83642 MERIDIAN	83861-83861 SAINT MARIES
83301-83301 TWIN FALLS	83462-83462 CARMEN	83643-83643 MESA	83862-83862 SAMUELS
83302-83302 ROGERSON	83463-83463 GIBBONSVILLE	83644-83644 MIDDLETON	83864-83864 SANDPOINT
83303-83303 TWIN FALLS	83464-83464 LEADORE	83645-83645 MIDVALE	83865-83865 COLBURN
83311-83311 ALBION	83465-83465 LEMHI	83647-83647 MOUNTAIN HOME	83866-83866 SANTA
83312-83312 ALMO	83466-83466 NORTH FORK	83648-83648 MOUNTAIN HOME A F B	83867-83867 SILVERTON
83313-83313 BELLEVUE	83467-83467 SALMON	83650-83650 MURPHY	83868-83868 SMELTERVILLE
83314-83314 BLISS	83468-83468 TENDOY	83651-83653 NAMPA	83869-83869 SPIRIT LAKE
83316-83316 BUHL	83469-83469 SHOUP	83654-83654 NEW MEADOWS	83870-83870 TENSED
83318-83318 BURLEY	83501-83501 LEWISTON	83655-83655 NEW PLYMOUTH	83871-83871 TROY
83320-83320 CAREY	83520-83520 AHSAHKA	83656-83656 NOTUS	83872-83872 VIOLA
83321-83321 CASTLEFORD	83522-83522 COTTONWOOD	83657-83657 OLA	83873-83873 WALLACE
83322-83322 CORRAL	83523-83523 CRAIGMONT	83660-83660 PARMA	83874-83874 MURRAY
83323-83323 DECLO	83524-83524 CULDESAC	83661-83661 PAYETTE	83876-83876 WORLEY
83324-83324 DIETRICH	83525-83525 ELK CITY	83666-83666 PLACERVILLE	83877-83877 POST FALLS
83325-83325 EDEN	83526-83526 FERDINAND	83669-83669 STAR	83888-83888 SANDPOINT

Illinois

General Help Numbers:

Governor's Office
222 S College, 1st Fl
Springfield, IL 62706
www.state.il.us/gov

217-782-0244
Fax 217-524-4049
8:30AM-5PM

Attorney General's Office
500 S 2nd St
Springfield, IL 62706
www.ag.state.il.us

217-782-1090
Fax 217-524-4701
8:45AM-4:45PM

State Court Administrator
222 N. Lasalle - 13th Floor
Chicago, IL 60601

312-793-3250
Fax 312-793-1335
8AM-5PM

State Archives
Archives Division
Norton Bldg, Capitol Complex
Springfield, IL 62756
www.sos.state.il.us/departments
/archives/archives.html

217-782-4682
Fax 217-524-3930
8AM-4:30PM M-F,
8AM-3:30PM SA

State Specifics:

Capital: Springfield
                             Sangamon County

Time Zone: CST

Number of Counties: 102

Population: 12,482,301

Web Site: http://www100.state.il.us

State Agencies

Criminal Records

Illinois State Police, Bureau of Identification, 260 N Chicago St, Joliet, IL 60432-4075; 815-740-5216, 8AM-4PM M-F.

www.isp.state.il.us

Note: Sex offender data is available online at http://samnet.isp.state.il.us/ispso2/sex_offenders/index.asp and may also be available at http://12.17.79.4

Indexing & Storage: Records are available from 1930's on. It takes 1 to 5 days before new records are available for inquiry. Records are indexed on microfilm, index cards, inhouse computer. 61% of all arrests in database have final dispositions recorded, 67% for those arrests within last 5 years.

Searching: Requester must use the state's Uniform Conviction Information Form ISP6-405B signed by person of record. Personal requests are honored per Illinois statute. Include the following in your request: the signed release, name, date of birth, sex, race. Fingerprint cards are an option; a fingerprint search using Form ISP6-404B is recommended in order to assure proper identification. No records are released without a disposition of conviction.

Access by: mail, in person, online.

Fee & Payment: The search fee is $12.00 per form. A fingerprint search is $14.00. Forms are available online at www.isp.state.il.us/ucia0002.html. There is also an automated name search available by modem; see online access below. Fee payee: Illinois State Police. Prepayment required. Modem users and ongoing UCIA requesters must prepay for records in groups of 35 at a time. Personal checks accepted. No credit cards accepted.

Mail search: Turnaround time: 6 to 12 weeks. No self addressed stamped envelope is required.

In person search: An in-person search saves mailing time only.

Online search: Online access costs $7.00 per name. Upon signing an interagency agreement with ISP and establishing a $200 escrow account, users can submit inquiries over modem. Replies with convictions are returned by mail. Clear records can be returned via e-mail, by request. Modem access is available from 7AM-4PM M-F, excluding holidays. Users must utilize LAPLINK version 6.0 or later. For more information on the Modem Porgram, call 815-740-5164.

Corporation Records
Limited Partnership Records
Trade Names
Assumed Name
Limited Liability Company Records

Department of Business Services, Corporate Department, 330 Howlett Bldg, 3rd Floor, Copy Section, Springfield, IL 62756 (Courier: 501 S 2nd St, Springfield, IL 62756); 217-782-7880, 217-782-9521 (Name Availability), 217-782-4528 (Fax), 8AM-4:30PM.

www.sos.state.il.us

Indexing & Storage: Records are available from mid-1800's on. Closed records are stored at the State Archives. Only limited information is available for corporations dissolved before 1986. New records are available for inquiry immediately. Records are indexed on inhouse computer.

Searching: Records are on micro-film from 1984. In-house computer has name of agent, state and date of incorporation, etc. Include the following in your request: full name of business, corporation file number. In addition to the articles of incorporation, corporation records include the following information: Annual Reports, Officers, Directors, Prior (merged) names, Assumed names, and Inactive names.

Access by: mail, phone, in person, online.

Fee & Payment: The search fee is $5.00 per name. Certification is $10.00 which includes search fee. Copies are $.50 per page after the initial $5.00. Fee payee: Secretary of State. Prepayment required. There is an additional $.50 charge to use a credit card. Personal checks accepted. Credit cards accepted: MasterCard, Visa, Discover.

Mail search: Turnaround time: 5 to 7 days. A self addressed stamped envelope is requested.

Phone search: Expedited copy service is available using a credit card.

In person search: Searching is available in person.

Online search: The web site gives free access to corporate and LLC records (no not-for-profit records). Search Corporate/LLC records at www.cyberdriveillinois.com/departments/business _services/corpstart.html. A commercial access program is also available. Fees vary. Potential users must submit in writing the purpose of the request. Submit to: Barbara Vincen, Dept. of Business Srvs, 330 Howlett Bldg, Springfield, IL 62756. Also, call 217-558-2116 for more information.

Other access: List or bulk file purchases are available. Call 217-558-2116 for more information.

Expedited service: Expedited service is available for mail, phone and fax searches. Turnaround time: 24 hours. Add $25.00 per business name.

Uniform Commercial Code
Federal Tax Liens

Secretary of State, UCC Division, 2nd & Edwards St, Howlett Bldg, Room 350 West, Springfield, IL 62756; 217-782-7518, 8AM-4:30PM.

www.cyberdriveillinois.com

Indexing & Storage: Records are available from 1962. Records are computerized since 1972.

Searching: Use search request form UCC-11. Request searches for federal tax liens on businesses since 1988 separately with a fee of $5.00. Federal tax liens on individuals and all state tax liens are filed at the county level. Include the following in your request: debtor name and address.

Access by: mail, in person.

Fee & Payment: A UCC search is $10.00 per debtor name. A federal tax lien search only is available for $5.00 plus $.50 per page of copies. Copies are $1.00 per page. Fee payee: Secretary of State. Prepayment required. Personal checks accepted. Credit cards accepted: MasterCard, Visa, Discover.

Mail search: Turnaround time: 48 hours. A self addressed stamped envelope is requested.

In person search: Documents can be viewed at no charge.

Other access: The entire database can be purchased and the state offers a CD update service for $250 per month.

State Tax Liens
Records not maintained by a state level agency.

Note: All state tax liens are filed at the county.

Sales Tax Registrations

Revenue Department, Taxpayer Services, PO Box 19044, Springfield, IL 62794-9044 (Courier: 101 W Jefferson, Springfield, IL 62702); 800-732-8866, 217-782-3336, 217-782-0985, 217-782-4217 (Fax), 8AM-5PM.

www.revenue.state.il.us

Indexing & Storage: Records are available for all active businesses with the state, records can go back to the 1930s.

Searching: This agency will only confirm that a business is registered if an Illinois business tax number is provided, often, the business name is not enough. They provide no other information. The state tax permit or federal tax ID is also helpful.

Access by: mail, phone, in person.

Fee & Payment: There is no fee.

Mail search: Turnaround time: 7 to 10 days. A self addressed stamped envelope is requested.

Phone search: Will do up to 5 confirmations at a time.

In person search: Searching is available in person.

Birth Certificates

IL Department of Public Health, Division of Vital Records, 605 W Jefferson St, Springfield, IL 62702-5097; 217-782-6554, 217-782-6553 (Instructions), 217-523-2648 (Fax), 8AM-5PM M-F.

www.idph.state.il.us/vital/vitalhome.htm

Indexing & Storage: Records are available from 1916 to present. It takes up to one month before new records are available for inquiry. Records are indexed on microfiche, inhouse computer.

Searching: Birth records are not considered public records. Copies are available to subject if 18 years old, parents, or legal guardian (with court order). Include the following in your request: full name, date of birth, place of birth, relationship to person of record, names of parents, mother's maiden name. Place of birth can be city or county. Include name of hospital, if known. The following data is not released: sealed records.

Access by: mail, phone, fax, in person.

Fee & Payment: Fees are $10.00 per name for a computer abstract and $15.00 per name for a certified copy of original. Add $2.00 for each additional copy. Add $6.00 service fee to use a credit card. Fee payee: Illinois Department of Public Health. Prepayment required. Personal checks accepted. Credit cards accepted: MasterCard, Visa, AmEx, Discover.

Mail search: Turnaround time: 15 days. No self addressed stamped envelope is required.

Phone search: Use of credit card is required for extra fee of $6.00. Normal turnaround time is 2 days.

Fax search: Same criteria as phone searching.

In person search: Turnaround time less than 1/2 hour.

Expedited service: Expedited service is available for mail, phone and fax searches. Add $6.00 for using a credit card, $13.00 for express delivery.

Death Records

IL Department of Public Health, Division of Vital Records, 605 W Jefferson St, Springfield, IL 62702-5097; 217-782-6554, 217-782-6553 (Instructions), 217-523-2648 (Fax), 8AM-5PM.

www.idph.state.il.us/vital/home.htm

Indexing & Storage: Records are available from 1916 to present. New records are available for inquiry immediately. Records are indexed on microfiche.

Searching: Death records are not considered public documents. Copies are available to person with property rights interest in the record. Once records are 20 years old, they are open for genealogical searches. Include the following in your request: full name, date of death, place of death, relationship to person of record, parents' names, reason for request.

Access by: mail, fax, in person, online.

Fee & Payment: Fees are $17.00 for a certified Death Certificate. Fee payee: Illinois Department of Public Health. Prepayment required. Personal checks accepted. Credit cards accepted: MasterCard, Visa, AmEx, Discover.

Mail search: Turnaround time: 1 month. No self addressed stamped envelope is required.

Fax search: Same criteria as phone searching.

In person search: There is one day waiting period. If ordered by 2PM, will be available the next day at 10AM.

Online search: No online access available from this agency. However, the state archives database of Illinois Death Certificates 1918 - 1950 is available free at www.cyberdriveillinois.com/departments/archives/genealogy/forms/idphdeathsrch.html

Expedited service: Expedited service is available for mail, phone and fax searches. The fee is $6.00 for the credit card use and $13.00 for express delivery. If you send your request in by express delivery, they will turnaround in one day.

Marriage Certificates

Divorce Records

Records not maintained by a state level agency.

Note: State will verify marriage or divorce from 1962-present but will not issue certificate. Verification requests must be in writing and there is a fee of $5.00 per event requested. Records of marriage and divorce are found at the county of issue. There is a free online search of a statewide Marriage Index for 1763-1900 found at the Illinois State Archives web site at www.cyberdriveillinois.com/departments/archives/marriage.html.

Workers' Compensation Records

Industrial Commission, 100 W Randolph, 8th Floor, Chicago, IL 60601; 312-814-6611, 8:30AM-5PM.

www.state.il.us/agency/iic

Note: The web site lists cases that are up for a hearing status.

Indexing & Storage: Records are available on computer from 1982 to present, on microfiche from 1927 to 1981. Settled file copies are stored in Springfield, but must be requested from Chicago. Data is indexed by name and file number. Records are indexed on file folders. Records are normally destroyed after five years.

Searching: Include the following in your request: claimant name, Social Security Number, date of accident. Include case number and company name.

Access by: mail, phone, in person.

Fee & Payment: There is no charge for a small file. For "large files," the office will contact you and suggest you use a record retrieval service. If your request is large enough to warrant the use of a copy service, the service will have its own fees that must be paid by you.

Mail search: Turnaround time: 2 weeks. Send a name as well as any other information you may have, such as company name and date of accident, to determine if any files existA self addressed stamped envelope is requested.

Phone search: Information about a case is accessed by the file number. The staff will do a name search if you have enough information for them to do so.

In person search: There are several public access terminals available in the office.

Driver Records

Abstract Information Unit, Drivers Services Department, 2701 S Dirksen Prky, Springfield, IL 62723; 217-782-2720, 8AM-4:30PM.

www.sos.state.il.us

Note: No personal identifiable information is provided on record unless requester is exempt. Exempt requesters include business representatives with a legitimate business need (e.g. insurance, financial institutions, employers, etc.).

Indexing & Storage: Records are available for 4 years for moving violations; 7 years for suspension; lifetime for DWI. Commercial Driver records can go back 10 years for serious violations. It takes 2 weeks before new records are available for inquiry.

Searching: Non-exempt requesters, with no consent, may receive records without personal information, but there is a 10 day waiting period while the state notifies the subject. Include the following in your request: full name, date of birth, sex. There is a 10 day waiting period when requesting an abstract of another individual's driving record unless the requester is "exempt." This is so the person of record can be informed of the name of the requesting individual.

Access by: mail, in person.

Fee & Payment: The fee is $6.00 per record, which includes certification. There is a full charge for a "no record found." Fee payee: Secretary of State. Prepayment required. Personal checks accepted. No credit cards accepted.

Mail search: Turnaround time: 10 days. No self addressed stamped envelope is required.

In person search: Up to five requests will be processed immediately if requester meets the access requirement (see above). Requests are available from any Driver Services Facility statewide.

Other access: Overnight magnetic tape processing is available to high volume users (there is a 200 request minimum per day). Call (217) 785-2384 for more information.

Vehicle Ownership

Vehicle Identification

Vehicle Services Department, Vehicle Record Inquiry, 501 S 2nd Street #408, Springfield, IL 62756; 217-782-6992, 217-524-0122 (Fax), 8AM-4:30PM.

www.sos.state.il.us

Indexing & Storage: Records are available generally for 10 years to present.

Searching: Personal information is not released for non-business purposes. Bulk sales are not permitted for solicitation purposes.

Access by: mail, in person.

Fee & Payment: The fee is $5.00 per record search. Fee payee: Secretary of State. Prepayment required. Personal checks accepted. MasterCard, Visa, Discover accepted.

Mail search: Turnaround time: 4 to 7 days. You may search by mail, but there is a 10 day delay if the requester is not "exempt."A self addressed stamped envelope is requested.

In person search: Walk-in requesters may retrieve data immediately; however, if requester is not exempt there is a 10 day delay.

Other access: The state will sell customized, bulk requests upon approval of purpose and with a signed contract.

Accident Reports (Crash Reports)

Illinois State Police, Patrol Records Unit, 500 Iles Park Place, Ste 200, Springfield, IL 62718; 217-785-0612, 8AM-5PM.

www.isp.state.il.us

Note: To request report if crash occurred on IL Tollway System, send check or money order payable to: IL Toll Highway Authority, Attn: State Police District 15, One Authority Drive, Downers Grove, IL 60515.

Indexing & Storage: Records are available from 1976 to present.

Searching: Crash reports are considered public record and are available without restriction. Items needed by the requester include date, names of drivers involved, report number, and an exact location.

Access by: mail, phone, in person.

Fee & Payment: The fee is $5.00 per report or $20.00 for a reconstruction report. Fee payee: Illinois State Police. Prepayment required. Personal checks accepted. No credit cards accepted.

Mail search: Turnaround time: 7 to 10 days. If requester provides express envelope & label, the request will be returned quicker. A self addressed stamped envelope is requested.

Phone search: You may call to get information, but copies of records are only released with written requests.

In person search: Turnaround time is immediate.

Vessel Ownership

Vessel Registration

Department of Natural Resources, 524 S. 2nd Street #210, Springfield, IL 62701; 800-382-1696, 217-557-0180, 217-782-5016 (Fax), 8AM-5PM.

http://dnr.state.il.us

Note: Lien information will show on the history report.

Indexing & Storage: Records are available from 1982 to the present. Snow mobile records are also available. Records are indexed on computer. All boats must be titled and registered unless if only used on a private lake.

Searching: To search, one of the following is required: name, hull id #, or registration #.

Access by: mail, phone.

Fee & Payment: There is a $5.00 fee for any search, including a title history search. Fee payee: IL Dept of Natural Resources. Prepayment required. Personal checks accepted. No credit cards accepted.

Mail search: Turnaround time: 4 to 6 weeks. No self addressed stamped envelope is required.

Phone search: They will give limited name search and verification information, time permitting.

Legislation Records

Illinois General Assembly, State House, House (or Senate) Bills Division, Springfield, IL 62706; 217-782-3944 (Bill Status Only), 217-782-7017 (Index Div-Older Bills), 217-782-5799 (House Bills), 217-782-9778 (Senate Bills), 217-524-6059 (Fax), 8AM-4:30PM.

www.legis.state.il.us

Note: Previous session bills must be obtained from: Senate 217-792-6970; House 217-782-7192. Cost is $.10 per page.

Indexing & Storage: Records are available from 1997 to present on computer. Records are indexed on microfiche.

Searching: Include the following in your request: bill number. For statutes, it is suggested to go to a local law library or visit the Internet site. Complete statutes are not available here.

Access by: mail, phone, in person, online.

Fee & Payment: All copies of documents are considered as certified. There is no search fee, copies are free if from the last two sessions, otherwise $0.10 each. Fee payee: Illinois General Assembly. Personal checks accepted. No credit cards accepted.

Mail search: No self addressed stamped envelope is required.

Phone search: Records are available by phone.

In person search: Searching is available in person.

Online search: The Legislative Information System is available for subscription through a standard modem. The sign-up fee is $500.00 which includes 100 free minutes of access. Thereafter, access time is billed at $1.00 per minute. The hours of availability are 8 AM - 10 PM when in session and 8 AM - 5 PM when not in session, M-F. Contact Craig Garret at 217-782-4083 to set-up an account. The Internet site offers free access but the state has a disclaimer which says the site should not be relied upon as an official record of action.

Other access: A prepayment of $500.00 is required to obtain a printed copy of all bills.

Voter Registration

Access to Records is Restricted

Board of Elections, 1020 S Spring, Springfield, IL 62704; 217-782-4141, 217-782-5959 (Fax), 8AM-4:30PM.

www.elections.state.il.us

Note: The data is not considered public record at the state level and is only available in bulk format to political committees and government agencies. County Clerks control the information at the local level.

GED Certificates

Access to Records is Restricted

State Board of Education, 100 N 1st St, Springfield, IL 62777; 217-782-4321 (Main Number).

Note: All GED information is kept at the county level. You must contact the county where the test was taken. If you need assistance determining which county, contact the State Board of Education at the number listed here.

Hunting License Information
Fishing License Information

Access to Records is Restricted

Note: They are just now creating a central database. At this time records are not available. The vendors hold license records for years prior to 2002.

Illinois State Licensing Agencies

Licenses Searchable Online

Architect #11	www.dpr.state.il.us/licenselookup/default.asp
Athletic Trainer #11	www.dpr.state.il.us/licenselookup/default.asp
Attorney #1	www.iardc.org/lawyersearch.html
Auctioneer #29	www.obre.state.il.us/lookup/ (site may be down)
Bank #29	www.obre.state.il.us/lookup/ (site may be down)
Barber #11	www.dpr.state.il.us/licenselookup/default.asp
Bilingual Teacher, Transitional #35	https://isbes1.isbe.net/tciscertificateinquiry/default.asp
Check Printer #29	www.obre.state.il.us/lookup/ (site may be down)
Chiropractor #11	www.dpr.state.il.us/licenselookup/default.asp
Collection Agency #11	www.dpr.state.il.us/licenselookup/default.asp
Controlled Substance Registrant #11	www.dpr.state.il.us/licenselookup/default.asp
Corporate Fiduciary #29	www.obre.state.il.us/lookup/ (site may be down)
Cosmetologist #11	www.dpr.state.il.us/licenselookup/default.asp
Counselor/Clinical Professional Counselor #11	www.dpr.state.il.us/licenselookup/default.asp
Dentist/Dental Hygienist #11	www.dpr.state.il.us/licenselookup/default.asp
Dietitian/Nutrition Counselor #11	www.dpr.state.il.us/licenselookup/default.asp
Drug Distributor, Wholesale #11	www.dpr.state.il.us/licenselookup/default.asp
Early Childhood Teacher #35	https://isbes1.isbe.net/tciscertificateinquiry/default.asp
Engineer #11	www.dpr.state.il.us/licenselookup/default.asp
Engineer, Structural #11	www.dpr.state.il.us/licenselookup/default.asp
Environmental Health Practitioner #11	www.dpr.state.il.us/licenselookup/default.asp
Esthetician #11	www.dpr.state.il.us/licenselookup/default.asp
Funeral Director/Embalmer #11	www.dpr.state.il.us/licenselookup/default.asp
High School Teacher #35	https://isbes1.isbe.net/tciscertificateinquiry/default.asp
HMO #4	www.state.il.us/INS/healthInsurance/HMO_by_County.htm
Insurance Producer #4	http://163.191.40.50:8080/ins/imsfor
Interior Designer #11	www.dpr.state.il.us/licenselookup/default.asp
Landscape Architect #11	www.dpr.state.il.us/licenselookup/default.asp
Lead Contractor #17	http://app.idph.state.il.us/Envhealth/Lead/Leadcnt.asp
Lead Risk Assessor/Inspector/Supervisor #17	http://app.idph.state.il.us/Envhealth/lead/Leadinsp.asp
Lead Training Provider #17	http://app.idph.state.il.us/Envhealth/lead/Leadinsp.asp
Liquor License, Retail/Dist./Mfg. #25	http://www2.state.il.us/lcc/license_search.asp
Lobbyist #32	www.cyberdriveillinois.com/cgi-bin/index/lobbysrch.s
Long Term Care Insurance Company #4	www.state.il.us/INS/ship/LTC_2002.pdf
Marriage & Family Therapist #11	www.dpr.state.il.us/licenselookup/default.asp
Medical Corporation #11	www.dpr.state.il.us/licenselookup/default.asp
Medical Doctor/Physician Assistant #11	www.dpr.state.il.us/licenselookup/default.asp
Mortgage Banker/Broker #29	www.obre.state.il.us/lookup/ (site may be down)
Nail Technician #11	www.dpr.state.il.us/licenselookup/default.asp
Naprapath #11	www.dpr.state.il.us/licenselookup/default.asp
Nurse #11	www.dpr.state.il.us/licenselookup/default.asp
Nursing Home Administrator #17	www.medicare.gov/Nursing/Overview.asp
Occupational Therapist #11	www.dpr.state.il.us/licenselookup/default.asp
Optometrist #11	www.dpr.state.il.us/licenselookup/default.asp
Osteopathic Physician #11	www.dpr.state.il.us/licenselookup/default.asp
Pawnbroker #29	www.obre.state.il.us/lookup/ (site may be down)
Pharmacist/Pharmacy #11	www.dpr.state.il.us/licenselookup/default.asp
Physical Therapist #11	www.dpr.state.il.us/licenselookup/default.asp
Podiatrist #11	www.dpr.state.il.us/licenselookup/default.asp
Polygraph - Deception Detection Examiner #11	www.dpr.state.il.us/licenselookup/default.asp
Private Detective #11	www.dpr.state.il.us/licenselookup/default.asp
Private Security Contractor #11	www.dpr.state.il.us/licenselookup/default.asp
Psychologist #11	www.dpr.state.il.us/licenselookup/default.asp
Public Accountant-CPA #11	www.dpr.state.il.us/licenselookup/default.asp
Real Estate Appraiser #29	www.obre.state.il.us/lookup/ (site may be down)
Real Estate Broker #29	www.obre.state.il.us/lookup/ (site may be down)
Real Estate Salesperson #29	www.obre.state.il.us/lookup/ (site may be down)
Roofer #11	www.dpr.state.il.us/licenselookup/default.asp
Sawmill #3	www.dnr.state.il.us/conservation/forestry/2002/SAWMILL.htm
Shorthand Reporter #11	www.dpr.state.il.us/licenselookup/default.asp
Social Worker #11	www.dpr.state.il.us/licenselookup/default.asp
Special Teacher #35	https://isbes1.isbe.net/tciscertificateinquiry/default.asp
Speech-Language Pathologist/Audiologist #11	www.dpr.state.il.us/licenselookup/default.asp

Substitute Teacher #35 .... https://isbes1.isbe.net/tciscertificateinquiry/default.asp
Surveyor, Land #11 .... www.dpr.state.il.us/licenselookup/default.asp
Teacher #35 .... https://isbes1.isbe.net/tciscertificateinquiry/default.asp
Timeshare/Land Sales #29 .... www.obre.state.il.us/lookup/
Trust Company #29 .... www.obre.state.il.us/CBT/REGENTY/BTREG.HTM
Veterinarian #11 .... www.dpr.state.il.us/licenselookup/default.asp

Licensing Quick Finder

Accident Reconstruction Specialist #19 217-782-4540
Alcohol Abuse Counselor #21 217-698-8110
Ambulance Service #13 217-785-2080
Animal Breeder #6 217-785-3423
Aquaculturist #6 217-785-3423
Architect #11 217-785-0800
Asbestos Contractor #17 217-782-3517
Athletic Trainer #11 217-785-0800
Attorney #1 217-522-6838
Auctioneer #29 312-793-8704
Auctioneer, Vehicle #30 217-782-7817
Automotive Parts Recycler #30 217-782-7817
Bank #29 312-793-3000
Barber #11 217-785-0800
Bilingual Teacher, Transitional #35 800-845-8749
Blacksmith #26 312-814-2600
Blaster #7 217-782-4970
Boat Operator #5 217-782-2138
Boiler Inspector #36 217-782-2696
Boxing/Wrestling Event/Profession #11 217-785-0800
Breath Analyzer Operator #13 217-782-1571
Check Printer #29 312-793-3000
Child Care Facility #2 217-785-2688
Chiropractor #11 217-785-0800
Coal Mine Worker #8 217-782-6791
Collection Agency #11 217-785-0800
Controlled Substance Registrant #11 ... 217-785-0800
Coroner (County) #19 217-782-4540
Corporate Fiduciary #29 312-793-3000
Correction Officer (County) #19 217-782-4540
Cosmetologist #11 217-785-0800
Counselor/Clinical Professional Counselor #11
.... 217-785-0800
Criminal Electronic Surveillance Officer #19
.... 217-782-4540
Cross-Connection Control Device Inspector #24
.... 217-782-1020
Day Care #2 217-785-2688
Dentist/Dental Hygienist #11 217-785-0800
Dietitian/Nutrition Counselor #11 217-785-0800
Distribution System (Public) Operator #24
.... 217-782-9720
Driving Instructor #31 847-437-3953
Drug Distributor, Wholesale #11 217-785-0800
Early Childhood Teacher #35 800-845-8749
Emergency Medical Technician #13 217-785-2080
Employee Leasing Company #4 217-782-6366
Employment Agency #23 312-793-2810
Engineer #11 217-785-0800
Engineer, Structural #11 217-785-0800
Environmental Health Practitioner #11 .. 217-785-0800
Esthetician #11 217-785-0800
Explosive Magazine Storage #8 217-782-9976
Explosive, General Use #8 217-782-9976
Firearms Regulation (Firearm Owner's Reg.) #27
.... 217-782-7980
Fish Dealer #6 217-785-3423
Fisherman, Commercial #6 217-785-3423
Food Processing Plant/Warehouse #13 217-785-2439
Food Service Sanitation Manager #13. 217-785-2439

Funeral Director/Embalmer #11 217-785-0800
Fur Buyer/Tanner/Dyer #5 217-785-3423
Gambling Addiction Counselor #21 217-698-8110
Gambling Employee #20 312-814-4702
Hearing Instrument Dispenser #15 217-782-4733
High School Teacher #35 800-845-8749
HMO #4 217-782-6366
Home Health Aide #13 217-782-7412
Home Health Care Agency #13 217-782-7412
Horseshoer #26 312-814-2600
Hospital #13 217-782-7412
Hunting Area Operator #5 217-785-3423
Industrial Radiographer #9 217-785-9913
Insurance Producer #4 217-782-6366
Interior Designer #11 217-785-0800
Investment Adviser #33 217-785-4929
Laboratory Analysis Technician #13 217-785-8820
Land Sale #11 217-785-0800
Landfill Chief Operator #24 217-782-9877
Landscape Architect #11 217-785-0800
Lead Contractor #17 217-782-3517
Lead Risk Assessor/Inspector/Supervisor #17
.... 217-782-3517
Lead Training Provider #17 217-782-3517
Liquor License, Retail/Dist./Mfg. #25 ... 312-814-3930
Lobbyist #32 217-782-0705
Long Term Care Insurance Company #4
.... 217-782-6366
Marriage & Family Therapist #11 217-785-0800
Medical Corporation #11 217-785-0800
Medical Doctor/Physician Assistant #11 217-785-0800
Mental Health Counselor #21 217-698-8110
Mine Engineer/Foreman #8 217-782-6791
Mine Rescue Supervisor/Assistant #8 .. 217-782-6791
Mine Supervisor #8 217-782-6791
Mortgage Banker/Broker #29 217-793-1409
Motor Vehicle Dealer, New #30 217-782-7817
Nail Technician #11 217-785-0800
Naprapath #11 217-785-0800
Notary Public #32 217-782-0641
Nuclear Medicine Technologist #9 217-785-9913
Nurse #11 217-785-0800
Nurses' Aide #13 217-785-5133
Nursing Agency #23 312-793-1718
Nursing Home #12 217-702-0545
Nursing Home Administrator #17 217-782-0514
Occupational Aide #12 217-782-0545
Occupational Therapist #11 217-785-0800
Optometrist #11 217-785-0800
Osteopathic Physician #11 217-785-0800
Pari-Mutuel Employee #26 312-814-2600
Pawnbroker #29 312-793-3000
Pest Control Technician/Business #17 . 217-782-4674
Pesticide Applicator #17 217-782-5830
Pharmacist/Pharmacy #11 217-785-0800
Physical Aide #12 217-782-0545
Physical Therapist #11 217-785-0800
Plumber #17 217-524-0791
Plumber Apprentice #13 217-785-1153
Podiatrist #11 217-785-0800

Polygraph - Deception Detection Examiner #11
.... 217-785-0800
Private Detective #11 217-785-0800
Private Security Contractor #11 217-785-0800
Psychologist #11 217-785-0800
Public Accountant-CPA #11 217-785-0800
Racetrack #26 312-814-2600
Radiation Therapist #10 217-785-9913
Radiographer #10 217-785-9913
Radon Measurement Specialist #10 217-785-9935
Real Estate Appraiser #29 312-793-8704
Real Estate Broker #29 312-793-8704
Real Estate Salesperson #29 312-793-8704
Rehabilitation Aide #12 217-782-0545
Restaurant & Retail Food Store #17 217-785-2439
Riverboat Employee #20 312-814-4702
Roofer #11 217-785-0800
Salvage Firm #13 217-785-2439
Savings & Loan Association #29 217-782-9043
Savings Bank #29 217-782-9043
Sawmill #3 217-782-6431
School Business Official #35 800-845-8749
School Guidance Counselor #35 800-845-8749
School Media Specialist/Librarian #35.. 800-845-8749
School Nurse #35 800-845-8749
School Principal/Super./Admin. #35 800-845-8749
School Psychologist #35 800-845-8749
Scrap Processor #30 217-782-7817
Securities Dealer/Salesperson #33 217-782-2256
Sewage System Contractor #17 217-782-5830
Sheriff Law Enforcement Officer #19 ... 217-782-4540
Shorthand Reporter #11 217-785-0800
Social Worker #11 217-785-0800
Special Teacher #35 800-845-8749
Speech-Language Pathologist/Audiologist #11
.... 217-785-0800
Stock Broker #33 217-782-2256
Substance Abuse Counselor #21 217-698-8110
Substitute Teacher #35 800-845-8749
Surveyor, Land #11 217-785-0800
Tanning Facility #17 217-785-2439
Taxidermist #6 217-785-3423
Teacher #35 800-845-8749
Timber Buyer #3 217-782-6431
Timeshare #11 217-785-0800
Timeshare/Land Sales #29 312-793-8704
Trust Company #29 312-793-3000
Underground Shot Firer #8 217-782-6791
Used Vehicle Dealer #30 217-782-7817
Vehicle Rebuilder/Repair #30 217-782-7817
Veterinarian #11 217-785-0800
Vision & Hearing Screening Technician #15
.... 217-782-4733
Waste Water Plant Operator #24 217-782-9720
Water Supply Operator #24 217-782-9720
Water Well & Pump Installation Contractor #17
.... 217-782-5830
Water Well Contractor/IDPH #17 217-782-5830
Weighing & Measuring Device Serviceman #22
.... 217-782-3817

Licensing Agency Information

#1 Attorney Registration & Disciplinary Commission of Supreme Court of IL, 700 E Adams St, Hilton Offices, #201, Springfield, IL 62701; 217-522-6838, Fax: 217-522-2417. www.iardc.org
Search database at www.iardc.org/lawyersearch.html

#2 Department of Children & Family Services, 406 E Monroe St, Springfield, IL 62701; 217-785-2509, Fax: 217-785-1052.

#3 Department of Natural Resources, Division of Forest Services, 524 S 2nd St, Springfield, IL 62701-1787; 217-782-6431, Fax: 217-785-8405. www.dnr.state.il.us

#4 Department of Insurance, 320 W Washington, Springfield, IL 62767-0001; 217-782-4515, Fax: 217-782-5020.
www.state.il.us/ins. Agency email: director@ins.state.il.us.

#5 Department of Natural Resources, 524 S 2nd St, Springfield, IL 62701; 217-782-2138, Fax: 217-782-5016.
http://dnr.state.il.us

#6 Department of Natural Resources, 524 S 2nd St, Springfield, IL 62701; 217-785-3423, Fax: 217-782-5016.
http://dnr.state.il.us

#8 Department of Natural Resources, Office of Mine & Minerals, 300 W Jefferson St, #300, Springfield, IL 62791; 217-782-6791, Fax: 217-524-4819.
http://dnr.state.il.us/mines/mines.htm

#9 Department of Nuclear Safety, 1035 Outer Park Dr, Springfield, IL 62704; 217-785-9900, Fax: 217-785-9962.
www.state.il.us/idns
Agency email: webmaster@idns.state.il.us.

#11 Department of Professional Regulation, Professions/Occupations/Entities, 320 W Washington, 3rd Fl, Springfield, IL 62786; 217-785-0800, Fax: 217-782-7645.
www.dpr.state.il.us
Agency email: netinfo@dpr084rl.state.il.us.
Search database at www.dpr.state.il.us/licenselookup/default.asp

#12 Department of Public Aid, Bureau of Long-Term Care, 201 S. Grand Ave, Springfield, IL 62763-0001; 217-782-0545, Fax: 217-524-7114.
Agency email: aidd2011@mail.idpa.state.il.us.

#13 Department of Public Health, Education & Training Section, 525 W Jefferson St 4th Fl, Springfield, IL 62761; 217-782-4977, Fax: 217-782-3987.
www.idph.state.il.us

#15 Department of Public Health, Division of Health Assessment & Screening, 535 W Jefferson St, Springfield, IL 62761; 217-782-4733, Fax: 217-524-2831.
www.idph.state.il.us
Agency email: gtanner@idph.state.il.us.

#17 Department of Public Health, Environmental Health, 525 W Jefferson St, 3rd Fl, Springfield, IL 62761; 217-782-5830, Fax: 217-785-0253.
www.idph.state.il.us. Agency email: mailus@idph.state.il.us.

#19 Law Enforcement & Standards Training Board, 600 S 2nd St, #300, Springfield, IL 62704; 217-782-4540, Fax: 217-524-5350.
www.ptb.state.il.us. Agency email: ptb@pop.state.il.us.

#20 Gaming Board, 160 N Lasalle #300, Chicago, IL 60601; 312-814-4700, Fax: 312-814-1581.
www.igb.state.il.us

#21 Counselor Certification Department, IAODAPCA, 1305 Wabash Ave #L, Springfield, IL 62704-4938; 217-698-8110, Fax: 217-698-8234.
www.iaodapca.org
Agency email: IAODAPCA@aol.com.

#22 Department of Agriculture, State Fairgrounds, PO Box 19281, Springfield, IL 62794-9281; 217-782-2172, Fax: 217-524-7801.
www.agr.state.il.us

#23 Department of Labor, State of Illinois Bldg., 160 N LaSalle, 13th Fl, #C1300, Chicago, IL 60601; 312-793-2800, Fax: 312-793-5257.
www.state.il.us/agency/idol
Agency email: idol@pop.state.il.us.

#24 Environmental Protection Agency, PO Box 19276 (1021 N Grand Ave E), Springfield, IL 62794-9276; 217-782-1020, Fax: 217-782-0075.
www.epa.state.il.us/water/index.html

#25 Freedom of Information Compliance Officer, Liquor Control Commission, 100 W Randolph, #5-300, Chicago, IL 60601; 312-814-2206, Fax: 312-814-2241.
www.state.il.us/lcc/default.htm
Agency email: lcc_webmaster@mail.state.il.us.
Search database at http://www2.state.il.us/lcc/license_search.asp

#26 Racing Board, 100 W Randolph, #11-100, Chicago, IL 60601; 312-814-2600, Fax: 312-814-5062.
www.state.il.us/agency/irb
Agency email: irb@pop.state.il.us.

#27 State Police, FOID, 100 Iles Park Pl, 103 Armory Bldg, Springfield, IL 62708; 217-782-7980, Fax: 217-785-2821.
www.isp.state.il.us

#29 Office of Banks & Real Estate, Bureaus of Res. Finance; Banks & Trusts; Real Estate Professions, 500 E Monroe, Springfield, IL 62701-1509; 217-782-3000, Fax: 217-524-5941.
www.obre.state.il.us
Agency email: obr_webmaster@pop.state.il.us.
Search database at www.obre.state.il.us/lookup/ (site may be down).

#30 Secretary of State, Howlett Bldg, Rm 069, Springfield, IL 62756; 217-782-7817, Fax: 217-524-0120.
www.sos.state.il.us. Agency email: secwhite@ccgate.sos.state.il.us.

#31 Secretary of State, Commercial Driver Training, 650 Roppolo Dr, Elk Grove, IL 60007; 847-437-3953, Fax: 847-437-3911.

#32 Secretary of State, Index Department, 111 E Monroe St, Springfield, IL 62756; 217-782-7017, Fax: 217-524-0930.
www.sos.state.il.us

#33 Secretary of State, Securities Department, 520 S 2nd St, Lincoln Tower, #200, Springfield, IL 62701; 217-782-2256, Fax: 217-524-2172.
www.sos.state.il.us
Search database at www.nasdr.com.

#35 Division of Professional Certification, Board of Education, 100 N 1st St, Springfield, IL 62777; 800-845-8749, 217 782-4321, Fax: 217 524-4928.
www.isbe.state.il.us/teachers/teachers.htm
Search database at https://isbes1.isbe.net/tcis certificateinquiry/default.asp

#36 State Fire Marshall, 1035 Stevenson Dr, Springfield, IL 62703; 217-785-0969, Fax: 217-782-1062.

#37 Department of Labor, Carnival & Amusement Ride Safety Division, 1 West Old State Capitol Plaza, #300, Springfield, IL 62701; 217-782-9347, Fax: 217-785-8776.
www.state.il.us/agency/idol/carn/index.htm

Illinois Federal Courts

The following list indicates the district and division name for each county in the state. If the bankruptcy court location is different from the district court, then the location of the bankruptcy court appears in parentheses.

County/Court Cross Reference

County	District	Division
Adams	Central	Springfield
Alexander	Southern	Benton
Bond	Southern	East St Louis
Boone	Northern	Rockford
Brown	Central	Springfield
Bureau	Central	Peoria
Calhoun	Southern	East St Louis
Carroll	Northern	Rockford
Cass	Central	Springfield
Champaign	Central	Danville/Urbana (Danville)
Christian	Central	Springfield
Clark	Southern	Benton (East St Louis)
Clay	Southern	Benton (East St Louis)
Clinton	Southern	East St Louis
Coles	Central	Danville/Urbana (Danville)
Cook	Northern	Chicago (Eastern)
Crawford	Southern	Benton (East St Louis)
Cumberland	Southern	Benton
De Kalb	Northern	Rockford
De Witt	Central	Springfield
Douglas	Central	Danville/Urbana (Danville)
Du Page	Northern	Chicago (Eastern)
Edgar	Central	Danville/Urbana (Danville)
Edwards	Southern	Benton
Effingham	Southern	Benton (East St Louis)
Fayette	Southern	East St Louis
Ford	Central	Danville/Urbana (Danville)
Franklin	Southern	Benton
Fulton	Central	Peoria
Gallatin	Southern	Benton
Greene	Central	Springfield
Grundy	Northern	Chicago (Eastern)
Hamilton	Southern	Benton
Hancock	Central	Peoria
Hardin	Southern	Benton
Henderson	Central	Rock Island (Peoria)
Henry	Central	Rock Island (Peoria)
Iroquois	Central	Danville/Urbana (Danville)
Jackson	Southern	Benton
Jasper	Southern	Benton (East St Louis)
Jefferson	Southern	Benton
Jersey	Southern	East St Louis
Jo Daviess	Northern	Rockford
Johnson	Southern	Benton
Kane	Northern	Chicago (Eastern)
Kankakee	Central	Danville/Urbana (Danville)
Kendall	Northern	Chicago (Eastern)
Knox	Central	Peoria
La Salle	Northern	Chicago (Eastern)
Lake	Northern	Chicago (Eastern)
Lawrence	Southern	Benton (East St Louis)
Lee	Northern	Rockford
Livingston	Central	Peoria (Danville)
Logan	Central	Springfield
Macon	Central	Danville/Urbana (Sprngfld)
Macoupin	Central	Springfield
Madison	Southern	East St Louis
Marion	Southern	East St Louis
Marshall	Central	Peoria
Mason	Central	Springfield
Massac	Southern	Benton
McDonough	Central	Peoria
McHenry	Northern	Rockford
McLean	Central	Peoria (Springfield)
Menard	Central	Springfield
Mercer	Central	Rock Island (Peoria)
Monroe	Southern	East St Louis
Montgomery	Central	Springfield
Morgan	Central	Springfield
Moultrie	Central	Danville/Urbana (Danville)
Ogle	Northern	Rockford
Peoria	Central	Peoria
Perry	Southern	Benton
Piatt	Central	Danville/Urbana (Danville)
Pike	Central	Springfield
Pope	Southern	Benton
Pulaski	Southern	Benton
Putnam	Central	Peoria
Randolph	Southern	East St Louis
Richland	Southern	Benton (East St Louis)
Rock Island	Central	Rock Island (Peoria)
Saline	Southern	Benton
Sangamon	Central	Springfield
Schuyler	Central	Springfield
Scott	Central	Springfield
Shelby	Central	Springfield
St. Clair	Southern	East St Louis
Stark	Central	Peoria
Stephenson	Northern	Rockford
Tazewell	Central	Peoria
Union	Southern	Benton
Vermilion	Central	Danville/Urbana (Danville)
Wabash	Southern	Benton
Warren	Central	Rock Island (Peoria)
Washington	Southern	East St Louis (Benton)
Wayne	Southern	Benton
White	Southern	Benton
Whiteside	Northern	Rockford
Will	Northern	Chicago (Eastern)
Williamson	Southern	Benton
Winnebago	Northern	Rockford
Woodford	Central	Peoria

Standards for Federal Courts: The search fee is $20.00 per item (one party name or case number). Certification fee is $7.00 per document. Copy fee is $.50 per page. All fees standard unless noted in profile. Mail Search: always enclose a stamped self addressed envelope unless otherwise noted. Before releasing records, all courts require prepayment unless noted in profile.

Open records are located at the court unless otherwise noted. District courts index by defendant and plaintiff as well as by case number. Bankruptcy courts usually index by debtor and case number. While most courts now have their indexes on computer, many still maintain index card files as well.

The universal PACER sign-up number is 800-676-6856. Find PACER and the Party/Case Index on the Web at http://pacer.psc.uscourts.gov. PACER dial-up access is $.60 per minute. Also, courts offering internet access via RACER, PACER, Web-PACER or the new CM-ECF charge $.07 per page fee unless noted as free.

US District Court

Central District of Illinois

Danville/Urbana Division 201 S Vine, Room 218, Urbana, IL 61801 (Courier Address: Use mail address for courier delivery), 217-373-5830.

www.ilcd.uscourts.gov

Counties: Champaign, Coles, Douglas, Edgar, Ford, Iroquois, Kankakee, Macon, Moultrie, Piatt, Vermilion.

Indexing & Storage: Cases are indexed by defendant, plaintiff, and case number. New cases are available in the index immediately after filing date. District wide searches are availiable for civil records from October 1989 and criminal records from April 1992 from this court.

Fee & Payment Notes: Payment may be made by money order, cashier check, business check. Personal checks are not accepted. Payee: Clerk, US District Court.

Phone Search: Only docket information is available by phone.

Mail Search: A stamped self addressed envelope is not required.

In Person Search: In person searching available.

PACER: Toll-free dial-up access: 800-258-3678. Local dial-up access: 217-492-4997. Case records are available back to 1995. Records are purged after 5-7 years. New records are available online after 1 day. PACER is available online at http://pacer.ilcd.uscourts.gov.

Peoria Division US District Clerk's Office, 309 Federal Bldg, 100 NE Monroe St, Peoria, IL 61602 (Courier Address: Use mail address for courier delivery), 309-671-7117.

www.ilcd.uscourts.gov

Counties: Bureau, Fulton, Hancock, Knox, Livingston, McDonough, McLean, Marshall, Peoria, Putnam, Stark, Tazewell, Woodford.

Indexing & Storage: Cases are indexed by defendant, plaintiff, and case number. New cases are available in the index immediately after filing date. District-wide searches are available for civil cases from November 1989 and for criminal

records from April 1992. Open records are located at this court.

Fee & Payment Notes: Payment may be made by money order, cashier check. Business checks are not accepted. Personal checks are not accepted. Law firm checks are accepted. Payee: Clerk, US District Court.

Phone Search: Searching not available by phone.

In Person Search: In person searching available.

PACER: Toll-free dial-up access: 800-258-3678. Local dial-up access: 217-492-4997. Case records are available back to 1995. Records are purged after 5-7 years. New records are available online after 1 day. PACER is available online at http://pacer.ilcd.uscourts.gov.

Rock Island Division US District Clerk's Office, Room 40, Post Office Bldg, 211 19th St, Rock Island, IL 61201 (Courier Address: Use mail address for courier delivery), 309-793-5778.

www.ilcd.uscourts.gov

Counties: Henderson, Henry, Mercer, Rock Island, Warren.

Indexing & Storage: Cases are indexed by defendant, plaintiff, and case number. New cases are available in the index immediately after filing date. Open records are located at this court.

Fee & Payment Notes: Payment may be made by money order, cashier check, business check. Personal checks are not accepted. Payee: Clerk of US District Court.

Phone Search: All information that is not sealed is available for release over the phone.

In Person Search: In person searching available.

PACER: Toll-free dial-up access: 800-258-3678. Local dial-up access: 217-492-4997. Case records are available back to 1995. Records are purged after 5-7 years. New records are available online after 1 day. PACER is available online at http://pacer.ilcd.uscourts.gov.

Springfield Division Clerk, 151 US Courthouse, 600 E Monroe, Springfield, IL 62701 (Courier Address: Use mail address for courier delivery), 217-492-4020.

www.ilcd.uscourts.gov

Counties: Adams, Brown, Cass, Christian, De Witt, Greene, Logan, Macoupin, Mason, Menard, Montgomery, Morgan, Pike, Sangamon, Schuyler, Scott, Shelby.

Indexing & Storage: Cases are indexed by defendant, plaintiff, and case number. New cases are available in the index immediately after filing date. District wide searches are available for civil records from November 1989 and criminal records from 1992 from this court.

Fee & Payment Notes: Payment may be made by money order, cashier check, business check. Personal checks are not accepted. Payee: US District Court Clerk. You are allowed to make your own copies. These copies cost $.50 per page.

Phone Search: Searching not available by phone.

Mail Search: A stamped self addressed envelope is not required.

In Person Search: In person searching available.

PACER: Toll-free dial-up access: 800-258-3678. Local dial-up access: 217-492-4997. Case records are available back to 1995. Records are purged after 5-7 years. New records are available online

after 1 day. PACER is available online at http://pacer.ilcd.uscourts.gov.

US Bankruptcy Court

Central District of Illinois

Danville Division 201 N Vermilion #130, Danville, IL 61832-4733 (Courier Address: Use mail address for courier delivery), 217-431-4820, Fax: 217-431-2694.

www.ilcb.uscourts.gov

Counties: Champaign, Coles, Douglas, Edgar, Ford, Iroquois, Kankakee, Livingston, Moultrie, Piatt, Vermilion.

Indexing & Storage: Cases are indexed by debtor as well as by case number. New cases are available in the index 24 hours after filing date. Open records are located at this court.

Fee & Payment Notes: Payment may be made by money order, cashier check, business check. Personal checks are not accepted. Payee: US Bankruptcy Court.

Phone Search: Docket information available by phone. An automated voice case information service (VCIS) is available. Call VCIS at 800-827-9005 or 217-492-4550.

Fax Search: You may request a fee quotation by fax. Court will add $25.00 if records are in Chicago. Will fax results for $15.00 plus other fees.

In Person Search: In person searching available.

PACER: Toll-free dial-up access: 800-454-9893. Local dial-up access: 217-492-4260. Case records are available back to 1989-90. Records are purged immediately when case is closed. New civil records are available online after 2 days. PACER is available online at http://pacer.ilcb.uscourts.gov.

Peoria Division 131 Federal Bldg, 100 NE Monroe, Peoria, IL 61602 (Courier Address: Use mail address for courier delivery), 309-671-7035, Fax: 309-671-7076.

www.ilcb.uscourts.gov

Counties: Bureau, Fulton, Hancock, Henderson, Henry, Knox, Marshall, McDonough, Mercer, Peoria, Putnam, Rock Island, Stark, Tazewell, Warren, Woodford.

Indexing & Storage: Cases are indexed by debtor as well as by case number. New cases are available in the index 24 hours after filing date. Open records are located at this court.

Fee & Payment Notes: Payment may be made by money order, cashier check, business check. Personal checks are not accepted. Will invoice for copy fees only. Payee: US Bankruptcy Court.

Phone Search: An automated voice case information service (VCIS) is available. Call VCIS at 800-827-9005 or 217-492-4550.

Fax Search: You may request a quotation of fees by fax.

In Person Search: In person searching available.

PACER: Toll-free dial-up access: 800-454-9893. Local dial-up access: 217-492-4260. Case records are available back to 1989-90. Records are purged immediately when case is closed. New civil records are available online after 2 days. PACER is available online at http://pacer.ilcb.uscourts.gov.

Springfield Division 226 US Courthouse, Springfield, IL 62701 (Courier Address: 600 E Monroe St., #226, Springfield, IL 62701), 217-492-4551, Fax: 217-492-4556.

www.ilcb.uscourts.gov

Counties: Adams, Brown, Cass, Christian, De Witt, Greene, Logan, Macon, Macoupin, Mason, McLean, Menard, Montgomery, Morgan, Pike, Sangamon, Schuyler, Scott, Shelby.

Indexing & Storage: Cases are indexed by debtor as well as by case number. New cases are available in the index 24 hours after filing date. Open records are located at this court.

Fee & Payment Notes: Payment may be made by money order, cashier check, business check. Personal checks are not accepted. Will invoice for copy fees only. Payee: US Bankruptcy Court.

Phone Search: An automated voice case information service (VCIS) is available. Call VCIS at 800-827-9005 or 217-492-4550.

Fax Search: Fax requests are handled the same as mail requests.

In Person Search: In person searching available.

PACER: Toll-free dial-up access: 800-454-9893. Local dial-up access: 217-492-4260. Case records are available back to 1989-90. Records are purged immediately when case is closed. New civil records are available online after 2 days. PACER is available online at http://pacer.ilcb.uscourts.gov.

US District Court

Northern District of Illinois

Chicago (Eastern) Division 20th Floor, 219 S Dearborn St, Chicago, IL 60604 (Courier Address: Use mail address for courier delivery), 312-435-5698.

www.ilnd.uscourts.gov

Counties: Cook, Du Page, Grundy, Kane, Kendall, Lake, La Salle, Will.

Indexing & Storage: Cases are indexed by defendant, plaintiff, and case number. New cases are available in the index 2 days after filing date. Records are also indexed on microfiche. Open records are located at this court.

Fee & Payment Notes: Payment may be made by money order, cashier check, personal check, Visa, Mastercard. Except for criminal bail bonds, all types of checks or money orders are accepted. Credit cards are only accepted in person. Payee: Clerk, US District Court. You are allowed to make your own copies. These copies cost $.25 per page.

Phone Search: Searching not available by phone. Only docket information is available by phone. Phone inquiries may be made from 8:15AM-5PM.

In Person Search: In person searching available.

PACER: Toll-free dial-up access: 800-621-7029. Local dial-up access: 312-408-7777. Case records are available back to 1988. Records are purged varies. New records are available online after 1-2 days. PACER is available online at http://pacer.ilnd.uscourts.gov. Document images available.

Rockford Division Room 211, 211 S Court St, Rockford, IL 61101 (Courier Address: Use mail address for courier delivery), 815-987-4355.

www.ilnd.uscourts.gov

Counties: Boone, Carroll, De Kalb, Jo Daviess, Lee, McHenry, Ogle, Stephenson, Whiteside, Winnebago.

Indexing & Storage: Cases are indexed by defendant, plaintiff, and case number. New cases are available in the index 1-3 days after filing date. Open records are located at this court.

Fee & Payment Notes: Payment may be made by money order, cashier check, personal check. Payee: Clerk, US District Court.

Phone Search: Searching not available by phone.

Mail Search: Any indictments, pending information, case numbers and docket sheets (if specifically requested) will be released. A stamped self addressed envelope is not required.

In Person Search: In person searching available.

PACER: Toll-free dial-up access: 800-621-7029. Local dial-up access: 312-408-7777. Case records are available back to 1988. Records are purged varies. New records are available online after 1-2 days. PACER is available online at http://pacer.ilnd.uscourts.gov. Document images available.

US Bankruptcy Court

Northern District of Illinois

Chicago (Eastern) Division 219 S Dearborn St, Chicago, IL 60604-1802 (Courier Address: Use mail address for courier delivery), 312-435-5694.

www.ilnb.uscourts.gov

Counties: Cook, Du Page, Grundy, Kane, Kendall, La Salle, Lake, Will.

Indexing & Storage: Cases are indexed by debtor as well as by case number. New cases are available in the index 1 day after filing date. Open records are located at this court.

Fee & Payment Notes: Payment may be made by money order, cashier check, business check. Personal checks are not accepted. Payee: Clerk, US Bankruptcy Court. You are allowed to make your own copies. These copies cost $.28 per page. Copies are available through Ikon Copy Service, 312-913-9508.

Phone Search: If the searcher has a case number, any information contained on the docket will be released. An automated voice case information service (VCIS) is available. Call VCIS at 888-232-6814 or 312-408-5089.

In Person Search: In person searching available.

PACER: Toll-free dial-up access: 888-541-1078. Local dial-up access: 312-408-5101. Document images available on Pacer. Case records are available back to July 1, 1993. Records are never purged. New civil records are available online after 1 day. Online access to PACER/RACER is available at the web site. Access fee is 7 cents per document.

Electronic Filing: (Currently in the process of implementing CM/ECF.)

Other Online Access: Case Image Viewing is available from 5 a.m. to 11:59 p.m. CST at www.ilnb.uscourts.gov/casenotice.htm.

Rockford Division Room 110, 211 S Court St, Rockford, IL 61101 (Courier Address: Use mail address for courier delivery), 815-987-4350, Fax: 815-987-4205.

www.ilnb.uscourts.gov

Counties: Boone, Carroll, De Kalb, Jo Daviess, Lee, McHenry, Ogle, Stephenson, Whiteside, Winnebago.

Indexing & Storage: Cases are indexed by debtor and creditors as well as by case number. New cases are available in the index immediately after filing date. Open records are located at this court.

Fee & Payment Notes: Payment may be made by money order, cashier check, personal check. Debtor's checks are not accepted. Payee: Clerk, US Bankruptcy Court.

Phone Search: Only docket information is available by phone. An automated voice case information service (VCIS) is available. Call VCIS at 815-987-4487.

In Person Search: In person searching available.

PACER: Local dial-up access: 815-987-4489, 815-987-4490. Case records are available back to 1992. New civil records are available online after 1 day. Online access to PACER/RACER is available at the web site. Document images available.

Electronic Filing: (Currently in the process of implementing CM/ECF.)

Other Online Access: Case Image Viewing is available from 5AM to 11:59PM CST at www.ilnb.uscourts.gov/casenotice.htm.

US District Court

Southern District of Illinois

Benton Division 301 W Main St, Benton, IL 62812 (Courier Address: Use mail address for courier delivery), 618-439-7760.

www.ilsd.uscourts.gov

Counties: Alexander, Clark, Clay, Crawford, Cumberland, Edwards, Effingham, Franklin, Gallatin, Hamilton, Hardin, Jackson, Jasper, Jefferson, Johnson, Lawrence, Massac, Perry, Pope, Pulaski, Richland, Saline, Union, Wabash, Wayne, White, Williamson. Cases mayalso be allocated to the Benton Division.

Indexing & Storage: Cases are indexed by defendant, plaintiff, and case number. New cases are available in the index immediately after filing date. The name and date are required to search for records. Records are also indexed on microfiche. Open records are located at this court.

Fee & Payment Notes: Payment may be made by money order, cashier check, personal check. Except in an emergency, Payee: Clerk, US District Court. You are allowed to make your own copies. These copies cost $.50 per page.

Phone Search: Docket information available by phone.

In Person Search: In person searching available.

PACER: Case records are available back to 1985. Records are purged when deemed necessary. New civil records are available online after 1 day. New criminal records are available online after 1-2 days. PACER is available online at http://pacer.ilsd.uscourts.gov.

East St Louis Division PO Box 249, East St Louis, IL 62202 (Courier Address: 750 Missouri Ave, East St Louis, IL 62201), 618-482-9371.

www.ilsd.uscourts.gov

Counties: Bond, Calhoun, Clinton, Fayette, Jersey, Madison, Marion, Monroe, Randolph, St. Clair, Washington. Cases for these counties may also be allocated to the Benton Division.

Indexing & Storage: Cases are indexed by defendant, plaintiff, and case number. New cases are available in the index immediately after filing date. Name and date are required to search for records. Records are also indexed on microfiche. Open records are located at this court.

Fee & Payment Notes: Payment may be made by money order, cashier check, personal check. Except in an emergency, Cash is also accepted. Payee: Clerk, US District Court.

Phone Search: Docket information available by phone.

In Person Search: In person searching available.

PACER:. Case records are available back to 1985. Records are purged when deemed necessary. New civil records are available online after 1 day. New criminal records are available online after 1-2 days. PACER is available online at http://pacer.ilsd.uscourts.gov.

US Bankruptcy Court

Southern District of Illinois

Benton Division 301 W Main, Benton, IL 62812 (Courier Address: Use mail address for courier delivery), 618-435-2200.

www.ilsb.uscourts.gov

Counties: Alexander, Edwards, Franklin, Gallatin, Hamilton, Hardin, Jackson, Jefferson, Johnson, Massac, Perry, Pope, Pulaski, Randolph, Saline, Union, Wabash, Washington, Wayne, White, Williamson.

Indexing & Storage: Cases are indexed by debtor as well as by case number. New cases are available in the index immediately after filing date. Open records are located at this court.

Fee & Payment Notes: Payment may be made by money order, cashier check, business check. Personal checks are not accepted. Payee: Clerk, US Bankruptcy Court.

Phone Search: An automated voice case information service (VCIS) is available. Call VCIS at 800-726-5622 or 618-482-9365.

In Person Search: In person searching available.

PACER:. Case records are available back to January 1989. Records are purged as deemed necessary. New civil records are available online after 1 day. PACER is available online at http://pacer.ilsb.uscourts.gov.

Electronic Filing: Information is available online at https://ecf.ilsb.uscourts.gov

East St Louis Division PO Box 309, East St Louis, IL 62202-0309 (Courier Address: 750 Missouri Ave, East St Louis, IL 62201), 618-482-9400.

www.ilsb.uscourts.gov

Counties: Bond, Calhoun, Clark, Clay, Clinton, Crawford, Cumberland, Effingham, Fayette, Jasper, Jersey, Lawrence, Madison, Marion, Monroe, Richland, St. Clair.

Indexing & Storage: Cases are indexed by debtor as well as by case number. New cases are available in the index 1 working day after filing date. Records are also indexed on microfiche. District wide searches are available from this court.

Fee & Payment Notes: Payment may be made by money order, cashier check, personal check. Debtor's checks are not accepted. Payee: Clerk, US Bankruptcy Court.

Phone Search: An automated voice case information service (VCIS) is available. Call VCIS at 800-726-5622 or 618-482-9365.

Mail Search: A stamped self addressed envelope is not required.

In Person Search: In person searching available.

PACER:. Case records are available back to January 1989. Records are purged as deemed necessary. New civil records are available online after 1 day. PACER is available online at http://pacer.ilsb.uscourts.gov.

Electronic Filing: Information is available online at https://ecf.ilsb.uscourts.gov

Illinois County Courts

Court	Jurisdiction	No. of Courts	How Organized
Circuit Courts*	General	106	22 Circuits

* Profiled in this Sourcebook.

CIVIL									
Court	Tort	Contract	Real Estate	Min. Claim	Max. Claim	Small Claims	Estate	Eviction	Domestic Relations
Circuit Courts*	X	X	X	$0	No Max	$5000	X	X	X

CRIMINAL					
Court	Felony	Misdemeanor	DWI/DUI	Preliminary Hearing	Juvenile
Circuit Courts*	X	X	X	X	X

ADMINISTRATION
Administative Office of Courts, 222 N LaSalle 13th Floor, Chicago, IL, 60601; 312-793-3250, Fax: 312-793-1335. www.state.il.us/court/

COURT STRUCTURE
Illinois is divided into 22 judicial circuits; 3 are single county: Cook, Du Page (18th Circuit) and Will (12th Circuit). The other 19 circuits consist of 2 or more contiguous counties. The Circuit Court of Cook County is the largest unified court system in the world. Its 2300-person staff handles approximately 2.4 million cases each year. The civil part of the various Circuit Courts in Cook County is divided as follows: under $30,000 are "civil cases" and over $30,000 are "civil law division cases."

Probate is handled by the Circuit Court in all counties.

ONLINE ACCESS
While there is no statewide public online system available, a number of Illinois Circuit Courts offer online access.

ADDITIONAL INFORMATION
The search fee is set by statute and has three levels based on the county population. The higher the population, the larger the fee. In most courts, both civil and criminal data is on computer from the same starting date. In most Illinois courts the search fee is charged on a per name per year basis.

Adams County

Circuit Court 521 Vermont St, Quincy, IL 62301; 217-277-2100; Fax: 217-277-2116. Hours: 8:15AM-4:30PM (CST). *Felony, Misdemeanor, Civil, Eviction, Small Claims, Probate.*
www.co.adams.il.us
Civil Records: Access: Phone, mail, fax, in person, online, email. Both court and visitors may perform in person searches. Search fee: $2.00 per name. Fee is $4.00 for years prior to 1987. Required to search: name, years to search. Civil cases indexed by defendant, plaintiff. Civil records on computer from 1987, books and index cards from 1920. Online access to 8th Circuit Clerk of Court records available free at www.circuitclerk.co.adams.il.us. Search by name, case or docket number.
Criminal Records: Access: Phone, mail, fax, in person, online, email. Both court and visitors may perform in person searches. Search fee: $2.00 per name. Fee is $4.00 for years prior to 1987. Required to search: name, years to search, DOB. Criminal records on computer from 1987, books and index cards from 1920. Online access to criminal records is the same as civil.
General Information: Public access terminal is available. No juvenile or adoption records released. SASE required. Turnaround time 2-3 days. Copy fee: $1.00 for first page, $.50 each add'l. Certification fee: $2.00. Fee payee: Clerk of Circuit Court. Personal checks accepted. Prepayment is required.

Alexander County

Circuit Court 2000 Washington Ave, Cairo, IL 62914; 618-734-0107; Fax: 618-734-7003. Hours: 8AM-4PM (CST). *Felony, Misdemeanor, Civil, Eviction, Small Claims, Probate.*
Civil Records: Access: Fax, mail, in person. Only the court may perform in person seraches. Search fee: $500 per name per year. Required to search: name, years to search. Civil cases indexed by defendant, plaintiff. Civil records on computer from 1987, books and index cards from 1800s.
Criminal Records: Access: Fax, mail, in person. Only the court may perform in person searches. Search fee: $5.00 per name per year. Required to search: name. Criminal records on computer from 1987, books and index cards from 1800s.
General Information: No juvenile or adoption records released. SASE required. Turnaround time 1 day. Copy fee: $1.00 for first page, $.50 each add'l. Certification fee: $2.50. Fee payee: Clerk of Circuit Court. Personal checks accepted. Prepayment is required.

Bond County

Circuit Court 200 W College Ave, Greenville, IL 62246; 618-664-3208; Fax: 618-664-2257. Hours: 8AM-4:30PM (CST). *Felony, Misdemeanor, Civil, Small Claims, Probate.*
www.johnkking.org

Civil Records: Access: Mail, in person. Both court and visitors may perform in person searches. Search fee: $4.00 per name per year. Required to search: name, years to search. Civil cases indexed by defendant, plaintiff. Civil records on computer back to 1/87 (and are limited); in index books from 1900s.
Criminal Records: Access: Mail, in person. Both court and visitors may perform in person searches. Search fee: $4.00 per name per year. Required to search: name, years to search, DOB. Criminal records on computer back to 1964; index books from 1900s.
General Information: Public access terminal is available. No juvenile or adoption records released. SASE required. Turnaround time 1-2 weeks. Copy fee: $.50 per page. Certification fee: $2.00 plus $.50 per page. Fee payee: Clerk of Circuit Court. Personal checks accepted. Prepayment is required.

Boone County

Circuit Court 601 N Main #303, Belvidere, IL 61008; 815-544-0371. Hours: 8:30AM-5PM (CST). *Felony, Misdemeanor, Civil, Eviction, Small Claims, Probate.*
Civil Records: Access: Mail, in person. Both court and visitors may perform in person searches. Search fee: $4.00 per name per year. Required to search: name, years to search. Civil cases indexed by defendant, plaintiff. Civil records on computer since August, 1993, on index books from 1800s.
Criminal Records: Access: Mail, in person. Both court and visitors may perform in person searches. Search

fee: $4.00 per name per year. Required to search: name, years to search, DOB; also helpful: SSN, signed release. Criminal records on computer since August, 1993, on index books from 1800s.

General Information: Public access terminal is available. No juvenile or adoption records released. SASE required. Turnaround time 1-2 days. Copy fee: $1.00 for first page, $.50 each add'l. Certification fee: $2.00. Fee payee: Clerk of Circuit Court. Person checks may be accepted. Prepayment is required.

Brown County

Circuit Court Brown County Courthouse, 200 Court St, Rm 5, Mt Sterling, IL 62353; 217-773-2713. Hours: 8:30AM-4:30PM (CST). *Felony, Misdemeanor, Civil, Eviction, Small Claims, Probate.*

Civil Records: Access: Phone, fax, mail, in person. Both court and visitors may perform in person searches. Search fee: $4.00 per name per year. Required to search: name, years to search. Civil cases indexed by defendant, plaintiff. Civil records on computer since 1994, on index books from 1830s.

Criminal Records: Access: Phone, fax, mail, in person. Both court and visitors may perform in person searches. Search fee: $4.00 per name per year. Required to search: name, years to search, DOB, signed release. Criminal records on computer since 1994, on index books from 1830s.

General Information: Public access terminal is available. No juvenile or adoption records released. SASE required. Turnaround time 1 week. Fax notes: $3.00 per page. Copy fee: $.35 per page. Certification fee: $2.00. Fee payee: Clerk of Circuit Court. Only cashiers checks and money orders accepted. Prepayment is required.

Bureau County

Circuit Court 702 S Main, Princeton, IL 61356; 815-872-2001; Fax: 815-872-0027. Hours: 8AM-4PM (CST). *Felony, Misdemeanor, Civil, Eviction, Small Claims, Probate.*

www.bccirclk.gov

Civil Records: Access: Online, in person. Visitors must perform in person searches for themselves. Required to search: name, years to search. Civil cases indexed by defendant, plaintiff. Civil records on computer from 8/1988, prior on index books. Online access to judicial circuit records is available to local attorney firms and retrievers. The service is free. Call Clerk's office for details, 815-872-0027.

Criminal Records: Access: Mail, fax, in person, online. Both court and visitors may perform in person searches. Search fee: $4.00 per name per year. Required to search: name, years to search, DOB. Criminal records on computer from 8/1988, prior on index books. Online access to criminal records is the same as civil.

General Information: Public access terminal is available. No juvenile or adoption records released. SASE required. Turnaround time 1 week. Fax notes: Fee to fax results is $2.00 1st pg; $1.00 each add'l. Copy fee: $.25 per page. Certification fee: $2.00. Fee payee: Bureau County Circuit Clerk. Personal checks accepted. Prepayment is required.

Calhoun County

Circuit Court PO Box 486, Hardin, IL 62047; 618-576-2451; Fax: 618-576-9541. Hours: 8:30AM-4:30PM (CST). *Felony, Misdemeanor, Civil, Eviction, Small Claims, Probate.*

Civil Records: Access: Phone, fax, mail, in person. Both court and visitors may perform in person searches. Search fee: $4.00 per name. Required to search: name, years to search. Civil cases indexed by defendant, plaintiff. Civil records on index books from 1800s, computerized since 07/98.

Criminal Records: Access: Phone, fax, mail, in person. Both court and visitors may perform in person searches. Search fee: $4.00 per name. Required to search: name, years to search, DOB. Criminal records on index books from 1800s, computerized since 07/98.

General Information: No juvenile or adoption records released. SASE required. Turnaround time 1-2 days. Fax notes: No fee to fax results. Copy fee: $1.00 for first page. $.50 per page, pages 2-19; $.25 each additional page. Certification fee: $2.00. Fee payee: Clerk of Circuit Court. Only cashiers checks and money orders accepted. Prepayment is required.

Carroll County

Circuit Court 301 N Main St, PO Box 32, Mt Carroll, IL 61053; 815-244-0230 X27; Fax: 815-244-3869. Hours: 8:30AM-4:30PM (CST). *Felony, Misdemeanor, Civil, Eviction, Small Claims, Probate.*

Civil Records: Access: Mail, in person, online. Both court and visitors may perform in person searches. Search fee: $4.00 per name per year. Required to search: name, years to search. Civil cases indexed by defendant. Civil records on computer from 1988, prior on index books. Free access to civil, small claims, probate and traffic records available at www.judici.com/IL008015J/index.html.

Criminal Records: Access: Mail, in person, online. Both court and visitors may perform in person searches. Search fee: $4.00 per name per year. Required to search: name, years to search, DOB. Criminal records on computer from 1988, prior on index books. Online access is available free at www.judici.com/IL008015J/index.html. Will respond by fax if possible.

General Information: Public access terminal is available. No juvenile, mental health or adoption records released. SASE required. Turnaround time 2-3 days. Copy fee: $1.00 for first page, $.50 each add'l. Certification fee: $2.00. Fee payee: Clerk of Circuit Court. Personal checks accepted. Prepayment required.

Cass County

Circuit Court PO Box 203, Virginia, IL 62691; 217-452-7225. 8:30AM-4:30PM (CST). *Felony, Misdemeanor, Civil, Eviction, Small Claims, Probate.*

Civil Records: Access: Mail, in person. Both court and visitors may perform in person searches. Search fee: $4.00 per name per year. Required to search: name, years to search. Civil cases indexed by defendant, plaintiff. Civil records on index books from 1800s.

Criminal Records: Access: Mail, in person, online. Both court and visitors may perform in person searches. Search fee: $4.00 per name per year. Required to search: name, years to search, DOB; also helpful: SSN. Criminal records on index books from 1800s, computerized since 08/98.

General Information: Public access terminal is available. No juvenile or adoption records released. SASE required. Turnaround time 1-2 weeks. Copy fee: $1.00 for first page, $.50 each add'l. Certification fee: $2.00. Fee payee: Cass County Circuit Clerk. Personal checks accepted. Prepayment is required.

Champaign County

Circuit Court 101 E Main, Urbana, IL 61801; Civil phone: 217-384-3725; Criminal phone: 217-384-3727; Fax: 217-384-3879. Hours: 8:30AM-4:30PM (CST). *Felony, Misdemeanor, Civil, Eviction, Small Claims, Probate.*

www.cccircuitclerk.com

Civil Records: Access: Mail, online, in person. Both court and visitors may perform in person searches. Search fee: $4.00 per name per year. Required to search: name, years to search. Civil cases indexed by defendant, plaintiff. Civil records on computer from 1986, index books from 1800s. Access to the remote online system called PASS requires a setup fee and

annual user fee. Online case records go back to '92. Fee is $200 per year plus $25 per user; there are separate reduced fees for law firms and non-profits organizations. Contact Jo Kelly at 217-384-3767 for subscription information.

Criminal Records: Access: Mail, online, in person. Both court and visitors may perform in person searches. Search fee: $4.00 per name per year. Required to search: name, years to search; also helpful: DOB, SSN. Criminal records on computer from 1988, index books from 1800s. Online access to criminal records is the same as civil.

General Information: Public access terminal is available. No juvenile or adoption records released. SASE required. Turnaround time 1-2 weeks. Copy fee: $.25 per page. Certification fee: $2.00. Fee payee: Clerk of Circuit Court. Personal checks accepted. Prepayment is required.

Christian County

Circuit Court PO Box 617, Taylorville, IL 62568; 217-824-4966; Fax: 217-824-5030. Hours: 8AM-4PM (CST). *Felony, Misdemeanor, Civil, Eviction, Small Claims, Probate.*

Civil Records: Access: Phone, mail, in person. Both court and visitors may perform in person searches. Search fee: $5.00 per name per year. Required to search: name; also helpful: years to search. Civil cases indexed by defendant, plaintiff. Civil records on computer from 1988, index books from 1840.

Criminal Records: Access: Phone, mail, in person. Both court and visitors may perform in person searches. Search fee: $5.00 per name per year. Required to search: name; also helpful: years to search, DOB. Criminal records on computer from 1988, index books from 1840.

General Information: No juvenile or adoption records released. SASE required. Turnaround time 1-2 days. Copy fee: $1.00 for first page, $.50 each add'l. Certification fee: $2.00. Fee payee: Clerk of Circuit Court. Business checks accepted. Prepayment required.

Clark County

Circuit Court PO Box 187, Marshall, IL 62441; 217-826-2811. Hours: 8AM-4PM (CST). *Felony, Misdemeanor, Civil, Eviction, Small Claims, Probate.*

Civil Records: Access: Mail, in person. Only the court may perform in person searches. Search fee: $4.00 per name per year. Required to search: name, years to search; also helpful: address. Civil cases indexed by defendant, plaintiff. Civil records on computer from 1989, index books from 1800s.

Criminal Records: Access: Mail, in person. Only the court may perform in person searches. Search fee: $4.00 per name per year. Required to search: name, years to search, DOB, signed release; also helpful: address, SSN. Criminal records on computer from 1989, index books from 1800s.

General Information: No juvenile, maternity, or adoption records released. Turnaround time 1 week. Copy fee: $1.00 for first page, $.50 each add'l. After 20 pages, fee is $.25 per page. Certification fee: $2.00. Fee payee: Clerk of Circuit Court. Only cashiers checks and money orders accepted.

Clay County

Circuit Court PO Box 100, Louisville, IL 62858; 618-665-3523; Fax: 618-665-3543. Hours: 8AM-4PM (CST). *Felony, Misdemeanor, Civil, Eviction, Small Claims, Probate.*

Civil Records: Access: Fax, mail, in person. Both court and visitors may perform in person searches. Search fee: $4.00 per name. Fee is $4.00 per year prior to 1988. Required to search: name, years to search. Civil cases indexed by defendant. Civil records on computer from 1988, index books from 1850s.

Criminal Records: Access: Fax, mail, in person. Both court and visitors may perform in person searches. Search fee: $4.00 per name. Fee is $4.00 per year prior to 1988. Required to search: name, years to search; also helpful: DOB. Criminal records on computer from 1988, index books from 1850s.
General Information: Public access terminal is available. No juvenile or adoption records released. SASE required. Turnaround time 2-3 days. Fax notes: $1.00 for first page, $.50 each add'l. Copy fee: $1.00 for first page, $.50 each add'l 19; $.25 each thereafter. Certification fee: $2.00. Fee payee: Clerk of Circuit Court. Personal checks accepted. Prepayment required.

Clinton County

Circuit Court County Courthouse, PO Box 407, Carlyle, IL 62231; 618-594-2464. Hours: 8AM-4PM (CST). *Felony, Misdemeanor, Civil, Eviction, Small Claims, Probate.*
Civil Records: Access: Mail, in person. Both court and visitors may perform in person searches. Search fee: $10.00 per name. Fee is for 10 year search. Required to search: name, years to search. Civil cases indexed by defendant, plaintiff. Civil records on computer from 1988, index books from 1825.
Criminal Records: Access: Mail, in person. Both court and visitors may perform in person searches. Search fee: $10.00 per name. Flat fee for 10 year search. Required to search: name, years to search, DOB. Criminal records on computer from 1988, index books from 1825.
General Information: Public access terminal is available. No juvenile or adoption records released. SASE required. Turnaround time 2-4 days. Copy fee: $.50 per page. Certification fee: $2.00. Fee payee: Clerk of Circuit Court. Personal checks accepted. Prepayment is required.

Coles County

Circuit Court PO Box 48, Charleston, IL 61920; 217-348-0516. Hours: 8:30AM-4:30PM (CST). *Felony, Misdemeanor, Civil, Eviction, Small Claims, Probate.*
Civil Records: Access: Fax, mail, in person. Both court and visitors may perform in person searches. Search fee: $5.00 per name. Required to search: name, years to search. Civil cases indexed by defendant, plaintiff. Civil records on computer from 1989, index books from 1800s.
Criminal Records: Access: Fax, mail, in person. Both court and visitors may perform in person searches. Search fee: $5.00 per name. Required to search: name, years to search, DOB; also helpful: SSN. Criminal records on computer from 1989, index books from 1800s.
General Information: Public access terminal is available. No juvenile or adoption records released. SASE required. Turnaround time 1-2 days. Copy fee: $.50 per page. Certification fee: $2.00. Fee payee: Clerk of Circuit Court. Personal checks accepted. Prepayment is required.

Cook County

Circuit Court - Criminal Division 2650 S California Ave, Chicago, IL 60608; Criminal phone: 773-869-3140; Fax: 773-869-4444. Hours: 8:30AM-4:30PM (CST). *Felony.*
www.cookcountyclerkofcourt.org
Note: Cases are heard in six district courts within the county and each court has a central index.
Criminal Records: Access: Mail, in person. Both court and visitors may perform in person searches. Search fee: $6.00 per name per year. Required to search: name, years to search, DOB; also helpful: SSN. Criminal records on computer since 1964; prior records on microfiche from 1800s.

General Information: Public access terminal is available. (Public access terminal for criminal in person searchers.) No juvenile or adoption records released. Copy fee: $2.00 for first page, $.50 each add'l. $.25 per page after 20. Certification fee: $6.00. Fee payee: Clerk of Circuit Court. Personal checks accepted. Personal checks accepted with drivers license# or attorney code. Prepayment is required.

Circuit Court - Chicago District 1 50 W Washington, Rm 601, Chicago, IL 60602; 312-603-5145; Civil phone: 312-603-5116 (admin); Criminal phone: 312-603-4641; Probate phone: 312-603-6441; Fax: 312-443-4557. Hours: 8:30AM-4:30PM (CST). *Misdemeanor, Civil Action Under $100,000, Eviction, Small Claims, Probate.*
www.cookcountyclerkofcourt.org
Note: Note: Cases are heard in six district courts within the county. Each court has a central index. Eventually all case files are maintained here. Probate is a separate division at the same address.
Civil Records: Access: Phone, mail, online, in person. Both court and visitors may perform in person searches. No search fee. Required to search: name, years to search. Civil cases indexed by defendant, plaintiff. Civil records on computer from 1983, index books from 1800s. Online case searching for limited case information - case snapshots - is available free online at www.cookcountyclerkofcourt.org/Terms/terms.html. Search by name, case number or court date. Information includes parties (up to 3), attorneys, case type, the filing date, the ad damnum (amount of damages sought), division and district, and most current court date. Phone inquiries to court to check status only. Phone record requests can be directed to the Computer Center at 312-603-7586 or 7.
Criminal Records: Access: Phone, mail, online, in person. Visitors must perform in person searches for themselves. Mail searches are directed to the Criminal Bureau, 2650 S California, Chicago 60608. Search fee is $6.00. Required to search: name, years to search, DOB. Misdemeanor records only. Search misdemeanors in person in Room 1006. For online information, see civil. Phone record requests can be directed to the Computer Ctr at 312-603-7586 or 7.
General Information: Public access terminal is available. No juvenile or adoption records released. SASE required. Turnaround time 1 week. Copy fee: $2.00 for first page, $.50 each add'l. Certification fee: $6.00. Fee payee: Clerk of Circuit Court. Personal checks accepted. Prepayment is required.

Bridgeview District 5 10220 S 76th Ave Rm 121, Bridgeview Court Bldg, Bridgeview, IL 60453; Civil phone: 708-974-6500; Criminal phone: 708-974-6404. *Felony, Civil Action Under $100,000, Eviction, Small Claims.*
www.cookcountyclerkofcourt.org
Note: Alsip, Bedford Park, Bridgeview, Burbank, Burr Ridge, Chicago Ridge, Countryside, Evergreen Pk, Forest View, Hickory Hills, Hinsdale, Hodgkins, Hometown, Indian Head Park, Justice, Lagrange, Lemont, Lyons, Merrionette Park, McCook, Oak Lawn, Orland Hills, Orland Park, Palos Heights, Palos Park, Stickney, Summit, Western Springs, West Haven, Willow Springs, Worth.
Civil Records: Access: Online, in person. Visitors must perform in person searches for themselves. No search fee. Required to search: name, years to search. Civil cases indexed by defendant, plaintiff. Civil records computerized since 1985, microfiche to early 1970s. Limited online case information is available; see Circuit Court - Chicago Division for details.
Criminal Records: Access: Online, in person. Mail searches are directed to the Criminal Bureau, 2650 S California, Chicago 60608. Visitors must perform in person searches for themselves. No search fee. Required

to search: name. Online access to criminal records is the same as civil.
General Information: Public access terminal is available. Copy fee: $2.00 for first page, $.50 each add'l. Certification fee: $6.00. Fee payee: Clerk of Circuit Court. Personal checks accepted.

Markham District 6 16501 S Kedzie Pkwy Rm119, Markham, IL 60426-5509; Civil phone: 708-210-4227; Criminal phone: 708-210-4588. *Felony, Civil Action Under $30,000, Eviction, Small Claims.*
www.cookcountyclerkofcourt.org
Note: Blue Is, Burnham, Calumet, Chicago Hgts, Crestwood, Crete, Dixmoor, Dolton, Flossmoor, Glenwood, Harvey, Hazelcrest, Homewood, Lansing, Lynwood, Markham, Matteson, Midlothian, Oak Forest, Posen, Riverdale, Robbins, Sauk Village, Tinley Pk.
Civil Records: Access: Online, in person. Visitors must perform in person searches for themselves. No search fee. Required to search: name. Civil cases indexed by defendant, plaintiff. Civil records computerized since 1989. Limited online case information is available; see Circuit Court - Chicago Division for details.
Criminal Records: Access: Mail, online, in person. Visitors must perform in person searches for themselves. Mail searches are directed to the Criminal Bureau, 2650 S California, Chicago 60608. $6.00 search fee. Required to search: name, years to search. Online access to criminal records is the same as civil.
General Information: Public access terminal is available. Turnaround time 2 weeks. Copy fee: $2.00 for first page, $.50 each add'l. Certification fee: $6.00. Fee payee: Clerk of Circuit Court. Personal checks accepted.

Maywood District 4 1500 S Maybrook Dr, Rm 236, Maywood, IL 60153-2410; Civil phone: 708-865-4973; Criminal phone: 708-865-6040. Hours: 9AM-5PM (CST). *Felony, Civil Action Under $100,000, Eviction, Small Claims.*
www.cookcountyclerkofcourt.org
Note: Bellwood, Berkeley, Berwyn, Broadview, Brookfield, Cicero, Elmwood Park, Forest Park, Franklin Park, Hillside, La Grange Park, Maywood, Melrose Park, Northlake, North Riverside, Oak Park, River Forest, River Grove, Riverside, Stone Park, Westchester.
Civil Records: Access: Mail, online, in person. Visitors must perform in person searches for themselves. No search fee. Required to search: name; also helpful: years to search. Civil cases indexed by defendant, plaintiff. Civil records computerized since 1982, docket books to 1970s, prior archived. Limited online case information is available; see Circuit Court - Chicago Division for details.
Criminal Records: Access: Online, in person. Mail searches are directed to the Criminal Bureau, 2650 S California, Chicago 60608. Visitors must perform in person searches for themselves. No search fee. Required to search: name, years to search, DOB. Online access to criminal records is same as civil.
General Information: Public access terminal is available. Turnaround time 1 week. Copy fee: $2.00 for first page, $.50 each add'l. Certification fee: $6.00. Fee payee: Clerk of Circuit Court. Personal checks accepted. Prepayment is required.

Rolling Meadows District 3 2121 Euclid Ave, Rolling Meadows, IL 60008-1566; Civil phone: 847-818-2300; Criminal phone: 847-818-2701. Hours: 8:30AM-4:30PM (CST). *Felony, Civil Action Under $100,000, Eviction, Small Claims.*
www.cookcountyclerkofcourt.org
Note: Arlington Hgts, Barrington, Bartlett, Bensonville, Buffalo Grove, Elgin, Elk Grove Village, Hanover Pk, Harwood Hgts, Inverness, Mt. Prospect, Norridge,

Palatine, Prospect Hgts, Rolling Meadows, Roselle, Rosemont, Schaumburg, Schiller Pk, Wheeling.

Civil Records: Access: Mail, online, in person. Visitors must perform in person searches for themselves. No search fee. Required to search: name; also helpful: years to search. Civil cases indexed by defendant, plaintiff. Civil records are computerized since 1986. Limited online case information is available; see Circuit Court - Chicago Division for details.

Criminal Records: Access: Online, in person. Mail searches are directed to the Criminal Bureau, 2650 S California, Chicago 60608.Visitors must perform in person searches for themselves. No search fee. Required to search: name, years to search; also helpful: DOB, SSN. Online access to criminal records is the same as civil.

General Information: Public access terminal is available. Turnaround time 2 weeks. Copy fee: $2.00 for first page, $.50 each add'l. Certification fee: $6.00. Fee payee: Clerk of Circuit Court. Personal checks accepted.

Skokie District 2 Skokie Court Bldg Rm 136, 5600 Old Orchard Rd, Skokie, IL 60076-1023; 847-470-7250. Hours: 8:30AM-4:30PM (CST). *Misdemeanor, Civil Action Under $100,000, Eviction, Small Claims.*

www.cookcountyclerkofcourt.org

Note: Deerfield, Des Plaines, Evanston, Glencoe, Glenview, Golf, Kenilworth, Lincolnwood, Morton Grove, Niles, Northbrook, Northfield, Park Ridge, Prospect Heights, Skokie, Wilmette, Winnetka.

Civil Records: Access: Phone, mail, online, in person. Visitors must perform in person searches for themselves. Search fee: $6.00 per name per year. Required to search: name, years to search. Civil cases indexed by defendant, plaintiff. Civil records computerized since 1983. Limited online case information is available; see Circuit Court - Chicago Division for details.

Criminal Records: Access: Phone, mail, online, in person. Mail searches are directed to the Criminal Bureau, 2650 S California, Chicago 60608. Both court and visitors may perform in person searches. Search fee: $6.00 per name per year. Required to search: name, years to search; also helpful: DOB, SSN. Online access to criminal records is same as civil.

General Information: Public access terminal is available. All records are public. SASE not required. Turnaround time 1 week to 1 month. Copy fee: $2.00 for first page, $.50 each add'l. Certification fee: $6.00. Fee payee: Clerk of Circuit Court. Personal checks accepted. Prepayment is required.

Crawford County

Circuit Court PO Box 655, Robinson, IL 62454-0655; 618-544-3512; Fax: 618-546-5628. Hours: 8AM-4PM (CST). *Felony, Misdemeanor, Civil, Eviction, Small Claims, Probate.*

Civil Records: Access: Fax, mail, in person. Both court and visitors may perform in person searches. Search fee: $4.00 per name per year. Required to search: name, years to search. Civil cases indexed by defendant, plaintiff. Civil records on computer from 1989, index books from 1800s.

Criminal Records: Access: Fax, mail, in person. Both court and visitors may perform in person searches. Search fee: $4.00 per name per year. Required to search: name, years to search, DOB. Criminal records on computer from 1989, index books from 1800s.

General Information: Public access terminal is available. No juvenile or adoption records released. SASE required. Turnaround time up to 1 week. Fax notes: $2.00 per page. Copy fee: $1.00 for first page, $.50 each add'l. Certification fee: $2.00. Fee payee: Circuit Clerk. Personal checks accepted. Prepayment is required.

Cumberland County

Circuit Court PO Box 145, Toledo, IL 62468; 217-849-3601; Fax: 217-849-2655. Hours: 8AM-4PM (CST). *Felony, Misdemeanor, Civil, Eviction, Small Claims, Probate.*

Civil Records: Access: Phone, fax, mail, in person. Both court and visitors may perform in person searches. Search fee: $4.00 per name per year. Required to search: name, years to search. Civil cases indexed by defendant, plaintiff. Civil records on computer from 1990, index books from 1885.

Criminal Records: Access: Phone, fax, mail, in person. Both court and visitors may perform in person searches. Search fee: $4.00 per name per year. Required to search: name, years to search; also helpful: DOB, SSN. Criminal records on computer from 1990, index books from 1885.

General Information: No juvenile or adoption records released. SASE required. Turnaround time up to 1 week. Copy fee: $1.00 for 1st page, $.50 per page next 19, then $.25 per page. Certification fee: $2.00. Fee payee: Clerk of Circuit Court. Only cashiers checks and money orders accepted. Prepayment is required.

De Kalb County

Circuit Court 133 W State St, Sycamore, IL 60178; Civil phone: 815-895-7131; Criminal phone: 815-895-7138; Fax: 815-895-7140. Hours: 8:30AM-4:30PM (CST). *Felony, Misdemeanor, Civil, Eviction, Small Claims, Probate.*

Civil Records: Access: Mail, in person. Both court and visitors may perform in person searches. Search fee: $4.00 per name per year. Required to search: name, years to search; also helpful: address. Civil cases indexed by defendant, plaintiff. Civil records on computer since 1987, records go back to 1858. Court planning to offer online access. Call 1-800-307-1100 for more information.

Criminal Records: Access: Mail, in person. Both court and visitors may perform in person searches. Search fee: $4.00 per name per year. Required to search: name, years to search, signed release; also helpful: address, DOB. Criminal records on computer since 9/91, on index books back 60 years. Court planning to offer online access to criminal records. Call 1-800-307-1100 for more information.

General Information: Public access terminal is available. No juvenile or adoption records released. SASE required. Turnaround time 2 weeks. Copy fee: $1.00 for first page, $.50 each add'l. After 20 pages, copies are $.25 each. Certification fee: $2.00. Fee payee: DeKalb County Circuit Clerk. Personal checks accepted. Credit cards accepted: Visa, MasterCard. Accepted in person only. Prepayment is required.

De Witt County

Circuit Court 201 Washington St, Clinton, IL 61727; 217-935-2195; Fax: 217-935-3310. Hours: 8:30AM-4:30PM (CST). *Felony, Misdemeanor, Civil, Eviction, Small Claims, Probate.*

Civil Records: Access: Mail, fax, in person. Both court and visitors may perform in person searches. Search fee: $4.00 per name per year. Required to search: name, years to search. Civil cases indexed by defendant. Civil records on computer from 1989, index books to 1839.

Criminal Records: Access: Mail, fax, in person. Both court and visitors may perform in person searches. Search fee: $4.00 per name per year. Required to search: name, years to search, DOB. Criminal records on computer from 1989, index books from 1839.

General Information: Public access terminal is available. No juvenile or adoption records released. SASE required. Turnaround time 1-2 weeks. Copy fee: $.50 for first page, $.25 each add'l. Certification fee: $2.00. Fee payee: Clerk of Circuit Court. Only cashiers

checks and money orders accepted. Prepayment is required.

Douglas County

Circuit Court PO Box 50, Tuscola, IL 61953; 217-253-2352. Hours: 8:30AM-4:30PM (CST). *Felony, Misdemeanor, Civil, Eviction, Small Claims, Probate.*

Civil Records: Access: Phone, fax, mail, in person. Both court and visitors may perform in person searches. Search fee: $4.00 per name per year. Required to search: name, years to search. Civil cases indexed by defendant, plaintiff. Civil records on computer from 1989, index books from 1859.

Criminal Records: Access: Mail, in person. Both court and visitors may perform in person searches. Search fee: $4.00 per name per year. Required to search: name, years to search: also helpful: DOB, SSN. Criminal records on computer from 1989, index books to 1859.

General Information: Public access terminal is available. No juvenile or adoption records released. SASE required. Turnaround time 1 week. Fax notes: $5.00 for 1st 4 pages; $1.00 each add'l. Copy fee: $1.00 for first page, $.50 each add'l. $.25 per pg after 20 pages. Certification fee: $2.00. Fee payee: Douglas County Circuit Clerk. Personal checks accepted. Prepayment is required.

Du Page County

Circuit Court 505 N County Farm Rd, Wheaton, IL 60187; Civil phone: 630-682-7100; Criminal phone: 630-682-7080; Fax: 630-682-7082. Hours: 8:30AM-4:30PM (CST). *Felony, Misdemeanor, Civil, Eviction, Small Claims, Probate.*

www.co.dupage.il.us/courtclerk

Civil Records: Access: Phone, mail, in person. Both court and visitors may perform in person searches. Search fee: $6.00 per name per year. Required to search: name, years to search. Civil cases indexed by defendant, plaintiff. Civil records online from 1976, microfilm records back to 1939, index records back to 1839. All document files after 01/01/92 are on optical disk.

Criminal Records: Access: Phone, mail, in person. Both court and visitors may perform in person searches. Search fee: $6.00 per name per year. Required to search: name, years to search, DOB. Criminal records online from 1976, microfilm records back to 1939, index records back to 1839. All document files after 01/01/92 are on optical disk.

General Information: Public access terminal is available. No juvenile or adoption records released. SASE required. Turnaround time 1 week. Copy fee: $2.00 for first page, $.50 each add'l. Certification fee: $6.00. Fee payee: Clerk of Circuit Court. Personal checks accepted. Credit cards accepted: Visa, MasterCard. Prepayment is required.

Edgar County

Circuit Court County Courthouse, 115 W Court, Paris, IL 61944; 217-466-7447. Hours: 8AM-4PM (CST). *Felony, Misdemeanor, Civil, Eviction, Small Claims, Probate.*

Civil Records: Access: Phone, mail, in person. Both court and visitors may perform in person searches. Search fee: $4.00 per name per year. Required to search: Name, years to search. Civil cases indexed by defendant, plaintiff. Civil records on computer from 1992, index books from 1823.

Criminal Records: Access: In person only. Both court and visitors may perform in person searches. Search fee: $4.00 per name per year. Required to search: Name, years to search, DOB. Criminal records on computer from 1992, index books from 1880.

General Information: No juvenile or adoption records released. SASE required. Turnaround time 1 week. Copy fee: $.50 per page. Certification fee: $1.00. Fee payee: Janis K. Nebergall, Circuit Clerk. Personal checks accepted. Prepayment is required.

Edwards County

Circuit Court County Courthouse, Albion, IL 62806; 618-445-2016; Fax: 618-445-4943. Hours: 8AM-4PM (CST). *Felony, Misdemeanor, Civil, Eviction, Small Claims, Probate.*

Civil Records: Access: Mail, in person. Both court and visitors may perform in person searches. Search fee: $4.00 per name per year. Required to search: name, years to search. Civil cases indexed by defendant. Civil records on computer from 1988, books and index cards from 1815.

Criminal Records: Access: Mail, in person. Both court and visitors may perform in person searches. Search fee: $4.00 per name per year. Required to search: name, years to search, DOB. Criminal records on computer from 1988, index books from 1815.

General Information: Public access terminal is available. No juvenile or adoption records released. SASE required. Turnaround time 1 week. Copy fee: $.30 per page. Certification fee: $2.00. Fee payee: Clerk of Circuit Court. Only cashiers checks and money orders accepted. Prepayment is required.

Effingham County

Circuit Court 100 E Jefferson, PO Box 586, Effingham, IL 62401; 217-342-4065; Fax: 217-342-6183. Hours: 8AM-4PM (CST). *Felony, Misdemeanor, Civil, Small Claims, Probate.*

Civil Records: Access: Mail, in person. Both court and visitors may perform in person searches. Search fee: $4.00 per name per year. Required to search: name, years to search; also helpful: address. Civil cases indexed by defendant, plaintiff. Civil records on computer from 1988, index books from 1800s.

Criminal Records: Access: Mail, in person. Both court and visitors may perform in person searches. Search fee: $4.00 per name per year. Required to search: name, years to search, DOB; also helpful: address. Criminal records on computer from 1988, index books to 1800s.

General Information: Public access terminal is available. No juvenile or adoption records released. SASE required. Turnaround time 1 week. Copy fee: $1.00 for first page, $.50 each add'l. $.25 per page after 20. Certification fee: $2.00. Fee payee: Effingham County Circuit Clerk. Business checks accepted. Prepayment is required.

Fayette County

Circuit Court 221 S 7th St, Vandalia, IL 62471; 618-283-5009. Hours: 8AM-4PM (CST). *Felony, Misdemeanor, Civil, Eviction, Small Claims, Probate.*

Civil Records: Access: Phone, mail, fax, in person. Both court and visitors may perform in person searches. Search fee: $4.00 per name per year. Required to search: name, years to search. Civil cases indexed by defendant. Civil records on computer from 1988, index books from 1800s.

Criminal Records: Access: Phone, mail, fax, in person. Both court and visitors may perform in person searches. Search fee: $4.00 per name per year. Required to search: name, years to search, DOB. Criminal records on computer from 1988, index books from 1800s.

General Information: Public access terminal is available. No juvenile, impounded or adoption records released. SASE required. Turnaround time 1 month. Copy fee: $1.00 for first page, $.50 each add'l. Certification fee: $1.00. Fee payee: Clerk of Circuit Court. Business checks accepted. Prepayment required.

Ford County

Circuit Court 200 W State St, Paxton, IL 60957; 217-379-2641; Fax: 217-379-3445. Hours: 8:30AM-4:30PM (CST). *Felony, Misdemeanor, Civil, Eviction, Small Claims, Probate.*

Civil Records: Access: Mail, fax, in person. Both court and visitors may perform in person searches. Search fee: $4.00 per name per year. Required to search: name, years to search. Civil cases indexed by defendant. Civil records on index books from 1800s; on computer back to 3/2000.

Criminal Records: Access: Mail, fax, in person. Both court and visitors may perform in person searches. Search fee: $4.00 per name per year. Required to search: name, years to search, DOB (signed release if for juvenile). Criminal records on index books from 1800s; on computer back to 3/2000.

General Information: Public access terminal is available. No juvenile or adoption records released. SASE required. Turnaround time 2 days. Copy fee: $1.00 for first page, $.50 each add'l. after 20 pages then $.25 per page. Certification fee: $2.00. Fee payee: Clerk of Circuit Court. Personal checks accepted. Prepayment is required.

Franklin County

Circuit Court County Courthouse, PO Box 485, Benton, IL 62812; Civil phone: 618-439-2011. Hours: 8AM-4PM (CST). *Felony, Misdemeanor, Civil, Small Claims, Probate, Entry and Detainer.*

Civil Records: Access: Mail, in person. Both court and visitors may perform in person searches. Search fee: $4.00 per name per year. Required to search: name, years to search. Civil cases indexed by defendant, plaintiff. Civil records on computer from 1987, index books from 1843.

Criminal Records: Access: Mail, in person. Both court and visitors may perform in person searches. Search fee: $4.00 per name per year. Required to search: name, years to search, DOB. Criminal records on computer from 1987, index books from 1843.

General Information: No juvenile or adoption records released. SASE required. Turnaround time 1 week. Copy fee: $1.00 for first page, $.50 each add'l. Certification fee: $2.00. Fee payee: Franklin County Circuit Clerk. Only cashiers checks and money orders accepted. Prepayment is required.

Fulton County

Circuit Court PO Box 152, Lewistown, IL 61542; 309-547-3041; Fax: 309-547-3674. Hours: 8AM-4PM (CST). *Felony, Misdemeanor, Civil, Eviction, Small Claims, Probate.*

Civil Records: Access: Phone, mail, fax, in person. Both court and visitors may perform in person searches. Search fee: $4.00 per name per year. Required to search: name, years to search. Civil cases indexed by defendant, plaintiff. Civil records on computer back to 1990, index books from 1900.

Criminal Records: Access: Mail, in person. Both court and visitors may perform in person searches. Search fee: $4.00 per name per year. Required to search: name, years to search; also helpful: DOB. Criminal records on computer back to 1990, index books from 1879.

General Information: Public access terminal is available. No juvenile, impounded or adoption records released. SASE required. Turnaround time 1-2 days; older, archived records require add'l 2-3 days. Copy fee: $1.00 for first page, $.50 each add'l. Certification fee: $2.00. Fee payee: Fulton County Circuit Clerk. Business checks accepted. Prepayment is required.

Gallatin County

Circuit Court County Courthouse, PO Box 249, Shawneetown, IL 62984; 618-269-3140; Fax: 618-269-4324. Hours: 8AM-4PM (CST). *Felony, Misdemeanor, Civil, Eviction, Small Claims, Probate.*

Civil Records: Access: Fax, mail, in person. Both the court and visitors may perform in person searches. Search fee: $4.00 per name, per year. Required to search: name, years to search. Civil cases indexed by defendant. Civil records on index books from 1800s; computerized records since 1992.

Criminal Records: Access: Fax, mail, in person. Both the court and visitors may perform in person searches. Search fee: $4.00 per name, per year. Required to search: name, years to search, DOB, signed release. Criminal records on index books from 1800s; computerized records since 1992.

General Information: No juvenile or adoption records released. SASE required. Turnaround time 1 week. Fax notes: $1.00 per page. Copy fee: $.25 per page. Certification fee: $1.00. Fee payee: Clerk of Circuit Court. Business checks accepted. Prepayment required.

Greene County

Circuit Court 519 N Main, County Courthouse, Carrollton, IL 62016; 217-942-3421; Fax: 217-942-6211. Hours: 8AM-4PM (CST). *Felony, Misdemeanor, Civil, Eviction, Small Claims, Probate.*

Civil Records: Access: Phone, mail, in person. Both court and visitors may perform in person searches. Search fee: $5.00 per name. Required to search: name, years to search. Civil cases indexed by defendant, plaintiff. Civil records on index books from 1830s; computerized since 2002.

Criminal Records: Access: Phone, fax, mail, in person. Both court and visitors may perform in person searches. Search fee: $5.00 per name. Required to search: name, years to search, DOB. Criminal records on index books from 1875; computerized since 2002. No felonies by phone. Include signed release with felony search requests.

General Information: No juvenile or adoption records released. SASE required. Turnaround time 1-2 days. Fax notes: $.25 per page. Copy fee: $.25 per page. Certification fee: $2.00. Fee payee: Clerk of Circuit Court. Personal checks accepted. Prepayment required.

Grundy County

Circuit Court PO Box 707, Morris, IL 60450; 815-941-3256; Fax: 815-942-2222. Hours: 8AM-4:30PM (CST). *Felony, Misdemeanor, Civil, Eviction, Small Claims, Probate.*

Civil Records: Access: Mail, online, in person. Both court and visitors may perform in person searches. Search fee: $4.00 per name per year. Required to search: name, years to search. Civil cases indexed by defendant, plaintiff. Civil records on computer back to 1988. Online access to judicial circuit records should be available in 2001 for local attorney firms and retrievers. Service is free. Call the Clerk's office at 815-941-3256 for details.

Criminal Records: Access: Mail, in person. Both court and visitors may perform in person searches. Search fee: $4.00 per name per year. Required to search: name, years to search, DOB, signed release. Criminal records on computer back to 1988.

General Information: Public access terminal is available. No juvenile or adoption records released. SASE required. Turnaround time 1-2 days. Copy fee: $.50 per page. Certification fee: $2.00. Fee payee: Clerk of Circuit Court. Personal checks accepted. Prepayment is required.

Hamilton County

Circuit Court County Courthouse, McLeansboro, IL 62859; 618-643-3224; Fax: 618-643-3455. Hours: 8AM-4:30PM (CST). *Felony, Misdemeanor, Civil, Eviction, Small Claims, Probate.*

Civil Records: Access: Mail, in person. Both court and visitors may perform in person searches. Search fee: $4.00 per name per year. Required to search: name, years to search. Civil cases indexed by defendant, plaintiff. Civil records on index books from 1800s; computer records go back to 1990.

Criminal Records: Access: Mail, in person. Both court and visitors may perform in person searches. Search fee: $4.00 per name per year. Required to search: name, years to search, DOB. Criminal records on index books from 1800s; computer records go back to 1990.

General Information: No juvenile or adoption records released. SASE required. Turnaround time 1-2 days. Copy fee: $.30 per page. Certification fee: $1.00 per page, $.50 per page for next 19 pages; additional pages $.25. Fee payee: Clerk of Circuit Court. No personal checks accepted. Prepayment is required.

Hancock County

Circuit Court PO Box 189, Carthage, IL 62321; 217-357-2616; Fax: 217-357-2231. Hours: 8AM-4PM (CST). *Felony, Misdemeanor, Civil, Eviction, Small Claims, Probate.*

Civil Records: Access: Mail, in person. Both court and visitors may perform in person searches. Search fee: $15.00 per name per year. Required to search: name, years to search. Civil cases indexed by defendant, plaintiff. Civil records on computer from 1992, index books from 1800s.

Criminal Records: Access: Mail, in person. Both court and visitors may perform in person searches. Search fee: $15.00 per name per year. Required to search: name, years to search, DOB; also helpful: SSN. Criminal records on computer from 1990, index books from 1970, archived to 1800s.

General Information: No juvenile or adoption records released. SASE required. Turnaround time 1 week. Copy fee: $.50 per page. Certification fee: $5.00. Fee payee: Clerk of Circuit Court. Personal checks accepted. Prepayment is required.

Hardin County

Circuit Court County Courthouse, Elizabethtown, IL 62931; 618-287-2735; Fax: 618-287-7833. Hours: 8AM-4PM (CST). *Felony, Misdemeanor, Civil, Eviction, Small Claims, Probate.*

Civil Records: Access: Mail, fax, in person. Both court and visitors may perform in person searches. Search fee: $4.00 per name per year. Required to search: name, years to search. Civil cases indexed by defendant, plaintiff. Civil records on computer back to 9/1992; on index books from 1800s.

Criminal Records: Access: Mail, fax, in person. Both court and visitors may perform in person searches. Search fee: $4.00 per name per year. Required to search: name, years to search, DOB. Criminal records on computer back to 9/1992; on index books from 1800s.

General Information: No juvenile or adoption records released. SASE required. Turnaround time 1 week. Fax notes: Fee to fax results is $2.00 for 1st 2 pages; $.50 each add'l page. Copy fee: $.25 per page. Certification fee: $1.00 plus $.50 each add'l page. Fee payee: Circuit Clerk. Only cashiers checks and money orders accepted. Prepayment is required.

Henderson County

Circuit Court County Courthouse, PO Box 546, Oquawka, IL 61469; 309-867-3121; Fax: 309-867-3207. Hours: 8AM-4PM (CST). *Felony, Misdemeanor, Civil, Eviction, Small Claims, Probate.*

Civil Records: Access: Phone, mail, in person. Both court and visitors may perform in person searches. No search fee. Required to search: name, years to search. Civil cases indexed by defendant, plaintiff. Civil records on computer from 1991, index books from 1800s.

Criminal Records: Access: Phone, mail, in person. Both court and visitors may perform in person searches. No search fee. Required to search: name, years to search, DOB; also helpful: SSN. Criminal records on computer from 1991, index books from 1800s.

General Information: Public access terminal is available. No juvenile or adoption records released. SASE required. Turnaround time 1 day to 1 week. Copy fee: $.25 per page. Certification fee: $1.00 plus $.50 each add'l page. Fee payee: Clerk of Circuit Court. Personal checks accepted. Prepayment is required.

Henry County

Circuit Court Henry County Courthouse, PO Box 9, Cambridge, IL 61238; 309-937-3572. Hours: 8AM-4:30PM (CST). *Felony, Misdemeanor, Civil, Eviction, Small Claims, Probate.*

Civil Records: Access: Mail, in person. Both court and visitors may perform in person searches. Search fee: $4.00 per name per year. Required to search: name, years to search. Civil cases indexed by defendant. Civil records on computer from 1989, index books from 1800s.

Criminal Records: Access: Mail, in person. Both court and visitors may perform in person searches. Search fee: $4.00 per name per year. Required to search: name, middle initial, years to search, DOB; also helpful-last known address. Criminal records on computer from 1989, index books from 1800s.

General Information: Public access terminal is available. No juvenile or adoption records released. SASE not required. Turnaround time 2 weeks. Copy fee: $.50 per page. Certification fee: $2.00. Fee payee: Clerk of Circuit Court. Only cashiers checks and money orders accepted. Prepayment is required.

Iroquois County

Circuit Court 550 S 10th St, Watseka, IL 60970; 815-432-6950 (6952 Traff) (6991 Ch Supp); Fax: 815-432-6953. Hours: 8:30AM-4:30PM (CST). *Felony, Misdemeanor, Civil, Eviction, Small Claims, Probate.*

Civil Records: Access: Fax, mail, in person. Both court and visitors may perform in person searches. Search fee: $4.00 per name per year. Required to search: name, years to search. Civil cases indexed by defendant. Civil records on index books from 1900, computerized since 1989.

Criminal Records: Access: Fax, mail, in person. Both court and visitors may perform in person searches. Search fee: $4.00 per name per year. Required to search: name, years to search, DOB. Criminal records on index books from 1820, computerized since 1989.

General Information: No juvenile or adoption records released. SASE required. Turnaround time 1-2 days. Fax notes: Fee to fax results is $4.00 per document. Copy fee: $.50 per page. Certification fee: $2.00. Fee payee: Clerk of Circuit Court. Personal checks accepted. Prepayment is required.

Jackson County

Circuit Court County Courthouse, 1001 Walnut, PO Box 730, Murphysboro, IL 62966; 618-687-7300. Hours: 8AM-4PM (CST). *Felony, Misdemeanor, Civil, Eviction, Small Claims, Probate.*

www.circuitclerk.co.jackson.il.us

Civil Records: Access: Mail, in person, online. Both court and visitors may perform in person searches. Search fee: $4.00 per name per year. Required to search: name, years to search. Civil cases indexed by defendant, plaintiff. Civil records on computer from 1986, index books from 1860. Free access to civil, small claims, probate and traffic records available at http://circuitclerk.co.jackson.il.us.

Criminal Records: Access: Mail, in person, online. Both court and visitors may perform in person searches. Search fee: $4.00 per name, per year. Required to search: name, years to search. Criminal records on computer from 1986, index books from 1860. Online access is available at http://circuitclerk.co.jackson.il.us.

General Information: Public access terminal is available. No juvenile or adoption records released. SASE required. Turnaround time 1-2 weeks. Copy fee: $.50 per page. Certification fee: $2.00. Fee payee: Circuit Clerk. Personal checks accepted. Prepayment is required.

Jasper County

Circuit Court 100 W Jourdan St, Newton, IL 62448; 618-783-2524. Hours: 8AM-4:30PM (CST). *Felony, Misdemeanor, Civil, Eviction, Small Claims, Probate.*

Civil Records: Access: Mail, in person. Both court and visitors may perform in person searches. Search fee: $4.00 per name. Required to search: name, years to search; also helpful: address. Civil cases indexed by defendant, plaintiff. Civil records on computer from 1988, index books from 1835.

Criminal Records: Access: Mail, in person. Both court and visitors may perform in person searches. Search fee: $4.00 per name. Required to search: name, years to search, DOB, sex, signed release. Criminal records on computer from 1988, index books from 1835.

General Information: No juvenile or adoption records released. SASE required. Turnaround time 1 week. Fax notes: Fee to fax results is $2.00 per document. Copy fee: $.50 per page. Certification fee: $2.00. Fee payee: Clerk of Circuit Court. Personal checks accepted. Prepayment is required.

Jefferson County

Circuit Court PO Box 1266, Mt Vernon, IL 62864; 618-244-8008; Fax: 618-244-8029. Hours: 8AM-5PM (CST). *Felony, Misdemeanor, Civil, Eviction, Small Claims, Probate.*

Civil Records: Access: Phone, fax, mail, in person. Both court and visitors may perform in person searches. Search fee: $8.00. Required to search: name, years to search. Civil cases indexed by defendant. Civil records on computer back to 1988, index books from 1800s. Fax requests must be followed by original by mail before being processed.

Criminal Records: Access: Phone, fax, mail, in person. Both court and visitors may perform in person searches. Search fee: $8.00. Required to search: name, years to search, DOB, SSN. Criminal records on computer back to 1988, index books from 1800s.

General Information: Sealed records not released. SASE required. Turnaround time 1-2 weeks. Fax notes: $.25 per page + phone charge. Copy fee: $.25 per page. Fee payee: Clerk of Circuit Court. Only cashiers checks and money orders accepted. Prepayment is required.

Jersey County

Circuit Court 201 W Pearl St, Jerseyville, IL 62052; 618-498-5571; Fax: 618-498-6128. Hours: 8:30AM-4:30PM (CST). *Felony, Misdemeanor, Civil, Eviction, Small Claims, Probate.*

Civil Records: Access: Fax, mail, in person. Both court and visitors may perform in person searches. Search fee: $5.00 per name. Required to search: name, years to search. Civil cases indexed by defendant. Civil records on computer from 1991, index books from 1800s.

Criminal Records: Access: Fax, mail, in person. Both court and visitors may perform in person searches. Search fee: $5.00 per name. Required to search: name, years to search, DOB. Criminal records on computer back to 1991, index books from 1800s.

General Information: No juvenile or adoption records released. SASE required. Turnaround time 1 week. Copy fee: $2 for 1st 2 pgs - $.50 each add'l. Certification fee: $6.00. Fee payee: Clerk of Circuit Court. Personal checks accepted. Prepayment required.

Jo Daviess County

Circuit Court 330 N Bench St, Galena, IL 61036; 815-777-2295/0037. Hours: 8AM-4PM (CST). *Felony, Misdemeanor, Civil, Eviction, Small Claims, Probate.*

Civil Records: Access: In person, online. Visitors must perform in person searches for themselves. No search fee. Required to search: name, years to search. Civil cases indexed by defendant, plaintiff. Civil records on computer since 1992, on index books from 1960; will and probate back to 1850. Free access to civil, small claims, probate and traffic records available at www.judici.com/IL043015J/index.html.

Criminal Records: Access: Mail, in person, online. Both court and visitors may perform in person searches. Search fee: $4.00 per name. Fee is for 1992 to present. Prior to 1992 $4.00 per name per year. Required to search: name, years to search, DOB. Criminal records on computer since 1992, on index books from 1960. Online access to court records is available free at www.judici.com/IL043015J/index.html.

General Information: Public access terminal is available. No juvenile or adoption records released. SASE required. Turnaround time 1 week. Fax notes: Will not fax results. Copy fee: $.25 per page. Certification fee: $2.00. Fee payee: Circuit Clerk. Business checks accepted. Prepayment is required.

Johnson County

Circuit Court PO Box 517, Vienna, IL 62995; 618-658-4751; Fax: 618-658-2908. Hours: 8AM-4PM (CST). *Felony, Misdemeanor, Civil, Eviction, Small Claims, Probate.*

Civil Records: Access: Mail, in person. Both court and visitors may perform in person searches. Search fee: $4.00 per name per year. Required to search: name, years to search. Civil cases indexed by defendant, plaintiff. Civil records on computer from 1987, index books from 1930s.

Criminal Records: Access: Mail, in person. Both court and visitors may perform in person searches. Search fee: $4.00 per name per year. Required to search: name, years to search, DOB. Criminal records on computer from 1987, index books from 1930s.

General Information: Public access terminal is available. No juvenile or adoption records released. SASE required. Turnaround time 1 week. Copy fee: $.50. Certification fee: $3.00. Fee payee: Circuit Clerk. Business checks accepted. Prepayment is required.

Kane County

Circuit Court PO Box 112, Geneva, IL 60134; 630-232-3413; Civil phone: 630-208-3323; Criminal phone: 630-208-3319; Fax: 630-208-2172. Hours: 8:30AM-4:30PM (CST). *Felony, Misdemeanor, Civil, Eviction, Small Claims, Probate.*

www.co.kane.il.us/circuitclerk

Civil Records: Access: Phone, fax, mail, in person. Both court and visitors may perform in person searches. Search fee: $4.00 per name per year. Fee is for past 5 years. $8.00 for past 6 years or more. Required to search: name, years to search. Civil cases indexed by defendant, plaintiff. Civil records on computer from 1986, index books from 1800s.

Criminal Records: Access: Phone, fax, mail, in person. Both court and visitors may perform in person searches. Search fee: $4.00 per name per year. Required to search: name, years to search, DOB. Criminal records on computer past 5-7 years, index books from 1800s. Same as civil.

General Information: Public access terminal is available. No juvenile, mental health or adoption records released. SASE required. Turnaround time 1 week. Fax notes: $2.00 for first page, $.50 each add'l. Copy fee: $2.00 for first page, $.50 each add'l. Certification fee: $4.00. Judgment orders certification fee $10.00. Fee payee: Clerk of Circuit Court. Personal checks accepted. Credit cards accepted: Visa, MasterCard, Discover card. Prepayment is required.

Kankakee County

Circuit Court 450 E Court St, County Courthouse, Kankakee, IL 60901; 815-937-2905; Fax: 815-939-8830. Hours: 8:30AM-4:30PM (CST). *Felony, Misdemeanor, Civil, Eviction, Small Claims, Probate.*

Civil Records: Access: Mail, in person. Both court and visitors may perform in person searches. Search fee: $4.00 per name per year. Required to search: name, years to search. Civil cases indexed by defendant, plaintiff. Civil records on computer from 1990, index books from 1800s.

Criminal Records: Access: Mail, in person. Both court and visitors may perform in person searches. Search fee: $4.00 per name per year. Required to search: name, years to search, DOB. Criminal records on computer from 1990, index books from 1800s.

General Information: Public access terminal is available. No juvenile, impounded, mental health, expunged or adoption records released. SASE required. Turnaround time 1-2 weeks. Copy fee: $1.00 for first page, $.50 each add'l. Certification fee: $2.00. Fee payee: Clerk of Circuit Court. Personal checks accepted. Prepayment is required.

Kendall County

Circuit Court PO Drawer M, 807 W John St, Yorkville, IL 60560; 630-553-4183. Hours: 8AM-4:30PM (CST). *Felony, Misdemeanor, Civil, Eviction, Small Claims, Probate.*

Civil Records: Access: Mail, in person. Both court and visitors may perform in person searches. Search fee: $4.00 per name per year. Required to search: name, years to search. Civil cases indexed by defendant, plaintiff. Civil records on computer since 1992, on index books from 1800s.

Criminal Records: Access: Mail, in person. Both court and visitors may perform in person searches. Search fee: $4.00 per name per year. Required to search: name, years to search, DOB. Criminal records on computer since 1992, on index books from 1800s.

General Information: Public access terminal is available. No juvenile or adoption records released. SASE required. Turnaround time 2-3 days. Copy fee: $1.00 for first page, $.50 each add'l. $2.00 per page when hard copy printouts when cases are maintained on an automated medium. Certification fee: $2.00. Fee payee: Clerk of Circuit Court. Only cashiers checks and money orders accepted. Prepayment is required.

Knox County

Circuit Court County Courthouse, Galesburg, IL 61401; 309-345-3817; Fax: 309-345-0098. Hours: 8:30AM-4:30PM (CST). *Felony, Misdemeanor, Civil, Eviction, Small Claims, Probate.*

Civil Records: Access: Fax, mail, in person. Both court and visitors may perform in person searches. Search fee: $4.00 per year per name. Required to search: name, years to search. Civil cases indexed by defendant, plaintiff. Civil records on index books from 1800s.

Criminal Records: Access: Fax, mail, in person. Both court and visitors may perform in person searches. Search fee: $4.00 per year per name. Required to search: name, years to search, DOB, sex. Criminal records on index books from 1800s.

General Information: No juvenile or adoption records released. SASE not required. Turnaround time 1 week. Copy fee: $1.00 for first page, $.50 each add'l. Certification fee: $2.00. Fee payee: Clerk of Circuit Court. Personal checks accepted. Prepayment is required.

La Salle County

Circuit Court - Civil Division PO Box 617, 707 Etna Road, Ottawa, IL 61350-0617; Civil phone: 815-434-8671; Criminal phone: 815-434-8271; Fax: 815-433-9198. Hours: 8AM-4:30PM (CST). *Civil, Eviction, Small Claims, Probate.*

Note: Criminal fax is 815-434-9299

Civil Records: Access: Mail, online, in person. Both court and visitors may perform in person searches. Search fee: $4.00 per name per year. Required to search: name, years to search. Civil cases indexed by defendant, plaintiff. Some records on computer since late 1980s; prior records on index books from 1800s. Online access to Judicial Circuit records requires a $200 setup fee (waived for not-for-profits) and $.10 per minute usage fee. Call the Clerk's office at 815-434-8671 for details.

General Information: Public access terminal is available. No juvenile or adoption records released. SASE required. Turnaround time 1-2 weeks. Fax notes: No fee to fax results. Copy fee: $1.00 for first page, $.50 each add'l. Certification fee: $2.00. Fee payee: Clerk of Circuit Court. Personal checks accepted. Credit cards accepted: Visa, MasterCard. Prepayment is required.

Circuit Court - Criminal Division 707 Etna Rd, Ottawa, IL 61360; 815-434-8271; Fax: 815-434-8299. 8AM-4:30PM (CST). *Felony, Misdemeanor.*

www.lasallecounty.com

Criminal Records: Access: Fax, mail, in person, online. Visitors must perform in person searches for themselves. No search fee. Required to search: name, years to search; also helpful: DOB. Online access to Judicial Circuit records requires a $200 setup fee (waived for not-for-profits) and $.10 per minute usage fee. Call the Clerk's office at 815-434-8671 for details.

General Information: Public access terminal is available. No juvenile or adoption records released. SASE required. Turnaround time 1-2 weeks. Fax notes: No fee to fax results. Copy fee: $1.00 for first page, $.50 each add'l. Certification fee: $2.00. Fee payee: Clerk of Circuit Court. Personal checks accepted. Credit cards accepted: Visa, MasterCard. Prepayment is required.

Lake County

Circuit Court 18 N County St, Waukegan, IL 60085; 847-360-6680. Hours: 8:30AM-5PM (CST). *Felony, Misdemeanor, Civil, Eviction, Small Claims, Probate.*

Civil Records: Access: Phone, mail, in person. Both court and visitors may perform in person searches. Search fee: $4.00 per name per year (first year free). Required to search: name, years to search. Civil cases indexed by defendant, plaintiff. Civil records on computer or microfiche from 1968, index books from 1800s.

Criminal Records: Access: Phone, mail, in person. Both court and visitors may perform in person searches. Search fee: $4.00 per name per year (first year free). Required to search: name, years to search, DOB. Criminal records on computer or microfiche from 1968, index books from 1800s.

General Information: Public access terminal is available. No juvenile or adoption records released.

SASE required. Turnaround time 1-2 days. Copy fee: $2.00 for first page, $.50 each add'l. Certification fee: $4.00. Fee payee: Circuit Clerk. No personal checks accepted. Credit cards accepted: Discover. Discover. Prepayment is required.

Lawrence County

Circuit Court County Courthouse, 1100 State St, Lawrenceville, IL 62439; 618-943-2815; Fax: 618-943-5205. Hours: 8AM-4PM (CST). *Felony, Misdemeanor, Civil, Eviction, Small Claims, Probate.*

Civil Records: Access: Mail, in person. Both court and visitors may perform in person searches. Search fee: $4.00 per name per year. Required to search: name, years to search, address. Civil cases indexed by defendant, plaintiff. Civil records on computer from 10/99, index books from 1800s.

Criminal Records: Access: Mail, in person. Both court and visitors may perform in person searches. Search fee: $4.00 per name per year. Required to search: name, years to search, address, DOB, SSN, signed release. Criminal records on computer from 10/99, index books from 1800s.

General Information: No juvenile or adoption records released. SASE required. Turnaround time 2-3 days. Copy fee: $1.00 for first page, $.50 each add'l. Certification fee: $2.00. Fee payee: Clerk of Circuit Court. Only cashiers checks and money orders accepted. Prepayment is required.

Lee County

Circuit Court PO Box 325, Dixon, IL 61021; 815-284-5234. Hours: 8:30AM-4:30PM (CST). *Felony, Misdemeanor, Civil, Eviction, Small Claims, Probate.*

Civil Records: Access: Mail, in person, online. Both court and visitors may perform in person searches. Search fee: $4.00 per name per year. Required to search: name, years to search. Civil cases indexed by defendant, plaintiff. Civil records on computer from 1989, index books from 1800s. Free access to civil, small claims, probate and traffic records available at www.judici.com/IL052025J/index.html.

Criminal Records: Access: Mail, in person, online. Both court and visitors may perform in person searches. Search fee: $4.00 per name per year. Required to search: name, years to search, DOB; also helpful: SSN. Criminal records on computer from 1989, index books from 1800s. Online access is available free at www.judici.com/IL052025J/index.html.

General Information: Public access terminal is available. No juvenile, impounded or adoption records released. SASE required. Turnaround time 1 week. Copy fee: $.50 per page. Certification fee: $2.00. Fee payee: Clerk of Circuit Court. Personal checks accepted. Prepayment is required.

Livingston County

Circuit Court 112 W Madison St, Box 320, Pontiac, IL 61764; 815-844-2602. Hours: 8AM-4:30PM (CST). *Felony, Misdemeanor, Civil, Eviction, Small Claims, Probate.*

Civil Records: Access: Mail, in person. Both court and visitors may perform in person searches. Search fee: $4.00 per name per year. Required to search: name, years to search; also helpful: address. Civil cases indexed by defendant, plaintiff. Civil records on computer from 1989 (child support since 1988), index books from 1837.

Criminal Records: Access: Mail, in person. Both court and visitors may perform in person searches. Search fee: $4.00 per name per year. Required to search: name, years to search, DOB, SSN; also helpful: address. Criminal records on computer from 1989 (child support since 1988), index books from 1837. Signed release required for juvenile cases.

General Information: Public access terminal is available. (Civil only) No juvenile, impound or adoption records released. SASE required. Turnaround time 3-5 days. Fax notes: Fee to fax results is $3.00 per fax. Copy fee: $1.00 for 1st pg; $.50 per pg, pages 2-19; $.25 each additional page. Certification fee: $2.00. Fee payee: Livingston County Circuit Clerk. Personal checks accepted. Prepayment is required.

Logan County

Circuit Court County Courthouse, PO Box 158, Lincoln, IL 62656; 217-735-2376; Fax: 217-732-1231. Hours: 8:30AM-4:30PM (CST). *Felony, Misdemeanor, Civil, Eviction, Small Claims, Probate.*
www.co.logan.il.us/circuit_clerk

Civil Records: Access: Mail, fax, in person, online. Both court and visitors may perform in person searches. Search fee: $4.00 per name per year. Required to search: name, years to search. Civil cases indexed by defendant, plaintiff. Civil records on computer back to 1990, index books from 1857. Online access to civil, small claims, probate and traffic records is available free at http://co.logan.il.us/circuit_clerk/. Click on search court cases.

Criminal Records: Access: Mail, fax, in person, online. Both court and visitors may perform in person searches. Search fee: $4.00 per name per year. Required to search: name, years to search, DOB; also helpful: sex. Criminal records on computer back to 1990, index books from 1857. Online access is available free at http://co.logan.il.us/circuit_clerk/. Click on search court cases.

General Information: Public access terminal is available. No juvenile or adoption records released. SASE not required. Turnaround time 1 week. Copy fee: $1.00 for first page, $.50 each add'l. After 20 pages, the fee is $.25 per page. Certification fee: $2.00. Fee payee: Carla Bender, Circuit Clerk. Business checks accepted. Prepayment is required.

Macon County

Circuit Court 253 E Wood St, Decatur, IL 62523; 217-424-1454; Fax: 217-424-1350. Hours: 8AM-4:30PM (CST). *Felony, Misdemeanor, Civil, Eviction, Small Claims, Probate.*
www.court.co.macon.il.us

Civil Records: Access: Phone, mail, online, in person. Both court and visitors may perform in person searches. Search fee: $4.00 per name per year. Required to search: name, years to search; also helpful: address. Civil cases indexed by defendant, plaintiff. Civil records on computer from 1989, index books from 1800s. Access to court records is available free online at the web site 24-hrs a day. Civil docket information is viewable back to 04/96.

Criminal Records: Access: Phone, mail, online, in person. Both court and visitors may perform in person searches. Search fee: $4.00 per name per year. Required to search: name, years to search; also helpful: address, DOB, SSN. Criminal records on computer from 1989, index books from 1800s. Access to court records is available free online at the web site 24-hrs a day. Search docket information back to 04/96.

General Information: Public access terminal is available. No juvenile or adoption records released. SASE required. Turnaround time 1 week. Copy fee: $1.00 for first page, $.50 each add'l. Certification fee: $2.00. Fee payee: Macon County Circuit Clerk. Business checks accepted. Prepayment is required.

Macoupin County

Circuit Court PO Box 197, Carlinville, IL 62626; 217-854-3211; Fax: 217-854-7361. Hours: 8:30AM-4:30PM (CST). *Felony, Misdemeanor, Civil, Eviction, Small Claims, Probate.*

Civil Records: Access: Mail, in person. Both court and visitors may perform in person searches. Search fee: $4.00 per name per year. Required to search: name, years to search. Civil cases indexed by defendant, plaintiff. Civil records on computer from 1994, index books from 1837.

Criminal Records: Access: Mail, in person. Both court and visitors may perform in person searches. Search fee: $4.00 per name per year. Required to search: name, years to search; also helpful: DOB, SSN. Criminal records on computer from 1994, index books to 1837.

General Information: Public access terminal is available. No juvenile or adoption records released. SASE required. Turnaround time 1 month to 6 weeks. Copy fee: $1.00 for first page, $.50 each add'l; $.25 for 20+ pages. Certification fee: $2.00. Fee payee: Mike Mathis Circuit Clerk. Personal checks accepted. Prepayment is required.

Madison County

Circuit Court 155 N Main St, Edwardsville, IL 62025; 618-692-6240; Fax: 618-692-0676. Hours: 8AM-5PM (CST). *Felony, Misdemeanor, Civil, Eviction, Small Claims, Probate.*

Civil Records: Access: Mail, in person. Both court and visitors may perform in person searches. Search fee: $4.00 per name per year. Required to search: name, years to search. Civil cases indexed by defendant, plaintiff. Civil records on computer from 1990, index books from 1800s.

Criminal Records: Access: Mail, in person. Both court and visitors may perform in person searches. Search fee: $4.00 per name per year. Required to search: name, years to search, DOB. Criminal records on computer from 1990, index books from 1800s.

General Information: Public access terminal is available. No juvenile, mental health, adoption records released. SASE required. Turnaround time 2-3 days. Copy fee: $2.00 for 1st pg; $.50 per pg for pgs 2-19; $.25 ea add'l pg. Certification fee: $4.00. Fee payee: Clerk of Circuit Court. Personal checks accepted. Prepayment is required.

Marion County

Circuit Court 100 E Main, PO Box 130, Salem, IL 62881; 618-548-3856; Fax: 618-548-2358. Hours: 8AM-4PM (CST). *Felony, Misdemeanor, Civil, Eviction, Small Claims, Probate.*

Civil Records: Access: In person only. Visitors must perform in person searches for themselves. No search fee. Required to search: name, years to search. Civil cases indexed by defendant, plaintiff. Civil records on computer from 1988, index books from 1800s.

Criminal Records: Access: In person only. Visitors must perform in person searches for themselves. No search fee. Required to search: name, years to search; also helpful: DOB, SSN. Criminal records on computer from 1988, index books from 1800s.

General Information: Public access terminal is available. No juvenile or adoption records released. Copy fee: $1.00 for first page, $.50 each add'l. Certification fee: $2.00. Fee payee: Clerk of Circuit Court. Only cashiers checks and money orders accepted. Will bill to attorneys.

Marshall County

Circuit Court PO Box 328, Lacon, IL 61540-0328; 309-246-6435; Fax: 309-246-2173. Hours: 8:30AM-Noon, 1-4:30PM (CST). *Felony, Misdemeanor, Civil, Eviction, Small Claims, Probate.*

Civil Records: Access: Mail, in person. Both court and visitors may perform in person searches. Search fee: $4.00 per name per year. Required to search: name, years to search. Civil cases indexed by defendant, plaintiff. Civil records on computer from 1988, microfiche since 1964, index books from 1800s.

Criminal Records: Access: Mail, in person. Both court and visitors may perform in person searches. Search fee: $4.00 per name per year. Required to search: name, years to search, DOB. Criminal records on computer from 1988, microfiche since 1964, index books from 1800s.

General Information: Public access terminal is available. No juvenile or adoption records released. SASE required. Turnaround time 1 week. Copy fee: $.50 per page. Certification fee: $2.00. Fee payee: Clerk of Circuit Court. Personal checks accepted. Prepayment is required.

Mason County

Circuit Court 125 N Plum, Havana, IL 62644; 309-543-6619; Fax: 309-543-4214. Hours: 8AM-4PM (CST). *Felony, Misdemeanor, Civil, Eviction, Small Claims, Probate.*

Civil Records: Access: Mail, in person. Both court and visitors may perform in person searches. Search fee: $4.00 per name per year. Required to search: name, years to search. Civil cases indexed by defendant, plaintiff. Civil records on computer from 1989; index books from 1800s.

Criminal Records: Access: Mail, in person. Both court and visitors may perform in person searches. Search fee: $4.00 per name per year. Required to search: name, years to search, DOB. Criminal records on computer from 1989, index books from 1800s.

General Information: Public access terminal is available. No juvenile or adoption records released. SASE required. Turnaround time 1 week. Copy fee: $1.00 for first page, $.50 each add'l. Certification fee: $2.00. Fee payee: Clerk of Circuit Court. Only cashiers checks and money orders accepted. Prepayment is required.

Massac County

Circuit Court PO Box 152, Metropolis, IL 62960; 618-524-9359; Fax: 618-524-4850. Hours: 8AM-Noon, 1-4PM (CST). *Felony, Misdemeanor, Civil, Eviction, Small Claims, Probate.*

Civil Records: Access: Phone, mail, in person. Both court and visitors may perform in person searches. Search fee: $4.00 per name per year. Required to search: name, years to search. Civil cases indexed by defendant. Civil records on computer from 1986, index books from 1800s.

Criminal Records: Access: Phone, mail, in person. Both court and visitors may perform in person searches. Search fee: $4.00 per name per year. Required to search: name, years to search, DOB, signed release. Criminal records on computer from 1986, index books from 1800s.

General Information: Public access terminal is available. No juvenile or adoption records released. SASE required. Turnaround time 5 business days. Copy fee: $.25 per page. Certification fee: $4.00. Fee payee: Clerk of Circuit Court. Only cashiers checks and money orders accepted. Prepayment is required.

McDonough County

Circuit Court County Courthouse, #1 Courthouse Sq, Macomb, IL 61455; 309-837-4889; Fax: 309-833-4493. Hours: 8AM-4PM (CST). *Felony, Misdemeanor, Civil, Eviction, Small Claims, Probate.*

Civil Records: Access: Phone, fax, mail, in person. Both court and visitors may perform in person searches. Search fee: $5.00 per name per year. Required to search: name, years to search. Civil cases indexed by defendant, plaintiff. Civil records on computer from 1991, index books from 1800s.

Criminal Records: Access: Phone, fax, mail, in person. Both court and visitors may perform in person searches. Search fee: $5.00 per name per year. Required to search: name, years to search; also helpful: SSN. Criminal records on computer from 1991, index books from 1800s.

General Information: Public access terminal is available. No juvenile or adoption records released. SASE required. Turnaround time 1 week. Fax notes: Fee to fax results is $1.50 per page. Copy fee: $1.00 1st pg; $.50 each add'l 19pgs; $.25 over 20 pgs. Certification fee: $2.00. Fee payee: Clerk of Circuit Court. Personal checks accepted. Prepayment required.

McHenry County

Circuit Court 2200 N Seminary Ave, Woodstock, IL 60098; 815-334-4307; Fax: 815-338-8583. Hours: 8AM-4:30PM (CST). *Felony, Misdemeanor, Civil, Eviction, Small Claims, Probate.*

www.mchenrycircuitclerk.org

Civil Records: Access: Phone, mail, online, in person. Both court and visitors may perform in person searches. Search fee: $4.00 per name per year. Required to search: name, years to search. Civil cases indexed by defendant, plaintiff. Civil records on computer from 1991, index books from 1800s. Access to records on the remote online system requires $750 license fee plus $50 per month. Records date back to 1991. Civil, criminal, probate, traffic, and domestic records are available. For more information, call 815-334-4193.

Criminal Records: Access: Phone, mail, online, in person. Both court and visitors may perform in person searches. Search fee: $4.00 per name per year. Required to search: name, years to search, DOB; also helpful: SSN. Criminal records on computer from 1990, index books from 1800s. Access to records on the remote online system requires $750 license fee plus $50 per month. Records date back to 1990. Civil, criminal, probate, traffic, and domestic records are available. For more information, call 815-334-4193.

General Information: Public access terminal is available. No juvenile or adoption records released. SASE required. Turnaround time 1 week; criminal same day. Copy fee: $2.00 for first page, $.50 each add'l. Over 20 copies then fee is $.25 per page. Certification fee: $4.00. Fee payee: Clerk of Circuit Court. Personal checks accepted. Credit cards accepted: Visa, MasterCard, Discover. Visa, MC, Discover. Prepayment is required.

McLean County

Circuit Court PO Box 2420, Bloomington, IL 61702-2420; Civil phone: 309-888-5341; Criminal phone: 309-888-5321. Hours: 8:30AM-4:30PM (CST). *Felony, Misdemeanor, Civil, Eviction, Small Claims, Probate.*

www.mclean.gov

Civil Records: Access: Mail, in person. Both court and visitors may perform in person searches. Search fee: $4.00 per name per year. Required to search: name, years to search. Civil cases indexed by defendant, plaintiff. Civil records on computer from 1991, index books from 1800s.

Criminal Records: Access: Mail, in person. Both court and visitors may perform in person searches. Search fee: $4.00 per name per year. Required to search: name, years to search, DOB; also helpful: address, SSN. Criminal records on computer from 1991, index books from 1800s.

General Information: Public access terminal is available. (Criminal only.) No juvenile or adoption records released. SASE required. Turnaround time 10 days. Copy fee: $1.00 for first page, $.50 each add'l. Certification fee: $2.00. Fee payee: McLean County Circuit Clerk. Personal checks accepted. Prepayment is required.

Menard County

Circuit Court PO Box 466, Petersburg, IL 62675; 217-632-2615. Hours: 8:30AM-4:30PM (CST). *Felony, Misdemeanor, Civil, Eviction, Small Claims, Probate.*

Civil Records: Access: Mail, in person. Both court and visitors may perform in person searches. Search fee: $4.00 per name per year. Required to search: name, years to search. Civil cases indexed by defendant. Civil records on computer from March, 1994, on index books from 1839.

Criminal Records: Access: Mail, in person. Both court and visitors may perform in person searches. Search fee: $4.00 per name per year. Required to search: name, years to search, DOB. Criminal records on computer from March, 1994, on index books from 1839.

General Information: No juvenile or adoption records released. SASE required. Turnaround time 2 days. Copy fee: $1.00 for first page, $.50 each add'l. Certification fee: $1.00. Fee payee: Clerk of Circuit Court. Only cashiers checks and money orders accepted. Prepayment is required.

Mercer County

Circuit Court PO Box 175, Aledo, IL 61231; 309-582-7122; Fax: 309-582-7121. Hours: 8AM-4PM (CST). *Felony, Misdemeanor, Civil, Eviction, Small Claims, Probate.*

www.mercercountycourthouse.com

Civil Records: Access: Fax, mail, in person. Both the court and visitors may perform in person searches. Search fee: $5.00 per name per year. Required to search: name, years to search. Civil cases indexed by defendant, plaintiff. Civil records on computer from 1988, index books from 1800s.

Criminal Records: Access: Phone, fax, mail, in person. Both the court and visitors may perform in person searches. Search fee: $5.00 per name per year. Required to search: name, years to search, DOB. Criminal records on computer from 1988, index books from 1800s.

General Information: Public access terminal is available. (1988 forward records are available.) No juvenile or adoption records released. SASE required. Turnaround time 2-3 days. Fax notes: Fee to fax results is $1.00 per page. Copy fee: $.25 per page. Certification fee: $3.00. Fee payee: Clerk of Circuit Court. Business checks accepted. Prepayment is required.

Monroe County

Circuit Court 100 S Main St, Waterloo, IL 62298; 618-939-8681; Fax: 618-939-5132. Hours: 8AM-4:30PM (CST). *Felony, Misdemeanor, Civil, Eviction, Small Claims, Probate.*

Civil Records: Access: Phone, fax, mail, in person. Both court and visitors may perform in person searches. Search fee: $4.00 per name per year. Required to search: name, years to search. Civil cases indexed by defendant, plaintiff. Civil records on computer from 1992, index books from 1818.

Criminal Records: Access: Phone, fax, mail, in person. Both court and visitors may perform in person searches. Search fee: $4.00 per name per year. Required to search: name, years to search, DOB. Criminal records on computer from 1992, index books from 1818.

General Information: Public access terminal is available. No juvenile or adoption records released. SASE required. Turnaround time 1 week. Fax notes: No fee to fax results. Copy fee: $1.00 for first page, $.50 each add'l. If over 20 pages, fee is $.25 per page (from 20 on). Certification fee: $2.00. Fee payee: Circuit Clerk. Business checks accepted.

Montgomery County

Circuit Court County Courthouse, PO Box C, Hillsboro, IL 62049; 217-532-9546. Hours: 8AM-4PM (CST). *Felony, Misdemeanor, Civil, Eviction, Small Claims, Probate.*

www.courts.montgomery.k12.il.us

Civil Records: Access: Mail, online, in person. Both court and visitors may perform in person searches. Search fee: $4.00 per name per year. Required to search: name, years to search. Civil cases indexed by defendant, plaintiff. Civil records on computer from 1988, index books from 1821, microfiche (probate only) since 1939. Online access to court records is at www.courts.montgomery.k12.il.us/CaseInfo.htm. Search by name or case number.

Criminal Records: Access: Mail, online, in person. Both court and visitors may perform in person searches. Search fee: $4.00 per name per year. Required to search: name, years to search, DOB. Criminal records on computer from 1988, index books from 1821, microfiche (probate only) since 1939. Online access to court records is available at www.courts.montgomery.k12.il.us/CaseInfo.htm. Search by name or case number.

General Information: Public access terminal is available. No juvenile or adoption records released. SASE required. Turnaround time 1 week. Copy fee: $1.00 for first page, $.50 each add'l. Certification fee: $4.00. Fee payee: Clerk of Circuit Court. Only cashiers checks and money orders accepted. Prepayment is required.

Morgan County

Circuit Court 300 W State St, Jacksonville, IL 62650; 217-243-5419; Fax: 217-243-2009. Hours: 8:30AM-4:30PM (CST). *Felony, Misdemeanor, Civil, Eviction, Small Claims, Probate.*

Civil Records: Access: Mail, in person. Both court and visitors may perform in person searches. Search fee: $4.00 per name per year. Required to search: name, years to search. Civil cases indexed by defendant. Civil records on computer from 1990, index books to 1890s.

Criminal Records: Access: Mail, in person. Both court and visitors may perform in person searches. Search fee: $4.00 per name per year. Required to search: name, years to search, DOB. Criminal records on computer from 1990, index books from 1890s.

General Information: Public access terminal is available. No juvenile or adoption records released. SASE required. Turnaround time 1 week. Fax notes: Fax fee $1.00 first page, $.50 per page thereafter. Copy fee: $1.00 first page, $.50 per page thereafter. Certification fee: $2.00. Fee payee: Clerk of Circuit Court. Only cashiers checks and money orders accepted. Prepayment is required.

Moultrie County

Moultrie County Courthouse 10 S Main, #7, Sullivan, IL 61951; 217-728-4622. Hours: 8:30AM-4:30PM (CST). *Felony, Misdemeanor, Civil, Eviction, Small Claims, Probate.*

www.circuit-clerk.moultrie.il.us

Civil Records: Access: Mail, in person. Both court and visitors may perform in person searches. Search fee:

$4.00 per name per year. Required to search: name, years to search. Civil cases indexed by defendant. Civil records on computer from 1990, index books to 1850.

Criminal Records: Access: Mail, in person. Both court and visitors may perform in person searches. Search fee: $4.00 per name per year. Required to search: name, years to search, DOB. Criminal records on computer from 1990, index books from 1850.

General Information: No juvenile or adoption records released. SASE required. Turnaround time 1 week. Copy fee: $.25 per page. Certification fee: $2.00. Fee payee: Clerk of Circuit Court. Business checks accepted. Prepayment is required.

Ogle County

Circuit Court PO Box 337, Oregon, IL 61061; 815-732-1130. Hours: 8:30AM-4:30PM (CST). *Felony, Misdemeanor, Civil, Eviction, Small Claims, Probate.*

www.oglecounty.org/marty/circuitclerk.html

Civil Records: Access: Mail, in person, online. Both court and visitors may perform in person searches. Search fee: $4.00 per name per year. Required to search: name, years to search. Civil cases indexed by defendant, plaintiff. Civil records on computer back to 1994; prior records on microfiche last 10 years, index books from 1836. Free access to civil, small claims, probate and traffic records available at www.oglecounty.org. Click on "Search for Case Information.".

Criminal Records: Access: Mail, online, in person. Both court and visitors may perform in person searches. Search fee: $4.00 per name per year. Required to search: name, years to search, DOB. Criminal records on computer back to 1989; prior records on microfiche last 10 years, index books from 1836. Online access is available free at www.oglecounty.org. Click on "Search for Case Information.".

General Information: Public access terminal is available. No juvenile or adoption records released. SASE required. Turnaround time 2-3 weeks. Copy fee: $1.00 for first page, $.50 each add'l. $.25 per page after 20. Certification fee: $2.00. Fee payee: Clerk of Circuit Court. Only cashiers checks and money orders accepted. Prepayment is required.

Peoria County

Circuit Court 324 Main St, Peoria, IL 61602; 309-672-6953; Fax: 309-677-6228. Hours: 8:30AM-5PM (CST). *Felony, Misdemeanor, Civil, Eviction, Small Claims, Probate.*

Civil Records: Access: Phone, mail, in person. Both court and visitors may perform in person searches. Search fee: $4.00 per name per year. Required to search: name, years to search. Civil cases indexed by defendant, plaintiff. Civil records on computer from 1986 (traffic), from 1987 (civil), archived from 1800s.

Criminal Records: Access: Phone, mail, in person. Both court and visitors may perform in person searches. Search fee: $4.00 per name per year. Required to search: name, years to search, DOB; also helpful: SSN. Criminal records on computer from 1978, archived from 1800s.

General Information: Public access terminal is available. No juvenile or adoption records released. SASE required. Turnaround time 1 week. Copy fee: $2.00 for first page, $.50 each add'l. Certification fee: $4.00. Fee payee: Clerk of Circuit Court. Personal checks accepted. Credit cards accepted: Visa, MasterCard. Prepayment is required.

Perry County

Circuit Court PO Box 219, Pinckneyville, IL 62274; 618-357-6726. 8AM-4PM (CST). *Felony, Misdemeanor, Civil, Eviction, Small Claims, Probate.*

Civil Records: Access: Mail, in person. Both court and visitors may perform in person searches. Search fee:

$4.00 per name per year. Required to search: name, years to search. Civil cases indexed by defendant, plaintiff. Civil records on computer from 1990, index books from 1800s.

Criminal Records: Access: Mail, in person. Both court and visitors may perform in person searches. Search fee: $4.00 per name per year. Required to search: name, years to search; also helpful: DOB. Criminal records on computer from 1990, index books from 1800s.

General Information: No juvenile or adoption records released. SASE required. Turnaround time 1 week. Copy fee: $.25 per page. Certification fee: $2.00. Fee payee: Clerk of Circuit Court. Only cashiers checks and money orders accepted. Prepayment is required.

Piatt County

Circuit Court PO Box 288, Monticello, IL 61856; 217-762-4966; Fax: 217-762-8394. Hours: 8:30AM-4:30PM (CST). *Felony, Misdemeanor, Civil, Eviction, Small Claims, Probate.*

Civil Records: Access: Phone, fax, mail, in person. Both court and visitors may perform in person searches. No search fee. Required to search: name, years to search. Civil cases indexed by defendant, plaintiff. Civil records on computer since 1988, index books from 1800s.

Criminal Records: Access: Phone, fax, mail, in person. Both court and visitors may perform in person searches. No search fee. Required to search: name, years to search, DOB; also helpful: SSN. Criminal records on computer since 1988, index books from 1800s.

General Information: Public access terminal is available. No juvenile or adoption records released. SASE not required. Turnaround time 2-3 days. Fax notes: $1.00 for first page, $.50 each add'l. Copy fee: $1.00 for first page, $.50 each add'l. Certification fee: $1.00 plus $.50 each add'l page. Fee payee: Clerk of Circuit Court. Business checks accepted. Prepayment is required.

Pike County

Circuit Court Pike County Courthouse, 100 E Washington St, Pittsfield, IL 62363; 217-285-6612; Fax: 217-285-4726. Hours: 8:30AM-4:30PM (CST). *Felony, Misdemeanor, Civil, Eviction, Small Claims, Probate.*

Civil Records: Access: Mail, in person, online. Both court and visitors may perform in person searches. Search fee: $4.00 per name per year. Required to search: name, years to search. Civil cases indexed by defendant, plaintiff. Civil records on computer since 1992, index books from 1800s. Free access to civil, small claims, probate and traffic records available at www.judici.com/IL075015J/index.html.

Criminal Records: Access: Mail, in person, online. Both court and visitors may perform in person searches. Search fee: $4.00 per name per year. Required to search: name, years to search; also helpful: SSN. Criminal records on computer since 1992, index books from 1800s. Online access is available free at www.judici.com/IL075015J/index.html.

General Information: Public access terminal is available. No juvenile or adoption records released. SASE required. Turnaround time as soon as possible. Copy fee: $1.00 for first page, $.50 each add'l. $.25 per page after 19 pages. Certification fee: $3.00. Fee payee: Circuit Clerk. Personal checks accepted. Prepayment is required.

Pope County

Circuit Court County Courthouse, Golconda, IL 62938; 618-683-3941; Fax: 618-683-3018. Hours: 8AM-4PM (CST). *Felony, Misdemeanor, Civil, Eviction, Small Claims, Probate.*

Civil Records: Access: Phone, fax, mail, in person. Both court and visitors may perform in person searches. Search fee: $4.00 per name per year. Required to search: name, years to search. Civil cases indexed by defendant. Civil records on computer from 1989, index books from 1800s.

Criminal Records: Access: Phone, fax, mail, in person. Both court and visitors may perform in person searches. Search fee: $4.00 per name per year. Required to search: name, years to search, DOB. Criminal records on computer from 1989, index books from 1800s.

General Information: Public access terminal is available. No juvenile or adoption records released. SASE required. Turnaround time 2-3 days. Fax notes: $.50 per page. Copy fee: $.25 per page. Certification fee: $2.00. Fee payee: Circuit Clerk. Business checks accepted. Prepayment is required.

Pulaski County

Circuit Court PO Box 88, Room C, Mound City, IL 62963; 618-748-9300; Fax: 618-748-9329. Hours: 8AM-4PM (CST). *Felony, Misdemeanor, Civil, Eviction, Small Claims, Probate.*

Civil Records: Access: Mail, in person. Both court and visitors may perform in person searches. Search fee: $4.00 per name. Required to search: name, years to search. Civil cases indexed by defendant, plaintiff. Civil records on computer since 1989, on books prior.

Criminal Records: Access: Mail, in person. Both court and visitors may perform in person searches. Search fee: $4.00 per name per year. Required to search: name, years to search, signed release; also helpful: DOB, SSN. Criminal records on computer since 1989, on books prior.

General Information: No juvenile, adoption records released. SASE required. Turnaround time 1 week. Copy fee: $1.00 for first page, $.50 each add'l. If over 20 pages, fee becomes $.25 per copy. Certification fee: $2.00. Fee payee: Clerk of Circuit Court. Only cashiers checks and money orders accepted. Prepayment is required.

Putnam County

Circuit Court 120 N 4th St, Hennepin, IL 61327; 815-925-7016; Fax: 815-925-7492. Hours: 9AM-4PM (CST). *Felony, Misdemeanor, Civil, Eviction, Small Claims, Probate.*

Civil Records: Access: Mail, in person. Both court and visitors may perform in person searches. Search fee: $5.00 per name. Fee is per 5 years searched. Required to search: name, years to search. Civil cases indexed by defendant. Civil records on computer from 1991, index books from 1836.

Criminal Records: Access: Mail, in person. Both court and visitors may perform in person searches. Search fee: $5.00 per name. Fee is per 5 years searched. Required to search: name, years to search, DOB. Criminal records on computer from 1991, index books from 1836. No criminal searches performed on Thursdays.

General Information: Public access terminal is available. No juvenile or adoption records released. SASE required. Turnaround time 3 days. Copy fee: $.50 per page. $.25 per page after 20. Certification fee: $2.00. Fee payee: Clerk of Circuit Court. Only cashiers checks and money orders accepted. Prepayment is required.

Randolph County

Circuit Court County Courthouse, Room 302, Chester, IL 62233; 618-826-5000 X150. Hours: 8AM-4PM (CST). *Felony, Misdemeanor, Civil, Eviction, Small Claims, Probate.*

Civil Records: Access: Mail, in person. Both court and visitors may perform in person searches. Search fee: $4.00 per name per year. Required to search: name, years to search. Civil cases indexed by defendant, plaintiff. Civil records on computer from 1992, index books from 1800s. Visitors can search both.

Criminal Records: Access: Mail, in person. Both court and visitors may perform in person searches. Search fee: $4.00 per name per year. Required to search: name, years to search, DOB. Criminal records on computer from 1992, index books from 1800s. Visitors can search both.

General Information: Public access terminal is available. No juvenile or adoption records released. SASE required. Turnaround time 1-2 days. Copy fee: $1.00 and $.50 each add'l page. Certification fee: $2.00 first page. Fee payee: Clerk of Circuit Court. Business checks accepted. Prepayment is required.

Richland County

Circuit Court 103 W Main #21, Olney, IL 62450; 618-392-2151; Fax: 618-392-5041. Hours: 8AM-4PM (CST). *Felony, Misdemeanor, Civil, Eviction, Small Claims, Probate.*

Civil Records: Access: Phone, mail, fax, in person. Both court and visitors may perform in person searches. Search fee: $4.00 per name per year. Required to search: name, years to search. Civil cases indexed by defendant. Civil records on index books from 1867; on computer back to 1999.

Criminal Records: Access: Mail, in person. Both court and visitors may perform in person searches. Search fee: $4.00 per name per year. Required to search: name, years to search, DOB. Criminal records on index books from 1867; on computer back to 1986.

General Information: Public access terminal is available. No juvenile or adoption records released. SASE required. Turnaround time 1-2 weeks. Copy fee: $1.00 for first page, $.50 each add'l. Certification fee: $.50. Fee payee: Clerk of Circuit Court. Only cashiers checks and money orders accepted. Prepayment is required.

Rock Island County

Circuit Court PO Box 5230 (210 15th St), Rock Island, IL 61204-5230; 309-786-4451; Fax: 309-786-3029. Hours: 8AM-4:30PM (CST). *Felony, Misdemeanor, Civil, Eviction, Small Claims, Probate.* www.co.rock-island.il.us/Government/CircuitClk/CircuitClk.html

Civil Records: Access: Mail, online, in person. Both court and visitors may perform in person searches. Search fee: $4.00 per name per year. Required to search: name, years to search. Civil cases indexed by defendant, plaintiff. Civil records on computer from 1989, index books from 1950s. Access to records on the remote online system requires $200 setup fee plus a $1.00 per minute for access. Civil, criminal, probate, traffic, and domestic records can be accessed by name or case number.

Criminal Records: Access: Mail, online, in person. Both court and visitors may perform in person searches. Search fee: $4.00 per name per year. Required to search: name, years to search, DOB; also helpful: SSN. Criminal records on computer from 1989, index books from 1950s. Online access to criminal records is the same as civil.

General Information: Public access terminal is available. No juvenile or adoption records released. SASE required. Turnaround time 1 week. Fax notes:

$1.00 for first page, $.50 each add'l. Copy fee: $1.00 for first page, $.50 each add'l. Certification fee: $2.00. Fee payee: Circuit Clerks Office. Money orders. Prepayment is required.

Saline County

Circuit Court County Courthouse, Harrisburg, IL 62946; 618-253-5096 & 253-3904; Fax: 618-252-8438. Hours: 8AM-4PM (CST). *Felony, Misdemeanor, Civil, Eviction, Small Claims, Probate.*

Civil Records: Access: Fax, mail, in person. Both court and visitors may perform in person searches. Search fee: $5.00 per name per year. Required to search: name, years to search. Civil cases indexed by defendant, plaintiff. Civil records on computer back to 1986, index books archived from 1886.

Criminal Records: Access: Fax, mail, in person. Both court and visitors may perform in person searches. Search fee: $5.00 per name per year. Required to search: name, years to search, DOB. Criminal records on computer back to 1986, index books archived from 1800s.

General Information: No juvenile or adoption records released. SASE required. Turnaround time 1-2 weeks. Fax notes: Fee to fax results is $2.00 1st page, $1.00 each add'l. Copy fee: $1.00 for first page, $.50 each add'l. Certification fee: $2.00. Fee payee: Clerk of Circuit Court. Business checks accepted. Prepayment is required.

Sangamon County

Circuit Court 200 S Ninth St Rm 405, Springfield, IL 62701; 217-753-6674; Fax: 217-753-6665. Hours: 8:30AM-4:30PM (CST). *Felony, Misdemeanor, Civil, Eviction, Small Claims, Probate.* www.co.sangamon.il.us/court/

Civil Records: Access: Fax, mail, in person. Both court and visitors may perform in person searches. Search fee: $4.00 per name per year. Required to search: name, years to search. Civil cases indexed by defendant, plaintiff. Civil records on computer from 1982, index books from 1800s.

Criminal Records: Access: Fax, mail, in person. Both court and visitors may perform in person searches. Search fee: $4.00 per name per year. Required to search: name, years to search, DOB. Criminal records on computer from 1982, index books from 1800s.

General Information: Public access terminal is available. No juvenile, mental health, adoption records released. SASE required. Turnaround time 1-2 weeks. Fax notes: No fee to fax results. Copy fee: $2.00 for first page, $.50 each add'l. $.25 per page after 19. Certification fee: $4.00. Fee payee: Circuit Clerk. Personal checks accepted.

Schuyler County

Circuit Court PO Box 80, Rushville, IL 62681; 217-322-4633; Fax: 217-322-6164. Hours: 8AM-4PM (CST). *Felony, Misdemeanor, Civil, Eviction, Small Claims, Probate.*

Civil Records: Access: Mail, in person. Both court and visitors may perform in person searches. Search fee: $4.00 per name per year. Required to search: name, years to search. Civil cases indexed by defendant. Civil records on computer from 1988, index books from 1800s.

Criminal Records: Access: Mail, in person. Both court and visitors may perform in person searches. Search fee: $4.00 per name per year. Required to search: name, years to search, DOB. Criminal records on computer from 1988, index books from 1800s.

General Information: No juvenile or adoption records released. SASE required. Turnaround time 1 week. Fax notes: Fee to fax results is $1.00 per page. Copy fee: $1.00 for first page, $.50 each add'l. $.25 after 20. Certification fee: $2.00. Fee payee: Clerk of Circuit

Court. Only cashiers checks and money orders accepted. Prepayment is required.

Scott County

Circuit Court 35 E Market St, Winchester, IL 62694; 217-742-5217; Fax: 217-742-5853. Hours: 8AM-Noon, 1-4PM (CST). *Felony, Misdemeanor, Civil, Eviction, Small Claims, Probate.*

Civil Records: Access: Mail, in person. Both court and visitors may perform in person searches. Search fee: $4.00 per name per year. Required to search: name, years to search. Civil cases indexed by defendant, plaintiff. Civil records on index books from 1800s.

Criminal Records: Access: Mail, in person. Both court and visitors may perform in person searches. Search fee: $4.00 per name per year. Required to search: name, years to search, DOB. Criminal records on index books from 1800s.

General Information: No juvenile or adoption records released. SASE required. Turnaround time 1 week. Copy fee: $1.00 for first page, $.50 each add'l. After 20 pages, copies are $.25 each. Certification fee: $2.00. Fee payee: Clerk of Circuit Court. Only cashiers checks and money orders accepted. Prepayment is required.

Shelby County

Circuit Court County Courthouse, PO Box 469, Shelbyville, IL 62565; 217-774-4212; Fax: 217-774-4109. Hours: 8AM-4PM (CST). *Felony, Misdemeanor, Civil, Eviction, Small Claims, Probate.*

Civil Records: Access: Fax, mail, in person. Search fee: $4.00 per name. Required to search: name, years to search. Civil cases indexed by defendant, plaintiff. Civil records on computer from 1988, index books to 1848.

Criminal Records: Access: Fax, mail, in person. Both court and visitors may perform in person searches. Search fee: $4.00 per name. Required to search: name, years to search, DOB. Criminal records on computer from 1988, index books from 1848.

General Information: Public access terminal is available. No juvenile or adoption records released. SASE required. Turnaround time 1-2 weeks. Copy fee: $1.00 for first page, $.50 each add'l. Certification fee: $2.00. Fee payee: Circuit Clerk.

St. Clair County

Circuit Court 10 Public Square, Belleville, IL 62220-1623; 618-277-6832; Fax: 618-277-1562. Hours: 8AM-4PM (CST). *Felony, Misdemeanor, Civil, Eviction, Small Claims, Probate.*

Civil Records: Access: Mail, phone, fax, in person. Both court and visitors may perform in person searches. Search fee: $4.00 per name per year. Required to search: name, years to search; also helpful: address. Civil cases indexed by defendant, plaintiff. Civil records on computer from 1990, microfiche from 1800s.

Criminal Records: Access: Mail, phone, fax, in person. Both court and visitors may perform in person searches. Search fee: $4.00 per name per year. Required to search: name, years to search, DOB. Criminal records on computer from 1990, microfiche from 1800s.

General Information: No juvenile or adoption records released. SASE required. Turnaround time 1-2 days. Copy fee: $2.00 for first page, $.50 each add'l. $.25 per pg after 19. Certification fee: $4.00. Fee payee: Clerk of Circuit Court. Only cashiers checks and money orders accepted. Prepayment is required.

Stark County

Circuit Court 130 W Main St, Toulon, IL 61483; 309-286-5941. Hours: 8AM-4:30PM (CST). *Felony, Misdemeanor, Civil, Eviction, Small Claims, Probate.*

Civil Records: Access: Mail, in person. Both court and visitors may perform in person searches. Search fee: $4.00 per name per year. Required to search: name,

years to search. Civil cases indexed by defendant. Civil records on index books from 1800s.

Criminal Records: Access: Mail, in person. Both court and visitors may perform in person searches. Search fee: $4.00 per name per year. Required to search: name, years to search, DOB. Criminal records on index books from 1800s.

General Information: Public access terminal is available. No juvenile or adoption records released. SASE required. Turnaround time 2-3 days. Copy fee: $1.00 for first page, $.50 each add'l. Certification fee: $2.00. Fee payee: Clerk of Circuit Court. Personal checks accepted. Prepayment is required.

Stephenson County

Circuit Court 15 N Galena Ave, Freeport, IL 61032; 815-235-8266. Hours: 8:30AM-4:30PM (CST). *Felony, Misdemeanor, Civil, Eviction, Small Claims, Probate.*

htto://www.judici.com

Civil Records: Access: Mail, in person, online. Both court and visitors may perform in person searches. Search fee: $4.00 per name per year. Required to search: name, years to search. Civil cases indexed by defendant, plaintiff. Civil records on computer from 8/1989, index books from 1875. Free access to civil, small claims, probate and traffic records available at www.judici.com/IL089015J/index.html.

Criminal Records: Access: Mail, in person, online. Both court and visitors may perform in person searches. Search fee: $4.00 per name per year. Required to search: name, years to search, DOB. Criminal records on computer from 8/1989, index books from 1875. Online access is available free at www.judici.com/IL089015J/index.html.

General Information: Public access terminal is available. No juvenile or adoption records released. SASE required. Turnaround time 5-15 days. Copy fee: $1.00 for first page, $.50 each add'l. Certification fee: $2.00. Fee payee: Clerk of Circuit Court. Business checks accepted. Prepayment is required.

Tazewell County

Circuit Court Courthouse, 4th & Court Sts, Pekin, IL 61554; 309-477-2214. Hours: 8:30AM-5PM (CST). *Felony, Misdemeanor, Civil, Small Claims, Probate.*

Civil Records: Access: Mail, in person. Both court and visitors may perform in person searches. Search fee: $4.00 per name per year. Required to search: name, years to search. Civil cases indexed by defendant, plaintiff. Civil records on computer from 02/89 index books from 1800s.

Criminal Records: Access: Mail, in person. Both court and visitors may perform in person searches. Search fee: $4.00 per name per year. Required to search: name, years to search, DOB, signed release. Criminal records on computer from 02/89 index books from 1800s.

General Information: Public access terminal is available. No juvenile or adoption records released. SASE required. Turnaround time 3-4 days. Copy fee: $1.00 for first page, $.50 each add'l. After 20 pages, $.10 per page. Certification fee: $2.00. Fee payee: Clerk of Circuit Court. Only cashiers checks and money orders accepted. Prepayment is required.

Union County

Circuit Court Union County Courthouse, 309 W Market, Rm 101, Jonesboro, IL 62952; 618-833-5913; Fax: 618-833-5223. Hours: 8AM-Noon,1-4PM (CST). *Felony, Misdemeanor, Civil, Eviction, Small Claims, Probate.*

Civil Records: Access: Fax, mail, in person. Both court and visitors may perform in person searches. Search fee: $4.00 per name per year. Required to search: name, years to search. Civil cases indexed by defendant, plaintiff. Civil records on computer from 1986, index

books from 1800s. Public can only search paper records up to 1986. Only court personnel have access to computer records.

Criminal Records: Access: Fax, mail, in person. Both court and visitors may perform in person searches. Search fee: $4.00 per name per year. Required to search: name, years to search; also helpful: DOB. Criminal records on computer from 1986, index books from 1800s. Same search procedures as civil.

General Information: No juvenile or adoption records released. SASE required. Turnaround time 1 week. Fee to fax results is $8.00. Copy fee: $1.00 first page, $.50 2-19th copy, $.25 thereafter. Certification fee: $1.00 first page, $.50 2-19th, $.25 thereafter. Fee payee: Lorraine Moreland, Circuit Clerk. Business checks accepted. Prepayment is required.

Vermilion County

Circuit Court 7 N Vermilion, Danville, IL 61832; 217-431-2534; Fax: 217-431-2538. Hours: 8:30AM-4:30PM (CST). *Felony, Misdemeanor, Civil, Eviction, Small Claims, Probate.*

Civil Records: Access: Phone, mail, in person. Both court and visitors may perform in person searches. Search fee: $4.00 per name per year. Required to search: name, years to search. Civil cases indexed by defendant, plaintiff. Civil records on computer from 1989; microfilm from March 1949 to May 1989; index books from 1800s.

Criminal Records: Access: Phone, mail, in person. Both court and visitors may perform in person searches. Search fee: $4.00 per name per year. Required to search: name, years to search, DOB; also helpful: SSN. Criminal records on computer from 1989; microfilm from March 1949 to May 1989; index books to 1800s.

General Information: Public access terminal is available. No juvenile, impounded, mental health or adoption records released. SASE required. Turnaround time 1 week. Copy fee: $1.00 for first page, $.50 each add'l. Certification fee: $4.00. Fee payee: Clerk of Circuit Court. Business checks accepted. Prepayment is required.

Wabash County

Circuit Court PO Box 997, 401 Market St, Mt Carmel, IL 62863; 618-262-5362; Fax: 618-263-4441. Hours: 8AM-5PM (CST). *Felony, Misdemeanor, Civil, Eviction, Small Claims, Probate.*

Civil Records: Access: Mail, in person. Both court and visitors may perform in person searches. Search fee: $4.00 per name per year. Required to search: name, years to search. Civil cases indexed by defendant, plaintiff. Civil records on computer from 1988, index books from 1800s.

Criminal Records: Access: Mail, in person. Both court and visitors may perform in person searches. Search fee: $4.00 per name per year. Required to search: name, years to search, DOB. Criminal records on computer from 1988, index books from 1800s.

General Information: Public access terminal is available. No juvenile or adoption records released. SASE required. Turnaround time 5 days. Fax notes: Will fax back if all fees prepaid. Copy fee: $.50 for 1st 20 pages; $.25 each add'l. Certification fee: $2.00. Fee payee: Clerk of Circuit Court. Only cashiers checks and money orders accepted. Prepayment is required.

Warren County

Circuit Court 100 W Broadway, Monmouth, IL 61462; 309-734-5179. Hours: 8AM-4:30PM (CST). *Felony, Misdemeanor, Civil, Eviction, Small Claims, Probate.*

Civil Records: Access: Mail, in person. Both court and visitors may perform in person searches. Search fee: $5.00 per name per year. Required to search: name, years to search. Civil cases indexed by defendant. Civil records on computer from 1990, index books from 1800s.

Criminal Records: Access: Mail, in person. Both court and visitors may perform in person searches. Search fee: $5.00 per name per year. Required to search: name, years to search, DOB. Criminal records on computer from 1990, index books from 1800s.

General Information: No juvenile or adoption records released. SASE required. Turnaround time 1-2 weeks. Copy fee: $.50 per page. Certification fee: $2.00. Fee payee: Clerk of Circuit Court. Only cashiers checks and money orders accepted. Prepayment is required.

Washington County

Circuit Court 101 E St Louis St, Nashville, IL 62263; 618-327-4800 X305; Fax: 618-327-3583. Hours: 8AM-4PM (CST). *Felony, Misdemeanor, Civil, Eviction, Small Claims, Probate.*

Civil Records: Access: Mail, in person. Both court and visitors may perform in person searches. Search fee: $5.00 per name per year. Required to search: name, years to search. Civil cases indexed by defendant, plaintiff. Civil records on computer since 1998; 1988 for child support; prior records on index books from 1800s.

Criminal Records: Access: Mail, in person. Both court and visitors may perform in person searches. Search fee: $5.00 per name per year. Required to search: name, years to search; also helpful: DOB. Criminal records on computer since 1998; 1988 for child support; prior records on index books from 1800s.

General Information: No juvenile or adoption records released. SASE required. Turnaround time 3-5 days. Copy fee: $1.00 per page. Certification fee: $2.00. Fee payee: Washington County Circuit Clerk. No personal checks accepted. Will bill to attorneys.

Wayne County

Circuit Court County Courthouse, PO Box 96, Fairfield, IL 62837; 618-842-7684; Fax: 618-842-2556. Hours: 8AM-4:30PM (CST). *Felony, Misdemeanor, Civil, Small Claims, Probate.*

Civil Records: Access: Mail, fax, in person. Both court and visitors may perform in person searches. Search fee: $4.00 per name per year. Required to search: name, years to search. Civil cases indexed by defendant, plaintiff. Civil records on computer back to 11/88, index books from 1800s.

Criminal Records: Access: Mail, fax, in person. Both court and visitors may perform in person searches. Search fee: $4.00 per name per year. Required to search: name, years to search, DOB. Criminal records computerized back 1/1990.

General Information: Public access terminal is available. No juvenile or adoption records released. SASE required. Turnaround time 1 week. Copy fee: $.50 per page. Certification fee: $2.00. Fee payee: Clerk of Circuit Court. Only cashiers checks and money orders accepted. Prepayment is required.

White County

Circuit Court PO Box 310, County Courthouse, Carmi, IL 62821; 618-382-2321; Fax: 618-382-2322. Hours: 8AM-4PM (CST). *Felony, Misdemeanor, Civil, Small Claims, Probate.*

Civil Records: Access: Fax, mail, in person. Both court and visitors may perform in person searches. Search fee: $4.00 per name per year. Required to search: name, years to search. Civil cases indexed by defendant, plaintiff. Civil records on computer from 1991, index books from 1800s.

Criminal Records: Access: Fax, mail, in person. Both court and visitors may perform in person searches. Search fee: $4.00 per name per year. Required to search: name, years to search; also helpful: DOB. Criminal records on computer from 1991, index books from 1800s.

General Information: Public access terminal is available. No juvenile or adoption records released. SASE required. Turnaround time 1-2 weeks. Fax notes: $2.00 per page. Copy fee: $.25 per page. Certification fee: $1.00 plus $.50 per add'l page. Fee payee: Clerk of Circuit Court. Personal checks accepted. Prepayment is required.

Whiteside County

Circuit Court 200 E Knox St, Morrison, IL 61270-2698; 815-772-5188; Fax: 815-772-5187. Hours: 8:30AM-4:30PM (CST). *Felony, Misdemeanor, Civil, Eviction, Small Claims, Probate.*

Civil Records: Access: Phone, fax, mail, in person. Both court and visitors may perform in person searches. Search fee: $4.00 per name. Required to search: name, years to search. Civil cases indexed by defendant. Civil records on computer from 1989, index books from 1800s.

Criminal Records: Access: Phone, fax, mail, in person. Both court and visitors may perform in person searches. Search fee: $4.00 per name. Required to search: name, years to search, DOB. Criminal records on computer from 1988, index books from 1800s.

General Information: Public access terminal is available. No juvenile or adoption records released. SASE required. Turnaround time 1 week. Fax notes: No fee to fax results. Local call only. Copy fee: $.25 per page. Certification fee: $2.00. Fee payee: Clerk of Circuit Court. Personal checks accepted. Prepayment is required.

Will County

Circuit Court 14 W Jefferson St, Joliet, IL 60432; 815-727-8592; Fax: 815-727-8896. Hours: 8:30AM-4:30PM (CST). *Felony, Misdemeanor, Civil, Eviction, Small Claims, Probate.*

www.willcountycircuitcourt.com

Civil Records: Access: Fax, mail, in person. Both court and visitors may perform in person searches. Search fee: $4.00 per name per year. Required to search: name, years to search. Civil cases indexed by defendant, plaintiff. Civil records on computer from 1989, index books from 1800s.

Criminal Records: Access: Fax, mail, in person. Both court and visitors may perform in person searches. Search fee: $4.00 per name per year. Required to search: name, years to search, DOB. Criminal records on computer from 1989, index books from 1800s.

General Information: Public access terminal is available. No juvenile, adoption, mental health records released. SASE required. Turnaround time 2 week. Copy fee: $2.00 for first page, $.50 each add'l. Certification fee: $4.00. Fee payee: Pamela J McGuire, Clerk of Circuit Court. Only cashiers checks and money orders accepted. Prepayment is required.

Williamson County

Circuit Court 200 W Jefferson St, Marion, IL 62959; 618-997-1301 X114. Hours: 8AM-4PM (CST). *Felony, Misdemeanor, Civil, Eviction, Small Claims, Probate.*

Civil Records: Access: Mail, in person. Both court and visitors may perform in person searches. Search fee: $4.00 per name per year. Required to search: name, years to search. Civil cases indexed by defendant,

plaintiff. Civil records on computer from 07/86, index books from 1800s.

Criminal Records: Access: Mail, in person. Both court and visitors may perform in person searches. Search fee: $4.00 per name per year. Required to search: name, years to search, DOB. Criminal records on computer from 07/86, index books from 1800s.

General Information: Public access terminal is available. No juvenile or adoption records released. SASE required. Turnaround time 1 week. Copy fee: $1.00 for first page, $.50 each add'l. Certification fee: $2.00. Fee payee: Clerk of Circuit Court. Business checks accepted. Prepayment is required.

Winnebago County

Circuit Court 400 W State St, Rockford, IL 61101; Civil phone: 815-987-2510; Criminal phone: 815-987-3079/3175; Fax: 815-987-3012. Hours: 8AM-5PM (CST). *Felony, Misdemeanor, Civil, Eviction, Small Claims, Probate.*

www.cc.co.winnebago.il.us

Civil Records: Access: Phone, mail, in person, online. Both court and visitors may perform in person searches. Search fee: $4.00 per name per year. Required to search: name, years to search. Civil cases indexed by defendant, plaintiff. Civil records on computer back to 1983; prior records on index books from 1800s. Online access to court records is via a subscription service; fee is $10 per month. Visit www.cc.co.winnebago.il.us/caseinfo.asp?P=I or call Wendi at 815- 987-3073 for information.

Criminal Records: Access: Phone, mail, in person, online. Both court and visitors may perform in person searches. Search fee: $4.00 per name per year. Required to search: name, years to search, DOB. Criminal records on computer back to 1983; prior records on index books from 1800s. Online access to court records is via a subscription service; fee is $10 per month. Visit www.cc.co.winnebago.il.us/caseinfo.asp?P=I or call Wendi at 815- 987-3073 for information.

General Information: Public access terminal is available. No juvenile, mental or adoption records released. SASE required. Turnaround time 1 week. Copy fee: $2.00 for first page, $.50 each add'l. After 20 pgs, fee is $.25 per pg. Certification fee: $4.00 plus $.50 per add'l page. Fee payee: Clerk of Circuit Court. Only cashiers checks and money orders accepted. Prepayment is required.

Woodford County

Circuit Court County Courthouse, PO Box 284, 115 N Main, Suite 201, Eureka, IL 61530; 309-467-3312. Hours: 8AM-5PM (CST). *Felony, Misdemeanor, Civil, Eviction, Small Claims, Probate.*

Civil Records: Access: Mail, in person. Both court and visitors may perform in person searches. Search fee: $4.00 per name per year. Required to search: name, years to search. Civil cases indexed by defendant, plaintiff. Civil records on computer from 1990, index books from 1800s.

Criminal Records: Access: Mail, in person. Both court and visitors may perform in person searches. Search fee: $4.00 per name per year. Required to search: name, years to search, DOB. Criminal records on computer from 1990, index books from 1800s.

General Information: Public access terminal is available. No juvenile or adoption records released. SASE required. Turnaround time 2-3 days. Copy fee: $.50 per page. Certification fee: $2.00. Fee payee: Woodford County Circuit Clerk. Personal checks accepted. Prepayment is required.

Illinois Recording Offices

ORGANIZATION: 102 counties, 103 recording offices. Cook County hads separate offices for real estate recording and UCC filing until June 30, 2001. As of that date the UCC filing office only searches for, and no longer takes new, UCC filings. The recording officer is Recorder of Deeds. Many counties utilize a grantor/grantee index containing all transactions. The entire state is in the Central Time Zone (CST).

REAL ESTATE RECORDS: Most counties will not perform real estate searches. Cost of certified copies varies widely, but many counties charge the same as the cost of recording the document. Tax records are usually located at the Treasurer's Office.

UCC RECORDS: Financing statements are filed at the state level except for real estate related filings which are filed with the County Recorder. (See above regarding Cook County.) Most counties will perform UCC searches. Use search request form UCC-11. Search fees are usually $10.00 per debtor name/address combination. Copies usually cost $1.00 per page.

TAX LIEN RECORDS: Federal tax liens on personal property of businesses are filed with the Secretary of State. Other federal and all state tax liens on personal property are filed with the County Recorder. Some counties will perform tax lien searches for $5.00-$10.00 per name (state and federal are separate searches in many of these counties) and $1.00 per page of copy.

OTHER LIENS: Judgments, mechanics, contractor, medical, lis pendens, oil & gas, mobile home.

ONLINE ACCESS: A limited number of counties offer online access. There is no statewide system.

Adams County

County Recorder, PO Box 1067, Quincy, IL 62306. County Recorder, R/E and UCC Recording 217-277-2125.
Will search UCC records. This agency will not do a tax lien search. Will not search real estate records. **Other Phone Numbers:** Assessor 217-277-2136; Treasurer 217-277-2248; Elections 217-277-2157; Vital Records 217-277-2158.

Alexander County

County Recorder, 2000 Washington Ave, Cairo, IL 62914. 618-734-7000; Fax 618-734-7002.
Will search UCC records. Tax liens not included in UCC search. Will not search real estate records. **Other Phone Numbers:** Assessor 618-734-7006; Treasurer 618-734-7009.

Bond County

County Recorder, 203 W. College Ave, Greenville, IL 62246. 618-664-0449; Fax 618-664-9414.
Will search UCC records. UCC search includes tax liens if requested. Will not search real estate records. **Other Phone Numbers:** Assessor 618-664-2848; Treasurer 618-664-0618.

Boone County

County Recorder, 601 N. Main St, Suite 202, Belvidere, IL 61008. 815-544-3103; Fax 815-547-8701.
Will search UCC records. This agency will not do a tax lien search. Will not search real estate records. **Other Phone Numbers:** Assessor 815-544-2958; Treasurer 815-544-2666; Elections 815-544-3103; Vital Records 815-544-3103.

Brown County

County Recorder, Courthouse - Room 4, #1 Court St, Mount Sterling, IL 62353-1285. County Recorder, R/E and UCC Recording 217-773-3421; Fax 217-773-2233.
Will search UCC records. UCC search includes tax liens if requested. Will not search real estate records. **Other Phone Numbers:** Assessor 217-773-3415; Treasurer 217-773-3133; Elections 217-773-3421; Vital Records 217-773-3421.

Bureau County

County Recorder, 700 S. Main St., Courthouse, Princeton, IL 61356. County Recorder, R/E and UCC Recording 815-875-3239; Fax 815-879-4803.
Will search UCC records. This agency will not do a tax lien search. Will not search real estate records. **Other Phone Numbers:** Assessor 815-875-6478; Treasurer 815-875-3241; Elections 815-875-2014; Vital Records 815-875-3239.

Calhoun County

County Clerk & Recorder, PO Box 187, Hardin, IL 62047. 618-576-2351; Fax 618-576-2895.
Will search UCC records. UCC search includes tax liens. Mortgage searches available. **Other Phones:** Assessor 618-576-8041; Treasurer 618-576-2421.

Carroll County

County Recorder, PO Box 152, Mount Carroll, IL 61053. 815-244-0223; Fax 815-244-3709.
Will search UCC records. This agency will not do a tax lien search. Will not search real estate records. **Other Phone Numbers:** Assessor 815-244-0238; Treasurer 815-244-0243.

Cass County

County Recorder, 100 E Springfield St, Virginia, IL 62691. 217-452-7217; Fax 217-452-7219.
Will search UCC records. UCC search includes tax liens. Will not search real estate records. **Other Phone Numbers:** Assessor 217-452-7249; Treasurer 217-452-7721.

Champaign County

County Recorder, 1776 E. Washington, Urbana, IL 61802. 217-384-3774; Fax 217-344-1663.
Will search UCC records. UCC search does not include state tax liens. Will not search real estate records. **Other Phone Numbers:** Assessor 217-384-3760; Treasurer 217-384-3743.

Christian County

County Recorder, PO Box 647, Taylorville, IL 62568. County Recorder, R/E and UCC Recording 217-824-4960; Fax 217-824-5105.
Will search UCC records. This agency will not do a tax lien search. Will not search real estate records. **Other Phone Numbers:** Assessor 217-824-5900; Treasurer 217-824-4889; Elections 217-824-4969; Vital Records 217-824-4969.

Clark County

County Recorder, Courthouse, Marshall, IL 62441. County Recorder, R/E and UCC Recording 217-826-8311.
Will search UCC records. This agency will not do a tax lien search. Will not search real estate records. **Other Phone Numbers:** Assessor 217-826-5815; Treasurer 217-826-5721; Elections 217-826-8311; Vital Records 217-826-8311.

Clay County

County Recorder, PO Box 160, Louisville, IL 62858-0160. County Recorder, R/E and UCC Recording 618-665-3626; Fax 618-665-3607.
Will search UCC records. UCC search includes tax liens. Real estate owner, mortgage, and property transfer searches available. **Other Phone Numbers:** Assessor 618-665-3370; Treasurer 618-665-3727; Elections 618-665-3626; Vital Records 618-665-3626.

Clinton County

County Recorder, PO Box 308, Carlyle, IL 62231. County Recorder, R/E and UCC Recording 618-594-2464 UCC Recording: 618-594-0142; Fax 618-594-0195. www.clintonco.org
Will search UCC records. UCC search includes tax liens if requested. Will not search real estate records. **Other Phone Numbers:** Assessor 618-594-3221; Treasurer 618-594-2464; Elections 618-594-2464; Vital Records 618-594-2464.

Coles County

County Recorder, 651 Jackson Ave., Room 122, Charleston, IL 61920. County Recorder, R/E and UCC Recording 217-348-7325; Fax 217-348-7337.
Will search UCC records. This agency will not do a tax lien search. Will not search real estate records.

Cook County Assessor

County Clerk, 118 N. Clark St, Room 120, Chicago, IL 60602-1387. 312-603-7524; Fax 312-603-5063. www.cookcountyassessor.com

Will search UCC records. This agency will not do a tax lien search. See Recorder for real estate records. **Online Access:** Property Tax Records. Records on the County Assessor Residential Assessment Search database are available free at www.cookcountyassessor.com/ startsearch.html. Search residential or non-residential properties. **Other Phones:** Assessor 312-443-7550.

Cook County Recorder

County Recorder, 118 N. Clark St. #120, Room 230, Chicago, IL 60602. 312-603-5134, 312-603-5050; Fax 312-603-5063.

There are no filings recorded at this office after June 30, 2001. Only records prior to this date can be searched. Will search UCC records, but only real estate related UCC filed here. **Online Access:** Recorder, Deed, Grantor/Grantee, Heir Records. Search the DIMS database of the recordings since 10/1985; registration and fees apply. Includes Treasurer's Current Year Tax System (APIN) and DuPageCounty Recorder. Registration response form is at www.cookctyrecorder.com/remoteform.htm. Also, you may purchase the real estate transfer list; $100 per year on disk ($50 if you pick-up at agency.) Also, search the treasurer's heirs database for free at www.cookcountytreasurer.com/info/estates. **Other Phone Numbers:** Assessor 312-443-7550; Treasurer 312-443-4436.

Crawford County

County Recorder, PO Box 602, Robinson, IL 62454-0602. County Recorder, R/E and UCC Recording 618-546-1212; Fax 618-546-0140. www.crawfordcountyclerk.com

Will search UCC records. This agency will not do a tax lien search. Will not search real estate records. **Other Phone Numbers:** Assessor 618-546-1212; Treasurer 618-546-1212; Elections 618-546-2590; Vital Records 618-546-1212.

Cumberland County

County Recorder, PO Box 146, Toledo, IL 62468. County Recorder, R/E and UCC Recording 217-849-2631; Fax 217-849-2968.

Will search UCC records. This agency will not do a tax lien search. Will not search real estate records. **Other Phone Numbers:** Assessor 217-849-3831; Treasurer 217-849-2321; Elections 217-849-2631; Vital Records 217-849-2631.

De Kalb County

County Recorder, 110 E. Sycamore St, Sycamore, IL 60178. 815-895-7156.

Will search UCC records. This agency will not do a tax lien search. Will not search real estate records. **Online Access:** Real Estate, Lien Records. The DeKalb County online system requires a $350 subscription fee, with a per minute charge of $.25, $.50 if printing. Records date back to 1980. Lending agency information is available. For further information, contact Sheila Larson at 815-895-7152. **Other Phone Numbers:** Assessor 815-895-7120; Treasurer 815-895-7112.

De Witt County

County Recorder, PO Box 439, Clinton, IL 61727-0439. 217-935-2119; Fax 217-935-4596.

Will search UCC records. This agency will not do a tax lien search. Will not search real estate records. **Other Phone Numbers:** Assessor 217-935-2242; Treasurer 217-935-2359; Appraiser/Auditor 217-935-2242.

Douglas County

County Recorder, PO Box 467, Tuscola, IL 61953-0467. County Recorder, R/E and UCC Recording 217-253-4410; Fax 217-253-2233.

Will search UCC records. This agency will not do a tax lien search. Will not search real estate records. **Other Phone Numbers:** Assessor 217-253-3031; Treasurer 217-253-4011; Elections 217-253-2411; Vital Records 217-253-2411.

Du Page County

County Recorder, PO Box 936, Wheaton, IL 60189. 630-682-7200; Fax 630-682-7204. www.dupageco.org/recorder/index.html

Will search UCC records. This agency will not do a tax lien search. Will not search real estate records. **Online Access:** Real Estate, Lien, Tax Assessor Records. For access to the Du Page County database one must lease a live interface telephone line from a carrier to establish a connection. Additionally, there is a fee of $.05 per transaction. Records date back to 1977. For information, contact Fred Kieltcka at 630-682-7030. Free access via the Internet may now be available; visit the web site. Online access to the sheriff's sex offenders, most wanted, and deadbeat parents lists are available free at www.co.dupage.il.us/sheriff. **Other Phone Numbers:** Assessor 630-682-7024; Treasurer 630-682-7012; Elections 630-682-7440; Vital Records 630-682-7035.

Edgar County

County Clerk and Recorder, 115 W Court St, Rm J, 115 W. Court St., Paris, IL 61944-1785. County Clerk and Recorder, R/E and UCC Recording 217-466-7433; Fax 217-466-7430.

Will search UCC records. UCC search includes tax liens if requested. Real estate owner, mortgage, and property transfer searches available. **Other Phones:** Assessor 217-466-5140; Treasurer 217-463-6050; Elections 217-466-7433; Vital Records 217-466-7433.

Edwards County

County Recorder, 50 E. Main St, Courthouse, Albion, IL 62806-1294. 618-445-2115; Fax 618-445-3505.

Will search UCC records. UCC search includes tax liens if requested. Real estate record owner searches available. **Other Phone Numbers:** Assessor 618-445-3591; Treasurer 618-445-3581; Elections 618-445-2115; Vital Records 618-445-2115.

Effingham County

County Clerk & Recorder, PO Box 628, Effingham, IL 62401-0628. County Clerk & Recorder, R/E and UCC Recording 217-342-6535; Fax 217-342-3577. http://co.effingham.il.us

Will search UCC records. Tax liens not included in UCC search. Will not search real estate records. **Other Phone Numbers:** Assessor 217-324-6711; Treasurer 217-342-6844; Elections 217-342-6535; Vital Records 217-342-6535.

Fayette County

County Recorder, PO Box 401, Vandalia, IL 62471-0401. County Recorder, R/E and UCC Recording 618-283-5000; Fax 618-283-5004.

Will search UCC records. This agency will not do a tax lien search. Will not search real estate records. **Other Phone Numbers:** Assessor 618-283-5020; Treasurer 618-283-5022; Elections 618-283-5000; Vital Records 618-283-5000.

Ford County

County Recorder, 200 W. State St, Room 101, Paxton, IL 60957. County Recorder, R/E and UCC Recording 217-379-2721; Fax 217-379-3258. www.prairienet.org

Will search UCC records. This agency will not do a tax lien search. Will not search real estate records. **Other**

Phone Numbers: Assessor 217-379-4132; Treasurer 217-379-2532.

Franklin County

County Clerk & Recorder, PO Box 607, Benton, IL 62812. County Clerk & Recorder, R/E and UCC Recording 618-438-3221; Fax 618-439-4119.

Will search UCC records. Tax liens not included in UCC search. Real estate record owner and mortgage searches available. **Other Phone Numbers:** Assessor 618-438-4331; Treasurer 618-438-7311; Elections 618-438-3403; Vital Records 618-438-3221.

Fulton County

County Recorder, PO Box 226, Lewistown, IL 61542. 309-547-3041 R/E Recording: 309-547-3041 x43 UCC Recording: 309-547-3041 x43.

Will search UCC records. This agency will not do a tax lien search. Will not search real estate records. **Other Phone Numbers:** Assessor 309-547-3041 x58; Treasurer 309-547-3041 x25; Elections 309-547-3041 x704; Vital Records 309-547-3041 x 42.

Gallatin County

County Recorder, PO Box 550, Shawneetown, IL 62984. County Recorder, R/E and UCC Recording 618-269-3025; Fax 618-269-3343.

Will search UCC records. This agency will not do a tax lien search. Will not search real estate records. **Online Access:** Property Records. Search for propety information on the GIS-mapping site for free at www.co.gallatin.mt.us/GIS/index.htm. No name searching. **Other Phone Numbers:** Assessor 618-269-3791; Treasurer 618-269-3022; Elections 618-269-3025; Vital Records 618-269-3025.

Greene County

County Recorder, 519 N. Main St, Courthouse, Carrollton, IL 62016-1033. 217-942-5443; Fax 217-942-9323.

Will search UCC records. Tax liens not included in UCC search. Will not search real estate records. **Other Phone Numbers:** Assessor 217-942-6412; Treasurer 217-942-5124.

Grundy County

County Recorder, PO Box 675, Morris, IL 60450-0675. 815-941-3224; Fax 815-942-2220.

Will search UCC records. UCC search includes tax liens if requested. Will not search real estate records. **Other Phone Numbers:** Assessor 815-941-3269; Treasurer 815-941-3215; Elections 815-941-3221; Vital Records 815-941-3222.

Hamilton County

County Recorder, Courthouse, 100 S Jackson St, Room 2, McLeansboro, IL 62859-1489. 618-643-2721.

Will search UCC records. UCC search includes tax liens if requested. Will not search real estate records. **Other Phone Numbers:** Treasurer 618-643-3313.

Hancock County

County Recorder, PO Box 39, Carthage, IL 62321-0039. County Recorder, R/E and UCC Recording 217-357-3911.

Will search UCC records. UCC search includes tax liens if requested. Will not search real estate records. **Other Phone Numbers:** Assessor 217-357-2615; Treasurer 217-357-2624; Elections 217-357-3911; Vital Records 217-357-3911.

Hardin County

County Recorder, PO Box 187, Elizabethtown, IL 62931. County Recorder, R/E and UCC Recording 618-287-2251; Fax 618-287-7833.

Will search UCC records. UCC search includes tax liens if requested. Real estate record owner and property searches available. **Other Phone Numbers:** Assessor 618-287-3551; Treasurer 618-287-2053; Elections 618-287-2251; Vital Records 618-287-2251; Other Fax 618-287-2661.

Henderson County

County Recorder, PO Box 308, Oquawka, IL 61469-0308. County Recorder, R/E and UCC Recording 309-867-2911; Fax 309-867-2033.

Will search UCC records. This agency will not do a tax lien search. Will not search real estate records. **Other Phone Numbers:** Assessor 309-867-3291; Treasurer 309-867-3121; Appraiser/Auditor 309-867-3291; Elections 309-867-2911; Vital Records 309-867-2911.

Henry County

County Recorder, 100 S. Main, Cambridge, IL 61238. 309-937-3585; Fax 309-937-2796. www.henrycty.com/recorder/index.html

Will search UCC records. This agency will not do a tax lien search. Will not search real estate records. **Online Access:** Assessor Records. Access to the assessor database is available for free at www.henrycty.com/assessor/search.asp. Also, the county most wanted/fugitive list is available at www.henrycty.com/sheriff/fugitives.html. **Other Phone Numbers:** Assessor 309-937-3570; Treasurer 309-937-3576; Elections 309-937-3492; Vital Records 309-937-3575.

Iroquois County

County Recorder, 1001 E. Grant St, Watseka, IL 60970. 815-432-6962; Fax 815-432-3894.

Will search UCC records. UCC search includes tax liens if requested. Will not search real estate records. **Other Phone Numbers:** Assessor 815-432-6978; Treasurer 815-432-6985.

Jackson County

County Recorder, 1001 Walnut, The Courthouse, Murphysboro, IL 62966. 618-687-7360.

Will search UCC records prior to 7/2001. This agency will not do a tax lien search. Will not search real estate records. **Other Phone Numbers:** Assessor 618-687-7220; Treasurer 618-687-3555.

Jasper County

County Recorder, 204 W Washington St #2, Newton, IL 62448. County Recorder, R/E and UCC Recording 618-783-3124; Fax 618-783-4137.

Will search UCC records. This agency will not do a tax lien search. Will not search real estate records. **Other Phone Numbers:** Assessor 618-783-8042; Treasurer 618-783-3211; Elections 618-783-3124; Vital Records 618-783-3124.

Jefferson County

County Recorder, Courthouse, 100 S. 10th St., Room 105, Mount Vernon, IL 62864. 618-244-8020.

Will search UCC records. This agency will not do a tax lien search. Will not search real estate records. **Other Phone Numbers:** Assessor 618-244-8016; Treasurer 618-244-8011.

Jersey County

County Recorder, 200 N Lafayette #2, Jerseyville, IL 62052. County Recorder, R/E and UCC Recording 618-498-5571 x117/8; Fax 618-498-6128.

Will search UCC records. Tax liens not included in UCC search. Will not search real estate records. **Other Phone Numbers:** Assessor 618-498-5571 x126; Treasurer 618-498-5571 x110; Elections 618-498-5571 x112; Vital Records 618-498-5571 x113.

Jo Daviess County

County Recorder, 330 N. Bench St, Galena, IL 61036. 815-777-9694; Fax 815-777-3688.

Will search UCC records. This agency will not do a tax lien search. Will do 20-year search regarding to liens for genealogy purposes. **Other Phone Numbers:** Assessor 815-777-1016; Treasurer 815-777-0355.

Johnson County

County Recorder, PO Box 96, Vienna, IL 62995. County Recorder, R/E and UCC Recording 618-658-3611; Fax 618-658-2908.

Will search UCC records. UCC search includes tax liens if requested. Real estate owner, mortgage, and property transfer searches available. **Other Phone Numbers:** Assessor 618-658-8010; Treasurer 618-658-8042; Elections 618-658-3611; Vital Records 618-658-3611.

Kane County

County Recorder, PO Box 71, Geneva, IL 60134. County Recorder, R/E and UCC Recording 630-232-5935; Fax 630-232-5945. www.co.kane.il.us

Will search UCC records. This agency will not do a tax lien search. Will not search real estate records. **Other Phone Numbers:** Assessor 630-232-3818; Treasurer 630-232-3565.

Kankakee County

County Recorder, 189 E. Court St, Kankakee, IL 60901. County Recorder, R/E and UCC Recording 815-937-2980; Fax 815-937-3657.

Will search UCC records. This agency will not do a tax lien search. Will not search real estate records. **Other Phone Numbers:** Assessor 815-937-2945; Treasurer 815-937-2960; Elections 815-937-2990; Vital Records 815-937-2990.

Kendall County

County Recorder, 111 W. Fox St, Yorkville, IL 60560. 630-553-4112; Fax 630-553-4119.

Will not search UCC records. Will not search tax liens. Will not search real estate records. **Other Phone Numbers:** Assessor 630-553-4146; Treasurer 630-553-4124; Appraiser/Auditor 630-553-4146; Elections 630-553-4105; Vital Records 630-553-4105.

Knox County

County Recorder, 200 S. Cherry, County Courthouse, Galesburg, IL 61401. 309-345-3818; Fax 309-343-7002.

Will search UCC records. This agency will not do a tax lien search. Will not search real estate records. **Other Phone Numbers:** Assessor 309-345-3806; Treasurer 309-345-3863.

La Salle County

County Recorder, PO Box 189, Ottawa, IL 61350. 815-434-8226; Fax 815-434-8260. www.lasallecounty.org/Final/contents2.htm

Will search UCC records. This agency will not do a tax lien search. Will not search real estate records. **Online Access:** Real Estate, Assessor Records. Assessor/property records on the County Assessor database are available online at www.lasallecounty.org/cidnet/asrpfull.htm. Registration and password required; there is a $200.00 per year fee, plus per minute charges. For information, phone 815-434-8233. Also, last two years assessment data can be accessed online free at www.lasallecounty.org/contents3.htm. Parcel number is required. **Other Phone Numbers:** Assessor 815-434-8280; Treasurer 815-434-8220; Elections 815-434-8202.

Lake County

County Recorder, 18 N. County St, Courthouse - 2nd Floor, Waukegan, IL 60085-4358. 847-377-2575 R/E Recording: 847-377-2040; Fax 847-625-7200. www.co.lake.il.us/recorder

Will search UCC records. This agency will not do a tax lien search. Will not search real estate records. **Other Phone Numbers:** Assessor 847-377-2050; Treasurer 847-377-2323; Elections 847-377-3610; Vital Records 847-377-3610.

Lawrence County

County Recorder, 100 State St, Courthouse, Lawrenceville, IL 62439. County Recorder, R/E and UCC Recording 618-943-5126; Fax 618-943-5205.

Will search UCC records. UCC search includes tax liens if requested. Will not search real estate records. **Other Phone Numbers:** Assessor 618-943-2719; Treasurer 618-943-2016; Elections 618-943-2346; Vital Records 618-943-2346.

Lee County

County Recorder, PO Box 329, Dixon, IL 61021-0329. 815-288-3309; Fax 815-288-6492.

Will search UCC records. This agency will not do a tax lien search. Will not search real estate records. **Other Phone Numbers:** Assessor 815-288-4483; Treasurer 815-288-4477.

Livingston County

County Recorder, 112 W. Madison, Pontiac, IL 61764-1871. 815-844-2006; Fax 815-842-1844.

Will search UCC records. Tax liens not included in UCC search. Will not search real estate records. **Other Phone Numbers:** Assessor 815-844-5166 x166-7; Treasurer 815-844-5166 x144.

Logan County

County Recorder, PO Box 278, Lincoln, IL 62656. 217-732-4148; Fax 217-732-6064.

Will search UCC records. UCC search includes tax liens if requested. Will not search real estate records. **Other Phone Numbers:** Assessor 217-732-9635; Treasurer 217-732-3761.

Macon County

County Recorder, 141 S. Main St., Room 201, Decatur, IL 62523-1293. County Recorder, R/E and UCC Recording 217-424-1359; Fax 217-428-2908.

Will search UCC records. UCC search includes tax liens if requested. Will not search real estate records. **Other Phone Numbers:** Assessor 217-424-1364; Treasurer 217-424-1426; Elections 217-424-1309; Vital Records 217-424-1305.

Macoupin County

County Recorder, PO Box 107, Carlinville, IL 62626. 217-854-3214; Fax 217-854-8461.

This agency will not perform searches. **Other Phones:** Assessor 217-854-8281; Treasurer 217-854-4014.

Madison County

County Recorder, PO Box 308, Edwardsville, IL 62025-0308. 618-692-7040 x4772; Fax 618-692-9843.

Will search UCC records. This agency will not do a tax lien searches. Will not search real estate records. **Other Phones:** Assessor 692-6270; Treasurer 692-6260.

Marion County

County Recorder, PO Box 637, Salem, IL 62881. 618-548-3400 R/E Recording: 618-548-3852 UCC Recording: 618-548-3852; Fax 618-548-2226.

Will search UCC records. Will not search real estate records. **Other Phone Numbers:** Assessor 618-548-3853; Treasurer 618-548-3858; Elections 618-548-3400; Vital Records 618-548-3850.

Marshall County

County Recorder, PO Box 328, Lacon, IL 61540. County Recorder, R/E and UCC Recording 309-246-6325; Fax 309-246-3667.

Will search UCC records. This agency will not do a tax lien search. Will not search real estate records. **Other Phone Numbers:** Assessor 309-246-2350; Treasurer 309-246-6085; Elections 309-246-6325; Vital Records 309-246-6325.

Mason County

County Recorder, PO Box 77, Havana, IL 62644. County Recorder, R/E and UCC Recording 309-543-6661; Fax 309-543-2085.

Will search UCC records. This agency will not do a tax lien search. Will not search real estate records. **Other Phone Numbers:** Assessor 309-543-4775; Treasurer 309-543-3359; Elections 309-543-6661; Vital Records 309-543-6661.

Massac County

County Recorder, PO Box 429, Metropolis, IL 62960. County Recorder, R/E and UCC Recording 618-524-5213; Fax 618-524-8514.

Will search UCC records. This agency will not do a tax lien search. Will not search real estate records. **Other Phone Numbers:** Assessor 618-524-9632; Treasurer 618-524-5121; Elections 618-524-5213; Vital Records 618-524-5213.

McDonough County

County Recorder, 1 Courthouse Square, Macomb, IL 61455. County Recorder, R/E and UCC Recording 309-833-2474; Fax 309-836-3368.

Will search UCC records. This agency will not do a tax lien search. Will not search real estate records. **Other Phone Numbers:** Assessor 309-833-5305; Treasurer 309-833-2032; Elections 309-833-4649; Vital Records 309-833-2474.

McHenry County

County Recorder, 2200 N. Seminary Ave, Room A280, Woodstock, IL 60098. 815-334-4110; Fax 815-338-9612.

Will search UCC records. This agency will not do a tax lien search. Will not search real estate records. **Online Access:** Assessor/Treasurer Records. Records on the County Treasurer Inquiry site are available free online at http://209.172.155.14/cidnet.publictre1.htm. **Other Phone Numbers:** Assessor 847-360-6378; Treasurer 815-334-2098.

McLean County

County Recorder, PO Box 2400, Bloomington, IL 61702-2400. 309-888-5170; Fax 309-888-5927. www.mclean.gov/

Will search UCC records and recorded deeds. This agency will not do a tax lien search. Will not search real estate records. **Online Access:** Assessor, Property, Treasurer Tax Bill, Sex Offender, Assumed Name Records. Access to the county Tax Bill Information Lookup data is available free at www.mclean.gov/Treasurer/2ndInstallmentSearch.asp. No name searching; parcel number or streetname and city required. Also, access to the Township of Normal assessor data is available at www.normaltownship.org/Assessor/ParcelSearch.php. No name searching; parcel number or address required. Also, search sex offender data at www.mclean.gov/sheriff/SexOffenderPage.htm. Also, search the assumed named list at www.mclean.gov/CountyClerk/CountyClerkAssumed NamesMain.asp. Search election officials by precinct at the web site. **Other Phone Numbers:** Assessor 309-888-5130; Treasurer 309-888-5180; Elections 309-888-5190.

Menard County

County Recorder, PO Box 465, Petersburg, IL 62675. 217-632-2415 R/E Recording: 217-632-3201 UCC Recording: 217-632-3201; Fax 217-632-4124.

Will search UCC records. This agency will not do a tax lien search. Will not search real estate records. **Other Phone Numbers:** Assessor 217-632-4461; Treasurer 217-632-2333; Appraiser/Auditor 217-632-4461; Elections 217-632-3201; Vital Records 217-632-3201.

Mercer County

County Recorder, PO Box 66, Aledo, IL 61231. 309-582-7021; Fax 309-582-7022.

Will search UCC records. This agency will not do a tax lien search. Will not search real estate records. **Other Phone Numbers:** Assessor 309-582-7814; Treasurer 309-582-2524.

Monroe County

County Recorder, 100 S. Main, Courthouse, Waterloo, IL 62298-1399. 618-939-8681; Fax 618-939-8639.

This agency will not perform searches. **Other Phone Numbers:** Assessor 618-939-8681 x211; Treasurer 618-939-8681 x213.

Montgomery County

County Recorder, Historic Courthouse, 1 Courthouse Square, Hillsboro, IL 62049-1196. County Recorder, R/E and UCC Recording 217-532-9532; Fax 217-532-9581. www.montgomeryco.com

Will search UCC records. UCC search includes tax liens if requested. Real estate owner, mortgage, and property transfer searches available. **Other Phones:** Assessor 217-532-9595; Treasurer 217-532-9521; Elections 217-532-9530; Vital Records 217-532-9537.

Morgan County

County Recorder, PO Box 1387, Jacksonville, IL 62651. County Recorder, R/E and UCC Recording 217-243-8581; Fax 217-243-8368.

Will search UCC records. UCC search includes tax liens if requested. Will not search real estate records. **Other Phone Numbers:** Assessor 217-243-8557; Treasurer 217-243-8581; Elections 217-243-8581; Vital Records 217-243-8581.

Moultrie County

County Recorder, Courthouse, Suite 6, 10 S. Main, Sullivan, IL 61951. County Recorder, R/E and UCC Recording 217-728-4389; Fax 217-728-8178.

Will search UCC records. Tax liens not included in UCC search. Will not search real estate records. **Other Phone Numbers:** Assessor 217-728-4951; Treasurer 217-728-4032; Elections 217-728-4389; Vital Records 217-728-4389.

Ogle County

County Recorder, PO Box 357, Oregon, IL 61061. 815-732-1115 x270/1.

Will search UCC records. UCC search includes tax liens if requested. Will not search real estate records. **Other Phone Numbers:** Assessor 815-732-1150 x239, 256, 257, 258 & 305; Treasurer 815-732-1100 x202/201/310 & 286; Elections 815-732-1110 x012/213/281/214 & 215; Vital Records 815-732-1110 x012/213/281/214 & 215.

Peoria County

County Recorder, County Courthouse - Room G04, 324 Main St, Peoria, IL 61602. County Recorder, R/E and UCC Recording 309-672-6090.

Will search UCC records. This agency will not do a tax lien search. Will not search real estate records. **Other Phone Numbers:** Assessor 309-672-6910; Treasurer 309-672-6065.

Perry County

County Recorder, PO Box 438, Pinckneyville, IL 62274. 618-357-5116; Fax 618-357-3194.

Will search UCC records. UCC search includes tax liens if requested. Will not search real estate records. **Other Phone Numbers:** Assessor 618-357-2209; Treasurer 618-357-5002.

Piatt County

County Recorder, PO Box 558, Monticello, IL 61856-0558. County Recorder, R/E and UCC Recording 217-762-9487; Fax 217-762-7563.

Will search UCC records. This agency will not do a tax lien search. Will not search real estate records. **Other Phones:** Assessor 217-762-4266; Treasurer 217-762-4866; Elections 762-9487; Vital Records 762-9487.

Pike County

County Recorder, Courthouse, 100 E. Washington St., Pittsfield, IL 62363. County Recorder, R/E and UCC Recording 217-285-6812; Fax 217-285-5820.

Will search UCC records. UCC search includes tax liens if requested. Will not search real estate records. **Other Phone Numbers:** Assessor 217-285-2382; Treasurer 217-285-4218; Elections 217-285-6812; Vital Records 217-285-6812.

Pope County

County Recorder, PO Box 216, Golconda, IL 62938. 618-683-4466; Fax 618-683-4466.

Will search UCC records. UCC search includes tax liens if requested. Will not search real estate records. **Other Phone Numbers:** Assessor 618-683-6231; Treasurer 618-683-5501.

Pulaski County

County Recorder, PO Box 118, Mound City, IL 62963. 618-748-9360; Fax 618-748-9305.

Will search UCC records. This agency will not do a tax lien search. Will not search real estate records. **Other Phone Numbers:** Assessor 618-748-9321; Treasurer 618-748-9322.

Putnam County

County Recorder, PO Box 236, Hennepin, IL 61327. County Recorder, R/E and UCC Recording 815-925-7129 UCC Recording: 815-925-7238; Fax 815-925-7549.

Will search UCC records. This agency will not do a tax lien search. Will not search real estate records. **Other Phone Numbers:** Assessor 815-925-7238; Treasurer 815-925-7226; Appraiser/Auditor 815-925-7238; Elections 815-925-7129; Vital Records 815-925-7129.

Randolph County

County Recorder, PO Box 309, Chester, IL 62233-0309. 618-826-5000 x191; Fax 618-826-3750.

Will search UCC records. Tax liens included with UCC search if requested. Will not search real estate records. **Other Phone Numbers:** Assessor 618-826-5000 x192; Treasurer 618-826-5000 x224.

Richland County

County Recorder, 103 W. Main, Courthouse, Olney, IL 62450. 618-392-3111; Fax 618-393-4005.

Will search UCC records. Tax liens not included in UCC search. Will not search real estate records. **Other Phone Numbers:** Assessor 618-395-4387; Treasurer 618-392-8341.

Rock Island County

County Recorder, PO Box 3067, Rock Island, IL 61204. 309-786-4451.

Will search UCC records. This agency will do a tax lien search. Will not search real estate records. **Other Phone**

Numbers: Assessor 309-786-4451; Treasurer 309-786-4451.

Saline County

County Recorder, 10 E. Poplar, Harrisburg, IL 62946. 618-253-8197 R/E Recording: 618-253-3073 UCC Recording: 618-253-3073; Fax 618-252-3073.
Will search UCC records. This agency will not do a tax lien search. Will not search real estate records. **Other Phone Numbers:** Assessor 618-252-0691; Treasurer 618-253-6915; Elections 618-253-8197; Vital Records 618-253-8197.

Sangamon County

County Recorder, P.O.Box 669, Springfield, IL 62705-0669. 217-535-3150; Fax 217-535-3159. www.co.sangamon.il.us
Will search UCC records. UCC search includes tax liens if requested. Will not search real estate records. **Other Phone Numbers:** Assessor 217-753-6615; Treasurer 217-753-6800.

Schuyler County

County Recorder, PO Box 200, Rushville, IL 62681. County Recorder, R/E and UCC Recording 217-322-4734; Fax 217-322-6164.
Will search UCC records. Tax liens not included in UCC search. Will not search real estate records. **Other Phone Numbers:** Assessor 217-322-4432; Treasurer 217-322-3830; Elections 217-322-4734; Vital Records 217-322-4734.

Scott County

County Recorder, Courthouse, Winchester, IL 62694. County Recorder, R/E and UCC Recording 217-742-3178; Fax 217-742-5853.
Will search UCC records. UCC search includes tax liens. Real estate owner, mortgage, and property transfer searches available. **Other Phone Numbers:** Assessor 217-742-5751; Treasurer 217-742-3368; Elections 217-742-3178; Vital Records 217-742-3178.

Shelby County

County Recorder, PO Box 230, Shelbyville, IL 62565. 217-774-4421; Fax 217-774-5291.
Will search UCC records. UCC search includes tax liens if requested. Will not search real estate records. **Other Phone Numbers:** Assessor 217-774-5579; Treasurer 217-774-3841.

St. Clair County

County Recorder, PO Box 543, Belleville, IL 62220. 618-277-6600 UCC Recording: 618-277-6600 x2484.
Will search UCC records. Tax liens not included in UCC search. Will not search real estate records. **Other Phone Numbers:** Assessor 618-277-6600 x2509; Treasurer 618-277-6600 x2448; Elections 770-531-6600 x2363.

Stark County

County Recorder, PO Box 97, Toulon, IL 61483. County Recorder, R/E and UCC Recording 309-286-5911; Fax 309-286-4039. www.starkcourt.org
Will search UCC records. This agency will not do a tax lien search. Will not search real estate records. **Online Access:** Unclaimed Funds Records. Access to the county clerk of courts unclaimed funds database are

avilable at www.starkcourt.org/cgi-bin/starkcrt/pdfarchive/uf_pdflist.cgi. File is in pdf format. **Other Phone Numbers:** Assessor 309-286-7172; Treasurer 309-286-5901; Elections 309-286-5911; Vital Records 309-286-5911.

Stephenson County

County Recorder, 15 N. Galena Ave., Suite 1, Freeport, IL 61032. 815-235-8385; Fax none.
Will search UCC records. Will not search real estate records. **Other Phone Numbers:** Assessor 815-235-8260; Treasurer 815-235-8264.

Tazewell County

County Recorder, PO Box 36, Pekin, IL 61555-0036. 309-477-2210; Fax 309-477-2321.
Will search UCC records. This agency will not do a tax lien search. Will not search real estate records. **Other Phone Numbers:** Assessor 309-477-2275; Treasurer 309-477-2284.

Union County

County Recorder, PO Box H, Jonesboro, IL 62952. 618-833-5711; Fax 618-833-8712.
Will search UCC records. This agency will not do a tax lien search. Will not search real estate records. **Other Phone Numbers:** Assessor 618-833-8051; Treasurer 618-833-5621.

Vermilion County

County Recorder, 6 N. Vermilion St, Danville, IL 61832-5877. 217-431-2604; Fax 217-431-7460.
Will search UCC records. This agency will not do a tax lien search. Will not search real estate records. **Other Phone Numbers:** Assessor 217-431-2634; Treasurer 217-431-2631.

Wabash County

County Recorder, PO Box 277, Mount Carmel, IL 62863. County Recorder, R/E and UCC Recording 618-262-4561.
Will search UCC records. Tax liens not included in UCC search. Real estate record owner searches available. **Other Phone Numbers:** Assessor 618-262-4463; Treasurer 618-262-5262.

Warren County

County Recorder, Courthouse, 100 W. Broadway, Monmouth, IL 61462-1797. 309-734-8592; Fax 309-734-7406.
Will search UCC records. UCC search includes tax liens if requested. Will not search real estate records. **Other Phone Numbers:** Assessor 309-734-8561; Treasurer 309-734-8536; Elections 309-734-4612; Vital Records 309-734-8592.

Washington County

County Recorder, County Courthouse, 101 E. St. Louis St, Nashville, IL 62263-1105. 618-327-4800 x300; Fax 618-327-3582.
Will search UCC records. UCC search includes tax liens if requested. Real estate owner, mortgage, and property transfer searches available. **Other Phone Numbers:** Assessor 618-327-4800 x325; Treasurer 618-327-4800 x315.

Wayne County

County Recorder, PO Box 187, Fairfield, IL 62837. County Recorder, R/E and UCC Recording 618-842-5182; Fax 618-842-6427. http://assessor.wayne.il.us/Index.html
Will search UCC records. UCC search includes tax liens if requested. Will not search real estate records. **Online Access:** Assessor, Property Records. Records on the Wayne Township Assessor Office database are available free online at http://assessor.wayne.il.us/OPID.html. Also, an advanced search feature (fee) is available for subscribers. This includes legal, assessment, sales history, buildings and other information. **Other Phone Numbers:** Assessor 618-842-2582; Treasurer 618-842-5087; Elections 618-842-5182; Vital Records 618-842-5182.

White County

County Recorder, PO Box 339, Carmi, IL 62821. 618-382-7211.
Will search UCC records. UCC search includes tax liens if requested. Will not search real estate records. **Other Phone Numbers:** Assessor 618-618-382-721182-2332; Treasurer 618-382-8122; Elections 618-382-7211; Vital Records 618-382-7211.

Whiteside County

County Recorder, 200 E. Knox, Morrison, IL 61270. 815-772-5192.
Will search UCC records. This agency will not do a tax lien search. Will not search real estate records. **Other Phone Numbers:** Assessor 815-772-5195; Treasurer 815-772-5196.

Will County

County Recorder, 58 E Clinton, Suite 100, Joliet, IL 60432. 815-740-4637; Fax 815-740-4697.
Will search UCC records. This agency will not do a tax lien search. Will not search real estate records.

Williamson County

County Recorder, PO Box 1108, Marion, IL 62959-1108. 618-997-1301 X121; Fax 618-993-2071.
Will search UCC records. This agency will not do a tax lien search. Will not search real estate records. **Other Phone Numbers:** Assessor 618-997-1301 x164; Treasurer 618-997-1301 x129.

Winnebago County

County Recorder, 404 Elm St., Room 405, Rockford, IL 61101. 815-987-3100; Fax 815-961-3261.
Will search UCC records. UCC search includes tax liens if requested. Will not search real estate records. **Online Access:** Property, UCC Records. Access to county land and UCC records is available free at www.landaccess.com. **Other Phone Numbers:** Assessor 815-987-3025; Treasurer 815-987-3010.

Woodford County

County Recorder, 115 N. Main, Courthouse, Room 202, Eureka, IL 61530-1273. County Recorder, R/E and UCC Recording 309-467-2822.
Will search UCC records. This agency will not do a tax lien search. Will not search real estate records. **Other Phone Numbers:** Assessor 309-467-3708; Treasurer 309-467-4621; Elections 309-467-2822; Vital Records 309-467-2822.

Illinois County Locator

You will usually be able to find the city name in the City/County Cross Reference below. In that case, it is a simple matter to determine the county from the cross reference. However, only the official US Postal Service city names are included in this index. There are an additional 40,000 place names that people use in their addresses. Therefore, we have also included a ZIP/City Cross Reference immediately following the City/County Cross Reference.

If you know the ZIP Code but the city name does not appear in the City/County Cross Reference index, look up the ZIP Code in the ZIP/City Cross Reference, find the city name, then look up the city name in the City/County Cross Reference. For example, you want to know the county for an address of Menands, NY 12204. There is no "Menands" in the City/County Cross Reference. The ZIP/City Cross Reference shows that ZIP Codes 12201-12288 are for the city of Albany. Looking back in the City/County Cross Reference, Albany is in Albany County.

City/County Cross Reference

ABINGDON (61410) Knox(97), Warren(2)
ADAIR McDonough
ADDIEVILLE Washington
ADDISON Du Page
ADRIAN Hancock
AKIN Franklin
ALBANY Whiteside
ALBERS Clinton
ALBION Edwards
ALDEN McHenry
ALEDO Mercer
ALEXANDER (62601) Morgan(93), Sangamon(6)
ALEXIS (61412) Mercer(80), Warren(19)
ALGONQUIN (60102) McHenry(81), Kane(18)
ALHAMBRA Madison
ALLENDALE Wabash
ALLERTON (61810) Vermilion(68), Douglas(14), Edgar(13), Champaign(3)
ALMA Marion
ALPHA Henry
ALSEY Scott
ALSIP Cook
ALTAMONT (62411) Effingham(98), Fayette(1)
ALTO PASS (62905) Union(78), Jackson(21)
ALTON (62002) Madison(98), Macoupin(1)
ALTONA (61414) Knox(68), Henry(31)
ALVIN Vermilion
AMBOY Lee
AMF OHARE Cook
ANCHOR (61720) McLean(76), Ford(23)
ANCONA Livingston
ANDALUSIA Rock Island
ANDOVER Henry
ANNA Union
ANNAPOLIS (62413) Crawford(93), Clark(6)
ANNAWAN Henry
ANTIOCH Lake
APPLE RIVER Jo Daviess
ARCOLA (61910) Douglas(88), Coles(11)
ARENZVILLE (62611) Cass(83), Morgan(16)
ARGENTA Macon
ARLINGTON Bureau
ARLINGTON HEIGHTS Cook
ARMINGTON (61721) Tazewell(92), Logan(7)
ARMSTRONG Vermilion
AROMA PARK Kankakee
ARROWSMITH McLean
ARTHUR (61911) Douglas(61), Moultrie(34), Coles(3)
ASHKUM Iroquois
ASHLAND (62612) Cass(68), Morgan(30)
ASHLEY (62808) Washington(81), Jefferson(18)
ASHMORE Coles
ASHTON (61006) Lee(71), Ogle(28)

ASSUMPTION (62510) Christian(86), Shelby(13)
ASTORIA Fulton
ATHENS (62613) Menard(94), Logan(4)
ATKINSON Henry
ATLANTA (61723) Logan(98), McLean(1)
ATWATER Macoupin
ATWOOD (61913) Douglas(91), Piatt(7), Moultrie(1)
AUBURN Sangamon
AUGUSTA (62311) Hancock(90), Schuyler(5), Adams(3)
AURORA Du Page
AVA Jackson
AVISTON Clinton
AVON (61415) Fulton(80), Warren(19)
BAILEYVILLE (61007) Ogle(72), Stephenson(27)
BALDWIN Randolph
BARDOLPH McDonough
BARNHILL Wayne
BARRINGTON Lake
BARRY (62312) Pike(85), Adams(14)
BARSTOW Rock Island
BARTELSO Clinton
BARTLETT (60103) Du Page(52), Cook(47)
BASCO Hancock
BATAVIA Kane
BATCHTOWN Calhoun
BATH Mason
BAYLIS (62314) Pike(74), Adams(24), Brown(1)
BEARDSTOWN Cass
BEASON (62512) Logan(93), De Witt(6)
BEAVERVILLE (60912) Kankakee(54), Iroquois(45)
BECKEMEYER Clinton
BEDFORD PARK Cook
BEECHER (60401) Will(97), Kankakee(2)
BEECHER CITY (62414) Effingham(62), Fayette(27), Shelby(9)
BELKNAP (62908) Massac(54), Johnson(45)
BELLE RIVE (62810) Jefferson(95), Hamilton(2), Wayne(2)
BELLEVILLE St. Clair
BELLFLOWER McLean
BELLMONT Wabash
BELLWOOD Cook
BELVIDERE Boone
BEMENT Piatt
BENLD Macoupin
BENSENVILLE Du Page
BENSON Woodford
BENTON Franklin
BERKELEY Cook
BERWICK Warren
BERWYN Cook
BETHALTO Madison
BETHANY (61914) Moultrie(97), Macon(2)
BIG ROCK (60511) Kane(94), De Kalb(5)
BIGGSVILLE Henderson

BINGHAM Fayette
BIRDS Lawrence
BISHOP HILL Henry
BISMARCK Vermilion
BLACKSTONE Livingston
BLANDINSVILLE (61420) McDonough(91), Hancock(8)
BLOOMINGDALE Du Page
BLOOMINGTON McLean
BLUE ISLAND Cook
BLUE MOUND (62513) Macon(76), Christian(23)
BLUFF SPRINGS Cass
BLUFFS (62621) Scott(94), Morgan(5)
BLUFORD (62814) Jefferson(98), Wayne(1)
BOLES Johnson
BOLINGBROOK Will
BONDVILLE Champaign
BONE GAP Edwards
BONFIELD Kankakee
BONNIE Jefferson
BOODY Macon
BOURBONNAIS Kankakee
BOWEN (62316) Hancock(97), Adams(2)
BRACEVILLE (60407) Will(58), Grundy(40), Kankakee(1)
BRADFORD (61421) Bureau(45), Stark(45), Marshall(9)
BRADLEY Kankakee
BRAIDWOOD Will
BREESE Clinton
BRIDGEPORT Lawrence
BRIDGEVIEW Cook
BRIGHTON (62012) Macoupin(59), Jersey(30), Madison(10)
BRIMFIELD Peoria
BRISTOL Kendall
BROADLANDS (61816) Champaign(96), Douglas(3)
BROADVIEW Cook
BROCTON (61917) Edgar(97), Douglas(2)
BROOKFIELD Cook
BROOKPORT (62910) Massac(96), Pope(3)
BROUGHTON Hamilton
BROWNING (62624) Schuyler(97), Fulton(2)
BROWNS (62818) Wabash(60), Edwards(39)
BROWNSTOWN Fayette
BRUSSELS Calhoun
BRYANT Fulton
BUCKINGHAM (60917) Kankakee(87), Livingston(11)
BUCKLEY Iroquois
BUCKNER Franklin
BUDA Bureau
BUFFALO Sangamon
BUFFALO GROVE (60089) Lake(58), Cook(41)
BUFFALO PRAIRIE Rock Island
BULPITT Christian

BUNCOMBE (62912) Johnson(55), Union(44)
BUNKER HILL Macoupin
BURBANK Cook
BUREAU Bureau
BURLINGTON Kane
BURNSIDE Hancock
BURNT PRAIRIE (62820) White(87), Wayne(12)
BUSHNELL McDonough
BUTLER Montgomery
BYRON Ogle
CABERY (60919) Kankakee(36), Livingston(36), Ford(27)
CACHE Alexander
CAIRO Alexander
CALEDONIA (61011) Boone(69), Winnebago(30)
CALHOUN Richland
CALUMET CITY Cook
CAMARGO Douglas
CAMBRIA Williamson
CAMBRIDGE Henry
CAMDEN Schuyler
CAMERON Warren
CAMP GROVE Marshall
CAMP POINT Adams
CAMPBELL HILL (62916) Jackson(77), Randolph(12), Perry(9)
CAMPUS Livingston
CANTON Fulton
CANTRALL Sangamon
CAPRON Boone
CARBON CLIFF Rock Island
CARBONDALE Jackson
CARLINVILLE Macoupin
CARLOCK (61725) McLean(82), Woodford(17)
CARLYLE Clinton
CARMAN Henderson
CARMI White
CAROL STREAM Du Page
CARPENTERSVILLE Kane
CARRIER MILLS (62917) Saline(88), Williamson(11)
CARROLLTON Greene
CARTERVILLE Williamson
CARTHAGE Hancock
CARY (60013) McHenry(94), Lake(5)
CASEY (62420) Clark(85), Cumberland(12), Coles(1)
CASEYVILLE St. Clair
CASTLETON Stark
CATLIN Vermilion
CAVE IN ROCK Hardin
CEDAR POINT La Salle
CEDARVILLE Stephenson
CENTRALIA (62801) Marion(67), Clinton(21), Washington(6), Jefferson(4)
CERRO GORDO (61818) Piatt(85), Macon(14)
CHADWICK (61014) Carroll(81), Whiteside(18)

CHAMBERSBURG (62323) Pike(91), Brown(8)
CHAMPAIGN Champaign
CHANA Ogle
CHANDLERVILLE (62627) Cass(68), Mason(31)
CHANNAHON (60410) Will(95), Grundy(4)
CHAPIN (62628) Morgan(88), Scott(11)
CHARLESTON Coles
CHATHAM Sangamon
CHATSWORTH (60921) Livingston(98), Ford(1)
CHEBANSE (60922) Kankakee(63), Iroquois(36)
CHENOA (61726) McLean(94), Livingston(5)
CHERRY Bureau
CHERRY VALLEY (61016) Winnebago(89), Boone(10)
CHESTER Randolph
CHESTERFIELD (62630) Macoupin(97), Greene(1)
CHESTNUT Logan
CHICAGO Cook
CHICAGO HEIGHTS Cook
CHICAGO RIDGE Cook
CHILLICOTHE (61523) Peoria(98), Marshall(1)
CHRISMAN Edgar
CHRISTOPHER Franklin
CICERO Cook
CISCO (61830) Piatt(71), Macon(28)
CISNE Wayne
CISSNA PARK Iroquois
CLARE De Kalb
CLAREMONT (62421) Richland(97), Crawford(1), Lawrence(1)
CLARENDON HILLS Du Page
CLAY CITY (62824) Clay(95), Wayne(4)
CLAYTON (62324) Adams(97), Brown(2)
CLAYTONVILLE Iroquois
CLIFTON Iroquois
CLINTON De Witt
COAL CITY Grundy
COAL VALLEY (61240) Rock Island(75), Henry(24)
COATSBURG Adams
COBDEN Union
COELLO Franklin
COFFEEN Montgomery
COLCHESTER (62326) McDonough(97), Hancock(2)
COLETA Whiteside
COLFAX McLean
COLLINSVILLE (62234) Madison(90), St. Clair(9)
COLLISON Vermilion
COLMAR McDonough
COLONA Henry
COLP Williamson
COLUMBIA (62236) Monroe(94), St. Clair(5)
COLUSA Hancock
COMPTON Lee
CONCORD Morgan
CONGERVILLE Woodford
COOKSVILLE McLean
CORDOVA Rock Island
CORNELL Livingston
CORNLAND Logan
CORTLAND De Kalb
COTTAGE HILLS Madison
COULTERVILLE (62237) Randolph(46), Washington(27), Perry(25)
COUNTRY CLUB HILLS Cook
COWDEN (62422) Shelby(73), Fayette(26)
CREAL SPRINGS (62922) Williamson(72), Johnson(27)
CRESCENT CITY Iroquois
CRESTON Ogle
CRETE Will
CREVE COEUR Tazewell

CROPSEY (61731) McLean(64), Ford(33), Livingston(1)
CROSSVILLE White
CRYSTAL LAKE McHenry
CUBA Fulton
CULLOM (60929) Livingston(83), Ford(16)
CUTLER (62238) Perry(97), Randolph(2)
CYPRESS (62923) Johnson(89), Pulaski(8), Union(1)
DAHINDA Knox
DAHLGREN (62828) Hamilton(97), Wayne(2)
DAKOTA Stephenson
DALE Hamilton
DALLAS CITY (62330) Hancock(92), Henderson(7)
DALTON CITY (61925) Macon(57), Moultrie(42)
DALZELL Bureau
DANA (61321) La Salle(85), Livingston(5), Woodford(5), Marshall(3)
DANFORTH Iroquois
DANVERS (61732) McLean(62), Tazewell(37)
DANVILLE Vermilion
DARIEN Du Page
DAVIS (61019) Stephenson(62), Winnebago(37)
DAVIS JUNCTION (61020) Ogle(94), Winnebago(5)
DAWSON Sangamon
DE KALB De Kalb
DE LAND Piatt
DE SOTO (62924) Jackson(80), Williamson(19)
DECATUR Macon
DEER CREEK Tazewell
DEER GROVE (61243) Whiteside(88), Bureau(5), Lee(5)
DEERE CO GROUP CLAIMS Rock Island
DEERFIELD Cook
DEKALB De Kalb
DELAVAN Tazewell
DENNISON (62423) Clark(90), Edgar(9)
DEPUE Bureau
DES PLAINES Cook
DEWEY (61840) Champaign(97), Ford(2)
DEWITT De Witt
DIETERICH (62424) Effingham(90), Jasper(9)
DIVERNON Sangamon
DIX (62830) Jefferson(95), Marion(4)
DIXON (61021) Lee(90), Ogle(9)
DOLTON Cook
DONGOLA (62926) Union(90), Pulaski(9)
DONNELLSON (62019) Montgomery(61), Bond(38)
DONOVAN Iroquois
DORSEY (62021) Madison(93), Macoupin(6)
DOVER Bureau
DOW Jersey
DOWELL Jackson
DOWNERS GROVE Du Page
DOWNS McLean
DU BOIS (62831) Washington(91), Perry(8)
DU QUOIN (62832) Perry(96), Jackson(3)
DUNDAS (62425) Richland(86), Jasper(13)
DUNDEE Kane
DUNFERMLINE Fulton
DUNLAP Peoria
DUPO St. Clair
DURAND Winnebago
DWIGHT (60420) Livingston(93), Grundy(6)
EAGARVILLE Macoupin
EARLVILLE (60518) La Salle(82), De Kalb(15), Lee(2)
EAST ALTON Madison
EAST CARONDELET (62240) St. Clair(97), Monroe(2)
EAST DUBUQUE Jo Daviess
EAST GALESBURG Knox

EAST LYNN Vermilion
EAST MOLINE Rock Island
EAST PEORIA (61611) Tazewell(86), Woodford(13)
EAST SAINT LOUIS St. Clair
EASTON Mason
EDDYVILLE Pope
EDELSTEIN (61526) Peoria(89), Marshall(8), Stark(1)
EDGEWOOD (62426) Effingham(60), Clay(34), Fayette(4)
EDINBURG Christian
EDWARDS Peoria
EDWARDSVILLE Madison
EFFINGHAM Effingham
EL PASO (61738) Woodford(96), McLean(2)
ELBURN Kane
ELCO Alexander
ELDENA Lee
ELDORADO (62930) Saline(98), Gallatin(1)
ELDRED Greene
ELEROY Stephenson
ELGIN Kane
ELIZABETH (61028) Jo Daviess(98), Carroll(1)
ELIZABETHTOWN (62931) Hardin(81), Gallatin(18)
ELK GROVE VILLAGE Cook
ELKHART Logan
ELKVILLE Jackson
ELLERY (62833) Edwards(56), Wayne(43)
ELLIOTT Ford
ELLIS GROVE Randolph
ELLISVILLE Fulton
ELLSWORTH McLean
ELMHURST Du Page
ELMWOOD (61529) Peoria(98), Knox(1)
ELMWOOD PARK Cook
ELSAH Jersey
ELVASTON Hancock
ELWIN Macon
ELWOOD Will
EMDEN (62635) Tazewell(93), Logan(6)
EMINGTON Livingston
EMMA White
ENERGY Williamson
ENFIELD (62835) White(94), Hamilton(5)
EOLA Du Page
EQUALITY (62934) Gallatin(67), Saline(32)
ERIE (61250) Whiteside(94), Henry(5)
ESMOND (60129) Ogle(60), De Kalb(39)
ESSEX (60935) Kankakee(98), Will(1)
EUREKA Woodford
EVANSTON Cook
EVANSVILLE Randolph
EVERGREEN PARK Cook
EWING (62836) Franklin(98), Jefferson(1)
FAIRBURY (61739) Livingston(89), McLean(10)
FAIRFIELD Wayne
FAIRMOUNT Vermilion
FAIRVIEW Fulton
FAIRVIEW HEIGHTS St. Clair
FARINA (62838) Fayette(54), Clay(29), Marion(14), Effingham(1)
FARMER CITY (61842) De Witt(89), McLean(9), Piatt(1)
FARMERSVILLE Montgomery
FARMINGTON (61531) Fulton(92), Peoria(5), Knox(1)
FENTON (61251) Whiteside(95), Rock Island(4)
FERRIS Hancock
FIATT Fulton
FIDELITY Jersey
FIELDON (62031) Jersey(97), Greene(2)
FILLMORE Montgomery
FINDLAY Shelby
FISHER (61843) Champaign(92), McLean(7)
FITHIAN Vermilion

FLANAGAN Livingston
FLAT ROCK (62427) Crawford(93), Lawrence(6)
FLORA Clay
FLOSSMOOR Cook
FOOSLAND (61845) Champaign(75), Ford(13), McLean(11)
FOREST CITY Mason
FOREST PARK Cook
FORREST Livingston
FORRESTON Ogle
FORSYTH Macon
FORT SHERIDAN Lake
FOWLER Adams
FOX LAKE Lake
FOX RIVER GROVE McHenry
FOX VALLEY Du Page
FRANKFORT Will
FRANKFORT HEIGHTS Franklin
FRANKLIN (62638) Morgan(98), Macoupin(1)
FRANKLIN GROVE (61031) Lee(94), Ogle(5)
FRANKLIN PARK Cook
FREDERICK Schuyler
FREEBURG St. Clair
FREEMAN SPUR Williamson
FREEPORT Stephenson
FULTON Whiteside
FULTS Monroe
GALATIA Saline
GALENA Jo Daviess
GALESBURG Knox
GALT Whiteside
GALVA (61434) Henry(97), Knox(1)
GARDEN PRAIRIE (61038) Boone(85), McHenry(14)
GARDNER Grundy
GAYS (61928) Moultrie(71), Coles(19), Shelby(9)
GEFF Wayne
GENESEO Henry
GENEVA Kane
GENOA De Kalb
GEORGETOWN Vermilion
GERLAW Warren
GERMAN VALLEY (61039) Stephenson(60), Ogle(39)
GERMANTOWN Clinton
GIBSON CITY (60936) Ford(98), Champaign(1)
GIFFORD Champaign
GILBERTS Kane
GILLESPIE Macoupin
GILMAN Iroquois
GILSON Knox
GIRARD (62640) Macoupin(89), Montgomery(10)
GLADSTONE Henderson
GLASFORD (61533) Peoria(77), Fulton(22)
GLEN CARBON Madison
GLEN ELLYN Du Page
GLENARM Sangamon
GLENCOE Cook
GLENDALE HEIGHTS Du Page
GLENVIEW Cook
GLENVIEW NAS Cook
GLENWOOD Cook
GODFREY (62035) Madison(94), Jersey(5)
GOLCONDA (62938) Pope(87), Massac(6), Hardin(5)
GOLDEN Adams
GOLDEN EAGLE Calhoun
GOLDEN GATE Wayne
GOLF Cook
GOOD HOPE McDonough
GOODFIELD Woodford
GOODWINE Iroquois
GOREVILLE (62939) Johnson(92), Williamson(4), Union(2)
GORHAM Jackson
GRAFTON Jersey

GRAND CHAIN (62941) Pulaski(60), Massac(39)
GRAND RIDGE La Salle
GRAND TOWER Jackson
GRANITE CITY Madison
GRANT PARK (60940) Kankakee(96), Will(3)
GRANTSBURG (62943) Johnson(79), Massac(16), Pope(3)
GRANVILLE (61326) Putnam(78), La Salle(21)
GRAYMONT Livingston
GRAYSLAKE Lake
GRAYVILLE (62844) White(57), Edwards(42)
GREAT LAKES Lake
GREEN VALLEY Tazewell
GREENFIELD (62044) Greene(87), Macoupin(12)
GREENUP Cumberland
GREENVIEW Menard
GREENVILLE Bond
GRIDLEY (61744) McLean(91), Livingston(8)
GRIGGSVILLE Pike
GROVELAND Tazewell
GURNEE Lake
HAGARSTOWN Fayette
HAMBURG Calhoun
HAMEL Madison
HAMILTON Hancock
HAMLETSBURG Pope
HAMMOND (61929) Piatt(98), Moultrie(1)
HAMPSHIRE Kane
HAMPTON Rock Island
HANNA CITY Peoria
HANOVER Jo Daviess
HANOVER PARK (60133) Cook(53), Du Page(46)
HARDIN Calhoun
HARMON (61042) Lee(98), Whiteside(1)
HARRISBURG Saline
HARRISTOWN Macon
HARTFORD Madison
HARTSBURG (62643) Montgomery(62), Logan(37)
HARVARD McHenry
HARVEL (62538) Montgomery(82), Christian(17)
HARVEY Cook
HARWOOD HEIGHTS Cook
HAVANA (62644) Mason(94), Fulton(5)
HAZEL CREST Cook
HEBRON McHenry
HECKER Monroe
HENDERSON Knox
HENNEPIN Putnam
HENNING Vermilion
HENRY Marshall
HERALD White
HEROD (62947) Saline(44), Hardin(31), Pope(24)
HERRICK (62431) Shelby(78), Fayette(21)
HERRIN Williamson
HERSCHER (60941) Kankakee(96), Iroquois(2), Ford(1)
HETTICK Macoupin
HEYWORTH (61745) McLean(96), De Witt(3)
HICKORY HILLS Cook
HIDALGO Jasper
HIGHLAND (62249) Madison(94), Clinton(4)
HIGHLAND PARK Lake
HIGHWOOD Lake
HILLSBORO Montgomery
HILLSDALE Rock Island
HILLSIDE Cook
HILLVIEW Greene
HINCKLEY De Kalb
HINDSBORO (61930) Douglas(83), Coles(16)

HINES Cook
HINSDALE Du Page
HOFFMAN Clinton
HOFFMAN ESTATES Cook
HOLCOMB Ogle
HOMER (61849) Champaign(78), Vermilion(21)
HOMETOWN Cook
HOMEWOOD Cook
HOOPESTON (60942) Vermilion(91), Iroquois(8)
HOOPPOLE Henry
HOPEDALE Tazewell
HOPKINS PARK Kankakee
HOYLETON Washington
HUDSON (61748) McLean(97), Woodford(2)
HUEY Clinton
HULL (62343) Pike(88), Adams(11)
HUMBOLDT Coles
HUME Edgar
HUNTLEY (60142) McHenry(76), Kane(23)
HUNTSVILLE Schuyler
HURST Williamson
HUTSONVILLE Crawford
ILLINOIS CITY (61259) Rock Island(98), Mercer(1)
ILLIOPOLIS (62539) Sangamon(93), Macon(5), Logan(1)
INA (62846) Jefferson(96), Franklin(3)
INDIANOLA (61850) Vermilion(98), Edgar(1)
INDUSTRY (61440) McDonough(97), Schuyler(2)
INGLESIDE Lake
INGRAHAM (62434) Jasper(83), Clay(16)
IOLA Clay
IPAVA Fulton
IROQUOIS Iroquois
IRVING Montgomery
IRVINGTON Washington
ISLAND LAKE (60042) Lake(52), McHenry(47)
ITASCA Du Page
IUKA Marion
IVESDALE (61851) Champaign(82), Piatt(13), Douglas(4)
JACKSONVILLE Morgan
JACOB Jackson
JANESVILLE Cumberland
JEFFERSON BANK Peoria
JERSEYVILLE Jersey
JEWETT (62436) Jasper(60), Cumberland(39)
JOHNSONVILLE Wayne
JOHNSTON CITY Williamson
JOLIET Will
JONESBORO Union
JOPPA Massac
JOY (61260) Mercer(93), Rock Island(6)
JUNCTION Gallatin
JUSTICE Cook
KAMPSVILLE (62053) Calhoun(97), Pike(2)
KANE (62054) Greene(60), Jersey(39)
KANEVILLE Kane
KANKAKEE Kankakee
KANSAS (61933) Edgar(85), Clark(12), Coles(2)
KARBERS RIDGE Hardin
KARNAK (62956) Massac(50), Pulaski(48)
KASBEER Bureau
KEENES (62851) Wayne(64), Jefferson(27), Marion(7)
KEENSBURG Wabash
KEITHSBURG (61442) Mercer(95), Henderson(4)
KELL (62853) Marion(98), Jefferson(1)
KEMPTON (60946) Ford(77), Livingston(22)
KENILWORTH Cook

KENNEY (61749) De Witt(69), Logan(17), Macon(12)
KENT (61044) Stephenson(72), Jo Daviess(27)
KEWANEE Henry
KEYESPORT (62253) Bond(59), Clinton(37), Fayette(3)
KILBOURNE Mason
KINCAID Christian
KINDERHOOK Pike
KINGS Ogle
KINGSTON (60145) De Kalb(94), Boone(5)
KINGSTON MINES Peoria
KINMUNDY (62854) Marion(97), Clay(1), Fayette(1)
KINSMAN (60437) Grundy(97), La Salle(2)
KIRKLAND (60146) De Kalb(90), Boone(7)
KIRKWOOD (61447) Warren(90), Henderson(9)
KNOXVILLE Knox
LA FAYETTE (61449) Knox(55), Stark(44)
LA GRANGE Cook
LA GRANGE PARK Cook
LA HARPE (61450) Hancock(58), McDonough(39), Henderson(2)
LA MOILLE (61330) Bureau(53), Lee(46)
LA PLACE Piatt
LA PRAIRIE (62346) Adams(75), Schuyler(15), Hancock(9)
LA ROSE Marshall
LA SALLE La Salle
LACON Marshall
LADD Bureau
LAFOX Kane
LAKE BLUFF Lake
LAKE FOREST Lake
LAKE FORK Logan
LAKE IN THE HILLS McHenry
LAKE VILLA Lake
LAKE ZURICH Lake
LAKEWOOD Shelby
LANARK Carroll
LANCASTER Wabash
LANE De Witt
LANSING Cook
LATHAM (62543) Logan(81), Macon(18)
LAURA (61451) Peoria(92), Stark(7)
LAWNDALE Logan
LAWRENCEVILLE Lawrence
LE ROY McLean
LEAF RIVER (61047) Ogle(96), Winnebago(1), Stephenson(1)
LEBANON St. Clair
LEE (60530) De Kalb(52), Lee(47)
LEE CENTER Lee
LELAND (60531) La Salle(68), De Kalb(31)
LEMONT (60439) Du Page(71), Cook(24), Will(3)
LENA (61048) Stephenson(97), Jo Daviess(2)
LENZBURG (62255) St. Clair(92), Washington(7)
LEONORE La Salle
LERNA (62440) Coles(71), Cumberland(28)
LEWISTOWN Fulton
LEXINGTON McLean
LIBERTY Adams
LIBERTYVILLE Lake
LIMA Adams
LINCOLN Logan
LINCOLN'S NEW SALEM Menard
LINCOLNSHIRE Lake
LINCOLNWOOD Cook
LINDENWOOD Ogle
LISLE Du Page
LITCHFIELD (62056) Montgomery(93), Macoupin(6)
LITERBERRY Morgan
LITTLE YORK (61453) Warren(87), Henderson(12)

LITTLETON (61452) Schuyler(83), McDonough(16)
LIVERPOOL Fulton
LIVINGSTON Madison
LOAMI Sangamon
LOCKPORT Will
LODA (60948) Iroquois(93), Ford(6)
LOGAN Franklin
LOMAX Henderson
LOMBARD Du Page
LONDON MILLS Fulton
LONG GROVE Lake
LONG POINT Livingston
LONGVIEW (61852) Champaign(83), Douglas(16)
LOOGOOTEE Fayette
LORAINE (62349) Adams(93), Hancock(6)
LOSTANT (61334) La Salle(95), Putnam(3)
LOUISVILLE Clay
LOVEJOY St. Clair
LOVES PARK Winnebago
LOVINGTON (61937) Moultrie(93), Macon(3), Piatt(2)
LOWDER Sangamon
LOWPOINT Woodford
LUDLOW (60949) Champaign(90), Ford(9)
LYNDON Whiteside
LYNN CENTER (61262) Henry(92), Mercer(7)
LYONS Cook
MACEDONIA (62860) Franklin(89), Hamilton(10)
MACHESNEY PARK Winnebago
MACKINAW Tazewell
MACOMB McDonough
MACON Macon
MADISON Madison
MAEYSTOWN Monroe
MAGNOLIA (61336) Putnam(94), Marshall(5)
MAHOMET (61853) Champaign(98), Piatt(1)
MAKANDA (62958) Jackson(70), Williamson(15), Union(13)
MALDEN Bureau
MALTA De Kalb
MANCHESTER Scott
MANHATTAN Will
MANITO (61546) Mason(89), Tazewell(10)
MANLIUS Bureau
MANSFIELD (61854) Piatt(96), McLean(3)
MANTENO (60950) Kankakee(97), Will(2)
MAPLE PARK (60151) Kane(85), De Kalb(14)
MAPLETON Peoria
MAQUON Knox
MARENGO McHenry
MARIETTA (61459) Fulton(59), McDonough(40)
MARINE Madison
MARION Williamson
MARISSA (62257) St. Clair(70), Washington(27), Randolph(1)
MARK Putnam
MAROA Macon
MARSEILLES La Salle
MARSHALL (62441) Clark(98), Edgar(1)
MARTINSVILLE (62442) Clark(98), Crawford(1)
MARTINTON Iroquois
MARYVILLE Madison
MASCOUTAH St. Clair
MASON (62443) Effingham(89), Clay(10)
MASON CITY Mason
MATHERVILLE Mercer
MATTESON Cook
MATTOON Coles
MAUNIE White
MAYWOOD Cook
MAZON Grundy
MC CLURE (62957) Alexander(64), Union(35)

MC CONNELL Stephenson
MC HENRY McHenry
MC LEAN (61754) McLean(96), Logan(3)
MC LEANSBORO Hamilton
MC NABB Putnam
MCHENRY McHenry
MECHANICSBURG (62545)
   Sangamon(61), Christian(38)
MEDIA (61460) Henderson(93), Warren(6)
MEDINAH Du Page
MEDORA (62063) Jersey(59),
   Macoupin(40)
MELROSE PARK Cook
MELVIN (60952) Ford(94), Livingston(5)
MENARD Randolph
MENDON (62351) Adams(81),
   Hancock(18)
MENDOTA (61342) La Salle(97),
   Bureau(1), Lee(1)
MEREDOSIA (62665) Morgan(94),
   Scott(3), Cass(2)
MERNA McLean
METAMORA Woodford
METCALF Edgar
METROPOLIS Massac
MICHAEL Calhoun
MIDDLETOWN (62666) Logan(84),
   Menard(15)
MIDLOTHIAN Cook
MILAN Rock Island
MILFORD Iroquois
MILL SHOALS White
MILLBROOK Kendall
MILLCREEK Union
MILLEDGEVILLE (61051) Carroll(93),
   Ogle(4), Whiteside(1)
MILLER CITY Alexander
MILLINGTON Kendall
MILLSTADT St. Clair
MILMINE Piatt
MILTON Pike
MINERAL (61344) Henry(73), Bureau(26)
MINIER Tazewell
MINONK (61760) Woodford(93),
   Marshall(6)
MINOOKA (60447) Grundy(44),
   Kendall(29), Will(26)
MOBIL OIL CREDIT CORP Du Page
MODE Shelby
MODESTO (62667) Macoupin(97),
   Morgan(2)
MODOC Randolph
MOKENA Will
MOLINE Rock Island
MOMENCE Kankakee
MONEE Will
MONMOUTH Warren
MONROE CENTER (61052) Ogle(91),
   Winnebago(4), De Kalb(3)
MONTGOMERY (60538) Kendall(56),
   Kane(43)
MONTGOMERY WARD Du Page
MONTICELLO Piatt
MONTROSE (62445) Jasper(55),
   Cumberland(34), Effingham(10)
MOOSEHEART Kane
MORO Madison
MORRIS Grundy
MORRISON Whiteside
MORRISONVILLE (62546) Christian(90),
   Montgomery(9)
MORTON Tazewell
MORTON GROVE Cook
MOSSVILLE Peoria
MOUND CITY Pulaski
MOUNDS Pulaski
MOUNT AUBURN (62547) Christian(97),
   Macon(2)
MOUNT CARMEL Wabash
MOUNT CARROLL (61053) Carroll(90), Jo
   Daviess(9)
MOUNT ERIE Wayne

MOUNT MORRIS Ogle
MOUNT OLIVE (62069) Macoupin(97),
   Montgomery(2)
MOUNT PROSPECT Cook
MOUNT PULASKI Logan
MOUNT STERLING Brown
MOUNT VERNON Jefferson
MOWEAQUA (62550) Christian(94),
   Shelby(5)
MOZIER Calhoun
MT ZION Macon
MUDDY Saline
MULBERRY GROVE (62262) Bond(87),
   Fayette(11), Montgomery(1)
MULKEYTOWN Franklin
MUNCIE Vermilion
MUNDELEIN Lake
MURDOCK Douglas
MURPHYSBORO Jackson
MURRAYVILLE Morgan
NACHUSA Lee
NAPERVILLE Du Page
NASHVILLE Washington
NASON Jefferson
NATIONAL STOCK YARDS St. Clair
NAUVOO Hancock
NEBO (62355) Pike(64), Calhoun(35)
NELSON Lee
NEOGA (62447) Cumberland(87),
   Shelby(11), Coles(1)
NEPONSET (61345) Bureau(96), Stark(3)
NEW ATHENS (62264) St. Clair(97),
   Monroe(2)
NEW BADEN (62265) Clinton(91), St.
   Clair(8)
NEW BEDFORD Bureau
NEW BERLIN Sangamon
NEW BOSTON Mercer
NEW BURNSIDE (62967) Johnson(86),
   Williamson(13)
NEW CANTON Pike
NEW DOUGLAS (62074) Madison(88),
   Bond(4), Macoupin(3), Montgomery(3)
NEW HAVEN (62867) Gallatin(59),
   White(40)
NEW HOLLAND (62671) Logan(92),
   Mason(7)
NEW LENOX Will
NEW MEMPHIS Clinton
NEW SALEM Pike
NEW WINDSOR (61465) Mercer(96),
   Henry(3)
NEWARK (60541) Kendall(90), Grundy(7),
   La Salle(2)
NEWMAN (61942) Douglas(93), Edgar(6)
NEWTON (62448) Jasper(97), Richland(2)
NIANTIC Macon
NILES Cook
NILWOOD Macoupin
NIOTA Hancock
NOBLE (62868) Richland(94), Clay(3),
   Wayne(1)
NOKOMIS (62075) Montgomery(95),
   Christian(4)
NORA Jo Daviess
NORMAL McLean
NORRIS Fulton
NORRIS CITY (62869) White(94),
   Gallatin(3), Hamilton(1)
NORTH AURORA Kane
NORTH CHICAGO Lake
NORTH HENDERSON (61466) Mercer(96),
   Warren(2)
NORTHBROOK Cook
O FALLON St. Clair
OAK FOREST Cook
OAK LAWN Cook
OAK PARK Cook
OAKDALE (62268) Washington(94),
   Perry(5)
OAKFORD (62673) Cass(51), Menard(48)

OAKLAND (61943) Coles(78), Douglas(14),
   Edgar(6)
OAKLEY Macon
OAKWOOD Vermilion
OBLONG (62449) Crawford(90), Jasper(8)
OCONEE (62553) Shelby(50),
   Christian(29), Montgomery(20)
ODELL Livingston
ODIN Marion
OGDEN (61859) Champaign(86),
   Vermilion(13)
OGLESBY La Salle
OHIO (61349) Cass(39), Bureau(38),
   Lee(21)
OHLMAN Montgomery
OKAWVILLE Washington
OLIVE BRANCH Alexander
OLMSTED Pulaski
OLNEY Richland
OLYMPIA FIELDS Cook
OMAHA Gallatin
ONARGA Iroquois
ONEIDA Knox
OPDYKE Jefferson
OPHEIM Henry
OQUAWKA Henderson
ORANGEVILLE Stephenson
ORAVILLE Jackson
OREANA Macon
OREGON Ogle
ORIENT Franklin
ORION (61273) Henry(63), Rock Island(36)
ORLAND PARK (60467) Cook(92), Will(7)
OSCO Henry
OSWEGO Kendall
OTTAWA La Salle
OWANECO (62555) Christian(94),
   Macon(5)
OZARK (62972) Johnson(96),
   Williamson(2), Pope(1)
PALATINE Cook
PALESTINE Crawford
PALMER Christian
PALMYRA Macoupin
PALOMA Adams
PALOS HEIGHTS Cook
PALOS HILLS Cook
PALOS PARK Cook
PANA (62557) Christian(92), Shelby(5),
   Montgomery(1)
PANAMA Montgomery
PAPINEAU Iroquois
PARIS Edgar
PARK FOREST (60466) Cook(55), Will(44)
PARK RIDGE Cook
PARKERSBURG Richland
PATOKA (62875) Marion(94), Fayette(5)
PATTERSON Greene
PAW PAW Lee
PAWNEE (62558) Sangamon(88),
   Christian(8), Montgomery(2)
PAXTON (60957) Ford(96), Champaign(3)
PAYSON Adams
PEARL (62361) Pike(97), Calhoun(2)
PEARL CITY (61062) Stephenson(93), Jo
   Daviess(5)
PECATONICA (61063) Winnebago(91),
   Stephenson(8)
PEKIN Tazewell
PENFIELD (61862) Champaign(80),
   Vermilion(19)
PEORIA Peoria
PEORIA HEIGHTS Peoria
PEOTONE (60468) Will(96), Kankakee(3)
PERCY (62272) Randolph(80), Perry(19)
PERKS Pulaski
PERRY Pike
PERU (61354) La Salle(98), Bureau(1)
PESOTUM Champaign
PETERSBURG Menard
PHILO Champaign
PIASA (62079) Macoupin(73), Jersey(26)

PIERRON Bond
PINCKNEYVILLE Perry
PIPER CITY (60959) Ford(93),
   Livingston(6)
PITTSBURG Williamson
PITTSFIELD Pike
PLAINFIELD Will
PLAINVIEW Macoupin
PLAINVILLE Adams
PLANO Kendall
PLATO CENTER Kane
PLEASANT HILL (62366) Pike(98),
   Calhoun(1)
PLEASANT PLAINS Sangamon
PLYMOUTH (62367) Hancock(51),
   McDonough(40), Schuyler(8)
POCAHONTAS (62275) Bond(67),
   Madison(23), Clinton(8)
POLO (61064) Ogle(97), Whiteside(1)
POMONA Jackson
PONTIAC Livingston
POPLAR GROVE Boone
PORT BYRON Rock Island
POSEN Cook
POTOMAC Vermilion
PRAIRIE CITY McDonough
PRAIRIE DU ROCHER (62277)
   Randolph(57), Monroe(43)
PREEMPTION Mercer
PRINCETON Bureau
PRINCEVILLE (61559) Peoria(95), Stark(4)
PROPHETSTOWN (61277) Whiteside(78),
   Henry(21)
PROSPECT HEIGHTS Cook
PULASKI Pulaski
PUTNAM (61560) Putnam(91), Bureau(5),
   Marshall(2)
QUINCY Adams
RADOM Washington
RALEIGH Saline
RAMSEY (62080) Fayette(91),
   Montgomery(7), Shelby(1)
RANKIN (60960) Vermilion(71), Ford(22),
   Iroquois(3), Champaign(2)
RANSOM (60470) La Salle(90), Grundy(5),
   Livingston(3)
RANTOUL Champaign
RAPIDS CITY Rock Island
RARITAN Henderson
RAYMOND (62560) Montgomery(90),
   Macoupin(9)
RED BUD (62278) Randolph(68),
   Monroe(31)
REDDICK (60961) Kankakee(82),
   Livingston(13), Grundy(3)
REDMON Edgar
RENAULT Monroe
REYNOLDS (61279) Rock Island(73),
   Mercer(26)
RICHMOND McHenry
RICHTON PARK Cook
RICHVIEW (62877) Washington(97),
   Jefferson(2)
RIDGE FARM (61870) Vermilion(93),
   Edgar(6)
RIDGWAY Gallatin
RIDOTT Stephenson
RINARD Wayne
RINGWOOD McHenry
RIO (61472) Knox(98), Mercer(1)
RIVER FOREST Cook
RIVER GROVE Cook
RIVERDALE Cook
RIVERSIDE Cook
RIVERTON Sangamon
ROANOKE Woodford
ROBBINS Cook
ROBERTS (60962) Ford(95), Livingston(4)
ROBINSON Crawford
ROCHELLE (61068) Ogle(96), Lee(3)
ROCHESTER (62563) Sangamon(82),
   Christian(17)

ROCK CITY Stephenson
ROCK FALLS Whiteside
ROCK ISLAND Rock Island
ROCKBRIDGE (62081) Greene(98), Jersey(2)
ROCKFORD Winnebago
ROCKPORT Pike
ROCKTON Winnebago
ROCKWOOD (62280) Jackson(58), Randolph(41)
ROLLING MEADOWS Cook
ROME Peoria
ROMEOVILLE Will
ROODHOUSE (62082) Greene(88), Scott(9), Morgan(1)
ROSAMOND (62083) Christian(59), Montgomery(40)
ROSCOE (61073) Winnebago(98), Boone(1)
ROSELLE (60172) Du Page(82), Cook(17)
ROSEVILLE (61473) McDonough(68), Warren(31)
ROSICLARE Hardin
ROSSVILLE Vermilion
ROUND LAKE Lake
ROXANA Madison
ROYAL Champaign
ROYALTON Franklin
RUSHVILLE Schuyler
RUSSELL Lake
RUTLAND (61358) La Salle(64), Marshall(35)
SADORUS (61872) Champaign(90), Douglas(9)
SAILOR SPRINGS Clay
SAINT ANNE (60964) Kankakee(94), Iroquois(5)
SAINT AUGUSTINE (61474) Knox(93), Warren(5), Fulton(1)
SAINT CHARLES Kane
SAINT DAVID Fulton
SAINT ELMO (62458) Fayette(91), Effingham(8)
SAINT FRANCISVILLE (62460) Lawrence(90), Wabash(9)
SAINT JACOB Madison
SAINT JOSEPH Champaign
SAINT LIBORY St. Clair
SAINT PETER Fayette
SAINTE MARIE Jasper
SALEM Marion
SAN JOSE (62682) Mason(81), Tazewell(9), Logan(9)
SANDOVAL (62882) Marion(91), Clinton(8)
SANDWICH (60548) De Kalb(77), La Salle(19), Kendall(3)
SAUNEMIN Livingston
SAVANNA (61074) Carroll(98), Jo Daviess(1)
SAVOY Champaign
SAWYERVILLE Macoupin
SAYBROOK McLean
SCALES MOUND Jo Daviess
SCHAUMBURG Cook
SCHELLER (62883) Jefferson(62), Franklin(29), Perry(7)
SCHILLER PARK Cook
SCIOTA (61475) McDonough(87), Warren(12)
SCIOTO MILLS Stephenson
SCIOTO MILLSX Stephenson
SCOTT AIR FORCE BASE St. Clair
SCOTTVILLE Macoupin
SEATON (61476) Mercer(88), Henderson(9), Warren(1)
SEATONVILLE Bureau
SECOR Woodford
SENECA (61360) La Salle(83), Grundy(16)
SERENA La Salle
SESSER Franklin
SEWARD Winnebago
SEYMOUR Champaign

SHABBONA De Kalb
SHANNON (61078) Carroll(80), Stephenson(12), Ogle(7)
SHATTUC Clinton
SHAWNEETOWN Gallatin
SHEFFIELD (61361) Henry(75), Bureau(24)
SHELBYVILLE Shelby
SHELDON Iroquois
SHERIDAN La Salle
SHERMAN Sangamon
SHERRARD Mercer
SHIPMAN Macoupin
SHIRLAND Winnebago
SHIRLEY McLean
SHOBONIER (62885) Fayette(95), Marion(4)
SHUMWAY (62461) Effingham(93), Shelby(6)
SIBLEY Ford
SIDELL (61876) Vermilion(81), Edgar(18)
SIDNEY Champaign
SIGEL (62462) Cumberland(60), Shelby(38), Effingham(1)
SILVIS Rock Island
SIMPSON (62985) Johnson(86), Pope(13)
SIMS Wayne
SKOKIE Cook
SMITHBORO Bond
SMITHFIELD Fulton
SMITHSHIRE (61478) Warren(94), Henderson(5)
SMITHTON St. Clair
SOLON MILLS McHenry
SOMONAUK (60552) De Kalb(52), La Salle(47)
SORENTO (62086) Bond(75), Montgomery(23), Madison(1)
SOUTH BELOIT (61080) Winnebago(93), Boone(6)
SOUTH ELGIN Kane
SOUTH HOLLAND Cook
SOUTH PEKIN Tazewell
SOUTH ROXANA Madison
SOUTH WILMINGTON Grundy
SPARLAND (61565) Marshall(98), Peoria(1)
SPARTA Randolph
SPEER Stark
SPRING GROVE (60081) McHenry(78), Lake(21)
SPRING VALLEY Bureau
SPRINGERTON (62887) White(77), Hamilton(22)
SPRINGFIELD Sangamon
STANDARD Putnam
STANDARD CITY Macoupin
STANFORD (61774) McLean(98), Tazewell(1)
STAUNTON (62088) Macoupin(85), Madison(14)
STEELEVILLE Randolph
STEGER Cook
STERLING (61081) Whiteside(97), Lee(2)
STEWARD (60553) Lee(98), De Kalb(1)
STEWARDSON Shelby
STILLMAN VALLEY (61084) Ogle(95), Winnebago(4)
STOCKLAND Iroquois
STOCKTON Jo Daviess
STONE PARK Cook
STONEFORT (62987) Saline(58), Williamson(34), Pope(7)
STONINGTON Christian
STOY Crawford
STRASBURG Shelby
STRAWN (61775) Livingston(90), Ford(9)
STREAMWOOD Cook
STREATOR (61364) La Salle(91), Livingston(8)
STRONGHURST Henderson
SUBLETTE Lee

SUGAR GROVE Kane
SULLIVAN (61951) Moultrie(98), Coles(1)
SUMMER HILL Pike
SUMMERFIELD St. Clair
SUMMIT ARGO Cook
SUMNER (62466) Lawrence(87), Crawford(6), Richland(5)
SUTTER (62373) Hancock(94), Adams(5)
SYCAMORE (60178) De Kalb(97), Kane(2)
TABLE GROVE (61482) Fulton(40), Knox(32), McDonough(26)
TALLULA Menard
TAMAROA Perry
TAMMS Alexander
TAMPICO (61283) Whiteside(49), Bureau(47), Henry(2)
TAYLOR RIDGE Rock Island
TAYLOR SPRINGS Montgomery
TAYLORVILLE Christian
TECHNY Cook
TENNESSEE (62374) McDonough(58), Hancock(41)
TEUTOPOLIS (62467) Effingham(85), Jasper(8), Cumberland(5)
TEXICO (62889) Jefferson(68), Marion(31)
THAWVILLE (60968) Iroquois(56), Ford(42), Livingston(1)
THAYER Sangamon
THEBES Alexander
THOMASBORO Champaign
THOMPSONVILLE (62890) Franklin(67), Williamson(24), Saline(6), Hamilton(1)
THOMSON Carroll
THORNTON Cook
TILDEN Randolph
TILTON Vermilion
TIMEWELL (62375) Brown(98), Adams(1)
TINLEY PARK (60477) Cook(95), Will(4)
TISKILWA Bureau
TOLEDO Cumberland
TOLONO Champaign
TOLUCA Marshall
TONICA La Salle
TOPEKA Mason
TOULON (61483) Stark(96), Henry(3)
TOVEY Christian
TOWANDA McLean
TOWER HILL Shelby
TREMONT Tazewell
TRENTON (62293) Clinton(76), St. Clair(14), Madison(9)
TRILLA (62469) Cumberland(77), Coles(22)
TRIUMPH La Salle
TRIVOLI (61569) Peoria(97), Fulton(2)
TROY Madison
TROY GROVE La Salle
TUNNEL HILL Johnson
TUSCOLA Douglas
ULLIN (62992) Pulaski(97), Alexander(2)
UNION McHenry
UNION HILL Kankakee
UNITY Alexander
URBANA Champaign
URSA Adams
UTICA La Salle
VALIER Franklin
VALMEYER Monroe
VAN ORIN Bureau
VANDALIA Fayette
VARNA Marshall
VENEDY Washington
VENICE (62090) Madison(97), St. Clair(2)
VERGENNES Jackson
VERMILION Edgar
VERMONT (61484) McDonough(81), Fulton(17), Schuyler(1)
VERNON (62892) Marion(90), Fayette(9)
VERNON HILLS Lake
VERONA Grundy
VERSAILLES Brown
VICTORIA Knox

VIENNA Johnson
VILLA GROVE (61956) Douglas(95), Champaign(4)
VILLA PARK Du Page
VILLA RIDGE Pulaski
VIOLA Mercer
VIRDEN (62690) Macoupin(89), Montgomery(5), Sangamon(4)
VIRGIL Kane
VIRGINIA Cass
WADSWORTH Lake
WAGGONER (62572) Montgomery(71), Macoupin(28)
WALNUT (61376) Bureau(92), Lee(7)
WALNUT HILL (62893) Marion(58), Jefferson(41)
WALSH Randolph
WALSHVILLE Montgomery
WALTONVILLE Jefferson
WAPELLA De Witt
WARREN (61087) Jo Daviess(98), Stephenson(1)
WARRENSBURG Macon
WARRENVILLE Du Page
WARSAW (62379) Hancock(95), Adams(4)
WASCO Kane
WASHBURN (61570) Woodford(74), Marshall(25)
WASHINGTON Tazewell
WATAGA Knox
WATERLOO (62298) Monroe(92), St. Clair(7)
WATERMAN De Kalb
WATSEKA Iroquois
WATSON Effingham
WAUCONDA Lake
WAUKEGAN Lake
WAVERLY (62692) Morgan(76), Sangamon(23)
WAYNE (60184) Du Page(61), Kane(38)
WAYNE CITY (62895) Wayne(95), Hamilton(4)
WAYNESVILLE De Witt
WEDRON La Salle
WELDON (61882) De Witt(90), Macon(8)
WELLINGTON Iroquois
WENONA (61377) Marshall(86), La Salle(13)
WEST BROOKLYN Lee
WEST CHICAGO Du Page
WEST FRANKFORT (62896) Franklin(94), Williamson(5)
WEST LIBERTY Jasper
WEST POINT Hancock
WEST SALEM (62476) Edwards(78), Wabash(18), Lawrence(1), Richland(1)
WEST UNION Clark
WEST YORK (62478) Clark(56), Crawford(43)
WESTCHESTER Cook
WESTERN SPRINGS Cook
WESTERVELT Shelby
WESTFIELD (62474) Clark(90), Coles(8)
WESTMONT Du Page
WESTVILLE Vermilion
WHEATON Du Page
WHEELER (62479) Jasper(97), Effingham(2)
WHEELING (60090) Cook(98), Lake(1)
WHITE HALL Greene
WHITE HEATH (61884) Piatt(77), Champaign(22)
WHITTINGTON Franklin
WILLIAMSFIELD (61489) Knox(88), Peoria(11)
WILLIAMSVILLE (62693) Sangamon(83), Logan(15)
WILLISVILLE Perry
WILLOW HILL Jasper
WILLOW SPRINGS Cook
WILLOWBROOK (60527) Du Page(91), Cook(8)

WILMETTE Cook
WILMINGTON (60481) Will(98), Grundy(1)
WILSONVILLE Macoupin
WINCHESTER (62694) Scott(86), Morgan(13)
WINDSOR Shelby
WINFIELD Du Page
WINNEBAGO Winnebago
WINNETKA Cook

WINSLOW Stephenson
WINTHROP HARBOR Lake
WITT Montgomery
WOLF LAKE Union
WONDER LAKE McHenry
WOOD DALE Du Page
WOOD RIVER Madison
WOODHULL (61490) McDonough(47), Henry(47), Knox(4)

WOODLAND Iroquois
WOODLAWN Jefferson
WOODRIDGE Du Page
WOODSON Morgan
WOODSTOCK McHenry
WOOSUNG Ogle
WORDEN Madison
WORTH Cook
WRIGHTS Greene

WYANET Bureau
WYOMING (61491) Stark(96), Marshall(3)
XENIA (62899) Clay(96), Marion(3)
YALE (62481) Jasper(97), Cumberland(2)
YATES CITY Knox
YORKVILLE Kendall
ZEIGLER Franklin
ZION Lake

ZIP/City Cross Reference

ZIP	City	ZIP	City	ZIP	City	ZIP	City
60000-60000	PALATINE	60087-60087	WAUKEGAN	60163-60163	BERKELEY	60450-60450	MORRIS
60001-60001	ALDEN	60088-60088	GREAT LAKES	60164-60164	MELROSE PARK	60451-60451	NEW LENOX
60002-60002	ANTIOCH	60089-60089	BUFFALO GROVE	60165-60165	STONE PARK	60452-60452	OAK FOREST
60004-60006	ARLINGTON HEIGHTS	60090-60090	WHEELING	60168-60168	SCHAUMBURG	60453-60454	OAK LAWN
60007-60007	ELK GROVE VILLAGE	60091-60091	WILMETTE	60170-60170	PLATO CENTER	60455-60455	BRIDGEVIEW
60008-60008	ROLLING MEADOWS	60092-60092	LIBERTYVILLE	60171-60171	RIVER GROVE	60456-60456	HOMETOWN
60009-60009	ELK GROVE VILLAGE	60093-60093	WINNETKA	60172-60172	ROSELLE	60457-60457	HICKORY HILLS
60010-60011	BARRINGTON	60094-60095	PALATINE	60173-60173	SCHAUMBURG	60458-60458	JUSTICE
60012-60012	CRYSTAL LAKE	60096-60096	WINTHROP HARBOR	60174-60175	SAINT CHARLES	60459-60459	BURBANK
60013-60013	CARY	60097-60097	WONDER LAKE	60176-60176	SCHILLER PARK	60460-60460	ODELL
60014-60014	CRYSTAL LAKE	60098-60098	WOODSTOCK	60177-60177	SOUTH ELGIN	60461-60461	OLYMPIA FIELDS
60015-60015	DEERFIELD	60099-60099	ZION	60178-60178	SYCAMORE	60462-60462	ORLAND PARK
60016-60019	DES PLAINES	60100-60100	CAROL STREAM	60179-60179	HOFFMAN ESTATES	60463-60463	PALOS HEIGHTS
60020-60020	FOX LAKE	60101-60101	ADDISON	60180-60180	UNION	60464-60464	PALOS PARK
60021-60021	FOX RIVER GROVE	60102-60102	ALGONQUIN	60181-60181	VILLA PARK	60465-60465	PALOS HILLS
60022-60022	GLENCOE	60103-60103	BARTLETT	60182-60182	VIRGIL	60466-60466	PARK FOREST
60025-60025	GLENVIEW	60104-60104	BELLWOOD	60183-60183	WASCO	60467-60467	ORLAND PARK
60026-60026	GLENVIEW NAS	60105-60106	BENSENVILLE	60184-60184	WAYNE	60468-60468	PEOTONE
60029-60029	GOLF	60107-60107	STREAMWOOD	60185-60186	WEST CHICAGO	60469-60469	POSEN
60030-60030	GRAYSLAKE	60108-60108	BLOOMINGDALE	60187-60187	WHEATON	60470-60470	RANSOM
60031-60031	GURNEE	60109-60109	BURLINGTON	60188-60188	CAROL STREAM	60471-60471	RICHTON PARK
60033-60033	HARVARD	60110-60110	CARPENTERSVILLE	60189-60189	WHEATON	60472-60472	ROBBINS
60034-60034	HEBRON	60111-60111	CLARE	60190-60190	WINFIELD	60473-60473	SOUTH HOLLAND
60035-60035	HIGHLAND PARK	60112-60112	CORTLAND	60191-60191	WOOD DALE	60474-60474	SOUTH WILMINGTON
60037-60037	FORT SHERIDAN	60113-60113	CRESTON	60192-60196	SCHAUMBURG	60475-60475	STEGER
60038-60038	PALATINE	60114-60114	ADDISON	60197-60199	CAROL STREAM	60476-60476	THORNTON
60039-60039	CRYSTAL LAKE	60115-60115	DE KALB	60201-60209	EVANSTON	60477-60477	TINLEY PARK
60040-60040	HIGHWOOD	60115-60115	DEKALB	60251-60251	PALATINE	60478-60478	COUNTRY CLUB HILLS
60041-60041	INGLESIDE	60116-60116	CAROL STREAM	60301-60304	OAK PARK	60479-60479	VERONA
60042-60042	ISLAND LAKE	60117-60117	BLOOMINGDALE	60305-60305	RIVER FOREST	60480-60480	WILLOW SPRINGS
60043-60043	KENILWORTH	60118-60118	DUNDEE	60351-60351	CAROL STREAM	60481-60481	WILMINGTON
60044-60044	LAKE BLUFF	60119-60119	ELBURN	60352-60352	MOBIL OIL CREDIT CORP	60482-60482	WORTH
60045-60045	LAKE FOREST	60120-60123	ELGIN	60353-60353	CAROL STREAM	60490-60490	BOLINGBROOK
60046-60046	LAKE VILLA	60125-60125	CAROL STREAM	60399-60399	BENSENVILLE	60499-60499	BEDFORD PARK
60047-60047	LAKE ZURICH	60126-60126	ELMHURST	60401-60401	BEECHER	60501-60501	SUMMIT ARGO
60048-60048	LIBERTYVILLE	60128-60128	CAROL STREAM	60402-60402	BERWYN	60504-60507	AURORA
60049-60049	LONG GROVE	60129-60129	ESMOND	60406-60406	BLUE ISLAND	60510-60510	BATAVIA
60050-60050	MC HENRY	60130-60130	FOREST PARK	60407-60407	BRACEVILLE	60511-60511	BIG ROCK
60050-60050	MCHENRY	60131-60131	FRANKLIN PARK	60408-60408	BRAIDWOOD	60512-60512	BRISTOL
60051-60051	MC HENRY	60132-60132	CAROL STREAM	60409-60409	CALUMET CITY	60513-60513	BROOKFIELD
60051-60051	MCHENRY	60133-60133	HANOVER PARK	60410-60410	CHANNAHON	60514-60514	CLARENDON HILLS
60053-60053	MORTON GROVE	60134-60134	GENEVA	60411-60412	CHICAGO HEIGHTS	60515-60516	DOWNERS GROVE
60055-60055	PALATINE	60135-60135	GENOA	60415-60415	CHICAGO RIDGE	60517-60517	WOODRIDGE
60056-60056	MOUNT PROSPECT	60136-60136	GILBERTS	60416-60416	COAL CITY	60518-60518	EARLVILLE
60060-60060	MUNDELEIN	60137-60138	GLEN ELLYN	60417-60417	CRETE	60519-60519	EOLA
60061-60061	VERNON HILLS	60139-60139	GLENDALE HEIGHTS	60419-60419	DOLTON	60520-60520	HINCKLEY
60062-60062	NORTHBROOK	60140-60140	HAMPSHIRE	60420-60420	DWIGHT	60521-60523	HINSDALE
60063-60063	DEERFIELD	60141-60141	HINES	60421-60421	ELWOOD	60525-60525	LA GRANGE
60064-60064	NORTH CHICAGO	60142-60142	HUNTLEY	60422-60422	FLOSSMOOR	60526-60526	LA GRANGE PARK
60065-60065	NORTHBROOK	60143-60143	ITASCA	60423-60423	FRANKFORT	60527-60527	HINSDALE
60067-60067	PALATINE	60144-60144	KANEVILLE	60424-60424	GARDNER	60527-60527	WILLOWBROOK
60068-60068	PARK RIDGE	60145-60145	KINGSTON	60425-60425	GLENWOOD	60530-60530	LEE
60069-60069	LINCOLNSHIRE	60146-60146	KIRKLAND	60426-60426	HARVEY	60531-60531	LELAND
60070-60070	PROSPECT HEIGHTS	60147-60147	LAFOX	60429-60429	HAZEL CREST	60532-60532	LISLE
60071-60071	RICHMOND	60148-60148	LOMBARD	60430-60430	HOMEWOOD	60534-60534	LYONS
60072-60072	RINGWOOD	60149-60149	MONTGOMERY WARD	60431-60436	JOLIET	60536-60536	MILLBROOK
60073-60073	ROUND LAKE	60150-60150	MALTA	60437-60437	KINSMAN	60537-60537	MILLINGTON
60074-60074	PALATINE	60151-60151	MAPLE PARK	60438-60438	LANSING	60538-60538	MONTGOMERY
60075-60075	RUSSELL	60152-60152	MARENGO	60439-60439	LEMONT	60539-60539	MOOSEHEART
60076-60077	SKOKIE	60153-60153	MAYWOOD	60440-60440	BOLINGBROOK	60540-60540	NAPERVILLE
60078-60078	PALATINE	60154-60154	WESTCHESTER	60441-60441	LOCKPORT	60541-60541	NEWARK
60079-60079	WAUKEGAN	60155-60155	CAROL STREAM	60442-60442	MANHATTAN	60542-60542	NORTH AURORA
60080-60080	SOLON MILLS	60155-60155	BROADVIEW	60443-60443	MATTESON	60543-60543	OSWEGO
60081-60081	SPRING GROVE	60156-60156	LAKE IN THE HILLS	60444-60444	MAZON	60544-60544	PLAINFIELD
60082-60082	TECHNY	60157-60157	MEDINAH	60445-60445	MIDLOTHIAN	60545-60545	PLANO
60083-60083	WADSWORTH	60158-60158	CAROL STREAM	60446-60446	ROMEOVILLE	60546-60546	RIVERSIDE
60084-60084	WAUCONDA	60159-60159	SCHAUMBURG	60447-60447	MINOOKA	60548-60548	SANDWICH
60085-60085	WAUKEGAN	60160-60161	MELROSE PARK	60448-60448	MOKENA	60549-60549	SERENA
60086-60086	NORTH CHICAGO	60162-60162	HILLSIDE	60449-60449	MONEE	60550-60550	SHABBONA

60551-60551 SHERIDAN	60962-60962 ROBERTS	61111-61111 LOVES PARK	61341-61341 MARSEILLES
60552-60552 SOMONAUK	60963-60963 ROSSVILLE	61112-61114 ROCKFORD	61342-61342 MENDOTA
60553-60553 STEWARD	60964-60964 SAINT ANNE	61115-61115 MACHESNEY PARK	61344-61344 MINERAL
60554-60554 SUGAR GROVE	60966-60966 SHELDON	61125-61126 ROCKFORD	61345-61345 NEPONSET
60555-60555 WARRENVILLE	60967-60967 STOCKLAND	61130-61132 LOVES PARK	61346-61346 NEW BEDFORD
60556-60556 WATERMAN	60968-60968 THAWVILLE	61201-61206 ROCK ISLAND	61348-61348 OGLESBY
60557-60557 WEDRON	60969-60969 UNION HILL	61230-61230 ALBANY	61349-61349 OHIO
60558-60558 WESTERN SPRINGS	60970-60970 WATSEKA	61231-61231 ALEDO	61350-61350 OTTAWA
60559-60559 WESTMONT	60973-60973 WELLINGTON	61232-61232 ANDALUSIA	61353-61353 PAW PAW
60560-60560 YORKVILLE	60974-60974 WOODLAND	61233-61233 ANDOVER	61354-61354 PERU
60561-60561 DARIEN	61001-61001 APPLE RIVER	61234-61234 ANNAWAN	61356-61356 PRINCETON
60563-60567 NAPERVILLE	61006-61006 ASHTON	61235-61235 ATKINSON	61358-61358 RUTLAND
60568-60568 AURORA	61007-61007 BAILEYVILLE	61236-61236 BARSTOW	61359-61359 SEATONVILLE
60570-60570 HINSDALE	61008-61008 BELVIDERE	61237-61237 BUFFALO PRAIRIE	61360-61360 SENECA
60572-60572 AURORA	61010-61010 BYRON	61238-61238 CAMBRIDGE	61361-61361 SHEFFIELD
60597-60597 FOX VALLEY	61011-61011 CALEDONIA	61239-61239 CARBON CLIFF	61362-61362 SPRING VALLEY
60598-60598 AURORA	61012-61012 CAPRON	61240-61240 COAL VALLEY	61363-61363 STANDARD
60599-60599 FOX VALLEY	61013-61013 CEDARVILLE	61241-61241 COLONA	61364-61364 STREATOR
60600-60626 CHICAGO	61014-61014 CHADWICK	61242-61242 CORDOVA	61367-61367 SUBLETTE
60627-60627 RIVERDALE	61015-61015 CHANA	61243-61243 DEER GROVE	61368-61368 TISKILWA
60628-60634 CHICAGO	61016-61016 CHERRY VALLEY	61244-61244 EAST MOLINE	61369-61369 TOLUCA
60635-60635 ELMWOOD PARK	61017-61017 COLETA	61249-61249 DEERE CO GROUP CLAIMS	61370-61370 TONICA
60636-60649 CHICAGO	61018-61018 DAKOTA	61250-61250 ERIE	61371-61371 TRIUMPH
60650-60650 CICERO	61019-61019 DAVIS	61251-61251 FENTON	61372-61372 TROY GROVE
60651-60665 CHICAGO	61020-61020 DAVIS JUNCTION	61252-61252 FULTON	61373-61373 UTICA
60666-60666 AMF OHARE	61021-61021 DIXON	61254-61254 GENESEO	61374-61374 VAN ORIN
60667-60701 CHICAGO	61024-61024 DURAND	61256-61256 HAMPTON	61375-61375 VARNA
60706-60706 HARWOOD HEIGHTS	61025-61025 EAST DUBUQUE	61257-61257 HILLSDALE	61376-61376 WALNUT
60707-60707 ELMWOOD PARK	61027-61027 ELEROY	61258-61258 HOOPPOLE	61377-61377 WENONA
60712-60712 LINCOLNWOOD	61028-61028 ELIZABETH	61259-61259 ILLINOIS CITY	61378-61378 WEST BROOKLYN
60714-60714 NILES	61030-61030 FORRESTON	61260-61260 JOY	61379-61379 WYANET
60799-60799 CHICAGO	61031-61031 FRANKLIN GROVE	61261-61261 LYNDON	61401-61402 GALESBURG
60803-60803 ALSIP	61032-61032 FREEPORT	61262-61262 LYNN CENTER	61410-61410 ABINGDON
60804-60804 CICERO	61036-61036 GALENA	61263-61263 MATHERVILLE	61411-61411 ADAIR
60805-60805 EVERGREEN PARK	61037-61037 GALT	61264-61264 MILAN	61412-61412 ALEXIS
60827-60827 RIVERDALE	61038-61038 GARDEN PRAIRIE	61265-61266 MOLINE	61413-61413 ALPHA
60901-60902 KANKAKEE	61039-61039 GERMAN VALLEY	61270-61270 MORRISON	61414-61414 ALTONA
60910-60910 AROMA PARK	61041-61041 HANOVER	61272-61272 NEW BOSTON	61415-61415 AVON
60911-60911 ASHKUM	61042-61042 HARMON	61273-61273 ORION	61416-61416 BARDOLPH
60912-60912 BEAVERVILLE	61043-61043 HOLCOMB	61274-61274 OSCO	61417-61417 BERWICK
60913-60913 BONFIELD	61044-61044 KENT	61275-61275 PORT BYRON	61418-61418 BIGGSVILLE
60914-60914 BOURBONNAIS	61045-61045 KINGS	61276-61276 PREEMPTION	61419-61419 BISHOP HILL
60915-60915 BRADLEY	61046-61046 LANARK	61277-61277 PROPHETSTOWN	61420-61420 BLANDINSVILLE
60917-60917 BUCKINGHAM	61047-61047 LEAF RIVER	61278-61278 RAPIDS CITY	61421-61421 BRADFORD
60918-60918 BUCKLEY	61048-61048 LENA	61279-61279 REYNOLDS	61422-61422 BUSHNELL
60919-60919 CABERY	61049-61049 LINDENWOOD	61281-61281 SHERRARD	61423-61423 CAMERON
60920-60920 CAMPUS	61050-61050 MC CONNELL	61282-61282 SILVIS	61424-61424 CAMP GROVE
60921-60921 CHATSWORTH	61051-61051 MILLEDGEVILLE	61283-61283 TAMPICO	61425-61425 CARMAN
60922-60922 CHEBANSE	61052-61052 MONROE CENTER	61284-61284 TAYLOR RIDGE	61426-61426 CASTLETON
60924-60924 CISSNA PARK	61053-61053 MOUNT CARROLL	61285-61285 THOMSON	61427-61427 CUBA
60926-60926 CLAYTONVILLE	61054-61054 MOUNT MORRIS	61299-61299 ROCK ISLAND	61428-61428 DAHINDA
60927-60927 CLIFTON	61057-61057 NACHUSA	61301-61301 LA SALLE	61430-61430 EAST GALESBURG
60928-60928 CRESCENT CITY	61058-61058 NELSON	61310-61310 AMBOY	61431-61431 ELLISVILLE
60929-60929 CULLOM	61059-61059 NORA	61311-61311 ANCONA	61432-61432 FAIRVIEW
60930-60930 DANFORTH	61060-61060 ORANGEVILLE	61312-61312 ARLINGTON	61433-61433 FIATT
60931-60931 DONOVAN	61061-61061 OREGON	61313-61313 BLACKSTONE	61434-61434 GALVA
60932-60932 EAST LYNN	61062-61062 PEARL CITY	61314-61314 BUDA	61435-61435 GERLAW
60933-60933 ELLIOTT	61063-61063 PECATONICA	61315-61315 BUREAU	61436-61436 GILSON
60934-60934 EMINGTON	61064-61064 POLO	61316-61316 CEDAR POINT	61437-61437 GLADSTONE
60935-60935 ESSEX	61065-61065 POPLAR GROVE	61317-61317 CHERRY	61438-61438 GOOD HOPE
60936-60936 GIBSON CITY	61067-61067 RIDOTT	61318-61318 COMPTON	61439-61439 HENDERSON
60938-60938 GILMAN	61068-61068 ROCHELLE	61319-61319 CORNELL	61440-61440 INDUSTRY
60939-60939 GOODWINE	61070-61070 ROCK CITY	61320-61320 DALZELL	61441-61441 IPAVA
60940-60940 GRANT PARK	61071-61071 ROCK FALLS	61321-61321 DANA	61442-61442 KEITHSBURG
60941-60941 HERSCHER	61072-61072 ROCKTON	61322-61322 DEPUE	61443-61443 KEWANEE
60942-60942 HOOPESTON	61073-61073 ROSCOE	61323-61323 DOVER	61447-61447 KIRKWOOD
60944-60944 HOPKINS PARK	61074-61074 SAVANNA	61324-61324 ELDENA	61448-61448 KNOXVILLE
60945-60945 IROQUOIS	61075-61075 SCALES MOUND	61325-61325 GRAND RIDGE	61449-61449 LA FAYETTE
60946-60946 KEMPTON	61076-61076 SCIOTO MILLS	61326-61326 GRANVILLE	61450-61450 LA HARPE
60948-60948 LODA	61076-61076 SCIOTO MILLSX	61327-61327 HENNEPIN	61451-61451 LAURA
60949-60949 LUDLOW	61077-61077 SEWARD	61328-61328 KASBEER	61452-61452 LITTLETON
60950-60950 MANTENO	61078-61078 SHANNON	61329-61329 LADD	61453-61453 LITTLE YORK
60951-60951 MARTINTON	61079-61079 SHIRLAND	61330-61330 LA MOILLE	61454-61454 LOMAX
60952-60952 MELVIN	61080-61080 SOUTH BELOIT	61331-61331 LEE CENTER	61455-61455 MACOMB
60953-60953 MILFORD	61081-61081 STERLING	61332-61332 LEONORE	61458-61458 MAQUON
60954-60954 MOMENCE	61084-61084 STILLMAN VALLEY	61333-61333 LONG POINT	61459-61459 MARIETTA
60955-60955 ONARGA	61085-61085 STOCKTON	61334-61334 LOSTANT	61460-61460 MEDIA
60956-60956 PAPINEAU	61087-61087 WARREN	61335-61335 MC NABB	61462-61462 MONMOUTH
60957-60957 PAXTON	61088-61088 WINNEBAGO	61336-61336 MAGNOLIA	61465-61465 NEW WINDSOR
60959-60959 PIPER CITY	61089-61089 WINSLOW	61337-61337 MALDEN	61466-61466 NORTH HENDERSON
60960-60960 RANKIN	61091-61091 WOOSUNG	61338-61338 MANLIUS	61467-61467 ONEIDA
60961-60961 REDDICK	61100-61110 ROCKFORD	61340-61340 MARK	61468-61468 OPHEIM

61469-61469 OQUAWKA	61726-61726 CHENOA	61858-61858 OAKWOOD	62046-62046 HAMEL
61470-61470 PRAIRIE CITY	61727-61727 CLINTON	61859-61859 OGDEN	62047-62047 HARDIN
61471-61471 RARITAN	61728-61728 COLFAX	61862-61862 PENFIELD	62048-62048 HARTFORD
61472-61472 RIO	61729-61729 CONGERVILLE	61863-61863 PESOTUM	62049-62049 HILLSBORO
61473-61473 ROSEVILLE	61730-61730 COOKSVILLE	61864-61864 PHILO	62050-62050 HILLVIEW
61474-61474 SAINT AUGUSTINE	61731-61731 CROPSEY	61865-61865 POTOMAC	62051-62051 IRVING
61475-61475 SCIOTA	61732-61732 DANVERS	61866-61868 RANTOUL	62052-62052 JERSEYVILLE
61476-61476 SEATON	61733-61733 DEER CREEK	61870-61870 RIDGE FARM	62053-62053 KAMPSVILLE
61477-61477 SMITHFIELD	61734-61734 DELAVAN	61871-61871 ROYAL	62054-62054 KANE
61478-61478 SMITHSHIRE	61735-61735 DEWITT	61872-61872 SADORUS	62056-62056 LITCHFIELD
61479-61479 SPEER	61736-61736 DOWNS	61873-61873 SAINT JOSEPH	62058-62058 LIVINGSTON
61480-61480 STRONGHURST	61737-61737 ELLSWORTH	61874-61874 SAVOY	62059-62059 LOVEJOY
61482-61482 TABLE GROVE	61738-61738 EL PASO	61875-61875 SEYMOUR	62060-62060 MADISON
61483-61483 TOULON	61739-61739 FAIRBURY	61876-61876 SIDELL	62061-62061 MARINE
61484-61484 VERMONT	61740-61740 FLANAGAN	61877-61877 SIDNEY	62062-62062 MARYVILLE
61485-61485 VICTORIA	61741-61741 FORREST	61878-61878 THOMASBORO	62063-62063 MEDORA
61486-61486 VIOLA	61742-61742 GOODFIELD	61880-61880 TOLONO	62065-62065 MICHAEL
61488-61488 WATAGA	61743-61743 GRAYMONT	61882-61882 WELDON	62067-62067 MORO
61489-61489 WILLIAMSFIELD	61744-61744 GRIDLEY	61883-61883 WESTVILLE	62069-62069 MOUNT OLIVE
61490-61490 WOODHULL	61745-61745 HEYWORTH	61884-61884 WHITE HEATH	62070-62070 MOZIER
61491-61491 WYOMING	61747-61747 HOPEDALE	61910-61910 ARCOLA	62071-62071 NATIONAL STOCK YARDS
61501-61501 ASTORIA	61748-61748 HUDSON	61911-61911 ARTHUR	62074-62074 NEW DOUGLAS
61516-61516 BENSON	61749-61749 KENNEY	61912-61912 ASHMORE	62075-62075 NOKOMIS
61517-61518 BRIMFIELD	61750-61750 LANE	61913-61913 ATWOOD	62076-62076 OHLMAN
61519-61519 BRYANT	61751-61751 LAWNDALE	61914-61914 BETHANY	62077-62077 PANAMA
61520-61520 CANTON	61752-61752 LE ROY	61917-61917 BROCTON	62078-62078 PATTERSON
61523-61523 CHILLICOTHE	61753-61753 LEXINGTON	61919-61919 CAMARGO	62079-62079 PIASA
61524-61524 DUNFERMLINE	61754-61754 MC LEAN	61920-61920 CHARLESTON	62080-62080 RAMSEY
61525-61525 DUNLAP	61755-61755 MACKINAW	61924-61924 CHRISMAN	62081-62081 ROCKBRIDGE
61526-61526 EDELSTEIN	61756-61756 MAROA	61925-61925 DALTON CITY	62082-62082 ROODHOUSE
61528-61528 EDWARDS	61758-61758 MERNA	61928-61928 GAYS	62083-62083 ROSAMOND
61529-61529 ELMWOOD	61759-61759 MINIER	61929-61929 HAMMOND	62084-62084 ROXANA
61530-61530 EUREKA	61760-61760 MINONK	61930-61930 HINDSBORO	62085-62085 SAWYERVILLE
61531-61531 FARMINGTON	61761-61761 NORMAL	61931-61931 HUMBOLDT	62086-62086 SORENTO
61532-61532 FOREST CITY	61764-61764 PONTIAC	61932-61932 HUME	62087-62087 SOUTH ROXANA
61533-61533 GLASFORD	61769-61769 SAUNEMIN	61933-61933 KANSAS	62088-62088 STAUNTON
61534-61534 GREEN VALLEY	61770-61770 SAYBROOK	61936-61936 LA PLACE	62089-62089 TAYLOR SPRINGS
61535-61535 GROVELAND	61771-61771 SECOR	61937-61937 LOVINGTON	62090-62090 VENICE
61536-61536 HANNA CITY	61772-61772 SHIRLEY	61938-61938 MATTOON	62091-62091 WALSHVILLE
61537-61537 HENRY	61773-61773 SIBLEY	61940-61940 METCALF	62092-62092 WHITE HALL
61539-61539 KINGSTON MINES	61774-61774 STANFORD	61941-61941 MURDOCK	62093-62093 WILSONVILLE
61540-61540 LACON	61775-61775 STRAWN	61942-61942 NEWMAN	62094-62094 WITT
61541-61541 LA ROSE	61776-61776 TOWANDA	61943-61943 OAKLAND	62095-62095 WOOD RIVER
61542-61542 LEWISTOWN	61777-61777 WAPELLA	61944-61944 PARIS	62097-62097 WORDEN
61543-61543 LIVERPOOL	61778-61778 WAYNESVILLE	61949-61949 REDMON	62098-62098 WRIGHTS
61544-61544 LONDON MILLS	61790-61790 NORMAL	61951-61951 SULLIVAN	62201-62207 EAST SAINT LOUIS
61545-61545 LOWPOINT	61791-61799 BLOOMINGTON	61953-61953 TUSCOLA	62208-62208 FAIRVIEW HEIGHTS
61546-61546 MANITO	61801-61803 URBANA	61955-61955 VERMILION	62214-62214 ADDIEVILLE
61547-61547 MAPLETON	61810-61810 ALLERTON	61956-61956 VILLA GROVE	62215-62215 ALBERS
61548-61548 METAMORA	61811-61811 ALVIN	61957-61957 WINDSOR	62216-62216 AVISTON
61550-61550 MORTON	61812-61812 ARMSTRONG	62001-62001 ALHAMBRA	62217-62217 BALDWIN
61552-61552 MOSSVILLE	61813-61813 BEMENT	62002-62002 ALTON	62218-62218 BARTELSO
61553-61553 NORRIS	61814-61814 BISMARCK	62006-62006 BATCHTOWN	62219-62219 BECKEMEYER
61554-61558 PEKIN	61815-61815 BONDVILLE	62009-62009 BENLD	62220-62223 BELLEVILLE
61559-61559 PRINCEVILLE	61816-61816 BROADLANDS	62010-62010 BETHALTO	62224-62224 MASCOUTAH
61560-61560 PUTNAM	61817-61817 CATLIN	62011-62011 BINGHAM	62225-62225 SCOTT AIR FORCE BASE
61561-61561 ROANOKE	61818-61818 CERRO GORDO	62012-62012 BRIGHTON	62226-62226 BELLEVILLE
61562-61562 ROME	61820-61826 CHAMPAIGN	62013-62013 BRUSSELS	62230-62230 BREESE
61563-61563 SAINT DAVID	61830-61830 CISCO	62014-62014 BUNKER HILL	62231-62231 CARLYLE
61564-61564 SOUTH PEKIN	61831-61831 COLLISON	62015-62015 BUTLER	62232-62232 CASEYVILLE
61565-61565 SPARLAND	61832-61832 DANVILLE	62016-62016 CARROLLTON	62233-62233 CHESTER
61567-61567 TOPEKA	61833-61833 TILTON	62017-62017 COFFEEN	62234-62234 COLLINSVILLE
61568-61568 TREMONT	61834-61834 DANVILLE	62018-62018 COTTAGE HILLS	62236-62236 COLUMBIA
61569-61569 TRIVOLI	61839-61839 DE LAND	62019-62019 DONNELLSON	62237-62237 COULTERVILLE
61570-61570 WASHBURN	61840-61840 DEWEY	62021-62021 DORSEY	62238-62238 CUTLER
61571-61571 WASHINGTON	61841-61841 FAIRMOUNT	62022-62022 DOW	62239-62239 DUPO
61572-61572 YATES CITY	61842-61842 FARMER CITY	62023-62023 EAGARVILLE	62240-62240 EAST CARONDELET
61600-61607 PEORIA	61843-61843 FISHER	62024-62024 EAST ALTON	62241-62241 ELLIS GROVE
61610-61610 CREVE COEUR	61844-61844 FITHIAN	62025-62026 EDWARDSVILLE	62242-62242 EVANSVILLE
61611-61611 EAST PEORIA	61845-61845 FOOSLAND	62027-62027 ELDRED	62243-62243 FREEBURG
61612-61615 PEORIA	61846-61846 GEORGETOWN	62028-62028 ELSAH	62244-62244 FULTS
61616-61616 PEORIA HEIGHTS	61847-61847 GIFFORD	62030-62030 FIDELITY	62245-62245 GERMANTOWN
61625-61644 PEORIA	61848-61848 HENNING	62031-62031 FIELDON	62246-62246 GREENVILLE
61649-61649 JEFFERSON BANK	61849-61849 HOMER	62032-62032 FILLMORE	62247-62247 HAGARSTOWN
61650-61656 PEORIA	61850-61850 INDIANOLA	62033-62033 GILLESPIE	62248-62248 HECKER
61701-61710 BLOOMINGTON	61851-61851 IVESDALE	62034-62034 GLEN CARBON	62249-62249 HIGHLAND
61720-61720 ANCHOR	61852-61852 LONGVIEW	62035-62035 GODFREY	62250-62250 HOFFMAN
61721-61721 ARMINGTON	61853-61853 MAHOMET	62036-62036 GOLDEN EAGLE	62252-62252 HUEY
61722-61722 ARROWSMITH	61854-61854 MANSFIELD	62037-62037 GRAFTON	62253-62253 KEYESPORT
61723-61723 ATLANTA	61855-61855 MILMINE	62040-62040 GRANITE CITY	62254-62254 LEBANON
61724-61724 BELLFLOWER	61856-61856 MONTICELLO	62044-62044 GREENFIELD	62255-62255 LENZBURG
61725-61725 CARLOCK	61857-61857 MUNCIE	62045-62045 HAMBURG	62256-62256 MAEYSTOWN

62257-62257 MARISSA	62365-62365 PLAINVILLE	62518-62518 CHESTNUT	62667-62667 MODESTO
62258-62258 MASCOUTAH	62366-62366 PLEASANT HILL	62519-62519 CORNLAND	62668-62668 MURRAYVILLE
62259-62259 MENARD	62367-62367 PLYMOUTH	62520-62520 DAWSON	62670-62670 NEW BERLIN
62260-62260 MILLSTADT	62370-62370 ROCKPORT	62521-62527 DECATUR	62671-62671 NEW HOLLAND
62261-62261 MODOC	62372-62372 SUMMER HILL	62530-62530 DIVERNON	62672-62672 NILWOOD
62262-62262 MULBERRY GROVE	62373-62373 SUTTER	62531-62531 EDINBURG	62673-62673 OAKFORD
62263-62263 NASHVILLE	62374-62374 TENNESSEE	62532-62532 ELWIN	62674-62674 PALMYRA
62264-62264 NEW ATHENS	62375-62375 TIMEWELL	62533-62533 FARMERSVILLE	62675-62675 PETERSBURG
62265-62265 NEW BADEN	62376-62376 URSA	62534-62534 FINDLAY	62676-62676 PLAINVIEW
62266-62266 NEW MEMPHIS	62378-62378 VERSAILLES	62535-62535 FORSYTH	62677-62677 PLEASANT PLAINS
62268-62268 OAKDALE	62379-62379 WARSAW	62536-62536 GLENARM	62681-62681 RUSHVILLE
62269-62269 O FALLON	62380-62380 WEST POINT	62537-62537 HARRISTOWN	62682-62682 SAN JOSE
62271-62271 OKAWVILLE	62401-62401 EFFINGHAM	62538-62538 HARVEL	62683-62683 SCOTTVILLE
62272-62272 PERCY	62410-62410 ALLENDALE	62539-62539 ILLIOPOLIS	62684-62684 SHERMAN
62273-62273 PIERRON	62411-62411 ALTAMONT	62540-62540 KINCAID	62685-62685 SHIPMAN
62274-62274 PINCKNEYVILLE	62413-62413 ANNAPOLIS	62541-62541 LAKE FORK	62686-62686 STANDARD CITY
62275-62275 POCAHONTAS	62414-62414 BEECHER CITY	62543-62543 LATHAM	62688-62688 TALLULA
62277-62277 PRAIRIE DU ROCHER	62415-62415 BIRDS	62544-62544 MACON	62689-62689 THAYER
62278-62278 RED BUD	62417-62417 BRIDGEPORT	62545-62545 MECHANICSBURG	62690-62690 VIRDEN
62279-62279 RENAULT	62418-62418 BROWNSTOWN	62546-62546 MORRISONVILLE	62691-62691 VIRGINIA
62280-62280 ROCKWOOD	62419-62419 CALHOUN	62547-62547 MOUNT AUBURN	62692-62692 WAVERLY
62281-62281 SAINT JACOB	62420-62420 CASEY	62548-62548 MOUNT PULASKI	62693-62693 WILLIAMSVILLE
62282-62282 SAINT LIBORY	62421-62421 CLAREMONT	62549-62549 MT ZION	62694-62694 WINCHESTER
62283-62283 SHATTUC	62422-62422 COWDEN	62550-62550 MOWEAQUA	62695-62695 WOODSON
62284-62284 SMITHBORO	62423-62423 DENNISON	62551-62551 NIANTIC	62700-62796 SPRINGFIELD
62285-62285 SMITHTON	62424-62424 DIETERICH	62552-62552 OAKLEY	62801-62801 CENTRALIA
62286-62286 SPARTA	62425-62425 DUNDAS	62553-62553 OCONEE	62803-62803 HOYLETON
62288-62288 STEELEVILLE	62426-62426 EDGEWOOD	62554-62554 OREANA	62805-62805 AKIN
62289-62289 SUMMERFIELD	62427-62427 FLAT ROCK	62555-62555 OWANECO	62806-62806 ALBION
62292-62292 TILDEN	62428-62428 GREENUP	62556-62556 PALMER	62807-62807 ALMA
62293-62293 TRENTON	62431-62431 HERRICK	62557-62557 PANA	62808-62808 ASHLEY
62294-62294 TROY	62432-62432 HIDALGO	62558-62558 PAWNEE	62809-62809 BARNHILL
62295-62295 VALMEYER	62433-62433 HUTSONVILLE	62560-62560 RAYMOND	62810-62810 BELLE RIVE
62296-62296 VENEDY	62434-62434 INGRAHAM	62561-62561 RIVERTON	62811-62811 BELLMONT
62297-62297 WALSH	62435-62435 JANESVILLE	62563-62563 ROCHESTER	62812-62812 BENTON
62298-62298 WATERLOO	62436-62436 JEWETT	62565-62565 SHELBYVILLE	62814-62814 BLUFORD
62301-62306 QUINCY	62438-62438 LAKEWOOD	62567-62567 STONINGTON	62815-62815 BONE GAP
62310-62310 ADRIAN	62439-62439 LAWRENCEVILLE	62568-62568 TAYLORVILLE	62816-62816 BONNIE
62311-62311 AUGUSTA	62440-62440 LERNA	62570-62570 TOVEY	62817-62817 BROUGHTON
62312-62312 BARRY	62441-62441 MARSHALL	62571-62571 TOWER HILL	62818-62818 BROWNS
62313-62313 BASCO	62442-62442 MARTINSVILLE	62572-62572 WAGGONER	62819-62819 BUCKNER
62314-62314 BAYLIS	62443-62443 MASON	62573-62573 WARRENSBURG	62820-62820 BURNT PRAIRIE
62316-62316 BOWEN	62444-62444 MODE	62574-62574 WESTERVELT	62821-62821 CARMI
62318-62318 BURNSIDE	62445-62445 MONTROSE	62601-62601 ALEXANDER	62822-62822 CHRISTOPHER
62319-62319 CAMDEN	62446-62446 MOUNT ERIE	62610-62610 ALSEY	62823-62823 CISNE
62320-62320 CAMP POINT	62447-62447 NEOGA	62611-62611 ARENZVILLE	62824-62824 CLAY CITY
62321-62321 CARTHAGE	62448-62448 NEWTON	62612-62612 ASHLAND	62825-62825 COELLO
62323-62323 CHAMBERSBURG	62449-62449 OBLONG	62613-62613 ATHENS	62827-62827 CROSSVILLE
62324-62324 CLAYTON	62450-62450 OLNEY	62615-62615 AUBURN	62828-62828 DAHLGREN
62325-62325 COATSBURG	62451-62451 PALESTINE	62617-62617 BATH	62829-62829 DALE
62326-62326 COLCHESTER	62452-62452 PARKERSBURG	62618-62618 BEARDSTOWN	62830-62830 DIX
62327-62327 COLMAR	62454-62454 ROBINSON	62621-62621 BLUFFS	62831-62831 DU BOIS
62328-62328 QUINCY	62458-62458 SAINT ELMO	62622-62622 BLUFF SPRINGS	62832-62832 DU QUOIN
62329-62329 COLUSA	62459-62459 SAINTE MARIE	62624-62624 BROWNING	62833-62833 ELLERY
62330-62330 DALLAS CITY	62460-62460 SAINT FRANCISVILLE	62625-62625 CANTRALL	62834-62834 EMMA
62332-62332 PITTSFIELD	62461-62461 SHUMWAY	62626-62626 CARLINVILLE	62835-62835 ENFIELD
62334-62334 ELVASTON	62462-62462 SIGEL	62627-62627 CHANDLERVILLE	62836-62836 EWING
62336-62336 FERRIS	62463-62463 STEWARDSON	62628-62628 CHAPIN	62837-62837 FAIRFIELD
62338-62338 FOWLER	62464-62464 STOY	62629-62629 CHATHAM	62838-62838 FARINA
62339-62339 GOLDEN	62465-62465 STRASBURG	62630-62630 CHESTERFIELD	62839-62839 FLORA
62340-62340 GRIGGSVILLE	62466-62466 SUMNER	62631-62631 CONCORD	62840-62840 FRANKFORT HEIGHTS
62341-62341 HAMILTON	62467-62467 TEUTOPOLIS	62633-62633 EASTON	62841-62841 FREEMAN SPUR
62343-62343 HULL	62468-62468 TOLEDO	62634-62634 ELKHART	62842-62842 GEFF
62344-62344 HUNTSVILLE	62469-62469 TRILLA	62635-62635 EMDEN	62843-62843 GOLDEN GATE
62345-62345 KINDERHOOK	62471-62471 VANDALIA	62638-62638 FRANKLIN	62844-62844 GRAYVILLE
62346-62346 LA PRAIRIE	62473-62473 WATSON	62639-62639 FREDERICK	62845-62845 HERALD
62347-62347 LIBERTY	62474-62474 WESTFIELD	62640-62640 GIRARD	62846-62846 INA
62348-62348 LIMA	62475-62475 WEST LIBERTY	62642-62642 GREENVIEW	62847-62847 IOLA
62349-62349 LORAINE	62476-62476 WEST SALEM	62643-62643 HARTSBURG	62848-62848 IRVINGTON
62351-62351 MENDON	62477-62477 WEST UNION	62644-62644 HAVANA	62849-62849 IUKA
62352-62352 MILTON	62478-62478 WEST YORK	62649-62649 HETTICK	62850-62850 JOHNSONVILLE
62353-62353 MOUNT STERLING	62479-62479 WHEELER	62650-62651 JACKSONVILLE	62851-62851 KEENES
62354-62354 NAUVOO	62480-62480 WILLOW HILL	62655-62655 KILBOURNE	62852-62852 KEENSBURG
62355-62355 NEBO	62481-62481 YALE	62656-62656 LINCOLN	62853-62853 KELL
62356-62356 NEW CANTON	62501-62501 ARGENTA	62659-62659 LINCOLN'S NEW SALEM	62854-62854 KINMUNDY
62357-62357 NEW SALEM	62510-62510 ASSUMPTION	62660-62660 LITERBERRY	62855-62855 LANCASTER
62358-62358 NIOTA	62511-62511 ATWATER	62661-62661 LOAMI	62856-62856 LOGAN
62359-62359 PALOMA	62512-62512 BEASON	62662-62662 LOWDER	62857-62857 LOOGOOTEE
62360-62360 PAYSON	62513-62513 BLUE MOUND	62663-62663 MANCHESTER	62858-62858 LOUISVILLE
62361-62361 PEARL	62514-62514 BOODY	62664-62664 MASON CITY	62859-62859 MC LEANSBORO
62362-62362 PERRY	62515-62515 BUFFALO	62665-62665 MEREDOSIA	62860-62860 MACEDONIA
62363-62363 PITTSFIELD	62517-62517 BULPITT	62666-62666 MIDDLETOWN	62861-62861 MAUNIE

62862-62862 MILL SHOALS	62894-62894 WALTONVILLE	62931-62931 ELIZABETHTOWN	62964-62964 MOUNDS
62863-62863 MOUNT CARMEL	62895-62895 WAYNE CITY	62932-62932 ELKVILLE	62965-62965 MUDDY
62864-62864 MOUNT VERNON	62896-62896 WEST FRANKFORT	62933-62933 ENERGY	62966-62966 MURPHYSBORO
62865-62865 MULKEYTOWN	62897-62897 WHITTINGTON	62934-62934 EQUALITY	62967-62967 NEW BURNSIDE
62866-62866 NASON	62898-62898 WOODLAWN	62935-62935 GALATIA	62969-62969 OLIVE BRANCH
62867-62867 NEW HAVEN	62899-62899 XENIA	62938-62938 GOLCONDA	62970-62970 OLMSTED
62868-62868 NOBLE	62901-62903 CARBONDALE	62939-62939 GOREVILLE	62971-62971 ORAVILLE
62869-62869 NORRIS CITY	62905-62905 ALTO PASS	62940-62940 GORHAM	62972-62972 OZARK
62870-62870 ODIN	62906-62906 ANNA	62941-62941 GRAND CHAIN	62973-62973 PERKS
62871-62871 OMAHA	62907-62907 AVA	62942-62942 GRAND TOWER	62974-62974 PITTSBURG
62872-62872 OPDYKE	62908-62908 BELKNAP	62943-62943 GRANTSBURG	62975-62975 POMONA
62874-62874 ORIENT	62909-62909 BOLES	62944-62944 HAMLETSBURG	62976-62976 PULASKI
62875-62875 PATOKA	62910-62910 BROOKPORT	62945-62945 GALATIA	62977-62977 RALEIGH
62876-62876 RADOM	62912-62912 BUNCOMBE	62946-62946 HARRISBURG	62979-62979 RIDGWAY
62877-62877 RICHVIEW	62913-62913 CACHE	62947-62947 HEROD	62982-62982 ROSICLARE
62878-62878 RINARD	62914-62914 CAIRO	62948-62948 HERRIN	62983-62983 ROYALTON
62879-62879 SAILOR SPRINGS	62915-62915 CAMBRIA	62949-62949 HURST	62984-62984 SHAWNEETOWN
62880-62880 SAINT PETER	62916-62916 CAMPBELL HILL	62950-62950 JACOB	62985-62985 SIMPSON
62881-62881 SALEM	62917-62917 CARRIER MILLS	62951-62951 JOHNSTON CITY	62987-62987 STONEFORT
62882-62882 SANDOVAL	62918-62918 CARTERVILLE	62952-62952 JONESBORO	62988-62988 TAMMS
62883-62883 SCHELLER	62919-62919 CAVE IN ROCK	62953-62953 JOPPA	62990-62990 THEBES
62884-62884 SESSER	62920-62920 COBDEN	62954-62954 JUNCTION	62991-62991 TUNNEL HILL
62885-62885 SHOBONIER	62921-62921 COLP	62955-62955 KARBERS RIDGE	62992-62992 ULLIN
62886-62886 SIMS	62922-62922 CREAL SPRINGS	62956-62956 KARNAK	62993-62993 UNITY
62887-62887 SPRINGERTON	62923-62923 CYPRESS	62957-62957 MC CLURE	62994-62994 VERGENNES
62888-62888 TAMAROA	62924-62924 DE SOTO	62958-62958 MAKANDA	62995-62995 VIENNA
62889-62889 TEXICO	62926-62926 DONGOLA	62959-62959 MARION	62996-62996 VILLA RIDGE
62890-62890 THOMPSONVILLE	62927-62927 DOWELL	62960-62960 METROPOLIS	62997-62997 WILLISVILLE
62891-62891 VALIER	62928-62928 EDDYVILLE	62961-62961 MILLCREEK	62998-62998 WOLF LAKE
62892-62892 VERNON	62929-62929 ELCO	62962-62962 MILLER CITY	62999-62999 ZEIGLER
62893-62893 WALNUT HILL	62930-62930 ELDORADO	62963-62963 MOUND CITY	

Indiana

General Help Numbers:

Governor's Office

206 State House   317-232-4567
Indianapolis, IN 46204-2797   Fax 317-232-3443
www.in.gov/gov   8AM-5PM

Attorney General's Office

402 W Washington   317-232-6201
Indianapolis, IN 46204   Fax 317-232-7979
www.in.gov/attorneygeneral   8:30AM-5PM

State Court Administrator

200 W Washington St, #312   317-232-2542
Indianapolis, IN 46204   Fax 317-232-8372
www.in.gov/judiciary/admin/   8:30AM-4:30PM

State Archives

Commission on Public Records   317-591-5222
6400 E 30th St   Fax 317-591-5324
Indianapolis, IN 46219   8AM-4:30PM
www.in.gov/icpr

State Specifics:

Capital: Indianapolis
Marion County

Time Zone: EST*

* Indiana's eleven northwestern-most counties are CST:
They are: Gibson, Jasper, Laporte, Lake, Newton, Porter, Posey, Spencer, Starke, Vanderburgh, Warrick.

Number of Counties: 92

Population: 6,114,745

Web Site: www.state.in.us

State Agencies

Criminal Records

Indiana State Police, Central Records, IGCN - 100 N Senate Ave Room 302, Indianapolis, IN 46204-2259; 317-232-8266, 8AM-4:30PM.

www.IN.gov/isp

Note: Sex offender data is available online at www.state.in.us/serv/cji_sor.

Indexing & Storage: Records are available from 1935. It takes 10 days before new records are available for inquiry. Records are indexed on inhouse computer. Approximately 10% of all arrests in database have final dispositions recorded, over 50% for those arrests within last 5 years. This agency now is notified when charges are made after fingerprints are submitted.

Searching: The release of records is governed by IC 5-2-5. A "Limited Criminal History" is available to designated entites including employers, licensing agencies, schools, and certain other designates. Use State Form 8053. Include the following in your request: full name, date of birth, sex, race. Submitting fingerprints is an option. 100% of the records are fingerprint-supported. Record will show all activity, including arrests, dismissals, and convictions. But, if a charge is over a year old with no disposition, then the record will not be released.

Access by: mail, in person, online.

Fee & Payment: The fee for employers is $7.00 per name if no fingerprints used. The fee for a fingerprint search is $10.00. If subject requests own record, fee is $10.00, and this is for a FULL record. Fee is $22.50 for online searches by non-government agencies. Fee payee: State of Indiana. Prepayment required. Cash, money orders, and certified checks are accepted. Ongoing requesters may open a monthly billing account. No credit cards accepted.

Mail search: Turnaround time: 5 to 10 working days. Use State Form 8053.

In person search: Requester must have picture ID, turnaround time is 30 minutes.

Online search: Subcribers to accessIndiana can obtain limited records for $22.50 per search. Go to www.in.gov/isp/lch/centralsearch.html

Corporation Records
Limited Partnerships
Fictitious Name
Assumed Name
Limited Liability Company Records
Limited Liability Partnerships

Corporation Division, Secretary of State, 302 W Washington St, Room E018, Indianapolis, IN 46204; 317-232-6576, 317-233-3387 (Fax), 8AM-5:30PM M-F.

www.IN.gov/sos

Note: This agency also holds Agricultural Cooperative and Business Trust records.

Indexing & Storage: Records are available for all active entities. Corporate reports prior to 1993 may take as long as 6 weeks to retrieve. New records are available for inquiry immediately. Records are indexed on microfilm, inhouse computer, and paper.

Searching: There are no restrictions, all information is public record. Include the following in your request: full name of business, specific records that you need copies of. Other records available include: Annual or Bi-annual Reports, Officers (when applicable), Prior (merged) names, Inactive and Reserved names, Assumed Business names, and Registered Agent and address. Directors information is available, but not by phone.

Access by: mail, phone, in person, online.

Fee & Payment: There is no search fee. Copies cost $1.00 per page plus $15.00 for document certification. Due & Diligent Searches may be ordered for information that cannot be found initially. Fee payee: Secretary of State. Prepayment required. The state will allow pre-paid accounts for filing only. Personal checks accepted. No credit cards accepted.

Mail search: Turnaround time: 4 to 7 days. No pre-payments accepted for mail requests. Due & Diligent searches take 10 business days. No self addressed stamped envelope is required.

Phone search: Limited verification information is available.

In person search: Turnaround time: In by noon, ready by noon the next day. Requests after 12 noon are ready within 2 business days.

Online search: This subscription service is available from the Access Indiana Information Network (AI) gateway on the Internet. There is no fee to view a partial record, but $1.00 to view a screen containing the registered agent and other information. Go to www.ai.org

Other access: Monthly lists of all new businesses are available online, as are bulk data and specialized searches.

Trademarks/Servicemarks

Secretary of State, Trademark Division, 302 W Washington St, IGC-South, Room E111, Indianapolis, IN 46204; 317-232-6540, 317-233-3675 (Fax), 8:AM-4:30PM.

www.in.gov/sos/business/trademarks.html

Note: These records are considered public and are available with no restrictions.

Indexing & Storage: Records are available for active trademarks. It takes 2 to 3 days before new records are available for inquiry.

Searching: Search requires trademark/servicemark name or file ID number. It generally takes 2 to 3 days to search for logo/designs, but name searches can be done immediately. If you have the file ID number, it will help.

Access by: mail, in person.

Fee & Payment: Copies cost $1.00 per page, copies returned by fax are an additional $1.00. Fee payee: Secretary of State. Prepayment required. Cash is not accepted. Personal checks accepted. No credit cards accepted.

Mail search: Turnaround time: 2 to 3 days. A self addressed stamped envelope is requested.

In person search: You may request information in person.

Uniform Commercial Code

UCC Division, Secretary of State, 302 West Washington St, Room E-018, Indianapolis, IN 46204; 317-233-3984, 317-233-3387 (Fax), 8AM-5:30PM.

www.in.gov/sos/business/ucc.html

Indexing & Storage: Records are available 1964, indexed on computer. It takes 3 days before new records are available for inquiry.

Searching: Use the state request form. All tax liens are filed at the county level. Include the following in your request: debtor name. Address is helpful.

Access by: mail, fax, in person, online.

Fee & Payment: The search fee of $5.00 per debtor name, which includes all copies. Fee payee: Secretary of State. Personal checks accepted. No credit cards accepted.

Mail search: Turnaround time: 2 days.

Fax search: Results are still mailed in 2 days.

In person search: Turnaround time is 2-5 days.

Online search: You may browse lien records at https://www.ai.org/sos/bus_service/online_ucc/browse/default.asp. There is no charge. An offical search may be performed online via an AccessIndiana account for $3.00 per record (plus $4.40 for use of credit card, if desired). Plans are underway to offer filing services also.

Federal Tax Liens
State Tax Liens

Records not maintained by a state level agency.

Note: All tax liens are found at the county level.

Sales Tax Registrations

Revenue Department, Taxpayer Services, Government Center N, 100 N Senate Ave, Room N105, Indianapolis, IN 46204; 317-233-4015, 317-232-2103 (Fax), 8:15AM-4:45PM.

www.in.gov/dor

Searching: This agency will only confirm whether a company is registered. No other information will be given about the company. The database is not available for purchase. Include the following in your request: name. They can also search by permit number or federal tax ID.

Access by: mail, phone.

Mail search: Turnaround time: 6 to 12 weeks. No fee for mail request.

Phone search: No fee for telephone request. This is very limited, only one search permitted.

Birth Certificates

State Department of Health, Vital Records Office, PO Box 7125, Indianapolis, IN 46206-7125 (Courier: 2 N. Meridian, Indianapolis, IN 46204); 317-233-2700, 317-233-7210 (Fax), 8:15AM-4:45PM.

www.in.gov/isdh/index.htm

Note: The information is also available at each local county health department.

Indexing & Storage: Records are available from October 1907 on and are computerized since 1978. It takes 12 weeks before new records are available for inquiry. Records are indexed on microfilm, index cards, books (volumes).

Searching: Must have a signed release form from person of record or be immediate family member or show direct need. Include the following in your request: full name, names of parents, mother's maiden name, date of birth, place of birth, relationship to person of record, reason for information request.

Access by: mail, fax, in person, online.

Fee & Payment: If exact date of birth is not known there is an additional fee of $4.00 for each 5 years searched. Add $1.00 per name requested for each additional copy of same record. Fee payee: Indiana State Department of Health. Prepayment required. Personal checks accepted. Credit cards accepted: MasterCard, Visa, AmEx, Discover.

Mail search: Turnaround time: 3 to 4 weeks. Must include a copy of a signature ID with your request. No self addressed stamped envelope is required. Search costs $6.00 for each name in request.

Fax search: The search costs $6.00 for each name in request, plus an additional $5.50 for the use of a credit card. Turnaround time is 5-10 days.

In person search: Search costs $6.00 for each name in request. It takes about 30 minutes to process the request.

Online search: Records may be ordered online via the web site, but the requester must still fax a photo copy of an ID before the record request is processed.

Expedited service: Expedited service is available for mail, online and fax searches. Turnaround time: 3 to 5 days. The expedited service requires use of a credit card and a $11.35 payment for overnight service.

Death Records

State Department of Health, Vital Records Office, PO Box 7125, Indianapolis, IN 46206-7125 (Courier: 2 N. Meridian, Indianapolis, IN 46204); 317-233-2700, 317-233-7210 (Fax), 8:15AM-4:45PM.

www.in.gov/isdh/index.htm

Indexing & Storage: Records are available from 1900 on. Records are indexed on microfilm, index cards, books (volumes).

Searching: This index is not for public review. You must have a signed release from immediate family member. Include a copy of your photo ID with your request. Include the following in your request: full name, date of death, place of death, relationship to person of record, reason for information request.

Access by: mail, fax, in person.

Fee & Payment: If exact date of death is not known, there is a $4.00 fee for each 5 years searched. Add $1.00 per name requested for each additional copy of same record. Fee payee: Indiana State Department of Health. Prepayment required. Personal checks accepted. Credit cards accepted: MasterCard, Visa, AmEx, Discover.

Mail search: Turnaround time: 1 month. No self addressed stamped envelope is required. Search costs $4.00 for each name in request.

Fax search: Search cost $4.00 for each name in request, plus an additional $5.50 fax fee for the use of a credit card.

In person search: Search costs $4.00 for each name in request.

Expedited service: Expedited service is available for fax searches. Turnaround time: 3 to 5 days. The expedited service requires use of a credit card and $11.35 payment for express delivery.

Marriage Certificates
Divorce Records

Records not maintained by a state level agency.

Note: Marriage and divorce records are found at county of issue. The state tells us that the index can also be found at the Indiana State Library.

Workers' Compensation Records

Workers Compensation Board, 402 W Washington St, Room W196, Indianapolis, IN 46204-2753; 317-232-3808, 8AM-4:30PM.

www.in.gov/workcomp/index.html

Indexing & Storage: Records are available for past 9 years. Records are indexed on inhouse computer.

Searching: Must have a notarized authorization release from claimant or a subpoena to obtain records from this agency. Requests are reviewed by the Executive Secretary who decides whether to release the information. Include the following in your request: claimant name, Social Security Number, date of accident, reason for information request.

Access by: mail.

Fee & Payment: Copies are $.10 per page, there is no search fee. Fee payee: Workers Compensation Board. Personal checks accepted. No credit cards accepted.

Mail search: Turnaround time: variable. No self addressed stamped envelope is required.

Driver Records

BMV-Driving Records, 100 N Senate Ave, Indiana Government Center North, Room N405, Indianapolis, IN 46204; 317-232-6000 x2, 8:15AM-4:30PM.

www.IN.gov/bmv

Note: Copies of tickets are available at the address listed above for a fee of $8.00 per ticket.

Indexing & Storage: Records are available for 7 years (10 years for habitual violators) for moving violations; 10 years for DWIs and suspensions. Accidents reported to the state police appear on the record. It takes 1-3 weeks before new records are available for inquiry.

Searching: Personal information is not disclosed to casual requesters. Further, a driver's Social Security Number, driver's license number or Federal ID number is not disclosed to all non-governmental requesters. The license number or name and DOB are required when ordering a record.

Access by: mail, in person, online.

Fee & Payment: The fee is $4.00 per record, except for online requests. The fee is $8.00 for a certified record. The fee is $12.00 for certified "complete" record and history. Turnaround time is 4 to 6 weeks for certified records. Fee payee: Bureau of Motor Vehicles. Prepayment required. Personal checks accepted. No credit cards accepted.

Mail search: Turnaround time: 7 to 10 days. No self addressed stamped envelope is required.

In person search: Up to seven requests are processed at one time for a walk-in requester at the Customer Service Center located at 531 Virginia Ave, Indianapolis.

Online search: Access Indiana Information Network (AIIN) is the state owned interactive information and communication system which provides batch and interactive access to driving records. There is an annual $50.00 fee. Online access costs $5.00 per record. For more information, call AIIN at 317-233-2010 or go to www.ai.org

Vehicle Ownership & Identification
Vessel Ownership & Registration

Bureau of Motor Vehicles, Records, 100 N Senate Ave, Room N404, Indianapolis, IN 46204; 317-233-6000, 8:15AM-4:45PM.

www.state.in.us/bmv

Indexing & Storage: Records are available for 3 years on computer and up to ten years on microfilm. All motor boats that were valued over $3,000 when new must be titled and registered.

Searching: Casual requesters can obtain records, but no personal information is released without consent. Vehicle owner's SSN, driver's license number, and Federal ID number cannot be disclosed to all non-governmental requesters. There are five types of records available for search; title inquiry, title history, registration inquiry, registration history, and registration copy. The title history will show liens. The title inquiry will show current listed lienholder, also.

Access by: mail, in person, online.

Fee & Payment: For vehicle, the fee is $4.00 per "inquiry" and $8.00 per "history." For watercraft, the fee is $4.00 for all title and registration searches. Fee payee: Bureau of Motor Vehicles. Prepayment required. Personal checks accepted. No credit cards accepted.

Mail search: Turnaround time: within 2 weeks. No self addressed stamped envelope is required.

In person search: The walk-in address for the Customer Service Center is 531 Virginia Ave, Indianapolis. Turnaround time depends on availability of personnel. Title histories are not provided on an immediate basis, they must be returned by mail or picked up later.

Online search: The Access Indiana Information network (AIIN) at 317-233-2010 is the state appointed vendor. The fee is $5.00 per record plus an annual fee of $50.00. Visit www.ai.org for more information.

Other access: Bulk record requests are not available from Indiana.

Accident Reports

State Police Department, Vehicle Crash Records Sections, Room N301, Indiana Government Center, Indianapolis, IN 46204; 317-232-8286, 317-232-0652 (Fax), 8AM-4PM.

Note: The only reports released are those of the officers. Indiana operator report forms are not released.

Indexing & Storage: Records are available from 20 years to present. Older records are archived on microfiche. It takes 2 weeks before new records are available for inquiry.

Searching: Include the following in your request: full name, date of accident, location of accident.

Access by: mail, phone, in person.

Fee & Payment: The fee is $3.00 per report. If you are requesting all reports on a per-name basis, there is a $6.81 per hour search fee in addition. Fee payee: Indiana State Police. Prepayment required. Personal checks accepted. No credit cards accepted.

Mail search: Turnaround time: 7 to 10 days. No self addressed stamped envelope is required.

Phone search: You can phone to see if a report is on file before the fee is sent.

In person search: Normal turnaround time is while you wait. If you are requesting all accidents on a "name," this request should be in writing and will take longer.

Other access: For information about bulk file purchasing, contact the Data Section at 317-232-8289.

Legislation Records

Legislative Services Agency, State House, 200 W Washington, Room 301, Indianapolis, IN 46204-2789; 317-232-9856, 8:15AM-4:45PM.

www.in.gov/legislative

Note: Sessions start in January. Long sessions (61 days) are in the odd years; short sessions (30 days) are in the even years. Bills prior to 1990 are stored in the State Law Library.

Indexing & Storage: Records are available from 1980 to present.

Searching: Include the following in your request: bill number. Can search on code citation also.

Access by: mail, phone, in person, online.

Fee & Payment: Fees are $.15 per copy plus postage. Fee payee: Legislative Services Agency. Prepayment required. Personal checks accepted. No credit cards accepted.

Mail search: Turnaround time: 1 to 4 days. No self addressed stamped envelope is required.

Phone search: You may request the cost of sending documents, but all requests must be prepaid.

In person search: Searching is available in person.

Online search: All legislative information is available over the Internet. The Indiana Code is also available.

Voter Registration
Access to Records is Restricted

Election Division, 302 Washington, Room E-204, Indianapolis, IN 46204-2767; 317-232-3939, 317-233-6793 (Fax), 8AM-4:30PM.

www.IN.gov/sos/elections

Note: This agency will not sell records for commercial or investigative reasons, but will sell data in bulk format for political purposes for $5,000. In general, the Circuit Court has records locally. Campaign finance reports are searchable at the web site, which is full of good information about elections in IN.

GED Certificates

Division of Adult Education, GED Testing, State House Rm 229, Indianapolis, IN 46204-2798; 317-232-0522, 317-233-0859 (Fax).

www.doe.state.in.us/adulted

Note: The suggested Release Form is available online at the web site.

Indexing & Storage: It takes six weeks before new records are available for inquiry.

Searching: To search, all of the following are required: a signed release, name, date/year of test, date of birth, Social Security Number, city of test, and a phone number where you can be reached.

Access by: mail, fax.

Fee & Payment: There is no fee. E-mail requests are accepted, but like all requests a signed release is required.

Mail search: Records are available by mail.

Fax search: Records are available by fax.

Hunting License Information
Fishing License Information
Records not maintained by a state level agency.

Note: They do not have a central database. Vendors keep all records.

Indiana State Licensing Agencies

Licenses Searchable Online

Athletic Trainer #9..www.state.in.us/hpb/mlvs/index.html
Audiologist #9 ....www.state.in.us/hpb/mlvs/index.html
Child Care Center #10 ....www.carefinderindiana.org/carefinder/LicStatus.htm
Child Care Home #10 ....www.carefinderindiana.org/carefinder/LicStatus.htm
Child Care Provider #10..www.carefinderindiana.org/carefinder/LicStatus.htm
Chiropractor #9 ....www.state.in.us/hpb/mlvs/index.html
Collection Agency #19 ....www.in.gov/serv/sos_securities
Dental Hygienist #9...www.state.in.us/hpb/mlvs/index.html
Dentist #9 ....www.state.in.us/hpb/mlvs/index.html
Dietitian #9..www.state.in.us/hpb/mlvs/index.html
Emergency Medical Technician #9 ....www.state.in.us/hpb/mlvs/index.html
Environmental Health #9..www.state.in.us/hpb/mlvs/index.html
Hazardous Waste Facility/Handler #5...................www.in.gov/idem/land/permits/lists/index.html
Health Services Administrator #9...........................www.state.in.us/hpb/mlvs/index.html
Hearing Aid Dealer #9 ....www.state.in.us/hpb/mlvs/index.html
Hypnotist #9..www.state.in.us/hpb/mlvs/index.html
Insurance Agent/Consultant #7.............................www.in.gov/idoi/
Investment Advisor #19 ....www.in.gov/serv/sos_securities
Loan Brokers #19 ....www.in.gov/serv/sos_securities
Marriage & Family Therapist #9.............................www.state.in.us/hpb/mlvs/index.html
Medical Doctor #9..www.state.in.us/hpb/mlvs/index.html
Mental Health Counselor #9 ....www.state.in.us/hpb/mlvs/index.html
Midwife Nurse #9 ....www.state.in.us/hpb/mlvs/index.html
Notary Public #17 ....www.ai.org/serv/sos_notary
Nurse #9 ....www.state.in.us/hpb/mlvs/index.html
Nurse-RN/LPN #9 ....www.state.in.us/hpb/mlvs/index.html
Nursing Home Administrator #9..............................www.state.in.us/hpb/mlvs/index.html
Occupational Therapist #9.....................................www.state.in.us/hpb/mlvs/index.html
Optometrist #9 ....www.state.in.us/hpb/mlvs/index.html
Osteopathic Physician #9 ....www.state.in.us/hpb/mlvs/index.html
Pharmacist/Pharmacist Intern #9..........................www.state.in.us/hpb/mlvs/index.html
Physical Therapist/Therapist Asst #9....................www.state.in.us/hpb/mlvs/index.html
Physician #9 ....www.state.in.us/hpb/mlvs/index.html
Physician Assistant #9...www.state.in.us/hpb/mlvs/index.html
Podiatrist #9...www.state.in.us/hpb/mlvs/index.html
Polygraph Examiner #21...www.indianapolygraphassociation.com
Psychologist #9..www.state.in.us/hpb/mlvs/index.html
Real Estate Appraiser #18 ....www.asc.gov/content/category1/appr_by_state.asp
Respiratory Care Practitioner #9............................www.state.in.us/hpb/mlvs/index.html
Securities Broker/Dealer #19 ....www.in.gov/serv/sos_securities
Securities Sales Agent #19....................................www.in.gov/serv/sos_securities
Social Worker #9 ....www.state.in.us/hpb/mlvs/index.html
Social Worker, Clinical #9 ....www.state.in.us/hpb/mlvs/index.html
Solid Waste Facility #5 ....www.in.gov/idem/land/permits/lists/index.html
Speech Pathologist #9...www.state.in.us/hpb/mlvs/index.html
Teacher #14 ....http://dew4.doe.state.in.us/LIC/license.html
Veterinarian #9 ....www.state.in.us/hpb/mlvs/index.html
Waste Tire Processor/Transporter #5....................www.in.gov/idem/land/permits/lists/index.html
Yard Waste Composting Facility #5.......................www.in.gov/idem/land/permits/lists/index.html

Licensing Quick Finder

Alcoholic Beverage Dist./Retailer/Employee #1
....317-232-2430
Amusement Ride #37 217-782-9347
Animal (Dead) Rendering #2................317-227-0345
Architect #18...317-232-2980
Asbestos Contractor #4 317-232-8232
Asbestos Disposal Manager/Worker #4317-232-8232

Asbestos Inspector/Supvr./Project Designer #4
....317-232-8232
Asbestos Training Course Provider #4 . 317-232-8232
Athletic Trainer #9 317-232-2960
Attorney #15 317-232-1930
Auctioneer #18 317-232-2980
Audiologist #9...317-232-2960
Bank & Trust Company #6 317-232-5846

Barber #18...317-232-2980
Boiler & Pressure Vessel Inspector #8 . 317-232-1921
Boxer #18...317-232-2980
Brands, Livestock #2............................317-227-0346
Building & Loan #6 317-232-5851
Check Casher #6.....................................317-232-3955
Child Care Center #10 317-232-4469
Child Care Home #10...........................317-232-4521

Child Care Provider #10	317-232-4521
Chiropractor #9	317-232-2960
Collection Agency #19	317-232-0093
Consumer Credit Grantor #6	317-232-5849
Cosmetologist #18	317-232-2980
Credit Union #6	317-232-5851
Dairy-related Occupation #2	317-227-0350
Dental Hygienist #9	317-232-2960
Dentist #9	317-232-2960
Dietitian #9	317-232-2960
Elevator Safety Contractor #8	317-232-6609
Emergency Medical Technician #9	317-233-6545
Engineer #18	317-232-2980
Environmental Health #9	317-232-2960
Funeral/Cemetery Director #18	317-232-2980
Grain Bank/Warehouse #12	317-232-1358
Grain Buyer #12	317-232-1360
Hazardous Waste Facility/Handler #5	317-232-8603
Health Services Administrator #9	317-232-2960
Hearing Aid Dealer #9	317-232-2960
Horse Racing #13	317-233-3119
Hypnotist #9	317-232-2960
Insurance Adjuster #7	317-232-2414
Insurance Agent/Consultant #7	317-232-2414
Investment Advisor #19	317-232-6681
Lender #6	317-232-3955
Livestock Dealer/market #2	317-227-0345

Livestock Transportation #2	317-227-0345
Loan Brokers #19	317-232-6681
Lottery Retailer #16	317-264-4800
Manufactured Home Builder #8	317-232-1408
Marriage & Family Therapist #9	317-232-2960
Meat & Poultry #2	317-227-0355
Medical Doctor #9	317-232-2960
Mental Health Counselor #9	317-232-2960
Midwife Nurse #9	317-232-2960
Money Transmitter #6	317-232-3955
Notary Public #17	317-232-6542
Nurse #9	317-232-2960
Nurse-RN/LPN #9	317-232-2960
Nursing Home Administrator #9	317-232-2960
Occupational Therapist #9	317-232-2960
Optometrist #9	317-232-2960
Osteopathic Physician #9	317-232-2960
Pawnbroker #6	317-232-3955
Pesticide Applicator #3	765-494-1594
Pesticide Technician/Consultant #3	765-494-1594
Pharmacist/Pharmacist Intern #9	317-232-2960
Physical Therapist/Therapist Asst #9	317-233-2960
Physician #9	317-232-2960
Physician Assistant #9	317-232-2960
Plumber #18	317-232-2980
Podiatrist #9	317-232-2960
Polygraph Examiner #21	317-232-8263

Private Detective #18	317-232-2980
Psychologist #9	317-232-2960
Public Accountant #18	317-232-2980
Radiologic Technologist #20	317-233-7565
Real Estate Agent #18	317-232-2980
Real Estate Appraiser #18	317-232-2980
Respiratory Care Practitioner #9	317-232-2960
School Administrator/Principal #14	317-232-9010
School Counselor #14	317-232-9010
Securities Broker/Dealer #19	317-232-6690
Securities Sales Agent #19	317-232-6690
Shorthand Reporter #11	219-756-0702
Social Worker #9	317-232-2960
Social Worker, Clinical #9	317-232-2960
Solid Waste Facility #5	317-232-8603
Speech Pathologist #9	317-232-2960
Surveyor, Land #18	317-232-2980
Teacher #14	317-232-9010
Underground Storage Tank #8	317-233-3560
Veterinarian #9	317-232-2960
Warehouse, Agricultural, etc. #12	317-232-1358
Waste Tire Processor/Transporter #5	317-232-8603
Waste Water Treatment Plant Operator #5	317-232-8666
Yard Waste Composting Facility #5	317-232-8603

Licensing Agency Information

#1 Alcoholic and Tobacco Commission, 302 W Washington St, Rm E114, Indianapolis, IN 46204; 317-233-3940, Fax: 317-233-6114.
www.in.gov/atc
Agency email: kchew@atc.state.in.us.

#2 Licensing & Compliance, Board of Animal Health, 805 Beachway Dr #50, Indianapolis, IN 46224; 317-227-0300, Fax: 317-227-0330.
www.state.in.us/boah. Agency email: dderrer@boah.state.in.us.

#3 Department of Biochemistry, Office of Chemist & Seed Commissioner, Purdue University, 1154 Biochemistry, West Lafayette, IN 47907-1154; 765-494-1492, Fax: 765-494-4331.
www.isco.purdue.edu
Agency email: walshm@isco.purdue.edu.

#4 Department of Environmental Management, Asbestos Department, 100 N. Senate, Indianapolis, IN 46204-6015; 317-232-8603, Fax: 317-232-8406.
www.IN.gov/idem
Agency email: webmaster@dem.state.in.us.

#5 Department of Environmental Management, Office of Land Quality, PO Box 6015, Indianapolis, IN 46204-6015; 317-232-8603, Fax: 317-232-8406.
www.in.gov/idem/land
Agency email: webmaster@dem.state.in.us.
Search database at
www.in.gov/idem/land/permits/lists/index.html

#6 Department of Financial Institutions, 402 W Washington St, IGC-S, Rm W066, Indianapolis, IN 46204-2759; 317-232-3955, Fax: 317-232-7655.
www.dfi.state.in.us

#7 Department of Insurance, 311 W Washington St #300, Indianapolis, IN 46204-2787; 317-232-2385, Fax: 317-232-5251.
www.in.gov/idol
Search database at www.in.gov/idol/licagent.html

#8 Fire & Building Services, 402 W Washington St, IGS-S, Rm W246, Indianapolis, IN 46204; 317-232-6609, Fax: 317-232-0146.

#9 Health Professions Bureau, 402 W Washington St, #041, Indianapolis, IN 46204-2739; 317-232-2960, Fax: 317-233-4236.
www.ai.org/hpb
Agency email: kburch@hpb.state.in.us.
Search database at
www.state.in.us/hpb/mlvs/index.html. To search online, you have to subscribe to AIIN. For more info on AIIN, visit
www.state.in.us/premium/about.html

#10 Family and Social Services Administration, Bureau of Child Development, 402 W. Washington St., Rm W386, Indianapolis, IN 46201; 317-232-1144.
www.ai.org/fssa/children
Agency email: cbigsbee2@fssa.state.in.us.
Search database at www.carefinderindiana.org

#11 ISRA President, Karen Price, PO Box 11270, Merrillville, IN 46411; 219-756-0702, Fax: 219-756-1766.

#12 Grain Buyers & Warehouse Licensing Agency, 150 W Market St, Rm 416, Indianapolis, IN 46204-2810; 317-232-1356, Fax: 317-232-1362.
www.IN.gov/igbwla
Agency email: dhenry@commerce.state.in.us.

#13 Horse Racing Licensing, 150 W Market St, Indianapolis, IN 46204; 317-233-3119, Fax: 317-233-4470.
www.IN.gov/ihrc. Agency email: hrc@state.in.us.

#14 Professional Standards Board, 101 W Ohio St, #300, Indianapolis, IN 46204; 317-232-9010, Fax: 317-232-9023.
www.state.in.us/psb
Agency email: webmaster@doe.state.in.us.

#15 Clerk of the Indiana Supreme Court, 217 State House, 20th Fl, Indianapolis, IN 46204; 317-232-1930, Fax: 317-232-8365.
www.IN.gov/judiciary/

#16 Lottery Commission of Indiana, 201 S Capitol Av #1100, Indianapolis, IN 46225; 317-264-4800, Fax: 317-264-4908.
www.hoosierlottery.com/yes.htm

#17 Business Services Division - Notary, Office of Secretary of State, Statehouse, #201, Indianapolis, IN 46204; 317-232-6542, Fax: 317-233-3283.
www.in.gov/sos/notary/index.html
Agency email: EMoore@sos.state.in.us.
Search database at www.ai.org/serv/sos_notary

#18 Professional Licensing Agency, Boards & Commissions, 302 W Washington St, Rm E034, Indianapolis, IN 46204; 317-232-2980, Fax: 317-232-2312.
www.IN.gov/pla/

#19 Secretary of State, Securities Division, 302 W Washington Rm E-111, Indianapolis, IN 46204; 317-232-6681, Fax: 317-233-3675.
www.in.gov/sos/securities/index.html
Search database at www.in.gov/serv/sos_securities

#20 Division of End. & Radiologic Health, Board of Health, 2 N Meridian St, 5F, Indianapolis, IN 46204-3003; 317-233-7150.

#21 State Police, 100 N Senate Ave, Government Center N, #302, Indianapolis, IN 46204-2259; 317-232-8263, Fax: 317-232-0652.
www.indianapolygraphassociation.com
Search database at
www.indianapolygraphassociation.com

Indiana Federal Courts

The following list indicates the district and division name for each county in the state. If the bankruptcy court location is different from the district court, then the location of the bankruptcy court appears in parentheses.

County/Court Cross Reference

County	District	Division
Adams	Northern	Fort Wayne
Allen	Northern	Fort Wayne
Bartholomew	Southern	Indianapolis
Benton	Northern	Lafayette (Hammond at Lafayette)
Blackford	Northern	Fort Wayne
Boone	Southern	Indianapolis
Brown	Southern	Indianapolis
Carroll	Northern	Lafayette (Hammond at Lafayette)
Cass	Northern	South Bend
Clark	Southern	New Albany
Clay	Southern	Terre Haute
Clinton	Southern	Indianapolis
Crawford	Southern	New Albany
Daviess	Southern	Evansville
DeKalb	Northern	Fort Wayne
Dearborn	Southern	New Albany
Decatur	Southern	Indianapolis
Delaware	Southern	Indianapolis
Dubois	Southern	Evansville
Elkhart	Northern	South Bend
Fayette	Southern	Indianapolis
Floyd	Southern	New Albany
Fountain	Southern	Indianapolis
Franklin	Southern	Indianapolis
Fulton	Northern	South Bend
Gibson	Southern	Evansville
Grant	Northern	Fort Wayne
Greene	Southern	Terre Haute
Hamilton	Southern	Indianapolis
Hancock	Southern	Indianapolis
Harrison	Southern	New Albany
Hendricks	Southern	Indianapolis
Henry	Southern	Indianapolis
Howard	Southern	Indianapolis
Huntington	Northern	Fort Wayne
Jackson	Southern	New Albany
Jasper	Northern	Lafayette (Hammond at Lafayette)
Jay	Northern	Fort Wayne
Jefferson	Southern	New Albany
Jennings	Southern	New Albany
Johnson	Southern	Indianapolis
Knox	Southern	Terre Haute
Kosciusko	Northern	South Bend
La Porte	Northern	South Bend
LaGrange	Northern	Fort Wayne
Lake	Northern	Hammond (Hammond. at Gary)
Lawrence	Southern	New Albany
Madison	Southern	Indianapolis
Marion	Southern	Indianapolis
Marshall	Northern	South Bend
Martin	Southern	Evansville
Miami	Northern	South Bend
Monroe	Southern	Indianapolis
Montgomery	Southern	Indianapolis
Morgan	Southern	Indianapolis
Newton	Northern	Lafayette (Hammond at Lafayette)
Noble	Northern	Fort Wayne
Ohio	Southern	New Albany
Orange	Southern	New Albany
Owen	Southern	Terre Haute
Parke	Southern	Terre Haute
Perry	Southern	Evansville
Pike	Southern	Evansville
Porter	Northern	Hammond (Hammond. at Gary)
Posey	Southern	Evansville
Pulaski	Northern	South Bend
Putnam	Southern	Terre Haute
Randolph	Southern	Indianapolis
Ripley	Southern	New Albany
Rush	Southern	Indianapolis
Scott	Southern	New Albany
Shelby	Southern	Indianapolis
Spencer	Southern	Evansville
St. Joseph	Northern	South Bend
Starke	Northern	South Bend
Steuben	Northern	Fort Wayne
Sullivan	Southern	Terre Haute
Switzerland	Southern	New Albany
Tippecanoe	Northern	Lafayette (Hammond at Lafayette)
Tipton	Southern	Indianapolis
Union	Southern	Indianapolis
Vanderburgh	Southern	Evansville
Vermillion	Southern	Terre Haute
Vigo	Southern	Terre Haute
Wabash	Northern	South Bend
Warren	Northern	Lafayette (Hammond at Lafayette)
Warrick	Southern	Evansville
Washington	Southern	New Albany
Wayne	Southern	Indianapolis
Wells	Northern	Fort Wayne
White	Northern	Lafayette (Hammond at Lafayette)
Whitley	Northern	Fort Wayne

Standards for Federal Courts: The search fee is $20.00 per item (one party name or case number). Certification fee is $7.00 per document. Copy fee is $.50 per page. All fees standard unless noted in profile. Mail Search: always enclose a stamped self addressed envelope unless otherwise noted. Before releasing records, all courts require prepayment unless noted in profile.

Open records are located at the court unless otherwise noted. District courts index by defendant and plaintiff as well as by case number. Bankruptcy courts usually index by debtor and case number. While most courts now have their indexes on computer, many still maintain index card files as well.

The universal PACER sign-up number is 800-676-6856. Find PACER and the Party/Case Index on the Web at http://pacer.psc.uscourts.gov. PACER dial-up access is $.60 per minute. Also, courts offering internet access via RACER, PACER, Web-PACER or the new CM-ECF charge $.07 per page fee unless noted as free.

US District Court

Northern District of Indiana

Fort Wayne Division Room 1108, Federal Bldg, 1300 S Harrison St, Fort Wayne, IN 46802 (Courier Address: Use mail address for courier delivery), 260-424-7360.

www.innd.uscourts.gov

Counties: Adams, Allen, Blackford, DeKalb, Grant, Huntington, Jay, Lagrange, Noble, Steuben, Wells, Whitley.

Indexing & Storage: Cases are indexed by defendant, plaintiff, and case number. New cases are available in the index 1-2 days after filing date. Open records are located at this court.

Fee & Payment Notes: Payment may be made by money order, cashier check, personal check. Payee: Clerk, US District Court.

Phone Search: Only case names and numbers will be released over the phone.

In Person Search: In person searching available.

PACER: Toll-free dial-up access: 800-371-8843. Local dial-up access: 574-246-8200. Case records are available back to 1994. Records are purged as deemed necessary. New records are available online after 2 days. PACER is available online at http://pacer.innd.uscourts.gov.

Hammond Division Room 101, 507 State St, Hammond, IN 46320 (Courier Address: Use mail address for courier delivery), 219-937-5235.

www.innd.uscourts.gov

Counties: Lake, Porter.

Indexing & Storage: Cases are indexed by defendant, plaintiff, and case number. New cases are available in the index 1-3 days after filing date. Open records are located at this court.

Fee & Payment Notes: Payment may be made by money order, cashier check, personal check. Payee: Clerk, US District Court.

Phone Search: Only docket information is available by phone.

In Person Search: In person searching available.

PACER: Toll-free dial-up access: 800-371-8843. Local dial-up access: 574-246-8200. Case records are available back to 1994. Records are purged as

deemed necessary. New records are available online after 2 days. PACER is available online at http://pacer.innd.uscourts.gov.

Lafayette Division PO Box 1498, Lafayette, IN 47902 (Courier Address: 230 N 4th St, Lafayette, IN 47901), 765-420-6250.

www.innd.uscourts.gov

Counties: Benton, Carroll, Jasper, Newton, Tippecanoe, Warren, White.

Indexing & Storage: Cases are indexed by defendant, plaintiff, and case number. New cases are available in the index 24 hours after filing date. Microfiche is also available. Open records are located at this court.

Fee & Payment Notes: Payment may be made by money order, cashier check, personal check. Payee: Clerk, US District Court.

Phone Search: Only docket information is available by phone.

Fax Search: Will accept fax only to ask if a person is a defendant or plaintiff in any cases.

In Person Search: In person searching available.

PACER: Toll-free dial-up access: 800-371-8843. Local dial-up access: 574-246-8200. Case records are available back to 1994. Records are purged as deemed necessary. New records are available online after 2 days. PACER is available online at http://pacer.innd.uscourts.gov.

South Bend Division Room 102, 204 S Main, South Bend, IN 46601 (Courier Address: Use mail address for courier delivery), 574-246-8000, Fax: 574-246-8002.

www.innd.uscourts.gov

Counties: Cass, Elkhart, Fulton, Kosciusko, La Porte, Marshall, Miami, Pulaski, St. Joseph, Starke, Wabash.

Indexing & Storage: Cases are indexed by defendant, plaintiff, and case number. New cases are available in the index 2 days after filing date. Open records are located at this court.

Fee & Payment Notes: Payment may be made by money order, cashier check, personal check. Payee: Clerk, US District Court.

Phone Search: Only docket information is available by phone.

In Person Search: In person searching available.

PACER: Toll-free dial-up access: 800-371-8843. Local dial-up access: 574-246-8200. Case records are available back to 1994. Records are purged as deemed necessary. New records are available online after 2 days. PACER is available online at http://pacer.innd.uscourts.gov.

US Bankruptcy Court

Northern District of Indiana

Fort Wayne Division PO Box 2547, Fort Wayne, IN 46801-2547 (Courier Address: 1188 Federal Bldg, 1300 S Harrison St, Fort Wayne, IN 46802), 260-420-5100.

www.innb.uscourts.gov

Counties: Adams, Allen, Blackford, DeKalb, Grant, Huntington, Jay, Lagrange, Noble, Steuben, Wells, Whitley.

Indexing & Storage: Cases are indexed by debtor and creditors as well as by case number. New

cases are available in the index 24 hours after filing date. A card index of debtor names is also maintained. Records in closed cases are only kept locally for a brief period. Records are shipped to the Chicago FRC annually. At the time a case is closed, both the date of filing and the date of closing are factors in determining when the case is shipped.

Fee & Payment Notes: Payment may be made by money order, cashier check, personal check. Debtor's checks are not accepted. Payee: Clerk, US Bankruptcy Court.

Phone Search: Only docket information is available by phone. An automated voice case information service (VCIS) is available. Call VCIS at 800-755-8393 or 574-236-8814.

In Person Search: In person searching available.

PACER: Toll-free dial-up access: 888-917-2237. Local dial-up access: 574-968-2270. Case records are available back to 1992. Records are purged every 6 months. New civil records are available online after 2 days. PACER is available online at http://pacer.innb.uscourts.gov.

Electronic Filing: (Currently in the process of implementing CM/ECF.)

Hammond at Gary Division 221 Federal Bldg, 610 Connecticut St, Gary, IN 46402-2595 (Courier Address: Use mail address for courier delivery), 219-881-3335, Fax: 219-881-3307.

www.innb.uscourts.gov

Counties: Lake, Porter.

Indexing & Storage: Cases are indexed by debtor and creditors as well as by case number. New cases are available in the index 24 hours after filing date. Records in closed cases are only kept locally for a brief period. Records are shipped to the FRC twice a year. At the time a case is closed, both the date of filing and the date of closing are factors in determining when the case is shipped.

Fee & Payment Notes: Payment may be made by money order, cashier check, personal check, Visa or Mastercard. Debtor's checks and credit cards are not accepted. Payee: Clerk, US Bankruptcy Court. You are allowed to make your own copies. These copies cost $.15 per page.

Phone Search: Only docket information is available by phone. An automated voice case information service (VCIS) is available. Call VCIS at 800-755-8393 or 574-236-8814.

In Person Search: In person searching available.

PACER: Toll-free dial-up access: 888-917-2237. Local dial-up access: 574-968-2270. Case records are available back to 1992. Records are purged every 6 months. New civil records are available online after 2 days. PACER is available online at http://pacer.innb.uscourts.gov.

Electronic Filing: (Currently in the process of implementing CM/ECF.)

Hammond at Lafayette Division c/o Fort Wayne Division, PO Box 2547, Fort Wayne, IN 46801-2547 (Courier Address: Use mail address for courier delivery), 260-420-5100.

www.innb.uscourts.gov

Counties: Benton, Carroll, Jasper, Newton, Tippecanoe, Warren, White.

Indexing & Storage: Cases are indexed by debtor and collector as well as by case number. New cases are available in the index after filing date. All the files for the Hammond Division at

Lafayette are physically kept in the Fort Wayne office. All papers pertaining to Hammond Division at Lafayette cases after the initial filing, including claims, should be sent to the Fort Wayne office. Open records are located at the Ft. Wayne Division.

Fee & Payment Notes: Payment may be made by money order, cashier check. Business checks are not accepted. Personal checks are not accepted.

Phone Search: An automated voice case information service (VCIS) is available. Call VCIS at 800-755-8393 or 574-236-8814.

In Person Search: In person searching available.

PACER: Toll-free dial-up access: 888-917-2237. Local dial-up access: 574-968-2270. Case records are available back to 1992. Records are purged every 6 months. New civil records are available online after 2 days. PACER is available online at http://pacer.innb.uscourts.gov.

Electronic Filing: (Currently in the process of implementing CM/ECF.)

South Bend Division PO Box 7003, South Bend, IN 46634-7003 (Courier Address: 401 S Michigan St, South Bend, IN 46601), 574-968-2100, Fax: 574-968-2205.

www.innb.uscourts.gov

Counties: Cass, Elkhart, Fulton, Kosciusko, La Porte, Marshall, Miami, Pulaski, St. Joseph, Starke, Wabash.

Indexing & Storage: Cases are indexed by debtor and creditors as well as by case number. New cases are available in the index 24 hours after filing date. Records in closed cases are only kept locally for a brief period. Records are shipped to the Chicago FRC semi-annually. At the time a case is closed, both the date of filing and the date of closing are factors in determining when the case is shipped.

Fee & Payment Notes: Payment may be made by money order, cashier check, personal check, Visa or Mastercard. Debtor's checks are not accepted. Payee: Clerk, US Bankruptcy Court. You are allowed to make your own copies. These copies cost $.15 per page. A self service copy machine is available.

Phone Search: Only docket information is available by phone. An automated voice case information service (VCIS) is available. Call VCIS at 800-755-8393 or 574-236-8814.

In Person Search: In person searching available.

PACER: Toll-free dial-up access: 888-917-2237. Local dial-up access: 574-968-2270. Case records are available back to 1992. Records are purged every 6 months. New civil records are available online after 2 days. PACER is available online at http://pacer.innb.uscourts.gov.

Electronic Filing: (Currently in the process of implementing CM/ECF.)

US District Court

Southern District of Indiana

Evansville Division 304 Federal Bldg, 101 NW Martin Luther King Blvd, Evansville, IN 47708 (Courier: Use mail address for courier delivery), 812-465-6426, Fax: 812-465-6428.

www.insd.uscourts.gov

Counties: Daviess, Dubois, Gibson, Martin, Perry, Pike, Posey, Spencer, Vanderburgh, Warrick.

Indexing & Storage: Cases are indexed by defendant, plaintiff, and case number. New cases are available in the index immediately after filing date. Cases prior to 1992 are indexed by name only on index cards. Open records are located at this court.

Fee & Payment Notes: Payment may be made by money order, cashier check, personal check. Payee: Clerk, US District Court.

Phone Search: Searching not available by phone.

Mail Search: A stamped self addressed envelope is not required.

In Person Search: In person searching available.

PACER: There is no PACER access to this court.

Electronic Filing: (Currently in the process of implementing CM/ECF.)

Other Online Access: Search records for free; visit www.insd.uscourts.gov/casesearch.htm to search. Court does not participate in the U.S. party case index.

Indianapolis Division Clerk, Room 105, 46 E Ohio St, Indianapolis, IN 46204 (Courier Address: Use mail address for courier delivery), 317-229-3700, Fax: 317-229-3959.

www.insd.uscourts.gov

Counties: Bartholomew, Boone, Brown, Clinton, Decatur, Delaware, Fayette, Fountain, Franklin, Hamilton, Hancock, Hendricks, Henry, Howard, Johnson, Madison, Marion, Monroe, Montgomery, Morgan, Randolph, Rush, Shelby, Tipton, Union, Wayne.

Indexing & Storage: Cases are indexed by defendant, plaintiff, and case number. New cases are available in the index 24 hours after filing date. District wide searches are available from this court for cases from 1996 to the present.

Fee & Payment Notes: Payment may be made by money order. Business checks are not accepted, Visa, Mastercard. Personal checks are not accepted. Payee: Clerk, US District Court.

Phone Search: Only information contained on the face of the docket sheet will be released over the phone. Anything from the remaining pages requires that the search fee be paid.

Mail Search: A stamped self addressed envelope is not required.

In Person Search: In person searching available.

PACER: There is no PACER access to this court.

Electronic Filing: (Currently in the process of implementing CM/ECF.)

Other Online Access: Search records for free visit www.insd.uscourts.gov/casesearch.htm to search. Court does not participate in the U.S. party case index.

New Albany Division Room 210, 121 W Spring St, New Albany, IN 47150 (Courier Address: Use mail address for courier delivery), 812-948-5238, Fax: 812-948-5246.

www.insd.uscourts.gov

Counties: Clark, Crawford, Dearborn, Floyd, Harrison, Jackson, Jefferson, Jennings, Lawrence, Ohio, Orange, Ripley, Scott, Switzerland, Washington.

Indexing & Storage: Cases are indexed by defendant, plaintiff, and case number. New cases are available in the index immediately after filing date. Files may also be in Indianapolis or Evansville.

Fee & Payment Notes: Payment may be made by money order, cashier check, personal check. Payee: Clerk, US District Court.

Phone Search: Searching not available by phone.

In Person Search: In person searching available.

PACER: There is no PACER access to this court.

Electronic Filing: (Currently in the process of implementing CM/ECF.)

Other Online Access: Search records for free; visit www.insd.uscourts.gov/casesearch.htm to search. Court does not participate in the U.S. party case index.

Terre Haute Division 207 Federal Bldg, 30 N 7th St, Terre Haute, IN 47808 (Courier Address: Use mail address for courier delivery), 812-234-9484.

www.insd.uscourts.gov

Counties: Clay, Greene, Knox, Owen, Parke, Putnam, Sullivan, Vermillion, Vigo.

Indexing & Storage: Cases are indexed by defendant, plaintiff, and case number. New cases are available in the index immediately after filing date. Open records are located at this court.

Fee & Payment Notes: Payment may be made by money order, cashier check, personal check. Payee: Clerk, US District Court.

Phone Search: All information that is not sealed is available for release over the phone.

In Person Search: In person searching available.

PACER: There is no PACER access to this court.

Electronic Filing: (Currently in the process of implementing CM/ECF.)

Other Online Access: Search records for free; visit www.insd.uscourts.gov/casesearch.htm to search. Court does not participate in the U.S. party case index.

US Bankruptcy Court

Southern District of Indiana

Evansville Division 352 Federal Building, 101 NW Martin Luther King Blvd, Evansville, IN 47708 (Courier: Use mail address for courier delivery), 812-465-6440, Fax: 812-465-6453.

www.insb.uscourts.gov

Counties: Daviess, Dubois, Gibson, Martin, Perry, Pike, Posey, Spencer, Vanderburgh, Warrick.

Indexing & Storage: Cases are indexed by debtor as well as by case number. New cases are available in the index 1-2 days after filing date. Open records are located at this court.

Fee & Payment Notes: Payment may be made by money order, cashier check, personal check. Debtor's checks are not accepted. Payee: Clerk, US Bankruptcy Court. You are allowed to make your own copies. These copies cost $.50 per page.

Phone Search: Only docket information is available by phone. An automated voice case information service (VCIS) is available. Call VCIS at 800-335-8003.

In Person Search: In person searching available.

PACER: Sign-up number is 317-229-3845. Case records are available back to 1988. Records are purged every 3 months. New civil records are available online after 2-3 days. PACER is now available at www.insb.uscourts.gov. Click on "Case Search." Registration and fees now required. The free case lookup system is no longer found.

Other Online Access: Court does not participate in the U.S. party case index.

Indianapolis Division US Courthouse, Rm 116, 46 E Ohio St, Indianapolis, IN 46204 (Courier Address: Use mail address for courier delivery), 317-229-3800, Fax: 317-229-3801.

www.insb.uscourts.gov

Counties: Bartholomew, Boone, Brown, Clinton, Decatur, Delaware, Fayette, Fountain, Franklin, Hamilton, Hancock, Hendricks, Henry, Howard, Johnson, Madison, Marion, Monroe, Montgomery, Morgan, Randolph, Rush, Shelby, Tipton, Union, Wayne.

Indexing & Storage: Cases are indexed by debtor as well as by case number. New cases are available in the index 48 hours after filing date. Records are stored electronically since 1986. Open records are located at this court.

Fee & Payment Notes: Payment may be made by money order, cashier check, personal check. Debtor's checks are not accepted. Payee: Clerk, US Bankruptcy Court (SDIN).

Phone Search: Only docket information is available by phone. An automated voice case information service (VCIS) is available. Call VCIS at 800-335-8003.

In Person Search: In person searching available.

PACER: Sign-up number is 317-229-3845. Case records are available back to 1988. Records are purged every 3 months. New civil records are available online after 2-3 days. PACER is now available at www.insb.uscourts.gov. Click on "Case Search." Registration and fees now

required. The free case lookup system is no longer found.

Other Online Access: Court does not participate in the U.S. party case index.

New Albany Division US Courthouse, Rm 110, 121 W Spring St, New Albany, IN 47150 (Courier Address: Use mail address for courier delivery), 812-948-5254, Fax: 812-948-5262.

www.insb.uscourts.gov

Counties: Clark, Crawford, Dearborn, Floyd, Harrison, Jackson, Jefferson, Jennings, Lawrence, Ohio, Orange, Ripley, Scott, Switzerland, Washington.

Indexing & Storage: Cases are indexed by debtor as well as by case number. New cases are available in the index 48 hours after filing date. Open records are located at this court.

Fee & Payment Notes: Payment may be made by money order, cashier check, personal check. Debtor's checks are not accepted. Payee: Clerk, US Bankruptcy Court (SDIN).

Phone Search: Only docket information is available by phone. An automated voice case information service (VCIS) is available. Call VCIS at 800-335-8003.

In Person Search: In person searching available.

PACER: Sign-up number is 317-229-3845. Case records are available back to 1988. Records are purged every 3 months. New civil records are available online after 2-3 days. PACER is now available at www.insb.uscourts.gov. Click on "Case Search." Registration and fees now required. The free case lookup system is no longer found.

Other Online Access: Court does not participate in the U.S. party case index.

Terre Haute Division Federal Bldg Rm 207, 30 N 7th St, Terre Haute, IN 47808 (Courier Address: Use mail address for courier delivery), 812-238-1550, Fax: 812-238-1831.

www.insb.uscourts.gov

Counties: Clay, Greene, Knox, Owen, Parke, Putnam, Sullivan, Vermillion, Vigo.

Indexing & Storage: Cases are indexed by debtor as well as by case number. New cases are available in the index 48 hours after filing date. Records are stored electronically since 1986. Open records are located at this court.

Fee & Payment Notes: Payment may be made by money order, cashier check, personal check. A search fee will only be charged if a detailed search is required. Personal checks are not accepted from debtors. Payee: Clerk, US Bankruptcy Court.

Phone Search: Only docket information is available by phone. An automated voice case information service (VCIS) is available. Call VCIS at 800-335-8003.

In Person Search: In person searching available.

PACER: Sign-up number is 317-229-3845. Case records are available back to 1988. Records are purged every 3 months. New civil records are available online after 2-3 days. PACER is now available at www.insb.uscourts.gov. Click on "Case Search." Registration and fees now required. The free case lookup system is no longer found.

Other Online Access: Court does not participate in the U.S. party case index.

Indiana County Courts

Court	Jurisdiction	No. of Courts	How Organized
Circuit Courts*	General	24	88 Circuits
Superior Courts*	General	4	
Combined Courts*		68	
County Courts*	Limited	Comb	
Combined Circuit/County*		4	
City Courts	Limited	48	
Small Claims -Marion County	Special	9	
Town Courts	Municipal	27	
Probate Court	Special	1	St. Joseph County

* Profiled in this Sourcebook.

Court	CIVIL								
	Tort	Contract	Real Estate	Min. Claim	Max. Claim	Small Claims	Estate	Eviction	Domestic Relations
Circuit Courts*	X	X	X	$0	No Max	$3000	X		X
Superior Courts*	X	X	X	$0	No Max	$3000	X		X
County Courts*	X	X	X	$0	$10,000	$3000		X	X
City Courts	X	X		$0	$2500			X	X
Small Claims - Marion County						$3000			
Town Courts									X
Probate Court							X		

Court	CRIMINAL				
	Felony	Misdemeanor	DWI/DUI	Preliminary Hearing	Juvenile
Circuit Courts*	X	X	X	X	X
Superior Courts*	X	X	X	X	X
County Courts*	X	X	X	X	
City Courts		X	X	X	
Small Claims - Marion County					
Town Courts		X	X	X	
Probate Court					X

ADMINISTRATION   State Court Administrator, 115 W Washington St Suite 1080, Indianapolis, IN, 46204; 317-232-2542, Fax: 317-233-6586. www.in.gov/judiciary

COURT STRUCTURE   There are 92 judicial circuits with Circuit Courts or Combined Circuit and Superior Courts. In addition, there are 48 City Courts and 27 Town Courts. County courts are gradually being restructured into divisions of the Superior Courts. Note that Small Claims in Marion County are heard at the township and records are maintained at that level. The phone number for the township offices are indicated in Marion County.

ONLINE ACCESS   No online access computer system, internal or external, is available, except for Marion County through CivicNet/Access Indiana Information Network, which is available on the Internet at www.civicnet.net. Account and password are required. No charge for civil court name searches, but fees range from $2.00 to $5.00 for civil case summaries, civil justice name searches, etc., criminal case summaries, and party booking details. There is a $4.50 charge for criminal record searches with use of credit card.

ADDITIONAL INFORMATION

The Circuit Court Clerk/County Clerk in every county is the same individual and is responsible for keeping all county judicial records. However, it is recommended that, when requesting a record, the request indicate which court heard the case (Circuit, Superior, or County).

Many courts are no longer performing searches, especially criminal searches, based on a 7/8/96 statement by the State Board of Accounts.

Certification and copy fees are set by statute as $1.00 per document plus copy fee for certification and $1.00 per page for copies.

Adams County

Circuit & Superior Court 112 S 2nd St, Decatur, IN 46733; 260-724-5309; Fax: 260-724-5313. Hours: 8AM-4:30PM (EST). *Felony, Misdemeanor, Civil, Eviction, Small Claims, Probate.*

Civil Records: Access: In person only. Visitors must perform in person searches for themselves. No search fee. Required to search: name, years to search. Civil cases indexed by defendant, plaintiff. Civil records on computer from 1992, archived from 1876. Some records on index cards.

Criminal Records: Access: In person only. Visitors must perform in person searches for themselves. No search fee. Required to search: name, years to search, DOB; also helpful: SSN. Criminal records on computer from 1992, archived from 1876. Some records on index cards.

General Information: Public access terminal is available. (Limited information available.) No juvenile, adoption, mental health or sealed records released. Copy fee: $1.00 per page. Certification fee: $2.00 per page. Fee payee: Adams County Clerk. Only cashiers checks and money orders accepted. Prepayment is required.

Allen County

Circuit & Superior Court 715 S. Calhoun St. Rm 200 Courthouse, Ft Wayne, IN 46802; 260-449-7245. Hours: 8AM-4:30PM (EST). *Felony, Misdemeanor, Civil, Eviction, Small Claims, Probate.*

www.co.allen.in.us

Civil Records: Access: In person only. Visitors must perform in person searches for themselves. No search fee. Required to search: name, years to search. Civil cases indexed by defendant, plaintiff. Recent civil cases on computer; prior records on microfiche, archived and index from 1824.

Criminal Records: Access: In person only. Visitors must perform in person searches for themselves. No search fee. Required to search: name, years to search; also helpful: DOB, SSN. Recent cases on computer; prior records on microfiche, archived and index to 1824.

General Information: Public access terminal is available. No juvenile, adoption or sealed records released. Copy fee: $1.00 per page. Certification fee: $1.00 per page. Fee payee: Clerk of Allen Circuit Court. Business checks accepted. Prepayment is required.

Bartholomew County

Circuit & Superior Court PO Box 924, Columbus, IN 47202-0924; 812-379-1600; Fax: 812-379-1675. Hours: 8AM-5PM (EST). *Felony, Misdemeanor, Civil, Eviction, Small Claims, Probate.*

Civil Records: Access: In person only. Visitors must perform in person searches for themselves. No search fee. Required to search: name. Civil cases indexed by plaintiff. Civil records on computer from 1985, on microfilm from 1940, on index from 1821.

Criminal Records: Access: Fax, mail, in person. Both court and visitors may perform in person searches. No search fee. Required to search: name, years to search,

DOB; also helpful: SSN, race, sex. Criminal records on computer from 1985, on microfilm from 1940, on index from 1821.

General Information: Public access terminal is available. No juvenile, mental health, adoption or sealed released. All searches 1985 to present. SASE required. Turnaround time 1 day. Fax notes: $5.00 per page. No fee to fax to 800 number. Copy fee: $1.00 per page. Certification fee: $1.00. Fee payee: Bartholomew County Clerk. Personal checks accepted. Prepayment is required.

Benton County

Circuit Court 706 E 5th St, #37, Fowler, IN 47944-1556; 765-884-0930; Fax: 765-884-0322. Hours: 8:30AM-4PM (EST). *Felony, Misdemeanor, Civil, Eviction, Small Claims, Probate.*

www.bentoncounty.org

Civil Records: Access: In person only. Visitors must perform in person searches for themselves. No search fee. Required to search: name, years to search. Civil cases indexed by defendant, plaintiff. Civil records on computer from 1992, on index books from 1860.

Criminal Records: Access: Mail, in person. Visitors must perform in person searches for themselves. Search fee: $5.00 per name; send search requests to attention of Melissa Williams in Clerk's office. Required to search: name, years to search, DOB. Criminal records on computer from 1992, on index books from 1860.

General Information: No juvenile, mental, adoption or sealed released. SASE required. Turnaround time 2-3 days. Copy fee: $1.00 per page. Certification fee: $1.00. Fee payee: Benton County Clerk. Only cashiers checks and money orders accepted. Prepayment is required.

Blackford County

Circuit & Superior Court 110 W Washington St, Hartford City, IN 47348; 765-348-1130. Hours: 8AM-4PM (EST). *Felony, Misdemeanor, Civil, Eviction, Small Claims, Probate.*

Civil Records: Access: Mail, in person. Both court and visitors may perform in person searches. No search fee. Required to search: name, years to search. Civil cases indexed by defendant, plaintiff. Civil records on computer from 1991, on index from 1800.

Criminal Records: Access: Mail, in person. Both court and visitors may perform in person searches. No search fee. Required to search: name, years to search, DOB; also helpful: SSN. court records on computer from 1991, on index from 1800.

General Information: No juvenile, mental, adoption or sealed released. Turnaround time 1 week. Fax notes: Fee to fax results is $1.00 per page. Copy fee: $1.00 per page. Certification fee: $2.00. Fee payee: Clerk of Blackford County. Business checks accepted. Prepayment is required.

Boone County

Circuit & Superior Court I & II Rm 212, Courthouse Sq, Lebanon, IN 46052; 765-482-3510. Hours: 7AM-4PM (EST). *Felony, Misdemeanor, Civil, Eviction, Small Claims, Probate.*

www.bccn.boone.in.us/bccn/Boone_Clerk.html

Civil Records: Access: Mail, in person. Both court and visitors may perform in person searches. No search fee. Required to search: name, years to search. Civil cases indexed by defendant, plaintiff. Civil records on index from 1900.

Criminal Records: Access: Mail, in person. Both court and visitors may perform in person searches. No search fee. Required to search: name, years to search; also helpful: SSN. Criminal records on index from 1900.

General Information: No juvenile, mental, adoption or sealed released. SASE required. Turnaround time 1 week. Copy fee: $1.00 per page. Certification fee: $1.00. Fee payee: Boone County Clerk. Business checks accepted. Prepayment is required.

Brown County

Circuit Court Box 85, Nashville, IN 47448; 812-988-5510; Fax: 812-988-5515. Hours: 8AM-4PM (EST). *Felony, Misdemeanor, Civil, Eviction, Small Claims, Probate.*

Civil Records: Access: In person only. Visitors must perform in person searches for themselves. No search fee. Required to search: name, years to search. Civil cases indexed by defendant, plaintiff. Civil records on open cases on computer from 1993, in entry books from early 1800s. Records are not indexed by SSN, but SSNs can be viewed.

Criminal Records: Access: In person only. Visitors must perform in person searches for themselves. No search fee. Required to search: name, years to search, DOB; also helpful: SSN. Criminal records on open cases on computer from 1993, in entry books from early 1800s. Records are not indexed by SSN, but SSNs can be viewed.

General Information: Public access terminal is available. No juvenile, mental, adoption or sealed records released. Copy fee: $1.00 per page. Certification fee: $2.00. Fee payee: County Clerk. Personal checks accepted. Prepayment is required.

Carroll County

Circuit & Superior Court Courthouse, 101 W Main, Delphi, IN 46923; 765-564-4485; Fax: 765-564-6907. Hours: 8AM-5PM M,T,Th,F; 8AM-Noon W (EST). *Felony, Misdemeanor, Civil, Eviction, Small Claims, Probate.*

Civil Records: Access: In person only. Both court and visitors may perform in person searches. No search fee. Required to search: name, years to search. Civil cases indexed by defendant, plaintiff. Civil records archived from 1981, on index from 1828.

Criminal Records: Access: In person only. Visitors must perform in person searches for themselves. No search fee. Required to search: name, years to search. Criminal records archived from 1981, on index to 1828.

General Information: No juvenile, mental, adoption or sealed released. Copy fee: $1.00 per page. Certification fee: $1.00. Fee payee: Carroll County Clerk. Personal checks accepted. Prepayment is required.

Cass County

Circuit & Superior Court 200 Court Park, Logansport, IN 46947; 574-753-7870. Hours: 8AM-4PM (EST). *Felony, Misdemeanor, Civil, Eviction, Small Claims, Probate.*

Civil Records: Access: Mail, in person. Both court and visitors may perform in person searches. No search fee. Required to search: name, years to search. Civil cases indexed by defendant, plaintiff. Civil records on computer from 1989, on index from 1830s.

Criminal Records: Access: Mail, in person. Both court and visitors may perform in person searches. No search fee. Required to search: name, years to search, DOB; also helpful: SSN, signed release. Criminal records on computer from 1989, on index from 1830s.

General Information: Public access terminal is available. No juvenile, mental, adoption or sealed released. SASE requested. Turnaround time 2 weeks. Fax notes: Fax fee $1.00 per page. Copy fee: $1.00 per page. Certification fee: $3.00. Fee payee: Cass County Clerk. Personal checks not accepted, use money order. Prepayment is required.

Clark County

Circuit, Superior & County Court 501 E Court, Rm 137, Jeffersonville, IN 47130; 812-285-6244. Hours: 8:30AM-4:30PM M-F, 8:30-Noon S (EST). *Felony, Misdemeanor, Civil, Eviction, Small Claims, Probate.*

www.clarkprosecutor.org/html/courts/courts.htm

Civil Records: Access: In person only. Visitors must perform in person searches for themselves. No search fee. Required to search: name, years to search; also helpful: address. Civil cases indexed by defendant, plaintiff. Civil records on computer since 8/92, on index cards from 1900.

Criminal Records: Access: In person only. Visitors must perform in person searches for themselves. No search fee. Required to search: name, years to search; also helpful: DOB, SSN. Criminal records on computer since 8/92, on index cards from 1900.

General Information: Public access terminal is available. No juvenile, mental, adoption or sealed released. Copy fee: $1.00 per page. Certification fee: $1.00. Fee payee: County Clerk. Business checks accepted. Prepayment is required.

Clay County

Circuit & Superior Court Box 33, Brazil, IN 47834; 812-448-9024. Hours: 8AM-4PM (EST). *Felony, Misdemeanor, Civil, Eviction, Small Claims, Probate.*

Civil Records: Access: Mail, in person. No search fee. Required to search: name, years to search; also helpful: address. Civil cases indexed by defendant, plaintiff. Civil records on index from 1850; on computer back to 1995.

Criminal Records: Access: Mail, in person. Visitors must perform in person searches for themselves. No search fee. Required to search: name, years to search, address, DOB; also helpful-SSN, signed release. Criminal records on index from 1850; on computer back to 1995.

General Information: No juvenile, mental, adoption or sealed released. SASE required. Turnaround time 1 week. Copy fee: $1.00 per page. Certification fee: $1.00. Fee payee: County Clerk. Business checks accepted. Prepayment is required.

Clinton County

Circuit & Superior Court 265 Courthouse Square, Frankfort, IN 46041; 765-659-6335. Hours: 8AM-4PM M-TH,8AM-5PM F (EST). *Felony, Misdemeanor, Civil, Eviction, Small Claims, Probate.*

Civil Records: Access: In person only. Visitors must perform in person searches for themselves. No search fee. Required to search: name, years to search. Civil cases indexed by defendant, plaintiff. Civil records on computer from 1991, on microfiche and index from 1900s.

Criminal Records: Access: In person only. Visitors must perform in person searches for themselves. Required to search: name, years to search, signed release; also helpful: DOB. Criminal records on computer from 1991, on microfiche and index from 1900s.

General Information: Public access terminal is available. No juvenile, mental, adoption or sealed released. Copy fee: $1.00 per page. Certification fee: $1.00. Fee payee: County Clerk. Business checks accepted. Prepayment is required.

Crawford County

Circuit Court Box 375, English, IN 47118; 812-338-2565; Fax: 812-338-2507. Hours: 8AM-4PM M,F; 8AM-6PM T-Th (EST). *Felony, Misdemeanor, Civil, Eviction, Small Claims, Probate.*

Civil Records: Access: In person only. Visitors must perform in person searches for themselves. No search fee. Required to search: name, years to search. Civil cases indexed by defendant, plaintiff. Civil records on index from 1900s.

Criminal Records: Access: Fax, mail, in person. Only the court performs in person searches; visitors may not. Search fee: $5.00 per name. Required to search: name, years to search, DOB, SSN, signed release. Criminal records on index from 1900s.

General Information: No juvenile, mental, adoption or sealed released. SASE required. Turnaround time 1 week. Fax notes: No fee to fax results. Copy fee: $1.00 per page. Fee is for criminal division only. Certification fee: $2.00. Fee payee: County Clerk. Business checks accepted. Prepayment is required.

Daviess County

Circuit & Superior Court PO Box 739, Washington, IN 47501; 812-254-8664; Fax: 812-254-8698. Hours: 8AM-4PM (EST). *Felony, Misdemeanor, Civil, Eviction, Small Claims, Probate.*

Civil Records: Access: Mail, in person. Both court and visitors may perform in person searches. No search fee. Required to search: name, years to search. Civil cases indexed by defendant, plaintiff. Civil records on index from 1900s; recent on computer.

Criminal Records: Access: Mail, in person. Both court and visitors may perform in person searches. No search fee. Required to search: name, years to search. Criminal records on index from 1900s; recent on computer.

General Information: Public access terminal is available. No juvenile, mental, adoption or sealed records released. SASE required. Turnaround time varies. Copy fee: $1.00 per page. Certification fee: $1.00. Fee payee: Daviess County Clerk. Business checks accepted. Prepayment is required.

Dearborn County

Circuit & Superior Court Courthouse, 215 W High St, Lawrenceburg, IN 47025; 812-537-8867; Fax: 812-537-4295. 8:30AM-4:30PM (EST). *Felony, Misdemeanor, Civil, Eviction, Small Claims, Probate.*

www.dearborncounty.org/datafiles/judges.html

Civil Records: Access: In person only. Visitors must perform in person searches for themselves. No search fee. Required to search: name, years to search. Civil

cases indexed by defendant, plaintiff. Civil records on computer from 1992, on index from 1970s.

Criminal Records: Access: In person only. Visitors must perform in person searches for themselves. No search fee. Required to search: name, years to search, DOB; also helpful: SSN. Criminal records on computer from 1992, on index from 1970s, archived to 1930.

General Information: Public access terminal is available. No juvenile, mental, adoption or sealed records released. Copy fee: $1.00 per page. Certification fee: $1.00. Fee payee: Circuit Court Clerk. Only cashiers checks and money orders accepted. Prepayment is required.

Decatur County

Circuit & Superior Court 150 Courthouse Square, #244, Greensburg, IN 47240; 812-663-8223/8642; Fax: 812-663-8642. Hours: 8AM-4PM, 8AM-5PM F (EST). *Felony, Misdemeanor, Civil, Eviction, Small Claims, Probate.*

www.decaturcounty.in.gov

Civil Records: Access: Phone, mail, in person. Visitors must perform in person searches for themselves. No search fee. Required to search: name, years to search. Civil cases indexed by defendant, plaintiff. Civil records on index from 1823; on computer back to 1998.

Criminal Records: Access: Mail, in person. Visitors must perform in person searches for themselves. No search fee. Required to search: name, years to search, DOB; also helpful: SSN. Criminal records on index from 1823; on computer back to 1998.

General Information: Public access terminal is available. No juvenile, mental, adoption or sealed released. Turnaround time 2-7 days. Copy fee: $1.00 per page. Certification fee: $1.00. Fee payee: Decatur County Clerk. Personal checks accepted. Prepayment is required.

DeKalb County

Circuit & Superior Court PO Box 230, Auburn, IN 46706; 260-925-0912; Fax: 219-925-5126. Hours: 8:30AM-4:30PM (EST). *Felony, Misdemeanor, Civil, Eviction, Small Claims, Probate.*

Civil Records: Access: In person only. Visitors must perform in person searches for themselves. No search fee. Required to search: name, years to search. Civil cases indexed by defendant, plaintiff. Civil records on computer back to 1987, on index from 1913.

Criminal Records: Access: In person only. Visitors must perform in person searches for themselves. No search fee. Required to search: name, years to search, DOB. Criminal records on computer back to 1987, on index from 1913.

General Information: Public access terminal is available. No juvenile, mental, adoption or sealed released. Fax notes: Fee to fax results is $1.00 per document plus $1.00 per page. Copy fee: $1.00 per page. Certification fee: $1.00. Fee payee: Court Clerk. Only cashiers checks and money orders accepted. Prepayment is required.

Delaware County

Circuit Court Box 1089, Muncie, IN 47308; 765-747-7726; Fax: 765-747-7768. Hours: 8:30AM-4:30PM (EST). *Felony, Misdemeanor, Civil, Small Claims, Probate.*

www.dcclerk.org

Civil Records: Access: Fax, mail, in person. Both court and visitors may perform in person searches. No search fee. Required to search: name, years to search. Civil cases indexed by defendant, plaintiff. Civil records on computer from 1989, on microfiche, archived and on index from 1800.

Criminal Records: Access: In person, online. Visitors must perform in person searches for themselves. No search fee. Required to search: name, years to search, DOB, SSN. Criminal records on computer from 1989, on microfiche, archived and on index from 1800. Online access to criminal records from 1850 to 1950 only is available free at www.munpl.org/Main_Pages/documents.htm the Muncie Public Library web site.

General Information: Public access terminal is available. No juvenile, mental, adoption or sealed released. Turnaround time 1-2 days. Fax notes: Fee to fax results is $2.00 per page. Copy fee: $.10 per page. Certification fee: $1.00. Fee payee: Court Clerk. Business checks accepted. Prepayment is required.

Dubois County

Circuit & Superior Court 1 Courthouse Square, Jasper, IN 47546; 812-481-7070/7035/7020; Fax: 812-481-7030. Hours: 8AM-4PM (EST). *Felony, Misdemeanor, Civil, Eviction, Small Claims, Probate.*

Civil Records: Access: In person only. Visitors must perform in person searches for themselves. No search fee. Required to search: name; also helpful: years to search. Civil cases indexed by defendant, plaintiff. Civil records on computer from 8\93, on index books from 1930.

Criminal Records: Access: In person only. Visitors must perform in person searches for themselves. No search fee. Required to search: name; also helpful: years to search. Criminal records on computer from 8\93, on index books from 1930.

General Information: Public access terminal is available. No juvenile, mental, adoption or sealed records released. Copy fee: $.25 per page. Certification fee: $1.00. Fee payee: Court Clerk. Personal checks accepted. Prepayment is required.

Elkhart County

Elkhart Superior Courts 1, 2, 5, 6 315 S Second St, Elkhart, IN 46516; 574-523-2233/2305/2007; Fax: 574-523-2323. Hours: 8AM-4PM M-Th, 8AM-5PM F (EST). *Felony, Misdemeanor, Civil, Eviction, Small Claims, Probate.*

Civil Records: Access: In person only. Visitors must perform in person searches for themselves. No search fee. Required to search: name, years to search. Civil cases indexed by defendant, plaintiff. Civil records archived from 1830; on computer since 1996. Some records on index books.

Criminal Records: Access: In person only. Visitors must perform in person searches for themselves. No search fee. Required to search: name, years to search, DOB; also helpful: SSN. Criminal records archived from 1830; on computer since 1996. Some records on index books.

General Information: Public access terminal is available. No juvenile, mental, adoption or sealed records released. Certification fee: $2.00. Fee payee: Court Clerk. Personal checks not accepted. Prepayment is required.

Goshen Circuit & Superior Courts 3, 4 Courthouse, 101 N. Main St, Goshen, IN 46526; 574-535-6431; Fax: 574-535-6471. Hours: 8AM-4PM M-Th, 8AM-5PM F (EST). *Felony, Misdemeanor, Civil, Eviction, Small Claims, Probate.*

Note: Includes Circuit Court (Rm 204) and Superior Court 3 (Rm 205) and 4 (Rm 105).

Civil Records: Access: In person only. Visitors must perform in person searches for themselves. No search fee. Required to search: name, years to search. Civil cases indexed by defendant, plaintiff. Civil records archived from 1830; on computer since 1996. Some records on index books.

Criminal Records: Access: In person only. Visitors must perform in person searches for themselves. No search fee. Required to search: name, years to search,

DOB; also helpful: SSN. Criminal records archived from 1830; on computer since 1996. Some records on index books.

General Information: Public access terminal is available. No juvenile, mental, adoption or sealed records released. Certification fee: $1.00. Fee payee: Court Clerk. Personal checks accepted. Prepayment is required.

Fayette County

Circuit & Superior Court PO Box 607, Connersville, IN 47331-0607; 765-825-1813. Hours: 8:30AM-4PM (5PM on Wed) (EST). *Felony, Misdemeanor, Civil, Eviction, Small Claims, Probate.*

http://courthouse.co.fayette.in.us

Civil Records: Access: In person only. Visitors must perform in person searches for themselves. No search fee. Required to search: name, years to search. Civil cases indexed by defendant, plaintiff. Civil records on computer from 1988 (Circuit), 1992 (Superior).

Criminal Records: Access: In person only. Visitors must perform in person searches for themselves. No search fee. Required to search: name, years to search. Criminal records on computer from 1988 (Circuit), 1992 (Superior).

General Information: Public access terminal is available. No juvenile, mental, adoption or sealed released. Copy fee: $1.00 per page. Certification fee: $1.00. Fee payee: Fayette County Clerk. Only cashiers checks and money orders accepted. Prepayment is required.

Floyd County

Circuit, Superior & County Court Box 1056, City County Bldg, New Albany, IN 47150; 812-948-5414; Fax: 812-948-4711. Hours: 8AM-4PM (EST). *Felony, Misdemeanor, Civil, Eviction, Small Claims, Probate.*

Civil Records: Access: Mail, in person. Visitors must perform in person searches. No search fee. Required to search: name, years to search. Civil cases indexed by defendant, plaintiff. Civil records on computer from 1988, archived from 1978, on index from 1819.

Criminal Records: Access: Mail, in person. Visitors must perform in person searches for themselves. Search fee: $5.00. Required to search: name, years to search; also helpful: SSN. Criminal records on computer from 1988, archived from 1978, on index from 1819.

General Information: Public access terminal is available. No juvenile, mental, adoption or sealed released. SASE required. Turnaround time 1-2 days. Copy fee: $.25 per page. Certification fee: $1.00. Fee payee: Court Clerk. Personal checks accepted. Prepayment is required.

Fountain County

Circuit Court Box 183, Covington, IN 47932; 765-793-2192; Fax: 765-793-5002. Hours: 8AM-4PM (EST). *Felony, Misdemeanor, Civil, Eviction, Small Claims, Probate.*

Civil Records: Access: Mail, in person. Both court and visitors may perform in person searches. No search fee. Required to search: name, years to search. Civil cases indexed by defendant, plaintiff. Civil records on computer from 1995.

Criminal Records: Access: Mail, in person. Both court and visitors may perform in person searches. No search fee. Required to search: name, years to search. Criminal records on computer from 1995.

General Information: Public access terminal is available. No juvenile, mental, adoption or sealed released. SASE required. Turnaround time 1-2 days if records after 1989, 4-5 days if prior. Copy fee: $1.00 per page. Certification fee: $2.00. Fee payee: Court Clerk. Personal checks accepted. Prepayment is required.

Franklin County

Circuit Court 459 Main, Brookville, IN 47012; 765-647-5111; Fax: 765-647-3224. Hours: 8:30AM-4PM (EST). *Felony, Misdemeanor, Civil, Eviction, Small Claims, Probate.*

Civil Records: Access: In person only. Visitors must perform in person searches for themselves. No search fee. Required to search: name, years to search. Civil cases indexed by defendant, plaintiff. Civil records on index from 1978.

Criminal Records: Access: In person only. Visitors must perform in person searches for themselves. No search fee. Required to search: name, years to search. Criminal records on index from 1950.

General Information: No juvenile, mental, adoption or sealed released. Copy fee: $.50 per page. Certification fee: $1.00. Fee payee: Court Clerk. Personal checks accepted. Prepayment is required.

Fulton County

Circuit Court 815 Main St, PO Box 524, Rochester, IN 46975; 574-223-2911; Fax: 574-223-8304. Hours: 8AM-4PM M-TH, 8AM-5PM F (EST). *Felony, Misdemeanor, Civil, Eviction, Small Claims, Probate.*

Civil Records: Access: Mail, in person. Both court and visitors may perform in person searches. No search fee. Required to search: name, years to search. Civil cases indexed by defendant, plaintiff. Civil records on computer from 1989, on microfiche, archived and on index from 1845.

Criminal Records: Access: Mail, in person. Both court and visitors may perform in person searches. No search fee. Required to search: name, years to search. Criminal records on computer from 1989, on microfiche, archived and on index from 1845.

General Information: Public access terminal is available. No juvenile, mental, adoption or sealed released. SASE Required. Turnaround time 3-4 days. Copy fee: $1.00 per page. Certification fee: $1.00. Fee payee: Court Clerk. Business checks accepted. Prepayment is required.

Gibson County

Circuit & Superior Court Courthouse, Princeton, IN 47670; 812-386-6474; Fax: 812-386-5025. Hours: 8AM-4PM (CST). *Felony, Misdemeanor, Civil, Eviction, Small Claims, Probate.*

Civil Records: Access: In person only. Visitors must perform in person searches for themselves. No search fee. Required to search: name, years to search. Civil cases indexed by defendant, plaintiff. Civil records on computer from 1996, on microfiche from 1940, on index from 1813.

Criminal Records: Access: In person only. Visitors must perform in person searches for themselves. No search fee. Required to search: name, years to search. Criminal records on computer from 1996, on microfiche from 1940, on index from 1813.

General Information: Public access terminal is available. No juvenile, mental, adoption or sealed records released. Fax notes: Fax fee $4.00 per document. Copy fee: $1.00 per page. Certification fee: $1.00. Fee payee: Court Clerk. Prepayment is required.

Grant County

Circuit & Superior Court Courthouse 101 E 4th St, Marion, IN 46952; 765-668-8121; Fax: 765-668-6541. Hours: 8AM-4PM (EST). *Felony, Misdemeanor, Civil, Eviction, Small Claims, Probate.*

Civil Records: Access: In person only. Visitors must perform in person searches for themselves. No search fee. Required to search: name, years to search; also helpful: address. Civil cases indexed by defendant, plaintiff. Civil records on computer from 1989, on index from 1881.

Criminal Records: Access: In person only. Visitors must perform in person searches for themselves. No search fee. Required to search: name, years to search; also helpful: DOB, SSN. Criminal records on computer from 1989, on index from 1881.

General Information: Public access terminal is available. No juvenile, adoption, mental health or sealed records released. Copy fee: $.10 per page. Certification fee: $1.00. Fee payee: Court Clerk. Personal checks accepted. Prepayment is required.

Greene County

Circuit & Superior Court PO Box 229, Bloomfield, IN 47424; 812-384-8532; Fax: 812-384-8458. Hours: 8AM-4PM (EST). *Felony, Misdemeanor, Civil, Eviction, Small Claims, Probate.*

Civil Records: Access: In person only. Visitors must perform in person searches for themselves. No search fee. Required to search: name, years to search. Civil cases indexed by defendant, plaintiff. Civil records on computer back to 1989, all other records in books.

Criminal Records: Access: In person only. Visitors must perform in person searches for themselves. No search fee. Required to search: name, years to search. Criminal records on computer back to 1989; prior in books.

General Information: Public access terminal is available. No juvenile, mental, adoption or sealed released. Copy fee: $1.00 per page. Certification fee: $1.00. Fee payee: Court Clerk. Only cashiers checks and money orders accepted. Prepayment is required.

Hamilton County

Circuit & Superior Court One Hamilton County Square, #106, Noblesville, IN 46060-2233; 317-776-9629; Fax: 317-776-9727. Hours: 8AM-4:30PM (EST). *Felony, Misdemeanor, Civil, Eviction, Small Claims, Probate.*

www.co.hamilton.in.us

Civil Records: Access: In person only. Visitors must perform in person searches for themselves. No search fee. Required to search: name, years to search. Civil cases indexed by defendant, plaintiff. Civil records on computer from 1987, on index from 1840s.

Criminal Records: Access: In person only. Visitors must perform in person searches for themselves. No search fee. Required to search: name, years to search. Criminal records on computer from 1987, on index from 1840s.

General Information: Public access terminal is available. No juvenile, mental, adoption or sealed released. Copy fee: $.50 per page. Certification fee: $1.00 plus $.50 per page. Fee payee: Court Clerk. Business checks accepted. Prepayment is required.

Hancock County

Circuit & Superior Court 9 E Main St, Rm 201, Greenfield, IN 46140; 317-462-1109; Fax: 317-462-1163. Hours: 8AM-4PM (EST). *Felony, Misdemeanor, Civil, Eviction, Small Claims, Probate.*

Civil Records: Access: Phone, mail, in person. Both court and visitors may perform in person searches. No search fee. Required to search: name, years to search. Civil cases indexed by defendant, plaintiff. Civil records on computer from 07/88, on index and archived from 1883.

Criminal Records: Access: Phone, mail, in person. Both court and visitors may perform in person searches. No search fee. Required to search: name, years to search, DOB; also helpful: SSN. Criminal records on computer from 07/88, on index and archived to 1883.

General Information: Public access terminal is available. No juvenile, mental, adoption or sealed released. SASE required. Turnaround time 3-7 days, same day or next for phone requests. Copy fee: $1.00 per page for case history, otherwise $.25 per page.

Certification fee: $1.00. Fee payee: Court Clerk. Personal checks accepted. Prepayment is required.

Harrison County

Circuit Court 300 N Capitol, Corydon, IN 47112; 812-738-4289. Hours: 8AM-4:30PM (EST). *Civil, Eviction, Probate.*

Civil Records: Access: Mail, in person. Visitors must perform in person searches for themselves. No search fee. Required to search: name, years to search. Civil cases indexed by defendant, plaintiff. Civil records on index from 1900; on computer back to 1992. Court personnel will only do record searching when they have time, strongly urge using a retriever.

Criminal Records: Access: Mail, in person. Visitors must perform in person searches for themselves. No search fee. Required to search: name, years to search, DOB; also helpful-SSN. Criminal records on index from 1900; on computer back to 1992. Court personnel only do record searching when they have time, suggest to use a retriever.

General Information: No juvenile, mental, adoption or sealed released. Turnaround - as time permits. Fax notes: Fee to fax results is $.50 per page. Copy fee: $.50 per page. Certification fee: $1.00 per document plus $1.00 per page. Fee payee: Court Clerk. Only cashiers checks and money orders accepted. Prepayment is required.

Superior Court 1145 Gardner Ln 3126, Corydon, IN 47112; 812-738-8149; Fax: 812-738-2459. Hours: 8AM-4:30PM. *Felony, Misdemeanor, Small Claims.*

Civil Records: Access: In person only. Visitors must perform in person searches for themselves. No search fee. Required to search: name, years to search. Civil cases indexed by defendant, plaintiff. Civil records on index from 1900; on computer back to 1992.

Criminal Records: Access: In person only. Visitors must perform in person searches for themselves. No search fee. Required to search: name, years to search, DOB; also helpful-SSN. Criminal records on index from 1900; on computer back to 1992.

General Information: Public access terminal is available. No juvenile, mental, adoption or sealed released. Copy fee: $.05 per page. Certification fee: $1.00 per document + $1.00 per page. Fee payee: Court Clerk. Only cashiers checks and money orders accepted. Prepayment is required.

Hendricks County

Circuit & Superior Court PO Box 599, Danville, IN 46122; 317-745-9231; Fax: 317-745-9306. Hours: 8AM-4PM (EST). *Felony, Misdemeanor, Civil, Eviction, Small Claims, Probate.*

Civil Records: Access: In person only. Visitors must perform in person searches for themselves. No search fee. Required to search: name, years to search. Civil cases indexed by defendant, plaintiff. Civil records on computer since late 1992, on index from 1800s.

Criminal Records: Access: In person only. Visitors must perform in person searches for themselves. No search fee. Required to search: name, years to search; also helpful: DOB, SSN. Criminal records on computer since late 1992, on index from 1800s.

General Information: No juvenile, mental, adoption or sealed released. Copy fee: $1.00 per page. Certification fee: $1.00. Fee payee: Court Clerk. Business checks accepted. Prepayment is required.

Henry County

Circuit & Superior Court PO Box B, New Castle, IN 47362; 765-529-6401. Hours: 8AM-4PM (EST). *Felony, Misdemeanor, Civil, Eviction, Small Claims, Probate.*

Civil Records: Access: Mail, fax, in person. Both court and visitors may perform in person searches. No search

fee. Required to search: name, years to search. Civil cases indexed by plaintiff. Civil records on computer from 1991, archived from 1979, on index from 1976.

Criminal Records: Access: Mail, fax, in person. Both court and visitors may perform in person searches. No search fee. Required to search: name, years to search. Criminal records on computer from 1991, archived from 1979, on index from 1976.

General Information: Public access terminal is available. No juvenile, mental, adoption or sealed released. SASE Required. Turnaround time 1-2 days. Fax notes: Fax fee $1.00 per document. Copy fee: $1.00 per page. Certification fee: $1.00. Fee payee: County Clerk. Only cashiers checks and money orders accepted. Prepayment is required.

Howard County

Circuit & Superior Court PO Box 9004, Kokomo, IN 46904; 765-456-2204; Fax: 765-456-2267. Hours: 8AM-4PM (EST). *Felony, Misdemeanor, Civil, Eviction, Small Claims, Probate.*

Civil Records: Access: In person only. Visitors must perform in person searches for themselves. Search fee: None. Required to search: name, years to search. Civil cases indexed by defendant, plaintiff. Civil records on computer since 1992 on microfiche from early 1800s.

Criminal Records: Access: In person only. Visitors must perform in person searches for themselves. No search fee. Required to search: name, years to search; also helpful: DOB, SSN. Criminal records on computer since 1992, on microfiche from early 1800s.

General Information: Public access terminal is available. No juvenile, mental, adoption or sealed records released. Copy fee: $.20 per page for any page printed. Certification fee: $1.00. Fee payee: County Clerk. Only cashiers checks and money orders accepted.

Huntington County

Circuit & Superior Court PO Box 228, Huntington, IN 46750; 260-358-4817. Hours: 8AM-4:30PM (EST). *Felony, Misdemeanor, Civil, Eviction, Small Claims, Probate.*

Civil Records: Access: Phone, mail, in person. Both court and visitors may perform in person searches. No search fee. Required to search: name, years to search. Civil cases indexed by defendant, plaintiff. Civil records on computer from 1990, on microfiche from 1970, on index and archived from 1800s.

Criminal Records: Access: In person only. Visitors must perform in person searches for themselves. No search fee. Required to search: name, years to search. Criminal records on computer from 1990, on microfiche from 1970, on index and archived from 1800s.

General Information: Public access terminal is available. No juvenile, mental, adoption or sealed released. SASE not required. Turnaround time 1-2 days. Copy fee: $1.00 per page. Certification fee: $1.00. Fee payee: County Clerk. Personal checks not accepted. Prepayment is required.

Jackson County

Circuit Court PO Box 318, Brownstown, IN 47220; 812-358-6117; Fax: 812-358-6187. Hours: 8AM-4:30PM (EST). *Felony, Misdemeanor, Civil, Eviction, Small Claims, Probate.*

Note: Will not perform searches for private companies.

Civil Records: Access: Fax, mail, in person. Both court and visitors may perform in person searches. Search fee: $5.00 per name. Required to search: name, years to search. Civil cases indexed by defendant, plaintiff. Civil records on computer from 1989, on index from 1800s.

Criminal Records: Access: In person only. Visitors must perform in person searches for themselves. No search fee. Required to search: name, years to search;

also helpful: DOB, SSN. Criminal records on computer from 1989, on index from 1800s. Will recommend local document retrievers to do searches for you.

General Information: Public access terminal is available. No juvenile, mental, adoption or sealed released. SASE required. Fax notes: $5.00 per document; no fee to toll-free number. Copy fee: $1.00 per page. Certification fee: $2.00. Fee payee: Jackson County Clerk. Personal checks accepted.

Superior Court PO Box 788, Seymour, IN 47274; 812-522-9676; Fax: 812-523-6065. Hours: 8AM-4:30PM (EST). *Felony, Misdemeanor, Civil, Eviction, Small Claims.*

Civil Records: Access: Fax, mail, in person. Both court and visitors may perform in person searches. No search fee. Required to search: name, years to search. Civil cases indexed by defendant, plaintiff. Civil records on computer from 1989, on index from 1800s.

Criminal Records: Access: Fax, mail, in person. Both court and visitors may perform in person searches. No search fee. Required to search: name, years to search; also helpful: DOB, SSN. Criminal records on computer from 1989, on index from 1800s.

General Information: No juvenile, mental, adoption or sealed released. SASE required. Turnaround time 2-3 days. Fax notes: $5.00 per document; no fee to toll-free number. Copy fee: $1.00 per page. Certification fee: $2.00. Fee payee: Jackson County Clerk. Personal checks accepted.

Jasper County

Circuit Court 115 W Washington, Rensselaer, IN 47978; 219-866-4941. Hours: 8AM-4PM (CST). *Felony, Misdemeanor, Civil, Eviction, Small Claims, Probate.*

Note: This court also handles juvenile, paternity and adoption.

Civil Records: Access: Mail, in person. Both court and visitors may perform in person searches. No search fee. Required to search: name, years to search. Civil cases indexed by defendant, plaintiff. County records on computer from 1976, circuit from 1989. Some records on index from 1900s.

Criminal Records: Access: Mail, in person. Both court and visitors may perform in person searches. No search fee. Required to search: name, years to search; also helpful: DOB, SSN. County records on computer from 1976, circuit from 1989. Some records on index from 1900s.

General Information: Public access terminal is available. No juvenile, mental, adoption or sealed released. SASE required. Turnaround time 1 day. Copy fee: $1.00 per page. Certification fee: $2.00. Fee payee: Jasper County Clerk. Business checks accepted. Prepayment is required.

Superior Court I 115 W Washington St, Rensselaer, IN 47978; 219-866-4922. Hours: 8AM-4PM (CST). *Felony, Misdemeanor, Civil, Probate.*

Civil Records: Access: Mail, in person. Both court and visitors may perform in person searches. No search fee. Required to search: name, years to search. Civil cases indexed by defendant, plaintiff. County records on computer from 1976, circuit from 1989. Some records on index from 1800s.

Criminal Records: Access: Mail, in person. Both court and visitors may perform in person searches. No search fee. Required to search: name, years to search. County records on computer from 1976, circuit from 1989. Some records on index from 1800s.

General Information: Public access terminal is available. No juvenile, mental, adoption or sealed released. SASE required. Turnaround time 1 day to 1 week. Copy fee: $.50 per page. Non-case related copies are $.10 per page. Certification fee: $1.00. Per page. Fee

payee: County Clerk. Only cashiers checks and money orders accepted. Prepayment is required.

Jay County

Circuit & Superior Court Courthouse, Portland, IN 47371; 260-726-4951. Hours: 8:30AM-4:30PM (EST). *Felony, Misdemeanor, Civil, Eviction, Small Claims, Probate.*

Civil Records: Access: Mail, fax, in person. Both court and visitors may perform in person searches. No search fee. Required to search: name, years to search; also helpful: address. Civil cases indexed by defendant, plaintiff. Civil records on computer from 8\94, prior on microfiche from 1979, on index books from 1900.

Criminal Records: Access: Mail, fax, in person. Both court and visitors may perform in person searches. No search fee. Required to search: name, years to search, DOB; also helpful: SSN, address. Criminal records on computer from 8\94, prior on microfiche from 1979, on index books from 1900.

General Information: Public access terminal is available. No juvenile, mental, adoption or sealed records released. SASE required. Turnaround time 1-2 days. Fax notes: Will not fax results. Copy fee: $1.00 per page. Certification fee: $1.00 per page. Fee payee: Court Clerk. Only cashiers checks and money orders accepted. Prepayment is required.

Jefferson County

Circuit & Superior Court Courthouse 300E Main St, Madison, IN 47250; 812-265-8923; Fax: 812-265-8950. Hours: 8AM-4PM (EST). *Felony, Misdemeanor, Civil, Eviction, Small Claims, Probate.*

Civil Records: Access: In person only. Visitors must perform in person searches for themselves. No search fee. Required to search: name, years to search. Civil cases indexed by defendant, plaintiff. Civil records on index from 1975, computerized since 1995.

Criminal Records: Access: In person only. Visitors must perform in person searches for themselves. No search fee. Required to search: Name, years to search, address, DOB, SSN, signed release. Criminal records on index from 1975, computerized since 1995.

General Information: Public access terminal is available. No juvenile, mental, adoption or sealed released. Fax notes: Fax fee $1.00 per page. Copy fee: $1.00 per page. Certification fee: $1.00. Fee payee: County Clerk. Only cashiers checks and money orders accepted. Prepayment is required.

Jennings County

Circuit Court Courthouse, PO Box 385, Vernon, IN 47282; 812-356-3070. Hours: 8AM-4PM (EST). *Felony, Misdemeanor, Civil, Eviction, Small Claims, Probate.*

Civil Records: Access: In person. Visitors must perform in person searches. No search fee. Required to search: name, years to search. Civil cases indexed by defendant, plaintiff. Civil records on index from 1930; computerized since 2000.

Criminal Records: Access: In person. Visitors must perform in person searches. No search fee. Required to search: name, years to search, DOB; also helpful: SSN. Criminal records on index from 1930; computerized since 2000.

General Information: Public access terminal is available. No juvenile, mental, adoption or sealed released. Copy fee: $.25 per page. Certification fee: $1.00. Fee payee: County Clerk. Personal checks accepted. Prepayment is required.

Johnson County

Circuit & Superior Court Courthouse, PO Box 368, Franklin, IN 46131; 317-736-3708; Fax: 317-736-3749. Hours: 8AM-4:30PM (EST). *Felony, Misdemeanor, Civil, Eviction, Small Claims, Probate.*

Civil Records: Access: Phone, fax, mail, in person. Both court and visitors may perform in person searches. No search fee. Required to search: name, years to search. Civil cases indexed by defendant, plaintiff. Civil records on computer back 10 years.

Criminal Records: Access: Phone, fax, mail, in person. Both court and visitors may perform in person searches. No search fee. Required to search: name, years to search; also helpful: DOB, SSN. Criminal records on computer back 10 years.

General Information: Public access terminal is available. No juvenile, mental, adoption or sealed released. Turnaround time 1-2 days. Fax notes: $.50 per page. Copy fee: $1.00 per page. Certification fee: $1.00. Fee payee: County Clerk. Business checks accepted. Prepayment is required.

Knox County

Circuit & Superior Court 101 N 7th St, Vincennes, IN 47591; 812-885-2521. Hours: 8AM-4PM (EST). *Felony, Misdemeanor, Civil, Eviction, Small Claims, Probate.*

Civil Records: Access: Mail, in person. Visitors must perform in person searches for themselves. No search fee. Required to search: name, years to search. Civil cases indexed by defendant, plaintiff. Civil records on index books from 1800s.

Criminal Records: Access: Mail, in person. Visitors must perform in person searches for themselves. No search fee. Required to search: name, years to search. Criminal records on index books from 1800s.

General Information: No juvenile, mental, adoption or sealed released. Turnaround time 1 week. Copy fee: $1.00 per page. Certification fee: $1.00. Fee payee: Knox County Clerk. Personal checks accepted.

Kosciusko County

Circuit & Superior Court 121 N Lake, Warsaw, IN 46580; 574-372-2331. Hours: 8AM-4PM (EST). *Felony, Misdemeanor, Civil, Eviction, Small Claims, Probate.*

www.indico.net/counties/KOSCIUSKO/GOVERNME NT/clerk.html

Civil Records: Access: Mail, in person. Both court and visitors may perform in person searches. No search fee. Required to search: name, years to search. Civil cases indexed by defendant, plaintiff. Civil records on computer from 10/1/93, general index from 1908.

Criminal Records: Access: Mail, in person. Both court and visitors may perform in person searches. No search fee. Required to search: name, years to search. Criminal records on computer from 10/1/93, general index from 1908.

General Information: Public access terminal is available. No juvenile, mental, adoption or sealed released. SASE required. Turnaround time 1-3 weeks. Copy fee: $1.00 per page. Certification fee: $1.00. Fee payee: County Clerk. Personal checks accepted. Prepayment is required.

La Porte County

Circuit & Superior Court 813 Lincolnway, La Porte, IN 46350; 219-326-6808; Fax: 219-326-6626. Hours: 8:00AM-4PM (CST). *Felony, Misdemeanor, Civil, Eviction, Probate.*

Civil Records: Access: In person only. Visitors must perform in person searches for themselves. No search fee. Required to search: name, years to search. Civil cases indexed by defendant, plaintiff. Civil records on microfiche and index from 1900.

Criminal Records: Access: In person only. Visitors must perform in person searches for themselves. No search fee. Required to search: name, years to search. Criminal records on microfiche and index from 1900.

General Information: Public access terminal is available. No juvenile, mental, adoption or sealed released. Copy fee: $1.00 per page. Certification fee: $1.00 per page. Fee payee: Court Clerk. Business checks accepted. Will bill dissolutions.

LaGrange County

Circuit & Superior Court 105 N Detroit St, Courthouse, LaGrange, IN 46761; 260-463-3442. Hours: 8AM-4PM M-TH, 8AM-5PM F (EST). *Felony, Misdemeanor, Civil, Eviction, Small Claims, Probate.*

Civil Records: Access: Phone, mail, in person. Vistors must perform in person searches. No search fee. Required to search: name, years to search. Civil cases indexed by defendant, plaintiff. Civil records on computer from 1990, on books from 1900.

Criminal Records: Access: Phone, mail, in person. Visitors must perform in person searches. No search fee. Required to search: name, years to search; also helpful: DOB, SSN. Criminal records on computer from 1990, on books from 1900.

General Information: Public access terminal is available. No juvenile, mental, adoption or sealed released. SASE requested. Turnaround time 1-2 days from 1/1/90. 30 days if prior to 1/1/90. Copy fee: $1.00 per page. Certification fee: $1.00. Fee payee: LaGrange County Clerk. Personal checks accepted. Prepayment is required.

Lake County

Circuit & Superior Court 2293 N Main St, Courthouse, Crown Point, IN 46307; 219-755-3000; Fax: 219-755-3781. Hours: 8:30AM-4:20PM (CST). *Felony, Misdemeanor, Civil, Eviction, Small Claims, Probate.*

Civil Records: Access: Mail, fax, n person. Both court and visitors may perform in person searches. No search fee. Required to search: name, years to search; also helpful: address. Civil cases indexed by defendant, plaintiff. Civil records go back to 1920s; on microfiche back to 1983; on computer back to 1990s. Fax requests must be on letterhead.

Criminal Records: Access: Mail, fax, in person. Only the court performs in person searches; visitors may not. No search fee. Required to search: name, years to search, DOB, SSN; also helpful: address. Criminal records go back to 1900s; on microfiche back to 1983; on computer back to 1990s. Fax requests must be on letterhead. Search requests for background checks are forwarded to the County Bureau of Identification, 219-775-3316.

General Information: Public access terminal is available. No juvenile, mental, adoption or sealed released. Turnaround time 1 week. Copy fee: $1.00 per page. Certification fee: $2.00. Fee payee: Lake County Clerk. Business checks accepted. Prepayment required.

Lawrence County

Circuit, Superior & County Court 31 Courthouse, 916 15th St RM31, Bedford, IN 47421; 812-275-7543; Fax: 812-277-2024. Hours: 8:30AM-4:30PM (EST). *Felony, Misdemeanor, Civil, Eviction, Small Claims, Probate.*

Note: Superior Court I is located at 1410 I Street, 812-275-3124. Superior Court II is located at 1420 I Street, 812-275-4161. All small claims are filed in Superior II.

Civil Records: Access: In person only. Visitors must perform in person searches for themselves. No search fee. Required to search: name, years to search. Civil cases indexed by plaintiff. Civil records on computer from 1987, on index from 1817.

Criminal Records: Access: In person only. Visitors must perform in person searches for themselves. No search fee. Required to search: name, years to search; also helpful: SSN. Criminal records on computer from 1987, on index from 1817.

General Information: No juvenile, mental, adoption or sealed released. Copy fee: $1.00 per page. Certification fee: $1.00. Fee payee: Lawrence County Clerk. Only cashiers checks and money orders accepted. Prepayment is required.

Madison County

Circuit, Superior & County Court PO Box 1277, Anderson, IN 46015-1277; 765-641-9443; Fax: 765-640-4203. Hours: 8AM-4PM (EST). *Felony, Misdemeanor, Civil, Eviction, Small Claims, Probate.*

http://madisoncty.com/courts/index.html

Civil Records: Access: In person only. Visitors must perform in person searches for themselves. No search fee. Required to search: name, years to search. Civil cases indexed by defendant. Civil records on microfiche and archived from 1950, on index from 1900.

Criminal Records: Access: In person only. Visitors must perform in person searches for themselves. No search fee. Required to search: name, years to search, signed release. Criminal records on microfiche and archived from 1950, on index from 1900.

General Information: Public access terminal is available. No juvenile, mental, adoption or sealed released. Copy fee: $1.00 per page. Certification fee: $1.00. Fee payee: County Clerk. Business checks accepted. Prepayment is required.

Marion County

Circuit & Superior Court 200 E Washington St, Indianapolis, IN 46204; 317-327-4740; Civil phone: 317-327-4733; Criminal phone: 317-327-4733. Hours: 8AM-4:30PM (EST). *Felony, Misdemeanor, Civil, Probate.*

www.indygov.org/clerk

Note: The Municipal Court of Marion County, once separate, is now part of Superior Court. All records are merged with the Superior Court.

Civil Records: Access: Mail, online, in person. Both court and visitors may perform in person searches. No search fee. Required to search: name, years to search. Civil cases indexed by defendant, plaintiff. Civil records on computer back to 1981, on microfiche, archived and on index from 1912. Small claims records are held by the township in which they were filed; the phone numbers are listed below. Access to the remote online system is available via the internet at www.civicnet.net. $50 setup fee. No charge for civil court name searches, but fees range from $2.00 to $5.00 for civil case summaries, civil justice name searches, etc.

Criminal Records: Access: Mail, online, in person. Both court and visitors may perform in person searches. Search fee: $7.00 per name. Fee is $3.00 for in person request. Required to search: name, years to search, DOB; also helpful: SSN. Criminal records on computer back to 1981, on microfiche, archived and on index from 1912. Small claims records are held by the township in which they were filed; the phone numbers are listed below. Online access to criminal records is at www.civicnet.net. There is a $4.50 search fee, credit card required. Criminal records go back to 1988.

General Information: Public access terminal is available. No juvenile, mental, adoption or sealed released. SASE not required. Turnaround time 1-2 days. Fax notes: Will not fax results. Copy fee: $1.00 per page. Certification fee: $1.00. Fee payee: County Clerk. Personal checks accepted.

Marshall County

Circuit & Superior Court 1 & 2 211 W Madison St, Plymouth, IN 46563; 574-936-8922; Fax: 574-936-8893. Hours: 8AM-4PM (EST). *Felony, Misdemeanor, Civil, Eviction, Small Claims, Probate.*

Civil Records: Access: In person only. Visitors must perform in person searches for themselves. No search fee. Required to search: name, years to search; also helpful: address. Civil cases indexed by defendant, plaintiff. Civil records on computer from 1989, on microfiche, archived and on index from 1835.

Criminal Records: Access: Mail, in person. Both court and visitors may perform in person searches. Search fee: $10.00 per name. Required to search: name, years to search, signed release; also helpful: address, DOB, SSN. Criminal records on computer from 1989, on microfiche, archived and on index from 1835.

General Information: Public access terminal is available. No juvenile, mental, adoption or sealed released. SASE required. Turnaround time within 1 week. Fax notes: Fee to fax results is $1.00 per page; certified 1st page is $2.00. Copy fee: $1.00 per page. Certification fee: $2.00. Fee payee: County Clerk. Business checks accepted. Prepayment is required.

Martin County

Circuit Court PO Box 120 (111 Main St), Shoals, IN 47581; 812-247-3651; Fax: 812-247-2791. Hours: 8AM-4PM (EST). *Felony, Misdemeanor, Civil, Eviction, Small Claims, Probate.*

Civil Records: Access: Phone, mail, fax, in person. Both court and visitors may perform in person searches. No search fee. Required to search: name, years to search. Civil cases indexed by defendant, plaintiff. Civil records on index books.

Criminal Records: Access: Phone, mail, fax, in person. Both court and visitors may perform in person searches. No search fee. Required to search: name, years to search, DOB or SSN. Criminal records on index books.

General Information: No juvenile, mental, adoption, or sealed records released. Turnaround time 4 days. Copy fee: $1.00 per page. Certification fee: $2.00. Fee payee: County Clerk. Business checks accepted. Prepayment is required.

Miami County

Circuit & Superior Court PO Box 184, Peru, IN 46970; 765-472-3901; Fax: 765-472-1778. Hours: 8AM-4PM (EST). *Felony, Misdemeanor, Civil, Eviction, Small Claims, Probate.*

Civil Records: Access: Fax, mail, in person. Both court and visitors may perform in person searches. Search fee: $10.00 per name. Required to search: name, years to search. Civil cases indexed by defendant, plaintiff. Civil records on computer back to 4/1998, archived from 1900s. Some records on docket books by case number and alpha.

Criminal Records: Access: Fax, mail, in person. Both court and visitors may perform in person searches. Search fee: $10.00 per name. Required to search: name, years to search, DOB, SSN, signed release. Criminal records on computer back to 4/1998; archived from 1900s. Some records on docket books by case number and alpha.

General Information: Public access terminal is available. No juvenile, mental, adoption, or sealed released. Turnaround time 1-2 days. Fax notes: $1.00 per page. No fee for toll free or local calls. Copy fee: $1.00 per page. Certification fee: $1.00. Fee payee: Miami County Clerk. Personal checks accepted. Prepayment is required.

Monroe County

Circuit Court PO Box 547, Bloomington, IN 47402; 812-349-2614; Fax: 812-349-2610. Hours: 8AM-4PM (EST). *Felony, Misdemeanor, Civil, Eviction, Small Claims, Probate.*

www.co.monroe.in.us/courts.html

Civil Records: Access: Mail, fax, in person. Both court and visitors may perform in person searches. No search fee. Required to search: name, years to search. Civil cases indexed by defendant, plaintiff. Civil records on computer from 1993. Some records on docket books by case number and alpha. In the process of putting records on microfiche.
Criminal Records: Access: Mail, fax, in person. Both court and visitors may perform in person searches. No search fee. Required to search: name, years to search, DOB; also helpful: SSN. Criminal records on computer from 1993. Some records on docket books by case number and alpha. In the process of putting records on microfiche.
General Information: Public access terminal is available. No juvenile, mental, adoption or sealed released. Turnaround time 48 hours. Fax notes: Fee to fax results is $1.00 per page. Copy fee: $1.00 per page. Certification fee: $1.00. Fee payee: Monroe County Clerk. Personal checks accepted. Prepayment required.

Montgomery County

Circuit, Superior & County Court PO Box 768, Crawfordsville, IN 47933; 765-364-6430; Fax: 765-364-6355. Hours: 8:30AM-4:30PM (EST). *Felony, Misdemeanor, Civil, Eviction, Small Claims, Probate.*

Civil Records: Access: Phone, fax, mail, in person. Both court and visitors may perform in person searches. No search fee. Required to search: name, years to search. Civil cases indexed by defendant, plaintiff. Civil records on computer from 1990, some on microfiche and docket books, and archived from 1800s. Indicate type(s) of cases sought in search request.
Criminal Records: Access: Mail, fax, in person. Both court and visitors may perform in person searches. No search fee. Required to search: name, years to search, DOB; also helpful: SSN. Criminal records on computer from 1990, some on microfiche and docket books, and archived from 1800s.
General Information: No juvenile, mental, adoption or sealed released. SASE required. Turnaround time 1 week. Fax notes: $1.00 per page. Additional fax fee $3.25. Copy fee: $1.00 per page. Certification fee: $2.00. Fee payee: Montgomery County Clerk. Prepayment is required.

Morgan County

Circuit & Superior Court PO Box 1556, Martinsville, IN 46151; 765-342-1025; Fax: 765-342-1111. Hours: 8AM-4PM (EST). *Felony, Misdemeanor, Civil, Eviction, Small Claims, Probate.*

Civil Records: Access: In person only. Visitors must perform in person searches for themselves. No search fee. Required to search: name, years to search. Civil cases indexed by defendant, plaintiff. Civil records archived from 1970; on computer back to 1993. Some records on index cards. In some instances, limited information is given over the phone if the docket number is known.
Criminal Records: Access: In person only. Visitors must perform in person searches for themselves. No search fee. Required to search: name, years to search, DOB; also helpful: SSN, signed release. Criminal records archived from 1970; on microfilm 1992-95, on computer back to 1993.
General Information: Public access terminal is available. No juvenile, mental, adoption or sealed released. Fax notes: Will not fax results. Copy fee: $.05

per page. Certification fee: $1.00 per page. Fee payee: Morgan County Clerk. Personal checks accepted. Prepayment is required.

Newton County

Circuit & Superior Court PO Box 49, Kentland, IN 47951; 219-474-6081. Hours: 8AM-4PM (CST). *Felony, Misdemeanor, Civil, Eviction, Small Claims, Probate.*

Civil Records: Access: Mail, in person. Both court and visitors may perform in person searches. Search fee: $3.00 per name. Required to search: name, years to search. Civil cases indexed by defendant, plaintiff. Civil records on index from 1950, partial on microfiche; on computer back to 1996.
Criminal Records: Access: Mail, in person. Both court and visitors may perform in person searches. Search fee: $3.00 per name. Required to search: name, years to search, DOB, signed release; also helpful: SSN. Criminal records on index from 1950, partial on microfiche; on computer back to 1996.
General Information: Public access terminal is available. No juvenile, mental, adoption or sealed records released. SASE required. Turnaround time 1-2 weeks. Copy fee: $1.00 per page. Certification fee: $2.00. Fee payee: Clerk of Newton Circuit Court. Business checks accepted. Prepayment is required.

Noble County

Circuit, Superior I & Superior II Court 101 N Orange St, Albion, IN 46701; 260-636-2736; Fax: 260-636-4000. Hours: 8AM-4PM (EST). *Felony, Misdemeanor, Civil, Eviction, Small Claims, Probate.*

Civil Records: Access: Fax, mail, in person. Both court and visitors may perform in person searches. No search fee. Required to search: name, years to search. Civil cases indexed by defendant, plaintiff. Civil records on index cards and docket books to 1856; on comptuer back to 1992.
Criminal Records: Access: Fax, mail, in person. Both court and visitors may perform in person searches. No search fee. Required to search: name, years to search; also helpful: DOB, SSN. Criminal records on index cards and docket books to 1856; on comptuer back to 1992. Criminal record searches are 10-year only.
General Information: Public access terminal is available. No juvenile, mental, adoption or sealed released. SASE required. Turnaround time 1 week. Fax notes: Will fax results to toll-free numbers. Copy fee: $1.00 per page. Certification fee: $1.00. Fee payee: Noble County Clerk. No personal checks accepted. Prepayment is required.

Ohio County

Circuit & Superior Court PO Box 185, Rising Sun, IN 47040; 812-438-2610; Fax: 812-438-4590. Hours: 9AM-4PM M,T,Th,F 9AM-Noon S (EST). *Felony, Misdemeanor, Civil, Eviction, Small Claims, Probate.*

Civil Records: Access: Phone, fax, mail, in person. Both court and visitors may perform in person searches. No search fee. Required to search: name, years to search. Civil cases indexed by defendant, plaintiff. Civil records archived from 1844; on computer back to 8/1999.
Criminal Records: Access: In person only. Visitors must perform in person searches for themselves. No search fee. Required to search: name, years to search. Criminal records on computer back to 8/1999.
General Information: Public access terminal is available. No juvenile, mental, adoption or sealed released. Fax notes: Fee to fax results is $3.00 1st page, $1.00 each add'l paid in advance. Copy fee: $1.00 per page. Certification fee: $2.00. Fee payee: Ohio County Clerk. Personal checks accepted. Prepayment is required.

Orange County

Circuit & County Court Courthouse, Court St, Paoli, IN 47454; 812-723-2649. Hours: 8AM-4PM (EST). *Felony, Misdemeanor, Civil, Eviction, Small Claims, Probate.*

Note: The physical location of the County Court is 205 E Main Street. The County Court handles misdemeanor, eviction and small claims.

Civil Records: Access: Mail, fax, in person. Both court and visitors may perform in person searches. No search fee. Required to search: name, years to search. Civil cases indexed by defendant, plaintiff. Civil records archived from 1874. Some records on docket books.
Criminal Records: Access: Mail, fax, in person. Both court and visitors may perform in person searches. No search fee. Required to search: name, years to search. Criminal records archived from 1874. Some records on docket books.
General Information: No juvenile, mental, adoption or sealed released. SASE required. Turnaround time 2 weeks. Copy fee: $1.00 per page. Certification fee: $2.00. Fee payee: Orange Circuit Clerk. Only cashiers checks and money orders accepted.

Owen County

Circuit Court PO Box 146, Courthouse, Spencer, IN 47460; 812-829-5015; Fax: 812-829-5147. Hours: 8AM-4PM (EST). *Felony, Misdemeanor, Civil, Eviction, Small Claims, Probate.*

Civil Records: Access: Fax, in person. Visitors must perform in person searches for themselves. Search fee: No search fee. Required to search: name, years to search. Civil cases indexed by defendant, plaintiff. Civil records archived from 1800s. Some records on docket books.
Criminal Records: Access: Fax, in person. Visitors must perform in person searches for themselves. Search fee: No search fee. Required to search: name, years to search. Criminal records archived from 1800s. Some records on docket books.
General Information: No juvenile, mental, adoption or sealed records released. Fax notes: No fee to fax results. Copy fee: $1.00 per page. Certification fee: $2.00. Fee payee: Owen County Clerk. Business checks accepted. Prepayment is required.

Parke County

Circuit Court 116 W High St, Rm 204, Rockville, IN 47872; 765-569-5132. Hours: 8AM-4PM (EST). *Felony, Misdemeanor, Civil, Eviction, Small Claims, Probate.*

Civil Records: Access: in person only. Visitors must perform in person searches for themselves. No search fee. Required to search: name, years to search. Civil cases indexed by defendant, plaintiff. Civil records archived from 1880s. Some records on docket books.
Criminal Records: Access: In person only. Visitors must perform in person searches for themselves. No search fee. Required to search: name, years to search. Criminal records archived from 1880s. Some records on docket books.
General Information: No juvenile, mental, adoption or sealed released. Copy fee: $1.00 per page. Certification fee: $2.00. Fee payee: Parke County Clerk. Personal checks not accepted.

Perry County

Circuit Court 2219 Payne St, Courthouse, Tell City, IN 47586; 812-547-3741. Hours: 8AM-4PM (EST). *Felony, Misdemeanor, Civil, Eviction, Small Claims, Probate.*

Civil Records: Access: In person only. Both court and visitors may perform in person searches. No search fee. Required to search: name, years to search. Civil cases indexed by defendant, plaintiff. Civil records archived from 1900s. Some records on dockets.

Criminal Records: Access: In person only. Both court and visitors may perform in person searches. No search fee. Required to search: name, years to search. Criminal records archived from 1900s. Some records on dockets.

General Information: No juvenile, mental, adoption or sealed released. Copy fee: $.50 per page. Certification fee: $1.00. Fee payee: Perry County Clerk. Business checks accepted. Prepayment is required.

Pike County

Circuit Court 801 Main St. Courthouse, Petersburg, IN 47567-1298; 812-354-6025; Fax: 812-354-3552. Hours: 8AM-4PM (EST). *Felony, Misdemeanor, Civil, Eviction, Small Claims, Probate.*

Civil Records: Access: Mail, in person. Both court and visitors may perform in person searches. No search fee. Required to search: name, years to search. Civil cases indexed by defendant, plaintiff. Civil records archived from 1817. Some records on docket books and index file; on computer since.

Criminal Records: Access: Mail, in person. Both court and visitors may perform in person searches. No search fee. Required to search: name, years to search, DOB. Criminal records archived from 1817. Some records on docket books and index file; on computer since.

General Information: No juvenile, mental, adoption or sealed released. SASE required. Turnaround time 1-2 days. Copy fee: $1.00 per page. Certification fee: $2.00. Fee payee: Pike County Clerk. Only cashiers checks and money orders accepted. Prepayment is required.

Porter County

Circuit Court Records Division, Courthouse, 16 E Lincolnway RM 217, Valparaiso, IN 46383-5659; 219-465-3453; Fax: 219-465-3592. Hours: 8:30AM-4:30PM (CST). *Felony, Misdemeanor, Civil, Eviction, Small Claims, Probate.*

Civil Records: Access: Mail, in person. Both court and visitors may perform in person searches. No search fee. Required to search: name, years to search. Civil cases indexed by defendant, plaintiff. Civil records on computer index from 1990. Circuit Court records kept from 1844, Superior Court records from 1895. Probate records from Circuit Court kept from 1853, Superior Court from 1900.

Criminal Records: Access: Mail, in person. Both court and visitors may perform in person searches. No search fee. Required to search: name, years to search. Criminal records on computer index since 1990. Circuit Court criminal records kept from 1877, Superior Court from 1895.

General Information: Public access terminal is available. No juvenile, mental, adoption or sealed released. SASE required. Turnaround time 1-2 weeks. Copy fee: $1.00 per page. Certification fee: $1.00. Fee payee: Porter County Clerk. Only cashiers checks and money orders accepted. Prepayment is required.

Superior Court 3560 Willow Creek Dr, Portage, IN 46368; 219-759-2501. Hours: 8:30AM-4:30PM (CST). *Misdemeanor, Civil, Small Claims, Probate.*

Civil Records: Access: Mail, in person. Both court and visitors may perform in person searches. No search fee. Required to search: name, years to search. Civil cases indexed by defendant, plaintiff. Civil records on computer since 1991; prior records on manual index.

Criminal Records: Access: Mail, in person. Both court and visitors may perform in person searches. No search fee. Required to search: name, years to search; also helpful: DOB, SSN. Criminal records on computer since 1991; prior records on manual index.

General Information: Public access terminal is available. No juvenile, mental, adoption or sealed records released. Fax notes: Fee to fax results is $.79 per

page. Copy fee: $2.00 per page. Certification fee: $1.00. Fee payee: Porter County Clerk. Only cashiers checks and money orders accepted. Prepayment is required.

Posey County

Circuit & Superior Court PO Box 606, 300 Main St, Mount Vernon, IN 47620-0606; 812-838-1306; Fax: 812-838-1307. Hours: 8AM-4PM (CST). *Felony, Misdemeanor, Civil, Eviction, Small Claims, Probate.*

http://members.sigecom.net/pcc/

Civil Records: Access: In person only. Visitors must perform in person searches for themselves. No search fee. Required to search: name, years to search; also helpful: address. Civil cases indexed by defendant, plaintiff. Civil records on computer since 8/88, prior on docket books.

Criminal Records: Access: In person only. Visitors must perform in person searches for themselves. No search fee. Required to search: name, years to search; also helpful: DOB, SSN. Criminal records on computer since 8/88, prior on docket books.

General Information: Public access terminal is available. (Available in Superior Court.) No juvenile, mental, adoption or sealed released. Copy fee: $1.00 per page. Certification fee: $1.00. Fee payee: Posey County Clerk. Only cashiers checks and money orders accepted. Prepayment is required.

Pulaski County

Circuit & Superior Court 112 E Main, Room 230, Winamac, IN 46996; 574-946-3313; Fax: 574-946-4953. Hours: 8AM-4PM (EST). *Felony, Misdemeanor, Civil, Eviction, Small Claims, Probate.*

Civil Records: Access: In person only. Visitors must perform in person searches for themselves. No search fee. Required to search: name, years to search. Civil cases indexed by defendant. Civil records archived from 1850s. Some records on docket books. On computer back to 10/2000.

Criminal Records: Access: In person only. Visitors must perform in person searches for themselves. No search fee. Required to search: name, years to search; also helpful: SSN. Criminal records archived from 1850s. Some records on docket books. On computer back to 10/2000.

General Information: Public access terminal is available. No juvenile, mental, adoption or sealed records released. Fax notes: Will not fax results. Copy fee: $.50 per page. Certification fee: $2.00. Fee payee: Pulaski County Clerk. Only cashiers checks and money orders accepted. Prepayment is required.

Putnam County

Circuit & Superior Court PO Box 546, Greencastle, IN 46135; 765-653-2648. Hours: 8AM-4PM (EST). *Felony, Misdemeanor, Civil, Eviction, Small Claims, Probate.*

Civil Records: Access: Mail, in person. Visitors must perform in person searches for themselves. No search fee. Required to search: name, years to search. Civil cases indexed by defendant, plaintiff. Civil records on index books from 1991, archived from 1800s. Some records on docket books.

Criminal Records: Access: In person only. Visitors must perform in person searches for themselves. No search fee. Required to search: name, years to search; also helpful: DOB, SSN. Criminal records on index books from 1991, archived from 1800s. Some records on docket books.

General Information: Public access terminal is available. No juvenile, mental, adoption or sealed released. Turnaround time 1 week. Copy fee: $1.00 per page. Certification fee: $1.00. Fee payee: Putnam County Clerk. Business checks accepted. Prepayment is required.

Randolph County

Circuit & Superior Court PO Box 230 Courthouse, Winchester, IN 47394-0230; 765-584-7070 X231; Fax: 765-584-2958. Hours: 8AM-4PM (EST). *Felony, Misdemeanor, Civil, Eviction, Small Claims, Probate.*

Civil Records: Access: Fax, mail, in person. Visitors must perform in person searches for themselves. No search fee. Required to search: name, years to search. Civil cases indexed by defendant, plaintiff. Civil records archived from early 1800s, computerized from 1994. Records on docket books and microfiche.

Criminal Records: Access: Fax, mail, in person. Visitors must perform in person searches for themselves. No search fee. Required to search: name, years to search. Criminal records archived from early 1800s, computerized since 1994. Records on docket books and microfiche.

General Information: Public access terminal is available. No juvenile, mental, adoption or sealed released. SASE required. Turnaround time 3 days. Fax notes: $4.00 for first page, $.75 each add'l. Copy fee: $1.00 per page. Certification fee: $1.00. Fee payee: Randolph County Clerk. Only cashiers checks and money orders accepted. Prepayment is required.

Ripley County

Circuit Court PO BOX 177, Versailles, IN 47042; 812-689-6115. Hours: 8AM-4PM (EST). *Felony, Misdemeanor, Civil, Eviction, Small Claims, Probate.*

Civil Records: Access: Phone, mail, in person. Both court and visitors may perform in person searches. No search fee. Required to search: name, years to search. Civil cases indexed by defendant, plaintiff. Civil records on computer since 1993, archived from 1800s. Some records on docket books.

Criminal Records: Access: Mail, in person. Both court and visitors may perform in person searches. No search fee. Required to search: name, years to search, DOB, signed release; also helpful: SSN. Criminal records on computer since 1993, archived from 1800s. Some records on docket books.

General Information: Public access terminal is available. No juvenile, mental, adoption or sealed records released. Turnaround time 1 week. Copy fee: $1.00 per page. Certification fee: $1.00. Fee payee: Clerk of Ripley Circuit Court. Personal checks accepted. Prepayment is required.

Rush County

Circuit & Superior Court PO Box 429, Rushville, IN 46173; 765-932-2086; Fax: 765-932-2357. Hours: 8AM-4PM (EST). *Felony, Misdemeanor, Civil, Eviction, Small Claims, Probate.*

Note: This office will not conduct general searches, but will pull files if the specific case number is given.

Civil Records: Access: In person only. Visitors must perform in person searches for themselves. No search fee. Required to search: name, years to search. Civil cases indexed by defendant, plaintiff. Civil records archived from 1822. Some records on docket books.

Criminal Records: Access: In person only. Visitors must perform in person searches for themselves. No search fee. Required to search: name, years to search, DOB; also helpful: SSN, cause number. Criminal records archived from 1822. Some records on docket books. Court will only search the status of an open case, and you need to provide the case number of it.

General Information: No juvenile, mental, adoption or sealed records released. Copy fee: $1.00 per page. Certification fee: $1.00. Fee payee: Rush County Clerk. Business checks accepted. Prepayment is required.

Scott County

Circuit & Superior Court 1 E McClain Ave, #120, Scottsburg, IN 47170; 812-752-8420; Fax: 812-752-5459. Hours: 8:30AM-4:30PM (EST). *Felony, Misdemeanor, Civil, Eviction, Small Claims, Probate.*

Civil Records: Access: In person only. Visitors must perform in person searches for themselves. No search fee. Required to search: name, years to search; also helpful: address. Civil cases indexed by defendant, plaintiff. Civil records on computer from 2/90, on docket books from 1970.

Criminal Records: Access: In person only. Visitors must perform in person searches for themselves. No search fee. Required to search: name, years to search; also helpful: DOB, SSN. Criminal records on computer from 2/90, on docket books from 1970.

General Information: Public access terminal is available. No juvenile, mental, adoption or sealed released. Copy fee: $1.00 per page. Certification fee: $2.00. Fee payee: Scott County Clerk. Business checks accepted. Prepayment is required.

Shelby County

Circuit & Superior Court PO Box 198, Shelbyville, IN 46176; 317-392-6320. Hours: 8AM-4PM (EST). *Felony, Misdemeanor, Civil, Eviction, Small Claims, Probate.*

Civil Records: Access: In person only. Visitors must perform in person searches for themselves. No search fee. Required to search: name, years to search. Civil cases indexed by defendant, plaintiff. Civil records on computer since 07/95.

Criminal Records: Access: In person only. Visitors must perform in person searches for themselves. No search fee. Required to search: name, years to search. Criminal records on computer since 07/95.

General Information: Public access terminal is available. No juvenile, mental, adoption or sealed released. Copy fee: $1.00 per page. Certification fee: $1.00. Fee payee: Clerk of Court. Personal checks not accepted. Prepayment is required.

Spencer County

Circuit Court PO Box 12, Rockport, IN 47635; 812-649-6027; Fax: 812-649-6030. Hours: 8AM-4PM (CST). *Felony, Misdemeanor, Civil, Eviction, Small Claims, Probate.*

Civil Records: Access: In person only. Visitors must perform in person searches for themselves. No search fee. Required to search: name, years to search. Civil cases indexed by defendant, plaintiff. Civil records archived from early 1900s. Some records on docket books. Child support cases on computer. Starting 02/02 all new cases are computerized.

Criminal Records: Access: In person only. Visitors must perform in person searches for themselves. No search fee. Required to search: name, years to search. Criminal records archived from early 1900s. Some records on docket books. Starting 02/02 all new cases are computerized.

General Information: Public access terminal is available. No juvenile, mental, adoption or sealed released. Copy fee: $1.00 per page. Certification fee: $1.00. Fee payee: Spencer Circuit Court. Only cashiers checks and money orders accepted. Prepayment is required.

St. Joseph County

Circuit & Superior Court 101 South Main St, South Bend, IN 46601; 574-235-9635; Fax: 574-235-9838. Hours: 8AM-4:30PM (EST). *Felony, Misdemeanor, Civil, Eviction, Small Claims, Probate.*

Civil Records: Access: Mail, in person. Both court and visitors may perform in person searches. No search fee. Required to search: name, years to search. Civil cases indexed by defendant, plaintiff. Civil records on general index from 1962, computerized since 1979.

Criminal Records: Access: In person only. Visitors must perform in person searches for themselves. No search fee. Required to search: name, years to search; also helpful: address, DOB, SSN. Criminal records on general index from 1962, computerized since 1979.

General Information: Public access terminal is available. No juvenile, mental, adoption or sealed released. SASE required. Turnaround time 1-2 days. Copy fee: $1.00 per page. Certification fee: $1.00. Fee payee: St Joseph County Clerk. Business checks accepted.

Starke County

Circuit Court Courthouse, 53 E Washington St, Knox, IN 46534; 574-772-9128. Hours: 8:30AM-4PM (CST). *Felony, Misdemeanor, Civil, Eviction, Small Claims, Probate.*

Civil Records: Access: In person only. Both the court and visitors may perform in person searches. No search fee. Required to search: name, years to search. Civil cases indexed by defendant, plaintiff. Civil records archived from 1850s. Some records on docket books.

Criminal Records: Access: In person only. Both the court and visitors may perform in person searches. No search fee. Required to search: name, years to search, DOB; also helpful: SSN. Criminal records archived from 1850s. Some records on docket books. Same as civil.

General Information: No juvenile, mental, adoption or sealed released. Copy fee: $1.00 per page. Certification fee: $2.00. Fee payee: Clerk of Stark Circuit Court. Business checks accepted. Prepayment is required.

Steuben County

Circuit & Superior Court Courthouse, 55 S. Public Square, Angola, IN 46703; 260-668-1000 X2240. Hours: 8AM-4:30PM (EST). *Felony, Misdemeanor, Civil, Eviction, Small Claims, Probate.*

Civil Records: Access: In person only. Visitors must perform in person searches for themselves. No search fee. Required to search: name, years to search. Civil cases indexed by defendant, plaintiff. Civil records archived from 1800s. Some records on docket books.

Criminal Records: Access: In person only. Visitors must perform in person searches for themselves. No search fee. Required to search: name, years to search. Criminal records archived from 1800s, computerized since 06/94. Some records on docket books.

General Information: Public access terminal is available. No juvenile, mental, adoption, some probate, or sealed released. Copy fee: $1.00 per page. Certification fee: $2.00. Fee payee: Steuben County Clerk. Only cashiers checks and money orders accepted. Prepayment is required.

Sullivan County

Circuit & Superior Court Courthouse, 3rd Fl, PO Box 370, Sullivan, IN 47882-0370; 812-268-4657. Hours: 8AM-4PM (EST). *Felony, Misdemeanor, Civil, Eviction, Small Claims, Probate.*

Civil Records: Access: In person only. Only visitors may perform in person searches. No search fee. Required to search: name, years to search; also helpful: address. Civil cases indexed by defendant, plaintiff. Civil records on docket books or general index from late 1800's; computerized from 1998.

Criminal Records: Access: In person only. Visitors must perform in person searches for themselves. No search fee. Required to search: name, years to search, DOB, signed release; also helpful: address, SSN. Criminal records on docket books or general index from late 1800's; computerized from 1998.

General Information: Public access terminal is available. No juvenile, mental, adoption or sealed released. Copy fee: $1.00 per page. Certification fee: $2.00 per page. Fee payee: Sullivan County. No Personal checks accepted. Prepayment is required.

Switzerland County

Circuit & Superior Court Courthouse, 212 W Main St, Vevay, IN 47043; 812-427-3175; Fax: 812-427-2017. Hours: 8:30-3:30PM M-W & F (EST). *Felony, Misdemeanor, Civil, Eviction, Small Claims, Probate.*

Civil Records: Access: in person only. Visitors must perform in person searches for themselves. No search fee. Required to search: name, years to search, DOB. Civil cases indexed by defendant, plaintiff. Civil records archived from 1900s. All records on docket books or general index.

Criminal Records: Access: n person only. Visitors must perform in person searches for themselves. No search fee. Required to search: name, years to search, DOB. Criminal records archived from 1900s. All records on docket books or general index.

General Information: No juvenile, mental, adoption or sealed records released. Fax notes: Fax fee $2.50 1st page, $.50 per page thereafter. Copy fee: $1.00 per page. Certification fee: $1.00. Fee payee: Switzerland County Clerk. Only cashiers checks and money orders accepted. Prepayment is required.

Tippecanoe County

Circuit, Superior & County Court PO Box 1665, Lafayette, IN 47902; 765-423-9326; Fax: 765-423-9194. Hours: 8AM-4:30PM (EST). *Felony, Misdemeanor, Civil, Eviction, Small Claims, Probate.* www.county.tippecanoe.in.us

Civil Records: Access: In person, online. Visitors must perform in person searches for themselves. No search fee. Required to search: name, years to search. Civil cases indexed by defendant, plaintiff. Civil records on computer from 1987, on microfiche from 1900. Some records on index and docket books. Online access to court records through CourtView are available free online at http://court.county.tippecanoe.in.us/pa/pa.htm.

Criminal Records: Access: In person, online. Visitors must perform in person searches for themselves. No search fee. Required to search: name, years to search; also helpful: DOB, SSN, sex, signed release. Criminal records on computer from 1987, on microfiche from 1900. Some records on index and docket books. Online access to criminal records is the same as civil.

General Information: Public access terminal is available. No juvenile, mental, adoption or sealed released. Copy fee: $.50 per page. Certification fee: $1.00. Fee payee: Tippecanoe County Clerk. Business checks accepted. Prepayment is required.

Tipton County

Circuit Court Tipton County Courthouse, Tipton, IN 46072; 765-675-2791; Fax: 765-675-7797. Hours: 8AM-4PM M-Th, 8AM-5PM F (EST). *Felony, Misdemeanor, Civil, Eviction, Small Claims, Probate.*

Civil Records: Access: In person only. Visitors must perform in person searches for themselves. No search fee. Required to search: name, years to search. Civil cases indexed by defendant, plaintiff. Civil records on card file and archived from 1930s.

Criminal Records: Access: In person only. Visitors must perform in person searches for themselves. No search fee. Required to search: name, years to search. Criminal records on card file and archived from 1930s.

General Information: No juvenile, mental, adoption or sealed released. Copy fee: $1.00 per page. Certification fee: $1.00. Fee payee: Tipton Counties Clerk. Personal checks accepted.

Union County

Circuit Court 26 W Union St, Liberty, IN 47353; 765-458-6121; Fax: 765-458-5263. Hours: 8AM-4PM (EST). *Felony, Misdemeanor, Civil, Eviction, Small Claims, Probate.*

Civil Records: Access: In person only. Both court and visitors may perform in person searches. No search fee. Required to search: name, years to search. Civil cases indexed by defendant, plaintiff. Civil records archived from 1821. Some records on docket books or entry books.

Criminal Records: Access: In person only. Both court and visitors may perform in person searches. No search fee. Required to search: name, years to search; also helpful: DOB, SSN. Criminal records archived from 1821. Some records on docket books or entry books.

General Information: No juvenile, mental, adoption or sealed records released. Copy fee: $.25 per page. Certification fee: $1.00. Fee payee: Union County Clerk. Only cashiers checks and money orders accepted. Prepayment is required.

Vanderburgh County

Circuit & Superior Court PO Box 3356 (Civic Center Courts Bldg - Rm 216), Evansville, IN 47732-3356; 812-435-5160; Fax: 812-435-5849. Hours: 8AM-5PM (CST). *Felony, Misdemeanor, Civil, Eviction, Small Claims, Probate.*

www.vanderburghgov.org/vander/countyclerk/index.htm

Civil Records: Access: In person only. Visitors must perform in person searches for themselves. No search fee. Required to search: name, years to search. Civil cases indexed by defendant, plaintiff. Civil records on computer back to 1991, archived from 1900s. Some records on index books.

Criminal Records: Access: In person only. Visitors must perform in person searches for themselves. No search fee. Required to search: name, years to search, DOB, SSN. Criminal records on computer back to 1991, archived from 1900s. Some records on index books.

General Information: Public access terminal is available. No juvenile, mental, adoption or sealed released. Fax notes: Fee to fax results is $2.00 per document plus $1.00 per page. Copy fee: $1.00 per page. Certification fee: $1.00. Fee payee: Vanderburgh County Clerk. Business checks accepted. Prepayment is required.

Vermillion County

Circuit Court PO Box 10, Newport, IN 47966-0010; 765-492-3500. Hours: 8AM-4PM (EST). *Felony, Misdemeanor, Civil, Eviction, Small Claims, Probate.*

Civil Records: Access: mail, in person. Both court and visitors may perform in person searches. Search fee: No search fee. Required to search: name. Civil cases indexed by defendant, plaintiff. Records on computer go back to 1994; archived from 1824. Some records on docket books.

Criminal Records: Access: In person only. Both court and visitors may perform in person searches. Search fee: No search fee. Required to search: name. Records on computer go back to 1994; archived from 1825. Some records on docket books.

General Information: No juvenile, mental, adoption or sealed released. Copy fee: $1.00 per page. Certification fee: $2.00. Fee payee: Vermillion County Clerk. Business checks accepted. Prepayment is required.

Vigo County

Circuit, Superior & County Court 2nd Fl, Courthouse, PO Box 8449, Terre Haute, IN 47807-8449; 812-462-3211. Hours: 8AM-4PM (EST). *Felony, Misdemeanor, Civil, Eviction, Small Claims, Probate.*

Civil Records: Access: In person only. Visitors must perform in person searches for themselves. No search fee. Required to search: name, years to search. Civil cases indexed by defendant, plaintiff. Civil records on index books; on computer back to 8/1996.

Criminal Records: Access: In person only. Visitors must perform in person searches for themselves. No search fee. Required to search: name, years to search; also helpful: DOB, SSN. Criminal records on index books; on computer back to 8/1996.

General Information: Public access terminal is available. No juvenile, mental, adoption or sealed released. Copy fee: $1.00 per page. Certification fee: $1.00. Fee payee: Vigo County Clerk. Only cashiers checks and money orders accepted. Prepayment is required.

Wabash County

Circuit & Superior Court 69 W Hill St, Wabash, IN 46992; 260-563-0661 X30 or X32; Fax: 260-563-3451. Hours: 8AM-4PM (EST). *Felony, Misdemeanor, Civil, Eviction, Small Claims, Probate.*

Civil Records: Access: In person only. Visitors must perform in person searches for themselves. Required to search: name, years to search. Civil cases indexed by defendant, plaintiff. Civil records archived from 1800s; on computer since 1989. Some judgments on fee books.

Criminal Records: Access: In person only. Visitors must perform in person searches for themselves. Required to search: name, years to search, DOB; also helpful: SSN. Criminal records archived from 1800s; on computer since 1989. Some judgments on fee books.

General Information: Public access terminal is available. No juvenile, mental, adoption or sealed records released. Copy fee: $1.00 per page. Certification fee: $1.00. Fee payee: Wabash County Clerk. Business checks accepted.

Warren County

Circuit Court Ste 11, 125 N Monroe, Williamsport, IN 47993; 765-762-3510; Fax: 765-762-7222. Hours: 8AM-4PM (EST). *Felony, Misdemeanor, Civil, Eviction, Small Claims, Probate.*

Civil Records: Access: In person only. Both court and visitors may perform in person searches. No search fee. Required to search: name, years to search. Civil cases indexed by defendant, plaintiff. Civil records archived from 1828. Some records on docket books.

Criminal Records: Access: In person only. Both court and visitors may perform in person searches. No search fee. Required to search: name, years to search, DOB; also helpful: SSN. Criminal records archived from 1828. Some records on docket books.

General Information: No juvenile, mental, adoption or sealed released. Fax notes: Fee to fax results is $1.00 per page. Copy fee: $1.00 per page. Certification fee: $1.00. Fee payee: Warren County Clerk. Personal checks accepted. Prepayment is required.

Warrick County

Circuit & Superior Court One County Square, #200, Boonville, IN 47601; 812-897-6160. Hours: 8AM-4PM (CST). *Felony, Misdemeanor, Civil, Eviction, Small Claims, Probate.*

Civil Records: Access: Phone, mail, in person. Both court and visitors may perform in person searches. No search fee. Required to search: name, years to search. Civil cases indexed by defendant, plaintiff. Civil records

on computer from 1987, archived from 1900s. Some records on index books.

Criminal Records: Access: Mail, in person. Both court and visitors may perform in person searches. No search fee. Required to search: name, years to search; also helpful: DOB, SSN. Criminal records on computer from 1987, archived from 1900s. Some records on index books.

General Information: No juvenile, mental, adoption or sealed released. SASE required. Turnaround time same day. Copy fee: $1.00 per page. Certification fee: $1.00. Fee payee: Warrick County Clerk. Business checks accepted. Prepayment is required.

Washington County

Circuit & Superior Court Courthouse, 99 Public Sq, Salem, IN 47167; 812-883-1634/5748; Fax: 812-883-8108. Hours: 8:30AM-4PM M-Th, 8:30AM-6PM F (EST). *Felony, Misdemeanor, Civil, Small Claims, Probate.*

Note: Will only return calls to toll-free numbers.

Civil Records: Access: In person only. Both court and visitors may perform in person searches. No search fee. Required to search: name, years to search; also helpful: address. Civil cases indexed by defendant, plaintiff. Civil records on books, archived from 1820. Some records on docket books.

Criminal Records: Access: Mail, fax, in person. Both court and visitors may perform in person searches. No search fee. Required to search: name, years to search, DOB; also helpful: address, SSN. Criminal index on computer from 1980, docket books and archived from 1820.

General Information: No juvenile, mental, adoption or sealed released; no information given out via telephone. SASE required. Turnaround time 1-5 days. Fax notes: Will return results to toll-free numbers. Copy fee: $1.00 per page. Certification fee: $1.00. Fee payee: Washington County Clerk. Only cashiers checks and money orders accepted. Prepayment is required.

Wayne County

Circuit & Superior Court Courthouse, 301 E Main Street, Richmond, IN 47374; 765-973-9200; Fax: 765-973-9490. Hours: 8:30AM-5PM M; 8:30AM-4:30PM T-F (EST). *Felony, Misdemeanor, Civil, Eviction, Small Claims, Probate.*

www.co.wayne.in.us/courts

Civil Records: Access: Mail, fax, in person. Both court and visitors may perform in person searches. No search fee. Required to search: name, years to search. Civil cases indexed by defendant, plaintiff. Civil records on computer from 4/90, circuit on microfiche from 1957, superior on microfiche from 1960 to 1971, all archived from 1800s. Some records on dockets. Fax request must be on letterhead.

Criminal Records: Access: Mail, fax, in person. Both court and visitors may perform in person searches. No search fee. Required to search: name, years to search, fax request on letterhead. Criminal records on computer from 4/90, circuit on microfiche from 1957, superior on microfiche from 1960 to 1971, all archived from 1800s. Some records on dockets. Fax request must be on letterhead.

General Information: Public access terminal is available. No juvenile, mental, adoption or sealed released. SASE required. Turnaround time 2-3 days. Fax notes: Will not fax results. Copy fee: $1.00 per page. Certification fee: $1.00. Fee payee: Wayne County Clerk. Personal checks accepted. Prepayment is required.

Wells County

Circuit & Superior Court 102 West Market, Rm 201, Bluffton, IN 46714; 260-824-6479. Hours: 8AM-4:30PM (EST). *Civil, Probate.*

Civil Records: Access: In person only. Visitors must perform in person searches for themselves. No search fee. Required to search: name, years to search. Civil cases indexed by defendant, plaintiff. Civil records archived from 1837. Some records on docket books.

Criminal Records: Access: In person only. Visitors must perform in person searches for themselves. No search fee. Required to search: name, years to search, DOB; also helpful: SSN. Criminal records archived from 1837. Some records on docket books.

General Information: No juvenile, mental, adoption or sealed released. Certification fee: $1.00. Fee payee: Wells County Clerk. Personal checks accepted. Prepayment is required.

White County

Circuit Court PO Box 350, 110 N Main, Monticello, IN 47960; 574-583-7032; Fax: 574-583-1532. Hours: 8AM-4PM (EST). *Civil, Probate.*

Civil Records: Access: Mail, fax, in person only. Both court and visitors may perform in person searches. No search fee. Required to search: name, years to search.

Civil cases indexed by defendant, plaintiff. Civil records on indexes and files, some records on docket books back to 1950s.

General Information: No juvenile, mental, adoption or sealed released. Copy fee: $1.00 per page. Certification fee: $1.00. Fee payee: White County Clerk. Personal checks accepted. Prepayment is required.

Superior Court PO Box 1005, 110 N Main, Monticello, IN 47960; 574-583-9520; Fax: 574-583-2437. Hours: 8AM-4PM (EST). *Felony, Misdemeanor, Eviction, Small Claims.*

Civil Records: Access: In person only. Both court and visitors may perform in person searches. Court will search only if a date is provided. No search fee. Required to search: name, years to search. Civil cases indexed by defendant, plaintiff. Civil records on indexes and files, some records on docket books.

Criminal Records: Access: In person only. Both court and visitors may perform in person searches. Court will search only if a date is provided. No search fee. Required to search: name, years to search. Criminal records on indexes and files, some records on docket books.

General Information: No juvenile, mental, adoption or sealed released. Copy fee: $1.00 per page. Certification fee: $1.00. Fee payee: White County Clerk. Personal checks accepted. Prepayment is required.

Whitley County

Circuit & Superior Court 101 W Van Buren, Rm 10, Columbia City, IN 46725; 260-248-3102; Fax: 260-248-3137. Hours: 8AM-4:30PM (EST). *Felony, Misdemeanor, Civil, Eviction, Small Claims, Probate.*

Civil Records: Access: In person only. Visitors must perform in person searches for themselves. No search fee. Required to search: name, years to search. Civil cases indexed by defendant, plaintiff. Civil records on computer from 1999. Some records on docket books.

Criminal Records: Access: In person only. Visitors must perform in person searches for themselves. No search fee. Required to search: name, years to search; also helpful: DOB. Criminal records on computer from 1999. Some records on docket books.

General Information: Public access terminal is available. No juvenile, mental, adoption or sealed released. Copy fee: $1.00 per page. Certification fee: $1.00. Fee payee: Whitley County Clerk. Only cashiers checks and money orders accepted. Prepayment is required.

Indiana Recording Offices

ORGANIZATION: 92 counties, 92 recording offices. The recording officer is County Recorder (Circuit Clerk for state tax liens on personal property). Many counties utilize a "Miscellaneous Index" for tax and other liens. 81 counties are in the Eastern Time Zone (EST), and 11 are in the Central Time Zone (CST).

REAL ESTATE RECORDS: Most counties will not perform real estate name searches. Copies usually cost $1.00 per page, and certification usually costs $5.00 per document.

UCC RECORDS: Financing statements are filed at the state level, except for real estate related collateral, which are filed with the County Recorder. However, prior to 07/2001, consumer goods collateral were also filed at the County Recorder and these older records can be searched there. Starting 07/2002, farm collateral will change from local to state centralized filing. All counties will perform UCC searches. Use search request form UCC-11. Search fees are usually $1.00 per debtor name. Copies usually cost $.50 per page. Most counties also charge $.50 for each financing statement reported on a search.

TAX LIEN RECORDS: All federal tax liens on personal property are filed with the County Recorder. State tax liens on personal property are filed with the Circuit Clerk, who is in a different office from the Recorder. Refer to the County Court section for information about Indiana Circuit Courts. Most counties will not perform tax lien searches.

OTHER LIENS: Judgments, mechanics, hospital, sewer, utility, innkeeper.

ONLINE ACCESS: Very few county agencies offer online access. The most notable is the subscription service offered by Marion County at www.civicnet.net

Adams County

County Recorder, Adams County Service Complex, 313 W. Jefferson, Room 240, Decatur, IN 46733. 260-724-2600 R/E Recording: 260-724-2600 x213; Fax 260-724-2815.
Will search UCC records. This agency will not do a federal tax lien search. Will not search real estate records. **Other Phone Numbers:** Assessor 260-724-2600 x225; Treasurer 260-724-2600 x215; Auditor 260-724-2600 x200.

Allen County

County Recorder, 1 E. Main St, City County Building Room 206, Fort Wayne, IN 46802-1890. County Recorder, R/E and UCC Recording 260-449-7165; Fax 260-449-3261.
Will search UCC records. This agency will not do a federal tax lien search. Will not search real estate records. **Other Phone Numbers:** Assessor 260-428-7123; Treasurer 260-428-7693; Elections 260-449-7329; Vital Records 260-449-7147.

Bartholomew County

County Recorder, PO Box 1121, Columbus, IN 47202-1121. 812-379-1520.
Will search UCC records. This agency will not do a federal tax lien search. Real estate record owner searches available.

Benton County

County Recorder, 706 E. 5th St, Suite 24, Fowler, IN 47944-1556. County Recorder, R/E and UCC Recording 765-884-1630; Fax 765-884-2013.
Will search UCC records. Will not search real estate records. **Other Phone Numbers:** Assessor 765-884-1205; Treasurer 765-884-1070; Elections 765-884-0930; Vital Records 765-884-1728.

Blackford County

County Recorder, 110 W. Washington St, Courthouse, Hartford City, IN 47348. County Recorder, R/E and UCC Recording 765-348-2207; Fax 765-348-7222.
Will search UCC records. This agency will not do a federal tax lien search. Will not search real estate records. **Other Phone Numbers:** Assessor 765-348-1707; Vital Records 765-348-2207.

Boone County

County Recorder, 202 Courthouse Square, Lebanon, IN 46052. 765-482-3070 R/E Recording: 765-482-2940.
Will search UCC records. This agency will not do a federal tax lien search. Will not search real estate records. **Other Phone Numbers:** Assessor 765-482-0140; Treasurer 765-482-2880; Elections 765-482-3510.

Brown County

County Recorder, PO Box 86, Nashville, IN 47448. County Recorder, R/E and UCC Recording 812-988-5462; Fax 812-988-5520.
Will search UCC records. This agency will not do a federal tax lien search. Will not search real estate records. **Other Phone Numbers:** Assessor 812-988-5466; Treasurer 812-988-5458.

Carroll County

County Recorder, Court House, 101 W. Main St, Delphi, IN 46923-1522. County Recorder, R/E and UCC Recording 765-564-2124; Fax 765-564-2576.
Will search UCC records. UCC search includes federal tax liens if requested. Will not search real estate records. **Other Phone Numbers:** Assessor 765-564-3444; Treasurer 765-564-3446; Elections 765-564-4485; Vital Records 765-564-3420.

Cass County

County Recorder, 200 Court Park, Logansport, IN 46947. 574-753-7810; www.in-map.net/counties/CASS/recorder/
Will search UCC records. This agency will not do a federal tax lien search. Will not search real estate records. **Other Phone Numbers:** Assessor 574-753-7720; Treasurer 574-753-7720.

Clark County

County Recorder, 501 E. Court Ave, Room 105, Jeffersonville, IN 47130. 812-285-6236.
Will search UCC records. This agency will not do a tax lien search. Will not search real estate records. **Other Phone Numbers:** Assessor 812-285-6224; Treasurer 812-285-6205.

Clay County

County Recorder, Courthouse, Room 111, 609 E National Ave., Brazil, IN 47834. County Recorder, R/E and UCC Recording 812-448-9005; Fax 812-446-5095.
Will search UCC records. This agency will not do a federal tax lien search. Will not search real estate records. **Other Phone Numbers:** Assessor 812-448-9013; Treasurer 812-448-9009; Elections 812-448-9023; Vital Records 812-448-9018.

Clinton County

County Recorder, 270 Courthouse Square, Frankfort, IN 46041-1957. 765-659-6320; Fax 765-659-6391.
Will search UCC records. This agency will not do a federal tax lien search. Will not search real estate records. **Other Phones:** Assessor 765-659-6315; Treasurer 765-659-6325; Elections 765-659-6335.

Crawford County

County Recorder, PO Box 214, English, IN 47118-0214. 812-338-2615; Fax 812-338-2507.
Will search UCC records. This agency will not do a federal tax lien search. Will not search real estate records. **Other Phone Numbers:** Assessor 812-338-2402; Treasurer 812-338-2651.

Daviess County

County Recorder, PO Box 793, Washington, IN 47501. 812-254-8675; Fax 812-254-8697.
Will search UCC records. This agency will not do a tax lien search. Will not search real estate records. **Other Phone Numbers:** Assessor 812-254-8660; Treasurer 812-254-8677.

Dearborn County

County Recorder, 215 B, W. High St, Lawrenceburg, IN 47025. 812-537-8837; Fax none.
Will search UCC records. This agency will not do a tax lien search. Will not search real estate records. **Other Phone Numbers:** Assessor 812-537-8809; Treasurer 812-537-8811.

Decatur County

County Recorder, 150 Courthouse Square, Suite 121, Greensburg, IN 47240. 812-663-4681; Fax 812-663-2407.
Will search UCC records. This agency will not do a federal tax lien search. Will not search real estate records. **Other Phone Numbers:** Assessor 812-663-4860; Treasurer 812-663-4190.

DeKalb County

County Recorder, PO Box 810, Auburn, IN 46706. County Recorder, R/E and UCC Recording 260-925-2112; Fax 260-925-5126.
Will search UCC records. This agency will not do a federal tax lien search. Will not search real estate records. **Other Phone Numbers:** Assessor 260-925-1824; Treasurer 260-925-2712; Elections 260-925-0912; Vital Records 260-925-2220.

Delaware County

County Recorder, PO Box 1008, Muncie, IN 47308. 765-747-7804.
Will search UCC records. This agency will not do a tax lien search. Will not search real estate records. **Other Phone Numbers:** Assessor 765-747-7715.

Dubois County

County Recorder, Room 101, 1 Courthouse Square, Jasper, IN 47546. 812-481-7067; Fax 812-481-7044.
Will search UCC records. This agency will not do a federal tax lien search. Will not search real estate records. **Other Phone Numbers:** Assessor 812-481-7010; Treasurer 812-481-7080.

Elkhart County

County Recorder, PO Box 837, Goshen, IN 46527. 574-535-6754 R/E Recording: 574-535-6756; www.elkhartcountygov.com/administrative
Will search UCC records. This agency will not do a federal tax lien search. Will not search real estate records. **Online Access:** Real Estate, Lien, Tax Assessor Records. Access to Elkhart County records is available for an annual fee of $50. plus a minimum of $20 per month of use. The minimum fee allows for 2 hours access, and additional use is billed at $10 per hour. Lending agency information is available. For information, call 574-535-6777. **Other Phone Numbers:** Assessor 574-535-6702; Treasurer 574-535-6759; Elections 574-535-6469; Vital Records 574-523-2107; Voter Registration 574-535-6775.

Fayette County

County Recorder, PO Box 324, Connersville, IN 47331-0324. 765-825-3051; www.indico.net/counties/FAYETTE/
Will search UCC records. This agency will not do a federal tax lien search. Will not search real estate records. **Other Phone Numbers:** Assessor 765-825-4931; Treasurer 765-825-1013.

Floyd County

County Recorder, PO Box 878, New Albany, IN 47151-0878. 812-948-5430; Fax 812-949-7727.
Will search UCC records. This agency will not do a federal tax lien search. Will not search real estate records. **Other Phone Numbers:** Assessor 812-948-5420; Treasurer 812-948-5477.

Fountain County

County Recorder, PO Box 55, Covington, IN 47932. 765-793-2431; Fax 765-793-5002.
Will search UCC records. This agency will not do a federal tax lien search. Will not search real estate records. **Other Phone Numbers:** Assessor 765-793-3481; Treasurer 765-793-4821.

Franklin County

County Recorder, 459 Main St, Brookville, IN 47012-1486. County Recorder, R/E and UCC Recording 765-647-5131.
Will search UCC records. Will not search real estate records. **Other Phone Numbers:** Assessor 765-647-4921; Treasurer 765-647-5121; Elections 765-647-5111; Vital Records 765-647-4322.

Fulton County

County Recorder, 125 E 9th St, Rochester, IN 46975. County Recorder, R/E and UCC Recording 574-223-2914; Fax 574-223-4734.
Will search UCC records. This agency will not do a federal tax lien search. Will not search real estate records. **Other Phones:** Assessor 574-223-2801; Treasurer 574-223-7705; Vital Records 574-223-2881.

Gibson County

County Recorder, PO Box 1078, Princeton, IN 47670. County Recorder, R/E and UCC Recording 812-385-3332; Fax 812-386-9502.
Will search UCC records. This agency will not do a federal tax lien search. Will not search real estate records. **Other Phone Numbers:** Assessor 812-385-5286; Treasurer 812-385-2540; Appraiser/Auditor 812-385-4927; Elections 812-385-8401; Vital Records 812-385-3831.

Grant County

County Recorder, 401 S. Adams St, Marion, IN 46953. 765-668-8871.
Will search UCC records. This agency will not do a tax lien search. Will not search real estate records. **Other Phone Numbers:** Assessor 765-668-8871; Treasurer 765-668-8871.

Greene County

County Recorder, PO Box 309, Bloomfield, IN 47424. County Recorder, R/E and UCC Recording 812-384-2020 UCC Recording: 812-384-2021; Fax 812-384-2044.
Will search UCC records. Real estate owner, mortgage, and property transfer searches available. **Other Phones:** Assessor 812-384-2003; Treasurer 812-384-4378; Elections 812-384-2015; Vital Records 812-384-2016.

Hamilton County

County Recorder, Courthouse, 33 N. 9th St, Suite 309, Noblesville, IN 46060. County Recorder, R/E and UCC Recording 317-776-9618 UCC Recording: 317-776-9688; Fax 317-776-8200.
Will search UCC records. This agency will not do a federal tax lien search. Will not search real estate records. **Other Phone Numbers:** Assessor 317-776-9614; Treasurer 317-776-9620.

Hancock County

County Recorder, 9 E. Main St, Courthouse, Room 204, Greenfield, IN 46140. 317-462-1142.
Will search UCC records. This agency will not do a tax lien search. Will not search real estate records. **Other Phone Numbers:** Assessor 317-462-1102; Treasurer 317-462-1152.

Harrison County

County Recorder, 300 Capitol Ave, Courthouse, Room 204, Corydon, IN 47112. County Recorder, R/E and UCC Recording 812-738-3788; Fax 812-738-1153.
Will search UCC records. This agency will not do a federal tax lien search. Will not search real estate records. **Other Phone Numbers:** Assessor 812-738-4280; Treasurer 812-738-2348; Elections 812-738-3126; Vital Records 812-738-3237.

Hendricks County

County Recorder, 355 S Washington, Danville, IN 46122. 317-745-9224.
Will search UCC records. This agency will not do a tax lien search. Will not search real estate records. **Other Phone Numbers:** Assessor 317-745-9207; Treasurer 317-745-9220.

Henry County

County Recorder, PO Box K, New Castle, IN 47362. County Recorder, R/E and UCC Recording 765-529-4304; Fax 765-521-7017.
Will search UCC records. This agency will not do a federal tax lien search. Will not search real estate records. **Other Phones:** Assessor 765-529-2104; Treasurer 765-529-4404; Elections 765-529-6401; Vital Records 765-521-7058; Auditor 765-529-2800.

Howard County

County Recorder, PO Box 733, Kokomo, IN 46903-0733. 765-456-2210; Fax 765-456-2056.
Will search UCC records. This agency will not do a tax lien search. Will not search real estate records. **Other Phone Numbers:** Assessor 317-456-2211; Treasurer 317-456-2213.

Huntington County

County Recorder, 201 N. Jefferson St., Room 101, Huntington, IN 46750-2841. County Recorder, R/E and UCC Recording 260-358-4848.
Will search UCC records. This agency will not do a federal tax lien search. Will not search real estate records. **Other Phone Numbers:** Assessor 260-358-4802; Treasurer 260-358-4860.

Jackson County

County Recorder, PO Box 75, Brownstown, IN 47220. 812-358-6113.
Will search UCC records. This agency will not do a tax lien search. Will not search real estate records. **Other Phone Numbers:** Assessor 812-358-6111; Treasurer 812-358-6125.

Jasper County

County Recorder, 115 W. Washington, Courthouse Box 4, Rensselaer, IN 47978-2891. 219-866-4923; Fax 219-866-4940.
Will search UCC records. This agency will not do a federal tax lien search. Will not search real estate records. **Other Phone Numbers:** Assessor 219-866-4194; Treasurer 219-866-4939.

Jay County

County Recorder, 120 W. Main St, Portland, IN 47371. County Recorder, R/E and UCC Recording 260-726-6940.
Will search UCC records. This agency will not do a federal tax lien search. Will not search real estate records. **Other Phone Numbers:** Assessor 260-726-6929; Treasurer 260-726-6925.

Jefferson County

County Recorder, Courthouse - Room 104, 300 E. Main St., Madison, IN 47250. County Recorder, R/E and UCC Recording 812-265-8902.
Will search UCC records. Will not search real estate records. **Other Phone Numbers:** Assessor 812-265-8905; Treasurer 812-265-8910.

Jennings County

County Recorder, PO Box 397, Vernon, IN 47282-0397. 812-346-3152 R/E Recording: 812-346-3053 UCC Recording: 812-346-3053; Fax 812-346-4605.
Will search UCC records. Will not search real estate records. **Other Phone Numbers:** Assessor 812-346-3013; Treasurer 812-346-3060; Appraiser/Auditor 812-

346-3021; Elections 812-346-3080; Vital Records 812-346-3024.

Johnson County

County Recorder, PO Box 475, Franklin, IN 46131. County Recorder, R/E and UCC Recording 317-736-3718; Fax 317-736-8066.

Will search UCC records. This agency will not do a federal tax lien search. Will not search real estate records. **Other Phone Numbers:** Assessor 317-736-3030; Treasurer 317-736-3711; Elections 317-736-3789; Vital Records 317-736-3775; Assessor County 317-736-3715.

Knox County

County Recorder, 101 N 7th St, Courthouse, Vincennes, IN 47591. 812-885-2508; Fax 812-886-2414.

Will search UCC records. This agency will not do a tax lien search. Will not search real estate records. **Other Phone Numbers:** Assessor 812-885-2513; Treasurer 812-885-2506.

Kosciusko County

County Recorder, 100 W. Center St, Courthouse Room 14, Warsaw, IN 46580. County Recorder, R/E and UCC Recording 574-372-2360; Fax 574-372-2469.

Will search UCC records. This agency will not do a federal tax lien search. Will not search real estate records. **Other Phone Numbers:** Assessor 574-372-2310; Treasurer 574-372-2370.

La Porte County

County Recorder, 813 Lincolnway, La Porte, IN 46350-3488. 219-326-6808 R/E Recording: 219-326-6808 x267 UCC Recording: 219-326-6808 x234; Fax 219-326-0828. www.laportecounty.org

Will search UCC records. This agency will not do a federal tax lien search. Will not search real estate records. **Other Phone Numbers:** Assessor 219-326-6808 x233; Treasurer 219-326-6808 x268; Elections 219-326-6808 x465; Vital Records 219-326-6808 x200.

LaGrange County

County Recorder, PO Box 214, LaGrange, IN 46761. County Recorder, R/E and UCC Recording 260-499-6320.

Will search UCC records. Will not search real estate records. **Other Phone Numbers:** Assessor 260-499-6319; Treasurer 260-499-6316.

Lake County

County Recorder, 2293 N Main St, Building A, 2nd Floor, Crown Point, IN 46307. 219-755-3730; Fax 219-755-3257.

Will search UCC records. UCC search does not include federal tax liens. Real estate owner, mortgage, and property transfer searches available. **Other Phone Numbers:** Assessor 219-755-3200; Treasurer 219-755-3760.

Lawrence County

County Recorder, 916 15th St, Rm 21, Room 21, Bedford, IN 47421. 812-275-3245; Fax 812-275-4138. Will search UCC records. This agency will not do a federal tax lien search. Will not search real estate records. **Other Phone Numbers:** Assessor 812-275-4135; Treasurer 812-275-2431.

Madison County

County Recorder, 16 E. 9th St, Anderson, IN 46016. 765-641-9618.

Will search UCC records. This agency will not do a tax lien search. Will not search real estate records. **Other Phone Numbers:** Assessor 765-641-9401; Treasurer 765-641-9645.

Marion County

County Recorder, 200 E. Washington, Suite 721, Indianapolis, IN 46204. 317-327-4020 R/E Recording: 317-327-4018 UCC Recording: 317-327-4015; Fax 317-327-3942.

Will search UCC records. UCC search includes federal tax liens if requested. Property transfer searches available. **Online Access:** Real Estate, Lien Records. Access to Marion County online records requires a $200 set up fee, plus an escrow balance of at least $100 must be maintained. Additional charges are $.50 per minute, $.25 display charge for first page; $.10 each add'l page. Records date back to 1987; images from 2/24/93. Federal tax liens and UCC information are available. For information, contact Mike Kerner at 317-327-4587. **Other Phone Numbers:** Assessor 317-327-4907; Treasurer 317-327-4040; Auditor 317-327-4646.

Marshall County

County Recorder, 112 W. Jefferson St, Room 201, Plymouth, IN 46563. County Recorder, R/E and UCC Recording 574-935-8515.

Will search UCC records. This agency will not do a federal tax lien search. Will not search real estate records. **Other Phones:** Assessor 574-935-8525.

Martin County

County Recorder, PO Box 147, Shoals, IN 47581. 812-247-2420; Fax 812-247-2756.

Will search UCC records. UCC search includes federal tax liens if requested. Will not search real estate records. **Other Phone Numbers:** Assessor 812-247-2070.

Miami County

County Recorder, PO Box 597, Peru, IN 46970. 765-472-3901; Fax 765-472-1412.

Will search UCC records. This agency will not do a federal tax lien search. Will not search real estate records.

Monroe County

County Recorder, PO Box 1634, Bloomington, IN 47402. County Recorder, R/E and UCC Recording 812-349-2520.

Will not search UCC records. This agency will not do a federal tax lien search. Will not search real estate records. **Other Phone Numbers:** Assessor 812-333-3502; Treasurer 812-333-3530.

Montgomery County

County Recorder, PO Box 865, Crawfordsville, IN 47933. 765-364-6415; Fax 765-364-6404.

Will search UCC records. This agency will not do a tax lien search. Will not search real estate records. **Other Phone Numbers:** Assessor 765-364-6420; Treasurer 765-364-6410.

Morgan County

County Recorder, PO Box 1653, Martinsville, IN 46151. County Recorder, R/E and UCC Recording 765-342-1077.

Will search UCC records. This agency will not do a federal tax lien search. Will not search real estate records. **Other Phone Numbers:** Assessor 765-342-1065; Treasurer 765-342-1048; Elections 765-342-1029; Vital Records 765-342-6621.

Newton County

County Recorder, 201 N 3rd St, Kentland, IN 47951. 219-474-6081.

Will search UCC records. This agency will not do a federal tax lien search. Mortgage searches available. **Other Phone Numbers:** Assessor 219-474-6081; Treasurer 219-474-6081.

Noble County

County Recorder, 101 N. Orange St, Albion, IN 46701. 260-636-2672; Fax 260-636-3264.

Will search UCC records. Will not search real estate records. **Other Phone Numbers:** Assessor 260-636-2297; Treasurer 260-636-2644.

Ohio County

County Recorder, Courthouse, 413 Main St., Rising Sun, IN 47040. County Recorder, R/E and UCC Recording 812-438-3369; Fax 812-438-4590.

Will search UCC records. This agency will not do a federal tax lien search. Will not search real estate records. **Other Phone Numbers:** Assessor 812-438-3264; Treasurer 812-438-2724; Elections 812-438-2610; Vital Records 812-438-2551.

Orange County

County Recorder, 205 E. Main St, Courthouse, Paoli, IN 47454. 812-723-3600.

Will search UCC records. This agency will not do a tax lien search. Will not search real estate records. **Other Phone Numbers:** Assessor 812-723-3600.

Owen County

County Recorder, Courthouse, Spencer, IN 47460. 812-829-5013; Fax 812-829-5014.

Will search UCC records. Will not search real estate records. **Other Phone Numbers:** Assessor 812-829-5018; Treasurer 812-829-5011.

Parke County

County Recorder, 116 W. High St., Room 102, Rockville, IN 47872-1787. County Recorder, R/E and UCC Recording 765-569-3419; Fax 765-569-4037.

Will search UCC records. This agency will not do a federal tax lien search. Will not search real estate records. **Other Phone Numbers:** Assessor 765-569-4036; Treasurer 765-569-3437.

Perry County

County Recorder, 2219 Payne St., Room W2, Tell City, IN 47586-2830. County Recorder, R/E and UCC Recording 812-547-4261; Fax 812-547-6428.

Will search UCC records. Will not search tax liens. Will not search real estate records. **Other Phone Numbers:** Assessor 812-547-5531; Treasurer 812-547-4816; Elections 812-547-3741; Vital Records 812-547-2746.

Pike County

County Recorder, Main St, Courthouse, Petersburg, IN 47567-1298. 812-354-6747; Fax 812-354-9431.

Will search UCC records. This agency will not do a federal tax lien search. Will not search real estate records. **Other Phone Numbers:** Assessor 812-354-6584; Treasurer 812-354-6363; Elections 812-354-6025; Vital Records 812-354-8797.

Porter County

County Recorder, 155 Indiana Ave, Suite 210, Valparaiso, IN 46383. County Recorder, R/E and UCC Recording 219-465-3465 UCC Recording: 219-465-3374; Fax 219-465-3592.

Will search UCC records. This agency will not do a federal tax lien search. Will not search real estate records. **Other Phone Numbers:** Assessor 219-465-3460; Treasurer 219-465-3470.

Posey County

County Recorder, 126 E 3rd St #215, Mount Vernon, IN 47620. County Recorder, R/E and UCC Recording 812-838-1314; Fax 812-838-8563.

Will search UCC records. This agency will not do a tax lien search. Will not search real estate records. **Other Phone Numbers:** Assessor 812-838-1309; Treasurer 812-838-1316.

Pulaski County

County Recorder, Courthouse - Room 220, 112 E. Main St., Winamac, IN 46996. County Recorder, R/E and UCC Recording 574-946-3844.
Will search UCC records. This agency will not do a state tax lien search. Will not search real estate records. **Other Phone Numbers:** Assessor 574-946-3845; Treasurer 574-946-3632; Elections 574-946-3313; Vital Records 574-946-6080.

Putnam County

County Recorder, Courthouse Square, Room 25, Greencastle, IN 46135. 765-653-5613.
Will search UCC records. Will not search real estate records. **Other Phone Numbers:** Assessor 765-653-4312; Treasurer 765-653-4510.

Randolph County

County Recorder, Courthouse, Room 101, 100 S. Main St., Winchester, IN 47394-1899. County Recorder, R/E and UCC Recording 765-584-7300.
Will search UCC records. This agency will not do a federal tax lien search. Will not search real estate records. **Other Phone Numbers:** Assessor 765-584-2427; Treasurer 765-584-0704; Appraiser/Auditor 765-584-7407; Elections 765-584-1155.

Ripley County

County Recorder, PO Box 404, Versailles, IN 47042. 812-689-5808 R/E Recording: 812-934-9498 UCC Recording: 812-934-9498; Fax 812-689-0048.
Will search UCC records. Will not search real estate records. **Other Phone Numbers:** Assessor 812-689-5656; Treasurer 812-689-6352.

Rush County

County Recorder, Courthouse, Room 208, Rushville, IN 46173. 765-932-2388.
Will search UCC records. This agency will not do a federal tax lien search. Will not search real estate records. **Other Phone Numbers:** Assessor 765-932-3242; Treasurer 765-932-2386.

Scott County

County Recorder, 1 E. McClain St., Suite 100, Scottsburg, IN 47170. 812-752-8442; Fax 812-752-2678.
Will search UCC records. This agency will not do a tax lien search. Will not search real estate records. **Other Phone Numbers:** Assessor 812-752-8436; Treasurer 812-752-8414.

Shelby County

County Recorder, 407 S. Harrison, Courthouse, Shelbyville, IN 46176. County Recorder, R/E and UCC Recording 317-392-6370; Fax 317-392-6393.
Will search UCC records. This agency will not do a federal tax lien search. Will not search real estate records. **Other Phone Numbers:** Assessor 317-392-5481; Treasurer 317-392-6375.

Spencer County

County Recorder, Courthouse, 200 Main, Rockport, IN 47635. 812-649-6013; Fax 812-649-6005.
Will search UCC records. This agency will not do a tax lien search. Will not search real estate records. **Other Phone Numbers:** Assessor 812-649-2381; Treasurer 812-649-4556.

St. Joseph County

County Recorder, 227 W Jefferson, Room 321, South Bend, IN 46601. Recorder, R/E and UCC Recording 574-235-9525; www.indico.net/counties/STJOSEPH/
Will search UCC records. This agency will not do a federal tax lien search. Will not search real estate records. **Online Access:** Land, Most Wanted Records. Access to county land information is available via a private company using Tapestry at https://www.landrecords.net. Registration and credit card required; casual requesters permitted. Also, access to the county sheriff most wanted list is at www.skyenet.net/cstoppers/mostwanted/mostwant.html . **Other Phone Numbers:** Assessor 574-235-9523; Treasurer 574-235-9531; Elections 574-235-9635; Vital Records 574-235-6719.

Starke County

County Recorder, PO Box 1, Knox, IN 46534. 574-772-9110 R/E Recording: 574-772-9109 UCC Recording: 574-772-9109; Fax 574-772-9178.
Will search UCC records. This agency will not do a federal tax lien search. Will not search real estate records. **Other Phone Numbers:** Assessor 574-772-9107; Treasurer 574-772-9113.

Steuben County

County Recorder, PO Box 397, Angola, IN 46703. County Recorder, R/E and UCC Recording 260-668-1000 x1700; Fax 260-665-8483.
Will search UCC records. This agency will not do a federal tax lien search. Will not search real estate records. **Other Phone Numbers:** Assessor 260-668-1000 x1000; Treasurer 260-668-1000 x1900; Elections 260-668-1000 x2220; Vital Records 260-668-1000 x1500.

Sullivan County

County Recorder, Room 205, 100 Court House Square, Sullivan, IN 47882-1565. 812-268-4844; Fax 812-268-0521.
Will search UCC records. This agency will not do a federal tax lien search. Will not search real estate records. **Other Phone Numbers:** Assessor 812-268-4657.

Switzerland County

County Recorder, Courthouse, 212 W. Main, Vevay, IN 47043. 812-427-2544.
Will search UCC records. This agency will not do a federal tax lien search. Will not search real estate records. **Other Phone Numbers:** Assessor 812-427-3379; Treasurer 812-427-3369; Auditor 812-427-3302.

Tippecanoe County

County Recorder, 20 N. 3rd St, Lafayette, IN 47901. 765-423-9353; Fax 765-423-9158. http://county.tippecanoe.in.us
Will search UCC records. This agency will not do a federal tax lien search. Will not search real estate records. **Online Access:** Property Records. Access to proeprty information on the county gis-mapping site is available free at http://gis.county.tippecanoe.in.us/gis/app12/index.html. **Other Phone Numbers:** Assessor 765-423-9255.

Tipton County

County Recorder, Courthouse, 101 E. Jefferson St., Tipton, IN 46072. 765-675-4614.
Will search UCC records. This agency will not do a tax lien search. Will not search real estate records. **Other Phone Numbers:** Assessor 765-675-2465; Treasurer 765-675-2742.

Union County

County Recorder, 26 W. Union St, Room 106, Liberty, IN 47353. County Recorder, R/E and UCC Recording 765-458-5434; Fax 765-458-5263.
Will search UCC records. This agency will not do a federal tax lien search. Will not search real estate records. **Other Phone Numbers:** Assessor 317-458-5331; Treasurer 317-458-6491.

Vanderburgh County

County Recorder, 231 City-County Admin. Building, 1 NW Martin Luther King, Jr. Blvd., Evansville, IN 47708-1881. County Recorder, R/E and UCC Recording 812-435-5215 UCC Recording: 812-435-5221; Fax 812-435-5580. www.assessor.evansville.net
Will search UCC records. This agency will not do a federal tax lien search. Will not search real estate records. **Online Access:** Property Records. Records on the County Assessor Property database are available free online at www.assessor.evansville.net/disclaim.htm. **Other Phone Numbers:** Assessor 812-435-5273; Treasurer 812-435-5248; Elections 812-435-5160; Vital Records 812-435-5681.

Vermillion County

County Recorder, PO Box 145, Newport, IN 47966-0145. 765-492-5003.
Will search UCC records. This agency will not do a federal tax lien search. Will not search real estate records. **Other Phones:** Assessor 765-492-5004.

Vigo County

County Recorder, 201 Cherry St, Terre Haute, IN 47807. County Recorder, R/E and UCC Recording 812-462-3301; Fax 812-232-2219.
Will search UCC records. This agency will not do a federal tax lien search. Will not search real estate records. **Other Phones:** Assessor 812-462-3358.

Wabash County

County Recorder, Courthouse, One W. Hill St., Wabash, IN 46992. County Recorder, R/E and UCC Recording 260-563-0661 x24.
Will search UCC records if their request form is used. This agency will not do a federal tax lien search. Will not search real estate records. **Other Phone Numbers:** Assessor 260-563-0661 x25; Treasurer 260-563-0661.

Warren County

County Recorder, 125 N. Monroe, Courthouse - Suite 10, Williamsport, IN 47993-1162. 765-762-3174; Fax 765-762-7222.
Will search UCC records. UCC search does not include federal tax liens. Will not search real estate records. **Other Phone Numbers:** Assessor 765-762-4528; Treasurer 765-762-3562.

Warrick County

County Recorder, PO Box 28, Boonville, IN 47601-0028. 812-897-6165; Fax 812-897-6168. www.warrickcounty.gov/departments/recorder.htm
Will search UCC records. This agency will not do a federal tax lien search. Will not search real estate records. **Other Phone Numbers:** Assessor 812-897-6125; Treasurer 812-897-6166.

Washington County

County Recorder, Courthouse, Salem, IN 47167. 812-883-4001; Fax 812-883-4020.
Will search UCC records. This agency will not do a federal tax lien search. Will not search real estate records. **Other Phone Numbers:** Assessor 812-883-4000; Treasurer 812-883-3307.

Wayne County

County Recorder, 401 E Main St, County Administration Bldg., 401 E. Main, Richmond, IN 47374. County Recorder, R/E and UCC Recording 765-973-9235; Fax 765-973-9321. www.co.wayne.in.us/offices

Will search UCC records. This agency will not do a tax lien search. Will not search real estate records. **Online Access:** Marriage Records. Marriage records are being added irregularly to the web site at www.co.wayne.in.us/marriage/retrieve.cgi. Records are from 1811 forward, with recent years being added. **Other Phone Numbers:** Assessor 765-973-9228; Treasurer 765-973-9238; Elections 765-973-9226; Vital Records 765-973-9245.

Wells County

County Recorder, Courthouse - Suite 203, 102 W. Market St., Bluffton, IN 46714. County Recorder, R/E and UCC Recording 260-824-6507.

Will search UCC records. This agency will not do a federal tax lien search. Will not search real estate records. **Other Phone Numbers:** Assessor 260-824-6476; Treasurer 260-824-6514; Appraiser/Auditor 260-824-6476; Elections 260-824-6482; Vital Records 260-824-6489; Auditor 260-824-6474.

White County

County Recorder, PO Box 127, Monticello, IN 47960. 574-583-5912; Fax 574-583-1521.

Will search UCC records. This agency will not do a tax lien search. Will not search real estate records. **Other Phone Numbers:** Assessor 574-583-7755.

Whitley County

County Recorder, Courthouse, 2nd Floor - Room 18, Columbia City, IN 46725. County Recorder, R/E and UCC Recording 260-248-3106; Fax 260-248-3137.

Will search UCC records. This agency will not do a federal tax lien search. Will not search real estate records. **Other Phone Numbers:** Assessor 260-248-3109.

Indiana County Locator

You will usually be able to find the city name in the City/County Cross Reference below. In that case, it is a simple matter to determine the county from the cross reference. However, only the official US Postal Service city names are included in this index. There are an additional 40,000 place names that people use in their addresses. Therefore, we have also included a ZIP/City Cross Reference immediately following the City/County Cross Reference.

If you know the ZIP Code but the city name does not appear in the City/County Cross Reference index, look up the ZIP Code in the ZIP/City Cross Reference, find the city name, then look up the city name in the City/County Cross Reference. For example, you want to know the county for an address of Menands, NY 12204. There is no "Menands" in the City/County Cross Reference. The ZIP/City Cross Reference shows that ZIP Codes 12201-12288 are for the city of Albany. Looking back in the City/County Cross Reference, Albany is in Albany County.

City/County Cross Reference

ADVANCE Boone
AKRON (46910) Fulton(60), Kosciusko(30), Miami(9)
ALAMO Montgomery
ALBANY (47320) Delaware(94), Randolph(4)
ALBION Noble
ALEXANDRIA (46001) Madison(97), Delaware(2)
AMBIA (47917) Warren(56), Benton(43)
AMBOY (46911) Miami(89), Wabash(10)
AMO Hendricks
ANDERSON Madison
ANDREWS (46702) Huntington(91), Wabash(8)
ANGOLA Steuben
ARCADIA Hamilton
ARCOLA Allen
ARGOS (46501) Marshall(96), Fulton(3)
ARLINGTON (46104) Rush(98), Shelby(1)
ASHLEY (46705) DeKalb(70), Steuben(29)
ATHENS Fulton
ATLANTA (46031) Hamilton(54), Tipton(45)
ATTICA (47918) Fountain(73), Warren(24), Tippecanoe(1)
ATWOOD Kosciusko
AUBURN DeKalb
AURORA Dearborn
AUSTIN (47102) Scott(84), Jackson(15)
AVILLA (46710) Noble(95), DeKalb(4)
AVOCA Lawrence
AVON Hendricks
BAINBRIDGE Putnam
BARGERSVILLE (46106) Johnson(94), Morgan(5)
BATESVILLE (47006) Franklin(68), Ripley(31)
BATH (47010) Franklin(67), Union(32)
BATTLE GROUND (47920) Tippecanoe(69), White(18), Carroll(12)
BEDFORD Lawrence
BEECH GROVE Marion
BELLMORE Parke
BENNINGTON (47011) Switzerland(55), Ohio(44)
BENTONVILLE Fayette
BERNE Adams
BETHLEHEM Clark
BEVERLY SHORES Porter
BICKNELL Knox
BIPPUS Huntington
BIRDSEYE (47513) Dubois(80), Crawford(13), Perry(4), Orange(1)
BLANFORD Vermillion
BLOOMFIELD Greene
BLOOMINGDALE Parke
BLOOMINGTON Monroe
BLUFFTON (46714) Wells(96), Adams(3)
BOGGSTOWN (46110) Shelby(93), Johnson(6)
BOONE GROVE Porter

BOONVILLE (47601) Warrick(98), Spencer(1)
BORDEN (47106) Clark(90), Washington(6), Floyd(3)
BOSTON Wayne
BOSWELL (47921) Benton(77), Warren(22)
BOURBON (46504) Marshall(96), Kosciusko(3)
BOWLING GREEN (47833) Clay(53), Owen(46)
BRADFORD Harrison
BRANCHVILLE Perry
BRAZIL (47834) Clay(92), Vigo(5), Parke(1)
BREMEN (46506) Marshall(88), St. Joseph(11)
BRIDGETON Parke
BRIMFIELD Noble
BRINGHURST Carroll
BRISTOL Elkhart
BRISTOW Perry
BROOK (47922) Newton(94), Jasper(5)
BROOKLYN Morgan
BROOKSTON (47923) White(89), Carroll(10)
BROOKVILLE Franklin
BROWNSBURG Hendricks
BROWNSTOWN Jackson
BROWNSVILLE (47325) Union(78), Fayette(18), Wayne(2)
BRUCEVILLE Knox
BRYANT (47326) Jay(96), Adams(2)
BUCK CREEK Tippecanoe
BUCKSKIN Gibson
BUFFALO White
BUNKER HILL Miami
BURKET Kosciusko
BURLINGTON Carroll
BURNETTSVILLE (47926) White(64), Carroll(33), Cass(1)
BURNEY Decatur
BURROWS Carroll
BUTLER DeKalb
BUTLERVILLE Jennings
CAMBRIDGE CITY (47327) Wayne(94), Henry(4)
CAMBY (46113) Morgan(67), Marion(19), Hendricks(12)
CAMDEN (46917) Carroll(98), Cass(1)
CAMPBELLSBURG (47108) Washington(91), Orange(8)
CANAAN (47224) Jefferson(98), Switzerland(1)
CANNELBURG Daviess
CANNELTON Perry
CARBON (47837) Clay(60), Parke(39)
CARLISLE Sullivan
CARMEL Hamilton
CARTERSBURG Hendricks
CARTHAGE (46115) Rush(94), Hancock(5)
CAYUGA Vermillion
CEDAR GROVE Franklin

CEDAR LAKE Lake
CELESTINE Dubois
CENTERPOINT (47840) Clay(96), Putnam(3)
CENTERVILLE Wayne
CENTRAL Harrison
CHALMERS White
CHANDLER Warrick
CHARLESTOWN Clark
CHARLOTTESVILLE (46117) Hancock(89), Henry(10)
CHESTERTON Porter
CHRISNEY Spencer
CHURUBUSCO (46723) Whitley(63), Allen(24), Noble(12)
CICERO Hamilton
CLARKS HILL (47930) Tippecanoe(71), Clinton(14), Montgomery(14)
CLARKSBURG Decatur
CLARKSVILLE Clark
CLAY CITY (47841) Clay(97), Owen(2)
CLAYPOOL Kosciusko
CLAYTON (46118) Hendricks(96), Morgan(3)
CLEAR CREEK Monroe
CLIFFORD Bartholomew
CLINTON Vermillion
CLOVERDALE (46120) Putnam(85), Owen(8), Morgan(6)
COAL CITY (47427) Owen(66), Clay(33)
COALMONT Clay
COATESVILLE (46121) Hendricks(56), Putnam(43)
COLBURN Tippecanoe
COLFAX (46035) Clinton(78), Boone(18), Montgomery(3)
COLUMBIA CITY (46725) Whitley(96), Noble(3)
COLUMBUS Bartholomew
COMMISKEY (47227) Jennings(81), Jefferson(18)
CONNERSVILLE Fayette
CONVERSE (46919) Grant(52), Miami(37), Howard(8)
CORTLAND Jackson
CORUNNA (46730) DeKalb(96), Noble(3)
CORY Clay
CORYDON Harrison
COVINGTON (47932) Fountain(89), Warren(5), Vermillion(4)
CRAIGVILLE (46731) Wells(90), Adams(9)
CRANDALL Harrison
CRANE Martin
CRAWFORDSVILLE Montgomery
CROMWELL (46732) Noble(57), Kosciusko(42)
CROSS PLAINS Ripley
CROTHERSVILLE (47229) Jackson(90), Jennings(9)
CROWN POINT Lake
CULVER (46511) Marshall(77), Starke(11), Fulton(9), Pulaski(1)

CUTLER Carroll
CYNTHIANA (47612) Posey(82), Gibson(17)
DALE (47523) Spencer(45), Dubois(37), Warrick(16)
DALEVILLE (47334) Delaware(98), Henry(1)
DANA Vermillion
DANVILLE Hendricks
DARLINGTON Montgomery
DAYTON Tippecanoe
DECATUR Adams
DECKER Knox
DEEDSVILLE Miami
DELONG Fulton
DELPHI Carroll
DEMOTTE (46310) Jasper(80), Newton(19)
DENHAM Pulaski
DENVER (46926) Miami(96), Cass(3)
DEPAUW Harrison
DEPUTY (47230) Jefferson(91), Jennings(8)
DERBY Perry
DILLSBORO Dearborn
DONALDSON Marshall
DUBLIN Wayne
DUBOIS Dubois
DUGGER (47848) Sullivan(96), Greene(3)
DUNKIRK (47336) Jay(63), Blackford(20), Delaware(16)
DUNREITH Henry
DUPONT (47231) Jefferson(74), Jennings(25)
DYER Lake
EARL PARK Benton
EAST CHICAGO Lake
EAST ENTERPRISE Switzerland
EATON (47338) Delaware(98), Blackford(1)
ECKERTY Crawford
ECONOMY Wayne
EDINBURGH (46124) Johnson(56), Bartholomew(25), Shelby(18)
EDWARDSPORT (47528) Knox(98), Sullivan(1)
ELBERFELD (47613) Warrick(90), Gibson(8), Vanderburgh(1)
ELIZABETH (47117) Harrison(97), Floyd(2)
ELIZABETHTOWN (47232) Bartholomew(69), Jennings(30)
ELKHART Elkhart
ELLETTSVILLE Monroe
ELNORA (47529) Daviess(96), Greene(3)
ELWOOD (46036) Madison(90), Tipton(8)
EMINENCE Morgan
EMISON Knox
ENGLISH (47118) Crawford(66), Orange(27), Perry(5)
ETNA GREEN (46524) Kosciusko(97), Marshall(2)
EVANSTON Spencer
EVANSVILLE Vanderburgh

FAIR OAKS (47943) Jasper(55), Newton(44)
FAIRBANKS Sullivan
FAIRLAND Shelby
FAIRMOUNT (46928) Grant(97), Madison(2)
FALMOUTH (46127) Rush(75), Fayette(24)
FARMERSBURG (47850) Sullivan(83), Vigo(16)
FARMLAND Randolph
FERDINAND (47532) Dubois(75), Perry(14), Spencer(9)
FILLMORE Putnam
FINLY Hancock
FISHERS Hamilton
FLAT ROCK (47234) Shelby(91), Bartholomew(8)
FLORA (46929) Carroll(91), Howard(8)
FLORENCE Switzerland
FLOYDS KNOBS (47119) Floyd(95), Clark(4)
FOLSOMVILLE Warrick
FONTANET Vigo
FOREST Clinton
FORT BRANCH Gibson
FORT RITNER Lawrence
FORT WAYNE Allen
FORTVILLE (46040) Hancock(74), Hamilton(18), Madison(7)
FOUNTAIN CITY (47341) Wayne(97), Randolph(2)
FOUNTAINTOWN (46130) Shelby(75), Hancock(24)
FOWLER Benton
FOWLERTON Grant
FRANCESVILLE (47946) Pulaski(83), Jasper(15)
FRANCISCO Gibson
FRANKFORT (46041) Clinton(98), Carroll(1)
FRANKLIN Johnson
FRANKTON Madison
FREDERICKSBURG (47120) Washington(97), Harrison(2)
FREEDOM Owen
FREELANDVILLE Knox
FREETOWN (47235) Jackson(71), Brown(28)
FREMONT Steuben
FRENCH LICK (47432) Orange(90), Dubois(9)
FRIENDSHIP Ripley
FULDA Spencer
FULTON Fulton
GALVESTON (46932) Cass(90), Miami(6), Howard(3)
GARRETT DeKalb
GARY Lake
GAS CITY Grant
GASTON (47342) Delaware(97), Grant(1)
GENEVA (46740) Adams(94), Wells(3), Jay(2)
GENTRYVILLE (47537) Spencer(86), Warrick(13)
GEORGETOWN (47122) Floyd(61), Harrison(38)
GLENWOOD (46133) Fayette(56), Rush(43)
GOLDSMITH Tipton
GOODLAND (47948) Newton(68), Jasper(20), Benton(11)
GOSHEN Elkhart
GOSPORT (47433) Owen(72), Monroe(16), Morgan(10)
GRABILL Allen
GRAMMER Bartholomew
GRANDVIEW Spencer
GRANGER (46530) St. Joseph(95), Elkhart(4)
GRANTSBURG Crawford
GRASS CREEK Fulton
GRAYSVILLE Sullivan

GREENCASTLE Putnam
GREENFIELD Hancock
GREENS FORK Wayne
GREENSBORO Henry
GREENSBURG Decatur
GREENTOWN Howard
GREENVILLE (47124) Floyd(73), Harrison(26)
GREENWOOD Johnson
GRIFFIN (47616) Posey(84), Gibson(15)
GRIFFITH Lake
GRISSOM AFB Miami
GRISSOM ARB Miami
GROVERTOWN (46531) Starke(98), Marshall(1)
GUILFORD Dearborn
GWYNNEVILLE Shelby
HAGERSTOWN (47346) Wayne(96), Henry(3)
HAMILTON (46742) Steuben(84), DeKalb(15)
HAMLET (46532) Starke(60), La Porte(39)
HAMMOND Lake
HANNA La Porte
HANOVER Jefferson
HARDINSBURG (47125) Orange(56), Washington(43)
HARLAN Allen
HARMONY Clay
HARRODSBURG Monroe
HARTFORD CITY Blackford
HARTSVILLE (47244) Bartholomew(79), Decatur(20)
HATFIELD Spencer
HAUBSTADT (47639) Gibson(77), Vanderburgh(21), Warrick(1)
HAYDEN Jennings
HAZLETON (47640) Gibson(70), Pike(29)
HEBRON (46341) Porter(80), Lake(17), Jasper(2)
HELMSBURG Brown
HELTONVILLE (47436) Lawrence(93), Monroe(6)
HEMLOCK Howard
HENRYVILLE (47126) Clark(94), Washington(3), Scott(1)
HIGHLAND Lake
HILLISBURG Clinton
HILLSBORO (47949) Fountain(98), Montgomery(1)
HILLSDALE Vermillion
HOAGLAND (46745) Allen(97), Adams(2)
HOBART (46342) Lake(97), Porter(2)
HOBBS Tipton
HOLLAND (47541) Dubois(80), Pike(16), Spencer(1), Warrick(1)
HOLTON (47023) Franklin(51), Ripley(47)
HOMER Rush
HOPE Bartholomew
HOWE LaGrange
HUDSON (46747) Steuben(77), LaGrange(13), DeKalb(8)
HUNTERTOWN (46748) Allen(96), DeKalb(2), Noble(1)
HUNTINGBURG Dubois
HUNTINGTON Huntington
HURON Lawrence
HYMERA Sullivan
IDAVILLE (47950) White(95), Carroll(4)
INDIANAPOLIS Marion
INGALLS Madison
INGLEFIELD Vanderburgh
IRELAND Dubois
JAMESTOWN (46147) Boone(91), Hendricks(8)
JASONVILLE (47438) Greene(74), Clay(23), Sullivan(1)
JASPER Dubois
JEFFERSONVILLE Clark
JONESBORO Grant
JONESVILLE Bartholomew
JUDSON Parke

KEMPTON (46049) Tipton(91), Clinton(8)
KENDALLVILLE Noble
KENNARD Henry
KENTLAND Newton
KEWANNA (46939) Fulton(87), Pulaski(12)
KEYSTONE Wells
KIMMELL Noble
KINGMAN (47952) Fountain(84), Parke(15)
KINGSBURY La Porte
KINGSFORD HEIGHTS La Porte
KIRKLIN (46050) Clinton(74), Boone(21), Tipton(3)
KNIGHTSTOWN (46148) Henry(84), Rush(15)
KNIGHTSVILLE Clay
KNOX Starke
KOKOMO Howard
KOLEEN Greene
KOUTS Porter
KURTZ Jackson
LA CROSSE (46348) La Porte(98), Porter(1)
LA FONTAINE (46940) Wabash(87), Huntington(8), Grant(3)
LA PORTE La Porte
LACONIA Harrison
LADOGA (47954) Montgomery(94), Putnam(4)
LAFAYETTE Tippecanoe
LAGRANGE (46761) LaGrange(95), Steuben(4)
LAGRO Wabash
LAKE CICOTT Cass
LAKE STATION Lake
LAKE VILLAGE Newton
LAKETON Wabash
LAKEVILLE (46536) St. Joseph(92), Marshall(7)
LAMAR Spencer
LANDESS Grant
LANESVILLE (47136) Harrison(81), Floyd(18)
LAOTTO (46763) Noble(86), DeKalb(13)
LAPAZ Marshall
LAPEL Madison
LARWILL (46764) Whitley(92), Noble(7)
LAUREL Franklin
LAWRENCEBURG Dearborn
LEAVENWORTH (47137) Crawford(96), Perry(3)
LEBANON Boone
LEESBURG Kosciusko
LEITERS FORD Fulton
LEO Allen
LEOPOLD Perry
LEROY Lake
LEWIS (47858) Clay(50), Vigo(32), Sullivan(17)
LEWISVILLE (47352) Rush(52), Henry(45), Fayette(1)
LEXINGTON (47138) Jefferson(53), Scott(45)
LIBERTY (47353) Union(94), Franklin(5)
LIBERTY CENTER (46766) Wells(98), Huntington(1)
LIBERTY MILLS Wabash
LIGONIER (46767) Noble(96), Elkhart(1), LaGrange(1)
LINCOLN CITY Spencer
LINDEN (47955) Montgomery(97), Tippecanoe(2)
LINN GROVE Adams
LINTON Greene
LITTLE YORK Washington
LIZTON Hendricks
LOGANSPORT (46947) Cass(97), Carroll(2)
LOOGOOTEE (47553) Martin(79), Daviess(20)
LOSANTVILLE (47354) Randolph(72), Henry(16), Delaware(6), Wayne(5)
LOWELL Lake

LUCERNE (46950) Cass(96), Fulton(3)
LYNN (47355) Randolph(99), Wayne(1)
LYNNVILLE (47619) Warrick(92), Gibson(6)
LYONS Greene
MACKEY Gibson
MACY (46951) Miami(75), Fulton(23)
MADISON (47250) Jefferson(96), Ripley(2), Switzerland(1)
MAGNET Perry
MANILLA (46150) Rush(93), Shelby(6)
MARENGO (47140) Orange(54), Crawford(45)
MARIAH HILL Spencer
MARION Grant
MARKLE (46770) Wells(79), Huntington(20)
MARKLEVILLE (46056) Madison(80), Hancock(15), Henry(3)
MARSHALL Parke
MARTINSVILLE Morgan
MARYSVILLE (47141) Clark(90), Scott(9)
MATTHEWS Grant
MAUCKPORT Harrison
MAXWELL Hancock
MAYS Rush
MC CORDSVILLE (46055) Hancock(81), Hamilton(18)
MECCA Parke
MEDARYVILLE (47957) Pulaski(90), Jasper(9)
MEDORA Jackson
MELLOTT Fountain
MEMPHIS Clark
MENTONE (46539) Kosciusko(91), Fulton(6), Marshall(2)
MEROM Sullivan
MERRILLVILLE Lake
METAMORA Franklin
MEXICO Miami
MIAMI Miami
MICHIGAN CITY La Porte
MICHIGANTOWN Clinton
MIDDLEBURY (46540) Elkhart(91), LaGrange(8)
MIDDLETOWN (47356) Henry(92), Madison(5), Delaware(1)
MIDLAND Greene
MILAN Ripley
MILFORD (46542) Kosciusko(95), Elkhart(4)
MILL CREEK La Porte
MILLERSBURG (46543) Elkhart(72), LaGrange(26), Noble(1)
MILLHOUSEN Decatur
MILLTOWN (47145) Crawford(96), Washington(3)
MILROY (46156) Rush(94), Decatur(5)
MILTON (47357) Wayne(71), Fayette(23), Madison(5)
MISHAWAKA St. Joseph
MITCHELL Lawrence
MODOC (47358) Randolph(98), Wayne(1)
MONGO LaGrange
MONON (47959) White(89), Jasper(7), Pulaski(2)
MONROE Adams
MONROE CITY Knox
MONROEVILLE (46773) Allen(90), Adams(9)
MONROVIA Morgan
MONTEREY (46960) Pulaski(64), Starke(28), Fulton(7)
MONTEZUMA Parke
MONTGOMERY Daviess
MONTICELLO (47960) White(90), Carroll(9)
MONTMORENCI Tippecanoe
MONTPELIER (47359) Blackford(87), Wells(11)
MOORELAND (47360) Henry(94), Wayne(3), Randolph(1)

MOORES HILL Dearborn
MOORESVILLE (46158) Morgan(90), Hendricks(9)
MORGANTOWN (46160) Brown(51), Morgan(29), Johnson(18)
MOROCCO Newton
MORRIS Ripley
MORRISTOWN (46161) Shelby(74), Hancock(18), Rush(7)
MOUNT AYR Newton
MOUNT PLEASANT Perry
MOUNT SAINT FRANCIS Floyd
MOUNT SUMMIT Henry
MOUNT VERNON Posey
MULBERRY (46058) Clinton(97), Tippecanoe(2)
MUNCIE Delaware
MUNSTER Lake
NABB (47147) Clark(41), Scott(32), Jefferson(25)
NAPOLEON Ripley
NAPPANEE (46550) Elkhart(83), Kosciusko(11), Marshall(4), St. Joseph(1)
NASHVILLE Brown
NEBRASKA Jennings
NEEDHAM (46162) Johnson(61), Shelby(39)
NEW ALBANY Floyd
NEW CARLISLE (46552) La Porte(57), St. Joseph(42)
NEW CASTLE Henry
NEW GOSHEN Vigo
NEW HARMONY Posey
NEW HAVEN Allen
NEW LEBANON Sullivan
NEW LISBON Henry
NEW MARKET Montgomery
NEW MIDDLETOWN Harrison
NEW PALESTINE (46163) Hancock(94), Shelby(5)
NEW PARIS Elkhart
NEW POINT Decatur
NEW RICHMOND (47967) Montgomery(92), Tippecanoe(7)
NEW ROSS (47968) Montgomery(86), Boone(8), Hendricks(4)
NEW SALISBURY Harrison
NEW TRENTON Franklin
NEW WASHINGTON Clark
NEW WAVERLY Cass
NEWBERRY (47449) Greene(93), Daviess(5), Martin(1)
NEWBURGH Warrick
NEWPORT Vermillion
NEWTOWN Fountain
NINEVEH (46164) Brown(70), Johnson(29)
NOBLESVILLE Hamilton
NORMAN (47264) Jackson(67), Lawrence(28), Monroe(3)
NORTH JUDSON (46366) Starke(93), Pulaski(6)
NORTH LIBERTY (46554) St. Joseph(97), La Porte(2)
NORTH MANCHESTER (46962) Wabash(94), Kosciusko(5)
NORTH SALEM (46165) Hendricks(98), Putnam(1)
NORTH VERNON Jennings
NORTH WEBSTER Kosciusko
NOTRE DAME St. Joseph
OAKFORD Howard
OAKLAND CITY (47660) Gibson(86), Pike(12)
OAKTOWN (47561) Knox(79), Sullivan(20)
OAKVILLE Delaware
ODON Daviess
OLDENBURG Franklin
ONWARD Cass
OOLITIC Lawrence
ORA Starke
ORESTES Madison

ORLAND (46776) Steuben(76), LaGrange(23)
ORLEANS (47452) Orange(91), Lawrence(7)
OSCEOLA (46561) St. Joseph(92), Elkhart(7)
OSGOOD Ripley
OSSIAN Wells
OTISCO Clark
OTTERBEIN (47970) Benton(43), Warren(43), Tippecanoe(12)
OTWELL (47564) Pike(89), Dubois(10)
OWENSBURG Greene
OWENSVILLE Gibson
OXFORD Benton
PALMYRA (47164) Harrison(72), Washington(26)
PAOLI Orange
PARAGON (46166) Morgan(95), Owen(4)
PARIS CROSSING (47270) Jennings(93), Jefferson(6)
PARKER CITY (47368) Randolph(85), Delaware(14)
PATOKA Gibson
PATRICKSBURG Owen
PATRIOT Switzerland
PAXTON Sullivan
PEKIN (47165) Washington(96), Clark(1), Floyd(1)
PENCE Warren
PENDLETON (46064) Madison(94), Hancock(4), Hamilton(1)
PENNVILLE (47369) Jay(95), Blackford(4)
PERRYSVILLE Vermillion
PERSHING Wayne
PERU (46970) Miami(93), Cass(3), Wabash(2)
PETERSBURG Pike
PETROLEUM Wells
PIERCETON (46562) Kosciusko(85), Noble(8), Whitley(6)
PIERCEVILLE Ripley
PIMENTO (47866) Vigo(92), Sullivan(7)
PINE VILLAGE (47975) Warren(95), Benton(4)
PITTSBORO (46167) Hendricks(98), Boone(1)
PLAINFIELD Hendricks
PLAINVILLE Daviess
PLEASANT LAKE Steuben
PLEASANT MILLS Adams
PLYMOUTH Marshall
POLAND (47868) Owen(83), Clay(13), Putnam(2)
PONETO Wells
PORTAGE Porter
PORTLAND Jay
POSEYVILLE (47633) Posey(93), Gibson(4), Vanderburgh(1)
PRAIRIE CREEK Vigo
PRAIRIETON Vigo
PREBLE Adams
PRINCETON Gibson
PUTNAMVILLE Putnam
QUINCY (47456) Owen(60), Morgan(35), Putnam(4)
RAGSDALE Knox
RAMSEY Harrison
REDKEY (47373) Jay(87), Randolph(12)
REELSVILLE (46171) Putnam(98), Clay(1)
REMINGTON (47977) Jasper(77), Benton(20), White(1)
RENSSELAER Jasper
REYNOLDS White
RICHLAND Spencer
RICHMOND Wayne
RIDGEVILLE (47380) Randolph(91), Jay(8)
RILEY Vigo
RISING SUN Ohio
ROACHDALE (46172) Putnam(96), Montgomery(3)
ROANN (46974) Wabash(61), Miami(38)

ROANOKE (46783) Huntington(54), Allen(35), Whitley(7), Wells(1)
ROCHESTER Fulton
ROCKFIELD Carroll
ROCKPORT Spencer
ROCKVILLE Parke
ROLLING PRAIRIE La Porte
ROME Perry
ROME CITY Noble
ROMNEY (47981) Tippecanoe(88), Montgomery(11)
ROSEDALE (47874) Vigo(53), Parke(41), Clay(5)
ROSELAWN Newton
ROSSVILLE (46065) Clinton(59), Carroll(40)
ROYAL CENTER (46978) Cass(93), Pulaski(3), White(3)
RUSHVILLE (46173) Rush(98), Franklin(1)
RUSSELLVILLE (46175) Putnam(89), Parke(7), Montgomery(3)
RUSSIAVILLE (46979) Howard(89), Clinton(4), Tipton(3), Carroll(2)
SAINT ANTHONY Dubois
SAINT BERNICE Vermillion
SAINT CROIX (47576) Perry(95), Crawford(4)
SAINT JOE DeKalb
SAINT JOHN Lake
SAINT MARY OF THE WOODS Vigo
SAINT MEINRAD (47577) Spencer(93), Perry(6)
SAINT PAUL (47272) Decatur(72), Shelby(26), Rush(1)
SALAMONIA Jay
SALEM Washington
SAN PIERRE (46374) Starke(88), Pulaski(11)
SANDBORN (47578) Knox(85), Greene(14)
SANDFORD Vigo
SANTA CLAUS Spencer
SARATOGA Randolph
SCHERERVILLE Lake
SCHNEIDER Lake
SCHNELLVILLE Dubois
SCIPIO Jennings
SCOTLAND Greene
SCOTTSBURG (47170) Scott(84), Washington(14)
SEDALIA Clinton
SEELYVILLE Vigo
SELLERSBURG (47172) Clark(92), Floyd(7)
SELMA Delaware
SERVIA Wabash
SEYMOUR (47274) Jackson(93), Bartholomew(3), Jennings(2)
SHARPSVILLE (46068) Tipton(90), Howard(9)
SHELBURN Sullivan
SHELBY Lake
SHELBYVILLE Shelby
SHEPARDSVILLE Vigo
SHERIDAN (46069) Hamilton(68), Boone(27), Clinton(4)
SHIPSHEWANA LaGrange
SHIRLEY (47384) Henry(72), Hancock(27)
SHOALS Martin
SIDNEY Kosciusko
SILVER LAKE (46982) Kosciusko(75), Wabash(20), Fulton(3)
SIMS Grant
SMITHVILLE Monroe
SOLSBERRY (47459) Greene(91), Owen(7)
SOMERSET Wabash
SOMERVILLE Gibson
SOUTH BEND St. Joseph
SOUTH MILFORD LaGrange
SOUTH WHITLEY (46787) Whitley(91), Kosciusko(7)
SPENCER (47460) Owen(96), Monroe(2)

SPENCERVILLE (46788) Allen(64), DeKalb(35)
SPICELAND Henry
SPRINGPORT (47386) Henry(97), Delaware(2)
SPRINGVILLE (47462) Lawrence(82), Monroe(9), Greene(8)
SPURGEON Pike
STANFORD Monroe
STAR CITY (46985) Pulaski(96), White(3)
STATE LINE Warren
STAUNTON Clay
STENDAL Pike
STILESVILLE (46180) Morgan(59), Hendricks(40)
STINESVILLE Monroe
STOCKWELL Tippecanoe
STRAUGHN (47387) Henry(98), Fayette(1)
STROH LaGrange
SULLIVAN Sullivan
SULPHUR Crawford
SULPHUR SPRINGS Henry
SUMAVA RESORTS Newton
SUMMITVILLE (46070) Madison(94), Delaware(3), Grant(2)
SUNMAN (47041) Ripley(61), Dearborn(38)
SWAYZEE (46986) Grant(98), Howard(1)
SWEETSER Grant
SWITZ CITY Greene
SYRACUSE (46567) Kosciusko(96), Elkhart(3)
TALBOT Benton
TANGIER Parke
TASWELL (47175) Crawford(91), Orange(8)
TAYLORSVILLE Bartholomew
TEFFT Jasper
TELL CITY Perry
TEMPLETON Benton
TENNYSON (47637) Warrick(87), Spencer(12)
TERRE HAUTE Vigo
THAYER Newton
THORNTOWN Boone
TIPPECANOE (46570) Marshall(88), Fulton(11)
TIPTON Tipton
TOBINSPORT Perry
TOPEKA (46571) LaGrange(98), Noble(1)
TRAFALGAR (46181) Johnson(83), Brown(16)
TROY (47588) Spencer(88), Perry(11)
TUNNELTON Lawrence
TWELVE MILE (46988) Cass(97), Fulton(2)
TYNER Marshall
UNDERWOOD (47177) Scott(57), Clark(42)
UNION CITY (47390) Randolph(95), Jay(4)
UNION MILLS La Porte
UNIONDALE Wells
UNIONVILLE (47468) Brown(51), Monroe(48)
UNIVERSAL Vermillion
UPLAND (46989) Grant(95), Blackford(2), Delaware(1)
URBANA Wabash
VALLONIA (47281) Jackson(58), Washington(41)
VALPARAISO Porter
VAN BUREN (46991) Grant(85), Huntington(12), Wells(2)
VEEDERSBURG Fountain
VELPEN (47590) Pike(89), Dubois(10)
VERNON Jennings
VERSAILLES Ripley
VEVAY (47043) Switzerland(97), Jefferson(2)
VINCENNES Knox
WABASH Wabash
WADESVILLE Posey
WAKARUSA (46573) Elkhart(72), St. Joseph(27)

WALDRON (46182) Shelby(81), Rush(18)
WALKERTON (46574) St. Joseph(38), Marshall(22), Starke(21), La Porte(17)
WALLACE Fountain
WALTON Cass
WANATAH La Porte
WARREN (46792) Huntington(81), Wells(18)
WARSAW Kosciusko
WASHINGTON Daviess
WATERLOO (46793) DeKalb(98), Steuben(1)
WAVELAND (47989) Montgomery(82), Parke(14), Putnam(2)
WAWAKA Noble
WAYNETOWN (47990) Montgomery(86), Fountain(13)
WEBSTER Wayne

WEST BADEN SPRINGS Orange
WEST COLLEGE CORNER (47003) Franklin(93), Union(6)
WEST HARRISON (47060) Dearborn(87), Franklin(12)
WEST LAFAYETTE Tippecanoe
WEST LEBANON Warren
WEST MIDDLETON Howard
WEST NEWTON Marion
WEST TERRE HAUTE Vigo
WESTFIELD Hamilton
WESTPHALIA Knox
WESTPOINT (47992) Tippecanoe(96), Fountain(3)
WESTPORT (47283) Decatur(92), Bartholomew(4), Jennings(3)
WESTVILLE (46391) La Porte(76), Porter(23)

WHEATFIELD Jasper
WHEATLAND Knox
WHEELER Porter
WHITELAND Johnson
WHITESTOWN Boone
WHITING Lake
WILKINSON (46186) Hancock(95), Henry(4)
WILLIAMS Lawrence
WILLIAMSBURG (47393) Wayne(71), Randolph(28)
WILLIAMSPORT Warren
WILLOW BRANCH Hancock
WINAMAC Pulaski
WINCHESTER Randolph
WINDFALL (46076) Tipton(94), Howard(5)
WINGATE (47994) Montgomery(77), Fountain(18), Tippecanoe(3)

WINONA LAKE Kosciusko
WINSLOW Pike
WOLCOTT (47995) White(72), Jasper(26)
WOLCOTTVILLE (46795) LaGrange(90), Noble(9)
WOLFLAKE Noble
WOODBURN Allen
WORTHINGTON (47471) Greene(90), Owen(9)
WYATT St. Joseph
YEOMAN Carroll
YODER (46798) Allen(92), Wells(7)
YORKTOWN Delaware
YOUNG AMERICA Cass
ZANESVILLE Allen
ZIONSVILLE (46077) Boone(91), Hamilton(6), Marion(1)

ZIP/City Cross Reference

46001-46001 ALEXANDRIA	46125-46125 EMINENCE	46340-46340 HANNA	46542-46542 MILFORD
46011-46018 ANDERSON	46126-46126 FAIRLAND	46341-46341 HEBRON	46543-46543 MILLERSBURG
46030-46030 ARCADIA	46127-46127 FALMOUTH	46342-46342 HOBART	46544-46546 MISHAWAKA
46031-46031 ATLANTA	46128-46128 FILLMORE	46345-46345 KINGSBURY	46550-46550 NAPPANEE
46032-46033 CARMEL	46129-46129 FINLY	46346-46346 KINGSFORD HEIGHTS	46552-46552 NEW CARLISLE
46034-46034 CICERO	46130-46130 FOUNTAINTOWN	46347-46347 KOUTS	46553-46553 NEW PARIS
46035-46035 COLFAX	46131-46131 FRANKLIN	46348-46348 LA CROSSE	46554-46554 NORTH LIBERTY
46036-46036 ELWOOD	46133-46133 GLENWOOD	46349-46349 LAKE VILLAGE	46555-46555 NORTH WEBSTER
46038-46038 FISHERS	46135-46135 GREENCASTLE	46350-46352 LA PORTE	46556-46556 NOTRE DAME
46039-46039 FOREST	46140-46140 GREENFIELD	46355-46355 LEROY	46561-46561 OSCEOLA
46040-46040 FORTVILLE	46142-46143 GREENWOOD	46356-46356 LOWELL	46562-46562 PIERCETON
46041-46041 FRANKFORT	46144-46144 GWYNNEVILLE	46360-46361 MICHIGAN CITY	46563-46563 PLYMOUTH
46044-46044 FRANKTON	46146-46146 HOMER	46365-46365 MILL CREEK	46565-46565 SHIPSHEWANA
46045-46045 GOLDSMITH	46147-46147 JAMESTOWN	46366-46366 NORTH JUDSON	46566-46566 SIDNEY
46046-46046 HILLISBURG	46148-46148 KNIGHTSTOWN	46367-46367 LA PORTE	46567-46567 SYRACUSE
46047-46047 HOBBS	46149-46149 LIZTON	46368-46368 PORTAGE	46570-46570 TIPPECANOE
46048-46048 INGALLS	46150-46150 MANILLA	46371-46371 ROLLING PRAIRIE	46571-46571 TOPEKA
46049-46049 KEMPTON	46151-46151 MARTINSVILLE	46372-46372 ROSELAWN	46572-46572 TYNER
46050-46050 KIRKLIN	46154-46154 MAXWELL	46373-46373 SAINT JOHN	46573-46573 WAKARUSA
46051-46051 LAPEL	46155-46155 MAYS	46374-46374 SAN PIERRE	46574-46574 WALKERTON
46052-46052 LEBANON	46156-46156 MILROY	46375-46375 SCHERERVILLE	46580-46582 WARSAW
46055-46055 MC CORDSVILLE	46157-46157 MONROVIA	46376-46376 SCHNEIDER	46590-46590 WINONA LAKE
46056-46056 MARKLEVILLE	46158-46158 MOORESVILLE	46377-46377 SHELBY	46595-46595 WYATT
46057-46057 MICHIGANTOWN	46160-46160 MORGANTOWN	46379-46379 SUMAVA RESORTS	46600-46699 SOUTH BEND
46058-46058 MULBERRY	46161-46161 MORRISTOWN	46380-46380 TEFFT	46701-46701 ALBION
46060-46061 NOBLESVILLE	46162-46162 NEEDHAM	46381-46381 THAYER	46702-46702 ANDREWS
46063-46063 ORESTES	46163-46163 NEW PALESTINE	46382-46382 UNION MILLS	46703-46703 ANGOLA
46064-46064 PENDLETON	46164-46164 NINEVEH	46383-46385 VALPARAISO	46704-46704 ARCOLA
46065-46065 ROSSVILLE	46165-46165 NORTH SALEM	46390-46390 WANATAH	46705-46705 ASHLEY
46067-46067 SEDALIA	46166-46166 PARAGON	46391-46391 WESTVILLE	46706-46706 AUBURN
46068-46068 SHARPSVILLE	46167-46167 PITTSBORO	46392-46392 WHEATFIELD	46710-46710 AVILLA
46069-46069 SHERIDAN	46168-46168 PLAINFIELD	46393-46393 WHEELER	46711-46711 BERNE
46070-46070 SUMMITVILLE	46170-46170 PUTNAMVILLE	46394-46394 WHITING	46713-46713 BIPPUS
46071-46071 THORNTOWN	46171-46171 REELSVILLE	46399-46399 LOWELL	46714-46714 BLUFFTON
46072-46072 TIPTON	46172-46172 ROACHDALE	46400-46404 GARY	46720-46720 BRIMFIELD
46074-46074 WESTFIELD	46173-46173 RUSHVILLE	46405-46405 LAKE STATION	46721-46721 BUTLER
46075-46075 WHITESTOWN	46175-46175 RUSSELLVILLE	46406-46409 GARY	46723-46723 CHURUBUSCO
46076-46076 WINDFALL	46176-46176 SHELBYVILLE	46410-46411 MERRILLVILLE	46725-46725 COLUMBIA CITY
46077-46077 ZIONSVILLE	46180-46180 STILESVILLE	46501-46501 ARGOS	46730-46730 CORUNNA
46082-46082 CARMEL	46181-46181 TRAFALGAR	46502-46502 ATWOOD	46731-46731 CRAIGVILLE
46102-46102 ADVANCE	46182-46182 WALDRON	46504-46504 BOURBON	46732-46732 CROMWELL
46103-46103 AMO	46183-46183 WEST NEWTON	46506-46506 BREMEN	46733-46733 DECATUR
46104-46104 ARLINGTON	46184-46184 WHITELAND	46507-46507 BRISTOL	46737-46737 FREMONT
46105-46105 BAINBRIDGE	46186-46186 WILKINSON	46508-46508 BURKET	46738-46738 GARRETT
46106-46106 BARGERSVILLE	46187-46187 WILLOW BRANCH	46510-46510 CLAYPOOL	46740-46740 GENEVA
46107-46107 BEECH GROVE	46200-46298 INDIANAPOLIS	46511-46511 CULVER	46741-46741 GRABILL
46110-46110 BOGGSTOWN	46301-46301 BEVERLY SHORES	46513-46513 DONALDSON	46742-46742 HAMILTON
46111-46111 BROOKLYN	46302-46302 BOONE GROVE	46514-46517 ELKHART	46743-46743 HARLAN
46112-46112 BROWNSBURG	46303-46303 CEDAR LAKE	46524-46524 ETNA GREEN	46744-46744 OSSIAN
46113-46113 CAMBY	46304-46304 CHESTERTON	46526-46528 GOSHEN	46745-46745 HOAGLAND
46114-46114 CARTERSBURG	46307-46308 CROWN POINT	46530-46530 GRANGER	46746-46746 HOWE
46115-46115 CARTHAGE	46310-46310 DEMOTTE	46531-46531 GROVERTOWN	46747-46747 HUDSON
46117-46117 CHARLOTTESVILLE	46311-46311 DYER	46532-46532 HAMLET	46748-46748 HUNTERTOWN
46118-46118 CLAYTON	46312-46312 EAST CHICAGO	46534-46534 KNOX	46750-46750 HUNTINGTON
46120-46120 CLOVERDALE	46319-46319 GRIFFITH	46536-46536 LAKEVILLE	46755-46755 KENDALLVILLE
46121-46121 COATESVILLE	46320-46320 HAMMOND	46537-46537 LAPAZ	46759-46759 KEYSTONE
46122-46122 DANVILLE	46321-46321 MUNSTER	46538-46538 LEESBURG	46760-46760 KIMMELL
46123-46123 AVON	46322-46322 HIGHLAND	46539-46539 MENTONE	46761-46761 LAGRANGE
46124-46124 EDINBURGH	46323-46327 HAMMOND	46540-46540 MIDDLEBURY	46763-46763 LAOTTO

46764-46764 LARWILL	46970-46970 PERU	47140-47140 MARENGO	47348-47348 HARTFORD CITY
46765-46765 LEO	46971-46971 GRISSOM AFB	47141-47141 MARYSVILLE	47351-47351 KENNARD
46766-46766 LIBERTY CENTER	46971-46971 GRISSOM ARB	47142-47142 MAUCKPORT	47352-47352 LEWISVILLE
46767-46767 LIGONIER	46974-46974 ROANN	47143-47143 MEMPHIS	47353-47353 LIBERTY
46769-46769 LINN GROVE	46975-46975 ROCHESTER	47144-47144 JEFFERSONVILLE	47354-47354 LOSANTVILLE
46770-46770 MARKLE	46977-46977 ROCKFIELD	47145-47145 MILLTOWN	47355-47355 LYNN
46771-46771 MONGO	46978-46978 ROYAL CENTER	47146-47146 MOUNT SAINT FRANCIS	47356-47356 MIDDLETOWN
46772-46772 MONROE	46979-46979 RUSSIAVILLE	47147-47147 NABB	47357-47357 MILTON
46773-46773 MONROEVILLE	46980-46980 SERVIA	47150-47151 NEW ALBANY	47358-47358 MODOC
46774-46774 NEW HAVEN	46982-46982 SILVER LAKE	47160-47160 NEW MIDDLETOWN	47359-47359 MONTPELIER
46776-46776 ORLAND	46983-46983 SIMS	47161-47161 NEW SALISBURY	47360-47360 MOORELAND
46777-46777 OSSIAN	46984-46984 SOMERSET	47162-47162 NEW WASHINGTON	47361-47361 MOUNT SUMMIT
46778-46778 PETROLEUM	46985-46985 STAR CITY	47163-47163 OTISCO	47362-47362 NEW CASTLE
46779-46779 PLEASANT LAKE	46986-46986 SWAYZEE	47164-47164 PALMYRA	47366-47366 NEW LISBON
46780-46780 PLEASANT MILLS	46987-46987 SWEETSER	47165-47165 PEKIN	47367-47367 OAKVILLE
46781-46781 PONETO	46988-46988 TWELVE MILE	47166-47166 RAMSEY	47368-47368 PARKER CITY
46782-46782 PREBLE	46989-46989 UPLAND	47167-47167 SALEM	47369-47369 PENNVILLE
46783-46783 ROANOKE	46990-46990 URBANA	47170-47170 SCOTTSBURG	47370-47370 PERSHING
46784-46784 ROME CITY	46991-46991 VAN BUREN	47172-47172 SELLERSBURG	47371-47371 PORTLAND
46785-46785 SAINT JOE	46992-46992 WABASH	47174-47174 SULPHUR	47373-47373 REDKEY
46786-46786 SOUTH MILFORD	46994-46994 WALTON	47175-47175 TASWELL	47374-47374 RICHMOND
46787-46787 SOUTH WHITLEY	46995-46995 WEST MIDDLETON	47177-47177 UNDERWOOD	47380-47380 RIDGEVILLE
46788-46788 SPENCERVILLE	46996-46996 WINAMAC	47199-47199 JEFFERSONVILLE	47381-47381 SALAMONIA
46789-46789 STROH	46998-46998 YOUNG AMERICA	47201-47203 COLUMBUS	47382-47382 SARATOGA
46790-46790 OSSIAN	47001-47001 AURORA	47220-47220 BROWNSTOWN	47383-47383 SELMA
46791-46791 UNIONDALE	47003-47003 WEST COLLEGE CORNER	47222-47222 BURNEY	47384-47384 SHIRLEY
46792-46792 WARREN	47006-47006 BATESVILLE	47223-47223 BUTLERVILLE	47385-47385 SPICELAND
46793-46793 WATERLOO	47010-47010 BATH	47224-47224 CANAAN	47386-47386 SPRINGPORT
46794-46794 WAWAKA	47011-47011 BENNINGTON	47225-47225 CLARKSBURG	47387-47387 STRAUGHN
46795-46795 WOLCOTTVILLE	47012-47012 BROOKVILLE	47226-47226 CLIFFORD	47388-47388 SULPHUR SPRINGS
46796-46796 WOLFLAKE	47016-47016 CEDAR GROVE	47227-47227 COMMISKEY	47390-47390 UNION CITY
46797-46797 WOODBURN	47017-47017 CROSS PLAINS	47228-47228 CORTLAND	47392-47392 WEBSTER
46798-46798 YODER	47018-47018 DILLSBORO	47229-47229 CROTHERSVILLE	47393-47393 WILLIAMSBURG
46799-46799 ZANESVILLE	47019-47019 EAST ENTERPRISE	47230-47230 DEPUTY	47394-47394 WINCHESTER
46800-46899 FORT WAYNE	47020-47020 FLORENCE	47231-47231 DUPONT	47396-47396 YORKTOWN
46901-46904 KOKOMO	47021-47021 FRIENDSHIP	47232-47232 ELIZABETHTOWN	47401-47403 BLOOMINGTON
46910-46910 AKRON	47022-47022 GUILFORD	47234-47234 FLAT ROCK	47420-47420 AVOCA
46911-46911 AMBOY	47023-47023 HOLTON	47235-47235 FREETOWN	47421-47421 BEDFORD
46912-46912 ATHENS	47024-47024 LAUREL	47236-47236 GRAMMER	47424-47424 BLOOMFIELD
46913-46913 BRINGHURST	47025-47025 LAWRENCEBURG	47240-47240 GREENSBURG	47426-47426 CLEAR CREEK
46914-46914 BUNKER HILL	47030-47030 METAMORA	47243-47243 HANOVER	47427-47427 COAL CITY
46915-46915 BURLINGTON	47031-47031 MILAN	47244-47244 HARTSVILLE	47429-47429 ELLETTSVILLE
46916-46916 BURROWS	47032-47032 MOORES HILL	47245-47245 HAYDEN	47430-47430 FORT RITNER
46917-46917 CAMDEN	47033-47033 MORRIS	47246-47246 HOPE	47431-47431 FREEDOM
46919-46919 CONVERSE	47034-47034 NAPOLEON	47247-47247 JONESVILLE	47432-47432 FRENCH LICK
46920-46920 CUTLER	47035-47035 NEW TRENTON	47249-47249 KURTZ	47433-47433 GOSPORT
46921-46921 DEEDSVILLE	47036-47036 OLDENBURG	47250-47250 MADISON	47434-47434 HARRODSBURG
46922-46922 DELONG	47037-47037 OSGOOD	47260-47260 MEDORA	47435-47435 HELMSBURG
46923-46923 DELPHI	47038-47038 PATRIOT	47261-47261 MILLHOUSEN	47436-47436 HELTONVILLE
46925-46925 DENHAM	47039-47039 PIERCEVILLE	47262-47262 NEBRASKA	47437-47437 HURON
46926-46926 DENVER	47040-47040 RISING SUN	47263-47263 NEW POINT	47438-47438 JASONVILLE
46928-46928 FAIRMOUNT	47041-47041 SUNMAN	47264-47264 NORMAN	47439-47439 KOLEEN
46929-46929 FLORA	47042-47042 VERSAILLES	47265-47265 NORTH VERNON	47441-47441 LINTON
46930-46930 FOWLERTON	47043-47043 VEVAY	47270-47270 PARIS CROSSING	47443-47443 LYONS
46931-46931 FULTON	47060-47060 WEST HARRISON	47272-47272 SAINT PAUL	47445-47445 MIDLAND
46932-46932 GALVESTON	47102-47102 AUSTIN	47273-47273 SCIPIO	47446-47446 MITCHELL
46933-46933 GAS CITY	47104-47104 BETHLEHEM	47274-47274 SEYMOUR	47448-47448 NASHVILLE
46935-46935 GRASS CREEK	47106-47106 BORDEN	47280-47280 TAYLORSVILLE	47449-47449 NEWBERRY
46936-46936 GREENTOWN	47107-47107 BRADFORD	47281-47281 VALLONIA	47451-47451 OOLITIC
46937-46937 HEMLOCK	47108-47108 CAMPBELLSBURG	47282-47282 VERNON	47452-47452 ORLEANS
46938-46938 JONESBORO	47110-47110 CENTRAL	47283-47283 WESTPORT	47453-47453 OWENSBURG
46939-46939 KEWANNA	47111-47111 CHARLESTOWN	47302-47308 MUNCIE	47454-47454 PAOLI
46940-46940 LA FONTAINE	47112-47112 CORYDON	47320-47320 ALBANY	47455-47455 PATRICKSBURG
46941-46941 LAGRO	47114-47114 CRANDALL	47322-47322 BENTONVILLE	47456-47456 QUINCY
46942-46942 LAKE CICOTT	47115-47115 DEPAUW	47324-47324 BOSTON	47457-47457 SCOTLAND
46943-46943 LAKETON	47116-47116 ECKERTY	47325-47325 BROWNSVILLE	47458-47458 SMITHVILLE
46944-46944 LANDESS	47117-47117 ELIZABETH	47326-47326 BRYANT	47459-47459 SOLSBERRY
46945-46945 LEITERS FORD	47118-47118 ENGLISH	47327-47327 CAMBRIDGE CITY	47460-47460 SPENCER
46946-46946 LIBERTY MILLS	47119-47119 FLOYDS KNOBS	47330-47330 CENTERVILLE	47462-47462 SPRINGVILLE
46947-46947 LOGANSPORT	47120-47120 FREDERICKSBURG	47331-47331 CONNERSVILLE	47463-47463 STANFORD
46950-46950 LUCERNE	47122-47122 GEORGETOWN	47334-47334 DALEVILLE	47464-47464 STINESVILLE
46951-46951 MACY	47123-47123 GRANTSBURG	47335-47335 DUBLIN	47465-47465 SWITZ CITY
46952-46953 MARION	47124-47124 GREENVILLE	47336-47336 DUNKIRK	47467-47467 TUNNELTON
46957-46957 MATTHEWS	47125-47125 HARDINSBURG	47337-47337 DUNREITH	47468-47468 UNIONVILLE
46958-46958 MEXICO	47126-47126 HENRYVILLE	47338-47338 EATON	47469-47469 WEST BADEN SPRINGS
46959-46959 MIAMI	47129-47129 CLARKSVILLE	47339-47339 ECONOMY	47470-47470 WILLIAMS
46960-46960 MONTEREY	47130-47134 JEFFERSONVILLE	47340-47340 FARMLAND	47471-47471 WORTHINGTON
46961-46961 NEW WAVERLY	47135-47135 LACONIA	47341-47341 FOUNTAIN CITY	47490-47490 BLOOMINGTON
46962-46962 NORTH MANCHESTER	47136-47136 LANESVILLE	47342-47342 GASTON	47501-47501 WASHINGTON
46965-46965 OAKFORD	47137-47137 LEAVENWORTH	47344-47344 GREENSBORO	47512-47512 BICKNELL
46967-46967 ONWARD	47138-47138 LEXINGTON	47345-47345 GREENS FORK	47513-47513 BIRDSEYE
46968-46968 ORA	47139-47139 LITTLE YORK	47346-47346 HAGERSTOWN	47514-47514 BRANCHVILLE

47515-47515	BRISTOW	47596-47596 WESTPHALIA	47851-47851 FONTANET	47940-47940 DARLINGTON
47516-47516	BRUCEVILLE	47597-47597 WHEATLAND	47852-47852 GRAYSVILLE	47941-47941 DAYTON
47519-47519	CANNELBURG	47598-47598 WINSLOW	47853-47853 HARMONY	47942-47942 EARL PARK
47520-47520	CANNELTON	47601-47601 BOONVILLE	47854-47854 HILLSDALE	47943-47943 FAIR OAKS
47521-47521	CELESTINE	47610-47610 CHANDLER	47855-47855 HYMERA	47944-47944 FOWLER
47522-47522	CRANE	47611-47611 CHRISNEY	47856-47856 JUDSON	47946-47946 FRANCESVILLE
47523-47523	DALE	47612-47612 CYNTHIANA	47857-47857 KNIGHTSVILLE	47948-47948 GOODLAND
47524-47524	DECKER	47613-47613 ELBERFELD	47858-47858 LEWIS	47949-47949 HILLSBORO
47525-47525	DERBY	47614-47614 FOLSOMVILLE	47859-47859 MARSHALL	47950-47950 IDAVILLE
47527-47527	DUBOIS	47615-47615 GRANDVIEW	47860-47860 MECCA	47951-47951 KENTLAND
47528-47528	EDWARDSPORT	47616-47616 GRIFFIN	47861-47861 MEROM	47952-47952 KINGMAN
47529-47529	ELNORA	47617-47617 HATFIELD	47862-47862 MONTEZUMA	47954-47954 LADOGA
47530-47530	EMISON	47618-47618 INGLEFIELD	47863-47863 NEW GOSHEN	47955-47955 LINDEN
47531-47531	EVANSTON	47619-47619 LYNNVILLE	47864-47864 NEW LEBANON	47957-47957 MEDARYVILLE
47532-47532	FERDINAND	47620-47620 MOUNT VERNON	47865-47865 PAXTON	47958-47958 MELLOTT
47535-47535	FREELANDVILLE	47629-47630 NEWBURGH	47866-47866 PIMENTO	47959-47959 MONON
47536-47536	FULDA	47631-47631 NEW HARMONY	47868-47868 POLAND	47960-47960 MONTICELLO
47537-47537	GENTRYVILLE	47633-47633 POSEYVILLE	47869-47869 PRAIRIE CREEK	47962-47962 MONTMORENCI
47541-47541	HOLLAND	47634-47634 RICHLAND	47870-47870 PRAIRIETON	47963-47963 MOROCCO
47542-47542	HUNTINGBURG	47635-47635 ROCKPORT	47871-47871 RILEY	47964-47964 MOUNT AYR
47545-47545	IRELAND	47637-47637 TENNYSON	47872-47872 ROCKVILLE	47965-47965 NEW MARKET
47546-47549	JASPER	47638-47638 WADESVILLE	47874-47874 ROSEDALE	47966-47966 NEWPORT
47550-47550	LAMAR	47639-47639 HAUBSTADT	47875-47875 SAINT BERNICE	47967-47967 NEW RICHMOND
47551-47551	LEOPOLD	47640-47640 HAZLETON	47876-47876 SAINT MARY OF THE	47968-47968 NEW ROSS
47552-47552	LINCOLN CITY	47647-47647 BUCKSKIN	WOODS	47969-47969 NEWTOWN
47553-47553	LOOGOOTEE	47648-47648 FORT BRANCH	47877-47877 SANDFORD	47970-47970 OTTERBEIN
47555-47555	MAGNET	47649-47649 FRANCISCO	47878-47878 SEELYVILLE	47971-47971 OXFORD
47556-47556	MARIAH HILL	47654-47654 MACKEY	47879-47879 SHELBURN	47973-47973 PENCE
47557-47557	MONROE CITY	47660-47660 OAKLAND CITY	47880-47880 SHEPARDSVILLE	47974-47974 PERRYSVILLE
47558-47558	MONTGOMERY	47665-47665 OWENSVILLE	47881-47881 STAUNTON	47975-47975 PINE VILLAGE
47559-47559	MOUNT PLEASANT	47666-47666 PATOKA	47882-47882 SULLIVAN	47976-47976 EARL PARK
47561-47561	OAKTOWN	47670-47671 PRINCETON	47884-47884 UNIVERSAL	47977-47977 REMINGTON
47562-47562	ODON	47683-47683 SOMERVILLE	47885-47885 WEST TERRE HAUTE	47978-47978 RENSSELAER
47564-47564	OTWELL	47700-47750 EVANSVILLE	47901-47905 LAFAYETTE	47980-47980 REYNOLDS
47567-47567	PETERSBURG	47801-47814 TERRE HAUTE	47906-47907 WEST LAFAYETTE	47981-47981 ROMNEY
47568-47568	PLAINVILLE	47830-47830 BELLMORE	47909-47909 LAFAYETTE	47982-47982 STATE LINE
47573-47573	RAGSDALE	47831-47831 BLANFORD	47916-47916 ALAMO	47983-47983 STOCKWELL
47574-47574	ROME	47832-47832 BLOOMINGDALE	47917-47917 AMBIA	47984-47984 TALBOT
47575-47575	SAINT ANTHONY	47833-47833 BOWLING GREEN	47918-47918 ATTICA	47985-47985 TANGIER
47576-47576	SAINT CROIX	47834-47834 BRAZIL	47920-47920 BATTLE GROUND	47986-47986 TEMPLETON
47577-47577	SAINT MEINRAD	47836-47836 BRIDGETON	47921-47921 BOSWELL	47987-47987 VEEDERSBURG
47578-47578	SANDBORN	47837-47837 CARBON	47922-47922 BROOK	47988-47988 WALLACE
47579-47579	SANTA CLAUS	47838-47838 CARLISLE	47923-47923 BROOKSTON	47989-47989 WAVELAND
47580-47580	SCHNELLVILLE	47840-47840 CENTERPOINT	47924-47924 BUCK CREEK	47990-47990 WAYNETOWN
47581-47581	SHOALS	47841-47841 CLAY CITY	47925-47925 BUFFALO	47991-47991 WEST LEBANON
47584-47584	SPURGEON	47842-47842 CLINTON	47926-47926 BURNETTSVILLE	47992-47992 WESTPOINT
47585-47585	STENDAL	47845-47845 COALMONT	47928-47928 CAYUGA	47993-47993 WILLIAMSPORT
47586-47586	TELL CITY	47846-47846 CORY	47929-47929 CHALMERS	47994-47994 WINGATE
47587-47587	TOBINSPORT	47847-47847 DANA	47930-47930 CLARKS HILL	47995-47995 WOLCOTT
47588-47588	TROY	47848-47848 DUGGER	47931-47931 COLBURN	47996-47996 WEST LAFAYETTE
47590-47590	VELPEN	47849-47849 FAIRBANKS	47932-47932 COVINGTON	47997-47997 YEOMAN
47591-47591	VINCENNES	47850-47850 FARMERSBURG	47933-47939 CRAWFORDSVILLE	

General Help Numbers:

Governor's Office
State Capitol Bldg   515-281-5211
Des Moines, IA 50319   Fax 515-281-6611
www.state.ia.us/governor   8AM-4:30PM

Attorney General's Office
Hoover Bldg   515-281-5164
1305 E Walnut St   Fax 515-281-4209
Des Moines, IA 50319   8AM-4:30PM
www.state.ia.us/government/ag

State Court Administrator
State Capitol Bldg   515-281-5241
Des Moines, IA 50319   Fax 515-242-0014
www.judicial.state.ia.us/courtadmin   8AM-4:30PM

State Archives
Library/Archives   515-281-5111
600 E. Locust   Fax 515-282-0502
Des Moines, IA 50319-0290   9AM-4:30PM TU-SA
www.iowahistory.org   & M (June-Aug)

State Specifics:

Capital: Des Moines
                                  Polk County

Time Zone: CST

Number of Counties: 99

Population: 2,923,179

Web Site: www.state.ia.us

State Agencies

Criminal Records

Division of Criminal Investigations, Bureau of Identification, Wallace State Office Bldg, Des Moines, IA 50309; 515-281-4776, 515-281-7996, 515-242-6297 (Fax), 8AM-4:30PM.

www.state.ia.us/government/dps/dci/crimhist.htm

Note: The Iowa Sex Offender Registry can be searched at www.state.ia.us/government/dps/dci/isor/ and www.iowasexoffender.com/default.asp. Only high-risk offenders listed; database may be searched at police or sheriff's offices.

Indexing & Storage: Records are available until the person is 80 years old or passes away, then records are deleted. There is a computerized index going back to 1935. It takes up to 10 days before new records are available for inquiry. Records are indexed on in house computer (100%). Records are normally destroyed after 4 years if there is no disposition. 91% of all arrests in database have final dispositions recorded, 91% for those arrests within last 5 years.

Searching: A signed release or waiver is not required, nor are fingerprints. But if release is included, the reports will show any arrest over 18 months old without a disposition, otherwise if no release is presented then only up to 18 months. Include the following in your request: date of birth, sex, Social Security Number. A signed release is an option. Be sure to give the full name. Request Form A is required for each surname. This form can be obtained from the web site, by fax, mail, or in person. A signed release by subject entitles requester to all records including those without dispositions (up to 4 years old). If the subject's signed release is not presented, then no arrest records over 18 months old without dispositions are released.

Access by: mail, fax, in person, online.

Fee & Payment: The fee for a record search is $13.00 per surname checked. If married and maiden names are checked, the fee would be $26.00. Iowa law requires employers to pay the fee for potential employees' record checks. Fee payee: Iowa Division of Criminal Investigation. Payment is required unless pre-arranged billing has been arranged. Ongoing requesters can set up an account with a $500 deposit. Personal checks accepted. Credit cards accepted: MasterCard, Visa.

Mail search: Turnaround time: 1 to 2 days. No self addressed stamped envelope is required.

Fax search: Only those requesters who have opened a pre-paid account may fax.

In person search: Only the subject or their attorney will receive the record while they wait, within 15 minutes.

Online search: Although this agency does not offer online access, there is online free access to the statewide Iowa Judicial System courts database at www.judicial.state.ia.us/online_records/.

Expedited service: Expedited service is available for fax searches. Account is required. Turnaround time: same day if possible.

Corporation Records
Limited Liability Company Records
Fictitious Name
Limited Partnership Records
Trademarks/Servicemarks

Secretary of State, Corporation Division, 2nd Floor, Hoover Bldg, Des Moines, IA 50319; 515-281-5204, 515-242-5953 (Fax), 8AM-4:30PM.

www.sos.state.ia.us

Indexing & Storage: Records are available from the late 1800s. New records are available for inquiry immediately. Records are indexed on microfilm, inhouse computer, on-line.

Searching: Include the following in your request: full name of business, specific records that you need copies of. In addition to the articles of incorporation, the following information is released: Annual/Biennial Reports, Officers, Directors, DBAs, Prior (merged) names, Inactive and Reserved names.

Access by: mail, phone, fax, in person, online.

Fee & Payment: Copies are $1.00 each, certificataion is $5.00. Fee payee: Secretary of State. Prepayment required. A charge account may be established for ongoing requesters. Call 515-281-5204 for more details. Personal checks accepted. Credit cards accepted: MasterCard, Visa.

Mail search: Turnaround time: 2 to 3 days. A self addressed stamped envelope is requested. No fee for mail request.

Phone search: No fee for telephone request. You are restricted to 3 requests per call.

Fax search: Add $1.00 for each page that is faxed. Turnaround time is 2 days.

In person search: No fee for request.

Online search: For free searching, go to www.sos.state.ia.us/corp/corp_search.asp

Other access: The state will sell the records in database format. Call the number listed above and ask for Karen Ubaldo for more information.

Uniform Commercial Code
Federal Tax Liens

UCC Division, Secretary of State, Hoover Bldg, 2nd Floor, Des Moines, IA 50319; 515-281-5204, 515-242-5953 (Other Fax Line), 515-242-6556 (Fax), 8AM-4:30PM.

www.sos.state.ia.us

Indexing & Storage: Records are available from 1966 and are computerized. All current records are on optical disk. It takes 1 to 3 days before new records are available for inquiry.

Searching: Use search request form UCC-11. Specify if you also want federal tax liens and include another search fee. Federal tax liens on individuals and all state tax liens are filed at the county level. Include the following in your request: debtor name. Copies of filings may be requested at time of search, but do not ask for copies with your initial request unless you have a charge account.

Access by: mail, phone, fax, in person, online.

Fee & Payment: The fee is $5.00 per debtor name, $6.00 for federal liens. Copies are $1.00 per page. Fee payee: Secretary of State. Prepayment required. Personal checks accepted. Credit cards accepted: MasterCard, Visa.

Mail search: Turnaround time: 1 to 2 days. A self addressed stamped envelope is requested.

Phone search: A telephone search is available with a prepaid or charge account, or with credit card.

Fax search: Turnaround time usually same day, fee is $1.00 per page.

In person search: Searching is available in person.

Online search: All computerized information on or before June 30, 2001 is available online at www.sos.state.ia.us/UCC_Search/UccOld_Search.asp. There is no fee at this "UCC Archive" site. For computerized records online from July 1, 2001 to present, you may search at www.sos.state.ia.us/UCC_Search/UCC_Search.asp

State Tax Liens
Records not maintained by a state level agency.

Note: Records are found at the county recorder's offices.

Sales Tax Registrations

Department of Revenue, Taxpayer Services Division, Hoover State Office Bldg, Des Moines, IA 50306-0465; 515-281-3114, 515-242-6487 (Fax), 8AM-4PM.

www.state.ia.us/tax

Indexing & Storage: Records are available for 5 years. Records are indexed on computer, microfiche.

Searching: This agency will provide any information found on the face of the Tax Permit-business name, business address, and tax permit number. Information not released includes telephone numbers, tax liabilities, taxes collected, officers, federal ID#s, etc. Include the following in your request: business name. They will also search by tax permit number.

Access by: mail, phone, in person, online.

Fee & Payment: There is no search fee; however, there is a $5.00 copy fee per document. Fee payee: Treasurer State of Iowa. Prepayment required. Personal checks accepted. No credit cards accepted.

Mail search: Turnaround time: 7 to 10 days. No self addressed stamped envelope is required.

Phone search: Limited information is available by phone.

In person search: Searching is available in person.

Online search: One may check the status of a permit online, but the permit number is needed (no name searching).

Other access: The agency will provide the database on lists, fees vary from $20.00 to $45.00.

Birth Certificates

Iowa Department of Public Health, Bureau of Vital Records, 321 E 12th St, Lucas Bldg, Des Moines, IA 50319-0075; 515-281-4944, 515-281-5871 (Message Recording), 7AM-4:45PM.

www.idph.state.ia.us

Note: All vital records are open for inspection at the county level, usually for a $10.00 fee.

Indexing & Storage: Records are available from 1880 to present. It takes 30 days to 6 weeks before new records are available for inquiry. Records are indexed on microfiche, inhouse computer.

Searching: Adoption records are not released. Include the following in your request: full name, names of parents, mother's maiden name, date of birth, place of birth, relationship to person of record, reason for information request. Must have copy of a photo ID (mail) or a photo ID (in person) to search.

Access by: mail, phone, in person.

Fee & Payment: The search fee is $10.00, There is an additional $5.00 fee to use a credit card. For records 1880 to 1915, a $10.00 per year fee is charged. Fee payee: Iowa Department of Public Health. Prepayment required. Personal checks accepted. Credit cards accepted: MasterCard, Visa, AmEx, Discover.

Mail search: Turnaround time: within 1 month.

Phone search: Records are available by phone.

In person search: Same day service is not available. Turnaround time is 48 hours.

Expedited service: Expedited mail service is available for phone searches. Add $11.00 per package. Must use a credit card which is an extra $5.00. Normal turnaround time is 10-14 days.

Death Records

Iowa Department of Public Health, Vital Records, 321 E 12th St, Lucas Bldg, Des Moines, IA 50319-0075; 515-281-4944, 515-281-5871 (Message Recording), 7AM-4:45PM.

www.idph.state.ia.us

Indexing & Storage: Records are available from 1880 to present. From 1880 to 1895 there is no index. It takes up to 60 days before new records are available for inquiry. Records are indexed on microfiche, inhouse computer.

Searching: Include the following in your request: full name, date of death, place of death, relationship to person of record, reason for information request. Must have a copy of a photo ID (mail) or a photo ID (in person) to search.

Access by: mail, phone, in person.

Fee & Payment: The search fee is $10.00 for each index searched. There is an additional $5.00 fee when using a credit card. Fee payee: Iowa Department of Public Health. Prepayment required. Personal checks accepted. Credit cards accepted: MasterCard, Visa, AmEx, Discover.

Mail search: Turnaround time: within 1 month. A self addressed stamped envelope is requested.

Phone search: Records are available by phone.

In person search: Same day service in not available. Turnaround time is 48 hours.

Expedited service: Expedited mail service is available phone searches. Add fee for express delivery. Also, be sure to include the extra credit card fee. Turnaround time is 7-10 days.

Marriage Certificates

Iowa Department of Public Health, Vital Records, 321 E 12th St, Lucas Bldg, Des Moines, IA 50319-0075; 515-281-4944, 515-281-5871 (Message Recording), 7AM-4:45PM.

www.idph.state.ia.us

Indexing & Storage: Records are available from 1880. Records from 1880 to 1915 have to be searched by year. 1916 forward are indexed. New records are available for inquiry immediately. Records are indexed on microfiche, inhouse computer.

Searching: Include the following in your request: names of husband and wife, date of marriage, place or county of marriage.

Access by: mail, phone, in person.

Fee & Payment: The search fee is $10.00 per index searched. There is an additional $5.00 fee when using a credit card. Fee payee: Iowa Department of Public Health. Prepayment required. Personal checks accepted. Credit cards accepted: MasterCard, Visa, AmEx, Discover.

Mail search: Turnaround time: within 1 month. A self addressed stamped envelope is requested.

Phone search: Records are available by phone.

In person search: Same day service is not available. Turnaround time is 48 hours.

Expedited service: Expedited mail service is available for phone searches. Add fee for express delivery. Also, there is an additional $5.00 for use of credit card. Turnaround time is 7-10 days.

Divorce Records

Records not maintained by a state level agency.

Note: Divorce records are found at the county court issuing the decree. In general records are available from 1880.

Workers' Compensation Records

Iowa Workforce Development, Division of Workers' Compensation, 1000 E Grand Ave, Des Moines, IA 50319; 515-281-5387, 515-281-6501 (Fax), 8AM-4:30PM.

www.state.ia.us/iwd/wc

Note: Regular, ongoing requesters may apply for charge accounts.

Indexing & Storage: Records are available from 1985 to present. It takes 2 weeks before new records are available for inquiry.

Searching: Include the following in your request: claimant name, Social Security Number, place of employment at time of accident. Older records may take as long as 6 weeks to research.

Access by: mail, phone, fax, in person.

Fee & Payment: There is no search fee, copies are $.50 per page. Fee payee: Workers' Compensation. Prepayment required. Personal checks accepted. No credit cards accepted.

Mail search: Turnaround time: 3 to 5 days. A self addressed stamped envelope is requested.

Phone search: No fee for telephone request. They will let you know if a record exists. Limit is 4 requests per day. Callers are required to provide their name, company, and SSN or FEIN (whichever applicable). These are permanently recorded.

Fax search: Response to fax requests is made by mail.

In person search: Files are available for personal viewing only if requested in advance.

Other access: This agency sells its entire database.

Driver Records

Department of Transportation, Driver Service Records Section, PO Box 9204, Des Moines, IA 50306-9204 (Courier: Park Fair Mall, 100 Euclid, Des Moines, IA 50306); 515-244-9124, 800-532-1121 (Iowa only), 515-237-3152 (Fax), 8AM-4:30PM.

www.dot.state.ia.us/mvd/ovs/index.htm

Note: Copies of tickets can be requested from this address for $.50 per copy.

Indexing & Storage: Records are available for 5 to 7 years for moving violations; 12 years for DWIs; 5 to 7 years after closed for suspensions. The driver's address is shown on the record. Accidents are listed, but fault is not shown. It takes 2 to 3 days before new records are available for inquiry.

Searching: Casual requesters receive records without personal information, unless written consent of the subject is presented. Include the following in your request: full name, driver's license number, date of birth. County sheriffs in Iowa are authorized to furnish copies of driving records, but not all do. There are DOT "Super Stations" in Cedar Rapids, Council Bluff, Davenport, and Sioux City that offer a public access terminal.

Access by: mail, in person.

Fee & Payment: The fee for certified mail-in or walk-in requests and tape-to-tape records is $5.50 per record. There is no charge for a no record found. Fee payee: Treasurer, State of Iowa.

Prepayment required. Personal checks accepted. No credit cards accepted.

Mail search: Turnaround time: 4 to 7 days. An account can be established for on-going requesters. No self addressed stamped envelope is required.

In person search: Iowa permits walk-in requesters to view driving records at a terminal. The fee for an on-screen look-up is $1.00 per record for the first 5 records viewed and $2.00 for each additional record viewed. These prints are not considered certified.

Other access: Iowa offers magnetic tape processing for high volume users. Iowa will sell the master data file, without driver history information, as well as a suspension/revocation file. Call Carol Padgett at 515-237-3146 for more information.

Vehicle Ownership
Vehicle Identification

Department of Transportation, Office of Vehicle Services, PO Box 9278, Des Moines, IA 50306-9278 (Courier: Park Fair Mall, 100 Euclid, Des Moines, IA 50306); 515-237-3110, 515-237-3049, 515-237-3181 (Fax), 8AM-4:30PM.

www.dot.state.ia.us/mvd/ovs/index.htm

Note: Vehicle lien information is not maintained by this department.

Indexing & Storage: Records are available from 1968-present for registration and title. Title records are indexed on computer from 1986-present.

Searching: Vehicle registration information is released to casual requesters, but personal information not given without consent. The state is in compliance with DPPA. Plate searches will release only the vehicle information.

Access by: mail, phone, fax, in person.

Fee & Payment: Fees: $.50 per certified record; photocopy of record is $.10 per copy; record search-$2.70 per quarter hour or fraction thereof. Fee payee: Iowa Department of Transportation. Prepayment required. Personal checks accepted. No credit cards accepted.

Mail search: Turnaround time: 3 to 5 days. No self addressed stamped envelope is required.

Phone search: Records are available by phone.

Fax search: Fax searching available.

In person search: You may request information in person.

Other access: Iowa makes the entire vehicle file or selected data available for purchase. Weekly updates are also available for those purchasers. For more information, call 515-237-3110.

Accident Reports

Department of Transportation, Office of Driver Services, Park Fair Mall, 100 Euclid, Des Moines, IA 50306; 515-244-9124, 800-532-1121, 515-239-1837 (Fax), 8AM-4:30PM.

www.dot.state.ia.us/mvd/ods/index.htm

Indexing & Storage: Records are available for five years.

Searching: Accident reports are available only to the person involved in accident or the person's insurance company or attorney. Include the following in your request: full name, date of accident, location of accident.

Access by: mail, fax, in person.

Fee & Payment: The fee is $4.00 per officer report. Fee payee: Treasurer, State of Iowa. Prepayment required. The state allows regular, ongoing requesters to open a deposit account. Personal checks accepted. No credit cards accepted.

Mail search: Turnaround time: 2 to 3 weeks. No self addressed stamped envelope is required.

Fax search: Same criteria as mail searches.

In person search: Turnaround time for walk-in requesters is generally immediate.

Vessel Ownership
Vessel Registration

Records not maintained by a state level agency.

Note: Vessels are registered at the county level.

Legislation Records

Iowa General Assembly, Legislative Information Office, State Capitol, Des Moines, IA 50319; 515-281-5129, 8AM-4:30PM.

www.legis.state.ia.us

Note: For copies of older bills, it is suggested to go to a local law library.

Indexing & Storage: Records are available for the current year. Records are indexed on inhouse computer.

Searching: Include the following in your request: bill number.

Access by: mail, phone, in person, online.

Fee & Payment: There is no fee for copies of current and pending legislation. Fee payee: Treasurer, State of Iowa. Prepayment required. Personal checks accepted. No credit cards accepted.

Mail search: Turnaround time: variable. A maximum of 20 bills will be sent by mail. No self addressed stamped envelope is required.

Phone search: You may request bills by phone or receive status information.

In person search: You may request bills in person.

Online search: Access is available through the Legislative Computer Support Bureau or through their web site.

Other access: The state sells a weekly summary called the Session Brief. The fee is $10.60.

Voter Registration

Secretary of State, Voter Registration Division, Lucas State Office Building, Des Moines, IA 50319; 515-281-5762, 515-242-5953 (Fax), 8AM-4:30PM.

www.sos.state.ia.us

Indexing & Storage: Records are available for active records and two elections back for inactive.

Searching: The following data is not released: Social Security Numbers or bulk information or lists for commercial purposes.

Access by: phone, in person.

Fee & Payment: There is no fee for confirmation. No searching by mail.

Phone search: Will only confirm.

In person search: Records may be viewed.

Other access: Information is available, on tape, cartridge, disk or CD for political purposes only. Data can be sorted by any field on the registration file. Fees are determined by cost of production.

GED Certificates

Department of Education, GED Records, Grimes State Office Building, Des Moines, IA 50319-0146; 515-281-7308, 515-281-3636, 515-281-6544 (Fax), 8AM-5PM.

Searching: Include the following in your request: signed release, Social Security Number, date of birth. The year and city of test are also helpful.

Access by: mail, phone, fax, in person.

Fee & Payment: There is a $5.00 fee for a copy (and $3.00 for 2nd copy) of a transcript or a diploma. There is no fee for a verification. Fee payee: IA Department of Education. Prepayment required. Money orders are accepted. No personal checks accepted. No credit cards accepted.

Mail search: Turnaround time: 1 to 3 days. A self addressed stamped envelope is requested.

Phone search: Limited information is available.

Fax search: They will return verification data by fax to local or toll-free numbers.

In person search: Searching is available in person.

Hunting License Information
Fishing License Information

Department of Natural Resources, Wallace Building, E 9th & Grand Ave, 4th Floor, Des Moines, IA 50319-0034; 515-281-8688, 515-281-6794 (Fax), 8:15AM-4:15PM.

www.state.ia.us

Indexing & Storage: Records are available for current year on computer, past years on microfiche. Records are indexed on inhouse computer.

Searching: Include the following in your request: full name, date of birth, Social Security Number. This agency only maintains records for deer (except bow & free landowners) and turkey.

Access by: mail, phone, in person.

Fee & Payment: There is no charge for a search of one record for personal use. Lists will incur a fee based on length and how search must be done. Fee payee: Iowa Department of Natural Resources. Personal checks accepted. No credit cards accepted.

Mail search: Turnaround time: 1 to 3 days. No self addressed stamped envelope is required.

Phone search: You may call for information.

In person search: You may request information in person.

Iowa State Licensing Agencies

Licenses Searchable Online

Acupuncturist #14 .... www.docboard.org/ia/find_ia.htm
Apiary #3 .... www.agriculture.state.ia.us/apiary.html
Architect #10 .... www.state.ia.us/government/com/prof/search.htm
Bank #4 .... www.idob.state.ia.us
Credit Union #6 .... www.iacudiv.state.ia.us/Public/fieldofmembership/membersearch.htm
Debt Management Company #4 .... www.idob.state.ia.us/license/lic_default.htm
Delayed Deposit Service Business #4 .... www.idob.state.ia.us/license/lic_default.htm
Engineer #10 .... www.state.ia.us/government/com/prof/search.htm
Finance Company #4 .... www.idob.state.ia.us/license/lic_default.htm
Landscape Architect #10 .... www.state.ia.us/government/com/prof/lands/lanscros.htm
Medical Doctor #14 .... www.docboard.org/ia/find_ia.htm
Money Transmitter #4 .... www.idob.state.ia.us/license/lic_default.htm
Mortgage Banker/Broker #4 .... www.idob.state.ia.us/license/lic_default.htm
Mortgage Loan Service #4 .... www.idob.state.ia.us/license/lic_default.htm
Notary Public #31 .... www.sos.state.ia.us/NotaryWeb
Nurse #15 .... www.state.ia.us/nursing/Licensure.html
Nurse, Advance Registered Practice #15 .... www.state.ia.us/nursing/Licensure.html
Nurse-LPN #15 .... www.state.ia.us/nursing/Licensure.html
Optometrist #22 .... www.odfinder.org/LicSearch.asp
Osteopathic Physician #14 .... www.docboard.org/ia/find_ia.htm
Public Accountant-CPA #10 .... www.state.ia.us/government/com/prof/search.htm
Real Estate Appraiser #32 .... www.state.ia.us/government/com/prof/search.htm
Real Estate Broker/Salesperson #10 .... www.state.ia.us/government/com/prof/search.htm
Surveyor, Land #10 .... www.state.ia.us/government/com/prof/search.htm
Trust Company #4 .... www.idob.state.ia.us/license/lic_default.htm

Licensing Quick Finder

Acupuncturist #14 515-281-5171
Adoption Investigator #18 515-281-6220
Alcoholic Beverage Retail/Whlse./Mfg. #5
.... 515-281-7430
Amusement Ride Inspection #27 515-281-5415
Apiary #3 515-281-5601
Architect #10 515-281-4126
Asbestos Abatement Contractor/Worker #27
.... 515-281-6175
Asbestos Inspector #27 515-281-6175
Asbestos Project Designer/Mgmt. Planner #27
.... 515-281-6175
Athletic Agent #31 515-281-5204
Athletic Trainer #22 515-281-4401
Attorney #30 515-281-5911
Audiologist #22 515-281-4408
Bail Enforcement Agent #25 515-281-7610
Bank #4 515-281-4014
Barber #22 515-281-4416
Boiler Inspector #27 515-281-6533
Bus Driver #34 515-237-3079
Chiropractor #22 515-281-4287
Contractor #27 515-281-6175
Controlled Substance Registrant #16 ... 515-281-5944
Cosmetologist #22 515-281-4416
Cosmetology Instructor #22 515-281-4416
Cosmetology Salon/School #22 515-281-4416
Credit Union #6 515-281-6514
Crematory #22 515-281-4287
Day Care #17 515-283-9106
Debt Management Company #4 515-281-4014
Delayed Deposit Service Business #4 .. 515-281-4014
Dental Hygienist #13 515-281-5157
Dentist #13 515-281-5157
Dietitian #22 515-281-6959
Drug Distributor/Whlse./Mfg. #16 515-281-5944

Electrologist #22 515-281-4416
Elevator Inspection #27 515-281-5415
Emergency Medical Technician-Paramedic #27
.... 515-281-3239
Engineer #10 515-281-5602
Esthetician #33 515-281-4031
Esthetician #22 515-281-4416
Family Foster Care #17 515-283-9106
Finance Company #4 515-281-4014
First Response Paramedic #27 515-281-4958
Funeral Director/Home #22 515-281-4287
Gambling Excursion #19 515-281-7352
Gambling Excursion Boat #19 515-281-7352
Group Foster Care #17 515-283-9106
Hearing Aid Dispenser/Dealer #22 515-281-6959
Instructional Schools #31 515-281-5204
Instructor, Com. College or Voc./Tech. School #12
.... 800-788-7856
Insurance Agency #7 515-281-7757
Insurance Company #7 515-281-7367
Insurance Producer #7 515-281-7757
Landfill Operator #20 515-281-8688
Landscape Architect #10 515-281-4126
Lottery Retailer #26 515-281-7900
Manicurist #33 515-281-4031
Manicurist/Nail Technician #22 515-281-4416
Marriage & Family Therapist #22 515-281-4422
Massage Therapist #22 515-281-6959
Medical Doctor #14 515-281-5171
Mental Health Counselor #22 515-281-4422
Money Transmitter #4 515-281-4014
Mortgage Banker/Broker #4 515-281-4014
Mortgage Loan Service #4 515-281-4014
Mortuary Science #22 515-281-4287
Nail Technologist #33 515-281-4031
Notary Public #31 515-281-5204

Nuclear Medicine Technologist #29 515-281-4942
Nurse #15 .... 515-281-3264 or 4826
Nurse, Advance Registered Practice #15
.... 515-281-3264 or 4826
Nurse-LPN #15 .... 515-281-3264 or 4826
Nursing Home Administrator #22 515-281-4401
Occupational Therapist/Assistant #22 .. 515-281-4401
Optometrist #22 515-281-4287
Osteopathic Physician #14 515-281-5171
Pari-Mutuel Wagering Facility #19 515-281-7352
Pesticide Commercial Applicator #3 515-281-5601
Pesticide Dealer/Applicator #3 515-281-5601
Pesticide Private Applicator #3 515-281-4339
Pharmacist/Pharmacist Tech/Intern #16 515-281-5944
Pharmacy #16 515-281-5944
Physical Therapist/Assistant #22 515-281-4401
Physician Assistant #22 515-242-4408
Podiatrist #22 515-242-4422
Post-Secondary School #31 515-281-5204
Private Investigator #25 515-281-7610
Private Security Guard #25 515-281-7610
Psychologist #22 515-281-4401
Public Accountant-CPA #10 515-281-4126
Racetrack Worker #19 515-281-7352
Radiation Therapist #29 515-281-4942
Radioactive Material #29 515-281-3478
Radiographer, Medical #29 515-281-4942
Radon Measurement Specialist #29 515-281-4928
Radon Mitigation Specialist #29 515-281-4928
Real Estate Appraiser #32 515-281-7393
Real Estate Broker/Salesperson #10 ... 515-281-5910
Respiratory Therapist #22 515-281-4501
Riverboat Gambling Worker #19 515-281-7352
School Coach #12 800-788-7856
School Counselor #12 800-788-7856
School Principal/Superintendent #12 800-788-7856

Securities Agent/Broker/Dealer #7	515-281-4441	Taxi Driver #34	515-237-3079	Voting Booth #1	515-281-0145
Sheep Dealer #2	515-281-8601	Teacher #12	800-788-7856	Voting Equipment #1	515-281-0145
Shorthand Reporter #30	515-246-8076	Transient Merchant #31	515-281-5204	Waste Water Lagoon/Treatment Operator #20	515-281-8688
Social Worker #22	515-281-4422	Travel Agency #31	515-281-5204	Water Distribution Operator #20	515-281-8688
Solid Waste Incinerator Operator #20	515-281-8688	Truck Driver #34	515-237-3079	Water Treatment Operator #20	515-281-8688
Speech Pathologist/Audiologist #22	515-281-3031	Trust Company #4	515-281-4014	Well Driller #20	515-281-8688
Surveyor, Land #10	515-281-5602	Veterinarian #2	515-281-8617		
Tattoo Artist #22	515-242-5149	Veterinary Technician #2	515-281-8617		

Licensing Agency Information

#1 Attn: Sandy Steinbach, Secretary of State's Office, Board of Voting Systems Examiners, Hoover Bldg, 2nd Fl, Des Moines, IA 50319; 515-281-0145, Fax: 515-242-5953.
www.sos.state.ia.us

#2 Department of Agriculture, Animal Industry Bureau, CP & RA, E 9th & Grand Ave, Wallace Bldg, 2nd Fl, Des Moines, IA 50319; 515-281-5305, Fax: 515-281-4282.
www.agriculture.state.ia.us/animalIndustry.htm

#3 Department of Agriculture, Pesticide Division, Wallace State Office Bldg, Des Moines, IA 50319; 515-281-5601, Fax: 515-242-6497.
www.agriculture.state.ia.us/pesticidebureau.htm.
Agency email: chuck.eckermann@idals.state.ia.us.
Search database at
www.agriculture.state.ia.us/apiary.html

#4 Department of Commerce, Iowa Division of Banking, 200 E Grand Ave, Des Moines, IA 50309; 515-281-4014, Fax: 515-281-4862.
www.idob.state.ia.us. Agency email:
www.idob.state.ia.us./email/email_form.asp.
Search database at
www.idob.state.ia.us/license/lic_default.htm

#5 Department of Commerce, Alcoholic Beverage Division, 1918 SE Hulsizer Ave, Ankeny, IA 50021; 515-281-7430, Fax: 515-281-7375.
www.iowaabd.com. Agency email:
judy.seibe@comm2.state.ia.us.

#6 Department of Commerce, Credit Union Division, 200 E Grand Ave #370, Des Moines, IA 50309; 515-281-6514, Fax: 515-281-7595.
www.iacudiv.state.ia.us
Search database at www.iacudiv.state.ia.us/Public/fieldofmembership/membersearch.htm

#7 IA Insurance Division, 330 Maple St, Des Moines, IA 50319-0065; 515-281-5705, Fax: 515-281-3059.
www.state.ia.us/government/com/ins/agent/agent.htm
Agency email: susan.white@comm6.state.ia.us.

#10 Department of Commerce, Professional Licensing Division, 1918 SE Hulsizer Ave, Ankeny, IA 50021; 515-281-3183, Fax: 515-281-7411.
www.state.ia.us/proflic
Search database at www.state.ia.us/government/com/prof/lands/lanscros.htm

#12 Department of Education, Board of Education Examiners, Grimes State Office Bldg, Des Moines, IA 50319-0147; 515-281-5849, Fax: 515-281-7669.
www.state.ia.us/educate/programs/boee

#13 Board of Dental Examiners, 400 SW 8th St, #D, Des Moines, IA 50309-4687; 515-281-5157, Fax: 515-281-7969.
www.state.ia.us/dentalboard
Agency email: ibde@bon.state.ia.us.

#14 Department of Health, Board of Medical Examiners, 400 SW 8th #C, Des Moines, IA 50309-4686; 515-281-5171, Fax: 515-242-5908.
www.docboard.org/ia/ia_home.htm. Agency email: ibme@bon.state.ia.us. Automated phone system verifications, call 515-281-5171. There is also direct access to their database (for a fee) at https://www.info.state.ia.us/sing/medicalmain.htm

#15 Department of Health, Board of Nursing, 1223 E Court Ave, Des Moines, IA 50319; 515-281-3255, Fax: 515-281-4825.
www.state.ia.us/government/nursing
Agency email: ibon@bon.state.ia.us.
Search database at
www.state.ia.us/nursing/Licensure.html

#16 Department of Health, Board of Pharmacy, 1209 E Court Ave, Executive Hills West, Des Moines, IA 50319-0187; 515-281-5944, Fax: 515-281-4609.

#17 Department of Human Services, Adult & Family Services, Hoover State Office Bldg, 5th Fl, Des Moines, IA 50319-0114; 515-281-5521, Fax: 515-281-4597.
www.dhs.state.ia.us

#18 Department of Human Services, Children & Family Services, Adoption Certifier, 1305 E Walnut, Des Moines, IA 50319-0114; 515-281-6220, Fax: 515-281-4597.

#19 Department of Inspections & Appeals, Racing & Gaming Commission, 717 E Court Av #B, Des Moines, IA 50309; 515-281-7352, Fax: 515-242-6560.
www3.state.ia.us/irgc/
Search database at www3.state.ia.us/irgc

#20 Department of Natural Resources, 502 E 9th St, Wallace State Office Bldg, Des Moines, IA 50319-0035; 515-281-8688, Fax: 515-281-6794.
www.state.ia.us/dnr. Agency email:
elonda.bacon@dnr.state.ia.us.

#22 Department of Public Health, Division of Professional Licensing, Lucas State Office Bldg, Des Moines, IA 50319; 515-281-7074, Fax: 515-281-3121.
www.idph.state.ia.us/idph_pl/

#25 Department of Public Safety, Wallace State Office Bldg, Des Moines, IA 50319; 515-281-7610, Fax: 515-281-8921.

#26 Department of Revenue & Finance, Lottery Board, 2015 Grand Av, Des Moines, IA 50312; 515-281-7900, Fax: 515-281-7882.
www.ialottery.com
Agency email: Web.Master@ilot.state.ia.us.

#27 Division of Labor, Workforce Development, 1000 E Grand Ave, Des Moines, IA 50319-0209; 515-281-6175, Fax: 515-281-7995.
www.state.ia.us/iwd/labor/index.html

#29 Department of Public Health, Bureau of Radiological Health, 321 E 12th St, Lucas State Office Bldg, Des Moines, IA 50319-0075; 515-281-3478, Fax: 515-242-6284.

#30 Supreme Court Clerk's Office, Legal Boards, Statehouse, Des Moines, IA 50319; 515-281-5911, Fax: 515-242-6164.
www.judicial.state.ia.us/regs

#31 Office of Secretary of State, Hoover Office Bldg, 2nd Fl, Des Moines, IA 50319; 515-281-5204, Fax: 515-242-5953 or 6556.
www.sos.state.ia.us
Agency email: sos@sos.state.ia.us.
Search database at www.sos.state.ia.us

#32 Real Estate Commission, 1918 SE Hulsizer, Ankeny, IA 50021-3941; 515-281-7393.
www.state.ia.us/government/com/prof/realappr/index.htm. Agency email: IAPP@max.state.ia.us.
Search database at
www.state.ia.us/government/com/prof/search.htm

#33 Bureau of Professional Licensure, Board of Cosmetology Arts & Sciences Examiners, 321 E 12th St, Lucas State Office Bldg 5th Fl, Des Moines, IA 50319-0075; 515-281-4287.

#34 Department of Transportation, Motor Vehicle Division, Office of Driver Svcs, 100 Euclid, Park Fair Mall, Des Moines, IA 50306-9204; 515-237-3079, Fax: 515-237-3152.
www.dot.state.ia.us/mvd/ods
Agency email: ods@max.state.ia.us.

Iowa Federal Courts

The following list indicates the district and division name for each county in the state. If the bankruptcy court location is different from the district court, then the location of the bankruptcy court appears in parentheses.

County/Court Cross Reference

County	District	Division
Adair	Southern	Council Bluffs (Des Moines)
Adams	Southern	Council Bluffs (Des Moines)
Allamakee	Northern	Dubuque (Cedar Rapids)
Appanoose	Southern	Des Moines (Central)
Audubon	Southern	Council Bluffs (Des Moines)
Benton	Northern	Cedar Rapids
Black Hawk	Northern	Dubuque (Cedar Rapids)
Boone	Southern	Des Moines (Central)
Bremer	Northern	Dubuque (Cedar Rapids)
Buchanan	Northern	Dubuque (Cedar Rapids)
Buena Vista	Northern	Sioux Cty (Cedar Rapids)
Butler	Northern	Sioux Cty (Cedar Rapids)
Calhoun	Northern	Sioux Cty (Cedar Rapids)
Carroll	Northern	Sioux Cty (Cedar Rapids)
Cass	Southern	Council Bluffs (Des Moines)
Cedar	Northern	Cedar Rapids
Cerro Gordo	Northern	Cedar Rapids
Cherokee	Northern	Sioux Cty (Cedar Rapids)
Chickasaw	Northern	Dubuque (Cedar Rapids)
Clarke	Southern	Council Bluffs (Des Moines)
Clay	Northern	Sioux Cty (Cedar Rapids)
Clayton	Northern	Dubuque (Cedar Rapids)
Clinton	Southern	Council Bluffs (Des Moines)
Crawford	Northern	Sioux Cty (Cedar Rapids)
Dallas	Southern	Des Moines (Central)
Davis	Southern	Des Moines (Central)
Decatur	Southern	Council Bluffs (Des Moines)
Delaware	Northern	Dubuque (Cedar Rapids)
Des Moines	Southern	Des Moines (Central)
Dickinson	Northern	Sioux Cty (Cedar Rapids)
Dubuque	Northern	Dubuque (Cedar Rapids)
Emmet	Northern	Sioux Cty (Cedar Rapids)
Fayette	Northern	Dubuque (Cedar Rapids)
Floyd	Northern	Dubuque (Cedar Rapids)
Franklin	Northern	Sioux Cty (Cedar Rapids)
Fremont	Southern	Council Bluffs (Des Moin
Greene	Southern	Des Moines (Central)
Grundy	Northern	Cedar Rapids
Guthrie	Southern	Des Moines (Central)
Hamilton	Northern	Sioux Cty (Cedar Rapids)
Hancock	Northern	Sioux Cty (Cedar Rapids)
Hardin	Northern	Cedar Rapids
Harrison	Southern	Council Bluffs (Des Moines)
Henry	Southern	Davenport (Des Moines)
Howard	Northern	Dubuque (Cedar Rapids)
Humboldt	Northern	Sioux Cty (Cedar Rapids)
Ida	Northern	Sioux Cty (Cedar Rapids)
Iowa	Northern	Cedar Rapids
Jackson	Northern	Dubuque (Cedar Rapids)
Jasper	Southern	Des Moines (Central)
Jefferson	Southern	Des Moines (Central)
Johnson	Southern	Davenport (Des Moines)
Jones	Northern	Cedar Rapids
Keokuk	Southern	Des Moines (Central)
Kossuth	Northern	Sioux Cty (Cedar Rapids)
Lee	Southern	Davenport (Des Moines)
Linn	Northern	Cedar Rapids
Louisa	Southern	Davenport (Des Moines)
Lucas	Southern	Council Bluffs (Des Moines)
Lyon	Northern	Sioux Cty (Cedar Rapids)
Madison	Southern	Des Moines (Central)
Mahaska	Southern	Des Moines (Central)
Marion	Southern	Des Moines (Central)
Marshall	Southern	Des Moines (Central)
Mills	Southern	Council Bluffs (Des Moines)
Mitchell	Northern	Dubuque (Cedar Rapids)
Monona	Northern	Sioux Cty (Cedar Rapids)
Monroe	Southern	Des Moines (Central)
Montgomery	Southern	Council Bluffs (Des Moines)
Muscatine	Southern	Davenport (Des Moines)
O'Brien	Northern	Sioux Cty (Cedar Rapids)
Osceola	Northern	Sioux Cty (Cedar Rapids)
Page	Southern	Council Bluffs (Des Moines)
Palo Alto	Northern	Sioux Cty (Cedar Rapids)
Plymouth	Northern	Sioux Cty (Cedar Rapids)
Pocahontas	Northern	Sioux Cty (Cedar Rapids)
Polk	Southern	Des Moines (Central)
Pottawattamie	Southern	Council Bluffs (Des Moines)
Poweshiek	Southern	Des Moines (Central)
Ringgold	Southern	Council Bluffs (Des Moines)
Sac	Northern	Sioux Cty (Cedar Rapids)
Scott	Southern	Davenport (Des Moines)
Shelby	Southern	Council Bluffs (Des Moines)
Sioux	Northern	Sioux Cty (Cedar Rapids)
Story	Southern	Des Moines (Central)
Tama	Northern	Cedar Rapids
Taylor	Southern	Council Bluffs (Des Moines)
Union	Southern	Council Bluffs (Des Moines)
Van Buren	Southern	Davenport (Des Moines)
Wapello	Southern	Des Moines (Central)
Warren	Southern	Des Moines (Central)
Washington	Southern	Davenport (Des Moines)
Wayne	Southern	Council Bluffs (Des Moines)
Webster	Northern	Sioux Cty (Cedar Rapids)
Winnebago	Northern	Sioux Cty (Cedar Rapids)
Winneshiek	Northern	Dubuque (Cedar Rapids)
Woodbury	Northern	Sioux Cty (Cedar Rapids)
Worth	Northern	Sioux Cty (Cedar Rapids)
Wright	Northern	Sioux Cty (Cedar Rapids)

Standards for Federal Courts: The search fee is $20.00 per item (one party name or case number). Certification fee is $7.00 per document. Copy fee is $.50 per page. All fees standard unless noted in profile. Mail Search: always enclose a stamped self addressed envelope unless otherwise noted. Before releasing records, all courts require prepayment unless noted in profile.

Open records are located at the court unless otherwise noted. District courts index by defendant and plaintiff as well as by case number. Bankruptcy courts usually index by debtor and case number. While most courts now have their indexes on computer, many still maintain index card files as well.

The universal PACER sign-up number is 800-676-6856. Find PACER and the Party/Case Index on the Web at http://pacer.psc.uscourts.gov. PACER dial-up access is $.60 per minute. Also, courts offering internet access via RACER, PACER, Web-PACER or the new CM-ECF charge $.07 per page fee unless noted as free.

US District Court

Northern District of Iowa

Cedar Rapids Division Court Clerk, PO Box 74710, Cedar Rapids, IA 52407-4710 (Courier Address: Federal Bldg, US Courthouse, 101 1st St SE, Room 313, Cedar Rapids, IA 52401), 319-286-2300.

www.iand.uscourts.gov

Counties: Benton, Cedar, Cerro Gordo, Grundy, Hardin, Iowa, Jones, Linn, Tama.

Indexing & Storage: Cases are indexed by defendant, plaintiff, and case number. New cases are available in the index immediately after filing date. Open records are located at this court.

Fee & Payment Notes: Payment may be made by money order, cashier check, personal check. Payee: Clerk, US District Court.

Phone Search: Anything that is public record will be released over the phone, but only for one name per call.

Mail Search: A stamped self addressed envelope is not required.

In Person Search: In person searching available.

PACER: Sign-up number is 800-676-5856. Toll-free dial-up access: 888-845-4528. Local dial-up access: 319-362-3256. Case records are available back to November 1992. New records are available online after 1 day. PACER is available online at http://pacer.iand.uscourts.gov.

Electronic Filing: (CM/ECF available late 2002)

Dubuque Division c/o Cedar Rapids Division, PO Box 74710, Cedar Rapids, IA 52407-4710 (Courier Address: Federal Bldg, US Courthouse, 101 1st St SE, Room 313, Cedar Rapids, IA 52401), 319-286-2300.

www.iand.uscourts.gov

Counties: Allamakee, Black Hawk, Bremer, Buchanan, Chickasaw, Clayton, Delaware, Dubuque, Fayette, Floyd, Howard, Jackson, Mitchell, Winneshiek.

Indexing & Storage: New cases are available in the index after filing date. Open records are located at the Cedar Rapids Division.

Fee & Payment Notes: Payment may be made by money order, cashier check. Business checks are not accepted. Personal checks are not accepted.

Phone Search: Searching not available by phone.

Mail Search: A stamped self addressed envelope is not required.

In Person Search: In person searching available.

PACER: Sign-up number is 800-676-5856. Toll-free dial-up access: 888-845-4528. Local dial-up access: 319-362-3256. Case records are available back to November 1992. New records are available online after 1 day. PACER is available online at http://pacer.iand.uscourts.gov.

Electronic Filing: (CM/ECF available late 2002)

Sioux City Division Room 301, Federal Bldg, 320 6th St, Sioux City, IA 51101 (Courier Address: Use mail address for courier delivery), 712-233-3900.

www.iand.uscourts.gov

Counties: Buena Vista, Cherokee, Clay, Crawford, Dickinson, Ida, Lyon, Monona, O'Brien, Osceola, Plymouth, Sac, Sioux, Woodbury.

Indexing & Storage: Cases are indexed by defendant, plaintiff, and case number. New cases are available in the index immediately after filing date. Open records are located at this court.

Fee & Payment Notes: Payment may be made by money order, cashier check, personal check. Payee: Clerk, US District Court.

Phone Search: Only docket information is available by phone.

In Person Search: In person searching available.

PACER: Sign-up number is 800-676-5856. Toll-free dial-up access: 888-845-4528. Local dial-up access: 319-362-3256. Case records are available back to November 1992. New records are available online after 1 day. PACER is available online at http://pacer.iand.uscourts.gov.

Electronic Filing: Information is available online at (CM/ECF available late, 2002)

US Bankruptcy Court

Northern District of Iowa

Cedar Rapids Division PO Box 74890, Cedar Rapids, IA 52407-4890 (Courier Address: 8th Floor, 425 2nd St SE, Cedar Rapids, IA 52401), 319-286-2200, Fax: 319-286-2280.

www.ianb.uscourts.gov

Counties: Allamakee, Benton, Black Hawk, Bremer, Buchanan, Buena Vista, Butler, Calhoun, Carroll, Cedar, Cerro Gordo, Cherokee, Chickasaw, Clay, Clayton, Crawford, Delaware, Dickinson, Dubuque, Emmet, Fayette, Floyd, Franklin, Grundy, Hamilton, Hancock, Hardin, Howard, Humboldt, Ida, Iowa, Jackson, Jones, Kossuth, Linn, Lyon, Mitchell, Monona, O'Brien, Osceola, Palo Alto, Plymouth, Pocahontas, Sac, Sioux, Tama, Webster, Winnebago, Winneshiek, Woodbury, Worth, Wright.

Indexing & Storage: Cases are indexed by debtor and creditors as well as by case number. New cases are available in the index immediately after filing date. District wide searches are available for information from 1988 to the present from this

court. This court handles records for the Sioux City division.

Fee & Payment Notes: Payment may be made by money order, cashier check, business check, Visa or Mastercard. Personal checks are not accepted. Checks are accepted from in-state law firms only. Payee: Clerk, US Bankruptcy Court. You are allowed to make your own copies. These copies cost $.25 per page.

Phone Search: Only minimal information will be released over the phone. Not all docket information will be released. An automated voice case information service (VCIS) is available. Call VCIS at 800-249-9859 or 319-362-9906.

In Person Search: In person searching available.

PACER: Sign-up number is. Access fee is. PACER is available online at http://pacer.ianb.uscourts.gov. Document images available.

Electronic Filing: Information is available online at https://ecf.ianb.uscourts.gov

US District Court

Southern District of Iowa

Council Bluffs (Western) Division PO Box 307, Council Bluffs, IA 51502 (Courier Address: Room 313, 8 S 6th St, Council Bluffs, IA 51501), 712-328-0283, Fax: 712-328-1241.

www.iasd.uscourts.gov

Counties: Audubon, Cass, Fremont, Harrison, Mills, Montgomery, Page, Pottawattamie, Shelby.

Indexing & Storage: Cases are indexed by defendant, plaintiff, and case number. New cases are available in the index immediately after filing date. Open records are located at this court.

Fee & Payment Notes: Payment may be made by money order, cashier check, personal check. The search fee will be charged only if the clerk's staff is required to spend more than 5 minutes searching. Payee: Clerk, US District Court. You are allowed to make your own copies. These copies cost $.50 per page.

Phone Search: All information available will be released over the phone.

In Person Search: In person searching available.

PACER: Local dial-up access: 515-284-6475, 515-284-6478. Case records are available back to mid 1989. Records are purged every six months. New records are available online after 3 days. PACER is available online at http://pacer.iasd.uscourts.gov. Document images available.

Other Online Access: The RACER system is now administered by PACER. Fee is $.07 per page.

Davenport (Eastern) Division PO Box 256, Davenport, IA 52805 (Courier Address: Room 215, 131 E 4th St, Davenport, IA 52801), 563-322-3223, Fax: 563-322-2962.

www.iasd.uscourts.gov

Counties: Henry, Johnson, Lee, Louisa, Muscatine, Scott, Van Buren, Washington.

Indexing & Storage: Cases are indexed by defendant, plaintiff, and case number. New cases are available in the index 1 week after filing date. All criminal cases are handled in Des Moines Division. Civil cases are handled here. Open records are located at this court.

Fee & Payment Notes: Payment may be made by money order, cashier check, personal check. Will bill fees. Payee: Clerk, US District Court. You are allowed to make your own copies. These copies cost $.50 per page. You are only allowed to search the index cards.

Phone Search: Docket information available by phone.

Fax Search: Fax requests are processed the same as mail searches. Will fax documents for $3.00 up to 9 pages and $5.00 if more, plus copy fees.

Mail Search: A stamped self addressed envelope is not required.

In Person Search: In person searching available.

PACER: Local dial-up access: 515-284-6475, 515-284-6478. Case records are available back to mid 1989. Records are purged every six months. New records are available online after 3 days. PACER is available online at http://pacer.iasd.uscourts.gov. Document images available.

Other Online Access: The RACER system is now administered by PACER. Fee of $.07 per page.

Des Moines (Central) Division PO Box 9344, Des Moines, IA 50306-9344 (Courier: 123 E. Walnut St., Rm. 300, Des Moines, IA 50306-9344), 515-284-6248, Fax: 515-284-6418.

www.iasd.uscourts.gov

Counties: Adair, Adams, Appanoose, Boone, Clarke, Clinton, Dallas, Davis, Decatur, Des Moines, Greene, Guthrie, Jasper, Jefferson, Keokuk, Lucas, Madison, Mahaska, Marion, Marshall, Monroe, Polk, Poweshiek, Ringgold, Story, Taylor, Union, Wapello, Warren, Wayne.

Indexing & Storage: Cases are indexed by defendant, plaintiff, and case number. New cases

are available in the index immediately after filing date. Records are stored by date filed and closed. Open records are located at this court.

Fee & Payment Notes: Payment may be made by money order, cashier check, personal check. A bill can be sent by mail. Payee: Clerk, US District Court.

Phone Search: Searching not available by phone. Requests for searches must be in writing.

Fax Search: Fax search handled same as mail. Will fax documents for $3.00 up to 9 pages and $5.00 if more, plus copy fee.

Mail Search: A stamped self addressed envelope is not required.

In Person Search: In person searching available.

PACER: Local dial-up access: 515-284-6475, 515-284-6478. Document images available. Case records are available back to mid 1989. Records are purged every six months. New records are available online after 3 days. PACER is available online at http://pacer.iasd.uscourts.gov. Document images available.

Other Online Access: The RACER system is now administered by PACER. Fee is $.07 per page.

US Bankruptcy Court

Southern District of Iowa

Des Moines Division PO Box 9264, Des Moines, IA 50306-9264 (Courier Address: 300 US Courthouse Annex, 110 East Court Ave, Des Moines, IA 50309), 515-284-6230, Fax: 515-284-6404.

www.iasb.uscourts.gov

Counties: Adair, Adams, Appanoose, Audubon, Boone, Cass, Clarke, Clinton, Dallas, Davis, Decatur, Des Moines, Fremont, Greene, Guthrie, Harrison, Henry, Jasper, Jefferson, Johnson, Keokuk, Lee, Louisa, Lucas, Madison, Mahaska, Marion, Marshall, Mills, Monroe,Montgomery, Muscatine, Page, Polk, Pottawattamie, Poweshiek, Ringgold, Scott, Shelby, Story, Taylor, Union, Van Buren, Wapello, Warren, Washington, Wayne.

Indexing & Storage: Cases are indexed by debtor as well as by case number. New cases are available in the index immediately after filing date. Open records are located at this court.

Fee & Payment Notes: Payment may be made by money order, cashier check, business check. Personal checks are not accepted. Payee: CopyCat Photocopy Center.

Phone Search: The information released over the phone is: name, case number, chapter date file, assets, attorney, attorney's telephone number, trustee, judge, status and discharge. Information is available from June 1987. An automated voice case information service (VCIS) is available. Call VCIS at 888-219-5534 or 515-284-6427.

In Person Search: In person searching available.

PACER: Toll-free dial-up access: 800-597-5917. Local dial-up access: 515-284-6466. Case records are available back to June 1987. Records are purged every six months. New civil records are available online after 1 day.

Electronic Filing: (Currently in the process of implementing CM/ECF.)

Other Online Access: Search records on the Internet using RACER at https://racer.iasb.uscourts.gov/perl/bkplog.html.

Iowa County Courts

Court	Jurisdiction	No. of Courts	How Organized
District Courts*	General	100	8 Districts

* Profiled in this Sourcebook.

Court	CIVIL								
	Tort	Contract	Real Estate	Min. Claim	Max. Claim	Small Claims	Estate	Eviction	Domestic Relations
District Courts*	X	X	X	$0	No Max	$4000	X	X	X

Court	CRIMINAL				
	Felony	Misdemeanor	DWI/DUI	Preliminary Hearing	Juvenile
District Courts*	X	X	X	X	X

ADMINISTRATION State Court Administrator, State Capitol, Des Moines, IA, 50319; 515-281-5241, Fax: 515-242-0014. www.judicial.state.ia.us

COURT STRUCTURE The District Court is the court of general jurisdiction. Effective 7/1/95, the Small Claims limit increased to $4000 from $3000.

Vital records were moved from courts to the County Recorder's office in each county.

ONLINE ACCESS Criminal, civil, probate, traffic and appellate information is now available from all 99 counties in Iowa at www.judicial.state.ia.us/online_records. The Iowa Courts Online site is providing basic case information for no charge; a more extensive fee portion will be available in the near future. Name searches are available on a statewide or specific county basis. While this is an excellent site with much information, there is one important consideration to keep in mind. Although records are updated daily, the historical records offered are not from the same starting date on a county-by-county basis. Over 40% of counties do not go back more than 7 years.

ADDITIONAL INFORMATION In most courts, the Certification Fee is $10.00 plus copy fee. Copy Fee is $.50 per page. Most courts do not do searches and recommend either in person searches or use of a record retriever.

Courts that accept written search requests usually require an SASE.

Most courts have a Public access terminal for access to that court's records.

Adair County

5th District Court PO Box L, Greenfield, IA 50849; 641-743-2445; Fax: 641-743-2974. Hours: 8AM-4:30PM (CST). *Felony, Misdemeanor, Civil, Eviction, Small Claims, Probate.*

Civil Records: Access: In person, online. Both court and visitors may perform in person searches. No search fee. Required to search: name, years to search. Civil cases indexed by defendant, plaintiff. Civil records on docket books from late 1800s, computerized since 1996. Civil, probate, and appellate information is available at www.judicial.state.ia.us/online_records.
Criminal Records: Access: In person, online. Both court and visitors may perform in person searches. No search fee. Required to search: name, years to search, DOB, signed release; also helpful: SSN. Criminal records on docket books from late 1800s, computerized since 1996. Criminal, traffic, and appellate information is available at www.judicial.state.ia.us/online_records.
General Information: Public access terminal is available. No juvenile, sealed, dissolution of marriage, mental health domestic abuse or deferred records released. Copy fee: $.50 per page. Certification fee: $10.00. Fee payee: Clerk of Court. Personal checks accepted. Prepayment is required.

Adams County

5th District Court Courthouse, PO Box 484, Corning, IA 50841; 641-322-4711; Fax: 641-322-4523. Hours: 8AM-4:30PM (CST). *Felony, Misdemeanor, Civil, Eviction, Small Claims, Probate.*

Civil Records: Access: In person, online. Visitors must perform in person searches for themselves. No search fee. Required to search: name, years to search. Civil cases indexed by defendant, plaintiff. Civil records on docket books from late 1800s. Civil, probate, and appellate information is available at www.judicial.state.ia.us/online_records.
Criminal Records: Access: In person, online. Visitors must perform in person searches for themselves. No search fee. Required to search: name, years to search, signed release. Criminal records on docket books from late 1800s. Criminal, traffic, and appellate information is available at www.judicial.state.ia.us/online_records.
General Information: Public access terminal is available. No sealed, dissolution of marriage, mental health, sealed or expunged records released. Copy fee: $.50 per page. Certification fee: $10.00. Fee payee: Clerk of Court. Personal checks accepted. Prepayment is required.

Allamakee County

1st District Court PO Box 248, Waukon, IA 52172; 563-568-6351. Hours: 8AM-4:30PM (CST). *Felony, Misdemeanor, Civil, Eviction, Small Claims, Probate.*

Civil Records: Access: In person, online. Visitors must perform in person searches for themselves. Court will perform not-for-profit searches only. No search fee. Required to search: name, years to search. Civil cases indexed by defendant, plaintiff. All judgments on computer back to 4/1997; on index books back to 1880, probate back to 1852. Civil, probate, and appellate information is available online at www.judicial.state.ia.us/online_records.
Criminal Records: Access: In person, online. Visitors must perform in person searches for themselves. No search fee. Required to search: name, years to search, signed release. Criminal records on docket books from 1800s; on computer back to 4/1997. Criminal, traffic, and appellate information is available online at www.judicial.state.ia.us/online_records.
General Information: Public access terminal is available. No juvenile, adoption, sealed, dissolution of marriage, mental health, domestic abuse or deferred records released. Copy fee: $.50 per page. Certification

fee: $10.00. Fee payee: Clerk of Court. Personal checks accepted. Prepayment is required.

Appanoose County

8th District Court PO Box 400, Centerville, IA 52544; 641-856-6101; Fax: 641-856-2282. Hours: 8AM-2:00 PM (CST). *Felony, Misdemeanor, Civil, Eviction, Small Claims, Probate.*

Civil Records: Access: In person, online. Visitors must perform in person searches for themselves. No search fee. Required to search: name, years to search. Civil cases indexed by defendant, plaintiff. Civil records on docket books from 1847. Civil, probate, and appellate information is available online at www.judicial.state.ia.us/online_records.
Criminal Records: Access: In person, online. Visitors must perform in person searches for themselves. No search fee. Required to search: name, years to search, signed release. Criminal records on docket books from 1847. Criminal, traffic, and appellate information is available at www.judicial.state.ia.us/online_records.
General Information: Public access terminal is available. No juvenile, sealed, dissolution of marriage, mental health, domestic abuse or deferred records released. Copy fee: $.25 per page. Certification fee: $10.00. Fee payee: Clerk of Court. Personal checks accepted. Prepayment is required.

Audubon County

4th District Court 318 Leroy St #6, Audubon, IA 50025; 712-563-4275; Fax: 712-563-4276. Hours: 8AM-4:30PM (CST). *Felony, Misdemeanor, Civil, Eviction, Small Claims, Probate.*

Civil Records: Access: In person, online. Visitors must perform in person searches for themselves. No search fee. Required to search: name, years to search; also helpful: address. Civil cases indexed by defendant, plaintiff. Civil records on docket books from 1930s, computerized since 1996. Civil, probate, and appellate information is available online at www.judicial.state.ia.us/online_records.
Criminal Records: Access: In person, online. Visitors must perform in person searches for themselves. No search fee. Required to search: name, years to search; also helpful: DOB, SSN, address. Criminal records on docket books from late 1800s. Criminal, traffic, and appellate information is available online at www.judicial.state.ia.us/online_records.
General Information: No juvenile, sealed, dissolution of marriage, mental health, domestic abuse or deferred records released. Copy fee: $.50 per page. Certification fee: $10.00. Fee payee: Clerk of Court. Prepayment is required.

Benton County

6th District Court PO Box 719, Vinton, IA 52349; 319-472-2766; Fax: 319-472-2747. Hours: 8AM-4:30PM (CST). *Felony, Misdemeanor, Civil, Eviction, Small Claims, Probate.*
www.iowacourtsonline.org
Civil Records: Access: In person, online. Visitors must perform in person searches for themselves. No search fee. Required to search: name, years to search. Civil cases indexed by defendant, plaintiff. Civil records on original record books from 1800s, index is on computer since 06/95. Civil, probate, and appellate information is available at www.judicial.state.ia.us/online_records.
Criminal Records: Access: In person, online. Visitors must perform in person searches for themselves. No search fee. Required to search: name, years to search. Criminal records on original record books from 1800s, index is on computer since 06/95. Criminal, traffic, and appellate information is available online at www.judicial.state.ia.us/online_records.
General Information: Public access terminal is available. No juvenile, sealed, dissolution of marriage,

mental health, domestic abuse or deferred records released. Copy fee: $.25 per page. Certification fee: $10.00. Fee payee: Clerk of Court. Personal checks accepted. Prepayment is required.

Black Hawk County

1st District Court 316 E 5th St, Waterloo, IA 50703; 319-833-3331. Hours: 8AM-4:30PM (CST). *Felony, Misdemeanor, Civil, Eviction, Small Claims, Probate.*

Civil Records: Access: In person, online. Visitors must perform in person searches for themselves. No search fee. Required to search: name, years to search. Civil cases indexed by defendant, plaintiff. Civil records on computer from 1992, docket books from early 1900s. Civil, probate, and appellate information is available online at www.judicial.state.ia.us/online_records.
Criminal Records: Access: In person, online. Visitors must perform in person searches for themselves. No search fee. Required to search: name, years to search; also helpful: DOB, SSN. Criminal records on computer from 1992, docket books from early 1900s. Criminal, traffic, and appellate information is available online at www.judicial.state.ia.us/online_records.
General Information: Public access terminal is available. No juvenile, sealed, dissolution of marriage, mental health, domestic abuse or deferred records released. Copy fee: $.50 per page. Certification fee: $10.00. Fee payee: District Court. Personal checks accepted. Prepayment is required.

Boone County

2nd District Court 201 State St, Boone, IA 50036; 515-433-0561; Fax: 515-433-0563. Hours: 8AM-4:30PM (CST). *Felony, Misdemeanor, Civil, Eviction, Small Claims, Probate.*

Civil Records: Access: In person, online. Visitors must perform in person searches for themselves. No search fee. Required to search: name, years to search. Civil cases indexed by defendant, plaintiff. Civil records on docket books from 1890s; computerized records go back to 1996. Civil, probate, and appellate information is available at www.judicial.state.ia.us/online_records.
Criminal Records: Access: In person, online. Visitors must perform in person searches for themselves. No search fee. Required to search: name, years to search, offense, date of offense. Criminal records on docket books from 1890s; computerized records go back to 1996. Criminal, traffic, and appellate information is available at www.judicial.state.ia.us/online_records.
General Information: Public access terminal is available. No juvenile, sealed, dissolution of marriage, mental health, domestic abuse or deferred records released. Copy fee: $.50 per page. Certification fee: $10.00. Fee payee: Clerk of Court. Personal checks accepted. Prepayment is required.

Bremer County

2nd District Court PO Box 328, Waverly, IA 50677; 319-352-5661; Fax: 319-352-1054. Hours: 8AM-4:30PM (CST). *Felony, Misdemeanor, Civil, Eviction, Small Claims, Probate.*

Note: Public access terminal has records since 1996 only.
Civil Records: Access: In person, online. Visitors must perform in person searches for themselves. No search fee. Required to search: name, years to search. Civil cases indexed by defendant, plaintiff. Civil records on computer since 07/97; prior records on docket books from 1900's. Civil, probate, and appellate information is available at www.judicial.state.ia.us/online_records.
Criminal Records: Access: In person, online. Visitors must perform in person searches for themselves. No search fee. Required to search: name, years to search. Criminal records go back to 1900's; computerized records go back to 1996. Criminal, traffic, and appellate

information is available online at www.judicial.state.ia.us/online_records.
General Information: Public access terminal is available. No juvenile, sealed, dissolution of marriage, mental health, domestic abuse or deferred records released. Copy fee: $.50 per page. Certification fee: $10.00. Fee payee: Clerk of Court. Personal checks accepted. Credit cards accepted: Visa, MasterCard. Prepayment is required.

Buchanan County

1st District Court PO Box 259, Independence, IA 50644; 319-334-2196; Fax: 319-334-7455. Hours: 9AM-Noon; 1PM-3:30PM (CST). *Felony, Misdemeanor, Civil, Eviction, Small Claims, Probate.*

Civil Records: Access: In person, online. Both court and visitors may perform in person searches. No search fee. Required to search: name, years to search. Civil cases indexed by defendant, plaintiff. Civil records on docket books from 1800s; computerized since 1996. Civil, probate, and appellate information is available online at www.judicial.state.ia.us/online_records.
Criminal Records: Access: Mail, in person, online. Both court and visitors may perform in person searches. No search fee. Required to search: name, years to search. Criminal records on docket books from 1800s; computerized since 1996. Criminal, traffic, and appellate information is available online at www.judicial.state.ia.us/online_records.
General Information: No juvenile, sealed, dissolution of marriage, mental health, domestic abuse or deferred records released. SASE required. Turnaround time 2 days. Copy fee: $.50 per page. Certification fee: $10.00. Fee payee: Clerk of Court. Personal checks accepted. Credit cards accepted: Visa, MasterCard. Prepayment is required.

Buena Vista County

3rd District Court PO Box 1186, Storm Lake, IA 50588; 712-749-2546; Fax: 712-749-2700. Hours: 8AM-4:30PM (CST). *Felony, Misdemeanor, Civil, Eviction, Small Claims, Probate.*

Civil Records: Access: In person, online. Visitors must perform in person searches for themselves. No search fee. Required to search: name, years to search. Civil cases indexed by defendant, plaintiff. Civil records on index cards from early 1900s; on computer back to 1996. Civil, probate, and appellate information is available at www.judicial.state.ia.us/online_records.
Criminal Records: Access: In person, online. Visitors must perform in person searches for themselves. No search fee. Required to search: name, years to search. Criminal records on index cards from early 1900s; on computer back to 1994. Criminal, traffic, and appellate information is available online at www.judicial.state.ia.us/online_records.
General Information: Public access terminal is available. No juvenile, sealed, dissolution of marriage, mental health, domestic abuse or deferred records released. Copy fee: $.50 per page. Certification fee: $10.00 per document. Fee payee: Clerk of Court. Personal checks accepted. Prepayment is required.

Butler County

2nd District Court PO Box 307, Allison, IA 50602; 319-267-2487; Fax: 319-267-2488. Hours: 9AM-3:30PM (CST). *Felony, Misdemeanor, Civil, Eviction, Small Claims, Probate.*

Civil Records: Access: In person, online. Visitors must perform in person searches for themselves. No search fee. Required to search: name, years to search. Civil cases indexed by defendant, plaintiff. Civil records on docket books from 1800s. Civil, probate, and appellate information is available online at www.judicial.state.ia.us/online_records.

Criminal Records: Access: In person, online. Visitors must perform in person searches for themselves. No search fee. Required to search: name, years to search. Criminal records on docket books from 1800s. Criminal, traffic, and appellate information is available online at www.judicial.state.ia.us/online_records.

General Information: Public access terminal is available. No juvenile, sealed, dissolution of marriage, mental health, domestic abuse or deferred records released. Copy fee: $1.00 for first page, $.50 each add'l. Certification fee: $10.00. Fee payee: Clerk of Court. Personal checks accepted. Prepayment is required.

Calhoun County

2nd District Court Box 273, Rockwell City, IA 50579; 712-297-8122; Fax: 712-297-5082. Hours: 9AM-3:30PM (CST). *Felony, Misdemeanor, Civil, Eviction, Small Claims, Probate.*

Civil Records: Access: In person, online. Visitors must perform in person searches for themselves. No search fee. Required to search: name, years to search. Civil cases indexed by defendant, plaintiff. Civil records on docket books from 1880s, computerized since 07/97. Civil, probate, and appellate information is available online at www.judicial.state.ia.us/online_records.

Criminal Records: Access: In person, online. Visitors must perform in person searches for themselves. No search fee. Required to search: name, years to search, DOB, signed release; also helpful: SSN. Criminal records on docket books from 1880s, computerized since 07/97. Criminal, traffic, and appellate information is available at www.judicial.state.ia.us/online_records.

General Information: Public access terminal is available. No juvenile, sealed, pending dissolution of marriage, mental health, domestic abuse or deferred records released. Fax notes: Fax fee is $1.00 per page (prepaid). Copy fee: $.50 per page. Certification fee: $10.00. Fee payee: Clerk of the Court. Personal checks accepted. Credit cards accepted: Visa, MasterCard. Prepayment is required.

Carroll County

2nd District Court PO Box 867, Carroll, IA 51401; 712-792-4327; Fax: 712-792-4328. Hours: 8AM-4:30PM (CST). *Felony, Misdemeanor, Civil, Eviction, Small Claims, Probate.*

Civil Records: Access: In person, online. Visitors must perform in person searches for themselves. No search fee. Required to search: name, years to search. Civil cases indexed by defendant, plaintiff. Civil records on index books from 1800s; computerized records go back to 1993. Civil, probate, and appellate information is available at www.judicial.state.ia.us/online_records.

Criminal Records: Access: In person, online. Visitors must perform in person searches for themselves. No search fee. Required to search: name, years to search. Criminal records on computer from June 1993, index books from 1800s. Criminal, traffic, and appellate information is available online at www.judicial.state.ia.us/online_records.

General Information: Public access terminal is available. No juvenile, sealed, dissolution of marriage, mental health, domestic abuse or deferred records released. Copy fee: $.50 per page. Certification fee: $10.00. Fee payee: Clerk of Court. Personal checks accepted. Credit cards accepted. Prepayment required.

Cass County

4th District Court 5 W 7th St, Courthouse, Atlantic, IA 50022; 712-243-2105. Hours: 8AM-4:30PM (CST). *Felony, Misdemeanor, Civil, Eviction, Small Claims, Probate.*

Civil Records: Access: In person, online. Visitors must perform in person searches for themselves. No search fee. Required to search: name, years to search. Civil cases indexed by defendant, plaintiff. Civil records on

docket books from early 1900s; on computer back to 11/1996. Civil, probate, and appellate information is available at www.judicial.state.ia.us/online_records.

Criminal Records: Access: In person, online. Visitors must perform in person searches for themselves. No search fee. Required to search: name, years to search, signed release; also helpful: DOB, SSN. Criminal records on docket books from 1880s; on computer back to 11/1996. Criminal, traffic, and appellate information is available at www.judicial.state.ia.us/online_records.

General Information: Public access terminal is available. No juvenile, sealed, dissolution of marriage, mental health, domestic abuse or deferred records released. Copy fee: $.50 per page. Certification fee: $10.00. Fee payee: Clerk of Court. Personal checks accepted. Prepayment is required.

Cedar County

7th District Court PO Box 111, Tipton, IA 52772; 563-886-3594. Hours: 8AM-4:30PM (CST). *Felony, Misdemeanor, Civil, Eviction, Small Claims, Probate.*

Civil Records: Access: Mail, in person, online. Both court and visitors may perform in person searches. Search fee: $10.00 per name. Required to search: name, years to search. Civil cases indexed by defendant, plaintiff. Civil records on computer since 1992; on microfiche and docket books from 1839. Civil, probate, and appellate information is available online at www.judicial.state.ia.us/online_records.

Criminal Records: Access: In person, online. Both court and visitors may perform in person searches. Search fee: $10.00 per name. Required to search: name, years to search; also helpful: DOB, SSN, signed release. Criminal records on computer since 1992; on microfiche and docket books from 1839. Criminal, traffic, and appellate information is available online at www.judicial.state.ia.us/online_records.

General Information: Public access terminal is available. No juvenile, sealed, dissolution of marriage, mental health, domestic abuse or deferred records released. SASE required. Turnaround time 1 week. Copy fee: $.50 per page. Certification fee: $10.00. Fee payee: Clerk of Court. Only cashiers checks and money orders accepted. Prepayment is required.

Cerro Gordo County

2nd District Court 220 W Washington, Mason City, IA 50401; 641-424-6431. Hours: 8AM-4:30PM (CST). *Felony, Misdemeanor, Civil, Eviction, Small Claims, Probate.*

Civil Records: Access: In person only. Visitors must perform in person searches for themselves. No search fee. Required to search: name, years to search. Civil cases indexed by defendant, plaintiff. Civil records on computer since 1996: prior records on docket books from early 1900s. Civil, probate, and appellate information is available online at www.judicial.state.ia.us/online_records.

Criminal Records: Access: In person, online. Visitors must perform in person searches for themselves. No search fee. Required to search: name, years to search; also helpful: DOB, SSN. Criminal records on computer since 4/95; prior records on index cards from 1977. Criminal, traffic, and appellate information is available online at www.judicial.state.ia.us/online_records.

General Information: Public access terminal is available. No juvenile, sealed, dissolution of marriage, mental health, domestic abuse or deferred records released. Copy fee: $.50 per page. Certification fee: $10.00. Fee payee: Clerk of Court. Personal checks accepted. Credit cards accepted. Prepayment required.

Cherokee County

3rd District Court Courthouse Drawer F, Cherokee, IA 51012; 712-225-6744; Fax: 712-225-6749. Hours: 8AM-4:30PM (CST). *Felony, Misdemeanor, Civil, Eviction, Small Claims, Probate.*

Civil Records: Access: In person, online. Visitors must perform in person searches for themselves. No search fee. Required to search: name, years to search. Civil cases indexed by defendant, plaintiff. Civil records on docket books from 1800s, indexed on computer since 1997. Civil, probate, and appellate information is available at www.judicial.state.ia.us/online_records.

Criminal Records: Access: In person, online. Visitors must perform in person searches for themselves. No search fee. Required to search: name, years to search. Criminal records index is computerized since 06/90. Criminal, traffic, and appellate information is available online at www.judicial.state.ia.us/online_records.

General Information: Public access terminal is available. No juvenile, sealed, dissolution of marriage, mental health, domestic abuse or deferred records released. Copy fee: $.50 per page. Certification fee: $10.00. Fee payee: Clerk of Court. Personal checks accepted. Prepayment is required.

Chickasaw County

1st District Court County Courthouse, 8 E Prospect, New Hampton, IA 50659; 641-394-2106; Fax: 641-394-5106. Hours: 8AM-4:30PM (CST). *Felony, Misdemeanor, Civil, Eviction, Small Claims, Probate.*

Civil Records: Access: In person, online. Visitors must perform in person searches for themselves. No search fee. Required to search: name, years to search. Civil cases indexed by defendant, plaintiff. Civil records on docket books from late 1800s; on computer back to 1996. Civil, probate, and appellate information is available at www.judicial.state.ia.us/online_records.

Criminal Records: Access: In person, online. Visitors must perform in person searches for themselves. No search fee. Required to search: name, years to search, signed release. Criminal records on docket books from late 1800s; on computer back to 1996. Criminal, traffic, and appellate information is available online at www.judicial.state.ia.us/online_records.

General Information: Public access terminal is available. No juvenile, sealed, dissolution of marriage, adoption, mental health, domestic abuse or deferred records released. Copy fee: $.50. $.25 per page after first 10. Certification fee: $10.00. Fee payee: Clerk of District Court. Personal checks accepted. Prepayment is required.

Clarke County

5th District Court 100 S Main St, Clarke County Courthouse, Osceola, IA 50213; 641-342-6096; Fax: 641-342-2463. Hours: 8AM-4:30PM (CST). *Felony, Misdemeanor, Civil, Eviction, Small Claims, Probate.*

Civil Records: Access: In person, online. Both court and visitors may perform in person searches. No search fee. Required to search: name, years to search. Civil cases indexed by defendant, plaintiff. Civil records on docket books from early 1900s. Civil, probate, and appellate information is available online at www.judicial.state.ia.us/online_records.

Criminal Records: Access: In person, online. Both court and visitors may perform in person searches. No search fee. Required to search: name, years to search; also helpful: SSN. Criminal records on docket books from early 1900s. Criminal, traffic, and appellate information is available online at www.judicial.state.ia.us/online_records.

General Information: Public access terminal is available. No juvenile, sealed, dissolution of marriage, mental health, domestic abuse or deferred records released. Copy fee: $.25 per page. Certification fee: $10.00. Fee payee: Clerk of Court. Personal checks accepted. Prepayment is required.

Clay County

3rd District Court Courthouse 215 W 4th St, Spencer, IA 51301; 712-262-4335. Hours: 8AM-4:30PM (CST). *Felony, Misdemeanor, Civil, Eviction, Small Claims, Probate.*

Civil Records: Access: In person, online. Visitors must perform in person searches for themselves. No search fee. Required to search: name, years to search. Civil cases indexed by defendant, plaintiff. Civil records on microfilm from 1972 to 1995, docket books from 1800s, on computer back to 8/18/97. Civil, probate, and appellate information is available online at www.judicial.state.ia.us/online_records.
Criminal Records: Access: In person, online. Visitors must perform in person searches for themselves. No search fee. Required to search: name, years to search. Criminal records on microfilm from to 1972 to 1995, docket books from 1800s, on comptuer back to 1/7/97. Criminal, traffic, and appellate information is available online at www.judicial.state.ia.us/online_records.
General Information: Public access terminal is available. No juvenile, sealed, pending dissolution of marriage, mental health, sealed domestic abuse or deferred records released. Copy fee: $.50 per page. Certification fee: $10.00. Fee payee: Clerk of Court. Personal checks accepted. Credit cards accepted: Visa, MasterCard.

Clayton County

1st District Court PO Box 418, Clayton County Courthouse, Elkader, IA 52043; 563-245-2204; Fax: 563-245-2825. Hours: 8AM-4:30PM (CST). *Felony, Misdemeanor, Civil, Eviction, Small Claims, Probate.*

Civil Records: Access: In person, online. Visitors must perform in person searches for themselves. No search fee. Required to search: name, years to search. Civil cases indexed by defendant, plaintiff. Civil records on docket books from late 1880s. Civil, probate, and appellate information is available online at www.judicial.state.ia.us/online_records.
Criminal Records: Access: In person, online. Visitors must perform in person searches for themselves. No search fee. Required to search: name, years to search. Criminal records on docket books from late 1880s. Criminal, traffic, and appellate information is available online at www.judicial.state.ia.us/online_records.
General Information: Public access terminal is available. No juvenile unless child is age 10 or older and offense is considered a public offense, sealed, dissolution of marriage, mental health, domestic abuse or deferred records released. Copy fee: $.50 per page. Certification fee: $10.00. Fee payee: Clerk of Court. Personal checks accepted. Prepayment is required.

Clinton County

7th District Court Courthouse (PO Box 2957), Clinton, IA 52733; 563-243-6210; Fax: 563-243-3655. Hours: 8AM-4:30PM (CST). *Felony, Misdemeanor, Civil, Eviction, Small Claims, Probate.*

Civil Records: Access: In person, online. Visitors must perform in person searches for themselves. No search fee. Required to search: name, years to search. Civil cases indexed by defendant. Civil records on computer since 1980, on docket books prior. Civil, probate, and appellate information is available online at www.judicial.state.ia.us/online_records.
Criminal Records: Access: In person, online. Visitors must perform in person searches for themselves. No search fee. Required to search: name, years to search, DOB, signed release; also helpful: SSN. Criminal records on computer since 1980, on docket books prior.

Criminal, traffic, and appellate information is available online at www.judicial.state.ia.us/online_records.
General Information: Public access terminal is available. No juvenile, adoption, sealed, dissolution of marriage before decree, mental health, domestic abuse or deferred records released. Copy fee: $.50 per page. Certification fee: $10.00. Fee payee: Clerk of Court. Personal checks accepted. Credit cards accepted: Visa, MasterCard. Prepayment is required.

Crawford County

3rd District Court 1202 Broadway, Denison, IA 51442; 712-263-2242; Fax: 712-263-5753. Hours: 9AM-4:30 M; 9AM-2PM T, W, TH; 8AM-4:30PM F (CST). *Felony, Misdemeanor, Civil, Eviction, Small Claims, Probate.*

Civil Records: Access: In person, online. Visitors must perform in person searches for themselves. No search fee. Required to search: name, years to search. Civil cases indexed by defendant, plaintiff. Civil records available since 1937, on docket books from 1869. Civil, probate, and appellate information is available online at www.judicial.state.ia.us/online_records.
Criminal Records: Access: In person, online. Visitors must perform in person searches for themselves. No search fee. Required to search: name, years to search. Criminal records available since 1937, on docket books from 1869. Criminal, traffic, and appellate information is available at www.judicial.state.ia.us/online_records.
General Information: Public access terminal is available. No juvenile, sealed, dissolution of marriage, mental health, domestic abuse or deferred records released. Copy fee: $.50 per page. Certification fee: $10.00. Fee payee: Clerk of Court. Personal checks accepted. Prepayment is required.

Dallas County

5th District Court 801 Court St, Adel, IA 50003; 515-993-5816; Fax: 515-993-4752. Hours: 9AM-3PM M,T,W; 8AM-4:30PM TH,F (CST). *Felony, Misdemeanor, Civil, Eviction, Small Claims, Probate.*

Civil Records: Access: In person, online. Visitors must perform in person searches for themselves. No search fee. Required to search: name, years to search. Civil cases indexed by defendant, plaintiff. Civil records on docket books from 1800s; computerized records since 1994. Civil, probate, and appellate information is available at www.judicial.state.ia.us/online_records.
Criminal Records: Access: In person, online. Visitors must perform in person searches for themselves. No search fee. Required to search: name, years to search. Criminal records on docket books from 1800s; computerized records since 1994. Criminal, traffic, and appellate information is available online at www.judicial.state.ia.us/online_records.
General Information: Public access terminal is available. No juvenile, sealed, dissolution of marriage, mental health, domestic abuse or deferred records released. Copy fee: $.50 per page. Certification fee: $10.00. Fee payee: Clerk of Court. Personal checks accepted. Prepayment is required.

Davis County

8th District Court Davis County Courthouse, Bloomfield, IA 52537; 641-664-2011; Fax: 641-664-2041. Hours: 8AM-2PM (CST). *Felony, Misdemeanor, Civil, Eviction, Small Claims, Probate.*

Civil Records: Access: In person, online. Visitors must perform in person searches for themselves. No search fee. Required to search: name, years to search. Civil cases indexed by defendant, plaintiff. Civil records on docket books from late 1800s; computerized since 1997. Civil, probate, and appellate information is available at www.judicial.state.ia.us/online_records.
Criminal Records: Access: In person, online. Visitors must perform in person searches for themselves. No

search fee. Required to search: name, years to search, DOB. Criminal records on docket books from late 1800s; computerized since 1997. Criminal, traffic, and appellate information is available online at www.judicial.state.ia.us/online_records.
General Information: Public access terminal is available. (Records available since 1997.) No juvenile, sealed, dissolution of marriage, mental health, domestic abuse or deferred records released. Copy fee: $.25 per page. Certification fee: $10.00. Fee payee: Clerk of Court. Personal checks accepted. Prepayment is required.

Decatur County

5th District Court 207 N Main St, Leon, IA 50144; 641-446-4331; Fax: 641-446-3759. Hours: 8AM-4:30PM (CST). *Felony, Misdemeanor, Civil, Eviction, Small Claims, Probate.*

Civil Records: Access: In person, online. Visitors must perform in person searches themselves. No search fee. Required to search: name, years to search. Civil cases indexed by defendant, plaintiff. Civil records on docket books since 1880; on computer back to 1996. Civil, probate, and appellate information is available online at www.judicial.state.ia.us/online_records.
Criminal Records: Access: In person, online. Visitors must perform in person searches themselves. No search fee. Required to search: name, years to search, DOB or SSN. Criminal records on docket books since 1880; on computer back to 1996. Criminal, traffic, and appellate information is available online at www.judicial.state.ia.us/online_records.
General Information: Public access terminal is available. No juvenile, sealed, dissolution of marriage, mental health, domestic abuse or deferred records released. Copy fee: $.50 per page. Certification fee: $10.00. Fee payee: Clerk of Court. Personal checks accepted.

Delaware County

District Court Delaware County Courthouse, PO Box 527, Manchester, IA 52057; 563-927-4942; Fax: 563-927-3074. Hours: 8AM-4:30PM (CST). *Felony, Misdemeanor, Civil, Eviction, Small Claims, Probate.*

Civil Records: Access: In person, online. Visitors must perform in person searches for themselves. No search fee. Required to search: name, years to search. Civil cases indexed by defendant, plaintiff. Civil records on docket books from late 1800s; on computer back to 1996. Civil, probate, and appellate information is available at www.judicial.state.ia.us/online_records.
Criminal Records: Access: In person, online. Visitors must perform in person searches for themselves. No search fee. Required to search: name, years to search. Criminal records on docket books from late 1800s; on computer back to 1996. Criminal, traffic, and appellate information is available online at www.judicial.state.ia.us/online_records.
General Information: Public access terminal is available. No juvenile, sealed, dissolution of marriage, mental health, domestic abuse or deferred records released. Copy fee: $.50 per page. Certification fee: $10.00. Fee payee: Clerk of Court. Personal checks accepted. Prepayment is required.

Des Moines County

8th District Court 513 Main St, PO Box 158, Burlington, IA 52601; 319-753-8262/8242; Fax: 319-753-8253. Hours: 8AM-3:30PM (CST). *Felony, Misdemeanor, Civil, Eviction, Small Claims, Probate.*

Civil Records: Access: In person, online. Visitors must perform in person searches for themselves. No search fee. Required to search: name, years to search; also helpful: address. Civil cases indexed by defendant, plaintiff. Civil records on computer from July, 1992, docket books prior. Civil, probate, and appellate information is available online at www.judicial.state.ia.us/online_records.

Criminal Records: Access: In person, online. Visitors must perform in person searches for themselves. No search fee. Required to search: name, years to search, aliases; also helpful: DOB, SSN. Criminal records on computer from July, 1992, docket books prior. Criminal, traffic, and appellate information is available online at www.judicial.state.ia.us/online_records.

General Information: Public access terminal is available. No juvenile, sealed, dissolution of marriage, mental health, domestic abuse or deferred records released. Copy fee: $.25 per page. Certification fee: $10.00. Fee payee: Clerk of Court. Personal checks accepted. Credit cards accepted: Visa, MasterCard.

Dickinson County

3rd District Court PO Drawer O N, Spirit Lake, IA 51360; 712-336-1138; Fax: 712-336-4005. Hours: 8AM-4:30PM (CST). *Felony, Misdemeanor, Civil, Eviction, Small Claims, Probate.*

Civil Records: Access: In person, online. Visitors must perform in person searches for themselves. No search fee. Required to search: name, years to search. Civil cases indexed by defendant, plaintiff. Early information on microfiche, docket books from 1800s; computerized back to 1992. Civil, probate, and appellate information is available at www.judicial.state.ia.us/online_records.
Criminal Records: Access: In person, online. Visitors must perform in person searches for themselves. No search fee. Required to search: name, years to search. Criminal records early information on microfiche, docket books from 1800s; computerized back to 1992. Criminal, traffic, and appellate information is available online at www.judicial.state.ia.us/online_records.
General Information: Public access terminal is available. No juvenile, sealed, dissolution of marriage, mental health, domestic abuse or deferred records released. Fax notes: No fee to fax results. Copy fee: $.50 per page. Certification fee: $10.00. Fee payee: Clerk of Court. Personal checks accepted.

Dubuque County

1st District Court 720 Central, Dubuque, IA 52001; 563-589-4418. Hours: 8AM-4:30PM (CST). *Felony, Misdemeanor, Civil, Eviction, Small Claims, Probate.*

Civil Records: Access: In person, online. Visitors must perform in person searches for themselves. No search fee. Required to search: name, years to search. Civil cases indexed by defendant, plaintiff. Civil records on computer since July, 1994, on docket books from 1900s. Civil, probate, and appellate information is available at www.judicial.state.ia.us/online_records.
Criminal Records: Access: In person, online. Visitors must perform in person searches for themselves. No search fee. Required to search: name, years to search; also helpful: DOB, SSN. Criminal records on computer since July, 1994, on docket books from 1900s. Criminal, traffic, and appellate information is available online at www.judicial.state.ia.us/online_records.
General Information: Public access terminal is available. No juvenile, sealed, dissolution of marriage, mental health, domestic abuse or expunged records released. Copy fee: $.50 per page. Certification fee: $10.00. Fee payee: Clerk of District Court. Local checks accepted. Credit cards accepted: Visa, MasterCard. Prepayment is required.

Emmet County

3rd District Court Emmet County, 609 1st Ave N, Estherville, IA 51334; 712-362-3325. Hours: 8AM-4:30PM M, T; 9AM-4:30PM TH, F (CST). *Felony, Misdemeanor, Civil, Eviction, Small Claims, Probate.*

Civil Records: Access: In person, online. Visitors must perform in person searches for themselves. No search

fee. Required to search: name, years to search. Civil cases indexed by defendant, plaintiff. Civil records on docket books from 1900s. Civil, probate, and appellate information is available online at www.judicial.state.ia.us/online_records.
Criminal Records: Access: In person, online. Visitors must perform in person searches for themselves. No search fee. Required to search: name, years to search. Criminal records on docket books from 1900s. Criminal, traffic, and appellate information is available online at www.judicial.state.ia.us/online_records.
General Information: Public access terminal is available. (Records available since 1996.) No juvenile, sealed, dissolution of marriage, mental health, domestic abuse or deferred records released. Copy fee: $.25 per page. Certification fee: $10.00. Fee payee: Clerk of Court. Personal checks accepted.

Fayette County

Fayette County District Court PO Box 458, West Union, IA 52175; 563-422-5694; Fax: 563-422-3137. Hours: 9AM-Noon, 1-3:30PM (CST). *Felony, Misdemeanor, Civil, Eviction, Small Claims, Probate, Traffic.*

Civil Records: Access: In person, online. Visitors must perform in person searches for themselves. Search fee: No search fee. Required to search: name, years to search. Civil cases indexed by defendant, plaintiff. Civil records on docket books from 1900s. Civil, probate, and appellate information is available online at www.judicial.state.ia.us/online_records.
Criminal Records: Access: In person, online. Visitors must perform in person searches for themselves. Search fee: No search fee. Required to search: name, years to search. Criminal records on docket books from 1900s; 1940-1960 on CD-ROM. Criminal, traffic, and appellate information is available online at www.judicial.state.ia.us/online_records. Hands-on retrieval: contact Fayette Co Abstract Co, West Union, IA 52175.
General Information: Public access terminal is available. No juvenile, sealed, dissolution of marriage, mental health, domestic abuse or deferred records released. Copy fee: $.50 per page. Certification fee: $10.00. Fee payee: Clerk of Court. Personal checks accepted. Prepayment is required.

Floyd County

2nd District Court 101 S Main St, Charles City, IA 50616; 641-228-7777; Fax: 641-228-7772. Hours: 8AM-4:30PM (CST). *Felony, Misdemeanor, Civil, Eviction, Small Claims, Probate.*

Civil Records: Access: In person, online. Visitors must perform in person searches for themselves. No search fee. Required to search: name, years to search. Civil cases indexed by defendant, plaintiff. Civil records in docket books, are computerized since 1996. Civil, probate, and appellate information is available online at www.judicial.state.ia.us/online_records.
Criminal Records: Access: In person, online. Visitors must perform in person searches for themselves. No search fee. Required to search: name, years to search, DOB, signed release; also helpful: SSN. Criminal records in docket books, are computerized since 1996. Criminal, traffic, and appellate information is available online at www.judicial.state.ia.us/online_records.
General Information: Public access terminal is available. No juvenile, sealed, dissolution of marriage, mental health, domestic abuse or deferred records released. Copy fee: $.50 per page. Certification fee: $10.00. Fee payee: Clerk of Court. Personal checks accepted. Credit cards accepted.

Franklin County

2nd Judicial District Court 12 1st Ave NW, PO Box 28, Hampton, IA 50441; 641-456-5626; Fax: 641-456-5628. Hours: 8AM-4:30PM (CST). *Felony, Misdemeanor, Civil, Eviction, Small Claims, Probate.*

Civil Records: Access: In person, online. Visitors must perform in person searches for themselves. No search fee. Required to search: name, years to search. Civil cases indexed by defendant, plaintiff. Civil records on microfiche and/or microfilm from 1860 to 1984, on docket books from 1984 to present. Civil, probate, and appellate information is available online at www.judicial.state.ia.us/online_records.
Criminal Records: Access: In person, online. Visitors must perform in person searches for themselves. No search fee. Required to search: name, years to search. Criminal records on microfiche and/or microfilm from 1860 to 1984, on docket books from 1984 to present. Criminal, traffic, and appellate information is available online at www.judicial.state.ia.us/online_records.
General Information: Public access terminal is available. No juvenile, sealed, dissolution of marriage, mental health, domestic abuse or deferred records released. Copy fee: $.50 per page. Certification fee: $10.00. Fee payee: Clerk of District Court. Personal checks accepted. Credit cards accepted: Visa, MasterCard. Credit cards accepted for traffic fees only. Prepayment is required.

Fremont County

4th District Court PO Box 549, Sidney, IA 51652; 712-374-2232; Fax: 712-374-3330. Hours: 8AM-4:30PM (CST). *Felony, Misdemeanor, Civil, Eviction, Small Claims, Probate.*

Civil Records: Access: In person, online. Visitors must perform in person searches for themselves. No search fee. Required to search: name. Civil cases indexed by defendant, plaintiff. Computerized from 11/96, civil records in docket books and microfiche from the 1930's. Civil, probate, and appellate information is available online at www.judicial.state.ia.us/online_records.
Criminal Records: Access: In person, online. Visitors must perform in person searches for themselves. No search fee. Required to search: name. Computerized from 11/96, criminal records in docket books and microfiche from the 1930's. Criminal, traffic, and appellate information is available online at www.judicial.state.ia.us/online_records.
General Information: Public access terminal is available. No juvenile, sealed, dissolution of marriage, mental health, domestic abuse or deferred records released. Fax notes: Fee to fax results is $3.00 per document. Copy fee: $.25 per page. Certification fee: $10.00. Fee payee: Clerk of Court. Personal checks accepted. Prepayment is required.

Greene County

2nd District Court Greene County Courthouse, 114 N Chestnut, Jefferson, IA 50129; 515-386-2516. Hours: 9AM-3:30PM (CST). *Felony, Misdemeanor, Civil, Eviction, Small Claims, Probate.*

Civil Records: Access: In person, online. Visitors must perform in person searches for themselves. No search fee. Required to search: name, years to search. Civil cases indexed by defendant, plaintiff. Civil records on microfiche from 1981 back to establishment of court, docket books from 1800s. Civil, probate, and appellate information is available online at www.judicial.state.ia.us/online_records.
Criminal Records: Access: In person, online. Visitors must perform in person searches for themselves. No search fee. Required to search: name, years to search. Criminal records on microfiche from 1981 back to establishment of court, docket books from 1800s.

Criminal, traffic, and appellate information is available online at www.judicial.state.ia.us/online_records.

General Information: Public access terminal is available. No juvenile, sealed, dissolution of marriage, mental health, domestic abuse or deferred records released. Copy fee: $.50 per page. Certification fee: $10.00. Fee payee: Clerk of Court. Personal checks accepted. Credit cards accepted: Visa, MasterCard. Credit cards accepted for traffic fees only. Prepayment is required.

Grundy County

1st District Court Grundy County Courthouse, 706 G Ave, Grundy Center, IA 50638; 319-824-5229; Fax: 319-824-3447. Hours: 8AM-4:30PM (CST). *Felony, Misdemeanor, Civil, Eviction, Small Claims, Probate.*

Civil Records: Access: In person, online. Visitors must perform in person searches for themselves. No search fee. Required to search: name, years to search. Civil cases indexed by defendant, plaintiff. Civil records on docket books from 1881. Civil, probate, and appellate information is available online at www.judicial.state.ia.us/online_records. Records complete back to 4/97.
Criminal Records: Access: In person, online. Visitors must perform in person searches for themselves. No search fee. Required to search: name, years to search. Criminal records on docket books from 1881. Criminal, traffic, and appellate information is available online at www.judicial.state.ia.us/online_records.
General Information: Public access terminal is available. No pending, confidential, juvenile, sealed, dissolution of marriage, mental health, or deferred records released. Copy fee: $.50 per page. Certification fee: $10.00. Fee payee: Clerk of Court. Personal checks accepted. Credit cards accepted: Visa, MasterCard. Prepayment is required.

Guthrie County

5th District Court Courthouse, 200 N 5th St, Guthrie Center, IA 50115; 641-747-3415. Hours: 8AM-4:30PM (CST). *Felony, Misdemeanor, Civil, Eviction, Small Claims, Probate.*

Civil Records: Access: In person, online. Visitors must perform in person searches for themselves. No search fee. Required to search: name, years to search. Civil cases indexed by defendant, plaintiff. Civil records on computer since 11/96; prior on docket books from 1880s. Civil, probate, and appellate information is available at www.judicial.state.ia.us/online_records.
Criminal Records: Access: In person, online. Visitors must perform in person searches for themselves. No search fee. Required to search: name, years to search. Criminal records on computer since 11/96; prior records on docket books from 1880s. Criminal, traffic, and appellate information is available online at www.judicial.state.ia.us/online_records.
General Information: Public access terminal is available. No juvenile, sealed, dissolution of marriage, mental health, domestic abuse or deferred records released. Copy fee: $.50 per page. Certification fee: $10.00. Fee payee: Clerk of Court. Personal checks accepted. Prepayment is required.

Hamilton County

2nd District Court Courthouse PO Box 845, Webster City, IA 50595; 515-832-9600. Hours: 8AM-4:30PM (CST). *Felony, Misdemeanor, Civil, Eviction, Small Claims, Probate.*

Civil Records: Access: In person, online. Visitors must perform in person searches for themselves. No search fee. Required to search: name, years to search. Civil cases indexed by defendant, plaintiff. Civil records on microfiche from 1939, docket books from 1880s. Civil,

probate, and appellate information is available online at www.judicial.state.ia.us/online_records.
Criminal Records: Access: In person, online. Visitors must perform in person searches for themselves. No search fee. Required to search: name, years to search. Criminal, traffic, and appellate information is available online at www.judicial.state.ia.us/online_records.
General Information: Public access terminal is available. No juvenile, sealed, dissolution of marriage, mental health, domestic abuse records released. Copy fee: $.50 per page. Certification fee: $10.00. Fee payee: Clerk of Court. Personal checks accepted. Credit cards accepted. Prepayment is required.

Hancock County

2nd District Court 855 State St, Garner, IA 50438; 641-923-2532; Fax: 641-923-3521. Hours: 8AM-4:30PM (CST). *Felony, Misdemeanor, Civil, Eviction, Small Claims, Probate.*

Civil Records: Access: In person, online. Visitors must perform in person searches for themselves. No search fee. Required to search: name, years to search. Civil cases indexed by defendant, plaintiff. Civil records on docket books from 1880s; on computer since 1997. Civil, probate, and appellate information is available online at www.judicial.state.ia.us/online_records.
Criminal Records: Access: In person, online. Visitors must perform in person searches for themselves. No search fee. Required to search: name, years to search. Criminal records on docket books from 1880s; on computer since 1997. Criminal, traffic, and appellate information is available online at www.judicial.state.ia.us/online_records.
General Information: Public access terminal is available. No juvenile, sealed, dissolution of marriage, mental health, domestic abuse or deferred records released. Fax notes: Fee to fax results is $1.00 per page. Copy fee: $.50 per page. Certification fee: $10.00. Fee payee: Clerk of Court. Personal checks accepted. Prepayment is required.

Hardin County

2nd District Court Courthouse, PO Box 495, Eldora, IA 50627; 641-858-2328; Fax: 641-858-2320. Hours: 8AM-4:30PM (CST). *Felony, Misdemeanor, Civil, Eviction, Small Claims, Probate.*

Civil Records: Access: In person, online. Visitors must perform in person searches for themselves. No search fee. Required to search: name, years to search. Civil cases indexed by defendant, plaintiff. Civil records on docket books from 1880s. Civil, probate, and appellate information is available online at www.judicial.state.ia.us/online_records.
Criminal Records: Access: In person, online. Visitors must perform in person searches for themselves. No search fee. Required to search: name, years to search. Criminal records on docket books from 1880s. Criminal, traffic, and appellate information is available online at www.judicial.state.ia.us/online_records.
General Information: Public access terminal is available. No juvenile, sealed, dissolution of marriage, mental health, domestic abuse or deferred records released. Copy fee: $.50 per page. Certification fee: $10.00. Fee payee: Clerk of Court. Personal checks accepted. Credit cards accepted: Visa, MasterCard. Prepayment is required.

Harrison County

District Court Court House, Logan, IA 51546; 712-644-2665. Hours: 8:30AM-3:30PM (CST). *Felony, Misdemeanor, Civil, Eviction, Small Claims, Probate.*

Civil Records: Access: In person, online. Visitors must perform in person searches for themselves. No search fee. Required to search: name, years to search. Civil cases indexed by defendant, plaintiff. Civil records on computer since 11/96; prior on docket books since

1840s in Recorder's office. Recent death and birth certificates on microfiche. Civil, probate, and appellate information is available online at www.judicial.state.ia.us/online_records.
Criminal Records: Access: In person, online. Visitors must perform in person searches for themselves. No search fee. Required to search: name, years to search. Criminal records on computer since 11/96, prior on docket books from 1840s in Recorder's office. Criminal, traffic, and appellate information is available online at www.judicial.state.ia.us/online_records.
General Information: Public access terminal is available. No juvenile, sealed, dissolution of marriage, mental health, domestic abuse or deferred records released. Copy fee: $.50 per page. Certification fee: $10.00. Fee payee: Clerk of Court. Personal checks accepted. Prepayment is required.

Henry County

8th District Court PO Box 176, Mount Pleasant, IA 52641; Civil phone: 319-385-2632; Criminal phone: 319-385-3150; Fax: 319-385-4144. Hours: 8AM-4:30PM (CST). *Felony, Misdemeanor, Civil, Eviction, Small Claims, Probate.*

Civil Records: Access: In person, online. Visitors must perform in person searches for themselves. No search fee. Required to search: name, years to search. Civil cases indexed by defendant, plaintiff. Civil records on docket books from 1880s. Civil, probate, and appellate information is available online at www.judicial.state.ia.us/online_records.
Criminal Records: Access: In person, online. Visitors must perform in person searches for themselves. No search fee. Required to search: name, years to search, DOB; also helpful: address, SSN. Criminal records on docket books from 1880s. Criminal, traffic, and appellate information is available online at www.judicial.state.ia.us/online_records.
General Information: Public access terminal is available. No juvenile, sealed, dissolution of marriage, mental health, domestic abuse or deferred records released. Copy fee: $.25 per page. Certification fee: $10.00. Fee payee: Clerk of Court. Personal checks accepted. Prepayment is required.

Howard County

1st District Court Courthouse, 137 N Elm St, Cresco, IA 52136; 563-547-2661. Hours: 8AM-4:30PM (CST). *Felony, Misdemeanor, Civil, Eviction, Small Claims, Probate.*

www.judicial.state.ia.us/district/d1.asp

Civil Records: Access: In person, online. Visitors must perform in person searches for themselves. No search fee. Required to search: name, years to search. Civil cases indexed by defendant, plaintiff. Civil records on docket books from 1900s. Civil, probate, and appellate information is available online at www.judicial.state.ia.us/online_records.
Criminal Records: Access: In person, online. Visitors must perform in person searches for themselves. No search fee. Required to search: name, years to search, DOB. Criminal records on docket books from 1900s. Criminal, traffic, and appellate information is available online at www.judicial.state.ia.us/online_records.
General Information: No juvenile, sealed, dissolution of marriage, mental health, domestic abuse or deferred records released. Copy fee: $.50 per page. Certification fee: $10.00. Fee payee: Clerk of Court. Personal checks accepted. Prepayment is required.

Humboldt County

2nd District Court PO Box 100, Dakota City, IA 50529; 515-332-1806; Fax: 515-332-7100. Hours: 8AM-4:30PM (CST). *Felony, Misdemeanor, Civil, Eviction, Small Claims, Probate.*

Civil Records: Access: In person, online. Visitors must perform in person searches for themselves. No search fee. Required to search: name, years to search. Civil cases indexed by defendant, plaintiff. Civil records on docket books from early 1900s; computerized records since 7/97. Civil, probate, and appellate information is available at www.judicial.state.ia.us/online_records.

Criminal Records: Access: In person, online. Visitors must perform in person searches for themselves. No search fee. Required to search: name, years to search. Criminal records on docket books from early 1900s; computerized records since 7/97. Criminal, traffic, and appellate information is available online at www.judicial.state.ia.us/online_records.

General Information: Public access terminal is available. No juvenile, sealed, dissolution of marriage, mental health, domestic abuse or deferred records released. Copy fee: $.50 per page. Certification fee: $10.00. Fee payee: Clerk of Court. Personal checks accepted. Prepayment is required.

Ida County

3rd District Court Courthouse, 401 Moorehead St, Ida Grove, IA 51445; 712-364-2628; Fax: 712-364-2699. Hours: AM-4:30PM T, TH, F (CST). *Felony, Misdemeanor, Civil, Eviction, Small Claims, Probate.*

Civil Records: Access: In person, online. Visitors must perform in person searches for themselves. No search fee. Required to search: name, years to search. Civil cases indexed by defendant, plaintiff. Civil records on docket books from early 1800s, computerized since 07/97. Civil, probate, and appellate information is available at www.judicial.state.ia.us/online_records.

Criminal Records: Access: In person, online. Visitors must perform in person searches for themselves. No search fee. Required to search: name, years to search. Criminal records on docket books from early 1800s, computerized since 07/97. Criminal, traffic, and appellate information is available online at www.judicial.state.ia.us/online_records.

General Information: Public access terminal is available. No juvenile, sealed, dissolution of marriage, mental health, domestic abuse or deferred records released. Copy fee: $.50 per page. Certification fee: $10.00. Fee payee: Clerk of Court. Personal checks accepted. Prepayment is required.

Iowa County

6th District Court PO Box 266, Marengo, IA 52301; 319-642-3914. Hours: 8AM-3:30PM (CST). *Felony, Misdemeanor, Civil, Eviction, Small Claims, Probate.*

Civil Records: Access: In person, online. Visitors must perform in person searches for themselves. No search fee. Required to search: name, years to search. Civil cases indexed by defendant, plaintiff. Civil records on docket books from early 1800s; on computer back to 2/97. Civil, probate, and appellate information is available at www.judicial.state.ia.us/online_records.

Criminal Records: Access: Mail, in person, online. Visitors must perform in person searches for themselves. No search fee. Required to search: name, years to search. Criminal records on docket books from early 1800s; on computer back to 2/1997. Criminal, traffic, and appellate information is available online at www.judicial.state.ia.us/online_records.

General Information: Public access terminal is available. No juvenile, sealed, dissolution of marriage, mental health, domestic abuse or deferred records released. Fax notes: Will not fax results. Copy fee: $.50

per page. Certification fee: $10.00. Fee payee: Clerk of Court. Personal checks accepted. Prepayment required.

Jackson County

7th District Court 201 West Platt, Maquoketa, IA 52060; 563-652-4946; Fax: 563-652-2708. Hours: 8AM-4:30PM (CST). *Felony, Misdemeanor, Civil, Eviction, Small Claims, Probate.*

Civil Records: Access: In person, online. Visitors must perform in person searches for themselves. No search fee. Required to search: name, years to search. Civil cases indexed by defendant, plaintiff. Civil records on computer since 1994, on docket books from 1900s. Civil, probate, and appellate information is available online at www.judicial.state.ia.us/online_records.

Criminal Records: Access: In person, online. Visitors must perform in person searches for themselves. No search fee. Required to search: name, years to search, DOB; also helpful: SSN. Criminal records on computer since 1994, on docket books from 1900s. Criminal, traffic, and appellate information is available online at www.judicial.state.ia.us/online_records.

General Information: Public access terminal is available. No juvenile, sealed, dissolution of marriage, mental health, domestic abuse or deferred records released. Copy fee: $.50 per page. Certification fee: $10.00. Fee payee: Clerk of Court. Personal checks accepted. Prepayment is required.

Jasper County

5th District Court 101 First Street North, Rm 104, Newton, IA 50208; Civil phone: 641-792-3255; Criminal phone: 641-792-9161; Fax: 641-792-2818. Hours: 8AM-4:30PM (CST). *Felony, Misdemeanor, Civil, Eviction, Small Claims, Probate.*

www.judicial.state.ia.us/decisions/district/d5.asp

Civil Records: Access: In person, online. Visitors must perform in person searches for themselves. No search fee. Required to search: name, years to search. Civil cases indexed by defendant, plaintiff. Civil records on computer since 1994, docket books from 1900s. Civil, probate, and appellate information is available online at www.judicial.state.ia.us/online_records.

Criminal Records: Access: In person, online. Visitors must perform in person searches for themselves. No search fee. Required to search: name, years to search. Criminal records on computer since 1994, docket books from 1900s. Criminal, traffic, and appellate information is available at www.judicial.state.ia.us/online_records.

General Information: Public access terminal is available. No juvenile, sealed, dissolution of marriage, mental health, or deferred records released. Copy fee: $.50 per page. Certification fee: $10.00 per document. Fee payee: Clerk of Court. Personal checks accepted. Prepayment is required.

Jefferson County

8th District Court PO Box 984, Fairfield, IA 52556; 641-472-3454; Fax: 641-472-9472. Hours: 8AM-3PM M; 8AM-2PM T-F (CST). *Felony, Misdemeanor, Civil, Eviction, Small Claims, Probate.*

Civil Records: Access: In person, online. Visitors must perform in person searches for themselves. No search fee. Required to search: name, years to search. Civil cases indexed by defendant, plaintiff. Civil records on docket books from 1800s. Civil, probate, and appellate information is available online at www.judicial.state.ia.us/online_records.

Criminal Records: Access: In person, online. Visitors must perform in person searches for themselves. No search fee. Required to search: name, years to search, DOB. Criminal records on docket books from 1800s. Criminal, traffic, and appellate information is available online at www.judicial.state.ia.us/online_records.

General Information: Public access terminal is available. No juvenile, sealed, dissolution of marriage,

mental health, domestic abuse or deferred records released. Copy fee: $.25 per page. Certification fee: $10.00. Fee payee: Clerk of Court. Personal checks accepted.

Johnson County

6th District Court PO Box 2510, Iowa City, IA 52244; 319-356-6060. Hours: 8AM-3:30PM (CST). *Felony, Misdemeanor, Civil, Eviction, Small Claims, Probate.*

Civil Records: Access: In person, online. Visitors must perform in person searches for themselves. No search fee. Required to search: name, years to search. Civil cases indexed by defendant, plaintiff. Civil records on docket books and microfilm from 1880s. Civil, probate, and appellate information is available online at www.judicial.state.ia.us/online_records.

Criminal Records: Access: In person, online. Visitors must perform in person searches for themselves. No search fee. Required to search: name, years to search; also helpful: address, DOB, SSN. Criminal records on docket books and microfilm from 1880s. Criminal, traffic, and appellate information is available online at www.judicial.state.ia.us/online_records.

General Information: Public access terminal is available. No juvenile, sealed, dissolution of marriage, mental health, domestic abuse or deferred records released. Copy fee: $.50 per page. Certification fee: $10.00. Fee payee: Clerk of Court. Personal checks accepted.

Jones County

6th District Court PO Box 19, Anamosa, IA 52205; 319-462-4341. Hours: 8AM-4:30PM (CST). *Felony, Misdemeanor, Civil, Eviction, Small Claims, Probate.*

Civil Records: Access: In person, online. Visitors must perform in person searches for themselves. No search fee. Required to search: name, years to search. Civil cases indexed by defendant, plaintiff. Civil records on docket books from mid 1800s; dockets on computer back to 6/1997. Civil, probate, and appellate information is available online at www.judicial.state.ia.us/online_records.

Criminal Records: Access: In person, online. Visitors must perform in person searches for themselves. No search fee. Required to search: name, years to search. Criminal records on docket books from early 1900s; dockets on computer back to 11/1996. Criminal, traffic, and appellate information is available online at www.judicial.state.ia.us/online_records.

General Information: Public access terminal is available. No juvenile, sealed, dissolution of marriage (prior to decree), mental health or deferred records released. Copy fee: $.50 per page. Certification fee: $10.00. Fee payee: Clerk of Court. Personal checks accepted. Prepayment is required.

Keokuk County

8th District Court 101 S. Main, Courthouse, Sigourney, IA 52591; 641-622-2210; Fax: 641-622-2171. Hours: 8AM-4:30PM (CST). *Felony, Misdemeanor, Civil, Eviction, Small Claims, Probate.*

Civil Records: Access: In person, online. Visitors must perform in person searches for themselves. No search fee. Required to search: name, years to search. Civil cases indexed by defendant, plaintiff. Civil records on docket books from 1888; on computer back to 2/1997. Civil, probate, and appellate information is available online at www.judicial.state.ia.us/online_records.

Criminal Records: Access: In person, online. Visitors must perform in person searches for themselves. No search fee. Required to search: name, years to search. Criminal records on docket books from 1888; on computer back to 2/1997. Criminal, traffic, and

appellate information is available online at www.judicial.state.ia.us/online_records.
General Information: Public access terminal is available. No juvenile, sealed, dissolution of marriage, mental health, domestic abuse or deferred records released. Copy fee: $.25 per page. Certification fee: $10.00. Fee payee: Clerk of Court. Personal checks accepted. Prepayment is required.

Kossuth County

3rd District Court Kossuth County Courthouse, 114 W State St, Algona, IA 50511; 515-295-3240. Hours: 8AM-4PM (CST). *Felony, Misdemeanor, Civil, Eviction, Small Claims, Probate.*

Civil Records: Access: In person, online. Visitors must perform in person searches for themselves. No search fee. Required to search: name, years to search. Civil cases indexed by defendant, plaintiff. Civil records on computer since 09/97; prior records on dockets. Civil, probate, and appellate information is available online at www.judicial.state.ia.us/online_records.
Criminal Records: Access: In person, online. Visitors must perform in person searches for themselves. No search fee. Required to search: name, years to search. Criminal records on computer since 09/97; prior records on dockets. Criminal, traffic, and appellate information is available at www.judicial.state.ia.us/online_records.
General Information: Public access terminal is available. No juvenile, sealed, dissolution of marriage, mental health, domestic abuse or deferred records released. Copy fee: $.50 per page. Certification fee: $10.00. Fee payee: Clerk of Court. Personal checks accepted. Prepayment is required.

Lee County

8th District Court PO Box 1443, Ft Madison, IA 52627; 319-372-3523. Hours: 8AM-4:30PM (CST). *Felony, Misdemeanor, Civil, Eviction, Small Claims, Probate.*

Civil Records: Access: In person, online. Visitors must perform in person searches for themselves. No search fee. Required to search: name, years to search. Civil cases indexed by defendant, plaintiff. Civil records on docket books from early 1800s; computerized from 1996. Civil, probate, and appellate information is available at www.judicial.state.ia.us/online_records.
Criminal Records: Access: In person, online. Visitors must perform in person searches for themselves. No search fee. Required to search: name, years to search. Criminal records on docket books from early 1800s; computerized from 1996. Criminal, traffic, and appellate information is available online at www.judicial.state.ia.us/online_records.
General Information: Public access terminal is available. No juvenile, sealed, dissolution of marriage, mental health, domestic abuse or deferred records released. Copy fee: $.25 per page. Certification fee: $10.00. Fee payee: Clerk of Court. Personal checks accepted. Prepayment is required.

Linn County

District Court Linn County Courthouse, PO Box 1468, Cedar Rapids, IA 52406-1468; 319-398-3411; Fax: 319-398-3964. Hours: 8AM-4:30PM (CST). *Felony, Misdemeanor, Civil, Eviction, Small Claims, Probate.*

Civil Records: Access: In person, online. Visitors must perform in person searches for themselves. No search fee. Required to search: name, years to search. Civil cases indexed by defendant, plaintiff. Civil records on computer from 1995, docket books from early 1900s. Civil, probate, and appellate information is available online at www.judicial.state.ia.us/online_records.
Criminal Records: Access: In person, online. Visitors must perform in person searches for themselves. No search fee. Required to search: name, years to search;

also helpful: address, DOB. Criminal records on computer since 1993. Criminal, traffic, and appellate information is available online at www.judicial.state.ia.us/online_records.
General Information: Public access terminal is available. No juvenile, sealed, pending dissolution of marriage, mental health, domestic abuse or deferred records released. Copy fee: $.50 per page. Certification fee: $10.00. Fee payee: Clerk of Court. Personal checks accepted. Prepayment is required.

Louisa County

8th District Court PO Box 268, Wapello, IA 52653; 319-523-4541; Fax: 319-523-4542. Hours: 8AM-2:30PM (CST). *Felony, Misdemeanor, Civil, Eviction, Small Claims, Probate.*

Civil Records: Access: In person, online. Both court and visitors may perform in person searches. No search fee. Required to search: name, years to search. Civil cases indexed by defendant, plaintiff. Civil records on docket books from 1920s, on computer since 02/97. Civil, probate, and appellate information is available online at www.judicial.state.ia.us/online_records.
Criminal Records: Access: In person, online. Both court and visitors may perform in person searches. No search fee. Required to search: name, years to search, DOB, signed release; also helpful: SSN. Criminal records on docket books from 1920s, on computer since 02/97. Criminal, traffic, and appellate information is available at www.judicial.state.ia.us/online_records.
General Information: Public access terminal is available. No juvenile, sealed, dissolution of marriage, mental health, domestic abuse or deferred records released. Copy fee: $.25 per page. Certification fee: $10.00. Fee payee: Clerk of Court. Personal checks accepted. Prepayment is required.

Lucas County

5th District Court Courthouse, 916 Braden, Chariton, IA 50049; 641-774-4421; Fax: 641-774-8669. Hours: 9AM-4PM, M-T; 12:30PM-4PM, W-TH-F (CST). *Felony, Misdemeanor, Civil, Eviction, Small Claims, Probate.*

Civil Records: Access: In person, online. Visitors must perform in person searches for themselves. No search fee. Required to search: name, years to search. Civil cases indexed by defendant, plaintiff. Civil records on docket books from 1880s; on computer back to 1997. Civil, probate, and appellate information is available online at www.judicial.state.ia.us/online_records.
Criminal Records: Access: In person, online. Visitors must perform in person searches for themselves. No search fee. Required to search: name, years to search, signed release; also helpful: SSN. Criminal records on docket books from 1880s; on computer back to 1997. Criminal, traffic, and appellate information is available online at www.judicial.state.ia.us/online_records.
General Information: Public access terminal is available. No juvenile, adoption, sealed, dissolution of marriage, mental health, domestic abuse or deferred records released. Fax notes: Fee to fax results is $1.00 per page. Copy fee: $.50 per page. Certification fee: $10.00. Fee payee: Clerk of District Court. Personal checks accepted. Credit cards accepted: Visa, MasterCard. Prepayment is required.

Lyon County

3rd District Court Courthouse, Rock Rapids, IA 51246; 712-472-2623; Fax: 712-472-2422. Hours: 8AM-4:30PM (CST). *Felony, Misdemeanor, Civil, Eviction, Small Claims, Probate.*

Civil Records: Access: In person, online. Visitors must perform in person searches for themselves. No search fee. Required to search: name, years to search. Civil cases indexed by defendant, plaintiff. Civil records on docket books from 1880s. Civil, probate, and appellate

information is available at www.judicial.state.ia.us/online_records.
Criminal Records: Access: In person, online. Visitors must perform in person searches for themselves. No search fee. Required to search: name, years to search. Criminal records on docket books from 1880s. Criminal, traffic, and appellate information is available online at www.judicial.state.ia.us/online_records.
General Information: Public access terminal is available. No juvenile, sealed, dissolution of marriage, mental health, domestic abuse or deferred records released. Copy fee: $.50 per page. Certification fee: $10.00. Fee payee: Clerk of Court. Personal checks accepted.

Madison County

5th District Court PO Box 152, Winterset, IA 50273; 515-462-4451; Fax: 515-462-9825. Hours: 8AM-4:30PM (CST). *Felony, Misdemeanor, Civil, Eviction, Small Claims, Probate.*

Civil Records: Access: In person, online. Visitors must perform in person searches for themselves. No search fee. Required to search: name, years to search. Civil cases indexed by plaintiff. Civil records on docket books from 1880s; computerized records since 1996. Misdemeanor records from 1974 to present. Other criminal same record keeping as civil. Civil, probate, and appellate information is available online at www.judicial.state.ia.us/online_records.
Criminal Records: Access: In person, online. Visitors must perform in person searches for themselves. No search fee. Required to search: name, years to search; also helpful: DOB. Criminal records on docket books from 1880s; computerized records since 1996. Misdemeanor records from 1974 to present. Other criminal same record keeping as civil. Criminal, traffic, and appellate information is available online at www.judicial.state.ia.us/online_records.
General Information: Public access terminal is available. No juvenile, sealed, dissolution of marriage, mental health, domestic abuse of deferred records released. Copy fee: $.25 per page. Certification fee: $10.00. Fee payee: Clerk of Court. Personal checks accepted. Prepayment is required.

Mahaska County

8th District Court Courthouse, 106 S 1st St, Oskaloosa, IA 52577; 641-673-7786; Fax: 641-672-1256. Hours: 8AM-4:30PM (CST). *Felony, Misdemeanor, Civil, Eviction, Small Claims, Probate.*

Civil Records: Access: In person, online. Visitors must perform in person searches for themselves. No search fee. Required to search: name, years to search. Civil cases indexed by defendant, plaintiff. Civil records on docket books from 1880s; computerized records since 1995. Civil, probate, and appellate information is available at www.judicial.state.ia.us/online_records.
Criminal Records: Access: In person, online. Visitors must perform in person searches for themselves. No search fee. Required to search: name, years to search. Criminal records on docket books from 1880s; computerized records since 1995. Criminal, traffic, and appellate information is available online at www.judicial.state.ia.us/online_records.
General Information: Public access terminal is available. No juvenile, sealed, dissolution of marriage, mental health, domestic abuse or deferred records released. Copy fee: $.25 per page. Docket Copy Fee: $1.00 per page. Certification fee: $10.00. Fee payee: Clerk of Court. Personal checks accepted. Prepayment is required.

Marion County

5th District Court PO Box 497, Knoxville, IA 50138; 641-828-2207; Fax: 641-828-7580. Hours: 8AM-4:30PM (CST). *Felony, Misdemeanor, Civil, Eviction, Small Claims, Probate.*

Civil Records: Access: In person, online. Visitors must perform in person searches for themselves. No search fee. Required to search: name, years to search. Civil cases indexed by defendant, plaintiff. Civil records on computer since 1992, docket books from 1896. Civil, probate, and appellate information is available online at www.judicial.state.ia.us/online_records.

Criminal Records: Access: In person, online. Visitors must perform in person searches for themselves. No search fee. Required to search: name, years to search. Criminal records on computer since 1992, docket books from 1896. Criminal, traffic, and appellate information is available at www.judicial.state.ia.us/online_records.

General Information: Public access terminal is available. No juvenile, sealed, dissolution of marriage, mental health, domestic abuse or deferred records released. Copy fee: $.50 per page. Certification fee: $10.00. Fee payee: Clerk of Court. Personal checks accepted. Prepayment is required.

Marshall County

2nd District Court Courthouse, Marshalltown, IA 50158; 641-754-1603; Fax: 641-754-1600. Hours: 8AM-4:30PM (CST). *Felony, Misdemeanor, Civil, Eviction, Small Claims, Probate.*

Civil Records: Access: In person, online. Visitors must perform in person searches for themselves. No search fee. Required to search: name, years to search. Civil cases indexed by defendant, plaintiff. Civil records on computer since June, 1994, docket books from late 1800s. Civil, probate, and appellate information is available at www.judicial.state.ia.us/online_records.

Criminal Records: Access: In person, online. Visitors must perform in person searches for themselves. No search fee. Required to search: name, years to search; also helpful: DOB, SSN. Criminal records on computer since August, 1992, docket books from late 1800s. Criminal, traffic, and appellate information is available online at www.judicial.state.ia.us/online_records.

General Information: Public access terminal is available. No juvenile, sealed, pending dissolution of marriage, mental health, domestic abuse and deferred records released. Copy fee: $.50 per page. Certification fee: $10.00. Fee payee: Clerk of Court. Personal checks accepted. Credit cards accepted. Prepayment is required.

Mills County

4th District Court 418 Sharp St, Courthouse, Glenwood, IA 51534; 712-527-4880; Fax: 712-527-4936. Hours: 8AM-4:30PM (CST). *Felony, Misdemeanor, Civil, Eviction, Small Claims, Probate.*

Civil Records: Access: In person, online. Both court and visitors may perform in person searches. Search fee: $6.00 per name. Required to search: name, years to search. Civil cases indexed by defendant, plaintiff. Civil records on docket books since 1880s; computerized records since 1996. Civil, probate, and appellate information is available online at www.judicial.state.ia.us/online_records.

Criminal Records: Access: In person, online. Both court and visitors may perform in person searches. Search fee: $6.00 per name. Required to search: name, years to search, DOB; also helpful: SSN. Criminal records on docket books since 1880s; computerized records since 1996. Criminal, traffic, and appellate information is available online at www.judicial.state.ia.us/online_records.

General Information: Public access terminal is available. No juvenile, sealed, dissolution of marriage,

mental health, domestic abuse or deferred records released. Copy fee: $.25 per page. Certification fee: $10.00. Fee payee: Clerk of Court. Personal checks accepted. Prepayment is required.

Mitchell County

2nd District Court 508 State St, Osage, IA 50461; 641-732-3726; Fax: 641-732-3728. Hours: 9AM-3:30PM (CST). *Felony, Misdemeanor, Civil, Eviction, Small Claims, Probate.*

Civil Records: Access: In person, online. Visitors must perform in person searches for themselves. No search fee. Required to search: name, years to search. Civil cases indexed by defendant, plaintiff. Civil records on docket books from 1880s, computerized since 1997. Civil, probate, and appellate information is available online at www.judicial.state.ia.us/online_records.

Criminal Records: Access: In person, online. Visitors must perform in person searches for themselves. No search fee. Required to search: name, years to search, signed release. Criminal records on docket books from 1880s, computerized since 1997. Criminal, traffic, and appellate information is available online at www.judicial.state.ia.us/online_records.

General Information: Public access terminal is available. No juvenile, sealed, dissolution of marriage, mental health, domestic abuse or deferred records released. Copy fee: $1.00 per page. Certification fee: $10.00 plus copy fee. Fee payee: Clerk of Court. Personal checks accepted. Prepayment is required.

Monona County

3rd District Court PO Box 14, Onawa, IA 51040; 712-423-2491. Hours: 8AM-4:30PM (closed Tues. & Th) (CST). *Felony, Misdemeanor, Civil, Eviction, Small Claims, Probate.*

www.iowacourtsonline.org

Civil Records: Access: In person, online. Visitors must perform in person searches for themselves. No search fee. Required to search: name, years to search. Civil cases indexed by defendant, plaintiff. Civil records on computer since 07/97; prior records on microfiche and docket books from 1880s. Civil, probate, and appellate information is available online at www.judicial.state.ia.us/online_records.

Criminal Records: Access: In person, online. Visitors must perform in person searches for themselves. No search fee. Required to search: name, years to search. Criminal records on computer since 07/97; prior records on microfiche and docket books from 1880s. Criminal, traffic, and appellate information is available online at www.judicial.state.ia.us/online_records.

General Information: Public access terminal is available. No juvenile, sealed, dissolution of marriage, mental health, domestic abuse or deferred records released. Copy fee: $.50 per page. Certification fee: $10.00. Fee payee: Clerk of Court. Personal checks accepted. Prepayment is required.

Monroe County

8th District Court Courthouse, 10 Benton Ave E, Albia, IA 52531; 641-932-5212; Fax: 641-932-3245. Hours: 8AM-4:30PM (CST). *Felony, Misdemeanor, Civil, Eviction, Small Claims, Probate.*

Civil Records: Access: In person, online. Visitors must perform in person searches for themselves. No search fee. Required to search: name, years to search. Civil cases indexed by defendant, plaintiff. Civil records on docket books from late 1800s. Civil, probate, and appellate information is available online at www.judicial.state.ia.us/online_records.

Criminal Records: Access: In person, online. Visitors must perform in person searches for themselves. No search fee. Required to search: name, years to search, DOB, signed release; also helpful: SSN. Criminal records on docket books from late 1800s. Criminal,

traffic, and appellate information is available online at www.judicial.state.ia.us/online_records.

General Information: Public access terminal is available. No juvenile, sealed, dissolution of marriage, mental health, domestic abuse or deferred records released. Certification fee: $10.00. Fee payee: Clerk of Court. Personal checks accepted. Prepayment is required.

Montgomery County

4th District Court PO Box 469, Red Oak, IA 51566; 712-623-4986. Hours: 8AM-4:30PM (CST). *Felony, Misdemeanor, Civil, Eviction, Small Claims, Probate.*

Civil Records: Access: In person, online. Visitors must perform in person searches for themselves. Search fee: No search fee. Required to search: name, years to search. Civil cases indexed by defendant, plaintiff. Civil records on docket books from 1940, microfiche prior. Civil, probate, and appellate information is available online at www.judicial.state.ia.us/online_records.

Criminal Records: Access: In person, online. Visitors must perform in person searches for themselves. Search fee: No search fee. Required to search: name, years to search. Criminal records on docket books from 1940, microfiche prior. Criminal, traffic, and appellate information is available at www.judicial.state.ia.us/online_records.

General Information: Public access terminal is available. No juvenile, sealed, dissolution of marriage, mental health or deferred records released. Copy fee: $.50 per page. Certification fee: $10.00. Fee payee: Clerk of Court. Personal checks accepted. Prepayment is required.

Muscatine County

7th District Court PO Box 8010, Courthouse, Muscatine, IA 52761; 563-263-6511; Criminal phone: 563-263-2447; Fax: 563-264-3622. Hours: 8AM-4:30PM (CST). *Felony, Misdemeanor, Civil, Eviction, Small Claims, Probate.*

Civil Records: Access: In person, online. Visitors must perform in person searches for themselves. No search fee. Required to search: name, years to search. Civil cases indexed by defendant, plaintiff. Civil records on docket books, on computer since 10/95. Civil, probate, and appellate information is available online at www.judicial.state.ia.us/online_records.

Criminal Records: Access: In person, online. Visitors must perform in person searches for themselves. No search fee. Required to search: name, years to search. Criminal Records are computerized since 04/94. Criminal, traffic, and appellate information is available online at www.judicial.state.ia.us/online_records.

General Information: Public access terminal is available. No juvenile, sealed, dissolutions of marriage, mental health, domestic abuse or deferred records released. Copy fee: $.50 per page. Certification fee: $10.00. Fee payee: Clerk of Court. Personal checks accepted. Prepayment is required.

O'Brien County

3rd District Court Courthouse Criminal Records, Primghar, IA 51245; 712-757-3255; Fax: 712-757-2965. Hours: 8AM-4:30PM (CST). *Felony, Misdemeanor, Civil, Eviction, Small Claims, Probate.*

www.obriencounty.com

Civil Records: Access: In person, online. Visitors must perform in person searches for themselves. No search fee. Required to search: name, years to search. Civil cases indexed by defendant, plaintiff. Civil records on docket books from late 1800s; computerized since 1997. Civil, probate, and appellate information is available at www.judicial.state.ia.us/online_records.

Criminal Records: Access: In person, online. Visitors must perform in person searches for themselves. No search fee. Required to search: name, years to search; also helpful: DOB, SSN. Criminal records on docket books from late 1800s; computerized since 1997. Criminal, traffic, and appellate information is available online at www.judicial.state.ia.us/online_records.

General Information: Public access terminal is available. No juvenile, sealed, dissolution of marriage, mental health, domestic abuse or deferred records released. Copy fee: $.50 per page. Certification fee: $10.00. Fee payee: Clerk of Court. Personal checks accepted. Prepayment is required.

Osceola County

3rd District Court Courthouse Criminal Records, Sibley, IA 51249; 712-754-3595; Fax: 712-754-2480. Hours: 8AM-4:30PM (may be closed Monday & Wednesday) (CST). *Felony, Misdemeanor, Civil, Eviction, Small Claims, Probate.*

Civil Records: Access: In person, online. Visitors must perform in person searches for themselves. No search fee. Required to search: name, years to search. Civil cases indexed by defendant, plaintiff. Civil records on docket books from 1883; on computer back to 1997. Civil, probate, and appellate information is available online at www.judicial.state.ia.us/online_records.

Criminal Records: Access: In person, online. Visitors must perform in person searches for themselves. No search fee. Required to search: name, years to search. Criminal records on docket books from 1883; on computer back to 1997. Criminal, traffic, and appellate information is available online at www.judicial.state.ia.us/online_records.

General Information: Public access terminal is available. No juvenile, sealed, dissolution of marriage, mental health, domestic abuse or deferred records released. Copy fee: $.50 per page. Certification fee: $10.00. Fee payee: Clerk of Court. Personal checks accepted.

Page County

4th District Court 112 E Main Box 263, Clarinda, IA 51632; 712-542-3214; Fax: 712-542-5460. Hours: 8AM-4:30PM (CST). *Felony, Misdemeanor, Civil, Eviction, Small Claims, Probate.*

Civil Records: Access: In person, online. Visitors must perform in person searches for themselves. No search fee. Required to search: name, years to search. Civil cases indexed by defendant, plaintiff. Civil records on docket books; on computer back to 1995. Civil, probate, and appellate information is available online at www.judicial.state.ia.us/online_records.

Criminal Records: Access: In person, online. Visitors must perform in person searches for themselves. No search fee. Required to search: name, years to search, DOB, SSN, signed release. Criminal records on docket books; on computer back to 1995. Criminal, traffic, and appellate information is available online at www.judicial.state.ia.us/online_records.

General Information: Public access terminal is available. No juvenile, sealed dissolution of marriage, mental health, domestic abuse or deferred records released. Copy fee: $.50 per page. Certification fee: $10.00. Fee payee: Clerk of District Court. Personal checks accepted. Prepayment is required.

Palo Alto County

3rd District Court PO Box 387, Emmetsburg, IA 50536; 712-852-3603. Hours: 8AM-4:30PM (CST). *Felony, Misdemeanor, Civil, Eviction, Small Claims, Probate.*

Civil Records: Access: In person, online. Visitors must perform in person searches for themselves. No search fee. Required to search: name, years to search. Civil cases indexed by defendant, plaintiff. Civil records on docket books from 1800s; computerized from 1997.

Civil, probate, and appellate information is available online at www.judicial.state.ia.us/online_records.

Criminal Records: Access: In person, online. Visitors must perform in person searches for themselves. No search fee. Required to search: name, years to search, DOB, SSN. Criminal records on docket books from 1800s; computerized from 1997. Criminal, traffic, and appellate information is available online at www.judicial.state.ia.us/online_records.

General Information: Public access terminal is available. No juvenile, sealed, dissolution of marriage, mental health, domestic abuse or deferred records released. Copy fee: $.50 per page. Certification fee: $10.00. Fee payee: Clerk of Court. Personal checks accepted. Prepayment is required.

Plymouth County

3rd District Court Courthouse 215-4th Ave SE, Le Mars, IA 51031; 712-546-4215. Hours: 8AM-4:30PM (CST). *Felony, Misdemeanor, Civil, Eviction, Small Claims, Probate.*

Civil Records: Access: In person, online. Visitors must perform in person searches for themselves. No search fee. Required to search: name, years to search. Civil cases indexed by defendant, plaintiff. Civil records on docket books from 1895 to 11/92, docket cards from 11/92 to 7/97. Civil, probate, and appellate information is available at www.judicial.state.ia.us/online_records.

Criminal Records: Access: In person, online. Visitors must perform in person searches for themselves. No search fee. Required to search: name, years to search. Criminal records on docket books from 1895 to 11/92, docket cards from 11/92 to 7/97. Criminal, traffic, and appellate information is available online at www.judicial.state.ia.us/online_records.

General Information: Public access terminal is available. No juvenile, sealed, dissolution of marriage, mental health, domestic abuse or deferred records released. Copy fee: $.50 per page. Certification fee: $10.00. Fee payee: Clerk of Court. Personal checks accepted. Prepayment is required.

Pocahontas County

2nd District Court Courthouse, 99 Court Square, Pocahontas, IA 50574; 712-335-4208; Fax: 712-335-5045. Hours: 9AM-3:30PM (CST). *Felony, Misdemeanor, Civil, Eviction, Small Claims, Probate.*

Civil Records: Access: In person, online. Visitors must perform in person searches for themselves. No search fee. Required to search: name, years to search. Civil cases indexed by defendant, plaintiff. Civil records on docket books from 1880s. Civil, probate, and appellate information is available online at www.judicial.state.ia.us/online_records.

Criminal Records: Access: In person, online. Visitors must perform in person searches for themselves. No search fee. Required to search: name, years to search, DOB. Criminal records on docket books from 1880s. Criminal, traffic, and appellate information is available online at www.judicial.state.ia.us/online_records.

General Information: Public access terminal is available. No juvenile, sealed, dissolution of marriage, mental health, domestic abuse or deferred records released. Copy fee: $.50 per page. Certification fee: $10.00. Fee payee: Clerk of Court. Personal checks accepted. Prepayment is required.

Polk County

District Court 500 Mulberry St, Rm 201, Des Moines, IA 50309; 515-286-3772; Fax: 515-286-3172 (Civil) 323-5250 (Criminal). Hours: 8AM-4:30PM (CST). *Felony, Misdemeanor, Civil, Eviction, Small Claims, Probate.*

www.judicial.state.ia.us

Civil Records: Access: Mail, in person, online. Visitors must perform in person searches for themselves. No

search fee. Required to search: name, years to search; also helpful: address. Civil cases indexed by defendant, plaintiff. Civil records on computer back to 1990; docket books and index cards from 1880s and microfilm prior to 1970. Civil, probate, and appellate information is available online at www.judicial.state.ia.us/online_records. Mail search requests are not recommended.

Criminal Records: Access: Mail, in person, online. Visitors must perform in person searches for themselves. No search fee. Required to search: name, years to search, address, DOB; also helpful: SSN. Criminal records on computer back to 1990; docket books and index cards from 1880s and microfilm prior to 1970. Criminal, traffic, and appellate information is available at www.judicial.state.ia.us/online_records. Mail search requests are not recommended.

General Information: Public access terminal is available. No juvenile, child, sealed, pending dissolution of marriage, mental health, expunged, domestic abuse or deferred records released. Copy fee: $.50 per page. Microfilm copy fee: $.50 per page. Certification fee: $10.00. Fee payee: Clerk of Court. Personal checks accepted. Credit cards accepted: Visa. Prepayment is required.

Pottawattamie County

4th District Court 227 S 6th St, Council Bluffs, IA 51501; 712-328-5604. Hours: 8:30AM-3:30PM (CST). *Felony, Misdemeanor, Civil, Eviction, Small Claims, Probate.*

Civil Records: Access: In person, online. Visitors must perform in person searches for themselves. No search fee. Required to search: name, years to search. Civil cases indexed by defendant, plaintiff. Civil records on computer from 1978, index books prior. Records are being microfilmed as load permits. Civil, probate, and appellate information is available online at www.judicial.state.ia.us/online_records.

Criminal Records: Access: In person, online. Visitors must perform in person searches for themselves. No search fee. Required to search: name, years to search. Criminal records on computer from 1978, index books prior. Records are being microfilmed as load permits. Criminal, traffic, and appellate information is available online at www.judicial.state.ia.us/online_records.

General Information: No juvenile, sealed, pending dissolution of marriage, mental health, domestic abuse or deferred records released. Copy fee: $.25 per page. Certification fee: $10.00. Fee payee: Clerk of Court. Personal checks accepted. Prepayment is required.

Poweshiek County

8th District Court PO Box 218, Montezuma, IA 50171; 641-623-5644; Fax: 641-623-5320. Hours: 8AM-4:30PM (CST). *Felony, Misdemeanor, Civil, Eviction, Small Claims, Probate.*

Civil Records: Access: In person, online. Visitors must perform in person searches for themselves. No search fee. Required to search: name, years to search. Civil cases indexed by defendant, plaintiff. Civil records on index cards from 1980, docket books from early 1900s, computer since 7/95. Civil, probate, and appellate information is available at www.judicial.state.ia.us/online_records.

Criminal Records: Access: In person, online. Visitors must perform in person searches for themselves. No search fee. Required to search: name, years to search. Criminal records on computer since 1995, index cards since 1980, docket books from early 1900s. Criminal, traffic, and appellate information is available online at www.judicial.state.ia.us/online_records.

General Information: Public access terminal is available. No juvenile, sealed, dissolution of marriage, mental health, domestic abuse or deferred records released. Copy fee: $.25 per page. Certification fee:

$10.00. Fee payee: Clerk of Court. Personal checks accepted.

Ringgold County

5th District Court 109 W Madison (PO Box 523), Mount Ayr, IA 50854; 641-464-3234; Fax: 641-464-2478. Hours: 8AM-4:30PM (CST). *Felony, Misdemeanor, Civil, Small Claims, Probate, Traffic.*

Civil Records: Access: In person, online. Visitors must perform in person searches for themselves. No search fee. Required to search: name, years to search. Civil cases indexed by defendant, plaintiff. Civil records on docket books and computer. Civil, probate, and appellate information is available online at www.judicial.state.ia.us/online_records.

Criminal Records: Access: In person, online. Visitors must perform in person searches for themselves. No search fee. Required to search: name, years to search. Criminal records on docket books and computer. Criminal, traffic, and appellate information is available online at www.judicial.state.ia.us/online_records.

General Information: Public access terminal is available. No juvenile, sealed, pending dissolution of marriage, mental health or deferred records released. Copy fee: $.50 per page. Certification fee: $10.00. Fee payee: Clerk of Court. Personal checks accepted.

Sac County

2nd District Court PO Box 368, Sac City, IA 50583; 712-662-7791. Hours: 9AM-3:30PM (CST). *Felony, Misdemeanor, Civil, Eviction, Small Claims, Probate.*

Civil Records: Access: In person, online. Visitors must perform in person searches for themselves. No search fee. Required to search: name. Civil cases indexed by defendant, plaintiff. Civil records go back to 1888; on computer back to 7/1997. Civil, probate, and appellate information is available online at www.judicial.state.ia.us/online_records.

Criminal Records: Access: In person, online. Visitors must perform in person searches for themselves. Court may assist in search, if necessary. No search fee. Required to search: name, approximate date. Criminal records go back to 1888; on computer back to 7/1997. Criminal, traffic, and appellate information is available online at www.judicial.state.ia.us/online_records.

General Information: Public access terminal is available. No juvenile, sealed, pending dissolution of marriage, mental health, domestic abuse or deferred records released. Copy fee: $.50 per page. Certification fee: $10.00. Fee payee: Clerk of Court. Personal checks accepted. Prepayment is required.

Scott County

7th District Court 416 W 4th St, Davenport, IA 52801; 563-326-8786. Hours: 8AM-4:30PM (CST). *Felony, Misdemeanor, Civil, Eviction, Small Claims, Probate.*

Civil Records: Access: In person, online. Visitors must perform in person searches for themselves. No search fee. Required to search: name, years to search. Civil cases indexed by defendant, plaintiff. Civil records on computer back to 11/1993, docket books prior. Civil, probate, and appellate information is available online at www.judicial.state.ia.us/online_records.

Criminal Records: Access: In person, online. Visitors must perform in person searches for themselves. No search fee. Required to search: name, years to search, DOB; also helpful: SSN. Criminal records on computer back to 1992, printouts and docket books prior. Criminal, traffic, and appellate information is available online at www.judicial.state.ia.us/online_records.

General Information: Public access terminal is available. No juvenile, sealed, dissolution of marriage, mental health, domestic abuse or deferred records released. Copy fee: $.50 per page. Certification fee:

$10.00. Fee payee: Clerk of Court. Personal checks accepted. Prepayment is required.

Shelby County

4th District Court PO Box 431, Harlan, IA 51537; 712-755-5543; Fax: 712-755-2667. Hours: 8AM-4:30PM (CST). *Felony, Misdemeanor, Civil, Eviction, Small Claims, Probate.*

www.shco.org

Civil Records: Access: In person, online. Visitors must perform in person searches for themselves. No search fee. Required to search: name, years to search. Civil cases indexed by defendant, plaintiff. Civil records on original files back to 1969, microfilm prior. Civil, probate, and appellate information is available online at www.judicial.state.ia.us/online_records.

Criminal Records: Access: In person, online. Visitors must perform in person searches for themselves. No search fee. Required to search: name, years to search; also helpful: DOB. Criminal records on original files back to 1980, microfilm prior. Criminal, traffic, and appellate information is available online at www.judicial.state.ia.us/online_records.

General Information: Public access terminal is available. No juvenile, sealed, dissolution of marriage, mental health, domestic abuse or deferred records released. Copy fee: $.50 per page. Certification fee: $10.00. Fee payee: Clerk of Court. Personal checks accepted. Prepayment is required.

Sioux County

3rd District Court PO Box 47, Courthouse, Orange City, IA 51041; 712-737-2286; Fax: 712-737-8908. Hours: 8AM-4:30PM (CST). *Felony, Misdemeanor, Civil, Eviction, Small Claims, Probate.*

Civil Records: Access: In person, online. Visitors must perform in person searches for themselves. No search fee. Required to search: name, years to search. Civil cases indexed by defendant, plaintiff. Civil records on docket books from 1800s; computerized records since 9/97. Civil, probate, and appellate information is available at www.judicial.state.ia.us/online_records.

Criminal Records: Access: In person, online. Visitors must perform in person searches for themselves. No search fee. Required to search: name, years to search, signed release. Criminal records on docket books from 1800s; computerized records since 9/97. Criminal, traffic, and appellate information is available online at www.judicial.state.ia.us/online_records.

General Information: Public access terminal is available. No juvenile, sealed, dissolution of marriage, mental health, domestic abuse or deferred records released. Copy fee: $.50 per page. Certification fee: $10.00. Fee payee: Clerk of Court. Personal checks accepted. Prepayment is required.

Story County

2nd District Court PO Box 408, Nevada, IA 50201; 515-382-7410. Hours: 8AM-4:30PM (CST). *Felony, Misdemeanor, Civil, Eviction, Small Claims, Probate.*

Civil Records: Access: In person, online. Visitors must perform in person searches for themselves. No search fee. Required to search: name, years to search. Civil cases indexed by defendant, plaintiff. Civil records on docket books from 1900s; on computer back to 1995. Civil, probate, and appellate information is available online at www.judicial.state.ia.us/online_records.

Criminal Records: Access: In person, online. Visitors must perform in person searches for themselves. No search fee. Required to search: name, years to search. Criminal records on computer since 1992, prior on docket books. Criminal, traffic, and appellate information is available online at www.judicial.state.ia.us/online_records.

General Information: Public access terminal is available. No juvenile, sealed, dissolution of marriage, mental health, domestic abuse or deferred records released. Copy fee: $.50 per page. Certification fee: $10.00. Fee payee: Clerk of Court. Personal checks accepted. Prepayment is required.

Tama County

6th Judicial District Court PO Box 306, Toledo, IA 52342; 641-484-3721; Fax: 641-484-6403. Hours: 8AM-4:30PM (CST). *Felony, Misdemeanor, Civil, Eviction, Small Claims, Probate.*

Civil Records: Access: In person, online. Visitors must perform in person searches for themselves. No search fee. Required to search: name, years to search. Civil cases indexed by defendant, plaintiff. Civil records on docket books from 1880s; computerized records since 1997. Magistrate dockets to 1972, prior to 1972, Justice of the Peace. Civil, probate, and appellate information is available at www.judicial.state.ia.us/online_records.

Criminal Records: Access: In person, online. Visitors must perform in person searches for themselves. No search fee. Required to search: name, years to search. Criminal records on docket books from 1880s; computerized records since 1995. Magistrate dockets to 1972, prior to 1972, Justice of the Peace. Criminal, traffic, and appellate information is available online at www.judicial.state.ia.us/online_records.

General Information: Public access terminal is available. No juvenile, sealed, dissolution of marriage, mental health, domestic abuse or deferred records released. Copy fee: $.25 per page. Certification fee: $10.00. Fee payee: Clerk of Court. Personal checks accepted. Prepayment is required.

Taylor County

5th District Court Courthouse, Bedford, IA 50833; 712-523-2095; Fax: 712-523-2936. Hours: 8AM-4:30PM (CST). *Felony, Misdemeanor, Civil, Eviction, Small Claims, Probate.*

Civil Records: Access: In person, online. Visitors must perform in person searches for themselves. No search fee. Required to search: name, years to search. Civil cases indexed by defendant, plaintiff. Civil records on computer since 11/01/96; prior to 1880s. Civil, probate, and appellate information is available online at www.judicial.state.ia.us/online_records.

Criminal Records: Access: In person, online. Visitors must perform in person searches for themselves. No search fee. Required to search: name, years to search. Criminal records on computer since 11/01/96; prior to 1880s. Criminal, traffic, and appellate information is available at www.judicial.state.ia.us/online_records.

General Information: Public access terminal is available. No juvenile, sealed, dissolution of marriage, mental health, domestic abuse or deferred records released. Fax notes: Fee to fax results is $3.00 per document and $.50 per pg. Copy fee: $.50 per page. Certification fee: $10.00. Fee payee: Clerk of Court. Personal checks accepted. Prepayment is required.

Union County

5th District Court Courthouse, Creston, IA 50801; 641-782-7315; Fax: 641-782-8241. Hours: 8AM-4:30PM (CST). *Felony, Misdemeanor, Civil, Eviction, Small Claims, Probate.*

Civil Records: Access: In person, online. Visitors must perform in person searches for themselves. No search fee. Required to search: name, years to search. Civil cases indexed by defendant, plaintiff. Civil records on docket books from 1900s; computerized back to 9/1996. Civil, probate, and appellate information is available at www.judicial.state.ia.us/online_records.

Criminal Records: Access: In person, online. Visitors must perform in person searches for themselves. No search fee. Required to search: name, years to search.

Criminal records on docket books from 1900s; computerized back to 9/996. Criminal, traffic, and appellate information is available online at www.judicial.state.ia.us/online_records.
General Information: Public access terminal is available. No juvenile, sealed, pending dissolution of marriage, mental health, domestic abuse or deferred records released. Fax notes: No fee to fax results. Copy fee: $.50 per page. Certification fee: $10.00. Fee payee: Clerk of Court. Personal checks accepted.

Van Buren County

8th District Court Courthouse Criminal Records, Keosauqua, IA 52565; 319-293-3108; Fax: 319-293-3811. Hours: 8AM-3:30PM (CST). *Felony, Misdemeanor, Civil, Eviction, Small Claims, Probate.*

Civil Records: Access: In person, online. Visitors must perform in person searches for themselves. Search fee: No search fee. Required to search: name, years to search. Civil cases indexed by defendant, plaintiff. Civil records on docket books from 1837, computerized since 1997. Civil, probate, and appellate information back to 1997 is available at www.judicial.state.ia.us/online_records.
Criminal Records: Access: In person, online. Visitors must perform in person searches for themselves. No search fee. Required to search: name, years to search, DOB. Criminal records on docket books from 1837, computerized since 1997. Criminal, traffic, and appellate information is available online at www.judicial.state.ia.us/online_records.
General Information: Public access terminal is available. No sealed, mental health, or sealed records released; will release un-sealed juvenile, marriage dissolution or DA records if after July, 2000. Copy fee: $.25 per page. Certification fee: $10.00. Fee payee: Clerk of Court. Personal checks accepted. Prepayment is required.

Wapello County

8th District Court 101 W 4th, Ottumwa, IA 52501; 641-683-0060. 8AM-3:30PM (CST). *Felony, Misdemeanor, Civil, Eviction, Small Claims, Probate.*
Note: SSNs are only maintained on a confidential sheet not available to the public.
Civil Records: Access: In person, online. Visitors must perform in person searches for themselves. No search fee. Required to search: name, years to search. Civil cases indexed by defendant, plaintiff. Civil records on computer (child support), docket books prior; computerized records since 5/1994. Civil, probate, and appellate information is available online at www.judicial.state.ia.us/online_records.
Criminal Records: Access: In person, online. Visitors must perform in person searches for themselves. No search fee. Required to search: name, years to search, DOB; also helpful: SSN. Criminal records on computer (for 6 months prior), docket books prior; computerized records since 5/1994. Criminal, traffic, and appellate information is available online at www.judicial.state.ia.us/online_records.
General Information: Public access terminal is available. No juvenile, sealed, dissolution of marriage, mental health, domestic abuse or deferred records released. Copy fee: $.25 per page. Certification fee: $10.00. Fee payee: Clerk of Court. Personal checks accepted. Prepayment is required.

Warren County

5th District Court PO Box 379, Indianola, IA 50125; 515-961-1033; Fax: 515-961-1071. Hours: 8AM-4:30PM (CST). *Felony, Misdemeanor, Civil, Eviction, Small Claims, Probate.*
Civil Records: Access: In person, online. Visitors may only perform in person searches. No search fee. Required to search: name, years to search. Civil cases

indexed by defendant, plaintiff. Civil records on computer back to 10/1995; prior on docket books to 1925. Civil, probate, and appellate information is available at www.judicial.state.ia.us/online_records.
Criminal Records: Access: In person, online. Visitors may only perform in person searches. No search fee. Required to search: name, years to search. Criminal records on computer back to 10/1995; prior on docket books to 1945. Criminal, traffic, and appellate information is available online at www.judicial.state.ia.us/online_records.
General Information: Public access terminal is available. No juvenile, sealed, dissolution of marriage, mental health, domestic abuse or deferred records released. Copy fee: $.50 per page. Certification fee: $10.00. Fee payee: Clerk of Court. Personal checks accepted. Credit cards accepted.

Washington County

8th District Court PO Box 391, Washington, IA 52353; 319-653-7741; Fax: 319-653-7787. Hours: 8AM-4:30PM (CST). *Felony, Misdemeanor, Civil, Eviction, Small Claims, Probate.*
Civil Records: Access: In person, online. Visitors must perform in person searches for themselves. No search fee. Required to search: name, years to search. Civil cases indexed by defendant, plaintiff. Civil records on computer back to 1997, microfilm from 1940, docket books since court inception. Civil, probate, and appellate information is available online at www.judicial.state.ia.us/online_records.
Criminal Records: Access: In person, online. Visitors must perform in person searches for themselves. No search fee. Required to search: name, years to search. Criminal records on computer back to 1997, microfilm from 1940, docket books since court inception. Criminal, traffic, and appellate information is available online at www.judicial.state.ia.us/online_records.
General Information: Public access terminal is available. No juvenile, sealed, dissolution of marriage, mental health, domestic abuse or deferred records released. Copy fee: $.25 per page. Certification fee: $10.00. Fee payee: Clerk of Court. Personal checks accepted. Prepayment is required.

Wayne County

5th District Court PO Box 424, Corydon, IA 50060; 641-872-2264; Fax: 641-872-2431. Hours: 8AM-4:30PM (CST). *Felony, Misdemeanor, Civil, Eviction, Small Claims, Probate.*
Civil Records: Access: In person, online. Visitors must perform in person searches for themselves. No search fee. Required to search: name, years to search. Civil cases indexed by defendant, plaintiff. Civil records on dockets from 1890. Civil, probate, and appellate information is available at www.judicial.state.ia.us/online_records.
Criminal Records: Access: In person, online. Visitors must perform in person searches for themselves. No search fee. Required to search: name, years to search, DOB. Criminal records on dockets from 1890. Criminal, traffic, and appellate information is available online at www.judicial.state.ia.us/online_records.
General Information: Public access terminal is available. No juvenile, sealed, dissolution of marriage, mental health, domestic abuse or deferred records released. Copy fee: $.50 per page. Certification fee: $10.00. Fee payee: Clerk of Court. Personal checks accepted. Prepayment is required.

Webster County

2nd District Court 701 Central Ave, Courthouse, Ft Dodge, IA 50501; 515-576-7115. Hours: 8AM-4:30PM (CST). *Felony, Misdemeanor, Civil, Eviction, Small Claims, Probate.*
Civil Records: Access: In person, online. Visitors must perform in person searches for themselves. No search fee. Required to search: name, years to search. Civil cases indexed by defendant, plaintiff. Civil records on docket books from 1800s, on computer since 1995. Civil, probate, and appellate information is available online at www.judicial.state.ia.us/online_records.
Criminal Records: Access: In person, online. Visitors must perform in person searches for themselves. No search fee. Required to search: name, years to search, signed release. Criminal records on docket books from 1800s, on computer since 1995. Criminal, traffic, and appellate information is available online at www.judicial.state.ia.us/online_records.
General Information: Public access terminal is available. No juvenile, sealed, dissolution of marriage, mental health, domestic abuse or deferred records released. Copy fee: $.50 per page. Certification fee: $10.00. Fee payee: Clerk of Court. Personal checks accepted. Prepayment is required.

Winnebago County

2nd District Court 126 W Clark, Box 468, Forest City, IA 50436; 641-585-4520; Fax: 641-585-2615. Hours: 9AM-3:30PM (CST). *Felony, Misdemeanor, Civil, Eviction, Small Claims, Probate.*
www.iowacourtsonline.org
Civil Records: Access: In person, online. Visitors must perform in person searches for themselves. No search fee. Required to search: name, years to search; also helpful: address. Civil cases indexed by defendant, plaintiff. Civil records on dockets from 1880s; on computer since 9/1997. Civil, probate, and appellate information is available online at www.judicial.state.ia.us/online_records.
Criminal Records: Access: In person, online. Visitors must perform in person searches for themselves. No search fee. Required to search: name, years to search, offense, date of offense; also helpful: address, DOB, aliases. Criminal records on dockets from 1940s; on computer since 9/1997. Criminal, traffic, and appellate information is available at www.judicial.state.ia.us/online_records.
General Information: Public access terminal is available. No juvenile, pending or dismissed dissolution of marriage, mental health, criminal deferred or substance abuse records released. Domestic abuse law change states that parts of the file may be public, depending on Judge's order. Copy fee: $.50 per page. Certification fee: $10.00. Fee payee: Clerk of Court. Personal checks accepted. Credit cards accepted: Visa, MasterCard. Prepayment is required.

Winneshiek County

1st District Court 201 W Main St, Decorah, IA 52101; 563-382-2469; Fax: 563-382-0603. Hours: 8AM-4:30PM (CST). *Felony, Misdemeanor, Civil, Eviction, Small Claims, Probate.*
Civil Records: Access: In person, online. Visitors must perform in person searches for themselves. No search fee. Required to search: name, years to search. Civil cases indexed by defendant, plaintiff. Civil records on computer since 1994, docket books since 1860s. Civil, probate, and appellate information is available online at www.judicial.state.ia.us/online_records.
Criminal Records: Access: In person, online. Visitors must perform in person searches for themselves. No search fee. Required to search: name, years to search, signed release. Criminal records on computer since 1992, docket books since 1860s. Criminal, traffic, and

appellate information is available online at www.judicial.state.ia.us/online_records.

General Information: Public access terminal is available. No juvenile, sealed, dissolution of marriage, mental health, domestic abuse or deferred records released. Copy fee: \$.50 per page. Certification fee: \$10.00. Fee payee: Clerk of Court. Personal checks accepted.

Woodbury County

3rd District Court 407 7th St, County Clerk at Law Enforcement Ctr, Sioux City, IA 51101; 712-279-6624. Hours: 8AM-4:30PM (CST). *Misdemeanor, Civil, Eviction, Small Claims.*

Civil Records: Access: In person, online. Visitors must perform in person searches for themselves. No search fee. Required to search: name, years to search. Civil cases indexed by defendant, plaintiff. Civil records on docket books from early 1900; on computer from 7/95. Civil, probate, and appellate information is available online at www.judicial.state.ia.us/online_records.

Criminal Records: Access: In person, online. Visitors must perform in person searches for themselves. No search fee. Required to search: name, years to search. Criminal Records indexed on computer since 1992; on computer from 7/92. Criminal, traffic, and appellate information is available online at www.judicial.state.ia.us/online_records.

General Information: Public access terminal is available. No juvenile records released. Copy fee: \$.50 per page. Certification fee: \$10.00. Fee payee: Clerk of Court. Personal checks accepted. Prepayment is required.

3rd District Court Woodbury County Courthouse, 620-Douglas, Rm 101, Sioux City, IA 51101-1248; 712-279-6611; Fax: 712-279-6021. Hours: 8AM-4:30PM (CST). *Felony, Civil, Eviction, Probate.*

Civil Records: Access: In person, online. Visitors must perform in person searches for themselves. No search fee. Required to search: name, years to search. Civil cases indexed by defendant, plaintiff. Civil records on index books from early 1900; on computer from 7/95. Civil, probate, and appellate information is available online at www.judicial.state.ia.us/online_records.

Criminal Records: Access: In person, online. Visitors must perform in person searches for themselves. No search fee. Required to search: name, years to search. Criminal records on index books from early 1900; on computer from 10/95. Criminal, traffic, and appellate information is available online at www.judicial.state.ia.us/online_records.

General Information: Public access terminal is available. No sealed, pending dissolution of marriage, mental health records released. Copy fee: \$.50 per page. Certification fee: \$10.00. Fee payee: Clerk of Court. Personal checks accepted. Prepayment is required.

Worth County

2nd District Court 1000 Central Ave, Northwood, IA 50459; 641-324-2840; Fax: 641-324-2360. Hours: 8AM-4:30PM (CST). *Felony, Misdemeanor, Civil, Eviction, Small Claims, Probate.*

Civil Records: Access: In person, online. Visitors must perform in person searches for themselves. No search fee. Required to search: name, years to search. Civil cases indexed by defendant, plaintiff. Civil records on computer and docket books. Civil, probate, and appellate information is available online at www.judicial.state.ia.us/online_records.

Criminal Records: Access: In person, online. Visitors must perform in person searches for themselves. No search fee. Required to search: name, years to search. Criminal records on computer and docket books. Criminal, traffic, and appellate information is available online at www.judicial.state.ia.us/online_records.

General Information: Public access terminal is available. No juvenile, sealed, dissolution of marriage, mental health, domestic abuse, dismissed, or deferred records released. Copy fee: \$.50 per page. Certification fee: \$10.00. Fee payee: Clerk of Court. Personal checks accepted. Prepayment is required.

Wright County

2nd District Court PO Box 306, Clarion, IA 50525; 515-532-3113; Fax: 515-532-2343. Hours: 9AM-3:30PM (CST). *Felony, Misdemeanor, Civil, Eviction, Small Claims, Probate.*

Civil Records: Access: In person, online. Visitors must perform in person searches for themselves. No search fee. Required to search: name, years to search. Civil cases indexed by defendant, plaintiff. Civil records on docket books from 1880; on computer since 1997. Civil, probate, and appellate information is available online at www.judicial.state.ia.us/online_records.

Criminal Records: Access: In person, online. Visitors must perform in person searches for themselves. No search fee. Required to search: name, years to search; also helpful: DOB, SSN. Criminal records on docket books from 1880s; on computer since 1997. Criminal, traffic, and appellate information is available online at www.judicial.state.ia.us/online_records.

General Information: Public access terminal is available. No juvenile, sealed, dissolution of marriage, mental health, domestic abuse or deferred records released. Copy fee: \$.50 per page. Certification fee: \$10.00. Fee payee: Clerk of Court. Personal checks accepted.

Iowa Recording Offices

ORGANIZATION: 99 counties, 100 recording offices. Lee County has two recording offices. The recording officer is the County Recorder. Many counties utilize a grantor/grantee index containing all transactions recorded with them. See the notes under the county for how to determine which office is appropriate to search. The entire state is in the Central Time Zone (CST).

REAL ESTATE RECORDS: Most counties are hesitant to perform real estate searches, but some will provide a listing from the grantor/grantee index with the understanding that it is not certified in the sense that a title search is. Certification of copies usually costs $2.00-5.00 per document.

UCC RECORDS: Financing statements are filed at the state level, except for real estate related collateral, which are filed with the County Recorder. However, prior to 07/2001, consumer goods were also filed at the County Recorder and these older records can be searched there. All counties will perform UCC searches. Use search request form UCC-11. Search fees are usually $5.00 per debtor name ($6.00 if the standard UCC-11 form is not used). Copies usually cost $1.00 per page.

TAX LIEN RECORDS: Federal tax liens on personal property of businesses are filed with the Secretary of State. Other federal and all state tax liens on personal property are filed with the County Recorder. County search practices vary widely, but most provide some sort of tax lien search for $6.00 per name.

OTHER LIENS: Home improvement, job service.

ONLINE ACCESS: A few counties offer online access. There is no statewide access to county recorder data.

Adair County

County Recorder, Courthouse, 400 Public Square, Greenfield, IA 50849. 641-743-2411; Fax 641-743-2565.
Will search UCC records. Tax liens not included in UCC search. Real estate record owner and mortgage searches available. **Other Phone Numbers:** Assessor 641-745-2531; Treasurer 641-743-2312; Vital Records 641-743-2411.

Adams County

County Recorder, PO Box 28, Corning, IA 50841. County Recorder, R/E and UCC Recording 641-322-3744; Fax 641-322-3744.
Will search UCC records. Tax liens not included in UCC search. Will not search real estate records. **Other Phone Numbers:** Assessor 641-322-4312; Treasurer 641-322-3210; Appraiser/Auditor 641-322-3340; Vital Records 641-322-3744.

Allamakee County

County Recorder, 110 Allamakee St, Courthouse, Waukon, IA 52172-1794. 563-568-2364; Fax 319-568-6419.
Will search UCC records. UCC search includes tax liens. Will not search real estate records. **Other Phone Numbers:** Assessor 563-568-3145; Treasurer 563-568-3793.

Appanoose County

County Recorder, Courthouse, Centerville, IA 52544. 641-856-6103; Fax 641-856-8023.
Will search UCC records. UCC search includes tax liens if requested. Will not search real estate records. **Other Phone Numbers:** Assessor 641-437-4529; Treasurer 641-856-3097.

Audubon County

County Recorder, 318 Leroy St. #7, Audubon, IA 50025-1255. County Recorder, R/E and UCC Recording 712-563-2119; Fax 712-563-4766.
Will search UCC records. Tax liens not included in UCC search. Will not search real estate records. **Other Phone Numbers:** Assessor 712-563-3418; Treasurer 712-563-2293; Vital Records 712-563-2119.

Benton County

County Recorder, Courthouse, Vinton, IA 52349. 319-472-3309; Fax 319-472-3309.
Will search UCC records. Will not search real estate records. **Other Phone Numbers:** Assessor 319-472-5211; Treasurer 319-472-2450.

Black Hawk County

County Recorder, 316 E. 5th St, Courthouse, Room 208, Waterloo, IA 50703-4774. 319-833-3171 R/E Recording: 319-833-3012 UCC Recording: 319-833-3012; Fax 319-833-3170.
Will search UCC records. Tax liens not included in UCC search. Real estate owner, mortgage, and property transfer searches available. **Other Phone Numbers:** Assessor 319-833-3006; Treasurer 319-833-3013; Elections 319-833-3123; Vital Records 319-833-3012.

Boone County

County Recorder, 201 State St, Boone, IA 50036-3987. County Recorder, R/E and UCC Recording 515-433-0514; Fax 515-432-8102.
Will search UCC records. Tax liens not included in UCC search. Mortgage searches available. **Other Phone Numbers:** Assessor 515-433-0508; Elections 515-433-0514; Vital Records 515-433-0514.

Bremer County

County Recorder, 415 E Bremer, 415 E. Bremer Ave., Waverly, IA 50677. 319-352-0401; Fax 319-352-0518.
Will search UCC records. Tax liens not included in UCC search. Real estate owner, mortgage, and property transfer searches available. **Other Phone Numbers:** Assessor 319-352-5040; Treasurer 319-352-5040.

Buchanan County

County Recorder, PO Box 298, Independence, IA 50644-0298. 319-334-4259 R/E Recording: 319-334-6887 UCC Recording: 319-334-6887; Fax 319-334-7453.
Will search UCC records. UCC search includes tax liens if requested. Will not search real estate records. **Other Phone Numbers:** Assessor 319-334-2706; Treasurer 319-334-4340; Elections 319-334-4109; Vital Records 319-334-6887.

Buena Vista County

County Recorder, PO Box 454, Storm Lake, IA 50588. 712-749-2539; Fax 712-749-2539.
Will search UCC records. UCC search includes tax liens. Will not search real estate records. **Online Access:** Property Assessor,Ag Sales, Jail Inmate, Accident, Incident Records. Search the property assessor and Ag sales databases for free at www.co.buena-vista.ia.us/assessors. No name searching. Also, search the jail inmates list for free at www.bvsheriff.com/jailroster/index.html. also, search accident/incident reports for free at www.bvsheriff.com/accident-incident/index.html.
Other Phone Numbers: Assessor 712-749-2543; Treasurer 712-749-5533.

Butler County

County Recorder, PO Box 346, Allison, IA 50602. 319-267-2735; Fax 319-267-2675.
Will search UCC records. Tax lien search included with UCC search. Will not search real estate records. **Other Phone Numbers:** Assessor 319-267-2264.

Calhoun County

County Recorder, Calhoun County Courthouse 416-4th St., Rockwell City, IA 50579. County Recorder, R/E and UCC Recording 712-297-8121.
Will search UCC records. Tax liens not included in UCC search. Will not search real estate records. **Other Phone Numbers:** Assessor 712-297-7500; Treasurer 712-297-7111; Vital Records 712-297-8121.

Carroll County

County Recorder, PO Box 782, Carroll, IA 51401-0782. 712-792-3328; Fax 712-792-9493.
Will search UCC records. Tax liens not included in UCC search. Will not search real estate records. **Other Phone Numbers:** Assessor 712-792-9973; Treasurer 712-792-1200.

Cass County

County Recorder, 5 West 7th, Atlantic, IA 50022-1492. 712-243-1692; Fax 712-243-4736.
Will search UCC records to 7/2001. This agency will not do a tax lien search. Will not search real estate records. **Other Phone Numbers:** Assessor 712-243-2005; Treasurer 712-243-5503.

Cedar County

County Recorder, 400 Cedar St, Courthouse, Tipton, IA 52772-1752. County Recorder, R/E and UCC Recording 563-886-2230; Fax 319-886-2095.
Will search UCC records. Will not search real estate records. **Other Phone Numbers:** Assessor 563-886-6413; Treasurer 563-886-2557; Elections 563-886-3168; Vital Records 563-886-2230.

Cerro Gordo County

County Recorder, 220 N. Washington, Mason City, IA 50401. County Recorder, R/E and UCC Recording 641-421-3056; Fax 641-421-3154.
Will search UCC records. Tax liens not included in UCC search. Real estate owner, mortgage, and property transfer searches available. **Other Phone Numbers:** Assessor 641-421-3065; Treasurer 641-421-3037; Elections 641-421-3027; Vital Records 641-421-3056.

Cherokee County

County Recorder, Drawer G, Cherokee, IA 51012. County Recorder, R/E and UCC Recording 712-225-6735; Fax 712-225-6754.
Will search UCC records. UCC search includes tax liens if requested. Real estate owner, mortgage, and property transfer searches available. **Other Phone Numbers:** Assessor 712-225-6701; Treasurer 712-225-4670; Appraiser/Auditor 712-225-6701; Elections 712-225-6704; Vital Records 712-225-6735.

Chickasaw County

County Recorder, PO Box 14, New Hampton, IA 50659. 641-394-2336; Fax 641-394-2816.
Will search UCC records. UCC search includes tax liens if requested. Real estate owner, mortgage, and property transfer searches available. **Other Phone Numbers:** Assessor 641-394-2813; Treasurer 641-394-2107.

Clarke County

County Recorder, 100 S Main, Courthouse, Osceola, IA 50213. 641-342-3313; Fax 641-342-3893.
Will search UCC records. Tax liens not included in UCC search. Separate combined tax lien search available. Mortgage searches available. **Other Phones:** Assessor 641-342-3817; Treasurer 641-342-3311.

Clay County

County Recorder, Administration Building, 300 W. 4th St, #3, Spencer, IA 51301-3806. County Recorder, R/E and UCC Recording 712-262-1081; Fax 712-264-3983.
Will search UCC records. Tax liens not included in UCC search. Will not search real estate records. **Other Phone Numbers:** Assessor 712-262-1986; Treasurer 712-262-2179; Appraiser/Auditor 712-262-1986; Elections 712-262-1569; Vital Records 712-262-1081.

Clayton County

County Recorder, PO Box 278, Elkader, IA 52043. County Recorder, R/E and UCC Recording 563-245-2710; Fax 319-245-2353.
Will search UCC records. Tax liens not included in UCC search. Real estate owner, mortgage, and property transfer searches available. **Other Phone Numbers:** Assessor 563-245-2533; Treasurer 563-245-1807; Elections 563-245-1106; Vital Records 563-245-2710.

Clinton County

County Recorder, PO Box 2957, Clinton, IA 52733-2957. 563-244-0565 x0544; Fax 563-242-8412.
Will search UCC records. Will not search real estate records. **Other Phone Numbers:** Assessor 563-242-0569; Treasurer 563-242-0573.

Crawford County

County Recorder, 1202 Broadway, Denison, IA 51442. County Recorder, R/E and UCC Recording 712-263-3643; Fax 712-263-3413.
Will search UCC records. UCC search includes tax liens if requested. Will not search real estate records. **Other Phone Numbers:** Assessor 712-263-3447; Treasurer 712-263-2648; Elections 712-263-3045; Vital Records 712-263-3643.

Dallas County

County Recorder, PO Box 38, Adel, IA 50003-0038. 515-993-5804; Fax 515-933-5790.
Will search UCC records. UCC search includes tax liens if requested. Real estate owner, mortgage, and property transfer searches available. **Other Phone Numbers:** Assessor 515-993-5802; Treasurer 515-993-5808.

Davis County

County Recorder, Courthouse, Bloomfield, IA 52537. County Recorder, R/E and UCC Recording 641-664-2321; Fax 641-664-3082.
Will search UCC records. UCC search includes tax liens if requested. Will not search real estate records. **Other Phone Numbers:** Assessor 641-664-3101; Treasurer 641-664-2155; Elections 641-664-2101; Vital Records 641-664-2321.

Decatur County

County Recorder, 207 N. Main St, Leon, IA 50144. 641-446-4322; Fax 641-446-7159.
Will search UCC records. Will not search real estate records. **Other Phone Numbers:** Assessor 641-446-4314.

Delaware County

County Recorder, Courthouse, 301 E. Main, Manchester, IA 52057. 563-927-4665; Fax 319-927-6423.
Will search UCC records. Tax liens not included in UCC search. Will not search real estate records. **Other Phone Numbers:** Assessor 563-927-2526; Treasurer 563-927-2845.

Des Moines County

County Recorder, PO Box 277, Burlington, IA 52601-0277. County Recorder, R/E and UCC Recording 319-753-8221; Fax 319-753-8721.
Will search UCC records. UCC search includes tax liens if requested. Will not search real estate records. **Other Phone Numbers:** Assessor 319-753-8224; Treasurer 319-753-8252; Appraiser/Auditor 319-753-8255; Elections 319-753-8266; Vital Records 319-753-8221; Motor Vehicle 319-753-8273.

Dickinson County

County Recorder, PO Box O.E., Spirit Lake, IA 51360. County Recorder, R/E and UCC Recording 712-336-1495; Fax 712-336-2677.
Will search UCC records. Tax liens not included in UCC search. Will not search real estate records. **Other Phone Numbers:** Assessor 712-336-2687; Treasurer 712-336-1205; Vital Records 712-336-1495.

Dubuque County

County Recorder, Courthouse, 720 Central #9, Dubuque, IA 52001. County Recorder, R/E and UCC Recording 563-589-4434; Fax 319-589-4484.
Will search UCC records. UCC search includes tax liens if requested. Will not search real estate records. **Other Phone Numbers:** Assessor 563-589-4432; Treasurer 563-589-4436; Elections 563-589-4458; Vital Records 563-589-4434.

Emmet County

County Recorder, 609 1st Ave North, Estherville, IA 51334. County Recorder, R/E and UCC Recording 712-362-4115; Fax 712-362-7454.
Will search UCC records. Tax liens not included in UCC search. Will not search real estate records. **Online Access:** Real Estate Records. Access to real estate records on the county database are available free at www.emmet.org/pmc. Also, the GIS mapping database may be searched. Includes parcel report, survey section grid, parcel maps, and more. Search the "Parcel Data" link by owner name, parcel ID, or address. **Other Phone Numbers:** Assessor 712-362-2609; Treasurer 712-362-3824; Appraiser/Auditor 712-362-2609; Elections 712-362-4261; Vital Records 712-362-4115.

Fayette County

County Recorder, PO Box 226, West Union, IA 52175-0226. 563-422-3687; Fax 319-422-9201.
Will search UCC records. Tax liens not included in UCC search. Will not search real estate records. **Other Phone Numbers:** Assessor 563-422-3397; Treasurer 563-422-3787.

Floyd County

County Recorder, Courthouse, 101 S. Main, Charles City, IA 50616. County Recorder, R/E and UCC Recording 641-257-6154; Fax 641-228-6458.
Will search UCC records. UCC search includes tax liens if requested. Real estate record owner and mortgage searches available. **Other Phone Numbers:** Assessor 641-257-6152; Treasurer 641-257-6118; Elections 641-257-6131; Vital Records 641-257-6154.

Franklin County

County Recorder, PO Box 26, Hampton, IA 50441. 641-456-5675; Fax 641-456-1990.
Will search UCC records. UCC search includes tax liens if requested. Real estate owner, mortgage, and property transfer searches available. **Other Phone Numbers:** Assessor 641-456-5118; Treasurer 641-456-5678.

Fremont County

County Recorder, PO Box 295, Sidney, IA 51652. County Recorder, R/E and UCC Recording 712-374-2315; Fax 712-374-2826.
Will search UCC records. Tax liens not included in UCC search. Will not search real estate records. **Other Phone Numbers:** Assessor 712-374-2631; Treasurer 712-374-2122; Elections 712-374-2031; Vital Records 712-374-2315.

Greene County

County Recorder, Courthouse, 114 N. Chestnut, Jefferson, IA 50129. 515-386-3716 R/E Recording: 515-386-5670 UCC Recording: 515-386-5670; Fax 515-386-5274.
Will search UCC records. UCC search includes tax liens if requested. Will not search real estate records. **Other Phones:** Assessor 515-386-5660; Treasurer 515-386-5675; Appraiser/Auditor 515-386-5680.

Grundy County

County Recorder, 706 G Ave, Grundy Center, IA 50638-1447. County Recorder, R/E and UCC Recording 319-824-3234.
Will search UCC records. Tax liens not included in UCC search. Will not search real estate records. **Other Phone Numbers:** Assessor 319-824-6216; Treasurer 319-824-3412; Elections 319-824-3122; Vital Records 319-824-3234.

Guthrie County

County Recorder, 200 N. 5th, Courthouse, Guthrie Center, IA 50115. County Recorder, R/E and UCC Recording 641-747-3412; Fax 641-747-3346.
Will search UCC records. This agency will not do a tax lien search. Will not search real estate records. **Other Phone Numbers:** Assessor 641-747-3319; Treasurer 641-747-3414; Appraiser/Auditor 641-747-3319; Elections 641-747-3619; Vital Records 641-747-3412.

Hamilton County

County Recorder, PO Box 126, Webster City, IA 50595-0126. 515-832-9535; Fax 515-833-9525.
Will search UCC records. UCC search includes federal tax liens if requested. **Other Phone Numbers:** Assessor 515-832-9505; Treasurer 515-832-9542.

Hancock County

County Recorder, 855 State St, Garner, IA 50438. County Recorder, R/E and UCC Recording 641-923-2464 UCC Recording: 641-923-2404; Fax 641-923-3912.
Will not search UCC records. Will not search real estate records. **Other Phone Numbers:** Assessor 641-923-2269; Treasurer 641-923-3122; Appraiser/Auditor 641-923-2269; Vital Records 641-923-2464.

Hardin County

County Recorder, PO Box 443, Eldora, IA 50627. 641-939-8178; Fax 641-939-8245.
Will search UCC records. Tax liens not included in UCC search. Real estate owner, mortgage, and property transfer searches available. **Other Phone Numbers:** Assessor 641-939-8100; Treasurer 641-939-8226; Appraiser/Auditor 641-939-8230; Drivers License 641-939-8328.

Harrison County

County Recorder, Courthouse, Logan, IA 51546. County Recorder, R/E and UCC Recording 712-644-2545; Fax 712-644-2643.
Will search UCC records. Tax liens not included in UCC search. Will not search real estate records. **Other Phone Numbers:** Assessor 712-644-3101; Treasurer 712-644-2750; Elections 712-644-2401; Vital Records 712-644-2545.

Henry County

County Recorder, PO Box 106, Mount Pleasant, IA 52641. 319-385-0765; Fax 319-385-3601.
Will search UCC records. Tax liens not included in UCC search. Will not search real estate records. **Other Phone Numbers:** Assessor 319-385-0750; Treasurer 319-385-0763; Elections 319-385-0756; Vital Records 319-385-0765.

Howard County

County Recorder, Court House, 137 N. Elm, Cresco, IA 52136. 563-547-3621; Fax 319-547-1103.
Will search UCC records. UCC search includes tax liens if requested. Real estate owner, mortgage, and property transfer searches available. **Other Phone Numbers:** Assessor 563-547-3409; Treasurer 563-547-3860.

Humboldt County

County Recorder, PO Box 100, Dakota City, IA 50529-0100. 515-332-3693; Fax 515-332-1738.
Will search UCC records. Tax liens not included in UCC search. Will not search real estate records. **Other Phone Numbers:** Assessor 515-332-1463; Treasurer 515-332-1681.

Ida County

County Recorder, 401 Moorehead, Courthouse, Ida Grove, IA 51445. County Recorder, R/E and UCC Recording 712-364-2220; Fax 712-364-2746.
Will search UCC records. Tax liens not included in UCC search. Will not search real estate records. **Other Phone Numbers:** Assessor 712-364-3622; Treasurer 712-364-2287; Elections 712-364-2620; Vital Records 712-364-2220.

Iowa County

County Recorder, PO Box 185, Marengo, IA 52301. County Recorder, R/E and UCC Recording 319-642-3622; Fax 319-642-5562.
Will search UCC records. UCC search includes tax liens if requested. Will not search real estate records. **Other Phone Numbers:** Assessor 319-642-3851; Treasurer 319-642-3672; Elections 319-642-3923; Vital Records 319-642-3622.

Jackson County

County Recorder, 201 W. Platt, Maquoketa, IA 52060. County Recorder, R/E and UCC Recording 563-652-2504; Fax 319-652-6460.
Will search UCC records. UCC search includes tax liens if requested. Real estate owner, mortgage, and property transfer searches available. **Other Phones:** Assessor 563-652-4935; Treasurer 563-652-5649; Elections 563-652-3144; Vital Records 563-652-2504.

Jasper County

County Recorder, PO Box 665, Newton, IA 50208. 641-792-5442; Fax 641-791-3680.
Will search UCC records. Will not search real estate records. **Other Phone Numbers:** Assessor 641-792-6195; Treasurer 641-792-6115.

Jefferson County

County Recorder, 51 W. Briggs, Fairfield, IA 52556-2820. 641-472-4331; Fax 641-472-6695.
Will search UCC records. UCC search includes tax liens if requested. State tax lien searches are uncertified and performed at no charge Will not search real estate records. **Other Phone Numbers:** Assessor 641-472-2849; Treasurer 641-472-2349.

Johnson County

County Recorder, 913 S. Dubuque St, Suite 202, Iowa City, IA 52240-4207. 319-356-6093; Fax 319-339-6181. www.johnson-county.com
Will search UCC records. Will not search real estate records. **Other Phones:** Assessor 319-356-6078; Treasurer 319-356-6087; Vital Records 319-356-6093.

Jones County

County Recorder, Courthouse, Room 116, 500 W. Main, Anamosa, IA 52205-1632. County Recorder, R/E and UCC Recording 319-462-2477; Fax 319-462-5802.
Will search UCC records. UCC search includes tax liens if requested. Real estate owner, mortgage, and property transfer searches available. **Other Phones:** Assessor 319-462-2671; Treasurer 319-462-3550; Elections 319-462-2282; Vital Records 319-462-2477.

Keokuk County

County Recorder, Courthouse, Sigourney, IA 52591. County Recorder, R/E and UCC Recording 641-622-2540; Fax 641-622-3789.
Will search UCC records. UCC search includes tax liens if requested. Will not search real estate records. **Other Phone Numbers:** Assessor 641-622-2560; Treasurer 641-622-2421; Elections 641-622-2320; Vital Records 641-622-2540.

Kossuth County

County Recorder, 114 W. State, Algona, IA 50511. 515-295-5660; Fax 515-295-9304.
Will search UCC records. Tax liens not included in UCC search. Will not search real estate records. **Other Phone Numbers:** Assessor 515-295-3857; Treasurer 515-295-3404.

Lee County (Northern District)

County Recorder, PO Box 322, Fort Madison, IA 52627-0322. 319-372-4662; Fax 319-372-7033.
Will search UCC records. Tax liens not included in UCC search. Will not search real estate records. **Other Phone Numbers:** Assessor 319-372-6302; Treasurer 319-372-3405; Elections 319-372-3705; Vital Records 319-372-4662.

Lee County (Southern District)

County Recorder, PO Box 160, Keokuk, IA 52632. 319-524-1126; Fax 319-524-1544.
Will search UCC records. Tax liens not included in UCC search. Will not search real estate records. **Other Phone Numbers:** Assessor 319-524-1375.

Linn County

County Recorder, PO Box 1406, Cedar Rapids, IA 52406-1406. County Recorder, R/E and UCC Recording 319-892-5420; Fax 319-892-5459. www.linncountyrecorder.com
Will search UCC records. Will not search real estate records. **Other Phone Numbers:** Assessor 319-892-5220; Treasurer 319-892-5550; Elections 319-892-5400; Vital Records 319-892-5445.

Louisa County

County Recorder, PO Box 264, Wapello, IA 52653-0264. 319-523-5361; Fax 319-523-5362.
Will search UCC records. This agency will not do a tax lien search. Will not search real estate records.

Lucas County

County Recorder, 916 Braden, Courthouse, Chariton, IA 50049. 641-774-2413; Fax 641-774-2993.
Will search UCC records. This agency will not do a tax lien search. **Other Phone Numbers:** Assessor 641-774-4411; Treasurer 641-774-5213.

Lyon County

County Recorder, 206 Second Ave, Courthouse, Rock Rapids, IA 51246. 712-472-2381; Fax 712-472-2381.
Will search UCC records. UCC search includes tax liens if requested. Will not search real estate records. **Other Phone Numbers:** Assessor 712-472-3592; Treasurer 712-472-3703.

Madison County

County Recorder, PO Box 152, Winterset, IA 50273-0152. County Recorder, R/E and UCC Recording 515-462-3771; Fax 515-462-5881.
Will search UCC records. Tax liens not included in UCC search. Will not search real estate records. **Other Phone Numbers:** Assessor 515-462-4303; Treasurer 515-462-1542; Elections 515-462-3914; Vital Records 515-462-3771.

Mahaska County

County Recorder, Courthouse, Oskaloosa, IA 52577. County Recorder, R/E and UCC Recording 641-673-8187.
Will search UCC records. UCC search includes tax liens if requested. Will not search real estate records. **Other Phone Numbers:** Assessor 641-673-5805; Treasurer 641-673-5482; Vital Records 641-673-8187.

Marion County

County Recorder, 214 E. Main St., Knoxville, IA 50138. County Recorder, R/E and UCC Recording 641-828-2211; Fax 641-842-3593.
Will search UCC records. UCC search includes tax liens if requested. Will not search real estate records. **Other Phone Numbers:** Assessor 641-828-2215; Treasurer 641-828-2211; Vital Records 641-828-2211.

Marshall County

County Recorder, Courthouse, 3rd Floor, 1 E. Main St., Marshalltown, IA 50158-4915. 6417546-355; Fax 641-754-6349. www.co.marshall.ia.us
Will search UCC records. UCC search includes tax liens if requested. Will not search real estate records. **Online Access:** Assessor, Property Records. Access to the accessor's property record card system is available free at www.co.marshall.ia.us/assessor/prcsystem.html. **Other Phone Numbers:** Assessor 641-754-6305; Treasurer 641-754-6366; Elections 641-754-6323; Vital Records 641-754-6355.

Mills County

County Recorder, Courthouse, 418 Sharp St., Glenwood, IA 51534. 712-527-9315.
Will search UCC records. This agency will not do a tax lien search. **Other Phone Numbers:** Assessor 712-527-4883; Treasurer 712-527-4419.

Mitchell County

County Recorder, 508 State St, Osage, IA 50461-1250. County Recorder, R/E and UCC Recording 641-732-5861; Fax 641-732-5218.
Will search UCC records. Tax liens not included in UCC search. Will not search real estate records. **Other Phone Numbers:** Assessor 641-732-5861; Treasurer 641-732-5861.

Monona County

County Recorder, PO Box 53, Onawa, IA 51040. County Recorder, R/E and UCC Recording 712-423-2575; Fax 712-423-3034.
Will search UCC records. UCC search includes tax liens if requested. Real estate record owner and mortgage searches available. **Other Phone Numbers:** Assessor 712-423-2271; Treasurer 712-423-2271; Elections 712-423-2191; Vital Records 712-423-2575.

Monroe County

County Recorder, Courthouse, 10 Benton Ave. East, Albia, IA 52531. 641-932-5164; Fax 641932-2863.
Will search UCC records. This agency will not do a tax lien search. Real estate owner, mortgage, and property transfer searches available. **Other Phone Numbers:** Assessor 641-932-2180; Treasurer 641-932-5011.

Montgomery County

County Recorder, PO Box 469, Red Oak, IA 51566. County Recorder, R/E and UCC Recording 712-623-4363; Fax 712-623-8915.
Will search UCC records. Tax liens not included in UCC search. Will not search real estate records. **Other Phone Numbers:** Assessor 712-623-4171; Treasurer 712-623-2392; Appraiser/Auditor 712-623-4171; Elections 712-623-5127; Vital Records 712-623-4363.

Muscatine County

County Recorder, 401 E. 3rd St, Courthouse, Muscatine, IA 52761-4166. County Recorder, R/E and UCC Recording 563-263-7741; Fax 563-263-7248.
Will search UCC records. Tax liens not included in UCC search. Federal tax lien copies are $5.00 per page. Real estate owner, mortgage, and property transfer searches available. **Other Phone Numbers:** Assessor 563-263-7061; Treasurer 563-263-7113; Elections 563-263-5821; Vital Records 563-263-7741.

O'Brien County

County Recorder, PO Box 340, Primghar, IA 51245-0340. County Recorder, R/E and UCC Recording 712-757-3045; Fax 712-757-3046. www.obriencounty.com/government/recorder.htm
Will search UCC records. Tax liens not included in UCC search. Will not search real estate records. **Other Phone Numbers:** Assessor 712-757-3205; Treasurer 712-757-3210 or 4185; Elections 712-757-3225; Vital Records 712-757-3045.

Osceola County

County Recorder, Courthouse, 300 7th St, Sibley, IA 51249-1695. County Recorder, R/E and UCC Recording 712-754-3345; Fax 712-754-2872. www.osceolaclerkcourt.org
Will search UCC records. UCC search includes tax liens if requested. Will not search real estate records. **Other Phone Numbers:** Assessor 712-754-3438; Treasurer 712-754-3217; Elections 712-754-2241; Vital Records 712-754-3345; Assessor 712-754-3438.

Page County

County Recorder, 112 E. Main St., Courthouse, Clarinda, IA 51632. 712-542-3130; Fax 712-542-5019.
Will search UCC records. UCC search includes tax liens if requested. Real estate owner, mortgage, and property transfer searches available. **Other Phones:** Assessor 712-542-2516; Treasurer 712-542-5322.

Palo Alto County

County Recorder, PO Box 248, Emmetsburg, IA 50536. County Recorder, R/E and UCC Recording 712-852-3701; Fax 712-852-3704.
Will search UCC records. Tax liens not included in UCC search. Will not search real estate records. **Other Phone Numbers:** Assessor 712-852-3823; Treasurer 712-852-3844; Elections 712-852-2924; Vital Records 712-852-3701.

Plymouth County

County Recorder, Courthouse, 215 4th Ave. SE, Le Mars, IA 51031. 712-546-4020.
Will search UCC records. Tax liens not included in UCC search. Will not search real estate records. **Other Phone Numbers:** Treasurer 712-546-4020.

Pocahontas County

County Recorder, 99 Court Square, Pocahontas, IA 50574-1621. County Recorder, R/E and UCC Recording 712-335-4404; Fax 712-335-4502.
Will search UCC records. Real estate owner, mortgage, and property transfer searches available. **Other Phone Numbers:** Assessor 712-335-3142; Treasurer 712-335-4334; Vital Records 712-335-4404.

Polk County

County Recorder, 111 Court Ave, Room 250, County Administration Building, Des Moines, IA 50309. County Recorder, R/E and UCC Recording 515-286-3160; Fax 515-323-5393. www.co.polk.ia.us
Will search UCC records. Tax liens not included in UCC search. Real estate record owner searches available. **Online Access:** Assessor, Property Records. Access to the Polk County assessor database is available free at www.co.polk.ia.us/departments/assessor/assessor.htm. Search by property or by sales. **Other Phone Numbers:** Assessor 515-286-3141; Treasurer 515-286-3041; Elections 515-286-3247; Vital Records 515-286-3781.

Pottawattamie County

County Recorder, 227 S. Sixth St, Council Bluffs, IA 51501. 712-328-5612; Fax 712-328-4738. www.pottco.org
Will search UCC records. Tax liens not included in UCC search. Will not search real estate records. **Online Access:** Real Estate, Property, Residential Sales Records. Records on the Pottawattamie County Courthouse/Council Bluffs property database are available free at www.pottco.org. Search by owner name, address, or parcel number. Records of the Pottawattamie County Assessor "Residential Sales" database are available free online at www.pottco.org/htdocs/assessor.html. **Other Phones:** Assessor 712-328-5617; Treasurer 712-328-5627.

Poweshiek County

County Recorder, PO Box 656, Montezuma, IA 50171-0656. County Recorder, R/E and UCC Recording 641-623-5434; Fax 641-623-2928.
Will search UCC records. This agency will not do a tax lien search. Will not search real estate records. **Other Phone Numbers:** Assessor 641-623-5445; Treasurer 641-623-5128; Elections 641-623-5434.

Ringgold County

County Recorder, 109 W Madison #204, Mount Ayr, IA 50854. County Recorder, R/E and UCC Recording 641-464-3231; Fax 641-464-2568.
Will search UCC records. UCC search includes tax liens if requested. Will not search real estate records. **Other Phone Numbers:** Assessor 641-464-3233; Treasurer 641-464-3230; Vital Records 641-464-3231.

Sac County

County Recorder, 100 NW State St., Sac City, IA 50583. 712-662-7789; Fax 712-662-6298. www.saccounty.org/Recorder.html
Will search UCC records. Tax liens not included in UCC search. Will not search real estate records. **Other Phone Numbers:** Assessor 712-662-4492; Treasurer 712-662-7411; Vital Records 712-662-7789.

Scott County

County Recorder, 416 W. 4th St, Davenport, IA 52801-1187. County Recorder, R/E and UCC Recording 563-326-8621; Fax 563-328-3225. www.scottcountyiowa.com
Will search UCC records. UCC search includes state tax liens if requested Real estate record owner and mortgage searches available. Record owner and mortgage search combined as UCC search **Other Phone Numbers:** Assessor 563-326-8635; Treasurer 563-326-8664; Elections 563-326-8631; Vital Records 563-326-8650.

Shelby County

County Recorder, PO Box 67, Harlan, IA 51537-0067. County Recorder, R/E and UCC Recording 712-755-5640; Fax 712-755-2519.
Will search UCC records. Tax liens not included in UCC search. Will not search real estate records. **Other Phone Numbers:** Assessor 712-755-5718; Treasurer 712-755-5898; Elections 712-755-3831; Vital Records 712-755-5640.

Sioux County

County Recorder, PO Box 48, Orange City, IA 51041. County Recorder, R/E and UCC Recording 712-737-2229; Fax 712-737-2230.
Will search UCC records. UCC search includes tax liens if requested. Will not search real estate records. **Online Access:** Tax Sales Records. Search the treasurer's delinquent tax list for free at www.courthouse.co.sioux.ia.us/pdf/taxlist.pdf. Site may be down. **Other Phone Numbers:** Assessor 712-737-4274; Treasurer 712-737-3505; Elections 712-737-2216; Vital Records 712-737-2229.

Story County

County Recorder, PO Box 55, Nevada, IA 50201-0055. 515-382-7230; Fax 515-382-7326. www.storycounty.com/departments.html Will search UCC records. UCC search includes tax liens if requested. Will not search real estate records. **Online Access:** Assessor Records. Records on the county assessor database are available free online at www.storyassessor.org/pmc/query.asp. **Other Phone Numbers:** Assessor 515-382-7320; Treasurer 515-382-7330; Appraiser/Auditor 515-382-7322; Elections 515-382-7217; Vital Records 515-382-7237; Deputy Assessor 515-382-7322.

Tama County

County Recorder, PO Box 82, Toledo, IA 52342. 641-484-3320. Will search UCC records. This agency will not do a tax lien search. Will not search real estate records. **Other Phone Numbers:** Assessor 641-484-3545; Treasurer 641-484-3141.

Taylor County

County Recorder, 405 Jefferson St., Courthouse, Bedford, IA 50833. 712-523-2275; Fax 712-523-2274. Will search UCC records. Tax liens not included in UCC search. Will not search real estate records. **Other Phone Numbers:** Assessor 712-523-2444; Treasurer 712-523-2080.

Union County

County Recorder, 301 N. Pine St, Creston, IA 50801. 641-782-1725; Fax 641-782-1709. Will search UCC records. This agency will not do a tax lien search. Real estate owner, mortgage, and property transfer searches available. **Other Phone Numbers:** Assessor 641-782-1735; Treasurer 641-782-1710.

Van Buren County

County Recorder, PO Box 455, Keosauqua, IA 52565. 319-293-3240; Fax 319-293-3828. Will search UCC records. UCC search includes tax liens. Will not search real estate records. **Other Phone Numbers:** Assessor 319-293-3001; Treasurer 319-293-3110; Vital Records 319-293-3240.

Wapello County

County Recorder, 101 W. 4th St, Ottumwa, IA 52501. 641-683-0045; Fax 641-683-0019. Will search UCC records. UCC search includes tax liens if requested. Will not search real estate records. **Other Phone Numbers:** Assessor 641-683-0088; Treasurer 641-683-0040.

Warren County

County Recorder, 301 N Buxton, #109, Indianola, IA 50125. 515-961-1089. Will search UCC records. Federal tax liens not included in UCC search Will not search real estate records. **Other Phone Numbers:** Assessor 515-961-1010; Treasurer 515-961-1110.

Washington County

County Recorder, PO Box 889, Washington, IA 52353-0889. County Recorder, R/E and UCC Recording 319-653-7727. Will search UCC records. Tax liens not included in UCC search. Mortgage searches available. **Other Phone Numbers:** Assessor 319-653-7709; Treasurer 319-653-7726; Elections 319-653-7777; Vital Records 319-653-7727.

Wayne County

County Recorder, PO Box 435, Corydon, IA 50060. County Recorder, R/E and UCC Recording 641-872-1676; Fax 641-872-2843. Will search UCC records. UCC search includes tax liens if requested. Real estate owner, mortgage, and property transfer searches available. **Other Phone Numbers:** Assessor 641-872-2663; Treasurer 641-872-2515; Vital Records 641-872-1676.

Webster County

County Recorder, PO Box 1253, Fort Dodge, IA 50501. County Recorder, R/E and UCC Recording 515-576-2401; Fax 515-574-3723. www.webstercountyia.org Will search UCC records. UCC search includes tax liens if requested. Will not search real estate records. **Other Phone Numbers:** Assessor 515-573-5871; Treasurer 515-576-2731; Elections 515-573-7175; Vital Records 515-576-2401.

Winnebago County

County Recorder, 126 S. Clark St, Courthouse, Forest City, IA 50436. County Recorder, R/E and UCC Recording 641-585-2094; Fax 641-585-2891. Will search UCC records. Tax liens not included in UCC search. Will not search real estate records. **Other Phone Numbers:** Assessor 641-585-2163; Treasurer 641-585-2322; Appraiser/Auditor 641-585-3412; Vital Records 641-585-2094.

Winneshiek County

County Recorder, 201 W. Main St, Decorah, IA 52101. 563-382-3486; Fax 319-387-4083. Will search UCC records. UCC search includes tax liens if requested. Will not search real estate records. **Other Phone Numbers:** Assessor 563-382-5356; Treasurer 563-382-3753.

Woodbury County

County Auditor & Recorder, 620 Douglas St, Room 106, Sioux City, IA 51101. County Auditor & Recorder, R/E and UCC Recording 712-279-6528; Fax 712-233-8946. Will search UCC records. Will not search real estate records. **Other Phone Numbers:** Assessor 712-279-6505 or 712-279-6535; Treasurer 712-279-6495; Elections 712-279-6465; Vital Records 712-279-6266.

Worth County

County Recorder, 1000 Central Ave, Northwood, IA 50459. County Recorder, R/E and UCC Recording 641-324-2734; Fax 641-324-2316. Will search UCC records. Tax liens not included in UCC search. Will not search real estate records. **Other Phone Numbers:** Assessor 641-324-1198; Treasurer 641-324-2942; Elections 641-324-2316; Vital Records 641-324-2734.

Wright County

County Recorder, PO Box 187, Clarion, IA 50525. County Recorder, R/E and UCC Recording 515-532-3204; www.wrightcounty.org/county_offices.htm Will search UCC records. Tax liens not included in UCC search. Real estate record owner and mortgage searches available. **Other Phone Numbers:** Assessor 515-532-3737; Treasurer 515-532-2691; Treasurer 515-532-2691.

Iowa County Locator

You will usually be able to find the city name in the City/County Cross Reference below. In that case, it is a simple matter to determine the county from the cross reference. However, only the official US Postal Service city names are included in this index. There are an additional 40,000 place names that people use in their addresses. Therefore, we have also included a ZIP/City Cross Reference immediately following the City/County Cross Reference.

If you know the ZIP Code but the city name does not appear in the City/County Cross Reference index, look up the ZIP Code in the ZIP/City Cross Reference, find the city name, then look up the city name in the City/County Cross Reference. For example, you want to know the county for an address of Menands, NY 12204. There is no "Menands" in the City/County Cross Reference. The ZIP/City Cross Reference shows that ZIP Codes 12201-12288 are for the city of Albany. Looking back in the City/County Cross Reference, Albany is in Albany County.

City/County Cross Reference

A C NIELSEN CO Clinton
ACKLEY (50601) Hardin(70), Franklin(12), Butler(9), Grundy(7)
ACKWORTH Warren
ADAIR (50002) Adair(67), Guthrie(31), Audubon(1)
ADEL Dallas
AFTON Union
AGENCY Wapello
AINSWORTH Washington
AKRON Plymouth
ALBERT CITY (50510) Buena Vista(84), Pocahontas(15)
ALBIA Monroe
ALBION Marshall
ALBURNETT Linn
ALDEN (50006) Hardin(84), Franklin(15)
ALEXANDER (50420) Franklin(84), Wright(10), Story(4)
ALGONA Kossuth
ALLEMAN Polk
ALLENDORF Osceola
ALLERTON Wayne
ALLISON Butler
ALPHA Fayette
ALTA Buena Vista
ALTA VISTA (50603) Chickasaw(86), Howard(12)
ALTON (51003) Sioux(98), Plymouth(1)
ALTOONA Polk
ALVORD Lyon
AMANA Iowa
AMES (50014) Story(96), Boone(3)
ANAMOSA Jones
ANDOVER Clinton
ANDREW Jackson
ANITA (50020) Cass(87), Adair(6), Audubon(4)
ANKENY Polk
ANTHON Woodbury
APLINGTON (50604) Butler(84), Grundy(15)
ARCADIA Carroll
ARCHER O'Brien
AREDALE (50605) Butler(62), Franklin(37)
ARGYLE Lee
ARION Crawford
ARISPE Union
ARLINGTON (50606) Fayette(94), Clayton(5)
ARMSTRONG (50514) Emmet(78), Kossuth(21)
ARNOLDS PARK Dickinson
ARTHUR (51431) Ida(87), Sac(12)
ASHTON (51232) Osceola(76), Lyon(20), O'Brien(2)
ASPINWALL Crawford
AT AND T Pottawattamie
ATALISSA (52720) Muscatine(78), Cedar(21)
ATKINS Benton
ATLANTIC (50022) Cass(98), Audubon(1)

AUBURN (51433) Sac(58), Calhoun(39), Carroll(1)
AUDUBON Audubon
AURELIA (51005) Cherokee(87), Buena Vista(12)
AURORA (50607) Buchanan(60), Fayette(39)
AUSTINVILLE Butler
AVOCA (51521) Pottawattamie(86), Shelby(13)
AYRSHIRE (50515) Palo Alto(82), Clay(17)
BADGER (50516) Webster(88), Humboldt(11)
BAGLEY (50026) Guthrie(70), Greene(29)
BALDWIN (52207) Jackson(90), Clinton(9)
BANCROFT Kossuth
BARNES CITY (50027) Mahaska(97), Poweshiek(2)
BARNUM Webster
BARTLETT Fremont
BATAVIA (52533) Jefferson(70), Wapello(29)
BATTLE CREEK (51006) Ida(90), Woodbury(9)
BAXTER Jasper
BAYARD (50029) Guthrie(96), Greene(3)
BEACON Mahaska
BEACONSFIELD Ringgold
BEAMAN (50609) Grundy(72), Marshall(21), Tama(5)
BEAVER Boone
BEDFORD Taylor
BELLE PLAINE (52208) Benton(93), Iowa(3), Tama(1)
BELLEVUE Jackson
BELMOND Wright
BENNETT Cedar
BENTON Ringgold
BERNARD (52032) Dubuque(54), Jackson(40), Jones(4)
BERWICK Polk
BETTENDORF Scott
BEVINGTON Madison
BIG ROCK Scott
BIRMINGHAM (52535) Van Buren(96), Jefferson(3)
BLAIRSBURG (50034) Hamilton(86), Wright(13)
BLAIRSTOWN (52209) Benton(96), Iowa(3)
BLAKESBURG (52536) Wapello(86), Monroe(11), Davis(2)
BLANCHARD Page
BLENCOE (51523) Monona(94), Harrison(5)
BLOCKTON Taylor
BLOOMFIELD (52537) Davis(94), Wapello(5)
BLUE GRASS (52726) Scott(91), Muscatine(8)
BODE (50519) Humboldt(68), Kossuth(31)
BONAPARTE Van Buren
BONDURANT Polk

BOONE Boone
BOONEVILLE Dallas
BOUTON (50039) Dallas(96), Boone(3)
BOXHOLM Boone
BOYDEN (51234) Sioux(96), Lyon(3)
BRADDYVILLE Page
BRADFORD Franklin
BRADGATE (50520) Humboldt(95), Pocahontas(4)
BRANDON Buchanan
BRAYTON (50042) Audubon(92), Cass(7)
BREDA (51436) Carroll(76), Sac(13), Crawford(10)
BRIDGEWATER (50837) Adair(74), Cass(19), Adams(6)
BRIGHTON (52540) Jefferson(52), Washington(47)
BRISTOW Butler
BRITT Hancock
BRONSON Woodbury
BROOKLYN Poweshiek
BRUNSVILLE Plymouth
BRYANT Clinton
BUCKEYE Hardin
BUCKINGHAM Tama
BUFFALO Scott
BUFFALO CENTER (50424) Winnebago(88), Kossuth(11)
BURLINGTON Des Moines
BURNSIDE Webster
BURR OAK Winneshiek
BURT Kossuth
BUSSEY (50044) Marion(72), Mahaska(20), Monroe(7)
CALAMUS Clinton
CALLENDER Webster
CALMAR (52132) Winneshiek(92), Howard(7)
CALUMET O'Brien
CAMANCHE Clinton
CAMBRIDGE (50046) Story(82), Polk(17)
CANTRIL Van Buren
CARBON Adams
CARLISLE (50047) Warren(79), Polk(20)
CARNARVON Sac
CARPENTER Mitchell
CARROLL Carroll
CARSON Pottawattamie
CARTER LAKE Pottawattamie
CASCADE (52033) Dubuque(61), Jones(38)
CASEY (50048) Guthrie(68), Adair(31)
CASTALIA (52133) Winneshiek(70), Fayette(29)
CASTANA Monona
CEDAR Mahaska
CEDAR FALLS Black Hawk
CEDAR RAPIDS Linn
CENTER JUNCTION Jones
CENTER POINT (52213) Linn(90), Benton(7), Scott(1)
CENTERVILLE Appanoose
CENTRAL CITY Linn

CHAPIN Franklin
CHARITON Lucas
CHARLES CITY Floyd
CHARLOTTE (52731) Clinton(91), Jackson(8)
CHARTER OAK Crawford
CHATSWORTH Sioux
CHELSEA (52215) Tama(82), Poweshiek(17)
CHEROKEE Cherokee
CHESTER Howard
CHILLICOTHE Wapello
CHURDAN Greene
CINCINNATI Appanoose
CLARE (50524) Webster(95), Pocahontas(2), Humboldt(1)
CLARENCE (52216) Cedar(87), Jones(12)
CLARINDA Page
CLARION Wright
CLARKSVILLE Butler
CLEAR LAKE Cerro Gordo
CLEARFIELD (50840) Taylor(97), Ringgold(2)
CLEGHORN (51014) Cherokee(98), O'Brien(1)
CLEMONS Marshall
CLERMONT (52135) Fayette(97), Clayton(2)
CLIMBING HILL Woodbury
CLINTON Clinton
CLIO Wayne
CLIVE (50325) Polk(89), Dallas(10)
CLUTIER Tama
COGGON (52218) Linn(86), Delaware(13)
COIN Page
COLESBURG (52035) Clayton(70), Delaware(19), Dubuque(10)
COLFAX Jasper
COLLEGE SPRINGS Page
COLLINS (50055) Story(67), Jasper(30), Marshall(2)
COLO Story
COLUMBIA Marion
COLUMBUS CITY Louisa
COLUMBUS JUNCTION (52738) Louisa(95), Washington(5)
COLWELL Floyd
CONESVILLE (52739) Louisa(66), Muscatine(33)
CONRAD (50621) Grundy(92), Marshall(7)
CONROY Iowa
COON RAPIDS (50058) Carroll(79), Guthrie(11), Audubon(4), Greene(3)
COOPER Greene
CORALVILLE Johnson
CORNING (50841) Adams(94), Taylor(5)
CORRECTIONVILLE (51016) Woodbury(94), Ida(5)
CORWITH (50430) Hancock(65), Kossuth(28), Humboldt(2), Wright(2)
CORYDON Wayne
COULTER Franklin

COUNCIL BLUFFS (51503) Pottawattamie(98), Mills(1)
CRAIG Plymouth
CRAWFORDSVILLE (52621) Washington(67), Louisa(30), Henry(1)
CRESCENT Pottawattamie
CRESCO (52136) Howard(92), Winneshiek(7)
CRESTON (50801) Union(96), Adair(1), Adams(1)
CROMWELL Union
CRYSTAL LAKE Hancock
CUMBERLAND (50843) Cass(96), Adams(3)
CUMMING (50061) Warren(37), Madison(24), Dallas(19), Polk(18)
CURLEW Palo Alto
CUSHING (51018) Woodbury(59), Ida(40)
CYLINDER Palo Alto
DAKOTA CITY Humboldt
DALLAS Marion
DALLAS CENTER Dallas
DANA (50064) Greene(88), Boone(11)
DANBURY (51019) Woodbury(82), Ida(8), Crawford(5), Monona(3)
DANVILLE (52623) Des Moines(91), Henry(8)
DAVENPORT Scott
DAVIS CITY Decatur
DAWSON Dallas
DAYTON (50530) Webster(95), Boone(4)
DE SOTO Dallas
DE WITT Clinton
DECATUR Decatur
DECORAH Winneshiek
DEDHAM (51440) Carroll(97), Audubon(2)
DEEP RIVER (52222) Poweshiek(74), Iowa(25)
DEFIANCE (51527) Shelby(84), Crawford(15)
DELAWARE Delaware
DELHI Delaware
DELMAR (52037) Clinton(94), Jackson(5)
DELOIT Crawford
DELPHOS Ringgold
DELTA (52550) Keokuk(98), Mahaska(1)
DENISON Crawford
DENMARK Lee
DENVER Bremer
DERBY (50068) Lucas(77), Wayne(22)
DES MOINES Polk
DEWAR Black Hawk
DEXTER (50070) Dallas(35), Guthrie(24), Madison(22), Adair(17)
DIAGONAL (50845) Ringgold(93), Union(6)
DICKENS (51333) Clay(97), Dickinson(2)
DIKE Grundy
DIXON Scott
DOLLIVER Emmet
DONAHUE Scott
DONNELLSON Lee
DOON (51235) Lyon(96), Sioux(3)
DORCHESTER (52140) Allamakee(93), Winneshiek(6)
DOUDS (52551) Van Buren(98), Davis(1)
DOUGHERTY (50433) Cerro Gordo(54), Floyd(18), Franklin(18), Butler(8)
DOW CITY Crawford
DOWS (50071) Wright(53), Franklin(46)
DRAKESVILLE (52552) Davis(95), Wapello(4)
DUBUQUE Dubuque
DUMONT (50625) Butler(92), Franklin(7)
DUNCOMBE (50532) Webster(94), Hamilton(5)
DUNDEE Delaware
DUNKERTON Black Hawk
DUNLAP (51529) Harrison(82), Crawford(8), Monona(6), Shelby(2)
DURANGO Dubuque
DURANT (52747) Cedar(78), Scott(21)

DYERSVILLE (52040) Dubuque(93), Delaware(6)
DYSART (52224) Tama(69), Benton(29)
EAGLE GROVE (50533) Wright(96), Humboldt(2), Webster(1)
EARLHAM (50072) Madison(78), Dallas(21)
EARLING Shelby
EARLVILLE Delaware
EARLY Sac
EDDYVILLE (52553) Wapello(43), Mahaska(36), Monroe(19)
EDGEWOOD (52042) Clayton(74), Delaware(25)
ELBERON (52225) Tama(80), Benton(19)
ELDON (52554) Wapello(89), Davis(4), Jefferson(3), Van Buren(2)
ELDORA (50627) Hardin(95), Grundy(4)
ELDRIDGE Scott
ELGIN (52141) Fayette(71), Clayton(28)
ELK HORN (51531) Shelby(85), Audubon(14)
ELKADER Clayton
ELKHART Polk
ELKPORT Clayton
ELLIOTT (51532) Montgomery(67), Pottawattamie(24), Cass(7)
ELLSTON (50074) Ringgold(63), Union(36)
ELLSWORTH (50075) Hamilton(89), Pocahontas(10)
ELMA (50628) Howard(97), Mitchell(2)
ELWOOD Clinton
ELY (52227) Linn(97), Johnson(2)
EMERSON (51533) Mills(60), Montgomery(39)
EMMETSBURG Palo Alto
EPWORTH Dubuque
ESSEX (51638) Page(97), Montgomery(2)
ESTHERVILLE (51334) Emmet(98), Dickinson(1)
EVANSDALE Black Hawk
EVERLY (51338) Clay(83), Dickinson(16)
EXIRA (50076) Audubon(98), Guthrie(1)
EXLINE Appanoose
FAIRBANK (50629) Buchanan(44), Fayette(27), Black Hawk(15), Bremer(11)
FAIRFAX (52228) Linn(79), Benton(11), Johnson(8)
FAIRFIELD Jefferson
FARLEY Dubuque
FARMERSBURG Clayton
FARMINGTON (52626) Van Buren(78), Lee(21)
FARNHAMVILLE (50538) Calhoun(91), Webster(8)
FARRAGUT Fremont
FAYETTE Fayette
FENTON (50539) Kossuth(79), Palo Alto(20)
FERGUSON Marshall
FERTILE (50434) Cerro Gordo(86), Worth(12)
FESTINA Winneshiek
FLORIS Davis
FLOYD Floyd
FONDA Pocahontas
FONTANELLE Adair
FOREST CITY (50436) Winnebago(91), Hancock(8)
FORT ATKINSON (52144) Winneshiek(78), Fayette(13), Chickasaw(8)
FORT DODGE Webster
FORT MADISON Lee
FOSTORIA Clay
FREDERICKSBURG (50630) Chickasaw(93), Bremer(6)
FREDERIKA Bremer
FREMONT (52561) Mahaska(72), Keokuk(15), Benton(12)
FRUITLAND Muscatine
GALT Wright

GALVA (51020) Ida(66), Sac(18), Cherokee(15)
GARBER Clayton
GARDEN CITY Hardin
GARDEN GROVE Decatur
GARNAVILLO Clayton
GARNER Hancock
GARRISON Benton
GARWIN (50632) Tama(87), Marshall(12)
GENEVA Franklin
GEORGE Lyon
GIBSON (50104) Keokuk(80), Poweshiek(14), Mahaska(5)
GIFFORD Hardin
GILBERT Story
GILBERTVILLE Black Hawk
GILLETT GROVE Clay
GILMAN (50106) Marshall(70), Jasper(16), Tama(8), Poweshiek(3)
GILMORE CITY (50541) Pocahontas(51), Humboldt(48)
GLADBROOK (50635) Tama(95), Marshall(4)
GLENWOOD Mills
GLIDDEN (51443) Carroll(98), Greene(1)
GOLDFIELD (50542) Wright(79), Humboldt(20)
GOODELL Hancock
GOOSE LAKE Clinton
GOWRIE (50543) Webster(96), Greene(3)
GRAETTINGER (51342) Palo Alto(79), Emmet(20)
GRAFTON (50440) Worth(98), Mitchell(1)
GRAND JUNCTION (50107) Greene(95), Boone(3)
GRAND MOUND Clinton
GRAND RIVER (50108) Decatur(90), Clarke(8), Ringgold(1)
GRANDVIEW Louisa
GRANGER (50109) Polk(60), Dallas(39)
GRANT Montgomery
GRANVILLE (51022) Sioux(58), O'Brien(41)
GRAVITY Taylor
GRAY Audubon
GREELEY (50050) Delaware(87), Clayton(12)
GREEN MOUNTAIN Marshall
GREENE (50636) Butler(83), Floyd(16)
GREENFIELD Adair
GREENVILLE Clay
GRIMES (50111) Polk(95), Dallas(4)
GRINNELL Poweshiek
GRISWOLD (51535) Cass(61), Pottawattamie(38)
GRUNDY CENTER Grundy
GRUVER Emmet
GUERNSEY (52221) Poweshiek(88), Iowa(11)
GUTHRIE CENTER Guthrie
GUTTENBERG (52052) Clayton(94), Dubuque(5)
HALBUR Carroll
HALE Jones
HAMBURG Fremont
HAMILTON Marion
HAMLIN (50117) Audubon(98), Guthrie(1)
HAMPTON Franklin
HANCOCK Pottawattamie
HANLONTOWN (50444) Worth(83), Cerro Gordo(15), Winnebago(1)
HANSELL Franklin
HARCOURT Webster
HARDY Humboldt
HARLAN Shelby
HARPER Keokuk
HARPERS FERRY Allamakee
HARRIS (51345) Osceola(94), Dickinson(5)
HARTFORD Warren
HARTLEY (51346) O'Brien(89), Osceola(6), Clay(3)

HARTWICK (52232) Poweshiek(85), Iowa(14)
HARVEY Marion
HASTINGS Mills
HAVELOCK (50546) Pocahontas(96), Palo Alto(3)
HAVERHILL Marshall
HAWARDEN Sioux
HAWKEYE Fayette
HAYESVILLE Keokuk
HAZLETON Buchanan
HEDRICK (52563) Keokuk(67), Wapello(31), Jefferson(1)
HENDERSON (51541) Mills(69), Pottawattamie(19), Montgomery(11)
HIAWATHA Linn
HIGHLANDVILLE Winneshiek
HILLS Johnson
HILLSBORO (52630) Van Buren(55), Henry(26), Lee(18)
HINTON Plymouth
HOLLAND Grundy
HOLSTEIN (51025) Ida(86), Cherokee(8), Woodbury(5)
HOLY CROSS (52053) Dubuque(79), Clayton(20)
HOMESTEAD (52236) Iowa(97), Johnson(2)
HONEY CREEK Pottawattamie
HOPKINTON (52237) Delaware(96), Dubuque(2), Jones(1)
HORNICK (51026) Woodbury(75), Monona(24)
HOSPERS (51238) Sioux(66), O'Brien(33)
HOUGHTON Lee
HUBBARD (50122) Hardin(98), Story(1)
HUDSON (50643) Black Hawk(93), Grundy(6)
HULL Sioux
HUMBOLDT (50548) Humboldt(98), Webster(1)
HUMESTON (50123) Wayne(91), Decatur(3), Lucas(3), Clarke(1)
HUXLEY (50124) Story(93), Polk(6)
IDA GROVE Ida
IMOGENE (51645) Fremont(64), Mills(24), Page(10), Montgomery(2)
INDEPENDENCE Buchanan
INDIANOLA Warren
INWOOD (51240) Lyon(90), Sioux(9)
IONIA (50645) Chickasaw(97), Floyd(2)
IOWA CITY Johnson
IOWA FALLS (50126) Hardin(97), Franklin(2)
IRA Jasper
IRETON (51027) Sioux(81), Plymouth(18)
IRWIN Shelby
JACKSON JUNCTION Winneshiek
JAMAICA (50128) Guthrie(62), Greene(25), Dallas(12)
JANESVILLE (50647) Bremer(55), Black Hawk(44)
JEFFERSON Greene
JESUP (50648) Buchanan(89), Black Hawk(10)
JEWELL Hamilton
JOHNSTON Polk
JOICE (50446) Worth(81), Winnebago(18)
JOLLEY Calhoun
KALONA (52247) Washington(66), Johnson(33)
KAMRAR Hamilton
KANAWHA (50447) Hancock(76), Wright(23)
KELLERTON (50133) Ringgold(93), Decatur(6)
KELLEY (50134) Story(78), Boone(21)
KELLOGG Jasper
KENSETT Worth
KENT (50850) Adams(50), Union(49)
KEOKUK Lee
KEOSAUQUA Van Buren

KEOTA (52248) Keokuk(76), Washington(23)
KESLEY Butler
KESWICK (50136) Keokuk(95), Iowa(3)
KEYSTONE Benton
KILLDUFF Jasper
KIMBALLTON (51543) Audubon(84), Shelby(15)
KINGSLEY (51028) Plymouth(81), Woodbury(18)
KINROSS Keokuk
KIRKMAN Shelby
KIRKVILLE Wapello
KIRON (51448) Crawford(64), Sac(19), Ida(15)
KLEMME (50449) Cerro Gordo(63), Hancock(36)
KNIERIM Calhoun
KNOXVILLE Marion
LA MOTTE (52054) Jackson(98), Dubuque(1)
LA PORTE CITY (50651) Black Hawk(93), Benton(6)
LACONA (50139) Warren(63), Marion(19), Lucas(16)
LADORA Iowa
LAKE CITY (51449) Calhoun(96), Carroll(3)
LAKE MILLS (50450) Winnebago(94), Worth(5)
LAKE PARK Dickinson
LAKE VIEW Sac
LAKOTA Kossuth
LAMONI Decatur
LAMONT (50650) Buchanan(70), Fayette(27), Delaware(2)
LANESBORO Carroll
LANGWORTHY Jones
LANSING Allamakee
LARCHWOOD Lyon
LARRABEE (51029) Cherokee(94), O'Brien(5)
LATIMER Franklin
LAUREL (50141) Marshall(53), Jasper(46)
LAURENS (50554) Pocahontas(96), Palo Alto(2)
LAWLER (52154) Chickasaw(94), Howard(5)
LAWTON Woodbury
LE CLAIRE Scott
LE GRAND Marshall
LE MARS Plymouth
LEDYARD Kossuth
LEHIGH Webster
LEIGHTON (50143) Mahaska(97), Marion(2)
LELAND Winnebago
LENOX (50851) Taylor(78), Adams(12), Union(8), Ringgold(1)
LEON Decatur
LESTER Lyon
LETTS (52754) Louisa(77), Muscatine(22)
LEWIS (51544) Cass(77), Pottawattamie(22)
LIBERTY CENTER Warren
LIBERTYVILLE (52567) Jefferson(85), Van Buren(14)
LIDDERDALE Carroll
LIME SPRINGS Howard
LINCOLN Tama
LINDEN (50146) Dallas(87), Guthrie(12)
LINEVILLE (50147) Wayne(81), Marion(18)
LINN GROVE (51033) Buena Vista(59), Clay(40)
LISBON (52253) Linn(70), Cedar(14), Jones(10), Johnson(4)
LISCOMB (50148) Marshall(88), Grundy(11)
LITTLE CEDAR Mitchell
LITTLE ROCK (51243) Lyon(91), Osceola(8)
LITTLE SIOUX (51545) Harrison(81), Monona(18)

LITTLEPORT Clayton
LIVERMORE (50558) Humboldt(57), Kossuth(42)
LOCKRIDGE (52635) Jefferson(73), Henry(26)
LOGAN Harrison
LOHRVILLE (51453) Calhoun(91), Carroll(7), Greene(1)
LONE ROCK Kossuth
LONE TREE (52755) Johnson(87), Louisa(11)
LONG GROVE (52756) Scott(98), Clinton(1)
LORIMOR (50149) Union(68), Madison(30)
LOST NATION Clinton
LOVILIA Monroe
LOW MOOR Clinton
LOWDEN (52255) Cedar(97), Clinton(2)
LU VERNE (50560) Kossuth(81), Humboldt(18)
LUANA (52156) Clayton(83), Allamakee(16)
LUCAS (50151) Warren(56), Lucas(40), Clarke(2)
LUTHER Boone
LUXEMBURG Dubuque
LUZERNE (52257) Benton(98), Iowa(1)
LYNNVILLE (50153) Jasper(90), Mahaska(6), Poweshiek(3)
LYTTON (50561) Calhoun(58), Sac(41)
MACEDONIA Pottawattamie
MACKSBURG (50155) Madison(94), Adair(4), Union(1)
MADRID (50156) Boone(96), Polk(2), Dallas(2)
MAGNOLIA Harrison
MALCOM Poweshiek
MALLARD (50562) Palo Alto(89), Pocahontas(10)
MALOY Ringgold
MALVERN (51551) Mills(98), Fremont(1)
MANCHESTER Delaware
MANILLA (51454) Crawford(68), Shelby(31)
MANLY (50456) Worth(95), Cerro Gordo(4)
MANNING (51455) Carroll(84), Crawford(7), Audubon(5), Shelby(1)
MANSON (50563) Calhoun(80), Pocahontas(16), Webster(3)
MAPLETON (51034) Monona(91), Woodbury(6), Crawford(1)
MAQUOKETA (52060) Jackson(98), Clinton(1)
MARATHON Buena Vista
MARBLE ROCK Floyd
MARCUS (51035) Cherokee(95), Plymouth(3)
MARENGO (52301) Iowa(98), Benton(1)
MARION Linn
MARNE (51552) Cass(83), Shelby(14), Pottawattamie(1)
MARQUETTE Clayton
MARSHALLTOWN Marshall
MARTELLE (52305) Jones(83), Linn(16)
MARTENSDALE Warren
MARTINSBURG Keokuk
MASON CITY Cerro Gordo
MASONVILLE (50654) Delaware(60), Buchanan(39)
MASSENA (50853) Cass(96), Adams(3)
MATLOCK Sioux
MAURICE Sioux
MAXWELL (50161) Story(57), Polk(41), Jasper(1)
MAY CITY Osceola
MAYNARD Fayette
MC CALLSBURG (50154) Story(90), Hardin(9)
MC CAUSLAND Scott
MC CLELLAND Pottawattamie
MC GREGOR Clayton
MC INTIRE Mitchell

MECHANICSVILLE (52306) Cedar(77), Jones(22)
MEDIAPOLIS Des Moines
MELBOURNE (50162) Marshall(97), Jasper(2)
MELCHER Marion
MELROSE (52569) Monroe(82), Appanoose(11), Wayne(5)
MELVIN (51350) Osceola(96), O'Brien(3)
MENLO (50164) Guthrie(70), Adair(29)
MERIDEN Cherokee
MERRILL Plymouth
MESERVEY (50457) Cerro Gordo(50), Hancock(22), Franklin(18), Wright(8)
MIDDLE AMANA Iowa
MIDDLETOWN Des Moines
MILES (52064) Jackson(93), Clinton(6)
MILFORD Dickinson
MILLERSBURG Iowa
MILLERTON Wayne
MILO Warren
MILTON (52570) Van Buren(85), Davis(14)
MINBURN Dallas
MINDEN Pottawattamie
MINEOLA Mills
MINGO (50168) Jasper(95), Polk(4)
MISSOURI VALLEY (51555) Harrison(80), Pottawattamie(19)
MITCHELLVILLE (50169) Polk(81), Jasper(18)
MODALE Harrison
MONDAMIN Harrison
MONMOUTH (52309) Jackson(73), Jones(26)
MONONA (52159) Clayton(75), Allamakee(24)
MONROE (50170) Jasper(87), Marion(12)
MONTEZUMA Poweshiek
MONTICELLO Jones
MONTOUR Tama
MONTPELIER Muscatine
MONTROSE Lee
MOORHEAD (51558) Monona(92), Harrison(7)
MOORLAND (50566) Webster(98), Calhoun(1)
MORAVIA (52571) Appanoose(90), Monroe(10)
MORLEY Jones
MORNING SUN (52640) Louisa(73), Des Moines(26)
MORRISON Grundy
MOSCOW (52760) Muscatine(60), Cedar(39)
MOULTON (52572) Appanoose(92), Davis(7)
MOUNT AUBURN Benton
MOUNT AYR Ringgold
MOUNT PLEASANT (52641) Henry(97), Washington(2)
MOUNT STERLING Van Buren
MOUNT UNION (52644) Henry(72), Des Moines(27)
MOUNT VERNON Linn
MOVILLE Woodbury
MURRAY (50174) Clarke(97), Union(2)
MUSCATINE (52761) Muscatine(96), Louisa(3)
MYSTIC Appanoose
NASHUA (50658) Chickasaw(84), Floyd(13), Bremer(2)
NEMAHA Sac
NEOLA (51559) Pottawattamie(96), Harrison(4)
NEVADA Story
NEW ALBIN Allamakee
NEW HAMPTON Chickasaw
NEW HARTFORD (50660) Butler(84), Grundy(15)
NEW LIBERTY (52765) Scott(86), Cedar(13)

NEW LONDON (52645) Henry(85), Des Moines(14)
NEW MARKET (51646) Taylor(98), Page(1)
NEW PROVIDENCE (50206) Hardin(89), Marshall(7), Story(3)
NEW SHARON (50207) Mahaska(98), Poweshiek(1)
NEW VIENNA (52065) Dubuque(83), Delaware(16)
NEW VIRGINIA (50210) Warren(78), Clarke(20), Madison(1)
NEWELL (50568) Buena Vista(90), Sac(8)
NEWHALL Benton
NEWTON Jasper
NICHOLS (52766) Muscatine(93), Johnson(6)
NODAWAY (50857) Adams(76), Taylor(20), Montgomery(4)
NORA SPRINGS (50458) Floyd(63), Cerro Gordo(32), Mitchell(4)
NORTH BUENA VISTA Clayton
NORTH ENGLISH (52316) Iowa(88), Keokuk(11)
NORTH LIBERTY Johnson
NORTH WASHINGTON Chickasaw
NORTHBORO (51647) Page(81), Fremont(18)
NORTHWOOD Worth
NORWALK Warren
NORWAY (52318) Benton(80), Iowa(19)
NUMA Appanoose
OAKDALE Johnson
OAKLAND Pottawattamie
OAKVILLE (52646) Louisa(52), Des Moines(47)
OCHEYEDAN Osceola
ODEBOLT Sac
OELWEIN Fayette
OGDEN Boone
OKOBOJI Dickinson
OLDS Henry
OLIN (52320) Jones(93), Cedar(6)
OLLIE (52576) Keokuk(98), Jefferson(1)
ONAWA Monona
ONSLOW Jones
ORAN Fayette
ORANGE CITY Sioux
ORCHARD (50460) Mitchell(72), Floyd(27)
ORIENT Adair
OSAGE Mitchell
OSCEOLA Clarke
OSKALOOSA Mahaska
OSSIAN (52161) Winneshiek(87), Fayette(12)
OTHO Webster
OTLEY (50214) Marion(97), Jasper(2)
OTO Woodbury
OTTOSEN (50570) Humboldt(61), Kossuth(37), Pocahontas(1)
OTTUMWA Wapello
OXFORD (52322) Johnson(97), Iowa(2)
OXFORD JUNCTION (52323) Jones(83), Clinton(7), Linn(4), Cedar(4)
OYENS Plymouth
PACIFIC JUNCTION Mills
PACKWOOD (52580) Jefferson(94), Keokuk(5)
PALMER Pocahontas
PALO (52324) Linn(96), Benton(3)
PANAMA (51562) Shelby(97), Harrison(2)
PANORA Guthrie
PARKERSBURG (50665) Butler(76), Grundy(23)
PARNELL (52325) Iowa(86), Johnson(13)
PATON (50217) Greene(80), Boone(13), Webster(5)
PATTERSON Madison
PAULLINA (51046) O'Brien(96), Cherokee(3)
PELLA (50219) Marion(94), Mahaska(5)
PEOSTA Dubuque

PERCIVAL Fremont
PERRY (50220) Dallas(93), Boone(5)
PERSHING Marion
PERSIA (51563) Harrison(97), Shelby(2)
PERU (50222) Madison(98), Clarke(1)
PETERSON (51047) Clay(69), Buena Vista(16), Cherokee(9), O'Brien(4)
PIERSON (51048) Woodbury(71), Cherokee(28)
PILOT GROVE Lee
PILOT MOUND Boone
PISGAH Harrison
PLAINFIELD (50666) Bremer(72), Butler(27)
PLANO (52581) Appanoose(95), Wayne(4)
PLEASANT VALLEY Scott
PLEASANTVILLE (50225) Marion(85), Warren(14)
PLOVER Pocahontas
PLYMOUTH (50464) Cerro Gordo(77), Worth(19), Mitchell(2)
POCAHONTAS Pocahontas
POLK CITY (50226) Polk(97), Boone(2)
POMEROY (50575) Calhoun(63), Pocahontas(36)
POPEJOY Franklin
PORTSMOUTH (51565) Shelby(79), Harrison(20)
POSTVILLE (52162) Allamakee(53), Clayton(33), Winneshiek(8), Fayette(4)
PRAIRIE CITY (50228) Jasper(96), Polk(2), Marion(1)
PRAIRIEBURG Linn
PRESCOTT (50859) Adams(97), Adair(2)
PRESTON (52069) Jackson(92), Clinton(7)
PRIMGHAR O'Brien
PRINCETON Scott
PROLE (50229) Warren(71), Madison(28)
PROMISE CITY Wayne
PROTIVIN Howard
PULASKI Davis
QUASQUETON Buchanan
QUIMBY Cherokee
RADCLIFFE (50230) Hardin(70), Hamilton(28), Story(1)
RAKE Winnebago
RALSTON Carroll
RANDALIA Fayette
RANDALL Hamilton
RANDOLPH (51649) Fremont(98), Mills(1)
RAYMOND Black Hawk
READLYN Bremer
REASNOR Jasper
RED OAK Montgomery
REDDING Ringgold
REDFIELD (50233) Dallas(88), Guthrie(11)
REINBECK (50669) Grundy(90), Tama(8), Black Hawk(1)
REMBRANDT Buena Vista
REMSEN (51050) Plymouth(98), Cherokee(1)
RENWICK (50577) Humboldt(69), Wright(30)
RHODES (50234) Marshall(77), Jasper(22)
RICEVILLE (50466) Howard(52), Mitchell(47)
RICHLAND (52585) Keokuk(61), Washington(28), Jefferson(9)
RICKETTS Crawford
RIDGEWAY Winneshiek
RINARD Calhoun
RINGSTED (50578) Emmet(92), Palo Alto(4), Kossuth(3)
RIPPEY (50235) Greene(92), Boone(5), Dallas(2)
RIVERSIDE (52327) Washington(67), Johnson(29), Louisa(2)
RIVERTON Fremont
ROBINS Linn
ROCK FALLS Cerro Gordo
ROCK RAPIDS Lyon
ROCK VALLEY (51247) Sioux(98), Lyon(1)

ROCKFORD (50468) Floyd(86), Cerro Gordo(13)
ROCKWELL Cerro Gordo
ROCKWELL CITY Calhoun
RODMAN Palo Alto
RODNEY (51051) Monona(91), Woodbury(8)
ROLAND (50236) Story(97), Hamilton(2)
ROLFE (50581) Pocahontas(98), Palo Alto(1)
ROME Henry
ROSE HILL (52586) Mahaska(92), Keokuk(7)
ROWAN (50470) Wright(95), Franklin(4)
ROWLEY Buchanan
ROYAL Clay
RUDD (50471) Floyd(94), Mitchell(5)
RUNNELLS (50237) Polk(92), Jasper(4), Marion(2)
RUSSELL (50238) Lucas(86), Wayne(13)
RUTHVEN (51358) Palo Alto(80), Clay(19)
RUTLAND Humboldt
RYAN Delaware
SABULA (52070) Jackson(89), Clinton(10)
SAC CITY Sac
SAINT ANSGAR (50472) Mitchell(95), Worth(4)
SAINT ANTHONY (50239) Marshall(87), Story(12)
SAINT CHARLES (50240) Madison(67), Warren(32)
SAINT DONATUS Jackson
SAINT LUCAS Fayette
SAINT MARYS Warren
SAINT OLAF Clayton
SAINT PAUL Lee
SALEM (52649) Henry(85), Lee(14)
SALIX Woodbury
SANBORN O'Brien
SCARVILLE Winnebago
SCHALLER (51053) Sac(91), Ida(6), Buena Vista(2)
SCHLESWIG (51461) Crawford(94), Ida(5)
SCOTCH GROVE Jones
SCRANTON (51462) Greene(97), Carroll(2)
SEARSBORO (50242) Poweshiek(94), Jasper(5)
SELMA (52588) Van Buren(74), Davis(24), Jefferson(1)
SERGEANT BLUFF Woodbury
SEYMOUR (52590) Wayne(90), Appanoose(9)
SHAMBAUGH Page
SHANNON CITY (50861) Union(91), Ringgold(8)
SHARPSBURG Taylor
SHEFFIELD (50475) Franklin(76), Cerro Gordo(23)
SHELBY (51570) Shelby(53), Pottawattamie(39), Harrison(6)
SHELDAHL Polk
SHELDON (51201) O'Brien(89), Sioux(10)
SHELL ROCK Butler
SHELLSBURG Benton
SHENANDOAH Page
SHERRILL (52073) Dubuque(96), Clayton(3)
SIBLEY Osceola
SIDNEY Fremont
SIGOURNEY Keokuk
SILVER CITY (51571) Mills(53), Pottawattamie(46)
SIOUX CENTER Sioux
SIOUX CITY Woodbury
SIOUX RAPIDS (50585) Buena Vista(69), Clay(30)
SLATER (50244) Story(71), Polk(26), Boone(2)
SLOAN (51055) Woodbury(66), Monona(33)

SMITHLAND (51056) Woodbury(92), Monona(7)
SOLDIER Monona
SOLON Johnson
SOMERS (50586) Calhoun(89), Webster(10)
SOUTH AMANA Iowa
SOUTH ENGLISH Keokuk
SPENCER Clay
SPERRY Des Moines
SPILLVILLE Winneshiek
SPIRIT LAKE Dickinson
SPRAGUEVILLE Jackson
SPRINGBROOK Jackson
SPRINGVILLE Linn
STACYVILLE Mitchell
STANHOPE Hamilton
STANLEY (50671) Fayette(67), Buchanan(32)
STANTON Montgomery
STANWOOD Cedar
STATE CENTER (50247) Marshall(94), Story(5)
STEAMBOAT ROCK (50672) Hardin(91), Grundy(8)
STOCKPORT (52651) Van Buren(91), Jefferson(8)
STOCKTON (52769) Scott(66), Muscatine(31), Henry(1)
STORM LAKE Buena Vista
STORY CITY (50248) Story(87), Hamilton(10), Boone(2)
STOUT Grundy
STRATFORD (50249) Hamilton(78), Webster(14), Boone(7)
STRAWBERRY POINT (52076) Clayton(94), Delaware(3), Fayette(1)
STRUBLE Plymouth
STUART (50250) Guthrie(74), Adair(25)
SULLY Jasper
SUMNER (50674) Bremer(66), Fayette(21), Chickasaw(12)
SUPERIOR Dickinson
SUTHERLAND (51058) O'Brien(95), Clay(2), Cherokee(1)
SWALEDALE Cerro Gordo
SWAN (50252) Warren(60), Marion(39)
SWEA CITY Kossuth
SWEDESBURG Henry
SWISHER (52338) Johnson(94), Linn(5)
TABOR (51653) Fremont(71), Mills(28)
TAINTOR Mahaska
TAMA Tama
TEEDS GROVE Clinton
TEMPLETON (51463) Carroll(98), Audubon(1)
TENNANT Shelby
TERRIL (51364) Dickinson(74), Clay(16), Emmet(9)
THAYER (50254) Union(97), Clarke(2)
THOMPSON Winnebago
THOR (50591) Humboldt(85), Webster(14)
THORNBURG Keokuk
THORNTON (50479) Cerro Gordo(88), Franklin(11)
THURMAN Fremont
TIFFIN Johnson
TINGLEY Ringgold
TIPTON Cedar
TITONKA (50480) Kossuth(94), Hancock(3), Winnebago(1)
TODDVILLE Linn
TOETERVILLE Mitchell
TOLEDO Tama
TORONTO Clinton
TRACY (50256) Marion(76), Mahaska(23)
TRAER Tama
TREYNOR Pottawattamie
TRIPOLI Bremer
TROY MILLS Linn
TRUESDALE Buena Vista

TRURO (50257) Madison(77), Clarke(16), Warren(6)
TURIN Monona
UDELL Appanoose
UNDERWOOD Pottawattamie
UNION (50258) Hardin(77), Marshall(21), Grundy(1)
UNIONVILLE (52594) Appanoose(67), Davis(32)
UNIVERSITY PARK Mahaska
URBANA Benton
URBANDALE (50323) Polk(59), Dallas(40)
UTE (51060) Monona(84), Crawford(15)
VAIL Crawford
VAN HORNE Benton
VAN METER (50261) Dallas(54), Madison(45)
VAN WERT Decatur
VARINA Pocahontas
VENTURA (50482) Cerro Gordo(87), Hancock(12)
VICTOR (52347) Iowa(79), Poweshiek(20)
VILLISCA (50864) Montgomery(85), Page(9), Taylor(2), Cass(1)
VINCENT Webster
VINING Tama
VINTON Benton
VIOLA Linn
VOLGA Clayton
WADENA (52169) Fayette(95), Clayton(4)
WALCOTT (52773) Scott(98), Muscatine(1)
WALFORD Benton
WALKER Linn
WALL LAKE (51466) Sac(92), Carroll(3), Crawford(3)
WALLINGFORD Emmet
WALNUT (51577) Pottawattamie(74), Shelby(24), Cass(1)
WAPELLO Louisa
WASHINGTON Washington
WASHTA (51061) Cherokee(78), Ida(20)
WATERLOO Black Hawk
WATERVILLE Allamakee
WATKINS Benton
WAUCOMA (52171) Fayette(70), Chickasaw(15), Winneshiek(13)
WAUKEE Dallas
WAUKON (52172) Allamakee(98), Winneshiek(1)
WAVERLY Bremer
WAYLAND (52654) Henry(84), Washington(14)
WEBB (51366) Clay(93), Buena Vista(6)
WEBSTER (52355) Keokuk(94), Iowa(5)
WEBSTER CITY Hamilton
WELDON (50264) Clarke(59), Decatur(40)
WELLMAN (52356) Washington(89), Iowa(8)
WELLSBURG (50680) Grundy(98), Hardin(1)
WELTON Clinton
WESLEY (50483) Kossuth(78), Hancock(21)
WEST AMANA Iowa
WEST BEND (50597) Kossuth(54), Palo Alto(43), Humboldt(1)
WEST BRANCH (52358) Cedar(83), Johnson(16)
WEST BURLINGTON Des Moines
WEST CHESTER Washington
WEST DES MOINES Polk
WEST GROVE Davis
WEST LIBERTY Muscatine
WEST POINT (52656) Lee(98), Henry(1)
WEST UNION Fayette
WESTFIELD Plymouth
WESTGATE Fayette
WESTPHALIA Shelby
WESTSIDE (51467) Crawford(70), Carroll(29)
WEVER (52658) Lee(87), Des Moines(12)

WHAT CHEER (50268) Keokuk(93), Mahaska(6)
WHEATLAND (52777) Clinton(93), Cedar(6)
WHITING Monona
WHITTEMORE (50598) Kossuth(76), Palo Alto(23)
WHITTEN Hardin
WILLIAMS (50271) Hamilton(90), Wright(8)

WILLIAMSBURG Iowa
WILLIAMSON Lucas
WILTON (52778) Muscatine(57), Cedar(42)
WINFIELD (52659) Henry(84), Louisa(15)
WINTERSET Madison
WINTHROP Buchanan
WIOTA Cass
WODEN (50484) Hancock(48), Winnebago(48), Kossuth(3)

WOODBINE Harrison
WOODBURN (50275) Clarke(92), Lucas(8)
WOODWARD (50276) Dallas(72), Boone(27)
WOOLSTOCK (50599) Wright(79), Hamilton(20)
WORTHINGTON (52078) Dubuque(74), Delaware(25)
WYOMING Jones

YALE (50277) Guthrie(84), Dallas(15)
YARMOUTH Des Moines
YORKTOWN Page
ZEARING Story
ZWINGLE (52079) Jackson(62), Dubuque(37)

ZIP/City Cross Reference

ZIP	City
50001-50001	ACKWORTH
50002-50002	ADAIR
50003-50003	ADEL
50005-50005	ALBION
50006-50006	ALDEN
50007-50007	ALLEMAN
50008-50008	ALLERTON
50009-50009	ALTOONA
50010-50014	AMES
50015-50015	ANKENY
50020-50020	ANITA
50021-50021	ANKENY
50022-50022	ATLANTIC
50025-50025	AUDUBON
50026-50026	BAGLEY
50027-50027	BARNES CITY
50028-50028	BAXTER
50029-50029	BAYARD
50030-50030	BEACONSFIELD
50031-50031	BEAVER
50032-50032	BERWICK
50033-50033	BEVINGTON
50034-50034	BLAIRSBURG
50035-50035	BONDURANT
50036-50037	BOONE
50038-50038	BOONEVILLE
50039-50039	BOUTON
50040-50040	BOXHOLM
50041-50041	BRADFORD
50042-50042	BRAYTON
50043-50043	BUCKEYE
50044-50044	BUSSEY
50046-50046	CAMBRIDGE
50047-50047	CARLISLE
50048-50048	CASEY
50049-50049	CHARITON
50050-50050	CHURDAN
50051-50051	CLEMONS
50052-50052	CLIO
50054-50054	COLFAX
50055-50055	COLLINS
50056-50056	COLO
50057-50057	COLUMBIA
50058-50058	COON RAPIDS
50059-50059	COOPER
50060-50060	CORYDON
50061-50061	CUMMING
50062-50062	DALLAS
50063-50063	DALLAS CENTER
50064-50064	DANA
50065-50065	DAVIS CITY
50066-50066	DAWSON
50067-50067	DECATUR
50068-50068	DERBY
50069-50069	DE SOTO
50070-50070	DEXTER
50071-50071	DOWS
50072-50072	EARLHAM
50073-50073	ELKHART
50074-50074	ELLSTON
50075-50075	ELLSWORTH
50076-50076	EXIRA
50077-50077	CHURDAN
50078-50078	FERGUSON
50101-50101	GALT
50102-50102	GARDEN CITY
50103-50103	GARDEN GROVE
50104-50104	GIBSON
50105-50105	GILBERT
50106-50106	GILMAN
50107-50107	GRAND JUNCTION
50108-50108	GRAND RIVER
50109-50109	GRANGER
50110-50110	GRAY
50111-50111	GRIMES
50112-50112	GRINNELL
50115-50115	GUTHRIE CENTER
50116-50116	HAMILTON
50117-50117	HAMLIN
50118-50118	HARTFORD
50119-50119	HARVEY
50120-50120	HAVERHILL
50122-50122	HUBBARD
50123-50123	HUMESTON
50124-50124	HUXLEY
50125-50125	INDIANOLA
50126-50126	IOWA FALLS
50127-50127	IRA
50128-50128	JAMAICA
50129-50129	JEFFERSON
50130-50130	JEWELL
50131-50131	JOHNSTON
50132-50132	KAMRAR
50133-50133	KELLERTON
50134-50134	KELLEY
50135-50135	KELLOGG
50136-50136	KESWICK
50137-50137	KILLDUFF
50138-50138	KNOXVILLE
50139-50139	LACONA
50140-50140	LAMONI
50141-50141	LAUREL
50142-50142	LE GRAND
50143-50143	LEIGHTON
50144-50144	LEON
50145-50145	LIBERTY CENTER
50146-50146	LINDEN
50147-50147	LINEVILLE
50148-50148	LISCOMB
50149-50149	LORIMOR
50150-50150	LOVILIA
50151-50151	LUCAS
50152-50152	LUTHER
50153-50153	LYNNVILLE
50154-50154	MC CALLSBURG
50155-50155	MACKSBURG
50156-50156	MADRID
50157-50157	MALCOM
50158-50158	MARSHALLTOWN
50160-50160	MARTENSDALE
50161-50161	MAXWELL
50162-50162	MELBOURNE
50163-50163	MELCHER
50164-50164	MENLO
50165-50165	MILLERTON
50166-50166	MILO
50167-50167	MINBURN
50168-50168	MINGO
50169-50169	MITCHELLVILLE
50170-50170	MONROE
50171-50172	MONTEZUMA
50173-50173	MONTOUR
50174-50174	MURRAY
50177-50177	GRINNELL
50197-50198	KNOXVILLE
50201-50201	NEVADA
50206-50206	NEW PROVIDENCE
50207-50207	NEW SHARON
50208-50208	NEWTON
50210-50210	NEW VIRGINIA
50211-50211	NORWALK
50212-50212	OGDEN
50213-50213	OSCEOLA
50214-50214	OTLEY
50216-50216	PANORA
50217-50217	PATON
50218-50218	PATTERSON
50219-50219	PELLA
50220-50220	PERRY
50221-50221	PERSHING
50222-50222	PERU
50223-50223	PILOT MOUND
50225-50225	PLEASANTVILLE
50226-50226	POLK CITY
50227-50227	POPEJOY
50228-50228	PRAIRIE CITY
50229-50229	PROLE
50230-50230	RADCLIFFE
50231-50231	RANDALL
50232-50232	REASNOR
50233-50233	REDFIELD
50234-50234	RHODES
50235-50235	RIPPEY
50236-50236	ROLAND
50237-50237	RUNNELLS
50238-50238	RUSSELL
50239-50239	SAINT ANTHONY
50240-50240	SAINT CHARLES
50241-50241	SAINT MARYS
50242-50242	SEARSBORO
50243-50243	SHELDAHL
50244-50244	SLATER
50246-50246	STANHOPE
50247-50247	STATE CENTER
50248-50248	STORY CITY
50249-50249	STRATFORD
50250-50250	STUART
50251-50251	SULLY
50252-50252	SWAN
50253-50253	TAINTOR
50254-50254	THAYER
50255-50255	THORNBURG
50256-50256	TRACY
50257-50257	TRURO
50258-50258	UNION
50259-50259	GIFFORD
50261-50261	VAN METER
50262-50262	VAN WERT
50263-50263	WAUKEE
50264-50264	WELDON
50265-50266	WEST DES MOINES
50268-50268	WHAT CHEER
50269-50269	WHITTEN
50271-50271	WILLIAMS
50272-50272	WILLIAMSON
50273-50273	WINTERSET
50274-50274	WIOTA
50275-50275	WOODBURN
50276-50276	WOODWARD
50277-50277	YALE
50278-50278	ZEARING
50300-50321	DES MOINES
50322-50323	URBANDALE
50325-50325	CLIVE
50327-50397	DES MOINES
50398-50398	WEST DES MOINES
50401-50402	MASON CITY
50420-50420	ALEXANDER
50421-50421	BELMOND
50423-50423	BRITT
50424-50424	BUFFALO CENTER
50426-50426	CARPENTER
50427-50427	CHAPIN
50428-50428	CLEAR LAKE
50430-50430	CORWITH
50431-50431	COULTER
50432-50432	CRYSTAL LAKE
50433-50433	DOUGHERTY
50434-50434	FERTILE
50435-50435	FLOYD
50436-50436	FOREST CITY
50438-50438	GARNER
50439-50439	GOODELL
50440-50440	GRAFTON
50441-50441	HAMPTON
50444-50444	HANLONTOWN
50446-50446	JOICE
50447-50447	KANAWHA
50448-50448	KENSETT
50449-50449	KLEMME
50450-50450	LAKE MILLS
50451-50451	LAKOTA
50452-50452	LATIMER
50453-50453	LELAND
50454-50454	LITTLE CEDAR
50455-50455	MC INTIRE
50456-50456	MANLY
50457-50457	MESERVEY
50458-50458	NORA SPRINGS
50459-50459	NORTHWOOD
50460-50460	ORCHARD
50461-50461	OSAGE
50464-50464	PLYMOUTH
50465-50465	RAKE
50466-50466	RICEVILLE
50467-50467	ROCK FALLS
50468-50468	ROCKFORD
50469-50469	ROCKWELL
50470-50470	ROWAN
50471-50471	RUDD
50472-50472	SAINT ANSGAR
50473-50473	SCARVILLE
50475-50475	SHEFFIELD
50476-50476	STACYVILLE
50477-50477	SWALEDALE
50478-50478	THOMPSON
50479-50479	THORNTON
50480-50480	TITONKA
50481-50481	TOETERVILLE
50482-50482	VENTURA
50483-50483	WESLEY
50484-50484	WODEN
50501-50501	FORT DODGE
50510-50510	ALBERT CITY
50511-50511	ALGONA
50514-50514	ARMSTRONG
50515-50515	AYRSHIRE
50516-50516	BADGER
50517-50517	BANCROFT
50518-50518	BARNUM
50519-50519	BODE
50520-50520	BRADGATE
50521-50521	BURNSIDE
50522-50522	BURT
50523-50523	CALLENDER
50524-50524	CLARE

ZIP Range	City	ZIP Range	City	ZIP Range	City	ZIP Range	City
50525-50526	CLARION	50625-50625	DUMONT	50861-50861	SHANNON CITY	51249-51249	SIBLEY
50527-50527	CURLEW	50626-50626	DUNKERTON	50862-50862	SHARPSBURG	51250-51250	SIOUX CENTER
50528-50528	CYLINDER	50627-50627	ELDORA	50863-50863	TINGLEY	51301-51301	SPENCER
50529-50529	DAKOTA CITY	50628-50628	ELMA	50864-50864	VILLISCA	51330-51330	ALLENDORF
50530-50530	DAYTON	50629-50629	FAIRBANK	50936-50981	DES MOINES	51331-51331	ARNOLDS PARK
50531-50531	DOLLIVER	50630-50630	FREDERICKSBURG	51001-51001	AKRON	51333-51333	DICKENS
50532-50532	DUNCOMBE	50631-50631	FREDERIKA	51002-51002	ALTA	51334-51334	ESTHERVILLE
50533-50533	EAGLE GROVE	50632-50632	GARWIN	51003-51003	ALTON	51338-51338	EVERLY
50535-50535	EARLY	50633-50633	GENEVA	51004-51004	ANTHON	51340-51340	FOSTORIA
50536-50536	EMMETSBURG	50634-50634	GILBERTVILLE	51005-51005	AURELIA	51341-51341	GILLETT GROVE
50538-50538	FARNHAMVILLE	50635-50635	GLADBROOK	51006-51006	BATTLE CREEK	51342-51342	GRAETTINGER
50539-50539	FENTON	50636-50636	GREENE	51007-51007	BRONSON	51343-51343	GREENVILLE
50540-50540	FONDA	50637-50637	GREEN MOUNTAIN	51008-51008	BRUNSVILLE	51344-51344	GRUVER
50541-50541	GILMORE CITY	50638-50638	GRUNDY CENTER	51009-51009	CALUMET	51345-51345	HARRIS
50542-50542	GOLDFIELD	50640-50640	HANSELL	51010-51010	CASTANA	51346-51346	HARTLEY
50543-50543	GOWRIE	50641-50641	HAZLETON	51011-51011	CHATSWORTH	51347-51347	LAKE PARK
50544-50544	HARCOURT	50642-50642	HOLLAND	51012-51012	CHEROKEE	51349-51349	MAY CITY
50545-50545	HARDY	50643-50643	HUDSON	51014-51014	CLEGHORN	51350-51350	MELVIN
50546-50546	HAVELOCK	50644-50644	INDEPENDENCE	51015-51015	CLIMBING HILL	51351-51351	MILFORD
50548-50548	HUMBOLDT	50645-50645	IONIA	51016-51016	CORRECTIONVILLE	51354-51354	OCHEYEDAN
50551-50551	JOLLEY	50647-50647	JANESVILLE	51017-51017	CRAIG	51355-51355	OKOBOJI
50552-50552	KNIERIM	50648-50648	JESUP	51018-51018	CUSHING	51357-51357	ROYAL
50553-50553	FONDA	50649-50649	KESLEY	51019-51019	DANBURY	51358-51358	RUTHVEN
50554-50554	LAURENS	50650-50650	LAMONT	51020-51020	GALVA	51360-51360	SPIRIT LAKE
50556-50556	LEDYARD	50651-50651	LA PORTE CITY	51022-51022	GRANVILLE	51363-51363	SUPERIOR
50557-50557	LEHIGH	50652-50652	LINCOLN	51023-51023	HAWARDEN	51364-51364	TERRIL
50558-50558	LIVERMORE	50653-50653	MARBLE ROCK	51024-51024	HINTON	51365-51365	WALLINGFORD
50559-50559	LONE ROCK	50654-50654	MASONVILLE	51025-51025	HOLSTEIN	51366-51366	WEBB
50560-50560	LU VERNE	50655-50655	MAYNARD	51026-51026	HORNICK	51401-51401	CARROLL
50561-50561	LYTTON	50657-50657	MORRISON	51027-51027	IRETON	51430-51430	ARCADIA
50562-50562	MALLARD	50658-50658	NASHUA	51028-51028	KINGSLEY	51431-51431	ARTHUR
50563-50563	MANSON	50659-50659	NEW HAMPTON	51029-51029	LARRABEE	51432-51432	ASPINWALL
50565-50565	MARATHON	50660-50660	NEW HARTFORD	51030-51030	LAWTON	51433-51433	AUBURN
50566-50566	MOORLAND	50661-50661	NORTH WASHINGTON	51031-51031	LE MARS	51436-51436	BREDA
50567-50567	NEMAHA	50662-50662	OELWEIN	51033-51033	LINN GROVE	51437-51437	CARNARVON
50568-50568	NEWELL	50664-50664	ORAN	51034-51034	MAPLETON	51439-51439	CHARTER OAK
50569-50569	OTHO	50665-50665	PARKERSBURG	51035-51035	MARCUS	51440-51440	DEDHAM
50570-50570	OTTOSEN	50666-50666	PLAINFIELD	51036-51036	MAURICE	51441-51441	DELOIT
50571-50571	PALMER	50667-50667	RAYMOND	51037-51037	MERIDEN	51442-51442	DENISON
50573-50573	PLOVER	50668-50668	READLYN	51038-51038	MERRILL	51443-51443	GLIDDEN
50574-50574	POCAHONTAS	50669-50669	REINBECK	51039-51039	MOVILLE	51444-51444	HALBUR
50575-50575	POMEROY	50670-50670	SHELL ROCK	51040-51040	ONAWA	51445-51445	IDA GROVE
50576-50576	REMBRANDT	50671-50671	STANLEY	51041-51041	ORANGE CITY	51446-51446	IRWIN
50577-50577	RENWICK	50672-50672	STEAMBOAT ROCK	51044-51044	OTO	51447-51447	KIRKMAN
50578-50578	RINGSTED	50673-50673	STOUT	51045-51045	OYENS	51448-51448	KIRON
50579-50579	ROCKWELL CITY	50674-50674	SUMNER	51046-51046	PAULLINA	51449-51449	LAKE CITY
50580-50580	RODMAN	50675-50675	TRAER	51047-51047	PETERSON	51450-51450	LAKE VIEW
50581-50581	ROLFE	50676-50676	TRIPOLI	51048-51048	PIERSON	51451-51451	LANESBORO
50582-50582	RUTLAND	50677-50677	WAVERLY	51049-51049	QUIMBY	51452-51452	LIDDERDALE
50583-50583	SAC CITY	50680-50680	WELLSBURG	51050-51050	REMSEN	51453-51453	LOHRVILLE
50585-50585	SIOUX RAPIDS	50681-50681	WESTGATE	51051-51051	RODNEY	51454-51454	MANILLA
50586-50586	SOMERS	50682-50682	WINTHROP	51052-51052	SALIX	51455-51455	MANNING
50587-50587	RINARD	50700-50706	WATERLOO	51053-51053	SCHALLER	51458-51458	ODEBOLT
50588-50588	STORM LAKE	50707-50707	EVANSDALE	51054-51054	SERGEANT BLUFF	51459-51459	RALSTON
50590-50590	SWEA CITY	50799-50799	WATERLOO	51055-51055	SLOAN	51460-51460	RICKETTS
50591-50591	THOR	50801-50801	CRESTON	51056-51056	SMITHLAND	51461-51461	SCHLESWIG
50592-50592	TRUESDALE	50830-50830	AFTON	51057-51057	STRUBLE	51462-51462	SCRANTON
50593-50593	VARINA	50831-50831	ARISPE	51058-51058	SUTHERLAND	51463-51463	TEMPLETON
50594-50594	VINCENT	50833-50833	BEDFORD	51059-51059	TURIN	51465-51465	VAIL
50595-50595	WEBSTER CITY	50835-50835	BENTON	51060-51060	UTE	51466-51466	WALL LAKE
50597-50597	WEST BEND	50836-50836	BLOCKTON	51061-51061	WASHTA	51467-51467	WESTSIDE
50598-50598	WHITTEMORE	50837-50837	BRIDGEWATER	51062-51062	WESTFIELD	51501-51503	COUNCIL BLUFFS
50599-50599	WOOLSTOCK	50839-50839	CARBON	51063-51063	WHITING	51510-51510	CARTER LAKE
50601-50601	ACKLEY	50840-50840	CLEARFIELD	51100-51111	SIOUX CITY	51519-51519	AT AND T
50602-50602	ALLISON	50841-50841	CORNING	51201-51201	SHELDON	51520-51520	ARION
50603-50603	ALTA VISTA	50842-50842	CROMWELL	51230-51230	ALVORD	51521-51521	AVOCA
50604-50604	APLINGTON	50843-50843	CUMBERLAND	51231-51231	ARCHER	51523-51523	BLENCOE
50605-50605	AREDALE	50844-50844	DELPHOS	51232-51232	ASHTON	51525-51525	CARSON
50606-50606	ARLINGTON	50845-50845	DIAGONAL	51234-51234	BOYDEN	51526-51526	CRESCENT
50607-50607	AURORA	50846-50846	FONTANELLE	51235-51235	DOON	51527-51527	DEFIANCE
50608-50608	AUSTINVILLE	50847-50847	GRANT	51237-51237	GEORGE	51528-51528	DOW CITY
50609-50609	BEAMAN	50848-50848	GRAVITY	51238-51238	HOSPERS	51529-51529	DUNLAP
50611-50611	BRISTOW	50849-50849	GREENFIELD	51239-51239	HULL	51530-51530	EARLING
50612-50612	BUCKINGHAM	50850-50850	KENT	51240-51240	INWOOD	51531-51531	ELK HORN
50613-50614	CEDAR FALLS	50851-50851	LENOX	51241-51241	LARCHWOOD	51532-51532	ELLIOTT
50616-50616	CHARLES CITY	50852-50852	MALOY	51242-51242	LESTER	51533-51533	EMERSON
50619-50619	CLARKSVILLE	50853-50853	MASSENA	51243-51243	LITTLE ROCK	51534-51534	GLENWOOD
50620-50620	COLWELL	50854-50854	MOUNT AYR	51244-51244	MATLOCK	51535-51535	GRISWOLD
50621-50621	CONRAD	50857-50857	NODAWAY	51245-51245	PRIMGHAR	51536-51536	HANCOCK
50622-50622	DENVER	50858-50858	ORIENT	51246-51246	ROCK RAPIDS	51537-51537	HARLAN
50623-50623	DEWAR	50859-50859	PRESCOTT	51247-51247	ROCK VALLEY	51540-51540	HASTINGS
50624-50624	DIKE	50860-50860	REDDING	51248-51248	SANBORN	51541-51541	HENDERSON

51542-51542 HONEY CREEK	52055-52055 LITTLEPORT	52227-52227 ELY	52501-52501 OTTUMWA
51543-51543 KIMBALLTON	52056-52056 LUXEMBURG	52228-52228 FAIRFAX	52530-52530 AGENCY
51544-51544 LEWIS	52057-52057 MANCHESTER	52229-52229 GARRISON	52531-52531 ALBIA
51545-51545 LITTLE SIOUX	52060-52060 MAQUOKETA	52230-52230 HALE	52533-52533 BATAVIA
51546-51546 LOGAN	52064-52064 MILES	52231-52231 HARPER	52534-52534 BEACON
51548-51548 MC CLELLAND	52065-52065 NEW VIENNA	52232-52232 HARTWICK	52535-52535 BIRMINGHAM
51549-51549 MACEDONIA	52066-52066 NORTH BUENA VISTA	52233-52233 HIAWATHA	52536-52536 BLAKESBURG
51550-51550 MAGNOLIA	52068-52068 PEOSTA	52235-52235 HILLS	52537-52537 BLOOMFIELD
51551-51551 MALVERN	52069-52069 PRESTON	52236-52236 HOMESTEAD	52538-52538 WEST GROVE
51552-51552 MARNE	52070-52070 SABULA	52237-52237 HOPKINTON	52540-52540 BRIGHTON
51553-51553 MINDEN	52071-52071 SAINT DONATUS	52240-52240 IOWA CITY	52542-52542 CANTRIL
51554-51554 MINEOLA	52072-52072 SAINT OLAF	52241-52241 CORALVILLE	52543-52543 CEDAR
51555-51555 MISSOURI VALLEY	52073-52073 SHERRILL	52242-52246 IOWA CITY	52544-52544 CENTERVILLE
51556-51556 MODALE	52074-52074 SPRAGUEVILLE	52247-52247 KALONA	52548-52548 CHILLICOTHE
51557-51557 MONDAMIN	52075-52075 SPRINGBROOK	52248-52248 KEOTA	52549-52549 CINCINNATI
51558-51558 MOORHEAD	52076-52076 STRAWBERRY POINT	52249-52249 KEYSTONE	52550-52550 DELTA
51559-51559 NEOLA	52077-52077 VOLGA	52250-52250 KINROSS	52551-52551 DOUDS
51560-51560 OAKLAND	52078-52078 WORTHINGTON	52251-52251 LADORA	52552-52552 DRAKESVILLE
51561-51561 PACIFIC JUNCTION	52079-52079 ZWINGLE	52252-52252 LANGWORTHY	52553-52553 EDDYVILLE
51562-51562 PANAMA	52099-52099 DUBUQUE	52253-52253 LISBON	52554-52554 ELDON
51563-51563 PERSIA	52101-52101 DECORAH	52254-52254 LOST NATION	52555-52555 EXLINE
51564-51564 PISGAH	52130-52130 ALPHA	52255-52255 LOWDEN	52556-52557 FAIRFIELD
51565-51565 PORTSMOUTH	52131-52131 BURR OAK	52257-52257 LUZERNE	52560-52560 FLORIS
51566-51566 RED OAK	52132-52132 CALMAR	52301-52301 MARENGO	52561-52561 FREMONT
51570-51570 SHELBY	52133-52133 CASTALIA	52302-52302 MARION	52562-52562 HAYESVILLE
51571-51571 SILVER CITY	52134-52134 CHESTER	52305-52305 MARTELLE	52563-52563 HEDRICK
51572-51572 SOLDIER	52135-52135 CLERMONT	52306-52306 MECHANICSVILLE	52565-52565 KEOSAUQUA
51573-51573 STANTON	52136-52136 CRESCO	52307-52307 MIDDLE AMANA	52566-52566 KIRKVILLE
51574-51574 TENNANT	52140-52140 DORCHESTER	52308-52308 MILLERSBURG	52567-52567 LIBERTYVILLE
51575-51575 TREYNOR	52141-52141 ELGIN	52309-52309 MONMOUTH	52568-52568 MARTINSBURG
51576-51576 UNDERWOOD	52142-52142 FAYETTE	52310-52310 MONTICELLO	52569-52569 MELROSE
51577-51577 WALNUT	52143-52143 FESTINA	52312-52312 MORLEY	52570-52570 MILTON
51578-51578 WESTPHALIA	52144-52144 FORT ATKINSON	52313-52313 MOUNT AUBURN	52571-52571 MORAVIA
51579-51579 WOODBINE	52146-52146 HARPERS FERRY	52314-52314 MOUNT VERNON	52572-52572 MOULTON
51591-51591 RED OAK	52147-52147 HAWKEYE	52315-52315 NEWHALL	52573-52573 MOUNT STERLING
51593-51593 HARLAN	52149-52149 HIGHLANDVILLE	52316-52316 NORTH ENGLISH	52574-52574 MYSTIC
51601-51603 SHENANDOAH	52150-52150 JACKSON JUNCTION	52317-52317 NORTH LIBERTY	52575-52575 NUMA
51630-51630 BLANCHARD	52151-52151 LANSING	52318-52318 NORWAY	52576-52576 OLLIE
51631-51631 BRADDYVILLE	52154-52154 LAWLER	52319-52319 OAKDALE	52577-52577 OSKALOOSA
51632-51632 CLARINDA	52155-52155 LIME SPRINGS	52320-52320 OLIN	52580-52580 PACKWOOD
51636-51636 COIN	52156-52156 LUANA	52321-52321 ONSLOW	52581-52581 PLANO
51637-51637 COLLEGE SPRINGS	52157-52157 MC GREGOR	52322-52322 OXFORD	52583-52583 PROMISE CITY
51638-51638 ESSEX	52158-52158 MARQUETTE	52323-52323 OXFORD JUNCTION	52584-52584 PULASKI
51639-51639 FARRAGUT	52159-52159 MONONA	52324-52324 PALO	52585-52585 RICHLAND
51640-51640 HAMBURG	52160-52160 NEW ALBIN	52325-52325 PARNELL	52586-52586 ROSE HILL
51645-51645 IMOGENE	52161-52161 OSSIAN	52326-52326 QUASQUETON	52588-52588 SELMA
51646-51646 NEW MARKET	52162-52162 POSTVILLE	52327-52327 RIVERSIDE	52590-52590 SEYMOUR
51647-51647 NORTHBORO	52163-52163 PROTIVIN	52328-52328 ROBINS	52591-52591 SIGOURNEY
51648-51648 PERCIVAL	52164-52164 RANDALIA	52329-52329 ROWLEY	52593-52593 UDELL
51649-51649 RANDOLPH	52165-52165 RIDGEWAY	52330-52330 RYAN	52594-52594 UNIONVILLE
51650-51650 RIVERTON	52166-52166 SAINT LUCAS	52331-52331 SCOTCH GROVE	52595-52595 UNIVERSITY PARK
51651-51651 SHAMBAUGH	52168-52168 SPILLVILLE	52332-52332 SHELLSBURG	52601-52601 BURLINGTON
51652-51652 SIDNEY	52169-52169 WADENA	52333-52333 SOLON	52619-52619 ARGYLE
51653-51653 TABOR	52170-52170 WATERVILLE	52334-52334 SOUTH AMANA	52620-52620 BONAPARTE
51654-51654 THURMAN	52171-52171 WAUCOMA	52335-52335 SOUTH ENGLISH	52621-52621 CRAWFORDSVILLE
51655-51655 BARTLETT	52172-52172 WAUKON	52336-52336 SPRINGVILLE	52623-52623 DANVILLE
51656-51656 YORKTOWN	52175-52175 WEST UNION	52337-52337 STANWOOD	52624-52624 DENMARK
51693-51693 SHENANDOAH	52201-52201 AINSWORTH	52338-52338 SWISHER	52625-52625 DONNELLSON
52001-52004 DUBUQUE	52202-52202 ALBURNETT	52339-52339 TAMA	52626-52626 FARMINGTON
52030-52030 ANDREW	52203-52204 AMANA	52340-52340 TIFFIN	52627-52627 FORT MADISON
52031-52031 BELLEVUE	52205-52205 ANAMOSA	52341-52341 TODDVILLE	52630-52630 HILLSBORO
52032-52032 BERNARD	52206-52206 ATKINS	52342-52342 TOLEDO	52631-52631 HOUGHTON
52033-52033 CASCADE	52207-52207 BALDWIN	52343-52343 TORONTO	52632-52632 KEOKUK
52035-52035 COLESBURG	52208-52208 BELLE PLAINE	52344-52344 TROY MILLS	52635-52635 LOCKRIDGE
52036-52036 DELAWARE	52209-52209 BLAIRSTOWN	52345-52345 URBANA	52637-52637 MEDIAPOLIS
52037-52037 DELMAR	52210-52210 BRANDON	52346-52346 VAN HORNE	52638-52638 MIDDLETOWN
52038-52038 DUNDEE	52211-52211 BROOKLYN	52347-52347 VICTOR	52639-52639 MONTROSE
52039-52039 DURANGO	52212-52212 CENTER JUNCTION	52348-52348 VINING	52640-52640 MORNING SUN
52040-52040 DYERSVILLE	52213-52213 CENTER POINT	52349-52349 VINTON	52641-52641 MOUNT PLEASANT
52041-52041 EARLVILLE	52214-52214 CENTRAL CITY	52350-52350 VIOLA	52642-52642 ROME
52042-52042 EDGEWOOD	52215-52215 CHELSEA	52351-52351 WALFORD	52644-52644 MOUNT UNION
52043-52043 ELKADER	52216-52216 CLARENCE	52352-52352 WALKER	52645-52645 NEW LONDON
52044-52044 ELKPORT	52217-52217 CLUTIER	52353-52353 WASHINGTON	52646-52646 OAKVILLE
52045-52045 EPWORTH	52218-52218 COGGON	52354-52354 WATKINS	52647-52647 OLDS
52046-52046 FARLEY	52219-52219 PRAIRIEBURG	52355-52355 WEBSTER	52648-52648 PILOT GROVE
52047-52047 FARMERSBURG	52220-52220 CONROY	52356-52356 WELLMAN	52649-52649 SALEM
52048-52048 GARBER	52221-52221 GUERNSEY	52357-52357 WEST AMANA	52650-52650 SPERRY
52049-52049 GARNAVILLO	52222-52222 DEEP RIVER	52358-52358 WEST BRANCH	52651-52651 STOCKPORT
52050-52050 GREELEY	52223-52223 DELHI	52359-52359 WEST CHESTER	52652-52652 SWEDESBURG
52052-52052 GUTTENBERG	52224-52224 DYSART	52361-52361 WILLIAMSBURG	52653-52653 WAPELLO
52053-52053 HOLY CROSS	52225-52225 ELBERON	52362-52362 WYOMING	52654-52654 WAYLAND
52054-52054 LA MOTTE	52226-52226 ELWOOD	52400-52499 CEDAR RAPIDS	52655-52655 WEST BURLINGTON

52656-52656 WEST POINT	52730-52730 CAMANCHE	52750-52750 GOOSE LAKE	52767-52767 PLEASANT VALLEY
52657-52657 SAINT PAUL	52731-52731 CHARLOTTE	52751-52751 GRAND MOUND	52768-52768 PRINCETON
52658-52658 WEVER	52732-52732 CLINTON	52752-52752 GRANDVIEW	52769-52769 STOCKTON
52659-52659 WINFIELD	52734-52734 A C NIELSEN CO	52753-52753 LE CLAIRE	52771-52771 TEEDS GROVE
52660-52660 YARMOUTH	52736-52736 CLINTON	52754-52754 LETTS	52772-52772 TIPTON
52701-52701 ANDOVER	52737-52737 COLUMBUS CITY	52755-52755 LONE TREE	52773-52773 WALCOTT
52720-52720 ATALISSA	52738-52738 COLUMBUS JUNCTION	52756-52756 LONG GROVE	52774-52774 WELTON
52721-52721 BENNETT	52739-52739 CONESVILLE	52757-52757 LOW MOOR	52776-52776 WEST LIBERTY
52722-52722 BETTENDORF	52742-52742 DE WITT	52758-52758 MC CAUSLAND	52777-52777 WHEATLAND
52725-52725 BIG ROCK	52745-52745 DIXON	52759-52759 MONTPELIER	52778-52778 WILTON
52726-52726 BLUE GRASS	52746-52746 DONAHUE	52760-52760 MOSCOW	52800-52809 DAVENPORT
52727-52727 BRYANT	52747-52747 DURANT	52761-52761 MUSCATINE	
52728-52728 BUFFALO	52748-52748 ELDRIDGE	52765-52765 NEW LIBERTY	
52729-52729 CALAMUS	52749-52749 FRUITLAND	52766-52766 NICHOLS	

Kansas

General Help Numbers:

Governor's Office
State Capitol Bldg, Room 212S   785-296-3232
Topeka, KS 66612-1590   Fax 785-296-7973
www.accesskansas.org/governor/   8AM-5PM

Attorney General's Office
Memorial Hall   785-296-2215
120 SW 10th Ave, 2nd Floor   Fax 785-296-6296
Topeka, KS 66612-1597   8AM-5PM
www.ink.org/public/ksag

State Court Administrator
Kansas Judicial Center, 301 SW 10th St   785-296-4873
Topeka, KS 66612-1507   Fax 785-296-7076
www.kscourts.org   8AM-5PM

State Archives
Library and Archives Division   785-272-8681
6425 SW 6th Ave   Fax 785-272-8682
Topeka, KS 66615-1099   9AM-4:30PM M-SA
http://hs4.kshs.org

State Specifics:

Capital: Topeka
Shawnee County

Time Zone: CST*
* Kansas' five western-most counties are MST:
They are: Greeley, Hamilton, Kearny, Sherman, Wallace,

Number of Counties: 105

Population: 2,694,641

Web Site: www.accesskansas.org

State Agencies

Criminal Records

Kansas Bureau of Investigation, Criminal Records Division, 1620 SW Tyler, Crim. History Record Sec., Topeka, KS 66612-1837; 785-296-8200, 785-296-6781 (Fax), 8AM-5PM.

www.kbi.state.ks.us

Note: Sex offender data is available online at https://www.accesskansas.org/apps/kbi.search. Contains infomrmation from 4/14/1994 forward.

Indexing & Storage: It takes up to 4 days before new records are available for inquiry. Records are indexed on Kansas Central Repository database, which is synchronized with the automated fingerprint ID system db. 46% of all arrests in database have final dispositions recorded, 57% for those arrests within last 5 years.

Searching: Non-criminal justice agencies, organizations, individuals and commercial companies are entitled to receive recorded conviction information. First time requesters must complete a user's agreement. Include the following in your request: full name, sex, race, date of birth, Social Security Number. Each request must be on a separate "Records Check Request Form." Fingerprints are optional. Approximately 85% of records are fingerprint supported. Turnaround time may be several weeks if the record is not currently automated; approximately 46% of records are automated. The following data is not released: expunged records, non-convictions or juvenile records except to Criminal justice agencies and agencies required by law. Arrests with no convictions over 12 months old are not shown; are shown if arrest is less than 12 months old.

Access by: mail, fax.

Fee & Payment: Fees: $10.00 for a name check; $17.00 for fingerprint search. All requests are allowed one additional alias name per person. However, add $5.00 per third and each additional alias name. Fee payee: KBI Records Fees Fund.

Prepayment required. Personal checks accepted. No credit cards accepted.

Mail search: Turnaround time: 2 to 4 weeks. A self addressed stamped envelope is requested.

Fax search: Prior arrangement is required, same criteria as mail.

Other access: Currently constructing web site that allows record checks with credit card payment system.

Corporation Records
Limited Partnerships
Limited Liability Company Records

Secretary of State, Memorial Hall, 120 SW 10th Ave, 1st Floor, Topeka, KS 66612-1594; 785-296-4564, 785-296-4570 (Fax), 8AM-5PM.

www.kssos.org/corpwelc.html

Indexing & Storage: Records are available since the applicable laws have been in effect. All Annual Reports before 1995 are at the Historical Society. New records are available for inquiry immediately. Records are indexed on inhouse computer.

Searching: Items not released include confidential annual report balance sheets and copies of extensions. Include the following in your request: full name of business, specific records that you need copies of. In addition to the articles of incorporation, corporation records include the following information: Annual Reports, Officers, Directors and Prior (merged) names. They do not keep Inactive or Reserved names.

Access by: mail, phone, fax, in person, online.

Fee & Payment: There is no search fee. Copies are $1.00 per page. A certificate of good standing is $7.50, a letter of status is $5.00. Fee payee: Secretary of State. Prepayment required. When requesting by mail, send check for $5.00 or $10.00. They will refund any excess. Prepaid accounts are available. Personal checks accepted. Credit cards accepted: MasterCard, Visa.

Mail search: Turnaround time: 2 to 3 days. No self addressed stamped envelope is required.

Phone search: General information is given without charge.

Fax search: Items can be returned by fax for an additional $2.00 for the first page and $1.00 each additional page.

In person search: No fee for request. Turnaround time 10 minutes.

Online search: Corporate data can be ordered from the AcessKansas, a state sponsored interface at www.accesskansas.org/corporations. You must have a subscription that entails a $60.00 annual fee. There is no fee to search or view records, but there is a fee to order copies of certificates or good standings. Search by individual or company name, key word, date, or organizational number.

Trademarks/Servicemarks

Secretary of State, Trademarks/Servicemarks Division, 120 SW 10th Ave, Rm 100, Topeka, KS 66612-1240; 785-296-4564, 785-296-4570 (Fax), 8AM-5PM.

www.kssos.org

Indexing & Storage: Records are available from the 1950s, all on computer. It takes 2 to 3 days before new records are available for inquiry.

Searching: All information recorded is available to the public. However, Kansas law prohibits the use of names and/or addresses derived from public record for solicitation purposes. Include the following in your request: trademark/servicemark name, name of owner. The search provides the names and addresses of owners, date of filing, and class code of filing.

Access by: mail, phone, fax, in person.

Fee & Payment: There is no search fee. Copies are $1.00 per page. Certification is $7.50 plus the copy fees. Fee payee: Secretary of State. Prepayment required. The Secretary of State's office offers prepaid accounts for all regular, ongoing requesters. Personal checks accepted. Credit cards accepted: MasterCard, Visa.

Mail search: Turnaround time: 1 to 2 days. A mail request must include the name of trademark/servicemark and/or the owner's name. No self addressed stamped envelope is required. No fee for mail request.

Phone search: No fee for telephone request. They will give you limited information from the computer index.

Fax search: Turnaround time 24 hours.

In person search: No fee for request. If you call ahead of time, they will have information ready when you come in.

Other access: For bulk file purchase, there is a $20-75 program set-up fee, plus $1.00 per page. Files are also available on CD for $40 and $20 program set-up fee.

Uniform Commercial Code
Federal Tax Liens
State Tax Liens

UCC Division, Secretary of State, Memorial Hall, 120 SW 10th Ave, Topeka, KS 66612; 785-296-1849, 785-296-3659 (Fax), 8AM-5PM.

www.kssos.org/uccwelc.html

Indexing & Storage: Records are available from 1966 on computer, from 1966 to present on microfiche with exception of electronic filings.

Searching: Use search request form UCC-3. The search includes federal tax liens on businesses. Federal tax liens on individuals can be filed here or at county, all state tax liens are filed at the county level. Include the following in your request: debtor name. You must order copies to receive collateral information. No collateral data is given over the phone.

Access by: mail, phone, fax, in person, online.

Fee & Payment: The search fee is $15.00 per name if written, $8.00 for electronic searches, and copies are $1.00 per page. Fee payee: Secretary of State. Prepayment required. Personal checks accepted. Credit cards accepted: MasterCard, Visa.

Mail search: Turnaround time: 1 day. A self addressed stamped envelope is requested. Search costs $8.00 per debtor name.

Phone search: Search costs $15.00 per debtor name.

Fax search: Same criteria as mail searching. You can have information returned by fax for an additional $2.00 for the first page and $1.00 each additional page.

In person search: Search costs $8.00 per debtor name. Copies cost $1.00 per page.

Online search: Online service is provided by AccessKaansas. The system is open 24 hours daily. There is an annual fee. Network charges are $.10 a minute unless access is through their Internet site at www.accesskansas.org which has no network fee. UCC records are $8.00 per record. This is the same online system used for corporation records. For more information, call at 800-4-KANSAS.

Other access: Access Kansas also provides records in a bulk or database format.

Sales Tax Registrations
Access to Records is Restricted

Kansas Department of Revenue, Customer Relations, 3rd Floor, Docking State Office Bldg, 915 SW Harrison, Topeka, KS 66612-1588; 785-368-8222, 785-291-3614 (Fax), 7AM-5PM.

www.ksrevenue.org/

Note: Sales tax registration information is considered confidential and not public record.

Birth Certificates

Kansas Department of Health & Environment, Office of Vital Statistics, 1000 SW Jackson, #120, Topeka, KS 66612-2221; 785-296-1400, 785-296-3253 (Credit Card Orders), 785-357-4332 (Fax), 8AM-5PM.

www.kdhe.state.ks.us/vital

Note: Vital records are not considered public records in Kansas.

Indexing & Storage: Records are available from July 1911 to present. Delayed birth registrations from the mid-1800s are available. Records are indexed on microfiche, index cards, inhouse computer.

Searching: Must have a signed release from person of record or have direct interest for personal or property right. Include the following in your request: full name, names of parents, mother's maiden name, date of birth, place of birth, relationship to person of record, reason for information request. Include a daytime phone number.

Access by: mail, phone, fax, in person.

Fee & Payment: The fee is $11.00 for first certified copy; add $6.00 for each additional copy of same record. Fee payee: Vital Statistics. Prepayment required. There is an additional $8.00 VitalChek fee with the use of a credit card. Personal checks accepted. Credit cards accepted: MasterCard, Visa, AmEx, Discover.

Mail search: Turnaround time: 2 to 3 weeks. Include copy of personal ID. A self addressed stamped envelope is requested.

Phone search: You must use a credit card for an additional $8.00 fee. Turnaround time is within 3 business days. Phone service hours are from 8am to 4pm.

Fax search: The fee must include $8.00 for use of a credit card. Turnaround time is within 3 business days.

In person search: You must complete an application and provide ID. Turnaround time: 20 to 30 minutes.

Expedited service: Expedited service is available for credit card searches. Turnaround time: overnight delivery. Overnight mail services for return of documents is available for an additional fee. Requests may require up to 24 business hours to process. Use of credit card required.

Death Records

Kansas State Department of Health & Environment, Office of Vital Statistics, 1000 SW Jackson, #120, Topeka, KS 66612-2221; 785-296-1400, 785-296-3253 (Credit Card Orders), 785-357-4332 (Fax), 8AM-5PM.

www.kdhe.state.ks.us/vital

Note: Vital records are not considered public records in Kansas.

Indexing & Storage: Records are available from July 1, 1911 to present. New records are available for inquiry immediately. Records are indexed on microfiche, index cards, inhouse computer.

Searching: Must have a signed release from immediate family member or show direct interest for personal or property right. Include the following in your request: full name, date of death, place of death, relationship to person of record, reason for information request. Please include a daytime phone number.

Access by: mail, phone, fax, in person.

Fee & Payment: The search fee is $12.00 for 1 certified copy; add $7.00 per copy requested at the same time. The search fee covers five years, if year not known. Fee payee: Vital Statistics. Prepayment required. Money orders are accepted. There is a $8.00 VitalChek fee for the use of a credit card. Personal checks accepted. Credit cards accepted: MasterCard, Visa, AmEx, Discover.

Mail search: Turnaround time: 3 to 5 days. Must include a personal ID. A self addressed stamped envelope is requested.

Phone search: Use a credit card required for an additional $8.00 fee. Turnaround time is within 3 business days.

Fax search: Same criteria as phone searches.

In person search: Must complete an application and provide personal ID. Turnaround time: 20 to 30 minutes.

Expedited service: Expedited service is available for credit card requests. Overnight service is available for an additional fee. Use of credit card required.

Marriage Certificates

Kansas State Department of Health & Environment, Office of Vital Statistics, 1000 SW Jackson, #120, Topeka, KS 66612-2221; 785-296-1400, 785-296-3253 (Credit Card Orders), 785-357-4332 (Fax), 8AM-5PM.

www.kdhe.state.ks.us/vital

Note: Vital records are not considered public records in Kansas.

Indexing & Storage: Records are available from May 1, 1913 to present. Records prior to 1913 are found at county of issue. Records are computerized from 1993. Records are indexed on microfiche, index cards, inhouse computer.

Searching: Must have a signed release from person of record or have direct interest in personal or property right. Include the following in your request: names of husband and wife, date of marriage, place or county of marriage, relationship to person of record, reason for information request, wife's maiden name. Include a daytime phone number.

Access by: mail, phone, fax, in person.

Fee & Payment: The search fee is $11.00 for 1 certified copy; add $6.00 per name for add'l copy. Fee payee: Vital Statistics. Prepayment required. Money orders are accepted. Personal checks accepted. Credit cards accepted: MasterCard, Visa, AmEx, Discover.

Mail search: Turnaround time: 3 to 5 days. Must include a personal ID number. A self addressed stamped envelope is requested.

Phone search: You must use a credit card for an additional $8.00 fee. Turnaround time is within 3 business days.

Fax search: Same criteria as phone searches.

In person search: Turnaround time 20 to 30 minutes.

Expedited service: Expedited service is available for credit card requests. Overnight mail service is available for an additional fee. Overnight requests may require up to 24 business hours to process. Use of credit card required.

Divorce Records

Kansas State Department of Health & Environment, Office of Vital Statistics, 1000 SW Jackson, #120, Topeka, KS 66612-2221; 785-296-1400, 785-296-3253 (Credit Card Orders), 785-357-4332 (Fax), 8AM-5PM.

www.kdhe.state.ks.us/vital

Note: The agency will issue a divorce certificate, but a copy of the decree must be ordered from the county of issue.

Indexing & Storage: Records are available from July 1, 1951 to present. Records prior to July 1, 1951 are found at county of issue. New records are available for inquiry immediately. Records are indexed on microfiche, index cards, inhouse computer.

Searching: Must have a signed release from person of record or show direct interest in personal or property right. Include the following in your request: names of husband and wife, date of divorce, relationship to person of record, reason for information request.

Access by: mail, phone, fax, in person.

Fee & Payment: The search fee is $11.00 for 1 certified copy; add $6.00 per additional copy. Fee payee: Vital Statistics. Prepayment required. Money orders are accepted. Personal checks accepted. Credit cards accepted: MasterCard, Visa, AmEx, Discover.

Mail search: Turnaround time: 3 to 5 days. A self addressed stamped envelope is requested.

Phone search: Must use a credit card for an additional $8.00 fee. Turnaround time is within 3 business days.

Fax search: Same criteria as phone searches.

In person search: Turnaround time is 20-30 minutes.

Expedited service: Expedited service is available for credit card requests. Overnight mail service is available for an additional fee and may require up to 24 business hours to process. Use of credit card required.

Workers' Compensation Records

Human Resources Department, Workers Compensation Division, 800 SW Jackson, Suite 600, Topeka, KS 66612-1227; 785-296-6762, 785-296-3430 (Fax), 8AM-5PM.

www.hr.state.ks.us/wc/html/wc.htm

Indexing & Storage: Records are available from the mid-1970's on. New records are available for inquiry immediately. Records are indexed on inhouse computer, file folders.

Searching: Information not released includes financial information submitted by employer, peer review records, and records related to safety inspections. Medical records are only released to those authorized by law, and are not open to the general public. Include the following in your request: claimant name, Social Security Number. All requests must be on Division Forms. Employers may receive medical records if a job has been conditionally offered and there is a signed release by the subject.

Access by: mail, phone, fax, in person.

Fee & Payment: There is no search fee.

Mail search: Turnaround time: 1 week to 10 days. No self addressed stamped envelope is required.

Phone search: Some records are available for verification by phone.

Fax search: Fax searching available.

In person search: Requests maintained off premises will take 2 days to obtain.

Driver Records
Accident Reports

Department of Revenue, Driver Control Bureau, PO Box 12021, Topeka, KS 66612-2021 (Courier: Docking State Office Building, 915 Harrison, Rm 100, Topeka, KS 66612); 785-296-3671, 785-296-6851 (Fax), 8AM-4:45PM.

www.ksrevenue.org/dmv/driverinfo.html

Indexing & Storage: Records are available for 3 years for minor violations and 5 years for DWIs. The state does not record speeding violations of 10 mph or less over in a 70 speed zone or 5 mph or less in all other speed zones. It takes 2 to 21 days before new records are available for inquiry.

Searching: Permissible use requesters should use Form TR/DL 302. Casual requesters must secure written consent from subject before any records are released. The driver license number and either full name or DOB are required when ordering a driving record. The driver's address will show on the record. For an accident report, include the full name, DOB and/or VIN number, and date of accident. The following data is not released: medical information.

Access by: mail, in person, online.

Fee & Payment: The fee is $5.00 for a walk-in or mail-in request for a driving record. An accident report is available for $5.00 per page. Fee payee:

Department of Revenue. Prepayment required. Personal checks accepted. No credit cards accepted.

Mail search: Turnaround time: 2 to 5 days. A self addressed stamped envelope is requested.

In person search: Walk-in requests are usually processed within 30 minutes. Local law enforcement agencies may also honor driving record requests at a higher cost.

Online search: Kansas has contracted with the AccessKansas (800-452-6727) to service all electronic media requests of driver license histories. They offer connection through an "800 number" or can be reached via the Internet at www.accesskansas.org. The fee per record is $4.00 for batch requests or $4.50 if single inquiry. There is an initial $75 subscription fee and an annual $60 fee. The system is open 24 hours a day, 7 days a week. Batch requests are available at 7:30 am (if ordered by 10 pm the previous day).

Other access: Tape-to-tape request records are available on an overnight basis through AccessKansas.

Vehicle Ownership
Vehicle Identification

Division of Vehicles, Title and Registration Bureau, 915 Harrison, Rm 155, Topeka, KS 66612; 785-296-3621, 785-296-3852 (Fax), 8AM-4:45PM.

www.ksrevenue.org/dmv

Indexing & Storage: Records are available from approximately 1940. Older records are on microfilm, on microfiche from 1970-1987, and computerized since 1988.

Searching: Casual requesters can obtain records, no personal information is released without consent. Records are restricted from purchase for the purpose of obtaining address mail lists for selling property or services. Mail and walk-in search requesters are asked to use Form TR/DL 302.

Access by: mail, in person, online.

Fee & Payment: The fee for a title/registration verification depends on the request mode, noted as below. Fee payee: Kansas Department of Revenue. Prepayment required. Personal checks accepted. No credit cards accepted.

Mail search: Turnaround time: 2 days. The fee for a title or registration verification is $5.00 ($3.50, if your own record). The fee for a title application copy of a vehicle title history is $10.00. A self addressed stamped envelope is requested.

In person search: Inquires are processed while you wait; however, requests must be in writing. Same fees as by mail.

Online search: Online batch inquires are $3.00 per record; online interactive requests are $4.00 per record. Visit www.accesskansas.org for a complete description of the AccessKansas (800-452-6727), the state authorized vendor. There is an initial $75 subscription fee and an annual $60 fee.

Other access: The state has several programs available to sell data in bulk format. Contact Donnita Thoma at the Dept of Revenue's Bureau of Policy and Research.

Vessel Ownership
Vessel Registration

Kansas Wildlife & Parks Department, Boat Registration, 512 SE 25th Ave, Pratt, KS 67124-8174; 620-672-5911, 620-672-3013 (Fax), 8AM-5PM M-F.

www.kdwp.state.ks.us

Note: Liens must be searched at the county level.

Indexing & Storage: Records are available from 1967 to present. Records are indexed on computer. Titles are not required. All motorized or sailboats must be registered.

Searching: All requests must be submitted in writing with specific reason given for the request. No information is released for solicitation purposes. To search, either the hull ID or name is required.

Access by: mail, fax, in person.

Fee & Payment: There is no search fee, unless extensive searching is requested.

Mail search: Turnaround time: 1-3 days. No self addressed stamped envelope is required.

Fax search: Same criteria as mail searching.

In person search: Searching is available in person.

Legislation Records

Kansas State Library, Capitol Bldg, 300 SW 10th Ave, Topeka, KS 66612; 785-296-2149, 785-296-6650 (Fax), 8AM-5PM.

www.ink.org

Note: A second URL is http://skways.lib.ks.us/ksl

Indexing & Storage: Records are available from 1908 to present. Records are on computer since 1991.

Searching: Include either bill number or bill topic.

Access by: mail, phone, fax, in person, online.

Fee & Payment: First 20 pages are free for all searches. Copies are $.10 a page. Fee payee: Kansas State Library. Personal checks accepted. No credit cards accepted.

Mail search: Turnaround time: 1 to 2 days. No self addressed stamped envelope is required. No fee for mail request.

Phone search: No fee for telephone request.

Fax search: Fax searching available.

In person search: No fee for request.

Online search: The web site has bill information for the current session. The site also contains access to the state statutes.

Voter Registration
Access to Records is Restricted

Secretary of State, Department of Elections, 120 SW 10th Street, Topeka, KS 66612; 785-296-4564, 785-291-3051 (Fax), 8AM-5PM.

www.kssos.org

Note: Individual records must be searched at the county level. This agency will sell the database on disk, CD or tape format only for political purposes.

GED Certificates

Kansas Board of Regents, GED Records, 1000 SW jackson St #520, Topeka, KS 66612-1368; 785-296-3191, 785-296-0983 (Fax).

www.kansasregents.com

Searching: Include the following in your request: Social Security Number, signed release. Also include the date of the test.

Access by: mail, fax.

Fee & Payment: There is no fee for a verification, the fee for a transcript is $5.00. Fee payee: Kansas Board of Regents. Prepayment required. Cash and money orders are accepted. No credit cards accepted.

Mail search: Turnaround time: 1 week. No self addressed stamped envelope is required.

Fax search: Same criteria as mail searching.

Fishing License Information
Records not maintained by a state level agency.

Hunting License Information

Dept of Wildlife & Parks, Operations Office, Fish & Wildlife, 512 SE 25th Ave, Pratt, KS 67124-8174; 620-672-5911, 620-672-3013 (Fax), 8AM-5PM.

www.kdwp.state.ks.us

Indexing & Storage: Records are available for 2 years. Boat statistics are available. Records are indexed on hard copy.

Searching: You can get big game information only. You must submit request in writing indicating what information you require and its intended use. Requests for information to be used for the sale of products or services will not be answered. Include the following in your request: full name, date of birth.

Access by: mail, in person.

Fee & Payment: You must have Department approval. The agency reserves the right to recover costs for voluminous requests.

Mail search: Turnaround time: 1 to 3 days. No self addressed stamped envelope is required.

In person search: You may request information in person.

Kansas State Licensing Agencies

Licenses Searchable Online

Alcohol/Drug Counselor #3	www.ksbsrb.org/verification.html
Architect #14	www.state.ks.us/public/ksbtp/roster.html
Athletic Trainer #10	www.docboard.org/ks/df/kssearch.htm
Chiropractor #10	www.docboard.org/ks/df/kssearch.htm
Counselor, Professional #3	www.ksbsrb.org/verification.html
Dental Hygienist #19	www.accesskansas.org/cgi-bin/dental/verification/index.cgi
Dentist/Dental Hygienist #19	www.accesskansas.org/cgi-bin/dental/verification/index.cgi
Engineer #14	www.state.ks.us/public/ksbtp/roster.html
Funeral Establishment #11	www.accesskansas.org/ksbma/listings.html
Geologist #14	www.state.ks.us/public/ksbtp/roster.html
Insurance Company #22	www.ksinsurance.org/company/main.html
Landscape Architect #14	www.state.ks.us/public/ksbtp/roster.html
Lobbyist #27	www.kssos.org/election/Lobbyist/lbSearch.asp
Marriage & Family Therapist #3	www.ksbsrb.org/verification.html
Medical Doctor #10	www.docboard.org/ks/df/kssearch.htm
Mortician #11	www.accesskansas.org/ksbma/listings.html
Occupational Therapist/Assistant #10	www.docboard.org/ks/df/kssearch.htm
Optometrist #26	www.odfinder.org/LicSearch.asp
Osteopathic Physician #10	www.docboard.org/ks/df/kssearch.htm
Physical Therapist/Assistant #10	www.docboard.org/ks/df/kssearch.htm
Physician Assistant #10	www.docboard.org/ks/df/kssearch.htm
Podiatrist #10	www.docboard.org/ks/df/kssearch.htm
Psychologist #3	www.ksbsrb.org/verification.html
Public Accountant-CPA #4	www.ink.org/public/ksboa
Real Estate Appraiser #28	www.ink.org/public/kreab/appraisdir.html
Respiratory Therapist #10	www.docboard.org/ks/df/kssearch.htm
Social Worker #3	www.ksbsrb.org/verification.html
Surveyor, Land #14	www.state.ks.us/public/ksbtp/roster.html

Licensing Quick Finder

Abstractor #1	316-544-2311
Adult Care Home Administrator #16	785-296-0061
Alcohol Vendor License #20	785-296-7015
Alcohol/Drug Counselor #3	785-296-3240
Ambulance Attendant #8	785-296-7299
Ambulance Service #8	785-296-7299
Animal Keeper #2	785-296-2326
Architect #14	785-296-3053
Athletic Trainer #10	785-296-7413
Attorney #18	785-296-8409
Audiologist #16	785-296-0061
Barber #5	785-296-2211
Body Piercer #6	785-296-3155
Child Care Attendant #30	785-296-1270
Chiropractor #10	785-296-7413
Contractor, General #21	785-296-4460
Cosmetic Facilities #6	785-296-3155
Cosmetologist #6	785-296-3155
Cosmetology School Instructor #6	785-296-3155
Counselor, Professional #3	785-296-3240
Dental Hygienist #19	785-273-0780
Dentist/Dental Hygienist #19	785-273-0780
Dietitian #16	785-296-0061
Electrologist #6	785-296-3155
Embalmer #11	785-296-3980
Emergency Medical Technician #8	785-296-7299
Engineer #14	785-296-3053
Esthetics #6	785-296-3155
Funeral Director/Assistant #11	785-296-3980
Funeral Establishment #11	785-296-3980
Geologist #14	785-296-3054
Hearing Aid Dispenser #9	620-263-0774
Home Health Aide #16	785-296-1250
Insurance Agent #22	785-296-7859
Insurance Company #22	785-296-7859
Investment Advisor #29	785-296-3307
Landscape Architect #14	785-296-3053
Livestock Brand #2	785-296-2326
Lobbyist #27	785-296-3488
Marriage & Family Therapist #3	785-296-3240
Medical Doctor #10	785-296-7413
Medication Aide #16	785-296-1250
Mortician #11	785-296-3980
Nail Technician #6	785-296-3155
Notary Public #27	785-296-2239
Nurse #12	785-296-4929
Nurses' Aide #16	785-296-1250
Nursing Home Administrator #16	785-296-0061
Occupational Therapist/Assistant #10	785-296-7413
Optometrist #26	785-832-9986
Osteopathic Physician #10	785-296-7413
Permanent Cosmetic Technician #6	785-296-3155
Pesticide Applicator #24	785-296-2263
Pesticide Dealer #24	785-296-2263
Pharmacist #13	785-296-8420
Physical Therapist/Assistant #10	785-296-7413
Physician Assistant #10	785-296-7413
Podiatrist #10	785-296-7413
Private Investigator #23	785-296-4436
Psychologist #3	785-296-3240
Public Accountant-CPA #4	785-296-2162
Racing & Wagering Equipment/Services #25	785-296-5800
Racing Concessionaire #25	785-296-5800
Racing Facility Owner/Manager #25	785-296-5800
Racing Occupation License #25	785-296-5800
Racing Organization #25	785-296-5800
Real Estate Agent/Salesperson #31	785-296-3411
Real Estate Appraiser #28	785-271-3373
Real Estate Broker #31	785-296-3411
Respiratory Therapist #10	785-296-7413
School Administrator #7	785-296-2288
School Counselor #7	785-296-2288
School Library Media Specialist #7	785-296-2288
School Nurse #7	785-296-2288
Securities Agent #29	785-296-3307
Securities Broker/Dealer #29	785-296-3307
Shorthand Reporter #17	785-296-8410
Social Worker #3	785-296-3240
Speech/Language Pathologist #16	785-296-0061
Surveyor, Land #14	785-296-3054
Tanning Facility #6	785-296-3155
Tattoo Artist #6	785-296-3155
Teacher #7	785-296-2288
Veterinarian #15	785-355-8781

Licensing Agency Information

#1 Abstracters Board of Examiners, 521 S. Main - PO Box 549, Hugoton, KS 67951-0549; 316-544-2311, Fax: 316-544-8029. Agency email: glen@pld.com.

#2 Animal Health Department, 708 S Jackson, Topeka, KS 66603-3714; 785-296-2326, Fax: 785-296-1765.

#3 Behavioral Sciences Regulatory Board, 712 S Kansas, Topeka, KS 66603; 785-296-3240, Fax: 785-296-3112.
www.ksbsrb.org. Agency email: lallen@ink.org.
Search database at
www.ksbsrb.org/verification.html

#4 Board of Accountancy, 900 SW Jackson, Topeka, KS 66612-1239; 785-296-2162.
www.ink.org/public/ksboa

#5 Board of Barbering, 700 SW Jackson #1002, Topeka, KS 66603; 785-296-2211, Fax: 785-368-7071.

#6 Board of Cosmetology, 714 SW Jackson St #100, Topeka, KS 66603-3722; 785-296-3155, Fax: 785-296-3002.
www.ink.org/public/KBOC

#7 Board of Education, 120 SE 10th Ave, Topeka, KS 66612-1182; 785-296-2288, Fax: 785-296-7933.
www.ksbe.state.ks.us/welcome.html

#8 Board of Emergency Medical Services, 109 SW 6th, Topeka, KS 66603-3826; 785-296-7299, Fax: 785-296-6212.
www.ksbems.org

#9 Board of Examiners for Hearing Aid Dispensers, 600 N St Francis, Wichita, KS 67201-0252; 620-263-0774, Fax: 620-264-2681.

#10 Board of Healing Arts, 235 S Topeka Blvd, Topeka, KS 66603-3059; 785-296-7413, Fax: 785-296-0852.
www.ksbha.org. Agency email: cabbot@ink.org.

#11 Board of Mortuary Arts, 700 SW Jackson, #904, Topeka, KS 66603-3733; 785-296-3980, Fax: 785-296-0891.
www.accesskansas.org/ksbma
Agency email: ksbma@cjnetworks.com.
Search database at
www.accesskansas.org/ksbma/listings.html

#12 Board of Nursing, 900 SW Jackson, Rm 551 S, Topeka, KS 66612-1230; 785-296-2967, Fax: 785-296-3929.
www.ksbn.org. Agency email: ksbn0@ink.org.
There is a searchable database of licenses available online for registered user of INK (Information Network of Kansas).

#13 Board of Pharmacy, 900 Jackson, Landon State Office Bldg, Rm 513, Topeka, KS 66612; 785-296-4056, Fax: 785-296-8420.

#14 Board of Technical Professions, 900 SW Jackson, Rm 507, Topeka, KS 66612-1257; 785-296-3053.
www.state.ks.us/public/ksbtp/roster.html
Search database at
www.state.ks.us/public/ksbtp/roster.html

#15 Board of Veterinary Examiners, PO Box 242 (1003 Lincoln), Wamego, KS 66547-0242; 785-456-8781, Fax: 785-456-8782.
www.ink.org/public/veterinary

#16 Department of Health & Environment, Bureau of Health Facilities, 900 SW Jackson #1051-S, Topeka, KS 66612-1290; 785-296-0056, Fax: 785-296-3075.
www.kdhe.state.ks.us/hoc/index.html

#17 Clerk of Appellate Court, 301 W 10th St, Topeka, KS 66612; 785-296-8410, Fax: 785-296-1028.
www.kscourts.org
Agency email: green@kscourts.org.

#18 Clerk of the Supreme Court, 301 SW 10th Ave, Topeka, KS 66612; 785-296-8409, Fax: 785-296-1028.
www.kscourts.org
Agency email: greenc@kscourts.org.

#19 Dental Board, 3601 SW 29th St #134, Topeka, KS 66614-2062; 785-273-0780, Fax: 785-273-7545.
www.accesskansas.org/kdb
Agency email: dental.ink.org.
Search database at www.accesskansas.org/cgi-bin/dental/verification/index.cgi

#20 Department of Revenue, Alcoholic Beverage Control, 200 SE 6th St, 4 Townsite Plaza, #210, Topeka, KS 66603-3512; 785-296-7015, Fax: 785-296-1279.
www.ink.org/public/kdor/abc
Agency email: abc_mail@kdor.state.ks.us.

#21 Department of Revenue, Robert B Docking, State Office Bldg, 915 SW Harrison St, Topeka, KS 66625-0001; 785-296-3160.
www.ink.org/public/kdor/main.html

#22 Insurance Department, 420 SW 9th, Topeka, KS 66612-1678; 785-296-7859, Fax: 785-368-7019.
www.ksinsurance.org
Search database at
www.ksinsurance.org/company/main.html

#23 Bureau of Investigation, 1620 SW Tyler, Topeka, KS 66612-1837; 785-296-8200, Fax: 785-296-6781.
www.ink.org/public/kbi
Agency email: meier@kbi.state.ks.us.

#24 Department of Agriculture, Records Ctr, 109 SW 9th St, Topeka, KS 66612; 785-296-2263, Fax: 785-296-0673.
www.ink.org/ii/?type=byserv&which=agencies

#25 Racing Commission, 3400 SW Van Buren, Topeka, KS 66611-2228; 785-296-5800, Fax: 785-296-0900.
www.ink.org/public/krc
Agency email: kracing@ynetworks.com.

#26 Board of Examiners in Optometry, 3111 W 6th #A, Lawrence, KS 66049; 785-832-9986, Fax: 785-832-9986.
www.terraworld.net/kssbeo
Agency email: kssbeo@terraworld.net.
Search database at
www.odfinder.org/LicSearch.asp

#27 Office of Secretary of State, Memorial Hall, Elections Div., 120 SW 10th Av, Topeka, KS 66612; 785-296-1848, Fax: 785-296-4570.
www.kssos.org

#28 Office of the Commissioner of Banks, Real Estate Appraisal Board, 4309 Mail Service Center (316 Edenton Rd), Topeka, KS 66604-3805; 785-271-3373, Fax: 785-271-3370.
www.ink.org/public/kreab
Agency email: kreab@cjnetworks.com.
Search database at
www.ink.org/public/kreab/appraisdir.html

#29 Securities Commissioner of Kansas, 618 S Kansas 2nd Fl, Topeka, KS 66603-3804; 785-296-3307, Fax: 785-296-6872.
www.ink.org/public/ksecom
Agency email: ksecom@cjnetworks.com.

#30 Child Care Licensing & Registration, 1000 SW Jackson #200, Topeka, KS 66612; 785-296-1240, Fax: 785-296-0803.

#31 Real Estate Commission, Licensing Board, 3 Townsite Plaza #200, 120 SE 6th, Topeka, KS 66603; 785-296-3411, Fax: 785-296-1771.
www.ink.org/public/krec/

Kansas Federal Courts

The following list indicates the district and division name for each county in the state. If the bankruptcy court location is different from the district court, then the location of the bankruptcy court appears in parentheses.

County/Court Cross Reference

County	Court		County	Court
Allen	Topeka		Linn	Kansas City
Anderson	Topeka		Logan	Wichita
Atchison	Kansas City		Lyon	Topeka
Barber	Wichita		Marion	Topeka
Barton	Wichita		Marshall	Kansas City
Bourbon	Kansas City		McPherson	Wichita
Brown	Kansas City		Meade	Wichita
Butler	Wichita		Miami	Kansas City
Chase	Topeka		Mitchell	Topeka
Chautauqua	Wichita		Montgomery	Wichita
Cherokee	Kansas City		Morris	Topeka
Cheyenne	Wichita		Morton	Wichita
Clark	Wichita		Nemaha	Kansas City
Clay	Topeka		Neosho	Topeka
Cloud	Topeka		Ness	Wichita
Coffey	Topeka		Norton	Wichita
Comanche	Kansas City (Wichita)		Osage	Topeka
Cowley	Wichita		Osborne	Wichita
Crawford	Kansas City		Ottawa	Topeka
Decatur	Wichita		Pawnee	Wichita
Dickinson	Topeka		Phillips	Wichita
Doniphan	Kansas City		Pottawatomie	Topeka
Douglas	Topeka		Pratt	Wichita
Edwards	Wichita		Rawlins	Wichita
Elk	Wichita		Reno	Wichita
Ellis	Wichita		Republic	Topeka
Ellsworth	Wichita		Rice	Wichita
Finney	Wichita		Riley	Topeka
Ford	Wichita		Rooks	Wichita
Franklin	Topeka		Rush	Wichita
Geary	Topeka		Russell	Wichita
Gove	Wichita		Saline	Topeka
Graham	Wichita		Scott	Wichita
Grant	Wichita		Sedgwick	Wichita
Gray	Wichita		Seward	Wichita
Greeley	Wichita		Shawnee	Topeka
Greenwood	Wichita		Sheridan	Wichita
Hamilton	Wichita		Sherman	Wichita
Harper	Wichita		Smith	Wichita
Harvey	Wichita		Stafford	Wichita
Haskell	Wichita		Stanton	Wichita
Hodgeman	Wichita		Stevens	Wichita
Jackson	Topeka		Sumner	Wichita
Jefferson	Wichita		Thomas	Wichita
Jewell	Topeka		Trego	Wichita
Johnson	Kansas City		Wabaunsee	Topeka
Kearny	Wichita		Wallace	Wichita
Kingman	Wichita		Washington	Topeka
Kiowa	Wichita		Wichita	Wichita
Labette	Kansas City		Wilson	Topeka
Lane	Wichita		Woodson	Topeka
Leavenworth	Kansas City		Wyandotte	Kansas City
Lincoln	Topeka			

Standards for Federal Courts: The search fee is $20.00 per item (one party name or case number). Certification fee is $7.00 per document. Copy fee is $.50 per page. All fees standard unless noted in profile. Mail Search: always enclose a stamped self addressed envelope unless otherwise noted. Before releasing records, all courts require prepayment unless noted in profile.

Open records are located at the court unless otherwise noted. District courts index by defendant and plaintiff as well as by case number. Bankruptcy courts usually index by debtor and case number. While most courts now have their indexes on computer, many still maintain index card files as well.

The universal PACER sign-up number is 800-676-6856. Find PACER and the Party/Case Index on the Web at http://pacer.psc.uscourts.gov. PACER dial-up access is $.60 per minute. Also, courts offering internet access via RACER, PACER, Web-PACER or the new CM-ECF charge $.07 per page fee unless noted as free.

US District Court

District of Kansas

Kansas City Division Clerk, 500 State Ave, Kansas City, KS 66101 (Courier Address: Use mail address for courier delivery), 913-551-6719.

www.ksd.uscourts.gov

Counties: Atchison, Bourbon, Brown, Cherokee, Crawford, Doniphan, Johnson, Labette,

Leavenworth, Linn, Marshall, Miami, Nemaha, Wyandotte.

Indexing & Storage: Cases are indexed by defendant, plaintiff, and case number. New cases are available in the index immediately after filing date. Records are also indexed on microfiche. Open records are located at this court.

Fee & Payment Notes: Payment may be made by money order, cashier check, personal check. No search fee is charged unless certification is required. All certification searches are conducted by the Wichita office. Payee: Clerk, US District Court.

Phone Search: Searching not available by phone. Only docket information will be released over the phone if you have a case number.

Mail Search: A stamped self addressed envelope is not required.

In Person Search: In person searching available.

PACER: Toll-free dial-up access: 800-898-3078. Local dial-up access: 316-269-6284. Case records are available back to 1991. Records are never purged. New civil records are available online after 2 days. New criminal records are available online after 3 days. PACER is available online at http://pacer.ksd.uscourts.gov.

Electronic Filing: (CM/ECF available late 2002)

Topeka Division Clerk, US District Court, Room 490, 444 SE Quincy, Topeka, KS 66683 (Courier Address: Use mail address for courier delivery), 785-295-2610.

www.ksd.uscourts.gov

Counties: Allen, Anderson, Chase, Clay, Cloud, Coffey, Dickinson, Douglas, Franklin, Geary, Jackson, Jewell, Lincoln, Lyon, Marion, Mitchell, Morris, Neosho, Osage, Ottawa, Pottawatomie, Republic, Riley, Saline, Shawnee, Wabaunsee, Washington, Wilson, Woodson.

Indexing & Storage: Cases are indexed by defendant, plaintiff, and case number. New cases are available in the index 24 hours after filing date. A full name, the case number and a date are very helpful to obtain records. Open records are located at this court.

Fee & Payment Notes: Payment may be made by money order, cashier check, personal check. Payee: Clerk of US District Court.

Phone Search: Docket information available by phone.

In Person Search: In person searching available.

PACER: Toll-free dial-up access: 800-898-3078. Local dial-up access: 316-269-6284. Case records are available back to 1991. Records are never purged. New civil records are available online after 2 days. New criminal records are available online after 3 days. PACER is available online at http://pacer.ksd.uscourts.gov.

Electronic Filing: (CM/ECF available late 2002)

Wichita Division 204 US Courthouse, 401 N Market, Wichita, KS 67202-2096 (Courier Address: Use mail address for courier delivery), 316-269-6491.

www.ksd.uscourts.gov

Counties: All counties in Kansas. Cases may be heard from counties in the other division.

Indexing & Storage: Cases are indexed by defendant, plaintiff, and case number. New cases are available in the index immediately after filing date. Records are indexed on the computer since

1990. Prior records are indexed on microfiche or index cards. District wide searches are available from this court.

Fee & Payment Notes: Payment may be made by money order, cashier check, personal check. Payee: Clerk, US District Court.

Phone Search: Will do computer search on one name over the phone.

In Person Search: In person searching available.

PACER: Toll-free dial-up access: 800-898-3078. Local dial-up access: 316-269-6284. Case records are available back to 1991. Records are never purged. New civil records are available online after 2 days. New criminal records are available online after 3 days. PACER is available online at http://pacer.ksd.uscourts.gov.

Electronic Filing: (CM/ECF available late 2002)

US Bankruptcy Court

District of Kansas

Kansas City Division 500 State Ave, Room 161, Kansas City, KS 66101 (Courier Address: Use mail address for courier delivery), 913-551-6732, Fax: 913-551-6715.

www.ksb.uscourts.gov

Counties: Atchison, Bourbon, Brown, Cherokee, Comanche, Crawford, Doniphan, Johnson, Labette, Leavenworth, Linn, Marshall, Miami, Nemaha, Wyandotte.

Indexing & Storage: Cases are indexed by debtor as well as by case number. New cases are available in the index 1 day after filing date. Approximate year of filing will also help in the search for files. Bankruptcy searches can be performed from any bankruptcy court in the district for case files from 1989 forward; master listing for pre-1989 cases are available from the Topeka Office. Open records are located at this court.

Fee & Payment Notes: Payment may be made by money order, cashier check, personal check. Debtor's checks are not accepted. Payee: Clerk of US Bankruptcy Court. You are allowed to make your own copies. These copies cost $.25 per page.

Phone Search: Only docket information is available by phone. An automated voice case information service (VCIS) is available. Call VCIS at 800-827-9028 or 316-269-6668.

In Person Search: In person searching available.

PACER: Toll-free dial-up access: 800-613-7052. Local dial-up access: 316-269-6258. Case records are available back to 1988. Records are purged every 6 months. New civil records are available online after 1 day. PACER is available online at http://pacer.ksb.uscourts.gov. Document images available.

Electronic Filing: (Currently in the process of implementing CM/ECF.)

Topeka Division 240 US Courthouse, 444 SE Quincy, Topeka, KS 66683 (Courier Address: Use mail address for courier delivery), 785-295-2750, Fax: 785-295-2964.

www.ksb.uscourts.gov

Counties: Allen, Anderson, Chase, Clay, Cloud, Coffey, Dickinson, Douglas, Franklin, Geary, Jackson, Jewell, Lincoln, Lyon, Marion, Mitchell, Morris, Neosho, Osage, Ottawa, Pottawatomie, Republic, Riley, Saline, Shawnee, Wabaunsee, Washington, Wilson, Woodson.

Indexing & Storage: Cases are indexed by debtor as well as by case number. New cases are available in the index 1 day after filing date. Approximate year of filing will also help in the search for files. Open records are located at this court.

Fee & Payment Notes: Payment may be made by money order, cashier check, personal check. Debtor's checks are not accepted. Payee: Clerk, US Bankruptcy Court. You are allowed to make your own copies. These copies cost $.25 per page.

Phone Search: Only docket information is available by phone. An automated voice case information service (VCIS) is available. Call VCIS at 800-827-9028 or 316-269-6668.

Mail Search: A stamped self addressed envelope is not required.

In Person Search: In person searching available.

PACER: Toll-free dial-up access: 800-613-7052. Local dial-up access: 316-269-6258. Case records are available back to 1988. Records are purged every 6 months. New civil records are available online after 1 day. PACER is available online at http://pacer.ksb.uscourts.gov. Document images available.

Electronic Filing: (Currently in the process of implementing CM/ECF.)

Wichita Division 167 US Courthouse, 401 N Market, Wichita, KS 67202 (Courier Address: Use mail address for courier delivery), 316-269-6486, Fax: 316-269-6181.

www.ksb.uscourts.gov

Counties: Barber, Barton, Butler, Chautauqua, Cheyenne, Clark, Comanche, Cowley, Decatur, Edwards, Elk, Ellis, Ellsworth, Finney, Ford, Gove, Graham, Grant, Gray, Greeley, Greenwood, Hamilton, Harper, Harvey, Haskell, Hodgeman, Jefferson, Kearny, Kingman, Kiowa,Lane, Logan, Mcpherson, Meade, Montgomery, Morton, Ness, Norton, Osborne, Pawnee, Phillips, Pratt, Rawlins, Reno, Rice, Rooks, Rush, Russell, Scott, Sedgwick, Seward, Sheridan, Smith, Stafford, Stanton, Stevens, Sumner, Thomas, Trego, Wallace, Wichita.

Indexing & Storage: Cases are indexed by debtor as well as by case number. New cases are available in the index 1 day after filing date. Records are also indexed on microfiche. District wide searches are available from this division.

Fee & Payment Notes: Payment may be made by money order, cashier check, personal check. Payee: Clerk, US Bankruptcy Court. You are allowed to make your own copies. These copies cost $.25 per page.

Phone Search: Only the attorneys, trustees, hearing dates and file dates will be released over the phone. An automated voice case information service (VCIS) is available. Call VCIS at 800-827-9028 or 316-269-6668.

Mail Search: A stamped self addressed envelope is not required.

In Person Search: In person searching available.

PACER: Toll-free dial-up access: 800-613-7052. Local dial-up access: 620-269-6258. Case records are available back to 1988. Records are purged every 6 months. New civil records are available online after 1 day. PACER is available online at http://pacer.ksb.uscourts.gov. Document images available.

Electronic Filing: (Currently in the process of implementing CM/ECF.)

Kansas County Courts

Court	Jurisdiction	No. of Courts	How Organized
District Courts*	General	109	31 Districts
Municipal Courts	Municipal	350	

* Profiled in this Sourcebook.

Court	CIVIL								
	Tort	Contract	Real Estate	Min. Claim	Max. Claim	Small Claims	Estate	Eviction	Domestic Relations
District Courts*	X	X	X	$0	No Max	$1800	X	X	
Municipal Courts									

Court	CRIMINAL				
	Felony	Misdemeanor	DWI/DUI	Preliminary Hearing	Juvenile
District Courts*	X	X	X	X	X
Municipal Courts			X		

ADMINISTRATION Judicial Administrator, Kansas Judicial Center, 301 SW 10th St, Topeka, KS, 66612; 785-296-2256, Fax: 785-296-7076. www.kscourts.org

COURT STRUCTURE The District Court is the court of general jurisdiction. There are 110 courts in 31 districts in 105 counties.

If an individual in Municipal Court wants a jury trial, the request must be filed de novo in a District Court.

ONLINE ACCESS Commercial online access is available for District Court Records in 4 counties - Johnson, Sedgwick, Shawnee, and Wyandotte - through Access Kansas, part of the Information Network of Kansas (INK) Services. Franklin and Finney counties may be available in 2003. A user may access INK at www.accesskansas.org or via a dial-up system. The INK subscription fee is $75.00, and the annual renewal fee is $60.00. There is no per minute connect charge, but there is a transaction fee. Other information from INK includes Drivers License, Title, Registration, Lien, and UCC searches. For additional information or a registration packet, call 800-4-KANSAS (800-452-6727).

The Kansas Appellate Courts offer free online access to case information at www.kscourts.org

ADDITIONAL INFORMATION Five counties - Cowley, Crawford, Labette, Montgomery, and Neosho - have two hearing locations but only one record center, which is the location included in this Sourcebook.

Many Kansas courts do not do criminal record searches and will refer any criminal requests to the Kansas Bureau of Investigation. The Kansas Legislature's Administrative Order 156 (Fall, 2000) allows Courts to charge up to $12.00 per hour for search services, though courts may set their own search fees, if any.

Allen County

District Court PO Box 630, Iola, KS 66749; 620-365-1425; Fax: 620-365-1429. Hours: 9AM-4PM (CST). *Felony, Misdemeanor, Civil, Eviction, Small Claims, Probate.*

Civil Records: Access: Phone, fax, mail, in person, email. Both court and visitors may perform in person searches. Search fee: $12.00 per hour. Required to search: name, years to search. Civil cases indexed by defendant, plaintiff. Civil records on computer from 1993, manual index from 1800s.

Criminal Records: Access: Fax, mail, in person, email. Both court and visitors may perform in person searches. Search fee: $12.00 per hour. Required to search: name, years to search. Criminal records on computer from 1993, manual index from 1800s.

General Information: Public access terminal is available. No juvenile (under the age of 15), mental health, sealed or expunged records released. Accepts requests via email, but cannot return results by email. SASE required. Turnaround time 1 week. Fax notes: Fee to fax results is $1.00 per page; $3.00 for 1st page. Copy fee: $.50 per page. Certification fee: $1.00. Fee payee: Clerk of Court. Personal checks accepted. Prepayment is required.

Anderson County

District Court PO Box 305, Garnett, KS 66032; 785-448-6886; Fax: 785-448-3230. Hours: 8AM-5PM (CST). *Felony, Misdemeanor, Civil, Eviction, Small Claims, Probate.*

www.kscourts.org/dstcts/4dstct.htm

Civil Records: Access: Fax, mail, in person, online. Both court and visitors may perform in person searches. No search fee. Required to search: name, years to search. Civil cases indexed by defendant, plaintiff. Civil records on computer from 1977, index books from 1800s. Current court calendars are available free online at www.kscourts.org/dstcts/4andckt.htm.

Criminal Records: Access: In person only. Visitors must perform in person searches for themselves. No search fee. Required to search: name, years to search. Criminal records on computer from 1977, index books from 1800s. Online access to criminal calendars is the same as civil. For criminal record searches, the court urges requesters to contact the KS Bureau of Investigations.

General Information: Public access terminal is available. (Not on statewide system.) No juvenile, mental health, sealed or expunged records released. SASE required. Turnaround time same day. Fax notes: $2.00 for first page, $.50 each add'l. Copy fee: $.25 per page. Certification fee: $1.00. Fee payee: District Court. Personal checks accepted.

Atchison County

District Court PO Box 408, Atchison, KS 66002; 913-367-7400; Fax: 913-367-1171. Hours: 8AM-5PM (CST). *Felony, Misdemeanor, Civil, Eviction, Small Claims, Probate.*

Civil Records: Access: Fax, mail, in person. Both court and visitors may perform in person searches. No search fee. Required to search: name, years to search. Civil cases indexed by defendant, plaintiff. Civil records on computer from 1991, index books from 1900s, archives from 1860s.

Criminal Records: Access: In person only. Visitors must perform in person searches for themselves. No search fee. Required to search: name, years to search; also helpful: SSN. Criminal records on computer from 1991, index books from 1900s, archives from 1860s.

General Information: Public access terminal is available. No juvenile, mental health, sealed or expunged records released. SASE required. Turnaround time 1-5 days. Fax notes: $1.25 per page. Copy fee: $.25 per page. Certification fee: $1.00. Fee payee: District Court. Personal checks accepted. Prepayment is required.

Barber County

District Court 118 E Washington, Medicine Lodge, KS 67104; 620-886-5639; Fax: 620-886-5854. Hours: 8AM-Noon,1-5PM (CST). *Felony, Misdemeanor, Civil, Eviction, Small Claims, Probate.*

Civil Records: Access: In person only. Visitors must perform in person searches for themselves. No search fee. Required to search: name, years to search. Civil cases indexed by defendant, plaintiff. Civil records on computer from 1990, microfiche from 1900-1976, index cards from 1800s.

Criminal Records: Access: In person only. Visitors must perform in person searches for themselves. No search fee. Required to search: name, years to search, SSN; also helpful: DOB. Criminal records on computer from 1990, microfiche from 1900-1976, index cards from 1800s.

General Information: Public access terminal is available. No juvenile, mental health, sealed or expunged records released. Copy fee: $.25 per page. Certification fee: $1.00. Fee payee: District Court. Personal checks accepted.

Barton County

District Court 1400 Main, Rm 306, Great Bend, KS 67530; 620-793-1856; Fax: 620-793-1860. Hours: 8AM-5PM (CST). *Felony, Misdemeanor, Civil, Eviction, Small Claims, Probate.*

Civil Records: Access: Fax, mail, in person. Both court and visitors may perform in person searches. Search fee: $12.00 per hour. Required to search: name, years to search. Civil cases indexed by defendant, plaintiff. Civil records on computer 1990, microfiche and archives from 1800s, index from 1987.

Criminal Records: Access: Fax, mail, in person. Both court and visitors may perform in person searches. Search fee: $12.00 per hour. Required to search: name, years to search. Criminal records on computer 1990, microfiche and archives from 1800s, index from 1987.

General Information: Public access terminal is available. No juvenile, mental health, sealed or expunged records released. Turnaround time 3 days. Fax notes: No fee to fax results. Copy fee: $.35 per page; $.50 for microfilm copies. Fee payee: Clerk of Court. Personal checks accepted. Prepayment is required.

Bourbon County

District Court PO Box 868, Ft Scott, KS 66701; 620-223-0780; Fax: 620-223-5303. Hours: 8:30AM-4:30PM (CST). *Felony, Misdemeanor, Civil, Eviction, Small Claims, Probate.*

Civil Records: Access: Fax, mail, in person. Both court and visitors may perform in person searches. Search fee: $12.00 per hour. Required to search: name, years to search. Civil cases indexed by defendant, plaintiff. Civil records on computer since 1990, index on computer since 1985.

Criminal Records: Access: Fax, mail, in person. Both court and visitors may perform in person searches. Search fee: $12.00 per hour. Required to search: name, years to search; also helpful: SSN. Criminal records on computer since 1990, index on computer since 1985.

General Information: Public access terminal is available. No juvenile, mental health, sealed or expunged records released. SASE required. Turnaround time 3 days. Fax notes: $1.00 per page. Copy fee: $.25 per page. Certification fee: $1.00. Fee payee: Clerk of Court. Personal checks accepted. Prepayment is required.

Brown County

District Court PO Box 417, Hiawatha, KS 66434; 785-742-7481; Fax: 785-742-3506. Hours: 8AM-5PM (CST). *Felony, Misdemeanor, Civil, Eviction, Small Claims, Probate.*

Civil Records: Access: Phone, fax, mail, in person. Both court and visitors may perform in person searches. Search fee: $12.00 per hour. Required to search: name, years to search. Civil cases indexed by defendant, plaintiff. Civil records on computer from 1982, microfiche from 1900s, index books from 1900s.

Criminal Records: Access: Phone, fax, mail, in person. Both court and visitors may perform in person searches. Search fee: $12.00 per hour. Required to search: name, years to search; also helpful: SSN. Criminal records on computer from 1982, microfiche and index books from 1900s.

General Information: Public access terminal is available. No juvenile, mental health, sealed or expunged records released. SASE required. Turnaround time 1-2 days. Fax notes: Fee to fax results is $1.00 per page. Copy fee: $.50 for first page, $.25 each add'l. Certification fee: $1.00. Fee payee: District Court. Personal checks accepted. Prepayment is required.

Butler County

District Court 121 S Gordy #102, El Dorado, KS 67042; 316-322-4370; Fax: 316-321-9486. Hours: 8:30AM-5PM (CST). *Felony, Misdemeanor, Civil, Eviction, Small Claims, Probate.*

Civil Records: Access: In person only. Visitors must perform in person searches for themselves. No search fee. Required to search: name, years to search. Civil cases indexed by defendant, plaintiff. Civil records on computer from 1992, index cards from 1800s.

Criminal Records: Access: In person only. Visitors must perform in person searches for themselves. No search fee. Required to search: name, years to search, SSN. Criminal records on computer from 1992, index cards from 1800s.

General Information: Public access terminal is available. No juvenile, mental health, sealed or expunged records released. Copy fee: $.25 per page. Certification fee: $1.00. Fee payee: Clerk of District Court. Personal checks accepted. Fax fees billed.

Chase County

District Court PO Box 529, Cottonwood Falls, KS 66845; 620-273-6319; Fax: 620-273-6890. Hours: 8AM-5PM (CST). *Felony, Misdemeanor, Civil, Eviction, Small Claims, Probate.*

Civil Records: Access: In person only. Visitors must perform in person searches for themselves. No search fee. Required to search: name, years to search. Civil cases indexed by defendant, plaintiff. Civil records on computer from late 1990, microfiche from 1860, index books from 1860; visitors may search the printed index desk copy.

Criminal Records: Access: In person only. Visitors must perform in person searches for themselves. No search fee. Required to search: name, years to search. Criminal records on computer from late 1990, microfiche from 1860, index books from 1860; visitors may search the printed index desk copy.

General Information: No juvenile, mental health, sealed or expunged records released. Copy fee: $.50 per page. Certification fee: $2.00. Fee payee: District Court. Personal checks accepted. Prepayment is required.

Chautauqua County

District Court 215 N Chautauqua, PO Box 306, Sedan, KS 67361; 620-725-5870; Fax: 620-725-3027. Hours: 8AM-5PM (CST). *Felony, Misdemeanor, Civil, Eviction, Small Claims, Probate.*

Civil Records: Access: Mail, in person. Both court and visitors may perform in person searches. Search fee: $12.00 per hour. Required to search: name, years to search. Civil cases indexed by defendant, plaintiff. Civil records on computer from 1990, archives from 1950, index cards from 1870.

Criminal Records: Access: Mail, in person. Both court and visitors may perform in person searches. Search fee: $12.00 per hour. Required to search: name, years to search; also helpful: DOB. Criminal records on computer from 1990, archives from 1950, index cards from 1870.

General Information: Public access terminal is available. No juvenile, mental health, sealed or expunged records released. SASE required. Turnaround time 1-2 weeks. Copy fee: $.25 per page. Certification fee: $1.00. Fee payee: District Court. Personal checks accepted.

Cherokee County

District Court PO Box 189, Columbus, KS 66725; 620-429-3880; Fax: 620-429-1130. Hours: 8AM-5PM (CST). *Felony, Misdemeanor, Civil, Eviction, Small Claims, Probate.*

Civil Records: Access: Mail, fax, in person. Visitors must perform in person searches for themselves. Search fee: $12.00 per hour. Required to search: name, years to search. Civil cases indexed by defendant, plaintiff. Civil records on computer back 10 years, index books from 1867.

Criminal Records: Access: Mail, fax, in person. Visitors must perform in person searches for themselves. Search fee: $12.00 per hour. Required to search: name, years to search; also helpful: SSN. Criminal records on computer back 10 years, index books from 1867.

General Information: Public access terminal is available. No juvenile, mental health, sealed or expunged records released. Certification fee: $1.00. Fee payee: District Court. Personal checks accepted. Prepayment is required.

Cheyenne County

District Court PO Box 646, St Francis, KS 67756; 785-332-8850; Fax: 785-332-8851. Hours: 8AM-Noon,1-5PM (CST). *Felony, Misdemeanor, Civil, Eviction, Small Claims, Probate.*

Civil Records: Access: Fax, mail, in person. Both court and visitors may perform in person searches. No search fee. Required to search: name, years to search. Civil cases indexed by defendant, plaintiff. Civil records on strip index from 1989, index cards from 1870.

Criminal Records: Access: Fax, mail, in person. Both court and visitors may perform in person searches. No search fee. Required to search: name, years to search. Criminal records on strip index from 1989, index cards from 1870.

General Information: No juvenile, adoptions, mental health, sealed or expunged records released. SASE not required. Turnaround time 2 days. Fax notes: $1.00 per page unless toll free line used. Copy fee: $.25 per page. Certification fee: $1.00. Fee payee: Clerk of Court. Personal checks accepted. Prepayment is required.

Clark County

District Court PO Box 790, Ashland, KS 67831; 620-635-2753; Fax: 620-635-2155. Hours: 8AM-5PM (CST). *Felony, Misdemeanor, Civil, Eviction, Small Claims, Probate.*

www.kscourts.org/dstcts/16dstct.htm

Civil Records: Access: Mail, fax, in person. Both court and visitors may perform in person searches. Search fee: $12.00 per hour. Required to search: name, years to search. Civil cases indexed by defendant, plaintiff. Civil records on computer from 1992 (Child support only), microfiche and archives from 1800s, index cards from 1800s.

Criminal Records: Access: Mail, fax, in person. Both court and visitors may perform in person searches. Search fee: $9.00 per hour (may be no fee if short and a name search). Required to search: name, years to search; also helpful: SSN. Criminal records on index cards.

General Information: No juvenile, mental health, sealed or expunged records released. SASE required. Turnaround time 1 day. Copy fee: $.25 per page. Certification fee: $1.25. Fee payee: District Court. Personal checks accepted. Prepayment is required.

Clay County

District Court PO Box 203, Clay Center, KS 67432; 785-632-3443; Fax: 785-632-2651. Hours: 8AM-5PM (CST). *Felony, Misdemeanor, Civil, Eviction, Small Claims, Probate.*

www.co.riley.ks.us/districtcourt

Civil Records: Access: Mail, in person. Visitors must perform in person searches for themselves. No search fee. Required to search: name, years to search. Civil cases indexed by defendant, plaintiff. Civil records on computer from July, 1994, index books from late 1800s.

Criminal Records: Access: In person only. Visitors must perform in person searches for themselves. No search fee. Required to search: name. Criminal records on computer from July, 1994, index books from late 1800s.

General Information: Public access terminal is available. No juvenile, adoption, mental health, sealed or expunged records released. SASE required. Turnaround time 2 days. Copy fee: $.25 per page. Certification fee: $1.00. Fee payee: Clerk of District Court. Personal checks accepted. Prepayment required.

Cloud County

District Court 811 Washington, Concordia, KS 66901; 785-243-8124; Fax: 785-243-8188. Hours: 8:00AM-5PM (CST). *Felony, Misdemeanor, Civil, Eviction, Small Claims, Probate.*

www.kscourts.org/dstcts/12dstct.htm

Civil Records: Access: Phone, fax, mail, in person. Visitors must perform in person searches for themselves. Search fee: $12.00 per hour. Required to search: name, years to search. Civil cases indexed by defendant, plaintiff. Civil records in print indexes from 1992, index books prior to 1992.

Criminal Records: Access: Fax, mail, in person. Both court and visitors may perform in person searches. Search fee: $12.00 per hour. Required to search: name, years to search; also helpful: SSN. Criminal records in print indexes from 1992, index books prior to 1992.

General Information: Public access terminal is available. No juvenile, mental health, sealed or expunged records released. SASE required. Turnaround time 3-4 days. Fax notes: $3.00 per page. Copy fee: $.25 per page. Certification fee: $1.00. Fee payee: Clerk of Court. Personal checks accepted. Prepayment is required.

Coffey County

District Court PO Box 330, Burlington, KS 66839; 620-364-8628; Fax: 620-364-8535. Hours: 8AM-4PM (CST). *Felony, Misdemeanor, Civil, Eviction, Small Claims, Probate.*

www.kscourts.org/dstcts/4dstct.htm

Civil Records: Access: Mail, fax, in person, email, online. Both court and visitors may perform in person searches. Search fee: $12.00 per hour. Required to search: name, years to search. Civil cases indexed by defendant, plaintiff. Civil records on computer back to 1800s, index cards from 1800s. Current court calendars are available free online at www.kscourts.org/dstcts/4codckt.htm. Probate and marriage records are accessible at the web site.

Criminal Records: Access: Mail, fax, in person, email, online. Both court and visitors may perform in person searches. Search fee: $12.00 per hour. Required to search: name, years to search, DOB. Criminal records on computer back to 1800s, index cards from 1800s. Online access to criminal records is the same as civil.

General Information: Public access terminal is available. No juvenile, mental health, sealed or expunged records released. SASE required. Turnaround time 3 days. Fax notes: Fee to fax results is $2.00 1st page; $.50 each add'l. Copy fee: $.25 per page. Certification fee: $1.00. Fee payee: Clerk of District Court. Personal checks accepted. Prepayment required.

Comanche County

District Court PO Box 722, Coldwater, KS 67029; 620-582-2182; Fax: 620-582-2603. Hours: 8AM-5PM (CST). *Felony, Misdemeanor, Civil, Eviction, Small Claims, Probate.*

www.kscourts.org/dstcts/16dstct.htm

Civil Records: Access: In person only. Both court and visitors may perform in person searches. No search fee. Required to search: name, years to search. Civil cases indexed by defendant, plaintiff. Civil records on computer since 1992 (child support only), index cards from 1886.

Criminal Records: Access: In person only. Both court and visitors may perform in person searches. No search fee. Required to search: name, years to search; also helpful: SSN. Criminal records on index cards from 1886.

General Information: No juvenile, mental health, sealed or expunged records released. Copy fee: $.25 per

page. Certification fee: $1.00. Fee payee: District Court. Personal checks accepted. Prepayment is required.

Cowley County

Arkansas City District Court PO Box 1152, Arkansas City, KS 67005; 620-441-4520; Fax: 620-442-7213. Hours: 8AM-Noon,1-4PM (CST). *Felony, Misdemeanor, Civil, Eviction, Small Claims, Probate.*

Note: This court covers the southern part of the county. All felony records are kept at Winfield.

Civil Records: Access: Mail, in person. Both court and visitors may perform in person searches. Search fee: $12.00 per hour. Required to search: name, years to search. Civil cases indexed by defendant, plaintiff. Civil records from 1977. This Court facility has only been in existence since 1977, so no records prior to that date, index cards only. Computer records commencing 1994.

Criminal Records: Access: Mail, in person. Both court and visitors may perform in person searches. Search fee: $12.00 per hour. Required to search: name, years to search, SSN. Criminal records from 1977. This Court facility has only been in existence since 1977, so no records prior to that date, index cards only. Computer records commencing 1994.

General Information: Public access terminal is available. No juvenile, mental health, sealed or expunged records released. SASE not required. Turnaround time 1 week. Copy fee: $.50 per page. Certification fee: $1.00. Fee payee: Clerk of Court. Personal checks accepted. Prepayment is required.

Winfield District Court PO Box 472, Winfield, KS 67156; 620-221-5470; Fax: 620-221-1097. Hours: 8AM-Noon,1-4PM (CST). *Felony, Misdemeanor, Civil, Eviction, Small Claims, Probate.*

Note: This court covers northern part of county.

Civil Records: Access: Fax, mail, in person. Both court and visitors may perform in person searches. Search fee: $12.00 per hour. Required to search: name, years to search. Civil cases indexed by defendant, plaintiff. Civil records on computer since 1994, index cards to 1874.

Criminal Records: Access: Fax, mail, in person. Both court and visitors may perform in person searches. Search fee: $12.00 per hour. Required to search: name, years to search. Criminal records on computer since 1994, index cards from 1874.

General Information: Public access terminal is available. No juvenile, mental health, sealed or expunged records released. SASE not required. Turnaround time 1 week. Copy fee: $.50 per page. Certification fee: $1.00. Fee payee: Clerk of Court. Personal checks accepted. Prepayment is required.

Crawford County

Girard District Court PO Box 69, Girard, KS 66743; 620-724-6211; Fax: 620-724-4987. Hours: 8AM-5PM *Felony, Misdemeanor, Civil, Probate.*

Note: Records on computer are maintained here for the Pittsburg District Court as well since 8/92. For prior cases, search both courts separately.

Civil Records: Access: Fax, mail, in person. Both court and visitors may perform in person searches. Search fee: $12.00 per hour. Required to search: name, years to search. Civil cases indexed by defendant, plaintiff. Civil records on computer since August, 1992, microfiche from 1977, index cards from 1977.

Criminal Records: Access: Phone, fax, in person. Both court and visitors may perform in person searches. Search fee: $12.00 per hour. Required to search: name, years to search. Criminal records on computer since August, 1992, microfiche from 1977, index cards from 1977. Employment/work-related mail inquires are referred to the Kansas Bureau of Investigation.

General Information: Public access terminal is available. No juvenile, mental health, sealed or expunged records released. SASE required. Turnaround time 3 days. Fax notes: $2.50 per page. Copy fee: $.25 per page. Certification fee: $1.00. Fee payee: Clerk of Court. Personal checks accepted. Prepayment is required.

Pittsburg District Court 602 N Locust, Pittsburg, KS 66762; 620-231-0391; Fax: 620-231-0316. Hours: 8AM-5PM (CST). *Misdemeanor, Civil, Eviction, Small Claims, Probate.*

Note: Records back to 8/92 can be searched at Girard District Court as well; Girard and Pittsburg share a computer system. For cases prior to 8/92, search both courts separately.

Civil Records: Access: Fax, mail, in person. Both court and visitors may perform in person searches. Search fee: $12.00 per hour. Required to search: name, years to search. Civil cases indexed by defendant, plaintiff. Civil records on computer since August, 1992, microfiche from 1977, index cards from 1977.

Criminal Records: Access: Phone, fax, in person. Both court and visitors may perform in person searches. Search fee: $12.00 per hour. Required to search: name, years to search. Criminal records on computer since August, 1992, microfiche from 1977, index cards from 1977. Employment/work-related mail inquires are referred to the Kansas Bureau of Investigation.

General Information: Public access terminal is available. No juvenile, mental health, sealed or expunged records released. SASE required. Turnaround time 3 days. Fax notes: $2.50 per page. Copy fee: $.25 per page. Certification fee: $1.00. Fee payee: Clerk of Court. Personal checks accepted. Prepayment required.

Decatur County

District Court PO Box 89, Oberlin, KS 67749; 785-475-8107; Fax: 785-475-8170. Hours: 8AM-5PM (CST). *Felony, Misdemeanor, Civil, Eviction, Small Claims, Probate.*

Civil Records: Access: In person only. Visitors must perform in person searches for themselves. No search fee. Required to search: name, years to search. Civil cases indexed by defendant, plaintiff. Civil records on index books from 1870.

Criminal Records: Access: In person only. Visitors must perform in person searches for themselves. No search fee. Required to search: name, years to search. Criminal records on index books from 1870.

General Information: No adoption, juvenile, mental health, sealed or expunged records released. Copy fee: $.25 per page. Certification fee: $1.00. Fee payee: Clerk of District Court.

Dickinson County

District Court PO Box 127, Abilene, KS 67410; 785-263-3142; Fax: 785-263-4407. Hours: 9AM-5PM (CST). *Felony, Misdemeanor, Civil, Eviction, Small Claims, Probate.*

Civil Records: Access: Mail, fax, in person, e-mail. Both court and visitors may perform in person searches. Search fee: $12.00 per hour. Required to search: name, years to search. Civil cases indexed by defendant, plaintiff. Civil records on computer since 7/92, on index books prior.

Criminal Records: Access: Mail, fax, in person, e-mail. Both court and visitors may perform in person searches. Search fee: $12.00 per hour. Required to search: name, years to search; also helpful: SSN. Criminal records on computer since 7/92, on index books prior.

General Information: Public access terminal is available. No juvenile, mental health, sealed or expunged records released. SASE required. Turnaround time 1 week. Fax notes: Fax fee $1.00 per page. Copy fee: $1.00. Fee for first 4 pages. Add $.25 per page thereafter. Certification fee: $1.00. Fee payee: Clerk of

District Court. Personal checks accepted. Prepayment is required.

Doniphan County

District Court PO Box 295, Troy, KS 66087; 785-985-3582; Fax: 785-985-2402. Hours: 8AM-5PM (CST). *Felony, Misdemeanor, Civil, Eviction, Small Claims, Probate.*

Civil Records: Access: Phone, fax, mail, in person. Both court and visitors may perform in person searches. Search fee: $12.00 per hour. Required to search: name, years to search. Civil cases indexed by defendant, plaintiff. Civil records on computer since 1992; index cards from 1856.

Criminal Records: Access: Phone, fax, mail, in person. Only the court performs in person searches; visitors may not. Search fee: $12.00 per hour. Required to search: name, years to search; also helpful: address, DOB. Criminal records on computer since 1992; index cards from 1852.

General Information: Public access terminal is available. No juvenile, mental health, sealed or expunged records released. SASE required. Turnaround time 1-2 days. Fax notes: Fee to fax results is $2.00 per page. Copy fee: $.50 for first page, $.25 each add'l. Certification fee: $1.00. Fee payee: Clerk of Court. Personal checks accepted.

Douglas County

District Court 111 E 11th St, Rm 144, Lawrence, KS 66044-2966; 785-841-7700 X141; Fax: 785-832-5174. Hours: 8:30AM-4PM (CST). *Felony, Misdemeanor, Civil, Eviction, Small Claims, Probate.*

www.douglas-county.com/District_Court/dc.asp

Civil Records: Access: Phone, fax, mail, in person, online. Both court and visitors may perform in person searches. Search fee: $12.00 per hour. Required to search: name, years to search. Civil cases indexed by defendant, plaintiff. Civil records on index cards from 1863, archived from 1865 on film, indexed on computer since 1989. Online access via Internet to district court records is available for $180.00 annual fee and $60.00 set-up fee. For further information and registration, contact Beverly at 785-832-5299. All written requests must include a phone number. In person requests take 48 hours to process, if court does search.

Criminal Records: Access: Phone, fax, mail, in person, online. Both court and visitors may perform in person searches. Search fee: $12.00 per hour. Required to search: name, years to search; also helpful: DOB, SSN. Criminal records on computer from 1989, index cards 1860, archived from 1865. Online access to criminal records is the same as civil. All other background check requests must be in writing.

General Information: Public access terminal is available. No juvenile, mental health, sealed or expunged records released. SASE not required. Turnaround time 3 days. Fax notes: Fee to fax results is $2.00 per document. Copy fee: $.25 per page. Certification fee: $1.00; Authentications are $2.00 each. Fee payee: Clerk of Court. Personal checks accepted. Prepayment is required.

Edwards County

District Court PO Box 232, Kinsley, KS 67547; 620-659-2442; Fax: 620-659-2998. Hours: 8AM-5PM (CST). *Felony, Misdemeanor, Civil, Eviction, Small Claims, Probate.*

www.kscourts.org/dstcts/24dstct.htm

Civil Records: Access: Mail, in person. Both court and visitors may perform in person searches. Search fee: $12.00 per hour. Required to search: name, years to search. Civil cases indexed by defendant, plaintiff. Civil records on index books from 1800s.

Criminal Records: Access: In person only. Visitors must perform in person searches for themselves. Required to search: name, years to search. Criminal records on index books from 1800s.

General Information: No juvenile, adoption, mental health, sealed or expunged records released. SASE required. Turnaround time 1-2 days. Copy fee: $.25 per page. Certification fee: $1.00. Fee payee: Clerk District Court. Personal checks accepted. Prepayment required.

Elk County

District Court PO Box 306, Howard, KS 67349; 620-374-2370; Fax: 620-374-3531. Hours: 8AM-4:30PM (CST). *Felony, Misdemeanor, Civil, Eviction, Small Claims, Probate.*

Civil Records: Access: Mail, in person. Both court and visitors may perform in person searches. Search fee: Depending on difficulty, clerk may charge $12 per hr search fee. Required to search: name, years to search. Civil cases indexed by defendant, plaintiff. Civil records on index books from 1907.

Criminal Records: Access: Mail, in person. Both court and visitors may perform in person searches. Search fee: Depending on difficulty, clerk may charge $12 per hr search fee. Required to search: name, years to search. Criminal records on index books from 1907; on comptuer back to 1984.

General Information: Public access terminal is available. No juvenile, mental health, sealed or expunged records released. Fax notes: Fee to fax results is $2 plus $.50 per page. Copy fee: $.25 per page. Certification fee: $1.00. Fee payee: Clerk of District Court. Personal checks accepted. Prepayment required.

Ellis County

District Court PO Box 8, Hays, KS 67601; 785-628-9415; Fax: 785-628-8415. Hours: 8AM-5PM (CST). *Felony, Misdemeanor, Civil, Eviction, Small Claims, Probate.*

Civil Records: Access: Mail, in person. Both court and visitors may perform in person searches. No search fee. Required to search: name, years to search. Civil cases indexed by defendant, plaintiff. Civil records on computer from 1991, microfiche from 1900s, index cards from 1800s, archives from 1800s.

Criminal Records: Access: In person only. Visitors must perform in person searches for themselves. No search fee. Required to search: name, years to search. Criminal records on computer from 1991, microfiche from 1900s, index cards from 1800s, archives from 1800s.

General Information: Public access terminal is available. No juvenile, mental health, sealed or expunged records released. SASE required. Turnaround time 7 days. Copy fee: $.25 per page. Certification fee: $1.00. Fee payee: Clerk of Court. Personal checks accepted. Prepayment is required.

Ellsworth County

District Court 210 N Kansas, Ellsworth, KS 67439-3118; 785-472-3832; Fax: 785-472-5712. Hours: 8AM-5PM (CST). *Felony, Misdemeanor, Civil, Eviction, Small Claims, Probate.*

Civil Records: Access: Phone, fax, mail, in person. Both court and visitors may perform in person searches. No search fee. Required to search: name, years to search. Civil cases indexed by defendant, plaintiff. Civil records on computer from 1994, microfiche from 1900s, books from late 1800s.

Criminal Records: Access: Phone, fax, mail, in person. Both court and visitors may perform in person searches. No search fee. Required to search: name, years to search; also helpful: SSN. Criminal records on computer from 1994, microfiche from 1900s, books from late 1800s.

General Information: No juvenile, mental health, sealed or expunged records released. SASE required. Turnaround time 1-2 days. Fax notes: $.50 per page. Copy fee: $.35 per page. Fee payee: District Court. Personal checks accepted. Prepayment is required.

Finney County

District Court PO Box 798, Garden City, KS 67846; Civil phone: 620-271-6121; Criminal phone: 620-271-6122; Fax: 620-271-6140. Hours: 8AM-4:30PM (CST). *Felony, Misdemeanor, Civil, Eviction, Small Claims, Probate.*

Civil Records: Access: In person only. Visitors must perform in person searches for themselves. No search fee. Required to search: name, years to search. Civil cases indexed by defendant, plaintiff. Civil records on computer from 1991, microfiche from 1900s, index books from 1900s.

Criminal Records: Access: In person only. Visitors must perform in person searches for themselves. No search fee. Required to search: name, years to search. Criminal records on computer from 1991, microfiche from 1900s, index books from 1900s.

General Information: Public access terminal is available. No juvenile, Mental health, sealed or expunged records released. Copy fee: $.25 per page. Certification fee: $1.00. Fee payee: District Court. Personal checks accepted. Prepayment is required.

Ford County

District Court 101 W Spruce, Dodge City, KS 67801; 620-227-4609; Civil phone: 620-227-4610; Criminal phone: 620-227-4608; Fax: 620-227-6799. Hours: 8AM-5PM (CST). *Felony, Misdemeanor, Civil, Eviction, Small Claims, Probate.*

www.kscourts.org/dstcts/16dstct.htm

Civil Records: Access: Fax, mail, in person. Both court and visitors may perform in person searches. Search fee: $12.00 per hour. Required to search: name, years to search. Civil cases indexed by defendant, plaintiff. Civil records on computer back to 10/1991, microfiche from 1900s, index books from 1900s.

Criminal Records: Access: Fax, mail, in person. Both court and visitors may perform in person searches. Search fee: $12 per hour. Required to search: name, years to search, DOB; also helpful: SSN. Criminal records on computer back to 10/1991, microfiche from 1900s, index books from 1900s.

General Information: Public access terminal is available. No juvenile, mental health, sealed or expunged records released. SASE required. Turnaround time 3 days. Fax notes: Fee to fax results is $1.00 per page. Copy fee: $.25 per page. Certification fee: $1.00. Fee payee: Clerk of District Court. Personal checks accepted. Prepayment is required.

Franklin County

District Court PO Box 637 (301 S Main), Ottawa, KS 66067; 785-242-6000; Fax: 785-242-5970. Hours: 8AM-12, 1PM-4PM (CST). *Felony, Misdemeanor, Civil, Eviction, Small Claims, Probate.*

www.kscourts.org/dstcts/4dstct.htm

Civil Records: Access: Mail, fax, in person, online. Both court and visitors may perform in person searches. Search fee: $12.00 per hour. Required to search: name, years to search. Civil cases indexed by defendant, plaintiff. Civil records on computer back to 1979, index books from 1800s. Current court calendars are available free online at www.kscourts.org/dstcts/4frdckt.htm.

Criminal Records: Access: In person, online. Visitors must perform in person searches for themselves. Required to search: name, years to search, SSN. Criminal records on computer back to 1980, index books from 1800s. Online access to criminal calendars is the same as civil.

General Information: Public access terminal is available. No juvenile, mental health, sealed or expunged records released. SASE required. Turnaround time 3-5 days. Copy fee: $.25 per page. Certification fee: $1.00. Fee payee: Clerk of District Court. Personal checks accepted. Prepayment is required.

Geary County

District Court PO Box 1147, Junction City, KS 66441; 785-762-5221; Fax: 785-762-4420. Hours: 8AM-5PM (CST). *Felony, Misdemeanor, Civil, Eviction, Small Claims, Probate.*

Civil Records: Access: Mail, in person, email. Both court and visitors may perform in person searches. Search fee: $12.00 per hour. Required to search: name, years to search. Civil cases indexed by defendant, plaintiff. Civil records on computer from 1992, microfiche, index books and archives from 1894.

Criminal Records: Access: Mail, in person, email. Both court and visitors may perform in person searches. Search fee: $12.00 per hour. Required to search: name, years to search; also helpful: SSN. Criminal records on computer from 1992, microfiche, index books and archives from 1894.

General Information: Public access terminal is available. No juvenile, adoption, mental health, sealed or expunged records released. SASE not required. Turnaround time 3 days. Fax notes: Fee to fax results is $2.00 per page. Copy fee: $.25 per page. Certification fee: $1.00. Fee payee: Clerk of Court. Personal checks accepted. Prepayment is required.

Gove County

District Court PO Box 97, Gove, KS 67736; 785-938-2310; Fax: 785-938-2312. Hours: 8AM-Noon, 1-5PM (CST). *Felony, Misdemeanor, Civil, Eviction, Small Claims, Probate.*

Civil Records: Access: Fax, mail, in person. Both court and visitors may perform in person searches. Search fee: $9.00 per hour. Required to search: name, years to search. Civil cases indexed by defendant, plaintiff. Civil records on computer from 1992, index books from 1890 through present.

Criminal Records: Access: Fax, mail, in person. Both court and visitors may perform in person searches. Search fee: $9.00 per hour. Required to search: name, years to search. Criminal records on computer from 1992, index books from 1890 through present.

General Information: No juvenile, mental health, sealed or expunged records released. SASE required. Turnaround time 1-2 days. Fax notes: Fee to fax results is $1.00 per page. Copy fee: $.25 per page. Certification fee: $1.00. Fee payee: Clerk of District Court. Personal checks accepted. Prepayment is required.

Graham County

District Court 410 N Pomeroy, Hill City, KS 67642; 785-421-3458; Fax: 785-421-5463. Hours: 8AM-5PM (CST). *Felony, Misdemeanor, Civil, Eviction, Small Claims, Probate.*

Civil Records: Access: In person. Visitors must perform in person searches for themselves. No search fee. Civil cases indexed by defendant, plaintiff. Civil records on index books from 1880s; computerized records go back to 2000.

Criminal Records: Access: In person. Visitors must perform in person searches for themselves. Required to search: name, years to search, DOB; also helpful: SSN, signed release. Criminal records on index books from 1880s; computerized records go back to 2000.

General Information: No juvenile, mental health, sealed or expunged records released. Copy fee: $.25 per page. Certification fee: $1.00. Fee payee: Clerk of District Court. Personal checks accepted. Prepayment is required.

Grant County

District Court 108 S Glenn, Ulysses, KS 67880; 620-356-1526; Fax: 620-353-2131. Hours: 8:30AM-5PM (CST). *Felony, Misdemeanor, Civil, Eviction, Small Claims, Probate.*

Civil Records: Access: In person only. Visitors must perform in person searches for themselves. No search fee. Required to search: name, years to search. Civil cases indexed by defendant, plaintiff. Civil records on computer from 1977, microfiche index from 1880s.

Criminal Records: Access: In person, mail. Visitors must perform in person searches for themselves. No search fee. Required to search: name, years to search. Criminal records on computer from 1977, microfiche index from 1880s. The court refers all searchers to the state Bureau of investigations, including in-person searchers.

General Information: Public access terminal is available. No juvenile, mental health, sealed or expunged records released. SASE required. Turnaround time same day. Copy fee: $.50 per page. Certification fee: $1.00. Fee payee: District Court. Personal checks accepted. Prepayment is required.

Gray County

District Court PO Box 487, Cimarron, KS 67835; 620-855-3812; Fax: 620-855-7037. Hours: 8AM-5PM (CST). *Felony, Misdemeanor, Civil, Eviction, Small Claims, Probate.*

www.kscourts.org/dstcts/16dstct.htm

Civil Records: Access: Fax, mail, in person. Visitors must perform in person searches for themselves. No search fee. Required to search: name; also helpful: years to search. Civil cases indexed by defendant, plaintiff. Civil records on computer from 1990, index books from 1800s. Fax requests must be pre-paid.

Criminal Records: Access: Fax, mail, in person. Visitors must perform in person searches for themselves. No search fee. Required to search: name, years to search; also helpful: address, DOB. Criminal records on computer from 1990, index books from 1800s. Fax requests must be pre-paid.

General Information: Public access terminal is available. No juvenile, mental health, sealed or expunged records released. Copy fee: $.50 per page. Certification fee: $1.00. Fee payee: Clerk of District Court. Personal checks accepted.

Greeley County

District Court PO Box 516, Tribune, KS 67879; 620-376-4292. Hours: 8AM-Noon, 1-5PM (MST). *Felony, Misdemeanor, Civil, Eviction, Small Claims, Probate.*

Civil Records: Access: In person only. Visitors must perform in person searches for themselves. No search fee. Required to search: name, years to search. Civil cases indexed by defendant, plaintiff. Civil records on hardcopy index from beginning.

Criminal Records: Access: In person only. Visitors must perform in person searches for themselves. No search fee. Required to search: name, years to search; also helpful: SSN. Criminal records on hardcopy index from beginning.

General Information: Public access terminal is available. No juvenile, mental health, sealed or expunged records released. Copy fee: $.50 per page. Certification fee: $1.00. Fee payee: Clerk of the District Court. Personal checks accepted. Prepayment required.

Greenwood County

District Court 311 N Main, Eureka, KS 67045; 620-583-8153; Fax: 620-583-6818. Hours: 8AM-5PM (CST). *Felony, Misdemeanor, Civil, Eviction, Small Claims, Probate.*

Civil Records: Access: Mail, in person. Both court and visitors may perform in person searches. Search fee: $12.00 per hour if search is conducted by court personnel. Required to search: name, years to search. Civil cases indexed by defendant, plaintiff. Civil records on computer from 1993, index cards from 1800s.

Criminal Records: Access: Mail, in person. Both court and visitors may perform in person searches. Search fee: $12.00 per hour if search is performed by court personnel. Required to search: name, years to search. Criminal records on computer from 1993, index cards from 1800s.

General Information: Public access terminal is available. No juvenile, mental health, sealed or expunged records released. SASE required. Turnaround time 1-2 days. Copy fee: $.25 per page. Certification fee: $1.00. Fee payee: Clerk of Court. Personal checks accepted. Prepayment is required.

Hamilton County

District Court PO Box 745, Syracuse, KS 67878; 620-384-5159; Fax: 620-384-7806. Hours: 8AM-5PM (MST). *Felony, Misdemeanor, Civil, Eviction, Small Claims, Probate.*

Civil Records: Access: In person only. Visitors must perform in person searches for themselves. No search fee. Required to search: name, years to search. Civil cases indexed by defendant, plaintiff. Civil records on computer from 1985, microfiche, archives and index cards from 1880s.

Criminal Records: Access: In person only. Visitors must perform in person searches for themselves. No search fee. Required to search: name, years to search. Criminal records on computer from 1985, microfiche, archives and index cards from 1880s.

General Information: Public access terminal is available. No juvenile, mental health, sealed or expunged records released. Fax notes: Fee to fax results is $1.00 per page. Copy fee: $.25 per page. Certification fee: $1.00. Fee payee: Clerk of District Court. Personal checks accepted. Prepayment is required.

Harper County

District Court PO Box 467, Anthony, KS 67003; 620-842-3721; Fax: 620-842-6025. Hours: 8AM-Noon, 1-5PM (CST). *Felony, Misdemeanor, Civil, Eviction, Small Claims, Probate.*

Civil Records: Access: Fax, mail, in person. Both court and visitors may perform in person searches. Search fee: $12.00 per hour. Required to search: name, years to search. Civil cases indexed by defendant, plaintiff. Civil records on computer from 1976, microfiche, index books and archives from 1887.

Criminal Records: Access: Fax, mail, in person. Both court and visitors may perform in person searches. Search fee: $12.00 per hour. Required to search: name, years to search, SSN. Criminal records on computer from 1976, microfiche, index books and archives from 1887.

General Information: Public access terminal is available. No juvenile, mental health, sealed or expunged records released. SAS required. Turnaround time same day. Fax notes: $1.00 per page. Copy fee: $.25 per page. Certification fee: $1.00. Fee payee: Clerk of District Court. Personal checks accepted.

Harvey County

District Court PO Box 665, Newton, KS 67114-0665; 316-284-6890; Civil phone: 316-284-6894; Criminal phone: 316-284-6896; Fax: 316-283-4601. Hours: 8AM-5PM (CST). *Felony, Misdemeanor, Civil, Eviction, Small Claims, Probate.*

Civil Records: Access: Mail, fax, in person, email. Both court and visitors may perform in person searches. Search fee: $12.00 per hour. Required to search: name, years to search. Civil cases indexed by defendant, plaintiff. Civil records on index books from 1800s; on computer back to mid 1970s.

Criminal Records: Access: Mail, fax, in person, email. Both court and visitors may perform in person searches. Search fee: $12.00 per hour. Required to search: name, years to search, DOB; also helpful-SSN, signed release. Criminal records computerized since 1960s, archived from 1800s. Call KBI for thorough search.

General Information: Public access terminal is available. No juvenile, mental health, sealed or expunged records released. SASE not required. Turnaround time 3-5 days. Copy fee: $.50 per page. Certification fee: $1.00. Fee payee: Clerk of District Court. Personal checks accepted.

Haskell County

District Court PO Box 146, Sublette, KS 67877; 620-675-2671; Fax: 620-675-8599. Hours: 8AM-5PM (CST). *Felony, Misdemeanor, Civil, Eviction, Small Claims, Probate.*

Civil Records: Access: Phone, mail, fax, in person. Both court and visitors may perform in person searches. Search fee: $12.00 per hour. Required to search: name, years to search. Civil cases indexed by defendant, plaintiff. Civil records on computer from 1990, index books from 1874.

Criminal Records: Access: Phone, mail, fax, in person. Visitors must perform in person searches for themselves. Search fee: $12.00 per hour. Required to search: name, years to search. Criminal records on computer from 1990, index books from 1874.

General Information: Public access terminal is available. No juvenile, mental health, sealed or expunged records released. SASE not required. Turnaround time same day. Fax notes: Fax fee is $.25 per page or $3.00 per document. Copy fee: $.25 per page. Certification fee: $1.00. Fee payee: Clerk of District Court. Personal checks accepted. Prepayment is required.

Hodgeman County

District Court PO Box 187, Jetmore, KS 67854; 620-357-6522; Fax: 620-357-6216. Hours: 8:30AM-5PM (CST). *Felony, Misdemeanor, Civil, Eviction, Small Claims, Probate.*

www.kscourts.org/dstcts/24dstct.htm

Civil Records: Access: Phone, fax, mail, in person. Both court and visitors may perform in person searches. Search fee: $12.00 per hour. Required to search: name, years to search. Civil cases indexed by defendant, plaintiff. Civil records on index cards and books from 1800s.

Criminal Records: Access: In person only. Visitors must perform in person searches for themselves. No search fee. Required to search: name, years to search; also helpful: SSN. Criminal records on index cards and books from 1800s.

General Information: No juvenile, mental health, sealed or expunged records released. SASE not required. Turnaround time 1-2 days. Fax notes: $.50 per page. Copy fee: $.25 per page. Certification fee: $1.00. Fee payee: Clerk of Court. Personal checks accepted. Must prepay for mail and fax.

Jackson County

District Court 400 New York Av #311, Holton, KS 66436; 785-364-2191; Fax: 785-364-3804. Hours: 8AM-4:30PM (CST). *Felony, Misdemeanor, Civil, Eviction, Small Claims, Probate.*

Civil Records: Access: In person only. Visitors must perform in person searches for themselves. No search fee. Required to search: name, years to search. Civil cases indexed by defendant, plaintiff. Civil records on index cards from 1800s (working on installation of computer at this time).

Criminal Records: Access: In person only. Visitors must perform in person searches for themselves. No search fee. Required to search: name, years to search. Criminal records on index cards from 1800s (working on installation of computer at this time).

General Information: No juvenile, mental health, sealed or expunged records released. Copy fee: $.25 per page. Certification fee: $1.00. Fee payee: Clerk of District Court. Personal checks accepted.

Jefferson County

District Court PO Box 327, Oskaloosa, KS 66066; 785-863-2461; Fax: 785-863-2369. Hours: 8AM-4:30PM (CST). *Felony, Misdemeanor, Civil, Eviction, Small Claims, Probate.*

Civil Records: Access: In person only. Visitors must perform in person searches for themselves. No search fee. Required to search: name, years to search. Civil cases indexed by defendant, plaintiff. Civil records on computer since 01/77, on index books from 1855.

Criminal Records: Access: In person only. Visitors must perform in person searches for themselves. No search fee. Required to search: name, years to search; also helpful: SSN. Criminal records on index books from 1855, computerized since 01/77.

General Information: Public access terminal is available. No juvenile, mental health, sealed or expunged records released. Copy fee: $.25 per page. Certification fee: $1.00. Fee payee: District Court. Personal checks accepted. Prepayment is required.

Jewell County

District Court 307 N Commercial, Mankato, KS 66956; 785-378-4030; Fax: 785-378-4035. Hours: 8AM-5PM (CST). *Felony, Misdemeanor, Civil, Eviction, Small Claims, Probate.*

www.kscourts.org/dstcts/12dstct.htm

Civil Records: Access: Phone, fax, mail, in person. Both court and visitors may perform in person searches. Search fee: $12.00 per hour. Required to search: name, years to search. Civil cases indexed by defendant, plaintiff. Civil records on index books from 1871.

Criminal Records: Access: Phone, fax, mail, in person. Both court and visitors may perform in person searches. Search fee: $12.00 per hour. Required to search: name, years to search. Criminal records on index books from 1871.

General Information: No juvenile, mental health, sealed or expunged records released. SASE required. Turnaround time 1-2 days. Fax notes: $3.00 per page. Copy fee: $.25 per page. Certification fee: $1.00. Fee payee: District Court. Personal checks accepted. Prepayment is required.

Johnson County

District Court 100 N Kansas, Olathe, KS 66061; 913-715-3500; Civil phone: 913-715-3400; Criminal phone: 913-715-3460; Fax: 913-715-3481. Hours: 8:30AM-4PM (CST). *Felony, Misdemeanor, Civil, Eviction, Small Claims, Probate.*

www.jocoks.com/jococourts/index.htm

Note: Search requests should be made to the Records Center, phone 913-715-3480.

Civil Records: Access: Fax, mail, online, in person. Both court and visitors may perform in person searches. Search fee: $12.00 per hour. Required to search: name, years to search. Civil cases indexed by defendant, plaintiff. Civil records on computer from 1980, microfiche, archives and index prior. Index online through INK of Kansas. See www.ink.org for subscription information.

Criminal Records: Access: Fax, mail, in person. Both court and visitors may perform in person searches. Search fee: $12.00 per hour. Required to search: name, years to search. Criminal records on computer from 1980, microfiche, archives and index prior. Criminal fax number is 913-715-3481.

General Information: Public access terminal is available. No juvenile, mental health, sealed or expunged records released. No employment searches. SASE required. Turnaround time 1-2 days if current records, 1-2 weeks for very old document. Fax notes: $2.50 per page. Copy fee: $.50 per page. Copy fee for records prior to 1993 $10.00 flat fee. Certification fee: $1.00. Fee payee: Clerk of the District Court. Only cashiers checks and money orders accepted. Prepayment is required.

Kearny County

District Court PO Box 64, Lakin, KS 67860; 620-355-6481; Fax: 620-355-7462. Hours: 8AM-Noon,1-5PM (CST). *Felony, Misdemeanor, Civil, Eviction, Small Claims, Probate.*

Civil Records: Access: Mail, in person. Visitors must perform in person searches for themselves. No search fee. Required to search: name, years to search. Civil cases indexed by defendant, plaintiff. Civil records on computer from 1991, index books from 1900s.

Criminal Records: Access: Mail, in person. Visitors must perform in person searches for themselves. No search fee. Required to search: name, years to search. Criminal records on computer from 1991, index books from 1900s. A case number must be provided with mail search requests.

General Information: Public access terminal is available. No juvenile, mental health, adoption, sealed or expunged records released. SASE required. Turnaround time 3 days. Copy fee: $.25 per page. Certification fee: $1.00. Fee payee: District Court. Personal checks accepted. Prepayment is required.

Kingman County

District Court PO Box 495 (130 N Spruce St), Kingman, KS 67068; 620-532-5151; Fax: 620-532-2952. Hours: 8AM-Noon, 1-5PM (CST). *Felony, Misdemeanor, Civil, Eviction, Small Claims, Probate.*

Civil Records: Access: Mail, fax, in person. Both court and visitors may perform in person searches. Search fee: $12.00 per hour. Required to search: name, years to search. Civil cases indexed by defendant, plaintiff. Civil records on computer from 1990, microfiche, archives and index cards from 1800s.

Criminal Records: Access: Mail, fax, in person. Both court and visitors may perform in person searches. Search fee: $12.00 per hour. Required to search: name, years to search; also helpful: case type. Criminal records on computer from 1990, microfiche, archives and index cards from 1800s.

General Information: Public access terminal is available. No juvenile, mental health, sealed or expunged records released. SASE required. Turnaround time 1-2 days. Fax notes: Fee to fax results is $1.00 per page. Copy fee: $.25 per page. Certification fee: $1.00. Fee payee: Clerk of Court. Personal checks accepted. Prepayment is required.

Kiowa County

District Court 211 E Florida, Greensburg, KS 67054; 620-723-3317; Fax: 620-723-2970. Hours: 8AM-5PM (CST). *Felony, Misdemeanor, Civil, Eviction, Small Claims, Probate.*

www.kscourts.org/dstcts/16dstct.htm

Civil Records: Access: Fax, mail, in person. Both court and visitors may perform in person searches. Search fee: $12.00 per hour. Required to search: name, years to search. Civil cases indexed by defendant, plaintiff. Civil records archived and on index books from 1800s; computerized back to 1980.

Criminal Records: Access: Fax, mail, in person. Both court and visitors may perform in person searches. Search fee: $12.00 per hour. Required to search: name, years to search, signed release; also helpful: DOB. Criminal records archived and on index books from 1800s; computerized back to 1940.

General Information: Public access terminal is available. No juvenile, mental health, sealed or expunged records released. SASE required. Turnaround time 7 days. Fax notes: Fee to fax results is $1.00 per page. Copy fee: $.25 per page. Certification fee: $1.00. Fee payee: Clerk of District Court. Personal checks accepted.

Labette County

District Court Courthouse, 501 Merchant PO Box 387, Oswego, KS 67356; 620-795-4533 X 245 (620-421-4120 Parsons); Fax: 620-795-3056 (316-421-3633 Parsons). Hours: 8AM-5PM (CST). *Felony, Misdemeanor, Civil, Eviction, Small Claims, Probate.*

Civil Records: Access: In person. Visitors must perform in person searches. No search fee. Required to search: name, years to search. Civil cases indexed by defendant, plaintiff. Civil records on computer since 1992.

Criminal Records: Access: In person. Visitors must perform In person searches. No search fee. Required to search: name, years to search; also helpful: DOB, SSN. Criminal records on computer since 1992.

General Information: Public access terminal is available. no juvenile, adoption, mental health, sealed or expunged records released. Copy fee: $.25 per page. Certification fee: $1.00. Fee payee: Clerk of District Court. Personal checks accepted. Prepayment is required.

District Court 201 South Central, Parsons, KS 67357; 620-421-4120; Fax: 620-421-3633. Hours: 8AM-5PM (CST). *Felony, Misdemeanor, Civil, Eviction, Small Claims, Probate.*

Civil Records: Access: Mail, in person. Both court and visitors may perform in person searches. No search fee. Required to search: name, years to search. Civil cases indexed by defendant, plaintiff. Civil records on computer from 1992, index books from 1874.

Criminal Records: Access: Mail, in person. Both court and visitors may perform in person searches. No search fee. Required to search: name, years to search. Criminal records on computer from 1992, index books from 1874.

General Information: Public access terminal is available. No juvenile, adoption, mental health, sealed or expunged records released. SASE required. Turnaround time 1-2 days. Copy fee: $.25 per page. Certification fee: $1.00. Fee payee: Clerk of District Court. Personal checks accepted. Prepayment required.

Lane County

District Court PO Box 188, Dighton, KS 67839; 620-397-2805; Fax: 620-397-5526. Hours: 8AM-5PM (CST). *Felony, Misdemeanor, Civil, Eviction, Small Claims, Probate.*

www.kscourts.org/dstcts/24dstct.htm

Civil Records: Access: Mail, in person. Both court and visitors may perform in person searches. Search fee: $12.00 per hour. Required to search: name, years to search. Civil cases indexed by defendant, plaintiff. Civil records on computer since 1993; prior records to 1800s.

Criminal Records: Access: Mail, in person. Visitors must perform in person searches for themselves. Search fee: $12.00 per hour. Required to search: name, years to search; also helpful: SSN. Criminal records on computer since 1993; prior records from 1800s.

General Information: No juvenile, mental health, sealed or expunged records released. SASE required. Turnaround time 1-2 weeks. Copy fee: $.25 per page. Certification fee: $1.00. Fee payee: Clerk of Court. Personal checks accepted. Prepayment is required.

Leavenworth County

District Court 601 S Third Street, Leavenworth, KS 66048; 913-684-0700; Civil phone: 913-684-0701; Criminal phone: 913-684-0704; Fax: 913-684-0492. Hours: 8AM-5PM (CST). *Felony, Misdemeanor, Civil, Eviction, Small Claims, Probate.*

Civil Records: Access: Mail, in person. Both court and visitors may perform in person searches. No search fee. Required to search: name, years to search. Civil cases indexed by defendant, plaintiff. Civil records on computer from 1990, microfiche and index books from 1960.

Criminal Records: Access: Mail, in person. Both court and visitors may perform in person searches. No search fee. Required to search: name, years to search; also helpful: SSN. Criminal records on computer from 1990, microfiche and index books from 1960.

General Information: Public access terminal is available. No juvenile, mental health, sealed or expunged records released. SASE required. Turnaround time 1-2 days. Copy fee: $.25 per page. Certification fee: $1.00. Fee payee: Clerk of District Court. Personal checks accepted. Prepayment is required.

Lincoln County

District Court 216 E Lincoln Ave, Lincoln, KS 67455; 785-524-4057; Fax: 785-524-3204. Hours: 8AM-12, 1-5PM (CST). *Felony, Misdemeanor, Civil, Eviction, Small Claims, Probate.*

www.kscourts.org/dstcts/12dstct.htm

Civil Records: Access: Fax, mail, in person. Both court and visitors may perform in person searches. Search fee: $9.00 per hour. Required to search: name; also helpful: years to search. Civil cases indexed by defendant, plaintiff. All records on computer.

Criminal Records: Access: Fax, mail, in person. Both court and visitors may perform in person searches. Search fee: $9.00 per hour. Required to search: name; also helpful: years to search, DOB, SSN. Criminal records on computer since 1980, on index cards from 1880.

General Information: No juvenile, mental health, sealed or expunged records released. SASE required. Turnaround time 3 days. Fax notes: $3.00 per page. Copy fee: $.25 per page. Certification fee: $1.00. Fee payee: Clerk of Court. Personal checks accepted. Prepayment is required.

Linn County

District Court PO Box 350, Mound City, KS 66056-0350; 913-795-2660; Fax: 913-795-2004. Hours: 8AM-5PM (CST). *Felony, Misdemeanor, Civil, Eviction, Small Claims, Probate.*

Civil Records: Access: In person only. Visitors must perform in person searches for themselves. No search fee. Required to search: name, years to search. Civil cases indexed by defendant, plaintiff. Civil records on computer from 1990, archives and index books from 1886.
Criminal Records: Access: In person only. Visitors must perform in person searches for themselves. No search fee. Required to search: name, years to search. Criminal records on computer from 1990, archives and index books from 1886.
General Information: Public access terminal is available. No juvenile, mental health, sealed or expunged records released. Copy fee: $.25 per page. Certification fee: $1.00. Fee payee: Clerk of District Court. Personal checks accepted. Prepayment required.

Logan County

District Court 710 W 2nd St, Oakley, KS 67748-1233; 785-672-3654; Fax: 785-672-3517. Hours: 8:30AM-Noon, 1-5PM (CST). *Felony, Misdemeanor, Civil, Eviction, Small Claims, Probate.*

Civil Records: Access: In person only. Visitors must perform in person searches for themselves. No search fee. Required to search: name; also helpful: years to search. Civil cases indexed by defendant, plaintiff. Civil records on computer from 1927, index cards from 1887.
Criminal Records: Access: In person only. Visitors must perform in person searches for themselves. No search fee. Required to search: name; also helpful: SSN, years to search. Criminal records on computer from 1927 index cards from 1887.
General Information: Public access terminal is available. No juvenile, mental health, sealed or expunged records released. Copy fee: $.25 per page. Certification fee: $1.00. Fee payee: Clerk of District Court. Personal checks accepted. Prepayment required.

Lyon County

District Court 430 Commercial St, Emporia, KS 66801; 620-341-3280; Fax: 620-341-3497. Hours: 8AM-4PM (CST). *Felony, Misdemeanor, Civil, Eviction, Small Claims, Probate.*

Civil Records: Access: Fax, mail, in person. Both court and visitors may perform in person searches. Search fee: $12.00 per hour. Required to search: name, years to search. Civil cases indexed by defendant, plaintiff.
Criminal Records: Access: Fax, mail, in person. Both court and visitors may perform in person searches. Search fee: $12.00 per hour. Required to search: name, years to search.
General Information: Public access terminal is available. (Has records 1998 to present.) No mental health, sealed or expunged records released. Turnaround time 3 days maximum. Fax notes: $1.00 per page. Copy fee: $.50 per page. Certification fee: $2.00. Fee payee: Clerk of District Court. Personal checks accepted. Prepayment required.

Marion County

District Court PO Box 298, Marion, KS 66861; 620-382-2104; Fax: 620-382-2259. Hours: 8AM-5PM; 9AM-5PM (open to public) (CST). *Felony, Misdemeanor, Civil, Eviction, Small Claims, Probate.*

Civil Records: Access: In person only. Visitors must perform in person searches for themselves. Required to search: name, years to search. Civil cases indexed by defendant, plaintiff. Civil records on computer from July, 1992, on index cards from 1800s.

Criminal Records: Access: In person only. Visitors must perform in person searches for themselves. Required to search: name, years to search. Criminal records on computer from July, 1992, on index cards from 1800s.
General Information: Public access terminal is available. No juvenile, mental health, sealed or expunged records released. Copy fee: $1.00 per page. Certification fee: $1.00. Fee payee: District Court. Personal checks accepted. Prepayment is required.

Marshall County

District Court PO Box 86, Marysville, KS 66508; 785-562-5301; Fax: 785-562-2458. Hours: 8AM-5PM; Search hours: 8:30AM-4:30PM (CST). *Felony, Misdemeanor, Civil, Eviction, Small Claims, Probate.*

Civil Records: Access: Fax, mail, in person. Both court and visitors may perform in person searches. Search fee: $12.00 per hour. Required to search: name, years to search. Civil cases indexed by defendant, plaintiff. Civil records on computer from 1990, microfiche from 1977 (earlier records on roll-marriage licenses on computer index 1860s, forward/naturalizations on computer index).
Criminal Records: Access: Fax, mail, in person. Both court and visitors may perform in person searches. Search fee: $12.00 per hour. Required to search: name, years to search. Criminal records on computer from 1986, microfiche from 1977.
General Information: Public access terminal is available. No juvenile, mental health, sealed or expunged records released. SASE required. Turnaround time 1-2 days. Fax notes: $2.00 for first page, $1.00 each add'l. Prepayment required. Copy fee: $.50 for first page, $.25 each add'l. Certification fee: $1.00. Fee payee: Clerk of Court. Personal checks accepted. Prepayment is required.

McPherson County

District Court PO Box 1106, McPherson, KS 67460; 620-241-3422; Fax: 620-241-1372. Hours: 8AM-5PM (CST). *Felony, Misdemeanor, Civil, Eviction, Small Claims, Probate.*

Civil Records: Access: Mail, in person. Both court and visitors may perform in person searches. Search fee: $12.00 per hour. Required to search: name, years to search. Civil cases indexed by defendant, plaintiff. Civil records on microfilm from 1953, index cards from 1900s.
Criminal Records: Access: Mail, in person. Both court and visitors may perform in person searches. Search fee: $12.00 per hour. Required to search: name, years to search; also helpful: SSN. Criminal records on microfilm from 1953, index cards from 1900s.
General Information: Public access terminal is available. No juvenile, mental health, sealed or expunged records released. SASE required. Turnaround time 1-3 days. Fax notes: Fax fee $1.00 per page. Copy fee: $.50 per page. Certification fee: $.50 per document. Fee payee: District Court. Personal checks accepted. Prepayment is required.

Meade County

Meade County District Court PO Box 623, Meade, KS 67864; 620-873-8750; Fax: 620-873-8759. Hours: 8AM-5PM (CST). *Felony, Misdemeanor, Civil, Eviction, Small Claims, Probate.*
www.kscourts.org/dstcts/16dstct.htm
Note: All employment background checks requested by mail, phone, or fax are referred to the KBI (state agency for criminal records).
Civil Records: Access: Mail, in person. Both court and visitors may perform in person searches. Search fee: $12.00 per hour. Required to search: name, years to search. Civil cases indexed by defendant, plaintiff. Civil records on computer from 1990, index cards from 1896.

Criminal Records: Access: Mail, in person. Both court and visitors may perform in person searches. Search fee: $12.00 per hour. Required to search: name, years to search. Criminal records on computer from 1990, index cards from 1896.
General Information: Public access terminal is available. No juvenile, mental health, sealed or expunged records released. SASE required. Turnaround time 1-2 days. Copy fee: $.25 per page. Certification fee: $1.00. Fee payee: Clerk of Court. Only cashiers checks and money orders accepted. Prepayment is required.

Miami County

District Court PO Box 187, Paola, KS 66071; 913-294-3326; Fax: 913-294-2535. Hours: 8AM-4:30PM (CST). *Felony, Misdemeanor, Civil, Eviction, Small Claims, Probate.*

Civil Records: Access: In person only. Both court and visitors may perform in person searches. No search fee. Required to search: name, years to search. Civil cases indexed by defendant, plaintiff. Civil records on computer from 1984, index cards from 1890s.
Criminal Records: Access: In person only. Both court and visitors may perform in person searches. No search fee. Required to search: name, years to search; also helpful: SSN. Criminal records on computer from 1984, index cards from 1890s.
General Information: Public access terminal is available. No juvenile, mental health, sealed or expunged records released. Copy fee: $.50 per page. Certification fee: $1.00. Fee payee: District Court. Personal checks accepted. Prepayment is required.

Mitchell County

District Court 115 S Hersey, Beloit, KS 67420; 785-738-3753; Fax: 785-738-4101. Hours: 8AM-5PM (CST). *Felony, Misdemeanor, Civil, Eviction, Small Claims, Probate.*
www.kscourts.org/dstcts/12dstct.htm
Civil Records: Access: Mail, in person. Both court and visitors may perform in person searches. Search fee: $10.00 per hour. Required to search: name, years to search. Civil cases indexed by defendant, plaintiff. Civil records on index cards from 1876.
Criminal Records: Access: Mail, in person. Both court and visitors may perform in person searches. Search fee: $10.00 per hour. Required to search: name, years to search. Criminal records on index cards from 1977, archived to 1870.
General Information: No juvenile, mental health, sealed or expunged records released. SASE required. Turnaround time 1-2 days. Copy fee: $.25 per page. Certification fee: $1.00. Fee payee: Clerk of Court. Personal checks accepted. Prepayment is required.

Montgomery County

Independence District Court 300 E Main St #201, Independence, KS 67301; 620-330-1070; Fax: 620-331-6120. Hours: 8AM-5PM (CST). *Felony, Misdemeanor, Civil, Eviction, Small Claims, Probate.*

Civil Records: Access: Fax, mail, in person. Both court and visitors may perform in person searches. Search fee: $12.80 per hour. $6.00 minimum. Required to search: name, years to search. Civil cases indexed by defendant, plaintiff. Civil records on computer since 1992, on microfiche from 1870-1930, archives 1930-1992, index cards from 1870. This court covers civil cases for the northern part of the county. It is suggested to search both courts.
Criminal Records: Access: Fax, mail, in person. Both court and visitors may perform in person searches. Search fee: $12.80 per hour. $6.00 minimum. Required to search: name, years to search; also helpful: SSN. Criminal records on computer since 1992, on

microfiche from 1870-1930, archives 1930-1992, index cards from 1870.

General Information: Public access terminal is available. No juvenile, adoptions, mental health, sealed or expunged records released. SASE not required. Turnaround time 72 hours. Fax notes: $5.00 for first page, $1.00 each add'l. Copy fee: $.25 per page. Certification fee: $1.00. Fee payee: Clerk of Court. Personal checks accepted. Prepayment is required.

Coffeyville District Court 102 W 7th St #A, Coffeyville, KS 67337; 620-251-1060; Fax: 620-251-2734. Hours: 8AM-5PM (CST). *Civil, Eviction, Small Claims, Probate.*

Note: This court covers civil cases for the southern part of the county, although cases can be filed in either court. It is recommended to search both courts

Civil Records: Access: Fax, mail, in person. Both court and visitors may perform in person searches. Search fee: $12.80 per hour; $6.00 minimum. Required to search: name, years to search. Civil cases indexed by defendant, plaintiff. Civil records on computer back to 1992, on paper, fiche, etc. since 1924.

General Information: Public access terminal is available. No juvenile, mental health, sealed, adoption, or expunged records released. Turnaround time 72 hours. Fax notes: Fee to fax results is $1.00 per page. Copy fee: $.25 per page. Certification fee: $1.00. Fee payee: Clerk of Court. Personal checks accepted.

Morris County

District Court County Courthouse, Council Grove, KS 66846; 620-767-6838; Fax: 620-767-6488. Hours: 8AM-5PM (CST). *Felony, Misdemeanor, Civil, Eviction, Small Claims, Probate.*

Civil Records: Access: Fax, mail, in person. Both court and visitors may perform in person searches. Search fee: $12.00 per hour. Required to search: name, years to search. Civil cases indexed by defendant, plaintiff. Civil records on computer since 1992, on microfiche, archives and index cards from 1860.

Criminal Records: Access: Fax, mail, in person. Both court and visitors may perform in person searches. Search fee: $12.00 per hour. Required to search: name, years to search. Criminal records on computer since 1992, on microfiche, archives and index cards from 1860.

General Information: Public access terminal is available. SASE required. Turnaround time 1-2 days. Fax notes: $1.00 per page. Copy fee: $.25 per page. Certification fee: $1.00. Fee payee: Clerk of Court. Personal checks accepted. Prepayment is required.

Morton County

District Court PO Box 825, Elkhart, KS 67950; 620-697-2563; Fax: 620-697-4289. Hours: 8AM-Noon, 1-5PM (CST). *Felony, Misdemeanor, Civil, Eviction, Small Claims, Probate.*

Civil Records: Access: Mail, fax, in person. Both court and visitors may perform in person searches. Search fee: $12.00 per hour. Required to search: name, years to search. Civil cases indexed by defendant, plaintiff. Civil records on computer from 1992, index cards from 1800s.

Criminal Records: Access: Mail, fax, in person. Both court and visitors may perform in person searches. Search fee: $12.00 per hour. Required to search: name, years to search. Criminal records on computer from 1977, index cards from 1800s.

General Information: Public access terminal is available. No juvenile, mental health, sealed or expunged records released. SASE not required. Turnaround time 1 day. Fax notes: Fee to fax results: $2.50 1st pg.; $.50 each add'l. Copy fee: $.25 per page. Certification fee: $1.00. Fee payee: Clerk of Court.

Personal checks accepted. Two party checks not accepted. Prepayment is required.

Nemaha County

District Court PO Box 213, Seneca, KS 66538; 785-336-2146; Fax: 785-336-6450. Hours: 8AM-5PM (CST). *Felony, Misdemeanor, Civil, Eviction, Small Claims, Probate.*

Civil Records: Access: Phone, mail, in person. Both court and visitors may perform in person searches. Search fee: $12.00 per hour. Required to search: name, years to search. Civil cases indexed by defendant, plaintiff. Civil records on computer from 1977, index cards from 1870.

Criminal Records: Access: Phone, mail, in person. Both court and visitors may perform in person searches. Search fee: $12.00 per hour. Required to search: name, years to search, SSN. Criminal records on computer from 1977, index cards from 1870.

General Information: Public access terminal is available. No juvenile, mental health, sealed or expunged records released. SASE required. Turnaround time 1-2 days. Fax notes: Fee to fax is $2.00 1st page, $1.00 each add'l. Copy fee: $.25 per page. Certification fee: $1.00. Fee payee: Clerk of District Court. Business checks accepted. Prepayment is required.

Neosho County

Chanute District Court 102 S Lincoln, PO Box 889, Chanute, KS 66720; 620-431-5700; Fax: 620-431-5710. *Felony, Misdemeanor, Civil, Eviction, Small Claims.*

Note: This is a branch court of Erie.

Civil Records: Access: Mail, in person. Both court and visitors may perform in person searches. Search fee: $12.00 per hour. Required to search: name, years to search. Civil cases indexed by defendant, plaintiff. Civil records on computer since 1993; prior back to 1955.

Criminal Records: Access: In person only. Visitors must perform in person searches for themselves. Required to search: name, years to search. Criminal records on computer since 1993; prior back to 1955.

General Information: Public access terminal is available. No juvenile, mental health, sealed or expunged records released. Turnaround time 1-3 days. Fax notes: Fee to fax results is $1.00 per page. Copy fee: $.50 per page. Certification fee: $1.00. Fee payee: Clerk of District Court. Personal checks accepted.

Erie District Court Neosho County Courthouse, PO Box 19, Erie, KS 66733; 620-244-3831; Fax: 620-244-3830. Hours: 8AM-noon, 1-4:30PM (CST). *Felony, Misdemeanor, Civil, Eviction, Small Claims, Probate.*

Note: This is the main court for the county.

Civil Records: Access: Fax, mail, in person. Both court and visitors may perform in person searches. Search fee: $12.00 per hour. Required to search: name, years to search. Civil cases indexed by defendant, plaintiff. Civil records on index cards from 1900s; on computer back to 1993.

Criminal Records: Access: In person only. Visitors must perform in person searches for themselves. Required to search: name, years to search, DOB. Criminal records on index cards from 1900s; on computer back to 1993.

General Information: Public access terminal is available. No juvenile, mental health, sealed or expunged records released. SASE required. Turnaround time 1-2 days. Fax notes: Fee to fax results is $1.00 per page. Copy fee: $.50 per page. Certification fee: $1.00. Fee payee: Clerk of Court. Personal checks accepted. Prepayment is required.

Ness County

District Court PO Box 445, Ness City, KS 67560; 785-798-3693; Fax: 785-798-3348. Hours: 8AM-5PM (CST). *Felony, Misdemeanor, Civil, Eviction, Small Claims, Probate.*

www.kscourts.org/dstcts/24dstct.htm

Civil Records: Access: Fax, mail, in person. Both court and visitors may perform in person searches. No search fee. Required to search: name, years to search. Civil cases indexed by defendant, plaintiff. Civil records on index books from 1885.

Criminal Records: Access: In person only. Visitors must perform in person searches for themselves. No search fee. Required to search: name, years to search. Criminal records on index books from 1885.

General Information: No juvenile, mental health, sealed or expunged records released. SASE not required. Turnaround time 3 days. Fax notes: $1.00 per page. Copy fee: $.25 per page. Certification fee: $1.00. Fee payee: Clerk of Court. Personal checks accepted. Prepayment is required.

Norton County

District Court PO Box 70, Norton, KS 67654; 785-877-5720; Fax: 785-877-5722. Hours: 8AM-5PM (CST). *Felony, Misdemeanor, Civil, Eviction, Small Claims, Probate.*

Civil Records: Access: Mail, in person. Both court and visitors may perform in person searches. Search fee: $12.00 per hour. Required to search: name, years to search. Civil cases indexed by defendant, plaintiff. Civil records on index from 1900s.

Criminal Records: Access: Mail, in person. Both court and visitors may perform in person searches. Search fee: $12.00 per hour. Required to search: name, years to search. Criminal records on index from 1900s.

General Information: No juvenile, mental health, sealed or expunged records released. SASE required. Turnaround time 1 week. Copy fee: $.25 per page. Certification fee: $1.00. Fee payee: Clerk of District Court. Personal checks accepted. Prepayment is required.

Osage County

District Court PO Box 549, Lyndon, KS 66451; 785-828-4514; Fax: 785-828-4704. Hours: 8AM-Noon,1-4PM (CST). *Felony, Misdemeanor, Civil, Eviction, Small Claims, Probate.*

www.kscourts.org/dstcts/4dstct.htm

Civil Records: Access: Mail, in person, online. Both court and visitors may perform in person searches. Search fee: $12.00 per hour. Required to search: name, years to search. Civil cases indexed by defendant, plaintiff. Civil records on computer from 1980, index cards from 1979. Current court calendars are available free online at www.kscourts.org/dstcts/4osdckt.htm.

Criminal Records: Access: Mail, in person, online. Both court and visitors may perform in person searches. Search fee: $12.00 per hour. Required to search: name, years to search. Criminal records on computer from 1980, index cards from 1979. Online access to criminal records is the same as civil.

General Information: Public access terminal is available. No juvenile, mental health, sealed or expunged records released. SASE required. Turnaround time 1-2 days. Copy fee: $.25 per page. Certification fee: $1.00. Fee payee: Clerk of Court. Business checks accepted. Prepayment is required.

Osborne County

District Court 423 W Main, PO Box 160, Osborne, KS 67473; 785-346-5911; Fax: 785-246-5992. Hours: 8:30AM-5PM (CST). *Felony, Misdemeanor, Civil, Eviction, Small Claims, Probate.*

Civil Records: Access: In person only. Visitors must perform in person searches for themselves. No search fee. Required to search: name, years to search. Civil cases indexed by defendant, plaintiff. Civil records on microfiche from 1872-1980, index books from 1981, index cards from 1872.

Criminal Records: Access: In person only. Visitors must perform in person searches for themselves. No search fee. Required to search: name, years to search; also helpful: SSN. Criminal records on microfiche from 1872-1980, index books from 1981, index cards from 1872.

General Information: No juvenile, mental health, sealed or expunged records released. Copy fee: $.25 per page. Certification fee: $1.00. Fee payee: Clerk of District Court. Personal checks accepted.

Ottawa County

District Court 307 N Concord, Minneapolis, KS 67467; 785-392-2917; Fax: 785-392-3626. Hours: 8:30AM-5PM (CST). *Felony, Misdemeanor, Civil, Eviction, Small Claims, Probate.*

Civil Records: Access: Mail, fax, in person. Both court and visitors may perform in person searches. Search fee: $9.00 per hour. Required to search: name, years to search. Civil cases indexed by defendant, plaintiff. Civil records on index from 1800s; computerized records since 1990.

Criminal Records: Access: Mail, in person. Both court and visitors may perform in person searches. Search fee: $9.00 per hour. Required to search: name, years to search; also helpful: SSN. Criminal records on index from 1800s; computerized records since 1990.

General Information: No juvenile, mental health, sealed or expunged records released. SASE required. Turnaround time 1 week. Copy fee: $1.00 for first page, $.25 each add'l. Certification fee: $1.00. Fee payee: Clerk of District Court. Personal checks accepted. Prepayment is required.

Pawnee County

District Court PO Box 270, Larned, KS 67550; 620-285-6937; Fax: 620-285-3665. Hours: 8AM-5PM (CST). *Felony, Misdemeanor, Civil, Eviction, Small Claims, Probate.*

www.kscourts.org/dstcts/24dstct.htm

Civil Records: Access: Fax, mail, in person. Both court and visitors may perform in person searches. Search fee: $12.00 an hour if done by court. Required to search: name, years to search. Civil cases indexed by defendant, plaintiff. Civil records on computer from 1991, index cards from 1900s.

Criminal Records: Access: In person only. Visitors must perform in person searches for themselves. Search fee: $12.00 an hour if done by court. Required to search: name, years to search; also helpful: SSN. Criminal records on computer from 1991, index cards from 1900s.

General Information: No juvenile, mental health, sealed or expunged records released. SASE not required. Turnaround time 1-2 days. Fax notes: $.50 per page. Copy fee: $.25 per page. Certification fee: $1.00. Fee payee: Clerk of District Court. Personal checks accepted. Prepayment is required.

Phillips County

District Court PO Box 564, Phillipsburg, KS 67661; 785-543-6830; Fax: 785-543-6832. Hours: 8AM-5PM (CST). *Felony, Misdemeanor, Civil, Eviction, Small Claims, Probate.*

Civil Records: Access: In person mail. Visitors must perform in person searches for themselves. Required to search: name, years to search. Civil cases indexed by defendant, plaintiff. Civil records on index from 1900s; on computer back to 1994.

Criminal Records: Access: In person, mail. Visitors must perform in person searches for themselves. Search fee: $12.00 per hour. Required to search: name, years to search; also helpful: DOB, SSN. Criminal records on index from 1900s; on computer back to 1994.

General Information: No juvenile, mental health, sealed or expunged records released. Fax notes: Fee to fax results is $.50 per page. Copy fee: $.25 per page. Certification fee: $1.00. Fee payee: Clerk of District Court. Personal checks accepted.

Pottawatomie County

District Court PO Box 129, Westmoreland, KS 66549; 785-457-3392; Fax: 785-457-2107. Hours: 8AM-4:30PM (CST). *Felony, Misdemeanor, Civil, Eviction, Small Claims, Probate.*

Civil Records: Access: In person. Visitors must perform in person searches No search fee. Required to search: name, years to search. Civil cases indexed by defendant, plaintiff. Civil records computerized since 1998, on microfiche from 1800s, index from 1800s.

Criminal Records: Access: In person. Visitors must perform in person searches No search fee. Required to search: name, years to search; also helpful: SSN. Criminal records computerized since 1998, on microfiche from 1800s, index from 1800s.

General Information: Public access terminal is available. (Records available back to 1995.) No juvenile, mental health, sealed or expunged records released. Copy fee: $.25 per page; $.10 per page self serve. Certification fee: $2.00. Fee payee: Clerk of District Court. Personal checks accepted.

Pratt County

District Court PO Box 984, Pratt, KS 67124; 620-672-4100; Fax: 620-672-2902. Hours: 8AM-Noon, 1-5PM (CST). *Felony, Misdemeanor, Civil, Eviction, Small Claims, Probate.*

Civil Records: Access: Mail, fax, in person. Both court and visitors may perform in person searches. Search fee: $12.00 per hour. Required to search: name, years to search. Civil cases indexed by defendant, plaintiff. Civil records on computer back to 1988, microfiche, archives, index from 1878.

Criminal Records: Access: Mail, fax, in person. Only the court performs in person searches; visitors may not. Search fee: $12.00 per hour. Required to search: name, years to search, DOB; also helpful: SSN, signed release. Criminal records on computer back to 1988, microfiche, archives, index from 1878.

General Information: Public access terminal is available. No juvenile, mental health, sealed or expunged records released. SASE required. Turnaround time 1-2 days. Fax notes: Fee to fax results is $1.00 per page. Copy fee: $.25 per page. Certification fee: $1.00. Fee payee: Clerk of District Court. Personal checks accepted. Prepayment is required.

Rawlins County

District Court PO Box 257, Atwood, KS 67730; 785-626-3465; Fax: 785-626-3350. Hours: 9AM-5PM (CST) *Felony, Misdemeanor, Civil, Eviction, Small Claims, Probate.*

Civil Records: Access: In person only. Visitors must perform in person searches for themselves. No search

fee. Required to search: name, years to search. Civil cases indexed by defendant, plaintiff. Civil records on index from 1900s.

Criminal Records: Access: In person only. Visitors must perform in person searches for themselves. No search fee. Required to search: name, years to search; also helpful: SSN. Criminal records on index from 1900s. This agency refers requesters to the Kansas Bureau of Investigations.

General Information: No juvenile, mental health, sealed or expunged records released. Copy fee: $.25 per page. Certification fee: $1.00. Fee payee: Clerk of District Court. Only in state checks accepted. Prepayment is required.

Reno County

District Court 206 W 1st, Hutchinson, KS 67501; 620-694-2956; Fax: 620-694-2958. Hours: 8AM-Noon, 1-5PM (CST). *Felony, Misdemeanor, Civil, Eviction, Small Claims, Probate.*

Civil Records: Access: Mail, in person. Only the court performs in person searches; visitors may not. Search fee: $9.50 per hour. Required to search: name, years to search. Civil cases indexed by defendant, plaintiff. Civil records on computer from 1992, index cards from 1900s.

Criminal Records: Access: Mail, in person. Only the court performs in person searches; visitors may not. Search fee: $9.50 per hour. Required to search: name, years to search, DOB, signed release; also helpful: address, SSN. Criminal records on computer from 1992, index cards from 1900s.

General Information: No mental health, juvenile (some), sealed or expunged records released. SASE required. Turnaround time 3-5 days (in-state); 3-10 days (out-of-state). Fax notes: Will not fax results. Copy fee: $.25 per page. Certification fee: $1.00. Fee payee: Clerk of District Court. Only cashiers checks and money orders accepted. Prepayment is required.

Republic County

District Court PO Box 8, Belleville, KS 66935; 785-527-5691; Fax: 785-527-5029. Hours: 8:30AM-5PM (CST). *Felony, Misdemeanor, Civil, Eviction, Small Claims, Probate.*

www.kscourts.org/dstcts/12dstct.htm

Civil Records: Access: Mail, in person. Both court and visitors may perform in person searches. No search fee. Required to search: name, years to search. Civil cases indexed by defendant, plaintiff. Civil records on computer from 1990, index cards from 1869 for probate.

Criminal Records: Access: In person only. Visitors must perform in person searches for themselves. No search fee. Required to search: name, years to search. Criminal records on computer from 1990, index cards from 1869 for probate.

General Information: No juvenile, mental health, sealed or expunged records released. SASE required. Turnaround time 2-4 weeks. Copy fee: $.25 per page. Certification fee: $1.00. Fee payee: Clerk of Court. Personal checks accepted. Prepayment is required.

Rice County

District Court 101 W Commercial, Lyons, KS 67554; 620-257-2383; Fax: 620-257-3826. Hours: 8:30AM-5PM (CST). *Felony, Misdemeanor, Civil, Eviction, Small Claims, Probate.*

Civil Records: Access: Fax, mail, in person. Both the court and visitors may perform in person searches. Search fee: $9.00 per hour. Required to search: name, years to search. Civil cases indexed by defendant, plaintiff. Civil records on computer from 1980, index cards from 1880.

Criminal Records: Access: Fax, mail, in person. Visitors must perform in person searches for themselves. Search fee: $9.00 per hour. Required to search: name, years to search; also helpful: SSN. Criminal records on computer from 1980, index cards from 1880. All criminal searches are referred to the KBI, 1620 SW Tyler, Topeka KS 66601.

General Information: Public access terminal is available. No juvenile, mental health, sealed or expunged records released. SASE required. Turnaround time 1-3 days. Fax notes: Fee to fax results is $.50 per page. Copy fee: $1.00 for first page, $.25 each add'l. Fee payee: Clerk of Court. Personal checks accepted. Prepayment is required.

Riley County

District Court PO Box 158, Manhattan, KS 66505-0158; 785-537-6364. Hours: 8:30AM-5PM (CST). *Felony, Misdemeanor, Civil, Eviction, Small Claims, Probate.*

www.co.riley.ks.us/districtcourt

Civil Records: Access: In person only. Visitors must perform in person searches for themselves. No search fee. Required to search: name, years to search. Civil cases indexed by defendant, plaintiff. Civil records on computer back to 10/93; prior records in index journals.

Criminal Records: Access: In person only. Visitors must perform in person searches for themselves. No search fee. Required to search: name, years to search; also helpful: DOB, SSN. Criminal records on computer back to 1986, microfiche, archives and index cards from 1900s.

General Information: Public access terminal is available. No mental health, sealed or expunged records released. Copy fee: $.25 per page. Certification fee: $1.00. Fee payee: Clerk of Court. Personal checks accepted. Prepayment is required.

Rooks County

District Court 115 N Walnut, PO Box 532, Stockton, KS 67669; 785-425-6718; Fax: 785-425-6568. Hours: 8AM-5PM (CST). *Felony, Misdemeanor, Civil, Eviction, Small Claims, Probate.*

Civil Records: Access: Mail, in person. Both court and visitors may perform in person searches. Search fee: $12.00 per hour. Required to search: name, years to search. Civil cases indexed by defendant, plaintiff. Civil records on index cards from 1888; on computer since.

Criminal Records: Access: Mail, in person. Both court and visitors may perform in person searches. Search fee: $12.00 per hour. Required to search: name, years to search; also helpful: DOB, SSN. Criminal records on index cards from 1888; on computer since.

General Information: Public access terminal is available. No juvenile, adoption, mental health, sealed or expunged records released. SASE required. Turnaround time 1-3 days. Fax notes: Fee to fax results is $1.00 per page. Copy fee: $.25 per page. Certification fee: $2.00. Fee payee: Clerk of Court. Personal checks accepted. Prepayment is required.

Rush County

District Court PO Box 387, La Crosse, KS 67548; 785-222-2718; Fax: 785-222-2748. Hours: 8AM-5PM (CST). *Felony, Misdemeanor, Civil, Eviction, Small Claims, Probate.*

www.kscourts.org/dstcts/24dstct.htm

Civil Records: Access: Phone, fax, mail, in person. Both court and visitors may perform in person searches. No search fee. Required to search: name, years to search. Civil cases indexed by defendant, plaintiff. Civil records on computer from April, 1994, on index from 1800s.

Criminal Records: Access: In person only. Visitors must perform in person searches for themselves. No search fee. Required to search: name, years to search;

also helpful: SSN. Criminal records on computer from April, 1994, on index from 1800s.

General Information: No juvenile, mental health, sealed or expunged records released. SASE required. Turnaround time 3 days. Fax notes: $.50 per page. Copy fee: $.25 per page. Certification fee: $1.00. Fee payee: Clerk of District Court. Personal checks accepted. Prepayment is required.

Russell County

District Court PO Box 876, Russell, KS 67665; 785-483-5641; Fax: 785-483-2448. Hours: 8AM-5PM (CST). *Felony, Misdemeanor, Civil, Eviction, Small Claims, Probate.*

Civil Records: Access: Fax, mail, in person. Both court and visitors may perform in person searches. Search fee: $12.00 per hour. Required to search: name, years to search. Civil cases indexed by defendant, plaintiff. Civil records on computer from 1990, index cards from 1900s.

Criminal Records: Access: Fax, mail, in person. Both court and visitors may perform in person searches. Search fee: $12.00 per hour. Required to search: name, years to search, DOB. Criminal records on computer from 1990, index cards from 1900s.

General Information: Public access terminal is available. No juvenile, mental health, sealed or expunged records released. SASE required. Turnaround time 3 days. Fax notes: Fee to fax results is $.50 per page. Copy fee: $.50 per page. Fee payee: Clerk of Court. Personal checks accepted. Prepayment is required.

Saline County

District Court PO Box 1760, Salina, KS 67402-1760; 785-826-6617; Fax: 785-826-7319. Hours: 8:30AM-4PM (CST). *Felony, Misdemeanor, Civil, Eviction, Small Claims, Probate.*

Civil Records: Access: Mail, in person. Both court and visitors may perform in person searches. Search fee: $12.00 per hour. Required to search: name, years to search, address. Civil cases indexed by defendant, plaintiff. Civil records on computer from 1990, index from early 1900s.

Criminal Records: Access: Mail, in person. Both court and visitors may perform in person searches. Search fee: $12.00 per hour. Required to search: name, years to search, address, DOB, SSN, signed release. Criminal records on computer from 1990, index from early 1900s.

General Information: No juvenile, mental health, sealed or expunged records released. SASE not required. Turnaround time 1 week. Copy fee: $.25 per page. Certification fee: $1.00. Fee payee: Clerk of District Court. Personal checks accepted. Prepayment is required.

Scott County

District Court 303 Court, Scott City, KS 67871; 620-872-7208. Hours: 8AM-Noon, 1-5PM (CST). *Felony, Misdemeanor, Civil, Eviction, Small Claims, Probate.*

Civil Records: Access: Mail, in person. No search fee. Required to search: name, years to search. Civil cases indexed by defendant, plaintiff. Civil records on computer back to 1992, index cards from 1980s.

Criminal Records: Access: In person only. Visitors must perform in person searches for themselves. No search fee. Required to search: name, years to search, DOB. Criminal records on computer back to 1992, index cards from 1980s.

General Information: Public access terminal is available. No juvenile, mental health, sealed or expunged records released. SASE required. Turnaround time 1-2 days. Fax notes: Fee to fax results is $1.00 per page. Copy fee: $.25 per page. Certification fee: $1.00.

Fee payee: Clerk of Court. Personal checks accepted. Prepayment is required.

Sedgwick County

District Court 525 N Main, Wichita, KS 67203; 316-383-7302; Civil phone: 316-383-7311; Criminal phone: 316-383-7253; Fax: 316-383-8070 (Civil) 383-8071 (Criminal). Hours: 8AM-5PM (CST). *Felony, Misdemeanor, Civil, Eviction, Small Claims, Probate.*

http://distcrt18.state.ks.us

Civil Records: Access: Fax, mail, online, in person. Both court and visitors may perform in person searches. Search fee: $12.00 per hour. Fee charged if more than 15 minutes. Required to search: name, years to search. Civil cases indexed by defendant, plaintiff. Civil records on computer from 1983, microfiche from 1982, archives from 1977 and index cards from 1900s. Access to the remote online system requires a $225 setup fee, $49 monthly fee and small transaction fee. The system also includes probate, traffic, domestic, and criminal cases. For more information, call 316-383-7563.

Criminal Records: Access: Fax, mail, online, in person. Both court and visitors may perform in person searches. Search fee: $12.00 per hour. Fee charged if more than 15 minutes. Required to search: name, years to search. Criminal records on computer from 1983, microfiche from 1982, archives from 1977 and index cards from 1900s. Online access to criminal records is the same as civil.

General Information: Public access terminal is available. No juvenile, adoption, mental health, sealed or expunged records released. SASE required. Turnaround time 7-10 days. Fax notes: $5.00 for first page, $2.00 each add'l. Copy fee: $.25 per page. Certification fee: $1.00. Fee payee: Clerk of Court. Personal checks accepted. Prepayment is required.

Seward County

District Court 415 N Washington #103, Liberal, KS 67901; 620-626-3265; Fax: 620-626-3302. Hours: 8:30AM-5PM (CST). *Felony, Misdemeanor, Civil, Eviction, Small Claims, Probate.*

Note: Court will do searches on occasion, fee is $12.00 per hour.

Civil Records: Access: In person only. Visitors must perform in person searches for themselves. No search fee. Required to search: name, years to search. Civil cases indexed by defendant, plaintiff. Civil records on computer back to 1977, index from 1900s.

Criminal Records: Access: In person only. Visitors must perform in person searches for themselves. No search fee. Required to search: name, years to search; also helpful: SSN. Criminal records on computer back to 1977, index from 1900s.

General Information: Public access terminal is available. No juvenile, mental health, sealed or expunged records released. Fax notes: Fee to fax results is $2.50 1st page, $.50 each add'l. Certification fee: $1.25. Fee payee: Clerk of District Court. Personal checks accepted. Prepayment is required.

Shawnee County

District Court 200 E 7th Rm 209, Topeka, KS 66603; 785-233-8200 X4327; Fax: 785-291-4911. Hours: 8AM-5PM (CST). *Felony, Misdemeanor, Civil, Eviction, Small Claims, Probate.*

www.shawneecourt.org

Civil Records: Access: Fax, mail, in person, online. Both court and visitors may perform in person searches. Search fee: $12.00 per hour. Required to search: name, years to search. Civil cases indexed by defendant, plaintiff. Civil records on computer from 1980, microfiche from 1950, archives and index from 1800s. Index online through INK of Kansas. See www.ink.org for subscription information. Also, online access to county court records available free at www.shawneecourt.org/pa_inst.htm. Also, online access to court record images is available free at www.shawneecourt.org/img_temp.htm.

Criminal Records: Access: Fax, mail, in person, online. Both court and visitors may perform in person searches. Search fee: $12.00 per hour. Required to search: name, years to search, DOB. Criminal records on computer from 1980, microfiche from 1950, archives and index from 1800s. Online access to criminal records is the same as civil.

General Information: Public access terminal is available. No juvenile, mental health, sealed or expunged records released. SASE not required. Turnaround time 3-4 days. Copy fee: $.50 per page. $1.50 per pg for microfilm copies. Certification fee: $2.25. Fee payee: Clerk of District Court. Personal checks accepted. Prepayment is required.

Sheridan County

District Court PO Box 753, Hoxie, KS 67740; 785-675-3451; Fax: 785-675-2256. Hours: 8AM-Noon, 1PM-5PM (CST). *Felony, Misdemeanor, Civil, Eviction, Small Claims, Probate.*

Civil Records: Access: Phone, fax, mail, in person. Both court and visitors may perform in person searches. Search fee: $12.00 per hour. Required to search: name, years to search. Civil cases indexed by defendant, plaintiff. Civil records on strip index from 1885. Mail requests require use of a special form.

Criminal Records: Access: Phone, fax, mail, in person. Both court and visitors may perform in person searches. Search fee: $12.00 per hour. Required to search: name, years to search, signed release. Criminal records on strip index from 1885; on computer since 1995.

General Information: No juvenile, mental health, sealed or expunged records released. SASE required. Turnaround time 1-2 days. Copy fee: $.20 per page. Certification fee: $1.00. Fee payee: Clerk of Court. Personal checks accepted. Prepayment is required.

Sherman County

District Court 813 Broadway Rm 201, Goodland, KS 67735; 785-899-4850; Fax: 785-899-4858. Hours: 8:30AM-5PM (MST). *Felony, Misdemeanor, Civil, Eviction, Small Claims, Probate.*

Civil Records: Access: In person only. Visitors must perform in person searches for themselves. No search fee. Required to search: name, years to search. Civil cases indexed by defendant, plaintiff. Civil records on docket books from 1900s.

Criminal Records: Access: In person only. Visitors must perform in person searches for themselves. No search fee. Required to search: name, years to search; also helpful: SSN. Criminal records on docket books from 1900s.

General Information: No juvenile, mental health, sealed or expunged records released. Copy fee: $.25 per page. Certification fee: $1.00. Fee payee: Clerk of District Court. Personal checks accepted.

Smith County

District Court PO Box 273, Smith Center, KS 66967; 785-282-5140/41; Fax: 785-282-5145. Hours: 8AM-5PM (CST). *Felony, Misdemeanor, Civil, Eviction, Small Claims, Probate.*

Civil Records: Access: In person only. Visitors must perform in person searches for themselves. No search fee. Required to search: name, years to search. Civil cases indexed by defendant, plaintiff. Civil records on index cards from 1873.

Criminal Records: Access: In person only. Visitors must perform in person searches for themselves. No search fee. Required to search: name, years to search;

also helpful: SSN. Criminal records on index cards from 1873.

General Information: No juvenile, mental health, sealed or expunged records released. Copy fee: $.25 per page. Certification fee: $1.00. Fee payee: Clerk of Court. Personal checks accepted. Prepayment is required.

Stafford County

District Court PO Box 365, St John, KS 67576; 620-549-3295; Fax: 620-549-3298. Hours: 8AM-5PM (CST). *Felony, Misdemeanor, Civil, Eviction, Small Claims, Probate.*

Civil Records: Access: Phone, mail, fax, in person, email. Both court and visitors may perform in person searches. No search fee. Required to search: name, years to search. Civil cases indexed by defendant, plaintiff. Civil records on computer from 1988, microfiche and index from 1900s.

Criminal Records: Access: In person only. Visitors must perform in person searches for themselves. No search fee. Required to search: name, years to search; also helpful: SSN, signed release. Criminal records on computer from 1988, microfiche and index from 1900s.

General Information: Public access terminal is available. No juvenile, mental health, sealed or expunged records released. SASE required. Turnaround time 1-3 days. Copy fee: $.15 per page. Fee payee: Clerk of District Court. Personal checks accepted. Prepayment is required.

Stanton County

District Court PO Box 913, Johnson, KS 67855; 620-492-2180; Fax: 620-492-6410. Hours: 8AM-5PM (CST). *Felony, Misdemeanor, Civil, Eviction, Small Claims, Probate.*

Civil Records: Access: Phone, fax, mail, in person. Both court and visitors may perform in person searches. Search fee: $12.00 per hour. Required to search: name, years to search. Civil cases indexed by defendant, plaintiff. Civil records on computer from 1977, index from 1887.

Criminal Records: Access: Phone, fax, mail, in person. Both court and visitors may perform in person searches. Search fee: $12.00 per hour. Required to search: name, years to search, DOB, SSN. Criminal records on computer from 1977, index from 1887.

General Information: Public access terminal is available. No juvenile, mental health, sealed or expunged records released. SASE required. Turnaround time 1-3 days. Fax notes: $2.50 for first page, $.50 each add'l. Copy fee: $.25 per page. Certification fee: $1.50. Fee payee: Clerk of District Court. Personal checks accepted. Prepayment is required.

Stevens County

District Court 200 E 6th, Hugoton, KS 67951; 620-544-2484; Fax: 620-544-2528. Hours: 8AM-5PM (CST). *Felony, Misdemeanor, Civil, Eviction, Small Claims, Probate.*

Civil Records: Access: Mail, in person. Both court and visitors may perform in person searches. Search fee: $12.00 per hour. Required to search: name, years to search. Civil cases indexed by defendant, plaintiff. Civil records on computer from 1991, microfiche, archives and index from 1887.

Criminal Records: Access: In person only. Visitors must perform in person searches for themselves. No search fee. Required to search: name, years to search; also helpful: SSN. Criminal records on computer from 1991, microfiche, archives and index from 1887.

General Information: Public access terminal is available. No juvenile, mental health, sealed or expunged records released. SASE required. Turnaround time 1-3 days. Fax notes: Fee to fax results is $3.00 plus $.25 per page. Copy fee: $.25 per page. Certification

fee: $1.25. Fee payee: Clerk of District Court. Personal checks accepted. Must prepay for fax and mail.

Sumner County

District Court PO Box 399, Sumner County Courthouse, Wellington, KS 67152; 620-326-5936; Fax: 620-326-5365. Hours: 8AM-Noon, 1-5PM (CST). *Felony, Misdemeanor, Civil, Eviction, Small Claims, Probate.*

Note: Court will not perform searches for "employment purposes" nor do they perform lien searches. The court prefers that you summit requests on their request form.

Civil Records: Access: Mail, fax in person. Both court and visitors may perform in person searches. Search fee: $12.00 per hour. Required to search: name, years to search. Civil cases indexed by defendant, plaintiff. Civil records on computer back to 1991, index cards from 1800s for probate.

Criminal Records: Access: Mail, fax, in person. Both court and visitors may perform in person searches. Search fee: $12.00 per hour. Required to search: name, years to search; also helpful: case number. Criminal records on computer back to 1991, index cards from 1800s for probate.

General Information: Public access terminal is available. No juvenile, mental health, sealed or expunged records released. SASE not required. Turnaround time 1-3 days. Copy fee: $.25 per page. Certification fee: $2.00. Fee payee: Clerk of Court. Personal checks accepted. Prepayment is preferred.

Thomas County

District Court PO Box 805, Colby, KS 67701; 785-462-4540; Fax: 785-462-2291. Hours: 8:30AM-5PM (CST). *Felony, Misdemeanor, Civil, Eviction, Small Claims, Probate.*

Civil Records: Access: Fax, mail, in person. Both court and visitors may perform in person searches. Search fee: $12.00 per hour. Required to search: name, years to search. Civil cases indexed by defendant, plaintiff. Civil records on index from 1887.

Criminal Records: Access: Fax, mail, in person. Both court and visitors may perform in person searches. Search fee: $12.00 per hour. Required to search: name, years to search, DOB, sex; also helpful: SSN. Criminal records on index from 1887.

General Information: Public access terminal is available. No juvenile, mental health, sealed or expunged records released. SASE required. Turnaround time varies. Fax notes: $1.00 per page. Copy fee: $.25 per page. Certification fee: $1.00. Fee payee: Clerk. Personal checks accepted. Prepayment is required.

Trego County

District Court 216 N Main, Wakeeney, KS 67672; 785-743-2148; Fax: 785-743-2726. Hours: 8:30AM-5PM (CST). *Felony, Misdemeanor, Civil, Eviction, Small Claims, Probate.*

Civil Records: Access: Phone, mail, fax, in person. Both court and visitors may perform in person searches. Search fee: $12.00 per hour. Required to search: name, years to search. Civil cases indexed by defendant, plaintiff. Civil records on computer since 1996; prior records on card index.

Criminal Records: Access: Mail, in person. Only the court performs in person searches; visitors may not. Search fee: $12.00 per hour. Required to search: name, years to search; also helpful: DOB, SSN, sex. Criminal records on computer since 1996; prior records on card index.

General Information: No juvenile, mental health, sealed or expunged records released. SASE required. Turnaround time 1-2 weeks. Fax notes: Fee to fax results is $5.00 per document. Copy fee: $.25 per page. Certification fee: $2.00. Fee payee: Clerk of Court. Personal checks accepted. Prepayment is required.

Wabaunsee County

District Court Courthouse, PO Box 278, Alma, KS 66401; 785-765-2406; Fax: 785-765-2487. Hours: 8:30AM-4:30PM (CST). *Felony, Misdemeanor, Civil, Eviction, Small Claims, Probate.*

Civil Records: Access: In person only. Visitors must perform in person searches for themselves. No search fee. Required to search: name, years to search. Civil cases indexed by defendant, plaintiff. Civil records on book index from 1800s; on computer back to 1996.
Criminal Records: Access: In person only. Visitors must perform in person searches for themselves. No search fee. Required to search: name, years to search; also helpful: SSN. Criminal records on book index from 1800s; on computer back to 1996.
General Information: Public access terminal is available. No juvenile, mental health, sealed or expunged records released. Copy fee: $.50 per page. Certification fee: $1.25. Fee payee: Clerk of District Court. Personal checks accepted.

Wallace County

District Court PO Box 8, Sharon Springs, KS 67758; 785-852-4289; Fax: 785-852-4271. Hours: 8AM-Noon,1-5PM (MST). *Felony, Misdemeanor, Civil, Eviction, Small Claims, Probate.*

Civil Records: Access: Mail, in person, fax. Both court and visitors may perform in person searches. Search fee: $12.00 per hour. Required to search: name; also helpful: years to search. Civil cases indexed by defendant, plaintiff. Civil records on index from 1887. By mail only if requested for a particular case, court will not do name searches.
Criminal Records: Access: In person only. Visitors must perform in person searches for themselves. No search fee. Required to search: name; also helpful: years to search. Criminal records on index from 1887.
General Information: No juvenile offender (under 14 years old), juvenile in need of care, adoption, mental health, sealed or expunged records released. SASE not required. Turnaround time 1-2 days. Copy fee: $.25 per page. Certification fee: $1.00. Fee payee: Clerk of Court. Personal checks accepted. Prepayment is required.

Washington County

District Court Courthouse, 214 C Street, Washington, KS 66968; 785-325-2381; Fax: 785-325-2557. Hours: 8AM-Noon,1-5PM (CST). *Felony, Misdemeanor, Civil, Eviction, Small Claims, Probate.*
www.kscourts.org/dstcts/12dstct.htm

Civil Records: Access: Fax, mail, in person. Both court and visitors may perform in person searches. Search fee: $12.00 per hour. Required to search: name, years to search. Civil cases indexed by defendant, plaintiff. Civil

records on card index from 1887; on computer back to 1995.
Criminal Records: Access: Fax, mail, in person. Both court and visitors may perform in person searches. Search fee: $12.00 per hour. Required to search: name, years to search. Criminal records on card index from 1887; on computer back to 1995.
General Information: No juvenile, mental health, sealed or expunged records released. SASE required. Turnaround time 1-3 days. Fax notes: Fee to fax results is $3.00 per page. Copy fee: $.25 per page. Certification fee: $1.00. Fee payee: Clerk of Court. Personal checks accepted. Prepayment is required.

Wichita County

District Court 206 S 4th St, PO Box 968, Leoti, KS 67861; 620-375-4454; Fax: 620-375-2999. Hours: 8AM-5PM (CST). *Felony, Misdemeanor, Civil, Eviction, Small Claims, Probate.*
Note: This court is not in Wichita, KS. Wichita, KS is in Sedgwick County.
Civil Records: Access: Mail, in person. Both court and visitors may perform in person searches. Search fee: $12.00 per hour. Required to search: name, years to search. Civil cases indexed by defendant, plaintiff. Civil records on computer back to 1986, on index from 1900.
Criminal Records: Access: In person only. Visitors must perform in person searches for themselves. Required to search: name, years to search. Criminal records on computer back to 1986, on index from 1900. Criminal records are available through the KBI.
General Information: Public access terminal is available. (Indexed only from 1991.) No juvenile, mental health, sealed or expunged records released. SASE required. Turnaround time 1 week. Copy fee: $.20 per page. Certification fee: $1.00. Fee payee: Clerk of District Court. Personal checks accepted. Prepayment is required.

Wilson County

District Court PO Box 246, Fredonia, KS 66736; 620-378-4533; Fax: 620-378-4531. Hours: 8:30AM-5PM (CST). *Felony, Misdemeanor, Civil, Eviction, Small Claims, Probate.*

Civil Records: Access: Fax, mail, in person. Both court and visitors may perform in person searches. Search fee: $12.00 per hour. Required to search: name, years to search. Civil cases indexed by defendant, plaintiff. Civil records on computer since 1993, index cards from 1864.
Criminal Records: Access: Fax, mail, in person. Both court and visitors may perform in person searches. Search fee: $12.00 per hour. Required to search: name, years to search; also helpful: SSN. Criminal records on computer since 1993, index cards from 1864.
General Information: Public access terminal is available. No juvenile, mental health, sealed or

expunged records released. SASE required. Turnaround time 1-3 weeks. Fax notes: Fee to fax results is $1.00 per page. Copy fee: $.25 per page. Certification fee: $.50. Fee payee: Clerk of Court. Personal checks accepted. Prepayment is required.

Woodson County

District Court PO Box 228, Yates Center, KS 66783; 620-625-8610; Fax: 620-625-8674. Hours: 8AM-Noon,1-5PM (CST). *Felony, Misdemeanor, Civil, Eviction, Small Claims, Probate.*

Civil Records: Access: Fax, mail, in person. Both court and visitors may perform in person searches. Search fee: $12.00 per hour. Required to search: name, years to search. Civil cases indexed by defendant, plaintiff. Civil records on index from 1880s, on computer since 1993.
Criminal Records: Access: In person only. Visitors must perform in person searches for themselves. Required to search: name, years to search. Criminal records on index from 1880s, on computer since 1993. Refer phone inquires to KBI at 785-296-8200.
General Information: Public access terminal is available. No juvenile (under age 14 years), mental health, sealed or expunged records released. SASE required. Turnaround time 1 day. Fax notes: Fee to fax results is $1.00 per page. Copy fee: $.50 per page. Certification fee: $1.00. Fee payee: District Court. Business checks accepted. Prepayment is required.

Wyandotte County

District Court 710 N 7th St, Kansas City, KS 66101; Civil phone: 913-573-2901; Criminal phone: 913-573-2905; Fax: 913-573-8177. Hours: 8AM-5PM (CST). *Felony, Misdemeanor, Civil, Eviction, Small Claims, Probate.*

Civil Records: Access: Phone, mail, online, in person. Both court and visitors may perform in person searches. No search fee. Required to search: name, years to search. Civil cases indexed by defendant, plaintiff. Civil records on computer from 1975, microfiche, archives and index from 1900s. Access to the remote online system requires specific software and $20 setup fee. Transactions are $.05 each. For more information call 913-573-2885.
Criminal Records: Access: Online, in person. Visitors must perform in person searches for themselves. No search fee. Required to search: name, years to search, DOB, SSN. Criminal records on computer from 1972, microfiche, archives and index from early 1900s. Online access to criminal records is the same as civil. Refer phone inquires to KBI at 785-296-8200.
General Information: No juvenile, mental health, sealed or expunged records released. SASE required. Turnaround time 1-3 days. Copy fee: $.25 per page. Certification fee: $1.00. Fee payee: Clerk of District Court. Personal checks accepted.

Kansas Recording Offices

ORGANIZATION: 105 counties, 105 recording offices. The recording officer is Register of Deeds. Many counties utilize a "Miscellaneous Index" for tax and other liens, separate from real estate records. 100 counties are in the Central Time Zone (CST) and 5 are in the Mountain Time Zone (MST).

REAL ESTATE RECORDS: Most counties will not perform real estate searches, although some will do as an accommodation with the understanding that they are not "certified." Some counties will also do a search based upon legal description to determine owner. Copy fees vary, and certification fees are usually $1.00 per document. Tax records are located at the Appraiser's Office.

UCC RECORDS: Financing statements are filed at the state level, except for real estate related collateral, which are filed with the Register of Deeds. However, prior to 07/2001, consumer goods collateral were also filed at the Register of Deeds and these older records can be searched there. All counties will perform UCC searches. Use search request form UCC-3. Search fees are usually $15.00 per debtor name. Copies usually cost $1.00 per page.

TAX LIEN RECORDS: Federal tax liens on personal property of businesses are filed with the Secretary of State. Other federal tax liens and all state tax liens on personal property are filed with the county Register of Deeds. Most counties automatically include tax liens on personal property with a UCC search. Tax liens on personal property may usually be searched separately for $8.00 per name.

OTHER LIENS: Mechanics, harvesters, lis pendens, threshers.

ONLINE ACCESS: A few counties have online access to recorder records; there is no statewide system.

Allen County

County Register of Deeds, PO Box 15, Iola, KS 66749. 620-365-1412; Fax 620-365-1414. www.ksrods.org Will search UCC records. UCC search includes tax liens. Will not search real estate records. **Other Phone Numbers:** Treasurer 620-365-1409; Appraiser/Auditor 620-365-1415; Elections 620-365-1407; Vital Records 785-296-1400 (Topeka); Clerk of District Court (Marriage, etc.) 620-365-1425; City of Iola Clerk (Birth & Death before 1911) 620-365-4910;

Anderson County

County Register of Deeds, Courthouse, 100 E. 4th St, Garnett, KS 66032-1503. Register of Deeds, R/E and UCC Recording 785-448-3715; Fax 785-448-5621. Will search UCC records. UCC search includes tax liens. Will not search real estate records. **Other Phone Numbers:** Assessor 785-448-6844; Treasurer 785-448-5824; Appraiser/Auditor 785-448-6844; Elections 785-448-6841; Vital Records 785-448-4564.

Atchison County

County Register of Deeds, 423 N. 5th St., Courthouse, Atchison, KS 66002-1861. Register of Deeds, R/E and UCC Recording 913-367-2568; Fax 913-367-0227. Will search UCC records. UCC search includes tax liens if requested. Real estate owner, mortgage, and property transfer searches available. **Other Phone Numbers:** Assessor 913-367-4400.

Barber County

County Register of Deeds, 120 E. Washington St, Courthouse, Medicine Lodge, KS 67104. 620-886-3981; Fax 620-886-5045. Will search UCC records. UCC search includes tax liens. Will search real estate records on a limited basis. **Other Phone Numbers:** Assessor 620-886-3723; Treasurer 620-886-3775; Elections 620-886-3961.

Barton County

County Register of Deeds, Courthouse, #205, 1400 Main St., Great Bend, KS 67530-4037. County Register of Deeds, R/E and UCC Recording 620-793-1849; Fax 620-793-1981. www.bartoncounty.org Will search UCC records. UCC search includes tax liens. Will not search real estate records. **Online Access:** Assessor Records. Access to the County 2002 Property value list by address and name is available at www.bartoncounty.org/values/Propvalues.htm. **Other Phones:** Assessor 793-1821; Treasurer 793-1827.

Bourbon County

County Register of Deeds, 210 S. National, Fort Scott, KS 66701. 620-223-3800 x17; Fax 620-223-5241. Will search UCC records. UCC search includes tax liens. Will not search real estate records. **Other Phone Numbers:** Assessor 620-223-3800 x16; Treasurer 620-223-3800 x29.

Brown County

County Register of Deeds, Courthouse, 601 Oregon, Hiawatha, KS 66434. County Register of Deeds, R/E and UCC Recording 785-742-3741; Fax 785-742-3255. Will search UCC records. UCC search includes tax liens. Real estate record owner and mortgage searches available. **Other Phone Numbers:** Assessor 785-742-7232; Treasurer 785-742-2051; Appraiser/Auditor 785-742-7232; Elections 785-742-2581.

Butler County

County Register of Deeds, 205 W. Central, Courthouse, Suite 104, El Dorado, KS 67042. County Register of Deeds, R/E and UCC Recording 316-322-4113 UCC Recording: 316-322-4111; Fax 316-321-1011. Will search UCC records. UCC search includes tax liens if requested. Will not search real estate records. **Other Phone Numbers:** Assessor 316-321-4220; Treasurer 316-322-4210; Appraiser/Auditor 316-322-4220; Elections 316-322-4233; Vital Records 785-296-1400 (State of Kansas).

Chase County

County Register of Deeds, PO Box 59, Cottonwood Falls, KS 66845-0059. County Register of Deeds, R/E and UCC Recording 620-273-6398; Fax 620-273-6617. Will search UCC records. UCC search includes tax liens if requested. Will not search real estate records. **Other Phones:** Assessor 620-273-6423; Treasurer 620-273-6493; Appraiser/Auditor 620-273-6306; Elections 620-273-6423; Vital Records 620-273-6398.

Chautauqua County

County Register of Deeds, 215 N. Chautauqua, Courthouse, Sedan, KS 67361. 620-725-5830; Fax 620-725-5831.

Will search UCC records. UCC search includes tax liens. Will not search real estate records. **Other Phone Numbers:** Assessor 620-725-3127; Treasurer 620-725-3666.

Cherokee County

County Register of Deeds, PO Box 228, Columbus, KS 66725. County Register of Deeds, R/E and UCC Recording 620-429-3777; Fax 620-429-1362. Will search UCC records. UCC search includes tax liens. Will not search real estate records. **Other Phone Numbers:** Assessor 620-429-3984; Treasurer 620-429-2418; Appraiser/Auditor 620-429-3984; Elections 620-429-8043.

Cheyenne County

County Register of Deeds, PO Box 907, St. Francis, KS 67756-0907. 785-332-8820; Fax 785-332-8825. Will search UCC records. UCC search includes tax liens. Will not search real estate records. **Other Phone Numbers:** Assessor 785-332-8830; Treasurer 785-332-8810; Appraiser/Auditor 785-332-8830; Elections 785-332-8830; Vital Records 785-332-8850.

Clark County

County Register of Deeds, PO Box 222, Ashland, KS 67831-0222. County Register of Deeds, R/E and UCC Recording 620-635-2812; Fax 620-635-2393. Will search UCC records. UCC search includes tax liens. Will not search real estate records. **Other Phone Numbers:** Assessor 620-635-2142; Treasurer 620-635-2745; Appraiser/Auditor 620-635-2142; Elections 620-635-2813.

Clay County

County Register of Deeds, PO Box 63, Clay Center, KS 67432. 785-632-3811; Fax 785-632-2651. Will search UCC records. UCC search includes tax liens. Real estate owner, mortgage, and property transfer searches available. **Other Phone Numbers:** Assessor 785-632-2800; Treasurer 785-632-3282.

Cloud County

County Register of Deeds, PO Box 96, Concordia, KS 66901-0096. 785-243-8121; Fax 785-243-8123. Will search UCC records. UCC search includes tax liens. Will not search real estate records. **Other Phone Numbers:** Assessor 785-243-8100.

Coffey County

County Register of Deeds, 110 S 6th St, Rm 205 - Courthouse, 110 S. 6th St., Burlington, KS 66839. 620-364-2423.
Will search UCC records. UCC search includes tax liens. Will not search real estate records. **Other Phone Numbers:** Assessor 620-364-8426; Treasurer 620-364-5532.

Comanche County

County Register of Deeds, PO Box 576, Coldwater, KS 67029-0576. County Register of Deeds, R/E and UCC Recording 620-582-2152; Fax 620-582-2390.
Will search UCC records. UCC search includes tax liens. Will not search real estate records but will help walk-ins. **Other Phone Numbers:** Assessor 620-582-2544; Treasurer 620-582-2964; Appraiser/Auditor 620-582-2544; Elections 620-582-2361.

Cowley County

County Register of Deeds, PO Box 741, Winfield, KS 67156-0471. 620-221-5461; Fax 620-221-5463.
Will search UCC records. UCC search includes tax liens. Will not search real estate records. **Other Phone Numbers:** Assessor 620-221-5430; Treasurer 620-221-5412.

Crawford County

County Register of Deeds, PO Box 44, Girard, KS 66743. 620-724-8218; Fax 620-724-8823.
Will search UCC records. UCC search includes tax liens. Real estate record owner and mortgage searches available. **Other Phone Numbers:** Assessor 620-724-6431.

Decatur County

County Register of Deeds, PO Box 167, Oberlin, KS 67749-0167. County Register of Deeds, R/E and UCC Recording 785-475-8105; Fax 785-475-8150.
Will search UCC records. UCC search includes tax liens. Will not search real estate records. **Other Phone Numbers:** Assessor 785-475-8109; Treasurer 785-475-8103; Appraiser/Auditor 785-475-8109; Elections 785-475-8102; Vital Records 785-475-8105; Clerk of District Court 785-475-8107; Decatur County Clerk 785-475-8102;

Dickinson County

County Register of Deeds, PO Box 517, Abilene, KS 67410. County Register of Deeds, R/E and UCC Recording 785-263-3073; Fax 785-263-1512.
Will search UCC records. UCC search includes tax liens if requested. Real estate owner, mortgage, and property transfer searches available. **Other Phone Numbers:** Assessor 785-263-4418; Treasurer 785-263-3231.

Doniphan County

County Register of Deeds, PO Box 73, Troy, KS 66087. 785-985-3932; Fax 785-985-3723.
Will search UCC records. UCC search includes tax liens if requested. Real estate owner, mortgage, and property transfer searches available. **Other Phone Numbers:** Assessor 785-985-3977; Treasurer 785-985-3831; Elections 785-985-3513.

Douglas County

County Register of Deeds, 1100 Massachusetts, Courthouse, Lawrence, KS 66044-3097. 785-832-5283; Fax 785-841-4036. www.douglas-county.com
Will search UCC records. UCC search includes tax liens. Will not search real estate records. **Online Access:** Property Appraiser, Real Estate Records. Two non-government Internet sites provide free access to records from the Douglas County Assessor. Find County Property Appraiser records at www.douglas-county.com/value. Douglas County property valuations can be found at http://hometown.lawrence.com/valuation/valuation.cgi. **Other Phone Numbers:** Assessor 785-841-7700 x107; Treasurer 785-841-7700.

Edwards County

County Register of Deeds, PO Box 264, Kinsley, KS 67547-0364. 620-659-3131; Fax 620-659-2583.
Will search UCC records. Will not search for tax liens. Will not search real estate records. **Other Phones:** Assessor 620-659-3100; Treasurer 620-659-3132.

Elk County

County Register of Deeds, PO Box 476, Howard, KS 67349-0476. County Register of Deeds, R/E and UCC Recording 620-374-2472; Fax 620-374-2771.
Will search UCC records. UCC search includes tax liens. Will not search real estate records. **Other Phone Numbers:** Assessor 620-374-2832; Treasurer 620-374-2256; Appraiser/Auditor 620-374-2832; Elections 620-374-2490; Vital Records 620-374-2370.

Ellis County

County Register of Deeds, PO Box 654, Hays, KS 67601. County Register of Deeds, R/E and UCC Recording 785-628-9450 UCC Recording: 785-628-9451; Fax 785-628-9451. www.ksrods.org
Will search UCC records. UCC search includes tax liens if requested. Will not search real estate records. **Other Phones:** Assessor 785-628-9400; Treasurer 785-628-9466; Appraiser/Auditor 785-628-9400; Elections 785-628-9410; Vital Records 785-628-9450.

Ellsworth County

County Register of Deeds, 210 N. Kansas, Courthouse, Ellsworth, KS 67439-3118. 785-472-3022; Fax 785-472-4912.
Will search UCC records. UCC search includes tax liens. Real estate owner, mortgage, and property transfer searches available. **Other Phone Numbers:** Assessor 785-472-3165; Treasurer 785-472-4152.

Finney County

County Register of Deeds, PO Box M, Garden City, KS 67846. County Register of Deeds, R/E and UCC Recording 620-272-3520; Fax 620-272-3624. www.finneycounty.org
Will search UCC records. UCC search includes tax liens. Will not search real estate records. **Other Phone Numbers:** Assessor 620-272-3517; Treasurer 620-373-3526; Appraiser/Auditor 620-272-3585; Elections 620-272-3523.

Ford County

County Register of Deeds, PO Box 1352, Dodge City, KS 67801-1352. County Register of Deeds, R/E and UCC Recording 620-227-4565 UCC Recording: 620-227-4568; Fax 620-227-4566.
Will search UCC records. UCC search includes tax liens. Real estate owner, mortgage, and property transfer searches available. **Other Phones:** Assessor 620-227-4516; Treasurer 620-227-4535; Appraiser 620-227-4570; Elections 620-227-4553.

Franklin County

County Register of Deeds, 315 S. Main, Courthouse, Room 103, Ottawa, KS 66067-2335. 785-229-3440; Fax 785-229-3419.
Will search UCC records. UCC search includes tax liens. Real estate record owner searches available. **Other Phone Numbers:** Assessor 785-242-2573; Treasurer 785-242-4201.

Geary County

County Register of Deeds, PO Box 927, Junction City, KS 66441-2591. 785-238-5531; Fax 785-238-5419.
Will search UCC records. UCC search includes tax liens. Will not search real estate records. **Other Phone Numbers:** Assessor 785-238-4407; Treasurer 785-238-3912.

Gove County

County Register of Deeds, PO Box 116, Gove, KS 67736. County Register of Deeds, R/E and UCC Recording 785-938-4465; Fax 785-938-4486.
Will search UCC records. UCC search includes tax liens if requested. Will search real estate records. **Other Phone Numbers:** Assessor 785-938-2301; Treasurer 785-938-2275; Appraiser/Auditor 785-938-2301; Elections 785-938-2300; Vital Records 785-938-4465.

Graham County

County Register of Deeds, 410 N. Pomeroy, Hill City, KS 67642. 785-421-2551; Fax 785-421-5463.
Will search UCC records. UCC search includes tax liens. Will not search real estate records. **Other Phone Numbers:** Assessor 785-674-2196; Treasurer 785-674-2331.

Grant County

County Register of Deeds, 108 S. Glenn, Lower Level, Courthouse, Ulysses, KS 67880. 620-356-1538; Fax 620-356-5379.
Will search UCC records. UCC search includes tax liens. Will not search real estate records. **Other Phone Numbers:** Assessor 620-356-3362; Treasurer 620-356-1551.

Gray County

County Register of Deeds, PO Box 487, Cimarron, KS 67835-0487. 620-855-3835; Fax 620-855-3107.
Will search UCC records. UCC search includes tax liens. Real estate owner, mortgage, and property transfer searches available. **Other Phones:** Assessor 620-855-3858; Treasurer 620-855-3861; Appraiser 620-855-3858; Elections 620-855-3618.

Greeley County

County Register of Deeds, PO Box 12, Tribune, KS 67879. 620-376-4275; Fax 620-376-2294.
Will search UCC records. UCC search includes tax liens. Will not search real estate records. **Other Phone Numbers:** Assessor 620-376-4057; Treasurer 620-376-4413.

Greenwood County

County Register of Deeds, Courthouse, 311 N. Main, Eureka, KS 67045-1311. 620-583-8162; Fax 620-583-8124.
Will search UCC records. UCC search includes tax liens. Will search real estate by legal description. **Other Phone Numbers:** Assessor 620-583-7431; Treasurer 620-583-8146.

Hamilton County

County Register of Deeds, PO Box 1167, Syracuse, KS 67878. 620-384-6925; Fax 620-384-5853.
Will search UCC records. UCC search includes tax liens. Will not search real estate records. **Other Phone Numbers:** Assessor 620-384-5451; Treasurer 620-384-5522.

Harper County

County Register of Deeds, Courthouse, 201 N. Jennings, Anthony, KS 67003. 620-842-5336; Fax 620-842-3455. www.harpercounty.org/departments.htm
Will search UCC records. UCC search includes tax liens. Will search real estate by record owner as a courtesy. **Other Phones:** Assessor 620-842-3718; Treasurer 620-842-5191; Elections 620-842-5555.

Harvey County

County Register of Deeds, PO Box 687, Newton, KS 67114-0687. County Register of Deeds, R/E and UCC Recording 316-284-6950; Fax 316-284-6951.
Will search UCC records. UCC search includes tax liens if requested. Real estate owner, mortgage, and property transfer searches available. **Other Phone Numbers:** Assessor 316-284-6815; Treasurer 316-284-6975; Appraiser/Auditor 316-284-6815; Elections 316-284-6842.

Haskell County

County Register of Deeds, PO Box 656, Sublette, KS 67877. 620-675-8343.
Will search UCC records. Tax liens included in UCC search and will search separately. Will not search real estate records. **Other Phone Numbers:** Assessor 620-675-8269; Treasurer 620-675-2265.

Hodgeman County

County Register of Deeds, PO Box 505, Jetmore, KS 67854-0505. 620-357-8536; Fax 620-357-8300.
Will search UCC records. UCC search includes tax liens. Will not search real estate records. **Other Phone Numbers:** Assessor 620-357-8366; Treasurer 620-357-6236.

Jackson County

County Register of Deeds, Courthouse, Room 203, 415 New York, Holton, KS 66436. 785-364-3591; Fax 785-364-3420.
Will search UCC records. UCC search includes tax liens. Will look up real estate last owner or mortgagor. **Other Phone Numbers:** Assessor 785-364-5256; Treasurer 785-364-3791.

Jefferson County

County Register of Deeds, PO Box 352, Oskaloosa, KS 66066-0352. County Register of Deeds, R/E and UCC Recording 785-863-2243; Fax 785-863-2602.
Will search UCC records. UCC search includes tax liens. Real estate record owner searches, but indexed by location. **Other Phone Numbers:** Assessor 785-863-2080; Treasurer 785-863-2691; Appraiser/Auditor 785-863-2552; Elections 785-863-2272.

Jewell County

County Register of Deeds, 307 N. Commercial St, Courthouse, Mankato, KS 66956-2093. County Register of Deeds, R/E and UCC Recording 785-378-4070; Fax 785-378-4075.
Will search UCC records. This agency will not do a tax lien search. Will not search real estate records. **Other Phone Numbers:** Assessor 785-378-4000; Treasurer 785-378-4090; Appraiser/Auditor 785-378-4000; Elections 785-378-4020.

Johnson County

County Register of Deeds, PO Box 700, Olathe, KS 66051. 913-715-2300 x5375; Fax 913-715-2310. www.jocoks.com
Will search UCC records. UCC search includes tax liens. Will not search real estate records. **Online Access:** Property Appraiser, Tax Sales, Land Records. Records on the Johnson County Kansas Land Records database are available free online at http://appraiser.jocoks.com/disclaim.html. At the bottom of the Disclaimer page, click on "Yes". No name searching. Also, search the tax sales list for free at www.jocoks.com/countyclerk/taxsale/salenone.htm.
Also, there is an online mapping service at http://aims.jocoks.com/products.htm. **Other Phones:** Assessor 913-829-9500; Treasurer 913-715-2600.

Kearny County

County Register of Deeds, PO Box 42, Lakin, KS 67860. County Register of Deeds, R/E and UCC Recording 620-355-6241; Fax 620-355-7382.
Will search UCC records. UCC search includes Federal tax liens Will not search real estate records. **Other Phone Numbers:** Assessor 620-355-6427; Treasurer 620-355-6372; Appraiser/Auditor 620-355-6427; Elections 620-355-6422.

Kingman County

County Register of Deeds, PO Box 461, Kingman, KS 67068. County Register of Deeds, R/E and UCC Recording 620-532-3211; Fax 620-532-2037.
Will search UCC records. Tax liens not included in UCC search. Will not search real estate records. **Other Phone Numbers:** Assessor 620-532-5119; Treasurer 620-532-3461; Appraiser/Auditor 620-532-5119; Elections 620-532-2521.

Kiowa County

County Register of Deeds, 211 East Florida, Greensburg, KS 67054. 620-723-2441; Fax 620-723-1033.
Will search UCC records. UCC search includes tax liens. Will not search real estate records. **Other Phone Numbers:** Assessor 620-723-3366; Treasurer 620-723-2681.

Labette County

County Register of Deeds, Courthouse, 521 Merchant, Oswego, KS 67356. County Register of Deeds, R/E and UCC Recording 620-795-4931; Fax 620-795-2928.
Will search UCC records. UCC search includes tax liens if requested. Will not search real estate records. **Other Phone Numbers:** Assessor 620-795-2548; Treasurer 620-795-2918; Appraiser/Auditor 620-795-2548; Elections 620-795-2138.

Lane County

County Register of Deeds, PO Box 805, Dighton, KS 67839-0805. County Register of Deeds, R/E and UCC Recording 620-397-2803; Fax 620-397-5937.
Will search UCC records. UCC search includes tax liens. Real estate owner, mortgage, and property transfer searches available. **Other Phones:** Assessor 620-397-2804; Treasurer 620-397-2802; Appraiser 620-397-2804; Elections 620-397-5356.

Leavenworth County

County Register of Deeds, 300 Walnut, Room 103, Courthouse, Leavenworth, KS 66048. 913-684-0424; Fax 913-684-0406.
Will search UCC records. UCC search includes tax liens if requested. Will not search real estate records. **Other Phone Numbers:** Assessor 913-684-0440; Treasurer 913-684-0430.

Lincoln County

County Register of Deeds, 216 E. Lincoln, Lincoln, KS 67455-2056. 785-524-4657; Fax 785-524-5008.
Will search UCC records. UCC search includes tax liens. Will not search real estate records. **Other Phone Numbers:** Treasurer 785-524-4190; Appraiser/Auditor 785-524-4958; Elections 785-524-4757.

Linn County

County Register of Deeds, PO Box 350, Mound City, KS 66056-0350. 913-795-2226 R/E Recording: 913-352-2226 UCC Recording: 913-352-2226; Fax 913-795-2889.
Will search UCC records. UCC search includes tax liens if requested. Will not search real estate records. **Other Phone Numbers:** Assessor 913-795-2536; Treasurer 913-795-2227.

Logan County

County Register of Deeds, 710 W. 2nd St, Courthouse, Oakley, KS 67748. County Register of Deeds, R/E and UCC Recording 785-672-4224; Fax 785-672-3517.
Will search UCC records. Tax liens not included in UCC search. Will not search real estate records. **Other Phone Numbers:** Assessor 785-672-4821; Treasurer 785-672-3216; Appraiser/Auditor 785-672-4821; Elections 785-672-4244; County Clerk 785-672-4244.

Lyon County

County Register of Deeds, 402 Commercial St, Emporia, KS 66801. County Register of Deeds, R/E and UCC Recording 620-341-3241; Fax 620-342-2652.
Will search UCC records. UCC search includes tax liens. Real estate record owner and mortgage searches available.

Marion County

County Register of Deeds, PO Box 158, Marion, KS 66861-0158. 620-382-2151; Fax 620-382-3420.
Will search UCC records. UCC search includes tax liens if requested. Will not search real estate records. **Other Phone Numbers:** Assessor 620-382-3715.

Marshall County

County Register of Deeds, 1201 Broadway, Courthouse, Marysville, KS 66508. County Register of Deeds, R/E and UCC Recording 785-562-3226; Fax 785-562-5685.
Will search UCC records. UCC search includes tax liens. Will not search real estate records. **Other Phones:** Assessor 785-562-3301; Treasurer 562-5363; Appraiser/Auditor 562-3301; Elections 785-562-5361.

McPherson County

County Register of Deeds, PO Box 86, McPherson, KS 67460. County Register of Deeds, R/E and UCC Recording 620-241-5050; Fax 620-241-5484.
Will search UCC records. UCC search includes tax liens. Real estate record owner and mortgage searches available. **Other Phone Numbers:** Assessor 620-241-5870; Treasurer 620-241-3664; Appraiser/Auditor 620-241-5870; Elections 620-241-3656.

Meade County

County Register of Deeds, PO Box 399, Meade, KS 67864-0399. 620-873-8705; Fax 620-873-8713.
Will search UCC records. UCC search includes tax liens. Will not search real estate records. **Other Phone Numbers:** Assessor 620-873-8710; Treasurer 620-873-8740; Appraiser 873-8710; Elections 620-873-8700.

Miami County

County Register of Deeds, 201 S. Pearl St. #101, Paola, KS 66071. 913-294-3716; Fax 913-294-9515.
Will search UCC records. This agency will not do a tax lien search. Will not search real estate records. **Other Phone Numbers:** Assessor 913-294-9311; Treasurer 913-294-2353.

Mitchell County

County Register of Deeds, PO Box 6, Beloit, KS 67420. 785-738-3854; Fax 785-738-5844.
Will search UCC records. UCC search includes tax liens if requested. Will search real estate by legal description. **Other Phone Numbers:** Assessor 785-738-5061; Treasurer 785-738-3411.

Montgomery County

County Register of Deeds, PO Box 647, Independence, KS 67301. 620-331-2180; Fax 620-331-2619.
Will search UCC records. This agency will not do a tax lien search. Will not search real estate records. **Other Phone Numbers:** Assessor 620-331-4510; Treasurer 620-331-3040.

Morris County

County Register of Deeds, Courthouse, Council Grove, KS 66846. 620-767-5614; Fax 620-767-6861.
Will search UCC records. UCC search includes tax liens if requested. Will not search real estate records. **Other Phone Numbers:** Assessor 620-767-5617; Treasurer 620-767-5614.

Morton County

County Register of Deeds, PO Box 756, Elkhart, KS 67950-0756. 620-697-2561; Fax 620-697-4386.
Will search UCC records. UCC search includes tax liens if requested. Will not search real estate records. **Other Phone Numbers:** Assessor 620-697-2106; Treasurer 620-697-2560.

Nemaha County

County Register of Deeds, PO Box 211, Seneca, KS 66538. County Register of Deeds, R/E and UCC Recording 785-336-2120; Fax 785-336-3373.
Will search UCC records. UCC search includes tax liens if requested. Will search real estate records. **Other Phone Numbers:** Assessor 785-336-2179; Treasurer 785-336-2106.

Neosho County

County Register of Deeds, PO Box 138, Erie, KS 66733-0138. 620-244-3858; Fax 620-244-3860.
Will search UCC records. UCC search includes tax liens if requested. Will not search real estate records. **Other Phone Numbers:** Assessor 620-244-3821; Treasurer 620-244-3800.

Ness County

County Register of Deeds, PO Box 127, Ness City, KS 67560. 785-798-3127; Fax 785-798-3829.
Will search UCC records. UCC search includes tax liens. Will not search real estate records. **Other Phone Numbers:** Assessor 785-798-2777.

Norton County

County Register of Deeds, PO Box 70, Norton, KS 67654. County Register of Deeds, R/E and UCC Recording 785-877-5765; Fax 785-877-5703.
Will search UCC records. Tax liens not included in UCC search. Real estate owner, mortgage, and property transfer searches available. **Other Phone Numbers:** Assessor 785-877-5700; Treasurer 785-877-5795.

Osage County

County Register of Deeds, PO Box 265, Lyndon, KS 66451-0265. 785-828-4523; Fax 785-828-4749. www.osageco.org
Will search UCC records. UCC search includes tax liens if requested. Will not search real estate records. **Other Phone Numbers:** Assessor 913-828-3124; Treasurer 913-828-4923.

Osborne County

County Register of Deeds, PO Box 160, Osborne, KS 67473-0160. 785-346-2452; Fax 785-346-5992.
Will search UCC records. UCC search includes tax liens. Real estate owner, mortgage, and property transfer searches available. **Other Phone Numbers:** Assessor 785-346-2310; Treasurer 785-346-2251; Appraiser/Auditor 785-346-2310.

Ottawa County

County Register of Deeds, Courthouse - Suite 220, 307 N. Concord, Minneapolis, KS 67467-2140. 785-392-2078; Fax 785-392-3605.
Will search UCC records. Will search real estate by name or legal description. **Other Phone Numbers:** Assessor 785-392-3037; Treasurer 785-392-3129.

Pawnee County

County Register of Deeds, Courthouse, 2nd Floor, 715 Broadway St., Larned, KS 67550-3097. County Register of Deeds, R/E and UCC Recording 620-285-3276; Fax 620-285-3802.
Will search UCC records. UCC search includes tax liens. Will look up last deed of record. **Other Phone Numbers:** Assessor 620-285-2915; Treasurer 620-285-3746; Appraiser/Auditor 620-285-2915; Elections 620-285-3721; Vital Records 620-285-6937.

Phillips County

County Register of Deeds, Courthouse, 301 State St., Phillipsburg, KS 67661. 785-543-6875; Fax 785-999-9999.
Will search UCC records. UCC search includes tax liens. Will not search real estate records. **Other Phone Numbers:** Assessor 785-543-6810; Treasurer 785-543-6895.

Pottawatomie County

County Register of Deeds, PO Box 186, Westmoreland, KS 66549. 785-457-3471; Fax 785-457-3577.
Will search UCC records. UCC search includes tax liens. Real estate record owner and mortgage searches not available. **Other Phone Numbers:** Assessor 785-457-3500; Treasurer 785-457-3681.

Pratt County

County Register of Deeds, PO Box 873, Pratt, KS 67124. County Register of Deeds, R/E and UCC Recording 620-672-4140; Fax 620-672-9541. www.prattcounty.org
Will search UCC records. This agency will not do a tax lien search. Will not search real estate records. **Other Phone Numbers:** Assessor 620-672-4112; Treasurer 620-672-4118; Appraiser/Auditor 620-672-4112; Elections 620-672-4110; District Court (probates & state tax liens) 620-672-4110.

Rawlins County

County Register of Deeds, PO Box 201, Atwood, KS 67730. County Register of Deeds, R/E and UCC Recording 785-626-3172; Fax 785-626-9481.
Will search UCC records. UCC search includes tax liens. Will not search real estate records. **Other Phone Numbers:** Assessor 785-626-3101; Treasurer 785-626-3331.

Reno County

County Register of Deeds, 206 W. First, Hutchinson, KS 67501. 620-694-2942; Fax 620-694-2944.
Will search UCC records. UCC search includes tax liens. Will not search real estate records. **Other Phone Numbers:** Assessor 620-694-2915; Treasurer 620-694-2938.

Republic County

County Register of Deeds, PO Box 429, Belleville, KS 66935. 785-527-5691 x224; Fax 785-527-2659.
Will search UCC records. UCC search includes tax liens. Real estate record owner and mortgage searches available. **Other Phone Numbers:** Assessor 785-527-5691; Treasurer 785-527-5691.

Rice County

County Register of Deeds, 101 W. Commercial, Lyons, KS 67554. 620-257-2931; Fax 620-257-3039.
Will search UCC records. UCC search includes tax liens. Real estate owner, mortgage, and property transfer searches available. **Other Phone Numbers:** Assessor 620-257-3611; Treasurer 620-257-2852.

Riley County

County Register of Deeds, 110 Courthouse Plaza, 5th & Humboldt Sts., Manhattan, KS 66502-6018. County Register of Deeds, R/E and UCC Recording 785-537-6340; Fax 785-537-6343. www.co.riley.ks.us/register/
Will search UCC records. This agency will not do a tax lien search. Will not search real estate records. **Other Phone Numbers:** Assessor 785-537-6310; Treasurer 785-537-6320; Appraiser/Auditor 785-537-6310.

Rooks County

County Register of Deeds, 115 N. Walnut St., Stockton, KS 67669. 785-425-6291.
Will search UCC records. Tax liens not included in UCC search. Will not search real estate records. **Other Phone Numbers:** Assessor 785-425-6262; Treasurer 785-425-6291.

Rush County

County Register of Deeds, PO Box 117, La Crosse, KS 67548. 785-222-3312; Fax 785-222-3559.
Will search UCC records. UCC search includes tax liens. Will give owner for a property. **Other Phones:** Assessor 785-222-2659; Treasurer 785-222-3416.

Russell County

County Register of Deeds, PO Box 191, Russell, KS 67665. County Register of Deeds, R/E and UCC Recording 785-483-4612; Fax 785-483-5725.
Will search UCC records. UCC search includes tax liens. **Other Phone Numbers:** Assessor 785-483-5551; Treasurer 785-483-2251; Appraiser/Auditor 785-483-5551; Elections 785-483-4641.

Saline County

County Register of Deeds, PO Box 5040, Salina, KS 67402-5040. 785-309-5855; Fax 785-309-5856. www.co.saline.ks.us
Will search UCC records. UCC search includes tax liens. Will not search real estate records. **Other Phone Numbers:** Assessor 785-309-5800; Treasurer 785-309-5860.

Scott County

County Register of Deeds, Courthouse, 303 Court St., Scott City, KS 67871. 620-872-3155; Fax 620-872-7145.
Will search UCC records. UCC search includes tax liens. Will do limited real estate searches. **Other Phone Numbers:** Assessor 620-872-5446; Treasurer 620-872-2640; Appraiser/Auditor 620-872-5446; Elections 620-872-2420.

Sedgwick County

County Register of Deeds, PO Box 3326, Wichita, KS 67201-3326. 316-383-7425 R/E Recording: 316-383-7511; Fax 316-383-8066. www.co.sedgwick.ks.us/dept.htm
Will search UCC records. UCC search includes tax liens if requested. Will not search real estate records. **Online Access:** Real Estate, Lien, Tax Assessor Records. Records are available two ways. Records on the Sedgwick County online system are available for a set up fee of $225, with a $49 monthly fee, and a per transaction charge of $.03-$.04. Lending agency information is available. For information, call John Zukovich at 316-383-7384. A sex offender registry list is available on the Web at the county departments page. County Treasurer & Appraiser database records are available free at www.co.sedgwick.ks.us/Appraiser/RealProperty.htm. Search by city, street numbers or street name for property tax/appraisal information. No name searching. **Other Phone Numbers:** Assessor 316-383-7461; Treasurer 316-383-7707; Appraiser/Auditor 316-383-7461; Elections 316-660-7100; County Clerk 316 383 7691.

Seward County

County Register of Deeds, 415 N. Washington, Courthouse, Suite 105, Liberal, KS 67901. County Register of Deeds, R/E and UCC Recording 620-626-3220; Fax 620-626-5031.
Will search UCC records. UCC search includes tax liens. Will not search real estate records. **Other Phone Numbers:** Treasurer 620-626-3216; Appraiser/Auditor 620-626-3252; Elections 620-626-3201.

Shawnee County

County Register of Deeds, 200 E. 7th St, Suite 108, Topeka, KS 66603-3932. 785-233-8200 x4021 R/E Recording: 785-233-8200 x4020; Fax 785-291-4912. www.co.shawnee.ks.us
Will search UCC records. Will not search real estate records. **Online Access:** Property Appraiser Records. Search residential/commercial property appraisal data at www.co.shawnee.ks.us/Appraiser_Web/appraiser.html. Search residential by name; commericial by address. **Other Phone Numbers:** Assessor 785-233-8200 x5151; Treasurer 785-233-8200 x5161; Appraiser/Auditor 785-233-2882 x6000; Elections 785-266-0285.

Sheridan County

County Register of Deeds, PO Box 899, Hoxie, KS 67740-0899. 785-675-3741; Fax 785-675-3050.
Will search UCC records. UCC search includes tax liens if requested. Real estate record owner searches available. **Other Phone Numbers:** Assessor 785-675-3932; Treasurer 785-675-3622.

Sherman County

County Register of Deeds, 813 Broadway, Room 104, Goodland, KS 67735-3097. 785-899-4845; Fax 785-899-4848.
Will search UCC records. UCC search includes tax liens. Will not search real estate records. **Other Phone Numbers:** Assessor 785-899-4825; Treasurer 785-899-4810; Appraiser/Auditor 785-899-4825; Elections 785-899-4800.

Smith County

County Register of Deeds, 218 S. Grant, Smith Center, KS 66967. 785-282-5160; Fax 785-282-6257.
Will search UCC records. Tax liens not included in UCC search. Real estate owner, mortgage, and property transfer searches available. **Other Phone Numbers:** Assessor 785-282-5100; Treasurer 785-282-5170; Appraiser/Auditor 785-282-5100; Elections 785-282-5110.

Stafford County

County Register of Deeds, 209 N. Broadway, Stafford County Courthouse, St. John, KS 67576. 620-549-3505.
Will search UCC records. UCC search includes tax liens. Will not search real estate records. **Other Phone Numbers:** Assessor 620-549-3540; Treasurer 620-549-3508; Appraiser/Auditor 620-549-3540.

Stanton County

County Register of Deeds, PO Box 716, Johnson, KS 67855. 620-492-2190; Fax 620-492-2688.
Will search UCC records. UCC search includes tax liens. Will not search real estate records. **Other Phone Numbers:** Assessor 620-492-6896; Treasurer 620-492-2160.

Stevens County

County Register of Deeds, 200 E. 6th, Hugoton, KS 67951. County Register of Deeds, R/E and UCC Recording 620-544-2630; Fax 620-544-4081.
Will search UCC records. UCC search includes tax liens if requested. Will search real estate records. **Other Phone Numbers:** Assessor 620-544-2993; Treasurer 620-544-2542; Appraiser/Auditor 620-544-2693; Elections 620-544-2541.

Sumner County

County Register of Deeds, PO Box 469, Wellington, KS 67152. County Register of Deeds, R/E and UCC Recording 620-326-2041; Fax 620-326-8172.
Will search UCC records. UCC search includes tax liens if requested. Real estate owner, mortgage, and property transfer searches available. **Other Phone Numbers:** Assessor 620-326-8986; Treasurer 620-326-3371; Appraiser/Auditor 620-326-8986; Elections 620-326-3395.

Thomas County

County Register of Deeds, 300 North Court, Colby, KS 67701. County Register of Deeds, R/E and UCC Recording 785-462-4535; Fax 785-462-4512.
Will search UCC records. UCC search includes tax liens. Will confirm property owner from legal description **Other Phone Numbers:** Assessor 785-462-4525; Treasurer 785-462-4520; Elections 785-462-4500.

Trego County

County Register of Deeds, 216 Main, WaKeeney, KS 67672-2189. County Register of Deeds, R/E and UCC Recording 785-743-6622; Fax 785-743-2461.
Will search UCC records. UCC search includes tax liens. Will give last owner from legal description. **Other Phone Numbers:** Assessor 785-743-5758; Treasurer 785-743-2001; Appraiser/Auditor 785-743-5758; Elections 785-743-5773.

Wabaunsee County

County Register of Deeds, PO Box 278, Alma, KS 66401-0278. County Register of Deeds, R/E and UCC Recording 785-765-3822; Fax 785-765-3992.
Will search UCC records. UCC search includes tax liens. Will not search real estate records. **Other Phone Numbers:** Assessor 785-765-3508; Treasurer 785-765-3812; Elections 785-765-2421; Vital Records 785-765-3822.

Wallace County

County Register of Deeds, PO Box 10, Sharon Springs, KS 67758-9998. County Register of Deeds, R/E and UCC Recording 785-852-4283; Fax 785-852-4783.

Will search UCC records. UCC search includes tax liens. Will not search real estate records. **Other Phone Numbers:** Assessor 785-852-4206; Treasurer 785-852-4281; Appraiser/Auditor 785-852-4206; Elections 785-852-4282.

Washington County

County Register of Deeds, 214 C St, Courthouse, Washington, KS 66968-1928. County Register of Deeds, R/E and UCC Recording 785-325-2286; Fax 785-325-2830.
Will search UCC records. UCC search includes tax liens. Will give real estate information at no charge. **Other Phone Numbers:** Assessor 785-325-2236; Treasurer 785-325-2461; Appraiser/Auditor 785-325-2236; Elections 785-325-2974; Vital Records 785-296-1400 (Topeka, KS).

Wichita County

County Register of Deeds, PO Box 472, Leoti, KS 67861-0472. County Register of Deeds, R/E and UCC Recording 620-375-2733; Fax 316-375-4350.
Will search UCC records. UCC search includes tax liens. Will not search real estate records. **Other Phone Numbers:** Assessor 620-375-4242; Treasurer 620-375-2715; Appraiser/Auditor 620-375-4242; Elections 620-375-2341.

Wilson County

County Register of Deeds, Courthouse, Room 106, Fredonia, KS 66736-1396. County Register of Deeds, R/E and UCC Recording 620-378-3662; Fax 620-378-4762.
Will search UCC records. UCC search includes tax liens. Real estate record owner and mortgage searches available. **Other Phones:** Assessor 620-378-2187.

Woodson County

County Register of Deeds, 105 W. Rutledge, Room 101, Yates Center, KS 66783-1499. 620-625-8635; Fax 620-625-8670.
Will search UCC records. UCC search includes tax liens. Will not search real estate records. **Other Phone Numbers:** Assessor 620-625-8600; Treasurer 620-625-8650.

Wyandotte County

County Register of Deeds, Courthouse, 710 N. 7th St., Kansas City, KS 66101-3084. 913-573-2841; Fax 913-321-3075.
Will search UCC records. UCC search includes tax liens. Will not search real estate records. **Online Access:** Real Estate, Lien, Property Appraisal Records. County records are available online, and property tax records are available on dial-up. The dial-up services requires a $20 set up fee, with a $5 monthly fee and $.05 each after the first 100 transactions. Lending agency information is available. For information, contact Louise Sachen at 913-573-2885. Records from the County Assessor Tax database are available free on the Internet at www.courthouseusa.com/wyanadd.htm. Search by street number and name, but no name searching. **Other Phone Numbers:** Assessor 913-287-2641.

Kansas County Locator

You will usually be able to find the city name in the City/County Cross Reference below. In that case, it is a simple matter to determine the county from the cross reference. However, only the official US Postal Service city names are included in this index. There are an additional 40,000 place names that people use in their addresses. Therefore, we have also included a ZIP/City Cross Reference immediately following the City/County Cross Reference.

If you know the ZIP Code but the city name does not appear in the City/County Cross Reference index, look up the ZIP Code in the ZIP/City Cross Reference, find the city name, then look up the city name in the City/County Cross Reference. For example, you want to know the county for an address of Menands, NY 12204. There is no "Menands" in the City/County Cross Reference. The ZIP/City Cross Reference shows that ZIP Codes 12201-12288 are for the city of Albany. Looking back in the City/County Cross Reference, Albany is in Albany County.

City/County Cross Reference

ABBYVILLE Reno
ABILENE Dickinson
ADA (67414) Ottawa(94), Lincoln(5)
ADMIRE Lyon
AGENDA Republic
AGRA Phillips
ALBERT (67511) Barton(56), Rush(43)
ALDEN (67512) Rice(94), Reno(5)
ALEXANDER (67513) Rush(95),
  Pawnee(5)
ALLEN Lyon
ALMA Wabaunsee
ALMENA Norton
ALTA VISTA (66834) Wabaunsee(49),
  Morris(20), Jackson(18), Geary(11)
ALTAMONT Labette
ALTON (67623) Osborne(98), Smith(1)
ALTOONA Wilson
AMERICUS Lyon
AMES Cloud
ANDALE Sedgwick
ANDOVER Butler
ANTHONY Harper
ARCADIA Bourbon
ARGONIA (67004) Sumner(85), Harper(13)
ARKANSAS CITY Cowley
ARLINGTON Reno
ARMA Crawford
ARNOLD (67515) Ness(83), Trego(16)
ASHLAND Clark
ASSARIA (67416) Saline(97),
  McPherson(2)
ATCHISON (66002) Atchison(93),
  Leavenworth(5), Jefferson(1)
ATHOL Smith
ATLANTA (67008) Cowley(70), Butler(29)
ATTICA (67009) Harper(97), Barber(2)
ATWOOD Rawlins
AUBURN (66402) Shawnee(98), Osage(1)
AUGUSTA Butler
AURORA Cloud
AXTELL (66403) Marshall(92), Nemaha(7)
BAILEYVILLE (66404) Nemaha(95),
  Marshall(4)
BALDWIN CITY (66006) Douglas(95),
  Franklin(4)
BARNARD (67418) Lincoln(91), Mitchell(8)
BARNES (66933) Washington(92), Riley(7)
BARTLETT Labette
BASEHOR Leavenworth
BAXTER SPRINGS Cherokee
BAZINE Ness
BEATTIE Marshall
BEAUMONT Butler
BEAVER Barton
BEELER (67518) Ness(74), Lane(25)
BELLE PLAINE Sumner
BELLEVILLE Republic
BELOIT (67420) Mitchell(98), Cloud(1)
BELPRE (67519) Edwards(89),
  Pawnee(10)
BELVIDERE Kiowa

BELVUE (66407) Wabaunsee(71),
  Pottawatomie(28)
BENDENA Doniphan
BENEDICT Wilson
BENNINGTON Ottawa
BENTLEY Sedgwick
BENTON (67017) Butler(89), Sedgwick(10)
BERN Nemaha
BERRYTON (66409) Shawnee(84),
  Douglas(12), Osage(3)
BEVERLY Lincoln
BIRD CITY Cheyenne
BISON Rush
BLUE MOUND (66010) Linn(96),
  Bourbon(2)
BLUE RAPIDS (66411) Marshall(97),
  Riley(2)
BLUFF CITY (67018) Harper(91),
  Sumner(8)
BOGUE Graham
BONNER SPRINGS (66012)
  Wyandotte(63), Leavenworth(36)
BREMEN (66412) Marshall(93),
  Washington(6)
BREWSTER (67732) Thomas(58),
  Sherman(32), Rawlins(7)
BRONSON (66716) Bourbon(94), Allen(5)
BROOKVILLE (67425) Saline(56),
  Ellsworth(42), Lincoln(1)
BROWNELL (67521) Ness(89), Trego(10)
BUCKLIN (67834) Ford(92), Clark(7)
BUCYRUS (66013) Johnson(53),
  Miami(46)
BUFFALO (66717) Wilson(96), Woodson(3)
BUHLER (67522) Reno(90), Harvey(9)
BUNKER HILL Russell
BURDEN Cowley
BURDETT (67523) Pawnee(92),
  Hodgeman(7)
BURDICK (66838) Morris(93), Marion(4),
  Chase(1)
BURLINGAME (66413) Osage(95),
  Lyon(3), Wabaunsee(1)
BURLINGTON Coffey
BURNS (66840) Butler(58), Marion(36),
  Chase(4)
BURR OAK Jewell
BURRTON (67020) Harvey(59), Reno(36),
  Sedgwick(4)
BUSHTON (67427) Rice(75), Ellsworth(24)
BYERS (67021) Pratt(94), Stafford(5)
CALDWELL Sumner
CAMBRIDGE Cowley
CANEY Montgomery
CANTON (67428) McPherson(94),
  Marion(5)
CARBONDALE Osage
CARLTON Dickinson
CASSODAY Butler
CATHARINE Ellis
CAWKER CITY (67430) Mitchell(74),
  Jewell(17), Osborne(4), Smith(2)
CEDAR Smith

CEDAR POINT (66843) Chase(97),
  Marion(2)
CEDAR VALE (67024) Chautauqua(77),
  Cowley(22)
CENTERVILLE (66014) Anderson(50),
  Linn(49)
CENTRALIA Nemaha
CHANUTE (66720) Neosho(96), Wilson(3)
CHAPMAN Dickinson
CHASE Rice
CHAUTAUQUA Chautauqua
CHENEY (67025) Sedgwick(72),
  Kingman(27)
CHEROKEE Crawford
CHERRYVALE (67335) Montgomery(84),
  Labette(13), Logan(1)
CHETOPA (67336) Labette(79),
  Cherokee(20)
CIMARRON Gray
CIRCLEVILLE Jackson
CLAFLIN (67525) Barton(96), Rice(3)
CLAY CENTER (67432) Clay(98),
  Ottawa(1)
CLAYTON (67629) Norton(81), Decatur(18)
CLEARVIEW CITY Johnson
CLEARWATER (67026) Sedgwick(96),
  Sumner(3)
CLIFTON (66937) Washington(82),
  Clay(17)
CLYDE (66938) Cloud(80),
  Washington(11), Republic(4), Clay(3)
COATS (67028) Pratt(57), Barber(25),
  Kiowa(17)
CODELL Rooks
COFFEYVILLE (67337) Montgomery(95),
  Labette(4)
COLBY Thomas
COLDWATER (67029) Comanche(97),
  Kiowa(2)
COLLYER (67631) Trego(73), Graham(22),
  Gove(3), Sheridan(1)
COLONY (66015) Anderson(79),
  Coffey(20)
COLUMBUS Cherokee
COLWICH Sedgwick
CONCORDIA (66901) Cloud(98),
  Republic(1)
CONWAY SPRINGS (67031) Sumner(96),
  Sedgwick(3)
COOLIDGE Hamilton
COPELAND (67837) Haskell(54), Gray(38),
  Meade(7)
CORNING Nemaha
COTTONWOOD FALLS Chase
COUNCIL GROVE (66846) Morris(94),
  Lyon(4)
COURTLAND (66939) Republic(91),
  Jewell(8)
COYVILLE Wilson
CRESTLINE Cherokee
CUBA (66940) Republic(98),
  Washington(1)
CUMMINGS Atchison

CUNNINGHAM (67035) Kingman(72),
  Pratt(18), Reno(9)
DAMAR (67632) Rooks(74), Graham(25)
DANVILLE Harper
DE SOTO Johnson
DEARING Montgomery
DEERFIELD (67838) Kearny(63),
  Finney(36)
DELIA Jackson
DELPHOS (67436) Ottawa(82), Cloud(17)
DENISON (66419) Jackson(84),
  Jefferson(15)
DENNIS Labette
DENNIS THE MENACE Sedgwick
DENTON Doniphan
DERBY Sedgwick
DEXTER Cowley
DIGHTON (67839) Lane(95), Gove(4)
DODGE CITY Ford
DORRANCE (67634) Russell(97),
  Barton(2)
DOUGLASS (67039) Butler(97), Cowley(2)
DOVER Shawnee
DOWNS (67437) Osborne(95), Smith(4)
DRESDEN (67635) Decatur(70),
  Sheridan(29)
DURHAM Marion
DWIGHT (66849) Morris(63), Geary(36)
EASTON Leavenworth
EDGERTON (66021) Johnson(71),
  Miami(25), Douglas(2)
EDMOND (67636) Norton(82), Graham(17)
EDNA Labette
EDSON Sherman
EDWARDSVILLE Wyandotte
EFFINGHAM Atchison
EL DORADO Butler
ELBING Butler
ELK CITY (67344) Montgomery(65),
  Chautauqua(27), Elk(6)
ELK FALLS Elk
ELKHART Morton
ELLINWOOD (67526) Barton(94), Rice(4),
  Stafford(1)
ELLIS (67637) Ellis(87), Trego(12)
ELLSWORTH Ellsworth
ELMDALE Chase
ELSMORE Allen
ELWOOD Doniphan
EMMETT (66422) Pottawatomie(53),
  Jackson(46)
EMPORIA Lyon
ENGLEWOOD Clark
ENSIGN (67841) Gray(74), Ford(25)
ENTERPRISE Dickinson
ERIE Neosho
ESBON Jewell
ESKRIDGE Wabaunsee
EUDORA (66025) Douglas(75),
  Johnson(24)
EUREKA Greenwood
EVEREST (66424) Brown(89),
  Atchison(10)

FAIRVIEW Brown
FALL RIVER (67047) Greenwood(62), Elk(21), Wilson(16)
FALUN (67442) Saline(97), McPherson(2)
FARLINGTON Crawford
FLORENCE Marion
FONTANA Miami
FORD Ford
FORMOSO (66942) Jewell(98), Republic(1)
FORT DODGE Ford
FORT LEAVENWORTH Leavenworth
FORT RILEY Geary
FORT SCOTT Bourbon
FOSTORIA Pottawatomie
FOWLER (67844) Meade(82), Ford(12), Gray(5)
FRANKFORT (66427) Marshall(97), Pottawatomie(2)
FRANKLIN Crawford
FREDONIA Wilson
FREEPORT (67049) Harper(89), Sumner(10)
FRONTENAC Crawford
FULTON (66738) Bourbon(97), Linn(2)
GALENA Cherokee
GALESBURG Neosho
GALVA McPherson
GARDEN CITY Finney
GARDEN PLAIN Sedgwick
GARDNER Johnson
GARFIELD Pawnee
GARLAND Bourbon
GARNETT Anderson
GAS Allen
GAYLORD (67638) Smith(93), Osborne(6)
GEM (67734) Thomas(66), Rawlins(33)
GENESEO (67444) Rice(71), Ellsworth(28)
GEUDA SPRINGS (67051) Sumner(83), Cowley(16)
GIRARD Crawford
GLADE Phillips
GLASCO (67445) Cloud(92), Ottawa(7)
GLEN ELDER (67446) Mitchell(91), Jewell(8)
GODDARD Sedgwick
GOESSEL Marion
GOFF Nemaha
GOODLAND Sherman
GORHAM (67640) Russell(73), Ellis(26)
GOVE Gove
GRAINFIELD (67737) Gove(76), Sheridan(23)
GRANTVILLE Jefferson
GREAT BEND (67530) Barton(98), Stafford(1)
GREELEY (66033) Anderson(62), Franklin(35), Linn(2)
GREEN (67447) Clay(90), Riley(9)
GREENLEAF Washington
GREENSBURG Kiowa
GREENWICH Sedgwick
GRENOLA (67346) Elk(58), Chautauqua(41)
GRIDLEY (66852) Coffey(82), Greenwood(10), Woodson(6)
GRINNELL (67738) Gove(73), Sheridan(26)
GYPSUM (67448) Saline(47), McPherson(26), Dickinson(22), Marion(3)
HADDAM (66944) Washington(96), Republic(3)
HALSTEAD Harvey
HAMILTON Greenwood
HANOVER Washington
HANSTON (67849) Hodgeman(97), Ness(2)
HARDTNER Barber
HARLAN Smith
HARPER (67058) Harper(97), Kingman(2)
HARTFORD (66854) Lyon(78), Coffey(20)

HARVEYVILLE (66431) Wabaunsee(93), Shawnee(6)
HAVANA (67347) Montgomery(62), Chautauqua(37)
HAVEN Reno
HAVENSVILLE (66432) Pottawatomie(77), Jackson(20), Nemaha(1)
HAVILAND (67059) Kiowa(70), Edwards(18), Pratt(11)
HAYS Ellis
HAYSVILLE Sedgwick
HAZELTON (67061) Barber(57), Harper(42)
HEALY (67850) Lane(87), Scott(10), Gove(1)
HEPLER (66746) Crawford(91), Bourbon(8)
HERINGTON (67449) Dickinson(81), Morris(17)
HERNDON (67739) Rawlins(89), Decatur(10)
HESSTON Harvey
HIAWATHA Brown
HIGHLAND Doniphan
HILL CITY Graham
HILLSBORO Marion
HILLSDALE Miami
HOISINGTON Barton
HOLCOMB Finney
HOLLENBERG Washington
HOLTON (66436) Jackson(97), Atchison(2)
HOLYROOD (67450) Ellsworth(82), Barton(15), Russell(1)
HOME Marshall
HOPE (67451) Dickinson(98), Marion(1)
HORTON (66439) Brown(84), Jackson(10), Atchison(5)
HOWARD Elk
HOXIE (67740) Sheridan(97), Graham(2)
HOYT Jackson
HUDSON Stafford
HUGOTON Stevens
HUMBOLDT Allen
HUNTER (67452) Lincoln(54), Mitchell(45)
HUTCHINSON Reno
INDEPENDENCE Montgomery
INGALLS (67853) Gray(91), Finney(8)
INMAN (67546) McPherson(86), Rice(8), Reno(3)
IOLA Allen
ISABEL (67065) Barber(58), Pratt(39), Kingman(2)
IUKA Pratt
JAMESTOWN (66948) Cloud(86), Republic(13)
JENNINGS (67643) Decatur(94), Sheridan(5)
JETMORE Hodgeman
JEWELL Jewell
JOHNSON (67855) Stanton(98), Grant(1)
JUNCTION CITY Geary
KALVESTA Finney
KANOPOLIS Ellsworth
KANORADO (67741) Sherman(95), Cheyenne(2), Wallace(1)
KANSAS CITY Wyandotte
KECHI Sedgwick
KENDALL (67857) Hamilton(57), Kearny(42)
KENSINGTON (66951) Smith(73), Phillips(26)
KINCAID (66039) Anderson(90), Allen(9)
KINGMAN (67068) Kingman(98), Reno(1)
KINGSDOWN (67858) Ford(90), Clark(9)
KINSLEY (67547) Edwards(97), Hodgeman(1)
KIOWA Barber
KIRWIN (67644) Phillips(92), Smith(3), Rooks(2)
KISMET Seward
LA CROSSE Rush
LA CYGNE Linn
LA HARPE Allen

LAKE CITY Barber
LAKIN Kearny
LAMONT Greenwood
LANCASTER Atchison
LANE Franklin
LANSING Leavenworth
LARNED (67550) Pawnee(97), Stafford(1)
LATHAM (67072) Butler(87), Cowley(12)
LAWRENCE Douglas
LE ROY Coffey
LEAVENWORTH Leavenworth
LEBANON (66952) Smith(95), Jewell(4)
LEBO (66856) Coffey(70), Osage(29)
LECOMPTON Douglas
LEHIGH Marion
LENEXA Johnson
LENORA (67645) Norton(64), Graham(35)
LEON Butler
LEONARDVILLE Riley
LEOTI (67861) Wichita(91), Logan(8)
LEVANT Thomas
LEWIS Edwards
LIBERAL Seward
LIBERTY (67351) Montgomery(88), Labette(11)
LIEBENTHAL Rush
LINCOLN Lincoln
LINCOLNVILLE (66858) Marion(97), Chase(2)
LINDSBORG (67456) McPherson(89), Saline(10)
LINN Washington
LINWOOD Leavenworth
LITTLE RIVER Rice
LOGAN (67646) Phillips(78), Rooks(9), Graham(7), Norton(4)
LONG ISLAND Phillips
LONGFORD (67458) Clay(84), Ottawa(15)
LONGTON (67352) Elk(82), Chautauqua(17)
LORRAINE Ellsworth
LOST SPRINGS (66859) Marion(86), Morris(13)
LOUISBURG Miami
LOUISVILLE Pottawatomie
LUCAS (67648) Russell(71), Osborne(22), Lincoln(6)
LUDELL Rawlins
LURAY (67649) Russell(64), Osborne(35)
LYNDON Osage
LYONS Rice
MACKSVILLE (67557) Stafford(58), Pawnee(18), Pratt(17), Edwards(5)
MADISON (66860) Greenwood(67), Lyon(32)
MAHASKA (66955) Washington(98), Republic(1)
MAIZE Sedgwick
MANCHESTER Dickinson
MANHATTAN Riley
MANKATO Jewell
MANTER (67862) Stanton(75), Morton(24)
MAPLE CITY Cowley
MAPLE HILL Wabaunsee
MAPLETON (66754) Bourbon(96), Linn(3)
MARIENTHAL Wichita
MARION Marion
MARQUETTE (67464) McPherson(65), Ellsworth(34)
MARYSVILLE Marshall
MATFIELD GREEN Chase
MAYETTA Jackson
MAYFIELD Sumner
MC CONNELL A F B Sedgwick
MC CRACKEN (67556) Rush(66), Ellis(17), Ness(16)
MC CUNE (66753) Crawford(95), Labette(4)
MC DONALD (67745) Rawlins(75), Cheyenne(25)
MC FARLAND Wabaunsee

MC LOUTH (66054) Jefferson(68), Leavenworth(31)
MCCONNELL AFB Sedgwick
MCPHERSON McPherson
MEADE Meade
MEDICINE LODGE Barber
MELVERN Osage
MENTOR Saline
MERIDEN (66512) Jefferson(90), Jackson(6), Shawnee(3)
MILAN Sumner
MILFORD Geary
MILTON (67106) Sumner(62), Sedgwick(35), Kingman(2)
MILTONVALE (67466) Cloud(56), Ottawa(27), Clay(16)
MINNEAPOLIS Ottawa
MINNEOLA (67865) Ford(64), Clark(35)
MISSION Johnson
MOLINE (67353) Elk(68), Chautauqua(31)
MONTEZUMA (67867) Gray(95), Meade(4)
MONUMENT (67747) Logan(91), Thomas(8)
MORAN (66755) Allen(98), Bourbon(1)
MORGANVILLE Clay
MORLAND Graham
MORRILL Brown
MORROWVILLE Washington
MOSCOW Stevens
MOUND CITY (66056) Linn(98), Atchison(1)
MOUND VALLEY Labette
MOUNDRIDGE (67107) McPherson(67), Harvey(32)
MOUNT HOPE (67108) Sedgwick(60), Reno(39)
MULBERRY Crawford
MULLINVILLE Kiowa
MULVANE (67110) Sedgwick(68), Sumner(30), Cowley(1)
MUNDEN Republic
MURDOCK Kingman
MUSCOTAH (66058) Jackson(66), Atchison(33)
NARKA (66960) Republic(97), Washington(2)
NASHVILLE (67112) Kingman(86), Barber(13)
NATOMA (67651) Osborne(72), Rooks(23), Ellis(4)
NEAL Greenwood
NEKOMA (67559) Rush(84), Pawnee(15)
NEODESHA (66757) Wilson(94), Montgomery(5)
NEOSHO FALLS (66758) Coffey(54), Woodson(41), Anderson(2), Allen(1)
NEOSHO RAPIDS (66864) Lyon(92), Coffey(7)
NESS CITY Ness
NETAWAKA (66516) Jackson(77), Brown(22)
NEW ALBANY Wilson
NEW ALMELO Norton
NEW CAMBRIA (67470) Saline(89), Ottawa(10)
NEW CENTURY Johnson
NEWTON (67114) Harvey(95), Butler(2), Marion(1)
NICKERSON Reno
NIOTAZE Chautauqua
NORCATUR (67653) Decatur(70), Norton(29)
NORTH NEWTON Harvey
NORTON Norton
NORTONVILLE (66060) Jefferson(50), Atchison(49)
NORWAY Republic
NORWICH (67118) Kingman(94), Sedgwick(2), Harper(1), Sumner(1)
OAKHILL (67472) Clay(70), Ottawa(29)
OAKLEY (67748) Logan(83), Thomas(11), Gove(4)

OBERLIN (67749) Decatur(98), Rawlins(1)
ODIN Barton
OFFERLE (67563) Edwards(56), Ford(39), Hodgeman(4)
OGALLAH (67656) Trego(91), Graham(8)
OGDEN Riley
OKETO Marshall
OLATHE Johnson
OLMITZ Barton
OLPE Lyon
OLSBURG Pottawatomie
ONAGA (66521) Pottawatomie(93), Nemaha(6)
ONEIDA Nemaha
OPOLIS Crawford
OSAGE CITY (66523) Osage(98), Lyon(1)
OSAWATOMIE (66064) Miami(94), Franklin(5)
OSBORNE Osborne
OSKALOOSA Jefferson
OSWEGO Labette
OTIS (67565) Rush(87), Barton(10), Russell(1)
OTTAWA Franklin
OVERBROOK (66524) Osage(57), Douglas(30), Shawnee(9), Franklin(2)
OVERLAND PARK Johnson
OXFORD (67119) Sumner(65), Cowley(34)
OZAWKIE Jefferson
PALCO (67657) Rooks(60), Graham(39)
PALMER (66962) Washington(79), Clay(20)
PAOLA Miami
PARADISE (67658) Osborne(61), Russell(38)
PARK (67751) Gove(68), Sheridan(31)
PARKER (66072) Linn(94), Miami(4)
PARSONS (67357) Labette(91), Neosho(8)
PARTRIDGE Reno
PAWNEE ROCK (67567) Barton(59), Pawnee(25), Stafford(9), Rush(5)
PAXICO Wabaunsee
PEABODY (66866) Marion(94), Harvey(5)
PECK (67120) Sedgwick(70), Sumner(29)
PENOKEE Graham
PERRY Jefferson
PERU Chautauqua
PFEIFER Ellis
PHILLIPSBURG Phillips
PIEDMONT (67122) Greenwood(67), Elk(32)
PIERCEVILLE Finney
PIQUA Woodson
PITTSBURG (66762) Crawford(97), Cherokee(2)
PLAINS Meade
PLAINVILLE Rooks
PLEASANTON Linn
PLEVNA Reno
POMONA Franklin
PORTIS (67474) Osborne(83), Smith(16)
POTTER Atchison
POTWIN Butler
POWHATTAN Brown
PRAIRIE VIEW (67664) Phillips(89), Norton(10)
PRATT Pratt
PRESCOTT Linn

PRETTY PRAIRIE (67570) Reno(88), Kingman(11)
PRINCETON Franklin
PROTECTION (67127) Comanche(87), Clark(12)
QUENEMO (66528) Osage(98), Franklin(1)
QUINTER (67752) Gove(91), Sheridan(8)
RAGO Kingman
RAMONA (67475) Marion(63), Dickinson(36)
RANDALL Jewell
RANDOLPH Riley
RANSOM (67572) Ness(83), Trego(16)
RANTOUL (66079) Franklin(94), Miami(5)
RAYMOND (67573) Rice(98), Barton(1)
READING (66868) Lyon(88), Osage(10)
REDFIELD Bourbon
REPUBLIC Republic
REXFORD (67753) Thomas(61), Sheridan(31), Rawlins(5), Wallace(1)
RICHFIELD Morton
RICHMOND (66080) Franklin(77), Anderson(22)
RILEY Riley
RIVERTON Cherokee
ROBINSON (66532) Brown(74), Doniphan(25)
ROCK (67131) Cowley(98), Butler(1)
ROLLA (67954) Morton(74), Stevens(25)
ROSALIA Butler
ROSE HILL (67133) Butler(98), Sedgwick(1)
ROSSVILLE (66533) Shawnee(96), Jackson(3)
ROXBURY McPherson
ROZEL Pawnee
RUSH CENTER (67575) Rush(97), Pawnee(2)
RUSSELL Russell
RUSSELL SPRINGS Logan
SABETHA (66534) Nemaha(92), Brown(7)
SAINT FRANCIS Cheyenne
SAINT GEORGE Pottawatomie
SAINT JOHN (67576) Stafford(96), Pratt(3)
SAINT MARYS (66536) Pottawatomie(94), Wabaunsee(2), Shawnee(2)
SAINT PAUL Neosho
SALINA Saline
SATANTA (67870) Haskell(82), Grant(17)
SAVONBURG (66772) Allen(97), Bourbon(2)
SAWYER (67134) Pratt(90), Barber(9)
SCAMMON Cherokee
SCANDIA Republic
SCHOENCHEN Ellis
SCOTT CITY (67871) Scott(97), Logan(1), Finney(1)
SCRANTON Osage
SEDAN Chautauqua
SEDGWICK (67135) Harvey(60), Sedgwick(39)
SELDEN (67757) Sheridan(57), Decatur(38), Thomas(4)
SENECA Nemaha
SEVERY (67137) Greenwood(88), Elk(12)
SEWARD Stafford
SHARON (67138) Barber(97), Harper(2)
SHARON SPRINGS Wallace

SHAWNEE Johnson
SHAWNEE MISSION Johnson
SHIELDS (67874) Lane(86), Gove(13)
SILVER LAKE (66539) Shawnee(98), Jackson(1)
SIMPSON Mitchell
SMITH CENTER Smith
SMOLAN Saline
SOLDIER (66540) Jackson(96), Nemaha(3)
SOLOMON (67480) Dickinson(57), Ottawa(29), Saline(13)
SOUTH HAVEN Sumner
SOUTH HUTCHINSON Reno
SPEARVILLE (67876) Ford(91), Hodgeman(8)
SPIVEY Kingman
SPRING HILL (66083) Johnson(61), Miami(38)
STAFFORD Stafford
STARK (66775) Neosho(98), Bourbon(1)
STERLING (67579) Rice(81), Reno(18)
STILWELL Johnson
STOCKTON Rooks
STRONG CITY Chase
STUDLEY (67759) Sheridan(89), Graham(10)
STUTTGART Phillips
SUBLETTE Haskell
SUMMERFIELD Marshall
SUN CITY Barber
SYCAMORE Montgomery
SYLVAN GROVE (67481) Lincoln(98), Russell(1)
SYLVIA Reno
SYRACUSE (67878) Hamilton(86), Stanton(13)
TALMAGE Dickinson
TAMPA Marion
TECUMSEH Shawnee
TESCOTT (67484) Ottawa(80), Saline(15), Lincoln(4)
THAYER (66776) Neosho(82), Wilson(16)
TIMKEN (67582) Rush(98), Pawnee(1)
TIPTON (67485) Osborne(53), Mitchell(46)
TONGANOXIE Leavenworth
TOPEKA Shawnee
TORONTO (66777) Woodson(91), Greenwood(6), Wilson(1)
TOWANDA Butler
TREECE Cherokee
TRIBUNE Greeley
TROY Doniphan
TURON (67583) Reno(50), Pratt(43), Stafford(5)
TYRO Montgomery
UDALL (67146) Cowley(93), Sumner(6)
ULYSSES (67880) Grant(98), Kearny(1)
UNIONTOWN Bourbon
UTICA (67584) Ness(56), Gove(23), Lane(10), Trego(9)
VALLEY CENTER (67147) Sedgwick(98), Harvey(1)
VALLEY FALLS (66088) Jefferson(97), Atchison(2)
VASSAR Osage
VERMILLION (66544) Marshall(95), Nemaha(4)
VICTORIA Ellis

VIOLA Sedgwick
VIRGIL (66870) Greenwood(96), Woodson(3)
VLIETS Marshall
WA KEENEY (67672) Trego(96), Graham(3)
WAKARUSA (66546) Shawnee(85), Osage(14)
WAKEFIELD (67487) Clay(90), Dickinson(6), Geary(2)
WALDO (67673) Russell(82), Osborne(17)
WALDRON Harper
WALKER Ellis
WALLACE (67761) Wallace(65), Logan(34)
WALNUT (66780) Bourbon(79), Crawford(19), Neosho(1)
WALTON (67151) Harvey(89), Marion(10)
WAMEGO (66547) Pottawatomie(88), Wabaunsee(11)
WASHINGTON Washington
WATERVILLE (66548) Marshall(97), Washington(1)
WATHENA Doniphan
WAVERLY (66871) Coffey(96), Osage(3)
WEBBER Jewell
WEIR Cherokee
WELDA (66091) Anderson(97), Franklin(2)
WELLINGTON Sumner
WELLS Ottawa
WELLSVILLE (66092) Franklin(66), Miami(25), Douglas(7)
WESKAN Wallace
WEST MINERAL Cherokee
WESTMORELAND Pottawatomie
WESTPHALIA (66093) Anderson(57), Coffey(42)
WETMORE (66550) Nemaha(80), Jackson(10), Brown(9)
WHEATON (66551) Pottawatomie(98), Marshall(1)
WHITE CITY (66872) Morris(96), Geary(3)
WHITE CLOUD (66094) Doniphan(98), Brown(1)
WHITEWATER (67154) Butler(94), Harvey(5)
WHITING Jackson
WICHITA Sedgwick
WILLIAMSBURG (66095) Franklin(88), Anderson(10)
WILMORE (67155) Comanche(85), Kiowa(14)
WILSEY Morris
WILSON (67490) Ellsworth(80), Russell(11), Lincoln(7)
WINCHESTER Jefferson
WINDOM (67491) McPherson(77), Rice(22)
WINFIELD Cowley
WINONA (67764) Logan(87), Thomas(12)
WOODBINE Dickinson
WOODSTON Rooks
WRIGHT Ford
YATES CENTER Woodson
YODER Reno
ZENDA (67159) Kingman(83), Harper(16)
ZURICH (67676) Rooks(90), Ellis(9)

ZIP/City Cross Reference

66002-66002 ATCHISON	66406-66406 BEATTIE	66714-66714 BENEDICT	66873-66873 WILSEY
66006-66006 BALDWIN CITY	66407-66407 BELVUE	66716-66716 BRONSON	66901-66901 CONCORDIA
66007-66007 BASEHOR	66408-66408 BERN	66717-66717 BUFFALO	66930-66930 AGENDA
66008-66008 BENDENA	66409-66409 BERRYTON	66720-66720 CHANUTE	66931-66931 AMES
66010-66010 BLUE MOUND	66411-66411 BLUE RAPIDS	66724-66724 CHEROKEE	66932-66932 ATHOL
66012-66012 BONNER SPRINGS	66412-66412 BREMEN	66725-66725 COLUMBUS	66933-66933 BARNES
66013-66013 BUCYRUS	66413-66413 BURLINGAME	66727-66727 COYVILLE	66935-66935 BELLEVILLE
66014-66014 CENTERVILLE	66414-66414 CARBONDALE	66728-66728 CRESTLINE	66936-66936 BURR OAK
66015-66015 COLONY	66415-66415 CENTRALIA	66732-66732 ELSMORE	66937-66937 CLIFTON
66016-66016 CUMMINGS	66416-66416 CIRCLEVILLE	66733-66733 ERIE	66938-66938 CLYDE
66017-66017 DENTON	66417-66417 CORNING	66734-66734 FARLINGTON	66939-66939 COURTLAND
66018-66018 DE SOTO	66418-66418 DELIA	66735-66735 FRANKLIN	66940-66940 CUBA
66019-66019 CLEARVIEW CITY	66419-66419 DENISON	66736-66736 FREDONIA	66941-66941 ESBON
66020-66020 EASTON	66420-66420 DOVER	66738-66738 FULTON	66942-66942 FORMOSO
66021-66021 EDGERTON	66422-66422 EMMETT	66739-66739 GALENA	66943-66943 GREENLEAF
66023-66023 EFFINGHAM	66423-66423 ESKRIDGE	66740-66740 GALESBURG	66944-66944 HADDAM
66024-66024 ELWOOD	66424-66424 EVEREST	66741-66741 GARLAND	66945-66945 HANOVER
66025-66025 EUDORA	66425-66425 FAIRVIEW	66741-66741 ARCADIA	66946-66946 HOLLENBERG
66026-66026 FONTANA	66426-66426 FOSTORIA	66742-66742 GAS	66948-66948 JAMESTOWN
66027-66027 FORT LEAVENWORTH	66427-66427 FRANKFORT	66743-66743 GIRARD	66949-66949 JEWELL
66030-66030 GARDNER	66428-66428 GOFF	66746-66746 HEPLER	66951-66951 KENSINGTON
66031-66031 NEW CENTURY	66429-66429 GRANTVILLE	66748-66748 HUMBOLDT	66952-66952 LEBANON
66032-66032 GARNETT	66431-66431 HARVEYVILLE	66749-66749 IOLA	66953-66953 LINN
66033-66033 GREELEY	66432-66432 HAVENSVILLE	66751-66751 LA HARPE	66955-66955 MAHASKA
66035-66035 HIGHLAND	66433-66433 MARYSVILLE	66753-66753 MC CUNE	66956-66956 MANKATO
66036-66036 HILLSDALE	66434-66434 HIAWATHA	66754-66754 MAPLETON	66958-66958 MORROWVILLE
66039-66039 KINCAID	66436-66436 HOLTON	66755-66755 MORAN	66959-66959 MUNDEN
66040-66040 LA CYGNE	66438-66438 HOME	66756-66756 MULBERRY	66960-66960 NARKA
66041-66041 LANCASTER	66439-66439 HORTON	66757-66757 NEODESHA	66961-66961 NORWAY
66042-66042 LANE	66440-66440 HOYT	66758-66758 NEOSHO FALLS	66962-66962 PALMER
66043-66043 LANSING	66441-66441 JUNCTION CITY	66759-66759 NEW ALBANY	66963-66963 RANDALL
66044-66047 LAWRENCE	66442-66442 FORT RILEY	66760-66760 OPOLIS	66964-66964 REPUBLIC
66048-66048 LEAVENWORTH	66449-66449 LEONARDVILLE	66761-66761 PIQUA	66966-66966 SCANDIA
66049-66049 LAWRENCE	66450-66450 LOUISVILLE	66762-66762 PITTSBURG	66967-66967 SMITH CENTER
66050-66050 LECOMPTON	66451-66451 LYNDON	66763-66763 FRONTENAC	66968-66968 WASHINGTON
66051-66051 OLATHE	66501-66501 MC FARLAND	66767-66767 PRESCOTT	66970-66970 WEBBER
66052-66052 LINWOOD	66502-66506 MANHATTAN	66769-66769 REDFIELD	67001-67001 ANDALE
66053-66053 LOUISBURG	66507-66507 MAPLE HILL	66770-66770 RIVERTON	67002-67002 ANDOVER
66054-66054 MC LOUTH	66508-66508 MARYSVILLE	66771-66771 SAINT PAUL	67003-67003 ANTHONY
66056-66056 MOUND CITY	66509-66509 MAYETTA	66772-66772 SAVONBURG	67004-67004 ARGONIA
66058-66058 MUSCOTAH	66510-66510 MELVERN	66773-66773 SCAMMON	67005-67005 ARKANSAS CITY
66060-66060 NORTONVILLE	66512-66512 MERIDEN	66775-66775 STARK	67008-67008 ATLANTA
66061-66063 OLATHE	66514-66514 MILFORD	66776-66776 THAYER	67009-67009 ATTICA
66064-66064 OSAWATOMIE	66515-66515 MORRILL	66777-66777 TORONTO	67010-67010 AUGUSTA
66066-66066 OSKALOOSA	66516-66516 NETAWAKA	66778-66778 TREECE	67012-67012 BEAUMONT
66067-66067 OTTAWA	66517-66517 OGDEN	66779-66779 UNIONTOWN	67013-67013 BELLE PLAINE
66070-66070 OZAWKIE	66518-66518 OKETO	66780-66780 WALNUT	67015-67015 BELVIDERE
66071-66071 PAOLA	66520-66520 OLSBURG	66781-66781 WEIR	67016-67016 BENTLEY
66072-66072 PARKER	66521-66521 ONAGA	66782-66782 WEST MINERAL	67017-67017 BENTON
66073-66073 PERRY	66522-66522 ONEIDA	66783-66783 YATES CENTER	67018-67018 BLUFF CITY
66075-66075 PLEASANTON	66523-66523 OSAGE CITY	66801-66801 EMPORIA	67019-67019 BURDEN
66076-66076 POMONA	66524-66524 OVERBROOK	66830-66830 ADMIRE	67020-67020 BURRTON
66077-66077 POTTER	66526-66526 PAXICO	66833-66833 ALLEN	67021-67021 BYERS
66078-66078 PRINCETON	66527-66527 POWHATTAN	66834-66834 ALTA VISTA	67022-67022 CALDWELL
66079-66079 RANTOUL	66528-66528 QUENEMO	66835-66835 AMERICUS	67023-67023 CAMBRIDGE
66080-66080 RICHMOND	66531-66531 RILEY	66838-66838 BURDICK	67024-67024 CEDAR VALE
66083-66083 SPRING HILL	66532-66532 ROBINSON	66839-66839 BURLINGTON	67025-67025 CHENEY
66085-66085 STILWELL	66533-66533 ROSSVILLE	66840-66840 BURNS	67026-67026 CLEARWATER
66086-66086 TONGANOXIE	66534-66534 SABETHA	66842-66842 CASSODAY	67028-67028 COATS
66087-66087 TROY	66535-66535 SAINT GEORGE	66843-66843 CEDAR POINT	67029-67029 COLDWATER
66088-66088 VALLEY FALLS	66536-66536 SAINT MARYS	66845-66845 COTTONWOOD FALLS	67030-67030 COLWICH
66090-66090 WATHENA	66537-66537 SCRANTON	66846-66846 COUNCIL GROVE	67031-67031 CONWAY SPRINGS
66091-66091 WELDA	66538-66538 SENECA	66849-66849 DWIGHT	67032-67032 CALDWELL
66092-66092 WELLSVILLE	66539-66539 SILVER LAKE	66850-66850 ELMDALE	67035-67035 CUNNINGHAM
66093-66093 WESTPHALIA	66540-66540 SOLDIER	66851-66851 FLORENCE	67036-67036 DANVILLE
66094-66094 WHITE CLOUD	66541-66541 SUMMERFIELD	66852-66852 GRIDLEY	67037-67037 DERBY
66095-66095 WILLIAMSBURG	66542-66542 TECUMSEH	66853-66853 HAMILTON	67038-67038 DEXTER
66097-66097 WINCHESTER	66543-66543 VASSAR	66854-66854 HARTFORD	67039-67039 DOUGLASS
66100-66112 KANSAS CITY	66544-66544 VERMILLION	66855-66855 LAMONT	67041-67041 ELBING
66113-66113 EDWARDSVILLE	66545-66545 VLIETS	66856-66856 LEBO	67042-67042 EL DORADO
66115-66160 KANSAS CITY	66546-66546 WAKARUSA	66857-66857 LE ROY	67045-67045 EUREKA
66200-66222 SHAWNEE MISSION	66547-66547 WAMEGO	66858-66858 LINCOLNVILLE	67047-67047 FALL RIVER
66222-66222 MISSION	66548-66548 WATERVILLE	66859-66859 LOST SPRINGS	67049-67049 FREEPORT
66223-66251 SHAWNEE MISSION	66549-66549 WESTMORELAND	66860-66860 MADISON	67050-67050 GARDEN PLAIN
66251-66251 OVERLAND PARK	66550-66550 WETMORE	66861-66861 MARION	67051-67051 GEUDA SPRINGS
66262-66283 SHAWNEE MISSION	66551-66551 WHEATON	66862-66862 MATFIELD GREEN	67052-67052 GODDARD
66283-66283 OVERLAND PARK	66552-66552 WHITING	66863-66863 NEAL	67053-67053 GOESSEL
66285-66285 SHAWNEE MISSION	66554-66554 RANDOLPH	66864-66864 NEOSHO RAPIDS	67054-67054 GREENSBURG
66285-66285 LENEXA	66555-66555 MARYSVILLE	66865-66865 OLPE	67055-67055 GREENWICH
66286-66286 SHAWNEE MISSION	66600-66699 TOPEKA	66866-66866 PEABODY	67056-67056 HALSTEAD
66286-66286 SHAWNEE	66701-66701 FORT SCOTT	66868-66868 READING	67057-67057 HARDTNER
66401-66401 ALMA	66710-66710 ALTOONA	66869-66869 STRONG CITY	67058-67058 HARPER
66402-66402 AUBURN	66711-66711 ARCADIA	66870-66870 VIRGIL	67059-67059 HAVILAND
66403-66403 AXTELL	66712-66712 ARMA	66871-66871 WAVERLY	67060-67060 HAYSVILLE
66404-66404 BAILEYVILLE	66713-66713 BAXTER SPRINGS	66872-66872 WHITE CITY	67061-67061 HAZELTON

ZIP Range	City	ZIP Range	City	ZIP Range	City	ZIP Range	City
67062-67062	HESSTON	67414-67414	ADA	67548-67548	LA CROSSE	67735-67735	GOODLAND
67063-67063	HILLSBORO	67416-67416	ASSARIA	67550-67550	LARNED	67736-67736	GOVE
67065-67065	ISABEL	67417-67417	AURORA	67552-67552	LEWIS	67737-67737	GRAINFIELD
67066-67066	IUKA	67418-67418	BARNARD	67553-67553	LIEBENTHAL	67738-67738	GRINNELL
67067-67067	KECHI	67420-67420	BELOIT	67554-67554	LYONS	67739-67739	HERNDON
67068-67068	KINGMAN	67422-67422	BENNINGTON	67556-67556	MC CRACKEN	67740-67740	HOXIE
67070-67070	KIOWA	67423-67423	BEVERLY	67557-67557	MACKSVILLE	67741-67741	KANORADO
67071-67071	LAKE CITY	67425-67425	BROOKVILLE	67559-67559	NEKOMA	67743-67743	LEVANT
67072-67072	LATHAM	67427-67427	BUSHTON	67560-67560	NESS CITY	67744-67744	LUDELL
67073-67073	LEHIGH	67428-67428	CANTON	67561-67561	NICKERSON	67745-67745	MC DONALD
67074-67074	LEON	67429-67429	CARLTON	67562-67562	ODIN	67747-67747	MONUMENT
67101-67101	MAIZE	67430-67430	CAWKER CITY	67563-67563	OFFERLE	67748-67748	OAKLEY
67102-67102	MAPLE CITY	67431-67431	CHAPMAN	67564-67564	OLMITZ	67749-67749	OBERLIN
67103-67103	MAYFIELD	67432-67432	CLAY CENTER	67565-67565	OTIS	67751-67751	PARK
67104-67104	MEDICINE LODGE	67436-67436	DELPHOS	67566-67566	PARTRIDGE	67752-67752	QUINTER
67105-67105	MILAN	67437-67437	DOWNS	67567-67567	PAWNEE ROCK	67753-67753	REXFORD
67106-67106	MILTON	67438-67438	DURHAM	67568-67568	PLEVNA	67755-67755	RUSSELL SPRINGS
67107-67107	MOUNDRIDGE	67439-67439	ELLSWORTH	67569-67569	TURON	67756-67756	SAINT FRANCIS
67108-67108	MOUNT HOPE	67441-67441	ENTERPRISE	67570-67570	PRETTY PRAIRIE	67757-67757	SELDEN
67109-67109	MULLINVILLE	67442-67442	FALUN	67572-67572	RANSOM	67758-67758	SHARON SPRINGS
67110-67110	MULVANE	67443-67443	GALVA	67573-67573	RAYMOND	67759-67759	STUDLEY
67111-67111	MURDOCK	67444-67444	GENESEO	67574-67574	ROZEL	67761-67761	WALLACE
67112-67112	NASHVILLE	67445-67445	GLASCO	67575-67575	RUSH CENTER	67762-67762	WESKAN
67114-67114	NEWTON	67446-67446	GLEN ELDER	67576-67576	SAINT JOHN	67764-67764	WINONA
67117-67117	NORTH NEWTON	67447-67447	GREEN	67577-67577	SEWARD	67801-67801	DODGE CITY
67118-67118	NORWICH	67448-67448	GYPSUM	67578-67578	STAFFORD	67831-67831	ASHLAND
67119-67119	OXFORD	67449-67449	HERINGTON	67579-67579	STERLING	67834-67834	BUCKLIN
67120-67120	PECK	67450-67450	HOLYROOD	67581-67581	SYLVIA	67835-67835	CIMARRON
67122-67122	PIEDMONT	67451-67451	HOPE	67582-67582	TIMKEN	67836-67836	COOLIDGE
67123-67123	POTWIN	67452-67452	HUNTER	67583-67583	TURON	67837-67837	COPELAND
67124-67124	PRATT	67454-67454	KANOPOLIS	67584-67584	UTICA	67838-67838	DEERFIELD
67127-67127	PROTECTION	67455-67455	LINCOLN	67585-67585	YODER	67839-67839	DIGHTON
67128-67128	RAGO	67456-67456	LINDSBORG	67601-67601	HAYS	67840-67840	ENGLEWOOD
67131-67131	ROCK	67457-67457	LITTLE RIVER	67621-67621	AGRA	67841-67841	ENSIGN
67132-67132	ROSALIA	67458-67458	LONGFORD	67622-67622	ALMENA	67842-67842	FORD
67133-67133	ROSE HILL	67459-67459	LORRAINE	67623-67623	ALTON	67843-67843	FORT DODGE
67134-67134	SAWYER	67460-67460	MCPHERSON	67625-67625	BOGUE	67844-67844	FOWLER
67135-67135	SEDGWICK	67463-67463	MANCHESTER	67626-67626	BUNKER HILL	67846-67846	GARDEN CITY
67137-67137	SEVERY	67464-67464	MARQUETTE	67627-67627	CATHARINE	67849-67849	HANSTON
67138-67138	SHARON	67465-67465	MENTOR	67628-67628	CEDAR	67850-67850	HEALY
67140-67140	SOUTH HAVEN	67466-67466	MILTONVALE	67629-67629	CLAYTON	67851-67851	HOLCOMB
67142-67142	SPIVEY	67467-67467	MINNEAPOLIS	67630-67630	CODELL	67853-67853	INGALLS
67143-67143	SUN CITY	67468-67468	MORGANVILLE	67631-67631	COLLYER	67854-67854	JETMORE
67144-67144	TOWANDA	67469-67469	ENTERPRISE	67632-67632	DAMAR	67855-67855	JOHNSON
67146-67146	UDALL	67470-67470	NEW CAMBRIA	67634-67634	DORRANCE	67856-67856	KALVESTA
67147-67147	VALLEY CENTER	67472-67472	OAKHILL	67635-67635	DRESDEN	67857-67857	KENDALL
67149-67149	VIOLA	67473-67473	OSBORNE	67636-67636	EDMOND	67858-67858	KINGSDOWN
67150-67150	WALDRON	67474-67474	PORTIS	67637-67637	ELLIS	67859-67859	KISMET
67151-67151	WALTON	67475-67475	RAMONA	67638-67638	GAYLORD	67860-67860	LAKIN
67152-67152	WELLINGTON	67476-67476	ROXBURY	67639-67639	GLADE	67861-67861	LEOTI
67154-67154	WHITEWATER	67478-67478	SIMPSON	67640-67640	GORHAM	67862-67862	MANTER
67155-67155	WILMORE	67479-67479	SMOLAN	67641-67641	HARLAN	67863-67863	MARIENTHAL
67156-67156	WINFIELD	67480-67480	SOLOMON	67642-67642	HILL CITY	67864-67864	MEADE
67159-67159	ZENDA	67481-67481	SYLVAN GROVE	67643-67643	JENNINGS	67865-67865	MINNEOLA
67200-67220	WICHITA	67482-67482	TALMAGE	67644-67644	KIRWIN	67867-67867	MONTEZUMA
67221-67221	MC CONNELL A F B	67483-67483	TAMPA	67645-67645	LENORA	67868-67868	PIERCEVILLE
67221-67221	MCCONNELL AFB	67484-67484	TESCOTT	67646-67646	LOGAN	67869-67869	PLAINS
67223-67236	WICHITA	67485-67485	TIPTON	67647-67647	LONG ISLAND	67870-67870	SATANTA
67240-67240	DENNIS THE MENACE	67487-67487	WAKEFIELD	67648-67648	LUCAS	67871-67871	SCOTT CITY
67251-67278	WICHITA	67488-67488	WELLS	67649-67649	LURAY	67874-67874	SHIELDS
67301-67301	INDEPENDENCE	67490-67490	WILSON	67650-67650	MORLAND	67876-67876	SPEARVILLE
67330-67330	ALTAMONT	67491-67491	WINDOM	67651-67651	NATOMA	67877-67877	SUBLETTE
67332-67332	BARTLETT	67492-67492	WOODBINE	67652-67652	NEW ALMELO	67878-67878	SYRACUSE
67333-67333	CANEY	67501-67504	HUTCHINSON	67653-67653	NORCATUR	67879-67879	TRIBUNE
67334-67334	CHAUTAUQUA	67505-67505	SOUTH HUTCHINSON	67654-67654	NORTON	67880-67880	ULYSSES
67335-67335	CHERRYVALE	67510-67510	ABBYVILLE	67656-67656	OGALLAH	67882-67882	WRIGHT
67336-67336	CHETOPA	67511-67511	ALBERT	67657-67657	PALCO	67901-67905	LIBERAL
67337-67337	COFFEYVILLE	67512-67512	ALDEN	67658-67658	PARADISE	67950-67950	ELKHART
67340-67340	DEARING	67513-67513	ALEXANDER	67659-67659	PENOKEE	67951-67951	HUGOTON
67341-67341	DENNIS	67514-67514	ARLINGTON	67660-67660	PFEIFER	67952-67952	MOSCOW
67342-67342	EDNA	67515-67515	ARNOLD	67661-67661	PHILLIPSBURG	67953-67953	RICHFIELD
67344-67344	ELK CITY	67516-67516	BAZINE	67663-67663	PLAINVILLE	67954-67954	ROLLA
67345-67345	ELK FALLS	67517-67517	BEAVER	67664-67664	PRAIRIE VIEW		
67346-67346	GRENOLA	67518-67518	BEELER	67665-67665	RUSSELL		
67347-67347	HAVANA	67519-67519	BELPRE	67667-67667	SCHOENCHEN		
67349-67349	HOWARD	67520-67520	BISON	67669-67669	STOCKTON		
67351-67351	LIBERTY	67521-67521	BROWNELL	67670-67670	STUTTGART		
67352-67352	LONGTON	67522-67522	BUHLER	67671-67671	VICTORIA		
67353-67353	MOLINE	67523-67523	BURDETT	67672-67672	WA KEENEY		
67354-67354	MOUND VALLEY	67524-67524	CHASE	67673-67673	WALDO		
67355-67355	NIOTAZE	67525-67525	CLAFLIN	67674-67674	WALKER		
67356-67356	OSWEGO	67526-67526	ELLINWOOD	67675-67675	WOODSTON		
67357-67357	PARSONS	67529-67529	GARFIELD	67676-67676	ZURICH		
67360-67360	PERU	67530-67530	GREAT BEND	67701-67701	COLBY		
67361-67361	SEDAN	67543-67543	HAVEN	67730-67730	ATWOOD		
67363-67363	SYCAMORE	67544-67544	HOISINGTON	67731-67731	BIRD CITY		
67364-67364	TYRO	67545-67545	HUDSON	67732-67732	BREWSTER		
67401-67402	SALINA	67546-67546	INMAN	67733-67733	EDSON		
67410-67410	ABILENE	67547-67547	KINSLEY	67734-67734	GEM		

Kentucky

General Help Numbers:

Governor's Office
700 Capitol Ave, Room 100
Frankfort, KY 40601
http://gov.state.ky.us

502-564-2611
Fax 502-564-2517
7:30AM-5PM

Attorney General's Office
700 Capitol Ave, Ste. 118
Frankfort, KY 40601
www..law.state.ky.us

502-696-5300
Fax 502-564-2894
8AM-5PM

State Court Administrator
100 Mill Creek Park
Frankfort, KY 40601
www..kycourts.net

502-573-2350
Fax 502-695-1759
8AM-4:30PM

State Archives
300 Coffee Tree Rd
Frankfort, KY 40601
www..kdla.state.ky.us

502-564-8300
Fax 502-564-5773
8AM-4PM T-SA

State Specifics:

Capital: Frankfort
                                          Franklin County

Time Zone: EST*
* Kentucky's forty western-most counties are CST: They are:
Adair, Allen, Ballard, Barren, Breckinridge, Butler, Caldwell,
Calloway, Carlisle, Christian, Clinton, Crittenden, Cumberland,
Daviess, Edmonson, Fulton, Graves, Grayson, Hancock, Hart,
Henderson, Hickman, Hopkins, Livingstone, Logan, Marshall,
McCracken, McLean, Metcalfe, Monroe, Muhlenberg, Ohio,Russell,
Simpson, Todd, Trigg, Union, Warren, Wayne, Webster.

Number of Counties: 120

Population: 4,065,556

Web Site: www.kydirect.net

State Agencies

Criminal Records

Kentucky State Police, Records Branch, 1250 Louisville Rd, Frankfort, KY 40601; 502-227-8713, 502-227-8734 (Fax), 8AM-4PM.

www.kentuckystatepolice.org

Note: Local Kentucky courts will not do criminal searches. They refer all requesters to the Administrative Office of Courts in Frankfort, KY; phone 502-573-2350. The state sexual offender list is available at http://kspsor.state.ky.us

Indexing & Storage: Records are available from 1952 on for criminal records. It takes a minimum of 30 days before new records are available for inquiry. Records are indexed on inhouse computer, fingerprint cards. Nearly 75% of records are automated. 69% of all arrests in database have final dispositions recorded, 59% for those arrests within last 5 years.

Searching: Per statute, requests are accepted for employment purposes for nursing, schools, lottery, EMT, YMCA, daycare, and adoptive/foster parent background searches. Other requesters are advised to submit requests through the court system. Include the following in your request: signed release from subject, full name, date of birth, Social Security Number, reason for information request. Fingerprints are not requested. Statistical information about criminal offenses and accidents is available from 1971 on. The following data is not released: juvenile records. Records without dispositions, including pending and dismissed cases, are not released.

Access by: mail, in person.

Fee & Payment: The fee is $10.00 per name. Fee payee: Kentucky State Treasurer. Prepayment required. Personal checks accepted. No credit cards accepted.

Mail search: Turnaround time: 2 to 3 weeks. A self addressed stamped envelope is requested.

In person search: Turnaround time is while you wait. There is a limit of 5 searches.

Corporation Records
Limited Partnerships
Assumed Name
Limited Liability Company Records

Secretary of State, Corporate Records, PO Box 718, Frankfort, KY 40602-0718 (Courier: 700 Capitol Ave, Room 156, Frankfort, KY 40601); 502-564-7330, 502-564-4075 (Fax), 8AM-4PM.

www.sos.state.ky.us

Indexing & Storage: Records are available from the 1977 forward on computer index. Hard copies are on microfilm. Records inactive by 1976 are archived and it takes 2 weeks to research. New records are available for inquiry immediately.

Searching: Computer records are limited, they contain name, dates, current registered agent and initial incorporators and initial directors. They do contain current lists of officers and directors when available. Include the following in your request: full name of business.

Access by: mail, phone, in person, online.

Fee & Payment: There is no search fee, but there is a $5.00 certification fee. Copies are $1.00 (minimum) for up to first to 10 pages, and $.10 per each additional page. Pages can be certified for $.50 each. A Certificate of Good Standing is $10.00. Fee payee: Secretary of State. Prepayment required. Send at least $1.00 in the mail for copies. If certified copies are needed, call first. Personal checks accepted. No credit cards accepted.

Mail search: Turnaround time: 2 to 3 days. No self addressed stamped envelope is required.

Phone search: Only information on the computer system is released over the phone.

In person search: Turnaround time while you wait. If you order 5 or more, they will mail the records to you.

Online search: The Internet site, open 24 hours, has a searchable database with over 340,000 KY businesses. The site also offers downloading of filing forms.

Other access: Monthly lists of new corporations are available for $50.00 per month.

Trademarks/Servicemarks

Secretary of State, Trademarks Section, 700 Capitol Ave, Suite 152, Frankfort, KY 40601; 502-564-2848 x442, 502-564-1484 (Fax), 8AM-4:30PM.

www.sos.state.ky.us

Indexing & Storage: Records are indexed on original documents on file in the office and online access to database.

Searching: Include the trademark/servicemark name or applicant name or certification number. Also, wordmark and description helps.

Access by: mail, phone, in person, online.

Fee & Payment: There is no fee.

Mail search: Turnaround time: 1 week. A self addressed stamped envelope is requested.

Phone search: Ask for Johnna Ballinger.

In person search: Searching is available in person.

Online search: Free, searchable database at www.kysos.com/trademarks/tmstart.asp

Uniform Commercial Code

UCC Division, Secretary of State, PO Box 1470, Frankfort, KY 40602-0718 (Courier: 363C Versailles Rd, Mare Manor, Frankfort, KY 40601); 502-573-0265, 502-573-0259 (Fax), 8AM-4:30PM.

www.kysos.com

Note: The state adopted Revised Article 9 effective July 1, 2001.

Searching: The Secretary of State maintains a searchable index for all active UCC records that provides for the retrieval of a record by the name of the debtor and by the file number of the initial financing statement to which the record relates. Include the following in your request: full debtor name. No partial name searches are permitted, except at web site. The state advises requesters to use Form UCC-11.

Access by: mail, in person, online.

Fee & Payment: $5.00 for a certified search. $.10 per page for copies of UCC records. Fee payee: KY State Treasurer. Personal checks accepted. No credit cards accepted.

Mail search: Turnaround time: 1-3 business days. Full names are required.

In person search: Searching is available in person.

Online search: UCC record searching is offered free of charge at the web site. Search by debtor name, or file number. SSNs are withheld from the online system. Pre-paid accounts may be established for those requiring copies or certified documents.

Federal Tax Liens
State Tax Liens
Records not maintained by a state level agency.

Note: All tax liens are at the county level.

Sales Tax Registrations

Revenue Cabinet, Tax Compliance Department, Sales Tax Section, Station 53, PO Box 181, Frankfort, KY 40602-0181 (Courier: 200 Fair Oaks, Bldg 2, Frankfort, KY 40602); 502-564-5170, 502-564-2041 (Fax), 8AM-4:30PM.

http://revenue.state.ky.us

Indexing & Storage: Records are available from the 1970's. Records are indexed on computer from 1996 to present, and on microfilm from 1985 to 1995.

Searching: This agency will only confirm if a business is registered, and they will confirm if a tax permit exists. They will provide no other information. Include the following in your request: business name, owner name and address, federal employer identification number. They will also search by tax permit number.

Access by: mail, in person.

Mail search: Turnaround time: 2 to 3 months. A self addressed stamped envelope is requested. No fee for mail request.

In person search: No fee for request.

Birth Certificates

Department for Public Health, Vital Statistics, 275 E Main St - IE-A, Frankfort, KY 40621-0001; 502-564-4212, 502-227-0032 (Fax), 8AM-4PM.

http://publichealth.state.ky.us/vital.htm

Indexing & Storage: Records are available from 1911 to present. It takes 1 month before new records are available for inquiry. Records are indexed on microfiche, inhouse computer, books (volumes).

Searching: Include the following in your request: full name, names of parents, mother's maiden name, date of birth, place of birth. Provide a daytime phone number.

Access by: mail, phone, fax, in person.

Fee & Payment: Searches are $9.00 per name. Add $5.00 if using a credit card. Fee payee: Kentucky State Treasurer. Prepayment required. Personal checks accepted. Credit cards accepted: MasterCard, Visa, AmEx, Discover.

Mail search: Turnaround time: 3 to 4 weeks. No self addressed stamped envelope is required.

Phone search: Must use a credit card (add $5.00 fee) for a phone request. Turnaround time is 3 to 5 days.

Fax search: Same fees as telephone search.

In person search: Turnaround time 1 1/2 hour.

Expedited service: Expedited service is available for mail, phone and fax searches. Turnaround time: overnight delivery. Add $11.75 per package. Also, be sure to include extra credit card use fee.

Death Records

Department for Public Health, Vital Statistics, 275 E Main St - IE-A, Frankfort, KY 40621-0001; 502-564-4212, 502-227-0032 (Fax), 8AM-3PM.

http://publichealth.state.ky.us/vital.htm

Indexing & Storage: Records are available from 1911 on. It takes 1 month before new records are available for inquiry. Records are indexed on microfiche, inhouse computer, books (volumes).

Searching: Include the following in your request: full name, date of death, place of death. Provide a daytime phone number.

Access by: mail, phone, fax, in person, online.

Fee & Payment: The fee is $6.00 per name. Fee payee: Kentucky State Treasurer. Prepayment required. Personal checks accepted. Credit cards accepted: MasterCard, Visa, AmEx, Discover.

Mail search: Turnaround time: 3 to 4 weeks. No self addressed stamped envelope is required.

Phone search: Must use a credit card (add $5.00 fee) to make phone request. Turnaround time is 2-3 days.

Fax search: Same fees and turnaround time as telephone requests.

In person search: Turnaround time 1 1/2 hour.

Online search: In cooperation with the University of Kentucky, there is a searchable death index at http://ukcc.uky.edu:80/~vitalrec/. This is for non-commercial use only. Records are from 1911 through 1992. Also, there is a free genealogy site at http://vitals.rootsweb.com/ky/death/search.cgi. Death Indexes from 1911-2000 are available. You may search by surname, given name, place of death, residence, or year.

Expedited service: Expedited service is available for mail, phone and fax searches. Turnaround time: overnight delivery. Add $11.75 per package. Also, be sure to include extra credit card use fee.

Marriage Certificates

Department for Public Health, Vital Statistics, 275 E Main St - IE-A, Frankfort, KY 40621-0001; 502-564-4212, 502-227-0032 (Fax), 8AM-3PM.

http://publichealth.state.ky.us/vital.htm

Indexing & Storage: Records are available from June 1958 to present. It takes 1 to 2 months before new records are available for inquiry. Records are indexed on microfiche, inhouse computer, books (volumes).

Searching: Include the following in your request: names of husband and wife, date of marriage, place or county of marriage. Must also include where marriage license was obtained and a daytime phone number.

Access by: mail, phone, fax, in person, online.

Fee & Payment: The fee is $6.00 per name. Fee payee: Kentucky State Treasurer. Prepayment required. Personal checks accepted. Credit cards accepted: MasterCard, Visa, AmEx, Discover.

Mail search: Turnaround time: 3 to 4 weeks. No self addressed stamped envelope is required.

Phone search: Must use a credit card (add $5.00 fee) for a phone request. Turnaround time is 3 to 5 days.

Fax search: Same criteria as phone orders.

In person search: Turnaround time 1 1/2 hour.

Online search: In cooperation with the University of Kentucky, a searchable index is available on the Internet at http://ukcc.uky.edu:80/~vitalrec/. The index runs from 1973 through 1993. This is for non-commercial use only.

Other access: Contact Libraries and Archives.

Expedited service: Expedited service is available for mail, phone and fax searches. Turnaround time: overnight delivery. Add $11.75 per package. Also, be sure to include extra credit card use fee.

Divorce Records

Department for Public Health, Vital Statistics, 275 E Main St - IE-A, Frankfort, KY 40621-0001; 502-564-4212, 502-227-0032 (Fax), 8AM-3PM.

http://publichealth.state.ky.us/vital.htm

Indexing & Storage: Records are available from June, 1958 to present. It takes 1 to 2 months before new records are available for inquiry. Records are indexed on microfiche, inhouse computer, books (volumes).

Searching: Include the following in your request: names of husband and wife, date of divorce, place of divorce. Provide a daytime phone number.

Access by: mail, phone, fax, in person, online.

Fee & Payment: The fee is $6.00 per name. Fee payee: Kentucky State Treasurer. Prepayment required. Personal checks accepted. Credit cards accepted: MasterCard, Visa, AmEx, Discover.

Mail search: Turnaround time: 3 to 4 weeks. No self addressed stamped envelope is required.

Phone search: Must use a credit card (add $5.00 fee) for a phone request. Turnaround time 3-5 days.

Fax search: Same criteria as phone requests.

In person search: Turnaround time 1 1/2 hour.

Online search: In cooperation with the University of Kentucky, there is a searchable index on the Internet at http://ukcc.uky.edu:80/~vitalrec/. This is for non-commercial use only. The index is for 1973-1993.

Other access: Contact Libraries and Archives.

Expedited service: Expedited service is available for mail, phone and fax searches. Turnaround time: overnight delivery. Add $11.75 per package.

Workers' Compensation Records

Kentucky Department of Workers' Claims, Provention Park, 657 Tobeannounced Ave, Frankfort, KY 40601; 502-564-5550, 502-564-5732 (Fax), 8AM-4:30PM.

www.state.ky.us/agencies/labor/workcomp.htm

Indexing & Storage: Records are available from 1982 to present on computer. New records are available for inquiry immediately.

Searching: Must have a signed release from claimant only for copies of first report. Otherwise, information is open to the public per KRS 61.870 through 61.884. Include the following in your request: claimant name, Social Security Number, date of accident, place of employment at time of accident. The following data is not released: Social Security Numbers, addresses or personal information (height, weight, sex, eye color, etc.).

Access by: mail, fax, in person.

Fee & Payment: Fees are $.50 per page from microfilm and photocopies are $.10 per page. Fee payee: Kentucky State Treasurer. Payment may be submitted at the time records are picked up. Otherwise, an invoice will be mailed at the end of the month. Personal checks accepted. No credit cards accepted.

Mail search: Turnaround time: 2 to 4 weeks. Requests are processed in order by the date received. A self addressed stamped envelope is requested.

Fax search: Fax requests are processed by date of receipt same as requests that are mailed.

In person search: The office will have the records ready for you if you call ahead first and make an appointment.

Other access: A listing of file contents may be requested. Call for details.

Driver Records

Division of Driver Licensing, State Office Bldg, MVRS, 501 High Street, 2nd Floor, Frankfort, KY 40622; 502-564-6800 x2250, 502-564-5787 (Fax), 8AM-4:30PM.

www.kytc.state.ky.us

Note: Requests for copies of tickets must be submitted in writing to; Cabinets Record Custodian, Department of Administrative Services, State Office Building, Frankfort 40622. There is a $.10 fee per document.

Indexing & Storage: Records are available for 3 years for moving violations, DWIs and suspensions. Accidents are not reported on 3 years records. Records are normally destroyed after five years.

Searching: Casual requesters can obtain record information, but personal information is "cloaked" unless written consent by subject is provided. The SSN or DL, the full name and DOB are needed when ordering. The driver's address is not included as part of the search report without a release from the driver.

Access by: mail, in person, online.

Fee & Payment: The fee is $3.00 per record. Fee payee: Kentucky State Treasurer. Business checks accepted.

Mail search: Turnaround time: 3 days.

In person search: Walk-in requesters may receive records immediately at the address listed above or at any one of 11 field offices in the state.

Online search: There are 2 systems. Permissible use requesters who need personal information can order by batch, minimum order is 150 requests per batch. Input received by 3 PM will be available the next morning. Fee is $3.00 per record and billing is monthly. Call for details to subscribe. Records without personal information can be obtained at www.kydirect.net. The $3.00 fee applies and up to 50 records can be ordered and received immediately.

Vehicle Ownership
Vehicle Identification

Department of Motor Vehicles, Division of Motor Vehicle Licensing, State Office Bldg, 3rd Floor, Frankfort, KY 40622; 502-564-4076 (Title History), 502-564-3298 (Other Requests), 502-564-1686 (Fax), 8AM-4:30PM.

www.kytc.state.ky.us

Indexing & Storage: Records are available from 1978 years to present, but generally only last 10 years released. Records are indexed on computer from 1983 to present, and on microfiche from 1978 to 1982. It takes 1-4 weeks before new records are available for inquiry.

Searching: Vehicle and ownership records are made available to the public; however, personal information is not released to the general public or for marketing purposes without consent. Vendors must submit either TC96-16 or TC96-325 when requesting data. This agency will not do a search by SSN.

Access by: mail, in person, online.

Fee & Payment: The fee is $2.00 per record request. The state reports current lien information. There is a full charge for a "no record found." Fee payee: Division of Motor Vehicle Licensing. Prepayment required. Cash and money orders are accepted. Personal checks accepted. No credit cards accepted.

Mail search: Turnaround time: 5 to 10 days. A self addressed stamped envelope is requested.

In person search: Turnaround time is while you wait (typically, 15 minutes to 1 hour).

Online search: Online access costs $2.00 per record. The online mode is interactive. Title, lien and registration searches are available. Records include those for mobile homes. For more information, contact Gale Warfield at 502-564-4076.

Other access: Kentucky has the ability to supply customized bulk delivery of vehicle registration information. The request must be in writing with the intended use outlined. For more information, call 502-564-3298.

Accident Reports

State Police, Records Branch, 1250 Louisville Rd, Frankfort, KY 40601; 502-226-7418, 502-227-8734 (Fax), 8AM-4:30PM.

www.kentuckystatepolice.org

Indexing & Storage: Records are available from 1996 at this location.

Searching: Requests must be made through "open records." Detailed listing of accidents at specific location without personal identifying information is available for a fee with a written request. For more information phone 502-226-2169 for details. Search requirements include the exact date, county, roadway and mile post. All requests must be in writing.

Access by: mail.

Fee & Payment: The charge is $.10 per page with a $.20 minimum. Fee payee: KY State Treasurer. Prepayment required. Personal checks accepted. No credit cards accepted.

Mail search: Turnaround time: 1 to 2 weeks. A self addressed stamped envelope is requested.

Other access: Specific accident statistics may be obtained by phoning the statistics coordinator.

Vessel Ownership
Vessel Registration

Division of Motor Vehicle Licensing, Vessel Titles and Registration, State Office Building, 3rd Floor, Frankfort, KY 40622; 502-564-5301, 8AM-5PM.

www.kytc.state.ky.us

Indexing & Storage: Records are available for titles from 1990, for registration from 1985. Prior records are kept by Circuit Clerks. Only motorized vessels must be titled and registered.

Searching: Personal information is not released to casual requesters. The hull number, title number or KY number must be submitted.

Access by: mail, in person.

Fee & Payment: The fee is $2.00 per record. Fee payee: Kentucky State Treasurer. Prepayment required. No credit cards accepted.

Mail search: Turnaround time: 1 week.

In person search: Most of the time results will be mailed.

Legislation Records

Kentucky General Assembly, Legislative Research Commission, 700 Capitol Ave, Room 300, Frankfort, KY 40601; 502-372-7181 (Bill Status Only), 502-564-8100 x323 (Bill Room), 502-564-8100 x340 (LRC Library), 502-223-5094 (Fax), 8AM-4:30PM.

www.lrc.state.ky.us

Indexing & Storage: Records are available from 1986 on computer, and from 1950 in hard copy. Kentucky Acts from 1820 to present are available in hard copy. Records are indexed on inhouse computer.

Searching: Include the following in your request: bill number, session year or subject matter.

Access by: mail, phone, fax, in person, online.

Fee & Payment: Minimum fee $1.00. Fees over $1.00 are invoiced. You pay postage/UPS charges over 8 ounces. Copies are $.15 each. Fee payee: LRC. Personal checks accepted. No credit cards accepted.

Mail search: Turnaround time: variable.

Phone search: Records are available by phone.

Fax search: The fee is $.65 per page.

In person search: Searching is available in person.

Online search: The web site has an extensive searching mechanism for bills, actions, summaries, and statutes.

Voter Registration

State Board of Elections, 140 Walnut, Frankfort, KY 40601; 502-573-7100, 502-573-4369 (Fax), 8AM-4:30PM.

www.kysos.com/index/main/elecdiv.asp

Note: Written requests are always required; agency is required to respond within 3 days. Bulk data is available for political purposes only. For individual searches, it is best to go to the county level.

Searching: The state will provide verification of records and voting histories upon receipt of a written request. The SSN or DOB is required when doing a verification. The following data is not released: Social Security Numbers, bulk information or information to ineligible persons, pursuant to state statutes.

Access by: mail, fax, in person.

Fee & Payment: There is no search fee. There is a $.10 per page copy fee.

Mail search: Turnaround time: 3 business days. Turnaround time is longer for information exempted by statute.

Fax search: Records are available by fax.

In person search: Records may be ordered (with written request) and picked up in person. Law allows for 3 business day turnaround. In person searching is not allowed.

Other access: Data is available on CD-rom, labels or lists for eligible persons, pursuant to state statutes

GED Certificates

Dept for Adult Education and Literacy, GED Program, Capitol Plaza Tower, 500 Mero St, 3rd Fl, Frankfort, KY 40601; 502-564-5117, 502-564-5436 (Fax).

http://adulted.state.ky.us

Searching: To verify or to get copy of transcript or diploma, all of the following is required: a signed release, name, date/year of test, date of birth, Social Security Number, and city of test.

Access by: mail, fax, in person.

Fee & Payment: There is no fee for verification. Copies of transcript or duplicate diplomas are $5.00 each. Fee payee: KY State Treasurer. Prepayment required. Money orders are accepted, personal checks are not. No credit cards accepted.

Mail search: Turnaround time is 1 week. No self addressed stamped envelope is required.

Fax search: Same criteria as mail searching.

In person search: In person searchers must bring a photo id. Turnaround time: Same day.

Hunting License Information
Fishing License Information

Fish & Wildlife Resources Department, Division of Administrative Services, 1 Game Farm Rd, Arnold Mitchell Bldg, Frankfort, KY 40601; 502-564-4224, 502-564-6508 (Fax), 8AM-4:30PM.

www.kdfwr.state.ky.us

Note: A database has been created, starting in 1996. Records are not released without written request and for good reason. Records are not available for commercial mail lists. Older records are archived in boxes. Record retrieval extremely difficult.

Indexing & Storage: Records are available for the past two years (actual copies). Prior records are archived and not readily available. It takes 16 days before new records are available for inquiry. Records are indexed on hard copy.

Searching: Requests must be in writing and addressed to the Commissioner's Office. The general public cannot receive records, beyond the type of license issued. Include the following in your request: full name, Social Security Number.

Access by: mail, in person.

Fee & Payment: Fees will vary by type of request.

Mail search: Records are available by mail.

In person search: Searching is available in person.

Kentucky State Licensing Agencies

Licenses Searchable Online

Alcohol/Drug Counselor #15	https://kyeasupt1.state.ky.us/OPB/BrdWebSearch.asp?BRD=4
Architect #7	http://kybera.com/roster.shtml
Art Therapist #15	https://kyeasupt1.state.ky.us/OPB/BrdWebSearch.asp?BRD=5
Athlete Agent #15	https://kyeasupt1.state.ky.us/OPB/BrdWebSearch.asp?BRD=19
Athletic Manager #15	https://kyeasupt1.state.ky.us/OPB/BrdWebSearch.asp?BRD=17
Athletic Trainer #15	https://kyeasupt1.state.ky.us/OPB/BrdWebSearch.asp?BRD=17
Auctioneer, Livestock, Limited #4	http://weba.state.ky.us/genericsearch/LicenseSearch.asp?AGY=3
Auctioneer, Tobacco, Limited #4	http://weba.state.ky.us/genericsearch/LicenseSearch.asp?AGY=3
Auctioneer/Auctioneer Apprentice #4	http://weba.state.ky.us/genericsearch/LicenseSearch.asp?AGY=3
Boxer/Boxing Professional #15	https://kyeasupt1.state.ky.us/OPB/BrdWebSearch.asp?BRD=17
Counselor, Pastoral #15	https://kyeasupt1.state.ky.us/OPB/BrdWebSearch.asp?BRD=3
Counselor, Professional #15	https://kyeasupt1.state.ky.us/OPB/BrdWebSearch.asp?BRD=6
Dental Hygienist #6	http://dentistry.state.ky.us/search.htm
Dentist #6	http://dentistry.state.ky.us/search.htm
Dietitian/Nutritionist #15	https://kyeasupt1.state.ky.us/OPB/BrdWebSearch.asp?BRD=8
Engineer #39	http://kyboels.state.ky.us/SearchRoster.asp
Engineer/Land Surveyor Firm #39	http://kyboels.state.ky.us/SearchRoster.asp
Geologist #15	www.state.ky.us/agencies/finance/boards/geology/pages/geol.html
Geologists, Recently Registered #15	www.state.ky.us/agencies/finance/boards/geology/pages/newgeo.htm
Hearing Instrument Specialist #15	https://kyeasupt1.state.ky.us/OPB/BrdWebSearch.asp?BRD=15
Insurance Agent #21	www.doi.state.ky.us/kentucky/search/agent/
Insurance CE Provider #21	www.doi.state.ky.us/kentucky/search/provider/
Insurance Company/Insurer #21	www.doi.state.ky.us/kentucky/search/company/
Marriage & Family Therapist #15	https://kyeasupt1.state.ky.us/OPB/BrdWebSearch.asp?BRD=9
Mortgage Broker #18	www.dfi.state.ky.us/aspscripts/mort_brokers.asp
Mortgage Loan Company #18	www.dfi.state.ky.us/aspscripts/mort_company.asp
Nursing Home Administrator #15	https://kyeasupt1.state.ky.us/OPB/BrdWebSearch.asp?BRD=10
Occupational Therapist/Assistant #15	https://kyeasupt1.state.ky.us/OPB/BrdWebSearch.asp?BRD=16
Ophthalmic Dispenser/Optician/Apprentice #10	https://kyeasupt1.state.ky.us/OPB/BrdWebSearch.asp?BRD=11
Optometrist #11	http://web.state.ky.us/GBC/LicenseSearch.asp?AGY=8
Proprietary Education School #15	https://kyeasupt1.state.ky.us/OPB/BrdWebSearch.asp?BRD=18
Psychologist #15	https://kyeasupt1.state.ky.us/OPB/BrdWebSearch.asp?BRD=7
Public Accountant-CPA #3	http://cpa.state.ky.us/Locate.html
Real Estate Appraiser #32	www.asc.gov/
Real Estate Broker #33	http://weba.state.ky.us/realestate/LicenseeLookUp.asp
Real Estate Brokerage/Firm #33	http://weba.state.ky.us/realestate/FirmLookUp.asp
Real Estate Sales Associate #33	http://weba.state.ky.us/realestate/LicenseeLookUp.asp
Social Worker #15	https://kyeasupt1.state.ky.us/OPB/BrdWebSearch.asp?BRD=2
Speech-Language Pathologist/Audiologist #15	https://kyeasupt1.state.ky.us/OPB/BrdWebSearch.asp?BRD=13
Surveyor, Land #39	http://kyboels.state.ky.us/SearchRoster.asp
Veterinarian #15	https://kyeasupt1.state.ky.us/OPB/BrdWebSearch.asp?BRD=14
Wrestler/Wrestling Professional #15	https://kyeasupt1.state.ky.us/OPB/BrdWebSearch.asp?BRD=17

Licensing Quick Finder

Alcohol/Drug Counselor #15	502-564-3296 x226	Blacksmith #31	859-246-2040	Dental Laboratory #6	502-423-0573
Animal Technician #15	502-564-3296	Boiler Contractor/Insp./Installer #26	502-564-8142	Dental Laboratory Technician #6	502-423-0573
Architect #7	859-246-2069	Boxer/Boxing Professional #15	502-564-3296	Dentist #6	502-423-0573
Art Therapist #15	502-564-3296 x230	Broker/Dealer Agent #18	502-573-3390	Dietitian/Nutritionist #15	502-564-3296 x227
Athlete Agent #15	502-564-3296 x222	Building Inspector #26	502-564-8090	Drinking Water Treatment/Dist. System Operator #29	
Athletic Manager #15	502-564-3296	Check Seller/Casher #18	502-573-3390		502-564-3410
Athletic Trainer #15	502-564-3296	Child Care Facility #13	502-564-2800	Driver Training Instructor #42	502-226-7404
Athletic Trainer (Medical) #41	502-429-8046	Chiropractor #35	270-651-2522	Drug Manufacturer/Wholesaler #12	502-573-1580
Attorney #2	502-564-3795	Compost Operator #24	502-565-6716	Electrical Contractor #26	502-564-8370
Auctioneer, Livestock, Limited #4	502-339-9453	Coroner #17	859-622-1328	Electrical Inspector #26	502-564-8370
Auctioneer, Tobacco, Limited #4	502-339-9453	Cosmetologist #37	502-564-4262	Elevator Inspector #26	502-564-8499
Auctioneer/Auctioneer Apprentice #4	502-339-9453	Counselor, Pastoral #15	502-564-3296 x226	Embalmer #36	502-241-3918
Bank #18	502-573-3390	Counselor, Professional #15	502-564-3296 x226	EMT, Basic #14	502-564-8963
Barber #5	502-429-8841	Dental Hygienist #6	502-423-0573	EMT, First Response #14	502-564-8963

Engineer #39 502-573-2680
Engineer/Land Surveyor Firm #39 502-573-2680
Exterminator #16 502-564-7274
Fire Alarm System Inspector #26 502-564-3626
Fire Protection Sprinkler Installer #26 ..502-564-3626
Fire Suppression System Inspector #26 502-564-8090
Fishing, Commercial #20 800-858-1549
Funeral Director #36 502-241-3918
Fur Buyer/Processor #20 800-858-1549
Geologist #15............................502-564-3296 x227
Geologists, Recently Registered #15 ...502-564-3296
x227
Guide, Hunting & Fishing #20 800-858-1549
Health Care Facility #13 502-564-2800
Hearing Instrument Specialist #15 502-564-3296x240
Horse Claiming License #31...................859-246-2040
Horse Farm Manager/Agent #31 859-246-2040
Horse Owner/Trainer/Asst. Trainer #31 829-246-2040
Horse Racing Occupational License #31859-246-2040
Horse Racing Official/Authorized Agent #31
....859-246-2040
Horse Veterinarian/Veterinary Assistant #31
....859-246-2040
Horse Veterinary Dental Technician #31859-246-2040
HVAC Contractor #26 502-564-1436
HVAC Journeyman/Master/Mechanic #26
....502-564-1436
Insurance Adjuster #21........................502-564-3630
Insurance Agent #21 502-564-3630
Insurance CE Provider #21 502-564-3630
Insurance Company/Insurer #21 502-564-3630
Insurance Consultant/Solicitor #21.......502-564-3630
Interpreters for the Deaf #15 ....502-564-3296 x239
Investment Advisor/Representative #18502-573-3390
Jockey Agent #31 859-246-2040
Jockey/Jockey Apprentice #31 859-246-2040
Lake Operator #20 800-858-1549
Landfarm Operator #24 502-564-6716
Landfill Operator/Manager #24.............502-564-6716
Law Enforcement Training Instructor #17
....859-622-1328

Liquor License #1 502-573-4850
Loan Company #18...............................502-573-3390
Malt Beverage Distributor #1................502-573-4850
Marriage & Family Therapist #15 . 502-564-3296 x239
Medical Doctor/Surgeon #41...............502-429-8046
Midwife Nurse #9 502-329-7000
Milk Sampler/Weigher/Tester #43........859-257-2785
Mine Safety Instructor #22 859-246-2026
Miner #22...859-246-2026
Mining Blaster #22 859-246-2026
Mining Fire Boss #22...........................859-246-2026
Mining Inspector/Foreman #22 859-246-2026
Mortgage Broker #18............................502-573-3390
Mortgage Loan Company #18 502-573-3390
Nail Technician #37..............................502-564-4262
Notary Public #30 502-564-3490
Nurse Anesthetist #9 502-329-7000
Nurse Clinical Specialist #9..................502-329-7000
Nurse-RN/LPN #9.................................502-329-7000
Nurses' Aide Instructor #9 502-329-7048
Nursing Home Administrator #15 . 502-564-3296 x222
Occupational Therapist/Assistant #15... 502-564-3296
Ophthalmic Dispenser/Optician/Apprentice #10
....502-564-3296 x227
Optometrist #11....................................859-246-2744
Osteopathic Physician #41...................502-429-8046
Paramedic #14 502-564-8963
Pari-Mutuel Employee #31 859-246-2040
Pesticide Applicator #16 502-564-7274
Pesticide Dealer #16 502-564-7274
Pharmacist #12.....................................502-573-1580
Pharmacy #12 502-573-1580
Physical Therapist #38 502-327-8497
Physical Therapist Assistant #38 502-327-8497
Physician Assistant #41 502-429-8046
Plans & Specifications Inspector #26... 502-564-8090
Plumber #26 502-564-3580
Podiatrist #27.......................................207-759-0007
Police Officer #17 859-622-1328
Polygraph Examiner/Examiner Trainee #28
....502-564-4756

Property Valuation Administrator #34 .. 502-564-8338
Proprietary Education School #15 502-564-4233
Psychologist #15 ....502-564-3296 x225
Public Accountant-CPA #3...................502-595-3037
Racetrack Occupation (vendors, etc.) #31
....859-246-2040
Racing Association Employee #31 859-246-2040
Racing Vendor/Vendor Employee #31.. 859-246-2040
Radiation Operator #44 502-564-3700
Radiation Producing Machine #44 502-564-3700
Radioactive Material Licensee #44 502-564-3700
Real Estate Appraiser #32 859-543-8943
Real Estate Broker #33 502-425-4273
Real Estate Brokerage/Firm #33...........502-425-4273
Real Estate Sales Associate #33.........502-425-4273
Rehabilitation Counselor #23 502-564-6745
Respiratory Care Practitioner #15........ 502-564-3296
Respiratory Therapist #15.....................502-564-3296
Sanitarian #45 502-564-7398
Savings & Loan #18.............................502-573-3390
School Administrator #25 502-573-4606
School Bus Driver #46 502-564-4718
School Guidance Counselor #25 502-573-4606
School Media Librarian #25 502-573-4606
School Nurse #25..................................502-573-4606
School Social Worker/Psychologist #25 502-573-4606
Securities Agent #18 502-573-3370
Securities Broker/Dealer #18 502-573-3370
Septic System Installer, Onsite #45 502-564-4856
Sexual Assault Nurse Examiner #9 502-329-7000
Social Worker #15.......................502-564-3296 x230
Speech-Language Pathologist/Audiologist #15
....502-564-3296 x240
Stable Employee #31 859-246-2040
Surveyor, Land #39..............................502-573-2680
Taxidermist #20....................................800-858-1549
Teacher #25 502-573-4606
Veterinarian #15...........................502-564-3296 x223
Waste Water System Operator #29 502-564-3410
Water Well Driller #29 502-564-3410
Wrestler/Wrestling Professional #15.... 502-564-3296

Licensing Agency Information

#1 Alcoholic Beverage Control Department, 1003 Twilight Trail, #A2, Frankfort, KY 40601; 502-564-4850, Fax: 502-564-1442.

#2 Bar Association, 514 W Main St, Frankfort, KY 40601-1883; 502-564-3795, Fax: 502-564-3225. www.kybar.org
Agency email: webmaster@kybar.org.

#3 Board of Accountancy, 332 W Broadway, #310, Louisville, KY 40202; 502-595-3037, Fax: 502-595-4281. http://cpa.state.ky.us
Agency email: debby.abell@mail.state.ky.us.
Search database at
http://cpa.state.ky.us/Locate.html

#4 Board of Auctioneers, 9112 Leesgate Rd, Louisville, KY 40222-5089; 502-339-9453, Fax: 502-423-1854.
http://auctioneers.state.ky.us
Agency email: auctioneers@mail.state.ky.us.

#5 Board of Barbering, 9114 Leesgate Rd, #6, Louisville, KY 40222-5055; 502-429-8841, Fax: 502-429-5223.

#6 Board of Dentistry, 10101 Linn Station Rd, #540, Louisville, KY 40223; 502-423-0573, Fax: 502-423-1239.
http://dentistry.state.ky.us
Search database at
http://dentistry.state.ky.us/search.htm

#7 Board of Examiners & Registration of Architects, 301 E Main St #860, Lexington, KY 40507; 859-246-2069, Fax: 859-246-2431.
http://kybera.com
Agency email: kybera@iglou.com.
Search database at http://kybera.com/roster.shtml

#9 Board of Nursing, 312 Whittington Pky, #300, Louisville, KY 40222-5172; 502-329-7000, Fax: 502-329-7011.
www.kbn.state.ky.us/index.htm
Agency email: kbn.webmaster@mail.state.ky.us.

#10 Division of Occupations and Professions, Board of Ophthalmic Dispensers, PO Box 456, Frankfort, KY 40602; 502-564-3296 x227, Fax: 502-564-4818.

#11 Board of Optometric Examiners, 301 E Main St #850, Lexington, KY 40507-1578; 859-246-2744, Fax: 859-246-2746.
http://optometry.state.ky.us
Agency email: ky.optometry@mail.state.ky.us.
Search database at http://web.state.ky.us/GBC/LicenseSearch.asp?AGY=8

#12 Board of Pharmacy, 23 Millcreek Park, Frankfort, KY 40601; 502-573-1580, Fax: 502-573-1582.
www.state.ky.us/boards/pharmacy/

#13 Division of Licensing & Regulations, Cabinet for Health Services, CHR Bldg, 5th Fl East, Frankfort, KY 40621-0001; 502-564-2800, Fax: 502-564-6546.
http://chs.state.ky.us
Agency email: fparrish@mail.state.ky.us.

#14 Board of Emergency Medical Services, 275 East Main Street, HS1E-F, Frankfort, KY 40621; 502-564-8963, Fax: 502-564-4687.
www.kbems.org

#15 Department of Administration, Division of Occupations & Professions, PO Box 1360, Frankfort, KY 40602; 502-564-3296, Fax: 502-564-4818.
www.state.ky.us/agencies/finance/occupations.

#16 Department of Agriculture, Division of Pesticide Regulation, 100 Fair Oak Ln, 5th Fl, Frankfort, KY 40601; 502-564-7274, Fax: 502-564-3773.
www.kyagr.com
Agency email: BillyRay.Smith@kyagr.com.

#17 Department of Criminal Justice Training, 521 Lancaster Ave, Richmond, KY 40475; 859-622-1328, Fax: 859-622-2740.
http://docjt.jus.state.ky.us
Agency email: pops@docjt.jus.state.ky.us.

#18 Department of Financial Institutions, Division of Law & Regulatory Compliance, 1025 Capitol Center Dr #200, Frankfort, KY 40601; 800-223-3390, Fax: 502-573-8787.
www.dfi.state.ky.us
Agency email: Becky.Mills@mail.state.ky.us.

#20 Department of Fish & Wildlife, 1 Game Farm Rd, Frankfort, KY 40601; 800-858-1549, Fax: 502-564-9136.
www.kdfwr.state.ky.us.

#21 Department of Insurance, Licensing Division, PO Box 517, 215 W Main St (40601), Frankfort, KY 40602-0517; 502-564-3630.
www.doi.state.ky.us/kentucky
Agency email: Randy.Donahue@mail.state.ky.us.
Search database at www.doi.state.ky.us/kentucky.

#22 Department of Mines & Minerals, PO Box 2244, Frankfort, KY 40602-2244; 502-573-0140, Fax: 502-573-0152.
www.caer.uky.edu
Agency email: JohnFranklin@mail.state.ky.us.

#23 Department of Vocational Rehabilitation, 209 St Clair St, Frankfort, KY 40601; 502-564-4440, Fax: 502-564-6742.
http://kydvr.state.ky.us
Agency email: flemingb@ihdi.uky.edu.

#24 Division of Waste Management, 14 Reilly Rd, Frankfort, KY 40601; 502-564-6716, Fax: 502-564-4049. www.nr.state.ky.us/nrepc/dep/waste/dwmhome.htm

#25 Education Department, Teacher Education/Certification Office, 1025 Capitol Center Dr, Frankfort, KY 40601; 502-573-4606, Fax: 502-573-4606.
www.kde.state.ky.us
Agency email: jbanta@kde.state.ky.us.

#26 Department of Housing, Buildings, and Construction, 1047 US 127 S, #1, Frankfort, KY 40601; 502-564-8044, Fax: 502-564-6799.
www.state.ky.us/agencies/cppr/dhbc.
Agency email: charlene.slemp@mail.state.ky.us.

#27 Board of Podiatry, 908 B South 12th St, Murray, KY 42071-2949; 270-759-0007, Fax: 270-753-0684.

#28 State Police, Polygraph Unit, 1250 Louisville Rd, Frankfort, KY 40601; 502-564-4756, Fax: 502-564-5956.
www.state.ky.us/agencies/ksp/ksphome.htm.
Agency email: kpayne@mail.state.ky.us.

#29 Division of Water, Natural Resources & Environmental Protection, 14 Reilly Rd, Frankfort Office Park, Frankfort, KY 40601; 502-564-3410, Fax: 502-564-9720.
http://water.nr.state.ky.us/dow/dwhome.htm

#30 Office of Secretary of State, Notary Commissions, Capitol Bldg, Frankfort, KY 40602-0821; 502-564-3490 x413, Fax: 502-564-4075.
www.kysos.com
Agency email: Kbagwell@mail.sos.state.ky.us.

#31 National Horse Center - Bldg B, Racing Commission, 4063 Iron Works Pike, Lexington, KY 40511; 859-246-2040, Fax: 859-246-2039.

#32 Real Estate Appraisers Board, 2480 Fortune Dr #120, Lexington, KY 40509; 859-543-8943, Fax: 859-543-0028.
www.kyappraisersboard.com
Agency email: sam.blackburn@mail.state.ky.us.
Search database at www.asc.gov

#33 Real Estate Commission, 10200 Linn Station Rd, #201, Louisville, KY 40223; 502-425-4273, Fax: 502-426-2717.
www.krec.net. Agency email: krecweb@uky.edu.
Search database at www.krec.net/index.html

#34 Department of Property Taxation, Revenue Cabinet, 200 Fair Oaks, Frankfort, KY 40620; 502-564-8338, Fax: 502-564-8368.
www.revenue.state.ky.ys/contact.htm
Agency email: revweb@mail.state.ky.us.

#35 Board of Chiropractic Examiners, 209 S Green St (PO Box 183), Glasgow, KY 42142-0183; 270-651-2522, Fax: 270-651-8784. Agency email: kychiro@glasgow-ky.com.

#36 Board of Embalmers & Funeral Directors, PO Box 324, Crestwood, KY 40014; 502-241-3918, Fax: 502-241-4297.

#37 Board of Hairdressers & Cosmetologists, 111 St James Court #A, Frankfort, KY 40601; 502-564-4262, Fax: 502-564-0481.

#38 Board of Physical Therapy, 9110 Leesgate Rd, #6, Louisville, KY 40222-5159; 502-327-8497, Fax: 502-423-0934.
http://kbpt.state.ky.us
Agency email: kybpt@mail.state.ky.us.

#39 Professional Engineers & Land Surveyors, Board of Licensure, 160 Democrat Dr, Frankfort, KY 40601; 502-573-2680, Fax: 502-573-6687.
http://kyboels.state.ky.us
Agency email: larry.perkins@mail.state.ky.us.
Search database at
http://kyboels.state.ky.us/SearchRoster.asp

#41 Board of Medical Licensure, 310 Whittington Pky, #1B, Louisville, KY 40222; 502-429-8046; dialup 1-900-555-6500, Fax: 502-429-9923.
www.kbml.org Use the fee dialup service only if you have a license or certification number.

#42 State Police Driver Testing Section, 919 Versailles Rd, Frankfort, KY 40601; 502-226-7404, Fax: 502-226-7412.

#43 Division of Regulatory Services, 103 Regulatory Service Bldg, Lexington, KY 40546-0275; 859-257-2785, Fax: 859-323-9931.
www.rs.uky.edu
Agency email: cthompso@ca.uky.edu.

#44 Radiation Health & Toxic Agents Branch, Department of Public Health, 275 E Main St, Frankfort, KY 40621; 502-564-3700, Fax: 502-564-1492.
http://publichealth.state.ky.us/radiation.htm

#45 Department for Public Health, Registered Sanitarian Examining Committee, 275 E Main, 2nd Fl E, HS 2EA, Frankfort, KY 40621; 502-564-7398, Fax: 502-564-6533.
http://chs.state.ky.us/publichealth/registered_sanitariancontent.htm
Agency email: guy.delius@mail.state.ky.us.

#46 Department of Education, Pupil Transportation, 500 Mero St 15th Fl, Frankfort, KY 40601; 502-564-4718, Fax: 502-564-9574.
www.kde.state.ky.us

Kentucky Federal Courts

The following list indicates the district and division name for each county in the state. If the bankruptcy court location is different from the district court, then the location of the bankruptcy court appears in parentheses.

County/Court Cross Reference

County	District	Division
Adair	Western	Bowling Green (Louisville)
Allen	Western	Bowling Green (Louisville)
Anderson	Eastern	Frankfort (Lexington)
Ballard	Western	Paducah (Louisville)
Barren	Western	Bowling Green (Louisville)
Bath	Eastern	Lexington
Bell	Eastern	London (Lexington)
Boone	Eastern	Covington (Lexington)
Bourbon	Eastern	Lexington
Boyd	Eastern	Ashland (Lexington)
Boyle	Eastern	Lexington
Bracken	Eastern	Covington (Lexington)
Breathitt	Eastern	Pikeville (Lexington)
Breckinridge	Western	Louisville
Bullitt	Western	Louisville
Butler	Western	Bowling Green (Louisville)
Caldwell	Western	Paducah (Louisville)
Calloway	Western	Paducah (Louisville)
Campbell	Eastern	Covington (Lexington)
Carlisle	Western	Paducah (Louisville)
Carroll	Eastern	Frankfort (Lexington)
Carter	Eastern	Ashland (Lexington)
Casey	Western	Bowling Green (Louisville)
Christian	Western	Paducah (Louisville)
Clark	Eastern	Lexington
Clay	Eastern	London (Lexington)
Clinton	Western	Bowling Green (Louisville)
Crittenden	Western	Paducah (Louisville)
Cumberland	Western	Bowling Green (Louisville)
Daviess	Western	Owensboro (Louisville)
Edmonson	Western	Bowling Green (Louisville)
Elliott	Eastern	Ashland (Lexington)
Estill	Eastern	Lexington
Fayette	Eastern	Lexington
Fleming	Eastern	Lexington
Floyd	Eastern	Pikeville (Lexington)
Franklin	Eastern	Frankfort (Lexington)
Fulton	Western	Paducah (Louisville)
Gallatin	Eastern	Covington (Lexington)
Garrard	Eastern	Lexington
Grant	Eastern	Covington (Lexington)
Graves	Western	Paducah (Louisville)
Grayson	Western	Owensboro (Louisville)
Green	Western	Bowling Green (Louisville)
Greenup	Eastern	Ashland (Lexington)
Hancock	Western	Owensboro (Louisville)
Hardin	Western	Louisville
Harlan	Eastern	London (Lexington)
Harrison	Eastern	Lexington
Hart	Western	Bowling Green (Louisville)
Henderson	Western	Owensboro (Louisville)
Henry	Eastern	Frankfort (Lexington)
Hickman	Western	Paducah (Louisville)
Hopkins	Western	Owensboro (Louisville)
Jackson	Eastern	London (Lexington)
Jefferson	Western	Louisville
Jessamine	Eastern	Lexington
Johnson	Eastern	Pikeville (Lexington)
Kenton	Eastern	Covington (Lexington)
Knott	Eastern	Pikeville (Lexington)
Knox	Eastern	London (Lexington)
Larue	Western	Louisville
Laurel	Eastern	London (Lexington)
Lawrence	Eastern	Ashland (Lexington)
Lee	Eastern	Lexington
Leslie	Eastern	London (Lexington)
Letcher	Eastern	Pikeville (Lexington)
Lewis	Eastern	Ashland (Lexington)
Lincoln	Eastern	Lexington
Livingston	Western	Paducah (Louisville)
Logan	Western	Bowling Green (Louisville)
Lyon	Western	Paducah (Louisville)
Madison	Eastern	Lexington
Magoffin	Eastern	Pikeville (Lexington)
Marion	Western	Louisville
Marshall	Western	Paducah (Louisville)
Martin	Eastern	Pikeville (Lexington)
Mason	Eastern	Covington (Lexington)
McCracken	Western	Paducah (Louisville)
McCreary	Eastern	London (Lexington)
McLean	Western	Owensboro (Louisville)
Meade	Western	Louisville
Menifee	Eastern	Lexington
Mercer	Eastern	Lexington
Metcalfe	Western	Bowling Green (Louisville)
Monroe	Western	Bowling Green (Louisville)
Montgomery	Eastern	Lexington
Morgan	Eastern	Ashland (Lexington)
Muhlenberg	Western	Owensboro (Louisville)
Nelson	Western	Louisville
Nicholas	Eastern	Lexington
Ohio	Western	Owensboro (Louisville)
Oldham	Western	Louisville
Owen	Eastern	Frankfort (Lexington)
Owsley	Eastern	London (Lexington)
Pendleton	Eastern	Covington (Lexington)
Perry	Eastern	Pikeville (Lexington)
Pike	Eastern	Pikeville (Lexington)
Powell	Eastern	Lexington
Pulaski	Eastern	London (Lexington)
Robertson	Eastern	Covington (Lexington)
Rockcastle	Eastern	London (Lexington)
Rowan	Eastern	Ashland (Lexington)
Russell	Western	Bowling Green (Louisville)
Scott	Eastern	Lexington
Shelby	Eastern	Frankfort (Lexington)
Simpson	Western	Bowling Green (Louisville)
Spencer	Western	Louisville
Taylor	Western	Bowling Green (Louisville)
Todd	Western	Bowling Green (Louisville)
Trigg	Western	Paducah (Louisville)
Trimble	Eastern	Frankfort (Lexington)
Union	Western	Owensboro (Louisville)
Warren	Western	Bowling Green (Louisville)
Washington	Western	Louisville
Wayne	Eastern	London (Lexington)
Webster	Western	Owensboro (Louisville)
Whitley	Eastern	London (Lexington)
Wolfe	Eastern	Lexington
Woodford	Eastern	Lexington

Standards for Federal Courts: The search fee is $20.00 per item (one party name or case number). Certification fee is $7.00 per document. Copy fee is $.50 per page. All fees standard unless noted in profile. Mail Search: always enclose a stamped self addressed envelope unless otherwise noted. Before releasing records, all courts require prepayment unless noted in profile.

Open records are located at the court unless otherwise noted. District courts index by defendant and plaintiff as well as by case number. Bankruptcy courts usually index by debtor and case number. While most courts now have their indexes on computer, many still maintain index card files as well.

The universal PACER sign-up number is 800-676-6856. Find PACER and the Party/Case Index on the Web at http://pacer.psc.uscourts.gov. PACER dial-up access is $.60 per minute. Also, courts offering internet access via RACER, PACER, Web-PACER or the new CM-ECF charge $.07 per page fee unless noted as free.

US District Court

Eastern District of Kentucky

Ashland Division Suite 336, 1405 Greenup Ave, Ashland, KY 41101 (Courier Address: Use mail address for courier delivery), 606-329-8652.

www.kyed.uscourts.gov

Counties: Boyd, Carter, Elliott, Greenup, Lawrence, Lewis, Morgan, Rowan.

Indexing & Storage: Cases are indexed by defendant, plaintiff, and case number. New cases are available in the index 1-2 days after filing date. Lexington Division has a master index for the district. The index is computerized from 1992. Open records are located at this court.

Fee & Payment Notes: Payment may be made by money order, cashier check, personal check. Payee: Clerk, USDC.

Phone Search: Only docket information from active cases will be released over the phone.

Mail Search: A stamped self addressed envelope is not required.

In Person Search: In person searching available.

PACER: Toll-free dial-up access: 800-361-0442. Local dial-up access: 606-233-2787. Case records are available back to September 1991. Records are never purged. New records are available online after 1 day. PACER is available online at http://pacer.kyed.uscourts.gov.

Covington Division Clerk, PO Box 1073, Covington, KY 41012 (Courier Address: US Courthouse, Room 201, 35 W 5th St, Covington, KY 41011), 859-392-7925.

www.kyed.uscourts.gov

Counties: Boone, Bracken, Campbell, Gallatin, Grant, Kenton, Mason, Pendleton, Robertson.

Indexing & Storage: Cases are indexed by defendant, plaintiff, and case number. New cases are available in the index immediately after filing date. Open records are located at this court.

Fee & Payment Notes: Payment may be made by money order, cashier check, personal check. The turnaround time for written requests varies. Payee: Clerk, US District Court.

Phone Search: Searching not available by phone.

In Person Search: In person searching available.

PACER: Toll-free dial-up access: 800-361-0442. Local dial-up access: 606-233-2787. Case records are available back to September 1991. Records are never purged. New records are available online after 1 day. PACER is available online at http://pacer.kyed.uscourts.gov.

Frankfort Division Room 313, 330 W Broadway, Frankfort, KY 40601 (Courier Address: Use mail address for courier delivery), 502-223-5225.

www.kyed.uscourts.gov

Counties: Anderson, Carroll, Franklin, Henry, Owen, Shelby, Trimble.

Indexing & Storage: Cases are indexed by defendant, plaintiff, and case number. New cases are available in the index immediately after filing date. Records have been indexed on computer since January, 1993. Open records are located at this court.

Fee & Payment Notes: Payment may be made by money order, cashier check, personal check. Payee: Clerk, US District Court.

Phone Search: Only docket information is available by phone.

Mail Search: A stamped self addressed envelope is not required.

In Person Search: In person searching available.

PACER: Toll-free dial-up access: 800-361-0442. Local dial-up access: 606-233-2787. Case records are available back to September 1991. Records are never purged. New records are available online after 1 day. PACER is available online at http://pacer.kyed.uscourts.gov.

Lexington Division PO Box 3074, Lexington, KY 40588 (Courier: Room 206, 101 Barr St, Lexington, KY 40507), 859-233-2503.

www.kyed.uscourts.gov

Counties: Bath, Bourbon, Boyle, Clark, Estill, Fayette, Fleming, Garrard, Harrison, Jessamine, Lee, Lincoln, Madison, Menifee, Mercer, Montgomery, Nicholas, Powell, Scott, Wolfe, Woodford. Lee and Wolfe counties were part of the Pikeville Divisionbefore 10/31/92. Perry became part of Pikeville after 1992.

Indexing & Storage: Cases are indexed by defendant, plaintiff, and case number. New cases are available in the index 24 hours after filing date. Civil cases filed after October 1, 1992 are on the computer. Cases prior to October 1992 are on index cards. Open records are located at this court.

Fee & Payment Notes: Payment may be made by money order, cashier check, personal check. Payee: Clerk, USDC.

Phone Search: Only docket information from active cases will be released over the phone.

Mail Search: A stamped self addressed envelope is not required.

In Person Search: In person searching available.

PACER: Toll-free dial-up access: 800-361-0442. Local dial-up access: 606-233-2787. Case records are available back to September 1991. Records are never purged. New records are available online after 1 day. PACER is available online at http://pacer.kyed.uscourts.gov.

London Division PO Box 5121, London, KY 40745-5121 (Courier Address: 124 US Courthouse, 300 S Main, London, KY 40741), 606-864-5137.

www.kyed.uscourts.gov

Counties: Bell, Clay, Harlan, Jackson, Knox, Laurel, Leslie, McCreary, Owsley, Pulaski, Rockcastle, Wayne, Whitley.

Indexing & Storage: Cases are indexed by defendant, plaintiff, and case number. New cases are available in the index 1 day after filing date. Open records are located at this court.

Fee & Payment Notes: Payment may be made by money order, cashier check, personal check. Payee: Clerk, USDC.

Phone Search: Only docket information is available by phone.

In Person Search: In person searching available.

PACER: Toll-free dial-up access: 800-361-0442. Local dial-up access: 606-233-2787. Case records are available back to September 1991. Records are never purged. New records are available online after 1 day. PACER is available online at http://pacer.kyed.uscourts.gov.

Pikeville Division Office of the clerk, 203 Federal Bldg, 110 Main St, Pikeville, KY 41501 (Courier Address: Use mail address for courier delivery), 606-437-6160.

www.kyed.uscourts.gov

Counties: Breathitt, Floyd, Johnson, Knott, Letcher, Magoffin, Martin, Perry, Pike. Lee and Wolfe Counties were part of this division until 10/31/92, when they were moved to the Lexington Division.

Indexing & Storage: Cases are indexed by defendant, plaintiff, and case number. New cases are available in the index immediately after filing date. Open records are located at this court.

Fee & Payment Notes: Payment may be made by money order, cashier check, personal check. Prepayment required except for Kentucky attorneys. Payee: Clerk, US District Court. You are allowed to make your own copies. These copies cost $.50 per page.

Phone Search: Only the date the case was filed and the status of the case will be released over the phone.

Mail Search: A stamped self addressed envelope is not required.

In Person Search: In person searching available.

PACER: Toll-free dial-up access: 800-361-0442. Local dial-up access: 606-233-2787. Case records are available back to September 1991. Records are never purged. New records are available online after 1 day. PACER is available online at http://pacer.kyed.uscourts.gov.

US Bankruptcy Court

Eastern District of Kentucky

Lexington Division PO Box 1111, Lexington, KY 40589-1111 (Courier Address: Community Trust Bldg, Suite 202, 100 E Vine St, Lexington, KY 40507), 859-233-2608.

www.kyeb.uscourts.gov

Counties: Anderson, Bath, Bell, Boone, Bourbon, Boyd, Boyle, Bracken, Breathitt, Campbell, Carroll, Carter, Clark, Clay, Elliott, Estill, Fayette, Fleming, Floyd, Franklin, Gallatin, Garrard, Grant, Greenup, Harlan, Harrison, Henry, Jackson, Jessamine, Johnson, Kenton, Knott, Knox, Laurel, Lawrence, Lee, Leslie, Letcher, Lewis, Lincoln,

Madison, Magoffin, Martin, Mason, McCreary, Menifee, Mercer, Montgomery, Morgan, Nicholas, Owen, Owsley, Pendleton, Perry, Pike, Powell, Pulaski, Robertson, Rockcastle, Rowan,Scott, Shelby, Trimble, Wayne, Whitley, Wolfe, Woodford.

Indexing & Storage: Cases are indexed by debtor as well as by case number. New cases are available in the index 3 days after filing date. Open records are located at this court.

Fee & Payment Notes: Payment may be made by money order, cashier check, business check. Personal checks are not accepted. Prepayment is required (excluding pauper filings). Payee: Clerk, US Bankruptcy Court. You are allowed to make your own copies. These copies cost $.15 per page.

Phone Search: Only docket information is available by phone. An automated voice case information service (VCIS) is available. Call VCIS at 800-998-2650 or 606-233-2657.

In Person Search: In person searching available.

PACER:. Case records are available back to July 1992. Records are purged every six months. New civil records are available online after 1 day. PACER is available online at http://pacer.kyeb.uscourts.gov.

Electronic Filing: Information is available online at https://ecf.kyeb.uscourts.gov/

US District Court

Western District of Kentucky

Bowling Green Division US District Court, 241 E Main St, Room 120, Bowling Green, KY 42101-2175 (Courier: Use mail address for courier delivery), 270-781-1110, Fax: 270-842-2836.

www.kywd.uscourts.gov

Counties: Adair, Allen, Barren, Butler, Casey, Clinton, Cumberland, Edmonson, Green, Hart, Logan, Metcalfe, Monroe, Russell, Simpson, Taylor, Todd, Warren.

Indexing & Storage: Cases are indexed by defendant, plaintiff, and case number. New cases are available in the index 1-2 days after filing date. Open records are located at this court.

Fee & Payment Notes: Payment may be made by money order, cashier check, personal check. Payee: Clerk, US District Court. You are allowed to make your own copies. These copies cost $.50 per page.

Phone Search: Only docket information is available by phone.

In Person Search: In person searching available.

PACER: Local dial-up access: 502-588-3260, 502-588-3261. Case records are available back to 1992. New records are available online after 1 day. Has converted the online WebPACER service over to nationwide PACER standards; click on "Court Records." Registration and fee required.

Electronic Filing: Information is available at www.kywd.uscourts.gov/scripts/usdckyw/ecf/ecf2.pl

Opinions Online: Court opinions are available online at www.kywd.uscourts.gov

Louisville Division Clerk, US District Court, 450 US Courthouse, 601 W Broadway, Louisville, KY 40202 (Courier: Use mail address for courier delivery), 502-625-3500, Fax: 502-625-3880.

www.kywd.uscourts.gov

Counties: Breckinridge, Bullitt, Hardin, Jefferson, Larue, Marion, Meade, Nelson, Oldham, Spencer, Washington.

Indexing & Storage: Cases are indexed by defendant, plaintiff, and case number. New cases are available in the index immediately after filing date. Records are indexed on index cards from 1938 to 1979. Records are indexed on microfiche from 1979 to 4/92. Records after 4/92 are on the automated system. District wide searches are available from this court for information from 1938.

Fee & Payment Notes: Payment may be made by money order, cashier check, personal check. Payee: Clerk, US District Court.

Phone Search: Searching not available by phone. Only docket information is available by phone.

In Person Search: In person searching available.

PACER: Local dial-up access: 502-588-3260, 502-588-3261. Case records are available back to 1992. New records are available online after 1 day. Has converted the online WebPACER service over to nationwide PACER standards; click on "Court Records" Registration and fee required.

Electronic Filing: Information is available at www.kywd.uscourts.gov/scripts/usdckyw/ecf/ecf2.pl

Opinions Online: Court opinions are available online at www.kywd.uscourts.gov

Owensboro Division Federal Bldg, Room 126, 423 Frederica St, Owensboro, KY 42301 (Courier Address: Use mail address for courier delivery), 270-683-0221, Fax: 502-685-4601.

www.kywd.uscourts.gov

Counties: Daviess, Grayson, Hancock, Henderson, Hopkins, McLean, Muhlenberg, Ohio, Union, Webster.

Indexing & Storage: Cases are indexed by defendant, plaintiff, and case number. New cases are available in the index 1-2 days after filing date. The court needs the correct name, date and/or criminal or civil case number to search for a record. Open records are located at this court.

Fee & Payment Notes: Payment may be made by money order, cashier check, personal check. The court will only bill to in state searchers. Payee: Clerk, US District Court. You are allowed to make your own copies. These copies cost $.50 per page.

Phone Search: Only docket information is available by phone.

Mail Search: A stamped self addressed envelope is not required.

In Person Search: In person searching available.

PACER: Local dial-up access: 502-588-3260, 502-588-3261. Case records are available back to 1992. New records are available online after 1 day. Has converted the online WebPACER service over to nationwide PACER standards; click on "Court Records." Registration and fee required.

Electronic Filing: Information is available at www.kywd.uscourts.gov/scripts/usdckyw/ecf/ecf2.pl

Opinions Online: Court opinions are available online at www.kywd.uscourts.gov

Paducah Division 127 Federal Building, 501 Broadway, Paducah, KY 42001 (Courier Address: Use mail address for courier delivery), 270-443-1337, Fax: 270-442-1919.

www.kywd.uscourts.gov

Counties: Ballard, Caldwell, Calloway, Carlisle, Christian, Crittenden, Fulton, Graves, Hickman, Livingston, Lyon, McCracken, Marshall, Trigg.

Indexing & Storage: Cases are indexed by defendant, plaintiff, and case number. New cases are available in the index 1-2 days after filing date. Open records are located at this court.

Fee & Payment Notes: Payment may be made by money order, cashier check, personal check. Payee: Clerk, US District Court. You are allowed to make your own copies. These copies cost $.50 per page.

Phone Search: Only docket information is available by phone.

Fax Search: You may fax for a fee quote.

In Person Search: In person searching available.

PACER: Local dial-up access: 502-588-3260, 502-588-3261. Case records are available back to 1992. New records are available online after 1 day. Has converted the online WebPACER service over to nationwide PACER standards; click on "Court Records." Registration and fee required.

Electronic Filing: Information is available at www.kywd.uscourts.gov/scripts/usdckyw/ecf/ecf2.pl

Opinions Online: Court opinions are available online at www.kywd.uscourts.gov

US Bankruptcy Court

Western District of Kentucky

Louisville Division 546 US Courthouse, 601 W Broadway, Louisville, KY 40202 (Courier Address: Use mail address for courier delivery), 502-627-5800.

www.kywb.uscourts.gov

Counties: Adair, Allen, Ballard, Barren, Breckinridge, Bullitt, Butler, Caldwell, Calloway, Carlisle, Casey, Christian, Clinton, Crittenden, Cumberland, Daviess, Edmonson, Fulton, Graves, Grayson, Green, Hancock, Hardin, Hart, Henderson, Hickman, Hopkins,Jefferson, Larue, Livingston, Logan, Lyon, Marion, Marshall, McCracken, McLean, Meade, Metcalfe, Monroe, Muhlenberg, Nelson, Ohio, Oldham, Russell, Simpson, Spencer, Taylor, Todd, Trigg, Union, Warren, Washington, Webster.

Indexing & Storage: Cases are indexed by debtor as well as by case number. New cases are available in the index 1-2 days after filing date. District wide searches are available from this division. This division maintains records for all of the divisions in this district.

Fee & Payment Notes: Payment may be made by money order, cashier check. Business checks are not accepted. Personal checks are not accepted. Payee: Clerk, US Bankruptcy Court.

Phone Search: Only docket information is available by phone. An automated voice case information service (VCIS) is available. Call VCIS at 800-263-9385 or 502-625-7391.

In Person Search: In person searching available.

PACER:. Case records are available back to July 1992. Records are purged every six months. New civil records are available online after 1-2 days. PACER is available online at http://pacer.kywb.uscourts.gov.

Electronic Filing: Information is available online at https://ecf.kywb.uscourts.gov/

Kentucky County Courts

Court	Jurisdiction	No. of Courts	How Organized
Circuit Courts*	General	19	56 Judicial Circuits
District Courts*	Limited	19	59 Judicial Districts
Combined*		102	

* Profiled in this Sourcebook.

Court	CIVIL								
	Tort	Contract	Real Estate	Min. Claim	Max. Claim	Small Claims	Estate	Eviction	Domestic Relations
Circuit Courts*	X	X	X	$4000	No Max				X
District Courts*	X	X	X	$0	$4000	$1500	X	X	X

Court	CRIMINAL				
	Felony	Misdemeanor	DWI/DUI	Preliminary Hearing	Juvenile
Circuit Courts*	X				
District Courts*		X	X	X	X

ADMINISTRATION Administrative Office of Courts, 100 Mill Creek Park, Frankfort, KY, 40601; 502-573-2350, Fax: 502-573-1448. www.kycourts.net

COURT STRUCTURE The Circuit Court is the court of general jurisdiction and the District Court is the limited jurisdiction court. Most of Kentucky's counties combined the courts into one location and records are co-mingled.

ONLINE ACCESS There are statewide, online computer systems called SUSTAIN and KyCourts available for internal judicial/state agency use only. No courts offer online access to records. However, you may search daily court calendars by county for free at http://dockets.ky courts.net. Also, you may search online for circuit court dockets (limited) on the supreme court search page at http://162.114.20.136/dockets. These are only the cases open before the Supreme Court.

ADDITIONAL INFORMATION Until 1978, county judges handled all cases; therefore, in many cases, District and Circuit Court records go back only to 1978. Records prior to that time are archived.

Many courts refer requests for criminal searches to the Administrative Office of Courts (AOC - 502-573-2350 or 800-928-6381) due to lack of personnel for searching at the court level. AOC maintains records on an internal system called COURTNET, which contains information on opening, closing, proceedings, disposition, and parties to including individual defendants. Felony convictions are accessible back to 1978, and Misdemeanors back five years. The required Release Form is available from the AOC at the numbers above. A check or money order for the Search Fee of $10.00 per requested individual ($5.00 fee if non-profit or if you are the individual) is payable to the State Treasurer of Kentucky. A SASE and a second postage-attached envelope must accompany the request.

Adair County

Circuit & District Court 500 Public Square, #6, Columbia, KY 42728; 270-384-2626; Fax: 270-384-4299. Hours: 8AM-4PM (CST). *Felony, Misdemeanor, Civil, Eviction, Small Claims, Probate.*

Civil Records: Access: In person only. Visitors must perform in person searches for themselves. No search fee. Required to search: name, years to search. Civil records on computer since June 1993, prior records on docket books since 1978.

Criminal Records: Access: Mail, in person. Visitors must perform in person searches for themselves. No search fee. Required to search: name, years to search, SSN. Criminal records on computer since June 1993, prior records on docket books since 1978. Mail requests must be made to Pretrial Services, 100 Millcreek Pk, Frankfort KY 40601, 800-928-6381.

General Information: Public access terminal is available. No adoption, mental, juvenile, or sealed records released. SASE required. Turnaround time same day. Copy fee: $.25 per page. Fee payee: Circuit Clerk. Personal checks accepted.

Allen County

Circuit & District Court Box 477, Scottsville, KY 42164; 270-237-3561. Hours: 8AM-4:30PM (CST). *Felony, Misdemeanor, Civil, Eviction, Small Claims, Probate.*

Civil Records: Access: In person only. Visitors must perform in person searches for themselves. Search fee: No search fee. Required to search: name, years to search. Civil cases indexed by defendant, plaintiff. Civil records on computer since 1992, records on index cards from 1980 to 1992, prior records on books.

Criminal Records: Access: In person only. Visitors must perform in person searches for themselves. Search fee: No search fee. Required to search: name, years to search; also helpful: SSN. Criminal records on computer back to 1992, records on index cards from 1978 to 1992, prior records on books. Court recommends that criminal search requests be directed to the State of Kentucky AOC, 502-573-2350.

General Information: Public access terminal is available. No adoption, mental, juvenile, or sealed records released. Fax notes: Fee to fax results is $1.00 for 1st page; $2.00 each add'l. Copy fee: $.25 per page. Certification fee: $5.00. Fee payee: Circuit Clerk. Personal checks accepted. Prepayment is required.

Anderson County

Circuit Court Courthouse 151 S Main St, Lawrenceburg, KY 40342; 502-839-3508. Hours: 8:30AM-5PM *Felony, Civil Actions Over $4,000.*

Civil Records: Access: In person only. Only the court performs in person searches; visitors may not. No search fee. Required to search: name, years to search. Civil cases indexed by defendant, plaintiff. Civil records on computer since August 1994, prior records on docket books since 1978.

Criminal Records: Access: In person only. Visitors must perform in person searches for themselves. No search fee. Required to search: name, years to search; also helpful: DOB, SSN. All record requests are referred to the state agency at 502-573-2350.

General Information: No adoption, mental, juvenile, or sealed records released. Copy fee: $.25 per page. Certification fee: $5.00. Fee payee: Clerk of Circuit Clerk. Personal checks accepted. Prepayment required.

District Court 151 S Main, Lawrenceburg, KY 40342; 502-839-5445. Hours: 8:30AM-5PM M-TH, 8:30AM-6PM F (EST). *Misdemeanor, Civil Actions Under $4,000, Eviction, Small Claims, Probate.*

Civil Records: Access: Phone, mail, fax, in person. Only the court performs in person searches; visitors

may not. Search fee: No search fee. Required to search: name, years to search. Civil cases indexed by defendant, plaintiff. Civil cases indexed by defendant, plaintiff. Civil cases indexed since 8/1994, prior records on index cards back to 1978.

Criminal Records: Access: In person only. Visitors must perform in person searches for themselves. No search fee. Required to search: name, years to search; also helpful: DOB, SSN. Criminal records on computer back to 1994; prior records on index cards back to 1978. All requests are referred to Pre-trial Services at 800-928-6381. Call them to perform the search for you.

General Information: No adoption, mental, juvenile, or sealed records released. Copy fee: $.25 per page. Certification fee: $5.00. Fee payee: Anderson County District Court. Business checks accepted. Prepayment is required.

Ballard County

Circuit & District Court Box 265, Wickliffe, KY 42087; 270-335-5123; Fax: 270-335-3849. Hours: 8AM-4PM (CST). *Felony, Misdemeanor, Civil, Eviction, Small Claims, Probate.*

Civil Records: Access: Mail, fax, in person. Both court and visitors may perform in person searches. No search fee. Required to search: name, years to search. Civil cases indexed by defendant, plaintiff. Civil records on computer since 1992, prior records on books to 1978.

Criminal Records: Access: In person only. Visitors must perform in person searches for themselves. No search fee. Required to search: name, years to search, DOB. Criminal records on computer since 1992, prior records on books to 1978.

General Information: Public access terminal is available. No adoption, mental, juvenile, or sealed records released. SASE required. Turnaround time 2 days. Fax notes: Fee to fax results is $2.00 per page. Copy fee: $.25 per page. Certification fee: $5.00. Fee payee: Circuit Clerk. Only cashiers checks and money orders accepted. Prepayment is required.

Barren County

Circuit & District Court PO Box 1359, Glasgow, KY 42142-1359; 270-651-3763; Fax: 270-651-6203. Hours: 8AM-4:30PM (CST). *Felony, Misdemeanor, Civil, Eviction, Small Claims, Probate.*

Civil Records: Access: In person only. Visitors must perform in person searches for themselves. No search fee. Required to search: name, years to search. Civil cases indexed by defendant, plaintiff. Civil records on computer back to 10/1991, prior records on index books since 1800s.

Criminal Records: Access: In person only. Visitors must perform in person searches for themselves. No search fee. Required to search: name, years to search, DOB; also helpful: SSN. Criminal records on computer back to 10/1991, prior records on index books since 1800s. Criminal record search requests should be directed to AOC Pre-Trial Services in Frankfort, 800-928-6381.

General Information: Public access terminal is available. No adoption, mental, juvenile, or sealed records released. Copy fee: $.25 per page. Certification fee: $5.00. Fee payee: Circuit Clerk. Personal checks accepted. Prepayment is required.

Bath County

Circuit & District Court Box 558, Owingsville, KY 40360; 606-674-2186 X6821; Fax: 606-674-3996. Hours: 8AM-4PM (EST). *Felony, Misdemeanor, Civil, Eviction, Small Claims, Probate.*

Civil Records: Access: In person only. Visitors must perform in person searches for themselves. No search fee. Required to search: name, years to search. Civil cases indexed by defendant, plaintiff. Civil records computerized since 1994, on docket books since 1978, prior records archived.

Criminal Records: Access: In person only. Visitors must perform in person searches for themselves. No search fee. Required to search: name, years to search, DOB, SSN. Criminal records computerized since 1994, on docket books since 1978, prior records archived.

General Information: Public access terminal is available. No adoption, mental, juvenile, or sealed records released. Copy fee: $.25 per page. Certification fee: $5.00. Fee payee: Circuit Clerk. Personal checks accepted. Prepayment is required.

Bell County

Circuit & District Court Box 307, Pineville, KY 40977; 606-337-2942/9900; Fax: 606-337-8850. Hours: 8:30AM-4PM (EST). *Felony, Misdemeanor, Civil, Eviction, Small Claims, Probate.*

Civil Records: Access: Phone, mail, in person. Both court and visitors may perform in person searches. No search fee. Required to search: name, years to search. Civil cases indexed by defendant, plaintiff. Civil records on computer since 1991, prior records on docket books since 1978.

Criminal Records: Access: Phone, mail, in person. Both court and visitors may perform in person searches. No search fee. Required to search: name, years to search. Criminal records on computer since 1991, prior records on docket books since 1978.

General Information: Public access terminal is available. No adoption, mental, juvenile, or sealed records released. SASE required. Copy fee: $.25 per page. Certification fee: $5.00. Fee payee: Circuit Clerk. Personal checks accepted. Prepayment is required.

Boone County

Circuit & District Court Box 480, Burlington, KY 41005; 859-334-2239; Fax: 859-586-9413. Hours: 8:30AM-4:30PM (EST). *Felony, Misdemeanor, Civil, Eviction, Small Claims, Probate.*

Civil Records: Access: Mail, in person. Both court and visitors may perform in person searches. Search fee: No search fee. Required to search: name, years to search. Civil cases indexed by defendant, plaintiff. Civil records on computer since July 1990, on index card file since 1978, prior records on books.

Criminal Records: Access: In person only. Visitors must perform in person searches for themselves. Search fee: No search fee. Required to search: name, years to search, DOB; also helpful: SSN. Criminal records on computer since July 1990, on index card file since 1978, prior records on books.

General Information: Public access terminal is available. No adoption, mental, juvenile, or sealed records released. SASE required. Fax notes: Fee to fax results is $3.00 per page. Copy fee: $.25 per page. Certification fee: $5.00. Fee payee: Circuit Clerk. Only cashiers checks and money orders accepted.

Bourbon County

Circuit & District Court Box 740, Paris, KY 40361; 859-987-2624. Hours: 8:30AM-4:30PM M-TH, 8:30AM-6PM F (EST). *Felony, Misdemeanor, Civil, Eviction, Small Claims, Probate.*

Civil Records: Access: In person only. Visitors must perform in person searches for themselves. No search fee. Required to search: name, years to search. Civil cases indexed by defendant, plaintiff. Civil records on computer since November 1991, prior records on books.

Criminal Records: Access: In person only. Visitors must perform in person searches for themselves. No search fee. Required to search: name, years to search; also helpful: SSN. Criminal records on computer since November 1991, prior records on books.

General Information: Public access terminal is available. No adoption, mental, juvenile, or sealed records released. Copy fee: $.25 per page. Certification fee: $5.00. Fee payee: Circuit Clerk. Personal checks accepted. Prepayment is required.

Boyd County

Circuit & District Court Box 694, Catlettsburg, KY 41129-0694; 606-739-4131; Fax: 606-739-5793. Hours: 8:30AM-4PM (EST). *Felony, Misdemeanor, Civil, Eviction, Small Claims, Probate.*

Civil Records: Access: In person only. Visitors must perform in person searches for themselves. No search fee. Required to search: name, years to search. Civil cases indexed by defendant, plaintiff. Civil records on computer since 1991, prior records on index cards since 1975.

Criminal Records: Access: In person only. Visitors must perform in person searches for themselves. No search fee. Required to search: name, years to search, signed release; also helpful: DOB, SSN. Criminal records on computer since 1991, on index cards since 1978; misdemeanor & traffic from 1987.

General Information: Public access terminal is available. No adoption, mental, juvenile, or sealed records released. Copy fee: $.25 per page. Certification fee: $5.00. Fee payee: Circuit Clerk. Personal checks accepted. Prepayment is required.

Boyle County

Circuit Court Courthouse, 321 Main St, Danville, KY 40422; 859-239-7442; Fax: 859-239-7000. Hours: 8AM-5PM (EST). *Felony, Civil Actions Over $4,000.*

Civil Records: Access: Fax, mail, in person. Both court and visitors may perform in person searches. No search fee. Required to search: name, years to search. Civil cases indexed by defendant, plaintiff. Civil records on computer since 08/91, prior records on index cards.

Criminal Records: Access: Fax, mail, in person. Both court and visitors may perform in person searches. No search fee. Required to search: name, years to search, DOB, SSN. Criminal records on computer since 08/91, prior records on index cards.

General Information: Public access terminal is available. No adoption, mental, juvenile, or sealed records released. SASE required. Turnaround time 2-4 days. Copy fee: $.25 per page. Certification fee: $5.00. Fee payee: Circuit Clerk. Personal checks accepted. Prepayment is required.

District Court Courthouse, 3rd Floor, Danville, KY 40422; 859-239-7362; Fax: 859-236-9807. Hours: 8AM-4:30PM (EST). *Misdemeanor, Civil Actions Under $4,000, Eviction, Small Claims, Probate.*

Civil Records: Access: Mail, fax, in person. Both court and visitors may perform in person searches. No search fee. Required to search: name, years to search. Civil cases indexed by defendant, plaintiff. Civil records on computer since 08/91, prior records on index cards since 1977.

Criminal Records: Access: Mail, fax, in person. Both court and visitors may perform in person searches. No search fee. Required to search: name, DOB, SSN. Criminal records on computer since 08/91; prior records on card index.

General Information: Public access terminal is available. No adoption, mental, juvenile, or sealed records released. SASE required. Turnaround time 3-4 days. Fax notes: Fee to fax results is $2.00 per page. Copy fee: $.25 per page. Certification fee: $5.00. Fee payee: District Clerk. Personal checks accepted. Prepayment is required.

Bracken County

Circuit & District Court PO Box 205, Brooksville, KY 41004-0205; 606-735-3328; Fax: 606-735-3900. Hours: 9AM-4PM M,T,TH,F, 9AM-Noon W & Sat (EST). *Felony, Misdemeanor, Civil, Eviction, Small Claims, Probate.*

Civil Records: Access: Mail, in person. Both court and visitors may perform in person searches. No search fee. Required to search: name, years to search. Civil cases indexed by defendant, plaintiff. Civil records on computer since 1993, prior records on docket books since the 1800s.

Criminal Records: Access: In person only. Visitors must perform in person searches for themselves. No search fee. Required to search: name, years to search; also helpful: SSN. Criminal records on computer since 1993, prior records on docket books since the 1800s.

General Information: Public access terminal is available. No adoption, mental, juvenile, or sealed records released. SASE required. Copy fee: $.25 per page. Certification fee: $5.00. Fee payee: Circuit Clerk. Prepayment is required.

Breathitt County

Circuit & District Court 1137 Main St, Jackson, KY 41339; 606-666-5768; Fax: 606-666-4893. Hours: 8AM-4PM M,T,TH,F; 8AM-Noon W; 9AM-Noon Sat (EST). *Felony, Misdemeanor, Civil, Eviction, Small Claims, Probate.*

Civil Records: Access: Phone, mail, in person. Both court and visitors may perform in person searches. No search fee. Required to search: name, years to search. Civil cases indexed by defendant, plaintiff. Civil records in files since 1987.

Criminal Records: Access: Phone, mail, in person. Both court and visitors may perform in person searches. No search fee. Required to search: name, years to search, DOB, SSN, signed release. Criminal records in files since 1987.

General Information: Public access terminal is available. No adoption, mental, juvenile, or sealed records released. SASE required. Turnaround time 2-3 days. Copy fee: $.25 per page. Certification fee: $5.00. Fee payee: Circuit Clerk. Personal checks accepted. Prepayment is required.

Breckinridge County

Circuit & District Court Box 111, Hardinsburg, KY 40143; 270-756-2239; Fax: 270-756-1129. Hours: 8AM-4PM (CST). *Felony, Misdemeanor, Civil, Eviction, Small Claims, Probate.*

Civil Records: Access: In person only. Visitors must perform in person searches for themselves. No search fee. Required to search: name, years to search. Civil cases indexed by defendant, plaintiff. Civil records on computer back to 8/1994, on index cards since 1978, prior records on docket books since the 1800s.

Criminal Records: Access: In person only. Visitors must perform in person searches for themselves. No search fee. Required to search: name, years to search, DOB, SSN. Criminal records on computer back to 8/1994, on index cards since 1978, prior records on docket books since the 1800s.

General Information: Public access terminal is available. No adoption, mental, juvenile, or sealed records released. Fax notes: Fee to fax results is $2.00 per page. Copy fee: $.25 per page. Certification fee: $5.00. Fee payee: Circuit Clerk. Personal checks accepted. Prepayment is required.

Bullitt County

Circuit & District Court Box 746, Shephardsville, KY 40165; 502-543-7104; Fax: 502-543-7158. Hours: 8AM-4PM (EST). *Felony, Misdemeanor, Civil, Eviction, Small Claims, Probate.*

Civil Records: Access: Fax, mail, in person. Both court and visitors may perform in person searches. Search fee: $1.00 per name. Required to search: name. Civil cases indexed by defendant, plaintiff. Civil records on computer since 11/91, prior records on index cards since the 1800s.

Criminal Records: Access: Fax, mail, in person. Both court and visitors may perform in person searches. Search fee: $1.00 per name. Required to search: name, years to search, DOB, SSN. Criminal records on computer since 11/91, prior records on index cards since the 1800s. Access by mail with authorization.

General Information: Public access terminal is available. No adoption, mental, juvenile, or sealed records released. SASE required. Turnaround time 1-2 days. Fax notes: Fee to fax results is $1.00 per page. Send copy of check with fax. Copy fee: $.25 per page. Certification fee: $5.00. Fee payee: Circuit Clerk. Personal checks accepted. Prepayment is required.

Butler County

Circuit & District Court Box 625, Morgantown, KY 42261; 270-526-5631. Hours: 8AM-4:30PM M-F; 9AM-Noon Sat (CST). *Felony, Misdemeanor, Civil, Eviction, Small Claims, Probate.*

Civil Records: Access: Mail, in person. No search fee. Required to search: name, years to search. Civil cases indexed by defendant, plaintiff. Civil records on computer since 1993, prior records on index cards since the 1800s.

Criminal Records: Access: Mail, in person. Both court and visitors may perform in person searches. No search fee. Required to search: name, years to search, DOB; also helpful: SSN. Criminal records on computer since 1993, prior records on index cards since the 1800s.

General Information: Public access terminal is available. No adoption, mental, juvenile, or sealed records released. SASE required. Turnaround time 1 week. Copy fee: $.25 per page. Fee payee: Circuit Clerk. Personal checks accepted. Prepayment is required.

Caldwell County

Circuit & District Court 105 West Court Sq, Princeton, KY 42445; 270-365-6884; Fax: 270-365-9171. Hours: 8AM-4PM (CST). *Felony, Misdemeanor, Civil, Eviction, Small Claims, Probate.*

Civil Records: Access: Mail, fax, in person. Visitors must perform in person searches for themselves. No search fee. Required to search: name, years to search. Civil cases indexed by defendant, plaintiff. Civil records on index cards; on computer back to 9/94.

Criminal Records: Access: In person only. Visitors must perform in person searches for themselves. No search fee. Required to search: name, years to search, DOB; also helpful: SSN. Criminal records on index cards; on computer back to 9/94.

General Information: Public access terminal is available. No adoption, mental, juvenile, or sealed records released. SASE required. Turnaround time 2 days. Fax notes: Fee to fax results is $2.00 for 1st page, $1.00 each add'l. Copy fee: $.25 per page. Copy request must include postage. Certification fee: $5.00. Fee payee: Circuit Clerk. Personal checks accepted. Prepayment is required.

Calloway County

Circuit & District Court 312 N 4th St, Murray, KY 42071; 270-753-2714; Fax: 270-759-9822. Hours: 8AM-4:30PM (CST). *Felony, Misdemeanor, Civil, Eviction, Small Claims, Probate.*

Civil Records: Access: Mail, in person. Both court and visitors may perform in person searches. No search fee. Required to search: name, years to search. Civil cases indexed by defendant, plaintiff. Civil records on computer since 06/92, on index cards since 1978. Prior to 1978 records are archived in Frankfurt.

Criminal Records: Access: In person only. Visitors must perform in person searches for themselves. No search fee. Required to search: name, years to search, DOB; also helpful: SSN. Criminal records on computer since 06/92, on index cards since 1978. Prior to 1978 records are archived in Frankfurt.

General Information: Public access terminal is available. No adoption, mental, juvenile, or sealed records released. SASE required. Turnaround time 2-4 days. Copy fee: $.25 per page. Certification fee: $5.00. Fee payee: Circuit Clerk. Personal checks accepted. Prepayment is required.

Campbell County

Circuit Court 330 York St Rm 8, Newport, KY 41071; 859-292-6314; Fax: 859-431-0816. Hours: 8:30AM-4PM (EST). *Felony, Civil Actions Over $4,000.*

Civil Records: Access: In person only. Visitors must perform in person searches for themselves. No search fee. Required to search: name, years to search. Civil cases indexed by defendant, plaintiff. Civil records on computer since 1992, prior records on index cards since 1978.

Criminal Records: Access: In person only. Visitors must perform in person searches for themselves. No search fee. Required to search: name, years to search; also helpful: SSN. Criminal records on computer since 1992, prior records on index cards since 1978.

General Information: Public access terminal is available. No adoption, mental, juvenile, or sealed records released. Copy fee: $.25 per page. Certification fee: $5.00. Fee payee: Campbell Circuit Court. Personal checks accepted. Prepayment is required.

District Court 600 Columbia St, Newport, KY 41071-1816; 859-292-6305; Fax: 859-292-6593. Hours: 8:30AM-4PM *Misdemeanor, Civil Actions Under $4,000, Eviction, Small Claims, Probate.*

Civil Records: Access: Mail, in person. Both court and visitors may perform in person searches. Search fee: $10.00 (probate searches only). Required to search: name, years to search. Civil cases indexed by defendant, plaintiff. Civil records on computer back to 1992, prior records on index cards to 1978.

Criminal Records: Access: In person only. Visitors must perform in person searches for themselves. Search fee: No search fee. Required to search: name, years to search, SSN. Criminal records on computer back to 1992, prior records on index cards to 1978.

General Information: Public access terminal is available. No adoption, mental, juvenile, or sealed records released. SASE required. Turnaround time 7 days. Copy fee: $.25 per page. Certification fee: $5.00. Fee payee: District Clerk (make probate checks to Tho. J Calme, Clerk). Business checks accepted. Prepayment is required.

Carlisle County

Circuit & District Court Box 337, Bardwell, KY 42023; 270-628-5425; Fax: 270-628-5456. Hours: 8AM-4PM (CST). *Felony, Misdemeanor, Civil, Eviction, Small Claims, Probate.*

Civil Records: Access: Phone, fax, mail, in person. Both court and visitors may perform in person searches. No search fee. Required to search: name, years to search. Civil cases indexed by defendant, plaintiff. Civil records on computer since May 1993, records on docket books since 1978, prior records archived.

Criminal Records: Access: Phone, fax, mail, in person. Both court and visitors may perform in person searches. No search fee. Required to search: name, years to search. Criminal records on computer since May 1993, records on docket books since 1978, prior records archived.

General Information: Public access terminal is available. No adoption, mental, juvenile, or sealed records released. SASE required. Turnaround time 1-5 days. Copy fee: $.25 per page. Certification fee: $5.00. Fee payee: Circuit Clerk. Personal checks accepted. Prepayment is required.

Carroll County

Circuit & District Court 802 Clay St, Carrollton, KY 41008; 502-732-4305. Hours: 8AM-4:30PM (EST). *Felony, Misdemeanor, Civil, Eviction, Small Claims, Probate.*

Civil Records: Access: Phone, mail, in person. Both court and visitors may perform in person searches. No search fee. Required to search: name, years to search. Civil cases indexed by defendant, plaintiff. Civil records on computer since 1994, on docket books since 1980. Records before 1980 are archived in Frankfurt.

Criminal Records: Access: Phone, mail, in person. Both court and visitors may perform in person searches. No search fee. Required to search: name, years to search, DOB; also helpful: SSN. Criminal records on computer since 1994, on docket books since 1980. Records before 1980 are archived in Frankfurt.

General Information: Public access terminal is available. No adoption, mental, juvenile, or sealed records released. SASE required. Turnaround time 2-4 days. Copy fee: $.25 per page. Certification fee: $5.00. Fee payee: Circuit Clerk. Personal checks accepted. Prepayment is required.

Carter County

Circuit Court 300 W Main St, Rm 308, Grayson, KY 41143; 606-474-5191; Fax: 606-474-8826. Hours: 8:30AM-4PM M-F; 9AM-Noon Sat (EST). *Felony, Civil Actions Over $4,000.*

Civil Records: Access: Mail, in person. Both court and visitors may perform in person searches. No search fee. Required to search: name, years to search. Civil cases indexed by defendant, plaintiff. Civil records on computer since 1994, records archived since 1978, prior records are archived.

Criminal Records: Access: In person only. Both court and visitors may perform in person searches. No search fee. Required to search: name, years to search, DOB, SSN. Criminal records on computer since 1994, records archived since 1978, prior records are archived.

General Information: Public access terminal is available. No adoption, mental, juvenile, or sealed records released. SASE required. Turnaround time 1-2 days. Copy fee: $.25 per page. Certification fee: $5.00. Fee payee: Carter County Circuit Clerk. Prepayment is required.

District Court Courthouse, Rm 203, 300 West Main, Grayson, KY 41143; 606-474-6572; Fax: 606-474-8584. Hours: 8AM-4PM (EST). *Misdemeanor, Civil Actions Under $4,000, Eviction, Small Claims, Probate.*

Civil Records: Access: Mail, in person. Both court and visitors may perform in person searches. No search fee. Required to search: name, years to search. Civil cases indexed by defendant, plaintiff. Civil records on computer since 1994, prior records on index cards.

Criminal Records: Access: In person only. Visitors must perform in person searches for themselves. No search fee. Required to search: name, years to search, DOB; also helpful: SSN. Criminal records on computer since 1994, prior records on index cards.

General Information: Public access terminal is available. No adoption, mental, juvenile, or sealed records released. SASE required. Turnaround time 2-4 days. Copy fee: $.25 per page. Certification fee: $5.00. Fee payee: District Clerk. Personal checks accepted. Prepayment is required.

Casey County

Circuit & District Court PO Box 147, Liberty, KY 42539; 606-787-6510. Hours: 8AM-4:30PM M & F, 8AM-4PM Tu-W-Th, 8AM-Noon Sat (EST). *Felony, Misdemeanor, Civil, Eviction, Small Claims, Probate.*

Note: This court asks all pre-trial record requests go to the Administrative office of the Courts in Frankfort.

Civil Records: Access: In person only. Visitors must perform in person searches for themselves. No search fee. Required to search: name, years to search. Civil cases indexed by defendant, plaintiff. Civil records on index cards since 1978, prior records archived, computerized from 1995.

Criminal Records: Access: In person only. Visitors must perform in person searches for themselves. No search fee. Required to search: name, years to search, DOB, SSN, signed release. Criminal records on index cards since 1978, prior records archived, computerized from 1995.

General Information: Public access terminal is available. No adoption, mental, juvenile, or sealed records released. Copy fee: $.25 per page. Certification fee: $5.00. Fee payee: Circuit Clerk. Personal checks accepted. Prepayment is required.

Christian County

Circuit & District Court 511 S Main St Rm 301, Hopkinsville, KY 42240-2368; 270-889-6539; Fax: 270-889-6564. Hours: 8AM-4:30PM (CST). *Felony, Misdemeanor, Civil, Eviction, Small Claims, Probate.*

Civil Records: Access: Mail, in person. Both court and visitors may perform in person searches. No search fee. Required to search: name, years to search. Civil cases indexed by defendant, plaintiff. Civil records on computer since 1991, prior records on index cards since 1978.

Criminal Records: Access: In person only. Visitors must perform in person searches for themselves. No search fee. Required to search: name, years to search; also helpful: DOB, SSN. Criminal records on computer since 1991, prior records on index cards since 1978.

General Information: Public access terminal is available. No adoption, mental, juvenile, or sealed records released. SASE required. Turnaround time 2-4 days. Copy fee: $.25 per page. Certification fee: $5.00. Fee payee: Circuit Clerk. Personal checks accepted. Prepayment is required.

Clark County

Circuit Court Box 687, Winchester, KY 40392; 859-737-7264. Hours: 8AM-4PM (EST). *Felony, Civil Actions Over $4,000.*

Civil Records: Access: Mail, in person. Both court and visitors may perform in person searches. No search fee. Required to search: name, years to search; also helpful: address. Civil cases indexed by defendant, plaintiff. Civil records on computer since 1989, on index cards since 1950, prior records archived since the 1700s.

Criminal Records: Access: In person only. Visitors must perform in person searches for themselves. No search fee. Required to search: name, years to search; also helpful: address, DOB, SSN. Criminal records on computer since 1989, on index cards since 1950, prior records archived since the 1700s.

General Information: Public access terminal is available. No adoption, mental, juvenile, or sealed records released. SASE required. Turnaround time 2-4 days. Copy fee: $.25 per page. Certification fee: $5.00. Fee payee: Circuit Clerk. Personal checks accepted. Prepayment is required.

District Court PO Box 687, Winchester, KY 40392-0687; 859-737-7141; Fax: 859-737-7005. Hours: 8AM-4PM (EST). *Misdemeanor, Civil Actions Under $4,000, Eviction, Small Claims, Probate.*

Civil Records: Access: Mail, fax, in person. Both court and visitors may perform in person searches. No search fee. Required to search: name, years to search. Civil cases indexed by defendant, plaintiff. Civil records on computer since 1989, on docket books since 1978, prior records on archived.

Criminal Records: Access: Mail, fax, in person. Both court and visitors may perform in person searches. No search fee. Required to search: name, years to search; also helpful: DOB, SSN. Criminal records on computer since 1989, on docket books since 1978, prior records on archived.

General Information: Public access terminal is available. No adoption, mental, juvenile, or sealed records released. SASE required. Turnaround time 1-3 days. Copy fee: $.25 per page. Certification fee: $5.00. Fee payee: District Clerk. Personal checks accepted. Prepayment is required.

Clay County

Circuit & District Court 79 Highway 80, Ste 3, Manchester, KY 40962; 606-598-3663; Fax: 606-598-4047. Hours: 7:30AM-4:30PM (EST). *Felony, Misdemeanor, Civil, Eviction, Small Claims, Probate.*

Civil Records: Access: In person only. Visitors must perform in person searches for themselves. No search fee. Required to search: name, years to search. Civil cases indexed by defendant, plaintiff. Civil records on computer back to 1992, on index cards since 1978, prior records archived.

Criminal Records: Access: In person only. Visitors must perform in person searches for themselves. No search fee. Required to search: name, years to search, DOB; also helpful: SSN. Criminal records on computer back to 1992, on index cards since 1978, prior records archived.

General Information: Public access terminal is available. No adoption, mental, juvenile, or sealed records released. Copy fee: $.25 per page. Certification fee: $5.00. Fee payee: Circuit Clerk. Personal checks accepted. Prepayment is required.

Clinton County

Circuit & District Court Courthouse 2nd Fl, Albany, KY 42602; 606-387-6424; Fax: 606-387-8154. Hours: 8AM-4PM M-F; 8AM-Noon Sat (CST). *Felony, Misdemeanor, Civil, Eviction, Small Claims, Probate.*

Civil Records: Access: Phone, mail, in person. Both court and visitors may perform in person searches. No search fee. Required to search: name, years to search. Civil cases indexed by defendant, plaintiff. Civil records on computer since 08/92, on docket books since 1978, prior records archived to 1865.

Criminal Records: Access: Phone, mail, in person. Both court and visitors may perform in person searches. No search fee. Required to search: name, years to search, SSN; also helpful: DOB. Criminal records on computer since 08/92, on docket books since 1978, prior records archive to 1865.

General Information: Public access terminal is available. No adoption, mental, juvenile, or sealed records released. SASE required. Turnaround time 5 days. Copy fee: $.25 per page. Certification fee: $5.00. Fee payee: Circuit Clerk. Personal checks accepted. Prepayment is required.

Crittenden County

Circuit & District Court 107 S Main, Marion, KY 42064; 270-965-4200. Hours: 8AM-4:30PM (CST). *Felony, Misdemeanor, Civil, Eviction, Small Claims, Probate.*

Civil Records: Access: Mail, in person. Visitors must perform in person searches for themselves. No search fee. Required to search: name, years to search. Civil cases indexed by defendant, plaintiff. Civil records on index cards since 1977; on computer back to 9/94.

Criminal Records: Access: In person only. Visitors must perform in person searches for themselves. No search fee. Required to search: name, years to search. Criminal records on index cards since 1977; on computer back to 9/94.

General Information: Public access terminal is available. No adoption, mental, juvenile, or sealed records released. SASE required. Turnaround time 10 days. Fax notes: Fee to fax results is $2.00 1st page; $1.00 each add'l. Copy fee: $.25 per page. Certification fee: $5.00. Fee payee: Circuit Clerk. Checks not accepted. Prepayment is required.

Cumberland County

Circuit & District Court Box 395, Burkesville, KY 42717; 270-864-2611. Hours: 8AM-4PM (CST). *Felony, Misdemeanor, Civil, Eviction, Small Claims, Probate.*

Civil Records: Access: Mail, fax, in person. Both court and visitors may perform in person searches. No search fee. Required to search: name, years to search. Civil cases indexed by defendant, plaintiff. Civil records on computer back to 06/93, on docket cards from 1978, prior records archived.

Criminal Records: Access: Mail, fax, in person. Both court and visitors may perform in person searches. No search fee. Required to search: name, years to search, DOB; also helpful: SSN. Criminal records on computer back to 06/93, on docket cards from 1978, prior records archived.

General Information: Public access terminal is available. No adoption, mental, juvenile, or sealed records released. SASE required. Turnaround time 3-5 days. Fax notes: Fee to fax results is $2.00 and $1.00 per page. Copy fee: $.25 per page. Certification fee: $5.00. Fee payee: Circuit Clerk. Personal checks accepted. Prepayment is required.

Daviess County

Circuit & District Court Box 277, Owensboro, KY 42302; 270-687-7333/7330. Hours: 8AM-4PM (CST). *Felony, Misdemeanor, Civil, Eviction, Small Claims, Probate.*

Civil Records: Access: In person only. Visitors must perform in person searches for themselves. No search fee. Required to search: name, years to search. Civil cases indexed by defendant, plaintiff. Civil records on computer since 04/91, on index cards since 1978, prior records on docket books since 1809. Search in person only on Tuesday or Thursday.

Criminal Records: Access: In person only. Visitors must perform in person searches for themselves. No search fee. Required to search: name, years to search, DOB, SSN. Criminal records on computer since 04/91, on index cards since 1978, prior records on docket books since 1809. Search in person only on Tuesday or Thursday.

General Information: Public access terminal is available. No adoption, mental, juvenile, or sealed records released. Copy fee: $.25 per page. Certification fee: $5.00. Fee payee: Circuit Clerk. Business checks accepted. Prepayment is required.

Edmonson County

Circuit & District Court Box 739, Brownsville, KY 42210; 270-597-2584; Fax: 270-597-2884. Hours: 8AM-4:30PM M-W,F; 8AM-Noon Th,S (CST). *Felony, Misdemeanor, Civil, Eviction, Small Claims, Probate.*

Civil Records: Access: In person only. Visitors must perform in person searches for themselves. No search fee. Required to search: name, years to search, address. Civil cases indexed by defendant, plaintiff. Civil records computerized since 1995, on index cards and docket books from 1800s.

Criminal Records: Access: In person only. Visitors must perform in person searches for themselves. No search fee. Required to search: name, years to search, DOB, SSN. Criminal records computerized since 1995, on index cards and docket books from 1800s.

General Information: No adoption, mental, juvenile, or sealed records released. Copy fee: $.25 per page. Certification fee: $5.00. Fee payee: Circuit Clerk. Personal checks accepted. Prepayment is required.

Elliott County

Circuit & District Court Box 788, Sandy Hook, KY 41171; 606-738-5238; Fax: 606-738-6962. Hours: 8AM-4PM M-F; 9AM-Noon Sat (EST). *Felony, Misdemeanor, Civil, Eviction, Small Claims, Probate.*

Civil Records: Access: In person only. Both court and visitors may perform in person searches. No search fee. Required to search: name, years to search. Civil cases indexed by defendant, plaintiff. Civil records on computer since October 1992, prior records on index cards since 1978.

Criminal Records: Access: In person only. Both court and visitors may perform in person searches. No search fee. Required to search: name, years to search; also helpful: SSN. Criminal records on computer since October 1992, prior records on index cards since 1978. Mail requests for criminal searches may be made to the state AOC.

General Information: Public access terminal is available. No adoption, mental, juvenile, or sealed records released. Copy fee: $.25 per page. Certification fee: $5.00. Fee payee: Circuit Clerk. Personal checks accepted. Prepayment is required.

Estill County

Circuit & District Court 130 Main St, Rm 207, Irvine, KY 40336; 606-723-3970; Fax: 606-723-1158. Hours: 8AM-4PM (EST). *Felony, Misdemeanor, Civil, Eviction, Small Claims, Probate.*

Civil Records: Access: Phone, fax, mail, in person. Both court and visitors may perform in person searches. No search fee. Required to search: name, years to search. Civil cases indexed by defendant, plaintiff. Civil records on index cards back to 1965; on computer back to 1994.

Criminal Records: Access: Phone, fax, mail, in person. Both court and visitors may perform in person searches. No search fee. Required to search: name, years to search, DOB, SSN. Criminal records on computer back to 1994.

General Information: Public access terminal is available. No adoption, mental, juvenile, or sealed records released. SASE required. Turnaround time 2-4 days. Fax notes: Fee to fax results is $1.00 per page. Copy fee: $.25 per page. Certification fee: $5.00. Fee payee: Circuit Clerk. Personal checks accepted. Prepayment is required.

Fayette County

Circuit Court - Criminal & Civil Divisions 120 N Limestone, Lexington, KY 40507; Civil phone: 859-246-2141; Criminal phone: 859-246-2224. Hours: 8:30AM-4:30PM (EST). *Felony, Civil Actions Over $4,000.*

Civil Records: Access: Mail, in person. Both court and visitors may perform in person searches. Search fee: $5.00 per name. Required to search: name, years to search. Civil cases indexed by defendant, plaintiff. Civil records on computer since April 1993, on index cards since 1978, prior records on books and archived.

Criminal Records: Access: Mail, in person. Both court and visitors may perform in person searches. Search fee: $5.00 per name. Required to search: name, years to search; also helpful: DOB, SSN. Criminal records on computer since April 1993, on index cards since 1978, prior records on books and archived.

General Information: Public access terminal is available. No adoption, juvenile, mental, or sealed records released. SASE required. Turnaround time 1-2 days. Copy fee: $.25 per page. Certification fee: $5.00. Fee payee: Fayette County Circuit Clerk. No personal checks accepted. Prepayment is required.

District Court - Criminal & Civil 150 N Limestone #0112, Lexington, KY 40507; Civil phone: 859-246-2240; Criminal phone: 859-246-2228. Hours: 8AM-4PM (EST). *Misdemeanor, Civil Actions Under $4,000, Eviction, Small Claims, Probate.*

Civil Records: Access: Mail, in person. Visitors must perform in person searches Search fee: $5.00 per name. Required to search: name, years to search. Civil cases indexed by defendant, plaintiff. Civil records on computer since 1992, prior records on index cards since 1977.

Criminal Records: Access: Mail, in person. Visitors must perform in person searches No search fee. Required to search: name, years to search, DOB; also helpful: SSN. Criminal records on computer since 1977.

General Information: Public access terminal is available. No adoption, mental, juvenile, or sealed records released. SASE required. Turnaround time 3 days. Copy fee: $.25 per page. Certification fee: $5.00. Fee payee: District Clerk. Personal checks accepted. Prepayment is required.

Fleming County

Circuit & District Court Courthouse 100 Court Square, Flemingsburg, KY 41041; 606-845-7011; Fax: 606-849-2400. Hours: 8AM-4:30PM (EST). *Felony, Misdemeanor, Civil, Eviction, Small Claims, Probate.*

Civil Records: Access: Phone, fax, mail, in person. Both court and visitors may perform in person searches. No search fee. Required to search: name, years to search. Civil cases indexed by defendant, plaintiff. Civil records on computer since May 1994, prior records on index cards since 1978.

Criminal Records: Access: In person only. Both court and visitors may perform in person searches. No search fee. Required to search: name, years to search, DOB; also helpful: SSN. Criminal records on computer since May 1994, prior records on index cards since 1978.

General Information: Public access terminal is available. No adoption, mental, juvenile, or sealed records released. SASE required. Turnaround time 1-2 days. Fax notes: Fee to fax results is $1.00 per page. Copy fee: $.25 per page. Certification fee: $5.00. Fee payee: Circuit Clerk. Personal checks accepted. Prepayment is required.

Floyd County

Circuit Court 127 S Lake Dr, Prestonsburg, KY 41653-3368; 606-886-3090; Fax: 606-886-9075. Hours: 8AM-4PM (EST). *Felony, Civil Actions Over $4,000.*

Civil Records: Access: Mail, in person. Both court and visitors may perform in person searches. No search fee. Required to search: name, years to search. Civil cases indexed by defendant, plaintiff. Civil records on computer since September 1991, prior records on index cards since 1978.

Criminal Records: Access: Mail, in person. Both court and visitors may perform in person searches. No search fee. Required to search: name, years to search, DOB, SSN. Criminal records on computer since September 1991, prior records on index cards since 1978.

General Information: No adoption, mental, juvenile, or sealed records released. SASE required. Turnaround time 2-4 days. Copy fee: $.25 per page. Certification fee: $5.00. Fee payee: Clerk of Circuit Court. Personal checks accepted. Prepayment is required.

District Court PO Box 3368, (127 S Lake Dr), Prestonsburg, KY 41653-3368; 606-886-9114. Hours: 8AM-4PM (EST). *Misdemeanor, Small Claims.*

Note: Small claims can be reached at 606-886-2124

Criminal Records: Access: Phone, mail, in person. Only the court performs in person searches; visitors may not. No search fee. Required to search: name, years to search; also helpful: SSN. Criminal records on computer since 1991, prior records in index cards since 1989. Records are only kept for five years in this office.

General Information: No adoption, mental, juvenile, or sealed records released. SASE required. Turnaround time 2-4 days. Copy fee: $.25 per page. Certification fee: $5.00. Fee payee: Floyd District Court. Personal checks accepted. Prepayment is required.

Franklin County

Circuit Court Box 678, Frankfort, KY 40602; 502-564-8380; Fax: 502-564-8188. Hours: 8AM-4:30PM (EST). *Felony, Civil Actions Over $4,000.*

Civil Records: Access: In person. Visitors must perform in person searches No search fee. Required to search: name, years to search. Civil cases indexed by defendant, plaintiff. Civil records on computer since 1990, prior records on index cards since 1978.

Criminal Records: Access: Fax, in person. Visitors must perform in person searches for themselves. No search fee. Required to search: name, years to search, DOB, SSN. Criminal records on computer since 1990,

prior records on index cards since 1978. All requests are referred to the state Administrator's Office of Courts.

General Information: Public access terminal is available. No adoption, mental, juvenile, or sealed records released. Fax notes: $2.00 for first page, $1.00 each add'l. Copy fee: $.25 per page. Certification fee: $5.00. Fee payee: Circuit Clerk. Personal checks accepted. Prepayment is required.

District Court Box 678, Frankfort, KY 40601; 502-564-7013; Fax: 502-564-8188. Hours: 8AM-4:30PM (EST). *Misdemeanor, Civil Actions Under $4,000, Eviction, Small Claims, Probate.*

Civil Records: Access: In person only. Visitors must perform in person searches for themselves. No search fee. Required to search: name, years to search. Civil cases indexed by defendant, plaintiff. Civil records on computer since 1990, records on index cards since 1978, prior records archived.

Criminal Records: Access: In person only. Visitors must perform in person searches for themselves. No search fee. Required to search: name, years to search, DOB. Criminal records on computer since 1990, records on index cards since 1978, prior records archived.

General Information: Public access terminal is available. No adoption, mental, juvenile, or sealed records released. Copy fee: $.25 per page. Certification fee: $5.00. Fee payee: Franklin Circuit Clerk. Personal checks accepted. Prepayment is required.

Fulton County

Circuit & District Court Box 198, Hickman, KY 42050; 270-236-3944; Fax: 270-236-3729. Hours: 8:30AM-4PM (CST). *Felony, Misdemeanor, Civil, Eviction, Small Claims, Probate.*

Civil Records: Access: Mail, in person. Both court and visitors may perform in person searches. No search fee. Required to search: name, years to search. Civil cases indexed by defendant, plaintiff. Civil records on index and archived since 1843.

Criminal Records: Access: In person only. Visitors must perform in person searches for themselves. No search fee. Required to search: name, years to search. Criminal records on index and archived since 1843.

General Information: Public access terminal is available. No adoption, mental, juvenile, or sealed records released. SASE required. Copy fee: $.25 per page. Certification fee: $5.00. Fee payee: Circuit Clerk. Personal checks accepted. Prepayment is required.

Gallatin County

Circuit Court Box 256, Warsaw, KY 41095; 859-567-5241. Hours: 8AM-5PM M,T,Th,F; Closed W (EST). *Felony, Civil Actions Over $4,000.*

Civil Records: Access: Mail, in person. Both court and visitors may perform in person searches. No search fee. Required to search: name, years to search. Civil cases indexed by defendant, plaintiff. Civil records go back to 1990. Computerized records go to 1993.

Criminal Records: Access: Mail, in person. Both court and visitors may perform in person searches. No search fee. Required to search: name, years to search; also helpful: SSN. Criminal records go back to 1990. Computerized records to 1993.

General Information: Public access terminal is available. No adoption, mental, juvenile, or sealed records released. SASE required. Turnaround time 4 days. Fax notes: Fax back fees $2.00 per page, $3.00 per document. Copy fee: $.25 per page. Certification fee: $5.00. Fee payee: Circuit Clerk. Personal checks accepted. Prepayment is required.

District Court Box 256, Warsaw, KY 41095; 859-567-2388. Hours: 8AM-5PM T,Th,F; 8AM-6PM M; 8AM-Noon Sat (EST). *Misdemeanor, Civil Actions Under $4,000, Eviction, Small Claims, Probate.*

Civil Records: Access: Mail, in person. Both court and visitors may perform in person searches. No search fee. Required to search: name, years to search. Civil cases indexed by defendant, plaintiff. Civil records on computer since November 1993, prior records on index cards since 1978.

Criminal Records: Access: Mail, in person. Both court and visitors may perform in person searches. No search fee. Required to search: name, years to search, DOB; also helpful: SSN. Criminal records on computer since November 1993, prior records on index cards since 1978.

General Information: Public access terminal is available. No adoption, mental, juvenile, or sealed records released. Turnaround time 1-2 days. Fax notes: Fee to fax results is $2.00 per page, $3.00 per document. Copy fee: $.25 per page. Certification fee: $5.00. Fee payee: District Clerk. Personal checks accepted. Prepayment is required.

Garrard County

Circuit & District Court 7 Public Square, Courthouse Annex, Lancaster, KY 40444; 859-792-6032; Fax: 859-792-6414. Hours: 8AM-4PM M,T,TH,F, 8AM-Noon Wed & Sat (EST). *Felony, Misdemeanor, Civil, Eviction, Small Claims, Probate.*

Civil Records: Access: In person only. Visitors must perform in person searches for themselves. Search fee: No search fee. Required to search: name, years to search. Civil cases indexed by defendant, plaintiff. Civil records in index since 1978.

Criminal Records: Access: In person only. Visitors must perform in person searches for themselves. No search fee. Required to search: name, years to search; also helpful: address, DOB, SSN. Criminal records in index since 1978.

General Information: Public access terminal is available. No adoption, mental, juvenile, or sealed records released. Copy fee: $.25 per page. Certification fee: $5.00. Fee payee: Circuit Clerk. Personal checks accepted. Prepayment is required.

Grant County

Circuit & District Court Courthouse 101 N Main, Williamstown, KY 41097; 859-824-4467. Hours: 8AM-4PM (EST). *Felony, Misdemeanor, Civil, Eviction, Small Claims, Probate.*

Civil Records: Access: In person only. Visitors must perform in person searches for themselves. No search fee. Required to search: name, years to search. Civil cases indexed by defendant, plaintiff. Civil records on computer back to 1992, prior records on index cards for District Court since 1978: Circuit Court since 1988.

Criminal Records: Access: In person only. Visitors must perform in person searches for themselves. No search fee. Required to search: name, years to search, DOB; also helpful: SSN. Criminal records on computer back to 1992, prior records on index cards since 1988.

General Information: Public access terminal is available. No adoption, mental, juvenile, or sealed records released. Copy fee: $.25 per page. Certification fee: $5.00. Fee payee: Circuit Clerk. Personal checks accepted. Prepayment is required.

Graves County

Circuit & District Court Courthouse 100 E Broadway, Mayfield, KY 42066; 270-247-1733; Fax: 270-247-7358. Hours: 8AM-4:30PM (CST). *Felony, Misdemeanor, Civil, Eviction, Small Claims, Probate.*

Civil Records: Access: In person only. Visitors must perform in person searches for themselves. No search

fee. Required to search: name, years to search. Civil cases indexed by defendant, plaintiff. Civil records on computer since June, 1994, prior records on index cards since 1978.

Criminal Records: Access: In person only. Visitors must perform in person searches for themselves. No search fee. Required to search: name, years to search, DOB; also helpful: SSN. Criminal records on computer since June, 1994, prior records on index cards since 1978.

General Information: Public access terminal is available. No adoption, mental, juvenile, or sealed records released. Copy fee: $.25 per page. Certification fee: $5.00. Fee payee: Circuit Clerk. Personal checks accepted. Prepayment is required.

Grayson County

Circuit & District Court 125 E White Oak, Leitchfield, KY 42754; 270-259-3040; Fax: 270-259-9866. Hours: 8AM-4PM M-F; 8AM-Noon Sat (CST). *Felony, Misdemeanor, Civil, Eviction, Small Claims, Probate.*

Civil Records: Access: Mail, in person. Both court and visitors may perform in person searches. Search fee: $10.00 per name. Required to search: name, years to search. Civil cases indexed by defendant, plaintiff. Civil records on computer since 05/94, prior records on index cards since 1978.

Criminal Records: Access: Mail, in person. Both court and visitors may perform in person searches. Search fee: $10.00. Required to search: name, years to search; also helpful: DOB, SSN. Criminal records on computer since 05/94, prior records on index cards since 1978.

General Information: Public access terminal is available. No adoption, mental, juvenile, or sealed records released. SASE required. Turnaround time 2 days. Copy fee: $.25 per page. Certification fee: $5.00. Fee payee: Circuit Clerk. Personal checks accepted. Prepayment is required.

Green County

Circuit & District Court 203 W Court St, Greensburg, KY 42743; 270-932-5631; Fax: 270-932-6468. Hours: 8AM-4PM M-W, F; 8AM-12:30PM Sat (EST). *Felony, Misdemeanor, Civil, Eviction, Small Claims, Probate.*

Civil Records: Access: Fax, mail, in person. Both court and visitors may perform in person searches. No search fee. Required to search: name, years to search; also helpful: address. Civil cases indexed by defendant, plaintiff. Civil records on index cards since 1978; computerized records since 1978.

Criminal Records: Access: Fax, mail, in person. Both court and visitors may perform in person searches. No search fee. Required to search: name, years to search; also helpful: address, DOB, SSN. Criminal records on index cards since 1978; computerized records since 1978.

General Information: Public access terminal is available. No adoption, mental, juvenile, or sealed records released. SASE required. Turnaround time 1-2 days. Fax notes: No fee to fax results; will only fax to 800 numbers. Copy fee: $.25 per page. Fee payee: Circuit Clerk. Personal checks accepted. Prepayment is required.

Greenup County

Circuit & District Court Courthouse Annex, Greenup, KY 41144; 606-473-9869; Fax: 606-473-7388. Hours: 9AM-4:30PM M-F (EST). *Felony, Misdemeanor, Civil, Eviction, Small Claims, Probate.*

Civil Records: Access: In person only. Both court and visitors may perform in person searches. No search fee. Required to search: name, years to search. Civil cases indexed by defendant, plaintiff. Civil records on

computer since 1990, prior records on index cards since 1978.

Criminal Records: Access: In person only. Visitors must perform in person searches for themselves. No search fee. Required to search: name, years to search, DOB; also helpful: SSN. Criminal records on computer since 1990, prior records on index cards since 1978.

General Information: Public access terminal is available. No adoption, mental, juvenile, or sealed records released. Fax notes: Fee to fax results is $3.00 1st page, $1.00 each add'l. Fee payee: $.25 per page. Certification fee: $5.00. Fee payee: Circuit Clerk. Personal checks accepted. Prepayment is required.

Hancock County

Circuit & District Court Courthouse, PO Box 250, Hawesville, KY 42348; 270-927-8144; Fax: 270-927-8629. Hours: 8AM-4PM M,T,W,F; 8AM-5:30PM Th (CST). *Felony, Misdemeanor, Civil, Eviction, Small Claims, Probate.*

Civil Records: Access: Mail, fax, in person. Both court and visitors may perform in person searches. No search fee. Required to search: name, years to search. Civil cases indexed by defendant, plaintiff. Civil records on computer since August, 1994, prior records on index cards.

Criminal Records: Access: Mail, fax, in person. Both court and visitors may perform in person searches. No search fee. Required to search: name, years to search, DOB; also helpful: SSN. Criminal records on computer since August, 1994, prior records on index cards.

General Information: Public access terminal is available. No adoption, mental, juvenile, or sealed records released. SASE required. Turnaround time 1-2 days. Fax notes: Fee to fax results is $2.00 for 1st page; $1.00 each add'l. Copy fee: $.25 per page. Certification fee: $5.00. Fee payee: Circuit Clerk. Personal checks accepted. Prepayment is required.

Hardin County

Circuit & District Court Hardin County Justice Center, 120 E Dixie Ave, Elizabethtown, KY 42701; 270-766-5000; Fax: 270-766-5243. Hours: 8AM-4:30PM; (EST). *Felony, Misdemeanor, Civil, Eviction, Small Claims, Probate.*

Civil Records: Access: In person only. Visitors must perform in person searches for themselves. No search fee. Required to search: name, years to search. Civil cases indexed by defendant, plaintiff. Civil records on computer since 03/28/94, prior records on index cards since 1978.

Criminal Records: Access: In person only. Visitors must perform in person searches for themselves. No search fee. Required to search: name, years to search, DOB. Criminal records on computer since 03/28/94, prior records on index cards since 1978.

General Information: No adoption, mental, juvenile, or sealed records released. Fax notes: Fee to fax results is $2.00 1st page; $1.00 each add'l. Copy fee: $.25 per page. Certification fee: $5.00. Fee payee: Circuit Clerk. Personal checks accepted. Prepayment is required.

Radcliff District Court 220 Freedom Way, Radcliff, KY 40160; 270-351-1299/4799; Fax: 270-351-1301. Hours: 8:30AM-12, 12:20-4PM (EST). *Probate, Eviction.*

Harlan County

Circuit & District Court Box 190, Harlan, KY 40831; 606-573-2680. Hours: 8AM-4:30PM (EST). *Felony, Misdemeanor, Civil, Eviction, Small Claims, Probate.*

Civil Records: Access: In person only. Visitors must perform in person searches for themselves. No search fee. Required to search: name, years to search. Civil cases indexed by defendant, plaintiff. Civil records on

computer since August, 1991, on index cards since 1978, records prior to 1988 are archived in Frankfort.
Criminal Records: Access: In person only. Visitors must perform in person searches for themselves. No search fee. Required to search: name, years to search, DOB; also helpful: SSN. Criminal records on computer since August, 1991, on index cards since 1978, records prior to 1988 are archived in Frankfort.
General Information: Public access terminal is available. No adoption, mental, juvenile, sealed or domestic violence records released. Fax notes: Fee to fax results is $2.00 for 1st page; $1.00 each add'l. Copy fee: $.25 per page. Certification fee: $5.00. Fee payee: Circuit Clerk. Only local personal checks accepted. Prepayment is required.

Harrison County

Circuit & District Court Courthouse Box 10, Cynthiana, KY 41031; 859-234-1914. Hours: 8:30AM-4:30PM M-F, 9AM-12PM Sat (EST). *Felony, Misdemeanor, Civil, Eviction, Small Claims, Probate.*

Note: Effective 8-1-02, copy fee is $.25 and certifictaion fee is $5.00.

Civil Records: Access: Mail, in person. Both court and visitors may perform in person searches. No search fee. Required to search: name, years to search. Civil cases indexed by defendant, plaintiff. Civil records on index cards since 1978 (circuit only); on computer back to 1995; others back to 1953.
Criminal Records: Access: In person only. Visitors must perform in person searches for themselves. No search fee. Required to search: name, years to search, DOB; also helpful: SSN. Criminal records on index cards since 1978 (circuit only); on computer back to 1995; others back to 1953.
General Information: Public access terminal is available. No adoption, mental, juvenile, or sealed records released. SASE required. Turnaround time 2-4 days. Copy fee: $.25 per page. Certification fee: $5.00. Fee payee: Circuit Clerk. Personal checks accepted. Prepayment is required.

Hart County

Circuit & District Court Box 248, Munfordville, KY 42765; 270-524-5181. Hours: 8AM-4PM M-F (CST). *Felony, Misdemeanor, Civil, Eviction, Small Claims, Probate.*

Civil Records: Access: In person only. Visitors must perform in person searches for themselves. No search fee. Required to search: name, years to search; also helpful: address. Civil cases indexed by defendant, plaintiff. Civil records on index cards since 1978, computerized since 03/95.
Criminal Records: Access: In person only. Visitors must perform in person searches for themselves. No search fee. Required to search: name, years to search, DOB, SSN; also helpful: address. Criminal records on index cards since 1978, computerized since 03/95.
General Information: Public access terminal is available. No adoption, mental, juvenile, or sealed records released. Copy fee: $.25 per page. Certification fee: $5.00. Fee payee: Circuit Clerk. Business checks accepted. Prepayment is required.

Henderson County

Circuit & District Court PO Box 675, Henderson, KY 42420; 270-826-2405/1566; Fax: 270-831-2710 (District). Hours: 8AM-6PM M; 8AM-4:30PM T-F (CST). *Felony, Civil Actions Over $4,000.*

Civil Records: Access: In person only. Visitors must perform in person searches for themselves. No search fee. Required to search: name, years to search. Civil cases indexed by defendant, plaintiff. Civil records on computer from March, 1991, records on index cards from 1978 to March, 1991.

Criminal Records: Access: In person only. Visitors must perform in person searches for themselves. No search fee. Required to search: name, years to search, DOB; also helpful: SSN. Criminal records on computer from March, 1991, records on index cards from 1978 to March, 1991.
General Information: No adoption, mental, juvenile, or sealed records released. Copy fee: $.25 per page. Certification fee: $5.00. Fee payee: Circuit Clerk. Personal checks accepted. Prepayment is required.

Henry County

Circuit & District Court PO Box 359, New Castle, KY 40050; 502-845-7551; Fax: 502-845-6738. Hours: 8AM-4:30PM M-F (EST). *Felony, Misdemeanor, Civil, Eviction, Small Claims, Probate.*

Civil Records: Access: In person only. Visitors must perform in person searches for themselves. No search fee. Required to search: name, years to search. Civil cases indexed by defendant, plaintiff. Civil records on computer since May, 1994, records on docket books since 1800s.
Criminal Records: Access: In person only. Visitors must perform in person searches for themselves. No search fee. Required to search: name, years to search; also helpful: SSN. Criminal records on computer since May, 1994, records on docket books since 1800s.
General Information: Public access terminal is available. No adoption, mental, juvenile, or sealed records released. Copy fee: $.25 per page. Certification fee: $5.00. Fee payee: Circuit Clerk. Personal checks accepted. Prepayment is required.

Hickman County

Circuit & District Court 109 S Washington St, Clinton, KY 42031; 270-653-3901; Fax: 270-653-3989. Hours: 8AM-4PM (CST). *Felony, Misdemeanor, Civil, Eviction, Small Claims, Probate.*

Civil Records: Access: Mail, in person. Both court and visitors may perform in person searches. No search fee. Required to search: name, years to search. Civil cases indexed by defendant, plaintiff. Civil records on computer from 06/94 to present, on index from 1978 to 06/94. If court does search, request must be in writing.
Criminal Records: Access: Mail, in person. Both court and visitors may perform in person searches. No search fee. Required to search: name, years to search, DOB; also helpful: SSN. Criminal records on computer from 06/94 to present, on index from 1978 to 06/94. Requests must be in writing.
General Information: Public access terminal is available. No adoption, mental, juvenile, or sealed records released. SASE required. Turnaround time same day. Fax notes: Fee to fax results is $2.00 1st pg; $1.00 each add'l. Copy fee: $.25 per page. Certification fee: $5.00. Fee payee: Circuit Clerk. Personal checks accepted. Prepayment is required.

Hopkins County

Circuit & District Court Courthouse 30 S Main St, Madisonville, KY 42431; 270-824-7502; Fax: 270-824-7032. Hours: 8AM-4PM (CST). *Felony, Misdemeanor, Civil, Eviction, Small Claims, Probate.*

Civil Records: Access: In person only. Visitors must perform in person searches for themselves. No search fee. Required to search: name, years to search. Civil cases indexed by defendant, plaintiff. Civil records on computer back to 6/1991; on index cards from 1978 to 1991.
Criminal Records: Access: In person only. Visitors must perform in person searches for themselves. No search fee. Required to search: name, years to search, signed release; also helpful: DOB, SSN. Criminal records on computer back to 6/1991, on index cards from 1978 to 1991, archived since 1800s.

Jackson County

Circuit Court PO Box 84, McKee, KY 40447; 606-287-7783; Fax: 606-287-3277. Hours: 8AM-4PM M-F 8AM-Noon Sat (EST). *Felony, Civil Actions Over $4,000.*

Civil Records: Access: Fax, mail, in person. Both court and visitors may perform in person searches. No search fee. Required to search: name, years to search; also helpful: address. Civil cases indexed by defendant, plaintiff. Civil records on computer from May, 1993 to present, on index cards from 1978 to 1993.
Criminal Records: Access: Fax, mail, in person. Both court and visitors may perform in person searches. No search fee. Required to search: name, years to search, DOB; also helpful: SSN. Criminal records on computer from May, 1993 to present, on index cards from 1978 to 1993.
General Information: Public access terminal is available. No adoption, mental, juvenile, or sealed records released. SASE required. Turnaround time 2 days. Fax notes: Fee to fax results is $1.00 per page. Copy fee: $.25 per page. Certification fee: $5.00. Fee payee: Jackson County Circuit Clerk. Personal checks accepted.

District Court PO Box 84, McKee, KY 40447; 606-287-8651; Fax: 606-287-3277. Hours: 8AM-4PM M-F; 8AM-Noon Sat (EST). *Misdemeanor, Civil Actions Under $4,000, Eviction, Small Claims, Probate.*

Civil Records: Access: Fax, mail, in person. Both court and visitors may perform in person searches. No search fee. Required to search: name, years to search. Civil cases indexed by defendant, plaintiff. Civil records on computer back to May, 1993, on index cards from 1978.
Criminal Records: Access: Fax, mail, in person. Both court and visitors may perform in person searches. No search fee. Required to search: name, years to search, DOB; also helpful: SSN. Criminal records on computer back to May, 1993; on index cards from 1990.
General Information: Public access terminal is available. No adoption, mental, juvenile, or sealed records released. SASE required. Turnaround time 1 week. Copy fee: $.25 per page. Certification fee: $5.00. Fee payee: Jackson County District Clerk. Personal checks accepted. Prepayment is required.

Jefferson County

Circuit & District Court Hall of Justice 600 W Jefferson St, Louisville, KY 40202; 502-595-3064; Civil phone: 502-595-3015; Criminal phone: 502-595-3042; Fax: 502-595-4629. *Felony, Misdemeanor, Civil, Eviction, Small Claims, Probate.*

Civil Records: Access: Phone, mail, in person. Visitors must perform in person seraches No search fee. Required to search: name, years to search. Civil cases indexed by defendant, plaintiff. Civil records on computer from 1988 to present, on index cards from 1978 to 1988.
Criminal Records: Access: Mail, in person. Visitors must perform in person searches No search fee. Required to search: name, years to search; also helpful: DOB, SSN. Criminal records on computer from 1988 to present, on index cards from 1978 to 1988.
General Information: Public access terminal is available. No adoption, mental, juvenile, or sealed records released. SASE not required. Turnaround time 3 days. Copy fee: $.25 per page. Certification fee: $5.00.

General Information: Public access terminal is available. No adoption, mental, juvenile, or sealed records released. Fax notes: Fee to fax results is $2.00 1st page; $1.00 each add'l. Copy fee: $.25 per page. Certification fee: $5.00. Fee payee: Circuit Clerk. Personal checks accepted. Prepayment is required.

Fee payee: Circuit Clerk. Personal checks accepted. Credit cards accepted. Accepted for District Criminal Traffic. Prepayment is required.

Jessamine County

Circuit Court 107 N Main St, Nicholasville, KY 40356; 859-885-4531. Hours: 8AM-4:30PM M-W, F; 8AM-12PM TH (EST). *Felony, Civil Actions Over $4,000.*

Civil Records: Access: Mail, in person. Visitors must perform in person searches No search fee. Required to search: name, years to search. Civil cases indexed by defendant, plaintiff. Civil records on computer from June, 1992 to present, on index cards from 1978 to 1992.

Criminal Records: Access: Mail, in person. Visitors must perform in person searches No search fee. Required to search: name, years to search, DOB; also helpful: SSN. Criminal records on computer from June, 1992 to present, on index cards from 1978 to 1992.

General Information: Public access terminal is available. No adoption, mental, juvenile, or sealed records released. SASE required. Turnaround time 1-2 days or refer to A.O.C. in Frankfort. Copy fee: $.25 per page. Certification fee: $5.00. Fee payee: Jessamine Circuit Clerk. Personal checks accepted. Prepayment is required.

District Court 107 N Main St, Nicholasville, KY 40356; 859-887-1005; Fax: 859-887-0425. Hours: 8AM-4:30PM M-W; 8AM-Noon TH; 8AM-4:30PM F (EST). *Misdemeanor, Civil Actions Under $4,000, Eviction, Small Claims, Probate.*

Civil Records: Access: Mail, in person. Both court and visitors may perform in person searches. No search fee. Required to search: name, years to search. Civil cases indexed by defendant, plaintiff. Civil records on computer since 1992, on file cards prior.

Criminal Records: Access: Mail, in person. Both court and visitors may perform in person searches. No search fee. Required to search: name, years to search; also helpful: DOB, SSN. Criminal records on computer since 1992, on file cards prior.

General Information: Public access terminal is available. No adoption, mental, juvenile, or sealed records released. SASE required. Turnaround time 2-4 days. Copy fee: $.25 per page. Certification fee: $5.00. Fee payee: Circuit Clerk. Personal checks accepted. Prepayment is required.

Johnson County

Circuit & District Court Box 1405, Paintsville, KY 41240; 606-789-5181; Fax: 606-789-4192. Hours: 8AM-4:30PM; 8:30AM-Noon Sat Driver's license only (EST). *Felony, Misdemeanor, Civil, Eviction, Small Claims, Probate.*

Civil Records: Access: Phone, mail, in person. Both court and visitors may perform in person searches. No search fee. Required to search: name, years to search. Civil cases indexed by defendant, plaintiff. Civil records on computer since 09/88, on index cards from 1978 to 1988, books from 1843 to 1978. From 1988 and prior files are at the archives in Frankfort.

Criminal Records: Access: In person only. Visitors must perform in person searches for themselves. No search fee. Required to search: name, years to search, DOB, SSN. Criminal records on computer since 09/88, on index cards from 1978 to 1988, books from 1843 to 1978. From 1988 and prior files are at the archives in Frankfort. Court will not conduct searches. Contact AOC for statewide search by mail.

General Information: Public access terminal is available. No adoption, mental, juvenile, or sealed records released. SASE required. Turnaround time at least 3 days. Copy fee: $.25 per page. Certification fee:

$5.00. Fee payee: Circuit Clerk. Personal checks accepted. Prepayment is required.

Kenton County

Circuit Court 230 Madison Ave (PO Box 669), Covington, KY 41011; 859-292-6521; Fax: 859-292-6611. Hours: 8AM-5PM (EST). *Felony, Civil Actions Over $4,000.*

www.aoc.state.ky.us/kenton

Civil Records: Access: Mail, in person. Both court and visitors may perform in person searches. Search fee: No search fee. Required to search: name, years to search. Civil cases indexed by defendant, plaintiff. Civil records on computer back to 06/89, on index cards from 1800s.

Criminal Records: Access: Mail, in person. Visitors must perform in person searches for themselves. No search fee. Required to search: name, years to search, DOB or SSN. Criminal records on computer back to 6/89.

General Information: Public access terminal is available. No adoption, mental, juvenile, or sealed records released. SASE required. Turnaround time 1-2 days. Copy fee: $.25 per page. Certification fee: $5.00. Fee payee: Kenton Circuit Clerk. Prepayment is required.

District Court 230 Madison Ave, 3rd Fl, Covington, KY 41011; 859-292-6523; Fax: 859-292-6611. Hours: 7AM-5PM (EST). *Misdemeanor, Civil Actions Under $4,000, Eviction, Small Claims, Probate.*

www.aoc.state.ky.us/kenton

Civil Records: Access: Mail, in person. Only the court performs in person searches; visitors may not. No search fee. Required to search: name, years to search. Civil cases indexed by defendant, plaintiff. Civil records on computer from 1989 to present, on index cards from 1983.

Criminal Records: Access: In person only. Visitors must perform in person searches for themselves. No search fee. Required to search: name, years to search DOB; also helpful: SSN. Criminal records on computer from 05/91 to present, index cards for the last 5 years.

General Information: Public access terminal is available. No adoption, mental, juvenile, or sealed records released. SASE required. Turnaround time 1 week. Fax notes: Fee to fax results is $3.00 per document. Copy fee: $.25 per page. Certification fee: $5.00. Fee payee: Circuit Clerk. Business checks accepted. Prepayment is required.

Knott County

Circuit & District Court PO Box 1317, Hindman, KY 41822; 606-785-5021. Hours: 8AM-4PM; 8AM-noon Sat. (EST). *Felony, Misdemeanor, Civil, Eviction, Small Claims, Probate.*

Civil Records: Access: Fax, mail, in person. Both court and visitors may perform in person searches. No search fee. Required to search: name, years to search. Civil cases indexed by defendant, plaintiff. Civil records in index files.

Criminal Records: Access: Phone, fax, mail, in person. Both court and visitors may perform in person searches. No search fee. Required to search: name, years to search, DOB; also helpful: SSN. Criminal records in index files; on computer back to 11/1994.

General Information: Public access terminal is available. No adoption, mental, juvenile, or sealed records released. SASE required. Turnaround time 2-4 days. Copy fee: $.25 per page. Certification fee: $5.00. Fee payee: Circuit Clerk. Personal checks accepted. Prepayment is required.

Knox County

Circuit & District Court PO Box 760, Barbourville, KY 40906; 606-546-3075 (Circuit) 546-3232 (Dist); Fax: 606-546-7949. Hours: 8AM-4:30PM M-F; 8:30AM-noon Sat (EST). *Felony, Misdemeanor, Civil, Eviction, Small Claims, Probate.*

Civil Records: Access: In person only. Visitors must perform in person searches for themselves. No search fee. Required to search: name, years to search. Civil cases indexed by defendant, plaintiff. Civil records go back to 1978; on computer back to 07/92.

Criminal Records: Access: In person only. Visitors must perform in person searches for themselves. No search fee. Required to search: name, years to search, DOB; also helpful: SSN. Criminal records go back to 1978; on computer back to 07/92.

General Information: Public access terminal is available. No adoption, mental, juvenile, or sealed records released. Fax notes: Fee to fax results is $.15 per page. Copy fee: $.25 per page. Certification fee: $5.00. Fee payee: Circuit Clerk. Personal checks accepted. Prepayment is required.

Larue County

Circuit & District Court Courthouse Annex, PO Box 191, Hodgenville, KY 42748; 270-358-3421; Fax: 270-358-3731. Hours: 8AM-4PM (EST). *Felony, Misdemeanor, Civil, Eviction, Small Claims, Probate.*

Civil Records: Access: Fax, mail, in person. Both court and visitors may perform in person searches. No search fee. Required to search: name, years to search. Civil cases indexed by defendant, plaintiff. Civil records on computer since 1995.

Criminal Records: Access: Fax, mail, in person. Both court and visitors may perform in person searches. No search fee. Required to search: name, years to search, DOB; also helpful: SSN. Criminal records on computer since 1995.

General Information: Public access terminal is available. No adoption, mental, juvenile, or sealed records released. SASE required. Turnaround time 2 days. Fax notes: No fee to fax results. Copy fee: $.25 per page. Fee payee: Circuit Clerk. Personal checks accepted. Prepayment is required.

Laurel County

Circuit & District Court Box 1798, London, KY 40743-1798; 606-864-2863; Fax: 606-864-8264. Hours: 8AM-4PM (EST). *Felony, Misdemeanor, Civil, Eviction, Small Claims, Probate.*

Civil Records: Access: In person only. Visitors must perform in person searches for themselves. No search fee. Required to search: name, years to search. Civil cases indexed by defendant, plaintiff. Civil records on computer and index books.

Criminal Records: Access: In person only. Visitors must perform in person searches for themselves. No search fee. Required to search: name, years to search, DOB, SSN. Criminal records on computer and index books.

General Information: Public access terminal is available. No adoption, mental, juvenile, or sealed records released. Copy fee: $.25 per page. Certification fee: $5.00. Fee payee: Circuit Clerk. Personal checks accepted. Prepayment is required.

Lawrence County

Circuit & District Court Courthouse, PO Box 212, Louisa, KY 41230; 606-638-4215; Fax: 606-638-0264. Hours: 8:30AM-4:30PM M-F 8:30AM-Noon Sat (EST). *Felony, Misdemeanor, Civil, Eviction, Small Claims, Probate.*

Note: Current docket information is available online on the statewide system at www.dockets.kycourts.net.

Civil Records: Access: Mail, fax, in person. Both court and visitors may perform in person searches. No search fee. Required to search: name, years to search. Civil cases indexed by defendant, plaintiff. Civil records on computer from 11/94, index cards from 1978.

Criminal Records: Access: Mail, fax, in person. Both court and visitors may perform in person searches. No search fee. Required to search: name, years to search; also helpful: DOB, SSN. Criminal records on computer from 11/94, index cards from 1978.

General Information: Public access terminal is available. No adoption, mental, juvenile, or sealed records released. SASE required. Turnaround time within 1 week. Fax notes: Fee to fax results is $2.00 per page. Copy fee: $.25 per page. Certification fee: $5.00. Fee payee: Circuit Clerk. Personal checks accepted.

Lee County

Circuit & District Court Box E, Beattyville, KY 41311; 606-464-8400; Fax: 606-464-0144. Hours: 8AM-4PM M-F; 8:30AM-11:30AM Sat (EST). *Felony, Misdemeanor, Civil, Eviction, Small Claims, Probate.*

Civil Records: Access: In person only. Visitors must perform in person searches for themselves. No search fee. Required to search: name, years to search. Civil cases indexed by defendant, plaintiff. Civil records on computer from 09/94 to present, on index cards from 1978.

Criminal Records: Access: In person only. Visitors must perform in person searches for themselves. No search fee. Required to search: name, years to search, DOB; also helpful: SSN. Criminal records on computer from 09/94 to present, on index cards from 1978.

General Information: Public access terminal is available. No adoption, mental, juvenile, or sealed records released. Copy fee: $.25 per page. Certification fee: $5.00. Fee payee: Circuit Clerk. Only cashiers checks and money orders accepted. Attorney checks accepted. Prepayment is required.

Leslie County

Circuit & District Court Box 1750, Hyden, KY 41749; 606-672-2505; Fax: 606-672-5128. Hours: 8AM-5PM M; 8AM-4PM T-F; 8AM-Noon Sat (EST). *Felony, Misdemeanor, Civil, Eviction, Small Claims, Probate.*

Civil Records: Access: In person. Visitors must perform in person seraches No search fee. Required to search: name, years to search. Civil cases indexed by plaintiff. Civil records on computer and index books.

Criminal Records: Access: In person only. Visitors must perform in person searches for themselves. No search fee. Required to search: name, years to search; also helpful: address, DOB, SSN. Criminal records on computer and index books.

General Information: Public access terminal is available. No adoption, mental, juvenile, or sealed records released. Fax notes: Fee to fax results is $2.00 for first page, $1.00 each add'l. Copy fee: $.25 per page. Certification fee: $5.00. Fee payee: Circuit Clerk. Personal checks accepted. Prepayment is required.

Letcher County

Circuit & District Court 156 W Main St, #201, Whitesburg, KY 41858; 606-633-7559/8810; Fax: 606-633-5864. Hours: 8:30AM-4PM M-F; 8:30AM-12PM first Sat of month (EST). *Felony, Misdemeanor, Civil, Eviction, Small Claims, Probate.*

Civil Records: Access: Fax, mail, in person. Both court and visitors may perform in person searches. No search fee. Required to search: name, years to search; also helpful: address. Civil cases indexed by defendant, plaintiff. Civil records on computer go back to 11/1991; on index books from 1986 to 1991. Files maintained in

office. Records from 1985 to 1800s in archives in Frankfort.

Criminal Records: Access: In person only. Visitors must perform in person searches for themselves. No search fee. Required to search: name, years to search, DOB, SSN; also helpful: address. Criminal records on computer go back to 11/1991; on index books from 1986 to 1991. Files maintained in office. Records from 1985 to 1800s in archives in Frankfort. Contact AOC 800-928-6381 for statewide search by mail.

General Information: Public access terminal is available. No adoption, mental, juvenile, or sealed records released. SASE required. Turnaround time 2-4 days. Fax notes: Fee to fax results is $2.00 for 1st page, $1.00 each add'l. Copy fee: $.25 per page. Certification fee: $5.00. Fee payee: Circuit Clerk. Personal checks accepted. Prepayment is required.

Lewis County

Circuit & District Court PO Box 70, Vanceburg, KY 41179; 606-796-3053; Fax: 606-796-3030. Hours: 8AM-4:30PM M,T,Th,F 8:30-Noon W,Sat (EST). *Felony, Misdemeanor, Civil, Eviction, Small Claims, Probate.*

Civil Records: Access: Phone, mail, in person. Both court and visitors may perform in person searches. No search fee. Required to search: name, years to search. Civil cases indexed by defendant, plaintiff. Computerized from 1994, civil records on index cards back to 1955.

Criminal Records: Access: Mail, in person. Both court and visitors may perform in person searches. No search fee. Required to search: name, years to search, DOB; also helpful: SSN. Computerized from 1994, criminal records on index cards back to 1960s.

General Information: Public access terminal is available. No adoption, mental, juvenile, or sealed records released. SASE required. Turnaround time within 1 week. Copy fee: $.25 per page. Certification fee: $5.00. Fee payee: Circuit Clerk. Personal checks accepted. Prepayment is required.

Lincoln County

Circuit & District Court 101 E Main, Stanford, KY 40484; 606-365-2535; Fax: 606-365-3389. Hours: 8AM-4PM; 9AM-12PM Sat. (EST). *Felony, Misdemeanor, Civil, Eviction, Small Claims, Probate.*

Civil Records: Access: In person only. Visitors must perform in person searches for themselves. No search fee. Required to search: name, years to search. Civil cases indexed by defendant, plaintiff. Civil records on computer from 05/94, index cards prior, archived from 978 to 1900.

Criminal Records: Access: In person only. Visitors must perform in person searches for themselves. No search fee. Required to search: name, years to search; also helpful: SSN. Criminal records on computer from 05/94, index cards prior, archived from 978 to 1900.

General Information: Public access terminal is available. No adoption, mental, juvenile, or sealed records released. Copy fee: $.25 per page. Fee payee: Circuit Clerk. Personal checks accepted.

Livingston County

Circuit & District Court PO Box 160, Smithland, KY 42081; 270-928-2172. Hours: 8AM-6PM M 8AM-4PM T-F (CST). *Felony, Misdemeanor, Civil, Eviction, Small Claims, Probate.*

Civil Records: Access: In person only. Visitors must perform in person searches for themselves. No search fee. Required to search: name, years to search. Civil cases indexed by defendant, plaintiff. Civil records on computer from 1993 to present, index cards prior, archived from 1799 to 1851.

Criminal Records: Access: In person only. Visitors must perform in person searches for themselves. No

search fee. Required to search: name, years to search, DOB; also helpful: SSN. Criminal records on computer from 1993 to present, index cards prior, archived from 1799 to 1851.

General Information: Public access terminal is available. No adoption, mental, juvenile, or sealed records released. Copy fee: $.25 per page. Certification fee: $5.00. Fee payee: Circuit Clerk. Personal checks accepted. Prepayment is required.

Logan County

Circuit Court Box 420, Russellville, KY 42276-0420; 270-726-2424; Fax: 270-726-7893. Hours: 8AM-4:30PM M-Th; 8AM-5PM F (CST). *Felony, Civil Actions Over $4,000.*

Civil Records: Access: In person only. Visitors must perform in person searches for themselves. No search fee. Required to search: name, years to search. Civil cases indexed by defendant, plaintiff. Civil records on computer from April, 1992 to present, on index card from 1978 to 1992.

Criminal Records: Access: In person only. Visitors must perform in person searches for themselves. No search fee. Required to search: name, years to search, DOB, SSN. Criminal records on computer from April, 1992 to present, on index card from 1978 to 1992.

General Information: Public access terminal is available. No adoptions, mental, juvenile or sealed records released. Copy fee: $.25 per page. Certification fee: $3.00. Fee payee: Circuit Clerk. Only cashiers checks and money orders accepted. Prepayment is required.

District Court Box 420, Russellville, KY 42276; 270-726-3107; Fax: 270-726-7893. Hours: 8AM-4:30PM (CST). *Misdemeanor, Civil Actions Under $4,000, Eviction, Small Claims, Probate.*

Civil Records: Access: In person only. Visitors must perform in person searches for themselves. No search fee. Required to search: name, years to search. Civil cases indexed by defendant, plaintiff. Civil records on computer since 1992, index cards from 1978 to 1992.

Criminal Records: Access: In person only. Visitors must perform in person searches for themselves. No search fee. Required to search: name, years to search, DOB; also helpful: SSN. Criminal records on computer since 1992, index cards from 1978 to 1992.

General Information: Public access terminal is available. No adoption, mental, juvenile, or sealed records released. Copy fee: $.25 per page. Certification fee: $5.00. Fee payee: Logan Circuit Clerk. Personal checks accepted. Prepayment is required.

Lyon County

Circuit & District Court Box 565, Eddyville, KY 42038; 270-388-7231. Hours: 8AM-4PM (CST). *Felony, Misdemeanor, Civil, Eviction, Small Claims, Probate.*

Note: This court also handles domestic violense, traffic, and juvenile cases.

Civil Records: Access: In person only. Both court and visitors may perform in person searches. No search fee. Required to search: name, years to search. Civil cases indexed by defendant, plaintiff. Civil records on computer from 11/94 to present, on index cards from 1978 to 1994.

Criminal Records: Access: In person only. Both court and visitors may perform in person searches. No search fee. Required to search: name, years to search, DOB; also helpful: SSN. Criminal records on computer from 11/94 to present. Circuit court records are on index cards from 1978 to 1994, but not District court records.

General Information: Public access terminal is available. No adoption, mental, juvenile, or sealed records released. Copy fee: $.25 per page. Certification fee: $5.00. Fee payee: Circuit Clerk. Personal checks accepted. Prepayment is required.

Madison County

Circuit Court PO Box 813, Richmond, KY 40476-0813; 859-624-4793. Hours: 8AM-4PM (EST). *Felony, Civil Actions Over $4,000.*

www.kycourts.net/Circuit/Circuit_Intro.shtm

Civil Records: Access: In person only. Visitors must perform in person searches for themselves. Search fee: No search fee. Required to search: name, years to search. Civil cases indexed by defendant, plaintiff. Civil records on computer back to 10/1990 to present, on index cards from 1978 to 1990.

Criminal Records: Access: In person only. Visitors must perform in person searches for themselves. No search fee. Required to search: name, years to search; also helpful: DOB, SSN. Criminal records on computer back to 10/1990 to present, on index cards from 1978 to 1990. Contact AOC for statewide searches by mail.

General Information: Public access terminal is available. No adoption, mental, juvenile, or sealed records released. Copy fee: $.25 per page. Certification fee: $5.00. Fee payee: Madison Circuit Clerk. Personal checks accepted. Prepayment is required.

District Court Madison Hall of Justice, 351 West Main St, Richmond, KY 40475; 859-624-4722; Fax: 859-624-4746. Hours: 8AM-4PM (EST). *Misdemeanor, Civil Actions Under $4,000, Eviction, Small Claims, Probate.*

Civil Records: Access: Fax, mail, in person. Both court and visitors may perform in person searches. No search fee. Required to search: name, years to search. Civil cases indexed by defendant, plaintiff. Civil records go back to 11/90; computerized records go back to 11/90.

Criminal Records: Access: In person only. Visitors may perform in person searches. No search fee. Required to search: name, years to search, DOB; also helpful: SSN. Criminal records go back to 11/90; computerized records go back to 11/90.

General Information: Public access terminal is available. No adoption, mental, juvenile, or sealed records released. SASE required. Turnaround time 1 week. Fax notes: Fee to fax results for $2.00 per page. Copy fee: $.25 per page. Certification fee: $5.00. Fee payee: Circuit Clerk. Personal checks accepted. Prepayment is required.

Magoffin County

Circuit & District Court Box 147, Salyersville, KY 41465; 606-349-2215; Fax: 606-349-2209. Hours: 8AM-4PM (EST). *Felony, Misdemeanor, Civil, Eviction, Small Claims, Probate.*

Civil Records: Access: Fax, mail, in person. Both court and visitors may perform in person searches. No search fee. Required to search: name, years to search. Civil cases indexed by defendant, plaintiff. Civil records on computer from March, 1993 to present, on index cards from 1978 to 1993.

Criminal Records: Access: Fax, mail, in person. Both court and visitors may perform in person searches. No search fee. Required to search: name, years to search, DOB; also helpful: SSN. Criminal records on computer from March, 1993 to present, on index cards from 1978 to 1993.

General Information: Public access terminal is available. No adoption, mental, juvenile, or sealed records released. SASE required. Turnaround time 3 days. Fax notes: Fee to fax results is $2.00 for 1st page, $1.00 each add'l. Copy fee: $.25 per page. Certification fee: $5.00. Fee payee: Circuit Clerk. Personal checks accepted. Prepayment is required.

Marion County

Circuit & District Court 120 W Main St, #B, Lebanon, KY 40033; 270-692-2681. Hours: 8:30AM-4:30PM M-F; 8:30AM-Noon Sat (EST). *Felony, Misdemeanor, Civil, Eviction, Small Claims, Probate.*

Civil Records: Access: In person only. Visitors must perform in person searches for themselves. No search fee. Required to search: name, years to search. Civil cases indexed by defendant, plaintiff. Civil records on computer from May, 1993 to present, on index cards from 1978 to 1993.

Criminal Records: Access: In person only. Visitors must perform in person searches for themselves. No search fee. Required to search: name, years to search; also helpful: SSN. Criminal records on computer from May, 1993 to present, on index cards from 1978 to 1993.

General Information: Public access terminal is available. No adoption, mental, juvenile, or sealed records released. Copy fee: $.25 per page. Certification fee: $5.00. Fee payee: Circuit Clerk. Personal checks accepted. Prepayment is required.

Marshall County

Circuit & District Court 1101 Main St, Benton, KY 42025; 270-527-3883/1721; Fax: 270-527-5865. Hours: 8AM-4:30PM (CST). *Felony, Misdemeanor, Civil, Eviction, Small Claims, Probate.*

Civil Records: Access: Phone, fax, mail, in person. Both court and visitors may perform in person searches. No search fee. Required to search: name, years to search. Civil cases indexed by defendant, plaintiff. Civil records on computer since August, 1992 to present, on index books from 1978 to 1992.

Criminal Records: Access: Phone, fax, mail, in person. Both court and visitors may perform in person searches. No search fee. Required to search: name, years to search, DOB; also helpful: SSN. Criminal records on computer since August, 1992 to present, on index books from 1978 to 1992.

General Information: Public access terminal is available. No adoption, mental, juvenile, or sealed records released. SASE required. Turnaround time 3 days. Fax notes: Fee to fax results is $2.00 for 1st page, $1.00 each add'l. Copy fee: $.25 per page. Certification fee: $5.00. Fee payee: Circuit Clerk. Personal checks accepted. Prepayment is required.

Martin County

Circuit & District Court Box 430, Inez, KY 41224; 606-298-3508; Fax: 606-298-4202. Hours: 8AM-4:30PM M-TH, 8AM-5:30PM F, 9AM-Noon Sat (EST). *Felony, Misdemeanor, Civil, Eviction, Small Claims, Probate.*

Civil Records: Access: Mail, in person. Both court and visitors may perform in person searches. No search fee. Required to search: name, years to search. Civil cases indexed by defendant, plaintiff. Civil records on computer since April, 1994, District on index books since 1987, Circuit on index books since 1978, prior records on docket books.

Criminal Records: Access: In person only. Visitors must perform in person searches for themselves. No search fee. Required to search: name, years to search; also helpful: DOB, SSN. Criminal records on computer since April, 1994, District on index books since 1987, Circuit on index books since 1978, prior records on docket books.

General Information: Public access terminal is available. No adoption, mental, juvenile, or sealed records released. SASE not required. Turnaround time 4 days. Copy fee: $.25 per page. Return postage required. Certification fee: $5.00. Fee payee: Circuit Clerk. Personal checks accepted. Prepayment is required.

Mason County

Circuit Court 100 W 3rd St, Maysville, KY 41056; 606-564-4340; Fax: 606-564-0932. Hours: 8:30AM-4:30PM (EST). *Felony, Civil Actions Over $4,000.*

Civil Records: Access: In person only. Visitors must perform in person searches for themselves. Search fee: No search fee. Required to search: name, years to search. Civil cases indexed by defendant, plaintiff. Civil records on computer back to 4/1994, records on index books since 1929, prior records archived from 1798.

Criminal Records: Access: In person only. Visitors must perform in person searches for themselves. Search fee: No search fee. Required to search: name, years to search, DOB. Criminal records on computer back to 4/1994, records on index books since 1929, prior records archived from 1798.

General Information: Public access terminal is available. No adoption, mental, juvenile, or sealed records released. Fax notes: Fee to fax results is $1.00 per page. Copy fee: $.25 per page. Certification fee: $5.00. Fee payee: Kentucky State Treasurer. Personal checks accepted. Prepayment is required.

District Court 100 W 3rd St, Maysville, KY 41056; 606-564-4011; Fax: 606-564-0932. Hours: 8:30AM-4:30PM (EST). *Misdemeanor, Civil Actions Under $4000, Eviction, Small Claims, Probate.*

Civil Records: Access: In person only. Visitors must perform in person searches for themselves. No search fee. Required to search: name, years to search. Civil cases indexed by defendant, plaintiff. Civil records on computer since April, 1994, prior records on index books from 1978.

Criminal Records: Access: In person only. Visitors must perform in person searches for themselves. No search fee. Required to search: name, years to search. Criminal records on computer since April, 1994, prior records on index books from 1983.

General Information: Public access terminal is available. No adoption, mental, juvenile, or sealed records released. Copy fee: $.25 per page. Certification fee: $5.00. Fee payee: Kentucky State Treasurer. Personal checks accepted. Prepayment is required.

McCracken County

Circuit Court Box 1455, Paducah, KY 42002-1455; 270-575-7280. Hours: 8:30AM-5:30PM M, 8:30AM-4:30PM T-F (CST). *Felony, Civil Actions Over $4,000.*

Note: Visitors may only search from 2PM-4PM on Thursday.

Civil Records: Access: Mail, in person. Both court and visitors may perform in person searches. No search fee. Required to search: name, years to search. Civil cases indexed by defendant, plaintiff. Civil records on computer since September 1991, prior records on index cards since 1978.

Criminal Records: Access: Mail, in person. Both court and visitors may perform in person searches. No search fee. Required to search: name, years to search; also helpful: DOB, SSN. Criminal records on computer since September 1991, prior records on index cards since 1978.

General Information: Public access terminal is available. No adoption, mental, juvenile, or sealed records released. SASE required. Turnaround time 1-2 days. Copy fee: $.25 per page. Certification fee: $5.00. Fee payee: Circuit Clerk. Personal checks accepted. Prepayment is required.

District Court Box 1436, Paducah, KY 42002; 270-575-7270. Hours: 8:30AM-4:30PM (CST). *Misdemeanor, Civil Actions Under $4,000, Eviction, Small Claims, Probate.*

Civil Records: Access: In person only. No search fee. Required to search: name, years to search. Civil cases indexed by defendant, plaintiff. Civil records on computer since 1991, on index books since 1978, prior records archived from the 1900s. Visitors may search only from 2PM to 4PM on Thursday.

Criminal Records: Access: In person only. Both court and visitors may perform in person searches. No search fee. Required to search: name, years to search; also helpful: SSN. Criminal records on computer since 1991, on index books since 1982, prior records archived from the 1900s.

General Information: Public access terminal is available. No adoption, mental, juvenile, or sealed records released. Copy fee: $.25 per page. Certification fee: $5.00. Fee payee: District Clerk. Personal checks accepted. Prepayment is required.

McCreary County

Circuit & District Court Box 40, Whitley City, KY 42653; 606-376-5041; Fax: 606-376-8844. Hours: 8AM-4:30PM (EST). *Felony, Misdemeanor, Civil, Eviction, Small Claims, Probate.*

Civil Records: Access: Mail, in person. Both court and visitors may perform in person searches. No search fee. Required to search: name, years to search; also helpful: address. Civil cases indexed by defendant, plaintiff. Civil records go back to 1992; on computer back to 1995.

Criminal Records: Access: Mail, in person. Both court and visitors may perform in person searches. No search fee. Required to search: name, years to search, DOB, SSN; also helpful: address. Criminal records go back to 1992; on computer back to 1995.

General Information: Public access terminal is available. No adoption, mental, juvenile, or sealed records released. SASE required. Copy fee: $.25 per page. Certification fee: $5.00 per document. Fee payee: Circuit Clerk. Personal checks accepted. Prepayment is required.

McLean County

Circuit & District Court Box 145, Calhoun, KY 42327; 270-273-3966; Fax: 270-273-5981. Hours: 8AM-4:30PM M-F; 9AM-Noon Sat (CST). *Felony, Misdemeanor, Civil, Eviction, Small Claims, Probate.*

Civil Records: Access: Mail, in person. Only the court performs in person searches; visitors may not. Search fee: No search fee. Required to search: name, years to search. Civil cases indexed by defendant, plaintiff. Civil records on computer since 1991, prior records on index cards since 1978.

Criminal Records: Access: In person only. Visitors must perform in person searches for themselves. Search fee: No search fee. Required to search: name, years to search, DOB; also helpful: SSN. Criminal records on computer since 1991, prior records on index cards since 1978. The court refers all written requests to the Administrative Office of Courts in Frankfort.

General Information: Public access terminal is available. No adoption, mental, juvenile, or sealed records released. SASE required. Turnaround time 7 days. Copy fee: $.25 per page. Certification fee: $5.00. Fee payee: Circuit Clerk. Personal checks accepted. Prepayment is required.

Meade County

Circuit & District Court Courthouse 516 Fairway Dr, Brandenburg, KY 40108; 270-422-4961; Fax: 270-422-2147. Hours: 8AM-4:30AM (EST). *Felony, Misdemeanor, Civil, Eviction, Small Claims, Probate.*

Note: This court asks all record requests go to the Administrative office of the Courts in Frankfort.

Civil Records: Access: In person, mail, fax. Visitors must perform in person searches for themselves. No search fee. Required to search: name, years to search. Civil cases indexed by defendant, plaintiff. Civil records on computer since 2/95, prior on index cards.

Criminal Records: Access: In perso, mail, fax. Visitors must perform in person searches for themselves. No search fee. Required to search: name, years to search. Criminal records on computer since 2/95, prior on index cards.

General Information: Public access terminal is available. No adoption, mental, juvenile, or sealed records released. Copy fee: $.25 per page. Fee payee: Circuit Clerk. Personal checks accepted.

Menifee County

Circuit & District Court Box 172, Frenchburg, KY 40322; 606-768-2461; Fax: 606-768-2462. Hours: 8:30AM-4PM (EST). *Felony, Misdemeanor, Civil, Eviction, Small Claims, Probate.*

Civil Records: Access: In person. Visitors must perform in person searches No search fee. Required to search: name, years to search. Civil cases indexed by defendant, plaintiff. Civil records on index cards from 1978 to present.

Criminal Records: Access: In person. Visitors must perform in person searches No search fee. Required to search: name, years to search. Criminal records on index cards from 1978 to present.

General Information: Public access terminal is available. No adoption, mental, juvenile, or sealed records released. Copy fee: $.25 per page. Court and visitors may not make copies. They will only show you the paperwork. Fee payee: Circuit Clerk. Prepayment is required.

Mercer County

Circuit & District Court Courthouse, 224 Main St S, Harrodsburg, KY 40330-1696; 859-734-6306; Fax: 859-734-9159. Hours: 8AM-4:30PM (EST). *Felony, Misdemeanor, Civil, Eviction, Small Claims, Probate.*

Civil Records: Access: In person only. Visitors must perform in person searches for themselves. No search fee. Required to search: name, years to search. Civil cases indexed by defendant, plaintiff. Civil records on computer back to 1993; prior in index books.

Criminal Records: Access: In person only. Visitors must perform in person searches for themselves. No search fee. Required to search: name, years to search; also helpful: DOB, SSN. Criminal records on computer back to 1993; prior in index books.

General Information: Public access terminal is available. No adoption, mental, juvenile, or sealed records released. Copy fee: $.25 per page. Certification fee: $5.00. Fee payee: Circuit Clerk. Personal checks accepted. Prepayment is required.

Metcalfe County

Circuit & District Court Box 485, Edmonton, KY 42129; 270-432-3663; Fax: 270-432-4437. Hours: 8AM-4PM (CST). *Felony, Misdemeanor, Civil, Eviction, Small Claims, Probate.*

Civil Records: Access: Phone, fax, mail, in person. Both court and visitors may perform in person searches. No search fee. Required to search: name, years to search. Civil cases indexed by defendant, plaintiff. Civil records on computer back to 1992, prior records on index cards since 1978.

Criminal Records: Access: Phone, fax, mail, in person. Both court and visitors may perform in person searches. No search fee. Required to search: name, years to search, DOB, SSN, signed release. Criminal records on computer back to 1992, prior records on index cards since 1980.

General Information: Public access terminal is available. No adoption, mental, juvenile, or sealed records released. SASE required. Turnaround time 1-2 days. Fax notes: Fee to fax results is $2.00 1st page; $1.00 each add'l. Copy fee: $.25 per page. Certification

fee: $5.00. Fee payee: Circuit Clerk. Personal checks accepted. Prepayment is required.

Monroe County

Circuit & District Court Box 245, Tompkinsville, KY 42167; 270-487-5480; Fax: 270-487-0068. Hours: 8AM-4PM (CST). *Felony, Misdemeanor, Civil, Eviction, Small Claims, Probate.*

Civil Records: Access: Phone, mail, in person. Both court and visitors may perform in person searches. No search fee. Required to search: name, years to search. Civil cases indexed by defendant, plaintiff. Civil records kept in files.

Criminal Records: Access: Phone, mail, in person. Both court and visitors may perform in person searches. No search fee. Required to search: name, years to search. Criminal records kept in files.

General Information: Public access terminal is available. No adoption, mental, juvenile, or sealed records released. SASE required. Turnaround time 1 week. Copy fee: $.25 per page. Certification fee: $5.00. Fee payee: Circuit Clerk. Personal checks accepted. Prepayment is required.

Montgomery County

Circuit & District Court Courthouse, One Court St (PO Box 327), Mt Sterling, KY 40353; 859-498-5966; Fax: 859-498-9341. Hours: 8:30AM-4PM (EST). *Felony, Misdemeanor, Civil, Eviction, Small Claims, Probate.*

Civil Records: Access: Mail, in person. Both court and visitors may perform in person searches. No search fee. Required to search: name, years to search. Civil cases indexed by defendant, plaintiff. Civil records on computer since August, 1991, on index cards from 1978-1991, prior records on docket books.

Criminal Records: Access: Mail, in person. Both court and visitors may perform in person searches. No search fee. Required to search: name, years to search. Criminal records on computer since August, 1991, on index cards from 1978-1991, prior records on docket books.

General Information: Public access terminal is available. No adoption, mental, juvenile, or sealed records released. SASE required. Turnaround time 1-2 days. Copy fee: $.25 per page. Certification fee: $5.00. Fee payee: Circuit Clerk. Personal checks accepted. Prepayment is required.

Morgan County

Circuit & District Court Box 85, West Liberty, KY 41472; 606-743-3763; Fax: 606-743-2633. Hours: 8AM-4PM (EST). *Felony, Misdemeanor, Civil, Eviction, Small Claims, Probate.*

Civil Records: Access: Mail, in person. Both court and visitors may perform in person searches. No search fee. Required to search: name, years to search. Civil cases indexed by defendant, plaintiff. Civil records on computer back to 9/1993; index books back to 1921.

Criminal Records: Access: Mail, in person. Both court and visitors may perform in person searches. No search fee. Required to search: name, years to search. Criminal records on computer back to 9/1993; index books back to 1921.

General Information: Public access terminal is available. No adoption, mental, juvenile, or sealed records released. Turnaround time 1 day. Fax notes: Will not fax results. Copy fee: $.25 per page. Certification fee: $5.00. Fee payee: Circuit Clerk. Personal checks accepted. Prepayment is required.

Muhlenberg County

Circuit Court Box 776, Greenville, KY 42345; 270-338-4850 (Felony); Fax: 270-338-0177. Hours: 8AM-4PM (CST). *Felony, Civil Actions Over $4,000.*

Note: Direct mail felony record requests to state AOC.

Civil Records: Access: In person only. Visitors must perform in person searches for themselves. No search fee. Required to search: name, years to search. Civil cases indexed by defendant, plaintiff. Civil records on computer since May, 1992, records on index since 1932, prior records archived since 1940.

Criminal Records: Access: In person only. Visitors must perform in person searches for themselves. No search fee. Required to search: name, years to search, SSN; also helpful: DOB. Criminal records on computer since May, 1992, records on index since 1932, prior records archived since 1940.

General Information: Public access terminal is available. No adoption, mental, juvenile, or sealed records released. Fax notes: Fee to fax results is $3. for 1st pg.; $1. each add'l. Copy fee: $.25 per page. Certification fee: $5.00. Fee payee: Circuit Clerk. Personal checks accepted. Prepayment is required.

District Court Box 274, Greenville, KY 42345; 270-338-0995; Fax: 270-338-7482. Hours: 8AM-4PM (CST). *Misdemeanor, Civil Actions Under $4,000, Eviction, Small Claims, Probate.*

Civil Records: Access: In person only. Both court and visitors may perform in person searches. No search fee. Required to search: name, years to search. Civil cases indexed by defendant, plaintiff. Civil records on computer since 1992, prior records on index books.

Criminal Records: Access: In person only. Visitors must perform in person searches for themselves. No search fee. Required to search: name, years to search. Criminal records on computer since 1992, prior records on index books.

General Information: Public access terminal is available. No adoption, mental, juvenile, or sealed records released. Copy fee: $.25 per page. Certification fee: $5.00. Fee payee: District Clerk. Personal checks accepted. Prepayment is required.

Nelson County

Circuit & District Court Box 845, Bardstown, KY 40004; 502-348-3648. Hours: 8:30AM-4:30PM (EST). *Felony, Misdemeanor, Civil, Eviction, Small Claims, Probate.*

Civil Records: Access: Mail, in person. Both court and visitors may perform in person searches. No search fee. Required to search: name, years to search. Civil cases indexed by defendant, plaintiff. Civil records on computer since 1990, on index since 1978, prior records archived from 1940.

Criminal Records: Access: Mail, in person. Both court and visitors may perform in person searches. No search fee. Required to search: name, years to search, DOB; also helpful: SSN. Criminal records on computer since 1990, on index since 1978, prior records archived from 1940.

General Information: Public access terminal is available. No adoption, mental, juvenile, domestic violence or sealed records released. Turnaround time 2 weeks. Copy fee: $.25 per page. Certification fee: $5.00. Fee payee: Circuit Clerk. Personal checks accepted. Prepayment is required.

Nicholas County

Circuit & District Court PO Box 109, Carlisle, KY 40311; 859-289-2336; Fax: 859-289-6141. Hours: 8:30AM-4:30PM M-F (EST). *Felony, Misdemeanor, Civil, Eviction, Small Claims, Probate.*

Civil Records: Access: Fax, mail, in person. Both court and visitors may perform in person searches. No search

fee. Required to search: name, years to search, written request. Civil cases indexed by defendant, plaintiff. Civil records on computer since March, 1993, prior records on index cards.

Criminal Records: Access: Fax, mail, in person. Both court and visitors may perform in person searches. No search fee. Required to search: name, years to search, written request. Criminal records on computer since March, 1993, prior records on index cards.

General Information: Public access terminal is available. No adoption, mental, juvenile, or sealed records released. SASE required. Turnaround time 1-2 days. Fax notes: No fee to fax results. Copy fee: $.25 per page. Certification fee: $5.00. Fee payee: Circuit Clerk. Personal checks accepted. Prepayment required.

Ohio County

Circuit & District Court 130 E Washington, Ste 300, Hartford, KY 42347; 270-298-3671; Fax: 270-298-9565. Hours: 8:30AM-4:30PM (CST). *Felony, Misdemeanor, Civil, Eviction, Small Claims, Probate.*

Civil Records: Access: In person only. Visitors must perform in person searches for themselves. No search fee. Required to search: name, years to search. Civil cases indexed by defendant, plaintiff. Civil records on computer since 10/91, Circuit court on index books since the 1800s, District court on index books since 1987 and prior records are archived.

Criminal Records: Access: In person only. Visitors must perform in person searches for themselves. No search fee. Required to search: name, years to search. Criminal records on computer since 10/91, Circuit court on index books since the 1800s, District court on index books since 1987 and prior records are archived.

General Information: Public access terminal is available. No adoption, mental, juvenile, or sealed records released. Copy fee: $.25 per page. Will not mail results. Certification fee: $5.00. Fee payee: Circuit Clerk. No personal checks accepted. Prepayment is required.

Oldham County

Circuit & District Court 100 W Main St, La Grange, KY 40031; 502-222-9837; Fax: 502-222-3047. Hours: 8AM-4PM (EST). *Felony, Misdemeanor, Civil, Eviction, Small Claims, Probate.*

Note: Criminal record requests are referred to the Administrative office of the Courts in Frankfort.

Civil Records: Access: In person only. Visitors must perform in person searches for themselves. No search fee. Required to search: name, years to search. Civil cases indexed by defendant, plaintiff. Civil records on computer since 1991, on index books since 1978, prior records archived since 1800s.

Criminal Records: Access: In person only. Visitors must perform in person searches for themselves. No search fee. Required to search: name, years to search; also helpful: SSN. Criminal records on computer since 1991, on index books since 1978, prior records archived since 1800s.

General Information: Public access terminal is available. No adoption, mental, juvenile, or sealed records released. Fax notes: Fee to fax results is $2.00 per page. Copy fee: $.25 per page. Certification fee: $5.00. Fee payee: Circuit Clerk. Personal checks accepted. Prepayment is required. Fee to fax results if $1.00 per document plus $.20 per page.

Owen County

Circuit & District Court Box 473, Owenton, KY 40359; 502-484-2232; Fax: 502-484-0625. Hours: 8AM-4PM (EST). *Felony, Misdemeanor, Civil, Eviction, Small Claims, Probate.*

Civil Records: Access: Fax, mail, in person. Both court and visitors may perform in person searches. No search fee. Required to search: name, years to search. Civil

cases indexed by defendant, plaintiff. Civil records on computer since 1992, prior records on index books since 1946. Cases before 1978 transferred to state archives.

Criminal Records: Access: Fax, mail, in person. Both court and visitors may perform in person searches. No search fee. Required to search: name, years to search, DOB, SSN. Criminal records on computer since 1992, prior records on index books since 1946. Cases before 1978 transferred to state archives. Court suggests statewide search through A.O.C. at 502-573-2350.

General Information: Public access terminal is available. No adoption, mental, juvenile, or sealed records released. Turnaround time 1 week. Copy fee: $.25 per page. Certification fee: $5.00. Fee payee: Circuit Clerk. Personal checks accepted. Prepayment is required.

Owsley County

Circuit & District Court Box 130, Booneville, KY 41314; 606-593-6226; Fax: 606-593-6343. Hours: 8AM-4PM M-F, 8AM-Noon Sat (EST). *Felony, Misdemeanor, Civil, Eviction, Small Claims, Probate.*

Civil Records: Access: In person only. Visitors must perform in person searches for themselves. No search fee. Required to search: name, years to search. Civil cases indexed by defendant, plaintiff. Civil records on computer since 10/1994, prior records on index cards since 1978.

Criminal Records: Access: In person only. Visitors must perform in person searches for themselves. No search fee. Required to search: name, years to search, DOB or SSN. Criminal records on computer since 10/1994, prior records on index cards since 1978.

General Information: Public access terminal is available. No adoption, mental, juvenile, or sealed records released. Fax notes: Fee to fax results is $2.00 1st page, $1.00 each add'l. Copy fee: $.25 per page. Certification fee: $5.00. Fee payee: Circuit Clerk. Personal checks accepted. Prepayment is required.

Pendleton County

Circuit & District Court PO Box 69, Falmouth, KY 41040; 859-654-3347. Hours: 8AM-4PM (EST). *Felony, Misdemeanor, Civil, Eviction, Small Claims, Probate.*

Civil Records: Access: Mail, in person. Both court and visitors may perform in person searches. No search fee. Required to search: name, years to search. Civil cases indexed by defendant, plaintiff. Civil records on computer since July, 1994, prior records on index books since 1978.

Criminal Records: Access: In person only. Both court and visitors may perform in person searches. No search fee. Required to search: name, years to search. Criminal records on computer since July, 1994, prior records on index books since 1978.

General Information: No adoption, mental, juvenile, or sealed records released. SASE not required. Copy fee: $.25 per page. Certification fee: $5.00. Fee payee: Circuit Clerk. Personal checks accepted. Prepayment is required.

Perry County

Circuit Court Box 7433, Hazard, KY 41701; 606-435-6000. Hours: 8AM-4PM (EST). *Felony, Civil Actions Over $4,000.*

Civil Records: Access: Phone, mail, in person. Both court and visitors may perform in person searches. No search fee. Required to search: name, years to search. Civil cases indexed by defendant, plaintiff. Civil records on computer since October, 1991, prior records on index cards since 1978.

Criminal Records: Access: Phone, mail, in person. Both court and visitors may perform in person searches. No search fee. Required to search: name, years to search. Criminal records on computer since October, 1991, prior records on index cards since 1978.

General Information: Public access terminal is available. No adoption, mental, juvenile, or sealed records released. SASE required. Turnaround time approximately 1 week. Copy fee: $.25 per page. Certification fee: $5.00. Fee payee: Circuit Clerk. Personal checks accepted. Prepayment is required.

District Court PO Box 7433, Hazard, KY 41702; 606-435-6002. Hours: 8AM-4PM (EST). *Misdemeanor, Civil Actions Under $4,000, Eviction, Small Claims, Probate.*

Civil Records: Access: In person. No search fee. Required to search: name, years to search. Civil cases indexed by defendant, plaintiff. Civil records on computer since 1991, records on index books since 1978, prior records archived since 1900s.

Criminal Records: Access: In person. Visitors must perform in person searches No search fee. Required to search: name, years to search. Criminal records on computer since 1991, records on index books since 1978, prior records archived since 1900s.

General Information: Public access terminal is available. No adoption, mental, juvenile, or sealed records released. Copy fee: $.25 per page. Certification fee: $5.00. Fee payee: District Clerk. Personal checks accepted. Prepayment is required.

Pike County

Circuit & District Court PO Box 1002, Pikeville, KY 41502; 606-433-7557; Fax: 606-433-7044. Hours: 8AM-4:30PM (EST). *Felony, Misdemeanor, Civil, Eviction, Small Claims, Probate.*

Civil Records: Access: Mail, in person. Both court and visitors may perform in person searches. No search fee. Required to search: name, years to search. Civil cases indexed by defendant, plaintiff. Civil records on computer since March, 1994, prior records on index cards from 1978.

Criminal Records: Access: In person only. Both the court and visitors may do in person searches. No search fee. Required to search: name, years to search. Criminal records on computer since March, 1994, prior records on index cards from 1978.

General Information: Public access terminal is available. No adoption, mental, juvenile, or sealed records released. SASE required. Turnaround time 3 days. Copy fee: $.25 per page. Certification fee: $5.00. Fee payee: Circuit Clerk. Personal checks accepted. Prepayment is required.

Powell County

Circuit & District Court Box 578, Stanton, KY 40380; 606-663-4141; Fax: 606-663-2710. Hours: 8AM-4PM M,T,W,F, 8AM-Noon Th & Sat (EST). *Felony, Misdemeanor, Civil, Eviction, Small Claims, Probate.*

Civil Records: Access: Mail, in person. Both court and visitors may perform in person searches. No search fee. Required to search: name, years to search. Civil cases indexed by defendant, plaintiff. Civil records on computer since 1993, prior records on index cards since 1978.

Criminal Records: Access: Mail, in person. Both court and visitors may perform in person searches. No search fee. Required to search: name, years to search, DOB; also helpful: SSN. Criminal records on computer since 1993, prior records on index cards since 1978.

General Information: Public access terminal is available. No adoption, mental, juvenile, or sealed records released. SASE required. Turnaround time varies. Copy fee: $.25 per page. Certification fee: $5.00. Fee payee: Circuit Clerk. Personal checks not accepted, money orders preferred. Prepayment is required.

Pulaski County

Circuit & District Court Box 664, Somerset, KY 42502; 606-677-4029; Fax: 606-677-4002. Hours: 8AM-4:30PM M-F, 8AM-Noon Sat (EST). *Felony, Misdemeanor, Civil, Eviction, Small Claims, Probate.*

Civil Records: Access: In person only. Visitors must perform in person searches for themselves. No search fee. Required to search: name, years to search. Civil cases indexed by defendant, plaintiff. Civil records on computer since 1991, prior records on index books from 1978.

Criminal Records: Access: In person only. Visitors must perform in person searches for themselves. No search fee. Required to search: name, years to search. Criminal records on computer since 1991, prior records on index books from 1978.

General Information: Public access terminal is available. No adoption, mental, juvenile, or sealed records released. Copy fee: $.25 per page. Certification fee: $5.00. Fee payee: Circuit Clerk. Personal checks accepted. Prepayment is required.

Robertson County

Circuit & District Court PO Box 63 (211 Court St), Mt Olivet, KY 41064; 606-724-5993; Fax: 606-724-5721. Hours: 8:30AM-4:30PM (EST). *Felony, Misdemeanor, Civil, Eviction, Small Claims, Probate.*

Note: The physical location is 211 Court Street.

Civil Records: Access: In person only. Visitors must perform in person searches for themselves. No search fee. Required to search: name, years to search. Civil cases indexed by defendant, plaintiff. Civil records on computer to 1995, previous on index cards.

Criminal Records: Access: In person only. Visitors must perform in person searches for themselves. No search fee. Required to search: name, years to search; also helpful: DOB, SSN. Criminal records on computer to 1995, previous on index cards.

General Information: Public access terminal is available. No adoption, mental, juvenile, or sealed records released. Copy fee: $.25 per page. Certification fee: $5.00. Fee payee: Circuit Clerk. Personal checks accepted. Prepayment is required.

Rockcastle County

Circuit & District Court Courthouse Annex, 1st Fl, 205 E Main St., Room 102, Mt Vernon, KY 40456; 606-256-2581. Hours: 8AM-4PM M-W & F; 8AM-6PM Th; 8:30AM-Noon Sat (EST). *Felony, Misdemeanor, Civil, Eviction, Small Claims, Probate.*

Civil Records: Access: In person. Visitors may perform in person searches. No search fee. Required to search: name, years to search. Civil cases indexed by defendant, plaintiff. Civil records on computer since 1991, index cards from 1978 to 1990, prior are archived at Frankfort.

Criminal Records: Access: In person only. Visitors must perform in person searches for themselves. No search fee. Required to search: name, years to search, DOB; also helpful: SSN. Criminal Records from 1991 to present are available. A form is available to request a criminal history through AOC, Retrieval Services. This court provides the form via mail if you provide them a SASE.

General Information: Public access terminal is available. No adoption, mental, juvenile, or sealed records released. Copy fee: $.25 per page. Certification fee: $5.00. Fee payee: Circuit Clerk. Personal checks accepted. Prepayment is required.

Rowan County

Circuit & District Court 627 E Main, Morehead, KY 40351-1398; 606-784-4574; Fax: 606-784-1899. Hours: 8:30AM-4:30PM M-F 8:30AM-12PM SAT (EST). *Felony, Misdemeanor, Civil, Eviction, Small Claims, Probate.*

www.kycourts.net

Civil Records: Access: In person only. Visitors must perform in person searches for themselves. No search fee. Required to search: name, years to search. Civil cases indexed by defendant, plaintiff. Civil records on computer from 1991, index cards from 1989, archived from 1900.

Criminal Records: Access: In person only. Visitors must perform in person searches for themselves. No search fee. Required to search: name, years to search. Criminal records on computer from 1991, index cards from 1989, archived from 1900.

General Information: Public access terminal is available. No adoption, mental, juvenile, or sealed records released. Copy fee: $.25 per page. Fee payee: Circuit Clerk. Only cashiers checks and money orders accepted. Prepayment is required.

Russell County

Circuit & District Court 410 Monument Square, #203, Jamestown, KY 42629; 270-343-2185; Fax: 270-343-5808. Hours: 8AM-4:30PM M-F 8AM-Noon Sat (CST). *Felony, Misdemeanor, Civil, Eviction, Small Claims, Probate.*

Civil Records: Access: In person only. Visitors must perform in person searches for themselves. No search fee. Required to search: name, years to search. Civil cases indexed by defendant, plaintiff. Civil records on computer from August, 1994, index cards from 1978-1994, prior archived at Frankfort.

Criminal Records: Access: In person only. Visitors must perform in person searches for themselves. No search fee. Required to search: name, years to search. Criminal records on computer from August, 1994, index cards from 1978-1994, prior archived at Frankfort.

General Information: Public access terminal is available. No adoption, mental, juvenile, or sealed records released. Copy fee: $.25 per page. Certification fee: $5.00. Fee payee: Circuit Clerk. Personal checks accepted. Prepayment is required.

Scott County

Circuit & District Court 119 N Hamilton, Georgetown, KY 40324; 502-863-0474. Hours: 8:30-4:30PM (EST). *Felony, Misdemeanor, Civil, Eviction, Small Claims, Probate.*

Civil Records: Access: Mail, in person. Both court and visitors may perform in person searches. No search fee. Required to search: name, years to search. Civil cases indexed by defendant, plaintiff. Civil records on computer since 1992, index cards from 1978 to 1992, in books prior.

Criminal Records: Access: Mail, in person. Both court and visitors may perform in person searches. No search fee. Required to search: name, years to search; also helpful: SSN. Criminal records on computer since 1992, index cards from 1978 to 1992, in books prior.

General Information: Public access terminal is available. No adoption, mental, juvenile, paternity and domestic violence records released. SASE required. Turnaround time varies. Copy fee: $.25 per page. Certification fee: $5.00. Fee payee: Circuit Clerk. Personal checks accepted. Prepayment is required.

Shelby County

Circuit & District Court 501 Main St, Shelbyville, KY 40065; 502-633-1289; Civil phone: 502-633-4736 (Dist Ct); Fax: 502-633-0146 (633-6421 Dist Ct fax). Hours: 8:30AM-4:30PM (EST). *Felony, Misdemeanor, Civil, Eviction, Small Claims, Probate.*

Civil Records: Access: Fax, mail, in person. Both court and visitors may perform in person searches. No search fee. Required to search: name, years to search. Civil cases indexed by defendant, plaintiff. Civil records on computer back to 1991; index cards from 1978 to 1991.
Criminal Records: Access: In person only. Visitors must perform in person searches for themselves. No search fee. Required to search: name, years to search, DOB. Criminal records on computer back to 1991; index cards from 1978 to 1991.
General Information: Public access terminal is available. No adoption, mental, juvenile, or sealed records released. SASE required. Turnaround time 3-5 days. Copy fee: $.25 per page. Certification fee: $5.00. Fee payee: Circuit Clerk. Personal checks accepted. Prepayment is required.

Simpson County

Circuit & District Court Box 261, Franklin, KY 42135-0261; 270-586-8910/4241; Fax: 270-586-0265. Hours: 8AM-4PM (CST). *Felony, Misdemeanor, Civil, Eviction, Small Claims, Probate.*

www.dockets.kycourts.net

Note: Weekly current court dockets are available at www.dockets.kycourts.net.
Civil Records: Access: Mail, in person. Both court and visitors may perform in person searches. No search fee. Required to search: name, years to search. Civil cases indexed by defendant, plaintiff. Civil records on computer since 11/92, manual prior to 1978.
Criminal Records: Access: Mail, in person. Visitors must perform in person searches themselves No search fee. Required to search: name, years to search, DOB, SSN. Criminal records on computer since 11/92, card index back to 1978.
General Information: Public access terminal is available. (Public access terminal available for criminal only.) No adoption, mental, juvenile, or sealed records released. SASE required. Turnaround time 1 week. Copy fee: $.25 per page. Certification fee: $5.00. Fee payee: Circuit Clerk. Only cashiers checks and money orders accepted. Prepayment is required.

Spencer County

Circuit & District Court Box 282, Taylorsville, KY 40071; 502-477-3220; Fax: 502-477-9368. Hours: 7:45AM-4PM (EST). *Felony, Misdemeanor, Civil, Eviction, Small Claims, Probate.*

Civil Records: Access: Mail, in person. Visitors must perform in person searches for themselves. No search fee. Required to search: name, years to search. Civil cases indexed by defendant, plaintiff. Civil records on computer from 08/94 to present, index cards from 1978 to 1994.
Criminal Records: Access: Mail, in person. Visitors must perform in person searches for themselves. No search fee. Required to search: name, years to search, DOB; also helpful: SSN. Criminal records on computer from 08/94 to present, index cards from 1978 to 1994.
General Information: Public access terminal is available. No adoption, mental, juvenile, or sealed records released. SASE required. Turnaround time 1-4 days. Copy fee: $.25 per page. Certification fee: $5.00. Fee payee: Circuit Clerk. Personal checks accepted. Prepayment is required.

Taylor County

Circuit & District Court 203 N Court Courthouse, Campbellsville, KY 42718; 270-465-6686; Fax: 270-789-4356. Hours: 8AM-4:30PM (EST). *Felony, Misdemeanor, Civil, Eviction, Small Claims, Probate.*

Civil Records: Access: In person only. Both court and visitors may perform in person searches. No search fee. Required to search: name, years to search. Civil cases indexed by defendant, plaintiff. Civil records on computer from 1993 to present, index cards from 1978 to 1993.
Criminal Records: Access: In person only. Visitors must perform in person searches for themselves. No search fee. Required to search: name, years to search, DOB, SSN. Criminal records on computer from 1993 to present, index cards from 1978 to 1993.
General Information: Public access terminal is available. No adoption, mental, juvenile, or sealed records released. Copy fee: $.25 per page. Certification fee: $5.00. Fee payee: Circuit Clerk. Personal checks accepted. Prepayment is required.

Todd County

Circuit & District Court Box 337, Elkton, KY 42220; 270-265-5631; Fax: 270-265-2122. Hours: 8AM-4:30PM (CST). *Felony, Misdemeanor, Civil, Eviction, Small Claims, Probate.*

Civil Records: Access: In person only. Visitors must perform in person searches for themselves. No search fee. Required to search: name, years to search. Civil cases indexed by defendant, plaintiff. Civil records on computer since January, 1993, index cards from 1978-1993, index books prior to 1978.
Criminal Records: Access: In person only. Visitors must perform in person searches for themselves. No search fee. Required to search: name, years to search. Criminal records on computer since January, 1993, index cards from 1978-1993, index books prior to 1978.
General Information: Public access terminal is available. No adoption, mental, juvenile, or sealed records released. Copy fee: $.25 per page. Certification fee: $5.00. Fee payee: Circuit Clerk. Personal checks accepted. Prepayment is required.

Trigg County

Circuit & District Court Box 673, Cadiz, KY 42211; 270-522-6270. Hours: 8AM-4PM M-F 9AM-11:30AM 1st SAT of each month (CST). *Felony, Misdemeanor, Civil, Eviction, Small Claims, Probate.*

Civil Records: Access: In person only. Visitors must perform in person searches for themselves. No search fee. Required to search: name, years to search. Civil cases indexed by defendant, plaintiff. Civil records on computer from 4/1993 to present, index cards from 1978 to 1993.
Criminal Records: Access: In person only. Visitors must perform in person searches for themselves. Search fee: No search fee. Required to search: name, years to search, DOB; also helpful: SSN. Criminal records on computer from 4/1993 to present, index cards from 1978 to 1993.
General Information: Public access terminal is available. No adoption, mental, juvenile, or sealed records released. Copy fee: $.25 per page. Certification fee: $5.00. Fee payee: Circuit Clerk. Only cashiers checks and money orders accepted.

Trimble County

Circuit & District Court Box 248, Bedford, KY 40006; 502-255-3213, 502-255-3525 (District); Fax: 502-255-4953. Hours: 8AM-4:30PM M,T,Th,F 8AM-Noon Sat (EST). *Felony, Misdemeanor, Civil, Eviction, Small Claims, Probate.*

Civil Records: Access: Mail, in person. Both court and visitors may perform in person searches. No search fee. Required to search: name, years to search. Civil cases indexed by defendant, plaintiff. Civil records on computer and in folders from 1993 to present, folders 1978 to 1992, archives prior to 1978.
Criminal Records: Access: In person only. Visitors must perform in person searches for themselves. No search fee. Required to search: name, years to search, DOB; also helpful: SSN. Criminal records on computer and in folders from 1993 to present, folders 1978 to 1992, archives prior to 1978.
General Information: Public access terminal is available. No adoption, mental, juvenile, or sealed records released. SASE required. Turnaround time 2-4 days. Copy fee: $.25 per page. Certification fee: $5.00. Fee payee: Circuit Clerk. Only cashiers checks and money orders accepted. Prepayment is required.

Union County

Circuit & District Court Box 59, Morganfield, KY 42437; 270-389-0800/0804; Fax: 270-389-9887. Hours: 8AM-4PM (No searches performed on Thursday) (CST). *Felony, Misdemeanor, Civil, Eviction, Small Claims, Probate.*

Civil Records: Access: Mail, in person. Both court and visitors may perform in person searches. No search fee. Required to search: name, years to search. Civil cases indexed by defendant, plaintiff. Civil records on computer since June, 1994 (new records only); prior on index cards and archived.
Criminal Records: Access: In person only. Visitors must perform in person searches for themselves. No search fee. Required to search: name, years to search, DOB, SSN. Criminal records on computer since June, 1994 (new records only); prior on index cards and archived. Contact AOC for statewide search by mail (criminal requests to be acquired through Pre-Trial Svcs, Frankfort).
General Information: Public access terminal is available. No adoption, mental, juvenile, or sealed records released. SASE required. Turnaround time 2-4 days. Copy fee: $.25 per page. Certification fee: $5.00. Fee payee: Circuit Clerk. Business checks accepted. Prepayment is required.

Warren County

Circuit & District Court 1001 Center St #102, Bowling Green, KY 42101-2184; 270-746-7400; Fax: 270-746-7501. Hours: 8:AM-4:30PM (CST). *Felony, Misdemeanor, Civil, Eviction, Small Claims, Probate.*

Civil Records: Access: In person only. Visitors must perform in person searches for themselves. No search fee. Required to search: name, years to search. Civil cases indexed by defendant, plaintiff. Civil records on computer since 1989.
Criminal Records: Access: In person only. Visitors must perform in person searches for themselves. No search fee. Required to search: name, years to search; also helpful: DOB, SSN. Criminal records on computer since 1990.
General Information: Public access terminal is available. No adoption, mental, juvenile, or sealed records released. Fax notes: Fee to fax results is $1.00 per page, $2.00 for 1st page. Copy fee: $.25 per page. Certification fee: $5.00. Fee payee: Circuit Clerk. Personal checks accepted. Prepayment is required.

Washington County

Circuit & District Court PO Box 346, Springfield, KY 40069; 859-336-3761; Fax: 859-336-9824. Hours: 8AM-4:30PM; 8:30-12 on Sat (EST). *Felony, Misdemeanor, Civil, Eviction, Small Claims, Probate.*

Civil Records: Access: Mail, in person. Both court and visitors may perform in person searches. No search fee. Required to search: name, years to search. Civil cases indexed by defendant, plaintiff. Civil records on computer, index cards and archived.

Criminal Records: Access: In person. Both court and visitors may perform in person searches. No search fee. Required to search: name, years to search, DOB. Criminal records on computer, index cards and archived. Mail requests must be made to Pretrial Services, 100 Millcreek Park., Frankfort, KY 40602, 800-928-6381.

General Information: Public access terminal is available. No adoption, mental, juvenile, or sealed records released. SASE not required. Turnaround time 2-4 days. Copy fee: $.25 per page. Return postage required. Certification fee: $5.00. Fee payee: Circuit Clerk. Personal checks accepted. Prepayment is required.

Wayne County

Circuit & District Court 109 N Main St, Monticello, KY 42633-1458; 606-348-5841; Fax: 606-348-4225. Hours: 8AM-4:15PM M-F; 8:30AM-Noon Sat (CST). *Felony, Misdemeanor, Civil, Eviction, Small Claims, Probate.*

Civil Records: Access: Mail, in person. Visitors must perform in person searches. No search fee. Required to search: name, years to search. Civil cases indexed by defendant, plaintiff. Civil records on computer from 10/92 to present, index cards from 1978 to 1992.

Criminal Records: Access: Mail, in person. Visitors must perform in person searches. No search fee. Required to search: name, years to search; also helpful: DOB, SSN. Criminal records on computer from 10/92 to present, index cards from 1978 to 1992.

General Information: Public access terminal is available. No adoption, mental, juvenile, or sealed records released. SASE required. Turnaround time 5 days. Copy fee: $.25 per page. Certification fee: $5.00. Fee payee: Circuit Clerk. Personal checks accepted. Prepayment is required.

Webster County

Circuit & District Court Box 290 (25 US Hiway 41A South), Dixon, KY 42409; 270-639-9160; Fax: 270-639-6757. Hours: 8AM-4PM (CST). *Felony, Misdemeanor, Civil, Eviction, Small Claims, Probate.*

Civil Records: Access: Fax, mail, in person. Both court and visitors may perform in person searches. No search fee. Required to search: name, years to search. Civil cases indexed by defendant, plaintiff. Civil records in office from 1987 to present, prior records are at Frankfort archives.

Criminal Records: Access: Fax, mail, in person. Both court and visitors may perform in person searches. No search fee. Required to search: name, years to search. Criminal records in office from 1987 to present, prior records are at Frankfort archives.

General Information: Public access terminal is available. No adoption, mental, juvenile, or sealed records released. SASE required. Turnaround time 1 day. Fax notes: Fee to fax results is $2.00 for 1st page, $1.00 each add'l. Copy fee: $.25 per page. Certification fee: $5.00. Fee payee: Circuit Clerk. Personal checks accepted. Prepayment is required.

Whitley County

Corbin Circuit & District Court 805 S Main St, Corbin, KY 40701; 606-523-1085; Fax: 606-523-2049. Hours: 8AM-4PM (EST). *Felony, Misdemeanor, Civil, Eviction, Small Claims, Probate.*

Civil Records: Access: In person only. Visitors must perform in person searches for themselves. No search fee. Required to search: name, years to search. Civil cases indexed by defendant, plaintiff. Civil records on computer from 1993 to present, index books prior.

Criminal Records: Access: In person only. Visitors must perform in person searches for themselves. No search fee. Required to search: name, years to search. Criminal records on computer from 1993 to present, index books prior.

General Information: Public access terminal is available. No adoption, mental, juvenile or sealed records released. Copy fee: $.25 per page. Certification fee: $5.00. Fee payee: Whitley District Court. Personal checks accepted.

Williamsburg Circuit & District Court Box 329, Williamsburg, KY 40769; 606-549-5162/2973. Hours: 8AM-4PM (EST). *Felony, Misdemeanor, Civil, Eviction, Small Claims, Probate.*

Civil Records: Access: In person only. Visitors must perform in person searches for themselves. No search fee. Required to search: name, years to search. Civil cases indexed by defendant, plaintiff. Civil records on computer from 1993 to present, index cards from 1978 to 1993.

Criminal Records: Access: In person only. Visitors must perform in person searches for themselves. No

search fee. Required to search: name, years to search; also helpful: DOB, SSN. Criminal records on computer from 1993 to present, index cards from 1978 to 1993.

General Information: Public access terminal is available. No adoption, mental, juvenile, or sealed records released. Copy fee: $.25 per page. Certification fee: $5.00. Fee payee: Whitley Circuit Clerk. Personal checks accepted. Prepayment is required.

Wolfe County

Circuit & District Court Box 296, Campton, KY 41301; 606-668-3736; Fax: 606-668-3198. Hours: 8:30AM-4:30PM (EST). *Felony, Misdemeanor, Civil, Eviction, Small Claims, Probate.*

Civil Records: Access: Mail, in person. Both court and visitors may perform in person searches. No search fee. Required to search: name, years to search. Civil cases indexed by defendant, plaintiff. Civil records on computer from 1992 to present, index books prior.

Criminal Records: Access: Mail, in person. Both court and visitors may perform in person searches. No search fee. Required to search: name, years to search; also helpful: DOB, SSN. Criminal records on computer from 1992 to present, index books prior. Mail requests should be directed to Pretrial Services, 100 Millcreek Park, Frankfort, KY 40601, 502-573-2350.

General Information: Public access terminal is available. No adoption, mental, juvenile, or sealed records released. SASE required. Turnaround time same day. Copy fee: $.25 per page. Certification fee: $5.00. Fee payee: Circuit Clerk. Personal checks accepted. Prepayment is required.

Woodford County

Circuit & District Court 130 Court St, Versailles, KY 40383; 859-873-3711. Hours: 8AM-4PM M-Th; 8AM-6PM F (EST). *Felony, Misdemeanor, Civil, Eviction, Small Claims, Probate.*

Civil Records: Access: In person only. Visitors must perform in person searches for themselves. No search fee. Required to search: name, years to search. Civil cases indexed by defendant, plaintiff. Civil records on computer from 02/91 to present, index cards from 1978 to 1991.

Criminal Records: Access: In person only. Visitors must perform in person searches for themselves. No search fee. Required to search: name, years to search; also helpful: SSN. Criminal records on computer from 02/91 to present, index cards from 1978 to 1991.

General Information: Public access terminal is available. No adoption, mental, juvenile, or sealed records released. Copy fee: $.25 per page. Certification fee: $5.00. Fee payee: Circuit Clerk. Personal checks accepted. Prepayment is required.

Kentucky Recording Offices

ORGANIZATION: 120 counties, 122 recording offices. The recording officer is County Clerk. Kenton County has two recording offices. Jefferson County hads a separate office for UCC filing until June 30, 2001; that office now only searches for filings up to that date. 80 counties are in the Eastern Time Zone (EST) and 40 are in the Central Time Zone (CST)

REAL ESTATE RECORDS: Most counties will not perform real estate searches. Copy fees vary. Certification fee is usually $5 per document. Tax records are maintained by the Property Valuation Administrator, designated "Assessor" in this section.

UCC RECORDS: Under revised Article 9, Kentucky changes from a "local filing state" to a "central filing state" with the Secretary Of State's office. Collateral on non-resident debtors were always filed at the state level. Rela estate related UCC is still found at the County Clerk's offcie. Many counties will not perform UCC searches. Use search request form UCC-11. Search fees are usually $5.00 per debtor name, and copy fees vary widely.

TAX LIEN RECORDS: All federal and state tax liens on personal property are filed with the County Clerk, often in an "Encumbrance Book." Most counties will not perform tax lien searches.

OTHER LIENS: Judgments, motor vehicle, mechanics, lis pendens, bail bond

ONLINE ACCESS: Three counties offer free access to assessor records. Several other counties offer commercial systems. There is no statewide system.

Adair County

County Clerk, 424 Public Square, Columbia, KY 42728. 270-384-2801; Fax 270-384-4805.
Will search UCC records. This agency will not do a tax lien search. Will not search real estate records. **Other Phone Numbers:** Assessor 270-384-3673.

Allen County

County Clerk, 201 W. Main St, Room 6, Scottsville, KY 42164. County Clerk, R/E and UCC Recording 270-237-3706; Fax 270-237-9206.
Will search UCC records. This agency will not do a tax lien search. Will not search real estate records. **Other Phone Numbers:** Assessor 270-237-3711.

Anderson County

County Clerk, 151 S. Main, Lawrenceburg, KY 40342. 502-839-3041; Fax 502-839-3043.
Will search UCC records. This agency will not do a tax lien search. Will not search real estate records. **Other Phone Numbers:** Assessor 502-839-4061.

Ballard County

County Clerk, PO Box 145, Wickliffe, KY 42087. County Clerk, R/E and UCC Recording 270-335-5168; Fax 270-335-3081.
Will search UCC records. UCC search includes tax liens if requested. Mortgage searches available. **Other Phone Numbers:** Assessor 270-335-3400; Treasurer 270-335-5176; Elections 270-335-5168; Vital Records 270-335-5123.

Barren County

County Clerk, 924 Happy Valley Rd., Suite A, Glasgow, KY 42141-2812. 270-651-5200; Fax 270-651-1083.
Will search UCC records. This agency will not do a tax lien search. Will not search real estate records. **Other Phone Numbers:** Assessor 270-651-2026.

Bath County

County Clerk, PO Box 609, Owingsville, KY 40360. 606-674-2613; Fax 606-674-9526.
Will not search UCC records. UCC search includes tax liens if requested. Real estate record owner and mortgage searches available. **Other Phone Numbers:** Assessor 606-674-6382.

Bell County

County Clerk, PO Box 156, Pineville, KY 40977. County Clerk, R/E and UCC Recording 606-337-6143; Fax 606-337-5415.
Will search UCC records. This agency will not do a tax lien search. Will not search real estate records. **Other Phone Numbers:** Assessor 606-337-2720; Treasurer 606-337-2497; Elections 606-337-6143.

Boone County

County Clerk, PO Box 874, Burlington, KY 41005. 859-334-2137;   Fax   859-334-2193. www.boonecountyclerk.com
Will search UCC records. This agency will not do a tax lien search. Will not search real estate records. **Online Access:** Real Estate, Lines, UCC, Assessor, Marriage Records. Access to the county clerk database is available through eCCLIX, a fee-based service; $200.00 sign-up and $65.00 monthly. Records go back to 1989; images to 1998. For information, see the web site or call 502-266-9445. **Other Phone Numbers:** Assessor 859-334-2236; Treasurer 859-334-2150.

Bourbon County

County Clerk, PO Box 312, Paris, KY 40362-0312. 859-987-2142; Fax 859-987-5660.
Will search UCC records. This agency will not do a tax lien search. Will not search real estate records. **Other Phone Numbers:** Assessor 859-987-2152.

Boyd County

County Clerk, PO Box 523, Catlettsburg, KY 41129. 606-739-5116; Fax 606-739-6357.
Will search UCC records. This agency will not do a tax lien search. Will not search real estate records. **Online Access:** Real Estate, Lien Records. Access to the County Clerk online records requires a $10 monthly usage fee. The system operates 24 hours daily; records date back to 1/1979. Lending agency information is available. For information, contact Maxine Selbee or Kathy Fisher at 606-739-5166. **Other Phones:** Assessor 606-739-5173; Treasurer 606-739-4242.

Boyle County

County Clerk, 321 W. Main St., Room 123, Danville, KY 40422-1837. County Clerk, R/E and UCC Recording 859-238-1112; Fax 859-238-1114.
Will search UCC records. UCC search includes tax liens if requested. Will not search real estate records. **Other Phones:** assessor 238-1104; treasurer 238-1118.

Bracken County

County Clerk, PO Box 147, Brooksville, KY 41004-0147. County Clerk, R/E and UCC Recording 606-735-2952; Fax 606-735-2925.
Will search UCC records. This agency will not do a tax lien search. Will not search real estate records. **Other Phone Numbers:** Assessor 606-735-2228; Treasurer 606-735-2125; Appraiser/Auditor 606-735-2228; Elections 606-735-2952606-735-2952.

Breathitt County

County Clerk, 1137 Main St, Jackson, KY 41339. County Clerk, R/E and UCC Recording 606-666-3810; Fax 606-666-3807.
Will search UCC records. This agency will not do a tax lien search. Will not search real estate records. **Other Phone Numbers:** Treasurer 606-666-4268; Elections 606-666-3810.

Breckinridge County

County Clerk, PO Box 538, Hardinsburg, KY 40143. County Clerk, R/E and UCC Recording 270-756-6166 UCC Recording: 270-756-2246; Fax 270-756-1569.
This agency will not perform searches. **Other Phone Numbers:** Assessor 270-756-5154; Treasurer 270-756-2269; Elections 270-756-2246.

Bullitt County

County Clerk, PO Box 6, Shepherdsville, KY 40165-0006. County Clerk, R/E and UCC Recording 502-543-2513; Fax 502-543-9121.
Will search UCC records. This agency will not do a tax lien search. Will not search real estate records. **Other Phone Numbers:** Assessor 502-543-7480; Treasurer 502-543-2262; Elections 502-543-2513; Vital Records 502-543-2415.

Butler County

County Clerk, PO Box 449, Morgantown, KY 42261. 270-526-5676; Fax 270-526-2658.
This agency will not perform searches.

Caldwell County

County Clerk, 100 E Market St, Rm 3, Courthouse - Room 3, Princeton, KY 42445. 270-365-6754; Fax 270-365-7447.
Will search UCC records. This agency will not do a tax lien search. Will not search real estate records. **Other Phone Numbers:** Assessor 270-365-7227; Treasurer 270-365-9776; Elections 270-365-6754.

Calloway County

County Clerk, 101 S. 5th St, Murray, KY 42071-2569. 270-753-3923; Fax 270-759-9611.
Will search UCC records. This agency will not do a tax lien search. Will not search real estate records. **Other Phone Numbers:** Assessor 270-753-3482.

Campbell County

County Clerk, 4th and York Streets, Courthouse, Newport, KY 41071. 859-292-3850 R/E Recording: 859-292-3845; Fax 859-292-3887.
Will search UCC records. This agency will not do a tax lien search. Will not search real estate records. **Other Phone Numbers:** Assessor 859-292-3871; Treasurer 859-292-3838; Appraiser/Auditor 859-292-3871; Elections 859-292-3885.

Carlisle County

County Clerk, PO Box 176, Bardwell, KY 42023. 270-628-3233; Fax 270-628-0191.
Will search UCC records. Will not search real estate records. **Other Phone Numbers:** Assessor 270-628-5498; Treasurer 270-628-3922.

Carroll County

County Clerk, 440 Main St, Court House, Carrollton, KY 41008. County Clerk, R/E and UCC Recording 502-732-7005; Fax 502-732-7007.
Will search UCC records. Tax liens not included in UCC search. Will not search real estate records. **Other Phone Numbers:** Assessor 502-732-5448; Treasurer 502-732-7000; Elections 502-732-7005.

Carter County

County Clerk, 300 W. Main St., Room 232, Grayson, KY 41143. County Clerk, R/E and UCC Recording 606-474-5188; Fax 606-474-6883.
Will search UCC records. This agency will not do a tax lien search. Will not search real estate records. **Other Phone Numbers:** Assessor 606-474-5663; Treasurer 606-474-9551; Elections 606-474-5188; Vital Records 606-474-5188.

Casey County

County Clerk, Box 310, Liberty, KY 42539. 606-787-6471; Fax 606-787-9155.
Will search UCC records. This agency will not do a tax lien search. Will not search real estate records. **Other Phone Numbers:** Assessor 606-787-7621.

Christian County

County Clerk, 511 S. Main, Hopkinsville, KY 42240. 270-887-4105 R/E Recording: 270-887-4109; Fax 270-887-4186.
Will search UCC records. This agency will not do a tax lien search. Will not search real estate records. **Other Phone Numbers:** Assessor 270-887-4115; Treasurer 270-887-4103; Appraiser/Auditor 270-887-4115; Elections 270-887-4105.

Clark County

County Clerk, PO Box 4060, Winchester, KY 40392. 859-745-0280 R/E Recording: 859-745-0282; Fax 859-745-4251.
Will search UCC records. This agency will not do a tax lien search. Will not search real estate records. **Other Phone Numbers:** Assessor 859-745-0270; Treasurer 859-745-0200; Elections 859-745-0280; Vital Records 859-745-0282.

Clay County

County Clerk, 316 Main St, Suite 143, Manchester, KY 40962. 606-598-2544; Fax 606-598-7199.
Will search UCC records. Will not search real estate records. **Other Phone Numbers:** Assessor 606-598-3832; Treasurer 606-598-2071.

Clinton County

County Clerk, 212 Washington St, Courthouse, Albany, KY 42602. County Clerk, R/E and UCC Recording 606-387-5943; Fax 606-387-5258.
Will search UCC records. This agency will not do a tax lien search. Will not search real estate records. **Other Phone Numbers:** Treasurer 606-387-5234; Elections 606-387-5943; Vital Records 606-387-5943.

Crittenden County

County Clerk, 107 S. Main, Courthouse, Suite 203, Marion, KY 42064. 270-965-3403; Fax 270-965-3447.
Will search UCC records. This agency will not do a tax lien search. Will not search real estate records. **Other Phone Numbers:** Assessor 270-965-4598.

Cumberland County

County Clerk, PO Box 275, Burkesville, KY 42717. County Clerk, R/E and UCC Recording 270-864-3726; Fax 270-864-5884.
Will search UCC records. This agency will not do a tax lien search. Will not search real estate records. **Other Phone Numbers:** Assessor 270-864-5161; Treasurer 270-864-3444; Elections 270-864-3726.

Daviess County

County Clerk, PO Box 609, Owensboro, KY 42302. 270-685-8420; Fax 270-685-2431.
Will search UCC records. This agency will not do a tax lien search. Will not search real estate records. **Other Phones:** Assessor 270-685-8474; Treasurer 685-8424.

Edmonson County

County Clerk, PO Box 830, Brownsville, KY 42210-0830. County Clerk, R/E and UCC Recording 270-597-2624; Fax 270-597-9714.
Will search UCC records. This agency will not do a tax lien search. Will not search real estate records. **Other Phones:** Assessor 270-597-2381; Treasurer 597-2819; Elections 270-597-2624; Vital Records 270-597-2624.

Elliott County

County Clerk, PO Box 225, Sandy Hook, KY 41171-0225. 606-738-5421; Fax 606-738-4462.
Will search UCC records. Tax liens not included in UCC search. Will not search real estate records. **Other Phones:** Assessor 738-5090; Treasurer 606-738-5821.

Estill County

County Clerk, PO BOX 59, Irvine, KY 40336. 606-723-5156; Fax 606-723-5108.
Will search UCC records. UCC search includes tax liens if requested. Real estate owner, mortgage, and property transfer searches available. **Other Phone Numbers:** Assessor 606-723-4569.

Fayette County

County Clerk, 162 E. Main St, Lexington, KY 40507-1334. 859-253-3344.
Will search UCC records. This agency will not do a tax lien search. Will not search real estate records. **Online Access:** Property, Crime Map Records. Search the GIS-property mapping site by address at http://arcims.lfucg.com/maps/zoning/viewer.htm. No name searching. Also, search the interactive crime map at http://crimewatch.lfucg.com. **Other Phones:** Assessor 859-254-2722; Treasurer 859-258-3300.

Fleming County

County Clerk, Court Square, Flemingsburg, KY 41041. County Clerk, R/E and UCC Recording 606-845-8461; Fax 606-845-0212.
Will search UCC records. This agency will not do a tax lien search. Will not search real estate records. **Other Phones:** Assessor 845-8801; Treasurer 606-845-8801; Elections 606-845-8461; Vital Records 606-845-8461.

Floyd County

County Clerk, PO Box 1089, Prestonsburg, KY 41653-5089. 606-886-3816; Fax 606-886-8089.
Will search UCC records. This agency will not do a tax lien search. Will not search real estate records. **Other Phone Numbers:** Assessor 606-886-9622.

Franklin County

County Clerk, PO Box 338, Frankfort, KY 40602. 502-875-8703 R/E Recording: 502-875-8710; Fax 502-875-8718. www.franklincountyclerk.org
Will search UCC records. This agency will not do a tax lien search. Will not search real estate records. **Other Phone Numbers:** Treasurer 502-875-8747; Elections 502-875-8704; Vital Records 502-875-8702.

Fulton County

County Clerk, PO Box 126, Hickman, KY 42050. 270-236-2061; Fax 270-236-2522.
Will search UCC records. Real estate owner, mortgage, and property transfer searches available. **Other Phones:** Assessor 270-236-2548; Treasurer 270-236-2594.

Gallatin County

County Clerk, PO Box 1309, Warsaw, KY 41095. 859-567-5411; Fax 859-567-5444.
Will search UCC records. This agency will not do a tax lien search. Will not search real estate records. **Other Phone Numbers:** Assessor 859-567-5621; Treasurer 859-567-5691; Elections 859-567-5411.

Garrard County

County Clerk, Courthouse Building, Lancaster, KY 40444. County Clerk, R/E and UCC Recording 859-792-3071; Fax 859-792-6751.
Berea, KY addresses may be in Madison County, and parts of Crab Orchard are in Lincoln County. Will search UCC records. UCC search includes tax liens if requested. Real estate owner, mortgage, and property transfer searches available. **Other Phone Numbers:** Assessor 859-792-3291.

Grant County

County Clerk, Courthouse Basement, Room 15, 101 N. Main St., Williamstown, KY 41097. 859-824-3321; Fax 859-824-3367.
Will search UCC records. This agency will not do a tax lien search. Will not search real estate records. **Other Phones:** Assessor 824-6511; Treasurer 859-824-7561.

Graves County

County Clerk, Courthouse, Mayfield, KY 42066. 270-247-1676 R/E Recording: 270-247-1697; Fax 270-247-1274.
Will search UCC records. Tax liens not included in UCC search. Will not search real estate records. **Other Phone Numbers:** Assessor 270-247-3301; Treasurer 270-247-3626; Elections 270-247-1676.

Grayson County

County Clerk, 10 Public Square, Leitchfield, KY 42754. County Clerk, R/E and UCC Recording 270-259-5295 UCC Recording: 270-259-3201; Fax 270-259-9264.
Will search UCC records. Will not search real estate records. **Other Phone Numbers:** Assessor 270-259-4838; Treasurer 270-259-5000; Elections 270-259-3201; Vital Records 270-259-5295.

Green County

County Clerk, 203 W. Court St, Greensburg, KY 42743. 270-932-5386; Fax 270-932-6241.
Will search UCC records. UCC search includes tax liens if requested. Will not search real estate records. **Other Phone Numbers:** Assessor 270-932-7518; Treasurer 270-932-4024.

Greenup County

County Clerk, PO Box 686, Greenup, KY 41144-0686. County Clerk, R/E and UCC Recording 606-473-7396; Fax 606-473-5354.
Will search UCC records. This agency will not do a tax lien search. Will not search real estate records. **Other Phone Numbers:** Assessor 606-473-9984; Treasurer 606-473-5350; Elections 606-473-7396; Vital Records 606-473-7396.

Hancock County

County Clerk, PO Box 146, Hawesville, KY 42348. 270-927-6117; Fax 270-927-8639.
Will search UCC records. This agency will not do a tax lien search. Will not search real estate records. **Other Phone Numbers:** Assessor 270-927-6846; Treasurer 270-927-8101.

Hardin County

County Clerk, PO Box 1030, Elizabethtown, KY 42702. 270-765-4116 R/E Recording: 270-765-2171; Fax 270-769-2682.
Will search UCC records. This agency will not do a tax lien search. Will not search real estate records. **Other Phone Numbers:** Assessor 270-765-2129; Treasurer 270-765-2350; Elections 270-765-6762; Vital Records 270-765-2171.

Harlan County

County Clerk, PO Box 670, Harlan, KY 40831-0670. County Clerk, R/E and UCC Recording 606-573-3636; Fax 606-573-0064.
Will search UCC records. This agency will not do a tax lien search. Will not search real estate records. **Other Phone Numbers:** Assessor 606-573-1990; Treasurer 606-573-4771.

Harrison County

County Clerk, 190 W. Pike St, Cynthiana, KY 41031-1397. 859-234-7130; Fax 859-234-8049.
Will search UCC records. This agency will not do a tax lien search. Will not search real estate records. **Other Phone Numbers:** Assessor 859-234-7113; Treasurer 859-234-7136.

Hart County

County Clerk, PO Box 277, Munfordville, KY 42765. County Clerk, R/E and UCC Recording 270-524-2751; Fax 270-524-0458.
Will search UCC records. This agency will not do a tax lien search. Will not search real estate records. **Other Phone Numbers:** Assessor 270-524-2321; Treasurer 270-524-9474.

Henderson County

County Clerk, PO Box 374, Henderson, KY 42419-0374. County Clerk, R/E and UCC Recording 270-826-3906; Fax 270-826-9677.
Will search UCC records. This agency will not do a tax lien search. Will not search real estate records. **Other Phone Numbers:** Assessor 270-827-6024; Treasurer 270-826-3233; Appraiser/Auditor 270-826-6024; Elections 270-826-3906.

Henry County

County Clerk, PO Box 615, New Castle, KY 40050-0615. 502-845-5705; Fax 502-845-5708.
Will search UCC records. This agency will not do a tax lien search. Will not search real estate records.

Hickman County

County Clerk, Courthouse, 110 E. Clay, Clinton, KY 42031-1296. 270-653-2131; Fax 270-653-4248.
Will search UCC records. This agency will not do a tax lien search. Will not search real estate records. **Other Phone Numbers:** Assessor 270-653-5521; Treasurer

270-653-6195; Elections 270-653-2131; Vital Records 270-653-6110.

Hopkins County

County Clerk, 10 S Main St, Madisonville, KY 42431. County Clerk, R/E and UCC Recording 270-821-7361 UCC Recording: 270-825-5001; Fax 270-825-7000.
Will search UCC records. This agency will not do a tax lien search. Will not search real estate records. **Other Phone Numbers:** Assessor 270-825-3092; Treasurer 270-825-2666.

Jackson County

County Clerk, PO Box 700, McKee, KY 40447-0700. 606-287-7800; Fax 606-287-4505.
Will search UCC records. This agency will not do a tax lien search. Will not search real estate records. **Other Phone Numbers:** Assessor 606-287-7634; Treasurer 606-287-8562.

Jefferson County Clerk

County Clerk, PO Box 35339, Louisville, KY 40232-5339. 502-574-6427; Fax 502-574-6041.
Will search UCC records. This agency will not do a tax lien search. See Recorder for real estate records. **Online Access:** Property, Assessor Records. Access to the county property valuation administrator's Assessment Roll is available free at www.pvalouky.org. **Other Phone Numbers:** Assessor 502-574-6380.

Jefferson County Recorder

County Clerk, 527 W Jefferson St, Rm 204, Louisville, KY 40202. County Clerk, R/E and UCC Recording 502-574-5785 UCC Recording: 502-574-6130; Fax 502-574-8130.
Will search UCC records, but only real estate related UCC filed here. This agency will not do a tax lien search. Will not search real estate records.

Jessamine County

County Clerk, 101 N. Main St, Nicholasville, KY 40356-1270. County Clerk, R/E and UCC Recording 859-885-4161; Fax 859-885-5837.
Will search UCC records. This agency will not do a tax lien search. Will not search real estate records. **Other Phone Numbers:** Assessor 859-885-4931; Treasurer 859-885-4500; Elections 859-885-4161.

Johnson County

County Clerk, Courthouse, Court St., Paintsville, KY 41240. 606-789-2557; Fax 606-789-2559.
Will search UCC records. UCC search includes tax liens. Real estate owner, mortgage, and property transfer searches available. **Other Phone Numbers:** Assessor 606-789-2564.

Kenton County (1st District)

County Clerk, PO Box 1109, Covington, KY 41012. 859-491-0702; Fax 859-491-4515. www.kentonpva.com
Will search UCC records. This agency will not do a tax lien search. Will not search real estate records. **Online Access:** Property Appraiser Records. Access to the county Property Valuation database is available at www.kentonpva.com. Click on "Property Data." Search for free by using "Guest Access." For full, professional property data you may subscribe; fee for user name/password is $50. per month. **Other Phone Numbers:** Assessor 859-491-2728; Treasurer 859-491-2800.

Kenton County (2nd District)

County Clerk, PO Box 38, Independence, KY 41051. 859-356-9272; Fax 859-356-9278. www.kentonpva.com
2nd District includes property south of Banklick Creek. 1st District includes property north of Banklick Creek. Will search UCC records. This agency will not do a tax

lien search. Will search real estate records. **Online Access:** Property Appraiser Records. Access to the county Property Valuation database is available free at www.kentonpva.com/pvacat/catsearch.htm. **Other Phone Numbers:** Assessor 859-491-2728; Treasurer 859-356-4942.

Knott County

County Clerk, PO Box 446, Hindman, KY 41822. 606-785-5651; Fax 606-785-0996.
Will search UCC records. UCC search includes tax liens if requested with extra fee Real estate owner, mortgage, and property transfer searches available. **Other Phone Numbers:** Assessor 606-785-5569; Treasurer 606-785-5592.

Knox County

County Clerk, 401 Court Square, Suite 102, Barbourville, KY 40906. County Clerk, R/E and UCC Recording 606-546-3568; Fax 606-546-3589.
Will search UCC records. This agency will not do a tax lien search. Will not search real estate records. **Other Phone Numbers:** Assessor 606-546-4113; Treasurer 546-6192; Elections 546-3568; Vital Recs 564-4212.

Larue County

County Clerk, 209 W. High St., Hodgenville, KY 42748. 270-358-3544; Fax 270-358-4528.
Will search UCC records. Tax liens not included in UCC search. Real estate owner, mortgage, and property transfer searches available. **Other Phone Numbers:** Assessor 270-358-4202; Treasurer 270-358-4400.

Laurel County

County Clerk, 101 S. Main, Courthouse, London, KY 40741. 606-864-5158; Fax 606-864-7369.
Will search UCC records. This agency will not do a tax lien search. Will not search real estate records. **Other Phone Numbers:** Assessor 606-864-2889.

Lawrence County

County Clerk, 122 S. Main Cross St, Louisa, KY 41230. County Clerk, R/E and UCC Recording 606-638-4108 UCC Recording: 606-638-0504; Fax 606-638-0638.
Will search UCC records. This agency will not do a tax lien search. Will not search real estate records. **Other Phones:** Assessor 638-4743; Treasurer 638-4102.

Lee County

County Clerk, PO Box 551, Beattyville, KY 41311. County Clerk, R/E and UCC Recording 606-464-4115; Fax 606-464-4102.
Will search UCC records. This agency will not do a tax lien search. Will search real estate records. **Other Phone Numbers:** Assessor 606-464-4105; Treasurer 606-464-4100; Elections 606-464-4115; Vital Records 606-464-4115; 2nd Main Number 606-464-4116.

Leslie County

County Clerk, PO Box 916, Hyden, KY 41749-0916. 606-672-2193; Fax 606-672-4264.
Will search UCC records. This agency will not do a tax lien search. Will not search real estate records. **Other Phone Numbers:** Assessor 606-672-2456.

Letcher County

County Clerk, PO Box 28, Whitesburg, KY 41858. 606-633-2432; Fax 606-632-9282.
Will search UCC records. This agency will not do a tax lien search. Will not search real estate records. **Other Phone Numbers:** Assessor 606-633-2182.

Lewis County

County Clerk, PO Box 129, Vanceburg, KY 41179-0129. County Clerk, R/E and UCC Recording 606-796-3062; Fax 606-796-6511.

Will search UCC records. UCC search includes tax liens if requested. Real estate record owner and mortgage searches available. **Other Phone Numbers:** Assessor 606-796-2622; Treasurer 606-796-2722; Elections 606-796-2311; Vital Records 606-796-3062.

Lincoln County

County Clerk, 102 E. Main, Courthouse, Stanford, KY 40484. 606-365-4570 R/E Recording: 606-365-4520; Fax 606-365-4572.

Will search UCC records. This agency will not do a tax lien search. Will not search real estate records. **Other Phone Numbers:** Assessor 606-365-4550; Treasurer 606-365-4590; Elections 606-365-4570.

Livingston County

County Clerk, PO Box 400, Smithland, KY 42081-0400. 270-928-2162; Fax 270-928-2162.

Will search UCC records. This agency will not do a tax lien search. Will not search real estate records. **Other Phone Numbers:** Assessor 270-928-2524.

Logan County

County Clerk, PO Box 358, Russellville, KY 42276-0358. 270-726-6061; Fax 270-726-4355.

Will search UCC records. UCC search includes tax liens if requested. Will not search real estate records. **Other Phone Numbers:** Assessor 270-726-8334; Treasurer 270-726-2167.

Lyon County

County Clerk, PO Box 310, Eddyville, KY 42038. County Clerk, R/E and UCC Recording 270-388-2331; Fax 270-388-0634.

Will search UCC records. This agency will not do a tax lien search. Will not search real estate records. **Other Phone Numbers:** Assessor 270-388-7271; Treasurer 270-388-7193; Elections 270-388-2331.

Madison County

County Clerk, 101 W. Main St, County Court House, Richmond, KY 40475-1415. 859-624-4704; Fax 859-624-8474.

Will search UCC records. This agency will not do a tax lien search. Will not search real estate records. **Other Phone Numbers:** Assessor 859-624-4704.

Magoffin County

County Clerk, PO Box 530, Salyersville, KY 41465. County Clerk, R/E and UCC Recording 606-349-2216; Fax 606-349-2328.

Will search UCC records. This agency will not do a tax lien search. Will not search real estate records. **Other Phone Numbers:** Assessor 606-349-6198; Treasurer 606-349-2313; Elections 606-349-6194; Vital Records 606-349-2216.

Marion County

County Clerk, Courthouse, Suite 3, 120 W. Main St., Lebanon, KY 40033. 270-692-2651; Fax 270-692-9811.

Will search UCC records. This agency will not do a tax lien search. Will not search real estate records. **Other Phone Numbers:** Assessor 270-692-3401; Treasurer 270-692-3451.

Marshall County

County Clerk, Courthouse, 1101 Main St., Benton, KY 42025. 270-527-4740; Fax 270-527-4738.

Will not search UCC records. Will not search real estate records. **Other Phone Numbers:** Assessor 270-527-4728.

Martin County

County Clerk, PO Box 460, Inez, KY 41224-0485. 606-298-2810; Fax 606-298-0143.

Will search UCC records. This agency will not do a tax lien search. Will not search real estate records. **Other Phone Numbers:** Assessor 606-298-2808.

Mason County

County Clerk, PO Box 234, Maysville, KY 41056. 606-564-3341; Fax 606-564-8979.

Will search UCC records. This agency will not do a tax lien search. Will not search real estate records. **Other Phone Numbers:** Assessor 606-564-3700; Treasurer 606-564-6381.

McCracken County

County Clerk, PO Box 609, Paducah, KY 42002-0609. 270-444-4700; Fax 270-444-4704.

Will search UCC records. This agency will not do a tax lien search. Will not search real estate records. **Other Phone Numbers:** Assessor 270-444-4712; Treasurer 270-444-4725.

McCreary County

County Clerk, PO Box 699, Whitley City, KY 42653. 606-376-2411; Fax 606-376-3898.

Will search UCC records. UCC search includes tax liens if requested. Will not search real estate records. **Other Phone Numbers:** Assessor 606-376-2514.

McLean County

County Clerk, PO Box 57, Calhoun, KY 42327-0057. County Clerk, R/E and UCC Recording 270-273-3082; Fax 270-273-5084.

Will search UCC records. This agency will not do a tax lien search. Will not search real estate records. **Other Phone Numbers:** Assessor 270-273-3291; Treasurer 270-273-9964; Elections 270-273-3082.

Meade County

County Clerk, PO Box 614, Brandenburg, KY 40108. 270-422-2152; Fax 270-422-2158.

Will search UCC records. This agency will not do a tax lien search. Will not search real estate records. **Other Phone Numbers:** Assessor 270-422-2178.

Menifee County

County Clerk, PO Box 123, Frenchburg, KY 40322-0123. County Clerk, R/E and UCC Recording 606-768-3512; Fax 606-768-2144.

Will search UCC records. This agency will not do a tax lien search. Will not search real estate records. **Other Phone Numbers:** Assessor 606-768-3514; Treasurer 606-768-3514; Elections 606-768-3512; Vital Records 606-768-3512.

Mercer County

County Clerk, PO Box 426, Harrodsburg, KY 40330. 859-734-6313; Fax 859-734-6309.

Will search UCC records. UCC search includes tax liens if requested. Will not search real estate records. **Other Phone Numbers:** Assessor 859-734-6330.

Metcalfe County

County Clerk, PO Box 25, Edmonton, KY 42129. 270-432-4821; Fax 270-432-5176.

Will search UCC records. This agency will not do a tax lien search. Will not search real estate records. **Other Phone Numbers:** Assessor 270-432-3162; Treasurer 270-432-3181.

Monroe County

County Clerk, PO Box 188, Tompkinsville, KY 42167. County Clerk, R/E and UCC Recording 270-487-5471; Fax 270-487-5976.

Will search UCC records. UCC search includes tax liens. Will not search real estate records. **Other Phone Numbers:** Assessor 270-487-6401; Treasurer 270-487-5505; Elections 270-487-5471.

Montgomery County

County Clerk, PO Box 414, Mount Sterling, KY 40353. County Clerk, R/E and UCC Recording 859-498-8700; Fax 859-498-8729.

Will search UCC records. This agency will not do a tax lien search. Will not search real estate records. **Other Phones:** Assessor 498-8710; Treasurer 859-498-8703.

Morgan County

County Clerk, PO Box 26, West Liberty, KY 41472. County Clerk, R/E and UCC Recording 606-743-3949; Fax 606-743-2111.

Will search UCC records. This agency will not do a tax lien search. Will not search real estate records. **Other Phone Numbers:** Assessor 606-743-3349; Treasurer 606-743-3195; Appraiser/Auditor 606-743-3349; Elections 606-743-3949; Vital Records 606-743-3949.

Muhlenberg County

County Clerk, PO Box 525, Greenville, KY 42345. 270-338-1441; Fax 270-338-1774.

Will search UCC records. UCC search includes tax liens if requested. Will not search real estate records. **Other Phone Numbers:** Assessor 270-338-4664.

Nelson County

County Clerk, PO Box 312, Bardstown, KY 40004. County Clerk, R/E and UCC Recording 502-348-1830 UCC Recording: 502-348-1828; Fax 502-348-1822.

Will search UCC records. Will not search real estate records. **Other Phone Numbers:** Assessor 502-348-1810; Treasurer 502-348-1800; Appraiser/Auditor 502-348-1810; Elections 502-348-1829; Vital Records 502-564-4212.

Nicholas County

County Clerk, PO Box 227, Carlisle, KY 40311. 859-289-3730; Fax 859-289-3709.

Will search UCC records. UCC search includes tax liens if requested. Will not search real estate records. **Other Phone Numbers:** Assessor 859-289-3735; Treasurer 859-289-3725; Elections 859-289-3730.

Ohio County

County Clerk, PO Box 85, Hartford, KY 42347. 270-298-4422; Fax 270-298-4425.

Will search UCC records. This agency will not do a tax lien search. Will not search real estate records. **Other Phone Numbers:** Assessor 270-298-3692.

Oldham County

County Clerk, 100 W. Jefferson St, LaGrange, KY 40031. County Clerk, R/E and UCC Recording 502-222-9311; Fax 502-222-3208. http://oldhamcounty.state.ky.us

Will search UCC records. This agency will not do a tax lien search. Will not search real estate records. **Online Access:** Real Estate, Lien, UCC, Assessor, Marriage Records. Access to the county clerk database is available through eCCLIX, a fee-based service; $200.00 sign-up and $65.00 monthly. Records go back, generally, to 1980. UCC images to 2/97. Real estate instruments back to 1/95. Marriages back to 1980. For information, see the web site or call 502-266-9445. **Other Phone Numbers:** Assessor 502-222-9320; Elections 502-222-0047.

Owen County

County Clerk, PO Box 338, Owenton, KY 40359-0338. County Clerk, R/E and UCC Recording 502-484-2213; Fax 502-484-1002.

Will search UCC records. This agency will not do a tax lien search. Will not search real estate records. **Other Phone Numbers:** Assessor 502-484-5172; Treasurer 502-484-3557; Elections 502-484-2213; Vital Records 502-484-2213.

Owsley County

County Clerk, PO Box 500, Booneville, KY 41314. 606-593-5735; Fax 606-593-5737.
Will search UCC records. UCC search includes tax liens if requested. Will not search real estate records. **Other Phone Numbers:** Assessor 606-593-6265; Treasurer 606-593-6202.

Pendleton County

County Clerk, PO Box 112, Falmouth, KY 41040. County Clerk, R/E and UCC Recording 859-654-3380; Fax 859-654-5600.
Will search UCC records. UCC search includes tax liens if requested. Will not search real estate records. **Other Phone Numbers:** Assessor 859-654-6055; Treasurer 859-654-4321; Appraiser/Auditor 859-654-3380; Elections 859-654-3380.

Perry County

County Clerk, PO Box 150, Hazard, KY 41702. County Clerk, R/E and UCC Recording 606-436-4614; Fax 606-439-0557.
Will search UCC records. Tax liens not included in UCC search. Will not search real estate records. **Other Phone Numbers:** Assessor 606-436-4914; Treasurer 606-436-1816.

Pike County

County Clerk, PO Box 631, Pikeville, KY 41502-0631. 606-432-6240; Fax 606-432-6222.
Will search UCC records. This agency will not do a tax lien search. Will not search real estate records. **Other Phone Numbers:** Assessor 606-432-6201.

Powell County

County Clerk, PO Box 548, Stanton, KY 40380. County Clerk, R/E and UCC Recording 606-663-6444; Fax 606-663-6406.
Will search UCC records. This agency will not do a tax lien search. Will not search real estate records. **Other Phone Numbers:** Assessor 606-663-4184; Treasurer 606-663-2834; Appraiser/Auditor 606-663-4184; Vital Records 502-564-4212.

Pulaski County

County Clerk, PO Box 724, Somerset, KY 42502. 606-679-3652 R/E Recording: 606-679-2042 UCC Recording: 606-679-2042; Fax 606-678-0073.
Will search UCC records. This agency will not do a tax lien search. Will not search real estate records. **Other Phones:** Assessor 606-679-1812; Treasurer 679-1311; Elections 606-679-3652; Vital Records 606-679-3652.

Robertson County

County Clerk, PO Box 75, Mount Olivet, KY 41064. 606-724-5212; Fax 606-724-5022.
Will search UCC records. UCC search includes tax liens if requested. Will not search real estate records. **Other Phone Numbers:** Assessor 606-724-5213; Treasurer 606-724-5403.

Rockcastle County

County Clerk, PO Box 365, Mount Vernon, KY 40456. 606-256-2831; Fax 606-256-4302.
Will search UCC records. This agency will not do a tax lien search. Will not search real estate records. **Other Phone Numbers:** Assessor 606-256-4194; Treasurer 606-256-3623.

Rowan County

County Clerk, Courthouse - 2nd Floor, 627 E. Main St, Morehead, KY 40351. County Clerk, R/E and UCC Recording 606-784-5212; Fax 606-784-2923.
Will search UCC records. This agency will not do a tax lien search. Will not search real estate records. **Other**

Phone Numbers: Assessor 606-784-5512; Treasurer 606-784-4211; Vital Records 502-564 4212.

Russell County

County Clerk, PO Box 579, Jamestown, KY 42629-0579. 270-343-2125; Fax 270-343-4700.
Will search UCC records. This agency will not do a tax lien search. Will not search real estate records. **Other Phone Numbers:** Assessor 270-343-4395; Treasurer 270-343-2112.

Scott County

County Clerk, Courthouse, 101 E. Main St., Georgetown, KY 40324-1794. 502-863-7875; Fax 502-863-7898.
Will search UCC records. This agency will not do a tax lien search. Will not search real estate records. **Other Phone Numbers:** Assessor 502-863-7885; Treasurer 502-863-7850.

Shelby County

County Clerk, PO Box 819, Shelbyville, KY 40066-0819. 502-633-4410; Fax 502-633-7887.
Will search UCC records. This agency will not do a tax lien search. Will not search real estate records. **Other Phone Numbers:** Assessor 502-633-4403; Treasurer 502-633-1220.

Simpson County

County Clerk, PO Box 268, Franklin, KY 42135-0268. 270-586-8161; Fax 270-586-6464.
Will search UCC records. This agency will not do a tax lien search. Will not search real estate records. **Other Phone Numbers:** Assessor 502-586-4261; Treasurer 502-586-7184.

Spencer County

County Clerk, PO Box 544, Taylorsville, KY 40071. 502-477-3215; Fax 502-477-3216.
Will search UCC records. This agency will not do a tax lien search. Will not search real estate records. **Other Phone Numbers:** Assessor 502-477-3207; Treasurer 502-477-3211.

Taylor County

County Clerk, 203 N. Court St, Suite # 5, Campbellsville, KY 42718-2298. County Clerk, R/E and UCC Recording 270-465-6677; Fax 270-789-1144. This agency will not perform searches. **Other Phone Numbers:** Assessor 270-465-5811; Treasurer 270-789-1008.

Todd County

County Clerk, PO Box 307, Elkton, KY 42220. 270-265-2363; Fax 270-265-2588.
Will search UCC records. This agency will not do a tax lien search. Will not search real estate records. **Other Phones:** Assessor 270-265-5614; Treasurer 265-2451.

Trigg County

County Clerk, PO Box 1310, Cadiz, KY 42211. 270-522-6661; Fax 270-522-6662.
Will search UCC records. This agency will not do a tax lien search. Will not search real estate records. **Other Phone Numbers:** Assessor 270-522-6661; Treasurer 270-522-8459.

Trimble County

County Clerk, PO Box 262, Bedford, KY 40006-0262. County Clerk, R/E and UCC Recording 502-255-7174; Fax 502-255-7045.
Will search UCC records. This agency will not do a tax lien search. Will not search real estate records. **Other Phone Numbers:** Assessor 502-255-3592; Elections 502-255-7174; Vital Records 502-255-7174.

Union County

County Clerk, PO Box 119, Morganfield, KY 42437-0119. 270-389-1334; Fax 270-389-9135.
Will search UCC records. This agency will not do a tax lien search. Will not search real estate records. **Other Phone Numbers:** Assessor 270-389-1933.

Warren County

County Clerk, PO Box 478, Bowling Green, KY 42102-0478. County Clerk, R/E and UCC Recording 270-842-9416; Fax 270-843-5319. http://warrencounty.state.ky.us
Will search UCC records. This agency will not do a tax lien search. Will not search real estate records. **Online Access:** Real Estate, Lien, UCC, Assessor, Marriage Records. Access to the county clerk database is available through eCCLIX, a fee-based service; $200.00 sign-up and $65.00 monthly. Records go back to 1989; images to 1998. For information, see the web site or call 502-266-9445. **Other Phone Numbers:** Assessor 270-842-3268; Treasurer 270-842-5805; Elections 270-842-5306; Vital Records 270-842-9416.

Washington County

County Clerk, PO Box 446, Springfield, KY 40069. 859-336-5425; Fax 859-336-5408.
Will search UCC records. Tax liens not included in UCC search. Real estate record owner and mortgage searches available. **Other Phone Numbers:** Assessor 859-336-5420.

Wayne County

County Clerk, PO Box 565, Monticello, KY 42633. County Clerk, R/E and UCC Recording 606-348-6661; Fax 606-348-8303.
Will search UCC records. This agency will not do a tax lien search. Will not search real estate records. **Other Phones:** Assessor 348-6621; Treasurer 606-348-8411.

Webster County

County Clerk, PO Box 19, Dixon, KY 42409-0019. 270-639-7006; Fax 270-639-7029.
Will search UCC records. This agency will not do a tax lien search. Will not search real estate records. **Other Phone Numbers:** Assessor 270-639-7016; Treasurer 270-639-5042.

Whitley County

County Clerk, PO Box 8, Williamsburg, KY 40769. County Clerk, R/E and UCC Recording 606-549-6002; Fax 606-549-2790.
Will search UCC records. This agency will not do a tax lien search. Will not search real estate records. **Other Phone Numbers:** Assessor 606-549-6008.

Wolfe County

County Clerk, PO Box 400, Campton, KY 41301. County Clerk, R/E and UCC Recording 606-668-3515; Fax 606-668-3492.
Will search UCC records. This agency will not do a tax lien search. Will not search real estate records. **Other Phone Numbers:** Assessor 606-668-6923; Treasurer 606-668-4060; Appraiser/Auditor 606-668-6925; Elections 606-668-3515; Vital Records 606-668-4212.

Woodford County

County Clerk, Courthouse - Room 120, 103 S. Main St., Versailles, KY 40383. 859-873-3421; Fax 859-873-6985.
Will search UCC records. This agency will not do a tax lien search. Will not search real estate records. **Other Phone Numbers:** Assessor 859-873-4101; Treasurer 859-873-6122; Elections 859-873-3421.

Kentucky County Locator

You will usually be able to find the city name in the City/County Cross Reference below. In that case, it is a simple matter to determine the county from the cross reference. However, only the official US Postal Service city names are included in this index. There are an additional 40,000 place names that people use in their addresses. Therefore, we have also included a ZIP/City Cross Reference immediately following the City/County Cross Reference.

If you know the ZIP Code but the city name does not appear in the City/County Cross Reference index, look up the ZIP Code in the ZIP/City Cross Reference, find the city name, then look up the city name in the City/County Cross Reference. For example, you want to know the county for an address of Menands, NY 12204. There is no "Menands" in the City/County Cross Reference. The ZIP/City Cross Reference shows that ZIP Codes 12201-12288 are for the city of Albany. Looking back in the City/County Cross Reference, Albany is in Albany County.

City/County Cross Reference

AARON (42601) Clinton(97), Russell(2)
ABERDEEN Butler
ACORN Pulaski
ADAIRVILLE (42202) Logan(97), Simpson(2)
ADAMS Lawrence
ADOLPHUS Allen
AGES BROOKSIDE Harlan
ALBANY Clinton
ALEXANDRIA Campbell
ALLEGRE Todd
ALLEN Floyd
ALLENSVILLE (42204) Todd(72), Logan(27)
ALLOCK Perry
ALMO Calloway
ALPHA (42603) Clinton(69), Wayne(30)
ALTRO Breathitt
ALVATON (42122) Warren(94), Allen(5)
AMBURGEY Knott
ANNVILLE Jackson
ARGILLITE Greenup
ARJAY Bell
ARLINGTON (42021) Carlisle(64), Hickman(35)
ARTEMUS Knox
ARY Perry
ASHCAMP Pike
ASHER Leslie
ASHLAND Boyd
ATHOL Breathitt
AUBURN (42206) Logan(92), Simpson(6), Warren(1)
AUGUSTA Bracken
AUSTIN Barren
AUXIER Floyd
AVAWAM Perry
AXTEL Breckinridge
BAGDAD (40003) Shelby(86), Franklin(13)
BAKERTON Cumberland
BANDANA Ballard
BANNER Floyd
BARBOURVILLE Knox
BARDSTOWN Nelson
BARDWELL Carlisle
BARLOW Ballard
BASKETT Henderson
BATTLETOWN Meade
BAXTER Harlan
BAYS Breathitt
BEAR BRANCH Leslie
BEATTYVILLE Lee
BEAUMONT Metcalfe
BEAUTY Martin
BEAVER Floyd
BEAVER DAM (42320) Ohio(98), Butler(1)
BEDFORD (40006) Trimble(97), Carroll(1)
BEE SPRING Edmonson
BEECH CREEK Muhlenberg
BEECH GROVE McLean
BEECHMONT Muhlenberg
BELCHER Pike
BELFRY Pike

BELLEVUE Campbell
BELTON Muhlenberg
BENHAM Harlan
BENTON (42025) Marshall(98), Calloway(1)
BEREA Madison
BERRY (41003) Grant(78), Harrison(17), Pendleton(3)
BETHANY Wolfe
BETHEL Bath
BETHELRIDGE Casey
BETHLEHEM Henry
BETSY LAYNE (41605) Floyd(97), Pike(2)
BEULAH HEIGHTS McCreary
BEVERLY (40913) Bell(94), Clay(5)
BEVINSVILLE Floyd
BIG CLIFTY (42712) Grayson(60), Hardin(39)
BIG CREEK Clay
BIG LAUREL (40808) Harlan(50), Leslie(50)
BIG SPRING (40106) Breckinridge(80), Hardin(20)
BIGHILL Madison
BIMBLE Knox
BLACKEY Letcher
BLACKFORD Webster
BLAINE Lawrence
BLANDVILLE Ballard
BLEDSOE (40810) Harlan(85), Leslie(14)
BLOOMFIELD (40008) Nelson(90), Spencer(9)
BLUE RIVER Floyd
BLUEHOLE Clay
BOAZ (42027) Graves(80), McCracken(19)
BOND Jackson
BONNIEVILLE Hart
BONNYMAN Perry
BOONEVILLE (41314) Owsley(66), Breathitt(33)
BOONS CAMP Johnson
BOSTON Nelson
BOW (42714) Cumberland(92), Clinton(7)
BOWEN Powell
BOWLING GREEN Warren
BRADFORDSVILLE (40009) Marion(78), Casey(13), Taylor(7)
BRANDENBURG Meade
BREEDING (42715) Adair(92), Metcalfe(6), Cumberland(2)
BREMEN Muhlenberg
BRINKLEY Knott
BRODHEAD (40409) Rockcastle(95), Lincoln(4)
BRONSTON (42518) Pulaski(96), Wayne(3)
BROOKLYN Butler
BROOKS (40109) Bullitt(97), Jefferson(2)
BROOKSVILLE Bracken
BROWDER Muhlenberg
BROWNS FORK Perry
BROWNSVILLE Edmonson
BRUIN Elliott

BRYANTS STORE Knox
BRYANTSVILLE Garrard
BUCKHORN Perry
BUCKNER Oldham
BUFFALO (42716) Larue(75), Green(19), Taylor(4)
BULAN (41722) Perry(66), Knott(33)
BURDINE Letcher
BURGIN Mercer
BURKESVILLE Cumberland
BURKHART Wolfe
BURLINGTON Boone
BURNA Livingston
BURNSIDE Pulaski
BURNWELL Pike
BUSH Laurel
BUSKIRK Morgan
BUSY (41723) Perry(75), Leslie(24)
BUTLER Pendleton
BYPRO Floyd
CADIZ Trigg
CALHOUN (42327) McLean(98), Daviess(1)
CALIFORNIA Campbell
CALVERT CITY Marshall
CALVIN Bell
CAMP DIX Lewis
CAMPBELLSBURG (40011) Henry(75), Trimble(19), Carroll(4)
CAMPBELLSVILLE Taylor
CAMPTON (41301) Wolfe(86), Breathitt(8), Lee(3)
CANADA Pike
CANE VALLEY Adair
CANEY Morgan
CANEYVILLE (42721) Grayson(88), Butler(7), Edmonson(3)
CANMER Hart
CANNEL CITY Morgan
CANNON Knox
CANOE Breathitt
CANTON Trigg
CARLISLE (40311) Nicholas(90), Bourbon(8), Bath(1)
CARRIE Knott
CARROLLTON Carroll
CARTER Carter
CARVER Magoffin
CASEY CREEK (42723) Adair(61), Taylor(31), Casey(6)
CASEY CREEKG (42723) Adair(61), Taylor(31), Casey(6)
CATLETTSBURG (41129) Boyd(96), Lawrence(3)
CAVE CITY (42127) Barren(92), Hart(7)
CAWOOD Harlan
CECILIA Hardin
CENTER (42214) Metcalfe(71), Green(28)
CENTERTOWN Ohio
CENTRAL CITY Muhlenberg
CERULEAN (42215) Trigg(57), Christian(42)
CHAPLIN Nelson

CHAPPELL Leslie
CHAVIES Perry
CINDA Leslie
CISCO Magoffin
CLARKSON Grayson
CLAY (42404) Webster(90), Union(9)
CLAY CITY Powell
CLAYHOLE Breathitt
CLEARFIELD Rowan
CLEATON Muhlenberg
CLERMONT Bullitt
CLIFTY Todd
CLINTON Hickman
CLOSPLINT Harlan
CLOVERPORT Breckinridge
COALGOOD Harlan
COBHILL Estill
COLDIRON Harlan
COLUMBIA Adair
COLUMBUS Hickman
COMBS Perry
CONCORD Lewis
CONFLUENCE Leslie
CONLEY Magoffin
CONSTANCE Boone
CONSTANTINE Breckinridge
CONWAY Rockcastle
COOPERSVILLE Wayne
CORBIN Whitley
CORINTH (41010) Grant(66), Owen(29), Harrison(2), Scott(1)
CORNETTSVILLE (41731) Perry(70), Letcher(30)
CORYDON Henderson
COTTLE Morgan
COVINGTON Kenton
COXS CREEK (40013) Nelson(80), Spencer(12), Bullitt(7)
CRAB ORCHARD (40419) Lincoln(53), Garrard(32), Rockcastle(9), Pulaski(4)
CRANKS Harlan
CRAYNE Crittenden
CRAYNOR Floyd
CRESTWOOD Oldham
CRITTENDEN (41030) Grant(71), Boone(28)
CROCKETT Morgan
CROFTON Christian
CROMONA Letcher
CROMWELL (42333) Ohio(86), Butler(13)
CROWN Letcher
CRYSTAL (40420) Lee(83), Estill(16)
CUB RUN (42729) Hart(79), Edmonson(20)
CULVER Elliott
CUMBERLAND (40823) Harlan(97), Letcher(2)
CUNDIFF Adair
CUNNINGHAM (42035) Carlisle(59), Graves(40)
CURDSVILLE Daviess
CUSTER Breckinridge
CUTSHIN Leslie
CYNTHIANA Harrison

DABOLT Jackson
DAISY Perry
DANA Floyd
DANVILLE Boyle
DAVID Floyd
DAWSON SPRINGS (42408) Hopkins(86), Caldwell(9), Christian(3)
DAYHOIT Harlan
DAYTON Campbell
DE MOSSVILLE Pendleton
DEANE (41812) Letcher(81), Knott(18)
DEBORD Martin
DECOY (41321) Knott(80), Breathitt(20)
DEFOE Henry
DELPHIA Perry
DELTA Wayne
DEMA Knott
DENNISTON Menifee
DENTON (41132) Carter(76), Lawrence(22), Boyd(1)
DENVER Johnson
DEWITT Knox
DEXTER (42036) Calloway(98), Marshall(1)
DICE Perry
DINGUS Morgan
DIXON Webster
DIZNEY Harlan
DORTON Pike
DOVER (41034) Mason(97), Bracken(2)
DRAFFIN Pike
DRAKE Warren
DRAKESBORO Muhlenberg
DREYFUS Madison
DRIFT Floyd
DRY RIDGE Grant
DUBRE (42731) Cumberland(74), Metcalfe(25)
DUNBAR Butler
DUNDEE Ohio
DUNMOR (42339) Muhlenberg(92), Butler(7)
DUNNVILLE (42528) Casey(96), Adair(2), Russell(1)
DWALE Floyd
DWARF Perry
DYCUSBURG Crittenden
EARLINGTON Hopkins
EAST BERNSTADT Laurel
EAST POINT (41216) Floyd(59), Johnson(40)
EASTERN Floyd
EASTVIEW Hardin
EASTWOOD Jefferson
EDDYVILLE Lyon
EDMONTON (42129) Metcalfe(93), Adair(6)
EDNA Magoffin
EGYPT Jackson
EIGHTY EIGHT Barren
EKRON Meade
ELIZABETHTOWN Hardin
ELIZAVILLE Fleming
ELK HORN (42733) Taylor(79), Casey(17), Adair(3)
ELKFORK Morgan
ELKHORN CITY Pike
ELKTON (42220) Todd(97), Muhlenberg(1)
ELLIOTTVILLE Rowan
ELSIE Magoffin
EMERSON Lewis
EMINENCE (40019) Henry(97), Shelby(2)
EMLYN Whitley
EMMA Floyd
EMMALENA Knott
ENDICOTT Floyd
EOLIA Letcher
ERILINE Clay
ERLANGER Kenton
ERMINE Letcher
ESSIE (40827) Leslie(96), Adair(3)
ESTILL Floyd

ETOILE Barren
EUBANK (42567) Pulaski(87), Lincoln(12)
EVARTS Harlan
EWING Fleming
EZEL Morgan
FAIRDALE Jefferson
FAIRFIELD Nelson
FAIRPLAY Adair
FAIRVIEW Christian
FALCON Magoffin
FALL ROCK Clay
FALLS OF ROUGH (40119) Grayson(58), Breckinridge(39), Ohio(2)
FALMOUTH Pendleton
FANCY FARM (42039) Graves(43), Carlisle(36), Hickman(20)
FARMERS Rowan
FARMINGTON (42040) Graves(76), Calloway(23)
FAUBUSH (42532) Pulaski(58), Russell(35), Wayne(6)
FEDSCREEK Pike
FERGUSON Pulaski
FILLMORE Lee
FINCHVILLE Shelby
FINLEY (42736) Taylor(56), Marion(43)
FIREBRICK Lewis
FISHERVILLE (40023) Spencer(53), Jefferson(45)
FISTY Knott
FLAT FORK Magoffin
FLAT LICK Knox
FLATGAP (41219) Johnson(95), Lawrence(4)
FLATWOODS Greenup
FLEMINGSBURG Fleming
FLORENCE Boone
FOGERTOWN Clay
FORD Clark
FORDS BRANCH Pike
FORDSVILLE (42343) Ohio(69), Hancock(30)
FOREST HILLS Pike
FORT CAMPBELL Christian
FORT KNOX (40121) Hardin(74), Meade(25)
FORT THOMAS Campbell
FOSTER Bracken
FOUNTAIN RUN (42133) Monroe(47), Barren(33), Allen(19)
FOURMILE (40939) Knox(65), Bell(34)
FRAKES (40940) Whitley(65), Bell(35)
FRANKFORT Franklin
FRANKLIN Simpson
FRAZER Wayne
FREDONIA (42411) Caldwell(57), Crittenden(37), Lyon(5)
FREDVILLE Magoffin
FREEBURN Pike
FRENCHBURG Menifee
FRITZ Magoffin
FT MITCHELL Kenton
FUGET Johnson
FULTON (42041) Fulton(72), Graves(16), Hickman(11)
GALVESTON Floyd
GAMALIEL Monroe
GAPVILLE Magoffin
GARFIELD (40140) Breckinridge(91), Hardin(8)
GARNER Knott
GARRARD Clay
GARRETT (41630) Knott(54), Floyd(45)
GARRISON (41141) Lewis(43), Carter(32), Greenup(24)
GAYS CREEK Perry
GEORGETOWN Scott
GERMANTOWN (41044) Mason(82), Bracken(17)
GHENT Carroll
GILBERTSVILLE Marshall
GILLMORE Wolfe

GIRDLER Knox
GLASGOW Barren
GLENCOE (41046) Grant(81), Gallatin(18)
GLENDALE Hardin
GLENS FORK (42741) Adair(94), Russell(5)
GLENVIEW Jefferson
GOODY Pike
GOOSE ROCK Clay
GORDON Letcher
GOSHEN Oldham
GRACEY (42232) Christian(78), Trigg(21)
GRADYVILLE Adair
GRAHAM Muhlenberg
GRAHN Carter
GRAND RIVERS Livingston
GRATZ Owen
GRAVEL SWITCH (40328) Marion(44), Boyle(32), Casey(21), Washington(1)
GRAY (40734) Knox(95), Laurel(4)
GRAY HAWK Jackson
GRAYS KNOB Harlan
GRAYSON Carter
GREEN HALL Owsley
GREEN ROAD Knox
GREENSBURG (42743) Green(98), Adair(1)
GREENUP Greenup
GREENVILLE Muhlenberg
GRETHEL Floyd
GULSTON Harlan
GUNLOCK Magoffin
GUSTON (40142) Meade(98), Breckinridge(1)
GUTHRIE Todd
GYPSY Magoffin
HADDIX Breathitt
HADLEY Warren
HAGERHILL Johnson
HALDEMAN Rowan
HALFWAY Allen
HALLIE Letcher
HALO Floyd
HAMLIN Calloway
HAMPTON Livingston
HANSON Hopkins
HAPPY Perry
HARDBURLY Perry
HARDIN (42048) Marshall(96), Calloway(3)
HARDINSBURG Breckinridge
HARDY Pike
HARDYVILLE (42746) Hart(80), Metcalfe(11), Green(7)
HARLAN Harlan
HARNED Breckinridge
HAROLD Floyd
HARRODS CREEK Jefferson
HARRODSBURG (40330) Mercer(95), Washington(4)
HARTFORD Ohio
HAWESVILLE (42348) Hancock(97), Daviess(2)
HAZARD Perry
HAZEL Calloway
HAZEL GREEN (41332) Morgan(79), Wolfe(20)
HEBRON Boone
HEIDELBERG Lee
HEIDRICK Knox
HELLIER Pike
HELTON (40840) Leslie(77), Harlan(22)
HENDERSON Henderson
HENDRICKS Magoffin
HERD Jackson
HERNDON (42236) Christian(85), Trigg(14)
HESTAND (42151) Monroe(90), Metcalfe(9)
HI HAT Floyd
HICKMAN Fulton
HICKORY Graves
HILLSBORO Fleming
HILLVIEW (40129) Jefferson(55), Bullitt(44)

HIMA Clay
HINDMAN Knott
HINKLE Knox
HIPPO Floyd
HISEVILLE Barren
HITCHINS Carter
HODGENVILLE Larue
HOLLAND Allen
HOLLYBUSH Knott
HOLMES MILL Harlan
HONAKER Floyd
HOPE (40334) Bath(88), Montgomery(11)
HOPKINSVILLE Christian
HORSE BRANCH (42349) Ohio(82), Grayson(17)
HORSE CAVE (42749) Hart(91), Metcalfe(6), Barren(2)
HOSKINSTON Leslie
HOWARDSTOWN (40028) Nelson(84), Larue(16)
HUDDY Pike
HUDSON Breckinridge
HUEYSVILLE (41640) Knott(76), Floyd(22)
HUFF Edmonson
HULEN Bell
HUNTER Floyd
HUNTSVILLE Butler
HUSTONVILLE (40437) Lincoln(69), Casey(30)
HYDEN Leslie
INDEPENDENCE Kenton
INEZ Martin
INGLE Pulaski
INGRAM Bell
INSKO Morgan
IRVINE (40336) Estill(97), Lee(1)
IRVINGTON (40146) Breckinridge(98), Meade(1)
ISLAND McLean
ISLAND CITY Owsley
ISOM Letcher
ISONVILLE Elliott
IVEL Floyd
IVYTON Magoffin
JACKHORN Letcher
JACKSON (41339) Breathitt(95), Knott(4)
JACOBS Carter
JAMBOREE Pike
JAMESTOWN Russell
JEFF Perry
JEFFERSONVILLE Montgomery
JENKINS (41537) Letcher(92), Pike(7)
JEREMIAH Letcher
JETSON Butler
JOB Martin
JOHNS RUN Carter
JONANCY Pike
JONESVILLE Grant
JUNCTION CITY Boyle
KEATON Johnson
KEAVY Laurel
KEENE Jessamine
KEITH Harlan
KENTON Kenton
KENVIR Harlan
KERBY KNOB Jackson
KETTLE Cumberland
KETTLE ISLAND Bell
KEVIL (42053) McCracken(58), Ballard(41)
KIMPER Pike
KINGS MOUNTAIN (40442) Lincoln(62), Casey(37)
KIRKSEY (42054) Calloway(79), Marshall(14), Graves(5)
KITE Knott
KNIFLEY Adair
KNOB LICK (42154) Metcalfe(86), Barren(13)
KONA Letcher
KRYPTON (41754) Perry(97), Leslie(2)
KUTTAWA Lyon
LA CENTER Ballard

LA FAYETTE Christian
LA GRANGE Oldham
LACKEY (41643) Knott(88), Floyd(11)
LAMB (42155) Barren(60), Monroe(39)
LAMBRIC Breathitt
LAMERO Rockcastle
LANCASTER Garrard
LANGLEY Floyd
LATONIA Kenton
LAWRENCEBURG Anderson
LEANDER Johnson
LEATHERWOOD Perry
LEBANON Marion
LEBANON JUNCTION (40150) Bullitt(95),
   Hardin(4)
LEBURN Knott
LEDBETTER Livingston
LEE CITY Wolfe
LEECO Lee
LEITCHFIELD Grayson
LEJUNIOR Harlan
LENOX Morgan
LEROSE Owsley
LETCHER Letcher
LEWISBURG (42256) Logan(85),
   Todd(11), Butler(2)
LEWISPORT (42351) Hancock(91),
   Daviess(8)
LEXINGTON Fayette
LIBERTY Casey
LICK CREEK Pike
LILY Laurel
LINDSEYVILLE Edmonson
LINEFORK Letcher
LITTCARR Knott
LITTLE Breathitt
LIVERMORE (42352) McLean(94), Ohio(5)
LIVINGSTON Rockcastle
LLOYD Greenup
LOCKPORT Henry
LOLA Livingston
LONDON Laurel
LONE Lee
LOOKOUT Pike
LORETTO (40037) Marion(73),
   Washington(15), Nelson(11)
LOST CREEK (41348) Breathitt(87),
   Perry(12)
LOUISA (41230) Lawrence(98), Martin(1)
LOUISVILLE (40299) Jefferson(98),
   Bullitt(1)
LOVELACEVILLE Ballard
LOVELY Martin
LOWES Graves
LOWMANSVILLE (41232) Lawrence(71),
   Johnson(28)
LOYALL Harlan
LUCAS Barren
LYNCH Harlan
LYNNVILLE Graves
MACEDONIA Breathitt
MACEO Daviess
MACKVILLE Washington
MADISONVILLE Hopkins
MAGNOLIA (42757) Larue(48), Hart(45),
   Green(6)
MAJESTIC Pike
MALLIE Knott
MALONE Morgan
MAMMOTH CAVE Edmonson
MANCHESTER Clay
MANITOU Hopkins
MANNSVILLE Taylor
MAPLE MOUNT Daviess
MARIBA Menifee
MARION (42064) Crittenden(98),
   Caldwell(1)
MARROWBONE Cumberland
MARSHALLVILLE Magoffin
MARSHES SIDING McCreary
MARTHA (41159) Lawrence(98),
   Johnson(1)

MARTIN Floyd
MARY ALICE Harlan
MARYDELL Laurel
MASON Grant
MASONIC HOME Jefferson
MAYFIELD Graves
MAYKING Letcher
MAYSLICK Mason
MAYSVILLE Mason
MAZIE Lawrence
MC ANDREWS Pike
MC CARR Pike
MC COMBS (41545) Pike(90), Floyd(10)
MC DANIELS Breckinridge
MC DOWELL Floyd
MC HENRY Ohio
MC KEE (40447) Jackson(96),
   Rockcastle(1), Estill(1)
MC KINNEY Lincoln
MC QUADY Breckinridge
MC ROBERTS Letcher
MC VEIGH Pike
MEALLY Johnson
MEANS (40346) Menifee(79), Bath(11),
   Montgomery(8)
MELBER (42069) Graves(78),
   McCracken(17), Carlisle(3)
MELBOURNE Campbell
MELVIN Floyd
MIDDLEBURG Casey
MIDDLESBORO Bell
MIDWAY (40347) Woodford(92),
   Franklin(3), Scott(3)
MIGRATE Fayette
MILBURN Carlisle
MILFORD Bracken
MILL SPRINGS Wayne
MILLERSBURG Bourbon
MILLS Knox
MILLSTONE Letcher
MILLTOWN Adair
MILLWOOD Grayson
MILTON (40045) Trimble(88), Carroll(11)
MIMA Morgan
MINERVA Mason
MINNIE Floyd
MIRACLE Bell
MISTLETOE Owsley
MITCHELLSBURG Boyle
MIZE Morgan
MONTICELLO Wayne
MONTPELIER Adair
MOON Morgan
MOOREFIELD Nicholas
MOORMAN Muhlenberg
MOREHEAD (40351) Rowan(98), Elliott(1)
MORGANFIELD (42437) Union(97),
   Webster(2)
MORGANTOWN Butler
MORNING VIEW Kenton
MORRILL Jackson
MORTONS GAP Hopkins
MOUNT EDEN (40046) Spencer(70),
   Anderson(24), Shelby(4)
MOUNT HERMON Monroe
MOUNT OLIVET Robertson
MOUNT SHERMAN (42764) Green(58),
   Larue(38), Hart(3)
MOUNT STERLING (40353)
   Montgomery(97), Clark(1)
MOUNT VERNON Rockcastle
MOUNT WASHINGTON Bullitt
MOUSIE Knott
MOUTHCARD Pike
MOZELLE Leslie
MULDRAUGH Meade
MUNFORDVILLE Hart
MURRAY Calloway
MUSES MILLS Fleming
MYRA Pike
NANCY (42544) Pulaski(73), Wayne(18),
   Russell(8)

NARROWS Ohio
NAZARETH Nelson
NEAFUS Grayson
NEBO (42441) Hopkins(94), Webster(5)
NELSE Pike
NEON Letcher
NERINX Marion
NEVISDALE Whitley
NEW CASTLE Henry
NEW CONCORD Calloway
NEW HAVEN (40051) Nelson(87),
   Larue(12)
NEW HOPE (40052) Nelson(92), Larue(5),
   Marion(1)
NEW LIBERTY Owen
NEWPORT Campbell
NICHOLASVILLE Jessamine
NOCTOR Breathitt
NORTH MIDDLETOWN Bourbon
NORTONVILLE (42442) Hopkins(98),
   Christian(1)
OAK GROVE Christian
OAKLAND Warren
OAKVILLE Logan
OFFUTT Johnson
OIL SPRINGS Johnson
OLATON (42361) Ohio(88), Grayson(11)
OLD LANDING Lee
OLDTOWN Greenup
OLIVE HILL (41164) Carter(97), Elliott(1)
OLLIE Edmonson
OLMSTEAD (42265) Logan(89), Todd(10)
OLYMPIA Bath
ONEIDA Clay
OPHIR Morgan
ORLANDO Rockcastle
OVEN FORK Letcher
OWENSBORO Daviess
OWENTON Owen
OWINGSVILLE (40360) Bath(93),
   Montgomery(6)
PADUCAH McCracken
PAINT LICK (40461) Garrard(81),
   Madison(18)
PAINTSVILLE Johnson
PARIS Bourbon
PARK CITY (42160) Barren(73),
   Edmonson(26)
PARKERS LAKE McCreary
PARKSVILLE (40464) Boyle(89),
   Casey(10)
PARROT Jackson
PARTRIDGE Letcher
PATHFORK Harlan
PAW PAW Pike
PAYNEVILLE Meade
PELLVILLE Hancock
PEMBROKE (42266) Christian(94),
   Todd(5)
PENDLETON (40055) Trimble(50),
   Henry(32), Oldham(16)
PENROD Muhlenberg
PEOPLES Jackson
PERRY PARK Owen
PERRYVILLE (40468) Boyle(93),
   Washington(4), Mercer(2)
PETERSBURG Boone
PEWEE VALLEY Oldham
PEYTONSBURG Cumberland
PHELPS Pike
PHILPOT (42366) Daviess(94),
   Hancock(3), Ohio(1)
PHYLLIS Pike
PIKEVILLE Pike
PILGRIM Martin
PINE KNOT McCreary
PINE RIDGE (41360) Wolfe(84), Powell(16)
PINE TOP Knott
PINEVILLE Bell
PINSONFORK Pike
PIPPA PASSES Knott
PITTSBURG Laurel

PLANK Clay
PLEASUREVILLE (40057) Henry(81),
   Shelby(18)
PLUMMERS LANDING Fleming
POMEROYTON Menifee
POOLE Webster
PORT ROYAL Henry
POWDERLY Muhlenberg
PREMIUM Letcher
PRESTON Bath
PRESTONSBURG Floyd
PRIMROSE Lee
PRINCETON (42445) Caldwell(93),
   Lyon(2), Hopkins(2), Trigg(1)
PRINTER Floyd
PROSPECT (40059) Jefferson(60),
   Oldham(39)
PROVIDENCE (42450) Webster(88),
   Hopkins(7), Crittenden(4)
PROVO Butler
PRYSE Estill
PUTNEY Harlan
QUALITY (42268) Butler(72), Logan(27)
QUICKSAND Breathitt
QUINCY Lewis
RACCOON Pike
RADCLIFF Hardin
RANSOM Pike
RAVEN Knott
RAVENNA Estill
RAYWICK Marion
REDFOX Knott
REED Henderson
REGINA Pike
RENFRO VALLEY Rockcastle
REVELO McCreary
REYNOLDS STATION (42368)
   Hancock(75), Ohio(24)
RHODELIA (40161) Meade(91),
   Breckinridge(8)
RICETOWN Owsley
RICHARDSON Lawrence
RICHARDSVILLE Warren
RICHMOND Madison
RINEYVILLE Hardin
RIVER (41254) Johnson(96), Lawrence(4)
ROARK Leslie
ROBARDS (42452) Henderson(84),
   Webster(15)
ROBINSON CREEK Pike
ROCHESTER Butler
ROCKFIELD (42274) Warren(92), Logan(7)
ROCKHOLDS (40759) Whitley(79),
   Knox(20)
ROCKHOUSE Pike
ROCKPORT Ohio
ROCKY HILL Edmonson
ROCKYBRANCH Wayne
ROGERS Wolfe
ROSINE Ohio
ROUNDHILL (42275) Butler(66),
   Edmonson(33)
ROUSSEAU Breathitt
ROWDY Perry
ROWLETTS Hart
ROXANA Letcher
ROYALTON Magoffin
RUMSEY McLean
RUSH (41168) Carter(62), Boyd(35),
   Lawrence(1)
RUSSELL Greenup
RUSSELL SPRINGS (42642) Russell(93),
   Adair(4), Casey(1)
RUSSELLVILLE Logan
SACRAMENTO (42372) McLean(51),
   Muhlenberg(48)
SADIEVILLE (40370) Scott(60),
   Harrison(39)
SAINT CATHARINE Washington
SAINT CHARLES Hopkins
SAINT FRANCIS Marion
SAINT HELENS Lee

SAINT JOSEPH Daviess
SAINT MARY Marion
SAINT PAUL Lewis
SALDEE Breathitt
SALEM (42078) Livingston(64), Crittenden(35)
SALT LICK (40371) Bath(88), Menifee(11)
SALVISA (40372) Mercer(94), Anderson(5)
SALYERSVILLE Magoffin
SANDERS Carroll
SANDGAP Jackson
SANDY HOOK Elliott
SASSAFRAS Knott
SAUL Perry
SAWYER McCreary
SCALF Knox
SCIENCE HILL Pulaski
SCOTTSVILLE Allen
SCUDDY Perry
SE REE Breckinridge
SEBREE Webster
SECO Letcher
SEDALIA Graves
SEITZ Magoffin
SEXTONS CREEK (40983) Clay(70), Owsley(30)
SHARON GROVE Todd
SHARPSBURG (40374) Bath(87), Nicholas(9), Bourbon(3)
SHELBIANA Pike
SHELBY GAP Pike
SHELBYVILLE Shelby
SHEPHERDSVILLE Bullitt
SHOPVILLE Pulaski
SIDNEY Pike
SILER (40763) Whitley(78), Bell(21)
SILVER GROVE Campbell
SILVERHILL Morgan
SIMPSONVILLE Shelby
SITKA Johnson
SIZEROCK Leslie
SLADE Powell
SLAUGHTERS (42456) Webster(72), Hopkins(27)
SLEMP Perry
SLOANS VALLEY Pulaski
SMILAX Leslie
SMITH Harlan
SMITH MILLS Henderson
SMITHFIELD (40068) Henry(87), Shelby(7), Oldham(4)
SMITHLAND Livingston
SMITHS GROVE (42171) Warren(43), Edmonson(32), Barren(24)
SOLDIER Carter
SOMERSET Pulaski
SONORA (42776) Hardin(68), Larue(31)
SOUTH CARROLLTON Muhlenberg
SOUTH PORTSMOUTH Greenup
SOUTH SHORE Greenup
SOUTH UNION Logan
SOUTH WILLIAMSON Pike

SPARTA (41086) Owen(74), Gallatin(25)
SPEIGHT Pike
SPOTTSVILLE Henderson
SPRING LICK Grayson
SPRINGFIELD (40069) Washington(98), Marion(1)
STAB Pulaski
STAFFORDSVILLE Johnson
STAMBAUGH Johnson
STAMPING GROUND (40379) Scott(75), Owen(20), Franklin(3)
STANFORD (40484) Lincoln(95), Garrard(3)
STANLEY Daviess
STANTON (40380) Powell(97), Estill(2)
STANVILLE (41659) Floyd(98), Pike(1)
STEARNS McCreary
STEELE Pike
STEFF Grayson
STEPHENS Elliott
STEPHENSBURG Hardin
STEPHENSPORT Breckinridge
STEUBENVILLE Wayne
STINNETT Leslie
STONE Pike
STONEY FORK (40988) Bell(53), Harlan(46)
STOPOVER Pike
STRUNK McCreary
STURGIS (42459) Union(93), Crittenden(6)
SULLIVAN Union
SULPHUR Henry
SUMMER SHADE (42166) Metcalfe(67), Monroe(18), Barren(14)
SUMMERSVILLE (42782) Green(93), Hart(6)
SUMMIT Hardin
SUNFISH Edmonson
SWAMP BRANCH Johnson
SWEEDEN Edmonson
SYMSONIA (42082) Graves(71), Marshall(23), McCracken(4)
TALBERT Breathitt
TALCUM (41765) Knott(85), Perry(14)
TALLEGA Lee
TATEVILLE Pulaski
TAYLORSVILLE (40071) Spencer(91), Bullitt(7), Shelby(1)
TEABERRY Floyd
THELMA Johnson
THORNTON Letcher
THOUSANDSTICKS Leslie
THREEFORKS Martin
TILINE Livingston
TOLER Pike
TOLLESBORO Lewis
TOLU Crittenden
TOMAHAWK Martin
TOMPKINSVILLE Monroe
TOPMOST Knott
TOTZ Harlan
TRAM Floyd

TRENTON (42286) Todd(96), Christian(4)
TROSPER Knox
TURKEY CREEK (41570) Pike(96), Martin(3)
TURNERS STATION (40075) Henry(77), Carroll(22)
TUTOR KEY Johnson
TYNER (40486) Jackson(97), Clay(2)
TYPO Perry
ULYSSES Lawrence
UNION Boone
UNION STAR (40171) Breckinridge(93), Meade(6)
UNIONTOWN (42461) Union(97), Henderson(2)
UPTON (42784) Hardin(51), Larue(29), Hart(19)
UTICA (42376) Daviess(72), Ohio(20), McLean(7)
VAN LEAR Johnson
VANCEBURG (41179) Lewis(95), Carter(3)
VANCLEVE Breathitt
VARNEY Pike
VENTRESS Hardin
VERONA Boone
VERSAILLES Woodford
VERTREES Hardin
VEST Knott
VICCO (41773) Perry(63), Knott(36)
VINCENT Owsley
VINE GROVE (40175) Hardin(54), Meade(44), Breckinridge(1)
VIPER Perry
VIRGIE Pike
VOLGA Johnson
WACO (40385) Madison(97), Estill(2)
WADDY (40076) Shelby(72), Franklin(15), Anderson(10), Spencer(1)
WALKER Knox
WALLINGFORD Fleming
WALLINS CREEK Harlan
WALNUT GROVE Pulaski
WALTON Boone
WANETA Jackson
WARBRANCH Leslie
WARFIELD Martin
WARSAW (41095) Gallatin(98), Boone(1)
WASHINGTON Mason
WATER VALLEY (42085) Graves(68), Hickman(31)
WATERVIEW Cumberland
WAVERLY (42462) Union(90), Henderson(9)
WAX Grayson
WAYLAND Floyd
WAYNESBURG (40489) Lincoln(92), Casey(7)
WEBBVILLE (41180) Carter(54), Lawrence(44)
WEBSTER (40176) Breckinridge(71), Meade(28)
WEEKSBURY Floyd

WELCHS CREEK Butler
WELLINGTON (40387) Menifee(91), Morgan(7), Wolfe(1)
WENDOVER Leslie
WEST LIBERTY Morgan
WEST LOUISVILLE Daviess
WEST PADUCAH McCracken
WEST POINT (40177) Hardin(87), Bullitt(9), Jefferson(3)
WEST PRESTONSBURG Floyd
WEST SOMERSET Pulaski
WEST VAN LEAR Johnson
WESTPORT Oldham
WESTVIEW Breckinridge
WHEATCROFT Webster
WHEATLEY Owen
WHEELWRIGHT Floyd
WHICK Breathitt
WHITE MILLS Hardin
WHITE OAK Morgan
WHITE PLAINS (42464) Hopkins(73), Muhlenberg(16), Christian(9)
WHITEHOUSE Johnson
WHITESBURG Letcher
WHITESVILLE (42378) Daviess(51), Ohio(48)
WHITLEY CITY McCreary
WICKLIFFE Ballard
WIDECREEK Breathitt
WILDIE Rockcastle
WILLARD Carter
WILLIAMSBURG Whitley
WILLIAMSPORT Johnson
WILLIAMSTOWN Grant
WILLISBURG (40078) Washington(96), Mercer(2), Anderson(1)
WILLOW SHADE Metcalfe
WILMORE (40390) Jessamine(98), Woodford(1)
WINCHESTER Clark
WIND CAVE Jackson
WINDSOR Casey
WINDY Wayne
WINGO (42088) Graves(84), Hickman(15)
WINSTON Estill
WITTENSVILLE Johnson
WOODBINE (40771) Knox(91), Whitley(8)
WOODBURN (42170) Warren(62), Simpson(37)
WOODBURY Butler
WOODMAN Pike
WOOLLUM Knox
WOOTON Leslie
WORTHINGTON Greenup
WORTHVILLE (41098) Owen(96), Carroll(3)
WRIGLEY Morgan
YEADDISS Leslie
YERKES Perry
YOSEMITE Casey
ZACHARIAH Lee
ZOE Lee

ZIP/City Cross Reference

40003-40003 BAGDAD	40023-40023 FISHERVILLE	40050-40050 NEW CASTLE	40070-40070 SULPHUR
40004-40004 BARDSTOWN	40025-40025 GLENVIEW	40051-40051 NEW HAVEN	40071-40071 TAYLORSVILLE
40006-40006 BEDFORD	40026-40026 GOSHEN	40052-40052 NEW HOPE	40075-40075 TURNERS STATION
40007-40007 BETHLEHEM	40027-40027 HARRODS CREEK	40055-40055 PENDLETON	40076-40076 WADDY
40008-40008 BLOOMFIELD	40028-40028 HOWARDSTOWN	40056-40056 PEWEE VALLEY	40077-40077 WESTPORT
40009-40009 BRADFORDSVILLE	40031-40032 LA GRANGE	40057-40057 PLEASUREVILLE	40078-40078 WILLISBURG
40010-40010 BUCKNER	40033-40033 LEBANON	40058-40058 PORT ROYAL	40103-40103 AXTEL
40011-40011 CAMPBELLSBURG	40036-40036 LOCKPORT	40059-40059 PROSPECT	40104-40104 BATTLETOWN
40012-40012 CHAPLIN	40037-40037 LORETTO	40060-40060 RAYWICK	40106-40106 BIG SPRING
40013-40013 COXS CREEK	40040-40040 MACKVILLE	40061-40061 SAINT CATHARINE	40107-40107 BOSTON
40014-40014 CRESTWOOD	40041-40041 MASONIC HOME	40062-40062 SAINT FRANCIS	40108-40108 BRANDENBURG
40017-40017 DEFOE	40045-40045 MILTON	40063-40063 SAINT MARY	40109-40109 BROOKS
40018-40018 EASTWOOD	40046-40046 MOUNT EDEN	40065-40066 SHELBYVILLE	40110-40110 CLERMONT
40019-40019 EMINENCE	40047-40047 MOUNT WASHINGTON	40067-40067 SIMPSONVILLE	40111-40111 CLOVERPORT
40020-40020 FAIRFIELD	40048-40048 NAZARETH	40068-40068 SMITHFIELD	40114-40114 CONSTANTINE
40022-40022 FINCHVILLE	40049-40049 NERINX	40069-40069 SPRINGFIELD	40115-40115 CUSTER

40117-40117 EKRON	40402-40402 ANNVILLE	40830-40830 GULSTON	41033-41033 DE MOSSVILLE
40118-40118 FAIRDALE	40403-40404 BEREA	40831-40831 HARLAN	41034-41034 DOVER
40119-40119 FALLS OF ROUGH	40405-40405 BIGHILL	40840-40840 HELTON	41035-41035 DRY RIDGE
40121-40121 FORT KNOX	40407-40407 BOND	40843-40843 HOLMES MILL	41037-41037 ELIZAVILLE
40129-40129 HILLVIEW	40409-40409 BRODHEAD	40844-40844 HOSKINSTON	41039-41039 EWING
40140-40140 GARFIELD	40410-40410 BRYANTSVILLE	40845-40845 HULEN	41040-41040 FALMOUTH
40142-40142 GUSTON	40415-40415 COBHILL	40846-40846 KEITH	41041-41041 FLEMINGSBURG
40143-40143 HARDINSBURG	40417-40417 CONWAY	40847-40847 KENVIR	41042-41042 FLORENCE
40144-40144 HARNED	40419-40419 CRAB ORCHARD	40849-40849 LEJUNIOR	41043-41043 FOSTER
40145-40145 HUDSON	40420-40420 CRYSTAL	40854-40854 LOYALL	41044-41044 GERMANTOWN
40146-40146 IRVINGTON	40421-40421 DABOLT	40855-40855 LYNCH	41045-41045 GHENT
40150-40150 LEBANON JUNCTION	40422-40423 DANVILLE	40856-40856 MIRACLE	41046-41046 GLENCOE
40152-40152 MC DANIELS	40426-40426 DREYFUS	40858-40858 MOZELLE	41048-41048 HEBRON
40153-40153 MC QUADY	40430-40430 EGYPT	40861-40861 OVEN FORK	41049-41049 HILLSBORO
40155-40155 MULDRAUGH	40434-40434 GRAY HAWK	40862-40862 PARTRIDGE	41051-41051 INDEPENDENCE
40157-40157 PAYNEVILLE	40435-40435 HERD	40863-40863 PATHFORK	41052-41052 JONESVILLE
40159-40160 RADCLIFF	40437-40437 HUSTONVILLE	40865-40865 PUTNEY	41053-41053 KENTON
40161-40161 RHODELIA	40440-40440 JUNCTION CITY	40867-40867 SMITH	41054-41054 MASON
40162-40162 RINEYVILLE	40441-40441 KERBY KNOB	40868-40868 STINNETT	41055-41055 MAYSLICK
40164-40164 SE REE	40442-40442 KINGS MOUNTAIN	40870-40870 TOTZ	41056-41056 MAYSVILLE
40165-40165 SHEPHERDSVILLE	40444-40444 LANCASTER	40873-40873 WALLINS CREEK	41059-41059 MELBOURNE
40170-40170 STEPHENSPORT	40445-40445 LIVINGSTON	40874-40874 WARBRANCH	41061-41061 MILFORD
40171-40171 UNION STAR	40446-40446 LANCASTER	40902-40902 ARJAY	41062-41062 MINERVA
40175-40175 VINE GROVE	40447-40447 MC KEE	40903-40903 ARTEMUS	41063-41063 MORNING VIEW
40176-40176 WEBSTER	40448-40448 MC KINNEY	40906-40911 BARBOURVILLE	41064-41064 MOUNT OLIVET
40177-40177 WEST POINT	40452-40452 MITCHELLSBURG	40913-40913 BEVERLY	41065-41065 MUSES MILLS
40178-40178 WESTVIEW	40455-40455 MORRILL	40914-40914 BIG CREEK	41071-41072 NEWPORT
40200-40299 LOUISVILLE	40456-40456 MOUNT VERNON	40915-40915 BIMBLE	41073-41073 BELLEVUE
40306-40306 BETHEL	40460-40460 ORLANDO	40917-40917 BLUEHOLE	41074-41074 DAYTON
40309-40309 BOWEN	40461-40461 PAINT LICK	40921-40921 BRYANTS STORE	41075-41075 FORT THOMAS
40310-40310 BURGIN	40464-40464 PARKSVILLE	40923-40923 CANNON	41076-41076 NEWPORT
40311-40311 CARLISLE	40465-40465 PARROT	40927-40927 CLOSPLINT	41080-41080 PETERSBURG
40312-40312 CLAY CITY	40467-40467 PEOPLES	40930-40930 DEWITT	41081-41081 PLUMMERS LANDING
40313-40313 CLEARFIELD	40468-40468 PERRYVILLE	40931-40931 ERILINE	41083-41083 SANDERS
40316-40316 DENNISTON	40471-40471 PRYSE	40932-40932 FALL ROCK	41085-41085 SILVER GROVE
40317-40317 ELLIOTTVILLE	40472-40472 RAVENNA	40935-40935 FLAT LICK	41086-41086 SPARTA
40319-40319 FARMERS	40473-40473 RENFRO VALLEY	40936-40936 FOGERTOWN	41091-41091 UNION
40320-40320 FORD	40475-40476 RICHMOND	40939-40939 FOURMILE	41092-41092 VERONA
40322-40322 FRENCHBURG	40481-40481 SANDGAP	40940-40940 FRAKES	41093-41093 WALLINGFORD
40324-40324 GEORGETOWN	40484-40484 STANFORD	40941-40941 GARRARD	41094-41094 WALTON
40327-40327 GRATZ	40486-40486 TYNER	40943-40943 GIRDLER	41095-41095 WARSAW
40328-40328 GRAVEL SWITCH	40488-40488 WANETA	40944-40944 GOOSE ROCK	41096-41096 WASHINGTON
40329-40329 HALDEMAN	40489-40489 WAYNESBURG	40946-40946 GREEN ROAD	41097-41097 WILLIAMSTOWN
40330-40330 HARRODSBURG	40492-40492 WILDIE	40949-40949 HEIDRICK	41098-41098 WORTHVILLE
40334-40334 HOPE	40494-40494 WIND CAVE	40951-40951 HIMA	41099-41099 NEWPORT
40336-40336 IRVINE	40495-40495 WINSTON	40953-40953 HINKLE	41101-41114 ASHLAND
40337-40337 JEFFERSONVILLE	40500-40598 LEXINGTON	40955-40955 INGRAM	41121-41121 ARGILLITE
40339-40339 KEENE	40601-40622 FRANKFORT	40958-40958 KETTLE ISLAND	41124-41124 BLAINE
40340-40340 NICHOLASVILLE	40701-40702 CORBIN	40962-40962 MANCHESTER	41125-41125 BRUIN
40341-40341 LAMERO	40724-40724 BUSH	40964-40964 MARY ALICE	41127-41127 CAMP DIX
40342-40342 LAWRENCEBURG	40729-40729 EAST BERNSTADT	40965-40965 MIDDLESBORO	41128-41128 CARTER
40345-40345 MARIBA	40730-40730 EMLYN	40970-40970 MILLS	41129-41129 CATLETTSBURG
40346-40346 MEANS	40734-40734 GRAY	40972-40972 ONEIDA	41131-41131 CONCORD
40347-40347 MIDWAY	40737-40737 KEAVY	40977-40977 PINEVILLE	41132-41132 DENTON
40348-40348 MILLERSBURG	40740-40740 LILY	40978-40978 PLANK	41135-41135 EMERSON
40350-40350 MOOREFIELD	40741-40748 LONDON	40979-40979 ROARK	41137-41137 FIREBRICK
40351-40351 MOREHEAD	40751-40751 MARYDELL	40981-40981 SAUL	41139-41139 FLATWOODS
40353-40353 MOUNT STERLING	40754-40754 NEVISDALE	40982-40982 SCALF	41141-41141 GARRISON
40355-40355 NEW LIBERTY	40755-40755 PITTSBURG	40983-40983 SEXTONS CREEK	41142-41142 GRAHN
40356-40356 NICHOLASVILLE	40759-40759 ROCKHOLDS	40988-40988 STONEY FORK	41143-41143 GRAYSON
40357-40357 NORTH MIDDLETOWN	40763-40763 SILER	40995-40995 TROSPER	41144-41144 GREENUP
40358-40358 OLYMPIA	40769-40769 WILLIAMSBURG	40997-40997 WALKER	41146-41146 HITCHINS
40359-40359 OWENTON	40771-40771 WOODBINE	40999-40999 WOOLLUM	41149-41149 ISONVILLE
40360-40360 OWINGSVILLE	40801-40801 AGES BROOKSIDE	41001-41001 ALEXANDRIA	41150-41150 JACOBS
40361-40362 PARIS	40803-40803 ASHER	41002-41002 AUGUSTA	41152-41152 JOHNS RUN
40363-40363 PERRY PARK	40806-40806 BAXTER	41003-41003 BERRY	41156-41156 LLOYD
40365-40365 POMEROYTON	40807-40807 BENHAM	41004-41004 BROOKSVILLE	41159-41159 MARTHA
40366-40366 PRESTON	40808-40808 BIG LAUREL	41005-41005 BURLINGTON	41160-41160 MAZIE
40370-40370 SADIEVILLE	40810-40810 BLEDSOE	41006-41006 BUTLER	41163-41163 OLDTOWN
40371-40371 SALT LICK	40813-40813 CALVIN	41007-41007 CALIFORNIA	41164-41164 OLIVE HILL
40372-40372 SALVISA	40815-40815 CAWOOD	41008-41008 CARROLLTON	41166-41166 QUINCY
40374-40374 SHARPSBURG	40816-40816 CHAPPELL	41009-41009 CONSTANCE	41168-41168 RUSH
40376-40376 SLADE	40818-40818 COALGOOD	41010-41010 CORINTH	41169-41169 RUSSELL
40379-40379 STAMPING GROUND	40819-40819 COLDIRON	41011-41014 COVINGTON	41170-41170 SAINT PAUL
40380-40380 STANTON	40820-40820 CRANKS	41015-41015 LATONIA	41171-41171 SANDY HOOK
40383-40384 VERSAILLES	40823-40823 CUMBERLAND	41016-41016 COVINGTON	41173-41173 SOLDIER
40385-40385 WACO	40824-40824 DAYHOIT	41017-41017 FT MITCHELL	41174-41174 SOUTH PORTSMOUTH
40386-40386 VERSAILLES	40825-40825 DIZNEY	41018-41018 ERLANGER	41175-41175 SOUTH SHORE
40387-40387 WELLINGTON	40826-40826 EOLIA	41019-41019 COVINGTON	41177-41177 STEPHENS
40389-40389 WHEATLEY	40827-40827 ESSIE	41022-41022 FLORENCE	41179-41179 VANCEBURG
40390-40390 WILMORE	40828-40828 EVARTS	41030-41030 CRITTENDEN	41180-41180 WEBBVILLE
40391-40392 WINCHESTER	40829-40829 GRAYS KNOB	41031-41031 CYNTHIANA	41181-41181 WILLARD

41183-41183 WORTHINGTON	41377-41377 TALBERT	41559-41559 REGINA	41745-41745 GAYS CREEK
41189-41189 TOLLESBORO	41378-41378 TALLEGA	41560-41560 ROBINSON CREEK	41746-41746 HAPPY
41201-41201 ADAMS	41385-41385 VANCLEVE	41561-41561 ROCKHOUSE	41747-41747 HARDBURLY
41203-41203 BEAUTY	41386-41386 VINCENT	41562-41562 SHELBIANA	41749-41749 HYDEN
41204-41204 BOONS CAMP	41390-41390 WHICK	41563-41563 SHELBY GAP	41751-41751 JEFF
41211-41211 CULVER	41391-41391 WIDECREEK	41564-41564 SIDNEY	41754-41754 KRYPTON
41214-41214 DEBORD	41396-41396 ZACHARIAH	41565-41565 SPEIGHT	41756-41756 LEATHERWOOD
41215-41215 DENVER	41397-41397 ZOE	41566-41566 STEELE	41759-41759 SASSAFRAS
41216-41216 EAST POINT	41406-41406 BUSKIRK	41567-41567 STONE	41760-41760 SCUDDY
41219-41219 FLATGAP	41407-41407 CANEY	41568-41568 STOPOVER	41762-41762 SIZEROCK
41220-41220 FUGET	41408-41408 CANNEL CITY	41569-41569 TOLER	41763-41763 SLEMP
41222-41222 HAGERHILL	41409-41409 CARVER	41570-41570 TURKEY CREEK	41764-41764 SMILAX
41224-41224 INEZ	41410-41410 CISCO	41571-41571 VARNEY	41765-41765 TALCUM
41225-41225 JOB	41411-41411 CONLEY	41572-41572 VIRGIE	41766-41766 THOUSANDSTICKS
41226-41226 KEATON	41412-41412 COTTLE	41574-41574 WOODMAN	41771-41771 TYPO
41228-41228 LEANDER	41413-41413 CROCKETT	41601-41601 ALLEN	41772-41772 VEST
41230-41230 LOUISA	41417-41417 DINGUS	41602-41602 AUXIER	41773-41773 VICCO
41231-41231 LOVELY	41419-41419 EDNA	41603-41603 BANNER	41774-41774 VIPER
41232-41232 LOWMANSVILLE	41421-41421 ELKFORK	41604-41604 BEAVER	41775-41775 WENDOVER
41234-41234 MEALLY	41422-41422 ELSIE	41605-41605 BETSY LAYNE	41776-41776 WOOTON
41237-41237 OFFUTT	41425-41425 EZEL	41606-41606 BEVINSVILLE	41777-41777 YEADDISS
41238-41238 OIL SPRINGS	41426-41426 FALCON	41607-41607 BLUE RIVER	41778-41778 YERKES
41240-41240 PAINTSVILLE	41427-41427 FLAT FORK	41612-41612 BYPRO	41801-41801 AMBURGEY
41250-41250 PILGRIM	41430-41430 FREDVILLE	41614-41614 CRAYNOR	41804-41804 BLACKEY
41253-41253 RICHARDSON	41431-41431 FRITZ	41615-41615 DANA	41805-41805 BRINKLEY
41254-41254 RIVER	41433-41433 GAPVILLE	41616-41616 DAVID	41810-41810 CROMONA
41255-41255 SITKA	41438-41438 GYPSY	41619-41619 DRIFT	41811-41811 CROWN
41256-41256 STAFFORDSVILLE	41441-41441 HENDRICKS	41621-41621 DWALE	41812-41812 DEANE
41257-41257 STAMBAUGH	41443-41443 INSKO	41622-41622 EASTERN	41815-41815 ERMINE
41258-41258 SWAMP BRANCH	41444-41444 IVYTON	41625-41625 EMMA	41817-41817 GARNER
41260-41260 THELMA	41447-41447 LENOX	41626-41626 ENDICOTT	41819-41819 GORDON
41261-41261 THREEFORKS	41451-41451 MALONE	41627-41627 ESTILL	41821-41821 HALLIE
41262-41262 TOMAHAWK	41452-41452 MARSHALLVILLE	41629-41629 GALVESTON	41822-41822 HINDMAN
41263-41263 TUTOR KEY	41456-41456 MIMA	41630-41630 GARRETT	41823-41823 HOLLYBUSH
41264-41264 ULYSSES	41457-41457 MOON	41631-41631 GRETHEL	41824-41824 ISOM
41265-41265 VAN LEAR	41459-41459 OPHIR	41632-41632 GUNLOCK	41825-41825 JACKHORN
41266-41266 VOLGA	41464-41464 ROYALTON	41633-41633 HALO	41826-41826 JEREMIAH
41267-41267 WARFIELD	41465-41465 SALYERSVILLE	41635-41635 HAROLD	41828-41828 KITE
41268-41268 WEST VAN LEAR	41466-41466 SEITZ	41636-41636 HI HAT	41829-41829 KONA
41269-41269 WHITEHOUSE	41467-41467 SILVERHILL	41637-41637 HIPPO	41831-41831 LEBURN
41271-41271 WILLIAMSPORT	41472-41472 WEST LIBERTY	41639-41639 HONAKER	41832-41832 LETCHER
41274-41274 WITTENSVILLE	41474-41474 WHITE OAK	41640-41640 HUEYSVILLE	41833-41833 LINEFORK
41301-41301 CAMPTON	41477-41477 WRIGLEY	41641-41641 HUNTER	41834-41834 LITTCARR
41306-41306 ALTRO	41501-41502 PIKEVILLE	41642-41642 IVEL	41835-41835 MC ROBERTS
41307-41307 ATHOL	41503-41503 SOUTH WILLIAMSON	41643-41643 LACKEY	41836-41836 MALLIE
41310-41310 BAYS	41512-41512 ASHCAMP	41645-41645 LANGLEY	41837-41837 MAYKING
41311-41311 BEATTYVILLE	41513-41513 BELCHER	41647-41647 MC DOWELL	41838-41838 MILLSTONE
41313-41313 BETHANY	41514-41514 BELFRY	41649-41649 MARTIN	41839-41839 MOUSIE
41314-41314 BOONEVILLE	41517-41517 BURDINE	41650-41650 MELVIN	41840-41840 NEON
41315-41315 BURKHART	41518-41518 BURNWELL	41651-41651 MINNIE	41843-41843 PINE TOP
41316-41316 CANOE	41519-41519 CANADA	41653-41653 PRESTONSBURG	41844-41844 PIPPA PASSES
41317-41317 CLAYHOLE	41520-41520 DORTON	41655-41655 PRINTER	41845-41845 PREMIUM
41321-41321 DECOY	41521-41521 DRAFFIN	41659-41659 STANVILLE	41847-41847 REDFOX
41323-41323 FILLMORE	41522-41522 ELKHORN CITY	41660-41660 TEABERRY	41848-41848 ROXANA
41327-41327 GILLMORE	41524-41524 FEDSCREEK	41663-41663 TRAM	41849-41849 SECO
41328-41328 GREEN HALL	41526-41526 FORDS BRANCH	41666-41666 WAYLAND	41855-41855 THORNTON
41331-41331 HADDIX	41527-41527 FOREST HILLS	41667-41667 WEEKSBURY	41858-41858 WHITESBURG
41332-41332 HAZEL GREEN	41528-41528 FREEBURN	41668-41668 WEST PRESTONSBURG	41859-41859 DEMA
41333-41333 HEIDELBERG	41529-41529 GOODY	41669-41669 WHEELWRIGHT	41861-41861 RAVEN
41338-41338 ISLAND CITY	41531-41531 HARDY	41701-41702 HAZARD	41862-41862 TOPMOST
41339-41339 JACKSON	41534-41534 HELLIER	41710-41710 ALLOCK	41901-41906 MIGRATE
41340-41340 LAMBRIC	41535-41535 HUDDY	41712-41712 ARY	42001-42003 PADUCAH
41342-41342 LEE CITY	41536-41536 JAMBOREE	41713-41713 AVAWAM	42020-42020 ALMO
41343-41343 LEECO	41537-41537 JENKINS	41714-41714 BEAR BRANCH	42021-42021 ARLINGTON
41344-41344 LEROSE	41538-41538 JONANCY	41719-41719 BONNYMAN	42022-42022 BANDANA
41346-41346 LITTLE	41539-41539 KIMPER	41720-41720 BROWNS FORK	42023-42023 BARDWELL
41347-41347 LONE	41540-41540 LICK CREEK	41721-41721 BUCKHORN	42024-42024 BARLOW
41348-41348 LOST CREEK	41542-41542 LOOKOUT	41722-41722 BULAN	42025-42025 BENTON
41351-41351 MISTLETOE	41543-41543 MC ANDREWS	41723-41723 BUSY	42026-42026 BLANDVILLE
41352-41352 MIZE	41544-41544 MC CARR	41725-41725 CARRIE	42027-42027 BOAZ
41357-41357 NOCTOR	41545-41545 MC COMBS	41727-41727 CHAVIES	42028-42028 BURNA
41358-41358 OLD LANDING	41546-41546 MC VEIGH	41728-41728 CINDA	42029-42029 CALVERT CITY
41360-41360 PINE RIDGE	41547-41547 MAJESTIC	41729-41729 COMBS	42031-42031 CLINTON
41362-41362 PRIMROSE	41548-41548 MOUTHCARD	41730-41730 CONFLUENCE	42032-42032 COLUMBUS
41363-41363 QUICKSAND	41549-41549 MYRA	41731-41731 CORNETTSVILLE	42033-42033 CRAYNE
41364-41364 RICETOWN	41550-41550 NELSE	41732-41732 CUTSHIN	42035-42035 CUNNINGHAM
41365-41365 ROGERS	41551-41551 PAW PAW	41733-41733 DAISY	42036-42036 DEXTER
41366-41366 ROUSSEAU	41553-41553 PHELPS	41735-41735 DELPHIA	42037-42037 DYCUSBURG
41367-41367 ROWDY	41554-41554 PHYLLIS	41736-41736 DICE	42038-42038 EDDYVILLE
41368-41368 SAINT HELENS	41555-41555 PINSONFORK	41739-41739 DWARF	42039-42039 FANCY FARM
41369-41369 SALDEE	41557-41557 RACCOON	41740-41740 EMMALENA	42040-42040 FARMINGTON
41370-41370 MACEDONIA	41558-41558 RANSOM	41743-41743 FISTY	42041-42041 FULTON

42044-42044 GILBERTSVILLE	42214-42214 CENTER	42366-42366 PHILPOT	42629-42629 JAMESTOWN
42045-42045 GRAND RIVERS	42215-42215 CERULEAN	42367-42367 POWDERLY	42631-42631 MARSHES SIDING
42046-42046 HAMLIN	42216-42216 CLIFTY	42368-42368 REYNOLDS STATION	42632-42632 MILL SPRINGS
42047-42047 HAMPTON	42217-42217 CROFTON	42369-42369 ROCKPORT	42633-42633 MONTICELLO
42048-42048 HARDIN	42219-42219 DUNBAR	42370-42370 ROSINE	42634-42634 PARKERS LAKE
42049-42049 HAZEL	42220-42220 ELKTON	42371-42371 RUMSEY	42635-42635 PINE KNOT
42050-42050 HICKMAN	42221-42221 FAIRVIEW	42372-42372 SACRAMENTO	42638-42638 REVELO
42051-42051 HICKORY	42223-42223 FORT CAMPBELL	42373-42373 SAINT JOSEPH	42640-42640 ROCKYBRANCH
42053-42053 KEVIL	42232-42232 GRACEY	42374-42374 SOUTH CARROLLTON	42642-42642 RUSSELL SPRINGS
42054-42054 KIRKSEY	42234-42234 GUTHRIE	42375-42375 STANLEY	42643-42643 SAWYER
42055-42055 KUTTAWA	42235-42235 HADLEY	42376-42376 UTICA	42647-42647 STEARNS
42056-42056 LA CENTER	42236-42236 HERNDON	42377-42377 WEST LOUISVILLE	42648-42648 STEUBENVILLE
42058-42058 LEDBETTER	42240-42241 HOPKINSVILLE	42378-42378 WHITESVILLE	42649-42649 STRUNK
42059-42059 LOLA	42250-42250 HUFF	42402-42402 BASKETT	42653-42653 WHITLEY CITY
42060-42060 LOVELACEVILLE	42251-42251 HUNTSVILLE	42403-42403 BLACKFORD	42655-42655 WINDY
42061-42061 LOWES	42252-42252 JETSON	42404-42404 CLAY	42701-42702 ELIZABETHTOWN
42063-42063 LYNNVILLE	42254-42254 LA FAYETTE	42406-42406 CORYDON	42711-42711 BAKERTON
42064-42064 MARION	42256-42256 LEWISBURG	42408-42408 DAWSON SPRINGS	42712-42712 BIG CLIFTY
42066-42066 MAYFIELD	42257-42257 LINDSEYVILLE	42409-42409 DIXON	42713-42713 BONNIEVILLE
42069-42069 MELBER	42259-42259 MAMMOTH CAVE	42410-42410 EARLINGTON	42714-42714 BOW
42070-42070 MILBURN	42261-42261 MORGANTOWN	42411-42411 FREDONIA	42715-42715 BREEDING
42071-42071 MURRAY	42262-42262 OAK GROVE	42413-42413 HANSON	42716-42716 BUFFALO
42076-42076 NEW CONCORD	42263-42263 OAKVILLE	42419-42420 HENDERSON	42717-42717 BURKESVILLE
42078-42078 SALEM	42264-42264 OLLIE	42431-42431 MADISONVILLE	42718-42719 CAMPBELLSVILLE
42079-42079 SEDALIA	42265-42265 OLMSTEAD	42436-42436 MANITOU	42720-42720 CANE VALLEY
42081-42081 SMITHLAND	42266-42266 PEMBROKE	42437-42437 MORGANFIELD	42721-42721 CANEYVILLE
42082-42082 SYMSONIA	42267-42267 PROVO	42440-42440 MORTONS GAP	42722-42722 CANMER
42083-42083 TILINE	42268-42268 QUALITY	42441-42441 NEBO	42723-42723 CASEY CREEKG
42084-42084 TOLU	42270-42270 RICHARDSVILLE	42442-42442 NORTONVILLE	42723-42723 CASEY CREEK
42085-42085 WATER VALLEY	42273-42273 ROCHESTER	42444-42444 POOLE	42724-42724 CECILIA
42086-42086 WEST PADUCAH	42274-42274 ROCKFIELD	42445-42445 PRINCETON	42726-42726 CLARKSON
42087-42087 WICKLIFFE	42275-42275 ROUNDHILL	42450-42450 PROVIDENCE	42728-42728 COLUMBIA
42088-42088 WINGO	42276-42276 RUSSELLVILLE	42451-42451 REED	42729-42729 CUB RUN
42101-42104 BOWLING GREEN	42280-42280 SHARON GROVE	42452-42452 ROBARDS	42730-42730 CUNDIFF
42120-42120 ADOLPHUS	42283-42283 SOUTH UNION	42453-42453 SAINT CHARLES	42731-42731 DUBRE
42122-42122 ALVATON	42284-42284 SUNFISH	42455-42455 SEBREE	42732-42732 EASTVIEW
42123-42123 AUSTIN	42285-42285 SWEEDEN	42456-42456 SLAUGHTERS	42733-42733 ELK HORN
42124-42124 BEAUMONT	42286-42286 TRENTON	42457-42457 SMITH MILLS	42735-42735 FAIRPLAY
42127-42127 CAVE CITY	42287-42287 WELCHS CREEK	42458-42458 SPOTTSVILLE	42736-42736 FINLEY
42128-42128 DRAKE	42288-42288 WOODBURY	42459-42459 STURGIS	42740-42740 GLENDALE
42129-42129 EDMONTON	42301-42304 OWENSBORO	42460-42460 SULLIVAN	42741-42741 GLENS FORK
42130-42130 EIGHTY EIGHT	42320-42320 BEAVER DAM	42461-42461 UNIONTOWN	42742-42742 GRADYVILLE
42131-42131 ETOILE	42321-42321 BEECH CREEK	42462-42462 WAVERLY	42743-42743 GREENSBURG
42133-42133 FOUNTAIN RUN	42322-42322 BEECH GROVE	42463-42463 WHEATCROFT	42746-42746 HARDYVILLE
42134-42135 FRANKLIN	42323-42323 BEECHMONT	42464-42464 WHITE PLAINS	42748-42748 HODGENVILLE
42140-42140 GAMALIEL	42324-42324 BELTON	42501-42503 SOMERSET	42749-42749 HORSE CAVE
42141-42142 GLASGOW	42325-42325 BREMEN	42510-42510 ACORN	42752-42752 KETTLE
42150-42150 HALFWAY	42326-42326 BROWDER	42516-42516 BETHELRIDGE	42753-42753 KNIFLEY
42151-42151 HESTAND	42327-42327 CALHOUN	42518-42518 BRONSTON	42754-42755 LEITCHFIELD
42152-42152 HISEVILLE	42328-42328 CENTERTOWN	42519-42519 BURNSIDE	42757-42757 MAGNOLIA
42153-42153 HOLLAND	42330-42330 CENTRAL CITY	42528-42528 DUNNVILLE	42758-42758 MANNSVILLE
42154-42154 KNOB LICK	42332-42332 CLEATON	42532-42532 FAUBUSH	42759-42759 MARROWBONE
42155-42155 LAMB	42333-42333 CROMWELL	42533-42533 FERGUSON	42761-42761 MILLTOWN
42156-42156 LUCAS	42334-42334 CURDSVILLE	42536-42536 INGLE	42762-42762 MILLWOOD
42157-42157 MOUNT HERMON	42337-42337 DRAKESBORO	42539-42539 LIBERTY	42763-42763 MONTPELIER
42159-42159 OAKLAND	42338-42338 DUNDEE	42541-42541 MIDDLEBURG	42764-42764 MOUNT SHERMAN
42160-42160 PARK CITY	42339-42339 DUNMOR	42544-42544 NANCY	42765-42765 MUNFORDVILLE
42163-42163 ROCKY HILL	42343-42343 FORDSVILLE	42553-42553 SCIENCE HILL	42766-42766 NEAFUS
42164-42164 SCOTTSVILLE	42344-42344 GRAHAM	42554-42554 SHOPVILLE	42768-42768 PEYTONSBURG
42166-42166 SUMMER SHADE	42345-42345 GREENVILLE	42555-42555 SLOANS VALLEY	42772-42772 ROWLETTS
42167-42167 TOMPKINSVILLE	42347-42347 HARTFORD	42557-42557 STAB	42776-42776 SONORA
42169-42169 WILLOW SHADE	42348-42348 HAWESVILLE	42558-42558 TATEVILLE	42779-42779 SPRING LICK
42170-42170 WOODBURN	42349-42349 HORSE BRANCH	42563-42563 WALNUT GROVE	42780-42780 STEFF
42171-42171 SMITHS GROVE	42350-42350 ISLAND	42564-42564 WEST SOMERSET	42781-42781 STEPHENSBURG
42201-42201 ABERDEEN	42351-42351 LEWISPORT	42565-42565 WINDSOR	42782-42782 SUMMERSVILLE
42202-42202 ADAIRVILLE	42352-42352 LIVERMORE	42566-42566 YOSEMITE	42783-42783 SUMMIT
42203-42203 ALLEGRE	42354-42354 MC HENRY	42567-42567 EUBANK	42784-42784 UPTON
42204-42204 ALLENSVILLE	42355-42355 MACEO	42601-42601 AARON	42785-42785 VENTRESS
42206-42206 AUBURN	42356-42356 MAPLE MOUNT	42602-42602 ALBANY	42785-42785 VERTREES
42207-42207 BEE SPRING	42357-42357 MOORMAN	42603-42603 ALPHA	42786-42786 WATERVIEW
42209-42209 BROOKLYN	42358-42358 NARROWS	42607-42607 BEULAH HEIGHTS	42787-42787 WAX
42210-42210 BROWNSVILLE	42361-42361 OLATON	42611-42611 COOPERSVILLE	42788-42788 WHITE MILLS
42211-42211 CADIZ	42364-42364 PELLVILLE	42613-42613 DELTA	
42212-42212 CANTON	42365-42365 PENROD	42618-42618 FRAZER	

Louisiana

General Help Numbers:

Governor's Office
PO Box 94004　　　　　　　　225-342-0991
Baton Rouge, LA 70804-9004　　Fax 225-342-7099
www.gov.state.la.us　　　　　　8AM-5PM

Attorney General's Office
LA Department of Justice　　　　225-342-7013
PO Box 94005　　　　　　　　Fax 225-342-7335
Baton Rouge, LA 70804-9005　　8:30AM-5PM
www.ag.state.la.us

State Court Administrator
Judicial Council of the Supreme Court　504-568-5747
1555 Poydras Street, Suite 1540
New Orleans, LA 70112-1814　　9AM-5PM
www.state.la.us/gov_judicial.htm

State Archives
Records Mgt, & History　　　　225-922-1000
3851 Essen Lane　　　　　　　Fax 225-922-0433
Baton Rouge, LA 70809-2137　　8AM-4:30PM,
www.sec.state.la.us/archives/　　9-5 SA 1-5 SU
archives/archives-index.htm

State Specifics:

Capital:　　　　　　　　　Baton Rouge
　　　　　　　　　East Baton Rouge Parish

Time Zone:　　　　　　　　CST

Number of Parishes:　　　　　64

Population:　　　　　　　4,465,430

Web Site:　　　　　　　www.state.la.us

State Agencies

Criminal Records
Access to Records is Restricted
State Police, Bureau of Criminal Identification, 265 S Foster, Baton Rouge, LA 70806; 225-925-6095, 225-925-7005 (Fax), 8AM-4:30PM.

www.lsp.org

Note: Sex offender and child predator data is available online at www.lasocpr.lsp.org/Static/Search.htm. Records are not available to the public in general.

Criminal records are available for employment screening purposes only if the employment statutorily requires a criminal record check (such as childcare or schools).

Corporation Records
Limited Partnership Records
Limited Liability Company Records
Trademarks/Servicemarks
Commercial Division, Corporation Department, PO Box 94125, Baton Rouge, LA 70804-9125 (Courier: 8549 United Plaze Blvd, Baton Rouge,

LA 70809); 225-925-4704, 225-925-4726 (Fax), 8AM-4:30PM.

www.sec.state.la.us

Note: Fictitious Names and Assumed Names are found at the parish level.

Indexing & Storage: Records are available from mid-1800s. New records are available for inquiry immediately. Records are indexed on microfilm, inhouse computer, index cards, on-line.

Searching: Include the following in your request: full name of business. In addition to the articles of incorporation, corporation records include the following information: Annual Reports, Officers, Directors, Prior (merged) names, Inactive names, Reserved names and (possibly) US Tax ID number.

Access by: mail, phone, fax, in person, online.

Fee & Payment: The search fee is $1.00. Copies cost $10.00 without amendments and $20.00 with amendments and a fee of $.25 per page after 40 pages for specific query searches on computer. Fee payee: Secretary of State. Prepayment required. Personal checks accepted. Credit cards accepted: MasterCard, Visa, AmEx, Discover.

Mail search: Turnaround time: 5 to 10 working days. No self addressed stamped envelope is required.

Phone search: You may call for information; however, only limited information is available.

Fax search: There is an additional $1.00 per page fee if returned by fax. Turnaround time is 5 to 10 working days.

In person search: There is a free public access terminal.

Online search: There are 2 ways to go: free on the Internet or pay. To view limited information on the web site, go to "Commercial Division, Corporations Section," then "Search Corporations Database." The pay system is $360 per year for unlimited access. Almost any communications software will work with up to a 14,400 baud rate. The system is open from 6:30 am to 11pm. For more information, call Brenda Wright at 225-922-2880.

Other access: The state offers corporation, LLC, partnership, and trademark information on tape cartridges. For more info, call 225-925-4792.

Expedited service: Expedited service is available for mail and phone searches. Turnaround time: 1 day. Add $20.00 per business name.

Uniform Commercial Code

Secretary of State, UCC Records, PO Box 94125, Baton Rouge, LA 70804-9125; 800-256-3758, 225-342-7011 (Fax), 8AM-4:30PM.

www.sec.state.la.us/comm/ucc-index.htm

Note: The statewide index of UCC filings is available in each parish office. All tax liens and financial statements are filed at the parish level. IRS liens show up on UCC records. Records CANNOT be obtained from this office, except via the online system.

Indexing & Storage: Records are available for all active listings. Records are indexed on computer since 1990. It takes 2 days before new records are available for inquiry.

Searching: All filing information including debtor names, property descriptions, and subsequent filings and amendments are available. Mail-in

requests are sent to any parish, as all searches reflect statewide information.

Access by: online.

Fee & Payment: Fees are only for the online service. Fee payee: Secretary of State. Prepayment required. The payment information outlined here applies only to online access. Personal checks accepted. Credit cards accepted: MasterCard, Visa.

Online search: An annual $400 fee gives unlimited access to UCC filing information. The dial-up service is open from 6:30 AM to 11 PM daily. Minimum baud rate is 14,400. Most any software communications program can be configured to work. For further information, call Brenda Wright at 225-922-2880, or visit the web site.

Federal Tax Liens
State Tax Liens
Records not maintained by a state level agency.

Note: Records are filed with the Clerk of Court at the parish level.

Sales Tax Registrations
Access to Records is Restricted

Revenue Department, Taxpayer Services Division, PO Box 201, Baton Rouge, LA 70821-0201 (Courier: 617 N 3rd St, Baton Rouge, LA 70802); 225-219-7356, 225-219-2210 (Fax), 8AM-4:30PM.

www.rev.state.la.us

Note: This agency will only provide registration information to the registrant itself.

Birth Certificates

Vital Records Registry, Office of Public Health, PO Box 60630, New Orleans, LA 70160 (Courier: 325 Loyola Ave Room 102, New Orleans, LA 70112); 504-568-5152, 504-568-5167 (For adoptions), 504-568-5391 (Fax), 8AM-4PM.

www.oph.dhh.state.la.us/recordsstatistics/vitalrecords

Note: Some certificates (all types of vital records) contain information at the bottom of the document that is confidential and not released to anyone. This information is used for statistical purposes and varies depending on legislative action.

Indexing & Storage: Records are available from 1914 on. Birth records for only the City of New Orleans are available from 1900 on. Records older than 100 years should be ordered from the State Archives. New records are available for inquiry immediately. Records are indexed on microfiche, index cards, inhouse computer.

Searching: Birth certificates are considered confidential for 100 years. Requesters must be related to the person of record or have a signed release. Include the following in your request: full name, names of parents, mother's maiden name, date of birth, place of birth, relationship to person of record, reason for information request. Older records must be searched at the State Archives 225-922-1184.

Access by: mail, fax, in person.

Fee & Payment: A "long form" birth certificate is $15.00, while a "birth card" is $9.00. Fee payee:

Vital Records Registry. Prepayment required. Credit cards are not accepted for mail requests. Personal checks accepted. Credit cards accepted: MasterCard, Visa.

Mail search: Turnaround time: 3 weeks. No self addressed stamped envelope is required.

Fax search: Fax requests are with a credit card number only. See expedited service.

In person search: Photo ID required, turnaround time immediate.

Expedited service: Expedited service is available for mail, fax, and phone searches. Turnaround time: 24 to 48 hours. Add $15.50 per package for overnight delivery. You must include written authorization to charge document fee and shipment fee to your credit card.

Death Records

Vital Records Registry, Office of Public Health, PO Box 60630, New Orleans, LA 70160 (Courier: 325 Loyola Ave Room 102, New Orleans, LA 70112); 504-568-5152, 504-568-5273 (Corrections), 504-568-5391 (Fax), 8AM-4PM.

www.dhh.state.la.us/OPH

Indexing & Storage: Records are available from 1950 on. Older records must be obtained from the State Archives. New records are available for inquiry immediately. Records are indexed on microfiche, index cards, inhouse computer.

Searching: Death records are considered confidential for 50 years. Must show how related or have a signed release from immediate family member if for investigative purposes. Include the following in your request: full name, date of death, place of death, relationship to person of record, reason for information request. Records older than 50 years must be searched at the State Archives 225-922-1184.

Access by: mail, fax, in person.

Fee & Payment: The search fee is $7.00. Fee payee: Department of Vital Records. Prepayment required. Credit cards accepted for fax and in person requests only. Personal checks accepted. Credit cards accepted: MasterCard, Visa.

Mail search: Turnaround time: 3 weeks. No self addressed stamped envelope is required.

Fax search: Fax requests require use of credit card and are charged expedited fees.

In person search: In person search requires a photo ID. Turnaround time usually 45 minutes.

Expedited service: Expedited service is available for mail and phone searches. Turnaround time: 24 to 48 hours. Add $15.50 per package. You must include written authorization to charge document fee and shipping fee to credit card.

Marriage Certificates
Divorce Records
Records not maintained by a state level agency.

Note: Only Orleans Parish marriage records are available from 1948 on at the VR Registry for a $5.00 fee same search criteria as others. Include bride name (maiden) groom and date of marriage. Other marriage and all divorce records are only found at parish of. Marriage Records older than 50 years are open to the public.

Workers' Compensation Records

Department of Labor, Office of Workers' Compensation, PO Box 94040, Baton Rouge, LA 70804-9040 (Courier: LA Department of Labor, Office of Workers' Compensation, Baton Rouge, LA 70802); 225-342-2056, 225-342-7582 (Fax), 8AM-5PM.

www.laworks.net

Note: For partial information, and to determine if a record exists, and if you have the name and SSN, see the Other Access section below.

Indexing & Storage: Records are available from 1983 to present on microfilm. Only cases on file are those where the employee lost 7 days or more of work and/or had disputed issues resolved or settlements approved. New records are available for inquiry immediately. Records are indexed on microfilm.

Searching: Most records are considered confidential. Public records include decisions, awards, or orders in disputed cases. No records are released until "copy" charges are paid. Include the following in your request: claimant name, Social Security Number, date of accident, reason for information request, specific records that you need copies of. Otherwise, signed release required. All record requests must be in writing. The following data is not released: pending records.

Access by: mail, phone, fax, in person.

Fee & Payment: Copies are $.25 per page, $1.00 to certify, there is no fee to search. Fee payee: Workers' Compensation Administrative Fund. Prepayment required. Cash is not accepted. Personal checks accepted. No credit cards accepted.

Mail search: Turnaround time: 7 to 10 days.

Phone search: With a name and SSN (required), you may use the "Easy Call" Interactive Voice Response System at 225-342-8731 for partial public information, especially to determine if a record exists.

Fax search: Records can be requested by fax at no extra fee.

In person search: If you request in person, the turnaround time is shortened only by the mail time.

Other access: With a name and SSN (required), you may use the "Easy Call" Interactive Voice Response System at 225-342-8731 for partial public information, especially to determine if a record exists. Enter 1-4-1-2-2 after the phone answers.

Driver Records

Dept of Public Safety and Corrections, Office of Motor Vehicles, PO Box 64886, Baton Rouge, LA 70896 (Courier: 109 S Foster Dr, Baton Rouge, LA 70806); 877-368-5463, 225-925-6388, 225-925-6915 (Fax), 8AM-4:30PM.

www.expresslane.org

Note: Copies of tickets may be obtained from the address listed above. The fee is $5.00 per page.

Indexing & Storage: Records are available for 3 years for moving violations, 10 years from date of conviction for DWIs and 5 or 10 years for suspensions. Accidents are reported, but fault is not shown. It takes 2 to 3 weeks before new records are available for inquiry.

Searching: Casual requesters can obtain driving records with proper release form signed by subject. Include the following in your request: driver's license number, full name, date of birth. It is sometimes helpful to include the race or sex when requesting a record.

Access by: mail, in person, online.

Fee & Payment: The fee for mail-in or walk-in requests is $15.00 per name. The fee for online or tape requests is $6.00. Fee payee: Office of Motor Vehicles. Prepayment required. No credit cards accepted.

Mail search: Turnaround time: 10 working days. No self addressed stamped envelope is required.

In person search: Walk-in requesters may "view" a record for no charge. Casual requesters must present signed form. The fee is for the hard copy. Records can be requested from the Motor Vehicle Offices in New Orleans, Lake Charles, Monroe, Baton Rouge, Shreveport, and Alexandria.

Online search: There are two methods. The commercial requester, interactive mode is available from 7 AM to 9:30 PM daily. There is a minimum order requirement of 2,000 requests per month. A bond or large deposit is required. Fee is $6.00 per record. For more information, call 225-925-6032. The 2nd method is for individuals to order their own record from the Internet site at www.expresslane.org. The fee is $16.40 and requires a credit card.

Other access: Tape ordering is available for batch delivery. Bulk database sales are available to permissible users.

Vehicle Ownership
Vehicle Identification

Department of Public Safety & Corrections, Office of Motor Vehicles, PO Box 64886, Baton Rouge, LA 70896 (Courier: 109 S Foster Dr, Baton Rouge, LA 70806); 225-922-6146, 877-368-5463, 225-925-3979 (Fax), 8AM-4PM.

www.dps.state.la.us/omv/home.html

Indexing & Storage: Records are available from the 1950's (only if plate or title is known). Records indexed on computer from 1970 to present and 1970 to 1998 on microfiche, if active.

Searching: Casual requesters can obtain records, but personal information is not released without consent of subject. The state requires a written request stating the nature of the inquiry. The following data is not released: Social Security Numbers.

Access by: mail.

Fee & Payment: The current fee for VIN, registration, and plate checks is $10.00 per record, which includes certification. Fee payee: Office of Motor Vehicles. Prepayment required. Personal checks accepted. No credit cards accepted.

Mail search: Turnaround time: 2 - 4 weeks. Mail searches require license plate number or vehicle identification number (VIN).

Accident Reports

Louisiana State Police, Accident Records, PO Box 66614, Baton Rouge, LA 70896 (Courier: 7919 Independence Blvd, Baton Rouge, LA 70806); 225-925-6157, 225-925-4922 (Fax), 8AM-4PM.

Indexing & Storage: Records are available from 1980's to present. It takes 2 to 3 weeks before new records are available for inquiry.

Searching: The driver name(s), date of accident and parish are needed when ordering.

Access by: mail, in person.

Fee & Payment: The fee is $7.50 per record. Fee payee: Louisiana State Police. Prepayment required. Personal checks are not accepted. No credit cards accepted.

Mail search: Turnaround time: 10 working days. A self addressed stamped envelope is requested.

In person search: Turnaround time is while you wait, if personnel not busy.

Vessel Ownership
Vessel Registration

Department of Wildlife & Fisheries, PO Box 14796, Baton Rouge, LA 70898 (Courier: 2000 Quail Road, Baton Rouge, LA 70898); 225-765-2898, 225-763-5421 (Fax), 8:15AM-4:15PM.

www.wlf.state.la.us

Note: Lien information is found at the parish level.

Indexing & Storage: Records are available from 1960 to present. Record are indexed on computer from the 1970s to present. All motorized boats and sailboats over 12 ft must be registered.

Searching: The hull ID # is not released. To search, one of the following is required: Louisiana #, name, or hull ID #, and from whom boat was acquired. Records are subject to DPPA and 14 permissible uses. Records are not released to the general public unless subject has given permission.

Access by: mail.

Fee & Payment: There is no fee. Fee payee: Department of Wildlife and Fisheries. Prepayment required. Payments are only required for list purchases. Personal checks accepted. No credit cards accepted.

Mail search: Turnaround time: 7 to 10 days. No self addressed stamped envelope is required.

Other access: Records can be purchased in bulk in a variety of media formats. There is a $100.00 minimum deposit, the fee is $.05 per record.

Legislation Records

Louisiana House (Senate) Representative, State Capitol, 2nd Floor, PO Box 44486, Baton Rouge, LA 70804; 225-342-2456 (Information Help Desk), 225-342-2365 (Senate Documents (Room 205)), 225-342-6458 (House Documents (Room 207)), 800-256-3793 (General Information, In-state), 8AM-5PM.

www.legis.state.la.us

Note: Sessions are from the last Monday in April for 60 days in even numbered years, In March for 85 days in odd numbered years. The PO Box above is for the House; the PO Box for Senate bills is 94183.

Indexing & Storage: Records are available from 1952 to present, 1997 forward is on Internet. Records are indexed on microfiche.

Searching: Include the following in your request: bill number, year. Call first on the passed bills for location on microfiche. Pending bills are available in hard copy.

Access by: mail, phone, fax, in person, online.

Fee & Payment: Copies are $.25 per page. Fee payee: LA Legislative Document Services. Will send invoices. Personal checks accepted. No credit cards accepted.

Mail search: Turnaround time: same day if possible. A minimum of $1.50 postage applies. No self addressed stamped envelope is required.

Phone search: A minimum of $1.50 for postage applies.

Fax search: The fee is $.25 per page for items returned by fax.

In person search: No fee for request.

Online search: The Internet site has a wealth of information about sessions and bills from 1997 forward.

Voter Registration

Department of Elections & Registration, PO Box 4729, Baton Rouge, LA 70821-4729; 225-925-7885, 225-925-1841 (Fax), 8AM-5PM.

www.laelections.org

Note: Although the information is public record, individual searching must be done at the parish level through the Parish Registrar of Voters.

Indexing & Storage: Records are available for all currently registered voters.

Searching: The following data is not released: Social Security Numbers or phone numbers.

Access by:. No searching by mail.

Other access: The state will sell the database statewide or by parish. Media formats include disk, tape, labels, CD, and lists. There are no restrictions regarding purchasing for marketing purposes. Call 225-925-7873 for more information.

GED Certificates

Division of Audit Education & Training, PO Box 94064, Baton Rouge, LA 70804-9064; 225-342-0444 (Main Number), 225-219-4439 (Fax).

Searching: You may verify a GED. To search, you must use their form, which may be requested via phone, fax, or mail.

Access by: mail, fax, in person.

Fee & Payment: There is no fee.

Mail search: Turnaround time 2 weeks. No self addressed stamped envelope is required.

Fax search: Results of a fax search will be mailed, same criteria as mail searches.

In person search: In person searchers must have a photo ID. Turnaround time: Immediate.

Hunting License Information
Fishing License Information

Wildlife & Fisheries Department, License Division, PO Box 98000, Baton Rouge, LA 70898-9000 (Courier: 2000 Quail Dr, Baton Rouge, LA 70808); 225-765-2881, 225-765-3150 (Fax), 8:AM-4:30PM.

www.wlf.state.la.us/apps/netgear/page1.asp

Note: Their central database has been modified an is now supplied by the DMV. All license information is subject to the DPPA under US Code 18. At present, not all 14 permissible uses are readily available and use of a subpoena is suggested.

Indexing & Storage: Records are available from 1987 and are on computer.

Searching: The following data is not released: Social Security Numbers.

Access by:. Records are available by mail.

Louisiana State Licensing Agencies

Licenses Searchable Online

Acupuncturist #20	www.lsbme.org/bmeSearch/licenseesearch.asp
Athletic Trainer #20	www.lsbme.org/bmeSearch/licenseesearch.asp
Bank #32	www.ofi.state.la.us/newbanks.htm
Bond For Deed Agency #32	www.ofi.state.la.us/newbfd.htm
Check Casher #32	www.ofi.state.la.us/newcheckcash.htm
Clinical Lab Personnel #20	www.lsbme.org/bmeSearch/licenseesearch.asp
Collection Agency #32	www.ofi.state.la.us/newcolagn.htm
Consumer Credit Grantor #32	www.ofi.state.la.us/newliclen.htm
Contractor, Commercial/Residential #30	www.lslbc.state.la.us/croster.asp
Contractor, General/Subcontractor #41	www.lslbc.state.la.us/croster.asp
Counselor, Professional (LPC) #46	www.lpcboard.org/lpc_alpha_list.htm
Credit Repair Agency #32	www.ofi.state.la.us/newcredrep.htm
Credit Union #32	www.ofi.state.la.us/newcus.htm
Dental Hygienist #9	www.lsbd.org/dentistsearch.asp
Dentist #9	www.lsbd.org/dentistsearch.asp
Dietitian #13	www.lbedn.org/licensee_database.asp
Drug Distributor, Wholesale #64	www.lsbwdd.org
Engineer #40	www.lapels.com/indv_reg.html
Exercise Physiologist, Clinical #20	www.lsbme.org/bmeSearch/licenseesearch.asp
Insurance Agent, LHA/PC #33	www.ldi.state.la.us/searchforms/searchform.asp
Insurance Agent/Broker #33	www.ldi.state.la.us/searchforms/searchform.asp
Land Surveyor #40	www.lapels.com/indv_reg.html
Lender #32	www.ofi.state.la.us/newliclen.htm
Lobbyist #66	www.ethics.state.la.us/lobs.htm
Medical Doctor #20	www.lsbme.org/bmeSearch/licenseesearch.asp
Midwife #20	www.lsbme.org/bmeSearch/licenseesearch.asp
Mortgage Lender/Broker, Residential #32	www.ofi.state.la.us/newrml.htm
Notary Public #54	www.sec.state.la.us/notary-pub/NTRINQ.htm
Notification Filer #32	www.ofi.state.la.us/newnotif.htm
Nutritionist #13	www.lbedn.org/licensee_database.asp
Occupational Therapist/Technologist #20	www.lsbme.org/bmeSearch/licenseesearch.asp
Optometrist #22	www.odfinder.org/LicSearch.asp
Osteopathic Physician #20	www.lsbme.org/bmeSearch/licenseesearch.asp
Pawnbroker #32	www.ofi.state.la.us/newpawn.htm
Physician Assistant #20	www.lsbme.org/bmeSearch/licenseesearch.asp
Podiatrist #20	www.lsbme.org/bmeSearch/licenseesearch.asp
Radiologic Technologist, Private #20	www.lsbme.org/bmeSearch/licenseesearch.asp
Real Estate Appraiser #29	www.lreasbc.state.la.us/appraiserinfo.htm
Respiratory Therapist/Therapy Technician #20	www.lsbme.org/bmeSearch/licenseesearch.asp
Savings & Loan #32	www.ofi.state.la.us/newcus.htm
Solicitor #33	www.ldi.state.la.us/searchforms/searchform.asp
Thrift & Loan Company #32	www.ofi.state.la.us/newthrift.htm
Vocational Rehabilitative Counselor #63	www.lrcboard.org/licensee_database.asp

Licensing Quick Finder

Acupuncturist #20 — 504-524-6820	Boiler Inspector/Installer #55 — 225-925-4344	Court Reporter #37 — 225-925-7671
Adult Day Care #35 — 225-022-0015	Bond For Deed Agency #32 — 225-925-4660	Credit Repair Agency #32 — 225-925-4660
Adult Education Instructor #42 — 225-342-3490	Boxing/Wrestling Personnel #27 — 337-828-7154	Credit Union #32 — 225-925-4660
Adult Residential Care #35 — 225-022-0015	Burglar Alarm Contractor #55 — 225-925-6766	Day Care Facilities #35 — 225-922-0015
Agricultural Consultant #56 — 225-925-3787	Cemetery #2 — 504-838-5267	Dental Hygienist #9 — 504-568-8574
Alarm/Security Company #26 — 225-272-2310	Check Casher #32 — 225-925-4660	Dentist #9 — 504-568-8574
Alcoholic Beverage Vendor #3 — 225-925-4041	Check Seller #32 — 225-925-4660	Dietitian #13 — 225-756-3490
Amusement Ride/Attraction Inspector #55 — 225-925-7045	Chemical Engineer #40 — 225-925-6291	Drug Distributor, Wholesale #64 — 225-295-8567
Amusement Ride/Attraction Owner/Operator #55 — 225-925-7045	Child Nutrition Program Supervisor #42 — 225-342-3490	Electrical Engineer — 225-925-6291
Arborist/Utility Arborist #39 — 225-925-7772	Child Residential Care #35 — 225-022-0015	Electrologist #10 — 318-463-6180
Architect/Architectural Firm #50 — 225-925-4802	Chiropractor #7 — 225-765-2322	Electronics Repairman #34 — 225-231-4710
Art Therapist #42 — 225-342-3490	Clinical Lab Personnel #20 — 504-524-6820	Embalmer #12 — 504-838-5109
Athletic Trainer #20 — 504-524-6820	Collection Agency #32 — 225-925-4660	Emergency Medical Technician #20 — 504-524-6820
Attorney #49 — 504-566-1600	Compulsive Gambler Counselor #28 — 225-927-7600	Emergency Shelter #35 — 225-922-0015
Auctioneer/Auction Company #44 — 225-922-2329	Construction Projects +$50,000 #41 — 225-765-2301	Engineer #40 — 225-925-6291
Bank #32 — 225-925-4660	Consumer Credit Grantor #32 — 225-925-4667	Engineer Intern #40 — 225-925-6291
Barber/Barber Shop/Instructor/School #4 — 225-925-1701	Contractor, Commercial/Residential #30 — 504-736-7125	Environmental Engineer #40 — 225-925-6291
Blood Alcohol Analyst #1 — 225-925-6216	Contractor, General/Subcontractor #41 — 225-765-2301	Equine Dentist #45 — 225-342-2176
	Cosmetologist/Cosmetology Instructor #8 — 225-756-3404	Esthetician #8 — 225-756-3404
	Counselor, Professional (LPC) #46 — 225-765-2515	Euthanasia Technician #45 — 225-342-2176
		Exercise Physiologist, Clinical #20 — 504-524-6820

Explosives Dealer/Handler #38 225-925-6178
Family Support #35.................................225-022-0015
Fire Alarm Contractor #55 225-925-6766
Fire Extinguisher Contractor #55............225-925-6766
Fire Protection Sprinkler Contractor #55 225-925-6766
Fire Suppression Contractor #55 225-925-6766
Florist, Retail/Wholesale #39.................225-925-7772
Foster Care/Adoption Care #35 225-922-0015
Funeral Director/Establishment #12 504-838-5109
Funeral Home Internship/Work Permit #12
....504-838-5109
Guidance Counselor #42.......................225-342-3490
Hearing Aid Dealer #19 318-362-3014
Horse Owner/Trainer #52 504-483-4000
Horse Racing #52...................................504-483-4000
Horse Racing-related Profession (Groom, Plater, etc.)
#52 504-483-4000
Horticulturist #39...................................225-925-7772
Infant Intervention Service #35.............225-022-0015
Insurance Agent, LHA/PC #33 225-342-0860
Insurance Agent/Broker #33.................225-342-0860
Interior Designer #14.............................225-298-1283
Investment Advisor #53 225-925-4660
Jockey/Apprentice/Jockey Agent #52 ..504-483-4000
Juvenile Detention #35..........................225-022-0015
Land Surveying Intern #40 225-925-6291
Land Surveyor #40 225-925-6291
Landscape Architect #39.......................225-925-7772
Landscape Contractor #39.....................225-925-7772
Lender #32..225-925-4660
Livestock Branding #43 225-925-3962
Loan Broker #32.....................................225-925-4660
Lobbyist #66 225-992-1400
Lottery #47..225-297-2000
Lottery Claims Center #48 504-889-0031
Manicurist #8 225-756-3404
Manufactured Home Installer/Developer #55
....225-925-4911
Manufactured Home Mfg #55...............225-925-4911
Manufactured Housing Dealer/Salesman #55
....225-925-4911
Massage Therapist #62 225-658-8941
Maternity Home #35 225-922-0015

Medical Doctor #20................................504-524-6820
Medical Gas Piping Installer #51..........504-826-2382
Midwife #20 504-524-6820
Montessori Teacher #42.........................225-342-3490
Mortgage Lender/Broker, Residential #32
....225-925-4662
Motor Vehicle Agent/Salesman #59.....504-838-5207
Motor Vehicle Dealer; New/Used #59 ..504-838-5207
Motor Vehicle Inspector #1...................225-925-6984
Motor Vehicle Leasing/Rental Company #59
....504-838-5207
Motor Vehicle Sales Finance Company #59
....504-838-5207
Music Therapist #42 225-342-3490
Notary Public #54 225-342-4981
Notification Filer #32..............................225-992-0634
Nuclear Engineer #40.............................225-925-6291
Nuclear Medicine Technologist #16......504-838-5231
Nurse #21 504-838-5332
Nurse (Practical) School #25.................504-568-6480
Nurse, Student #21 504-838-5332
Nurse-LPN #25.......................................504-568-6480
Nurses' Aide #36 225-925-4132
Nursing Home Administrator #36 225-925-4132
Nursing School #21................................504-838-5332
Nutritionist #13.......................................225-756-3490
Occupational Therapist/Tech. #20 504-524-6820
Optometrist #22......................................318-335-2989
Osteopathic Physician #20....................504-524-6820
Pari-Mutuel Employee #52....................504-483-4000
Pawnbroker #32......................................225-925-4660
Payday Lender #32.................................225-925-4660
Personal Care Attendant #35................225-922-0015
Pesticide Applicator #56........................225-925-3796
Pesticide Dealer/Operator #56 225-925-3796
Pharmacist/Pharmacy #23 225-925-6496
Physical Therapist/Therapist Asst #24. 337-262-1043
Physician Assistant #20.........................504-524-6820
Plumber Journeyman/Master #51 504-826-2382
Podiatrist #20..504-524-6820
Polygraph Examiner #57 225-389-3836
Prevention Specialist (Social Work) #28 225-927-7600
Private Investigator/PI Company #58.....225-763-3556

Private Security #26 225-272-2310
Psychologist #15 225-763-3935
Public Accountant-CPA #5 504-566-1244
Radiation Therapy Technologist #16 ... 504-838-5231
Radio & TV Technician #40 225-925-6291
Radiographer #16...................................504-838-5231
Radiologic Technologist #16..................504-838-5231
Radiologic Technologist, Private #20 ... 504-524-6820
Reading Specialist #42 225-342-3490
Real Estate Appraiser #29 225-925-4771
Real Estate Broker/Salesperson #60 ... 225-925-4771
Respiratory Therapist/Therapy Technician #20
....504-524-6820
Respite Care #35 225-022-0015
Sanitarian #17 225-925-7204
Satellite Technician #34 225-231-4710
Savings & Loan #32................................225-925-4660
School Counselor/Librarian/Nurse/Principal #42
....225-342-3490
School Psychologist #42 225-342-3490
School Superintendent, Parish/City #42 225-342-3490
School Therapist #42 225-342-3490
Securities Dealer/Salesperson #53.......225-925-4660
Security Guard #26 225-272-2310
Shorthand Reporter #37.........................225-925-7671
Social Worker #6 225-763-5470
Solicitor #33..225-342-0860
Speech Pathologist/Audiologist #18 225-763-5480
Speech/Language/Hearing Teacher #42
....225-342-3490
Substance Abuse Counselor #28 225-927-7600
Supervised Independent Living #35..... 225-022-0015
Surveyor, Land #40................................225-925-6291
Teacher, Temporary #42........................225-342-3490
Teacher/Teacher's Aide #11 225-342-3490
Thrift & Loan Company #32 225-925-4660
Timeshare Interest Salesperson #60 ... 225-925-4771
TV-Radio Technician #34........................225-231-4710
Used Vehicle Salesperson #61.............225-925-3870
Veterinarian/Veterinary Technician #45 225-342-2176
Vocational Rehabilitative Counselor #63 225-922-1435
Water Supply Piping #51.......................504-826-2382

Licensing Agency Information

#1 State Police Safety & Enforcement, PO Box 66614, Baton Rouge, LA 70896; 225-925-6984, Fax: 225-925-3966.

#2 Cemetery Board, 2901 Ridgelake Dr, #101, Metairie, LA 70002-4946; 504-838-5267, Fax: 504-838-5289.

#3 Board of Alcohol & Tobacco, 8549 United Plaza Blvd, Baton Rouge, LA 70809; 225-925-4041, Fax: 225-925-3975.
www.atc.rev.state.la.us/atcweb/home.htm
Agency email: info@atcla.com.

#4 Board of Barber Examiners, PO Box 14029, Baton Rouge, LA 70898-4029; 225-925-1701, Fax: 225-925-1703. www.barber-cosmos.com

#5 Board of Certified Public Accountants, 601 Poydras St, #1770, New Orleans, LA 70130; 504-566-1244, Fax: 504-566-1252.

#6 Board of Certified Social Work Examiners, 11930 Perkins Rd, #B, Baton Rouge, LA 70810; 225-763-5470, Fax: 225-763-5400.
www.labswe.org
Agency email: socialwork@labswe.org.

#7 Board of Chiropractic Examiners, 8621 Summa Ave, Baton Rouge, LA 70809; 225-765-2322, Fax: 225-765-2640.
www.dhh.state.la.us/boards.htm
Agency email: lsbce@eatel.net.

#8 Board of Cosmetology, 11622 Sunbelt Court, Baton Rouge, LA 70809; 225-756-3404, Fax: 225-756-3410/3109.

#9 Board of Dentistry, 365 Canal St, #2680, New Orleans, LA 70112; 504-568-8574, Fax: 504-568-8598. www.lsbd.org
Agency email: webmaster@lsbd.org.
Search database at www.lsbd.org/dentistsearch.asp

#10 Board of Electrolysis Examiners, PO Box 67, DeRidder, LA 70634-0067; 318-463-6180, Fax: 318-463-3991
Agency email: istatebrdee@aol.com.

#11 Board of Elementary & Secondary Education, 626 N 4th St, Baton Rouge, LA 70804-9064; 225-342-3490, Fax: 225-342-3499.
www.doe.state.la.us

#12 Board of Embalmers & Funeral Directors, 3500 N Causeway Blvd, #1232, New Orleans, LA 70002; 504-838-5109, Fax: 504-838-5112.
www.lsbefd.state.la.us
Agency email: webmaster@lsbefd.state.la.us or labefd@ix.netcom.com.

#13 Board of Examiners of Dietitics & Nutrition, 11930 Perkins Rd, #B, Baton Rouge, LA 70810; 225-756-3490, Fax: 225-756-3472.
www.lbedn.org. Agency email: admin@lbedn.org.

#14 Board of Examiners of Interior Designers, 2900 Westfork Dr #200, Baton Rouge, LA 70827-0004; 225-298-1283, Fax: 225-925-1892.

#15 Board of Examiners of Psychologists, 8280 YMCA Plaza Dr, Bldg 8B, Baton Rouge, LA 70810; 225-763-3935, Fax: 225-763-3968.
www.lsbep.org. Agency email: lsbep@cmq.net.
Search database at www.lsbep.org

#16 Board of Examiners of Radiologic Technologists, 3108 Cleary Ave, #207, Metairie, LA 70002; 504-838-5231, Fax: 504-780-1740.
Agency email: larabrd@bellsouth.net.

#17 Board of Examiners of Sanitarians, 1772 Wooddale Blvd, Baton Rouge, LA 70806; 225-925-7204, Fax: 225-925-7245.
www.lsbes.org
Agency email: dkuhns@dhh.state.la.us.

#18 Board of Examiners of Speech/Language Pathology & Audiology, 11930 Perkins Rd, #B, Baton Rouge, LA 70810; 225-763-5480, Fax: 225-763-5400. www.lbespa.org
Agency email: speech@ibespa.org.

#19 Board of Hearing Aid Dealers, 2200 Justice St, Monroe, LA 71201; 318-362-3014, Fax: 318-362-3019.

#20 Executive Director, Board of Medical Examiners, 630 Camp St, New Orleans, LA

70130; 504-524-6820, auto response: dial 1, Fax: 504-568-8893. www.lsbme.org
Agency email: lsbmever@lsbme.org.
Search database at
www.lsbme.org/bmeSearch/licenseesearch.asp

#21 Board of Nursing, 3510 N Causeway Blvd, #501, Metairie, LA 70002; 504-838-5332, Fax: 504-838-5349. www.lsbn.state.la.us
Agency email: lsbn@lsbn.state.la.us.

#22 Board of Optometry Examiners, 115 B N 13th St, Oakdale, LA 71463; 318-335-2989, Fax: 318-335-2989. Search database at www.odfinder.org/LicSearch.asp

#23 Board of Pharmacy, 5615 Corporate Blvd, #8E, Baton Rouge, LA 70808; 225-925-6496, Fax: 225-925-6499.
www.labp.com. Agency email: labp@labp.com.

#24 Board of Physical Therapy Examiners, 714 E Kaliste Saloom Rd #D2, Lafayette, LA 70508; 337-262-1043, Fax: 337-262-1054.
www.laptboard.org
Agency email: lsbpte@iamerica.net.

#25 Board of Practical Nurse Examiners, 3421 N Causeway Blvd #203, Metairie, LA 70002-3711; 504-838-5791, Fax: 504-838-5279.
www.lsbpne.com

#26 Board of Private Security Examiners, 15703 Old Hammond Hwy, Baton Rouge, LA 70816; 225-272-2310, Fax: 225-272-5816.

#27 Boxing & Wrestling Commission, PO Box 251, Franklin, LA 70538; 337-828-7154.

#28 Board of Certification for Substance Abuse Counselors, 4637 Jamestown #2A, Baton Rouge, LA 70808; 225-927-7600, Fax: 225-927-8150.
www.lsbcsac.org

#29 Real Estate Appraisers State Board of Certification, 9071 Interline Ave, Baton Rouge, LA 70898; 225-925-4771, 800-821-4529, Fax: 225-925-4431.
www.lreasbc.state.la.us
Agency email: info@lreasbc.state.la.us.
Search database at
www.lreasbc.state.la.us/appraiserinfo.htm

#30 Contractors Licensing Board (New Orleans), 1221 Elmwood Pk Blvd, New Orleans, LA 70141; 504-736-7125, Fax: 504-736-7125 *Key.
www.lslbc.state.la.us. Search database at
www.lslbc.state.la.us/croster.asp

#32 Department of Economic Development, Office of Financial Institutions, 8660 United Plaza Blvd, 2nd Floor, Baton Rouge, LA 70809; 225-925-4660, Fax: 225-925-4548.
www.ofi.state.la.us
Agency email: ofila@ofi.state.la.us.

#33 Department of Insurance, Agent's License Division, 950 N 5th, Baton Rouge, LA 70802; 225-342-0860, Fax: 225-342-3078.
www.ldi.state.la.us

#34 Radio And Television Technicians Board, 6554 Florida Boulevard #109, Baton Rouge, LA 70806; 225-231-4710, Fax: 225-231-4711.

#35 Department of Social Services, Bureau of Licensing, PO Box 3078, Baton Rouge, LA 70821; 225-922-0015, Fax: 225-922-0014.
www.dss.state.la.us/offos/html/licensing.html

#36 Examiners of Nursing Facility Administrators, 5615 Corporate Blvd, #8D, Baton Rouge, LA

70808; 225-922-0009, Fax: 225-922-0006
Agency email: kempwright@compuserve.com.

#37 Examiners of Certified Shorthand Reporters, PO Box 3257, Baton Rouge, LA 70821-3257; 225-925-7671, Fax: 225-925-7672.
www.lacourtreporterboard.com. Agency email: courtreporter@lacourtreporterboard.com.

#38 Explosives Control Unit, PO Box 66614, Mail Stop 21, Baton Rouge, LA 70896; 225-925-6178 x208, Fax: 225-925-4048. www.dps.state.la.us/lsp

#39 Department of Agriculture, Horticulture Commission, PO Box 3596, Baton Rouge, LA 70821-3596; 225-925-7772, Fax: 225-925-3760.

#40 Professional Engineers & Land Surveying Board, 9643 Brookline Ave #121, Baton Rouge, LA 70809-1433; 225-925-6291, Fax: 225-925-6292. www.lapels.com
Search database at www.lapels.com/indv_reg.html

#41 Licensing Board for Contractors, PO Box 14419, Baton Rouge, LA 70898-4419; 225-765-2301, Fax: 225-765-2431. www.lslbc.state.la.us
Agency email: info@lslbc.state.la.us.

#42 Department of Education, Licensing Bureau of Higher Education Certification, 626 N 4th St, Baton Rouge, LA 70804-9064; 225-342-3490, Fax: 225-342-3499. www.doe.state.la.us

#43 LA Dept of Agriculture & Forestry, Livestock Brand Commission, PO Box 1951 (5825 Florida Blvd, 70806), Baton Rouge, LA 70821; 225-925-3962, Fax: 225-925-4103.
www.ldaf.state.la.us
Agency email: liz_b@ldaf.state.la.us.

#44 Auctioneers Licensing Board, 8017 Jefferson Hwy, #A-2, Baton Rouge, LA 70809; 225-922-2329, Fax: 225-925-1892
Agency email: auctionboard@eatel.net.

#45 Board of Veterinary Medicine, 263 3rd St, #104, Baton Rouge, LA 70801; 225-342-2176, Fax: 225-342-2142.
www.lsbvm.org. Agency email: lbvm@eatel.net.

#46 Licensed Professional Counselors, Board of Examiners, 8631 Summa Ave, #A, Baton Rouge, LA 70809; 225-765-2515, Fax: 225-765-2514.
www.lpcboard.org
Agency email: lpcboard@eatel.net.
Search database at
www.lpcboard.org/lpc_alpha_list.htm

#47 Lottery Corporation, State Headquarters, 11200 Industriplex, #190, Baton Rouge, LA 70809; 225-297-2000, Fax: 225-297-2005.
www.lalottery.com

#48 Lottery Corporation, 2222 Clearview Parkway, Metairie, LA 70001; 504-889-0031, Fax: 504-889-0490.
www.louisianalottery.com

#49 State Bar Association, 601 St Charles Av, New Orleans, LA 70130; 504-566-1600, Fax: 504-566-0930.
www.lsba.org. Agency email: lsbainfo@lsba.org.

#50 Board of Architectural Examiners, 8017 Jefferson Hwy B-2, Baton Rouge, LA 70809; 225-925-4802, Fax: 225-925-4804.
www.lastbdarchs.com
Agency email: lastbdarchs@eatel.net.
Search database at
www.lastbdarchs.com/roster.htm

#51 Plumbing Board, 2714 Canal St, #512, New Orleans, LA 70119; 504-826-2382, Fax: 504-826-2175.

#52 Racing Commission, 320 N Carrollton Ave, #2B, New Orleans, LA 70119-5100; 504-483-4000, Fax: 504-483-4898.
www.lded.state.la.us/new/lrc/lrcmain.htm
Agency email: webmaster@lded.state.la.us.

#53 Securities, Office of Financial Institutions, PO Box 94095 (8660 United Plaza Blvd, 2nd Fl), Baton Rouge, LA 70804; 225-925-4660, Fax: 225-925-4548. www.ofi.state.la.us

#54 Office of Secretary of State, PO Box 94125, Baton Rouge, LA 70804-9125; 225-342-4981, Fax: 225-342-2066.
www.sec.state.la.us/notary-pub/notary.htm
Search database at www.sec.state.la.us/notary-pub/NTRINQ.htm

#55 Office of the State Fire Marshall, 5150 Florida Blvd, Baton Rouge, LA 70806; 225-925-4911; 800-256-5452, Fax: 225-925-4241.
www.dps.state.la.us/sfm

#56 Agricultural & Environmental Sciences, Pest Control Commission, PO Box 3596 (5825 Florida Blvd), Baton Rouge, LA 70821; 225-925-3796, 225-925-3770, Fax: 225-925-3760.
www.ldaf.state.la.us/divisions/aes/default.asp.
Agency email: bobby_s@ldaf.state.la.us.

#57 Baton Rouge Police Dept., Polygraph Board, PO Box 2406, Baton Rouge, LA 70821; 225-389-3836.

#58 Board of Private Investigators Examiners, 2051 Silverside Dr. #109, Baton Rouge, LA 70808; 225-763-3556, Fax: 225-763-3536.
www.lsbpie.com
Agency email: lsbpie@intersurf.com.

#59 Motor Vehicle Commission, 3519 12th Street, Metairie, LA 70002-3427; 504-838-5207.

#60 Real Estate Commission, 9071 Interline Ave, Baton Rouge, LA 70809; 225-925-4771, Fax: 225-925-4431. www.lrec.state.la.us
Agency email: info@lrec.state.la.us.

#61 Used Motor Vehicle & Parts Commission, 3132 Valley Creek Drive, Baton Rouge, LA 70808; 225-925-3870, Fax: 225-925-3869.
www.lumvpc.state.la.us

#62 Professional Licensing Boards, Board of Massage Therapy, 4707 Main St, Zachary, LA 70791; 225-658-8941, Fax: 225-658-8946.
www.lsbmt.org. Agency email: lsbmt@eatel.net.

#63 Board of Examiners, Board of Vocational Rehabilitative Counselors, PO Box 41594, Baton Rouge, LA 70801; 225-922-1435, Fax: 225-922-1352. www.lrcboard.org
Agency email: lrcboard@eatel.net.

#64 Board of Wholesale Drug Distributors, 12046 Justice Ave, #C, Baton Rouge, LA 70816; 225-295-8567, Fax: 225-295-8568.
www.lsbwdd.org
Agency email: info@lsbwdd.org.
Search database at www.lsbwdd.org

#66 Ethics Board, 8401 United Plaza Blvd #200, Baton Rouge, LA 70809; 225-992-1400 1-800-842-6630, Fax: 225-922-1414.
www.ethics.state.la.us
Search database at www.ethics.state.la.us/lobs.htm

Louisiana Federal Courts

The following list indicates the district and division name for each Parish in the state. If the bankruptcy court location is different from the district court, then the location of the bankruptcy court appears in parentheses.

Parish/Court Cross Reference

Parish	District	Division
Acadia Parish	Western	Lafayette (Lafayette-Opelousas)
Allen Parish	Western	Lake Charles
Ascension Parish	Middle	Baton Rouge
Assumption Parish	Eastern	New Orleans
Avoyelles Parish	Western	Alexandria
Beauregard Parish	Western	Lake Charles
Bienville Parish	Western	Shreveport
Bossier Parish	Western	Shreveport
Caddo Parish	Western	Shreveport
Calcasieu Parish	Western	Lake Charles
Caldwell Parish	Western	Monroe
Cameron Parish	Western	Lake Charles
Catahoula Parish	Western	Alexandria
Claiborne Parish	Western	Shreveport
Concordia Parish	Western	Alexandria
De Soto Parish	Western	Shreveport
East Baton Rouge Parish	Parish	Middle Baton Rouge
East Carroll Parish	Western	Monroe
East Feliciana Parish	Middle	Baton Rouge
Evangeline Parish	Western	Lafayette (Lafayette-Opelousas)
Franklin Parish	Western	Monroe
Grant Parish	Western	Alexandria
Iberia Parish	Western	Lafayette (Lafayette-Opelousas)
Iberville Parish	Middle	Baton Rouge
Jackson Parish	Western	Monroe
Jefferson Davis Parish	Western	Lake Charles
Jefferson Parish	Eastern	New Orleans
La Salle Parish	Western	Alexandria
Lafayette Parish	Western	Lafayette (Lafayette-Opelousas)
Lafourche Parish	Eastern	New Orleans
Lincoln Parish	Western	Monroe
Livingston Parish	Middle	Baton Rouge
Madison Parish	Western	Monroe
Morehouse Parish	Western	Monroe
Natchitoches Parish	Western	Alexandria
Orleans Parish	Eastern	New Orleans
Ouachita Parish	Western	Monroe
Plaquemines Parish	Eastern	New Orleans
Pointe Coupee Parish	Middle	Baton Rouge
Rapides Parish	Western	Alexandria
Red River Parish	Western	Shreveport
Richland Parish	Western	Monroe
Sabine Parish	Western	Shreveport
St. Bernard Parish	Eastern	New Orleans
St. Charles Parish	Eastern	New Orleans
St. Helena Parish	Middle	Baton Rouge
St. James Parish	Eastern	New Orleans
St. John the Baptist Parish	Parish	EasternNew Orleans
St. Landry Parish	Western	Lafayette (Lafayette-Opelousas)
St. Martin Parish	Western	Lafayette (Lafayette-Opelousas)
St. Mary Parish	Western	Lafayette (Lafayette-Opelousas)
St. Tammany Parish	Eastern	New Orleans
Tangipahoa Parish	Eastern	New Orleans
Tensas Parish	Western	Monroe
Terrebonne Parish	Eastern	New Orleans
Union Parish	Western	Monroe
Vermilion Parish	Western	Lafayette (Lafayette-Opelousas)
Vernon Parish	Western	Alexandria
Washington Parish	Eastern	New Orleans
Webster Parish	Western	Shreveport
West Baton Rouge Parish	Parish	Middle Baton Rouge
West Carroll Parish	Western	Monroe
West Feliciana Parish	Middle	Baton Rouge
Winn Parish	Western	Alexandria

Standards for Federal Courts: The search fee is $20.00 per item (one party name or case number). Certification fee is $7.00 per document. Copy fee is $.50 per page. All fees standard unless noted in profile. Mail Search: always enclose a stamped self addressed envelope unless otherwise noted. Before releasing records, all courts require prepayment unless noted in profile.

Open records are located at the court unless otherwise noted. District courts index by defendant and plaintiff as well as by case number. Bankruptcy courts usually index by debtor and case number. While most courts now have their indexes on computer, many still maintain index card files as well.

The universal PACER sign-up number is 800-676-6856. Find PACER and the Party/Case Index on the Web at http://pacer.psc.uscourts.gov. PACER dial-up access is $.60 per minute. Also, courts offering internet access via RACER, PACER, Web-PACER or the new CM-ECF charge $.07 per page fee unless noted as free.

US District Court

Eastern District of Louisiana

New Orleans Division Clerk, Room 151, 500 Camp St, New Orleans, LA 70130 (Courier Address: Use mail address for courier delivery), 504-589-7650, Fax: 504-589-7189.

www.laed.uscourts.gov

Parishes: Assumption Parish, Jefferson Parish, Lafourche Parish, Orleans Parish, Plaquemines Parish, St. Bernard Parish, St. Charles Parish, St. James Parish, St. John the Baptist Parish, St. Tammany Parish, Tangipahoa Parish, Terrebonne Parish, Washington Parish.

Indexing & Storage: Cases are indexed by defendant, plaintiff, and case number. New cases are available in the index 1-2 days after filing date. Open records are located at this court.

Fee & Payment Notes: Payment may be made by money order, cashier check, personal check. Payee: Clerk, US District Court.

Phone Search: Searching not available by phone. Only docket information is available by phone.

In Person Search: In person searching available.

PACER: Toll-free dial-up access: 888-257-1175. Local dial-up access: 504-589-6714. Case records are available back to 1989. Records are purged every six months. New records are available online after 1-2 days. PACER is available online at http://pacer.laed.uscourts.gov. Document images available.

US Bankruptcy Court

Eastern District of Louisiana

New Orleans Division Hale Boggs Federal Bldg, 501 Magazine St, #601, New Orleans, LA 70130 (Courier Address: Use mail address for courier delivery), 504-589-7878.

www.laeb.uscourts.gov

Parishes: Assumption Parish, Jefferson Parish, Lafourche Parish, Orleans Parish, Plaquemines Parish, St. Bernard Parish, St. Charles Parish, St. James Parish, St. John the Baptist Parish, St. Tammany Parish, Tangipahoa Parish, Terrebonne Parish, Washington Parish.

Indexing & Storage: Cases are indexed by debtor as well as by case number. New cases are available in the index 2 days after filing date. Records are also indexed on microfiche. District wide searches are available from this court from November 1985 for information in the computer and from 1979 to 1985 on card index.

Fee & Payment Notes: Payment may be made by money order, cashier check, business check. Personal checks are not accepted. Payee: Clerk, US Bankruptcy Court.

Phone Search: Information is available from 9:00 to 10:30 a.m. and 1:00 to 2:30 p.m. over the phone. There is no fee for case status information. Only docket information will be released. An automated voice case information service (VCIS) is available. Call VCIS at 504-589-7879.

In Person Search: In person searching available.

PACER:. Case records are available back to 1985. Records are purged every six months. New civil records are available online after 2 days. PACER is available at http://pacer.laeb.uscourts.gov.

Electronic Filing: Information is available online at https://ecf.laeb.uscourts.gov

US District Court

Middle District of Louisiana

Baton Rouge Division PO Box 2630, Baton Rouge, LA 70821-2630 (Courier Address: 777 Florida St., #139, Baton Rouge, LA 70801), 225-389-3500, Fax: 225-389-3501.

www.lamd.uscourts.gov

Parishes: Ascension Parish, East Baton Rouge Parish, East Feliciana Parish, Iberville Parish, Livingston Parish, Pointe Coupee Parish, St. Helena Parish, West Baton Rouge Parish, West Feliciana Parish.

Indexing & Storage: Cases are indexed by defendant, plaintiff, and case number. New cases are available in the index immediately after filing date. Index prior to 1992 is on microfiche and computer. Open records are located at this court.

Fee & Payment Notes: Payment may be made by money order, cashier check, business check, Visa, Mastercard. Personal checks are not accepted. The court has no billing procedures. Payee: Clerk, US District Court. You are allowed to make your own copies. These copies cost $.25 per page. A coin operated copier is installed for the public.

Phone Search: Only docket information is available by phone. If the information is at the Federal Records Center, the court will provide the information needed to review a record.

Mail Search: A stamped self addressed envelope is not required.

In Person Search: In person searching available.

PACER: Toll-free dial-up access: 800-616-8757. Local dial-up access: 225-389-3547. Case records are available back to October 1993. New records are available online after 1 day. PACER is available online at http://pacer.lamd.uscourts.gov. Document images available.

US Bankruptcy Court

Middle District of Louisiana

Baton Rouge Division Room 119, 707 Florida St, Baton Rouge, LA 70801 (Courier

Address: Use mail address for courier delivery), 225-389-0211.

www.lamb.uscourts.gov

Parishes: Ascension Parish, East Baton Rouge Parish, East Feliciana Parish, Iberville Parish, Livingston Parish, Pointe Coupee Parish, St. Helena Parish, West Baton Rouge Parish, West Feliciana Parish.

Indexing & Storage: Cases are indexed by debtor and creditors as well as by case number. New cases are available in the index immediately after filing date. Open records are located at this court.

Fee & Payment Notes: Payment may be made by money order, cashier check, business check. Personal checks are not accepted. Payee: Clerk, US Bankruptcy Court. You are allowed to make your own copies. These copies cost $.25 per page.

Phone Search: Only docket information is available by phone. An automated voice case information service (VCIS) is available. Call VCIS at 504-382-2175.

In Person Search: In person searching available.

PACER: Access fee is. Case records are available back to May 15, 1992. New civil records are available online after 1 day. PACER is available online at http://pacer.lamb.uscourts.gov.

Electronic Filing: Information is available online at https://ecf.lamb.uscourts.gov

US District Court

Western District of Louisiana

Alexandria Division PO Box 1269, Alexandria, LA 71309 (Courier Address: 515 Murray, Alexandria, LA 71301), 318-473-7415, Fax: 318-473-7345.

www.lawd.uscourts.gov

Parishes: Avoyelles Parish, Catahoula Parish, Concordia Parish, Grant Parish, La Salle Parish, Natchitoches Parish, Rapides Parish, Winn Parish.

Indexing & Storage: Cases are indexed by defendant, plaintiff, and case number. New cases are available in the index 3 days after filing date. Open records are located at this court.

Fee & Payment Notes: Payment may be made by money order, cashier check, personal check. Payee: Clerk, US District Court.

Phone Search: Only docket information is available by phone.

In Person Search: In person searching available.

PACER: Toll-free dial-up access: 888-263-2679. Local dial-up access: 318-676-3958. Case records are available back to October 1993. Records are purged as deemed necessary. New records are available online after 1 day. PACER is available online at https://pacer.lawd.uscourts.gov. Document images available.

Lafayette Division Room 113, Federal Bldg, 705 Jefferson St, Lafayette, LA 70501 (Courier Address: Use mail address for courier delivery), 337-593-5000.

www.lawd.uscourts.gov

Parishes: Acadia Parish, Evangeline Parish, Iberia Parish, Lafayette Parish, St. Landry Parish, St. Martin Parish, St. Mary Parish, Vermilion Parish.

Indexing & Storage: Cases are indexed by defendant, plaintiff, and case number. New cases

are available in the index 1 day after filing date. Open records are located at this court.

Fee & Payment Notes: Payment may be made by money order, cashier check, business check. Personal checks are not accepted. Payee: Clerk, US District Court.

Phone Search: Only docket information is available by phone.

Mail Search: Certified name searches can only be performed from the Shreveport office. A stamped self addressed envelope is not required.

In Person Search: In person searching available.

PACER: Toll-free dial-up access: 888-263-2679. Local dial-up access: 318-676-3958. Document images available on Pacer. Case records are available back to October 1993. Records are purged as deemed necessary. New records are available online after 1 day. PACER is available online at https://pacer.lawd.uscourts.gov. Document images available.

Lake Charles Division 611 Broad St, Suite 188, Lake Charles, LA 70601 (Courier: Use mail address for courier delivery), 337-437-3870.

www.lawd.uscourts.gov

Parishes: Allen Parish, Beauregard Parish, Calcasieu Parish, Cameron Parish, Jefferson Davis Parish, Vernon Parish.

Indexing & Storage: Cases are indexed by defendant, plaintiff, and case number. New cases are available in the index 3 days after filing date. Open records are located at this court.

Fee & Payment Notes: Payment may be made by money order, cashier check, business check. Personal checks are not accepted. Payee: Clerk, US District Court.

Phone Search: Only docket information is available by phone.

In Person Search: In person searching available.

PACER: Toll-free dial-up access: 888-263-2679. Local dial-up access: 318-676-3958. Case records are available back to October 1993. Records are purged as deemed necessary. New records are available online after 1 day. PACER is available online at https://pacer.lawd.uscourts.gov. Document images available.

Monroe Division PO Drawer 3087, Monroe, LA 71210 (Courier Address: Room 215, 201 Jackson St, Monroe, LA 71201), 318-322-6740.

www.lawd.uscourts.gov

Parishes: Caldwell Parish, East Carroll Parish, Franklin Parish, Jackson Parish, Lincoln Parish, Madison Parish, Morehouse Parish, Ouachita Parish, Richland Parish, Tensas Parish, Union Parish, West Carroll Parish.

Indexing & Storage: Cases are indexed by defendant, plaintiff, and case number. New cases are available in the index 3 days after filing date. The Shreveport computerized index is used for searching. This division has been without a judge since 1996, and may not be getting one. Therefore, there are very few. Case records held here any longer. It is recommended to search at the Shreveport division.

Fee & Payment Notes: Payment may be made by money order, cashier check, business check. Personal checks are not accepted. Payee: Clerk, US District Court.

Phone Search: Only docket information is available by phone.

In Person Search: In person searching available.

PACER: Toll-free dial-up access: 888-263-2679. Local dial-up access: 318-676-3958. Case records are available back to October 1993. Records are purged as deemed necessary. New records are available online after 1 day. PACER is available online at https://pacer.lawd.uscourts.gov. Document images available.

Shreveport Division US Courthouse, Suite 1167, 300 Fannin St, Shreveport, LA 71101-3083 (Courier Address: Use mail address for courier delivery), 318-676-4273.

www.lawd.uscourts.gov

Parishes: Bienville Parish, Bossier Parish, Caddo Parish, Claiborne Parish, De Soto Parish, Red River Parish, Sabine Parish, Webster Parish.

Indexing & Storage: Cases are indexed by defendant, plaintiff, and case number. New cases are available in the index immediately after filing date. On computer are cases that were filed in 1977 or later. Copies from closed records in cases filed in 1977 or later are available from microfiche located at this court. Open records are located at this court.

Fee & Payment Notes: Payment may be made by money order, cashier check, business check. Personal checks are not accepted. Payee: Clerk, US District Court.

Phone Search: Only docket information is available by phone. If the information is at the Federal Records Center, the court will provide the information needed to review a record.

Mail Search: A stamped self addressed envelope is not required.

In Person Search: In person searching available.

PACER: Toll-free dial-up access: 888-263-2679. Local dial-up access: 318-676-3958. Case records are available back to October 1993. Records are purged as deemed necessary. New records are available online after 1 day. PACER is available online at https://pacer.lawd.uscourts.gov. Document images available.

US Bankruptcy Court

Western District of Louisiana

Alexandria Division 300 Jackson St, Suite 116, Alexandria, LA 71301-8357 (Courier Address: Hemenway Bldg, 300 Jackson St, Alexandria, LA 71301), 318-445-1890.

www.lawb.uscourts.gov

Parishes: Avoyelles Parish, Catahoula Parish, Concordia Parish, Grant Parish, La Salle Parish, Natchitoches Parish, Rapides Parish, Vernon Parish, Winn Parish.

Indexing & Storage: Cases are indexed by debtor as well as by case number. New cases are available in the index 1 day after filing date. Chapter 7 and 11 cases from the Monroe Division are now at this court. Chapter 12 and Chapter 13 continue to be handled by Shreveport. Open records are located at this court.

Fee & Payment Notes: Payment may be made by money order, cashier check, personal check. A copy service will also do the search and copies at $5.00 for the search fee and $.25 per page plus cost of postage. The copy service will bill law firms. Payee: Clerk, US Bankruptcy Court or copy

service. The fee for copies made by court personnel is $.50 per page.

Phone Search: Only docket information is available by phone. An automated voice case information service (VCIS) is available. Call VCIS at 800-326-4026 or 318-676-4234.

Mail Search: A stamped self addressed envelope is not required.

In Person Search: In person searching available.

PACER: Toll-free dial-up access: 888-523-1976. Local dial-up access: 318-676-4235. Case records are available back to 1992. New civil records are available online after 1 day. PACER is available online at http://pacer.lawb.uscourts.gov. Document images available.

Electronic Filing: (Currently in the process of implementing CM/ECF.)

Lafayette-Opelousas Division PO Box J, Opelousas, LA 70571-1909 (Courier Address: Room 205, 231 S Union, Opelousas, LA 70570), 318-948-3451, Fax: 318-948-4426.

www.lawb.uscourts.gov

Parishes: Acadia Parish, Evangeline Parish, Iberia Parish, Lafayette Parish, St. Landry Parish, St. Martin Parish, St. Mary Parish, Vermilion Parish.

Indexing & Storage: Cases are indexed by debtor as well as by case number. New cases are available in the index 1 day after filing date. Records are indexed on index cards for pre-1987 files only. Records are also indexed on microfiche. District wide searches are available for information from January 1, 1986 from this division. This office handles case records for the Lake Charles also.

Fee & Payment Notes: Payment may be made by money order, cashier check, business check. Personal checks are not accepted. Payee: Clerk, US Bankruptcy Court.

Phone Search: Only docket information is available by phone. An automated voice case information service (VCIS) is available. Call VCIS at 800-326-4026 or 318-676-4234.

Mail Search: A stamped self addressed envelope is not required.

In Person Search: In person searching available.

PACER: Toll-free dial-up access: 888-523-1976. Local dial-up access: 318-676-4235. Case records are available back to 1992. New civil records are available online after 1 day. PACER is available online at http://pacer.lawb.uscourts.gov.

Electronic Filing: (Currently in the process of implementing CM/ECF.)

Lake Charles Division c/o Lafayette-Opelousas Division, PO Box J, Opelousas, LA 70571-1909 (Courier Address: Room 205, 250 S Union, Opelousas, LA 70570), 318-948-3451.

www.lawb.uscourts.gov

Parishes: Allen Parish, Beauregard Parish, Calcasieu Parish, Cameron Parish, Jefferson Davis Parish.

Indexing & Storage: New cases are available in the index after filing date. Open records are located at the Division.

Fee & Payment Notes: Payment may be made by money order, cashier check. Business checks are not accepted. Personal checks are not accepted.

Phone Search: An automated voice case information service (VCIS) is available. Call VCIS at 800-326-4026 or 318-676-4234.

Mail Search: A stamped self addressed envelope is not required.

In Person Search: In person searching available.

PACER: Toll-free dial-up access: 888-523-1976. Local dial-up access: 318-676-4235. Case records are available back to 1992. New civil records are available online after 1 day. PACER is available online at http://pacer.lawb.uscourts.gov. Document images available.

Electronic Filing: (Currently in the process of implementing CM/ECF.)

Monroe Division c/o Shreveport Division, Suite 2201, 300 Fannin St, Shreveport, LA 71101 (Courier Address: Use mail address for courier delivery), 318-676-4267.

www.lawb.uscourts.gov

Parishes: Caldwell Parish, East Carroll Parish, Franklin Parish, Jackson Parish, Lincoln Parish, Madison Parish, Morehouse Parish, Ouachita Parish, Richland Parish, Tensas Parish, Union Parish, West Carroll Parish.

Indexing & Storage: New cases are available in the index after filing date. This court is an unmanned office. Cases are housed as follows: Chapter 7 and Chapter 11 cases to Alexandria; Chapter 12 and Chapter 13 cases to Shreveport. Open records are located at Shreveport Division.

Fee & Payment Notes: Payment may be made by money order. Business checks are not accepted. Personal checks are not accepted.

Phone Search: An automated voice case information service (VCIS) is available. Call VCIS at 800-326-4026 or 318-676-4234.

In Person Search: In person searching available.

PACER: Toll-free dial-up access: 888-523-1976. Local dial-up access: 318-676-4235. Case records are available back to 1992. New civil records are available online after 1 day. PACER is available online at http://pacer.lawb.uscourts.gov.

Electronic Filing: (Currently in the process of implementing CM/ECF.)

Shreveport Division Suite 2201, 300 Fannin St, Shreveport, LA 71101-3089 (Courier: Use mail address for courier delivery), 318-676-4267.

www.lawb.uscourts.gov

Parishes: Bienville Parish, Bossier Parish, Caddo Parish, Claiborne Parish, De Soto Parish, Red River Parish, Sabine Parish, Webster Parish.

Indexing & Storage: New cases are available in the index immediately after filing date. Open records are located at this court.

Fee & Payment Notes: Payment may be made by money order, business check. Personal checks are not accepted. Debtor's checks are not accepted. Payee: Clerk, US Bankruptcy Court.

Phone Search: An automated voice case information service (VCIS) is available. Call VCIS at 800-326-4026 or 318-676-4234.

In Person Search: In person searching available.

PACER: Toll-free dial-up access: 888-523-1976. Local dial-up access: 318-676-4235. Case records are available back to 1992. New civil records are available online after 1 day. PACER is available online at http://pacer.lawb.uscourts.gov.

Electronic Filing: (Currently in the process of implementing CM/ECF.)

Louisiana Parish Courts

Court	Jurisdiction	No. of Courts	How Organized
District Courts*	General	65	42 Districts
City Courts*	Limited	4	City Boundaries
Parish Courts	Limited	48	
Justice of the Peace Courts	Municipal	390	
Mayor's Courts	Municipal	250	
Family Court	Special	1	East Baton Rouge
Juvenile Courts	Special	4	

* Profiled in this Sourcebook.

	CIVIL								
Court	Tort	Contract	Real Estate	Min. Claim	Max. Claim	Small Claims	Estate	Eviction	Domestic Relations
District Courts*	X	X	X	$0	No Max		X		X
City Courts*	X	X	X	$0	$20,000	$3000			X
City and Parish Courts	X	X	X	$0	$10,000	$3000		X	X
Justice of the Peace Courts	X	X	X	$0	$3000	$3000		X	
Mayor's Courts									
Family Court									X
Juvenile Courts									X

	CRIMINAL				
Court	Felony	Misdemeanor	DWI/DUI	Preliminary Hearing	Juvenile
District Courts*	X	X	X		X
City Courts*		X	X	X	X
Parish Courts		X	X	X	X
Justice of the Peace Courts					
Mayor's Courts					
Family Court					X
Juvenile Courts					X

ADMINISTRATION Judicial Administrator, Judicial Council of the Supreme Court, 1555 Poydras St #1540, New Orleans, LA, 70112; 504-568-5747, Fax: 504-568-5687; www.lasc.org

COURT STRUCTURE A District Court Clerk in each Parish holds all the records for that Parish. Each Parish has its own clerk and courthouse. A municipality may have a Mayor's Court; the mayor may hold trials, but nothing over $30.00, and there are no records.

ONLINE ACCESS The online computer system, Case Management Information System (CMIS), is operating and development is continuing. It is for internal use only; there is no plan to permit online public access. However, Supreme Court and Appellate opinions are currently available.

There are a number of Parishes that offer a means of remote online access to the public.

Acadia Parish

15th District Court PO Box 922, Crowley, LA 70527; 337-788-8881; Fax: 337-788-1048. 8:30AM-4:30PM (CST). *Felony, Misdemeanor, Civil, Probate.*

www.acadiaparishclerk.com

Civil Records: Access: Phone, fax, mail, in person. Both court and visitors may perform in person searches. Search fee: $11.00 per name per year. Required to search: name, years to search. Civil cases indexed by defendant, plaintiff. Civil records on computer from 1979, archived from 1800s.
Criminal Records: Access: Phone, fax, mail, in person. Both court and visitors may perform in person searches. Search fee: $11.00 per name per year. Required to search: name, years to search, DOB; also helpful: SSN. Criminal records on computer from 1979, archived from 1800s. Copy of check must be included in the fax request. Copy of check must be faxed with request.
General Information: No adoption or juvenile records released. SASE required. Turnaround time 1-2 days. Fax notes: Fee to fax results is $6.00 1st page, $2.00 for any add'l pages. Copy fee: $2.00 per page. Certification fee: $6.00. Fee payee: Acadia Parish Clerk of Court. Personal checks accepted. Prepayment is required.

Allen Parish

33rd District Court PO Box 248, Oberlin, LA 70655; 337-639-4351; Fax: 337-639-2030. Hours: 8AM-4:30PM *Felony, Misdemeanor, Civil, Probate.*

Civil Records: Access: Fax, mail, in person. Both court and visitors may perform in person searches. Search fee: $10.00 per name. Fee is for a 10 year search. Required to search: name, years to search. Civil cases indexed by defendant, plaintiff. Civil records archived back to 1913; on computer back to 1985.
Criminal Records: Access: Mail, in person. Both court and visitors may perform in person searches. Search fee: $10.00 per name. Fee is for a 10 year search. Required to search: name, years to search, DOB, SSN. Criminal records archived back to 1913; on computer back to 7/94.
General Information: Public access terminal is available. No adoption or juvenile records released. SASE requested. Turnaround time 2 days. Fax notes: Fee to fax results is $2.00 per page. Copy fee: $1.00 per page. Certification fee: $2.00. Fee payee: Allen Parish Clerk of Court. Personal checks accepted. Prepayment is required.

Ascension Parish

23rd District Court PO Box 192, Donaldsonville, LA 70346; 225-473-9866; Fax: 225-473-8641. Hours: 8:30AM-4:30PM (CST). *Felony, Misdemeanor, Civil, Probate.*

Civil Records: Access: Fax, mail, in person. Both court and visitors may perform in person searches. Search fee: $10.00 per name. Required to search: name, years to search. Civil cases indexed by defendant, plaintiff. Civil records on computer from 1987, index books back to 1800s, property tax to 1994, mortgage since 11/77.
Criminal Records: Access: Fax, mail, in person. Both court and visitors may perform in person searches. Search fee: $10.00 per name. Required to search: name, years to search, DOB; also helpful: SSN. Criminal Records go back to 1800's; computerized records since 11/86.
General Information: Public access terminal is available. No adoption or juvenile records released. SASE requested. Turnaround time 2 days. Fax notes: $5.00 for first page, $1.00 each add'l. Add $5.00 on search fee if request by fax. Copy fee: $1.00 per page. Certification fee: $3.00. Fee payee: Ascension Parish Clerk of Court. Personal checks accepted. Prepayment is required.

Assumption Parish

23rd District Court PO Box 249, Napoleonville, LA 70390; 985-369-6653; Fax: 985-369-2032. Hours: 8:30AM-4:30PM (CST). *Felony, Misdemeanor, Civil, Probate.*

Civil Records: Access: Fax, mail, in person. Both court and visitors may perform in person searches. Search fee: $10.00 per name. Required to search: name, years to search. Civil cases indexed by defendant, plaintiff. Civil records archived back to 1800s; on computer back to 1994.
Criminal Records: Access: Fax, mail, in person. Both court and visitors may perform in person searches. Search fee: $10.00 per name. Required to search: name, years to search, DOB. Criminal records archived back to 1800s; on computer back to 1994.
General Information: Public access terminal is available. No adoption or juvenile records released. SASE requested. Turnaround time 1 day. Fax notes: $2.00 for first page, $1.00 each add'l. Copy fee: $1.00 per page. Certification fee: $4.00. Fee payee: Assumption Parish Clerk of Court. Personal checks accepted. Prepayment is required.

Avoyelles Parish

12th District Court PO Box 219, Marksville, LA 71351; 318-253-7523. Hours: 8:30AM-4:30PM (CST). *Felony, Misdemeanor, Civil, Probate.*

Civil Records: Access: Mail, in person. Both court and visitors may perform in person searches. Search fee: $10.00 per name. Required to search: name, years to search. Civil cases indexed by defendant, plaintiff. Civil records on computer from 1985, microfiche to 1800s.
Criminal Records: Access: Mail, in person. Both court and visitors may perform in person searches. Search fee: $10.00 per name. Required to search: name, years to search, DOB; also helpful: SSN. Criminal records on computer from 1985, microfiche back to 1800s.
General Information: No adoption or juvenile records released. SASE not required. Turnaround time 1 day. Copy fee: $1.00 per page. Certification fee: $3.00 per page. Fee payee: Clerk of Court. Personal checks accepted. Prepayment is required.

Beauregard Parish

36th District Court PO Box 100, DeRidder, LA 70634; 337-463-8595; Fax: 337-462-3916. Hours: 8AM-4:30PM *Felony, Misdemeanor, Civil, Probate.*

Civil Records: Access: Mail, in person. Both court and visitors may perform in person searches. Search fee: $15.00 per name. Fee is per 10 years searched. Required to search: name, years to search. Civil cases indexed by defendant, plaintiff. Civil records on computer since 1985, archived from 1913.
Criminal Records: Access: Mail, in person. Both court and visitors may perform in person searches. Search fee: $15.00 per name. Fee is per 10 years searched. Required to search: name, years to search, DOB; also helpful: SSN. Criminal records on computer since 1985, archived from 1913.
General Information: No adoption or juvenile records released. SASE required. Turnaround time 1 wk. Copy fee: $1.25 per page. Certification fee: $5.00. Fee payee: Clerk of Court. Personal checks accepted. Prepayment is required.

Bienville Parish

2nd District Court 100 Courthouse Dr, Rm 100, Arcadia, LA 71001; 318-263-2123; Fax: 318-263-7426. Hours: 8:30AM-4:30PM (CST). *Felony, Misdemeanor, Civil, Probate.*

www.bienvilleparish.org/clerk

Civil Records: Access: Fax, mail, in person. Both court and visitors may perform in person searches. Search fee: $10.00 per name. Required to search: name, years

to search. Civil cases indexed by defendant, plaintiff. Civil records on computer from 1991, index books prior.
Criminal Records: Access: Fax, mail, in person. Both court and visitors may perform in person searches. Search fee: $10.00 per name. Required to search: name, years to search, DOB; also helpful: SSN. Criminal records on computer from 1991, index books prior.
General Information: No adoption or juvenile records released. SASE not required. Turnaround time 2-3 days. Fax notes: $3.00 fee plus $.50 per page. Copy fee: $.50 per page. Certification fee: $2.50. Fee payee: Clerk of Court. Personal checks accepted. Prepayment required.

Bossier Parish

26th District Court PO Box 430, Benton, LA 71006; 318-965-2336; Fax: 318-965-2713. Hours: 8:30AM-4:30PM (CST). *Felony, Misdemeanor, Civil, Probate.*

www.ebrclerkofcourt.org

Civil Records: Access: Mail, online, in person. Both court and visitors may perform in person searches. Search fee: $15.00 per name. Required to search: name, years to search. Civil cases indexed by defendant, plaintiff. Civil records on computer from 1987, index books back to 1843. Access to the Parish Clerk of Court online records requires $50 setup fee and a $35 monthly flat fee. Civil, criminal, probate (1988 forward), traffic and domestic index information iavailable by name or case number. Call 318-965-2336 for more information.
Criminal Records: Access: Mail, online, in person. Both court and visitors may perform in person searches. Search fee: $15.00 per name. Required to search: name, years to search. Criminal records on computer since 1982. Online access to criminal records is the same as civil.
General Information: Public access terminal is available. No adoption or juvenile records released. SASE requested. Turnaround time 4-5 days. Copy fee: $.50 per page. Certification fee: $2.00. Fee payee: Clerk of Court. Business checks accepted. Prepayment is required.

Caddo Parish

1st District Court 501 Texas St, Rm 103, Shreveport, LA 71101-5408; 318-226-6780; Fax: 318-227-9080. Hours: 8:30AM-5PM (CST). *Felony, Misdemeanor, Civil, Probate.*

www.caddoclerk.com

Civil Records: Access: Mail, in person, online. Both court and visitors may perform in person searches. Search fee: $10.00 per name. Fee is $5.00 for second name on same search request. Required to search: name, years to search. Civil cases indexed by defendant, plaintiff. Civil records on computer from 1984. Online access to civil records back to 1994 and name index back to 1984 are available through county dial-up service. Registration and $50 set-up fee and $30 monthly usage fee is required. Marriage and recording information is also available. For information and sign-up, call 318-226-6523.
Criminal Records: Access: Mail, in person, online. Both court and visitors may perform in person searches. Search fee: $10.00 per name. Fee is $5.00 for second name on same search request. For criminal computer printouts, fee is $2.00 for first page and $1.00 each add'l.. Required to search: name, years to search, DOB; also helpful: SSN. Criminal records on computer from 1984. Online access to criminal records is the same as civil. Online criminal name index goes back to '80; minutes to '84. Current calendar is also available.
General Information: Public access terminal is available. No adoption or juvenile records released. SASE required. Turnaround time 1-2 days. Copy fee: $.50 per page. Certification fee: $2.00. Fee payee: Clerk

of Court. Personal checks accepted. Prepayment is required.

Shreveport City Court 1244 Texas, Shreveport, LA 71101; 318-673-5800. Hours: 8AM-5PM (CST). *Civil Actions Under $15,000, Small Claims.*

Civil Records: Access: Mail, in person. Visitors must perform in person searches for themselves. No search fee. Must have case number for mail searches.Required to search: name, years to search. Civil cases indexed by defendant, plaintiff. Civil records on computer back to 1965.

General Information: Public access terminal is available. No sealed records released. Turnaround time 2-15 days. Copy fee: $.50 per page. Certification fee: $1.50. Fee payee: Shreveport City Court. Personal checks accepted. Prepayment is required.

Calcasieu Parish

14th District Court PO Box 1030, Lake Charles, LA 70602; 337-437-3550; Fax: 337-437-3350/3833. Hours: 8:30AM-4:30PM (CST). *Felony, Misdemeanor, Civil, Probate.*

Civil Records: Access: Fax, mail, in person. Both court and visitors may perform in person searches. Search fee: $10.00 per name. Additional fee of $1.00 per year after 1st 10 years. Required to search: name, years to search. Civil cases indexed by defendant, plaintiff. Civil records on computer since 1987.

Criminal Records: Access: Mail, in person. Both court and visitors may perform in person searches. Search fee: $10.00 per name. Additional fee of $2.00 per year after 1st 10 years. Required to search: name, DOB; also helpful: SSN. Criminal records on computer since 1987.

General Information: Public access terminal is available. No adoption or juvenile records released. SASE required. Turnaround time 1 wk. Fax notes: $7.00 for first page, $2.00 each add'l. Fax available for civil division only. Copy fee: $1.00 per page. Certification fee: $10.00. Fee payee: Clerk of Court. Personal checks accepted. Prepayment is required.

Lake Charles City Court PO Box 1664, Lake Charles, LA 70602; 337-491-1564. Hours: 8:30AM-4PM (CST). *Civil Actions Under $20,000, Small Claims.*

www.lakecharlescitycourt.com

Civil Records: Access: Mail, in person. Visitors must perform in person searches for themselves.No search fee. Required to search: name, years to search. Civil cases indexed by defendant, plaintiff. Civil records kept on paper for 10 years, older records archived on computer.

General Information: Public access terminal is available. No sealed records released.. Turnaround time 2-5 days. Copy fee: $1.50 per page. Certification fee: $1.50. Fee payee: lake Charles City Court. Personal checks accepted. Prepayment is required.

Caldwell Parish

37th District Court PO Box 1327, Columbia, LA 71418; 318-649-2272; Fax: 318-649-2037. Hours: 8AM-4:30PM *Felony, Misdemeanor, Civil, Probate.*

Note: All record requests must be in writing.

Civil Records: Access: Fax, mail, in person. Both court and visitors may perform in person searches. Search fee: $10.00 per name. Required to search: name, years to search. Civil cases indexed by defendant, plaintiff. Civil records on books from 1838, computerized since 1996.

Criminal Records: Access: Mail, in person. Both court and visitors may perform in person searches. Search fee: $10.00 per name. Required to search: name, years to search, DOB; also helpful: SSN. Criminal Records kept on books since 1970.

General Information: No adoption or juvenile records released. SASE not required. Turnaround time 1 week. Fax notes: $3.00 for first page, $1.00 each add'l. Copy fee: $1.00 per page. Certification fee: $2.00 plus $1.00 per page. Fee payee: Clerk of Court. Personal checks accepted. Prepayment is required.

Cameron Parish

38th District Court PO Box 549, Cameron, LA 70631; 337-775-5316; Fax: 337-775-7172. Hours: 8:30AM-4:30PM (CST). *Felony, Misdemeanor, Civil, Probate.*

Civil Records: Access: Phone, mail, fax, in person. Both court and visitors may perform in person searches. Search fee: $10.00. Required to search: name, years to search. Civil cases indexed by defendant, plaintiff. Civil records from 1874; on computer back to 7/1994.

Criminal Records: Access: Fax, mail, in person. Only the court performs in person searches; visitors may not. Search fee: $10.00 per name. Required to search: name, years to search, DOB. Criminal records from 1874; on computer back to 1968.

General Information: No adoption, interdiction or juvenile records released. SASE required. Turnaround time 2 days. Fax notes: Fee to fax results $1.00 per page plus cert fee. Copy fee: $1.00 per page. Certification fee: $5.00. Fee payee: Cameron Parish Clerk of Court. Personal checks accepted.

Catahoula Parish

7th District Court PO Box 654, Harrisonburg, LA 71340; 318-744-5222; Fax: 318-744-5488. Hours: 8AM-4:30PM *Felony, Misdemeanor, Civil, Probate.*

Civil Records: Access: Mail, in person. Both court and visitors may perform in person searches. Search fee: $25.00 per name. Fee is for 10 year search. Required to search: name, years to search. Civil cases indexed by defendant, plaintiff. Civil records minute entries back to 1800s.

Criminal Records: Access: Mail, in person. Both court and visitors may perform in person searches. Search fee: $25.00 per name. Fee is for 10 year search. Required to search: name, years to search, DOB. Criminal records minute entries back to 1800s.

General Information: No adoption or juvenile records released. SASE required. Turnaround time 1-2 weeks. Copy fee: $1.00 per page. Certification fee: $5.00. Fee payee: Clerk of Court. Personal checks accepted. Prepayment is required.

Claiborne Parish

2nd District Court PO Box 330, Homer, LA 71040; 318-927-9601; Fax: 318-927-2345. Hours: 8:30AM-4:30PM (CST). *Felony, Misdemeanor, Civil, Probate.*

Civil Records: Access: Mail, in person. Both court and visitors may perform in person searches. Search fee: $10.00 per name. Required to search: name, years to search. Civil cases indexed by defendant, plaintiff. Civil records on index books back to early 1900s.

Criminal Records: Access: Mail, in person. Both court and visitors may perform in person searches. Search fee: $10.00 per name. Required to search: name, years to search, DOB; also helpful: SSN. Criminal records on computer 1993 forward.

General Information: No adoption or juvenile records released. SASE required. Turnaround time 1-2 days. Fax notes: Fee to fax results is $10.00 per document. Copy fee: $1.00 per page. Certification fee: $5.00. Fee payee: Clerk of Court. Personal checks accepted. Prepayment is required.

Concordia Parish

7th District Court PO Box 790, Vidalia, LA 71373; 318-336-4204; Fax: 318-336-8217. Hours: 8:30AM-4:30PM (CST). *Felony, Misdemeanor, Civil, Probate.*

Civil Records: Access: Mail, in person. Visitors must perform in person searches. Search fee: $25.00 per name. Required to search: name, years to search. Civil cases indexed by defendant, plaintiff. Civil records on computer from 1983, index books back to 1800s.

Criminal Records: Access: Mail, in person. Visitors must perform in person searches. Search fee: $15.00 per name. Required to search: name, years to search, DOB; also helpful: SSN. Criminal records on computer from 1983, index books back to 1800s.

General Information: No adoption or juvenile records released. SASE not required. Turnaround time 3-4 days. Fax notes: $5.00 per document. Fax available for civil division only. Copy fee: $1.00 per page. Certification fee: $5.50. Fee payee: Clerk of Court. Personal checks accepted. Prepayment is required.

De Soto Parish

11th District Court PO Box 1206, Mansfield, LA 71052; 318-872-3110; Criminal phone: 318-872-3181; Fax: 318-872-4202. Hours: 8AM-4:30PM (CST). *Felony, Misdemeanor, Civil, Probate.*

Civil Records: Access: Mail, in person. Both court and visitors may perform in person searches. Search fee: $10.00 per name. Required to search: name, years to search. Civil cases indexed by defendant, plaintiff. Civil records on computer from 1991, index books back to 1843.

Criminal Records: Access: Mail, in person. Both court and visitors may perform in person searches. Search fee: $10.00 per name. Required to search: name, years to search, DOB. Criminal records on computer since 1991, archived or in books to 1950's.

General Information: Public access terminal is available. No adoption or juvenile records released. SASE Required. Turnaround time 1-2 days. Fax notes: Fee to fax results is $5.00 plus $1.00 per page. Copy fee: $1.00 per page. Certification fee: $3.50 plus $1.00 per page. Fee payee: Clerk of Court. Prepayment is required.

East Baton Rouge Parish

19th District Court PO Box 1991, Baton Rouge, LA 70821; 225-389-3950; Fax: 225-389-3392. Hours: 7:30AM-5:30PM (CST). *Felony, Misdemeanor, Civil, Probate.*

www.ebrclerkofcourt.org

Civil Records: Access: Fax, mail, online, in person. Both court and visitors may perform in person searches. Search fee: Search fee is determined by the years searched. Required to search: name, years to search. Civil cases indexed by defendant, plaintiff. Civil records in index books from 1942. Online access to the clerk's database is available by subscription. Civil record indexes go back to '88; case tracking of civil and probate back to 1991. Setup fee is $100.00 plus $15.00 per month plus per-minute usage charges. VS Com software required. Call the MIS Dept at 225-389-5295 for information or visit the web site.

Criminal Records: Access: Mail, online, in person. Both court and visitors may perform in person searches. Search fee: $20.00 per name. Required to search: name, years to search, DOB; also helpful: SSN. Criminal records in index books from 1942; on computer back to 1990. Online access to criminal records is the same as civil. Criminal case tracking goes back to 8/1990.

General Information: Public access terminal is available. No adoption or juvenile records released. Fax notes: Fee to fax results is $5.00 per document and $.50

per page. Copy fee: $.50 per page. Criminal record copy fee is $1.00 per page. Certification fee: $2.20.

Baton Rouge City Court 233 St Louis St, Baton Rouge, LA 70802; 225-389-5279; Fax: 225-389-5260. Hours: 8:30AM-4PM (CST). *Civil Actions Under $20,000, Small Claims.*

Civil Records: Access: Mail, in person, fax. Visitors must perform in person searches for themselves.. No search fee. Required to search: name, years to search. Civil cases indexed by defendant, plaintiff. Civil records on computer back to 1985, microfiche to 1980.
General Information: Public access terminal is available. No sealed records released. Turnaround time 2 - 5 days. Copy fee: $.50 per page. Certification fee: $1.00. Fee payee: Baton Rouge City Court. Personal checks accepted. Credit cards accepted: Visa, MasterCard, but 5% surcharge. Prepayment is required.

East Carroll Parish

6th District Court 400 1st St, Lake Providence, LA 71254; 318-559-2399. Hours: 8:30AM-4:30PM (CST). *Felony, Misdemeanor, Civil, Probate.*

Civil Records: Access: Mail, in person. Both court and visitors may perform in person searches. Search fee: $10.00 per name. Required to search: name, years to search. Civil cases indexed by defendant, plaintiff. Civil records on index books back to 1832.
Criminal Records: Access: Mail, in person. Both court and visitors may perform in person searches. Search fee: $10.00 per name. Required to search: name, years to search, DOB; also helpful: SSN. Criminal records on index books back to 1832.
General Information: No adoption or juvenile records released. SASE required. Turnaround time same day. Copy fee: $2.00 per page. Certification fee: $5.00. Fee payee: Clerk of Court. Personal checks accepted. Prepayment is required.

East Feliciana Parish

20th District Court PO Box 599, Clinton, LA 70722; 225-683-5145; Fax: 225-683-3556. Hours: 8AM-4:30PM (CST). *Felony, Misdemeanor, Civil, Probate.*

Civil Records: Access: Mail, in person. Both court and visitors may perform in person searches. Search fee: $10.00 per name per ten years. Required to search: name, years to search; also helpful: address. Civil cases indexed by defendant, plaintiff. Civil records on computer from 1980, index books back to 1825. State which years to search.
Criminal Records: Access: Fax, mail, in person. Both court and visitors may perform in person searches. Search fee: $10.00 per name. Required to search: name, years to search, DOB, SNN. Criminal records on computer from 1990, index books back to 1825. State which years to search.
General Information: Public access terminal is available. No adoption or juvenile records released. SASE required. Turnaround time 1-2 days. Fax notes: $5.00 for first page, $1.00 each add'l. Copy fee: $1.00 per page. Certification fee: $5.00. Fee payee: Clerk of Court. Personal checks accepted. Prepayment required.

Evangeline Parish

13th District Court PO Drawer 347, Ville Platte, LA 70586; 337-363-5671; Fax: 337-363-5780. Hours: 8AM-4:30PM (CST). *Felony, Misdemeanor, Civil, Probate.*

Civil Records: Access: Fax, mail, in person. Both court and visitors may perform in person searches. Search fee: $10.00 per name. Fee is for first 7 years searched. Add $2.00 per additional year. Required to search: name, years to search. Civil cases indexed by defendant, plaintiff. Civil records on computer back to 1989; prior records archived from 1911.

Criminal Records: Access: Fax, mail, in person. Both court and visitors may perform in person searches. Search fee: $10.00 per name. Fee is for first 7 years searched. Add $2.00 per additional year. Required to search: name, years to search; also helpful: DOB, SSN. Criminal records on computer back to 1989, prior records archived from 1911.
General Information: Public access terminal is available. No adoption or juvenile records released. Turnaround time 1-2 days. Fax notes: $5.00 for first page, $2.00 each add'l. Copy fee: $.75 per page; $5.00 minimum. Certification fee: $2.00 per page. Fee payee: Clerk of Court. Personal checks accepted. Prepayment is required.

Franklin Parish

5th District Court PO Box 1564, Winnsboro, LA 71295; 318-435-5133; Fax: 318-435-5134. Hours: 8:30AM-4:30PM (CST). *Felony, Misdemeanor, Civil, Probate.*

Civil Records: Access: Mail, in person. Both court and visitors may perform in person searches. Search fee: $10.00 per name. Required to search: name, years to search. Civil cases indexed by defendant, plaintiff. Civil records on computer from 1988, index books back to 1843.
Criminal Records: Access: Mail, in person. Both court and visitors may perform in person searches. Search fee: $10.00 per name. Fee includes 10 year search. Required to search: name, years to search, DOB; also helpful: SSN. Criminal records on computer since 1995.
General Information: No adoption or juvenile records released. SASE required. Turnaround time 1-2 days. Fax notes: $5.00 for first page, $1.00 each add'l. Copy fee: $1.00 per page. Certification fee: $5.00. Fee payee: Clerk of Court. Business checks accepted. Prepayment is required.

Grant Parish

35th District Court PO Box 263, Colfax, LA 71417; 318-627-3246; Fax: 318-627-3201. Hours: 8:30AM-4:30PM (CST). *Felony, Misdemeanor, Civil, Probate.*

Civil Records: Access: Phone, fax, mail, in person. Both court and visitors may perform in person searches. Search fee: $5.00 per name. Required to search: name, years to search. Civil cases indexed by defendant, plaintiff. Civil records on computer back to 1990; index books back to 1878.
Criminal Records: Access: Phone, fax, mail, in person. Both court and visitors may perform in person searches. Search fee: $5.00 per name. Required to search: name, years to search, DOB; also helpful: SSN. Criminal records go back to 1904; on computer back to 1996.
General Information: No adoption or juvenile records released without approval of a judge. SASE required. Turnaround time 1-2 days. Copy fee: $1.00 per page. Certification fee: $5.00. Fee payee: Grant Parish Clerk of Court. Personal checks accepted.

Iberia Parish

16th District Court PO Drawer 12010, New Iberia, LA 70562-2010; 337-365-7282; Fax: 337-365-0737. Hours: 8:30AM-4:30PM (CST). *Felony, Misdemeanor, Civil, Probate.*

Civil Records: Access: In person. Visitors must perform in person searches for themselves. No search fee. Required to search: name, years to search; also helpful: address. Civil cases indexed by defendant, plaintiff. Civil records on computer back to 1974, index books back to 1800s.
Criminal Records: Access: In person. Visitors must perform in person searches for themselves. No search fee. Required to search: name, years to search, DOB;

also helpful: address, SSN. Criminal records on computer back to 1974, index books back to 1800s.
General Information: Public access terminal is available. No adoption or juvenile records released. Copy fee: $.50 per page. Certification fee: $5.50. Fee payee: Clerk of Court. Personal checks accepted. Prepayment is required.

Iberville Parish

18th District Court PO Box 423, Plaquemine, LA 70764; 225-687-5160; Fax: 225-687-5260. Hours: 8:30AM-4:30PM (CST). *Felony, Misdemeanor, Civil, Probate.*

Civil Records: Access: Fax, mail, in person. Both court and visitors may perform in person searches. Search fee: $10.00 per name. Required to search: name, years to search. Civil cases indexed by defendant, plaintiff. Civil records on books back to 1800s.
Criminal Records: Access: Fax, mail, in person. Both court and visitors may perform in person searches. Search fee: $10.00 per name. Required to search: name, years to search, DOB; also helpful: SSN. Criminal records on books back to 1800s.
General Information: No adoption or juvenile records released. SASE required. Turnaround time 1-2 days. Fax notes: Fee to fax results is $5.00 1st page, $2.00 each add'l. Copy fee: $.75 per page. Certification fee: $4.00. Fee payee: Clerk of Court. Personal checks accepted. Prepayment is required.

Jackson Parish

2nd District Court PO Drawer 730, Jonesboro, LA 71251; 318-259-2424; Fax: 318-395-0386. Hours: 8:30AM-4:30PM (CST). *Felony, Misdemeanor, Civil, Probate.*

Civil Records: Access: Phone, mail, in person. Both court and visitors may perform in person searches. Search fee: $10.00 per name. Fee is per 10 years searched. Required to search: name, years to search. Civil cases indexed by defendant, plaintiff. Civil records on index books from 1880 and on computer since 1988.
Criminal Records: Access: Phone, mail, in person. Both court and visitors may perform in person searches. Search fee: $10.00 per name. Fee is per 10 years searched. Required to search: name, years to search, DOB; also helpful: SSN. Criminal records on computer since 1988.
General Information: Public access terminal is available. No adoption or juvenile records released. SASE required. Turnaround time 1-2 days. Copy fee: $1.00 per page. Certification fee: $2.50. Fee payee: Clerk of Court. Personal checks accepted. Prepayment is required.

Jefferson Davis Parish

31st District Court PO Box 799, Jennings, LA 70546; 337-824-1160; Fax: 337-824-1354. Hours: 8:30AM-4:30PM (CST). *Felony, Misdemeanor, Civil, Probate.*

Civil Records: Access: Mail, in person. Both court and visitors may perform in person searches. Search fee: $10.00 per name. Required to search: name, years to search; also helpful: address. Civil cases indexed by defendant, plaintiff. Civil records archived from 1913, on computer back to 1991.
Criminal Records: Access: Mail, in person. Both court and visitors may perform in person searches. Search fee: $10.00 per name. Required to search: name, years to search; also helpful: DOB, SSN. Criminal records archived from 1913, on computer back to 1991. Include city of residence of subject in your search request.
General Information: No adoption or juvenile records released. SASE not required. Turnaround time 2 days. Fax notes: Fee to fax results is $1.00 per page. Copy fee: $1.00 per page. Certification fee: $5.00. Fee payee:

Clerk of Court. Personal checks accepted. Prepayment is required.

Jefferson Parish

24th District Court PO Box 10, Gretna, LA 70053; 504-364-2992; Fax: 504-364-3797. Hours: 8:30AM-4:30PM (CST). *Felony, Misdemeanor, Civil, Probate.*

www.clerkofcourt.co.jefferson.la.us

Civil Records: Access: Fax, mail, online, in person. Both court and visitors may perform in person searches. Search fee: $20.00 per name per year. Required to search: name, years to search. Civil cases indexed by defendant, plaintiff. Civil records on computer from 1986, in index books back to 1972, prior records archived. Online access is available through dial-up service. Initiation fee is $200, plus $85.00 monthly and $.25 per minute usage fee. Includes recordings, marriage index, and assessor rolls. For further information and sign-up, call 504-364-2908 or visit the web site and click on "Jeffnet.".

Criminal Records: Access: Fax, mail, online, in person. Both court and visitors may perform in person searches. Search fee: $10.00 per name. Required to search: name, years to search, DOB; also helpful: SSN. Criminal records on computer from 1994 to present, active cases are in books from 1972. Online access is via a dial-up service, see civil.

General Information: Public access terminal is available. No adoption, juvenile or grand jury records released. Turnaround time 1-2 days. Fax notes: $5.00 for first page, $1.00 each add'l. Copy fee: $.75 per page. Add postage. Certification fee: $1.25 per page. Fee payee: Clerk of Court. Personal checks accepted. Out of state personal checks not accepted. Prepayment is required.

La Salle Parish

28th District Court PO Box 1316, Jena, LA 71342; 318-992-2158; Fax: 318-992-2157. Hours: 8:30AM-4:30PM (CST). *Felony, Misdemeanor, Civil, Probate.*

Civil Records: Access: Phone, fax, mail, in person. Both court and visitors may perform in person searches. Search fee: $20.00 1st name, $10.00 additional name. Fee is for 10 year search per name with certificate. Required to search: name, years to search. Civil cases indexed by defendant, plaintiff. Civil records archived from 1916; on computer since 1993.

Criminal Records: Access: Phone, fax, mail, in person. Both court and visitors may perform in person searches. Search fee: $20.00 1st name, $10.00 additional name. Fee is for 10 year search per name with certificate. Required to search: name, years to search, DOB; also helpful: SSN. Criminal records archived from 1916; on computer since 1993.

General Information: Public access terminal is available. No adoption or juvenile records released. SASE not required. Turnaround time 1-2 wks, will release info sooner by phone. Fax notes: Fee to fax results is $10.00 per document. Copy fee: $1.00 per page. Certification fee: $5.00 per page. Fee payee: Clerk of Court. Personal checks accepted. Prepayment is required.

Lafayette Parish

15th District Court PO Box 2009, c/o Clerk of Court, Lafayette, LA 70502; 337-291-6400; Fax: 337-291-6392. Hours: 8:30AM-4:30PM (CST). *Felony, Misdemeanor, Civil, Probate.*

www.lafayetteparishclerk.com

Civil Records: Access: Phone, fax, mail, online, in person. Both court and visitors may perform in person searches. Search fee: $11.00 per name. Required to search: name, years to search. Civil cases indexed by

defendant, plaintiff. Civil records archived from 1923; on computer back to 1986. Access to the remote online system requires $100 setup fee plus $15 per month and $.50 per minute. Civil index goes back to 1986. For more information, call Derek Comeaux at 337-291-6433.

Criminal Records: Access: Phone, fax, mail, online, in person. Both court and visitors may perform in person searches. Search fee: $11.00 per name. Required to search: name, years to search, DOB. Criminal records archived from 1966; on computer back to 1986. Online access to criminal records is the same as civil.

General Information: Public access terminal is available. No adoption or juvenile records released. SASE not required. Turnaround time 1-2 days. Copy fee: $.50 per page. Certification fee: The fee is $1.00 for criminal records and $5.50 for civil. Fee payee: Clerk of Court. Personal checks accepted. Prepayment required.

Lafourche Parish

17th District Court PO Box 818, Thibodaux, LA 70302; 985-447-4841; Fax: 985-447-5800. Hours: 8:30AM-4:30PM (CST). *Felony, Misdemeanor, Civil, Probate.*

Civil Records: Access: Fax, mail, in person. Both court and visitors may perform in person searches. Search fee: $20.00 per name. Fee is for 10 year search. Required to search: name, years to search. Civil cases indexed by defendant, plaintiff. Civil records on computer back to 7/1982, microfiche from 1968, index books back to 1800s.

Criminal Records: Access: Fax, mail, in person. Both court and visitors may perform in person searches. Search fee: $20.00 per name. Fee is for 10 year search. Required to search: name, years to search, DOB; also helpful: SSN, race, sex. Criminal records on computer back to 7/1982, microfiche from 1968, index books back to 1800s.

General Information: No adoption or juvenile records released. SASE requested. Turnaround time 1-2 days. Fax notes: Fee to fax results is $2.00 per page. Copy fee: $1.00 per page. Certification fee: Minimum certification fee with copies is $5.00. Fee payee: Lafourche Parish Clerk of Court. Personal checks accepted. Prepayment is required.

Lincoln Parish

3rd District Court PO Box 924, Ruston, LA 71273-0924; 318-251-5130; Fax: 318-255-6004. Hours: 8:30AM-4:30PM (CST). *Felony, Misdemeanor, Civil, Probate.*

Civil Records: Access: Mail, in person. Both court and visitors may perform in person searches. Search fee: $10.00 per name. Fee is per 10 years searched. Required to search: name, years to search. Civil cases indexed by defendant, plaintiff. Civil records on computer since 1985, index books back to 1800s.

Criminal Records: Access: Mail, in person. Both court and visitors may perform in person searches. Search fee: $10.00 per name. Fee is per 10 years searched. Required to search: name, years to search, DOB; also helpful: SSN. Criminal records on computer since 1992.

General Information: Public access terminal is available. No adoption or juvenile records released. SASE not required. Turnaround time 1-2 days. Fax notes: Fee to fax results is $5.00 for 1st page, $1.00 each add'l. Copy fee: $1.00 per page. Certification fee: $5.00. Fee payee: Clerk of Court. Personal checks accepted. Prepayment is required.

Livingston Parish

21st District Court PO Box 1150, Livingston, LA 70754; 225-686-2216. Hours: 8AM-4:30PM (CST). *Felony, Misdemeanor, Civil, Probate.*

Civil Records: Access: Mail, In person. Visitors must perform in person searches for themselves. Search fee:

$25.00. Required to search: name, years to search. Civil cases indexed by defendant, plaintiff. Civil records on index books since 1800s; computerized records past 10 years.

Criminal Records: Access: In person, mail. Visitors must perform in person searches for themselves. Search fee: $25.00. Required to search: name, years to search, DOB; also helpful: SSN, race, sex. Criminal records on index books since 1800s; computerized records past 10 years.

General Information: Public access terminal is available. No adoption or juvenile records released. Copy fee: $1.00 per page. Certification fee: $5.00. Fee payee: 21st District Court. Personal checks accepted. Prepayment is required.

Madison Parish

6th District Court PO Box 1710, Tallulah, LA 71282; 318-574-0655; Fax: 318-574-0656. Hours: 8:30AM-4:30PM (CST). *Felony, Misdemeanor, Civil, Probate.*

Civil Records: Access: Phone, mail, in person. Both court and visitors may perform in person searches. Search fee: $10.00 per name. Required to search: name, years to search. Civil cases indexed by defendant, plaintiff. Civil records kept on computer since 7/93.

Criminal Records: Access: Phone, mail, in person. Both court and visitors may perform in person searches. Search fee: $10.00 per name. Required to search: name, years to search, DOB; also helpful: SSN. Criminal records on index.

General Information: No adoption or juvenile records released. SASE required. Turnaround time 1-2 days. No copy fee. Certification fee: $5.50. Fee does not include any copy fees. Fee payee: Clerk of Court. Personal checks accepted. Prepayment is required.

Morehouse Parish

4th District Court PO Box 1543, Bastrop, LA 71221; 318-281-3343/3346/3349; Fax: 318-281-3775. Hours: 8:30AM-4:30PM (CST). *Felony, Misdemeanor, Civil, Probate.*

Civil Records: Access: Phone, fax, mail, in person. Both court and visitors may perform in person searches. Search fee: $15.00 per name. Fee is per 10 years searched. Required to search: name, years to search; also helpful: address. Civil cases indexed by defendant, plaintiff. Civil records on computer since 1987, in books since 1898, some on microfilm.

Criminal Records: Access: Phone, fax, mail, in person. Both court and visitors may perform in person searches. Search fee: $15.00 per name. Fee is per 10 years searched. Required to search: name, years to search, DOB; also helpful: address, SSN. Criminal records in books since 1926 and on microfilm since 1974; computerized records go back to 1994.

General Information: Public access terminal is available. No adoption, juvenile or judicial commitment records released. SASE required. Turnaround time 2-3 days. Fax notes: $5.00 for first page, $1.00 each add'l. Copy fee: $1.00 per page. Certification fee: $5.00. Fee payee: Clerk of Court. Personal checks accepted. Prepayment is required.

Natchitoches Parish

10th District Court PO Box 476, Natchitoches, LA 71458; 318-352-8152; Fax: 318-352-9321. Hours: 8:15AM-4:30PM (CST). *Felony, Misdemeanor, Civil, Probate, Small Claims.*

Civil Records: Access: Phone, fax, mail, in person. Both court and visitors may perform in person searches. Search fee: $10.00 per name. Required to search: name, years to search. Civil cases indexed by defendant, plaintiff. Civil records on computer back to 6/1991, archived from 1950, index books back to 1800s.

Criminal Records: Access: Phone, fax, mail, in person. Both court and visitors may perform in person searches. Search fee: $10.00 per name. Required to search: name, years to search, DOB; also helpful: SSN. Criminal records on computer back to 6/1991, archived from 1950, index books back to 1800s.

General Information: Public access terminal is available. No adoption or juvenile records released. SASE required. Turnaround time 1 week. Fax notes: $5.00 1st page, $2.00 each add'l. Fax available for civil division only. Copy fee: $1.00 per page. Certification fee: $5.00. Fee payee: Clerk of Court. Personal checks accepted. Prepayment is required.

Orleans Parish

Civil District Court 421 Loyola Ave, Rm 402, New Orleans, LA 70112; 504-592-9100 X122; Fax: 504-592-9128. Hours: 8AM-5PM (CST). *Civil, Probate.*

www.orleanscdc.gov

Civil Records: Access: Phone, mail, online, in person. Both court and visitors may perform in person searches. No search fee. Required to search: name, years to search. Civil cases indexed by defendant, plaintiff. Civil records on computer since 1985, in books back to early 1800s. CDC Remote provides access to civil cases from 1985 and First City Court cases as well as parish mortgage and conveyance indexes. The fee is $250 per year. Call 504-592-9264 for more information.

General Information: Public access terminal is available. No adoptions or juvenile released. SASE required. Turnaround time 1-2 days. Copy fee: $.75 per page. Certification fee: $2.00 per document. Fee payee: Clerk of Court. Only cashiers checks and money orders accepted. Prepayment is required.

Criminal District Court 2700 Tulane Ave, Rm 115, New Orleans, LA 70119; 504-827-3546; Fax: 504-827-3385. Hours: 8:15AM-3:30PM (CST). *Felony, Misdemeanor.*

Criminal Records: Access: Mail, in person. Both court and visitors may perform in person searches. Search fee: $10.00 per name. Required to search: name, years to search, DOB; also helpful: SSN. Criminal records on computer past 8 years, books and files go back to early 1900s.

General Information: No adoption or juvenile records released. SASE required. Turnaround time 2 days. No copy fee. Fee payee: Clerk of Court. Business checks accepted. Prepayment is required.

New Orleans City Court 421 Loyola Ave, Rm 201, New Orleans, LA 70112; 504-592-9155; Fax: 504-592-9281. Hours: 8:30AM-4PM (CST). *Civil Actions Under $20,000, Small Claims.*

www.orleanscdc.gov/fcc.htm

Note: a 2nd City Court is located at 225 Morgan Street, Rm 206, new Orleans, LA 70114, 504-368-4245.

Civil Records: Access: Mail, online, in person. Both court and visitors may perform in person searches. No search fee. Required to search: name, years to search. Civil cases indexed by defendant, plaintiff. Civil records on computer back to 1988. CDC Remote provides access to First City Court cases from 1988 as well as civil cases, parish mortgage and conveyance indexes. The fee is $250 per year. Call 504-592-9264 for more information.

General Information: Public access terminal is available. No sealed records released. SASE requested. Turnaround time 5-10 days. Copy fee: $1.00 per page. Certification fee: $3.00. Fee payee: New Orleans First City Court. Personal checks accepted. Credit cards accepted: Visa, MasterCard. Prepayment is required.

Ouachita Parish

4th District Court PO Box 1862, Monroe, LA 71210-1862; 318-327-1444; Fax: 318-327-1462. Hours: 8:30AM-5PM (CST). *Felony, Misdemeanor, Civil, Probate.*

Civil Records: Access: Fax, mail, in person. Both court and visitors may perform in person searches. Search fee: $10.00 per name. Required to search: name, years to search. Civil cases indexed by defendant, plaintiff. Civil records on computer from 1991, index books back to 1800s.

Criminal Records: Access: Fax, mail, in person. Both court and visitors may perform in person searches. Search fee: $10.00 per name. Required to search: name, years to search, DOB; also helpful: SSN. Criminal records on computer from 1991, index books back to 1800s.

General Information: No adoption or juvenile records released. SASE required. Turnaround time 1-2 days. Fax notes: $2.00 for first page, $1.00 each add'l. Copy fee: $.50 per page. Certification fee: $2.00. Fee payee: Clerk of Court. Business checks accepted. Checks accepted up to $50.00. Prepayment is required.

Plaquemines Parish

25th District Court PO Box 40 (8346 Highway 23, Region 1 Bldg, 2nd Fl), Clerk of Court - 25th JDC, Belle Chasse, LA 70037; 504-392-4969. Hours: 8:30AM-4:30PM (CST). *Felony, Misdemeanor, Civil, Probate.*

Civil Records: Access: In person only. Visitors must perform in person searches for themselves. No search fee. Required to search: name, years to search. Civil cases indexed by defendant, plaintiff. Civil records on index books back to 1800s; computerized since 1/91. Court will search probate records; fee is $10 per name.

Criminal Records: Access: In person only. Visitors must perform in person searches for themselves. No search fee. Required to search: name, years to search, DOB. Criminal records on index books back to 1966; computerized records go back to 1/91. The county sex offender database is available free online at www.lasocpr.lsp.org/Static/Search.htm. Contact the Plaquemines Sheriff's Office (18039 Hwy 15, Pointe-a-LaHache 70082) for a criminal search, 985-333-5002, fax-985-333-9238.

General Information: Public access terminal is available. No adoption or juvenile records released. Copy fee: $.50 per page. Certification fee: $5.00. Fee payee: Clerk of Court. Personal checks accepted. Prepayment is required.

Pointe Coupee Parish

18th District Court PO Box 86, New Roads, LA 70760; 225-638-9596. Hours: 8:30AM-4:30PM (CST). *Felony, Misdemeanor, Civil, Probate.*

Civil Records: Access: Mail, in person. Both court and visitors may perform in person searches. No search fee. Required to search: name, years to search. Civil cases indexed by defendant, plaintiff. Civil records on index books back to 1800s.

Criminal Records: Access: In person only. Visitors must perform in person searches for themselves. No search fee. Required to search: name, years to search, DOB; also helpful: SSN. Criminal records on index books back to 1800s.

General Information: No adoption or juvenile records released. SASE not required. Turnaround time 2 weeks. Copy fee: $1.25 per page. Certification fee: $5.00. Fee payee: Clerk of Court. Personal checks accepted. Prepayment is required.

Rapides Parish

9th District Court PO Box 952, Alexandria, LA 71309; 318-473-8153; Fax: 318-473-4667. Hours: 8:30AM-4:30PM (CST). *Felony, Misdemeanor, Civil, Probate.*

Civil Records: Access: Mail, in person. Both court and visitors may perform in person searches. Search fee: $11.00 per name. Fee is per separate index. Required to search: name, years to search. Civil cases indexed by defendant, plaintiff. Civil records on index books since 1864, civil in computer since 10/84.

Criminal Records: Access: Mail, in person. Both court and visitors may perform in person searches. Search fee: $11.00 per name. Fee is per separate index. Required to search: name, years to search, DOB; also helpful: SSN. Criminal records on computer since 1984; prior records in index books back to 1864.

General Information: Public access terminal is available. No adoption, juvenile, or judicial commitment records released. SASE not required. Turnaround time 2-4 days. Copy fee: $1.00 per page. Certification fee: $5.00. Fee payee: Rapides Parish Clerk of Court. Personal checks accepted. Prepayment is required.

Red River Parish

39th District Court PO Box 485, Coushatta, LA 71019; 318-932-6741. Hours: 8:30AM-4:30PM (CST). *Felony, Misdemeanor, Civil, Probate.*

Civil Records: Access: Mail, in person. Both court and visitors may perform in person searches. Search fee: $10.00 per name. Required to search: name, years to search. Civil cases indexed by defendant, plaintiff. Civil records on index books.

Criminal Records: Access: Mail, in person. Only the court performs in person searches; visitors may not. Search fee: $10.00 per name. Required to search: name, years to search, DOB; also helpful: SSN. The index is kept in the DA's office.

General Information: No adoption or juvenile records released. SASE required. Turnaround time 1-2 days. Copy fee: $1.00 per page. Certification fee: $5.00. Fee payee: Clerk of Court. Personal checks accepted. Prepayment is required.

Richland Parish

5th District Court PO Box 119, Rayville, LA 71269; 318-728-4171. Hours: 8:30AM-4:30PM (CST). *Felony, Misdemeanor, Civil, Probate.*

Civil Records: Access: Mail, in person. Both court and visitors may perform in person searches. Search fee: $10.00 per name. Required to search: name, years to search. Civil cases indexed by defendant, plaintiff. Civil records on since 1/94, prior on books to 1800s.

Criminal Records: Access: Mail, in person. Both court and visitors may perform in person searches. Search fee: $10.00 per name. Required to search: name, years to search, DOB, SSN. Criminal records on since 1/94, prior on books to 1800s.

General Information: No adoption or juvenile records released. SASE required. Turnaround time 1-2 days. Copy fee: $1.00 per page. Certification fee: $5.00. Fee payee: Clerk of Court. Personal checks accepted. Prepayment is required.

Sabine Parish

11th District Court PO Box 419, Many, LA 71449; 318-256-6223; Fax: 318-256-9037. Hours: 8AM-4:30PM (CST). *Felony, Misdemeanor, Civil, Probate.*

Civil Records: Access: Fax, mail, in person. Both court and visitors may perform in person searches. Search fee: $20.00 per name. Required to search: name, years to search. Civil cases indexed by defendant, plaintiff. Civil records on index books back to 1843's.

Criminal Records: Access: Fax, mail, in person. Both court and visitors may perform in person searches. Search fee: $20.00 per name. Required to search: name, years to search. Criminal Records available for 10 years.

General Information: Public access terminal is available. (Only civil cases are available.) No adoption or juvenile records released. SASE required. Turnaround time 5-10 days. Fax notes: $5.00 for first page, $2.00 each add'l. Copy fee: $1.25 per page. Certification fee: $25.00. Fee payee: Sabine Parish Clerk. Personal checks accepted. Prepayment required.

St. Bernard Parish

34th District Court PO Box 1746, Chalmette, LA 70044; 504-271-3434. Hours: 8:30AM-4:30PM (CST). *Felony, Misdemeanor, Civil, Probate.*

Civil Records: Access: Mail, in person. Both court and visitors may perform in person searches. Search fee: $5.00 per name. Fee is per 10 years searched. Required to search: name, years to search. Civil cases indexed by defendant, plaintiff. Civil records on index books back to 1800s, on computer since 1989.

Criminal Records: Access: Mail, in person. Both court and visitors may perform in person searches. Search fee: $10.00 per name. Fee is per 10 years searched. Required to search: name, years to search, DOB; also helpful: SSN. Criminal records on index books back to 1800s, on computer since 1989.

General Information: Public access terminal is available. No adoption or juvenile. SASE required. Turnaround time 2-3 days. Copy fee: $1.00 per page. Certification fee: $5.00. Fee payee: Clerk of Court. Personal checks accepted. Prepayment is required.

St. Charles Parish

29th District Court PO Box 424, Hahnville, LA 70057; 985-783-6632; Fax: 985-783-2005. Hours: 8:30AM-4:30PM (CST). *Felony, Misdemeanor, Civil, Probate.*

Civil Records: Access: Mail, in person. Both court and visitors may perform in person searches. Search fee: $5.00 per name. Required to search: name, years to search. Civil cases indexed by defendant, plaintiff. Civil records on computer back to 1982, on index books back to 1890.

Criminal Records: Access: Mail, in person. Both court and visitors may perform in person searches. Search fee: $5.00 per name. Required to search: name, years to search, DOB; also helpful: SSN, race, sex. Criminal records on computer back to 1981, on index books back to 1900s.

General Information: Public access terminal is available. No adoption or juvenile records released. Turnaround time 1 day. Fax notes: Fee to fax results is $4.00 per document. Copy fee: $.50 per page. Certification fee: $2.00 per page. Fee payee: Clerk of Court. Personal checks accepted. Prepayment required.

St. Helena Parish

21st District Court PO Box 308, Greensburg, LA 70441; 225-222-4514. Hours: 8:30AM-4:30PM (CST). *Felony, Misdemeanor, Civil, Probate.*

Civil Records: Access: Phone, mail, fax, in person. Both court and visitors may perform in person searches. Search fee: $10.00 per name. Required to search: name, years to search. Civil cases indexed by defendant, plaintiff. Civil records on index books back to 1800s.

Criminal Records: Access: Mail, in person. Both court and visitors may perform in person searches. Search fee: $10.00 per name. Required to search: name, years to search, DOB; also helpful: SSN. Criminal records on index books back to 1800s.

General Information: No adoption or juvenile records released. SASE required. Turnaround time 1-2 days. Fax notes: Fee to fax results is $2.00 per page. No copy

fee. Certification fee: $5.00. Fee payee: Clerk of Court. Personal checks accepted.

St. James Parish

23rd District Court PO Box 63, Convent, LA 70723; 225-562-7496; Fax: 504-562-2383. Hours: 8AM-4:30PM (CST). *Felony, Misdemeanor, Civil, Probate.*

Civil Records: Access: Mail, in person. Both court and visitors may perform in person searches. Search fee: $15.00 per name. Required to search: name, years to search. Civil cases indexed by defendant, plaintiff. Civil records on index books back to early 1900s; on computer back to 1988.

Criminal Records: Access: Mail, in person. Both court and visitors may perform in person searches. Search fee: $15.00 per name. Required to search: name, years to search, DOB. Criminal records on index books back to early 1900s; on computer back to 1990.

General Information: Public access terminal is available. No adoption or juvenile records released. SASE required. Turnaround time 1-2 days. Copy fee: $.75 per page. Certification fee: $5.00. Fee payee: Clerk of Court. Only cashiers checks and money orders accepted. Prepayment is required.

St. John the Baptist Parish

40th District Court PO Box 280, Edgard, LA 70049; 985-497-3331; Fax: 985-497-3972. Hours: 8:30AM-4:30PM (CST). *Felony, Misdemeanor, Civil, Probate.*

Civil Records: Access: Mail, fax, in person. Both court and visitors may perform in person searches. Search fee: $5.00 per name. Fee is for first 5 years. Add $1.00 per additional year. Required to search: name, years to search. Civil cases indexed by defendant, plaintiff. Civil records on computer since 1983.

Criminal Records: Access: Mail, fax, in person. Both court and visitors may perform in person searches. Search fee: $5.00 per name. Fee is for first 5 years. Add $1.00 per additional year. Required to search: name, years to search, DOB; also helpful: SSN. Felony records on computer since 1983, misdemeanors since 3/91.

General Information: Public access terminal is available. No adoption or juvenile records released. SASE required. Turnaround time 3-4 days. Fax notes: Fee to fax results is $5.00 per page. Copy fee: $1.00 per page. Certification fee: $5.50. Fee payee: Clerk of Court. Personal checks accepted. Prepayment is required.

St. Landry Parish

27th District Court PO Box 750, Courtthouse, Opelousas, LA 70570; 337-942-5606; Fax: 337-948-1653. Hours: 8AM-4:30PM (CST). *Felony, Misdemeanor, Civil, Probate.*

www.stlandry.org

Civil Records: Access: Mail, fax, in person, online. Both court and visitors may perform in person searches. Search fee: $15.00 per name. Additional $1.00 fee per year after 1st 10 years. Required to search: name, years to search. Civil cases indexed by defendant, plaintiff. Civil records on index books back to 1800s, on computer back to 1992. Access to civil indexes and images is to be available at www.stlandry.org. Index and images go back to 1998.

Criminal Records: Access: Mail, fax, in person. Both court and visitors may perform in person searches. Search fee: $15.00 per name. Additional $1.00 fee per year after 1st 10 years. Required to search: name, years to search, DOB; also helpful: SSN. Criminal records on index books back to 1800s, on computer back to 1992.

General Information: Public access terminal is available. (Public terminal only allows access to civil records.) No adoption or juvenile records released.

SASE required. Turnaround time 1-2 days. Fax notes: Fee to fax results is $5.00 1st page, $1.00 each add'l. Copy fee: $.75 per page. Certification fee: $5.50. Fee payee: Clerk of Court. Personal checks accepted. Prepayment is required.

St. Martin Parish

16th District Court PO Box 308, St. Martinville, LA 70582; 337-394-2210; Fax: 337-394-7772. Hours: 8:30AM-4:30PM (CST). *Felony, Misdemeanor, Civil, Probate.*

Civil Records: Access: Fax, mail, in person. Both court and visitors may perform in person searches. Search fee: $10.00 per name. Required to search: name, years to search; also helpful: address. Civil cases indexed by defendant, plaintiff. Civil records archived from 1760, on computer since 1990.

Criminal Records: Access: Fax, mail, in person. Both court and visitors may perform in person searches. Search fee: $10.00 per name. Required to search: name, years to search, DOB; also helpful: address, SSN. Criminal records archived from 1760, on computer since 1990.

General Information: Public access terminal is available. No adoption, sealed records, expunged or juvenile records released. SASE required. Turnaround time 1-2 days. Fax notes: $.75 per page. Copy fee: $.50 per page. Certification fee: $6.00. Fee payee: Clerk of Court. Personal checks accepted. Prepayment required.

St. Mary Parish

16th District Court PO Box 1231, Franklin, LA 70538; 337-828-4100 X200; Fax: 337-828-2509. Hours: 8:30AM-4:30PM (CST). *Felony, Misdemeanor, Civil, Probate.*

Civil Records: Access: In person only. Visitors must perform in person searches for themselves. No search fee. Required to search: name, years to search. Civil cases indexed by defendant, plaintiff. Civil records on index books back to 1800s.

Criminal Records: Access: In person only. Visitors must perform in person searches for themselves. No search fee. Required to search: name, years to search, DOB; also helpful: SSN. Criminal records on index books back to 1800s.

General Information: No adoption or juvenile records released. Copy fee: $1.00 per page. Certification fee: $5.00. Fee payee: St. Mary Parish Clerk of Court. Personal checks accepted. Prepayment is required.

St. Tammany Parish

22nd District Court PO Box 1090, Covington, LA 70434; 985-898-2430. Hours: 8:30AM-4:30PM (CST). *Felony, Misdemeanor, Civil, Probate.*

Civil Records: Access: Mail, in person, online. Both court and visitors may perform in person searches. Search fee: $10.00 per name. Required to search: name, years to search. Civil cases indexed by defendant, plaintiff. Civil records on index books back to 1800s, on computer since 1967. Remote online access to civil records is available from the Clerk of Court; fee is $.20 per minute with $100 initial setup fee. Modem and PC Anywhere is required. For information, call Kristie Howell at 985-898-2491.

Criminal Records: Access: Mail, in person, online. Both court and visitors may perform in person searches. Search fee: $10.00 per name. Required to search: name, years to search, DOB; also helpful: SSN. Criminal records on computer since 10/87. Remote online access to criminal records is the same as civil.

General Information: Public access terminal is available. No adoption or juvenile records released. SASE required. Turnaround time 2-3 days. Copy fee: $1.00 per page. Certification fee: $2.00 per document. Fee payee: Clerk of Court. Personal checks accepted. Prepayment is required.

Tangipahoa Parish

21st District Court PO Box 667, Amite, LA 70422; 985-748-4146; Fax: 985-748-6503. 8:30AM-4:30PM (CST). *Felony, Misdemeanor, Civil, Probate.* www.tangiclerk.org

Civil Records: Access: Mail, in person, online. Both court and visitors may perform in person searches. Search fee: $10.00 per name per 10 years. Required to search: name, years to search. Civil cases indexed by defendant, plaintiff. Civil records archived back to early 1900s; on computer back to 1980s. Online access to Parish notarial index records is available by free subscription (subject to change; expect fee for images and usage); images go back to 1/1990. Visit www.tangiclerk.org/OnlineServices/onlineservices.asp for information or call Alison Theard: 985-748-7404.

Criminal Records: Access: Mail, in person. Both court and visitors may perform in person searches. Search fee: $10.00 per name. Required to search: name, years to search, DOB, SSN. Criminal records archived back to early 1900s; on computer back to 1993.

General Information: Public access terminal is available. No adoption or juvenile records released. SASE required. Turnaround time 3-4 days. Fax notes: Fee to fax results is $5.00 1st page, $1.00 each add'l. Copy fee: $1.00 per page. Certification fee: $5.50. Fee payee: Clerk of Court. Personal checks accepted. Prepayment is required.

Tensas Parish

6th District Court PO Box 78, St. Joseph, LA 71366; 318-766-3921. Hours: 8:30AM-4:30PM (CST). *Felony, Misdemeanor, Civil, Probate.*

Civil Records: Access: In person only. Visitors must perform in person searches for themselves. No search fee. Required to search: name, years to search. Civil cases indexed by defendant, plaintiff. Civil records archived back to 1800s, on computer since mid-1998.

Criminal Records: Access: In person only. Visitors must perform in person searches for themselves. No search fee. Required to search: name, years to search; also helpful: DOB, SSN. Criminal records on computer since 1998; archived back to 1800s.

General Information: No adoption or juvenile records released. Fax notes: Fee to fax results is $5.00 per document. Certification fee: $5.50. Fee payee: Clerk of Court. Personal checks accepted. Prepayment is required.

Terrebonne Parish

32nd District Court PO Box 1569, Houma, LA 70361; 985-868-5660. Hours: 8:30AM-4:30PM (CST). *Felony, Misdemeanor, Civil, Probate.*

Civil Records: Access: Mail, in person. Both court and visitors may perform in person searches. Search fee: $15.00 per name. Required to search: name, years to search. Civil cases indexed by defendant, plaintiff. Civil records on computer since 1986, in books to 1823.

Criminal Records: Access: Mail, in person. Both court and visitors may perform in person searches. Search fee: $15.00 per name. Required to search: name, years to search, DOB; also helpful: SSN, race, sex. Criminal records archived to 1800s.

General Information: No adoption or juvenile records released. SASE required. Turnaround time 2-3 days. Fax notes: Fee to fax results is $2.00 per page. Copy fee: $.75 per page. Certification fee: $6.00. Fee payee: Terrebonne Parish Clerk of Court. Personal checks accepted. Prepayment is required.

Union Parish

3rd District Court Courthouse Bldg, 100 E Bayou #105, Farmerville, LA 71241; 318-368-3055; Fax: 318-368-2487. Hours: 8:30AM-4:30PM (CST). *Felony, Misdemeanor, Civil, Probate.*

Civil Records: Access: Mail, in person. Search fee: $5.00 per name. Required to search: name, years to search. Civil cases indexed by defendant, plaintiff. Civil records on index books back to 1839.

Criminal Records: Access: Mail, fax, in person. Both court and visitors may perform in person searches. Search fee: $10.00 per name. Required to search: name, years to search, SSN. Criminal records on index books back to 1839; computerized records go back to 1982.

General Information: No adoption or juvenile records released. SASE required. Turnaround time 2-3 days. Fax notes: $5.00 fee per document. Copy fee: $.75 per page. Certification fee: $3.00. Payee: Clerk of Court. Personal checks accepted. Prepayment is required.

Vermilion Parish

15th District Court 100 N. State St, #101, Abbeville, LA 70511-0790; 337-898-1992; Fax: 337-898-0404. Hours: 8:30AM-4:30PM (CST). *Felony, Misdemeanor, Civil, Probate.*

Civil Records: Access: Phone, fax, mail, in person. Both court and visitors may perform in person searches. Search fee: $12.00 per name. Fee for second name on same search request is $6.50. Required to search: name, years to search. Civil cases indexed by defendant, plaintiff. Civil records on computer since 1982, in books since 1885, on microfilm since 1885.

Criminal Records: Access: Phone, fax, mail, in person. Both court and visitors may perform in person searches. Search fee: $12.00 per name. Fee for second name on same search request is $6.50. Required to search: name, years to search, DOB; also helpful: SSN, race, sex. Criminal records on computer since 1982, in books since 1885, on microfilm since 1885.

General Information: Public access terminal is available. No adoption or juvenile records released. SASE required. Turnaround time 1-2 days after payment. Fax notes: $2.00 for first page, $1.00 each add'l. Copy fee: $1.00 per page. Certification fee: $5.00. Fee payee: Vermilion Parish Clerk of Court. Personal checks accepted. Prepayment is required.

Vernon Parish

30th District Court PO Box 40, Leesville, LA 71496; 337-238-1384; Fax: 337-238-9902. Hours: 8AM-4:30PM *Felony, Misdemeanor, Civil, Probate.*

Civil Records: Access: Mail, fax, in person. Both court and visitors may perform in person searches. Search fee: $10.00 per name. Required to search: name, years to search. Civil cases indexed by defendant, plaintiff. Civil records on computer from November 1985, archived back to 1900.

Criminal Records: Access: Mail, in person. Both court and visitors may perform in person searches. Search fee: $10.00 per name. Required to search: name, years to search, DOB, SNN. Criminal records on computer from November 1985, archived back to 1900.

General Information: Public access terminal is available. No adoption or juvenile records released. SASE required. Turnaround time same day. Copy fee: $1.25 per page. Certification fee: $5.00. Fee payee: Clerk of Court. Personal checks accepted. Prepayment is required.

Washington Parish

22nd District Court PO Box 607, Franklinton, LA 70438; 985-839-4663/7821. Hours: 8AM-4:30PM (CST). *Felony, Misdemeanor, Civil, Probate.*

Civil Records: Access: Mail, in person. Both court and visitors may perform in person searches. Search fee: $10.00 per name. Required to search: name, years to search. Civil cases indexed by defendant, plaintiff. Civil records on computer from 1993, archived April 1967, index books back to 1800s.

Criminal Records: Access: Mail, in person. Both court and visitors may perform in person searches. Search fee: $10.00 per name. Required to search: name, years to search, DOB, SSN. Criminal records on computer from 1993, archived April 1967, index books back to 1800s.

General Information: No adoption or juvenile records released. SASE requested. Turnaround time 1-2 days. Copy fee: $1.00 per page. Certification fee: $5.00. Fee payee: Washington Parish Clerk of Court. Personal checks accepted. Prepayment is required.

Webster Parish

26th District Court PO Box 370, Minden, LA 71058-0370; 318-371-0366; Fax: 318-371-0226. Hours: 8:30AM-4:30PM (CST). *Felony, Misdemeanor, Civil, Probate.*

Civil Records: Access: Fax, mail, in person. Both court and visitors may perform in person searches. Search fee: $10.00 per name. Required to search: name, years to search. Civil cases indexed by defendant, plaintiff. Civil records archived back to 1800s, on computer since 1986.

Criminal Records: Access: Fax, mail, in person. Both court and visitors may perform in person searches. Search fee: $10.00 per name. Required to search: name; also helpful: years to search. Criminal records not on computer, in books to 1800s.

General Information: Public access terminal is available. No adoption or juvenile records released. SASE not required. Turnaround time 2-3 days. Fax notes: $5.00 per page. Copy fee: $1.00 per page. Certification fee: $5.00. Fee payee: Clerk of Court. Personal checks accepted. Prepayment is required.

West Baton Rouge Parish

18th District Court PO Box 107, Port Allen, LA 70767; 225-383-0378. Hours: 8:30AM-4:30PM (CST). *Felony, Misdemeanor, Civil, Probate.*

Civil Records: Access: Phone, mail, in person. Both court and visitors may perform in person searches. Search fee: $10.00 per name. Required to search: name, years to search. Civil cases indexed by defendant, plaintiff. Civil records on computer from 1983.

Criminal Records: Access: Phone, mail, in person. Both court and visitors may perform in person searches. Search fee: $10.00 per name. Required to search: name, years to search, DOB; also helpful: SSN. Criminal records on computer from 1983.

General Information: Public access terminal is available. No adoption or juvenile records released. SASE required. Turnaround time 1-2 days. Copy fee: $1.00 per page. Certification fee: $2.00. Fee payee: Clerk of Court. Personal checks accepted. Prepayment is required.

West Carroll Parish

5th District Court PO Box 1078, Oak Grove, LA 71263; 318-428-3281. Hours: 8:30AM-4:30PM (CST). *Felony, Misdemeanor, Civil, Probate.*

Civil Records: Access: Mail, in person. Both court and visitors may perform in person searches. Search fee: $1.00 per name per year. Required to search: name, years to search. Civil cases indexed by defendant, plaintiff. Civil records on index books back to 1800s.

Criminal Records: Access: Mail, in person. Both court and visitors may perform in person searches. Search fee: $1.00 per name per year. Required to search: name, years to search, DOB. Criminal records on index books back to 1800s.

General Information: No adoption or juvenile records released. SASE required. Turnaround time 1-2 days. Copy fee: $1.00 per page. Certification fee: $5.00. Fee payee: Clerk of Court. Only cashiers checks and money orders accepted. Prepayment is required.

West Feliciana Parish

20th District Court PO Box 1843, St Francisville, LA 70775; 225-635-3794; Fax: 225-635-3770. Hours: 8:30AM-4:30PM (CST). *Felony, Misdemeanor, Civil, Probate.*

Civil Records: Access: Mail, in person. Both court and visitors may perform in person searches. Search fee: $10.00 per name. Fee is per 5 years searched. Required to search: name, years to search; also helpful: address. Civil cases indexed by defendant, plaintiff. Civil records on computer from 1984, index books back to 1800s.

Criminal Records: Access: Mail, in person. Both court and visitors may perform in person searches. Search fee: $10.00 per name. Fee is per 5 years searched. Required to search: name, years to search, DOB; also helpful: address. Criminal records on computer since 1992; prior on cards and dockets back to 1800s.

General Information: No adoption, juvenile or juvenile records released. SASE required. Turnaround time 3-5 days. Copy fee: $1.00 per page. Certification fee: $5.00. Fee payee: Clerk of Court. Business checks accepted. Prepayment is required.

Winn Parish

8th District Court 100 Main St, #103, Winnfield, LA 71483; 318-628-3515. Hours: 8AM-4:30PM (CST). *Felony, Misdemeanor, Civil, Probate.*

Civil Records: Access: Mail, in person. Both court and visitors may perform in person searches. Search fee: $15.00 per name. Fee is for 10 year search. Required to search: name, years to search, address. Civil cases indexed by defendant, plaintiff. Civil records on books from 1886 to present, on computer from 1988, mortgages since 1981, conveyances since 1993.

Criminal Records: Access: Mail, in person. Both court and visitors may perform in person searches. Search fee: $15.00 per name. Fee is for 10 year search. Required to search: name, years to search, address, DOB; also helpful: SSN. Criminal records in books since 1886, computerized since 1997.

General Information: No adoption or juvenile records released. SASE required. Turnaround time 2-3 days. Fax notes: Fee to fax results is $5.00 per document and $1.00 per page. Copy fee: $1.00 per page. Certification fee: $5.00. Fee payee: Winn Parish Clerk of Court. Personal checks accepted. Prepayment is required.

Louisiana Recording Offices

ORGANIZATION: 64 parishes (not counties), 64 recording offices. One parish, St. Martin, has two non-contiguous segments. The recording officer is the Clerk of Court. Many parishes include tax and other non-UCC liens in their mortgage records. The entire state is in the Central Time Zone (CST).

REAL ESTATE RECORDS: Most parishes will perform a mortgage search. Some will provide a record owner search. Copy and certification fees vary widely.

UCC RECORDS: Financing statements are filed with the Clerk of Court in any parish in the state and are entered onto a statewide computerized database of UCC financing statements available for searching at any parish office. All parishes perform UCC searches for $15.00 per debtor name. Use search request form UCC-11. Copy fees are $.50-1.00 per page.

TAX LIEN RECORDS: All federal and state tax liens are filed with the Clerk of Court. Parishes usually file tax liens on personal property in their UCC or mortgage records, and most will perform tax lien searches for varying fees. Some parishes will automatically include tax liens on personal property in a mortgage certificate search.

OTHER LIENS: Judgments, labor, material, hospital.

ONLINE ACCESS: A number of Parrishes offer online access to recorded documents, most are commercial fee systems.

Acadia Parish

Clerk of Court, PO Box 922, Crowley, LA 70526. 337-788-8881; Fax 337-788-1048. www.acadiaparishclerk.com
Will search UCC records. This agency will not do a tax lien search. Will provide mortgage certificates. **Other Phone Numbers:** Assessor 337-788-8871; Treasurer 337-788-8800.

Allen Parish

Clerk of Court, PO Box 248, Oberlin, LA 70655. 337-639-4351; Fax 337-639-2030.
Will search UCC records. Tax liens not included in UCC search. Real estate owner, mortgage, and property transfer searches available. **Other Phone Numbers:** Assessor 337-639-4391.

Ascension Parish

Clerk of Court, PO Box 192, Donaldsonville, LA 70346. Clerk of Court, R/E and UCC Recording 225-473-9866; Fax 225-473-8641.
Will search UCC records. UCC search includes tax liens if requested. Real estate record owner and mortgage searches available. **Other Phone Numbers:** Assessor 225-473-9239.

Assumption Parish

Clerk of Court, PO Drawer 249, Napoleonville, LA 70390. 985-369-6653; Fax 985-369-2032.
Will search UCC records. UCC search includes tax liens if requested. Real estate record owner and mortgage searches available. **Other Phone Numbers:** Assessor 985-369-6385; Register of Voters 985-369-7347.

Avoyelles Parish

Clerk of Court, PO Box 219, Marksville, LA 71351. Clerk of Court, R/E and UCC Recording 318-253-7523; Fax 318-253-4614.
Will search UCC records. UCC search includes tax liens if requested. Will not search real estate records. **Other Phone Numbers:** Assessor 318-253-4507; Treasurer 318-253-9208.

Beauregard Parish

Clerk of Court, PO Box 100, De Ridder, LA 70634. 337-463-8595; Fax 337-462-3916.
Will search UCC records. Tax liens not included in UCC search. Real estate owner, mortgage, and property transfer searches available. **Other Phone Numbers:** Assessor 337-463-8945.

Bienville Parish

Clerk of Court, 100 Courthouse Dr, Rm 100, Room 100, Arcadia, LA 71001-3600. 318-263-2123; Fax 318-263-7426.
Will search UCC records. Tax liens not included in UCC search. Real estate owner, mortgage, and property transfer searches available. **Other Phone Numbers:** Assessor 318-263-2214; Treasurer 318-263-2019.

Bossier Parish

Clerk of Court, PO Box 430, Benton, LA 71006. 318-965-2336.
Will search UCC records. UCC search includes tax liens. Mortgage searches available. **Other Phone Numbers:** Assessor 318-965-2213.

Caddo Parish

Clerk of Court, 501 Texas St, Room 103, Shreveport, LA 71101-5408. 318-226-6783 R/E Recording: 318-226-6790; Fax 318-227-9080. www.caddoclerk.com
Will search UCC records. Tax liens not included in UCC search. Will not search real estate records. **Online Access:** Real Estate, Lien, Marriage Records. Access to the Parish online records requires a $50 set up fee plus a $30 monthly fee. Mortgages and indirect conveyances date back to 1981; direct conveyances date back to 1914. Lending agency information available. UCCs are at Sec. of State. Marriage licenses go back to 1937. For system information, contact Susan Twohig at 318-226-6523. **Other Phones:** Assessor 318-226-6702; Treasurer 318-226-6900; Elections 318-226-6788.

Calcasieu Parish

Clerk of Court, PO Box 1030, Lake Charles, LA 70601-1030. 337-437-3550; Fax 337-437-3350.
Will search UCC records. UCC search includes tax liens. Real estate record owner and mortgage searches available. **Other Phone Numbers:** Assessor 337-437-3461; Treasurer 337-437-3680.

Caldwell Parish

Clerk of Court, PO Box 1327, Columbia, LA 71418. 318-649-2272; Fax 318-649-2037.
Will search UCC records. Tax liens not included in UCC search. Mortgage searches available. **Other Phone Numbers:** Assessor 318-649-2636; Treasurer 318-649-2681.

Cameron Parish

Clerk of Court, PO Box 549, Cameron, LA 70631. Clerk of Court, R/E and UCC Recording 337-775-5316; Fax 337-775-7172.

Will search UCC records. UCC search includes tax liens if requested. Real estate owner, mortgage, and property transfer searches available. **Other Phones:** Assessor 337-775-5416; Treasurer 337-775-5718; Elections 337-775-5316; Vital Records 337-775-5316.

Catahoula Parish

Clerk of Court, PO Box 198, Harrisonburg, LA 71340. 318-744-5497; Fax 318-744-5488.
Will search UCC records. Tax liens not included in UCC search. Mortgage searches available. **Other Phone Numbers:** Assessor 318-744-5291.

Claiborne Parish

Clerk of Court, PO Box 330, Homer, LA 71040. 318-927-9601; Fax 318-927-2345.
Will search UCC records. Tax liens not included in UCC search. Mortgage certificate searches including tax liens available. **Other Phone Numbers:** Assessor 318-927-3022; Treasurer 318-927-2222.

Concordia Parish

Clerk of Court, Courthouse, PO Box 790, Vidalia, LA 71373. 318-336-4204.
Will search UCC records. UCC search includes tax liens. Mortgage searches available. **Other Phone Numbers:** Assessor 318-336-5122.

De Soto Parish

Clerk of Court, PO Box 1206, Mansfield, LA 71052. Clerk of Court, R/E and UCC Recording 318-872-3110; Fax 318-872-4202.
Will search UCC records. UCC search includes tax liens if requested. Real estate owner, mortgage, and property transfer searches available. **Other Phone Numbers:** Assessor 318-872-3610; Elections 318-872-3110; Criminal 318-872-3181.

East Baton Rouge Parish

Clerk of Court, PO Box 1991, Baton Rouge, LA 70821-1991. 225-389-3985; Fax 225-389-3392. www.ebrclerkofcourt.org
Will search UCC records. UCC search includes tax liens if requested. Real estate owner, mortgage, and property transfer searches available. **Online Access:** Real Estate, Lien Records. Access to online records requires a $100 set up fee with a $5 monthly fee and $.33 per minute of use. Four years worth of data is kept active on the system. Lending agency information is available. For information, contact Wendy Gibbs at 225-398-5295. UCC information is located at the Secretary of State. **Other Phone Numbers:** Assessor 225-389-3920; Treasurer 225-389-3276.

East Carroll Parish

Clerk of Court, 400 First St, Lake Providence, LA 71254. 318-559-2399.
Will search UCC records. Tax liens not included in UCC search. Real estate owner, mortgage, and property transfer searches available. **Other Phone Numbers:** Assessor 318-559-2850; Treasurer 318-559-2000.

East Feliciana Parish

Clerk of Court, PO Drawer 599, Clinton, LA 70722. 225-683-5145; Fax 225-683-3556.
Will search UCC records. Tax liens not included in UCC search. Mortgage searches available. Property description required **Other Phone Numbers:** Assessor 225-683-8945.

Evangeline Parish

Clerk of Court, PO Drawer 347, Ville Platte, LA 70586. Clerk of Court, R/E and UCC Recording 337-363-5671; Fax 337-363-5780.
Will search UCC records. Tax liens not included in UCC search. Mortgage searches available. **Other Phone Numbers:** Assessor 337-363-4310; Treasurer 337-363-5651.

Franklin Parish

Clerk of Court, PO Box 1564, Winnsboro, LA 71295. Clerk of Court, R/E and UCC Recording 318-435-5133; Fax 318-435-5134.
Will search UCC records. Tax liens not included in UCC search. Mortgage searches available. Property description required **Other Phone Numbers:** Assessor 318-435-5390.

Grant Parish

Clerk of Court, PO Box 263, Colfax, LA 71417. Clerk of Court, R/E and UCC Recording 318-627-3246; Fax 318-627-3201.
Will search UCC records. Tax liens not included in UCC search. Mortgage searches available. **Other Phone Numbers:** Assessor 318-627-5471; Treasurer 318-627-3157; Elections 318-627-3246.

Iberia Parish

Clerk of Court, PO Drawer 12010, New Iberia, LA 70562-2010. 337-365-7282; Fax 337-365-0737.
Will search UCC records. Tax liens not included in UCC search. Real estate owner, mortgage, and property transfer searches available. **Online Access:** Real Estate, Lien, Marriage, Divorce Records. Access to the Parish online records requires a $50 monthly usage fee. Records date back to 1959. Lending agency information is available. System includes court records. For information, contact Mike Thibodeaux at 337-365-7282. **Other Phone Numbers:** Assessor 337-369-4415; Treasurer 337-685-4720.

Iberville Parish

Clerk of Court, PO Box 423, Plaquemine, LA 70765-0423. 225-687-5160; Fax 225-687-5260.
Will search UCC records. Tax liens not included in UCC search. Mortgage searches available. **Other Phone Numbers:** Assessor 225-687-3568.

Jackson Parish

Clerk of Court, PO Drawer 730, Jonesboro, LA 71251. Clerk of Court, R/E and UCC Recording 318-259-2424; Fax 318-395-0386.
Will search UCC records. Tax liens not included in UCC search. Tax liens will automatically show on a mortgage certificate. Real estate record owner and mortgage searches available. **Other Phone Numbers:** Assessor 318-259-2151; Elections 318-259-2424; Police Jury 318-259-2361.

Jefferson Davis Parish

Clerk of Court, PO Box 799, Jennings, LA 70546-0799. 337-824-1160/1161.
Will search UCC records. UCC search includes tax liens if requested. Real estate record owner and mortgage searches available. **Other Phone Numbers:** Assessor 337-824-3451.

Jefferson Parish

Clerk of Court, PO Box 10, Gretna, LA 70054-0010. 504-364-2907; Fax 504-364-3836.
www.clerkofcourt.co.jefferson.la.us
Will search UCC records. Tax liens not included in UCC search, but tax liens are included with other lien searches. Mortgage and property transfer searches available. **Online Access:** Real Estate, Assessor, Marriage, Civil Records. Access to the clerk's JeffNet database is available by subscription; set-up fee is $200.00 plus $8.50 monthly and $.25 per minute. Mortgage and convenyance images go back to 1990; index to 1967. Marriage and assessor records go back to 1992. For information, visit online at www.clerkofcourt.co.jefferson.la.us/jeffnet.htm or call the Court Information Systems at 504-364-2908.

La Salle Parish

Clerk of Court, PO Box 1316, Jena, LA 71342. Clerk of Court, R/E and UCC Recording 318-992-2158; Fax 318-992-2157.
Will search UCC records. UCC search includes tax liens if requested. Separate combined tax lien search available. Real estate record owner and mortgage searches available. **Other Phone Numbers:** Assessor 318-992-8256; Appraiser/Auditor 318-992-2211; Elections 318-992-2158; Vital Records 318-992-2158.

Lafayette Parish

Clerk of Court, PO Box 2009, Lafayette, LA 70502. 337-291-6400 R/E Recording: 337-291-6310 UCC Recording: 337-291-6310; Fax 337-291-6392.
www.lafayetteparishclerk.com
Will search UCC records. Mortgage searches available. **Online Access:** Real Estate, Lien Records. Access to Parish online records requires a $100 set up fee plus $15 per month and $.50 per minute. Conveyances date back to 1936; mortgages to 1948; other records to 1986. Lending agency information is available. For information, contact Derek Comeaux at 337-291-6433. Tax and UCC lien information is for this parish only. **Other Phones:** Assessor 337-291-7080; Elections 337-291-6454; Vital Records 337-262-5616 x139.

Lafourche Parish

Clerk of Court, PO Box 818, Thibodaux, LA 70302. Clerk of Court, R/E and UCC Recording 985-447-4841; Fax 985-447-5800.
Will search UCC records. Tax liens not included in UCC search. Will not search real estate records. **Other Phone Numbers:** Assessor 985-447-7242; Treasurer 985-447-4841; Elections 985-447-4841.

Lincoln Parish

Clerk of Court, PO Box 924, Ruston, LA 71273-0924. Clerk of Court, R/E and UCC Recording 318-251-5130; Fax 318-255-6004.
Will search UCC records. Tax liens not included in UCC search. Separate combined tax lien search available. Mortgage searches available. **Other Phone Numbers:** Assessor 318-251-5140.

Livingston Parish

Clerk of Court, PO Box 1150, Livingston, LA 70754. 225-686-2216; Fax 225-686-1867.
Will search UCC records. UCC search includes tax liens if requested. Will not search real estate records. **Other Phone Numbers:** Assessor 225-686-7278.

Madison Parish

Clerk of Court, PO Box 1710, Tallulah, LA 71282. 318-574-0655; Fax 318-574-3961.
Will search UCC records. This agency will not do a tax lien search. Mortgage searches available. **Other Phone Numbers:** Assessor 318-574-0117.

Morehouse Parish

Clerk of Court, PO Box 1543, Bastrop, LA 71221-1543. Clerk of Court, R/E and UCC Recording 318-281-3343; Fax 318-281-3775.
Will search UCC records. Tax liens not included in UCC search. Real estate record owner and mortgage searches available. **Online Access:** Real Estate, Lien Records. Remote online access will be available in 2001. The service and fees will be similar to the Lafayette Parish. **Other Phone Numbers:** Assessor 318-281-1802; Vital Records 318-568-5050.

Natchitoches Parish

Clerk of Court, PO Box 476, Natchitoches, LA 71458-0476. 318-352-8152; Fax 318-352-9321.
Will search UCC records. Tax liens not included in UCC search. Real estate owner, mortgage, and property transfer searches available. **Other Phone Numbers:** Assessor 318-352-2377; Vital Records 318-357-2243; Civil 318-357-2293 or 2294.

Orleans Parish

Clerk of Court, 421 Loyola Ave, B-1, Civil Court Building, New Orleans, LA 70112. 504-592-9189; Fax 504-592-9192.
Will search UCC records. UCC search includes tax liens. Additional $5.00 fee for general combined and state tax lien searches Real estate record owner and property transfer searches available. **Online Access:** Real Estate, Lien Records. Access to the Parish online records requires a set up fee and $300 deposit for 1,200 minutes of usage, plus $.25 per minute. Records date back to 9/1987. No lending agency information is available. For information, contact John Rabb at 504-592-9264. **Other Phones:** Assessor 504-592-7050.

Ouachita Parish

Clerk of Court, PO Box 1862, Monroe, LA 71210-1862. 318-327-1444; Fax 318-327-1462.
Will search UCC records. UCC search includes tax liens. Mortgage searches available. **Other Phone Numbers:** Assessor 318-327-1300.

Plaquemines Parish

Clerk of Court, PO Box 129, Pointe a la Hache, LA 70082. 504-392-4969 R/E Recording: 985-333-4377 UCC Recording: 985-333-4377.
Will search UCC records. UCC search includes tax liens. Real estate record owner and property searches available. **Other Phone Numbers:** Assessor 985-333-4331; Elections 985-333-4377.

Pointe Coupee Parish

Clerk of Court, PO Box 86, New Roads, LA 70760. Clerk of Court, R/E and UCC Recording 225-638-9596; Fax 225-638-9590.
Will search UCC records. Tax liens not included in UCC search. Real estate owner, mortgage, and property transfer searches available. **Other Phone Numbers:** Assessor 225-638-7077; Treasurer 504-638-9556.

Rapides Parish

Clerk of Court, PO Box 952, Alexandria, LA 71309. Clerk of Court, R/E and UCC Recording 318-473-8153; Fax 318-473-4667.
Will search UCC records. UCC search includes tax liens if requested. Real estate record owner and mortgage searches available. **Other Phone Numbers:** Assessor 318-448-8511; Elections 318-473-6770.

Red River Parish

Clerk of Court, PO Box 485, Coushatta, LA 71019-0485. 318-932-6741; Fax 318-932-3126.
Will search UCC records. UCC search does not include tax liens. Mortgage searches available; includes tax liens. **Other Phone Numbers:** Assessor 318-932-4922.

Richland Parish

Clerk of Court, PO Box 119, Rayville, LA 71269. 318-728-4171; Fax 318-728-7020.
Will search UCC records. UCC search includes tax liens if requested. Mortgage searches available. **Other Phone Numbers:** Assessor 318-728-4491.

Sabine Parish

Clerk of Court, PO Box 419, Many, LA 71449. Clerk of Court, R/E and UCC Recording 318-256-6223; Fax 318-256-9037.
Will search UCC records. Tax liens not included in UCC search. Real estate owner, mortgage, and property transfer searches available. **Other Phone Numbers:** Assessor 318-256-3482; Treasurer 318-256-5637; Sheriff 318-256-9241.

St. Bernard Parish

Clerk of Court, PO Box 1746, Chalmette, LA 70044. Clerk of Court, R/E and UCC Recording 504-271-3434.
Will search UCC records. UCC search includes tax liens if requested. Mortgage and property transfer searches available. **Other Phone Numbers:** Assessor 504-279-6379; Elections 504-271-3434.

St. Charles Parish

Clerk of Court, PO Box 424, Hahnville, LA 70057. Clerk of Court, R/E and UCC Recording 985-783-6632; Fax 985-783-2005.
Will search UCC records. UCC search includes tax liens if requested. Separate combined tax lien search available. Mortgage searches available. **Other Phone Numbers:** Assessor 985-783-6281.

St. Helena Parish

Clerk of Court, PO Box 308, Greensburg, LA 70441-0308. 225-222-4514; Fax 225-222-3443.
Will search UCC records. UCC search includes tax liens if requested. Real estate record owner searches available. **Other Phones:** Assessor 225-222-4540.

St. James Parish

Clerk of Court, PO Box 63, Convent, LA 70723. 225-562-2270 R/E Recording: 225-562-7496 UCC Recording: 225-562-7496; Fax 225-562-2383.
Will search UCC records. Tax liens not included in UCC search. Real estate owner, mortgage, and property transfer searches available. **Other Phone Numbers:** Assessor 225-562-2250; Treasurer 504-562-2300; Elections 225-562-7496.

St. John the Baptist Parish

Clerk of Court, PO Box 280, Edgard, LA 70049-0280. 985-497-3331 R/E Recording: 985-497-8836 x246 UCC Recording: 985-497-8836 x249; Fax 985-497-3972.
Will search UCC records. Tax liens not included in UCC search. Separate combined tax lien search available. Real estate owner, mortgage, and property transfer searches available. **Other Phone Numbers:** Assessor 985-497-8788.

St. Landry Parish

Clerk of Court, PO Box 750, Opelousas, LA 70571-0750. 337-942-5606 R/E Recording: 337-942-5606 x121 UCC Recording: 337-942-5606 x122; Fax 337-948-7265. www.stlandry.org/index.htm

Will search UCC records. Tax liens not included in UCC search. Separate combined tax lien search available. Real estate owner, mortgage, and property transfer searches available. **Online Access:** Recording, Deed, Judgment, Civil Court Records. Access to conveyances data is to be available free at www.stlandry.org. Document images 1978-present. **Other Phone Numbers:** Assessor 337-942-2316; Treasurer 337-948-6516; Elections 337-942-5606 x133; Vital Records 337-942-5606 x122.

St. Martin Parish

Clerk of Court, PO Box 308, St. Martinville, LA 70582. 337-394-2210; Fax 337-394-7772.
Will search UCC records. Tax liens not included in UCC search. Real estate owner, mortgage, and property transfer searches available. **Other Phone Numbers:** Assessor 337-394-2208; Treasurer 337-394-2200; Elections 337-394-2210; Vital Records 337-394-2210.

St. Mary Parish

Clerk of Court, PO Box 1231, Franklin, LA 70538. 318-828-4100 x200; Fax 318-828-2509.
Will search UCC records. UCC search includes tax liens. Real estate owner, mortgage, and property transfer searches available. **Other Phone Numbers:** Assessor 318-828-4100 x250.

St. Tammany Parish

Clerk of Court, PO Box 1090, Covington, LA 70434. 985-898-2430.
Will search UCC records. Tax liens not included in UCC search. Separate combined tax lien search available. Real estate owner, mortgage, and property transfer searches available. **Online Access:** Real Estate, Lien Records. Access to online records requires a $100 set up fee, plus $.30 per minute of use. Records date back to 1961; viewable images on conveyances back to 1985; mortgages to 8/93. For information, contact Mark Cohn at 504-898-2890 or Christy Howell at 504-898-2491. UCC lien information is with the Secretary of State. **Other Phones:** Assessor 985-892-6150.

Tangipahoa Parish

Clerk of Court, PO Box 667, Amite, LA 70422. 985-549-1611 R/E Recording: 985-549-1612; Fax 985-748-6503. www.tangiclerk.org
Will search UCC records. Tax liens not included in UCC search. Separate combined tax lien search available. Mortgage searches available. **Online Access:** Real Estate, Lien, Recording, Civil Records. Access to Parish online records requires registration and a $55 monthly fee. Record dates vary though most indexes go back to 1990. Lending agency information is available. For information, contact Alison Carona at 504-549-1611. Also, a free mapping feature is being developed.

Tensas Parish

Clerk of Court, PO Box 78, St. Joseph, LA 71366. 225-766-3921; Fax 225-222-3443.
Will search UCC records. Tax liens not included in UCC search. Real estate owner, mortgage, and property transfer searches available. **Other Phone Numbers:** Assessor 225-766-3501.

Terrebonne Parish

Clerk of Court, PO Box 1569, Houma, LA 70361. 985-868-5660 UCC Recording: 985-868-5660 x15.
Will search UCC records. Tax liens not included in UCC search. Real estate owner, mortgage, and property transfer searches available. **Other Phone Numbers:** Assessor 985-876-6620.

Union Parish

Clerk of Court, Courthouse, 100 E. Bayou, Suite 105, Farmerville, LA 71241. 318-368-3055; Fax 318-368-3861.

Will search UCC records. Tax liens not included in UCC search. Real estate record owner and mortgage searches available. **Other Phone Numbers:** Assessor 318-368-3232.

Vermilion Parish

Clerk of Court, 100 N State St #101, Abbeville, LA 70510. Clerk of Court, R/E and UCC Recording 337-898-1992; Fax 337-898-0404.
Will search UCC records. Tax liens not included in UCC search. Real estate owner, mortgage, and property transfer searches available. **Other Phone Numbers:** Assessor 337-893-2837; Treasurer 337-898-4300; Appraiser/Auditor 337-898-2837; Elections 337-898-1992; Vital Records 337-898-1992.

Vernon Parish

Clerk of Court, PO Box 40, Leesville, LA 71496-0040. 337-238-1384 R/E Recording: 337-238-4824; Fax 337-238-9902.
Will search UCC records. UCC search includes tax liens if requested. Mortgage searches available. **Other Phone Numbers:** Assessor 337-293-2167; Elections 337-238-1384.

Washington Parish

Clerk of Court, PO Box 607, Franklinton, LA 70438. 985-839-4663.
Will search UCC records. Tax liens not included in UCC search. Real estate owner, mortgage, and property transfer searches available. **Other Phone Numbers:** Assessor 985-839-2280.

Webster Parish

Clerk of Court, PO Box 370, Minden, LA 71058-0370. Clerk of Court, R/E and UCC Recording 318-371-0366; Fax 318-371-0226.
Will search UCC records. UCC search includes tax liens if requested. Separate combined tax lien search available. Real estate record owner searches available. **Other Phone Numbers:** Assessor 318-377-9311; Elections 318-371-0366.

West Baton Rouge Parish

Clerk of Court, PO Box 107, Port Allen, LA 70767. Clerk of Court, R/E and UCC Recording 225-383-0378; Fax 225-383-3694.
Will search UCC records. Tax liens not included in UCC search. Real estate owner, mortgage, and property transfer searches available. **Other Phone Numbers:** Assessor 225-344-6777.

West Carroll Parish

Clerk of Court, PO Box 1078, Oak Grove, LA 71263. Clerk of Court, R/E and UCC Recording 318-428-3281; Fax 318-428-9896.
Will search UCC records. UCC search includes tax liens. Mortgage searches available. **Other Phone Numbers:** Assessor 318-428-2371.

West Feliciana Parish

Clerk of Court, PO Box 1843, St. Francisville, LA 70775. 225-635-3794; Fax 225-635-3770.
Will search UCC records. Tax liens not included in UCC search. Real estate owner, mortgage, and property transfer searches available. **Other Phone Numbers:** Assessor 225-635-3350.

Winn Parish

Clerk of Court, Courthouse, Room 103, 100 Main St., Winnfield, LA 71483. Clerk of Court, R/E and UCC Recording 318-628-3515; Fax 318-628-2753.
Will search UCC records. Tax liens not included in UCC search. Real estate owner, mortgage, and property transfer searches available. **Other Phone Numbers:** Assessor 318-628-3267; Treasurer 318-628-5824.

Louisiana County Locator

You will usually be able to find the city name in the City/Parish Cross Reference below. In that case, it is a simple matter to determine the county from the cross reference. However, only the official US Postal Service city names are included in this index. There are an additional 40,000 place names that people use in their addresses. Therefore, we have also included a ZIP/City Cross Reference immediately following the City/Parish Cross Reference.

If you know the ZIP Code but the city name does not appear in the City/Parish Cross Reference index, look up the ZIP Code in the ZIP/City Cross Reference, find the city name, then look up the city name in the City/Parish Cross Reference. For example, you want to know the county for an address of Menands, NY 12204. There is no "Menands" in the City/Parish Cross Reference. The ZIP/City Cross Reference shows that ZIP Codes 12201-12288 are for the city of Albany. Looking back in the City/Parish Cross Reference, Albany is in Albany Parish.

City/Parish Cross Reference

ABBEVILLE Vermilion Parish
ABITA SPRINGS St. Tammany Parish
ACME Concordia Parish
ADDIS West Baton Rouge Parish
AIMWELL Catahoula Parish
AKERS Tangipahoa Parish
ALBANY Livingston Parish
ALEXANDRIA Rapides Parish
AMA St. Charles Parish
AMELIA St. Mary Parish
AMITE (70422) Tangipahoa Parish(70), St. Helena Parish(29)
ANACOCO (71403) Vernon Parish(97), Sabine Parish(2)
ANGIE Washington Parish
ANGOLA West Feliciana Parish
ARABI St. Bernard Parish
ARCADIA (71001) Bienville Parish(80), Lincoln Parish(9), Claiborne Parish(9)
ARCHIBALD Richland Parish
ARNAUDVILLE (70512) St. Landry Parish(59), St. Martin Parish(40)
ASHLAND Natchitoches Parish
ATHENS Claiborne Parish
ATLANTA (71404) Grant Parish(50), Winn Parish(49)
AVERY ISLAND Iberia Parish
BAKER East Baton Rouge Parish
BALDWIN St. Mary Parish
BALL Rapides Parish
BARATARIA Jefferson Parish
BARKSDALE AFB Bossier Parish
BASILE (70515) Acadia Parish(63), Evangeline Parish(36)
BASKIN Franklin Parish
BASTROP Morehouse Parish
BATCHELOR Pointe Coupee Parish
BATON ROUGE East Baton Rouge Parish
BAYOU GOULA Iberville Parish
BELCHER Caddo Parish
BELL CITY (70630) Calcasieu Parish(67), Cameron Parish(32)
BELLE CHASSE Plaquemines Parish
BELLE ROSE Assumption Parish
BELMONT Sabine Parish
BENTLEY Grant Parish
BENTON Bossier Parish
BERNICE (71222) Union Parish(80), Claiborne Parish(19)
BERWICK St. Mary Parish
BETHANY Caddo Parish
BIENVILLE Bienville Parish
BIG BEND Avoyelles Parish
BLANCHARD Caddo Parish
BLANKS Pointe Coupee Parish
BOGALUSA Washington Parish
BONITA Morehouse Parish
BOOTHVILLE Plaquemines Parish
BORDELONVILLE Avoyelles Parish
BOSSIER CITY Bossier Parish
BOURG (70343) Terrebonne Parish(82), Lafourche Parish(17)
BOUTTE St. Charles Parish

BOYCE Rapides Parish
BRAITHWAITE Plaquemines Parish
BRANCH Acadia Parish
BREAUX BRIDGE St. Martin Parish
BRITTANY Ascension Parish
BROUSSARD (70518) Lafayette Parish(88), St. Martin Parish(7), Iberia Parish(4)
BRUSLY West Baton Rouge Parish
BRYCELAND Bienville Parish
BUCKEYE Rapides Parish
BUECHE West Baton Rouge Parish
BUNKIE (71322) Avoyelles Parish(86), St. Landry Parish(12), Rapides Parish(1)
BURAS Plaquemines Parish
BURNSIDE Ascension Parish
BUSH St. Tammany Parish
CADE St. Martin Parish
CALHOUN Ouachita Parish
CALVIN Winn Parish
CAMERON Cameron Parish
CAMPTI Natchitoches Parish
CARENCRO (70520) Lafayette Parish(98), St. Landry Parish(1)
CARLISLE Plaquemines Parish
CARVILLE Iberville Parish
CASTOR Bienville Parish
CECILIA St. Martin Parish
CENTER POINT (71323) Avoyelles Parish(98), Rapides Parish(1)
CENTERVILLE St. Mary Parish
CHALMETTE St. Bernard Parish
CHARENTON St. Mary Parish
CHASE Franklin Parish
CHATAIGNIER Evangeline Parish
CHATHAM Jackson Parish
CHAUVIN Terrebonne Parish
CHENEYVILLE (71325) Rapides Parish(68), Evangeline Parish(31)
CHOPIN Natchitoches Parish
CHOUDRANT (71227) Lincoln Parish(64), Jackson Parish(28), Ouachita Parish(7)
CHURCH POINT (70525) Acadia Parish(82), St. Landry Parish(17)
CLARENCE Natchitoches Parish
CLARKS Caldwell Parish
CLAYTON (71326) Concordia Parish(54), Catahoula Parish(44), Tensas Parish(1)
CLINTON (70722) East Feliciana Parish(96), East Baton Rouge Parish(3)
CLOUTIERVILLE Natchitoches Parish
COLFAX Grant Parish
COLLINSTON (71229) Morehouse Parish(81), Ouachita Parish(18)
COLUMBIA (71418) Caldwell Parish(86), Richland Parish(8), Ouachita Parish(3), Catahoula Parish(1)
CONVENT St. James Parish
CONVERSE (71419) Sabine Parish(85), De Soto Parish(14)
COTTON VALLEY (71018) Webster Parish(86), Bossier Parish(13)
COTTONPORT Avoyelles Parish

COUSHATTA (71019) Red River Parish(87), Natchitoches Parish(12)
COVINGTON St. Tammany Parish
CREOLE Cameron Parish
CRESTON Natchitoches Parish
CROWLEY Acadia Parish
CROWVILLE Franklin Parish
CULLEN Webster Parish
CUT OFF Lafourche Parish
CYPRESS Natchitoches Parish
DARROW Ascension Parish
DAVANT Plaquemines Parish
DELCAMBRE (70528) Vermilion Parish(91), Iberia Parish(8)
DELHI (71232) Richland Parish(60), Franklin Parish(20), Madison Parish(19)
DELTA Madison Parish
DENHAM SPRINGS Livingston Parish
DEQUINCY Calcasieu Parish
DERIDDER (70634) Beauregard Parish(92), Vernon Parish(7)
DERRY Natchitoches Parish
DES ALLEMANDS (70030) St. Charles Parish(88), Lafourche Parish(11)
DESTREHAN St. Charles Parish
DEVILLE (71328) Rapides Parish(86), Avoyelles Parish(13)
DODSON Winn Parish
DONALDSONVILLE Ascension Parish
DONNER Terrebonne Parish
DOWNSVILLE (71234) Union Parish(80), Ouachita Parish(14), Lincoln Parish(5)
DOYLINE Webster Parish
DRY CREEK (70637) Beauregard Parish(73), Allen Parish(26)
DRY PRONG (71423) Grant Parish(96), Rapides Parish(3)
DUBACH (71235) Lincoln Parish(97), Claiborne Parish(1)
DUBBERLY Webster Parish
DULAC Terrebonne Parish
DUPLESSIS Ascension Parish
DUPONT Avoyelles Parish
DUSON Lafayette Parish
EAST POINT Red River Parish
ECHO Rapides Parish
EDGARD St. John the Baptist Parish
EFFIE Avoyelles Parish
EGAN Acadia Parish
ELIZABETH Allen Parish
ELM GROVE Bossier Parish
ELMER Rapides Parish
ELTON (70532) Jefferson Davis Parish(79), Allen Parish(20)
EMPIRE Plaquemines Parish
ENTERPRISE (71425) Catahoula Parish(70), Rapides Parish(29)
EPPS (71237) West Carroll Parish(83), Madison Parish(13), East Carroll Parish(3)
ERATH Vermilion Parish
EROS (71238) Ouachita Parish(52), Jackson Parish(47)

ERWINVILLE (70729) West Baton Rouge Parish(89), Pointe Coupee Parish(10)
ESTHERWOOD Acadia Parish
ETHEL East Feliciana Parish
EUNICE (70535) St. Landry Parish(94), Acadia Parish(4)
EVANGELINE Acadia Parish
EVANS Vernon Parish
EVERGREEN Avoyelles Parish
EXTENSION Franklin Parish
FAIRBANKS Ouachita Parish
FARMERVILLE Union Parish
FENTON Jefferson Davis Parish
FERRIDAY Concordia Parish
FISHER Sabine Parish
FLATWOODS (71427) Rapides Parish(75), Natchitoches Parish(24)
FLORA Natchitoches Parish
FLORIEN Sabine Parish
FLUKER (70436) Tangipahoa Parish(89), St. Helena Parish(10)
FOLSOM St. Tammany Parish
FORDOCHE Pointe Coupee Parish
FOREST West Carroll Parish
FOREST HILL Rapides Parish
FORT NECESSITY Franklin Parish
FRANKLIN St. Mary Parish
FRANKLINTON Washington Parish
FRENCH SETTLEMENT Livingston Parish
FRIERSON De Soto Parish
FROGMORE Concordia Parish
FULLERTON Vernon Parish
GALLIANO Lafourche Parish
GARDEN CITY St. Mary Parish
GARDNER Rapides Parish
GARYVILLE St. John the Baptist Parish
GEISMAR Ascension Parish
GEORGETOWN Grant Parish
GHEENS Lafourche Parish
GIBSLAND Bienville Parish
GIBSON Terrebonne Parish
GILBERT Franklin Parish
GILLIAM Caddo Parish
GLENMORA (71433) Rapides Parish(98), Allen Parish(1)
GLOSTER De Soto Parish
GLYNN (70736) Pointe Coupee Parish(98), West Baton Rouge Parish(1)
GOLDEN MEADOW Lafourche Parish
GOLDONNA (71031) Natchitoches Parish(53), Winn Parish(46)
GONZALES Ascension Parish
GORUM Natchitoches Parish
GOUDEAU Avoyelles Parish
GRAMBLING Lincoln Parish
GRAMERCY St. James Parish
GRAND CANE De Soto Parish
GRAND CHENIER Cameron Parish
GRAND COTEAU St. Landry Parish
GRAND ISLE Jefferson Parish
GRANT Allen Parish
GRAY Terrebonne Parish

GRAYSON (71435) Caldwell Parish(98), Catahoula Parish(1)
GREENSBURG St. Helena Parish
GREENWELL SPRINGS East Baton Rouge Parish
GREENWOOD Caddo Parish
GRETNA Jefferson Parish
GROSSE TETE Iberville Parish
GUEYDAN (70542) Vermilion Parish(95), Cameron Parish(4)
HACKBERRY Cameron Parish
HAHNVILLE St. Charles Parish
HALL SUMMIT Red River Parish
HAMBURG Avoyelles Parish
HAMMOND Tangipahoa Parish
HARMON Red River Parish
HARRISONBURG Catahoula Parish
HARVEY Jefferson Parish
HAUGHTON Bossier Parish
HAYES Calcasieu Parish
HAYNESVILLE Claiborne Parish
HEBERT Caldwell Parish
HEFLIN (71039) Webster Parish(79), Bienville Parish(20)
HESSMER Avoyelles Parish
HESTER St. James Parish
HICKS Vernon Parish
HINESTON (71438) Rapides Parish(82), Vernon Parish(17)
HODGE Jackson Parish
HOLDEN (70744) Livingston Parish(95), St. Helena Parish(4)
HOMER Claiborne Parish
HORNBECK (71439) Vernon Parish(78), Sabine Parish(21)
HOSSTON Caddo Parish
HOUMA (70364) Terrebonne Parish(82), Lafourche Parish(17)
HUSSER Tangipahoa Parish
IDA Caddo Parish
INDEPENDENCE (70443) Tangipahoa Parish(49), Livingston Parish(31), St. Helena Parish(18)
INNIS Pointe Coupee Parish
IOTA Acadia Parish
IOWA Calcasieu Parish
JACKSON (70748) East Feliciana Parish(75), West Feliciana Parish(21), East Baton Rouge Parish(2)
JAMESTOWN Bienville Parish
JARREAU Pointe Coupee Parish
JEANERETTE (70544) Iberia Parish(85), St. Mary Parish(14)
JENA La Salle Parish
JENNINGS (70546) Jefferson Davis Parish(97), Acadia Parish(2)
JIGGER Franklin Parish
JONES Morehouse Parish
JONESBORO (71251) Jackson Parish(94), Bienville Parish(5)
JONESVILLE (71343) Catahoula Parish(88), Concordia Parish(11)
JOYCE Winn Parish
KAPLAN Vermilion Parish
KEATCHIE De Soto Parish
KEITHVILLE Caddo Parish
KELLY (71441) Caldwell Parish(82), La Salle Parish(17)
KENNER Jefferson Parish
KENTWOOD (70444) Tangipahoa Parish(85), St. Helena Parish(14)
KILBOURNE West Carroll Parish
KILLONA St. Charles Parish
KINDER (70648) Allen Parish(98), Jefferson Davis Parish(1)
KRAEMER Lafourche Parish
KROTZ SPRINGS St. Landry Parish
KURTHWOOD Vernon Parish
LA PLACE St. John the Baptist Parish
LABADIEVILLE Assumption Parish
LABARRE Pointe Coupee Parish
LACAMP Vernon Parish

LACASSINE Jefferson Davis Parish
LACOMBE St. Tammany Parish
LAFAYETTE Lafayette Parish
LAFITTE Jefferson Parish
LAKE ARTHUR (70549) Jefferson Davis Parish(97), Cameron Parish(2)
LAKE CHARLES Calcasieu Parish
LAKE PROVIDENCE East Carroll Parish
LAKELAND Pointe Coupee Parish
LAROSE Lafourche Parish
LARTO Catahoula Parish
LAWTELL St. Landry Parish
LE MOYEN St. Landry Parish
LEANDER Vernon Parish
LEBEAU St. Landry Parish
LEBLANC Allen Parish
LECOMPTE Rapides Parish
LEESVILLE Vernon Parish
LENA (71447) Rapides Parish(53), Natchitoches Parish(46)
LEONVILLE St. Landry Parish
LETTSWORTH Pointe Coupee Parish
LIBUSE Rapides Parish
LILLIE (71256) Union Parish(95), Claiborne Parish(4)
LISBON Claiborne Parish
LIVINGSTON Livingston Parish
LIVONIA Pointe Coupee Parish
LOCKPORT Lafourche Parish
LOGANSPORT De Soto Parish
LONGLEAF Rapides Parish
LONGSTREET De Soto Parish
LONGVILLE Beauregard Parish
LORANGER Tangipahoa Parish
LOREAUVILLE Iberia Parish
LOTTIE Pointe Coupee Parish
LULING St. Charles Parish
LUTCHER St. James Parish
LYDIA Iberia Parish
MADISONVILLE St. Tammany Parish
MAMOU Evangeline Parish
MANDEVILLE St. Tammany Parish
MANGHAM Richland Parish
MANSFIELD De Soto Parish
MANSURA Avoyelles Parish
MANY Sabine Parish
MARINGOUIN Iberville Parish
MARION Union Parish
MARKSVILLE Avoyelles Parish
MARRERO Jefferson Parish
MARTHAVILLE (71450) Natchitoches Parish(67), Sabine Parish(32)
MATHEWS Lafourche Parish
MAUREPAS (70449) Livingston Parish(98), Ascension Parish(1)
MAURICE (70555) Vermilion Parish(96), Lafayette Parish(3)
MELDER Rapides Parish
MELROSE Natchitoches Parish
MELVILLE St. Landry Parish
MER ROUGE Morehouse Parish
MERAUX St. Bernard Parish
MERMENTAU Acadia Parish
MERRYVILLE Beauregard Parish
METAIRIE Jefferson Parish
MILTON Lafayette Parish
MINDEN Webster Parish
MIRA Caddo Parish
MITTIE Allen Parish
MODESTE Ascension Parish
MONROE Ouachita Parish
MONTEGUT (70377) Terrebonne Parish(89), Lafourche Parish(10)
MONTEREY Concordia Parish
MONTGOMERY (71454) Grant Parish(81), Winn Parish(18)
MOORINGSPORT Caddo Parish
MORA (71455) Rapides Parish(98), Natchitoches Parish(1)
MOREAUVILLE Avoyelles Parish
MORGAN CITY St. Mary Parish
MORGANZA Pointe Coupee Parish

MORROW (71356) St. Landry Parish(55), Avoyelles Parish(44)
MORSE Acadia Parish
MOUNT AIRY St. John the Baptist Parish
MOUNT HERMON Washington Parish
NAPOLEONVILLE Assumption Parish
NATALBANY Tangipahoa Parish
NATCHEZ Natchitoches Parish
NATCHITOCHES Natchitoches Parish
NEGREET Sabine Parish
NEW IBERIA Iberia Parish
NEW ORLEANS Orleans Parish
NEW ROADS Pointe Coupee Parish
NEW SARPY St. Charles Parish
NEWELLTON Tensas Parish
NEWLLANO Vernon Parish
NOBLE Sabine Parish
NORCO St. Charles Parish
NORWOOD East Feliciana Parish
OAK GROVE West Carroll Parish
OAK RIDGE (71264) Morehouse Parish(78), Richland Parish(21)
OAKDALE (71463) Allen Parish(89), Evangeline Parish(6), Rapides Parish(4)
OBERLIN Allen Parish
OIL CITY Caddo Parish
OLLA (71465) La Salle Parish(86), Winn Parish(10), Caldwell Parish(2)
OPELOUSAS St. Landry Parish
OSCAR Pointe Coupee Parish
OTIS Rapides Parish
PAINCOURTVILLE Assumption Parish
PALMETTO St. Landry Parish
PARADIS St. Charles Parish
PATTERSON St. Mary Parish
PAULINA St. James Parish
PEARL RIVER St. Tammany Parish
PELICAN De Soto Parish
PERRY Vermilion Parish
PIERRE PART (70339) Assumption Parish(92), St. Martin Parish(7)
PILOTTOWN Plaquemines Parish
PINE GROVE (70453) St. Helena Parish(85), Livingston Parish(14)
PINE PRAIRIE Evangeline Parish
PINEVILLE Rapides Parish
PIONEER West Carroll Parish
PITKIN (70656) Vernon Parish(59), Rapides Parish(22), Allen Parish(18)
PLAIN DEALING Bossier Parish
PLAQUEMINE Iberville Parish
PLATTENVILLE Assumption Parish
PLAUCHEVILLE Avoyelles Parish
PLEASANT HILL (71065) Sabine Parish(97), Natchitoches Parish(2)
POINTE A LA HACHE Plaquemines Parish
POLLOCK Grant Parish
PONCHATOULA Tangipahoa Parish
PORT ALLEN West Baton Rouge Parish
PORT BARRE St. Landry Parish
PORT SULPHUR Plaquemines Parish
POWHATAN Natchitoches Parish
PRAIRIEVILLE Ascension Parish
PRIDE East Baton Rouge Parish
PRINCETON Bossier Parish
PROVENCAL Natchitoches Parish
QUITMAN (71268) Jackson Parish(79), Bienville Parish(20)
RACELAND Lafourche Parish
RAGLEY (70657) Beauregard Parish(85), Allen Parish(13)
RAYNE (70578) Acadia Parish(90), Vermilion Parish(5), Lafayette Parish(4)
RAYVILLE Richland Parish
REDDELL Evangeline Parish
REEVES Allen Parish
RESERVE St. John the Baptist Parish
RHINEHART Catahoula Parish
RINGGOLD (71068) Bienville Parish(93), Red River Parish(6)
ROANOKE Jefferson Davis Parish

ROBELINE (71469) Natchitoches Parish(76), Sabine Parish(23)
ROBERT Tangipahoa Parish
RODESSA Caddo Parish
ROSA St. Landry Parish
ROSEDALE Iberville Parish
ROSELAND Tangipahoa Parish
ROSEPINE Vernon Parish
ROUGON Pointe Coupee Parish
RUBY Rapides Parish
RUSTON Lincoln Parish
SAINT AMANT Ascension Parish
SAINT BENEDICT St. Tammany Parish
SAINT BERNARD St. Bernard Parish
SAINT FRANCISVILLE West Feliciana Parish
SAINT GABRIEL Iberville Parish
SAINT JAMES St. James Parish
SAINT JOSEPH Tensas Parish
SAINT LANDRY Evangeline Parish
SAINT MARTINVILLE St. Martin Parish
SAINT MAURICE Winn Parish
SAINT ROSE St. Charles Parish
SALINE (71070) Natchitoches Parish(61), Bienville Parish(38)
SAREPTA (71071) Webster Parish(95), Bossier Parish(4)
SCHRIEVER Terrebonne Parish
SCOTT (70583) Lafayette Parish(94), Acadia Parish(5)
SHONGALOO Webster Parish
SHREVEPORT Caddo Parish
SIBLEY Webster Parish
SICILY ISLAND Catahoula Parish
SIEPER Rapides Parish
SIKES Winn Parish
SIMMESPORT Avoyelles Parish
SIMPSON Vernon Parish
SIMSBORO (71275) Lincoln Parish(85), Bienville Parish(14)
SINGER Beauregard Parish
SLAGLE Vernon Parish
SLAUGHTER East Feliciana Parish
SLIDELL St. Tammany Parish
SONDHEIMER (71276) East Carroll Parish(95), Madison Parish(4)
SORRENTO Ascension Parish
SPEARSVILLE Union Parish
SPRINGFIELD (70462) Livingston Parish(88), Tangipahoa Parish(11)
SPRINGHILL (71075) Webster Parish(96), Bossier Parish(3)
STARKS Calcasieu Parish
START Richland Parish
STERLINGTON (71280) Ouachita Parish(52), Union Parish(47)
STONEWALL De Soto Parish
SUGARTOWN Beauregard Parish
SULPHUR Calcasieu Parish
SUMMERFIELD Claiborne Parish
SUN St. Tammany Parish
SUNSET St. Landry Parish
SUNSHINE Iberville Parish
SWARTZ Ouachita Parish
TALISHEEK St. Tammany Parish
TALLULAH Madison Parish
TANGIPAHOA Tangipahoa Parish
TAYLOR Bienville Parish
THERIOT Terrebonne Parish
THIBODAUX Lafourche Parish
TICKFAW Tangipahoa Parish
TIOGA Rapides Parish
TORBERT Pointe Coupee Parish
TRANSYLVANIA East Carroll Parish
TROUT La Salle Parish
TULLOS (71479) Winn Parish(65), La Salle Parish(34)
TUNICA West Feliciana Parish
TURKEY CREEK Evangeline Parish
UNCLE SAM St. James Parish
URANIA La Salle Parish

VACHERIE (70090) St. James Parish(76), St. John the Baptist Parish(23)
VENICE Plaquemines Parish
VENTRESS Pointe Coupee Parish
VERDA Grant Parish
VICK Avoyelles Parish
VIDALIA Concordia Parish
VILLE PLATTE Evangeline Parish
VINTON Calcasieu Parish

VIOLET St. Bernard Parish
VIVIAN Caddo Parish
WAKEFIELD West Feliciana Parish
WALKER Livingston Parish
WASHINGTON (70589) St. Landry Parish(91), Evangeline Parish(8)
WATERPROOF Tensas Parish
WATSON Livingston Parish
WELSH Jefferson Davis Parish

WEST MONROE Ouachita Parish
WESTLAKE Calcasieu Parish
WESTWEGO Jefferson Parish
WEYANOKE West Feliciana Parish
WHITE CASTLE Iberville Parish
WILDSVILLE Concordia Parish
WILSON East Feliciana Parish
WINNFIELD Winn Parish
WINNSBORO Franklin Parish

WISNER Franklin Parish
WOODWORTH Rapides Parish
YOUNGSVILLE (70592) Lafayette Parish(80), Vermilion Parish(12), Iberia Parish(6)
ZACHARY East Baton Rouge Parish
ZWOLLE Sabine Parish

ZIP/City Cross Reference

ZIP Range	City
70001-70011	METAIRIE
70030-70030	DES ALLEMANDS
70031-70031	AMA
70032-70032	ARABI
70033-70033	METAIRIE
70036-70036	BARATARIA
70037-70037	BELLE CHASSE
70038-70038	BOOTHVILLE
70039-70039	BOUTTE
70040-70040	BRAITHWAITE
70041-70041	BURAS
70042-70042	CARLISLE
70043-70044	CHALMETTE
70046-70046	DAVANT
70047-70047	DESTREHAN
70049-70049	EDGARD
70050-70050	EMPIRE
70051-70051	GARYVILLE
70052-70052	GRAMERCY
70053-70054	GRETNA
70055-70055	METAIRIE
70056-70056	GRETNA
70057-70057	HAHNVILLE
70058-70059	HARVEY
70060-70060	METAIRIE
70062-70065	KENNER
70066-70066	KILLONA
70067-70067	LAFITTE
70068-70069	LA PLACE
70070-70070	LULING
70071-70071	LUTCHER
70072-70073	MARRERO
70075-70075	MERAUX
70076-70076	MOUNT AIRY
70078-70078	NEW SARPY
70079-70079	NORCO
70080-70080	PARADIS
70081-70081	PILOTTOWN
70082-70082	POINTE A LA HACHE
70083-70083	PORT SULPHUR
70084-70084	RESERVE
70085-70085	SAINT BERNARD
70086-70086	SAINT JAMES
70087-70087	SAINT ROSE
70090-70090	VACHERIE
70091-70091	VENICE
70092-70092	VIOLET
70094-70096	WESTWEGO
70100-70195	NEW ORLEANS
70301-70310	THIBODAUX
70339-70339	PIERRE PART
70340-70340	AMELIA
70341-70341	BELLE ROSE
70342-70342	BERWICK
70343-70343	BOURG
70344-70344	CHAUVIN
70345-70345	CUT OFF
70346-70346	DONALDSONVILLE
70352-70352	DONNER
70353-70353	DULAC
70354-70354	GALLIANO
70355-70355	GHEENS
70356-70356	GIBSON
70357-70357	GOLDEN MEADOW
70358-70358	GRAND ISLE
70359-70359	GRAY
70360-70364	HOUMA
70371-70371	KRAEMER
70372-70372	LABADIEVILLE
70373-70373	LAROSE
70374-70374	LOCKPORT
70375-70375	MATHEWS
70376-70376	MODESTE
70377-70377	MONTEGUT
70380-70381	MORGAN CITY
70390-70390	NAPOLEONVILLE
70391-70391	PAINCOURTVILLE
70392-70392	PATTERSON
70393-70393	PLATTENVILLE
70394-70394	RACELAND
70395-70395	SCHRIEVER
70397-70397	THERIOT
70401-70404	HAMMOND
70420-70420	ABITA SPRINGS
70421-70421	AKERS
70422-70422	AMITE
70426-70426	ANGIE
70427-70429	BOGALUSA
70431-70431	BUSH
70433-70435	COVINGTON
70436-70436	FLUKER
70437-70437	FOLSOM
70438-70438	FRANKLINTON
70441-70441	GREENSBURG
70442-70442	HUSSER
70443-70443	INDEPENDENCE
70444-70444	KENTWOOD
70445-70445	LACOMBE
70446-70446	LORANGER
70447-70447	MADISONVILLE
70448-70448	MANDEVILLE
70449-70449	MAUREPAS
70450-70450	MOUNT HERMON
70451-70451	NATALBANY
70452-70452	PEARL RIVER
70453-70453	PINE GROVE
70454-70454	PONCHATOULA
70455-70455	ROBERT
70456-70456	ROSELAND
70457-70457	SAINT BENEDICT
70458-70461	SLIDELL
70462-70462	SPRINGFIELD
70463-70463	SUN
70464-70464	TALISHEEK
70465-70465	TANGIPAHOA
70466-70466	TICKFAW
70467-70467	ANGIE
70469-70469	SLIDELL
70470-70471	MANDEVILLE
70501-70509	LAFAYETTE
70510-70511	ABBEVILLE
70512-70512	ARNAUDVILLE
70513-70513	AVERY ISLAND
70514-70514	BALDWIN
70515-70515	BASILE
70516-70516	BRANCH
70517-70517	BREAUX BRIDGE
70518-70518	BROUSSARD
70519-70519	CADE
70520-70520	CARENCRO
70521-70521	CECILIA
70522-70522	CENTERVILLE
70523-70523	CHARENTON
70524-70524	CHATAIGNIER
70525-70525	CHURCH POINT
70526-70527	CROWLEY
70528-70528	DELCAMBRE
70529-70529	DUSON
70531-70531	EGAN
70532-70532	ELTON
70533-70533	ERATH
70534-70534	ESTHERWOOD
70535-70535	EUNICE
70537-70537	EVANGELINE
70538-70538	FRANKLIN
70540-70540	GARDEN CITY
70541-70541	GRAND COTEAU
70542-70542	GUEYDAN
70543-70543	IOTA
70544-70544	JEANERETTE
70546-70546	JENNINGS
70548-70548	KAPLAN
70549-70549	LAKE ARTHUR
70550-70550	LAWTELL
70551-70551	LEONVILLE
70552-70552	LOREAUVILLE
70554-70554	MAMOU
70555-70555	MAURICE
70556-70556	MERMENTAU
70558-70558	MILTON
70559-70559	MORSE
70560-70563	NEW IBERIA
70569-70569	LYDIA
70570-70571	OPELOUSAS
70575-70575	PERRY
70576-70576	PINE PRAIRIE
70577-70577	PORT BARRE
70578-70578	RAYNE
70580-70580	REDDELL
70581-70581	ROANOKE
70582-70582	SAINT MARTINVILLE
70583-70583	SCOTT
70584-70584	SUNSET
70585-70585	TURKEY CREEK
70586-70586	VILLE PLATTE
70589-70589	WASHINGTON
70591-70591	WELSH
70592-70592	YOUNGSVILLE
70593-70598	LAFAYETTE
70601-70629	LAKE CHARLES
70630-70630	BELL CITY
70631-70631	CAMERON
70632-70632	CREOLE
70633-70633	DEQUINCY
70634-70634	DERIDDER
70637-70637	DRY CREEK
70638-70638	ELIZABETH
70639-70639	EVANS
70640-70640	FENTON
70642-70642	FULLERTON
70643-70643	GRAND CHENIER
70644-70644	GRANT
70645-70645	HACKBERRY
70646-70646	HAYES
70647-70647	IOWA
70648-70648	KINDER
70650-70650	LACASSINE
70651-70651	LEBLANC
70652-70652	LONGVILLE
70653-70653	MERRYVILLE
70654-70654	MITTIE
70655-70655	OBERLIN
70656-70656	PITKIN
70657-70657	RAGLEY
70658-70658	REEVES
70659-70659	ROSEPINE
70660-70660	SINGER
70661-70661	STARKS
70662-70662	SUGARTOWN
70663-70665	SULPHUR
70668-70668	VINTON
70669-70669	WESTLAKE
70704-70704	BAKER
70706-70706	DENHAM SPRINGS
70707-70707	GONZALES
70710-70710	ADDIS
70711-70711	ALBANY
70712-70712	ANGOLA
70714-70714	BAKER
70715-70715	BATCHELOR
70716-70716	BAYOU GOULA
70717-70717	BLANKS
70718-70718	BRITTANY
70719-70719	BRUSLY
70720-70720	BUECHE
70721-70721	CARVILLE
70722-70722	CLINTON
70723-70723	CONVENT
70725-70725	DARROW
70726-70727	DENHAM SPRINGS
70728-70728	DUPLESSIS
70729-70729	ERWINVILLE
70730-70730	ETHEL
70732-70732	FORDOCHE
70733-70733	FRENCH SETTLEMENT
70734-70734	GEISMAR
70736-70736	GLYNN
70737-70737	GONZALES
70738-70738	BURNSIDE
70739-70739	GREENWELL SPRINGS
70740-70740	GROSSE TETE
70743-70743	HESTER
70744-70744	HOLDEN
70747-70747	INNIS
70748-70748	JACKSON
70749-70749	JARREAU
70750-70750	KROTZ SPRINGS
70751-70751	LABARRE
70752-70752	LAKELAND
70753-70753	LETTSWORTH
70754-70754	LIVINGSTON
70755-70755	LIVONIA
70756-70756	LOTTIE
70757-70757	MARINGOUIN
70759-70759	MORGANZA
70760-70760	NEW ROADS
70761-70761	NORWOOD
70762-70762	OSCAR
70763-70763	PAULINA
70764-70765	PLAQUEMINE
70767-70767	PORT ALLEN
70769-70769	PRAIRIEVILLE
70770-70770	PRIDE
70772-70772	ROSEDALE
70773-70773	ROUGON
70774-70774	SAINT AMANT
70775-70775	SAINT FRANCISVILLE
70776-70776	SAINT GABRIEL
70777-70777	SLAUGHTER
70778-70778	SORRENTO
70780-70780	SUNSHINE
70781-70781	TORBERT
70782-70782	TUNICA
70783-70783	VENTRESS
70784-70784	WAKEFIELD
70785-70785	WALKER

70786-70786 WATSON	71078-71078 STONEWALL	71322-71322 BUNKIE	71419-71419 CONVERSE
70787-70787 WEYANOKE	71079-71079 SUMMERFIELD	71323-71323 CENTER POINT	71420-71420 CYPRESS
70788-70788 WHITE CASTLE	71080-71080 TAYLOR	71324-71324 CHASE	71421-71421 DERRY
70789-70789 WILSON	71082-71082 VIVIAN	71325-71325 CHENEYVILLE	71422-71422 DODSON
70791-70791 ZACHARY	71101-71109 SHREVEPORT	71326-71326 CLAYTON	71423-71423 DRY PRONG
70792-70792 UNCLE SAM	71110-71110 BARKSDALE AFB	71327-71327 COTTONPORT	71424-71424 ELMER
70800-70898 BATON ROUGE	71111-71113 BOSSIER CITY	71328-71328 DEVILLE	71425-71425 ENTERPRISE
71001-71001 ARCADIA	71115-71166 SHREVEPORT	71329-71329 DUPONT	71426-71426 FISHER
71002-71002 ASHLAND	71171-71172 BOSSIER CITY	71330-71330 ECHO	71427-71427 FLATWOODS
71003-71003 ATHENS	71201-71213 MONROE	71331-71331 EFFIE	71428-71428 FLORA
71004-71004 BELCHER	71218-71218 ARCHIBALD	71333-71333 EVERGREEN	71429-71429 FLORIEN
71006-71006 BENTON	71219-71219 BASKIN	71334-71334 FERRIDAY	71430-71430 FOREST HILL
71007-71007 BETHANY	71220-71221 BASTROP	71335-71335 FROGMORE	71431-71431 GARDNER
71008-71008 BIENVILLE	71222-71222 BERNICE	71336-71336 GILBERT	71432-71432 GEORGETOWN
71009-71009 BLANCHARD	71223-71223 BONITA	71338-71338 GOUDEAU	71433-71433 GLENMORA
71014-71014 BRYCELAND	71225-71225 CALHOUN	71339-71339 HAMBURG	71434-71434 GORUM
71016-71016 CASTOR	71226-71226 CHATHAM	71340-71340 HARRISONBURG	71435-71435 GRAYSON
71018-71018 COTTON VALLEY	71227-71227 CHOUDRANT	71341-71341 HESSMER	71436-71436 HEBERT
71019-71019 COUSHATTA	71229-71229 COLLINSTON	71342-71342 JENA	71437-71437 HICKS
71020-71020 CRESTON	71230-71230 CROWVILLE	71343-71343 JONESVILLE	71438-71438 HINESTON
71021-71021 CULLEN	71232-71232 DELHI	71344-71344 LARTO	71439-71439 HORNBECK
71023-71023 DOYLINE	71233-71233 DELTA	71345-71345 LEBEAU	71440-71440 JOYCE
71024-71024 DUBBERLY	71234-71234 DOWNSVILLE	71346-71346 LECOMPTE	71441-71441 KELLY
71025-71025 EAST POINT	71235-71235 DUBACH	71347-71347 LE MOYEN	71443-71443 KURTHWOOD
71027-71027 FRIERSON	71237-71237 EPPS	71348-71348 LIBUSE	71444-71444 LACAMP
71028-71028 GIBSLAND	71238-71238 EROS	71350-71350 MANSURA	71445-71445 LEANDER
71029-71029 GILLIAM	71239-71239 EXTENSION	71351-71351 MARKSVILLE	71446-71446 LEESVILLE
71030-71030 GLOSTER	71240-71240 FAIRBANKS	71353-71353 MELVILLE	71447-71447 LENA
71031-71031 GOLDONNA	71241-71241 FARMERVILLE	71354-71354 MONTEREY	71448-71448 LONGLEAF
71032-71032 GRAND CANE	71242-71242 FOREST	71355-71355 MOREAUVILLE	71449-71449 MANY
71033-71033 GREENWOOD	71243-71243 FORT NECESSITY	71356-71356 MORROW	71450-71450 MARTHAVILLE
71034-71034 HALL SUMMIT	71245-71245 GRAMBLING	71357-71357 NEWELLTON	71451-71451 MELDER
71036-71036 HARMON	71247-71247 HODGE	71358-71358 PALMETTO	71452-71452 MELROSE
71037-71037 HAUGHTON	71249-71249 JIGGER	71359-71361 PINEVILLE	71454-71454 MONTGOMERY
71038-71038 HAYNESVILLE	71250-71250 JONES	71362-71362 PLAUCHEVILLE	71455-71455 MORA
71039-71039 HEFLIN	71251-71251 JONESBORO	71363-71363 RHINEHART	71456-71456 NATCHEZ
71040-71040 HOMER	71253-71253 KILBOURNE	71364-71364 ROSA	71457-71458 NATCHITOCHES
71043-71043 HOSSTON	71254-71254 LAKE PROVIDENCE	71365-71365 RUBY	71459-71459 LEESVILLE
71044-71044 IDA	71256-71256 LILLIE	71366-71366 SAINT JOSEPH	71460-71460 NEGREET
71045-71045 JAMESTOWN	71259-71259 MANGHAM	71367-71367 SAINT LANDRY	71461-71461 NEWLLANO
71046-71046 KEATCHIE	71260-71260 MARION	71368-71368 SICILY ISLAND	71462-71462 NOBLE
71047-71047 KEITHVILLE	71261-71261 MER ROUGE	71369-71369 SIMMESPORT	71463-71463 OAKDALE
71048-71048 LISBON	71263-71263 OAK GROVE	71371-71371 TROUT	71465-71465 OLLA
71049-71049 LOGANSPORT	71264-71264 OAK RIDGE	71372-71372 VICK	71466-71466 OTIS
71050-71050 LONGSTREET	71266-71266 PIONEER	71373-71373 VIDALIA	71467-71467 POLLOCK
71051-71051 ELM GROVE	71268-71268 QUITMAN	71375-71375 WATERPROOF	71468-71468 PROVENCAL
71052-71052 MANSFIELD	71269-71269 RAYVILLE	71377-71377 WILDSVILLE	71469-71469 ROBELINE
71055-71058 MINDEN	71270-71273 RUSTON	71378-71378 WISNER	71471-71471 SAINT MAURICE
71059-71059 MIRA	71275-71275 SIMSBORO	71401-71401 AIMWELL	71472-71472 SIEPER
71060-71060 MOORINGSPORT	71276-71276 SONDHEIMER	71403-71403 ANACOCO	71473-71473 SIKES
71061-71061 OIL CITY	71277-71277 SPEARSVILLE	71404-71404 ATLANTA	71474-71474 SIMPSON
71063-71063 PELICAN	71279-71279 START	71405-71405 BALL	71475-71475 SLAGLE
71064-71064 PLAIN DEALING	71280-71280 STERLINGTON	71406-71406 BELMONT	71477-71477 TIOGA
71065-71065 PLEASANT HILL	71281-71281 SWARTZ	71407-71407 BENTLEY	71479-71479 TULLOS
71066-71066 POWHATAN	71282-71284 TALLULAH	71409-71409 BOYCE	71480-71480 URANIA
71067-71067 PRINCETON	71286-71286 TRANSYLVANIA	71410-71410 CALVIN	71481-71481 VERDA
71068-71068 RINGGOLD	71291-71294 WEST MONROE	71411-71411 CAMPTI	71483-71483 WINNFIELD
71069-71069 RODESSA	71295-71295 WINNSBORO	71412-71412 CHOPIN	71485-71485 WOODWORTH
71070-71070 SALINE	71301-71315 ALEXANDRIA	71414-71414 CLARENCE	71486-71486 ZWOLLE
71071-71071 SAREPTA	71316-71316 ACME	71415-71415 CLARKS	71496-71496 LEESVILLE
71072-71072 SHONGALOO	71318-71318 BIG BEND	71416-71416 CLOUTIERVILLE	71497-71497 NATCHITOCHES
71073-71073 SIBLEY	71320-71320 BORDELONVILLE	71417-71417 COLFAX	
71075-71075 SPRINGHILL	71321-71321 BUCKEYE	71418-71418 COLUMBIA	

General Help Numbers:

Governor's Office

1 State House Station, Room 236   207-287-3531
Augusta, ME 04333-0001   Fax 207-287-1034
www.state.me.us/governor   7:30AM-5:30PM

Attorney General's Office

6 State House Station   207-626-8800
Augusta, ME 04333   Fax 207-626-8828
www.state.me.us/ag   8AM-5PM

State Court Administrator

PO Box 4820   207-822-0792
Portland, ME 04112   Fax 207-822-0781
www.courts.state.me.us   8AM-4PM

State Archives

84 State House Station   207-287-5795
Augusta, ME 04333-0084   Fax 207-287-5739
www.state.me.us/sos/arc   8:30AM-4PM

State Specifics:

Capital: Augusta
                                         Kennebec County

Time Zone: EST

Number of Counties: 16

Population: 1,286,670

Web Site: www.state.me.us

State Agencies

Criminal Records

Maine State Police, State Bureau of Identification, 42 State House Station, Augusta, ME 04333; 207-624-7009, 207-624-7088 (Fax), 8AM-5PM.

www.state.me.us/dps/

Note: The sex offender registry can be requested by fax; no fee required. The registry should be available electonically in late 2002 or early 2003.

Indexing & Storage: Records are available from 1937 on. It takes 1 to 2 days before new records are available for inquiry. Records are indexed on computer (43%) and court index cards. Records are normally destroyed after 99 years, if no activity within last five years. 90% of all arrests in database have final dispositions recorded, 90% for those arrests within last 5 years.

Searching: Requests must be in writing. Submit one name per page (otherwise list could be held or sent back). Will not do FBI fingerprint checks. Include the following in your request: name, date of birth, any aliases. Fingerprints are optional. Include maiden name for females. Also include purpose of the inquiry and name and address of requester. 35% of the records are fingerprint-supported. Fingerprints are not submitted with arrest information to this agency by the courts or police. The following data is not released: juvenile records. All convictions and all pending cases less than 1 year old are reported, or if the case has not yet been adjudicated in court.

Access by: mail, in person.

Fee & Payment: The search fee is $8.00 per individual. Fee payee: Treasurer, State of Maine. Personal checks accepted. No credit cards accepted.

Mail search: Normal turnaround time is less than one week, those records with "hits" may take slightly longer to process. A self addressed stamped envelope is requested. Search costs $8.00 per individual.

In person search: This only saves mail-in time; records are returned by mail.

Corporation Records
Limited Partnerships
Trademarks/Servicemarks
Assumed Name
Limited Liability Company
Records
Limited Liability
Partnerships

Secretary of State, Reports & Information Division, 101 State House Station, Augusta, ME 04333-0101; 207-624-7752, 207-624-7736 (Main Number), 207-287-5874 (Fax), 8AM-5PM.

www.state.me.us/sos/cec/corp

Indexing & Storage: Records are available from 1700's on. The older records are in law books. Records on the in-house computer are for all active and some inactive corporations. New records are available for inquiry immediately. Records are indexed on index cards, inhouse computer.

Searching: Include the following in your request: full name of business, specific records that you need copies of. In addition to the articles of incorporation, corporation records include the following information: Annual Reports (back to 1972), Officers, Directors, Prior (merged) names, Inactive and Reserved names.

Access by: mail, phone, in person, online.

Fee & Payment: Copies are $2.00 per page if plain and $5.00 if certified. A Good Standing is $25.00 short form, $35.00 long form and $10.00 if not for profit. Fee payee: Secretary of State. They will invoice for copies. Personal checks accepted. No credit cards accepted.

Mail search: Turnaround time: 1 week. No self addressed stamped envelope is required.

Phone search: They will provide names and addresses of officers and directors over the phone.

In person search: Searching is available in person.

Online search: The Internet site gives basic information about the entity including address, corp ID, agent, and status.

Other access: Lists of new entities filed with this office are available monthly.

Expedited service: Expedited service is available for mail and phone searches. Turnaround time: 24 hours. Add $50.00 per business name. For immediate service, the fee is $100.00.

Uniform Commercial Code
Federal Tax Liens
State Tax Liens

UCC Filing Section, Secretary of State, 101 State House Station, Augusta, ME 04333-0101 (Courier: Burton McCross State Office Bldg, 109 Sewell St, 4th Fl, Augusta, ME 04333); 207-624-7760, 207-287-5874 (Fax), 8AM-5PM.

www.state.me.us/sos/cec/corp/ucc.htm#fi111

Indexing & Storage: Records are available from 1964. Records are computerized since 1993. Records are indexed on inhouse computer.

Searching: Use search request form UCC-11 when needed for certification or a form fabricated by this office. The search includes both federal and state tax liens. Include the following in your request: debtor name. Try to include a middle initial in your request. Searching is done by index number or debtor name only. They will not search by address or collateral or secured party.

Access by: mail, phone, fax, in person, online.

Fee & Payment: Searches cost $20.00 per name. Certification is $5.00. Fee payee: State Treasurer. Prepayment required. Ongoing requesters may make arrangements for invoicing. Personal checks accepted. No credit cards accepted.

Mail search: Turnaround time: a maximum of 5 days. If update or certain dates requested, state boldly. No self addressed stamped envelope is required.

Phone search: Limited information is available by phone.

Fax search: Same criteria as mail requests. Up to 15 pages will be returned as long as request is in writing.

In person search: There are 3 public access terminals. If copies are needed, written request required and fees apply.

Online search: Online access is available at https://www.informe.org/ucc/search/begin.shtml. There is a free name search, and reports may be ordered online, also.

Other access: Farm products - buyers reports, secured party available in bulk.

Expedited service: Expedited service is available for mail and phone searches. Turnaround time: 1 day. Add $10.00 per name. Write and highlight the word "Expedite" on the search request. For immediate turnaround, the fee is $25.00.

Sales Tax Registrations

Maine Revenue Services, Sales, Fuel & Special Tax Division, 24 State House Station, Augusta, ME 04333; 207-624-9693, 207-287-6628 (Fax), 8AM-4PM.

www.state.me.us/revenue

Indexing & Storage: Records are available from 1993, on computer. It takes up to 2 months before new records are available for inquiry.

Searching: This agency will only confirm that a business is registered. They will provide no other information. Include the following in your request: business name. They will also search by tax permit number or federal ID.

Access by: mail, phone, fax, in person.

Mail search: Turnaround time: 7 to 10 days. A self addressed stamped envelope is requested. No fee for mail request.

Phone search: No fee for telephone request.

Fax search: Same criteria as mail searching.

In person search: No fee for request.

Birth Certificates

Maine Department of Human Services, Vital Records, 221 State St, Station 11, Augusta, ME 04333-0011; 207-287-3181, 877-523-2659 (VitalChek), 207-287-1093 (Fax), 8AM-5PM.

www.state.me.us/dhs/welcome.htm

Note: The web site has a link to VitalChek for online ordering.

Indexing & Storage: Records are available from 1923 to present. Maine State Archives has records prior to 1923 (call 207-287-5795). Records are indexed on computer from 1975 to present, and on microfiche from 1892 to present. Records are indexed on books (volumes).

Searching: Must give relationship to person of record and reason for request. Confidential information will not be released except to the person listed on the birth certificate. Include the following in your request: full name, names of parents, mother's maiden name, date of birth, place of birth. Also include your daytime phone number with the request. The following data is not released: illegitimate births or adoption records.

Access by: mail, phone, in person, online.

Fee & Payment: $10.00 fee for certified copy, add $4.00 per name for additional copy of same record. Add $5.00 if using VitalChek. Fee payee: Treasurer, State of Maine. Prepayment required. Personal checks accepted. Credit cards accepted: MasterCard, Visa, AmEx, Discover.

Mail search: Turnaround time: 1 to 2 weeks. Specific dates are needed to search as well as names (if available).

Phone search: See expedited service.

In person search: Turnaround time is while you wait.

Online search: Pre-1892 records are available at the Internet at www.state.me.us/sos/geneology/homepage.html

Other access: Birth lists are available, excluding restricted information.

Expedited service: Expedited service is available for mail, phone and fax searches. Turnaround time: overnight delivery. Add $15.50 courier fee. Use of credit card is required.

Death Records

Maine Department of Human Services, Vital Records, 221 State St, Station 11, Augusta, ME 04333-0011; 207-287-3181, 877-523-2659 (VitalChek), 207-287-1093 (Fax), 8AM-5PM.

www.state.me.us/dhs/welcome.htm

Note: The web site has a link to VitalChek for online ordering.

Indexing & Storage: Records are available from 1923 to present. Maine State Archives has records prior to 1923 (call 207-287-5795). Records are indexed on computer from 1975 to present, and on microfiche from 1892 to present. Records are indexed on books (volumes).

Searching: Access to cause of death is restricted to those with a legitimate interest in the information. All information on certificate of death is confidential, except name, age, date of death, as well as city/town where death occurred. Include the following in your request: full name, date of death, place of death, relationship to person of record.

Access by: mail, in person, online.

Fee & Payment: $10.00 fee for certified copy, add $4.00 per name for additional copy of same record. Add $5.00 if using VitalChek. Fee payee: Treasurer, State of Maine. Prepayment required. Personal checks accepted. Credit cards accepted: MasterCard, Visa, AmEx, Discover.

Mail search: Turnaround time: 1 to 2 weeks. When requesting a search, keep in mind that records are filed by the date of the death, and then by name.

In person search: Turnaround time is while you wait.

Online search: Both old and newer records are available at www.state.me.us/sos/arc/geneology/homepage.html. Death History records from the Maine State Archives are also available at http://thor.ddp.state.me.us/archives.plsql/archdev.death_archinve.search_form. Also, a free genealogy site at http://vitals.rootsweb.com/me/death/search.cgi has Death Indexes from 1960-1997. Search by surname, given name, place or year.

Other access: Bulk file purchases are available, with the exclusion of restricted data.

Expedited service: Expedited service is available for mail, phone and fax searches. Turnaround time: overnight delivery. Add $15.50 for delivery. Use of credit card required.

Marriage Certificates

Maine Department of Human Services, Vital Records, 221 State St, Station 11, Augusta, ME 04333-0011; 207-287-3181, 877-523-2659 (VitalChek), 207-287-1093 (Fax), 8AM-5PM.

www.state.me.us/dhs/welcome.htm

Note: The web site has a link to VitalChek for online ordering.

Indexing & Storage: Records are available from 1923 to present. Maine State Archives has records prior to 1923 (call 207-287-5795). Records are indexed on microfiche from 1892 to present. Records are indexed on books (volumes).

Searching: Must give relationship to persons of record and reason for request. Data recorded in the section of the certificate specified as confidential is not released (i.e. race, education, etc.). Include the following in your request: names of husband and wife, date of marriage, place or county of marriage.

Access by: mail, phone, in person, online.

Fee & Payment: $10.00 fee for certified copy, add $4.00 per name for additional copy of same record. Add $5.00 if using VitalChek. Fee payee: Treasurer, State of Maine. Prepayment required. Personal checks accepted. Credit cards accepted: MasterCard, Visa, AmEx, Discover.

Mail search: Turnaround time: 1 to 2 weeks.

Phone search: See expedited service.

In person search: Turnaround time is while you wait.

Online search: Records are available at www.state.me.us/sos/arc/geneology/homepage.html from 1892-1966 and 1976-1996. Marriage History records from the Maine State Archives are available at http://thor/ddp/state.me.us

Other access: Bulk file purchasing is available, with restricted data excluded.

Expedited service: Expedited service is available for mail, phone and fax searches. Turnaround time: overnight delivery. Add $15.50 for courier per package. Use of credit card is required. Make this check out to Federal Express.

Divorce Records

Maine Department of Human Services, Office of Vital Records, 221 State St, Station 11, Augusta, ME 04333-0011; 207-287-3181, 877-523-2659 (VitalChek), 207-287-1093 (Fax), 8AM-5PM.

www.state.me.us/dhs/welcome.htm

Note: The web site has a link to VitalChek for online ordering.

Indexing & Storage: Records are available from 1923 to present. Maine State Archives has records prior to 1923, call 207-287-5795. It takes 1 week before new records are available for inquiry. Records are indexed on books (volumes).

Searching: Must give relationship to persons of record and reason for request. Include the following in your request: names of husband and wife, date of divorce, place of divorce.

Access by: mail, phone, in person.

Fee & Payment: $10.00 fee for certified copy, add $4.00 per name for additional copy of same record. Add $5.00 if using VitalChek. Fee payee: Treasurer, State of Maine. Prepayment required. Personal checks accepted. Credit cards accepted: MasterCard, Visa, AmEx, Discover.

Mail search: Turnaround time: 1 to 2 weeks.

Phone search: See expedited service.

In person search: Turnaround time is while you wait.

Other access: Index information is available for bulk purchase.

Expedited service: Expedited service is available for phone requests. Turnaround time: overnight delivery. Add courier charge of $15.50 per package. Use of credit card required.

Workers' Compensation Records

Workers Compensation Board, 27 State House Station, Augusta, ME 04333-0027; 207-287-7071, 207-287-5895 (Fax), 7:30AM-5PM.

www.state.me.us

Indexing & Storage: Records are available from 1984, indexed on computer.

Searching: Records are considered confidential and are released "on a need-to-know basis." Include purpose of your request. Include the following in your request: claimant name, Social Security Number, reason for information request. The following data is not released: personal information (height, weight, sex, eye color, etc.) or Social Security Numbers.

Access by: mail, in person.

Fee & Payment: The research fee is $5.00. Copies are $.50 per page. Fee payee: State of Maine, Workers' Compensation Board. When remitting payment, please include invoice number on your check. Personal checks accepted. No credit cards accepted.

Mail search: Turnaround time: 3 to 4 weeks. Requests should be addressed to: Linda Larrabee,

Workers' Compensation Board, 27 State House Station, Augusta, ME 04333-0027. A self addressed stamped envelope is requested.

In person search: Requests must still be in writing and prior approval is suggested.

Other access: Computer data is available, but requests are screened for purpose.

Driver Records

Bureau of Motor Vehicles, Driver License Services, 29 State House Station, Augusta, ME 04333-0029; 207-624-9000, 8AM-5PM.

www.state.me.us/sos/bmv

Indexing & Storage: Records are available for 3 years for moving violations, DWIs and 3 years after the reinstatement of suspensions. Accidents are indicated on the record. It takes up to 30 days before new records are available for inquiry.

Searching: Driving records and ticket information is released per DPPA guidelines. Personal information is not available to the general public unless the subject opts in, or a signed release is presented. The full name and DOB are required for a search. The driver's license number is optional. The following data is not released: medical information.

Access by: mail, fax, in person, online.

Fee & Payment: The fee is $5.00 for a non-certified record and $6.00 for a certified record. A "no record found" incurs a full charge, except for walk-in requesters. Fee payee: Secretary of State. Prepayment required. Personal checks accepted. No credit cards accepted.

Mail search: Turnaround time: 3 days. No self addressed stamped envelope is required.

Fax search: The cost is $7.00 and results are returned by mail.

In person search: Up to 5 requests can be obtained in-person immediately; additional requests are available the next day.

Online search: Access is through InforME via the Internet. There is a $50.00 annual fee and records are $5.00 per request. Visit the web site for details and sign-up or call 207-621-2600. The state offers "Driver Cross Check" - a program of notification when activity occurs on a specific record.

Other access: Maine will sell statewide or customized lists of license drivers via magnetic tape and other media for high volume users. Call 207-621-2600 for details.

Vehicle Ownership Vehicle Identification

Department of Motor Vehicles, Registration Section, 29 State House Station, Augusta, ME 04333-0029; 207-624-9000 x52149, 207-624-9204 (Fax), 8AM-5PM M-F.

www.state.me.us/sos/bmv/

Indexing & Storage: Records are available from 1977. It takes up to 30 days before new records are available for inquiry.

Searching: Casual requesters can obtain records, but personal information is not included unless the subject given authorization. Opt-in is available. Include the following in your request: full name, VIN, license plate number. The vehicle owner's DOB is helpful when requesting ownership information.

Access by: mail, phone, fax, in person, online.

Fee & Payment: Fees: $6.00 for certified record; $5.00 for uncertified record. Will also fax record back for an additional $2.00. Fee payee: Secretary of State. Prepayment required. Personal checks accepted. No credit cards accepted.

Mail search: Turnaround time: 5 days. No self addressed stamped envelope is required.

Phone search: Telephone searching is available for parties who establish an account. They are billed monthly.

Fax search: Established accounts may order by fax, and then have data returned by fax for an additional $2.00.

In person search: Searching is available in person.

Online search: Maine offers online access to title and registration records via PC and modem. The system is open 24 hours daily. To set up an account, call 207-624-9264. Fee is $5.00 per record, annual registration is $50.00.

Accident Reports

Maine State Police, Traffic Division, Station 20, Augusta, ME 04333-0020 (Courier: 397 Water St, Gardiner, ME 04345); 207-624-8944, 207-624-8945 (Fax), 7:30AM-4PM.

www.state.me.us/dps/msp

Note: Accidents must be reported involving death, injury, or property damage in excess of $1000.00.

Indexing & Storage: Records are available from 1975. Most records are on microfilm. It takes up to 30 days before new records are available for inquiry.

Searching: Most accident records are public information. All requests must be in writing. Include the following in your request: full name, date of birth, date of accident, location of accident. Be sure to order by the operator's name, not by vehicle owner name.

Access by: mail, in person.

Fee & Payment: The fee is $5.00 per copy for Police Traffic report, $10.00 for an Officers Investigative Report (fatality involved), $10.00 for an Accident Reconstruction Report, and $10.00 for a Vehicle Autopsy Report. Fee payee: Maine State Police. Prepayment required. Personal checks accepted. No credit cards accepted.

Mail search: Turnaround time: 7 days. No self addressed stamped envelope is required.

In person search: Turnaround time is usually immediate for walk-in requesters.

Vessel Ownership
Vessel Registration

Dept of Inland Fisheries & Wildlife, 41 State House Station, Augusta, ME 04333-0041; 207-287-5231, 207-287-8094 (Fax), 8AM-5PM.

www.state.me.us/ifw

Note: Liens are not recorded here and must be searched with UCCs.

Indexing & Storage: Records are available from 1993 to present for registrations that have been continuously renewed. Older records on microfiche are archived, and require payment of a $25.00 search fee. There are no titles, all motorized boats must be registered. Records are indexed on computer. Older records on microfiche and archived.

Searching: Submit the name, registration number and serial number.

Access by: mail, phone, fax, in person.

Fee & Payment: The search fee is $5.00 per record if done by staff, $2.00 if you do in person (per copy). A boat history fee is $25.00. Fee payee: Treasurer, State of Maine. Prepayment required. Credit cards accepted: MasterCard, Visa.

Mail search: Turnaround time: 2-3 weeks. No self addressed stamped envelope is required.

Phone search: Results will only be given verbally, unless payment is arranged using a credit card.

Fax search: Turnaround time is within 72 hours. A credit card must be used for all fax searches.

In person search: There is no search fee, but copies are $2.00 each.

Other access: The agency offers record access via tape, labels or printed lists.

Legislation Records

Maine Legislature, 2 State House Station, Legislative Document Room, Augusta, ME 04333-0002; 207-287-1692 (Bill Status or LD #), 207-287-1408 (Document Room), 207-287-1456 (Fax), 8AM-5PM.

http://janus.state.me.us/legis

Note: Older passed bills are found at the State Law Library, 207-287-1600.

Indexing & Storage: Records are available for the current session only.

Searching: Include the following in your request: bill number. A paid document service is available. Will express any results at searcher's expense.

Access by: mail, phone, in person, online.

Fee & Payment: There is no search fee or copy fee.

Mail search: Turnaround time: variable. No self addressed stamped envelope is required.

Phone search: There is a limit of 15 bills per phone call.

In person search: Searching is available in person.

Online search: The web site offers bills, status, and access to text of state laws.

Other access: A weekly list of LDs (legislative documents) is available.

Voter Registration

Records not maintained by a state level agency.

Note: The data is considered public record in Maine but can only be accessed at the municipality level.

GED Certificates

Dept of Education, Attn: GED, 23 State House Station, Augusta, ME 04333; 207-624-6752, 207-624-6731 (Fax).

http://janus.state.me.us/education

Searching: Requests for transcripts must be in writing. To verify, all of the following is required: name, date of birth, and Social Security Number. For transcripts, a signed release is required.

Access by: mail, phone, fax, in person, online.

Fee & Payment: There are no fees.

Mail search: Turnaround time 1-2 days. No self addressed stamped envelope is required.

Phone search: You can do a verification over the phone.

Fax search: Turnaround time 1-2 days.

In person search: Turnaround time: Immediate.

Online search: E-mail requests can be made by sending e-mail to: lisa.taylor@state&me.us

Hunting License Information
Fishing License Information

Inland Fisheries & Wildlife Department, Licensing Division, 284 State St, Augusta, ME 04333; 207-287-5209, 207-287-8094 (Fax), 8AM-5PM.

www.state.me.us/ifw

Note: The state is in the process of computerizing license data. Licenses are issued by Town Clerks and approved businesses and forwarded monthly to this department.

Indexing & Storage: Records are available from 1996 to present. It takes at least 3 months before new records are available for inquiry. Records are indexed on inhouse computer.

Searching: All information is considered open to the public. Include the following in your request: full name, date of birth, address.

Access by: mail, phone, in person.

Fee & Payment: Individual searches are completed for $5.00 each. Fee payee: Treasurer, State of Maine. Prepayment required. Credit cards accepted: MasterCard, Visa.

Mail search: Turnaround time: 7 business days. No self addressed stamped envelope is required.

Phone search: Credit card required.

In person search: Searching is available in person.

Other access: Bulk data purchases are available at a cost of $.05 per name. Call InforME at 207-621-2600.

Maine State Licensing Agencies

Licenses Searchable Online

Acupuncturist #13 .... http://pfr.informe.org/webquery/LicLookup.aspx
Aesthetician #13 .... http://pfr.informe.org/webquery/LicLookup.aspx
Alcohol/Drug Abuse Counselor #13 .... http://pfr.informe.org/webquery/LicLookup.aspx
Animal Medical Technician #13 .... http://pfr.informe.org/webquery/LicLookup.aspx
Appraiser, Residential Real Estate #13 .... http://pfr.informe.org/webquery/LicLookup.aspx
Architect #13 .... http://pfr.informe.org/webquery/LicLookup.aspx
Athletic Trainer #13 .... http://pfr.informe.org/webquery/LicLookup.aspx
ATV-All-Terrain Vehicle #11 .... www.state.me.us/ifw/index.html
Auctioneer #13 .... http://pfr.informe.org/webquery/LicLookup.aspx
Bank #14 .... www.state.me.us/pfr/bkg/mebanks.htm
Barber #13 .... http://pfr.informe.org/webquery/LicLookup.aspx
Boiler Contractor #13 .... http://pfr.informe.org/webquery/LicLookup.aspx
Boxer #13 .... http://pfr.informe.org/webquery/LicLookup.aspx
Charitable Solicitation #13 .... http://pfr.informe.org/webquery/LicLookup.aspx
Chiropractor #13 .... http://pfr.informe.org/webquery/LicLookup.aspx
Cosmetologist #13 .... http://pfr.informe.org/webquery/LicLookup.aspx
Counselor #13 .... http://pfr.informe.org/webquery/LicLookup.aspx
Credit Union #14 .... www.state.me.us/pfr/bkg/mebanks.htm
Dental Hygienist #16 .... www.mainedental.org/search.htm
Dental Radiographer #16 .... www.mainedental.org/search.htm
Dentist #16 .... www.mainedental.org/search.htm
Denturist #16 .... www.mainedental.org/search.htm
Dietitian #13 .... http://pfr.informe.org/webquery/LicLookup.aspx
Electrician #13 .... http://pfr.informe.org/webquery/LicLookup.aspx
Elevator/Tramway Contractor #13 .... http://pfr.informe.org/webquery/LicLookup.aspx
Employee Leasing Company #15 .... www.state.me.us/pfr/ins/emplease.htm
Engineer #17 .... http://professionals.maineusa.com/engineers/database.html
Forester #13 .... http://pfr.informe.org/webquery/LicLookup.aspx
Fund Raiser #13 .... http://pfr.informe.org/webquery/LicLookup.aspx
Funeral Home #13 .... http://pfr.informe.org/webquery/LicLookup.aspx
Funeral Service #13 .... http://pfr.informe.org/webquery/LicLookup.aspx
Geologist #13 .... http://pfr.informe.org/webquery/LicLookup.aspx
Hearing Aid Dealer/Fitter #13 .... http://pfr.informe.org/webquery/LicLookup.aspx
HMO #15 .... www.state.me.us/pfr/ins/inshmo.htm
Insurance Advisor #13 .... http://pfr.informe.org/webquery/LicLookup.aspx
Insurance Agent #13 .... http://pfr.informe.org/webquery/LicLookup.aspx
Insurance Company #15 .... http://pfr.informe.org/webquery/LicLookup.aspx
Interior Designer #13 .... http://pfr.informe.org/webquery/LicLookup.aspx
Interpreter #13 .... http://pfr.informe.org/webquery/LicLookup.aspx
Kickboxer #13 .... http://pfr.informe.org/webquery/LicLookup.aspx
Landscape Architect #13 .... http://pfr.informe.org/webquery/LicLookup.aspx
Manicurist #13 .... http://pfr.informe.org/webquery/LicLookup.aspx
Manufactured Housing #13 .... http://pfr.informe.org/webquery/LicLookup.aspx
Marriage & Family Therapist #13 .... http://pfr.informe.org/webquery/LicLookup.aspx
Massage Therapist #13 .... http://pfr.informe.org/webquery/LicLookup.aspx
Medical Doctor #23 .... www.docboard.org/me/df/mesearch.htm
Naturopathic Physician #13 .... http://pfr.informe.org/webquery/LicLookup.aspx
Notary Public #24 .... www.state.me.us/sos/cec/rcn/notary/notlist.htm
Nursing Home Administrator #13 .... http://pfr.informe.org/webquery/LicLookup.aspx
Occupational Therapist #13 .... http://pfr.informe.org/webquery/LicLookup.aspx
Oil & Solid Fuel #13 .... http://pfr.informe.org/webquery/LicLookup.aspx
Optometrist #18 .... http://pfr.informe.org/webquery/LicLooKup.aspx
Osteo. Physician/Physician Assist. #26 .... www.docboard.org/me-osteo/df/index.htm
Osteopathic Resident/Intern #26 .... www.docboard.org/me-osteo/df/index.htm
Pastoral Counselor #13 .... http://pfr.informe.org/webquery/LicLookup.aspx
Pharmacist #13 .... http://pfr.informe.org/webquery/LicLookup.aspx
Physical Therapist #13 .... http://pfr.informe.org/webquery/LicLookup.aspx
Physician Assistant #23 .... www.docboard.org/me/df/mesearch.htm
Plumber #13 .... http://pfr.informe.org/webquery/LicLookup.aspx
Podiatrist #13 .... http://pfr.informe.org/webquery/LicLookup.aspx
Preferred Provider Organization #15 .... www.state.me.us/pfr/ins/insppo.htm
Psychologist #13 .... http://pfr.informe.org/webquery/LicLookup.aspx

Public Accountant-CPA #13................http://pfr.informe.org/webquery/LicLookup.aspx
Radiologic Technician #13.................http://pfr.informe.org/webquery/LicLookup.aspx
Real Estate Appraiser, General #13 ....http://pfr.informe.org/webquery/LicLookup.aspx
Real Estate Appraiser/Trainee #13 ....http://pfr.informe.org/webquery/LicLookup.aspx
Real Estate Broker #13.....................http://pfr.informe.org/webquery/LicLookup.aspx
Re-insurer, Approved #15..................http://pfr.informe.org/webquery/LicLookup.aspx
Respiratory Care Therapist #13............http://pfr.informe.org/webquery/LicLookup.aspx
Savings & Loan #14.........................www.state.me.us/pfr/bkg/mebanks.htm
Snowmobile #11 ....www.state.me.us/ifw/index.html
Social Worker #13 ....http://pfr.informe.org/webquery/LicLookup.aspx
Soil Scientist #13 ....http://pfr.informe.org/webquery/LicLookup.aspx
Speech Pathologist/Audiologist #13 ....http://pfr.informe.org/webquery/LicLookup.aspx
Substance Abuse Counselor #13 ....http://pfr.informe.org/webquery/LicLookup.aspx
Surplus Lines Company #15................http://pfr.informe.org/webquery/LicLookup.aspx
Surveyor, Land #13 ....http://pfr.informe.org/webquery/LicLookup.aspx
Trust Company #14 ....www.state.me.us/pfr/bkg/mebanks.htm
Utilization Review Entity #15................www.state.me.us/pfr/ins/insmedur.htm
Vendor, Itinerant/Transient #13 ....http://pfr.informe.org/webquery/LicLookup.aspx
Veterinarian #13 ....http://pfr.informe.org/webquery/LicLookup.aspx
Veterinary Technician #13 ....http://pfr.informe.org/webquery/LicLookup.aspx
Watercraft #11 ....www.state.me.us/ifw/index.html
Wrestler #13 ....http://pfr.informe.org/webquery/LicLookup.aspx

Licensing Quick Finder

Acupuncturist #13................207-624-8603
Adult Care Home #9 207-624-5250
Adult Day Service #9 207-624-5250
Aesthetician #13.................207-624-8603
Air Quality Control (Business) #5 ...207-287-2437
Alcohol/Drug Abuse Counselor #13 207-624-8603
Alcoholic Beverage Distributor #21 207-624-8745
Ambulance Attendant #20 207-287-3953
Ambulatory Surgical Center #9 207-624-5443
Animal Medical Technician #13...........207-624-8603
Appraiser, Residential Real Estate #13.207-624-8616
Architect #13...................207-624-8522
Assisted Living Facility #9 207-624-5250
Athletic Trainer #13...............207-624-8624
Attorney #22 207-623-1121
ATV-All-Terrain Vehicle #11 207-287-2043
Auctioneer #13..................207-624-8521
Bank #14.......................207-624-8648
Barber #13.....................207-624-8620
Bedding/Upholstering/Furniture/Stuffed Toy Mfg. #12
..........................207-624-6411
Beekeeper #3 207-287-3117
Boiler Contractor #13.............207-624-8615
Boxer #13......................207-624-8603
Charitable Solicitation #13.................207-624-8624
Chiropractor #13.................207-624-8634
Commercial Shellfish #27.........207-624-6550
Cosmetologist #13...............207-624-8620
Counselor #13 207-624-8626
Credit Union #14.................207-624-8648
Dental Hygienist #16 207-287-4746
Dental Radiographer #16 207-287-4746
Dentist #16.....................207-287-4746
Denturist #16...................207-287-4746
Dietitian #13....................207-624-8611
Drug Analyzer #7 207-287-3201
Electrician #13..................207-624-8611
Electrologist #7.................207-287-5338
Elevator/Tramway Contractor #13...207-624-8615
Emergency Medical Technician #10 207-287-3953
Employee Leasing Company #15 207-624-8475
Engineer #17 207-287-3236
Firearm Permit (Non-resident, Concealed) #25
..........................207-624-8775
Firearm Permit (Resident, Concealed) #25
..........................207-624-8775
First Responder #10 207-287-3953
Forester #13 207-624-8628
Fund Raiser #13 207-624-8624

Funeral Home #13...............207-624-8603
Funeral Service #13 207-624-8611
Geologist #13 207-624-8616
Hazardous Material/Solid Waste Operator #6
..........................207-287-7865
Hearing Aid Dealer/Fitter #13.............207-624-8628
HMO #15 207-624-8475
Home Health Agency #9 207-624-5443
Home Health Care Service Agency #9 . 207-624-5443
Hospice #9.....................207-624-5443
Hospital #9 207-624-5443
Insurance Advisor #13............207-624-8603
Insurance Agent #13.............207-624-8603
Insurance Company #15..........207-624-8475
Interior Designer #13.............207-624-8522
Intermediate Care Facility for the Mentally Retarded
    #9 207-624-5443
Interpreter #13.................207-624-8624
Investment Advisor #13...........207-624-8603
Kickboxer #13..................207-624-8603
Landscape Architect #13.................207-624-8616
Library Media Specialist #4 207-624-6603
Loan Broker #13................207-624-8603
Lobbyist #1 207-287-6221
Lobster Harvester #27............207-624-6550
Lottery Combined Vendor #21 207-287-6824
Lottery Retailer #2 207-287-6824
Lottery Vending #21 207-287-6824
Manicurist #13..................207-624-8603
Manufactured Housing #13 207-582-8612
Marine Worm Digger #27 207-624-6550
Marriage & Family Therapist #13 207-624-8634
Massage Therapist #13............207-624-8624
Medical Doctor #23..............207-287-3601
Naturopathic Physician #13........207-624-8603
Notary Public #24...............207-624-7650
Nurse #8 207-287-1133
Nursing Home #9................207-624-5443
Nursing Home Administrator #13 207-624-8611
Occupational Therapist #13........207-624-8616
Oil & Solid Fuel #13..............207-624-8631
Optometrist #18 207-624-8691
Osteopathic Physician Extender #26 207-287-2480
Osteopath Physician/Phys. Assist. #26. 207-287-2480
Osteopathic Resident/Intern #26.........207-287-2480
Paramedic #10 207-287-3953
Pastoral Counselor #13 207-624-8634
Pesticide Applicator #3............207-287-2731
Pesticide Dealer #3 207-287-2731

Pharmacist #13 207-624-8616
Physical Therapist #13...........207-624-8628
Physician Assistant #23 207-287-3601
Pilot #13.......................207-624-8620
Plumber #13 207-624-8628
Podiatrist #13 207-624-8626
Polygraph Examiner #20 207-624-7074
Preferred Provider Organization #15 ... 207-624-8475
Private Investigator #25 207-624-8775
Propane/LPGas Operator/Delivery #13 207-624-8610
Propane/LPGas Technician #13.........207-624-8610
Psychologist #13 207-624-8628
Public Accountant-CPA #13.........207-582-8627
Radiologic Technician #13.........207-624-8628
Real Estate Appraiser, General #13 207-624-8616
Real Estate Appraiser/Trainee #13...... 207-624-8616
Real Estate Broker #13...........207-624-8603
Re-insurer, Approved #15.........207-624-8475
Renal Disease (End Stage) Facility #9 . 207-624-5443
Residential Child Care Provider #7 207-287-5060
Respiratory Care Therapist #13.........207-624-8628
Savings & Loan #14..............207-624-8648
School Guidance Counselor #4 207-624-6603
School Library Media Specialist #4...... 207-624-6603
School Principal/Superintendent #4...... 207-624-6603
Sea Urchin Harvester #27.........207-624-6550
Seaweed Harvester #27...........207-624-6550
Security Company, Guard/Alarm #25 ... 207-624-8775
Self Insurance Company #15.........207-624-8475
Snowmobile #11................207-287-2043
Social Worker #13 207-624-8631
Soil Scientist #13................207-624-8603
Speech Pathologist/Audiologist #13 ... 207-624-8634
Sprinkler Inspector #20 207-287-3473
Substance Abuse Counselor #13 207-624-8634
Surplus Lines Company #15........207-624-8475
Surveyor, Land #13..............207-624-8611
Tattoo Artist #7.................207-287-3201
Taxidermist #11.................207-287-2751
Teacher #4 207-624-6603
Trust Company #14..............207-624-8648
Utilization Review Entity #15.........207-624-8475
Vendor, Itinerant/Transient #13 207-624-8624
Veterinarian #13................207-624-8628
Veterinary Technician #13 207-624-8603
Watercraft #11 207-287-2043
Wrestler #13 207-624-8603

Licensing Agency Information

#1 Registrar, Commission on Governmental Ethics & Elections, State House Station 135, Augusta, ME 04333; 207-287-6221, Fax: 207-287-6775. www.state.me.us/ethics

#2 Department of Administrative & Financial Services, Bureau of Alcoholic Beverages & Lottery Operations, 8 State House Station, Augusta, ME 04333-0008; 207-287-6824, Fax: 207-287-6769. www.mainelottery.com

#3 Department of Agriculture, Food & Rural Resources, Board of Pesticides Control, 280 State House Station, Augusta, ME 04332-0028; 207-287-2731, Fax: 207-287-7548. www.state.me.us/agriculture/pesticides Agency email: gary.fish@state.me.us.

#4 Department of Education, Certification Office, 23 State House Station, Augusta Complex, Augusta, ME 04333-0023; 207-624-6603, Fax: 207-624-6604. www.state.me.us/education/homepage.htm. Agency email: Pat.Julien@state.me.us. Make labels for school mailing lists at www.state.me.us/education/labels/labels.htm

#5 Department of Environmental Protection, Bureau of Air Quality Control, 17 State House Station, Augusta, ME 04333-0017; 207-287-2437, Fax: 207-287-7641. www.state.me.us/dep/home.htm

#6 Department of Environmental Protection, Bureau/Hazardous Materials & Solid Waste Control, State House Station 17, Augusta, ME 04333; 207-287-7865, Fax: 207-287-7826. www.state.me.us/agencies.htm

#7 Department of Human Services, 221 State St, 11 State House Station, Augusta, ME 04333-0011; 207-287-5060, Fax: 207-287-5282. www.state.me.us/dhs/

#8 Department of Professional & Financial Regulation, Board of Nursing, 24 Stone Street, # 158 State House Station, Augusta, ME 04333-0158; 207-287-1133, Fax: 207-287-1149. www.state.me.us/nursingbd Agency email: virginia.e.delormier@state.me.us.

#9 Department of Human Services, Division of Licensure, 35 SHS, Augusta, ME 04333; 207-624-5443, Fax: 207-624-5378. www.state.me.us/pfr/olr/

#10 Department of Public Safety, Main Emergency Medical Svcs, 16 Edison Dr, Augusta, ME 04333; 207-287-3953, Fax: 207-289-6251. www.state.me.us/dps/ems. Agency email: maine.ems@state.me.us.

#11 Department of Inland Fisheries & Wildlife, Licensing & Registration Division, 284 State St, 41 Statehouse Station, Augusta, ME 04333-0041; 207-287-8000, Fax: 207-287-8094. www.state.me.us/ifw/index.html Agency email: ifw@state.me.us. Search database at www.state.me.us/ifw/index.html

#12 Department of Labor, 45 State House Station, Augusta, ME 04333-0045; 207-624-6411, Fax: 207-624-6449. www.state.me.us/labor Agency email: webmaster_bls@state.me.us.

#13 Department of Professional & Financial Regulation, Bureau of Licensing, 35 State House Station, Augusta, ME 04333-0035; 207-624-8500, Fax: 207-624-8637. www.state.me.us/pfr/olr Agency email: jeri.l.betts@state.me.us. Search database at http://pfr.informe.org/webquery/LicLookup.aspx

#14 Department of Professional & Financial Regulation, Bureau of Banking, 36 State House Station, Augusta, ME 04333-0036; 207-624-8570, Fax: 207-624-8590. www.mainebankingreg.org

#15 Department of Professional & Financial Regulation, Bureau of Insurance, State House Station 34, Augusta, ME 04333-0034; 207-624-8475, Fax: 207-624-8599. www.state.me.us/pfr/ins/inshome2.htm Agency email: webmaster_pfr@state.me.us.

#16 Board of Dental Examiners, 143 Statehouse Station, 2 Bangor St, Augusta, ME 04333-0143; 207-287-3333/4746, Fax: 207-287-8140. www.licenseverification.com/medental Agency email: anita.c.merrow@state.me.us or ale.e.tripp@state.me.us. Search database www.mainedental.org/search.htm

#17 Department of Professional & Financial Regulation, Professional Engineers Reg. Board, 92 State House Station, Augusta, ME 04333; 207-287-3236, Fax: 207-626-2309. www.state.me.us/pfr/auxboards/enghome.htm. Agency email: pengineers@ctel.net. Search database at http://professionals.maineusa.com/engineers/database.html

#18 Department of Professional & Financial Regulation, Bureau of Optometry, 113 State House Station, Augusta, ME 04333; 207-624-8691, Fax: 207-624-8691. www.state.me.us/pfr/auxboards/optometry. Agency email: susan.a.giampetruzzi@state.me.us.

Search database at http://pfr.informe.org/webquery/LicLooKup.aspx. The alternative search site is www.odfinder.org/LicSearch.asp

#20 Department of Public Safety, 18 Meadow Rd, 104 State House Station, Augusta, ME 04333-0042; 207-624-7094, Fax: 207-624-7088. www.state.me.us/dps

#21 Department of Public Safety, Licensing & Inspection-Liquor, 164 State House Station, Augusta, ME 04333; 207-624-8745, Fax: 207-624-8767.

#22 Board of Overseers of the Bar, PO Box 527 (97 Winthrop St), Augusta, ME 04332; 207-623-1121, Fax: 207-623-4175. www.mebaroverseers.org Agency email: board@mebaroverseers.org.

#23 Medical Doctor & Physician Assistant Licensing & Investigation, Board of Licensure in Medicine, 137 State House Station, 2 Bangor St, Augusta, ME 04333; 207-287-3601, Fax: 207-287-6590. www.docboard.org/me/me_home.htm Agency email: Tim.E.Terranova@state.me.us. Search database at www.docboard.org/me/df/mesearch.htm

#24 Secretary of State, Div of Elections & Commissions, Notary Public Section, 101 State House Station, Augusta, ME 04333-0101; 207-624-7650, Fax: 207-287-6545. www.state.me.us/sos/cec/rcn/notary/not.htm Search database at www.state.me.us/sos/cec/rcn/notary/not.htm

#25 State Police Licensing Division, 164 State House Station, Augusta, ME 04333; 207-624-8775, Fax: 207-624-8767.

#26 State of Maine, Board of Osteopathic Licensure, 142 State House Station, Augusta, ME 04333-0142; 207-287-2480, Fax: 207-287-2480. www.docboard.org/me-osteo Agency email: susan.e.strout@state.me.us. Search database at www.docboard.org/me-osteo/df/index.htm

#27 Department of Marine Resources, Bureau of Marine Patrol, Licensing Division, 21 State House Station, Hallowell Annex-Baker Bldg, Augusta, ME 04333-0021; 207-624-6550, Fax: 207-624-6550.

Maine Federal Courts

The following list indicates the district and division name for each county in the state. If the bankruptcy court location is different from the district court, then the location of the bankruptcy court appears in parentheses.

County/Court Cross Reference

Androscoggin	Portland	Oxford	Portland
Aroostook	Bangor	Penobscot	Bangor
Cumberland	Portland	Piscataquis	Bangor
Franklin	Bangor	Sagadahoc	Portland
Hancock	Bangor	Somerset	Bangor
Kennebec	Bangor	Waldo	Bangor
Knox	Portland (Bangor)	Washington	Bangor
Lincoln	Portland (Bangor)	York	Portland

Standards for Federal Courts: The search fee is $20.00 per item (one party name or case number). Certification fee is $7.00 per document. Copy fee is $.50 per page. All fees standard unless noted in profile. Mail Search: always enclose a stamped self addressed envelope unless otherwise noted. Before releasing records, all courts require prepayment unless noted in profile.

Open records are located at the court unless otherwise noted. District courts index by defendant and plaintiff as well as by case number. Bankruptcy courts usually index by debtor and case number. While most courts now have their indexes on computer, many still maintain index card files as well.

The universal PACER sign-up number is 800-676-6856. Find PACER and the Party/Case Index on the Web at http://pacer.psc.uscourts.gov. PACER dial-up access is $.60 per minute. Also, courts offering internet access via RACER, PACER, Web-PACER or the new CM-ECF charge $.07 per page fee unless noted as free.

US District Court

District of Maine

Bangor Division Court Clerk, PO Box 1007, Bangor, ME 04402-1007 (Courier Address: Room 357, 202 Harlow St, Bangor, ME 04401), 207-945-0575, Fax: 207-945-0362.

www.med.uscourts.gov

Counties: Aroostook, Franklin, Hancock, Kennebec, Penobscot, Piscataquis, Somerset, Waldo, Washington.

Indexing & Storage: Cases are indexed by defendant, plaintiff, and case number. New cases are available in the index immediately after filing date. Records are indexed and stored by year, then docket number for case files and by name for electronic index system. Open records are located at this court.

Fee & Payment Notes: Payment may be made by money order, cashier check, personal check. Payee: Clerk, US District Court.

Phone Search: Any public record information will be released over the phone including accession #.

Mail Search: A SASE is not required.

In Person Search: In person searching available.

PACER:. Case records are available back to August 1991. Records are purged every 6 months. New records are available online after 1 day. PACER is at https://pacer.med.uscourts.gov.

Electronic Filing: (CM/ECF available late 2002)

Portland Division Court Clerk, 156 Federal St, Portland, ME 04101 (Courier Address: Use mail address for courier delivery), 207-780-3356, Fax: 207-780-3772.

www.med.uscourts.gov

Counties: Androscoggin, Cumberland, Knox, Lincoln, Oxford, Sagadahoc, York.

Indexing & Storage: Cases are indexed by defendant, plaintiff, and case number. New cases are available in the index immediately after filing date. Records are indexed and stored by year, then docket number for case files and by name for electronic index system. Open records are located at this court.

Fee & Payment Notes: Payment may be made by money order, cashier check, personal check. Payee: Clerk, US District Court.

Phone Search: Any public record information will be released over the phone including accession numbers.

Mail Search: A stamped self addressed envelope is not required.

In Person Search: In person searching available.

PACER:. Case records are available back to August 1991. Records are purged every 6 months. New records are available online after 1 day. PACER is available online at https://pacer.med.uscourts.gov.

Electronic Filing: (CM/ECF available late 2002)

US Bankruptcy Court

District of Maine

Bangor Division PO Box 1109, Bangor, ME 04402-1109 (Courier: 202 Harlow St, Bangor, ME 04401), 207-945-0348, Fax: 207-945-0304.

www.meb.uscourts.gov

Counties: Aroostook, Franklin, Hancock, Kennebec, Knox, Lincoln, Penobscot, Piscataquis, Somerset, Waldo, Washington.

Indexing & Storage: Cases are indexed by debtor as well as by case number. New cases are available in the index immediately after filing date. Archived records are available within 2 weeks of shipment to the archives. The length of time records are retained depends on space; files are usually retained 3 years before being sent to the Boston Federal Records Center.

Fee & Payment Notes: Payment may be made by money order, cashier check, business check. Personal checks are not accepted. Payee: United States Courts.

Phone Search: An automated voice case information service (VCIS) is available. Call VCIS at 800-650-7253 or 207-780-3755.

Mail Search: A stamped self addressed envelope is not required.

In Person Search: In person searching available.

PACER: Toll-free dial-up access: 800-733-8797. Local dial-up access: 207-780-3268. Case records are available back to December 1988. Records are purged every two years. New civil records are available online after 1 day. PACER is available online at http://pacer.meb.uscourts.gov.

Electronic Filing: Information is available online at https://ecf.meb.uscourts.gov

Portland Division 537 Congress St, Portland, ME 04101 (Courier Address: P.O. Box 17575, Portland, ME 04112-8575), 207-780-3482, Fax: 207-780-3679.

www.meb.uscourts.gov

Counties: Androscoggin, Cumberland, Oxford, Sagadahoc, York.

Indexing & Storage: Cases are indexed by debtor as well as by case number. New cases are available in the index immediately after filing date. Searches for cases filed prior to 1988 require the debtor's name. Automated searches require either the case number or debtor's name. Records from the court are available from the court immediately after docketing. Information through VCIS and Pacer is available 24 hours after docketing. Open records are located at this court.

Fee & Payment Notes: Payment may be made by money order, cashier check, business check. Personal checks are not accepted. Prepayment is required for individual requesters. Payee: US Bankruptcy Court.

Phone Search: Only docket information is available by phone. An automated voice case information service (VCIS) is available. Call VCIS at 800-650-7253 or 207-780-3755.

In Person Search: In person searching available.

PACER: Toll-free dial-up access: 800-733-8797. Local dial-up access: 207-780-3268. Case records are available back to December 1988. Records are purged every two years. New civil records are available online after 1 day. PACER is available online at http://pacer.meb.uscourts.gov.

Electronic Filing: Information is available online at https://ecf.meb.uscourts.gov

Maine County Courts

Court	Jurisdiction	No. of Courts	How Organized
Superior Courts*	General	17	16 Counties
District Courts*	Limited	31	13 Districts
Probate Courts*	Special	16	

* Profiled in this Sourcebook.

Court	CIVIL								
	Tort	Contract	Real Estate	Min. Claim	Max. Claim	Small Claims	Estate	Eviction	Domestic Relations
Superior Courts*	X	X	X	No Min	No Max				X
District Courts*	X	X	X	No Min	No Max	$4500		X	X
Probate Courts*							X		X

Court	CRIMINAL				
	Felony	Misdemeanor	DWI/DUI	Preliminary Hearing	Juvenile
Superior Courts*	X	X	X	X	
District Courts*	X	X	X	X	X
Probate Courts*					

ADMINISTRATION

State Court Administrator, PO Box 4820, Portland, ME, 04112; 207-822-0792, Fax: 207-822-0781. www.state.me.us/courts

COURT STRUCTURE

The Superior Court is the court of general jurisdiction. Prior to year 2001, District Courts accepted civil cases involving claims less than $30,000. Now, District Courts have jurisdiction concurrent with that of the Superior Court for all civil actions except those cases vested in the Superior Court by statute.

Both Superior and District Courts handle "misdemeanor" and "felony" cases, with jury trials being held in Superior Court only. Superior Court has exclusive jurisdiction over pleas or trials for murder cases.

The small claims limit was raised from $3000 to $4500 as of 7/1/1997.

ONLINE ACCESS

Development of a judicial computer system is in use statewide for all criminal and certain civil case types. The remainder of civil case types will be available statewide in the near future. The system is initially for judicial and law enforcement agencies and will not include public access in the near term.

Some counties are online through a private vendor.

ADDITIONAL INFORMATION

Mail requests for full criminal history record information are returned to the sender, referring them to the State Bureau of Investigation or the Bureau of Motor Vehicles, in most courts. Mail requests that make a specific inquiry related to an identified case are responded to in writing, with appropriate copy and attestation fees.

Telephone requests for information will only be provided to parties to the case and criminal justice agencies.

PROBATE COURTS

Probate Courts are part of the county court system, not the state system. Even though the Probate Court may be housed with other state courts, it is on a different phone system and calls may not be transferred.

Androscoggin County

Androscoggin Superior Court PO Box 3660, Auburn, ME 04212-3660; 207-783-5450. Hours: 8AM-4:30PM (EST). *Felony, Misdemeanor, Civil Actions.*

Civil Records: Access: Phone, mail, in person. Only the court performs in person searches; visitors may not. No search fee. Required to search: name, years to search; also helpful: address. Civil cases indexed by defendant, plaintiff. Civil records on index cards since 1977, docket books from 1961-1977.

Criminal Records: Access: In person only. Visitors must perform in person searches for themselves. No search fee. Required to search: name, years to search; also helpful: DOB. Criminal records go back to 1920s; on computer back to 1997.

General Information: No adoption, juvenile, impounded by judge, certain domestic matters. SASE required. Turnaround time 1 week. Copy fee: $1.00 per page. Certification fee: $1.00. Fee payee: Androscoggin Superior Court. Personal checks accepted. Prepayment is required.

Lewiston District Court - South 8 PO Box 1345, 85 Park St, Lewiston, ME 04243; 207-783-5401. Hours: 8AM-4PM (EST). *Misdemeanor, Civil Actions, Eviction, Small Claims.*

Civil Records: Access: Mail, in person. Both court and visitors may perform in person searches. No search fee. Required to search: name, years to search; also helpful: address. Civil cases indexed by defendant. Civil records on docket books from 1956-1987; on computer back to 1987.

Criminal Records: Access: Mail, in person. Both court and visitors may perform in person searches. No search fee. Required to search: name, years to search, DOB; also helpful: address, SSN. Criminal records on computer back to 1987, docket books from 1956-1987.

General Information: Public access terminal is available. No juvenile, protective custody records released. SASE required. Turnaround time 1-2 days. Fax notes: Fee to fax results is $1.00 per page. Copy fee: $1.00 per page. Certification fee: $1.00. Fee payee: Maine District Court. Personal checks accepted. Prepayment is required.

North Androscoggin District Court 11 2 Main St, Livermore Falls, ME 04254; 207-897-3800. Hours: 8AM-4PM T-Th (EST). *Misdemeanor, Civil Actions, Eviction, Small Claims.*

Civil Records: Access: Mail, in person. Both court and visitors may perform in person searches. No search fee. Required to search: name, years to search, DOB. Civil cases indexed by defendant. Civil records on docket books.

Criminal Records: Access: Mail, in person. Only the court performs in person searches; visitors may not. No search fee. Required to search: name, years to search; also helpful: DOB. Criminal records on computer since 1988, prior on docket books.

General Information: No juvenile, protective custody records released. SASE requested. Turnaround time up to 1 week. Copy fee: $1.00 per page. Certification fee: $1.00. Fee payee: Maine District Court. Personal checks accepted. Prepayment is required.

Probate Court 2 Turner St, Auburn, ME 04210; 207-782-0281; Fax: 207-782-1135. Hours: 8:30AM-5PM (EST). *Probate.*

Aroostook County

Caribou Superior Court 144 Sweden St, #101, Caribou, ME 04736; 207-498-8125. Hours: 8AM-4PM (EST). *Felony, Misdemeanor, Civil Actions.*

Civil Records: Access: Mail, in person. Only the court performs in person searches; visitors may not. No search fee. Required to search: name, years to search. Civil cases indexed by defendant, plaintiff. Civil records on docket books since 1951. All cases 1990 forward stored in Caribou Court.

Criminal Records: Access: Mail, in person. Only the court performs in person searches; visitors may not. No search fee. Required to search: name, years to search; also helpful: DOB. Criminal records on docket books since 1951. All cases 1990 forward stored in Caribou Court.

General Information: No juvenile, protective custody records released. SASE required. Turnaround time 1 week. Copy fee: $1.00 per page. Certification fee: $2.00. Fee payee: Treasurer, State of Maine or Superior Court. Personal checks accepted. Prepayment is required.

Houlton Superior Court PO Box 457, Houlton, ME 04730; 207-532-6563. Hours: 8AM-4PM (EST). *Felony, Misdemeanor, Civil Actions.*

Civil Records: Access: Mail, in person. Both court and visitors may perform in person searches. No search fee. Required to search: name, years to search. Civil cases indexed by defendant, plaintiff. Civil records on docket books 1960-89. Non-pending closed case records are stored at the Houlton Court 1960-89.

Criminal Records: Access: Mail, in person. Both court and visitors may perform in person searches. No search fee. Required to search: name, years to search, DOB. Criminal records on docket books 1960-89. Non-pending closed case records are stored at the Houlton Court 1960-89.

General Information: No juvenile or protective custody records released. SASE required. Turnaround time 2-3 days. Copy fee: $2.00 for first page, $.50 each add'l. Certification fee: $2.00. Fee payee: Maine Superior Court. No personal checks accepted. Prepayment is required.

Caribou District Court - East 1 144 Sweden St, Caribou, ME 04736; 207-493-3144. Hours: 8AM-4PM (EST). *Misdemeanor, Civil Actions, Eviction, Small Claims.*

Civil Records: Access: Mail, in person. Only the court performs in person searches; visitors may not. No search fee. Required to search: name, years to search. Civil cases indexed by defendant. Civil records on docket books since 1963, on computer from 10/01.

Criminal Records: Access: In person only. Visitors must perform in person searches for themselves. No search fee. Required to search: name, years to search; also helpful: DOB. Criminal records on computer since 1987 (includes traffic), docket books since 1963.

General Information: Public access terminal is available. (Public access for criminal records only.) No juvenile or child protective records released. SASE required. Turnaround time 1 week. Copy fee: $1.00 per page. Certification fee: $2.00 plus $1.00 each additional page. Fee payee: Maine District Court. Personal checks accepted. Prepayment is required.

District Court 2 PO Box 794 (27 Riverside Dr), Presque Isle, ME 04769; 207-764-2055. Hours: 8AM-4PM (EST). *Misdemeanor, Civil Actions, Eviction, Small Claims.*

Civil Records: Access: Mail, in person. Both court and visitors may perform in person searches. No search fee. Required to search: name, years to search. Civil cases indexed by defendant. Civil records on computer since 1987, docket books since 1962.

Criminal Records: Access: In person only. Visitors must perform in person searches for themselves. No search fee. Required to search: name, years to search; also helpful: DOB. Criminal records on computer since 1987, docket books since 1962.

General Information: Public access terminal is available. No juvenile or child protective records released. SASE required. Turnaround time 1 week. Copy fee: $1.00 per page. Include $1.00 for postage or SASE. Certification fee: $1.00. Fee payee: Maine District Court. Personal checks accepted. Prepayment is required.

Fort Kent District Court - District 1 Division of Western Aroostook, PO Box 473, Fort Kent, ME 04743; 207-834-5003. Hours: 8AM-4PM (EST). *Misdemeanor, Civil Actions, Eviction, Small Claims.*

Civil Records: Access: Phone, mail, in person. Both court and visitors may perform in person searches. No search fee. Required to search: name, years to search. Civil cases indexed by defendant, plaintiff. Few civil records are computerized.

Criminal Records: Access: Phone, mail, in person. Both court and visitors may perform in person searches. No search fee. Required to search: name, years to search. Criminal records on computer from 1988, on docket books from 1960-1988.

General Information: No juvenile, protective custody, impounded, mental health records released. SASE required. Turnaround time 2-3 days. Copy fee: $1.00 per page. Certification fee: $1.00. Fee payee: Maine District Court. Personal checks accepted. Prepayment is required.

Houlton District Court - South 2 PO Box 457, Houlton, ME 04730; 207-532-2147. Hours: 8AM-4PM (EST). *Misdemeanor, Civil Actions, Eviction, Small Claims.*

Civil Records: Access: Mail, in person. Both court and visitors may perform in person searches. No search fee. Required to search: name, years to search; also helpful: address. Civil cases indexed by defendant, plaintiff. Civil records on docket books since 1960.

Criminal Records: Access: In person only. No search fee. Required to search: name, years to search; also helpful: address, DOB. Criminal records on computer since June 1987, docket books since 1960.

General Information: Public access terminal is available. (Records available since June 1987.) No Juvenile or protective custody records released. SASE required. Turnaround time 2-3 days. Copy fee: $1.00 per page. Certification fee: $1.00. Fee payee: Maine District Court. Personal checks accepted. Prepayment is required.

Madawaska District Court - West PO Box 127, 645 E Main St, Madawaska, ME 04756; 207-728-4700. Hours: 8AM-4PM M,T,F (EST). *Misdemeanor, Civil Actions, Eviction, Small Claims.*

Civil Records: Access: Phone, mail, in person. Only the court performs in person searches; visitors may not. No search fee. Required to search: name, years to search. Civil cases indexed by defendant, plaintiff. Civil records on docket books from 1967; on comptuer back to 8/2001.

Criminal Records: Access: Phone, mail, in person. Only the court performs in person searches; visitors may not. No search fee. Required to search: name, years to search, DOB. Criminal records on computer back to 1988, docket books from 1965.

General Information: No juvenile, protected custody, impounded or mental health records released. SASE required. Turnaround time 2-3 days. Copy fee: $1.00 per page. Additional fee $1.00 if no SASE. Certification fee: $1.00. Fee payee: Maine District Court. Personal checks accepted. Prepayment is required.

Probate Court 26 Court St #103, Houlton, ME 04730; 207-532-1502. Hours: 8AM-4:30PM (EST). *Probate.*

Cumberland County

Superior Court - Civil PO Box 287-DTS, Portland, ME 04112; 207-822-4105. Hours: 8AM-4:30PM (EST). *Civil Actions.*

Civil Records: Access: In person only. Both court and visitors may perform in person searches. No search fee. Required to search: name, years to search. Civil cases indexed by defendant, plaintiff. Civil records on index cards since 1975, prior records archived. They will only answer general questions on filing and hearing dates by phone or mail.
General Information: No juvenile, medical malpractice, impounded records released. SASE required. Turnaround time 1 day to 1 week. Copy fee: $1.00 per page. Include $1.00 for postage unless pre-paid envelope already enclosed. Certification fee: $1.00. Fee payee: Superior Court. Personal checks accepted. Prepayment is required.

Superior Court - Criminal PO Box 287, Portland, ME 04112; 207-822-4113. Hours: 8AM-4:30PM (EST). *Felony, Misdemeanor.*

Criminal Records: Access: In person only. Both court and visitors may perform in person searches. No search fee. Required to search: name, years to search, DOB. Criminal records on index cards since 1900s, some records form 08/98 to present are computerized.
General Information: No juvenile records released. SASE required. Turnaround time 2-3 days. Fax notes: Fee to fax results is $1.00 per page. Copy fee: $1.00 per page. Certification fee: $1.00. Fee payee: Clerk of Courts. Personal checks accepted. Prepayment is required.

Portland District Court - South 9 Civil PO Box 412, 205 Newbury St, Portland, ME 04112; 207-822-4200. Hours: 8AM-4:30PM (EST). *Civil Actions, Eviction, Small Claims.*

Note: Also see Sagadahoc District Court, which handles cases from eastern Cumberland County. Also see Brighton District Court which handles cases from western Cumberland County.
Civil Records: Access: In person. Both court and visitors may perform in person searches. No search fee. Required to search: name, years to search. Civil cases indexed by defendant. Civil records go back ten years, small claims and eviction five years.
General Information: No child custody records released. SASE required. Turnaround time 1 week. Copy fee: $1.00 per page. Certification fee: $1.00. Fee payee: Maine District Court. Personal checks accepted. Prepayment is required.

Portland District Court - South 9 Criminal PO Box 412, Portland, ME 04112; 207-822-4204. Hours: 8AM-4:30PM (EST). *Misdemeanor.*

Criminal Records: Access: In person only. Visitors may perform in person searches for themselves. Search fee: No search fee. Required to search: name, years to search, DOB, offense, date of offense. Criminal records on computer back to 09/86, prior records archived.
General Information: No impounded records released. SASE required. Turnaround time 3-4 days. Fax notes: Will not fax results. Copy fee: $1.00 per page. Certification fee: $1.00. Fee payee: Maine District Court. Personal checks accepted. Prepayment is required.

Bath District Court - East 6 RR 1, Box 310, New Meadows Rd, Bath, ME 04530; 207-442-0200. *Misdemeanor, Civil Actions, Eviction, Small Claims.*

Note: Combined with West Bath District Court 6 in Sagadahoc County.

Bridgton District Court - North 9 2 Chase Common, Bridgton, ME 04009; 207-647-3535. Hours: 8AM-4PM (EST). *Misdemeanor, Civil Actions, Eviction, Small Claims.*

Civil Records: Access: Phone, mail, in person. Visitors must perform in person searches for themselves. Search fee: $1.00 per page (copy fee). Required to search: name, years to search. Civil cases indexed by defendant. Civil records go back to 1965; on computer back to 2001.
Criminal Records: Access: Phone, mail, in person. Visitors must perform in person searches for themselves. Search fee: $1.00 per page (copy fee). Required to search: name, years to search; also helpful: DOB. Criminal records on computer back to 1986, records go back to 1965.
General Information: Public access terminal is available. (Criminal only.) No juvenile, protective custody, financial affidavits, impounded or domestic records released. Copy fee: $1.00 per page. Certification fee: $1.00. Fee payee: Maine District Court. Personal checks accepted. Prepayment is required.

Probate Court 142 Federal St, Portland, ME 04101-4196; 207-871-8382. Hours: 8:30AM-4:30PM (EST). *Probate.*

www.cumberlandcounty.org

Franklin County

Superior Court 140 Main St, Farmington, ME 04938; 207-778-3346; Fax: 207-778-8261. Hours: 8AM-4PM (EST). *Felony, Misdemeanor, Civil Actions.*

Civil Records: Access: Mail, in person. Both court and visitors may perform in person searches. No search fee. Required to search: name, years to search. Civil cases indexed by defendant, plaintiff. Civil records on docket books and index cards since 1900s.
Criminal Records: Access: In person only. No search fee. Required to search: name, years to search; also helpful: DOB, SSN. Criminal records on docket books and index cards since 1900s.
General Information: No juvenile, impounded or medical malpractice records released. Copy fee: $1.00 per page. Certification fee: $1.00. Fee payee: Superior Court. Personal checks accepted. Prepayment is required.

Franklin District Court 12 129 Main St, Farmington, ME 04938; 207-778-8200. Hours: 8AM-4PM (EST). *Misdemeanor, Civil Actions, Eviction, Small Claims.*

Civil Records: Access: In person only. Visitors must perform in person searches for themselves. No search fee. Required to search: name, years to search. Civil cases indexed by defendant. Civil records on docket books since 1965 (index cards in front).
Criminal Records: Access: In person. Visitors must perform in person searches for themselves. No search fee. Required to search: name, years to search, DOB. Criminal records on computer since 1987, on docket books since 1965 (index cards in front).
General Information: No impounded records released. Copy fee: $1.00 per page. Certification fee: $1.00. Fee payee: Maine District Court. Personal checks accepted. Prepayment is required.

Probate Court County Courthouse, 140 Main St, Farmington, ME 04938; 207-778-5888; Fax: 207-778-5899. Hours: 8:30AM-4PM (EST). *Probate.*

Hancock County

Superior Court 50 State St, Ellsworth, ME 04605-1926; 207-667-7176. Hours: 8AM-4PM (EST). *Felony, Misdemeanor, Civil Actions.*

Civil Records: Access: In person. Only the court performs in person searches; visitors may not. No search fee. Required to search: name, years to search. Civil cases indexed by defendant, plaintiff. Civil records on card files since 1960.
Criminal Records: Access: In person. Only the court performs in person searches; visitors may not. No search fee. Required to search: name, years to search, DOB. Criminal records on card files since 1960.
General Information: No protective custody records released. Copy fee: $1.00 per page. Certification fee: $1.00. Fee payee: State of Maine. Personal checks accepted. Prepayment is required.

Bar Harbor District Court - South 5 93 Cottage St, Bar Harbor, ME 04609; 207-288-3082. Hours: 8AM-4PM (EST). *Misdemeanor, Civil Actions, Eviction, Small Claims.*

Civil Records: Access: Mail, in person. Court may perform in person searches. No search fee. Required to search: name, years to search. Civil cases indexed by defendant, plaintiff. Civil records on docket books since 1970.
Criminal Records: Access: Mail, in person. Court may perform in person searches. No search fee. Required to search: name, years to search, DOB. Criminal records on computer since 1987, on docket books since 1970.
General Information: No juvenile or impounded records released. SASE required. Turnaround time 2-3 days. Copy fee: $1.00 per page. Certification fee: $1.00. Fee payee: Maine District Court. Personal checks accepted. Prepayment is required.

Ellsworth District Court - Central 5 50 State St #2, Ellsworth, ME 04605; 207-667-7141. Hours: 8AM-4PM (EST). *Misdemeanor, Civil Actions, Eviction, Small Claims.*

Civil Records: Access: Mail, in person. Both court and visitors may perform in person searches. No search fee. Required to search: name, years to search. Civil cases indexed by defendant, plaintiff. Need to know names of both parties to search. Civil records on docket books since 1965; on computer back to 5/1987.
Criminal Records: Access: Mail, in person. Both court and visitors may perform in person searches. No search fee. Required to search: name, years to search, DOB. Criminal records on computer back to 1987, docket books since 1965. The court will allow no access to criminal records.
General Information: No juvenile, child protection, adoption or mental health records released. SASE required. Turnaround time 1 week. Fax notes: Will not fax results. Copy fee: $1.00 per page. Certification fee: $2.00. Fee payee: Maine District Court. Personal checks accepted. Prepayment is required.

Probate Court 50 State St, Ellsworth, ME 04605; 207-667-8434. Hours: 8:30AM-4PM (EST). *Probate.*

Kennebec County

Superior Court 95 State St, Clerk of Court, Augusta, ME 04330; 207-622-9357. Hours: 8AM-4PM (EST). *Felony, Misdemeanor, Civil Actions.*

Civil Records: Access: Mail, in person. Only the court performs in person searches; visitors may not. No search fee. Required to search: name, years to search. Civil cases indexed by defendant, plaintiff. Civil records on index cards since 1977, docket books since 1950, on computer 2 years.

Criminal Records: Access: In person only. Visitors must perform in person searches for themselves. No search fee. Required to search: name, years to search; also helpful: DOB, docket number. Criminal records on index cards since 1977, docket books since 1950, on computer 2 years.

General Information: No protective custody records released. SASE not required. Turnaround time 1 week. Copy fee: $1.00 per page. Certification fee: $1.00. Fee payee: Treasurer State of Maine. Personal checks accepted. Prepayment is required.

Maine District Court 7 Division of Southern Kennebec, 145 State St, Augusta, ME 04330-7495; 207-287-8075. Hours: 8AM-4PM (EST). *Misdemeanor, Civil Actions, Eviction, Small Claims.*

Civil Records: Access: Mail, in person. Both court and visitors may perform in person searches. No search fee. Required to search: name, years to search. Civil cases indexed by defendant. Civil records kept 10 years.

Criminal Records: Access: Mail, in person. Only the court may perform in person searches No search fee. Required to search: name, years to search, DOB; also helpful: SSN. Criminal records on computer back to 1987, docket books since 1963.

General Information: No juvenile, mental health, protective custody and closed proceeding case records released. Turnaround time 1 week. Copy fee: $1.00 per page. Certification fee: $1.00. Fee payee: Maine District Court. Personal checks accepted. Prepayment is required.

Waterville District Court - District 7 18 Colby St, PO Box 397, Waterville, ME 04903; 207-873-2103. Hours: 8AM-4PM (EST). *Misdemeanor, Civil Actions, Eviction, Small Claims.*

Civil Records: Access: Mail, in person. Both court and visitors may perform in person searches. No search fee. Required to search: name, years to search; also helpful: address. Civil cases indexed by defendant. Civil records on docket books from 1979-1998; on computer since 2001.

Criminal Records: Access: Mail, in person. Both court and visitors may perform in person searches. No search fee. Required to search: name, years to search, DOB; also helpful: address, SSN. Criminal records on computer since 1987, docket books from 1979-1987.

General Information: No juvenile, protective custody records released. Court reserves the right to restrict the number of record requests. SASE required. Turnaround time 1 week. Copy fee: $1.00 per page. Certification fee: $1.00. Fee payee: Maine. Personal checks accepted. Prepayment is required.

Probate Court 95 State St, Augusta, ME 04330; 207-622-7558 or 207-622-7559; Fax: 207-621-1639. Hours: 8AM-4PM (EST). *Probate.*

www.datamaine.com/probate

Knox County

Superior Court 62 Union St, Rockland, ME 04841-2836; 207-594-2576. Hours: 8AM-4PM (EST). *Felony, Misdemeanor, Civil Actions.*

Civil Records: Access: Phone, mail, in person. Both court and visitors may perform in person searches. No search fee. Required to search: name, years to search. Civil cases indexed by defendant, plaintiff. Civil records on docket books since 1930s, index cards (in office) since mid-1970s; on computer back to 1999.

Criminal Records: Access: In person only. Visitors must perform in person searches for themselves. No search fee. Required to search: name, years to search; also helpful: DOB. Criminal records on docket books since 1930s, index cards (in office) since mid-1970s; on computer back to 1999.

General Information: No Impounded or pre-sentence records released. SASE not required. Turnaround time 1 week. Fax notes: Will not fax results. Copy fee: $1.00 per page. Certification fee: $1.00 per document. Fee payee: State Treasurer. Personal checks accepted. Prepayment is required.

District Court 6 62 Union St, Rockland, ME 04841; 207-596-2240. Hours: 8AM-4PM (EST). *Misdemeanor, Civil Actions, Eviction, Small Claims.*

Civil Records: Access: In person. Court may perform in person searches. No search fee. Required to search: name, years to search. Civil cases indexed by defendant, plaintiff. Civil records on docket books.

Criminal Records: Access: In person. Court may perform in person searches. No search fee. Required to search: name, years to search, DOB. Criminal records on docket books.

General Information: No impounded records released. Copy fee: $1.00 per page. Certification fee: $1.00. Fee payee: Maine District Court. Personal checks accepted. Prepayment is required.

Probate Court 62 Union St, Rockland, ME 04841; 207-594-0427; Fax: 207-594-0443. Hours: 8AM-4PM (EST). *Probate.*

http://knoxcounty.midcoast.com

Lincoln County

Lincoln County Superior Court High St, PO Box 249, Wiscasset, ME 04578; 207-882-7517; Fax: 207-882-7741. Hours: 8AM-4PM (EST). *Felony, Misdemeanor, Civil Actions.*

www.co.lincoln.me.us

Civil Records: Access: Mail, in person. Only the court performs in person searches; visitors may not. No search fee. Required to search: name, years to search. Civil cases indexed by defendant, plaintiff. Civil records on docket books and index cards since 1960s.

Criminal Records: Access: Mail, in person. Only the court performs in person searches; visitors may not. No search fee. Required to search: name, years to search, DOB. Criminal records on docket books and index cards since 1960s.

General Information: No protective custody records released. SASE not required. Copy fee: $1.00 per page. Certification fee: $2.00. Personal checks accepted. Prepayment is required.

District Court 6 32 High St, PO Box 249, Wiscasset, ME 04578; 207-882-6363; Fax: 207-882-5980. Hours: 8AM-4PM (EST). *Misdemeanor, Civil Actions, Eviction, Small Claims.*

www.co.lincoln.me.us

Civil Records: Access: Phone, mail, in person. Both court and visitors may perform in person searches. No search fee. Required to search: name, years to search. Civil cases indexed by defendant, plaintiff. Civil records on docket books since 1965; on computer back to 1987.

Criminal Records: Access: Mail, in person. Only the court performs in person searches; visitors may not. No search fee. Required to search: name, years to search, DOB or SSN. Criminal records on computer back to 1987, docket books since 1960.

General Information: No juvenile, child protective or impounded records released. SASE required. Turnaround time 1 week. Copy fee: $1.00 per page. Certification fee: $5.00. Fee payee: Maine District Court. Personal checks accepted. Prepayment required.

Probate Court High St, PO Box 249, Wiscasset, ME 04578; 207-882-7392; Fax: 207-882-4324. Hours: 8AM-4PM (EST). *Probate.*

www.co.lincoln.me.us/dep.html

Oxford County

Superior Court Courthouse, 26 Western Ave, PO Box 179, South Paris, ME 04281-0179; 207-743-8936; Fax: 207-743-0544. Hours: 8AM-4PM (EST). *Felony, Misdemeanor, Civil Actions.*

Civil Records: Access: Mail, in person. Visitors must perform in person searches for themselves. No search fee. Required to search: name, years to search, DOB. Civil cases indexed by defendant, plaintiff. Criminal records on computer back to 1998; on docket books since 1980.

Criminal Records: Access: In person only. Visitors must perform in person searches for themselves. No search fee. Required to search: name, years to search, DOB. Criminal records on docket books since 1960.

General Information: No protective custody or protection from abuse records released. SASE required. Turnaround time 3-4 days. Copy fee: $1.00 per page. Certification fee: $1.00. Fee payee: Clerk of Superior Court. Personal checks accepted.

Rumford District Court - North 11 Municipal Bldg, 145 Congress St, Rumford, ME 04276; 207-364-7171. Hours: 8AM-4PM (EST). *Misdemeanor, Civil Actions, Eviction, Small Claims.*

Civil Records: Access: Mail, in person. Both court and visitors may perform in person searches. No search fee. Required to search: name, years to search. Civil cases indexed by defendant, plaintiff. Civil records on docket books since 1966.

Criminal Records: Access: Mail, in person. Both court and visitors may perform in person searches. No search fee. Required to search: name, years to search, DOB. Criminal records on computer since March 1988, docket books since 1966.

General Information: No impounded records released. SASE required. Turnaround time 1 week. Copy fee: $1.00 per page. Certification fee: $2.00. Fee payee: Maine District Court. Personal checks accepted.

South Paris District Court - South 11 26 Western Ave, South Paris, ME 04281; 207-743-8942. Hours: 8AM-4PM (EST). *Misdemeanor, Civil Actions, Eviction, Small Claims.*

Civil Records: Access: Mail, in person. Only the court performs in person searches; visitors may not. No search fee. Required to search: name, years to search. Civil cases indexed by defendant. Civil records on docket books back 5 years.

Criminal Records: Access: Mail, in person. Both court and visitors may perform in person searches. No search fee. Required to search: name, years to search; also helpful: DOB. Criminal records on computer 1988-4/1999, docket books back 5 years. Records after 4/99 cannot be accessed on the public access computer; request a search in writing.

General Information: Public access terminal is available. (Criminal only.) No juvenile or child protective records released. SASE required. Turnaround time 1-2 days. Copy fee: $1.00 per page. Certification fee: $1.00. Fee payee: Maine District Court. Personal checks accepted. Prepayment is required.

Probate Court 26 Western Ave, PO Box 179, South Paris, ME 04281; 207-743-6671; Fax: 207-743-2656. Hours: 8AM-4PM (EST). *Probate.*

Penobscot County

Superior Court 97 Hammond St, Bangor, ME 04401; 207-561-2300. Hours: 8AM-4:30PM (EST). *Felony, Misdemeanor, Civil Actions.*

Civil Records: Access: Mail, in person. Only the court performs in person searches; visitors may not. No search fee. Required to search: name, years to search. Civil cases indexed by defendant, plaintiff. Civil records on docket books since 1975; on computer back to 1998; archived back to 1927.

Criminal Records: Access: In person only. Only the court performs in person searches; visitors may not. No search fee. Required to search: name, years to search, DOB. Criminal records on docket books since 1975; on computer back to 1998; archived back to 1927.

General Information: No impounded records released. SASE required. Copy fee: $1.00 per page. Certification fee: $1.00. Fee payee: Treasurer, State of Maine. Personal checks accepted. Prepayment is required.

Bangor District Court 73 Hammond St, Bangor, ME 04401; 207-941-3040. Hours: 8AM-4PM (EST). *Misdemeanor, Civil Actions, Eviction, Small Claims.*

Civil Records: Access: Mail, in person. Both court and visitors may perform in person searches. No search fee. Required to search: name, years to search. Civil cases indexed by defendant. Civil records on docket books since 1962. Court suggests using central state repository.

Criminal Records: Access: Mail, in person. Both court and visitors may perform in person searches. No search fee. Required to search: name, years to search; also helpful: DOB. Criminal records on computer since late 1986, docket books since 1962.

General Information: Public access terminal is available. (Criminal only.) No protective custody records released. SASE required. Turnaround time 1 week. Copy fee: $1.00 per page. Certification fee: $1.00. Fee payee: Maine District Court. Personal checks accepted. Prepayment is required.

Central District Court - Central 13 66 Maine St, Lincoln, ME 04457; 207-794-8512. Hours: 8AM-4PM (EST). *Misdemeanor, Civil Actions, Eviction, Small Claims.*

Civil Records: Access: In person only. Only the court performs in person searches; visitors may not. No search fee. Required to search: name, years to search. Civil cases indexed by defendant. Civil records on docket books since 1964.

Criminal Records: Access: In person only. Only the court performs in person searches; visitors may not. No search fee. Required to search: name, years to search, DOB. Criminal records on computer since 1987, docket books since 1964.

General Information: No juvenile or protective custody records released. Copy fee: $1.00 per page. Certification fee: $1.00. Fee payee: Maine District Court. Personal checks accepted. Prepayment required.

Millinocket District Court - North 13 207 Penobscot Ave, Millinocket, ME 04462; 207-723-4786. Hours: 8AM-4PM (EST). *Misdemeanor, Civil Actions, Eviction, Small Claims.*

Civil Records: Access: In person. Both the court and visitors may perform in person searches. No search fee. Required to search: name, years to search. Civil cases indexed by defendant, plaintiff. Civil records on docket books since 1964; computerized records since 1987.

Criminal Records: Access: In person. Both court and visitors may perform in person searches. No search fee. Required to search: name, years to search, DOB. Criminal records on computer since 1987, docket books since 1964.

General Information: No juvenile or protective custody records released. Copy fee: $1.00 per page. Certification fee: $1.00. Fee payee: Maine District Court. Personal checks accepted. Prepayment is required.

Newport District Court - West 3 12 Water St, Newport, ME 04953; 207-368-5778. Hours: 8AM-4PM (EST). *Misdemeanor, Civil Actions, Eviction, Small Claims.*

Civil Records: Access: Mail, in person. Both court and visitors may perform in person searches. No search fee. Required to search: name, years to search. Civil cases indexed by defendant, plaintiff. Civil records on docket books back to 1965; computerized back to 2001.

Criminal Records: Access: Mail, in person. Both court and visitors may perform in person searches. No search fee. Required to search: name, years to search, DOB. Criminal records on computer back to 1987, docket books since 1965.

General Information: Public access terminal is available. No impounded records released. SASE required. Turnaround time 1 week. Copy fee: $1.00 per page. Certification fee: $1.00. Fee payee: Maine District Court. Personal checks accepted. Prepayment required.

Probate Court 97 Hammond St, Bangor, ME 04401-4996; 207-942-8769; Fax: 207-941-8499. Hours: 8AM-4:30PM (EST). *Probate.*

Piscataquis County

Superior Court 159 E Main St, Dover-Foxcroft, ME 04426; 207-564-8419; Fax: 207-564-3363. Hours: 8AM-4PM (EST). *Felony, Misdemeanor, Civil Actions.*

Civil Records: Access: Mail, in person. Only the court performs in person searches; visitors may not. No search fee. Required to search: name, years to search. Civil cases indexed by defendant, plaintiff. Civil records on docket books since 1960; computerized records since 1998.

Criminal Records: Access: Mail, in person. Only the court performs in person searches; visitors may not. No search fee. Required to search: name, years to search; also helpful: DOB. Criminal records on docket books since 1960; computerized records since 1998.

General Information: No pre-sentence report records released. SASE required. Turnaround time 1 week. Copy fee: $1.00 per page. Certification fee: $1.00. Fee payee: State of Maine Superior Court. Personal checks accepted. Prepayment is required.

District Court 13 59 E Main St, Dover-Foxcroft, ME 04426; 207-564-2240. Hours: 8AM-4PM (EST). *Misdemeanor, Civil Actions, Eviction, Small Claims.*

Civil Records: Access: Mail, in person. Both court and visitors may perform in person searches. No search fee. Required to search: name, years to search. Civil cases indexed by defendant, plaintiff. Civil records on docket books since 1963.

Criminal Records: Access: Mail, in person. Both court and visitors may perform in person searches. No search fee. Required to search: name, years to search; also helpful: DOB. Criminal records on computer since 1987, docket books since 1963.

General Information: No protective custody or juvenile records released. SASE required. Turnaround time 1 week. Copy fee: $1.00 per page. Certification fee: $1.00. Fee payee: Maine District Court. Personal checks accepted. Prepayment is required.

Probate Court 51 E Main St, Dover-Foxcroft, ME 04426; 207-564-2431; Fax: 207-564-3022. Hours: 8:30AM-4PM (EST). *Probate.*

Sagadahoc County

Superior Court 752 High St, PO Box 246, Bath, ME 04530; 207-443-9733. Hours: 8AM-4:30PM (EST). *Felony, Misdemeanor, Civil Actions.*

Civil Records: Access: Mail, in person. Both court and visitors may perform in person searches. Search fee: $5.00 per name. Required to search: name, years to search. Civil cases indexed by defendant, plaintiff. Civil records on docket books since 1900s; on comptuer back to 1999.

Criminal Records: Access: Mail, in person. Both court and visitors may perform in person searches. Search fee: $5.00 per name. Required to search: name, years to search, DOB. Criminal records on docket books since 1900s; on computer back to 1999.

General Information: No impounded records released. SASE required. Copy fee: $1.00 per page. Certification fee: $1.00. Fee payee: Clerk of Superior Court. Cash, checks and money orders accepted. Prepayment is required.

West Bath District Court 6 RR 1, Box 310, New Meadows Rd, Bath, ME 04530; 207-442-0200. Hours: 8AM-4PM (EST). *Misdemeanor, Civil Actions, Eviction, Small Claims.*

Note: This court handles the eastern part of Cumberland County and all of Sagadahoc County.

Civil Records: Access: In person only. Both court and visitors may perform in person searches. No search fee. Required to search: name, years to search. Civil cases indexed by defendant, plaintiff. Civil records on docket books since 1980's; prior archived.

Criminal Records: Access: In person only. Both court and visitors may perform in person searches. No search fee. Required to search: name, years to search; also helpful: DOB. Criminal records on computer since 1987, docket books back to 1975; prior archived. Search requests are referred to central state repository.

General Information: No protective custody or juvenile records released. Copy fee: $1.00 per page. Certification fee: $1.00. Fee payee: Maine District Court. Personal checks accepted. Prepayment is required.

Probate Court 752 High St, PO Box 246, Bath, ME 04530; 207-443-8218; Fax: 207-443-8217. Hours: 8:30AM-4:30PM (EST). *Probate.*

Somerset County

Superior Court PO Box 725, Skowhegan, ME 04976; 207-474-5161. Hours: 8AM-4PM (EST). *Felony, Misdemeanor, Civil Actions.*

Civil Records: Access: In person only. Visitors must perform in person searches for themselves. No search fee. Required to search: name, years to search. Civil cases indexed by defendant, plaintiff. Civil records archived in Augusta back to 1800s, docket books and index cards back to 1900s.

Criminal Records: Access: In person only. Visitors must perform in person searches for themselves. No search fee. Required to search: name, years to search; also helpful: DOB. Criminal records archived in Augusta back to 1800s, docket books and index cards back to 1900s; on computer back to 1998.

General Information: No impounded, present investigations, psychological evaluations or child support records released. Copy fee: $1.00 per page. Certification fee: $1.00. Fee payee: Clerk of Superior Court. Personal checks accepted. Prepayment required.

District Court 12 PO Box 525, 47 Court St, Skowhegan, ME 04976; 207-474-9518. Hours: 8AM-

4PM (EST). *Misdemeanor, Civil Actions, Eviction, Small Claims.*

Civil Records: Access: Mail, in person. Both court and visitors may perform in person searches. No search fee. Required to search: name, years to search. Civil cases indexed by defendant. Civil records on docket books since 1960s, divorces since 1970s.

Criminal Records: Access: Mail, in person. Both court and visitors may perform in person searches. No search fee. Required to search: name, years to search; also helpful: DOB. Criminal records on computer since 1987, docket books since 1960s.

General Information: Public access terminal is available. (Criminal only.) No juvenile records released. SASE required. Turnaround time 2-4 weeks. Copy fee: $1.00 per page. Certification fee: $1.00. Fee payee: Maine District Court. Personal checks accepted. Prepayment is required.

Probate Court 41 Court St, Skowhegan, ME 04976; 207-474-3322. Hours: 8:30AM-4:30PM (EST). *Probate.*

Waldo County

Superior Court 137 Church St, PO Box 188, Belfast, ME 04915; 207-338-1940; Fax: 207-338-1086. Hours: 8AM-4PM (EST). *Felony, Misdemeanor, Civil Actions.*

Civil Records: Access: Mail, fax, in person. Only the court performs in person searches; visitors may not. No search fee. Required to search: name, years to search. Civil cases indexed by defendant, plaintiff. Civil records archived back to 1980 (not in office), on docket books since 1980; on computer back to 1998.

Criminal Records: Access: Mail, fax, in person. Only the court performs in person searches; visitors may not. No search fee. Required to search: name, years to search, DOB. Criminal records archived back to 1975 (not in office), on docket books since 1975; on computer back to 1998.

General Information: No protective custody records released. SASE required. Turnaround time 1 week. Fax notes: Will fax results to toll free numbers only. Copy fee: $1.00 per page. Certification fee: $1.00 per document. Fee payee: State Treasurer. Personal checks accepted. Prepayment is required.

District Court 5 PO Box 382, 103 Church St, Belfast, ME 04915; 207-338-3107. Hours: 8AM-4PM (EST). *Misdemeanor, Civil Actions, Eviction, Small Claims.*

Civil Records: Access: Mail, in person. Both court and visitors may perform in person searches. No search fee. Required to search: name, years to search. Civil cases indexed by defendant, plaintiff. Civil records on docket books since 1966, computerized since 2001.

Criminal Records: Access: Mail, in person. Both court and visitors may perform in person searches. No search fee. Required to search: name, years to search, DOB. Criminal records on computer since 1987, docket books since 1966.

General Information: No juvenile or impounded records released. SASE required. Turnaround time 1 week. Copy fee: $1.00 per page. Certification fee: $1.00. Fee payee: Maine District Court. Personal checks accepted.

Probate Court 172 High St, PO Box 323, Belfast, ME 04915-0323; 207-338-2780; Fax: 207-338-6360. Hours: 8AM-4PM (EST). *Probate.*

Note: This office will move to a new location approximately July 2002. The PO Box and phone numbers will remain the same.

Washington County

Superior Court Clerk of Court, PO Box 526, Machias, ME 04654; 207-255-3326. Hours: 8AM-4PM (EST). *Felony, Misdemeanor, Civil.*

Civil Records: Access: Mail, in person. Both court and visitors may perform in person searches. No search fee. Required to search: name, years to search. Civil cases indexed by defendant, plaintiff. Civil records on docket books and index cards since 1930s.

Criminal Records: Access: Mail, in person. Both court and visitors may perform in person searches. No search fee. Required to search: name, years to search, DOB. Criminal records on docket books and index cards since 1930s.

General Information: No impounded records released. SASE required. Turnaround time 1 week. Copy fee: $1.00 per page. Certification fee: $1.00. Fee payee: Treasurer, State of Maine. Personal checks accepted. Prepayment is required.

Calais District Court - North 4 PO Box 929, Calais, ME 04619; 207-454-2055; TTY# 207-454-0085. Hours: 8AM-4PM (EST). *Misdemeanor, Civil Actions, Eviction, Small Claims.*

Civil Records: Access: In person only. Visitors must perform in person searches for themselves. No search fee. Required to search: name, years to search. Civil cases indexed by defendant, plaintiff. Civil records on docket books since 1964.

Criminal Records: Access: In person only. Visitors must perform in person searches for themselves. No search fee. Required to search: name, years to search, DOB. Criminal records on computer since 1987, docket books since 1964.

General Information: Public access terminal is available. No juvenile or protective custody records released. Copy fee: $1.00 per page. Certification fee: $1.00. Fee payee: Maine District Court. Personal checks accepted. Prepayment is required.

Maine District Court 4 47 Court St, PO Box 297, Machias, ME 04654; 207-255-3044. Hours: 8AM-4PM (EST). *Misdemeanor, Civil Actions, Eviction, Small Claims.*

Civil Records: Access: Mail, in person. Both court and visitors may perform in person searches. No search fee. Required to search: name, years to search. Civil cases indexed by defendant, plaintiff. Civil records on docket books since 1964; on computer 1987-1999.

Criminal Records: Access: Mail, in person. Both court and visitors may perform in person searches. No search fee. Required to search: name, years to search, DOB. Criminal records on computer 1987-1999, docket books since 1964.

General Information: Public access terminal is available. (Public access terminal access for civil in person searches.) No protective custody or juvenile records released. SASE required. Turnaround time 4 days. Copy fee: $1.00 per page. Add $1.00 processing fee. Certification fee: $1.00. Fee payee: Maine District Court. Personal checks accepted. Prepayment required.

Probate Court PO Box 297, Machias, ME 04654; 207-255-6591. Hours: 8AM-4PM (EST). *Probate.*

York County

Superior Court Clerk of Court, PO Box 160, Alfred, ME 04002; 207-324-5122. Hours: 8AM-4:30PM (EST). *Felony, Misdemeanor, Civil Actions.*

Civil Records: Access: Mail, in person. Visitors must perform in person searches for themselves. No search fee. Required to search: name, years to search. Civil cases indexed by defendant, plaintiff. Civil records on docket books since 1960; computerized records go back to 2002.

Criminal Records: Access: Mail, in person. Visitors must perform in person searches for themselves. No search fee. Required to search: name, years to search, DOB. Criminal records on docket books since 1966; computerized records go back to 1998.

General Information: Public access terminal is available. (Terminal available in late 2002.) No juvenile, or protective custody records released. Copy fee: $1.00 per page. Add $1.00 handling fee. Certification fee: $1.00. Fee payee: Clerk of Courts. Only cashiers checks and money orders accepted. Prepayment is required.

Biddeford District Court - East 10 25 Adams St, Biddeford, ME 04005; 207-283-1147. Hours: 8AM-4PM (EST). *Misdemeanor, Civil Actions, Eviction, Small Claims.*

Civil Records: Access: In person only. Visitors must perform in person searches for themselves. No search fee. Required to search: name, years to search. Civil cases indexed by defendant. Civil records on docket books since 1989. Court will do up to 3 searches.

Criminal Records: Access: In person only. Visitors must perform in person searches for themselves. No search fee. Required to search: name, years to search; also helpful: DOB. Criminal records on computer since 1986. Court will do up to 3 searches.

General Information: No child protection or juvenile records released. Copy fee: $1.00 per page. Certification fee: $1.00. Fee payee: Maine District Court. Personal checks accepted. Prepayment is required.

Springvale District Court - West 10 447 Main St, Springvale, ME 04083; 207-459-1400. Hours: 8AM-4PM (EST). *Misdemeanor, Civil Actions, Eviction, Small Claims.*

Civil Records: Access: In person only. Both court and visitors may perform in person searches Search fee: $1.00 per page. Required to search: name, years to search. Civil cases indexed by defendant. Civil records on computer since 1985, docket books since 1985.

Criminal Records: Access: Mail, in person. Both court and visitors may perform in person searches No search fee. Required to search: name, years to search, DOB. Criminal records on computer since 1997, dockets books since 1980.

General Information: No impounded, juvenile, mental health or protective custody records released. SASE required. Turnaround time 3-4 days. Copy fee: $1.00 per page. Certification fee: $1.00. Fee payee: Maine District Court. Personal checks accepted. Prepayment is required.

York District Court - South 10 PO Box 770, Chase's Pond Rd, York, ME 03909-0770; 207-363-1230. Hours: 8AM-4PM (EST). *Misdemeanor, Civil Actions, Eviction, Small Claims.*

Civil Records: Access: Mail, in person. Visitors must perform in person searches for themselves. Search fee: Court will perform search if name, year and book are provided; no fee except for copies. Required to search: name, years to search. Civil cases indexed by defendant, plaintiff. Civil records on docket books since 1975; on computer back to 1985.

Criminal Records: Access: In person only. Visitors must perform in person searches for themselves. Search fee: Court will perform search if name, year and book are provided; no fee except for copies. Required to search: name, years to search, DOB. Criminal records on computer back to 1985, docket books since 1975.

General Information: No impounded, juvenile and protective custody records released. Copy fee: $1.00 per page. Certification fee: $2.00. Fee payee: Maine District Court. Personal checks accepted. Prepayment required.

Probate Court PO Box 399, 45 Kennebunk Rd, Alfred, ME 04002; 207-324-1577; Fax: 207-324-0163. Hours: 8:30AM-4:30PM (EST). *Probate.*

Maine Recording Offices

ORGANIZATION: 16 counties, 17 recording offices. The recording officer is County Register of Deeds. Counties maintain a general index of all transactions recorded. Aroostock and Oxford Counties each have two recording offices. There are no county assessors; each town has its own. The entire state is in the Eastern Time Zone (EST).

REAL ESTATE RECORDS: Counties do not usually perform real estate name searches, but some will look up a name informally. Copy and certification fees vary widely. Assessor and tax records are located at the town/city level.

UCC RECORDS: Financing statements are filed at the state level, except for real estate related filings, which are filed only with the Register of Deeds. Counties do not perform UCC searches. Copy fees are usually $1.00 per page.

TAX LIEN RECORDS: All tax liens on personal property are filed with the Secretary of State. All tax liens on real property are filed with the Register of Deeds.

OTHER LIENS: Municipal, bail bond, mechanics.

ONLINE ACCESS: There is no statewide system. However, a private vendor has placed assessor records from a number of towns on the Internet. Visit http://data.visionappraisal.com

Androscoggin County

County Register of Deeds, 2 Turner St, Courthouse, Auburn, ME 04210-5978. County Register of Deeds, R/E and UCC Recording 207-782-0191; Fax 207-784-3163.
This agency will not perform searches. **Online Access:** Real Estate, Tax Lien Records. Access to the Registry index is available for a $50.00 annual fee and $.25 per minute. Indexes go back to 1976. For information and sign-up, contact Jeanine at 207-782-0191. **Other Phone Numbers:** Treasurer 207-784-7491.

Aroostook County (Northern Dist.)

County Register of Deeds, PO Box 47, Fort Kent, ME 04743. County Register of Deeds, R/E and UCC Recording 207-834-3925; Fax 207-834-3138. www.aroostook.me.us/indexhome.html
This agency will not perform searches. **Other Phone Numbers:** Assessor 207-834-3090; Treasurer 207-834-3318; Vital Records 207-834-3090.

Aroostook County (Southern Dist.)

County Register of Deeds, 26 Court St., Suite 102, Houlton, ME 04730. 207-532-1500 R/E Recording: 207-834-3925; Fax 207-532-1506. www.aroostook.me.us/indexhome.html
All locations from New Sweden south file in this office. This agency will not perform searches.

Cumberland County

County Register of Deeds, PO Box 7230, Portland, ME 04112. County Register of Deeds, R/E and UCC Recording 207-871-8389; Fax 207-772-4162.
This agency will not perform searches. **Online Access:** Assessor, Property Sales Records. Records on the Cape Elizabeth Town Assessor database are available free online at www.capeelizabeth.com/taxdata.html. Search by owner name, road and house number for Cape Elizabeth Town. Records on the Freeport Town Assessor property databases are available free online at www.freeportmaine.com/assessor/sendform.html. Also, search the Town of South Portland assessor database at http://data.visionappraisal.com/SouthPortlandME. Also, search the Town of Cumberland assessor data at http://data.visionappraisal.com/CumberlandME. The Gorham assessor is at http://data.visionappraisal.com/GorhamME. **Other Phone Numbers:** Assessor 207-874-8486; Treasurer 207-871-8392.

Franklin County

County Register of Deeds, 140 Main St, Courthouse, Farmington, ME 04938-1818. 207-778-5889; Fax 207-778-5899.
This agency will not perform searches.

Hancock County

County Register of Deeds, PO Box 784, Ellsworth, ME 04605. County Register of Deeds, R/E and UCC Recording 207-667-8353; Fax 207-667-1410. www.co.hancock.me.us/deeds2.html
Will search UCC records. This agency will not do a tax lien search. Will not search real estate records. **Online Access:** Real Estate, Lines, UCC, Recording Records. Access to the county registry of deeds database at www.registryofdeeds.com requires registration. Viewing of records back to 1790 is free, but $1.25 per page to print. Register online. This site has had hacker problems; site of the infamous 3-monkeys. For information, visit www.registryofdeeds.com or call 888-833-3979.

Kennebec County

County Register of Deeds, PO Box 1053, Augusta, ME 04332-1053. 207-622-0431; Fax 207-622-1598.
Will search UCC records. This agency will not do a tax lien search. Will not search real estate records. **Online Access:** Assessor Records. Records on the Winslow Town Property Records database are available free online at www.winslowmaine.org. Records on the Town of Waterville Assessor's Database are available free online at http://data.visionappraisal.com/WatervilleME. User ID is required; registration is free.

Knox County

County Register of Deeds, 62 Union St, Rockland, ME 04841. 207-594-0422; Fax 207-594-0446.
This agency will not perform searches. **Other Phone Numbers:** Assessor 207-594-0420.

Lincoln County

County Register of Deeds, PO Box 249, 32 High St., Wiscasset, ME 04578-0249. 207-882-7515; Fax 207-882-4061.
Will search UCC records. This agency will not do a tax lien search. Will not search real estate records.

Oxford County

County Register of Deeds, PO Box 179, South Paris, ME 04281-0179. 207-743-6211; Fax 207-743-2656.
File in this office for all towns EXCEPT the following: Brownfield, Denmark, Fryeburg, Hiram, Lovell, Porter, Stoneham, Stow, and Sweden. Will search UCC records. This agency will not do a tax lien search. Will not search real estate records. **Other Phone Numbers:** Assessor 207-539-4431.

Penobscot County

County Register of Deeds, PO Box 2070, Bangor, ME 04402-2070. 207-942-8797; Fax 207-945-4920.
This agency will not perform searches.

Piscataquis County

County Register of Deeds, 51 E. Main St, Dover-Foxcroft, ME 04426. 207-564-2411; Fax 207-564-7708.
This agency will not perform searches. **Other Phone Numbers:** Assessor 207-564-3318.

Sagadahoc County

County Register of Deeds, PO Box 246, Bath, ME 04530. 207-443-8214; Fax 207-443-8216. www.cityofbath.com
Will not search UCC records. Will check a name for recent recording. This agency will not do a tax lien search. Will not search real estate records. **Online Access:** Assessor Records. Records on the City of Bath Assessor database are available free online at www.cityofbath.com/assessing/INDEX.htm.

Somerset County

County Register of Deeds, PO Box 248, Skowhegan, ME 04976-0248. 207-474-3421; Fax 207-474-2793.
This agency will not perform searches.

Waldo County

County Register of Deeds, PO Box D, Belfast, ME 04915. 207-338-1710; Fax 207-338-6360.
This agency will not perform searches.

Washington County

County Register of Deeds, PO Box 297, Machias, ME 04654-0297. 207-255-6512; Fax 207-255-3838.
Will search UCC records. This agency will not do a tax lien search. Will not search real estate records. **Other Phone Numbers:** Assessor 207-255-6621.

York County

County Register of Deeds, PO Box 339, Alfred, ME 04002-0339. 207-324-1576; Fax 207-324-2886. www.raynorshyn.com/yorknet
This agency will not perform searches. **Online Access:** Assessor, Property Records. Search the Town of Kennebunk assessor data free at www.kennebunk.maine.org/assessing/database/database.html. Search the Town of Eliot assessor data at http://data.visionappraisal.com/EliotME. Search Town of York assessor data at www.yorkmaine.org/assess/accsel.html. There is also an avdanced search feature with land value and acres. Town of York assessor data is also available at http://data.visionappraisal.com/YorkME. Free registration is required. **Other Phone Numbers:** Treasurer 207-324-1571.

Maine County Locator

You will usually be able to find the city name in the City/County Cross. Reference below. In that case, it is a simple matter to determine the county from the cross reference. However, only the official US Postal Service city names are included in this index. There are an additional 40,000 place names that people use in their addresses. Therefore, we have also included a ZIP/City Cross. Reference immediately following the City/County Cross. Reference.

If you know the ZIP Code but the city name does not appear in the City/County Cross. Reference index, look up the ZIP Code in the ZIP/City Cross. Reference, find the city name, then look up the city name in the City/County Cross. Reference. For example, you want to know the county for an address of Menands, NY 12204. There is no "Menands" in the City/County Cross. Reference. The ZIP/City Cross. Reference shows that ZIP Codes 12201-12288 are for the city of Albany. Looking back in the City/County Cross. Reference, Albany is in Albany County.

City/County Cross Reference

ABBOT Piscataquis
ABBOT VILLAGE Piscataquis
ACTON York
ADDISON Washington
ALBION Kennebec
ALFRED York
ALNA Lincoln
ANDOVER Oxford
ANSON Somerset
ASHLAND Aroostook
ATHENS Somerset
ATLANTIC Hancock
AUBURN Androscoggin
AUGUSTA Kennebec
AURORA Hancock
BAILEY ISLAND Cumberland
BAILEYVILLE Washington
BANGOR Penobscot
BAR HARBOR Hancock
BAR MILLS York
BASS HARBOR Hancock
BATH Sagadahoc
BAYVILLE Lincoln
BEALS Washington
BELFAST Waldo
BELGRADE Kennebec
BELGRADE LAKES Kennebec
BENEDICTA Aroostook
BERNARD Hancock
BERWICK York
BETHEL Oxford
BIDDEFORD York
BIDDEFORD POOL York
BINGHAM Somerset
BIRCH HARBOR Hancock
BLAINE Aroostook
BLUE HILL Hancock
BLUE HILL FALLS Hancock
BOOTHBAY Lincoln
BOOTHBAY HARBOR Lincoln
BOWDOIN Sagadahoc
BOWDOINHAM Sagadahoc
BRADFORD Penobscot
BRADLEY Penobscot
BREMEN Lincoln
BREWER Penobscot
BRIDGEWATER Aroostook
BRIDGTON Cumberland
BRISTOL Lincoln
BROOKLIN Hancock
BROOKS Waldo
BROOKSVILLE Hancock
BROOKTON Washington
BROWNFIELD Oxford
BROWNVILLE Piscataquis
BROWNVILLE JUNCTION Piscataquis
BRUNSWICK Cumberland
BRYANT POND Oxford
BUCKFIELD Oxford
BUCKS HARBOR Washington
BUCKSPORT (04416) Waldo(55), Hancock(44)
BURLINGTON Penobscot

BURNHAM Waldo
BUSTINS ISLAND Cumberland
BUXTON York
CALAIS Washington
CAMBRIDGE Somerset
CAMDEN Knox
CANAAN Somerset
CANTON Oxford
CAPE ELIZABETH Cumberland
CAPE NEDDICK York
CAPE PORPOISE York
CARATUNK Somerset
CARDVILLE Penobscot
CARIBOU Aroostook
CARMEL Penobscot
CASCO Cumberland
CASTINE Hancock
CENTER LOVELL Oxford
CHAMBERLAIN Lincoln
CHARLESTON Penobscot
CHEBEAGUE ISLAND Cumberland
CHERRYFIELD Washington
CHINA Kennebec
CHINA VILLAGE Kennebec
CLAYTON LAKE Aroostook
CLIFF ISLAND Cumberland
CLINTON Kennebec
COLUMBIA FALLS Washington
COOPERS MILLS Lincoln
COREA Hancock
CORINNA Penobscot
CORINTH Penobscot
CORNISH York
COSTIGAN Penobscot
CRANBERRY ISLES Hancock
CROUSEVILLE Aroostook
CUMBERLAND CENTER Cumberland
CUMBERLAND FORESIDE Cumberland
CUSHING Knox
CUTLER Washington
DAMARISCOTTA Lincoln
DANFORTH Washington
DANVILLE Androscoggin
DEER ISLE Hancock
DENMARK Oxford
DENNYSVILLE Washington
DETROIT Somerset
DEXTER (04930) Penobscot(97), Somerset(2)
DIXFIELD Oxford
DIXMONT Penobscot
DOVER FOXCROFT Piscataquis
DRESDEN Lincoln
DRYDEN Franklin
DURHAM Androscoggin
EAGLE LAKE Aroostook
EAST ANDOVER Oxford
EAST BALDWIN Cumberland
EAST BLUE HILL Hancock
EAST BOOTHBAY Lincoln
EAST CORINTH Penobscot
EAST DIXFIELD Franklin
EAST LIVERMORE Androscoggin

EAST MACHIAS Washington
EAST MILLINOCKET Penobscot
EAST NEWPORT Penobscot
EAST ORLAND Hancock
EAST PARSONFIELD York
EAST POLAND Androscoggin
EAST STONEHAM Oxford
EAST VASSALBORO Kennebec
EAST WATERBORO York
EAST WATERFORD Oxford
EAST WILTON Franklin
EAST WINTHROP Kennebec
EASTON Aroostook
EASTPORT Washington
EDDINGTON Penobscot
EDGECOMB Lincoln
ELIOT York
ELLSWORTH Hancock
ENFIELD Penobscot
ESTCOURT STATION Aroostook
ETNA Penobscot
EUSTIS Franklin
EXETER Penobscot
FAIRFIELD (04937) Kennebec(97), Somerset(2)
FALMOUTH Cumberland
FARMINGDALE Kennebec
FARMINGTON Franklin
FARMINGTON FALLS Franklin
FORT FAIRFIELD Aroostook
FORT KENT Aroostook
FORT KENT MILLS Aroostook
FRANKFORT Waldo
FRANKLIN Hancock
FREEDOM Waldo
FREEPORT Cumberland
FRENCHBORO Hancock
FRENCHVILLE Aroostook
FRIENDSHIP Knox
FRYE Oxford
FRYEBURG Oxford
GARDINER Kennebec
GARLAND Penobscot
GEORGETOWN Sagadahoc
GLEN COVE Knox
GORHAM Cumberland
GOULDSBORO Hancock
GRAND ISLE Aroostook
GRAND LAKE STREAM Washington
GRAY Cumberland
GREENBUSH Penobscot
GREENE Androscoggin
GREENVILLE Piscataquis
GREENVILLE JUNCTION (04442) Piscataquis(85), Somerset(14)
GREENWOOD Oxford
GROVE Washington
GUILFORD Piscataquis
HALLOWELL Kennebec
HAMPDEN Penobscot
HANCOCK Hancock
HANOVER Oxford
HARBORSIDE Hancock

HARMONY Somerset
HARPSWELL Cumberland
HARRINGTON Washington
HARRISON Cumberland
HARTLAND Somerset
HAYNESVILLE Aroostook
HEBRON Oxford
HINCKLEY Somerset
HIRAM Oxford
HOLDEN (04429) Penobscot(97), Hancock(2)
HOLLIS CENTER York
HOPE Knox
HOULTON Aroostook
HOWLAND Penobscot
HUDSON Penobscot
HULLS COVE Hancock
ISLAND FALLS Aroostook
ISLE AU HAUT Knox
ISLE OF SPRINGS Lincoln
ISLESBORO Waldo
ISLESFORD Hancock
JACKMAN Somerset
JAY Franklin
JEFFERSON Lincoln
JONESBORO Washington
JONESPORT Washington
KENDUSKEAG Penobscot
KENNEBUNK York
KENNEBUNKPORT York
KENTS HILL Kennebec
KINGFIELD Franklin
KINGMAN Penobscot
KITTERY York
KITTERY POINT York
LAGRANGE (04453) Penobscot(97), Piscataquis(2)
LAMBERT LAKE Washington
LEBANON York
LEE Penobscot
LEEDS Androscoggin
LEVANT Penobscot
LEWISTON Androscoggin
LIBERTY (04949) Waldo(87), Knox(12)
LILLE Aroostook
LIMERICK York
LIMESTONE Aroostook
LIMINGTON York
LINCOLN Penobscot
LINCOLN CENTER Penobscot
LINCOLNVILLE Waldo
LINCOLNVILLE CENTER Waldo
LISBON Androscoggin
LISBON CENTER Androscoggin
LISBON FALLS Androscoggin
LITCHFIELD Kennebec
LITTLE DEER ISLE Hancock
LIVERMORE Androscoggin
LIVERMORE FALLS Androscoggin
LOCKE MILLS Oxford
LONG ISLAND Cumberland
LOVELL Oxford
LUBEC Washington

MACHIAS Washington
MACHIASPORT Washington
MADAWASKA Aroostook
MADISON Somerset
MANCHESTER Kennebec
MANSET Hancock
MAPLETON Aroostook
MARS HILL Aroostook
MASARDIS Aroostook
MATINICUS Knox
MATTAWAMKEAG Penobscot
MECHANIC FALLS Androscoggin
MEDDYBEMPS Washington
MEDWAY Penobscot
MEREPOINT Cumberland
MEXICO Oxford
MILBRIDGE Washington
MILFORD Penobscot
MILLINOCKET Penobscot
MILO Piscataquis
MINOT Androscoggin
MINTURN Hancock
MONHEGAN Lincoln
MONMOUTH Kennebec
MONROE Waldo
MONSON Piscataquis
MONTICELLO Aroostook
MOODY York
MORRILL Waldo
MOUNT DESERT Hancock
MOUNT VERNON Kennebec
NAPLES Cumberland
NEW GLOUCESTER Cumberland
NEW HARBOR Lincoln
NEW LIMERICK Aroostook
NEW PORTLAND Somerset
NEW SHARON Franklin
NEW SWEDEN Aroostook
NEW VINEYARD Franklin
NEWAGEN Lincoln
NEWCASTLE Lincoln
NEWFIELD York
NEWPORT Penobscot
NEWRY Oxford
NOBLEBORO Lincoln
NORRIDGEWOCK Somerset
NORTH AMITY Aroostook
NORTH ANSON Somerset
NORTH BERWICK York
NORTH BRIDGTON Cumberland
NORTH BROOKLIN Hancock
NORTH FRYEBURG Oxford
NORTH HAVEN Knox
NORTH JAY Franklin
NORTH MONMOUTH Kennebec
NORTH NEW PORTLAND Somerset
NORTH SHAPLEIGH York
NORTH TURNER Androscoggin
NORTH VASSALBORO Kennebec
NORTH WATERBORO York
NORTH WATERFORD Oxford
NORTH YARMOUTH Cumberland
NORTHEAST HARBOR Hancock
NORWAY Oxford
OAKFIELD Aroostook
OAKLAND Kennebec
OCEAN PARK York
OGUNQUIT York

OLAMON Penobscot
OLD ORCHARD BEACH York
OLD TOWN Penobscot
OQUOSSOC Franklin
ORIENT Aroostook
ORLAND Hancock
ORONO Penobscot
ORRINGTON Penobscot
ORRS ISLAND Cumberland
OTTER CREEK Hancock
OWLS HEAD Knox
OXBOW Aroostook
OXFORD Oxford
PALERMO Waldo
PALMYRA Somerset
PARIS Oxford
PARSONSFIELD York
PASSADUMKEAG Penobscot
PATTEN Penobscot
PEAKS ISLAND Cumberland
PEJEPSCOT Sagadahoc
PEMAQUID Lincoln
PEMBROKE Washington
PENOBSCOT Hancock
PERHAM Aroostook
PERRY Washington
PERU Oxford
PHILLIPS Franklin
PHIPPSBURG Sagadahoc
PITTSFIELD Somerset
PLAISTED Aroostook
PLYMOUTH Penobscot
POLAND Androscoggin
PORT CLYDE Knox
PORTAGE Aroostook
PORTER Oxford
PORTLAND Cumberland
POWNAL Cumberland
PRESQUE ISLE Aroostook
PRINCETON Washington
PROSPECT HARBOR Hancock
QUIMBY Aroostook
RANDOLPH Kennebec
RANGELEY Franklin
RAYMOND Cumberland
READFIELD Kennebec
RICHMOND Sagadahoc
ROBBINSTON Washington
ROCKLAND Knox
ROCKPORT Knox
ROCKWOOD (04478) Somerset(86),
    Piscataquis(13)
ROUND POND Lincoln
ROXBURY Oxford
RUMFORD Oxford
RUMFORD CENTER Oxford
RUMFORD POINT Oxford
SABATTUS Androscoggin
SACO York
SAINT AGATHA Aroostook
SAINT ALBANS Somerset
SAINT DAVID Aroostook
SAINT FRANCIS Aroostook
SAINT GEORGE Knox
SALSBURY COVE Hancock
SANDY POINT Waldo
SANFORD York
SANGERVILLE Piscataquis

SARGENTVILLE Hancock
SCARBOROUGH Cumberland
SEAL COVE Hancock
SEAL HARBOR Hancock
SEARSMONT Waldo
SEARSPORT Waldo
SEBAGO Cumberland
SEBAGO LAKE Cumberland
SEBASCO ESTATES Sagadahoc
SEBEC Piscataquis
SEBEC LAKE Piscataquis
SEDGWICK Hancock
SHAPLEIGH York
SHAWMUT Somerset
SHERIDAN Aroostook
SHERMAN MILLS Aroostook
SHERMAN STATION (04777)
    Penobscot(84), Aroostook(15)
SHIRLEY MILLS Piscataquis
SINCLAIR Aroostook
SKOWHEGAN Somerset
SMALL POINT Sagadahoc
SMITHFIELD Somerset
SMYRNA MILLS Aroostook
SOLDIER POND Aroostook
SOLON Somerset
SORRENTO Hancock
SOUTH BERWICK York
SOUTH BRISTOL Lincoln
SOUTH CASCO Cumberland
SOUTH CHINA Kennebec
SOUTH FREEPORT Cumberland
SOUTH GARDINER Kennebec
SOUTH GOULDSBORO Hancock
SOUTH HIRAM Oxford
SOUTH PARIS Oxford
SOUTH PORTLAND Cumberland
SOUTH THOMASTON Knox
SOUTH WATERFORD Oxford
SOUTH WINDHAM Cumberland
SOUTHPORT Lincoln
SOUTHWEST HARBOR Hancock
SPRINGFIELD Penobscot
SPRINGVALE York
SPRUCE HEAD Knox
SQUIRREL ISLAND Lincoln
STACYVILLE Penobscot
STANDISH Cumberland
STEEP FALLS Cumberland
STETSON Penobscot
STEUBEN Washington
STILLWATER Penobscot
STOCKHOLM Aroostook
STOCKTON SPRINGS Waldo
STONEHAM Oxford
STONINGTON Hancock
STRATTON Franklin
STRONG Franklin
SULLIVAN Hancock
SUMNER Oxford
SUNSET Hancock
SURRY Hancock
SWANS ISLAND Hancock
TEMPLE Franklin
TENANTS HARBOR Knox
THOMASTON Knox
THORNDIKE Waldo
TOPSFIELD Washington

TOPSHAM Sagadahoc
TREVETT Lincoln
TROY Waldo
TURNER Androscoggin
TURNER CENTER Androscoggin
UNION Knox
UNITY Waldo
UPPER FRENCHVILLE Aroostook
VAN BUREN Aroostook
VANCEBORO Washington
VASSALBORO Kennebec
VIENNA Kennebec
VINALHAVEN Knox
WAITE Washington
WALDOBORO Lincoln
WALLAGRASS Aroostook
WALPOLE Lincoln
WARREN Knox
WASHBURN Aroostook
WASHINGTON Knox
WATERBORO York
WATERFORD Oxford
WATERVILLE Kennebec
WAYNE Kennebec
WEEKS MILLS Kennebec
WELD Franklin
WELLS York
WESLEY Washington
WEST BALDWIN Cumberland
WEST BETHEL Oxford
WEST BOOTHBAY HARBOR Lincoln
WEST BOWDOIN Sagadahoc
WEST BUXTON York
WEST ENFIELD Penobscot
WEST FARMINGTON Franklin
WEST FORKS Somerset
WEST KENNEBUNK York
WEST MINOT Androscoggin
WEST NEWFIELD York
WEST PARIS Oxford
WEST POLAND Androscoggin
WEST ROCKPORT Knox
WEST SOUTHPORT Lincoln
WEST TREMONT Hancock
WESTBROOK Cumberland
WESTFIELD Aroostook
WHITEFIELD Lincoln
WHITING Washington
WHITNEYVILLE Washington
WILEYS CORNER Knox
WILTON Franklin
WINDHAM Cumberland
WINDSOR Kennebec
WINN Penobscot
WINTER HARBOR Hancock
WINTERPORT Waldo
WINTERVILLE Aroostook
WINTHROP Kennebec
WISCASSET Lincoln
WOODLAND Washington
WOOLWICH Sagadahoc
WYTOPITLOCK Aroostook
YARMOUTH Cumberland
YORK York
YORK BEACH York
YORK HARBOR York

ZIP/City Cross Reference

ZIP	City
03901-03901	BERWICK
03902-03902	CAPE NEDDICK
03903-03903	ELIOT
03904-03904	KITTERY
03905-03905	KITTERY POINT
03906-03906	NORTH BERWICK
03907-03907	OGUNQUIT
03908-03908	SOUTH BERWICK
03909-03909	YORK
03910-03910	YORK BEACH
03911-03911	YORK HARBOR
04001-04001	ACTON
04002-04002	ALFRED
04003-04003	BAILEY ISLAND
04004-04004	BAR MILLS
04005-04005	BIDDEFORD
04006-04006	BIDDEFORD POOL
04007-04007	BIDDEFORD
04008-04008	BOWDOINHAM
04009-04009	BRIDGTON
04010-04010	BROWNFIELD
04011-04011	BRUNSWICK
04013-04013	BUSTINS ISLAND
04014-04014	CAPE PORPOISE
04015-04015	CASCO
04016-04016	CENTER LOVELL
04017-04017	CHEBEAGUE ISLAND
04019-04019	CLIFF ISLAND
04020-04020	CORNISH
04021-04021	CUMBERLAND CENTER
04022-04022	DENMARK
04024-04024	EAST BALDWIN
04027-04027	LEBANON
04028-04028	EAST PARSONFIELD
04029-04029	SEBAGO
04030-04030	EAST WATERBORO
04032-04034	FREEPORT
04037-04037	FRYEBURG
04038-04038	GORHAM
04039-04039	GRAY
04040-04040	HARRISON
04041-04041	HIRAM
04042-04042	HOLLIS CENTER
04043-04043	KENNEBUNK
04046-04046	KENNEBUNKPORT
04047-04047	PARSONSFIELD
04048-04048	LIMERICK
04049-04049	LIMINGTON
04050-04050	LONG ISLAND
04051-04051	LOVELL
04053-04053	MEREPOINT
04054-04054	MOODY
04055-04055	NAPLES
04056-04056	NEWFIELD
04057-04057	NORTH BRIDGTON
04058-04058	NORTH FRYEBURG
04060-04060	NORTH SHAPLEIGH
04061-04061	NORTH WATERBORO
04062-04062	WINDHAM
04063-04063	OCEAN PARK
04064-04064	OLD ORCHARD BEACH
04066-04066	ORRS ISLAND
04067-04067	PEJEPSCOT
04068-04068	PORTER
04069-04069	POWNAL
04070-04070	SCARBOROUGH
04071-04071	RAYMOND
04072-04072	SACO
04073-04073	SANFORD
04074-04074	SCARBOROUGH
04075-04075	SEBAGO LAKE
04076-04076	SHAPLEIGH
04077-04077	SOUTH CASCO
04078-04078	SOUTH FREEPORT
04079-04079	HARPSWELL
04080-04080	SOUTH HIRAM
04081-04081	SOUTH WATERFORD
04082-04082	SOUTH WINDHAM
04083-04083	SPRINGVALE
04084-04084	STANDISH
04085-04085	STEEP FALLS
04086-04086	TOPSHAM
04087-04087	WATERBORO
04088-04088	WATERFORD
04090-04090	WELLS
04091-04091	WEST BALDWIN
04092-04092	WESTBROOK
04093-04093	WEST BUXTON
04093-04093	BUXTON
04094-04094	WEST KENNEBUNK
04095-04095	WEST NEWFIELD
04096-04096	YARMOUTH
04097-04097	NORTH YARMOUTH
04098-04098	WESTBROOK
04100-04104	PORTLAND
04105-04105	FALMOUTH
04106-04106	SOUTH PORTLAND
04107-04107	CAPE ELIZABETH
04108-04108	PEAKS ISLAND
04109-04109	PORTLAND
04110-04110	CUMBERLAND FORESIDE
04112-04112	PORTLAND
04116-04116	SOUTH PORTLAND
04122-04124	PORTLAND
04210-04212	AUBURN
04216-04216	ANDOVER
04217-04217	BETHEL
04219-04219	BRYANT POND
04220-04220	BUCKFIELD
04221-04221	CANTON
04222-04222	DURHAM
04223-04223	DANVILLE
04224-04224	DIXFIELD
04225-04225	DRYDEN
04226-04226	EAST ANDOVER
04227-04227	EAST DIXFIELD
04228-04228	EAST LIVERMORE
04230-04230	EAST POLAND
04231-04231	EAST STONEHAM
04231-04231	STONEHAM
04233-04233	EAST WATERFORD
04234-04234	EAST WILTON
04235-04235	FRYE
04236-04236	GREENE
04237-04237	HANOVER
04238-04238	HEBRON
04239-04239	JAY
04240-04243	LEWISTON
04250-04250	LISBON
04251-04251	LISBON CENTER
04252-04252	LISBON FALLS
04253-04253	LIVERMORE
04254-04254	LIVERMORE FALLS
04255-04255	LOCKE MILLS
04255-04255	GREENWOOD
04256-04256	MECHANIC FALLS
04257-04257	MEXICO
04258-04258	MINOT
04259-04259	MONMOUTH
04260-04260	NEW GLOUCESTER
04261-04261	NEWRY
04262-04262	NORTH JAY
04263-04263	LEEDS
04265-04265	NORTH MONMOUTH
04266-04266	NORTH TURNER
04267-04267	NORTH WATERFORD
04268-04268	NORWAY
04270-04270	OXFORD
04271-04271	PARIS
04273-04274	POLAND
04275-04275	ROXBURY
04276-04276	RUMFORD
04278-04278	RUMFORD CENTER
04279-04279	RUMFORD POINT
04280-04280	SABATTUS
04281-04281	SOUTH PARIS
04282-04282	TURNER
04283-04283	TURNER CENTER
04284-04284	WAYNE
04285-04285	WELD
04286-04286	WEST BETHEL
04287-04287	WEST BOWDOIN
04287-04287	BOWDOIN
04288-04288	WEST MINOT
04289-04289	WEST PARIS
04290-04290	PERU
04291-04291	WEST POLAND
04292-04292	SUMNER
04294-04294	WILTON
04330-04338	AUGUSTA
04341-04341	COOPERS MILLS
04342-04342	DRESDEN
04343-04343	EAST WINTHROP
04344-04344	FARMINGDALE
04345-04345	GARDINER
04346-04346	RANDOLPH
04347-04347	HALLOWELL
04348-04348	JEFFERSON
04349-04349	KENTS HILL
04350-04350	LITCHFIELD
04351-04351	MANCHESTER
04352-04352	MOUNT VERNON
04353-04353	WHITEFIELD
04354-04354	PALERMO
04355-04355	READFIELD
04357-04357	RICHMOND
04358-04358	SOUTH CHINA
04359-04359	SOUTH GARDINER
04360-04360	VIENNA
04361-04361	WEEKS MILLS
04362-04362	WHITEFIELD
04363-04363	WINDSOR
04364-04364	WINTHROP
04401-04402	BANGOR
04406-04406	ABBOT VILLAGE
04406-04406	ABBOT
04408-04408	AURORA
04410-04410	BRADFORD
04411-04411	BRADLEY
04412-04412	BREWER
04413-04413	BROOKTON
04414-04414	BROWNVILLE
04415-04415	BROWNVILLE JUNCTION
04416-04416	BUCKSPORT
04417-04417	BURLINGTON
04418-04418	CARDVILLE
04418-04418	GREENBUSH
04419-04419	CARMEL
04420-04421	CASTINE
04422-04422	CHARLESTON
04423-04423	COSTIGAN
04424-04424	DANFORTH
04426-04426	DOVER FOXCROFT
04427-04427	EAST CORINTH
04427-04427	CORINTH
04428-04428	EDDINGTON
04429-04429	HOLDEN
04430-04430	EAST MILLINOCKET
04431-04431	EAST ORLAND
04433-04433	ENFIELD
04434-04434	ETNA
04435-04435	EXETER
04438-04438	FRANKFORT
04441-04441	GREENVILLE
04442-04442	GREENVILLE JUNCTION
04443-04443	GUILFORD
04444-04444	HAMPDEN
04446-04446	HAYNESVILLE
04448-04448	HOWLAND
04449-04449	HUDSON
04450-04450	KENDUSKEAG
04451-04451	KINGMAN
04453-04453	LAGRANGE
04454-04454	LAMBERT LAKE
04455-04455	LEE
04456-04456	LEVANT
04457-04457	LINCOLN
04458-04458	LINCOLN CENTER
04459-04459	MATTAWAMKEAG
04460-04460	MEDWAY
04461-04461	MILFORD
04462-04462	MILLINOCKET
04463-04463	MILO
04464-04464	MONSON
04465-04465	NORTH AMITY
04467-04467	OLAMON
04468-04468	OLD TOWN
04469-04469	ORONO
04471-04471	ORIENT
04472-04472	ORLAND
04473-04473	ORONO
04474-04474	ORRINGTON
04475-04475	PASSADUMKEAG
04476-04476	PENOBSCOT
04478-04478	ROCKWOOD
04479-04479	SANGERVILLE
04481-04481	SEBEC
04482-04482	GUILFORD
04482-04482	SEBEC LAKE
04485-04485	SHIRLEY MILLS
04487-04487	SPRINGFIELD
04488-04488	STETSON
04489-04489	STILLWATER
04490-04490	TOPSFIELD
04491-04491	VANCEBORO
04492-04492	WAITE
04493-04493	WEST ENFIELD
04495-04495	WINN
04496-04496	WINTERPORT
04497-04497	WYTOPITLOCK
04530-04530	BATH
04535-04535	ALNA
04536-04536	BAYVILLE
04537-04537	BOOTHBAY
04538-04538	BOOTHBAY HARBOR
04539-04539	BRISTOL
04541-04541	CHAMBERLAIN
04543-04543	DAMARISCOTTA
04544-04544	EAST BOOTHBAY
04547-04547	FRIENDSHIP
04548-04548	GEORGETOWN
04549-04549	ISLE OF SPRINGS
04551-04551	BREMEN
04552-04552	NEWAGEN
04553-04553	NEWCASTLE
04554-04554	NEW HARBOR
04555-04555	NOBLEBORO
04556-04556	EDGECOMB
04558-04558	PEMAQUID
04562-04562	PHIPPSBURG
04563-04563	CUSHING
04564-04564	ROUND POND
04565-04565	SEBASCO ESTATES
04567-04567	SMALL POINT
04568-04568	SOUTH BRISTOL
04570-04570	SQUIRREL ISLAND
04571-04571	TREVETT
04572-04572	WALDOBORO
04573-04573	WALPOLE
04574-04574	WASHINGTON
04575-04575	WEST BOOTHBAY HARBOR
04576-04576	WEST SOUTHPORT
04576-04576	SOUTHPORT
04578-04578	WISCASSET
04579-04579	WOOLWICH
04605-04605	ELLSWORTH
04606-04606	ADDISON
04607-04607	GOULDSBORO
04608-04608	ATLANTIC
04609-04609	BAR HARBOR
04611-04611	BEALS
04612-04612	BERNARD

04613-04613 BIRCH HARBOR	04678-04678 SOUTH GOULDSBORO	04779-04779 SINCLAIR	04933-04933 EAST NEWPORT
04614-04614 BLUE HILL	04679-04679 SOUTHWEST HARBOR	04780-04780 SMYRNA MILLS	04935-04935 EAST VASSALBORO
04615-04615 BLUE HILL FALLS	04680-04680 STEUBEN	04781-04781 SOLDIER POND	04936-04936 EUSTIS
04616-04616 BROOKLIN	04681-04681 STONINGTON	04781-04781 WALLAGRASS	04937-04937 FAIRFIELD
04617-04617 BROOKSVILLE	04683-04683 SUNSET	04782-04782 STACYVILLE	04938-04938 FARMINGTON
04618-04618 BUCKS HARBOR	04684-04684 SURRY	04783-04783 STOCKHOLM	04939-04939 GARLAND
04619-04619 CALAIS	04685-04685 SWANS ISLAND	04784-04784 UPPER FRENCHVILLE	04940-04940 FARMINGTON FALLS
04622-04622 CHERRYFIELD	04686-04686 WESLEY	04785-04785 VAN BUREN	04941-04941 FREEDOM
04623-04623 COLUMBIA FALLS	04690-04690 WEST TREMONT	04786-04786 WASHBURN	04942-04942 HARMONY
04624-04624 COREA	04691-04691 WHITING	04787-04787 WESTFIELD	04943-04943 HARTLAND
04625-04625 CRANBERRY ISLES	04692-04692 WHITNEYVILLE	04788-04788 WINTERVILLE	04944-04944 HINCKLEY
04626-04626 CUTLER	04693-04693 WINTER HARBOR	04841-04841 ROCKLAND	04945-04945 JACKMAN
04627-04627 DEER ISLE	04694-04694 WOODLAND	04843-04843 CAMDEN	04947-04947 KINGFIELD
04628-04628 DENNYSVILLE	04694-04694 BAILEYVILLE	04846-04846 GLEN COVE	04949-04949 LIBERTY
04629-04629 EAST BLUE HILL	04730-04730 HOULTON	04847-04847 HOPE	04950-04950 MADISON
04630-04630 EAST MACHIAS	04732-04732 ASHLAND	04848-04848 ISLESBORO	04951-04951 MONROE
04631-04631 EASTPORT	04733-04733 BENEDICTA	04849-04849 LINCOLNVILLE	04952-04952 MORRILL
04634-04634 FRANKLIN	04734-04734 BLAINE	04850-04850 LINCOLNVILLE CENTER	04953-04953 NEWPORT
04635-04635 FRENCHBORO	04735-04735 BRIDGEWATER	04851-04851 MATINICUS	04954-04954 NEW PORTLAND
04637-04637 GRAND LAKE STREAM	04736-04736 CARIBOU	04852-04852 MONHEGAN	04955-04955 NEW SHARON
04638-04638 GROVE	04737-04737 CLAYTON LAKE	04853-04853 NORTH HAVEN	04956-04956 NEW VINEYARD
04640-04640 HANCOCK	04738-04738 CROUSEVILLE	04854-04854 OWLS HEAD	04957-04957 NORRIDGEWOCK
04642-04642 HARBORSIDE	04739-04739 EAGLE LAKE	04855-04855 PORT CLYDE	04958-04958 NORTH ANSON
04643-04643 HARRINGTON	04740-04740 EASTON	04856-04856 ROCKPORT	04961-04961 NORTH NEW PORTLAND
04644-04644 HULLS COVE	04741-04741 ESTCOURT STATION	04857-04857 SAINT GEORGE	04961-04961 NEW PORTLAND
04645-04645 ISLE AU HAUT	04742-04742 FORT FAIRFIELD	04857-04857 WILEYS CORNER	04962-04962 NORTH VASSALBORO
04646-04646 ISLESFORD	04743-04743 FORT KENT	04858-04858 SOUTH THOMASTON	04963-04963 OAKLAND
04648-04648 JONESBORO	04744-04744 FORT KENT MILLS	04859-04859 SPRUCE HEAD	04964-04964 OQUOSSOC
04649-04649 JONESPORT	04745-04745 FRENCHVILLE	04860-04860 TENANTS HARBOR	04965-04965 PALMYRA
04650-04650 LITTLE DEER ISLE	04746-04746 GRAND ISLE	04861-04861 THOMASTON	04966-04966 PHILLIPS
04652-04652 LUBEC	04747-04747 ISLAND FALLS	04862-04862 UNION	04967-04967 PITTSFIELD
04653-04653 BASS HARBOR	04749-04749 LILLE	04863-04863 VINALHAVEN	04969-04969 PLYMOUTH
04654-04654 MACHIAS	04750-04751 LIMESTONE	04864-04864 WARREN	04970-04970 RANGELEY
04655-04655 MACHIASPORT	04756-04756 MADAWASKA	04865-04865 WEST ROCKPORT	04971-04971 SAINT ALBANS
04656-04656 MANSET	04757-04757 MAPLETON	04901-04903 WATERVILLE	04972-04972 SANDY POINT
04657-04657 MEDDYBEMPS	04758-04758 MARS HILL	04910-04910 ALBION	04973-04973 SEARSMONT
04658-04658 MILBRIDGE	04759-04759 MASARDIS	04911-04911 ANSON	04974-04974 SEARSPORT
04659-04659 MINTURN	04760-04760 MONTICELLO	04912-04912 ATHENS	04975-04975 SHAWMUT
04660-04660 MOUNT DESERT	04761-04761 NEW LIMERICK	04915-04915 BELFAST	04976-04976 SKOWHEGAN
04661-04661 NORTH BROOKLIN	04762-04762 NEW SWEDEN	04917-04917 BELGRADE	04978-04978 SMITHFIELD
04662-04662 NORTHEAST HARBOR	04763-04763 OAKFIELD	04918-04918 BELGRADE LAKES	04979-04979 SOLON
04664-04664 SULLIVAN	04764-04764 OXBOW	04920-04920 BINGHAM	04981-04981 STOCKTON SPRINGS
04665-04665 OTTER CREEK	04765-04765 PATTEN	04921-04921 BROOKS	04982-04982 STRATTON
04666-04666 PEMBROKE	04766-04766 PERHAM	04922-04922 BURNHAM	04983-04983 STRONG
04667-04667 PERRY	04767-04767 PLAISTED	04923-04923 CAMBRIDGE	04984-04984 TEMPLE
04668-04668 PRINCETON	04768-04768 PORTAGE	04924-04924 CANAAN	04985-04985 WEST FORKS
04669-04669 PROSPECT HARBOR	04769-04769 PRESQUE ISLE	04925-04925 CARATUNK	04986-04986 THORNDIKE
04671-04671 ROBBINSTON	04770-04770 QUIMBY	04926-04926 CHINA	04987-04987 TROY
04672-04672 SALSBURY COVE	04772-04772 SAINT AGATHA	04926-04926 CHINA VILLAGE	04988-04988 UNITY
04673-04673 SARGENTVILLE	04773-04773 SAINT DAVID	04927-04927 CLINTON	04989-04989 VASSALBORO
04674-04674 SEAL COVE	04774-04774 SAINT FRANCIS	04928-04928 CORINNA	04992-04992 WEST FARMINGTON
04675-04675 SEAL HARBOR	04775-04775 SHERIDAN	04929-04929 DETROIT	
04676-04676 SEDGWICK	04776-04776 SHERMAN MILLS	04930-04930 DEXTER	
04677-04677 SORRENTO	04777-04777 SHERMAN STATION	04932-04932 DIXMONT	

Maryland

General Help Numbers:

Governor's **Office**

State House, 100 State Circle
Annapolis, MD 21401
www.gov.state.md.us

410-974-3901
Fax 410-974-3275
9AM-5PM

Attorney General's Office

200 St Paul Place
Baltimore, MD 21202
www.oag.state.md.us

410-576-6300
Fax 410-576-6404
8AM-5PM

State Court Administrator

580 Taylor Ave
Annapolis, MD 21401
www.courts.state.md.us

410-260-1400
Fax 410-974-2169
8AM-5PM

State Archives

Hall of Records
350 Rowe Blvd
Annapolis, MD 21401
www.mdarchives.state.md.us

410-260-6400
Fax 410-974-2525
8AM-4:30PM TU-FR;
8:30-4:30 SA

State Specifics:

Capital:	Annapolis Anne Arundel County
Time Zone:	EST
Number of Counties:	23
Population:	5,375,156
Web Site:	www.mec.state.md.us

State Agencies

Criminal Records

Criminal Justice Information System, Public Safety & Correctional Records, PO Box 5743, Pikeville, MD 21282-5743 (Courier: 6776 Reisterstown Rd, Rm 200, Pikeville, MD 21208); 410-764-4501, 888-795-0011, 7:30AM-5:00PM.

www.dpscs.state.md.us

Note: The Sexual Offender registry can be obtained by email, sor@dpscs.state.md.us. Visit www.dpscs.state.md.us/sor/ for instructions.

Indexing & Storage: Records are available from 1978. It takes a week if not submitted electornically. before new records are available for inquiry. Records are indexed on in-house computer (90+%). Approximately 80% of all arrests in database have final dispositions recorded.

Searching: Release of criminal records is somewhat restricted. All private parties must first write to this office and receive a "petition package," then apply for a petition number. Employers and investigative firms are eligible to

apply for this petition number. Include the following in your request: signed release, set of fingerprints, photo ID of requester. 100% of the records are fingerprint-supported. All records are released to law enforcement; public receives records with dispositions only.

Access by: mail, online.

Fee & Payment: The fee is $18.00 per request. If a statutorily-required FBI fingerpint check is required, add $24.00. Fee payee: CJIS. Prepayment required. Money orders and cashier's checks are preferred. Personal checks accepted. No credit cards accepted.

Mail search: Turnaround time: 2 to 4 weeks.

Online search: The State Court Administrator's office has online access to criminal records from all state district courts, 3 circuit courts, and 1 city court. The system is available 24 hours daily. There is a one-time $50 fee to register and a $5.00 per hour fee. Land records may also be accessed from this system. Call 410-260-1031 for a sign-up package.

Corporation Records
Limited Partnerships
Trade Names
Limited Liability Company Records
Fictitious Name
Limited Liability Partnerships

Department of Assessments and Taxation, Corporations Division, 301 W Preston St, Room 801, Baltimore, MD 21201; 410-767-1340, 410-767-1330 (Charter Information), 410-333-7097 (Fax), 8AM-4:30PM.

www.dat.state.md.us/bsfd

Indexing & Storage: Records are available from 1908 on. New records are available for inquiry immediately. Records are indexed on inhouse computer.

Searching: Officers and directors info is not immediately available. Include the following in your request: full name of business, corporation file number. The following is available; the Articles of Incorporation, Annual Reports, Officers, Directors, DBA's, Prior (merged) names, Inactive and Reserved names.

Access by: mail, phone, fax, in person, online.

Fee & Payment: An abstract of corporate records is $6.00, A Good Standing is $6.00 or $12.00 if long form is needed. Copies are $1.00 per page plus $6.00 to certify. Fee payee: SDAT. Prepayment required. Personal checks accepted. Credit cards accepted: MasterCard, Visa.

Mail search: Turnaround time: 7 days. Officer and director information takes 2 weeks. Expedited service will improve turnaround time for mail or fax requests. No self addressed stamped envelope is required.

Phone search: Charter information includes date of incorporation, agent, and status. They will let you know how many pages if you wish to order copies.

Fax search: This is considered expedited service, see below.

In person search: The office closes at 5 PM for searchers. Public access terminals are available.

Online search: The web site offers free searching for corporate name and trade name records. The site also includes real estate (cannot search by name) and UCC records.

Other access: The state will release information in a bulk output format. Call 410-561-9600 for details.

Expedited service: Expedited service is available for mail, phone and fax searches. Turnaround time: 2 days. There is an additional $20.00 fee to expedite a copy or $9.00 to expedite a certificate. A credit card must be used if requesting by fax.

Trademarks/Servicemarks

Secretary of State, Trademarks Division, State House, Annapolis, MD 21401; 410-974-5531 x2, 410-974-5527 (Fax), 9AM-5PM.

www.sos.state.md.us

Indexing & Storage: Records are available for the past 10 years. New records are available for inquiry immediately. Records are indexed on inhouse computer.

Searching: Include the following in your request: trademark/servicemark name.

Access by: mail, phone, fax, in person, online.

Fee & Payment: There is no search fee. Certification is $5.00, copies are $.30 per page. Fee payee: Secretary of State. Prepayment required. Personal checks accepted. No credit cards accepted.

Mail search: Turnaround time: 1 week. No fee for mail request.

Phone search: No fee for telephone request. Only limited information is available.

Fax search: Will return information by mail in 1 week.

In person: No fee for request. Call before visiting.

Online search: Online searching is available at the Internet site. Search can be by keyword in the description field, the service or product, the owner, the classification, or the mark name or keyword in the mark name. The site offers application forms to register, renew, or assign trade and service marks, and general information about registration. Click on "Trade & Service Marks."

Other access: A computer printout of all marks registered, renewed or assigned within a 3 month period is available for $.05 per trademark.

Uniform Commercial Code

UCC Division-Taxpayer's Services, Department of Assessments & Taxation, 301 West Preston St, Baltimore, MD 21201; 410-767-1340, 410-333-7097 (Fax), 8AM-4:30PM.

http://sdatcert3.resiusa.org/ucc-charter

Note: This agency will not do a general name or entity search, you must come in person, hire a retriever, use the Internet, or buy the database.

Indexing & Storage: Records are available for all active files.

Searching: Tax liens are not filed here, but are filed with the clerk of the circuit court of the debtor's jurisdiction. For help, e-mail charterhelp@dat.state.md.us.

Access by: mail, phone, in person, online.

Fee & Payment: There is no search fee. The copy fee is $1.00 per page. Fee payee: Department of Assessments & Taxation Prepayment required. Personal checks accepted. No credit cards accepted.

Mail search: Will not do name searching, but will make copies if exact number of pages paid in advance.

Phone search: Yuou can call to find the number of pages of a specific document, but data is not released.

In person search: Records can be viewed at no charge on public access terminals.

Online search: The Internet site above offers free access to UCC index information. Also, there is a related site offering access to real property data for the whole state at www.dat.state.md.us/realprop

Other access: The agency has available for sale copies of public release master data files including corporation, real estate, and UCC. In addition, they can produce customized files on paper or disk. Visit the web site for more information.

Federal Tax Liens
State Tax Liens

Records not maintained by a state level agency.

Note: All tax liens are filed at the county level.

Sales Tax Registrations

Taxpayer Services, Revenue Administration Division, 301 W Preston St #206, Baltimore, MD 21201; 410-767-1313, 410-767-1571 (Fax), 8AM-5PM.

www.comp.state.md.us

Indexing & Storage: Records are available on a computer index for the past 4 years of applicants.

Searching: This agency will only confirm that a business's number is valid and confirm the name and address of the business. They will provide no other information. The business name and federal ID# or SSN of owner is required to search.

Access by: mail, phone.

Fee & Payment: There are no fees.

Mail search: Turnaround time: 7 working days. Records are not returned by mail, they will call you. No self addressed stamped envelope is required.

Phone search: Call only if you have the permit number.

Birth Certificates

Department of Health, Division of Vital Records, PO Box 68760, Baltimore, MD 21215-0020 (Courier: 6550 Reisterstown Plaza, Baltimore, MD 21215); 410-764-3038, 410-764-3170 (Order), 410-318-6119 (Recording), 410-358-7381 (Fax), 8AM-4PM M-F; 3rd Saturday of each month.

www.dhmh.state.md.us

Indexing & Storage: Records are available from 1898 to present for all counties and 1910 to present for City of Baltimore. For prior records, contact the State Archives or city of Baltimore. It takes 6-8 weeks before new records are available for inquiry. Records are indexed on index cards.

Searching: Must have a notarized signed release form from person of record or mother or father, unless requester is parent or guardian. Include the following in your request: full name, names of parents, mother's maiden name, date of birth, place of birth, relationship to person of record.

Access by: mail, phone, fax, in person.

Fee & Payment: The search fee is $6.00. Only fax, phone and expedited requesters may use a credit card and there is an additional $7.00 fee. Fee payee: Division of Vital Records. Prepayment required. Cash is accepted for walk in requesters only. Personal checks accepted. Credit cards accepted: MasterCard, Visa, AmEx, Discover.

Mail search: Turnaround time: 2 to 3 weeks. A self addressed stamped envelope is requested.

Phone search: Credit card prepayment required. Turnaround time is 2-3 days.

Fax search: Same criteria as phone searches.

In person search: Turnaround time is same day (typically, 45 minutes to 1 hour). Walk in requesters may pay with cash. Presentation of photo ID is required for walk in requesters.

Other access: Records may be ordered over the web at www.vitalchek.com

Expedited service: Expedited service is available for mail, phone and fax searches. Turnaround time: 2 days. Add $12.00 per package plus charge for use of credit card.

Death Records

Department of Health, Division of Vital Records, PO Box 68760, Baltimore, MD 21215-0020 (Courier: 6550 Reisterstown Plaza, Baltimore, MD 21215); 410-764-3038, 410-764-3170 (Order), 410-318-6119 (Recording), 410-358-7381 (Fax), 8AM-4PM M-F; 3rd Saturday of each month.

www.dhmh.state.md.us

Indexing & Storage: Records are available from 1969 to present. For records prior to 1969 contact Maryland State Archives, 410-260-6429. New records are available for inquiry immediately. Records are indexed on index cards.

Searching: Must have a signed release form from immediate family member. A signature is required from the requester. Include the following in your request: full name, date of death, place of death, relationship to person of record, reason for information request. Request must be signed. Include copy of photo ID with request.

Access by: mail, phone, fax, in person.

Fee & Payment: The search fee is $6.00. Only phone, fax and expedited requesters may use a credit card for an extra $7.00 fee. Fee payee: Division of Vital Records. Prepayment required. Personal checks, M.O.s accepted. Credit cards accepted: MasterCard, Visa, AmEx, Discover.

Mail search: Turnaround time: 2 to 4 weeks. A self addressed stamped envelope is requested.

Phone search: Credit card pre-payment required. Turnaround time is 2-3 days.

Fax search: Same criteria as phone searches.

In person search: Turnaround time is same day.

Other access: Records may be ordered from www.vitalchek.com

Expedited service: Expedited service is available for mail, phone and fax searches. Turnaround time: 2 days. Add $12.00 per package for express delivery. Use of credit card and fee is required, also.

Marriage Certificates

Department of Health, Division of Vital Records, PO Box 68760, Baltimore, MD 21215-0020 (Courier: 6550 Reisterstown Plaza, Baltimore, MD 21215); 410-764-3038, 410-764-3170 (Order), 410-318-6119 (Recording), 410-358-7381 (Fax), 8AM-4PM M-F; 3rd Saturday of each month.

www.dhmh.state.md.us

Indexing & Storage: Records are available from June 1951 to present. Prior records must be obtained form the court of record. Also, marriages

from 1973, 1974, 1978, and 1979 are unavailable from this location and must be searched at local level. It takes 6 months before new records are available for inquiry. Records are indexed on computer.

Searching: Must have a notarized signed release form from persons of record or authorized representative. Include the following in your request: names of husband and wife, date of marriage, place or county of marriage, besides permission letter. Include copy of photo ID with request.

Access by: mail, phone, fax, in person.

Fee & Payment: The search fee is $6.00. Only phone, fax and expedited requesters may use a credit card for an additional fee of $7.00. Fee payee: Division of Vital Records. Prepayment required. Personal checks & M.O.s accepted. Credit cards accepted: MasterCard, Visa, AmEx, Discover.

Mail search: Turnaround time: 2 to 3 weeks. A self addressed stamped envelope is requested.

Phone search: Credit Card prepayment required. Turnaround time is 2-3 days.

Fax search: Same search criteria as phone searches.

In person search: Turnaround time same day.

Other access: Onlien ordering available at www.vitalchek.com

Expedited service: Expedited service is available for mail, phone and fax searches. Turnaround time: 2 days. Add $12.00 per package for express delivery. Use of credit card and fee is required, also.

Divorce Records

Department of Health, Division of Vital Records, PO Box 68760, Baltimore, MD 21215-0020 (Courier: 6550 Reisterstown Plaza, Baltimore, MD 21215); 410-764-3038, 410-318-6119 (Recording), 800-832-3277, 410-358-7381 (Fax), 8AM-4PM M-F; 3rd Saturday of each month.

www.dhmh.state.md.us

Note: This office does not issue a certificate of divorce, but can verify those names involved. The divorce decree must be obtained from the circuit court granting the divorce.

Indexing & Storage: Records are available from July 1961 to present. New records are available for inquiry immediately. Records are indexed on index cards. 1983-84 indexes are not available for searching.

Searching: Must have a notarized release form from persons of record or authorized agent. Include the following in your request: names of husband and wife (maiden name), date of divorce.

Access by: mail, fax, in person.

Fee & Payment: There is no fee to receive a Verification of Report of Divorce and Absolute Annulment. The clerk of the court issuing the decree holds the actual hard copy record.

Mail search: Turnaround time: 2 to 3 weeks.

Fax search: No searching by fax.

In person search: Turnaround time same day.

Workers' Compensation Records

Workers Compensation Commission, 10 E Baltimore St, Baltimore, MD 21202; 410-864-5100, 410-864-5101 (Fax), 8AM-4:30PM.

www.charm.net/~wcc

Indexing & Storage: Records are available for past 10 years are on computer. New records are available for inquiry immediately. Records are indexed on microfilm, inhouse computer.

Searching: Include the following in your request: claimant name, Social Security Number, date of accident, place of employment at time of accident. The claim number helps. The following data is not released: medical records.

Access by: mail, phone, in person, online.

Fee & Payment: Fee for copies is $.50 per page. There is no search fee. Fee payee: Workers Compensation Commission. Prepayment required. Personal checks accepted. No credit cards accepted.

Mail search: Turnaround time: 1 week. For copies of documents, the claimant's authorization is needed. A self addressed stamped envelope is requested.

Phone search: Limited verification information is available by phone for three names only per call.

In person: Turnaround time while you wait.

Online search: Request for online hook-up must be in writing on letterhead. There is no search fee, but there is a $7.00 set-up fee, $5.00 monthly fee and a $.01-03 per minute connect fee assessed by Verizon or other provider. The system is open 24 hours a day to only in-state accounts. Write to the Commission at address above, care of Information Technology Division, or call Lili Joseph at 410-864-5119.

Other access: This agency will sell its entire database depending on the use of the purchaser. Contact the commission for further information.

Driver Records

MVA, Driver Records Unit, 6601 Ritchie Hwy, NE, Glen Burnie, MD 21062; 410-787-7758, 8:15AM-4:30PM.

www.mva.state.md.us

Note: Copies of tickets can be obtained from the MD District Court/MATS, 1750 Forest Dr, Annapolis, 21401. There is no charge for ticket copies, but a self addressed stamped envelope is advised.

Indexing & Storage: Records are available for 3 years for moving violations, 10 years for DWIs, and 5 years for suspensions. Law requires a request from the driver to have violations purged from the driving record. Accidents are indicated. It takes 5 to 10 days before new records are available for inquiry.

Searching: Casual requesters may obtain records with personal information only with consent of subject. Records may not be resold or used for direct mail advertising or selling. The driver's license number or the name and DOB are needed for a search. Permissible use requesters must submit form DR-057 if an account has not been established.

Access by: mail, in person, online.

Fee & Payment: The fee for a driving record is $7.00. There is an additional $3.00 if you wish to have the record certified. Fee payee: MVA. Prepayment required. Credit cards are not accepted for mail requests. Personal checks accepted. Credit cards accepted: MasterCard, Visa.

Mail search: Turnaround time: 2 to 3 days. MVA offices statewide will also accept mail-in requests for records. A self addressed stamped envelope is requested.

In person search: Up to 20 requests will be processed in-person, additional requests are available the next day. In-person inquires may be processed at over 25 Motor Vehicle offices throughout the state.

Online search: The network is available 6 days a week, twenty-four hours a day to qualified and bonded individuals and businesses. Access is through PC and modem. The communication network is the Public Data Network (Bell Atlantic). Fee is $7.00 per record. Call Ms. Barbara Bentley at 410-768-7234 for account information.

Vehicle Ownership
Vehicle Identification

Department of Motor Vehicles, Vehicle Registration Division, Room 204, 6601 Ritchie Hwy, NE, Glen Burnie, MD 21062; 410-768-7520, 410-768-7653 (Fax), 8:15AM-4:30PM.

www.mva.state.md.us

Indexing & Storage: Records are available from 1920. It takes 3 to 5 days before new records are available for inquiry.

Searching: All vehicle/ownership records are open to the public; however, personal information is not released to casual requesters without consent of subject. The following data is not released: medical information.

Access by: mail, in person, online.

Fee & Payment: Fees are $7.00 for non-certified records and $10.00 for certified records. Fee payee: MVA. Prepayment required. Credit cards are only accepted for walk-in requesters. Personal checks accepted. Credit cards accepted: MasterCard, Visa.

Mail search: Turnaround time: 3 to 5 days. Requester can provide prepaid express mail package for faster service. No self addressed stamped envelope is required.

In person search: Turnaround time is generally in a few minutes.

Online search: The state offers vehicle and ownership data over the same online network utilized for driving record searches. Fee is $7.00 per record and line charges will be incurred. For more information, call 410-768-7234.

Accident Reports

Maryland State Police, Central Records Division, 1711 Belmont Ave, Baltimore, MD 21244; 410-298-3390, 410-298-3198 (Fax), 8AM-5PM.

Note: This agency does not have reports for the City of Baltimore. Call 410-396-2359 for those reports.

Indexing & Storage: Records are available for 5 years. Records are computer indexed from 1996 to present.

Searching: If a fatality was involved, please so state in the request. Copies of accident reports investigated by the state police and other police

agencies may be requested by giving the date of incident and driver name(s).

Access by: mail, in person.

Fee & Payment: The search fee is $4.00 which includes all copies and is non-refundable. Fee payee: Maryland State Police. Prepayment required. Personal checks accepted. No credit cards accepted.

Mail search: Turnaround time: 3 to 4 weeks. A self addressed stamped envelope is requested.

In person: Searching is available in person.

Vessel Ownership
Vessel Registration

Dept of Natural Resources, Licensing & Registration Service, 580 Taylor Ave, Annapolis, MD 21401; 410-260-8200, 8:30AM-4:30PM.

www.dnr.state.md.us

Indexing & Storage: Records are available from the 1960s to the present. This is a title state: all motorized boats must be titled and registered. Records are on indexed on microfiche from the 1960s to the present, and on computer for the last 4 years.

Searching: Lien records are not searchable. However, the Department will indicate with a "yes" or "no" when asked if a lien exists. To search, one of the following is required: Maryland boat #, tidal fish license #, or name and address of boat owner/license holder. There are five additional Regional Service Centers in the state that will process record requests.

Access by: mail, in person.

Fee & Payment: Certified true copies are $10.00 each. Microfiche history files are $5.00 each. Current computer file copies are $5.00 each. Fee payee: DNR. Prepayment required. Personal checks accepted. No credit cards accepted.

Mail search: Turnaround time: 7 to 10 days. No self addressed stamped envelope is required.

In person search: Turnaround time is immediate, unless historical records needed.

Other access: Bulk lists are available through Marine Trades Assoc. of MD at 410-269-0741.

Legislation Records

Maryland General Assembly, Dept of Legislative Services, 90 State Circle, Annapolis, MD 21401-1991; 410-946-5400 (Bill Status Only), 410-946-5010, 800-492-7122 (In-state), 410-946-5405 (Fax), 8AM-5PM.

http://mlis.state.md.us

Indexing & Storage: Records are available from 1991 to present on computer and to 1990 on hard copy only. Records are indexed on inhouse computer, hard copy.

Searching: Include the following in your request: bill number.

Access by: mail, phone, in person, online.

Fee & Payment: The copy fee is $.15 per page. Fee payee: Maryland General Assembly. Prepayment required. Personal checks accepted. No credit cards accepted.

Mail search: Turnaround time: variable. The first 10 pages are free. No fee for mail request.

Phone search: No fee for telephone request.

In person search: No fee for request.

Online search: The Internet site has complete information regarding bills and status.

Voter Registration
Access to Records is Restricted

State Board of Elections, PO Box 6486, Annapolis, MD 21401-0486 (Courier: 151 West Street, #200, Annapolis, MD 21401); 410-269-2840, 800-222-8683, 410-974-2019 (Fax), 8AM-5PM.

www.elections.state.md.us

Note: This agency is authorized to sell voter registration lists in bulk media format for 5 of its 24 local jurisdictions. Purchaser must be a MD registered voter. Lists cannot be used for commercial solicitation. The web site offers a wealth of information, including access to the campaign finance database.

GED Certificates

State Department of Education, GED Office, 200 W Baltimore St, Baltimore, MD 21201; 410-767-0538, 410-333-8435 (Fax), 8:30AM-5PM.

www.research.umbc.edu/~ira

Indexing & Storage: It takes 30 days before new records are available for inquiry.

Searching: Include the following in your request: date of birth, Social Security Number, signed release.

Access by: mail, fax, in person.

Fee & Payment: The fee is $5.00 for a copy of a transcript. Fee payee: GED Office. Prepayment required. Personal checks accepted. No credit cards accepted.

Mail search: Turnaround time: 3 to 5 days. No self addressed stamped envelope is required.

Fax search: Results are returned by mail.

In person search: Results can be picked up at office (around the corner) at 4 N Liberty, between the hours of 10AM and 1PM.

Hunting License Information
Fishing License Information

Department of Natural Resources, Licensing & Registration Service, 580 Taylor Ave, Annapolis, MD 21401; 410-260-8200, 410-260-8217 (Fax), 8:30AM-4:30PM.

www.dnr.state.md.us

Note: They have a central computer database.

Indexing & Storage: Records are available since 1999. It takes 1-2 days before new records are available for inquiry.

Searching: Requests must be in writing, submit as many identifiers as possible.

Access by: mail, in person.

Fee & Payment: There is a $5.00 fee per name. Fee payee: Department of Natural Resources. Personal checks accpeted.

Mail search: Searching is available by mail.

In person search: No fee for request.

Other access: The agency will sell an annual tape of commercial fishing licenses, including names and addresses. The fee is $175.00. Licensees have the option of opting out. Call Mrs. Johnston at 410-260-8237 for details.

Maryland State Licensing Agencies

Licenses Searchable Online

Architectural Partnership/Corporation #12 .... www.dllr.state.md.us/query/arch.html
Barber #8 .... www.dllr.state.md.us/query/barber.html
Charity #28 .... www.sos.state.md.us/sos/charity/html/search.html
Contractor #10 .... www.dllr.state.md.us/query/home_imprv.html
Cosmetologist #8 .... www.dllr.state.md.us/query/cosmet.html
Electrician, Master #12 .... www.dllr.state.md.us/query/master_elec.html
Engineer, Examining #12 .... www.dllr.state.md.us/query/stat_eng.html
Engineer, Professional #12 .... www.dllr.state.md.us/query/prof_eng.html
Esthetician #8 .... www.dllr.state.md.us/query/cosmet.html
Forester #12 .... www.dllr.state.md.us/query/forester.html
Fund Raising Counsel #28 .... www.sos.state.md.us/sos/charity/html/psfrclist.html
Home Improvement #12 .... www.dllr.state.md.us/query/home_imprv.html
Home Improvement Salesperson #10 .... www.dllr.state.md.us/query/home_imprv.html
HVACR Contractor #12 .... www.dllr.state.md.us/query/hvacr.html
Interior Designer #12 .... www.dllr.state.md.us/query/cert_int_des.html
Land Surveyor #12 .... www.dllr.state.md.us/query/land_surv.html
Landscape Architect #12 .... www.dllr.state.md.us/query/land_arch.html
Makeup Artist #8 .... www.dllr.state.md.us/query/cosmet.html
Medical Doctor #22 .... www.docboard.org/md/df/mdsearch.htm
Nail Technician #8 .... www.dllr.state.md.us/query/cosmet.html
Nurse-RN/LPN #24 .... http://63.72.31.185/
Nursing Assistant #24 .... http://63.72.31.185/
Optometrist #22 .... www.odfinder.org/LicSearch.asp
Plumber #12 .... www.dllr.state.md.us/query/plumb.html
Polygraph Examiner #32 .... http://polygraph.org/states/mpa/Members.htm
Precious Metals & Gem Dealer/Secondhand #12 .... www.dllr.state.md.us/query/sec_hand_deal.html
Public Accountant-CPA #12 .... www.dllr.state.md.us/query/cpa.html
Real Estate Agent #15 .... www.dllr.state.md.us/query/real_est.html
Real Estate Appraiser #11 .... www.dllr.state.md.us/query/real_est_app.html
Solicitor, Professional #28 .... www.sos.state.md.us/sos/charity/html/psfrclist.html
Subcontractor #10 .... www.dllr.state.md.us/query/home_imprv.html

Licensing Quick Finder

Acupuncturist #22 410-764-4766
Airport #19 410-859-7064
Airport License (Public & Private Regis.) #19
.... 410-859-7064
Alarm Technician #27 410-799-0191
Architect #30 410-230-6322
Architectural Partnership/Corporation #12
.... 410-333-6322
Asbestos Abatement Company #6 410-631-3200
Athletic Agent #16 410-333-6315
Attorney #3 410-260-1950
Audiologist #22 410-764-4725
Bail Bondsman #21 410-468-2383
Barber #8 410-230-6320
Boxer/Boxing Professional #17 410-333-6315
Charity #28 410-974-5534
Chiropractor/Chiropractic Assistant #22 410-764-2965
Collection Agency #14 410-333-6820
Contractor #10 410-230-6231
Cosmetologist #8 410-230-6320
Counselor #22 410-764-4732
Day Care Provider #2 410-321-2216
Dental Assistant #22 410-764-4730
Dental Hygienist #22 410-764-4730
Dentist #22 410-764-4730
Dietitian/Nutritionist #22 410-764-4733
Electrician, Master #12 410-230-6231

Electrologist #7 410-764-4702
Embalmer #22 410-764-4792
Engineer, Examining #12 410-230-6231
Engineer, Professional #12 410-333-6322
Esthetician #8 410-230-6320
Forester #12 410-230-6231
Franchises, Bus. Opportunities, Multi-level Mktng
Programs #29 410-576-7785
Fund Raising Counsel #28 410-974-5534
Funeral Director #22 410-764-4792
Funeral Establishment #22 410-764-4792
Grain Dealer #4 410-841-5710
Guidance Counselor #5 410-767-0412
Handgun Permittee #27 410-799-0191
Harness Racing #9 410-230-6330
Hazardous Waste #6 410-631-3344
Hearing Aid Dispenser #22 410-764-4792
Home Improvement #12 410-333-6200
Home Improvement Salesperson #10 .. 410-230-6231
Horse Racing #9 410-230-6330
HVACR Contractor #12 410-333-6200
Insurance Agent #21 410-468-2383
Insurance Broker/Advisor #21 410-468-2383
Interior Designer #12 410-333-6322
Investment Adviser/Representative #29 410-576-7784
Land Surveyor #12 410-333-6322
Landscape Architect #12 410-333-6322

Lead Inspectors/Contractors #6 410-631-3167
Makeup Artist #8 410-230-6320
Massage Therapist #22 410-764-2431
Medical Doctor #22 410-764-4761
Mining Foreman/Fire Boss #6 410-631-3609
Mortgage Broker #13 410-333-6830
Mortician #22 410-764-4792
Nail Technician #8 410-230-6320
Notary Public #28 410-974-5520
Nurse-RN/LPN #24 410-585-1979
Nursing Assistant #24 410-585-1990
Nursing Home Administrator #22 410-764-4750
Occupational Therapist/Assistant #22 .. 410-764-2964
Optometrist #22 410-764-4725
Pesticide Applicator/Operator #4 410-841-5710
Pesticide Business/Dealer #4 410-841-5710
Pesticide Consultant #4 410-841-5710
Pesticide, Private Applicator #4 410-841-5710
Pharmacist #22 410-764-4755
Physical Therapist #22 410-764-4752
Physical Therapist Assistant #22 410-764-4752
Pilot #12 410-333-6329
Plant Broker/Dealer #4 410-841-5710
Plumber #12 410-230-6231
Podiatrist #22 410-764-4785
Police Officer, Special #27 410-799-0191
Polygraph Examiner #32 410-987-6665

Precious Metals & Gem Dealer/Secondhand #12 410-333-4640	Real Estate Appraiser #11 410-230-6231	Social Worker #22............................... 410-764-4788
Private Investigator #27......................410-799-0191	Referee #14.. 410-333-6315	Solicitor, Professional #28................... 410-974-5534
Psychologist #22................................410-764-4787	Respiratory Care Practitioner #22........ 410-764-4775	Speech Pathologist #22 410-764-4725
Psychometrist (Education) #5 410-767-0412	Sanitarian #6 410-631-3167	Subcontractor #10............................... 410-230-6231
Public Accountant-CPA #12 410-333-6325	School Admin./Superintendent #5......... 410-767-0412	Taxicab #31... 410-767-8107
Pump Installer #6...............................410-631-3167	School Library Media Generalist/Specialist #5	Teacher #5 410-767-0412
Pupil Personnel Worker #5..................410-767-0412	 410-767-0412	Veterinarian #1 410-841-5862
Radiation Therapy Technician #22.......410-764-4775	School Psychologist #5 410-767-0412	Veterinary Hospital #1........................ 410-841-5862
Reading Specialist #5 410-767-0412	Securities Broker/Dealer #29 410-576-6494	Waste Water Treatment Plant Superintendent #6
Reading Teacher #5 410-767-0412	Securities Sales Agent #29 410-576-6494	 410-631-3609
Real Estate Agent #15........................410-333-6230	Security Guard #27.............................. 410-799-0191	Water Conditioner Installer #6 410-631-3167
	Sewage Treatment #6 410-631-3609	Well Driller #6 410-631-3167

Licensing Agency Information

#1 Board of Veterinary Medical Examiners, 50 Harry S Truman Pky, Annapolis, MD 21401; 410-841-5862, Fax: 410-841-5999. www.mda.state.md.us/vet/begin.htm

#2 Child Care Administration, Region 3, 409 Washighton Ave LL8, Towson, MD 21204; 410-321-2216, Fax: 410-321-2240. www.dhr.state.md.us/cca-home.htm Agency email: rhayes@dhr.state.md.us.

#3 Client Security Trust Fund, Robert F Sweeney Dist Ct Bldg, 251 Rowe Blvd 3rd Fl, Annapolis, MD 21401; 410-260-1950, Fax: 410-260-1954. The MSBA and the CSTF are separate organizations. The MSBA phone number is 410-685-7878, fax 410-685-1016; 520 W Fayette St, Balt. MD 21201.

#4 Department of Agriculture, Pesticide Regulation Section, 50 Harry S Truman Pky, Annapolis, MD 21401; 410-841-5710, Fax: 410-841-2765. www.mda.state.md.us/geninfo/genera10.htm. Agency email: howarddw@mda.state.md.us.

#5 Department of Education, Division of Certification & Accreditation, 200 W Baltimore St, Baltimore, MD 21201-2595; 410-767-0412, Fax: 410-333-8963. www.msde.state.md.us/certification/certification.html Search database at www.msde.state.md.us/certification/certification.html

#6 Department of Environment, 2500 Broenig Hwy, Baltimore, MD 21224; 410-631-3000, Fax: 410-633-0456. www.mde.state.md.us

#7 Department of Health & Mental Hygiene, Boards & Commissions, 4201 Patterson Av Room 316, Baltimore, MD 21215; 410-764-4702, Fax: 410-358-0836.

#8 Department of Labor, Licensing & Regulation, Board of Barbers & Cosmetologists, 500 N Calvert St, 3rd Fl, Rm 307, Baltimore, MD 21202; 410-230-6320, Fax: 410-230-6314. www.dllr.state.md.us/license/occprof/barber.html. Agency email: mbrown@dllr.state.md.us. Search database at www.dllr.state.md.us/query/barber.html (or) cosmet.html

#9 Department of Labor, Licensing & Regulation, Racing Commission, 500 N Calvert St #201, Baltimore, MD 21202; 410-230-6330, Fax: 410-333-8308. www.dllr.state.md.us/racing Agency email: mhopkins@dllr.state.md.us.

#10 Department of Licensing & Regulation, Home Improvement Commission, 500 N Calvert St, #306, Baltimore, MD 21202-3651; 410-333-6200. www.dllr.state.md.us/occprof/homeim.html. Agency email: krosenthal@dllr.state.md.us. Search database at www.dllr.state.md.us/query/home_imprv.html

#11 Department of Labor, Licensing & Regulation, Board of Real Estate Appraisers, 500 N Calvert St, Baltimore, MD 21202; 410-333-6200, Fax: 410-333-1229. www.dllr.state.md.us/occprof/reappr.html. Agency email: pschott@dllr.state.md.us. Search database at www.dllr.state.md.us/query/real_est_app.html

#12 Department of Licensing & Regulation, Occupational Boards, 500 N Calvert St, Baltimore, MD 21202; 410-333-6200, Fax: 410-333-1229. Agency email: twhite@dllr.state.md.us.

#13 Department of Licensing & Regulation, Office of Financial Regulations, 500 N Calvert St, #402, Baltimore, MD 21202; 410-333-6200, Fax: 410-333-1229. www.dllr.state.md.us/license/fin_reg/mortlend/md finreg.html

#14 Department of Licensing & Regulation, Office of the Secretary, 500 N Calvert St, 4th Fl, Baltimore, MD 21202; 410-333-6200, Fax: 410-333-1229. www.dllr.state.md.us

#15 Department of Licensing & Regulation, Real Estate Commission, 500 N Calvert St, 3rd Fl, Baltimore, MD 21202-3551; 410-333-6230, Fax: 410-333-0023. www.dllr.state.md.us/license/occprof/recomm.html. Agency email: mrec@dllr.state.md.us. Search database at www.dllr.state.md.us/query/real_est.html

#16 Department of Licensing & Regulation, Athletic Commission, 500 N Calvert St, Rm 304, Baltimore, MD 21202; 410-230-6271, Fax: 410-333-1229. www.dllr.state.md.us/license/occprof/sportag.html

#17 Department of Licensing & Regulation, Athletic Commission, 500 N Calvert St, 2nd Fl, Baltimore, MD 21202; 410-333-6200, Fax: 410-333-6314. www.dllr.state.md.us/license/occprof/athlet.html

#19 Department of Transportation, Aviation Administration, PO Box 8766, BW1 Airport, Baltimore, MD 21240; 410-859-7064, Fax: 410-859-7287.

#21 Licensing & Regulation, Insurance Agent/Brokers Licensing & Investigation, 525 St Paul Pl, Baltimore, MD 21202; 410-468-2383, Fax: 410-468-2399. www.mdinsurance.state.md.us

#22 Licensing Boards, 4201 Patterson Ave, Baltimore, MD 21215-2299; 410-764-2431, Fax: 410-358-6571. Agency email: jchull@dhmh.state.md.us. Search database at www.docboard.org/md/df/mdsearch.htm

#24 Board of Nursing, 4140 Patterson Ave, Baltimore, MD 21215; 410-585-1900, Fax: 410-358-3530. www.dhmh.state.md.us/mbn Search database at http://63.72.31.185 A telephone voice response system called IVR is available; 410-585-1978.

#27 State Police, Licensing Division, 7751 Washington Blvd, Jessup, MD 20794; 410-799-0191, Fax: 410-799-5934. www.inform.umd.edu/UMS+State/MD_Resources/MDSP/

#28 Office of Secretary of State, Statehouse (16 Francis St), Annapolis, MD 21401; 410-974-5521, Fax: 410-974-5190. www.sos.state.md.us Agency email: mdsos@sos.state.md.us.

#29 Securities Division, Attorney General's Office, 200 St. Paul Place, 25th Fl, Baltimore, MD 21202; 410-576-6360, Fax: 410-576-6532. www.oag.state.md.us/Securities/index.htm. Agency email: securities@oag.state.md.us.

#30 Board of Architects, 500 N Calvert St 3rd Fl, Baltimore, MD 21202-2272; 410-333-6322.

#31 Public Service Commission, 6 St Paul St, Baltimore, MD 21202; 410-767-8000, Fax: 410-333-6088.

#32 Polygraph Association, PO Box 882, Millersville, MD 21108; 410-987-6665. http://polygraph.org/states/mpa Agency email: mdmicj@aol.com. Search database at http://polygraph.org/states/mpa/Members.htm

Maryland Federal Courts

The following list indicates the district and division name for each county in the state. If the bankruptcy court location is different from the district court, then the location of the bankruptcy court appears in parentheses.

County/Court Cross Reference

Allegany	Baltimore	Harford	Baltimore
Anne Arundel	Baltimore	Howard	Baltimore
Baltimore	Baltimore	Kent	Baltimore
Baltimore City City	Baltimore	Montgomery	Greenbelt
Calvert	Greenbelt	Prince George's	Greenbelt
Caroline	Baltimore	Queen Anne's	Baltimore
Carroll	Baltimore	Somerset	Baltimore
Cecil	Baltimore	St. Mary's	Greenbelt
Charles	Greenbelt	Talbot	Baltimore
Dorchester	Baltimore	Washington	Baltimore
Frederick	Baltimore	Wicomico	Baltimore
Garrett	Baltimore	Worcester	Baltimore

Standards for Federal Courts: The search fee is $20.00 per item (one party name or case number). Certification fee is $7.00 per document. Copy fee is $.50 per page. All fees standard unless noted in profile. Mail Search: always enclose a stamped self addressed envelope unless otherwise noted. Before releasing records, all courts require prepayment unless noted in profile.

Open records are located at the court unless otherwise noted. District courts index by defendant and plaintiff as well as by case number. Bankruptcy courts usually index by debtor and case number. While most courts now have their indexes on computer, many still maintain index card files as well.

The universal PACER sign-up number is 800-676-6856. Find PACER and the Party/Case Index on the Web at http://pacer.psc.uscourts.gov. PACER dial-up access is $.60 per minute. Also, courts offering internet access via RACER, PACER, Web-PACER or the new CM-ECF charge $.07 per page fee unless noted as free.

US District Court

Northern District of Maryland

Baltimore Division Clerk, 4th Floor, Room 4415, 101 W Lombard St, Baltimore, MD 21201 (Courier Address: Use mail address for courier delivery), 410-962-2600.

www.mdd.uscourts.gov

Counties: Allegany, Anne Arundel, Baltimore, City of Baltimore, Caroline, Carroll, Cecil, Dorchester, Frederick, Garrett, Harford, Howard, Kent, Queen Anne's, Somerset, Talbot, Washington, Wicomico, Worcester.

Indexing & Storage: Cases are indexed by defendant, plaintiff, and case number. New cases are available in the index 1-2 days after filing date. Open records are located at this court.

Fee & Payment Notes: Payment may be made by money order, cashier check, personal check. Payee: Clerk, USDC.

Phone Search: The court will verify questions over the phone, but will not read long dockets.

In Person Search: In person searching available.

PACER: Toll-free dial-up access: 800-241-2259. Local dial-up access: 410-962-1812. Case records are available back to October 1990. Records are purged every six months. New records are available online after 1 day. PACER is available online at http://pacer.mdd.uscourts.gov.

Electronic Filing: (CM/ECF available late 2002)

Opinions Online: Court opinions are available online at www.mdd.uscourts.gov

US Bankruptcy Court

Northern District of Maryland

Baltimore Division 8308 US Courthouse, 101 W Lombard St, Baltimore, MD 21201 (Courier Address: Use mail address for courier delivery), 410-962-2688.

www.mdb.uscourts.gov

Counties: Anne Arundel, Baltimore, City of Baltimore, Caroline, Carroll, Cecil, Dorchester, Harford, Howard, Kent, Queen Anne's, Somerset, Talbot, Wicomico, Worcester.

Indexing & Storage: Cases are indexed by debtor as well as by case number. New cases are available in the index 2 days after filing date. The name and/or case number of the debtor(s) as well as specific identification of the pleading involved are required to search for a record. Closed files are retained for the existing year as well as the previous calendar year.

Fee & Payment Notes: Payment may be made by money order, cashier check. Business checks are not accepted. Personal checks are not accepted.

Non-certified copy work is available from an on-site vendor, Document Technology, which charges $.30 per page for copies. Call 410-837-0409 for information. Payee: Clerk, US Bankruptcy Court.

Phone Search: Only docket information is available by phone. An automated voice case information service (VCIS) is available. Call VCIS at 800-829-0145 or 410-962-0733.

Mail Search: A stamped self addressed envelope is not required.

In Person Search: In person searching available.

PACER: Toll-free dial-up access: 800-927-0474. Local dial-up access: 410-962-0776. Case records are available back to mid 1991. Records are purged every six months. New civil records are available online after 2 days. PACER is available online at http://pacer.mdb.uscourts.gov.

Electronic Filing: (Currently in the process of implementing CM/ECF.)

US District Court

Southern District of Maryland

Greenbelt Division Clerk, Room 240, 6500 Cherrywood Lane, Greenbelt, MD 20770 (Courier Address: Use mail address for courier delivery), 301-344-0660.

www.mdd.uscourts.gov

Counties: Calvert, Charles, Montgomery, Prince George's, St. Mary's.

Indexing & Storage: Cases are indexed by defendant, plaintiff, and case number. New cases are available in the index 3 days after filing date. Both computer and card indexes are maintained. Case records indexed on computer since 1990. Open records are located at this court.

Fee & Payment Notes: Payment may be made by money order, cashier check, personal check. Payee: Clerk, USDC.

Phone Search: The court will verify information over the phone, but will not read long dockets.

Fax Search: To arrange a fax request, contact the court's copy service, Office Solutions, at 301-982-4682.

Mail Search: An outside copy service, Office Solutions, 301-982-4682, is contracted to do all searching and copies. Always enclose a stamped self addressed envelope.

In Person Search: In person searching available.

PACER: Toll-free dial-up access: 800-241-2259. Local dial-up access: 410-962-1812. Case records are available back to October 1990. Records are purged every six months. New records are available online after 1 day. PACER is available online at http://pacer.mdd.uscourts.gov.

Electronic Filing: (CM/ECF available late 2002)

Opinions Online: Court opinions are available online at www.mdd.uscourts.gov

US Bankruptcy Court

Southern District of Maryland

Greenbelt Division 6500 Cherrywood Ln, #300, Greenbelt, MD 20770 (Courier Address: Use mail address for courier delivery), 301-344-8018.

www.mdb.uscourts.gov

Counties: Allegany, Calvert, Charles, Frederick, Garrett, Montgomery, Prince George's, St. Mary's, Washington.

Indexing & Storage: Cases are indexed by debtor as well as by case number. New cases are available in the index 2-3 days after filing date. The name and/or case number of the debtor(s) as well as specific identification of the pleading involved are required to search for a record. Open records are located at this court.

Fee & Payment Notes: Payment may be made by money order, cashier check, personal check. The copy fee for in house copy work (4 pages or less

and copies that need to be certified) is $.50 per page and is done on an "as time permits" basis. Copy work of 5 pages or more is done off premises at a cost of $.35 per page

. Payee: Clerk, US Bankruptcy Court.

Phone Search: Only docket information is available by phone. An automated voice case information service (VCIS) is available. Call VCIS at 800-829-0145 or 410-962-0733.

Mail Search: Open cases are searched by IKON Office Solutions, 301-982-4682. A stamped self addressed envelope is not required.

In Person Search: In person searching available.

PACER: Toll-free dial-up access: 800-927-0474. Local dial-up access: 410-962-0776. Case records are available back to mid 1991. Records are purged every six months. New civil records are available online after 2 days. PACER is available online at http://pacer.mdb.uscourts.gov.

Electronic Filing: (Currently in the process of implementing CM/ECF.)

Maryland County Courts

Court	Jurisdiction	No. of Courts	How Organized
Circuit Courts*	General	25	8 Circuits
District Courts*	Limited	26	12 Districts
Orphan's Courts*	Probate	24	Register of Wills

* Profiled in this Sourcebook.

Court	CIVIL								
	Tort	Contract	Real Estate	Min. Claim	Max. Claim	Small Claims	Estate	Eviction	Domestic Relations
Circuit Courts*	X	X	X	$25000	No Max				X
District Courts*	X	X	X	$2500	$25000	$2500		X	X
Orphan's Court*							X		

Court	CRIMINAL				
	Felony	Misdemeanor	DWI/DUI	Preliminary Hearing	Juvenile
Circuit Courts*	X	X			X
District Courts*		X	X	X	X
Orphan's Court*					

ADMINISTRATION Court Administrator, Administrative Office of the Courts, 361 Rowe Blvd, Courts of Appeal Building, Annapolis, MD, 21401; 410-260-1400, Fax: 410-974-2169.
www.courts.state.md.us

COURT STRUCTURE The Ciruit court is the highest court of record. Effective 10/1/98, the civil judgment limit increased from $20,000 to $25,000 at the District Court level.

Certain categories of minor felonies are handled by the District Courts. However, all misdemeanors and felonies that require a jury trial are handled by Circuit Courts.

ONLINE ACCESS An online computer system called the Judicial Information System (JIS) or (SJIS) provides access to civil and criminal case information from the following:

> All District Courts - All civil and all misdemeanors

> Circuit Courts Civil - All Circuit Courts are online through JIS except Montgomery and Prince George who have their own systems.

> Circuit Courts Criminal - Three courts are on JIS - Anne Arundel, Carroll county, and Baltimore City Court

Inquiries may be made to: the District Court traffic system for case information data, calendar information data, court schedule data, or officer schedule data; the District Court criminal system for case information data or calendar caseload data; the District Court civil system for case information data, attorney name and address data; the land records system for land and plat records. There is an annual fee for JIS of $50.00, which must be included with the application. For additional information or to receive a registration packet, write or call Judicial Information Systems, Security Administrator, 2661 Riva Rd., Suite 900, Annapolis, MD 21401, 410-260-1031, or visit the web site.

PROBATE COURTS The Circuit Court handles Probate in Montgomery and Harford counties. In other counties, probate is handled by the Register of Wills and is a county, not a court, function.

📖 📖 📖 📖 📖 📖 📖

Allegany County

4th Judicial Circuit Court 30 Washington St, PO Box 359, Cumberland, MD 21502; 301-777-5922; Fax: 301-777-2100. Hours: 8AM-4:30PM (EST). *Felony, Misdemeanor, Civil Actions Over $25,000.*
Civil Records: Access: Phone, fax, mail, online, in person. Visitors must perform in person searches for themselves. No search fee. Required to search: name, years to search. Civil cases indexed by defendant, plaintiff. Civil records on computer since 11/92, archived and indexed from 1790. Online access available through SJIS. See state introduction or visit www.courts.state.md.us.
Criminal Records: Access: In person only. Visitors must perform in person searches for themselves. No search fee. Required to search: name, years to search; also helpful: DOB. Criminal records on computer since 9/99, archived and indexed from 1790.
General Information: Public access terminal is available. No adoptions, juvenile, sealed, expunged or mental records released. SASE required. Copy fee: $.50 per page. Certification fee: $5.00 per instrument. Fee payee: Circuit Court. Personal checks accepted. Prepayment is required.

District Court 3 Pershing St, 2nd Floor, Cumberland, MD 21502; 301-777-2105. Hours: 8:30AM-4:30PM (EST). *Misdemeanor, Civil Actions Under $25,000, Eviction, Small Claims.*

Civil Records: Access: Mail, online, in person. Both court and visitors may perform in person searches. No search fee. Required to search: name, years to search. Civil cases indexed by defendant. Civil records on computer from 1990, on index books from 1970. Online access available through SJIS. See state introduction or visit www.courts.state.md.us. Court will only conduct a search if requester provides case number.

Criminal Records: Access: Mail, online, in person. Both court and visitors may perform in person searches. No search fee. Required to search: name, years to search, signed release; also helpful: SSN. Criminal records on computer from 1980, index books. Online access available through SJIS; see www.courts.state.md.us. Court requires a case number for a search.

General Information: No adoptions, juvenile, sealed, expunged or mental records released. SASE required. Turnaround time 7 days. Copy fee: $.25 per page. Certification fee: $5.00 per page. Fee payee: District Court of MD. Personal checks accepted. Prepayment is required.

Register of Wills Courthouse, 30 Washington St, Rm 2, Cumberland, MD 21502; 301-724-3760, 888-724-0148 in MD; Fax: 301-724-1249. Hours: 8AM-4:30PM (EST). *Probate.*

www.registers.state.md.us/county/al/html/allegany.html

Anne Arundel County

5th Judicial Circuit Court Box 71, Annapolis, MD 21404; 410-222-1397; Civil phone: 410-222-1420. Hours: 8:30AM-4:30PM (EST). *Felony, Misdemeanor, Civil Actions Over $25,000.*

Civil Records: Access: Phone, mail, online, in person. Both court and visitors may perform in person searches. No search fee. Required to search: name, years to search. Civil cases indexed by defendant, plaintiff. Civil records on computer from 1991, on index from 1900. Online access available through SJIS. See state introduction or visit www.courts.state.md.us.

Criminal Records: Access: Online, in person. Both court and visitors may perform in person searches. No search fee. Required to search: name, years to search; also helpful: SSN. Criminal records on computer from 1988, indexed from 1960, archived from 1900. Online access available through SJIS; see www.courts.state.md.us.

General Information: Public access terminal is available. No adoptions, juvenile, sealed, expunged or mental records released. SASE required. Turnaround time 1 week. Copy fee: $.50 per page. Certification fee: $5.00. Fee payee: Clerk of Circuit Court. Personal checks accepted. Prepayment is required.

District Court 251 Rowe Blvd, #141, Annapolis, MD 21401; 410-260-1370. Hours: 8:30AM-4:30PM (EST). *Misdemeanor, Civil Actions Under $25,000, Eviction, Small Claims.*

Civil Records: Access: Mail, online, in person. Both court and visitors may perform in person searches. No search fee. Required to search: name, years to search. Civil cases indexed by defendant. Civil records on computer from 1982, archived and indexed from 1900s. Online access available through SJIS. See state introduction or visit www.courts.state.md.us.

Criminal Records: Access: Mail, online, in person. Both court and visitors may perform in person searches. No search fee. Required to search: name, years to search. Criminal records on computer from 1982,

archived and indexed from 1900s. Online access available through SJIS; see www.courts.state.md.us.

General Information: Public access terminal is available. SASE required. Turnaround time 5 days. Copy fee: $.25 per page. Certification fee: $5.00. Fee payee: District Court. Personal checks accepted. Prepayment is required.

Register of Wills PO Box 2368, Circuit Courthouse-Church Circle #403, Annapolis, MD 21404-2368; 410-222-1430, 800-679-6665 in MD; Fax: 410-222-1467. Hours: 8:30AM-4:30PM (EST). *Probate.*

www.registers.state.md.us/county/aa/html/annearundel.html

Note: Wills only, no genealogy searches .

Baltimore County

3rd Judicial Circuit Court 401 Bosley Ave, 2nd Floor, Towson, MD 21204; 410-887-2601. Hours: 8:30AM-4:30PM (EST). *Felony, Misdemeanor, Civil Actions Over $25,000.*

Civil Records: Access: Online, in person. Visitors must perform in person searches for themselves. No search fee. Required to search: name, years to search; also helpful: address. Civil cases indexed by defendant, plaintiff. Civil records in books, file jackets. Online access available through SJIS. See state introduction or visit www.courts.state.md.us.

Criminal Records: Access: In person only. Visitors must perform in person searches for themselves. No search fee. Required to search: name, years to search; also helpful: address, DOB, SSN. Criminal records on computer from 1984, prior on books.

General Information: Public access terminal is available. (Civil only.) No adoptions, juvenile, sealed, expunged or mental records released. Copy fee: $.50 per page. Certification fee: $5.00 per page. Fee payee: Suzanne Mensh, Clerk. Personal checks accepted. Out of state checks not accepted. Prepayment is required.

District Court 120 E Chesapeake Ave, Towson, MD 21286-5307; 410-512-2000; Criminal phone: 410-512-2101. Hours: 8:30AM-4:30PM (EST). *Misdemeanor, Civil Actions Under $25,000, Eviction, Small Claims.*

Civil Records: Access: Online, in person. Visitors must perform in person searches for themselves. No search fee. Required to search: name, years to search; also helpful: address. Civil cases indexed by defendant, plaintiff. Civil records on computer from 1985, on microfiche from 1971, archived from 1970, on card index from 1971. Online access available through SJIS. See state introduction or visit www.courts.state.md.us.

Criminal Records: Access: Online, in person. Visitors must perform in person searches for themselves. No search fee. Required to search: name, years to search. Criminal records on computer since 1981. Online access available through SJIS; see www.courts.state.md.us.

General Information: Public access terminal is available. No adoptions, juvenile, sealed, expunged or mental records released. Copy fee: $.25 per page. Certification fee: $5.00. Fee payee: District Court of MD. Personal checks accepted. Prepayment is required.

Register of Wills 401 Bosley Ave, Mail Stop 3507, Towson, MD 21204-4403; 410-887-6685, 888-642-5387 in MD; Fax: 410-583-2517. Hours: 8AM-4:30PM (EST). *Probate.*

www.registers.state.md.us/county/ba/html/baltimore.html

Baltimore City

8th Judicial Circuit Court - Civil Division 111 N Calvert, Rm 409, Baltimore, MD 21202; 410-333-3716. Hours: 8:30AM-4:30PM (EST). *Civil Actions Over $25,000.*

Civil Records: Access: Phone, mail, online, in person. Both court and visitors may perform in person searches. No search fee. Required to search: name, years to search; also helpful: address. Civil cases indexed by defendant. Civil records on computer from 1983. Online access available through SJIS. See state introduction or visit www.courts.state.md.us. Court conducts searches on a limited basis.

General Information: Public access terminal is available. No adoptions, juvenile, sealed, expunged or mental records released. SASE not required. Turnaround time 5 days. Copy fee: $.50 per page. Certification fee: $5.00. Fee payee: Clerk of the Circuit Court. Business checks accepted. Prepayment is required.

8th Judicial Circuit Court - Criminal Division 110 N Calvert Rm 200, Baltimore, MD 21202; 410-333-3750. Hours: 8:30AM-4:30PM (EST). *Felony, Misdemeanor.*

Criminal Records: Access: Online, in person. Visitors must perform in person searches for themselves. No search fee. Required to search: name, years to search; also helpful: address, DOB. Criminal records on computer from 1994, on microfilm from 1973. Online access available through SJIS; see www.courts.state.md.us.

General Information: Public access terminal is available. No adoptions, juvenile, sealed, expunged or mental records released. Copy fee: $.50 per page. Certification fee: $5.00. Fee payee: Clerk of Circuit Court. Business checks accepted.

District Court - Civil Division 501 E Fayette St, Baltimore, MD 21202; 410-878-8900. Hours: 8:30AM-4:30PM (EST). *Civil Actions Under $25,000, Eviction, Small Claims.*

Civil Records: Access: Mail, online, in person. No search fee. Required to search: name, years to search. Civil cases indexed by defendant. Civil records on computer from 1986, on card index from 1971. Online access available through SJIS. See state introduction or visit www.courts.state.md.us.

General Information: Public access terminal is available. No medical or sealed records released. SASE required. Turnaround time 1-2 days. Copy fee: $.25 per page. Certification fee: $5.00. Fee payee: District Court of MD. Personal checks accepted. Prepayment is required.

District Court - Criminal Division 5800 Wabash Ave, Baltimore, MD 21215; 410-878-8000. Hours: 8AM-4:30PM (EST). *Misdemeanor.*

Criminal Records: Access: Mail, online, in person. Both court and visitors may perform in person searches. No search fee. Required to search: name, years to search; also helpful: SSN. Criminal records on computer from 1983, prior on index cards from 1970. Online access available through SJIS; see www.courts.state.md.us.

General Information: No adoptions, juvenile, sealed, expunged, medical or mental records released. SASE required. Turnaround time 1 week. Copy fee: $.25 per page. Certification fee: $5.00. Fee payee: District Court. Personal checks accepted. Prepayment is required.

Register of Wills Courthouse East, 111 N Calvert St, Rm 352, Baltimore, MD 21202; 410-752-5131, 888-876-0035 in MD; Fax: 410-752-3494. Hours: 8AM-4:30PM (EST). *Probate.*

www.registers.state.md.us/city/bc/html/baltimorecity.html

Calvert County

7th Judicial Circuit Court 175 Main St Courthouse, Prince Frederick, MD 20678; 410-535-1660. Hours: 8:30AM-4:30PM (EST). *Felony, Misdemeanor, Civil Actions Over $25,000.*

www.courts.state.md.us/clerks/calvert

Civil Records: Access: Online, in person. Visitors must perform in person searches for themselves. No search fee. Required to search: name, years to search. Civil cases indexed by defendant, plaintiff. Civil records on computer back to 10/1997, prior on index books back to 1959. Online access available through JIS. See state introduction or visit www.courts.state.md.us.

Criminal Records: Access: In person only. Visitors must perform in person searches for themselves. No search fee. Required to search: name, years to search; also helpful: SSN. Criminal records on computer from 4/2000; prior in books back to 1967.

General Information: Public access terminal is available. No adoptions, juvenile, sealed, expunged or mental records released. Copy fee: $.50 per page. Certification fee: $5.00. Fee payee: Clerk of Circuit Court. Personal checks accepted. Prepayment is required.

District Court 200 Duke St Rm 2200, Prince Frederick, MD 20678; 410-535-8800. Hours: 8:30AM-4:30PM (EST). *Misdemeanor, Civil Actions Under $25,000, Eviction, Small Claims.*

Civil Records: Access: Mail, in person. Visitors must perform in person searches for themselves. No search fee. Required to search: name; also helpful: address. Civil cases indexed by defendant. Civil records on computer from mid-80s, archived from 1971 to 1981, prior on Cott index. Online access available through SJIS. See state introduction or visit www.courts.state.md.us.

Criminal Records: Access: In person only. Visitors must perform in person searches for themselves. No search fee. Required to search: name; also helpful: address, DOB. Criminal records on computer from 1981, archived from 1971-1981, prior on cott index. Online access available through SJIS; see www.courts.state.md.us.

General Information: Public access terminal is available. No adoptions, juvenile, sealed, expunged or mental records released. SASE required. Turnaround time 1-3o days. Copy fee: $.25 per page. Certification fee: $5.00. Fee payee: District Court of Maryland. Personal checks accepted. Prepayment is required.

Register of Wills Courthouse, 175 Main St, Prince Frederick, MD 20678; 410-535-0121, 888-374-0015 in MD; Fax: 410-414-3952. Hours: 8:30AM-4:30PM (EST). *Probate.*

www.registers.state.md.us/county/cv/html/calvert.html

Caroline County

2nd Judicial Circuit Court Box 458, Denton, MD 21629; 410-479-1811; Fax: 410-479-1142. Hours: 8:30AM-4:30PM (EST). *Felony, Misdemeanor, Civil Actions Over $25,000.*

Note: Misdemeanor case records held at District Court until appealed, then stored at Circuit Court.

Civil Records: Access: Online, in person. Visitors must perform in person searches for themselves. No search fee. Required to search: name, years to search; also helpful: address. Civil cases indexed by defendant, plaintiff. Civil records on computer from 10/98, card index from 1774. Online access available through SJIS. See state introduction or visit www.courts.state.md.us.

Criminal Records: Access: In person only. Visitors must perform in person searches for themselves. No search fee. Required to search: name, years to search;

also helpful: address, DOB, SSN. Criminal records on computer from 2000, card index from 1774.

General Information: Public access terminal is available. No adoptions, juvenile, sealed, expunged or mental records released. Copy fee: $.50 per page; $.25 self serve. Certification fee: $5.00. Fee payee: F Dale Minner, Clerk. Personal checks accepted. Prepayment is required.

District Court 207 S 3rd St, Denton, MD 21629; 410-479-5800; Fax: 410-479-5808. Hours: 8AM-4:30PM (EST). *Misdemeanor, Civil Actions Under $25,000, Eviction, Small Claims.*

Civil Records: Access: Online, in person. Visitors must perform in person searches for themselves. No search fee. Required to search: name, years to search; also helpful: address. Civil cases indexed by defendant. Civil records on cards from 1971, archived. Online access available through SJIS. See state introduction or visit www.courts.state.md.us.

Criminal Records: Access: Online, in person. Visitors must perform in person searches for themselves. No search fee. Required to search: name, years to search; also helpful: address, DOB, SSN. Criminal records on cards from 1971, archived. Online access available through SJIS; see www.courts.state.md.us.

General Information: No adoptions, juvenile, sealed, expunged or mental records released. Certification fee: $5.00. Fee payee: District Court. Personal checks accepted. Prepayment is required.

Register of Wills County Courthouse, 109 Market St, Rm 108, PO Box 416, Denton, MD 21629; 410-479-0717, 888-786-0019 in MD; Fax: 410-479-4983. Hours: 8AM-4:30PM (EST). *Probate.*

www.registers.state.md.us/county/ca/html/caroline.html

Carroll County

5th Judicial Circuit Court 55 N Court Street, Westminster, MD 21157; 410-386-2642; Fax: 410-876-0822. Hours: 8:30AM-4:30PM (EST). *Felony, Misdemeanor, Civil Actions Over $25,000.*

Civil Records: Access: Online, in person. Visitors must perform in person searches for themselves. No search fee. Required to search: name; also helpful: years to search. Civil cases indexed by defendant, plaintiff. Civil records on computer from 1990, on card books from 1837 to 1990. Online access available through SJIS. See state introduction or visit www.courts.state.md.us.

Criminal Records: Access: Online, in person. Visitors must perform in person searches for themselves. No search fee. Required to search: name; also helpful: years to search. Criminal records on computer from 1990, on card books from 1837 to 1990. Online access available through SJIS; see www.courts.state.md.us.

General Information: Public access terminal is available. No adoptions, juvenile, sealed, expunged or mental records released. Copy fee: $.50 per page. Certification fee: $5.00 per document. Fee payee: Clerk of Court. Personal checks accepted. Credit cards accepted: Visa, MasterCard.

District Court 55 N Court St, Westminster, MD 21157; 410-386-2365. Hours: 8:30AM-4:30PM (EST). *Misdemeanor, Civil Actions Under $25,000, Eviction, Small Claims.*

Civil Records: Access: Online, in person. Visitors must perform in person searches for themselves. No search fee. Required to search: name, years to search. Civil cases indexed by defendant, plaintiff. Civil records on computer back to 1984; on card index from 1971. Online access available through SJIS. See state introduction or visit www.courts.state.md.us.

Criminal Records: Access: Online, in person. Visitors must perform in person searches for themselves. No search fee. Required to search: name, years to search; also helpful: DOB, SSN. Criminal records on computer

back to 1984; on card index from 1971. Online access available through SJIS; see www.courts.state.md.us.

General Information: Public access terminal is available. No adoptions, juvenile, sealed, expunged or mental records released. Copy fee: $.25 per page. Certification fee: $5.00 per document. Fee payee: District Court. Personal checks accepted. Prepayment is required.

Register of Wills 55 N Court St, Rm 104, Westminster, MD 21157; 410-848-2586, 888-876-0034 in MD; Fax: 410-876-0657. Hours: 8:30AM-4:30PM (EST). *Probate.*

www.registers.state.md.us/county/cr/html/carroll.html

Cecil County

2nd Judicial Circuit Court 129 E Main St, Rm 108, Elkton, MD 21921; 410-996-5373; Civil phone: 410-996-5369; Fax: 410-392-6032. Hours: 8:30AM-4:30PM (EST). *Felony, Misdemeanor, Civil Actions Over $25,000.*

Civil Records: Access: Online, in person. Visitors must perform in person searches for themselves. No search fee. Required to search: name, years to search. Civil cases indexed by defendant. Civil records on card index from 1948. Online access available through SJIS. See state introduction or visit www.courts.state.md.us.

Criminal Records: Access: In person only. Visitors must perform in person searches for themselves. No search fee. Required to search: name, years to search; also helpful: DOB, SSN. Criminal records on card index from 1948; computerized records since 1993.

General Information: Public access terminal is available. No adoptions, juvenile, sealed, expunged or mental records released. Certification fee: $5.00 per page. Fee payee: Clerk of Court. Personal checks accepted. Prepayment is required.

District Court 170 E Main St, Elkton, MD 21921; 410-996-0700. Hours: 8:30AM-4:30PM (EST). *Misdemeanor, Civil Actions Under $25,000, Eviction, Small Claims.*

Civil Records: Access: Online, in person. Visitors must perform in person searches for themselves. No search fee. Required to search: name, years to search. Civil cases indexed by defendant. Civil records on computer from 1987, on card index from 1971. Online access available through SJIS. See state introduction or visit www.courts.state.md.us.

Criminal Records: Access: Online, in person. Visitors must perform in person searches for themselves. No search fee. Required to search: name, years to search. Criminal records on computer from 1981, on card index from 1971. Online access available through SJIS; see www.courts.state.md.us.

General Information: Public access terminal is available. No adoptions, juvenile, sealed, expunged or mental records released. Copy fee: $.25 per page. Certification fee: $5.00. Fee payee: District Court. Personal checks accepted. Prepayment is required.

Register of Wills County Courthouse, #101, PO Box 468, Elkton, MD 21922; 410-398-2737, 888-398-0301 in MD; Fax: 410-620-3849. Hours: 8:30AM-4:30PM (EST). *Probate.*

www.registers.state.md.us/county/ce/html/cecil.html

Charles County

Circuit Court for Charles County PO Box 970, La Plata, MD 20646; 301-932-3201. Hours: 8:30AM-4:30PM (EST). *Felony, Misdemeanor, Civil Actions Over $25,000.*

Civil Records: Access: Online, in person. Visitors must perform in person searches for themselves. No search fee. Required to search: name, years to search. Civil cases indexed by defendant, plaintiff. Civil records on index books from 1950, on computer back to 1996. Online access available through SJIS. See state introduction or visit www.courts.state.md.us.

Criminal Records: Access: In person only. Visitors must perform in person searches for themselves. No search fee. Required to search: name, years to search. Criminal records on index books from 1950, on computer back to 1996.

General Information: Public access terminal is available. No adoptions, juvenile, sealed, expunged or medical records released. Copy fee: $.50 per page. Certification fee: $5.00. Fee payee: Clerk of the Circuit Court. Personal checks accepted. Prepayment is required.

District Court PO Box 3070, La Plata, MD 20646; 301-932-3300; Civil phone: 301-932-3290; Criminal phone: 301-932-3295. Hours: 8:30AM-4:30PM (EST). *Misdemeanor, Civil Actions Under $25,000, Eviction, Small Claims.*

Civil Records: Access: Online, in person. Visitors must perform in person searches for themselves. No search fee. Required to search: name, years to search. Civil cases indexed by defendant, plaintiff. Civil records on computer from 1987, on card index from 1980. Online access available through SJIS. See state introduction or visit www.courts.state.md.us.

Criminal Records: Access: Online, in person. Visitors must perform in person searches for themselves. No search fee. Required to search: name, years to search. Criminal records on computer from 1984, on card index from 1980, from 09/98 on public access terminal. Online access available through SJIS; see www.courts.state.md.us.

General Information: Public access terminal is available. (For civil inquiry.) No confidential info, unserved warrants, medical records released. Copy fee: $.25 per page. Certification fee: $5.00. Fee payee: District Court. Personal checks accepted. Prepayment is required.

Register of Wills Box 3080 (Courthouse, 200 E Charles St), La Plata, MD 20646; 301-932-3345, 888-256-0054 in MD; Fax: 301-932-3349. Hours: 8:30AM-4:30PM (EST). *Probate.*

www.registers.state.md.us/county/ch/html/charles.html

Dorchester County

1st Judicial Circuit Court Box 150, Cambridge, MD 21613; 410-228-0481. Hours: 8:30AM-4:30PM (EST). *Felony, Misdemeanor, Civil Actions Over $25,000.*

Civil Records: Access: Online, in person. Visitors must perform in person searches for themselves. No search fee. Required to search: name, years to search. Civil cases indexed by defendant, plaintiff. Civil records on computer from 1993. Online access available through SJIS. See state introduction or visit www.courts.state.md.us.

Criminal Records: Access: In person only. Visitors must perform in person searches for themselves. No search fee. Required to search: name, years to search. Criminal records on computer from 1993.

General Information: Public access terminal is available. No adoptions, juvenile, sealed, expunged or mental records released. Copy fee: $.25 per page. Certification fee: $5.00. Fee payee: Clerk of Circuit Court.

District Court 310 Gay St, Cambridge, MD 21613; 410-901-1420. Hours: 8:30AM-4:30PM (EST). *Misdemeanor, Civil Actions Under $25,000, Eviction, Small Claims.*

Civil Records: Access: Online, in person. Visitors must perform in person searches for themselves. No search fee. Required to search: name, years to search; also helpful: address. Civil cases indexed by defendant. Civil

records archived and indexed from 1971; computerized records since 1985. Online access available through SJIS. See state introduction or visit www.courts.state.md.us.

Criminal Records: Access: Online, in person. Visitors must perform in person searches for themselves. No search fee. Required to search: name, years to search; also helpful: address, DOB, SSN. Criminal records on card index from 1971; computerized records since 1985. Online access available through SJIS; see www.courts.state.md.us.

General Information: Public access terminal is available. No adoptions, sealed, juvenile, expunged or mental records released. Copy fee: $.25 per page. Certification fee: $5.00 per page. Fee payee: District Court. Personal checks accepted. Prepayment is required.

Register of Wills 206 High St, Cambridge, MD 21613; 410-228-4181, 888-242-6257 in MD; Fax: 410-228-4988. Hours: 8AM-4:30PM; Public hours 8:30AM-4:30PM (EST). *Probate.*

www.registers.state.md.us/county/do/html/dorchester.html

Frederick County

6th Judicial Circuit Court 100 W Patrick St, Frederick, MD 21701; 301-694-1972. Hours: 8AM-4:30PM (EST). *Felony, Misdemeanor, Civil Actions Over $25,000.*

Civil Records: Access: Online, in person. Visitors must perform in person searches for themselves. No search fee. Required to search: name, years to search. Civil cases indexed by defendant, plaintiff. Civil records on computer from 08/94, prior on card books. Online access available through SJIS. See state introduction or visit www.courts.state.md.us.

Criminal Records: Access: In person only. Visitors must perform in person searches for themselves. No search fee. Required to search: name, years to search. Criminal records on computer from 12/81, prior on index books.

General Information: Public access terminal is available. No adoptions, juvenile, sealed, expunged or mental records released. Copy fee: $.50 per page. Certification fee: $5.00. Fee payee: Clerk of Circuit Court. Personal checks accepted. Prepayment is required.

District Court 100 W Patrick St, Frederick, MD 21701; 301-694-2000. Hours: 8:30AM-4:30PM (EST). *Misdemeanor, Civil Actions Under $25,000, Eviction, Small Claims.*

Civil Records: Access: Online, in person. Visitors must perform in person searches No search fee. Required to search: name; also helpful: years to search. Civil cases indexed by defendant, plaintiff. Civil records on computer and microfiche from 1982, archived and on card index from 1971. Online access available through SJIS. See state introduction or visit www.courts.state.md.us.

Criminal Records: Access: Online, in person. Visitors must perform in person searches. No search fee. Required to search: name, DOB; also helpful: years to search. Criminal records on computer and microfiche from 1982, archived and on card index from 1971. Online access available through SJIS; see www.courts.state.md.us.

General Information: Public access terminal is available. No adoptions, juvenile, sealed, expunged or mental records released. Copy fee: $.25 per page. Certification fee: $5.00. Fee payee: District Court. Personal checks accepted. Credit cards accepted: Visa, MasterCard, AmEx. Prepayment is required.

Register of Wills 100 W Patrick St, Frederick, MD 21701; 301-663-3722, 888-258-0526; Fax: 301-846-0744. Hours: 8AM-4:30PM (EST). *Probate.*

www.registers.state.md.us/county/fr/html/frederick.html

Garrett County

4th Judicial Circuit Court PO Box 447, Oakland, MD 21550; 301-334-1937; Fax: 301-334-5017. Hours: 8:30AM-4:30PM (EST). *Felony, Misdemeanor, Civil Actions Over $25,000.*

Civil Records: Access: Mail, online, in person. No search fee. Required to search: name, years to search. Civil cases indexed by defendant, plaintiff. Civil records on computer since 11/97. Online access available through SJIS. See state introduction or visit www.courts.state.md.us.

Criminal Records: Access: Mail, in person. Both court and visitors may perform in person searches. No search fee. Required to search: name, years to search, DOB. Criminal records on computer since 11/97.

General Information: Public access terminal is available. No adoptions, juvenile, sealed, expunged or mental records released. SASE not required. Turnaround time 1 day. Copy fee: $.50 per page. Certification fee: $5.00 per page. Fee payee: David K Martin, Clerk. Personal checks accepted. Prepayment is required.

District Court 205 S 3rd St, Oakland, MD 21550; 301-334-8164. Hours: 8:30AM-4:30PM (EST). *Misdemeanor, Civil Actions Under $25,000, Eviction, Small Claims.*

www.courts.state.md.us/district/dcgarrett.html

Civil Records: Access: Mail, online, in person. Both court and visitors may perform in person searches. No search fee. Required to search: name, years to search. Civil cases indexed by defendant. Civil records on computer from 1990, on index books from 1971. Online access available through SJIS. See state introduction or visit www.courts.state.md.us.

Criminal Records: Access: Online, in person. Visitors must perform in person searches for themselves. No search fee. Required to search: name, years to search, DOB. Criminal records on computer from 1981. Online access available through SJIS; see www.courts.state.md.us.

General Information: No adoptions, juvenile, sealed, expunged or mental records released. SASE required. Turnaround time 1 week. Copy fee: $.25 per page. Certification fee: $5.00 per page. Fee payee: District Court. Personal checks accepted. Prepayment is required.

Register of Wills Courthouse, 313 E Alder St, Room 103, Oakland, MD 21550; 301-334-1999, 888-334-2203 in MD; Fax: 301-334-1984. Hours: 8AM-4:30PM (EST). *Probate.*

www.registers.state.md.us/county/ga/html/garrett.html

Harford County

3rd Judicial Circuit 20 W Courtland St, Bel Air, MD 21014; 410-638-3426. Hours: 8:30AM-4:30PM (EST). *Felony, Misdemeanor, Civil Actions Over $25,000.*

www.courts.state.md.us/harford.html

Civil Records: Access: Online, in person. Visitors must perform in person searches for themselves. No search fee. Required to search: name, years to search; also helpful: address. Civil cases indexed by defendant, plaintiff. Civil records on computer since 08/92 and on books prior. Online access available through SJIS. See state introduction or visit www.courts.state.md.us.

Criminal Records: Access: In person only. Visitors must perform in person searches for themselves. No search fee. Required to search: name, years to search;

also helpful: DOB. Criminal records on computer since 08/92 and on books prior.

General Information: Public access terminal is available. No adoptions, presentence investigations, juvenile, sealed, expunged or mental records released. Copy fee: $.50 per page. Certification fee: $5.00. Fee payee: Clerk of the Circuit Court. Only cashiers checks and money orders accepted. Prepayment is required.

District Court 2 S Bond St, Bel Air, MD 21014; 410-838-2300. Hours: 8:30AM-4:30PM (EST). *Misdemeanor, Civil Actions Under $25,000, Eviction, Small Claims.*

Civil Records: Access: Mail, online, in person. Both court and visitors may perform in person searches. No search fee. Required to search: name, years to search. Civil cases indexed by defendant. Civil records on computer from 1981, on microfiche from 1972, archived from 1900. Online access available through SJIS. See state introduction or visit www.courts.state.md.us.

Criminal Records: Access: Mail, online, in person. Visitors must perform in person searches for themselves. No search fee. Required to search: name, years to search; also helpful: address, DOB. Criminal records on computer from 1981, on microfiche from 1972, archived from 1900. Online access available through SJIS; see www.courts.state.md.us.

General Information: Public access terminal is available. No adoptions, motor vehicle, juvenile, sealed, expunged or mental records released. SASE required. Turnaround time 3-4 days. Copy fee: $.25 per page. Certification fee: $5.00. Fee payee: District Court of MD. Personal checks accepted. Credit cards accepted: Visa, MC, Amex. Prepayment is required.

Register of Wills 20 W Courtland St, Room 304, Court House, Bel Air, MD 21014; 410-638-3275, 888-258-0525 in MD; Fax: 410-893-3177. Hours: 8:30AM-4:30PM (EST). *Probate.*

www.registers.state.md.us/county/ha/html/harford.html

Howard County

5th Judicial Circuit Court 8360 Court Ave, Ellicott City, MD 21043; 410-313-2111. Hours: 8:30AM-4:30PM (EST). *Felony, Misdemeanor, Civil Actions Over $25,000.*

Civil Records: Access: Online, in person. Visitors must perform in person searches for themselves. No search fee. Required to search: name, years to search; also helpful: address. Civil cases indexed by defendant, plaintiff. Civil records on computer from 1984, archived from 1900, on card index from 1900. Online access available through SJIS. See state introduction or visit www.courts.state.md.us.

Criminal Records: Access: In person only. Visitors must perform in person searches for themselves. No search fee. Required to search: name, years to search; also helpful: address, DOB, SSN. Criminal records on card index to 1840, on computer since 1984.

General Information: Public access terminal is available. No adoptions, juvenile, sealed, expunged or mental records released. Certification fee: $5.00 per page. Fee payee: Office of Clerk. Personal checks accepted.

District Court 3451 Courthouse Dr, Ellicott City, MD 21043; 410-461-0200. Hours: 8:30AM-4:30PM (EST). *Misdemeanor, Civil Actions Under $25,000, Eviction, Small Claims.*

Civil Records: Access: Mail, online, in person. Both court and visitors may perform in person searches. No search fee. Required to search: name, years to search. Civil cases indexed by defendant. Civil records on computer from 1996, on card index prior. Online access available through SJIS. See state introduction or visit www.courts.state.md.us.

Criminal Records: Access: Mail, online, in person. Both court and visitors may perform in person searches. No search fee. Required to search: name, years to search. Criminal records on computer from 1996, on card index prior. Online access available through SJIS; see www.courts.state.md.us.

General Information: Public access terminal is available. No adoptions, juvenile, sealed, expunged or mental records released. SASE required if return receipt requested. Turnaround time before 1989 4-6 weeks, 1989-present 7 days. Copy fee: $.25 per page. Certification fee: $5.00. Fee payee: District Court of MD. Personal checks accepted. Credit cards accepted: Visa.

Register of Wills 8360 Court Ave, Ellicott City, MD 21043; 410-313-2133, 888-848-0136 in MD; Fax: 410-313-3409. Hours: 8:30AM-4:30PM (EST). *Probate.*

www.registers.state.md.us/county/ho/html/howard.html

Kent County

2nd Judicial Circuit Court 103 N Cross St Courthouse, Chestertown, MD 21620; 410-778-7460; Fax: 410-778-7412. Hours: 8:30AM-4:30PM (EST). *Felony, Misdemeanor, Civil Actions Over $25,000.*

www.courts.state.md.us/clerks/kent/records.html

Civil Records: Access: Online, in person. Visitors must perform in person searches for themselves. No search fee. Required to search: name, years to search. Civil cases indexed by defendant, plaintiff. Civil records on computer from 1991, on card index from 1656. Online access available through SJIS. See state introduction or visit www.courts.state.md.us.

Criminal Records: Access: In person only. Visitors must perform in person searches for themselves. No search fee. Required to search: name, years to search; also helpful: DOB, SSN. Criminal records on computer from 1991, on card index from 1656.

General Information: Public access terminal is available. No adoptions, juvenile, sealed, expunged or mental records released. Copy fee: $.50 per page. Certification fee: $5.00. Fee payee: Mark L Mumford, Clerk. Personal checks accepted. Prepayment is required.

District Court 103 N Cross St, Chestertown, MD 21620; 410-810-3362; Fax: 410-810-3361. Hours: 8:30AM-4:30PM (EST). *Misdemeanor, Civil Actions Under $25,000, Eviction, Small Claims.*

Civil Records: Access: Online, in person. Visitors must perform in person searches for themselves. No search fee. Required to search: name, years to search. Civil cases indexed by defendant. Civil records on computer from 1989; on card index from 1971. Online access available through SJIS. See state introduction or visit www.courts.state.md.us.

Criminal Records: Access: Online, in person. Visitors must perform in person searches for themselves. No search fee. Required to search: name, years to search, DOB. Criminal records on computer from 1988, on card index from 1971. Online access available through SJIS; see www.courts.state.md.us.

General Information: No sealed, expunged, mental records or judge's notes released. Copy fee: $.25 per page. Certification fee: $5.00 per page. Fee payee: District Court of MD. Personal checks accepted. Credit cards accepted: Visa, Discover.

Register of Wills 103 N Cross St, Chestertown, MD 21620; 410-778-7466, 888-778-0179 in MD; Fax: 410-778-2466. Hours: 8AM-4:30PM (EST). *Probate.*

www.registers.state.md.us/county/ke/html/kent.html

Montgomery County

6th Judicial Circuit Court 50 Maryland Ave, Rockville, MD 20850; 240-777-9466. Hours: 8:30AM-4:30PM (EST). *Felony, Misdemeanor, Civil Actions Over $25,000.*

www.co.mo.md.us/judicial

Civil Records: Access: Phone, mail, fax, in person. Both court and visitors may perform in person searches. No search fee. Required to search: name, years to search; also helpful: case number. Civil cases indexed by defendant, plaintiff. Civil records on computer from 1973, archived from 1900, on card index from 1977.

Criminal Records: Access: Phone, mail, fax, in person. Both court and visitors may perform in person searches. No search fee. Required to search: name, years to search; also helpful: case number. Criminal records on computer from 1973, archived from 1900, on card index from 1977.

General Information: Public access terminal is available. No adoptions, juvenile, sealed, expunged or mental records released. Copy fee: $.50. Certification fee: $5.00. Plus $.50 per page. Fee payee: Clerk of Circuit Court. Personal checks accepted. Prepayment is required.

District Court 8665 Georgia Ave, Silver Spring, MD 20910; 301-608-0660. Hours: 8:30AM-4:30PM (EST). *Misdemeanor, Civil Actions Under $25,000, Eviction, Small Claims.*

Civil Records: Access: Mail, online, in person. Both court and visitors may perform in person searches. No search fee. Required to search: name, years to search. Civil cases indexed by defendant, plaintiff. Civil records on computer from 1986, on card index and case folder. Online access available through SJIS. See state introduction or visit www.courts.state.md.us.

Criminal Records: Access: Mail, online, in person. Both court and visitors may perform in person searches. No search fee. Required to search: name, years to search. Criminal records on computer, index book and case folder. Online access available through SJIS; see www.courts.state.md.us.

General Information: Public access terminal is available. No juvenile, sealed, expunged or mental records or judge's notes released. SASE required. Turnaround time 2-4 weeks. Copy fee: $.25 per page. Certification fee: $5.00. Fee payee: District Court. Personal checks accepted. Prepayment is required.

Rockville District Court 27 Courthouse Square, Rockville, MD 20850; Civil phone: 301-279-1500; Criminal phone: 301-279-1565. Hours: 8:30AM-4:30PM (EST). *Misdemeanor, Civil Actions Under $25,000, Eviction, Small Claims.*

Civil Records: Access: Mail, online, in person. Both court and visitors may perform in person searches. No search fee. Required to search: name, years to search. Civil cases indexed by defendant. Civil records go back to 1971; on computer back to 1990, prior in case folder. Online access available through SJIS. See state introduction or visit www.courts.state.md.us.

Criminal Records: Access: Mail, online, in person. Both court and visitors may perform in person searches. No search fee. Required to search: name, years to search; also helpful: DOB, SSN. Criminal records go back to 1971; on computer back to 1987. Online access to criminal records is the same as civil.

General Information: Public access terminal is available. No juvenile, sealed, expunged, mental records or judge's notes released. SASE required. Turnaround time 2-4 weeks. Copy fee: $.25 per page. Certification fee: $5.00 per page. Fee payee: District Court. Personal checks accepted. Prepayment is required.

Register of Wills Judicial Center, 50 Maryland Ave, #322, Rockville, MD 20850; 240-777-9600. Hours: 8:30AM-4:30PM (EST). *Probate.*

www.registers.state.md.us/county/mo/html/montgomery.html

Prince George's County

7th Judicial Circuit Court 14735 Main St, Upper Marlboro, MD 20772; Civil phone: 301-952-3240; Criminal phone: 301-952-3344. Hours: 8:30AM-4:30PM (EST). *Felony, Misdemeanor, Civil Actions Over $25,000.*

Civil Records: Access: In person. Visitors must perform in person searches for themselves. No search fee. Required to search: name, years to search. Civil cases indexed by defendant, plaintiff. Civil records on computer from 1981, on microfiche from 1979, on card index prior.

Criminal Records: Access: In person. Visitors must perform in person searches for themselves. No search fee. Required to search: name, years to search, DOB; also helpful: SSN. Criminal records on computer from 1981, on microfiche from 1979, on card index prior.

General Information: No adoptions, juvenile, sealed, expunged or mental records released. Copy fee: $.50 per page. Certification fee: $5.00 per page. Fee payee: Clerk of Circuit Court. Personal checks accepted. Prepayment is required.

District Court 14735 Main St, Rm 173B, Upper Marlboro, MD 20772; 301-952-4080. Hours: 8:30AM-4:30PM (EST). *Misdemeanor, Civil Actions Under $25,000, Eviction, Small Claims.*

Civil Records: Access: Mail, online, in person. No search fee. Required to search: name, years to search. Civil cases indexed by defendant. Civil records on computer from 1988, on card index from 1970. Online access available through SJIS. See state introduction or visit www.courts.state.md.us.

Criminal Records: Access: Mail, online, in person. Visitors must perform in person searches for themselves. No search fee. Required to search: name, years to search. Criminal records on computer from 1984, on cards from 1970. Online access available through SJIS; see www.courts.state.md.us.

General Information: Public access terminal is available. No adoptions, juvenile, sealed, expunged or mental records released. SASE required. Turnaround time 1-2 weeks. Copy fee: $.25 per page. Certification fee: $5.00 per page. Fee payee: District Court of Maryland. Personal checks accepted. Prepayment is required.

Register of Wills PO Box 1729, Upper Marlboro, MD 20773; 301-952-3250, 888-464-4219 in MD; Fax: 301-952-4489. Hours: 8:30AM-4:30PM (EST). *Probate.*

www.registers.state.md.us/county/pg/html/princegeorges.html

Queen Anne's County

2nd Judicial Circuit Court Courthouse, 100 Courthouse Sq, Centreville, MD 21617; 410-758-1773. Hours: 8:30AM-4:30PM (EST). *Felony, Misdemeanor, Civil Actions Over $25,000.*

Note: Misdemeanor case records held at District Court until appealed, then stored at Circuit Court.

Civil Records: Access: Online, in person. Visitors must perform in person searches for themselves. No search fee. Required to search: name, years to search. Civil cases indexed by defendant, plaintiff. Civil records on computer from 11/92; on index books from 1978. Online access available through SJIS. See state introduction or visit www.courts.state.md.us.

Criminal Records: Access: In person only.. Visitors must perform in person searches for themselves. No

search fee. Required to search: name, years to search, SSN. Criminal records on computer from 11/92; on index books from 1978.

General Information: Public access terminal is available. No adoptions, juvenile, sealed, expunged or mental records released. Certification fee: $5.00. Fee payee: Clerk of Circuit Court. Personal checks accepted. Prepayment is required.

District Court 120 Broadway, Centreville, MD 21617; 410-758-5200. Hours: 8:30AM-4:30PM (EST). *Misdemeanor, Civil Actions Under $25,000, Eviction, Small Claims.*

Civil Records: Access: Online, in person. Visitors must perform in person searches for themselves. No search fee. Required to search: name, years to search; also helpful: address. Civil cases indexed by defendant. Civil records on computer from 1988, archived from 1974, prior on index books. Online access available through SJIS. See state introduction or visit www.courts.state.md.us.

Criminal Records: Access: Online, in person. Visitors must perform in person searches for themselves. No search fee. Required to search: name, years to search; also helpful: address, DOB, SSN. Criminal records on computer from 1981, prior on index books. Online access available through SJIS; see www.courts.state.md.us.

General Information: No adoptions, juvenile, sealed, expunged or mental records released. Certification fee: $5.00. Fee payee: District Court of Maryland. Personal checks accepted. Credit cards accepted: Visa, Discover. Prepayment is required.

Register of Wills Liberty Bldg, 107 N Liberty St #220, PO Box 59, Centreville, MD 21617; 410-758-0585, 888-758-0010 in MD; Fax: 410-758-4408. Hours: 8AM-4:30PM (EST). *Probate.*

www.registers.state.md.us/county/qa/html/queenannes.html

Somerset County

1st Judicial Circuit Court PO Box 99, Princess Anne, MD 21853; 410-651-1555; Fax: 410-651-1048. Hours: 8:30AM-4:30PM (EST). *Felony, Misdemeanor, Civil Actions Over $25,000.*

Civil Records: Access: Online, in person. Visitors must perform in person searches for themselves. No search fee. Required to search: name, years to search; also helpful: address. Civil cases indexed by defendant, plaintiff. Civil records on computer from 9/93; prior archived and on index books. Online access available through SJIS. See state introduction or visit www.courts.state.md.us.

Criminal Records: Access: In person only. Visitors must perform in person searches for themselves. No search fee. Required to search: name, years to search; also helpful: address, DOB, SSN. Criminal records on computer from 9/93; prior archived and on index books.

General Information: Public access terminal is available. No adoptions, juvenile, sealed, expunged or mental records released. Copy fee: $.50 per page. Certification fee: $5.00. Fee payee: Clerk of Circuit Court. Personal checks accepted. Prepayment is required.

District Court 11774 Somerset Ave, Princess Anne, MD 21853; 410-651-2713. Hours: 8:30AM-4:30PM (EST). *Misdemeanor, Civil Actions Under $25,000, Eviction, Small Claims.*

Note: Misdemeanor cases go to Circuit Court if preliminary hearing waived. Records held at court where trial heard.

Civil Records: Access: Online, in person. Visitors must perform in person searches for themselves. No search fee. Required to search: name, years to search. Civil cases indexed by defendant, plaintiff. Civil records on computer from 1987, archived and on index books from

1971. Online access available through SJIS. See state introduction or visit www.courts.state.md.us.

Criminal Records: Access: Online, in person. Visitors must perform in person searches for themselves. No search fee. Required to search: name, years to search; also helpful: SSN. Criminal records on computer from 1987, archived and on index books from 1971. Online access available through SJIS; see www.courts.state.md.us.

General Information: No adoptions, juvenile, sealed, expunged or mental records released. Copy fee: $.25per page. Certification fee: $5.00. Fee payee: District Court. Personal checks accepted. Prepayment is required.

Register of Wills 30512 Prince William St, Princess Anne, MD 21853; 410-651-1696, 888-758-0039 in MD; Fax: 410-651-3873. Hours: 8:30AM-4:30PM (EST). *Probate.*

www.registers.state.md.us/county/so/html/somerset.html

St. Mary's County

7th Judicial Circuit Court PO Box 676, Leonardtown, MD 20650; 301-475-5621. Hours: 8:30AM-4:30PM (EST). *Felony, Misdemeanor, Civil Actions Over $25,000.*

Civil Records: Access: Online, in person. Visitors must perform in person searches for themselves. No search fee. Required to search: name, years to search. Civil cases indexed by defendant, plaintiff. Civil records on computer from 1987, on card index from 1970. Online access available through SJIS. See state introduction or visit www.courts.state.md.us.

Criminal Records: Access: In person only. Visitors must perform in person searches for themselves. No search fee. Required to search: name, years to search; also helpful: SSN. Criminal records on computer from 1987, on card index from 1970.

General Information: Public access terminal is available. No adoptions, juvenile, sealed, expunged or mental records released. Copy fee: $.50 per page. Certification fee: $5.00. Fee payee: Clerk of the Circuit Court. Personal checks accepted. Prepayment is required.

District Court Carter State Office Bldg, 23110 Leonard Hall Dr, PO Box 653, Leonardtown, MD 20650; 301-475-4530; Fax: 301-475-4535. Hours: 8:30AM-4:30PM (EST). *Misdemeanor, Civil Actions Under $25,000, Eviction, Small Claims.*

Civil Records: Access: Online, in person. Visitors must perform in person searches for themselves. No search fee. Required to search: name, years to search. Civil cases indexed by defendant. Civil records on computer from 1985, archived from 1979. Online access available through SJIS. See state introduction or visit www.courts.state.md.us.

Criminal Records: Access: Online, in person. Visitors must perform in person searches for themselves. No search fee. Required to search: name, years to search; also helpful: DOB. Criminal records on computer from 1985, archived from 1979. Online access available through SJIS; see www.courts.state.md.us.

General Information: Public access terminal is available. No adoptions, juvenile, sealed, expunged or mental records released. Copy fee: $.25 per page. Certification fee: $10.00. Fee payee: District Court of Maryland. Personal checks accepted.

Register of Wills 41605 Court House Drive, Leonardtown, MD 20650; 301-475-5566, 888-475-4821 in MD; Fax: 301-475-4968. Hours: 8:30AM-4:30PM (EST). *Probate.*

www.registers.state.md.us/county/sm/html/stmarys.html

Talbot County

Circuit Court PO Box 723, Easton, MD 21601; 410-822-2611; Fax: 410-820-8168. Hours: 8:30AM-4:30PM (EST). *Felony, Misdemeanor, Civil Actions Over $25,000.*

Civil Records: Access: Online, in person. Visitors must perform in person searches for themselves. No search fee. Required to search: name, years to search; also helpful: address. Civil cases indexed by defendant, plaintiff. Civil records on card index from 1993. Online access available through SJIS. See state introduction or visit www.courts.state.md.us.

Criminal Records: Access: In person only. Visitors must perform in person searches for themselves. No search fee. Required to search: name, years to search; also helpful: address, DOB, SSN. Criminal records on card index from 1993.

General Information: Public access terminal is available. No adoptions, juvenile, sealed, expunged or mental records released. Copy fee: $.50 per page. Certification fee: $5.00. Fee payee: Maryann Shorall, Clerk of Court. Personal checks accepted. Prepayment is required.

District Court 108 W Dover St, Easton, MD 21601; 410-819-5850; Fax: 410-819-5853. Hours: 8:30AM-4:30PM (EST). *Misdemeanor, Civil Actions Under $25,000, Eviction, Small Claims.*

Civil Records: Access: Online, in person. Visitors must perform in person searches for themselves. No search fee. Required to search: name, years to search. Civil cases indexed by defendant. Civil records go back to 1971; on computer back to 1988. Online access available through SJIS. See state introduction or visit www.courts.state.md.us.

Criminal Records: Access: Online, in person. Visitors must perform in person searches for themselves. No search fee. Required to search: name, years to search. Criminal records go back to 1971; on computer back to 1984. Online access available through SJIS; see www.courts.state.md.us.

General Information: Public access terminal is available. No adoptions, juvenile, sealed, expunged or mental records released. Copy fee: $.25 per page. Certification fee: $5.00. Fee payee: District Court of MD. Personal checks accepted.

Register of Wills Courthouse, 11 N Washington St, Easton, MD 21601; 410-770-6700, 888-822-0039 in MD; Fax: 410-822-5452. Hours: 8AM-4:30PM (EST). *Probate.*

www.registers.state.md.us/county/ta/html/talbot.html

Washington County

Washington County Circuit Court Box 229, Hagerstown, MD 21741; 301-733-8660; Fax: 301-791-1151. Hours: 8:30AM-4:30PM (EST). *Felony, Misdemeanor, Civil Actions Over $25,000.*

Civil Records: Access: Online, in person. Visitors must perform in person searches for themselves. Search fee: No search fee. Required to search: name, years to search. Civil cases indexed by defendant. Civil records on case files, docket books to 1900; on computer back to 1985. Online access available through SJIS. See state introduction or visit www.courts.state.md.us.

Criminal Records: Access: In person only. Visitors must perform in person searches for themselves. Search fee: No search fee. Required to search: name, years to search; also helpful: DOB. Criminal records on case files, docket books to 1900; on coputer back to 1985.

General Information: Public access terminal is available. No adoptions, juvenile, sealed, expunged or mental records released. Copy fee: $.25 per page.

Certification fee: $5.00. Fee payee: Clerk of Circuit Court. Personal checks accepted. Prepayment is required.

District Court 36 W Antietam St, Hagerstown, MD 21740; 240-420-4600. Hours: 8:30AM-4:30PM (EST). *Misdemeanor, Civil Actions Under $25,000, Eviction, Small Claims.*

Civil Records: Access: Phone, mail, online, in person. Both court and visitors may perform in person searches. No search fee. Required to search: name, years to search; also helpful: address. Civil cases indexed by defendant. Civil records on computer from 1986, archived and on index books from 1971. Online access available through SJIS. See state introduction or visit www.courts.state.md.us.

Criminal Records: Access: Online, in person. Visitors must perform in person searches for themselves. No search fee. Required to search: name, years to search; also helpful: address, DOB, SSN, case number. Criminal records on computer from 1982, on index books from 1971. Online access available through SJIS; see www.courts.state.md.us.

General Information: Public access terminal is available. No adoptions, juvenile, sealed, expunged or mental records released. SASE required. Turnaround time less than 30 days. Copy fee: $.25 per page. Certification fee: $5.00. Fee payee: District Court. Personal checks accepted. Credit cards accepted: Visa, Discover. Prepayment is required.

Register of Wills 95 W Washington, Hagerstown, MD 21740; 301-739-3612, 888-739-0013 in MD; Fax: 301-733-8636. Hours: 8:30AM-4:30PM (EST). *Probate.*

www.registers.state.md.us/county/wa/html/washington.html

Wicomico County

1st Judicial Circuit Court PO Box 198, Salisbury, MD 21803-0198; 410-543-6551; Fax: 410-548-5150. Hours: 8:30AM-4:30PM (EST). *Felony, Misdemeanor, Civil Actions Over $25,000.*

Civil Records: Access: Phone, mail, online, in person. Both court and visitors may perform in person searches. No search fee. Required to search: name, years to search. Civil cases indexed by defendant, plaintiff. Civil records on books since 1867, cases filed after 05/93 on computer. Online access available through SJIS. See state introduction or visit www.courts.state.md.us. All phone requests must include case number.

Criminal Records: Access: Phone, mail, in person. Both court and visitors may perform in person searches. No search fee. Required to search: name, years to search; also helpful: DOB, SSN. Criminal records on books since 1867, cases filed after 05/93 on computer. Phone requests must include case number.

General Information: Public access terminal is available. No adoptions, juvenile, sealed, expunged or mental records released. SASE not required. Turnaround time 1-2 days. Copy fee: $.50 per page. Certification fee: $5.00. Fee payee: Clerk of Circuit Court. Personal checks accepted. Out of state checks not accepted. Prepayment is required.

District Court 201 Baptist St, Salisbury, MD 21801; 410-543-6600. Hours: 8:30AM-4:30PM (EST). *Misdemeanor, Civil Actions Under $25,000, Eviction, Small Claims.*

Civil Records: Access: Online, in person. Visitors must perform in person searches for themselves. No search fee. Required to search: name, years to search; also helpful: address. Civil cases indexed by defendant, plaintiff. Civil records on computer go back to 1985, archived from 1984, on card index from 1976. Online

access available through SJIS. See state introduction or visit www.courts.state.md.us.

Criminal Records: Access: Online, in person. Visitors must perform in person searches for themselves. No search fee. Required to search: name, years to search; also helpful: address, DOB. Criminal records go back to 1971; on computer back 1983. Online access available through SJIS; see www.courts.state.md.us.

General Information: Public access terminal is available. No adoptions, juvenile, sealed, expunged or mental records released. Copy fee: $.50. Certification fee: $5.00. Fee payee: District Court. Personal checks accepted. Prepayment is required.

Register of Wills 101 N Division St, Room 102, Salisbury, MD 21801; 410-543-6635, 888-786-0018 in MD; Fax: 410-334-3440. Hours: 8:30AM-4:30PM (EST). *Probate.*

www.registers.state.md.us/county/wi/html/wicomico.html

Worcester County

1st Judicial Circuit Court Box 40, Snow Hill, MD 21863; Civil phone: 410-632-1222; Criminal phone: 410-632-1235. Hours: 8:30AM-4:30PM (EST). *Felony, Misdemeanor, Civil Actions Over $25,000.*

Civil Records: Access: Online, in person. Visitors must perform in person searches for themselves. No search fee. Required to search: name, years to search. Civil cases indexed by defendant. Civil records on computer since 7/93, on docket books prior. Online access available through JIS. See state introduction or visit www.courts.state.md.us.

Criminal Records: Access: In person only. Visitors must perform in person searches for themselves. No search fee. Required to search: name, years to search. Criminal records on computer since 7/93, on docket books prior.

General Information: Public access terminal is available. No adoptions, juvenile, sealed or expunged records released. Copy fee: $.50 per page. Certification fee: $5.00. Fee payee: Clerk of Circuit Court. Personal checks accepted. Will bill copy fees to Maryland attorneys.

District Court 301 Commerce St, Snow Hill, MD 21863-1007; 410-219-7830; Fax: 410-219-7840. Hours: 8:30AM-4:30PM (EST). *Misdemeanor, Civil Actions Under $25,000, Eviction, Small Claims.*

Civil Records: Access: Online, in person. Visitors must perform in person searches for themselves. No search fee. Required to search: name, years to search; also helpful: address. Civil cases indexed by defendant. Civil records on computer since 1988. Online access available through SJIS. See state introduction or visit www.courts.state.md.us.

Criminal Records: Access: Online, in person. Visitors must perform in person searches for themselves. No search fee. Required to search: name, years to search; also helpful: address, DOB, SSN. Criminal records on computer since 1982. Online access available through SJIS; see www.courts.state.md.us.

General Information: Public access terminal is available. No sealed or juvenile records released. Copy fee: $1.00 per page. Certification fee: $5.00 per page. Fee payee: District Court. Personal checks accepted. Prepayment is required.

Register of Wills Courthouse, 1 W Market St, Room 102, Snow Hill, MD 21863-1074; 410-632-1529, 888-256-0047 in MD; Fax: 410-632-5600. Hours: 8AM-4:30PM (EST). *Probate.*

www.registers.state.md.us/county/wo/html/worcester.html

Maryland Recording Offices

ORGANIZATION: 23 counties and one independent city, 24 recording offices. The recording officer is Clerk of the Circuit Court. Baltimore City has a recording office separate from the county of Baltimore. See the City/County Locator section at the end of this chapter for ZIP Codes that include both the city and the county. The entire state is in the Eastern Time Zone (EST).

REAL ESTATE RECORDS: Counties will not perform real estate searches. Copies usually cost $.50 per page, and certification fees $5.00 per document.

UCC RECORDS: This was a dual filing state until July 1995. As of July 1995, all new UCC filings except for consumer goods, farm related and real estate related filings were submitted only to the central filing office. Starting July 2001, only real estate related filing are submitted to the Clerk of Circuit Court,

TAX LIEN RECORDS: All tax liens are filed with the county Clerk of Circuit Court. Counties will not perform name searches.

OTHER LIENS: Judgment, mechanics, county, hospital, condominium.

ONLINE ACCESS: Search statewide property records data free online at http://sdatcert3.resiusa.org/rp_rewrite/. There is no name searching.

Also, online access to county tax records is available at www.taxrecords.com. Land survey, condominium and survey plats is available free by county at www.plats.net. Use username "Plato" and password "plato#". No name searching. Another option for online access to county tax records is available at www.taxrecords.com

Also, the Maryland State Dept. of Planning offers MDPropertyview with property maps/parcels and assessments on the web or CD-Rom. Registration required; visit www.mdp.state.md.us data/mdview.htm or call 410-767-4614 or 410-767-4474. There is no name searching.

Allegany County

County Clerk of the Circuit Court, PO Box 359, Cumberland, MD 21502. 301-777-5922; Fax 301-777-2100.
Will search UCC records. This agency will not do a tax lien search. Will not search real estate records. **Online Access:** Real Property, Land Survey/Plat Records. Online search data at http://sdatcert3.resiusa.org/rp_rewrite. No name searching. Also, see state introduction for add'l land records online from www.plats.net (use username "Plato" and password "plato#") and MDPropertyview at www.mdp.state.md.us/data/mdview.htm. No name searching. **Other Phone Numbers:** Assessor 301-777-2108; Treasurer 301-777-5965.

Anne Arundel County

County Clerk of the Circuit Court, PO Box 71, Annapolis, MD 21404. 410-222-1425; Fax 410-222-1087.
Will search UCC records. This agency will not do a tax lien search. Will not search real estate records. **Online Access:** Real Property, Land Survey/Plat Records. Online search data at http://sdatcert3.resiusa.org/rp_rewrite. No name searching. Also, see state introduction for add'l land records online from www.plats.net (use username "Plato" and password "plato#") and MDPropertyview at www.mdp.state.md.us/data/mdview.htm. No name searching. **Other Phones:** Assessor 410-974-5727.

Baltimore City

City Clerk, 100 N. Calvert St, Room 610, Baltimore, MD 21202. 410-333-3760.
Will search UCC records. This agency will not do a tax lien search. Will not search real estate records. **Online Access:** Real Property, Land Survey/Plat Records. Online search data at http://sdatcert3.resiusa.org/rp_rewrite. No name searching. Also, see state introduction for add'l land records online from MDPropertyview at www.mdp.state.md.us/data/mdview.htm. No name searching. **Other Phone Numbers:** Assessor 401-512-4900.

Baltimore County

County Clerk of the Circuit Court, PO Box 6754, Baltimore, MD 21285. 410-887-2652; Fax 410-887-3062.
This agency will not perform searches. **Online Access:** Real Property, Land Survey/Plat Records. Online search data at http://sdatcert3.resiusa.org/rp_rewrite. No name searching. Also, see state introduction for add'l land records online from www.plats.net (use username "Plato" and password "plato#") and MDPropertyview at www.mdp.state.md.us/data/mdview.htm. No name searching. **Other Phone Numbers:** Assessor 410-512-4906; Treasurer 410-887-2416; Elections 410-887-5700; Vital Records 410-764-3038.

Calvert County

County Clerk of the Circuit Court, 175 Main St, Courthouse, Prince Frederick, MD 20678. 410-535-1660 R/E Recording: 410-535-1600 x269 UCC Recording: 410-535-1600 x269.
Will search UCC records. This agency will not do a tax lien search. Will not search real estate records. **Online Access:** Real Property, Land Survey/Plat Records. Online search data at http://sdatcert3.resiusa.org/rp_rewrite. No name searching. Also, see state introduction for add'l land records online from www.plats.net (use username "Plato" and password "plato#") and at MDPropertyview at www.mdp.state.md.us/data/mdview.htm. No name searching. **Other Phone Numbers:** Assessor 410-535-8850; Treasurer 410-535-1600 x272.

Caroline County

County Clerk of the Circuit Court, PO Box 458, Denton, MD 21629. County Clerk of the Circuit Court, R/E and UCC Recording 410-479-1811; Fax 410-479-1142.
Will search UCC records. This agency will not do a tax lien search. Will not search real estate records. **Online Access:** Real Property, Land Survey/Plat Records. Online search data at http://sdatcert3.resiusa.org/rp_rewrite. No name searching. Also, see state introduction for add'l land records online from www.plats.net (use username "Plato" and password

"plato#") and also at MDPropertyview at www.mdp.state.md.us/data/mdview.htm. No name searching. **Other Phone Numbers:** Assessor 410-479-5950; Treasurer 410-479-0410.

Carroll County

County Clerk of the Circuit Court, 55 N. Court St, Room G8, Westminster, MD 21157. 410-386-2022; Fax 410-876-0822.
Will search UCC records. This agency will not do a tax lien search. Will not search real estate records. **Online Access:** Real Property, Land Survey/Plat Records. Online search data at http://sdatcert3.resiusa.org/rp_rewrite. No name searching. Also, see state introduction for add'l land records online from www.plats.net (use username "Plato" and password "plato#") and at MDPropertyview at www.mdp.state.md.us/data/mdview.htm. No name searching. **Other Phone Numbers:** Assessor 410-857-0600; Treasurer 410-386-2971; Appraiser/Auditor 410-857-0600.

Cecil County

County Clerk of the Circuit Court, 129 E. Main St., Room 108, Elkton, MD 21921-5971. 410-996-5375.
Will search UCC records. This agency will not do a tax lien search. Will not search real estate records. **Online Access:** Real Property, Land Survey/Plat Records. Online search data at http://sdatcert3.resiusa.org/rp_rewrite/ No name searching. Also, see state introduction for add'l land records online from www.plats.net (use username "Plato" and password "plato#") and at MDPropertyview at www.mdp.state.md.us/data/mdview.htm. No name searching. **Other Phone Numbers:** Assessor 410-996-0525; Treasurer 410-996-5394.

Charles County

County Clerk of the Circuit Court, PO Box 970, La Plata, MD 20646. 301-932-3255.
This agency will not perform searches. **Online Access:** Real Property, Land Survey/Plat Records. Online search data at http://sdatcert3.resiusa.org/rp_rewrite. No name searching. Also, see state introduction for add'l land records online from www.plats.net (use username

"Plato" and password "plato#") and MDPropertyview at www.mdp.state.md.us/data/mdview.htm. No name searching. **Other Phone Numbers:** Assessor 301-932-2440; Treasurer 645-0685; Elections 934-8962.

Dorchester County

County Clerk of the Circuit Court, PO Box 150, Cambridge, MD 21613. 410-228-0481 R/E Recording: 410-228-0480 UCC Recording: 410-228-0480.

Will search UCC records. This agency will not do a tax lien search. Will not search real estate records. **Online Access:** Real Property, Land Survey/Plat Records. Online search data at http://sdatcert3.resiusa.org/rp_rewrite. No name searching. Also, see state introduction for add'l land records online from www.plats.net (use username "Plato" and password "plato#") and at MDPropertyview at www.mdp.state.md.us/data/mdview.htm. No name searching. **Other Phone Numbers:** Assessor 410-228-3380; Treasurer 410-228-4343 (County).

Frederick County

County Clerk of the Circuit Court, 100 W. Patrick St, Frederick, MD 21701. 301-694-1964; Fax 301-846-2245.

Will search UCC records. This agency will not do a tax lien search. Will not search real estate records. **Online Access:** Real Property, Land Survey/Plat Records. Online search data at http://sdatcert3.resiusa.org/rp_rewrite. No name searching. Also, see state introduction for add'l land records online from www.plats.net (use username "Plato" and password "plato#") and at MDPropertyview at www.mdp.state.md.us/data/mdview.htm. No name searching. **Other Phone Numbers:** Assessor 301-694-2040; Treasurer 301-694-1111.

Garrett County

County Clerk of the Circuit Court, PO Box 447, Oakland, MD 21550-0447. 301-334-1937 R/E Recording: 301-334-1938 UCC Recording: 301-334-5016; Fax 301-334-5017.

Will search UCC records. This agency will not do a tax lien search. Will not search real estate records. **Online Access:** Real Property, Land Survey/Plat Records. Online search data at http://sdatcert3.resiusa.org/rp_rewrite. No name searching. Also, see state introduction for add'l land records online from www.plats.net (use username "Plato" and password "plato#") and at MDPropertyview at www.mdp.state.md.us/data/mdview.htm. No name searching. **Other Phone Numbers:** Assessor 301-334-1950; Treasurer 334-1965; Elections 301-334-1962.

Harford County

County Clerk of the Circuit Court, 20 W. Courtland St, Bel Air, MD 21014. 410-638-3244.

This agency will not perform searches. **Online Access:** Real Property, Land Survey/Plat Records. Online search data at http://sdatcert3.resiusa.org/rp_rewrite. No name searching. Also, see state introduction for add'l land records online from www.plats.net (use username "Plato" and password "plato#") and MDPropertyview at www.mdp.state.md.us/data/mdview.htm. No name searching. **Other Phone Numbers:** Assessor 410-838-4800; Treasurer 410-638-3269.

Howard County

County Clerk of the Circuit Court, 8360 Court Ave, Ellicott City, MD 21043. 410-313-2111.

Will search UCC records. This agency will not do a tax lien search. Will not search real estate records. **Online Access:** Real Property, Land Survey/Plat Records. Online search data at http://sdatcert3.resiusa.org/p_rewrite. No name searching. Also, see state introduction for add'l land records online from www.plats.net (use username "Plato" and password

"plato#") and at MDPropertyview at www.mdp.state.md.us/data/mdview.htm. No name searching. **Other Phones:** Assessor 410-461-0135.

Kent County

Clerk of the Circuit Court, 103 N. Cross St., Chestertown, MD 21620. 410-778-7431 R/E Recording: 410-778-7460.

This agency will not perform searches. **Online Access:** Real Property, Land Survey/Plat Records. Online search data at http://sdatcert3.resiusa.org/rp_rewrite. No name searching. Also, see state introduction for add'l land records online from www.plats.net (use username "Plato" and password "plato#") and MDPropertyview at www.mdp.state.md.us/data/mdview.htm. No name searching. **Other Phones:** Assessor 410-778-7447; Treasurer 410-778-7443; Elections 410-778-0038.

Montgomery County

County Clerk of the Circuit Court, 50 Maryland Ave., County Courthouse, Rockville, MD 20850. 240-777-9470; Fax 240-777-9486. www.co.mo.md.us/judicial

This agency will not perform searches. **Online Access:** Real Property, Land Survey/Plat Records. Access to clerk records is available via JIS Dialup Access; contact Mary Hutchins 410-260-1031. Also, online search real property data at http://sdatcert3.resiusa.org/rp_rewrite. No name searching. Also, see state introduction for add'l land records online from www.plats.net (use username "Plato" and password "plato#") and at MDPropertyview at www.mdp.state.md.us/data/mdview.htm. No name searching. **Other Phone Numbers:** Assessor 301-279-1701; Treasurer 240-777-8995; Vital Records 240-777-1755.

Prince George's County

County Clerk of the Circuit Court, 14735 Main St, Upper Marlboro, MD 20772. 301-952-3352.

Will search UCC records. This agency will not do a tax lien search. Will not search real estate records. **Online Access:** Real Property, Land Survey/Plat Records. Online search data at http://sdatcert3.resiusa.org/rp_rewrite. No name searching. Also, see state introduction for add'l land records online from www.plats.net (use username "Plato" and password "plato#") and at MDPropertyview at www.mdp.state.md.us/data/mdview.htm. No name searching. **Other Phone Numbers:** Assessor 301-952-2500; Treasurer 301-952-3946.

Queen Anne's County

County Clerk of the Circuit Court, 100 Court House Square, Centreville, MD 21617. 410-758-1773.

Will search UCC records. This agency will not do a tax lien search. Will not search real estate records. **Online Access:** Real Property, Land Survey/Plat Records. Online search data at http://sdatcert3.resiusa.org/rp_rewrite. No name searching. Also, see state introduction for add'l land records online from www.plats.net (use username "Plato" and password "plato#") and at MDPropertyview at www.mdp.state.md.us/data/mdview.htm. No name searching. **Other Phone Numbers:** Assessor 410-758-5030; Treasurer 410-758-0414.

Somerset County

County Clerk of the Circuit Court, PO Box 99, Princess Anne, MD 21853. 410-651-1555; Fax 410-651-1048.

Will search UCC records. This agency will not do a tax lien search. Will not search real estate records. **Online Access:** Real Property, Land Survey/Plat Records. Online search data at http://sdatcert3.resiusa.org/rp_rewrite. No name searching. Also, see state introduction for add'l land records online from www.plats.net (use username "Plato" and password "plato#") and at MDPropertyview at www.mdp.state.md.us/data/mdview.htm. No name

searching. **Other Phone Numbers:** Assessor 410-651-0868; Treasurer 651-0440; Vital Records 651-1555.

St. Mary's County

County Clerk of the Circuit Court, PO Box 676, Leonardtown, MD 20650. 301-475-4567 R/E Recording: 301-475-4554.

Will search UCC records. This agency will not do a tax lien search. Will not search real estate records. **Online Access:** Real Property, Land Survey/Plat Records. Online search data at http://sdatcert3.resiusa.org/rp_rewrite. No name searching. Also, see state introduction for add'l land records online from www.plats.net (use username "Plato" and password "plato#") and at www.mdp.state.md.us/data/mdview.htm. No name searching. **Other Phone Numbers:** Assessor 301-475-4610; Treasurer 301-475-4473.

Talbot County

County Clerk of the Circuit Court, PO Box 723, Easton, MD 21601. 410-822-2611; Fax 410-820-8168. www.courts.state.md.us/clerks/talbot/index.html

This agency will not perform searches. **Online Access:** Real Property, Land Survey/Plat Records. Online search data at http://sdatcert3.resiusa.org/rp_rewrite. No name searching. Also, see state introduction for add'l land records online from www.plats.net (use username "Plato" and password "plato#") and MDPropertyview at www.mdp.state.md.us/data/mdview.htm. No name searching. **Other Phone Numbers:** Assessor 410-819-5920; Treasurer 410-770-8020; Elections 410-770-8099; Vital Records 410-764-3038.

Washington County

Clerk of the Circuit Court, PO Box 229, Hagerstown, MD 21741-0229. Clerk of the Circuit Court, R/E and UCC Recording 301-733-8660; Fax 301-791-1151. www.courts.state.md.us/washington.html

This agency will not perform searches. **Online Access:** Real Property, Land Survey/Plat Records. Search real property data at http://sdatcert3.resiusa.org/rp_rewrite. No name searching. Also, see state introduction for add'l land records online from www.plats.net (use username "Plato" and password "plato#") and at MDPropertyview at www.mdp.state.md.us/data/mdview.htm. No name searching. **Other Phone Numbers:** Assessor 301-791-3050; Treasurer 240-313-2110; Elections 313-2050; Vital Records 733-8660.

Wicomico County

County Clerk of the Circuit Court, PO Box 198, Salisbury, MD 21803-0198. 410-543-6551.

Will search UCC records. This agency will not do a tax lien search. Will not search real estate records. **Online Access:** Real Property, Land Survey/Plat Records. Online search data at http://sdatcert3.resiusa.org/rp_rewrite. No name searching. Also, see state introduction for add'l land records online from www.plats.net (use username "Plato" and password "plato#") and at MDPropertyview at www.mdp.state.md.us/data/mdview.htm. No name searching. **Other Phones:** Assessor 410-543-6623.

Worcester County

County Clerk of the Circuit Court, PO Box 40, Snow Hill, MD 21863-0040. 410-632-1221.

This agency will not perform searches. **Online Access:** Real Property, Land Survey/Plat Records. Online search data at http://sdatcert3.resiusa.org/rp_rewrite. No name searching. Also, see state introduction for add'l land records online from www.plats.net (use username "Plato" and password "plato#") and at MDPropertyview at www.mdp.state.md.us/data/mdview.htm. No name searching. **Other Phone Numbers:** Assessor 410-632-1194.

Maryland County Locator

You will usually be able to find the city name in the City/County Cross Reference below. In that case, it is a simple matter to determine the county from the cross reference. However, only the official US Postal Service city names are included in this index. There are an additional 40,000 place names that people use in their addresses. Therefore, we have also included a ZIP/City Cross Reference immediately following the City/County Cross Reference.

If you know the ZIP Code but the city name does not appear in the City/County Cross Reference index, look up the ZIP Code in the ZIP/City Cross Reference, find the city name, then look up the city name in the City/County Cross. Reference. For example, you want to know the county for an address of Menands, NY 12204. There is no "Menands" in the City/County Cross Reference. The ZIP/City Cross Reference shows that ZIP Codes 12201-12288 are for the city of Albany. Looking back in the City/County Cross Reference, Albany is in Albany County.

City/County Cross Reference

ABELL St. Mary's
ABERDEEN Harford
ABERDEEN PROVING GROUND Harford
ABINGDON Harford
ACCIDENT Garrett
ACCOKEEK Prince George's
ADAMSTOWN Frederick
ALESIA (21107) Carroll(59), Baltimore(40)
ALLEN Wicomico
ANDREWS AIR FORCE BASE Prince George's
ANNAPOLIS Anne Arundel
ANNAPOLIS JUNCTION (20701) Howard(79), Anne Arundel(20)
AQUASCO Prince George's
ARNOLD Anne Arundel
ASHTON Montgomery
AVENUE St. Mary's
BALDWIN (21013) Baltimore(69), Harford(30)
BALTIMORE Baltimore City
BARCLAY Queen Anne's
BARNESVILLE Montgomery
BARSTOW Calvert
BARTON (21521) Allegany(73), Garrett(26)
BEALLSVILLE Montgomery
BEL AIR Harford
BEL ALTON Charles
BELCAMP Harford
BELTSVILLE Prince George's
BENEDICT Charles
BENSON Harford
BERLIN Worcester
BETHESDA Montgomery
BETHLEHEM Caroline
BETTERTON Kent
BIG POOL Washington
BISHOPVILLE Worcester
BITTINGER Garrett
BIVALVE Wicomico
BLADENSBURG Prince George's
BLOOMINGTON Garrett
BOONSBORO Washington
BORING Baltimore
BOWIE Prince George's
BOYDS Montgomery
BOZMAN Talbot
BRADDOCK HEIGHTS Frederick
BRADSHAW Baltimore
BRANDYWINE (20613) Prince George's(88), Charles(11)
BRENTWOOD Prince George's
BRINKLOW Montgomery
BROOKEVILLE (20833) Montgomery(96), Howard(3)
BROOKLANDVILLE Baltimore
BROOKLYN (21225) Baltimore City(54), Anne Arundel(45)
BROOMES ISLAND Calvert
BROWNSVILLE Washington
BRUNSWICK Frederick
BRYANS ROAD Charles
BRYANTOWN Charles

BUCKEYSTOWN Frederick
BURKITTSVILLE Frederick
BURTONSVILLE Montgomery
BUSHWOOD St. Mary's
BUTLER Baltimore
CABIN JOHN Montgomery
CALIFORNIA St. Mary's
CALLAWAY St. Mary's
CAMBRIDGE Dorchester
CAPITOL HEIGHTS Prince George's
CARDIFF Harford
CASCADE (21719) Washington(98), Frederick(1)
CATONSVILLE Baltimore
CAVETOWN Washington
CECILTON Cecil
CENTREVILLE Queen Anne's
CHANCE Somerset
CHAPTICO St. Mary's
CHARLESTOWN Cecil
CHARLOTTE HALL (20622) Charles(63), St. Mary's(36)
CHASE Baltimore
CHELTENHAM Prince George's
CHESAPEAKE BEACH Calvert
CHESAPEAKE CITY Cecil
CHESTER Queen Anne's
CHESTERTOWN Queen Anne's
CHEVY CHASE Montgomery
CHEWSVILLE Washington
CHILDS Cecil
CHURCH CREEK Dorchester
CHURCH HILL Queen Anne's
CHURCHTON Anne Arundel
CHURCHVILLE Harford
CLAIBORNE Talbot
CLARKSBURG (20871) Montgomery(90), Frederick(9)
CLARKSVILLE Howard
CLEAR SPRING Washington
CLEMENTS St. Mary's
CLINTON Prince George's
COBB ISLAND Charles
COCKEYSVILLE Baltimore
COLLEGE PARK Prince George's
COLORA Cecil
COLTONS POINT St. Mary's
COLUMBIA Howard
COMPTON St. Mary's
CONOWINGO Cecil
COOKSVILLE Howard
CORDOVA Talbot
CORRIGANVILLE Allegany
CRAPO Dorchester
CRISFIELD Somerset
CROCHERON Dorchester
CROFTON Anne Arundel
CROWNSVILLE Anne Arundel
CRUMPTON Queen Anne's
CUMBERLAND Allegany
CURTIS BAY (21226) Baltimore City(57), Anne Arundel(42)
DAMASCUS Montgomery

DAMERON St. Mary's
DAMES QUARTER Somerset
DARLINGTON Harford
DAVIDSONVILLE Anne Arundel
DAYTON Howard
DEAL ISLAND Somerset
DEALE Anne Arundel
DELMAR Wicomico
DENTON Caroline
DERWOOD Montgomery
DETOUR Carroll
DICKERSON (20842) Montgomery(82), Frederick(17)
DISTRICT HEIGHTS Prince George's
DOWELL Calvert
DRAYDEN St. Mary's
DUNDALK (21222) Baltimore(97), Baltimore City(2)
DUNKIRK (20754) Calvert(89), Anne Arundel(10)
EARLEVILLE Cecil
EAST NEW MARKET Dorchester
EASTON Talbot
ECKHART MINES Allegany
EDEN (21822) Worcester(96), Somerset(3)
EDGEWATER Anne Arundel
EDGEWOOD Harford
ELK MILLS Cecil
ELKRIDGE Howard
ELKTON Cecil
ELLERSLIE Allegany
ELLICOTT CITY (21043) Howard(97), Baltimore(2)
EMMITSBURG Frederick
ESSEX Baltimore
EWELL Somerset
FAIRPLAY Washington
FALLSTON Harford
FAULKNER Charles
FEDERALSBURG Caroline
FINKSBURG Carroll
FISHING CREEK Dorchester
FLINTSTONE Allegany
FOREST HILL Harford
FORK Baltimore
FORT GEORGE G MEADE Anne Arundel
FORT HOWARD Baltimore
FORT WASHINGTON Prince George's
FREDERICK Frederick
FREELAND (21107) Carroll(59), Baltimore(40)
FRIENDSHIP Anne Arundel
FRIENDSVILLE Garrett
FROSTBURG (21532) Allegany(84), Garrett(15)
FRUITLAND Wicomico
FULTON Howard
FUNKSTOWN Washington
GAITHER Carroll
GAITHERSBURG Montgomery
GALENA Kent
GALESVILLE Anne Arundel
GAMBRILLS Anne Arundel

GAPLAND Washington
GARRETT PARK Montgomery
GARRISON Baltimore
GEORGETOWN Cecil
GERMANTOWN Montgomery
GIBSON ISLAND Anne Arundel
GIRDLETREE Worcester
GLEN ARM Baltimore
GLEN BURNIE Anne Arundel
GLEN ECHO Montgomery
GLENELG Howard
GLENN DALE Prince George's
GLENWOOD Howard
GLYNDON Baltimore
GOLDSBORO Caroline
GRANTSVILLE Garrett
GRASONVILLE Queen Anne's
GREAT MILLS St. Mary's
GREENBELT Prince George's
GREENSBORO Caroline
GUNPOWDER Harford
GWYNN OAK Baltimore
HAGERSTOWN Washington
HALETHORPE (21227) Baltimore(95), Baltimore City(4)
HAMPSTEAD Carroll
HANCOCK Washington
HANOVER Anne Arundel
HARMANS Anne Arundel
HARWOOD Anne Arundel
HAVRE DE GRACE Harford
HEBRON Wicomico
HELEN St. Mary's
HENDERSON Caroline
HENRYTON Carroll
HIGHLAND (20777) Howard(95), Montgomery(4)
HILLSBORO Caroline
HOLLYWOOD St. Mary's
HUGHESVILLE Charles
HUNT VALLEY Baltimore
HUNTINGTOWN Calvert
HURLOCK Dorchester
HYATTSVILLE Prince George's
HYDES (21082) Baltimore(96), Harford(3)
IJAMSVILLE Frederick
INDIAN HEAD Charles
INGLESIDE Queen Anne's
IRONSIDES Charles
ISSUE Charles
JARRETTSVILLE Harford
JEFFERSON Frederick
JESSUP (20794) Howard(80), Anne Arundel(19)
JOPPA Harford
KEEDYSVILLE Washington
KENNEDYVILLE Kent
KENSINGTON Montgomery
KEYMAR (21757) Frederick(50), Carroll(49)
KINGSVILLE (21087) Baltimore(84), Harford(15)
KITZMILLER Garrett

KNOXVILLE (21758) Washington(50), Frederick(49)
LA PLATA Charles
LADIESBURG Frederick
LANHAM Prince George's
LAUREL Prince George's
LEONARDTOWN St. Mary's
LEXINGTON PARK St. Mary's
LIBERTYTOWN Frederick
LINEBORO Carroll
LINKWOOD Dorchester
LINTHICUM HEIGHTS Anne Arundel
LINWOOD Carroll
LISBON Howard
LITTLE ORLEANS Allegany
LONACONING (21539) Allegany(67), Garrett(32)
LONG GREEN Baltimore
LOTHIAN Anne Arundel
LOVEVILLE St. Mary's
LUKE Allegany
LUSBY Calvert
LUTHERVILLE TIMONIUM Baltimore
LYNCH Kent
MADISON Dorchester
MAGNOLIA Harford
MANCHESTER (21102) Carroll(98), Baltimore(1)
MANOKIN Somerset
MARBURY Charles
MARDELA SPRINGS Wicomico
MARION STATION Somerset
MARRIOTTSVILLE (21104) Carroll(55), Howard(35), Baltimore(9)
MARYDEL Caroline
MARYLAND LINE Baltimore
MASSEY Kent
MAUGANSVILLE Washington
MAYO Anne Arundel
MC HENRY Garrett
MCDANIEL Talbot
MECHANICSVILLE (20659) St. Mary's(97), Charles(2)
MIDDLE RIVER Baltimore
MIDDLEBURG Carroll
MIDDLETOWN Frederick
MIDLAND Allegany
MIDLOTHIAN Allegany
MILLERS (21107) Carroll(59), Baltimore(40)
MILLERSVILLE Anne Arundel
MILLINGTON Kent
MONKTON (21111) Baltimore(87), Harford(12)
MONROVIA Frederick
MONTGOMERY VILLAGE Montgomery
MORGANZA St. Mary's
MOUNT AIRY (21771) Frederick(47), Carroll(38), Howard(12), Montgomery(1)
MOUNT RAINIER Prince George's
MOUNT SAVAGE Allegany

MOUNT VICTORIA Charles
MYERSVILLE Frederick
NANJEMOY Charles
NANTICOKE Wicomico
NEAVITT Talbot
NEW MARKET Frederick
NEW MIDWAY Frederick
NEW WINDSOR (21776) Carroll(81), Frederick(18)
NEWARK Worcester
NEWBURG Charles
NEWCOMB Talbot
NIKEP Allegany
NORTH BEACH (20714) Calvert(86), Anne Arundel(13)
NORTH EAST Cecil
NOTTINGHAM Baltimore
OAKLAND Garrett
OCEAN CITY Worcester
ODENTON Anne Arundel
OLDTOWN Allegany
OLNEY Montgomery
OWINGS Calvert
OWINGS MILLS Baltimore
OXFORD Talbot
OXON HILL Prince George's
PARK HALL St. Mary's
PARKTON Baltimore
PARKVILLE (21234) Baltimore(89), Baltimore City(10)
PARSONSBURG Wicomico
PASADENA Anne Arundel
PATUXENT RIVER St. Mary's
PERRY HALL Baltimore
PERRY POINT Cecil
PERRYMAN Harford
PERRYVILLE Cecil
PHOENIX Baltimore
PIKESVILLE (21208) Baltimore(93), Baltimore City(6)
PINEY POINT St. Mary's
PINTO Allegany
PITTSVILLE Wicomico
POCOMOKE CITY (21851) Worcester(87), Somerset(12)
POINT OF ROCKS Frederick
POMFRET Charles
POOLESVILLE Montgomery
PORT DEPOSIT Cecil
PORT REPUBLIC Calvert
PORT TOBACCO Charles
POTOMAC Montgomery
POWELLVILLE Wicomico
PRESTON Caroline
PRINCE FREDERICK Calvert
PRINCESS ANNE Somerset
PYLESVILLE Harford
QUANTICO Wicomico
QUEEN ANNE Queen Anne's
QUEENSTOWN Queen Anne's
RANDALLSTOWN Baltimore

RAWLINGS Allegany
REHOBETH Somerset
REISTERSTOWN (21136) Baltimore(97), Carroll(2)
RHODES POINT Somerset
RHODESDALE Dorchester
RIDERWOOD Baltimore
RIDGE St. Mary's
RIDGELY Caroline
RISING SUN Cecil
RIVA Anne Arundel
RIVERDALE Prince George's
ROCK HALL Kent
ROCK POINT Charles
ROCKVILLE Montgomery
ROCKY RIDGE Frederick
ROHRERSVILLE Washington
ROSEDALE (21237) Baltimore(96), Baltimore City(3)
ROYAL OAK Talbot
SABILLASVILLE (21780) Frederick(94), Washington(5)
SAINT INIGOES St. Mary's
SAINT JAMES Washington
SAINT LEONARD Calvert
SAINT MARYS CITY St. Mary's
SAINT MICHAELS Talbot
SALISBURY Wicomico
SANDY SPRING Montgomery
SAVAGE Howard
SCOTLAND St. Mary's
SECRETARY Dorchester
SEVERN Anne Arundel
SEVERNA PARK Anne Arundel
SHADY SIDE Anne Arundel
SHARPSBURG Washington
SHARPTOWN Wicomico
SHERWOOD Talbot
SHOWELL Worcester
SILVER SPRING Montgomery
SIMPSONVILLE Howard
SMITHSBURG (21783) Washington(78), Frederick(21)
SNOW HILL Worcester
SOLOMONS Calvert
SOUTHERN MD FACILITY Prince George's
SPARKS GLENCOE Baltimore
SPARROWS POINT Baltimore
SPENCERVILLE Montgomery
SPRING GAP Allegany
STEVENSON Baltimore
STEVENSVILLE Queen Anne's
STILL POND Kent
STOCKTON Worcester
STREET Harford
SUBURB MARYLAND FAC Montgomery
SUDLERSVILLE Queen Anne's
SUITLAND Prince George's
SUNDERLAND Calvert
SWANTON Garrett

SYKESVILLE (21784) Carroll(94), Howard(5)
TAKOMA PARK Prince George's
TALL TIMBERS St. Mary's
TANEYTOWN (21787) Carroll(93), Frederick(6)
TAYLORS ISLAND Dorchester
TEMPLE HILLS Prince George's
TEMPLEVILLE Caroline
THURMONT Frederick
TILGHMAN Talbot
TODDVILLE Dorchester
TOWSON Baltimore
TRACYS LANDING Anne Arundel
TRAPPE Talbot
TUSCARORA Frederick
TYASKIN Wicomico
TYLERTON Somerset
UNION BRIDGE (21791) Carroll(52), Frederick(47)
UNIONVILLE Frederick
UPPER FAIRMOUNT Somerset
UPPER FALLS Baltimore
UPPER HILL Somerset
UPPER MARLBORO Prince George's
UPPERCO (21155) Baltimore(90), Carroll(9)
VALLEY LEE St. Mary's
VIENNA Dorchester
WALDORF Charles
WALKERSVILLE Frederick
WARWICK Cecil
WASHINGTON Prince George's
WASHINGTON GROVE Montgomery
WELCOME Charles
WENONA Somerset
WEST FRIENDSHIP Howard
WEST RIVER Anne Arundel
WESTERNPORT Allegany
WESTMINSTER Carroll
WESTOVER Somerset
WHALEYVILLE Worcester
WHITE HALL (21161) Baltimore(57), Harford(42)
WHITE MARSH Baltimore
WHITE PLAINS Charles
WHITEFORD Harford
WILLARDS Wicomico
WILLIAMSPORT Washington
WINDSOR MILL Baltimore
WINGATE Dorchester
WITTMAN Talbot
WOODBINE (21797) Howard(58), Carroll(41)
WOODSBORO Frederick
WOODSTOCK (21163) Baltimore(52), Howard(47)
WOOLFORD Dorchester
WORTON Kent
WYE MILLS Talbot

ZIP/City Cross Reference

20331-20331	WASHINGTON	20731-20731	CAPITOL HEIGHTS
20601-20604	WALDORF	20732-20732	CHESAPEAKE BEACH
20606-20606	ABELL	20733-20733	CHURCHTON
20607-20607	ACCOKEEK	20735-20735	CLINTON
20608-20608	AQUASCO	20736-20736	OWINGS
20609-20609	AVENUE	20737-20738	RIVERDALE
20610-20610	BARSTOW	20740-20742	COLLEGE PARK
20611-20611	BEL ALTON	20743-20743	CAPITOL HEIGHTS
20612-20612	BENEDICT	20744-20744	FORT WASHINGTON
20613-20613	BRANDYWINE	20745-20745	OXON HILL
20615-20615	BROOMES ISLAND	20746-20746	SUITLAND
20616-20616	BRYANS ROAD	20747-20747	DISTRICT HEIGHTS
20617-20617	BRYANTOWN	20748-20748	TEMPLE HILLS
20618-20618	BUSHWOOD	20749-20749	FORT WASHINGTON
20619-20619	CALIFORNIA	20750-20750	OXON HILL
20620-20620	CALLAWAY	20751-20751	DEALE
20621-20621	CHAPTICO	20752-20752	SUITLAND
20622-20622	CHARLOTTE HALL	20753-20753	DISTRICT HEIGHTS
20623-20623	CHELTENHAM	20754-20754	DUNKIRK
20624-20624	CLEMENTS	20755-20755	FORT GEORGE G MEADE
20625-20625	COBB ISLAND	20757-20757	TEMPLE HILLS
20626-20626	COLTONS POINT	20758-20758	FRIENDSHIP
20627-20627	COMPTON	20759-20759	FULTON
20628-20628	DAMERON	20762-20762	ANDREWS AIR FORCE
20629-20629	DOWELL		BASE
20630-20630	DRAYDEN	20763-20763	SAVAGE
20632-20632	FAULKNER	20764-20764	SHADY SIDE
20634-20634	GREAT MILLS	20765-20765	GALESVILLE
20635-20635	HELEN	20768-20768	GREENBELT
20636-20636	HOLLYWOOD	20769-20769	GLENN DALE
20637-20637	HUGHESVILLE	20770-20770	GREENBELT
20639-20639	HUNTINGTOWN	20772-20775	UPPER MARLBORO
20640-20640	INDIAN HEAD	20776-20776	HARWOOD
20643-20643	IRONSIDES	20777-20777	HIGHLAND
20645-20645	ISSUE	20778-20778	WEST RIVER
20646-20646	LA PLATA	20779-20779	TRACYS LANDING
20650-20650	LEONARDTOWN	20780-20789	HYATTSVILLE
20653-20653	LEXINGTON PARK	20790-20791	CAPITOL HEIGHTS
20656-20656	LOVEVILLE	20792-20792	UPPER MARLBORO
20657-20657	LUSBY	20794-20794	JESSUP
20658-20658	MARBURY	20797-20797	SOUTHERN MD FACILITY
20659-20659	MECHANICSVILLE	20799-20799	CAPITOL HEIGHTS
20660-20660	MORGANZA	20800-20800	SUBURB MARYLAND FAC
20661-20661	MOUNT VICTORIA	20812-20812	GLEN ECHO
20662-20662	NANJEMOY	20813-20814	BETHESDA
20664-20664	NEWBURG	20815-20815	CHEVY CHASE
20667-20667	PARK HALL	20816-20817	BETHESDA
20670-20670	PATUXENT RIVER	20818-20818	CABIN JOHN
20674-20674	PINEY POINT	20824-20824	BETHESDA
20675-20675	POMFRET	20825-20825	CHEVY CHASE
20676-20676	PORT REPUBLIC	20827-20827	BETHESDA
20677-20677	PORT TOBACCO	20830-20832	OLNEY
20678-20678	PRINCE FREDERICK	20833-20833	BROOKEVILLE
20680-20680	RIDGE	20837-20837	POOLESVILLE
20682-20682	ROCK POINT	20838-20838	BARNESVILLE
20684-20684	SAINT INIGOES	20839-20839	BEALLSVILLE
20685-20685	SAINT LEONARD	20841-20841	BOYDS
20686-20686	SAINT MARYS CITY	20842-20842	DICKERSON
20687-20687	SCOTLAND	20847-20853	ROCKVILLE
20688-20688	SOLOMONS	20854-20854	POTOMAC
20689-20689	SUNDERLAND	20855-20855	DERWOOD
20690-20690	TALL TIMBERS	20856-20858	ROCKVILLE
20692-20692	VALLEY LEE	20858-20858	SILVER SPRING
20693-20693	WELCOME	20859-20859	POTOMAC
20695-20695	WHITE PLAINS	20860-20860	SANDY SPRING
20697-20697	SOUTHERN MD FACILITY	20861-20861	ASHTON
20701-20701	ANNAPOLIS JUNCTION	20862-20862	BRINKLOW
20703-20703	LANHAM	20866-20866	BURTONSVILLE
20704-20705	BELTSVILLE	20868-20868	SPENCERVILLE
20706-20706	LANHAM	20871-20871	CLARKSBURG
20707-20709	LAUREL	20872-20872	DAMASCUS
20710-20710	BLADENSBURG	20874-20876	GERMANTOWN
20711-20711	LOTHIAN	20877-20879	GAITHERSBURG
20712-20712	MOUNT RAINIER	20880-20880	WASHINGTON GROVE
20714-20714	NORTH BEACH	20882-20885	GAITHERSBURG
20715-20721	BOWIE	20886-20886	MONTGOMERY VILLAGE
20722-20722	BRENTWOOD	20889-20889	BETHESDA
20723-20726	LAUREL	20890-20890	SUBURB MARYLAND FAC

20891-20891	KENSINGTON	21120-21120	PARKTON
20892-20894	BETHESDA	21122-21123	PASADENA
20895-20895	KENSINGTON	21128-21128	PERRY HALL
20896-20896	GARRETT PARK	21130-21130	PERRYMAN
20897-20897	SUBURB MARYLAND FAC	21131-21131	PHOENIX
20898-20899	GAITHERSBURG	21132-21132	PYLESVILLE
20900-20911	SILVER SPRING	21133-21133	RANDALLSTOWN
20912-20913	TAKOMA PARK	21136-21136	REISTERSTOWN
20914-20997	SILVER SPRING	21139-21139	RIDERWOOD
21001-21001	ABERDEEN	21140-21140	RIVA
21005-21005	ABERDEEN PROVING	21144-21144	SEVERN
	GROUND	21146-21146	SEVERNA PARK
21009-21009	ABINGDON	21150-21150	SIMPSONVILLE
21010-21010	GUNPOWDER	21152-21152	SPARKS GLENCOE
21012-21012	ARNOLD	21153-21153	STEVENSON
21013-21013	BALDWIN	21154-21154	STREET
21014-21015	BEL AIR	21155-21155	UPPERCO
21017-21017	BELCAMP	21156-21156	UPPER FALLS
21018-21018	BENSON	21157-21158	WESTMINSTER
21020-21020	BORING	21160-21160	WHITEFORD
21021-21021	BRADSHAW	21161-21161	WHITE HALL
21022-21022	BROOKLANDVILLE	21162-21162	WHITE MARSH
21023-21023	BUTLER	21163-21163	WOODSTOCK
21024-21024	CARDIFF	21200-21203	BALTIMORE
21027-21027	CHASE	21204-21204	TOWSON
21028-21028	CHURCHVILLE	21205-21206	BALTIMORE
21029-21029	CLARKSVILLE	21207-21207	GWYNN OAK
21030-21030	COCKEYSVILLE	21208-21208	PIKESVILLE
21031-21031	HUNT VALLEY	21209-21218	BALTIMORE
21032-21032	CROWNSVILLE	21219-21219	SPARROWS POINT
21034-21034	DARLINGTON	21220-21220	MIDDLE RIVER
21035-21035	DAVIDSONVILLE	21221-21221	ESSEX
21036-21036	DAYTON	21222-21222	DUNDALK
21037-21037	EDGEWATER	21223-21224	BALTIMORE
21040-21040	EDGEWOOD	21225-21225	BROOKLYN
21041-21043	ELLICOTT CITY	21226-21226	CURTIS BAY
21044-21046	COLUMBIA	21227-21227	HALETHORPE
21047-21047	FALLSTON	21228-21228	CATONSVILLE
21048-21048	FINKSBURG	21229-21233	BALTIMORE
21050-21050	FOREST HILL	21234-21234	PARKVILLE
21051-21051	FORK	21235-21235	BALTIMORE
21052-21052	FORT HOWARD	21236-21236	NOTTINGHAM
21053-21053	FREELAND	21237-21237	ROSEDALE
21054-21054	GAMBRILLS	21239-21241	BALTIMORE
21055-21055	GARRISON	21244-21244	GWYNN OAK
21056-21056	GIBSON ISLAND	21244-21244	WINDSOR MILL
21057-21057	GLEN ARM	21250-21285	BALTIMORE
21060-21062	GLEN BURNIE	21286-21286	TOWSON
21065-21065	COCKEYSVILLE	21287-21299	BALTIMORE
21071-21071	GLYNDON	21400-21412	ANNAPOLIS
21074-21074	HAMPSTEAD	21501-21505	CUMBERLAND
21075-21075	ELKRIDGE	21520-21520	ACCIDENT
21076-21076	HANOVER	21521-21521	BARTON
21077-21077	HARMANS	21522-21522	BITTINGER
21078-21078	HAVRE DE GRACE	21523-21523	BLOOMINGTON
21080-21080	HENRYTON	21524-21524	CORRIGANVILLE
21082-21082	HYDES	21528-21528	ECKHART MINES
21084-21084	JARRETTSVILLE	21529-21529	ELLERSLIE
21085-21085	JOPPA	21530-21530	FLINTSTONE
21087-21087	KINGSVILLE	21531-21531	FRIENDSVILLE
21088-21088	LINEBORO	21532-21532	FROSTBURG
21090-21090	LINTHICUM HEIGHTS	21536-21536	GRANTSVILLE
21092-21092	LONG GREEN	21538-21538	KITZMILLER
21093-21094	LUTHERVILLE TIMONIUM	21539-21539	LONACONING
21098-21098	HANOVER	21540-21540	LUKE
21101-21101	MAGNOLIA	21541-21541	MC HENRY
21102-21102	MANCHESTER	21542-21542	MIDLAND
21104-21104	MARRIOTTSVILLE	21543-21543	MIDLOTHIAN
21105-21105	MARYLAND LINE	21545-21545	MOUNT SAVAGE
21106-21106	MAYO	21546-21546	NIKEP
21107-21107	ALESIA	21550-21550	OAKLAND
21107-21107	FREELAND	21555-21555	OLDTOWN
21107-21107	MILLERS	21556-21556	PINTO
21108-21108	MILLERSVILLE	21557-21557	RAWLINGS
21111-21111	MONKTON	21560-21560	SPRING GAP
21113-21113	ODENTON	21561-21561	SWANTON
21114-21114	CROFTON	21562-21562	WESTERNPORT
21117-21117	OWINGS MILLS	21601-21606	EASTON

Code	Place	Code	Place	Code	Place	Code	Place
21607-21607	BARCLAY	21664-21664	SECRETARY	21762-21762	LIBERTYTOWN	21837-21837	MARDELA SPRINGS
21609-21609	BETHLEHEM	21665-21665	SHERWOOD	21764-21764	LINWOOD	21838-21838	MARION STATION
21610-21610	BETTERTON	21666-21666	STEVENSVILLE	21765-21765	LISBON	21840-21840	NANTICOKE
21612-21612	BOZMAN	21667-21667	STILL POND	21766-21766	LITTLE ORLEANS	21841-21841	NEWARK
21613-21613	CAMBRIDGE	21668-21668	SUDLERSVILLE	21767-21767	MAUGANSVILLE	21842-21843	OCEAN CITY
21617-21617	CENTREVILLE	21669-21669	TAYLORS ISLAND	21768-21768	MIDDLEBURG	21849-21849	PARSONSBURG
21619-21619	CHESTER	21670-21670	TEMPLEVILLE	21769-21769	MIDDLETOWN	21850-21850	PITTSVILLE
21620-21620	CHESTERTOWN	21671-21671	TILGHMAN	21770-21770	MONROVIA	21851-21851	POCOMOKE CITY
21622-21622	CHURCH CREEK	21672-21672	TODDVILLE	21771-21771	MOUNT AIRY	21852-21852	POWELLVILLE
21623-21623	CHURCH HILL	21673-21673	TRAPPE	21773-21773	MYERSVILLE	21853-21853	PRINCESS ANNE
21624-21624	CLAIBORNE	21675-21675	WINGATE	21774-21774	NEW MARKET	21856-21856	QUANTICO
21625-21625	CORDOVA	21676-21676	WITTMAN	21775-21775	NEW MIDWAY	21857-21857	REHOBETH
21626-21626	CRAPO	21677-21677	WOOLFORD	21776-21776	NEW WINDSOR	21858-21858	RHODES POINT
21627-21627	CROCHERON	21678-21678	WORTON	21777-21777	POINT OF ROCKS	21861-21861	SHARPTOWN
21628-21628	CRUMPTON	21679-21679	WYE MILLS	21778-21778	ROCKY RIDGE	21862-21862	SHOWELL
21629-21629	DENTON	21681-21688	RIDGELY	21779-21779	ROHRERSVILLE	21863-21863	SNOW HILL
21631-21631	EAST NEW MARKET	21690-21690	CHESTERTOWN	21780-21780	SABILLASVILLE	21864-21864	STOCKTON
21632-21632	FEDERALSBURG	21701-21709	FREDERICK	21781-21781	SAINT JAMES	21865-21865	TYASKIN
21634-21634	FISHING CREEK	21710-21710	ADAMSTOWN	21782-21782	SHARPSBURG	21866-21866	TYLERTON
21635-21635	GALENA	21711-21711	BIG POOL	21783-21783	SMITHSBURG	21867-21867	UPPER FAIRMOUNT
21636-21636	GOLDSBORO	21713-21713	BOONSBORO	21784-21784	SYKESVILLE	21868-21868	UPPER HILL
21637-21637	GALENA	21714-21714	BRADDOCK HEIGHTS	21787-21787	TANEYTOWN	21869-21869	VIENNA
21638-21638	GRASONVILLE	21715-21715	BROWNSVILLE	21788-21788	THURMONT	21870-21870	WENONA
21639-21639	GREENSBORO	21716-21716	BRUNSWICK	21790-21790	TUSCARORA	21871-21871	WESTOVER
21640-21640	HENDERSON	21717-21717	BUCKEYSTOWN	21791-21791	UNION BRIDGE	21872-21872	WHALEYVILLE
21641-21641	HILLSBORO	21718-21718	BURKITTSVILLE	21792-21792	UNIONVILLE	21874-21874	WILLARDS
21643-21643	HURLOCK	21719-21719	CASCADE	21793-21793	WALKERSVILLE	21875-21875	DELMAR
21644-21644	INGLESIDE	21720-21720	CAVETOWN	21794-21794	WEST FRIENDSHIP	21890-21890	WESTOVER
21645-21645	KENNEDYVILLE	21721-21721	CHEWSVILLE	21795-21795	WILLIAMSPORT	21901-21901	NORTH EAST
21646-21646	LYNCH	21722-21722	CLEAR SPRING	21797-21797	WOODBINE	21902-21902	PERRY POINT
21647-21647	MCDANIEL	21723-21723	COOKSVILLE	21798-21798	WOODSBORO	21903-21903	PERRYVILLE
21648-21648	MADISON	21725-21725	DETOUR	21801-21804	SALISBURY	21904-21904	PORT DEPOSIT
21649-21649	MARYDEL	21727-21727	EMMITSBURG	21810-21810	ALLEN	21911-21911	RISING SUN
21650-21650	MASSEY	21733-21733	FAIRPLAY	21811-21811	BERLIN	21912-21912	WARWICK
21651-21651	MILLINGTON	21734-21734	FUNKSTOWN	21813-21813	BISHOPVILLE	21913-21913	CECILTON
21652-21652	NEAVITT	21735-21735	GAITHER	21814-21814	BIVALVE	21914-21914	CHARLESTOWN
21653-21653	NEWCOMB	21736-21736	GAPLAND	21816-21816	CHANCE	21915-21915	CHESAPEAKE CITY
21654-21654	OXFORD	21737-21737	GLENELG	21817-21817	CRISFIELD	21916-21916	CHILDS
21655-21655	PRESTON	21738-21738	GLENWOOD	21820-21820	DAMES QUARTER	21917-21917	COLORA
21656-21656	CHURCH HILL	21740-21749	HAGERSTOWN	21821-21821	DEAL ISLAND	21918-21918	CONOWINGO
21657-21657	QUEEN ANNE	21750-21750	HANCOCK	21822-21822	EDEN	21919-21919	EARLEVILLE
21658-21658	QUEENSTOWN	21754-21754	IJAMSVILLE	21824-21824	EWELL	21920-21920	ELK MILLS
21659-21659	RHODESDALE	21755-21755	JEFFERSON	21826-21826	FRUITLAND	21921-21922	ELKTON
21660-21660	RIDGELY	21756-21756	KEEDYSVILLE	21829-21829	GIRDLETREE	21930-21930	GEORGETOWN
21661-21661	ROCK HALL	21757-21757	KEYMAR	21830-21830	HEBRON		
21662-21662	ROYAL OAK	21758-21758	KNOXVILLE	21835-21835	LINKWOOD		
21663-21663	SAINT MICHAELS	21759-21759	LADIESBURG	21836-21836	MANOKIN		

Massachusetts

General Help Numbers:

Governor's Office

State House, Room 360
Boston, MA 02133
www.state.ma.us/gov

617-727-6250
Fax 617-727-9725
8AM-6PM

Attorney General's Office

One Ashburton Place, Room 2010
Boston, MA 02108-1698
www.ago.state.ma.us

617-727-2200
Fax 617-727-5768
9AM-5PM

State Court Administrator

2 Center Plaza, Room 540
Boston, MA 02108
www.state.ma.us/courts/admin/index.html

617-742-8575
Fax 617-742-0968
8:30AM-5PM

State Archives

Archives Division
220 Morrissey Blvd
Boston, MA 02125
www.state.ma.us/sec/arc

617-727-2816
Fax 617-288-8429
9AM-5PM M-F; 9-3 SA

State Specifics:

Capital:	Boston
	Suffolk County
Time Zone:	EST
Number of Counties:	14
Population:	6,379,304
Web Site:	www.mass.gov/portal/index.jsp

State Agencies

Criminal Records

Criminal History Systems Board, 200 Arlington Street, #2200, Chelsea, MA 02150; 617-660-4600, 617-660-4613 (Fax), 9AM-5PM.

www.state.ma.us/chsb

Note: These searches are offered: 1) Personal, 2) Certified Agency, 3) Publicly Accessible (PUBAC). Certified Agency requests are pre-approved via statute or the Board. PUBAC is open to the public; data is limited. Online sex offender registry is not maintained

Indexing & Storage: Records are available for at least 50 years. It takes 1 day before new records are available for inquiry. Records are indexed on inhouse computer, file folders. 100% of PUBAC records have final dispositions recorded.

Searching: PUBAC requesters are limited to adult records; the crime must include a sentence of 5 years or more OR sentenced and convicted for any term if, at the time of request, the subject is on probation or has been released within 2 years of felony conviction. Include the following in your request: name, date of birth. The Personal request

(on one's self) requires a notarized signature. A "certified agency" search may include youth organizations, child care providers, and others approved by CHSB. This agency does not conduct FBI fingerprint searches. The following data is not released: pending cases; misdemeanor convictions or incarcerations beyond five years old. A Certified Agency record includes all conviction and all open or pending actions. A PUBAC record contains only convictions.

Access by: mail.

Fee & Payment: The Personal request is free. The Certified Agency request is $10.00. The PUBAC request is $25.00. No fingerprint requests are permitted, thus no fingerprint fees. In fact, 0% of the records are fingerprint-supported. Fee payee: The Commonwealth of Massachusetts. Prepayment required. Personal checks accepted. No credit cards accepted.

Mail search: Turnaround time: 2 weeks. A self addressed stamped envelope is required.

Corporation Records
Trademarks/Servicemarks
Limited Liability
Partnerships
Limited Partnerships
Limited Liability Companys

Secretary of the Commonwealth, Corporation Division, One Ashburton Pl, 17th Floor, Boston, MA 02108; 617-727-9640 (Corporations), 617-727-2850 (Records), 617-727-8329 (Trademarks), 617-727-9440 (Forms request line), 617-742-4538 (Fax), 8:45AM-5PM.

www.state.ma.us/sec/cor/coridx.htm

Indexing & Storage: Records are available for corporations and business entities organized since 1978 on computer. Corporations and business entities organized prior to 1978 may or may not be available. Annual reports are maintained for 10 years. New records are available for inquiry immediately. Records are indexed on microfilm, inhouse computer.

Searching: Include the following in your request: full name of business. In addition to the articles of incorporation, corporation records include the following information: Annual Reports, Officers and Directors names and addresses, Prior (merged) names, Inactive and Reserved names and US Tax ID numbers.

Access by: mail, phone, in person, online.

Fee & Payment: Uncertified copies cost $.30 per page. Certified copies cost $7.00 for the first page and $2.00 for each additional page. Certified copies of articles of incorporation are $12.00 per organization. Fee payee: Commonwealth of Massachusetts. Prepayment required. Personal checks accepted. No credit cards accepted.

Mail search: Turnaround time: 3 to 5 days. A self addressed stamped envelope is requested.

Phone search: No fee for telephone request. Telephone room hours are 8:45AM-5PM.

In person search: Turnaround time: while you wait.

Online search: There is a free Internet lookup at http://corp.sec.state.ma.us/Portal/Functionality/Search.htm. This site also provides UCC information. The agency offers a commercial system called "Direct Access." The annual subscription fee is $149.00 and there is a $.40 a minute access fee. System is available from 8 AM to 10 PM. Call 617-727-7655 for a sign-up packet.

Uniform Commercial Code
State Tax Liens

UCC Division, Secretary of the Commonwealth, One Ashburton Pl, Room 1711, Boston, MA 02108; 617-727-2860, 900-555-4500 (Computer Prints), 900-555-4600 (Copies), 8:45AM-5PM.

www.state.ma.us/sec

Indexing & Storage: Records are available from 09/01/81 on computer and 01/01/84 on microfiche. It takes 24 hours before new records are available for inquiry. Records are indexed on inhouse computer.

Searching: Use search request form UCC-11. Federal tax liens are filed at the US District Courts, PO & Courthouse Bldg, Boston, MA 02109 (617-233-9152). A list of state tax liens is available here, but must be searched in person separately from UCC filings. Include the following in your request: debtor name. Only active filings are available.

Access by: mail, phone, fax, in person, online.

Fee & Payment: Information listing only is $10.00. Search with copies is $305.00 for first 15 pages, $1.00 per page of copies after 15. State tax liens cost $0.20 per copy made. The state does not certify any state tax lien. Fee payee: Commonwealth of Massachusetts. Prepayment required. Credit cards accepted for fax and online searches. Personal checks accepted.

Mail search: Turnaround time: 2 days. Information requests are available.

Phone search: See expedited service.

Fax search: Results can be returned by fax, if arrangements are made, only by 900 calls. Call number above for more information. Essentially the fee is $20.00 per search.

In person search: You may request information in person, but turnaround time for certified documents is 24 hours. You may search on an inhouse public terminal.

Online search: Free access to records is available at http://corp.sec.state.ma.us/Portal/Functionality/Search.htm. "Direct Access" is the commercial systems available for $149 per year plus a $.40 per minute network fee. The system is open from 8 AM to 9:50 PM. Call 617-727-7655 to obtain information packet.

Other access: Microfiche may be purchased.

Expedited service: Expedited service is available for fax and phone searches, but only until December 2002. Turnaround time: 24 hours. A 24 hours express search of financial statements (900-555-4600) is $50.00. An express search of computer printouts is $25.00 per debtor name (900-555-4500), from 10AM-4PM.

Sales Tax Registrations

Revenue Department, Taxpayer Assistance Office, PO Box 7010, Boston, MA 02204 (Courier: 200 Arlington Street, 4th Floor, Chelsea, MA 02150); 617-887-6100, 8AM-5PM.

www.dor.state.ma.us

Note: There are actually 6 offices in the state that will allow walk-in researchers. The office in Chelsea will not let you in the building.

Searching: This agency will only confirm that a business is registered. They will provide no other information. Include the following in your request:

business name. They will also search by tax permit number.

Access by: mail, phone, fax, in person.

Mail search: Turnaround time: 5 to 10 days. A self addressed stamped envelope is requested. No fee for mail request.

Phone search: No fee for telephone request.

Fax search: They ask that you call first to get the number, they do not wish to publish their fax number.

In person search: No fee for request. Call to find closest office.

Birth Certificates

Registry of Vital Records and Statistics, 150 Mt. Vernon St, 1st FL, Dorchester, MA 02125; 617-740-2600, 617-740-2606, 617-825-7755 (Fax), 8:45AM-4:45PM.

www.state.ma.us/dph/bhsre/rvr/vrcopies.htm

Indexing & Storage: Records are available from 1906 to present. Records from 1841 to 1905 are located at the Massachusetts Archives, 220 Morrissey Blvd., Boston, MA 02125. Records prior to 1841 are located at the town/city level. It takes 6 months before new records are available for inquiry.

Searching: Access to out-of-wedlock birth records and health information is strictly limited. A court order is required for adopted children's records. Otherwise, records are open. Include the following in your request: full name, names of parents, mother's maiden name, date of birth, place of birth. Must present a photo ID or provide a copy of a photo ID to search. Phone and fax searchers must give exact place and date of event.

Access by: mail, phone, fax, in person.

Fee & Payment: Prepayment required. Fees vary by access mode. Fee payee: Commonwealth of Massachusetts. Personal checks accepted. Credit cards accepted: MasterCard, Visa, AmEx, Discover.

Mail search: Turnaround time: 3 to 4 weeks. A self addressed stamped envelope is requested. Search costs $11.00 for each 10 years searched.

Phone search: Search costs $19.50 for each 10 years searched. Must use a credit card.

Fax search: Search costs $19.50 for each 10 years searched. Must use a credit card.

In person search: Search costs $6.00 for each 10 years searched. Turnaround time is immediate. You can also do your own searching of records. First 20 minutes is free, then there is a $3.00 fee. The research center is open 9AM-12PM and 2PM-4:30PM, M-F.

Expedited service: Expedited service is available for mail, phone and fax searches. Turnaround time: 2 days. Use of credit card required, add $16.00 for express delivery.

Death Records

Registry of Vital Records and Statistics, 150 Mt Vernon St, 1st FL, Dorchester, MA 02125; 617-740-2600, 617-740-2606, 617-825-7755 (Fax), 8:45AM-4:45PM.

www.state.ma.us/dph/bhsre/rvr/vrcopies.htm

Indexing & Storage: Records are available from 1906 to present. Prior records at State Archives to 1841. It takes 4 months before new records are available for inquiry.

Searching: Fetal death records are not available. A court order is required to access the originals of amended records. Include the following in your request: full name, date of death, place of death. Name of spouse and age at time of death will help facilitate the search. Phone and fax requesters must supply exact place and date of event.

Access by: mail, phone, fax, in person.

Fee & Payment: Prepayment required. Fees vary by access mode. Fee payee: Commonwealth of Massachusetts. Personal checks accepted. Credit cards accepted: MasterCard, Visa, AmEx, Discover.

Mail search: Turnaround time: 3 to 4 weeks. A self addressed stamped envelope is requested. Search costs $11.00 for each 10 years searched.

Phone search: Search costs $19.50 per record. You must use a credit card.

Fax search: Same criteria as phone searches.

In person search: Search costs $6.00 for each 10 years searched. There is a research center open 9AM-12PM and 2PM-4:30PM M-F. Searching is free the first 20 minutes, then it is $3.00 per hour.

Expedited service: Expedited service is available for mail, phone and fax searches. Turnaround time: 2 days. Add $16.00 for express delivery. Use of credit card required.

Marriage Certificates

Registry of Vital Records and Statistics, 150 Mt Vernon St, 1st FL, Dorchester, MA 02125; 617-740-2600, 617-740-2606, 617-825-7755 (Fax), 8:45AM-4:45PM.

www.state.ma.us/dph/bhsre/rvr/vrcopies.htm

Indexing & Storage: Records are available from 1906 to present. Prior records to 1841 are at State Archives. It takes 5 months before new records are available for inquiry.

Searching: A court order is required for originals of amended records. Include the following in your request: names of husband and wife, date of marriage, place or county of marriage. Phone or fax searchers must submit exact place and date of event. Also helpful is parents' names.

Access by: mail, phone, fax, in person.

Fee & Payment: Prepayment required. Fees vary by access mode. Fee payee: Commonwealth of Massachusetts. Personal checks accepted. Credit cards accepted: MasterCard, Visa, AmEx, Discover.

Mail search: Turnaround time: 3 to 4 weeks. A self addressed stamped envelope is requested. Search costs $11.00 for each 10 years searched.

Phone search: Search costs $19.50 per record. You must use a credit card.

Fax search: Same search criteria as phone searching.

In person search: Search costs $6.00 for each 10 years searched. There is a research center open from 9AM-12PM and 2PM-4:30PM, M-F. The first 20 minutes are free, then a $3.00 per hour fee is charged.

Expedited service: Expedited service is available for mail, phone and fax searches. Turnaround time: 2 days. Add $16.00 for express delivery. Use of credit card required.

Divorce Records

Registry of Vital Records and Statistics, 150 Mt. Vernon St, 1st FL, Dorchester, MA 02125; 617-740-2600, 617-740-2606.

www.state.ma.us/dph/bhsre/rvr/vrcopies.htm

Note: Divorce records are found at county of issue. However, this agency maintains an index from 1952 to present. The state will do a search for free by mail only to determine the county.

Workers' Compensation Records

Keeper of Records, Department of Industrial Accidents, 600 Washington St, 7th Floor, Boston, MA 02111; 617-727-4900 x301,209, 617-727-4440 (Fax), 8AM-4PM.

www.state.ma.us/dia

Indexing & Storage: Records are available from 1994 on, and prior records located at State Archives. The index is computerized since 1981. Earlier records may be researched via microfiche for an index number. It takes 2 weeks before new records are available for inquiry. Records are indexed on inhouse computer.

Searching: You need a signed release from claimant to receive data regarding medical records, DOB, and SSN. Include the following in your request: claimant name, Social Security Number, date of injury, employer, insurance carrier, and other pertinent information. E-mail address is infodesk@dia.state.ma.us. The following data is not released: medical records, date of birth or Social Security Numbers.

Access by: mail, in person.

Fee & Payment: There is a standard fee of $3.00 prior to release of record(s). Add $.20 per page and $.50 per page if computer generated. Fee payee: Commonwealth of Massachusetts. Prepayment required. Personal checks accepted. No credit cards accepted.

Mail search: Turnaround time: 2 weeks. No self addressed stamped envelope is required.

In person search: All requests must be in writing.

Driver Records-Registry

Registry of Motor Vehicles, Driver Control Unit, Box 199150, Roxbury, MA 02119-1950; 617-351-9213 (Registry), 617-351-9219 (Fax), 8AM-4:30PM M-T-W-F; 8AM-7PM TH.

www.state.ma.us/rmv

Note: The driving records provided by the Registry are for employment or general business use. Both the Registry and the Merit Rating Board use the same database of driving record histories.

Indexing & Storage: Records are available for 6 years plus current year for moving violations. It takes 1 week before new records are available for inquiry.

Searching: Casual requesters can only obtain records without personal information. Include the following in your request: full name, driver's license number, date of birth. The address of the requester should also be included. The following data is not released: bulk information or lists for commercial purposes.

Access by: mail, phone, in person.

Fee & Payment: The fee is $10.00 per record. Fee payee: Registry of Motor Vehicles. Prepayment

required. Personal checks accepted. No credit cards accepted.

Mail search: Turnaround time: 8 working days. No self addressed stamped envelope is required.

Phone search: For pre-approved accounts, the Registry offers a phone-in request line at 617-351-9213. Orders can be paid with a credit card, results are mailed.

In person search: Up to 10 requests will be processed immediately; the rest are available the next day. You may request a record from any field office.

Driver Records-Insurance

Merit Rating Board, Attn: Driving Records, PO Box 199100, Boston, MA 02119-9100 (Courier: 630 Washington St, Boston, MA 02108); 617-351-4400, 617-351-9660 (Fax), 8:45AM-5:00PM.

www.state.ma.us/rmv

Note: The Merit Rating Board processes driving records for the insurance industry in accordance with state statutes.

Indexing & Storage: Records are available for 6 years for moving violations and at fault accidents (process date). The license number and name are validated against the Registry license file.

Searching: These records do not show revocation or suspension action. Include the following in your request: driver's license number, full name, date of birth. All requests must be on the agency form.

Access by: mail, in person, online.

Fee & Payment: The fee is $10.00 per record. Fee payee: Commonwealth of Massachusetts. Prepayment required. Personal checks accepted. No credit cards accepted.

Mail search: Turnaround time: 2 days. No self addressed stamped envelope is required.

In person search: Turnaround time while you wait.

Online search: The Merit Rating Board provides both online and tape inquiry to the insurance industry for rating and issuance of new and renewal automobile insurance policies. Per statute, this method of retrieval is not open to the general public.

Vehicle Ownership
Vehicle Identification

Registry of Motor Vehicles, Document Control, PO Box 199100, Boston, MA 02119-9100; 617-351-9458, 617-351-9524 (Fax), 8AM-4:30PM.

www.state.ma.us/rmv

Note: In general, license, ownership, and registration information is available to the public. Personal information is not available to casual requesters without consent.

Indexing & Storage: Records are available from the 1940's for licenses, from 1963 for registrations and names. Records are computerized from 1986.

Searching: Requesters with a DPPA permissible use should use "A Request for Personal Information In RMV Records for Multiple Records." Casual requesters should use "A Request for Personal Information In RMV Records for Individual." The state does not do VIN look-ups. Lien information is provided as part of the record.

Access by: mail, fax, in person, online.

Fee & Payment: The current fee is $5.00 for per record request if on computer, $10.00 if on microfiche. Fee payee: Commonwealth of Massachusetts. Prepayment required. Personal checks accepted. No credit cards accepted.

Mail search: Turnaround time: 7 to 10 days. A self addressed stamped envelope is requested.

Fax search: Records are available by fax.

In person search: In person requesters may get computer records immediately, microfiche records take 3 days.

Online search: Searching is limited to Massachusetts based insurance companies and agents for the purpose of issuing or renewing insurance. This system is not open to the public. There is no fee, but line charges will be incurred.

Other access: The state offers an extensive array of customized bulk record requests to authorzied users. For further information, contact the Production Control Office.

Accident Reports

Crash Records, Registry of Motor Vehicles, PO Box 199100, Roxbury, MA 02119-9100; 617-351-9434, 617-351-9401 (Fax), 8:45AM-5PM.

www.state.ma.us/rmv

Note: Accident reports may also be obtained from the local police department in the investigating jurisdiction. Normal fee is $1.00 per page.

Indexing & Storage: Records are available for 2 years to present. Records are indexed on computer.

Searching: Criminal Offender Record Information (CORI) will not be released. Items required for search include; full name, date of accident, location of accident, and license or registration number.

Access by: mail, in person.

Fee & Payment: The charge is $10.00 per report. Fee payee: Registry of Motor Vehicles. Prepayment required. Personal checks accepted. No credit cards accepted.

Mail search: Turnaround time: 7 to 10 days.

In person search: Walk-in location is Copley Place, Tower One, 5th Floor, Boston, MA 02116. Turnaround time is immediate if on system.

Vessel Ownership
Vessel Registration

Massachusetts Environmental Police, 251 Causeway Street, #101, Boston, MA 02114; 617-626-1610, 617-626-1630 (Fax), 8:45AM-5PM.

Indexing & Storage: Records are available from 1988 to present. All motor powered boats and jet skis must be registered with this agency. All boats over 14ft must be titled. Records are indexed on computer.

Searching: To search, you need name and registration or hull number. The following data is not released: Social Security Numbers or phone numbers.

Access by: mail, fax.

Fee & Payment: There is no search fee.

Mail search: Turnaround time: 1 week. No self addressed stamped envelope is required.

Fax search: Turnaround time is usually 5 minutes.

Other access: To obtain printed lists or tapes, contact Andy Petrie.

Legislation Records

Massachusetts General Court, State House, Beacon St, Room 428 (Document Room), Boston, MA 02133; 617-722-2860 (Document Room), 9AM-5PM.

www.state.ma.us/legis

Indexing & Storage: Records are available for usually two years on computer. Older years are available from the State House Library at 617-727-2590. Records are computer indexed from 1995 to present.

Searching: The document room only has information on current bills. Include the following in your request: bill number, date of debate.

Access by: mail, phone, in person, online.

Fee & Payment: There is no fee.

Mail search: Turnaround time: same day if possible. A self addressed stamped envelope is requested.

Phone search: Records are available by phone.

In person search: Turnaround time same day.

Online search: The web site has bill information for the current session and the previous session.

Other access: The state does make available a listing of all bills filed and several bulletins; call 617-722-2860 for more information.

Voter Registration

Records not maintained by a state level agency.

Note: Records are maintained at the local city and town level. In general they are open to the public.

GED Certificates

Massachusetts Dept of Education, GED Processing, 350 Main St, Malden, MA 02148; 781-338-6636, 781-338-3391, 781-338-3391 (Fax).

www.doe.mass.edu/ged

Searching: They will not release copies of transcripts (you must go to the educational institution). This agency will verify or confirm receipt of GED diploma information. All of the following are required: a signed release, date of birth, and Social Security Number. The year and the name of institution are also helpful.

Access by: mail, fax, in person.

Fee & Payment: The fee is $5.00 per verification or letter of certification. Fee payee: Commonwealth of Massachusetts. Prepayment required. Only money orders or business checks are accepted. No credit cards accepted.

Mail search: Turnaround time 2-5 days. No self addressed stamped envelope is required.

Fax search: Fax is only available to companies and educational institutions.

In person search: Turnaround time can be immediate, depending on workload.

Hunting License Information
Fishing License Information

Division of Fisheries & Wildlife, 251 Causeway St #S400, Boston, MA 02114-2104; 617-626-1590, 617-626-1517 (Fax), 8:45AM-5PM.

www.state.ma.us/dfwele

Indexing & Storage: Records are available for 1 year back only. Older records are maintained at one of several locations off premises and take longer to research.

Searching: All requests must be in writing and on their form. You may call to request the form. Need to know the store where license was purchased and month it was purchased. They are filed by license number only.

Access by: mail, in person.

Fee & Payment: There is no search fee.

Mail search: Turnaround time: same day if possible. No self addressed stamped envelope is required.

In person search: You must complete their form.

Massachusetts State Licensing Agencies

Licenses Searchable Online

Adoption Center #52......................................www.qualitychildcare.org/adoption_search_a.asp
Alarm Installer, Burglar/Fire #7 ....http://license.reg.state.ma.us/pubLic/licque.asp?color=red&Board=EL
Allied Health Profession #7...........................http://license.reg.state.ma.us/pubLic/licque.asp?color=red&Board=AH
Allied Mental Health & Human Svcs Prof. #7
....http://license.reg.state.ma.us/pubLic/licque.asp?query=personal&color=red&board=MH
Amusement Device Inspector #27 ....www.state.ma.us/dps/Lic_srch.htm
Architect #42...http://license.reg.state.ma.us/pubLic/licque.asp?color=red&Board=AR
Athletic Trainer #7...http://license.reg.state.ma.us/pubLic/licque.asp?color=red&Board=AH
Attorney #2 ....www.state.ma.us/obcbbo/bboreg/
Auctioneer School #43..................................www.state.ma.us/standards/auc-sch.htm
Bank & Savings Institution #35 ....http://db.state.ma.us/dob/in-choose.asp
Barber/Barber Shop #7.................................http://license.reg.state.ma.us/pubLic/licque.asp?color=red&Board=BR
Boilers/Pressure Vessels Inspector #27 ......www.state.ma.us/dps/Lic_srch.htm
Boxer #50 ....www.state.ma.us/mbc/ranking.htm
Building Inspector/Local Inspector #3 ....www.state.ma.us/bbrs/bocert.PDF
Building Producer #3 ....www.state.ma.us/bbrs/mfg98.pdf
Chiropractor #7 ....http://license.reg.state.ma.us/pubLic/licque.asp?color=red&Board=CH
Concrete Technician #3.................................www.state.ma.us/bbrs/programs.htm
Concrete Testing Laboratory #3 ....www.state.ma.us/bbrs/programs.htm
Construction Supervisor #18.........................www.state.ma.us/bbrs/cslsearch.htm
Cosmetologist/Manicurist/Aesthetician #7 ...http://license.reg.state.ma.us/pubLic/licque.asp?color=red&Board=HD
Credit Union #35..http://db.state.ma.us/dob/in-choose.asp
Day Care Center #52.....................................www.qualitychildcare.org/
Dental Hygienist #7.......................................http://license.reg.state.ma.us/pubLic/licque.asp?color=red&Board=DN
Dentist #7 ....http://license.reg.state.ma.us/pubLic/licque.asp?color=red&Board=DN
Educational Psychologist #7 ....http://license.reg.state.ma.us/pubLic/licque.asp?query=personal&color=red&board=MH
Electrician #7 ....http://license.reg.state.ma.us/pubLic/licque.asp?color=red&Board=EL
Electrologist #7 ....http://license.reg.state.ma.us/pubLic/licque.asp?color=red&Board=ET
Embalmer #40 ....http://license.reg.state.ma.us/pubLic/licque.asp?color=red&Board=EM
Engineer #7 ....http://license.reg.state.ma.us/pubLic/licque.asp?color=red&Board=EN
Family Child Care Provider #52 ....www.qualitychildcare.org/
Fire Protection Sprinkler Sys. Contr./Fitter #27
....www.state.ma.us/dps/Lic_srch.htm
Firemen / Engineer #27 ....www.state.ma.us/dps/Lic_srch.htm
Foster Care Provider #52 ....www.qualitychildcare.org/adoption_search_fc.asp
Funeral Director #40 ....http://license.reg.state.ma.us/pubLic/licque.asp?color=red&Board=EM
Gas Fitter #7..http://license.reg.state.ma.us/pubLic/licque.asp?color=red&Board=PL
Health Officer (Certified) #12 ....http://license.reg.state.ma.us/pubLic/licque.asp?color=red&Board=HO
HMO #38 ....www.state.ma.us/doi/Consumer/css_health_HMO.html
Hoisting Machinery (Forklift, Crane) Operator #27
....www.state.ma.us/dps/Lic_srch.htm
Home Improvement Contractor #18............www.state.ma.us/bbrs/Hicsearch.htm
Insurance, Domestic/Foreign Company #38.www.state.ma.us/doi/companies/companies_home.html
Land Surveyor #7 ....http://license.reg.state.ma.us/pubLic/licque.asp?color=red&Board=EN
Landscape Architect #42 ....http://license.reg.state.ma.us/pubLic/licque.asp?color=red&Board=LA
Lobbyist/Lobbyist Employer #21 ....http://db.state.ma.us/SEC/PRE/search.asp
Lumber Producer, Native #3 ....www.state.ma.us/bbrs/lumber99.PDF
Marriage & Family Therapist #7...................http://license.reg.state.ma.us/pubLic/licque.asp?query=personal&color=red&board=MH
Medical Doctor #53.......................................www.docboard.org/ma/df/name.html
Mental Health Counselor #7 ....http://license.reg.state.ma.us/pubLic/licque.asp?query=personal&color=red&board=MH
Nuclear Power Plant Engr./Operator #27.....www.state.ma.us/dps/Lic_srch.htm
Nurse (LPN, RN, Midwife) #7.......................http://license.reg.state.ma.us/pubLic/licque.asp?color=red&Board=RN
Nursing Home Administrator #12.................http://license.reg.state.ma.us/pubLic/licque.asp?color=red&Board=NH
Nursing Home/Rest Home #45 ....www.medicare.gov/nhcompare/home.asp
Occupational Therapist/Assistant #7 ....http://license.reg.state.ma.us/pubLic/licque.asp?color=red&Board=AH
Oil Burner Technician/Contractor #27..........www.state.ma.us/dps/Lic_srch.htm
Optician #0 ....http://license.reg.state.ma.us/pubLic/licque.asp?query=personal&color=red&board=DO

Optician, Dispensing #7 ....http://license.reg.state.ma.us/pubLic/licque.asp?color=red&Board=DO
Optometrist #7 ....http://license.reg.state.ma.us/pubLic/licque.asp?color=red&Board=OP
Pharmacist #7...http://license.reg.state.ma.us/pubLic/licque.asp?color=red&Board=PH
Physical Therapist/Assistant #7 ....http://license.reg.state.ma.us/pubLic/licque.asp?color=red&Board=AH
Physician Assistant #13.............................http://license.reg.state.ma.us/pubLic/licque.asp?color=red&Board=AP
Pipefitter #27...www.state.ma.us/dps/Lic_srch.htm
Plumber #7 ....http://license.reg.state.ma.us/pubLic/licque.asp?color=red&Board=PL
Podiatrist #7..http://license.reg.state.ma.us/pubLic/licque.asp?color=red&Board=PD
Psychologist/Provider #13 ....http://license.reg.state.ma.us/pubLic/licque.asp?color=red&Board=PY
Public Accountant-CPA #7.........................http://license.reg.state.ma.us/pubLic/licque.asp?color=red&Board=PA
Radio & TV Repair Technician #7...............http://license.reg.state.ma.us/pubLic/licque.asp?color=red&Board=TV
Real Estate Appraiser #7 ....http://license.reg.state.ma.us/pubLic/licque.asp?color=red&Board=RA
Real Estate Broker/Salesperson #7 ....http://license.reg.state.ma.us/pubLic/licque.asp?color=red&Board=RE
Refrigeration Technician/Contractor #27 .....www.state.ma.us/dps/Lic_srch.htm
Rehabilitation Therapist #7 ....http://license.reg.state.ma.us/pubLic/licque.asp?query=personal&color=red&board=MH
Residential Care, Youth #52 ....www.qualitychildcare.org/residential_search.asp
Respiratory Care Therapist #7 ....http://license.reg.state.ma.us/pubLic/licque.asp?color=red&Board=RC
Sanitarian #42...http://license.reg.state.ma.us/pubLic/licque.asp?color=red&Board=SA
Social Worker #7 ....http://license.reg.state.ma.us/pubLic/licque.asp?color=red&Board=SW
Speech-Language Pathologist/Audiologist #7
....http://license.reg.state.ma.us/pubLic/licque.asp?color=red&Board=SP
Veterinarian #7 ....http://license.reg.state.ma.us/pubLic/licque.asp?color=red&Board=VT
Water Supply Facility Operator #7 ....http://license.reg.state.ma.us/pubLic/licque.asp?color=red&Board=DW

Licensing Quick Finder

Acupuncturist #5 617-727-3086
Adoption Center #52.............................617-626-2069
Aerial Passenger Cable Car #27..617-727-3200 x662
Aesthetician #7......................................617-727-9940
Agent, Entertainment #27......................617-727-3296
Aircraft #46 617-973-8883
Airport Manager #46 617-973-8883
Alarm Installer, Burglar/Fire #7.............617-727-9931
Alcoholic Bev./Wine Sales/Broker/Whlse #1
....617-727-3040
Alcoholic Bev/Wine Transportation Permit #1
....617-727-3040
Alcoholism/Drug Facility #15 617-624-5111
Alcoholism/Drug Program #15...............617-624-5111
Allied Health Profession #7 617-727-3071
Allied Mental Health & Human Svcs Prof. #7
....617-727-3071
Ambulance Service #14.........................617-284-8300
Ambulatory Surgical Center #45 617-753-8000
Amusement Device Inspector #27 617-727-3200 x607
Architect #42...617-727-3072
Asbestos/Lead Abatement #24 617-727-7047
Athletic Trainer #7................................617-727-3071
Attorney #2 617-728-8800
Auctioneer #43......................................617-727-3480
Auctioneer School #43 617-727-3480
Automobile Dealer #48 ....617-956-1500 X501
Automobile Sales Finance Company #48
....617-956-1500 X501
Bank & Savings Institution #35............617-956-1500
Bank, Cooperative #35..........................617-956-1500
Barber/Barber Shop #7.........................617-727-7367
Birthing Center #45................................617-753-8000
Blood Bank #45......................................617-753-8000
Boiler Engineer #27 617-727-3200
Boilers/Pressure Vessels Inspector #27
....617-727-3200 x607
Boxer #50 ....617-727-3200 x657
Boxing Physician #50 ....617-727-3200 x657
Boxing Professional #50.............617-727-3200 x657
Brewery/Pub/Sacramental Wine #1 617-727-3040
Brewery/Winery Storage/Farmer #1.....617-727-3040
Brokerage Firm #49 617-727-3548
Building Inspector/Local Inspector #3 ...617-727-7532
Building Producer #3 617-727-7532

Bus/Motor Coach Driver #31 617-305-3559
Cattle Dealer/Transporter #19.....617-727-3018 x158
Chair Lift #27 ....617-727-3200 x662
Chiropractor #7......................................617-727-3093
Cigarette Seller #32..............................617-887-5090
Clinic #45..617-753-8000
Collection Agency #35...........................617-956-1500
Concrete Technician #3 617-727-7532
Concrete Testing Laboratory #3...........617-727-7532
Construction Supervisor #18 ...617-727-7532 x25205
Consumer Credit Grantor #35 617-956-1500
Cosmetologist (Hairdresser, Manicurist, Aesthetician)
#7 617-727-9940
Credit Union #35....................................617-956-1500
Day Care Center #52 617-626-2069
Day Care Center Teacher/Director #52 617-626-2069
Dental Examiner #41 617-727-9928
Dental Hygienist #7 617-727-9928
Dentist #7 617-727-9928
Domestics Agency #22..........................617-727-3696
Educational Psychologist #7 617-727-3071
Electrician #7 617-727-9931
Electrologist #7 617-727-9957
Elevator Construction/Maintenance #27
....617-727-3200 x25238
Elevator Operator #27 ....617-727-3200 x25238
Embalmer #40 617-727-1718
Emergency Medical Technician #14 617-284-8300
Employment Agency, Placement/Temporary #22
....617-727-3696
Engineer #7 617-727-9957
Exterminator #19 ....617-727-3020 x104
Family Child Care Assistant #52 617-626-2069
Family Child Care Provider #52 617-626-2069
Finfishing, Commercial #34...................617-626-1520
Fire Protection Sprinkler System Contractor/Fitter #27
....617-727-3200 x607
Firemen / Engineer #27...............617-727-3200 x607
Foster Care Provider #52 617-626-2069
Funeral Director #40..............................617-727-1718
Fur Buyer #34..617-626-1590
Gas Fitter #7 617-727-9952
Gas Station Owner #43 617-727-3480
Guard Dog/Hearing Dog Business #19
....617-727-3018 x157

Hairdresser #7......................................617-727-9940
Health Officer (Certified) #12 617-727-9925
HMO #38..617-521-7794
Hoisting Machinery (Forklift, Hydraulic, Crane) Operator
#27...617-727-3200 x607
Home Health Care Provider #22..........617-727-3696
Home Improvement Contractor #18.....617-727-7532
x25207
Horse (Equine) Dealer #19 ....617-727-3018 x168
Horse/Greyhound #16...........................617-568-3336
Hospice #45 617-753-8000
Hospital #45 617-753-8000
Insurance Advisor/Adjuster #38............617-727-7189
Insurance Agent/Broker #38 617-727-7189
Insurance, Domestic/Foreign Company #38
....617-321-7391
Investment Advisor #49.........................617-727-3548
Jockey #16 617-568-3336
Justice of the Peace #44................617-727-2795 X3
Laboratory, Medical-related #45 617-753-8000
Land Surveyor #7..................................617-727-9957
Landscape Architect #42 617-727-3072
Lead Inspector #24 617-727-7047
Library Media Specialist #17 .....781-338-3000 x6600
Loan Company, Small #48.........617-956-1500 x501
Lobbyist/Lobbyist Employer #21 617-878-3434
Lobstering #34.......................................617-626-1520
Lumber Producer, Native #3 617-727-3636
Mammography Radiologic Technologist #26
....617-727-6214
Manicurist #7 617-727-9940
Marriage & Family Therapist #7 617-727-3071
Medical Doctor #53 617-727-3086
Mental Health Counselor #7.................617-727-3071
Milk Plant #19 ....617-727-3018 x174
Modeling Industry/Agency #22 617-727-3696
Mortgage Broker/Lender #48 ......617-956-1500 x501
Motion Picture Operator #27 ...617-727-3200 x25223
Motor Vehicle Repair Shop (Auto Body/Glass/etc.) #43
....617-727-3480
Nanny Agency #22 617-727-3696
Notary Public #44 ....617-727-2795 X1
Nuclear Medicine Technologist (Radiologic
Technologist-Nuclear Medicine) #26 ... 617-727-6214

Nuclear Power Plant Engineer/Operator #27
.... 617-727-3200 x607
Nurse, LPN/RN/Midwife #7................... 617-727-9961
Nursery #19 617-626-1801
Nursery Agent #19............................... 617-626-1801
Nurses' Aide in Long Term Care Facility #45
.... 617-753-8143
Nursing Home Administrator #12 617-727-9925
Nursing Home/Rest Home #45............. 617-753-8000
Occupational Therapist/Assistant #7..... 617-727-3071
Oil Burner Technician/Contractor #27
.... 617-727-3200 x607
Optician, Dispensing #7....................... 617-727-3093
Optometrist #7 617-727-3093
Out-Patient Rehabilitation Facility #45 .. 617-753-8000
Owner/Trainer, Horse/Greyhound #16 .. 617-568-3336
Pasteurization Plant #19.............. 617-727-3018 x174
Peddler/Hawker #43 617-727-3480
Personal Agent #27 .... 617-727-3200 x637
Pesticide Applicator/Dealer #19 617-626-1777
Pet Shop #19.............................. 617-727-3018 x158
Pharmacist #7 617-727-9953
Physical Therapist/Assistant #7 617-727-3071
Physician Assistant #13....................... 617-727-3069
Pipefitter #27 .... 617-727-3200 x607
Plumber #7 617-727-9952
Podiatrist #7 617-727-1747
Private Detective #33 978-538-6128

Private Investigator #33...................... 978-538-6128
Psychologist/Provider #13.................... 617-727-9925
Public Accountant-CPA #7 617-727-1806
Racetrack, Horse/Greyhound #16........ 617-727-2581
Radiation Therapy/Radiologic Technologist #26
.... 617-727-6214
Radio & TV Repair Technician #7........ 617-727-3074
Radiographer #26................................ 617-727-6214
Radiologic Technologist #26 617-727-6214
Radon Specialist #26 617-727-6214
Real Estate Appraiser #7 617-727-3055
Real Estate Broker/Salesperson #7 617-727-2373
Refrigeration Technician/Contractor #27
.... 617-727-3200 x607
Rehabilitation Therapist #7................... 617-727-3071
Renal Dialysis (End Stage) #45 617-753-8000
Residential Care, Youth #52 617-626-2069
Respiratory Care Therapist #7 617-727-1747
Riding Instructor #19 .... 617-727-3018 x161
Riding School #19 .... 617-727-3018 x161
Sales Finance Company #48 ...... 617-956-1500 X501
Sanitarian #42 617-727-3072
School Administrator #17 .... 781-338-3000 x6600
School Bus #31 617-305-3559
School Guidance Counselor #17 781-338-3000x6600
Seafood Dealer #34 617-626-1520
Securities Agent #49 617-727-3548
Securities Broker/Dealer #49 617-727-3548

Security Guard Agency #33 978-538-6128
Shellfishing, Commercial #34 617-626-1520
Simulcast & Inter-Track Wagering #16 . 617-727-2581
Ski Tow #27................................. 617-727-3200 x662
Skimobile #27.............................. 617-727-3200 x662
Social Worker #7................................. 617-727-3073
Speech-Language Pathologist/Audiologist #7
.... 617-727-1747
Stable (Horse & Buggy Operator) #19
.... 617-727-3018 x161
Stock Broker #49................................. 617-727-3548
Swine Dealer #19........................ 617-727-3018 x158
Taxidermist #34................................... 617-626-1590
Teacher #17 .... 781-338-3000 x6600
Theatrical Booking Agent #27 ..... 617-727-3200 x637
Ticket Broker #27 617-727-3296
Ticket Reseller #27.................... 617-727-3200 x637
Tramway Inspector #27............. 617-727-3200 x662
Trapping #34 617-626-1590
Trust Company #35.............................. 617-956-1500
Vending Machine #25 617-522-6712
Vendor, Transient #43.......................... 617-727-3480
Veterinarian #7.................................... 617-727-3080
Water Supply Facility Operator #7 617-727-3074
Weights & Measures #43...................... 617-727-3480
Wine & Malt Beverage Permit #1......... 617-727-3040

Licensing Agency Information

#1 Alcoholic Beverages Control Commission, 239 Causeway St #200, Boston, MA 02114-2130; 617-727-3040, Fax: 617-727-1258.
www.state.ms.us/abcc
Agency email: errol.flynn@state.ma.us.

#2 Board of Overseers Registry Dept, Board of Bar Examiners, 75 Federal St, 5th Fl, Boston, MA 02110; 617-728-8800, Fax: 617-357-1872.
www.state.ma.us/obcbbo/bboreg/
Search database at
www.state.ma.us/obcbbo/bboreg

#3 Board of Building Regulations & Standards, Construction-related Licensing Programs, 1 Ashburton Place, Rm 2133, Boston, MA 02108; 617-727-7532, Fax: 617-727-1754.
www.state.ma.us/eops/index.htm
Agency email: david.bratton@eps.state.ma.us.
Search database at
www.state.ma.us/bbrs/programs.htm

#5 Committee on Acupuncture, Board of Registration in Medicine, 10 West St, 3rd Fl, Boston, MA 02111; 617-727-3086, Fax: 617-357-8453.
www.massmedboard.org/acupuncture.htm.
Agency email: nick@docboard.org.
Search database at
www.docboard.org/ma/df/masearch.htm

#7 Division of Registration, Boards of Registration & Examination, 239 Causeway St #400, Boston, MA 02114-2130; 617-727-3074, Fax: 617-727-2197.
www.state.ma.us/reg/home.htm
Agency email: REG.WebMaster@State.ma.us.
Search database at
http://license.reg.state.ma.us/pubLic/licque.asp

#12 Division of Registration, Boards of Registration of Nursing Home Admin., 239 Causeway St #400, Boston, MA 02114-2130; 617-727-9925, Fax: 617-727-2366.
www.state.ma.us/reg/home.htm
Search database at
www.state.ma.us/reg/apps/reg15.htm

#13 Division of Registration, Boards of Registration of Physicians Assistants, 100 Cambridge St, 15th Fl, Boston, MA 02202; 617-727-3074, Fax: 617-727-2197.
www.state.ma.us/reg/boards.htm#P
Search database at
http://license.reg.state.ma.us/pubLic/licque.asp

#14 Office of Emergency Medical Services, 56 Roland St, Boston, MA 02129; 617-284-8300, Fax: 617-284-8350.
www.state.ma.us/dph/oems

#15 Department of Public Health, Bureau of Substance Abuse Services, 250 Washington St, 3rd Fl, Boston, MA 02108; 617-624-5111, Fax: 617-624-5185.
www.state.ma.us/dph/bsas
Agency email: bsas.questions@state.ma.us.

#16 Consumer Department, Racing Commission, 1 Ashburton Place, 13th Fl, Rm 1313, Boston, MA 02108; 617-727-2581, Fax: 617-227-6062.
www.state.ma.us/src

#17 Division of Educational Personnel, Department of Education & Arts, 350 Main St, Malven, MA 02148; 781-338-3000 x6600, Fax: 781-338-3391.
www.doe.mass.edu/cert

#18 Home Improvement Contractor/Construction Supervisor Licensing, Board of Build Regulations and Standards, 1 Ashburton Pl, Rm 1301, Boston, MA 02108; 617-727-7532.
www.state.ma.us/bbrs/programs.htm
Search database at
www.state.ma.us/bbrs/programs.htm

#19 Department of Food & Agriculture, Pesticide Bureau, 251 Causeway St, 5th Fl, Boston, MA 02114-2151; 617-626-1700, Fax: 617-626-1850.
www.massdfa.org/pesticide.htm
Agency email: Mark.Buffone@state.ma.us.

#21 Secretary of the Commonwealth, Lobbyist & Lobbyist Employer Directory, One Ashburton Place, Room 1719, Boston, MA 02108; 617-878-3434, Fax: 617-727-5914.
www.state.ma.us/sec/pre/prelob
Agency email: lob@sec.state.ma.us.
Search database at
http://db.state.ma.us/SEC/PRE/search.asp

#22 Department of Labor & Industries, Employment Agency Program, 399 Washington St, 5th Fl, Boston, MA 02108; 617-727-3696, Fax: 617-727-7568.
www.state.ma.us/dos/pages/employ.htm

#24 Department of Occupational Safety, Licensing Division, Labor & Workforce Development, 399 Washington St, 5th Fl, Boston, MA 02100-5212; 617-727-7047, Fax: 617-727-7568.
www.state.ma.us/dos

#25 Department of Public Health, 305 S St, Jamaica Plain, MA 02130; 617-522-3700, Fax: 617-753-8436.
www.state.ma.us/dph
Agency email: mark.leccese@state.ma.us.

#26 Radiation Control Program, Department of Public Health, 305 South St, Jamaica Plain, MA 02130; 617-522-3700, Fax: 617-727-2098. www.state.ma.us/dph

#27 Department of Public Safety, 1 Ashburton Pl, 13th Fl, Rm 1301, Boston, MA 02108; 617-727-3200 x623, Fax: 617-248-0813. www.state.ma.us/dps Agency email: MailBox.DPS@state.ma.us.

#31 Department of Telecommunications and Energy, Transportation Division, 1 South Sta #2, Boston, MA 02110-2208; 617-305-3559, Fax: 617-478-2598.

#32 Department of Revenue, Excises Unit, PO Box 7012, Boston, MA 02204; 617-887-5090, Fax: 617-887-5039. www.dor.state.ma.us Agency email: dortsd@shore.net.

#33 Department of State Police, Certification Unit, 485 Maple St, Danvers, MA 01923; 978-538-6128, Fax: 978-538-6021. www.state.ma.us/msp Agency email: webmaster@eps.state.ma.us.

#34 Department of Fisheries, Wildlife & Environmental Enforcement, Division of Fish & Wildlife, 251 Causeway St #S-400, Boston, MA 02114-2104; 617-626-1500, Fax: 617-626-1505. www.state.ma.us/dfwele/dpt_toc.htm Agency email: steve.mcrae@state.ma.us.

#35 Division of Banks & Loan Agencies, 1 South Station, 3rd FL, Boston, MA 02110; 617-956-1500, Fax: 617-956-1597. www.state.ma.us/dob Agency email: bernard.n.waxman@state.ma.us. Search database at http://db.state.ma.us/dob/in-choose.asp

#38 Division of Insurance, 470 Atlantic Ave, Boston, MA 02110-2223; 617-521-7794, Fax: 617-521-7772. www.state.ma.us/doi Agency email: Franklin.Holt@state.ma.us. Search database at www.state.ma.us/doi/doi_site_alt.html

#40 Division of Registration, Board of Funeral Directors & Embalmers, 239 Causeway St #400, Boston, MA 02114-2130; 617-727-3074, Fax: 617-727-2197. www.state.ma.us/reg/boards/em/default.htm Search database at http://license.reg.state.ma.us/pubLic/licque.asp?color=red&Board=EM

#42 Division of Regulation of Architecture, 239 Causeway St #500, Boston, MA 02114; 617-727-3072, Fax: 617-727-2197. www.state.ma.us/reg/boards/ar/default.htm. Agency email: REG.Webmaster@State.ma.us. Search database at http://license.reg.state.ma.us/pubLic/licque.asp?color=red&Board=AR

#43 Executive Office of Public Safety, Division of Standards, 1 Ashburton Pl, Boston, MA 02108; 617-727-3480, Fax: 617-727-5705. www.state.ma.us/standards Search database at www.state.ma.us/standards/license.htm

#44 Governor's Council, State House, Rm 184, Boston, MA 02133; 617-727-2795. www.state.ma.us/gov/govco.htm

#45 Department of Public Health, Health Care Quality, 10 West St, 5th Fl, Boston, MA 02111; 617-753-8000, Fax: 617-753-8095. www.state.ma.us/dph/hcqskel.htm

#46 Massachusetts Aeronautics Commission, 10 Park Plaza, Rm 6620, Boston, MA 02116-3966; 617-973-8881, Fax: 617-973-8889.

#48 Consumer Compliance Unit, Division of Banks, 1 South Station, 3rd Fl, Boston, MA 02110; 617-956-1500 x501, Fax: 617-956-1599. www.state.ma.us/dob

#49 Securities Division, Licensing and Registration Section, 1 Ashburton Place, 17th Fl, Boston, MA 02108; 617-727-3548, Fax: 617-248-0177. www.state.ma.us/sec/sct/sctidx.htm. Agency email: securities@sec.state.ma.us.

#50 Boxing Commission, 1 Ashburton Pl Rm 1301, Boston, MA 02108; 617-727-3200 x657, Fax: 617-727-5732. www.state.ma.us/dps/Boxing.htm Search database at www.state.ma.us/mbc/ranking.htm

#52 Executive Office of Human Svcs, Office for Children, Staff Qualifications, 1 Ashburton Pl Rm 1105, Boston, MA 02108-1518; 617-626-2069, Fax: 617-626-2027. www.qualitychildcare.org Search database at www.qualitychildcare.org/childcare_finding.asp

#53 Board of Registration in Medicine, 10 West St, Boston, MA 02111; 617-727-3086, Fax: 617-426-9358. www.massmedboard.org Agency email: webmaster@massmedboard.org.

Massachusetts Federal Courts

The following list indicates the district and division name for each county in the state. If the bankruptcy court location is different from the district court, then the location of the bankruptcy court appears in parentheses.

County/Court Cross Reference

Barnstable	Boston	Hampshire	Springfield (Worcester)
Berkshire	Springfield (Worcester)	Middlesex	Boston
Bristol	Boston	Nantucket	Boston
Dukes	Boston	Norfolk	Boston
Essex	Boston	Plymouth	Boston
Franklin	Springfield (Worcester)	Suffolk	Boston
Hampden	Springfield (Worcester)	Worcester	Worcester

Standards for Federal Courts: The search fee is $20.00 per item (one party name or case number). Certification fee is $7.00 per document. Copy fee is $.50 per page. All fees standard unless noted in profile. Mail Search: always enclose a stamped self addressed envelope unless otherwise noted. Before releasing records, all courts require prepayment unless noted in profile.

Open records are located at the court unless otherwise noted. District courts index by defendant and plaintiff as well as by case number. Bankruptcy courts usually index by debtor and case number. While most courts now have their indexes on computer, many still maintain index card files as well.

The universal PACER sign-up number is 800-676-6856. Find PACER and the Party/Case Index on the Web at http://pacer.psc.uscourts.gov. PACER dial-up access is $.60 per minute. Also, courts offering internet access via RACER, PACER, Web-PACER or the new CM-ECF charge $.07 per page fee unless noted as free.

US District Court

District of Massachusetts

Boston Division US Courthouse, 1 Courthouse Way, Boston, MA 02210 (Courier Address: Use mail address for courier delivery), 617-748-9152, Fax: 617-748-9096.

www.mad.uscourts.gov

Counties: Barnstable, Bristol, Dukes, Essex, Middlesex, Nantucket, Norfolk, Plymouth, Suffolk.

Indexing & Storage: Cases are indexed by defendant, plaintiff, and case number. New cases are available in the index 1 day to 1 week after filing date. The civil and criminal database dates from the early 1900's until the present. Records are available when they are not in the possession of the judge or his/her clerks. Open records are located at this court.

Fee & Payment Notes: Payment may be made by money order, cashier check, personal check. Payee: Clerk, US District Court. You are allowed to make your own copies. These copies cost $.25 per page.

Phone Search: Searching not available by phone.

Mail Search: A stamped self addressed envelope is not required.

In Person Search: In person searching available.

PACER: Toll-free dial-up access: 888-399-4639. Local dial-up access: 617-748-4294. Case records are available back to January 1990. Records are purged every 12 months. New records are available online after 1 day. PACER is available online at http://pacer.mad.uscourts.gov. Document images available.

Electronic Filing: (CM/ECF available late 2002)

Springfield Division 1550 Main St, Springfield, MA 01103 (Courier Address: Use mail address for courier delivery), 413-785-0214, Fax: 413-785-0204.

www.mad.uscourts.gov

Counties: Berkshire, Franklin, Hampden, Hampshire.

Indexing & Storage: Cases are indexed by defendant, plaintiff, and case number. New cases are available in the index immediately after filing date. There is a microfiche index for pre-1989 cases. The civil and criminal database dates from July 1979. Records are not available when they are in the possession of a judge or a judge's clerk.

Fee & Payment Notes: Payment may be made by money order, cashier check, personal check. Will bill if total fee is less than $25.00. Payee: Clerk, US District Court.

Phone Search: Docket information available over the phone if Clerk has time.

Fax Search: Will charge for fax search request only if copies and certification requested. Will fax results at $.50 per page.

Mail Search: A stamped self addressed envelope is not required.

In Person Search: In person searching available.

PACER: Toll-free dial-up access: 888-399-4639. Local dial-up access: 617-748-4294. Case records are available back to January 1990. Records are purged every 12 months. New records are available online after 1 day. PACER is available online at http://pacer.mad.uscourts.gov. Document images available.

Electronic Filing: (CM/ECF available late 2002)

Worcester Division 595 Main St., Room 502, Worcester, MA 01608 (Courier Address: Use mail address for courier delivery), 508-793-0552.

www.mad.uscourts.gov

Counties: Worcester.

Indexing & Storage: Cases are indexed by defendant, plaintiff, and case number. New cases are available in the index immediately after filing date. Indexes are on computer from 1988 and on microfiche from 1981. Earlier indexes are in storage from the early 1900's. Records are not available when in the possession of a judge or the judge's clerks.

Fee & Payment Notes: Payment may be made by money order, cashier check, personal check. Payee: Clerk, US District Court.

Phone Search: Only docket information available by telephone.

Fax Search: Invoice will be sent with copies of records for a fax request.

In Person Search: In person searching available.

PACER: Toll-free dial-up access: 888-399-4639. Local dial-up access: 617-748-4294. Case records are available back to January 1990. Records are purged every 12 months. New records are available online after 1 day. PACER is available online at http://pacer.mad.uscourts.gov. Document images available.

Electronic Filing: (CM/ECF available late 2002)

US Bankruptcy Court

District of Massachusetts

Boston Division Room 1101, 10 Causeway, Boston, MA 02222-1074 (Courier Address: Use mail address for courier delivery), 617-565-6051, Fax: 617-565-6087.

www.mab.uscourts.gov

Counties: Barnstable, Bristol, Dukes, Essex (except towns assigned to Worcester Division), Nantucket, Norfolk (except towns assigned to Worcester Division), Plymouth, Suffolk, and the following towns in Middlesex: Arlington,

Belmont, Burlington, Everett,Lexington, Malden, Medford, Melrose, Newton, North Reading, Reading, Stoneham, Wakefield, Waltham, Watertown, Wilmington, Winchester and Woburn.

Indexing & Storage: Cases are indexed by debtor as well as by case number. New cases are available in the index immediately after filing date. Open records are located at this court.

Fee & Payment Notes: Payment may be made by money order, cashier check, personal check. Copy fees will be billed after the search is completed. Checks are not accepted from debtors. Payee: US Bankruptcy Court. You are allowed to make your own copies. These copies cost $.50 per page.

Phone Search: Only general information will be released over the phone. An automated voice case information service (VCIS) is available. Call VCIS at 888-201-3572 or 617-565-6025.

Fax Search: Fax requests are processed the same as mail requests.

In Person Search: In person searching available.

PACER: Toll-free dial-up access: 888-201-3571. Local dial-up access: 617-565-6021. Case records are available back to April 1, 1987. Records are purged every 12 months. New civil records are available online after 1 day. PACER is available online at http://pacer.mab.uscourts.gov. Document images available.

Electronic Filing: (Currently in the process of implementing CM/ECF.)

Worcester Division 595 Main St, Room 211, Worcester, MA 01608 (Courier Address: Use mail address for courier delivery), 508-770-8900, Fax: 508-793-0541.

www.mab.uscourts.gov

Counties: Berkshire, Franklin, Hampden, Hampshire, Middlesex (except the towns assigned to the Boston Division), Worcester and the following towns: in Essex-Andover, Haverhill, Lawrence, Methuen and North Andover; in Norfolk-Bellingham, Franklin, Medway,Millis and Norfolk.

Indexing & Storage: Cases are indexed by debtor as well as by case number. New cases are available in the index immediately after filing date. Open records are located at this court.

Fee & Payment Notes: Payment may be made by money order, cashier check, personal check. Checks are not accepted from debtors. Payee: US Bankruptcy Court. You are allowed to make your own copies. These copies cost $.25 per page.

Phone Search: Only docket information is available by phone. An automated voice case information service (VCIS) is available. Call VCIS at 888-201-3572 or 617-565-6025.

Mail Search: A stamped self addressed envelope is not required.

In Person Search: In person searching available.

PACER: Toll-free dial-up access: 888-201-3571. Local dial-up access: 617-565-6021. Case records are available back to April 1, 1987. Records are purged every 12 months. New civil records are available online after 1 day. PACER is available online at http://pacer.mab.uscourts.gov. Document images available.

Electronic Filing: (Currently in the process of implementing CM/ECF.)

Massachusetts County Courts

Court	Jurisdiction	No. of Courts	How Organized
Superior Courts*	General	19	14 Counties
District Courts*	General	68	68 Geographic Divisions
Boston Municipal Court*	General	1	
Housing Courts	General	7	
Probate and Family Courts*	Probate	15	14 Counties
Juvenile Courts	Special	7	
Land Court	Special	1	

* Profiled in this Sourcebook.

Court	CIVIL								
	Tort	Contract	Real Estate	Min. Claim	Max. Claim	Small Claims	Estate	Eviction	Domestic Relations
Superior Courts*	X	X	X	$25,000	No Max				
District Courts*	X	X	X	$0	No Max	$2000	X	X	X
Boston Municipal Court*	X	X	X	$0	No Max	$2000			X
Housing Courts			X	$0	No Max	$2000			
Probate and Family Courts*							X		X
Juvenile Courts									
Land Court			X						

Court	CRIMINAL				
	Felony	Misdemeanor	DWI/DUI	Preliminary Hearing	Juvenile
Superior Courts*	X				
District Courts*	X	X	X	X	X
Boston Municipal Court*		X	X		
Housing Courts		X		X	
Probate and Family Courts*					
Juvenile Courts					X
Land Court					

ADMINISTRATION Chief Justice for Administration and Management, 2 Center Plaza, Room 540, Boston, MA, 02108; 617-742-8575, Fax: 617-742-0968. www.state.ma.us/courts/admin/index.html

COURT STRUCTURE The various court sections are called "Departments." While Superior and District Courts have concurrent jurisdiction in civil cases, the practice is to assign cases less than $25,000 to the District Court and those over $25,000 to Superior Court. In addition to misdemeanors, District Courts and Boston Municipal Courts have jurisdiction over certain minor felonies.

ONLINE ACCESS Online access to records on the statewide Trial Courts Information Center web site is available to attorneys and law firms at www.ma-trialcourts.org/tcic/welcome.jsp. Contact Peter Nylin by email: nylin_p@jud.state.ma.us. Site updated daily.

PROBATE COURTS There are more than 20 Probate and Family Court locations in MA - one per county plus two each in Bristol, plus a Middlesex satellite in Cambridge and Lawrence.

Barnstable County

Superior Court 3195 Main St, PO Box 425, Barnstable, MA 02630; 508-375-6684. Hours: 8:30AM-4:30PM (EST). *Felony, Civil Actions Over $25,000.*

Note: Their public access terminal is connected to the statewide Superior Court system.

Civil Records: Access: Mail, in person. Visitors must perform in person searches for themselves. No search fee. Required to search: name, years to search; also helpful: address. Civil cases indexed by defendant, plaintiff. Civil records on computer back to 1/2001; on index cards from 1985 and books from 1830s.

Criminal Records: Access: Mail, in person, online. Visitors must perform in person searches for themselves. No search fee. Required to search: name, years to search, DOB; also helpful: address, SSN. Criminal records on computer back to 1/2001; on index cards from 1985 and books from 1830s. Online access to records on the Trial Courts Information Center web site available to attorneys and law firms at www.ma-trialcourts.org. See state introduction for more information.

General Information: Public access terminal is available. No victims names released. SASE not required. Copy fee: $.50 per page. Certification fee: $1.50. Fee payee: Barnstable Superior Court. Business checks accepted. Prepayment is required.

Barnstable District Court Route 6A, PO Box 427, Barnstable, MA 02630; 508-362-2511. Hours: 8:30AM-4:30PM (EST). *Felony, Misdemeanor, Civil, Eviction, Small Claims.*

Civil Records: Access: Phone, mail, in person. Only the court performs in person searches; visitors may not. No search fee. Required to search: name, years to search. Civil cases indexed by defendant, plaintiff. Civil records on index cards and docket books.

Criminal Records: Access: Phone, mail, in person. Only the court performs in person searches; visitors may not. No search fee. Required to search: name, years to search; also helpful: DOB. Criminal records on computer since 1996; prior records on index cards and docket books.

General Information: No impounded records released. Turnaround time 1-2 weeks. Copy fee: $.50 per page. Certification fee: $1.50. Fee payee: District Court. Only cashiers checks and money orders accepted. Prepayment is required.

Orleans District Court 237 Rock Harbor Rd, Orleans, MA 02653; 508-255-4700. Hours: 8:30AM-4:30PM (EST). *Felony, Misdemeanor, Civil, Eviction, Small Claims.*

Note: Includes Brewster, Chatham, Dennis, Eastham, Orleans, Truro, Wellfleet, Harwich, and Provincetown.

Civil Records: Access: In person only. Visitors must perform in person searches for themselves. No search fee. Required to search: name, years to search. Civil cases indexed by defendant, plaintiff. Civil records kept in storage from 1978. Some prior records destroyed.

Criminal Records: Access: In person only. Visitors must perform in person searches for themselves. No search fee. Required to search: name, years to search. Criminal records kept in storage from 1978. Some prior records destroyed.

General Information: No impounded records released. Copy fee: $.50 per page. Certification fee: $1.50. Fee payee: Orleans District Court. Personal checks accepted. Prepayment is required.

Falmouth District Court 161 Jones Rd, Falmouth, MA 02540; 508-495-1500. Hours: 8:30AM-4:30PM (EST). *Felony, Misdemeanor, Civil, Eviction, Small Claims.*

Note: Includes Includes Falmouth, Mashpee, and Bourne.

Civil Records: Access: Phone, in person. Only the court performs in person searches; visitors may not. No search fee. Required to search: name, years to search. Civil cases indexed by defendant, plaintiff. Civil records kept on computer since 1996.

Criminal Records: Access: Phone, in person. Only the court performs in person searches; visitors may not. No search fee. Required to search: name, years to search. Civil cases indexed by defendant, plaintiff. Records kept on computer since 1996.

General Information: No impounded records released. Copy fee: $.50 per page. Certification fee: $1.50. Fee payee: Falmouth District Court. Personal checks accepted. Prepayment is required.

Probate & Family Court PO Box 346, Barnstable, MA 02630; 508-375-6600; Fax: 508-362-3662. Hours: 8AM-4PM (EST). *Probate.*

Berkshire County

Superior Court 76 East St, Pittsfield, MA 01201; 413-499-7487; Fax: 413-442-9190. Hours: 8:30AM-4:30PM (EST). *Felony, Civil Actions Over $25,000.*

Civil Records: Access: Mail, in person. Both court and visitors may perform in person searches. No search fee. Required to search: name, years to search. Civil cases indexed by defendant, plaintiff. Civil records on index cards from 1900s, on computer back to 2000.

Criminal Records: Access: Mail, in person. Both court and visitors may perform in person searches. No search fee. Required to search: name, years to search. Criminal records on index cards from 1900s, on computer back to 2000. Because their index does not contain DOBs or SSNs, they cannot verify the subject, thus they recommend you contact the Criminal History Board in Boston, MA.

General Information: No impounded records released. Turnaround time 1-2 weeks. Fax notes: Will not fax results. Copy fee: $.50 per page. Certification fee: $1.50 per document. Fee payee: Berkshire Superior Court. Personal checks accepted. Prepayment is required.

North Berkshire District Court #28 City Hall - 10 Main St, North Adams, MA 01247; 413-663-5339; Fax: 413-664-7209. Hours: 8AM-4:30PM (EST). *Felony, Misdemeanor, Civil, Eviction, Small Claims.*

Note: Handles cases for Clarksburg, Florida, Hancock, New Ashford, North Adams, and Williamstown.

Civil Records: Access: Phone, fax, mail, in person. Only the court performs in person searches; visitors may not. No search fee. Required to search: name, years to search. Civil cases indexed by defendant, plaintiff. Civil records on index cards from 1983, docket books to 1900.

Criminal Records: Access: Phone, fax, mail, in person. Only the court performs in person searches; visitors may not. No search fee. Required to search: name, years to search; also helpful: DOB, SSN. Criminal records on index cards from 1983, docket books to 1900.

General Information: No impounded records released. Turnaround time 1-2 weeks. Copy fee: $.50 per page. Certification fee: $1.50. Fee payee: District Court. Business checks accepted. Prepayment is required.

North Berkshire District Court #30 65 Park St, Adams, MA 01220; 413-743-0021; Fax: 413-743-4848. Hours: 8AM-4:30PM (EST). *Felony, Misdemeanor, Civil, Eviction, Small Claims.*

Note: Handles cases for Adams, Cheshire, Savoy, and Windsor.

Civil Records: Access: Mail, fax, in person. Both the court and visitors may perform in person searches. No search fee. Required to search: name, years to search; also helpful: address. Civil cases indexed by defendant, plaintiff. Civil records on index cards from 1990, small claims from 1988. Prior stored.

Criminal Records: Access: Mail, fax, in person. Both court and visitors may perform in person searches. No search fee. Required to search: name, years to search, docket #; also helpful: DOB, SSN. Criminal records on computer since 1976/77, lists on docket books until 1985.

General Information: No juvenile, mental health, impounded case records released. SASE required. Turnaround time 7 days. Copy fee: $.50 per page. Certification fee: $1.50. Fee payee: District Court. No personal checks accepted. Prepayment is required.

Pittsfield District Court #27 24 Wendell Ave, Pittsfield, MA 01201; 413-442-5468; Fax: 413-499-7327. Hours: 8:30AM-4:30PM (EST). *Felony, Misdemeanor, Civil, Eviction, Small Claims.*

Civil Records: Access: Phone, mail, in person. Only the court performs in person searches; visitors may not. No search fee. Required to search: name, years to search. Civil cases indexed by defendant, plaintiff. Civil records on docket books.

Criminal Records: Access: Phone, mail, in person. Only the court performs in person searches; visitors may not. No search fee. Required to search: name, years to search; also helpful: DOB. Criminal records on docket books.

General Information: No juvenile or sealed records released. SASE required. Turnaround time 1-2 weeks. Copy fee: $.50 per page. Certification fee: $1.50. Fee payee: Pittsfield District Court. Personal checks accepted. Prepayment is required.

South Berkshire District Court 9 Gilmore Ave, Great Barrington, MA 01230; 413-528-3520; Fax: 413-528-0757. Hours: 8AM-4PM (EST). *Felony, Misdemeanor, Civil, Eviction, Small Claims.*

Civil Records: Access: Fax, mail, in person. Both court and visitors may perform in person searches. No search fee. Required to search: name, years to search. Civil cases indexed by defendant, plaintiff. Civil records on index cards from 1984, docket books to 1900. Court will only perform search if given the docket number.

Criminal Records: Access: Fax, mail, in person. Only the court performs in person searches; visitors may not. No search fee. Required to search: name, years to search. Criminal records on index cards from 1984, docket books to 1900. Court will only do search if given docket number.

General Information: No juvenile, impounded records released. SASE required. Turnaround time 1-2 weeks. Copy fee: $.50 per page. Certification fee: $1.50. Fee payee: District Court. Personal checks accepted. Prepayment is required.

Probate & Family Court 44 Bank Row, Pittsfield, MA 01201; 413-442-6941; Fax: 413-443-3430. Hours: 8:30AM-4PM (EST). *Probate.*

Bristol County

Superior Court - Taunton 9 Court St, Taunton, MA 02780; 508-823-6588 X1. Hours: 8AM-4:30PM (EST). *Felony, Civil Actions Over $25,000.*

Civil Records: Access: Mail, in person. Both court and visitors may perform in person searches. No search fee. Required to search: name, years to search. Civil cases indexed by defendant, plaintiff. Civil records on computer link to Boston from 1985, index books from 1935.

Criminal Records: Access: Mail, in person. Both court and visitors may perform in person searches. No search fee. Required to search: name, years to search; also helpful: DOB. Criminal records on computer link to Boston from 1985, index books from 1935.

General Information: Public access terminal is available. No impounded records released. Turnaround time 2 weeks. Copy fee: $.50 per page. Certification fee: $1.50. Fee payee: Clerk of Superior Court of Bristol County. Personal checks accepted. Prepayment is required.

Attleboro District Court 34 Courthouse, 88 N Main St, Attleboro, MA 02703; 508-222-5900; Fax: 508-223-3916. Hours: 8AM-4:30PM (EST). *Felony, Misdemeanor, Civil, Eviction, Small Claims.*

Note: Includes Attleboro, Mansfield, North Attleboro, and Norton.

Civil Records: Access: Phone, mail, in person. Only the court performs in person searches; visitors may not. No search fee. Required to search: name, years to search. Civil cases indexed by defendant, plaintiff. Civil records on computer since 1995; prior records on index cards from 1983, docket books from 1900.

Criminal Records: Access: Phone, mail, in person. Only the court performs in person searches; visitors may not. No search fee. Required to search: name, years to search, DOB, SSN. Criminal records on computer since 1995; prior records on index cards from 1983, docket books from 1900.

General Information: No impounded records released. Turnaround time 1-2 weeks. Copy fee: $.50 per page. Certification fee: $1.50. Fee payee: District Court, Attleboro District Court. Business checks accepted. Prepayment is required.

Fall River District Court 45 Rock St, Fall River, MA 02720; 508-679-8161; Fax: 508-675-5477. Hours: 8AM-4:30PM (EST). *Felony, Misdemeanor, Civil, Eviction, Small Claims.*

Civil Records: Access: Mail, in person. Both court and visitors may perform in person searches. No search fee. Required to search: name, years to search. Civil cases indexed by defendant, plaintiff. Civil records on index on computer from 1989, on docket books in vault from 1985.

Criminal Records: Access: Mail, in person. Both court and visitors may perform in person searches. No search fee. Required to search: name, years to search, DOB or SSN. Criminal records on index on computer from 1991, on docket books in vault from 1985.

General Information: No sealed, minor, confidential address records released. SASE requested. Turnaround time 1-2 weeks. Fax notes: Fee to fax results is $.50 per page. Copy fee: $.50 per page. Certification fee: $1.00 per page. Fee payee: District Court. Only cashiers checks and money orders accepted. Prepayment is required.

New Bedford District Court 33 75 N 6th St, New Bedford, MA 02740; 508-999-9700. Hours: 8:30AM-4PM (EST). *Felony, Misdemeanor, Civil, Eviction, Small Claims.*

Civil Records: Access: Mail, in person. Only the court performs in person searches; visitors may not. No search fee. Required to search: name, years to search.

Civil cases indexed by defendant, plaintiff. Civil records filed from 1989, prior on docket books; on computer back to 1995.

Criminal Records: Access: Mail, in person. Only the court performs in person searches; visitors may not. No search fee. Required to search: name, years to search, DOB; also helpful: SSN. Criminal records filed from 1989, prior on docket books; on computer back to 1995. Searches are limited to pending charges, this agency recommends searching elsewhere for closed case files.

General Information: No impounded records released. Turnaround time 1-2 weeks. Copy fee: $.50 per page. Certification fee: $1.50. Fee payee: District Court. Business checks accepted. Prepayment is required.

Taunton District Court 15 Court St, Taunton, MA 02780; 508-824-4032; Fax: 508-824-2282. Hours: 8:30AM-4:30PM (EST). *Felony, Misdemeanor, Civil, Eviction, Small Claims.*

Civil Records: Access: Phone, mail, in person. Visitors must perform in person searches No search fee. Required to search: name, years to search. Civil cases indexed by defendant, plaintiff. Civil records on index cards for 6 years; computerized records since 1980's.

Criminal Records: Access: Phone, mail, in person. Visitors must perform in person searches No search fee. Required to search: name, years to search, DOB. Criminal records on index cards for 6 years; computerized records since 1980's.

General Information: Turnaround time 1-2 days. Copy fee: $.50 per page. Certification fee: $1.50. Fee payee: District Court. Personal checks accepted. Prepayment is required.

New Bedford Probate & Family Court 505 Pleasant St, New Bedford, MA 02740; 508-999-5249; Fax: 508-991-7421. Hours: 8AM-4:30PM (EST). *Probate.*

Taunton Probate & Family Court 11 Court St, PO Box 567, Taunton, MA 02780; 508-824-4004. Hours: 8AM-4:30PM (EST). *Probate.*

Dukes County

Superior Court PO Box 1267, Edgartown, MA 02539; 508-627-4668. Hours: 8AM-4PM (EST). *Felony, Civil Actions Over $25,000.*

Civil Records: Access: Mail, in person. Both court and visitors may perform in person searches. No search fee. Required to search: name, years to search. Civil cases indexed by defendant, plaintiff. Civil records on index cards from 1976 and books from 1695.

Criminal Records: Access: Mail, in person. Both court and visitors may perform in person searches. No search fee. Required to search: name, years to search. Criminal records on index cards from 1976 and books from 1695.

General Information: Public access terminal is available. No sealed records released. SASE required. Turnaround time 1-2 days. Copy fee: $.50 per page. Certification fee: $1.50. Fee payee: Clerk of Superior Court. Personal checks accepted. Prepayment required.

Edgartown District Court PO Box 1284, Courthouse, 81 Main St, Edgartown, MA 02539-1284; 508-627-3751/4622. Hours: 8:30AM-4:30PM (EST). *Felony, Misdemeanor, Civil, Eviction, Small Claims.*

Civil Records: Access: In person only. Both court and visitors may perform in person searches. No search fee. Required to search: name, years to search. Civil cases indexed by defendant, plaintiff. Civil records on index cards from 1983, docket books to 1900.

Criminal Records: Access: In person only. Both court and visitors may perform in person searches. No search fee. Required to search: name, years to search, DOB; also helpful: SSN. Criminal records on index cards from 1983, docket books to 1900.

General Information: No sealed records released. Copy fee: $.50 per page. Certification fee: $1.50. Fee payee: District Court. Personal checks accepted. Prepayment is required.

Probate & Family Court PO Box 237, Rm 104, 1st Fl, Edgartown, MA 02539; 508-627-4703; Fax: 508-627-7664. 8:30AM-4:30PM (EST). *Probate.*

Essex County

Superior Court - Lawrence 43 Appleton Way, Lawrence, MA 01840; 978-687-7463. Hours: 8AM-4:30PM (EST). *Civil Actions Over $25,000.*

Note: Index cards are found in the Salem office (records prior to 1985)

Civil Records: Access: Mail, in person. Both court and visitors may perform in person searches. No search fee. Required to search: name, years to search. Civil cases indexed by defendant, plaintiff. Civil records on computer since 1985; prior records on index cards in Salem office.

General Information: Public access terminal is available. No impounded records released. Turnaround time 1-2 days. Copy fee: $.50 per page. Certification fee: $1.50. Fee payee: Clerk of Superior Court. Personal checks accepted. Prepayment is required.

Superior Court - Newburyport 145 High St, Newburyport, MA 01950; 978-462-4474. Hours: 8AM-4:30PM (EST). *Felony, Civil Actions Over $25,000.*

Note: All finished criminal record files are in Salem and civil case records Session A in Salem, Session B in Newburyport and Session C & D in Lawrence.

Civil Records: Access: Mail, in person. Both court and visitors may perform in person searches. No search fee. Required to search: name, years to search. Civil cases indexed by defendant, plaintiff. Civil records on computer back to 1988.

Criminal Records: Access: Mail, in person. Both court and visitors may perform in person searches. No search fee. Required to search: name, years to search.

General Information: No impounded records released. Turnaround time 1-2 days. Copy fee: $.50 per page. Certification fee: $1.50. Fee payee: Clerk of Superior Court. Personal checks accepted. Prepayment is required.

Superior Court - Salem 34 Federal St, Salem, MA 01970; 978-744-5500; Civil phone: X223; Criminal phone: X343; Fax: 978-741-0691 (civ); 978-825-9989 (crim). Hours: 8:00AM-4:30PM (EST). *Felony, Civil Actions Over $25,000.*

Civil Records: Access: Mail, in person. Visitors must perform in person searches for themselves. No search fee. Required to search: name, years to search. Civil cases indexed by defendant, plaintiff. Civil records are entered on computer for civil actions from all three Superior courts in this county. Computer records go back to 1985.

Criminal Records: Access: In person only. Visitors must perform in person searches for themselves. No search fee. Required to search: name, years to search. Criminal records are entered on computer for civil actions from all three Superior courts in this county. Computer records go back to 1985.

General Information: Public access terminal is available. Impounded cases are not released. Turnaround time 1-2 days. Fax notes: Fee to fax results is $1.50 per page. Copy fee: $.50 per page. Certification fee: $1.50. Fee payee: Clerk of Superior Court. Personal checks accepted. Prepayment is required.

Haverhill District Court PO Box 1389, Haverhill, MA 01831; 978-373-4151; Fax: 978-521-6886. Hours: 8:30AM-4:30PM (EST). *Felony, Misdemeanor, Civil, Eviction, Small Claims.*

Civil Records: Access: Phone, fax, mail, in person. Only the court performs in person searches; visitors may not. No search fee. Required to search: name, years to search. Civil cases indexed by defendant, plaintiff. Civil records on index cards from 1983. Non-active in storage.

Criminal Records: Access: Phone, fax, mail, in person. Only the court performs in person searches; visitors may not. No search fee. Required to search: name, years to search; also helpful: DOB. Criminal records on index cards from 1992, computerized since 2000. Non-active in storage.

General Information: No juvenile, sealed cases, confidential records released. SASE required. Turnaround time 1-2 weeks. Copy fee: $.50 per page. Certification fee: $1.50. Fee payee: District Court. Personal checks accepted. Prepayment is required.

Ipswich District Court 30 South Main St, PO Box 246, Ipswich, MA 01938; 978-356-2681; Fax: 978-356-4396. Hours: 8:30AM-4:30PM (EST). *Felony, Misdemeanor, Civil, Eviction, Small Claims.*

Civil Records: Access: In person only. Visitors must perform in person searches for themselves. No search fee. Required to search: name, years to search. Civil cases indexed by defendant, plaintiff. Civil records on index cards, small claims from 1984, civil from 1964. Civil on docket books from 1970.

Criminal Records: Access: In person only. Visitors must perform in person searches for themselves. No search fee. Required to search: name, years to search; also helpful: DOB. Criminal records on index cards from 1979.

General Information: No juvenile records released. Copy fee: $.50 per page. Certification fee: Certification fee is $1.50 per page. Fee payee: District Court. Personal checks accepted. Prepayment is required.

Lawrence District Court 381 Common St, Lawrence, MA 01840; 978-687-7184; Civil phone: 978-689-2810. Hours: 8AM-4:30PM (EST). *Felony, Misdemeanor, Civil, Eviction, Small Claims.*

Civil Records: Access: In person. Visitors must perform in person searches No search fee. Required to search: name, years to search. Civil cases indexed by defendant, plaintiff. Civil records on index cards from 1983, docket books from 1900, on computer since 1990.

Criminal Records: Access: Mail, in person. Both court and visitors may perform in person searches No search fee. Required to search: name, years to search, DOB; also helpful: address, SSN. Criminal records on index cards from 1983, docket books from 1900, on computer since 1990.

General Information: No medical, police reports, impounded, juvenile records released. SASE requested. Turnaround time 1-2 weeks. Copy fee: $.50 per page. Certification fee: $1.50. Fee payee: District Court. Personal checks accepted. Prepayment is required.

Lynn District Court 580 Essex St, Lynn, MA 01901; 781-598-5200. Hours: 8AM-4:30PM (EST). *Felony, Misdemeanor, Civil, Eviction, Small Claims.*

Civil Records: Access: Mail, in person. Visitors must perform in person searches No search fee. Required to search: name, years to search. Civil cases indexed by defendant, plaintiff. Civil records on index cards from 1983, docket books from approx 1900. Records older than 15 years are difficult to find and may take longer.

Criminal Records: Access: Mail, in person. Visitors must perform in person searches No search fee. Required to search: name, years to search; also helpful: DOB, SSN. Criminal records on index cards from 1983, docket books from approx 1900. Records older than 15 years are difficult to find and may take longer.

General Information: No juvenile, impounded or sealed records released. Copy fee: $.50 per page.

Certification fee: $1.50. Fee payee: District Court. Personal checks accepted. Prepayment is required.

Newburyport District Court 22 188 State St, Newburyport, MA 01950; 978-462-2652. Hours: 8:30AM-4:30PM (EST). *Felony, Misdemeanor, Civil, Eviction, Small Claims.*

Civil Records: Access: Mail, in person. Only the court may perform in person searches No search fee. Required to search: name, years to search. Civil cases indexed by defendant, plaintiff. Civil records on index cards from 1983, prior archived in Worcester.

Criminal Records: Access: Mail, in person. Only the court performs in person searches; visitors may not. No search fee. Required to search: name, years to search, DOB. Criminal records on index cards from 1983, prior archived in Worcester.

General Information: No juvenile or impounded records released. Turnaround time 1-2 weeks. Copy fee: $.50 per page. Certification fee: $1.50. Fee payee: District Court. Personal checks accepted. Prepayment is required.

Peabody District Court 86 PO Box 666, Peabody, MA 01960; 978-532-3100. Hours: 8:30AM-4:30PM (EST). *Felony, Misdemeanor, Civil, Eviction, Small Claims.*

Civil Records: Access: In person. Visitors must perform in person searches No search fee. Required to search: name, years to search. Civil cases indexed by defendant, plaintiff. Civil records stored in office for 10 years, prior stored in basement and are difficult to find.

Criminal Records: Access: In person. Visitors must perform in person searches No search fee. Required to search: name, years to search, DOB. Criminal records stored in office for 10 years, prior stored in basement and are difficult to find.

General Information: No juvenile or impounded records released. Turnaround time 1-2 weeks. Copy fee: $.50 per page. Certification fee: $1.50. Fee payee: District Court. Personal checks accepted. Prepayment is required.

Salem District Court 36 65 Washington St, Salem, MA 01970; 978-744-1167. Hours: 8:30AM-4:30PM (EST). *Felony, Misdemeanor, Civil, Eviction, Small Claims.*

Civil Records: Access: In person. Visitors must perform in person searches on Thursday or Friday 2Pm-4:30PM No search fee. Required to search: name, years to search. Civil cases indexed by defendant, plaintiff. Civil records on index cards and docket books.

Criminal Records: Access: In person. Visitors must perform in person searches on Thursday or Friday 2PM-4:30PM No search fee. Required to search: name, years to search, DOB, SSN. Criminal records on index cards and docket books.

General Information: No juvenile or impounded records released. Turnaround time 1-2 weeks. Copy fee: $.50 per page. Certification fee: $1.50. Fee payee: District Court. Personal checks accepted. Prepayment is required.

Probate & Family Court 36 Federal St, Salem, MA 01970; 978-744-1020; Fax: 978-741-2957. Hours: 8:00AM-4:30PM (EST). *Probate.*

Franklin County

Superior Court PO Box 1573, Greenfield, MA 01302; 413-774-5535; Fax: 413-774-4770. Hours: 8:30AM-4:30PM (EST). *Felony, Civil Actions Over $25,000.*

Civil Records: Access: Fax, in person. Both court and visitors may perform in person searches. No search fee. Required to search: name, years to search. Civil cases indexed by defendant, plaintiff. Civil records in files; on computer back 2 years.

Criminal Records: Access: Fax, in person. Only the court performs in person searches; visitors may not. No search fee. Required to search: name, years to search, DOB. Criminal records in files; on computer back 2 years.

General Information: Public access terminal is available. No impounded or juvenile records released. Fax notes: Fee to fax results is $1.50 per page. Copy fee: $.50 per page. Certification fee: $1.50 per page. Fee payee: Franklin County Superior Court. Personal checks accepted. Prepayment is required.

Greenfield District Court 425 Main St, Greenfield, MA 01301; 413-774-5533; Fax: 413-774-5328. Hours: 8:30AM-4:30PM (EST). *Felony, Misdemeanor, Civil, Eviction, Small Claims.*

Civil Records: Access: In person only. Both court and visitors may perform in person searches. No search fee. Required to search: name, years to search. Civil cases indexed by defendant, plaintiff. Civil records on docket books or index cards; on computer back to 1998.

Criminal Records: Access: In person only. Both court and visitors may perform in person searches. No search fee. Required to search: name, years to search, DOB. Criminal records on docket books or index cards; on computer back to 1994.

General Information: No juvenile records released. Copy fee: $.50 per page. Certification fee: $1.50. Fee payee: Greenfield District Court. Personal checks accepted. Prepayment is required.

Orange District Court #42 One Court Square, Orange, MA 01364; 978-544-8277; Fax: 978-544-5204. Hours: 8:30AM-4:30PM (EST). *Felony, Misdemeanor, Civil, Eviction, Small Claims.*

Civil Records: Access: Phone, mail, in person. Both court and visitors may perform in person searches. No search fee. Required to search: name, years to search. Civil cases indexed by defendant, plaintiff. Civil records on docket books from 1975.

Criminal Records: Access: Phone, mail, in person. Only the court performs in person searches; visitors may not. No search fee. Required to search: name, years to search. Criminal records on docket books from 1975.

General Information: No juvenile records released. Turnaround time 1-2 weeks. Copy fee: $.50 per page. Certification fee: $1.50 per page. Fee payee: District Court. Personal checks accepted. Prepayment is required.

Probate & Family Court PO Box 590, Greenfield, MA 01302; 413-774-7011; Fax: 413-774-3829. Hours: 8AM-4:30PM (EST). *Probate.*

www.fcpfc.com

Hampden County

Superior Court 50 State St, PO Box 559, Springfield, MA 01102-0559; 413-735-6016; Fax: 413-737-1611. Hours: 8:30AM-4:30PM (EST). *Felony, Civil Actions Over $25,000.*

Civil Records: Access: Phone, mail, in person. Both court and visitors may perform in person searches. No search fee. Required to search: name, years to search. Civil cases indexed by defendant, plaintiff. Civil records on computer from 1989 to present; prior on index cards from 1930s, books from 1812.

Criminal Records: Access: In person only. Both court and visitors may perform in person searches. No search fee. Required to search: name, years to search. Criminal records on computer from 1992 to present; prior on index cards from 1930s, books from 1812.

General Information: Public access terminal is available. No impounded case records released. SASE requested. Turnaround time 1 week. Copy fee: $.50 per page. Certification fee: $1.50. Fee payee: Clerk of Superior Court. Personal checks accepted. Prepayment is required.

Chicopee District Court #20 30 Church St, Chicopee, MA 01020; 413-598-0099; Fax: 413-598-8176. Hours: 8AM-4PM (EST). *Felony, Misdemeanor, Civil, Eviction, Small Claims.*

Civil Records: Access: Phone, fax, mail, in person. Only visitors may perform in person searches. No search fee. Required to search: name, years to search. Civil cases indexed by defendant, plaintiff. Civil records on index cards from 1983, docket books to 1960; computerized since 2001.

Criminal Records: Access: Phone, mail, in person. Both court and visitors may perform in person searches. No search fee. Required to search: name, years to search, DOB. Criminal records on index cards from 1983, docket books to 1900.

General Information: No juvenile records released. Turnaround time 1-2 weeks. Fax notes: Fee to fax results is $.50 per page. Copy fee: $.50 per page. Certification fee: $1.50. Fee payee: District Court. Personal checks accepted. Prepayment is required.

Holyoke District Court 20 Court Sq, Holyoke, MA 01041-5075; 413-538-9710; Fax: 413-533-7165. Hours: 8:30AM-4:30PM (EST). *Felony, Misdemeanor, Civil, Eviction, Small Claims.*

Civil Records: Access: Phone, mail, fax, in person. Both court and visitors may perform in person searches. No search fee. Required to search: name, years to search. Civil cases indexed by defendant, plaintiff. Civil records on index cards and docket books back to 1989.

Criminal Records: Access: Fax, mail, in person. Both court and visitors may perform in person searches. No search fee. Required to search: name, years to search, DOB or SSN, signed release. Criminal records on index cards and docket books since 1976; on computer back to 1986.

General Information: No juvenile, sealed records released. SASE requested. Turnaround time 1-2 weeks. Copy fee: $.50 per page. Certification fee: $1.50. Fee payee: District Court. Only cashiers checks and money orders accepted. Prepayment is required.

Palmer District Court 235 Sykes St, Palmer, MA 01069; 413-283-8916; Fax: 413-283-6775. Hours: 8:15AM-4:15PM (EST). *Felony, Misdemeanor, Civil, Eviction, Small Claims.*

Civil Records: Access: In person only. Visitors must perform in person searches for themselves. No search fee. Required to search: name, years to search. Civil cases indexed by defendant, plaintiff. Civil records on index cards back to 1982.

Criminal Records: Access: In person only. Visitors must perform in person searches for themselves. No search fee. Required to search: name, years to search. Criminal records on index cards for 10 years; on computer back to 1995.

General Information: No sealed or juvenile records released. Copy fee: $.50 per page. Certification fee: $1.50. Fee payee: Palmer District Court. Personal checks accepted. Prepayment is required.

Springfield District Court 50 State St, Springfield, MA 01103; 413-748-7613; Civil phone: 413-748-8659; Criminal phone: 413-748-7982; Fax: 413-747-4841. Hours: 8:00AM-4:30PM (EST). *Felony, Misdemeanor, Civil, Eviction, Small Claims.*

Civil Records: Access: In person. Visitors must perform in person searches No search fee. Required to search: name, years to search. Civil cases indexed by defendant, plaintiff. Civil records on index cards; computerized records since 1992.

Criminal Records: Access: In person. Visitors must perform in person searches No search fee. Required to search: name, years to search. Criminal records on index cards; computerized records since 1992.

General Information: No sealed, expunged, or adoption records released. Turnaround time 1-2 weeks.

Copy fee: $.50 per page. Certification fee: $1.50. Fee payee: District Court. Business checks accepted. Prepayment is required.

Westfield District Court 224 Elm St, Westfield, MA 01085; 413-568-8946; Fax: 413-568-4863. Hours: 8AM-4PM (EST). *Felony, Misdemeanor, Civil, Eviction, Small Claims.*

Civil Records: Access: Mail, in person. Both court and visitors may perform in person searches. No search fee. Required to search: name, years to search. Civil cases indexed by defendant, plaintiff. Civil records on index cards and in files.

Criminal Records: Access: Mail, in person. Both court and visitors may perform in person searches. No search fee. Required to search: name, years to search. Criminal records on index cards and in files.

General Information: No sealed or juvenile records released. Turnaround time 1-2 weeks. Copy fee: $.50 per page. Certification fee: $1.50. Fee payee: District Court. Personal checks accepted. Prepayment is required.

Probate & Family Court 50 State St, Springfield, MA 01103-0559; 413-748-7759; Fax: 413-781-5605. Hours: 8AM-4:25PM (EST). *Probate.*

Hampshire County

Superior Court PO Box 1119, Northampton, MA 01061; 413-584-5810 x331; Fax: 413-586-8217. Hours: 9AM-4PM (EST). *Felony, Civil Actions Over $25,000.*

Civil Records: Access: Mail, fax, in person. Both court and visitors may perform in person searches. No search fee. Required to search: name, years to search. Civil cases indexed by defendant, plaintiff. Civil records in files, index cards from 1800s; on computer back to 1983.

Criminal Records: Access: Mail, fax, in person. Both court and visitors may perform in person searches. No search fee. Required to search: name, years to search. Criminal records in files, index cards from 1800s; on computer back to 1983.

General Information: Public access terminal is available. (Civil only.) No impounded case records released. Turnaround time 1 week. Copy fee: $.50 per page. Certification fee: $10.00. Fee payee: Clerk of Superior Court. Personal checks accepted. Prepayment is required.

Northampton District Court Courthouse, 15 Gothic St, Northampton, MA 01060; 413-584-7400/7405 413-584-7776; Criminal phone: 413-584-7400; Fax: 413-586-1980. Hours: 8:30AM-4PM (EST). *Felony, Misdemeanor, Civil, Eviction, Small Claims.*

Civil Records: Access: Fax, mail, in person. Only the court performs in person searches; visitors may not. No search fee. Required to search: name, years to search, address. Civil cases indexed by defendant, plaintiff. Civil records on index cards and docket books back 20 years.

Criminal Records: Access: Fax, mail, in person. Both court and visitors may perform in person searches. No search fee. Required to search: name, years to search, DOB, SSN. Criminal records on docket books go back 7 years.

General Information: Public access terminal is available. (Only civil records back to 6/4/02 are available.) No CHINS-care & protection, show cause-mental health records released. SASE requested. Turnaround time 1-2 weeks. Fax notes: No fee to fax results. Copy fee: $.50 per page. Certification fee: $1.50 per page. Fee payee: District Court. Personal checks accepted. Prepayment is required.

Ware District Court PO Box 300, Ware, MA 01082; 413-967-3301; Fax: 413-967-7986. Hours: 8AM-4:30PM (EST). *Felony, Misdemeanor, Civil, Eviction, Small Claims.*

Civil Records: Access: Fax, mail, in person. Only the court performs in person searches; visitors may not. No search fee. Required to search: name, years to search. Civil cases indexed by defendant, plaintiff. Civil records on index cards or docket books back to 1960. Some records sent to archives in Worcester.

Criminal Records: Access: Phone, fax, mail, in person. Only the court performs in person searches; visitors may not. No search fee. Required to search: name, years to search, DOB, SSN. Criminal records on index cards or docket books back to 1920; on computer back to 1996. Some records sent to archives in Worcester.

General Information: No sealed, impounded, confidential or juvenile records released. Turnaround time 1-2 weeks. Copy fee: $.50 per page. Certification fee: $1.50. Fee payee: Ware District Court. Personal checks accepted. Prepayment is required.

Probate & Family Court 33 King St #3, Northampton, MA 01060; 413-586-8500; Fax: 413-584-1132. Hours: 8:45AM-4:30PM (EST). *Probate.*

Middlesex County

Superior Court - East Cambridge 40 Thorndike St, Edward J Sullivan Courthouse, East Cambridge, MA 02141; 617-494-4010. Hours: 8:30AM-4:30PM (EST). *Felony, Civil Actions Over $25,000.*

Civil Records: Access: Mail, in person. Both court and visitors may perform in person searches. No search fee. Required to search: name, years to search; also helpful: address. Civil cases indexed by defendant, plaintiff. Civil records on computer from 1986, rest on card indexes to 1986. The court is planning to have Internet access.

Criminal Records: Access: Mail, in person. Both court and visitors may perform in person searches. No search fee. Required to search: name, years to search; also helpful: address. Criminal records on computer back to 1991, rest on card indexes to 1986. The court is planning to have Internet access.

General Information: Public access terminal is available. No impounded or those restricted by statute records released. Turnaround time 3-5 days for criminal records. Copy fee: $.50 per page. Certification fee: $1.50. Fee payee: Clerk of Superior Court. Personal checks accepted. Prepayment is required.

Superior Court - Lowell 360 Gorham St, Lowell, MA 01852; 978-453-0201. Hours: 8:30AM-4:30PM (EST). *Felony, Civil Actions Over $25,000.*

Civil Records: Access: Mail, in person. Both court and visitors may perform in person searches. No search fee. Required to search: name, years to search. Civil cases indexed by defendant, plaintiff. Civil records on computer since 1990; prior records kept at East Cambridge Middlesex Superior Court, 40 Thorndike, Cambridge, MA 02141.

Criminal Records: Access: Mail, in person. Both court and visitors may perform in person searches. No search fee. Required to search: name, years to search. Criminal records on computer since 1990; prior records kept at East Cambridge Middlesex Superior Court, 40 Thorndike, Cambridge, MA 02141.

General Information: Turnaround time 1-2 days. Copy fee: $.50 per page. Certification fee: $1.50. Fee payee: Clerk of Superior Court. Personal checks accepted. Prepayment is required.

Ayer District Court 25 E Main St, Ayer, MA 01432; 978-772-2100; Fax: 978-772-5345. Hours:

8:30AM-4:30PM (EST). *Felony, Misdemeanor, Civil, Eviction, Small Claims.*

Civil Records: Access: Mail, in person. No search fee. Required to search: name, years to search. Civil cases indexed by defendant, plaintiff. Civil records on index cards from 1977 to present; only required to keep records 20 years. DOB required on subject.

Criminal Records: Access: Phone, mail, in person. Both court and visitors may perform in person searches. No search fee. Required to search: name, years to search, DOB. Criminal records on index cards from 1977 to 1995, computerized 1996 forward; Only required to keep records 10 years. Access by phone may be limited.

General Information: Juvenile records not released. Turnaround time 1-2 weeks. Copy fee: $.50 per page. Certification fee: $1.50. Fee payee: Ayer District Court. Personal checks accepted. Prepayment is required.

Cambridge District Court 52 PO Box 338, East Cambridge, MA 02141; 617-494-4095; Civil phone: 617-494-4095 X502; Criminal phone: 617-494-4095 X501; Probate phone: 617-494-5233. Hours: 8:30AM-4:30PM (EST). *Felony, Misdemeanor, Civil, Eviction, Small Claims, Probate.*

Civil Records: Access: In person. Visitors must perform in person searches No search fee. Required to search: name, years to search. Civil cases indexed by defendant, plaintiff. Civil records on index cards or docket books. State law requires records be retained for 10 years.

Criminal Records: Access: In person, mail. Visitors must perform in person searches for themselves. No search fee. Required to search: name, years to search, DOB. Criminal records on index cards or docket books; computerized records since 1997. State law requires records be retained for 10 years.

General Information: No sealed or juvenile records released. Turnaround time 1-2 weeks. Copy fee: $.50 per page. Certification fee: $1.50. Fee payee: District Court. Personal checks accepted. Prepayment is required.

Concord District Court 47 305 Walden St, Concord, MA 01742; 978-369-0500. Hours: 8:30AM-4:30PM (EST). *Felony, Misdemeanor, Civil, Eviction, Small Claims.*

Civil Records: Access: Mail, in person. Both court and visitors may perform in person searches. No search fee. Required to search: name, years to search; also helpful: address. Civil cases indexed by defendant, plaintiff. Civil records on computer from 1991, index cards and books from 1950, archived from 1643. In person searches performed from 1-2PM only.

Criminal Records: Access: Mail, in person. Both court and visitors may perform in person searches. No search fee. Required to search: name, years to search; also helpful: address, DOB, SSN. Criminal records on computer from 1991, index cards and books from 1950, archived from 1643. In person searches performed from 1-2PM only.

General Information: No impounded files released. SASE requested. Turnaround time 1 week. Copy fee: $.50 per page. Certification fee: $1.50. Fee payee: Commonwealth of Massachusetts. Personal checks accepted. Prepayment is required.

Framingham District Court 600 Concord St (PO Box 1669), Framingham, MA 01701; 508-875-7461. Hours: 8:30AM-4:30PM (EST). *Felony, Misdemeanor, Civil, Eviction, Small Claims.*

Civil Records: Access: Mail, in person. Both court and visitors may perform in person searches. No search fee. Required to search: name, years to search. Civil cases indexed by defendant, plaintiff. Civil records on index cards or docket books back to 1900; on computer back to 1986. Special form required for mail request.

Criminal Records: Access: Mail, in person. Both court and visitors may perform in person searches. No search fee. Required to search: name, years to search. Criminal records on index cards or docket books back to 1900; on computer back to 1986. Special form required for mail request.

General Information: No sealed, expunged or juvenile records released. Copy fee: $1.50 per page. Certification fee: $1.50 per page. Fee payee: District Court. Only cashiers checks and money orders accepted. Prepayment is required.

Lowell District Court 41 Hurd St, Lowell, MA 01852; 978-459-4101; Civil phone: x235; Criminal phone: X204. Hours: 8:30AM-4:30PM (EST). *Felony, Misdemeanor, Civil, Eviction, Small Claims.*

Civil Records: Access: In person only. Visitors must perform in person searches for themselves. No search fee. Required to search: name, years to search. Civil cases indexed by defendant, plaintiff. Civil records on index cards or docket books. Records retained for 10 years.

Criminal Records: Access: Mail, in person. Visitors must perform in person searches for themselves. No search fee. Required to search: name, years to search, DOB. Criminal records on index cards or docket books. Records retained for 10 years.

General Information: No impounded records released. Copy fee: $.50 per page. Certification fee: $1.50. Fee payee: District Court, Lowell Division. Business checks accepted. Prepayment is required.

Malden District Court 89 Summer St., Malden, MA 02148; 781-322-7500. Hours: 8:30AM-4:30PM (EST). *Felony, Misdemeanor, Civil, Eviction, Small Claims.*

Civil Records: Access: Phone, mail, in person. Only the court performs in person searches; visitors may not. No search fee. Required to search: name, years to search. Civil cases indexed by defendant, plaintiff. Civil records on index cards or docket books back to 1970; on computer back to 1992.

Criminal Records: Access: Phone, mail, in person. Both court and visitors may perform in person searches. No search fee. Required to search: name, years to search, DOB. Criminal records on index cards or docket books back to 1970; on computer back to 1992.

General Information: No juvenile records released. Turnaround time 1-2 weeks. Copy fee: $.50 per page. Certification fee: $10.00. Fee payee: District Court. Personal checks accepted. Prepayment is required.

Marlborough District Court 21 45 Williams St, Marlborough, MA 01752; 508-485-3700. Hours: 8AM-4:30PM (EST). *Felony, Misdemeanor, Civil, Eviction, Small Claims.*

Civil Records: Access: Phone, mail, in person. Both court and visitors may perform in person searches. No search fee. Required to search: name, years to search. Civil cases indexed by defendant, plaintiff. Civil records on index cards or docket books. State law requires records be retained for 10 years.

Criminal Records: Access: Phone, mail, in person. Both court and visitors may perform in person searches. No search fee. Required to search: name, years to search, DOB. Criminal records on index cards or docket books. State law requires records be retained for 10 years.

General Information: No juvenile records released. Turnaround time 1-2 weeks. Copy fee: $.50 per page. Certification fee: $1.50. Fee payee: District Court. Personal checks accepted. Prepayment is required.

Natick District Court 117 E Central, Natick, MA 01760; 508-653-4332. Hours: 8:30AM-4:30PM (EST). *Felony, Misdemeanor, Civil, Eviction, Small Claims.*

Civil Records: Access: In person. Visitors must perform in person searches on Friday 3PM-4:30PM No search fee. Required to search: name, years to search. Civil cases indexed by defendant, plaintiff. Civil records on index cards and docket books, back for 10 years.

Criminal Records: Access: In person. Visitors must perform in person searches on Friday 3PM-4:30PM No search fee. Required to search: name, years to search, DOB. Criminal records on index cards and docket books, back for 10 years.

General Information: No juvenile records released. Turnaround time 1-2 weeks. Copy fee: $.50 per page. Certification fee: $1.50. Fee payee: District Court. Personal checks accepted. Prepayment is required.

Newton District Court 121 Third St, East Cambridge, MA 02141; 617-494-0102. Hours: 8:30AM-4:30PM (EST). *Felony, Misdemeanor, Civil, Eviction, Small Claims.*

www.state.ma.us/courts/courtsandjudges/courts/newton districtmain.html

Note: After renovations, the court is expected to return to 1309 Washington, West Newton 02141 on or near June 4, 2003.

Civil Records: Access: Phone, mail, in person. Both court and visitors may perform in person searches. No search fee. Required to search: name, years to search. Civil cases indexed by defendant, plaintiff. Civil records on index cards back to 1930.

Criminal Records: Access: Phone, mail, in person. Both court and visitors may perform in person searches. No search fee. Required to search: name, years to search. Criminal records on index books back to 1930.

General Information: No juvenile, (some) 209-A cases or mental health records released. Turnaround time 1 week. Copy fee: $.50 per page. Certification fee: $1.50. Fee payee: District Court of Newton. Personal checks accepted.

Somerville District Court 175 Fellsway, Somerville, MA 02145; 617-666-8000. Hours: 8:30AM-4:30PM (EST). *Felony, Misdemeanor, Civil, Eviction, Small Claims.*

Civil Records: Access: In person. Visitors must perform in person searches No search fee. Required to search: name, years to search. Civil cases indexed by defendant, plaintiff. Civil records on index cards or docket books. State law requires records be retained for 10 years.

Criminal Records: Access: In person. Visitors must perform in person searches No search fee. Required to search: name, years to search, DOB. Criminal records on computer since 1997; prior records on index cards or docket books. State law requires records be retained for 10 years.

General Information: No juvenile or impounded records released. Turnaround time 1-2 weeks. Copy fee: $.50 per page. Certification fee: $1.50. Fee payee: District Court. Personal checks accepted. Prepayment is required.

Waltham District Court 51 38 Linden St, Waltham, MA 02154; 781-894-4500. Hours: 8:30AM-4:30PM (EST). *Felony, Misdemeanor, Civil, Eviction, Small Claims.*

Civil Records: Access: Mail, in person. Both court and visitors may perform in person searches. No search fee. Required to search: name, years to search. Civil cases indexed by defendant, plaintiff. Civil records on index cards and docket books, back for 10 years.

Criminal Records: Access: Mail, in person. Both court and visitors may perform in person searches. No search fee. Required to search: name, years to search; also helpful: DOB. Criminal records on index cards and docket books, back for 10 years.

General Information: Public access terminal is available. No juvenile records released. Turnaround time 1 week. Copy fee: $.50 per page. Certification fee:

$1.50. Fee payee: District Court. No personal checks. Prepayment is required.

Woburn District Court 53 30 Pleasant St, Woburn, MA 01801; 781-935-4000. Hours: 8:30AM-4:30PM (EST). *Felony, Misdemeanor, Civil, Eviction, Small Claims.*

Civil Records: Access: Mail, in person. Both court and visitors may perform in person searches. No search fee. Required to search: name, years to search. Civil cases indexed by defendant, plaintiff. Civil records on index cards, computer listing or docket books back 30 years.
Criminal Records: Access: Mail, in person. Only the court performs in person searches; visitors may not. No search fee. Required to search: name, years to search; also helpful: DOB. Criminal records on index cards, computer listing or docket books back 30 years.
General Information: Public access terminal is available. (For records since 1996.) No statutorily non-public records released. SASE requested. Turnaround time 1-2 weeks. Copy fee: $.50 per page. Certification fee: $1.50. Fee payee: District Court. Personal checks accepted. Prepayment is required.

Probate & Family Court 208 Cambridge St, PO Box 410480, East Cambridge, MA 02141-0005; 617-768-5800; Fax: 617-225-0781. Hours: 8AM-4PM (EST). *Probate.*

Nantucket County

Superior Court PO Box 967, Nantucket, MA 02554; 508-228-2559; Fax: 508-228-3725. Hours: 8:30AM-4PM (EST). *Felony, Civil Actions Over $25,000.*
Civil Records: Access: Phone, fax, mail, in person. Both court and visitors may perform in person searches. No search fee. Required to search: name, years to search. Civil cases indexed by defendant, plaintiff. Civil records on index books from 1762.
Criminal Records: Access: Phone, fax, mail, in person. Both court and visitors may perform in person searches. No search fee. Required to search: name, years to search. Criminal records on index books from 1762.
General Information: No impounded records released. SASE required. Turnaround time 1 week. Fax notes: No fee to fax results. In-state faxing only. Copy fee: $.50 per page. Certification fee: $1.50. Fee payee: Nantucket Superior Court. Personal checks accepted. Prepayment is required.

Nantucket District Court 16 Broad Street, PO Box 1800, Nantucket, MA 02554; 508-228-0460. Hours: 8AM-4PM (EST). *Felony, Misdemeanor, Civil, Eviction, Small Claims.*

Civil Records: Access: In person only. Visitors must perform in person searches for themselves. No search fee. Required to search: name, years to search. Civil cases indexed by defendant, plaintiff. Civil records on index cards or docket books. State law requires records be retained for 10 years.
Criminal Records: Access: In person only. Visitors must perform in person searches for themselves. No search fee. Required to search: name, years to search. Criminal records on index cards or docket books back to 1917. State law requires records be retained for 10 years.
General Information: Copy fee: $.50 per page. Certification fee: $1.50. Fee payee: Nantucket District Court. Prepayment is required.

Probate & Family Court PO Box 1116, Nantucket, MA 02554; 508-228-2669; Fax: 508-228-3662. Hours: 8:30AM-4PM (EST). *Probate.*

Norfolk County

Superior Court 650 High St, Dedham, MA 02026; 781-326-1600; Civil phone: X1; Criminal phone: X2; Fax: 781-326-3871(Civ); 781-320-9726(Crim). Hours: 8:30AM-4:30PM (EST). *Felony, Civil Actions Over $25,000.*
Civil Records: Access: Phone, mail, in person. Both court and visitors may perform in person searches. No search fee. Required to search: name, years to search. Civil cases indexed by defendant, plaintiff. Civil records on index books from 1900, on computer back to 9/2000.
Criminal Records: Access: Mail, in person. Visitors must perform in person searches for themselves. No search fee. Required to search: name, years to search; also helpful: address, DOB, SSN. Criminal records on index books from 1900; on computer back to 9/2000.
General Information: Public access terminal is available. No impounded records released. No one may view a file of a sex-related crime without authorization from a judge. SASE not required. Turnaround time 1 week, 1-2 days for criminal phone in requests. Copy fee: $.50 per page. Certification fee: $1.50. Fee payee: Clerk of Superior Court. Personal checks accepted for copies only. Prepayment is required.

Brookline District Court 360 Washington St, Brookline, MA 02146; 617-232-4660; Fax: 617-739-0734. Hours: 8:30AM-4:30PM (EST). *Felony, Misdemeanor, Civil, Eviction, Small Claims.*

Civil Records: Access: Mail, in person. Both court and visitors may perform in person searches. No search fee. Required to search: name, years to search. Civil cases indexed by defendant, plaintiff. Civil records on index cards and docket books back for 10 years.
Criminal Records: Access: Mail, in person. Only the court performs in person searches; visitors may not. No search fee. Required to search: name, years to search; also helpful: DOB. Criminal records on index cards and docket books back for 10 years.
General Information: No sealed case records released. Turnaround time 1-2 weeks. Copy fee: $.50 per page. Certification fee: $1.50. Fee payee: Brookline District Court. Personal checks accepted. Prepayment is required.

Dedham District Court 631 High St, Dedham, MA 02026; 781-329-4777. Hours: 8:15AM-4:30PM (EST). *Felony, Misdemeanor, Civil, Eviction, Small Claims.*

Civil Records: Access: In person only. Visitors must perform in person searches for themselves. No search fee. Required to search: name, years to search. Civil cases indexed by defendant, plaintiff. Civil records on computer since 1997, and on index cards or docket books prior to that. State law requires records be retained for 10 years.
Criminal Records: Access: In person only. Visitors must perform in person searches for themselves. No search fee. Required to search: name, years to search. Criminal records on computer since 1997, and on index cards or docket books prior to that. State law requires records be retained for 10 years. Access is available after 10AM.
General Information: No juvenile records released. Copy fee: $.50 per page. Certification fee: $1.50. Fee payee: District Court. Personal checks accepted. Prepayment is required.

Quincy District Court One Dennis Ryan Parkway, Quincy, MA 02169; 617-471-1650. Hours: 8:30AM-4:30PM (EST). *Felony, Misdemeanor, Civil, Eviction, Small Claims.*

Civil Records: Access: In person only. Visitors must perform in person searches for themselves. No search fee. Required to search: name, years to search. Civil

cases indexed by defendant, plaintiff. Civil records on index cards or docket books. State law requires records be retained for 10 years.
Criminal Records: Access: In person only. Visitors must perform in person searches for themselves. No search fee. Required to search: name, years to search; also helpful: DOB. Criminal records on computer since 1996; prior records on index cards or docket books. State law requires records be retained for 10 years.
General Information: No juvenile records released. Copy fee: $.50 per page. Certification fee: $1.50. Fee payee: District Court. Only cashiers checks and money orders accepted. Prepayment is required.

Stoughton District Court 1288 Central St, Stoughton, MA 02072; 781-344-2131. Hours: 8:30AM-4:30PM (EST). *Felony, Misdemeanor, Civil, Eviction, Small Claims.*

Civil Records: Access: Mail, in person. Both court and visitors may perform in person searches. No search fee. Required to search: name, years to search. Civil cases indexed by defendant, plaintiff. Civil records on index cards or docket books for 10 years or more.
Criminal Records: Access: Mail, in person. Only the court performs in person searches; visitors may not. No search fee. Required to search: name, years to search; also helpful: DOB. Criminal records on computer since 1996; prior records on index cards or docket books for 10 years or more.
General Information: No juvenile records released. Turnaround time 1 week. Copy fee: $.50 per page. Certification fee: $1.50. Fee payee: District Court. Personal checks accepted. Prepayment is required.

Wrentham District Court 60 East Street, Wrentham, MA 02093; 508-384-3106; Fax: 508-384-5052. Hours: 8:30AM-4:30PM (EST). *Felony, Misdemeanor, Civil, Eviction, Small Claims.*

Civil Records: Access: In person. Both court and visitors may perform in person searches. No search fee. Required to search: name, years to search. Civil cases indexed by defendant, plaintiff. Criminal records retained 20 years. Physical records go back to 1985; pre-1985 on docket books.
Criminal Records: Access: In person. Both court and visitors may perform in person searches. No search fee. Required to search: name, years to search; also helpful: DOB, Criminal records retained 20 years. Physical records go back to 1985; on computer back to 1999; pre-1985 on docket books.
General Information: No show cause hearing or juvenile records released. Mail requests not accepted. Copy fee: $.50 per page. Certification fee: $1.50 per page. Fee payee: District Court. Personal checks accepted. Prepayment is required.

Probate & Family Court 649 High St, PO Box 269, Dedham, MA 02027; 781-326-7200; Fax: 781-326-5575. Hours: 8AM-4:30PM (EST). *Probate.*

Plymouth County

Superior Court - Brockton 72 Belmont St, Brockton, MA 02401; 508-583-8250. Hours: 8:30AM-4:30PM (EST). *Felony, Civil Actions Over $25,000.*
Civil Records: Access: In person only. Visitors must perform in person searches No search fee. Required to search: name, years to search. Civil cases indexed by defendant, plaintiff. Civil records for current civil cases are here, closed case are in Plymouth, some pending; computerized records since 2000.
Criminal Records: Access: In person only. Visitors must perform in person searches No search fee. Required to search: name, years to search. Criminal records for current civil cases are here, closed case are in Plymouth, some pending; computerized records since 2000.

General Information: Public access terminal is available. No impounded records released. Copy fee: $.50 per page. Certification fee: $1.50. Fee payee: Clerk of Superior Court. Personal checks accepted. Prepayment is required.

Superior Court - Plymouth Court St, Plymouth, MA 02360; 508-747-6911. Hours: 8:30AM-4:30PM (EST). *Felony, Civil Actions Over $25,000.*

Civil Records: Access: Phone, mail, in person. Only the court performs in person searches; visitors may not. No search fee. Required to search: name, years to search. Civil cases indexed by defendant, plaintiff. Civil records for all closed cases are kept here; computerized records since 1977.

Criminal Records: Access: In person only, with exception. No search fee. Required to search: name, years to search. Criminal records 10 years or older are here; for recent cases go to the Brockton Superior Court. This court's criminal records under ten years old can be searched in person only at Brockton Superior Court, 72 Belmont St, Brockton, 508-583-8250.

General Information: No impounded records released. Turnaround time 1 week, immediate four phone requests. Copy fee: $.50 per page. Certification fee: $1.50. Fee payee: Clerk of Superior Court. Personal checks accepted. Prepayment is required.

Brockton District Court PO Box 7610 (215 Main St.), Brockton, MA 02303-7610; 508-587-8000. Hours: 8:30AM-4:30PM (EST). *Felony, Misdemeanor, Civil, Eviction, Small Claims.*

Civil Records: Access: Mail, in person. Both court and visitors may perform in person searches. No search fee. Required to search: name, years to search. Civil cases indexed by defendant, plaintiff. Civil records on index cards or docket books, retained for 10 years.

Criminal Records: Access: Mail, in person. Both court and visitors may perform in person searches. No search fee. Required to search: name, years to search; also helpful: DOB. Criminal records on index cards or docket books, retained for 10 years.

General Information: Public access terminal is available. No juvenile or impounded records released. Turnaround time 1-2 weeks. Copy fee: $.50 per page. Certification fee: $1.50. Fee payee: District Court. Personal checks accepted. Prepayment is required.

Hingham District Court 28 George Washington Blvd, Hingham, MA 02043; 781-749-7000; Fax: 781-740-8390. Hours: 8:30AM-4:30PM (EST). *Felony, Misdemeanor, Civil, Eviction, Small Claims.*

Civil Records: Access: Mail, in person. Only the court performs in person searches; visitors may not. No search fee. Required to search: name, years to search. Civil cases indexed by defendant, plaintiff. Civil records on index cards or docket books, retained for 10 years or more.

Criminal Records: Access: Mail, in person. Only the court performs in person searches; visitors may not. No search fee. Required to search: name, years to search; also helpful: DOB. Criminal records on index cards or docket books, retained for 10 years or more.

General Information: No juvenile records released. Turnaround time 1-2 weeks. Copy fee: $.50 per page. Certification fee: $1.50. Fee payee: District Court. Personal checks accepted. Prepayment is required.

Plymouth 3rd District Court Courthouse, South Russell St, Plymouth, MA 02360; 508-747-0500. Hours: 8:30AM-4:30PM (EST). *Felony, Misdemeanor, Civil, Eviction, Small Claims.*

Civil Records: Access: Mail, in person. Both court and visitors may perform in person searches. No search fee. Required to search: name, years to search. Civil cases indexed by defendant, plaintiff. Civil records on index cards or docket books. State law requires records be

retained for 10 years. Visitors can only access the index cards.

Criminal Records: Access: Mail, in person. Both court and visitors may perform in person searches. No search fee. Required to search: name, years to search; also helpful: DOB. Criminal records on index cards or docket books. State law requires records be retained for 10 years. Visitors can only access the index cards.

General Information: No juvenile or impounded records released. Turnaround time 3-4 days. Copy fee: $.50 per page. Certification fee: $1.50. Fee payee: Plymouth District Court. Personal checks accepted. Prepayment is required.

Wareham District Court 2200 Cranberry Hwy, Junction Routes 28 & 58, West Wareham, MA 02576; 508-295-8300; Fax: 508-291-6376. Hours: 8:30AM-4:30PM (EST). *Felony, Misdemeanor, Civil, Eviction, Small Claims.*

Civil Records: Access: Phone, mail, in person. Both court and visitors may perform in person searches. No search fee. Required to search: name, years to search. Civil cases indexed by defendant, plaintiff. Criminal records back to 1960. Computerized records back to 1995.

Criminal Records: Access: Phone, mail, in person. Only the court performs in person searches; visitors may not. No search fee. Required to search: name, years to search; also helpful: DOB. Criminal records back to 1960. Computerized records back to 1995.

General Information: No juvenile records released. SASE requested. Turnaround time 1-2 weeks. Copy fee: $.50 per page. Certification fee: $1.50. Fee payee: District Court. Personal checks accepted. Prepayment is required.

Probate & Family Court 11 Russell, PO Box 3640, Plymouth, MA 02361; 508-747-6204; Fax: 508-746-6846. Hours: 8:30AM-4PM (EST). *Probate.*

Suffolk County

Superior Court - Civil 90 Devonshire St, Rm 807, Copy Dept, Boston, MA 02109; 617-788-7677. Hours: 8:30AM-5PM (EST). *Civil.*

Civil Records: Access: Mail, in person. Both court and visitors may perform in person searches. No search fee. Required to search: name, years to search. Civil cases indexed by defendant, plaintiff. Civil records on computer from 1991, index cards and books from 1860.

General Information: Public access terminal is available. No impounded records released. Turnaround time 1 week. Copy fee: $.50 per page. Certification fee: $1.50. Fee payee: Clerk of Superior Court. Business checks accepted. Prepayment is required.

Superior Court - Criminal 90 Devonshire St #607, USPO & Courthouse, Boston, MA 02109; 617-788-8160; Fax: 617-788-7798. Hours: 9AM-5PM (EST). *Felony.*

Criminal Records: Access: Mail, in person. Both court and visitors may perform in person searches. No search fee. Required to search: name, years to search. Criminal records on computer back to 1991, index cards and books from 1950, archived from 1864.

General Information: Public access terminal is available. Turnaround time 1-2 weeks. Copy fee: $.50 per page. Certification fee: $1.50. Fee payee: Superior Court. Personal checks accepted. Prepayment is required.

Boston Municipal Court Civil Clerk's Office, 90 Devonshire St, Boston, MA 02109; 617-725-8000. Hours: 8:30AM-4:30PM (EST). *Misdemeanor, Civil, Small Claims.*

Civil Records: Access: Mail, in person. Both court and visitors may perform in person searches. No search fee. Required to search: name, years to search. Civil cases

indexed by defendant, plaintiff. Civil records on computer from 1995 to present, and only court searches those records. Public can search prior records on index cards and look-up. State law requires records be retained for 10 years.

Criminal Records: Access: Mail, in person. Both court and visitors may perform in person searches. No search fee. Required to search: name, years to search; also helpful: DOB. Criminal records on computer from 1995 to present, and only court searches those records. Public can search prior records on index cards and look-up. State law requires records be retained for 10 years.

General Information: No impounded records released. Turnaround time 1-2 weeks. Copy fee: $.50 per page. Certification fee: $1.50. Fee payee: District Court. Personal checks accepted. Prepayment is required.

Brighton District Court 52 Academy Hill Rd, Brighton, MA 02135; 617-782-6521; Fax: 617-254-2127. Hours: 8:30AM-4:30PM (EST). *Felony, Misdemeanor, Civil, Eviction, Small Claims.*

Civil Records: Access: In person only. Visitors must perform in person searches for themselves. No search fee. Required to search: name, years to search. Civil cases indexed by defendant, plaintiff. Civil records on index cards or docket books back to 1980. State law requires records be retained for 10 years.

Criminal Records: Access: Phone, mail, in person. Visitors must perform in person searches for themselves. No search fee. Required to search: name, years to search, DOB. Computerized records from 1990, criminal records on index cards or docket books back to 1978. State law requires records be retained for 10 years.

General Information: No sealed or impounded records released. Turnaround time 1-2 weeks. Copy fee: $.50 per page. Certification fee: $1.50 per page. Fee payee: District Court. Personal checks accepted. Prepayment is required.

Charlestown District Court 3 City Square, Charlestown, MA 02129; 617-242-5400; Fax: 617-242-1677. Hours: 8:30AM-4:30PM (EST). *Felony, Misdemeanor, Civil, Eviction, Small Claims.*

Civil Records: Access: Fax, mail, in person. Only the court performs in person searches; visitors may not. No search fee. Required to search: name, years to search. Civil cases indexed by defendant, plaintiff. Civil records on index cards or docket books. State law requires records be retained for 10 years.

Criminal Records: Access: Fax, mail, in person. Only the court performs in person searches; visitors may not. No search fee. Required to search: name, years to search; also helpful: DOB. Criminal records on index cards or docket books. State law requires records be retained for 10 years.

General Information: No juvenile records released. Turnaround time 1-2 weeks. Copy fee: $.50 per page. Certification fee: $1.50. Fee payee: District Court. Personal checks accepted. Prepayment is required.

Chelsea District Court 120 Broadway, Chelsea, MA 02150-2606; 617-660-9400; Fax: 617-621-9215. Hours: 8:30AM-4:30PM (EST). *Felony, Misdemeanor, Civil, Eviction, Small Claims.*

Civil Records: Access: Phone, mail, in person. Both court and visitors may perform in person searches. No search fee. Required to search: name, years to search. Civil cases indexed by defendant, plaintiff. Civil records on index cards or docket books back to 1900; on computer back to 1990.

Criminal Records: Access: Phone, mail, in person. Both court and visitors may perform in person searches. No search fee. Required to search: name, years to search; also helpful: address, DOB. Criminal records on index cards or docket books back to 1900; on computer back to 1990.

General Information: No closed cases, impounded, sealed, mental health commitment, alcoholic or victim of sexual offense records released. SASE required. Turnaround time 1-2 weeks. Copy fee: $.50 per page. Certification fee: $1.50. Fee payee: District Court. Personal checks accepted. Prepayment is required.

Dorchester District Court 510 Washington St, Dorchester, MA 02124; 617-288-9500. Hours: 8:30AM-4:30PM (EST). *Felony, Misdemeanor, Civil, Eviction, Small Claims.*

Civil Records: Access: Mail, in person. Both court and visitors may perform in person searches. No search fee. Required to search: name, years to search. Civil cases indexed by defendant, plaintiff. Civil records on index cards or docket books from 1970. State law requires records be retained for 20 years.
Criminal Records: Access: Mail, in person. Only the court performs in person searches; visitors may not. No search fee. Required to search: name, years to search, DOB. Criminal records on index cards or docket books to 1950's; on computer since 1998. State law requires records be retained for 20 years.
General Information: No juvenile records released. Turnaround time 1-2 weeks. Copy fee: $.50 per page. Certification fee: $1.50. Fee payee: District Court. Personal checks accepted. Prepayment is required.

East Boston District Court 37 Meridian St, East Boston, MA 02128; 617-569-7550; Fax: 617-561-4988. Hours: 8:30AM-4:30PM (EST). *Misdemeanor, Civil Actions Under $25,000, Eviction, Small Claims.*

Civil Records: Access: In person. Both court and visitors may perform in person searches. No search fee. Required to search: name, years to search. Civil cases indexed by defendant, plaintiff. Civil records on index cards or docket books since 1965, computerized since 1988. State law requires records be retained for 20 years.
Criminal Records: Access: In person. Both court and visitors may perform in person searches. No search fee. Required to search: name, years to search. Criminal records on index cards or docket books, computerized since 1988. State law requires records be retained for 20 years.
General Information: No juvenile records released. Copy fee: $.50 per page. Certification fee: $1.50. Fee payee: District Court. Personal checks accepted. Prepayment is required.

Roxbury District Court 85 Warren St, Roxbury, MA 02119; 617-427-7000; Fax: 617-442-0615. Hours: 8:30AM-4:30PM (EST). *Felony, Misdemeanor, Civil, Eviction, Small Claims.*

Civil Records: Access: Phone, fax, mail, in person. Both court and visitors may perform in person searches. No search fee. Required to search: name, years to search. Civil cases indexed by defendant, plaintiff. Civil records on index cards or docket books since 1981; on computer back to 1999. State law requires records be retained for 10 years.
Criminal Records: Access: Phone, fax, mail, in person. Both court and visitors may perform in person searches. No search fee. Required to search: name, years to search, DOB; also helpful: address. Criminal records on index cards or docket books since 1981; on computer back to 1999. State law requires records be retained for 10 years.
General Information: Public access terminal is available. No juvenile records released. Turnaround time 1-2 weeks. Fax notes: Fee to fax results is $1.00 per page. Copy fee: $1.00 per page. Certification fee: $1.50. Fee payee: District Court. Prepayment is required.

South Boston District Court 535 East Broadway, South Boston, MA 02127; 617-268-9292/9293; Fax: 617-268-7321. Hours: 8:30AM-

4:30PM (EST). *Felony, Misdemeanor, Civil, Eviction, Small Claims.*

Civil Records: Access: In person only. Visitors must perform in person searches for themselves. No search fee. Required to search: name, years to search, address. Civil cases indexed by defendant, plaintiff. Civil records on index cards or docket books. Records go back 20 years.
Criminal Records: Access: In person only. Visitors must perform in person searches for themselves. No search fee. Required to search: name, years to search, address, DOB. Criminal records on index cards or docket books. Records go back 20 years; from 2000 on computer.
General Information: No juvenile or medical records released. Copy fee: $.50 per page. Certification fee: $1.50. Fee payee: District Court. Personal checks accepted. Prepayment is required.

West Roxbury District Court Courthouse, 445 Arborway, Jamaica Plain, MA 02130; 617-971-1200. Hours: 8:30AM-4:30PM (EST). *Felony, Misdemeanor, Civil, Eviction, Small Claims.*

Civil Records: Access: In person. Only the visitor may perform in person searches. No search fee. Required to search: name, years to search; also helpful: address. Civil cases indexed by defendant, plaintiff. Civil records on index cards or docket books. State law requires records be retained for 10 years. Include type of civil action to be searched.
Criminal Records: Access: In person. Only the visitor may perform in person searches. No search fee. Required to search: name, years to search; also helpful: DOB. Criminal records on index cards or docket books. State law requires records be retained for 10 years.
General Information: No juvenile records released. Turnaround time 1-2 weeks. Copy fee: $.50 per page. Certification fee: $1.50. Fee payee: District Court. Personal checks accepted. Prepayment is required.

Probate & Family Court 24 New Chardon St, Boston, MA 02114-4703; 617-788-8300; Fax: 617-788-8926. Hours: 8:30AM-4:30PM (EST). *Probate.*

Worcester County

Superior Court 2 Main St Rm 21, Worcester, MA 01608; 508-770-1899. Hours: 8AM-4:30PM (EST). *Felony, Civil Actions Over $25,000.*

Civil Records: Access: Mail, in person. Both court and visitors may perform in person searches. No search fee. Required to search: name, years to search. Civil cases indexed by defendant, plaintiff. Civil records on computer from 1990, index books from 1900.
Criminal Records: Access: Mail, in person, online. Both court and visitors may perform in person searches. No search fee. Required to search: name, years to search. Criminal records on computer from 1990, index books from 1900. The online access is restricted to only attorneys. Call the court for details.
General Information: Public access terminal is available. No impounded or juvenile records released. Turnaround time 1 week. Copy fee: $.50 per page. Certification fee: $1.50. Fee payee: Clerk of Superior Court. Personal checks accepted. Prepayment is required.

Clinton District Court 300 Boylston St, Clinton, MA 01510; 978-368-7811; Fax: 978-368-7827. Hours: 8:30AM-4:30PM (EST). *Felony, Misdemeanor, Civil, Eviction, Small Claims.*

Civil Records: Access: Mail, in person. Only the court performs in person searches; visitors may not. No search fee. Required to search: name, years to search; also helpful: DOB, SSN. Civil cases indexed by defendant, plaintiff. Civil records on index cards or docket books back to 1968. State law requires records be retained for 20 years.

Criminal Records: Access: Mail, in person. Only the court performs in person searches; visitors may not. No search fee. Required to search: name, years to search, address, DOB, SSN, signed release. Criminal records on index cards or docket books back to 1978. State law requires records be retained for 20 years.
General Information: No juvenile records released. SASE required. Turnaround time 1-2 weeks. Copy fee: $1.00 per page. Certification fee: $1.50 per page. Fee payee: District Court Clerk Magistrate. Prepayment is required.

Dudley District Court 64 PO Box 100, Dudley, MA 01571; 508-943-7123; Fax: 508-949-0015. Hours: 8AM-4:30PM (EST). *Felony, Misdemeanor, Civil, Eviction, Small Claims.*

Civil Records: Access: Phone, fax, mail, in person. Both court and visitors may perform in person searches. No search fee. Required to search: name, years to search. Civil cases indexed by defendant, plaintiff. Civil records on computer back to 2002; prior on index cards or docket books; records retained for 10 years.
Criminal Records: Access: Phone, fax, mail, in person. Both court and visitors may perform in person searches. No search fee. Required to search: name, years to search, DOB. Criminal records on computer back to 06/96; prior records on index cards or docket books; records retained for 10 years.
General Information: Public access terminal is available. (Only civil records available.) No juvenile records released. SASE not required. Turnaround time 1-2 weeks. Copy fee: $.50 per page. Certification fee: $1.50. Fee payee: District Court. Business checks accepted. Prepayment is required.

East Brookfield District Court 544 E Main St, East Brookfield, MA 01515-1701; 508-885-6305/6306; Fax: 508-885-7623. Hours: 8:30AM-4:30PM (EST). *Felony, Misdemeanor, Civil, Eviction, Small Claims.*

Civil Records: Access: Mail, in person. Both court and visitors may perform in person searches. No search fee. Required to search: name, years to search. Civil cases indexed by defendant, plaintiff. Civil records on index cards or docket books. State law requires records be retained for 10 years.
Criminal Records: Access: Mail, in person. Both court and visitors may perform in person searches. No search fee. Required to search: name, years to search; also helpful: DOB. Criminal records on index cards or docket books. State law requires records be retained for 10 years.
General Information: No juvenile, mental health records released. SASE requested. Turnaround time 1-2 weeks, strongly suggest to use a retriever when possible. Copy fee: $.50 per page. Certification fee: $1.50. Fee payee: District Court. Personal checks accepted. Prepayment is required.

Fitchburg District Court 16 100 Elm St, Fitchburg, MA 01420; 978-345-2111; Fax: 978-342-2461. Hours: 8:30AM-4:30PM (EST). *Felony, Misdemeanor, Civil, Eviction, Small Claims.*

Civil Records: Access: In person only. Visitors must perform in person searches for themselves. No search fee. Required to search: name, years to search. Civil cases indexed by defendant, plaintiff. Civil records on index cards or docket books back 10 years.
Criminal Records: Access: In person only. Visitors must perform in person searches for themselves. No search fee. Required to search: name, years to search. Criminal records on index cards or docket books back 10 years; on computer back to 1994.
General Information: No juvenile or mental health records released. Copy fee: $.50 per page. Certification fee: $1.50. Fee payee: District Court. Personal checks accepted. Prepayment is required.

Gardner District Court 108 Matthews St, PO Box 40, Gardner, MA 01440-0040; 978-632-2373; Fax: 978-630-3902. Hours: 8:30AM-4:30PM (EST). *Felony, Misdemeanor, Civil, Small Claims.*

Civil Records: Access: Phone, fax, mail, in person. Both court and visitors may perform in person searches. No search fee. Required to search: name, years to search, address. Civil cases indexed by defendant, plaintiff. Civil records on index cards or docket books. State law requires records be retained for 10 years.

Criminal Records: Access: Phone, fax, mail, in person. Both court and visitors may perform in person searches. No search fee. Required to search: name, years to search, DOB. Criminal records on index cards or docket books. State law requires records be retained for 10 years.

General Information: No juvenile records released. Turnaround time 1-2 weeks, quicker for phone and FAX verifications. Fax notes: No fee to fax results. Copy fee: $.50 per page. Certification fee: $1.50. Fee payee: District Court. Personal checks accepted. Prepayment is required.

Leominster District Court 25 School St, Leominster, MA 01453; 978-537-3722; Fax: 978-537-3970. Hours: 8:30AM-4:30PM (EST). *Felony, Misdemeanor, Civil, Eviction, Small Claims.*

Civil Records: Access: Phone, mail, in person. Both court and visitors may perform in person searches. No search fee. Required to search: name, years to search. Civil cases indexed by defendant, plaintiff. Civil records on index cards or docket books. State law requires records be retained for 10 years.

Criminal Records: Access: Phone, mail, in person. Both court and visitors may perform in person searches. No search fee. Required to search: name, years to search; also helpful: DOB. Criminal records on computer since 1987; Prior records on index cards or docket books. State law requires records be retained for 10 years.

General Information: No juvenile or impounded records released. Turnaround time 1-2 weeks. Copy fee: $.50 per page. Certification fee: $1.50. Fee payee: District Court. Personal checks accepted. Prepayment is required.

Milford District Court PO Box 370, Milford, MA 01757; 508-473-1260. Hours: 8:30AM-4:30PM (EST). *Felony, Misdemeanor, Civil, Eviction, Small Claims.*

Civil Records: Access: In person only. Both court and visitors may perform in person searches. No search fee. Required to search: name, years to search. Civil cases indexed by defendant, plaintiff. Civil records on index

cards or docket books. State law requires records be retained for 10 years. Some indexes can only be searches by court.

Criminal Records: Access: In person only. Both court and visitors may perform in person searches. No search fee. Required to search: name, years to search, DOB; also helpful: SSN, aliases. Criminal records on computer since 1995; prior records on index cards & docket books; some indexes only searchable by court.

General Information: No mental health, impounded, alcohol, commitment, sexual abuse victim, waivers of fees or costs for indigents, delinquency, C & P, CHINS, 209A minor or 209A address records released. Copy fee: $.50 per page. Certification fee: $1.50. Fee payee: District Court. Business checks accepted. Prepayment is required.

Uxbridge District Court PO Box 580, Uxbridge, MA 01569; 508-278-2454; Fax: 508-278-2929. Hours: 8:30AM-4:30PM (EST). *Felony, Misdemeanor, Civil, Eviction, Small Claims.*

Civil Records: Access: Mail, in person. Only the court performs in person searches; visitors may not. No search fee. Required to search: name, years to search. Civil cases indexed by defendant, plaintiff. Civil records on index cards or docket books. State law requires records be retained for 10 years.

Criminal Records: Access: Mail, in person. Only the court performs in person searches; visitors may not. No search fee. Required to search: name, years to search; also helpful: DOB. Criminal records on index cards or docket books. State law requires records be retained for 10 years.

General Information: Turnaround time 1-2 weeks. Copy fee: $.50 per page. Certification fee: $1.50. Fee payee: District Court. Personal checks accepted. Prepayment is required.

Westborough District Court 175 Milk St, Westborough, MA 01581; 508-366-8266; Fax: 508-366-8268. Hours: 8AM-4:30PM (EST). *Felony, Misdemeanor, Civil, Eviction, Small Claims.*

Civil Records: Access: Mail, in person. Both court and visitors may perform in person searches. No search fee. Required to search: name, years to search. Civil cases indexed by defendant, plaintiff. Civil records go back to 1986, on books and cards.

Criminal Records: Access: Mail, in person. Both court and visitors may perform in person searches. No search fee. Required to search: name, years to search; also helpful: DOB. Criminal records go back to 1986, on books and cards.

General Information: No impounded, juvenile records released. SASE required. Turnaround time 5 days. Copy fee: $.50 per page. Certification fee: $1.50. Fee payee: District Court Westborough Division. Personal checks accepted. Prepayment is required.

Winchendon District Court 80 Central St, Winchendon, MA 01475; 978-297-0156; Fax: 978-297-0161. Hours: 8:30AM-4:30PM (EST). *Felony, Misdemeanor, Civil, Eviction, Small Claims.*

Civil Records: Access: Phone, mail, in person. Both court and visitors may perform in person searches. No search fee. Required to search: name, years to search. Civil cases indexed by defendant, plaintiff. Civil records on index cards or docket books. State law requires records be retained for 10 years.

Criminal Records: Access: Phone, mail, in person. Both court and visitors may perform in person searches. No search fee. Required to search: name, years to search; also helpful: DOB. Criminal records on index cards or docket books. State law requires records be retained for 10 years.

General Information: Turnaround time 1-2 weeks. Copy fee: $.50 per page. Certification fee: $1.50 per page. Fee payee: District Court. Personal checks accepted. Prepayment is required.

Worcester District Court 50 Harvard St, Worcester, MA 01608; 508-757-8350; Fax: 508-797-0716. Hours: 8AM-4:30PM (EST). *Felony, Misdemeanor, Civil, Eviction, Small Claims.*

Civil Records: Access: Mail, in person. Only the court performs in person searches; visitors may not. No search fee. Required to search: name, years to search. Civil cases indexed by defendant, plaintiff. Civil records on index cards or docket books since 1982. State law requires records be retained for 10 years.

Criminal Records: Access: Mail, in person. Only the court performs in person searches; visitors may not. No search fee. Required to search: name, years to search. Criminal records on computer since 1996; prior records on docket books since 1982.

General Information: No sealed, expunged, adoption or sex offense records released. Turnaround time 1-2 weeks. Copy fee: $.50 per page. Certification fee: $1.50. Fee payee: District Court. Personal checks accepted. Prepayment is required.

Probate & Family Court 2 Main St, Worcester, MA 01608; 508-770-0825 x217; Fax: 508-752-6138. Hours: 8AM-4:30PM (EST). *Probate.*

Massachusetts Recording Offices

ORGANIZATION: 14 counties, 312 towns, and 39 cities; 21 recording offices and 365 UCC filing offices. Each town/city profile indicates the county in which the town/city is located. Filing locations vary depending upon the type of document, as noted below. Berkshire and Bristol counties each has three recording offices. Essex, Middlesex and Worcester counties each has two recording offices. Cities/towns bearing the same name as a county are Barnstable, Essex, Franklin, Hampden, Nantucket, Norfolk, Plymouth, and Worcester. Some UCC financing statements on personal property collateral are were submitted to cities/towns until June 30, 2001, while real estate recording is handled by the counties. Recording officers are Town/City Clerk (UCC), County Register of Deeds (real estate), and Clerk of US District Court (federal tax liens). The entire state is in the Eastern Time Zone (EST).

REAL ESTATE RECORDS: Real estate records are located at the county level. Each town/city profile indicates the county in which the town/city is located. Counties will not perform searches. Copy fee with certification is usually $.75 per page. Each town also has Assessor/Tax Collector/Treasurer offices from which real estate ownership and tax information is available.

UCC RECORDS: This was a dual filing state. Until July 1, 2001, financing statements were usually filed both with the Town/City clerk and at the state level, except for real estate related collateral, which is recorded at the county Register of Deeds. Now, all filing are at the state except for the real estate related collateral. Most all recording offices perform searches. Use search request form UCC-11. Search fees are usually $10.00 per debtor name. Copy fees vary widely.

TAX LIEN RECORDS: Federal tax liens on personal property were filed with the Town/City Clerks prior to 1970. Since that time, federal tax liens on personal property are filed with the US District Court in Boston as well as with the towns/cities. Following is how to search the central index for federal tax liens - Address:

    US District Court (617-748-9152)

    1 Courthouse Way.

    Boston, MA 02110

The federal tax liens are indexed here on a computer system. Searches are available by mail or in person. Do not use the telephone. The court suggests including the Social Security number and/or address of individual names in your search request in order to narrow the results. A mail search costs $15.00 and will take about two weeks. Copies are included. Make your check payable to Clerk, US District Court. You can do the search yourself at no charge on their public computer terminal.

State tax liens on personal property are filed with the Town/City Clerk or Tax Collector. All tax liens against real estate are filed with the county Register of Deeds. Some towns file state tax liens on personal property with the UCC index and include tax liens on personal property automatically with a UCC search. Others will perform a separate state tax lien search, usually for a fee of $10.00 plus $1.00 per page of copies.

OTHER LIENS: Medical, town/city tax, child support.

ONLINE ACCESS: A large number of towns and several counties offer online access to assessor records via the Internet for no charge. Also, a private vendor has placed on the Internet the assessor records from a number of towns. Visit http://data.visionappraisal.com

Abington Town

Town Clerk, 500 Gliniewicz Way, Abington, MA 02351. 781-982-2112 R/E Recording: 781-982-2107; Fax 781-982-2138.
Will search UCC records. This agency will not do a tax lien search. Real estate records located in Plymouth County. **Other Phone Numbers:** Assessor 781-982-2107; Treasurer 781-982-2131; Appraiser/Auditor 781-982-2107; Elections 781-982-2112; Vital Records 781-982-2112.

Acton Town

Town Clerk, 472 Main St, Town Hall, Acton, MA 01720. 978-264-9615 R/E Recording: 978-264-9618; Fax 978-264-9630. www.town.acton.ma.us
Will search UCC records. UCC search includes tax liens. Real estate records located in Middlesex County. **Other Phone Numbers:** Assessor 978-264-9622; Treasurer 978-264-9612; Vital Records 978-264-9615.

Acushnet Town

Town Clerk, 122 Main St, Town Hall, Acushnet, MA 02743. 508-998-0215; Fax 508-998-0203.
Will search UCC records. Tax liens not included in UCC search. Real estate records located in Bristol County. **Other Phones:** Assessor 508-998-0205; Treasurer 508-998-0212; Vital Records 508-998-0215.

Adams Town

Town Clerk, 8 Park St, Adams, MA 01220. 413-743-8320; Fax 413-743-8316.
Will search UCC records. Tax liens not included in UCC search. Real estate records located in Berkshire County. **Other Phones:** Assessor 413-743-8350.

Agawam Town

Town Clerk, 36 Main St., Agawam, MA 01001-1837. 413-786-0400 x215; Fax 413-786-9927.
Will search UCC records. This agency will not do a tax lien search. Real estate records located in Hampden County. **Online Access:** Property Assessment Data

Records. Access to Property Assessment Data is available free at www.patriotproperties.com/agawam/Default.asp?br=exp&vr=5. **Other Phone Numbers:** Assessor 413-786-0400 x205; Treasurer 413-786-0400 x221; Elections 413-786-0400 x215; Vital Records 413-786-0400 x216.

Alford Town

Town Clerk, Town Hall, 5 Alford Center Road, Alford, MA 01230-8914. 413-528-4536; Fax 413-528-4581.
Will search UCC records. This agency will not do a tax lien search. Real estate records located in Berkshire County. **Other Phones:** Assessor 413-528-4536 x2.

Amesbury Town

Town Clerk, 62 Friend St, Town Hall, Amesbury, MA 01913. 978-388-8100; Fax 978-388-8150.
Will search UCC records prior to 7/2001 only. This agency will not do a tax lien search. Real estate records located in Essex County. **Other Phone Numbers:** Assessor 978-388-8102; Treasurer 978-388-8105; Elections 978-388-8100; Vital Records 978-388-8100.

Amherst Town

Town Clerk, Town Hall, 4 Boltwood Ave., Amherst, MA 01002. 413-256-4035; Fax 413-256-2504.
Will search UCC records. This agency will do a tax lien search. Real estate records located in Hampshire County. **Other Phones:** Assessor 413-256-4024; Treasurer 413-256-4020; Appraiser/Auditor 413-256-4024; Elections 256-4035; Vital Records 256-4035.

Andover Town

Town Clerk, 36 Bartlet St, Andover, MA 01810-3882. 978-623-8256 R/E Recording: 978-623-8200 UCC Recording: 978-623-8200; Fax 978-623-8221. www.town.andover.ma.us
Will search UCC records. This agency will not do a tax lien search. Real estate records located in Essex County. **Online Access:** Assessor, Land, Grantor/Grantee, Recording Records. Property tax records on the Assessor's database are available free online at www.town.andover.ma.us/assess/values.htm. Also, search the county recorder database for free at www.lawrencedeeds.com/dsSearch.asp. **Other Phone Numbers:** Assessor 978-623-8200; Treasurer 978-623-8200; Appraiser/Auditor 978-623-8200; Elections 978-623-8200; Vital Records 978-623-8200.

Arlington Town

Town Clerk, 730 Mass Ave, Town Hall, Arlington, MA 02476-9109. 781-316-3073 R/E Recording: 781-316-3051 UCC Recording: 781-316-3051; Fax 781-316-3079. www.town.arlington.ma.us/arthalli.htm
Will search UCC records. Tax liens included in UCC search. Real estate records located in Middlesex County. **Online Access:** Assessor Records. Search the town assessor database for free at http://arlserver.town.arlington.ma.us/property.html. **Other Phone Numbers:** Assessor 781-316-3051; Treasurer 781-316-3031; Appraiser/Auditor 781-316-3051; Elections 781-316-3070; Vital Records 781-316-3070.

Ashburnham Town

Town Clerk, 54 Willard Rd., Ashburnham, MA 01430. 978-827-4102; Fax 978-827-4105.
Will search UCC records. UCC search includes tax liens if requested. Real estate records located in Worcester County. **Other Phone Numbers:** Assessor 978-827-4100; Treasurer 978-827-4102; Appraiser/Auditor 978-827-4101; Elections 978-827-4102; Vital Records 978-827-4102.

Ashby Town

Town Clerk, 895 Main St., Ashby, MA 01431. 978-386-2424; Fax 978-386-2490.
Will search UCC records. This agency will not do a tax lien search. Real estate records located in Middlesex County. **Other Phone Numbers:** Assessor 978-386-2427; Treasurer 978-386-2424.

Ashfield Town

Town Clerk, PO Box 595, Ashfield, MA 01330-0595. 413-628-4441; Fax 413-628-4588.
Will search UCC records. UCC search includes tax liens if requested. Real estate records located in Franklin County. **Other Phone Numbers:** Assessor 413-628-4439; Treasurer 413-628-4441; Elections 413-628-4441; Vital Records 413-628-4441.

Ashland Town

Town Clerk, 101 Main St, Town Hall, Ashland, MA 01721. 508-881-0101; Fax 508-881-0102. www.ashlandmass.com
Will search UCC records. UCC search includes tax liens. Real estate records located in Middlesex County. **Other Phone Numbers:** Assessor 508-881-0104;

Treasurer 508-881-0107; Elections 508-881-0101; Vital Records 508-881-0101.

Athol Town

Town Clerk, 584 Main St, Athol, MA 01331. 978-249-4551; Fax 978-249-2491.
Will search UCC records. UCC search includes tax liens. Real estate records located in Worcester County. **Other Phone Numbers:** Assessor 978-249-3880; Treasurer 978-249-3374; Elections 978-249-4551; Vital Records 978-249-4551.

Attleboro City

City Clerk, 77 Park St, City Hall, Attleboro, MA 02703. 508-223-2222; Fax 508-222-3046.
Will search UCC records. UCC search includes tax liens if requested. Real estate records located in Bristol County. **Online Access:** Property Assessor Records. Search the city assessor data at http://data.visionappraisal.com/attleboroMA. Free registration for full data. Non-registered users can access a limited set of data. **Other Phone Numbers:** Assessor 508-223-2222 x3135; Treasurer 508-223-2222 x3214; Elections 508-223-2222 x3271; Vital Records 508-223-2222 x3111.

Auburn Town

Town Clerk, 104 Central St, Auburn, MA 01501. 508-832-7701; Fax 508-832-7702.
Will search UCC records. UCC search includes tax liens. Real estate records located in Worcester County. **Other Phone Numbers:** Assessor 508-832-7708; Treasurer 508-832-7700.

Avon Town

Town Clerk, Buckley Center, Avon, MA 02322. 508-588-0414; Fax 508-559-0209.
Will search UCC records. UCC search includes tax liens. Real estate records located in Norfolk County. **Other Phone Numbers:** Assessor 508-588-0414; Treasurer 508-588-0414.

Ayer Town

Town Clerk, PO Box 308, Ayer, MA 01432. 978-772-8215; Fax 978-772-8222.
Will search UCC records. Tax liens included in UCC search if requested. Real estate records located in Middlesex County. **Other Phone Numbers:** Assessor 978-772-8211; Treasurer 978-772-8216.

Barnstable County

County Register of Deeds, PO Box 368, Barnstable, MA 02630. 508-362-7733; Fax 508-362-5065. www.bcrd.co.barnstable.ma.us
Will search UCC records, but only real estate related UCC filed here. Tax liens included in UCC search if requested. Will not search real estate records. **Online Access:** Real Estate, Lien Records. Access to County records requires a $50 annual fee, plus $.50 per minute of use. Records date back to 1976. Lending agency information is available. For information, contact Janet Hoben at 508-362-7733. **Other Phone Numbers:** Assessor 508-362-4022; Treasurer 508-362-4653.

Barnstable Town

Town Clerk, 367 Main St., Hyannis, MA 02601. 508-862-4044 R/E Recording: 508-362-7733 UCC Recording: 508-862-4094; Fax 508-790-6326. www.town.barnstable.ma.us
Hyannis, ZIP Code 02601, is located here, as well as the villages of Barnstable, West Barnstable, Centerville, Cotuit, Osterville and Marstons Mills. Will search UCC records. Tax liens included in UCC search if requested. Real estate records located in Barnstable County. **Online Access:** Assessor Records. Town of Barnstable Assessor records are available free online at http://town.barnstable.ma.us/Information_01/Assessme

nt/asse_online_db.htm. Email questions or comments to webadm@town.barnstable.ma.us or call the Assessing Dept. at 508-862-4022. **Other Phone Numbers:** Assessor 508-862-4022; Treasurer 508-862-4653; Elections 508-862-4044; Vital Records 508-862-4095.

Barre Town

Town Clerk, PO Box 418, Barre, MA 01005. 978-355-5003; Fax 978-355-5032.
Will search UCC records. UCC search includes tax liens if requested. Real estate records located in Worcester County. **Other Phone Numbers:** Assessor 978-355-5010; Treasurer 978-355-5000; Elections 978-355-5003; Vital Records 978-355-5003.

Becket Town

Town Clerk, Virginia Andrews, 557 Main St., Becket, MA 01223. 413-623-8934; Fax 413-623-6036.
Will search UCC records. UCC search includes tax liens if requested. Real estate records located in Berkshire County. **Other Phone Numbers:** Assessor 413-623-8934; Treasurer 413-623-8934; Appraiser/Auditor 413-623-8934; Elections 413-623-8934; Vital Records 413-623-8934.

Bedford Town

Town Clerk, 10 Mudge Way, Town Hall, Bedford, MA 01730-0083. 781-275-0083; Fax 781-687-6157.
Will search UCC records. UCC search includes tax liens if requested. Real estate records located in Middlesex County. **Other Phone Numbers:** Assessor 781-275-0046; Treasurer 781-275-8996.

Belchertown Town

Town Clerk, PO Box 607, Belchertown, MA 01007-0607. 413-323-0400 R/E Recording: 413-584-3637; Fax 413-323-0411. www.belchertown.org
Will search UCC records. UCC search includes tax liens if requested. Real estate records located in Hampshire County. **Other Phones:** Assessor 413-323-0413; Treasurer 413-323-0400; Appraiser/Auditor 413-323-0413; Elections 413-323-0400; Vital Records 413-323-0400.

Bellingham Town

Town Clerk, PO Box 367, Bellingham, MA 02019-0367. 508-966-5827; Fax 508-966-5804.
Will search UCC records. This agency will not do a tax lien search. Real estate records located in Norfolk County. **Other Phone Numbers:** Assessor 508-966-5825; Treasurer 508-966-5828; Elections 508-966-5827; Vital Records 508-966-5827.

Belmont Town

Town Clerk, 455 Concord Ave, Town Hall, Belmont, MA 02178-2514. 617-489-8201 UCC Recording: 617-489-8200; Fax 617-489-2185. www.belmont.ma.us
Will search UCC records. This agency will not do a tax lien search. Real estate records located in Middlesex County. **Other Phone Numbers:** Assessor 617-489-8231; Treasurer 617-489-8234; Elections 617-489-8201; Vital Records 617-489-8200.

Berkley Town

Town Clerk, 1 N. Main St, Berkley, MA 02779. 508-822-3348; Fax 508-822-3511.
Will search UCC records. UCC search includes tax liens if requested. Real estate records located in Bristol County. **Other Phone Numbers:** Assessor 508-822-7955.

Berkshire County (Middle District)

County Register of Deeds, 44 Bank Row, Pittsfield, MA 01201. 413-443-7438; Fax 413-448-6025.
This agency will not perform searches. **Online Access:** Real Estate, Lien Records. Online search: see Berkshire

County Southern District. **Other Phone Numbers:** Assessor 413-443-5502.

Berkshire County (Northern District)

County Register of Deeds, 65 Park St, Suite 1, Adams, MA 01220. 413-743-0035; Fax 413-743-1003. www.bcn.net/~nbrd
Will not search UCC records, but only real estate related UCC filed here. This agency will not do a tax lien search. Will not search real estate records. **Online Access:** Real Estate, Lien Records. Online search: see Berkshire County Southern District. **Other Phone Numbers:** Assessor 413-743-8350 (Town of Adams); Treasurer 413-743-8390 (Town of Adams); Vital Records 413-743-8320 (Town of Adams).

Berkshire County (Southern District)

County Register of Deeds, 334 Main St, Great Barrington, MA 01230. 413-528-0146; Fax 413-528-6878.
Will search UCC records, but only real estate related UCC filed here. This agency will not do a tax lien search. Will not search real estate records. **Online Access:** Real Estate, Lien Records. Searching of Titlesearch records requires a one-time $100 signup and $.50 per minute of use. System provides access to all three District Recorder's records; records date back to 1985. Searchable indices: recorded land, plans, registered land. Lending agency information available. For information, contact Sharon Henault at 413-443-7438. **Other Phones:** Assessor 413-637-5502.

Berlin Town

Town Clerk, 23 Linden St, Box 8, Berlin, MA 01503. 978-838-2931; Fax 978-838-0014.
Will search UCC records. UCC search includes tax liens if requested. Real estate records located in Worcester County. **Other Phone Numbers:** Assessor 978-838-2256; Treasurer 978-838-0344; Tax Collector 978-838-2765.

Bernardston Town

Town Clerk, PO Box 504, Bernardston, MA 01337-0435. 413-648-5400 R/E Recording: 413-648-5407; Fax 413-648-5408.
Will search UCC records. UCC search includes tax liens if requested. Real estate records located in Franklin County. **Other Phones:** Assessor 413-648-5407; Treasurer 413-648-5400; Elections 413-648-5400; Vital Records 413-648-5400; Tax Collector 413-648-5401.

Beverly City

City Clerk, 191 Cabot St, Beverly, MA 01915-1031. 978-921-6000 x164; Fax 978-921-8511.
Will search UCC records. This agency will not do a tax lien search. Real estate records located in Essex County. **Other Phone Numbers:** Assessor 978-921-6003; Treasurer 978-921-6135.

Billerica Town

Town Clerk, 365 Boston Road, Town Hall, Billerica, MA 01821-1885. 978-671-0924; Fax 978-663-6510.
Will search UCC records. This agency will not do a tax lien search. Real estate records located in Middlesex County.

Blackstone Town

Town Clerk, Municipal Center, 15 St. Paul St, Blackstone, MA 01504-2295. 508-883-1500 x146; Fax 508-883-7043.
Will search UCC records. Tax liens not included in UCC search. Real estate records located in Worcester County.

Blandford Town

Town Clerk, PO Box 101, Blandford, MA 01008. 413-848-2747 UCC Recording: 413-848-0054; Fax 413-848-0908.
Will search UCC records. UCC search includes tax liens if requested. Real estate records located in Hampden County. **Other Phone Numbers:** Assessor 413-848-2791; Treasurer 413-848-2782; Elections 413-848-0054; Vital Records 413-848-0054.

Bolton Town

Town Clerk, PO Box 278, Bolton, MA 01740. 978-779-2771; Fax 978-779-5461. www.bolton.ma.us
Will search UCC records. Tax liens not included in UCC search. Real estate records located in Worcester County. **Other Phone Numbers:** Assessor 978-779-5556.

Boston City

City Clerk, City Hall, Room 601, 1 City Hall Plaza, Boston, MA 02201. 617-635-4600 R/E Recording: 617-788-8575 UCC Recording: 617-635-2689; Fax 617-635-4658. www.ci.boston.ma.us/assessing
Will search UCC records. UCC search includes tax liens if requested. Real estate records located in Suffolk County. **Online Access:** Assessor Records. Records on the City of Boston Assessor database are available free online at www.ci.boston.ma.us/assessing/search.asp. **Other Phones:** Assessor 617-635-4287; Treasurer 617-535-4138; Appraiser/Auditor 617-635-4287; Elections 617-635-4634; Vital Records 617-635-4175.

Bourne Town

Town Clerk, 24 Perry Ave, Town Hall, Buzzards Bay, MA 02532. 508-759-0613 UCC Recording: 508-759-0600; Fax 508-759-8026.
Will search UCC records. UCC search includes tax liens if requested. Real estate records located in Barnstable County. **Other Phone Numbers:** Assessor 508-759-0600; Treasurer 508-759-0600; Appraiser/Auditor 508-759-0600; Elections 508-759-0600; Vital Records 508-759-0600.

Boxborough Town

Town Clerk, 29 Middle Road, Boxborough, MA 01719-1499. Town Clerk, R/E and UCC Recording 978-263-1116; Fax 978-264-3127.
Will search UCC records. UCC search includes tax liens. Real estate records located in Middlesex County. **Other Phone Numbers:** Assessor 978-263-1116; Treasurer 978-263-1116; Appraiser/Auditor 978-263-1116; Elections 978-263-1116; Vital Records 978-263-1116.

Boxford Town

Town Clerk, 28 Middleton Road, Boxford, MA 01921. 978-887-0806; Fax 978-887-3546.
Will search UCC records. UCC search includes tax liens if requested. Real estate records located in Essex County. **Other Phone Numbers:** Assessor 978-887-3674; Treasurer 978-887-0806.

Boylston Town

Town Clerk, 45 Main St, Boylston, MA 01505. 508-869-2234; Fax 508-869-6210.
Will search UCC records. Tax liens included in UCC search if requested. Real estate records located in Worcester County. **Other Phone Numbers:** Assessor 508-869-6543; Treasurer 508-869-2972; Elections 508-869-2234.

Braintree Town

Town Clerk, 1 JFK Memorial Drive, Braintree, MA 02184-6498. 781-794-8000 x8241 UCC Recording: 781-794-8000; Fax 781-794-8259.

Will search UCC records. UCC search includes tax liens if requested. Real estate records located in Norfolk County. **Other Phones:** Assessor 781-794-8050.

Brewster Town

Town Clerk, 2198 Main St, Brewster, MA 02631. 508-896-4506; Fax 508-896-8089.
Will search UCC records. UCC search includes tax liens if requested. Real estate records located in Barnstable County. **Other Phone Numbers:** Assessor 508-896-3701 x22; Treasurer 508-896-3701 x112; Elections 508-896-4506; Vital Records 508-896-4506.

Bridgewater Town

Town Clerk, Town Hall, 64 Central Square, Bridgewater, MA 02324. Town Clerk, R/E and UCC Recording 508-697-0921; Fax 508-697-0941.
Will search UCC records. UCC search includes tax liens. Real estate records located in Plymouth County. **Other Phone Numbers:** Assessor 508-697-0928; Treasurer 508-697-0923; Elections 508-697-0922; Vital Records 508-697-0921.

Brimfield Town

Town Clerk, PO Box 508, Brimfield, MA 01010. 413-245-4101; Fax 413-245-4107.
Will search UCC records. UCC search includes tax liens if requested. Real estate records located in Hampden County. **Other Phone Numbers:** Assessor 413-245-4100.

Bristol County (Fall River District)

County Register of Deeds, 441 N. Main St, Fall River, MA 02720. County Register of Deeds, R/E and UCC Recording 508-673-1651; Fax 508-673-7633.
This agency will not perform searches. **Online Access:** Real Estate, Lien Records. Online search: see Bristol County Southern District. **Other Phone Numbers:** Assessor 508-324-2302.

Bristol County (Northern District)

County Register of Deeds, 11 Court St, Taunton, MA 02780-0248. 508-822-0502; Fax 508-880-4975.
Will search UCC records, but only real estate related UCC filed here. This agency will not do a tax lien search. Will not search real estate records. **Online Access:** Real Estate, Lien Records. Online search: see Bristol County Southern District. **Other Phone Numbers:** Treasurer 508-824-4028.

Bristol County Southern District)

County Register of Deeds, 25 N. 6th St, New Bedford, MA 02740. 508-993-2605; Fax 508-997-4250.
Will search UCC records, but only real estate related UCC filed here. This agency will not do a tax lien search. Will not search real estate records. **Online Access:** Real Estate, Lien Records. Access to County records requires a $100 set up fee and $.50 per minute of use. All three districts are on this system; the record dates vary by district. Lending agency information is available. For information, contact Rosemary at 508-993-2605.

Brockton City

City Clerk, 45 School St, Brockton, MA 02401. 508-580-7114; Fax 508-580-7104.
Will search UCC records. This agency will not do a tax lien search. Real estate records located in Plymouth County. **Other Phone Numbers:** Assessor 508-580-7194.

Brookfield Town

Town Clerk, 6 Central St., Brookfield, MA 01506. 508-867-8004 R/E Recording: 508-867-3171; Fax 508-867-5091.
Will search UCC records. Tax liens included in UCC search if requested. Real estate records located in Worcester County. **Other Phone Numbers:** Assessor 508-867-3171; Treasurer 508-867-8004; Elections 508-867-8004; Vital Records 508-867-8004.

Brookline Town

Town Clerk, 333 Washington St, Town Hall, Brookline, MA 02445. 617-730-2010 R/E Recording: 617-730-2020; Fax 617-730-2043. www.town.brookline.ma.us/Assessors
Will search UCC records. Tax liens included in UCC search if requested. Real estate records located in Norfolk County. **Online Access:** Assessor, Property Records. Records on the Town of Brookline Assessors database are available free online at www.townofbrooklinemass.com/assessors/propertyloo kup.asp. **Other Phone Numbers:** Assessor 617-730-2060; Treasurer 617-730-2020; Elections 617-730-2010; Vital Records 617-730-2010.

Buckland Town

Town Clerk, PO Box 159, Buckland, MA 01338. 413-625-8572; Fax 413-625-8570.
Postal designation "Shelburne Falls" is not a town. It refers either to Shelburne or Buckland. Will search UCC records. This agency will not do a tax lien search. Real estate records located in Franklin County. **Other Phone Numbers:** Assessor 413-625-2335; Treasurer 413-625-9474; Elections 413-625-8572; Vital Records 413-625-8572.

Burlington Town

Town Clerk, 29 Center St, Town Hall, Burlington, MA 01803. 781-270-1660; Fax 781-270-1608. www.burlington.org/clerk
Will search UCC records. UCC search includes tax liens if requested. Real estate records located in Middlesex County. **Other Phone Numbers:** Assessor 781-270-1650; Treasurer 781-270-1622.

Cambridge City

City Clerk, 795 Massachusetts Ave., City Hall, Room 103, Cambridge, MA 02139. 617-349-4260; Fax 617-349-4269. http://www2.ci.cambridge.ma.us/assessor
Will search UCC records. This agency will not do a tax lien search. Real estate records located in Middlesex County. **Online Access:** Assessor Records. Records on the City of Cambridge Assessor database are available free online at www2.ci.cambridge.ma.us/assessor/index.html. **Other Phone Numbers:** Assessor 617-349-4343; Treasurer 617-349-4212; Elections 617-349-4361; Vital Records 617-349-4260.

Canton Town

Town Clerk, 801 Washington St, Memorial Hall, Canton, MA 02021. 781-821-5013; Fax 781-821-5016.
Will search UCC records. Tax liens included in UCC search if requested. Real estate records located in Norfolk County. **Other Phone Numbers:** Assessor 781-821-5008; Treasurer 781-821-5006; Elections 781-821-5013; Vital Records 781-821-5013.

Carlisle Town

Town Clerk, PO Box 827, Carlisle, MA 01741. 978-369-6155; Fax 978-371-0594.
Will search UCC records. This agency will not do a tax lien search. Real estate records located in Middlesex County. **Other Phone Numbers:** Assessor 978-369-0392; Treasurer 978-369-5557; Appraiser/Auditor 978-369-0392; Elections 978-369-6155; Vital Records 978-369-6155.

Carver Town

Town Clerk, 108 Main St, Carver, MA 02330. 508-866-3403 UCC Recording: 508-86-3403; Fax 508-866-3408.
Will search UCC records. This agency will not do a tax lien search, records kept in Treasurer's Office Real estate records located in Plymouth County. **Other Phone Numbers:** Assessor 508-86-3410; Treasurer 508-866-3435; Elections 508-86-3403; Vital Records 508-86-3403.

Charlemont Town

Town Clerk, PO Box 605, Charlemont, MA 01339-0605. 413-625-6157; Fax 413-339-0329.
Will search UCC records. This agency will not do a tax lien search. Real estate records located in Franklin County. **Other Phone Numbers:** Assessor 413-339-8586; Treasurer 413-625-1097; Elections 413-625-6157; Vital Records 413-625-6157; Tax Lien/Tax Collector 413-339-5707.

Charlton Town

Town Clerk, 37 Main St, Charlton, MA 01507. 508-248-2249; Fax 508-248-2073.
Will search UCC records. UCC search includes tax liens if requested. Real estate records located in Worcester County.

Chatham Town

Town Clerk, 549 Main St, Chatham, MA 02633. 508-945-5101; Fax 508-945-3550.
Will search UCC records. Telephone requests for UCC searches cannot be honored. Tax liens included in UCC search if requested. Real estate records located in Barnstable County. **Other Phone Numbers:** Assessor 508-945-5103; Treasurer 508-945-5108; Vital Records 508-945-5101.

Chelmsford Town

Town Clerk, 50 Billerica Road, Chelmsford, MA 01824. 978-250-5205; Fax 978-840-5208. www.townhall.chelmsford.ma.us
Will search UCC records. Tax liens not included in UCC search. Real estate records located in Middlesex County. **Other Phone Numbers:** Assessor 978-250-5220; Treasurer 978-250-5210; Elections 978-250-5205; Vital Records 978-250-5205.

Chelsea City

City Clerk, 500 Broadway, City Hall Room 209, Chelsea, MA 02150. 617-889-8226 R/E Recording: 617-889-8213; Fax 617-889-8367.
Will search UCC records. Tax liens included in UCC search if requested. Real estate records located in Suffolk County. **Online Access:** Assessor Records. Search the city assessor database at http://data.visionappraisal.com/ChelseaMA. Free registration for full data. **Other Phone Numbers:** Assessor 617-889-8213; Treasurer 617-889-8210; Appraiser/Auditor 617-889-8213; Elections 617-889-8226; Vital Records 617-889-8226.

Cheshire Town

Town Clerk, 80 Church St, PO Box S, Cheshire, MA 01225. 413-743-1690; Fax 413-743-0389.
Will search UCC records. This agency will not do a tax lien search. Real estate records located in Berkshire County. **Other Phones:** Assessor 413-743-1690.

Chester Town

Town Clerk, Town Hall, Chester, MA 01011. 413-354-6603; Fax 413-354-2268.
Will search UCC records. This agency will not do a tax lien search. Real estate records located in Hampden County. **Other Phone Numbers:** Assessor 413-354-6357; Treasurer 413-354-7761.

Chesterfield Town

Town Clerk, Davenport Bldg., 422 Main Rd., Chesterfield, MA 01012-0033. 413-296-4741; Fax 413-296-4394.
Will search UCC records. UCC search includes tax liens. Real estate records located in Hampshire County. **Other Phone Numbers:** Assessor 413-296-4010; Treasurer 413-296-4771; Elections 413-296-4741; Vital Records 413-296-4741.

Chicopee City

City Clerk, 17 Springfield St, City Hall, Chicopee, MA 01013. 413-594-1466; Fax 413-594-2057.
Will search UCC records. UCC search includes tax liens. Real estate records located in Hampden County. **Other Phone Numbers:** Assessor 413-594-1430; Treasurer 413-594-1560; Appraiser/Auditor 413-594-1410; Elections 413-594-1550.

Chilmark Town

Town Clerk, PO Box 119, Chilmark, MA 02535-0119. 508-645-2107; Fax 508-645-2110. www.ci.chilmark.ma.us
Will search UCC records. This agency will not do a tax lien search. Real estate records located in Dukes County. **Other Phones:** Assessor 508-645-2102.

Clarksburg Town

Town Clerk, 111 River Road, Town Hall, Clarksburg, MA 01247. 413-663-8247; Fax 413-664-6575.
Will search UCC records. UCC search includes tax liens. Real estate records located in Berkshire County. **Other Phone Numbers:** Assessor 413-663-8255; Treasurer 413-663-7940; Elections 413-663-7940; Vital Records 413-663-8247.

Clinton Town

Town Clerk, 242 Church St, Clinton, MA 01510. 978-365-4119; Fax 978-895-4130.
Will search UCC records. Tax liens included in UCC search if requested. Real estate records located in Worcester County. **Other Phone Numbers:** Assessor 978-365-4117; Treasurer 978-365-4129; Elections 978-365-4119; Vital Records 978-365-4119.

Cohasset Town

Town Clerk, 41 Highland Ave, Cohasset, MA 02025-1814. 781-383-4100; Fax 781-383-1561.
Will search UCC records. This agency will not do a tax lien search. Real estate records located in Norfolk County. **Other Phone Numbers:** Assessor 781-383-4114; Treasurer 781-383-4102; Elections 781-383-4100; Vital Records 781-383-4100.

Colrain Town

Town Clerk, PO Box 31, Colrain, MA 01340-0031. 413-624-3454; Fax 413-624-8852.
Will search UCC records. Tax liens included in UCC search. Real estate records located in Franklin County. **Other Phone Numbers:** Assessor 413-624-3356; Treasurer 413-624-3454; Elections 413-624-3454; Vital Records 413-624-3454.

Concord Town

Town Clerk, PO Box 535, Concord, MA 01742. 978-318-3080; Fax 978-318-3093. www.concordnet.org
Will search UCC records. UCC search includes tax liens. Real estate records located in Middlesex County. **Online Access:** Assessor values. Visit http://www.concordnet.org/assessor/fy01value_main.ht m, no name searching. **Other Phone Numbers:** Assessor 978-318-3070; Treasurer 978-318-3050; Appraiser/Auditor 978-318-3070; Elections 978-318-3080; Vital Records 978-318-3080.

Conway Town

Town Clerk, PO Box 240, Conway, MA 01341. 413-369-4235; Fax 413-369-4237.
Will search UCC records. This agency will not do a tax lien search. Real estate records located in Franklin County. **Other Phone Numbers:** Assessor 413-369-4773; Treasurer 413-369-4235.

Cummington Town

Town Clerk, 585 Berkshire Trail, Cummington, MA 01026. 413-634-5458; Fax 413-634-5568.
Will search UCC records. Tax liens not included in UCC search. Real estate records located in Hampshire County. **Other Phones:** Assessor 413-634-5354; Elections 413-634-5458; Vital Records 413-634-5457.

Dalton Town

Town Clerk, 462 Main St, Town Hall, Dalton, MA 01226. 413-684-6103 x14; Fax 413-684-6107.
Will search UCC records. UCC search includes tax liens. Real estate records located in Berkshire County. **Other Phone Numbers:** Assessor 413-684-6105; Treasurer 413-684-6111 x18; Elections 413-684-6103 x15; Vital Records 413-684-6103 x15.

Danvers Town

Town Clerk, 1 Sylvan St, Town Hall, Danvers, MA 01923. 978-777-0001; Fax 978-777-1025.
Will search UCC records. This agency will not do a tax lien search. Real estate records located in Essex County.

Dartmouth Town

Town Clerk, PO Box 79399, Dartmouth, MA 02747. Town Clerk, R/E and UCC Recording 508-910-1809 UCC Recording: 508-910-1800; Fax 508-910-1894. www.town.dartmouth.ma.us/town_hall.htm
Will search UCC records. Tax liens not included in UCC search. Real estate records located in Bristol County. **Online Access:** Assessor Records. Search the town assessor database at http://data.visionappraisal.com/DartmouthMA. Free registration for full data. **Other Phone Numbers:** Assessor 508-910-1809; Treasurer 508-910-1802; Elections 508-910-1800; Vital Records 508-910-1800.

Dedham Town

Town Clerk, PO Box 306, Dedham, MA 02027. 781-326-1638 UCC Recording: 781-326-8247; Fax 781-461-5992.
Will search UCC records. This agency will not do a tax lien search. Real estate records located in Norfolk County. **Online Access:** Assessor Records. Property records on the Assessor's database are available free online at http://data.visionappraisal.com/dedhamma. Registration is required for full access; registration is free. **Other Phone Numbers:** Assessor 781-326-8247.

Deerfield Town

Town Clerk, 8 Conway St., South Deerfield, MA 01373. 413-665-2130; Fax 413-665-7275.
Will not search UCC records. Real estate records located in Franklin County. **Other Phone Numbers:** Assessor 413-665-7184; Treasurer 413-665-2130.

Dennis Town

Town Clerk, PO Box 1419, South Dennis, MA 02660-1419. 508-760-6115 R/E Recording: 508-362-2511 UCC Recording: 508-760-6112; Fax 508-394-8309.
Will search UCC records. Tax liens not included in UCC search. Real estate records located in Barnstable County. **Other Phone Numbers:** Assessor 508-760-6142; Treasurer 508-760-6117; Appraiser/Auditor 508-760-6141; Elections 508-760-6112; Vital Records 508-760-6112.

Dighton Town

Town Clerk, 979 Somerset Ave, Dighton, MA 02715-0465. Town Clerk, R/E and UCC Recording 508-669-5411; Fax 508-669-5667.
Will search UCC records. This agency will not do a tax lien search. Real estate records located in Bristol County. **Other Phone Numbers:** Assessor 508-669-5043; Treasurer 508-669-5411; Elections 508-669-5411; Vital Records 508-669-5411.

Douglas Town

Town Clerk, 29 Depot St., Municipal Center, Douglas, MA 01516. 508-476-4000 x355 R/E Recording: 508-476-4000 x353; Fax 508-476-4012.
Will search UCC records. Tax liens not included in UCC search. Real estate records located in Worcester County. **Other Phone Numbers:** Assessor 508-476-4000 x353; Treasurer 508-476-4000 x356; Elections 508-476-4000 x355; Vital Records 508-476-4000 x355.

Dover Town

Town Clerk, PO Box 250, Dover, MA 02030-0250. 508-785-1719 R/E Recording: 508-785-0726; Fax 508-785-2341. http://doverma.org/townclerk.shtml
Will search UCC records. Tax liens not included in UCC search. Real estate records located in Norfolk County. **Other Phone Numbers:** Assessor 508-785-0726; Treasurer 508-785-0057; Elections 508-785-1719; Vital Records 508-785-1719.

Dracut Town

Town Clerk, 62 Arlington St, Room 4, Dracut, MA 01826. 978-453-0951; Fax 978-452-7924.
Will not search UCC records. Tax liens not included in UCC search. Real estate records located in Middlesex County. **Online Access:** Assessor Records. Search the town assessor data at http://data.visionappraisal.com/DracutMA. Free registration for full data. **Other Phone Numbers:** Assessor 978-453-2451.

Dudley Town

Town Clerk, 40 Schofield Ave, Town Hall, 40 Schofield Ave., Dudley, MA 01571. 508-949-8004; Fax 508-949-7115.
Will search UCC records. UCC search includes tax liens. Real estate records located in Worcester County. **Online Access:** Assessor Records. Search the town assessor database at http://data.visionappraisal.com/DudleyMA. Free registration for full data. **Other Phone Numbers:** Assessor 508-949-8006; Treasurer 508-949-8002; Appraiser/Auditor 508-949-8001; Elections 508-949-8004; Vital Records 508-949-8004.

Dukes County

County Register of Deeds, PO Box 5231, Edgartown, MA 02539. County Register of Deeds, R/E and UCC Recording 508-627-4025; Fax 508-627-7821.
This county is comprised of 6 towns-there is no County Assessor, Appraiser, Elections, etc. This agency will not perform searches.

Dunstable Town

Town Clerk, 511 Main St., Dunstable, MA 01827. 978-649-4514; Fax 978-649-2205.
Will search UCC records. This agency will not do a tax lien search. Real estate records located in Middlesex County. **Other Phone Numbers:** Assessor 978-649-3257; Treasurer 978-649-3257; Elections 978-649-4514; Vital Records 978-649-4514.

Duxbury Town

Town Clerk, 878 Tremont St, Duxbury, MA 02332-4499. 781-934-1100; Fax 781-934-9278.
Will search UCC records. UCC search includes tax liens if requested. Include $5.00 search fee Real estate records located in Plymouth County. **Online Access:**

Property Assessor Records. Search the town public documents free at http://duxburyma.virtualtownhall.net/Public_Documents/Search. **Other Phone Numbers:** Assessor 781-934-1109; Treasurer 781-934-1102.

East Bridgewater Town

Town Clerk, PO Box 387, East Bridgewater, MA 02333. 508-378-1606; Fax 508-378-1638.
Will search UCC records. UCC search includes tax liens. Real estate records located in Plymouth County.

East Brookfield Town

Town Clerk, Town Hall, East Brookfield, MA 01515. Town Clerk, R/E and UCC Recording 508-867-6769; Fax 508-867-4190.
Will search UCC records. This agency will not do a tax lien search. Real estate records located in Worcester County. **Other Phone Numbers:** Assessor 508-867-6769; Treasurer 508-867-6769; Elections 508-867-6769; Vital Records 508-867-6769.

East Longmeadow Town

Town Clerk, 60 Center Square, East Longmeadow, MA 01028-2446. 413-525-5400; Fax 413-525-1025. www.eastlongmeadow.org
Will search UCC records. Tax liens not included in UCC search. Real estate records located in Hampden County. **Other Phone Numbers:** Assessor 413-525-5425; Treasurer 413-525-5400.

Eastham Town

Town Clerk, 2500 State Highway, Eastham, MA 02642. 508-240-5900 x223.
Will search UCC records. UCC search includes tax liens if requested. Real estate records located in Barnstable County. **Other Phone Numbers:** Assessor 508-255-0333.

Easthampton City

City Clerk, 43 Main St, Town Hall, Room 1, Easthampton, MA 01027. 413-529-1460 R/E Recording: 413-529-1401; Fax 413-529-1488.
Will search UCC records. UCC search includes tax liens if requested. Real estate records located in Hampshire County. **Other Phone Numbers:** Assessor 413-529-1401; Treasurer 413-529-1416; Elections 413-529-1460; Vital Records 413-529-1460.

Easton Town

Town Clerk, 136 Elm St, North Easton, MA 02356-0129. 508-230-3335 R/E Recording: 508-230-3416; Fax 508-230-3438. www.easton.ma.us
Will search UCC records. Tax liens included in UCC search if requested. Real estate records located in Bristol County. **Other Phone Numbers:** Assessor 508-230-3416; Treasurer 508-230-3358; Elections 508-230-3335; Vital Records 508-230-3335.

Edgartown Town

Town Clerk, P.O.Box 35, Edgartown, MA 02539-0035. 508-627-6110 R/E Recording: 508-627-4025; Fax 508-627-6123.
Will search UCC records. UCC search includes tax liens if requested. Real estate records located in Dukes County. **Online Access:** Real Estate, Property Tax Records. Search the Town assessor's database at http://data.visionappraisal.com/EdgartownMA. Free registration for full data. **Other Phone Numbers:** Assessor 508-627-6140; Treasurer 508-627-6130; Elections 508-627-6110; Vital Records 508-627-6110.

Egremont Town

Town Clerk, PO Box 56, North Egremont/ So. Egremont, MA 01258-0056. 413-528-0182; Fax 413-528-5465.
Will search UCC records. UCC search includes tax liens if requested. Real estate records located in

Berkshire County. **Other Phone Numbers:** Assessor 413-528-0182.

Erving Town

Town Clerk, Town Hall, 12 E. Main St., Erving, MA 01344. 978-544-3636 X102; Fax 978-544-5436.
Will search UCC records. UCC search includes tax liens if requested. Real estate records located in Franklin County. **Other Phone Numbers:** Assessor 978-544-3636 X107; Treasurer 978-544-3636 X104.

Essex County (Northern District)

County Register of Deeds, 381 Common St, Lawrence, MA 01840. 978-683-2745; Fax 978-688-4679. www.lawrencedeeds.com
Will search UCC records, but only real estate related UCC filed here. Tax liens included in UCC search if requested. Will not search real estate records. **Online Access:** Real Estate, Lien, Grantor/Grantee, Recording Records. Search the county recorder database for free at www.lawrencedeeds.com/dsSearch.asp. Also see Andover Town and Essex County Southern District. **Other Phone Numbers:** Assessor 978-683-2745; Treasurer 978-683-2745.

Essex County (Southern District)

County Register of Deeds, 36 Federal St, Salem, MA 01970. 978-741-0201; Fax 978-744-5865.
Will search UCC records, but only real estate related UCC filed here. This agency will not do a tax lien search. Will not search real estate records. **Online Access:** Real Estate, Lien, Deed Records. Access to the Essex County online records requires a $25 deposit, with a $.25 per minute charge for use. Records date back to 1981. Lending agency information is available. For information, contact David Burke at 978-683-2745. Records on the Essex County South Registry of Deeds database are available free on the Internet at www.salemdeeds.com. Click on "Deeds online". Images start 1/1992; records back to 1/1984. Search by grantee/grantor, town & date, street, or book & page. **Other Phone Numbers:** Assessor 978-741-0200.

Essex Town

Town Clerk, Town Hall, Martin St., Essex, MA 01929. 978-768-7111.
Do not confuse Essex Town with Essex County. UCC records are filed with the Town/City Clerk, real estate records are at the county level with the Register of Deeds. Will search UCC records. This agency will not do a tax lien search. Real estate records located in Essex County.

Everett City

City Clerk, City Hall, Room 10, Everett, MA 02149. 617-394-2228; Fax 617-387-5770.
Will search UCC records. Tax liens not included in UCC search. Real estate records located in Middlesex County. **Other Phones:** Assessor 617-394-2205; Treasurer 617-394-2315; Elections 617-394-2229; Vital Records 394-2225; Registrar of Voters 394-2295.

Fairhaven Town

Town Clerk, 40 Center St, Fairhaven, MA 02719-2999. 508-979-4025; Fax 508-979-4079.
Will search UCC records. UCC search includes tax liens. Real estate records located in Bristol County. **Other Phone Numbers:** Assessor 508-979-4018; Treasurer 508-979-4026; Elections 508-979-4025; Vital Records 508-979-4025.

Fall River City

City Clerk, One Government Center, Fall River, MA 02722. 508-324-2220; Fax 508-324-2211.

Will search UCC records. Tax liens not included in UCC search. Real estate records located in Bristol County. **Other Phone Numbers:** Assessor 508-324-2300; Treasurer 508-324-2260; Elections 508-324-2630; Vital Records 508-324-2220.

Falmouth Town

Town Clerk, PO Box 904, Falmouth, MA 02541. 508-548-7611 R/E Recording: 508-495-7675 UCC Recording: 508-495-7357; Fax 508-457-2511. www.town.falmouth.ma.us
Will search UCC records. This agency will not do a tax lien search. Real estate records located in Barnstable County. **Online Access:** Assessor Records. Records on the Town of Falmouth Assessor database are available free by experiment on the Internet at www.town.falmouth.ma.us/propinq.html. Provides owner, address, and valuation only. **Other Phone Numbers:** Assessor 508-495-7377; Treasurer 508-495-7362; Elections 508-495-7358; Vital Records 508-495-7357; Switchboard 508-548-7611.

Fitchburg City

City Clerk, 718 Main St, Fitchburg, MA 01420-3198. 978-345-9592; Fax 978-345-9595.
Will search UCC records. This agency will not do a tax lien search. Real estate records located in Worcester County. **Other Phones:** Assessor 978-345-9562.

Florida Town

Town Clerk, Town Hall, 20 South St, Drury, MA 01343. 413-664-6685; Fax 413-664-8640.
Will search UCC records. UCC search includes tax liens if requested. Real estate records located in Berkshire County. **Other Phone Numbers:** Assessor 413-662-2448; Treasurer 413-663-9851.

Foxborough Town

Town Clerk, 40 South St, Foxborough, MA 02035-2397. 508-543-1208 R/E Recording: 508-543-1215; Fax 508-543-6278.
Will search UCC records. UCC search includes tax liens. Real estate records located in Norfolk County. **Other Phone Numbers:** Assessor 508-543-1215; Treasurer 508-543-1216; Elections 508-543-1208; Vital Records 508-543-1208; Main Number 508-543-1200.

Framingham Town

Town Clerk, Memorial Building - Room 105, 150 Concord St., Framingham, MA 01702-8374. 508-620-4863; Fax 508-628-1358. www.framinghamma.org
Will search UCC records. UCC search includes tax liens if requested. Real estate records located in Middlesex County. **Other Phone Numbers:** Assessor 508-620-4858; Treasurer 508-628-1311; Elections 508-620-4863; Vital Records 508-620-4863.

Franklin County

County Register of Deeds, PO Box 1495, Greenfield, MA 01302-1495. 413-772-0239; Fax 413-774-7150.
This agency will not perform searches. **Other Phone Numbers:** Treasurer 413-774-4804.

Franklin Town

Town Clerk, Municipal Building, 150 Emmons St, Franklin, MA 02038. 508-520-4900; Fax 508-520-4903.
Will search UCC records. Tax liens included in UCC search. Real estate records located in Franklin County. **Other Phone Numbers:** Assessor 508-520-4920; Treasurer 508-520-4950.

Freetown Town

Town Clerk, PO Box 438, Assonet, MA 02702. 508-644-2203 R/E Recording: 508-644-2205; Fax 508-644-9826. http://town.freetown.ma.us/tg/

Will search UCC records. Real estate records located in Bristol County. **Other Phone Numbers:** Assessor 508-644-2205; Treasurer 508-644-2204; Appraiser/Auditor 508-644-2205; Elections 508-644-2203; Vital Records 508-644-2203.

Gardner City

City Clerk, 95 Pleasant St, City Hall Room 118, Gardner, MA 01440. 978-630-4008; Fax 978-630-2520.
Will search UCC records. Tax liens included in UCC search if requested. Real estate records located in Worcester County. **Other Phone Numbers:** Assessor 978-630-4004; Treasurer 978-630-4016.

Gay Head Town

Town Clerk, 65 State Rd, Aquinnah, MA 02535. 508-645-2306; Fax 508-645-2310.
The Town of Aquinnah was formerly known as Gay Head. Will search UCC records. This agency will not do a tax lien search. Real estate records located in Dukes County.

Georgetown Town

Town Clerk, 1 Library St, Georgetown, MA 01833. 978-352-5711 R/E Recording: 978-352-5708; Fax 978-352-5725.
Will search UCC records. This agency will not do a tax lien search. Real estate records located in Essex County. **Other Phones:** Appraiser/Auditor 978-352-5708; Elections 978-352-5711; Vital Records 978-352-5711.

Gill Town

Town Clerk, Town Clerk's Office, 325 Main Road, Gill, MA 01376. 413-863-8103; Fax 413-863-9347.
Will search UCC records. This agency will not do a tax lien search. Real estate records located in Franklin County. **Other Phones:** Assessor 413-863-8103.

Gloucester City

City Clerk, 9 Dale Ave, Gloucester, MA 01930-5998. 978-281-9720; Fax 978-281-8472. www.ci.gloucester.ma.us
Will search UCC records. UCC search includes tax liens if requested. Real estate records located in Essex County. **Other Phone Numbers:** Assessor 978-281-9715; Treasurer 978-281-9707; Elections 978-281-9720; Vital Records 978-281-9720.

Goshen Town

Town Clerk, PO Box 124, Goshen, MA 01032-0124. 413-268-8236; Fax 413-268-8237.
Will search UCC records. This agency will not do a tax lien search. Real estate records located in Hampshire County. **Other Phone Numbers:** Assessor 413-268-7856; Treasurer 413-268-7760; Elections 413-268-8236; Vital Records 413-268-8236.

Gosnold Town

Town Clerk, Town Hall, Gosnold, MA 02713. Town Clerk, R/E and UCC Recording 508-990-7408; Fax 508-990-7408.
Will search UCC records. This agency will not do a tax lien search. Real estate records located in Dukes County. **Other Phones:** Assessor 508-990-7408; Treasurer 508-990-7408; Appraiser/Auditor 508-990-7408; Elections 990-7408; Vital Records 990-7408.

Grafton Town

Town Clerk, Municipal Center, 30 Providence Road, Grafton, MA 01519-1186. 508-839-4722 UCC Recording: 508-839-5335 x195; Fax 508-839-4602.
Will search UCC records. UCC search includes tax liens. Real estate records located in Worcester County. **Other Phone Numbers:** Assessor 508-839-5335 x165; Treasurer 508-839-5335 x170

508-839-5335 x170; Elections 508-839-5335 x195; Vital Records 508-839-5335 x195.

Granby Town

Town Clerk, 250 State St., Kellogg Hall, Granby, MA 01033. 413-467-7178 R/E Recording: 413-584-3637; Fax 413-467-2080.

Will search UCC records. This agency will not do a tax lien search. Real estate records located in Hampshire County. **Other Phone Numbers:** Assessor 413-467-7196; Treasurer 413-467-7176; Elections 413-467-7178; Vital Records 413-467-7178.

Granville Town

Town Clerk, PO Box 247, Granville, MA 01034-0247. Town Clerk, R/E and UCC Recording 413-357-8585; Fax 413-357-6002.

Will search UCC records. UCC search includes tax liens. Real estate records located in Hampden County. **Other Phone Numbers:** Assessor 413-357-8585; Treasurer 413-357-8585; Elections 413-357-8585; Vital Records 413-357-8585.

Great Barrington Town

Town Clerk, 334 Main St, Great Barrington, MA 01230-1802. 413-528-3140 R/E Recording: 413-528-0146; Fax 413-528-2290.

Will search UCC records. This agency will not do a tax lien search. Real estate records located in Berkshire County. **Other Phone Numbers:** Assessor 413-528-2220; Treasurer 413-528-1025; Elections 413-528-3140; Vital Records 413-528-3140; Selectman 413-528-1619.

Greenfield Town

Town Clerk, 14 Court Square, Town Hall, Greenfield, MA 01301. 413-772-1555; Fax 413-772-1542.

Will search UCC records. UCC search includes tax liens if requested. Real estate records located in Franklin County. **Other Phones:** Assessor 413-772-1506.

Groton Town

Town Clerk, Town Hall, 173 Main St., Groton, MA 01450. 978-448-1100; Fax 978-448-2030. www.groton.ma.us

Will search UCC records. This agency will not do a tax lien search. Real estate records located in Middlesex County. **Other Phone Numbers:** Assessor 978-448-1127; Treasurer 978-448-1103; Elections 978-448-1100; Vital Records 978-448-1100.

Groveland Town

Town Clerk, Town Hall, Groveland, MA 01830. Town Clerk, R/E and UCC Recording 978-372-6861 UCC Recording: 978-372-5005; Fax 978-469-5006.

Will search UCC records. This agency will not do a tax lien search. Real estate records located in Essex County. **Other Phone Numbers:** Assessor 978-372-8528; Treasurer 978-372-6861; Elections 978-372-5005; Vital Records 978-372-5005.

Hadley Town

Town Clerk, 100 Middle St, Hadley, MA 01035-9517. 413-584-1590; Fax 413-586-5661. www.hadleyma.org
Will search UCC records. UCC search includes tax liens if requested. Real estate records located in Hampshire County. **Other Phone Numbers:** Assessor 413-586-6320; Treasurer 413-586-3354.

Halifax Town

Town Clerk, 499 Plymouth St, Halifax, MA 02338-1395. 781-293-7970; Fax 781-294-7684.

Will search UCC records. Tax liens not included in UCC search. Real estate records located in Plymouth County. **Other Phone Numbers:** Assessor 781-293-5960; Treasurer 781-293-8348; Appraiser/Auditor 781-

293-5960; Elections 781-293-7970; Vital Records 781-293-7970.

Hamilton Town

Town Clerk, PO Box 429, Hamilton, MA 01936. 978-468-5570; Fax 978-468-2682. www.town.hamilton.ma.us

Will search UCC records. UCC search includes tax liens if requested. Real estate records located in Essex County. **Other Phone Numbers:** Assessor 508-468-5574; Treasurer 508-468-5575; Appraiser/Auditor 508-468-5574; Elections 508-468-5570; Vital Records 508-468-5570; Selectmen 508-468-5572.

Hampden County

County Register of Deeds, 50 State St, Hall of Justice, Springfield, MA 01103. 413-755-1722; Fax 413-731-8190.

Will search UCC records, but only real estate related UCC filed here. This agency will not do a tax lien search. Will not search real estate records. **Online Access:** Real Estate, Lien Records. Access to County online records requires a $50 annual fee and $.50 per minute of use. Records date back to 1962. Lending agency information is available. Searchable indexes are bankruptcy (from PACER), unregistered land site and registered land site. For information, contact Donna Brown or Mary Caron at 413-755-1722 x121.

Hampden Town

Town Clerk, PO Box 351, Hampden, MA 01036. 413-566-3214; Fax 413-566-2010.

Will search UCC records. Tax liens included in UCC search if requested. Real estate records located in Hampden County. **Other Phone Numbers:** Assessor 413-566-3223; Treasurer 413-566-2401.

Hampshire County

County Register of Deeds, 33 King St, Hall of Records, Northampton, MA 01060. 413-584-3637; Fax 413-584-4136.

This agency will not perform searches. **Online Access:** Real Estate, Lien Records. Access to County Register of Deeds online records requires a $100 annual fee and $.50 per minute of use, $.60 for out-of-state. Records date back to 9/2/1986. Lending agency information is available. For information, contact MaryAnn Foster at 413-584-3637.

Hancock Town

Town Clerk, 3650 Hancock Rd., Hancock, MA 01237-1097. Town Clerk, R/E and UCC Recording 413-738-5225; Fax 413-738-5310.

Will search UCC records. Tax liens included in UCC search if requested. Real estate records located in Berkshire County. **Other Phone Numbers:** Assessor 413-738-5225; Treasurer 413-738-5225; Elections 413-738-5225; Vital Records 413-738-5225.

Hanover Town

Town Clerk, 550 Hanover St, Hanover, MA 02339-2217. 781-826-2691; Fax 781-826-5950.

Will search UCC records. This agency will not do a tax lien search. Real estate records located in Plymouth County. **Other Phones:** Assessor 781-826-6401; Treasurer 781-826-3571; Vital Records 781-826-2691.

Hanson Town

Town Clerk, Town Hall, 542 Liberty St., Hanson, MA 02341. 781-293-2772; Fax 781-294-0884.

Will search UCC records. Tax liens not included in UCC search. Real estate records located in Plymouth County. **Other Phone Numbers:** Assessor 781-293-5259; Treasurer 781-293-2422; Appraiser/Auditor 781-293-5259; Elections 781-293-2772; Vital Records 781-293-2772.

Hardwick Town

Town Clerk, PO Box 575, Gilbertville, MA 01031-0575. 413-477-6197; Fax 413-477-6703.

Will search UCC records. UCC search includes tax liens if requested. Real estate records located in Worcester County. **Other Phone Numbers:** Assessor 413-477-6197 x102; Treasurer 413-477-6197 x105.

Harvard Town

Town Clerk, Town Hall, 13 Ayer Rd., Harvard, MA 01451-1458. 978-456-4100 UCC Recording: 978-456-4100 extention 16; Fax 978-456-4113. www.harvard.ma.us/townclerk.htm

The Village of Still River is in the Town of Harvard. UCC records are filed with the Town/City Clerk, real estate records are at the county level with the Register of Deeds. Will search UCC records. UCC search includes tax liens. Real estate records located in Worcester County. **Other Phone Numbers:** Assessor 978-456-4100; Treasurer 978-456-4100; Elections 978-456-4100 x16; Vital Records 978-456-4100 x16.

Harwich Town

Town Clerk, 732 Main St, Harwich, MA 02645-2717. Town Clerk, R/E and UCC Recording 508-430-7516; Fax 508-432-5039.

Will search UCC records. This agency will not do a tax lien search. Real estate records located in Barnstable County. **Other Phone Numbers:** Assessor 508-430-7503; Treasurer 508-430-7501; Appraiser/Auditor 508-430-7503; Elections 508-430-7516; Vital Records 508-430-7516; Board of Selectmen 508-430-7513.

Hatfield Town

Town Clerk, 59 Main St, Hatfield, MA 01038-9702. 413-247-0492; Fax 413-347-5029.

Will search UCC records. UCC search includes tax liens. Real estate records located in Hampshire County. **Other Phone Numbers:** Assessor 413-247-0322.

Haverhill City

City Clerk, 4 Summer St, City Hall, Room 118, Haverhill, MA 01830-5880. 978-374-2312; Fax 978-373-8490.

Will search UCC records. UCC search includes tax liens if requested. Real estate records located in Essex County. **Other Phone Numbers:** Assessor 978-347-2316; Treasurer 978-374-2320; Elections 978-374-2312; Vital Records 978-374-2312.

Hawley Town

Town Clerk, Town Hall, Hawley, MA 01339. 413-339-5518; Fax 413-339-4959.

Will search UCC records. This agency will not do a tax lien search. Real estate records located in Franklin County. **Other Phone Numbers:** Assessor 413-339-5518; Treasurer 413-339-4231; Elections 413-339-5531; Vital Records 413-339-5531.

Heath Town

Town Clerk, Town Hall, 1 E. Main St., Heath, MA 01346. 413-337-4934; Fax 413-337-8542.

Will search UCC records. Tax liens included in UCC search if requested. Real estate records located in Franklin County. **Other Phone Numbers:** Assessor 413-337-4934; Treasurer 413-337-4934.

Hingham Town

Town Clerk, 210 Central St, Hingham, MA 02043. 781-741-1410; Fax 781-740-0239.

Will search UCC records. This agency will not do a tax lien search. Real estate records located in Plymouth County. **Online Access:** Property Assessor Records. Search the property rolls for free at www.hingham-ma.com/html/assessment_data.html. Click on "Click here to view data.". **Other Phone Numbers:** Assessor

781-741-1455; Treasurer 781-741-1408; Appraiser/Auditor 781-741-1455; Elections 781-741-1410; Vital Records 781-741-1410.

Hinsdale Town

Town Clerk, Town Hall, PO Box 803, Hinsdale, MA 01235. 413-655-2301 R/E Recording: 413-443-7438; Fax 413-655-8807.
Will search UCC records. Tax liens included in UCC search if requested. Real estate records located in Berkshire County. **Other Phone Numbers:** Assessor 413-655-2300; Treasurer 413-655-2306; Appraiser/Auditor 413-655-2300; Elections 413-655-2301; Vital Records 413-655-2301.

Holbrook Town

Town Clerk, Town Hall, Holbrook, MA 02343-1502. 781-767-4314; Fax 781-767-0705.
Will search UCC records. This agency will not do a tax lien search. Real estate records located in Norfolk County. **Other Phone Numbers:** Assessor 781-767-4315; Treasurer 781-767-4316; Elections 781-767-4314; Vital Records 781-767-4314.

Holden Town

Town Clerk, 1196 Main St, Town Hall, Holden, MA 01520-1092. 508-829-0265; Fax 508-829-0252.
Will search UCC records. Tax liens included in UCC search if requested. Real estate records located in Worcester County. **Online Access:** Real Estate, Property Tax Records. Search the Town assessor's data free at http://data.visionappraisal.com/HOLDENMA. Registration is required; sign-up is free. **Other Phones:** Assessor 508-829-0223; Treasurer 508-829-0235.

Holland Town

Town Clerk, 27 Sturbridge Rd, Holland, MA 01521-9712. 413-245-7108; Fax 413-245-7037.
Will search UCC records. This agency will not do a tax lien search. Real estate records located in Hampden County.

Holliston Town

Town Clerk, 703 Washington St, Holliston, MA 01746. 508-429-0601; Fax 508-429-0684. www.holliston.ma.us
Will search UCC records. UCC search includes tax liens. Real estate records located in Middlesex County. **Other Phone Numbers:** Assessor 508-429-0604; Treasurer 508-429-0602; Vital Records 508-429-0601.

Holyoke City

City Clerk, City Hall, Holyoke, MA 01040. 413-534-2166; Fax 413-534-2322. www.ci.holyoke.ma.us
Will search UCC records. UCC search includes tax liens if requested. Real estate records located in Hampden County. **Online Access:** Tax Assessor Records. Access to property valuations on the tax accessor database are available free at www.ci.holyoke.ma.us/Assesment.asp. No name searching. **Other Phone Numbers:** Assessor 413-534-2180; Treasurer 413-534-2153; Appraiser/Auditor 413-534-2166; Elections 413-534-2166.

Hopedale Town

Town Clerk, PO Box 7, Hopedale, MA 01747. 508-634-2211; Fax 508-634-2200.
Will search UCC records. UCC search includes tax liens if requested. Real estate records located in Worcester County. **Other Phones:** Assessor 508-634-2201; Treasurer 508-634-2203; Elections 634-2211.

Hopkinton Town

Town Clerk, 18 Main St, Hopkinton, MA 01748-1260. 508-497-9710; Fax 508-497-9702.
Will search UCC records. Tax liens not included in UCC search. Real estate records located in Middlesex

County. **Other Phone Numbers:** Assessor 508-497-9720.

Hubbardston Town

Town Clerk, PO Box H, Hubbardston, MA 01452. 978-928-5244; Fax 978-928-1402.
Will search UCC records. Tax liens not included in UCC search. Real estate records located in Worcester County. **Other Phone Numbers:** Assessor 978-928-1400; Treasurer 978-928-1401; Elections 978-928-5244; Vital Records 978-928-5244.

Hudson Town

Town Clerk, 78 Main St, Town Hall, Hudson, MA 01749. 978-568-9615.
Will search UCC records. UCC search includes tax liens. Real estate records located in Middlesex County. **Other Phone Numbers:** Assessor 978-568-9620; Treasurer 978-568-9605; Elections 978-568-9615; Vital Records 978-568-9615.

Hull Town

Town Clerk, Town Hall, Hull, MA 02045. 781-925-2262; Fax 781-925-0224.
Will search UCC records. Tax liens not included in UCC search. Real estate records located in Plymouth County. **Other Phones:** Assessor 781-925-2205.

Huntington Town

Town Clerk, Office of Town Clerk, 50 Searle Rd., Huntington, MA 01050. 413-667-3186; Fax 413-667-3507.
Will search UCC records. UCC search includes tax liens if requested. Real estate records located in Hampshire County. **Other Phone Numbers:** Assessor 413-667-3501; Treasurer 413-667-3500.

Ipswich Town

Town Clerk, 25 Green St, 30 S. Main St., Ipswich, MA 01938-2357. 978-356-6600; Fax 978-356-6616.
Will search UCC records. Tax liens not included in UCC search. Real estate records located in Essex County. **Other Phones:** Assessor 978-356-6603; Treasurer 978-356-6601; Elections 978-356-6600.

Kingston Town

Town Clerk, PO Drawer E, Kingston, MA 02364. 781-585-0502; Fax 781-585-0542.
Will search UCC records. Real estate records located in Plymouth County. **Other Phone Numbers:** Assessor 781-585-0509; Treasurer 781-585-0508; Elections 781-585-0502; Vital Records 781-585-0502.

Lakeville Town

Town Clerk, 346 Bedford St, Lakeville, MA 02347. 508-946-8814; Fax 508-946-0112.
Will search UCC records. UCC search includes tax liens if requested. Real estate records located in Plymouth County. **Other Phone Numbers:** Assessor 508-947-4428; Treasurer 508-946-8801; Appraiser/Auditor 508-947-4428.

Lancaster Town

Town Clerk, Town Hall, Box 97, 695 Main St., Lancaster, MA 01523-0097. 978-365-2542 R/E Recording: 978-365-9562; Fax 978-368-4005.
Will search UCC records. This agency will not do a tax lien search. Real estate records located in Worcester County. **Other Phone Numbers:** Assessor 978-365-9562; Treasurer 978-365-6115; Appraiser/Auditor 978-365-9562; Elections 978-365-2542; Vital Records 978-365-2542.

Lanesborough Town

Town Clerk, PO Box 1492, Lanesborough, MA 01237. 413-442-1351; Fax 413-443-5811.

Will search UCC records. UCC search includes tax liens if requested. Real estate records located in Berkshire County. **Other Phone Numbers:** Assessor 413-442-8622; Treasurer 413-442-1167; Elections 413-442-1351; Vital Records 413-442-1351.

Lawrence City

City Clerk, 200 Common St, Lawrence, MA 01840. 978-794-5803 R/E Recording: 978-683-2745; Fax 978-557-0285. www.cityoflawrence.com/Departments.asp
Will search UCC records. This agency will not do a tax lien search. Real estate records located in Essex County. **Online Access:** land, Grantor/Grantee, Recording Records. Search the county recorder database for free at www.lawrencedeeds.com/dsSearch.asp. **Other Phone Numbers:** Assessor 978-794-5790; Treasurer 978-794-5843; Elections 794-5807; Vital Records 794-5803.

Lee Town

Town Clerk, Town Hall, 32 Main St., Lee, MA 01238. 413-243-5505; Fax 413-243-5507.
Will search UCC records. UCC search includes tax liens. Real estate records located in Berkshire County. **Other Phone Numbers:** Assessor 413-243-5512; Treasurer 413-243-5506; Elections 413-243-5505; Vital Records 413-243-5505.

Leicester Town

Town Clerk, 3 Washburn Square, Leicester, MA 01524. 508-892-7011; Fax 508-892-7070.
Will search UCC records. Tax liens included in UCC search if requested. Real estate records located in Worcester County. **Other Phone Numbers:** Assessor 508-892-7001; Treasurer 508-892-7002.

Lenox Town

Town Clerk, 6 Walker St, Town Hall, Lenox, MA 01240-2718. 413-637-5506; Fax 413-637-5518.
Will search UCC records. This agency will not do a tax lien search. Real estate records located in Berkshire County. **Other Phone Numbers:** Assessor 413-637-5502; Treasurer 413-637-5506; Elections 413-637-5506; Vital Records 413-637-5506.

Leominster City

City Clerk, 25 West St, Leominster, MA 01453. 978-534-7536; Fax 978-534-7546.
Will search UCC records. UCC search includes tax liens if requested. Real estate records located in Worcester County. **Online Access:** Assessor Records. Search the assessor's database at http://data.visionappraisal.com/leominsterma. Free registration for full data. **Other Phone Numbers:** Assessor 978-534-7531.

Leverett Town

Town Clerk, PO Box 178, Leverett, MA 01054. 413-548-9150 R/E Recording: 413-548-9699; Fax 413-548-9150.
Will search UCC records. This agency will not do a tax lien search. Real estate records located in Franklin County. **Other Phones:** Assessor 413-548-4945.

Lexington Town

Town Clerk, 1625 Massachusetts Ave, Town Office Building, Lexington, MA 02420. 781-862-0500 x270; Fax 781-861-2754.
Will search UCC records. Tax liens not included in UCC search. Real estate records located in Middlesex County. **Other Phone Numbers:** Assessor 781-862-0500 x203.

Leyden Town

Town Clerk, Town Hall, Leyden, MA 01337. 413-774-7769; Fax 413-772-0146.
Will search UCC records. UCC search includes tax liens if requested. Real estate records located in Franklin

County. **Other Phone Numbers:** Assessor 413-774-4111; Treasurer 413-774-4111; Elections 413-774-7769; Vital Records 413-774-7769.

Lincoln Town

Town Clerk, PO Box 6353, Lincoln Center, MA 01773-6353. 781-259-2607; Fax 781-259-1677. www.state.ma.us/cc/lincoln.html
Will search UCC records. This agency will not do a tax lien search. Real estate records located in Middlesex County. **Other Phone Numbers:** Assessor 781-259-2611; Treasurer 781-259-2606; Elections 781-259-2607; Vital Records 781-259-2607.

Littleton Town

Town Clerk, PO Box 1305, Littleton, MA 01460. 978-952-2314; Fax 978-952-2321. www.littletonma.org
Will search UCC records. UCC search includes tax liens if requested. Real estate records located in Middlesex County. **Other Phone Numbers:** Assessor 978-952-2309; Treasurer 978-952-2306; Elections 978-952-2314; Vital Records 978-952-2314.

Longmeadow Town

Town Clerk, Town Hall, 20 Williams St, Longmeadow, MA 01106. 413-567-1066; Fax 413-565-4112. www.longmeadow.org
Will search UCC records. UCC search includes tax liens. Real estate records located in Hampden County. **Online Access:** Assessor Records. Access to tax records is available free at http://data.visionappraisal.com/LONGMEADOWMA. Free registration for full data. **Other Phone Numbers:** Assessor 413-565-4115; Treasurer 413-567-1066; Elections 413-567-1066; Vital Records 413-567-1066.

Lowell City

City Clerk, City Hall, 375 Merrimack St, Lowell, MA 01852. 978-970-4161 R/E Recording: 978-970-4224 UCC Recording: 978-970-4159; Fax 978-970-4162.
Will search UCC records. UCC search includes tax liens if requested. Real estate records located in Middlesex County. **Online Access:** Assessor Records. Search the Assessor's database at http://data.visionappraisal.com/LowellMA. Free registration for full data. **Other Phone Numbers:** Assessor 978-970-4200; Treasurer 978-970-4224; Appraiser/Auditor 978-970-4200; Elections 978-970-4046; Vital Records 978-970-4161.

Ludlow Town

Town Clerk, 488 Chapin St, Ludlow, MA 01056. 413-583-5610 R/E Recording: 413-583-5608; Fax 413-583-5603.
Will search UCC records. Tax liens included in UCC search if requested. Real estate records located in Hampden County. **Other Phone Numbers:** Assessor 413-583-5608; Treasurer 413-583-5616; Elections 413-583-5610; Vital Records 413-583-5610.

Lunenburg Town

Town Clerk, PO Box 135, Lunenburg, MA 01462. 978-582-4131; Fax 978-582-4148.
Will search UCC records. Tax liens not included in UCC search. Real estate records located in Worcester County. **Other Phone Numbers:** Assessor 978-582-4145; Treasurer 978-582-4130; Elections 978-582-4132; Vital Records 978-582-4131.

Lynn City

City Clerk, 3 City Hall Square, Lynn, MA 01901. 781-598-4000; Fax 781-477-7032.
Will search UCC records. Tax liens at Tax Collector's Office. Real estate records located in Essex County. **Other Phone Numbers:** Assessor 781-598-4000.

Lynnfield Town

Town Clerk, 55 Summer St, Lynnfield, MA 01940-1823. 781-334-3128; Fax 781-334-0014.
Will search UCC records. Tax liens included in UCC search if requested. Real estate records located in Essex County. **Other Phone Numbers:** Assessor 781-334-2231; Treasurer 781-334-7663; Elections 781-334-3128; Vital Records 781-334-3128.

Malden City

City Clerk, 200 Pleasant St, City Hall, Malden, MA 02148. 781-397-7116; Fax 781-388-0610.
Will search UCC records. Tax liens not included in UCC search. Real estate records located in Middlesex County. **Other Phones:** Assessor 781-397-7100.

Manchester-by-the-Sea Town

Town Clerk, Town Hall, 10 Central St, Manchester-by-the-Sea, MA 01944-1399. 978-526-2040; Fax 978-526-2001. www.manchester.ma.us
Will search UCC records. This agency will not do a tax lien search. Real estate records located in Essex County. **Online Access:** Property Assessor Records. Search the property assessment data at www.patriotproperties.com/manchester. **Other Phone Numbers:** Assessor 978-526-2010; Treasurer 978-526-2030; Elections 978-526-2040; Vital Records 978-526-2040.

Mansfield Town

Town Clerk, Town Hall, 6 Park Row, Mansfield, MA 02048-2433. 508-261-7345; Fax 508-261-1083.
Will search UCC records. UCC search includes tax liens. Real estate records located in Bristol County. **Other Phone Numbers:** Assessor 508-261-7350; Treasurer 508-261-7340; Appraiser/Auditor 508-261-7350; Elections 508-261-7345; Vital Records 508-261-7345.

Marblehead Town

Town Clerk, Abbot Hall, Marblehead, MA 01945. 781-631-0528; Fax 781-631-8571.
Will search UCC records. This agency will not do a tax lien search. Real estate records located in Essex County. **Other Phone Numbers:** Assessor 781-631-0236; Treasurer 781-631-1033.

Marion Town

Town Clerk, 2 Spring St, Marion, MA 02738. 508-748-3502; Fax 508-748-2845. www.townofmarion.org
Will search UCC records. Tax liens included in UCC search if requested. Real estate records located in Plymouth County. **Other Phone Numbers:** Assessor 508-748-3510; Treasurer 508-748-3505.

Marlborough City

City Clerk, 140 Main St, Marlborough, MA 01752-3812. 508-460-3775; Fax 508-624-6504.
Will search UCC records. This agency will not do a tax lien search. Real estate records located in Middlesex County. **Other Phone Numbers:** Assessor 508-460-3779; Treasurer 508-460-3730; Appraiser/Auditor 508-460-3779; Elections 508-460-3775; Vital Records 508-460-3775.

Marshfield Town

Town Clerk, Town Hall, Marshfield, MA 02050. 781-834-5540; Fax 781-837-7163.
Will search UCC records. UCC search includes tax liens. Real estate records located in Plymouth County. **Other Phone Numbers:** Assessor 781-834-5585; Treasurer 781-834-5545; Elections 781-834-5540; Vital Records 781-834-5540.

Mashpee Town

Town Clerk, Town Hall, 16 Great Neck Rd. N., Mashpee, MA 02649. 508-539-1400 x561 R/E Recording: 508-539-1400 x537; Fax 508-539-1403. www.ci.mashpee.ma.us
Will search UCC records. UCC search includes tax liens if requested. Real estate records located in Barnstable County. **Online Access:** Assessor Records. Records on the Town of Mashpee Assessor database are available free online at www.capecode.com/mashpee/search.asp. **Other Phone Numbers:** Assessor 508-539-1400 x529; Treasurer 508-539-1400 x537; Appraiser/Auditor 508-539-1400 x529; Elections 508-539-1400 x561; Vital Records 508-539-1400 x561.

Mattapoisett Town

Town Clerk, PO Box 89, Mattapoisett, MA 02739-0089. 508-758-4103; Fax 508-758-3030. www.mattapoisett.net
Will search UCC records. Tax liens included in UCC search if requested. Real estate records located in Plymouth County. **Other Phone Numbers:** Assessor 508-758-4106; Treasurer 508-758-4108; Elections 508-758-4103; Vital Records 508-758-4103.

Maynard Town

Town Clerk, 195 Main St, Town Hall, Maynard, MA 01754-2575. 978-897-1000 R/E Recording: 978-897-1005; Fax 978-897-8457.
Will search UCC records. Tax liens not included in UCC search. Real estate records located in Middlesex County. **Other Phones:** Assessor 978-897-1004; Treasurer 978-897-1005; Appraiser/Auditor 978-897-1007; Elections 978-897-1000; Vital Records 978-897-1000.

Medfield Town

Town Clerk, Town Hall, 459 Main St., Medfield, MA 02052. 508-359-8505 R/E Recording: 508-359-8505 x630; Fax 508-359-6182. www.town.medfield.net
Will search UCC records. UCC search includes tax liens if requested. Real estate records located in Norfolk County. **Other Phones:** Treasurer 508-359-8505 X625.

Medford City

City Clerk, 85 George P. Hassett Drive, City Clerk, Medford, MA 02155. 781-393-2425; Fax 781-391-1895. www.medford.org
Will search UCC records. This agency will not do a tax lien search. Real estate records located in Middlesex County. **Online Access:** Property Assessor Records. Seach the city assessor database at http://data.visionappraisal.com/MedfordMA. Free registration for full data. **Other Phone Numbers:** Assessor 781-393-2435; Treasurer 781-393-2550; Elections 781-393-2491; Vital Records 781-393-2425.

Medway Town

Town Clerk, 155 Village St., Medway, MA 02053. 508-533-3204; Fax 508-533-3287.
Will search UCC records. UCC searchdoes not include tax liens. Real estate records located in Norfolk County. **Other Phone Numbers:** Assessor 508-533-3203; Treasurer 508-533-3205.

Melrose City

City Clerk, PO Box C, Melrose, MA 02176. 781-797-4114; Fax 781-65-6877. www.cityofmelrose.org
Will search UCC records. This agency will not do a tax lien search. Real estate records located in Middlesex County. **Other Phone Numbers:** Assessor 781-979-4104; Treasurer 781-979-4160; Elections 781-979-4125; Vital Records 781-979-4114.

Mendon Town

Town Clerk, PO Box 54, Mendon, MA 01756-0054. 508-473-1085; Fax 508-478-8241. www.mendonma.net
Will search UCC records. UCC search includes tax liens if requested. Real estate records located in Worcester County. **Other Phone Numbers:** Assessor 508-473-2738; Treasurer 508-473-6410; Elections 508-473-1085; Vital Records 508-473-1085.

Merrimac Town

Town Clerk, 2 School St, Merrimac, MA 01860. 978-346-8013; Fax 978-346-0522.
Will search UCC records. UCC search includes tax liens if requested. Real estate records located in Essex County. **Other Phone Numbers:** Assessor 978-346-9022.

Methuen City

City Clerk, 41 Pleasant St., Room 112, Methuen, MA 01844. 978-794-3213 R/E Recording: 978-794-3219; Fax 978-794-7509. www.ci.methuen.ma.us
Will search UCC records. UCC search includes tax liens if requested. Real estate records located in Essex County at Northern Essex Register of Deeds, Lawrence, MA. **Online Access:** Property Assessor, Land, Grantor/Grantee, Recording Records. Search the property assessment data free at http://host229.ci.methuen.ma.us. Also, search the county recorder database for free at www.lawrencedeeds.com/dsSearch.asp. **Other Phone Numbers:** Assessor 978-794-3219; Treasurer 978-794-3205; Appraiser/Auditor 978-794-3220; Elections 978-794-3213; Vital Records 978-794-3213.

Middleborough Town

Town Clerk, 20 Centre St., 1st Floor, Middleborough, MA 02346. 508-946-2415 R/E Recording: 508-946-2410; Fax 508-946-2308.
Will search UCC records. This agency will not do a tax lien search. Real estate records located in Plymouth County. **Other Phone Numbers:** Assessor 508-946-2410; Treasurer 508-946-2411; Appraiser/Auditor 508-946-2410; Elections 508-946-2415; Vital Records 508-946-2415.

Middlefield Town

Town Clerk, PO Box 265, Middlefield, MA 01243. Town Clerk, R/E and UCC Recording 413-623-8966; Fax 413-623-6108.
Will search UCC records. This agency will not do a tax lien search. Real estate records located in Hampshire County. **Other Phone Numbers:** Assessor 413-623-8966; Treasurer 413-623-8966; Appraiser/Auditor 413-623-8966; Elections 413-623-8966.

Middlesex County (Northern District)

County Register of Deeds, 360 Gorham St, Lowell, MA 01852. 978-322-9000; Fax 978-322-9001. www.lowelldeeds.com
This agency will not perform searches. **Online Access:** Real Estate, Lien, Grantor/Grantee Records. The Telesearch subscription online system with North District records has been replaced with free internet access at http://216.60.44.25/MA25017/namesearch.jsp or the main web site. **Other Phone Numbers:** Assessor 978-970-4200.

Middlesex County (Southern District)

County Register of Deeds, 208 Cambridge St, Cambridge, MA 02141. 617-679-6300; Fax 617-494-9083.
This agency will not perform searches. **Online Access:** Real Estate, Lien Records. Access to the LandTrack online system with Southern District records requires a $100 annual fee, plus $.50 per minute of use. Lending agency information is available as is a fax back service for documents. No new customers are being accepted and the system will be replaced by free web access late 2002.

Middleton Town

Town Clerk, Memorial Hall, Middleton, MA 01949. 978-774-6927.
Will search UCC records. This agency will not do a tax lien search. Real estate records located in Essex County. **Other Phone Numbers:** Assessor 978-774-2099; Treasurer 978-774-8327; Elections 978-774-6927; Vital Records 978-774-6927.

Milford Town

Town Clerk, 52 Main St, Milford, MA 01757. 508-634-2307; Fax 508-634-2324.
Will search UCC records. UCC search includes tax liens if requested. Real estate records located in Worcester County. **Other Phone Numbers:** Assessor 508-634-2306.

Millbury Town

Town Clerk, 127 Elm St, Municipal Office Building, Millbury, MA 01527. 508-865-9110 R/E Recording: 508-865-9121.
Will search UCC records. UCC search includes tax liens. Real estate records located in Worcester County. **Other Phone Numbers:** Assessor 508-865-4732; Treasurer 508-865-8040; Elections 508-865-9110; Vital Records 508-865-9110.

Millis Town

Town Clerk, PO Box 181, Millis, MA 02054. 508-376-7046; Fax 508-376-7053.
Will search UCC records. This agency will not do a tax lien search. Real estate records located in Norfolk County. **Other Phones:** Assessor 508-376-7049.

Millville Town

Town Clerk, PO Box 703, Millville, MA 01529-0703. 508-883-5849; Fax 508-883-2994.
Will search UCC records. UCC search includes tax liens if requested. Real estate records located in Worcester County. **Other Phone Numbers:** Assessor 508-883-5031; Treasurer 508-883-7449; Elections 508-883-5849; Vital Records 508-883-5849.

Milton Town

Town Clerk, 525 Canton Ave, Town Hall, Milton, MA 02186. 617-696-5414.
Will search UCC records. Tax liens included in UCC search if requested. Real estate records located in Norfolk County. **Other Phone Numbers:** Assessor 617-696-5703; Treasurer 617-696-5409.

Monroe Town

Town Clerk, PO Box 6, Monroe, MA 01350. Town Clerk, R/E and UCC Recording 413-424-5272; Fax 413-424-5272.
Will search UCC records. Tax liens included in UCC search if requested. Real estate records located in Franklin County. **Other Phone Numbers:** Assessor 413-424-5272; Treasurer 413-424-5272.

Monson Town

Town Clerk, 110 Main St. #4, Monson, MA 01057-1332. 413-267-4115; Fax 413-267-3726.
Will search UCC records. UCC search includes tax liens if requested. Real estate records located in Hampden County. **Other Phone Numbers:** Assessor 413-267-4120; Treasurer 413-267-4125; Appraiser/Auditor 413-267-4120; Elections 413-267-4115; Vital Records 413-267-4115.

Montague Town

Town Clerk, 1 Avenue A, Turners Falls, MA 01376-1128. 413-863-3211; Fax 413-863-3224.
Will search UCC records. Tax liens included in UCC search if requested. Real estate records located in Franklin County. **Other Phone Numbers:** Assessor 413-863-4654; Treasurer 413-863-3207; Elections 413-863-3211; Vital Records 413-863-3211.

Monterey Town

Town Clerk, Town Hall, Monterey, MA 01245. 413-528-5175; Fax 413-528-9452.
Will search UCC records. Tax liens included in UCC search if requested. Real estate records located in Berkshire County. **Other Phone Numbers:** Assessor 413-528-6481; Treasurer 413-528-1443; Elections 413-528-5175; Vital Records 413-528-5175.

Montgomery Town

Town Clerk, Town Hall, Montgomery, MA 01085. 413-862-4478; Fax 413-862-3204.
Will search UCC records. This agency will not do a tax lien search. Real estate records located in Hampden County. **Other Phone Numbers:** Assessor 413-862-3386; Treasurer 413-862-3386.

Mt. Washington Town

Town Clerk, 118 East St., Mt. Washington, MA 01258. 413-528-2839; Fax 413-528-2839.
Will search UCC records. This agency will not do a tax lien search. Real estate records located in Berkshire County. **Other Phone Numbers:** Assessor 413-528-2839; Treasurer 413-528-2839; Elections 413-528-2839; Vital Records 413-528-2839.

Nahant Town

Town Clerk, Town Hall, Nahant, MA 01908-0075. 781-581-0018; Fax 781-593-0340.
Will search UCC records. UCC search includes tax liens. Real estate records located in Essex County. **Other Phone Numbers:** Assessor 781-581-0212; Treasurer 781-581-0018; Appraiser/Auditor 781-581-0212; Elections 781-581-0018; Town Accountant 781-581-0099.

Nantucket County

County Register of Deeds, 16 Broad St, Nantucket, MA 02554. 508-228-7250; Fax 508-325-5331. www.nantucketdeeds.com
Will not search UCC records, but only real estate related UCC filed here. This agency will not do a tax lien search. Will not search real estate records. **Other Phone Numbers:** Assessor 508-228-7211; Treasurer 508-228-7265; Elections 508-228-7217; Vital Records 508-228-7217.

Nantucket Town

Town Clerk, Town & County Building, 16 Broad St, Nantucket, MA 02554. 508-228-7217 R/E Recording: 508-228-7250; Fax 508-325-5313. www.town.nantucket.ma.us
Will search UCC records. UCC search includes tax liens if requested. Real estate records located in Nantucket County. **Other Phone Numbers:** Assessor 508-228-7211; Treasurer 508-325-5314; Elections 508-228-7217; Vital Records 508-228-7255; 508-228-7255.

Natick Town

Town Clerk, 13 E. Central St, Natick, MA 01760. 508-647-6400 UCC Recording: 508-647-6430.
Will search UCC records. UCC search includes tax liens. Real estate records located in Middlesex County. **Online Access:** Assessor, Property Records. Search town assessments free at www.natickma.org/assess/cama.asp. **Other Phone Numbers:** Assessor 508-647-6420; Treasurer 508-647-6425;

Appraiser/Auditor 508-647-6420; Elections 508-647-6430; Vital Records 508-647-6430.

Needham Town

Town Clerk, PO Box 663, Needham, MA 02192. 781-455-7510; Fax 781-449-4569. www.town.needham.ma.us
Will search UCC records. This agency will not do a tax lien search. Real estate records located in Norfolk County. **Other Phone Numbers:** Assessor 781-455-7507; Treasurer 781-455-7504; Appraiser/Auditor 781-455-7507; Elections 781-455-7501; Vital Records 781-455-7501.

New Ashford Town

Town Clerk, 142 Beach Hill Road, New Ashford, MA 01237. 413-458-5461; Fax 413-458-5461.
Will search UCC records. UCC search includes tax liens if requested. Real estate records located in Berkshire County. **Other Phone Numbers:** Assessor 413-743-9154.

New Bedford City

City Clerk, 133 William St, New Bedford, MA 02740. 508-979-1450; Fax 508-991-6225. www.ci.new-bedford.ma.us/Nav3.htm
Will search UCC records. Tax liens not included in UCC search. Real estate records located in Bristol County. **Online Access:** Property, Assessor Records. Access to the assessor's proeprty database is available free at www.ci.new-bedford.ma.us/Assessors/RealPropertyLookup.htm. **Other Phone Numbers:** Assessor 508-979-1440; Treasurer 508-979-1430.

New Braintree Town

Town Clerk, 20 Memorial Dr Rm 5, New Braintree, MA 01531. 508-867-4952; Fax 508-867-6316.
Will not search UCC records. Real estate records located in Worcester County. **Other Phone Numbers:** Assessor 508-867-4467; Treasurer 508-867-2581.

New Marlborough Town

Town Clerk, PO Box 99, Mill River, MA 01244. 413-229-8116; Fax 413-229-6674.
Will search UCC records. This agency will not do a tax lien search. Real estate records located in Berkshire County. **Other Phones:** Assessor 413-229-8926; Treasurer 413-229-8963; Vital Records 413-229-8116.

New Salem Town

Town Clerk, Town Hall, 15 S. Main St., New Salem, MA 01355. 978-544-2731; Fax 978-544-5775.
Will search UCC records. Tax liens included in UCC search if requested. Real estate records located in Franklin County.

Newbury Town

Town Clerk, 25 High Road, Newbury, MA 01951-4799. 978-462-2332; Fax 978-465-3064.
Will search UCC records. UCC search includes tax liens if requested. Real estate records located in Essex County. **Other Phone Numbers:** Assessor 978-465-0211; Treasurer 978-465-0862.

Newburyport City

City Clerk, 60 Pleasant St, Newburyport, MA 01950. 978-465-4407; Fax 978-465-4452.
Will search UCC records. Real estate records located in Essex County. **Online Access:** Assessor Records. Search the city assessor database at http://data.visionappraisal.com/NewBURYPORTMA. Free registration for full data. **Other Phone Numbers:** Assessor 978-465-4403; Treasurer 978-465-4415; Elections 978-465-4407; Vital Records 978-465-4407.

Newton City

City Clerk, 1000 Commonwealth Ave, Newton Center, MA 02159. 617-552-7030; Fax 617-964-2333. www.ci.newton.ma.us
Will search UCC records. Tax liens included in UCC search if requested. Real estate records located in Middlesex County. **Online Access:** Assessor Records. Records on the City of Newton Fiscal 1998 Assessment database are available free at www.ci.newton.ma.us/GIS/Assessors/Default.asp. Data represents market value as of 1/1/1997. **Other Phone Numbers:** Assessor 617-552-7065; Treasurer 617-552-7080.

Norfolk County

County Register of Deeds, PO Box 69, Dedham, MA 02027-0069. County Register of Deeds, R/E and UCC Recording 781-461-6122; Fax 781-326-4742. www.norfolkdeeds.org
Will not search UCC records, but only real estate related UCC filed here. This agency will not do a tax lien search. Will not search real estate records. **Online Access:** Real Estate, Lien Records. Access to county online records requires a $25 set up fee, plus $1 fee for the first minute and $.50 per minute thereafter per session. The system is only accessible in Massachusetts. Lending agency information is available. For information, contact Pam at 781-461-6116.

Norfolk Town

Town Clerk, PO Box 216, Norfolk, MA 02056. 508-528-1400 R/E Recording: 781-461-6100 UCC Recording: 617-727-9180; Fax 508-520-3250.
Will search UCC records. Real estate records located in Norfolk County. **Other Phone Numbers:** Assessor 508-528-1120; Treasurer 508-528-0058; Vital Records 508-528-1400.

North Adams City

City Clerk, 10 Main St, North Adams, MA 01247. 413-662-3015 R/E Recording: 413-743-0035 North; 443-7438 Cent.; 528-0146 South.
Will search UCC records. UCC Form 11 must accompany a search request. Real estate records located in Berkshire County. **Other Phone Numbers:** Assessor 413-662-3012; Treasurer 413-662-3044; Elections 413-662-3015; Vital Records 413-662-3015.

North Andover Town

Town Clerk, 120 Main St, North Andover, MA 01845. 978-688-9501; Fax 978-688-9556. www.townofnorthandover.com
Will search UCC records. UCC search includes tax liens if requested. Real estate records located in Essex County. **Online Access:** Land, Grantor/Grantee, Recording Records. Search the county recorder database for free at www.lawrencedeeds.com/dsSearch.asp. **Other Phone Numbers:** Assessor 978-688-9565; Treasurer 978-688-9565; Elections 978-688-9501; Vital Records 978-688-9501.

North Attleborough Town

Town Clerk, PO Box 871, North Attleborough, MA 02761-0871. 508-699-0108 R/E Recording: 508-822-3081; Fax 508-699-2354.
Will search UCC records. UCC search includes tax liens if requested. Real estate records located in Bristol County. **Online Access:** Assessor Records. Search the town assessor database online at http://data.visionappraisal.com/NorthAttleboroMA. Free registration for full data. **Other Phone Numbers:** Assessor 508-699-0117; Treasurer 508-699-0114; Elections 508-699-0106; Vital Records 508-699-0108.

North Brookfield Town

Town Clerk, 185 No. Main St., North Brookfield, MA 01535. 508-867-0203; Fax 508-867-0249.

Will search UCC records. UCC search includes tax liens if requested. Real estate records located in Worcester County. **Other Phone Numbers:** Assessor 508-867-0209; Treasurer 508-867-0204; Elections 508-867-0203; Vital Records 508-867-0203.

North Reading Town

Town Clerk, 235 N. St, North Reading, MA 01864-1294. 978-664-6030 R/E Recording: 978-664-6021; Fax 978-664-6048.
Will search UCC records. This agency will not do a tax lien search. Real estate records located in Middlesex County. **Other Phone Numbers:** Assessor 978-664-6021; Treasurer 978-664-6019; Appraiser/Auditor 978-664-6021; Elections 978-664-6030; Vital Records 978-664-6030.

Northampton City

City Clerk, 210 Main St, Northampton, MA 01060. 413-587-1224; Fax 413-587-1264.
Will search UCC records. UCC search includes tax liens if requested. Real estate records located in Hampshire County. **Other Phone Numbers:** Assessor 413-587-1200; Treasurer 413-587-1297; Elections 413-587-1224; Vital Records 413-587-1224.

Northborough Town

Town Clerk, 63 Main St, Northborough, MA 01532-1994. 508-393-5001; Fax 508-393-6996.
Will search UCC records. UCC search includes tax liens if requested. Real estate records located in Worcester County. **Other Phone Numbers:** Assessor 508-393-5005; Treasurer 508-393-5045.

Northbridge Town

Town Clerk, Town Hall, 7 Main St., Whitinsville, MA 01588. 508-234-2001 R/E Recording: 508-234-5432; Fax 508-234-7640.
Will search UCC records. UCC search includes tax liens if requested. Real estate records located in Worcester County. **Other Phones:** Assessor 508-234-2740; Treasurer 508-234-5432; Appraiser/Auditor 508-234-2740; Elections 508-234-2001.

Northfield Town

Town Clerk, Town Hall, Northfield, MA 01360. 413-498-2901; Fax 413-498-5103.
Will search UCC records. Tax liens included in UCC search. Real estate records located in Franklin County. **Other Phone Numbers:** Assessor 413-498-2901; Treasurer 413-498-2901.

Norton Town

Town Clerk, 70 E. Main St, Town Hall, Norton, MA 02766. 508-285-0231; Fax 508-285-0297.
Will search UCC records. Tax liens included in UCC search if requested. Real estate records located in Bristol County. **Other Phones:** Assessor 508-285-0270; Treasurer 508-285-0223; Vital Records 508-285-0230.

Norwell Town

Town Clerk, PO Box 295, Norwell, MA 02061-0295. 781-659-8072 R/E Recording: 781-659-8014; Fax 781-659-7795.
Will search UCC records. Tax liens included in UCC search if requested. Real estate records located in Plymouth County. **Other Phone Numbers:** Assessor 781-659-8014; Treasurer 781-659-8070; Elections 781-659-8072; Vital Records 781-659-8072.

Norwood Town

Town Clerk, PO Box 40, Norwood, MA 02062. 781-762-1240 x193 UCC Recording: 781-762-1240; Fax 781-762-0954.
Will search UCC records. Tax liens included in UCC search if requested. Real estate records located in Norfolk County. **Other Phone Numbers:** Assessor

781-762-1240; Treasurer 781-762-1240; Elections 781-762-1240; Vital Records 781-762-1240.

Oak Bluffs Town

Town Clerk, PO Box 2490, Oak Bluffs, MA 02557-2490. 508-693-5515; Fax 508-696-7736.
Will search UCC records. Tax liens not included in UCC search. Real estate records located in Dukes County. **Online Access:** Assessor Records. Search the town assessor database at http://data.visionappraisal.com/OakBluffsMA. Free registration for full data. **Other Phone Numbers:** Assessor 508-693-5519; Treasurer 508-693-5514; Elections 508-693-5515; Vital Records 508-693-5515.

Oakham Town

Town Clerk, PO Box 222, Oakham, MA 01068-0222. 508-882-5549; Fax 508-882-3060.
Will search UCC records. This agency will not do a tax lien search. Real estate records located in Worcester County. **Other Phone Numbers:** Assessor 508-882-5549; Treasurer 508-882-5549.

Orange Town

Town Clerk, 6 Prospect St, Orange, MA 01364. 978-544-2254; Fax 978-544-1120.
Will search UCC records. This agency will not do a tax lien search. Real estate records located in Franklin County. **Other Phone Numbers:** Assessor 978-544-1108; Treasurer 978-544-1103; Elections 978-544-2254; Vital Records 978-544-2254.

Orleans Town

Town Clerk, 19 School Road, Orleans, MA 02653-3699. 508-240-3700 UCC Recording: 508-240-3700 x304; Fax 508-240-3388.
Will search UCC records. UCC search includes tax liens if requested. Real estate records located in Barnstable County. **Other Phone Numbers:** Assessor 508-240-3700 x331; Treasurer 508-240-3700 x323.

Otis Town

Town Clerk, PO Box 237, Otis, MA 01253. 413-269-0101; Fax 413-269-0111.
Will search UCC records. This agency will not do a tax lien search. Real estate records located in Berkshire County. **Other Phone Numbers:** Assessor 413-269-0102; Treasurer 413-269-0108; Elections 413-269-0101; Vital Records 413-269-0101.

Oxford Town

Town Clerk, 325 Main St, Oxford, MA 01540. 508-987-6032; Fax 508-987-6048. www.town.oxford.ma.us
Will search UCC records. Tax liens included in UCC search if requested. Real estate records located in Worcester County. **Online Access:** Property Assessor Records. Search the property assessments by street name for free at www.town.oxford.ma.us/Assessor/Assessor.htm. **Other Phone Numbers:** Assessor 508-987-6036; Treasurer 508-987-6038; Elections 508-987-6032; Vital Records 508-987-6032.

Palmer Town

Town Clerk, Palmer Town Building, Palmer, MA 01069-1198. 413-283-2608 R/E Recording: 413-283-2607; Fax 413-283-2637.
Will search UCC records. Real estate records located in Hampden County. **Other Phone Numbers:** Assessor 413-283-2607; Treasurer 413-283-2600; Elections 413-283-2608; Vital Records 413-283-2608.

Paxton Town

Town Clerk, 697 Pleasant St, Paxton, MA 01612. 508-799-7347 x13; Fax 508-797-0966.
Will search UCC records. UCC search includes tax liens if requested. Real estate records located in

Worcester County. **Other Phone Numbers:** Assessor 508-799-7231 x16.

Peabody City

City Clerk, 24 Lowell St, City Hall, Peabody, MA 01960. 978-538-5900 UCC Recording: 978-538-5753; Fax 978-538-5985. www.ci.peabody.ma.us
Will search UCC records. This agency will not do a tax lien search. Real estate records located in Essex County. **Other Phone Numbers:** Assessor 978-538-5729; Treasurer 978-538-5764; Appraiser/Auditor 978-538-5726; Elections 978-538-5750; Vital Records 978-538-5752 or 5751.

Pelham Town

Town Clerk, Rhodes Building, 351 Amherst Rd., Pelham, MA 01002-9753. 413-253-7129; Fax 413-256-1061.
Will search UCC records. UCC search includes tax liens if requested. Real estate records located in Hampshire County. **Other Phone Numbers:** Assessor 413-253-7129; Treasurer 413-253-2267; Elections 413-253-7129; Vital Records 413-253-7129.

Pembroke Town

Town Clerk, 100 Center St, Pembroke, MA 02359. 781-293-7211.
Will search UCC records. This agency will not do a tax lien search. Real estate records located in Plymouth County. **Other Phone Numbers:** Assessor 781-293-2393; Treasurer 781-293-3893; Appraiser/Auditor 781-293-2393; Elections 781-293-7211; Vital Records 781-293-7211; Town Administrator 781-293-3844.

Pepperell Town

Town Clerk, 1 Main St, Town Hall, Pepperell, MA 01463-1644. 978-433-0339; Fax 978-433-0338. www.town.pepperell.ma.us
Will search UCC records. UCC search includes tax liens if requested. Real estate records located in Middlesex County. **Other Phone Numbers:** Assessor 978-433-0322; Treasurer 978-433-0337; Elections 978-433-0339; Vital Records 978-433-0339.

Peru Town

Town Clerk, 4 North Rd, Peru, MA 01235-9803. 413-655-8326 UCC Recording: 413-655-8312; Fax 413-655-8312.
Will search UCC records. Tax liens not included in UCC search. Real estate records located in Berkshire County. **Other Phone Numbers:** Assessor 413-655-8312; Treasurer 413-655-8312; Elections 413-655-8326; Vital Records 413-655-8326.

Petersham Town

Town Clerk, PO Box 486, Petersham, MA 01366. 978-724-6649; Fax 978-724-3501.
Will search UCC records. This agency will not do a tax lien search. Real estate records located in Worcester County. **Other Phone Numbers:** Assessor 978-724-6658; Treasurer 978-724-8813; Elections 978-724-6649; Vital Records 978-724-6649.

Phillipston Town

Town Clerk, 50 The Common, Phillipston, MA 01331. 978-249-1733 R/E Recording: 978-249-1732; Fax 978-249-3356.
Will search UCC records. This agency will not do a tax lien search. Real estate records located in Worcester County. **Other Phone Numbers:** Assessor 978-249-1732; Treasurer 978-249-3415; Appraiser/Auditor 978-249-1732; Elections 978-249-1733; Vital Records 978-249-1733; General Town Hall 978-249-6828.

Pittsfield City

City Clerk, 70 Allen St, City Hall, Pittsfield, MA 01201. 413-499-9361; Fax 413-499-9363. www.pittsfield-ma.org
Will search UCC records. UCC search includes tax liens if requested. Real estate records located in Berkshire County. **Other Phone Numbers:** Assessor 413-499-9445; Treasurer 413-499-9466; Elections 413-499-9460; Vital Records 413-499-9361.

Plainfield Town

Town Clerk, 344 Main St, Plainfield, MA 01070. 413-634-5417; Fax 413-634-5683.
Will search UCC records. This agency will not do a tax lien search. Real estate records located in Hampshire County. **Other Phone Numbers:** Assessor 413-634-5420; Treasurer 413-634-5420; Elections 413-634-5417; Vital Records 413-634-5417.

Plainville Town

Town Clerk, PO Box 1717, Plainville, MA 02762. 508-695-3142 x20 R/E Recording: 508-695-3142 x14 UCC Recording: 508-695-3142 x19; Fax 508-695-1857.
Will search UCC records. Tax liens included in UCC search if requested. Real estate records located in Norfolk County. **Other Phone Numbers:** Assessor 508-695-3142 x14; Treasurer 508-695-3142 x17,18; Elections 508-695-3142 x19; Vital Records 508-695-3142 x19.

Plymouth County

County Register of Deeds, PO Box 3535, Plymouth, MA 02361. 508-830-9200; Fax 508-830-9280.
This agency will not perform searches. **Online Access:** Real Estate, Lien, Judgment Records. Access to Online Titleview for Plymouth County records requires a usage charge of $.60 per minute of use. Records date back to 1971. Lending agency information is available. A fax back service is $3 plus $1 per page in county, $5. plus $1 per page, outside. For information, call 508-830-9287.

Plymouth Town

Town Clerk, 11 Lincoln St, Plymouth, MA 02360-3386. 508-830-4050; Fax 508-830-4062.
Will search UCC records. UCC search includes tax liens if requested. Real estate records located in Plymouth County. **Other Phone Numbers:** Assessor 508-830-4020; Treasurer 508-830-4051; Elections 508-830-4050; Vital Records 508-830-4052.

Plympton Town

Town Clerk, PO Box 153, Plympton, MA 02367-0153. 781-585-3220; Fax 781-582-1505.
Will search UCC records. This agency will not do a tax lien search. Real estate records located in Plymouth County. **Other Phone Numbers:** Assessor 781-585-3227; Treasurer 781-585-0409.

Princeton Town

Town Clerk, 6 Town Hall Drive, Princeton, MA 01541-1137. 978-464-2103; Fax 978-464-2106. http://town.princeton.ma.us
Will search UCC records. Tax liens included in UCC search if requested. Real estate records located in Worcester County. **Other Phone Numbers:** Assessor 978-464-2104; Treasurer 978-464-2105; Elections 978-464-2103; Vital Records 978-464-2103; Switchboard 978-464-2100.

Provincetown Town

Town Clerk, 260 Commercial St, Provincetown, MA 02657. 508-487-7013; Fax 508-487-9560. www.provincetowngov.org
Will search UCC records. UCC search includes tax liens if requested. Real estate records located in

Barnstable County. **Online Access:** Assessor, Property Sales Records. Records on the Provincetown Assessor database are available free online at www.provincetowngov.org/assessor.html. **Other Phone Numbers:** Assessor 508-487-7017; Treasurer 508-487-7015; Elections 508-487-7013; Vital Records 508-487-7013.

Quincy City

City Clerk, 1305 Hancock St, City Hall, Quincy, MA 02169. 617-376-1136; Fax 617-376-1139.
Will search UCC records. UCC search includes tax liens. Real estate records located in Norfolk County. **Other Phone Numbers:** Assessor 617-376-1178.

Randolph Town

Town Clerk, 41 S. Main St., Randolph, MA 02368. 781-961-0900; Fax 781-961-0919.
Will search UCC records. This agency will not do a tax lien search. Real estate records located in Norfolk County. **Other Phone Numbers:** Assessor 781-961-0906; Treasurer 781-961-0934.

Raynham Town

Town Clerk, 53 Orchard St, Raynham, MA 02767-1320. 508-824-2700; Fax 508-823-1812.
Will search UCC records. This agency will not do a tax lien search. Real estate records located in Bristol County. **Other Phones:** Assessor 508-824-2704; Treasurer 508-824-2702; Vital Records 508-824-2701.

Reading Town

Town Clerk, 16 Lowell St, Reading, MA 01867. 781-942-9050 UCC Recording: 781-942-9049; Fax 781-942-9070. www.ci.reading.ma.us/depts.htm
Will search UCC records. Real estate records located in Middlesex County. **Online Access:** Assessor Records. Records on the Town of Reading Assessor database are available free online at www.ziplink.net/~reading1/assessor.htm. **Other Phone Numbers:** Assessor 781-942-9027; Treasurer 781-942-9032; Elections 781-942-9050; Vital Records 781-942-9048.

Rehoboth Town

Town Clerk, 148 Peck St, Rehoboth, MA 02769-3099. 508-252-6502; Fax 508-252-5342.
Will search UCC records. UCC search includes tax liens if requested. Real estate records located in Bristol County. **Other Phones:** Assessor 508-252-3352.

Revere City

City Clerk, 281 Broadway, City Hall, Revere, MA 02151-5087. 781-286-8160; Fax 781-286-8135.
Will search UCC records. Tax liens included in UCC search if requested. Real estate records located in Suffolk County. **Online Access:** Assessor Records. Search the town assessor database at http://data.visionappraisal.com/RevereMA. Free registration for full data. **Other Phone Numbers:** Assessor 781-286-8169; Treasurer 781-286-8136.

Richmond Town

Town Clerk, PO Box 81, Richmond, MA 01254. 413-698-3315; Fax 413-698-3272.
Will search UCC records. Real estate records located in Berkshire County. **Other Phones:** Treasurer 698-3355.

Rochester Town

Town Clerk, Town Hall, 1 Constitution Way, Rochester, MA 02770. 508-763-3871; Fax 508-763-4892.
Will search UCC records. Tax liens not included in UCC search. Real estate records located in Plymouth County.

Rockland Town

Town Clerk, 242 Union St, Rockland, MA 02370. 781-871-1892 R/E Recording: 781-871-0137.
Will search UCC records. This agency will not do a tax lien search. Real estate records located in Plymouth County. **Other Phones:** Assessor 781-871-0137; Treasurer 781-871-1895; Appraiser/Auditor 781-871-0137; Elections 871-1892; Vital Records 871-1892.

Rockport Town

Town Clerk, PO Box 429, Rockport, MA 01966. 978-546-6894; Fax 978-546-3562.
Will search UCC records. This agency will not do a tax lien search. Real estate records located in Essex County. **Other Phone Numbers:** Assessor 978-546-2011; Treasurer 978-546-6648.

Rowe Town

Town Clerk, Town Hall, Rowe, MA 01367. 413-339-5520; Fax 413-339-5316.
Will search UCC records. UCC search includes tax liens if requested. Real estate records located in Berkshire County. **Other Phone Numbers:** Assessor 413-339-5520; Treasurer 413-339-5520; Vital Records 413-339-4446.

Rowley Town

Town Clerk, PO Box 351, Rowley, MA 01969-0351. 978-948-2081; Fax 978-948-2162.
Will not search UCC records. This agency will not do a tax lien search. Real estate records located in Essex County. **Other Phone Numbers:** Assessor 978-948-2021; Treasurer 978-948-2631; Elections 978-948-2081; Vital Records 978-948-2081.

Royalston Town

Town Clerk, PO Box 118, Royalston, MA 01368-0118. 978-249-0493; Fax 978-575-0493.
Will search UCC records. This agency will not do a tax lien search. Real estate records located in Worcester County.

Russell Town

Town Clerk, Town Hall, Russell, MA 01071. 413-862-3265; Fax 413-862-3103.
Will search UCC records. This agency will not do a tax lien search. Real estate records located in Hampden County.

Rutland Town

Town Clerk, 250 Main St, Rutland, MA 01543. 508-886-4104; Fax 508-886-2929.
Will search UCC records. This agency will not do a tax lien search. Real estate records located in Worcester County. **Other Phone Numbers:** Assessor 508-886-4101; Treasurer 508-886-4103.

Salem City

City Clerk, City Hall, 93 Washington, Salem, MA 01970-3593. 978-745-9595; Fax 978-740-9209.
Will search UCC records. This agency will not do a tax lien search. Real estate records located in Essex County. **Other Phone Numbers:** Assessor 978-745-9595 x261.

Salisbury Town

Town Clerk, 5 Beach Rd, Salisbury, MA 01952. 978-462-7591; Fax 978-462-4176.
Will search UCC records. This agency will not do a tax lien search. Real estate records located in Essex County. **Other Phone Numbers:** Assessor 978-462-7591; Treasurer 978-465-0331; Vital Records 978-462-7591.

Sandisfield Town

Town Clerk, PO Box 163, Sandisfield, MA 01255. 413-258-4711 R/E Recording: 413-258-4701 UCC Recording: 413-258-4075; Fax 413-258-4225.

Will search UCC records. Tax liens not included in UCC search. **Other Phone Numbers:** Assessor 413-258-4701; Treasurer 413-258-8102; Appraiser/Auditor 413-258-4701; Elections 413-258-4075; Vital Records 413-258-4075; Selectmen 413-258-4711.

Sandwich Town

Town Clerk, 145 Main St, Sandwich, MA 02563. 508-888-0340; Fax 508-888-2497.
Will search UCC records. UCC search includes tax liens if requested. Real estate records located in Barnstable County. **Other Phone Numbers:** Assessor 508-888-0157; Treasurer 508-888-6508; Elections 508-888-0340; Vital Records 508-888-0340.

Saugus Town

Town Clerk, 298 Central St, Town Hall, Saugus, MA 01906. 781-231-4101; Fax 781-231-4109. www.saugus.net
Will search UCC records. This agency will not do a tax lien search. Real estate records located in Essex County. **Other Phone Numbers:** Assessor 781-231-4130; Treasurer 781-231-4135.

Savoy Town

Town Clerk, 720 Main Rd., Savoy, MA 01256. 413-743-3759; Fax 413-743-4292.
Will search UCC records. This agency will not do a tax lien search. Real estate records located in Berkshire County. **Other Phone Numbers:** Assessor 413-743-4290; Treasurer 413-743-4290; Elections 413-743-3759; Vital Records 413-743-3759.

Scituate Town

Town Clerk, Town Hall, 600 C. J. Cushing Way, Scituate, MA 02066. 781-545-8744; Fax 781-545-8704.
Will search UCC records. Real estate records located in Plymouth County. **Other Phone Numbers:** Assessor 781-545-8713.

Seekonk Town

Town Clerk, 100 Peck St, Seekonk, MA 02771. 508-336-2920; Fax 508-336-0764.
Will search UCC records. Tax liens included in UCC search. Real estate records located in Bristol County.

Sharon Town

Town Clerk, 90 S. Main St, Town Hall, Sharon, MA 02067. 781-784-1505; Fax 781-784-1503.
Will search UCC records. UCC search includes tax liens. Real estate records located in Norfolk County. **Other Phone Numbers:** Assessor 781-784-1507; Treasurer 781-784-1500; Elections 781-784-1505; Vital Records 781-784-1505.

Sheffield Town

Town Clerk, PO Box 175, Sheffield, MA 01257. 413-229-8752; Fax 413-229-7010.
Will search UCC records. This agency will not do a tax lien search. Real estate records located in Berkshire County. **Other Phone Numbers:** Assessor 413-229-7001; Treasurer 413-229-7007; Elections 413-229-8752; Vital Records 413-229-8752.

Shelburne Town

Town Clerk, Town Hall, 51 Bridge St., Shelburne, MA 01370. 413-625-0301; Fax 413-625-0303.
Will search UCC records. Tax liens included in UCC search if requested. Real estate records located in Franklin County. **Other Phone Numbers:** Assessor 413-625-0301; Treasurer 413-625-0301.

Sherborn Town

Town Clerk, PO Box 186, Sherborn, MA 01770-0186. 508-651-7853; Fax 508-651-7854. http://members.aol.com/sherbornma
Will search UCC records. UCC search includes tax liens if requested. Real estate records located in Middlesex County. **Other Phones:** Assessor 508-651-7857; Treasurer 508-651-7859; Appraiser/Auditor 508-651-7857; Elections 508-651-7853; Vital Records 508-651-7853.

Shirley Town

Town Clerk, PO Box 782, Shirley, MA 01464. 978-425-2610; Fax 978-425-2602.
Will search UCC records. Tax liens included in UCC search if requested. Real estate records located in Middlesex County. **Other Phone Numbers:** Assessor 978-425-2613; Treasurer 978-425-2604; Vital Records 978-425-2610.

Shrewsbury Town

Town Clerk, 100 Maple Ave, Town Hall, Shrewsbury, MA 01545. 508-841-8507; Fax 508-842-0587.
Will search UCC records. UCC search includes tax liens. Real estate records located in Worcester County. **Other Phone Numbers:** Assessor 508-841-8501; Treasurer 508-841-8509; Elections 508-841-8507; Vital Records 508-841-8507.

Shutesbury Town

Town Clerk, PO Box 326, Shutesbury, MA 01072-0326. 413-259-1204 R/E Recording: 413-259-3790; Fax 413-259-1107. www.shutesbury.org
Will search UCC records. This agency will not do a tax lien search. Real estate records located in Franklin County. **Other Phone Numbers:** Assessor 413-259-3790; Treasurer 413-259-1801; Elections 413-259-1204; Vital Records 413-259-1204.

Somerset Town

Town Clerk, 140 Wood St, Somerset, MA 02726. 508-646-2818; Fax 508-646-2802.
Will search UCC records. This agency will not do a tax lien search. Real estate records located in Bristol County. **Other Phones:** Assessor 508-646-2824; Treasurer 508-646-2822; Vital Records 508-646-2818.

Somerville City

City Clerk, 93 Highland Ave, Somerville, MA 02143. 617-625-6600 x4100; Fax 617-625-4239.
Will search UCC records. This agency will not do a tax lien search. Real estate records located in Middlesex County. **Online Access:** Assessor Records. Search the city assessor database at http://data.visionappraisal.com/SomervilleMA. Free registration for full data. **Other Phone Numbers:** Assessor 617-625-6600 x3100; Vital Records 617-625-6600 x4100.

South Hadley Town

Town Clerk, 116 Main St, South Hadley, MA 01075-2833. 413-538-5023; Fax 413-538-7565.
Will search UCC records. Real estate records located in Hampshire County. **Other Phone Numbers:** Assessor 413-538-5027.

Southampton Town

Town Clerk, PO Box 276, Southampton, MA 01073. 413-527-8392; Fax 413-529-1006.
Will search UCC records. Tax liens not included in UCC search. Real estate records located in Hampshire County. **Other Phone Numbers:** Assessor 413-527-4741; Treasurer 413-527-4920; Elections 413-527-8392; Selectman 413-529-0106.

Southborough Town

Town Clerk, 17 Common St, Town Hall, Southborough, MA 01772-9109. 508-485-0710; Fax 508-480-0161.
Will search UCC records. UCC search includes tax liens if requested. Real estate records located in Worcester County. **Other Phone Numbers:** Assessor 508-485-0710; Treasurer 508-485-0710; Elections 508-485-0710; Vital Records 508-485-0710.

Southbridge Town

Town Clerk, 41 Elm St, Southbridge, MA 01550. 508-764-5408; Fax 508-764-5425.
Will search UCC records. This agency will not do a tax lien search. Real estate records located in Worcester County. **Other Phone Numbers:** Assessor 508-764-5404; Treasurer 508-764-5401; Elections 508-764-5408; Vital Records 508-764-5408.

Southwick Town

Town Clerk, Town Hall, 11 Depot St., Southwick, MA 01077. 413-569-5504; Fax 413-569-5001.
Will search UCC records prior to 7/2001. UCC search includes tax liens if requested. Real estate records located in Hampden County. **Online Access:** Assessor Records. Search the town assessor database at http://data.visionappraisal.com/SouthwickMA. Free registration for full data. **Other Phone Numbers:** Assessor 413-569-0565.

Spencer Town

Town Clerk, 157 Main St, Town Hall, Spencer, MA 01562-2197. 508-885-7500; Fax 508-885-7528.
Will search UCC records. Tax liens included in UCC search. Real estate records located in Worcester County. **Other Phone Numbers:** Assessor 508-885-7520; Treasurer 508-885-7510; Elections 508-885-7500; Vital Records 508-885-7500.

Springfield City

City Clerk, 36 Court St, Springfield, MA 01103. 413-787-6094.
Will search UCC records. Real estate records located in Hampden County. **Other Phone Numbers:** Assessor 413-787-6160; Treasurer 413-787-6130.

Sterling Town

Town Clerk, Mary Ellen Butterick Municipal Bldg, 1 Park St., Sterling, MA 01564. 978-422-8111; Fax 978-422-0289.
Will search UCC records. UCC search includes tax liens if requested. Real estate records located in Worcester County. **Other Phone Numbers:** Assessor 978-422-8113; Treasurer 978-422-3028; Elections 978-422-8111; Vital Records 978-422-8111.

Stockbridge Town

Town Clerk, PO Box 417, Stockbridge, MA 01262-0417. 413-298-4568; Fax 413-298-4485.
Will search UCC records. UCC search includes tax liens if requested. Real estate records located in Berkshire County. **Other Phone Numbers:** Assessor 413-298-3509; Treasurer 413-298-4534; Elections 413-298-4568; Vital Records 413-298-4568.

Stoneham Town

Town Clerk, 35 Central St, Stoneham, MA 02180. 781-279-2650; Fax 781-279-2653.
Will search UCC records prior to 7/2001. Real estate records located in Middlesex County. **Other Phone Numbers:** Assessor 781-279-2640.

Stoughton Town

Town Clerk, 10 Pearl St, Town Hall, Stoughton, MA 02072. 781-341-1300; Fax 781-341-1032.

Will search UCC records. Tax liens included in UCC search if requested. Real estate records located in Norfolk County. **Other Phone Numbers:** Assessor 781-341-1300; Treasurer 781-341-1300.

Stow Town

Town Clerk, Town Building, 380 Great Road, Stow, MA 01775. 978-897-4514; Fax 978-897-4534.
Will search UCC records. UCC search includes tax liens if requested. Real estate records located in Middlesex County. **Other Phone Numbers:** Assessor 978-897-4597; Treasurer 978-897-2834.

Sturbridge Town

Town Clerk, 308 Main, Sturbridge, MA 01566. 508-347-2510 R/E Recording: 508-347-2503; Fax 508-347-5886.
Will search UCC records. UCC search includes tax liens if requested. Real estate records located in Worcester County. **Other Phone Numbers:** Assessor 508-347-2503; Treasurer 508-347-2509; Elections 508-347-2510; Vital Records 508-347-2510.

Sudbury Town

Town Clerk, 322 Concord Road, Sudbury, MA 01776-1800. 978-443-8891 x351; Fax 978-443-0264. www.town.sudbury.ma.us/services
Will search UCC records. This agency will not do a tax lien search. Real estate records located in Middlesex County. **Other Phone Numbers:** Assessor 978-443-8891 x393.

Suffolk County

County Register of Deeds, P. O. Box 9660, Boston, MA 02114-9660. County Register of Deeds, R/E and UCC Recording 617-788-8575; Fax 617-720-4163. www.suffolkdeeds.com
This agency will not perform searches. **Online Access:** Real Estate, Lien, Deed, Property Assessor Records. Searchs on the Registry of Deeds site are free; real estate/liens on the county online system is not. Access to the County online system requires a written request submitted to Register of Deeds, POB 9660, Boston MA 02114. Online charges are $.50 per minute. A fax back service is available. Records on the County Registry of Deeds database are available free on the Internet at www.suffolkdeeds.com/search/default.asp. Search by name, corporation, and grantor/grantee. Recorded land records begin 1979; Registered land, 1983. Also, search the Boston assessor property records for free at www.cityofboston.gov/assessing/search.asp. City property taxes are also available, but no name searching. **Other Phones:** Assessor 617-788-8575; Treasurer 617-788-8575; Appraiser/Auditor 617-788-8575; Elections 788-8575; Vital Records 788-8575.

Sunderland Town

Town Clerk, 12 School St., Sunderland, MA 01375-9503. 413-665-1442 R/E Recording: 413-665-1445; Fax 413-665-1446.
Will search UCC records. UCC search includes tax liens if requested. Real estate records located in Franklin County. **Other Phone Numbers:** Assessor 413-665-1445; Treasurer 413-665-1444; Elections 413-665-1442; Vital Records 413-665-1442.

Sutton Town

Town Clerk, Town Hall, 4 Uxbridge Rd., Sutton, MA 01590. 508-865-8725; Fax 508-865-8721.
Will search UCC records. This agency will not do a tax lien search. Real estate records located in Worcester County.

Swampscott Town

Town Clerk, Town Hall, 22 Monument Ave., Swampscott, MA 01907. 781-596-8856; Fax 781-596-8870. www.swampscott.org/government.htm

Will search UCC records. Tax liens not included in UCC search. Real estate records located in Essex County. **Online Access:** Assessor, Real Estate Records. Access to the Assessor's Property Valuation List fy-2002 is available free at www.swampscott.org. Click on "Assessors Valuation Book". Search the name column: Contol+F then enter name information, then "Find Next." Site may be temporarily down. **Other Phone Numbers:** Assessor 781-596-8858; Elections 781-596-8855; Vital Records 781-596-8856.

Swansea Town

Town Clerk, 81 Main St, Town Hall, Swansea, MA 02777. 508-678-9389.
Will search UCC records. UCC search includes tax liens if requested. Real estate records located in Bristol County. **Other Phone Numbers:** Assessor 508-678-6702; Treasurer 508-678-6489; Elections 508-678-9389; Vital Records 508-678-9389.

Taunton City

City Clerk, 15 Summer St, City Hall, Taunton, MA 02780. 508-821-1024 R/E Recording: 508-822-0502; Fax 508-821-1098.
Will search UCC records. UCC search includes tax liens if requested. Real estate records located in Bristol County. **Other Phone Numbers:** Assessor 508-821-1011; Treasurer 508-821-1057; Elections 508-821-1044; Vital Records 508-821-1024.

Templeton Town

Town Clerk, Town Office Building, 9 Main St., Baldwinville, MA 01436. 978-939-8466; Fax 978-939-8327.
Will search UCC records. UCC search includes tax liens if requested. Real estate records located in Worcester County. **Other Phone Numbers:** Assessor 978-939-2793; Treasurer 978-939-4475; Elections 978-939-8466; Vital Records 978-939-8466; Tax Collector 978-939-2216.

Tewksbury Town

Town Clerk, 1009 Main St, Town Hall, Tewksbury, MA 01876-2796. 978-640-4355; Fax 978-640-4302.
Will search UCC records. UCC search includes tax liens. Real estate records located in Middlesex County. **Other Phone Numbers:** Assessor 978-640-4330; Treasurer 978-640-4340; Elections 978-640-4355; Vital Records 978-640-4355.

Tisbury Town

Town Clerk, PO Box 606, Tisbury, MA 02568-0606. 508-696-4215; Fax 508-693-5876. www.ci.tisbury.ma.us
Will search UCC records. This agency will not do a tax lien search. Real estate records located in Dukes County. **Online Access:** Assessor Records. Search the town assessor database at http://data.visionappraisal.com/TisburyMA. Free registration for full data. **Other Phone Numbers:** Assessor 508-696-4206; Treasurer 508-696-4250; Elections 508-696-4215; Vital Records 508-696-4215.

Tolland Town

Town Clerk, 241 W. Granville Rd, Tolland, MA 01034. 413-259-4794; Fax 413-258-4048.
Will search UCC records. This agency will not do a tax lien search. Real estate records located in Hampden County. **Other Phone Numbers:** Assessor 413-259-4794; Treasurer 413-259-4794; Elections 413-259-4794; Vital Records 413-259-4794.

Topsfield Town

Town Clerk, 8 W. Common St, Town Hall, Topsfield, MA 01983. 978-887-1505; Fax 978-887-1502.

Will search UCC records. Tax liens not included in UCC search. Real estate records located in Essex County. **Other Phones:** Assessor 978-887-1514.

Townsend Town

Town Clerk, Memorial Hall, 272 Main St, Townsend, MA 01469. 978-597-1704; Fax 978-597-8135.
Will search UCC records. UCC search includes tax liens if requested. Real estate records located in Middlesex County. **Other Phone Numbers:** Assessor 978-597-6612; Treasurer 978-597-1708; Elections 978-597-1704; Vital Records 978-597-1704.

Truro Town

Town Clerk, PO Box 2012, Truro, MA 02666-2012. 508-349-3860; Fax 508-349-7720.
Will search UCC records. Real estate records located in Barnstable County. **Other Phone Numbers:** Assessor 508-349-9248; Treasurer 508-349-3860.

Tyngsborough Town

Town Clerk, 25 Bryants Lane, Tyngsborough, MA 01879. 978-649-2300 x129; Fax 978-649-2301.
Will search UCC records. This agency will not do a tax lien search. Real estate records located in Middlesex County. **Other Phone Numbers:** Assessor 978-649-2300 x121; Treasurer 978-649-2300 x125; Elections 978-649-2300 x129.

Tyringham Town

Town Clerk, Main Road, Tyringham, MA 01264. 413-243-1749; Fax 413-243-4942.
Will search UCC records. This agency will not do a tax lien search. Real estate records located in Berkshire County.

Upton Town

Town Clerk, Box 969, Upton, MA 01568. Town Clerk, R/E and UCC Recording 508-529-3565; Fax 508-529-1010. www.upton.ma.us
Will search UCC records. This agency will not do a tax lien search. Real estate records located in Worcester County. **Other Phone Numbers:** Assessor 508-529-1002; Treasurer 508-529-3737; Elections 508-529-3565; Vital Records 508-529-3565.

Uxbridge Town

Town Clerk, 21 S. Main St, Uxbridge, MA 01569. 508-278-8608; Fax 508-278-8605.
Will search UCC records. UCC search includes tax liens if requested. Real estate records located in Worcester County.

Wakefield Town

Town Clerk, 1 Lafayette St, Town Hall, Wakefield, MA 01880-2383. 781-246-6383 R/E Recording: 781-246-6380; Fax 781-246-4155.
Will search UCC records. Tax liens not included in UCC search. Real estate records located in Middlesex County. **Other Phone Numbers:** Assessor 781-246-5159; Treasurer 781-246-6340; Elections 781-246-6384; Vital Records 781-246-6383; Town Adm./Selectmen 781-246-6390.

Wales Town

Town Clerk, PO Box 834, Wales, MA 01081-0834. 413-245-7571; Fax 413-245-3261.
Will search UCC records. UCC search includes tax liens if requested. Real estate records located in Hampden County. **Other Phone Numbers:** Assessor 413-245-3260; Treasurer 413-245-3260; Vital Records 413-245-7571.

Walpole Town

Town Clerk, 135 School St, Town Hall, Walpole, MA 02081-2898. 508-660-7297 UCC Recording: 508-660-7296; Fax 508-660-7303. www.walpole.ma.us

Will search UCC records. UCC search includes tax liens. Real estate records located in Norfolk County. **Online Access:** Property Assessor Records. Search the town assessor database at http://data.visionappraisal.com/WalpoleMA. Free registration for full data. **Other Phone Numbers:** Assessor 508-660-7314; Treasurer 508-660-7311; Elections 508-660-7296; Vital Records 508-660-7296.

Waltham City

City Clerk, 610 Main St, Waltham, MA 02452. 781-314-3120; Fax 781-314-3130. www.city.waltham.ma.us
Will search UCC records. UCC search includes tax liens. Real estate records located in Middlesex County. **Online Access:** Assessor Records. Records on the City of Waltham Assessor database are available free online at www.city.waltham.ma.us/assessors/caveat.htm. **Other Phone Numbers:** Assessor 781-314-3200; Treasurer 781-314-3250; Elections 781-314-3120; Vital Records 781-314-3120.

Ware Town

Town Clerk, 126 Main St, Ware, MA 01082. 413-967-4471 UCC Recording: 413-967-4471 x104; Fax 413-967-9600.
Will search UCC records. This agency will not do a tax lien search. Real estate records located in Hampshire County. **Other Phone Numbers:** Assessor 413-967-9610; Treasurer 413-967-4471; Vital Records 413-967-4471 x104.

Wareham Town

Town Clerk, 54 Marion Road, Wareham, MA 02571. 508-291-3140 R/E Recording: 508-830-9200; Fax 508-291-3116.
Will search UCC records. Tax liens included in UCC search if requested. Real estate records located in Plymouth County. **Other Phone Numbers:** Assessor 508-291-3160; Treasurer 508-291-3100 x3146; Elections 508-291-3140; Vital Records 508-291-3140.

Warren Town

Town Clerk, PO Box 603, Warren, MA 01083-0603. 413-436-5702; Fax 413-436-9754.
Will not search UCC records. Tax lien searches contact the tax collector. Real estate records located in Middlesex County. **Other Phones:** Assessor 413-436-5703; Treasurer 436-5700; Tax Collector 436-5709.

Warwick Town

Town Clerk, Town Hall, 12 Athol Rd., Warwick, MA 01378. 978-544-8304; Fax 978-544-6499.
Will search UCC records. This agency will not do a tax lien search. Real estate records located in Franklin County. **Other Phones:** Assessor 978-544-8304; Treasurer 978-544-3845; Vital Records 978-544-8304.

Washington Town

Town Clerk, Town Hall Route 8, GA094, Washington, MA 01223. 413-623-8878; Fax 413-623-2116. http://town.washington.ma.us
Will search UCC records. UCC search includes tax liens if requested. Real estate records located in Berkshire County. **Other Phone Numbers:** Assessor 413-623-6446; Treasurer 413-623-8878; Elections 413-623-2185; Vital Records 413-623-2185.

Watertown Town

Town Clerk, 149 Main St, Administration Building, Watertown, MA 02472. 617-972-6486; Fax 617-972-6595.
Will search UCC records. This agency will not do a tax lien search. Real estate records located in Middlesex County. **Online Access:** Assessor Records. Records on the Watertown Town Online Assessed Values site are available free online at www.townonline.com/

watertown/realestate/assessments/index.html.   **Other Phones:** Assessor 617-972-6410; Treasurer 617-972-6450; Elections 972-6488; Vital Records 972-6486.

Wayland Town

Town Clerk, 41 Cochituate Road, Wayland, MA 01778-2697. 508-358-3630; Fax 508-358-3627. www.wayland.ma.us/townadministration.html
Will search UCC records. This agency will not do a tax lien search. Real estate records located in Middlesex County. **Online Access:** Assessor Records. Property tax records on the Assessor's database are available free online at www.wayland.ma.us/assess-reval99.htm. Also, the read only tax assessor information is available through a private company's site at www.mypropertyrecords.com/univers. **Other Phone Numbers:** Assessor 508-358-3658; Treasurer 508-358-3635; Appraiser/Auditor 508-358-3658; Elections 508-358-3631; Vital Records 508-358-3630.

Webster Town

Town Clerk, PO Box 193, Webster, MA 01570. 508-949-3850 R/E Recording: 508-949-3810; Fax 508-949-3888.
Will search UCC records. UCC search includes tax liens if requested. Real estate records located in Worcester County. **Other Phone Numbers:** Assessor 508-949-3810; Treasurer 508-949-3820; Elections 508-949-3850; Vital Records 508-949-3850.

Wellesley Town

Town Clerk, 525 Washington St, Wellesley, MA 02482. 781-431-1019 x250; Fax 781-239-1043. www.ci.wellesley.ma.us/town/index.html
Will search UCC records. Real estate records located in Norfolk County. **Online Access:** Assessor Records. Property tax records on the Assessor's database are available free online at www.ci.wellesley.ma.us/asr/index.html. **Other Phone Numbers:** Assessor 781-431-1019; Elections 781-431-1019 x253; Vital Records 781-431-1019 x252.

Wellfleet Town

Town Clerk, 300 Main St, Wellfleet, MA 02667. 508-349-0301; Fax 508-349-0317.
Will search UCC records. UCC search includes tax liens if requested. Real estate records located in Barnstable County. **Other Phone Numbers:** Assessor 508-349-0304.

Wendell Town

Town Clerk, 270 Wendell Depot Rd., Wendell Depot, MA 01380. 978-544-6682.
Will search UCC records. This agency will not do a tax lien search. Real estate records located in Franklin County.

Wenham Town

Town Clerk, Town Hall, 138 Main St., Wenham, MA 01984. 978-468-5520; Fax 978-468-6164.
Will search UCC records. Tax liens included with UCC search if requested. Real estate records located in Essex County. **Other Phone Numbers:** Assessor 978-468-5524; Treasurer 978-468-5525; Elections 978-468-5520; Vital Records 978-468-5520.

West Boylston Town

Town Clerk, 120 Prescott St, West Boylston, MA 01583. Town Clerk, R/E and UCC Recording 508-835-6240; Fax 508-835-4102. www.westboylston.com
Will search UCC records. This agency will not do a tax lien search. Real estate records located in Worcester County. **Online Access:** Assessor Records. Search the town assessor Valuations Listings for free at www.westboylston.com/ASSESS/Assessors1.htm. Files are searchable by street and include owner names. **Other Phone Numbers:** Assessor 508-835-6093;

Treasurer 508-835-6092; Elections 508-835-6240; Vital Records 508-835-6240.

West Bridgewater Town

Town Clerk, 65 N. Main St, Town Hall, West Bridgewater, MA 02379-1734. 508-894-1200; Fax 508-894-1210.
Bridgewater, East Bridgewater and West Bridgewater are separate towns. UCC records are filed with the Town/City Clerk, real estate records are at the county level with the Register of Deeds. Will search UCC records. This agency will not do a tax lien search. Real estate records located in Plymouth County.

West Brookfield Town

Town Clerk, PO Box 372, West Brookfield, MA 01585. 508-867-1415; Fax 508-867-1401.
Will search UCC records. UCC search includes tax liens if requested. Real estate records located in Worcester County. **Other Phone Numbers:** Assessor 508-867-1402.

West Newbury Town

Town Clerk, Town Office Bldg., 381 Main St., West Newbury, MA 01985-1499. 978-363-1100 x15 UCC Recording: 978-363-1100 x10; Fax 978-363-1117.
Will search UCC records. UCC search includes tax liens if requested. Real estate records located in Essex County. **Other Phone Numbers:** Assessor 978-363-1100 x17; Treasurer 978-363-1100 x13; Elections 978-363-1100 x15; Vital Records 978-363-1100 x10.

West Springfield Town

Town Clerk, 26 Central St, Town Hall, West Springfield, MA 01089-2779. 413-263-3012 R/E Recording: 413-263-3055.
Will search UCC records. This agency will not do a tax lien search. Real estate records located in Hampden County. **Online Access:** Assessor Records. Search the town assessor database at http://data.visionappraisal.com/WestSpringfieldMA. Free registration for full data. **Other Phone Numbers:** Assessor 413-263-3055; Treasurer 413-263-3004; Elections 413-263-3012; Vital Records 413-263-3012.

West Stockbridge Town

Town Clerk, PO Box 163, West Stockbridge, MA 01266. 413-232-0300; Fax 413-232-0318.
Will search UCC records. UCC search includes tax liens if requested. Real estate records located in Berkshire County. **Other Phone Numbers:** Assessor 413-232-0303; Treasurer 413-232-0316; Elections 413-232-0300; Vital Records 413-232-0300.

West Tisbury Town

Town Clerk, Box 278, West Tisbury, MA 02575-0278. 508-696-0148; Fax 508-696-0103.
Will search UCC records. UCC search includes tax liens. Real estate records located in Dukes County. **Other Phone Numbers:** Assessor 508-693-9733; Treasurer 508-696-0108; Elections 508-696-0148; Vital Records 508-696-0148.

Westborough Town

Town Clerk, 34 W. Main St, Town Hall, Westborough, MA 01581-1998. 508-366-3020; Fax 508-366-3099.
Will search UCC records. UCC search includes tax liens if requested. Real estate records located in Worcester County. **Other Phone Numbers:** Assessor 508-366-3010; Treasurer 508-366-3025; Elections 508-366-3020; Vital Records 508-366-3020.

Westfield City

City Clerk, 59 Court St, Westfield, MA 01085-3574. 413-572-6235;   Fax   413-564-3114. www.ci.westfield.ma.us
Will search UCC records. This agency will not do a tax lien search. Real estate records located in Hampden County. **Online Access:** Assessor Records. Property tax records on the Assessor's database are available free online at www.ci.westfield.ma.us/realest/rea00.htm. **Other Phones:** Assessor 413-572-6222; Treasurer 413-572-6230; Appraiser/Auditor 413-572-6222; Elections 413-572-6266; Vital Records 413-572-6236.

Westford Town

Town Clerk, 55 Main St, Town Hall, Westford, MA 01886. 978-692-5515; Fax 978-692-9607.
Will search UCC records. UCC search includes tax liens if requested. Real estate records located in Middlesex County. **Other Phone Numbers:** Assessor 978-692-5504; Treasurer 978-692-5506; Elections 978-692-5515; Vital Records 978-652-5515.

Westhampton Town

Town Clerk, Town Hall, Westhampton, MA 01027. 413-527-0463; Fax 413-527-8655.
Will search UCC records. This agency will not do a tax lien search. Real estate records located in Hampshire County.

Westminster Town

Town Clerk, PO Box 456, Westminster, MA 01473. 978-874-7406; Fax 978-874-7411. www.westminster-ma.org
Will search UCC records. Tax liens included in UCC search. Real estate records located in Worcester County. **Other Phone Numbers:** Assessor 978-874-7401; Treasurer 978-874-7403; Elections 978-874-7406; Vital Records 978-874-7406.

Weston Town

Town Clerk, PO Box 378, Weston, MA 02493. 781-893-7320; Fax 781-891-3697. www.weston.org
Will search UCC records. This agency will not do a tax lien search. Real estate records located in Registry of Deeds, Southern Middlesex District located at 208 Cambridge St, Cambridge, MA 02141-0001. **Other Phone Numbers:** Assessor 781-893-7320 x313; Treasurer 781-893-7320 x316; Elections 781-893-7320 x303; Vital Records 781-893-7320 x303.

Westport Town

Town Clerk, Town Hall, 816 Main Rd., Westport, MA 02790. 508-636-1000 R/E Recording: 508-993-2605 (Registry of Deeds in New Bedford); Fax 508-636-1147.
Will search UCC records. Tax liens not included in UCC search. Real estate records located in Bristol County. **Other Phones:** Assessor 508-636-1012; Treasurer 508-636-1007; Elections 508-636-1001; Vital Records 508-636-1000; Selectmen 508-636-1003.

Westwood Town

Town Clerk, 580 High St, Westwood, MA 02090. 781-326-3964; Fax 781-329-8030.
Will search UCC records. Tax liens not included in UCC search. Real estate records located in Norfolk County. **Other Phones:** Assessor 781-326-6450.

Weymouth Town

Town Clerk, 75 Middle St, Town Hall, East Weymouth, MA 02189. 781-335-2000; Fax 781-335-3283.
Will search UCC records. Real estate records located in Norfolk County. **Other Phone Numbers:** Assessor 781-335-2000; Treasurer 781-335-2000.

Whately Town

Town Clerk, 218 Chestnut Plain Rd., Whately, MA 01093-0002. 413-665-0054; Fax 413-665-9560.
Will search UCC records. UCC search includes tax liens if requested. Real estate records located in Franklin County. **Other Phone Numbers:** Assessor 413-665-3470; Treasurer 413-665-2595; Elections 413-665-0054; Vital Records 413-665-0054.

Whitman Town

Town Clerk, PO Box 426, Whitman, MA 02382. 781-447-7607; Fax 781-447-7318.
Will search UCC records. UCC search includes tax liens if requested. Real estate records located in Plymouth County. **Other Phone Numbers:** Assessor 781-447-7617; Treasurer 781-447-7609.

Wilbraham Town

Town Clerk, 240 Springfield St, Wilbraham, MA 01095. 413-596-2809; Fax 413-596-2830.
Will search UCC records. UCC search includes tax liens if requested. Real estate records located in Hampden County. **Other Phone Numbers:** Assessor 413-596-2818.

Williamsburg Town

Town Clerk, PO Box 447, Haydenville, MA 01039-0447. 413-268-8402; Fax 413-268-8409.
Will search UCC records. Real estate records located in Hampshire County. **Other Phone Numbers:** Assessor 413-268-8403; Treasurer 413-268-8419.

Williamstown Town

Town Clerk, 31 North St, Williamstown, MA 01267. 413-458-9341 R/E Recording: 413-743-0035; Fax 413-458-4839. www.williamstown.net
Will search UCC records. UCC search includes tax liens. Real estate records located in Berkshire County. **Other Phone Numbers:** Assessor 413-458-9342; Treasurer 413-458-9342; Elections 413-458-9341; Vital Records 413-458-9341.

Wilmington Town

Town Clerk, 121 Glen Road, Town Hall, Wilmington, MA 01887. 978-658-2030 R/E Recording: 978-658-3531; Fax 978-658-3334. www.town.wilmington.ma.us
Will search UCC records. Tax liens included in UCC search if requested. Real estate records located in Middlesex County. **Other Phones:** Assessor 978-658-3675; Treasurer 978-658-3531; Appraiser/Auditor 978-658-3675; Elections 978-658-2030.

Winchendon Town

Town Clerk, 109 Front St, Winchendon, MA 01475. 978-297-2766; Fax 978-297-1616.
Will search UCC records. Tax liens not included in UCC search. Real estate records located in Worcester County. **Other Phone Numbers:** Assessor 978-297-0155; Treasurer 978-297-0152.

Winchester Town

Town Clerk, 71 Mount Vernon St, Town Hall, Winchester, MA 01890. 781-721-7130; Fax 781-721-1153.
Will search UCC records. Real estate records located in Middlesex County. **Other Phone Numbers:** Assessor 781-721-7111; Treasurer 781-721-7123.

Windsor Town

Town Clerk, 3 Hinsdale Rd., Windsor, MA 01270. 413-684-3977; Fax 413-684-1585.
Will search UCC records. This agency will not do a tax lien search. Real estate records located in Berkshire County. **Other Phone Numbers:** Assessor 413-684-3811; Treasurer 413-684-3811; Appraiser/Auditor 413-684-3811; Elections 413-684-3977; Vital Records 413-684-3977.

Winthrop Town

Town Clerk, Town Hall, Winthrop, MA 02152-3156. 617-846-1742; Fax 617-846-5458.
Will search UCC records. Tax liens included in UCC search if requested. Real estate records located in Suffolk County. **Other Phone Numbers:** Assessor 617-846-2716; Treasurer 617-846-3226; Elections 617-846-1742; Vital Records 617-846-1742; Municipal Tax Liens 617-846-1750.

Woburn City

City Clerk, 10 Common St, Woburn, MA 01801-4197. 781-932-4453; Fax 781-932-4455.
Will search UCC records. UCC search includes tax liens. Real estate records located in Middlesex County.

Worcester City

City Clerk, 455 Main St, City Hall - Room 206, Worcester, MA 01608. 508-799-1121; Fax 508-799-1194.
Will search UCC records. Real estate records located in Worcester County. **Online Access:** Real Estate, Lien, Assessor Records. Data is available online in 2 ways. Online access to the City Assessor Valuation Search database is available free at www.ci.worcester.ma.us/assessing/index.html. And, access to the "Landtrack System" for Worcester District records requires a $50 annual fee plus $.25 per minute of use. Index records date back to 1966. Images are viewable from 1974 onward. Lending agency info is available. Fax back service is available for $.50 per page. For information, contact Joe Ursoleo at 508-798-7713 X233. **Other Phone Numbers:** Assessor 508-799-1112; Treasurer 508-799-1077.

Worcester County (Northern District)

County Register of Deeds, PO Box 983, Fitchburg, MA 01420. 978-342-2637; Fax 978-345-2865. www.state.ma.us/nwrod
This agency will not perform searches. **Online Access:** Real Estate, Lien Records. Access to the "Northfield" online service requires $50 annually, plus $.25 per minute of use. Records date back to 1983. Viewable images are available back to 1995. Lending agency information is available. A fax back service is available. For information, contact Ruth Piermarini at 978-342-2637. **Other Phone Numbers:** Assessor 508-799-1098.

Worcester County (Worcester District)

County Register of Deeds, 2 Main St, Courthouse, Worcester, MA 01608. 508-798-7717; Fax 508-753-1338.
This agency will not perform searches. **Online Access:** Real Estate, Property Tax Records. Records on the Town of Holden assessor's database are available free online at http://data.visionappraisal.com/HOLDENMA. Registration is required; sign-up is free. **Other Phones:** Assessor 508-799-1000; Treasurer 508-798-2441.

Worthington Town

Town Clerk, Town Hall, Worthington, MA 01098-0247. 413-238-5578; Fax 413-238-5579.
Will search UCC records. This agency will not do a tax lien search. Real estate records located in Hampshire County. **Other Phone Numbers:** Assessor 413-238-5578; Treasurer 413-238-5577.

Wrentham Town

Town Clerk, 79 South St, Wrentham, MA 02093. 508-384-5415; Fax 508-384-5434.
Will search UCC records. This agency will not do a tax lien search. Real estate records located in Norfolk County. **Other Phone Numbers:** Assessor 508-384-5408; Treasurer 508-384-5413; Elections 508-384-5415; Vital Records 508-384-5415.

Yarmouth Town

Town Clerk, 1146 Route 28, Town Hall, South Yarmouth, MA 02664. 508-398-2231 R/E Recording: 508-362-7733 x106 UCC Recording: 508-398-2231 x216; Fax 508-398-2365. www.yarmouthcapecod.org
Will search UCC records. Tax liens included in UCC search if requested. Real estate records located in Barnstable County. **Online Access:** Assessor Records. Records on the Assessor's database are available free online at http://data.visionappraisal.com/yarmouthma. Free registration for full data. Non-registered users can access a limited set of data. **Other Phone Numbers:** Assessor 508-398-2231 x221; Treasurer 508-398-2231 x219; Elections 508-398-2231 x216; Vital Records 508-398-2231 x216.

Massachusetts County Locator

You will usually be able to find the city name in the City/County Cross Reference below. In that case, it is a simple matter to determine the county from the cross reference. However, only the official US Postal Service city names are included in this index. There are an additional 40,000 place names that people use in their addresses. Therefore, we have also included a ZIP/City Cross Reference immediately following the City/County Cross Reference.

If you know the ZIP Code but the city name does not appear in the City/County Cross Reference index, look up the ZIP Code in the ZIP/City Cross Reference, find the city name, then look up the city name in the City/County Cross Reference. For example, you want to know the county for an address of Menands, NY 12204. There is no "Menands" in the City/County Cross Reference. The ZIP/City Cross Reference shows that ZIP Codes 12201-12288 are for the city of Albany. Looking back in the City/County Cross Reference, Albany is in Albany County.

City/County Cross Reference

ABINGTON Plymouth
ACCORD Plymouth
ACTON Middlesex
ACUSHNET Bristol
ADAMS Berkshire
AGAWAM Hampden
ALLSTON Suffolk
AMESBURY Essex
AMHERST Hampshire
ANDOVER Essex
ARLINGTON Middlesex
ARLINGTON HEIGHTS Middlesex
ASHBURNHAM Worcester
ASHBY Middlesex
ASHFIELD Franklin
ASHLAND Middlesex
ASHLEY FALLS Berkshire
ASSONET Bristol
ATHOL Worcester
ATTLEBORO Bristol
ATTLEBORO FALLS Bristol
AUBURN Worcester
AUBURNDALE Middlesex
AVON Norfolk
AYER (01432) Middlesex(80),
   Worcester(19)
BABSON PARK Norfolk
BALDWINVILLE Worcester
BAR CODE MCCORMACK Suffolk
BARNSTABLE Barnstable
BARRE Worcester
BECKET Berkshire
BEDFORD Middlesex
BELCHERTOWN Hampshire
BELLINGHAM Norfolk
BELMONT Middlesex
BERKLEY Bristol
BERKSHIRE Berkshire
BERLIN Worcester
BERNARDSTON Franklin
BEVERLY Essex
BILLERICA Middlesex
BLACKSTONE Worcester
BLANDFORD Hampden
BOLTON Worcester
BONDSVILLE Hampden
BOSTON Suffolk
BOXBOROUGH Middlesex
BOXFORD Essex
BOYLSTON Worcester
BRAINTREE Norfolk
BRANT ROCK Plymouth
BREWSTER Barnstable
BRIDGEWATER Plymouth
BRIGHTON Suffolk
BRIMFIELD Hampden
BROCKTON Plymouth
BROOKFIELD Worcester
BROOKLINE Norfolk
BROOKLINE VILLAGE Norfolk
BRYANTVILLE Plymouth
BUCKLAND Franklin
BURLINGTON Middlesex

BUZZARDS BAY Barnstable
BYFIELD Essex
CAMBRIDGE Middlesex
CANTON Norfolk
CARLISLE Middlesex
CARVER Plymouth
CATAUMET Barnstable
CENTERVILLE Barnstable
CHARLEMONT Franklin
CHARLESTOWN Suffolk
CHARLTON Worcester
CHARLTON CITY Worcester
CHARLTON DEPOT Worcester
CHARTLEY Bristol
CHATHAM Barnstable
CHELMSFORD Middlesex
CHELSEA Suffolk
CHERRY VALLEY Worcester
CHESHIRE Berkshire
CHESTER (01011) Hampden(94),
   Berkshire(5)
CHESTERFIELD Hampshire
CHESTNUT HILL Middlesex
CHICOPEE Hampden
CHILMARK Dukes
CLINTON Worcester
COHASSET Norfolk
COLRAIN Franklin
CONCORD Middlesex
CONWAY Franklin
COTUIT Barnstable
CUMMAQUID Barnstable
CUMMINGTON Hampshire
CUTTYHUNK Dukes
DALTON Berkshire
DANVERS Essex
DARTMOUTH Bristol
DEDHAM Norfolk
DEERFIELD Franklin
DENNIS Barnstable
DENNIS PORT Barnstable
DIGHTON Bristol
DOUGLAS Worcester
DOVER Norfolk
DRACUT Middlesex
DRURY Berkshire
DUDLEY Worcester
DUNSTABLE Middlesex
DUXBURY Plymouth
EAST BOSTON Suffolk
EAST BRIDGEWATER Plymouth
EAST BROOKFIELD Worcester
EAST DENNIS Barnstable
EAST FALMOUTH Barnstable
EAST FREETOWN Bristol
EAST LONGMEADOW Hampden
EAST MANSFIELD Bristol
EAST ORLEANS Barnstable
EAST OTIS Berkshire
EAST PRINCETON Worcester
EAST SANDWICH Barnstable
EAST TAUNTON Bristol
EAST TEMPLETON Worcester

EAST WALPOLE Norfolk
EAST WAREHAM Plymouth
EASTHAM Barnstable
EASTHAMPTON Hampshire
EASTON Bristol
EDGARTOWN Dukes
ELMWOOD Plymouth
ERVING Franklin
ESSEX Essex
EVERETT Middlesex
FAIRHAVEN Bristol
FALL RIVER Bristol
FALMOUTH Barnstable
FAYVILLE Worcester
FEEDING HILLS Hampden
FISKDALE Worcester
FITCHBURG Worcester
FLORENCE Hampshire
FORESTDALE Barnstable
FORT DEVENS (01433) Worcester(53),
   Middlesex(46)
FOXBORO Norfolk
FRAMINGHAM Middlesex
FRANKLIN Norfolk
GARDNER Worcester
GEORGETOWN Essex
GILBERTVILLE Worcester
GLENDALE Berkshire
GLOUCESTER Essex
GOSHEN Hampshire
GRAFTON Worcester
GRANBY Hampshire
GRANVILLE Hampden
GREAT BARRINGTON Berkshire
GREEN HARBOR Plymouth
GREENBUSH Plymouth
GREENFIELD Franklin
GROTON Middlesex
GROVELAND Essex
HADLEY Hampshire
HALIFAX Plymouth
HAMILTON Essex
HAMPDEN Hampden
HANOVER Plymouth
HANSCOM AFB Middlesex
HANSON Plymouth
HARDWICK Worcester
HARVARD Worcester
HARWICH Barnstable
HARWICH PORT Barnstable
HATFIELD Hampshire
HATHORNE Essex
HAVERHILL Essex
HAYDENVILLE Hampshire
HEATH Franklin
HINGHAM Plymouth
HINSDALE Berkshire
HOLBROOK Norfolk
HOLDEN Worcester
HOLLAND Hampden
HOLLISTON Middlesex
HOLYOKE Hampden
HOPEDALE Worcester

HOPKINTON Middlesex
HOUSATONIC Berkshire
HUBBARDSTON Worcester
HUDSON Middlesex
HULL Plymouth
HUMAROCK Plymouth
HUNTINGTON (01050) Hampshire(98),
   Hampden(1)
HYANNIS Barnstable
HYANNIS PORT Barnstable
HYDE PARK Suffolk
INDIAN ORCHARD Hampden
IPSWICH Essex
JAMAICA PLAIN Suffolk
JEFFERSON Worcester
KINGSTON Plymouth
LAKE PLEASANT Franklin
LAKEVILLE Plymouth
LANCASTER Worcester
LANESBORO Berkshire
LAWRENCE Essex
LEE Berkshire
LEEDS Hampshire
LEICESTER Worcester
LENOX Berkshire
LENOX DALE Berkshire
LEOMINSTER Worcester
LEVERETT Franklin
LEXINGTON Middlesex
LINCOLN Middlesex
LINWOOD Worcester
LITTLETON Middlesex
LONGMEADOW Hampden
LOWELL Middlesex
LUDLOW Hampden
LUNENBURG Worcester
LYNN Essex
LYNNFIELD Essex
MALDEN Middlesex
MANCHAUG Worcester
MANCHESTER Essex
MANOMET Plymouth
MANSFIELD Bristol
MARBLEHEAD Essex
MARION Plymouth
MARLBOROUGH Middlesex
MARSHFIELD Plymouth
MARSHFIELD HILLS Plymouth
MARSTONS MILLS Barnstable
MASHPEE Barnstable
MATTAPAN Suffolk
MATTAPOISETT Plymouth
MAYNARD Middlesex
MEDFIELD Norfolk
MEDFORD Middlesex
MEDWAY Norfolk
MELROSE Middlesex
MENDON Worcester
MENEMSHA Dukes
MERRIMAC Essex
METHUEN Essex
MIDDLEBORO Plymouth
MIDDLEFIELD Hampshire

MIDDLETON Essex
MILFORD Worcester
MILL RIVER Berkshire
MILLBURY Worcester
MILLIS Norfolk
MILLVILLE Worcester
MILTON Norfolk
MILTON VILLAGE Norfolk
MINOT Plymouth
MONPONSETT Plymouth
MONROE BRIDGE Franklin
MONSON Hampden
MONTAGUE Franklin
MONTEREY Berkshire
MONUMENT BEACH (02553)
   Barnstable(50), Barnstable(50)
NAHANT Essex
NANTUCKET Nantucket
NATICK Middlesex
NEEDHAM Norfolk
NEW BEDFORD Bristol
NEW BRAINTREE Worcester
NEW SALEM Franklin
NEW TOWN Middlesex
NEWBURY Essex
NEWBURYPORT Essex
NEWTON Middlesex
NEWTON CENTER Middlesex
NEWTON HIGHLANDS Middlesex
NEWTON LOWER FALLS Middlesex
NEWTON UPPER FALLS Middlesex
NEWTONVILLE Middlesex
NONANTUM Middlesex
NORFOLK Norfolk
NORTH ADAMS Berkshire
NORTH AMHERST Hampshire
NORTH ANDOVER Essex
NORTH ATTLEBORO Bristol
NORTH BILLERICA Middlesex
NORTH BROOKFIELD Worcester
NORTH CARVER Plymouth
NORTH CHATHAM Barnstable
NORTH CHELMSFORD Middlesex
NORTH DARTMOUTH Bristol
NORTH DIGHTON Bristol
NORTH EASTHAM Barnstable
NORTH EASTON Bristol
NORTH EGREMONT Berkshire
NORTH FALMOUTH Barnstable
NORTH GRAFTON Worcester
NORTH HATFIELD Hampshire
NORTH MARSHFIELD Plymouth
NORTH OXFORD Worcester
NORTH PEMBROKE Plymouth
NORTH READING Middlesex
NORTH SCITUATE Plymouth
NORTH TRURO Barnstable
NORTH UXBRIDGE Worcester
NORTH WALTHAM Middlesex
NORTHAMPTON Hampshire
NORTHBOROUGH Worcester
NORTHBRIDGE Worcester
NORTHFIELD Franklin
NORTON Bristol
NORWELL Plymouth
NORWOOD Norfolk
NUTTING LAKE Middlesex

OAK BLUFFS Dukes
OAKDALE Worcester
OAKHAM Worcester
OCEAN BLUFF Plymouth
ONSET Plymouth
ORANGE Franklin
ORLEANS Barnstable
OSTERVILLE Barnstable
OTIS Berkshire
OXFORD Worcester
PALMER Hampden
PAXTON Worcester
PEABODY Essex
PEMBROKE Plymouth
PEPPERELL Middlesex
PETERSHAM (01366) Franklin(51),
   Worcester(48)
PINEHURST Middlesex
PITTSFIELD Berkshire
PLAINFIELD Hampshire
PLAINVILLE (02762) Norfolk(98), Bristol(1)
PLYMOUTH Plymouth
PLYMPTON Plymouth
POCASSET Barnstable
PRIDES CROSSING Essex
PRINCETON Worcester
PROVINCETOWN Barnstable
QUINCY Norfolk
RANDOLPH Norfolk
RAYNHAM Bristol
RAYNHAM CENTER Bristol
READING Middlesex
READVILLE Suffolk
REHOBOTH Bristol
REVERE Suffolk
RICHMOND Berkshire
ROCHDALE Worcester
ROCHESTER (02770) Plymouth(98),
   Bristol(1)
ROCKLAND Plymouth
ROCKPORT Essex
ROSLINDALE Suffolk
ROWE Franklin
ROWLEY Essex
ROYALSTON Worcester
RUSSELL Hampden
RUTLAND Worcester
SAGAMORE Barnstable
SAGAMORE BEACH Barnstable
SALEM Essex
SALISBURY Essex
SANDISFIELD Berkshire
SANDWICH Barnstable
SAUGUS Essex
SAVOY Berkshire
SCITUATE Plymouth
SEARS ROEBUCK Suffolk
SEEKONK Bristol
SHARON Norfolk
SHATTUCKVILLE Franklin
SHEFFIELD Berkshire
SHELBURNE FALLS Franklin
SHELDONVILLE Norfolk
SHERBORN Middlesex
SHIRLEY Middlesex
SHREWSBURY Worcester
SHUTESBURY Franklin

SIASCONSET Nantucket
SILVER BEACH Barnstable
SOMERSET Bristol
SOMERVILLE Middlesex
SOUTH BARRE Worcester
SOUTH CARVER Plymouth
SOUTH CHATHAM Barnstable
SOUTH DARTMOUTH Bristol
SOUTH DEERFIELD Franklin
SOUTH DENNIS Barnstable
SOUTH EASTON Bristol
SOUTH EGREMONT Berkshire
SOUTH GRAFTON Worcester
SOUTH HADLEY Hampshire
SOUTH HAMILTON Essex
SOUTH HARWICH Barnstable
SOUTH LANCASTER Worcester
SOUTH LEE Berkshire
SOUTH ORLEANS Barnstable
SOUTH WALPOLE Norfolk
SOUTH WELLFLEET Barnstable
SOUTH YARMOUTH Barnstable
SOUTHAMPTON Hampshire
SOUTHBOROUGH Worcester
SOUTHBRIDGE Worcester
SOUTHFIELD Berkshire
SOUTHWICK Hampden
SPENCER Worcester
SPRINGFIELD Hampden
STERLING Worcester
STILL RIVER Worcester
STOCKBRIDGE Berkshire
STONEHAM Middlesex
STOUGHTON Norfolk
STOW Middlesex
STURBRIDGE Worcester
SUDBURY Middlesex
SUNDERLAND Franklin
SUTTON Worcester
SWAMPSCOTT Essex
SWANSEA Bristol
TAUNTON Bristol
TEMPLETON Worcester
TEWKSBURY Middlesex
THORNDIKE Hampden
THREE RIVERS Hampden
TOPSFIELD Essex
TOWNSEND Middlesex
TRURO Barnstable
TURNERS FALLS Franklin
TYNGSBORO Middlesex
TYRINGHAM Berkshire
UPTON Worcester
UXBRIDGE Worcester
VILLAGE OF NAGOG WOODS Middlesex
VINEYARD HAVEN Dukes
WABAN Middlesex
WAKEFIELD Middlesex
WALES Hampden
WALPOLE Norfolk
WALTHAM Middlesex
WARE Hampshire
WAREHAM Plymouth
WARREN Worcester
WARWICK Franklin
WATERTOWN Middlesex
WAVERLEY Middlesex

WAYLAND Middlesex
WEBSTER Worcester
WELLESLEY Norfolk
WELLESLEY HILLS Norfolk
WELLFLEET Barnstable
WENDELL Franklin
WENDELL DEPOT Franklin
WENHAM Essex
WEST BARNSTABLE Barnstable
WEST BOXFORD Essex
WEST BOYLSTON Worcester
WEST BRIDGEWATER Plymouth
WEST BROOKFIELD Worcester
WEST CHATHAM Barnstable
WEST CHESTERFIELD Hampshire
WEST DENNIS Barnstable
WEST FALMOUTH Barnstable
WEST GROTON Middlesex
WEST HARWICH Barnstable
WEST HATFIELD (01088) Worcester(98),
   Hampshire(1)
WEST HYANNISPORT Barnstable
WEST MEDFORD Middlesex
WEST MILLBURY Worcester
WEST NEWBURY Essex
WEST NEWTON Middlesex
WEST ROXBURY Suffolk
WEST SPRINGFIELD Hampden
WEST STOCKBRIDGE Berkshire
WEST TISBURY Dukes
WEST TOWNSEND Middlesex
WEST WAREHAM Plymouth
WEST WARREN Worcester
WEST YARMOUTH Barnstable
WESTBOROUGH Worcester
WESTFIELD Hampden
WESTFORD Middlesex
WESTMINSTER Worcester
WESTON Middlesex
WESTPORT Bristol
WESTPORT POINT Bristol
WESTWOOD Norfolk
WEYMOUTH Norfolk
WHATELY Franklin
WHEELWRIGHT Worcester
WHITE HORSE BEACH Plymouth
WHITINSVILLE Worcester
WHITMAN Plymouth
WILBRAHAM Hampden
WILLIAMSBURG Hampshire
WILLIAMSTOWN Berkshire
WILMINGTON Middlesex
WINCHENDON Worcester
WINCHENDON SPRINGS Worcester
WINCHESTER Middlesex
WINDSOR (01270) Franklin(95),
   Berkshire(4)
WINTHROP Suffolk
WOBURN Middlesex
WOODS HOLE Barnstable
WOODVILLE Middlesex
WORCESTER Worcester
WORONOCO Hampden
WORTHINGTON Hampshire
WRENTHAM Norfolk
YARMOUTH PORT Barnstable

ZIP/City Cross Reference

01001-01001	AGAWAM
01002-01004	AMHERST
01005-01005	BARRE
01007-01007	BELCHERTOWN
01008-01008	BLANDFORD
01009-01009	BONDSVILLE
01010-01010	BRIMFIELD
01011-01011	CHESTER
01012-01012	CHESTERFIELD
01013-01022	CHICOPEE
01026-01026	CUMMINGTON
01027-01027	EASTHAMPTON
01028-01028	EAST LONGMEADOW
01029-01029	EAST OTIS
01030-01030	FEEDING HILLS
01031-01031	GILBERTVILLE
01032-01032	GOSHEN
01033-01033	GRANBY
01034-01034	GRANVILLE
01035-01035	HADLEY
01036-01036	HAMPDEN
01037-01037	HARDWICK
01038-01038	HATFIELD
01039-01039	HAYDENVILLE
01040-01041	HOLYOKE
01050-01050	HUNTINGTON
01053-01053	LEEDS
01054-01054	LEVERETT
01056-01056	LUDLOW
01057-01057	MONSON
01059-01059	NORTH AMHERST
01060-01061	NORTHAMPTON
01062-01062	FLORENCE
01063-01063	NORTHAMPTON
01066-01066	NORTH HATFIELD
01068-01068	OAKHAM
01069-01069	PALMER
01070-01070	PLAINFIELD
01071-01071	RUSSELL
01072-01072	SHUTESBURY
01073-01073	SOUTHAMPTON
01074-01074	SOUTH BARRE
01075-01075	SOUTH HADLEY
01077-01077	SOUTHWICK
01079-01079	THORNDIKE
01080-01080	THREE RIVERS
01081-01081	WALES
01082-01082	WARE
01083-01083	WARREN
01084-01084	WEST CHESTERFIELD
01085-01086	WESTFIELD
01088-01088	WEST HATFIELD
01089-01090	WEST SPRINGFIELD
01092-01092	WEST WARREN
01093-01093	WHATELY
01094-01094	WHEELWRIGHT
01095-01095	WILBRAHAM
01096-01096	WILLIAMSBURG
01097-01097	WORONOCO
01098-01098	WORTHINGTON
01101-01105	SPRINGFIELD
01106-01106	LONGMEADOW
01107-01115	SPRINGFIELD
01116-01116	LONGMEADOW
01118-01144	SPRINGFIELD
01151-01151	INDIAN ORCHARD
01152-01199	SPRINGFIELD
01201-01203	PITTSFIELD
01220-01220	ADAMS
01222-01222	ASHLEY FALLS
01223-01223	BECKET
01224-01224	BERKSHIRE
01225-01225	CHESHIRE
01226-01227	DALTON
01229-01229	GLENDALE
01230-01230	GREAT BARRINGTON
01235-01235	HINSDALE
01236-01236	HOUSATONIC
01237-01237	LANESBORO
01238-01238	LEE

01240-01240	LENOX
01242-01242	LENOX DALE
01243-01243	MIDDLEFIELD
01244-01244	MILL RIVER
01245-01245	MONTEREY
01247-01247	NORTH ADAMS
01252-01252	NORTH EGREMONT
01253-01253	OTIS
01254-01254	RICHMOND
01255-01255	SANDISFIELD
01256-01256	SAVOY
01257-01257	SHEFFIELD
01258-01258	SOUTH EGREMONT
01259-01259	SOUTHFIELD
01260-01260	SOUTH LEE
01262-01263	STOCKBRIDGE
01264-01264	TYRINGHAM
01266-01266	WEST STOCKBRIDGE
01267-01267	WILLIAMSTOWN
01270-01270	WINDSOR
01301-01302	GREENFIELD
01330-01330	ASHFIELD
01331-01331	ATHOL
01337-01337	BERNARDSTON
01338-01338	BUCKLAND
01339-01339	CHARLEMONT
01340-01340	COLRAIN
01341-01341	CONWAY
01342-01342	DEERFIELD
01343-01343	DRURY
01344-01344	ERVING
01346-01346	HEATH
01347-01347	LAKE PLEASANT
01349-01349	TURNERS FALLS
01350-01350	MONROE BRIDGE
01351-01351	MONTAGUE
01354-01354	NORTHFIELD
01355-01355	NEW SALEM
01360-01360	NORTHFIELD
01364-01364	ORANGE
01366-01366	PETERSHAM
01367-01367	ROWE
01368-01368	ROYALSTON
01369-01369	SHATTUCKVILLE
01370-01370	SHELBURNE FALLS
01373-01373	SOUTH DEERFIELD
01375-01375	SUNDERLAND
01376-01376	TURNERS FALLS
01378-01378	WARWICK
01379-01379	WENDELL
01380-01380	WENDELL DEPOT
01420-01420	FITCHBURG
01430-01430	ASHBURNHAM
01431-01431	ASHBY
01432-01432	AYER
01433-01433	FORT DEVENS
01436-01436	BALDWINVILLE
01438-01438	EAST TEMPLETON
01440-01441	GARDNER
01441-01441	WESTMINSTER
01450-01450	GROTON
01451-01451	HARVARD
01452-01452	HUBBARDSTON
01453-01453	LEOMINSTER
01460-01460	LITTLETON
01462-01462	LUNENBURG
01463-01463	PEPPERELL
01464-01464	SHIRLEY
01466-01466	ASHBURNHAM
01467-01467	STILL RIVER
01468-01468	TEMPLETON
01469-01469	TOWNSEND
01470-01471	GROTON
01472-01472	WEST GROTON
01473-01473	WESTMINSTER
01474-01474	WEST TOWNSEND
01475-01475	WINCHENDON
01477-01477	WINCHENDON SPRINGS
01501-01501	AUBURN
01503-01503	BERLIN

01504-01504	BLACKSTONE
01505-01505	BOYLSTON
01506-01506	BROOKFIELD
01507-01507	CHARLTON
01508-01508	CHARLTON CITY
01509-01509	CHARLTON DEPOT
01510-01510	CLINTON
01515-01515	EAST BROOKFIELD
01516-01516	DOUGLAS
01517-01517	EAST PRINCETON
01518-01518	FISKDALE
01519-01519	GRAFTON
01520-01520	HOLDEN
01521-01521	HOLLAND
01522-01522	JEFFERSON
01523-01523	LANCASTER
01524-01524	LEICESTER
01525-01525	LINWOOD
01526-01526	MANCHAUG
01527-01527	MILLBURY
01529-01529	MILLVILLE
01531-01531	NEW BRAINTREE
01532-01532	NORTHBOROUGH
01534-01534	NORTHBRIDGE
01535-01535	NORTH BROOKFIELD
01536-01536	NORTH GRAFTON
01537-01537	NORTH OXFORD
01538-01538	NORTH UXBRIDGE
01539-01539	OAKDALE
01540-01540	OXFORD
01541-01541	PRINCETON
01542-01542	ROCHDALE
01543-01543	RUTLAND
01545-01546	SHREWSBURY
01549-01549	BERLIN
01550-01550	SOUTHBRIDGE
01560-01560	SOUTH GRAFTON
01561-01561	SOUTH LANCASTER
01562-01562	SPENCER
01564-01564	STERLING
01566-01566	STURBRIDGE
01568-01568	UPTON
01569-01569	UXBRIDGE
01570-01570	WEBSTER
01571-01571	DUDLEY
01580-01582	WESTBOROUGH
01583-01583	WEST BOYLSTON
01585-01585	WEST BROOKFIELD
01586-01586	WEST MILLBURY
01587-01587	UPTON
01588-01588	WHITINSVILLE
01590-01590	SUTTON
01600-01610	WORCESTER
01611-01611	CHERRY VALLEY
01612-01612	PAXTON
01613-01655	WORCESTER
01701-01705	FRAMINGHAM
01718-01718	VILLAGE OF NAGOG WOODS
01719-01719	BOXBOROUGH
01720-01720	ACTON
01721-01721	ASHLAND
01730-01730	BEDFORD
01731-01731	HANSCOM AFB
01740-01740	BOLTON
01741-01741	CARLISLE
01742-01742	CONCORD
01745-01745	FAYVILLE
01746-01746	HOLLISTON
01747-01747	HOPEDALE
01748-01748	HOPKINTON
01749-01749	HUDSON
01752-01752	MARLBOROUGH
01754-01754	MAYNARD
01756-01756	MENDON
01757-01757	MILFORD
01760-01760	NATICK
01770-01770	SHERBORN
01772-01772	SOUTHBOROUGH
01773-01773	LINCOLN

01775-01775	STOW
01776-01776	SUDBURY
01778-01778	WAYLAND
01784-01784	WOODVILLE
01801-01801	WOBURN
01803-01805	BURLINGTON
01806-01808	WOBURN
01810-01812	ANDOVER
01813-01815	WOBURN
01821-01822	BILLERICA
01824-01824	CHELMSFORD
01826-01826	DRACUT
01827-01827	DUNSTABLE
01830-01832	HAVERHILL
01833-01833	GEORGETOWN
01834-01834	GROVELAND
01835-01835	HAVERHILL
01840-01843	LAWRENCE
01844-01844	METHUEN
01845-01845	NORTH ANDOVER
01850-01854	LOWELL
01860-01860	MERRIMAC
01862-01862	NORTH BILLERICA
01863-01863	NORTH CHELMSFORD
01864-01864	NORTH READING
01865-01865	NUTTING LAKE
01866-01866	PINEHURST
01867-01867	READING
01876-01876	TEWKSBURY
01879-01879	TYNGSBORO
01880-01880	WAKEFIELD
01885-01885	WEST BOXFORD
01886-01886	WESTFORD
01887-01887	WILMINGTON
01888-01888	WOBURN
01889-01889	NORTH READING
01890-01890	WINCHESTER
01899-01899	ANDOVER
01901-01905	LYNN
01906-01906	SAUGUS
01907-01907	SWAMPSCOTT
01908-01908	NAHANT
01910-01910	LYNN
01913-01913	AMESBURY
01915-01915	BEVERLY
01921-01921	BOXFORD
01922-01922	BYFIELD
01923-01923	DANVERS
01929-01929	ESSEX
01930-01931	GLOUCESTER
01936-01936	HAMILTON
01937-01937	HATHORNE
01938-01938	IPSWICH
01940-01940	LYNNFIELD
01944-01944	MANCHESTER
01945-01945	MARBLEHEAD
01947-01947	SALEM
01949-01949	MIDDLETON
01950-01951	NEWBURYPORT
01951-01951	NEWBURY
01952-01952	SALISBURY
01960-01964	PEABODY
01965-01965	PRIDES CROSSING
01966-01966	ROCKPORT
01969-01969	ROWLEY
01970-01971	SALEM
01982-01982	SOUTH HAMILTON
01983-01983	TOPSFIELD
01984-01984	WENHAM
01985-01985	WEST NEWBURY
02018-02018	ACCORD
02019-02019	BELLINGHAM
02020-02020	BRANT ROCK
02021-02021	CANTON
02025-02025	COHASSET
02026-02027	DEDHAM
02030-02030	DOVER
02031-02031	EAST MANSFIELD
02032-02032	EAST WALPOLE
02035-02035	FOXBORO

ZIP Range	City	ZIP Range	City	ZIP Range	City	ZIP Range	City
02038-02038	FRANKLIN	02179-02179	WAVERLEY	02458-02458	NEWTON	02643-02643	EAST ORLEANS
02040-02040	GREENBUSH	02180-02180	STONEHAM	02459-02459	NEWTON CENTER	02644-02644	FORESTDALE
02041-02041	GREEN HARBOR	02181-02181	WELLESLEY	02460-02460	NEWTONVILLE	02645-02645	HARWICH
02043-02044	HINGHAM	02184-02185	BRAINTREE	02461-02461	NEWTON HIGHLANDS	02646-02646	HARWICH PORT
02045-02045	HULL	02186-02186	MILTON	02462-02462	NEWTON LOWER FALLS	02647-02647	HYANNIS PORT
02047-02047	HUMAROCK	02187-02187	MILTON VILLAGE	02464-02464	NEWTON UPPER FALLS	02648-02648	MARSTONS MILLS
02048-02048	MANSFIELD	02188-02191	WEYMOUTH	02465-02465	WEST NEWTON	02649-02649	MASHPEE
02050-02050	MARSHFIELD	02192-02192	NEEDHAM	02466-02466	AUBURNDALE	02650-02650	NORTH CHATHAM
02051-02051	MARSHFIELD HILLS	02193-02193	WESTON	02467-02467	CHESTNUT HILL	02651-02651	NORTH EASTHAM
02052-02052	MEDFIELD	02194-02194	NEEDHAM	02468-02468	WABAN	02652-02652	NORTH TRURO
02053-02053	MEDWAY	02195-02195	NEWTON	02471-02472	WATERTOWN	02653-02653	ORLEANS
02054-02054	MILLIS	02196-02222	BOSTON	02474-02474	ARLINGTON	02655-02655	OSTERVILLE
02055-02055	MINOT	02228-02228	EAST BOSTON	02475-02475	ARLINGTON HEIGHTS	02657-02657	PROVINCETOWN
02056-02056	NORFOLK	02238-02239	CAMBRIDGE	02476-02476	ARLINGTON	02659-02659	SOUTH CHATHAM
02059-02059	NORTH MARSHFIELD	02241-02241	BOSTON	02477-02477	WATERTOWN	02660-02660	SOUTH DENNIS
02060-02060	NORTH SCITUATE	02254-02254	WALTHAM	02478-02478	BELMONT	02661-02661	SOUTH HARWICH
02061-02061	NORWELL	02258-02258	NEWTON	02479-02479	WAVERLEY	02662-02662	SOUTH ORLEANS
02062-02062	NORWOOD	02266-02266	BOSTON	02481-02481	WELLESLEY HILLS	02663-02663	SOUTH WELLFLEET
02065-02065	OCEAN BLUFF	02269-02269	QUINCY	02482-02482	WELLESLEY	02664-02664	SOUTH YARMOUTH
02066-02066	SCITUATE	02272-02277	WATERTOWN	02492-02492	NEEDHAM	02666-02666	TRURO
02067-02067	SHARON	02283-02293	BOSTON	02493-02493	WESTON	02667-02667	WELLFLEET
02070-02070	SHELDONVILLE	02294-02294	SEARS ROEBUCK	02494-02494	NEEDHAM	02668-02668	WEST BARNSTABLE
02071-02071	SOUTH WALPOLE	02295-02297	BOSTON	02495-02495	NONANTUM	02669-02669	WEST CHATHAM
02072-02072	STOUGHTON	02299-02299	BAR CODE MCCORMACK	02499-02499	BROCKTON	02670-02670	WEST DENNIS
02081-02081	WALPOLE	02301-02305	BROCKTON	02532-02532	BUZZARDS BAY	02671-02671	WEST HARWICH
02090-02090	WESTWOOD	02322-02322	AVON	02534-02534	CATAUMET	02672-02672	WEST HYANNISPORT
02093-02093	WRENTHAM	02324-02325	BRIDGEWATER	02535-02535	CHILMARK	02673-02673	WEST YARMOUTH
02100-02125	BOSTON	02327-02327	BRYANTVILLE	02536-02536	EAST FALMOUTH	02675-02675	YARMOUTH PORT
02126-02126	MATTAPAN	02330-02330	CARVER	02537-02537	EAST SANDWICH	02702-02702	ASSONET
02127-02128	BOSTON	02331-02332	DUXBURY	02538-02538	EAST WAREHAM	02703-02703	ATTLEBORO
02129-02129	CHARLESTOWN	02333-02333	EAST BRIDGEWATER	02539-02539	EDGARTOWN	02712-02712	CHARTLEY
02130-02130	JAMAICA PLAIN	02334-02334	EASTON	02540-02541	FALMOUTH	02713-02713	CUTTYHUNK
02131-02131	ROSLINDALE	02337-02337	ELMWOOD	02542-02542	BUZZARDS BAY	02714-02714	DARTMOUTH
02132-02132	WEST ROXBURY	02338-02338	HALIFAX	02543-02543	WOODS HOLE	02715-02715	DIGHTON
02133-02133	BOSTON	02339-02340	HANOVER	02552-02552	MENEMSHA	02717-02717	EAST FREETOWN
02134-02134	ALLSTON	02341-02341	HANSON	02553-02553	MONUMENT BEACH	02718-02718	EAST TAUNTON
02135-02135	BRIGHTON	02343-02343	HOLBROOK	02554-02554	NANTUCKET	02719-02719	FAIRHAVEN
02136-02136	HYDE PARK	02344-02344	MIDDLEBORO	02556-02556	NORTH FALMOUTH	02720-02724	FALL RIVER
02137-02137	READVILLE	02345-02345	MANOMET	02557-02557	OAK BLUFFS	02725-02726	SOMERSET
02138-02142	CAMBRIDGE	02346-02346	MIDDLEBORO	02558-02558	ONSET	02738-02738	MARION
02143-02145	SOMERVILLE	02347-02347	LAKEVILLE	02559-02559	POCASSET	02739-02739	MATTAPOISETT
02146-02146	BROOKLINE	02348-02349	MIDDLEBORO	02561-02561	SAGAMORE	02740-02742	NEW BEDFORD
02147-02147	BROOKLINE VILLAGE	02350-02350	MONPONSETT	02562-02562	SAGAMORE BEACH	02743-02743	ACUSHNET
02148-02148	MALDEN	02351-02351	ABINGTON	02563-02563	SANDWICH	02744-02746	NEW BEDFORD
02149-02149	EVERETT	02355-02355	NORTH CARVER	02564-02564	SIASCONSET	02747-02747	NORTH DARTMOUTH
02150-02150	CHELSEA	02356-02357	NORTH EASTON	02565-02565	SILVER BEACH	02748-02748	SOUTH DARTMOUTH
02151-02151	REVERE	02358-02358	NORTH PEMBROKE	02568-02568	VINEYARD HAVEN	02754-02754	NORTH DIGHTON
02152-02152	WINTHROP	02359-02359	PEMBROKE	02571-02571	WAREHAM	02760-02761	NORTH ATTLEBORO
02153-02153	MEDFORD	02360-02363	PLYMOUTH	02573-02573	VINEYARD HAVEN	02762-02762	PLAINVILLE
02154-02154	WALTHAM	02364-02364	KINGSTON	02574-02574	WEST FALMOUTH	02763-02763	ATTLEBORO FALLS
02155-02155	MEDFORD	02366-02366	SOUTH CARVER	02575-02575	WEST TISBURY	02764-02764	NORTH DIGHTON
02156-02156	WEST MEDFORD	02367-02367	PLYMPTON	02576-02576	WEST WAREHAM	02766-02766	NORTON
02157-02157	BABSON PARK	02368-02368	RANDOLPH	02584-02584	NANTUCKET	02767-02767	RAYNHAM
02158-02162	NEWTON	02370-02371	ROCKLAND	02601-02601	HYANNIS	02768-02768	RAYNHAM CENTER
02163-02163	BOSTON	02375-02375	SOUTH EASTON	02630-02630	BARNSTABLE	02769-02769	REHOBOTH
02164-02165	NEWTON	02379-02379	WEST BRIDGEWATER	02631-02631	BREWSTER	02770-02770	ROCHESTER
02166-02166	AUBURNDALE	02381-02381	WHITE HORSE BEACH	02632-02632	CENTERVILLE	02771-02771	SEEKONK
02167-02167	CHESTNUT HILL	02382-02382	WHITMAN	02633-02633	CHATHAM	02777-02777	SWANSEA
02168-02168	WABAN	02401-02411	BROCKTON	02634-02634	CENTERVILLE	02779-02779	BERKLEY
02169-02171	QUINCY	02420-02421	LEXINGTON	02635-02635	COTUIT	02780-02783	TAUNTON
02172-02172	WATERTOWN	02445-02446	BROOKLINE	02636-02636	CENTERVILLE	02790-02790	WESTPORT
02173-02173	LEXINGTON	02447-02447	BROOKLINE VILLAGE	02637-02637	CUMMAQUID	02791-02791	WESTPORT POINT
02174-02174	ARLINGTON	02451-02454	WALTHAM	02638-02638	DENNIS	05501-05544	ANDOVER
02175-02175	ARLINGTON HEIGHTS	02455-02455	NORTH WALTHAM	02639-02639	DENNIS PORT		
02176-02177	MELROSE	02456-02456	NEW TOWN	02641-02641	EAST DENNIS		
02178-02178	BELMONT	02457-02457	BABSON PARK	02642-02642	EASTHAM		

Michigan

General Help Numbers:

Governor's Office

PO Box 30013
Lansing, MI 48909
www.michigan.gov/gov

517-373-7858
Fax 517-335-6863
8AM-5PM

Attorney General's Office

PO Box 30212
Lansing, MI 48909
www.ag.state.mi.us

517-373-1110
Fax 517-373-3042
8AM-5PM

State Court Administrator

309 N Washington Sq
Lansing, MI 48909
http://courts.michigan.gov

517-373-2222
Fax 517-373-2112
8:30AM-5PM

State Archives

Michigan Historical Center
Michigan Library & Historical Ctr
717 W Allegan
Lansing, MI 48918-1837
www.sos.state.mi.us/history/archive

517-373-1408
Fax 517-241-1658
10AM-4PM

State Specifics:

Capital: Lansing
Ingham County

Time Zone: EST*

* Four north-western Michigan counties are CST:
They are: Dickinson, Gogebic, Iron, Menominee.

Number of Counties: 83

Population: 9,990,817

Web Site: www.state.mi.us

State Agencies

Criminal Records

Michigan State Police, Ident. Section, Criminal Justice Information Center, 7150 Harris Dr, Lansing, MI 48913; 517-322-5531, 517-322-0635 (Fax), 8AM-5PM.

www.msp.state.mi.us

Note: Non-profit organizations may submit a copy of Federal Form 501C3 in lieu of payment for a name search. Sex offender data is available online at www.mipsor.state.mi.us

Indexing & Storage: Records are available until the subject's DOB indicates 99 years or a death is reported. It takes up to 30 days before new records are available for inquiry. Records are indexed on inhouse computer. 76% of all arrests in database have final dispositions recorded.

Searching: Include the following in your request: full name, sex, race, date of birth. A SSN or maiden name/previous name is very helpful. Records can be searched with or without a fingerprint card. The following data is not released: non-conviction information. Records without dispositions are not released.

Access by: mail, fax, online.

Fee & Payment: The search fee is $5.00 per name without a fingerprint card, $15.00 with a fingerprint card, and $39.00 with state and FBI fingerprint cards. Registered users may be eligible for a fee waiver. Fee payee: State of Michigan. Prepayment required. Payment required in advance unless a prepaid account has been arranged with Division cashier. Personal checks accepted. Credit cards will be accepted for online access.

Mail search: Turnaround time: 2 to 4 weeks.

Fax search: The state will permit ongoing requesters to set up a pre-paid account and submit requests by fax, but this may be discontinued.

Online search: Online access is limited to businesses that are ongoing requesters. Access is via the Internet, credit cards are required. To set up an account, call 517-322-5546.

Corporation Records
Limited Liability Company Records
Limited Partnership Records
Assumed Name

Department of Consumer & Industry Svcs, bureau of Commercial Services, PO Box 30054, Lansing, MI 48909-7554 (Courier: 6546 Mercantile Way, Lansing, MI 48910); 517-241-6470, 517-241-0538 (Fax), 8AM-noon, 1-5PM.

http://michigan.gov/cis/0,1607,7-154-10557_12901---,00.html

Note: Forms, policies, and procedures may be viewed at their web site. The fax listed above is for record requests. The fax for copies or certificates is 517-241-0537.

Indexing & Storage: Records are available from the first corporation in Michigan. Older records were indexed on cards. The index to records for active entities are maintained on computer. It takes 24 hours or less before new records are available for inquiry.

Searching: Include the following in your request: full name of business, corporation file number. The directors are only listed on the annual report.

Access by: mail, phone, fax, in person, online.

Fee & Payment: There is no search fee. The minimum charge for copies is $6.00 per record and $1.00 per page if over 6 pages. The minimum charge for a certificate is $10.00. Fee payee: State of Michigan. Credit cards are accepted for in person requests only. Personal checks accepted. Credit cards accepted: MasterCard, Visa.

Mail search: Turnaround time: 5 to 7 days. There is no fee unless copies or certificates are needed, then there is a minimum $6.00 fee. No self addressed stamped envelope is required. Copies cost $1.00 per page.

Phone search: You can order copies or certificates.

Fax search: Same criteria as mail searches.

In person search: The agency has a public access terminal for viewing records.

Online search: At the web site, search by company name or file number for records of domestic corporations, limited liability companies, and limited partnerships and of foreign corporations, and limited partnerships qualified to transact business in the state.

Other access: The database is for sale on tape or microfiche.

Trademarks/Servicemarks

Bureua of Commercial Services, Trademarks & Service Marks, PO Box 30054, Lansing, MI 48909-7554 (Courier: 6546 Mercantile Way, Lansing, MI 48910); 517-241-6470, 8AM-5PM (closed at noon for 1 hr).

www.cis.state.mi.us/bcs/corp/forms.htm

Indexing & Storage: Records are available for current records. The index is available since 1990.

Access by: mail, phone, in person, online.

Fee & Payment: The fee is $5.00 if this agency does the search.

Mail search: They suggest to use the web instead.

Phone search: No fee for telephone request. Search is limited, they will let you know if a wording exists.

In person search: No fee for request. There is a public access terminal.

Online search: Free searching is available at www.cis.state.mi.us/bcs/corp/pdf/markcom.pdf. This is a search of a PDF file of their system. It is very tricky to get to on the web.

Uniform Commercial Code
Federal Tax Liens
State Tax Liens

UCC Section, Department of State, PO Box 30197, Lansing, MI 48909-7697 (Courier: 7064 Crowner Dr, Dimondale, MI 48821); 517-322-1144, 517-322-5434 (Fax), 8AM-5PM.

www.michigan.gov/sos

Note: To find information at the web site on UCC, click on the Services to Businesses tab.

Indexing & Storage: Records are available from 1964. Records are computerized since 1990. It takes 7 to 10 days before new records are available for inquiry.

Searching: Use search request form UCC-11. The search includes federal and state tax liens on businesses. Federal and state tax liens on individuals are filed at the county level. Include the following in your request: debtor name.

Access by: mail, phone, fax, in person.

Fee & Payment: The search fee is $6.00. The copy fee is $2.00. Certification (official seal) is an additional $6.00. Fee payee: State of Michigan. Prepayment required. Personal checks accepted. No credit cards accepted.

Mail search: Turnaround time: 1 week. A self addressed stamped envelope is requested.

Phone search: Phone searching is available on a prepaid account basis, results are returned by mail.

Fax search: See expedited services.

In person search: Must be scheduled in advance and subject to availability of equipment.

Expedited service: Expedited service is available for an additional $25.00 fee. Expedited searches are provided on a prepaid account basis at $25.00 + $6.00 per debtor name. If request is received by 11 AM, search is mailed that same day.

Sales Tax Registrations

Michigan Dept of Treasury, Sales, Use, Withholding Tax Division, Lansing, MI 48922; 517-636-4770, 517-373-0884, 517-335-1135 (Fax), 8AM-5PM.

www.treas.state.mi.us

Note: The agency will only verify or confirm data.

Birth Certificates

Department of Community Health, Vital Records Requests, PO Box 30721, Lansing, MI 48909 (Courier: 3423 Martin Luther King, Jr Blvd, Lansing, MI 48909); 517-335-8656 (Instructions), 517-335-8666 (Request Unit), 517-321-5884 (Fax), 8AM-5PM.

www.mdch.state.mi.us/Pha/Osr/vitframe.htm

Note: Note: Any Michigan vital record can be "verified" for a fee of $4.00. Verification is only for names, date and place of filing.

Indexing & Storage: Records are available from 1867 on. It takes 90 to 120 days after birth before new records are available for inquiry. Records are indexed on microfiche, inhouse computer.

Searching:. Records over 110 yrs old are open to public. Otherwise, certified copies of birth records are only issued to the individual to whom the record pertains, the parent(s) named on the record, an heir, legal guardian or legal rep. of an eligible person, or through court order Include the following in your request: full name, names of parents, mother's maiden name, date of birth, place of birth, relationship to person of record. The signature and relationship to the subject are required items on the request form. The following data is not released: sealed records.

Access by: mail, phone, in person, online.

Fee & Payment: The fee is $13.00 per name for every 3 years searched. The fee is $4.00 for each additional year. Additional copies of the same record are $4.00 each. Use of a credit card is additional $5.00. An "Authenticated Copy" is available for $16.00. Fee payee: State of Michigan. Prepayment required. Personal checks accepted. Credit cards accepted: MasterCard, Visa, AmEx, Discover.

Mail search: Turnaround time: 2 to 3 weeks. No self addressed stamped envelope is required.

Phone search: You can use a credit card when ordering by phone.

In person search: Turnaround time up to 3 hours. Counter closes at 3:30 PM.

Online search: Records may be ordered from the web site. Step-by-step instructions given, use of credit card required.

Expedited service: Expedited service is available for mail, phone, and online searches. The total fee is $32.50 (includes express delivery) and payment must be on credit card. Turnaround is next day if ordered by noon.

Death Records

Department of Health, Vital Records Requests, PO Box 30721, Lansing, MI 48909 (Courier: 3423 Martin Luther King, Jr Blvd, Lansing, MI 48909); 517-335-8656 (Instructions), 517-335-8666 (Request Unit), 517-321-5884 (Fax), 8AM-5PM.

www.mdch.state.mi.us/pha/osr/vitframe.htm

Indexing & Storage: Records are available from 1867 to present. New records are available for inquiry immediately. Records are indexed on microfiche, inhouse computer.

Searching: Records are open to the public. Include the following in your request: full name, date of death, place of death, relationship to person of record. The following data is not released: sealed records.

Access by: mail, phone, in person, online.

Fee & Payment: The fee for a certified copy is $13.00 for a 3 year search, add $4.00 for each additional year searched. Add $4.00 per name per copy for additional copies. Use of credit card is additional $5.00 fee. Fee payee: State of Michigan. Prepayment required. Personal checks, money orders accepted. Credit cards accepted: MasterCard, Visa, AmEx, Discover.

Mail search: Turnaround time: 2 to 3 weeks. No self addressed stamped envelope is required.

Phone search: Credit cards are accepted over the phone for an additional fee.

In person search: Turnaround time 2-3 hours. Counter closes at 3:30 PM.

Online search: Records may be ordered from the web. Use of a credit card is required. Records are returned by mail or express delivery. If problems, call 800-255-2414.

Expedited service: Expedited service is available for mail, phone and online searches. The total fee is $32.50 (includes express delivery) and a credit card is required. Turnaround time is 24 hours if order in by noon.

Marriage Certificates

Department of Health, Vital Records Requests, PO Box 30721, Lansing, MI 48909 (Courier: 3423 Martin Luther King, Jr Blvd, Lansing, MI 48909); 517-335-8656 (Instructions), 517-335-8666 (Requests Unit), 517-321-5884 (Fax), 8AM-5PM.

www.mdch.state.mi.us/pha/osr/vitframe.htm

Indexing & Storage: Records are available from 1867 to present. New records are available for inquiry immediately. Records are indexed on microfiche, inhouse computer.

Searching: Records are open to the public. There is no bride index for the years 1950 thru 1975. Include the following in your request: names of husband and wife, date of marriage, place or county of marriage, relationship to person of record. The following data is not released: sealed records.

Access by: mail, phone, in person, online.

Fee & Payment: The fee for a certified copy is $13.00 which includes 3 years searched. Each additional year searched is another $4.00. Additional copies of the same records are $4.00 each. use of credit card is an additional $5.00 fee. Fee payee: State of Michigan. Prepayment required. Personal checks accepted. Credit cards accepted: MasterCard, Visa, AmEx, Discover.

Mail search: Turnaround time: 2 to 3 weeks. No self addressed stamped envelope is required.

Phone search: You can order by credit card over the phone.

In person search: Turnaround time up to 3 hours minutes. Counter closes at 3:30 PM.

Online search: Records can be ordered from the web site, credit card is required.

Expedited service: Expedited service is available for mail and phone searches. The total fee is $32.50 (includes express delivery) and use of a credit card is required. Turnaround time is 24 hours if ordered by noon.

Divorce Records

Department of Health, Vital Records Requests, PO Box 30721, Lansing, MI 48909 (Courier: 3423 Martin Luther King, Jr Blvd, Lansing, MI 48909); 517-335-8656 (Instructions), 517-335-8666 (Requests Unit), 517-321-5884 (Fax), 8AM-5PM.

www.mdch.state.mi.us/pha/osr/vitframe.htm

Indexing & Storage: Records are available from 1897 to present. New records are available for inquiry immediately. Records are indexed on microfiche, inhouse computer.

Searching: Records are open to the public. There are no divorce records for Detroit for 1973 and 1974. There is no "wife index" available prior to 1978. Include the following in your request: names of husband and wife, date of divorce, year divorce case began, case number (if known), relationship to person of record.

Access by: mail, phone, in person.

Fee & Payment: The fee for a certified copy is $13.00, which includes 3 years searched. Each additional year is another $4.00. Extra copies of the same record are $4.00 each. Use of a credit card is an additional $5.00. Fee payee: State of Michigan. Prepayment required. Personal checks accepted. Credit cards accepted: MasterCard, Visa, AmEx, Discover.

Mail search: Turnaround time: 2 to 3 weeks. No self addressed stamped envelope is required.

Phone search: You can order over the phone by credit card.

In person search: Turnaround time 45 minutes. Counter closes at 3:30 PM.

Expedited service: Expedited service is available for mail, phone and fax searches. The total fee is $32.50 (includes express delivery), use of credit card is required. Turnaround time is overnight if ordered by noon.

Workers' Compensation Records

Department of Consumer & Industry Services, Bureau of Workers & Unemployment Compensation, 7150 Harris Dr, Lansing, MI 48909; 517-322-1884, 888-396-5041, 517-322-1808 (Fax), 8AM-5PM.

www.michigan.gov/cis

Note: In person requests are discouraged due to confidentiality of records and records may not be on site. Injured employee may review their own records, but should call first and make arrangements.

Indexing & Storage: Records are available from 1981 on computer and from 1976 to 1981 records on microfilm. You can request by fax, but results are mailed.

Searching: Request must be in writing and cannot be for pre-employment screening. Only litigated cases are released. Include the following in your request: claimant name, Social Security Number.

Access by: mail, online.

Fee & Payment: Fee is $.25 per page plus postage and research labor cost if over 30 pages. Fee payee: Consumer & Industry Services, Bureau of Workers Unemp Comp. Personal checks accepted. No credit cards accepted.

Mail search: Turnaround time: 1 to 2 weeks. Turnaround time may be longer if records must be searched at archives. No self addressed stamped envelope is required.

Online search: Go to the web site and follow the links to see if an employer has coverage. The site does not allow searching by employee name.

Driver Records

Department of State Police, Record Look-up Unit, 7064 Crowner Dr, Lansing, MI 48918; 517-322-1624, 517-322-1181 (Fax), 8AM-4:45PM.

www.sos.state.mi.us/dv

Note: Copies of court abstracts of convictions may be purchased at the same address for a fee of $6.55 per copy. Copies of tickets must be obtained from the courts involved.

Indexing & Storage: Records are available for 7 years from conviction date; unless there is an alcohol or controlled substance conviction which will remain on record for 10 years. Accidents are reported on the record only if the driver is cited. It takes 14 days before new records are available for inquiry.

Searching: The state is in compliance with DPPA. Casual requesters must submit form BDVR-154, with written consent of subject, to receive records with personal information. Otherwise, records without personal information are released.

Access by: mail, phone, fax, in person, online.

Fee & Payment: The fee for obtaining a record is $6.55 per search. If certification is needed, there is an additional $1.00 fee. Fee payee: State of Michigan. The fee may accompany the request for mail-in, or a bill can be sent with the records. There is a full charge for a "no record found." Credit cards are accepted for fax and phone requests only. Personal checks accepted. Credit cards accepted: MasterCard, Visa.

Mail search: Turnaround time: 10 working days. No self addressed stamped envelope is required.

Phone search: Phone requesting is available for pre-approved accounts and government agencies or with a credit card.

Fax search: Established accounts can order by fax, results are returned by mail.

In person search: Search costs $6.55 per record. Turnaround time is up to 14 days (they mail the record back) unless you are the actual driver, then the record is immediately available.

Online search: Online ordering is available on an interactive basis. The system is open 7 days a week. Ordering is by DL or name and DOB. An account must be established and billing is monthly. Access is also available from the Internet. Fee is $6.55 per record. For more information, call 517-322-1591.

Other access: Magnetic tape inquiry is available. Also, the state offers the license file for bulk purchase. Customized runs are $64 per thousand records; the complete database can be purchased for $16 per thousand. A $10,000 surety bond is required.

Vehicle Ownership & Identification
Vessel Ownership & Registration

Department of State Police, Record Look-up Unit, 7064 Crowner Dr, Lansing, MI 48918; 517-322-1624, 517-322-1181 (Fax), 8AM-4:45PM.

www.sos.state.mi.us/dv

Indexing & Storage: Records are available for 10 years to present for vehicle information and 3 years to present for registration information. Vessel titles are on computer since 1974. All motorized boats must be registered, if 20 ft or over they must also be titled. It takes 14 days before new records are available for inquiry.

Searching: Requests for vehicle and ownership records must be submitted in writing with a statement of intended use. Large volume users or fax requesters must be pre-approved. There is no opt out provision.

Access by: mail, phone, fax, in person, online.

Fee & Payment: The fee is $6.55 per transaction. Normal searching requires the plate or VIN number. Records to be accessed include mobile homes and boats. Copy fee is $1.00 per record. Fee payee: State of Michigan. The fee may accompany the request for mail-in, or a bill can be sent with the records. Requests made by fax will be sent a bill with the records. There is a full charge for a "no record found." Personal checks accepted. Credit cards accepted: MasterCard, Visa.

Mail search: Turnaround time: 10 days. A self addressed stamped envelope is requested.

Phone search: Call-in requests are for established, approved accounts only. Records may be mailed or faxed back. They will usually also accept a credit card.

Fax search: Established accounts may order by fax and receive results by fax.

In person search: You can make your request in person, but they will mail back the records in 4 or 5 days. Requests must be in writing.

Online search: Online searching is single inquiry and requires a VIN or plate number. A $25,000 surety bond is required. Fee is $6.55 per record. Direct dialup or Internet access is offered. For more information, call 517-322-1591.

Other access: Michigan offers bulk retrieval from the VIN and plate database. A written request letter, stating purpose, must be submitted and approved. A surety bond is required upon approval. Please call 517-322-3454.

Accident Reports

Department of State Police, Criminal Justice Information Center, 7150 Harris Dr, Lansing, MI 48913; 517-322-5509, 517-323-5350 (Fax), 8AM-5PM.

www.msp.state.mi.us

Indexing & Storage: Records are available from 1983 to present for state police records. UD10's for all law enforcement agencies in Michigan are available for the current year plus 2 years back, first page only. It takes 3 to 4 weeks before new records are available for inquiry.

Searching: Include the following in your request: full name, date of accident, location of accident.

Access by: mail, in person.

Fee & Payment: Fee is $5.00 per report. Fee payee: State of Michigan. Prepayment required. Personal checks accepted. No credit cards accepted.

Mail search: Turnaround time: 10 days. A self addressed stamped envelope is requested.

In person search: You may request information in person, but it is discouraged.

Legislation Records

Michigan Legislature Document Room, State Capitol, PO Box 30036, Lansing, MI 48909 (Courier: North Capitol Annex, Lansing, MI 48909); 517-373-0169, 8:30AM-5PM.

www.michiganlegislature.org

Note: Older passed bills found at the State Law Library, 517-373-0630.

Indexing & Storage: Records are available from 1997 on computer.

Searching: Search by bill number, sponsor or subject.

Access by: mail, phone, in person, online.

Fee & Payment: There are no fees involved. No credit cards accepted.

Mail search: Turnaround time: 1 day. No self addressed stamped envelope is required.

Phone search: Only current and past session information is available.

In person search: Searching is available in person.

Online search: Access is available from their Internet site. Adobe Acrobat Reader is required. Information available includes status of bills, bill text, joint resolution text, journals, calendars, session and committee schedules, and MI complied laws.

Voter Registration

Bureau of Elections, Qualified Voter File, 208 n Capitol Ave, 3rd Fl, Lansing, MI 48918; 517-373-2540, 517-373-0941 (Fax), 8AM-5PM.

www.michiganlegislature.org

Note: Older passed bills found at the State Law Library, 517-373-0630.

Indexing & Storage: Records are available from from 08/98 forward.

Searching: In general, the records are open to the public.

Access by: mail.

Fee & Payment: The fee is The fee is $6.55 per name. No credit cards accepted.

Mail search: Turnaround time: 2-3 days. No self addressed stamped envelope is required.

GED Certificates

MI Department of Career Development, Adult Education - GED Testing, PO Box 30714, Lansing, MI 48909 (Courier: 201 N Washington Square, 3rd Fl, Lansing, MI 48933-8214); 517-373-1692, 517-335-3461 (Fax), 8AM-5PM.

www.michigan.gov/mdcd

Indexing & Storage: Records are available 3/1969 to present.

Searching: To search, include the SSN, DOB and date and location of test. For a copy of a transcript, also include a signed release.

Access by: mail, phone, fax, in person.

Fee & Payment: There are no fees.

Mail search: Turnaround time: 1 week. No self addressed stamped envelope is required.

Phone search: You request a verification by leaving a message and the agency will call back with the information.

Fax search: Same criteria as mail searching.

In person search: The building is also known as the Victor Building

Hunting License Information
Fishing License Information
Access to Records is Restricted

Dept of Natural Resources, E-Commerce, PO Box 30181, Lansing, MI 48909 (Courier: 530 W Allegan St, Lansing, MI 48933); 517-373-1204, 517-373-0784 (Fax), 8AM-5PM.

Note: Hunting and fishing license information is no longer released. All FOIA requests are now being denied because it is personal information.

Michigan State Licensing Agencies

Licenses Searchable Online

Airport Manager #24 .... www.michigan.gov/documents/MGRLST_17899_7.pdf
Ambulance Attendant #10 .... www.michigan.gov/cis/0,1607,7-154-10557---,00.html
Amusement Ride #8 .... www.cis.state.mi.us/verify.htm
Appraiser, Real Estate #8 .... www.cis.state.mi.us/verify.htm
Architect #8 .... www.cis.state.mi.us/verify.htm
Assessor #25 .... www.michigan.gov/documents/CertificationLevel_3022_7.pdf
Athletic Control #8 .... www.michigan.gov/cis/0,1607,7-154-10557---,00.html
Attorney (State Bar) #27 .... www.michbar.org/framemaker.cfm?content_dir=member&content=content.html
Aviation Medical Examiner #24 .... www.michigan.gov/aero/0,1607,7-145-6775_7027---,00.html
Bank & Trust Company #14 .... www.michigan.gov/cis/1,1607,7-154--22352--,00.html
Barber #8 .... www.cis.state.mi.us/verify.htm
Boxing Occupation #8 .... www.cis.state.mi.us/verify.htm
Builder #8 .... www.cis.state.mi.us/verify.htm
Camp, Children/Adult Foster Care #13 .... www.michigan.gov/cis/0,1607,7-154-10568_17846_17885---,00.html
Carnival #8 .... www.cis.state.mi.us/verify.htm
Cemetery #8 .... www.cis.state.mi.us/verify.htm
Check Seller #3 .... www.michigan.gov/cis/0,1607,7-154-10555_13251_13257---,00.html
Child Caring Institution #26 .... www.michigan.gov/cis/0,1607,7-154-10568_17846---,00.html
Child Court Operated Facility #26 .... www.michigan.gov/cis/0,1607,7-154-10568_17846---,00.html
Child Day Care #13 .... www.michigan.gov/cis/0,1607,7-154-10568_17949---,00.html
Child Welfare Agency (Child Placing) #26 ... www.michigan.gov/cis/0,1607,7-154-10568_17846---,00.html
Chiropractor #15 .... www.cis.state.mi.us/verify.htm
Collection Manager #8 .... www.cis.state.mi.us/verify.htm
Community Planner #8 .... www.cis.state.mi.us/verify.htm
Consumer Financial Service #3 .... www.michigan.gov/cis/0,1607,7-154-10555_13251_13257---,00.html
Cosmetologist #8 .... www.cis.state.mi.us/verify.htm
Counselor #15 .... www.cis.state.mi.us/verify.htm
Credit Card Issuer #3 .... www.michigan.gov/cis/0,1607,7-154-10555_13251_13257---,00.html
Credit Union #14 .... www.michigan.gov/cis/1,1607,7-154--22352--,00.html
Dentist/Dental Assistant #15 .... www.michigan.gov/cis/1,1607,7-154--22352--,00.html
Emergency Medical Personnel #15 .... www.michigan.gov/cis/1,1607,7-154--22352--,00.html
EMT Advanced/Specialist/Instructor #10 ... www.michigan.gov/cis/0,1607,7-154-10557---,00.html
Employment Agency #8 .... www.michigan.gov/cis/0,1607,7-154-10557---,00.html
Engineer #9 .... www.michigan.gov/cis/0,1607,7-154-10557---,00.html
Flight School #24 .... www.michigan.gov/aero/0,1607,7-145-6774_6887---,00.html
Forester #8 .... www.cis.state.mi.us/verify.htm
Foster Care Facility/Adult Camp #13 .... www.michigan.gov/emi/1,1303,7-102-117_401_459---CI,00.html
Foster Care Program #21 .... www.michigan.gov/cis/0,1607,7-154-10568_17801---,00.html
Foster Care, Child #13 .... www.michigan.gov/cis/0,1607,7-154-10568_17846_17865---,00.html
Foster Family Home #21 .... www.michigan.gov/cis/0,1607,7-154-10568_17801---,00.html
Funeral Salesperson (prepaid contract Reg.) #9 ..... www.michigan.gov/cis/0,1607,7-154-10557---,00.html
Funeral Home #8 .... www.cis.state.mi.us/verify.htm
Grain Dealer #2 .... www.mda.state.mi.us/prodag/GrainDealers/dealers.html
Health Facilities/Laboratory #15 .... www.michigan.gov/cis/1,1607,7-154--22352--,00.html
Hearing Aid Dealer #8 .... www.cis.state.mi.us/verify.htm
HMO #5 .... www.michigan.gov/cis/0,1607,7-154-10555_13251_13262---,00.html
Hygenist, Dental #15 .... www.michigan.gov/cis/1,1607,7-154--22352--,00.html
Insurance Adjuster #5 .... www.michigan.gov/cis/0,1607,7-154-10555_13251_13262---,00.html
Insurance Agent/Counselor/Solicitor/Admin. #5
.... www.michigan.gov/cis/0,1607,7-154-10555_13251_13262---,00.html
Insurance-related Entity #5 .... www.michigan.gov/cis/0,1607,7-154-10555_13251_13262---,00.html
Landscape Architect #8 .... www.cis.state.mi.us/verify.htm
Liquor License #6 .... www.michigan.gov/cis/0,1607,7-154-10570_12905---,00.html
Living Care Facility #12 .... www.michigan.gov/cis/0,1607,7-154-10555_13251---,00.html
Long Term Care Company #5 .... www.cis.state.mi.us/verify.htm
Mammography Facility #15 .... www.cis.state.mi.us/verify.htm
Marriage & Family Therapist #15 .... www.cis.state.mi.us/verify.htm
Medical Doctor #15 .... www.cis.state.mi.us/verify.htm
Medical First Responder #10 .... www.michigan.gov/cis/0,1607,7-154-10557---,00.html
Mortgage Licensee #3 .... www.michigan.gov/cis/0,1607,7-154-10555_13251_13257---,00.html
Mortuary Science #8 .... www.cis.state.mi.us/verify.htm
Motor Vehicle Installment Seller #3 .... www.michigan.gov/cis/0,1607,7-154-10555_13251_13257---,00.html

Motor Vehicle Sales Financer #3 ....www.michigan.gov/cis/0,1607,7-154-10555_13251_13257---,00.html
Notary Public #22 ....www.sos.state.mi.us/greatse/notaries/notaries.html
Nurse #15 ....www.cis.state.mi.us/verify.htm
Nursery Dealer/Grower #2 ....www.mda.state.mi.us/industry/Nursery/license/index.html
Nurses' Aide #15 ....www.cis.state.mi.us/verify.htm
Nursing Home #8 ....www.cis.state.mi.us/verify.htm
Nursing Home Administrator #8 ....www.cis.state.mi.us/verify.htm
Occularist #8 ....www.cis.state.mi.us/verify.htm
Optometrist #15 ....www.cis.state.mi.us/verify.htm
Osteopathic Physician #15 ....www.cis.state.mi.us/verify.htm
Paramedic #10...................................www.michigan.gov/cis/0,1607,7-154-10557---,00.html
Pesticide Applicator Company #2 ....www.michigan.gov/mda/0,1607,7-125-1569_2459-13075--,00.html
Pharmacist #15..................................www.michigan.gov/cis/1,1607,7-154--22352--,00.html
Physical Therapist #15 ....www.cis.state.mi.us/verify.htm
Physician Assistant #15 ....www.cis.state.mi.us/verify.htm
Pilot Examiner #24.............................www.michigan.gov/aero/0,1607,7-145-6775_7029-30993--,00.html
Podiatrist #15 ....www.cis.state.mi.us/verify.htm
Polygraph Examiner #8.......................www.cis.state.mi.us/verify.htm
Potato Dealer #2................................www.michigan.gov/mda/0,1607,7-125-1566_1733_2321-11149--,00.html
Psychologist #15................................www.cis.state.mi.us/verify.htm
Public Accountant-CPA #8..................www.cis.state.mi.us/verify.htm
Real Estate Broker/Salesperson #9 ....www.michigan.gov/cis/0,1607,7-154-10557---,00.html
Regulatory Loan Licensee #3 ....www.michigan.gov/cis/0,1607,7-154-10555_13251_13257---,00.html
Sanitarian #15...................................www.cis.state.mi.us/verify.htm
Savings Bank #14..............................www.michigan.gov/cis/1,1607,7-154--22352--,00.html
Social Worker #15 ....www.michigan.gov/cis/1,1607,7-154--22352--,00.html
Surety Company #5 ....www.michigan.gov/cis/0,1607,7-154-10555_13251_13262---,00.html
Surplus Line Broker #5 ....www.michigan.gov/cis/0,1607,7-154-10555_13251_13262---,00.html
Surveyor, Professional #9..................www.michigan.gov/cis/0,1607,7-154-10557---,00.html
Third-Party Administrator #5 ....www.michigan.gov/cis/0,1607,7-154-10555_13251_13262---,00.html
Veterinarian/Veterinary Tech. #15 ....www.michigan.gov/cis/1,1607,7-154--22352--,00.html

Licensing Quick Finder

Adoption Service #13 517-373-4021
Aircraft/Aeronautics #24 517-335-9283
Airport Manager #24.............................517-335-9283
Alarm System Service #23 517-336-3440
Ambulance Attendant #10.....................517-241-3018
Amusement Ride #8..............................517-241-9265
Animal (Dead) Renderer #2.............800-292-3939
Animal Control Officer #2 800-292-3939
Animal Feed (Commercial) #2..............800-292-3939
Animal Shelter #2 800-292-3939
Aquaculture Facility #2 800-292-3939
Architect #8 517-241-9253
Asbestos Accreditation, Individual #11..517-322-1320
Asbestos License #11 517-322-1320
Assessor #25 517-373-8320
Athletic Control #8 517-241-9246
Attorney (State Bar) #27......................517-372-9030
Automobile Dealer/Mechanic/Repair Facility #28
....517-373-9082
Aviation Medical Examiner #24 517-335-9283
Bank & Trust Company #14 517-373-6950
Barber #8 517-241-9261
BIDCO #14 517-373-6930
Bingo Operation, Special or Weekly #1.517-335-5781
Boiler Repairer #7...............................517-241-9334
Boilermaker (Installer) #7 517-241-9334
Camp, Children/Adult Foster Care #13.517-373-8300
Carnival #8 517-241-9265
Cemetery #8 517-241-9244
Charitable Gaming (Supplier) #1 517-335-5781
Check Seller #3 517-373-0220
Child Caring Institution #26 517-373-8383
Child Court Operated Facility #26 517-373-8383
Child Day Care #13 517-373-8300
Child Welfare Agency (Child Placing Agency) #26
....517-373-8383
Chiropractor #15..................................900-555-8374

Collection Manager #8 517-241-9258
Community Planner #8..........................517-241-9253
Consumer Financial Service #3 517-373-0220
Corrections Officer #18 517-335-1426
Cosmetologist #8.................................517-373-9234
Counselor #15 900-555-8374
Credit Card Issuer #3 517-373-0220
Credit Union #14..................................517-373-6930
Debt Management Firm #12..................517-373-0220
Dentist/Dental Assistant #15 900-555-8374
Electrician (various types) #7...............517-241-9320
Elevator Service #7..............................517-241-9337
Emergency Medical Personnel #15 900-555-8374
Emergency Medical Technician/Advanced/Specialist/
  Instructor #10.................................900-555-8374
Employment Agency #8 517-241-9246
Engineer #9 517-241-9253
Family/Group Day Care #13..................517-373-8300
Fieldperson (Dairy/Farm related) #2 800-292-3939
Flight School #24.................................517-335-9283
Foster Care Facility/Adult Camp #13 ...517-373-8300
Foster Care Program #21.....................517-335-6108
Foster Care, Child #13 517-373-8300
Foster Family Home #21 517-335-6108
Funeral Salesperson (Prepaid Funeral Contract Reg.)
  #9...517-241-9252
Gasoline Seller (Retail) #2 800-292-3939
Grain Dealer #2...................................800-292-3939
Grain Trucker #2..................................800-292-3939
Guidance Counselor #19.....................517-373-6505
Health Facilities/Laboratory #15...........517-241-2648
Hearing Aid Dealer #8 517-241-9234
HMO #5 517-373-0234
Hygenist, Dental #15 900-555-8374
Insurance Adjuster #5 517-373-0234
Insurance Agent/Counselor/Solicitor/Admin. #5
....517-373-0234

Insurance-related Entity #5 517-373-0234
Investment Adviser #12.........................517-373-0220
Liquor Dist./Whlse./Mfg. #6 517-322-1420
Liquor License #6................................517-322-1408
Liquor Licensing Director #6 517-322-1408
Livestock Dealer #2.............................800-292-3939
Living Care Facility #12........................517-373-0220
Long Term Care Company #5 517-373-0234
Lottery Retailer #1...............................517-335-5619
Mammography Facility #15.................517-241-1989
Manufactured Home Community #16 ..517-241-6300
Manufactured Home Installer/Svcs./Retailer #16
....517-241-6300
Marriage & Family Therapist #15.........900-555-8374
Mechanical Construction #7.................517-241-9325
Medical Doctor #15 900-555-8374
Medical First Responder #10 900-555-8374
Milk Distributor #2...............................800-292-3939
Milk Facility/Wash Facility #2 800-292-3939
Milk Plant/Hauler/Installer #2 800-292-3939
Millionaire Party/Vegas Night Gaming #1
....517-335-5781
Mortgage Licensee #3.........................517-373-0220
Mortuary Science #8 517-241-9252
Motor Vehicle Installment Seller #3 517-373-0220
Motor Vehicle Sales Financer #3 517-373-0220
Notary Public #22................................517-373-2531
Nurse #15..900-555-8374
Nursery Dealer/Grower #2 800-292-3939
Nurses' Aide #15 900-555-8374
Nursing Home #8 517-335-4403
Nursing Home Administrator #8............517-335-4403
Occularist #8 517-241-9234
Optometrist #15...................................900-555-8374
Osteopathic Physician #15...................900-555-8374
Paramedic #10 900-555-8374
Pesticide Applicator Company #2 800-292-3939

Pesticide Applicator/Technician #2 800-292-3939
Pet Shop #2 800-292-3939
Pharmacist #15 900-555-8374
Physical Therapist #15 900-555-8374
Physician Assistant #15......................... 900-555-8374
Pilot Examiner #24................................. 517-335-9283
Plumber #7 517-241-9304
Podiatrist #15.. 900-555-8374
Polygraph Examiner #8 517-241-9234
Potato Dealer #2 800-292-3939
Private Detective #23 517-336-3440

Private Security/Security Arrest Authority #23
.... 517-336-3440
Psychologist #15 900-555-8374
Public Accountant-CPA #8 517-373-0682
Race Track Employee #4 734-462-2400
Racing Professional #4 734-462-2400
Raffle #1 517-335-5781
Railroad Commission #23 517-336-3440
Real Estate Broker/Salesperson #9 517-241-9288
Regulatory Loan Licensee #3................ 517-373-0220
Riding Stable #2 800-292-3939
Sanitarian #15 900-555-8374

Savings Bank #14 517-373-6930
School Librarian #19 517-373-6505

Securities Agent #12 517-373-0220
Securities Broker/Dealer #12 517-373-0220
Social Worker #15 900-555-8374
Surety Company #5 517-373-0234
Surplus Line Broker #5.......................... 517-373-0234
Surveyor, Professional #9 517-241-9253
Teacher #19 517-373-6505
Third-Party Administrator #5 517-373-0234
Veterinarian/Veterinary Tech. #15 900-555-8374

Licensing Agency Information

#1 Bureau of State Lottery, PO Box 3023 (101 E Hillsdale), Lansing, MI 48909; 517-335-5781, Fax: 517-373-6863.
www.state.mi.us/milottery

#2 Department of Agriculture, Licensing, Certification & Registration, PO Box 30017 (525 W Alegan, 4th Fl), Lansing, MI 48909; 800-292-3939. www.michigan.gov/mda
Agency email: mdainfo@state.mi.us. Food establishment licensing is at the local/county level.

#3 Department of Consumer & Industry Services, Consumer Finance Division, PO Box 30220 (611 Ottawa, 2nd Fl), Lansing, MI 48909; 517-373-0220. www.michigan.gov/cis
Agency email: ofis-fin-info@michigan.gov.
Search database at www.michigan.gov/cis/0,1607,7-154-10555_13251_13257---,00.html

#4 Department of Agriculture, Office of Racing Commissioner, 37650 Professional Center Dr, Livonia, MI 48154-1100; 734-462-2400, Fax: 734-462-2429.
www.mda.state.mi.us/racing/

#5 Department of Commerce, Financial and Insurance Services, PO Box 30220 (611 W Ottawa, 2nd Fl), Lansing, MI 48909; 517-373-0234, Fax: 517-335-4978.
www.michigan.gov/cis
Agency email: ofis-ins-info@michigan.gov.
Search database at www.michigan.gov/cis/0,1607,7-154-10555_13251_13262---,00.html

#6 Department of Consumer & Industry Services, Liquor Control Commission, PO Box 30005 (7150 Harris Dr), Lansing, MI 48909-7505; 517-322-1345, Fax: 517-322-6137.
www.michigan.gov/cis
Agency email: lccinfo@cis.state.mi.us.
Search database at www.michigan.gov/cis/0,1607,7-154-10570_12905---,00.html

#7 Department of Consumer & Industry Services, Bureau of Construction Codes, PO Box 30255, Lansing, MI 48909; 517-241-9302, Fax: 517-241-9308. www.cis.state.mi.us/bcc/director.htm

#8 Department of Consumer & Industry Services, Commercial Services/Licensing Division, PO Box 30018, Lansing, MI 48909; 517-241-9288, Fax: 517-241-9280. www.michigan.gov/cis/0,1607,7-154-10557---,00.html

#9 Department of Consumer & Industry Services, Commercial Services/Licensing Division, 2501 Woodlake Cir, Okemos, MI 48864; 517-241-9254, Fax: 517-241-9280.
www.michigan.gov/cis/

Search database at www.michigan.gov/cis/0,1607,7-154-10557---,00.html

#10 Department of Consumer & Industry Services, Division of Emergency Medical Services, 525 W Ottawa, Lansing, MI 48909; 517-335-0918, Fax: 517-373-2179.
www.michigan.gov/cis/
Search database at www.michigan.gov/cis/0,1607,7-154-10557---,00.html

#11 Department of Consumer & Industry Services, Occupational Health Division, PO Box 30671, Lansing, MI 48909-8171; 517-322-1320, Fax: 517-322-1713. www.cis.state.mi.us/bsr/divisions/occ/asbestos.htm

#12 Department of Consumer & Industry Services, Securities Division, OFIS, PO Box 30220 (611 Ottawa, 2nd Fl), Lansing, MI 48909; 517-373-0220, Fax: 517-335-4978.
www.michigan.gov/cis
Agency email: ofis-sec-info@michigan.gov.

#13 Department of Consumer & Industry Services, Health and Human Services, 525 W Ottawa, Lansing, MI 48909; 517-373-1820, Fax: 517-333-6121.
www.michigan.gov/cis/

#14 Department of Consumer & Industry Services, Office of Financial & Insurance Services, PO Box 30224 (333 S. Capitol Ave, #A) (611 W Ottawa St), Lansing, MI 48933; 517-373-3460, Fax: 517-373-9475.
www.michigan.gov/cis
Agency email: ofis-fin-info@michigan.gov.
Search database at www.cis.state.mi.us/fis/ind_srch/cht_bank/state_charter_bank_criteria.asp

#15 Department of Consumer & Industry Services, Health Services Licensing Division, 611 W Ottawa, 1st Fl, Lansing, MI 48909-8170; 517-335-0918, Fax: 517-373-2179.
www.michigan.gov/cis/
Search database at www.michigan.gov/cis/1,1607,7-154--22352--,00.html

#16 Department of Consumer & Industry Services, Manufactured Home & Land Development Division, PO Box 30703, Lansing, MI 48909; 517-241-6300, Fax: 517-241-6301.
www.michigan.gov/cis
Search database at www.cis.state.mi.us/bcs_free

#18 Department of Corrections, 206 E Michigan Ave, Lansing, MI 48933; 517-335-1426.

#19 Departmen of Education, Office of Professional Preparation & Certification, Hannah Bldg, 3rd Fl, Lansing, MI 48909; 517-373-3310, Fax: 517-373-0542.

www.state.mi.us/mde/off/ppc/

#21 Department of Consumer & Industry Services, Bureau of Regulatory Services-Div of Child Welfare Licensing/Child Foster Home Licensing, 7109 W Saginaw, 2nd Floor, Lansing, MI 48909-8150; 517-335-6108.
www.michigan.gov/cis/
Search database at www.michigan.gov/cis/0,1607,7-154-10568_17801---,00.html

#22 Department of State, Office of the Great Seal, 717 W Allegan St, Lansing, MI 48918; 517-373-2531, Fax: 517-373-3706.
www.michigan.gov.sos Search database at www.sos.state.mi.us/greatse/notaries/notaries.html

#23 Department of State Police, Private Security & Investigator Unit, 4000 Collins Rd, Lansing, MI 48909; 517-336-3440, Fax: 517-336-3441.
www.voyager.net/msp
Agency email: msppsiunit@state.mi.us.

#24 Department of Transportation, Bureau of Aeronautics, 2700 E Airport Service Dr, Lansing, MI 48906; 517-335-9283, Fax: 517-321-6522.
www.mdot.state.mi.us/aero
Agency email: krashent@state.mi.us.

#25 Department of Treasury, Treasury Bldg, Lansing, MI 48922; 517-373-3200, Fax: 517-373-3553.
www.michigan.gov/treasury/0,1607,7-121-1751_2220---,00.html
Search database at www.michigan.gov/documents/CertificationLevel_3022_7.pdf

#26 Department of Consumer & Industry Services, Bureau of Regulatory Services, 7109 W Saginaw, 2nd Fl, Lansing, MI 48909-8150; 517-373-8383, Fax: 517-335-6121.
www.michigan.gov/cis/
Search database at www.michigan.gov/cis/0,1607,7-154-10568_17846---,00.html

#27 State Bar, 306 Townsend, Lansing, MI 48933; 517-372-9030, Fax: 517-482-6248.
www.michbar.org
Search database at www.michbar.org/framemaker.cfm?content_dir=member&content=content.html

#28 Business Licensing Section, Bureau of Automobile Regulation, 208 N Capitol Ave, Lansing, MI 48918; 517-373-9082, Fax: 517-373-0964.
www.michigan.gov/sos

Michigan Federal Courts

The following list indicates the district and division name for each county in the state. If the bankruptcy court location is different from the district court, then the location of the bankruptcy court appears in parentheses.

County/Court Cross Reference

County	District	Division
Alcona	Eastern	Bay City
Alger	Western	Marquette-Northern (Marquette)
Allegan	Western	Kalamazoo (Grand Rapids)
Alpena	Eastern	Bay City
Antrim	Western	Grand Rapids
Arenac	Eastern	Bay City
Baraga	Western	Marquette-Northern (Marquette)
Barry	Western	Grand Rapids
Bay	Eastern	Bay City
Benzie	Western	Grand Rapids
Berrien	Western	Kalamazoo (Grand Rapids)
Branch	Western	Lansing (Grand Rapids)
Calhoun	Western	Kalamazoo (Grand Rapids)
Cass	Western	Kalamazoo (Grand Rapids)
Charlevoix	Western	Grand Rapids
Cheboygan	Eastern	Bay City
Chippewa	Western	Marquette-Northern (Marquette)
Clare	Eastern	Bay City
Clinton	Western	Lansing (Grand Rapids)
Crawford	Eastern	Bay City
Delta	Western	Marquette-Northern (Marquette)
Dickinson	Western	Marquette-Northern (Marquette)
Eaton	Western	Lansing (Grand Rapids)
Emmet	Western	Grand Rapids
Genesee	Eastern	Flint
Gladwin	Eastern	Bay City
Gogebic	Western	Marquette-Northern (Marquette)
Grand Traverse	Western	Grand Rapids
Gratiot	Eastern	Bay City
Hillsdale	Western	Lansing (Grand Rapids)
Houghton	Western	Marquette-Northern (Marquette)
Huron	Eastern	Bay City
Ingham	Western	Lansing (Grand Rapids)
Ionia	Western	Grand Rapids
Iosco	Eastern	Bay City
Iron	Western	Marquette-Northern (Marquette)
Isabella	Eastern	Bay City
Jackson	Eastern	Ann Arbor (Detroit)
Kalamazoo	Western	Kalamazoo (Grand Rapids)
Kalkaska	Western	Grand Rapids
Kent	Western	Grand Rapids
Keweenaw	Western	Marquette-Northern (Marquette)
Lake	Western	Grand Rapids
Lapeer	Eastern	Flint
Leelanau	Western	Grand Rapids
Lenawee	Eastern	Ann Arbor (Detroit)
Livingston	Eastern	Flint
Luce	Western	Marquette-Northern (Marquette)
Mackinac	Western	Marquette-Northern (Marquette)
Macomb	Eastern	Detroit
Manistee	Western	Grand Rapids
Marquette	Western	Marquette-Northern (Marquette)
Mason	Western	Grand Rapids
Mecosta	Western	Grand Rapids
Menominee	Western	Marquette-Northern (Marquette)
Midland	Eastern	Bay City
Missaukee	Western	Grand Rapids
Monroe	Eastern	Ann Arbor (Detroit)
Montcalm	Western	Grand Rapids
Montmorency	Eastern	Bay City
Muskegon	Western	Grand Rapids
Newaygo	Western	Grand Rapids
Oakland	Eastern	Ann Arbor (Detroit)
Oceana	Western	Grand Rapids
Ogemaw	Eastern	Bay City
Ontonagon	Western	Marquette-Northern (Marquette)
Osceola	Western	Grand Rapids
Oscoda	Eastern	Bay City
Otsego	Eastern	Bay City
Ottawa	Western	Grand Rapids
Presque Isle	Eastern	Bay City
Roscommon	Eastern	Bay City
Saginaw	Eastern	Bay City
Sanilac	Eastern	Detroit
Schoolcraft	Western	Marquette-Northern (Marquette)
Shiawassee	Eastern	Flint
St. Clair	Eastern	Detroit
St. Joseph	Western	Kalamazoo (Grand Rapids)
Tuscola	Eastern	Bay City
Van Buren	Western	Kalamazoo (Grand Rapids)
Washtenaw	Eastern	Ann Arbor (Detroit)
Wayne	Eastern	Detroit
Wexford	Western	Grand Rapids

Standards for Federal Courts: The search fee is $20.00 per item (one party name or case number). Certification fee is $7.00 per document. Copy fee is $.50 per page. All fees standard unless noted in profile. Mail Search: always enclose a stamped self addressed envelope unless otherwise noted. Before releasing records, all courts require prepayment unless noted in profile.

Open records are located at the court unless otherwise noted. District courts index by defendant and plaintiff as well as by case number. Bankruptcy courts usually index by debtor and case number. While most courts now have their indexes on computer, many still maintain index card files as well.

The universal PACER sign-up number is 800-676-6856. Find PACER and the Party/Case Index on the Web at http://pacer.psc.uscourts.gov. PACER dial-up access is $.60 per minute. Also, courts offering internet access via RACER, PACER, Web-PACER or the new CM-ECF charge $.07 per page fee unless noted as free.

US District Court

Eastern District of Michigan

Ann Arbor Division PO Box 8199, Ann Arbor, MI 48107 (Courier Address: 200 E Liberty, Room 120, Ann Arbor, MI 48104), 734-741-2380, Fax: 734-741-2065.

www.mied.uscourts.gov

Counties: Jackson, Lenawee, Monroe, Oakland, Washtenaw, Wayne. Civil cases in these counties are assigned randomly to the Detroit, Flint or Port Huron Divisions. Case files are maintained where the case is assigned.

Indexing & Storage: Cases are indexed by defendant, plaintiff, and case number. New cases are available in the index immediately after filing date. Open records are located at this court.

Fee & Payment Notes: Payment may be made by money order, cashier check, personal check. Payee: Clerk, US District Court.

Phone Search: Only docket information is available by phone.

In Person Search: In person searching available.

PACER: Toll-free dial-up access: 800-229-8015. Local dial-up access: 313-234-5376. Case records are available back to 1988. New records are available online after 2 days. PACER is available online at http://pacer.mied.uscourts.gov.

Bay City Division 1000 Washington Ave Rm 304, PO Box 913, Bay City, MI 48707 (Courier Address: Use mail address for courier delivery), 989-894-8800, Fax: 989-894-8804.

www.mied.uscourts.gov

Counties: Alcona, Alpena, Arenac, Bay, Cheboygan, Clare, Crawford, Gladwin, Gratiot, Huron, Iosco, Isabella, Midland, Montmorency, Ogemaw, Oscoda, Otsego, Presque Isle, Roscommon, Saginaw, Tuscola.

Indexing & Storage: Cases are indexed by defendant, plaintiff, and case number. New cases are available in the index 24 hours after filing date. Records are also indexed on microfiche. District wide searches are available for information from 1985 from this division.

Fee & Payment Notes: Payment may be made by money order, cashier check, personal check. Payee: Clerk, US District Court.

Phone Search: Only docket information is available by phone.

In Person Search: In person searching available.

PACER: Toll-free dial-up access: 800-229-8015. Local dial-up access: 313-234-5376. Case records are available back to 1988. New records are available online after 2 days. PACER is available online at http://pacer.mied.uscourts.gov.

Detroit Division 231 W Lafayette Blvd, Detroit, MI 48226 (Courier Address: Use mail address for courier delivery), 313-234-5050, Fax: 313-234-5393.

www.mied.uscourts.gov

Counties: Macomb, St. Clair, Sanilac. Civil cases for these counties are assigned randomly among the Flint, Ann Arbor and Detroit divisions. Port Huron cases may also be assigned here. Case files are kept where the case is assigned.

Indexing & Storage: Cases are indexed by defendant, plaintiff, and case number. New cases

are available in the index 2 days after filing date. A card index is maintained for older cases. Court is in process of adding older records to the PACER system.

Fee & Payment Notes: Payment may be made by money order, cashier check, personal check. Prepayment is required for all copying. All checks should be made out for the exact amount. Payee: Clerk, US District Court.

Phone Search: Only docket information on active cases will be released over the phone.

Fax Search: Court will call with costs.

Mail Search: A stamped self addressed envelope is not required.

In Person Search: In person searching available.

PACER: Toll-free dial-up access: 800-229-8015. Local dial-up access: 313-234-5376. Case records are available back to 1988. New records are available online after 2 days. PACER is available online at http://pacer.mied.uscourts.gov.

Flint Division Clerk, Federal Bldg, Room 140, 600 Church St, Flint, MI 48502 (Courier: Use mail address for courier delivery), 810-341-7840.

www.mied.uscourts.gov

Counties: Genesee, Lapeer, Livingston, Shiawassee. This office handles all criminal cases for these counties. Civil cases are assigned randomly among the Detroit, Ann Arbor and Flint divisions.

Indexing & Storage: Cases are indexed by defendant, plaintiff, and case number. New cases are available in the index 2-5 days after filing date. As of July 3, 1995, cases from these counties may also be assigned to Detroit, Ann Arbor or Port Huron. Case files are maintained where the case is handled. Records are also indexed on microfiche. The only records indexed on index cards are old Flint cases. District wide searches are available from this division. The date the information is available varies.

Fee & Payment Notes: Payment may be made by money order, cashier check, personal check. Payee: Clerk, US District Court.

Phone Search: Only general information and a reasonable number of requests will be released over the phone. All docket information will not be released.

Mail Search: A stamped self addressed envelope is not required.

In Person Search: In person searching available.

PACER: Toll-free dial-up access: 800-229-8015. Local dial-up access: 313-234-5376. Case records are available back to 1988. New records are available online after 2 days. PACER is available online at http://pacer.mied.uscourts.gov.

US Bankruptcy Court

Eastern District of Michigan

Bay City Division PO Box 911, Bay City, MI 48707 (Courier Address: 111 1st St, Bay City, MI 48708), 989-894-8840.

www.mieb.uscourts.gov

Counties: Alcona, Alpena, Arenac, Bay, Cheboygan, Clare, Crawford, Gladwin, Gratiot, Huron, Iosco, Isabella, Midland, Montmorency, Ogemaw, Oscoda, Otsego, Presque Isle, Roscommon, Saginaw, Tuscola.

Indexing & Storage: Cases are indexed by debtor as well as by case number. New cases are available in the index immediately after filing date. District wide searches are available from this division for records filed on or after 10/1/92.

Fee & Payment Notes: Payment may be made by money order, cashier check, personal check. Payee: US Bankruptcy Court.

Phone Search: Use VCIS to obtain docket information. An automated voice case information service (VCIS) is available. Call VCIS at 877-422-3066 or 313-961-4940.

In Person Search: In person searching available.

PACER: Toll-free dial-up access: 800-498-5061. Local dial-up access: 313-961-4934. Case records are available back to October 1, 1992. New civil records are available online after 1-2 days. PACER is available online at http://pacer.mieb.uscourts.gov.

Detroit Division Clerk, 21st Floor, 211 W Fort St, Detroit, MI 48226 (Courier Address: Use mail address for courier delivery), 313-234-0065.

www.mieb.uscourts.gov

Counties: Jackson, Lenawee, Macomb, Monroe, Oakland, Sanilac, St. Clair, Washtenaw, Wayne.

Indexing & Storage: Cases are indexed by debtor as well as by case number. New cases are available in the index immediately after filing date. District wide searches are available from this division for records filed on or after 10/1/92.

Fee & Payment Notes: Payment may be made by money order, cashier check, business check. Personal checks are not accepted. Payee: US Bankruptcy Court.

Phone Search: Only the case number, case name, filing date, chapter, 341 date, attorney and trustee names will be released. An automated voice case information service (VCIS) is available. Call VCIS at 877-422-3066 or 313-961-4940.

In Person Search: In person searching available.

PACER: Toll-free dial-up access: 800-498-5061. Local dial-up access: 313-961-4934. Case records are available back to October 1, 1992. New civil records are available online after 1-2 days. PACER is available online at http://pacer.mieb.uscourts.gov.

Flint Division 226 W 2nd St, Flint, MI 48502 (Courier Address: Use mail address for courier delivery), 810-235-4126.

www.mieb.uscourts.gov

Counties: Genesee, Lapeer, Livingston, Shiawassee.

Indexing & Storage: Cases are indexed by debtor as well as by case number. New cases are available in the index immediately after filing date. District wide searches are available from this division for records filed on or after 10/1/92.

Fee & Payment Notes: Payment may be made by money order, cashier check, business check. Personal checks are not accepted. Payee: Clerk, US Bankruptcy Court.

Phone Search: Only the case number, case name, filing date, chapter, 341 date, attorney and trustee names will be released. An automated voice case information service (VCIS) is available. Call VCIS at 877-422-3066 or 313-961-4940.

In Person Search: In person searching available.

PACER: Toll-free dial-up access: 800-498-5061. Local dial-up access: 313-961-4934. Case records are available back to October 1, 1992. New civil records are available online after 1-2 days. PACER is online at http://pacer.mieb.uscourts.gov.

US District Court

Western District of Michigan

Grand Rapids Division PO Box 3310, Grand Rapids, MI 49501 (Courier Address: Gerald Ford Federal Building, 110 Michigan St NW, Rm 299, Grand Rapids, MI 49503), 616-456-2693.

www.miwd.uscourts.gov

Counties: Antrim, Barry, Benzie, Charlevoix, Emmet, Grand Traverse, Ionia, Kalkaska, Kent, Lake, Leelanau, Manistee, Mason, Mecosta, Missaukee, Montcalm, Muskegon, Newaygo, Oceana, Osceola, Ottawa, Wexford. The Lansing and Kalamazoo Divisions also handle casesfrom these counties.

Indexing & Storage: Cases are indexed by defendant, plaintiff, and case number. New cases are available in the index 24-48 hours after filing date. Cases in these counties may also be tried in the Kalamazoo or Lansing courts.

Fee & Payment Notes: Payment may be made by money order, cashier check, personal check. Will bill businesses and law firms for search and copy fees only; otherwise, Payee: Clerk, US District Court.

Phone Search: Only docket information is available by phone.

In Person Search: In person searching available.

PACER: Toll-free dial-up access: 800-547-6398. Local dial-up access: 616-732-2765. Case records are available back to September 1989. Records are never purged. New records are available online after 1-2 days. PACER is available online at http://pacer.miwd.uscourts.gov.

Electronic Filing: Information is available online at https://ecf.miwd.uscourts.gov

Kalamazoo Division 410 W Michigan, Rm B-35, Kalamazoo, MI 49007 (Courier: Use mail address for courier delivery), 269-349-2922.

www.miwd.uscourts.gov

Counties: Allegan, Berrien, Calhoun, Cass, Kalamazoo, St. Joseph, Van Buren. Also handle cases from the counties in Grand Rapids Division.

Indexing & Storage: Cases are indexed by defendant, plaintiff, and case number. New cases are available in the index 24-48 hours after filing date. Open records are located at this court.

Fee & Payment Notes: Payment may be made by money order, cashier check, personal check, Visa, Mastercard. Prepayment is required, except for law firms. Payee: Clerk, US District Court.

Phone Search: Only docket information is available by phone.

In Person Search: In person searching available.

PACER: Toll-free dial-up access: 800-547-6398. Local dial-up access: 616-732-2765. Case records are available back to September 1989. Records are never purged. New records are available online after 1-2 days. PACER is available online at http://pacer.miwd.uscourts.gov.

Electronic Filing: Information is available online at https://ecf.miwd.uscourts.gov

Lansing Division 113 Federal Building, 315 W Allegan, Rm 101, Lansing, MI 48933 (Use mail address for courier delivery), 517-377-1559.

www.miwd.uscourts.gov

Counties: Branch, Clinton, Eaton, Hillsdale, Ingham. Also handle cases from the counties in the Grand Rapids Division.

Indexing & Storage: Cases are indexed by defendant, plaintiff, and case number. New cases are available in the index 24-48 hours after filing date. Open records are located at this court.

Fee & Payment Notes: Payment may be made by money order, cashier check, personal check, Visa, Mastercard. Prepayment is required except from businesses and law firms. Payee: Clerk, US District Court.

Phone Search: Only docket information is available by phone.

In Person Search: In person searching available.

PACER: Toll-free dial-up access: 800-547-6398. Local dial-up access: 616-732-2765. Case records are available back to September 1989. Records are never purged. New records are available online after 1-2 days. PACER is available online at http://pacer.miwd.uscourts.gov.

Electronic Filing: Information is available online at https://ecf.miwd.uscourts.gov

Marquette-Northern Division PO Box 909, Marquette, MI 49855 (Courier Address: 202 W Washington, Room 229, Marquette, MI 49855), 906-226-2117, Fax: 906-226-6735.

www.miwd.uscourts.gov

Counties: Alger, Baraga, Chippewa, Delta, Dickinson, Gogebic, Houghton, Iron, Keweenaw, Luce, Mackinac, Marquette, Menominee, Ontonagon, Schoolcraft.

Indexing & Storage: Cases are indexed by defendant, plaintiff, and case number. New cases are available in the index 24-48 hours after filing date. Open records are located at this court.

Fee & Payment Notes: Payment may be made by money order, cashier check, personal check, Visa, Mastercard. Prepayment is required, except from businesses and law firms. Payee: Clerk, US District Court.

Phone Search: Use a credit card for telephone searching. Copies will be mailed.

Mail Search: A SASE is not required.

In Person Search: In person searching available.

PACER: Toll-free dial-up access: 800-547-6398. Local dial-up access: 616-732-2765. Case records are available back to September 1989. Records are never purged. New records are available online after 1-2 days. PACER is available online at http://pacer.miwd.uscourts.gov.

Electronic Filing: Information is available online at https://ecf.miwd.uscourts.gov

US Bankruptcy Court

Western District of Michigan

Grand Rapids Division PO Box 3310, Grand Rapids, MI 49501 (Courier Address: 110 Michigan NW, Grand Rapids, MI 49503), 616-456-2693, Fax: 616-456-2919.

www.miwb.uscourts.gov

Counties: Allegan, Antrim, Barry, Benzie, Berrien, Branch, Calhoun, Cass, Charlevoix, Clinton, Eaton, Emmet, Grand Traverse, Hillsdale, Ingham, Ionia, Kalamazoo, Kalkaska, Kent, Lake, Leelanau, Manistee, Mason, Mecosta, Missaukee, Montcalm, Muskegon, Newaygo,Oceana, Osceola, Ottawa, St. Joseph, Van Buren, Wexford.

Indexing & Storage: Cases are indexed by debtor and creditors as well as by case number. New cases are available in the index immediately after filing date. Records are on the computer from 1990. Open records are located at this court.

Fee & Payment Notes: Payment may be made by money order, cashier check, personal check, Visa or Mastercard. Will bill for charges less than $10.00. Checks will not be accepted from debtors. Payee: US Bankruptcy Court.

Phone Search: The court will only verify by phone whether a case was filed. An automated voice case information service (VCIS) is available. Call VCIS at 616-456-2075.

Fax Search: Will accept fax requests for $15.00 in advance. Will fax back results of a search.

In Person Search: In person searching available.

PACER: Toll-free dial-up access: 800-526-0342. Local dial-up access: 616-456-2415. Case records are available back to September 1989. Records are purged six months after case closed. New civil records are available online after 1 day. PACER is available online at http://pacer.miwb.uscourts.gov.

Electronic Filing: (Currently in the process of implementing CM/ECF.)

Marquette Division PO Box 909, Marquette, MI 49855 (Courier Address: 202 W Washington, Room 314, Marquette, MI 49855), 906-226-2117, Fax: 906-226-7388.

www.miwb.uscourts.gov

Counties: Alger, Baraga, Chippewa, Delta, Dickinson, Gogebic, Houghton, Iron, Keweenaw, Luce, Mackinac, Marquette, Menominee, Ontonagon, Schoolcraft.

Indexing & Storage: Cases are indexed by debtor as well as by case number. New cases are available in the index immediately after filing date. Records are on computer from 1990.

Fee & Payment Notes: Payment may be made by money order, cashier check, personal check, Visa or Mastercard. Court will bill for charges totaling less than $10.00. Checks from a debtor are not accepted. Payee: US Bankruptcy Court.

Phone Search: The court will only verify by phone if a case is filed. An automated voice case information service (VCIS) is available. Call VCIS at 616-456-2075.

Fax Search: Will accept searches by fax with a credit card. Will fax copies at $.50 per page plus search fee.

Mail Search: For the fee, the following items will be sent: Case number, list of creditors, and when the first meeting of creditors is scheduled. A stamped self addressed envelope is not required.

In Person Search: In person searching available.

PACER: Toll-free dial-up access: 800-526-0342. Local dial-up access: 616-456-2415. Case records are available back to September 1989. Records are purged six months after case closed. New civil records are available online after 1 day. PACER is available online at http://pacer.miwb.uscourts.gov.

Electronic Filing: (Currently in the process of implementing CM/ECF.)

Michigan County Courts

Court	Jurisdiction	No. of Courts	How Organized
Circuit Courts*	General	83	57 Circuits
District Courts*	Limited	104	98 Districts
Municipal Courts	Municipal	5	
Probate Courts*	Probate	78	83 Counties

* Profiled in this Sourcebook.

Court	CIVIL								
	Tort	Contract	Real Estate	Min. Claim	Max. Claim	Small Claims	Estate	Eviction	Domestic Relations
Circuit Courts*	X	X	X	$25,000	No Max				X
District Courts*	X	X	X	$0	$25,000	$3000		X	
Municipal Courts	X	X	X	$0	$3000				
Probate Courts*							X		

Court	CRIMINAL				
	Felony	Misdemeanor	DWI/DUI	Preliminary Hearing	Juvenile
Circuit Courts*	X				X
District Courts*		X	X	X	
Municipal Courts		X	X	X	
Probate Courts*					

ADMINISTRATION

State Court Administrator, 309 N. Washington Sq, PO Box 30048, Lansing, MI, 48909; 517-373-2222, Fax: 517-373-2112. http://courts.michigan.gov/scao/

COURT STRUCTURE

The Circuit Court is the court of general jurisdiction. District Courts and Municipal Courts have jurisdiction over certain minor felonies and handle all preliminary hearings.

There is a Court of Claims in Lansing that is a function of the 30th Circuit Court with jurisdiction over claims against the state of Michigan. A Recorder's Court in Detroit was abolished as of October 1, 1997.

As of January 1, 1998, the Family Division of the Circuit Court was created. Domestic relations actions and juvenile cases, including criminal and abuse/neglect, formerly adjudicated in the Probate Court, were transferred to the Family Division of the Circuit Court. Mental health and estate cases continue to be handled by the Probate Courts.

Several counties (Barry, Berrien, Iron, Isabella, Lake, and Washtenaw) and the 46th Circuit Court are participating in a "Demonstration" pilot project designed to streamline court services and consolidate case management. These courts may refer to themselves as County Trial Courts.

ONLINE ACCESS

There is a wide range of online computerization of the judicial system from "none" to "fairly complete," but there is no statewide court records network. Some Michigan courts provide public access terminals in clerk's offices, and some courts are developing off-site electronic filing and searching capability. A few offer remote online to the public. The Criminal Justice Information Center (CJIC), the repository for Michigan criminal record info, offers online access, but the requester must be a business. Results are available in seconds; fee is $5.00 per name. For more information, call 517-322-5546.

ADDITIONAL INFORMATION

Court records are considered public except for specific categories: controlled substances, spousal abuse, Holmes youthful trainee, parental kidnapping, set aside convictions and probation, and sealed records. Courts will, however, affirm that cases exist and provide case numbers.

Some courts will not perform criminal searches. Rather, they refer requests to the State Police.

Note that costs, search requirements, and procedures vary widely because each jurisdiction may create its own administrative orders.

Alcona County

26th Circuit Court PO Box 308, Harrisville, MI 48740; 989-724-6807; Fax: 989-724-5838. Hours: 8:30AM-Noon, 1-4:30PM (EST). *Felony, Civil Actions Over $25,000.*

Civil Records: Access: Phone, mail, in person. Only the court performs in person searches; visitors may not. No search fee. Required to search: name, years to search. Civil cases indexed by defendant, plaintiff. Civil records on computer since 1990, pleading headings in books since 1869.

Criminal Records: Access: Phone, mail, in person. Only the court performs in person searches; visitors may not. No search fee. Required to search: name, years to search, DOB. Criminal records on computer since 1990, pleading headings in books since 1869.

General Information: No suppressed, juvenile, sex offenders, mental health, or adoption records released. SASE required. Turnaround time 1-2 days. Copy fee: $1.00 per page. Certification fee: $10.00 plus $1.00 per page after first. Fee payee: Alcona County Clerk. Personal checks accepted. Prepayment is required.

82nd District Court PO Box 385, Harrisville, MI 48740; 989-724-5313; Fax: 989-724-5397. Hours: 8:30AM-4:30PM (EST). *Misdemeanor, Civil Actions Under $25,000, Eviction, Small Claims.*

Civil Records: Access: Phone, fax, mail, in person. Both court and visitors may perform in person searches. Search fee: $2.00. Required to search: name, years to search. Civil cases indexed by defendant, plaintiff. Civil records on books since 1980; on computer back to 1997.

Criminal Records: Access: Fax, mail, in person. Both court and visitors may perform in person searches. Search fee: $2.00. Required to search: name, years to search, DOB; also helpful: SSN. Criminal records on books since 1980; on computer back to 1997.

General Information: No suppressed, juvenile, sex offenders, mental health, or adoption records released. SASE required. Turnaround time 1 week. Fax notes: Fee to fax results is $10.00 1st page, $1.00 each add'l. Copy fee: $1.00 per page. Certification fee: $15.00. Fee payee: 82nd District Court. Personal checks accepted. Prepayment is required.

Probate Court PO Box 328, Harrisville, MI 48740; 989-724-6880; Fax: 989-724-6196. Hours: 8:30AM-4:30PM (EST). *Probate.*

Alger County

11th Circuit Court 101 Court St, PO Box 538, Munising, MI 49862; 906-387-2076; Fax: 906-387-2156. Hours: 8AM-4PM (EST). *Felony, Civil Actions Over $25,000.*

Civil Records: Access: Phone, mail, in person. Both court and visitors may perform in person searches. No search fee. Required to search: name, years to search. Civil cases indexed by defendant, plaintiff. Civil records on index books back to 1884; on computer back to 2000.

Criminal Records: Access: Phone, mail, in person. Both court and visitors may perform in person searches. No search fee. Required to search: name, years to search. Criminal records on index books back to 1884; on computer back to 2000.

General Information: No juvenile, sex offenders, mental health, or adoption records released. Turnaround time 1 week. Copy fee: $1.00 per page. Certification fee: $10.00 plus $1.00 per page after first. Fee payee: Alger County Clerk. Personal checks accepted.

93rd District Court PO Box 186, Munising, MI 49862; 906-387-3879; Fax: 906-387-2688. Hours: 8AM-4PM (EST). *Misdemeanor, Civil Actions Under $25,000, Eviction, Small Claims.*

Civil Records: Access: Mail, in person. Only the court performs in person searches; visitors may not. Search fee: $10.00 per name. Required to search: name, years to search. Civil cases indexed by defendant, plaintiff. Civil records on index books from 1988; on computer back to 2000.

Criminal Records: Access: Fax, mail, in person. Only the court performs in person searches; visitors may not. Search fee: $10.00 per name. Required to search: name, years to search, DOB. Criminal records on index books from 1988; on computer back to 2000.

General Information: No suppressed records released. SASE required. Turnaround time 5-7 days. Copy fee: $.25 per page. Certification fee: $15.00. Fee payee: District Court. Business checks accepted.

Probate Court 101 Court St, Munising, MI 49862; 906-387-2080; Fax: 906-387-4134. Hours: 8AM-Noon, 1-4PM (EST). *Probate.*

Allegan County

48th Circuit Court 113 Chestnut St, Allegan, MI 49010; 269-673-0300; Fax: 269-673-0298. Hours: 8AM-5PM (EST). *Felony, Civil Actions Over $25,000.*

Civil Records: Access: Mail, in person. Only the court performs in person searches; visitors may not. No search fee. Required to search: name, years to search. Civil cases indexed by defendant, plaintiff. Civil records on computer since 1985.

Criminal Records: Access: Mail, in person. Only the court performs in person searches; visitors may not. No search fee. Required to search: name, years to search, DOB; also helpful: SSN. Criminal records on computer since 1985.

General Information: No suppressed, juvenile, sex offenders, mental health, or adoption records released. SASE required. Turnaround time 1-7 days. Copy fee: $1.00 per page. Certification fee: $10.00. Fee payee: Allegan County Clerk. Personal checks accepted. Visa, MasterCard accepted for fax filings only. Prepayment is required.

57th District Court 113 Chestnut St, Allegan, MI 49010; 269-673-0400. Hours: 8AM-5PM (EST). *Misdemeanor, Civil Actions Under $25,000, Eviction, Small Claims.*

Civil Records: Access: In person only. Both court and visitors may perform in person searches. No search fee. Required to search: name, years to search. Civil cases indexed by defendant, plaintiff. Civil records on index books.

Criminal Records: Access: In person only. Both court and visitors may perform in person searches. No search fee. Required to search: name, years to search, DOB. Criminal records on index books.

General Information: Public access terminal is available. No suppressed or sex offenders records released. Copy fee: $1.00 per page.

Probate Court 2243 33rd St, Allegan, MI 49010; 269-673-0250; Fax: 269-673-2200. Hours: 8AM-5PM (EST). *Probate.*

Alpena County

26th Circuit Court 720 West Chisholm #2, Alpena, MI 49707; 989-354-9520; Fax: 989-356-9644. Hours: 8:30AM-4:30PM (EST). *Felony, Civil Actions Over $25,000.*

Civil Records: Access: Fax, mail, in person. Only the court performs in person searches; visitors may not. Search fee: $5.00 per name. Required to search: name, years to search. Civil cases indexed by defendant, plaintiff. Civil records on computer since 1988, prior on docket books.

Criminal Records: Access: Fax, mail, in person. Only the court performs in person searches; visitors may not. Search fee: $5.00 per name. Required to search: name, years to search. Criminal records on computer since 1988; prior on docket books.

General Information: No suppressed, juvenile, sex offenders, mental health, or adoption records released. SASE required. Turnaround time 3-4 days. Fax notes: Fax fee $5.00 per document plus $1.00 per page. Copy fee: $1.00 per page. Certification fee: $10.00 plus $1.00 per page after first. Fee payee: County Clerk. Personal checks accepted. Prepayment is required.

88th District Court 719 West Chisholm #3, Alpena, MI 49707; 989-354-9785; Fax: 989-354-9678. Hours: 8:30AM-4:30PM (EST). *Misdemeanor, Civil Actions Under $25,000, Eviction, Small Claims.*

Civil Records: Access: Fax, mail, in person. Only the court performs in person searches; visitors may not. No search fee. Required to search: name, years to search. Civil cases indexed by defendant, plaintiff. Civil records on computer back to 1989, prior on cards back to 1970s.

Criminal Records: Access: Fax, mail, in person. Only the court performs in person searches; visitors may not. No search fee. Required to search: name, years to search, DOB; also helpful: SSN. Criminal records on computer back to 1989, prior on cards back to 1970s.

General Information: No suppressed, juvenile, sex offenders, mental health, or adoption records released. SASE required. Turnaround time 1-2 days. Copy fee: $1.00 per page. Fee payee: 88th District Court. Only cashiers checks and money orders accepted. Prepayment is required.

Probate Court 719 West Chisholm St, Alpena, MI 49707; 989-354-8785; Fax: 989-356-3665. Hours: 8:30AM-4:30PM (EST). *Probate.*

Antrim County

13th Circuit Court PO Box 520, Bellaire, MI 49615; 231-533-6353; Fax: 231-533-6935. Hours: 8:30AM-5PM (EST). *Felony, Civil Actions Over $25,000.*

Civil Records: Access: Fax, mail, in person. Both court and visitors may perform in person searches. Search fee: $5.00 per name. Required to search: name, years to search. Civil cases indexed by defendant, plaintiff. Civil records on computer since 1977, prior on books. Only court can search on computer, in person searchers may look at old records on docket books.

Criminal Records: Access: Fax, mail, in person. Both court and visitors may perform in person searches. Search fee: $5.00 per name. Required to search: name, years to search; also helpful: SSN, DOB. Criminal records on books from 1800s, on computer since 1997. Only court can search on computer, in person searchers may review old docket books.

General Information: No suppressed, juvenile, sex offenders, mental health, or adoption records released. SASE required. Turnaround time 1 week. Fax notes: $5.00 per document. Copy fee: $1.00 per page. Certification fee: $10.00 plus $1.00 per page. Fee payee: Antrim County Clerk. Prepayment is required.

86th District Court PO Box 597, Bellaire, MI 49615; 231-533-6441; Fax: 231-533-6322. Hours: 8AM-4:30PM (EST). *Misdemeanor, Civil Actions Under $25,000, Eviction, Small Claims.*

Civil Records: Access: Fax, mail, in person. Only the court performs in person searches; visitors may not. No search fee. Required to search: name, years to search. Civil cases indexed by defendant, plaintiff. Civil records on computer since 1985, prior on cards.

Criminal Records: Access: Fax, mail, in person. Only the court performs in person searches; visitors may not. No search fee. Required to search: name, years to search, DOB; also helpful: SSN. Criminal records on computer since 1985, prior on cards.

General Information: No suppressed, sex offenders records released. SASE not required. Turnaround time same day. Copy fee: $.30 per page. Certification fee: $10.00. Fee payee: District Court. Business checks accepted. Prepayment is required.

Probate Court 205 Cayuga St, PO Box 130, Bellaire, MI 49615; 231-533-6681; Fax: 231-533-6600. Hours: 8:30AM-4:30PM (EST). *Probate.*

Arenac County

34th Circuit Court 120 N Grove St, PO Box 747, Standish, MI 48658; 989-846-9186; Fax: 989-846-6757. Hours: 8:30AM-5PM (EST). *Felony, Civil Actions Over $25,000.*

Civil Records: Access: Mail, in person. Both court and visitors may perform in person searches. Search fee: $5.00 per name. Required to search: name, years to search. Civil cases indexed by defendant, plaintiff. Civil records go back to 1883, civil records on computer back to 1991, prior on index books.

Criminal Records: Access: Mail, in person. Both court and visitors may perform in person searches. Search fee: $5.00 per name. Required to search: name, years to search, DOB; also helpful: SSN. Criminal records go back to 1883, criminal records on computer back to 1991, prior on index books.

General Information: Public access terminal is available. No suppressed, juvenile, mental health, or adoption records released. SASE required. Turnaround time 1-5 days. Fax notes: Will not fax results. Copy fee: $1.00 per page. Certification fee: $10.00 plus $1.00 per page after first. Fee payee: Arenac County Clerk. Personal checks accepted. Prepayment is required.

81st District Court PO Box 129, Standish, MI 48658; 989-846-9538; Fax: 989-846-2008. Hours: 8:30AM-5PM (EST). *Misdemeanor, Civil Actions Under $25,000, Eviction, Small Claims.*

Civil Records: Access: Phone, fax, mail, in person. Only the court performs in person searches; visitors may not. Search fee: $5.00. Required to search: name, years to search. Civil cases indexed by defendant, plaintiff. Civil records on computer since 1990, prior on docket books.

Criminal Records: Access: Phone, fax, mail, in person. Only the court performs in person searches; visitors may not. Search fee: $5.00. Required to search: name, years to search, DOB; also helpful: SSN. Criminal records on computer since 1990, prior on cards by name.

General Information: No suppressed, juvenile, sex offenders, mental health, or adoption records released. SASE required. Turnaround time 5 days. Fax notes: $2.00 for first page, $.50 each add'l. No charge for fax cover sheet. Copy fee: $.25 per page. Fee payee: 81st District Court. Personal checks accepted. Prepayment is required.

Probate Court 120 N Grove, PO Box 666, Standish, MI 48658; 989-846-6941; Fax: 989-846-6757. Hours: 9AM-5PM (EST). *Probate.*

Baraga County

12th Circuit Court 16 North 3rd St, L'Anse, MI 49946; 906-524-6183; Fax: 906-524-6186. Hours: 8:30AM-4:30PM (EST). *Felony, Civil Actions Over $25,000.*

Civil Records: Access: Phone, mail, in person. Both court and visitors may perform in person searches. No search fee. Required to search: name, years to search. Civil cases indexed by defendant, plaintiff. Civil records on docket books, are computerized since 1998.

Criminal Records: Access: Phone, mail, in person. Both court and visitors may perform in person searches. No search fee. Required to search: name, years to search, DOB; also helpful: SSN. Criminal records on docket books, are computerized since 1998.

General Information: No suppressed records released. SASE required. Turnaround time same day. Copy fee: $2.00 per page. Certification fee: $10.00 plus $2.00 per page after first. Fee payee: County Clerk. Personal checks accepted. Prepayment is required.

97th District Court 16 North 3rd St, L'Anse, MI 49946; 906-524-6109; Fax: 906-524-7017. Hours: 8:30AM-Noon,1-4:30PM (EST). *Misdemeanor, Civil Actions Under $25,000, Eviction, Small Claims.*

Civil Records: Access: Mail, in person. Only the court performs in person searches; visitors may not. Search fee: $10.00 per name. Required to search: name, years to search. Civil cases indexed by defendant, plaintiff. Civil records listed on docket books since 1968.

Criminal Records: Access: Mail, in person. Only the court performs in person searches; visitors may not. Search fee: $10.00 per name. Required to search: name, years to search, DOB; also helpful: SSN. Criminal records listed on docket books since 1968.

General Information: No suppressed, sex offenders records released. SASE requested. Turnaround time 2-3 days. Copy fee: $1.00 per page. Certification fee: $10.00 plus $1.00 per page after first. Fee payee: 97th District Court. Personal checks accepted. Prepayment is required.

Probate Court County Courthouse, 16 N 3rd St, L'Anse, MI 49946; 906-524-6390; Fax: 906-524-6186. Hours: 8:30AM-Noon, 1-4:30PM (EST). *Probate.*

Barry County

5th Circuit Court 220 West State St, Hastings, MI 49058; 269-945-1286; Fax: 269-945-1299. Hours: 8AM-5PM (EST). *Felony, Civil Actions Over $25,000.*

Civil Records: Access: Fax, mail, in person. Only the court performs in person searches; visitors may not. Search fee: $5.00 per name. Required to search: name, years to search. Civil cases indexed by defendant, plaintiff. Civil records on computer since 1992, card index back to 1977, prior on books.

Criminal Records: Access: Fax, mail, in person. Only the court performs in person searches; visitors may not. Search fee: $5.00 per name. Required to search: name, years to search, DOB; also helpful: SSN. Criminal records on computer since 1992, card index back to 1977, prior on books.

General Information: No suppressed, juvenile, sex offenders, mental health, or adoption records released. SASE required. Turnaround time 2 days. Fax notes: $1.00 per page. Copy fee: $1.00 per page. Certification fee: $10.00. Fee payee: County Clerk. Personal checks accepted. Prepayment is required.

56B District Court 206 W Court St #202, Hastings, MI 49058; 269-945-1404; Fax: 269-948-3314. Hours: 8AM-5PM (EST). *Misdemeanor, Civil Actions Under $25,000, Eviction, Small Claims.*

Note: Court will remain at the old address 220 West Court St, #202 until 1/1/03.

Civil Records: Access: Phone, fax, mail, in person. Only the court performs in person searches; visitors may not. Search fee: $5.00 per name. Required to search: name, years to search. Civil cases indexed by defendant, plaintiff. Civil records on computer since 1990, prior on index books.

Criminal Records: Access: Phone, fax, mail, in person. Only the court performs in person searches; visitors may not. Search fee: $5.00 per name. Required to search: name, years to search, DOB; also helpful: SSN. Criminal records on computer since 1990, prior on index books.

General Information: No suppressed, sex offenders, or mental health records released. SASE required. Turnaround time 2 days. Fax notes: $1.00 per page. Copy fee: $.25 per page. Certification fee: $10.00 plus

$1.00 per page after first. Fee payee: 56B District Court. Personal checks accepted. Prepayment is required.

Probate Court 220 West Court St, #302, Hastings, MI 49058; 269-948-4842; Fax: 269-948-3322. Hours: 8AM-5PM (EST). *Probate.*

Bay County

18th Circuit Court 1230 Washington Ave #725, Bay City, MI 48708-5737; 989-895-2066; Fax: 989-895-46254. Hours: 8AM-5PM (EST). *Felony, Civil Actions Over $25,000.*

Civil Records: Access: Phone, fax, mail, in person. The court and public may perform in person searches. No search fee. Required to search: name, years to search. Civil cases indexed by defendant, plaintiff. Civil records on computer for the last since 1986.

Criminal Records: Access: Phone, fax, mail, in person. The court and public may performs in person searches. No search fee. Required to search: name, years to search, DOB. Criminal records on computer for the last since 1986.

General Information: Public access terminal is available. No suppressed records released. SASE requested. Turnaround time same day. Copy fee: $.25 per page. Certification fee: $10.00. Fee payee: County Clerk. Personal checks accepted. Prepayment required.

74th District Court 1230 Washington Ave, Bay City, MI 48708; 989-895-4232; Fax: 989-895-4233. Hours: 8AM-5PM (EST). *Misdemeanor, Civil Actions Under $25,000, Eviction, Small Claims.*

Civil Records: Access: In person only. Visitors must perform in person searches for themselves. No search fee. Required to search: name, years to search. Civil cases indexed by defendant, plaintiff. Civil records on computer since 1992, listed on index cards prior.

Criminal Records: Access: In person only. Visitors must perform in person searches for themselves. No search fee. Required to search: name, years to search, DOB; also helpful: SSN. Criminal records on computer since 1992, listed on index cards prior.

General Information: No suppressed, juvenile, sex offenders, mental health, or adoption records released. Copy fee: $1.00 per page. Certification fee: $10.00. Fee payee: 74th District Court. Personal checks accepted. Prepayment is required.

Probate Court 1230 Washington, Ste 715, Bay City, MI 48708; 989-895-4205; Fax: 989-895-4194. Hours: 8AM-5PM (EST). *Probate.*

Benzie County

19th Circuit Court PO Box 377, Beulah, MI 49617; 231-882-9671 & 800-315-3593; Fax: 231-882-5941. Hours: 8AM-5PM (EST). *Felony, Civil Actions Over $25,000.*

Civil Records: Access: Phone, fax, mail, in person. Both court and visitors may perform in person searches. No search fee. Required to search: name, years to search. Civil cases indexed by defendant, plaintiff. Civil records on computer since 1980, records go back to 1869.

Criminal Records: Access: Phone, fax, mail, in person. Both court and visitors may perform in person searches. No search fee. Required to search: name, years to search. Criminal records on computer since 1980, records go back to 1869.

General Information: Public access terminal is available. No suppressed or home-youthful training case records released. SASE not required. Turnaround time 1-2 days. Fax notes: $3.00 for first page, $1.00 each add'l. Copy fee: $.50 per page. Certification fee: $10.00 plus $1.00 per page after first. Fee payee: Benzie County Clerk. Personal checks accepted. Prepayment is required.

85th District Court PO Box 377, Beulah, MI 49617; 800-759-5175 231-882-0019; Fax: 231-882-0022. Hours: 9AM-5PM (EST). *Misdemeanor, Civil Actions Under $25,000, Eviction, Small Claims.*

Civil Records: Access: Fax, mail, in person. Only the court performs in person name searches; visitors may not. Search fee: $3.00 per name. Required to search: name, years to search. Civil cases indexed by defendant, plaintiff. Civil records on computer back to 1990, prior on cards to 1965.

Criminal Records: Access: Fax, mail, in person. Only the court performs in person name searches; visitors may not. Search fee: $3.00 per name. Required to search: name, years to search, DOB; also helpful: SSN. Criminal records on computer back to 1990, prior on cards to 1965.

General Information: Public access terminal is available. (The public access terminal can be used to look up by case number.) No suppressed, juvenile, sex offenders, mental health, or adoption records released. SASE required. Turnaround time 1 week. Fax notes: $3.00 for first page, $1.00 each add'l. Copy fee: $1.00 per page. Certification fee: $10.00. Fee payee: 85th District Court. Personal checks accepted. Out of state checks not accepted. Prepayment is required.

Probate Court 448 Court Place, County Gov't Ctr., PO Box 377, Beulah, MI 49617; 231-882-9675; Fax: 231-882-5987. 8:30AM-Noon, 1-5PM (EST). *Probate.*

Berrien County

2nd Circuit Court 811 Port St, St Joseph, MI 49085; 269-983-7111 X8574; Fax: 269-982-8647. Hours: 8:30AM-5PM (EST). *Felony, Civil Actions Over $25,000.*

Civil Records: Access: Mail, in person. Only the court performs in person searches; visitors may not. Search fee: $10.00 per name. Required to search: name, years to search. Civil cases indexed by defendant, plaintiff. Civil records on computer since 1981, prior on books (domestic) back to 1835, (civil & criminal) to 1837.

Criminal Records: Access: Mail, in person. Only the court performs in person searches; visitors may not. Search fee: $10.00 per name. Required to search: name, years to search, DOB; also helpful: SSN. Criminal records on computer since 1981, prior on books (domestic) back to 1835, (civil & criminal) back to 1837.

General Information: No suppressed, juvenile, sex offenders, mental health, or adoption records released. SASE required. Turnaround time 2-3 days. Copy fee: $1.00 per page. Certification fee: $13.00 plus $1.00 per page after first. Fee payee: Berrien County Clerk. Personal checks accepted. Prepayment is required.

5th District Court - Trial Court Criminal Division Attn: Records, 811 Port St, St Joseph, MI 49085; 269-983-7111; Fax: 269-982-8643. Hours: 8:30AM-4PM (EST). *Misdemeanor, Civil Actions Under $25,000, Eviction, Small Claims.*

www.berriencounty.org

Civil Records: Access: Mail, in person. Both court and visitors may perform in person searches. In person requesters must call ahead five days in advance; records held for 3 add'l days. Search fee: $10.00 per name. Required to search: name, years to search; also helpful: address. Civil cases indexed by defendant, plaintiff. Civil records on computer since 1988, on logs from 1976-87, on index cards from 1969-75. Will do civil record check searches for only seven years.

Criminal Records: Access: Mail, in person. Only the court performs in person searches; visitors may not. In person requesters must call ahead five days in advance; records held for 3 add'l days. Search fee: $10.00 per name. Required to search: name, years to search, DOB or SSN; also helpful: signed release, address. Criminal

records on computer back ten years, on microfiche back to 1970.

General Information: No suppressed or mental health records released. SASE not required. Turnaround time 5 days. Copy fee: $1.00 per page; microfilm copies are $2.00 per page. Certification fee: $10.00 plus $1.00 per page after first; no charge if search fee is paid. Fee payee: 5th District Court. Personal checks accepted. Prepayment is required.

Probate Court 811 Port St., St Joseph, MI 49085; 269-983-7111 X8365; Fax: 269-982-8644. Hours: 8:30AM-5PM (EST). *Probate.*

Branch County

15th Circuit Court 31 Division St, Coldwater, MI 49036; 517-279-4306; Fax: 517-278-5627. Hours: 9AM-5PM (EST). *Felony, Civil Actions Over $25,000.*

www.co.branch.mi.us

Civil Records: Access: Mail, in person. Both court and visitors may perform in person searches. Search fee: $10.00 for 10 year search; $1.00 per name per each add'l year. Required to search: name, years to search. Civil cases indexed by defendant, plaintiff. Civil records on computer since 1988, prior in books back to 1830s.

Criminal Records: Access: Mail, in person. Both court and visitors may perform in person searches. Search fee: $10.00 for 10 year search; $1.00 per name per each add'l year. Required to search: name, years to search, DOB. Criminal records on computer since 1988, prior in books back to 1830s.

General Information: No suppressed records released. SASE not required. Turnaround time 1-5 days. Copy fee: $1.00 per page. Certification fee: $10.00 plus $1.00 per page. Fee payee: Branch County Clerk. Business checks accepted. Prepayment is required.

3A District Court 31 Division St., Coldwater, MI 49036; 517-279-4308; Fax: 517-279-4333. Hours: 8AM-5PM (EST). *Misdemeanor, Civil Actions Under $25,000, Eviction, Small Claims.*

www.branchcountycourts.com

Civil Records: Access: Phone, mail, in person. Only the court performs in person searches; visitors may not. Search fee: $10.00 per name. Required to search: name, years to search. Civil cases indexed by defendant, plaintiff. Civil records on computer since June 1991, prior on index books.

Criminal Records: Access: Phone, mail, in person. Only the court performs in person searches; visitors may not. Search fee: $10.00 per name. Required to search: name, years to search, DOB; also helpful: SSN. Criminal records on computer since Oct. 1988.

General Information: No suppressed, juvenile, sex offenders, mental health, or adoption records released. SASE requested. Turnaround time immediate if possible, otherwise 2-3 days. Copy fee: $1.00 per page. Certification fee: $10.00. Fee payee: 3A District Court. Personal checks accepted. Credit cards accepted. Prepayment is required.

Probate Court 31 Division St., Coldwater, MI 49036; 517-279-4318; Fax: 517-279-0516. Hours: 9AM-Noon, 1-5PM (EST). *Probate.*

Calhoun County

37th Circuit Court 161 East Michigan, Battle Creek, MI 49014-4066; 269-969-6518. Hours: 8AM-5PM (EST). *Felony, Civil Actions Over $25,000.*

http://courts.co.calhoun.mi.us

Civil Records: Access: Mail, in person. Both court and visitors may perform in person searches. Search fee: $5.00 per name. Required to search: name, years to search. Civil cases indexed by defendant, plaintiff. Civil records on computer since 1984, prior on microfilm. The court will provide case number, filed date, case

title, case status, and date of final judgment for the search fee.

Criminal Records: Access: In person only. Both court and visitors may perform in person searches. Search fee: $5.00 per name. Required to search: name, years to search, DOB; also helpful: SSN. Criminal records on computer since 1984, prior on microfilm. The court refers requests to the State Police (517-322-5531). Searcher may view public court file if case number known.

General Information: No suppressed, juvenile, sex offenders, mental health, or adoption records released. SASE required. Turnaround time 1 week. Copy fee: $1.00 per page. Certification fee: $10.00 plus $1.00 per page after first. Fee payee: 37th Circuit Court Clerk. Personal checks accepted. Prepayment is required.

10th District Court 161 E Michigan Ave, Battle Creek, MI 49014; 269-969-6666; Fax: 269-969-6663. Hours: 8:00AM-4PM (EST). *Misdemeanor, Civil Actions Under $25,000, Eviction, Small Claims.*

http://courts.co.calhoun.mi.us

Note: The 10th District Court Marshall Branch's records and administration is now housed here.

Civil Records: Access: Mail, fax, in person. Visitors must perform in person searches for themselves. No search fee. Required to search: name, years to search. Civil cases indexed by defendant, plaintiff. Civil records on computer back to 1986, prior on docket books. Public access terminal searches back to 10/1997. Fax requests must be signed.

Criminal Records: Access: Fax, in person. Visitors must perform in person searches for themselves. No search fee. Required to search: name, years to search, DOB. Criminal records on computer back to 1986, prior on docket books. Public access terminal searches back to 10/1997. Fax requests must be signed.

General Information: Public access terminal is available. No suppressed, juvenile, sex offenders, mental health, or adoption records released. Copy fee: $.25 per page. Certification fee: $10.00 plus $1.00 per page after first. Fee payee: 10th District Court. Personal checks accepted. Credit cards accepted: Visa, MasterCard. Prepayment is required.

Probate Court Justice Center, 161 E Michigan Ave, Battle Creek, MI 49014; 269-969-6795; Fax: 269-969-6797. Hours: 8AM-5PM (EST). *Probate.*

http://courts.co.calhoun.mi.us

Cass County

43rd Circuit Court 120 North Broadway, File Room, Cassopolis, MI 49031; 269-445-4416 X3201; Fax: 269-445-4406. Hours: 8AM-5PM (EST). *Felony, Civil Actions Over $25,000.*

Civil Records: Access: Phone, fax, mail, in person. Both court and visitors may perform in person searches. No search fee. Required to search: name, years to search. Civil cases indexed by defendant, plaintiff. Civil records on computer back to 1988; books since 1963.

Criminal Records: Access: Fax, mail, in person. Only the court performs in person searches; visitors may not. No search fee. Required to search: name, years to search, DOB; also helpful: SSN. Criminal records on computer back to 1988; books since 1963.

General Information: No suppressed, juvenile, sex offenders, mental health, or adoption records released. SASE helpful. Turnaround time 2 weeks. Fax notes: No fee to fax back to an 800 number. Copy fee: $1.00 per page. Certification fee: $10.00. Fee payee: Cass County Clerk. Business checks accepted. Prepayment required.

4th District Court 110 North Broadway, Cassopolis, MI 49031; 269-445-4424; Fax: 269-445-4486. Hours: 8AM-5PM (EST). *Misdemeanor, Civil Actions Under $25,000, Eviction, Small Claims.*

Civil Records: Access: Phone, mail, in person. Court may perform in person searches. No search fee. Required to search: name, years to search; also helpful: address. Civil cases indexed by defendant, plaintiff. Civil records on computer since 1988, indexed on cards prior back to 1969. You can fax requests, but results will not be returned by fax.

Criminal Records: Access: Phone, mail, in person. Court may perform in person searches. No search fee. Required to search: name, years to search, DOB; also helpful: address. Criminal records on computer since 1988, indexed on cards prior back to 1969. You can fax requests, but results will not be returned by fax.

General Information: No suppressed, juvenile, sex offenders, mental health, or adoption records released. SASE not required. Turnaround time 2 weeks. Copy fee: $1.00 for first page, $.10 each add'l. Certification fee: $10.00 plus $1.00 per page after first. Fee payee: 4th District Court. Personal checks accepted. Prepayment is required.

Probate Court 110 North Broadway, Rm 202, Cassopolis, MI 49031; 269-445-4454; Fax: 269-445-4453. Hours: 8AM-Noon, 1-5PM (EST). *Probate.*

Charlevoix County

33rd Circuit Court 203 Antrim St, Charlevoix, MI 49720; 231-547-7200; Fax: 231-547-7217. Hours: 9AM-5PM (EST). *Felony, Civil Actions Over $25,000.*

Civil Records: Access: Mail, in person. Only the court performs in person searches; visitors may not. No search fee. Required to search: name, years to search. Civil cases indexed by defendant, plaintiff. Civil records on computer from 1991, microfiche and archives from 1868.

Criminal Records: Access: Mail, in person. Only the court performs in person searches; visitors may not. No search fee. Required to search: name, years to search, DOB; also helpful: SSN. Criminal records on computer from 1991, microfiche and archives from 1868.

General Information: No suppressed, juvenile, adoption records released. SASE requested. Turnaround time 1 week. Copy fee: $1.00 per page. Certification fee: $10.00. Fee payee: Charlevoix County Clerk. Personal checks accepted. Prepayment is required.

90th District Court 301 State St, Court Bldg, Charlevoix, MI 49720; 231-547-7227; Fax: 231-547-7253. Hours: 9AM-5PM (EST). *Misdemeanor, Civil Actions Under $25,000, Eviction, Small Claims.*

Civil Records: Access: Phone, mail, fax, in person. Both court and visitors may perform in person searches. No search fee. Required to search: name, years to search. Civil cases indexed by defendant, plaintiff. Civil records on computer back to 1987, listed on index cards to 1963.

Criminal Records: Access: Mail, fax, in person. Both court and visitors may perform in person searches. No search fee. Required to search: name, years to search, DOB. Criminal records on computer back to 1987, listed on index cards to 1963.

General Information: Public access terminal is available. No suppressed records released. SASE helpful. Turnaround time 1-2 days. Copy fee: $1.00 per page. Fee payee: 90th District Court. Personal checks accepted. Prepayment is required.

Probate Court 301 State St, County Bldg, Charlevoix, MI 49720; 231-547-7214; 547-7215; Fax: 231-547-7256. Hours: 9AM-5PM (EST). *Probate.*

Note: Shares the same judge with Emmet County Probate Court.

Cheboygan County

53rd Circuit Court PO Box 70, Cheboygan, MI 49721; 231-627-8808. Hours: 8:30AM-5PM (EST). *Felony, Civil Actions Over $25,000.*

Civil Records: Access: Phone, mail, in person. Only the court performs in person searches; visitors may not. No search fee. Required to search: name, years to search. Civil cases indexed by defendant, plaintiff. Civil records on computer from 1985, index cards from 1886.

Criminal Records: Access: Phone, mail, in person. Only the court performs in person searches; visitors may not. No search fee. Required to search: name, years to search, DOB. Criminal records on computer from 1985, index cards from 1886.

General Information: No suppressed records released. SASE requested. Turnaround time 3-4 days. Copy fee: $1.00 for first page, $.20 each add'l. Certification fee: $10.00 plus $1.00 each additional page. Fee payee: County Clerk. Personal checks accepted. Prepayment is required.

89th District Court PO Box 70, Cheboygan, MI 49721; 231-627-8809; Fax: 231-627-8444. Hours: 8:30AM-4PM (EST). *Misdemeanor, Civil Actions Under $25,000, Eviction, Small Claims.*

Civil Records: Access: Phone, fax, mail, in person. Only the court performs in person searches; visitors may not. No search fee. Required to search: name, years to search. Civil cases indexed by defendant, plaintiff. Civil records on computer back to 1988, microfilmed prior.

Criminal Records: Access: Phone, fax, mail, in person. Only the court performs in person searches; visitors may not. No search fee. Required to search: name, years to search, DOB. Criminal records on computer back to 1986.

General Information: No suppressed, juvenile, sex offenders, mental health, or adoption records released. SASE required. Turnaround time 3-4 days. Fax notes: No fee to fax results. Copy fee: $1.00 per page. Certification fee: $10.00 plus $1.00 per page after first. Fee payee: 89th District Court. Personal checks accepted. Prepayment is required.

Probate Court 870 S Main St, PO Box 70, Cheboygan, MI 49721; 231-627-8823; Fax: 231-627-8868. Hours: 8:30AM-4:30PM (EST). *Probate.*

Chippewa County

50th Circuit Court 319 Court St, Sault Ste Marie, MI 49783; 906-635-6300; Fax: 906-635-6851. Hours: 8AM-5PM (EST). *Felony, Civil Actions Over $25,000.*

Civil Records: Access: Mail, in person. Only the court performs in person searches; visitors may not. Search fee: $5.00 per name. Fee is for 10 year search. Required to search: name, years to search. Civil cases indexed by defendant, plaintiff. Civil records on computer since 1990, prior on index books to late 1800s.

Criminal Records: Access: Mail, in person. Only the court performs in person searches; visitors may not. Search fee: $5.00 per name. Fee is for 10 year search. Required to search: name, years to search, DOB; also helpful: SSN. Criminal records on computer since 1990, prior on index books to late 1800s.

General Information: No suppressed, juvenile, sex offenders, mental health, or adoption records released. SASA not required. Turnaround time 1-2 days. Copy fee: $1.00 per page. Certification fee: $10.00 plus $1.00 per page after first. Fee payee: County Clerk. Personal checks accepted. Prepayment is required.

91st District Court 325 Court St, Sault Ste Marie, MI 49783; 906-635-6320; Fax: 906-635-7605. Hours: 9AM-4:30PM (EST). *Misdemeanor, Civil Actions Under $25,000, Eviction, Small Claims.*

Note: Call before faxing for instructions.

Civil Records: Access: Mail, fax, in person. Both court and visitors may perform in person searches. Search fee: $5.00 per name. Required to search: name, years to search. Civil cases indexed by defendant, plaintiff. Civil records on computer since 1989, prior on index books to 1968.

Criminal Records: Access: Mail, fax, in person. Both court and visitors may perform in person searches. Search fee: $5.00 per name. Required to search: name, years to search, DOB; also helpful: SSN. Criminal records on computer since 1989, prior on index books to 1968.

General Information: Public access terminal is available. No suppressed, juvenile, sex offenders, mental health, or adoption records released. SASE required. Turnaround time 10 days. Copy fee: $1.00 per page. Certification fee: $10.00. Only cashiers checks and money orders accepted. Prepayment is required.

Probate Court 319 Court St., Sault Ste Marie, MI 49783; 906-635-6314; Fax: 906-635-6852. Hours: 9AM-5PM (EST). *Probate.*

Clare County

55th Circuit Court 225 West Main St, PO Box 438, Harrison, MI 48625; 989-539-7131; Fax: 989-539-6616. Hours: 8AM-4:30PM (EST). *Felony, Civil Actions Over $25,000.*

Civil Records: Access: Mail, in person. Only the court performs in person searches; visitors may not. Search fee: $5.00 per name. Add $1.00 per year if more than five. Required to search: name, years to search DOB. Civil cases indexed by defendant, plaintiff. Civil records on computer since 1992, on books from 1925.

Criminal Records: Access: Mail, in person. Only the court performs in person searches; visitors may not. Search fee: $5.00 per name. Add $1.00 per year if more than five. Required to search: name, years to search, DOB; also helpful: SSN. Criminal records on computer since 1992, on books from 1925.

General Information: No suppressed, juvenile, sex offenders, mental health, or adoption records released. SASE required. Turnaround time 1-5 days. Copy fee: $1.00 per page. Certification fee: $10.00 per document plus $1.00 per page. Fee payee: Clare County Clerk. Personal checks accepted. Prepayment is required.

80th District Court 225 W. Main St, Harrison, MI 48625; 989-539-7173; Fax: 989-539-4036. Hours: 8AM-4:30PM (EST). *Misdemeanor, Civil Actions Under $25,000, Eviction, Small Claims.*

Civil Records: Access: Mail, fax, in person. Only the court performs in person searches. Visitors may not. No search fee. Required to search: name, years to search. Civil cases indexed by defendant, plaintiff. Civil records go back to 1969; on computer back to 1988.

Criminal Records: Access: Mail, fax, in person. Only the court performs in person searches; visitors may not. No search fee. Required to search: name, years to search, DOB, SSN. Criminal records go back to 1969; on computer back to 1988.

General Information: No suppressed, juvenile, sex offenders, mental health, or adoption records released. SASE required. Turnaround time 1-2 days. Copy fee: $1.00 per page. Certification fee: $10.00. Fee payee: 80th District Court. Personal checks accepted. Prepayment is required.

Probate Court 225 W. Main St., PO Box 96, Harrison, MI 48625; 989-539-7109. Hours: 8AM-4:30PM (EST). *Probate.*

Note: This is combined with Gladwin County Probate Court.

Clinton County

29th Circuit Court PO Box 69, St Johns, MI 48879-0069; 989-224-5140; Fax: 989-224-5254. Hours: 8AM-5PM (EST). *Felony, Civil Actions Over $25,000.*

www.clinton-county.org

Civil Records: Access: Mail, in person. Both court and visitors may perform in person searches. Search fee: $10.00 per name. Fee is for 10 year search. Required to search: name, years to search. Civil cases indexed by defendant, plaintiff. Civil records in calendar books since 1800s, some on microfiche; on computer since 1996.
Criminal Records: Access: Mail, in person. Both court and visitors may perform in person searches. Search fee: $10.00 per name. Fee is for 10 year search. Required to search: name, years to search; also helpful: DOB. Criminal records in calendar books since 1800s, some on microfiche; on computer since 1996.
General Information: No suppressed or non public records released. SASE required. Turnaround time 24 hrs. Copy fee: $1.00 per page. Certification fee: $10.00 plus $1.00 per page. Fee payee: Clinton County Clerk. Personal checks accepted. Prepayment is required.

65th District Court 100 E State St, #3400, St Johns, MI 48879-1571; 989-224-5150; Fax: 989-224-5154. Hours: 8AM-5PM (EST). *Misdemeanor, Civil Actions Under $25,000, Eviction, Small Claims.*

Civil Records: Access: Mail, in person. Both court and visitors may perform in person searches. No search fee. Required to search: name, years to search. Civil cases indexed by defendant, plaintiff. Civil records on computer since 1989-90.
Criminal Records: Access: Mail, in person. Both court and visitors may perform in person searches. No search fee. Required to search: name, years to search, DOB, SSN. Criminal records on computer since 1986.
General Information: Public access terminal is available. No suppressed, juvenile, sex offenders, mental health, or adoption records released. SASE required. Turnaround time 1 week. Copy fee: $.25 per page. Fee payee: 65th District Court. Personal checks accepted. Prepayment is required.

Probate Court 101 E State St #4300, St Johns, MI 48879; 989-224-5190; Fax: 989-224-5102. Hours: 8AM-5PM (EST). *Probate.*

www.clinton-county.org

Crawford County

46th Circuit Court 200 West Michigan Ave, Grayling, MI 49738; 989-348-2841; Fax: 989-344-3223. Hours: 8:30AM-4:30PM (EST). *Felony, Civil Actions Over $25,000.*

www.Circuit46.org

Civil Records: Access: Mail, in person, online. Only the court performs in person searches; visitors may not. No search fee. Required to search: name, years to search. Civil cases indexed by defendant, plaintiff. Civil records on computer since 1990, prior on books to 1930s. Online access to court case records (open or closed cases for 90 days only) available free at www.circuit46.org/Cases/cases.html. Search by name.
Criminal Records: Access: Mail, in person, online. Only the court performs in person searches; visitors may not. No search fee. Required to search: name, years to search, DOB. Criminal records on computer since 1990, prior on books to 1960. Online access to criminal records is the same as civil.
General Information: No suppressed records released. SASE required. Turnaround time 2-3 days. Copy fee: $1.00 per page. Certification fee: $10.00 plus $1.00 per page after first. Fee payee: Crawford County. Personal checks accepted. Prepayment is required.

83rd District Court 200 West Michigan Ave., Grayling, MI 49738; 989-348-2841 X242; Fax: 989-344-3290. Hours: 8AM-4:30PM (EST). *Misdemeanor, Civil Actions Under $25,000, Eviction, Small Claims.*

www.Circuit46.org

Civil Records: Access: Phone, mail, fax, in person, online. Only the court performs in person searches; visitors may not. No search fee. Required to search: name, years to search. Civil cases indexed by defendant, plaintiff. Civil records on computer since 1990, books from 1969. Online access to court case records (open or closed cases for 90 days only) available free at www.circuit46.org/Cases/cases.html. Search by name.
Criminal Records: Access: Phone, mail, fax, in person, online. Only the court performs in person searches; visitors may not. No search fee. Required to search: name, years to search, DOB. Criminal records on computer since 1989. Online access to criminal records is the same as civil.
General Information: No suppressed, juvenile, sex offenders, mental health, or adoption records released. SASE not required. Turnaround time 1-4 days. Copy fee: $.25 per page. Certification fee: $10.00 plus $1.00 each additional page. Fee payee: Crawford County 83rd District Court. Personal checks accepted. Credit cards accepted: Visa, MasterCard. Prepayment is required.

Probate Court 200 W Michigan Ave, Grayling, MI 49738; 989-344-3237; Fax: 989-344-3277. Hours: 8:30AM-4:30PM (EST). *Probate.*

www.Circuit46.org

Note: Search cases by name free at www.circuit46.org/Cases/cases.html.

Delta County

47th Circuit Court 310 Ludington St, Escanaba, MI 49829; 906-789-5105; Fax: 906-789-5196. Hours: 8AM-4PM (EST). *Felony, Civil Actions Over $25,000.*

Civil Records: Access: Mail, in person. Both court and visitors may perform in person searches. Search fee: $5.00 per name. Required to search: name; also helpful: years to search, address. Civil cases indexed by defendant, plaintiff. Civil records on computer from 1986, archived into 1800s.
Criminal Records: Access: Mail, in person. Both court and visitors may perform in person searches. Search fee: $5.00 per name. Required to search: name; also helpful: years to search, DOB, SSN. Criminal records on computer from 1989, archived into 1800s.
General Information: No suppressed, juvenile, sex offenders, mental health, or adoption records released. SASE required. Turnaround time same day. Copy fee: $.25 per page. Certification fee: $10.00 plus $1.00 per page after first. Fee payee: Delta County. Personal checks accepted. Prepayment is required.

94th District Court 310 Ludington St., Escanaba, MI 49829; 906-789-5106; Fax: 906-789-5198. Hours: 8AM-4PM (EST). *Misdemeanor, Civil Actions Under $25,000, Eviction, Small Claims.*

Civil Records: Access: Mail, in person. Only the court performs in person searches; visitors may not. No search fee. Required to search: name, years to search; also helpful: address. Civil cases indexed by defendant, plaintiff. Civil records on computer back to 1988, prior on books to 1968.
Criminal Records: Access: Mail, in person. Only the court performs in person searches; visitors may not. Search fee: $5.00 per name. Required to search: name, years to search, DOB; also helpful: address, SSN. Criminal records on computer back to 1988, prior on books to 1968.
General Information: No suppressed, juvenile, sex offenders, mental health, or adoption records released. SASE required. Turnaround time 3 days. Copy fee: $.25 per page. Certification fee: $10.00. Fee payee: 94th

District Court. Personal checks accepted. Prepayment is required.

Probate Court 310 Ludington St., Escanaba, MI 49829; 906-789-5112; Fax: 906-789-5140. Hours: 8AM-Noon, 1-4PM (EST). *Probate.*

Dickinson County

41st Circuit Court PO Box 609, Iron Mountain, MI 49801; 906-774-0988; Fax: 906-779-0587. Hours: 8AM-4:30PM (CST). *Felony, Civil Actions Over $25,000.*

Civil Records: Access: Mail, in person. Both court and visitors may perform in person searches. Search fee: $15.00 per name. Fee is for 10 year search. Required to search: name, years to search. Civil cases indexed by defendant, plaintiff. Civil records on docket books since 1891; on computer since.
Criminal Records: Access: Mail, in person. Both court and visitors may perform in person searches. Search fee: $5.00 per name. Fee is for 10 year search. Required to search: name, years to search, DOB; also helpful: SSN. Criminal records on docket books since 1891; on computer since.
General Information: No suppressed, juvenile, sex offenders, mental health, or adoption records released. SASE required. Turnaround time 1-2 days. Fax notes: Fee to fax results is $1.50 per page. Copy fee: $.15 per page. Certification fee: $10.00 plus $1.00 per page. Fee payee: County Clerk. Business checks accepted. Prepayment is required.

95 B District Court County Courthouse, PO Box 609, Iron Mountain, MI 49801; 906-774-0506; Fax: 906-774-8560. Hours: 8AM-4:30PM (CST). *Misdemeanor, Civil Actions Under $25,000, Eviction, Small Claims.*

Note: May require a signed release for certain records.

Civil Records: Access: Phone, mail, fax. Only the court may perform in person searches. Search fee: $5.00 per name if pre-2/1995. Required to search: name, years to search; also helpful: address. Civil cases indexed by defendant, plaintiff. Civil records on index cards from 1981; on computer back to 2/1995.
Criminal Records: Access: Mail, fax, in person. Only the court may perform in person searches. Search fee: $5.00 per name if pre-2/1995. Required to search: name, years to search, DOB; also helpful: address, SSN. Criminal records on index cards from 1981; on computer back to 2/1995.
General Information: No suppressed, juvenile, sex offenders, mental health, or adoption records released. Turnaround time 1 week. Copy fee: $1.00 per page. Certification fee: $10.00. Fee payee: 95-B District Court. Only cashiers checks and money orders accepted. Prepayment is required.

Probate Court PO Box 609, Iron Mountain, MI 49801; 906-774-1555; Fax: 906-774-1561. Hours: 8AM-4:30PM (CST). *Probate.*

Eaton County

56th Circuit Court 1045 Independence Blvd, Charlotte, MI 48813; 517-543-7500 X396; Fax: 517-543-4475. Hours: 8AM-5PM (EST). *Felony, Civil Actions Over $25,000.*

www.co.eaton.mi.us/COURTS/COURTS.HTM

Civil Records: Access: Phone, fax, mail, in person. Both court and visitors may perform in person searches. Search fee: $5.00 per name. Required to search: name, years to search. Civil cases indexed by defendant, plaintiff. Civil records on computer back to 1988, microfilm since 1930s, books from 1848.
Criminal Records: Access: Fax, mail, in person. Both court and visitors may perform in person searches. Search fee: $5.00 per name. Required to search: name,

years to search, DOB; also helpful: SSN. Criminal records on computer back to 1985, microfilm since 1930s, books from 1860s.

General Information: No suppressed, juvenile, sex offenders, mental health, or adoption records released. SASE required. Turnaround time 1-3 days. Copy fee: $1.00 for first page, $.50 each add'l. Certification fee: $10.00. Fee payee: Eaton County Circuit Court Clerk. Personal checks accepted. Prepayment is required.

56A District Court 1045 Independence Blvd, Charlotte, MI 48813; 517-543-7500; Civil phone: X294; Criminal phone: X282; Fax: 517-543-7377. Hours: 8AM-5PM (EST). *Misdemeanor, Civil Actions Under $25,000, Eviction, Small Claims.*

www.co.eaton.mi.us/courts/courts.htm

Note: A more complete criminal record check may be requested in writing through Mich. State Police Central Records Bureau, call 517-322-5531 for further information.

Civil Records: Access: Mail, fax, in person. Visitors must perform in person searches for themselves. Search fee: No search fee. Required to search: name, years to search. Civil records on computer back to 1990; prior in books.

Criminal Records: Access: In person only. Visitors must perform in person searches for themselves. No search fee. Required to search: name, years to search, DOB; also helpful: SSN. Criminal records on computer back to 1990.

General Information: Public access terminal is available. No suppressed, sex offenders, mental health, or adoption records released. SASE required. Copy fee: $.25 per page. Certification fee: $10.00. Fee payee: 56A District Court. Personal checks accepted. Prepayment is required.

Emmet County

57th Circuit Court 200 Division St, Petoskey, MI 49770; 231-348-1744; Fax: 231-348-0602. Hours: 8AM-5PM (EST). *Felony, Civil Actions Over $25,000.*

www.co.emmet.mi.us/emmetsite.nsf?Opendatabase

Civil Records: Access: Mail, in person. Only the court performs in person searches; visitors may not. Search fee: $5.00 per name. Required to search: name, years to search. Civil cases indexed by defendant, plaintiff. Civil records on computer from 1867 to present.

Criminal Records: Access: Mail, in person. Only the court performs in person searches; visitors may not. Search fee: $5.00 per name. Required to search: name, years to search, DOB. Criminal records on computer from 1867 to present.

General Information: No suppressed records released. SASE required. Turnaround time 5 days. Copy fee: $.50 per page. Certification fee: $10.00 plus $1.00 per page. Fee payee: Emmet County Clerk. Personal checks accepted. Credit cards accepted: Visa, MasterCard. Prepayment is required.

90th District Court 200 Division St., Petoskey, MI 49770; 231-348-1750; Fax: 231-348-0616. Hours: 8AM-5PM (EST). *Misdemeanor, Civil Actions Under $25,000, Eviction, Small Claims.*

Civil Records: Access: Fax, mail, in person. Only the court performs in person searches; visitors may not. No search fee. Required to search: name, years to search. Civil cases indexed by defendant, plaintiff. Civil records on computer since 1981, prior listed in books.

Criminal Records: Access: Fax, mail, in person. Only the court performs in person searches; visitors may not. No search fee. Required to search: name, years to search, DOB; also helpful: SSN. Criminal records on computer since 1981, prior listed in books.

General Information: No suppressed, juvenile, sex offenders, mental health, or adoption records released. Turnaround time 2-3 days. Fax notes: $6.00 for first page, $1.00 each add'l. Copy fee: $2.00 per page. Fee is for non-parties. Certification fee: $10.00. Fee payee: 90th District Court. Business checks accepted. Prepayment is required.

Probate Court 200 Division St., Petoskey, MI 49770; 231-348-1707; Fax: 231-348-0672. Hours: 8AM-5PM (EST). *Probate.*

Note: Shares the same judge with Charlevoix County Probate Court.

Genesee County

7th Circuit Court 900 South Saginaw, Flint, MI 48502; 810-257-3220. Hours: 8AM-5PM (EST). *Felony, Civil Actions Over $25,000.*

www.co.genesee.mi.us

Civil Records: Access: Mail, in person, online. Both court and visitors may perform in person searches. Search fee: $5.00 per name. Required to search: name, years to search. Civil cases indexed by defendant, plaintiff. Civil records on computer since 1978, prior on index cards. Online access to court records is available free at the web site; click on "Circuit Court Records.".

Criminal Records: Access: Mail, in person, online. Both court and visitors may perform in person searches. Search fee: $5.00 per name. Required to search: name, years to search, DOB; also helpful: SSN, sex. Criminal records on computer since 1978, prior on index cards. Online access to criminal records is the same as civil.

General Information: Public access terminal is available. No suppressed, juvenile, adoption, or mental health records released. SASE required. Turnaround time 1-2 weeks. Copy fee: $1.00 per page. Certification fee: $10.00. Fee payee: Genesee County Clerk. Prepayment is required.

67th District Court 630 South Saginaw, Flint, MI 48502; 810-257-3170. Hours: 8AM-4PM (EST). *Misdemeanor, Civil Actions Under $25,000, Eviction, Small Claims.*

www.co.genesee.mi.us

Civil Records: Access: Mail, in person. Only the court performs in person searches; visitors may not. No search fee. Required to search: name, years to search; also helpful: address. Civil cases indexed by defendant, plaintiff. Civil records on computer since 1983, on microfilm since 1969, prior archived.

Criminal Records: Access: Mail, in person. Only the court performs in person searches; visitors may not. No search fee. Required to search: name, years to search, DOB, offense; also helpful: address, SSN. Criminal records on computer since 1983, on microfilm since 1969, prior archived.

General Information: No drug related case records released. SASE helpful. Turnaround time 1 week. Copy fee: $1.00 per page. Certification fee: $10.00. Fee payee: 67th District Court. Only cashiers checks and money orders accepted. Prepayment is required.

Probate Court 900 S Saginaw St #502, Flint, MI 48502; 810-257-3528; Fax: 810-257-2713. Hours: 8AM-4PM (EST). *Probate.*

Gladwin County

55th Circuit Court 401 West Cedar, Gladwin, MI 48624; 989-426-7351; Fax: 989-426-6917. Hours: 8:30AM-4:30PM (EST). *Felony, Civil Actions Over $25,000.*

Civil Records: Access: Fax, mail, in person. Both court and visitors may perform in person searches. No search fee. Required to search: name, years to search. Civil cases indexed by defendant, plaintiff. Civil records on computer since 1994, prior on books.

Criminal Records: Access: Fax, mail, in person. Both court and visitors may perform in person searches. No search fee. Required to search: name, years to search,

DOB; also helpful: SSN. Criminal records on computer since 1994, prior on books.

General Information: No suppressed, juvenile, sex offenders, mental health, or adoption records released. SASE required. Turnaround time 2-3 days. Copy fee: $1.00 per page. Certification fee: $10.00 plus $1.00 per page after first. Fee payee: Gladwin County Clerk. Personal checks accepted. Prepayment is required.

80th District Court 401 West Cedar, Gladwin, MI 48624; 989-426-9207; Fax: 989-246-0894. Hours: 8:30AM-4:30PM (EST). *Misdemeanor, Civil Actions Under $25,000, Eviction, Small Claims.*

Civil Records: Access: Mail, fax, in person. Only the court performs in person searches; visitors may not. No search fee. Required to search: name, years to search. Civil cases indexed by defendant, plaintiff. Civil records on computer since 1988, prior on index cards and docket books, archived to late 1968.

Criminal Records: Access: Mail, fax, in person. Only the court performs in person searches; visitors may not. No search fee. Required to search: name, years to search, DOB; also helpful: SSN. Criminal records on computer since 1988, prior on index cards and docket books, archived to late 1968.

General Information: No suppressed, juvenile, sex offenders, mental health, or adoption records released. SASE required. Turnaround time same day when possible. Copy fee: $2.00 per page. Certification fee: $10.00 plus $1.00 per page after first. Fee payee: 80th District Court. Personal checks accepted. Prepayment is required.

Probate Court 401 West Cedar, Gladwin, MI 48624; 989-426-7451; Fax: 989-426-5478. Hours: 8:30AM-4:30PM (EST). *Probate.*

Note: This is combined with Clare County Probate Court.

Gogebic County

32nd Circuit Court 200 North Moore St, Bessemer, MI 49911; 906-663-4518; Fax: 906-663-4660. Hours: 8:30AM-4:30PM (CST). *Felony, Civil Actions Over $25,000.*

Civil Records: Access: Mail, in person. Both court and visitors may perform in person searches. Search fee: $5.00 per name. Required to search: name, years to search. Civil cases indexed by defendant, plaintiff. Civil records in books since 1887.

Criminal Records: Access: Mail, in person. Both court and visitors may perform in person searches. Search fee: $5.00 per name. Required to search: name, years to search, DOB; also helpful: SSN. Criminal records in books since 1887.

General Information: No suppressed, juvenile, sex offenders, mental health, or adoption records released. SASE requested. Turnaround time 1-2 days. Copy fee: $1.00 per page. Certification fee: $10.00. Fee payee: Gogebic County Clerk's Office. Personal checks accepted. Prepayment is required.

98th District Court 200 North Moore St, Bessemer, MI 49911; 906-663-4611; Fax: 906-663-4660. Hours: 8:30AM-4:30PM (CST). *Misdemeanor, Civil Actions Under $25,000, Eviction, Small Claims.*

Civil Records: Access: Mail, in person. Only the court performs in person searches; visitors may not. Search fee: $5.00 per name. Required to search: name, years to search. Civil cases indexed by defendant, plaintiff. Civil records on computer since 6/88.

Criminal Records: Access: Mail, in person. Only the court performs in person searches; visitors may not. Search fee: $5.00 per name. Required to search: name, years to search, DOB, SSN. Criminal records on computer since 6/88.

General Information: No suppressed, juvenile, sex offenders, mental health, or adoption records released.

SASE not required. Turnaround time 10 days. Copy fee: $1.00 per page. Certification fee: $10.00 per document. Fee payee: District Court. Business checks accepted. Prepayment is required.

Probate Court 200 North Moore St., Bessemer, MI 49911; 906-667-0421; Fax: 906-663-4660. Hours: 8:30AM-Noon, 1-4:30PM (CST). *Probate.*

Grand Traverse County

13th Circuit Court 328 Washington St, Traverse City, MI 49684; 231-922-4710. Hours: 8AM-5PM (EST). *Felony, Civil Actions Over $25,000.*

Civil Records: Access: Phone, mail, in person. Both court and visitors may perform in person searches. Search fee: None, but if record is on microfilm, fee is $10.00. Required to search: name, years to search. Civil cases indexed by defendant, plaintiff. Civil records on computer since 1971, prior on books since 1859.
Criminal Records: Access: Phone, mail, in person. Both court and visitors may perform in person searches. Search fee: None, but if record is on microfilm, fee is $10.00. Required to search: name, years to search; also helpful: DOB, SSN. Criminal records on computer since 1981.
General Information: No suppressed records released. SASE required. Turnaround time 1 week. Copy fee: $1.00 for first page, $.25 each add'l. Certification fee: $10.00 plus $1.00 per page after first. Fee payee: 13th Circuit Court. Personal checks accepted. Prepayment is required.

86th District Court 328 Washington St., Traverse City, MI 49684; 231-922-4580; Fax: 231-922-4454. Hours: 8AM-5PM (EST). *Misdemeanor, Civil Actions Under $25,000, Eviction, Small Claims.*

Civil Records: Access: Phone, mail, in person. Only the court performs in person searches; visitors may not. No search fee. Required to search: name, years to search. Civil cases indexed by defendant, plaintiff. Civil records on computer since 1988, prior on books.
Criminal Records: Access: Phone, mail, in person. Only the court performs in person searches; visitors may not. No search fee. Required to search: name, years to search, DOB; also helpful: SSN. Most criminal records on computer.
General Information: No suppressed, juvenile, sex offenders, mental health, or adoption records released. SASE required. Turnaround time 2-3 days. Copy fee: $.25 per page. Certification fee: $10.00. Fee payee: 86th District Court. Business checks accepted. Prepayment is required.

Probate Court 400 Boardman Av, Traverse City, MI 49684; 231-922-6862; Fax: 231-922-4458. Hours: 8AM-5PM (EST). *Probate.*

Gratiot County

29th Circuit Court 214 East Center St, Ithaca, MI 48847; 989-875-5215. Hours: 8:00AM-Noon, 1:00PM-4:30PM (EST). *Felony, Civil Actions Over $25,000.*

Civil Records: Access: Mail, in person. Only the court performs in person searches; visitors may not. Search fee: $10.00 per name. Fee is for 5 years, $1.00 each additional year. Required to search: name, years to search. Civil cases indexed by defendant, plaintiff.
Criminal Records: Access: Mail, in person. Only the court performs in person searches; visitors may not. Search fee: $10.00 per name. Fee is for 5 years, $1.00 each additional year. Required to search: name, years to search.
General Information: No suppressed, juvenile, sex offenders, mental health, or adoption records released. SASE required. Turnaround time 1-3 days. Copy fee: $1.00 per page. Certification fee: $10.00. Fee payee: Gratiot County Clerk. Personal checks accepted. Prepayment is required.

65-B District Court 245 East Newark St, Ithaca, MI 48847; 989-875-5240; Fax: 989-875-5290. Hours: 8AM-4:30PM (EST). *Misdemeanor, Civil Actions Under $25,000, Eviction, Small Claims.*

Civil Records: Access: In person only. Visitors must perform in person searches for themselves. No search fee. Required to search: name, years to search. Civil cases indexed by defendant, plaintiff. Civil records on index books from 1969 to present, computerized since 1996.
Criminal Records: Access: In person only. Visitors must perform in person searches for themselves. No search fee. Required to search: name, years to search, DOB; also helpful: SSN. Criminal records on computer since 02/20/96, in books since 1969.
General Information: Public access terminal is available. No non-public records released. Copy fee: $1.00 per page. Certification fee: $10.00 plus $1.00 per page after first. Fee payee: 65B District Court. Personal checks accepted. Prepayment is required.

Probate Court 214 E Center St, PO Box 217, Ithaca, MI 48847; 989-875-5231; Fax: 989-875-5331. Hours: 8:30AM-5PM (EST). *Probate.*

Hillsdale County

1st Circuit Court 29 North Howell, Hillsdale, MI 49242; 517-437-3391; Fax: 517-437-3392. Hours: 8:30AM-5PM (EST). *Felony, Civil Actions Over $25,000.*

Civil Records: Access: Mail, in person. Only the court performs in person searches; visitors may not. Search fee: $1.00 per name per year. Required to search: name, years to search. Civil cases indexed by defendant, plaintiff. Civil records on computer back to 1985, prior on docket books, archived to 1844.
Criminal Records: Access: Mail, in person. Only the court performs in person searches; visitors may not. Search fee: $1.00 per name per year. Required to search: name, years to search, DOB; also helpful: SSN. Criminal records on computer back to 1985, prior on docket books, archived to 1844.
General Information: No suppressed, juvenile, sex offenders, mental health, or adoption records released. SASE required. Turnaround time 2-3 days. Copy fee: $1.00 per page. Certification fee: $10.00. Fee payee: Hillsdale County Clerk. Personal checks accepted. Out-of-state personal checks not accepted. Prepayment is required.

2nd District Court 49 North Howell, Hillsdale, MI 49242; 517-437-7329; Fax: 517-437-2908. Hours: 8AM-4:30PM; 8AM-5PM Traffic (EST). *Misdemeanor, Civil Actions Under $25,000, Eviction, Small Claims.*

Civil Records: Access: Phone, mail, in person. Both court and visitors may perform in person searches. Search fee: $10.00. Required to search: name, years to search. Civil cases indexed by defendant, plaintiff. Civil records kept in docket books back to 1969; on computer back to 2001. A request in writing may be required.
Criminal Records: Access: Phone, mail, in person. Only the court performs in person searches; visitors may not. Search fee: $10.00. Required to search: name, years to search, DOB; also helpful: SSN. Criminal records kept in docket books back to 1969; on computer back to 2001.
General Information: No suppressed records released. Turnaround time 1 week. Copy fee: $.15 per page. Certification fee: $10.00 plus $1.00 each add'l page. Fee payee: Hillsdale District Court. Personal checks accepted. Prepayment is required.

Probate Court 29 North Howell, Hillsdale, MI 49242; 517-437-4643. Hours: 8:30AM-Noon, 1-5PM (EST). *Probate.*

Houghton County

12th Circuit Court 401 East Houghton Ave, Houghton, MI 49931; 906-482-5420. Hours: 8AM-4:30PM (EST). *Felony, Civil Actions Over $25,000.*

Civil Records: Access: Mail, in person. Only the court performs in person searches; visitors may not. Search fee: $10.00 per name. Required to search: name, years to search. Civil cases indexed by defendant, plaintiff. Civil records kept on docket books, cards since 6/76; are computerized as of 1997.
Criminal Records: Access: Mail, in person. Only the court performs in person searches; visitors may not. Search fee: $10.00 per name. Required to search: name, years to search, DOB; also helpful: SSN. Criminal records kept on docket books, cards since 11/63; are computerized as of 1997.
General Information: No suppressed, juvenile, sex offenders, mental health, or adoption records released. SASE required. Turnaround time 1-2 days. Copy fee: $1.00 per page. Certification fee: $10.00 plus $1.00 per page after first. Fee payee: Clerk of Circuit Court. Personal checks accepted. Prepayment is required.

97th District Court 401 East Houghton Ave., Houghton, MI 49931; 906-482-4980; Fax: 906-482-5270. Hours: 8AM-4:30PM (EST). *Misdemeanor, Civil Actions Under $25,000, Eviction, Small Claims.*

Civil Records: Access: Mail, fax, in person. Only the court may perform in person searches. Search fee: $10.00 per name. Required to search: name, years to search; also helpful: address. Civil cases indexed by defendant, plaintiff. Civil records listed in "Registers of Actions." Records on computer back to 1998; others back to 1969.
Criminal Records: Access: Mail, fax, in person. Only the court may perform in person searches. Search fee: $10.00 per name. Required to search: name, years to search, DOB, SSN; also helpful: address, signed release. Criminal records listed in "Registers of Actions." Records on computer back to 1998; others back to 1969.
General Information: No conviction records released. SASE required. Turnaround time up to 1 week. Copy fee: $1.00 for first page, $.25 each add'l. Certification fee: $10.00 plus $1.00 per page after first. Fee payee: 97th District Court. Business checks accepted. Prepayment is required.

Probate Court 401 E. Houghton Ave., Houghton, MI 49931; 906-482-3120; Fax: 906-487-5964. Hours: 8AM-4:30PM (EST). *Probate.*

Huron County

52nd Circuit Court 250 East Huron Ave, Bad Axe, MI 48413; 989-269-9942; Fax: 989-269-6160. Hours: 8:30AM-5PM (EST). *Felony, Civil Actions Over $25,000.*

Civil Records: Access: Phone, mail, in person. Both court and visitors may perform in person searches. Search fee: $5.00 per name. Required to search: name, years to search. Civil cases indexed by defendant, plaintiff. Civil records on computer since 1992, prior on books to 1867.
Criminal Records: Access: Phone, mail, in person. Both court and visitors may perform in person searches. Search fee: $5.00 per name. Required to search: name, years to search, DOB; also helpful: SSN. Criminal records on computer since 1992, prior on books to 1867.
General Information: No suppressed, juvenile, sex offenders, mental health, or adoption records released. SASE required. Turnaround time 2-3 days. Copy fee: $1.00 per page. Certification fee: $10.00 plus $1.00 per page after first. Fee payee: Huron County Clerk. Personal checks accepted. Prepayment is required.

73B District Court 250 East Huron Ave., Bad Axe, MI 48413; 989-269-9987; Fax: 989-269-6167. Hours: 8:30AM-5PM (EST). *Misdemeanor, Civil Actions Under $25,000, Eviction, Small Claims.*

Civil Records: Access: Phone, fax, mail, in person. Only the court performs in person searches; visitors may not. Search fee: $5.00 per name. Required to search: name, years to search. Civil cases indexed by defendant, plaintiff. Civil records on computer since June 1992, prior on books since 1969.

Criminal Records: Access: Phone, fax, mail, in person. Only the court performs in person searches; visitors may not. Search fee: $5.00 per name. Required to search: name, years to search, DOB; also helpful: SSN. Criminal records on computer since June 1992, prior on books since 1969.

General Information: No suppressed, juvenile, sex offenders, mental health, or adoption records released. SASE required. Turnaround time 1-5 days. Fax notes: No fee to fax results. Copy fee: $1.00 per page. Fee payee: 73B District Court. Business checks accepted. Prepayment is required.

Probate Court 250 E. Huron Ave., Bad Axe, MI 48413; 989-269-9944; Fax: 989-269-0004. Hours: 8:30AM-Noon, 1-5PM (EST). *Probate.*

Ingham County

30th Circuit Court 313 W. Kalamazoo (PO Box 40771), Lansing, MI 48933; 517-483-6500; Fax: 517-483-6501. Hours: 8:00AM-5:00PM M-F (EST). *Felony, Civil Actions Over $25,000.*

Civil Records: Access: Phone, mail, in person. Both court and visitors may perform in person searches. No search fee. Required to search: name, years to search. Civil cases indexed by defendant, plaintiff. Civil records on computer since 1986.

Criminal Records: Access: Phone, mail, in person. Both court and visitors may perform in person searches. Search fee: $8.00 per name. Required to search: name, years to search; also helpful: DOB. Criminal records on computer since 1986.

General Information: Public access terminal is available. All circuit Court files are public record unless specifically suppressed by Judge. SASE not required. Turnaround time 1-2 days, unless file is in storage then 1 week. Copy fee: $5.00 for any # of copies up to 10 copies, over 10 are $5.00 for first 10 plus $.50 a page thereafter. Certification fee: $10.00 plus $1.00 per page after first. Fee payee: Ingham County Circuit Court. Personal checks accepted. Prepayment is required.

54 A District Court 124 West Michigan Ave, Lansing, MI 48933; 517-483-4433; Civil phone: 517-483-4426; Criminal phone: 517-483-4445; Fax: 517-483-4108. Hours: 8AM-4:30PM (EST). *Misdemeanor, Civil Actions Under $25,000, Eviction, Small Claims.*

Note: This court covers the City of Lansing.

Civil Records: Access: In person only. Visitors must perform in person searches for themselves. No search fee. Required to search: name, years to search. Civil cases indexed by defendant, plaintiff. Civil records on computer since 1990, microfiche from 1985, prior archived.

Criminal Records: Access: In person only. Visitors must perform in person searches for themselves. No search fee. Required to search: name, years to search, DOB, offense, date of offense; also helpful: SSN. Criminal records on computer since 1990, microfiche from 1985, prior archived.

General Information: Public access terminal is available. No suppressed, juvenile, sex offenders, mental health, or adoption, non-public records released. Copy fee: $.50 per page. Certification fee: $10.00 plus $1.00 per page after first. Fee payee: 54A District Court.

No personal checks accepted. Credit cards accepted: Visa, MasterCard. Prepayment is required.

54 B District Court 101 Linden, East Lansing, MI 48823; 517-351-7000; Civil phone: 517-351-1730; Criminal phone: 517-336-8630; Fax: 517-351-3371. Hours: 8AM-4:30PM (EST). *Misdemeanor, Civil Actions Under $25,000, Eviction, Small Claims.*

Note: This court covers the City of East Lansing.

Civil Records: Access: Mail, in person. Both court and visitors may perform in person searches. No search fee. Required to search: name, years to search. Civil cases indexed by defendant, plaintiff. Civil records on computer since 1991, ROA's are kept indefinitely.

Criminal Records: Access: Mail, in person. Both court and visitors may perform in person searches. No search fee. Required to search: name, years to search, DOB; also helpful: case number. Criminal records on computer since 1989, files stored prior.

General Information: Public access terminal is available. No suppressed, juvenile, sex offenders, mental health, or adoption records released. Turnaround time up 1 hour to 1 week, depends on availability. Copy fee: $.25 per page. Certification fee: $10.00 plus $1.00 per page after first. Fee payee: 54-B District Court. Personal checks accepted. Two party or payroll checks not allowed. Credit cards accepted: Visa, MC, Discover. Debit card. Prepayment is required.

55th District Court 700 Buhl, Mason, MI 48854; 517-676-8400. Hours: 8:30AM-4:30PM (EST). *Misdemeanor, Civil Actions Under $25,000, Eviction, Small Claims.*

Note: This court covers all of Ingham County except for Lansing and East Lansing.

Civil Records: Access: Mail, in person. Both court and visitors may perform in person searches. No search fee. Required to search: name, years to search. Civil records on computer since 11/91, prior listed in index books.

Criminal Records: Access: Mail, in person. Both court and visitors may perform in person searches. No search fee. Required to search: name, years to search, DOB; case number; also helpful: SSN. Criminal records on computer since 1994, prior on books.

General Information: No suppressed, juvenile, sex offenders, mental health, or adoption records released. SASE required. Turnaround time 5 days. Copy fee: $1.00 per page. Certification fee: $10.00 plus $1.00 each additional page. Fee payee: 55th District Court. Personal checks accepted. Prepayment is required.

Ingham County Probate Court PO Box 176, Mason, MI 48854; 517-676-7276; Fax: 517-676-7344. Hours: 8AM-Noon, 1-5PM (EST). *Probate.*

Lansing Probate Court 313 West Kalamazoo, Lansing, MI 48933; 517-483-6300; Fax: 517-483-6150. Hours: 8AM-Noon, 1-5PM (EST). *Probate.*

Ionia County

8th Circuit Court 100 Main, Ionia, MI 48846; 616-527-5322; Fax: 616-527-8201. Hours: 8:30AM-5PM (EST). *Felony, Civil Actions Over $25,000.*

www.ioniacounty.org

Civil Records: Access: Phone, fax, mail, in person. Only the court performs in person searches; visitors may not. No search fee. Required to search: name, years to search. Civil cases indexed by defendant, plaintiff. Civil records on computer since 1990; prior records kept in books and files, archived to 1800s.

Criminal Records: Access: Phone, fax, mail, in person. Only the court performs in person searches; visitors may not. No search fee. Required to search: name, years to search; also helpful: DOB, SSN. Criminal records on computer since 6/84; in books and files prior.

General Information: No suppressed records released. SASE not required. Turnaround time 1 week. Fax notes: $1.00 per page. Copy fee: $1.00 per page. Certification fee: $10.00 plus $1.00 per page after first. Fee payee: Ionia County Clerk. Personal checks accepted. Prepayment is required.

64 A District Court 101 West Main, Ionia, MI 48846; 616-527-5346; Fax: 616-527-5343. Hours: 7:45AM-5:30PM (EST). *Misdemeanor, Civil Actions Under $25,000, Eviction, Small Claims.*

Civil Records: Access: Fax, mail, in person. Only the court performs in person searches; visitors may not. Search fee: $3.00 per name. Required to search: name, years to search. Civil cases indexed by defendant, plaintiff. Civil records in files and books available since 1969. Fax request must be followed up by originals.

Criminal Records: Access: Fax, mail, in person. Only the court performs in person searches; visitors may not. Search fee: $3.00 per name. Required to search: name, years to search, DOB; also helpful: address. Criminal records in files and books available since 1969. Fax must be followed up by originals.

General Information: No suppressed, juvenile, sex offenders, mental health, or adoption records released. SASE requested. Turnaround time 10 days. Copy fee: $.50 per page. Certification fee: $10.00 plus $1.00 per page after first. Fee payee: 64-A District Court. Personal checks accepted. Prepayment is required.

Probate Court 100 Main, Ionia, MI 48846; 616-527-5326; Fax: 616-527-5321. Hours: 8:30AM-5PM (EST). *Probate.*

Iosco County

23rd Circuit Court PO Box 838, Tawas City, MI 48764; 989-362-3497; Fax: 989-984-1012. Hours: 9AM-5PM (EST). *Felony, Civil Actions Over $25,000.*

Civil Records: Access: Phone, mail, in person. Both court and visitors may perform in person searches. No search fee. Required to search: name, years to search. Civil records on computer since 1987, prior on books.

Criminal Records: Access: Phone, mail, in person. Both court and visitors may perform in person searches. No search fee. Required to search: name, years to search, DOB; also helpful: SSN. Criminal records on computer since 1983.

General Information: No suppressed, parental waivers, mental health, or adoption records released. SASE not required. Turnaround time 1 week. Copy fee: $.25 per page. Certification fee: $10.00 plus $1.00 per page after first. Fee payee: Iosco County Clerk. Only cashiers checks and money orders accepted. Prepayment is required.

81st District Court PO Box 388, Tawas City, MI 48764; 989-362-4441; Fax: 989-362-3494. Hours: 8AM-5PM (EST). *Misdemeanor, Civil Actions Under $25,000, Eviction, Small Claims.*

Civil Records: Access: Mail, in person. Only the court performs in person searches; visitors may not. Search fee: $5.00. Required to search: name, years to search. Civil cases indexed by defendant, plaintiff. Civil records on computer since 1987, prior on books.

Criminal Records: Access: Mail, in person. Only the court performs in person searches; visitors may not. Search fee: $5.00. Required to search: name, years to search, DOB; also helpful: SSN. Criminal records on computer since 1987, prior on books.

General Information: No suppressed, juvenile, sex offenders, mental health, or adoption records released. SASE required. Turnaround time 2-3 days. Copy fee: $2.00 for first page, $.50 each add'l. Certification fee: $10.00 plus $1.00 per page after first. Fee payee: 81st District Court. Personal checks accepted. Prepayment is required.

Probate Court PO Box 421, Tawas City, MI 48764; 989-362-3991, 989-984-1037; Fax: 989-984-1035. Hours: 8AM-5PM (EST). *Probate.*

Iron County

41st Circuit Court 2 South 6th St, Crystal Falls, MI 49920; 906-875-3221; Fax: 906-875-6675. Hours: 8AM-4PM (CST). *Felony, Civil Actions Over $25,000.*

Civil Records: Access: Fax, mail, in person. Only the court performs in person searches; visitors may not. Search fee: $6.00 per name. Required to search: name, years to search. Civil cases indexed by defendant, plaintiff. Most records on books, on microfiche 1958-67.

Criminal Records: Access: Fax, mail, in person. Only the court performs in person searches; visitors may not. Search fee: $6.00 per name. Required to search: name, years to search, DOB; also helpful: SSN. Most records on books, on microfiche 1958-67.

General Information: No suppressed, juvenile, sex offenders, mental health, or adoption records released. SASE required. Turnaround time 2-3 days. Fax notes: $1.50 per page. Copy fee: $.25 per page. Certification fee: $10.00 plus $1.00 per page after first. Fee payee: Iron County Clerk. Personal checks accepted. Prepayment is required.

95 B District Court 2 South 6th St., Crystal Falls, MI 49920; 906-875-0619; Fax: 906-875-6775. Hours: 8AM-4PM (CST). *Misdemeanor, Civil Actions Under $25,000, Eviction, Small Claims.*

Civil Records: Access: Mail, in person. Only the court performs in person searches; visitors may not. Search fee: $5.00. Required to search: name, years to search. Civil cases indexed by defendant, plaintiff. Civil records computerized since 1999, earlier records index kept on cards, accessible from 1970.

Criminal Records: Access: Mail, in person. Only the court performs in person searches; visitors may not. Search fee: $5.00. Required to search: name, years to search, DOB; also helpful: SSN. Criminal records computerized since 1999, earlier records index kept on cards, accessible from 1970.

General Information: No suppressed, juvenile, sex offenders, mental health, or adoption records released. SASE required. Turnaround time 1 week. Copy fee: $.25 per page. Certification fee: $10.00 plus $1.00 per page after first. Fee payee: 95-B District Court. Personal checks accepted. Prepayment is required.

Probate Court 2 South 6th St, #10, Crystal Falls, MI 49920; 906-875-0659; Fax: 906-875-0656. Hours: 8AM-Noon, 12:30-4PM (CST). *Probate.*

www.iron.org

Isabella County

21st Circuit Court 200 North Main St, Mount Pleasant, MI 48858; 989-772-0911 X259. Hours: 8AM-4:30PM (EST). *Felony, Civil Actions Over $25,000.*

Civil Records: Access: Mail, in person. Both court and visitors may perform in person searches. Search fee: $5.00 from 1980 to present. Prior years $1.00 per year. Required to search: name, years to search. Civil cases indexed by defendant, plaintiff. Civil records on computer since 1980, archived from 1900.

Criminal Records: Access: Mail, in person. Only the court performs in person searches; visitors may not. Search fee: $5.00 from 1980 to present. Prior years $1.00 per year. Required to search: name, years to search, DOB; also helpful: SSN. Criminal records on computer since 1980, archived from 1900.

General Information: No suppressed, juvenile, sex offenders, mental health, or adoption records released. Turnaround time 1-2 weeks. Copy fee: $1.00 per page. Certification fee: $10.00 plus $1.00 per page after first.

Fee payee: sabella County Trial Court. Personal checks accepted. Prepayment is required.

76th District Court 200 North Main St., Mount Pleasant, MI 48858; 989-772-0911 X268; Fax: 989-773-2419. Hours: 8AM-4:30PM (EST). *Misdemeanor, Civil Actions Under $25,000, Eviction, Small Claims.*

Civil Records: Access: Mail, in person. Both court and visitors may perform in person searches. Search fee: $5.00 per name. Required to search: name, years to search. Civil cases indexed by defendant, plaintiff. Civil records on computer since 1988, on books since 1960s.

Criminal Records: Access: Mail, in person. Both court and visitors may perform in person searches. Search fee: $5.00 per name. Required to search: name, years to search, DOB; also helpful: SSN. Criminal records on computer since 1988, on books since 1960s.

General Information: No suppressed, juvenile, sex offenders, mental health, or adoption records released. SASE required. Turnaround time 5-7 days. Copy fee: $1.00 per page. Certification fee: $10.00 pler document. Fee payee: 76th District Court. Business checks accepted. Prepayment is required.

Probate Court 300 N Main St, Mount Pleasant, MI 48858; 989-772-0911 x316 (or x276); Fax: 989-779-8022. Hours: 8AM-4:30PM (EST). *Probate.*

www.isabellacounty.org

Jackson County

4th Circuit Court 312 South Jackson St, Jackson, MI 49201; 517-788-4268. Hours: 8AM-5PM (EST). *Felony, Civil Actions Over $25,000.*

www.co.jackson.mi.us

Civil Records: Access: Phone, mail, in person. Only the court performs in person searches; visitors may not. Search fee: $10.50 per hour. Required to search: name, years to search. Civil cases indexed by defendant, plaintiff. Civil records on computer since 1980, prior on index cards and docket books since 1800s.

Criminal Records: Access: Phone, mail, in person. Only the court performs in person searches; visitors may not. Search fee: $10.50 per hour. Required to search: name, years to search; also helpful: DOB, SSN. Criminal records on computer since 1980, prior on index cards and docket books since 1800s.

General Information: No adoption or juvenile records released. Turnaround time 1 week. Fax notes: Fax back fee $3.00 per page. Copy fee: $.50 per page. Certification fee: $10.00 plus $2.00 per page after first. Fee payee: Jackson County Clerk. Only cashiers checks and money orders accepted. Credit cards accepted: Visa, MasterCard. Prepayment of fax and mail service required. Fees billed to attorneys.

12th District Court 312 South Jackson St., Jackson, MI 49201; 517-788-4260; Fax: 517-788-4262. Hours: 7AM-6PM (EST). *Misdemeanor, Civil Actions Under $25,000, Eviction, Small Claims.*

www.d12.com

Civil Records: Access: Fax, mail, in person. Only the court performs in person searches; visitors may not. No search fee. Required to search: name, years to search. Civil cases indexed by defendant, plaintiff. Civil records on computer since 1986; microfilm to 1969.

Criminal Records: Access: Fax, mail, in person. Only the court performs in person searches; visitors may not. No search fee. Required to search: name, years to search, DOB; also helpful: SSN. Criminal records on computer since 1986; microfilm from 1969.

General Information: No suppressed, juvenile, sex offenders, mental health, or probation records released. Turnaround time 5 days. Fax notes: $5.00 for first page, $1.00 each add'l. Copy fee: $.25 per page. Certification fee: $10.00 plus $1.00 per page after first. Fee payee:

12th District Court. Personal checks accepted. Third party checks not allowed. Prepayment is required.

Probate Court 312 S Jackson St, 1st Fl, Jackson, MI 49201; 517-788-4290. Hours: 8AM-5PM (EST). *Probate.*

Kalamazoo County

9th Circuit Court 227 West Michigan Ave, Kalamazoo, MI 49007; 269-383-8837. Hours: 9AM-4PM (EST). *Felony, Civil Actions Over $25,000.*

Civil Records: Access: Mail, in person. Visitors must perform in person searches for themselves. Search fee: $1.00. Required to search: name, years to search. Civil cases indexed by defendant, plaintiff. Civil records stored as hard copies, some records kept off-site; computerized records go back to 1984.

Criminal Records: Access: Mail, in person. Visitors must perform in person searches for themselves. Search fee: $1.00. Required to search: name, years to search, DOB. Criminal records stored as hard copies, some records kept off-site; computerized records go back to 1984.

General Information: Public access terminal is available. No suppressed or non-public records released. Turnaround time 2 days. Copy fee: $1.00 per page. Certification fee: $13.00. Fee payee: Circuit Court Clerk. Personal checks accepted. Prepayment is required.

8th District Court - Central 416 S. Rose, Kalamazoo, MI 49007; 269-384-8020; Fax: 269-383-8899. Hours: 8AM-4PM (EST). *Misdemeanor, Civil Actions Under $25,000, Eviction, Small Claims.*

Note: This court covers City of Kalamazoo.

Civil Records: Access: Fax, mail, in person. Both court and visitors may perform in person searches. No search fee. Required to search: name, years to search. Civil cases indexed by defendant, plaintiff. Civil records on computer back to 1998, prior on index books to 1969.

Criminal Records: Access: Fax, mail, in person. Both court and visitors may perform in person searches. No search fee. Required to search: name, years to search, DOB; also helpful: SSN. Criminal records on computer back to 1998, prior on index books to 1969.

General Information: Public access terminal is available. No suppressed records released. SASE not required. Turnaround time 1-3 days. Copy fee: $.50 per page. Certification fee: $10.00. Fee payee: 8th District Court. Personal checks accepted. Credit cards accepted: Visa, MasterCard.

8th District Court - North 227 West Michigan St., Kalamazoo, MI 49007; 269-384-8171; Fax: 269-384-8047. Hours: 8:30AM-4PM (EST). *Misdemeanor, Civil Actions Under $25,000, Eviction, Small Claims.*

Note: This court covers Kalamazoo County.

Civil Records: Access: Fax, mail, in person, fax. Both court and visitors may perform in person searches. No search fee. Required to search: name, years to search, address. Civil cases indexed by defendant, plaintiff. Civil records on computer back to 1991, prior on books to 1969.

Criminal Records: Access: Fax, mail, in person. Both court and visitors may perform in person searches. No search fee. Required to search: name, years to search, DOB; also helpful: SSN. Criminal records on computer back to 1991, prior on books to 1969.

General Information: Public access terminal is available. No suppressed or non-public records released. SASE requested. Turnaround time 2 days. Fax notes: No fee to fax results. Copy fee: $.50 per page. Certification fee: $10.00. Fee payee: 8th District Court. Personal checks accepted. Credit cards accepted: Visa, MasterCard. Prepayment is required.

8th District Court - South 7810 Shaver Rd., Portage, MI 49002; 269-383-6460; Fax: 269-321-3645. Hours: 8AM-4:30PM (EST). *Misdemeanor, Civil Actions Under $25,000, Eviction, Small Claims.*

Note: This court covers Kalamazoo County South of N Avenue (Kilgore Rd).

Civil Records: Access: Mail, in person. Both the court and visitors may perform in person searches. Search fee: $20.00 per name if prior to 1992. Required to search: name, years to search. Civil cases indexed by defendant, plaintiff. Civil records on computer back to 1991, prior on index books to 1969.

Criminal Records: Access: Mail, in person. Both the court and visitors may perform in person searches. Search fee: $20.00 per name if prior to 1992. Required to search: name, years to search, DOB; also helpful: SSN. Criminal records on computer back to 1991, prior on index books to 1969.

General Information: Public access terminal is available. No suppressed, juvenile, sex offenders, mental health, or adoption records released. SASE required. Turnaround time 5 days. Fax notes: Fee to fax results is $1.00 per page. Copy fee: $.50 per page. Certification fee: $10.00 plus $1.00 per page after first. Fee payee: 8th District Court. Personal checks accepted. Prepayment is required.

Probate Court 227 West Michigan Ave., Kalamazoo, MI 49007; 269-383-8666/8933; Fax: 269-383-8685. Hours: 9AM-Noon, 1-5PM M; 8AM-Noon, 1-5PM T-F (EST). *Probate.*

Kalkaska County

46th Circuit Court PO Box 10, Kalkaska, MI 49646; 231-258-3300. Hours: 9AM-5PM (EST). *Felony, Civil Actions Over $25,000.*

www.Circuit46.org

Civil Records: Access: Mail, in person, online. Only the court performs in person searches; visitors may not. Search fee: $5.00 per name. Required to search: name, years to search. Civil cases indexed by defendant, plaintiff. Civil records on computer since 1989, prior on books, indexed to 1800s. Online access to court case records (open or closed cases for 90 days only) available free at www.circuit46.org/Cases/cases.html.

Criminal Records: Access: Mail, in person, online. Only the court performs in person searches; visitors may not. Search fee: $5.00 per name. Required to search: name, years to search, DOB; also helpful: SSN. Criminal records on computer since 1989, prior on books, indexed to 1800s. Online access to criminal records is the same as civil.

General Information: No suppressed records released. SASE required. Turnaround time 2-3 days. Copy fee: $.30 per page. Certification fee: $10.00 plus $1.00 per page. Fee payee: County Clerk. Personal checks accepted. Prepayment is required.

46th Circuit Trial Court - District Court PO Box 780, Kalkaska, MI 49646; 231-258-9031; Fax: 231-258-2424. Hours: 8AM-4:30PM (EST). *Misdemeanor, Civil Actions Under $25,000, Eviction, Small Claims.*

www.Circuit46.org

Civil Records: Access: Phone, mail, in person, online. Only the court performs in person searches; visitors may not. No search fee. Required to search: name, years to search. Civil cases indexed by defendant, plaintiff. Civil records on computer since 1989, prior on books. Online access to court case records (open or closed cases for 90 days only) available free at www.circuit46.org/Cases/cases.html. Search by name.

Criminal Records: Access: Phone, mail, in person, online. Only the court performs in person searches; visitors may not. No search fee. Required to search: name, years to search, DOB. Criminal records on computer since 1989, prior on books. Online access to criminal records is the same as civil.

General Information: Public access terminal is in a secured area, available by appointment only. No suppressed records released. SASE required. Turnaround time 4 days. Copy fee: $1.00 per page. Certification fee: $10.00 plus $1.00 per page after first. Fee payee: 46th Circuit Trial Court. Personal checks accepted. Prepayment is required.

Circuit Trial Court - Probate Division 605 North Birch, PO Box 780, Kalkaska, MI 49646; 231-258-3330; Fax: 231-258-3329. Hours: 9AM-Noon, 1-5PM (EST). *Probate.*

www.Circuit46.org

Note: Search cases by name free at www.circuit46.org/Cases/cases.html.

Kent County

17th Circuit Court 333 Monroe Ave NW, Grand Rapids, MI 49503; 616-632-5480; Fax: 616-632-5458. Hours: 8AM-5PM (EST). *Felony, Civil Actions Over $25,000.*

Civil Records: Access: Mail, in person. Only the court performs in person searches; visitors may not. Search fee: $5.00 per name. Required to search: name, years to search. Civil cases indexed by defendant, plaintiff. Civil records on computer since 1986, prior on books.

Criminal Records: Access: Mail, in person. Only the court performs in person searches; visitors may not. Search fee: $5.00 per name. Required to search: name, years to search, DOB. Criminal records on computer since 1986, prior on books.

General Information: No suppressed records released. SASE not required. Turnaround time 2-3 days. Copy fee: $1.00 per page. Certification fee: $10.00 plus $1.00 per page after first. Fee payee: Kent County Clerk. Personal checks accepted. Prepayment is required.

59th District Court - Grandville & Walker 3181 Wilson Ave SW, Grandville, MI 49418; 616-538-9660; Fax: 616-538-5144. Hours: 8:30AM--5PM (EST). *Misdemeanor, Civil Actions Under $25,000, Eviction, Small Claims.*

Civil Records: Access: Mail, in person. Only the court performs in person searches; visitors may not. Search fee: $1.00 per name. Add $.50 per year requested. Required to search: name, years to search; also helpful: address. Civil cases indexed by defendant, plaintiff. Civil records on computer from 1986, docket books and cards prior.

Criminal Records: Access: Mail, in person. Only the court performs in person searches; visitors may not. Search fee: $1.00 per name. Add $.50 per year requested. Required to search: name, years to search, DOB; also helpful: address, SSN. Criminal records on computer from 1986, docket books and cards prior.

General Information: No suppressed, juvenile, sex offenders, mental health, or adoption records released. SASE required. Turnaround time varies. Copy fee: $1.00 per page. Certification fee: $10.00 plus $1.00 per page after first. Fee payee: 59th District Court. Personal checks accepted. Prepayment is required.

61st District Court - Grand Rapids 180 Ottawa Ave NW #1400, Kent County Courthouse, Grand Rapids, MI 49503; 616-632-5525; Fax: 616-632-5582. Hours: 7:45AM-4:45PM (EST). *Misdemeanor, Civil Actions Under $25,000, Eviction, Small Claims.*

Civil Records: Access: Mail, in person. Visitors must perform in person searchs for themselves. No search fee. Required to search: name, years to search. Civil cases indexed by defendant, plaintiff. Civil records kept in files and books.

Criminal Records: Access: Mail, in person. Visitors must perform in person searchs for themselves. Search fee: $1.00 per name per year. Required to search: name,

years to search, DOB; also helpful: SSN. Criminal records are automated from 1985, microfiche from 1980.

General Information: Public access terminal is available. (All records from 10/1999 to present available.) No suppressed, juvenile, sex offenders, mental health, or adoption records released. SASE not required. Turnaround time 7-10 days. Copy fee: $1.00 for first page, $.50 each add'l. Certification fee: $10.00 plus $1.00 per page after first. Fee payee: 61st District Court. Personal checks accepted. Prepayment of mail service required.

62 A District Court - Wyoming 2650 De Hoop Ave SW, Wyoming, MI 49509; 616-530-7385; Fax: 616-249-3419. Hours: 8AM-5PM (EST). *Misdemeanor, Civil Actions Under $25,000, Eviction, Small Claims.*

www.ci.wyoming.mi.us/courts.htm

Civil Records: Access: Mail, fax, in person. Both court and visitors may perform in person searches. Search fee: $1.00 per name & $.50 per year. Required to search: name, years to search. Civil cases indexed by defendant, plaintiff. Civil records kept on docket books since 1980; on computer back to 1997. The judge must approve all requests from collection agencies.

Criminal Records: Access: Mail, fax, in person. Both court and visitors may perform in person searches. Search fee: $1.00 per name & $.50 per year. Required to search: name, years to search, DOB; also helpful: SSN. Criminal records kept on docket books since 1980; on computer back to 1997. The court suggests mail requests be sent to the state police.

General Information: Public access terminal is available. No suppressed, juvenile, sex offenders, mental health, or adoption records released. SASE required. Turnaround time 2-3 days. Fax notes: Will not fax results. Copy fee: $1.00 per page. Certification fee: $10.00 plus $1.00 per page after first. Fee payee: 62 A District Court. Personal checks accepted. Credit cards accepted: Visa. Accepted in person only. Prepayment is required.

62 B District Court - Kentwood PO Box 8848, Kentwood, MI 49518; 616-698-9310; Fax: 616-698-8199. Hours: 8AM-5PM (EST). *Misdemeanor, Civil Actions Under $25,000, Eviction, Small Claims.*

Civil Records: Access: Mail, in person. Only the court performs in person searches; visitors may not. Search fee: $5.00 per name. Required to search: name, years to search. Civil cases indexed by defendant, plaintiff. Civil records on computer since 11/88, prior on books.

Criminal Records: Access: Mail, in person. Only the court performs in person searches; visitors may not. Search fee: $5.00 per name. Required to search: name, years to search, DOB. Criminal records on computer since 11/88, prior on books.

General Information: No suppressed, juvenile, sex offenders, mental health, or adoption records released. SASE required. Turnaround time 1-2 days. Copy fee: $2.00 for first page, $.25 each add'l. Certification fee: $10.00. Fee payee: 62 B District Court. Personal checks accepted. Prepayment is required.

63rd District Court - 1st Division 105 Maple St, Rockford, MI 49341; 616-866-1576; Fax: 616-866-3080. Hours: 8AM-5PM (EST). *Misdemeanor, Civil Actions Under $25,000, Eviction, Small Claims.*

Civil Records: Access: Mail, in person. Both court and visitors may perform in person searches. No search fee. Required to search: name, years to search. Civil cases indexed by defendant, plaintiff. Civil records on computer since 8/94, prior on books.

Criminal Records: Access: Mail, in person. Both court and visitors may perform in person searches. No search fee. Required to search: name, years to search, DOB;

also helpful: SSN. Criminal records on computer since 8/94, prior on books.

General Information: Public access terminal is available. No suppressed, juvenile, sex offenders, mental health, or adoption records released. SASE required. Turnaround time 1 week. Copy fee: $1.00 per page. Certification fee: $10.00. Fee payee: 63rd District Court. Personal checks accepted. Prepayment is required.

Probate Court 180 Ottawa Ave NW #2500, Grand Rapids, MI 49503; 616-632-5440; Fax: 616-632-5430. Hours: 8:30AM-5PM (EST). *Probate.*

Keweenaw County

12th Circuit Court HCI Box 607, Eagle River, MI 49950-9744; 906-337-2229; Fax: 906-337-2795. Hours: 9AM-4PM (EST). *Felony, Civil Actions Over $25,000.*

Civil Records: Access: Mail, in person. Only the court performs in person searches; visitors may not. No search fee. Required to search: name, years to search. Civil cases indexed by defendant, plaintiff. Civil records kept on index books since 1963.

Criminal Records: Access: Mail, in person. Only the court performs in person searches; visitors may not. Search fee: $10.00. Required to search: name, years to search, DOB. Criminal records kept on index books since 1964.

General Information: No suppressed, juvenile, sex offenders, mental health, or adoption records released. SASE required. Turnaround time 1-2 days. Copy fee: $.50 per page. Certification fee: $10.00. Fee payee: Keweenaw County. Personal checks accepted. Prepayment is required.

97th District Court HCI Box 607, Eagle River, MI 49950; 906-337-2229; Fax: 906-337-2795. Hours: 9AM-4PM (EST). *Misdemeanor, Civil Actions Under $25,000, Eviction, Small Claims.*

Civil Records: Access: Fax, mail, in person. Only the court performs in person searches; visitors may not. Search fee: $10.00 per name. Required to search: name, years to search. Civil cases indexed by defendant, plaintiff. Civil records kept on books to 1970's. Results cannot be faxed.

Criminal Records: Access: Fax, mail, in person. Only the court performs in person searches; visitors may not. Search fee: $10.00 per name. Required to search: name, years to search, DOB; also helpful: SSN. Criminal records kept on books to 1970's. Results cannot be faxed.

General Information: No suppressed, juvenile, sex offenders, mental health, or adoption records released. SASE required. Turnaround time 1-2 days. Copy fee: $.50 per page. Certification fee: $10.00. Fee payee: Keweenaw County. Personal checks accepted. Prepayment is required.

Probate Court HC1 Box 607, Courthouse, Eagle River, MI 49950; 906-337-1927; Fax: 906-337-2795. Hours: 9AM-4PM (EST). *Probate.*

Lake County

Lake County Trial Court PO Box 1330, Baldwin, MI 49304; 231-745-4614. Hours: 8AM-Noon, 1-5PM (EST). *Felony, Misdemeanor, Civil Actions, Eviction, Small Claims.*

Civil Records: Access: Mail, in person. Only the court performs in person searches; visitors may not. Search fee: $5.00 per name per year. Required to search: name, years to search. Civil cases indexed by defendant, plaintiff. Civil records on computer since 7/89, prior on books.

Criminal Records: Access: Mail, in person. Only the court performs in person searches; visitors may not. Search fee: $5.00 per name per year. Required to

search: name, years to search, DOB; also helpful: SSN. Criminal records on computer since 7/89, prior on books.

General Information: No suppressed, juvenile, sex offenders, mental health, or adoption records released. SASE not required. Turnaround time 1-2 days. Fax notes: Fee to fax results is $1.00 per document. Copy fee: $1.00 per page. Certification fee: $10.00. Fee payee: Lake County Trial Court. Personal checks accepted. Prepayment is required.

Lake County Trial Court PO Box 1330, Baldwin, MI 49304; 231-745-4614; Fax: 231-745-2241. Hours: 8:30AM-5PM (EST). *Probate.*

Lapeer County

40th Circuit Court 255 Clay St, Lapeer, MI 48446; 810-667-0358. Hours: 8AM-5PM (EST). *Felony, Civil Actions Over $25,000.*

Civil Records: Access: Mail, in person. Visitors must perform in person searches for themselves. Search fee: $5.00 search fee covers 10 year span. Required to search: name, years to search. Civil cases indexed by defendant, plaintiff. Civil records on computer since 1994, prior on index cards.

Criminal Records: Access: Mail, in person. Visitors must perform in person searches for themselves. Search fee: $5.00 search fee covers 10 year span. Required to search: name, years to search, DOB, sex. Criminal records on computer since 1996, prior on index cards.

General Information: Public access terminal is available. No suppressed records released. SASE required. Turnaround time 1-3 days. Copy fee: $1.00 per page. Certification fee: $10.00 plus $1.00 per page after first. Fee payee: 40th Circuit Court. Personal checks accepted. Prepayment is required.

71 A District Court 255 Clay St., Lapeer, MI 48446; 810-667-0314. Hours: 8AM-5PM (EST). *Misdemeanor, Civil Actions Under $25,000, Eviction, Small Claims.*

Civil Records: Access: Mail, in person. Only the court performs in person searches; visitors may not. Search fee: $5.00 per name. Required to search: name, years to search. Civil cases indexed by defendant, plaintiff. Civil records on computer since 1992, cards and dockets from 1969.

Criminal Records: Access: Mail, in person. Only the court performs in person searches; visitors may not. Search fee: $5.00 per name. Required to search: name, years to search, DOB; also helpful: SSN. Criminal records on computer since 1992, cards and dockets from 1969.

General Information: No suppressed, juvenile, sex offenders, mental health, or adoption records released. SASE requires. Turnaround time 10 days. Copy fee: $1.00 per page. Certification fee: $10.00 plus $1.00 per page after first. Fee payee: 71 A District Court. Personal checks accepted. Third party checks not accepted. Prepayment is required.

Probate Court 255 Clay St., Lapeer, MI 48446; 810-667-0261; Fax: 810-667-0271. Hours: 8AM-5PM (EST). *Probate.*

Leelanau County

13th Circuit Court PO Box 467, Leland, MI 49654; 231-256-9824; Fax: 231-256-8295. Hours: 9AM-5PM (EST). *Felony, Civil Actions Over $25,000.*

Civil Records: Access: Mail, fax, in person. Both court and visitors may perform in person searches. Search fee: $3.00 per name. Required to search: name, years to search. Civil cases indexed by defendant, plaintiff. Civil records on computer since 1/93, prior on docket books.

Criminal Records: Access: Mail, fax, in person. Both court and visitors may perform in person searches. Search fee: $3.00 per name. Required to search: name,

years to search. Criminal records on computer since 1/97; prior records on books.

General Information: No suppressed, juvenile, sex offenders, mental health, or adoption records released. SASE required. Turnaround time 2-3 days. Copy fee: $.50 per page. Certification fee: $10.00 plus $1.00 per page after first. Fee payee: County Clerk. Personal checks accepted. Prepayment is required.

86th District Court PO Box 486, Leland, MI 49654; 231-256-8250; Fax: 231-256-8275. Hours: 8AM-4PM (EST). *Misdemeanor, Civil Actions Under $25,000, Eviction, Small Claims.*

Civil Records: Access: Fax, mail, in person. Only the court performs in person searches; visitors may not. No search fee. Required to search: name, years to search. Civil cases indexed by defendant, plaintiff. Civil records on computer since 1991, prior on books to 1969.

Criminal Records: Access: Phone, fax, mail, in person. Only the court performs in person searches; visitors may not. No search fee. Required to search: name, years to search, DOB; also helpful: SSN. Criminal records on computer since 1991, prior on books to 1969.

General Information: No suppressed, sex offenders records released. SASE requested. Turnaround time 3 days. Fax notes: $.25 per page. Copy fee: $.25 per page. Certification fee: $10.00. Fee payee: 86th District Court. Business checks accepted. Prepayment is required.

Family Court PO Box 595, Leland, MI 49654; 231-256-9803; Fax: 231-256-9845. Hours: 9AM-5PM (EST). *Probate.*

Lenawee County

39th Circuit Court 425 North Main St, Adrian, MI 49221; 517-264-4597. Hours: 8AM-4:30PM (EST). *Felony, Civil Actions Over $25,000.*

Civil Records: Access: Mail, in person. Only the court performs in person searches; visitors may not. Search fee: $10.00 per name. Fee is for ten years. Required to search: name, years to search. Civil records on computer back to 1/89, prior on books.

Criminal Records: Access: Mail, in person. Only the court performs in person searches; visitors may not. Search fee: $10.00 per name. Fee is for 10 years. Required to search: name, years to search. Criminal records on computer back to 1/89, prior on books.

General Information: No suppressed, juvenile, sex offenders, mental health, or adoption records released. SASE helpful. Turnaround time 1-2 days. Copy fee: $.50 per page. Certification fee: $10.00. Fee payee: Lenawee County Clerk or 39th Circuit Court. Personal checks accepted. Prepayment is required.

2A District Court 425 North Main St., Adrian, MI 49221; 517-264-4673 & 264-4668; Fax: 517-264-4665 Probation; 264-4681. Hours: 8AM-4:30PM (EST). *Misdemeanor, Civil Actions Under $25,000, Eviction, Small Claims.*

Civil Records: Access: Fax, mail, in person. Both court and visitors may perform in person searches. Search fee: $10.00 per name. Required to search: name, years to search. Civil cases indexed by defendant, plaintiff. Civil records on computer since 1988, prior on index books, cards and microfilm back to 1969.

Criminal Records: Access: In person only. Both court and visitors may perform in person searches. Search fee: $10.00 per name. Required to search: name, years to search, DOB. Criminal records on computer since 1988, prior on index books, cards and microfilm back to 1969.

General Information: No suppressed, juvenile, sex offenders, mental health, or adoption records released. SASE required. Turnaround time 1 week. Copy fee: $.25 per page. Certification fee: $10.00. Fee payee: 2A

District Court. Personal checks accepted. Prepayment is required.

Probate Court 425 North Main St., Adrian, MI 49221; 517-264-4614; Fax: 517-264-4616. Hours: 8AM-4:30PM (EST). *Probate.*

Livingston County

44th Circuit Court 204 South Highlander Way #4, Howell, MI 48843; 517-546-9816. Hours: 8AM-5PM (EST). *Felony, Civil Actions Over $25,000.*

Note: Juvenile Unit records are at 517-546-1500.

Civil Records: Access: Mail, in person. Both court and visitors may perform in person searches. No search fee. Required to search: name, years to search. Civil cases indexed by defendant, plaintiff. Civil records computerized from 1987, on microfiche and archived from 1900s.
Criminal Records: Access: Mail, in person. Both court and visitors may perform in person searches. No search fee. Required to search: name, years to search. Criminal records computerized from 1987, microfiche and archived from 1900s.
General Information: Public access terminal is available. All records released, none are restricted. SASE required. Turnaround time 5 days. Copy fee: $1.00 per page. Certification fee: $10.00 plus $1.00 ea add'l pg. Fee payee: Livingston County Clerk. Personal checks accepted. Out of state checks not accepted. Prepayment is required.

53 A District Court 204 South Highlander Way #1, Howell, MI 48843; 517-548-1000; Civil ext. 369; Criminal ext. 379; Fax: 517-548-9445. Hours: 8AM-5PM (EST). *Misdemeanor, Civil Actions Under $25,000, Eviction, Small Claims.*

http://co.livingston.mi.us/DistrictCourt

Civil Records: Access: Mail, in person. Visitors must perform in person searchs for themselves. No search fee. Required to search: name, years to search; also helpful: address. Civil cases indexed by defendant, plaintiff. Civil records on computer since 1982.
Criminal Records: Access: Mail, in person. Visitors must perform in person searchs for themselves. No search fee. Required to search: name, years to search, DOB; also helpful: address, SSN. Criminal records on computer since 1982.
General Information: Public access terminal is available. No suppressed, juvenile, sex offenders, mental health, or adoption records released. SASE preferred. Turnaround time 1 week. Copy fee: $1.00 for first page, $.50 each add'l. Certification fee: $10.00. Fee payee: 53 District Court. Personal checks accepted. Prepayment is required.

53 B District Court 224 N First, Brighton, MI 48116; 810-229-6615; Fax: 810-229-1770. Hours: 8AM-5PM (EST). *Misdemeanor, Civil Actions Under $25,000, Eviction, Small Claims.*

http://co.livingston.mi.us/DistrictCourt/brighton.htm

Note: This court is being renovated and will temporarily move to 200 E Grand River, Howell MI 48843 from 07/5/02 to 2/3/03.
Civil Records: Access: Mail, in person. Only the court performs in person searches; visitors may not. No search fee. Required to search: name, years to search. Civil cases indexed by defendant, plaintiff. Civil records on computer since 1985, prior on index books.
Criminal Records: Access: Mail, in person. Only the court performs in person searches; visitors may not. No search fee. Required to search: name, years to search, DOB; also helpful: SSN. Criminal records on computer since 1985, prior on index books.
General Information: No suppressed, juvenile, sex offenders, mental health, or adoption records released. SASE required. Turnaround time 1 week. Copy fee:

$1.00 for first page, $.50 each add'l. Certification fee: $10.00. Fee payee: 53rd District Court. Personal checks accepted.

Probate Court 204 Highlander Way #2, Howell, MI 48843; 517-546-3750; Fax: 517-552-2510. Hours: 8AM-5PM (EST). *Probate.*

Luce County

11th Circuit Court 407 W Harrie, Newberry, MI 49868; 906-293-5521; Fax: 906-293-0050. Hours: 8AM-4PM (EST). *Felony, Civil Actions Over $25,000.*

Civil Records: Access: Mail, in person. Only the court performs in person searches; visitors may not. No search fee. Required to search: name, years to search. Civil cases indexed by defendant, plaintiff. Civil records listed on cards since 1876.
Criminal Records: Access: Mail, in person. Only the court performs in person searches; visitors may not. No search fee. Required to search: name, years to search, DOB. Criminal records listed on cards since 1876.
General Information: No suppressed, juvenile, sex offenders, mental health, or adoption records released. SASE required. Turnaround time 4-5 days. Copy fee: $1.00 per page. Certification fee: $10.00. Fee payee: 11th Circuit Court. Personal checks accepted. Prepayment is required.

92nd District Court 407 W Harrie, Newberry, MI 49868; 906-293-5531; Fax: 906-293-3581. Hours: 8AM-4PM (EST). *Misdemeanor, Civil Actions Under $25,000, Eviction, Small Claims.*

Civil Records: Access: Phone, fax, mail, in person. Only the court performs in person searches; visitors may not. No search fee. Required to search: name, years to search. Civil cases indexed by defendant, plaintiff. Civil records to 1969, some on computer.
Criminal Records: Access: Phone, fax, mail, in person. Only the court performs in person searches; visitors may not. No search fee. Required to search: name, years to search, DOB; also helpful: SSN. Criminal records to 1969, some on computer.
General Information: SASE preferred. Turnaround time 1 week. Fax notes: $1.00 per page. Copy fee: $1.00 per page. Fee payee: 92nd District Court. In-state personal checks accepted. Prepayment is required.

Probate Court 407 W. Harrie, Newberry, MI 49868; 906-293-5601; Fax: 906-293-3581. Hours: 8AM-Noon, 1-4PM (EST). *Probate.*

Note: This is a combined court with Mackinac County Probate Court.

Mackinac County

50th Circuit Court 100 S Marley St, Rm 10, St Ignace, MI 49781; 906-643-7300; Fax: 906-643-7302. Hours: 8:30AM-4:30PM (EST). *Felony, Civil Actions Over $25,000.*

Civil Records: Access: Mail, in person. Both court and visitors may perform in person searches. No search fee. Required to search: name, years to search. Civil cases indexed by defendant, plaintiff. Civil records on docket book; on computer back to 1998.
Criminal Records: Access: In person only. Visitors must perform in person searches for themselves. Search fee: Record checks are referred to the state police. Required to search: name, years to search, DOB. Criminal records on docket book; on computer back to 1998.
General Information: No suppressed, juvenile, sex offenders, mental health, or adoption records released. SASE required. Turnaround time 10 days. Copy fee: $1.00 per page. Certification fee: $10.00 plus $1.00 per page after first. Fee payee: County Clerk. Personal checks accepted. Prepayment is required.

92nd District Court 100 South Marley, Room 55, St Ignace, MI 49781; 906-643-7321; Fax: 906-643-7302. Hours: 8:30AM-4:30PM (EST). *Misdemeanor, Civil Actions Under $25,000, Eviction, Small Claims.*

Civil Records: Access: Mail, in person, fax, phone. No search fee. Required to search: name, years to search. Civil cases indexed by defendant. Civil records on computer since 11/92, prior in files to 1980.
Criminal Records: Access: Mail, in person. Both court and visitors may perform in person searches. No search fee. Required to search: name, years to search, DOB. Criminal records on computer since 11/92, prior in files to 1970.
General Information: No suppressed, juvenile, sex offenders, mental health, or adoption records released. SASE required. Turnaround time 1 week. No copy fee. Personal checks accepted.

Probate Court 100 S Marley St, St Ignace, MI 49781; 906-643-7303; Fax: 906-643-8861. Hours: 8:30AM-Noon, 1-4:30PM (EST). *Probate.*

Note: This is a combined court with Luce County Probate Court.

Macomb County

16th Circuit Court 40 N Main St, Mount Clemens, MI 48043; 586-469-5120. Hours: 8AM-4:30PM (EST). *Felony, Civil Actions Over $25,000.*

www.co.macomb.mi.us/circuitcourt

Civil Records: Access: Mail, in person. Both court and visitors may perform in person searches. Search fee: $1.00 per name per year. Required to search: name, years to search. Civil cases indexed by defendant, plaintiff. Civil records on computer since 1977, on microfiche to 1969, prior to 1800s archived.
Criminal Records: Access: Mail, in person. Both court and visitors may perform in person searches. Search fee: $1.00 per name per year. Required to search: name, years to search; also helpful: DOB. Criminal records on computer since 1970, on microfiche to 1969, prior to 1800s archived.
General Information: Public access terminal is available. No suppressed, juvenile, sex offenders, mental health, or adoption records released. Turnaround time 1 week. Copy fee: $.40 per page. Certification fee: $10.00 plus $1.00 per page after first. Fee payee: Macomb County Clerk. Personal checks accepted, most credit cards accepted. Prepayment is required.

37th District Court - Warren & Center Line 8300 Common Rd., Warren, MI 48093; 586-574-4928; Fax: 586-574-4932. Hours: 8:30AM-4:30PM (EST). *Misdemeanor, Civil Actions Under $25,000, Eviction, Small Claims.*

Civil Records: Access: Mail, in person. Only the court performs in person searches; visitors may not. Search fee: $10.00 per name. Required to search: name, years to search. Civil cases indexed by defendant, plaintiff. Civil records on computer since 1992, prior on cards.
Criminal Records: Access: Mail, in person. Only the court performs in person searches; visitors may not. Search fee: $10.00 per name. Required to search: name, years to search, DOB; also helpful: SSN. Criminal records on computer since 1992, prior on index cards.
General Information: No suppressed, juvenile, sex offenders, mental health, or adoption records released. SASE not required. Turnaround time 2 weeks. Copy fee: $.25 per page. Certification fee: $10.00. Fee payee: 37th District Court. Personal checks accepted. Prepayment is required.

39th District Court - Roseville & Frasier

29733 Gratiot Ave, Roseville, MI 48066; 586-773-2010; Fax: 586-774-3310. Hours: 8AM-4:30PM (EST). *Misdemeanor, Civil Actions Under $25,000, Eviction, Small Claims.*

Civil Records: Access: Mail, in person. Only the court performs in person searches; visitors may not. No search fee. Required to search: name, years to search. Civil cases indexed by defendant, plaintiff. Civil records on computer since 1985, prior on microfilm.

Criminal Records: Access: Mail, in person. Only the court performs in person searches; visitors may not. No search fee. Required to search: name, years to search, DOB; also helpful: SSN. Criminal records on computer since 1985, prior on microfilm.

General Information: No suppressed, juvenile, sex offenders, mental health, or adoption records released. SASE not required. Turnaround time 1-2 days. Copy fee: $2.00 per page. Fee payee: 39th District Court. Personal checks accepted.

40th District Court - St. Clair Shores

27701 Jefferson, St. Clair Shores, MI 48081; 586-445-5281; Civil phone: 586-445-5282; Criminal phone: 586-445-5281; Fax: 586-445-4003. Hours: 8:30AM-4:30PM (EST). *Misdemeanor, Civil Actions Under $25,000, Eviction, Small Claims.*

Civil Records: Access: Mail, in person. Only the court performs in person searches; visitors may not. Search fee-$10.00. Required to search: name, years to search. Civil cases indexed by defendant, plaintiff. Civil records on computer since 1991; prior records on index books. The court has a request form that must be used with all searches.

Criminal Records: Access: Mail, in person. Only the court performs in person searches; visitors may not. Search fee-$10.00. Required to search: name, years to search, DOB; also helpful: SSN. Criminal records on computer since 1991; prior records on index books. Mail requests must have case number. The court has a request form that must be used with all searches.

General Information: No suppressed, juvenile, sex offenders, mental health, or adoption records released. Turnaround time 2 weeks. Copy fee: $1.00 for first page. Certification fee: $10.00. Fee payee: 40th District Court. Personal checks accepted. Prepayment of mail search required.

41 A District Court - Shelby

51660 Van Dyke, Shelby Township, MI 48316; 586-739-7325; Fax: 586-726-4555; 997-6172 (Civil). Hours: 8AM-4:30PM (EST). *Misdemeanor, Civil Actions Under $25,000, Eviction, Small Claims.*

Civil Records: Access: Mail, in person. Both court and visitors may perform in person searches. No search fee. Required to search: name, years to search. Civil cases indexed by defendant, plaintiff. Civil records on computer since 1992, prior on index cards.

Criminal Records: Access: Mail, in person. Both court and visitors may perform in person searches. No search fee. Required to search: name, years to search, DOB. Criminal records on computer since 1992, prior on index cards.

General Information: Public access terminal is available. (Available Friday afternoons by appointment only.) No suppressed, sex offenders, mental health records released. SASE required. Turnaround time 10 days. Copy fee: $.50 per page. Certification fee: $10.00. Fee payee: 41A District Court. Personal checks accepted. Credit cards accepted. Prepayment is required.

41 A District Court - Sterling Heights

40111 Dodge Park, Sterling Heights, MI 48313; 586-446-2500. Hours: 8:30AM-4:30PM (EST). *Misdemeanor, Civil Actions Under $25,000, Eviction, Small Claims.*

Civil Records: Access: Mail, in person. Only the court performs in person searches; visitors may not. No search fee. Required to search: name, years to search. Civil cases indexed by defendant, plaintiff. Civil records on computer since 1986; prior records on books.

Criminal Records: Access: Mail, in person. Only the court performs in person searches; visitors may not. No search fee. Required to search: name, years to search, DOB; also helpful: SSN. Criminal records on computer since 1986; prior records on books.

General Information: No suppressed, juvenile, sex offenders, mental health, or adoption records released. SASE required. Turnaround time 1 week. Copy fee: $.50 per page. Certification fee: $10.00. Fee payee: Clerk of Court. Personal checks accepted. Prepayment is required.

41 B District Court - Clinton TWP

40700 Romeo Plank Rd, Clinton Township, MI 48038-2951; 586-286-8010; Fax: 586-228-2555. Hours: 8:30AM-4:30PM (EST). *Misdemeanor, Civil Actions Under $25,000, Eviction, Small Claims.*

Civil Records: Access: Mail, in person. Only the court performs in person searches; visitors may not. No search fee. Required to search: name, years to search. Civil cases indexed by defendant, plaintiff. Civil records on computer back to 1993, prior on microfilm to 1970s.

Criminal Records: Access: Mail, in person. Only the court performs in person searches; visitors may not. No search fee. Required to search: name, years to search, DOB; also helpful: SSN. Criminal records on computer back to 1993, prior on microfilm to 1970s.

General Information: No suppressed, juvenile, sex offenders, mental health, or adoption records released. SASE required. Copy fee: $.50 per page. Certification fee: $10.00. Fee payee: 41 B District Court. Only cashiers checks and money orders accepted. Credit cards accepted: Visa, MasterCard. Prepayment is required.

42nd District Court Division 1

14713 Thirty-three Mile Rd., PO Box 6, Romeo, MI 48065; 586-752-9679; Fax: 586-469-5515. Hours: 8:30AM-5PM (EST). *Misdemeanor, Civil Actions Under $25,000, Eviction, Small Claims.*

Civil Records: Access: Mail, in person. Only the court performs in person searches; visitors may not. Search fee: $10.00 per name. Required to search: name, years to search. Civil cases indexed by defendant, plaintiff. Civil records on computer since 1990, prior on index books.

Criminal Records: Access: Mail, in person. Only the court performs in person searches; visitors may not. Search fee: $10.00 per name. Required to search: name, years to search, DOB; also helpful: SSN, sex, signed release. Criminal records on computer since 1990, prior on index books.

General Information: SASE requested. Turnaround time 2-3 days. Copy fee: $.35 per page. Certification fee: $10.00. Fee payee: 42-1 District Court. Personal checks accepted. Prepayment is required.

42nd District Court Division 2

36540 Green St, New Baltimore, MI 48047; Civil phone: 586-725-9266; Criminal phone: 586-725-9520; Fax: 586-469-5516. Hours: 8:30AM-5PM (EST). *Misdemeanor, Civil Actions Under $25,000, Eviction, Small Claims.*

Note: Includes City of New Baltimore, Village of New Haven, and townships of Lenox and Chesterfield.

Civil Records: Access: Mail, in person. Only the court performs in person searches; visitors may not. No search fee. Required to search: name, years to search.

Civil cases indexed by defendant, plaintiff. Civil records on computer back to 1990.

Criminal Records: Access: Mail, in person. Only the court performs in person searches; visitors may not. No search fee. Required to search: name, years to search, DOB; also helpful: SSN. Criminal records on computer back to 1990.

General Information: SASE required. Turnaround time 1 week. Copy fee: $.50 per page. Fee payee: 42nd District Court. Personal checks accepted. Prepayment of mail search required.

41 B District Court - Mt Clemens

1 Crocker Blvd, Mount Clemens, MI 48043; 586-469-6870; Fax: 586-469-5037. Hours: 8AM-4:30PM (EST). *Civil Actions Under $25,000, Eviction, Small Claims.*

Civil Records: Access: Mail, fax, in person. Only the court performs in person searches; visitors may not. No search fee. Required to search: name, years to search; also helpful-DOB, case number. Civil cases indexed by defendant, plaintiff. Civil records on computer back to 1996; prior on books back to 1930's.

General Information: No suppressed, juvenile, sex offenders, mental health, or adoption records released. SASE required. Turnaround time 3 days. Copy fee: $.25 per page. Fee payee: 41 B District Court. Business checks accepted. Credit cards accepted. Prepayment is required.

Probate Court 21850 Dumham, Mount Clemens, MI 48043-1075; 586-469-5290; Fax: 586-783-0971. Hours: 8:30AM-5PM (EST). *Probate.*

Manistee County

19th Circuit Court

415 3rd St, Manistee, MI 49660; 231-723-3331; Fax: 231-723-1492. Hours: 8:30AM-Noon, 1-5PM (EST). *Felony, Civil Actions Over $25,000.*

Civil Records: Access: Mail, in person. Only the court performs in person searches; visitors may not. Search fee: $5.00 per name. Required to search: name, years to search. Civil cases indexed by defendant, plaintiff. Civil records on computer since 7/90, index books from 1867.

Criminal Records: Access: Mail, in person. Only the court performs in person searches; visitors may not. Search fee: $5.00 per name. Required to search: name, years to search, DOB. Criminal records on computer since 7/90, index books from 1867.

General Information: No suppressed, juvenile, sex offenders, mental health, or adoption records released. SASE required. Turnaround time 2-3 days. Fax notes: Fee to fax results is $1.00 per page. Copy fee: $.25 per page. Certification fee: $10.00 plus $1.00 each add'l page. Fee payee: Manistee County Clerk. Personal checks accepted. Prepayment is required.

85th District Court

415 3rd St, Manistee, MI 49660; 231-723-5010; Fax: 231-723-1491. Hours: 8:30AM-5PM (EST). *Misdemeanor, Civil Actions Under $25,000, Eviction, Small Claims.*

Civil Records: Access: Fax, mail, in person. Both court and visitors may perform in person searches. Search fee: $1.00 per name. Required to search: name, years to search. Civil cases indexed by defendant, plaintiff. Civil records on computer since 4/89, prior on index books.

Criminal Records: Access: Fax, mail, in person. Both court and visitors may perform in person searches. Search fee: $1.00 per name. Required to search: name, years to search, DOB. Criminal records on computer since 4/89, prior on index books.

General Information: No suppressed, juvenile, sex offenders, mental health, or adoption records released. SASE required. Turnaround time 5-7 days. Copy fee: $1.00 per page. Certification fee: $10.00. Fee payee: 85th District Court. Personal checks accepted. Prepayment is required.

Probate Court 415 3rd St, Manistee, MI 49660; 231-723-3261; Fax: 231-723-1492. Hours: 8:30AM-Noon, 1-5PM (EST). *Probate.*

Marquette County

25th Circuit Court 234 W Baraga, Marquette, MI 49855; 906-225-8330; Fax: 906-228-1572. Hours: 8AM-5PM (EST). *Felony, Civil Actions Over $25,000.*

Civil Records: Access: Mail, in person. Only the court performs in person searches; visitors may not. Search fee: $5.00 per name. Required to search: name, years to search. Civil cases indexed by defendant, plaintiff. Civil records on books since 1852, on computer from 04/95.

Criminal Records: Access: Mail, in person. Only the court performs in person searches; visitors may not. Search fee: $5.00 per name. Required to search: name, years to search, DOB. Criminal records on books since 1852, on computer from 04/95.

General Information: No suppressed, juvenile, sex offenders, mental health, or adoption records released. Turnaround time 2-3 business days. Copy fee: $1.00 per page. Certification fee: $10.00 plus $1.00 per page after first. Fee payee: County Clerk. Personal checks accepted. Prepayment is required.

96th District Court County Courthouse, Marquette, MI 49855; 906-225-8235; Fax: 906-225-8255. Hours: 8:00AM-5PM (EST). *Misdemeanor, Civil Actions Under $25,000, Eviction, Small Claims.*

Civil Records: Access: Fax, mail, in person. Both court and visitors may perform in person searches. Search fee: $5.00 per name. Required to search: name, years to search; also helpful: address. Civil records indexed by defendant, plaintiff. Civil records on computer since 1987, prior on docket books.

Criminal Records: Access: Fax, mail, in person. Both court and visitors may perform in person searches. Search fee: $5.00 per name. Required to search: name, years to search, DOB; also helpful: offense. Criminal records on computer since 1987, prior on docket books.

General Information: Public access terminal is available. No suppressed records released. SASE required. Turnaround time 1-2 weeks. Fax notes: No fee to fax results. Copy fee: $1.00 per page. Certification fee: $10.00 plus $1.00 per page after first. Fee payee: 96th District Court. Business checks accepted. Prepayment is required.

Probate Court 234 W Baraga, Marquette, MI 49855; 906-225-8300; Fax: 906-225-8293. Hours: 8AM-5PM (EST). *Probate.*

Mason County

51st Circuit Court 304 E Ludington Ave, Ludington, MI 49431; 231-845-1445; Fax: 231-843-1972. Hours: 9AM-5PM (EST). *Felony, Civil Actions Over $25,000.*

Civil Records: Access: Phone, mail, in person. Only the court performs in person searches; visitors may not. No search fee. Required to search: name, years to search. Civil cases indexed by defendant, plaintiff. Civil records on file since 1867.

Criminal Records: Access: Phone, mail, in person. Only the court performs in person searches; visitors may not. No search fee. Required to search: name, years to search, DOB; also helpful: SSN. Criminal records on file since 1867.

General Information: No suppressed, juvenile, sex offenders, mental health, or adoption records released. SASE required. Turnaround time 1 week. Copy fee: $1.00 per page. Certification fee: $10.00. Fee payee: Mason County Clerk. Personal checks accepted. Prepayment of mail service required.

79th District Court County Court, Ludington, MI 49431; 231-843-4130; Fax: 231-845-7779. Hours:

8AM-5PM (EST). *Misdemeanor, Civil Actions Under $25,000, Eviction, Small Claims.*

Civil Records: Access: Fax, mail, in person. Only the court performs in person searches; visitors may not. Search fee: $5.00 per name. Required to search: name, years to search. Civil cases indexed by defendant, plaintiff. Civil records on Register of Action Docket Cards, computerized since 10/96.

Criminal Records: Access: Fax, mail, in person. Only the court performs in person searches; visitors may not. Search fee: $5.00 per name. Required to search: name, years to search, DOB. Criminal records on Register of Action Docket Cards, computerized since 10/96.

General Information: No suppressed, juvenile, sex offenders, mental health, or adoption records released. SASE required. Turnaround time 2 days. Fax notes: No fee to fax results. Local calls only. Copy fee: $1.00 per page. Certification fee: $10.00 plus $1.00 per page after first. Fee payee: 79th District Court. Only cashiers checks and money orders accepted.

Probate Court 304 E Ludington Ave, Ludington, MI 49431; 231-843-8666; Fax: 231-843-1972. Hours: 9AM-Noon, 1-5PM (EST). *Probate.*

Mecosta County

49th Circuit Court 400 Elm, Big Rapids, MI 49307; 231-592-0783; Fax: 231-592-0193. Hours: 8:30AM-5PM (EST). *Felony, Civil Actions Over $25,000.*

Civil Records: Access: Fax, mail, in person. Only the court performs in person searches; visitors may not. Search fee: $5.00 per name. Required to search: name, years to search. Civil cases indexed by defendant, plaintiff. Civil records on computer since 10/70, archived and microfiche since 1900s.

Criminal Records: Access: Fax, mail, in person. Only the court performs in person searches; visitors may not. Search fee: $5.00 per name. Required to search: name, years to search. Criminal records on computer since 10/70, archived and microfiche since 1900s.

General Information: No suppressed, juvenile, mental health, or adoption records released. SASE requested. Turnaround time 1 week. Copy fee: $1.00 per page. Certification fee: $10.00. Fee payee: Mecosta County Clerk. Personal checks not accepted, money orders and cashiers checks preferred. Prepayment is required.

77th District Court 400 Elm, Big Rapids, MI 49307; 231-592-0799; Fax: 231-796-2180. Hours: 8:30AM-4:30PM (EST). *Misdemeanor, Civil Actions Under $25,000, Eviction, Small Claims.*

Civil Records: Access: Mail, fax. Only the court performs in person searches; visitors may not. Search fee: $10.00 per name. Required to search: name, years to search. Civil cases indexed by defendant, plaintiff. Civil records on computer to 1992, archived and microfiche prior.

Criminal Records: Access: Mail, in person. Only the court performs in person searches; visitors may not. Search fee: $10.00 per name. Required to search: name, years to search, DOB. Criminal records on computer for 10 years, archived and microfiche prior. Signed release required for employment screening.

General Information: No suppressed, juvenile, sex offenders, mental health, or adoption records released. SASE not required. Turnaround time 7 days. Copy fee: $1.00 per page. Certification fee: $10.00. Fee payee: 77th District Court. Business checks accepted. Prepayment is required.

Probate Court 400 Elm St, PO Box 820, Big Rapids, MI 49307; 231-592-0135; Fax: 231-592-0191. Hours: 8:30AM-5PM (EST). *Probate.*

Note: Shares the same judge with Osceola County Probate Court.

Menominee County

41st Circuit Court 839 10th Ave, Menominee, MI 49858; 906-863-9968; Fax: 906-863-8839. Hours: 8AM-4:30PM (CST). *Felony, Civil Actions Over $25,000.*

Civil Records: Access: Mail, in person. Only the court performs in person searches; visitors may not. Search fee: $1.00 per name per year. Required to search: name, years to search. Civil cases indexed by defendant, plaintiff. Civil records kept by docket entry in file folders, archived to 1900, computerized since 1998.

Criminal Records: Access: Mail, in person. Only the court performs in person searches; visitors may not. Search fee: $5.00 per name for first 7 years, then $1.00 each additional year. Required to search: name, years to search, DOB; also helpful: SSN. Criminal records kept by docket entry in file folders to 1900; on computer back to 1998.

General Information: No suppressed, juvenile, sex offenders, mental health, or adoption records released. Turnaround time 2-3 days. Fax notes: Fee to fax results is $3.00 1st page, $1.00 each add'l. Copy fee: $1.00 per page. Certification fee: $10.00 plus $1.00 per page after first. Fee payee: 41st Circuit Court. Personal checks accepted. Prepayment is required.

95 A District Court 839 10th Ave, Menominee, MI 49858; 906-863-8532; Fax: 906-863-2023. Hours: 8AM-4:30PM (CST). *Misdemeanor, Civil Actions Under $25,000, Eviction, Small Claims.*

Civil Records: Access: Fax, mail, in person. Both court and visitors may perform in person searches. Search fee: $5.00 per name. Required to search: name, years to search. Civil cases indexed by defendant, plaintiff. Civil records on index books since 1969.

Criminal Records: Access: Fax, mail, in person. Only the court performs in person searches; visitors may not. Search fee: $5.00 per name. Required to search: name, years to search, DOB. Criminal records on index books since 1969.

General Information: No suppressed, juvenile, sex offenders, mental health, or adoption records released. SASE required. Turnaround time 1 week. Fax notes: $.20 per page. Copy fee: $.20 per page. Certification fee: $10.00. Fee payee: District Court 95A. Personal checks accepted. Prepayment is required.

Probate Court 839 10th Ave., Menominee, MI 49858; 906-863-2634; Fax: 906-863-8839. Hours: 8AM-4:30PM (CST). *Probate.*

Midland County

42nd Circuit Court Courthouse, 301 W Main St, Midland, MI 48640; 989-832-6735; Fax: 989-832-6610. Hours: 8AM-5PM (EST). *Felony, Civil Actions Over $25,000.*

Civil Records: Access: Phone, mail, in person. Only the court performs in person searches; visitors may not. No search fee. Required to search: name, years to search. Civil cases indexed by defendant, plaintiff. Civil records on computer from 1985, prior on books since 1800s.

Criminal Records: Access: Phone, mail, in person. Only the court performs in person searches; visitors may not. No search fee. Required to search: name, years to search, DOB. Criminal records on computer from 1985, prior on books since 1800s.

General Information: No suppressed records released. SASE required. Turnaround time same day. Copy fee: $10.00 per doc. + $1.00 per page. Certification fee: $10.00 plus $1.00 per page after first. Fee payee: Clerk of Circuit Court. Personal checks accepted. Prepayment is required.

75th District Court - Civil Division 301 W Main St, Midland, MI 48640; 989-832-6701. Hours:

8:30AM-4:30PM (EST). *Civil Actions Under $25,000, Eviction, Small Claims.*

Note: Small Claims can be reached at 989-832-6717

Civil Records: Access: Mail, in person. Both court and visitors may perform in person searches. Search fee: $1.00 per name per year. Required to search: name, years to search; also helpful: address. Civil cases indexed by defendant, plaintiff. Civil records on computer since 06/89; on index books until 06/89.

General Information: No suppressed, juvenile, sex offenders, mental health, or adoption records released. SASE not required. Turnaround time 5-7 days. Copy fee: $.25 per page. Certification fee: Certification $10.00 for the first page, additional pages $1.00 each. Fee payee: 75th District Court. Personal checks accepted. Prepayment is required.

75th District Court - Criminal Division 301 W Main St, Midland, MI 48640-5183; 989-832-6702 (6714-traffic). Hours: 8:30AM-4:30PM (EST). *Misdemeanor.*

Criminal Records: Access: Mail, in person. Only the court performs in person searches; visitors may not. Search fee: $1.00 per name per year. $5.00 minimum. Required to search: name, years to search, DOB. Criminal records on computer since 1991, prior on docket books and paper index.

General Information: No suppressed, sex offenders or mental health records released. SASE not required. Turnaround time 2 weeks. Copy fee: $1.00 per page. Certification fee: $10.00. Fee payee: 75th District Court. Personal checks accepted.

Probate Court 301 W Main St, Midland, MI 48640; 989-832-6880; Fax: 989-832-6607. Hours: 8AM-5PM (EST). *Probate.*

www.midlandcounty.org

Missaukee County

28th Circuit Court PO Box 800, Lake City, MI 49651; 231-839-4967; Fax: 231-839-3684. Hours: 9AM-5PM (EST). *Felony, Civil Actions Over $25,000.*

Civil Records: Access: Phone, fax, mail, in person. Both court and visitors may perform in person searches. Search fee: $5.00 per name. Required to search: name, years to search. Civil cases indexed by defendant, plaintiff. Civil records on computer since 1990, prior on books.

Criminal Records: Access: Phone, fax, mail, in person. Both court and visitors may perform in person searches. Search fee: $5.00 per name. Required to search: name, years to search; also helpful: DOB, SSN. Criminal records on computer since 1990, prior on books.

General Information: Public access terminal is available. No suppressed, juvenile, sex offenders, mental health, or adoption records released. SASE not required. Turnaround time 2 days. Fax notes: $5.00 for first page, $1.00 each add'l. Copy fee: $1.00 per page. Certification fee: $10.00. Fee payee: Missaukee County Clerk. Personal checks accepted. Prepayment is required.

84th District Court PO Box 800, Lake City, MI 49651; 231-839-4590. Hours: 9AM-5PM (EST). *Misdemeanor, Civil Actions Under $25,000, Eviction, Small Claims.*

Civil Records: Access: Mail, in person. Both court and visitors may perform in person searches. Search fee: $5.00 per name. Required to search: name, years to search. Civil cases indexed by defendant, plaintiff. Civil records on computer since 1989.

Criminal Records: Access: Mail, in person. Both court and visitors may perform in person searches. Search fee: $5.00 per name. Required to search: name, years to

search, DOB, SSN. Criminal records on computer since 1988.

General Information: No suppressed, juvenile, sex offenders, mental health, or adoption records released. SASE required. Turnaround time 1 week. Copy fee: $1.00 per page. Certification fee: $10.00 plus $1.00 per page after first. Fee payee: District Court. Personal checks accepted. Prepayment is required.

Probate Court PO Box 800, Lake City, MI 49651; 231-839-2266; Fax: 231-839-5856. Hours: 9AM-Noon, 1-5PM (EST). *Probate.*

Monroe County

38th Circuit Court 106 E 1st St, Monroe, MI 48161; 734-240-7020; Fax: 734-240-7266. Hours: 8:30AM-5PM *Felony, Civil Actions Over $25,000.*

www.co.monroe.mi.us/Courts/index.html

Civil Records: Access: Mail, fax, in person. Both court and visitors may perform in person searches. Search fee: $8.00 per name. Fee is per name per 5 years. Required to search: name, years to search. Civil cases indexed by defendant, plaintiff. Civil records on computer back to 1990; prior on docket books.

Criminal Records: Access: Mail, fax, in person. Both court and visitors may perform in person searches. Search fee: $8.00 per name. Fee is per name per 5 years. Required to search: name, years to search, DOB. Criminal records on computer back to 1990; prior on docket books.

General Information: Public access terminal is available. No suppressed records released. SASE required. Turnaround time same day. Copy fee: $1.00 per page. Certification fee: $10.00. Fee payee: 38th Circuit Court. Personal checks accepted. Prepayment is required.

1st District Court 106 E 1st St, Monroe, MI 48161; 734-240-7075; Fax: 734-240-7098. Hours: 8AM-5PM (EST). *Misdemeanor, Civil Actions Under $25,000, Eviction, Small Claims.*

www.co.monroe.mi.us/DistrictCourt/index.html

Civil Records: Access: Mail, in person. Only the court performs in person searches; visitors may not. No search fee. Required to search: name, years to search, address. Civil cases indexed by defendant, plaintiff. Civil records on computer since 1993; prior records to 1969 on microfiche.

Criminal Records: Access: Mail, in person. Only the court performs in person searches; visitors may not. No search fee. Required to search: name, years to search, DOB; also helpful: address, SSN. Criminal records on computer since 1993; prior records to 1969 on microfiche.

General Information: No suppressed, juvenile, sex offenders, mental health, or adoption records released. Turnaround time 1 week. Copy fee: $1.00 per page. Certification fee: $10.00 per page. Fee payee: 1st District Court. Business checks accepted. Prepayment is required.

Probate Court 106 E 1st St, Monroe, MI 48161; 734-243-7018. Hours: 8AM-Noon, 1-5PM (EST). *Probate.*

www.co.monroe.mi.us/Courts/index.html

Montcalm County

8th Circuit Court PO Box 368, Stanton, MI 48888; 989-831-7339; Fax: 989-831-7474. Hours: 8AM-5PM (EST). *Felony, Civil Actions Over $25,000.*

Note: The office closes for lunch for one hour.

Civil Records: Access: Mail, in person. Only the court performs in person searches; visitors may not. Search fee: $5.00 for 5 years then $1.00 for each additional year searched. Required to search: name, years to search. Civil cases indexed by defendant, plaintiff. Civil

records on docket books to 1867, computerized since 1990.

Criminal Records: Access: Mail, in person. Only the court performs in person searches; visitors may not. Search fee: Same fees as civil. Required to search: name, years to search, DOB. Criminal records on docket books to 1867, computerized since 1990.

General Information: No suppressed, juvenile, sex offenders, mental health, adoption, birth or DD214 records released. Turnaround time 1-3 days. Copy fee: $1.00 per page. Certification fee: $10.00 plus $1.00 per page after first. Fee payee: Montcalm County Clerk. Personal checks accepted. Prepayment is required.

64 B District Court 617 N State Rd #D, Stanton, MI 48888; 989-831-7450; Fax: 989-831-4747. Hours: 8AM-5PM (EST). *Misdemeanor, Civil Actions Under $25,000, Eviction, Small Claims.*

Civil Records: Access: Mail, in person. Only the court performs in person searches; visitors may not. No search fee. Required to search: name, years to search. Civil cases indexed by defendant, plaintiff. Civil records on computer since 1989, prior on books and microfiche.

Criminal Records: Access: Mail, in person. Only the court performs in person searches; visitors may not. No search fee. Required to search: name, years to search, DOB; also helpful: SSN. Criminal records on computer since 1989, prior on books and microfiche.

General Information: No suppressed records released. SASE required. Turnaround time 14 days. Copy fee: $.10 per page. Certification fee: $10.00 plus $1.00 each add'l pg. Fee payee: 64 B District Court. Personal checks accepted. Prepayment is required.

Probate Court 211 W Main St, PO Box 309, Stanton, MI 48888; 989-831-7316; Fax: 989-831-7314. Hours: 8AM-5PM (EST). *Probate.*

Montmorency County

26th Circuit Court PO Box 789, Atlanta, MI 49709; 989-785-8022; Fax: 989-785-8028. Hours: 8:30AM-Noon, 1-4:30PM (EST). *Felony, Civil Actions Over $25,000.*

Note: A Board ruling regarding search fee changes is pending.

Civil Records: Access: Phone, fax, mail, in person. Both court and visitors may perform in person searches. No search fee. Required to search: name, years to search. Civil cases indexed by defendant, plaintiff. Civil records on computer since 1990, prior on books since 1940s, microfiche to 1970. For in person searches, call ahead two days in advance.

Criminal Records: Access: Phone, fax, mail, in person. Both court and visitors may perform in person searches. No search fee. Required to search: name, years to search; also helpful: DOB. Criminal records on computer since 1990, prior on books since 1940s. For in person searches, call ahead two days in advance.

General Information: No suppressed, mental health, birth certificate (except to heir or parent) adoption records released. Turnaround time 7-10 days. Fax notes: Fee to fax results is $1.00 per page. Copy fee: $1.00 per page. Certification fee: $10.00 plus $1.00 each additional page. Fee payee: County Clerk. Personal checks accepted. Prepayment is required.

88th District Court County Courthouse, PO Box 789, Atlanta, MI 49709; 989-785-8035; Fax: 989-785-8036. Hours: 8:30AM-Noon, 1-4:30PM (EST). *Misdemeanor, Civil Actions Under $25,000, Eviction, Small Claims.*

Civil Records: Access: Mail, fax, in person. Only the court performs in person searches; visitors may not. Search fee: $5.00 per name. Required to search: name, years to search; also helpful: address. Civil cases indexed by defendant, plaintiff. Civil records on computer back to 1990, prior on books and card file since 1969.

Criminal Records: Access: Mail, fax, in person. Only the court performs in person searches; visitors may not. Search fee: $5.00 per name. Required to search: name, years to search, DOB; also helpful: address, SSN, signed release. Criminal records on computer back to 1990, prior on books and card file since 1969.

General Information: No suppressed, juvenile, sex offenders, mental health, or adoption records released. SASE required. Turnaround time 1-3 days. Fax notes: Fee to fax results is $1.00 per document plus $1.00 per page. Copy fee: $1.00 per page. Certification fee: $10.00. Fee payee: 88th District Court-Montmorency County. Personal checks accepted, credit card payments accepted. Prepayment is required.

Probate Court PO Box 789, Atlanta, MI 49709-0789; 989-785-4403; Fax: 989-785-2605. *Probate.*

Muskegon County

14th Circuit Court County Bldg, 6th Floor, 990 Terrace St, Muskegon, MI 49442; 231-724-6251; Fax: 231-724-6695. Hours: 8AM-5PM (EST). *Felony, Civil Actions Over $25,000.*

Civil Records: Access: Phone, mail, fax, in person. Both court and visitors may perform in person searches. No search fee. Required to search: name, years to search. Civil cases indexed by defendant, plaintiff. Civil records on computer back to 1984, prior on books since 1853.

Criminal Records: Access: Phone, mail, fax, in person. Both court and visitors may perform in person searches. No search fee. Required to search: name, years to search, DOB; also helpful: SSN. Criminal records on computer back to 1984, prior on books since 1853.

General Information: Public access terminal is available. No suppressed, juvenile, sex offenders, mental health, or adoption records released. SASE requires. Turnaround time 2-3 days. Fax notes: Fee to fax results is $1.00 per page. Copy fee: $1.00 per page. Certification fee: $10.00 plus $1.00 per page after first. Fee payee: Circuit Court Records. Personal checks accepted. Prepayment is required.

60th District Court 990 Terrace, 1st Floor, Muskegon, MI 49442; 231-724-6250; Fax: 231-724-3489. Hours: 8:30AM-4:45PM (EST). *Misdemeanor, Civil Actions Under $25,000, Eviction, Small Claims.*

www.co.muskegon.mi.us/60thdistrict

Civil Records: Access: Mail, in person. Both court and visitors may perform in person searches. No search fee. Required to search: name, years to search. Civil cases indexed by defendant, plaintiff. Civil records on computer since 5/93, prior on hard copy. Online access to the court weekly docket is available free at www.co.muskegon.mi.us/60thdistrict/docket.htm.

Criminal Records: Access: Mail, in person. Only the court performs in person searches; visitors may not. No search fee. Required to search: name, years to search, DOB. Criminal records on computer since 5/93, prior on hard copy. Online access to the court weekly docket is at www.co.muskegon.mi.us/60thdistrict/docket.htm.

General Information: Public access terminal is available. No suppressed, juvenile, sex offenders, mental health, or adoption records released. SASE required. Turnaround time 3 days. Copy fee: $1.00 per page. Certification fee: $10.00. Fee payee: 60th District Court. Personal checks accepted. Prepayment is required.

Probate Court 990 Terrace St, 5th Floor, Muskegon, MI 49442; 231-724-6241; Fax: 231-724-6232. Hours: 8AM-5PM (EST). *Probate.*

Newaygo County

27th Circuit Court PO Box 885, White Cloud, MI 49349-0885; 231-689-7269; Fax: 231-689-7007. Hours: 8AM-noon; 1-5PM (EST). *Felony, Civil Actions Over $25,000.*

Civil Records: Access: Mail, fax, in person. Only the court performs in person searches; visitors may not. No search fee. Required to search: name, years to search. Civil cases indexed by defendant, plaintiff. Civil records archived since 1880s; on computer since 7/1994.

Criminal Records: Access: Mail, fax, in person. Only the court performs in person searches; visitors may not. No search fee. Required to search: name, years to search; also helpful: DOB. Criminal records archived since 1880s; on computer since 7/1994.

General Information: No suppressed records released. SASE requested. Turnaround time 2-5 days. Fax notes: Will fax results to toll-free numbers only. Copy fee: $1.00 per page. Certification fee: $10.00 plus $1.00 per page after first. Fee payee: Newaygo County Circuit Court. Personal checks accepted. Prepayment is required.

78th District Court 1092 Newell St, White Cloud, MI 49349; 231-689-7257; Fax: 231-689-7258. Hours: 8AM-noon, 1-5PM (EST). *Misdemeanor, Civil Actions Under $25,000, Eviction, Small Claims.*

Civil Records: Access: Fax, mail, in person. Both court and visitors may perform in person searches. No search fee. Required to search: name, years to search; also helpful: address. Civil cases indexed by defendant, plaintiff. Civil records on computer since 7/27/89, prior in folders.

Criminal Records: Access: Fax, mail, in person. Both court and visitors may perform in person searches. No search fee. Required to search: name, years to search, DOB; also helpful: address, SSN. Criminal records on computer since 7/27/89, prior in folders.

General Information: Public access terminal is available. No suppressed records released. SASE required. Turnaround time 7-10 days. Fax notes: No fee to fax results. Copy fee: $1.00 per page. Certification fee: $10.00 plus $1.00 per page after first. Fee payee: 78th District Court. Personal checks accepted. Prepayment is required.

Probate Court PO Box 885 (1092 Newell St.), White Cloud, MI 49349; 231-689-7270; Fax: 231-689-7276. Hours: 8AM-Noon, 1-5PM (EST). *Probate.*

Oakland County

6th Circuit Court 1200 N Telegraph Rd, Pontiac, MI 48341; 248-858-0581. Hours: 8:30AM-4:30PM (EST). *Felony, Civil Actions Over $25,000.*

www.co.oakland.mi.us/arc/c_serv/ccourt

Civil Records: Access: Mail, in person. Both court and visitors may perform in person searches. Search fee: $1.00 per name. Required to search: name, years to search. Civil cases indexed by defendant, plaintiff. Civil records on computer since 1963, prior on microfilm & books.

Criminal Records: Access: Mail, in person. Both court and visitors may perform in person searches. Search fee: $1.00 per name. Required to search: name; also helpful: years to search, DOB, SSN. Criminal records on computer since 1963, prior on microfilm & books.

General Information: Public access terminal is available. No suppressed, non-public, sex offenders or mental health records released. SASE required. Turnaround time 7 days. Copy fee: $1.00 per page. Certification fee: $10.00 plus $1.00 per page after first.

Fee payee: Circuit Court. Personal checks not accepted, but most credit cards are.

43rd District Court 43 E Nine Mile Rd, Hazel Park, MI 48030; 248-547-3034; Fax: 248-546-4088. Hours: 8:30AM-5PM (EST). *Misdemeanor, Civil Actions Under $25,000, Eviction, Small Claims.*

Civil Records: Access: Mail, in person. Both court and visitors may perform in person searches. No search fee. Required to search: name, years to search. Civil cases indexed by defendant, plaintiff. Civil records on computer since 1989, prior on books since 1970.

Criminal Records: Access: Mail, in person. Both court and visitors may perform in person searches. No search fee. Required to search: name, years to search, DOB; also helpful: SSN. Criminal records on computer since 1989, prior on books since 1970.

General Information: No suppressed, juvenile, sex offenders, mental health, or adoption records released. SASE not required. Turnaround time 3-7 days. Copy fee: $.25 per page. Certification fee: $10.00. Fee payee: 43rd District Court. Only cashiers checks, cash or money orders accepted. Prepayment is required.

44th District Court - Royal Oak 400 E Eleven Mile Rd, Box 20, Royal Oak, MI 48068; 248-246-3600; Fax: 248-246-3601. Hours: 8AM-4:30PM (EST). *Misdemeanor, Civil Actions Under $25,000, Eviction, Small Claims.*

Civil Records: Access: Mail, in person. Both court and visitors may perform in person searches. Search fee: $10.00 per name. Required to search: name, years to search. Civil cases indexed by defendant, plaintiff. Civil records on computer since 1983s, prior on docket books and index cards.

Criminal Records: Access: Mail, in person. Both court and visitors may perform in person searches. Search fee: $10.00 per name. Required to search: name, years to search, DOB, signed release, offense; also helpful: address. Criminal records on computer since 1983s, prior on docket books and index cards.

General Information: No suppressed, juvenile, sex offenders, mental health, or adoption records released. SASE required. Turnaround time 5 days. Copy fee: $1.00 per page. Certification fee: $10.00 plus $1.00 per page after first. Fee payee: 44th District Court. Personal checks accepted. Prepayment is required.

45 A District Court - Berkley 3338 Coolidge, Berkley, MI 48072; 248-544-3300; Fax: 248-546-2416. Hours: 8:30AM-4:45PM (EST). *Misdemeanor, Civil Actions Under $25,000, Eviction, Small Claims.*

Civil Records: Access: Mail, in person. Only the court performs in person searches; visitors may not. Search fee: $1.00 per name. Required to search: name, years to search. Civil cases indexed by defendant, plaintiff. Civil records on computer since 1986, prior on books.

Criminal Records: Access: Mail, in person. Only the court performs in person searches; visitors may not. No search fee. Required to search: name, years to search, DOB; also helpful: SSN. Criminal records on computer since 1986, prior on books.

General Information: No suppressed records released. SASE required. Turnaround time 1 week. Copy fee: $1.00 per page. Certification fee: $10.00. Fee payee: 45 A District Court. Personal checks accepted. Prepayment is required.

45 B District Court 13600 Oak Park Blvd, Oak Park, MI 48237; 248-691-7440; Fax: 248-691-7158. Hours: 9AM-5PM (EST). *Misdemeanor, Civil Actions Under $25,000, Eviction, Small Claims.*

Note: Court covers Huntington Woods, Oak Park, Pleasant Ridge, and Royal Oak Township.

Civil Records: Access: Mail, in person. Both court and visitors may perform in person searches. No search fee. Required to search: name, years to search. Civil cases indexed by defendant, plaintiff. Civil records on computer back to 1988. Docket books and index cards back to 1987.

Criminal Records: Access: Mail, in person. Both court and visitors may perform in person searches. No search fee. Required to search: name, years to search, DOB; also helpful: SSN. Criminal records on computer back to 1988. Docket books and index cards go back to 1988.

General Information: Public access terminal is available. No suppressed records released. Turnaround time varies. Copy fee: $1.00 per page. Certification fee: $10.00. Fee payee: 45 B District Court. Business checks accepted.

46th District Court
26000 Evergreen Rd, Southfield, MI 48076; 248-354-9506; Civil phone: 248-354-9370; Criminal phone: 248-354-9368; Fax: 248-354-5315. Hours: 8AM-4:45PM (counter) (EST). *Misdemeanor, Civil Actions Under $25,000, Eviction, Small Claims.*

www.cityofsouthfield.com/46court

Civil Records: Access: Mail, in person. Both court and visitors may perform in person searches. No search fee. Required to search: name, years to search. Civil cases indexed by defendant, plaintiff. Civil records prior to 1990 are on microfilm; most recent records are computerized.

Criminal Records: Access: Mail, in person. Both court and visitors may perform in person searches. Court will search only 1990 to present with case # provided. No search fee. Required to search: name, years to search, DOB. Criminal records on computer since 1991, prior on microfiche.

General Information: No suppressed, juvenile, sex offenders, mental health, or adoption records released. SASE requested. Turnaround time varies. Copy fee: $.25 per page. Certification fee: $10.00 plus $1.00 per page after first. Fee payee: 46th District Court. Personal checks accepted. Credit cards accepted: M/C, Visa, Prepayment is required.

47th District Court - Farmington, Farmington Hills
32795 W Ten Mile Rd, Farmington, MI 48336; 248-477-5630; Fax: 248-477-2441. Hours: 8:30AM-4:30PM; 'til 6:30PM 3rd Tues each month (EST). *Misdemeanor, Civil Actions Under $25,000, Eviction, Small Claims.*

Civil Records: Access: Mail, fax, in person. No search fee. Required to search: name, years to search, case number. Civil cases indexed by defendant, plaintiff. Civil records on computer since 7/19/93; prior on microfiche since 1975.

Criminal Records: Access: Mail, fax, in person. Visitors must perform in person searches for themselves. No search fee. Required to search: name, years to search, case number DOB; also helpful: SSN, offense. Criminal records on computer since 7/19/93; prior on microfiche since 1975.

General Information: Public access terminal is available. No suppressed, sex offenders or mental health records released. SASE required. Turnaround time varies. Copy fee: $1.00 per page. Certification fee: $10.00 plus $1.00 per page after first. Fee payee: 47th District Court. Personal checks accepted. Credit cards accepted: Visa, MasterCard.

48th District Court
4280 Telegraph Rd, Bloomfield Hills, MI 48302; 248-647-1141; Fax: 248-647-8955. Hours: 8:30AM-4:30PM (EST). *Misdemeanor, Civil Actions Under $25,000, Eviction, Small Claims.*

Civil Records: Access: Phone, mail, in person. Both court and visitors may perform in person searches. No search fee. Required to search: name, years to search, address. Civil cases indexed by defendant, plaintiff. Civil records on computer since 1980, prior on index cards.

Criminal Records: Access: Phone, mail, in person. Both court and visitors may perform in person searches. No search fee. Required to search: name, years to search, address, DOB; also helpful: SSN. Criminal records on computer since 1980, prior on index cards.

General Information: Public access terminal is available. No suppressed, juvenile, sex offenders, mental health, victim or adoption records released. Turnaround time varies. Copy fee: $.50 per page. Certification fee: $10.00 plus $1.00 per page after first. Fee payee: 48th District Court. Personal checks accepted. Credit cards accepted: Visa, MasterCard, AmEx. Debit Card accepted. Prepayment is required.

51st District Court - Waterford
5100 Civic Center Dr, Waterford, MI 48329; 248-674-4655. Hours: 8:30AM-4:45PM (EST). *Misdemeanor, Civil Actions Under $25,000, Eviction, Small Claims.*

Civil Records: Access: Mail, in person. Only the court performs in person searches; visitors may not. Search fee: $2.00 per name. Required to search: name, years to search. Civil cases indexed by defendant, plaintiff. Civil records on computer since 1980s, prior on docket books and index cards to 1969.

Criminal Records: Access: Mail, in person. Only the court performs in person searches; visitors may not. No search fee. Required to search: name, years to search, DOB; also helpful: SSN. Criminal records on computer since 1980s, prior on docket books and index cards to 1969. Search hours are 10-11AM and 2-4PM.

General Information: No suppressed, juvenile, sex offenders, mental health, or adoption records released. Turnaround time 10 days. Copy fee: $.25 per page. Certification fee: $10.00. Fee payee: 51st District Court. Personal checks accepted. Credit cards accepted: Visa, MasterCard. Prepayment is required.

52nd District Court - Division 1
48150 Grand River, Novi, MI 48374; Civil phone: 248-305-6080; Criminal phone: 248-305-6460. Hours: 8:30AM-4:30PM (EST). *Misdemeanor, Civil Actions Under $25,000, Eviction, Small Claims.*

www.52-1districtcourt.com

Civil Records: Access: Phone, mail, in person. Only the court performs in person searches; visitors may not. No search fee. For multiple name searching, please search on Tuesday or Friday. Required to search: name, years to search. Civil cases indexed by defendant, plaintiff. Civil records on computer since 1984, prior on books.

Criminal Records: Access: Phone, mail, in person. Only the court performs in person searches; visitors may not. No search fee. For multiple name searching, please search on Wednesday or Thursday. Required to search: name, years to search; also helpful: DOB. Criminal records on computer since 1984, prior on books.

General Information: No suppressed, juvenile, sex offenders or mental health records released. SASE required. Turnaround time 1 month. Copy fee: $1.00 per page. Certification fee: $10.00. Fee payee: 52-1 District Court. Personal checks accepted. Credit cards accepted: Visa, MasterCard. In state only. Prepayment is required.

52nd District Court - Division 2
5850 Lorac, Clarkston, MI 48346; Civil phone: 248-625-4994; Criminal phone: 248-625-4888; Fax: 248-625-5602. Hours: 8:30AM-4:30PM (EST). *Misdemeanor, Civil Actions Under $25,000, Eviction, Small Claims.*

Note: Court covers Springfield, Holly, Groveland, Brandon, Independence, Clarkston & Ortonville.

Civil Records: Access: Phone, fax, mail, in person. Only the court performs in person searches; visitors may not. No search fee. Required to search: name, years to search. Civil cases indexed by defendant, plaintiff.

Civil records on computer since 1982, prior on microfiche since 1976.

Criminal Records: Access: Phone, fax, mail, in person. Only the court performs in person searches; visitors may not. No search fee. Required to search: name, years to search, DOB; also helpful: SSN. Criminal records on computer since 1982, prior on microfiche since 1976.

General Information: No suppressed, juvenile or sex offender records released. Turnaround time 3-5 days. Copy fee: $1.00 per page. Certification fee: $10.00. Fee payee: 52-2 District Court. Personal checks accepted. Credit cards accepted: Visa, MasterCard. Prepayment is required.

52nd District Court - Division 3
135 Barclay Circle, Rochester Hills, MI 48307; 248-853-5553; Fax: 248-853-3277. Hours: 8:30AM-4:30PM (EST). *Misdemeanor, Civil Actions Under $25,000, Eviction, Small Claims.*

Civil Records: Access: Phone, fax, mail, in person. Only the court performs in person searches; visitors may not. No search fee. Required to search: name; also helpful: years to search. Civil cases indexed by defendant, plaintiff. Civil records on computer for 10 years, prior on docket books and index cards.

Criminal Records: Access: Phone, fax, mail, in person. Only the court performs in person searches; visitors may not. No search fee. Required to search: name, DOB; also helpful: years to search. Criminal records on computer for 10 years, prior on docket books and index cards.

General Information: No suppressed records released. Turnaround time varies. Copy fee: $1.00 per page. Certification fee: $10.00. Fee payee: 52-3 District Court. Personal checks accepted. Credit cards accepted: Visa, MasterCard. In person only. Prepayment is required.

52nd District Court - Division 4 (Troy, Clawson)
520 W Big Beaver Rd, Troy, MI 48084; 248-528-0400; Fax: 248-528-3588. Hours: 8:15AM-4:15PM (EST). *Misdemeanor, Civil Actions Under $25,000, Eviction, Small Claims.*

Civil Records: Access: Mail, fax, in person. Only the court may perform in person searches. No search fee. Required to search: name, years to search. Civil cases indexed by defendant, plaintiff.

Criminal Records: Access: Fax, mail, in person. Only the court performs in person searches; visitors may not. No search fee. Required to search: name; also helpful: years to search, DOB, SSN. Criminal records.

General Information: No suppressed, juvenile, sex offenders, mental health, or adoption records released. SASE required. Turnaround time 1 week. Fax notes: No fee to fax results. Fax for criminal records and local calls only. Copy fee: $1.00 per page. Fee payee: 52-4 District Court. Personal checks accepted. Credit cards accepted: Visa, MasterCard. Prepayment is required.

50th District Court - Pontiac Civil Division
70 N Saginaw, Pontiac, MI 48342; 248-857-8090; Fax: 248-857-6028. Hours: 8:30AM-5PM *Civil Actions Under $25,000, Eviction, Small Claims.*

Civil Records: Access: Mail, in person. Both court and visitors may perform in person searches. No search fee. Required to search: name, years to search. Civil cases indexed by defendant, plaintiff. Civil records on computer since 1985.

General Information: Public access terminal is available. No suppressed, juvenile, sex offenders, mental health, or adoption records released. Turnaround time 3-4 days. Copy fee: $1.00 1st page, $.10 each add'l page. Fee payee: 50th District Court. Personal checks accepted. Prepayment is required.

50th District Court - Pontiac Criminal Division
70 N Saginaw, Pontiac, MI 48342; 248-

857-8027; Fax: 248-857-6028. Hours: 8:30AM-5PM (EST). *Misdemeanor.*

Criminal Records: Access: Mail, fax, in person. Both court and visitors may perform in person searches. No search fee. Required to search: name, years to search, DOB; also helpful: SSN. Criminal records on computer since 1984, prior on index cards since 1975.

General Information: Public access terminal is available. No suppressed, juvenile, sex offenders, mental health, or adoption records released. Turnaround time 2-3 days. Copy fee: $1.00 first page, $.10 thereafter. Certification fee: $10.00. Fee payee: 50th District Court. Business checks accepted. Prepayment is required.

Probate Court 1200 N Telegraph Rd, 1st Fl, Oakland County Complex, East Wing, Pontiac, MI 48341; 248-858-0260; Fax: 248-452-2016. Hours: 8AM-5PM (EST). *Probate.*

Oceana County

27th Circuit Court 100 State Street, #M-34, Hart, MI 49420; 231-873-3977. Hours: 9AM-5PM (EST). *Felony, Civil Actions Over $25,000.*

Civil Records: Access: Mail, in person. Only the court performs in person searches; visitors may not. Search fee: $5.00 per name. Required to search: name, years to search. Civil cases indexed by defendant, plaintiff. Civil records on computer since 1994, paper records to 1800's.

Criminal Records: Access: Mail, in person. Only the court performs in person searches; visitors may not. Search fee: $5.00 per name. Required to search: name, years to search; also helpful: DOB. Criminal records on computer since 1994, paper records to 1800's.

General Information: No suppressed, juvenile, sex offenders, mental health, or adoption records released. SASE requested. Turnaround time same day. Copy fee: $10.00 for first page, $1.00 each add'l. Certification fee: $10.00 plus $1.00 per page after first. Fee payee: Oceana County Circuit Court. Personal checks accepted. Prepayment is required.

79th District Court PO Box 471, Hart, MI 49420; 231-873-4530; Fax: 231-873-1861. Hours: 8AM-5PM (EST). *Misdemeanor, Civil Actions Under $25,000, Eviction, Small Claims.*

Civil Records: Access: Mail, in person. Only the court performs in person searches; visitors may not. Search fee: $5.00 per name. Required to search: name, years to search. Civil cases indexed by plaintiff. Civil records on file cards and in file folders since 1967; on computer back to 1999.

Criminal Records: Access: Mail, in person. Only the court performs in person searches; visitors may not. Search fee: $5.00 per name. Required to search: name, years to search, DOB. Criminal records on file cards and in file folders since 1967; on computer back to 1999.

General Information: No suppressed records released. SASE not required. Turnaround time same day. Copy fee: $1.00 per page. Certification fee: $10.00 plus $1.00 per page after first. Fee payee: 79th District Court. No personal checks accepted. Prepayment is required.

Probate Court County Bldg, 100 S State St, Suite M-34, Hart, MI 49420; 231-873-3666; Fax: 231-873-5914. Hours: 9AM-Noon, 1-5PM (EST). *Probate.*

Ogemaw County

34th Circuit Court 806 W Houghton, West Branch, MI 48661; 989-345-0215; Fax: 989-345-7223. Hours: 8:30AM-4:30PM (EST). *Felony, Civil Actions Over $25,000.*

Civil Records: Access: Phone, fax, mail, in person. Only the court performs in person searches; visitors may not. Search fee: $10.00 per name. Fee is for search

prior to 1993. Required to search: name, years to search. Civil cases indexed by defendant, plaintiff. Civil records on index cards since 1970, library books in vault since 1960; on computer back to 1993.

Criminal Records: Access: Phone, fax, mail, in person. Only the court performs in person searches; visitors may not. Search fee: $10.00 per name. Fee is for search prior to 1993. Required to search: name, years to search, DOB; also helpful: SSN. Criminal records on index cards since 1970, library books in vault since 1960; on computer back to 1993.

General Information: No suppressed, juvenile, sex offenders, mental health, or adoption records released. SASE required. Turnaround time 1-3 weeks. Fax notes: $2.00 for first page, $1.00 each add'l. Copy fee: $.50 per page. Certification fee: $10.00 plus $1.00 per page. Fee payee: 34th Circuit Court. Personal checks accepted. Prepayment is required.

82nd District Court PO Box 365, West Branch, MI 48661; 989-345-5040; Fax: 989-345-5910. Hours: 8:30AM-4:30PM (EST). *Misdemeanor, Civil Actions Under $25,000, Eviction, Small Claims.*

Civil Records: Access: Fax, mail, in person. Only the court performs in person searches; visitors may not. Search fee: $2.00 per name. Required to search: name, years to search. Civil cases indexed by defendant, plaintiff. Civil records on computer since 1990, prior on books since 1969.

Criminal Records: Access: Fax, mail, in person. Only the court performs in person searches; visitors may not. Search fee: $2.00 per name. Required to search: name, years to search, DOB. Criminal records on computer since 1990, prior on books since 1969.

General Information: No suppressed records released. SASE requested. Turnaround time 2-3 days. Fax notes: No fee to fax results. Copy fee: $.50 per page. Certification fee: $10.00. Fee payee: 82nd District Court. Personal checks accepted. Prepayment of mail search required.

Probate Court County Courthouse, Rm 203, 806 W Houghton Ave, West Branch, MI 48661; 989-345-0145; Fax: 989-345-5901. Hours: 8:30AM-Noon, 1-4:30PM (EST). *Probate.*

Ontonagon County

32nd Circuit Court 725 Greenland Rd, Ontonagon, MI 49953; 906-884-4255; Fax: 906-884-2916. Hours: 8:30AM-4:30PM (EST). *Felony, Civil Actions Over $25,000.*

Civil Records: Access: Mail, fax, in person. Both court and visitors may perform in person searches. Search fee: $5.00 per name. Required to search: name, years to search. Civil cases indexed by defendant, plaintiff. Civil records on index cards and in folders.

Criminal Records: Access: Mail, fax, in person. Both court and visitors may perform in person searches. Search fee: $5.00 per name. Required to search: name, years to search. Criminal records in folders.

General Information: Public access terminal is available. No suppressed records released. SASE not required. Turnaround time 2-3 days. Copy fee: $1.00 per page. Certification fee: $10.00. Fee payee: County Clerk. Personal checks accepted. Prepayment is required.

98th District Court 725 Greenland Rd, Ontonagon, MI 49953; 906-884-2865; Fax: 906-884-2916. Hours: 8:30AM-4:30PM (EST). *Misdemeanor, Civil Actions Under $25,000, Eviction, Small Claims.*

Civil Records: Access: Mail. Only the court performs in person searches; visitors may not. Search fee: $5.00 each name. Required to search: name, years to search. Civil cases indexed by defendant, plaintiff. Civil records kept for 10 years the destroyed.

Criminal Records: Access: Mail, in person. Only the court performs in person searches; visitors may not. Search fee: $5.00 each name. Required to search: name, years to search, DOB. Criminal records kept for 10 years the destroyed.

General Information: No suppressed records released. SASE required. Turnaround time 1 week. Fax notes: Fee to fax results is $5.00 per document. Copy fee: $1.00 per page. Certification fee: $10.00 plus $1.00 per page. Fee payee: 98th District Court. Business checks accepted.

Probate Court 725 Greenland Rd, Ontonagon, MI 49953; 906-884-4117; Fax: 906-884-2916. Hours: 8:30AM-4:30PM (EST). *Probate.*

Osceola County

49th Circuit Court 301 W Upton, Reed City, MI 49677; 231-832-6103; Fax: 231-832-6149. Hours: 9AM-5PM (EST). *Felony, Civil Actions Over $25,000.*

Civil Records: Access: Phone, fax, mail, in person. Both court and visitors may perform in person searches. No search fee. Required to search: name, years to search. Civil cases indexed by defendant, plaintiff. Civil records on computer since 1992, prior on docket books.

Criminal Records: Access: Phone, fax, mail, in person. Both court and visitors may perform in person searches. No search fee. Required to search: name, years to search, DOB. Criminal records on computer since 1992, prior on docket books back to 1967.

General Information: No suppressed or adoption records released. SASE required. Turnaround time 1-2 days. Fax notes: Fax fee $1.00 1st 5 pages, each additional page $.50. Copy fee: $1.00 per page. Certification fee: $10.00 plus $1.00 per page after first. Fee payee: 49th Circuit Court. Personal checks accepted. Prepayment is required.

77th District Court 410 W Upton, Reed City, MI 49677; 231-832-6155; Fax: 231-832-9190. Hours: 8:30AM-4:30PM (EST). *Misdemeanor, Civil Actions Under $25,000, Eviction, Small Claims.*

Civil Records: Access: Phone, mail, fax, in person. Only the court performs in person searches; visitors may not. No search fee. Required to search: name, years to search. Civil cases indexed by defendant, plaintiff. Civil records on computer since 6/91; on cards to 1987.

Criminal Records: Access: Phone, mail, fax, in person. Only the court performs in person searches; visitors may not. No search fee. Required to search: name, years to search, DOB. Criminal records on computer since 6/91; on index cards back to 1987.

General Information: No suppressed records released. SASE required. Turnaround time 2 days. Copy fee: $1.00 per page. Certification fee: $10.00. Fee payee: 77th District Court. Only cashiers checks and money orders accepted. Prepayment is required.

Probate Court 410 W Upton, Reed City, MI 49677; 231-832-6124; Fax: 231-832-6181. Hours: 8:30AM-Noon, 1-4:30PM (EST). *Probate.*

Note: Shares the same judge with Mecosta County Probate Court.

Oscoda County

23rd Circuit Court PO Box 399, 311 Morenci Ave, Mio, MI 48647; 989-826-1110; Fax: 989-826-1136. Hours: 8:30AM-4:30PM (EST). *Felony, Civil Actions Over $25,000.*

Civil Records: Access: Mail, in person. Only the court performs in person searches; visitors may not. Search fee: $15.00 per name per year. Required to search: name, years to search. Civil cases indexed by defendant, plaintiff. Civil records on computer since 1989, prior on docket books to 1880s.

Criminal Records: Access: Mail, in person. Only the court performs in person searches; visitors may not.

Search fee: $15.00 per name per year. Required to search: name, years to search, DOB. Criminal records on computer since 1989, prior on docket books to 1880s.

General Information: No suppressed records released. SASE required. Turnaround time 2-3 weeks. Copy fee: $.25 per page. Certification fee: $10.00 plus $1.00 per page after first. Fee payee: Oscoda County Clerk. Personal checks accepted. Prepayment is required.

82nd District Court
PO Box 625, Mio, MI 48647; 989-826-1106. Hours: 8:30AM-4:30PM (EST). *Misdemeanor, Civil Actions Under $25,000, Eviction, Small Claims.*

Civil Records: Access: Mail, in person. Only the court performs in person searches; visitors may not. Search fee: $2.00 per name. Required to search: name, years to search. Civil cases indexed by defendant, plaintiff. Civil records on computer back to 1990, prior on index cards.
Criminal Records: Access: Mail, in person. Only the court performs in person searches; visitors may not. Search fee: $2.00 per name. Required to search: name, years to search, DOB; also helpful: SSN. Criminal records on computer back to 1990, prior on index cards.
General Information: No suppressed records released. SASE required. Turnaround time 1-2 days. Copy fee: $.50 per page. Certification fee: $10.00 plus $1.00 per page after first. Fee payee: 82nd District Court. Personal checks accepted.

Probate Court
PO Box 399, Mio, MI 48647; 989-826-1107; Fax: 989-826-1158. Hours: 8:30AM-Noon, 1-4:30PM (EST). *Probate.*

Otsego County

46th Circuit Court
225 Main St, Gaylord, MI 49735; 989-732-6484; Fax: 989-732-1562. Hours: 8AM-4:30PM *Felony, Civil Actions Over $25,000.*

www.Circuit46.org

Civil Records: Access: Phone, mail, in person, online. Both court and visitors may perform in person searches. No search fee. Required to search: name, years to search. Civil records on computer since 1988, prior on indexes since 1800s. Online access to court case records (closed cases for 90 days only) available free at www.circuit46.org/Cases/cases.html. Search by name.
Criminal Records: Access: Phone, mail, in person, online. Both court and visitors may perform in person searches. No search fee. Required to search: name, years to search, DOB. Criminal records on computer since 1988, prior on indexes since 1800s. Online access to criminal records is the same as civil.
General Information: Public access terminal is available. No suppressed, juvenile, mental health, or adoption records released. SASE required. Turnaround time varies. Copy fee: $1.00 per page. Certification fee: $10.00. Fee payee: Otsego County Clerk. Personal checks accepted. Prepayment is required.

46th Circuit Trial Court - District Court
800 Livingston Blvd, #1C, Gaylord, MI 49735; 989-732-6486; Fax: 989-732-5130. Hours: 8AM-4:30PM (EST). *Misdemeanor, Civil Actions Under $25,000, Eviction, Small Claims.*

www.circuit46.org

Civil Records: Access: Mail, in person, online. Both court and visitors may perform in person searches. No search fee. Required to search: name, years to search. Civil cases indexed by defendant, plaintiff. Civil records on computer since 1985, prior index cards. Online access to court case records (closed cases for 90 days only) available free at www.circuit46.org/ Cases/cases.html. Search by name.
Criminal Records: Access: Mail, in person, online. Both court and visitors may perform in person searches. No search fee. Required to search: name, years to search, DOB. Criminal records on computer since 1985,

prior index cards. Online access to criminal records is the same as civil.
General Information: Public access terminal is available. No suppressed records released. SASE required. Turnaround time 4 days. Copy fee: $1.00 per page. Certification fee: $10.00 plus $1.00 per page after first. Fee payee: 87th District Court. Personal checks accepted. Prepayment is required.

Probate Court
800 Livingston Blvd, #1C, Gaylord, MI 49735; 989-731-0204, 989-732-1586; Fax: 989-705-1562. Hours: 8AM-4:30PM (EST). *Probate.*

www.Circuit46.org

Probate Note: Search cases by name free at www.circuit46.org/Cases/cases.html.

Ottawa County

20th Circuit Court
414 Washington Ave, Grand Haven, MI 49417; 616-846-8136; Fax: 616-846-8138. Hours: 8AM-5PM (EST). *Felony, Civil Actions Over $25,000.*

www.co.ottawa.mi.us/Courts/courts.htm

Civil Records: Access: Mail, fax, in person. Visitors may perform in person searches. No search fee. Required to search: name, years to search. Civil cases indexed by defendant, plaintiff. Civil records on computer since June, 1984.
Criminal Records: Access: Mail, in person. Visitors may perform in person searches. No search fee. Required to search: name, years to search, DOB; also helpful: SSN. Criminal records on computer since 1990.
General Information: Public access terminal is available. No suppressed, juvenile, sex offenders, mental health, or adoption records released. SASE requested. Turnaround time 2-3 days, phone search turnaround time 24 hours. Copy fee: $.50 per page. Certification fee: $10.00 plus $1.00 per page. Fee payee: Ottawa County Clerk. Personal checks accepted. Prepayment is required.

58th District Court - Grand Haven
414 Washington Ave, Grand Haven, MI 49417; 616-846-8280; Fax: 616-846-8291. Hours: 8AM-5PM (EST). *Misdemeanor, Civil Actions Under $25,000, Eviction, Small Claims.*

www.co.ottawa.mi.us/Courts/courts.htm

Civil Records: Access: Mail, in person. Both the court and visitors may perform in person searches. No search fee. Required to search: name, years to search. Civil cases indexed by defendant, plaintiff. Civil records on computer back to 1993, prior on index cards since 1969.
Criminal Records: Access: Mail, in person. Both the court and visitors may perform in person searches. No search fee. Required to search: name, years to search, DOB. Criminal records on computer back to 1990, prior on index cards since 1969.
General Information: Public access terminal is available. No suppressed records released. SASE required. Turnaround time 4 days. Fax notes: Fee to fax results is $.25 per page. Copy fee: $.25 per page. Certification fee: $10.00 plus $1.00 per page after first. Fee payee: 58th District Court. Personal checks accepted. Out of state checks not accepted. Prepayment is required.

58th District Court - Holland
57 W 8th St, Holland, MI 49423; 616-392-6991; Fax: 616-392-5013. Hours: 8AM-5PM (EST). *Misdemeanor, Civil Actions Under $25,000, Eviction, Small Claims.*

www.co.ottawa.mi.us/Courts/courts.htm

Civil Records: Access: Mail, in person. Only the court performs in person searches; visitors may not. No search fee. Required to search: name, years to search. Civil cases indexed by defendant, plaintiff. Civil records on computer since 1988, prior on books since 1969.

Criminal Records: Access: Mail, in person. Only the court performs in person searches; visitors may not. No search fee. Required to search: name, years to search, DOB; also helpful: SSN. Criminal records on computer since 1988, prior on books since 1969.
General Information: No suppressed records released. SASE required. Turnaround time varies. Copy fee: $.25 per page. Certification fee: $10.00 per document. Fee payee: 58th District Court. Personal checks accepted. Out of state checks not accepted. Prepayment required.

58th District Court - Hudsonville
3100 Port Sheldon, Hudsonville, MI 49426; 616-662-3100; Fax: 616-669-2950. Hours: 8AM-noon; 1-5PM (EST). *Misdemeanor, Civil Actions Under $25,000, Eviction, Small Claims.*

www.co.ottawa.mi.us/Courts/courts.htm

Civil Records: Access: Mail, in person. Only the court performs in person searches; visitors may not. No search fee. Required to search: name, years to search; also helpful: address. Civil cases indexed by defendant, plaintiff. Civil records on computer since July, 1993, prior on index file.
Criminal Records: Access: Mail, in person. Only the court performs in person searches; visitors may not. No search fee. Required to search: name, years to search, DOB; also helpful: address. Criminal records on computer since 1990.
General Information: No suppressed records released. SASE not required. Turnaround time 2 days. Copy fee: $.25 per page. Certification fee: $10.00. Fee payee: 58th District Court. Personal checks accepted.

Probate Court
12120 Fillmore St, West Olive, MI 49460; 616-786-4110; Fax: 616-786-4154. Hours: 8AM-5PM (EST). *Probate.*

www.co.ottawa.mi.us/Courts/Probate/probate.htm

Presque Isle County

26th Circuit Court
PO Box 110, Rogers City, MI 49779; 989-734-3288; Fax: 989-734-7635. Hours: 9AM-5PM (EST). *Felony, Civil Actions Over $25,000.*

Civil Records: Access: Phone, fax, mail, in person. Only the court performs in person searches; visitors may not. No search fee. Required to search: name, years to search. Civil cases indexed by defendant, plaintiff. Civil records on docket books since 1800s.
Criminal Records: Access: Phone, fax, mail, in person. Only the court performs in person searches; visitors may not. No search fee. Required to search: name, years to search, DOB. Criminal records on docket books since 1800s.
General Information: No suppressed, juvenile, sex offenders, mental health, or adoption records released. SASE required. Turnaround time 1 week. Copy fee: $1.00 per page. Certification fee: $10.00 plus $1.00 per page after first. Fee payee: Presque Isle County Clerk. Personal checks accepted. Prepayment is required.

89th District Court
PO Box 110, Rogers City, MI 49779; 989-734-2411; Fax: 989-734-3400. Hours: 8:30AM-4:30PM (EST). *Misdemeanor, Civil Actions Under $25,000, Eviction, Small Claims.*

Civil Records: Access: Mail, in person. Only the court performs in person searches; visitors may not. No search fee. Required to search: name, years to search. Civil cases indexed by defendant, plaintiff. Civil records on computer since 6/94, prior on index books.
Criminal Records: Access: Mail, in person. Only the court performs in person searches; visitors may not. No search fee. Required to search: name, years to search, DOB. Criminal records on computer since 6/94, prior on index books.
General Information: No suppressed records released. SASE required. Turnaround time 2 weeks. Copy fee: $1.00 for first page, $.25 each add'l. Certification fee:

$10.00 plus $1.00 per page after first. Fee payee: 89th District Court. Personal checks accepted.

Probate Court 151 Huron Ave, PO Box 110, Rogers City, MI 49779; 989-734-3268; Fax: 989-734-4420. Hours: 8:30AM-4:30PM (EST). *Probate.*

Roscommon County

34th Circuit Court PO Box 98, Roscommon, MI 48653; 989-275-1902; Fax: 989-275-0602. Hours: 8:30AM-4:30PM (EST). *Felony, Civil Actions Over $25,000.*

Civil Records: Access: Fax, mail, in person. Only the court performs in person searches; visitors may not. Search fee: $5.00 per name. Required to search: name, years to search. Civil records on computer since 3/94, prior on docket books and cards.

Criminal Records: Access: Fax, mail, in person. Only the court performs in person searches; visitors may not. Search fee: $5.00 per name. Required to search: name, years to search, DOB. Criminal records on computer since 3/94, prior on docket books and cards.

General Information: No suppressed, sex offenders or mental health records released. SASE required. Turnaround time 24 hours. Fax notes: Fee to fax results is $3.00 1st page, $1.00 each add'l. Copy fee: $.50 per page. Certification fee: $10.00 plus $1.00 per page after first. Fee payee: 34th Circuit Court. Personal checks accepted. Prepayment is required.

83rd District Court PO Box 189, Roscommon, MI 48653; 989-275-5312; Fax: 989-275-6033. Hours: 8:30AM-4:30PM (EST). *Misdemeanor, Civil Actions Under $25,000, Eviction, Small Claims.*

Civil Records: Access: Phone, fax, mail, in person. Only the court performs in person searches; visitors may not. No search fee. Required to search: name, years to search. Civil cases indexed by defendant, plaintiff. Civil records on computer since 1988, prior on index cards since 1969.

Criminal Records: Access: Phone, fax, mail, in person. Only the court performs in person searches; visitors may not. No search fee. Required to search: name, years to search, DOB; also helpful: SSN. Criminal records on computer since 1988, prior on index cards since 1969.

General Information: No suppressed, juvenile, sex offenders, mental health, or adoption records released. Turnaround time same day. Fax notes: No fee to fax results. Copy fee: $.50 per page. Fee payee: 83rd District Court. Personal checks accepted. Prepayment is required.

Probate Court PO Box 607, Roscommon, MI 48653; 989-275-5221; Fax: 989-275-8537. Hours: 8:30AM-4:30PM (EST). *Probate.*

Saginaw County

10th Circuit Court 111 S Michigan Ave, Saginaw, MI 48602; 989-790-5541; Fax: 989-790-8254. Hours: 8AM-5:00PM (EST). *Felony, Civil Actions Over $25,000.*

www.saginawcounty.com/clerk/court/index.html

Civil Records: Access: Mail, in person. Both court and visitors may perform in person searches. Search fee: None at this time. Required to search: name, years to search. Civil cases indexed by defendant, plaintiff (no SSNs or ID #s). Civil records on computer since 1985, prior on index books, microfilm.

Criminal Records: Access: Mail, in person. Both court and visitors may perform in person searches. Search fee: None at this time. Required to search: name, years to search, DOB; also helpful: SSN. Criminal records on computer since 1994, prior on index books.

General Information: No suppressed, sex offenders, mental health or guardianship records released. SASE required. Turnaround time 2 days. Copy fee: $1.00 per page. Certification fee: $10.00 plus $.25 per docket page after first. Fee payee: Saginaw County Clerk. No personal checks accepted.

70th District Court - Civil Division 111 S Michigan Ave, Saginaw, MI 48602; 989-790-5380; Fax: 989-790-5589. Hours: 8AM-4:45PM (EST). *Civil Actions Under $25,000, Eviction, Small Claims.*

Civil Records: Access: Mail, in person. Only the court performs in person searches; visitors may not. Search fee: $5.00 per name. Required to search: name, years to search. Civil cases indexed by defendant, plaintiff. Civil records on computer since 1982, prior on docket books.

General Information: No suppressed records released. SASE required. Turnaround time 1 week. Copy fee: $1.00 per page. Certification fee: $10.00. Fee payee: 70th District court. Personal checks accepted. Prepayment is required.

70th District Court - Criminal Division 111 S Michigan Ave, Saginaw, MI 48602; 989-790-5385; Fax: 989-790-5589. Hours: 8AM-4:45PM (EST). *Misdemeanor.*

Criminal Records: Access: Fax, mail, in person. Only the court performs in person searches; visitors may not. Search fee: $5.00 per name. Required to search: name, years to search, DOB, signed release; also helpful: address. Criminal records on computer back to 1987, prior on microfiche since 1972. Fax information received only if pre-paid. They must receive $5.00 fee before they fax out information.

General Information: No suppressed, juvenile, sex offenders, mental health, or adoption records released. SASE required. Turnaround time 1 week. Copy fee: $1.00 per page. Certification fee: $10.00. Fee payee: 70th District Court. Business checks accepted. Credit cards accepted: Visa, MasterCard. Prepayment is required.

Probate/Family Court 111 S Michigan St, Saginaw, MI 48602; 989-790-5320; Fax: 989-790-5328. Hours: 8AM-5PM (EST). *Probate.*

Sanilac County

24th Circuit Court 60 W Sanilac, Rm 203, Sandusky, MI 48471; 810-648-3212; Fax: 810-648-5466. Hours: 8AM-4:30PM (EST). *Felony, Civil Actions Over $25,000.*

Civil Records: Access: Mail, in person. Both court and visitors may perform in person searches. Search fee: $10.00 per name. Required to search: name, years to search. Civil cases indexed by defendant, plaintiff. Civil records on computer since 1993.

Criminal Records: Access: Mail, in person. Both court and visitors may perform in person searches. Search fee: $10.00 per name. Required to search: name, years to search. Criminal records on computer since 1993.

General Information: Public access terminal is available. No suppressed, juvenile, sex offenders, mental health, or adoption records released. SASE required. Turnaround time 2-3 days. Copy fee: $1.00 per page. Certification fee: $10.00. Fee payee: Sanilac County Clerk. Personal checks accepted. Prepayment is required.

73rd District Court 60 W Sanilac, Sandusky, MI 48471; 810-648-3250. Hours: 8AM-4:30PM (EST). *Misdemeanor, Civil Actions Under $25,000, Eviction, Small Claims.*

Civil Records: Access: Mail, in person. Only the court performs in person searches; visitors may not. Search fee: $1.00 per name per year. Required to search: name, years to search; also helpful: address. Civil cases indexed by defendant, plaintiff. Civil records on computer back to 1989, prior on docket books to 1969.

Criminal Records: Access: Mail, in person. Only the court performs in person searches; visitors may not.

Search fee: $1.00 per name per year. Required to search: name, years to search, DOB; also helpful: address. Criminal records on computer back to 1989, prior on docket books to 1969.

General Information: No suppressed records released. SASE required. Turnaround time 1 week. Copy fee: $1.00 per page. Certification fee: $10.00 plus $1.00 per page after first. Fee payee: 73rd District Court. Personal checks accepted. Prepayment is required.

Probate Court 60 W Sanilac Ave., Room 106, Sandusky, MI 48471-1096; 810-648-3221; Fax: 810-648-2900. Hours: 8AM-Noon, 1-4:30PM *Probate.*

Schoolcraft County

11th Circuit Court 300 Walnut St, Rm 164, Manistique, MI 49854; 906-341-3618. Hours: 8AM-4PM (EST). *Felony, Civil Actions Over $25,000.*

Civil Records: Access: Phone, fax, mail, in person. Both court and visitors may perform in person searches. No search fee. Required to search: name, years to search. Civil cases indexed by defendant, plaintiff. Civil records on docket books and index since 1881.

Criminal Records: Access: Phone, fax, mail, in person. Only the court may perform in person searches. No search fee. Required to search: name, years to search. Criminal records on docket books and index since 1881.

General Information: No suppressed, juvenile, sex offenders, mental health, or adoption records released. SASE requested. Turnaround time 2-3 days. Copy fee: $1.00 per page. Certification fee: $10.00. Fee payee: Schoolcraft County Clerk. Personal checks accepted. Prepayment is required.

93rd District Court 300 Walnut St, Rm 135, Manistique, MI 49854; 906-341-3630; Fax: 906-341-8006. Hours: 8AM-4PM (EST). *Misdemeanor, Civil Actions Under $25,000, Eviction, Small Claims.*

Civil Records: Access: Mail, in person. Both court and visitors may perform in person searches. Search fee: $10.00. Required to search: name, years to search. Civil cases indexed by defendant, plaintiff. Civil records kept on index cards.

Criminal Records: Access: Mail, in person. Only the court performs in person searches; visitors may not. Search fee: $10.00. Required to search: name, years to search, DOB; also helpful: SSN. Criminal records kept on index cards.

General Information: No suppressed, sex offenders or mental health records released. SASE required. Turnaround time 2-3 days. Copy fee: $.25 per page. Certification fee: $10.00 plus $1.00 per page after first. Fee payee: 93rd District Court. Business checks accepted. Prepayment is required.

Probate Court 300 Walnut St, Manistique, MI 49854; 906-341-3641; Fax: 906-341-3627. Hours: 8AM-Noon, 1-4PM (EST). *Probate.*

Shiawassee County

35th Circuit Court 208 N Shiawassee St, Corunna, MI 48817; 989-743-2262; Fax: 989-743-2241. Hours: 8AM-5PM (EST). *Felony, Civil Actions Over $25,000.*

Civil Records: Access: Phone, fax, mail, in person. Both court and visitors may perform in person searches. Search fee: $1.00 per name per year. Required to search: name, years to search. Civil cases indexed by defendant, plaintiff. Civil records on computer since 09/87, prior on docket books and cards.

Criminal Records: Access: Phone, fax, mail, in person. Both court and visitors may perform in person searches. Search fee: $10.00 for up to 10 years. Required to search: name, years to search, DOB. Criminal records on computer since 10/93.

General Information: No suppressed records released. SASE required. Turnaround time 1 week. Copy fee: $1.00 per page. Certification fee: $10.00. Fee payee: 35th Circuit Court. Personal checks accepted. Prepayment is required.

66th District Court 110 E Mack St, Corunna, MI 48817; 989-743-2395; Fax: 989-743-2469. Hours: 8AM-5PM (EST). *Misdemeanor, Civil Actions Under $25,000, Eviction, Small Claims.*
Civil Records: Access: Phone, fax, mail, in person. Only the court performs in person searches; visitors may not. No search fee. Required to search: name, years to search; also helpful: DOB, SSN. Civil cases indexed by defendant, plaintiff. Civil records on computer back to 1995, prior on microfiche.
Criminal Records: Access: Phone, fax, mail, in person. Only the court performs in person searches; visitors may not. No search fee. Required to search: name, years to search, DOB. Case number required for pre-1995 research. Criminal records on computer back to 1995, prior on microfiche to 1969.
General Information: No suppressed records released. SASE required. Turnaround time 1 week. Fax notes: Friday is their day to fax results. Copy fee: $1.00 per page. Certification fee: $10.00. Fee payee: 66th District Court. Personal checks accepted.

Probate Court 110 E Mack St, Corunna, MI 48817; 989-743-2211; Fax: 989-743-2349. Hours: 8AM-5PM (EST). *Probate.*

St. Clair County

31st Circuit Court 201 McMorran Blvd, Port Huron, MI 48060; 810-985-2200; Fax: 810-985-4796. Hours: 8AM-4:30PM (EST). *Felony, Civil Actions Over $25,000.*
Civil Records: Access: Mail, fax, in person. Both court and visitors may perform in person searches. No search fee. Required to search: name, years to search; also helpful: address. Civil cases indexed by defendant, plaintiff. Civil records on computer back to 1987, non computerzied records back to 1936.
Criminal Records: Access: Mail, fax, in person. Both court and visitors may perform in person searches. No search fee. Required to search: name, years to search, DOB; also helpful: address. Criminal records on computer back to 1987, non computerized records back to 1936.
General Information: Public access terminal is available. No suppressed, juvenile, mental health, or adoption records released. SASE required. Turnaround time 24 hours. Copy fee: $1.00 per page. Certification fee: $10.00. Fee payee: St. Clair Clerk of Court. Only cashiers checks and money orders accepted. In state checks allowed. Prepayment is required.

72nd District Court 201 McMorran Rd, Port Huron, MI 48060; Civil phone: 810-985-2077; Criminal phone: 810-985-2072. Hours: 8AM-4:30PM (EST). *Misdemeanor, Civil Actions Under $25,000, Eviction, Small Claims.*
Civil Records: Access: In person only. Visitors must perform in person searches for themselves. No search fee. Required to search: name, years to search. Civil cases indexed by defendant, plaintiff. Civil records on computer since 1987, prior on docket books back to 1969.
Criminal Records: Access: in person only. Visitors must perform in person searches for themselves. No search fee. Required to search: name, years to search, DOB; also helpful: SSN. Criminal records on computer since 1987, prior on docket books back to 1969.
General Information: No suppressed records released. Copy fee: $1.00 per page. Certification fee: $10.00. Fee payee: 72nd District Court. Personal checks accepted. Prepayment is required.

Probate Court 201 McMorran Blvd Rm 2600, Port Huron, MI 48060; 810-985-2066; Fax: 810-985-2179. Hours: 8AM-4:30PM (EST). *Probate.*

St. Joseph County

45th Circuit Court PO Box 189, Centreville, MI 49032; 269-467-5531; Fax: 269-467-5628. Hours: 9AM-5PM (EST). *Felony, Civil Actions Over $25,000.*
Civil Records: Access: Mail, in person. Only the court performs in person searches; visitors may not. Search fee: $1.00 per name per year. For records prior to 1988, fee is $1.00 per year searched. Required to search: name, years to search. Civil cases indexed by defendant, plaintiff. Civil records on computer since 1988, prior on books from 1900, earlier in archives.
Criminal Records: Access: Mail, in person. Only the court performs in person searches; visitors may not. Search fee: $1.00 per name per year. For records prior to 1988, fee is $10.00 per year searched. Required to search: name, years to search. Criminal records on computer since 1988, prior on books from 1900, earlier in archives.
General Information: No suppressed records released. SASE not required. Turnaround time same day. Copy fee: $1.00 per page. Certification fee: $10.00. Fee payee: St. Joseph County Clerk. Business checks accepted. Prepayment is required.

3-B District Court PO Box 67, Centreville, MI 49032; 269-467-5627. Hours: 8AM-5PM (EST). *Misdemeanor, Civil Actions Under $25,000, Eviction, Small Claims.*
Civil Records: Access: Phone, mail, in person. Both court and visitors may perform in person computer searches. No search fee. Required to search: name, years to search; also helpful: address. Civil cases indexed by defendant, plaintiff. Civil records on computer since 1987, prior in archives. Phone search access limited.
Criminal Records: Access: Fax, mail, in person. Both court and visitors may perform in person computer searches. No search fee. Required to search: name, years to search, DOB, date of offense. Criminal records on computer since 1987, prior in archives. Signed release required for some searches.
General Information: Public access terminal is available. No suppressed records released. Turnaround time 2 weeks. Copy fee: $.15 per page. Certification fee: $10.00 plus $1.00 each additional page. Fee payee: 3-B District Court. Business checks accepted.

Probate Court PO Box 190, Centreville, MI 49032; 269-467-5538; Fax: 269-467-5560. Hours: 8AM-5PM (EST). *Probate.*

Tuscola County

54th Circuit Court 440 N State St, Caro, MI 48723; 989-672-3780; Fax: 989-672-4266. Hours: 8AM-Noon, 1-3:30PM (EST). *Felony, Civil Actions Over $25,000.*
Civil Records: Access: Mail, in person. Only the court performs in person searches; visitors may not. Search fee: $5.00 per name. Fee is $1.00 for each year prior to 1989. Required to search: name, years to search. Civil cases indexed by defendant, plaintiff. Civil records on computer since 1989, prior on books since beginning.
Criminal Records: Access: Mail, in person. Only the court performs in person searches; visitors may not. Search fee: $5.00 per name. Fee is $1.00 for each year prior to 1989. Required to search: name, years to search, DOB; also helpful: SSN. Criminal records on computer since 1989, prior on books since beginning.
General Information: No suppressed, juvenile, sex offenders, mental health, or adoption records released. SASE required. Turnaround time 3-4 days. Copy fee: $1.00 per page. Certification fee: $10.00 plus $1.00 per

page after first. Fee payee: County Clerk. Personal checks not accepted. Prepayment is required.

71 B District Court 440 N State St., Caro, MI 48723; 989-672-3800; Fax: 989-673-0451. Hours: 8AM-4:30PM (EST). *Misdemeanor, Civil Actions Under $25,000, Eviction, Small Claims.*
Civil Records: Access: Phone, mail, in person. Both court and visitors may perform in person searches. No search fee. Required to search: name, years to search. Civil cases indexed by defendant, plaintiff. Civil records on computer since 1991, prior on cards.
Criminal Records: Access: Phone, mail, in person. Both court and visitors may perform in person searches. No search fee. Required to search: name, years to search, DOB; also helpful: SSN. Criminal records on computer since 1991; others back to 1969.
General Information: No suppressed records released. SASE not required. Copy fee: $.50 per page. Certification fee: $10.00 plus $1.00 per page after first. Fee payee: 71 B District Court. Personal checks accepted.

Probate Court 440 N State St, Caro, MI 48723; 989-672-3850; Fax: 989-672-4266. Hours: 8AM-Noon, 1-4:30PM (EST). *Probate.*

Van Buren County

36th Circuit Court 212 Paw Paw St #101, Paw Paw, MI 49079; 269-657-8218. Hours: 8:30AM-5PM (EST). *Felony, Civil Actions Over $25,000.*
Civil Records: Access: Mail, in person. Only the court performs in person searches; visitors may not. Search fee: $1.00 per name per year. Fee includes combined civil and criminal search. Required to search: name, years to search. Civil cases indexed by defendant, plaintiff. Civil records on computer back to 1990, prior on docket books since 1800s.
Criminal Records: Access: Mail, in person. Only the court performs in person searches; visitors may not. Search fee: $1.00 per name per year. Required to search: name, years to search, DOB, signed release. Criminal records on computer back to 1990, prior on docket books since 1800s.
General Information: No suppressed, sex offender records released. SASE required. Turnaround time 1 day. Fax notes: Will phone with results if a toll-free number is provided. Copy fee: $1.00 per page. Certification fee: $10.00 plus $1.00 per page after first. Fee payee: Van Buren County Clerk. Personal checks accepted. Prepayment is required.

7th District Court 212 Paw Paw St, Paw Paw, MI 49079; 269-657-8222; Fax: 269-657-8223. Hours: 9AM-4:30PM (EST). *Misdemeanor, Civil Actions Under $25,000, Eviction, Small Claims.*
Civil Records: Access: Mail,fax, in person. Both court and visitors may perform in person searches. No search fee. Required to search: name, years to search. Civil cases indexed by defendant, plaintiff. Civil records kept in file folder; computerized records since 1999.
Criminal Records: Access: Mail, in person. Both court and visitors may perform in person searches. No search fee. Required to search: name, years to search, DOB, SSN. Criminal records kept in file folder; computerized since 1999.
General Information: No suppressed records released. SASE required. Turnaround time 1-2 days. Copy fee: $1.00 per page. Certification fee: $10.00. Fee payee: 7th District Court. No personal checks accepted. Prepayment is required.

7th District Court - West Division 1007 E Wells, PO Box 311, South Haven, MI 49090; 269-637-5258; Fax: 269-637-9169. Hours: 8:30AM-4:30PM (EST). *Misdemeanor, Civil Actions Under $25,000, Eviction, Small Claims.*

Civil Records: Access: Mail, in person. Only the court performs in person searches; visitors may not. Search fee: $1.00 per name. Required to search: name, years to search. Civil cases indexed by defendant, plaintiff. Civil records on computer since 1991, prior on index cards since 1982.

Criminal Records: Access: Mail, in person. Only the court performs in person searches; visitors may not. Search fee: $1.00 per name. Required to search: name, years to search, DOB; also helpful: SSN. Criminal records on computer since 1991, prior on index cards since 1982.

General Information: No suppressed, juvenile, sex offenders, mental health, or adoption records released. Turnaround time 3 days. Copy fee: $.25 per page. Certification fee: $10.00 plus $1.00 per page after first. Fee payee: 7th District Court. Personal checks accepted. Prepayment is required.

Probate Court 212 Paw Paw St, Paw Paw, MI 49079; 269-657-8225; Fax: 269-657-7573. Hours: 8:30AM-5PM (EST). *Probate.*

Washtenaw County

22nd Circuit Court PO Box 8645, Ann Arbor, MI 48107-8645; 734-222-3001. Hours: 8:30AM-4:30PM (EST). *Felony, Civil Actions Over $25,000.*

www.co.washtenaw.mi.us/depts/courts/index.htm

Civil Records: Access: Mail, in person. Both court and visitors may perform in person searches. Search fee: $5.00 per name from 1979 to present; $1.00 per name per year prior to 1979. Required to search: name, years to search. Civil cases indexed by defendant, plaintiff. Civil records kept as originals in file folders, records go back to 1900; computerized since 1979.

Criminal Records: Access: Mail, in person. Both court and visitors may perform in person searches. Search fee: Same fees as civil. Required to search: name, years to search, DOB. Criminal records kept as originals in file folders, records go back to 1900; computerized since 1979.

General Information: Public access terminal is available. No suppressed records released. SASE required. Turnaround time 2 or 3 days. Copy fee: $.25 per page. Certification fee: $10.00 plus $1.00 per page. Fee payee: Circuit Court Clerk. Personal checks accepted. Prepayment is required.

14A-1 District Court 4133 Washtenaw, Ann Arbor, MI 48107-8645; 734-971-6050; Fax: 734-971-5018. Hours: 8AM-4:30PM (EST). *Misdemeanor, Civil Actions Under $25,000, Eviction, Small Claims.*

Civil Records: Access: Mail, in person. Both court and visitors may perform in person searches. No search fee. Required to search: name, years to search. Civil cases indexed by defendant, plaintiff. Civil records on computer since 1985, prior on index cards.

Criminal Records: Access: Mail, in person. Both court and visitors may perform in person searches. No search fee. Required to search: name, years to search, DOB, SSN. Criminal records on computer since 1985, prior on index cards.

General Information: Public access terminal is available. No suppressed records released. SASE required. Turnaround time 1-2 weeks. Copy fee: $.25 per page. Certification fee: $10.00 plus $1.00 per page. Fee payee: 14 A-1 District Court. Personal checks accepted. Prepayment is required.

14th District Court A-2 415 W Michigan Ave, Ypsilanti, MI 48197; 734-484-6690; Fax: 734-484-

6697. Hours: 8AM-4:30PM (EST). *Misdemeanor, Civil Actions Under $25,000, Eviction, Small Claims.*

Civil Records: Access: Mail, in person. Only the court performs in person searches; visitors may not. No search fee. Required to search: name, years to search. Civil cases indexed by defendant, plaintiff. Civil records on computer since 1985, prior on file cards since 1969. Specific docket information must be given, the court will not do name searches.

Criminal Records: Access: Mail, in person. Only the court performs in person searches; visitors may not. No search fee. Required to search: name, years to search, DOB; also helpful: SSN. Criminal records on computer since 1985, prior on file cards since 1969. The court will not do name searches.

General Information: No suppressed, juvenile, sex offenders, mental health, or adoption records released. SASE requested. Turnaround time 1 week, phone turnaround time immediate to 2 days. Copy fee: $.25 per page. Certification fee: $10.00 plus $1.00 per page. Fee payee: 14 A-2 District Court. Personal checks accepted. Prepayment is required.

14th District Court A-3 122 S Main St, Chelsea, MI 48118; 734-475-8606; Fax: 734-475-0460. Hours: 8AM-4:30PM (EST). *Misdemeanor, Civil Actions Under $25,000, Eviction, Small Claims.*

Civil Records: Access: Mail, fax, in person. Only the court (time permitting) performs in person searches; visitors may not. No search fee. Required to search: name, years to search. Civil cases indexed by defendant, plaintiff. Civil records on computer since 1986; prior on index cards.

Criminal Records: Access: Mail, fax, in person. Only the court (time permitting) performs in person searches; visitors may not. No search fee. Required to search: name, years to search, DOB; also helpful: SSN. Criminal records on computer since 1986; prior on index cards.

General Information: No suppressed records released. SASE required. Copy fee: $.25 per page. Certification fee: $10.00. Fee payee: 14th District Court. Personal checks accepted. Prepayment is required.

14th District Court A-4 122 S Main, Chelsea, MI 48118; 734-475-8606; Fax: 734-475-0460. Hours: 8AM-4:30PM M-F (Office), 8AM-3:30PM M-F (Phone) (EST). *Misdemeanor, Civil Actions Under $25,000, Eviction, Small Claims.*

Civil Records: Access: Mail, fax, in person. Only the court performs in person searches; visitors may not. No search fee. Required to search: name, years to search. Civil cases indexed by defendant, plaintiff. Civil records on computer since 1986, prior on index cards.

Criminal Records: Access: Mail, fax, in person. Only the court performs in person searches; visitors may not. No search fee. Required to search: name, years to search, DOB; also helpful: SSN. Criminal records on computer since 1986, prior on index cards.

General Information: No suppressed records released. SASE required. Turnaround time 1 week. Copy fee: $.25 per page. Certification fee: $11.00. Fee payee: 14 A-4 District Court. Personal checks accepted. Credit cards accepted. Prepayment is required.

14th District Court B - Civil Division 7200 S Huron River Dr, Ypsilanti, MI 48197; 734-483-5300; Fax: 734-483-3630. Hours: 8AM-5PM (EST). *Civil Actions Under $25,000, Eviction, Small Claims.*

Civil Records: Access: Mail, in person. Only the court performs in person searches; visitors may not. No search fee. Required to search: name, years to search. Civil cases indexed by defendant, plaintiff. Civil records on computer since 1990, prior on card files from 1985-1989.

General Information: No suppressed, juvenile, sex offenders, probation, mental health, or adoption records

released. SASE not required. Turnaround time 1 week, phone turnaround time 1 day. Copy fee: $.50 per page. Certification fee: $10.00. Fee payee: 14-B District Court. Business checks accepted. Credit cards accepted. Prepayment is required.

14th District Court B - Criminal Division 7200 S Huron River Dr, Ypsilanti, MI 48197; 734-483-1333; Fax: 734-483-3630. Hours: 8AM-5PM (EST). *Misdemeanor.*

Criminal Records: Access: Mail, in person. Only the court performs in person searches; visitors may not. No search fee. Required to search: name, years to search, DOB; also helpful: SSN. Criminal records on computer since 1990, prior records kept by name.

General Information: No suppressed, probation, juvenile, sex offenders, probation, mental health, or adoption records released. SASE not required. Turnaround time 1 week, phone turnaround time 1 day. Copy fee: $.50 per page. Certification fee: $10.00. Fee payee: 14-B District Court. Personal checks accepted. Credit cards accepted.

15th District Court - Civil Division 101 E Huron, Box 8650, Ann Arbor, MI 48107; 734-994-2749; Fax: 734-994-2617. Hours: 8:30AM-4:30PM (EST). *Civil Actions Under $25,000, Eviction, Small Claims.*

www.co.washtenaw.mi.us/depts/courts/index.htm

Civil Records: Access: Phone, fax, mail, in person. Both court and visitors may perform in person searches. No search fee. Required to search: name, years to search. Civil cases indexed by defendant, plaintiff. Civil records on computer since 1990, prior on docket books.

General Information: No suppressed records released. SASE required. Turnaround time 2-3 days. Copy fee: $.25 per page. Certification fee: $10.00. Fee payee: 15th District Court. Personal checks accepted. Credit cards accepted: Visa, MasterCard, Discover. Prepayment is required.

15th District Court - Criminal Division 101 E Huron, Box 8650, Ann Arbor, MI 48107-8650; 734-222-3380; Civil phone: 734-222-3389; Criminal phone: 734-994-2746; Fax: 734-222-3335. Hours: 8AM-4:30PM (EST). *Misdemeanor, Traffic.*

www.co.washtenaw.mi.us/depts/courts/index.htm

Criminal Records: Access: Mail, fax, in person. Both court and visitors may perform in person searches. No search fee. Required to search: name, years to search, DOB; also helpful: SSN, offense. Criminal records on computer since 1996; prior on docket cards since 1965. The court will not do a name search. Either a case number or charge and incident date is required.

General Information: Public access terminal is available. (Limited information available.) No suppressed, juvenile, sex offenders, mental health, or adoption records released. SASE required. Turnaround time 2-3 days. Copy fee: $.25 per page. Certification fee: $10.00. Fee payee: 15th District Court. Check, cashiers checks and money orders accepted. Credit cards accepted: Visa, MasterCard, Discover. Prepayment is required.

Probate Court PO Box 8645, Ann Arbor, MI 48107; 734-994-2474; Fax: 734-222-3019. Hours: 8:30AM-4:30PM (EST). *Probate.*

www.co.washtenaw.mi.us/depts/courts/index.htm

Wayne County

3rd Circuit Court 201 Coleman A Young Municipal Center, Detroit, MI 48226; 313-224-5509. Hours: 8AM-4:30PM (EST). *Civil Actions Over $25,000.*

Civil Records: Access: Phone, mail, in person. Both court and visitors may perform in person searches. No search fee. Required to search: name, years to search. Civil cases indexed by defendant, plaintiff. Civil records on computer since 1984, prior on index cards.

General Information: Public access terminal is available. No suppressed records released. Turnaround time 1 week. Copy fee: $2.25 per page. Certification fee: $10.00 plus $1.00 per page. Fee payee: 3rd Circuit Court. Business checks accepted. Prepayment is required.

Frank Murphy Hall of Justice 1441 St Antoine, Detroit, MI 48226; 313-224-2500; Fax: 313-224-2786. Hours: 8AM-4:30PM (EST). *Felony.*

Criminal Records: Access: Mail, in person. Both court and visitors may perform in person searches. Search fee: $2.25 per name. Required to search: name, years to search, DOB; also helpful: SSN, city where crime occurred, aliases. Criminal records on computer since mid 1974, prior on microfiche through 1976, archives off-site 1800s to 1995.

General Information: Public access terminal is available. No suppressed, juvenile, sex offenders, mental health, or adoption records released. SASE required. Turnaround time 3-4 days. Fax notes: Fee to fax results is $2.00 per page. Copy fee: $1.00 per page. Certification fee: $10.00 plus $1.00 per page after 1st. Fee payee: Wayne County Clerk. Prepayment is required.

36th District Court - Civil (Detroit) 421 Madison Ave, Detroit, MI 48226; 313-965-5794; Civil phone: 313-965-5794; Fax: 313-965-4059. Hours: 8AM-4:30PM (EST). *Civil Actions Under $25,000, Eviction, Small Claims.*

Civil Records: Access: In person only. Visitors must perform in person searches for themselves. No search fee. Required to search: name, years to search, address. Civil cases indexed by defendant, plaintiff. Civil records on computer since 1985, prior kept in file folders.

General Information: Public access terminal is available. No suppressed records released. Copy fee: $1.00 per page. Certification fee: $10.00 plus $1.00 per page after first. Fee payee: 36th District Court. Personal checks accepted. Credit cards accepted: Visa, MasterCard.

16th District Court 15140 Farmington Rd, Livonia, MI 48154-5498; 734-466-2500; 466-2550 Probation; Civil phone: X3541; Criminal phone: X3452. Hours: 8:30AM-4:30PM (EST). *Misdemeanor, Civil Actions Under $25,000, Eviction, Small Claims.*

Civil Records: Access: Mail, in person. Both court and visitors may perform in person searches. No search fee. Required to search: name, years to search. Civil cases indexed by defendant, plaintiff. Civil records on computer since 1990, prior on microfiche.

Criminal Records: Access: In person only. Visitors must perform in person searches for themselves. No search fee. Required to search: name, years to search, DOB; also helpful: offense, date of offense, case number. Criminal records on computer since 1991, prior on microfiche. General searches are not performed.

General Information: Public access terminal is available. (Civil only.) No suppressed records released. SASE required. Turnaround time 1 week. Copy fee: $1.00 per page. Certification fee: $10.00. Fee payee: 16th District Court. Personal checks accepted. Prepayment is required.

17th District Court 15111 Beech-Daly Rd, Redford, MI 48239; 313-387-2790; Fax: 313-538-3468. Hours: 8:30AM-4:15PM (EST). *Misdemeanor, Civil Actions Under $25,000, Eviction, Small Claims.*

Civil Records: Access: Mail, in person. Only the court performs in person searches; visitors may not. No search fee. Required to search: name, years to search. Civil cases indexed by defendant, plaintiff. Civil records on computer since 1990, prior on index cards.

Criminal Records: Access: Mail, in person. Only the court performs in person searches; visitors may not. No search fee. Required to search: name, years to search, DOB, SSN. Criminal records on computer since 1990, prior on index cards.

General Information: No suppressed, child and spousal abuse records released. SASE required. Turnaround time 2 days. Copy fee: $1.00 per page. Certification fee: $10.00. Fee payee: 17th District Court. Personal checks accepted. Credit cards accepted: Visa, MasterCard. ATM cards accepted. Prepayment is required.

18th District Court 36675 Ford Rd, Westland, MI 48185; 734-595-8720; Fax: 734-595-0160. Hours: 8:30AM-4PM M,F; 8:30AM-5:30PM T,W; 8:30AM-5:30PM Th (EST). *Misdemeanor, Civil Actions Under $25,000, Eviction, Small Claims.*

www.18thdistrictcourt.com

Civil Records: Access: Mail, fax, in person. Only the court performs in person searches; visitors may not. Search fee: $10.00 per name. Required to search: name, years to search; also helpful: case number or title. Civil cases indexed by defendant, plaintiff. Civil records on computer since 1987, prior on microfilm back to 1969.

Criminal Records: Access: Mail, in person. Only the court performs in person searches; visitors may not. Search fee: $10.00 per name. Required to search: name, years to search, DOB; also helpful: case number. Criminal records on computer since 1992, prior on microfilm back to 1969.

General Information: No suppressed records released. SASE required. Turnaround time 1-2 weeks. Copy fee: $1.00 per page. Certification fee: $10.00. Fee payee: 18th District Court. Personal checks accepted. Prepayment is required.

19th District Court 16077 Michigan Ave, Dearborn, MI 48126; 313-943-2056; Fax: 313-943-3071. Hours: 8AM-4:30PM (EST). *Misdemeanor, Civil Actions Under $25,000, Eviction, Small Claims.*

www.cityofdearborn.org

Civil Records: Access: Fax, mail, in person. Only the court performs in person searches; visitors may not. No search fee. Required to search: name, years to search. Civil cases indexed by defendant, plaintiff. Civil records on computer since 1986.

Criminal Records: Access: Fax, mail, in person. Only the court performs in person searches; visitors may not. No search fee. Required to search: name, years to search, DOB, offense, date of offense. Criminal records on computer since 1987, prior on docket books.

General Information: No suppressed records released. SASE helpful. Copy fee: $1.00 per page. Certification fee: $10.00. Fee payee: 19th District Court. Only cashiers checks and money orders accepted. Credit cards accepted: Visa, MasterCard. Prepayment is required.

20th District Court 6045 Fenton, Dearborn Heights, MI 48127; 313-277-7480; Fax: 313-277-7141. Hours: 9AM-5PM (EST). *Misdemeanor, Civil Actions Under $25,000, Eviction, Small Claims.*

Civil Records: Access: Mail, in person. Only the court performs in person searches; visitors may not. No search fee. Required to search: name, years to search; also helpful: address. Civil cases indexed by defendant,

plaintiff. Civil records on computer since April 1991, prior records on microfiche or books.

Criminal Records: Access: Mail, in person. Only the court performs in person searches; visitors may not. No search fee. Required to search: name, years to search, DOB; also helpful: SSN. Criminal records on computer since April 1991, prior on microfiche or books.

General Information: No suppressed, juvenile, sex offenders, mental health, or adoption records released. SASE required. Turnaround time 1 week-10 days. Copy fee: $1.00 per page. Certification fee: $10.00. Fee payee: 20th District Court. Business checks accepted. Credit cards accepted: Visa, MasterCard. Prepayment is required.

21st District Court 6000 Middlebelt Rd, Garden City, MI 48135; 734-525-8805; Fax: 734-421-4797. Hours: 8:30AM-4:30PM (EST). *Misdemeanor, Civil Actions Under $25,000, Eviction, Small Claims.*

Civil Records: Access: Mail, in person. Only the court performs in person searches; visitors may not. No search fee. Required to search: name, years to search. Civil cases indexed by defendant, plaintiff. Civil records on computer back to 1989, prior on books, microfilm, and cards. In person searchers must fill out a "File/copy Request Form.".

Criminal Records: Access: Mail, in person. Only the court performs in person searches; visitors may not. No search fee. Required to search: name, years to search, DOB; also helpful: SSN. Criminal records on computer back to 1989, prior on books, microfilm, and cards. In person searchers must fill out a "File/copy Request Form.".

General Information: No suppressed records released. SASE required. Turnaround time 1-2 days. Copy fee: $1.00 per page. Fee payee: 21st District Court. Personal checks accepted. Prepayment is required.

22nd District Court 27331 S River Park Dr, Inkster, MI 48141; 313-277-8200; Fax: 313-277-8221. Hours: 8:30AM-4:30PM (EST). *Misdemeanor, Civil Actions Under $25,000, Eviction, Small Claims.*

Civil Records: Access: Mail, in person. Only the court performs in person searches; visitors may not. No search fee. Required to search: name, years to search. Civil cases indexed by defendant, plaintiff. Civil records on computer since 1985, prior on docket books.

Criminal Records: Access: Mail, in person. Only the court performs in person searches; visitors may not. No search fee. Required to search: name, years to search, DOB; also helpful: SSN. Criminal records on computer since 1985, prior on books.

General Information: No suppressed records released. SASE required. Turnaround time 2 weeks. Copy fee: $.25 per page. Certification fee: $10.00 first page plus $1.00 per page thereafter. Fee payee: 22nd District Court. Personal checks accepted. Prepayment required.

23rd District Court 23511 Goddard Rd, Taylor, MI 48180; 734-374-1334; Fax: 734-374-1303. Hours: 8:15AM-4:30PM (EST). *Misdemeanor, Civil Actions Under $25,000, Eviction, Small Claims.*

Civil Records: Access: Mail, in person. Only the court performs in person searches; visitors may not. No search fee. Required to search: name, years to search. Civil cases indexed by defendant, plaintiff. Civil records on computer since 1993, prior on books.

Criminal Records: Access: Mail, in person. Only the court performs in person searches; visitors may not. No search fee. Required to search: name, years to search, DOB; also helpful: SSN. Criminal records on computer since 1993, prior on index cards.

General Information: No suppressed, sexual abuse or drug abuse records released. SASE not required. Turnaround time 1-2 days. Copy fee: $1.00 per page. Certification fee: $10.00. Fee payee: 23rd District Court. Personal checks accepted. Prepayment required.

24th District Court - Allen Park & Melvindale
6515 Roosevelt, Allen Park, MI 48101-2524; 313-928-0535; Fax: 313-928-1860. Hours: 8:30AM-4:30PM (EST). *Misdemeanor, Civil Actions Under $25,000, Eviction, Small Claims.*

www.24thdiscourt.org

Civil Records: Access: Phone, mail, fax, in person. Only the court performs in person searches; visitors may not. No search fee. Required to search: name, years to search. Civil cases indexed by defendant, plaintiff. Civil records on computer since 1992, prior records stored as hard-copies.

Criminal Records: Access: Fax, mail, in person. Only the court performs in person searches; visitors may not. No search fee. Required to search: name, years to search, DOB; also helpful: SSN. Criminal records on computer since 1993, prior records stored as hard-copies.

General Information: No non-public records, including driving and probation records, released. SASE required if return mail requested. Turnaround time 1 week. Copy fee: $.50 per page. Certification fee: $10.00. Fee payee: 24th District Court. Personal checks accepted. Prepayment is required.

25th District Court
1475 Cleophus, Lincoln Park, MI 48146; 313-382-8603; Civil phone: 313-382-9317; Criminal phone: 313-382-8600; Fax: 313-382-9361. Hours: 9AM-4:30PM (EST). *Misdemeanor, Civil Actions Under $25,000, Eviction, Small Claims.*

Civil Records: Access: Mail, in person. Only the court performs in person searches; visitors may not. No search fee. Required to search: name, years to search. Civil cases indexed by defendant, plaintiff. Civil records on computer since 1988, prior records stored as hard-copies.

Criminal Records: Access: Mail, in person. Only the court performs in person searches; visitors may not. No search fee. Required to search: name, years to search, DOB. Criminal records on computer since 1987, prior on docket books and cards.

General Information: No suppressed or expunged records released. SASE required. Turnaround time 1 week. Copy fee: $1.00 per page. Certification fee: $11.00. Fee payee: 25th District Court. Personal checks accepted. Credit cards accepted: Visa, MasterCard. Prepayment is required.

26-1 District Court
10600 W Jefferson, River Rouge, MI 48218; 313-842-7819; Fax: 313-842-5923. Hours: 8:30AM-4:30PM (EST). *Misdemeanor, Civil Actions Under $25,000, Eviction, Small Claims.*

Civil Records: Access: Mail, in person. Only the court performs in person searches; visitors may not. No search fee. Required to search: name, years to search. Civil cases indexed by defendant, plaintiff. Civil records on computer since 11/93; prior records on cards.

Criminal Records: Access: Mail, in person. Only the court performs in person searches; visitors may not. No search fee. Required to search: name, years to search, DOB. Criminal records on computer since 1993, prior on index cards.

General Information: No suppressed records released. SASE required. Turnaround time 1 week. Copy fee: $1.00 per page. Fee payee: 26-1 District Court. No personal checks accepted. Prepayment is required.

26-2 District Court
3869 W Jefferson, Ecorse, MI 48229; 313-386-7900; Fax: 313-928-5956. Hours: 9AM-4PM (EST). *Misdemeanor, Civil Actions Under $25,000, Eviction, Small Claims.*

Civil Records: Access: Mail, fax, in person. Only the court performs in person searches; visitors may not. Search fee: $25.00. Required to search: name, years to search. Civil cases indexed by defendant, plaintiff. Civil records on computer back to 1992, prior on index cards.

Criminal Records: Access: Mail, fax, in person. Only the court performs in person searches; visitors may not. Search fee: $25.00. Required to search: name, years to search, DOB; also helpful: SSN. Criminal records on computer back to 1992, prior on index cards.

General Information: No suppressed records released. SASE not required. Turnaround time 1 week. Copy fee: $.50 per page. Certification fee: $10.00. Fee payee: 26-2 District Court. Business checks accepted.

27-1 District Court
2015 Biddle Ave, Wyandotte, MI 48192; 734-324-4475; Fax: 734-324-4472. Hours: 8:30AM-4:30PM (EST). *Misdemeanor, Civil Actions Under $25,000, Eviction, Small Claims.*

Civil Records: Access: Mail, in person. Only the court performs in person searches; visitors may not. Search fee: $1.00. Required to search: name, years to search. Civil cases indexed by defendant, plaintiff. Civil records on computer since 1988, prior on index cards.

Criminal Records: Access: Mail, in person. Only the court performs in person searches; visitors may not. Search fee: $1.00. Required to search: name, years to search, DOB. Criminal records on computer since 1988, prior on index cards.

General Information: No suppressed records released. SASE required. Turnaround time 1 week. Copy fee: $1.00 per page. Certification fee: $10.00 plus $1.00 per page after first. Fee payee: 27-1 District Court. Money order or in person cash or money order. Prepayment is required.

27-2 District Court
14100 Civic Park Dr, Riverview, MI 48192; 734-281-4204. Hours: 8:30AM-4:30PM (EST). *Misdemeanor, Civil Actions Under $25,000, Eviction, Small Claims.*

Note: As of 12/31/02, this court will be merged with the 27th District Court in Wyandotte.

Civil Records: Access: Mail, in person. Both court and visitors may perform in person searches. No search fee. Required to search: name, years to search. Civil cases indexed by defendant, plaintiff. Civil records on computer since 1993.

Criminal Records: Access: Mail, in person. Both court and visitors may perform in person searches. No search fee. Required to search: name, years to search, DOB. Criminal records on computer since 1993.

General Information: No suppressed records released. Turnaround time 1 week. Copy fee: $1.00 per page. Certification fee: $10.00 plus $1.00 per page after first. Fee payee: 27-2 District Court. Personal checks accepted. Prepayment is required.

28th District Court
14720 Reaume Parkway, Southgate, MI 48195; Civil phone: 734-246-1360 X3632; Criminal phone: 734-246-1360 X3631; Fax: 734-246-1405. Hours: 8:30AM-4:30PM (EST). *Misdemeanor, Civil Actions Under $25,000, Eviction, Small Claims.*

Civil Records: Access: In person only. Both court and visitors may perform in person searches. No search fee. Required to search: name, years to search; also helpful: address. Civil cases indexed by defendant, plaintiff. Civil records on computer back to 1987, prior on card files by party back to 1979.

Criminal Records: Access: In person only. Only the court performs in person searches; visitors may not. No search fee. Required to search: name, years to search, DOB; also helpful: address, SSN, case number. Criminal records go back to 1979; on computer back to 1986.

General Information: No suppressed, probation, juvenile, sex offenders, mental health, or adoption records released. Copy fee: $1.00 per page. Certification fee: $10.00. Fee payee: 28th District Court. Only cash, cashiers checks and money orders accepted. Credit cards accepted: Visa, MasterCard and Discover. In person only. Prepayment is required.

29th District Court
34808 Sims Ave, Wayne, MI 48184; 734-722-5220; Fax: 734-722-7003. Hours: 8AM-4:30PM (EST). *Misdemeanor, Civil Actions Under $25,000, Eviction, Small Claims.*

Civil Records: Access: Mail, in person. Only the court performs in person searches; visitors may not. No search fee. Required to search: name, years to search. Civil cases indexed by defendant, plaintiff. Civil records on computer since 1990.

Criminal Records: Access: Mail, in person. Only the court performs in person searches; visitors may not. No search fee. Required to search: name, years to search, DOB; also helpful: address, SSN. Criminal records on computer since 1990.

General Information: No suppressed, juvenile, sex offenders, mental health, or adoption records released. SASE required. Turnaround time 1 week, phone turnaround time 1 day. Copy fee: $.50 per page. Certification fee: $25.00. Fee payee: 29th District Court. Personal checks accepted. Credit cards accepted: Visa, MasterCard. Prepayment is required.

30th District Court
28 Gerard Ave, Highland Park, MI 48203; 313-252-0300; Fax: 313-865-1115. Hours: 8AM-4:30PM (EST). *Misdemeanor, Civil Actions Under $25,000, Eviction, Small Claims.*

Civil Records: Access: Mail, in person. Both court and visitors may perform in person searches. Search fee: $5.00 per name. Required to search: name, years to search. Civil cases indexed by defendant, plaintiff. Civil records on computer since 1989, prior on index cards or docket books.

Criminal Records: Access: Mail, in person. Both court and visitors may perform in person searches. Search fee: $5.00 per name. Required to search: name, years to search, DOB. Criminal records on computer since 1989, prior on index cards or docket books.

General Information: No suppressed records released. SASE required. Turnaround time 1 week. Copy fee: $1.00 per page. Certification fee: $5.00. Fee payee: 30th District Court. Prepayment is required.

31st District Court
3401 Evaline Ave, Hamtramck, MI 48212; 313-876-7710; Fax: 313-876-7724. Hours: 8AM-4PM (EST). *Misdemeanor, Civil Actions Under $25,000, Eviction, Small Claims.*

Civil Records: Access: Mail, in person. Only the court performs in person searches; visitors may not. No search fee. Required to search: name, years to search. Civil cases indexed by defendant, plaintiff. Civil records on computer since 1989, prior on index cards.

Criminal Records: Access: Mail, in person. Only the court performs in person searches; visitors may not. No search fee. Required to search: name, years to search, DOB. Criminal records on computer since 1989, prior on index cards.

General Information: No suppressed records released. SASE required. Turnaround time 1-2 days. Copy fee: $1.00 per page. Certification fee: $10.00 plus $1.00 per page after first. Fee payee: 31st District Court. Personal checks accepted. Prepayment is required.

32 A District Court
19617 Harper Ave, Harper Woods, MI 48225; 313-343-2590; Fax: 313-343-2594. Hours: 8:30AM-4:30PM (EST). *Misdemeanor, Civil Actions Under $25,000, Small Claims.*

Civil Records: Access: Phone, fax, mail, in person. Only the court performs in person searches; visitors may not. No search fee. Required to search: name, years to search. Civil cases indexed by defendant, plaintiff. Civil records indexed by name and case number on computer, microfiche, and paper.

Criminal Records: Access: Phone, fax, mail, in person. Only the court performs in person searches; visitors may not. No search fee. Required to search: name, years to search. Criminal records indexed by name and case number on computer, microfiche, and paper.

General Information: No suppressed records released. SASE requested. Turnaround time same day. Fax notes: No fee to fax results. Copy fee: $.50 per page. Certification fee: $11.00. Fee payee: 32A District Court. Personal checks accepted. Credit cards accepted: Visa, MasterCard. Prepayment is required.

33rd District Court 19000 Van Horn Rd, Woodhaven, MI 48183; Civil phone: 734-671-0225; Criminal phone: 734-671-0201; Fax: 734-671-0307. Hours: 8:30AM-4:30PM (EST). *Misdemeanor, Civil Actions Under $25,000, Eviction, Small Claims.*

Civil Records: Access: Mail, fax, in person. Only the court performs in person searches; visitors may not. No search fee. Required to search: name, years to search; also helpful: address. Civil cases indexed by defendant, plaintiff. Civil records on computer since 1995, prior on microfilm and microfiche.

Criminal Records: Access: Mail, fax, in person. Only the court performs in person searches; visitors may not. No search fee. Required to search: name, years to search, DOB; also helpful: address. Criminal records on computer since 1995, prior on microfilm and microfiche.

General Information: No suppressed records released. SASE required. Turnaround time 1-5 days. Copy fee: $.25 per page. Certification fee: $10.00 plus $1.00 per page after first. Fee payee: 33rd District Court. Business checks accepted. Credit cards accepted: Visa, MasterCard. Prepayment is required.

34th District Court 11131 S Wayne Rd, Romulus, MI 48174; 734-941-4462; Fax: 734-941-7530. Hours: 8:30AM-4PM (EST). *Misdemeanor, Civil Actions Under $25,000, Eviction, Small Claims.*

Civil Records: Access: Mail, in person. Only the court performs in person searches; visitors may not. No search fee. Required to search: name, years to search. Civil cases indexed by defendant, plaintiff. Civil records on computer since 1984, prior on index cards and docket books.

Criminal Records: Access: Mail, in person. Only the court performs in person searches; visitors may not. No search fee. Required to search: name, years to search, DOB; also helpful: SSN. Criminal records on computer since 1984, prior on index cards and docket books.

General Information: No suppressed records released. SASE required. Turnaround time 1 week. Copy fee: $1.00 per page. Certification fee: $10.00 per page. Fee payee: 34th District Court. Personal checks accepted. Prepayment is required.

35th District Court 660 Plymouth Rd, Plymouth, MI 48170; 734-459-4740; Fax: 734-454-9303. Hours: 8:30AM-4:25PM (EST). *Misdemeanor, Civil Infractions, Civil Actions Under $25,000, Landlord Tenant, Small Claims, Juvenile.*

www.35thdistrictcourt.org

Civil Records: Access: Mail, in person. Both court and visitors may perform in person searches. No search fee. Required to search: name, years to search. Civil cases indexed by defendant, plaintiff. Civil records on computer since 1990; prior records archived.

Criminal Records: Access: Mail, in person. Both court and visitors may perform in person searches. No search fee. Required to search: name, years to search, DOB; also helpful: SSN, sex, signed release. Criminal records on computer since 1990; prior records archived.

General Information: Public access terminal is available. No suppressed, juvenile, sex offenders, mental health, or adoption records released. Turnaround time 1 week. Fax notes: Fee to fax results is $1.00 per document. Copy fee: $1.00 per page. Certification fee: $10.00. Fee payee: 35th District Court. Personal checks accepted. Third party checks not allowed. Debit cards accepted. Prepayment is required.

Wexford County

28th Circuit Court PO Box 490, Cadillac, MI 49601; 231-779-9450. Hours: 8:30AM-5PM (EST). *Felony, Civil Actions Over $25,000.*

Civil Records: Access: Mail, in person. Only the court performs in person searches; visitors may not. Search fee: $1.00 per name. Required to search: name, years to

search. Civil cases indexed by defendant, plaintiff. Civil records go back to 1868, civil records on computer since 1977.

Criminal Records: Access: Mail, in person. Only the court performs in person searches; visitors may not. Search fee: $1.00 per name. Required to search: name, years to search. Criminal records go back to 1868, criminal records on computer since 1977.

General Information: No suppressed, YTA files, juvenile, sex offenders, mental health, or adoption records released. SASE required. Turnaround time same day. Copy fee: $1.00 per page. Certification fee: $10.00. Fee payee: Wexford County Clerk. Only cashiers checks and money orders accepted. Prepayment is required.

84th District Court 501 S Garfield, Cadillac, MI 49601; 231-779-9515; Fax: 231-779-9485. Hours: 8:30AM-5PM (EST). *Misdemeanor, Civil Actions Under $25,000, Eviction, Small Claims.*

Civil Records: Access: Phone, fax, mail, in person. Both court and visitors may perform in person searches. Search fee: $1.00 per name. Required to search: name, years to search. Civil cases indexed by defendant, plaintiff. Civil records on computer since 1984; on index from 1969 to 1984.

Criminal Records: Access: Mail, fax, in person. Both court and visitors may perform in person searches. Search fee: $1.00 per name. Required to search: name, years to search, DOB; also helpful: SSN. Criminal records on computer since 1984; prior records on blue cards.

General Information: No suppressed, juvenile, sex offenders, mental health, or adoption records released. SASE required. Turnaround time 1 week. Copy fee: $1.00 per page. Certification fee: $10.00. Fee payee: 84th District Court. Personal checks accepted. Prepayment is required.

Probate Court 503 S Garfield, Cadillac, MI 49601; 231-779-9510; Fax: 231-779-9485. Hours: 8:30AM-5PM (EST). *Probate.*

Michigan Recording Offices

ORGANIZATION: 83 counties, 83 recording offices. The recording officer is County Register of Deeds. 79 counties are in the Eastern Time Zone (EST) and 4 are in the Central Time Zone (CST).

REAL ESTATE RECORDS: Some counties will perform real estate searches. Copies usually cost $1.00 per page. and certification fees vary. Ownership records are located at the Equalization Office, designated "Assessor" in this section. Tax records are located at the Treasurer's Office.

UCC RECORDS: Financing statements are filed at the state level, except for real estate related collateral, which are filed with the County Register. However, prior to 07/2001, consumer goods and farm collateral were also filed at the County Register and these older records can be searched there. All counties will perform UCC searches. Use search request form UCC-11. Search fees are usually $3.00 per debtor name if federal tax identification number or Social Security Number are given, or $6.00 without a number. Copies usually cost $1.00 per page.

TAX LIEN RECORDS: Federal and state tax liens on personal property of businesses are filed with the Secretary of State. Other federal and state tax liens are filed with the Register of Deeds. Most counties search each tax lien index separately. Some charge one fee to search both, while others charge a separate fee for each one. When combining a UCC and tax lien search, total fee is usually $9.00 for all three searches. Some counties require tax identification number as well as name to do a search. Copy fees are usually $1.00 per page.

OTHER LIENS: Construction, lis pendens.

ONLINE ACCESS: There is no statewide online access, but a number of counties, including Wayne, offer free access to assessor and register of deeds records.

Alcona County

County Register of Deeds, PO Box 269, Harrisville, MI 48740-0269. County Register of Deeds, R/E and UCC Recording 989-724-6802; Fax 989-724-5684.
Will search UCC records prior to 7/2001. UCC search includes tax liens if requested. Will not search real estate records. **Other Phone Numbers:** Assessor 989-724-6223; Treasurer 989-724-5140; Elections 989-724-6807; Vital Records 989-724-6807.

Alger County

County Register of Deeds, PO Box 538, Munising, MI 49862. 906-387-2076; Fax 906-387-2156.
Will search UCC records prior to 7/2001 and current fixture (land) files. UCC search includes tax liens if requested. Will not search real estate records. **Other Phones:** Assessor 906-387-2567; Treasurer 387-4535.

Allegan County

County Register of Deeds, 113 Chestnut St, County Court House, Allegan, MI 49010-1360. County Register of Deeds, R/E and UCC Recording 269-673-0390 UCC Recording: 269-673-0390 x3280; Fax 269-673-0289.
Will search UCC records. UCC search includes tax liens if requested. Will not search real estate records. **Other Phone Numbers:** Assessor 269-673-0230.

Alpena County

County Register of Deeds, 720 W. Chisholm St, Courthouse, Alpena, MI 49707-2487. 989-356-3887; Fax 989-356-6559.
Will search UCC records prior to 7/2001 and current fixture (land) files. UCC search includes tax liens if requested. Will not search real estate records. **Other Phones:** Assessor 989-356-2015; Treasurer 356-1751.

Antrim County

County Register of Deeds, PO Box 376, Bellaire, MI 49615. County Register of Deeds, R/E and UCC Recording 231-533-6683; Fax 231-533-8317.
Will search UCC records prior to 7/2001 and current fixture (land) files. UCC search includes tax liens if requested. Will not search real estate records. **Other Phone Numbers:** Assessor 231-533-6320; Treasurer 231-533-6720.

Arenac County

County Register of Deeds, PO Box 296, Standish, MI 48658. 989-846-9201 R/E Recording: 517-846-9201.
Will search UCC records prior to 7/2001 and current fixture (land) files. This agency will not do a tax lien search. Will not search real estate records. **Other Phone Numbers:** Assessor 517-846-6246.

Baraga County

County Register of Deeds, Courthouse, 16 N. 3rd St., L'Anse, MI 49946-1085. 906-524-6183; Fax 906-524-6186.
Will search UCC records prior to 7/2001 and current fixture (land) files. UCC search includes tax liens if requested. Will not search real estate records. **Other Phone Numbers:** Assessor 906-524-7331; Treasurer 906-524-7773; Elections 906-524-6183; Vital Records 906-524-6183.

Barry County

County Register of Deeds, PO Box 7, Hastings, MI 49058-0007. County Register of Deeds, R/E and UCC Recording 269-948-4824; Fax 269-948-4820. www.barrycounty.org
Will search UCC records prior to 7/2001 and current fixture (land) files. UCC search includes tax liens. Will not search real estate records. **Other Phone Numbers:** Assessor 269-948-4821; Treasurer 269-948-4818; Elections 269-948-4810; Vital Records 269-948-4810.

Bay County

County Register of Deeds, 515 Center Ave, Bay City, MI 48708-5994. County Register of Deeds, R/E and UCC Recording 989-895-4228; Fax 989-895-4296.
Will search UCC records. UCC search includes tax liens. Will not search real estate records. **Other Phone Numbers:** Assessor 989-895-4075; Treasurer 989-895-4285; Vital Records 989-895-4280.

Benzie County

County Register of Deeds, PO Box 398, Beulah, MI 49617. 231-882-0016; Fax 231-882-0167.
Will search UCC records prior to 7/2001 and current fixture (land) files. Tax liens not included in UCC search. Will not search real estate records unless specific document specified. **Other Phone Numbers:**
Assessor 231-882-0015; Treasurer 231-882-0011; Elections 231-882-0001; Vital Records 231-882-0001.

Berrien County

County Register of Deeds, Berrien County Administration Center, 701 Main St., St. Joseph, MI 49085. 616-983-7111 x8562; Fax 616-982-8659.
Will search UCC records prior to 7/2001 and current fixture (land) files. UCC search includes tax liens if requested. **Other Phone Numbers:** Assessor 616-983-7111 x8215; Treasurer 616-983-7111 x8208.

Branch County

County Register of Deeds, 570 Marshall Rd, Ste. C, Coldwater, MI 49036. County Register of Deeds, R/E and UCC Recording 517-279-4320.
Will search UCC records prior to 7/2001 and current fixture (land) files. UCC search includes tax liens. Will not search real estate records. **Other Phone Numbers:** Assessor 517-279-4312; Treasurer 517-279-8411.

Calhoun County

County Register of Deeds, 315 W. Green St, Marshall, MI 49068. 269-781-0718; Fax 269-781-0721. http://co.calhoun.mi.us
Will search UCC records prior to 7/2001 and current fixture (land) files. UCC search includes tax liens if requested. Will not search real estate records. **Other Phone Numbers:** Assessor 269-781-0745; Treasurer 269-969-6910/616-781-0807; Elections 269-781-0988; Vital Records 269-781-0718.

Cass County

County Register of Deeds, PO Box 355, Cassopolis, MI 49031-0355. County Register of Deeds, R/E and UCC Recording 269-445-4464; Fax 269-445-4406. www.casscountymi.org
Will search UCC records prior to 7/2001 and current fixture (land) files. UCC search includes tax liens if requested with extra fee Will not search real estate records. **Other Phone Numbers:** Assessor 269-445-4432; Treasurer 269-445-4468; Elections 269-445-4464; Vital Records 269-445-4464.

Charlevoix County

County Register of Deeds, 301 State St, County Building, Charlevoix, MI 49720. 231-547-7204; Fax 231-547-7246.

Will search UCC records prior to 7/2001 and current fixture (land) files. UCC search includes tax liens if requested. Will not search real estate records. **Other Phone Numbers:** Assessor 231-547-7230; Treasurer 231-547-7202.

Cheboygan County

County Register of Deeds, PO Box 70, Cheboygan, MI 49721. 231-627-8866; Fax 231-627-8453.

Will search UCC records prior to 7/2001 and current fixture (land) files. Will not search real estate records. **Other Phone Numbers:** Assessor 231-627-8845; Treasurer 231-627-8821; Elections 231-627-8808; Vital Records 231-627-8808.

Chippewa County

County Register of Deeds, Courthouse, 319 Court St., Sault Ste. Marie, MI 49783. County Register of Deeds, R/E and UCC Recording 906-635-6312; Fax 906-635-6855.

Will search UCC records prior to 7/2001 and current fixture (land) files. UCC search includes tax liens if requested with $6.00 extra per type of tax lien Will not search real estate records. **Other Phone Numbers:** Assessor 906-635-6304; Treasurer 906-635-6308; Elections 906-635-6300; Vital Records 906-635-6300.

Clare County

County Register of Deeds, PO Box 438, Harrison, MI 48625. County Register of Deeds, R/E and UCC Recording 989-539-7131; Fax 989-539-6616.

Will search UCC records. UCC search includes tax liens if requested. Mortgage searches available. **Other Phone Numbers:** Assessor 989-539-7894; Treasurer 989-539-7801; Elections 989-539-7131; Vital Records 989-539-7131.

Clinton County

County Register of Deeds, PO Box 435, St. Johns, MI 48879-0435. County Register of Deeds, R/E and UCC Recording 989-224-5270; Fax 989-224-5102.

Will search UCC records prior to 7/2001 and current fixture (land) files. UCC search includes tax liens if requested, with extra fees Will not search real estate records. **Other Phone Numbers:** Assessor 989-224-5170; Treasurer 989-224-5280.

Crawford County

County Register of Deeds, 200 W. Michigan, Grayling, MI 49738. 989-348-2841 R/E Recording: 989-344-3203 UCC Recording: 989-344-3203; Fax 989-344-3223.

Will search UCC records prior to 7/2001 and current fixture (land) files. UCC search includes tax liens if requested. Will not search real estate records. **Other Phone Numbers:** Assessor 989-344-3235; Treasurer 989-344-3229; Appraiser/Auditor 989-344-3234; Elections 989-344-3200; Vital Records 989-344-3207.

Delta County

County Register of Deeds, 310 Ludington St, Suite 104, Escanaba, MI 49829-4039. County Register of Deeds, R/E and UCC Recording 906-789-5116; Fax 906-789-5196.

Will search UCC records. Tax liens not included in UCC search. Real estate owner, mortgage, and property transfer searches available. **Other Phone Numbers:** Assessor 906-789-5109; Treasurer 906-789-5117; Appraiser/Auditor 906-789-5109; Elections 906-789-5105; Vital Records 906-789-5105.

Dickinson County

County Register of Deeds, PO Box 609, Iron Mountain, MI 49801. 906-774-0955; Fax 906-774-4660.

Will search UCC records prior to 7/2001 and current fixture (land) files. UCC search includes tax liens if requested. Will not search real estate records. **Other Phone Numbers:** Assessor 906-774-2515; Treasurer 906-774-8130.

Eaton County

County Register of Deeds, 1045 Independence Blvd., Room 104, Charlotte, MI 48813-1095. 517-543-7500 x232 R/E Recording: 517-543-7500; Fax 517-543-7377. www.co.eaton.mi.us/cntsrv/online.htm

Will search UCC records prior to 7/2001 and current fixture (land) files. UCC search includes tax liens. Will not search real estate records. **Online Access:** Assessor, Tax Records. Two levels of service are available on the County Online Data Service site. For free information, click on the Free Limited Public Information on the main page; then, on the Access System Page, at "User" enter PUBLIC. For "password," enter PUBLIC. The more sophisticated, restricted "Enhanced Records Access" requires registration, a password, and an associated fee. Access fees are billable monthly and can be prepaid to cover usage for any length of time. Also,search the Delta Charter Township assessments free at www.township.delta.mi.us/Assessing/BSALink.htm. **Other Phone Numbers:** Assessor 517-543-7500 x236; Treasurer 517-543-7500 x210.

Emmet County

County Register of Deeds, 200 Division, Petoskey, MI 49770. 231-348-1761; Fax 231-348-0633.

Will search UCC records prior to 7/2001 and current fixture (land) files. UCC search includes tax liens if requested. Will not search real estate records. **Other Phone Numbers:** Assessor 231-348-1708; Treasurer 231-348-1715.

Genesee County

County Register of Deeds, 1101 Beach St, Administration Building, Flint, MI 48502. County Register of Deeds, R/E and UCC Recording 810-257-3060; Fax 810-768-7965. www.co.genesee.mi.us

Will search UCC records prior to 7/2001 and current fixture (land) files. UCC search includes tax liens if requested. Will not search real estate records. **Online Access:** Recording, Property, Deed, Marriage, Death Records. Access to Register of Deeds database is available free at www.co.genesee.mi.us/rod. But to view documents back to 10/2000, there is a fee, and user ID and password required. Also, online access to the county clerk's marriage (back to 1963) and death (back to 1930) indexes are available free at www.co.genesee.mi.us/vitalrec. **Other Phones:** Assessor 810-257-3017; Treasurer 810-257-3059; Elections 810-257-3283; Vital Records 810-257-3225.

Gladwin County

County Register of Deeds, 401 W. Cedar Ave., Ste 7, Gladwin, MI 48624-2093. 989-426-7551.

Will search UCC records prior to 7/2001 and current fixture (land) files. UCC search includes tax liens if requested. Will not search real estate records. **Other Phones:** Assessor 989-426-9327; Treasurer 426-7351.

Gogebic County

County Register of Deeds, Courthouse, 200 N. Moore St., Bessemer, MI 49911. County Register of Deeds, R/E and UCC Recording 906-667-0381; Fax 906-663-4660.

Will search UCC records prior to 7/2001 and current fixture (land) files. UCC search includes tax liens if requested. Real estate owner, mortgage, and property transfer searches available. **Other Phone Numbers:**

Assessor 906-663-4414; Treasurer 906-667-4517; Elections 906-667-4518; Vital Records 906-667-4518.

Grand Traverse County

County Register of Deeds, 400 Boardman Ave, Traverse City, MI 49684-2577. 231-922-4750; Fax 231-922-4658.

Will search UCC records prior to 7/2001 and current fixture (land) files. Tax liens not included in UCC search. Will search grantor/grantee or mortgagor/mortgagee records. **Other Phone Numbers:** Assessor 231-922-4772; Treasurer 231-922-4735.

Gratiot County

County Register of Deeds, PO Box 5, Ithaca, MI 48847. 989-875-5217.

Will search UCC records. Real estate record owner searches available. **Other Phone Numbers:** Assessor 989-875-5203; Treasurer 989-875-5220.

Hillsdale County

County Register of Deeds, Courthouse, 29 N Howell, Rm 3, 29 N. Howell, Room 3, Hillsdale, MI 49242. 517-437-2231; Fax 517-437-3139. www.co.hillsdale.mi.us

Will search UCC records prior to 7/2001 and current fixture (land) files. UCC search includes tax liens if requested. Will not search real estate records. **Other Phone Numbers:** Assessor 517-439-9166; Treasurer 517-437-4700; Elections 517-437-3391; Vital Records 517-437-3391.

Houghton County

County Register of Deeds, 401 E. Houghton Ave, Houghton, MI 49931. 906-482-1311; Fax 906-483-0364.

Will search UCC records prior to 7/2001. UCC search includes tax liens if requested for an extra fee. Will search for last owner by property location. **Other Phone Numbers:** Assessor 906-482-0250; Treasurer 906-482-0560.

Huron County

County Register of Deeds, 250 E Huron Ave, Bad Axe, MI 48413. 989-269-9941.

Will search UCC records prior to 7/2001 and current fixture (land) files. UCC search includes tax liens if requested. Will not search real estate records. **Other Phone Numbers:** Assessor 989-269-6497; Treasurer 989-269-9238.

Ingham County

County Register of Deeds, PO Box 195, Mason, MI 48854-0195. County Register of Deeds, R/E and UCC Recording 517-676-7216 UCC Recording: 517-676-7224; Fax 517-676-7287. www.ingham.org/rd/rodindex.htm

Will search UCC records prior to 7/2001 and current fixture (land) files. This agency will not do a tax lien search. Will not search real estate records. **Online Access:** Assumed Business Name Records. County DBA and co-partnership listings are available free online at www.ingham.org/CL/dbalists.htm. **Other Phone Numbers:** Assessor 517-676-7212; Treasurer 517-676-7220; Elections 517-676-7205; Vital Records 517-676-7201.

Ionia County

County Register of Deeds, PO Box 35, Ionia, MI 48846. 616-527-5320; Fax 616-527-5380. www.ioniacounty.org

Will search UCC records prior to 7/2001 and current fixture (land) files. UCC search includes tax liens if requested. Will not search real estate records. **Other Phone Numbers:** Assessor 616-527-5376; Treasurer 616-527-5329.

Iosco County

County Register of Deeds, PO Box 367, Tawas City, MI 48764. County Register of Deeds, R/E and UCC Recording 989-362-2021; Fax 989-984-1101.

Will search UCC records prior to 7/2001 and current fixture (land) files. UCC search includes tax liens if requested. Real estate owner, mortgage, and property transfer searches available only over phone or in person **Other Phone Numbers:** Assessor 989-362-5801; Treasurer 989-362-4409; Elections 989-362-3497; Vital Records 989-362-3497.

Iron County

County Register of Deeds, 2 S. Sixth St, Ste. 11, Courthouse Annex, Suite 11, Crystal Falls, MI 49920-1413. 906-875-3321; Fax 906-875-0658.

Will search UCC records prior to 7/2001 and current fixture (land) files. UCC search includes tax liens if requested. Will not search real estate records. **Other Phone Numbers:** Assessor 906-875-6502; Treasurer 906-875-3362.

Isabella County

County Register of Deeds, 200 N. Main St, Mt. Pleasant, MI 48858. County Register of Deeds, R/E and UCC Recording 989-772-0911 x253; Fax 989-773-7431.

Will search UCC records prior to 7/2001 and current fixture (land) files. UCC search includes tax liens if requested. Will not search real estate records. **Other Phone Numbers:** Assessor 989-772-0911 x242; Treasurer 989-772-0911 x254; Elections 989-772-0911 x259; Vital Records 989-772-0911 x259.

Jackson County

County Register of Deeds, 120 W. Michigan Ave, 11th Floor, Jackson, MI 49201. 517-788-4350; Fax 517-788-4686. www.co.jackson.mi.us

Will search UCC records prior to 7/2001 and current fixture (land) files. UCC search includes tax liens if requested. Will not search real estate records. **Online Access:** Real Estate, Lien, Deed Records. Access to county online records requires pre-payment and $1 per minute of use (this may be revised). Records date back to 1985. Indexes include grantor/grantee, deeds, mortgage information. Lending agency information is available. Vital records will be added to the system when it is upgraded. For information, contact Mindy at 517-768-6682. Also, online access to deeds should be available free at www.co.jackson.mi.us/officials/elected/reilly/deeds.htm. **Other Phone Numbers:** Assessor 517-788-4378; Treasurer 517-788-4418.

Kalamazoo County

County Register of Deeds, 201 W. Kalamazoo Ave, Kalamazoo, MI 49007. 269-383-8970.

Will search UCC records prior to 7/2001 and current fixture (land) files. This agency will not do a tax lien search. Will not search real estate records. **Other Phone Numbers:** Assessor 269-383-8960; Treasurer 269-383-8124.

Kalkaska County

County Register of Deeds, 605 N. Birch St, Kalkaska, MI 49646. County Register of Deeds, R/E and UCC Recording 231-258-3315; Fax 231-258-3318.

Will search UCC records prior to 7/2001 and current fixture (land) files. UCC search includes tax liens. Mortgage searches available. **Other Phone Numbers:** Assessor 231-258-3340; Treasurer 231-258-3310; Vital Records 231-258-3300.

Kent County

County Register of Deeds, 300 Monroe Ave NW, Grand Rapids, MI 49503-2286. 616-336-3558; www.co.kent.mi.us/government/departments/

Will search UCC records prior to 7/2001 and current fixture (land) files. UCC search includes tax liens. Will not search real estate records. **Online Access:** Assessor, Property Records. Records on the Walker City Assessing Dept. database are available free online at www.ci.walker.mi.us/Services/Assessor/AssessingData/DataIntro.html. In most cases, sales and permit histories go back to 1993. Database contains residential assessment and structural information. Also, records on the Alpine Charter Township Assessment database are available free online at http://alpine.data-web.net. Search by parcel number or street name. **Other Phone Numbers:** Assessor 616-336-3527; Treasurer 616-336-0762.

Keweenaw County

County Register of Deeds, HC 1 Box 607, Eagle River, MI 49924-9700. County Register of Deeds, R/E and UCC Recording 906-337-2229; Fax 906-337-2795.

Will search UCC records. UCC search includes tax liens if requested. Will not search real estate records. **Other Phone Numbers:** Assessor 906-337-3471; Treasurer 906-337-1625.

Lake County

County Register of Deeds, Drawer B, Baldwin, MI 49304. County Register of Deeds, R/E and UCC Recording 231-745-4641; Fax 231-745-2241. www.michigan.gov

Will search UCC records prior to 7/2001 and current fixture (land) files. UCC search includes tax liens if requested. Will not search real estate records. **Other Phone Numbers:** Assessor 231-745-2723; Treasurer 231-745-4622; Appraiser/Auditor 231-745-4641; Elections 231-745-4641; Vital Records 231-745-2725.

Lapeer County

County Register of Deeds, 279 N. Court St, Lapeer, MI 48446. 810-667-0211; Fax 810-667-0293.

Will search UCC records prior to 7/2001 and current fixture (land) files. UCC search includes tax liens if requested. Will not search real estate records. **Other Phones:** Assessor 810-667-0228; Treasurer 667-0239.

Leelanau County

County Register of Deeds, PO Box 595, Leland, MI 49654. 231-256-9682; Fax 231-256-8149.

Will search UCC records prior to 7/2001 and current fixture (land) files. UCC search includes tax liens if requested. Will not search real estate records. **Other Phones:** Assessor 231-256-9823; Treasurer 256-9838.

Lenawee County

County Register of Deeds, 301 N. Main St., Adrian, MI 49221. County Register of Deeds, R/E and UCC Recording 517-264-4538 UCC Recording: 517-264-4540; Fax 517-264-4543.

Will search UCC records. UCC search includes tax liens if requested. Will not search real estate records. **Other Phone Numbers:** Assessor 517-264-4522; Treasurer 517-264-4554.

Livingston County

County Register of Deeds, PO Box 197, Howell, MI 48844. 517-546-0270; Fax 517-546-5966.

Will search UCC records prior to 7/2001 and current fixture (land) files. UCC search includes tax liens. Will not search real estate records. **Online Access:** Real Estate, Lien, Tax Assessor Records. Access to county online records is available for occasional users, and a dedicated line is available for $1200 for professional users. Annual fee for occasional use is $400, plus $.000043 per second. Records date back to 1984. Lending agency information is available. For information, contact Judy Epley at 517-546-2530. **Other Phone Numbers:** Assessor 517-546-4182; Treasurer 517-546-7010.

Luce County

County Register of Deeds, County Government Building, Newberry, MI 49868. County Register of Deeds, R/E and UCC Recording 906-293-5521; Fax 906-293-0050.

Will search UCC records. Real estate record owner and mortgage searches available. **Other Phone Numbers:** Assessor 906-293-5611; Treasurer 906-293-8171; Elections 906-293-5521; Vital Records 906-293-5521.

Mackinac County

County Register of Deeds, 100 Marley St, Saint Ignace, MI 49781. 906-643-7306; Fax 906-643-7302.

Will search UCC records prior to 7/2001 and current fixture (land) files. UCC search includes tax liens if requested. Will not search real estate records. **Other Phone Numbers:** Assessor 906-643-7310; Treasurer 906-643-7317.

Macomb County

County Register of Deeds, 10 N. Main, Mt. Clemens, MI 48043. County Register of Deeds, R/E and UCC Recording 586-469-5342; Fax 586-469-5130. www.co.macomb.mi.us

Will search UCC records prior to 7/2001 and current fixture (land) files. UCC search includes tax liens. Real estate record owner and mortgage searching available. **Online Access:** Business Registration, Death Records. Business registration information - owner name, address, type and filing date - is available free online at http://macomb.mcntv.com/businessnames. Search by full or partial company name. County death records are available free online at http://macomb.mcntv.com/deathrecords. Search by name or apx. date. Also, County Recorder records are available from a private online source at www.landaccess.com; Fees and registration required. Also, Clinton Township Assessor records are available at www.clintontownship.com/assprd.htm. Enter user name: "clintwp" and password "assessor". **Other Phone Numbers:** Assessor 586-469-5190; Treasurer 586-469-5190; Elections 586-469-5209; Vital Records 586-469-5120.

Manistee County

County Register of Deeds, 415 Third St, Courthouse, Manistee, MI 49660-1606. 231-723-2146; Fax 231-398-3544.

Will search UCC records prior to 7/2001 and current fixture (land) files. Tax liens not included in UCC search. Will not search real estate records. **Other Phone Numbers:** Assessor 231-723-5957.

Marquette County

County Register of Deeds, 234 W. Baraga Ave, C-105, Marquette, MI 49855. County Register of Deeds, R/E and UCC Recording 906-225-8415; Fax 906-225-8420. www.co.marquette.mi.us

Will search UCC records prior to 7/2001 and current fixture (land) files. UCC search includes tax liens if requested. Will not search real estate records. **Online Access:** Warrant List Records. Access to the sheriff's warrants list is available at www.co.marquette.mi.us/Sheriff/WARRANTS.htm. **Other Phones:** Assessor 906-225-8405; Treasurer 906-225-8425; Appraiser/Auditor 906-225-8405; Elections 906-225-8330; Vital Records 906-225-8330.

Mason County

County Register of Deeds, PO Box 57, Ludington, MI 49431-0057. 231-843-4466; Fax 231-843-1972.

Will search UCC records prior to 7/2001 and current fixture (land) files. Will not search real estate records. **Other Phone Numbers:** Assessor 231-845-6288; Treasurer 231-845-8411.

Mecosta County

County Register of Deeds, PO Box 718, Big Rapids, MI 49307. 231-592-0148.
Will search UCC records prior to 7/2001 and current fixture (land) files. UCC search includes tax liens if requested. Will not search real estate records. **Online Access:** Assessor, Property Records. Search the City of Big Rapids assessing and tax page for free at www.ci.big-rapids.mi.us/Assessing/onlinesearch.htm. **Other Phone Numbers:** Assessor 231-592-0108; Treasurer 231-592-0169.

Menominee County

Register of Deeds, 839 10th Ave, 839 10th Ave., Menominee, MI 49858. 906-863-2822; Fax 906-863-8839.
Will search UCC records prior to 7/2001 and current fixture (land) files. Tax liens not included in UCC search. Property transfer searches available. **Other Phone Numbers:** Assessor 906-863-2685; Treasurer 906-863-5548; Elections 906-863-9968; Vital Records 906-863-9968.

Midland County

County Register of Deeds, 220 W. Ellsworth St, County Services Building, Midland, MI 48640-5194. 989-832-6820; Fax 989-832-6608.
Will search UCC records prior to 7/2001 and current fixture (land) files. This agency will not do a tax lien search. Will not search real estate records. **Other Phone Numbers:** Assessor 989-837-3334; Treasurer 989-832-6850; Elections 989-832-6739; Vital Records 989-832-6739.

Missaukee County

County Register of Deeds, PO Box 800, Lake City, MI 49651. 231-839-4967; Fax 231-839-3684.
Will search UCC records prior to 7/2001 and current fixture (land) files. UCC search includes tax liens if requested. Will search real estate records 1990 forward on computer. **Other Phone Numbers:** Assessor 231-839-2702; Treasurer 231-839-2169.

Monroe County

County Register of Deeds, 51 S Macomb St, Monroe, MI 48161. 734-240-7390.
Will search UCC records prior to 7/2001 and current fixture (land) files. UCC search includes tax liens if requested. Will not search real estate records. **Other Phone Numbers:** Assessor 734-240-7235; Treasurer 734-240-7365.

Montcalm County

County Register of Deeds, PO Box 368, Stanton, MI 48888. 989-831-7337 R/E Recording: 989-831-7337; Fax 989-831-7320.
Will search UCC records prior to 7/2001 and current fixture (land) files. UCC search includes tax liens if requested. Will search for records after 1/88 for last owner from property location. **Online Access:** Real Estate, Lien Records. Two sources are available. To view the index, the monthly fee is $250. To view both the index and document image, the monthly fee is $650. Records date back to 1/1/1988. Lending agency information is available. For information, call 989-831-7321. **Other Phone Numbers:** Assessor 989-831-5226 x203; Treasurer 989-831-5226 x234.

Montmorency County

County Register of Deeds, PO Box 789, Atlanta, MI 49709. County Register of Deeds, R/E and UCC Recording 989-785-3374; Fax 989-785-2825.
Will search UCC records prior to 7/2001 and current fixture (land) files. UCC search includes tax liens if requested. Will not search real estate records. **Other Phone Numbers:** Assessor 989-785-3411; Treasurer 989-785-4769; Elections 989-785-3374; Vital Records 989-785-3374.

Muskegon County

County Register of Deeds, 990 Terrace St., Muskegon, MI 49442. 231-724-6271; Fax 231-724-6842.
Will search UCC records prior to 7/2001 and current fixture (land) files. UCC search includes tax liens if requested. Real estate record owner and mortgage searches available. **Other Phone Numbers:** Assessor 231-724-6386; Treasurer 231-724-6261.

Newaygo County

County Register of Deeds, PO Box 885, White Cloud, MI 49349. County Register of Deeds, R/E and UCC Recording 231-689-7246; Fax 231-689-7205.
Will search UCC records prior to 7/2001 and current fixture (land) files. UCC search includes tax liens if requested. Will not search real estate records. **Other Phone Numbers:** Assessor 231-689-7240; Treasurer 231-689-7230; Elections 231-689-7235; Vital Records 231-689-7235.

Oakland County

County Register of Deeds, 1200 N. Telegraph Road, Dept 480, Pontiac, MI 48341-0480. 248-858-0599 R/E Recording: 248-858-0581; www.co.oakland.mi.us
Will search UCC records prior to 7/2001 and current fixture (land) files. UCC search includes tax liens if requested. Will not search real estate records. **Online Access:** Real Estate, Property Tax, Tax Lien Records. Access to Access Oakland property information is available by subscription. Available monthly or per use. For information or sign-up, visit www.co.oakland.mi.us (click on "@cess Oakland") or call Information Services at 248-858-0861. Also, County Recorder records are accessible through a private online service at www.landaccess.com; Fees and registration are required. **Other Phone Numbers:** Assessor 248-858-0740; Treasurer 248-858-0599.

Oceana County

County Register of Deeds, PO Box 111, Hart, MI 49420. County Register of Deeds, R/E and UCC Recording 231-873-4158; Fax 231-873-9218.
Will search UCC records prior to 7/2001 and current fixture (land) files. UCC search includes tax liens if requested. Will not search real estate records. **Other Phone Numbers:** Assessor 231-873-4609; Treasurer 231-873-3980; Elections 231-873-4328; Vital Records 231-873-1748.

Ogemaw County

County Register of Deeds, 806 W. Houghton Ave, Room 104, West Branch, MI 48661. County Register of Deeds, R/E and UCC Recording 989-345-0728; Fax 989-345-6221.
Will search UCC records prior to 7/2001 and current fixture (land) files. UCC search includes tax liens if requested. Will not search real estate records. **Other Phones:** Assessor 989-345-0328; Treasurer 989-345-0084; Elections 345-0215; Vital Records 345-0215.

Ontonagon County

County Register of Deeds, 725 Greenland Road, Ontonagon, MI 49953-1492. County Register of Deeds, R/E and UCC Recording 906-884-4255; Fax 906-884-2916.
Will search UCC records prior to 7/2001 and current fixture (land) files. UCC search includes tax liens. Will search real estate name index. **Other Phone Numbers:** Assessor 906-884-2765; Treasurer 906-884-4665; Appraiser/Auditor 906-884-2765; Elections 906-884-4255; Vital Records 906-884-2806.

Osceola County

County Register of Deeds, 301 W Upton Ave., Reed City, MI 49677-0208. 231-832-6113.
Will search UCC records prior to 7/2001 and current fixture (land) files. UCC search includes tax liens. Will not search real estate records. **Other Phone Numbers:** Assessor 231-832-6119; Treasurer 231-832-6110.

Oscoda County

County Register of Deeds, PO Box 399, Mio, MI 48647. 989-826-1116; Fax 989-826-1136.
Will search UCC records prior to 7/2001 and current fixture (land) files. Tax liens not included in UCC search. Will not search real estate records. **Other Phone Numbers:** Assessor 989-826-1113; Treasurer 989-826-3241 x112.

Otsego County

County Register of Deeds, 225 W. Main St, Rm 110, Room 108, Gaylord, MI 49735. 989-732-6484 x301/2 R/E Recording: 989-732-6484 x301; Fax 989-732-1562.
Will search UCC records prior to 7/2001 and current fixture (land) files. Tax liens included in UCC search with extra fees. Will not search real estate records. **Other Phone Numbers:** Assessor 989-732-6484 x315; Treasurer 989-732-6484 x311; Elections 989-732-6484 x392; Vital Records 989-732-6484 x303.

Ottawa County

County Register of Deeds, PO Box 265, Grand Haven, MI 49417-0265. 616-846-8240 R/E Recording: 616-846-8310; Fax 616-846-8131. www.co.ottawa.mi.us
Will search UCC records prior to 7/2001 and current fixture (land) files. UCC search includes tax liens if requested. Will not search real estate records. **Other Phone Numbers:** Assessor 616-738-4826; Treasurer 616-846-8230; Elections 616-846-8231; Vital Records 616-846-8231.

Presque Isle County

County Register of Deeds, PO Box 110, Rogers City, MI 49779-0110. 989-734-2676 R/E Recording: 989-734-4941; Fax 989-734-0506.
Will search UCC records prior to 7/2001 and current fixture (land) files. UCC search includes tax liens if requested. Will not search real estate records. **Other Phone Numbers:** Assessor 989-734-3810; Treasurer 989-734-4075.

Roscommon County

County Register of Deeds, PO Box 98, Roscommon, MI 48653. 989-275-5931 R/E Recording: 517-275-5931; Fax 989-275-8640.
Will search UCC records prior to 7/2001 and current fixture (land) files. UCC search includes tax liens if requested. Will not search real estate records. **Other Phone Numbers:** Assessor 989-275-8121 x5754; Treasurer 989-275-5823; Elections 989-275-5923; Vital Records 989-275-5923.

Saginaw County

County Register of Deeds, 111 S. Michigan Ave, Saginaw, MI 48602. 989-790-5270; Fax 989-790-5278.
Will search UCC records prior to 7/2001 and current fixture (land) files. UCC search includes tax liens if requested. Real estate record owner searches available. **Online Access:** Assessor, Assumed Business Name, Marriage, Death, Elections, Notary Records. Access to the county clerks database is available free at www.saginawcounty.com/clerk/search/index.html. Records go back to 1995. Also, records on the Saginaw Charter Township Assessor's Property Data Page are available free online at www.sagtwp.org/pt_scripts/search.cfm. Search by address, tax roll number, or

owner name. **Other Phone Numbers:** Assessor 989-790-5260; Treasurer 989-790-5225.

Sanilac County

County Register of Deeds, Box 168, Sandusky, MI 48471-0168. County Register of Deeds, R/E and UCC Recording 810-648-2313 UCC Recording: 810-648-1213; Fax 810-648-5461.

Will search UCC records prior to 7/2001 and current fixture (land) files. UCC search includes tax liens if requested. Real estate record owner and property searches available. **Other Phone Numbers:** Assessor 810-648-2955; Treasurer 810-648-2127; Elections 810-648-3212; Vital Records 810-648-3212.

Schoolcraft County

County Register of Deeds, 300 Walnut St, Room 164, Manistique, MI 49854. 906-341-3618; Fax 906-341-5680.

This agency will not perform searches. **Other Phones:** Assessor 906-341-3677; Treasurer 906-341-3622.

Shiawassee County

County Register of Deeds, PO Box 103, Corunna, MI 48817. 989-743-2216 R/E Recording: 517-743-2216; Fax 989-743-2459.

Will search UCC records prior to 7/2001 and current fixture (land) files. UCC search includes tax liens if requested. Will not search real estate records. **Other Phone Numbers:** Assessor 989-743-2263; Treasurer 989-743-2224.

St. Clair County

County Register of Deeds, 201 McMorran Blvd., Room 116, Port Huron, MI 48060. 810-985-2275; Fax 810-985-4297.

Will search UCC records prior to 7/2001 and current fixture (land) files. UCC search includes tax liens if requested. Will not search real estate records. **Other Phone Numbers:** Assessor 810-985-6925; Treasurer 810-985-2295.

St. Joseph County

County Register of Deeds, PO Box 388, Centreville, MI 49032-0388. 269-467-5552 x552 R/E Recording: 269-467-5552 UCC Recording: 269-467-5552; Fax 269-467-5628.

Will search UCC records prior to 7/2001 and current fixture (land) files. UCC search includes tax liens if requested. Tax number required Will not search real estate records. **Other Phone Numbers:** Assessor 269-467-5576; Treasurer 269-467-5581.

Tuscola County

Register of Deeds, 440 N. State St, Caro, MI 48723. 989-672-3840; Fax 989-672-4266. www.tuscolacounty.org

Will search UCC records prior to 7/2001. UCC search includes tax liens if requested. Will not search real estate records.

Van Buren County

County Register of Deeds, 219 Paw Paw St, #102, Paw Paw, MI 49079. County Register of Deeds, R/E and UCC Recording 269-657-8242; Fax 269-657-7573.

Will search UCC records prior to 7/2001 and current fixture (land) files. UCC search includes tax liens if requested. Will not search real estate records. **Other Phone Numbers:** Assessor 269-657-8234; Treasurer 269-657-8228; Elections 269-657-8218; Vital Records 269-657-8218.

Washtenaw County

County Register of Deeds, PO Box 8645, Ann Arbor, MI 48107. 734-222-6700 R/E Recording: 734-222-6710 UCC Recording: 734-222-6710; Fax 734-222-6528.

www.co.washtenaw.mi.us/DEPTS/CLERK.HTM

Will search UCC records prior to 7/2001 and current fixture (land) files. UCC search includes tax liens if requested. Will not search real estate records. **Other Phone Numbers:** Assessor 734-994-2511; Treasurer 734-994-2520; Elections 734-222-6730; Vital Records 734-222-6700.

Wayne County

County Register of Deeds, 400 Monroe, Room 620, Detroit, MI 48226. 313-224-5860 R/E Recording: 313-224-5854; Fax 313-224-5884.

Will search UCC records prior to 7/2001 and current fixture (land) files. UCC search includes tax liens if requested. Real estate owner, mortgage, and property transfer searches available. **Online Access:** Assessor, Recording, Deed, Judgment, Lien, Tax Sales, Assumed Name Records. Search the recorders land records database for free at http://208.246.137.57/default.asp. A full data on-demand or business service is also available; all 313-967-6857 or visit http://208.246.137.57/RODC/Default.asp. Search the recorders assumed names index at www.waynecounty.com/clerk/default_names.htm. Also, two county property auction listings are available free at www.waynecounty.com/property/default.htm and http://208.246.137.55/wcop. Records on the City of Dearborn Residential Property Assessment Database are available free online at http://65.186.162.37/dbnassessor. Search by street name and number. **Other Phone Numbers:** Assessor 313-224-2326; Treasurer 313-224-5990.

Wexford County

County Register of Deeds, 437 E. Division St, Cadillac, MI 49601. 231-779-9455; Fax 231-779-0292.

Will search UCC records prior to 7/2001 and current fixture (land) files. UCC search includes tax liens if requested. Will not search real estate records. **Other Phone Numbers:** Assessor 231-779-9531; Treasurer 231-779-9475.

Michigan County Locator

You will usually be able to find the city name in the City/County Cross Reference below. In that case, it is a simple matter to determine the county from the cross reference. However, only the official US Postal Service city names are included in this index. There are an additional 40,000 place names that people use in their addresses. Therefore, we have also included a ZIP/City Cross Reference immediately following the City/County Cross Reference.

If you know the ZIP Code but the city name does not appear in the City/County Cross Reference index, look up the ZIP Code in the ZIP/City Cross Reference, find the city name, then look up the city name in the City/County Cross Reference. For example, you want to know the county for an address of Menands, NY 12204. There is no "Menands" in the City/County Cross Reference. The ZIP/City Cross Reference shows that ZIP Codes 12201-12288 are for the city of Albany. Looking back in the City/County Cross Reference, Albany is in Albany County.

City/County Cross Reference

ACME Grand Traverse
ADA Kent
ADDISON Lenawee
ADRIAN Lenawee
AFTON Cheboygan
AHMEEK Keweenaw
AKRON Tuscola
ALANSON (49706) Emmet(82),
    Cheboygan(17)
ALBA Antrim
ALBION Calhoun
ALDEN (49612) Antrim(71), Kalkaska(28)
ALGER (48610) Ogemaw(34), Arenac(33),
    Gladwin(31)
ALGONAC St. Clair
ALLEGAN Allegan
ALLEN Hillsdale
ALLEN PARK Wayne
ALLENDALE Ottawa
ALLENTON St. Clair
ALLOUEZ Keweenaw
ALMA Gratiot
ALMONT Lapeer
ALPENA (49707) Alpena(97), Presque
    Isle(2)
ALPHA Iron
ALTO Kent
AMASA Iron
ANCHORVILLE St. Clair
ANN ARBOR Washtenaw
APPLEGATE Sanilac
ARCADIA (49613) Manistee(79),
    Benzie(20)
ARGYLE Sanilac
ARMADA (48005) Macomb(96), St. Clair(3)
ARNOLD Marquette
ASHLEY Gratiot
ATHENS (49011) Calhoun(96), St.
    Joseph(1), Branch(1)
ATLANTA Montmorency
ATLANTIC MINE Houghton
ATLAS Genesee
ATTICA Lapeer
AU GRES Arenac
AU TRAIN Alger
AUBURN Bay
AUBURN HILLS Oakland
AUGUSTA Kalamazoo
AVOCA St. Clair
AZALIA Monroe
BAD AXE Huron
BAILEY (49303) Muskegon(85),
    Newaygo(13)
BALDWIN Lake
BANCROFT Shiawassee
BANGOR Van Buren
BANNISTER (48807) Gratiot(65),
    Saginaw(32), Clinton(1)
BARAGA Baraga
BARBEAU Chippewa
BARK RIVER (49807) Delta(46),
    Dickinson(34), Menominee(19)
BARODA Berrien

BARRYTON (49305) Mecosta(92),
    Isabella(7)
BARTON CITY Alcona
BATH Clinton
BATTLE CREEK Calhoun
BAY CITY Bay
BAY PORT Huron
BAY SHORE Charlevoix
BEAR LAKE Manistee
BEAVER ISLAND Charlevoix
BEAVERTON (48612) Gladwin(96),
    Clare(1), Midland(1)
BEDFORD Calhoun
BELDING (48809) Ionia(90), Kent(9)
BELLAIRE Antrim
BELLEVILLE Wayne
BELLEVUE (49021) Eaton(63), Barry(27),
    Calhoun(8)
BELMONT Kent
BENTLEY (48613) Bay(88), Gladwin(10),
    Arenac(1)
BENTON HARBOR Berrien
BENZONIA (49616) Benzie(98),
    Manistee(1)
BERGLAND Ontonagon
BERKLEY Oakland
BERRIEN CENTER (49102) Berrien(97),
    Cass(2)
BERRIEN SPRINGS Berrien
BESSEMER Gogebic
BEULAH Benzie
BIG BAY Marquette
BIG RAPIDS (49307) Mecosta(97),
    Newaygo(2)
BIRCH RUN (48415) Saginaw(97),
    Tuscola(1), Genesee(1)
BIRMINGHAM Oakland
BITELY (49309) Newaygo(90), Lake(9)
BLACK RIVER Alcona
BLANCHARD (49310) Isabella(62),
    Mecosta(34), Montcalm(3)
BLISSFIELD Lenawee
BLOOMFIELD HILLS Oakland
BLOOMINGDALE (49026) Van Buren(89),
    Allegan(10)
BOON Wexford
BOYNE CITY (49712) Charlevoix(97),
    Antrim(2)
BOYNE FALLS (49713) Charlevoix(92),
    Emmet(8)
BRADLEY Allegan
BRANCH (49402) Lake(50), Mason(44),
    Oceana(4)
BRANT Saginaw
BRECKENRIDGE (48615) Gratiot(74),
    Midland(25)
BREEDSVILLE Van Buren
BRETHREN Manistee
BRIDGEPORT Saginaw
BRIDGEWATER Washtenaw
BRIDGMAN Berrien
BRIGHTON Livingston
BRIMLEY Chippewa

BRITTON (49229) Lenawee(89),
    Monroe(8), Washtenaw(1)
BROHMAN Newaygo
BRONSON Branch
BROOKLYN Jackson
BROWN CITY (48416) Sanilac(57),
    Lapeer(37), St. Clair(4)
BRUCE CROSSING Ontonagon
BRUNSWICK (49313) Muskegon(77),
    Newaygo(22)
BRUTUS (49716) Emmet(55),
    Cheboygan(44)
BUCHANAN Berrien
BUCKLEY (49620) Wexford(57), Grand
    Traverse(42)
BURLINGTON Calhoun
BURNIPS Allegan
BURR OAK (49030) St. Joseph(90),
    Branch(9)
BURT Saginaw
BURT LAKE Cheboygan
BURTON Genesee
BYRON (48418) Shiawassee(63),
    Genesee(28), Livingston(8)
BYRON CENTER (49315) Kent(93),
    Ottawa(4), Allegan(2)
CADILLAC (49601) Wexford(98),
    Missaukee(2)
CADMUS Lenawee
CALEDONIA (49316) Kent(87), Allegan(8),
    Barry(4)
CALUMET Houghton
CAMDEN Hillsdale
CANNONSBURG Kent
CANTON Wayne
CAPAC (48014) St. Clair(98), Lapeer(1)
CARLETON Monroe
CARNEY Menominee
CARO Tuscola
CARP LAKE (49718) Emmet(70),
    Cheboygan(29)
CARROLLTON Saginaw
CARSON CITY (48811) Montcalm(73),
    Gratiot(26)
CARSONVILLE Sanilac
CASCO St. Clair
CASEVILLE Huron
CASNOVIA (49318) Muskegon(67),
    Newaygo(21), Kent(11)
CASPIAN Iron
CASS CITY (48726) Tuscola(84),
    Sanilac(12), Huron(3)
CASSOPOLIS Cass
CEDAR Leelanau
CEDAR LAKE Montcalm
CEDAR RIVER Menominee
CEDAR SPRINGS Kent
CEDARVILLE Mackinac
CEMENT CITY (49233) Lenawee(76),
    Jackson(23)
CENTER LINE Macomb
CENTRAL LAKE Antrim
CENTREVILLE St. Joseph

CERESCO Calhoun
CHAMPION Marquette
CHANNING Dickinson
CHARLEVOIX (49720) Charlevoix(98),
    Antrim(1)
CHARLOTTE Eaton
CHASE Lake
CHASSELL Houghton
CHATHAM Alger
CHEBOYGAN Cheboygan
CHELSEA Washtenaw
CHESANING Saginaw
CHIPPEWA LAKE Mecosta
CLARE (48617) Clare(78), Isabella(21)
CLARKLAKE Jackson
CLARKSTON Oakland
CLARKSVILLE (48815) Ionia(96), Kent(3)
CLAWSON Oakland
CLAYTON Lenawee
CLIFFORD (48727) Lapeer(51),
    Tuscola(48)
CLIMAX Kalamazoo
CLINTON (49236) Lenawee(82),
    Washtenaw(17)
CLINTON TOWNSHIP Macomb
CLIO (48420) Genesee(98), Tuscola(1)
CLOVERDALE Barry
COHOCTAH Livingston
COLDWATER Branch
COLEMAN (48618) Midland(83),
    Isabella(13), Gladwin(2)
COLOMA (49038) Berrien(94), Van
    Buren(5)
COLON St. Joseph
COLUMBIAVILLE (48421) Lapeer(95),
    Genesee(4)
COLUMBUS St. Clair
COMINS (48619) Oscoda(78),
    Montmorency(21)
COMMERCE TOWNSHIP Oakland
COMSTOCK Kalamazoo
COMSTOCK PARK Kent
CONCORD Jackson
CONKLIN (49403) Ottawa(91),
    Muskegon(4), Kent(3)
CONSTANTINE (49042) St. Joseph(98),
    Cass(1)
CONWAY Emmet
COOKS (49817) Schoolcraft(81), Delta(18)
COOPERSVILLE (49404) Ottawa(96),
    Muskegon(3)
COPEMISH (49625) Manistee(92),
    Wexford(7)
COPPER CITY Houghton
COPPER HARBOR Keweenaw
CORAL Montcalm
CORNELL (49818) Delta(88),
    Marquette(11)
CORUNNA Shiawassee
COVERT Van Buren
COVINGTON Baraga
CROSS VILLAGE Emmet
CROSWELL Sanilac

CRYSTAL Montcalm
CRYSTAL FALLS Iron
CURRAN (48728) Alcona(86), Oscoda(13)
CURTIS Mackinac
CUSTER Mason
DAFTER Chippewa
DAGGETT Menominee
DANSVILLE Ingham
DAVISBURG Oakland
DAVISON Genesee
DE TOUR VILLAGE Chippewa
DEARBORN Wayne
DEARBORN HEIGHTS Wayne
DECATUR (49045) Van Buren(91), Cass(8)
DECKER (48426) Sanilac(92), Tuscola(7)
DECKERVILLE Sanilac
DEERFIELD Lenawee
DEERTON (49822) Alger(96), Marquette(3)
DEFORD (48729) Tuscola(98), Sanilac(1)
DELTON Barry
DETROIT Wayne
DEWITT Clinton
DEXTER Washtenaw
DIMONDALE (48821) Eaton(94), Ingham(5)
DODGEVILLE Houghton
DOLLAR BAY Houghton
DORR (49323) Allegan(97), Ottawa(1)
DOUGLAS Allegan
DOWAGIAC (49047) Cass(93), Van Buren(6)
DOWLING Barry
DRAYTON PLAINS Oakland
DRUMMOND ISLAND Chippewa
DRYDEN Lapeer
DUNDEE Monroe
DURAND (48429) Shiawassee(98), Genesee(1)
EAGLE Clinton
EAGLE RIVER Keweenaw
EAST CHINA St. Clair
EAST JORDAN (49727) Charlevoix(67), Antrim(32)
EAST LANSING Ingham
EAST LEROY Calhoun
EAST TAWAS Iosco
EASTLAKE Manistee
EASTPOINTE Macomb
EASTPORT Antrim
EATON RAPIDS (48827) Eaton(93), Ingham(6)
EAU CLAIRE (49111) Berrien(89), Cass(10)
EBEN JUNCTION Alger
ECKERMAN Chippewa
ECORSE Wayne
EDENVILLE Midland
EDMORE (48829) Montcalm(98), Isabella(1)
EDWARDSBURG Cass
ELBERTA Benzie
ELK RAPIDS Antrim
ELKTON Huron
ELLSWORTH (49729) Antrim(88), Charlevoix(11)
ELM HALL Gratiot
ELMIRA (49730) Antrim(70), Otsego(22), Charlevoix(6)
ELSIE (48831) Clinton(57), Shiawassee(21), Saginaw(17), Gratiot(3)
ELWELL Gratiot
EMMETT St. Clair
EMPIRE (49630) Leelanau(98), Benzie(1)
ENGADINE Mackinac
ERIE Monroe
ESCANABA Delta
ESSEXVILLE Bay
EUREKA Clinton
EVART (49631) Osceola(91), Mecosta(8)
EWEN Ontonagon
FAIR HAVEN St. Clair
FAIRGROVE Tuscola

FAIRVIEW Oscoda
FALMOUTH Missaukee
FARMINGTON Oakland
FARWELL (48622) Clare(80), Isabella(19)
FELCH (49831) Dickinson(81), Marquette(18)
FENNVILLE Allegan
FENTON (48430) Genesee(76), Livingston(18), Oakland(4)
FENWICK (48834) Montcalm(65), Ionia(34)
FERNDALE Oakland
FERRYSBURG Ottawa
FIFE LAKE (49633) Kalkaska(60), Grand Traverse(31), Wexford(4), Missaukee(2)
FILER CITY Manistee
FILION Huron
FLAT ROCK Wayne
FLINT Genesee
FLUSHING Genesee
FORESTVILLE Sanilac
FORT GRATIOT St. Clair
FOSTER CITY Dickinson
FOSTORIA (48435) Tuscola(57), Lapeer(42)
FOUNTAIN Mason
FOWLER (48835) Clinton(98), Gratiot(1)
FOWLERVILLE Livingston
FRANKENMUTH Saginaw
FRANKFORT Benzie
FRANKLIN Oakland
FRASER Macomb
FREDERIC (49733) Crawford(77), Otsego(22)
FREE SOIL (49411) Mason(98), Manistee(1)
FREELAND (48623) Saginaw(81), Midland(10), Bay(8)
FREEPORT (49325) Barry(76), Ionia(13), Kent(9)
FREMONT Newaygo
FRONTIER Hillsdale
FRUITPORT (49415) Muskegon(89), Ottawa(10)
FULTON (49052) Kalamazoo(77), Calhoun(18), St. Joseph(4)
GAASTRA Iron
GAGETOWN (48735) Tuscola(63), Huron(36)
GAINES (48436) Genesee(93), Shiawassee(6)
GALESBURG Kalamazoo
GALIEN Berrien
GARDEN Delta
GARDEN CITY Wayne
GAYLORD Otsego
GENESEE Genesee
GERMFASK (49836) Schoolcraft(53), Mackinac(46)
GILFORD Tuscola
GLADSTONE Delta
GLADWIN (48624) Gladwin(92), Clare(4), Roscommon(1)
GLEN ARBOR Leelanau
GLENN Allegan
GLENNIE (48737) Alcona(89), Iosco(10)
GOBLES (49055) Van Buren(92), Allegan(7)
GOETZVILLE Chippewa
GOOD HART Emmet
GOODELLS St. Clair
GOODRICH (48438) Genesee(81), Lapeer(18)
GOULD CITY Mackinac
GOWEN (49326) Kent(69), Montcalm(30)
GRAND BLANC Genesee
GRAND HAVEN Ottawa
GRAND JUNCTION (49056) Van Buren(74), Allegan(25)
GRAND LEDGE (48837) Eaton(89), Clinton(9)
GRAND MARAIS Alger
GRAND RAPIDS Kent

GRANDVILLE Kent
GRANT Newaygo
GRASS LAKE (49240) Jackson(91), Washtenaw(8)
GRAWN Grand Traverse
GRAYLING Crawford
GREENBUSH (48738) Alcona(90), Iosco(9)
GREENLAND Ontonagon
GREENVILLE (48838) Montcalm(89), Kent(10)
GREGORY (48137) Livingston(98), Washtenaw(1)
GROSSE ILE Wayne
GROSSE POINTE Wayne
GULLIVER Schoolcraft
GWINN Marquette
HADLEY Lapeer
HAGAR SHORES Berrien
HALE (48739) Iosco(75), Ogemaw(24)
HAMBURG Livingston
HAMILTON Allegan
HAMTRAMCK Wayne
HANCOCK Houghton
HANOVER Jackson
HARBERT Berrien
HARBOR BEACH Huron
HARBOR SPRINGS Emmet
HARPER WOODS Wayne
HARRIETTA (49638) Wexford(90), Manistee(9)
HARRIS Menominee
HARRISON Clare
HARRISON TOWNSHIP Macomb
HARRISVILLE Alcona
HARSENS ISLAND St. Clair
HART Oceana
HARTFORD Van Buren
HARTLAND Livingston
HASLETT (48840) Ingham(94), Clinton(5)
HASTINGS Barry
HAWKS Presque Isle
HAZEL PARK Oakland
HEMLOCK (48626) Saginaw(94), Midland(5)
HENDERSON (48841) Shiawassee(82), Saginaw(17)
HERMANSVILLE Menominee
HERRON Alpena
HERSEY (49639) Osceola(77), Mecosta(22)
HESPERIA (49421) Oceana(71), Newaygo(28)
HESSEL Mackinac
HICKORY CORNERS (49060) Barry(96), Kalamazoo(3)
HIGGINS LAKE Roscommon
HIGHLAND Oakland
HIGHLAND PARK Wayne
HILLMAN (49746) Montmorency(88), Alpena(11)
HILLSDALE Hillsdale
HOLLAND Ottawa
HOLLY (48442) Oakland(96), Genesee(2)
HOLT Ingham
HOLTON (49425) Muskegon(81), Oceana(11), Newaygo(6)
HOMER Calhoun
HONOR Benzie
HOPE (48628) Midland(82), Gladwin(17)
HOPKINS Allegan
HORTON (49246) Jackson(95), Hillsdale(4)
HOUGHTON Houghton
HOUGHTON LAKE Roscommon
HOUGHTON LAKE HEIGHTS Roscommon
HOWARD CITY (49329) Montcalm(84), Newaygo(15)
HOWELL Livingston
HUBBARD LAKE (49747) Alpena(54), Alcona(45)
HUBBARDSTON (48845) Ionia(58), Clinton(19), Montcalm(15), Gratiot(6)
HUBBELL Houghton

HUDSON (49247) Lenawee(71), Hillsdale(28)
HUDSONVILLE Ottawa
HULBERT Chippewa
HUNTINGTON WOODS Oakland
IDA Monroe
IDLEWILD Lake
IMLAY CITY (48444) Lapeer(98), St. Clair(1)
INDIAN RIVER Cheboygan
INGALLS Menominee
INKSTER Wayne
INTERLOCHEN (49643) Grand Traverse(68), Benzie(31)
IONIA Ionia
IRON MOUNTAIN Dickinson
IRON RIVER Iron
IRONS (49644) Lake(81), Manistee(18)
IRONWOOD Gogebic
ISHPEMING Marquette
ITHACA Gratiot
JACKSON Jackson
JAMESTOWN Ottawa
JASPER Lenawee
JEDDO (48032) St. Clair(81), Sanilac(18)
JENISON Ottawa
JEROME (49249) Hillsdale(95), Jackson(4)
JOHANNESBURG (49751) Otsego(93), Montmorency(6)
JONES Cass
JONESVILLE Hillsdale
KALAMAZOO Kalamazoo
KALEVA Manistee
KALKASKA Kalkaska
KARLIN Grand Traverse
KAWKAWLIN Bay
KEARSARGE Houghton
KEEGO HARBOR Oakland
KENDALL Van Buren
KENT CITY (49330) Kent(92), Newaygo(5), Ottawa(1), Muskegon(1)
KENTON Houghton
KEWADIN Antrim
KINCHELOE Chippewa
KINDE Huron
KINGSFORD Dickinson
KINGSLEY (49649) Grand Traverse(95), Wexford(4)
KINGSTON (48741) Tuscola(94), Sanilac(5)
KINROSS Chippewa
LA SALLE Monroe
LACHINE Alpena
LACOTA Van Buren
LAINGSBURG (48848) Shiawassee(67), Clinton(32)
LAKE (48632) Clare(76), Isabella(21), Osceola(1)
LAKE ANN Benzie
LAKE CITY Missaukee
LAKE GEORGE Clare
LAKE LEELANAU Leelanau
LAKE LINDEN (49945) Houghton(97), Keweenaw(2)
LAKE ODESSA (48849) Ionia(81), Barry(15), Eaton(3)
LAKE ORION Oakland
LAKELAND Livingston
LAKESIDE Berrien
LAKEVIEW (48850) Montcalm(81), Mecosta(18)
LAKEVILLE Oakland
LAMBERTVILLE Monroe
LAMONT Ottawa
LANSE Baraga
LANSING Ingham
LAPEER Lapeer
LAWRENCE Van Buren
LAWTON Van Buren
LELAND Leelanau
LENNON (48449) Shiawassee(54), Genesee(45)

LEONARD Oakland
LEONIDAS St. Joseph
LEROY (49655) Osceola(93), Lake(6)
LESLIE Ingham
LEVERING (49755) Emmet(63),
   Cheboygan(36)
LEWISTON (49756) Montmorency(51),
   Oscoda(47), Otsego(1)
LEXINGTON Sanilac
LINCOLN Alcona
LINCOLN PARK Wayne
LINDEN (48451) Genesee(89),
   Livingston(10)
LINWOOD Bay
LITCHFIELD Hillsdale
LITTLE LAKE Marquette
LIVONIA Wayne
LONG LAKE (48743) Iosco(91),
   Ogemaw(8)
LORETTO Dickinson
LOWELL (49331) Kent(89), Ionia(10)
LUDINGTON Mason
LUNA PIER Monroe
LUPTON Ogemaw
LUTHER Lake
LUZERNE Oscoda
LYONS Ionia
MACATAWA Ottawa
MACKINAC ISLAND Mackinac
MACKINAW CITY Cheboygan
MACOMB Macomb
MADISON HEIGHTS Oakland
MANCELONA (49659) Antrim(78),
   Kalkaska(21)
MANCHESTER Washtenaw
MANISTEE (49660) Manistee(96),
   Mason(3)
MANISTIQUE (49854) Schoolcraft(98),
   Delta(1)
MANITOU BEACH Lenawee
MANTON (49663) Wexford(79),
   Missaukee(20)
MAPLE CITY Leelanau
MAPLE RAPIDS Clinton
MARCELLUS (49067) Cass(63), St.
   Joseph(24), Van Buren(12)
MARENISCO (49947) Gogebic(64),
   Ontonagon(35)
MARINE CITY St. Clair
MARION (49665) Osceola(83), Clare(11),
   Missaukee(4)
MARLETTE (48453) Sanilac(95),
   Tuscola(4)
MARNE (49435) Ottawa(96), Kent(3)
MARQUETTE Marquette
MARSHALL Calhoun
MARTIN Allegan
MARYSVILLE St. Clair
MASON Ingham
MASS CITY Ontonagon
MATTAWAN (49071) Van Buren(84),
   Kalamazoo(15)
MAYBEE Monroe
MAYFIELD Grand Traverse
MAYVILLE (48744) Tuscola(88),
   Lapeer(11)
MC BAIN Missaukee
MC MILLAN (49853) Luce(98), Mackinac(1)
MCBRIDES Montcalm
MEARS Oceana
MECOSTA Mecosta
MELVIN Sanilac
MELVINDALE Wayne
MEMPHIS (48041) St. Clair(74),
   Macomb(25)
MENDON St. Joseph
MENOMINEE Menominee
MERRILL (48637) Saginaw(72),
   Midland(14), Gratiot(12)
MERRITT Missaukee
MESICK (49668) Wexford(98), Manistee(1)
METAMORA Lapeer

MICHIGAMME (49861) Baraga(60),
   Marquette(40)
MICHIGAN CENTER Jackson
MIDDLETON Gratiot
MIDDLEVILLE (49333) Barry(97), Kent(2)
MIDLAND Midland
MIKADO (48745) Alcona(94), Iosco(5)
MILAN (48160) Monroe(96), Washtenaw(3)
MILFORD Oakland
MILLBROOK Mecosta
MILLERSBURG Presque Isle
MILLINGTON (48746) Tuscola(91),
   Genesee(8)
MINDEN CITY (48456) Sanilac(78),
   Huron(21)
MIO Oscoda
MOHAWK Keweenaw
MOLINE Allegan
MONROE Monroe
MONTAGUE (49437) Muskegon(85),
   Oceana(14)
MONTGOMERY (49255) Branch(96),
   Hillsdale(3)
MONTROSE (48457) Genesee(77),
   Saginaw(22)
MORAN Mackinac
MORENCI Lenawee
MORLEY (49336) Mecosta(91),
   Montcalm(8)
MORRICE Shiawassee
MOSCOW Hillsdale
MOSHERVILLE Hillsdale
MOUNT CLEMENS Macomb
MOUNT MORRIS Genesee
MOUNT PLEASANT Isabella
MUIR Ionia
MULLETT LAKE Cheboygan
MULLIKEN (48861) Eaton(89), Ionia(10)
MUNGER (48747) Bay(96), Saginaw(3)
MUNISING Alger
MUNITH Jackson
MUSKEGON Muskegon
NADEAU Menominee
NAHMA Delta
NAPOLEON Jackson
NASHVILLE (49073) Barry(90), Eaton(9)
NATIONAL CITY Iosco
NATIONAL MINE Marquette
NAUBINWAY Mackinac
NAZARETH Kalamazoo
NEGAUNEE Marquette
NEW BALTIMORE Macomb
NEW BOSTON Wayne
NEW BUFFALO Berrien
NEW ERA Oceana
NEW HAVEN Macomb
NEW HUDSON Oakland
NEW LOTHROP (48460) Shiawassee(60),
   Saginaw(37), Genesee(1)
NEW RICHMOND Allegan
NEW TROY Berrien
NEWAYGO (49337) Newaygo(96),
   Montcalm(2), Mecosta(1)
NEWBERRY Luce
NEWPORT Monroe
NILES Berrien
NISULA Houghton
NORTH ADAMS Hillsdale
NORTH BRANCH Lapeer
NORTH STAR Gratiot
NORTH STREET St. Clair
NORTHLAND Marquette
NORTHPORT Leelanau
NORTHVILLE (48167) Wayne(67),
   Oakland(28), Washtenaw(4)
NORVELL Jackson
NORWAY Dickinson
NOTTAWA St. Joseph
NOVI Oakland
NUNICA (49448) Ottawa(85),
   Muskegon(14)
OAK GROVE Livingston

OAK PARK Oakland
OAKLAND Oakland
OAKLEY (48649) Saginaw(94),
   Shiawassee(5)
ODEN Emmet
OKEMOS Ingham
OLD MISSION Grand Traverse
OLIVET (49076) Eaton(71), Calhoun(28)
OMENA Leelanau
OMER Arenac
ONAWAY (49765) Presque Isle(66),
   Cheboygan(33)
ONEKAMA Manistee
ONONDAGA (49264) Ingham(65),
   Jackson(30), Eaton(4)
ONSTED Lenawee
ONTONAGON Ontonagon
ORLEANS Ionia
ORTONVILLE (48462) Oakland(95),
   Lapeer(3), Genesee(1)
OSCODA Iosco
OSHTEMO Kalamazoo
OSSEO Hillsdale
OSSINEKE Alpena
OTISVILLE (48463) Genesee(98),
   Lapeer(1)
OTSEGO (49078) Allegan(92),
   Kalamazoo(5), Van Buren(2)
OTTAWA LAKE (49267) Monroe(89),
   Lenawee(10)
OTTER LAKE (48464) Lapeer(79),
   Genesee(11), Tuscola(9)
OVID (48866) Clinton(65), Shiawassee(34)
OWENDALE Huron
OWOSSO Shiawassee
OXFORD (48371) Oakland(93), Lapeer(6)
PAINESDALE Houghton
PALMER Marquette
PALMS Sanilac
PALMYRA Lenawee
PALO Ionia
PARADISE Chippewa
PARIS (49338) Mecosta(64), Newaygo(30),
   Osceola(4)
PARMA Jackson
PAW PAW Van Buren
PECK Sanilac
PELKIE (49958) Houghton(79), Baraga(20)
PELLSTON (49769) Emmet(85),
   Cheboygan(14)
PENTWATER (49449) Oceana(79),
   Mason(20)
PERKINS Delta
PERRINTON Gratiot
PERRONVILLE (49873) Menominee(87),
   Dickinson(12)
PERRY (48872) Shiawassee(91),
   Ingham(6), Livingston(1)
PETERSBURG Monroe
PETOSKEY Emmet
PEWAMO (48873) Ionia(72), Clinton(27)
PICKFORD (49774) Chippewa(90),
   Mackinac(9)
PIERSON Montcalm
PIGEON Huron
PINCKNEY Livingston
PINCONNING (48650) Bay(95), Arenac(4)
PITTSFORD Hillsdale
PLAINWELL (49080) Allegan(68),
   Barry(21), Kalamazoo(10)
PLEASANT LAKE Jackson
PLEASANT RIDGE Oakland
PLYMOUTH (48170) Wayne(95),
   Washtenaw(4)
POINTE AUX PINS Mackinac
POMPEII Gratiot
PONTIAC Oakland
PORT AUSTIN Huron
PORT HOPE Huron
PORT HURON St. Clair
PORT SANILAC Sanilac
PORTAGE Kalamazoo

PORTLAND (48875) Ionia(93), Clinton(6)
POSEN (49776) Presque Isle(73),
   Alpena(26)
POTTERVILLE Eaton
POWERS Menominee
PRATTVILLE Hillsdale
PRESCOTT Ogemaw
PRESQUE ISLE Presque Isle
PRUDENVILLE Roscommon
PULLMAN Allegan
QUINCY (49082) Branch(92), Hillsdale(7)
QUINNESEC Dickinson
RALPH Dickinson
RAMSAY Gogebic
RAPID CITY (49676) Kalkaska(60),
   Antrim(39)
RAPID RIVER (49878) Delta(91), Alger(8)
RAVENNA (49451) Muskegon(96),
   Ottawa(3)
RAY Macomb
READING Hillsdale
REDFORD Wayne
REED CITY (49677) Osceola(82),
   Lake(14), Newaygo(2)
REESE (48757) Tuscola(67), Saginaw(28),
   Bay(3)
REMUS (49340) Mecosta(66), Isabella(33)
REPUBLIC Marquette
RHODES (48652) Gladwin(59), Bay(23),
   Midland(16)
RICHLAND Kalamazoo
RICHMOND Macomb
RICHVILLE Tuscola
RIDGEWAY Lenawee
RIGA (49276) Lenawee(70), Monroe(29)
RIVER ROUGE Wayne
RIVERDALE (48877) Gratiot(57),
   Montcalm(32), Isabella(9)
RIVERSIDE Berrien
RIVES JUNCTION Jackson
ROCHESTER Oakland
ROCK (49880) Delta(68), Marquette(31)
ROCKFORD Kent
ROCKLAND Ontonagon
ROCKWOOD Wayne
RODNEY Mecosta
ROGERS CITY Presque Isle
ROLLIN Lenawee
ROMEO Macomb
ROMULUS Wayne
ROSCOMMON (48653) Roscommon(79),
   Crawford(20)
ROSE CITY (48654) Ogemaw(81),
   Oscoda(18)
ROSEBUSH Isabella
ROSEVILLE Macomb
ROTHBURY Oceana
ROYAL OAK Oakland
RUDYARD (49780) Chippewa(94),
   Mackinac(5)
RUMELY Alger
RUTH (48470) Huron(97), Sanilac(2)
SAGINAW Saginaw
SAGOLA Dickinson
SAINT CHARLES Saginaw
SAINT CLAIR St. Clair
SAINT CLAIR SHORES Macomb
SAINT HELEN Roscommon
SAINT IGNACE Mackinac
SAINT JOHNS Clinton
SAINT JOSEPH Berrien
SAINT LOUIS (48880) Gratiot(92),
   Midland(7)
SALEM Washtenaw
SALINE Washtenaw
SAMARIA Monroe
SAND CREEK Lenawee
SAND LAKE (49343) Kent(60),
   Newaygo(23), Montcalm(16)
SANDUSKY Sanilac
SANFORD Midland
SARANAC Ionia

SAUGATUCK Allegan
SAULT SAINTE MARIE Chippewa
SAWYER Berrien
SCHOOLCRAFT (49087) Kalamazoo(96), Van Buren(2)
SCOTTS Kalamazoo
SCOTTVILLE Mason
SEARS Osceola
SEBEWAING (48759) Huron(98), Tuscola(1)
SENECA Lenawee
SENEY (49883) Schoolcraft(53), Alger(46)
SHAFTSBURG Shiawassee
SHELBY Oceana
SHELBYVILLE (49344) Barry(50), Allegan(49)
SHEPHERD (48883) Isabella(74), Midland(24), Gratiot(1)
SHERIDAN Montcalm
SHERWOOD Branch
SHINGLETON (49884) Alger(97), Schoolcraft(2)
SIDNAW Houghton
SIDNEY Montcalm
SILVERWOOD (48760) Tuscola(62), Lapeer(37)
SIX LAKES (48886) Montcalm(97), Mecosta(2)
SKANDIA (49885) Marquette(78), Alger(21)
SKANEE Baraga
SMITHS CREEK St. Clair
SMYRNA Ionia
SNOVER Sanilac
SODUS Berrien
SOMERSET Hillsdale
SOMERSET CENTER Hillsdale
SOUTH BOARDMAN Kalkaska
SOUTH BRANCH (48761) Iosco(43), Ogemaw(27), Alcona(27), Oscoda(2)
SOUTH HAVEN (49090) Van Buren(95), Allegan(4)
SOUTH LYON (48178) Oakland(67), Livingston(20), Washtenaw(12)
SOUTH RANGE Houghton
SOUTH ROCKWOOD Monroe
SOUTHFIELD Oakland

SOUTHGATE Wayne
SPALDING Menominee
SPARTA Kent
SPRING ARBOR Jackson
SPRING LAKE (49456) Ottawa(95), Muskegon(4)
SPRINGPORT (49284) Jackson(60), Calhoun(29), Eaton(9)
SPRUCE (48762) Alcona(87), Alpena(12)
STALWART Chippewa
STAMBAUGH Iron
STANDISH (48658) Arenac(95), Bay(4)
STANTON Montcalm
STANWOOD Mecosta
STEPHENSON Menominee
STERLING (48659) Arenac(96), Bay(3)
STERLING HEIGHTS Macomb
STEVENSVILLE Berrien
STOCKBRIDGE (49285) Ingham(86), Jackson(5), Livingston(4), Washtenaw(3)
STRONGS Chippewa
STURGIS St. Joseph
SUMNER (48889) Gratiot(98), Montcalm(1)
SUNFIELD (48890) Eaton(63), Ionia(36)
SUTTONS BAY Leelanau
SWARTZ CREEK Genesee
TAWAS CITY Iosco
TAYLOR Wayne
TECUMSEH Lenawee
TEKONSHA (49092) Calhoun(81), Branch(18)
TEMPERANCE Monroe
THOMPSONVILLE (49683) Benzie(61), Manistee(31), Grand Traverse(6)
THREE OAKS Berrien
THREE RIVERS St. Joseph
TIPTON Lenawee
TOIVOLA (49965) Houghton(94), Ontonagon(5)
TOPINABEE Cheboygan
TOWER Cheboygan
TRAUNIK Alger
TRAVERSE CITY Grand Traverse
TRENARY Alger
TRENTON Wayne

TROUT CREEK (49967) Ontonagon(58), Houghton(34), Iron(6)
TROUT LAKE Chippewa
TROY Oakland
TRUFANT (49347) Montcalm(94), Kent(5)
TURNER (48765) Arenac(67), Iosco(32)
TUSCOLA Tuscola
TUSTIN (49688) Osceola(91), Lake(5), Wexford(2)
TWIN LAKE Muskegon
TWINING (48766) Arenac(96), Iosco(3)
UBLY (48475) Huron(61), Sanilac(38)
UNION Cass
UNION CITY (49094) Branch(97), Calhoun(2)
UNION LAKE Oakland
UNION PIER Berrien
UNIONVILLE (48767) Tuscola(97), Huron(2)
UNIVERSITY CENTER Bay
UTICA Macomb
VANDALIA Cass
VANDERBILT (49795) Otsego(80), Cheboygan(16), Charlevoix(2)
VASSAR Tuscola
VERMONTVILLE Eaton
VERNON Shiawassee
VESTABURG Montcalm
VICKSBURG (49097) Kalamazoo(97), St. Joseph(2)
VULCAN (49892) Dickinson(76), Menominee(23)
WABANINGO Muskegon
WAKEFIELD Gogebic
WALDRON Hillsdale
WALHALLA Mason
WALKERVILLE (49459) Oceana(90), Newaygo(9)
WALLACE Menominee
WALLED LAKE Oakland
WALLOON LAKE Charlevoix
WARREN Macomb
WASHINGTON Macomb
WATERFORD Oakland
WATERS Otsego
WATERSMEET Gogebic

WATERVLIET (49098) Berrien(90), Van Buren(9)
WATTON Baraga
WAYLAND (49348) Allegan(79), Barry(20)
WAYNE Wayne
WEBBERVILLE (48892) Ingham(77), Livingston(22)
WEIDMAN Isabella
WELLS Delta
WELLSTON (49689) Manistee(85), Wexford(14)
WEST BLOOMFIELD Oakland
WEST BRANCH Ogemaw
WEST OLIVE Ottawa
WESTLAND Wayne
WESTON Lenawee
WESTPHALIA Clinton
WETMORE (49895) Alger(70), Delta(24), Schoolcraft(5)
WHEELER (48662) Gratiot(86), Midland(13)
WHITE CLOUD Newaygo
WHITE LAKE Oakland
WHITE PIGEON (49099) St. Joseph(87), Cass(12)
WHITE PINE Ontonagon
WHITEHALL Muskegon
WHITMORE LAKE (48189) Washtenaw(56), Livingston(43)
WHITTAKER Washtenaw
WHITTEMORE (48770) Iosco(96), Arenac(2), Ogemaw(1)
WILLIAMSBURG (49690) Grand Traverse(89), Antrim(5), Kalkaska(4)
WILLIAMSTON Ingham
WILLIS Washtenaw
WILSON Menominee
WINN Isabella
WIXOM Oakland
WOLVERINE Cheboygan
WOODLAND Barry
WYANDOTTE Wayne
YALE (48097) St. Clair(82), Sanilac(17)
YPSILANTI Washtenaw
ZEELAND Ottawa

ZIP/City Cross Reference

ZIP Range	City		ZIP Range	City		ZIP Range	City		ZIP Range	City
48001-48001	ALGONAC		48046-48046	MOUNT CLEMENS		48098-48099	TROY		48146-48146	LINCOLN PARK
48002-48002	ALLENTON		48047-48047	NEW BALTIMORE		48101-48101	ALLEN PARK		48150-48154	LIVONIA
48003-48003	ALMONT		48048-48048	NEW HAVEN		48103-48109	ANN ARBOR		48157-48157	LUNA PIER
48004-48004	ANCHORVILLE		48049-48049	NORTH STREET		48110-48110	AZALIA		48158-48158	MANCHESTER
48005-48005	ARMADA		48050-48050	NEW HAVEN		48111-48112	BELLEVILLE		48159-48159	MAYBEE
48006-48006	AVOCA		48051-48051	NEW BALTIMORE		48113-48113	ANN ARBOR		48160-48160	MILAN
48007-48007	TROY		48052-48052	ALGONAC		48114-48114	BRIGHTON		48161-48162	MONROE
48009-48012	BIRMINGHAM		48054-48054	EAST CHINA		48115-48115	BRIDGEWATER		48164-48164	NEW BOSTON
48014-48014	CAPAC		48059-48059	FORT GRATIOT		48116-48116	BRIGHTON		48165-48165	NEW HUDSON
48015-48015	CENTER LINE		48060-48061	PORT HURON		48117-48117	CARLETON		48166-48166	NEWPORT
48017-48017	CLAWSON		48062-48062	RICHMOND		48118-48118	CHELSEA		48167-48167	NORTHVILLE
48021-48021	EASTPOINTE		48063-48063	COLUMBUS		48120-48121	DEARBORN		48169-48169	PINCKNEY
48022-48022	EMMETT		48064-48064	CASCO		48122-48122	MELVINDALE		48170-48170	PLYMOUTH
48023-48023	FAIR HAVEN		48065-48065	ROMEO		48123-48124	DEARBORN		48173-48173	ROCKWOOD
48025-48025	FRANKLIN		48066-48066	ROSEVILLE		48125-48125	DEARBORN HEIGHTS		48174-48174	ROMULUS
48026-48026	FRASER		48067-48068	ROYAL OAK		48126-48126	DEARBORN		48175-48175	SALEM
48027-48027	GOODELLS		48069-48069	PLEASANT RIDGE		48127-48127	DEARBORN HEIGHTS		48176-48176	SALINE
48028-48028	HARSENS ISLAND		48070-48070	HUNTINGTON WOODS		48128-48128	DEARBORN		48177-48177	SAMARIA
48030-48030	HAZEL PARK		48071-48071	MADISON HEIGHTS		48130-48130	DEXTER		48178-48178	SOUTH LYON
48032-48032	JEDDO		48072-48072	BERKLEY		48131-48131	DUNDEE		48179-48179	SOUTH ROCKWOOD
48034-48034	SOUTHFIELD		48073-48073	ROYAL OAK		48133-48133	ERIE		48180-48180	TAYLOR
48035-48036	CLINTON TOWNSHIP		48074-48074	SMITHS CREEK		48134-48134	FLAT ROCK		48182-48182	TEMPERANCE
48037-48037	SOUTHFIELD		48075-48076	SOUTHFIELD		48135-48136	GARDEN CITY		48183-48183	TRENTON
48038-48038	CLINTON TOWNSHIP		48079-48079	SAINT CLAIR		48137-48137	GREGORY		48184-48184	WAYNE
48039-48039	MARINE CITY		48080-48082	SAINT CLAIR SHORES		48138-48138	GROSSE ILE		48185-48186	WESTLAND
48040-48040	MARYSVILLE		48083-48085	TROY		48139-48139	HAMBURG		48188-48188	CANTON
48041-48041	MEMPHIS		48086-48086	SOUTHFIELD		48140-48140	IDA		48189-48189	WHITMORE LAKE
48042-48042	MACOMB		48088-48093	WARREN		48141-48141	INKSTER		48190-48190	WHITTAKER
48043-48043	MOUNT CLEMENS		48094-48095	WASHINGTON		48143-48143	LAKELAND		48191-48191	WILLIS
48044-48044	MACOMB		48096-48096	RAY		48144-48144	LAMBERTVILLE		48192-48192	WYANDOTTE
48045-48045	HARRISON TOWNSHIP		48097-48097	YALE		48145-48145	LA SALLE		48195-48195	SOUTHGATE

48197-48198 YPSILANTI	48445-48445 KINDE	48720-48720 BAY PORT	48845-48845 HUBBARDSTON
48200-48202 DETROIT	48446-48446 LAPEER	48721-48721 BLACK RIVER	48846-48846 IONIA
48203-48203 HIGHLAND PARK	48449-48449 LENNON	48722-48722 BRIDGEPORT	48847-48847 ITHACA
48204-48211 DETROIT	48450-48450 LEXINGTON	48723-48723 CARO	48848-48848 LAINGSBURG
48212-48212 HAMTRAMCK	48451-48451 LINDEN	48724-48724 CARROLLTON	48849-48849 LAKE ODESSA
48213-48217 DETROIT	48452-48452 ATTICA	48725-48725 CASEVILLE	48850-48850 LAKEVIEW
48218-48218 RIVER ROUGE	48453-48453 MARLETTE	48726-48726 CASS CITY	48851-48851 LYONS
48219-48219 DETROIT	48454-48454 MELVIN	48727-48727 CLIFFORD	48852-48852 MCBRIDES
48220-48220 FERNDALE	48455-48455 METAMORA	48728-48728 CURRAN	48853-48853 MAPLE RAPIDS
48221-48224 DETROIT	48456-48456 MINDEN CITY	48729-48729 DEFORD	48854-48854 MASON
48225-48225 HARPER WOODS	48457-48457 MONTROSE	48730-48730 EAST TAWAS	48856-48856 MIDDLETON
48226-48228 DETROIT	48458-48458 MOUNT MORRIS	48731-48731 ELKTON	48857-48857 MORRICE
48229-48229 ECORSE	48460-48460 NEW LOTHROP	48732-48732 ESSEXVILLE	48858-48859 MOUNT PLEASANT
48230-48230 GROSSE POINTE	48461-48461 NORTH BRANCH	48733-48733 FAIRGROVE	48860-48860 MUIR
48231-48235 DETROIT	48462-48462 ORTONVILLE	48734-48734 FRANKENMUTH	48861-48861 MULLIKEN
48236-48236 GROSSE POINTE	48463-48463 OTISVILLE	48735-48735 GAGETOWN	48862-48862 NORTH STAR
48237-48237 OAK PARK	48464-48464 OTTER LAKE	48736-48736 GILFORD	48863-48863 OAK GROVE
48238-48238 DETROIT	48465-48465 PALMS	48737-48737 GLENNIE	48864-48864 OKEMOS
48239-48240 REDFORD	48466-48466 PECK	48738-48738 GREENBUSH	48865-48865 ORLEANS
48242-48299 DETROIT	48467-48467 PORT AUSTIN	48739-48739 HALE	48866-48866 OVID
48301-48304 BLOOMFIELD HILLS	48468-48468 PORT HOPE	48740-48740 HARRISVILLE	48867-48867 OWOSSO
48306-48309 ROCHESTER	48469-48469 PORT SANILAC	48741-48741 KINGSTON	48870-48870 PALO
48310-48314 STERLING HEIGHTS	48470-48470 RUTH	48742-48742 LINCOLN	48871-48871 PERRINTON
48315-48318 UTICA	48471-48471 SANDUSKY	48743-48743 LONG LAKE	48872-48872 PERRY
48320-48320 KEEGO HARBOR	48472-48472 SNOVER	48744-48744 MAYVILLE	48873-48873 PEWAMO
48321-48321 AUBURN HILLS	48473-48473 SWARTZ CREEK	48745-48745 MIKADO	48874-48874 POMPEII
48322-48325 WEST BLOOMFIELD	48475-48475 UBLY	48746-48746 MILLINGTON	48875-48875 PORTLAND
48326-48326 AUBURN HILLS	48476-48476 VERNON	48747-48747 MUNGER	48876-48876 POTTERVILLE
48327-48329 WATERFORD	48500-48507 FLINT	48748-48748 NATIONAL CITY	48877-48877 RIVERDALE
48330-48330 DRAYTON PLAINS	48509-48529 BURTON	48749-48749 OMER	48878-48878 ROSEBUSH
48331-48336 FARMINGTON	48531-48559 FLINT	48750-48753 OSCODA	48879-48879 SAINT JOHNS
48340-48343 PONTIAC	48601-48609 SAGINAW	48754-48754 OWENDALE	48880-48880 SAINT LOUIS
48346-48348 CLARKSTON	48610-48610 ALGER	48755-48755 PIGEON	48881-48881 SARANAC
48350-48350 DAVISBURG	48611-48611 AUBURN	48756-48756 PRESCOTT	48882-48882 SHAFTSBURG
48353-48353 HARTLAND	48612-48612 BEAVERTON	48757-48757 REESE	48883-48883 SHEPHERD
48356-48357 HIGHLAND	48613-48613 BENTLEY	48758-48758 RICHVILLE	48884-48884 SHERIDAN
48359-48362 LAKE ORION	48614-48614 BRANT	48759-48759 SEBEWAING	48885-48885 SIDNEY
48363-48363 OAKLAND	48615-48615 BRECKENRIDGE	48760-48760 SILVERWOOD	48886-48886 SIX LAKES
48366-48366 LAKEVILLE	48616-48616 CHESANING	48761-48761 SOUTH BRANCH	48887-48887 SMYRNA
48367-48367 LEONARD	48617-48617 CLARE	48762-48762 SPRUCE	48888-48888 STANTON
48370-48371 OXFORD	48618-48618 COLEMAN	48763-48764 TAWAS CITY	48889-48889 SUMNER
48374-48374 NOVI	48619-48619 COMINS	48765-48765 TURNER	48890-48890 SUNFIELD
48380-48381 MILFORD	48620-48620 EDENVILLE	48766-48766 TWINING	48891-48891 VESTABURG
48382-48382 COMMERCE TOWNSHIP	48621-48621 FAIRVIEW	48767-48767 UNIONVILLE	48892-48892 WEBBERVILLE
48383-48386 WHITE LAKE	48622-48622 FARWELL	48768-48768 VASSAR	48893-48893 WEIDMAN
48387-48387 UNION LAKE	48623-48623 FREELAND	48769-48769 TUSCOLA	48894-48894 WESTPHALIA
48390-48391 WALLED LAKE	48624-48624 GLADWIN	48770-48770 WHITTEMORE	48895-48895 WILLIAMSTON
48393-48393 WIXOM	48625-48625 HARRISON	48787-48787 FRANKENMUTH	48896-48896 WINN
48397-48397 WARREN	48626-48626 HEMLOCK	48801-48802 ALMA	48897-48897 WOODLAND
48398-48398 CLAWSON	48627-48627 HIGGINS LAKE	48804-48804 MOUNT PLEASANT	48900-48980 LANSING
48401-48401 APPLEGATE	48628-48628 HOPE	48805-48805 OKEMOS	49001-49001 KALAMAZOO
48410-48410 ARGYLE	48629-48629 HOUGHTON LAKE	48806-48806 ASHLEY	49002-49002 PORTAGE
48411-48411 ATLAS	48630-48630 HOUGHTON LAKE HEIGHTS	48807-48807 BANNISTER	49003-49009 KALAMAZOO
48412-48412 ATTICA	48631-48631 KAWKAWLIN	48808-48808 BATH	49010-49010 ALLEGAN
48413-48413 BAD AXE	48632-48632 LAKE	48809-48809 BELDING	49011-49011 ATHENS
48414-48414 BANCROFT	48633-48633 LAKE GEORGE	48811-48811 CARSON CITY	49012-49012 AUGUSTA
48415-48415 BIRCH RUN	48634-48634 LINWOOD	48812-48812 CEDAR LAKE	49013-49013 BANGOR
48416-48416 BROWN CITY	48635-48635 LUPTON	48813-48813 CHARLOTTE	49014-49018 BATTLE CREEK
48417-48417 BURT	48636-48636 LUZERNE	48815-48815 CLARKSVILLE	49019-49019 KALAMAZOO
48418-48418 BYRON	48637-48637 MERRILL	48816-48816 COHOCTAH	49020-49020 BEDFORD
48419-48419 CARSONVILLE	48640-48642 MIDLAND	48817-48817 CORUNNA	49021-49021 BELLEVUE
48420-48420 CLIO	48647-48647 MIO	48818-48818 CRYSTAL	49022-49023 BENTON HARBOR
48421-48421 COLUMBIAVILLE	48649-48649 OAKLEY	48819-48819 DANSVILLE	49024-49024 PORTAGE
48422-48422 CROSWELL	48650-48650 PINCONNING	48820-48820 DEWITT	49026-49026 BLOOMINGDALE
48423-48423 DAVISON	48651-48651 PRUDENVILLE	48821-48821 DIMONDALE	49027-49027 BREEDSVILLE
48426-48426 DECKER	48652-48652 RHODES	48822-48822 EAGLE	49028-49028 BRONSON
48427-48427 DECKERVILLE	48653-48653 ROSCOMMON	48823-48826 EAST LANSING	49029-49029 BURLINGTON
48428-48428 DRYDEN	48654-48654 ROSE CITY	48827-48827 EATON RAPIDS	49030-49030 BURR OAK
48429-48429 DURAND	48655-48655 SAINT CHARLES	48829-48829 EDMORE	49031-49031 CASSOPOLIS
48430-48430 FENTON	48656-48656 SAINT HELEN	48830-48830 ELM HALL	49032-49032 CENTREVILLE
48432-48432 FILION	48657-48657 SANFORD	48831-48831 ELSIE	49033-49033 CERESCO
48433-48433 FLUSHING	48658-48658 STANDISH	48832-48832 ELWELL	49034-49034 CLIMAX
48434-48434 FORESTVILLE	48659-48659 STERLING	48833-48833 EUREKA	49035-49035 CLOVERDALE
48435-48435 FOSTORIA	48661-48661 WEST BRANCH	48834-48834 FENWICK	49036-49036 COLDWATER
48436-48436 GAINES	48662-48662 WHEELER	48835-48835 FOWLER	49038-49038 COLOMA
48437-48437 GENESEE	48663-48663 SAGINAW	48836-48836 FOWLERVILLE	49039-49039 HAGAR SHORES
48438-48438 GOODRICH	48667-48686 MIDLAND	48837-48837 GRAND LEDGE	49040-49040 COLON
48439-48439 GRAND BLANC	48701-48701 AKRON	48838-48838 GREENVILLE	49041-49041 COMSTOCK
48440-48440 HADLEY	48703-48703 AU GRES	48840-48840 HASLETT	49042-49042 CONSTANTINE
48441-48441 HARBOR BEACH	48705-48705 BARTON CITY	48841-48841 HENDERSON	49043-49043 COVERT
48442-48442 HOLLY	48706-48708 BAY CITY	48842-48842 HOLT	49045-49045 DECATUR
48444-48444 IMLAY CITY	48710-48710 UNIVERSITY CENTER	48843-48844 HOWELL	49046-49046 DELTON

Zip Range	City	Zip Range	City	Zip Range	City	Zip Range	City
49047-49047	DOWAGIAC	49238-49238	DEERFIELD	49336-49336	MORLEY	49626-49626	EASTLAKE
49048-49048	KALAMAZOO	49239-49239	FRONTIER	49337-49337	NEWAYGO	49627-49627	EASTPORT
49050-49050	DOWLING	49240-49240	GRASS LAKE	49338-49338	PARIS	49628-49628	ELBERTA
49051-49051	EAST LEROY	49241-49241	HANOVER	49339-49339	PIERSON	49629-49629	ELK RAPIDS
49052-49052	FULTON	49242-49242	HILLSDALE	49340-49340	REMUS	49630-49630	EMPIRE
49053-49053	GALESBURG	49245-49245	HOMER	49341-49341	ROCKFORD	49631-49631	EVART
49055-49055	GOBLES	49246-49246	HORTON	49342-49342	RODNEY	49632-49632	FALMOUTH
49056-49056	GRAND JUNCTION	49247-49247	HUDSON	49343-49343	SAND LAKE	49633-49633	FIFE LAKE
49057-49057	HARTFORD	49248-49248	JASPER	49344-49344	SHELBYVILLE	49634-49634	FILER CITY
49058-49058	HASTINGS	49249-49249	JEROME	49345-49345	SPARTA	49635-49635	FRANKFORT
49060-49060	HICKORY CORNERS	49250-49250	JONESVILLE	49346-49346	STANWOOD	49636-49636	GLEN ARBOR
49061-49061	JONES	49251-49251	LESLIE	49347-49347	TRUFANT	49637-49637	GRAWN
49062-49062	KENDALL	49252-49252	LITCHFIELD	49348-49348	WAYLAND	49638-49638	HARRIETTA
49063-49063	LACOTA	49253-49253	MANITOU BEACH	49349-49349	WHITE CLOUD	49639-49639	HERSEY
49064-49064	LAWRENCE	49254-49254	MICHIGAN CENTER	49351-49351	ROCKFORD	49640-49640	HONOR
49065-49065	LAWTON	49255-49255	MONTGOMERY	49355-49357	ADA	49642-49642	IDLEWILD
49066-49066	LEONIDAS	49256-49256	MORENCI	49401-49401	ALLENDALE	49643-49643	INTERLOCHEN
49067-49067	MARCELLUS	49257-49257	MOSCOW	49402-49402	BRANCH	49644-49644	IRONS
49068-49069	MARSHALL	49258-49258	MOSHERVILLE	49403-49403	CONKLIN	49645-49645	KALEVA
49070-49070	MARTIN	49259-49259	MUNITH	49404-49404	COOPERSVILLE	49646-49646	KALKASKA
49071-49071	MATTAWAN	49261-49261	NAPOLEON	49405-49405	CUSTER	49647-49647	KARLIN
49072-49072	MENDON	49262-49262	NORTH ADAMS	49406-49406	DOUGLAS	49648-49648	KEWADIN
49073-49073	NASHVILLE	49263-49263	NORVELL	49408-49408	FENNVILLE	49649-49649	KINGSLEY
49074-49074	NAZARETH	49264-49264	ONONDAGA	49409-49409	FERRYSBURG	49650-49650	LAKE ANN
49075-49075	NOTTAWA	49265-49265	ONSTED	49410-49410	FOUNTAIN	49651-49651	LAKE CITY
49076-49076	OLIVET	49266-49266	OSSEO	49411-49411	FREE SOIL	49653-49653	LAKE LEELANAU
49077-49077	OSHTEMO	49267-49267	OTTAWA LAKE	49412-49413	FREMONT	49654-49654	LELAND
49078-49078	OTSEGO	49268-49268	PALMYRA	49415-49415	FRUITPORT	49655-49655	LEROY
49079-49079	PAW PAW	49269-49269	PARMA	49416-49416	GLENN	49656-49656	LUTHER
49080-49080	PLAINWELL	49270-49270	PETERSBURG	49417-49417	GRAND HAVEN	49657-49657	MC BAIN
49081-49081	PORTAGE	49271-49271	PITTSFORD	49418-49418	GRANDVILLE	49659-49659	MANCELONA
49082-49082	QUINCY	49272-49272	PLEASANT LAKE	49419-49419	HAMILTON	49660-49660	MANISTEE
49083-49083	RICHLAND	49273-49273	PRATTVILLE	49420-49420	HART	49663-49663	MANTON
49084-49084	RIVERSIDE	49274-49274	READING	49421-49421	HESPERIA	49664-49664	MAPLE CITY
49085-49085	SAINT JOSEPH	49275-49275	RIDGEWAY	49422-49424	HOLLAND	49665-49665	MARION
49087-49087	SCHOOLCRAFT	49276-49276	RIGA	49425-49425	HOLTON	49666-49666	MAYFIELD
49088-49088	SCOTTS	49277-49277	RIVES JUNCTION	49426-49426	HUDSONVILLE	49667-49667	MERRITT
49089-49089	SHERWOOD	49278-49278	ROLLIN	49427-49427	JAMESTOWN	49668-49668	MESICK
49090-49090	SOUTH HAVEN	49279-49279	SAND CREEK	49428-49429	JENISON	49670-49670	NORTHPORT
49091-49091	STURGIS	49280-49280	SENECA	49430-49430	LAMONT	49673-49673	OLD MISSION
49092-49092	TEKONSHA	49281-49281	SOMERSET	49431-49431	LUDINGTON	49674-49674	OMENA
49093-49093	THREE RIVERS	49282-49282	SOMERSET CENTER	49434-49434	MACATAWA	49675-49675	ONEKAMA
49094-49094	UNION CITY	49283-49283	SPRING ARBOR	49435-49435	MARNE	49676-49676	RAPID CITY
49095-49095	VANDALIA	49284-49284	SPRINGPORT	49436-49436	MEARS	49677-49677	REED CITY
49096-49096	VERMONTVILLE	49285-49285	STOCKBRIDGE	49437-49437	MONTAGUE	49679-49679	SEARS
49097-49097	VICKSBURG	49286-49286	TECUMSEH	49440-49445	MUSKEGON	49680-49680	SOUTH BOARDMAN
49098-49098	WATERVLIET	49287-49287	TIPTON	49446-49446	NEW ERA	49682-49682	SUTTONS BAY
49099-49099	WHITE PIGEON	49288-49288	WALDRON	49447-49447	NEW RICHMOND	49683-49683	THOMPSONVILLE
49101-49101	BARODA	49289-49289	WESTON	49448-49448	NUNICA	49684-49686	TRAVERSE CITY
49102-49102	BERRIEN CENTER	49301-49301	ADA	49449-49449	PENTWATER	49688-49688	TUSTIN
49103-49104	BERRIEN SPRINGS	49302-49302	ALTO	49450-49450	PULLMAN	49689-49689	WELLSTON
49106-49106	BRIDGMAN	49303-49303	BAILEY	49451-49451	RAVENNA	49690-49690	WILLIAMSBURG
49107-49107	BUCHANAN	49304-49304	BALDWIN	49452-49452	ROTHBURY	49696-49696	TRAVERSE CITY
49111-49111	EAU CLAIRE	49305-49305	BARRYTON	49453-49453	SAUGATUCK	49701-49701	MACKINAW CITY
49112-49112	EDWARDSBURG	49306-49306	BELMONT	49454-49454	SCOTTVILLE	49705-49705	AFTON
49113-49113	GALIEN	49307-49307	BIG RAPIDS	49455-49455	SHELBY	49706-49706	ALANSON
49115-49115	HARBERT	49309-49309	BITELY	49456-49456	SPRING LAKE	49707-49707	ALPENA
49116-49116	LAKESIDE	49310-49310	BLANCHARD	49457-49457	TWIN LAKE	49709-49709	ATLANTA
49117-49117	NEW BUFFALO	49311-49311	BRADLEY	49458-49458	WALHALLA	49710-49710	BARBEAU
49119-49119	NEW TROY	49312-49312	BROHMAN	49459-49459	WALKERVILLE	49711-49711	BAY SHORE
49120-49121	NILES	49313-49313	BRUNSWICK	49460-49460	WEST OLIVE	49712-49712	BOYNE CITY
49125-49125	SAWYER	49314-49314	BURNIPS	49461-49461	WHITEHALL	49713-49713	BOYNE FALLS
49126-49126	SODUS	49315-49315	BYRON CENTER	49463-49463	WABANINGO	49715-49715	BRIMLEY
49127-49127	STEVENSVILLE	49316-49316	CALEDONIA	49464-49464	ZEELAND	49716-49716	BRUTUS
49128-49128	THREE OAKS	49317-49317	CANNONSBURG	49468-49468	GRANDVILLE	49717-49717	BURT LAKE
49129-49129	UNION PIER	49318-49318	CASNOVIA	49500-49599	GRAND RAPIDS	49718-49718	CARP LAKE
49130-49130	UNION	49319-49319	CEDAR SPRINGS	49601-49601	CADILLAC	49719-49719	CEDARVILLE
49201-49204	JACKSON	49320-49320	CHIPPEWA LAKE	49610-49610	ACME	49720-49720	CHARLEVOIX
49220-49220	ADDISON	49321-49321	COMSTOCK PARK	49611-49611	ALBA	49721-49721	CHEBOYGAN
49221-49221	ADRIAN	49322-49322	CORAL	49612-49612	ALDEN	49722-49722	CONWAY
49224-49224	ALBION	49323-49323	DORR	49613-49613	ARCADIA	49723-49723	CROSS VILLAGE
49227-49227	ALLEN	49325-49325	FREEPORT	49614-49614	BEAR LAKE	49724-49724	DAFTER
49228-49228	BLISSFIELD	49326-49326	GOWEN	49615-49615	BELLAIRE	49725-49725	DE TOUR VILLAGE
49229-49229	BRITTON	49327-49327	GRANT	49616-49616	BENZONIA	49726-49726	DRUMMOND ISLAND
49230-49230	BROOKLYN	49328-49328	HOPKINS	49617-49617	BEULAH	49727-49727	EAST JORDAN
49231-49231	CADMUS	49329-49329	HOWARD CITY	49618-49618	BOON	49728-49728	ECKERMAN
49232-49232	CAMDEN	49330-49330	KENT CITY	49619-49619	BRETHREN	49729-49729	ELLSWORTH
49233-49233	CEMENT CITY	49331-49331	LOWELL	49620-49620	BUCKLEY	49730-49730	ELMIRA
49234-49234	CLARKLAKE	49332-49332	MECOSTA	49621-49621	CEDAR	49733-49733	FREDERIC
49235-49235	CLAYTON	49333-49333	MIDDLEVILLE	49622-49622	CENTRAL LAKE	49734-49735	GAYLORD
49236-49236	CLINTON	49334-49334	MILLBROOK	49623-49623	CHASE	49736-49736	GOETZVILLE
49237-49237	CONCORD	49335-49335	MOLINE	49625-49625	COPEMISH	49737-49737	GOOD HART

49738-49739	GRAYLING
49740-49740	HARBOR SPRINGS
49743-49743	HAWKS
49744-49744	HERRON
49745-49745	HESSEL
49746-49746	HILLMAN
49747-49747	HUBBARD LAKE
49748-49748	HULBERT
49749-49749	INDIAN RIVER
49751-49751	JOHANNESBURG
49752-49752	KINROSS
49753-49753	LACHINE
49755-49755	LEVERING
49756-49756	LEWISTON
49757-49757	MACKINAC ISLAND
49759-49759	MILLERSBURG
49760-49760	MORAN
49761-49761	MULLETT LAKE
49762-49762	NAUBINWAY
49764-49764	ODEN
49765-49765	ONAWAY
49766-49766	OSSINEKE
49768-49768	PARADISE
49769-49769	PELLSTON
49770-49770	PETOSKEY
49774-49774	PICKFORD
49775-49775	POINTE AUX PINS
49776-49776	POSEN
49777-49777	PRESQUE ISLE
49778-49778	BRIMLEY
49779-49779	ROGERS CITY
49780-49780	RUDYARD
49781-49781	SAINT IGNACE
49782-49782	BEAVER ISLAND
49783-49783	SAULT SAINTE MARIE
49784-49788	KINCHELOE
49789-49789	STALWART
49790-49790	STRONGS
49791-49791	TOPINABEE
49792-49792	TOWER
49793-49793	TROUT LAKE
49795-49795	VANDERBILT
49796-49796	WALLOON LAKE
49797-49797	WATERS
49799-49799	WOLVERINE
49801-49801	IRON MOUNTAIN
49802-49802	KINGSFORD
49805-49805	ALLOUEZ
49806-49806	AU TRAIN
49807-49807	BARK RIVER
49808-49808	BIG BAY
49812-49812	CARNEY
49813-49813	CEDAR RIVER
49814-49814	CHAMPION
49815-49815	CHANNING
49816-49816	CHATHAM
49817-49817	COOKS
49818-49818	CORNELL
49819-49819	ARNOLD
49820-49820	CURTIS
49821-49821	DAGGETT
49822-49822	DEERTON
49825-49825	EBEN JUNCTION
49826-49826	RUMELY
49827-49827	ENGADINE
49829-49829	ESCANABA
49831-49831	FELCH
49833-49833	LITTLE LAKE
49834-49834	FOSTER CITY
49835-49835	GARDEN
49836-49836	GERMFASK
49837-49837	GLADSTONE
49838-49838	GOULD CITY
49839-49839	GRAND MARAIS
49840-49840	GULLIVER
49841-49843	GWINN
49845-49845	HARRIS
49847-49847	HERMANSVILLE
49848-49848	INGALLS
49849-49849	ISHPEMING
49852-49852	LORETTO
49853-49853	MC MILLAN
49854-49854	MANISTIQUE
49855-49855	MARQUETTE
49858-49858	MENOMINEE
49861-49861	MICHIGAMME
49862-49862	MUNISING
49863-49863	NADEAU
49864-49864	NAHMA
49865-49865	NATIONAL MINE
49866-49866	NEGAUNEE
49868-49868	NEWBERRY
49869-49869	NORTHLAND
49870-49870	NORWAY
49871-49871	PALMER
49872-49872	PERKINS
49873-49873	PERRONVILLE
49874-49874	POWERS
49876-49876	QUINNESEC
49877-49877	RALPH
49878-49878	RAPID RIVER
49879-49879	REPUBLIC
49880-49880	ROCK
49881-49881	SAGOLA
49883-49883	SENEY
49884-49884	SHINGLETON
49885-49885	SKANDIA
49886-49886	SPALDING
49887-49887	STEPHENSON
49890-49890	TRAUNIK
49891-49891	TRENARY
49892-49892	VULCAN
49893-49893	WALLACE
49894-49894	WELLS
49895-49895	WETMORE
49896-49896	WILSON
49901-49901	AHMEEK
49902-49902	ALPHA
49903-49903	AMASA
49905-49905	ATLANTIC MINE
49908-49908	BARAGA
49909-49909	IRON RIVER
49910-49910	BERGLAND
49911-49911	BESSEMER
49912-49912	BRUCE CROSSING
49913-49913	CALUMET
49915-49915	CASPIAN
49916-49916	CHASSELL
49917-49917	COPPER CITY
49918-49918	COPPER HARBOR
49919-49919	COVINGTON
49920-49920	CRYSTAL FALLS
49921-49921	DODGEVILLE
49922-49922	DOLLAR BAY
49924-49924	EAGLE RIVER
49925-49925	EWEN
49927-49927	GAASTRA
49929-49929	GREENLAND
49930-49930	HANCOCK
49931-49931	HOUGHTON
49934-49934	HUBBELL
49935-49935	IRON RIVER
49938-49938	IRONWOOD
49942-49942	KEARSARGE
49943-49943	KENTON
49945-49945	LAKE LINDEN
49946-49946	LANSE
49947-49947	MARENISCO
49948-49948	MASS CITY
49950-49950	MOHAWK
49952-49952	NISULA
49953-49953	ONTONAGON
49955-49955	PAINESDALE
49958-49958	PELKIE
49959-49959	RAMSAY
49960-49960	ROCKLAND
49961-49961	SIDNAW
49962-49962	SKANEE
49963-49963	SOUTH RANGE
49964-49964	STAMBAUGH
49965-49965	TOIVOLA
49967-49967	TROUT CREEK
49968-49968	WAKEFIELD
49969-49969	WATERSMEET
49970-49970	WATTON
49971-49971	WHITE PINE

Minnesota

General Help Numbers:

Governor's Office
130 State Capitol Bldg, 75 Constitution Ave 651-296-3391
St Paul, MN 55155   Fax 651-296-2089
www.governor.state.mn.us   7:30AM-5PM

Attorney General's Office
1400 NCL Tower   651-296-3353
445 Minnesota St   Fax 651-297-4193
St Paul, MN 55101   8AM-5PM
www.ag.state.mn.us

State Court Administrator
135 Minnesota Judicial Center, 25 Constitution Ave   651-296-2474
St Paul, MN 55155   Fax 651-297-5636
www.courts.state.mn.us   8AM-4:30PM

State Archives
Division of Library & Archives   651-296-6126
345 Kellogg Blvd West   Fax 651-297-7436
St Paul, MN 55102-1906   9AM-5PM M-SA;
www.mnhs.org   till 9PM TU

State Specifics:

Capital:	St. Paul
	Ramsey County
Time Zone:	CST
Number of Counties:	87
Population:	4,972,294
Web Site:	www.state.mn.us

State Agencies

Criminal Records

Bureau of Criminal Apprehension, Criminal Justice Information Systems, 1246 University Ave, St Paul, MN 55104; 651-642-0670, 8:15AM-4PM.

www.dps.state.mn.us/bca

Note: Search the Level 3 sexual offenders registry at www.doc.state.mn.us/level3/Search.asp

Indexing & Storage: Records are available from 1924. It takes 1 day before new records are available for inquiry. Records are indexed on inhouse computer, microfilm and digital disc. 72% of all arrests in database have final dispositions recorded, 63% for those arrests within last 5 years.

Searching: For most requesters, to obtain the entire adult history, including all arrests, you must have a notarized release form signed by person of record. To get a 15-year record of convictions only, a consent form is not required. Include the following in your request: name, date of birth, and sex. Fingerprint searches are not permitted.

However, 100% of records are fingerprint-supported. The following data is not released: juvenile records. With consent, all records, including those without dispositions, are released. If no consent, then only conviction records released. Targeted misdemeanors (violent, DV, DUI, etc., where a jail sentence may be imposed) are released; other misdemeanors are not.

Access by: mail, in person.

Fee & Payment: The fee for the full adult history is $15.00, for non-profits the fee is $8.00. The fee for the 15-year public record is $4.00. Non-profits have a reduced fee, call first. Fee payee: BCA. Prepayment required. Business checks, personal checks, money orders and certified funds are accepted. No credit cards accepted.

Mail search: Turnaround time: 1 to 2 weeks. A self addressed stamped envelope is requested.

In person search: Turnaround time is 2 days, unless you are the person of record, then it is immediate. Public access (15-year search) is also immediate.

Other access: A public database is available on CD-ROM. Monthly updates can be purchased. Data is in ASCII format and is raw data. Fee is $250.00.

Corporation Records
Limited Liability Company Records
Assumed Name
Trademarks/Servicemarks
Limited Partnerships

Business Records Services, Secretary of State, 180 State Office Bldg, 100 Constitution Ave, St Paul, MN 55155-1299; 651-296-2803 (Information), 651-297-7067 (Fax), 8AM-4:30PM.

www.sos.state.mn.us

Indexing & Storage: Records are available from 1850's on. All records are indexed together. It takes one day before new records are available for inquiry. Records are indexed on computer and microfilm.

Searching: Part II of foreign corporation annual reports are not released. Include the following in your request: full name of business, corporation file number. In addition to articles of incorporation, corporation records include the following information: Annual Reports, Prior (merged) names, Inactive and Reserved names.

Access by: mail, phone, in person, online.

Fee & Payment: Certification is $5.00 per copy. Copies are $1.00 per page. Fee payee: Secretary of State. Prepayment required. Personal checks accepted. No credit cards accepted.

Mail search: Turnaround time: 1 to 2 days. No self addressed stamped envelope is required.

Phone search: Limited verification information, only on corporation data, is given over the phone.

In person search: You may make copies at $3.00 per business name. There is no fee to view the database or microfilm. However, if you walk-in and wish copies immediately, there is an additional $20.00 fee.

Online search: The Internet site permits free look-ups of "business" names. Also, a commercial program called Direct Access is available 24 hours. There is an annual subscription fee of $50.00. Records are $1-4, depending on item needed. Please call 651-296-2803 or 877-551-6767 for more information.

Other access: Information can be purchased in bulk format. Call 651-298-4059 for more information.

Uniform Commercial Code
Federal Tax Liens
State Tax Liens

UCC Division, Secretary of State, 180 State Office Bldg, St Paul, MN 55155-1299; 651-296-2803, 651-215-1009 (Fax), 8AM-4:30PM.

www.sos.state.mn.us

Indexing & Storage: Records are available from 1987 on computer. Records on microfiche from 1966 to present. It takes 5 days before new records are available for inquiry. Records are indexed on inhouse computer.

Searching: Use search request form UCC-11 for UCC filings. Use a separate UCC-12 request form to obtain federal and state tax liens on businesses. All tax liens on individuals are filed at the county level. Include the following in your request: debtor name.

Access by: mail, fax, in person, online.

Fee & Payment: Search fee is $20.00 per name. The search fee includes all copies. Fee payee: Secretary of State. Prepayment required. Personal checks accepted. Credit cards accepted.

Mail search: Turnaround time: 2 days.

Fax search: Same criteria as mail searches.

In person search: A free public access terminal is available.

Online search: There is a free look-up by filing number available from the web site. A comprehensive commercial program called Direct Access is available 24 hours. There is an annual subscription fee of $50.00 per year, plus $4.00 per debtor name. Call 651-296-2803 for more information.

Other access: The state will provide information in bulk form on paper, CD or disk. Call 651-296-2803 or 877-551-6767 for more information.

Sales Tax Registrations

Minnesota Department of Revenue, Corporate Sales Tax Division, 600 N Robert Street MS:6330, St Paul, MN 55146-6330; 651-296-6181, 651-282-5225 (To Register), 651-296-1938 (Fax), 7:30AM-4:30PM.

www.taxes.state.mn.us

Indexing & Storage: Records are available from 1992 on computer.

Searching: This agency will only confirm that a business is registered, business name and location, and date permit was issued. They will provide no other information. Include the following in your request: business name and MN business identification number.

Access by: mail, phone, fax, in person.

Fee & Payment: There is no fee. No credit cards accepted.

Mail search: Turnaround time: 7 days. No self addressed stamped envelope is required.

Phone search: Turnaround time for a written reply is approximately 7 days from the request date.

Fax search: Fax searching available.

In person search: Searching is available in person.

Birth Certificates

Minnesota Department of Health, Vital Records, PO Box 9441, Minneapolis, MN 55440-9441 (Courier: 717 Delaware St SE, Minneapolis, MN 55414); 612-676-5120, 612-331-5776 (Fax), 8AM-4:30PM.

www.health.state.mn.us

Note: For information pertaining to adoption records, call 612-676-5129,

Indexing & Storage: Records are available from 1900 on. Prior records must be obtained from the county level. It takes 3 months before new records are available for inquiry. Records are indexed on microfiche, inhouse computer, depending on years.

Searching: As of 08/01/2000, only those with a "tangible interest" may request a certified record, anyone may order a non-certified record. Out of wedlock birth certificates require a notarized release from parent or child if 18 years or older. Include the following in your request: full name, date of birth, place of birth, names of parents, mother's maiden name. Also, requester's signature must be notarized.

Access by: mail, fax.

Fee & Payment: Fees are $10.00 for a non-certified copy, $13.00 for a certified copy and $7.00 for an additional certified copy of the same name. Fee payee: Minnesota Department of Health. Prepayment required. Credit cards may be used for fax requesters. Personal checks accepted. Credit cards accepted: MasterCard, Visa, AmEx, Discover.

Mail search: Turnaround time: 2 to 3 weeks. No self addressed stamped envelope is required.

Fax search: See expedited services.

Expedited service: Expedited service is available for fax searches. Turnaround time: 4 weeks. Use of credit card required. Add $5.00 for use of credit card and $14.00 for overnight delivery.

Death Records

Minnesota Department of Health, Section of Vital Records, PO Box 9441, Minneapolis, MN 55440-9441 (Courier: 717 Delaware St SE, Minneapolis, MN 55414); 612-676-5120, 612-331-5776 (Fax), 8AM-4:30PM.

www.health.state.mn.us

Indexing & Storage: Records are available from 1908 on. Prior records must be obtained at the county level. It takes 3 months before new records are available for inquiry.

Searching: As of 08/01/2000, only those with a "tangible interest" may request a certified record. Those without such interest made receive non-certified. Include the following in your request: full name, date of death, place of death. Also, requester's signature must be notarized. If date or place not known, include last year known to be alive.

Access by: mail, fax.

Fee & Payment: The search fees are $13.00 for a certified record or $1.00 for a non-certified, and $5.00 for additional identical copy of same name. Fee payee: Minnesota Department of Health. Prepayment required. Credit cards may be used for ordering by fax only. Personal checks accepted. Credit cards accepted: MasterCard, Visa, AmEx, Discover.

Mail search: Turnaround time: 2 to 3 weeks. No self addressed stamped envelope is required.

Fax search: See expedited services.

Expedited service: Expedited service is available for fax searches. Turnaround time: 4 weeks. Use of credit card is required. Add $5.00 for credit card and $14.00 for overnight express.

Marriage Certificates
Divorce Records

Records not maintained by a state level agency.

Note: Marriage and divorce records are found at the county level. The Section of Vital Records has an index and they will direct you to the proper county (Marriage since 1958, Divorce since 1970). Call the Section of Vital Records at 651-676-5120.

Workers' Compensation Records

Labor & Industry Department, Workers Compensation Division - File Review, 443 Lafayette Rd, St Paul, MN 55155; 651-284-5435, 651-215-0170 (Fax), 8AM-4:30PM.

www.doli.state.mn.us/workcomp.html

Indexing & Storage: Records are available on microfilm or image and paper for 18 years after file closure. New records are available for inquiry immediately. Records are indexed on microfilm, microfiche, inhouse computer. Records are normally destroyed after 19 years old or more.

Searching: Must have a signed release from claimant to obtain all files. Include the following in your request: claimant name, Social Security Number. Include any and all dates of injury in your authorized request.

Access by: mail, phone, in person.

Fee & Payment: There is no search fee. Copies are $.65 each. Add 6.5% tax and postage. There is a $6.00 fee for records retrieved from archives. Fee payee: Department of Labor & Industry. Prepayment required. Personal checks accepted. No credit cards accepted.

Mail search: Turnaround time: 2 to 4 weeks. No self addressed stamped envelope is required.

Phone search: Phone searching is limited to employees involved within a case.

In person search: If you request in person, they will mail requested copies.

Driver Records

Driver & Vehicle Services, Records Section, 445 Minnesota St, #180, St Paul, MN 55101; 651-296-6911, 8AM-4:30PM.

www.dps.state.mn.us/dvs/index.html

Note: Copies of tickets can be requested from the same address. The fee is $4.00 per record, $5.00 if certified.

Indexing & Storage: Records are available for 5 years minimum for moving violations and suspensions; 10 years for open revocation; retained indefinitely for DWIs for 2 or more convictions. Accidents and up to 10 mph over in a 55 zone on interstate roads are not shown. It takes no more than 15 days before new records are available for inquiry.

Searching: A casual requester can only receive the driver's address with consent of driver. The driver's license number or full name and DOB is required for a search. Surrendered licenses will be purged after one year if clear; after five years if the record has convictions. The following data is not released: medical information.

Access by: mail, in person, online.

Fee & Payment: Fees: $5.50 per certified record; $4.50 per non-certified record. Fee payee: Department of Public Safety. Prepayment required. Personal checks accepted. No credit cards accepted.

Mail search: Turnaround time: 1 week. No self addressed stamped envelope is required.

In person search: Up to 3 requests will be processed for walk-in requesters, the rest are available the next day.

Online search: Online access costs $2.50 per record. Online inquiries can be processed either as interactive or as batch files (overnight) 24 hours a day, 7 days a week. Requesters operate from a "bank." Records are accessed by either DL number or full name and DOB. Call 651-297-1714 for more information.

Other access: Minnesota will sell its entire database of driving record information with monthly updates. Customized request sorts are available. Fees vary by type with programming and computer time and are quite reasonable.

Vehicle Ownership
Vehicle Identification

Driver & Vehicle Services, Vehicle Record Requests, 445 Minnesota St, #180, St Paul, MN 55101; 651-296-6911 (General Information), 8AM-4:30PM.

www.dps.state.mn.us/dvs/index.html

Note: Their "Record Request Form" can be downloaded from the web site.

Indexing & Storage: Records are available for past 7 years. It takes 5 days before new records are available for inquiry.

Searching: The state adopted the 14 permissible uses of DPPA. Casual requesters can obtain records without personal information. If consent is given, then personal information is released.

Access by: mail, in person, online.

Fee & Payment: The fee is $1.50 for a vehicle title document or vehicle registration document. Certification is an additional $1.00. Fee payee: Department of Public Safety. Prepayment required. Personal checks accepted. No credit cards accepted.

Mail search: Turnaround time: 1 week. A self addressed stamped envelope is requested.

In person search: Turnaround time is immediate for walk-in requesters.

Online search: Online access costs $2.50 per record. There is an additional monthly charge for dial-in access. The system is the same as described for driving record requests. It is open 24 hours a day, 7 days a week. Lien information is included. Call 651-297-1714 for more information.

Accident Reports

Driver & Vehicle Services, Accident Records, 445 Minnesota St, Suite 181, St Paul, MN 55101-5181; 651-296-2060, 651-282-2360 (Fax), 8AM-4:30PM.

www.dps.state.mn.us/dvs

Indexing & Storage: Records are available from 1993 to 1997 on microfilm, and from 1998 to present records are electronically imaged. It takes 3 weeks from date of accident before new records are available for inquiry.

Searching: Police reports may be obtained with the written and signed authorization from the person involved in the accident. Include the following in your request: date of accident, full name, date of birth, driver's license number. Records are indexed by driver names.

Access by: mail, fax, in person.

Fee & Payment: The fee is $4.00 per police report. Fee payee: DVS. Prepayment required. Personal checks accepted. No credit cards accepted.

Mail search: Turnaround time: 1 week. A self addressed stamped envelope is requested.

Fax search: Fax requests require an account with the agency. Turnaround time 3 days if the request is received after the file has become available.

In person search: Walk-in requesters may obtain copies of accident reports with the authorization of the individual(s) involved in the accident. Turnaround time: while you wait (typically, 5 to 10 minutes).

Vessel Ownership
Vessel Registration

Department of Natural Resources, Information, Education & Licensing Bureau, 500 Lafayette Rd, St Paul, MN 55155-4026; 651-296-2316, 800-285-2000, 651-297-8851 (Fax), 8AM-4:30PM.

www.dnr.state.mn.us

Note: Lien information shows on title records obtained at this agency.

Indexing & Storage: Records are available for the last 15 years. Records are maintained for watercraft, snow mobiles, and off-highway vehicles (all terrain) and off-highway motorcycles. A watercraft must be titled if over 16 ft and 1980 model or newer, registered if over 9 ft.

Searching: The name and hull number or registration number is required to complete a search.

Access by: mail, phone, fax, in person.

Fee & Payment: There is no search fee.

Mail search: Turnaround time: 2 weeks.

Phone search: Up to 2 names may be searched over the phone.

Fax search: Same criteria as mail searching.

In person search: Turnaround time is usually immediate.

Other access: Bulk requests are offered in several media types. Call 651-297-4928 for more information.

Legislation Records

Minnesota Legislature, State Capitol, House-Room 211, Senate-Room 231, St Paul, MN 55155; 651-296-2887 (Senate Bills), 651-296-6646 (House Bill Status), 651-296-2314 (House Bill Copies), 651-296-2146 (House Information), 651-296-1563 (Fax), 8AM-5PM.

www.leg.state.mn.us

Note: When sessions, the hours are extended to 5:30 PM. Sessions start in January in odd numbered years and in February in even numbered years.

Indexing & Storage: Records are available for current session only. For Senate bill status & general legis. questions, call 651-296-0504; Senate bill copies, 651-296-2343. For historical records, call the legislative reference library at 612-296-3398, and there will be a fee involved. Records are indexed on inhouse computer, hard copy.

Searching: Include the following in your request: bill number.

Access by: mail, phone, in person, online.

Fee & Payment: There is no search fee. There is no expedited service; however, they will help requesters who have their own Federal Express account.

Mail search: Turnaround time: variable. No self addressed stamped envelope is required.

Phone search: No fee for telephone request.

In person search: No fee for request.

Online search: Information available through the Internet site includes full text of bills, status, previous 4 years of bills, and bill tracking.

Voter Registration

Access to Records is Restricted

Secretary of State, Election Division, 180 State Office Bldg, 100 Constitution Ave, St Paul, MN 55155; 651-215-1440, 651-296-9073 (Fax), 8AM-4:30PM.

www.sos.state.mn.us/election

Note: Records are sold by the state only for political, election, or law enforcement purposes and only to MN registered voters. Some counties will honor record requests.

GED Certificates

Department of Children, Families & Learning, GED Testing, 1500 Highway 36 West, Roseville, MN 55113; 651-582-8446, 651-582-8458 (Fax), 7AM-3:30PM.

http://cfl.state.mn.us

Searching: The SSN, DOB, and year of the test are helpful to search. A signed release is needed for a copy of a transcript, scores or graduation verification.

Access by: mail, phone, fax.

Mail search: Turnaround time: 1 to 2 days. No self addressed stamped envelope is required. No fee for mail request.

Phone search: No fee for telephone request. For verification only.

Fax search: Same criteria as mail searching.

Hunting License Information
Fishing License Information

Fish & Wildlife Division, DNR Information Center, 500 Lafayette Rd, St Paul, MN 55155-4040; 651-296-6157, 888-646-6367, 651-297-3618 (Fax), 8AM-4:30PM.

www.dnr.state.mn.us

Indexing & Storage: Records are available on computer from 1979 for doe, turkey - Spring permits; 1985 for moose, 1982 for bear and 1990 for turkey-Fall permits.

Searching: Records are open to public; all information is released. Include the following in your request: full name, date of birth. The driver's license is also helpful.

Access by: mail, phone, fax, in person.

Fee & Payment: There is no search fee. Fee payee: DNR. Prepayment required. Personal checks accepted. No credit cards accepted.

Mail search: Turnaround time: 1 to 3 days. No self addressed stamped envelope is required.

Phone search: They will confirm information over the phone.

Fax search: They will confirm information, turnaround time is 1 week.

In person search: Searching is available in person.

Other access: They have mailing lists available for purchase. Call 651-296-0930 for details.

Minnesota State Licensing Agencies

Licenses Searchable Online

Acupuncturist #9 .... www.docboard.org/mn/df/mndf.htm

Alarm & Com. System Contr./Installer #6 .... www.electricity.state.mn.us/Elec_lic/index.html

Ambulance Service/Personnel #28 .... www.emsrb.state.mn.us/cert.asp?p=s

Athletic Trainer #9... www.docboard.org/mn/df/mndf.htm

Auditor #39 .... www.boa.state.mn.us/

Bingo Operation #35.. www.gcb.state.mn.us/

Building Contractors, Residential #23 .... www.commerce.state.mn.us/pages/Contractors/BuilderList.htm

Chiropractor #4 .... www.mn-chiroboard.state.mn.us/main-licensing.htm

Consumer Credit/Payday Lender #24.................... www.commerce.state.mn.us/pages/FinService/FSLicensees/SL.HTM

Credit Union #24.. www.commerce.state.mn.us/pages/FinService/FSLicensees/CU.HTM

Debt Prorate Company #24 .... www.commerce.state.mn.us/pages/FinService/FSLicensees/DP.HTM

Electrician #6 .... www.electricity.state.mn.us/Elec_lic/index.html

Emergency Medical Technician #28 .... www.emsrb.state.mn.us/cert.asp?p=s

EMS Examiner #28... www.emsrb.state.mn.us/examiner.asp?p=s

Funeral Establishment #27 .... www.health.state.mn.us/divs/hpsc/mortsci/mortsciselect.cfm

Gambling Equipment Distributor #35 .... www.gcb.state.mn.us/

Gambling Equipment Mfg. #35 .... www.gcb.state.mn.us/

Gambling, Lawful Organization #35 .... www.gcb.state.mn.us/

Grain Licensing #21... http://www2.mda.state.mn.us/webapp/lis/default.jsp

Industr. Loan/Thrift Company #24 .... www.commerce.state.mn.us/pages/FinService/FSLicensees/IL.HTM

Insurance Agent/Salesman #23............................. licensing.commerce@state.mn.us

Liquor On-sale Retail #34 .... www.dps.state.mn.us/alcgamb/alcenf/liquorlic/liquorlic.html

Liquor Store, On-sale Retail Municipal #34............. www.dps.state.mn.us/alcgamb/alcenf/liquorlic/liquorlic.html

Livestock Dealer/Market #21 .... http://www2.mda.state.mn.us/webapp/lis/default.jsp

Livestock Weighing #21 .... http://www2.mda.state.mn.us/webapp/lis/default.jsp

Loan Company #24 .... www.commerce.state.mn.us/pages/FinService/FSLicensees/RL.HTM

Lobbyist #19 .... www.cfboard.state.mn.us/lobby/index.html

Lottery Retailer #42 .... www.lottery.state.mn.us/retailer/lookup.html

LPA #39.. www.boa.state.mn.us/

Medical Doctor #9.. www.docboard.org/mn/df/mndf.htm

Midwife #9.. www.docboard.org/mn/df/mndf.htm

Mortgage Originators/Servicers, Residential. #24.... www.commerce.state.mn.us/pages/FinService/MOList.htm

Mortician #27 .... www.health.state.mn.us/divs/hpsc/mortsci/mortsciselect.cfm

Motor Vehicle Financer #24 .... www.commerce.state.mn.us/pages/FinService/FSLicensees/MV.HTM

Notary Public #23 .... licensing.commerce@state.mn.us

Optometrist #11 .... www.odfinder.org/LicSearch.asp

Pesticide Applicator Company #22 .... http://www2.mda.state.mn.us/webapp/lis/pestappdefault.jsp

Pesticide Applicator, Private #22 .... www.mda.state.mn.us/privapp/default.asp

Physical Therapist #9 .... www.docboard.org/mn/df/mndf.htm

Physician Assistant #9... www.docboard.org/mn/df/mndf.htm

Political Candidate #19 .... www.cfboard.state.mn.us/legcand.html

Public Accountant-CPA #39................................... www.boa.state.mn.us/

Real Estate Broker/Dealer #23 .... license.commerce@state.mn.us

Respiratory Care Practitioner #9........................... www.docboard.org/mn/df/mndf.htm

Securities/Investment Advisor #23......................... securities.commerce@state.mn.us

Surgeon #9 .... www.docboard.org/mn/df/mndf.htm

Teacher #17 .... http://cfl.state.mn.us/licen/licinfo.html

Underground Storage Tank Contr./Supervisor #43.. www.pca.state.mn.us/cleanup/ust.html#certification

Weather Modifier #21 .... http://www2.mda.state.mn.us/webapp/lis/default.jsp

Licensing Quick Finder

Abstractor/Abstractor Company #25 800-657-3978
Acupuncturist #9 612-617-2130
Adoption/Guardianship Agency #31 651-296-0584
Alarm & Com. System Contr./Installer #6
.... 651-642-0800
Alcohol/Drug Counselor #29 651-282-5619
All-Terrain Vehicle Registration #32 .. 651-296-2316
Ambulance Service/Personnel #28 612-627-6000
Applicant Background Study & Investigation #30
.... 651-296-3971
Architect #37 651-297-2208
Asbestos Abatement Contractor/Worker #26
.... 651-215-0900
Assessor, Senior Accredited #1 651-296-0209
Assessor, State Accredited #1 651-296-0209
Assessor/Assessor Specialist #1 651-296-0209
Athletic Trainer #9 612-617-2130
Attorney #40 651-296-2254
Audiologist #29 651-282-5629
Auditor #39 651-296-7937
Bank #24 651-297-3779
Barber #2 651-642-0489
Bingo Operation #35 651-639-4000
Boat & Canoe Registration #32 651-296-2316
Boat Title #32 651-297-2316
Boats for Hire #36 651-289-5080
Boiler Inspector #36 651-296-4531
Bondsman (Insurance) #23 651-296-6319
Building Contractors, Residential #23 .. 651-296-6319
Chemical Dependency Professional #30
.... 651-582-1832
Child Care Facility #31 651-296-3971
Children's Service #30 651-297-3840
Chiropractor #4 612-617-2223
Consumer Credit/Payday Lender #24 ... 651-296-2297
Contractor/Remodeler, Residential #23 651-296-6319
Cosmetologist #23 651-296-6319
Cosmetology School/Shop #23 651-296-6319
County Fair #41 952-496-7950
Credit Union #24 651-296-2297
Crematory #27 651-282-3829
Debt Prorate Company #24 651-296-2297
Dental Assistant #5 612-617-2250
Dental Hygienist #5 612-617-2250
Dentist #5 612-617-2250
Developmental Disabilities Licensing #30
.... 651-582-1998
Dietitian #46 612-617-2175
Electrician #6 651-642-0800
Elevator Inspector #36 651-297-1644
Emergency Medical Technician #28 612-627-6000

Employment Agency Counselor #36 651-296-2282
Employment Agency Manager #36 651-296-2282
Engineer #37 651-296-2388
Esthetician #23 651-296-6319
Food Manager #26 651-215-0870
Foster Care Program #31 651-296-3971
Funeral Director #27 651-282-3829
Funeral Establishment #27 651-282-3829
Gambling Equipment Distributor #35 ... 651-639-4000
Gambling Equipment Mfg. #35 651-639-4000
Gambling, Lawful Organization #35 651-639-4000
Geologist #37 651-296-2388
Grain Licensing #21 651-296-2980
Hearing Aid Dispenser #29 651-282-5620
High Pressure Inspector #36 651-296-4531
Industr. Loan/Thrift Company #24 651-296-2297
Insurance Agent/Salesman #23 651-296-6319
Interior Designer #37 651-296-2388
Landscape Architect #37 651-296-2388
Liquor and Wine Offsale Retail #34 651-296-9519
Liquor Consumption & Display Information #34
.... 651-296-6439
Liquor On-sale Retail #34 651-296-6939
Liquor Store, On-sale Retail Municipal #34
.... 651-215-6209
Liquor Wholesaler/Mfg./Labeler/Importer #34
.... 651-296-6939
Livestock Dealer/Market #21 651-297-5509
Livestock Weighing #21 651-296-2980
Loan Company #24 651-296-2297
Lobbyist #19 651-296-5148
Lottery Retailer #42 651-635-8119
LPA #39 651-296-7937
Manicurist #23 800-657-3978
Manufactured Home Installer #38 651-296-8458
Manufactured Home Mfg./Dealer #38 .. 651-296-4628
Manufactured Structures Section #38 .. 651-296-4628
Marriage & Family Therapist #8 612-617-2220
Medical Doctor #9 612-617-2130
Mental Health Practitioners, Unlicensed #29
.... 651-282-5621
Mental Health, Chemical Dependency #30
.... 651-582-1990
Midwife #9 612-617-2130
Mortgage Originators/Servicers, Resi. #24
.... 651-282-9855
Mortician #27 651-282-3829
Motor Vehicle Financer #24 651-296-2297
Notary Public #23 651-296-6319
Nurse-LPN #10 612-617-2270
Nurse-RN #10 612-617-2270

Nursing Home Administrator #7 612-617-2117
Nutritionist #46 612-617-2175
Occupational Therapist/Assistant #29 .. 651-282-5624
Off-Highway Motorcycle #32 651-296-2316
Off-Road Vehicle #32 651-296-2316
Optometrist #11 612-617-2173
Pesticide Applicator Company #22 651-296-6121
Pesticide Applicator, Private #22 651-296-6121
Pharmacist #13 612-617-2201
Physical Therapist #9 612-617-2130
Physician Assistant #9 612-617-2130
Plumber #26 651-215-0836
Podiatrist #14 612-617-2200
Police (Peace) Officer, Full/Part Time #12
.... 651-643-3060
Political Candidate #19 651-296-5148
Private Detective #44 651-215-1753
Private Investigator #44 651-215-1753
Psychological Practitioner #15 651-617-2230
Psychologist #15 651-617-2230
Public Accountant-CPA #39 651-296-7937
Racetrack/Card Club Operator #41 952-496-7950
Racing (Racing Class "A"- Owners of Track) #41
.... 952-496-7950
Racing/Card Club Occupational #41 952-496-7950
Real Estate Broker/Dealer #23 651-296-6319
Respiratory Care Practitioner #9 612-617-2130
Sanitarian #26 651-215-0870
Securities/Investment Advisor #23 651-296-2083
Security Agent/Protective Agent #44 ... 651-215-1753
Snowmobile Registration #32 651-296-2316
Social Worker #16 612-617-2100
Soil Scientist #37 651-296-2388
Speech-Language Pathologist #29 651-282-5629
Surgeon #9 612-617-2130
Surveyor, Land #37 651-296-2388
Teacher #17 651-582-8691
Underground Storage Tank Contr./Spvr. #43
.... 651-297-8616
Veterinarian #18 612-617-2170
Waste Disposal Facility Inspector #43 . 651-296-7162
Waste Water Disposal Facility Operator #43
.... 651-296-7162
Water Conditioning Installer/Contractor #26
.... 651-215-0836
Water Supply Operator #26 651-215-0770
Water Well Contractor #26 651-215-0811
Watercraft #32 651-296-2316
Weather Modifier #21 651-296-0591
X-ray Operator #20 651-643-2151

Licensing Agency Information

#1 Board of Assessors, Mail Station 3340, St Paul, MN 55146-3340; 651-296-0209, Fax: 651-297-2166.

#2 Board of Barber Examiners, 1885 University Ave W, #335, St Paul, MN 55104-3403; 651-642-0489, Fax: 651-649-5997.

#3 Department of Commerce, Board of Boxing (Abolished in 2001), 85 East 7th St #170, Golden Rule Bldg, St Paul, MN 55101.

#4 Board of Chiropractic Examiners, 2829 University Ave SE, Minneapolis, MN 55414-3220; 612-617-2222, Fax: 612-617-2224.
www.mn-chiroboard.state.mn.us
Agency email: karen.dorff@state.mn.us.

Search database at www.mn-chiroboard.state.mn.us/main-licensing.htm

#5 Board of Dentistry, 2829 University Ave SE, #450, Minneapolis, MN 55414; 612-617-2250, Fax: 612-617-2260.
www.dentalboard.state.mn.us

#6 Board of Electricity, 1821 University - RM S-128, St Paul, MN 55104; 651-642-0800, Fax: 651-642-0441.
www.electricity.state.mn.us
Search database at www.electricity.state.mn.us/Elec_lic/index.html

#7 Board of Examiners for Nursing Home Administrators, 2829 University Ave SE #440,

Minneapolis, MN 55414; 612-617-2117, Fax: 612-617-2119.
www.benha.state.mn.us.
Agency email: benha@state.mn.us

#8 Board of Marriage & Family Therapy, 2829 University Ave SE #330, Minneapolis, MN 55414-3222; 612-617-2220, Fax: 612-617-2221.
www.bmft.state.mn.us
Agency email: robert.butler@state.mn.us.

#9 Board of Medical Practice, 2829 University Ave SE, #400, Minneapolis, MN 55414-3246; 612-617-2130, Fax: 612-617-2166.
www.bmp.state.mn.us
Agency email: webmaster@bmp.state.mn.us.
Search database at www.docboard.org/mn/df/mndf.htm

#10 Board of Nursing, 2829 University Ave SE, #500, Minneapolis, MN 55414-3253; 612-617-2181, Fax: 612-617-2190.
www.nursingboard.state.mn.us
Agency email: nursing.board@state.mn.us.

#11 Board of Optometry, 2829 University Av SE #550, Minneapolis, MN 55414; 612-617-2173, Fax: 612-617-2174.
www.odfinder.org/LicSearch.asp
Agency email: optometry.board@state.mn.us.
Search database at
www.odfinder.org/LicSearch.asp

#12 Board of Peace Officers Standards & Training, 1600 University Av #200, St Paul, MN 55104-3825; 651-643-3060, Fax: 651-643-3072.
www.dps.state.mn.us/newpost. Agency email: neil.melton@state.mn.us.

#13 Board of Pharmacy, 2829 University Ave SE, #530, Minneapolis, MN 55414-3251; 612-617-2201, Fax: 651-617-2212.
www.phcybrd.state.mn.us
Agency email: pharmacy.board@state.mn.us.

#14 Board of Podiatric Medicine, 2829 University Av SE #430, Minneapolis, MN 55414; 612-617-2200, Fax: 612-617-2698.
www.podiatry.state.mn.us
Agency email: benesh.pod@state.mn.us.

#15 Board of Psychology, 2829 University Ave. SE, #320, Minneapolis, MN 55414-3237; 612-612-2230, Fax: 612-617-2240.

#16 Board of Social Work, 2829 University Ave SE, #340, Minneapolis, MN 55414-3239; 612-617-2100, Fax: 612-617-2103.
www.socialwork.state.mn.us
Agency email: social.work@state.mn.us.

#17 Licensing Unit, Board of Teaching, 1500 Highway 36 W, Roseville, MN 55113-4266; 651-582-8691, Fax: 651-582-8809.
http://cfl.state.mn.us/teachbrd
Agency email: personnellicensing@state.mn.us.
Search database at
http://cfl.state.mn.us/licen/licinfo.html

#18 Board of Veterinary Medicine, 2829 University Ave SE, Minneapolis, MN 55414; 612-617-2170, Fax: 612-617-2172.
www.vetmed.state.mn.us
Agency email: vet.med@state.mn.us.

#19 Division of Plant Health, Campaign Finance Board, 658 Cedar St, Centennial Bld, 1st Fl, St Paul, MN 55155; 651-296-5148, Fax: 651-296-1722.
www.cfboard.state.mn.us. Agency email: cf.board@state.mn.us.
Search database at www.cfboard.state.mn.us

#20 Department of Health, Radiation Control, 1645 Energy Park Dr #300, St Paul, MN 55108; 651-643-2151, Fax: 651-613-2152.
www.health.state.mn.us/divs/eh/radiation/

#21 Department of Agriculture, Livestock Weighing & Licensing, 90 W Plato Blvd, St Paul, MN 55107; 651-297-2980, Fax: 651-297-2504.
www.mda.state.mn.us
Search database at http://www2.mda.state.mn.us/webapp/lis/default.jsp

#22 Department of Agriculture, Pesticide Registration, 90 W Plato Blvd, St Paul, MN 55107; 651-296-6121, Fax: 651-297-2271.
www.mda.state.mn.us
Search database at
www.mda.state.mn.us/lis/default.htm

#23 Department of Commerce, 85 7th Pl E #500, St Paul, MN 55101-2198; 800-657-3978, Fax: 651-296-8591.
www.commerce.state.mn.us
Agency email: licensing.commerce@state.mn.us.

#24 Department of Commerce, Division of Financial Examinations, 85 7th Place E #500, St Paul, MN 55101; 651-298-4026, Fax: 651-296-8591.
www.commerce.state.mn.us
Agency email: commerce@state.mn.us.
Search database at www.commerce.state.mn.us/pages/FinService/FSLicensees.htm

#25 Department of Commerce, Licensing Unit for Abstractors, 85 7th Pl E #600, St Paul, MN 55101-2198; 800-657-3978. www.commerce.state.mn.us/pages/RealEstateMain.htm

#26 Department of Health, Environmental Health Division, 121 E 7th Pl #230, St Paul, MN 55164-0975; 651-215-0900, Fax: 651-215-0975.
www.health.state.mn.us/divs/eh/eh.html

#27 Department of Health, Mortuary Science Section, PO Box 64975, St Paul, MN 55164-0975; 651-282-3829, Fax: 651-282-3839.
www.health.state.mn.us/divs/hpsc/mortsci/mortsci.htm. Agency email: mortsci@health.state.mn.us.
Search database at www.health.state.mn.us/divs/hpsc/mortsci/finda.htm

#28 Emergency Medical Services, Regulatory Board, 2829 University Av SE #310, Minneapolis, MN 55414-3222; 612-627-6000, Fax: 612-627-5442.
www.emsrb.state.mn.us
Search database at www.emsrb.state.mn.us

#29 Health Occupation Programs, Health Policy & Systems Compliance, 121 E 7th Pl #450, Metro Square Bldg, St Paul, MN 55164-0975; 651-282-6366, Fax: 651-282-5628.
www.health.state.mn.us/divs/hpsc/hop/home/homepg.html
Search database at
www.health.state.mn.us/divs/hpsc/hop/home/homepg.html. Online searching is under construction at the web site.

#30 Department of Human Services, 444 Lafayette Rd, St Paul, MN 55155; 651-296-6117, Fax: 651-297-1490.
www.dhs.state.mn.us

#31 Department of Human Services, 444 Lafayette Rd, St Paul, MN 55155; 651-296-6117, Fax: 651-297-1490.
www.dhs.state.mn.us

#32 Department of Natural Resources, License Bureau, 500 Lafayette Rd, St Paul, MN 55155; 651-296-2316, Fax: 651-297-8851.
www.dnr.state.mn.us/license_bureau/licenses.html
Agency email: info@dnr.state.mn.us.

#34 Department of Public Safety, Alcohol & Gambling Enforcement, 444 Cedar St #133, St Paul, MN 55101-5133; 651-296-6159, Fax: 651-297-5259.
www.dps.state.mn.us/alcgamb/alcenf/alcenf.html.
Agency email: dps.webmaster@state.mn.us.
Search database at
www.dps.state.mn.us/alcgamb/alcenf/liquorlic/liquorlic.html. Also, search the liquor license database at www.dps.state.mn.us/alcgamb/New_Folder/search1.asp

#35 Gambling Control Board, 1711 W County B, #300 South, Roseville, MN 55113; 651-639-4000.
www.gcb.state.mn.us
Search database at www.gcb.state.mn.us

#36 Labor & Industry, Code & Inspection Services, 443 Lafayette Rd, St Paul, MN 55155-4304; 651-296-4531, Fax: 651-296-1140.
www.doli.state.mn.us

#37 Board of AELSLAGID, Licensing Boards, 85 E 7th Pl #160, St Paul, MN 55101; 651-296-2388, Fax: 651-297-5310.

#38 Building Codes & Standards Division, Manufactured Structures Section, 408 Metro Square Bldg, 121 7th Pl E, St Paul, MN 55101-2181; 800-657-3944, 651-297-7081, Fax: 651-297-1973.
www.admin.state.mn.us/buildingcodes

#39 Board of Accountancy, 8 SE 7th Pl #125, St Paul, MN 55101; 651-296-7937, Fax: 651-282-2644.
www.boa.state.mn.us

#40 Judicial Center, Board of Law Examiners, 380 Jackson St #201, St Paul, MN 55101; 651-297-1800, Fax: 651-296-5866.
www.ble.state.mn.us

#41 Racing Commission, PO Box 630, Shakopee, MN 55379; 952-496-7950, Fax: 952-496-7954.
www.mnrace.commission.state.mn.us
Agency email: colleen.hurlbert@state.mn.us.

#42 State Lottery, 2645 Long Lake Rd, Roseville, MN 55113; 651-635-8100, Fax: 651-297-7498.
www.lottery.state.mn.us
Agency email: drewv@msl.state.mn.us.
Search database at
www.lottery.state.mn.us/retailer/lookup.html

#43 Pollution Control Agency, 520 Lafayette Rd N, St Paul, MN 55155-4194; 651-297-8367, Fax: 651-282-6247.
www.pca.state.mn.us/netscape4.html. Agency email: webmaster@pca.state.mn.us.

#44 Private Detective & Protective Agent Services Board, 445 Minnesota St, St Paul, MN 55101-5530; 651-215-1753, Fax: 651-296-7096.
www.dps.state.mn.us/pdb. Agency email: private.detective.board@state.mn.us.

#46 Board of Dietetics & Nutrition Practice, 2829 University Ave SE #555, Minneapolis, MN 55414-3250; 612-617-2175.

Minnesota Federal Courts

The following list indicates the district and division name for each county in the state. If the bankruptcy court location is different from the district court, then the location of the bankruptcy court appears in parentheses.

County/Court Cross Reference

County	Court	County	Court
Aitkin	Duluth	Martin	Minneapolis (St Paul)
Anoka	Minneapolis	McLeod	Minneapolis
Becker	Minneapolis (Fergus Falls)	Meeker	Minneapolis
Beltrami	Minneapolis (Fergus Falls)	Mille Lacs	Duluth
Benton	Duluth	Morrison	Duluth
Big Stone	Minneapolis (Fergus Falls)	Mower	Minneapolis (St Paul)
Blue Earth	Minneapolis (St Paul)	Murray	Minneapolis (St Paul)
Brown	Minneapolis (St Paul)	Nicollet	Minneapolis (St Paul)
Carlton	Duluth	Nobles	Minneapolis (St Paul)
Carver	Minneapolis	Norman	Minneapolis (Fergus Falls)
Cass	Duluth	Olmsted	Minneapolis (St Paul)
Chippewa	Minneapolis	Otter Tail	Minneapolis (Fergus Falls)
Chisago	Minneapolis (St Paul)	Pennington	Minneapolis (Fergus Falls)
Clay	Minneapolis (Fergus Falls)	Pine	Duluth
Clearwater	Minneapolis (Fergus Falls)	Pipestone	Minneapolis (St Paul)
Cook	Duluth	Polk	Minneapolis (Fergus Falls)
Cottonwood	Minneapolis (St Paul)	Pope	Minneapolis (Fergus Falls)
Crow Wing	Duluth	Ramsey	St Paul
Dakota	Minneapolis (St Paul)	Red Lake	Minneapolis (Fergus Falls)
Dodge	Minneapolis (St Paul)	Redwood	Minneapolis (St Paul)
Douglas	Minneapolis (Fergus Falls)	Renville	Minneapolis
Faribault	Minneapolis (St Paul)	Rice	Minneapolis (St Paul)
Fillmore	Minneapolis (St Paul)	Rock	Minneapolis (St Paul)
Freeborn	Minneapolis (St Paul)	Roseau	Minneapolis (Fergus Falls)
Goodhue	Minneapolis (St Paul)	Scott	Minneapolis (St Paul)
Grant	Minneapolis (Fergus Falls)	Sherburne	Minneapolis
Hennepin	Minneapolis	Sibley	Minneapolis (St Paul)
Houston	Minneapolis (St Paul)	St. Louis	Duluth
Hubbard	Minneapolis (Fergus Falls)	Stearns	Minneapolis (Fergus Falls)
Isanti	Minneapolis	Steele	Minneapolis (St Paul)
Itasca	Duluth	Stevens	Minneapolis (Fergus Falls)
Jackson	Minneapolis (St Paul)	Swift	Minneapolis
Kanabec	Duluth	Todd	Minneapolis (Fergus Falls)
Kandiyohi	Minneapolis	Traverse	Minneapolis (Fergus Falls)
Kittson	Minneapolis (Fergus Falls)	Wabasha	Minneapolis (St Paul)
Koochiching	Duluth	Wadena	Minneapolis (Fergus Falls)
Lac qui Parle	Minneapolis (St Paul)	Waseca	Minneapolis (St Paul)
Lake	Duluth	Washington	Minneapolis (St Paul)
Lake of the Woods	Minneapolis (Fergus Falls)	Watonwan	Minneapolis (St Paul)
Le Sueur	Minneapolis (St Paul)	Wilkin	Minneapolis (Fergus Falls)
Lincoln	Minneapolis (St Paul)	Winona	Minneapolis (St Paul)
Lyon	Minneapolis (St Paul)	Wright	Minneapolis
Mahnomen	Minneapolis (Fergus Falls)	Yellow Medicine	Minneapolis (St Paul)
Marshall	Minneapolis (Fergus Falls)		

Standards for Federal Courts: The search fee is $20.00 per item (one party name or case number). Certification fee is $7.00 per document. Copy fee is $.50 per page. All fees standard unless noted in profile. Mail Search: always enclose a stamped self addressed envelope unless otherwise noted. Before releasing records, all courts require prepayment unless noted in profile.

Open records are located at the court unless otherwise noted. District courts index by defendant and plaintiff as well as by case number. Bankruptcy courts usually index by debtor and case number. While most courts now have their indexes on computer, many still maintain index card files as well.

The universal PACER sign-up number is 800-676-6856. Find PACER and the Party/Case Index on the Web at http://pacer.psc.uscourts.gov. PACER dial-up access is $.60 per minute. Also, courts offering internet access via RACER, PACER, Web-PACER or the new CM-ECF charge $.07 per page fee unless noted as free.

US District Court

District of Minnesota

Duluth Division Clerk's Office, 417 Federal Bldg, Duluth, MN 55802 (Courier Address: Use mail address for courier delivery), 218-529-3500, Fax: 218-529-3505.

www.mnd.uscourts.gov

Counties: Aitkin, Becker*, Beltrami*, Benton, Big Stone*, Carlton, Cass, Clay*, Clearwater*, Cook, Crow Wing, Douglas*, Grant*, Hubbard*, Itasca, Kanabec, Kittson*, Koochiching, Lake, Lake of the Woods*, Mahnomen*, Marshall*, Mille Lacs, Morrison, Norman*, Otter*,Tail, Pennington*, Pine, Polk*, Pope*, Red Lake*, Roseau*, Stearns*, Stevens*, St. Louis, Todd*, Traverse*, Wadena*, Wilkin*. From March 1, 1995, to 1998, cases from the counties marked with an asterisk (*) were heard here.Before and after that period, cases were and are allocated between St. Paul and Minneapolis.

Indexing & Storage: Cases are indexed by defendant, plaintiff, and case number. New cases are available in the index immediately after filing date. Open records are located at this court.

Fee & Payment Notes: Payment may be made by money order, cashier check, personal check. Payee: Clerk, US District Court.

Phone Search: Only docket information is available by phone.

Mail Search: A stamped self addressed envelope is not required.

In Person Search: In person searching available.

PACER: Access fee is. Case records are available back to February 1990. New records are available online after 1 day. PACER is available online at http://pacer.mnd.uscourts.gov.

Minneapolis Division Court Clerk, Room 202, 300 S 4th St, Minneapolis, MN 55415 (Courier Address: Use mail address for courier delivery), 612-664-5000, Fax: 612-664-5033.

www.mnd.uscourts.gov

Counties: All counties not covered by the Duluth Division. Cases are allocated between Minneapolis and St Paul.

Indexing & Storage: Cases are indexed by defendant, plaintiff, and case number. New cases are available in the index immediately after filing date. Records are also indexed on microfiche. Open records are located at this court.

Fee & Payment Notes: Payment may be made by money order, cashier check, personal check. Payee: Clerk, US District Court.

Phone Search: The case number and parties involved will be released over the phone.

Mail Search: A stamped self addressed envelope is not required.

In Person Search: In person searching available.

PACER: Access fee is. Case records are available back to February 1990. New records are available online after 1 day. PACER is available online at http://pacer.mnd.uscourts.gov.

St Paul Division 700 Federal Bldg, 316 N Robert, St Paul, MN 55101 (Courier Address: Use mail address for courier delivery), 651-848-1100, Fax: 651-848-1109.

www.mnd.uscourts.gov

Counties: All counties not covered by the Duluth Division. Cases are allocated between Minneapolis and St Paul.

Indexing & Storage: Cases are indexed by defendant, plaintiff, and case number. New cases are available in the index immediately after filing date. Records are also indexed on microfiche. Open records are located at this court.

Fee & Payment Notes: Payment may be made by money order, cashier check, personal check. Payee: Clerk, US District Court.

Phone Search: Only the case number and parties involved will be released over the phone.

Fax Search: Fax requests will be accepted, but results that involve copies will not be faxed or mailed back until after payment has been received.

Mail Search: A stamped self addressed envelope is not required.

In Person Search: In person searching available.

PACER: Access fee is. Case records are available back to February 1990. New records are available online after 1 day. PACER is available online at http://pacer.mnd.uscourts.gov.

US Bankruptcy Court

District of Minnesota

Duluth Division 416 US Courthouse, 515 W 1st St, Duluth, MN 55802 (Courier Address: Use mail address for courier delivery), 218-529-3600.

www.mnb.uscourts.gov

Counties: Aitkin, Benton, Carlton, Cass, Cook, Crow Wing, Itasca, Kanabec, Koochiching, Lake, Mille Lacs, Morrison, Pine, St. Louis. A petition commencing Chapter 11 or 12 proceedings may initially be filed in any of the four divisons, but may be assigned toanother division.

Indexing & Storage: Cases are indexed by debtor as well as by case number. New cases are available in the index 1-2 days after filing date. Chapter 7 and 13 cases in Benton, Kanabec, Mille Lacs, Morrison and Pine may also be filed in St. Paul. Open records are located at this court.

Fee & Payment Notes: Payment may be made by money order, personal check. Payee: Clerk, US

Bankruptcy Court. You are allowed to make your own copies. These copies cost $.15 per page.

Phone Search: Only basic information is released over the phone. An automated voice case information service (VCIS) is available. Call VCIS at 800-959-9002 or 612-664-5302.

Mail Search: A stamped self addressed envelope is not required.

In Person Search: In person searching available.

PACER: Local dial-up access: 651-848-1096. Case records are available back to January 1993. Records are purged up to April 1996. New civil records are available online after 1 day.

Other Online Access: Search records using the Internet. Searching is currently free. Images go back to 1997.

Fergus Falls Division 204 US Courthouse, 118 S Mill St, Fergus Falls, MN 56537 (Courier Address: Use mail address for courier delivery), 218-739-4671.

www.mnb.uscourts.gov

Counties: Becker, Beltrami, Big Stone, Clay, Clearwater, Douglas, Grant, Hubbard, Kittson, Lake of the Woods, Mahnomen, Marshall, Norman, Otter Tail, Pennington, Polk, Pope, Red Lake, Roseau, Stearns, Stevens, Todd, Traverse, Wadena, Wilkin. A petition commencingChapter 11 or 12 proceedings may be filed initially in any of the four divisions, but may then be assigned to another division.

Indexing & Storage: Cases are indexed by debtor as well as by case number. New cases are available in the index immediately after filing date. Open records are located at this court.

Fee & Payment Notes: Payment may be made by money order, cashier check, personal check. Payee: US Bankruptcy Court.

Phone Search: Only docket information is available by phone. An automated voice case information service (VCIS) is available. Call VCIS at 800-959-9002 or 612-664-5302.

Mail Search: A stamped self addressed envelope is not required.

In Person Search: In person searching available.

PACER: Local dial-up access: 651-848-1096. Case records are available back to January 1993. Records are purged up to April 1996. New civil records are available online after 1 day.

Other Online Access: Search records using the Internet. Searching is currently free. Images go back to 1997.

Minneapolis Division 301 US Courthouse, 300 S 4th St, Minneapolis, MN 55415 (Courier Address: Use mail address for courier delivery), 612-664-5200.

www.mnb.uscourts.gov

Counties: Anoka, Carver, Chippewa, Hennepin, Isanti, Kandiyohi, McLeod, Meeker, Renville, Sherburne, Swift, Wright. Initial petitions for Chapter 11 or 12 may be filed initially at any of the four divisions, but may then be assigned to a judge in another division.

Indexing & Storage: New cases are available in the index immediately after filing date. Records are also indexed on microfiche. District wide searches are available for information from January 2, 1992 from this court. This division holds closed cases from St. Paul for 4 years (no indexing available at this office).

Fee & Payment Notes: Payment may be made by money order, cashier check, personal check. Payee: Clerk, US Bankruptcy Court. You are allowed to make your own copies. These copies cost $.15 per page.

Phone Search: Only basic information is released over the phone. An automated voice case information service (VCIS) is available. Call VCIS at 800-959-9002 or 612-664-5302.

Mail Search: A stamped self addressed envelope is not required.

In Person Search: In person searching available.

PACER: Local dial-up access: 651-848-1096. Case records are available back to January 1993. Records are purged up to April 1996. New civil records are available online after 1 day.

Other Online Access: Search records using the Internet. Searching is currently free. Images go back to 1997.

St Paul Division 200 US Courthouse, 316 N Robert St, St Paul, MN 55101 (Courier Address: Use mail address for courier delivery), 651-848-1000.

www.mnb.uscourts.gov

Counties: Blue Earth, Brown, Chisago, Cottonwood, Dakota, Dodge, Faribault, Fillmore, Freeborn, Goodhue, Houston, Jackson, Lac qui Parle, Le Sueur, Lincoln, Lyon, Martin, Mower, Murray, Nicollet, Nobles, Olmsted, Pipestone, Ramsey, Redwood, Rice, Rock, Scott,Sibley, Steele, Wabasha, Waseca, Washington, Watonwan, Winona, Yellow Medicine. Cases from Benton, Kanabec, Mille Lacs, Morrison and Pine may also be heard here. A petition commencing Chapter 11 or 12 proceedings may be filed initially with any of the four divisions, but may then be assigned to another division.

Indexing & Storage: Cases are indexed by debtor as well as by case number. New cases are available in the index 1 day after filing date. Open records are located at this court.

Fee & Payment Notes: Payment may be made by money order, cashier check, personal check. Payee: Clerk, US Bankruptcy Court. You are allowed to make your own copies. These copies cost $.15 per page.

Phone Search: Only docket information is available by phone. An automated voice case information service (VCIS) is available. Call VCIS at 800-959-9002 or 612-664-5302.

Mail Search: A stamped self addressed envelope is not required.

In Person Search: In person searching available.

PACER: Local dial-up access: 651-848-1096. Case records are available back to January 1993. Records are purged up to April 1996. New civil records are available online after 1 day.

Other Online Access: Search records using the Internet. Searching is currently free. Images go back to 1997.

Minnesota County Courts

Court	Jurisdiction	No. of Courts	How Organized
District Courts*	General	97	10 Districts

* Profiled in this Sourcebook.

Court	CIVIL								
	Tort	Contract	Real Estate	Min. Claim	Max. Claim	Small Claims	Estate	Eviction	Domestic Relations
District Courts*	X	X	X	$0	No Max	$7500	X	X	X

Court	CRIMINAL				
	Felony	Misdemeanor	DWI/DUI	Preliminary Hearing	Juvenile
District Courts*	X	X	X		X

ADMINISTRATION   State Court Adminstrator, 135 Minn. Judicial Center, 25 Constitution Ave, St Paul, MN, 55155; 651-296-2474, Fax: 651-297-5636. www.courts.state.mn.us

COURT STRUCTURE   There are 97 District Courts comprising 10 judicial districts. Effective July 1, 1996, the limit for small claims was raised from $5000 to $7500.

ONLINE ACCESS   There is an online system in place that allows internal and external access. Some criminal information is available online from St Paul through the Bureau of Criminal Apprehension (BCA), 1246 University Ave, St. Paul, MN 55104. Additional information is available from BCA by calling 651-642-0670.

ADDITIONAL INFORMATION   Statewide certification and copy fees are as follows: Certification Fee: $10.00 per document, Copy Fee: $5.00 per document (not per page).

An exact name is required to search, e.g., a request for "Robert Smith" will not result in finding "Bob Smith." The requester must request both names and pay two search and copy fees.

When a search is permitted by "plaintiff or defendant," most jurisdictions stated that a case is indexed by only the 1st plaintiff or defendant, and a 2nd or 3rd party would not be sufficient to search.

The 3rd, 5th, 8th and 10th Judicial Districts no longer will perform criminal record searches for the public.

Most courts take personal checks. Exceptions are noted.

Aitkin County

9th Judicial District Court 209 Second St NW, Aitkin, MN 56431; 218-927-7350; Fax: 218-927-4535. Hours: 8AM-4:30PM (CST). *Felony, Misdemeanor, Civil, Eviction, Small Claims, Probate.*

Civil Records: Access: Mail, in person. Both court and visitors may perform in person searches. Search fee: $5.00 per name. Required to search: name, years to search. Civil cases indexed by defendant. Civil records on computer from 2/90, cards to 1982, index books prior.

Criminal Records: Access: Mail, in person. Both court and visitors may perform in person searches. Search fee: $5.00 per name. Required to search: name, years to search, DOB. Criminal records on computer from 2/90, cards to 1982, index books prior.

General Information: Public access terminal is available. No adoption, juvenile, sex offender or sealed records released. SASE required. Turnaround time 1 week. Copy fee: $5.00 per document. Certification fee: $10.00. Fee payee: Aitkin District Court. Personal checks accepted. Prepayment is required.

Anoka County

10th Judicial District Court 325 E Main St, Anoka, MN 55303; 763-422-7350; Criminal phone: 763-422-7385; Fax: 763-422-6919. Hours: 8AM-4:30PM (CST). *Felony, Misdemeanor, Civil, Eviction, Small Claims, Probate.*

Civil Records: Access: In person only. Visitors must perform in person searches for themselves. Search fee: No search fee. Required to search: name, years to search. Civil cases indexed by defendant, plaintiff. Civil records on computer from 1985, prior on microfiche.

Criminal Records: Access: In person only. Visitors must perform in person searches for themselves. Search fee: No search fee. Required to search: name, years to search, DOB; also helpful: SSN. Criminal records on computer from 1985, prior on microfiche.

General Information: Public access terminal is available. No adoption, juvenile, sex offender or sealed records released. Copy fee: $5.00 per document. Certification fee: $10.00. Fee payee: Court Administrator. Personal checks accepted. Credit cards accepted: Visa, MasterCard. Prepayment is required.

Becker County

7th Judicial District Court PO Box 787, Detroit Lakes, MN 56502; 218-846-7305; Fax: 218-847-7620. Hours: 8AM-4:30PM (CST). *Felony, Misdemeanor, Civil, Eviction, Small Claims, Probate.*

Civil Records: Access: Phone, fax, mail, in person. Both court and visitors may perform in person searches. No search fee. Required to search: name; also helpful: years to search, plaintiff. Civil cases indexed by defendant, plaintiff. Civil records on computer from 8/86, prior on books from 1891.

Criminal Records: Access: In person only. Visitors must perform in person searches for themselves. No search fee. Required to search: name, years to search. Criminal records on computer from 8/86, prior on books from 1891.

General Information: Public access terminal is available. No adoption, juvenile, sex offender or sealed records released. SASE required. Turnaround time same day. Fax notes: $5.00 per document. Copy fee: $5.00 per document. Certification fee: $10.00. Fee payee: Becker County. Personal checks accepted. Prepayment is required.

Beltrami County

District Court 619 Beltrami Ave NW, #10, Bemidji, MN 56601-3068; 218-759-4531; Fax: 218-759-4209. Hours: 8AM-4:30PM (CST). *Felony, Misdemeanor, Civil, Eviction, Small Claims, Probate.*

Civil Records: Access: Mail, in person. Both court and visitors may perform in person searches. Search fee: $5.00 per name. Required to search: name, years to search. Civil cases indexed by defendant, plaintiff. Civil records on computer back to 1983.

Criminal Records: Access: Mail, in person. Both court and visitors may perform in person searches. Search fee: $5.00 per name. Required to search: name, years to search, DOB. Criminal records on computer back to 1983.

General Information: Public access terminal is available. No adoption, juvenile, sex offender or sealed records released. SASE not required. Turnaround time 1-5 days. Copy fee: $5.00 per document. Certification fee: $10.00. Fee payee: Court Administrator. Personal checks accepted. Prepayment is required.

Benton County

7th Judicial District Court 615 Highway 23, PO Box 189, Foley, MN 56329-0189; 320-968-5205; Fax: 320-968-5353. Hours: 8AM-4:30PM (CST). *Felony, Misdemeanor, Civil, Eviction, Small Claims, Probate.*

Civil Records: Access: In person only. Visitors must perform in person searches for themselves. No search fee. Required to search: name, years to search. Civil cases indexed by defendant, plaintiff. Civil records on computer from 1986.

Criminal Records: Access: In person only. Visitors must perform in person searches for themselves. No search fee. Required to search: name, years to search, DOB. Criminal records on computer from 1986.

General Information: Public access terminal is available. No adoption, juvenile records released. Copy fee: $5.00 per document. Certification fee: $10.00. Fee payee: Court Administrator. Personal checks accepted. Prepayment is required.

Big Stone County

8th Judicial District Court 20 SE 2nd St, Ortonville, MN 56278; 320-839-2536; Fax: 320-839-2537. Hours: 8AM-4:30PM (CST). *Felony, Misdemeanor, Civil, Eviction, Small Claims, Probate.*

Civil Records: Access: Mail, in person. Both court and visitors may perform in person searches. Search fee: $5.00. Required to search: name, years to search. Civil cases indexed by defendant, plaintiff. Civil records on computer from 1989, prior on cards and in books.

Criminal Records: Access: In person only. Visitors must perform in person searches for themselves. No search fee. Required to search: name, years to search, DOB; also helpful: SSN. Criminal records on computer from 1989, prior on cards and in books.

General Information: Public access terminal is available. No adoption, juvenile, sex offender or sealed records released. SASE required. Turnaround time 3 days. Copy fee: $5.00 per document. Certification fee: $10.00. Fee payee: Court Administrator. Personal checks accepted. Prepayment is required.

Blue Earth County

5th Judicial District Court 204 S 5th St (PO Box 0347), Mankato, MN 56002-0347; 507-389-8310; Fax: 507-389-8437. Hours: 8AM-5PM (CST). *Felony, Misdemeanor, Civil, Eviction, Small Claims, Probate.*

Civil Records: Access: Mail, in person. Both court and visitors may perform in person searches. No search fee. Required to search: name, years to search. Civil cases indexed by defendant, plaintiff. Civil records on computer from 8/85, prior in books and cards.

Criminal Records: Access: In person only. Visitors must perform in person searches for themselves. No search fee. Required to search: name, years to search; also helpful: DOB. Criminal records on computer from 8/85, prior in books and cards. The county forwards mail requests to the state Bureau of Criminal Apprehension.

General Information: Public access terminal is available. No juvenile, adoption, sealed records released. SASE not required. Turnaround time is same day. Copy fee: $5.00 per document. Certification fee: $10.00. Fee payee: Court Administrator. Personal checks accepted. Prepayment is required.

Brown County

5th Judicial District Court PO Box 248, New Ulm, MN 56073-0248; 507-233-6670; Fax: 507-359-9562. Hours: 8AM-5PM (CST). *Felony, Misdemeanor, Civil, Eviction, Small Claims, Probate.*

Civil Records: Access: Mail, in person. Both court and visitors may perform in person searches. Search fee: $5.00. Required to search: name, years to search. Civil cases indexed by defendant, plaintiff. Civil records on computer from 1988, microfiche 1981-1988, prior on books.

Criminal Records: Access: In person only. Visitors must perform in person searches for themselves. No search fee. Required to search: name, years to search. Criminal records on computer from 1988, microfiche 1981-1988, prior on books. Requests must be made to the state Bureau of Criminal Apprehension.

General Information: Public access terminal is available. No adoption, juvenile, sex offender or sealed records released. SASE required. Turnaround time 3 days. Fax notes: Fee to fax results is $5.00. Copy fee: $5.00 per document. Certification fee: $10.00. Fee payee: Court Administrator. Personal checks accepted. Credit cards accepted: Visa, MasterCard. Prepayment is required.

Carlton County

6th Judicial District Court PO Box 190 (301 Walnut St), Carlton, MN 55718; 218-384-4281; Fax: 218-384-9182. Hours: 8AM-4PM (CST). *Felony, Misdemeanor, Civil, Eviction, Small Claims, Probate.*

www.courts.state.mn.us/districts/sixth/index.html

Civil Records: Access: Mail, fax, in person. Both court and visitors may perform in person searches. No search fee. Required to search: name, years to search; also helpful: address. Civil cases indexed by defendant, plaintiff. Civil records on computer from 1985, in books from 1982.

Criminal Records: Access: In person only. Visitors must perform in person searches for themselves. No search fee. Required to search: name, years to search; also helpful: address, DOB. Criminal records on computer from 1985, in books from 1972.

General Information: Public access terminal is available. No adoption, juvenile, sex offender or sealed records released. SASE required. Turnaround time 1 day. Copy fee: $5.00 per document. Certification fee: $10.00. Fee payee: Court Administrator. Personal checks accepted. Prepayment is required.

Carver County

1st Judicial District Court 604 E 4th St, Box 4, Chaska, MN 55318-2183; 952-361-1420; Fax: 952-361-1491. Hours: 8AM-4:30PM (CST). *Felony, Misdemeanor, Civil, Eviction, Small Claims, Probate.*

www.co.carver.mn.us/depts.htm

Civil Records: Access: Mail, in person. Both court and visitors may perform in person searches. Search fee: $5.00 per name. Required to search: name, years to search. Civil cases indexed by defendant, plaintiff. Civil records on computer from 2/92, prior on books.

Criminal Records: Access: Mail, in person. Both court and visitors may perform in person searches. Search fee: $5.00 per name. Required to search: name, years to search, DOB. Criminal records on computer from 2/92, prior on books.

General Information: Public access terminal is available. No adoption, juvenile, sex offender or sealed records released. SASE not required. Turnaround time 3-4 days. Copy fee: $5.00 per document. Certification fee: $10.00 per document. Fee payee: Court Administrator. Personal checks accepted. Prepayment is required.

Cass County

9th Judicial District Court 300 Minnesota Ave, PO Box 3000, Walker, MN 56484; 218-547-7200; Fax: 218-547-1904. Hours: 8AM-4:30PM (CST). *Felony, Misdemeanor, Civil, Eviction, Small Claims, Probate.*

Civil Records: Access: Mail, in person. Both court and visitors may perform in person searches. Search fee: $5.00 per name. Required to search: name, years to search; also helpful: address. Civil cases indexed by defendant, plaintiff. Civil records on computer from mid-1990, on index cards from 1983-1990, on books to 1983, cards to 1900.

Criminal Records: Access: Mail, in person. Both court and visitors may perform in person searches. Search fee: $5.00 per name. Required to search: name, years to search, DOB; also helpful: address. Criminal records on computer from mid-1990, on index cards from 1983-1990, on books to 1983; cards to 1900.

General Information: Public access terminal is available. No adoption, juvenile or sealed records released. SASE required. Turnaround time up to 2 weeks. Fax notes: Fee to fax results is $5.00 per document. Copy fee: $5.00 per document. Certification fee: $10.00. Fee payee: District Court. Personal checks accepted. Prepayment is required.

Chippewa County

8th Judicial District Court Chippewa County Court Administor, PO Box 697, Montevideo, MN 56265; 320-269-7774; Fax: 320-269-7733. Hours: 8AM-4:30PM (CST). *Felony, Misdemeanor, Civil, Eviction, Small Claims, Probate.*

Civil Records: Access: Mail, in person. Only the court performs in person searches; visitors may not. No search fee. Required to search: name, years to search. Civil cases indexed by defendant, plaintiff. Civil records on computer from 1988, in books from 1870.

Criminal Records: Access: In person only. Visitors must perform in person searches for themselves. No search fee. Required to search: name, years to search, DOB. Criminal records on computer from 1988, in books from 1870.

General Information: No adoption, juvenile, sex offender or sealed records released. SASE required. Turnaround time same day. Copy fee: $5.00 document. Certification fee: $10.00 per document. Fee payee: Court Administrator. Personal checks accepted. Prepayment is required.

Chisago County

10th Judicial District Court 313 N Main St, Rm 358, Center City, MN 55012; 651-257-1300; Fax: 651-257-0359. Hours: 8AM-4:30PM (CST). *Felony, Misdemeanor, Civil, Eviction, Small Claims, Probate.*

Civil Records: Access: Mail, in person. Both court and visitors may perform in person searches. No search fee. Required to search: name, years to search. Civil cases indexed by defendant, plaintiff. Civil records on computer from 1984, prior on index cards.

Criminal Records: Access: In person only. Visitors must perform in person searches for themselves. No search fee. Required to search: name, years to search;

also helpful: DOB. Criminal records on computer from 1984, prior on index cards.

General Information: Public access terminal is available. No adoption, juvenile, sex offender or sealed records released. SASE required. Turnaround time 1-2 days. Copy fee: $.25 per page. Certification fee: $10.00. Fee payee: Court Administrator. Personal checks accepted. Prepayment is required.

Clay County

7th Judicial District Court PO Box 280, Moorhead, MN 56561; 218-299-5065; Fax: 218-299-7307. Hours: 8AM-4:30PM (CST). *Felony, Misdemeanor, Civil, Eviction, Small Claims, Probate.*

Civil Records: Access: Fax, mail, in person. Both court and visitors may perform in person searches. Search fee: $5.00. Required to search: name; also helpful: years to search. Civil cases indexed by defendant, plaintiff. Civil records on computer back to 1982; prior on microfiche and microfilm.

Criminal Records: Access: In person only. Visitors must perform in person searches for themselves. Search fee: No search fee. Required to search: name, years to seach, DOB. Criminal records on computer back to 1982; prior on microfiche and microfilm. Court no longer performs searches as of July 1, 1997.

General Information: Public access terminal is available. No adoption or sealed records released. SASE required. Turnaround time 3 days. Copy fee: $5.00 per document. Certification fee: $10.00. Fee payee: Court Administrator. Personal checks accepted. Prepayment is required.

Clearwater County

9th Judicial District Court 213 Main Ave North, Bagley, MN 56621; 218-694-6177; Fax: 218-694-6213. Hours: 8AM-4:30PM (CST). *Felony, Misdemeanor, Civil, Eviction, Small Claims, Probate.*

Civil Records: Access: Mail, in person. Both court and visitors may perform in person searches. Search fee: $5.00 per name, by court. Required to search: name, years to search. Civil cases indexed by defendant, plaintiff. Civil records on computer from 1990, on cards and books prior back to 1903.

Criminal Records: Access: Mail, in person. Both court and visitors may perform in person searches. Search fee: $5.00 per name, by court. Required to search: name, years to search; also helpful: DOB. Criminal records on computer from 1990, on cards and books prior back to 1903.

General Information: Public access terminal is available. No adoption, juvenile or sealed records released. SASE not required. Turnaround time 3-5 days. Copy fee: $5.00 per document. Certification fee: $10.00. Fee payee: Court Administrator. Personal checks accepted. Prepayment is required.

Cook County

6th Judicial District Court PO Box 1150, Grand Marais, MN 55604-1150; 218-387-3000; Fax: 218-387-3007. Hours: 8AM-4PM (CST). *Felony, Misdemeanor, Civil, Eviction, Small Claims, Probate.*

www.6courts.com

Civil Records: Access: In person only. Visitors must perform in person searches for themselves. No search fee. Required to search: name, years to search. Civil cases indexed by defendant, plaintiff. Civil records on computer back to 2/91, prior on card files.

Criminal Records: Access: In person only. Visitors must perform in person searches for themselves. No search fee. Required to search: name, years to search, DOB. Criminal records on computer back to 2/91, prior on card files.

General Information: Public access terminal is available. No adoption, juvenile, sex offender or sealed records released. Fax notes: Fee to fax results is $5.00

per document. Copy fee: $5.00 per document. Certification fee: $10.00. Fee payee: Court Administrator. Business checks accepted. Prepayment is required.

Cottonwood County

5th Judicial District Court PO Box 97, Windom, MN 56101; 507-831-4551; Fax: 507-831-1425. Hours: 8AM-4:30PM (CST). *Felony, Misdemeanor, Civil, Eviction, Small Claims, Probate.*

Civil Records: Access: Mail, fax, in person. Only the court performs in person searches; visitors may not. Search fee: $10.00 per name. Required to search: name; also helpful: years to search. Civil cases indexed by defendant, plaintiff. Civil records on computer back to 1989; probate on microfilm. There is a $5 fee to certify a judgment search done on computer.

Criminal Records: Access: Mail, fax, in person. Both court and visitors may perform in person searches. Search fee: $10.00 per name. Required to search: name, years to search, DOB; also helpful: SSN. Criminal records on computer back to 1989; prior records on card file. Court will only do searches if caseload permits.

General Information: Public access terminal is available. No adoption, juvenile, sex offender or sealed records released. SASE required. Turnaround time 2-3 days. Copy fee: $5.00 per document. Certification fee: $10.00. Fee payee: Court Administrator. Personal checks accepted. Prepayment is required.

Crow Wing County

District Court 326 Laurel St, Brainerd, MN 56401; 218-824-1310; Fax: 218-824-1311. Hours: 8AM-5PM (CST). *Felony, Misdemeanor, Civil, Eviction, Small Claims, Probate.*

Civil Records: Access: Mail, in person. Both court and visitors may perform in person searches. Search fee: $5.00 per name. Required to search: name, years to search. Civil cases indexed by defendant, plaintiff. Civil records on computer from 1989, prior in books from 1873.

Criminal Records: Access: Mail, in person. Both court and visitors may perform in person searches. Search fee: $5.00 per name. Required to search: name, years to search; also helpful: DOB. Criminal records on computer from 1989, prior in books from 1873.

General Information: Public access terminal is available. No adoption, juvenile, sex offender or sealed records released. SASE required. Turnaround time 7-14 days. Copy fee: $5.00 per document. Certification fee: $10.00. Fee payee: Court Administrator. Personal checks accepted. Prepayment is required.

Dakota County

1st Judicial District Court - Apple Valley 14955 Galaxie Ave, Apple Valley, MN 55124; 952-891-7256; Fax: 952-891-7285. Hours: 8AM-4:30PM (CST). *Misdemeanor, Civil, Eviction, Small Claims.*

www.co.dakota.mn.us/courts/index.htm

Civil Records: Access: In person only. Visitors must perform in person searches for themselves. Search fee: No search fee. Required to search: name, years to search. Civil cases indexed by defendant, plaintiff. Civil records on computer back to 1988, prior in files in index books back to 1969.

Criminal Records: Access: In person only. Visitors must perform in person searches for themselves. Search fee: No search fee. Required to search: name, years to search, DOB; also helpful: SSN. Criminal records on computer back to 1988, prior in files to 1987 if not destroyed.

General Information: Public access terminal is available. No adoption, juvenile, sex offender or sealed records released. Fax notes: Will not fax results. Copy fee: $5.00 per document. Certification fee: $10.00 per

document. Fee payee: District Court. Personal checks accepted. Prepayment is required.

1st Judicial District Court - Division 3 1 Mendota Rd West, #140, West St Paul, MN 55118; 651-554-6200; Fax: 651-554-6226. Hours: 8AM-4:30PM (CST). *Felony, Misdemeanor, Civil, Eviction, Small Claims, Probate.*

www.co.dakota.mn.us/courts/index.htm

Formerly located at 125 3rd Ave North, S. St. Paul.

Civil Records: Access: In person only. Visitors must perform in person searches for themselves. No search fee. Required to search: name, years to search. Civil records on computer from 12/87, prior on ledgers.

Criminal Records: Access: In person only. Visitors must perform in person searches for themselves. No search fee. Required to search: name, years to search. Criminal records on computer from 12/87, prior on ledgers.

General Information: No adoption, juvenile, sex offender or sealed records released. Copy fee: $5.00 per document. Certification fee: $10.00. Fee payee: Court Administrator. Personal checks accepted. Prepayment is required.

District Court Judicial Center, 1560 Hwy 55, Hastings, MN 55033; 651-438-8100; Fax: 651-438-8162. Hours: 8AM-4:30PM (CST). *Felony, Misdemeanor, Civil, Eviction, Small Claims, Probate.*

www.co.dakota.mn.us/courts

Civil Records: Access: In person only. Visitors must perform in person searches for themselves. No search fee. Required to search: name, years to search. Civil cases indexed by defendant, plaintiff. Civil records on computer from 1/88, on ledgers prior.

Criminal Records: Access: In person only. Visitors must perform in person searches for themselves. No search fee. Required to search: name, years to search. Criminal records on computer from 1/88, on ledgers prior.

General Information: Public access terminal is available. No adoption, juvenile, sealed records released. Copy fee: $5.00 per document. Certification fee: $10.00. Fee payee: District Court. Personal checks accepted. Prepayment is required.

Dodge County

3rd Judicial District Court 22 Sixth St SE #12, Mantorville, MN 55955; 507-635-6260; Fax: 507-635-6271. Hours: 8AM-4:30PM (CST). *Felony, Misdemeanor, Civil, Eviction, Small Claims, Probate.*

www.courts.state.mn.us/districts/third

Civil Records: Access: Fax, mail, in person. Both court and visitors may perform in person searches. No search fee. Required to search: name, years to search. Civil cases indexed by defendant, plaintiff. Civil records on computer back to 1984, on cards from 1984, on books from 1972.

Criminal Records: Access: In person only. Visitors must perform in person searches for themselves. No search fee. Required to search: name, years to search, DOB. Criminal records on computer back to 1984, on cards from 1984, on books from 1972.

General Information: Public access terminal is available. No adoption, juvenile, sex offender or sealed records released. SASE required. Turnaround time 1-2 days. Fax notes: Fee to fax results is $5.00 per document. Copy fee: $5.00 per document. Certification fee: $10.00. Fee payee: Court Administrator. Personal checks accepted. Prepayment is required.

Douglas County

7th Judicial District Court 305 8th Ave West, Alexandria, MN 56308; 320-762-3882; Fax: 320-762-8863. Hours: 8AM-4:30PM (CST). *Felony, Misdemeanor, Civil, Eviction, Small Claims, Probate.*

Civil Records: Access: Mail, in person. Both court and visitors may perform in person searches. Search fee: $5.00 per name. Required to search: name, years to search. Civil cases indexed by defendant, plaintiff. Civil records on computer from 1987, on microfiche from 1951, books prior. The books are grouped by letter, but not alphabetized.

Criminal Records: Access: In person only. Both court and visitors may perform in person searches. Search fee: $5.00 per name. Required to search: name. Criminal records on computer from 1987, on microfiche from 1951, books prior. The books are grouped by letter, but not alphabetized.

General Information: Public access terminal is available. No adoption, juvenile or sealed records released. SASE required. Turnaround time 1-7 days. Copy fee: $5.00 per document. Certification fee: $10.00. Fee payee: Court Administrator. Personal checks accepted. Prepayment is required.

Faribault County

5th Judicial District Court PO Box 130, Blue Earth, MN 56013; 507-526-6273; Fax: 507-526-3054. Hours: 8AM-4:30PM (CST). *Felony, Misdemeanor, Civil, Eviction, Small Claims, Probate.*

Civil Records: Access: Mail, in person. Only the court performs in person searches; visitors may not. No search fee. Required to search: name, years to search. Civil cases indexed by defendant, plaintiff. Civil records on computer from 1989, in books from 1870.

Criminal Records: Access: In person only. Visitors must perform in person searches for themselves. No search fee. Required to search: name, years to search; also helpful: DOB. Criminal records on computer from 1989, in books from 1870. The county suggests sending requests to the state Bureau of Criminal Apprehension.

General Information: Public access terminal is available. No adoption, juvenile, sex offender or sealed records released. SASE required. Turnaround time 7 days or less. Copy fee: $5.00 per document. Certification fee: $10.00. Fee payee: Court Administrator. Personal checks accepted. Prepayment is required.

Fillmore County

3rd Judicial District Court 101 Fillmore St, PO Box 436, Preston, MN 55965; 507-765-4483; Fax: 507-765-4571. Hours: 8AM-4:30PM (CST). *Felony, Misdemeanor, Civil, Eviction, Small Claims, Probate.*

www.courts.state.mn.us/districts/third

Civil Records: Access: Mail, in person. Both court and visitors may perform in person searches. Search fee: No search fee. Required to search: name, years to search. Civil cases indexed by defendant, plaintiff. Civil records on computer from 1990, books from 1860s.

Criminal Records: Access: In person only. Visitors must perform in person searches for themselves. Search fee: No search fee. Required to search: name, years to search, DOB. Criminal records on computer from 1990, books from 1860s.

General Information: Public access terminal is available. No adoption, juvenile or sealed records released. SASE not required. Turnaround time 1-2 days. Copy fee: $5.00 per document. Certification fee: $10.00. Fee payee: Court Administrator. Personal checks accepted. Prepayment is required.

Freeborn County

3rd Judicial District Court 411 S Broadway, Albert Lea, MN 56007; 507-377-5153; Fax: 507-377-5260. Hours: 8AM-5PM (CST). *Felony, Misdemeanor, Civil, Eviction, Small Claims, Probate.*

www.courts.state.mn.us/districts/third

Civil Records: Access: Mail, in person. Both court and visitors may perform in person searches. Search fee:

$5.00. Required to search: name, years to search. Civil cases indexed by defendant, plaintiff. Civil records on computer from 11/89.

Criminal Records: Access: In person only. Visitors must perform in person searches for themselves. Required to search: name, years to search, DOB. Criminal records on computer from 11/89.

General Information: Public access terminal is available. No adoption, juvenile, sex offender or sealed records released. SASE required. Turnaround time 3-5 days. Copy fee: $5.00 per document. Certification fee: $10.00. Fee payee: Court Administrator. Personal checks accepted. Prepayment is required.

Goodhue County

1st Judicial District Court PO Box 408 (454 W 6th St), Red Wing, MN 55066; 651-267-4800; Fax: 651-267-4989. Hours: 8AM-4:30PM (CST). *Felony, Misdemeanor, Civil, Eviction, Small Claims, Probate.*

Civil Records: Access: Mail, in person. Both court and visitors may perform in person searches. No search fee. Required to search: name, years to search. Civil cases indexed by defendant, plaintiff. Civil records on computer from 3/92, prior records on docket books.

Criminal Records: Access: In person only. Visitors must perform in person searches for themselves. No search fee. Required to search: name. Criminal records on computer from 3/92, prior records on docket books.

General Information: Public access terminal is available. No adoption, juvenile, sex offender or sealed records released. SASE required. Turnaround time same day. Copy fee: $5.00 per document. Certification fee: $10.00. Fee payee: Court Administrator. Personal checks accepted. Prepayment is required.

Grant County

8th Judicial District Court PO Box 1007 (10 2nd St NE), Elbow Lake, MN 56531; 218-685-4825. Hours: 8AM-4PM (CST). *Felony, Misdemeanor, Civil, Eviction, Small Claims, Probate.*

Civil Records: Access: Mail, in person. Visitors must perform in person searches for themselves. No search fee. Required to search: name, years to search. Civil cases indexed by defendant, plaintiff. Civil records on computer from 6/89, on cards from 1930, prior at Historical Society.

Criminal Records: Access: In person only. Visitors must perform in person searches for themselves. No search fee. Required to search: name, years to search; also helpful: DOB. Criminal records on computer from 6/89, on cards from 1930, prior at Historical Society.

General Information: Public access terminal is available. No adoption, juvenile, sex offender or sealed records released. SASE required. Turnaround time 1-2 days. Fax notes: Fee to fax results is $5.00 per document. Copy fee: $5.00 per document. Certification fee: $10.00. Fee payee: Court Administrator. Personal checks accepted. Prepayment is required.

Hennepin County

4th Judicial District Court - Division 1
Civil 1251 C Government Center, 300 S 6th St, Minneapolis, MN 55487; 612-348-3164; Fax: 612-348-2131. Hours: 8AM-4:30PM (CST). *Civil.*

www.co.hennepin.mn.us/courts/court.htm

Civil Records: Access: Fax, mail, in person. Both court and visitors may perform in person searches. No search fee. Required to search: name, years to search. Civil cases indexed by defendant, plaintiff. Civil records on computer from 1978, prior on microfilm.

General Information: Public access terminal is available. No sex offender or sealed records released, domestic abuse and paternity cases are limited. SASE required. Turnaround time 7-10 days. Copy fee: $.50 per document. Certification fee: $10.00. Fee payee:

Court Administrator. Personal checks accepted. Prepayment is required.

4th Judicial District Court - Division 1
Criminal 300 S 6th St, Minneapolis, MN 55487; 612-348-2612; Fax: 612-348-6099. Hours: 8AM-4:30PM (CST). *Felony, Misdemeanor.*

www.co.hennepin.mn.us/courts/court.htm

Criminal Records: Access: Fax, mail, in person. Both court and visitors may perform in person searches. Search fee: $5.00 per name if no record found; otherwise $10.00 per name. Required to search: name, years to search, DOB. Overall records go back to 1886. Computerized records back to 1978.

General Information: Public access terminal is available. No adoption, juvenile, sex offender or sealed records released. SASE required. Turnaround time 7-10 days. Copy fee: $5.00 per document. Certification fee: $10.00. Fee payee: Court Administrator. Personal checks accepted. Prepayment is required.

4th Judicial District Court - Division 2
Brookdale 4139 Regent Ave N #132, Brooklyn Center, MN 55430; 763-569-2799; Fax: 763-569-3697. Hours: 7:45AM-4:30PM (CST). *Misdemeanor, Eviction, Small Claims.*

www.co.hennepin.mn.us/courts/court.htm

Civil Records: Access: Mail, fax, in person. Search fee: $5.00 per name. Required to search: name, years to search. Civil cases indexed by defendant.

Criminal Records: Access: Mail, fax, in person. Both court and visitors may perform in person searches. Search fee: $5.00 per name. Required to search: name, years to search, DOB. Criminal records on computer since 1987.

General Information: Public access terminal is available. No juvenile court, unlawful detainers or sealed records released. SASE required. Turnaround time 1-7 days. Copy fee: $5.00 per document. Certification fee: $10.00. Fee payee: Hennepin County District Court. Personal checks accepted. Prepayment is required.

4th Judicial District Court - Division 3
Ridgedale 12601 Ridgedale Dr, Minnetonka, MN 55305; 952-541-7000; Fax: 952-541-6297. Hours: 8AM-4:30PM (CST). *Misdemeanor, Eviction, Small Claims.*

www.co.hennepin.mn.us/courts/court.htm

Civil Records: Access: Mail, in person. Both court and visitors may perform in person searches. Search fee: $5.00 per name. Required to search: name, years to search. Civil cases indexed by defendant. Civil records on computer.

Criminal Records: Access: Mail, in person. Both court and visitors may perform in person searches. Search fee: $5.00 per name. Required to search: name, years to search; also helpful: DOB. Criminal records on computer since 1989; prior records on microfiche.

General Information: Public access terminal is available. (Limited information available.) No police reports, juvenile or sealed records released. SASE required. Turnaround time 3-4 weeks. Copy fee: $5.00 per document. Certification fee: $10.00. Fee payee: Hennepin County District Court. Personal checks accepted. Prepayment is required.

4th Judicial District Court - Division 4
Southdale 7009 York Ave South, Edina, MN 55435; 952-830-4877; Fax: 952-830-4993. Hours: 8AM-4:30PM (CST). *Misdemeanor.*

www.co.hennepin.mn.us/courts/court.htm

Criminal Records: Access: Mail, fax, in person. Visitors must perform in person searches for themselves. No search fee. Required to search: name, years to search, DOB; also helpful: offense, date of offense. Criminal records on computer since late 1970s, felonies on computer earlier. In person search with court assistance $10.00.

General Information: Public access terminal is available. (Criminal & Traffic.) No juvenile or sealed records released. Copy fee: $5.00 per document. Certification fee: $10.00. Fee payee: Hennepin County District Court. Personal checks accepted. Prepayment is required.

4th Judicial District Court - Division 1
C400 Government Center, 300 S 6th St, Minneapolis, MN 55487; 612-348-3244; Fax: 612-348-5799. Hours: 7AM-5PM (CST). *Probate.*

www.co.hennepin.mn.us/courts/court.htm

Houston County

3rd Judicial District Court 304 S Marshall, Rm 204, Caledonia, MN 55921; 507-725-5806; Fax: 507-725-5550. Hours: 8AM-4:30PM (CST). *Felony, Misdemeanor, Civil, Eviction, Small Claims, Probate.*

www.courts.state.mn.us/districts/third

Civil Records: Access: Mail, in person. Visitors must perform in person searches for themselves. No search fee. Required to search: name, years to search, DOB. Civil cases indexed by defendant, plaintiff. Civil records on computer back to 8/89, prior on cards and books. Probate on microfilm to 1990.

Criminal Records: Access: In person only. Visitors must perform in person searches for themselves. No search fee. Required to search: name, years to search; also helpful: DOB. Criminal records on computer back to 8/89, prior on cards and books.

General Information: Public access terminal is available. No adoption, juvenile, sex offender or sealed records released. SASE required. Turnaround time 2 days. Fax notes: Fee to fax results is $5.00 per document. Copy fee: $5.00 per document. Certification fee: $10.00. Fee payee: Court Administrator. Personal checks accepted. Prepayment is required.

Hubbard County

9th Judicial District Court 301 Court St, Park Rapids, MN 56470; 218-732-3573; Fax: 218-732-0137. Hours: 8AM-4:30PM (CST). *Felony, Misdemeanor, Civil, Eviction, Small Claims, Probate.*

Civil Records: Access: Mail, in person. Both court and visitors may perform in person searches. Search fee: $5.00 per name. Required to search: name, years to search. Civil cases indexed by defendant, plaintiff. Civil records on computer since 1990, prior on index cards.

Criminal Records: Access: Mail, in person. Both court and visitors may perform in person searches. Search fee: $5.00 per name. Required to search: name, DOB. Criminal records on computer since 1990, prior on index cards.

General Information: Public access terminal is available. No adoption, juvenile, sex offender or sealed records released. SASE required. Turnaround time 1 week. Copy fee: $5.00 per document. Certification fee: $10.00. Fee payee: Court Administrator. Personal checks accepted. Prepayment is required.

Isanti County

10th Judicial District Court 555 18th Ave SW, Cambridge, MN 55008-9386; 763-689-2292; Fax: 763-689-8340. Hours: 8AM-4:30PM (CST). *Felony, Misdemeanor, Civil, Eviction, Small Claims, Probate.*

Civil Records: Access: Mail, in person. Visitors must perform in person searches for themselves. Search fee: No search fee. Required to search: name, years to search. Civil cases indexed by defendant, plaintiff. Civil records on computer from 12/84, prior on microfiche.

Criminal Records: Access: In person only. Visitors must perform in person searches for themselves. Search fee: No search fee. Required to search: name, years to

search. Criminal records on computer from 12/84, prior on microfiche.

General Information: Public access terminal is available. No adoption, juvenile, sex offender or sealed records released. SASE required. Turnaround time up to 10 days. Fax notes: Will fax free to local or toll-free numbers. Copy fee: $5.00 per document. Certification fee: $10.00. Fee payee: Court Administrator. Personal checks accepted. Prepayment is required.

Itasca County

9th Judicial District Court 123 4th St NE, Grand Rapids, MN 55744-2600; 218-327-2870; Fax: 218-327-2897. Hours: 8AM-4PM (CST). *Felony, Misdemeanor, Civil, Eviction, Small Claims, Probate.*

Civil Records: Access: Mail, in person. Both court and visitors may perform in person searches. Search fee: $5.00 per name. Required to search: name, years to search, DOB. Civil cases indexed by defendant, plaintiff. Civil records on computer from 4-87, on microfiche to 1982, on books prior.

Criminal Records: Access: Mail, in person. Both court and visitors may perform in person searches. Search fee: $5.00 per name. Required to search: name, years to search, DOB. Criminal records on computer from 4-87, on microfiche to 1982, on books prior.

General Information: Public access terminal is available. No adoption, juvenile or sealed records released. SASE not required. Turnaround time 7-14 days, 24 hours required to pull from off-site storage. Fax notes: Fee to fax results is additional $5.00 per document. Copy fee: $5.00 per document. Certification fee: $10.00. Fee payee: Court Administrator. Personal checks accepted. Prepayment is required.

Jackson County

5th Judicial District Court PO Box 177, Jackson, MN 56143; 507-847-4400; Fax: 507-847-5433. Hours: 8:30AM-4:30PM (CST). *Felony, Misdemeanor, Civil, Eviction, Small Claims, Probate.*

Civil Records: Access: Fax, mail, in person. Both court and visitors may perform in person searches. Search fee: $10.00 per name. Required to search: name, years to search, address. Civil cases indexed by defendant, plaintiff. Civil records on computer from 5/89. Probate on microfiche from 1870.

Criminal Records: Access: Fax, mail, in person. Visitors must perform in person searches for themselves. Search fee: $15.00 per name if referred to state agency. Required to search: name, years to search, DOB. Criminal records on computer from 5/89. Probate on microfiche from 1870.

General Information: Public access terminal is available. No adoption, juvenile, sex offender or sealed records released. SASE required. Turnaround time 2-3 days. Fax notes: Fax fee 1-5 pages $5.00, each additional page $1.00. Copy fee: $5.00 per document. Certification fee: $10.00. Fee payee: Court Administrator. Personal checks accepted. Prepayment is required.

Kanabec County

10th Judicial District Court 18 North Vine, Suite 318, Mora, MN 55051-1385; 320-679-6400; Fax: 320-679-6411. Hours: 8AM-4:30PM (CST). *Felony, Misdemeanor, Civil, Eviction, Small Claims, Probate.*

Civil Records: Access: In person only. Visitors must perform in person searches for themselves. No search fee. Required to search: name, years to search. Civil cases indexed by defendant, plaintiff. Civil records on computer from 1986, prior on books and microfiche.

Criminal Records: Access: In person only. Visitors must perform in person searches for themselves. No search fee. Required to search: name, years to search; also helpful: DOB. Criminal records on computer from 1986, prior on books and microfiche.

General Information: Public access terminal is available. No adoption, juvenile or sealed records released. Copy fee: $5.00 per document. Certification fee: $10.00. Fee payee: Court Administrator. Personal checks accepted. Prepayment is required.

Kandiyohi County

8th Judicial District Court 505 Becker Ave SW, Willmar, MN 56201; 320-231-6206; Fax: 320-231-6276. Hours: 8AM-4:30PM (CST). *Felony, Misdemeanor, Civil, Eviction, Small Claims, Probate.*

Civil Records: Access: In person only. Both court and visitors may perform in person searches. No search fee. Required to search: name, years to search. Civil cases indexed by defendant, plaintiff. Civil records on computer from 1986, prior on microfilm.

Criminal Records: Access: In person only. Visitors must perform in person searches for themselves. No search fee. Required to search: name, years to search, DOB; also helpful: SSN. Criminal records on computer from 1986, prior on microfilm.

General Information: Public access terminal is available. No adoption, juvenile, sex offender or sealed records released. Copy fee: $5.00 per document. Certification fee: $10.00. Fee payee: Court Administrator. Personal checks accepted. Prepayment is required.

Kittson County

9th Judicial District Court PO Box 39, Hallock, MN 56728; 218-843-3632; Fax: 218-843-3634. Hours: 8:00AM-4:30PM (CST). *Felony, Misdemeanor, Civil, Eviction, Small Claims, Probate.*

Civil Records: Access: Fax, mail, in person. Both court and visitors may perform in person searches. Search fee: $5.00 per name. Will charge $20.00 per hour for extensive searches. Required to search: name, years to search. Civil cases indexed by defendant, plaintiff. Civil records on computer from 9/90, prior on books and index cards. Visitors may look at judgment docket.

Criminal Records: Access: Fax, mail, in person. Only the court performs in person searches; visitors may not. Search fee: $5.00 per name. Will charge $20.00 per hour for extensive searches. Required to search: name, years to search, DOB, offense. Criminal records on computer from 9/90, prior on books and index cards.

General Information: Public access terminal is available. No adoption, juvenile, sex offender or sealed records released. SASE required. Turnaround time 1-2 days. Fax notes: No fee to fax results. Copy fee: $5.00 per document. Certification fee: $10.00. Fee payee: Court Administrator. Personal checks accepted. Prepayment is required.

Koochiching County

9th Judicial District Court Court House, 715 4th St, International Falls, MN 56649; 218-283-1160; Fax: 218-283-1162. Hours: 8AM-4PM (CST). *Felony, Misdemeanor, Civil, Eviction, Small Claims, Probate.*

Civil Records: Access: Mail, in person. Both court and visitors may perform in person searches. Search fee: $5.00 per name. Required to search: name, years to search. Civil cases indexed by defendant, plaintiff. Civil records on computer from 5/90, on TCIS cards from 1984, on books from 1906.

Criminal Records: Access: Mail, in person, fax. Both court and visitors may perform in person searches. Search fee: $5.00 per name. Required to search: name, years to search, DOB. Criminal records on computer from 5/90, on TCIS cards from 1984, on books from 1906.

General Information: Public access terminal is available. No adoption, juvenile, sex offender or sealed records released. SASE required. Turnaround time 1 week. Fax notes: Fee to fax results is $5.00 per document. Copy fee: $5.00 per document. Certification fee: $10.00. Fee payee: Court Administrator. Personal checks accepted. Prepayment is required.

Lac qui Parle County

8th Judicial District Court PO Box 36 (600 6th St), Madison, MN 56256; 320-598-3536; Fax: 320-598-3915. Hours: 8:30AM-4:30PM (CST). *Felony, Misdemeanor, Civil, Eviction, Small Claims, Probate.*

www.courts.state.mn.us/districts/eighth/dist08.htm

Civil Records: Access: Fax, phone, mail, in person. Only the court performs in person searches; visitors may not. Search fee: $5.00 per name. Required to search: name, years to search. Civil cases indexed by defendant, plaintiff. Civil records on computer from 1988, prior on index cards.

Criminal Records: Access: In person only. Mail, in person. No search fee. Required to search: name, years to search, DOB; also helpful: SSN. Criminal records on computer from 1988, prior on index cards. Court may refer criminal searches requests to the sheriff's office, 320-598-3720. Sheriff address is 600 6th St.

General Information: No adoption, juvenile, sex offender or sealed records released. SASE required. Turnaround time 1-3 days. Fax notes: $5.00 per document. Copy fee: $5.00 per document. Certification fee: $10.00. Fee payee: Court Administrator. Personal checks accepted. Prepayment is required.

Lake County

6th Judicial District Court 601 3rd Ave, Two Harbors, MN 55616; 218-834-8330; Fax: 218-834-8397. Hours: 8AM-4:30PM (CST). *Felony, Misdemeanor, Civil, Eviction, Small Claims, Probate.*

www.6courts.com

Civil Records: Access: Fax, mail, in person. Both court and visitors may perform in person searches. No search fee. Required to search: name, years to search. Civil cases indexed by defendant, plaintiff. Civil records on computer back to 1991, prior on index cards.

Criminal Records: Access: In person only. Visitors must perform in person searches for themselves. No search fee. Required to search: name, years to search, DOB. Criminal records on computer back to 1991, prior on index cards.

General Information: Public access terminal is available. No adoption, juvenile, sex offender or sealed records released. SASE required. Turnaround time 1 day. Fax notes: Fee to fax results is $5.00 per document. Copy fee: $5.00 per document. Certification fee: $10.00. Fee payee: Court Administrator. Personal checks accepted. Credit cards accepted: Visa, MasterCard. Prepayment is required.

Lake of the Woods County

9th Judicial District Court PO Box 808, Baudette, MN 56623; 218-634-1451; Fax: 218-634-9444. Hours: 7:30AM-4PM (CST). *Felony, Misdemeanor, Civil, Eviction, Small Claims, Probate.*

Civil Records: Access: Fax, mail, in person. Both court and visitors may perform in person searches. Search fee: $10.00 per name. Required to search: name, years to search. Civil records on computer back to 1990; on microfilm to 1923.

Criminal Records: Access: Fax, mail, in person. Only the court performs in person searches; visitors may not. Search fee: $10.00 per name. Required to search: name, years to search, DOB. Criminal records on computer back to 1990; on microfilm back to 1923.

General Information: No adoption, juvenile, sex offender or sealed records released. SASE not required. Turnaround time 2 days, no phone searches. Fax notes: No fee to fax results. Copy fee: $5.00 per document. Certification fee: $10.00. Fee payee: Court

Administrator. Personal checks accepted. Prepayment is required.

Le Sueur County

1st Judicial District Court 88 S Park Ave, Le Center, MN 56057; 507-357-2251; Fax: 507-357-6375. Hours: 8AM-4:30PM (CST). *Felony, Misdemeanor, Civil, Eviction, Small Claims, Probate.*

Civil Records: Access: In person only. Visitors must perform in person searches for themselves. No search fee. Required to search: name, years to search. Civil cases indexed by defendant, plaintiff. Civil records on computer from 1992, prior on books.

Criminal Records: Access: In person only. Visitors must perform in person searches for themselves. No search fee. Required to search: name, years to search, DOB, signed release. Criminal records on computer from 1992, prior on books.

General Information: Public access terminal is available. No adoption, juvenile, sex offender or sealed records released. Fax notes: No fee to fax results. Copy fee: $5.00 per document. Certification fee: $10.00. Fee payee: Court Administrator. Personal checks accepted. Prepayment is required.

Lincoln County

5th Judicial District Court PO Box 15, Ivanhoe, MN 56142-0015; 507-694-1355; Fax: 507-694-1717. Hours: 8:30AM-Noon,1-4:30PM (CST). *Felony, Misdemeanor, Civil, Eviction, Small Claims, Probate.*

Civil Records: Access: Mail, in person. Only the court performs in person searches; visitors may not. No search fee. Required to search: name, years to search. Civil cases indexed by defendant, plaintiff. Civil records on computer from 1989, on TCIS from 12/82, on books from late 1800.

Criminal Records: Access: In person only. Visitors must perform in person searches for themselves. No search fee. Required to search: name, years to search, DOB. Criminal records on computer from 1989, on TCIS from 12/82, on books from late 1800. All written requests for criminal record information is referred to Bureau of Criminal Apprehension (state agency). Call first for form, 650-642-0670.

General Information: Public access terminal is available. No adoption, juvenile, sex offender or sealed records released. SASE required. Turnaround time 1 week. Fax notes: Fee to fax results is $5.00 per document. Copy fee: $5.00 per document. Certification fee: $10.00. Fee payee: Court Administrator. Personal checks accepted. Prepayment is required.

Lyon County

5th Judicial District Court 607 W Main, Marshall, MN 56258; 507-537-6734; Fax: 507-537-6150. Hours: 8:30AM-4:30PM (CST). *Felony, Misdemeanor, Civil, Eviction, Small Claims, Probate.*

Civil Records: Access: Mail, in person. Both court and visitors may perform in person searches. No search fee. Required to search: name, years to search. Civil cases indexed by defendant, plaintiff. Civil records on computer from 1987, prior on index cards.

Criminal Records: Access: In person only. Visitors must perform in person searches for themselves. No search fee. The court requires sending requests to the state Bureau of Criminal Apprehension.

General Information: Public access terminal is available. No adoption, juvenile, sex offender or sealed records released. SASE required. Copy fee: $5.00 per document. Certification fee: $10.00. Fee payee: Court Administrator. Personal checks accepted. Credit cards accepted: Visa, MasterCard. Prepayment is required.

Mahnomen County

9th Judicial District Court PO Box 459, Mahnomen, MN 56557; 218-935-2251; Fax: 218-935-2851. Hours: 8AM-4:30PM (CST). *Felony, Misdemeanor, Civil, Eviction, Small Claims, Probate.*

Civil Records: Access: Mail, in person. Both the court and visitor may perform in person searches. Search fee: $5.00 per name. Required to search: name, years to search. Civil cases indexed by defendant, plaintiff. Civil records on computer from 8/90, prior on books from 1907.

Criminal Records: Access: Mail, in person. Both the court and visitor may perform in person searches Search fee: $5.00 per name. Required to search: name, years to search. Criminal records on computer from 8/90, prior on books from 1907.

General Information: Public access terminal is available. No adoption, juvenile, sex offender or sealed records released. SASE required. Turnaround time 1-5 days. Copy fee: $5.00 per document. Certification fee: $10.00. Fee payee: Court Administrator. Personal checks accepted. Prepayment is required.

Marshall County

9th Judicial District Court 208 E Colvin, Warren, MN 56762; 218-745-4921; Fax: 218-745-4343. Hours: 8AM-4:30PM (CST). *Felony, Misdemeanor, Civil, Eviction, Small Claims, Probate.*

Civil Records: Access: Mail, in person. Both court and visitors may perform in person searches. Search fee: $5.00 per name. Required to search: name, years to search; also helpful: address. Civil cases indexed by defendant, plaintiff. Civil records on computer from 5/90, on cards from 1982, on books from 1885.

Criminal Records: Access: Mail, in person. Both court and visitors may perform in person searches. Search fee: $5.00 per name. Required to search: name, years to search; also helpful: address, DOB. Criminal records on computer from 5/90, on cards from 1982, on books from 1885.

General Information: Public access terminal is available. No adoption, juvenile, sex offender or sealed records released. SASE required. Turnaround time same day. Copy fee: $5.00 per document. Certification fee: $10.00. Fee payee: Court Administrator. Personal checks accepted. Prepayment is required.

Martin County

5th Judicial District Court 201 Lake Ave, Rm 304, Martin County Court Administration, Fairmont, MN 56031; 507-238-3205; Fax: 507-238-1913. Hours: 8AM-5PM (CST). *Felony, Misdemeanor, Civil, Eviction, Small Claims, Probate.*

Civil Records: Access: Mail, in person. Both court and visitors may perform in person searches. Search fee: $10.00. Required to search: name, years to search; also helpful: address. Civil cases indexed by defendant, plaintiff. Civil records on computer from 7/89, on cards from 1986, on books from 1800s.

Criminal Records: Access: In person only. Visitors must perform in person searches for themselves. No search fee. Required to search: name, years to search, DOB; also helpful: address, SSN. Criminal records on computer from 7/89, on cards from 1986, on books from 1800s. The court suggests sending requests to the state Bureau of Criminal Apprehension.

General Information: Public access terminal is available. No adoption, juvenile, sex offender or sealed records released. SASE required. Turnaround time 1-2 weeks. Copy fee: $5.00 per document. Certification fee: $10.00. Fee payee: Court Administrator. Personal checks accepted. Credit cards accepted: Visa, MasterCard. Prepayment is required.

McLeod County

1st Judicial District Court 830 E 11th, Glencoe, MN 55336; 320-864-5551. Hours: 8AM-4:30PM (CST). *Felony, Misdemeanor, Civil, Eviction, Small Claims, Probate.*

Civil Records: Access: Mail, in person. No search fee. Required to search: name, years to search. Civil records on computer from 4/92, prior on books.

Criminal Records: Access: In person only. Visitors must perform in person searches for themselves. No search fee. Required to search: name, years to search. Criminal records on computer from 4/92, prior on books.

General Information: Public access terminal is available. No adoption, juvenile, sex offender or sealed records released. SASE required. Copy fee: $5.00 per document. Certification fee: $10.00. Fee payee: Court Administrator. Personal checks accepted. Prepayment is required.

Meeker County

8th Judicial District Court 325 N Sibley, Litchfield, MN 55355; 320-693-5230; Fax: 320-693-5254. Hours: 8AM-4:30PM (CST). *Felony, Misdemeanor, Civil, Eviction, Small Claims, Probate.*

Civil Records: Access: Fax, mail, in person. Both court and visitors may perform in person searches. Search fee: $5.00 per name. Required to search: name; also helpful: years to search, address. Civil cases indexed by defendant, plaintiff. Civil records on computer from 11/88, prior on index cards.

Criminal Records: Access: In person only. Visitors must perform in person searches for themselves. No search fee. Required to search: name; also helpful: years to search, DOB. Criminal records on computer from 11/88, prior on index cards back to 1880s.

General Information: Public access terminal is available. No adoption, juvenile, sex offender or sealed records released. SASE required. Turnaround time 3 days. Fax notes: $5.00 per document. Copy fee: $5.00 per document. Certification fee: $10.00. Fee payee: Court Administrator. Personal checks accepted. Prepayment is required.

Mille Lacs County

7th Judicial District Court Courthouse, Milaca, MN 56353; 320-983-8313; Fax: 320-983-8384. Hours: 8AM-4:30PM (CST). *Felony, Misdemeanor, Civil, Eviction, Small Claims, Probate.*

Civil Records: Access: Fax, mail, in person. Both court and visitors may perform in person searches. Search fee: $5.00. Required to search: name, years to search. Civil records on computer from 4/86, cards from 1981, books prior.

Criminal Records: Access: Fax, in person. Visitors must perform in person searches for themselves. No search fee. Required to search: name, years to search. Criminal records on computer from 4/86, cards from 1981, books prior.

General Information: Public access terminal is available. No adoption, juvenile, sex offender or sealed records released. SASE required. Turnaround time 1 week. Fax notes: $5.00 per document. Copy fee: $5.00 per document. Certification fee: $10.00. Fee payee: District Court. Personal checks accepted. Prepayment is required.

Morrison County

7th Judicial District Court 213 SE 1st Ave, Little Falls, MN 56345; 320-632-0325; Fax: 320-632-0340. Hours: 8AM-4:30PM (CST). *Felony, Misdemeanor, Civil, Eviction, Small Claims, Probate.*

Civil Records: Access: Fax, mail, in person. Both court and visitors may perform in person searches. Search fee: $5.00. Required to search: name, years to search.

Civil cases indexed by defendant, plaintiff. Civil records on computer from 5/86, prior on cards and books.

Criminal Records: Access: In person only. Visitors must perform in person searches for themselves. Required to search: name, years to search, DOB. Criminal records on computer from 5/86, prior on cards and books.

General Information: Public access terminal is available. No adoption, juvenile, sex offender or sealed records released. SASE required. Turnaround time 2-3 days. Fax notes: $5.00 per document. Copy fee: $5.00 per document. Certification fee: $10.00. Fee payee: Court Administrator. Personal checks accepted. Prepayment is required.

Mower County

Mower County District Court 201 1st St NE, Austin, MN 55912; 507-437-9465; Fax: 507-437-9471. Hours: 8AM-5PM (CST). *Felony, Misdemeanor, Civil, Eviction, Small Claims, Probate.*

Civil Records: Access: Mail, in person. Both court and visitors may perform in person searches. No search fee. Required to search: name, years to search. Civil cases indexed by defendant, plaintiff. Civil records on computer from 1989.

Criminal Records: Access: In person only. Visitors must perform in person searches for themselves. No search fee. Required to search: name, years to search, DOB. Criminal records on computer from 1989. Effective July 1, 1997, this court will no longer conduct criminal record searches.

General Information: No adoption, juvenile, paternity or sealed records released. SASE required. Turnaround time 2-3 weeks for civil, 3-4 days for criminal. Copy fee: $5.00 per document. Certification fee: $10.00. Fee payee: Court Administrator. Personal checks accepted. Prepayment is required.

Murray County

5th Judicial District Court PO Box 57, Slayton, MN 56172-0057; 507-836-6163; Fax: 507-836-6019. Hours: 8AM-5PM (CST). *Felony, Misdemeanor, Civil, Eviction, Small Claims, Probate.*

Civil Records: Access: Fax, mail, in person. Both court and visitors may perform in person searches. No search fee. Required to search: name, years to search. Civil cases indexed by defendant, plaintiff. Civil records on computer from 7/88.

Criminal Records: Access: In person only. Visitors must perform in person searches for themselves. No search fee. Required to search: name, years to search; also helpful: SSN. Criminal records on computer from 7/88. The court suggests sending requests to the state Bureau of Criminal Apprehension.

General Information: No adoption, juvenile, or sealed records released. SASE required. Turnaround time 5 days. Fax notes: $5.00 per document. Copy fee: $5.00 per document. Certification fee: $10.00. Fee payee: Court Administrator. Personal checks accepted. Prepayment is required.

Nicollet County

5th Judicial District Court PO Box 496, St Peter, MN 56082; 507-931-6800; Fax: 507-931-4278. Hours: 8AM-5PM (CST). *Felony, Misdemeanor, Civil, Eviction, Small Claims, Probate.*

Note: Records for this county can also be found at the District Court Branch in North Mankato.

Civil Records: Access: Mail, in person. Both court and visitors may perform in person searches. No search fee. Required to search: name, years to search. Civil cases indexed by defendant, plaintiff. Civil records on computer from 9/25/88, on books from 1890. The civil records prior to 9/25/88 for the entire county are located here.

Criminal Records: Access: In person only. Both court and visitors may perform in person searches. No search fee. Required to search: name, years to search, DOB. Criminal records on computer since 9/25/88. Prior records for this court only are located here on books and cards.

General Information: Public access terminal is available. No adoption, juvenile, sex offender or sealed records released. SASE required. Turnaround time 2 days. Copy fee: $5.00 per document. Certification fee: $10.00. Fee payee: Court Administrator. Personal checks accepted. Prepayment is required.

District Court - Branch PO Box 2055, North Mankato, MN 56002-2055; 507-625-3149; Fax: 507-345-1273. Hours: 8AM-5PM (CST). *Felony, Misdemeanor, Civil, Eviction, Small Claims, Probate.*

Note: Phone number for traffic is 507-625-7795.

Civil Records: Access: Mail, in person. Both court and visitors may perform in person searches. No search fee. Required to search: name, years to search. Civil cases indexed by defendant, plaintiff. Civil records on computer from 10/2/1988, prior in St Peters office.

Criminal Records: Access: In person only. Visitors must perform in person searches for themselves. No search fee. Required to search: name, years to search, DOB; also helpful: SSN. Criminal records for both courts are on computer since 9/25/88. Prior records are here for only this branch.

General Information: Public access terminal is available. No adoption, juvenile, sex offender or sealed records released. SASE required. Turnaround time 2 days. Copy fee: $5.00 per document. Certification fee: $10.00. Fee payee: District Court. Personal checks accepted. Prepayment is required.

Nobles County

5th Judicial District Court PO Box 547, Worthington, MN 56187; 507-372-8263; Fax: 507-372-4994. Hours: 8AM-4:30PM (CST). *Felony, Misdemeanor, Civil, Eviction, Small Claims, Probate.*

Civil Records: Access: Mail, in person. Both court and visitors may perform in person searches. Search fee: $5.00 per name. Required to search: name, years to search. Civil cases indexed by defendant, plaintiff. Civil records on computer from 7/88, on books and index cards prior.

Criminal Records: Access: In person only. Visitors must perform in person searches for themselves. No search fee. Required to search: name, years to search; also helpful: SSN. Criminal records on computer from 7/88, on books and index cards prior. The court suggests sending requests to the state Bureau of Criminal Apprehension.

General Information: Public access terminal is available. No adoption, juvenile, sex offender or sealed records released. SASE required. Turnaround time 1 week. Copy fee: $5.00 per document. Certification fee: $10.00. Fee payee: Court Administrator. Personal checks accepted. Credit cards accepted: Visa, MasterCard. In person only. Prepayment is required.

Norman County

9th Judicial District Court 16 3rd Ave E, Ada, MN 56510-0146; 218-784-5458; Fax: 218-784-3110. Hours: 8AM-4:30PM (CST). *Felony, Misdemeanor, Civil, Eviction, Small Claims, Probate.*

Civil Records: Access: Mail, in person. Both court and visitors may perform in person searches. Search fee: $5.00 per name. Required to search: name, years to search. Civil records on computer since 5/90, prior on index cards.

Criminal Records: Access: Mail, in person. Both court and visitors may perform in person searches. Search fee: $5.00 per name. Required to search: name, years to

search, DOB. Criminal records on computer since 5/90, prior on index cards.

General Information: No adoption, juvenile, sex offender or sealed records released. SASE required. Turnaround time 1-5 days. Copy fee: $5.00 per document. Certification fee: $10.00. Fee payee: Court Administrator. Business checks accepted. Prepayment is required.

Olmsted County

Olmsted County District Court 151 4th St SE, Rochester, MN 55904; 507-285-8210; Fax: 507-285-8996. 8AM-5PM (CST). *Felony, Misdemeanor, Civil, Eviction, Small Claims, Probate, Juvenile.*

www.courts.state.mn.us/districts/third

Civil Records: Access: Mail, in person. Both court and visitors may perform in person searches. No search fee. Required to search: name, years to search. Civil cases indexed by defendant, plaintiff. Civil records on computer from mid-1989, prior to 1856 on index cards.

Criminal Records: Access: In person only. Visitors must perform in person searches for themselves. No search fee. Required to search: name, DOB. Criminal records on computer from mid-1989, prior to 1856 on ndex cards.

General Information: Public access terminal is available. No adoption, juvenile, sex offender or sealed records released. SASE required. Turnaround time 2-7 days. Copy fee: $5.00 per document. Certification fee: $10.00. Fee payee: Court Administrator. Personal checks accepted. Credit cards accepted: Visa, MasterCard, Discover. Prepayment is required.

Otter Tail County

Otter Tail County District Court PO Box 417, Fergus Falls, MN 56538-0417; 218-739-2271; Fax: 218-739-4983. Hours: 8AM-5PM (CST). *Felony, Misdemeanor, Civil, Eviction, Small Claims, Probate.*

Civil Records: Access: Mail, in person. Both court and visitors may perform in person searches. No search fee. Required to search: name; also helpful: years to search. Civil cases indexed by defendant, plaintiff. Civil records on computer from 1987, prior on index books.

Criminal Records: Access: In person only. Visitors must perform in person searches for themselves. No search fee. Required to search: name, years to search, DOB; also helpful: address. Criminal records on computer from 1987, prior on index books.

General Information: Public access terminal is available. No adoption, juvenile, sex offender or sealed records released. SASE required. Turnaround time 2-3 days. Copy fee: $5.00 per document. Certification fee: $10.00. Fee payee: Court Administrator. Personal checks accepted. Prepayment is required.

Pennington County

9th Judicial District Court PO Box 619, Thief River Falls, MN 56701; 218-681-7023; Fax: 218-681-0907. Hours: 8AM-4:30PM (CST). *Felony, Misdemeanor, Civil, Eviction, Small Claims, Probate.*

Civil Records: Access: Mail, in person. Both court and visitors may perform in person searches. Search fee: $5.00 per name. Required to search: name, years to search. Civil cases indexed by defendant, plaintiff. Civil records on computer back to 1990, prior on TCIS cards and books to 1911.

Criminal Records: Access: Mail, in person. Both court and visitors may perform in person searches. Search fee: $5.00 per name. Required to search: name, years to search, DOB. Criminal records on computer back to 1990, prior on TCIS cards and books to 1911.

General Information: Public access terminal is available. No adoption, juvenile, sex offender or sealed records released. SASE required. Turnaround time 1 day. Copy fee: $5.00 per document. Certification fec:

$10.00. Fee payee: Court Administrator. Personal checks accepted. Prepayment is required.

Pine County

10th Judicial District Court 315 Main St S., Pine City, MN 55063; 320-629-5634. Hours: 8AM-4:30PM (CST). *Felony, Misdemeanor, Civil, Eviction, Small Claims, Probate.*

Civil Records: Access: Mail, in person. Visitors must perform in person searches for themselves. No search fee. Required to search: name, years to search. Civil records on computer from 2/85.

Criminal Records: Access: In person only. Visitors must perform in person searches for themselves. No search fee. Required to search: name, years to search. Criminal records on computer from 2/85.

General Information: Public access terminal is available. No adoption, juvenile, sex offender or sealed records released. SASE required. Turnaround time 7-9 days. Copy fee: $5.00 per document. Certification fee: $10.00. Fee payee: Court Administrator. Personal checks accepted. Prepayment is required.

Pipestone County

5th Judicial District Court 416 S Hiawatha Ave (PO Box 337), Pipestone, MN 56164; 507-825-6730; Fax: 507-825-6733. Hours: 8:30AM-4:30PM (CST). *Felony, Misdemeanor, Civil, Eviction, Small Claims, Probate.*

Civil Records: Access: Mail, in person. Both court and visitors may perform in person searches. No search fee. Required to search: name, years to search. Civil cases indexed by defendant, plaintiff. Civil records on computer from 1989, prior on books.

Criminal Records: Access: In person only. Visitors must perform in person searches for themselves. No search fee. Required to search: name, years to search. Criminal records on computer from 1989, prior on books. The court suggests sending requests to the state Bureau of Criminal Apprehension.

General Information: Public access terminal is available. No adoption, juvenile, sex offender victims or sealed records released. SASE required. Turnaround time 1 week. Copy fee: $5.00 per document. Certification fee: $10.00. Fee payee: Court Administrator. Personal checks accepted. Prepayment is required.

Polk County

9th Judicial District Court Court Administrator, 612 N Broadway #301, Crookston, MN 56716; 218-281-2332; Fax: 218-281-2204. Hours: 8AM-4:30PM (CST). *Felony, Misdemeanor, Civil, Eviction, Small Claims, Probate.*

Note: Child protection and child service cases are available as of 7/1/2002.

Civil Records: Access: Mail, in person. Both court and visitors may perform in person searches. Search fee: $5.00 per name. Required to search: name, years to search. Civil cases indexed by defendant, plaintiff. Civil records on computer from 1990, prior on index cards or books.

Criminal Records: Access: Mail, in person. Both court and visitors may perform in person searches. Search fee: $5.00 per name. Required to search: name, years to search, DOB. Criminal records on computer from 1990, prior on index cards or books.

General Information: Public access terminal is available. No adoption, non-felony under age 16 juvenile or sealed records released. SASE required. Turnaround time 3-5 days. Copy fee: $5.00 per document. Certification fee: $10.00. Fee payee: Court Administrator. Personal checks accepted. Credit cards accepted. Prepayment is required.

Pope County

8th Judicial District Court 130 E Minnesota Ave, Glenwood, MN 56334; 320-634-5222. Hours: 8AM-4:30PM (CST). *Felony, Misdemeanor, Civil, Eviction, Small Claims, Probate.*

www.courts.state.mn.us/districts/eighth/default.htm

Civil Records: Access: Mail, in person. No search fee. Required to search: name, years to search. Civil cases indexed by defendant, plaintiff. Civil records on computer from 2/89, prior on TCIS cards ad books.

Criminal Records: Access: In person only. Visitors must perform in person searches for themselves. No search fee. Required to search: name, years to search. Criminal records on computer from 2/89, prior on TCIS cards ad books.

General Information: Public access terminal is available. No adoption, juvenile, sex offender or sealed records released. SASE required. Turnaround time 1-2 days. Copy fee: $5.00 per document. Certification fee: $10.00. Fee payee: Court Administrator. Personal checks accepted. Prepayment is required.

Ramsey County

2nd Judicial District Court 15 W Kellogg, Rm 1700, St Paul, MN 55102; Civil phone: 651-266-8253; Criminal phone: 651-266-8180; Fax: 651-266-8278 civil; 266-8172 crim. Hours: 8AM-4:30PM (CST). *Felony, Misdemeanor, Civil, Probate.*

www.ramsey.courts.state.mn.us

Civil Records: Access: Mail, in person. Both court and visitors may perform in person searches. Search fee: $10.00 per name. Required to search: name, years to search. Civil cases indexed by defendant. Civil records on computer from 5/88, prior on books.

Criminal Records: Access: In person only. Visitors must perform in person searches for themselves. Required to search: name, years to search, DOB. Felony records on computer go back to 1987; misdemeanors go back to 1985, prior on books to 1932.

General Information: Public access terminal is available. No juvenile, sex offender or sealed records released. SASE required. Turnaround time 3-5 days. Copy fee: $5.00 per document. Certification fee: $10.00. Fee payee: Court Administrator. Personal checks accepted. Prepayment is required.

2nd Judicial District Court - Maplewood Area 2785 White Bear Ave, Maplewood, MN 55109; 651-777-9111; Fax: 651-777-3970. Hours: 8AM-4:30PM (CST). *Misdemeanor.*

www.co.ramsey.mn.us/courts/index.htm

Criminal Records: Access: In person only. Visitors must perform in person searches for themselves. No search fee. Required to search: name; also helpful: address, DOB, offense, date of offense. Criminal records on computer from 11/90, prior on books or index cards.

General Information: Public access terminal is available. No adoption, juvenile, sex offender victim, sealed or medical records released. Copy fee: $5.00 per document. Certification fee: $10.00. Fee payee: Ramsey County District Court. Personal checks accepted. Credit cards accepted: Visa, MasterCard, Discover. Not accepted over the phone. Prepayment is required.

2nd Judicial District Court - New Brighton Area 2785 White Bear Ave, Maplewood, MN 55109; 651-777-9111; Fax: 651-777-3970. Hours: 8AM-4:30PM (CST). *Misdemeanor.*

Note: The New Brighton Court is no longer in operation; records are at Maplewood Branch, address and phone above.

Red Lake County

9th Judicial District Court PO Box 339, Red Lake Falls, MN 56750; 218-253-4281; Fax: 218-253-4287. Hours: 8AM-4:30PM (CST). *Felony, Misdemeanor, Civil, Eviction, Small Claims, Probate.*

Civil Records: Access: Mail, in person. Both court and visitors may perform in person searches. Search fee: $5.00 per name. Required to search: name, years to search. Civil cases indexed by defendant, plaintiff. Civil records on computer and microfiche from 1990, on books from 1897.

Criminal Records: Access: Mail, in person. Both the court and visitors may perform in person searches. Search fee: $5.00 per name. Required to search: name, years to search, DOB. Criminal records on computer and microfiche from 1990, on books from 1897.

General Information: Public access terminal is available. (Only civil records available.) No adoption, juvenile, sex offender or sealed records released. SASE required. Turnaround time 1 week. Copy fee: $5.00 per document. Certification fee: $10.00. Fee payee: Court Administrator. Personal checks accepted. Prepayment is required.

Redwood County

5th Judicial District Court PO Box 130, Redwood Falls, MN 56283; 507-637-4020; Fax: 507-637-4021. Hours: 8AM-4:30PM (CST). *Felony, Misdemeanor, Civil, Eviction, Small Claims, Probate.*

Civil Records: Access: Mail, in person. Both court and visitors may perform in person searches. Search fee: $5.00 per name. Required to search: name, years to search. Civil cases indexed by defendant, plaintiff. Civil records on computer from 11/88, prior on card and books.

Criminal Records: Access: In person only. Visitors must perform in person searches for themselves. No search fee. Required to search: name, years to search. Criminal records on computer from 11/88, prior on card and books. No felony or gross misdemeanor searches will be performed.

General Information: Public access terminal is available. No adoption, juvenile, sex offender or sealed records released. SASE required. Turnaround time 2-3 days. Copy fee: $5.00 per document. Certification fee: $10.00. Fee payee: Court Administrator. Personal checks accepted. Prepayment is required.

Renville County

8th Judicial District Court 500 E DePue Ave, 3rd level, Olivia, MN 56277; 320-523-3680; Fax: 320-523-3689. Hours: 8AM-4:30PM (CST). *Felony, Misdemeanor, Civil, Eviction, Small Claims, Probate.*

Civil Records: Access: Mail, in person. Visitors must perform in person searches for themselves. No search fee. Required to search: name, years to search. Civil cases indexed by defendant, plaintiff. Civil records on computer from 1988, prior on index cards.

Criminal Records: Access: In person only. Visitors must perform in person searches for themselves. No search fee. Required to search: name. Criminal records on computer from 1988, prior on index cards.

General Information: Public access terminal is available. No adoption, juvenile, sex offender, criminal or sealed records released. SASE required. Turnaround time 1-5 days. Copy fee: $5.00 per document. Certification fee: $10.00. Fee payee: Court Administrator. Personal checks accepted. Prepayment is required.

Rice County

3rd Judicial District Court 218 NW 3rd St, Faribault, MN 55021; 507-332-6107; Fax: 507-332-6199. Hours: 8AM-4:30PM (CST). *Felony, Misdemeanor, Civil, Eviction, Small Claims, Probate.*

www.courts.state.mn.us/districts/third

Civil Records: Access: Mail, in person. Both court and visitors may perform in person searches. Search fee: $5.00. Required to search: name, years to search. Civil cases indexed by defendant, plaintiff. Civil records on computer from 1990, prior on index cards.

Criminal Records: Access: In person only. Visitors must perform in person searches for themselves. Required to search: name, years to search; also helpful: SSN. Criminal records on computer from 1990, prior on index cards.

General Information: Public access terminal is available. No adoption, juvenile, sex offender or sealed records released. SASE required. Turnaround time 1-2 days. Copy fee: $5.00 per document. Certification fee: $10.00. Fee payee: Court Administrator. Personal checks accepted. Prepayment is required.

Rock County

5th Judicial District Court PO Box 745, Luverne, MN 56156; 507-283-5020; Fax: 507-283-5017. Hours: 8AM-5PM (CST). *Felony, Misdemeanor, Civil, Eviction, Small Claims, Probate.*

Civil Records: Access: Mail, in person. Only the court performs in person searches on computer; visitors may not. Visitors may search in books for records prior to 1985. Search fee: $10.00 per name. Required to search: name, years to search. Civil cases indexed by defendant, plaintiff. Civil records on computer from 1989, prior on books.

Criminal Records: Access: Mail, in person. Only the court performs in person searches on computer; visitors may not. Visitors may search in books for records prior to 1985. Search fee: $10.00 per name. Required to search: name, years to search; also helpful: SSN. Criminal records on computer from 1989, prior on books. The court will provide address for the state Bureau of Criminal Apprehension for complete record searches.

General Information: No adoption, juvenile, sex offender or sealed records released. SASE required. Turnaround time same day if possible. Copy fee: $5.00 per document. Certification fee: $10.00. Fee payee: Court Administrator. Personal checks accepted. Prepayment is required.

Roseau County

9th Judicial District Court 606 5th Ave SW Rm 20, Roseau, MN 56751; 218-463-2541; Fax: 218-463-1889. Hours: 8AM-4:30PM (CST). *Felony, Misdemeanor, Civil, Eviction, Small Claims, Probate.*

Civil Records: Access: Mail, in person. Both court and visitors may perform in person searches. Search fee: $5.00 per name. Required to search: name, years to search. Civil cases indexed by defendant, plaintiff. Civil records on computer back to 1990, prior on index cards.

Criminal Records: Access: Mail, in person. Both court and visitors may perform in person searches. Search fee: $5.00 per name. Required to search: name, years to search; also helpful: DOB. Criminal records on computer back to 1990, prior on index cards.

General Information: Public access terminal is available. No adoption, juvenile, paternity or sealed records released. SASE required. Turnaround time same day if possible. Copy fee: $5.00 per document. Certification fee: $10.00. Fee payee: Court Administrator. Personal checks accepted. Prepayment is required.

Scott County

1st Judicial District Court Scott County Justice Center, 200 Fourth Ave W, Shakopee, MN 55379; 952-496-8200; Fax: 952-496-8211. Hours: 8AM-4:30PM (CST). *Felony, Misdemeanor, Civil, Eviction, Small Claims, Probate.*

Civil Records: Access: Mail, in person. Both court and visitors may perform in person searches. No search fee. Required to search: name, years to search. Civil cases indexed by defendant, plaintiff. Civil records on computer from 1981, prior on books.

Criminal Records: Access: In person only. Visitors must perform in person searches for themselves. No search fee. Required to search: name, years to search, DOB. Criminal records on computer from 1981, prior on books.

General Information: Public access terminal is available. No adoption, juvenile or sealed records released. SASE required. Turnaround time 1-2 days. Copy fee: $5.00 per document. Certification fee: $10.00. Fee payee: Scott County. Personal checks accepted. Prepayment is required.

Sherburne County

10th Judicial District Court Sherburne County Government Center, 13880 Hwy #10, Elk River, MN 55330-4608; 763-241-2800; Fax: 763-241-2816. Hours: 8AM-5PM (CST). *Felony, Misdemeanor, Civil, Eviction, Small Claims, Probate.*

Civil Records: Access: Mail, in person. Both court and visitors may perform in person searches. Search fee: $5.00. Required to search: name, years to search. Civil cases indexed by defendant, plaintiff. Civil records on computer from 02/85, prior on books.

Criminal Records: Access: In person only. Both court and visitors may perform in person searches. Search fee: $5.00. Required to search: name, years to search, DOB. Criminal records on computer from 02/85, prior on books back to 1930s.

General Information: Public access terminal is available. No adoption, juvenile, confidential or sealed records released. SASE required. Turnaround time 5 days. Copy fee: $5.00 per document. Certification fee: $10.00. Fee payee: Court Administrator. Personal checks accepted. Prepayment is required.

Sibley County

1st Judicial District Court PO Box 867, Gaylord, MN 55334; 507-237-4051; Fax: 507-237-4062. Hours: 8AM-5PM (CST). *Felony, Misdemeanor, Civil, Eviction, Small Claims, Probate.*

Civil Records: Access: Mail, in person. Both court and visitors may perform in person searches. Search fee: $5.00 per name. Required to search: name, years to search. Civil cases indexed by defendant, plaintiff. Civil records on computer from 5/92, prior on books to 1800's.

Criminal Records: Access: Mail, in person. Both court and visitors may perform in person searches. Search fee: $5.00 per name. Required to search: name, years to search, DOB. Criminal records on computer from 5/92, prior on books to 1800's.

General Information: Public access terminal is available. No adoption, juvenile or sealed records released. SASE required. Turnaround time 2-3 week. Fax notes: Fee to fax results is $5.00 per document. Copy fee: $5.00 per document. Certification fee: $10.00 per document. Fee payee: Court Administrator. Personal checks accepted. Prepayment is required.

St. Louis County

6th Judicial District Court 100 N 5th Ave W, Rm 320, Duluth, MN 55802-1294; 218-726-2460; Civil phone: 218-726-2431; Criminal phone: 218-726-2460; Probate phone: 218-726-2500; Fax: 218-726-2473. Hours: 8AM-4:30PM (CST). *Felony, Misdemeanor, Civil, Eviction, Small Claims, Probate.*

www.6courts.com

Note: All three St Louis County courts can access computer records for the county and direct you to the appropriate court to get the physical file.

Civil Records: Access: Mail, in person. No search fee. Required to search: name, years to search. Civil records on computer from 1976.

Criminal Records: Access: In person only. Visitors must perform in person searches for themselves. No search fee. Required to search: name. Criminal records on computer from 1976.

General Information: Public access terminal is available. No adoption, juvenile, juvenile victim of sex offense, sealed records released. SASE not required. Turnaround time 5 days. Copy fee: $5.00 per document. Certification fee: $10.00. Fee payee: Court Administrator. Personal checks accepted. Prepayment is required.

6th Judicial District Court - Hibbing Branch 1810 12th Ave East, Hibbing, MN 55746; 218-262-0100; Fax: 218-262-0219. Hours: 8AM-4:30PM (CST). *Felony, Misdemeanor, Civil, Eviction, Small Claims, Probate.*

www.courts.state.mn.us/districts/sixth/index.html

Note: All three St Louis County courts can access county computer records and direct you to the appropriate court for the physical file.

Civil Records: Access: Mail, in person. Both court and visitors may perform in person searches. Search fee: $5.00 per name/per judgment. Required to search: name, years to search. Civil cases indexed by defendant, plaintiff. Civil records on computer from 1985, prior on card or books.

Criminal Records: Access: Mail, in person. Visitors must perform in person searches for themselves. No search fee. Required to search: name, years to search. Criminal records on computer from 1985, prior on card or books. Mail requests are forwarded to MN BCA for processing.

General Information: Public access terminal is available. No adoption, juvenile, sex offender or sealed records released. SASE required. Turnaround time 2 days. Copy fee: $5.00 per document. Certification fee: $10.00. Fee payee: Court Administrator. Personal checks accepted. Prepayment is required.

6th Judicial District Court - Virginia Branch 300 S 5th Ave, Virginia, MN 55792; 218-749-7106; Fax: 218-749-7109. Hours: 8AM-4:30PM (CST). *Felony, Misdemeanor, Civil, Eviction, Small Claims, Probate.*

www.6courts.com

Note: All three St Louis County courts can access computer records for the county and direct you to the appropriate court for the physical files.

Civil Records: Access: Mail, in person. Both court and visitors may perform in person searches. No search fee. Required to search: name, years to search. Civil cases indexed by defendant, plaintiff. Civil records on computer back to 1991, prior on books.

Criminal Records: Access: In person only. Visitors must perform in person searches for themselves. No search fee. Required to search: name, years to search, DOB. Criminal records on computer back to 1991, prior on books.

General Information: Public access terminal is available. No adoption, juvenile, sex offender or sealed records released. SASE required. Turnaround time 2-3 days. Copy fee: $5.00 per document. Certification fee: $10.00. Fee payee: Court Administrator. Personal checks accepted. Prepayment is required.

Stearns County

Stearns County District Court 725 Courthouse Square, St Cloud, MN 56303; 320-656-3620; Fax: 320-656-6335. Hours: 8AM-4:30PM (CST). *Felony, Misdemeanor, Civil, Small Claims, Eviction, Probate.*

www.co.stearns.mn.us/departments/other/court/index.htm

Civil Records: Access: Mail, in person. Both court and visitors may perform in person searches. Search fee: $5.00 per name. Required to search: name, years to search. Civil cases indexed by defendant, plaintiff. Civil records on computer baclt to 1984, on books from the 1920s.

Criminal Records: Access: In person only. Visitors must perform in person searches for themselves. Required to search: name, years to search, DOB. Criminal records on computer back to 1984, on books from the 1920s.

General Information: Public access terminal is available. No adoption, juvenile, sex offender or sealed records released without court petition. SASE not required. Turnaround time 1-2 days. Copy fee: $5.00 per document. Certification fee: $10.00. Fee payee: District Court. Personal checks accepted. Credit cards accepted: Visa, MasterCard, Discover. Prepayment is required.

Steele County

3rd Judicial District Court PO Box 487 (111 E Main St), Owatonna, MN 55060; 507-444-7700; Fax: 507-444-7491. Hours: 8AM-5PM (CST). *Felony, Misdemeanor, Civil, Eviction, Small Claims, Probate.*

www.courts.state.mn.us/districts/third

Civil Records: Access: Mail, in person. Both court and visitors may perform in person searches. Search fee: $5.00. Required to search: name, years to search. Civil cases indexed by defendant, plaintiff. Civil records on computer from 1990, on books from 1870.

Criminal Records: Access: In person only. Visitors must perform in person searches for themselves. Required to search: name, years to search; also helpful: SSN. Criminal records on computer from 1990, on books from 1870.

General Information: Public access terminal is available. No adoption, juvenile, sex offender or sealed records released. SASE required. Turnaround time 1-3 days. Copy fee: $5.00 per document. Certification fee: $10.00. Fee payee: Court Administrator. Personal checks accepted. Prepayment is required.

Stevens County

8th Judicial District Court PO Box 530, Morris, MN 56267; 320-589-7287; Fax: 320-589-7288. Hours: 8AM-4:30PM (8AM-4PM Summer hours) (CST). *Felony, Misdemeanor, Civil, Eviction, Small Claims, Probate.*

Civil Records: Access: Mail, in person. Only the court performs in person searches; visitors may not. Search fee: $5.00 per name. Required to search: name, years to search. Civil cases indexed by defendant, plaintiff. Civil records on computer from 2/89, on cards from 5/86, on books from 1900.

Criminal Records: Access: In person only. Only the court performs in person searches; visitors may not. No search fee. Required to search: name, years to search. Criminal records on computer from 2/89, on cards from 5/86, on books from 1900. For access to criminal

history information, the court recommends the BCA at 651-642-0610.

General Information: No adoption, juvenile, sex offender or sealed records released. SASE required. Turnaround time 1-2 days. Copy fee: $5.00 per document. Certification fee: $10.00. Fee payee: Court Administrator. Personal checks accepted. Prepayment is required.

Swift County

8th Judicial District Court PO Box 110, Benson, MN 56215; 320-843-2744; Fax: 320-843-4124. Hours: 8AM-4:30PM (CST). *Felony, Misdemeanor, Civil, Eviction, Small Claims, Probate.*

Civil Records: Access: Phone, fax, mail, in person. Both court and visitors may perform in person searches. No search fee. Required to search: name, years to search. Civil cases indexed by defendant, plaintiff. Civil records on computer back to 8/1988, prior in files and books from 1800s.

Criminal Records: Access: In person only. Visitors must perform in person searches for themselves. No search fee. Required to search: name, years to search; also helpful: DOB. Criminal records on computer back to 1988, prior in files and books from 1800s.

General Information: No adoption, juvenile, minor victim of sex offense, sealed records released. SASE required. Turnaround time 1 week. Copy fee: $5.00 per document. Certification fee: $10.00. Fee payee: Court Administrator. Personal checks accepted. Prepayment is required.

Todd County

7th Judicial District Court 221 1st Ave South, Long Prairie, MN 56347; 320-732-7800; Fax: 320-732-2506. Hours: 8AM-4:30PM (CST). *Felony, Misdemeanor, Civil, Eviction, Small Claims, Probate.*

Civil Records: Access: Mail, in person. Both court and visitors may perform in person searches. No search fee. Required to search: name, years to search, address. Civil cases indexed by defendant, plaintiff. Civil records on computer 7/86, prior on index cards and books.

Criminal Records: Access: In person, mail. Both the court and visitors may perform in person searches. Search fee: $5.00. Required to search: name, years to search, address, DOB; also helpful: SSN. Criminal records on computer 7/86, prior on index cards and books.

General Information: Public access terminal is available. No adoption, juvenile or sealed records released. SASE required. Turnaround time 3-4 days. Fax notes: Fee to fax results is $5.00 per document. Copy fee: $5.00 per document. Certification fee: $10.00. Fee payee: Court Administrator. Personal checks accepted. Prepayment is required.

Traverse County

8th Judicial District Court 702 2nd Ave N, PO Box 867, Wheaton, MN 56296; 320-563-4343; Fax: 320-563-4311. Hours: 8AM-Noon, 12:30-4:30PM (CST). *Felony, Misdemeanor, Civil, Eviction, Small Claims, Probate.*

Civil Records: Access: Mail, in person. Both court and visitors may perform in person searches. No search fee. Required to search: name, years to search. Civil cases indexed by defendant, plaintiff. Civil records on computer from 6/89, prior on index cards and books. Only judgment searches accepted by mail.

Criminal Records: Access: In person only. Visitors must perform in person searches for themselves. No search fee. Required to search: name, years to search. Criminal records on computer from 6/89, prior on index cards and books.

General Information: No adoption, juvenile, sex offender or sealed records released. SASE required. Turnaround time 1 day. Copy fee: $5.00 per document.

Certification fee: $10.00. Fee payee: Court Administrator. Personal checks accepted. Prepayment is required.

Wabasha County

3rd Judicial District Court 625 Jefferson Ave, Wabasha, MN 55981; 651-565-3579; Fax: 651-565-3160. Hours: 8AM-4PM (CST). *Felony, Misdemeanor, Civil, Eviction, Small Claims, Probate.*

www.courts.state.mn.us/districts/third

Civil Records: Access: Phone, fax, mail, in person. Both court and visitors may perform in person searches. No search fee. Required to search: name, years to search. Civil cases indexed by defendant, plaintiff. Civil records on computer from 6/89, prior on index cards and books.
Criminal Records: Access: In person only. Visitors must perform in person searches for themselves. No search fee. Required to search: name, years to search; also helpful: DOB. Criminal records on computer from 6/89, prior on index cards and books.
General Information: Public access terminal is available. No adoption, juvenile, sex offender or sealed records released. SASE required. Turnaround time same day usually. Fax notes: Fee to fax results is $5.00 first page; $1.00 each add'l. Copy fee: $5.00 per document. Certification fee: $10.00. Fee payee: Wabasha District Court. Personal checks accepted. Prepayment is required.

Wadena County

7th Judicial District Court County Courthouse, 415 South Jefferson St, Wadena, MN 56482; 218-631-7634; Fax: 218-631-7635. Hours: 8AM-4:30PM (CST). *Felony, Misdemeanor, Civil, Eviction, Small Claims, Probate.*

Civil Records: Access: In person only. Both court and visitors may perform in person searches. No search fee. Required to search: name, years to search. Civil cases indexed by defendant, plaintiff. Civil records on computer from 7/86; prior on books, cards and microfiche.
Criminal Records: Access: In person only. Visitors must perform in person searches for themselves. No search fee. Required to search: name, years to search, DOB; also helpful: address. Criminal records on computer from 7/86; prior on books, cards and microfiche.
General Information: Public access terminal is available. No adoption, juvenile, or sealed records released. Copy fee: $5.00 per document. Certification fee: $10.00. Fee payee: Court Administrator. Personal checks accepted. Prepayment is required.

Waseca County

3rd Judicial District Court 307 N State St, Waseca, MN 56093; 507-835-0540; Fax: 507-835-0633. Hours: 8AM-4:30PM (CST). *Felony, Misdemeanor, Civil, Eviction, Small Claims, Probate.*

www.courts.state.mn.us/districts/third

Civil Records: Access: Mail, in person. Both court and visitors may perform in person searches. No search fee. Required to search: name, years to search. Civil cases indexed by defendant, plaintiff. Civil records on computer from 1990, prior on TCIS cards and books.
Criminal Records: Access: In person only. Visitors must perform in person searches for themselves. No search fee. Required to search: name, years to search, DOB. Criminal records on computer from 1990, prior on TCIS cards and books.
General Information: Public access terminal is available. No adoption, juvenile, sex offender victim or sealed records released. SASE required. Turnaround time 2 days. Copy fee: $5.00 per document.

Certification fee: $10.00. Fee payee: Court Administrator. Personal checks accepted. Prepayment is required.

Washington County

10th Judicial District Court 14949 62nd St North, PO Box 3802, Stillwater, MN 55082-3802; 651-430-6263; Fax: 651-430-6300. Hours: 7:30AM-5PM (CST). *Felony, Misdemeanor, Civil, Eviction, Small Claims, Probate.*

www.co.washington.mn.us/crtadmn.htm

Civil Records: Access: Mail, in person. Both court and visitors may perform in person searches. No search fee. Required to search: name, years to search. Civil cases indexed by defendant, plaintiff. Civil records on computer back to 12/83, prior on books.
Criminal Records: Access: In person only. Visitors must perform in person searches for themselves. No search fee. Required to search: name, years to search, DOB. Criminal records on computer back to 12/83, prior on books. Fax & mail access limited to statute requirements.
General Information: Public access terminal is available. No adoption, juvenile, sex offender or sealed records released. SASE required. Turnaround time 1 week. Copy fee: $5.00 per document. Certification fee: $10.00. Fee payee: Court Administrator. Personal checks accepted. Credit cards accepted: Visa, MasterCard. Prepayment is required.

Watonwan County

5th Judicial District Court PO Box 518, St James, MN 56081; 507-375-1236; Fax: 507-375-5010. Hours: 8AM-5PM (CST). *Felony, Misdemeanor, Civil, Eviction, Small Claims, Probate.*

Civil Records: Access: Mail, in person. Both court and visitors may perform in person searches. Search fee: $10.00. Required to search: name, years to search. Civil cases indexed by defendant, plaintiff. Civil records on computer from 5/89, prior on index cards.
Criminal Records: Access: In person only. Visitors must perform in person searches for themselves. Required to search: name, years to search; also helpful: DOB. Criminal records on computer from 5/89, prior on index cards. A signed release is necessary if court does search.
General Information: Public access terminal is available. No adoption, juvenile, sex offender or sealed records released. SASE required. Fax notes: Fee to fax is $5.00 per page. Copy fee: $5.00 per document. Certification fee: $10.00. Fee payee: Court Administrator. Personal checks accepted. Prepayment is required.

Wilkin County

8th Judicial District Court PO Box 219, Breckenridge, MN 56520; 218-643-7172; Fax: 218-643-7167. Hours: 8AM-4:30PM (CST). *Felony, Misdemeanor, Civil, Eviction, Small Claims, Probate.*

Civil Records: Access: Mail, in person. Both court and visitors may perform in person searches. No search fee. Required to search: name; also helpful: years to search. Civil cases indexed by defendant, plaintiff. Civil records on computer from 1989, prior on books.
Criminal Records: Access: In person only. The court must perform in person searches. No search fee. Required to search: name; also helpful: years to search. Criminal records on computer from 1989, prior on books.
General Information: No adoption, juvenile, sex offender or sealed records released. SASE required. Turnaround time 3-5 days. Copy fee: $5.00 per document. Certification fee: $10.00. Fee payee: Court

Administrator. Personal checks accepted. Prepayment is required.

Winona County

3rd Judicial District Court 171 West 3rd St, Winona, MN 55987; 507-457-6386; Fax: 507-457-6392. Hours: 8AM-4:30PM (CST). *Felony, Misdemeanor, Civil, Eviction, Small Claims, Probate.*

www.courts.state.mn.us/districts/third/winona.htm

Civil Records: Access: Mail, in person. Both court and visitors may perform in person searches. Search fee: $10.00 per hour. Required to search: name, years to search. Civil cases indexed by defendant, plaintiff. Civil records on computer from 1986, on books from 1888.
Criminal Records: Access: In person only. Visitors must perform in person searches for themselves. No search fee. Required to search: name, years to search, DOB. Criminal records on computer from 1986, on books from 1888. Criminal searchers are usually referred to the MN State BCA.
General Information: Public access terminal is available. No adoption, juvenile, sex offender or sealed records released. SASE not required. Turnaround time 5-10 working days. Copy fee: $10.00 per document. Certification fee: $10.00. Fee payee: Court Administrator. Personal checks accepted. Prepayment is required.

Wright County

10th Judicial District Court 10 NW 2nd St, Room 201, Buffalo, MN 55313-1192; 763-682-7549; Fax: 763-682-7300. Hours: 8AM-4:30PM (CST). *Felony, Misdemeanor, Civil, Eviction, Small Claims, Probate.*

Civil Records: Access: In person, mail. Visitors must perform in person searches for themselves. Search fee: $5.00 per name. Required to search: name, years to search. Civil cases indexed by defendant, plaintiff. Civil records on computer from 8/84, prior on books, cards & microfiche. Certificates for outstanding docketed money judgments may be requested by mail. Each name variation requires fee.
Criminal Records: Access: In person only. Visitors must perform in person searches for themselves. No search fee. Required to search: name, years to search; also helpful: DOB. Criminal records on computer from 8/84, prior on books, cards & microfiche.
General Information: Public access terminal is available. No adoption, juvenile, confidential or sealed records released. Copy fee: $5.00 per document. Certification fee: $10.00. Fee payee: Court Administrator. Personal checks accepted. Prepayment is required.

Yellow Medicine County

8th Judicial District Court 415 9th Ave, Granite Falls, MN 56241; 320-564-3325; Fax: 320-564-4435. Hours: 8AM-4PM (CST). *Felony, Misdemeanor, Civil, Eviction, Small Claims, Probate.*

Civil Records: Access: Mail, in person. Both court and visitors may perform in person searches. No search fee. Required to search: name, years to search; also helpful: address. Civil cases indexed by defendant, plaintiff. Civil records on computer from 1988.
Criminal Records: Access: In person only. Visitors must perform in person searches for themselves. No search fee. Required to search: name, years to search. Criminal records on computer from 1988.
General Information: Public access terminal is available. No adoption, juvenile or sealed records released. SASE required. Turnaround time 2-3 days. Copy fee: $5.00 per document. Certification fee: $10.00. Fee payee: Court Administrator. Personal checks accepted. Prepayment is required.

Minnesota Recording Offices

ORGANIZATION: 87 counties, 87 recording offices. The recording officer is County Recorder. The entire state is in the Central Time Zone (CST).

REAL ESTATE RECORDS: Many Minnesota counties will perform real estate searches, especially short questions over the telephone. Copy fees vary, but do not apply to certified copies. Certification fees are usually $1.00 per page with a minimum of $5.00.

UCC RECORDS: Until July 2001, Minnesota maintained a centralized database of financing statements filed at the state level and all counties entered all non-real estate filings into the central statewide database which was accessible from any county office. Now, the only filings recorded by the County Recorder are real estate related collateral. All counties will perform UCC searches. Use search request form UCC-11. Search fees are usually $15.00 per debtor name if the standard UCC-12 request form is used, or $20.00 if a nonstandard form is used. A UCC search can include tax liens. The search fee usually includes 10 listings or copies. Additional copies usually cost $1.00 per page.

TAX LIEN RECORDS: Federal and state tax liens on personal property of businesses are filed with the Secretary of State. Other federal and state tax liens are filed with the County Recorder. A special search form UCC-12 is used for separate tax lien searches. Some counties search each tax lien index separately. Some charge one $15.00 fee to search both indexes, but others charge a separate fee for each index searched. Search and copy fees vary widely.

OTHER LIENS: Mechanics, hospital, judgment, attorneys.

ONLINE ACCESS: There is no statewide system, but a number of counties offer web access to assessor data and recorded deeds.

Aitkin County

County Recorder, 209 Second St NW, Aitkin, MN 56431. County Recorder, R/E and UCC Recording 218-927-7336; Fax 218-927-7324.
Will search UCC records. Tax liens not included in UCC search. Real estate owner, mortgage, and property transfer searches available. **Other Phone Numbers:** Assessor 218-927-7327; Treasurer 218-927-7325; Elections 218-927-7354; Vital Records 218-927-7336; Marriage Records 218-927-7325.

Anoka County

County Recorder, 2100 3rd Ave., Anoka, MN 55303-2265. 763-323-5416 R/E Recording: 763-323-5413; Fax 763-323-5421. www.co.anoka.mn.us
Will search UCC records. UCC search includes tax liens if requested. Will not search real estate records. **Online Access:** Real Estate, Tax Assessor Records. Access to the County online records requires an annual fee of $35 and a $25 monthly fee and $.25 per transaction. Records date back to 1995. Lending agency information is available. For information, contact Pam LeBlanc at 763-323-5424. Also, you may access property information at https://anoka.mn.ezgov.com/ezproperty/review_search.jsp. No name searching. There is also a dial-up property information system at 763-323-5400. **Other Phone Numbers:** Assessor 763-323-5400; Treasurer 763-323-5400.

Becker County

County Recorder, PO Box 595, Detroit Lakes, MN 56502-0595. County Recorder, R/E and UCC Recording 218-846-7304; Fax 218-846-7323. www.beckercounty.com
Will search UCC records. Standard form is UCC-11. UCC search includes tax liens if requested. Real estate owner, mortgage, and property searches available by phone (very restricted) **Other Phone Numbers:** Assessor 218-846-7300; Treasurer 218-846-7311; Elections 218-846-7301; Vital Records 218-846-7304.

Beltrami County

County Recorder, 619 Beltrami Ave. NW, Bemidji, MN 56601. 218-759-4170; Fax 218-759-4527.
Will search UCC records. UCC search includes tax liens if requested. Will not search real estate records. **Other Phone Numbers:** Assessor 218-759-4114; Treasurer 218-759-4175.

Benton County

County Recorder, PO Box 129, Foley, MN 56329. 320-968-5037 R/E Recording: 320-968-6254; Fax 320-968-5329.
Will search UCC records. UCC search includes tax liens if requested. Will not search real estate records. **Other Phone Numbers:** Assessor 320-968-5019; Treasurer 320-968-5006; Vital Records 320-968-5037.

Big Stone County

County Recorder, PO Box 218, Ortonville, MN 56278. 320-839-2308; Fax 320-839-2308.
Will search UCC records. UCC tax liens will be done on UCC 12 form. Will not search real estate records. **Other Phone Numbers:** Assessor 320-839-3272; Treasurer 320-839-3445.

Blue Earth County

County Recorder, PO Box 3567, Mankato, MN 56002-3567. 507-389-8251 R/E Recording: 507-389-8222; Fax 507-389-8808.
Will search UCC records. Tax liens not included in UCC search. Real estate owner, mortgage, and property transfer searches available. Legal description required **Other Phone Numbers:** Assessor 507-389-8257; Treasurer 507-389-8237.

Brown County

County Recorder, PO Box 248, New Ulm, MN 56073-0248. County Recorder, R/E and UCC Recording 507-233-6653 UCC Recording: 507-233-6657; Fax 507-359-1430. www.co.brown.mn.us
Will search UCC records. Tax liens not included in UCC search. Real estate owner, mortgage, and property transfer searches available. **Other Phone Numbers:**

Assessor 507-233-6609; Treasurer 507-233-6617; Appraiser/Auditor 507-233-6609; Elections 507-233-6617; Vital Records 507-233-6657.

Carlton County

County Recorder, Box 70, Carlton, MN 55718. 218-384-9122 R/E Recording: 218-384-9126 UCC Recording: 218-384-9156; Fax 218-384-9157.
Will search UCC records. Tax liens not included in UCC search. Real estate owner, mortgage, and property transfer searches available. Legal description required **Other Phone Numbers:** Assessor 218-384-4281; Treasurer 218-384-4281; Vital Records 218-384-9156.

Carver County

County Recorder, Carver County Govt Center, Admin Bldg, 600 E. Fourth St, Chaska, MN 55318-2158. 952-361-1930 R/E Recording: 952-361-1935; Fax 952-361-1931. www.co.carver.mn.us
Will search UCC records. Tax liens not included in UCC search. Will not search real estate records. **Online Access:** Property Tax Records. Records on the County Property Tax Information database are available free online at www.co.carvr.mn.us/Prop_Tax/default.asp. Information is updated bi-monthly. **Other Phones:** Assessor 952-361-1960; Treasurer 952-361-1980.

Cass County

County Recorder, PO Box 3000, Walker, MN 56484. County Recorder, R/E and UCC Recording 218-547-7381 UCC Recording: 218-547-7233; Fax 218-547-7292. www.mncasscounty.com
Will search UCC records. Requests must be on approved forms. Tax liens not included in UCC search. Will search real estate records. Will go back 2 years only (verbal). **Other Phone Numbers:** Assessor 218-547-7298; Treasurer 218-547-7247; Elections 218-547-7281; Vital Records 218-547-7293.

Chippewa County

County Recorder, 629 No. 11th St., Montevideo, MN 56265. 320-269-9431 R/E Recording: 320-269-7447; Fax 320-269-7168.

Will search UCC records. Tax liens not included in UCC search. Real estate owner, mortgage, and property transfer searches available. **Other Phone Numbers:** Assessor 320-269-7696; Treasurer 320-269-7347; Vital Records 320-269-9431.

Chisago County

County Recorder, Government Center, Room/Box 277, 313 N. Main St., Center City, MN 55012-9663. 651-213-0438 R/E Recording: 651-257-1300; Fax 651-213-0454.

Will search UCC records. Tax liens not included in UCC search. Will not search real estate records. **Other Phone Numbers:** Assessor 651-213-0401.

Clay County

County Recorder, PO Box 280, Moorhead, MN 56561-0280. County Recorder, R/E and UCC Recording 218-299-5031; Fax 218-299-7500. www.co.clay.mn.us

Will search UCC records. Requests must be on approved forms. Tax liens not included in UCC search. Will not search real estate records. **Online Access:** Real Estate Records. The county online GIS mapping service provides property record searching, but by parcel number only. County Recorder records may be available at the web site in the near future. **Other Phone Numbers:** Assessor 218-299-5017; Treasurer 218-299-5011; Elections 218-299-5006; Vital Records 218-299-5031.

Clearwater County

County Recorder, 213 Main Ave North, Dept. 207, Bagley, MN 56621. County Recorder, R/E and UCC Recording 218-694-6129; Fax 218-694-6179.

Will search UCC records. UCC search includes tax liens if requested. Real estate record owner searches available. **Other Phone Numbers:** Assessor 218-694-6260; Treasurer 218-694-6130.

Cook County

County Recorder, PO Box 1150, Grand Marais, MN 55604-1150. 218-387-3000 R/E Recording: 218-387-2282 UCC Recording: 218-387-3000 x160/161; Fax 218-387-2610.

Will search UCC records. Real estate owner, mortgage, and property transfer searches available. **Other Phones:** Assessor 218-387-3000 x150-153; Treasurer 218-387-3000; Vital Records 218-387-3000 x160/161.

Cottonwood County

County Recorder, PO Box 326, Windom, MN 56101. 507-831-1458 R/E Recording: 507-831-1905; Fax 507-831-3675.

Will search UCC records. Tax liens not included in UCC search. Real estate owner, mortgage, and property transfer searches available. **Other Phone Numbers:** Assessor 507-831-2458; Treasurer 507-831-1342; Elections 507-831-1905; Vital Records 507-831-1458.

Crow Wing County

County Recorder, PO Box 383, Brainerd, MN 56401. 218-828-3965; Fax 218-825-1808.

Will search UCC records. Tax liens not included in UCC search. Real estate owner, mortgage, and property transfer searches available. **Other Phone Numbers:** Assessor 218-828-3954; Treasurer 218-828-3953.

Dakota County

County Recorder, 1590 Highway 55, Hastings, MN 55033. 651-438-4355; Fax 651-438-8176. www.co.dakota.mn.us

Will search UCC records. Tax liens not included in UCC search. No charge for verbal search. Will not search real estate records. **Online Access:** Real Estate, Assessor Records. Records on the County Real Estate Inquiry database are available free online at www.co.dakota.mn.us/assessor/real_estate_inquiry.htm.

Information includes items such as address, estimated value, taxes, last sale price, building details. **Other Phone Numbers:** Assessor 651-438-4200; Treasurer 651-438-4360.

Dodge County

County Recorder, PO Box 128, Mantorville, MN 55955-0128. County Recorder, R/E and UCC Recording 507-635-6250; Fax 507-635-6265. www.co.dodge.mn.us

Will search UCC records. UCC search includes tax liens if requested. Real estate record owner and mortgage searches available. **Other Phone Numbers:** Assessor 507-635-6245; Treasurer 507-635-6240; Vital Records 507-635-6250.

Douglas County

County Recorder, 305 8th Ave West, Courthouse, Alexandria, MN 56308. 320-762-3877 R/E Recording: 320-762-2381; Fax 320-762-2389.

Will search UCC records. Tax liens not included in UCC search. Property transfer searches available. Legal description required. **Other Phone Numbers:** Assessor 320-762-3854; Treasurer 320-762-3077; Vital Records 320-762-3877.

Faribault County

County Recorder, PO Box 130, Blue Earth, MN 56013. 507-526-6252 R/E Recording: 507-526-5147; Fax 507-526-6227.

Will search UCC records. UCC search includes tax liens if requested. Will give last document of record. **Other Phones:** Assessor 507-526-6201; Treasurer 507-526-6260; Appraiser/Auditor 507-526-6201; Elections 507-526-6212; Vital Records 507-526-6252.

Fillmore County

County Recorder, Box 465, Preston, MN 55965-0465. 507-765-3852 R/E Recording: 507-765-4701; Fax 507-765-4571.

Will search UCC records. This agency will do a tax lien search, fee is $5.00 per name. Real estate owner, mortgage, and property transfer searches available. **Other Phone Numbers:** Assessor 507-765-3868; Treasurer 507-765-3811; Elections 507-765-4701; Vital Records 507-765-5339.

Freeborn County

County Recorder, 411 S. Broadway, Court House, Albert Lea, MN 56007-4506. 507-377-5130 R/E Recording: 507-377-5116; Fax 507-377-5265. www.co.freeborn.mn.us/recorder.html

Will not search UCC records. Tax liens not included in UCC search. Will not search real estate records. **Other Phone Numbers:** Assessor 507-377-5176; Treasurer 507-377-5117.

Goodhue County

County Recorder, Box 408, Red Wing, MN 55066. 651-385-3149 R/E Recording: 651-385-8261; Fax 651-385-3039.

Will search UCC records. Tax liens not included in UCC search. Will not search real estate records. **Other Phone Numbers:** Assessor 651-385-3006; Treasurer 651-385-3032.

Grant County

County Recorder, 10th Second St NE, Courthouse, Elbow Lake, MN 56531-4300. County Recorder, R/E and UCC Recording 218-685-4133; Fax 218-685-4521.

Will search UCC records. Tax liens not included in UCC search. Real estate owner, mortgage, and property transfer searches available. Legal description required **Other Phone Numbers:** Assessor 218-685-4644.

Hennepin County

County Recorder, 300 S. 6th St, 8-A Government Center, Minneapolis, MN 55487. 612-348-3049 R/E Recording: 612-348-3050; www.co.hennepin.mn.us

Will not search UCC records. Will not search real estate records. **Online Access:** Real Estate, Lien Records. Three sources available. Access to Hennepin County online records requires a $35 annual fee with a charge of $5 per hour from 7AM-7PM, or $4.15 per hour at other times. Records date back to 1988. Only UCC & lending agency information is available. Property tax info is at the Treasurer office. For information, contact Jerry Erickson at 612-348-3856. Also, records on the County Property Information Search database are available free on the Internet at www2.co.hennepin.mn.us/pins. Search by Property ID #, address, or addition name. An Automated phone system is also available; 612-348-3011. **Other Phone Numbers:** Assessor 612-348-3046.

Houston County

County Recorder, PO Box 29, Caledonia, MN 55921-0029. County Recorder, R/E and UCC Recording 507-725-5813; Fax 507-725-2647.

Will search UCC records. UCC search includes tax liens if requested. Real estate owner, mortgage, and property transfer searches available. **Other Phones:** Assessor 507-725-5801; Treasurer 507-725-5815; Elections 507-725-5803; Vital Records 507-725-5813.

Hubbard County

County Recorder, Courthouse, Park Rapids, MN 56470. 218-732-3552 R/E Recording: 218-732-3196. Will search UCC records. Real estate owner, mortgage, and property transfer searches available. Legal description required **Other Phone Numbers:** Assessor 218-732-3452; Treasurer 218-732-4348.

Isanti County

County Recorder, 555 18th Ave SW, Courthouse, Cambridge, MN 55008. 763-689-1191 R/E Recording: 612-689-1191; Fax none.

Will search UCC records. Tax liens not included in UCC search. Property transfer searches available. Legal description required. **Other Phone Numbers:** Assessor 763-689-2752.

Itasca County

County Recorder, 123 NE 4th St, Grand Rapids, MN 55744-2600. County Recorder, R/E and UCC Recording 218-327-2856; Fax 218-327-0689.

Will search UCC records. Tax liens not included in UCC search. Real estate record owner and mortgage searches available. **Other Phone Numbers:** Assessor 218-327-2861; Appraiser/Auditor 218-327-2860; Vital Records 218-327-2856.

Jackson County

County Recorder, Jackson County Recorder PO Box 209, Jackson, MN 56143. County Recorder, R/E and UCC Recording 507-847-2580; Fax 507-847-4718.

Will search UCC records. UCC search includes tax liens if requested. Real estate owner, mortgage, and property transfer searches available. Legal description required **Other Phone Numbers:** Assessor 507-847-4033; Treasurer 507-847-2763; Elections 507-847-2763; Vital Records 507-847-2580.

Kanabec County

County Recorder, 18 N. Vine St, Mora, MN 55051. 320-679-6466 R/E Recording: 320-679-1441; Fax 320-679-6431.

Will search UCC records. Tax liens not included in UCC search. Real estate owner, mortgage, and property transfer searches available. Legal description required

Other Phone Numbers: Assessor 320-679-3381; Treasurer 320-679-1951.

Kandiyohi County

County Recorder, PO Box 736, Willmar, MN 56201-0736. County Recorder, R/E and UCC Recording 320-231-6223 UCC Recording: 320-231-6224; Fax 320-231-6284.

Will search UCC records. This agency will not do a tax lien search. Will search real estate records. **Other Phone Numbers:** Assessor 320-231-6200; Treasurer 320-231-6202; Appraiser/Auditor 320-231-6202; Vital Records 320-231-6532.

Kittson County

County Recorder, PO Box 639, Hallock, MN 56728. 218-843-2842; Fax 218-843-2020.

Will search UCC records. Tax liens not included in UCC search. Real estate owner, mortgage, and property transfer searches available. Legal description required **Other Phone Numbers:** Assessor 218-843-3615; Treasurer 218-843-3432.

Koochiching County

County Recorder, Courthouse, 715 4th St., International Falls, MN 56649. 218-283-1190 R/E Recording: 218-283-6290 UCC Recording: 218-283-1193; Fax 218-283-1194.

Will search UCC records. Tax liens not included in UCC search. Will not search real estate records. **Other Phone Numbers:** Assessor 218-283-1120; Treasurer 218-283-1112; Elections 218-283-1101; Vital Records 218-283-1190.

Lac qui Parle County

County Recorder, PO Box 132, Madison, MN 56256-0132. 320-598-3724.

Will search UCC records. Tax liens not included in UCC search. Real estate owner, mortgage, and property transfer searches available. **Other Phone Numbers:** Assessor 320-598-3187; Treasurer 320-598-3648.

Lake County

County Recorder, 601 Third Ave, Two Harbors, MN 55616. County Recorder, R/E and UCC Recording 218-834-8347; Fax 218-834-8365.

Will search UCC records. UCC search includes tax liens if requested. Will not search real estate records. **Other Phone Numbers:** Assessor 218-834-8313; Treasurer 218-834-8344; Elections 218-834-8318; Vital Records 218-834-8301.

Lake of the Woods County

County Recorder, PO Box 808, Baudette, MN 56623. 218-634-1902; Fax 218-634-2509.

Will search UCC records. Tax liens not included in UCC search. Will not search real estate records. **Other Phones:** Assessor 218-634-2536; Treasurer 634-2361.

Le Sueur County

County Recorder, 88 S. Park Ave, Courthouse, Le Center, MN 56057-1620. 507-357-2251; Fax 507-357-6375.

Will search UCC records. Tax liens not included in UCC search. Real estate record owner and mortgage searches available. **Other Phone Numbers:** Assessor 507-357-2257.

Lincoln County

County Recorder, PO Box 119, Ivanhoe, MN 56142. County Recorder, R/E and UCC Recording 507-694-1360; Fax 507-694-1198.

Will search UCC records. UCC search includes tax liens if requested. Real estate owner, mortgage, and property transfer searches available. **Other Phone Numbers:** Assessor 507-694-1522; Treasurer 507-694-1550.

Lyon County

County Recorder, 607 W. Main St, Marshall, MN 56258. County Recorder, R/E and UCC Recording 507-537-6722; Fax 507-537-7988.

Will search UCC records. UCC search includes tax liens if requested. Only telephone searches performed for real estate records. **Other Phone Numbers:** Assessor 507-537-6731.

Mahnomen County

County Recorder, PO Box 380, Mahnomen, MN 56557. County Recorder, R/E and UCC Recording 218-935-5528; Fax 218-935-5946.

Will search UCC records. Tax liens not included in UCC search. Real estate owner, mortgage, and property transfer searches available. **Other Phone Numbers:** Assessor 218-935-2417.

Marshall County

County Recorder, 208 East Colvin, Warren, MN 56762. 218-745-4801 R/E Recording: 218-745-4851; Fax 218-745-4343.

Will search UCC records. Tax liens not included in UCC search. Will search real estate records. **Other Phone Numbers:** Assessor 218-745-5331; Treasurer 218-745-4831.

Martin County

County Recorder, PO Box 785, Fairmont, MN 56031-0785. 507-238-3213; Fax 507-235-8537.

Will search UCC records. Tax liens not included in UCC search. Real estate owner, mortgage, and property transfer searches available. Legal description required **Online Access:** Property Records. Access to Martin County property records are available for a fee at https://www.landrecords.net. Search fee is $3.99 plus $.50 per image. **Other Phone Numbers:** Assessor 507-238-3210; Treasurer 507-238-3211.

McLeod County

County Recorder, PO Box 127, Glencoe, MN 55336. 320-864-5551; Fax 320-864-1295.

Will search UCC records. Tax liens not included in UCC search. Real estate owner, mortgage, and property transfer searches available. **Other Phone Numbers:** Assessor 320-864-1254; Treasurer 320-864-1203; Vital Records 320-864-1234.

Meeker County

County Recorder, 325 N. Sibley Ave, Courthouse, Litchfield, MN 55355. 320-693-5440 R/E Recording: 320-693-6112; Fax 320-693-5444.

Will search UCC records. Tax liens not included in UCC search. Real estate owner, mortgage, and property transfer searches available. **Other Phone Numbers:** Assessor 320-693-5205; Treasurer 320-693-5345; Elections 320-693-5212; Vital Records 320-693-5345.

Mille Lacs County

County Recorder, 635 2nd St S.E., Milaca, MN 56353. 320-983-8309 R/E Recording: 320-983-3146 UCC Recording: 320-983-8326; Fax 320-983-8388.

Will search UCC records with written UCCII request. Tax liens not included in UCC search. Will not search real estate records. **Other Phone Numbers:** Assessor 320-983-8311; Treasurer 320-983-8310; Appraiser/Auditor 320-983-8281; Elections 320-983-8301; Vital Records 320-983-8236.

Morrison County

County Recorder, Administration Building, 213 SE 1st Ave., Little Falls, MN 56345. 320-632-0145 R/E Recording: 320-632-2941 UCC Recording: 320-632-0142; Fax 320-632-0141. www.co.morrison.mn.us/wsite/index.htm

Will search UCC records. Tax liens not included in UCC search. Real estate owner, mortgage, and property transfer searches available. **Other Phone Numbers:** Assessor 320-632-0100; Treasurer 320-632-0151; Appraiser/Auditor 320-632-0101; Elections 320-632-0132; Vital Records 320-632-0146.

Mower County

County Recorder, 201 First St NE, Austin, MN 55912-3475. 507-437-9446 R/E Recording: 507-437-9535; Fax 507-437-9471.

Payments must be paid in advance or an account set up with a security deposit for copies mailed or faxed. Will search UCC records. This agency will do a tax lien search, fee is $15.00 per name. Will not search real estate records. **Other Phone Numbers:** Assessor 507-437-9440; Treasurer 507-437-9456; Appraiser/Auditor 507-437-9440; Elections 507-437-9536; Vital Records 507-437-9456; Information 507-437-9493.

Murray County

County Recorder, PO Box 57, Slayton, MN 56172-0057. 507-836-6148 x144; Fax 507-836-8904.

Will search UCC records. Tax liens not included in UCC search. Real estate owner, mortgage, and property transfer searches available. **Other Phone Numbers:** Assessor 507-836-6148 x151; Treasurer 507-836-6148 x149; Elections 507-836-6148 x147; Vital Records 507-836-6148 x149.

Nicollet County

County Recorder, PO Box 493, St. Peter, MN 56082-0493. County Recorder, R/E and UCC Recording 507-931-6800; Fax 507-931-9220.

Will search UCC records. Tax liens not included in UCC search. Will search real estate records, but only tract information for one year. **Other Phone Numbers:** Assessor 507-931-6800; Treasurer 507-931-6800; Elections 507-931-6800.

Nobles County

County Recorder, PO Box 757, Worthington, MN 56187. 507-372-8236; Fax 507-372-8223.

Will search UCC records. Tax liens not included in UCC search. Will not search real estate records. **Other Phone Numbers:** Assessor 507-372-8234; Treasurer 507-372-8231.

Norman County

County Recorder, PO Box 146, Ada, MN 56510. 218-784-5481 R/E Recording: 218-784-4422; Fax 218-784-2399.

Will search UCC records. UCC search includes tax liens if requested. Real estate owner, mortgage, and property transfer searches available. **Other Phone Numbers:** Assessor 218-784-5487; Treasurer 218-784-5473; Elections 218-784-5471; Vital Records 218-784-5481.

Olmsted County

Property Records & Licensing, 151 4th St. SE, Rochester, MN 55904. 507-285-8194 R/E Recording: 507-285-8195 UCC Recording: 507-285-8204; Fax 507-287-7186. www.olmstedcounty.com

Will search UCC records. Real estate owner, mortgage, and property transfer searches available. **Other Phone Numbers:** Assessor 507-285-8124; Treasurer 507-285-8197; Elections 287-2118; Vital Records 287-1444.

Otter Tail County

County Recorder, PO Box 867, Fergus Falls, MN 56538. County Recorder, R/E and UCC Recording 218-739-2271.

Will search UCC records. Tax liens not included in UCC search. Real estate owner, mortgage, and property transfer searches available. **Other Phone Numbers:** Assessor 218-739-2271.

Pennington County

County Recorder, PO Box 616, Thief River Falls, MN 56701. 218-683-7027; Fax 218-683-7026.
Will search UCC records. Tax liens not included in UCC search. Will give recent real estate documents related to a property location. **Other Phone Numbers:** Assessor 218-683-7029; Treasurer 218-683-7022; Vital Records 218-683-7027.

Pine County

County Recorder, Courthouse, 315 Sixth St., Suite 3, Pine City, MN 55063. 320-629-5665 R/E Recording: 320-629-6781; Fax 320-629-7319.
Will search UCC records. Tax liens not included in UCC search. Will not search real estate records. **Other Phone Numbers:** Assessor 320-629-6781 x150; Treasurer 320-629-6781 x138.

Pipestone County

County Recorder, 416 Hiawatha Ave. S., Pipestone, MN 56164. County Recorder, R/E and UCC Recording 507-825-6755; Fax 507-825-6767.
Will search UCC records. Tax liens not included in UCC search. Will search real estate records with specific legal description. **Other Phone Numbers:** Assessor 507-825-6750; Treasurer 507-825-6745; Elections 507-825-6740; Vital Records 507-825-6755.

Polk County

County Recorder, PO Box 397, Crookston, MN 56716. 218-281-3464; Fax 218-281-2204.
Will search UCC records. Tax liens not included in UCC search. Will not search real estate records. **Other Phone Numbers:** Assessor 218-281-4186.

Pope County

County Recorder, 130 E. Minnesota, Glenwood, MN 56334. 320-634-5723; Fax 320-634-5717. www.mncounties.org/pope/
Will search UCC records. Tax liens not included in UCC search. Real estate owner, mortgage, and property transfer searches available. **Other Phone Numbers:** Assessor 320-634-5728; Treasurer 320-634-5705; Appraiser/Auditor 320-634-5728; Elections 320-634-5705; Vital Records 320-634-5723.

Ramsey County

County Recorder, 50 W. Kellogg Blvd., Suite 812 RCGC-W, St. Paul, MN 55102-1693. 651-266-2060 R/E Recording: 612-266-2060.
Will not search UCC records. This agency will not do a tax lien search. Will give owner for a property location. **Online Access:** Property Assessor Records. Search the property assessment rolls free at www.co.ramsey.mn.us/prr/propertytax/index.asp. No name searching. **Other Phone Numbers:** Assessor 612-266-2000.

Red Lake County

County Recorder, Box 3, Red Lake Falls, MN 56750-0003. County Recorder, R/E and UCC Recording 218-253-2997; Fax 218-253-4894.
Will search UCC records. Tax liens not included in UCC search. Real estate owner, mortgage, and property transfer searches available. **Other Phone Numbers:** Assessor 218-253-2596; Treasurer 218-253-2797; Vital Records 218-253-2997.

Redwood County

County Recorder, PO Box 130, Redwood Falls, MN 56283. 507-637-4032 R/E Recording: 507-637-8325; Fax 507-637-4064.
Will search UCC records. UCC search includes tax liens if requested. Will not search real estate records. **Other Phone Numbers:** Assessor 507-637-5345.

Renville County

County Recorder, Olivia, MN 56277-1396. County Recorder, R/E and UCC Recording 320-523-3669; Fax 320-523-3679. www.co.renville.mn.us/dept.html
Will search UCC records. Tax liens not included in UCC search. Will not search real estate records. **Other Phone Numbers:** Assessor 320-523-3645; Treasurer 320-523-3676; Appraiser/Auditor 320-523-3645; Elections 320-523-2071; Vital Records 320-523-3669.

Rice County

County Recorder, 320 NW 3rd St., Suite 10, Faribault, MN 55021-6146. 507-332-6114 R/E Recording: 507-332-6100; Fax 507-332-5999.
Will search UCC records. UCC search includes tax liens if requested. Real estate owner, mortgage, and property transfer searches available. **Online Access:** Property Assessor, Property Sales Records. Search parcel information and residential/commercial sales data free at www.minnesotaassessors.com/rice. No name searching. **Other Phone Numbers:** Assessor 507-332-6102; Treasurer 507-332-6104; Appraiser/Auditor 507-332-6102; Elections 507-332-6104; Vital Records 507-332-6114.

Rock County

County Recorder, PO Box 509, Luverne, MN 56156. 507-283-5014 R/E Recording: 507-283-9177; Fax 507-283-1343.
Will search UCC records. UCC search includes tax liens if requested. Real estate owner and mortgage searches available. **Other Phone Numbers:** Assessor 507-283-5022; Treasurer 507-283-5055; Elections 507-283-5060; Vital Records 507-283-5060.

Roseau County

County Recorder, 606 5th Ave. SW, Room 170, Roseau, MN 56751-1477. County Recorder, R/E and UCC Recording 218-463-2061.
Will search UCC records. Tax liens not included in UCC search. Will not search real estate records. **Other Phone Numbers:** Assessor 218-463-1861; Treasurer 218-463-1215; Elections 218-463-1282; Vital Records 218-463-1215.

Scott County

County Recorder, 200 Fourth Ave West, Shakopee, MN 55379. County Recorder, R/E and UCC Recording 952-496-8150; Fax 952-496-8138. www.co.scott.mn.us
Will search UCC records. Tax liens not included in UCC search. Will not search real estate records. **Online Access:** Land, Property Tax Records. Search the county property databases free at www.co.scott.mn.us/xpedio/groups/public/documents/web_files/scottcounty webframe.hcsp. There is also a free online document subscription service and GIS mapping. **Other Phone Numbers:** Assessor 952-496-8150; Treasurer 952-496-8150; Appraiser/Auditor 952-496-8150; Elections 952-496-8161; Vital Records 952-496-8150.

Sherburne County

County Recorder, 13880 Highway 10, Elk River, MN 55330. 763-241-2915 R/E Recording: 800-719-2826 UCC Recording: 800-719-2826; Fax 763-241-2995. www.co.sherburne.mn.us
Will search UCC records. UCC search includes tax liens if requested. Real estate owner, mortgage, and property transfer searches available. **Online Access:** Real Estate, Tax Assessor Records. Records from the county tax assessor database are available free online at www.hometimes.com/Communities/Taxes/TaxSearch/Shurburne/index.html. **Other Phone Numbers:** Assessor 800-438-0577; Treasurer 800-438-0575; Vital Records 800-719-2826.

Sibley County

County Recorder, PO Box 44, Gaylord, MN 55334-0044. 507-237-4080 R/E Recording: 507-237-2369; Fax 507-237-4062. http://co.sibley.mn.us
Will search UCC records. UCC search includes tax liens if requested. Real estate record owner searches available. **Other Phone Numbers:** Assessor 507-237-5541; Treasurer 507-237-2820; Elections 507-237-4070; Vital Records 507-237-4080.

St. Louis County

County Recorder, PO Box 157, Duluth, MN 55801-0157. County Recorder, R/E and UCC Recording 218-726-2677; Fax 218-725-5052.
Will search UCC records. Tax liens not included in UCC search. Will not search real estate records. **Online Access:** Real Estate, Property Tax Records. Access to the Auditor and Recorder's tax records for tax professionals database is available by subscription. Fee is $100 quarterly; password provided. For information or sign-up, contact Pam Palen at 218-726-2380 or email to palenp@co.st-louis.mn.us or visit www.co.st-louis.mn.us/auditorsoffice/subscription.pdf. Also, search the City of Duluth property assessor data free at www.ci.duluth.mn.us/city/assessor/index.htm. **Other Phone Numbers:** Assessor 218-726-2304; Treasurer 218-726-2380; Appraiser/Auditor 218-726-2304; Elections 218-726-2304; Vital Records 218-726-2559; Torrens Division 218-726-2680.

Stearns County

County Recorder, 705 Courthouse Square, Administration Center, Room 131, St. Cloud, MN 56303. 320-656-3855 R/E Recording: 320-259-3855; Fax 320-656-3916.
Will search UCC records. Tax liens not included in UCC search. Will not search real estate records. **Online Access:** Real Estate, Tax Assessor Records. Records from the county tax assessor database are available free online at www.hometimes.com/Communities/Taxes/TaxSearch/index.html. **Other Phone Numbers:** Assessor 320-656-3680; Treasurer 320-656-3870.

Steele County

County Recorder, PO Box 890, Owatonna, MN 55060. County Recorder, R/E and UCC Recording 507-444-7450; Fax 507-444-7470.
Will search UCC records. Tax liens not included in UCC search. Will not search real estate records. **Other Phone Numbers:** Assessor 507-444-7435; Treasurer 507-444-7420; Elections 507-444-7410; Vital Records 507-444-7490.

Stevens County

County Recorder, PO Box 530, Morris, MN 56267. 320-589-7414; Fax 320-589-2036.
Will search UCC records. Tax liens not included in UCC search. Real estate owner, mortgage, and property transfer searches available. **Other Phone Numbers:** Assessor 320-589-7407; Treasurer 320-589-7418.

Swift County

County Recorder, PO Box 246, Benson, MN 56215. 320-843-3377 R/E Recording: 612-843-3377; Fax 320-843-2275.
Will search UCC records. Tax liens not included in UCC search. Will not search real estate records. **Other Phone Numbers:** Assessor 320-842-5891.

Todd County

County Recorder, 221 First Ave South, Suite 300, Long Prairie, MN 56347-1391. County Recorder, R/E and UCC Recording 320-732-4428; Fax 320-732-4001. www.co.todd.mn.us/contacts.htm
Will search UCC records. Tax liens not included in UCC search. Will not search real estate records. **Other**

Phone Numbers: Assessor 320-732-4430; Treasurer 320-732-4471; Vital Records 320-732-4428.

Traverse County

County Recorder, PO Box 487, Wheaton, MN 56296-0487. 320-563-4622 R/E Recording: 320-563-4242; Fax 320-563-4424.
Will search UCC records. Tax liens not included in UCC search. Real estate owner, mortgage, and property transfer searches available. **Other Phone Numbers:** Assessor 320-563-4113; Treasurer 320-563-4616.

Wabasha County

County Recorder, 625 Jefferson Ave, Wabasha, MN 55981. 651-565-3623 R/E Recording: 612-565-3623; Fax 651-565-2774.
Will search UCC records. UCC search includes tax liens if requested. Real estate record owner and mortgage searches available. **Other Phone Numbers:** Assessor 651-565-3669; Treasurer 651-565-3669.

Wadena County

County Recorder, PO Box 415, Wadena, MN 56482. 218-631-7622 R/E Recording: 218-631-2425; Fax 218-631-5709. www.co.wadena.mn.us/record.htm
Will search UCC records. Tax liens not included in UCC search. Will not search real estate records. **Other Phone Numbers:** Assessor 218-631-7628; Treasurer 218-631-7621; Appraiser/Auditor 218-631-7628; Elections 218-631-7650; Vital Records 218-631-7788; Auditor 218-631-7785.

Waseca County

County Recorder, 307 N. State St, Waseca, MN 56093. 507-835-0670 R/E Recording: 5-7-835-0670; Fax 507-835-0633.
Will search UCC records. Tax liens not included in UCC search. Will not search real estate records. **Other Phone Numbers:** Assessor 507-835-0640.

Washington County

County Recorder, 14900 N. 61st St, PO Box 6, Stillwater, MN 55082. 651-430-6755; Fax 651-430-6753. www.co.washington.mn.us
Will search UCC records. Tax liens not included in UCC search. Real estate owner, mortgage, and property transfer searches available. **Online Access:** Real Estate, Lien, Tax Assessor Records. Access to county online records requires a $250 set up fee; no fees apply to Recorder office information. Records date back 3 years. Lending agency information is available, but UCC information is on a separate system. For information, contact Larry Haseman at 651-430-6423. Also, online access to property tax records is available free at https://washington.mn.ezgov.com/ezproperty/review_search.jsp; no name searching - property ID or address required. **Other Phone Numbers:** Assessor 651-430-6090; Treasurer 651-430-6175.

Watonwan County

County Recorder, PO Box 518, St. James, MN 56081. 507-375-1216 R/E Recording: 507-375-3341.
Will search UCC records. Tax liens not included in UCC search. Real estate owner, mortgage, and property transfer searches available. **Other Phone Numbers:** Assessor 507-375-1205; Treasurer 507-375-1213.

Wilkin County

County Recorder, PO Box 29, Breckenridge, MN 56520. 218-643-7164 R/E Recording: 218-643-4012; Fax 218-643-7170. www.co.wilkin.mn.us/recorder.asp
Will search UCC records. Tax liens not included in UCC search. Real estate owner, mortgage, and property transfer searches available. **Other Phone Numbers:** Assessor 218-643-7162; Treasurer 218-643-7112; Vital Records 218-643-7164.

Winona County

County Recorder, 171 W. 3rd St, Winona, MN 55987-3102. 507-457-6340; Fax 507-457-6469.
Will search UCC records. Tax liens not included in UCC search. Real estate owner, mortgage, and property transfer searches available. **Other Phone Numbers:** Assessor 507-457-6300; Treasurer 507-457-6450.

Wright County

County Recorder, 10 2nd St NW, Room 210, Buffalo, MN 55313-1196. 763-682-7357 R/E Recording: 763-682-3900 UCC Recording: 763-682-7360; Fax 763-684-4558. www.co.wright.mn.us
Will search UCC records. Tax liens not included in UCC search. Real estate owner, mortgage, and property transfer searches available. **Other Phone Numbers:** Assessor 763-682-7368; Treasurer 763-682-7573.

Yellow Medicine County

County Recorder, 415 9th Ave, Courthouse, Granite Falls, MN 56241. 320-564-2529 R/E Recording: 320-564-3132; Fax 320-564-3670.
Will search UCC records. Tax liens not included in UCC search. Will not search real estate records. **Other Phone Numbers:** Assessor 320-564-3678; Treasurer 320-564-3231.

Minnesota County Locator

You will usually be able to find the city name in the City/County Cross Reference below. In that case, it is a simple matter to determine the county from the cross reference. However, only the official US Postal Service city names are included in this index. There are an additional 40,000 place names that people use in their addresses. Therefore, we have also included a ZIP/City Cross Reference immediately following the City/County Cross Reference.

If you know the ZIP Code but the city name does not appear in the City/County Cross Reference index, look up the ZIP Code in the ZIP/City Cross Reference, find the city name, then look up the city name in the City/County Cross Reference. For example, you want to know the county for an address of Menands, NY 12204. There is no "Menands" in the City/County Cross Reference. The ZIP/City Cross Reference shows that ZIP Codes 12201-12288 are for the city of Albany. Looking back in the City/County Cross Reference, Albany is in Albany County.

City/County Cross Reference

ADA Norman
ADAMS Mower
ADOLPH St. Louis
ADRIAN Nobles
AFTON Washington
AH GWAH CHING Cass
AITKIN (56431) Aitkin(75), Crow Wing(24)
AKELEY (56433) Hubbard(74), Cass(25)
ALBANY Stearns
ALBERT LEA Freeborn
ALBERTA (56207) Stevens(98), Swift(1)
ALBERTVILLE Wright
ALBORN St. Louis
ALDEN Freeborn
ALDRICH (56434) Wadena(54), Todd(45)
ALEXANDRIA Douglas
ALMELUND Chisago
ALPHA (56111) Jackson(53), Martin(46)
ALTURA (55910) Winona(77), Wabasha(22)
ALVARADO (56710) Marshall(93), Polk(6)
AMBOY (56010) Blue Earth(97), Faribault(1), Martin(1)
AMIRET Lyon
ANGLE INLET Lake of the Woods
ANGORA St. Louis
ANGUS Polk
ANNANDALE Wright
ANOKA Anoka
APPLETON (56208) Swift(93), Lac qui Parle(2), Big Stone(2)
ARCO (56113) Lincoln(93), Lyon(6)
ARGYLE Marshall
ARLINGTON Sibley
ASHBY (56309) Grant(67), Otter Tail(27), Douglas(5)
ASKOV Pine
ATWATER (56209) Kandiyohi(83), Meeker(16)
AUDUBON Becker
AURORA St. Louis
AUSTIN (55912) Mower(94), Freeborn(5)
AVOCA Murray
AVON Stearns
BABBITT St. Louis
BACKUS (56435) Cass(96), Crow Wing(3)
BADGER Roseau
BAGLEY (56621) Clearwater(98), Polk(1)
BAKER Clay
BALATON (56115) Lyon(55), Murray(44)
BANGOR Pope
BARNESVILLE (56514) Clay(84), Wilkin(14), Otter Tail(1)
BARNUM Carlton
BARRETT Grant
BARRY Big Stone
BATTLE LAKE Otter Tail
BAUDETTE (56623) Lake of the Woods(83), Koochiching(16)
BAXTER (56425) Crow Wing(98), Cass(1)
BAYPORT Washington
BEARDSLEY (56211) Big Stone(82), Traverse(17)

BEAVER BAY Lake
BEAVER CREEK Rock
BECIDA Hubbard
BECKER Sherburne
BEJOU (56516) Mahnomen(85), Norman(14)
BELGRADE (56312) Stearns(66), Kandiyohi(34)
BELLE PLAINE (56011) Scott(78), Sibley(14), Le Sueur(4), Carver(2)
BELLINGHAM Lac qui Parle
BELTRAMI (56517) Polk(95), Norman(4)
BELVIEW (56214) Redwood(88), Yellow Medicine(11)
BEMIDJI Beltrami
BENA Cass
BENEDICT Hubbard
BENSON (56215) Swift(94), Pope(5)
BEROUN Pine
BERTHA (56437) Todd(86), Otter Tail(13)
BETHEL (55005) Anoka(96), Isanti(3)
BIG FALLS Koochiching
BIG LAKE Sherburne
BIGELOW (56117) Nobles(76), Sibley(23)
BIGFORK Itasca
BINGHAM LAKE (56118) Cottonwood(91), Jackson(8)
BIRCHDALE Koochiching
BIRD ISLAND Renville
BIWABIK St. Louis
BLACKDUCK (56630) Itasca(37), Aitkin(31), Beltrami(31)
BLOMKEST Kandiyohi
BLOOMING PRAIRIE (55917) Steele(64), Dodge(19), Mower(9), Freeborn(6)
BLUE EARTH (56013) Faribault(97), Martin(2)
BLUFFTON Otter Tail
BOCK Mille Lacs
BORUP (56519) Norman(58), Clay(41)
BOVEY Itasca
BOWLUS (56314) Morrison(95), Stearns(4)
BOWSTRING Itasca
BOY RIVER Cass
BOYD (56218) Yellow Medicine(51), Lac qui Parle(48)
BRAHAM (55006) Isanti(60), Kanabec(18), Pine(13), Chisago(8)
BRAINERD (56401) Crow Wing(93), Cass(6)
BRANDON (56315) Douglas(93), Otter Tail(6)
BRECKENRIDGE Wilkin
BREWSTER (56119) Nobles(56), Jackson(43)
BRICELYN Faribault
BRIMSON (55602) St. Louis(94), Lake(5)
BRITT St. Louis
BROOK PARK (55007) Pine(98), Kanabec(1)
BROOKS (56715) Red Lake(96), Polk(3)
BROOKSTON St. Louis

BROOTEN (56316) Stearns(81), Kandiyohi(10), Pope(8)
BROWERVILLE Todd
BROWNS VALLEY (56219) Traverse(93), Big Stone(5)
BROWNSDALE Mower
BROWNSVILLE Houston
BROWNTON (55312) McLeod(98), Sibley(1)
BRUNO Pine
BUCKMAN Morrison
BUFFALO Wright
BUFFALO LAKE (55314) Renville(80), Sibley(19)
BUHL St. Louis
BURNSVILLE Dakota
BURTRUM (56318) Todd(78), Morrison(21)
BUTTERFIELD (56120) Watonwan(98), Cottonwood(1)
BYRON (55920) Olmsted(98), Dodge(1)
CALEDONIA Houston
CALLAWAY Becker
CALUMET Itasca
CAMBRIDGE Isanti
CAMPBELL (56522) Wilkin(87), Otter Tail(10), Grant(2)
CANBY (56220) Yellow Medicine(88), Lac qui Parle(7), Lincoln(4)
CANNON FALLS (55009) Goodhue(91), Dakota(8)
CANTON Fillmore
CANYON St. Louis
CARLOS (56319) Douglas(91), Todd(8)
CARLTON Carlton
CARVER Carver
CASS LAKE (56633) Cass(67), Beltrami(25), Hubbard(6)
CASTLE ROCK Dakota
CEDAR Anoka
CENTER CITY Chisago
CEYLON Martin
CHAMPLIN Hennepin
CHANDLER Murray
CHANHASSEN Carver
CHASKA Carver
CHATFIELD (55923) Fillmore(52), Olmsted(47)
CHISAGO CITY Chisago
CHISHOLM St. Louis
CHOKIO (56221) Stevens(90), Big Stone(8)
CIRCLE PINES Anoka
CLARA CITY Chippewa
CLAREMONT (55924) Dodge(72), Steele(27)
CLARISSA Todd
CLARKFIELD Yellow Medicine
CLARKS GROVE Freeborn
CLEAR LAKE Sherburne
CLEARBROOK (56634) Clearwater(55), Polk(44)
CLEARWATER (55320) Wright(80), Stearns(19)

CLEMENTS Redwood
CLEVELAND Le Sueur
CLIMAX Polk
CLINTON Big Stone
CLITHERALL Otter Tail
CLONTARF (56226) Swift(82), Pope(17)
CLOQUET (55720) Carlton(90), St. Louis(9)
COHASSET Itasca
COKATO Wright
COLD SPRING Stearns
COLERAINE Itasca
COLLEGEVILLE Stearns
COLOGNE Carver
COMFREY (56019) Brown(68), Cottonwood(29), Watonwan(1)
COMSTOCK Clay
CONGER Freeborn
COOK (55788) Itasca(77), St. Louis(22)
CORRELL Big Stone
COSMOS (56228) Meeker(93), Renville(6)
COTTAGE GROVE Washington
COTTON St. Louis
COTTONWOOD (56229) Lyon(78), Yellow Medicine(21)
COURTLAND (56021) Nicollet(98), Aitkin(1)
CRANE LAKE St. Louis
CROMWELL Carlton
CROOKSTON Polk
CROSBY Crow Wing
CROSSLAKE Crow Wing
CRYSTAL BAY Hennepin
CULVER St. Louis
CURRIE Murray
CUSHING (56443) Morrison(73), Todd(26)
CYRUS (56323) Pope(85), Stevens(14)
DAKOTA Winona
DALBO Isanti
DALTON (56324) Otter Tail(97), Grant(2)
DANUBE Renville
DANVERS Swift
DARFUR Watonwan
DARWIN Meeker
DASSEL (55325) Meeker(96), Wright(3)
DAWSON Lac qui Parle
DAYTON Hennepin
DE GRAFF (56233) Swift(82), Chippewa(17)
DEBS Beltrami
DEER CREEK Otter Tail
DEER RIVER (56636) Itasca(92), Cass(7)
DEERWOOD Crow Wing
DELANO (55328) Wright(90), Hennepin(5), Carver(4)
DELAVAN Faribault
DELFT Cottonwood
DENHAM St. Louis
DENNISON (55018) Goodhue(86), Rice(12), Dakota(1)
DENT Otter Tail
DETROIT LAKES Becker
DEXTER Mower

DILWORTH Clay
DODGE CENTER Dodge
DONALDSON Kittson
DONNELLY (56235) Grant(53), Stevens(46)
DOVER Olmsted
DOVRAY Murray
DULUTH St. Louis
DUMONT (56236) Traverse(54), Big Stone(45)
DUNDAS Rice
DUNDEE (56126) Nobles(65), Cottonwood(18), Murray(12), Jackson(3)
DUNNELL (56127) Martin(98), Jackson(2)
DUQUETTE Pine
EAGLE BEND (56446) Todd(92), Douglas(5), Otter Tail(2)
EAGLE LAKE Blue Earth
EAST GRAND FORKS Polk
EASTON (56025) Faribault(98), Blue Earth(1)
ECHO Yellow Medicine
EDEN PRAIRIE Hennepin
EDEN VALLEY (55329) Stearns(65), Meeker(34)
EDGERTON (56128) Pipestone(76), Nobles(14), Rock(5), Murray(3)
EFFIE (56639) Itasca(93), Koochiching(6)
EITZEN Houston
ELBOW LAKE Grant
ELGIN (55932) Wabasha(52), Olmsted(47)
ELIZABETH Otter Tail
ELK RIVER (55330) Sherburne(74), Wright(19), Anoka(6)
ELKO Scott
ELKTON Mower
ELLENDALE (56026) Steele(44), Freeborn(41), Olmsted(12), Waseca(1)
ELLSWORTH (56129) Nobles(85), Rock(13), Lyon(1)
ELMORE (56027) Faribault(66), Olmsted(31), Martin(2)
ELROSA Stearns
ELY (55731) St. Louis(88), Lake(11)
ELYSIAN (56028) Le Sueur(91), Waseca(8)
EMBARRASS St. Louis
EMILY Crow Wing
EMMONS Freeborn
ERHARD Otter Tail
ERSKINE (56535) Polk(96), Red Lake(3)
ESKO (55733) Carlton(96), St. Louis(3)
ESSIG Brown
EUCLID Polk
EVAN (56238) Redwood(75), Brown(25)
EVANSVILLE (56326) Douglas(78), Otter Tail(17), Grant(3)
EVELETH St. Louis
EXCELSIOR (55331) Hennepin(78), Carver(21)
EYOTA Olmsted
FAIRFAX (55332) Renville(81), Nicollet(13), Sibley(4)
FAIRMONT Martin
FARIBAULT Rice
FARMINGTON Dakota
FARWELL (56327) Douglas(53), Pope(46)
FEDERAL DAM Cass
FELTON Clay
FERGUS FALLS Otter Tail
FERTILE (56540) Polk(90), Norman(9)
FIFTY LAKES Crow Wing
FINLAND Lake
FINLAYSON (55735) Pine(72), Aitkin(27)
FISHER Polk
FLENSBURG Morrison
FLOM Norman
FLOODWOOD (55736) St. Louis(93), Itasca(6)
FOLEY (56329) Benton(93), Morrison(6)
FORBES St. Louis

FOREST LAKE (55025) Washington(77), Anoka(12), Chisago(9)
FORESTON (56330) Mille Lacs(75), Benton(24)
FORT RIPLEY (56449) Crow Wing(83), Morrison(16)
FOSSTON (56542) Polk(88), Mahnomen(11)
FOUNTAIN Fillmore
FOXHOME Wilkin
FRANKLIN (55333) Renville(91), Redwood(7), Brown(1)
FRAZEE (56544) Becker(80), Otter Tail(20)
FREEBORN Freeborn
FREEPORT (56331) Stearns(98), Todd(1)
FRONTENAC Goodhue
FROST Faribault
FULDA (56131) Murray(84), Nobles(10), Cottonwood(4)
GARDEN CITY Blue Earth
GARFIELD Douglas
GARRISON (56450) Crow Wing(60), Mille Lacs(39)
GARVIN (56132) Lyon(81), Murray(18)
GARY Norman
GATZKE Marshall
GAYLORD (55334) Sibley(93), Nicollet(5)
GENEVA Freeborn
GEORGETOWN Clay
GHENT Lyon
GIBBON (55335) Sibley(77), Nicollet(22)
GILBERT St. Louis
GILMAN Benton
GLENCOE (55336) McLeod(93), Sibley(6)
GLENVILLE Freeborn
GLENWOOD Pope
GLYNDON Clay
GONVICK (56644) Clearwater(96), Polk(4)
GOOD THUNDER Blue Earth
GOODHUE (55027) Goodhue(96), Wabasha(3)
GOODLAND Itasca
GOODRIDGE (56725) Pennington(72), Marshall(27)
GRACEVILLE (56240) Big Stone(88), Traverse(11)
GRANADA (56039) Martin(97), Faribault(2)
GRAND MARAIS Cook
GRAND MEADOW Mower
GRAND PORTAGE (55605) Cook(73), Lyon(26)
GRAND RAPIDS Itasca
GRANDY Isanti
GRANGER Fillmore
GRANITE FALLS (56241) Yellow Medicine(79), Chippewa(14), Renville(6)
GRASSTON (55030) Pine(90), Kanabec(9)
GREEN ISLE (55338) Sibley(93), Carver(6)
GREENBUSH Roseau
GREENWALD Stearns
GREY EAGLE Todd
GROVE CITY Meeker
GRYGLA (56727) Beltrami(59), Marshall(40)
GULLY (56646) Polk(91), Clearwater(8)
HACKENSACK Cass
HADLEY Murray
HALLOCK Kittson
HALMA Kittson
HALSTAD Norman
HAMBURG (55339) Carver(73), Sibley(25)
HAMEL Hennepin
HAMMOND Wabasha
HAMPTON Dakota
HANCOCK (56244) Stevens(67), Pope(29), Swift(2)
HANLEY FALLS Yellow Medicine
HANOVER (55341) Wright(96), Hennepin(3)
HANSKA Brown
HARDWICK Rock
HARMONY Fillmore

HARRIS Chisago
HARTLAND (56042) Freeborn(95), Waseca(4)
HASTINGS (55033) Dakota(92), Washington(7)
HAWICK Kandiyohi
HAWLEY Clay
HAYFIELD (55940) Dodge(81), Olmsted(16), Mower(1)
HAYWARD Freeborn
HAZEL RUN Yellow Medicine
HECTOR (55342) Renville(96), Sibley(2)
HENDERSON (56044) Sibley(87), Le Sueur(10), Scott(2)
HENDRICKS (56136) Lincoln(82), Dodge(17)
HENDRUM Norman
HENNING Otter Tail
HENRIETTE Pine
HERMAN (56248) Grant(90), Stevens(5), Traverse(3)
HERON LAKE (56137) Jackson(60), Cottonwood(25), Nobles(14)
HEWITT (56453) Todd(75), Otter Tail(25)
HIBBING St. Louis
HILL CITY (55748) Aitkin(68), Itasca(31)
HILLMAN (56338) Morrison(95), Crow Wing(4)
HILLS (56138) Rock(98), Mower(1)
HINCKLEY (55037) Pine(96), Kanabec(3)
HINES Beltrami
HITTERDAL (56552) Clay(78), Becker(21)
HOFFMAN (56339) Grant(90), Douglas(9)
HOKAH Houston
HOLDINGFORD Stearns
HOLLAND Pipestone
HOLLANDALE Freeborn
HOLLOWAY Swift
HOLMES CITY Douglas
HOLYOKE (55749) Carlton(91), Pine(8)
HOMER Winona
HOPE Steele
HOPKINS Hennepin
HOUSTON (55943) Houston(94), Winona(5)
HOVLAND Cook
HOWARD LAKE Hennepin
HOYT LAKES St. Louis
HUGO (55038) Washington(59), Anoka(40)
HUMBOLDT Kittson
HUNTLEY Faribault
HUTCHINSON (55350) McLeod(91), Renville(5), Meeker(3)
IHLEN Pipestone
INTERNATIONAL FALLS Koochiching
INVER GROVE HEIGHTS Dakota
IONA (56141) Murray(90), Nobles(9)
IRON St. Louis
IRONTON Crow Wing
ISABELLA Lake
ISANTI Isanti
ISLE (56342) Mille Lacs(68), Kanabec(18), Aitkin(12)
IVANHOE Lincoln
JACKSON Jackson
JACOBSON (55752) Itasca(81), Aitkin(18)
JANESVILLE (56048) Waseca(98), Blue Earth(1)
JASPER (56144) Rock(59), Pipestone(35), Murray(4), Mower(1)
JEFFERS Cottonwood
JENKINS Crow Wing
JOHNSON (56250) Big Stone(70), Traverse(29)
JORDAN Scott
KANARANZI (56146) Nobles(95), Rock(5)
KANDIYOHI Kandiyohi
KARLSTAD (56732) Kittson(88), Marshall(8), Roseau(3)
KASOTA (56050) Le Sueur(97), Blue Earth(2)
KASSON (55944) Dodge(96), Olmsted(3)

KEEWATIN Itasca
KELLIHER Beltrami
KELLOGG Wabasha
KELSEY St. Louis
KENNEDY Kittson
KENNETH (56147) Rock(66), Nobles(33)
KENSINGTON (56343) Douglas(64), Pope(20), Stevens(9), Grant(6)
KENT Wilkin
KENYON (55946) Goodhue(82), Rice(12), Dodge(3), Steele(1)
KERKHOVEN (56252) Kandiyohi(57), Swift(32), Chippewa(9)
KERRICK Pine
KETTLE RIVER Carlton
KIESTER (56051) Faribault(97), Freeborn(2)
KILKENNY (56052) Rice(66), Le Sueur(33)
KIMBALL (55353) Stearns(95), Meeker(4)
KINNEY St. Louis
KLOSSNER Nicollet
KNIFE RIVER Lake
LA CRESCENT (55947) Houston(90), Winona(9)
LA SALLE Watonwan
LAFAYETTE (56054) Nicollet(89), Sibley(10)
LAKE BENTON (56149) Lincoln(95), Pipestone(4)
LAKE BRONSON Kittson
LAKE CITY (55041) Wabasha(83), Goodhue(16)
LAKE CRYSTAL Blue Earth
LAKE ELMO Washington
LAKE GEORGE Hubbard
LAKE HUBERT Crow Wing
LAKE ITASCA Clearwater
LAKE LILLIAN Kandiyohi
LAKE PARK (56554) Becker(93), Clay(6)
LAKE WILSON Murray
LAKEFIELD Jackson
LAKELAND Washington
LAKEVILLE (55044) Dakota(86), Scott(13)
LAMBERTON (56152) Redwood(80), Cottonwood(19)
LANCASTER (56735) Kittson(98), Roseau(1)
LANESBORO Fillmore
LANSING Mower
LAPORTE (56461) Hubbard(95), Cass(4)
LASTRUP Morrison
LE CENTER Le Sueur
LE ROY (55951) Mower(92), Fillmore(5), Rice(1)
LE SUEUR (56058) Le Sueur(82), Sibley(13), Nicollet(3)
LENGBY (56651) Mahnomen(81), Polk(18)
LEONARD (56652) Clearwater(97), Beltrami(2)
LEOTA Nobles
LESTER PRAIRIE McLeod
LEWISTON Winona
LEWISVILLE (56060) Watonwan(93), Blue Earth(6)
LINDSTROM Chisago
LISMORE Nobles
LITCHFIELD Meeker
LITTLE FALLS Morrison
LITTLEFORK Koochiching
LOMAN Koochiching
LONDON Freeborn
LONG LAKE Hennepin
LONG PRAIRIE (56347) Todd(98), Morrison(1)
LONGVILLE Cass
LONSDALE Rice
LORETTO Hennepin
LOUISBURG Lac qui Parle
LOWRY (56349) Pope(83), Douglas(16)
LUCAN Redwood
LUTSEN Cook
LUVERNE Rock

LYLE (55953) Mower(79), Rice(15), Freeborn(4)
LYND Lyon
MABEL (55954) Fillmore(89), Houston(10)
MADELIA (56062) Watonwan(82), Brown(11), Blue Earth(6)
MADISON Lac qui Parle
MADISON LAKE (56063) Blue Earth(62), Waseca(19), Le Sueur(18)
MAGNOLIA (56158) Rock(61), Nobles(38)
MAHNOMEN (56557) Mahnomen(96), Clearwater(1), Norman(1)
MAHTOWA Carlton
MAKINEN St. Louis
MANCHESTER Freeborn
MANHATTAN BEACH Crow Wing
MANKATO Blue Earth
MANTORVILLE Dodge
MAPLE LAKE Wright
MAPLE PLAIN Hennepin
MAPLETON (56065) Blue Earth(56), Faribault(32), Waseca(11)
MARBLE Itasca
MARCELL Itasca
MARGIE Koochiching
MARIETTA (56257) Lac qui Parle(97), Grant(2)
MARINE ON SAINT CROIX Washington
MARSHALL Lyon
MAX Itasca
MAYER Carver
MAYNARD (56260) Chippewa(70), Renville(29)
MAZEPPA (55956) Wabasha(74), Goodhue(24), Olmsted(1)
MC GRATH Aitkin
MC KINLEY St. Louis
MCGREGOR Aitkin
MCINTOSH Polk
MEADOWLANDS St. Louis
MEDFORD (55049) Steele(88), Rice(11)
MELROSE Stearns
MELRUDE St. Louis
MENAHGA (56464) Wadena(51), Becker(30), Hubbard(15), Otter Tail(2)
MENDOTA Dakota
MENTOR (56736) Polk(88), Red Lake(11)
MERIDEN (56067) Waseca(69), Steele(30)
MERRIFIELD Crow Wing
MIDDLE RIVER Marshall
MILACA (56353) Mille Lacs(97), Isanti(1)
MILAN (56262) Chippewa(84), Swift(15)
MILLVILLE Wabasha
MILROY (56263) Redwood(83), Lyon(16)
MILTONA Douglas
MINNEAPOLIS Hennepin
MINNEOTA (56264) Lyon(88), Yellow Medicine(11)
MINNESOTA CITY Winona
MINNESOTA LAKE (56068) Waseca(44), Faribault(43), Blue Earth(12)
MINNETONKA Hennepin
MINNETONKA BEACH Hennepin
MIZPAH Koochiching
MONTEVIDEO (56265) Chippewa(91), Lac qui Parle(4), Yellow Medicine(3)
MONTGOMERY (56069) Le Sueur(63), Rice(36)
MONTICELLO Wright
MONTROSE (55363) Wright(98), Carver(1)
MOORHEAD Clay
MOOSE LAKE (55767) Carlton(75), Pine(24)
MORA Kanabec
MORGAN (56266) Redwood(90), Brown(9)
MORRIS Stevens
MORRISTOWN (55052) Rice(93), Waseca(6)
MORTON (56270) Renville(53), Redwood(46)
MOTLEY (56466) Morrison(46), Cass(41), Todd(12)

MOUND Hennepin
MOUNTAIN IRON St. Louis
MOUNTAIN LAKE (56159) Cottonwood(94), Jackson(5)
MURDOCK (56271) Swift(83), Chippewa(16)
MYRTLE Freeborn
NASHUA (56565) Wilkin(80), Grant(19)
NASHWAUK Itasca
NASSAU Lac qui Parle
NAVARRE Hennepin
NAYTAHWAUSH Mahnomen
NELSON Douglas
NERSTRAND (55053) Rice(80), Goodhue(19)
NETT LAKE St. Louis
NEVIS Hubbard
NEW AUBURN Sibley
NEW GERMANY Carver
NEW LONDON Kandiyohi
NEW MARKET Scott
NEW MUNICH Stearns
NEW PRAGUE (56071) Scott(49), Le Sueur(47), Rice(3)
NEW RICHLAND (56072) Waseca(90), Freeborn(8)
NEW ULM (56073) Brown(86), Nicollet(12), Blue Earth(1)
NEW YORK MILLS Otter Tail
NEWFOLDEN Marshall
NEWPORT Washington
NICOLLET Nicollet
NIELSVILLE (56568) Polk(87), Norman(12)
NIMROD Wadena
NISSWA (56468) Crow Wing(69), Cass(30)
NORCROSS (56274) Grant(80), Traverse(19)
NORTH BRANCH (55056) Chisago(79), Isanti(20)
NORTHFIELD (55057) Rice(81), Dakota(18)
NORTHOME (56661) Itasca(52), Koochiching(34), Beltrami(13)
NORTHROP Martin
NORWOOD Carver
NOYES Kittson
OAK ISLAND Lake of the Woods
OAK PARK Benton
OAKLAND Freeborn
ODESSA (56276) Big Stone(76), Lac qui Parle(23)
ODIN (56160) Watonwan(35), Martin(33), Jackson(31)
OGEMA Becker
OGILVIE (56358) Kanabec(88), Mille Lacs(11)
OKABENA Jackson
OKLEE (56742) Red Lake(49), Pennington(48), Polk(1)
OLIVIA Renville
ONAMIA Mille Lacs
ORMSBY (56162) Martin(65), Watonwan(34)
ORONOCO Olmsted
ORR (55771) St. Louis(91), Koochiching(8)
ORTONVILLE Big Stone
OSAGE Becker
OSAKIS (56360) Todd(67), Douglas(31)
OSLO (56744) Marshall(88), Polk(11)
OSSEO Hennepin
OSTRANDER (55961) Mower(70), Fillmore(29)
OTISCO Waseca
OTTERTAIL Otter Tail
OUTING Cass
OWATONNA Steele
PALISADE Aitkin
PARK RAPIDS (56470) Hubbard(88), Becker(11)
PARKERS PRAIRIE (56361) Otter Tail(73), Douglas(26)
PARKVILLE St. Louis

PAYNESVILLE (56362) Stearns(89), Meeker(6), Kandiyohi(3)
PEASE Mille Lacs
PELICAN RAPIDS (56572) Otter Tail(95), Becker(2), Clay(1)
PEMBERTON (56078) Waseca(74), Blue Earth(25)
PENGILLY Itasca
PENNINGTON Beltrami
PENNOCK Kandiyohi
PEQUOT LAKES (56472) Crow Wing(77), Cass(22)
PERHAM Otter Tail
PERLEY (56574) Norman(95), Clay(4)
PETERSON (55962) Fillmore(93), Winona(6)
PIERZ (56364) Morrison(97), Crow Wing(2)
PILLAGER Cass
PINE CITY Pine
PINE ISLAND (55963) Goodhue(47), Olmsted(33), Dodge(19)
PINE RIVER (56474) Cass(92), Crow Wing(7)
PIPESTONE (56164) Pipestone(95), Murray(4)
PITT Lake of the Woods
PLAINVIEW (55964) Wabasha(95), Olmsted(2), Winona(1)
PLATO McLeod
PLUMMER (56748) Red Lake(68), Pennington(31)
PONEMAH Beltrami
PONSFORD Becker
PORTER (56280) Yellow Medicine(75), Lincoln(24)
PRESTON Fillmore
PRINCETON (55371) Mille Lacs(57), Sherburne(23), Isanti(16), Benton(1)
PRINSBURG Kandiyohi
PRIOR LAKE Scott
PUPOSKY Beltrami
RACINE Mower
RANDALL Morrison
RANDOLPH Dakota
RANIER Koochiching
RAY (56669) Koochiching(61), St. Louis(38)
RAYMOND (56282) Kandiyohi(81), Chippewa(18)
READING Nobles
READS LANDING Wabasha
RED LAKE FALLS (56750) Red Lake(91), Pennington(5), Polk(3)
RED WING Goodhue
REDBY Beltrami
REDLAKE Beltrami
REDWOOD FALLS (56283) Redwood(93), Renville(6)
REMER Cass
RENVILLE (56284) Renville(85), Kandiyohi(11), Redwood(2)
REVERE (56166) Redwood(59), Cottonwood(40)
RICE (56367) Benton(81), Stearns(18)
RICHMOND Stearns
RICHVILLE Otter Tail
RICHWOOD Becker
ROCHERT Becker
ROCHESTER Olmsted
ROCK CREEK Pine
ROCKFORD (55373) Wright(64), Hennepin(35)
ROCKVILLE Stearns
ROGERS (55374) Hennepin(94), Wright(5)
ROLLINGSTONE Winona
ROOSEVELT (56673) Roseau(82), Lake of the Woods(17)
ROSCOE Stearns
ROSE CREEK Mower
ROSEAU Roseau
ROSEMOUNT Dakota

ROTHSAY (56579) Wilkin(63), Otter Tail(36)
ROUND LAKE (56167) Jackson(58), Nobles(41)
ROYALTON (56373) Morrison(89), Benton(10)
RUSH CITY (55069) Chisago(95), Pine(4)
RUSHFORD (55971) Fillmore(80), Houston(12), Winona(7)
RUSHMORE Nobles
RUSSELL Lyon
RUTHTON (56170) Pipestone(67), Murray(18), Lyon(11), Lincoln(1)
RUTLEDGE Pine
SABIN Clay
SACRED HEART Renville
SAGINAW St. Louis
SAINT BONIFACIUS Hennepin
SAINT CHARLES (55972) Winona(86), Olmsted(13)
SAINT CLAIR Blue Earth
SAINT CLOUD Stearns
SAINT FRANCIS (55070) Anoka(90), Isanti(10)
SAINT HILAIRE (56754) Pennington(95), Red Lake(4)
SAINT JAMES (56081) Watonwan(96), Brown(3)
SAINT JOSEPH Stearns
SAINT LEO Yellow Medicine
SAINT MARTIN Stearns
SAINT MICHAEL Wright
SAINT PAUL Ramsey
SAINT PAUL PARK Washington
SAINT PETER (56082) Nicollet(88), Le Sueur(11)
SAINT STEPHEN Stearns
SAINT VINCENT Kittson
SALOL Roseau
SANBORN (56083) Redwood(53), Cottonwood(30), Brown(16)
SANDSTONE (55072) Pine(78), Kanabec(21)
SANTIAGO Sherburne
SARGEANT (55973) Mower(96), Dodge(3)
SARTELL (56377) Stearns(78), Benton(21)
SAUK CENTRE (56378) Stearns(71), Todd(28)
SAUK RAPIDS (56379) Benton(98), Stearns(1)
SAUM Beltrami
SAVAGE Scott
SAWYER Carlton
SCANDIA (55073) Washington(62), Chisago(37)
SCHROEDER Cook
SEAFORTH Redwood
SEARLES Brown
SEBEKA (56477) Wadena(77), Otter Tail(21)
SEDAN Pope
SHAFER Chisago
SHAKOPEE Scott
SHELLY Norman
SHERBURN Martin
SHEVLIN (56676) Beltrami(63), Clearwater(36)
SIDE LAKE St. Louis
SILVER BAY Lake
SILVER CREEK Wright
SILVER LAKE McLeod
SLAYTON Murray
SLEEPY EYE (56085) Brown(97), Redwood(2)
SOLWAY (56678) Hubbard(65), Beltrami(33)
SOUDAN St. Louis
SOUTH HAVEN (55382) Stearns(47), Wright(46), Meeker(6)
SOUTH INTERNATIONAL FALLS Koochiching
SOUTH SAINT PAUL Dakota

SPICER Kandiyohi
SPRING GROVE (55974) Houston(98), Fillmore(1)
SPRING LAKE Itasca
SPRING PARK Hennepin
SPRING VALLEY (55975) Fillmore(87), Mower(12)
SPRINGFIELD (56087) Brown(90), Redwood(9)
SQUAW LAKE Itasca
STACY (55079) Chisago(50), Anoka(29), Isanti(19)
STANCHFIELD (55080) Isanti(62), Chisago(37)
STAPLES (56479) Todd(62), Wadena(34), Cass(3)
STARBUCK Pope
STEEN (56173) Rock(76), Lyon(23)
STEPHEN (56757) Marshall(98), Kittson(1)
STEWART (55385) McLeod(51), Renville(34), Sibley(13)
STEWARTVILLE (55976) Olmsted(96), Mower(2), Fillmore(1)
STILLWATER Washington
STOCKTON Winona
STORDEN Cottonwood
STRANDQUIST Marshall
STRATHCONA (56759) Roseau(59), Marshall(40)
STURGEON LAKE (55783) Pine(96), Carlton(2)
SUNBURG (56289) Kandiyohi(75), Swift(22), Pope(1)
SWAN RIVER Itasca
SWANVILLE (56382) Todd(50), Morrison(49)
SWATARA (55785) Cass(51), Aitkin(48)
SWIFT Roseau
TACONITE Itasca
TALMOON Itasca
TAMARACK (55787) Aitkin(78), Carlton(21)
TAOPI Mower
TAUNTON (56291) Lyon(52), Yellow Medicine(38), Lincoln(9)

TAYLORS FALLS Chisago
TENSTRIKE Beltrami
THEILMAN Wabasha
THIEF RIVER FALLS (56701) Pennington(92), Marshall(6)
TINTAH (56583) Wilkin(54), Traverse(45)
TOFTE Cook
TOWER St. Louis
TRACY (56175) Lyon(82), Redwood(10), Murray(6)
TRAIL (56684) Pennington(66), Polk(28), Red Lake(5)
TRIMONT Martin
TROSKY Pipestone
TRUMAN (56088) Martin(82), Watonwan(12), Blue Earth(4)
TWIG St. Louis
TWIN LAKES Freeborn
TWIN VALLEY Norman
TWO HARBORS Lake
TYLER (56178) Lincoln(91), Lyon(8)
ULEN (56585) Clay(72), Becker(26), Norman(1)
UNDERWOOD Otter Tail
UPSALA Morrison
UTICA (55979) Winona(96), Fillmore(3)
VERDI (56179) Lincoln(92), Pipestone(7)
VERGAS Otter Tail
VERMILLION Dakota
VERNDALE (56481) Wadena(77), Todd(19), Cass(2)
VERNON CENTER Blue Earth
VESTA (56292) Redwood(97), Yellow Medicine(2)
VICTORIA Carver
VIKING (56760) Marshall(97), Pennington(2)
VILLARD (56385) Pope(61), Stearns(33), Douglas(5)
VINING Otter Tail
VIRGINIA St. Louis
WABASHA Wabasha
WABASSO Redwood

WACONIA (55387) Carver(97), Hennepin(2)
WADENA (56482) Wadena(77), Otter Tail(21)
WAHKON Mille Lacs
WAITE PARK Stearns
WALDORF Waseca
WALKER Cass
WALNUT GROVE (56180) Redwood(63), Murray(19), Cottonwood(16)
WALTERS (56092) Faribault(92), Freeborn(7)
WALTHAM (55982) Mower(98), Dodge(1)
WANAMINGO Goodhue
WANDA Redwood
WANNASKA (56761) Roseau(96), Marshall(3)
WARBA Itasca
WARREN (56762) Marshall(85), Polk(14)
WARROAD Roseau
WARSAW Rice
WASECA (56093) Waseca(96), Steele(3)
WASKISH Beltrami
WATERTOWN (55388) Carver(85), Wright(12), Hennepin(2)
WATERVILLE (56096) Le Sueur(82), Waseca(9), Rice(7)
WATKINS (55389) Meeker(79), Stearns(20)
WATSON Chippewa
WAUBUN (56589) Becker(69), Mahnomen(30)
WAVERLY Wright
WAWINA Itasca
WAYZATA Hennepin
WEBSTER (55088) Rice(68), Scott(30)
WELCH (55089) Goodhue(88), Dakota(11)
WELCOME Martin
WELLS (56097) Faribault(85), Freeborn(11), Waseca(2)
WENDELL (56590) Grant(98), Otter Tail(1)
WEST CONCORD Dodge
WEST UNION Todd

WESTBROOK (56183) Cottonwood(93), Murray(6)
WHALAN Fillmore
WHEATON Traverse
WHIPHOLT Cass
WHITE EARTH Becker
WILLERNIE Washington
WILLIAMS Lake of the Woods
WILLMAR Kandiyohi
WILLOW RIVER Pine
WILMONT Nobles
WILTON Beltrami
WINDOM (56101) Cottonwood(81), Jackson(18)
WINGER (56592) Polk(89), Mahnomen(9), Norman(1)
WINNEBAGO (56098) Faribault(90), Martin(9)
WINONA Winona
WINSTED (55395) McLeod(93), Carver(6)
WINTHROP Sibley
WINTON St. Louis
WIRT Itasca
WOLF LAKE Becker
WOLVERTON Wilkin
WOOD LAKE (56297) Yellow Medicine(94), Redwood(3), Lyon(2)
WOODSTOCK (56186) Murray(74), Pipestone(25)
WORTHINGTON (56187) Nobles(97), Jackson(2)
WRENSHALL (55797) Carlton(82), Pine(17)
WRIGHT Carlton
WYKOFF Fillmore
WYOMING (55092) Chisago(59), Anoka(40)
YOUNG AMERICA Carver
ZIM St. Louis
ZIMMERMAN (55398) Sherburne(90), Isanti(9)
ZUMBRO FALLS (55991) Wabasha(89), Olmsted(10)
ZUMBROTA Goodhue

ZIP/City Cross Reference

ZIP	City
55001-55001	AFTON
55002-55002	ALMELUND
55003-55003	BAYPORT
55004-55004	BEROUN
55005-55005	BETHEL
55006-55006	BRAHAM
55007-55007	BROOK PARK
55008-55008	CAMBRIDGE
55009-55009	CANNON FALLS
55010-55010	CASTLE ROCK
55011-55011	CEDAR
55012-55012	CENTER CITY
55013-55013	CHISAGO CITY
55014-55014	CIRCLE PINES
55016-55016	COTTAGE GROVE
55017-55017	DALBO
55018-55018	DENNISON
55019-55019	DUNDAS
55020-55020	ELKO
55021-55021	FARIBAULT
55024-55024	FARMINGTON
55025-55025	FOREST LAKE
55026-55026	FRONTENAC
55027-55027	GOODHUE
55029-55029	GRANDY
55030-55030	GRASSTON
55031-55031	HAMPTON
55032-55032	HARRIS
55033-55033	HASTINGS
55036-55036	HENRIETTE
55037-55037	HINCKLEY
55038-55038	HUGO
55040-55040	ISANTI
55041-55041	LAKE CITY
55042-55042	LAKE ELMO
55043-55043	LAKELAND
55044-55044	LAKEVILLE
55045-55045	LINDSTROM
55046-55046	LONSDALE
55047-55047	MARINE ON SAINT CROIX
55049-55049	MEDFORD
55051-55051	MORA
55052-55052	MORRISTOWN
55053-55053	NERSTRAND
55054-55054	NEW MARKET
55055-55055	NEWPORT
55056-55056	NORTH BRANCH
55057-55057	NORTHFIELD
55060-55060	OWATONNA
55063-55063	PINE CITY
55065-55065	RANDOLPH
55066-55066	RED WING
55067-55067	ROCK CREEK
55068-55068	ROSEMOUNT
55069-55069	RUSH CITY
55070-55070	SAINT FRANCIS
55071-55071	SAINT PAUL PARK
55072-55072	SANDSTONE
55073-55073	SCANDIA
55074-55074	SHAFER
55075-55075	SOUTH SAINT PAUL
55076-55077	INVER GROVE HEIGHTS
55078-55078	STACY
55080-55080	STANCHFIELD
55082-55083	STILLWATER
55084-55084	TAYLORS FALLS
55085-55085	VERMILLION
55087-55087	WARSAW
55088-55088	WEBSTER
55089-55089	WELCH
55090-55090	WILLERNIE
55092-55092	WYOMING
55100-55146	SAINT PAUL
55150-55150	MENDOTA
55155-55191	SAINT PAUL
55301-55301	ALBERTVILLE
55302-55302	ANNANDALE
55303-55304	ANOKA
55305-55305	HOPKINS
55306-55306	BURNSVILLE
55307-55307	ARLINGTON
55308-55308	BECKER
55309-55309	BIG LAKE
55310-55310	BIRD ISLAND
55311-55311	OSSEO
55312-55312	BROWNTON
55313-55313	BUFFALO
55314-55314	BUFFALO LAKE
55315-55315	CARVER
55316-55316	CHAMPLIN
55317-55317	CHANHASSEN
55318-55318	CHASKA
55319-55319	CLEAR LAKE
55320-55320	CLEARWATER
55321-55321	COKATO
55322-55322	COLOGNE
55323-55323	CRYSTAL BAY
55324-55324	DARWIN
55325-55325	DASSEL
55327-55327	DAYTON
55328-55328	DELANO
55329-55329	EDEN VALLEY
55330-55330	ELK RIVER
55331-55331	EXCELSIOR
55332-55332	FAIRFAX
55333-55333	FRANKLIN
55334-55334	GAYLORD
55335-55335	GIBBON
55336-55336	GLENCOE
55337-55337	BURNSVILLE
55338-55338	GREEN ISLE
55339-55339	HAMBURG
55340-55340	HAMEL
55341-55341	HANOVER
55342-55342	HECTOR
55343-55343	HOPKINS
55344-55344	EDEN PRAIRIE
55345-55345	MINNETONKA
55346-55347	EDEN PRAIRIE
55348-55348	MAPLE PLAIN
55349-55349	HOWARD LAKE
55350-55350	HUTCHINSON
55351-55351	YOUNG AMERICA
55352-55352	JORDAN
55353-55353	KIMBALL
55354-55354	LESTER PRAIRIE
55355-55355	LITCHFIELD
55356-55356	LONG LAKE
55357-55357	LORETTO
55358-55358	MAPLE LAKE
55359-55359	MAPLE PLAIN
55360-55360	MAYER
55361-55361	MINNETONKA BEACH
55362-55362	MONTICELLO
55363-55363	MONTROSE
55364-55364	MOUND

Zip Range	City	Zip Range	City	Zip Range	City	Zip Range	City
55365-55365	MONTICELLO	55713-55713	BUHL	55918-55918	BROWNSDALE	56025-56025	EASTON
55366-55366	NEW AUBURN	55716-55716	CALUMET	55919-55919	BROWNSVILLE	56026-56026	ELLENDALE
55367-55367	NEW GERMANY	55717-55717	CANYON	55920-55920	BYRON	56027-56027	ELMORE
55368-55368	NORWOOD	55718-55718	CARLTON	55921-55921	CALEDONIA	56028-56028	ELYSIAN
55369-55369	OSSEO	55719-55719	CHISHOLM	55922-55922	CANTON	56029-56029	EMMONS
55370-55370	PLATO	55720-55720	CLOQUET	55923-55923	CHATFIELD	56030-56030	ESSIG
55371-55371	PRINCETON	55721-55721	COHASSET	55924-55924	CLAREMONT	56031-56031	FAIRMONT
55372-55372	PRIOR LAKE	55722-55722	COLERAINE	55925-55925	DAKOTA	56032-56032	FREEBORN
55373-55373	ROCKFORD	55723-55723	COOK	55926-55926	DEXTER	56033-56033	FROST
55374-55374	ROGERS	55724-55724	COTTON	55927-55927	DODGE CENTER	56034-56034	GARDEN CITY
55375-55375	SAINT BONIFACIUS	55725-55725	CRANE LAKE	55929-55929	DOVER	56035-56035	GENEVA
55376-55376	SAINT MICHAEL	55726-55726	CROMWELL	55931-55931	EITZEN	56036-56036	GLENVILLE
55377-55377	SANTIAGO	55727-55727	CULVER	55932-55932	ELGIN	56037-56037	GOOD THUNDER
55378-55378	SAVAGE	55728-55728	DENHAM	55933-55933	ELKTON	56039-56039	GRANADA
55379-55379	SHAKOPEE	55729-55729	DUQUETTE	55934-55934	EYOTA	56041-56041	HANSKA
55380-55380	SILVER CREEK	55730-55730	GRAND RAPIDS	55935-55935	FOUNTAIN	56042-56042	HARTLAND
55381-55381	SILVER LAKE	55731-55731	ELY	55936-55936	GRAND MEADOW	56043-56043	HAYWARD
55382-55382	SOUTH HAVEN	55732-55732	EMBARRASS	55937-55937	GRANGER	56044-56044	HENDERSON
55383-55383	NORWOOD	55733-55733	ESKO	55938-55938	HAMMOND	56045-56045	HOLLANDALE
55384-55384	SPRING PARK	55734-55734	EVELETH	55939-55939	HARMONY	56046-56046	HOPE
55385-55385	STEWART	55735-55735	FINLAYSON	55940-55940	HAYFIELD	56047-56047	HUNTLEY
55386-55386	VICTORIA	55736-55736	FLOODWOOD	55941-55941	HOKAH	56048-56048	JANESVILLE
55387-55387	WACONIA	55738-55738	FORBES	55942-55942	HOMER	56050-56050	KASOTA
55388-55388	WATERTOWN	55740-55740	DENHAM	55943-55943	HOUSTON	56051-56051	KIESTER
55389-55389	WATKINS	55741-55741	GILBERT	55944-55944	KASSON	56052-56052	KILKENNY
55390-55390	WAVERLY	55742-55742	GOODLAND	55945-55945	KELLOGG	56053-56053	KLOSSNER
55391-55391	WAYZATA	55744-55745	GRAND RAPIDS	55946-55946	KENYON	56054-56054	LAFAYETTE
55392-55392	NAVARRE	55746-55747	HIBBING	55947-55947	LA CRESCENT	56055-56055	LAKE CRYSTAL
55393-55393	MAPLE PLAIN	55748-55748	HILL CITY	55949-55949	LANESBORO	56056-56056	LA SALLE
55394-55394	YOUNG AMERICA	55749-55749	HOLYOKE	55950-55950	LANSING	56057-56057	LE CENTER
55395-55395	WINSTED	55750-55750	HOYT LAKES	55951-55951	LE ROY	56058-56058	LE SUEUR
55396-55396	WINTHROP	55751-55751	IRON	55952-55952	LEWISTON	56060-56060	LEWISVILLE
55397-55397	YOUNG AMERICA	55752-55752	JACOBSON	55953-55953	LYLE	56061-56061	LONDON
55398-55398	ZIMMERMAN	55753-55753	KEEWATIN	55954-55954	MABEL	56062-56062	MADELIA
55399-55399	YOUNG AMERICA	55754-55754	HIBBING	55955-55955	MANTORVILLE	56063-56063	MADISON LAKE
55400-55488	MINNEAPOLIS	55755-55755	KELSEY	55956-55956	MAZEPPA	56064-56064	MANCHESTER
55550-55554	YOUNG AMERICA	55756-55756	KERRICK	55957-55957	MILLVILLE	56065-56065	MAPLETON
55554-55554	NORWOOD	55757-55757	KETTLE RIVER	55959-55959	MINNESOTA CITY	56067-56067	MERIDEN
55555-55560	YOUNG AMERICA	55758-55758	KINNEY	55960-55960	ORONOCO	56068-56068	MINNESOTA LAKE
55561-55561	MONTICELLO	55760-55760	MCGREGOR	55961-55961	OSTRANDER	56069-56069	MONTGOMERY
55562-55562	YOUNG AMERICA	55761-55761	MC KINLEY	55962-55962	PETERSON	56070-56070	MYRTLE
55563-55563	MONTICELLO	55762-55762	MAHTOWA	55963-55963	PINE ISLAND	56071-56071	NEW PRAGUE
55564-55564	YOUNG AMERICA	55763-55763	MAKINEN	55964-55964	PLAINVIEW	56072-56072	NEW RICHLAND
55565-55565	MONTICELLO	55764-55764	MARBLE	55965-55965	PRESTON	56073-56073	NEW ULM
55566-55568	YOUNG AMERICA	55765-55765	MEADOWLANDS	55967-55967	RACINE	56074-56074	NICOLLET
55569-55569	OSSEO	55766-55766	MELRUDE	55968-55968	READS LANDING	56075-56075	NORTHROP
55570-55572	MAPLE PLAIN	55767-55767	MOOSE LAKE	55969-55969	ROLLINGSTONE	56076-56076	OAKLAND
55573-55573	YOUNG AMERICA	55768-55768	MOUNTAIN IRON	55970-55970	ROSE CREEK	56077-56077	OTISCO
55574-55574	MAPLE PLAIN	55769-55769	NASHWAUK	55971-55971	RUSHFORD	56078-56078	PEMBERTON
55575-55575	HOWARD LAKE	55771-55771	ORR	55972-55972	SAINT CHARLES	56080-56080	SAINT CLAIR
55576-55579	MAPLE PLAIN	55772-55772	NETT LAKE	55973-55973	SARGEANT	56081-56081	SAINT JAMES
55580-55582	MONTICELLO	55773-55773	PARKVILLE	55974-55974	SPRING GROVE	56082-56082	SAINT PETER
55583-55583	NORWOOD	55775-55775	PENGILLY	55975-55975	SPRING VALLEY	56083-56083	SANBORN
55584-55591	MONTICELLO	55777-55777	VIRGINIA	55976-55976	STEWARTVILLE	56084-56084	SEARLES
55592-55593	MAPLE PLAIN	55778-55778	RUTLEDGE	55977-55977	TAOPI	56085-56085	SLEEPY EYE
55594-55594	YOUNG AMERICA	55779-55779	SAGINAW	55978-55978	THEILMAN	56087-56087	SPRINGFIELD
55595-55599	LORETTO	55780-55780	SAWYER	55979-55979	UTICA	56088-56088	TRUMAN
55601-55601	BEAVER BAY	55781-55781	SIDE LAKE	55981-55981	WABASHA	56089-56089	TWIN LAKES
55602-55602	BRIMSON	55782-55782	SOUDAN	55982-55982	WALTHAM	56090-56090	VERNON CENTER
55603-55603	FINLAND	55783-55783	STURGEON LAKE	55983-55983	WANAMINGO	56091-56091	WALDORF
55604-55604	GRAND MARAIS	55784-55784	SWAN RIVER	55985-55985	WEST CONCORD	56092-56092	WALTERS
55605-55605	GRAND PORTAGE	55785-55785	SWATARA	55986-55986	WHALAN	56093-56093	WASECA
55606-55606	HOVLAND	55786-55786	TACONITE	55987-55987	WINONA	56096-56096	WATERVILLE
55607-55607	ISABELLA	55787-55787	TAMARACK	55988-55988	STOCKTON	56097-56097	WELLS
55609-55609	KNIFE RIVER	55788-55788	COOK	55990-55990	WYKOFF	56098-56098	WINNEBAGO
55612-55612	LUTSEN	55789-55789	MEADOWLANDS	55991-55991	ZUMBRO FALLS	56101-56101	WINDOM
55613-55613	SCHROEDER	55790-55790	TOWER	55992-55992	ZUMBROTA	56110-56110	ADRIAN
55614-55614	SILVER BAY	55791-55791	TWIG	56001-56006	MANKATO	56111-56111	ALPHA
55615-55615	TOFTE	55792-55792	VIRGINIA	56007-56007	ALBERT LEA	56112-56112	AMIRET
55616-55616	TWO HARBORS	55793-55793	WARBA	56009-56009	ALDEN	56113-56113	ARCO
55701-55701	ADOLPH	55794-55794	WAWINA	56010-56010	AMBOY	56114-56114	AVOCA
55702-55702	ALBORN	55795-55795	WILLOW RIVER	56011-56011	BELLE PLAINE	56115-56115	BALATON
55703-55703	ANGORA	55796-55796	WINTON	56013-56013	BLUE EARTH	56116-56116	BEAVER CREEK
55704-55704	ASKOV	55797-55797	WRENSHALL	56014-56014	BRICELYN	56117-56117	BIGELOW
55705-55705	AURORA	55798-55798	WRIGHT	56016-56016	CLARKS GROVE	56118-56118	BINGHAM LAKE
55706-55706	BABBITT	55799-55799	ZIM	56017-56017	CLEVELAND	56119-56119	BREWSTER
55707-55707	BARNUM	55800-55816	DULUTH	56019-56019	COMFREY	56120-56120	BUTTERFIELD
55708-55708	BIWABIK	55901-55906	ROCHESTER	56020-56020	CONGER	56121-56121	CEYLON
55709-55709	BOVEY	55909-55909	ADAMS	56021-56021	COURTLAND	56122-56122	CHANDLER
55710-55710	BRITT	55910-55910	ALTURA	56022-56022	DARFUR	56123-56123	CURRIE
55711-55711	BROOKSTON	55912-55912	AUSTIN	56023-56023	DELAVAN	56124-56124	DELFT
55712-55712	BRUNO	55917-55917	BLOOMING PRAIRIE	56024-56024	EAGLE LAKE	56125-56125	DOVRAY

56126-56126 DUNDEE	56236-56236 DUMONT	56334-56334 GLENWOOD	56468-56468 NISSWA
56127-56127 DUNNELL	56237-56237 ECHO	56335-56335 GREENWALD	56469-56469 PALISADE
56128-56128 EDGERTON	56238-56238 EVAN	56336-56336 GREY EAGLE	56470-56470 PARK RAPIDS
56129-56129 ELLSWORTH	56239-56239 GHENT	56338-56338 HILLMAN	56472-56472 PEQUOT LAKES
56131-56131 FULDA	56240-56240 GRACEVILLE	56339-56339 HOFFMAN	56473-56473 PILLAGER
56132-56132 GARVIN	56241-56241 GRANITE FALLS	56340-56340 HOLDINGFORD	56474-56474 PINE RIVER
56133-56133 HADLEY	56243-56243 GROVE CITY	56341-56341 HOLMES CITY	56475-56475 RANDALL
56134-56134 HARDWICK	56244-56244 HANCOCK	56342-56342 ISLE	56477-56477 SEBEKA
56136-56136 HENDRICKS	56245-56245 HANLEY FALLS	56343-56343 KENSINGTON	56478-56478 NIMROD
56137-56137 HERON LAKE	56246-56246 HAWICK	56344-56344 LASTRUP	56479-56479 STAPLES
56138-56138 HILLS	56247-56247 HAZEL RUN	56345-56345 LITTLE FALLS	56481-56481 VERNDALE
56139-56139 HOLLAND	56248-56248 HERMAN	56346-56347 LONG PRAIRIE	56482-56482 WADENA
56140-56140 IHLEN	56249-56249 HOLLOWAY	56349-56349 LOWRY	56484-56484 WALKER
56141-56141 IONA	56250-56250 JOHNSON	56350-56350 MC GRATH	56485-56485 WHIPHOLT
56142-56142 IVANHOE	56251-56251 KANDIYOHI	56352-56352 MELROSE	56501-56502 DETROIT LAKES
56143-56143 JACKSON	56252-56252 KERKHOVEN	56353-56353 MILACA	56510-56510 ADA
56144-56144 JASPER	56253-56253 LAKE LILLIAN	56354-56354 MILTONA	56511-56511 AUDUBON
56145-56145 JEFFERS	56254-56254 LOUISBURG	56355-56355 NELSON	56513-56513 BAKER
56146-56146 KANARANZI	56255-56255 LUCAN	56356-56356 NEW MUNICH	56514-56514 BARNESVILLE
56147-56147 KENNETH	56256-56256 MADISON	56357-56357 OAK PARK	56515-56515 BATTLE LAKE
56149-56149 LAKE BENTON	56257-56257 MARIETTA	56358-56358 OGILVIE	56516-56516 BEJOU
56150-56150 LAKEFIELD	56258-56258 MARSHALL	56359-56359 ONAMIA	56517-56517 BELTRAMI
56151-56151 LAKE WILSON	56260-56260 MAYNARD	56360-56360 OSAKIS	56518-56518 BLUFFTON
56152-56152 LAMBERTON	56262-56262 MILAN	56361-56361 PARKERS PRAIRIE	56519-56519 BORUP
56153-56153 LEOTA	56263-56263 MILROY	56362-56362 PAYNESVILLE	56520-56520 BRECKENRIDGE
56155-56155 LISMORE	56264-56264 MINNEOTA	56363-56363 PEASE	56521-56521 CALLAWAY
56156-56156 LUVERNE	56265-56265 MONTEVIDEO	56364-56364 PIERZ	56522-56522 CAMPBELL
56157-56157 LYND	56266-56266 MORGAN	56367-56367 RICE	56523-56523 CLIMAX
56158-56158 MAGNOLIA	56267-56267 MORRIS	56368-56368 RICHMOND	56524-56524 CLITHERALL
56159-56159 MOUNTAIN LAKE	56270-56270 MORTON	56369-56369 ROCKVILLE	56525-56525 COMSTOCK
56160-56160 ODIN	56271-56271 MURDOCK	56371-56371 ROSCOE	56527-56527 DEER CREEK
56161-56161 OKABENA	56272-56272 NASSAU	56372-56372 SAINT CLOUD	56528-56528 DENT
56162-56162 ORMSBY	56273-56273 NEW LONDON	56373-56373 ROYALTON	56529-56529 DILWORTH
56164-56164 PIPESTONE	56274-56274 NORCROSS	56374-56374 SAINT JOSEPH	56531-56531 ELBOW LAKE
56165-56165 READING	56276-56276 ODESSA	56375-56375 SAINT STEPHEN	56533-56533 ELIZABETH
56166-56166 REVERE	56277-56277 OLIVIA	56376-56376 SAINT MARTIN	56534-56534 ERHARD
56167-56167 ROUND LAKE	56278-56278 ORTONVILLE	56377-56377 SARTELL	56535-56535 ERSKINE
56168-56168 RUSHMORE	56279-56279 PENNOCK	56378-56378 SAUK CENTRE	56536-56536 FELTON
56169-56169 RUSSELL	56280-56280 PORTER	56379-56379 SAUK RAPIDS	56537-56538 FERGUS FALLS
56170-56170 RUTHTON	56281-56281 PRINSBURG	56380-56380 BANGOR	56540-56540 FERTILE
56171-56171 SHERBURN	56282-56282 RAYMOND	56380-56380 SEDAN	56541-56541 FLOM
56172-56172 SLAYTON	56283-56283 REDWOOD FALLS	56381-56381 STARBUCK	56542-56542 FOSSTON
56173-56173 STEEN	56284-56284 RENVILLE	56382-56382 SWANVILLE	56543-56543 FOXHOME
56174-56174 STORDEN	56285-56285 SACRED HEART	56384-56384 UPSALA	56544-56544 FRAZEE
56175-56175 TRACY	56286-56286 SAINT LEO	56385-56385 VILLARD	56545-56545 GARY
56176-56176 TRIMONT	56287-56287 SEAFORTH	56386-56386 WAHKON	56546-56546 GEORGETOWN
56177-56177 TROSKY	56288-56288 SPICER	56387-56388 WAITE PARK	56547-56547 GLYNDON
56178-56178 TYLER	56289-56289 SUNBURG	56389-56389 WEST UNION	56548-56548 HALSTAD
56179-56179 VERDI	56291-56291 TAUNTON	56393-56399 SAINT CLOUD	56549-56549 HAWLEY
56180-56180 WALNUT GROVE	56292-56292 VESTA	56401-56401 BRAINERD	56550-56550 HENDRUM
56181-56181 WELCOME	56293-56293 WABASSO	56425-56425 BAXTER	56551-56551 HENNING
56183-56183 WESTBROOK	56294-56294 WANDA	56430-56430 AH GWAH CHING	56552-56552 HITTERDAL
56185-56185 WILMONT	56295-56295 WATSON	56431-56431 AITKIN	56553-56553 KENT
56186-56186 WOODSTOCK	56296-56296 WHEATON	56433-56433 AKELEY	56554-56554 LAKE PARK
56187-56187 WORTHINGTON	56297-56297 WOOD LAKE	56434-56434 ALDRICH	56556-56556 MCINTOSH
56201-56201 WILLMAR	56301-56304 SAINT CLOUD	56435-56435 BACKUS	56557-56557 MAHNOMEN
56207-56207 ALBERTA	56307-56307 ALBANY	56436-56436 BENEDICT	56560-56563 MOORHEAD
56208-56208 APPLETON	56308-56308 ALEXANDRIA	56437-56437 BERTHA	56565-56565 NASHUA
56209-56209 ATWATER	56309-56309 ASHBY	56438-56438 BROWERVILLE	56566-56566 NAYTAHWAUSH
56210-56210 BARRY	56310-56310 AVON	56440-56440 CLARISSA	56567-56567 NEW YORK MILLS
56211-56211 BEARDSLEY	56311-56311 BARRETT	56441-56441 CROSBY	56568-56568 NIELSVILLE
56212-56212 BELLINGHAM	56312-56312 BELGRADE	56442-56442 CROSSLAKE	56569-56569 OGEMA
56214-56214 BELVIEW	56313-56313 BOCK	56443-56443 CUSHING	56570-56570 OSAGE
56215-56215 BENSON	56314-56314 BOWLUS	56444-56444 DEERWOOD	56571-56571 OTTERTAIL
56216-56216 BLOMKEST	56315-56315 BRANDON	56446-56446 EAGLE BEND	56572-56572 PELICAN RAPIDS
56218-56218 BOYD	56316-56316 BROOTEN	56447-56447 EMILY	56573-56573 PERHAM
56219-56219 BROWNS VALLEY	56317-56317 BUCKMAN	56448-56448 FIFTY LAKES	56574-56574 PERLEY
56220-56220 CANBY	56318-56318 BURTRUM	56449-56449 FORT RIPLEY	56575-56575 PONSFORD
56221-56221 CHOKIO	56319-56319 CARLOS	56450-56450 GARRISON	56576-56576 RICHVILLE
56222-56222 CLARA CITY	56320-56320 COLD SPRING	56452-56452 HACKENSACK	56577-56577 RICHWOOD
56223-56223 CLARKFIELD	56321-56321 COLLEGEVILLE	56453-56453 HEWITT	56578-56578 ROCHERT
56224-56224 CLEMENTS	56323-56323 CYRUS	56455-56455 IRONTON	56579-56579 ROTHSAY
56225-56225 CLINTON	56324-56324 DALTON	56456-56456 JENKINS	56580-56580 SABIN
56226-56226 CLONTARF	56325-56325 ELROSA	56458-56458 LAKE GEORGE	56581-56581 SHELLY
56227-56227 CORRELL	56326-56326 EVANSVILLE	56459-56459 LAKE HUBERT	56583-56583 TINTAH
56228-56228 COSMOS	56327-56327 FARWELL	56460-56460 LAKE ITASCA	56584-56584 TWIN VALLEY
56229-56229 COTTONWOOD	56328-56328 FLENSBURG	56461-56461 LAPORTE	56585-56585 ULEN
56230-56230 DANUBE	56329-56329 FOLEY	56463-56463 MANHATTAN BEACH	56586-56586 UNDERWOOD
56231-56231 DANVERS	56330-56330 FORESTON	56464-56464 MENAHGA	56587-56587 VERGAS
56232-56232 DAWSON	56331-56331 FREEPORT	56465-56465 MERRIFIELD	56588-56588 VINING
56233-56233 DE GRAFF	56332-56332 GARFIELD	56466-56466 MOTLEY	56589-56589 WAUBUN
56235-56235 DONNELLY	56333-56333 GILMAN	56467-56467 NEVIS	56590-56590 WENDELL

56591-56591	WHITE EARTH
56592-56592	WINGER
56593-56593	WOLF LAKE
56594-56594	WOLVERTON
56601-56619	BEMIDJI
56621-56621	BAGLEY
56623-56623	BAUDETTE
56625-56625	BECIDA
56626-56626	BENA
56627-56627	BIG FALLS
56628-56628	BIGFORK
56629-56629	BIRCHDALE
56630-56630	BLACKDUCK
56631-56631	BOWSTRING
56632-56632	BOY RIVER
56633-56633	CASS LAKE
56634-56634	CLEARBROOK
56636-56636	DEER RIVER
56637-56637	TALMOON
56639-56639	EFFIE
56641-56641	FEDERAL DAM
56644-56644	GONVICK
56646-56646	GULLY
56647-56647	HINES
56649-56649	INTERNATIONAL FALLS
56650-56650	KELLIHER
56651-56651	LENGBY

56652-56652	LEONARD
56653-56653	LITTLEFORK
56654-56654	LOMAN
56655-56655	LONGVILLE
56657-56657	MARCELL
56658-56658	MARGIE
56659-56659	MAX
56660-56660	MIZPAH
56661-56661	NORTHOME
56662-56662	OUTING
56663-56663	PENNINGTON
56664-56664	DEBS
56665-56665	PITT
56666-56666	PONEMAH
56667-56667	PUPOSKY
56668-56668	RANIER
56669-56669	RAY
56670-56670	REDBY
56671-56671	REDLAKE
56672-56672	REMER
56673-56673	ROOSEVELT
56674-56674	SAUM
56676-56676	SHEVLIN
56678-56678	SOLWAY
56679-56679	SOUTH INTERNATIONAL FALLS
56680-56680	SPRING LAKE

56681-56681	SQUAW LAKE
56682-56682	SWIFT
56683-56683	TENSTRIKE
56684-56684	TRAIL
56685-56685	WASKISH
56686-56686	WILLIAMS
56687-56687	WILTON
56688-56688	WIRT
56701-56701	THIEF RIVER FALLS
56710-56710	ALVARADO
56711-56711	ANGLE INLET
56712-56712	ANGUS
56713-56713	ARGYLE
56714-56714	BADGER
56715-56715	BROOKS
56716-56716	CROOKSTON
56720-56720	DONALDSON
56721-56721	EAST GRAND FORKS
56722-56722	EUCLID
56723-56723	FISHER
56724-56724	GATZKE
56725-56725	GOODRIDGE
56726-56726	GREENBUSH
56727-56727	GRYGLA
56728-56728	HALLOCK
56729-56729	HALMA
56731-56731	HUMBOLDT

56732-56732	KARLSTAD
56733-56733	KENNEDY
56734-56734	LAKE BRONSON
56735-56735	LANCASTER
56736-56736	MENTOR
56737-56737	MIDDLE RIVER
56738-56738	NEWFOLDEN
56740-56740	NOYES
56741-56741	OAK ISLAND
56742-56742	OKLEE
56744-56744	OSLO
56748-56748	PLUMMER
56750-56750	RED LAKE FALLS
56751-56751	ROSEAU
56754-56754	SAINT HILAIRE
56755-56755	SAINT VINCENT
56756-56756	SALOL
56757-56757	STEPHEN
56758-56758	STRANDQUIST
56759-56759	STRATHCONA
56760-56760	VIKING
56761-56761	WANNASKA
56762-56762	WARREN
56763-56763	WARROAD

Mississippi

General Help Numbers:

Governor's Office

PO Box 139
Jackson, MS 39205-0139
www.governor.state.ms.us

601-359-3100
Fax 601-359-3741
8AM-5PM

Attorney General's Office

PO Box 220
Jackson, MS 39205
www.ago.state.ms.us

601-359-3680
Fax 601-359-3796
8AM-5PM

State Court Administrator

Supreme Court, Box 117
Jackson, MS 39205
www.mssc.state.ms.us

601-354-7406
Fax 601-354-7459
8AM-5PM

State Archives

Archives & Library Division
PO Box 571
Jackson, MS 39205-0571
www.mdah.state.ms.us

601-359-6850
Fax 601-359-6975

8AM-5PM TU-F;
8AM-1PM SA

State Specifics:

Capital:	Jackson
	Hinds County
Time Zone:	CST
Number of Counties:	82
Population:	2,858,029
Web Site:	www.ms.gov

State Agencies

Criminal Records
Access to Records is Restricted

Criminal Information Center, Dept. of Public Safety, PO Box 958, Jackson, MS 39205; 601-933-2600.

Note: Mississippi does not permit the public to access their central state repository of criminal records, except for pre-approved entities with purposes provided for by state statute such as health care, banking/finance, military, childcare and schools. They suggest that you obtain information at the county level. The records on file are 100% fingerprint supported. 40% of the records contain dispositions. The state Sex Offender Registry can be access at www.sor.mdps.state.ms.us

Criminal Records
Access From Courts

The state Court Administrator's Office offers a fax request search mode for statewide criminal record searches. Fees include a $25.00 start-up fee and $5.00 per name. The full name, DOB and SSN are required. Turnaround time is 24 hours. Fax 601-354-7459 or call 601-354-7449 for details.

Corporation Records
Limited Partnership Records
Limited Liability Company Records
Trademarks/Servicemarks

Corporation Commission, Secretary of State, PO Box 136, Jackson, MS 39205-0136 (Courier: 202 N Congress, Suite 601, Jackson, MS 39201); 601-359-1633, 800-256-3494, 601-359-1607 (Fax), 8AM-5PM.

www.sos.state.ms.us

Indexing & Storage: Records are available from the 1800's, computerized since 1995. New records are available for inquiry immediately. Records are indexed on microfilm, inhouse computer.

Searching: Include the following in your request: full name of business. In addition to the articles of incorporation, corporation records include the following information: Annual Reports, Officers, Directors, Prior (merged) names, Inactive and Reserved names. The following data is not released: federal id numbers or phone numbers.

Access by: mail, phone, fax, in person, online.

Fee & Payment: There is no search fee. The certification fee is $10.00 per package. Copies are $1.00 per page. Fee payee: Secretary of State. Prepayment required. You must prepay if the invoice amount is over $50.00. If under $50.00 they will invoice. Personal checks accepted. Credit cards accepted: MasterCard, Visa.

Mail search: Turnaround time: 1 to 2 days.

Phone search: Will only verify if record exists.

Fax search: Requests only are accepted, will return to toll-free fax numbers.

In person search: Computer screen prints are free.

Online search: The system is called "CorpSnap" and is available online at www.sos.state.ms.us/busserv/corpsnap/index.html. There is no fee to view records, including officers and registered agents.

Other access: The Data Division offers bulk release of information on paper or disk.

Uniform Commercial Code
Federal Tax Liens

Business Services Division, Secretary of State, PO Box 136, Jackson, MS 39205-0136 (Courier: 202 N Congress St, Suite 601, Union Planters Bank Bldg, Jackson, MS 39201); 601-359-1633, 800-256-3494, 601-359-1607 (Fax), 8AM-5PM.

www.sos.state.ms.us

Indexing & Storage: Records are available from 1968. Records are computerized since 1987. Records are indexed on inhouse computer.

Searching: Use search request form UCC-11. The search includes federal tax liens on businesses. Federal tax liens on individuals and all state tax liens are filed at the county level. Include the following in your request: debtor name.

Access by: mail, phone, fax, in person, online.

Fee & Payment: The search fee is $5.00, copies are $2.00 each, financing statements are $2.00 each. Fee payee: Secretary of State. Prepayment required. The state offers ACH accounts for regular requesters. Personal checks accepted. Credit cards accepted: MasterCard, Visa.

Mail search: Turnaround time: 1 day. No self addressed stamped envelope is required.

Phone search: Limited information is released over the phone.

Fax search: Requester must first set-up a prepaid account.

In person search: Searching is available in person.

Online search: Two systems available. Free searching for UCC debtors is at www.sos.state.ms.us/busserv/ucc/soskb/SearchStandardRA9.asp. Also, the commerical system called "Success" is open 24 hours daily. There is a $250 set-up fee and usage fee of $.10 per screen. Users can access via the Internet to avoid any toll charges. Customers are billed quarterly. For more information, call Burrell Brown at 601-359-1633.

Other access: A monthly list of farm liens is available for purchase.

State Tax Liens

Records not maintained by a state level agency.

Note: All state tax liens are filed at the county level.

Sales Tax Registrations

Revenue Bureau, Sales Tax Division, PO Box 22828, Jackson, MS 39225-2828 (Courier: 1577 Springridge Rd, Raymond, MS 39154); 601-923-7000, 8AM-5PM.

www.mstc.state.ms.us

Indexing & Storage: Records are available for the most current 3 years and are computerized.

Searching: The agency will only verify if a business is registered and will not release ownership data. Include the following in your request: business name. They will also search by tax permit number.

Access by: mail, phone, fax, in person.

Fee & Payment: Prepayment required. Fee payee: Revenue Bureau. Personal checks accepted. No credit cards accepted.

Mail search: Turnaround time: 5 to 10 working days. No self addressed stamped envelope is required. No fee for mail request. Copies cost $2.00 per page.

Phone search: No fee for telephone request.

Fax search: Same criteria as phone or mail searches.

In person search: No fee for request. Copies cost $2.00 per page.

Birth Certificates

State Department of Health, Vital Statistics & Records, PO Box 1700, Jackson, MS 39215-1700 (Courier: 571 Stadium Dr, Jackson, MS 39216); 601-576-7960, 601-576-7988, 601-576-7505 (Fax), 7:30AM-5PM.

www.msdh.state.ms.us/phs/index.htm

Indexing & Storage: Records are available from November 1, 1912 to present. New records are available for inquiry immediately. Records are indexed on microfiche, inhouse computer.

Searching: Employers need written release form from person of record. Records are not public access documents, they are only available to persons with legitimate and tangible interest. Include the following in your request: full name, names of parents, mother's maiden name, date of birth, place of birth, relationship to person of record, reason for information request. The following data is not released: original records of adoption.

Access by: mail, phone, fax, in person.

Fee & Payment: The $7.00 fee is for the short form. The fee for the long form certified is $12.00, plus is a $3.00 per for each additional copy. There is a $7.00 charge for no record found. Fee payee: Mississippi State Department of Health. Prepayment required. Use credit card for phone and/or expedited service only. Personal checks accepted only if in-state. Credit cards accepted: MasterCard, Visa, AmEx, Discover.

Mail search: Turnaround time: 7 to 10 days. No self addressed stamped envelope is required.

Phone search: Must use a credit card for an additional $5.00 fee. Turnaround time is same or next day.

Fax search: Same criteria as phone searches.

In person search: Turnaround time for Short Form-while you wait, Long Form-next day mail.

Expedited service: Expedited service is available for mail, phone and fax searches. Turnaround time: overnight delivery. Add a $5.00 credit card fee and $12.75 for overnight shipping.

Death Records

State Department of Health, Vital Statistics & Records, PO Box 1700, Jackson, MS 39215-1700 (Courier: 571 Stadium Dr, Jackson, MS 39216); 601-576-7960, 601-576-7988, 601-576-7505 (Fax), 7:30AM-5PM.

www.msdh.state.ms.us/phs/index.htm

Indexing & Storage: Records are available from November 1, 1912 to present. New records are available for inquiry immediately. Records are indexed on microfiche, inhouse computer.

Searching: Employers need written release form from immediate family member. Records are not considered public access documents. They are only available to persons with legitimate and tangible interest. Include the following in your request: full name, date of death, place of death, Social Security Number, relationship to person of record, reason for information request.

Access by: mail, phone, fax, in person.

Fee & Payment: Fee is $10.00 if you want a certified copy, and an additional $2.00 for each additional copy ordered at same time. If no record is found, the fee is $6.00. Fee payee: Mississippi State Department of Health. Prepayment required. Use credit cards for phone, fax and/or expedited service only. Credit cards accepted: MasterCard, Visa, AmEx, Discover.

Mail search: Turnaround time: 7 to 10 days. No self addressed stamped envelope is required.

Phone search: Turnaround time 2-3 days. Must use a credit card for an additional fee of $5.00.

Fax search: Same criteria as phone searching.

In person search: Turnaround time next day mail.

Expedited service: Expedited service is available for mail, phone and fax searches. Turnaround time: 1 day. Add $5.00 for use of credit card and $12.75 for overnight shipping.

Marriage Certificates

State Department of Health, Vital Statistics & Records, PO Box 1700, Jackson, MS 39215-1700 (Courier: 571 Stadium Dr, Jackson, MS 39216); 601-576-7960, 601-576-7988, 601-576-7505 (Fax), 7:30AM-5PM.

www.msdh.state.ms.us/phs/index.htm

Note: Records are also available at the county level, including those records from 1938 to 1942.

Indexing & Storage: Records are available from January 1926 to June 1938 and January 1942 to present. New records are available for inquiry immediately. Records are indexed on microfiche, inhouse computer.

Searching: Employers need written release from persons of record. Records are not considered public access documents. They are only available to persons with legitimate and tangible interest. Include the following in your request: names of husband and wife, date of marriage, place or county of marriage, relationship to person of record, reason for information request, wife's maiden name.

Access by: mail, phone, fax, in person.

Fee & Payment: The fee is $10.00 and $2.00 for each additional copy ordered at same time. If record not found fee is $6.00. Fee payee: Mississippi State Department of Health. Prepayment required. Use credit cards for phone, fax and/or expedited service only. Personal checks accepted only if in-state. Credit cards accepted: MasterCard, Visa, AmEx, Discover.

Mail search: Turnaround time: 4 to 7 days. No self addressed stamped envelope is required.

Phone search: Turnaround time 2-3 days. Must use a credit card for an additional $5.00 fee.

Fax search: Same criteria as phone searching.

In person search: Search costs $10.00 per request. Turnaround time next day mail.

Expedited service: Expedited service is available for mail, phone and fax searches. Turnaround time: 1 day. Add $5.00 for use of credit card and $12.75 for overnight delivery.

Divorce Records

State Department of Health, Vital Statistics, PO Box 1700, Jackson, MS 39215-1700 (Courier: 571 Stadium Dr, Jackson, MS 39216); 601-576-7960, 601-576-7988, 601-576-7505 (Fax), 7:30AM-5PM.

www.msdh.state.ms.us/phs/index.htm

Note: The state maintains a state-wide index and can refer to book and page number in county records. Requests for copies must be made to the county of record.

Indexing & Storage: Records are available from 1930 to present in county of record. This office will only confirm that a record exists and where. New records are available for inquiry immediately. Records are indexed on microfiche, inhouse computer.

Searching: Employers need written release form from person of record. Records are not public access documents and are available only to persons with legitimate and tangible interest. Include the following in your request: names of

husband and wife, date of divorce, year divorce case began, case number (if known), relationship to person of record, reason for information request.

Access by: mail, phone, fax, in person.

Fee & Payment: The fee to do an index search is $6.00. Copies are not released from this agency. Fee payee: Mississippi State Department of Health. Prepayment required. Personal checks accepted if in-state. Credit cards accepted: MasterCard, Visa, AmEx, Discover.

Mail search: Turnaround time: 1 to 3 days. No self addressed stamped envelope is required.

Phone search: Use of credit card, for an additional $5.00 fee, required.

Fax search: Same criteria as phone searching.

In person search: Turnaround time next day mail.

Expedited service: Expedited service is available for mail, phone and fax searches. Turnaround time: 1 day. Add $5.00 for use of credit card and $12.75 for overnight delivery.

Workers' Compensation Records

Workers Compensation Commission, PO Box 5300, Jackson, MS 39296-5300 (Courier: 1428 Lakeland Dr, Jackson, MS 39216); 601-987-4200, 8AM-5PM.

www.mwcc.state.ms.us

Indexing & Storage: Records are available for 10 years back to present. New records are available for inquiry immediately. Records are indexed on inhouse computer.

Searching: All requests must be in writing. Claimant's attorney must have contract or medical authorization. Employer/carrier must be party to action to obtain records. They do not conduct searches for pre-employment screening. Include the following in your request: claimant name, Social Security Number, docket number, place of employment at time of accident.

Access by: mail, in person, online.

Fee & Payment: Copy fee is $.50 with a $5.00 minimum, there is no search fee. Fee payee: Mississippi Workers' Compensation Commission. They will invoice. Personal checks accepted. No credit cards accepted.

Mail search: Turnaround time: 3 to 4 working days. No self addressed stamped envelope is required.

In person search: Anyone can come in to view. Medical information is not made available and copies cannot be made unless there is written authorization by party of record.

Online search: The First Report of Injury is available via the web. There is no fee, but users must register.

Other access: A first report of injury database is available on CD-ROM for $500.00.

Driver Records

Department of Public Safety, Driver Records, PO Box 958, Jackson, MS 39205 (Courier: 1900 E Woodrow Wilson, Jackson, MS 39216); 601-987-1274, 8AM-5PM.

www.dps.state.ms.us

Note: Copies of tickets may be obtained from the same address for a fee of $5.00 per record. A pre-addressed, stamped envelope is advised.

Indexing & Storage: Records are available for 3 years for moving violations, DUIs and suspensions. Accidents appear on driving records. The driver's address is provided on the record. It takes 45 days or more before new records are available for inquiry.

Searching: Casual requesters can obtain personal information only with consent of subject. The state adopted the provisions of the DPPA. The driver's full name, license number, and/or DOB are needed when ordering. The magnetic tape system requires only the driver's last name and number (first name and DOB are optional). Surrendered license records can only be obtained by a manual search.

Access by: mail, in person, online.

Fee & Payment: The fee is $7.00 per request. Fee payee: Department of Public Safety. Prepayment required. Personal checks accepted. No credit cards accepted.

Mail search: Turnaround time: 2 days. A self addressed stamped envelope is requested.

In person search: Walk-in requesters may submit up to 10 requests for immediate delivery; the rest are available the next day.

Online search: Both interactive and batch delivery is offer for high volume users only. Billing is monthly. Hook-up is through the Advantis System, fees apply. Lookup is by name only-not by driver license number. Fee is $7.00 per record. For more information, call 601-987-1337.

Other access: Overnight batch delivery by tape is available.

Accident Reports

Safety Responsibility, Accident Records, PO Box 958, Jackson, MS 39205 (Courier: 1900 E Woodrow Wilson, Jackson, MS 39216); 601-987-1278, 601-987-1261 (Fax), 8AM-5PM.

www.dps.state.ms.us

Note: The above address is for Highway Patrol accident investigations only. Reports require authorization from person involved. You must go to the agency that did the investigation for reports not found with the Highway Patrol.

Indexing & Storage: Records are available for 3 years to present on computer. Records are on microfiche from 1990 to present.

Searching: Must have authorization from individuals involved in the accident. Accident reports are only available to persons involved, their legal counsel and their insurance representative. Include the following in your request: date of accident, location of accident, full name, written authorization. SSN is helpful. Requests must be in writing.

Access by: mail.

Fee & Payment: The fee is $10.00 per record. Fee payee: Department of Public Safety. Prepayment required. Personal checks accepted. No credit cards accepted.

Mail search: Turnaround time: 5 days. A self addressed stamped envelope is requested.

Vehicle Ownership
Vehicle Identification

Mississippi State Tax Commission, Registration Department, PO Box 1140, Jackson, MS 39215 (Courier: 1577 Springridge Rd, Raymond, MS 39154); 601-923-7100 (Registration), 601-923-7200 (Titles), 601-923-7134 (Fax), 8AM-5PM.

www.mstc.state.ms.us/mvl/main.htm

Note: Please note that title information (liens, histories) requests are processed by a different section than registration information. For mail requests, use PO Box 1033 for the Title Department.

Indexing & Storage: Records are available from July 1, 1969 to present. Title records are computer indexed from July 1, 1969 to present, and on microfiche from July 1, 1969 to present.

Searching: Personal information is not released to casual requesters without consent from the subject. The turnaround time will be one week longer if the request requires a search farther back than 5 years.

Access by: mail, in person.

Fee & Payment: Fees are $4.50 per search for title, $1.00 per search for VIN or registration, and $2.00 for lien history. Fee payee: Mississippi State Tax Commission. Prepayment required. No cash will be accepted for mail requests. Personal checks accepted. No credit cards accepted.

Mail search: Turnaround time: 2 days. A self addressed stamped envelope is requested.

In person search: Turnaround time is immediate.

Other access: Mississippi offers some standardized files as well as some customization for bulk requesters of VIN and registration information. For more information, contact MLVB at the address listed above.

Vessel Ownership
Vessel Registration

Dept of Wildlife, Fisheries, & Parks, PO Box 451, Jackson, MS 39205; 601-432-2186, 601-432-2071 (Fax), 8AM-5PM.

www.mdwfp.com

Note: Liens are recorded if the vessel has been titled. Starting July 1998, boats are titled at the option of the owner/lender.

Indexing & Storage: Records are available from 1981 to present. Records are indexed on computer from 1985 to present. All motorized boats and all sailboats must be registered. It takes 2 weeks or so before new records are available for inquiry.

Searching: The name or DL number or MS number or hull number is required to search.

Access by: mail, phone, fax, in person.

Fee & Payment: There is no search fee.

Mail search: Turnaround time is the same day, except during the summer, which can take 3-4 weeks. A self addressed stamped envelope is requested.

Phone search: Records are available by phone.

Fax search: Results will be mailed back usually the same day.

In person search: Turnaround time is usually immediate.

Other access: The state makes records available on printed lists and magnetic tapes. Fees vary.

Legislation Records

Mississippi Legislature, PO Box 1018, Jackson, MS 39215 (Courier: New Capitol, 3rd Floor, Jackson, MS 39215-1018), 601-359-3229 (Senate), 601-359-3358 (House), 8:30AM-5PM.

www.ls.state.ms.us

Note: The room number for Senate documents is 308, the room number for House documents is 305. The session begins the 1st Tuesday after the 1st Monday in January and usually lasts 3 months.

Indexing & Storage: Records are available from the beginning of the Legislature. Bills from 1991 to present are on computer, prior bills are in file books. New records are available for inquiry immediately. Records are indexed on inhouse computer, books (volumes).

Searching: Include the following in your request: bill number.

Access by: mail, phone, fax, in person, online.

Fee & Payment: No charges for copies or searches.

Mail search: Turnaround time: same day. No self addressed stamped envelope is required.

Phone search: Records are available by phone.

Fax search: Same day fax-back service is available.

In person search: Searching is available in person.

Online search: The Internet site has an excellent bill status and measure information program. Data includes current and the previous year.

Voter Registration

Secretary of State, Elections Division, PO Box 136, Jackson, MS 39205-0136; 800-829-6786, 601-359-1350, 601-359-5019 (Fax), 8AM-5PM.

www.sos.state.ms.us/elections/elections.asp

Note: Records are open to the public, but must be individually searched at the county level.

Access by: online. Records are available by mail.

Online search: County Voter Rolls are available to download free online at www.sos.state.ms.us/elections/voter_registration_downloads/voter_reg_main.asp. Individual county files are in delimited text and may be downloaded to a database program.

GED Certificates

State Board for Community & Jr Colleges, GED Office, 3825 Ridgewood Rd, Jackson, MS 39211; 601-432-6338, 601-432-6363 (Fax), 8AM-5PM.

www.sbcjc.cc.ms.us

Searching: Transcripts are only available by written request. To search, all of the following is required: a signed release, name, date of birth, and Social Security Number. If known, the diploma number is helpful.

Access by: mail, fax, in person.

Fee & Payment: There is no fee for either a verification or a transcript.

Mail search: Turnaround time is 3 days. No self addressed stamped envelope is required.

Fax search: Same criteria as mail searching.

In person search: In person searchers must have a picture ID. Turnaround time: 2-3 minutes for a verification.

Hunting License Information
Fishing License Information

Department of Wildlife, Fisheries & Parks, PO Box 451, Jackson, MS 39205; 601-432-2055 (License Division), 601-432-2041 (Data Processing Div), 601-432-2071 (Fax), 8AM-5PM.

www.mdwfp.com

Indexing & Storage: Records are available for present data only.

Searching: Records are open to the public. They hold records on "sportsman" license holders which is a combination of hunting and fishing. Temporary license information is not maintained. You can search using the name or driver's license number.

Access by: mail, phone, fax, in person.

Fee & Payment: There is no search fee.

Mail search: Turnaround time: 10 days. No self addressed stamped envelope is required.

Phone search: Records are available by phone.

Fax search: Same criteria as mail searches.

In person search: You can make the request in person but they will mail back your response.

Other access: They offer bulk sale of various license groups in a variety of media methods. Visit the web site for more information, or call 601-432-2025.

Mississippi State Licensing Agencies

Licenses Searchable Online

Architect #3...www.archbd.state.ms.us/roster_tmp.htm
Attorney #27 ....www.msbar.org/lawyerdirectory.htm
Attorney Firm #27 ....www.msbar.org/lawyerdirectory.htm
Camp, Youth #40....................................www.msdh.state.ms.us/msdhsite/index.cfm/15,0,81,html
Charity #32 ....www.sos.state.ms.us/regenf/charities/charannrpt/index.asp
Child Care Facility #40............................www.msdh.state.ms.us/msdhsite/index.cfm/15,0,81,html
Contractor, General #6 ....www.msboc.state.ms.us/Search.cfm
Dental Hygienist #8................................www.msbde.state.ms.us
Dental Radiologist #8..............................www.msbde.state.ms.us
Dentist #8 ....www.msbde.state.ms.us
Engineer #9 ....http://dsitspe01.its.state.ms.us/pepls/EngSurveyors.nsf
Fund Raiser #32 ....www.sos.state.ms.us/regenf/charities/charannrpt/index.asp
HMO #25 ....www.doi.state.ms.us/hmolist.pdf
Insurance Company #25..........................www.doi.state.ms.us/compdir.html
Landscape Architect #3 ....www.archbd.state.ms.us/roster_tmp.htm
Lobbyist #31 ....www.sos.state.ms.us/elections/Lobbying/Lobbyist_Dir.asp
Long Term Care Insurance Company #25...www.doi.state.ms.us/ltclist.html
Notary Public #31 ....www.sos.state.ms.us/regenf/notaries/notaries.asp
Optometrist #15......................................www.odfinder.org/LicSearch.asp
Real Estate Appraiser #30.......................www.mrec.state.ms.us/asp/findappraiser.asp
Real Estate Broker #34............................www.mrec.state.ms.us/asp/findrealtor.asp
Real Estate Salesperson #34 ....www.mrec.state.ms.us/asp/findrealtor.asp
Surveyor, Land #9 ....http://dsitspe01.its.state.ms.us/pepls/EngSurveyors.nsf

Licensing Quick Finder

Air Monitor #22 601-961-5100
Alcohol Beverage Employee #26 601-856-1330
Alcoholic Beverage Retailer #2 601-856-1330
Animal/Veterinary Technician #29.......662-324-9380
Architect #3............................601-359-6020
Asbestos Contractor/Inspector/Supv #22
....601-961-5100
Asbestos Project Designer/Mgmt. Planner #22
....601-961-5100
Asbestos Worker #22 601-961-5100
Athletic Trainer #37.................601-576-7260
Attorney #27 601-948-4471
Attorney Firm #27 601-948-4471
Bank #4...................................601-359-1031
Barber Instructor/School #5.................601-359-1015
Barber/Barber Shop #5.............601-359-1015
Beauty Shop/Salon #7..............601-987-6837
Boiler & Pressure Vessel Inspector #37 601-576-7917
Camp, Youth #40......................601-576-7613
Charity #32 601-359-1371
Child Care Facility #40...............601-576-7613
Chiropractor #35......................662-773-4478
Contractor, General #6 601-354-6161
Cosmetologist #7 601-987-6837
Cosmetology Instructor #7......601-987-6837
Counselor, Licensed Professional #10..662-716-3932
CPA-Certified Public Accountant #19....601-354-7320
Dental Hygienist #8.................601-944-9622
Dental Radiologist #8 601-944-9622
Dentist #8...............................601-944-9622
Dietitian #37..........................601-576-7260

Educator, Citizen/Emergency/Non-Licensed #36
....601-359-3483
Emergency Medical Technician #37 601-576-7681
Engineer #9 601-359-6160
Esthetician #7 601-987-6837
Eye Enucleator #37 601-576-7260
Finance Company #4 601-359-1031
Fishing, Commercial #24..........601-432-2400
Fund Raiser #32 601-359-1371
Funeral Director #11................601-354-6903
Funeral Preneed Contractor #32...601-359-6271
Funeral Service Practitioner #11...601-354-6903
Gaming #26 601-351-2800
Health Facility #41...................601-576-7300
Hearing Aid Dealer (Specialist) #37 601-576-7260
HMO #25 601-359-3582
Insurance Agent/Solicitor/Advisor #25 . 601-359-3582
Insurance Company #25 601-359-3582
Investment Advisor #32............601-359-6363
Landscape Architect #3 601-359-6020
Liquor Control #2.....................601-856-1310
Lobbyist #31 601-359-6353
Long Term Care Insurance Company #25
....601-359-3582
Manicurist #7 601-987-6837
Marriage & Family Therapist #28 601-987-6806
Medical Doctor #12..................601-987-3079
Mortgage Lender/Company #4 601-359-1031
Notary Public #31 601-359-1615
Nurse #13...............................601-987-6858
Nurse-LPN #13........................601-987-6858
Nursing Home Administrator #14 601-364-2310

Occupational Therapist/Assistant #33 .. 601-576-7260
Optometrist #15......................601-853-4338
Osteopathic Physician #12.......601-987-3079
Pawn Shop #4.........................601-359-1031
Pharmacist #16 601-345-6750
Pharmacy #16 601-345-6750
Pharmacy Intern/Technician #16 601-345-6750
Physical Therapist/Assistant #33.........601-576-7260
Podiatrist #12 601-987-3079
Polygraph Examiner #17...........601-987-1596
Psychologist #18.....................601-321-4621
Radiation Technician #37..........601-576-7260
Real Estate Appraiser #30........601-932-6770
Real Estate Broker #34.............601-932-9191
Real Estate Salesperson #34 ...601-932-9191
Savings Institution #4...............601-359-1031
School Administrator #36..........601-359-3483
Securities Agent #32................601-359-6363
Securities Broker/Dealer #32....601-359-6363
Septic Tank Installer #37..........601-576-7260
Shorthand Reporter #20...........601-354-6580
Social Worker #28....................601-987-6806
Speech Pathologist/Audiologist #39 601-987-4153
Speech-Language Pathologist/Audiologist #21
....601-576-7260
Surveyor, Land #9 601-359-6160
Tattoo Artist #37.....................601-576-7260
Teacher #36 601-359-3483
Title & Loan Company #4..........601-359-1031
Veterinarian #29 662-324-9380
Veterinary Facility #29.............662-324-9380

Licensing Agency Information

#2 Office of Alcoholic Beverage Control, PO Box 540, Madison, MS 39110-0540; 601-856-1330, Fax: 601-856-1390.
www.mstc.state.ms.us
Agency email: bsmith@mstc.state.ms.us.

#3 Board of Architecture, 400 Legacy Park Dr #B, Ridgeland, MS 39157; 601-899-9071, Fax: 601-899-9171.
www.archbd.state.ms.us
Agency email: msboa@archbd.state.ms.us.
Search database at
www.archbd.state.ms.us/roster_tmp.htm

#4 Department of Banking & Consumer Finance, Board of Banking Review, 501 NW St, 901 Woolfolk Bldg, Ste. A, Jackson, MS 39202; 601-359-1031, Fax: 601-359-3557.
www.dbcf.state.ms.us/review.htm

#5 Board of Barber Examiners, 510 George St, Rm 240, Jackson, MS 39205; 601-359-1015, Fax: 601-359-1050.

#6 Board of Contractors, 2001 Airport Rd. #101, Jackson, MS 39208; 601-354-6161, Fax: 601-354-6715. www.state.nu.us/vetbo
Search database at
www.msboc.state.ms.us/Search.cfm

#7 Board of Cosmetology, PO Box 55689, Jackson, MS 39296-5689; 601-987-6837, Fax: 601-987-6840.

#8 Board of Dental Examiners, 600 E Amitest #100, Jackson, MS 39060; 601-944-9622, Fax: 601-924-9623 or 9624.
www.msbde.state.ms.us
Search database at www.msbde.state.ms.us

#9 Board of Engineers & Land Surveyors, 239 N Lamar St, 501 Robert E Lee Bldg, Jackson, MS 39201; 601-359-6160, Fax: 601-359-6159.
www.pepls.state.ms.us
Agency email: information@pepls.state.ms.us.
Search database at http://dsitspe01.its.state.ms.us/pepls/EngSurveyors.nsf

#10 Board of Examiners for Licensed Professional Counselors, 319 S Main St, Yazoo City, MS 39194; 662-716-3932, Fax: 662-751-4628.
www.lpc.state.ms.us
Agency email: acox@maminc.net.

#11 Board of Funeral Service, 7 River Bend Place, Ste. A, Flowood, MS 39208; 601-932-1973, Fax: 601-932-1901.
www.msfuneralboard.com. Agency email: msfuneralboard@msfuneralboard.com. The web site will soon list funeral homes.

#12 Board of Medical Licensure, 2600 Insurance Center Dr #2008, Jackson, MS 39216; 601-987-3079, Fax: 601-987-4159.
www.msbml.state.ms.us
Agency email: mboard@msbml.state.ms.us.

#13 Board of Nursing, 1935 Lakeland Dr #B, Jackson, MS 39216; 601-987-4188, Fax: 601-364-2352.

#14 Board of Nursing Home Administrators, 1400 Lakeover Rd #120, Jackson, MS 39213; 601-364-2310, Fax: 601-364-2306.

#15 Board of Optometry, PO Box 12370, Jackson, MS 39236; 601-853-4338, Fax: 601-853-0336.
www.msoptometry.org
Search database at
www.odfinder.org/LicSearch.asp

#16 Board of Pharmacy, 625 N State St, #202, Jackson, MS 39225-4507; 601-354-6750, Fax: 601-354-6071.
www.mbp.state.ms.us
Agency email: sstovall@mbp.state.ms.us.

#17 Board of Polygraph Examiners, PO Box 958, Jackson, MS 39205; 601-987-1596.

#18 Board of Psychology, 4273 I-55 N. #104, Jackson, MS 39206-6157; 601-321-4621, Fax: 601-321-4628.

#19 Board of Public Accountancy, 653 N State St, Jackson, MS 39202; 601-354-7320, Fax: 601-354-7290.
www.msbpa.state.ms.us

#20 Board of Certified Court Reporters, PO Box 369 (656 N State St, Jackson, MS 39205; 601-354-6580, Fax: 601-354-6058.
www.mssc.state.ms.us
Agency email: tgraves@mssc,state.ms.us.

#21 Department of Health, Council of Advisors in Speech Pathology/Audiology, PO Box 1700 (570 Woodrow Wilson, 39216), Jackson, MS 39215-1700; 601-576-7260, Fax: 601-576-7267.
www.msdh.state.ms.us
Agency email: squilter@msdh.state.ms.us.

#22 Department of Environmental Quality, Pollution Control, PO Box 10385, Jackson, MS 39289-0385; 601-961-5171, Fax: 601-354-6612.
www.deq.state.ms.us/domino/pcweb.nsf

#24 Department of Wildlife, Fisheries & Parks, 1505 Eastover Dr, Jackson, MS 39211-6322; 601-432-2400, Fax: 601-432-2024.
www.mdwfp.com

#25 Insurance Department, Licensing Division, PO Box 79, Jackson, MS 39205; 601-359-3582, Fax: 601-359-1951.
www.doi.state.ms.us/agents.html. Agency email: licensing@mid.state.ms.us.

#26 Gaming Commission, 200 E Pearl St, Jackson, MS 39205; 601-351-2800, Fax: 601-351-2817. www.msgaming.com

#27 Board of Bar Admissions, PO Box 2168, Jackson, MS 39225; 601-948-4471, Fax: 601-355-8635. www.msbar.org
Search database at
www.msbar.org/lawyerdirectory.htm

#28 Marriage & Family Therapists, Board of Examiners for Social Workers, PO Box 4508, Jackson, MS 39296-4508; 601-987-6806, Fax: 601-987-6808
Agency email: mboe@swmft.state.ms.us.

#29 Board of Veterinary Medicine, 209 S Lafayette, Starkville, MS 39759; 662-324-9380, Fax: 662-324-9380.

#30 Real Estate Appraiser, Licensing & Certification Board, 5176 Keele St, Jackson, MS 39236-2685; 601-932-6770, Fax: 601-932-2990.
www.mrec.state.ms.us/default.asp
Search database at
www.mrec.state.ms.us/asp/findappraiser.asp

#31 Office of Secretary of State, PO Box 136, Jackson, MS 39205-0136; 601-359-1350, Fax: 601-359-1499.
www.sos.state.ms.us
Search database at www.sos.state.ms.us

#32 Office of Secretary of State, Business Regulation & Enforcement Division, PO Box 136 (202 N Congress), Jackson, MS 39205-0136; 601-359-6363, Fax: 601-359-2663.
www.sos.state.ms.us
Agency email: administrator@sos.state.ms.us.

#33 Professional Licensure Division, MSDH, PO Box 1700, Jackson, MS 39215-1700; 601-576-7260, Fax: 601-576-7267
Agency email: sjones@msdh.state.ms.us.

#34 Real Estate Commission, Licensing & Certification Board, PO Box 12685 (2506 Lakeland Dr, #300), Jackson, MS 39236; 601-932-9191, Fax: 601-932-2990.
www.mrec.state.ms.us/default.asp
Search database at
www.mrec.state.ms.us/asp/findrealtor.asp

#35 Board of Chiropractic Examiners, PO Box 775, Louisville, MS 39339; 662-773-4478, Fax: 662-773-4433.

#36 Department of Education, Teacher Licensure/Certification, PO Box 771 (359 N West Street), Jackson, MS 39205; 601-359-3483, Fax: 601-359-2778.
www.mde.k12.ms.us
Agency email: cchester@mde.k12.ms.us.

#37 Department of Health, (Licensing Division), 570 E Woodrow Wilson, Jackson, MS 39215; 601-576-7917, Fax: 601-576-7923.
www.msdh.state.ms.us

#40 Department of Health, (Childcare Board), 570 E Woodrow Wilson, Jackson, MS 39215; 601-576-7613.
www.msdh.state.ms.us
Search database at www.msdh.state.ms.us/msdhsite/index.cfm/15,0,81,html.

#41 Department of Health, Health Facilities Licensure & Certification, 570 E Woodrow Wilson Blvd, (PO Box 1700), Jackson, MS 39215-1700; 601-576-7300, Fax: 601-576-7350.
www.msdh.state.ms.us

Mississippi Federal Courts

The following list indicates the district and division name for each county in the state. If the bankruptcy court location is different from the district court, then the location of the bankruptcy court appears in parentheses.

County/Court Cross Reference

County	District	Division
Adams	Southern	Vicksburg (Jackson)
Alcorn	Northern	Aberdeen-Eastern (Aberdeen)
Amite	Southern	Jackson
Attala	Northern	Aberdeen-Eastern (Aberdeen)
Benton	Northern	Oxford-Northern (Aberdeen)
Bolivar	Northern	Clarksdale/Delta (Aberdeen)
Calhoun	Northern	Oxford-Northern (Aberdeen)
Carroll	Northern	Greenville (Aberdeen)
Chickasaw	Northern	Aberdeen-Eastern (Aberdeen)
Choctaw	Northern	Aberdeen-Eastern (Aberdeen)
Claiborne	Southern	Vicksburg (Jackson)
Clarke	Southern	Meridian (Biloxi)
Clay	Northern	Aberdeen-Eastern (Aberdeen)
Coahoma	Northern	Clarksdale/Delta (Aberdeen)
Copiah	Southern	Jackson
Covington	Southern	Hattiesburg (Biloxi)
De Soto	Northern	Clarksdale/Delta (Aberdeen)
Forrest	Southern	Hattiesburg (Biloxi)
Franklin	Southern	Jackson
George	Southern	Biloxi-Southern (Biloxi)
Greene	Southern	Hattiesburg (Biloxi)
Grenada	Northern	Oxford-Northern (Aberdeen)
Hancock	Southern	Biloxi-Southern (Biloxi)
Harrison	Southern	Biloxi-Southern (Biloxi)
Hinds	Southern	Jackson
Holmes	Southern	Jackson
Humphreys	Northern	Greenville (Aberdeen)
Issaquena	Southern	Vicksburg (Jackson)
Itawamba	Northern	Aberdeen-Eastern (Aberdeen)
Jackson	Southern	Biloxi-Southern (Biloxi)
Jasper	Southern	Meridian (Biloxi)
Jefferson	Southern	Vicksburg (Jackson)
Jefferson Davis	Southern	Hattiesburg (Biloxi)
Jones	Southern	Hattiesburg (Biloxi)
Kemper	Southern	Meridian (Biloxi)
Lafayette	Northern	Oxford-Northern (Aberdeen)
Lamar	Southern	Hattiesburg (Biloxi)
Lauderdale	Southern	Meridian (Biloxi)
Lawrence	Southern	Hattiesburg (Biloxi)
Leake	Southern	Jackson
Lee	Northern	Aberdeen-Eastern (Aberdeen)
Leflore	Northern	Greenville (Aberdeen)
Lincoln	Southern	Jackson
Lowndes	Northern	Aberdeen-Eastern (Aberdeen)
Madison	Southern	Jackson
Marion	Southern	Hattiesburg (Jackson)
Marshall	Northern	Oxford-Northern (Aberdeen)
Monroe	Northern	Aberdeen-Eastern (Aberdeen)
Montgomery	Northern	Oxford-Northern (Aberdeen)
Neshoba	Southern	Meridian (Biloxi)
Newton	Southern	Meridian (Biloxi)
Noxubee	Southern	Meridian (Biloxi)
Oktibbeha	Northern	Aberdeen-Eastern (Aberdeen)
Panola	Northern	Clarksdale/Delta (Aberdeen)
Pearl River	Southern	Biloxi-Southern (Biloxi)
Perry	Southern	Hattiesburg (Biloxi)
Pike	Southern	Jackson
Pontotoc	Northern	Oxford-Northern (Aberdeen)
Prentiss	Northern	Aberdeen-Eastern (Aberdeen)
Quitman	Northern	Clarksdale/Delta (Aberdeen)
Rankin	Southern	Jackson
Scott	Southern	Jackson
Sharkey	Southern	Vicksburg (Jackson)
Simpson	Southern	Jackson
Smith	Southern	Jackson
Stone	Southern	Biloxi-Southern (Biloxi)
Sunflower	Northern	Greenville (Aberdeen)
Tallahatchie	Northern	Clarksdale/Delta (Aberdeen)
Tate	Northern	Clarksdale/Delta (Aberdeen)
Tippah	Northern	Oxford-Northern (Aberdeen)
Tishomingo	Northern	Aberdeen-Eastern (Aberdeen)
Tunica	Northern	Clarksdale/Delta (Aberdeen)
Union	Northern	Oxford-Northern (Aberdeen)
Walthall	Southern	Hattiesburg (Biloxi)
Warren	Southern	Vicksburg (Jackson)
Washington	Northern	Greenville (Aberdeen)
Wayne	Southern	Meridian (Biloxi)
Webster	Northern	Oxford-Northern (Aberdeen)
Wilkinson	Southern	Vicksburg (Jackson)
Winston	Northern	Aberdeen-Eastern (Aberdeen)
Yalobusha	Northern	Oxford-Northern (Aberdeen)
Yazoo	Southern	Vicksburg (Jackson)

Standards for Federal Courts: The search fee is $20.00 per item (one party name or case number). Certification fee is $7.00 per document. Copy fee is $.50 per page. All fees standard unless noted in profile. Mail Search: always enclose a stamped self addressed envelope unless otherwise noted. Before releasing records, all courts require prepayment unless noted in profile.

Open records are located at the court unless otherwise noted. District courts index by defendant and plaintiff as well as by case number. Bankruptcy courts usually index by debtor and case number. While most courts now have their indexes on computer, many still maintain index card files as well.

The universal PACER sign-up number is 800-676-6856. Find PACER and the Party/Case Index on the Web at http://pacer.psc.uscourts.gov. PACER dial-up access is $.60 per minute. Also, courts offering internet access via RACER, PACER, Web-PACER or the new CM-ECF charge $.07 per page fee unless noted as free.

US District Court

Northern District of Mississippi

Aberdeen-Eastern Division PO Box 704, Aberdeen, MS 39730 (Courier Address: 301 W Commerce, Room 310, Aberdeen, MS 39730), 662-369-4952.

www.msnd.uscourts.gov

Counties: Alcorn, Attala, Chickasaw, Choctaw, Clay, Itawamba, Lee, Lowndes, Monroe, Oktibbeha, Prentiss, Tishomingo, Winston.

Indexing & Storage: Cases are indexed by defendant, plaintiff, and case number. New cases are available in the index 48 hours after filing date. Open records are located at this court.

Fee & Payment Notes: Payment may be made by money order, cashier check, personal check. Payee: Clerk, US District Court. You are allowed to make your own copies. These copies cost $.25 per page.

Phone Search: Searching not available by phone. If a case number is provided over the phone, the court will verify that the case number is correct.

In Person Search: In person searching available.

PACER:. Case records are available back to 1990. Records are purged every six months. New records are available online after 1 day. PACER is available online at http://pacer.msnd.uscourts.gov.

Opinions Online: Court opinions are available online at http://sunset.backbone.olemiss.edu/~llibcoll/ndms

Clarksdale/Delta Division c/o Oxford-Northern Division, PO Box 727, Oxford, MS 38655 (Courier Address: Suite 369, 911 Jackson Ave, Oxford, MS 38655), 662-234-1971.

www.msnd.uscourts.gov

Counties: Bolivar, Coahoma, De Soto, Panola, Quitman, Tallahatchie, Tate, Tunica.

Indexing & Storage: New cases are available in the index after filing date. Open records are located at the Oxford-Northern Division.

Fee & Payment Notes: Payment may be made by money order, cashier check. Business checks are not accepted. Personal checks are not accepted.

Phone Search: Searching not available by phone.

In Person Search: In person searching available.

PACER:. Case records are available back to 1990. Records are purged every six months. New records are available online after 1 day. PACER is available online at http://pacer.msnd.uscourts.gov.

Opinions Online: Court opinions are available online at http://sunset.backbone.olemiss.edu/~llibcoll/ndms

Greenville Division PO Box 190, Greenville, MS 38702-0190 (Courier Address: US Post Office & Federal Bldg, 305 Main, Greenville, MS 38701), 662-335-1651, Fax: 662-332-4292.

www.msnd.uscourts.gov

Counties: Carroll, Humphreys, Leflore, Sunflower, Washington.

Indexing & Storage: Cases are indexed by defendant, plaintiff, and case number. New cases are available in the index immediately after filing date. Open records are located at this court.

Fee & Payment Notes: Payment may be made by money order, cashier check, personal check. Payee: Clerk, US District Court. You are allowed to make your own copies. These copies cost $.25 per page.

Phone Search: Only docket information based on case number is available by phone.

In Person Search: In person searching available.

PACER:. Case records are available back to 1990. Records are purged every six months. New records are available online after 1 day. PACER is available online at http://pacer.msnd.uscourts.gov.

Opinions Online: Court opinions are available online at http://sunset.backbone.olemiss.edu/~llibcoll/ndms

Oxford-Northern Division PO Box 727, Oxford, MS 38655 (Courier Address: Suite 369, 911 Jackson Ave, Oxford, MS 38655), 662-234-1971.

www.msnd.uscourts.gov

Counties: Benton, Calhoun, Grenada, Lafayette, Marshall, Montgomery, Pontotoc, Tippah, Union, Webster, Yalobusha.

Indexing & Storage: Cases are indexed by defendant, plaintiff, and case number. New cases are available in the index 48 hours after filing date. Records are also indexed on microfiche. Civil records are sent to the Atlanta Federal Records Center 5 years after closing. Criminal records are sent to the Atlanta Federal Records Ce10 years after closing. All criminal records for the Delta Division (Clarksdale) are maintained in this office.

Fee & Payment Notes: Payment may be made by money order, cashier check, personal check. Payee: Clerk, US District Court. You are allowed to make your own copies. These copies cost $.25 per page.

Phone Search: Searching not available by phone. If a case number is provided over the phone, the court will verify that the case number is correct.

In Person Search: In person searching available.

PACER:. Case records are available back to 1990. Records are purged every six months. New records are available online after 1 day. PACER is available online at http://pacer.msnd.uscourts.gov.

Opinions Online: Court opinions are available online at http://sunset.backbone.olemiss.edu/~llibcoll/ndms

US Bankruptcy Court

Northern District of Mississippi

Aberdeen Division PO Drawer 867, Aberdeen, MS 39730-0867 (Courier Address: 205 Federal Bldg, 301 W. Commerce St, Aberdeen, MS 39730), 662-369-2596.

www.msnb.uscourts.gov

Counties: Alcorn, Attala, Benton, Bolivar, Calhoun, Carroll, Chickasaw, Choctaw, Clay, Coahoma, De Soto, Grenada, Humphreys, Itawamba, Lafayette, Lee, Leflore, Lowndes, Marshall, Monroe, Montgomery, Oktibbeha, Panola, Pontotoc, Prentiss, Quitman, Sunflower, Tallahatchie, Tate, Tippah, Tishomingo, Tunica, Union, Washington, Webster, Winston, Yalobusha.

Indexing & Storage: Cases are indexed by debtor as well as by case number. New cases are available in the index 1-2 days after filing date. Open records are located at this court.

Fee & Payment Notes: Payment may be made by money order, cashier check, personal check. Payee: Clerk, US Bankruptcy Court, Northern District. You are allowed to make your own copies. These copies cost $.50 per page. The $15.00 charge is per name or item. You may not take case files from the court for copies.

Phone Search: Only docket information is available by phone. An automated voice case information service (VCIS) is available. Call VCIS at 800-392-8653 or 662-369-8147.

In Person Search: In person searching available.

PACER: Toll-free dial-up access: 888-372-5709. Local dial-up access: 662-369-9805. Case records are available back to April 1, 1987. Records are purged every 6 months. New civil records are available online after 2 days. PACER is available online at http://pacer.msnb.uscourts.gov.

Electronic Filing: (Currently in the process of implementing CM/ECF.)

US District Court

Southern District of Mississippi

Biloxi-Southern Division Room 243, 725 Dr. Martin Luther King Jr. Blvd, Biloxi, MS 39530 (Courier Address: Use mail address for courier delivery), 228-432-8623, Fax: 601-436-9632.

www.mssd.uscourts.gov

Counties: George, Hancock, Harrison, Jackson, Pearl River, Stone.

Indexing & Storage: Cases are indexed by defendant, plaintiff, and case number. New cases are available in the index 48 hours after filing date. Open records are located at this court.

Fee & Payment Notes: Payment may be made by money order, cashier check, personal check. Payee: Clerk, US District Court. You are allowed to make your own copies. These copies cost $.25 per page.

Phone Search: Searching not available by phone. Only docket information is available by phone.

In Person Search: In person searching available.

PACER: Access fee is. Toll-free dial-up access: 800-839-6425. Local dial-up access: 601-965-5141. Case records are available back to 1992.

New records are available online after 2 days. PACER is available online at http://pacer.mssd.uscourts.gov.

Hattiesburg Division Suite 200, 701 Main St, Hattiesburg, MS 39401 (Courier Address: Use mail address for courier delivery), 601-583-2433.

www.mssd.uscourts.gov

Counties: Covington, Forrest, Greene, Jefferson Davis, Jones, Lamar, Lawrence, Marion, Perry, Walthall.

Indexing & Storage: Cases are indexed by defendant, plaintiff, and case number. New cases are available in the index 48 hours after filing date. Open records are located at this court.

Fee & Payment Notes: Payment may be made by money order, cashier check, personal check. Payee: Clerk, US District Court. You are allowed to make your own copies. These copies cost $.25 per page.

Phone Search: Only docket information is available by case number over the phone.

In Person Search: In person searching available.

PACER: Access fee is. Toll-free dial-up access: 800-839-6425. Local dial-up access: 601-965-5141. Case records are available back to 1992. New records are available online after 2 days. PACER is available online at http://pacer.mssd.uscourts.gov.

Jackson Division Suite 316, 245 E Capitol St, Jackson, MS 39201 (Courier Address: Use mail address for courier delivery), 601-965-4439.

www.mssd.uscourts.gov

Counties: Amite, Copiah, Franklin, Hinds, Holmes, Leake, Lincoln, Madison, Pike, Rankin, Scott, Simpson, Smith.

Indexing & Storage: Cases are indexed by defendant, plaintiff, and case number. New cases are available in the index 48 hours after filing date. Microfiche index also maintained. Open records are located at this court.

Fee & Payment Notes: Payment may be made by money order, cashier check, personal check. Payee: Clerk, US District Court. You are allowed to make your own copies. These copies cost $.25 per page.

Phone Search: Searching not available by phone.

In Person Search: In person searching available.

PACER: Access fee is. Toll-free dial-up access: 800-839-6425. Local dial-up access: 601-965-5141. Case records are available back to 1992. New records are available online after 2 days. PACER is available online at http://pacer.mssd.uscourts.gov.

Meridian Division c/o Jackson Division, Suite 316, 245 E Capitol St, Jackson, MS 39201 (Courier Address: Use mail address for courier delivery), 601-965-4439.

www.mssd.uscourts.gov

Counties: Clarke, Jasper, Kemper, Lauderdale, Neshoba, Newton, Noxubee, Wayne.

Indexing & Storage: Cases are indexed by defendant, plaintiff, and case number. New cases are available in the index after filing date. Open records are located at the Jackson Division.

Fee & Payment Notes: Payment may be made by money order, cashier check. Business checks are not accepted. Personal checks are not accepted.

Phone Search: Searching not available by phone.

In Person Search: In person searching available.

PACER: Access fee is. Toll-free dial-up access: 800-839-6425. Local dial-up access: 601-965-5141. Case records are available back to 1992. New records are available online after 2 days. PACER is available online at http://pacer.mssd.uscourts.gov.

Vicksburg Division c/o Jackson Division, Suite 316, 245 E Capitol St, Jackson, MS 39201 (Courier Address: Use mail address for courier delivery), 601-965-4439.

www.mssd.uscourts.gov

Counties: Adams, Claiborne, Issaquena, Jefferson, Sharkey, Warren, Wilkinson, Yazoo.

Indexing & Storage: New cases are available in the index after filing date. Open records are located at the Jackson Division.

Fee & Payment Notes: Payment may be made by money order, cashier check. Business checks are not accepted. Personal checks are not accepted.

Phone Search: Searching not available by phone.

In Person Search: In person searching available.

PACER: Access fee is. Toll-free dial-up access: 800-839-6425. Local dial-up access: 601-965-5141. Case records are available back to 1992. New records are available online after 2 days. PACER is available online at http://pacer.mssd.uscourts.gov.

US Bankruptcy Court

Southern District of Mississippi

Biloxi Division Room 117, 725 Dr. Martin Luther King Jr. Blvd, Biloxi, MS 39530 (Courier Address: Use mail address for courier delivery), 228-432-5542.

www.mssb.uscourts.gov

Counties: Clarke, Covington, Forrest, George, Greene, Hancock, Harrison, Jackson, Jasper, Jefferson Davis, Jones, Kemper, Lamar, Lauderdale, Lawrence, Marion, Neshoba, Newton, Noxubee, Pearl River, Perry, Stone, Walthall, Wayne.

Indexing & Storage: Cases are indexed by debtor as well as by case number. New cases are available in the index a few hours after filing date. Open records are located at this court.

Fee & Payment Notes: Payment may be made by money order, cashier check, personal check. Payee: Clerk, US Bankruptcy Court.

Phone Search: An automated voice case information service (VCIS) is available. Call VCIS at 800-293-2723 or 601-435-2905.

In Person Search: In person searching available.

PACER: Toll-free dial-up access: 800-223-1078. Local dial-up access: 601-965-6103. Use of PC Anywhere V4.0 recommended. Case records are available back to 1986. New civil records are available online after 1 day.

Jackson Division PO Box 2448, Jackson, MS 39225-2448 (Courier Address: 100 E Capitol St, Jackson, MS 39201), 601-965-5301.

www.mssb.uscourts.gov

Counties: Adams, Amite, Claiborne, Copiah, Franklin, Hinds, Holmes, Issaquena, Jefferson, Leake, Lincoln, Madison, Pike, Rankin, Scott, Sharkey, Simpson, Smith, Warren, Wilkinson, Yazoo.

Indexing & Storage: Cases are indexed by debtor as well as by case number. New cases are available in the index a few hours after filing date. Open records are located at this court.

Fee & Payment Notes: Payment may be made by money order, cashier check, personal check. Payee: Clerk, US Bankruptcy Court.

Phone Search: An automated voice case information service (VCIS) is available. Call VCIS at 800-601-8859 or 601-965-6106.

In Person Search: In person searching available.

PACER: Toll-free dial-up access: 800-223-1078. Local dial-up access: 601-965-6103. Use of PC Anywhere V4.0 recommended.

Mississippi County Courts

Court	Jurisdiction	No. of Courts	How Organized
Circuit Courts*	General	70	22 Districts
County Courts*	Limited	3	19 Counties
Combined Courts*		20	
Chancery Courts*	General	91	20 Districts
Justice Courts	Limited	88	
Municipal Courts	Municipal	154	
Family Court	Special	1	

* Profiled in this Sourcebook.

Court	Tort	Contract	Real Estate	Min. Claim	Max. Claim	Small Claims	Estate	Eviction	Domestic Relations
Circuit Courts*	X	X	X	$2500	No Max			X	X
County Courts*	X	X	X	$0	$75,000			X	X
Combined Courts*									
Chancery Court*	X	X	X	$0	No Max		X		X
Justice Courts*	X	X	X	$0	$2500	$2500		X	
Municipal Courts								X	
Family Court									X

Court	Felony	Misdemeanor	DWI/DUI	Preliminary Hearing	Juvenile
Circuit Courts*	X				
County Courts*		X	X	X	X
Combined Courts*					
Chancery Court*					X
Justice Courts*		X	X	X	
Municipal Courts		X	X	X	
Family Court					X

ADMINISTRATION Court Administrator, Supreme Court, Box 117, Jackson, MS, 39205; 601-359-3697, Fax: 601-359-2443. www.mssc.state.ms.us

COURT STRUCTURE The court of general jurisdiction is the Circuit Court with 70 courts in 22 districts. Justice Courts were first created in 1984, replacing the Justice of the Peace. Prior to 1984, records were kept separately by each Justice of the Peace, so the location of such records today is often unknown. Probate is handled by the Chancery Courts, as are property matters.

ONLINE ACCESS A statewide online computer system is in use internally for court personnel. There are plans underway to make this system available to the public, but this was put on hold in 2002.

ADDITIONAL INFORMATION A number of Mississippi counties have two Circuit Court Districts. A search of either court in such a county will include the index from the other court.

Full Name is a search requirement for all courts. DOB and SSN are very helpful for differentiating between like-named individuals.

CRIMINAL RECORDS The Administrative Office of Courts offers a statewide search via fax requesting with a 24 hour turnaround time. There is a $25.00 start-up fee and a $5.00 per name search fee. Call 601-354-7449 or fax 601-354-7459 for details.

Adams County

Circuit & County Court PO Box 1224, Natchez, MS 39121; 601-446-6326; Fax: 601-445-7955. Hours: 8AM-5PM (CST). *Felony, Misdemeanor, Civil Actions Over $2,500.*

Civil Records: Access: Fax, mail, in person. Both court and visitors may perform in person searches. Search fee: $10.00 per name. Required to search: name, years to search. Civil cases indexed by defendant, plaintiff. Civil records on computer; docket books to 1950s; records stored in basement to 1799.

Criminal Records: Access: Mail, fax, in person. Both court and visitors may perform in person searches. Search fee: $10.00 per name. Required to search: name, years to search; also helpful: SSN. Criminal records on computer; docket books to 1950s; records stored in basement to 1799.

General Information: No sealed, adoptions, mental health, juvenile, sex, or expunged records released. Turnaround time 1-2 days if on computer. Copy fee: $1.00 per page. Certification fee: $2.00. Fee payee: Circuit Clerk. Personal checks accepted. Prepayment is required.

Justice Court 115 S Wall, Natchez, MS 39120; 601-446-6326; Fax: 601-445-7955. Hours: 8AM-5PM (CST). *Misdemeanor, Civil Actions Under $2,500, Eviction, Small Claims.*

Chancery Court PO Box 1006, Natchez, MS 39121; 601-446-6684; Fax: 601-445-7913. Hours: 8AM-5PM (CST). *Probate.*

Alcorn County

Circuit Court PO Box 430 Attn: Circuit Clerk, Corinth, MS 38835; 662-286-7740; Fax: 662-286-7767. Hours: 8AM-5PM (CST). *Felony, Civil Actions Over $2,500.*

Civil Records: Access: Mail, fax, in person. Both court and visitors may perform in person searches. Search fee: $10.00 per name. Required to search: name, years to search. Civil cases indexed by defendant, plaintiff. Civil records on docket books from the 1930s.

Criminal Records: Access: Mail, fax, in person. Both court and visitors may perform in person searches. Search fee: $10.00 per name. Required to search: name, years to search, DOB; also helpful: SSN, sex. Criminal records on docket books from the 1930s.

General Information: No sealed, adoptions, mental health, juvenile, sex, or expunged records released. SASE required. Turnaround time varies. Fax notes: Fee to fax results is $10.00 per document. Copy fee: $.50 per page. Fee payee: Circuit Clerk. Personal checks accepted. Prepayment is required.

Justice Court PO Box 226, Corinth, MS 38834; 662-286-7776; Fax: 662-286-2157. Hours: 8AM-5PM (CST). *Misdemeanor, Civil Actions Under $2,500, Eviction, Small Claims.*

Chancery Court PO Box 69, Corinth, MS 38835-0069; 662-286-7702; Fax: 662-286-7706. *Probate.*

Amite County

Circuit Court PO Box 312, Liberty, MS 39645; 601-657-8932; Fax: 601-657-1082. Hours: 8AM-5PM (CST). *Felony, Civil Actions Over $2,500.*

Civil Records: Access: Phone, fax, mail, in person. Both court and visitors may perform in person searches. Search fee: $10.00 per name. Required to search: name, years to search. Civil cases indexed by defendant, plaintiff. Civil records on docket books since 1976; on computer back to 1990.

Criminal Records: Access: Fax, mail, in person. Both court and visitors may perform in person searches. Search fee: $10.00 per name. Required to search: name,

years to search, DOB; also helpful: SSN. Criminal records on docket books since 1976; on computer back to 1990.

General Information: No sealed, adoptions, mental health, juvenile, sex, or expunged records released. SASE required. Turnaround time same day. Fax notes: $3.00. Copy fee: $1.00 per page. Certification fee: $10.00. Fee payee: Circuit Clerk. Personal checks accepted.

Justice Court PO Box 362, Liberty, MS 39645; 601-657-4527; Fax: 601-657-8604. Hours: 8AM-5PM (CST). *Misdemeanor, Civil Actions Under $2,500, Eviction, Small Claims.*

Chancery Court PO Box 680, Liberty, MS 39645; 601-657-8022; Fax: 601-657-8288. Hours: 8AM-5PM (CST). *Probate.*

Attala County

Circuit Court Courthouse, Kosciusko, MS 39090; 662-289-1471; Fax: 662-289-7666. Hours: 8AM-5PM (CST). *Felony, Civil Actions Over $2,500.*

Civil Records: Access: Fax, mail, in person. Both court and visitors may perform in person searches. Search fee: $10.00 per name. Required to search: name, years to search. Civil cases indexed by defendant, plaintiff. Civil records kept on docket books since 1915.

Criminal Records: Access: Fax, mail, in person. Both court and visitors may perform in person searches. Search fee: $10.00 per name. Required to search: name, years to search, DOB; also helpful: SSN. Criminal records kept on docket books since 1915.

General Information: No sealed, adoptions, mental health, juvenile, sex, or expunged records released. SASE required. Turnaround time same day. Fax notes: $.50 per page. Copy fee: $.50 per page. Certification fee: $1.00. Fee payee: Circuit Clerk. Business checks accepted. Prepayment is required.

Justice Court 100 Courthouse, #4, Kosciusko, MS 39090; 662-289-7272; Fax: 662-289-0105. Hours: 8AM-5PM (CST). *Misdemeanor, Civil Actions Under $2,500, Eviction, Small Claims.*

Chancery Court 230 W. Washington, Kosciusko, MS 39090; 662-289-2921; Fax: 662-289-7662. Hours: 8AM-5PM (CST). *Probate.*

Benton County

Circuit Court PO Box 262, Ashland, MS 38603; 662-224-6310; Fax: 662-224-6312. Hours: 8AM-5PM (CST). *Felony, Civil Actions Over $2,500.*

Civil Records: Access: Mail, in person. Both court and visitors may perform in person searches. Search fee: $10.00 per name. Required to search: name, years to search, address. Civil cases indexed by defendant, plaintiff. Civil records kept on index books since 1871.

Criminal Records: Access: Mail, in person. Both court and visitors may perform in person searches. Search fee: $10.00 per name. Required to search: name, years to search, DOB; also helpful: SSN. Criminal records kept on index books since 1871.

General Information: No sealed, adoptions, mental health, juvenile, sex, or expunged records released. Turnaround time same day. Copy fee: $.50 per page. Certification fee: $1.00. Fee payee: Circuit Court. Only cashiers checks and money orders accepted. Prepayment is required.

Justice Court PO Box 152, Ashland, MS 38603; 662-224-6320; Fax: 662-224-6313. Hours: 8AM-5PM (CST). *Misdemeanor, Civil Actions Under $2,500, Eviction, Small Claims.*

Chancery Court PO Box 218, Ashland, MS 38603; 662-224-6300; Fax: 662-224-6303. Hours: 8AM-5PM (CST). *Probate.*

Bolivar County

Circuit & County Court - 1st District PO Box 205, Rosedale, MS 38769; 662-759-6521. Hours: 8AM-5PM (CST). *Felony, Misdemeanor, Civil.*

Civil Records: Access: In person only. Visitors must perform in person searches for themselves. No search fee. Required to search: name, years to search. Civil cases indexed by defendant, plaintiff. Civil records on docket books since 1900s.

Criminal Records: Access: Mail, in person. Both court and visitors may perform in person searches. Search fee: $10.00 per name. Fee is for 7 year search. Required to search: name, years to search. Criminal records on docket books since 1900s.

General Information: No sealed, juvenile, sex, or expunged records released. Turnaround time 2-3 days. Copy fee: $.50 per page. Certification fee: $1.50. Fee payee: Circuit Clerk. Personal checks accepted. Prepayment is required.

Circuit & County Court - 2nd District PO Box 670, Cleveland, MS 38732; 662-843-2061; Fax: 662-846-2943. Hours: 8AM-5PM (CST). *Felony, Misdemeanor, Civil.*

Civil Records: Access: In person only. Visitors must perform in person searches for themselves. No search fee. Required to search: name, years to search. Civil cases indexed by defendant, plaintiff. Civil records on docket books since 1940.

Criminal Records: Access: Mail, in person. Both court and visitors may perform in person searches. Search fee: $10.00 per name. Fee is for 7 year search. Required to search: name, years to search. Criminal records on docket books since 1940.

General Information: No sealed, juvenile or expunged records released. Turnaround time 2-3 days. Copy fee: $.50 per page. Certification fee: $1.50. Fee payee: Circuit Clerk. Personal checks accepted. Prepayment is required.

Justice Court PO Box 1507, Cleveland, MS 38732; 662-843-4008; Fax: 662-846-6783. Hours: 8:00AM-5:00PM (CST). *Misdemeanor, Civil Actions Under $2,500, Eviction, Small Claims.*

Cleveland Chancery Court PO Box 789, Cleveland, MS 38732; 662-843-2071; Fax: 662-846-5880. Hours: 8AM-5PM (CST). *Probate.*

Rosedale Chancery Court PO Box 238, Rosedale, MS 38769; 662-759-3762; Fax: 662-759-3467. Hours: 8AM-Noon, 1-5PM (CST). *Probate.*

Calhoun County

Circuit Court PO Box 25, Pittsboro, MS 38951; 662-412-3101; Fax: 662-412-3103. Hours: 8AM-5PM (CST). *Felony, Civil Actions Over $2,500.*

Civil Records: Access: Mail, in person. Both court and visitors may perform in person searches. Search fee: $10.00 per name. Required to search: name, years to search. Civil cases indexed by defendant, plaintiff. Civil records on docket books since 1922; computerized records go back to 1922.

Criminal Records: Access: Mail, in person. Both court and visitors may perform in person searches. Search fee: $10.00 per name. Required to search: name, years to search, DOB; also helpful: SSN. Criminal records on docket books since 1922; computerized records go back to 1922.

General Information: No sealed, adoptions, mental health, juvenile, sex, or expunged records released. SASE not required. Turnaround time same day, phone search info released when payment is received. Fax notes: Fee to fax results is $2.00 per page. Copy fee: $1.00 per page. Certification fee: $1.50. Fee payee:

Circuit Clerk. Personal checks accepted. Prepayment is required.

Justice Court PO Box 7, Pittsboro, MS 38951; 662-412-3134; Fax: 662-412-3136. Hours: 8AM-5PM (CST). *Misdemeanor, Civil Actions Under $2,500, Eviction, Small Claims.*

Chancery Court PO Box 8, Pittsboro, MS 38951; 662-412-3117; Fax: 662-412-3128. Hours: 8AM-5PM (CST). *Probate.*

Carroll County

Circuit Court PO Box 6, Vaiden, MS 39176; 662-464-5476; Fax: 662-464-7745. Hours: 8AM-5PM (CST). *Felony, Civil Actions Over $2,500.*

Civil Records: Access: Mail, in person. Both court and visitors may perform in person searches. Search fee: $10.00 per name. Required to search: name, years to search. Civil cases indexed by defendant, plaintiff. Civil records on books since 1900s.

Criminal Records: Access: Mail, in person. Both court and visitors may perform in person searches. Search fee: $10.00 per name. Required to search: name, years to search; also helpful: SSN. Criminal records on books since 1900s.

General Information: No adoptions, mental health or juvenile records released. Turnaround time 2 days. Copy fee: $.50 per page. Certification fee: $2.00. Fee payee: Circuit Court. Personal checks accepted. Prepayment is required.

Justice Court PO Box 10, Carrollton, MS 38917; 662-237-9285; Fax: 662-237-9286. Hours: 8AM-4PM (CST). *Misdemeanor, Civil Actions Under $2,500, Eviction, Small Claims.*

Chancery Court PO Box 60, Carrollton, MS 38917; 662-237-9274; Fax: 662-237-9642. Hours: 8AM-12; 1-5PM (CST). *Probate.*

Chickasaw County

Circuit Court - 1st District 1 Pinson Sq, Rm 2, Houston, MS 38851; 662-456-2331; Fax: 662-456-5295. Hours: 8AM-5PM (CST). *Felony, Civil Actions Over $2,500.*

Civil Records: Access: Fax, mail, in person. Both court and visitors may perform in person searches. Search fee: $10.00 per name. There is no fee if the visitor performs the search. Required to search: name, years to search; also helpful: address. Civil cases indexed by defendant, plaintiff. Civil records on docket books since mid-1800s.

Criminal Records: Access: Fax, mail, in person. Both court and visitors may perform in person searches. Search fee: $10.00 per name. Required to search: name, years to search, DOB; also helpful: address, SSN. Criminal records on docket books since mid-1800s.

General Information: Public access terminal is available. (For civil records only.) No sealed, adoptions, mental health, juvenile, sex, or expunged records released. SASE required. Turnaround time 2-3 days. Fax notes: $1.00 per page. Copy fee: $.25 if visitor does; $1.00 if court does. Certification fee: $1.00 plus $.50 per page after first. Fee payee: Circuit Clerk. Business checks accepted. Prepayment is required.

Circuit Court - 2nd District Courthouse, Okolona, MS 38860; 662-447-2838; Fax: 662-447-5024. Hours: 8AM-5PM (CST). *Felony, Civil Actions Over $2,500.*

Civil Records: Access: Fax, mail, in person. Both court and visitors may perform in person searches. Search fee: $10.00 per name. Required to search: name, years to search; also helpful: address. Civil cases indexed by defendant, plaintiff. Civil records on docket books.

Criminal Records: Access: Fax, mail, in person. Both court and visitors may perform in person searches. Search fee: $10.00 per name. Required to search: name, years to search, DOB; also helpful: SSN. Criminal records on docket books.

General Information: No sealed, adoptions, mental health, juvenile, sex, or expunged records released. SASE required. Turnaround time 2-3 days. Copy fee: $.50 per page. Certification fee: $1.00 plus $.50 per page after first. Fee payee: Circuit Clerk. Business checks accepted. Prepayment is required.

Justice Court Courthouse, 1 Pinson Sq, Houston, MS 38851; 662-456-3941; Fax: 662-448-8122. Hours: 8AM-5PM (CST). *Misdemeanor, Civil Actions Under $2,500, Eviction, Small Claims.*

Justice Court District 2 234 W Main, Rm 207, Okolona, MS 38860; 662-447-3402. *Misdemeanor, Civil Actions Under $2,500, Eviction, Small Claims.*

Chancery Court Courthouse Bldg, 1 Pinson Square, Houston, MS 38851; 662-456-2513; Fax: 662-456-5295. *Probate.*

Chancery Court 234 W Main, Rm 201, Okolona, MS 38860-1438; 662-447-2092; Fax: 662-447-5024. *Probate.*

Choctaw County

Circuit Court PO Box 34, Ackerman, MS 39735; 662-285-6245; Fax: 662-285-2196. Hours: 8AM-5PM (CST). *Felony, Civil Actions Over $2,500.*

Civil Records: Access: Mail, in person. Both court and visitors may perform in person searches. Search fee: $10.00 per name. Required to search: name, years to search. Civil cases indexed by defendant, plaintiff. Civil records in books back to 1926.

Criminal Records: Access: Mail, in person. Both court and visitors may perform in person searches. Search fee: $10.00 per name. Same fee for in person search. Required to search: name, years to search; also helpful: DOB, SSN. Criminal records in books back to 1926.

General Information: No sealed, adoptions, mental health, juvenile, sex, or expunged records released. SASE required. Turnaround time 14 days legal maximum. Copy fee: $1.00 per page. Certification fee: $1.00. Fee payee: Choctaw County Circuit Clerk. Personal checks accepted. Prepayment is required.

Justice Court PO Box 357, Ackerman, MS 39735; 662-285-3599; Fax: 662-285-9039. Hours: 8AM-5PM (CST). *Misdemeanor, Civil Actions Under $2,500, Eviction, Small Claims.*

Chancery Court PO Box 250, Ackerman, MS 39735; 662-285-6329; Fax: 662-285-3444. Hours: 8AM-5PM (CST). *Probate.*

Claiborne County

Circuit Court PO Box 549, Port Gibson, MS 39150; 601-437-5841. Hours: 8AM-5PM (CST). *Felony, Civil Actions Over $2,500.*

Civil Records: Access: Mail, in person. Both court and visitors may perform in person searches. Search fee: $10.00 per name. Required to search: name, years to search, address. Civil cases indexed by defendant, plaintiff. Civil records on docket books since 1820.

Criminal Records: Access: Mail, in person. Both court and visitors may perform in person searches. Search fee: $10.00 per name. Required to search: name, years to search, address, DOB, signed release. Criminal records on docket books since 1820.

General Information: No sealed, adoptions, mental health, juvenile, sex, or expunged records released. Turnaround time varies. Copy fee: $1.00 per page. Certification fee: $1.50. Fee payee: Sammie L Good,

Circuit Clerk. Personal checks accepted. Prepayment is required.

Justice Court PO Box 497, Port Gibson, MS 39150; 601-437-4478. Hours: 8AM-5PM (CST). *Misdemeanor, Civil Actions Under $2,500, Eviction, Small Claims.*

Chancery Court PO Box 449, Port Gibson, MS 39150; 601-437-4992; Fax: 601-437-3137. Hours: 8AM-5PM (CST). *Probate, Small Claims.*

Clarke County

Circuit Court PO Box 216, Quitman, MS 39355; 601-776-3111; Fax: 601-776-1001. Hours: 8AM-5PM (CST). *Felony, Civil Actions Over $2,500.*

Civil Records: Access: Fax, mail, in person. Both court and visitors may perform in person searches. Search fee: $10.00 per name. Required to search: name, years to search; also helpful: address. Civil cases indexed by defendant, plaintiff. Civil records kept on docket books since 1950s.

Criminal Records: Access: Fax, mail, in person. Both court and visitors may perform in person searches. Search fee: $10.00 per name. Required to search: name, years to search; also helpful: address, DOB, SSN, sex. Criminal records kept on docket books since 1950s.

General Information: No sealed, adoptions, mental health, juvenile, sex, or expunged records released. Turnaround time 1 day. Fax notes: No fee to fax results. No copy fee. Certification fee: $1.50. Fee payee: Circuit Clerk. Personal checks accepted. Prepayment is required.

Justice Court PO Box 4, Quitman, MS 39355; 601-776-5371. Hours: 8AM-5PM (CST). *Misdemeanor, Civil Actions Under $2,500, Eviction, Small Claims.*

Chancery Court PO Box 689, Quitman, MS 39355; 601-776-2126. Hours: 8AM-5PM (CST). *Probate.*

Clay County

Circuit Court PO Box 364, West Point, MS 39773; 662-494-3384; Fax: 662-495-2057. Hours: 8AM-5PM (CST). *Felony, Civil Actions Over $2,500.*

Civil Records: Access: Phone, mail, in person, online. Both court and visitors may perform in person searches. Search fee: $10.00 per name. Required to search: name, years to search. Civil cases indexed by defendant, plaintiff. Civil records on docket books back to 1962; archived since mid-1800s. Online access to circuit court dockets available by subscription at www.recordsusa.com/Mississippi/ClayCnMS.htm. Credit card, username and password is required; choose either monthly or per-use plan. Visit the web site or call Lisa at 601-264-7701 for information.

Criminal Records: Access: Mail, in person, online. Both court and visitors may perform in person searches. Search fee: $10.00 per name. Required to search: name, years to search, address, DOB; also helpful: SSN. Criminal records on docket books back to 1962; archived since mid-1800s. Online access to criminal dockets is the same as civil.

General Information: No sealed, adoptions, mental health, juvenile, sex, or expunged records released. SASE required. Turnaround time same day. Copy fee: $.50 per page. Certification fee: $10.00. Fee payee: Clay County Circuit Clerk. Personal checks accepted. Prepayment is required.

Justice Court PO Box 674, West Point, MS 39773; 662-494-6141; Fax: 662-494-4034. Hours: 8AM-5PM (CST). *Misdemeanor, Civil Actions Under $2,500, Eviction, Small Claims.*

Chancery Court PO Box 815, West Point, MS 39773; 662-494-3124. Hours: 8AM-5PM (CST). *Probate.*

Coahoma County

Circuit & County Court PO Box 849, Clarksdale, MS 38614-0849; 662-624-3014; Fax: 662-624-3075. Hours: 8AM-5PM (CST). *Felony, Civil.*

Civil Records: Access: Fax, mail, in person. Both court and visitors may perform in person searches. Search fee: $10.00 per name. Required to search: name, years to search, address. Civil cases indexed by defendant, plaintiff. Civil records on dockets since 1950, archived since 1836.

Criminal Records: Access: Fax, mail, in person. Both court and visitors may perform in person searches. Search fee: $10.00 per name. Required to search: name, years to search, DOB, signed release; also helpful: address, SSN. Criminal records on dockets since 1910, archived since 1836.

General Information: No sealed, adoptions, mental health, juvenile, sex, or expunged records released. SASE not required. Turnaround time 2 days. Fax notes: No fee to fax results. Copy fee: $1.00 per page. Certification fee: $1.00. Fee payee: Circuit Clerk. Personal checks accepted. Prepayment is required.

Justice Court 144 Ritch, Clarksdale, MS 38614; 662-624-3060. Hours: 8AM-5PM (CST). *Misdemeanor, Civil Actions Under $2,500, Eviction, Small Claims.*

Chancery Court PO Box 98, Clarksdale, MS 38614; 662-624-3000; Fax: 662-624-3029. Hours: 8AM-5PM (CST). *Probate.*

Copiah County

Circuit Court PO Box 467, Hazlehurst, MS 39083; 601-894-1241; Fax: 601-894-3026. Hours: 8AM-5PM (CST). *Felony, Civil Actions Over $2,500.*

Civil Records: Access: Fax, mail, in person. Both court and visitors may perform in person searches. Search fee: $10.00 per name. Required to search: name, years to search. Civil cases indexed by defendant. Civil records on docket books since late 1800s.

Criminal Records: Access: Fax, mail, in person. Both court and visitors may perform in person searches. Search fee: $10.00 per name. Required to search: name, years to search; also helpful: DOB, SSN. Criminal records on docket books since late 1800s.

General Information: No sealed, adoptions, mental health, juvenile, sex, or expunged records released. Turnaround time 1-2 days. Fax notes: No fee to fax results. Copy fee: $.50 per page. Certification fee: $1.50. Fee payee: Circuit Clerk. Business checks accepted. Prepayment is required.

Justice Court PO Box 798, Hazlehurst, MS 39083; 601-894-3218; Fax: 601-894-6038. Hours: 8:00AM-5:00PM (CST). *Misdemeanor, Civil Actions Under $2,500, Eviction, Small Claims.*

Chancery Court 122 S Lowe St, Hazlehurst, MS 39083; 601-894-3021; Fax: 601-894-4081. Hours: 8AM-5PM (CST). *Probate.*

Covington County

Circuit Court PO Box 667, Collins, MS 39428; 601-765-6506; Fax: 601-765-5012. Hours: 8AM-5PM (CST). *Felony, Civil Actions Over $2,500.*

Civil Records: Access: Fax, mail, in person. Both court and visitors may perform in person searches. Search fee: $10.00 per name. Required to search: name, years to search. Civil cases indexed by defendant, plaintiff. Civil records on docket books since 1915.

Criminal Records: Access: Fax, mail, in person. Both court and visitors may perform in person searches. Search fee: $10.00 per name. Required to search: name, years to search, DOB; also helpful: SSN. Criminal records on docket books since 1915.

General Information: No sealed, adoptions, mental health, juvenile, sex, or expunged records released. Turnaround time 2-3 days. Fax notes: No fee to fax results. Copy fee: $.50 per page. Certification fee: $3.00. Fee payee: Circuit Clerk. Personal checks accepted. Prepayment is required.

Justice Court PO Box 665, Collins, MS 39428; 601-765-6581. Hours: 8AM-5PM (CST). *Misdemeanor, Civil Actions Under $2,500, Eviction, Small Claims.*

Chancery Court PO Box 1679, Collins, MS 39428; 601-765-4242; Fax: 601-765-1052. Hours: 8AM-5PM (CST). *Probate.*

De Soto County

Circuit & County Court 2535 Hwy 51 South, Hernando, MS 38632; 662-429-1325. Hours: 8AM-5PM (CST). *Felony, Misdemeanor, Civil.*

Civil Records: Access: Fax, mail, in person. Both court and visitors may perform in person searches. Search fee: $10.00 per name. Required to search: name, years to search; also helpful: address. Civil cases indexed by defendant, plaintiff. Civil records on docket books since 1972.

Criminal Records: Access: Fax, mail, in person. Both court and visitors may perform in person searches. Search fee: $10.00 per name. Required to search: name, years to search, DOB; also helpful: SSN. Criminal records on docket books since 1972.

General Information: No sealed, adoptions, mental health, juvenile, sex, or expunged records released. Turnaround time 1-2 days. Copy fee: $.50 per page. Certification fee: $2.50. Fee payee: Circuit Clerk. Personal checks accepted. Prepayment is required.

Justice Court 8525 Highway 51 North, Southaven, MS 38671; 662-393-5810; Fax: 662-393-5859. Hours: 8AM-5PM (CST). *Misdemeanor, Civil Actions Under $2,500, Eviction, Small Claims.*

Chancery Court, Rm 100 2535 Hwy 51 South, (PO Box 949), Hernando, MS 38632; 662-429-1320; Fax: 662-449-1420. Hours: 8AM-5PM (CST). *Probate.*

Forrest County

Circuit & County Court PO Box 992, Hattiesburg, MS 39403; 601-582-3213; Fax: 601-545-6065. Hours: 8AM-5PM (CST). *Felony, Misdemeanor, Civil.*

Civil Records: Access: Phone, mail, in person. Both court and visitors may perform in person searches. Search fee: $10.00 per name. Required to search: name, years to search; also helpful: address. Civil cases indexed by defendant, plaintiff. Civil records on docket books since 1900s. Limited phone access.

Criminal Records: Access: Mail, in person. Both court and visitors may perform in person searches. Search fee: $10.00 per name. Required to search: name, years to search, DOB, SSN; also helpful: address. Criminal records on docket books since 1900s; on computer since 1995.

General Information: No juvenile or expunged records released. Turnaround time 10 days. Copy fee: $.50 per page. Certification fee: $1.50. Fee payee: Circuit Clerk. Business checks accepted. Attorney's checks accepted. Prior approval required.

Justice Court 316 Forrest St, Hattiesburg, MS 39401; 601-544-3136; Fax: 601-545-6114. Hours: 8AM-5PM (CST). *Misdemeanor, Civil Actions Under $2,500, Eviction, Small Claims.*

Note: No searches are performed by the court on Monday, Wednesday, or Friday.

Chancery Court PO Box 951, Hattiesburg, MS 39403; 601-545-6040. Hours: 8AM-5PM (CST). *Probate.*

Franklin County

Circuit Court PO Box 267, Meadville, MS 39653; 601-384-2320; Fax: 601-384-8244. Hours: 8AM-5PM (CST). *Felony, Civil Actions Over $2,500.*

Civil Records: Access: Phone, fax, mail, in person. Both court and visitors may perform in person searches. Search fee: $10.00 per name. Required to search: name, years to search. Civil cases indexed by defendant, plaintiff. Civil records on books since 1944.

Criminal Records: Access: Fax, mail, in person. Both court and visitors may perform in person searches. Search fee: $10.00 per name. Required to search: name, years to search, DOB or SSN; also helpful: address. Criminal records on books since 1944.

General Information: No sealed, adoptions, mental health, juvenile, sex, or expunged records released. Turnaround time 2-3 days. Copy fee: $1.00 per page. Certification fee: $.50. Fee payee: Circuit Clerk. Personal checks accepted. Prepayment is required.

Justice Court PO Box 365, Meadville, MS 39653; 601-384-2002. Hours: 8AM-5PM (CST). *Misdemeanor, Civil Actions Under $2,500, Eviction, Small Claims.*

Chancery Court PO Box 297, Meadville, MS 39653; 601-384-2330; Fax: 601-384-5864. Hours: 8AM-5PM (CST). *Probate.*

George County

Circuit Court 355 Cox St, #C, Lucedale, MS 39452; 601-947-4881; Fax: 601-947-8804. Hours: 8AM-5PM M-F, 9AM-12PM Sat (CST). *Felony, Civil Actions Over $2,500.*

Civil Records: Access: Fax, mail, in person. Both court and visitors may perform in person searches. Search fee: $10.00 per name. Required to search: name, years to search. Civil cases indexed by defendant, plaintiff. Civil records on docket books since 1910.

Criminal Records: Access: Fax, mail, in person. Both court and visitors may perform in person searches. Search fee: $10.00 per name. Required to search: name, years to search; also helpful: SSN. Criminal records on docket books since 1910.

General Information: No sealed, adoptions, mental health, juvenile, sex, or expunged records released. SASE requested. Turnaround time 1-2 days. Fax notes: No fee to fax results. Copy fee: $.50 per page. Certification fee: $2.00. Fee payee: Circuit Clerk. Personal checks accepted.

Justice Court 356 A Cox St, Lucedale, MS 39452; 601-947-4834; Fax: 601-947-1911. Hours: 8AM-5PM (CST). *Misdemeanor, Civil Actions Under $2,500, Eviction, Small Claims.*

Note: Records on computer (5/92 forward) are 41.00 per name. Prior to 5/92, searhces are $20 for first 1/2 hour then $5.00 each 1/4 hour.

Chancery Court 355 Cox St, #A, Lucedale, MS 39452; 601-947-4801; Fax: 601-947-1300. Hours: 8AM-5PM (CST). *Probate.*

Greene County

Circuit Court PO Box 310, Leakesville, MS 39451; 601-394-2379; Fax: 601-394-2334. Hours: 8AM-5PM M-F (CST). *Felony, Civil Actions Over $2,500.*

Civil Records: Access: Phone, fax, mail, in person. Both court and visitors may perform in person searches. Search fee: $10.00 per name. Required to search: name, years to search; also helpful: address. Civil cases indexed by defendant, plaintiff. Civil records on docket books since early 1900s.

Criminal Records: Access: Phone, fax, mail, in person. Both court and visitors may perform in person searches. Search fee: $10.00 per name. Required to search: name, years to search; also helpful: SSN. Criminal records on docket books since early 1900s. Misdemeanor records are kept in Greene County Justice Court, 601-394-2347.

General Information: No sealed, adoptions, mental health, juvenile, sex, or expunged records released. SASE requested. Turnaround time 1-2 days. Fax notes: No fee to fax results. Copy fee: $.50 per page. Certification fee: $1.00. Fee payee: Circuit Clerk. Personal checks accepted. Prepayment is required.

Justice Court PO Box 547, Leakesville, MS 39451; 601-394-2347; Fax: 601-394-2114. Hours: 8AM-5PM (CST). *Misdemeanor, Civil Actions Under $2,500, Eviction, Small Claims.*

Chancery Court PO Box 610, Leakesville, MS 39451; 601-394-2377. 8AM-5PM (CST). *Probate.*

Grenada County

Circuit Court PO Box 1517, Grenada, MS 38902-1517; 662-226-1941; Fax: 662-227-2865. Hours: 8AM-5PM (CST). *Felony, Civil Actions Over $2,500.*

Civil Records: Access: In person only. Visitors must perform in person searches for themselves. No search fee. Required to search: name, years to search. Civil cases indexed by defendant, plaintiff. Civil records on docket books since mid-1970s.

Criminal Records: Access: In person only. Visitors must perform in person searches for themselves. No search fee. Required to search: name, years to search. Criminal records on docket books since mid-1970s.

General Information: Public access terminal is available. (Judgment roll on terminal from 1996.) No sealed, juvenile, or expunged records released. Copy fee: $.50 per page. Certification fee: $1.50. Fee payee: Circuit Clerk. No personal checks accepted. Prepayment is required.

Justice Court 16 First St, Grenada, MS 38901; 662-226-3331; Fax: 662-227-5513. Hours: 8AM-5PM (CST). *Misdemeanor, Civil Actions Under $2,500, Eviction, Small Claims.*

Chancery Court PO Box 1208, Grenada, MS 38902; 662-226-1821; Fax: 662-226-0427. Hours: 8AM-5PM (CST). *Probate.*

Hancock County

Circuit Court PO Box 249, 152 Main Street, Bay St. Louis, MS 39520; 228-467-5265; Fax: 228-467-2779. Hours: 8AM-5PM (CST). *Felony, Civil Actions Over $2,500.*

Civil Records: Access: Mail, in person. Both court and visitors may perform in person searches. Search fee: $10.00 per name. Required to search: name, years to search. Civil cases indexed by defendant, plaintiff. Civil records on docket books since 1975.

Criminal Records: Access: Mail, in person. Both court and visitors may perform in person searches. Search fee: $10.00 per name. Required to search: name, years to search, DOB; also helpful: SSN. Criminal records on docket books since 1970.

General Information: No sealed, adoptions, mental health, juvenile, sex, or expunged records released. Turnaround time 1 week. Copy fee: $.50 per page. Certification fee: $1.50 per page. Fee payee: Circuit Clerk. Personal checks accepted. Prepayment is required.

Justice Court 306 Hwy 90, Bay St. Louis, MS 39520; 228-467-5573; Fax: 228-467-3126. Hours:

8AM-5PM (CST). *Misdemeanor, Civil Actions Under $2,500, Eviction, Small Claims.*

Chancery Court PO Box 429 Bay St., Bay St. Louis, MS 39520; 228-467-5404; Fax: 228-467-3159. Hours: 8AM-5PM (CST). *Probate.*

Harrison County

Circuit Court - 1st District PO Box 998, Gulfport, MS 39502; 228-865-4147; Fax: 228-865-4009. Hours: 8AM-5PM (CST). *Felony, Civil Actions Over $75,000.*

Civil Records: Access: Mail, in person. Both court and visitors may perform in person searches. Search fee: $10.00 per name. Required to search: name, years to search. Civil cases indexed by defendant, plaintiff. Civil records on computer back to 7/1991, prior on docket books, older records are archived.

Criminal Records: Access: Mail, in person. Both court and visitors may perform in person searches. Search fee: $10.00 per name. Required to search: name, years to search, DOB; also helpful: SSN. Criminal records on computer back to 7/1991, prior on docket books, older records are archived.

General Information: Public access terminal is available. No sealed, adoptions, mental health, juvenile, sex, or expunged records released. SASE requested. Turnaround time 1-2 days. Copy fee: $.50 per page. Certification fee: $1.00. Fee payee: Circuit Clerk. Business checks accepted. Prepayment is required.

Circuit Court - 2nd District PO Box 235, Biloxi, MS 39533; 228-435-8258; Fax: 228-435-8277. Hours: 8AM-5PM (CST). *Felony, Civil Actions Over $75,000.*

Civil Records: Access: Fax, mail, in person. Both court and visitors may perform in person searches. Search fee: $10.00 per name. Required to search: name, years to search. Civil cases indexed by defendant, plaintiff. Civil records on computer since July 1991.

Criminal Records: Access: Fax, mail, in person. Both court and visitors may perform in person searches. Search fee: $10.00 per name. Required to search: name, years to search, DOB; also helpful: SSN. Criminal records on computer since July 1991.

General Information: Public access terminal is available. No sealed or expunged records released. SASE required. Turnaround time 3 days. Fax notes: $.50 per page. Copy fee: $.50 per page. Certification fee: $1.00. Fee payee: Circuit Clerk. Business checks accepted. Attorney's checks accepted. Prepayment is required.

County Court - 1st District PO Box 998, Gulfport, MS 39502; 228-865-4097; Fax: 228-865-4009. Hours: 8AM-5PM (CST). *Misdemeanor, Civil Actions Under $75,000.*

Civil Records: Access: Mail, in person. Both court and visitors may perform in person searches. Search fee: $10.00 per name. Required to search: name, years to search. Civil cases indexed by defendant, plaintiff. Civil records on computer since 1991, prior on docket books since early 1900s.

Criminal Records: Access: Mail, in person. Both court and visitors may perform in person searches. Search fee: $10.00 per name. Required to search: name, years to search; also helpful: DOB. Criminal records on computer since 1991, prior on docket books since early 1900s.

General Information: Public access terminal is available. No sealed, adoptions, mental health, juvenile, sex, or expunged records released. Turnaround time 1-2 days. Copy fee: $.50 per page. Certification fee: $1.00. Fee payee: County Clerk. Business checks accepted. Prepayment is required.

County Court - 2nd District PO Box 235, Biloxi, MS 39533; 228-435-8294/8232; Fax: 228-435-8277. Hours: 8AM-5PM (CST). *Misdemeanor, Civil Actions Under $75,000.*

Civil Records: Access: Fax, mail, in person. Both court and visitors may perform in person searches. Search fee: $10.00 per name. Required to search: name, years to search. Civil cases indexed by defendant, plaintiff. Civil records on computer since July 1991, prior on books.

Criminal Records: Access: Fax, mail, in person. Both court and visitors may perform in person searches. Search fee: $10.00 per name. Required to search: name, years to search, DOB; also helpful: SSN, aliases. Criminal records on computer since July 1991, prior on books.

General Information: Public access terminal is available. No sealed or expunged records released. SASE required. Turnaround time 3 days. Fax notes: No fee to fax results. Copy fee: $.50 per page. Certification fee: $1.00. Fee payee: Circuit Clerk. Business checks accepted. Attorney's checks accepted. Prepayment is required.

Justice Court PO Box 1754, Gulfport, MS 39502; Civil phone: 228-865-4193; Criminal phone: 228-865-4214; Fax: 228-865-4216. Hours: 8AM-5PM (CST). *Misdemeanor, Civil Actions Under $2,500, Eviction, Small Claims.*

Biloxi Chancery Court PO Box 544, Biloxi, MS 39533; 228-435-8220; Fax: 228-435-8251. Hours: 8AM-Noon, 1-5PM (CST). *Probate.*

Gulfport Chancery Court PO Drawer CC, Gulfport, MS 39502; 228-865-4092, 865-4095; Fax: 228-865-1646. 8AM-Noon, 1-5PM (CST). *Probate.*

Hinds County

Circuit & County Court - 1st District PO Box 327, Jackson, MS 39205; 601-968-6628. Hours: 8AM-5PM (CST). *Felony, Misdemeanor, Civil.*

Civil Records: Access: Mail, in person. Both court and visitors may perform in person searches. Search fee: $9.00 per name. Required to search: name, years to search. Civil cases indexed by defendant, plaintiff. Civil records on docket books back to 1900s.

Criminal Records: Access: Mail, in person. Both court and visitors may perform in person searches. Search fee: $9.00 per name. Required to search: name, years to search, DOB; also helpful: SSN. Criminal records on docket books back to 1900s.

General Information: Public access terminal is available. No sealed, adoptions, mental health, juvenile, sex, or expunged records released. Turnaround time 14 days. Copy fee: $.50 per page. Fee payee: Circuit Clerk. Personal checks accepted. Prepayment is required.

Circuit & County Court - 2nd District PO Box 999, Raymond, MS 39154; 601-968-6653. Hours: 8AM-Noon, 1-5PM (CST). *Felony, Misdemeanor, Civil.*

Civil Records: Access: Mail, in person. Both court and visitors may perform in person searches. Search fee: $9.00 per name. Required to search: name, years to search. Civil cases indexed by defendant, plaintiff. Civil records on computer since 1994, prior on docket books since late 1800s.

Criminal Records: Access: Mail, in person. Both court and visitors may perform in person searches. Search fee: $9.00 per name. Required to search: name, years to search; also helpful: DOB, SSN. Criminal records on computer since 1994, prior on docket books since late 1800s.

General Information: No sealed, adoptions, mental health, juvenile, sex, expunged or some preliminary criminal records released. SASE requested. Turnaround time 1 week. Copy fee: $.50 per page. Certification fee: $1.50. Fee payee: Circuit Clerk. Personal checks accepted. Prepayment is required.

Justice Court 407 E Pascagoula, 3rd floor, PO Box 3490, Jackson, MS 39207; 601-968-6781; Fax: 601-973-5532. Hours: 8AM-Noon, 1-5PM (CST). *Misdemeanor, Civil Actions Under $2,500, Eviction, Small Claims.*

Jackson Chancery Court PO Box 686, Jackson, MS 39205; 601-968-6540; Fax: 601-973-5554. Hours: 8AM-5PM (CST). *Probate.*

Raymond Chancery Court PO Box 88, Raymond, MS 39154; 601-857-8055; Fax: 601-857-4953. Hours: 8AM-5PM (CST). *Probate.*

Holmes County

Circuit Court PO Box 718, Lexington, MS 39095; 662-834-2476; Fax: 662-834-3870. Hours: 8AM-5PM (CST). *Felony, Civil Actions Over $2,500.*

Civil Records: Access: Fax, mail, in person. Both court and visitors may perform in person searches. Search fee: $10.00 per name. Required to search: name, years to search. Civil cases indexed by defendant, plaintiff. Civil records on docket books since 1940s.
Criminal Records: Access: Fax, mail, in person. Both court and visitors may perform in person searches. Search fee: $10.00 per name. Required to search: name, years to search; also helpful: DOB, SSN. Criminal records on docket books since 1940s.
General Information: Public access terminal is available. No sealed or expunged records released. Turnaround time 1-2 days. Fax notes: No fee to fax results. Copy fee: $1.00 per page. Certification fee: $1.50. Fee payee: Holmes County Circuit Clerk. Business checks accepted. Prepayment is required.

Justice Court PO Box 99, Lexington, MS 39095; 662-834-4565. Hours: 8AM-Noon, 1-5PM (CST). *Misdemeanor, Civil Actions Under $2,500, Eviction, Small Claims.*

Chancery Court PO Box 239, Lexington, MS 39095; 662-834-2508; Fax: 662-834-3020. Hours: 8AM-5PM (CST). *Probate.*

Humphreys County

Circuit Court PO Box 696, Belzoni, MS 39038; 662-247-3065; Fax: 662-247-3906. Hours: 8AM-5PM (CST). *Felony, Civil Actions Over $2,500.*

Civil Records: Access: Fax, mail, in person. Both court and visitors may perform in person searches. Search fee: $10.00 per name. Required to search: name, years to search. Civil cases indexed by defendant, plaintiff. Civil records on books since 1918.
Criminal Records: Access: Fax, mail, in person. Both court and visitors may perform in person searches. Search fee: $10.00 per name. Required to search: name, years to search; also helpful: DOB, SSN. Criminal records on books since 1918.
General Information: No sealed, adoptions, mental health, juvenile, sex, or expunged records released. SASE not required. Turnaround time 1 day, phone turnaround 30 minutes. Fax notes: $.50 per page. Copy fee: $1.00 per page. Certification fee: Certification is included in search fee, unless you do search yourself then $1.00. Fee payee: Circuit Clerk. Personal checks accepted. Prepayment is required.

Justice Court 102 Castleman St, Belzoni, MS 39038; 662-247-4337; Fax: 662-247-1095. Hours: 8AM-Noon, 1-5PM (CST). *Misdemeanor, Civil Actions Under $2,500, Eviction, Small Claims.*

Chancery Court PO Box 547, Belzoni, MS 39038; 662-247-1740; Fax: 662-247-1010. Hours: 8AM-Noon, 1-5PM (CST). *Probate.*

Issaquena County

Circuit Court PO Box 27, Mayersville, MS 39113; 662-873-2761; Fax: 662-873-2061. Hours: 8AM-5PM (CST). *Felony, Civil Actions Over $2,500.*

Civil Records: Access: Mail, in person. Both court and visitors may perform in person searches. Search fee: $20.00 per name. Required to search: name, years to search. Civil cases indexed by defendant, plaintiff. Civil records on docket books since 1846.
Criminal Records: Access: Mail, in person. Both court and visitors may perform in person searches. Search fee: $20.00 per name. Required to search: name, years to search; also helpful: DOB, SSN. Criminal records on docket books since 1846.
General Information: No sealed, adoptions, mental health, juvenile, sex, or expunged records released. Turnaround time 1 week. Copy fee: $.50 per page. Certification fee: $1.00. Fee payee: Circuit Clerk. Personal checks accepted. Prepayment is required.

Justice Court PO Box 58, Mayersville, MS 39113; 662-873-6287. Hours: 8AM-Noon, 1-5PM (CST). *Misdemeanor, Civil Actions Under $2,500, Eviction, Small Claims.*

Chancery Court PO Box 27, Mayersville, MS 39113; 662-873-2761; Fax: 662-873-2061. Hours: 8AM-5PM (CST). *Probate.*

Itawamba County

Circuit Court 201 W Main, Fulton, MS 38843; 662-862-3511; Fax: 662-862-4006. Hours: 8AM-5PM (CST). *Felony, Civil Actions Over $2,500.*

Civil Records: Access: Phone, fax, mail, in person. Both court and visitors may perform in person searches. No search fee. Required to search: name, years to search. Civil cases indexed by defendant, plaintiff. Civil records on books since 1940s.
Criminal Records: Access: Phone, fax, mail, in person. Both court and visitors may perform in person searches. No search fee. Required to search: name, years to search, DOB; also helpful: SSN. Criminal records on books since 1940s.
General Information: Public access terminal is available. sex or expunged records released. SASE required. Turnaround time 1 day. Fax notes: No fee to fax results. No copy fee. Business checks accepted.

Justice Court 201 W Main, Fulton, MS 38843; 662-862-4315; Fax: 662-862-5805. Hours: 8AM-Noon, 1-5PM (CST). *Misdemeanor, Civil Actions Under $2,500, Eviction, Small Claims.*

Chancery Court 201 W Main, Fulton, MS 38843; 662-862-3421; Fax: 662-862-3421. Hours: 8AM-5PM M-F; 8AM-Noon Sat (CST). *Probate.*

Jackson County

Circuit Court PO Box 998, Pascagoula, MS 39568-0998; 228-769-3025; Fax: 228-769-3180. Hours: 8AM-5PM (CST). *Felony, Civil.*
www.co.jackson.ms.us/Dept_Pages/Dept_Courts.htm
Civil Records: Access: Mail, in person, online. Both court and visitors may perform in person searches. Search fee: $10.00 per name per 10 years searched. Required to search: name, years to search. Civil cases indexed by defendant, plaintiff. Civil records on computer back to 1993, prior on docket books since 1920s. Online access to courts records is to be available free at www.co.jackson.ms.us/Dept_Pages/Dept_Circuit_Court_Docket.htm. Click on "Circuit Court Dockets.".

Criminal Records: Access: Mail, in person, online. Both court and visitors may perform in person searches. Search fee: $10.00 per name, per 10 years searched. Required to search: name, years to search, DOB; also helpful: SSN. Criminal records on computer back to 1992, prior on docket books since 1920s. Online access to criminal records is the same as civil.
General Information: Public access terminal is available. No sealed or expunged records released. SASE required. Turnaround time varies. Fax notes: Fee to fax results is $2.00 per page. Copy fee: $1.0 per page. Certification fee: $2.50. Fee payee: Circuit Clerk. Business checks accepted. Prepayment is required.

County Court PO Box 998 (3104 Magnolia St), Pascagoula, MS 39568; 228-769-3181. Hours: 8AM-5PM (CST). *Misdemeanor, Civil Actions Under $75,000.*
www.co.jackson.ms.us/Dept_Pages/Dept_Courts.htm
Civil Records: Access: Mail, in person. Both court and visitors may perform in person searches. Search fee: $10.00 per name. Required to search: name, years to search. Civil cases indexed by defendant, plaintiff. Civil records files go back 10 years; on computer back to 2001.
Criminal Records: Access: Mail, in person. Both court and visitors may perform in person searches. Search fee: $10.00 per name. Required to search: name, years to search, DOB. Criminal records go back 20 years; on computer back to 2000.
General Information: Public access terminal is available. No sealed, adoptions, mental health, juvenile, sex, or expunged records released. Turnaround time 1 week. Copy fee: $1.00 per page. Certification fee: $2.50. Fee payee: Clerk of County Court. Only cashiers checks and money orders accepted. Prepayment is required.

Justice Court 5343 Jefferson St, Moss Point, MS 39563; 228-769-3080; Civil phone: 228-769-3087; Criminal phone: 228-769-3089; Fax: 228-769-3364. Hours: 8AM-5PM (CST). *Misdemeanor, Civil Actions Under $2,500, Eviction, Small Claims.*
www.co.jackson.ms.us/Dept_Pages/Dept_Courts.htm

Chancery Court PO Box 998, Pascagoula, MS 39568; 228-769-3124; 769-3124; Fax: 228-769-3397. Hours: 8AM-5PM (CST). *Probate.*
www.co.jackson.ms.us/Dept_Pages/Dept_Chancery_Court.htm
Note: Dockets are available free online at www.co.jackson.ms.us/Dept_Pages/Dept_Courts.htm

Jasper County

Circuit Court - 1st District PO Box 58, Paulding, MS 39348; 601-727-4941; Fax: 601-727-4475. Hours: 8AM-5PM (CST). *Felony, Civil Actions Over $2,500.*

Civil Records: Access: Fax, mail, in person. Both court and visitors may perform in person searches. Search fee: $10.00 per name. Fee includes a search of both districts in the county. Required to search: name, years to search. Civil cases indexed by defendant, plaintiff. Civil records on docket books since 1932.
Criminal Records: Access: Fax, mail, in person. Both court and visitors may perform in person searches. Search fee: $10.00 per name. Fee includes a search of both districts in the county. Required to search: name, years to search; also helpful: DOB, SSN. Criminal records on docket books since 1932.
General Information: No sealed or expunged records released. Turnaround time 1 week. Fax notes: $5.00 per document. Copy fee: $.50 per page. Certification fee: $1.50. Fee payee: Circuit Clerk. Personal checks accepted. Prepayment is required.

Circuit Court - 2nd District PO Box 447, Bay Springs, MS 39422; 601-764-2245; Fax: 601-764-3078. Hours: 8AM-5PM (CST). *Felony, Civil Actions Over $2,500.*

Civil Records: Access: Mail, in person. Both court and visitors may perform in person searches. Search fee: $10.00 per name. Fee includes a search of both districts in the county. Required to search: name, years to search. Civil cases indexed by defendant, plaintiff. Civil records on docket books since 1932.

Criminal Records: Access: Mail, in person. Both court and visitors may perform in person searches. Search fee: $10.00 per name. Fee includes a search of both districts in the county. Required to search: name, years to search; also helpful: SSN. Criminal records on docket books since 1932.

General Information: No sealed, adoptions, mental health, juvenile, sex, or expunged records released. SASE requested. Turnaround time 1 day. Copy fee: $.50 per page. Certification fee: $1.50. Fee payee: Circuit Clerk. Personal checks accepted.

Justice Court PO Box 1054, Bay Springs, MS 39422; 601-764-2065; Fax: 601-764-3402. Hours: 8AM-Noon, 1-5PM (CST). *Misdemeanor, Civil Actions Under $2,500, Eviction, Small Claims.*

Note: This Justice Court houses all the Justices for Jasper County.

Bay Springs Chancery Court PO Box 1047, Bay Springs, MS 39422; 601-764-3368; Fax: 601-764-3999. Hours: 8AM-5PM (CST). *Probate.*

Paulding Chancery Court PO Box 38, Paulding, MS 39348; 601-727-4941; Fax: 601-727-4475. Hours: 8AM-5PM (CST). *Probate.*

Jefferson County

Circuit Court PO Box 305, Fayette, MS 39069; 601-786-3422; Fax: 601-786-9676. Hours: 8AM-5PM (CST). *Felony, Civil Actions Over $2,500.*

Civil Records: Access: Phone, mail, in person. Both court and visitors may perform in person searches. Search fee: $10.00 per name. Required to search: name, years to search, DOB; also helpful: SSN, sex, signed release. Civil cases indexed by defendant, plaintiff. Civil records on docket books since 1966, prior archived.

Criminal Records: Access: Phone, mail, in person. Both court and visitors may perform in person searches. Search fee: $10.00 per name. Required to search: name, years to search, DOB; also helpful: SSN. Criminal records on docket books since 1971, prior archived.

General Information: No sealed, adoptions, mental health, juvenile, sex, or expunged records released. SASE required. Turnaround time same day. Copy fee: $.50 per page. Certification fee: $1.50. Fee payee: Jefferson County Circuit Court. Business checks accepted. Prepayment is required.

Justice Court 307 Main St, 2nd Floor, Fayette, MS 39069; 601-786-8594; Fax: 601-786-6017. Hours: 8AM-5PM (CST). *Misdemeanor, Civil Actions Under $2,500, Eviction, Small Claims.*

Chancery Court PO Box 145, Fayette, MS 39069; 601-786-3021; Fax: 601-786-6009. Hours: 8AM-5PM (CST). *Probate.*

Jefferson Davis County

Circuit Court PO Box 1082, Prentiss, MS 39474; 601-792-4231; Fax: 601-792-4957. Hours: 8AM-5PM (CST). *Felony, Civil Actions Over $2,500.*

Civil Records: Access: Phone, fax, mail, in person. Both court and visitors may perform in person searches. Search fee: $10.00 per name. Required to search: name, years to search. Civil cases indexed by defendant, plaintiff. Civil records on docket books since 1906.

Criminal Records: Access: Phone, fax, mail, in person. Both court and visitors may perform in person searches. Search fee: $10.00 per name. Required to search: name, years to search; also helpful: SSN. Criminal records on docket books since 1906.

General Information: No sealed, adoptions, mental health, juvenile, sex, or expunged records released. Turnaround time 1-2 days. Fax notes: Fee to fax results is $1.00 per page. Copy fee: $1.00 per page. Certification fee: $2.00. Fee payee: Circuit Clerk. Personal checks accepted. Prepayment is required.

Justice Court PO Box 1407, Prentiss, MS 39474; 601-792-5129. Hours: 8AM-Noon, 1-5PM (CST). *Misdemeanor, Civil Actions Under $2,500, Eviction, Small Claims.*

Chancery Court PO Box 1137, Prentiss, MS 39474; 601-792-4204; Fax: 601-792-2894. Hours: 8AM-5PM (CST). *Probate.*

Jones County

Circuit & County Court - 1st District 101 N. Court St., #B, Ellisville, MS 39437; 601-477-8538. Hours: 8AM-5PM (CST). *Felony, Misdemeanor, Civil.*

Civil Records: Access: In person only. Visitors must perform in person searches for themselves. No search fee. Required to search: name, years to search. Civil cases indexed by defendant, plaintiff. Civil records on docket books since 1960s.

Criminal Records: Access: Mail, fax, in person. Both court and visitors may perform in person searches. Search fee: $10.00 per name. Required to search: name, years to search. Criminal records on docket books since 1960s.

General Information: No sealed, adoptions, mental health, juvenile, sex, or expunged records released. Turnaround time 1-2 days. Copy fee: $.50 per page. Certification fee: $1.00. Fee payee: Circuit Clerk. Personal checks accepted. Prepayment is required.

Circuit & County Court - 2nd District PO Box 1336, Laurel, MS 39441; 601-425-2556. Hours: 8AM-5PM (CST). *Felony, Misdemeanor, Civil.*

Civil Records: Access: In person only. Visitors must perform in person searches for themselves. No search fee. Required to search: name, years to search. Civil cases indexed by defendant, plaintiff. Civil records on docket books since 1960s.

Criminal Records: Access: Mail, in person. Both court and visitors may perform in person searches. Search fee: $10.00 per name. Fee is per district. Required to search: name, years to search; also helpful: SSN. Criminal records on docket books since 1960s.

General Information: No sealed or Juvenile Youth Court records released. Turnaround time 2 days. Copy fee: $.50 per page. Certification fee: $1.00. Fee payee: Jones County Circuit Clerk. Personal checks accepted. Prepayment is required.

Justice Court PO Box 1997, Laurel, MS 39441; 601-428-3137; Fax: 601-428-0526. Hours: 8AM--5PM M-F (CST). *Misdemeanor, Civil Actions Under $2,500, Eviction, Small Claims.*

Note: This Justice Court houses all the Justices for Jones County.

Ellisville Chancery Court 101-D Court St., Ellisville, MS 39437; 601-477-3307. Hours: 8AM-Noon, 1-5PM (CST). *Probate.*

Laurel Chancery Court PO Box 1468, Laurel, MS 39441; 601-428-0527; Probate phone: 602-428-3182; Fax: 601-428-3610. Hours: 8AM-5PM (CST). *Probate.*

www.chancery19thms.com

Kemper County

Circuit Court PO Box 130, De Kalb, MS 39328; 601-743-2224; Fax: 601-743-4173. Hours: 8AM-5PM (CST). *Felony, Civil Actions Over $2,500.*

Civil Records: Access: Phone, fax, mail, in person. Both court and visitors may perform in person searches. Search fee: $10.00 per name. Required to search: name, years to search, address. Civil cases indexed by defendant, plaintiff. Civil records on docket books since 1960s, archived since 1912.

Criminal Records: Access: Phone, fax, mail, in person. Both court and visitors may perform in person searches. Search fee: $10.00 per name. Required to search: name, years to search, address, DOB; also helpful: SSN. Criminal records on docket books since 1960s, archived since 1912.

General Information: No sealed, adoptions, mental health, juvenile, sex, or expunged records released. Turnaround time 1 week. Fax notes: $.25 per page. Copy fee: $.25 per page. Fee payee: Circuit Clerk. Business checks accepted. Prepayment is required.

Justice Court PO Box 661, De Kalb, MS 39328; 601-743-2793; Fax: 601-743-4893. Hours: 8AM-5PM (CST). *Misdemeanor, Civil Actions Under $2,500, Eviction, Small Claims.*

Chancery Court PO Box 188, De Kalb, MS 39328; 601-743-2460; Fax: 601-743-2789. Hours: 8AM-5PM (CST). *Probate.*

Lafayette County

Circuit Court LaFayette County Courthouse, One Courethouse Sq, Suite 201, Oxford, MS 38655; 662-234-4951; Fax: 662-236-0238. Hours: 8AM-5PM (CST). *Felony, Civil Actions Over $2,500.*

Civil Records: Access: Mail, in person. Both court and visitors may perform in person searches. Search fee: $10.00 per name. Fee is per 10 years searched. Required to search: name, years to search; also helpful: address. Civil cases indexed by defendant, plaintiff. Civil records on docket books from 1900; on computer back to 1995.

Criminal Records: Access: Mail, in person. Both court and visitors may perform in person searches. Search fee: $10.00 per name. Fee is per 10 years searched. Required to search: name, years to search, DOB; also helpful: address, SSN. Criminal records on docket books from 1900, on computer back to 1995.

General Information: Public access terminal is available. No sealed, adoptions, mental health, juvenile, sex, or expunged records released. Turnaround time 1-2 days. Copy fee: $1.00 per page. Certification fee: $1.50. Fee payee: Circuit Clerk. Business checks accepted. Prepayment is required.

Justice Court 713 Jackson Ave E, Oxford, MS 38655; 662-234-1545; Fax: 662-238-7990. Hours: 8AM-5PM (CST). *Misdemeanor, Civil Actions Under $2,500, Eviction, Small Claims.*

Chancery Court PO Box 1240, Oxford, MS 38655; 662-234-2131; Fax: 662-234-5402. Hours: 8AM-5PM (CST). *Probate.*

Lamar County

Circuit Court PO Box 369, Purvis, MS 39475; 601-794-8504; Fax: 601-794-3905. Hours: 8AM-5PM (CST). *Felony, Civil Actions Over $2,500.*

Civil Records: Access: Mail, in person. Both court and visitors may perform in person searches. Search fee: $10.00 per name. Required to search: name, years to search. Civil cases indexed by defendant, plaintiff. Civil records on docket books since 1904.

Criminal Records: Access: Mail, in person. Both court and visitors may perform in person searches. Search

fee: $10.00 per name. Required to search: name, years to search; also helpful: SSN. Criminal records on docket books since 1904.

General Information: No sealed, adoptions, mental health, juvenile, sex, or expunged records released. SASE requested. Turnaround time 1-2 days. Copy fee: $1.00 per page. Fee payee: Circuit Clerk. Business checks accepted. Prepayment is required.

Justice Court PO Box 1010, Purvis, MS 39475; 601-794-2950; Fax: 601-794-1076. Hours: 8AM-5PM (CST). *Misdemeanor, Civil Actions Under $2,500, Eviction, Small Claims.*

Chancery Court PO Box 247, Purvis, MS 39475; 601-794-8504; Fax: 601-794-3903. Hours: 8AM-5PM (CST). *Probate.*

Lauderdale County

Circuit & County Court PO Box 1005, Meridian, MS 39302-1005; 601-482-9738; Fax: 601-484-3970. Hours: 8AM-5PM (CST). *Felony, Civil Actions Over $2,500.*

Note: County Court can be reached at 601-482-9715.

Civil Records: Access: Phone, mail, fax, in person. Both court and visitors may perform in person searches. Search fee: $10.00 per name. Required to search: name, years to search, SSN. Civil cases indexed by defendant, plaintiff. Civil records on docket books back to 1950s, on computer back to 1992. Court will only search computer records.

Criminal Records: Access: Mail, fax, in person. Both court and visitors may perform in person searches. Search fee: $10.00 per name. Required to search: name, years to search, DOB; also helpful: SSN. Criminal records on computer (Felony) back to 1965.

General Information: Public access terminal is available. No sealed, adoptions, mental health, juvenile, sex, or expunged records released. SASE not required. Turnaround time 1 week, phone turnaround time 1 week. Fax notes: Will not fax results. Copy fee: $.50 per page. Fee payee: Circuit Clerk. Business checks accepted. Will bill complete files to attorneys.

Justice Court PO Box 5126, Meridian, MS 39302; 601-482-9879; Fax: 601-482-9813. Hours: 8AM-5PM (CST). *Misdemeanor, Civil Actions Under $2,500, Eviction, Small Claims.*

Chancery Court PO Box 1587, Meridian, MS 39302; 601-482-9701; Fax: 601-486-4920. Hours: 8AM-Noon, 1-5PM (CST). *Probate.*

Lawrence County

Circuit Court PO Box 1249, Monticello, MS 39654; 601-587-4791; Fax: 601-587-0750. Hours: 8AM-5PM (CST). *Felony, Civil Actions Over $2,500.*

Civil Records: Access: Phone, fax, mail, in person. Both court and visitors may perform in person searches. Search fee: $10.00 per name. Required to search: name, years to search; also helpful: address. Civil cases indexed by defendant, plaintiff. Civil records on docket books since 1977. For fax request send copy of check for fee.

Criminal Records: Access: Phone, fax, mail, in person. Both court and visitors may perform in person searches. Search fee: $10.00 per name. Required to search: name, years to search, DOB; also helpful: address, SSN. Criminal records on docket books since 1977. For fax request send copy of check for fee.

General Information: No sealed, adoptions, mental health, juvenile, sex, or expunged records released. SASE requested. Turnaround time 1 week, phone turnaround time 1-2 days. Fax notes: $10.00 per document. No copy fee. Certification fee: $1.50. Fee payee: Circuit Clerk. Personal checks accepted. Prepayment is required.

Justice Court PO Box 903, Monticello, MS 39654; 601-587-7183; Fax: 601-587-0755. Hours: 8AM-5PM (CST). *Misdemeanor, Civil Actions Under $2,500, Eviction, Small Claims.*

Chancery Court 517 Broad St, Courthouse Sq, PO Box 821, Monticello, MS 39654; 601-587-7162; Fax: 601-587-0767. Hours: 8AM-5PM (CST). *Probate.*

Leake County

Circuit Court PO Box 67, Carthage, MS 39051; 601-267-8357; Fax: 601-267-8889. Hours: 8AM-5PM (CST). *Felony, Civil Actions Over $2,500.*

Civil Records: Access: In person only. Visitors must perform in person searches for themselves. No search fee. Required to search: name, years to search. Civil cases indexed by defendant, plaintiff. Civil records on docket books since 1970s.

Criminal Records: Access: Mail, in person. Both court and visitors may perform in person searches. Search fee: $10.00 per name. Required to search: name, years to search, DOB; also helpful: SSN. Criminal records on docket books since 1977.

General Information: Public access terminal is available. (Voting & Judgments only.) No sealed, adoptions, mental health, juvenile, sex, or expunged records released. SASE required. Turnaround time 1-2 days. Copy fee: $.50 per page. Certification fee: $1.50. Fee payee: Circuit Clerk. Prepayment is required.

Justice Court PO Box 69, Carthage, MS 39051; 601-267-5677; Fax: 601-267-6134. Hours: 8:00AM-5:00PM (CST). *Misdemeanor, Civil Actions Under $2,500, Eviction, Small Claims.*

Chancery Court PO Box 72, Carthage, MS 39051; 601-267-7371; Fax: 601-267-6137. Hours: 8AM-5PM (CST). *Probate.*

Lee County

Circuit & County Court Circuit Court - PO Box 762, County Court - PO Box 736, Tupelo, MS 38802; 662-841-9022/9023(Circuit) 9730 (County); Fax: 662-680-6079. Hours: 8AM-5PM (CST). *Felony, Civil Actions Over $2,500.*

Civil Records: Access: Mail, in person. Both court and visitors may perform in person searches. Search fee: $10.00 per name. Required to search: name, years to search. Civil cases indexed by defendant, plaintiff. Circuit records on computer since 1990, others on docket books since 1987. County records not on computer.

Criminal Records: Access: Mail, in person. Both court and visitors may perform in person searches. Search fee: $10.00 per name. Required to search: name, years to search; also helpful: DOB, SSN. Circuit records on computer since 1990, others on docket books since 1987. County records not on computer.

General Information: No sealed or expunged records released. SASE required. Turnaround time 1-2 days. Copy fee: $.25 per page. Certification fee: $1.50. Fee payee: Lee County & Circuit Court. Business checks accepted. Prepayment is required.

Justice Court PO Box 108, Tupelo, MS 38802; 662-841-9014; Fax: 662-680-6021. Hours: 8AM-5PM (CST). *Misdemeanor, Civil Actions Under $2,500, Eviction, Small Claims.*

Chancery Court PO Box 7127, Tupelo, MS 38802; 662-841-9100; Fax: 662-680-6091. Hours: 8AM-5PM (CST). *Probate.*

Leflore County

Circuit & County Court PO Box 1953, Greenwood, MS 38935-1953; 662-453-1041; Fax: 662-455-1278. Hours: 8AM-5PM (CST). *Felony, Civil Actions Over $2,500.*

Civil Records: Access: Phone, fax, mail, in person. Both court and visitors may perform in person searches. Search fee: $10.00 per name. Required to search: name, years to search. Civil cases indexed by defendant, plaintiff. Civil records on computer index goes back 10 years; prior records on docket books since mid-1800s.

Criminal Records: Access: Fax, mail, in person. Both court and visitors may perform in person searches. Search fee: $10.00 per name. Required to search: name, years to search; also helpful: DOB, SSN. Criminal records on computer index goes back 10 years; prior records on docket books since mid-1800s.

General Information: Public access terminal is available. No sealed or expunged records released. Turnaround time 1-2 days. Fax notes: Call for fax fee. Copy fee: $1.00 per page. Certification fee: $1.50. Fee payee: Circuit Clerk. Personal checks accepted. Prepayment is required.

Justice Court PO Box 8056, Greenwood, MS 38935; 662-453-1605. Hours: 8AM-5PM (CST). *Misdemeanor, Civil Actions Under $2,500, Eviction, Small Claims.*

Chancery Court PO Box 250, Greenwood, MS 38935-0250; 662-453-1041; 453-1432 (court admin); Fax: 662-455-7959. Hours: 8AM-5PM (CST). *Probate.*

Lincoln County

Circuit Court PO Box 357, Brookhaven, MS 39602; 601-835-3435; Fax: 601-835-3482. Hours: 8AM-5PM (CST). *Felony, Civil Actions Over $2,500.*

Civil Records: Access: Fax, mail, in person. Both court and visitors may perform in person searches. Search fee: $10.00 per name. Required to search: name, years to search. Civil cases indexed by defendant, plaintiff. Civil records on computer since 1986, prior on docket books.

Criminal Records: Access: Fax, mail, in person. Both court and visitors may perform in person searches. Search fee: $10.00 per name. Required to search: name, years to search; also helpful: DOB, SSN. Criminal records on computer since 1982, prior on docket books.

General Information: Public access terminal is available. No sealed or expunged records released. Turnaround time 1-2 days. Fax notes: $10.00 per document. Copy fee: $.50 per page. Certification fee: $1.00. Fee payee: Circuit Clerk. Personal checks accepted. Out of state checks not accepted. Prepayment is required.

Justice Court PO Box 767, Brookhaven, MS 39602; 601-835-3474. Hours: 8:00AM-5:00PM (CST). *Misdemeanor, Civil Actions Under $2,500, Eviction, Small Claims.*

Chancery Court PO Box 555, Brookhaven, MS 39602; 601-835-3412; Fax: 601-835-3423. Hours: 8AM-5PM (CST). *Probate.*

www.15thchancerydistrictms.org

Lowndes County

Circuit & County Court PO Box 31, Columbus, MS 39703; 662-329-5900. Hours: 8AM-5PM (CST). *Felony, Civil.*

Civil Records: Access: Mail, in person. Both court and visitors may perform in person searches. Search fee: $10.00 per name. Required to search: name, years to search. Civil cases indexed by defendant, plaintiff. Civil records on computer from 2/94, on docket books from 1900s.

Criminal Records: Access: Mail, in person. Both court and visitors may perform in person searches. Search fee: $10.00 per name per year. Required to search: name, years to search, DOB; also helpful: SSN. Criminal records on computer since 11/93; prior on docket books.

General Information: Public access terminal is available. No sealed, adoption, mental health, juvenile, sex or expunged cases released. Copy fee: $1.00 per page. Certification fee: $1.00. Fee payee: Clerk of Court. Personal checks accepted. Prepayment is required.

Justice Court 11 Airline Rd, Columbus, MS 39702; 662-329-5929; Fax: 662-245-4619. Hours: 8AM-5PM (CST). *Misdemeanor, Civil Actions Under $2,500, Eviction, Small Claims.*

Chancery Court PO Box 684, Columbus, MS 39703; 662-329-5800. 8AM-5PM (CST). *Probate.*

Madison County

Circuit & County Court PO Box 1626, Canton, MS 39046; 601-859-4365; Fax: 601-859-8555. Hours: 8AM-5PM (CST). *Felony, Civil.*

Civil Records: Access: Phone, fax, mail, in person. Both court and visitors may perform in person searches. No search fee. Required to search: name, years to search. Civil cases indexed by defendant, plaintiff. Civil records on computer since 1987, prior on docket books since 1950.

Criminal Records: Access: Mail, in person. Both court and visitors may perform in person searches. Search fee: $10.00 per name. Required to search: name, years to search. Criminal records on computer since 1992, prior on docket books since 1945.

General Information: Public access terminal is available. No sealed, adoptions, mental health, juvenile, sex, or expunged records released. SASE requested. Turnaround time 1 week. Copy fee: $.25 per page. Certification fee: $1.00. Fee payee: Circuit Clerk. Personal checks accepted. Prepayment is required.

Justice Court 175 N Union, Canton, MS 39046; 601-859-6337; Fax: 601-859-5878. Hours: 8AM-5PM (CST). *Misdemeanor, Civil Actions Under $2,500, Eviction, Small Claims.*

Note: Request for history must be in writing with a $6.00 fee made out to Madison County Justice Court.

Chancery Court PO Box 404, Canton, MS 39046; 601-859-1177; Fax: 601-859-5875. Hours: 8AM-5PM (CST). *Probate.*

Marion County

Circuit Court 250 Broad St, #1, Columbia, MS 39429; 601-736-8246. Hours: 8AM-5PM (CST). *Felony, Civil Actions Over $2,500.*

Civil Records: Access: Mail, in person, online. Both court and visitors may perform in person searches. Search fee: $10.00 per name. Required to search: name, years to search. Civil cases indexed by defendant, plaintiff. Civil records on docket books since 1800s. Online access to circuit court dockets available by subscription at www.recordsusa.com/Mississippi/MarionCnMS.htm. Credit card, username and password is required; choose either monthly or per-use plan. Visit the web site for sign-up or call Lisa at 601-264-7701 for information.

Criminal Records: Access: Mail, in person, online. Both court and visitors may perform in person searches. Search fee: $10.00 per name. Required to search: name, years to search; also helpful: SSN. Criminal records on docket books since 1800s. Online access to criminal court dockets is the same as civil.

General Information: No sealed, adoptions, mental health, juvenile, sex, or expunged records released.

SASE required. Turnaround time 1-2 days. Copy fee: No search fee. Fee payee: Circuit Clerk. Personal checks accepted. Prepayment is required.

Justice Court 500 Courthouse Square, Columbia, MS 39429; 601-736-2572; Fax: 601-731-3781. Hours: 8AM-5PM (CST). *Misdemeanor, Civil Actions Under $2,500, Eviction, Small Claims.*

Chancery Court 250 Broad St, #2, Columbia, MS 39429; 601-444-0205; Fax: 601-444-0206. Hours: 8AM-5PM (CST). *Probate.*

Marshall County

Circuit Court PO Box 459, Holly Springs, MS 38635; 662-252-3434; Fax: 662-252-0004 & 252-5951. Hours: 8AM-5PM (CST). *Felony, Civil Actions Over $2,500.*

Civil Records: Access: Fax, mail, in person. Both court and visitors may perform in person searches. Search fee: $10.00 per name. Required to search: name, years to search. Civil cases indexed by defendant, plaintiff. Civil records on docket books since 1960s; computerized records go back to 1999.

Criminal Records: Access: Mail, in person. Both court and visitors may perform in person searches. Search fee: $10.00 per name. Required to search: name, years to search; also helpful: DOB, SSN. Criminal records on docket books since 1960s; computerized records go back to 1999.

General Information: Public access terminal is available. No sealed or expunged records released. Turnaround time 1-2 days. Fax notes: No fee to fax results. Fax copy of search fee check. Copy fee: $.50 per page. Fee payee: Circuit Court Clerk. Personal checks accepted. Prepayment is required.

Justice Court - North & South Districts PO Box 729, Holly Springs, MS 38635; 662-252-3585. Hours: 8AM-5PM (CST). *Misdemeanor, Civil Actions Under $2,500, Eviction, Small Claims.*

Chancery Court PO Box 219, Holly Springs, MS 38635; 662-252-4431; Fax: 662-252-0004. Hours: 8AM-5PM (CST). *Probate.*

Monroe County

Circuit Court PO Box 843, Aberdeen, MS 39730; 662-369-8695; Fax: 662-369-3684. Hours: 8AM-5PM (CST). *Felony, Civil Actions Over $2,500.*

Civil Records: Access: In person only. Visitors must perform in person searches for themselves. No search fee. Required to search: name, years to search; also helpful: address. Civil cases indexed by defendant, plaintiff. Civil records on docket books since 1821.

Criminal Records: Access: In person only. Visitors must perform in person searches for themselves. No search fee. Required to search: name, years to search, DOB; also helpful: address, SSN. Criminal records on docket books since 1821.

General Information: No sealed, adoptions, mental health, juvenile, sex, or expunged records released. Copy fee: $.50 per page. Certification fee: $3.00. Fee payee: Monroe County Circuit Clerk. Only cashiers checks and money orders accepted. Prepayment is required.

Justice Court - District 1, 2, 3 PO Box 518 (101 9th St), Amory, MS 38821; 662-256-8493; Fax: 662-256-7876. *Misdemeanor, Civil Actions Under $2,500, Eviction, Small Claims.*

Justice Court - District 2 PO Box 518, Amory, MS 38821; 662-256-8493. *Misdemeanor, Civil Actions Under $2,500, Eviction, Small Claims.*

Note: Aberdeen Justice Court Dist. 2 is closed; records now at Amory Justice Court 1 & 2.

Chancery Court PO Box 578, Aberdeen, MS 39730; 662-369-8143; Fax: 662-369-7928. Hours: 8AM-5PM (CST). *Probate.*

Montgomery County

Circuit Court PO Box 765, Winona, MS 38967; 662-283-4161; Fax: 662-283-2233. Hours: 8AM-5PM (CST). *Felony, Civil Actions Over $2,500.*

Civil Records: Access: Mail, in person. Both court and visitors may perform in person searches. Search fee: $10.00 per name. Required to search: name, years to search. Civil cases indexed by defendant, plaintiff. Civil records on docket books since early 1900s.

Criminal Records: Access: Mail, in person. Both court and visitors may perform in person searches. Search fee: $10.00 per name. Required to search: name, years to search. Criminal records on docket books since early 1900s.

General Information: No sealed or expunged records released. SASE required. Turnaround time 1-2 days. Copy fee: $.25 per page. Certification fee: $2.00. Fee payee: Circuit Clerk. Personal checks accepted. Prepayment is required.

Justice Court PO Box 229, Winona, MS 38967; 662-283-2290; Fax: 662-283-2233. Hours: 8AM-5PM (CST). *Misdemeanor, Civil Actions Under $2,500, Eviction, Small Claims.*

Chancery Court PO Box 71, Winona, MS 38967; 662-283-2333; Fax: 662-283-2233. Hours: 8AM-5PM (CST). *Probate.*

Neshoba County

Circuit Court 401 E Beacon St #110, Philadelphia, MS 39350; 601-656-4781; Fax: 601-650-3997. Hours: 8AM-5PM (CST). *Felony, Civil Actions Over $2,500.*

Civil Records: Access: Mail, in person. Both court and visitors may perform in person searches. Search fee: $10.00 per name. Required to search: name, years to search. Civil cases indexed by defendant.

Criminal Records: Access: Mail, in person. Both court and visitors may perform in person searches. Search fee: $10.00 per name. Required to search: name, years to search, DOB; also helpful: SSN. Criminal records on docket books since 1877.

General Information: No sealed, adoptions, mental health, juvenile, sex, or expunged records released. Turnaround time 1 day. Copy fee: $.50 per page. Certification fee: $2.00. Fee payee: Circuit Clerk. Business checks accepted.

Justice Court 401 E Beacon St #209, Philadelphia, MS 39350; 601-656-5361/1101; Fax: 601-656-6482. *Misdemeanor, Civil Actions Under $2,500, Eviction, Small Claims.*

Chancery Court 401 Beacon St #107, Philadelphia, MS 39350; 601-656-3581; Fax: 601-650-3280. Hours: 8AM-5PM (CST). *Probate.*

Newton County

Circuit Court PO Box 447, Decatur, MS 39327; 601-635-2368; Fax: 601-635-3210. Hours: 8AM-5PM (CST). *Felony, Civil Actions Over $2,500.*

Civil Records: Access: Mil, in person. Both court and visitors may perform in person searches. Search fee: $10.00 per name. Required to search: name, years to search. Civil cases indexed by defendant, plaintiff. Civil records on docket books since 1968.

Criminal Records: Access: Mail, in person. Both court and visitors may perform in person searches. Search fee: $10.00 per name. Required to search: name, years to search, DOB; also helpful: SSN. Criminal records on docket books since 1968.

General Information: No sealed, adoptions, mental health, juvenile, sex, or expunged records released. SASE required. Turnaround time same day. Copy fee: $.50 per page. Certification fee: $1.50. Fee payee: Circuit Court. Personal checks accepted. Prepayment is required.

Justice Court PO Box 69, Decatur, MS 39327; 601-635-2740. Hours: 8AM-5PM (CST). *Misdemeanor, Civil Actions Under $2,500, Eviction, Small Claims.*

Chancery Clerk Office PO Box 68, Decatur, MS 39327; 601-635-2367. 8AM-5PM (CST). *Probate.*

Noxubee County

Circuit Court PO Box 431, Macon, MS 39341; 662-726-5737; Fax: 662-726-6041. Hours: 8AM-5PM (CST). *Felony, Civil Actions Over $2,500.*

Civil Records: Access: Mail, fax, in person. Both court and visitors may perform in person searches. Search fee: $10.00 per name. Required to search: name, years to search. Civil cases indexed by defendant. Civil records on docket books since 1800s.

Criminal Records: Access: Mail, fax, in person. Both court and visitors may perform in person searches. Search fee: $10.00 per name. Required to search: name, years to search; also helpful: SSN. Criminal records on docket books since 1800s.

General Information: No sealed, adoptions, mental health, juvenile, sex, or expunged records released. SASE required. Turnaround time 1 week. Copy fee: $.50 per page. Certification fee: $5.00. Fee payee: Circuit Clerk. Business checks accepted. Prepayment is required.

Justice Court - North & South Districts 507 S Jefferson, PO Box 550, Macon, MS 39341; 662-726-5834; Fax: 662-726-2944. Hours: 8AM-5PM (CST). *Misdemeanor, Civil Actions Under $2,500, Eviction, Small Claims.*

Chancery Court PO Box 147, Macon, MS 39341; 662-726-4243; Fax: 662-726-2272. Hours: 8AM-5PM (CST). *Probate.*

Oktibbeha County

Circuit Court Courthouse, 101 E Main, Starkville, MS 39759; 662-323-1356. Hours: 8AM-5PM (CST). *Felony, Civil Actions Over $2,500.*

Civil Records: Access: Mail, fax, in person. Both court and visitors may perform in person searches. Search fee: $10.00 per name. Required to search: name, years to search; also helpful: address. Civil cases indexed by defendant, plaintiff. Civil records on docket books since 1938.

Criminal Records: Access: Mail, fax, in person. Both court and visitors may perform in person searches. Search fee: $10.00 per name. Required to search: name, years to search; also helpful: DOB, SSN. Criminal records on docket since 1950.

General Information: Public access terminal is available. No sealed, adoptions, mental health, juvenile, sex, or expunged records released. Turnaround time 1 week. Copy fee: $1.00 per page. Certification fee: $1.50. Fee payee: Circuit Clerk. Personal checks accepted. Prepayment is required.

Justice Court - Districts 1-3 104 Felix Long Dr, Starkville, MS 39759; 662-324-3032; Fax: 662-338-1078. Hours: 8AM-5PM (CST). *Misdemeanor, Civil Actions Under $2,500, Eviction, Small Claims.*

Chancery Court Courthouse, 101 E Main, Starkville, MS 39759; 662-323-5834. Hours: 8AM-5PM (CST). *Probate.*

Panola County

Circuit Court - 1st District PO Box 130, Sardis, MS 38666; 662-487-2073; Fax: 662-487-3595. Hours: 8AM-5PM (CST). *Felony, Civil Actions Over $2,500.*

Civil Records: Access: Fax, mail, in person. Both court and visitors may perform in person searches. Search fee: $10.00 per name. Fee is for dual district search. Required to search: name, years to search. Civil cases indexed by defendant, plaintiff. Civil records on docket books since 170s, archived since 1925.

Criminal Records: Access: Fax, mail, in person. Both court and visitors may perform in person searches. Search fee: $10.00 per name. Fee is for dual district search. Required to search: name, years to search, DOB; also helpful: SSN. Criminal records on docket books since 1970, archived since 1925, records are not computerized.

General Information: No sealed, adoptions, mental health, juvenile, sex, or expunged records released. SASE required. Turnaround time varies. Fax notes: No fee to fax results. Fax copy of the search fee check. Copy fee: $.50 per page. Certification fee: $1.50. Fee payee: Circuit Clerk. Business checks accepted. Prepayment is required.

Circuit Court - 2nd District PO Box 346, Batesville, MS 38606; 662-563-6210; Fax: 662-563-8233. Hours: 8AM-5PM (CST). *Felony, Civil Actions Over $2,500.*

Civil Records: Access: Phone, fax, mail, in person. Both court and visitors may perform in person searches. Search fee: $10.00 per name. Fee is per district. Required to search: name, years to search. Civil cases indexed by defendant, plaintiff. Civil records on docket books since 1900.

Criminal Records: Access: Phone, fax, mail, in person. Both court and visitors may perform in person searches. Search fee: $10.00 per name. Fee is per district. Required to search: name, years to search, address, DOB; also helpful: SSN. Criminal records on docket books since 1900.

General Information: No sealed, adoptions, mental health, juvenile, sex, or expunged records released. Turnaround time same day. Fax notes: $1.00 per page. Copy fee: $.25 per page. Certification fee: $10.00. Fee payee: Circuit Clerk's Office. Personal checks accepted. Prepayment is required.

Justice Court PO Box 249, Sardis, MS 38666; 662-487-2080. Hours: 8AM-5PM (CST). *Misdemeanor, Civil Actions Under $2,500, Eviction, Small Claims.*

Note: This Justice Court houses all the Justices for Panola County.

Panola County Chancery Clerk 151 Public Square, Batesville, MS 38606; 662-563-6205; Fax: 662-563-8233. Hours: 8AM-5PM (CST). *Probate.*

Sardis Chancery Court PO Box 130, Sardis, MS 38666; 662-487-2070; Fax: 662-487-3595. Hours: 8AM-Noon, 1-5PM (CST). *Probate.*

Pearl River County

Circuit Court Courthouse, Poplarville, MS 39470; 601-795-3059; Fax: 601-795-3084. Hours: 8AM-5PM (CST). *Felony, Civil Actions Over $2,500.*

Civil Records: Access: Mail, fax, in person. Both court and visitors may perform in person searches. Search fee: $10.00 per name. Required to search: name, years to search, DOB, SSN. Civil cases indexed by defendant, plaintiff. Civil records on docket books since 1890.

Criminal Records: Access: Mail, fax, in person. Both court and visitors may perform in person searches. Search fee: $10.00 per name. Required to search: name,

years to search. Criminal records on computer since late 1960s, prior on docket books since 1890.

General Information: No sealed, adoptions, mental health, juvenile, sex, or expunged records released. Turnaround time 1-2 days. Copy fee: $.50 per page. Certification fee: $2.50. Fee payee: Circuit Clerk. Personal checks accepted. Prepayment is required.

Justice Court - Northern, Southeastern & Southwestern Districts 204 Julia St, Poplarville, MS 39470; 601-795-8018; Fax: 601-795-3063. Hours: 8AM-5PM (CST). *Misdemeanor, Civil Actions Under $2,500, Eviction, Small Claims.*

Chancery Court PO Box 431, Poplarville, MS 39470; 601-795-2238; Fax: 601-795-3093. Hours: 8AM-5PM (CST). *Probate.*

Perry County

Circuit Court PO Box 198, New Augusta, MS 39462; 601-964-8663; Fax: 601-964-8740. Hours: 8AM-5PM (CST). *Felony, Civil Actions Over $2,500.*

Civil Records: Access: Mail, fax, in person. Both court and visitors may perform in person searches. Search fee: $10.00 per name. Fee is per 10 years searched. Required to search: name, years to search. Civil cases indexed by defendant, plaintiff. Civil records on docket books since 1980.

Criminal Records: Access: Mail, fax, in person. Both court and visitors may perform in person searches. Search fee: $10.00 per name. Fee is per 10 years searched. Required to search: name, years to search, DOB; also helpful: SSN, sex, signed release. Criminal records on docket books since 1971; on computer since.

General Information: No sealed, adoptions, mental health, juvenile, sex, or expunged records released. Turnaround time 1-2 days. Copy fee: $.50 per page. Certification fee: $2.50. Fee payee: Circuit Clerk. Personal checks accepted. Prepayment is required.

Justice Court PO Box 455, New Augusta, MS 39462; 601-964-8366. Hours: 8AM-5PM (CST). *Misdemeanor, Civil Actions Under $2,500, Eviction, Small Claims.*

Chancery Court PO Box 198, New Augusta, MS 39462; 601-964-8398; Fax: 601-964-8746. Hours: 8AM-5PM (CST). *Probate.*

Pike County

Circuit & County Court PO Drawer 31, Magnolia, MS 39652; 601-783-2581; Fax: 601-783-4101. Hours: 8AM-5PM (CST). *Felony, Misdemeanor, Civil.*

Civil Records: Access: Fax, mail, in person. Both court and visitors may perform in person searches. Search fee: $6.00 per name. Required to search: name, years to search. Civil cases indexed by defendant, plaintiff. Civil records on docket books since 1950s; on computer back to 1984.

Criminal Records: Access: Fax, mail, in person. Both court and visitors may perform in person searches. Search fee: $6.00 per name. Required to search: name, years to search, DOB; also helpful: SSN. Criminal records on docket books since 1950s; on computer back to 1984.

General Information: Public access terminal is available. No sealed, adoptions, mental health, juvenile, sex, or expunged records released. SASE required. Turnaround time 1-2 days. Copy fee: $1.00 per page. Certification fee: $1.50. Fee payee: Circuit Clerk. Personal checks accepted. Prepayment is required.

Justice Court - Divisions 1-3 PO Box 509, Magnolia, MS 39652; 601-783-5333; Fax: 601-783-4181. Hours: 8AM-5PM (CST). *Misdemeanor, Civil Actions Under $2,500, Eviction, Small Claims.*

Chancery Court PO Box 309, Magnolia, MS 39652; 601-783-3362; Fax: 601-783-4101. Hours: 8AM-5PM (CST). *Probate, Civil.*

Pontotoc County

Circuit Court PO Box 428, Pontotoc, MS 38863; 662-489-3908. Hours: 8AM-5PM (CST). *Felony, Civil Actions Over $2,500.*

Civil Records: Access: Mail, in person. Both court and visitors may perform in person searches. Search fee: $5.00 per name. Required to search: name, years to search. Civil cases indexed by defendant, plaintiff. Civil records on books from 1849.

Criminal Records: Access: Mail, in person. Both court and visitors may perform in person searches. Search fee: $5.00 per name. Required to search: name, years to search, DOB; also helpful: SSN. Criminal records on books from 1849. Records are not computerized.

General Information: No sealed, adoptions, mental health, juvenile, sex, or expunged records released. SASE required. Turnaround time 1 week. Copy fee: $.50 per page. Fee payee: Circuit Clerk. Prepayment is required.

Justice Court - East & West Districts 29 E Washington St, Pontotoc, MS 38863-2923; 662-489-3920; Fax: 662-489-3921. Hours: 8AM-5PM (CST). *Misdemeanor, Civil Actions Under $2,500, Eviction, Small Claims.*

Chancery Court 11East Washington, PO Box 209, Pontotoc, MS 38863; 662-489-3900; Fax: 662-489-3940. Hours: 8AM-5PM (CST). *Probate.*

Prentiss County

Circuit Court PO Box 727, 101 N Main St, Booneville, MS 38829; 662-728-4611; Fax: 662-728-2006. Hours: 8AM-5PM (CST). *Felony, Civil Actions Over $2,500.*

Civil Records: Access: Mail, in person. Both court and visitors may perform in person searches. Search fee: $10.00 per name. Required to search: name, years to search. Civil cases indexed by defendant, plaintiff. Civil records on docket books from 1880, only judgments are on computer since 1985.

Criminal Records: Access: Fax, mail, in person. Both court and visitors may perform in person searches. Search fee: $10.00 per name. Required to search: name, years to search; also helpful: DOB, SSN. Criminal records on docket books from 1880, computerized since 1985. Prepaid account is required for fax access.

General Information: No sealed, adoptions, mental health, juvenile, sex, or expunged records released. SASE required. Turnaround time varies. Copy fee: $.50 per page. Certification fee: $2.00. Fee payee: Circuit Clerk. Personal checks accepted. Accounts available.

Justice Court 1901C East Chambers Dr, Booneville, MS 38829; 662-728-8696; Fax: 662-728-2009. Hours: 8AM-5PM (CST). *Misdemeanor, Civil Actions Under $2,500, Eviction, Small Claims.*

Chancery Court PO Box 477, Booneville, MS 38829; 662-728-8151; Fax: 662-728-2007. Hours: 8AM-5PM (CST). *Probate.*

Quitman County

Circuit Court Courthouse, 230 Chestnut St, Marks, MS 38646; 662-326-8003; Fax: 662-326-8004. Hours: 8AM-5PM (CST). *Felony, Civil Actions Over $2,500.*

Civil Records: Access: Fax, mail, in person. Both court and visitors may perform in person searches. Search fee: $10.00 per name. Required to search: name, years to search. Civil cases indexed by defendant, plaintiff. Civil records on books and files since 1890.

Criminal Records: Access: Fax, mail, in person. Both court and visitors may perform in person searches. Search fee: $10.00 per name. Required to search: name, years to search, DOB; also helpful: SSN. Criminal records on books and files since 1890.

General Information: No sealed, adoptions, mental health, juvenile, sex, or expunged records released. SASE not required. Turnaround time 2 days, phone turnaround time 10 minutes. Fax notes: No fax fee when $10.00 has been paid. Copy fee: $.50 per page. Certification fee: $1.50. Fee payee: Circuit Clerk. Business checks accepted. Prepayment is required.

Justice Court - Districts 1 & 2 PO Box 100, Marks, MS 38646; 662-326-2104/7906; Fax: 662-326-2330. Hours: 8AM-5PM (CST). *Misdemeanor, Civil Actions Under $2,500, Eviction, Small Claims.*

Chancery Court 230 Chestnut St, Marks, MS 38646; 662-326-2661; Fax: 662-326-8004. Hours: 8AM-Noon, 1-5PM (CST). *Probate.*

Rankin County

Circuit & County Court PO Drawer 1599, Brandon, MS 39043; 601-825-1466. Hours: 8AM-5PM (CST). *Felony, Misdemeanor, Civil.*

www.rankincounty.org

Civil Records: Access: Mail, in person. Both court and visitors may perform in person searches. Search fee: $5.00 per name. Required to search: name, years to search. Civil cases indexed by defendant, plaintiff. Civil records on computer since 1990, prior on docket books.

Criminal Records: Access: Mail, in person. Both court and visitors may perform in person searches. Search fee: $5.00 per name. Required to search: name, years to search; also helpful: DOB, SSN. Criminal records on computer since 1990, prior on docket books.

General Information: Public access terminal is available. No sealed or expunged records released. Turnaround time 1-2 days. Copy fee: $.50 per page. Certification fee: $1.50. Fee payee: Circuit Clerk. Personal checks accepted. Prepayment is required.

Justice Court - Districts 1-4 110 Paul Truitt Lane, Pearl, MS 39208; 601-939-1885; Fax: 601-939-2320. Hours: 8AM-5PM (CST). *Misdemeanor, Civil Actions Under $2,500, Eviction, Small Claims.*

Chancery Court 203 Town Sq, PO Box 700, Brandon, MS 39042; 601-825-1649; Fax: 601-824-2450. Hours: 8AM-5PM (CST). *Probate, Civil.*

www.rankincounty.org

Scott County

Circuit Court PO Box 371, Forest, MS 39074; 601-469-3601. Hours: 8AM-5PM (CST). *Felony, Civil Actions Over $2,500.*

Note: The court began computerization of records in 2002.

Civil Records: Access: Mail, in person. Both court and visitors may perform in person searches. Search fee: $10.00 per name. Fee is for 7 year search. Required to search: name, years to search. Civil cases indexed by defendant, plaintiff. Civil records on docket books since 1865.

Criminal Records: Access: Mail, in person. Both court and visitors may perform in person searches. Search fee: $10.00 per name. Fee is for 7 year search. Required to search: name, years to search, DOB; also helpful: SSN. Criminal records on docket books since 1865.

General Information: No sealed, adoptions, mental health, juvenile, sex, or expunged records released. SASE required. Turnaround time 1 week. Copy fee: $.50 per page. Certification fee: $1.50. Fee payee: Circuit Clerk. Personal checks accepted. Prepayment is required.

Justice Court PO Box 371, Forest, MS 39074; 601-469-4555; Fax: 601-469-5193. Hours: 8AM-5PM (CST). *Misdemeanor, Civil Actions Under $2,500, Eviction, Small Claims.*

Chancery Court 100 Main St, PO Box 630, Forest, MS 39074; 601-469-1922, 601-469-1927; Fax: 601-469-5180. Hours: 8AM-5PM (CST). *Probate.*

Sharkey County

Circuit Court PO Box 218 (400 Locust St), Rolling Fork, MS 39159; 662-873-2766; Fax: 662-873-6045. Hours: 8AM-Noon, 1-5PM (CST). *Felony, Civil Actions Over $2,500.*

Civil Records: Access: Fax, mail, in person. Both court and visitors may perform in person searches. Search fee: $10.00 per name. Required to search: name, years to search. Civil cases indexed by defendant, plaintiff. Civil records on docket books since 1893.

Criminal Records: Access: Fax, mail, in person. Both court and visitors may perform in person searches. Search fee: $10.00 per name. Required to search: name, years to search, DOB; also helpful: SSN. Criminal records on docket books since 1893.

General Information: No sealed, adoptions, mental health, juvenile, sex, or expunged records released. Turnaround time 1 week. Fax notes: Fee to fax results is $1.00 per page. Copy fee: $.50 per page; $.25 if self-serve. Certification fee: $2.00 per page. Fee payee: Circuit Clerk. Business checks accepted. Prepayment is required.

Justice Court PO Box 218, Rolling Fork, MS 39159; 662-873-6140. Hours: 8AM-5PM (CST). *Misdemeanor, Civil Actions Under $2,500, Eviction, Small Claims.*

Chancery Court 120 Locust St, PO Box 218, Rolling Fork, MS 39159; 662-873-2755; Fax: 662-873-6045. Hours: 8AM-Noon,1-5PM (CST). *Probate.*

Simpson County

Circuit Court PO Box 307, Mendenhall, MS 39114; 601-847-2474; Fax: 601-847-4011. Hours: 8AM-5PM (CST). *Felony, Civil Actions Over $2,500.*

Civil Records: Access: Fax, mail, in person. Both court and visitors may perform in person searches. Search fee: $10.00 per name. Required to search: name, years to search. Civil cases indexed by defendant, plaintiff. Civil records on docket books since 1978.

Criminal Records: Access: Fax, mail, in person. Both court and visitors may perform in person searches. Search fee: $10.00 per name. Required to search: name, years to search; also helpful: DOB, SSN. Criminal records on docket books since 1978.

General Information: No sealed or expunged records released. Turnaround time 1-2 days. Fax notes: No fee to fax results. Copy fee: $.50 per page. Certification fee: $1.50. Fee payee: Circuit Clerk. Business checks accepted. Prepayment is required.

Justice Court 159 Court Ave, Mendenhall, MS 39114; 601-847-5848; Fax: 601-847-5856. Hours: 8AM-5PM (CST). *Misdemeanor, Civil Actions Under $2,500, Eviction, Small Claims.*

Chancery Court Chancery Building, PO Box 367, Mendenhall, MS 39114; 601-847-2626. Hours: 8AM-5PM (CST). *Probate.*

Smith County

Circuit Court PO Box 517, Raleigh, MS 39153; 601-782-4751; Fax: 601-782-4007. Hours: 8AM-5PM (CST). *Felony, Civil Actions Over $2,500.*

Civil Records: Access: Mail, in person. Both court and visitors may perform in person searches. Search fee: $10.00 per name. Required to search: name, years to

search. Civil cases indexed by defendant, plaintiff. Civil records on docket books since 1912.

Criminal Records: Access: Mail, in person. Both court and visitors may perform in person searches. Search fee: $10.00 per name. Required to search: name, years to search, DOB; also helpful: SSN. Criminal records on docket books since 1912.

General Information: No sealed, adoptions, mental health, juvenile, sex, or expunged records released. SASE required. Turnaround time 2 days. Fax notes: Fee to fax results is $.50 per page. Copy fee: $.50 per page. Certification fee: $5.00. Fee payee: Circuit Clerk. Personal checks accepted.

Justice Court PO Box 171, Raleigh, MS 39153; 601-782-4334; Fax: 601-782-4005. Hours: 8AM-5PM (CST). *Misdemeanor, Civil Actions Under $2,500, Eviction, Small Claims.*

Chancery Court 123 Main St, PO Box 39, Raleigh, MS 39153; 601-782-9811; Fax: 601-782-4690. Hours: 8AM-5PM (CST). *Probate.*

Stone County

Circuit Court Courthouse, 323 Cavers Ave, Wiggins, MS 39577; 601-928-5246; Fax: 601-928-5248. Hours: 8AM-5PM (CST). *Felony, Civil Actions Over $2,500.*

Civil Records: Access: Fax, mail, in person. Both court and visitors may perform in person searches. Search fee: $10.00 per name. Required to search: name, years to search. Civil cases indexed by defendant, plaintiff. Civil records on docket books since 1945.

Criminal Records: Access: Fax, mail, in person. Both court and visitors may perform in person searches. Search fee: $10.00 per name. Required to search: name, years to search, DOB, notarized release; also helpful: SSN. Criminal records on docket books since 1945.

General Information: No sealed, adoptions, mental health, juvenile, sex, or expunged records released. Turnaround time same day. Fax notes: $3.00 for first page, $.50 each add'l. Copy fee: $.50 per page. Certification fee: $1.50. Fee payee: Circuit Clerk. Business checks accepted. Prepayment is required.

Justice Court 231 3rd Street, Wiggins, MS 39577; 601-928-4415; Fax: 601-928-2114. Hours: 8AM-5PM (CST). *Misdemeanor, Civil Actions Under $2,500, Eviction, Small Claims.*

Justice Court - West District 231 3rd St, Wiggins, MS 39577; 601-928-4415. Hours: 8AM-5PM (CST). *Misdemeanor, Civil Actions Under $2,500, Eviction, Small Claims.*

Chancery Court 323 E Cavers, PO Drawer 7, Wiggins, MS 39577; 601-928-5266; Fax: 601-928-6464. Hours: 8AM-5PM (CST). *Probate.*

Sunflower County

Circuit Court PO Box 576, Indianola, MS 38751; 662-887-1252; Fax: 662-887-7077. Hours: 8AM-5PM (CST). *Felony, Civil Actions Over $2,500.*

Civil Records: Access: Mail, in person. Both court and visitors may perform in person searches. Search fee: $10.00 per name. Fee is for 7 year search. Required to search: name, years to search. Civil cases indexed by defendant, plaintiff. Civil records on docket books since 1881; on computer since 2000.

Criminal Records: Access: Mail, in person. Both court and visitors may perform in person searches. Search fee: $10.00 per name. Fee is for 7 year search. Required to search: name, years to search, DOB; also helpful: SSN. Criminal records on docket books since 1913; on computer since 2000.

General Information: Public access terminal is available. No sealed, adoptions, mental health, juvenile,

sex, or expunged records released. Turnaround time 1-3 days. Fax notes: Fee to fax results $1.00 per page. Copy fee: $.50 per page. Certification fee: $1.50. Fee payee: Circuit Clerk. Personal checks accepted. Prepayment is required.

Justice Court - Northern District PO Box 52, Ruleville, MS 38771; 662-756-2835. Hours: 8AM-Noon, 1-5PM (CST). *Misdemeanor, Civil Actions Under $2,500, Eviction, Small Claims.*

Justice Court - Southern District PO Box 487, Indianola, MS 38751; 662-887-6921. Hours: 8AM-5PM (CST). *Misdemeanor, Civil Actions Under $2,500, Eviction, Small Claims.*

Chancery Court 200 Main St, PO Box 988, Indianola, MS 38751; 662-887-4703; Fax: 662-887-7054. Hours: 8AM-5PM (CST). *Probate.*

Tallahatchie County

Charleston Circuit Court PO Box 86, Charleston, MS 38921; 662-647-8758; Fax: 662-647-8490. Hours: 8AM-5PM (CST). *Felony, Civil Actions Over $2,500.*

Civil Records: Access: Mail, in person. Both court and visitors may perform in person searches. Search fee: $10.00 per name. Required to search: name, years to search. Civil cases indexed by defendant, plaintiff. Civil records on books since 1920s.

Criminal Records: Access: Mail, in person. Both court and visitors may perform in person searches. Search fee: $10.00 per name. Required to search: name, years to search, DOB; also helpful: SSN. Criminal records on books since 1920s.

General Information: No sealed, adoptions, mental health, juvenile, sex, or expunged records released. SASE requested. Turnaround time 3 days. Copy fee: $2.00 per page. Certification fee: $3.00. Fee payee: Circuit Clerk. Personal checks accepted. Prepayment is required.

Charleston Justice Court PO Box 440, Charleston, MS 38921; 662-647-3477; Fax: 662-647-3478. Hours: 8AM-5PM (CST). *Misdemeanor, Civil Actions Under $2,500, Eviction, Small Claims.*

Note: Court is located upstairs of the Charleston Circuit Court; records are not comingled.

Sumner Justice Court PO Box 155, Sumner, MS 38957; 662-375-9452; Fax: 662-375-8200. Hours: 8AM-Noon; 1PM-5PM (CST). *Misdemeanor, Civil Actions Under $2,500, Eviction, Small Claims.*

Chancery Court #1 Main St, PO Box 350, Charleston, MS 38921; 662-647-5551; Fax: 662-647-8490. Hours: 8AM-5PM (CST). *Probate.*

Chancery Court PO Box 180, Sumner, MS 38957; 662-375-8731; Fax: 662-375-7252. Hours: 8AM-Noon, 1-5PM (CST). *Probate.*

Tate County

Circuit Court 201 Ward St, Senatobia, MS 38668; 662-562-5211; Fax: 662-562-7486. Hours: 8AM-5PM (CST). *Felony, Civil Actions Over $2,500.*

Civil Records: Access: Mail, in person. Both court and visitors may perform in person searches. Search fee: $10.00 per name. Required to search: name, years to search. Civil cases indexed by defendant, plaintiff. Civil records on books since 1872.

Criminal Records: Access: Mail, in person. Both court and visitors may perform in person searches. Search fee: $10.00 per name. Required to search: name, years to search; also helpful: SSN. Criminal records on books since 1872.

General Information: No sealed, adoptions, mental health, juvenile, sex, or expunged records released.

SASE requested. Turnaround time same day. Copy fee: $.50 for first page, $.25 each add'l. Certification fee: $1.50. Fee payee: Circuit Clerk. Personal checks accepted. Prepayment is required.

Justice Court 111 Court St, Senatobia, MS 38668; 662-562-7626. Hours: 8AM-5PM (CST). *Misdemeanor, Civil Actions Under $2,500, Eviction, Small Claims.*

Chancery Court 201 Ward St, Senatobia, MS 38668; 662-562-5661; Fax: 662-562-7486. Hours: 8AM-5PM (CST). *Probate.*

Tippah County

Circuit Court Courthouse, Ripley, MS 38663; 662-837-7370; Fax: 662-837-1030. Hours: 8AM-5PM (CST). *Felony, Civil Actions Over $2,500.*

Civil Records: Access: Phone, fax, mail, in person. Both court and visitors may perform in person searches. Search fee: $5.00 per name. Required to search: name, years to search. Civil cases indexed by defendant. Civil records on docket books since 1800s.

Criminal Records: Access: Phone, fax, mail, in person. Both court and visitors may perform in person searches. Search fee: $5.00 per name. Required to search: name, years to search, DOB; also helpful: SSN. Criminal records on docket books since 1800s.

General Information: No sealed, adoptions, mental health, juvenile, sex or expunged records released. SASE not required. Turnaround time 1 week, phone turnaround time 30 minutes. Fax notes: $1.00 per page. Copy fee: $.50 per page. Fee payee: Circuit Clerk. Personal checks accepted. All fees may be billed.

Justice Court Justice Court, 205-B Spring Ave, Ripley, MS 38663; 662-837-8842; Fax: 662-837-1398. Hours: 8AM-5PM (CST). *Misdemeanor, Civil Actions Under $2,500, Eviction, Small Claims.*

Chancery Court PO Box 99, Ripley, MS 38663; 662-837-7374; Probate phone: 662-837-3607; Fax: 662-837-7148. Hours: 8AM-5PM (CST). *Probate.*

Tishomingo County

Circuit Court 1008 Battleground Dr, Iuka, MS 38852; 662-423-7026; Fax: 662-423-1667. Hours: 8AM-5PM (CST). *Felony, Civil Actions Over $2,500.*

Civil Records: Access: Mail, in person. Both court and visitors may perform in person searches. Search fee: $10.00 per name. Required to search: name, years to search. Civil cases indexed by defendant, plaintiff. Civil records on computer back to 2000, in docket books since 1950s, others in storage.

Criminal Records: Access: Mail, in person. Both court and visitors may perform in person searches. Search fee: $10.00 per name. Required to search: name, years to search, DOB; also helpful: SSN, signed release. Criminal records on computer back to 2000, in docket books since 1950s, others in storage.

General Information: Public access terminal is available. No sealed, adoptions, mental health, juvenile, sex, or expunged records released. SASE requested. Turnaround time 1-2 days. Copy fee: $.25 per page. Certification fee: $1.00. Fee payee: Circuit Clerk. Business checks accepted. Prepayment is required.

Justice Court - Northern & Southern Districts 1008 Battleground Drive, Room 212, Iuka, MS 38852; 662-423-7033; Fax: 662-423-7050. Hours: 8AM-5PM (CST). *Misdemeanor, Civil Actions Under $2,500, Eviction, Small Claims.*

Chancery Court 1008 Battleground Dr, Iuka, MS 38852; 662-423-7010; Fax: 662-423-7005. Hours: 8AM-5PM (CST). *Probate.*

Tunica County

Circuit Court PO Box 184, Tunica, MS 38676; 662-363-2842. Hours: 8AM-5PM (CST). *Felony, Civil Actions Over $2,500.*

Civil Records: Access: Mail, in person. Both court and visitors may perform in person searches. Search fee: $10.00 per name. Required to search: name, years to search. Civil cases indexed by defendant, plaintiff. Civil records on docket books for 10 years; archived prior.

Criminal Records: Access: Mail, in person. Both court and visitors may perform in person searches. Search fee: $10.00 per name. Required to search: name, years to search, DOB; also helpful: SSN. Criminal records on docket books for 10 years.

General Information: No sealed, adoptions, mental health, juvenile, sex, or expunged records released. SASE requested. Turnaround time 1 week. Copy fee: $.50 per page. Add postage. Certification fee: $1.50. Fee payee: Circuit Clerk. Personal checks accepted. Prepayment is required.

Justice Court 5130 Old Moon Landing, Tunica, MS 38676; 662-363-2178; Fax: 662-363-4234. Hours: 8AM-5PM (CST). *Misdemeanor, Civil Actions Under $2,500, Eviction, Small Claims.*

Chancery Court PO Box 217, Tunica, MS 38676; 662-363-2451; Fax: 662-357-5934. Hours: 8AM-Noon, 1-5PM (CST). *Probate.*

Union County

Circuit Court PO Box 298, New Albany, MS 38652; 662-534-1910; Fax: 662-534-2059. Hours: 8AM-5PM (CST). *Felony, Civil Actions Over $2,500.*

Civil Records: Access: Fax, mail, in person. Both court and visitors may perform in person searches. Search fee: $10.00 per name. Includes certification fee. Required to search: name, years to search, address. Civil cases indexed by defendant, plaintiff. Civil records on docket books since early 1900s.

Criminal Records: Access: Fax, mail, in person. Both court and visitors may perform in person searches. Search fee: $10.00 per name. Fee includes certification. Required to search: name, years to search, DOB; also helpful: SSN. Criminal records on docket books since early 1900s.

General Information: No adoptions, mental health or juvenile records released. SASE requested. Turnaround time 1 week. Fax notes: No fee to fax results. Copy fee: $.50 per page. Certification fee: $5.00. Fee payee: Union County Circuit Clerk. Personal checks accepted. Prepayment is required.

Justice Court - East & West Posts PO Box 27, New Albany, MS 38652; 662-534-1951; Fax: 662-534-1935. Hours: 8AM-5PM (CST). *Misdemeanor, Civil Actions Under $2,500, Eviction, Small Claims.*

Chancery Court PO Box 847, New Albany, MS 38652; 662-534-1900; Fax: 662-534-1907. Hours: 8AM-5PM (CST). *Probate.*

Walthall County

Circuit Court 200 Ball Ave, Tylertown, MS 39667; 601-876-5677; Fax: 601-876-4077. Hours: 8AM-Noon; 1-5PM (CST). *Felony, Civil Actions Over $2,500.*

Civil Records: Access: Mail, in person. Both court and visitors may perform in person searches. Search fee: $10.00 per name. Required to search: name, years to search. Civil cases indexed by defendant, plaintiff. Civil records on docket books since 1914.

Criminal Records: Access: Mail, in person. Both court and visitors may perform in person searches. Search fee: $10.00 per name. Required to search: name, years to search; also helpful: SSN. Criminal records on docket books since 1914.

General Information: No sealed, adoptions, mental health, juvenile, sex, or expunged records released. Turnaround time 1-2 days. Copy fee: $.25 per page. Certification fee: $1.50 plus $.50 per page. Fee payee: Circuit Clerk. Personal checks accepted. Prepayment is required.

Justice Court - Districts 1 & 2 PO Box 507, Tylertown, MS 39667; 601-876-2311. Hours: 8AM-5PM (CST). *Misdemeanor, Civil Actions Under $2,500, Eviction, Small Claims.*

Chancery Court PO Box 351, Tylertown, MS 39667; 601-876-3553; Fax: 601-876-6026. Hours: 8AM-5PM (CST). *Probate.*

Warren County

Circuit & County Court PO Box 351, Vicksburg, MS 39181; 601-636-3961; Fax: 601-630-4100. 8AM-5PM (CST). *Felony, Misdemeanor, Civil.*

Civil Records: Access: Mail, in person. Both court and visitors may perform in person searches. Search fee: $10.00 per name. Required to search: name, years to search. Civil cases indexed by defendant, plaintiff. Civil records on books since 1970s.

Criminal Records: Access: Mail, in person. Both court and visitors may perform in person searches. Search fee: $10.00 per name. Required to search: name, years to search; also helpful: DOB, SSN. Criminal records on books since 1970s.

General Information: No sealed or expunged records released. SASE required. Turnaround time 1 day. Copy fee: $1.00 per page. Certification fee: $5.00 per page. Fee payee: Circuit Clerk. Personal checks accepted. Prepayment is required.

Justice Court - Northern, Central & Southern Districts PO Box 1598, Vicksburg, MS 39181; 601-634-6402. Hours: 8AM-5PM (CST). *Misdemeanor, Civil Actions Under $2,500, Eviction, Small Claims.*

Chancery Court PO Box 351, Vicksburg, MS 39181; 601-636-4415; Fax: 601-630-8016. Hours: 8AM-5PM (CST). *Probate.*

Washington County

Circuit & County Court PO Box 1276, Greenville, MS 38702; 662-378-2747; Fax: 662-334-2698. Hours: 8AM-5PM (CST). *Felony, Misdemeanor, Civil.*

Civil Records: Access: Fax, mail, in person. Both court and visitors may perform in person searches. Search fee: $10.00 per name. Required to search: name, years to search. Civil cases indexed by defendant, plaintiff. Civil records on books since 1964.

Criminal Records: Access: Fax, mail, in person. Both court and visitors may perform in person searches. Search fee: $10.00 per name for 7 years, $1.00 each add'l year. Required to search: name, years to search; also helpful: DOB, SSN. Criminal records on books since 1964.

General Information: No sealed or expunged records released. SASE required. Turnaround time 5-10 days. Fax notes: No fee to fax results. Copy fee: $1.00 per page. Certification fee: $1.50. Fee payee: Circuit Clerk. Business checks accepted. Prepayment is required.

Justice Court - Districts 1-3 905 W Alexander, Greenville, MS 38701; 662-332-0633. Hours: 8AM-5PM (CST). *Misdemeanor, Civil Actions Under $2,500, Eviction, Small Claims.*

Chancery Court PO Box 309, Greenville, MS 38702-0309; 662-332-1595; Fax: 662-334-2725. Hours: 8AM-5PM (CST). *Probate.*

Wayne County

Circuit Court PO Box 428, Waynesboro, MS 39367; 601-735-1171; Fax: 601-735-6261. Hours: 8AM-5PM (CST). *Felony, Civil Actions Over $2,500.*

Note: This court is in process of computerizing their records.

Civil Records: Access: Phone, fax, mail, in person. Both court and visitors may perform in person searches. Search fee: $10.00 per name. Required to search: name, years to search. Civil cases indexed by defendant, plaintiff. Civil records on docket books since 1980, others in storage.

Criminal Records: Access: Fax, mail, in person. Both court and visitors may perform in person searches. Search fee: $10.00 per name. Required to search: name, years to search; also helpful: DOB, SSN, signed release. Criminal records on docket books since 1980, others in storage.

General Information: No sealed or expunged records released. Turnaround time 1-2 days. Fax notes: Fee to fax results is $1.00 per page. Copy fee: $.50 per page. Certification fee: $1.50. Fee payee: Circuit Clerk. Business checks accepted.

Justice Court - Posts 1 & 2 810 Chickasawhay St, #C, Waynesboro, MS 39367; 601-735-3118; Fax: 601-735-6266. *Misdemeanor, Civil Actions Under $2,500, Eviction, Small Claims.*

Chancery Court Courthouse, 609 Azalea Dr, Waynesboro, MS 39367; 601-735-2873; Fax: 601-735-6248. Hours: 8AM-5PM (CST). *Probate.*

Webster County

Circuit Court PO Box 308, Walthall, MS 39771; 662-258-6287; Fax: 662-258-7686. Hours: 8AM-5PM (CST). *Felony, Civil Actions Over $2,500.*

Civil Records: Access: Phone, fax, mail, in person. Both court and visitors may perform in person searches. Search fee: $10.00 per name. Required to search: name, years to search. Civil cases indexed by defendant, plaintiff. Civil records on docket books since 1874.

Criminal Records: Access: Fax, mail, in person. Both court and visitors may perform in person searches. Search fee: $10.00 per name. Required to search: name, years to search, DOB; also helpful: SSN. Criminal records on docket books since 1874.

General Information: Public access terminal is available. No sealed, adoptions, mental health, juvenile, sex, or expunged records released. Turnaround time 1-2 days. Fax notes: No fee to fax results. Copy fee: $.50 per page. Certification fee: $1.00. Fee payee: Circuit Clerk. Business checks accepted. Prepayment required.

Justice Court - Districts 1 & 2 114 Hwy 9 N, Eupora, MS 39744; 662-258-2590; Fax: 662-258-3093. Hours: 8AM-5PM (CST). *Misdemeanor, Civil Actions Under $2,500, Eviction, Small Claims.*

Chancery Court PO Box 398, Walthall, MS 39771; 662-258-4131; Fax: 662-258-6657. Hours: 8AM-5PM (CST). *Probate.*

Wilkinson County

Circuit Court PO Box 327, Woodville, MS 39669; 601-888-6697; Fax: 601-888-6984. Hours: 8:00AM-5:00PM (CST). *Felony, Civil Actions Over $2,500.*

Civil Records: Access: Mail, in person. Both court and visitors may perform in person searches. Search fee: $10.00 per name. Required to search: name, years to search. Civil cases indexed by defendant, plaintiff. Civil records on docket books since 1940s.

Criminal Records: Access: Mail, in person. Both court and visitors may perform in person searches. Search fee: $10.00 per name. Required to search: name, years

to search; also helpful: DOB, SSN. Criminal records on docket books since 1940s.

General Information: No sealed or expunged records released. Turnaround time 1-2 days. Copy fee: $.50 per page. Certification fee: $5.00. Fee payee: Circuit Clerk. Personal checks accepted. Prepayment is required.

Justice Court - East & West Districts PO Box 40, Woodville, MS 39669; 601-888-3538, 601-888-3972; Fax: 601-888-6776. Hours: 8AM-5PM (CST). *Misdemeanor, Civil Actions Under $2,500, Eviction, Small Claims.*

Chancery Court PO Box 516, Woodville, MS 39669; 601-888-4381; Fax: 601-888-6776. Hours: 8AM-5PM (CST). *Probate.*

Winston County

Circuit Court PO Drawer 785, Louisville, MS 39339; 662-773-3581; Fax: 662-773-8825. Hours: 8AM-5PM (CST). *Felony, Civil Actions Over $2,500.*

Civil Records: Access: Phone, fax, mail, in person. Both court and visitors may perform in person searches. Search fee: $10.00 per name. Required to search: name, years to search. Civil cases indexed by defendant, plaintiff. Civil records on docket books since early 1950s; on computer back to 1994.

Criminal Records: Access: Fax, mail, in person. Both court and visitors may perform in person searches. Search fee: $10.00 per name. Required to search: name, years to search, DOB; also helpful: SSN. Criminal records on docket books since early 1800s; on computer back to 1994.

General Information: No sealed, adoptions, mental health, juvenile or expunged records released. SASE requested. Turnaround time 14 days. Fax notes: $5.00 for first page, $1.00 each add'l. Copy fee: $1.00 per page. Certification fee: $1.50. Fee payee: Circuit Clerk. Personal checks accepted. Prepayment is required.

Justice Court PO Box 327, Louisville, MS 39339; 662-773-6016; Fax: 662-773-8817. Hours: 8AM-5PM (CST). *Misdemeanor, Civil Actions Under $2,500, Eviction, Small Claims.*

Chancery Court PO Drawer 69, Louisville, MS 39339; 662-773-3631; Fax: 662-773-8825. Hours: 8AM-5PM (CST). *Probate.*

Yalobusha County

Coffeeville Circuit Court PO Box 260, Coffeeville, MS 38922; 662-675-8187; Fax: 662-675-8004. Hours: 8AM-5PM (CST). *Felony, Civil Actions Over $2,500.*

Civil Records: Access: Phone, fax, mail, in person. Both court and visitors may perform in person searches. Search fee: $10.00 per name. May mail request with check or fax request with copy of check to be mailed. Required to search: name, years to search. Civil cases indexed by defendant, plaintiff. Civil records on docket books since 1930s.

Criminal Records: Access: Phone, fax, mail, in person. Both court and visitors may perform in person searches. Search fee: $10.00 per name. May mail request with check or fax request with copy of check to be mailed. Required to search: name, years to search; also helpful: DOB. Criminal records on docket books since 1930s.

General Information: No sealed, adoptions, mental health, juvenile, sex, or expunged records released. SASE requested. Turnaround time 1-2 days. Copy fee: $.25 per page. Certification fee: $10.00. Fee payee: Circuit Clerk. Personal checks accepted. Prepayment is required.

Water Valley Circuit Court PO Box 1431, Water Valley, MS 38965; 662-473-1341; Fax: 662-473-5020. Hours: 8AM-5PM (CST). *Felony, Civil Actions Over $2,500.*

Civil Records: Access: Fax, mail, in person. Both court and visitors may perform in person searches. Search fee: $10.00 per name. Includes certification fee. Required to search: name, years to search. Civil cases indexed by defendant, plaintiff. Civil records on docket books since 1930s.

Criminal Records: Access: Fax, mail, in person. Both court and visitors may perform in person searches. Search fee: $10.00 per name. Fee includes certification. Required to search: name, years to search, DOB; also helpful: SSN. Criminal records on docket books since 1930s.

General Information: No sealed, adoptions, mental health, juvenile, sex, or expunged records released. Turnaround time 1 week. Fax notes: No fee to fax results. Copy fee: $.50 per page. Certification fee: $10.00 per docket. Fee payee: Circuit Clerk. Personal checks accepted.

Justice Court - District 1 PO Box 218, Coffeeville, MS 38922; 662-675-8115; Fax: 662-675-8452. Hours: 8AM-5PM (CST). *Misdemeanor, Civil Actions Under $2,500, Eviction, Small Claims.*

Justice Court - Division 2 PO Box 918, Water Valley, MS 38965; 662-473-4502. Hours: 8AM-5PM (CST). *Misdemeanor, Civil Actions Under $2,500, Eviction, Small Claims.*

Chancery Court PO Box 664, Water Valley, MS 38965; 662-473-2091; Fax: 662-473-5020. Hours: 8AM-5PM (CST). *Probate.*

Chancery Court PO Box 260, Coffeeville, MS 38922; 662-675-2716; Fax: 662-675-8004. Hours: 8AM-Noon, 1-5PM (CST). *Probate.*

Yazoo County

Circuit & County Court PO Box 108, Yazoo City, MS 39194; 662-746-1872. Hours: 8AM-5PM (CST). *Felony, Misdemeanor, Civil.*

Civil Records: Access: Mail, in person. Both court and visitors may perform in person searches. Search fee: $10.00 per name. Required to search: name, years to search. Civil cases indexed by defendant, plaintiff. Civil records for Civil Circuit on docket books since 1973; for Civil County on docket books since 1977.

Criminal Records: Access: Mail, in person. Both court and visitors may perform in person searches. Search fee: $10.00 per name. Required to search: name, years to search, DOB; also helpful: SSN. Criminal records for Criminal Circuit from 1975; Criminal County on docket books since 1975.

General Information: No sealed, adoptions, mental health, juvenile, sex, or expunged records released. SASE required. Turnaround time 1 day. Copy fee: $.50 per page. Certification fee: $1.00. Fee payee: Circuit Clerk. Business checks accepted. Prepayment is required.

Justice Court - Northern & Southern Districts PO Box 798, Yazoo City, MS 39194; 662-746-8181; Fax: 662-746-2186. Hours: 8AM-5PM (CST). *Misdemeanor, Civil Actions Under $2,500, Eviction, Small Claims.*

Chancery Court PO Box 68, Yazoo City, MS 39194; 662-746-2661; Fax: 662-746-3893. Hours: 8AM-5PM (CST). *Probate.*

Mississippi Recording Offices

ORGANIZATION: 82 counties, 92 recording offices. The recording officers are Chancery Clerk and Clerk of Circuit Court (state tax liens). Ten counties have two separate recording offices - Bolivar, Carroll, Chickasaw, Craighead, Harrison, Hinds, Jasper, Jones, Panola, Tallahatchie, and Yalobusha. See the notes under each county for how to determine which office is appropriate to search. The entire state is in the Central Time Zone (CST).

REAL ESTATE RECORDS: A few counties will perform real estate searches. Copies usually cost $.50 per page and certification fees $1.00 per document. The Assessor maintains tax records.

UCC RECORDS: This was a dual filing state. Until 07/2001, financing statements were filed both at the state level and with the Chancery Clerk, except for consumer goods, farm related and real estate related filings, which were filed only with the Chancery Clerk. Now, only real estate related filings are filed at the county level. Nearly all counties will perform UCC searches. Use search request form UCC-11. Search fees are usually $5.00 per debtor name. Copy fees vary from $.25 to $2.00 per page.

TAX LIEN RECORDS: Federal tax liens on personal property of businesses are filed with the Secretary of State. Federal tax liens on personal property of individuals are filed with the county Chancery Clerk. State tax liens on personal property are filed with the county Clerk of Circuit Court. Refer to the County Court section for information about Mississippi Circuit Courts. State tax liens on real property are filed with the Chancery Clerk. Most Chancery Clerk offices will perform a federal tax lien search for a fee of $5.00 per name. Copy fees vary.

OTHER LIENS: Mechanics, lis pendens, judgment (Circuit Court), construction.

ONLINE ACCESS: A limited number of counties offer online access to records, there is no statewide system except for the Secretary of State's UCC access – see State Agencies section.

Adams County

Chancery Clerk, PO Box 1006, Natchez, MS 39121. Chancery Clerk, R/E and UCC Recording 601-446-6684; Fax 601-445-7913.
Will search UCC records. Will not search real estate records. **Other Phone Numbers:** Assessor 601-442-6732; Elections 601-446-6326.

Alcorn County

Chancery Clerk, PO Box 69, Corinth, MS 38835-0069. Chancery Clerk, R/E and UCC Recording 662-286-7700; Fax 662-286-7706.
Will search UCC records. Will not search real estate records. **Online Access:** Property Tax, Appraisal Records. Access is available free at www.deltacomputersystems.com/MS/MS02/index.html. **Other Phones:** Assessor 662-286-7733; Elections 662-286-7740.

Amite County

Chancery Clerk, PO Box 680, Liberty, MS 39645-0680. 601-657-8022; Fax 601-657-8288.
Will search UCC records. Will not search real estate records. **Other Phones:** Assessor 601-657-8973; Treasurer 601-657-8932; Elections 601-657-8932.

Attala County

Chancery Clerk, Chancery Court Bldg., 230 W. Washington St., Kosciusko, MS 39090. 662-289-2921; Fax 662-289-7662.
Will search UCC records. Will not search real estate records. **Other Phone Numbers:** Assessor 662-289-5731; Elections 662-289-1471.

Benton County

Chancery Clerk, PO Box 218, Ashland, MS 38603. 662-224-6300; Fax 662-224-6303.
Will search UCC records. Will not search real estate records. **Other Phone Numbers:** Assessor 662-224-6315; Elections 662-224-6310.

Bolivar County (1st District)

Chancery Clerk, PO Box 238, Rosedale, MS 38769-0238. 662-759-3762; Fax 662-759-3467.
Will search UCC records. Will not search real estate records. **Other Phones:** Assessor 662-843-3826; Treasurer 662-843-2531; Elections 662-843-2061.

Bolivar County (2nd District)

Chancery Clerk, PO Box 789, Cleveland, MS 38732. Chancery Clerk, R/E and UCC Recording 662-843-2071; Fax 662-846-2940.
Will search UCC records prior to 1/2002. Will not search real estate records. **Other Phone Numbers:** Assessor 662-843-3926; Treasurer 662-843-2071; Elections 662-843-2061.

Calhoun County

Chancery Clerk, PO Box 8, Pittsboro, MS 38951. Chancery Clerk, R/E and UCC Recording 662-412-3117 UCC Recording: 662-412-3121; Fax 662-412-3128.
Will search UCC records. This agency will not do a federal tax lien search. Will not search real estate records. **Other Phones:** Assessor 662-412-3140; Treasurer 662-412-3117; Appraiser/Auditor 662-412-3146; Elections 662-412-3101; Vital Records 662-412-3101.

Carroll County (1st District)

Chancery Clerk, PO Box 60, Carrollton, MS 38917. 662-237-9274; Fax 662-237-9642.
Will search UCC records. Will not search real estate records. **Other Phone Numbers:** Assessor 662-237-9217; Elections 662-464-5476.

Carroll County (2nd District)

Chancery Clerk, PO Box 6, Vaiden, MS 39176. 662-464-5476; Fax 662-464-5407.
The 2nd district is split by section, township and range. Will not search UCC records. This agency will not do a federal tax lien search. Will not search real estate records. **Other Phone Numbers:** Assessor 662-464-8852; Elections 662-464-5476.

Chickasaw County (1st District)

Chancery Clerk, Courthouse, Houston, MS 38851. 662-456-2513; Fax 662-456-5295.
Will search UCC records. Will not search real estate records. **Other Phones:** Assessor 662-456-3327; Treasurer 662-456-3941; Elections 662-456-2331.

Chickasaw County (2nd District)

Chancery Clerk, 234 Main St, Room 201, Okolona, MS 38860-1438. 662-447-2092; Fax 662-447-5024.
Will search UCC records. Will not search real estate records. **Other Phones:** Assessor 662-447-2242; Treasurer 662-456-2513; Elections 662-456-2331.

Choctaw County

Chancery Clerk, PO Box 250, Ackerman, MS 39735-0250. 662-285-6329; Fax 662-285-3444.
Will search UCC records. Will not search real estate records. **Other Phone Numbers:** Assessor 662-285-6320; Elections 662-285-6245.

Claiborne County

Chancery Clerk, PO Box 449, Port Gibson, MS 39150. Chancery Clerk, R/E and UCC Recording 601-437-4992; Fax 601-437-3731.
Will search UCC records. UCC search includes federal tax liens if requested. Will not search real estate records. **Other Phone Numbers:** Assessor 601-437-5591; Treasurer 601-437-4992; Appraiser/Auditor 601-437-5591; Elections 601-437-5841.

Clarke County

Chancery Clerk, PO Box 689, Quitman, MS 39355. Chancery Clerk, R/E and UCC Recording 601-776-2126; Fax 601-776-1001.
Will search UCC records. This agency will not do a federal tax lien search. Will not search real estate records. **Other Phone Numbers:** Assessor 601-776-6931; Treasurer 601-776-2126; Appraiser/Auditor 601-776-1021; Elections 601-776-3111.

Clay County

Chancery Clerk, PO Box 815, West Point, MS 39773. Chancery Clerk, R/E and UCC Recording 662-494-3124.
Will search UCC records prior to 1/2002. UCC search does not include federal tax liens. Will not search real estate records. **Other Phone Numbers:** Assessor 662-494-3432; Appraiser/Auditor 662-494-3432; Elections 662-494-3384.

Coahoma County

Chancery Clerk, PO Box 98, Clarksdale, MS 38614. Chancery Clerk, R/E and UCC Recording 662-624-3000; Fax 662-624-3040.
Will search UCC records. Will not search real estate records. **Other Phone Numbers:** Assessor 662-624-3006; Treasurer 662-624-3020; Elections 662-624-3014; Vital Records 662-624-3014.

Copiah County

Chancery Clerk, PO Box 507, Hazlehurst, MS 39083-0507. 601-894-3021; Fax 601-894-3026.
Will search UCC records. **Other Phone Numbers:** Assessor 601-894-2721; Elections 601-894-1241.

Covington County

Chancery Clerk, PO Box 1679, Collins, MS 39428. 601-765-4242; Fax 601-765-5016.
Will search UCC records. UCC search includes federal tax liens. Will not search real estate records. **Other Phones:** Assessor 601-756-6402; Elections 765-6506.

De Soto County

Chancery Clerk, PO Box 949, Hernando, MS 38632. Chancery Clerk, R/E and UCC Recording 662-429-1318.
Will search UCC records. UCC search does not include federal tax liens. Will not search real estate records. **Other Phone Numbers:** Assessor 662-429-1335; Elections 662-429-1325.

Forrest County

Chancery Clerk, PO Box 951, Hattiesburg, MS 39401. 601-545-6014; Fax 601-545-6095.
Will search UCC records. Will not search real estate records. **Other Phone Numbers:** Assessor 601-582-8228; Elections 601-582-3213.

Franklin County

Chancery Clerk, PO Box 297, Meadville, MS 39653-0297. 601-384-2330; Fax 601-384-5864.
Will search UCC records. **Other Phone Numbers:** Assessor 601-384-2359; Elections 601-384-2320; Tax Collector 601-384-2359.

George County

Chancery Clerk, 355 Cox St, Lucedale, MS 39452. Chancery Clerk, R/E and UCC Recording 601-947-4801; Fax 601-947-1300.
Will search UCC records. UCC search includes federal tax liens if requested. Will not search real estate records. **Other Phone Numbers:** Assessor 601-947-7541; Treasurer 601-947-3766; Appraiser/Auditor 601-947-7541; Elections 601-947-4881.

Greene County

Chancery Clerk, PO Box 610, Leakesville, MS 39451. 601-394-2377.
Will search UCC records. UCC search includes federal tax liens if requested. Real estate owner, mortgage, and property transfer searches available. **Other Phone Numbers:** Assessor 601-394-2377; Treasurer 601-394-2377; Elections 601-394-2379.

Grenada County

Chancery Clerk, PO Drawer 1208, Grenada, MS 38902-1208. 662-226-1821; Fax 662-226-0427.
Will not search UCC records. This agency will not do a federal tax lien search. Will not search real estate records. **Other Phones:** Treasurer 662-226-1741; Elections 662-226-1941; Tax Collector 662-226-1741.

Hancock County

Chancery Clerk, PO Box 429, Bay Saint Louis, MS 39520. Chancery Clerk, R/E and UCC Recording 228-467-5404 UCC Recording: 228-467-2252; Fax 228-467-3159.
Will search UCC records. Will not search real estate records. **Other Phone Numbers:** Assessor 228-467-5727; Treasurer 228-467-4425; Appraiser/Auditor 228-467-0130; Elections 228-467-5265; Tax Collector 228-467-4425.

Harrison County (1st District)

Chancery Clerk, PO Drawer CC, Gulfport, MS 39502. 228-865-4195 R/E Recording: 228-865-4036; Fax 228-868-1480.
Will search UCC records. Will not search real estate records. **Online Access:** Property, Deed, Recording, UCC, Tax Sales Records. Access is available free at www.deltacomputersystems.com/MS/MS24DELTA/DATALINK.html. Also, search the delinquent tax sales list for free at www.co.harrison.ms.us/departments/chancery/delinquent.html. **Other Phone Numbers:** Assessor 228-865-4043; Treasurer 228-865-4040; Appraiser/Auditor 228-865-4044; Elections 228-865-4049; Vital Records 228-960-7400.

Harrison County (2nd District)

Chancery Clerk, PO Box 544, Biloxi, MS 39533. 228-435-8220; Fax 228-435-8292.
Will search UCC records. Will not search real estate records. **Online Access:** Property, Deed, Recording, UCC, Tax Sales Records. Access is available free at www.deltacomputersystems.com/MS/MS24DELTA/DATALINK.html. Also, search the delinquent tax sales list for free at www.co.harrison.ms.us/departments/chancery/delinquent.html. **Other Phones:** Assessor 228-435-8265; Elections 228-865-4167.

Hinds County (1st District)

Chancery Clerk, PO Box 686, Jackson, MS 39205-0686. 601-968-6516 R/E Recording: 601-968-6508; Fax 601-973-5535. www.co.hinds.ms.us/pgs/elected/chanceryclerk.asp
Will search UCC records. Will not search real estate records. **Online Access:** Real Estate, Grantor/Grantee, Judgment, Lien, Assessor, Condominium, Acreage Records. Access to the county records databases are available free at www.co.hinds.ms.us/pgs/apps/gindex.asp. Also, search the assessor landrolls for free at www.co.hinds.ms.us/pgs/apps/landroll_query.asp.
Other Phone Numbers: Treasurer 601-968-6588; Elections 601-968-6628; Tax Collector 601-968-6588.

Hinds County (2nd District)

Chancery Clerk, PO Box 88, Raymond, MS 39154. 601-857-8055; www.co.hinds.ms.us
The 2nd District consists of all towns/cities outside the limits of Jackson, including Bolton, part of Clinton, Edwards, Learned, Raymond, part of Terry, and Utica. Will search UCC records. UCC search does not include federal tax liens. Will not search real estate records. **Online Access:** Real Estate, Assessor, Grantor/Grantee, Judgment Records. Access to the county clerk database is available free at www.co.hinds.ms.us/pgs/apps/gindex.asp. Chose to search general index, landroll, judgments, acreage, subdivision, condominiums. **Other Phone Numbers:** Assessor

601-857-8787; Treasurer 601-857-5574; Elections 601-968-6628; Tax Collector 601-857-5574.

Holmes County

Chancery Clerk, PO Box 239, Lexington, MS 39095. 662-834-2508 R/E Recording: 662-834-0005 UCC Recording: 662-834-0005; Fax 662-834-3020.
Will search UCC records. Will not search real estate records. **Other Phones:** Assessor 662-834-2865; Treasurer 662-834-0005; Appraiser/Auditor 662-834-3737; Elections 834-2476; Vital Records 834-2476.

Humphreys County

Chancery Clerk, PO Box 547, Belzoni, MS 39038. 662-247-1740; Fax 662-247-0101.
Will search UCC records. UCC search includes federal tax liens if requested. Mortgage and property transfer searches available. **Other Phones:** Assessor 662-247-3174; Treasurer 662-247-2552; Appraiser/Auditor 662-247-0106; Elections 662-247-3065; Tax Collector 662-247-2552.

Issaquena County

Chancery Clerk, PO Box 27, Mayersville, MS 39113-0027. Chancery Clerk, R/E and UCC Recording 662-873-2761; Fax 662-873-2061.
Will search UCC records. **Other Phones:** Assessor 662-873-4665; Treasurer 662-873-2761; Elections 662-873-2761; Marriages/Divorces 662-873-2761.

Itawamba County

Chancery Clerk, PO Box 776, Fulton, MS 38843. Chancery Clerk, R/E and UCC Recording 662-862-3421; Fax 662-862-3421.
Will search UCC records. Will not search real estate records. **Other Phone Numbers:** Assessor 662-862-7598; Appraiser/Auditor 662-862-7598; Elections 662-862-3511; Vital Records 662-862-3511.

Jackson County

Chancery Clerk, PO Box 998, Pascagoula, MS 39568. 228-769-3131; Fax 228-769-3135.
Will search UCC records. Will not search real estate records. **Other Phones:** Assessor 228-769-3070; Treasurer 228-769-3131; Elections 228-769-3040.

Jasper County (1st District)

Chancery Clerk, PO Box 38, Paulding, MS 39348-0038. 601-727-4941; Fax 601-727-4475.
Will search UCC records. This agency will not do a federal tax lien search. Will not search real estate records. **Other Phone Numbers:** Assessor 601-764-2813; Elections 601-764-2245.

Jasper County (2nd District)

Chancery Clerk, PO Box 1047, Bay Springs, MS 39422. 601-764-3026; Fax 601-764-3999.
Will search UCC records. Will not search real estate records. **Other Phones:** Assessor 601-764-2813; Treasurer 601-764-3469; Elections 601-764-2245.

Jefferson County

Chancery Clerk, PO Box 145, Fayette, MS 39069. Chancery Clerk, R/E and UCC Recording 601-786-3021 UCC Recording: 601-359-1350; Fax 601-786-6009.
Will search UCC records. Will not search real estate records. **Other Phone Numbers:** Assessor 601-786-3781; Appraiser/Auditor 601-786-3781; Elections 601-786-3422; Tax Collector 601-786-3781.

Jefferson Davis County

Chancery Clerk, PO Box 1137, Prentiss, MS 39474. 601-792-4204; Fax 601-792-2894.
Will search UCC records. Will not search real estate records. **Other Phones:** Assessor 601-792-4291; Treasurer 601-792-4204; Elections 601-792-4231.

Jones County (1st District)

Chancery Clerk, Court St, Jones County Courthouse, Ellisville, MS 39437. 601-477-3307.
Will search UCC records. This agency will not do a federal tax lien search. Will not search real estate records. **Other Phone Numbers:** Assessor 601-477-3250; Elections 601-425-2556.

Jones County (2nd District)

Chancery Clerk, PO Box 1468, Laurel, MS 39441. Chancery Clerk, R/E and UCC Recording 601-428-0527 UCC Recording: 601-428-3131; Fax 601-428-3602.
Will search UCC records. Will not search real estate records. **Other Phones:** Assessor 601-428-3248; Treasurer 501-428-3128; Appraiser: 601-649-1896; Elections 601-425-2556; Vital Records 601-576-7981.

Kemper County

Chancery Clerk, PO Box 188, De Kalb, MS 39328. Chancery Clerk, R/E and UCC Recording 601-743-2460; Fax 601-743-2789.
Will search UCC records. Will not search real estate records. **Other Phones:** Assessor 601-743-2693; Treasurer 601-743-4290; Appraiser/Auditor 601-743-2693; Elections 743-2224; Vital Records 743-2224.

Lafayette County

Chancery Clerk, PO Box 1240, Oxford, MS 38655. Chancery Clerk, R/E and UCC Recording 662-234-2131; Fax 662-234-5402.
Will search UCC records. This agency will not do a federal tax lien search. Will not search real estate records. **Other Phones:** Assessor 662-234-6006; Appraiser/Auditor 234-5562; Elections 234-4951.

Lamar County

Chancery Clerk, PO Box 247, Purvis, MS 39475. 601-794-8504; Fax 601-794-3903.
Will search UCC records. Will not search real estate records. **Online Access:** Property Tax, Appraisal Records. Access is available free at www.deltacomputersystems.com/MS/MS37/INDEX.html.
Other Phone Numbers: Elections 601-794-8504.

Lauderdale County

Chancery Clerk, PO Box 1587, Meridian, MS 39302-1587. 601-482-9701.
Will search UCC records. UCC search includes federal tax liens if requested. Will not search real estate records. **Online Access:** Property Tax, Appraisal Records. Access is available free at www.deltacomputersystems.com/MS/MS38/INDEX.html. **Other Phone Numbers:** Assessor 601-482-9779; Treasurer 601-482-4701; Elections 601-482-9731.

Lawrence County

Chancery Clerk, PO Box 821, Monticello, MS 39654. Chancery Clerk, R/E and UCC Recording 601-587-7162; Fax 601-587-0767.
Will search UCC records. Will not search real estate records. **Other Phones:** Treasurer 601-587-2211; Elections 601-587-4791; Tax Collector 601-587-2211.

Leake County

Chancery Clerk, PO Box 72, Carthage, MS 39051. 601-267-7371; Fax 601-267-6137.
Will search UCC records. Will not search real estate records. **Other Phones:** Assessor 601-267-3021; Treasurer 601-267-7371; Elections 601-267-8357.

Lee County

Chancery Clerk, PO Box 7127, Tupelo, MS 38802. 662-841-9100; Fax 662-680-6091.
Will search UCC records. Will not search real estate records. **Online Access:** Property Tax, Appraisal

Records. Access is available free at www.deltacomputersystems.com/MS/MS41/INDEX.html. **Other Phone Numbers:** Assessor 662-841-9030; Treasurer 662-841-9100; Elections 662-841-9024.

Leflore County

Chancery Clerk, PO Box 250, Greenwood, MS 38935-0250. 662-455-7913; Fax 662-455-7965.
Will search UCC records. Will not search real estate records. **Other Phone Numbers:** Assessor 662-453-1041; Elections 662-453-1435.

Lincoln County

Chancery Clerk, PO Box 555, Brookhaven, MS 39602. 601-835-3416.
Will search UCC records. UCC search includes federal tax liens if requested. Will not search real estate records. **Other Phone Numbers:** Assessor 601-835-3428; Treasurer 601-835-3412; Elections 601-835-3435.

Lowndes County

Chancery Clerk, PO Box 684, Columbus, MS 39703. 662-329-5800 R/E Recording: 662-329-5809 or 5806 UCC Recording: 662-329-5807.
Will search UCC records. UCC search does not include federal tax liens. Will not search real estate records. **Other Phone Numbers:** Assessor 662-329-5700; Treasurer 662-329-5700; Appraiser/Auditor 662-329-5701; Elections 662-329-5900.

Madison County

Chancery Clerk, PO Box 404, Canton, MS 39046. 601-859-1177; http://mcatax.com
Will search UCC records. UCC search does not include federal tax liens. Will not search real estate records. **Online Access:** Real Estate, Tax Assessor Records. Records from the county Assessor office are available free online. At www.mcatax.com/mcasearch.asp, click on "Search The Database." Records include parcel number, address, legal description, value information, and tax district. **Other Phone Numbers:** Assessor 601-859-1921; Elections 601-352-2049.

Marion County

Chancery Clerk, 250 Broad St, Suite 2, Columbia, MS 39429. Chancery Clerk, R/E and UCC Recording 601-736-2691; Fax 601-736-1232.
Will search UCC records. **Other Phone Numbers:** Assessor 601-736-8256; Elections 601-736-8246.

Marshall County

Chancery Clerk, PO Box 219, Holly Springs, MS 38635. 662-252-4431; Fax 662-252-0004.
Will search UCC records. Will not search real estate records. **Online Access:** Property Tax, Appraisal Records. Access is available free at www.deltacomputersystems.com/MS/MS47/INDEX.html. **Other Phone Numbers:** Assessor 662-252-3661; Elections 662-252-3434.

Monroe County

Chancery Clerk, PO Box 578, Aberdeen, MS 39730. 662-369-8143; Fax 662-369-7928.
Will search UCC records. Will not search real estate records. **Other Phones:** Assessor 662-369-2033; Treasurer 662-369-8143; Elections 662-369-8695.

Montgomery County

Chancery Clerk, PO Box 71, Winona, MS 38967. 662-283-2333; Fax 662-283-2233.
Will search UCC records. Will not search real estate records. **Other Phone Numbers:** Assessor 662-283-2112; Elections 662-283-4161.

Neshoba County

Chancery Clerk, 401 Beacon St, Suite 107, Philadelphia, MS 39350. 601-656-3581.

Will search UCC records. This agency will not do a federal tax lien search. Will not search real estate records. **Other Phones:** Elections 601-656-4781.

Newton County

Chancery Clerk, PO Box 68, Decatur, MS 39327. 601-635-2367; Fax 601-635-3210.
Will search UCC records. Will not search real estate records. **Other Phone Numbers:** Assessor 601-635-2367; Elections 601-635-2368.

Noxubee County

Chancery Clerk, PO Box 147, Macon, MS 39341. Chancery Clerk, R/E and UCC Recording 662-726-4243; Fax 662-726-2272.
Will search UCC records. UCC search does not include federal tax liens. Will not search real estate records. **Other Phone Numbers:** Assessor 662-726-4744; Elections 662-726-5737.

Oktibbeha County

Chancery Clerk, 101 E. Main, Courthouse, Starkville, MS 39759. Chancery Clerk, R/E and UCC Recording 662-323-5834; Fax 662-338-1064.
Will search UCC records. This agency will not do a tax lien search. Will not search real estate records. **Other Phones:** Assessor 662-323-1273; Appraiser/Auditor 662-323-1273; Elections 662-323-1356.

Panola County (1st District)

Chancery Clerk, PO Box 130, Sardis, MS 38666. 662-487-2070; Fax 662-487-3595.
Will search UCC records. Will not search real estate records. **Other Phones:** Assessor 662-487-2093; Treasurer 662-487-6215; Tax Collector 662-487-6215.

Panola County (2nd District)

Chancery Clerk, 151 Public Square, Batesville, MS 38606. 662-563-6205; Fax 662-563-8233.
Will search UCC records. Will not search real estate records. **Other Phones:** Assessor 662-563-6270; Treasurer 662-563-6215; Elections 662-563-6210.

Pearl River County

Chancery Clerk, PO Box 431, Poplarville, MS 39470. 601-795-2237; Fax 601-795-3093.
This agency will not search real estate or UCC records. **Online Access:** Property Tax, Appraiser Records. Access is available free at www.deltacomputersystems.com/MS/MS55/INDEX.html. **Other Phones:** Assessor 601-795-4081; Elections 601-795-4911.

Perry County

Chancery Clerk, PO Box 198, New Augusta, MS 39462. Chancery Clerk, R/E and UCC Recording 601-964-8398; Fax 601-964-8265.
Will search UCC records. **Other Phone Numbers:** Assessor 601-964-3398; Appraiser/Auditor 601-964-3400; Elections 601-964-8663.

Pike County

Chancery Clerk, PO Box 309, Magnolia, MS 39652. 601-783-3362; Fax 601-783-2001.
Will search UCC records. Will not search real estate records. **Other Phone Numbers:** Assessor 601-783-5511; Elections 601-783-2581.

Pontotoc County

Chancery Clerk, PO Box 209, Pontotoc, MS 38863. 662-489-3900.
Will search UCC records. UCC search does not include federal tax liens. Will not search real estate records. **Other Phones:** Assessor 662-489-3903; Treasurer 662-489-3904; Appraiser/Auditor 662-489-3903; Elections 662-489-3908; Tax Collector 662-489-3904.

Prentiss County

Chancery Clerk, PO Box 477, Booneville, MS 38829. Chancery Clerk, R/E and UCC Recording 662-728-8151; Fax 662-728-2007.
Will search UCC records. Will not search real estate records. **Other Phone Numbers:** Assessor 662-728-5044; Treasurer 662-728-8151; Appraiser/Auditor 662-728-4349; Elections 662-728-4611.

Quitman County

Chancery Clerk, Chestnut St, Courthouse, Marks, MS 38646. Chancery Clerk, R/E and UCC Recording 662-326-2661; Fax 662-326-8004.
Will search UCC records. Will not search real estate records. **Other Phone Numbers:** Assessor 662-326-8928; Treasurer 662-326-2661; Appraiser/Auditor 662-326-8928; Elections 662-326-8003.

Rankin County

Chancery Clerk, PO Box 700, Brandon, MS 39043. 601-825-1469; Fax 601-824-7116. www.rankincounty.org
Will search UCC records. Will not search real estate records. **Online Access:** Real Estate, Tax Assessor Records. Records on the county Land Roll database are at www.rankincounty.org/TA/interact_LandRoll.asp. **Other Phone Numbers:** Assessor 601-825-1470; Treasurer 601-825-1366; Elections 601-825-1466.

Scott County

Chancery Clerk, PO Box 630, Forest, MS 39074. 601-469-1922; Fax 601-469-5180.
Will search UCC records. Will not search real estate records. **Other Phone Numbers:** Elections 601-469-3601; Tax Collector 601-469-4051.

Sharkey County

Chancery Clerk, PO Box 218, Rolling Fork, MS 39159. 662-873-2755; Fax 662-873-6045.
Will search UCC records. Will search tax liens-$5.00 per name. Will not search real estate records. **Other Phone Numbers:** Elections 662-873-2755; Tax Collector 662-873-4317.

Simpson County

Chancery Clerk, PO Box 367, Mendenhall, MS 39114. 601-847-2626 R/E Recording: 601-847-2624; Fax 601-847-7016.
Will search UCC records. Will not search real estate records. **Other Phone Numbers:** Assessor 601-847-1744; Elections 601-847-2474.

Smith County

Chancery Clerk, PO Box 39, Raleigh, MS 39153. 601-782-9811; Fax 601-782-4690.
Will search UCC records. Will not search real estate records. **Other Phones:** Assessor 601-782-9803; Treasurer 601-782-9811; Elections 601-782-4751.

Stone County

Chancery Clerk, PO Drawer 7, Wiggins, MS 39577. 601-928-5266; Fax 601-928-5248.
Will search UCC records. Will not search real estate records. **Other Phones:** Assessor 601-928-3121; Treasurer 601-928-5266; Elections 601-928-5246.

Sunflower County

Chancery Clerk, PO Box 988, Indianola, MS 38751-0988. Chancery Clerk, R/E and UCC Recording 662-887-4703; Fax 662-887-7054.
Will search UCC records. Will not search real estate records. **Other Phone Numbers:** Assessor 662-887-1454; Treasurer 662-887-4703; Appraiser/Auditor 662-887-1454; Elections 662-887-1252; Vital Records 662-887-1252.

Tallahatchie County (1st District)

Chancery Clerk, PO Box 350, Charleston, MS 38921. Chancery Clerk, R/E and UCC Recording 662-647-5551; Fax 662-647-8490.
Will search UCC records. This agency will not do a federal tax lien search. Will not search real estate records. **Other Phone Numbers:** Assessor 662-647-8922; Elections 662-647-8758.

Tallahatchie County (2nd District)

Chancery Clerk, PO Box 180, Sumner, MS 38957. Chancery Clerk, R/E and UCC Recording 662-375-8731; Fax 662-375-7252.
Will search UCC records. UCC search does not include federal tax liens. Will not search real estate records. **Other Phone Numbers:** Assessor 662-375-8386; Elections 662-375-8515.

Tate County

Chancery Clerk, 201 Ward St, Senatobia, MS 38668. Chancery Clerk, R/E and UCC Recording 662-562-5661; Fax 662-560-6205.
Will search UCC records. Will not search real estate records. **Other Phone Numbers:** Assessor 662-562-6011; Elections 662-562-5211.

Tippah County

Chancery Clerk, PO Box 99, Ripley, MS 38663. 662-837-7374; Fax 662-837-1030.
Will search UCC records. Will not search real estate records. **Other Phone Numbers:** Assessor 662-837-9410; Elections 662-837-7370.

Tishomingo County

Chancery Clerk, 1008 Battleground Dr., Courthouse, Iuka, MS 38852. 662-423-7010; Fax 662-423-7005.
Will search UCC records. Will not search real estate records. **Other Phone Numbers:** Assessor 662-423-7048; Treasurer 662-423-7032; Elections 662-423-7026.

Tunica County

Chancery Clerk, PO Box 217, Tunica, MS 38676. 662-363-2451.
Will search UCC records. UCC search includes federal tax liens if requested. Real estate owner, mortgage, and property transfer searches available. **Other Phone Numbers:** Assessor 662-363-1266; Treasurer 662-363-1465; Elections 662-363-2842.

Union County

Chancery Clerk, PO Box 847, New Albany, MS 38652. Chancery Clerk, R/E and UCC Recording 662-534-1900; Fax 662-534-1907.
Will search UCC records. Will not search real estate records. **Other Phone Numbers:** Assessor 662-534-1972; Treasurer 662-534-1973; Elections 662-534-1910; Tax Collector 662-534-1973.

Walthall County

Chancery Clerk, PO Box 351, Tylertown, MS 39667. Chancery Clerk, R/E and UCC Recording 601-876-3553; Fax 601-876-6026.
Will search UCC records. Will not search real estate records. **Other Phones:** Assessor 601-876-4349; Appraiser/Auditor 876-4349; Elections 601-876-5677.

Warren County

Chancery Clerk, PO Box 351, Vicksburg, MS 39181. Chancery Clerk, R/E and UCC Recording 601-636-4415; Fax 601-634-4815. www.co.warren.ms.us
Will search UCC records. Will not search real estate records. **Online Access:** Property Tax, Appraisal Records. Access is available free at www.deltacomputersystems.com/MS/MS75/INDEX.html. **Other Phones:** Assessor 601-638-6161; Treasurer

601-638-6181; Appraiser/Auditor 601-638-6161; Elections 601-636-3961; Tax Collector 601-638-6181.

Washington County

Chancery Clerk, PO Box 309, Greenville, MS 38702-0309. Chancery Clerk, R/E and UCC Recording 662-332-1595; Fax 662-334-2725.
Will search UCC records. UCC search includes federal tax liens if requested. Will not search real estate records. **Online Access:** Property Tax, Appraisal Records. Access is free at www.deltacomputersystems.com/MS/MS76/INDEX.html. **Other Phones:** Assessor 662-332-2651; Treasurer 662-332-2922; Appraiser/Auditor 662-332-2651; Elections 662-378-2747.

Wayne County

Chancery Clerk, Wayne Co. Courthouse, 609 Azalea Dr., Waynesboro, MS 39367. Chancery Clerk, R/E and UCC Recording 601-735-2873; Fax 601-735-6224.
Will search UCC records. Will not search real estate records. **Other Phone Numbers:** Assessor 601-735-3381; Treasurer 601-735-2588; Appraiser/Auditor 601-735-3381; Elections 601-735-1171.

Webster County

Chancery Clerk, PO Box 398, Walthall, MS 39771. 662-258-4131; Fax 662-258-6657.
Will search UCC records. Will not search real estate records. **Other Phone Numbers:** Assessor 662-258-6446; Elections 662-258-6287.

Wilkinson County

Chancery Clerk, PO Box 516, Woodville, MS 39669. Chancery Clerk, R/E and UCC Recording 601-888-4381; Fax 601-888-6776.
Will search UCC records. Will not search real estate records. **Other Phone Numbers:** Assessor 601-888-4562; Treasurer 601-888-4562; Appraiser/Auditor 601-888-6146; Elections 601-888-6697; Vital Records 601-960-7960.

Winston County

Chancery Clerk, PO Drawer 69, Louisville, MS 39339. 662-773-3631; Fax 662-773-8831.
Will search UCC records. Will not search real estate records. **Other Phones:** Assessor 662-773-3694; Treasurer 662-773-3631; Elections 662-773-3581.

Yalobusha County (1st District)

Chancery Clerk, PO Box 260, Coffeeville, MS 38922. 662-675-2716 R/E Recording: 662-675-2091 UCC Recording: 662-675-2091; Fax 662-675-8004.
Will search UCC records. Will not search real estate records. **Other Phone Numbers:** Assessor 662-473-1235; Treasurer 662-675-2091; Appraiser/Auditor 662-675-1235; Elections 662-675-1341.

Yalobusha County (2nd District)

Chancery Clerk, PO Box 664, Water Valley, MS 38965. Chancery Clerk, R/E and UCC Recording 662-473-2091; Fax 662-473-5020.
Will search UCC records. Will not search real estate records. **Other Phone Numbers:** Assessor 662-473-1235; Treasurer 662-473-2092; Appraiser/Auditor 662-473-1341; Elections 662-473-1341.

Yazoo County

Chancery Clerk, PO Box 68, Yazoo City, MS 39194. Chancery Clerk, R/E and UCC Recording 662-746-2661; Fax 662-746-3893.
Will search UCC records. UCC search includes federal tax liens if requested. Real estate record owner and mortgage searches available. **Other Phone Numbers:** Assessor 662-746-1583; Treasurer 662-746-2661; Appraiser/Auditor 662-746-1583; Elections 662-746-1872.

Mississippi County Locator

You will usually be able to find the city name in the City/County Cross Reference below. In that case, it is a simple matter to determine the county from the cross reference. However, only the official US Postal Service city names are included in this index. There are an additional 40,000 place names that people use in their addresses. Therefore, we have also included a ZIP/City Cross Reference immediately following the City/County Cross Reference.

If you know the ZIP Code but the city name does not appear in the City/County Cross Reference index, look up the ZIP Code in the ZIP/City Cross Reference, find the city name, then look up the city name in the City/County Cross Reference. For example, you want to know the county for an address of Menands, NY 12204. There is no "Menands" in the City/County Cross Reference. The ZIP/City Cross Reference shows that ZIP Codes 12201-12288 are for the city of Albany. Looking back in the City/County Cross Reference, Albany is in Albany County.

City/County Cross Reference

ABBEVILLE Lafayette
ABERDEEN Monroe
ACKERMAN Choctaw
ALGOMA Pontotoc
ALLIGATOR (38720) Bolivar(63), Coahoma(36)
AMORY Monroe
ANGUILLA Sharkey
ARCOLA Washington
ARKABUTLA Tate
ARTESIA Lowndes
ASHLAND Benton
AVALON Carroll
AVON Washington
BAILEY (39320) Lauderdale(80), Kemper(19)
BALDWYN (38824) Lee(75), Prentiss(23)
BANNER (38913) Calhoun(96), Lafayette(3)
BASSFIELD (39421) Jefferson Davis(72), Marion(27)
BATESVILLE Panola
BAY SAINT LOUIS Hancock
BAY SPRINGS (39422) Jasper(91), Smith(8)
BEAUMONT Perry
BECKER Monroe
BELDEN Lee
BELEN Quitman
BELLEFONTAINE Webster
BELMONT Tishomingo
BELZONI Humphreys
BENOIT Bolivar
BENTON Yazoo
BENTONIA Yazoo
BEULAH Bolivar
BIG CREEK Calhoun
BIGBEE VALLEY Noxubee
BILOXI Harrison
BLUE MOUNTAIN (38610) Tippah(91), Union(7), Benton(1)
BLUE SPRINGS Union
BOGUE CHITTO Lincoln
BOLTON Hinds
BOONEVILLE Prentiss
BOYLE Bolivar
BRANDON Rankin
BRAXTON (39044) Rankin(52), Simpson(47)
BROOKHAVEN Lincoln
BROOKLYN (39425) Forrest(55), Perry(44)
BROOKSVILLE Noxubee
BRUCE Calhoun
BUCKATUNNA Wayne
BUDE Franklin
BURNSVILLE Tishomingo
BYHALIA (38611) Marshall(81), De Soto(18)
BYRAM Hinds
CALEDONIA (39740) Monroe(92), Montgomery(7)
CALHOUN CITY (38916) Calhoun(97), Webster(2)

CAMDEN Madison
CANTON Madison
CARLISLE Claiborne
CARRIERE Pearl River
CARROLLTON Carroll
CARSON Jefferson Davis
CARTHAGE Leake
CARY Sharkey
CASCILLA Tallahatchie
CEDARBLUFF Clay
CENTREVILLE (39631) Wilkinson(77), Amite(22)
CHARLESTON Tallahatchie
CHATAWA Pike
CHATHAM Washington
CHUNKY (39323) Newton(79), Lauderdale(20)
CHURCH HILL Jefferson
CLARA Wayne
CLARKSDALE Coahoma
CLEVELAND Bolivar
CLINTON Hinds
COAHOMA Coahoma
COFFEEVILLE (38922) Yalobusha(96), Grenada(3)
COILA Carroll
COLDWATER Tate
COLLINS Covington
COLLINSVILLE (39325) Lauderdale(75), Newton(12), Kemper(9), Neshoba(2)
COLUMBIA Marion
COLUMBUS Lowndes
COMO (38619) Panola(97), Lafayette(2)
CONEHATTA (39057) Newton(84), Scott(15)
CORINTH Alcorn
COURTLAND Panola
CRAWFORD (39743) Lowndes(73), Oktibbeha(25), Noxubee(1)
CRENSHAW (38621) Panola(98), Quitman(1)
CROSBY Amite
CROWDER Quitman
CRUGER (38924) Holmes(92), Carroll(5), Leflore(2)
CRYSTAL SPRINGS (39059) Copiah(96), Hinds(3)
D LO Simpson
DALEVILLE (39326) Lauderdale(71), Kemper(28)
DARLING Quitman
DE KALB Kemper
DECATUR Newton
DELTA CITY Sharkey
DENNIS Tishomingo
DERMA Calhoun
DIAMONDHEAD Hancock
DIBERVILLE Harrison
DODDSVILLE (38736) Sunflower(61), Leflore(38)
DREW (38737) Sunflower(98), Tallahatchie(1)
DUBLIN Coahoma

DUCK HILL (38925) Montgomery(69), Grenada(30)
DUMAS (38625) Tippah(84), Union(15)
DUNCAN Bolivar
DUNDEE (38626) Tunica(74), Coahoma(25)
DURANT Holmes
EASTABUCHIE Jones
EBENEZER Holmes
ECRU Pontotoc
EDWARDS Hinds
ELLIOTT Grenada
ELLISVILLE Jones
ENID (38927) Tallahatchie(96), Panola(3)
ENTERPRISE (39330) Clarke(86), Lauderdale(13)
ESCATAWPA Jackson
ETHEL Attala
ETTA Union
EUPORA Webster
FALCON Quitman
FALKNER (38629) Tippah(96), Benton(3)
FARRELL Coahoma
FAYETTE Jefferson
FERNWOOD Pike
FITLER Issaquena
FLORA (39071) Madison(98), Hinds(1)
FLORENCE Rankin
FLOWOOD Rankin
FOREST (39074) Scott(98), Smith(1)
FORKVILLE Scott
FOXWORTH Marion
FRENCH CAMP Choctaw
FRIARS POINT Coahoma
FULTON Itawamba
GALLMAN Copiah
GATTMAN (38844) Alcorn(82), Monroe(17)
GAUTIER Jackson
GEORGETOWN Copiah
GLEN (38846) Alcorn(79), Tishomingo(20)
GLEN ALLAN Washington
GLENDORA Tallahatchie
GLOSTER Amite
GOLDEN (38847) Itawamba(96), Tishomingo(3)
GOODMAN (39079) Madison(92), Holmes(4), Attala(3)
GORE SPRINGS (38929) Grenada(92), Webster(6), Calhoun(1)
GRACE Issaquena
GREENVILLE Bolivar
GREENWOOD Leflore
GREENWOOD SPRINGS Monroe
GRENADA Grenada
GULFPORT Harrison
GUNNISON Bolivar
GUNTOWN Lee
HAMILTON Monroe
HARPERVILLE Scott
HARRISTON Jefferson
HARRISVILLE Simpson
HATTIESBURG Forrest
HAZLEHURST Copiah

HEIDELBERG (39439) Jasper(69), Clarke(26), Jones(4)
HERMANVILLE (39086) Copiah(60), Claiborne(39)
HERNANDO De Soto
HICKORY (39332) Newton(89), Jasper(10)
HICKORY FLAT (38633) Benton(91), Union(8)
HILLSBORO Scott
HOLCOMB (38940) Grenada(93), Tallahatchie(3), Carroll(3)
HOLLANDALE (38748) Washington(97), Sharkey(2)
HOLLY BLUFF Yazoo
HOLLY RIDGE Sunflower
HOLLY SPRINGS (38635) Marshall(98), Benton(1)
HORN LAKE De Soto
HOULKA Chickasaw
HOUSTON Chickasaw
HURLEY Jackson
INDEPENDENCE Tate
INDIANOLA Sunflower
INVERNESS (38753) Sunflower(93), Humphreys(6)
ISOLA (38754) Humphreys(98), Sunflower(1)
ITTA BENA Leflore
IUKA Tishomingo
JACKSON Rankin
JAYESS (39641) Lawrence(91), Walthall(8)
JONESTOWN Coahoma
KILMICHAEL Montgomery
KILN Hancock
KOKOMO (39643) Marion(86), Walthall(13)
KOSCIUSKO (39090) Attala(96), Leake(3)
LAKE (39092) Newton(93), Scott(5)
LAKE CORMORANT De Soto
LAKESHORE Hancock
LAMAR (38642) Marshall(98), Benton(1)
LAMBERT Quitman
LAUDERDALE (39335) Lauderdale(93), Kemper(6)
LAUREL (39443) Jones(95), Wayne(3), Jasper(2)
LAWRENCE Newton
LEAKESVILLE Greene
LELAND Washington
LENA (39094) Leake(54), Scott(37), Rankin(8)
LEXINGTON (39095) Holmes(84), Yazoo(14)
LIBERTY Amite
LITTLE ROCK Newton
LONG BEACH Harrison
LORMAN (39096) Claiborne(62), Jefferson(37)
LOUIN (39338) Jasper(60), Smith(39)
LOUISE Humphreys
LOUISVILLE Winston
LUCEDALE (39452) George(83), Jackson(16)
LUDLOW Scott

LULA Coahoma
LUMBERTON (39455) Lamar(44), Pearl River(42), Stone(11), Marion(1)
LYON (38645) Coahoma(95), Quitman(4)
MABEN Webster
MACON (39341) Noxubee(88), Winston(11)
MADDEN Leake
MADISON Madison
MAGEE (39111) Simpson(96), Smith(3)
MAGNOLIA Pike
MANTACHIE Itawamba
MANTEE Calhoun
MARIETTA (38856) Prentiss(93), Itawamba(6)
MARION Lauderdale
MARKS Quitman
MATHISTON Webster
MATTSON Coahoma
MAYERSVILLE Issaquena
MAYHEW Lowndes
MC ADAMS Attala
MC CALL CREEK (39647) Franklin(98), Lincoln(1)
MC CARLEY Carroll
MC COMB Pike
MC CONDY Chickasaw
MC COOL (39108) Winston(41), Attala(36), Choctaw(22)
MC HENRY Stone
MC LAIN (39456) Greene(69), Perry(30)
MC NEILL Pearl River
MEADVILLE (39653) Franklin(98), Amite(1)
MENDENHALL (39114) Simpson(96), Rankin(2)
MERIDIAN Lauderdale
MERIGOLD (38759) Sunflower(84), Bolivar(15)
METCALFE Washington
MICHIGAN CITY Benton
MIDNIGHT Humphreys
MINERAL WELLS De Soto
MINTER CITY Leflore
MISSISSIPPI STATE Oktibbeha
MIZE Smith
MONEY Leflore
MONTICELLO Lawrence
MONTPELIER Clay
MOOREVILLE Lee
MOORHEAD Sunflower
MORGAN CITY Leflore
MORGANTOWN Marion
MORTON (39117) Scott(92), Smith(4), Rankin(3)
MOSELLE Jones
MOSS Jasper
MOSS POINT Jackson
MOUND BAYOU Bolivar
MOUNT OLIVE (39119) Covington(85), Smith(6), Simpson(4), Jefferson Davis(2)
MOUNT PLEASANT Marshall
MYRTLE (38650) Union(97), Benton(1), Tippah(1)
NATCHEZ Adams
NEELY Greene
NESBIT De Soto
NETTLETON (38858) Itawamba(41), Monroe(31), Lee(27)
NEW ALBANY Union
NEW AUGUSTA Perry
NEW SITE Prentiss
NEWHEBRON (39140) Lawrence(88), Jefferson Davis(11)
NEWTON Newton
NICHOLSON Pearl River
NITTA YUMA Sharkey

NORTH CARROLLTON Carroll
NOXAPATER Winston
OAK VALE (39656) Lawrence(66), Jefferson Davis(33)
OAKLAND (38948) Yalobusha(89), Tallahatchie(10)
OCEAN SPRINGS Jackson
OKOLONA (38860) Chickasaw(92), Lee(7)
OLIVE BRANCH De Soto
OSYKA Pike
OVETT (39464) Perry(97), Jones(2)
OXFORD Lafayette
PACE Bolivar
PACHUTA (39347) Jasper(71), Clarke(28)
PANTHER BURN Sharkey
PARCHMAN Sunflower
PARIS Lafayette
PASCAGOULA Jackson
PASS CHRISTIAN (39571) Harrison(97), Hancock(2)
PATTISON (39144) Claiborne(50), Copiah(44), Jefferson(4)
PAULDING Jasper
PEARL Rankin
PEARLINGTON Hancock
PELAHATCHIE (39145) Rankin(95), Scott(4)
PERKINSTON (39573) Stone(62), Hancock(26), George(4), Pearl River(3)
PETAL (39465) Forrest(89), Perry(10)
PHEBA (39755) Clay(62), Oktibbeha(37)
PHILADELPHIA Neshoba
PHILIPP Tallahatchie
PICAYUNE Pearl River
PICKENS (39146) Yazoo(64), Madison(32), Holmes(3)
PINEY WOODS Rankin
PINOLA Simpson
PITTSBORO Calhoun
PLANTERSVILLE Lee
PLEASANT GROVE Panola
POCAHONTAS Hinds
PONTOTOC Pontotoc
POPE Panola
POPLARVILLE (39470) Pearl River(98), Hancock(1)
PORT GIBSON Claiborne
PORTERVILLE Kemper
POTTS CAMP (38659) Marshall(97), Benton(2)
PRAIRIE (39756) Clay(96), Monroe(2)
PRAIRIE POINT Noxubee
PRENTISS Jefferson Davis
PRESTON (39354) Kemper(66), Winston(26), Neshoba(5), Noxubee(1)
PUCKETT Rankin
PULASKI (39152) Scott(57), Smith(42)
PURVIS Lamar
QUITMAN Clarke
RALEIGH Smith
RANDOLPH (38864) Pontotoc(93), Calhoun(6)
RAYMOND Hinds
RED BANKS Marshall
REDWOOD Warren
REFORM Choctaw
RENA LARA Coahoma
RICH Coahoma
RICHTON (39476) Perry(93), Wayne(5)
RIDGELAND Madison
RIENZI Alcorn
RIPLEY Tippah
ROBINSONVILLE Tunica
ROLLING FORK (39159) Sharkey(93), Issaquena(5)
ROME Sunflower

ROSE HILL Jasper
ROSEDALE Bolivar
ROXIE (39661) Franklin(89), Adams(9), Jefferson(1)
RULEVILLE Sunflower
RUTH (39662) Lincoln(76), Lawrence(20), Pike(3)
SALLIS (39160) Attala(97), Leake(2)
SALTILLO Lee
SANATORIUM Simpson
SANDERSVILLE Jones
SANDHILL Rankin
SANDY HOOK (39478) Marion(86), Walthall(13)
SARAH (38665) Panola(91), Tate(8)
SARDIS Panola
SATARTIA (39162) Warren(96), Yazoo(3)
SAUCIER Harrison
SCHLATER Leflore
SCOBEY (38953) Yalobusha(53), Grenada(32), Tallahatchie(13)
SCOOBA Kemper
SCOTT Bolivar
SEBASTOPOL Scott
SEMINARY (39479) Covington(97), Jones(2)
SENATOBIA Tate
SHANNON (38868) Lee(86), Pontotoc(8), Chickasaw(3)
SHARON Madison
SHAW (38773) Bolivar(75), Sunflower(24)
SHELBY Bolivar
SHERARD Coahoma
SHERMAN Pontotoc
SHUBUTA (39360) Clarke(76), Wayne(23)
SHUQUALAK Noxubee
SIBLEY Adams
SIDON (38954) Leflore(85), Carroll(14)
SILVER CITY Humphreys
SILVER CREEK (39663) Lawrence(96), Jefferson Davis(3)
SKENE Bolivar
SLATE SPRING Calhoun
SLEDGE (38670) Tunica(82), Quitman(17)
SMITHDALE (39664) Amite(76), Franklin(15), Lincoln(8)
SMITHVILLE Monroe
SONTAG (39665) Lawrence(80), Lincoln(19)
SOSO (39480) Jones(97), Smith(2)
SOUTHAVEN De Soto
STAR Rankin
STARKVILLE Oktibbeha
STATE LINE (39362) Greene(68), Wayne(31)
STEENS Lowndes
STENNIS SPACE CENTER Hancock
STEWART Montgomery
STONEVILLE Washington
STONEWALL Clarke
STRINGER Jasper
STURGIS (39769) Oktibbeha(87), Winston(12)
SUMMIT (39666) Pike(70), Lincoln(23), Amite(6)
SUMNER Tallahatchie
SUMRALL (39482) Lamar(94), Jefferson Davis(3), Marion(2)
SUNFLOWER Sunflower
SWAN LAKE Tallahatchie
SWIFTOWN Leflore
TAYLOR Lafayette
TAYLORSVILLE (39168) Smith(97), Covington(2)
TCHULA Holmes
TERRY Hinds

THAXTON (38871) Pontotoc(86), Lafayette(8), Union(5)
THOMASTOWN Leake
THORNTON Holmes
TIE PLANT Grenada
TILLATOBA (38961) Yalobusha(91), Tallahatchie(8)
TINSLEY Yazoo
TIPLERSVILLE Tippah
TIPPO Tallahatchie
TISHOMINGO Tishomingo
TOCCOPOLA Lafayette
TOOMSUBA Lauderdale
TOUGALOO (39174) Hinds(91), Madison(8)
TREBLOC Chickasaw
TREMONT Itawamba
TRIBBETT Washington
TULA Lafayette
TUNICA Tunica
TUPELO (38804) Lee(98), Itawamba(1)
TUTWILER (38963) Coahoma(78), Tallahatchie(18), Sunflower(2)
TYLERTOWN Walthall
UNION (39365) Neshoba(70), Newton(28)
UNION CHURCH (39668) Jefferson(97), Franklin(1)
UNIVERSITY Lafayette
UTICA (39175) Hinds(91), Copiah(8)
VAIDEN (39176) Carroll(44), Montgomery(41), Attala(13)
VALLEY PARK Issaquena
VAN VLEET Chickasaw
VANCE Quitman
VARDAMAN (38878) Calhoun(98), Chickasaw(1)
VAUGHAN Yazoo
VERONA Lee
VICKSBURG Warren
VICTORIA Marshall
VOSSBURG (39366) Clarke(64), Jasper(35)
WALLS De Soto
WALNUT (38683) Tippah(82), Alcorn(13), Benton(4)
WALNUT GROVE (39189) Leake(79), Scott(20)
WALTHALL Webster
WASHINGTON Adams
WATER VALLEY (38965) Yalobusha(96), Lafayette(2), Calhoun(1)
WATERFORD (38685) Marshall(90), Lafayette(9)
WAVELAND Hancock
WAYNESBORO (39367) Wayne(97), Clarke(2)
WAYSIDE Washington
WEBB Tallahatchie
WEIR Choctaw
WESSON (39191) Copiah(58), Lincoln(41)
WEST (39192) Holmes(69), Attala(28), Carroll(2)
WEST POINT (39773) Clay(97), Monroe(2)
WHEELER Prentiss
WHITFIELD Rankin
WIGGINS (39577) Stone(87), Forrest(12)
WINONA (38967) Montgomery(96), Carroll(3)
WINSTONVILLE Bolivar
WINTERVILLE Washington
WOODLAND Chickasaw
WOODVILLE Wilkinson
YAZOO CITY Yazoo

ZIP/City Cross Reference

ZIP Range	City	ZIP Range	City	ZIP Range	City	ZIP Range	City
38601-38601	ABBEVILLE	38739-38739	DUBLIN	38878-38878	VARDAMAN	39077-39077	GALLMAN
38602-38602	ARKABUTLA	38740-38740	DUNCAN	38879-38879	VERONA	39078-39078	GEORGETOWN
38603-38603	ASHLAND	38744-38744	GLEN ALLAN	38880-38880	WHEELER	39079-39079	GOODMAN
38606-38606	BATESVILLE	38745-38745	GRACE	38901-38902	GRENADA	39080-39080	HARPERVILLE
38609-38609	BELEN	38746-38746	GUNNISON	38912-38912	AVALON	39081-39081	HARRISTON
38610-38610	BLUE MOUNTAIN	38748-38748	HOLLANDALE	38913-38913	BANNER	39082-39082	HARRISVILLE
38611-38611	BYHALIA	38749-38749	HOLLY RIDGE	38914-38914	BIG CREEK	39083-39083	HAZLEHURST
38614-38614	CLARKSDALE	38751-38751	INDIANOLA	38915-38915	BRUCE	39086-39086	HERMANVILLE
38617-38617	COAHOMA	38753-38753	INVERNESS	38916-38916	CALHOUN CITY	39087-39087	HILLSBORO
38618-38618	COLDWATER	38754-38754	ISOLA	38917-38917	CARROLLTON	39088-39088	HOLLY BLUFF
38619-38619	COMO	38755-38755	GREENVILLE	38920-38920	CASCILLA	39090-39090	KOSCIUSKO
38620-38620	COURTLAND	38756-38756	LELAND	38921-38921	CHARLESTON	39092-39092	LAKE
38621-38621	CRENSHAW	38758-38758	MATTSON	38922-38922	COFFEEVILLE	39094-39094	LENA
38622-38622	CROWDER	38759-38759	MERIGOLD	38923-38923	COILA	39095-39095	LEXINGTON
38623-38623	DARLING	38760-38760	METCALFE	38924-38924	CRUGER	39096-39096	LORMAN
38625-38625	DUMAS	38761-38761	MOORHEAD	38925-38925	DUCK HILL	39097-39097	LOUISE
38626-38626	DUNDEE	38762-38762	MOUND BAYOU	38926-38926	ELLIOTT	39098-39098	LUDLOW
38627-38627	ETTA	38763-38763	NITTA YUMA	38927-38927	ENID	39107-39107	MC ADAMS
38628-38628	FALCON	38764-38764	PACE	38928-38928	GLENDORA	39108-39108	MC COOL
38629-38629	FALKNER	38765-38765	PANTHER BURN	38929-38929	GORE SPRINGS	39109-39109	MADDEN
38630-38630	FARRELL	38767-38767	RENA LARA	38930-38935	GREENWOOD	39110-39110	MADISON
38631-38631	FRIARS POINT	38768-38768	ROME	38940-38940	HOLCOMB	39111-39111	MAGEE
38632-38632	HERNANDO	38769-38769	ROSEDALE	38941-38941	ITTA BENA	39112-39112	SANATORIUM
38633-38633	HICKORY FLAT	38771-38771	RULEVILLE	38943-38943	MC CARLEY	39113-39113	MAYERSVILLE
38634-38635	HOLLY SPRINGS	38772-38772	SCOTT	38944-38944	MINTER CITY	39114-39114	MENDENHALL
38637-38637	HORN LAKE	38773-38773	SHAW	38945-38945	MONEY	39115-39115	MIDNIGHT
38638-38638	INDEPENDENCE	38774-38774	SHELBY	38946-38946	MORGAN CITY	39116-39116	MIZE
38639-38639	JONESTOWN	38775-38775	SKENE	38947-38947	NORTH CARROLLTON	39117-39117	MORTON
38641-38641	LAKE CORMORANT	38776-38776	STONEVILLE	38948-38948	OAKLAND	39119-39119	MOUNT OLIVE
38642-38642	LAMAR	38778-38778	SUNFLOWER	38949-38949	PARIS	39120-39122	NATCHEZ
38643-38643	LAMBERT	38779-38779	TRIBBETT	38950-38950	PHILIPP	39130-39130	MADISON
38644-38644	LULA	38780-38780	WAYSIDE	38951-38951	PITTSBORO	39140-39140	NEWHEBRON
38645-38645	LYON	38781-38781	WINSTONVILLE	38952-38952	SCHLATER	39144-39144	PATTISON
38646-38646	MARKS	38782-38782	WINTERVILLE	38953-38953	SCOBEY	39145-39145	PELAHATCHIE
38647-38647	MICHIGAN CITY	38801-38804	TUPELO	38954-38954	SIDON	39146-39146	PICKENS
38648-38648	MINERAL WELLS	38820-38820	ALGOMA	38955-38955	SLATE SPRING	39148-39148	PINEY WOODS
38649-38649	MOUNT PLEASANT	38821-38821	AMORY	38957-38957	SUMNER	39149-39149	PINOLA
38650-38650	MYRTLE	38824-38824	BALDWYN	38958-38958	SWAN LAKE	39150-39150	PORT GIBSON
38651-38651	NESBIT	38825-38825	BECKER	38959-38959	SWIFTOWN	39151-39151	PUCKETT
38652-38652	NEW ALBANY	38826-38826	BELDEN	38960-38960	TIE PLANT	39152-39152	PULASKI
38654-38654	OLIVE BRANCH	38827-38827	BELMONT	38961-38961	TILLATOBA	39153-39153	RALEIGH
38655-38655	OXFORD	38828-38828	BLUE SPRINGS	38962-38962	TIPPO	39154-39154	RAYMOND
38657-38657	PLEASANT GROVE	38829-38829	BOONEVILLE	38963-38963	TUTWILER	39156-39156	REDWOOD
38658-38658	POPE	38833-38833	BURNSVILLE	38964-38964	VANCE	39157-39158	RIDGELAND
38659-38659	POTTS CAMP	38834-38835	CORINTH	38965-38965	WATER VALLEY	39159-39159	ROLLING FORK
38661-38661	RED BANKS	38838-38838	DENNIS	38966-38966	WEBB	39160-39160	SALLIS
38662-38662	RICH	38839-38839	DERMA	38967-38967	WINONA	39161-39161	SANDHILL
38663-38663	RIPLEY	38841-38841	ECRU	39038-39038	BELZONI	39162-39162	SATARTIA
38664-38664	ROBINSONVILLE	38843-38843	FULTON	39039-39039	BENTON	39163-39163	SHARON
38665-38665	SARAH	38844-38844	GATTMAN	39040-39040	BENTONIA	39165-39165	SIBLEY
38666-38666	SARDIS	38846-38846	GLEN	39041-39041	BOLTON	39166-39166	SILVER CITY
38668-38668	SENATOBIA	38847-38847	GOLDEN	39042-39043	BRANDON	39167-39167	STAR
38669-38669	SHERARD	38848-38848	GREENWOOD SPRINGS	39044-39044	BRAXTON	39168-39168	TAYLORSVILLE
38670-38670	SLEDGE	38849-38849	GUNTOWN	39045-39045	CAMDEN	39169-39169	TCHULA
38671-38672	SOUTHAVEN	38850-38850	HOULKA	39046-39046	CANTON	39170-39170	TERRY
38673-38673	TAYLOR	38851-38851	HOUSTON	39047-39047	BRANDON	39171-39171	THOMASTOWN
38674-38674	TIPLERSVILLE	38852-38852	IUKA	39049-39049	CARLISLE	39172-39172	THORNTON
38675-38675	TULA	38854-38854	MC CONDY	39051-39051	CARTHAGE	39173-39173	TINSLEY
38676-38676	TUNICA	38855-38855	MANTACHIE	39054-39054	CARY	39174-39174	TOUGALOO
38677-38677	UNIVERSITY	38856-38856	MARIETTA	39055-39055	CHURCH HILL	39175-39175	UTICA
38679-38679	VICTORIA	38857-38857	MOOREVILLE	39056-39056	CLINTON	39176-39176	VAIDEN
38680-38680	WALLS	38858-38858	NETTLETON	39057-39057	CONEHATTA	39177-39177	VALLEY PARK
38683-38683	WALNUT	38859-38859	NEW SITE	39058-39058	CLINTON	39179-39179	VAUGHAN
38685-38685	WATERFORD	38860-38860	OKOLONA	39059-39059	CRYSTAL SPRINGS	39180-39183	VICKSBURG
38686-38686	WALLS	38862-38862	PLANTERSVILLE	39060-39060	CLINTON	39189-39189	WALNUT GROVE
38701-38704	GREENVILLE	38863-38863	PONTOTOC	39061-39061	DELTA CITY	39190-39190	WASHINGTON
38720-38720	ALLIGATOR	38864-38864	RANDOLPH	39062-39062	D LO	39191-39191	WESSON
38721-38721	ANGUILLA	38865-38865	RIENZI	39063-39063	DURANT	39192-39192	WEST
38722-38722	ARCOLA	38866-38866	SALTILLO	39064-39064	EBENEZER	39193-39193	WHITFIELD
38723-38723	AVON	38868-38868	SHANNON	39066-39066	EDWARDS	39194-39194	YAZOO CITY
38725-38725	BENOIT	38869-38869	SHERMAN	39067-39067	ETHEL	39200-39208	JACKSON
38726-38726	BEULAH	38870-38870	SMITHVILLE	39069-39069	FAYETTE	39208-39208	PEARL
38730-38730	BOYLE	38871-38871	THAXTON	39070-39070	FITLER	39209-39232	JACKSON
38731-38731	CHATHAM	38873-38873	TISHOMINGO	39071-39071	FLORA	39232-39232	FLOWOOD
38732-38733	CLEVELAND	38874-38874	TOCCOPOLA	39072-39072	POCAHONTAS	39235-39272	JACKSON
38736-38736	DODDSVILLE	38875-38875	TREBLOC	39073-39073	FLORENCE	39272-39272	BYRAM
38737-38737	DREW	38876-38876	TREMONT	39074-39074	FOREST	39282-39298	JACKSON
38738-38738	PARCHMAN	38877-38877	VAN VLEET	39076-39076	FORKVILLE	39301-39309	MERIDIAN

ZIP Range	City
39320-39320	BAILEY
39322-39322	BUCKATUNNA
39323-39323	CHUNKY
39324-39324	CLARA
39325-39325	COLLINSVILLE
39326-39326	DALEVILLE
39327-39327	DECATUR
39328-39328	DE KALB
39330-39330	ENTERPRISE
39332-39332	HICKORY
39335-39335	LAUDERDALE
39336-39336	LAWRENCE
39337-39337	LITTLE ROCK
39338-39338	LOUIN
39339-39339	LOUISVILLE
39341-39341	MACON
39342-39342	MARION
39345-39345	NEWTON
39346-39346	NOXAPATER
39347-39347	PACHUTA
39348-39348	PAULDING
39350-39350	PHILADELPHIA
39352-39352	PORTERVILLE
39353-39353	PRAIRIE POINT
39354-39354	PRESTON
39355-39355	QUITMAN
39356-39356	ROSE HILL
39358-39358	SCOOBA
39359-39359	SEBASTOPOL
39360-39360	SHUBUTA
39361-39361	SHUQUALAK
39362-39362	STATE LINE
39363-39363	STONEWALL
39364-39364	TOOMSUBA
39365-39365	UNION
39366-39366	VOSSBURG
39367-39367	WAYNESBORO
39400-39407	HATTIESBURG
39421-39421	BASSFIELD
39422-39422	BAY SPRINGS
39423-39423	BEAUMONT
39425-39425	BROOKLYN
39426-39426	CARRIERE
39427-39427	CARSON
39428-39428	COLLINS
39429-39429	COLUMBIA
39436-39436	EASTABUCHIE
39437-39437	ELLISVILLE
39439-39439	HEIDELBERG
39440-39443	LAUREL
39451-39451	LEAKESVILLE
39452-39452	LUCEDALE
39455-39455	LUMBERTON
39456-39456	MC LAIN
39457-39457	MC NEILL
39459-39459	MOSELLE
39460-39460	MOSS
39461-39461	NEELY
39462-39462	NEW AUGUSTA
39463-39463	NICHOLSON
39464-39464	OVETT
39465-39465	PETAL
39466-39466	PICAYUNE
39470-39470	POPLARVILLE
39474-39474	PRENTISS
39475-39475	PURVIS
39476-39476	RICHTON
39477-39477	SANDERSVILLE
39478-39478	SANDY HOOK
39479-39479	SEMINARY
39480-39480	SOSO
39481-39481	STRINGER
39482-39482	SUMRALL
39483-39483	FOXWORTH
39484-39484	MORGANTOWN
39500-39507	GULFPORT
39520-39522	BAY SAINT LOUIS
39522-39522	STENNIS SPACE CENTER
39525-39525	DIAMONDHEAD
39529-39529	BAY SAINT LOUIS
39530-39535	BILOXI
39540-39540	DIBERVILLE
39552-39552	ESCATAWPA
39553-39553	GAUTIER
39555-39555	HURLEY
39556-39556	KILN
39558-39558	LAKESHORE
39560-39560	LONG BEACH
39561-39561	MC HENRY
39562-39563	MOSS POINT
39564-39566	OCEAN SPRINGS
39567-39569	PASCAGOULA
39571-39571	PASS CHRISTIAN
39572-39572	PEARLINGTON
39573-39573	PERKINSTON
39574-39574	SAUCIER
39576-39576	WAVELAND
39577-39577	WIGGINS
39581-39595	PASCAGOULA
39601-39603	BROOKHAVEN
39629-39629	BOGUE CHITTO
39630-39630	BUDE
39631-39631	CENTREVILLE
39632-39632	CHATAWA
39633-39633	CROSBY
39635-39635	FERNWOOD
39638-39638	GLOSTER
39641-39641	JAYESS
39643-39643	KOKOMO
39645-39645	LIBERTY
39647-39647	MC CALL CREEK
39648-39649	MC COMB
39652-39652	MAGNOLIA
39653-39653	MEADVILLE
39654-39654	MONTICELLO
39656-39656	OAK VALE
39657-39657	OSYKA
39661-39661	ROXIE
39662-39662	RUTH
39663-39663	SILVER CREEK
39664-39664	SMITHDALE
39665-39665	SONTAG
39666-39666	SUMMIT
39667-39667	TYLERTOWN
39668-39668	UNION CHURCH
39669-39669	WOODVILLE
39701-39710	COLUMBUS
39730-39730	ABERDEEN
39735-39735	ACKERMAN
39736-39736	ARTESIA
39737-39737	BELLEFONTAINE
39738-39738	BIGBEE VALLEY
39739-39739	BROOKSVILLE
39740-39740	CALEDONIA
39741-39741	CEDARBLUFF
39743-39743	CRAWFORD
39744-39744	EUPORA
39745-39745	FRENCH CAMP
39746-39746	HAMILTON
39747-39747	KILMICHAEL
39750-39750	MABEN
39751-39751	MANTEE
39752-39752	MATHISTON
39753-39753	MAYHEW
39754-39754	MONTPELIER
39755-39755	PHEBA
39756-39756	PRAIRIE
39757-39757	REFORM
39759-39760	STARKVILLE
39762-39762	MISSISSIPPI STATE
39766-39766	STEENS
39767-39767	STEWART
39769-39769	STURGIS
39771-39771	WALTHALL
39772-39772	WEIR
39773-39773	WEST POINT
39776-39776	WOODLAND

Missouri

General Help Numbers:

Governor's Office
PO Box 720
Jefferson City, MO 65102-0720
www.gov.state.mo.us

573-751-3222
Fax 573-751-1495
8AM-5PM

Attorney General's Office
PO Box 899
Jefferson City, MO 65102
www.ago.state.mo.us

573-751-3321
Fax 573-751-0774
8AM-5PM

State Court Administrator
2112 Industrial Drive - PO Box 104480
Jefferson City, MO 65110
www.osca.state.mo.us

573-751-4377
Fax 573-751-5540
8AM-5PM

State Archives
Archives Division
PO Box 1747
Jefferson City, MO 65102-1747
www.sos.state.mo.us/archives/

573-751-3280
Fax 573-526-7333
8-5 M-F
(till 9PM on Th);
8:30-3:30 SA

State Specifics:

Capital:

Jefferson City
Cole County

Time Zone:

CST

Number of Counties:

114

Population:

5,629,707

Web Site:

www.state.mo.us

State Agencies

Criminal Records

Missouri State Highway Patrol, Criminal Record & Identification Division, PO Box 568, Jefferson City, MO 65102-0568 (Courier: 1510 E Elm St, Jefferson City, MO 65102); 573-526-6153, 573-751-9382 (Fax), 8AM-5PM.

www.mshp.state.mo.us

Note: The sex offender registry is not available online. Qualified entites may obtain sex offender info pursunat to Sect. 43.500, RSMO. Registry information is available from the sheriff in the county where the offender resides.

Indexing & Storage: Records are available from 1970 on. It takes 5 weeks before new records are available for inquiry. Records are indexed on inhouse computer (84%) including images. Records are normally destroyed after (records maintained indefinitely). 64% of all arrests in database have final dispositions recorded, 62% for those arrests within last 5 years.

Searching: Youth service providers must have signature of the subject. Include the following in your request: full name, date of birth, sex, race, Social Security Number. Fingerprints are an option. A request form can be downloaded from the web site. Records are 100% fingerprint-supported. Open records are accessible by the public. These are convictions, or arrests less than 30 days old unless charges are sought, or suspended imposition of sentence during probation period. Certain entites may access closed record files in accordance with state statute, with the submission of fingerprints and required fee.

Access by: mail, in person.

Fee & Payment: The search fee is $5.00 per individual for a name search. Searches by fingerprint cost $14.00 each, add $22.00 if the fingerprint search to include an FBI fingerprint check. Fee payee: State of Missouri. Prepayment required. Personal checks accepted. No credit cards accepted.

Mail search: Turnaround time: 3-4 weeks. No self addressed stamped envelope is required.

In person search: Turnaround time is while you wait for one search only.

Corporation Records
Fictitious Name
Limited Partnership Records
Assumed Name
Trademarks/Servicemarks
Limited Liability Company Records

Secretary of State, Corporation Services, PO Box 778, Jefferson City, MO 65102 (Courier: 600 W Main, Jefferson City, MO 65101); 573-751-4153, 573-751-5841 (Fax), 8AM-5PM.

www.sos.state.mo.us

Note: Trademarks and servicemarks are handled by the Commissions Division within Sec. of State and can be reached at 573-751-4756.

Indexing & Storage: Records are available from the 1800s. New records are available for inquiry immediately. Records are indexed on microfilm, inhouse computer, hard copy.

Searching: Include the following in your request: full name of business, specific records that you need copies of. In addition to the articles of incorporation, corporation records include the following information: Annual Reports, Officers, Directors, DBAs, Prior (merged) names, Inactive and Reserved names.

Access by: mail, phone, fax, in person, online.

Fee & Payment: An uncertified copy of a record is $.50 per page, a certified copy of a record is $10.00 certification fee plus $.50 per page. The fee for an officers and directors list is $10.00. A Good Standing is $10.00. A trademark or servicemark search is $5.00. Fee payee: Secretary of State. Prepayment required. They will invoice. Personal checks accepted. Credit cards accepted: MasterCard, Visa.

Mail search: Turnaround time: 2 to 3 days. No self addressed stamped envelope is required.

Phone search: Status information is given over the phone at no charge.

Fax search: Same criteria as mail searching. Records are returned by mail.

In person search: Results are returned by mail.

Online search: Search free online at www.sos.state.mo.us/BusinessEntity. The corporate name, the agent name or the charter number is required to search. The site will indicate the currency of the data. Many business entity type searches are available.

Uniform Commercial Code

UCC Division, Secretary of State, PO Box 1159, Jefferson City, MO 65102 (Courier: 600 W Main St, Rm 302, Jefferson City, MO 65101); 573-751-2360, 573-522-2057 (Fax), 8AM-5PM.

www.sos.state.mo.us/ucc/

Indexing & Storage: Records are available from 1965. Records are on microfiche from 7-1-80 to present.

Searching: Use search request form UCC-11. Please note that all tax liens are filed at the county level only. Include the following in your request: debtor name.

Access by: mail, phone, in person, online.

Fee & Payment: A UCC-11 search is $27.00 plus $1.00 per page for copies. UCC-3's are not listed on the summary; order copies to review them. Fee payee: Secretary of State. Prepayment required. Personal checks accepted. Credit cards accepted: MasterCard, Visa.

Mail search: Turnaround time: 2 weeks.

Phone search: General information is available without charge.

In person search: You may request information in person.

Online search: Free searching for debtor names is available on the Internet. Images are available.

Other access: The agency will release information for bulk purchase, call for procedures and pricing.

Federal Tax Liens
State Tax Liens

Records not maintained by a state level agency.

Note: All tax liens are filed at the county level.

Sales Tax Registrations

Access to Records is Restricted

Department of Revenue, Sales Tax Administration Bureau, PO Box 3300, Jefferson City, MO 65105-3300; 573-751-5860, 573-751-2836, 573-522-1722 (Fax), 7:45AM-4:45PM.

www.dor.state.mo.us/tax

Note: This agency will neither confirm nor supply any information. Confidential information is only released to owners or corporate officers registered with the Department. They suggest other requesters to check at the city level.

Birth Certificates

Department of Health, Bureau of Vital Records, PO Box 570, Jefferson City, MO 65102-0570 (Courier: 930 Wildwood, Jefferson City, MO 65109); 573-751-6387, 573-751-6400 (Message Number), 573-526-3846 (Fax), 8AM-5PM.

www.health.state.mo.us

Indexing & Storage: Records are available from 1910 on. New records are available for inquiry immediately. Records are indexed on microfiche, inhouse computer.

Searching: Records are only released to person of record or legal representative of immediate family member. Must have a signed release form from person of record or immediate family member for investigative purposes. Include the following in your request: full name, names of parents,

mother's maiden name, date of birth, place of birth, relationship to person of record, reason for information request.

Access by: mail, phone, in person.

Fee & Payment: Search fee is $10.00 per 5 years searched. Fee is charged regardless if record is found. Emergency requests using a credit card pay an additional $5.50 fee. Fee payee: Missouri Department of Health. Prepayment required. Personal checks accepted. Credit cards accepted: MasterCard, Visa, AmEx, Discover.

Mail search: Turnaround time: 2 to 3 weeks. No self addressed stamped envelope is required.

Phone search: This service is only available for emergencies.

In person search: Turnaround time 10 minutes.

Death Records

Department of Health, Bureau of Vital Records, PO Box 570, Jefferson City, MO 65102-0570 (Courier: 930 Wildwood, Jefferson City, MO 65109); 573-751-6370, 573-751-6400 (Message Number), 573-526-3846 (Fax), 8AM-5PM.

www.health.state.mo.us

Indexing & Storage: Records are available from 1910 on. New records are available for inquiry immediately. Records are indexed on microfiche, inhouse computer.

Searching: Records are only released to legal representative of person of record or immediate family member. Must have a signed release form from immediate family member for investigative purposes. Include the following in your request: full name, date of death, place of death, relationship to person of record, reason for information request.

Access by: mail, in person.

Fee & Payment: The $10.00 search fee is for 5 years searched. Use of credit card is additional $5.50. Fee payee: Missouri Department of Health. Prepayment required. Personal checks accepted.

Mail search: Turnaround time: 2 to 3 weeks. No self addressed stamped envelope is required.

In person search: Turnaround time 10 minutes.

Expedited service: Expedited service is available for mail and phone searches. This is for emergency use only. Add fee for use of credit ($5.50) and fee for express delivery.

Marriage Certificates
Divorce Records

Department of Health, Bureau of Vital Records, PO Box 570, Jefferson City, MO 65102-0570 (Courier: 930 Wildwood, Jefferson City, MO 65109); 573-751-6382, 573-751-6400 (Message Number), 573-526-3846 (Fax), 8AM-5PM.

www.health.state.mo.us

Note: Actual marriage and divorce records are found at county of issue. This agency will issue a certificate of statement only.

Indexing & Storage: Records are available from July 1, 1948 to present on microfiche.

Searching: Include names, year of occurrence and county in your request.

Access by: mail, in person.

Fee & Payment: The fee is $10.00 for each 5 years searched. Use of credit card is additional

$5.50. Fee payee: Missouri Department of Health. Prepayment required. Personal checks accepted.

Mail search: Turnaround time: 1 to 2 weeks. No self addressed stamped envelope is required.

In person search: The agency personnel do the searching.

Expedited service: Expedited service is available for fax searches. Add fee for use of credit ($5.50) and fee for express delivery.

Workers' Compensation Records

Labor & Industrial Relations Department, Workers Compensation Division, PO Box 58, Jefferson City, MO 65102-0058 (Courier: 3315 W Truman Blvd, Jefferson City, MO 65101); 573-751-4231, 573-751-2012 (Fax), 8AM-4:30PM.

www.dolir.state.mo.us

Indexing & Storage: Records are available from 1945. Records are computerized since 1994. Records are indexed on inhouse computer.

Searching: Report of injury and medical records released only with a release form. All other records are open. Include the following in your request: claimant name, Social Security Number, date of accident.

Access by: mail, fax, in person.

Fee & Payment: The search fee is $5.00. Fee payee: Workers Compensation Division. Personal checks accepted. No credit cards accepted.

Mail search: Turnaround time: 1 to 2 days. No self addressed stamped envelope is required.

Fax search: The initial fax must include a written request for the search. Turnaround time is 1 to 2 days.

In person search: To search in person, you must be party to the case in question or possess written authorization.

Driver Records

Department of Revenue, Driver and Vehicle Services Bureau, PO Box 200, Jefferson City, MO 65105-0200 (Courier: Harry S Truman Bldg, 301 W High St, Room 470, Jefferson City, MO 65105); 573-751-400, 573-526-4769 (Fax), 7:45AM-4:45PM.

www.dor.state.mo.us/mvdl/drivers

Note: Copies of tickets are available from the same address. Requests must be in writing, include the name, DOB, license number, and specific violation information. The cost is $3.75 per ticket.

Indexing & Storage: Records are available for 5 years for moving violations and suspensions, permanent for DWI's. Zero point violations are not shown on the record. Accidents are stored in the state computer, but are not shown on the driving record, unless suspension/revocation action taken.

Searching: The state complies with DPPA. Frequent requesters should establish an account for electronic access. Casual requesters can receive records without personal information, unless written consent of subject is provided.

Access by: mail, phone, fax, in person, online.

Fee & Payment: The fee is $1.25 per record for walk-in or mail-in requests, $4.00 if certified. The fee for online retrieval is $1.25 per record plus network line charges. Fee payee: Department of Revenue. Prepayment required. Cashier's check

and money orders preferred. Personal checks accepted. No credit cards accepted.

Mail search: Turnaround time: 2 days. A self addressed stamped envelope is requested.

Phone search: Pre-approved accounts may request records for 24 hour mail or fax return. To establish an account, call 573-751-4300.

Fax search: Pre-approved accounts may order records by phone and receive by fax for $2.75 per record.

In person search: You may request information in person.

Online search: Online access costs $1.25 per record. Online inquiries can be put in Missouri's "mailbox" any time of the day. These inquiries are then picked up at 2 AM the following morning, and the resulting MVR's are sent back to each customer's "mailbox" approximately two hours later.

Other access: The tape-to-tape process has been replaced by the online system. The entire license file can be purchased, with updates. Call 573-751-5579 for more information.

Vehicle Ownership & Identification
Vessel Ownership & Registration

Department of Revenue, Driver and Vehicle Services Bureau, PO Box 100, Jefferson City, MO 65105-0100 (Courier: Harry S Truman Bldg, 301 W High St, Jefferson City, MO 65105); 573-526-3669, 573-751-4509, 573-751-7060 (Fax), 7:45AM-4:45PM.

www.dor.state.mo.us/mvdl/default.htm

Note: Lien information shows on the title records.

Indexing & Storage: Records are available from 1968 to present. Records are indexed on microfiche from 1968 to present, and microfilm from 1981 to present. Records include boats and mobile homes. All motorized boats 12 ft or longer must be titled and registered.

Searching: Ownership and vehicle information is available with no restrictions to access, if request is of a legal nature. Casual requesters must have consent of subject to obtain records with personal information, other this data is blocked. Current registration/title records are on computer. Records are purged from the computer files after 2 years of no activity. However, the records will remain on microfiche.

Access by: mail, phone, fax, in person.

Fee & Payment: The fee for a record search is $4.50 and a complete title history is $8.00. There is an additional $3.00 for certification. Fee payee: Department of Revenue. Prepayment required. Pre-approved accounts may be billed. Personal checks accepted. No credit cards accepted.

Mail search: Turnaround time: 2 to 4 weeks.

Phone search: The state offers a phone-in service for title verification and lien holder information ONLY for dealers and lienholders. The fee is $1.50 per record. For more information, call 573-526-3669 or 751-4509.

Fax search: To have results returned by fax costs an additional $.50 per page.

In person search: You may request records in person.

Other access: Missouri has an extensive range of records and information available on magnetic tape, labels or paper. Besides offering license, vehicle, title, dealer, and marine records, specific public report data is also available.

Accident Reports

Missouri Highway Patrol, Traffic Division, PO Box 568, Jefferson City, MO 65102-0568 (Courier: 1510 E Elm St, Jefferson City, MO 65101); 573-526-6113, 573-751-9921 (Fax), 8AM-5PM.

www.mshp.state.mo.us

Indexing & Storage: Records are available for 5 years to present on computer. Records are available within 2 weeks. Records are indexed on an in-house computer. Records are on a document imaging system or microfilm from 1941.

Searching: Record requests must be in writing. Generally, these records are open to the public. The first 60 days after the accident, records are restricted to only family members or those involved or their representatives. Include the following in your request: full name, date of accident, location of accident, relationship of requester to the subject. There is no telephone searching, but you can call to determine if an accident is on file.

Access by: mail, in person.

Fee & Payment: At present, due to restrictions imposed by legislation, the $5.00 fee for reports has not been implemented.

Mail search: Turnaround time: 3 to 4 working days. A self addressed stamped envelope is requested.

In person search: Turnaround time is immediate.

Legislation Records

Legislative Library, 117A State Capitol, Jefferson City, MO 65101; 573-751-4633 (Bill Status Only), 8:30AM-4:30PM.

www.moga.state.mo.us

Note: Sessions are from January to May.

Indexing & Storage: Records are available from 1993 to present on computer, from 1909-1972 and 1985 to 2000 on microfiche, and from 1973 to 1984 in books. Records are indexed on microfiche, books (volumes).

Searching: Include the following in your request: bill number, year.

Access by: mail, phone, in person, online.

Fee & Payment: There is no search fee, but there is a $.10 copy fee per page. Fees must be paid in advance.

Mail search: Turnaround time: 1 week to 10 days. No self addressed stamped envelope is required.

Phone search: No fee for telephone request. If the requests involves much time/paper, it will be refused.

In person search: Searching is available in person.

Online search: The web site offers access to bills and statutes. One can search or track bills by key words, bill number, or sponsors. Request can be made via e-mail to library@mail.state.mo.us

Voter Registration

Access to Records is Restricted

Secretary of State, Division of Elections, PO Box 1767, Jefferson City, MO 65102; 573-751-2301, 573-526-3242 (Fax), 8AM-5PM.

www.sos.state.mo.us/section4.asp

Note: For individual look-ups, the agency recommends searching at the county level by the County Clerks.

GED Certificates

GED Office, PO Box 480, Jefferson City, MO 65102; 573-751-3504, 8AM-4:30PM.

www.dese.state.mo.us/divvoced

Indexing & Storage: Records are available from 1960 to present. It takes 2 to 3 weeks before new records are available for inquiry.

Searching: Include the following in your request: signed release, date of birth, Social Security Number. The year and location of the test are very helpful and should also be included in the request.

Access by: mail, in person.

Fee & Payment: The fee is $2.00 for either a verification or a transcript. Fee payee: Treasurer, State of Missouri. Prepayment required. Personal checks accepted.

Mail search: Turnaround time: same day. No self addressed stamped envelope is required.

In person search: $2.00 fee per request.

Hunting License Information
Fishing License Information

Conservation Department, Fiscal Services, PO Box 180, Jefferson City, MO 65102-0180 (Courier: 2901 W Truman Blvd, Jefferson City, MO 65102); 573-751-4115, 573-751-4864 (Fax), 8AM-5PM.

www.conservation.state.mo.us

Indexing & Storage: Records are available for since 1/1/99. Records are indexed on inhouse computer, hard copy.

Searching: Records are only released to the permitee. Otherwise, they are not released until the reason for the request is reviewed by the Department's General Counsel. Names and addresses may be released, if request is approved. Include the following in your request: full name. For older records, you will need the permittee's name, date of birth, and type of permit.

Access by: mail.

Fee & Payment: Prepayment required. Fee payee: Conservation Department. Price is based upon type of service provided. Personal checks accepted. Credit cards accepted: MasterCard, Visa.

Mail search: No self addressed stamped envelope is required.

Other access: Mailing lists of the hunting and fishing permit vendors are available. The cost is about $100.

Missouri State Licensing Agencies

Licenses Searchable Online

Architect #2	http://riversrun.ded.state.mo.us/cgi-bin/professionalregistration.pl
Athletic Trainer #28	http://showme.ded.state.mo.us/dynded/pronline.form1
Attorney #40	www.mobar.org/directory/index.htm
Audiologist, Clinical #16	http://riversrun.ded.state.mo.us/cgi-bin/professionalregistration.pl
Audiologist/Speech (combined), Clinical #16	http://riversrun.ded.state.mo.us/cgi-bin/professionalregistration.pl
Barber Instructor/School #3	http://riversrun.ded.state.mo.us/cgi-bin/professionalregistration.pl
Barber/Barber Shop #3	http://riversrun.ded.state.mo.us/cgi-bin/professionalregistration.pl
Beauty Shop #5	http://riversrun.ded.state.mo.us/cgi-bin/professionalregistration.pl
Boxer/Boxing Professional #44	http://riversrun.ded.state.mo.us/cgi-bin/professionalregistration.pl
Cemetery (Endowed Care Cemetery) #25	www.ecodev.state.mo.us/pr/endowed.html
Chiropractor #4	http://riversrun.ded.state.mo.us/cgi-bin/professionalregistration.pl
Cosmetologist #5	http://riversrun.ded.state.mo.us/cgi-bin/professionalregistration.pl
Cosmetology School/Instructor #5	http://riversrun.ded.state.mo.us/cgi-bin/professionalregistration.pl
Cosmetology Shop #5	http://riversrun.ded.state.mo.us/cgi-bin/professionalregistration.pl
Counselor, Professional #23	http://riversrun.ded.state.mo.us/cgi-bin/professionalregistration.pl
Dental Hygienist #17	http://riversrun.ded.state.mo.us/cgi-bin/professionalregistration.pl
Dental Specialist #17	http://riversrun.ded.state.mo.us/cgi-bin/professionalregistration.pl
Dentist #17	http://riversrun.ded.state.mo.us/cgi-bin/professionalregistration.pl
Drug Distribution #9	http://riversrun.ded.state.mo.us/cgi-bin/professionalregistration.pl
Embalmer #6	http://riversrun.ded.state.mo.us/cgi-bin/professionalregistration.pl
Engineer #2	http://riversrun.ded.state.mo.us/cgi-bin/professionalregistration.pl
Funeral Director #6	http://riversrun.ded.state.mo.us/cgi-bin/professionalregistration.pl
Funeral Establishment #6	http://riversrun.ded.state.mo.us/cgi-bin/professionalregistration.pl
Funeral Preneed Provider/Seller #6	http://riversrun.ded.state.mo.us/cgi-bin/professionalregistration.pl
Geologist #47	http://riversrun.ded.state.mo.us/cgi-bin/professionalregistration.pl
Geologist Registrant in Training #47	http://riversrun.ded.state.mo.us/cgi-bin/professionalregistration.pl
Insurance Agent/Broker #20	www.insurance.state.mo.us/industry/agtstatus.htm
Interpreter for the Deaf #46	http://riversrun.ded.state.mo.us/cgi-bin/professionalregistration.pl
Land Surveyor #2	http://riversrun.ded.state.mo.us/cgi-bin/professionalregistration.pl
Landfill #37	www.dnr.state.mo.us/deq/swmp/availpub.htm
Landscape Architect #26	http://riversrun.ded.state.mo.us/cgi-bin/professionalregistration.pl
Landscape Architect Corp./or/Partnership #26	http://riversrun.ded.state.mo.us/cgi-bin/professionalregistration.pl
Manicurist #5	http://riversrun.ded.state.mo.us/cgi-bin/professionalregistration.pl
Marital & Family Therapist #43	http://riversrun.ded.state.mo.us/cgi-bin/professionalregistration.pl
Martial Artist/Martial Arts Professional #44	http://riversrun.ded.state.mo.us/cgi-bin/professionalregistration.pl
Medical Doctor #11	http://riversrun.ded.state.mo.us/cgi-bin/professionalregistration.pl
Nurse, Advanced Practical #7	http://riversrun.ded.state.mo.us/cgi-bin/professionalregistration.pl
Nurse, Registered #7	http://riversrun.ded.state.mo.us/cgi-bin/professionalregistration.pl
Nurse-LPN #7	http://riversrun.ded.state.mo.us/cgi-bin/professionalregistration.pl
Nursing School #7	http://riversrun.ded.state.mo.us/cgi-bin/professionalregistration.pl
Occupational Therapist #41	http://riversrun.ded.state.mo.us/cgi-bin/professionalregistration.pl
Occupational Therapist Assistant #41	http://riversrun.ded.state.mo.us/cgi-bin/professionalregistration.pl
Optometrist #8	http://riversrun.ded.state.mo.us/cgi-bin/professionalregistration.pl
Osteopathic Physician #11	http://riversrun.ded.state.mo.us/cgi-bin/professionalregistration.pl
Perfusionist #11	http://riversrun.ded.state.mo.us/cgi-bin/professionalregistration.pl
Pharmacist/Pharmacy Intern #9	http://riversrun.ded.state.mo.us/cgi-bin/professionalregistration.pl
Pharmacy #9	http://riversrun.ded.state.mo.us/cgi-bin/professionalregistration.pl
Pharmacy Technician #9	http://riversrun.ded.state.mo.us/cgi-bin/professionalregistration.pl
Physical Therapist #11	http://riversrun.ded.state.mo.us/cgi-bin/professionalregistration.pl
Physician Assistant #11	http://riversrun.ded.state.mo.us/cgi-bin/professionalregistration.pl
Podiatrist #10	http://riversrun.ded.state.mo.us/cgi-bin/professionalregistration.pl

Podiatrist Temporary #10..http://riversrun.ded.state.mo.us/cgi-bin/professionalregistration.pl
Podiatrist/Ankle #10..http://riversrun.ded.state.mo.us/cgi-bin/professionalregistration.pl
Psychologist #36...http://riversrun.ded.state.mo.us/cgi-bin/professionalregistration.pl
Public Accountant Partnership #1 ....http://riversrun.ded.state.mo.us/cgi-bin/professionalregistration.pl
Public Accountant-CPA #1...http://riversrun.ded.state.mo.us/cgi-bin/professionalregistration.pl
Real Estate Appraiser #14 ....http://riversrun.ded.state.mo.us/cgi-bin/professionalregistration.pl
Real Estate Broker/Partner/Associate #35...............http://riversrun.ded.state.mo.us/cgi-bin/professionalregistration.pl
Real Estate Instructor #35 ....http://riversrun.ded.state.mo.us/cgi-bin/professionalregistration.pl
Real Estate Officer/Corp/Association #35..................http://riversrun.ded.state.mo.us/cgi-bin/professionalregistration.pl
Real Estate Sales Agent #35 ....http://riversrun.ded.state.mo.us/cgi-bin/professionalregistration.pl
Respiratory Care Practitioner #42..............................http://riversrun.ded.state.mo.us/cgi-bin/professionalregistration.pl
Social Worker, Clinical #15 ....http://riversrun.ded.state.mo.us/cgi-bin/professionalregistration.pl
Speech-Language Pathologist/Audiologist #16 ......http://riversrun.ded.state.mo.us/cgi-bin/professionalregistration.pl
Transfer Station #37 ....www.dnr.state.mo.us/deq/swmp/tranlist.htm
Veterinarian #31 ....http://riversrun.ded.state.mo.us/cgi-bin/professionalregistration.pl
Veterinary Technician #31 ....http://riversrun.ded.state.mo.us/cgi-bin/professionalregistration.pl
Waste Tire End User #37 ....www.dnr.state.mo.us/deq/swmp/tireend.htm
Waste Tire Hauler #37 ....www.dnr.state.mo.us/deq/swmp/tirehaul.htm
Waste Tire Processor/Site #37 ....www.dnr.state.mo.us/deq/swmp/tireend.htm
Wrestler/Wrestling Professional #44 ....http://riversrun.ded.state.mo.us/cgi-bin/professionalregistration.pl

Licensing Quick Finder

Architect #2....................................573-751-0047
Athletic Trainer #28........................573-751-0171
Attorney #40 573-635-4128
Audiologist, Clinical #16 573-751-0171
Audiologist/Speech (Combined), Clinical #16
....573-751-0171
Barber Instructor/School #3...........573-751-0805
Barber/Barber Shop #3..................573-751-0805
Beauty Shop #5..............................573-751-1052
Bingo Worker/Officer/Operation #30 573-526-5370
Boxer/Boxing Professional #44 573-751-0243
Cemetery (Endowed Care Cemetery) #25
....573-751-0849
Child Care Facility #29 573-751-2450
Chiropractor #4..............................573-751-2104
Cosmetologist #5...........................573-751-1052
Cosmetology School/Instructor #5 573-751-1052
Cosmetology Shop #5....................573-751-1052
Counselor, Professional #23 573-751-0018
Court Reporter #12.........................573-751-4144
Dental Hygienist #17......................573-751-0040
Dental Specialist #17.....................573-751-0040
Dentist #17.....................................573-751-0040
Drug Distribution #9.......................573-751-0091
Embalmer #6 573-751-0813
Emergency Medical Technician, Basic #19
....573-751-6356
Engineer #2....................................573-751-0047
Funeral Director #6 573-751-0813
Funeral Establishment #6..............573-751-0813
Funeral Preneed Provider/Seller #6 573-751-0813
Gaming Occupational License #30 573-526-4092
Gaming Property, Boat #30.............573-526-4092
Gaming Supply #30 573-526-4092
Geologist #47.................................573-526-7625

Geologist Registrant in Training #47......73-526-7625
Horse Racing #30 573-526-4083
Insurance Agent/Broker #20.................573-751-3518
Interpreter for the Deaf #46...........573-526-7787
Investment Advisor #34..................573-751-4136
Land Surveyor #2 573-751-0047
Landfill #37......................................573-751-5401
Landfill Operator #37......................573-751-5401
Landscape Architect #26................573-751-0039
Landscape Architect Corp./or/Partnership #26
....573-751-0039
Liquor Control #21..........................573-751-2333
Manicurist #5 573-751-1052
Marital & Family Therapist #43 573-751-0870
Martial Artist/Martial Arts Professional #44
....573-751-0243
Medical Doctor #11.........................573-751-0108
Notary Public #33...........................573-751-2783
Nurse, Advanced Practical #7 573-751-0681
Nurse, Registered #7 573-751-0681
Nurse-LPN #7.................................573-751-0681
Nursing Home Administrator #32 573-751-3511
Nursing School #7 573-751-0681
Occupational Therapist #41 573-751-0877
Occupational Therapist Assistant #41..573-751-0877
Optometrist #8................................573-751-0814
Osteopathic Physician #11.............573-751-0108
Perfusionist #11..............................573-751-0108
Pesticide Applicator #18.................573-751-5504
Pesticide Dealer #18......................573-751-5504
Pesticide Technician #18 573-751-9298
Pharmacist/Pharmacy Intern #9...........573-751-0091
Pharmacy #9 573-751-0091
Pharmacy Technician #9.................573-751-0091
Physical Therapist #11 573-751-0171

Physician Assistant #11 573-751-0171
Podiatrist #10 573-751-0873
Podiatrist Temporary #10...............573-751-0873
Podiatrist/Ankle #10 573-751-0873
Prevention Specialist (Social Work) #39573-751-9211
Psychologist #36............................573-751-0099
Public Accountant Partnership #1 573-751-0012
Public Accountant-CPA #1..............573-751-0012
Real Estate Appraiser #14 573-751-0038
Real Estate Broker/Partner/Associate #35
....573-751-2628
Real Estate Instructor #35..............573-751-2628
Real Estate Officer/Corp/Association #35
....573-751-2628
Real Estate Sales Agent #35 573-751-2628
Respiratory Care Practitioner #42........573-522-2864
School Commissioner Assistant #24 ...573-526-4900
School Librarian #24 573-526-4900
Securities Agent #34 573-751-4136
Securities Broker/Dealer #34 573-751-4136
Social Worker, Clinical #15 573-751-0885
Speech-Language Pathologist/Audiologist #16
....573-751-0171
Substance Abuse Assoc-in-Training #39573-751-9211
Substance Abuse Counselor #39 573-751-9211
Transfer Station #37.......................573-751-5401
Veterinarian #31.............................573-751-0031
Veterinary Technician #31 573-751-0031
Waste Tire End User #37 573-751-5401
Waste Tire Hauler #37 573-751-5401
Waste Tire Processor/Site #37 573-751-5401
Waste Water System Operator #38.....573-526-6627
Water Supply Operator #38 573-526-6627
Wrestler/Wrestling Professional #44....573-751-0243

Licensing Agency Information

#1 Board of Accountancy, 3605 Missouri Blvd, Jefferson City, MO 65102-0613; 573-751-1052, Fax: 573-751-0890. www.ecodev.state.mo.us/pr/account. Agency email: boa@mail.state.mo.us. Search database at http://riversrun.ded.state. mo.us/cgi-bin/professionalregistration.pl. Lists are available at www.ecodev.state.mo.us/pr/ftp4.htm

#2 Engineers & Land Survey, Board of Architects, 3605 Missouri Blvd, #380, Jefferson City, MO 65102; 573-751-0047, Fax: 573-751-8046. www.ecodev.state.mo.us/moapels. Agency email: moapels@mail.state.mo.us. Search database at http://riversrun.ded.state. mo.us/cgi-bin/professionalregistration.pl. Lists are available at www.ecodev.state.mo.us/pr/ftp4.htm

#3 Board of Barber Examiners, 3605 Missouri Blvd, Jefferson City, MO 65102-1335; 573-751-0805, Fax: 573-751-8167. www.ecodev.state.mo.us/pr/barber. Agency email: barber@mail.state.mo.us. Search database at http://riversrun.ded.state.mo. us/cgi-bin/professionalregistration.pl. Lists are available at www.ecodev.state.mo.us/pr/ftp4.htm

#4 Board of Chiropractic Examiners, 3605 Missouri Blvd, Jefferson City, MO 65102-0672; 573-751-2104, Fax: 573-751-0735. www.ecodev.state.mo.us/pr/chiro. Agency email: chiro@mail.state.mo.us. Search database at http://riversrun.ded.state.mo. us/cgi-bin/professionalregistration.pl. Lists are available at www.ecodev.state.mo.us/pr/ftp4.htm

#5 Board of Cosmetology, 3605 Missouri Blvd, Jefferson City, MO 65102; 573-751-1052, Fax: 573-751-8167. www.ecodev.state.mo.us/pr/cosmo. Agency email: cosmo@mail.state.mo.us. Search database at http://riversrun.ded.state. mo.us/cgi-bin/professionalregistration.pl. Lists are available at www.ecodev.state.mo.us/pr/ftp4.htm

#6 Board of Embalmers & Funeral Directors, 3605 Missouri Blvd, Jefferson City, MO 65102-0625; 573-751-0813, Fax: 573-751-1155. www.ecodev.state.mo.us/pr/embalm. Agency email: emblamer@mail.state.mo.us. Search database at http://riversrun.ded.state. mo.us/cgi-bin/professionalregistration.pl. Lists are available at www.ecodev.state.mo.us/pr/ftp4.htm

#7 Board of Nursing, 3605 Missouri Blvd, Jefferson City, MO 65102; 573-751-0681, Fax: 573-751-0075. www.ecodev.state.mo.us/pr/nursing. Agency email: nursing@mail.state.mo.us. Search database at http://riversrun.ded.state. mo.us/cgi-bin/professionalregistration.pl. Nursing lists are available at www.ecodev.state.mo.us/pr/nursingdown.html

#8 Board of Optometry, PO Box 1335 (3605 Missouri Blvd), Jefferson City, MO 65102-0423; 573-751-0814, Fax: 573-751-0735. www.ecodev.state.mo.us/pr/optom. Agency email: optom@mail.state.mo.us. Search database at http://riversrun.ded.state. mo.us/cgi-bin/professionalregistration.pl. Lists are available at www.ecodev.state.mo.us/pr/ftp4.htm

#9 Board of Pharmacy, 3605 Missouri Blvd, Jefferson City, MO 65102; 573-751-0091, Fax: 573-526-3464.

www.ecodev.state.mo.us/pr/pharmacy. Agency email: pharmacy@mail.state.mo.us. Search database at http://riversrun.ded.state. mo.us/cgi-bin/professionalregistration.pl. Lists are available at www.ecodev.state.mo.us/pr/ftp4.htm

#10 Board of Podiatric Medicine, 3605 Missouri Blvd, Jefferson City, MO 65102; 573-751-0873, Fax: 573-751-1155. www.ecodev.state.mo.us/pr/podiatry. Agency email: podiatry@mail.state.mo.us. Search database at http://riversrun.ded.state.mo. us/cgi-bin/professionalregistration.pl. Lists are available at www.ecodev.state.mo.us/pr/ftp4.htm

#11 Board of Registration for Healing Arts, 3605 Missouri Blvd, Jefferson City, MO 65102; 573-751-0098, Fax: 573-751-3166. www.ecodev.state.mo.us/pr/healarts. Agency email: healarts@mail.state.mo.us. Search database at http://riversrun.ded.state.mo. us/cgi-bin/professionalregistration.pl. Lists are available at www.ecodev.state.mo.us/pr/healingdown.html

#14 Commission of Real Estate Appraisers, 3605 Missouri Blvd, Jefferson City, MO 65109; 573-751-0038, Fax: 573-526-3489. www.ecodev.state.mo.us/pr/rea. Agency email: reacom@mail.state.mo.us. Search database at http://riversrun.ded.state.mo. us/cgi-bin/professionalregistration.pl. Lists are available at www.ecodev.state.mo.us/pr/ftp4.htm

#15 Division of Professional Registration, Committee for Licensed Clinical Social Workers, 3605 Missouri Blvd, Jefferson City, MO 65102; 573-751-0885, Fax: 573-751-0890. www.ecodev.state.mo.us/pr/social. Agency email: lcsw@mail.state.mo.us. Search database at http://riversrun.ded.state. mo.us/cgi-bin/professionalregistration.pl. List are available at www.ecodev.state.mo.us/pr/ftp4.htm

#16 Committee of Speech Pathology & Audiology, 3605 Missouri Blvd, Jefferson City, MO 65102; 573-751-0098, Fax: 573-751-3166. www.ecodev.state.mo.us/pr/healarts. Agency email: healarts@mail.state.mo.us. Search database at http://riversrun.ded.state.mo. us/cgi-bin/professionalregistration.pl. Lists are available at www.ecodev.state.mo.us/pr/healingdown.html

#17 Dental Board, 3605 Missouri Blvd, Jefferson City, MO 65102; 573-751-0040, Fax: 573-751-8216. www.ecodev.state.mo.us/pr/dental. Agency email: dental@mail.state.mo.us. Search database at http://riversrun.ded.state.mo. us/cgi-bin/professionalregistration.pl. Lists are available at www.ecodev.state.mo.us/pr/ftp4.htm

#18 Department of Agriculture, Division of Plant Industries, Bureau of Pesticide, 1616 Missouri Blvd, Jefferson City, MO 65102; 573-751-2462, Fax: 573-751-0005. www.mda.state.mo.us/d.htm. Agency email: paul_bailey@mail.meda.state.mo.us.

#19 Department of Health, Emergency Medical Services, PO Box 570 (912 Wildwood Dr), Jefferson City, MO 65102-0570; 573-751-6356, Fax: 573-526-4102. www.health.state.mo.us.

#20 Department of Insurance, Licensing Section, PO Box 690 (301 W High St), Jefferson City, MO 65102-0690; 573-751-4126, Fax: 573-526-3416. www.insurance.state.mo.us. Agency email: mdimedia@mail.state.mo.us. Search database at www.insurance.state.mo.us/industry/agtstatus.htm

#21 Department of Public Safety, Division of Liquor Control, Truman Bldg, Rm 870, Jefferson City, MO 65102-0837; 573-751-5445, Fax: 573-526-4540. www.mdlc.state.mo.us. Agency email: liquor@mail.state.mo.us.

#23 Division of Professional Regulation, Committee for Professional Counselors, PO Box 1335 (3605 Missouri Blvd), Jefferson City, MO 65102-1335; 573-751-0018, Fax: 573-526-3489. www.ecodev.state.mo.us/pr/counselr. Agency email: couns@mail.state.ma.us. Search database at http://riversrun.ded.state.mo. us/cgi-bin/professionalregistration.pl. Lists are available at www.ecodev.state.mo.us/pr/ftp4.htm

#24 Education, Elementary & Secondary Instruction, Div of School Improvement, 205 Jefferson St, Jefferson City, MO 65102-0480; 573-751-4234, Fax: 573-751-9434. www.dese.state.mo.us

#25 Endowed Care Cemeteries, 3605 Missouri Blvd (PO Box 1335, 65102), Jefferson City, MO 65102-1335; 573-751-0849, Fax: 573-751-0878. www.ecodev.state.mo.us/pr/endowed. Agency email: endocare@mail.state.mo.us. Search database at www.ecodev.state.mo.us/pr/endowed.html

#26 Landscape Architectural Council, 3605 Missouri Blvd, Jefferson City, MO 65102-1339; 573-751-0039, Fax: 573-751-2831. www.ecodev.state.mo.us/pr/landarch. Agency email: landarch@mail.state.mo.us. Search database at http://riversrun.ded.state.mo. us/cgi-bin/professionalregistration.pl. Lists are available at www.ecodev.state.mo.us/pr/ftp4.htm

#29 Department of Health, Bureau of Child Care Safety & Licensure, 1715 South Ridge, Jefferson City, MO 65109; 573-751-2450, Fax: 573-526-5345. www.health.state.mo.us/AbouttheDepartment/BofCC.html

#30 Gaming Commission, 3417 Knipp Dr, Jefferson City, MO 65102; 573-526-4080, Fax: 573-526-1999. www.mgc.state.mo.us. Agency email: hbailey@mail.state.mo.us.

#31 Veterinary Medical Board, 3605 Missouri Blvd, Jefferson City, MO 65102-0633; 573-751-0031, Fax: 573-751-3856. www.ecodev.state.mo.us/pr/vet. Agency email: vets@mail.state.mo.us. Search database at http://riversrun.ded.state.mo. us/cgi-bin/professionalregistration.pl. Lists are available at www.ecodev.state.mo.us/pr/ftp4.htm

#32 Board of Nursing Home Administrators, 2033 St Mary's Blvd (PO Box 570), Jefferson City, MO 65102; 573-751-3511, Fax: 573-573-4314. Agency email: loveqbl@state.mo.us.

#33 Office of Secretary of State, State Capitol Rm 208, Jefferson City, MO 65101; 573-751-4936, Fax: 573-526-3489.
www.sos.state.mo.us

#34 Secretary of State, Securities Division, 600 W Main St #229, Jefferson City, MO 65101; 573-751-4136, Fax: 573-526-3124.
http://mosl.sos.state.mo.us/sos-sec/sossec.html

#35 Real Estate Commission, PO Box 1339 (3605 Missouri Blvd), Jefferson City, MO 65102-1339; 573-751-2628, Fax: 573-751-2777.
www.ecodev.state.mo.us/pr/restate.
Agency email: realesta@mail.state.mo.us.
Search database at http://riversrun.ded.state.mo.us/cgi-bin/professionalregistration.pl. Lists are available at www.ecodev.state.mo.us/pr/new.html

#36 Committee of Psychology, 3605 Missouri Blvd, Jefferson City, MO 65102-1335; 573-751-0099, Fax: 573-526-3489.
www.ecodev.state.mo.us/pr/psych.
Agency email: scop@mail.state.mo.us.
Search database at http://riversrun.ded.state.mo.us/cgi-bin/professionalregistration.pl. Lists are available at www.ecodev.state.mo.us/pr/ftp4.htm

#37 Department of Natural Resources, Div of Environmental Quality, Solid Waste Mgmt, 1738 E Elm, PO Box 176, Jefferson City, MO 65102-0176; 573-751-5401, Fax: 573-526-3902.
www.dnr.state.mo.us.
Agency email: nrmars.b2@mail.dnr.state.mo.us.

#38 Department of Natural Resources, Technical Assistance Program, PO Box 176 (1659 Elm St), Jefferson City, MO 65102; 573-526-6627, Fax: 573-526-5808.
www.dnr.state.mo.us/deq/tap/oprtrain.htm

#39 Abuse Counselors Certification Board, 1706 E Elm, Jefferson City, MO 65102; 573-751-9211, Fax: 573-526-3489.
www.modmh.state.mo.us/msaccb.
Agency email: msaccb@mail.dmh.state.mo.us.

#40 The Missouri Bar, PO Box 119 (326 Monroe St), Jefferson City, MO 65102-0119; 573-635-4128, Fax: 573-635-2811.
www.mobar.org
Search database at
www.mobar.org/directory/index.htm

#41 Division of Professional Registration, Board of Occupational Therapy, PO Box 1335 (3605 Missouri Blvd, 65109), Jefferson City, MO 65102-1335; 573-751-0877, Fax: 573-526-3489.
www.ecodev.state.mo.us/pr/octherap.
Agency email: ot@mail.state.mo.us.
Search database at http://riversrun.ded.state.mo.us/cgi-bin/professionalregistration.pl. Lists are available at www.ecodev.state.mo.us/pr/ftp4.htm

#42 Board for Respiratory Care, 3605 Missouri Blvd, Jefferson City, MO 65102-1335; 573-522-5864, Fax: 573-526-4176.
www.ecodev.state.mo.us/pr/mbrc.
Agency email: rcp@mail.state.mo.us.
Search database at http://riversrun.ded.state.mo.us/cgi-bin/professionalregistration.pl. Lists are available at www.ecodev.state.mo.us/pr/ftp4.htm

#43 Committee of Marital & Family Therapists, 3605 Missouri Blvd, Jefferson City, MO 65102-1335; 573-751-0870, Fax: 573-526-3489.
www.ecodev.state.mo.us/pr/mft. Agency email: mfts@mail.state.mo.us.
Search database at
http://riversrun.ded.state.mo.us/cgi-bin/professionalregistration.pl. Lists are available at www.ecodev.state.mo.us/pr/ftp4.htm

#44 Office of Athletics, 3605 Missouri Blvd, Jefferson City, MO 65102-1335; 573-751-0243, Fax: 573-751-5649.
www.ecodev.state.mo.us/pr/athletic.
Agency email: athletic@mail.state.mo.us.
Search database at http://riversrun.ded.state.mo.us/cgi-bin/professionalregistration.pl

#46 Committee of Interpreters, PO Box 1335 (3605 Missouri Blvd), Jefferson City, MO 65102-1335; 573-526-7787, Fax: 573-526-3489.
www.ecodev.state.mo.us/pr/inter.
Agency email: interp@mail.state.mo.us.
Search database at http://riversrun.ded.state.mo.us/cgi-bin/professionalregistration.pl. Lists are available at www.ecodev.state.mo.us/pr/ftp4.htm

#47 Board of Geologist Registration, 3605 Missouri Blvd, PO Box 1335, Jefferson City, MO 65102; 573-526-7625, Fax: 573-526-3489.
www.ecodev.state.mo.us/pr/geo.
Agency email: geo@mail.state.mo.us.
Search database at http://riversrun.ded.state.mo.us/cgi-bin/professionalregistration.pl. Lists are available at www.ecodev.state.mo.us/pr/ftp4.htm

Missouri Federal Courts

The following list indicates the district and division name for each county in the state. If the bankruptcy court location is different from the district court, then the location of the bankruptcy court appears in parentheses.

County/Court Cross Reference

County	District	Division
Adair	Eastern	Hannibal (St Louis)
Andrew	Western	St Joseph (Kansas City - Western)
Atchison	Western	St Joseph (Kansas City - Western)
Audrain	Eastern	Hannibal (St Louis)
Barry	Western	Joplin-Southwestern (Kansas City)
Barton	Western	Joplin-Southwestern (Kansas City)
Bates	Western	Kansas City - Western
Benton	Western	Jefferson City-Central (Kansas City)
Bollinger	Eastern	Cape Girardeau (St Louis)
Boone	Western	Jefferson City-Central (Kansas City)
Buchanan	Western	St Joseph (Kansas City - Western)
Butler	Eastern	Cape Girardeau (St Louis)
Caldwell	Western	St Joseph (Kansas City - Western)
Callaway	Western	Jefferson City-Central (Kansas City)
Camden	Western	Jefferson City-Central (Kansas City)
Cape Girardeau	Eastern	Cape Girardeau (St Louis)
Carroll	Western	Kansas City - Western
Carter	Eastern	Cape Girardeau (St Louis)
Cass	Western	Kansas City - Western
Cedar	Western	Springfield-Southern (Kansas City)
Chariton	Eastern	Hannibal (St Louis)
Christian	Western	Springfield-Southern (Kansas City)
Clark	Eastern	Hannibal (St Louis)
Clay	Western	Kansas City - Western
Clinton	Western	St Joseph (Kansas City - Western)
Cole	Western	Jefferson City-Central (Kansas City)
Cooper	Western	Jefferson City-Central (Kansas City)
Crawford	Eastern	St Louis
Dade	Western	Springfield-Southern (Kansas City)
Dallas	Western	Springfield-Southern (Kansas City)
Daviess	Western	St Joseph (Kansas City - Western)
De Kalb	Western	St Joseph (Kansas City - Western)
Dent	Eastern	St Louis
Douglas	Western	Springfield-Southern ((Kansas City)
Dunklin	Eastern	Cape Girardeau (St Louis)
Franklin	Eastern	St Louis
Gasconade	Eastern	St Louis
Gentry	Western	St Joseph (Kansas City - Western)
Greene	Western	Springfield-Southern (Kansas City)
Grundy	Western	St Joseph (Kansas City - Western)
Harrison	Western	St Joseph (Kansas City - Western)
Henry	Western	Kansas City - Western
Hickory	Western	Jefferson City-Central (Kansas City)
Holt	Western	St Joseph (Kansas City - Western)
Howard	Western	Jefferson City-Central (Kansas City)
Howell	Western	Springfield-Southern (Kansas City)
Iron	Eastern	St Louis
Jackson	Western	Kansas City – Western
Jasper	Western	Joplin-Southwestern (Kansas City)
Jefferson	Eastern	St Louis
Johnson	Western	Kansas City - Western
Knox	Eastern	Hannibal (St Louis)
Laclede	Western	Springfield-Southern (Kansas City
Lafayette	Western	Kansas City - Western
Lawrence	Western	Joplin-Southwestern (Kansas City)
Lewis	Eastern	Hannibal (St Louis)
Lincoln	Eastern	St Louis
Linn	Eastern	Hannibal (St Louis)
Livingston	Western	St Joseph (Kansas City - Western)
Macon	Eastern	Hannibal (St Louis)
Madison	Eastern	Cape Girardeau (St Louis)
Maries	Eastern	St Louis
Marion	Eastern	Hannibal (St Louis)
McDonald	Western	Joplin-Southwestern (Kansas City)
Mercer	Western	St Joseph (Kansas City - Western)
Miller	Western	Jefferson City-Central (Kansas City)
Mississippi	Eastern	Cape Girardeau (St Louis)
Moniteau	Western	Jefferson City-Central (Kansas City)
Monroe	Eastern	Hannibal (St Louis)
Montgomery	Eastern	Hannibal (St Louis)
Morgan	Western	Jefferson City-Central (Kansas City)
New Madrid	Eastern	Cape Girardeau (St Louis)
Newton	Western	Joplin-Southwestern (Kansas City)
Nodaway	Western	St Joseph (Kansas City - Western)
Oregon	Western	Springfield-Southern (Kansas City)
Osage	Western	Jefferson City-Central (Kansas City)
Ozark	Western	Springfield-Southern (Kansas City)
Pemiscot	Eastern	Cape Girardeau (St Louis)
Perry	Eastern	Cape Girardeau (St Louis)
Pettis	Western	Jefferson City-Central (Kansas City)
Phelps	Eastern	St Louis
Pike	Eastern	Hannibal (St Louis)
Platte	Western	St Joseph (Kansas City - Western)
Polk	Western	Springfield-Southern (Kansas City)

Pulaski	Western	Springfield-Southern (Kansas City)
Putnam	Western	St Joseph (Kansas City - Western)
Ralls	Eastern	Hannibal (St Louis)
Randolph	Eastern	Hannibal (St Louis)
Ray	Western	Kansas City - Western)
Reynolds	Eastern	Cape Girardeau (St Louis)
Ripley	Eastern	Cape Girardeau (St Louis)
Saline	Western	Kansas City - Western
Schuyler	Eastern	Hannibal (St Louis)
Scotland	Eastern	Hannibal (St Louis)
Scott	Eastern	Cape Girardeau (St Louis)
Shannon	Eastern	Cape Girardeau (St Louis)
Shelby	Eastern	Hannibal (St Louis)
St. Charles	Eastern	St Louis
St. Clair	Western	Kansas City - Western
St. Francois	Eastern	St Louis

St. Louis	Eastern	St Louis
St. Louis City City	Eastern	St Louis
Ste. Genevieve	Eastern	St Louis
Stoddard	Eastern	Cape Girardeau (St Louis)
Stone	Western	Joplin-Southwestern (Kansas City)
Sullivan	Western	St Joseph (Kansas City - Western)
Taney	Western	Springfield-Southern (Kansas City)
Texas	Western	Springfield-Southern (Kansas City)
Vernon	Western	Joplin-Southwestern (Kansas City)
Warren	Eastern	St Louis
Washington	Eastern	St Louis
Wayne	Eastern	Cape Girardeau (St Louis)
Webster	Western	Springfield-Southern (Kansas City)
Worth	Western	St Joseph (Kansas City - Western)
Wright	Western	Springfield-Southern (Kansas City)

Standards for Federal Courts: The search fee is $20.00 per item (one party name or case number). Certification fee is $7.00 per document. Copy fee is $.50 per page. All fees standard unless noted in profile. Mail Search: always enclose a stamped self addressed envelope unless otherwise noted. Before releasing records, all courts require prepayment unless noted in profile.

Open records are located at the court unless otherwise noted. District courts index by defendant and plaintiff as well as by case number. Bankruptcy courts usually index by debtor and case number. While most courts now have their indexes on computer, many still maintain index card files as well.

The universal PACER sign-up number is 800-676-6856. Find PACER and the Party/Case Index on the Web at http://pacer.psc.uscourts.gov. PACER dial-up access is $.60 per minute. Also, courts offering internet access via RACER, PACER, Web-PACER or the new CM-ECF charge $.07 per page fee unless noted as free.

US District Court

Eastern District of Missouri

Cape Girardeau Division 339 Broadway, Room 240, Cape Girardeau, MO 63701 (Courier Address: Use mail address for courier delivery), 573-335-8538, Fax: 573-335-0379.

www.moed.uscourts.gov

Counties: Bollinger, Butler, Cape Girardeau, Carter, Dunklin, Madison, Mississippi, New Madrid, Pemiscot, Perry, Reynolds, Ripley, Scott, Shannon, Stoddard, Wayne.

Indexing & Storage: Cases are indexed by defendant, plaintiff, and case number. New cases are available in the index 1-2 days after filing date. Computerized records are available from January 1, 1992. Open records are located at this court.

Fee & Payment Notes: Payment may be made by money order, cashier check, personal check. Payee: Clerk, US District Court.

Phone Search: Only docket information is available by phone.

Mail Search: A stamped self addressed envelope is not required.

In Person Search: In person searching available.

PACER: Toll-free dial-up access: 800-533-8105. Local dial-up access: 314-244-7775. Case records are available back to 1992. Records are never purged. New records are available online after 4-5 days. PACER is available online at http://pacer.moed.uscourts.gov.

Hannibal Division 801 Broadway, Hannibal, MO 63401 (Courier Address: Use mail address for courier delivery), 573-221-0757.

www.moed.uscourts.gov

Counties: Adair, Audrain, Chariton, Clark, Knox, Lewis, Linn, Macon, Marion, Monroe, Montgomery, Pike, Ralls, Randolph, Schuyler, Scotland, Shelby.

Indexing & Storage: Cases are indexed by defendant, plaintiff, and case number. New cases are available in the index after filing date. Open records are located at the Division.

Fee & Payment Notes: Payment may be made by money order, cashier check. Business checks are not accepted. Personal checks are not accepted.

Phone Search: Searching not available by phone.

Mail Search: A stamped self addressed envelope is not required.

In Person Search: In person searching available.

PACER: Toll-free dial-up access: 800-533-8105. Local dial-up access: 314-244-7775. Case records are available back to 1992. Records are never purged. New records are available online after 4-5 days. PACER is available online at http://pacer.moed.uscourts.gov.

St Louis Division 111 S. 10th St, Ste 3.300, St Louis, MO 63102 (Courier Address: Use mail address for courier delivery), 314-244-7900, Fax: 314-244-7909.

www.moed.uscourts.gov

Counties: Crawford, Dent, Franklin, Gasconade, Iron, Jefferson, Lincoln, Maries, Phelps, St. Charles, Ste. Genevieve, St. Francois, St. Louis, Warren, Washington, City of St. Louis.

Indexing & Storage: Cases are indexed by defendant, plaintiff, and case number. New cases are available in the index immediately after filing date. Open records are located at this court.

Fee & Payment Notes: Payment may be made by money order, cashier check, personal check. Payee: Clerk, US District Court.

Phone Search: Only docket information is available by phone.

Mail Search: A stamped self addressed envelope is not required.

In Person Search: In person searching available.

PACER: Toll-free dial-up access: 800-533-8105. Local dial-up access: 314-244-7775. Case records are available back to 1992. Records are never purged. New records are available online after 4-5 days. PACER is available online at http://pacer.moed.uscourts.gov.

US Bankruptcy Court

Eastern District of Missouri

St Louis Division 4th Floor, 110 S. 10th St, St Louis, MO 63102-2734 (Courier Address: Use mail address for courier delivery), 314-244-4500, Fax: 314-244-4990.

www.moeb.uscourts.gov

Counties: Adair, Audrain, Bollinger, Butler, Cape Girardeau, Carter, Chariton, Clark, Crawford, Dent, Dunklin, Franklin, Gasconade, Iron, Jefferson, Knox, Lewis, Lincoln, Linn, Macon, Madison, Maries, Marion, Mississippi, Monroe, Montgomery, New Madrid, Pemiscot,Perry, Phelps, Pike, Ralls, Randolph, Reynolds, Ripley, Schuyler, Scotland, Scott, Shannon, Shelby, St. Charles, St. Francois, St. Louis, St.Louis City, Ste. Genevieve, Stoddard, Warren, Washington, Wayne.

Indexing & Storage: Cases are indexed by debtor as well as by case number. New cases are available in the index 24 hours after filing date. Open records are located at this court.

Fee & Payment Notes: Payment may be made by money order, cashier check, personal check. Payee: Clerk, US Bankruptcy Court.

Phone Search: Docket information is available by phone. An automated voice case information service (VCIS) is available. Call VCIS at 888-223-6431 or 314-425-4054.

Mail Search: A stamped self addressed envelope is not required.

In Person Search: In person searching available.

PACER: Toll-free dial-up access: 888-577-1668. Local dial-up access: 314-244-4998. Case records are available back to January 1991. Records are purged every six months. New civil records are available online after 1 day. PACER is available online at http://pacer.moeb.uscourts.gov.

Electronic Filing: (Currently in the process of implementing CM/ECF.)

Other Online Access: Search records on the Internet using RACER at http://racer.moeb.uscourts.gov/perl/bkplog.html.

US District Court

Western District of Missouri

Jefferson City-Central Division 131 W High St, Jefferson City, MO 65101 (Courier Address: Use mail address for courier delivery), 573-636-4015, Fax: 573-636-3456.

www.mow.uscourts.gov

Counties: Benton, Boone, Callaway, Camden, Cole, Cooper, Hickory, Howard, Miller, Moniteau, Morgan, Osage, Pettis.

Indexing & Storage: Cases are indexed by defendant, plaintiff, and case number. New cases are available in the index 1-2 days after filing date. Open records are located at this court.

Fee & Payment Notes: Payment may be made by money order, cashier check, personal check. Payee: Clerk, US District Court.

Phone Search: Only docket information is available by phone.

In Person Search: In person searching available.

PACER: Access fee is. Case records are available back to May 1, 1989. Records are purged as deemed necessary. New records are available online after 1 day. PACER is available online at http://pacer.mowd.uscourts.gov.

Electronic Filing: Information is available online at https://ecf.mowd.uscourts.gov/

Joplin-Southwestern Division c/o Kansas City Division, Charles Evans Whitttaker Courthouse, 400 E 9th St, Kansas City, MO 64106 (Courier Address: Use mail address for courier delivery), 816-512-5000, Fax: 816-512-5078.

www.mow.uscourts.gov

Counties: Barry, Barton, Jasper, Lawrence, McDonald, Newton, Stone, Vernon.

Indexing & Storage: Cases are indexed by defendant, plaintiff, and case number. New cases are available in the index after filing date. Open records are located at the Kansas City Division.

Fee & Payment Notes: Payment may be made by money order, cashier check. Business checks are not accepted. Personal checks are not accepted.

Phone Search: Searching not available by phone. Searching not available by phone.

Mail Search: A stamped self addressed envelope is not required.

In Person Search: In person searching available.

PACER: Access fee is. Case records are available back to May 1, 1989. Records are purged as deemed necessary. New records are available online after 1 day. PACER is available online at http://pacer.mowd.uscourts.gov.

Electronic Filing: Information is available online at https://ecf.mowd.uscourts.gov/

Kansas City-Western Division Clerk of Court, 201 US Courthouse, Rm 1056, 400 E 9th St, Kansas City, MO 64106 (Courier Address: Use mail address for courier delivery), 816-512-5000, Fax: 816-512-5078.

www.mow.uscourts.gov

Counties: Bates, Carroll, Cass, Clay, Henry, Jackson, Johnson, Lafayette, Ray, St. Clair, Saline.

Indexing & Storage: Cases are indexed by defendant, plaintiff, and case number. New cases are available in the index 1-2 days after filing date.

Records are indexed on computer and microfiche. Open records are located at this court.

Fee & Payment Notes: Payment may be made by money order, cashier check, personal check. Payee: US District Court Clerk.

Phone Search: Only docket information is available by phone.

Fax Search: Will accept fax requests.

Mail Search: A stamped self addressed envelope is not required.

In Person Search: In person searching available.

PACER: Access fee is. Case records are available back to May 1, 1989. Records are purged as deemed necessary. New records are available online after 1 day. PACER is available online at http://pacer.mowd.uscourts.gov.

Electronic Filing: Information is available online at https://ecf.mowd.uscourts.gov/

Springfield-Southern Division 222 N John Q Hammons Pkwy, Suite 1400, Springfield, MO 65806 (Courier Address: Use mail address for courier delivery), 417-865-3869, Fax: 417-865-7719.

www.mow.uscourts.gov

Counties: Cedar, Christian, Dade, Dallas, Douglas, Greene, Howell, Laclede, Oregon, Ozark, Polk, Pulaski, Taney, Texas, Webster, Wright.

Indexing & Storage: Cases are indexed by defendant, plaintiff, and case number. New cases are available in the index immediately after filing date. Open records are located at this court.

Fee & Payment Notes: Payment may be made by money order, cashier check, personal check. Payee: Clerk, US District Court.

Phone Search: Only docket information is available by phone.

In Person Search: In person searching available.

PACER: Access fee is. Case records are available back to May 1, 1989. Records are purged as deemed necessary. New records are available online after 1 day. PACER is available online at http://pacer.mowd.uscourts.gov.

Electronic Filing: Information is available online at https://ecf.mowb.uscourts.gov/

St Joseph Division PO Box 387, 201 S 8th St, St Joseph, MO 64501 (Courier Address: Use mail address for courier delivery), Fax: 816-279-0177.

www.mow.uscourts.gov

Counties: Andrew, Atchison, Buchanan, Caldwell, Clinton, Daviess, De Kalb, Gentry, Grundy, Harrison, Holt, Livingston, Mercer, Nodaway, Platte, Putnam, Sullivan, Worth.

Indexing & Storage: Cases are indexed by defendant, plaintiff, and case number. New cases are available in the index immediately after filing date. Open records are located at this court.

Fee & Payment Notes: Payment may be made by money order, cashier check, personal check. Payee: Clerk, US District Court.

Phone Search: Only docket information is available by phone.

Mail Search: A stamped self addressed envelope is not required.

In Person Search: In person searching available.

PACER: Access fee is. Case records are available back to May 1, 1989. Records are purged as deemed necessary. New records are available online after 1 day. PACER is available online at http://pacer.mowd.uscourts.gov.

Electronic Filing: Information is available online at https://ecf.mowd.uscourts.gov/

US Bankruptcy Court

Western District of Missouri

Kansas City-Western Division Room 1510, 400 E 9th st, Kansas City, MO 64106 (Courier Address: Use mail address for courier delivery), 816-512-1800.

www.mow.uscourt.gov

Counties: Andrew, Atchison, Barry, Barton, Bates, Benton, Boone, Buchanan, Caldwell, Callaway, Camden, Carroll, Cass, Cedar, Christian, Clay, Clinton, Cole, Cooper, Dade, Dallas, Daviess, De Kalb, Douglas, Gentry, Greene, Grundy, Harrison, Henry, Hickory, Holt,Howard, Howell, Jackson, Jasper, Johnson, Laclede, Lafayette, Lawrence, Livingston, McDonald, Mercer, Miller, Moniteau, Morgan, Newton, Nodaway, Oregon, Osage, Ozark, Pettis, Platte, Polk, Pulaski, Putnam, Ray, Saline, St. Clair, Stone, Sullivan, Taney,Texas, Vernon, Webster, Worth, Wright.

Indexing & Storage: Cases are indexed by debtor and creditors as well as by case number. New cases are available in the index 24 hours after filing date. Older records are indexed on microfiche. District wide searches are available from June 1989 from this division.

Fee & Payment Notes: Payment may be made by money order, cashier check, personal check. Payee: Clerk, US Bankruptcy Court. You are allowed to make your own copies. These copies cost \$.10 per page. There is no search fee for in person searchers.

Phone Search: Use VCIS for docket information. In addition to numbers given, call 816-426-2913 for information on cases closed prior to October 1995. An automated voice case information service (VCIS) is available. Call VCIS at 888-205-2527 or 816-426-5822.

In Person Search: In person searching available.

PACER: Access fee is. PACER is available online at http://pacer.mowb.uscourts.gov/bc/index.html.

Electronic Filing: Information is available online at https://ecf.mowb.uscourts.gov

Missouri County Courts

Court	Jurisdiction	No. of Courts	How Organized
Circuit Courts*	General	115	45 Circuits
Associate Circuit Courts*	Limited	114	45 Circuits
Combined Courts*		7	
Probate Courts*	Probate	5	
Municipal Courts	Municipal	406	
Family Courts	Special	8	

* Profiled in this Sourcebook.

Court	CIVIL								
	Tort	Contract	Real Estate	Min. Claim	Max. Claim	Small Claims	Estate	Eviction	Domestic Relations
Circuit Courts*	X	X	X	$25,000	No Max				X
Associate Circuit Courts*	X	X	X	$0	$25,000	$3000		X	
Municipal Courts									
Probate Courts*							X		
Family Courts									X

Court	CRIMINAL				
	Felony	Misdemeanor	DWI/DUI	Preliminary Hearing	Juvenile
Circuit Courts*	X				X
Associate Circuit Courts*		X	X	X	
Probate Courts*					
Family Courts					X

ADMINISTRATION

State Court Administrator, 2112 Industrial Dr., PO Box 104480, Jefferson City, MO, 65109; 573-751-4377, Fax: 573-751-5540. www.osca.state.mo.us

COURT STRUCTURE

The Circuit Court is the court of general jurisdiction. There are 45 circuits comprised of 114 county circuit courts and one independent city court. There are also Associate Circuit Courts with limited jurisdiction and some counties have Combined Courts. Municipal Courts only have jurisdiction over traffic and ordinance violations.

ONLINE ACCESS

Available at http://casenet.osca.state.mo.us/casenet is Casenet, a limited but growing online system. The system includes 44 counties (with more projected) as well as the Eastern, Western, and Southern Appellate Courts, the Supreme Court, and Fine Collection Center. Cases can be searched case number, filing date, or litigant name.

ADDITIONAL INFORMATION

While the Missouri State Statutes set the Civil Case limit at $25,000 for the Associate Courts, and over $25,000 for the Circuit Courts, a great many Missouri County Courts have adopted their own Local Court Rules regarding civil cases and the monetary limits. Presumably, Local Court's Rules are setup to allow the county to choose which court - Circuit or Associate - to send a case. This may depend on the court's case load, but generally, the cases are assigned more by "the nature of the case" and less by the monetary amount involved. Often, Local Court Rules are found where both the Circuit and the Associate Court are located in the same building, or share the same offices and perhaps the same phones. A solution for court record searches is to use this source to find a telephone number of a County's Court Clerk, and call to determine the court location of the case.

Adair County

Circuit Court PO Box 690, Kirksville, MO 63501; 660-665-2552; Fax: 660-665-3420. Hours: 8AM-5PM (CST). *Felony, Misdemeanor, Civil Actions Over $25,000.*

Civil Records: Access: In person. Only the court performs in person searches; visitors may not. No search fee. Required to search: name, years to search. Civil cases indexed by defendant, plaintiff. Prior on index cards.

Criminal Records: Access: In person only. Visitors must perform in person searches for themselves. No search fee. Required to search: name, years to search. Criminal records on computer since 1991, prior on index cards. All written requests referred to State Highway Patrol.

General Information: No juvenile, mental, expunged, sealed, dismissed or suspended records released. Copy fee: $.10 per page. Certification fee: $1.00. Fee payee: Circuit Clerk. Personal checks accepted. Prepayment is required.

Associate Circuit Court

Associate Circuit Court Courthouse, Kirksville, MO 63501; 660-665-3877; Fax: 660-785-3222. Hours: 8AM-5PM (CST). *Misdemeanor, Civil Actions Under $25,000, Eviction, Small Claims, Probate.*

Civil Records: Access: Phone, fax, mail, in person. Only the court performs in person searches; visitors may not. No search fee. Required to search: name, years to search. Civil cases indexed by defendant, plaintiff. Civil records on computer back to 1990; probate records on microfilm since 1840.

Criminal Records: Access: Phone, fax, mail, in person. Only the court performs in person searches; visitors may not. No search fee. Required to search: name, years to search, DOB, SSN. Criminal records on computer back to 1990; prior records in files. Signed release required for closed cases.

General Information: No juvenile, mental, expunged, sealed, dismissed or suspended imposition of case records released. SASE required. Turnaround time 1 day. Fax notes: $1.50 per page. Copy fee: $.25 per page. Fee payee: Associate Circuit Court. Personal checks accepted. Prepayment is required.

Andrew County

Circuit Court PO Box 208 Division I, Savannah, MO 64485; 816-324-4221; Fax: 816-324-5667. Hours: 8AM-5PM (CST). *Felony, Misdemeanor, Civil Actions Over $45,000.*

Civil Records: Access: Phone, fax, mail, in person, online. Both court and visitors may perform in person searches. No search fee. Required to search: name, years to search. Civil cases indexed by defendant, plaintiff. Civil records on index cards since 1976, archived since 1850. Participates in the free state online court record system at http://casenet.osca.state.mo.us/casenet. Online records go back to 1993.

Criminal Records: Access: In person, online. Visitors must perform in person searches for themselves. No search fee. Required to search: name, years to search; also helpful: DOB. Criminal records on computer since mid-1993. Online access to criminal records is the same as civil.

General Information: No juvenile, mental, expunged, sealed, dismissed or suspended imposition of sentence records released. Turnaround time 1-2 days. Copy fee: $.25 per page. Certification fee: $2.50. Fee payee: Andrew County Circuit Clerk. Personal checks accepted. Prepayment is required.

Associate Circuit Court PO Box 49, Savannah, MO 64485; 816-324-3921; Fax: 816-324-5667. Hours: 8AM-5PM (CST). *Misdemeanor, Civil Actions Under $45,000, Eviction, Small Claims, Probate.*

Civil Records: Access: Mail, in person, online. Both court and visitors may perform in person searches. No search fee. Required to search: name, years to search. Civil cases indexed by defendant, plaintiff. Civil records on card file, archived from 1950. Participates in the free state online court record system at http://casenet.osca.state.mo.us/casenet. Online records go back to 1993.

Criminal Records: Access: Mail, in person, online. Both court and visitors may perform in person searches. No search fee. Required to search: name, years to search. Criminal records on computer since mid-1993. Online access to criminal records is the same as civil.

General Information: No juvenile, mental, expunged, sealed, dismissed or suspended imposition of sentence records released. SASE required. Turnaround time varies. Copy fee: $.25 per page. Certification fee: $1.50 plus additional pages for $.25 each. Fee payee: Associate Circuit Court. Personal checks accepted. Prepayment is required.

Atchison County

Circuit Court PO Box 280, Rock Port, MO 64482; 660-744-2707; Fax: 660-744-5705. Hours: 8:30AM-4:30PM (CST). *Felony, Misdemeanor, Civil Actions Over $25,000.*

Civil Records: Access: Mail, in person. Visitors must perform in person searches for themselves. No search fee. Required to search: name, years to search. Civil cases indexed by defendant, plaintiff. Civil records on index books, and archived from 1845.

Criminal Records: Access: Mail, in person. Both court and visitors may perform in person searches. Search fee: $4.00 per name. Required to search: name, years to search. Criminal records on index books, and archived from 1845.

General Information: No juvenile, mental, expunged, sealed, dismissed or suspended imposition of sentence records released. Turnaround time 1 day. Copy fee: $1.00 per page. Certification fee: $1.00. Fee payee: Circuit Clerk. Personal checks accepted. Prepayment is required.

Associate Division PO Box 187, Rock Port, MO 64482; 660-744-2700; Fax: 660-744-5705. Hours: 8AM-4:30PM (CST). *Misdemeanor, Civil Actions Under $25,000, Eviction, Small Claims, Probate.*

Civil Records: Access: Fax, mail, in person. Both court and visitors may perform in person searches. Search fee: $4.00 per name. Required to search: name, years to search; also helpful: address. Civil cases indexed by defendant, plaintiff. Civil records on books and cardex system, archived since 1845.

Criminal Records: Access: Fax, mail, in person. Both court and visitors may perform in person searches. Search fee: $4.00 per name. Required to search: name, years to search; also helpful: address, DOB, SSN, offense. Criminal records on computer since mid 1980s; prior on books and cardex system.

General Information: No juvenile, mental, expunged, sealed, dismissed or suspended imposition of sentence records released. SASE required. Turnaround time 7 days. Fax notes: $2.00 per page. Copy fee: $1.00 per page. Certification fee: $1.50. Fee payee: Circuit Court Division II. Personal checks accepted. Prepayment is required.

Audrain County

Circuit Court Courthouse, 101 N Jefferson, Mexico, MO 65265; 573-473-5840; Fax: 573-581-3237. Hours: 8AM-5PM (CST). *Felony, Misdemeanor, Civil Actions Over $25,000.*

www.audrain-county.org

Civil Records: Access: In person only. Visitors must perform in person searches for themselves. No search fee. Required to search: name, years to search. Civil cases indexed by defendant, plaintiff. Civil records on computer since 8/92, prior on index cards, older records archived at Genealogy Club in Mexico, MO.

Criminal Records: Access: In person only. Visitors must perform in person searches for themselves. No search fee. Required to search: name, years to search; also SSN, case number. Criminal records on computer since 8/92, stored for 25 years on site then archived (back to 1800s).

General Information: Public access terminal is available. No juvenile, mental, expunged, sealed, dismissed or suspended imposition of sentence records released. Fax notes: Fee to fax results is $5.00. Copy fee: $.25 per page. Certification fee: $1.50 for first 2 pages; $.25 each add'l. Fee payee: Circuit Clerk. Prepayment is required.

Associate Circuit Court Courthouse, 101 N Jefferson, Rm 205, Mexico, MO 65265; 573-473-5850; Probate phone: 573-473-5854; Fax: 573-581-3237. Hours: 8AM-5PM (CST). *Misdemeanor, Civil Actions Under $25,000, Eviction, Small Claims, Probate.*

Civil Records: Access: Mail, in person. Both court and visitors may perform in person searches. No search fee. Required to search: name, years to search. Civil cases indexed by defendant, plaintiff. Civil records on computer since 9/93, prior on cards, archived to 1800s.

Criminal Records: Access: Mail, in person. Only the court performs in person searches; visitors may not. No search fee. Required to search: name, years to search, DOB, SSN, signed release. Criminal records on computer since 9/93, prior on cards, archived to 1800s.

General Information: No juvenile, mental, expunged, sealed, dismissed or suspended imposition of sentence records released. Turnaround time 1 week. Copy fee: $.15 per page. Certification fee: $1.50 first page, $1.00 each additional. Fee payee: Circuit Court Division II. Only cashiers checks and money orders accepted. Prepayment is required.

Barry County

Circuit Court Barry County Courthouse, 700 Main, Ste 1, Cassville, MO 65625; 417-847-2361. Hours: 8AM-4PM (CST). *Felony, Misdemeanor, Civil Actions Over $25,000.*

Civil Records: Access: Mail, in person. Both court and visitors may perform in person searches. Search fee: $4.00 per name. Required to search: name, years to search. Civil cases indexed by defendant, plaintiff. Civil records on index cards, archived since mid-1800s.

Criminal Records: Access: Mail, in person. Both court and visitors may perform in person searches. Search fee: $4.00 per name. Required to search: name, years to search. Criminal records on index cards, archived since mid-1800s.

General Information: No juvenile, mental expunged, sealed, dismissed or suspended imposition of sentence records released. SASE required. Turnaround time 1-3 days. Copy fee: $.25 per page. Certification fee: $1.00. Fee payee: Circuit Clerk. Personal checks accepted. Prepayment is required.

Associate Circuit Court Barry County Courthouse, #8, Cassville, MO 65625; Civil phone: 417-847-2127; Criminal phone: 417-847-6557. Hours: 7:30AM-4PM (CST). *Misdemeanor, Civil Actions Under $25,000, Eviction, Small Claims, Probate.*

Civil Records: Access: Mail, in person. Both court and visitors may perform in person searches. No search fee. Required to search: name, years to search. Civil cases indexed by defendant, plaintiff. Civil records on index cards since 1982; prior records on index books to mid 1800s.

Criminal Records: Access: Mail, in person. Both court and visitors may perform in person searches. No search fee. Required to search: name, years to search. Criminal records on computer since 1996; prior records on index books to mid 1800s.

General Information: No juvenile, mental, expunged, sealed, dismissed or suspended imposition of sentence records released. Turnaround time 1-3 days. Copy fee: $.50 per page. Fee payee: Barry County. Personal checks accepted. Prepayment is required.

Barton County

Circuit & Associate Court Courthouse, 1007 Broadway, Lamar, MO 64759; 417-682-2444/5754; Fax: 417-682-2960. 8AM-4:30PM (CST). *Felony, Misdemeanor, Civil, Eviction, Small Claims, Probate.*

Civil Records: Access: Mail, online, in person. Both court and visitors may perform in person searches. No search fee. Required to search: name, years to search; also helpful: address. Civil cases indexed by defendant, plaintiff. Civil records on computer since 1999; prior from 1880 on books or archived. Participates in the free state online court record system at http://casenet.osca.state.mo.us/casenet. Online records go back to 9/20/1999.

Criminal Records: Access: Mail, online, in person. Both court and visitors may perform in person searches. No search fee. Required to search: name, years to search; also helpful: address, DOB, SSN. Criminal records on computer since 1993; prior from 1880 on books or archived. Online access to criminal records is the same as civil.

General Information: Public access terminal is available. No juvenile, mental, expunged, dismissed, or suspended imposition of sentence records released. SASE required. Turnaround time 1 week. Fax notes: Fee to fax is $2.00 per document. Copy fee: $1.00 per page. Certification fee: $1.50. Fee payee: Circuit Court. Personal checks accepted. Prepayment is required.

Bates County

Circuit Court Bates County Courthouse, Butler, MO 64730; 660-679-5171; Fax: 660-679-4446. Hours: 8AM-4:30PM (CST). *Felony, Misdemeanor, Civil Actions Over $25,000.*

Civil Records: Access: Fax, mail, in person. Both court and visitors may perform in person searches. No search fee. Required to search: name, years to search. Civil cases indexed by defendant, plaintiff. Civil records on computer since 9/1/92, prior on books since 1858.

Criminal Records: Access: Fax, mail, in person. Both court and visitors may perform in person searches. No search fee. Required to search: name, years to search. Criminal records on computer since 9/1/92, prior on books since 1858.

General Information: No juvenile, mental, expunged, dismissed, or suspended imposition of sentence records released. SASE required. Turnaround time varies. Fax notes: No fee to fax results. Copy fee: $.25 per page. Certification fee: $1.50. Fee payee: Circuit Court. Only cashiers checks and money orders accepted. Prepayment is required.

Associate Circuit Court Courthouse, Butler, MO 64730; 660-679-3311. Hours: 8:30AM-4PM (CST). *Misdemeanor, Civil Actions Under $25,000, Eviction, Small Claims, Probate.*

Civil Records: Access: Mail, in person. Both court and visitors may perform in person searches, though visitors are limited. No search fee. Required to search: name, years to search. Civil cases indexed by defendant, plaintiff. Civil records on index cards (unsure of starting date).

Criminal Records: Access: Mail, in person. Only the court performs in person searches; visitors may not. No search fee. Required to search: name, years to search, DOB; also helpful: SSN. Criminal records on computer since 1992, prior on index cards.

General Information: No juvenile, mental, expunged, dismissed, or suspended imposition of sentence records released. SASE required. Turnaround time 1 week. Copy fee: $.50 per page. Certification fee: $1.50. Fee payee: Associate Circuit Court. Only cashiers checks and money orders accepted.

Benton County

Circuit & Associate Court PO Box 37, Warsaw, MO 65355; 660-438-7712; Fax: 660-438-5755. 8AM-4:30PM (CST). *Felony, Misdemeanor, Civil Actions, Eviction, Small Claims, Probate.*

www.positech.net/~dcourt

Note: Associate court clerk phone is 660-438-6231.

Civil Records: Access: Mail, fax, in person, online. Visitors must perform in person searches for themselves. Search fee: No search fee. Required to search: name, years to search. Civil cases indexed by defendant, plaintiff. Civil records on computer since 1993, prior on index cards since 1800. Participates in the statewide Casenet system at http://casenet.osca.state.mo.us/casenet/.

Criminal Records: Access: In person, online. Visitors must perform in person searches for themselves, however, court may conduct search if time permits. Search fee: No search fee. Required to search: name, years to search, DOB; also helpful: SSN. Criminal records on computer since 1993, prior on index cards since 1800. Participates in the statewide Casenet system at http://casenet.osca.state.mo.us/casenet/. The court will only indicate if subject is on probation or has open case. For criminal searches contact Jefferson City Highway Patrol.

General Information: Public access terminal is available. No juvenile, mental, expunged, dismissed, or suspended imposition of sentence records released. Copy fee: $1.00 for first page, $.25 each add'l. Certification fee: $2.50. Fee payee: Clerk of Circuit Court. Personal checks accepted. Prepayment is required.

Bollinger County

Circuit Court PO Box 949, Marble Hill, MO 63764; 573-238-2710; Fax: 573-238-2773. Hours: 8AM-4PM (CST). *Felony, Misdemeanor, Civil Actions Over $25,000.*

Civil Records: Access: Mail, in person, online. Only the court performs in person searches; visitors may not. No search fee. Required to search: name, years to search. Civil cases indexed by defendant, plaintiff. Civil records on computer since 1990, prior on index cards 1976-1990. Access to civil records available free at http://casenet.osca.state.mo.us/casenet/. At the web site, select the judicial district, then search by name, case # or date. Online records go back to 7/1/2001.

Criminal Records: Access: In person, online. Only the court performs in person searches; visitors may not. No search fee. Required to search: name, years to search. Criminal records on computer since 1990, prior on index cards 1976-1990. Online access to criminal records is the same as civil. Online public case records go back to 7/1/2001; judgments to 8/23/1993.

General Information: No juvenile, mental, expunged, dismissed, or suspended imposition of sentence records released. SASE required. Turnaround time 1 day to 1 week. Copy fee: $1.00 for first page, $.50 each add'l. Certification fee: $1.00. Fee payee: Circuit Clerk and Recorder's Office. Personal checks accepted. Prepayment is required.

Associate Circuit Court PO Box 1040, Marble Hill, MO 63764-1040; 573-238-2900 ext 4; Fax: 573-238-4511. Hours: 8AM-4PM (CST). *Misdemeanor, Civil Actions Under $25,000, Eviction, Small Claims, Probate.*

Civil Records: Access: In person, online. Visitors must perform in person searches for themselves. No search fee. Required to search: name, years to search. Civil cases indexed by defendant, plaintiff. Civil records on computer back to 1995, prior on books, archived to 1890. Participates in the free state online Banner court record system at http://casenet.osca.state.mo.us/casenet. Online records go back to 7/1/2001.

Criminal Records: Access: In person, online. Visitors must perform in person searches for themselves. No search fee. Required to search: name, years to search. Criminal records on computer back to 1995, prior on books, archived to 1890. Online access to criminal records is the same as civil. Online public case records go back to 7/1/2001; judgments to 8/23/1993.

General Information: Public access terminal is available. No juvenile, mental, expunged, dismissed, or suspended imposition of sentence records released. Copy fee: $1.00 per page. Certification fee: $1.50. Fee payee: Circuit Court Division IV. Personal checks accepted. Prepayment is required.

Boone County

Circuit and Associate Court 705 E Walnut, Columbia, MO 65201; 573-886-4000; Fax: 573-886-4044. Hours: 8AM-5PM (CST). *Felony, Misdemeanor, Civil, Eviction, Small Claims, Probate.*

Civil Records: Access: Phone, mail, online, in person. Both court and visitors may perform in person searches. No search fee. Required to search: name, years to search. Civil cases indexed by defendant, plaintiff. Civil records on computer for recent cases, others on books. Participates in the free state online court record system at http://casenet.osca.state.mo.us/casenet. Civil records go back to 3/23/79. Probate records back to 2/23/1956 are also available online.

Criminal Records: Access: Online, in person. Visitors must perform in person searches for themselves. No search fee. Required to search: name, years to search, DOB. Criminal records on computer for recent cases, others on books. Online access to criminal records is the same as civil. Online criminal records go back to 7/7/1953.

General Information: Public access terminal is available. No juvenile, mental, paternity, expunged, dismissed, or suspended imposition of sentence records released. SASE required. Turnaround time varies. Copy fee: $.25 per page. Certification fee: $1.00. Fee payee: Boone County Circuit Clerk. Business checks accepted. Prepayment is required.

Buchanan County

Circuit & Associate Court 411 Jules St, Rm 331, St Joseph, MO 64501; 816-271-1462; Fax: 816-271-1538. Hours: 8AM-5PM (CST). *Felony, Misdemeanor, Civil, Eviction, Small Claims.*

Civil Records: Access: In person, online. Visitors must perform in person searches for themselves. No search fee. Required to search: name, years to search. Civil cases indexed by defendant, plaintiff. Civil records on computer since 2/92, on index cards since 1976, prior archived. Participates in the free state online court record system at http://casenet.osca.state.mo.us/casenet. Online records go back to 1992.

Criminal Records: Access: In person, online. Visitors must perform in person searches for themselves. No search fee. Required to search: name, years to search. Criminal records on computer since 2/92, on index cards since 1976, prior archived. Online access to criminal records is the same as civil. County Case.net records go back to 1992.

General Information: Public access terminal is available. No juvenile, mental, expunged, dismissed, or suspended imposition of sentence records released. Copy fee: $.25 per page. Certification fee: $2.50. Fee payee: Buchanan Circuit Clerk. Personal checks accepted.

Probate Court Buchanan County Courthouse, 411 Jules St, Room 333, St Joseph, MO 64501; 816-271-1477; Fax: 816-271-1538. 8AM-5PM (CST). *Probate.*

Butler County

Circuit Court Courthouse, Poplar Bluff, MO 63901; 573-686-8082; Fax: 573-686-8094. Hours: 7:30AM-4PM (CST). *Felony, Misdemeanor, Civil Actions Over $25,000.*

Civil Records: Access: Fax, mail, in person. Visitors must perform in person searches. Search fee: $1.00 per name per year. Required to search: name, years to search. Civil cases indexed by defendant, plaintiff. Civil records on computer since 9/91, prior on cards and books since 1865.

Criminal Records: Access: Fax, mail, in person. Visitors must perform in person searches. Search fee: $1.00 per name per year. Required to search: name, years to search. Criminal records on computer since 9/91, prior on cards and books since 1865.

General Information: Public access terminal is available. No juvenile, mental, expunged, dismissed, or suspended imposition of sentence records released. SASE not required. Turnaround time 1-2 days. Fax notes: $1.00 per page. Copy fee: $.25 per page. Certification fee: $2.50. Fee payee: Clerk of Circuit Court. Business checks accepted. Prepayment is required.

Associate Circuit Court Courthouse, Poplar Bluff, MO 63901; 573-686-8087; Probate phone: 573-686-8073; Fax: 573-686-8093. Hours: 7:30AM-4PM (CST). *Misdemeanor, Civil Actions Under $25,000, Eviction, Small Claims, Probate.*

Note: Probate records are in a separate office at the courthouse.

Civil Records: Access: Phone, fax, mail, in person. Both court and visitors may perform in person searches. No search fee. Required to search: name, years to search. Civil cases indexed by defendant, plaintiff. Civil records on cards since 1976, and index books since 1900s.

Criminal Records: Access: Fax, mail, in person. Only the court performs in person searches; visitors may not. No search fee. Required to search: name, years to search, signed release. Criminal records on cards since 1976, and index books since early 1990s, computer back to 1991.

General Information: No juvenile, mental, expunged, dismissed, or suspended imposition of sentence records released. SASE required. Turnaround time varies. Fax notes: Fee to fax results is $.25 per page. Copy fee: $.25 per page. Certification fee: $2.50. Fee payee: Circuit Court Division II. Business checks accepted. Prepayment is required.

Caldwell County

Circuit Court PO Box 86, Kingston, MO 64650; 816-586-2581; Fax: 816-586-2705. Hours: 8:30AM-4:30PM (CST). *Felony, Misdemeanor, Civil Actions Over $45,000.*

Civil Records: Access: Phone, mail, in person. Both court and visitors may perform in person searches. No search fee. Required to search: name, years to search. Civil cases indexed by defendant, plaintiff. Civil records archived since 1860; on computer back to 1995.

Criminal Records: Access: Phone, mail, in person. Both court and visitors may perform in person searches. No search fee. Required to search: name, years to search. Criminal records archived since 1860; on computer back to 1995.

General Information: No juvenile, mental, expunged, dismissed, or suspended imposition of sentence records released. SASE required. Turnaround time 3 days, phone turnaround time 1 day. Copy fee: $1.00 per page. Certification fee: $.50 per page. Fee payee: Circuit Clerk. Personal checks accepted. Prepayment is required.

Associate Circuit Court PO Box 5, Kingston, MO 64650; 816-586-2771; Fax: 816-586-2333. Hours: 8AM-4:30PM (CST). *Misdemeanor, Civil Actions Under $45,000, Eviction, Small Claims, Probate.*

Civil Records: Access: In person only. Visitors must perform in person searches for themselves. No search fee. Required to search: name, years to search. Civil cases indexed by defendant, plaintiff. Records prior to 1992 on index cards back to 1970s.

Criminal Records: Access: In person only. Visitors must perform in person searches for themselves. No search fee. Required to search: name, years to search; also helpful: DOB, SSN. Criminal records on computer since 1992; prior records on index cards back to 1970s.

General Information: No juvenile, mental, expunged, dismissed, or suspended imposition of sentence records released. Copy fee: $.25 per page. Legal Size Copy Fee: $.50 per page. Certification fee: $1.50. Fee payee: Associate Circuit Court. Only cashiers checks and money orders accepted. Prepayment is required.

Callaway County

Circuit Court 10 E 5th St, Fulton, MO 65251; 573-642-0780; Fax: 573-642-0700. Hours: 8AM-5PM (CST). *Felony, Misdemeanor, Civil Actions Over $25,000.*

www.osca.state.mo.us

Civil Records: Access: Fax, mail, in person, online. Both court and visitors may perform in person searches. Court will only perform searches as time permits No search fee. Required to search: name, years to search. Civil cases indexed by defendant, plaintiff. Civil records on index books and cards since 1821. Participates in the free state online court record system at http://casenet.osca.state.mo.us/casenet. Online public cases go back to 2000; online probate to 1977.

Criminal Records: Access: In person, online. Visitors must perform in person searches for themselves. No search fee. Required to search: name, years to search; also helpful: DOB, SSN. Criminal records on computer since 1993, prior on index books and cards since 1821. Online access to criminal records is the same as civil.

General Information: Public access terminal is available. No juvenile, mental, expunged, dismissed, or suspended imposition of sentence records released. SASE not required. Turnaround time 3 days. Fax notes: $.25 per page. Copy fee: $.25 per page. Certification fee: $1.00. Fee payee: Circuit Clerk. Business checks accepted. Attorney & Law Firm checks accepted.

Associate Circuit Court Courthouse, Fulton, MO 65251; 573-642-0777; Fax: 573-642-0700. Hours:

8AM-5PM (CST). *Misdemeanor, Civil Actions Under $25,000, Eviction, Small Claims, Probate.*

Civil Records: Access: Mail, in person, online. Both court and visitors may perform in person searches. No search fee. Required to search: name, years to search. Civil cases indexed by defendant, plaintiff. Civil records on computer go back 10 years, archived since 1821. Participates in the free state online court record system at http://casenet.osca.state.mo.us/casenet.

Criminal Records: Access: Mail, in person, online. Both court and visitors may perform in person searches. No search fee. Required to search: name, years to search; also helpful: DOB. Criminal records on computer go back 10 years, prior on index cards since 1979. Online access to criminal records is the same as civil.

General Information: No juvenile, mental, expunged, dismissed, or suspended imposition of sentence records released. SASE requested. Turnaround time 2 days. No copy fee.

Camden County

Circuit Court 1 Court Circle, Camdenton, MO 65020; 573-346-4440 X289; Fax: 573-346-5422. Hours: 8:30AM-4:30PM (CST). *Felony, Misdemeanor, Civil Actions Over $25,000.*

Civil Records: Access: Mail, in person. Both court and visitors may perform in person searches. No search fee. Required to search: name, years to search. Civil cases indexed by defendant, plaintiff. Civil records on computer since 1989, on index cards from 1965 to 1989, prior on index books since 1903.

Criminal Records: Access: Mail, in person. Both court and visitors may perform in person searches. No search fee. Required to search: name, years to search; also helpful: DOB, SSN. Criminal records on computer since 1989, on index cards from 1965 to 1989, prior on index books since 1903.

General Information: No juvenile, mental, expunged, dismissed, or suspended imposition of sentence records released. SASE required. Turnaround time 7 days. No copy fee. Only cashiers checks and money orders accepted.

Associate Circuit Court 1 Court Circle #8, Camdenton, MO 65020; 573-346-4440; Civil phone: X242; Criminal phone: X243; Fax: 573-346-5422. Hours: 8:00AM-5:00PM (CST). *Misdemeanor, Civil Actions Under $25,000, Eviction, Small Claims, Probate.*

Civil Records: Access: In person only. Visitors must perform in person searches for themselves. No search fee. Required to search: name, years to search. Civil cases indexed by defendant, plaintiff. Civil records on index cards since 1976; on computer back to 1989.

Criminal Records: Access: Mail, in person. Only the court performs in person searches; visitors may not. No search fee. Required to search: name, years to search, DOB; also helpful: SSN. Criminal records on computer back to 1989, prior on index cards since 1980.

General Information: Public access terminal is available. No juvenile, mental, expunged, dismissed, or suspended imposition of sentence records released. SASE required. Turnaround time 1-2 weeks. No copy fee. Personal checks accepted.

Cape Girardeau County

Circuit & Associate Circuit Court - Civil Division 44 N Lorimier, PO Box 2047, Cape Girardeau, MO 63702; 573-335-8253; Fax: 573-331-2565. Hours: 8AM-4:30PM (CST). *Civil.*

Civil Records: Access: Mail, in person, online. Both court and visitors may perform in person searches. No search fee. Required to search: name, years to search. Civil cases indexed by defendant, plaintiff. Civil records on computer since 1994, prior on index cards since

10/75. Access to civil records available free at http://casenet.osca.state.mo.us/casenet/. At the web site, select the judicial district, then search by name, case # or date. Online records go back to 7/1/2001.
General Information: Public access terminal is available. No juvenile, mental, expunged, dismissed, or suspended imposition of sentence, paternity, cases where one party on AFDC records released. SASE required. Turnaround time 1 week. Copy fee: $1.00 for first page, $.50 each add'l. Certification fee: $1.00. Fee payee: Circuit Clerk. Personal checks accepted. Prepayment is required.

Circuit Court - Criminal Division I & II
100 Court St, Jackson, MO 63755; 573-243-8446 (misdemeanors); Criminal phone: 573-243-1755 (felo.); Fax: 573-204-2367. Hours: 8AM-4:30PM (CST). *Felony, Misdemeanor.*
Criminal Records: Access: Mail, in person, online. Both court and visitors may perform in person searches. Search fee: $10.00 per name. Required to search: name, years to search. Criminal records on computer since 1991, prior on books. Access to criminal records available free at http://casenet.osca.state.mo.us/casenet/. At the web site, select the judicial district, then search by name, case # or date. Online public case records go back to 7/1/01; Circuit court judgments to 8/23/1993.
General Information: No juvenile, mental, expunged, dismissed, or suspended imposition of sentence records released. SASE required. Turnaround time 1 week. Copy fee: $1.00 for first page, $.50 each add'l. Certification fee: $1.00. Fee payee: Circuit Clerk. Personal checks accepted. Prepayment is required.

Carroll County

Circuit Court
PO Box 245, Carrollton, MO 64633; 660-542-1466; Fax: 660-542-1444. Hours: 8:30AM-4:30PM (CST). *Felony, Misdemeanor, Civil Actions Over $25,000.*
Civil Records: Access: Fax, mail, in person. Both court and visitors may perform in person searches. No search fee. Required to search: name, years to search. Civil cases indexed by defendant, plaintiff. Civil records on books since 1833.
Criminal Records: Access: Fax, mail, in person. Both court and visitors may perform in person searches. No search fee. Required to search: name, years to search. Criminal records on books since 1833.
General Information: No juvenile, mental, expunged, dismissed, or suspended imposition of sentence records released. SASE not required. Turnaround time varies. Fax notes: No fee to fax results. No copy fee. Certification fee: $2.00. Fee payee: Circuit Clerk. Personal checks accepted. Prepayment is required.

Associate Circuit Court
Courthouse, 8 S Main, Suite 1, Carrollton, MO 64633; 660-542-1818; Fax: 660-542-1877. Hours: 8:30AM-4:30PM (CST). *Misdemeanor, Civil Actions Under $25,000, Eviction, Small Claims, Probate.*
Civil Records: Access: Mail, in person. Visitors must perform in person searches for themselves. No search fee. Required to search: name, years to search, address. Civil cases indexed by defendant, plaintiff. Civil records go back to 1990; on computer back to 12/2001.
Criminal Records: Access: In person only. Visitors must perform in person searches for themselves. No search fee. Required to search: name, years to search, address, DOB. Criminal records go back to 1990; on computer back to 12/2001.
General Information: Public access terminal is available. No juvenile, mental, expunged, dismissed, or suspended imposition of sentence records released. Copy fee: $.35 per page. Certification fee: $2.50. Fee payee: Associate Circuit Court. Only cashiers checks and money orders accepted. Prepayment is required.

Carter County

Circuit Court
PO Box 578, Van Buren, MO 63965; 573-323-4513; Fax: 573-323-4885. Hours: 8AM-4PM (CST). *Felony, Misdemeanor, Civil Actions Over $45,000.*
Civil Records: Access: Fax, mail, in person, online. Both court and visitors may perform in person searches. No search fee. Required to search: name, years to search. Civil cases indexed by defendant, plaintiff. Civil records on computer since 1979, on index cards since 1988, archived since late-1800s. Participates in the free state online court record system at http://casenet.osca.state.mo.us/casenet. Online records go back to 4/17/2000.
Criminal Records: Access: Fax, mail, in person, online. Both court and visitors may perform in person searches. No search fee. Required to search: name, years to search. Criminal records on computer since 1979, on index cards since 1988, archived since late-1800s. Online access to criminal records is the same as civil.
General Information: No juvenile, mental, paternity, expunged, dismissed, or suspended imposition of sentence records released. SASE required. Turnaround time 1 day. Copy fee: $.25 per page. Certification fee: $1.00. Fee payee: Circuit Clerk. Personal checks accepted.

Associate Circuit Court
PO Box 328, Van Buren, MO 63965; 573-323-4344; Fax: 573-323-8914. Hours: 8AM-4PM (CST). *Misdemeanor, Civil Actions Under $45,000, Eviction, Small Claims, Probate.*
Civil Records: Access: Phone, fax, mail, in person, online. Only the court performs in person searches; visitors may not. Search fee: $5.00 per name. Required to search: name, years to search. Civil cases indexed by defendant, plaintiff. Civil records on index since 1979, prior on docket sheets. Participates in the free state online court record system at http://casenet.osca.state.mo.us/casenet. Online records go back to 4/17/2000.
Criminal Records: Access: Phone, fax, mail, in person, online. Only the court performs in person searches; visitors may not. Search fee: $5.00 per name. Required to search: name, years to search. Criminal records on index since 1979, prior on docket sheets. Online access to criminal records is the same as civil.
General Information: No juvenile, mental, expunged, dismissed, or suspended imposition of sentence records released. SASE required. Turnaround time varies. Copy fee: $.25 per page. Fee payee: Circuit Court Division II. Personal checks accepted. Prepayment is required.

Cass County

Circuit Court
102 E Wall, Harrisonville, MO 64701; 816-380-8226; Fax: 816-380-8225. Hours: 8AM-4:30PM (CST). *Felony, Misdemeanor, Civil Actions Over $25,000.*
Civil Records: Access: Phone, mail, in person. Both court and visitors must perform in person searches. No search fee. Required to search: name, years to search. Civil cases indexed by defendant, plaintiff. Civil records on computer since 1992, on index cards since 1976, prior on judgment books since 1800s.
Criminal Records: Access: Phone, mail, in person. Both court and visitors must perform in person searches. No search fee. Required to search: name, years to search. Criminal records on computer since 1992, on index cards since 1976, prior on judgment books since 1800s.
General Information: Public access terminal is available. No juvenile, mental, expunged, dismissed, or suspended imposition of sentence records released. SASE required. Turnaround time 1 week. Copy fee: $.25 per page. Certification fee: $1.50. Fee payee: Cass

County Circuit Clerk. Personal checks accepted. Prepayment is required.

Associate Circuit Court
PO Box 384, Harrisonville, MO 64701; 816-380-8100; Fax: 816-380-8195. Hours: 8AM-4:30PM (CST). *Misdemeanor, Civil Actions Under $25,000, Eviction, Small Claims, Felony.*
Civil Records: Access: Mail, in person. Visitors must perform in person searches for themselves. No search fee. Required to search: name, years to search. Civil cases indexed by defendant, plaintiff. Civil records go back to 1960s; on index cards since 1983; on computer back to 1995.
Criminal Records: Access: Mail, in person. Visitors must perform in person searches for themselves. No search fee. Required to search: name, years to search, signed release. Criminal records go back to 1960s; on index cards since 1983; on computer back to 1995.
General Information: Public access terminal is available. No juvenile, mental, expunged, dismissed, or suspended imposition of sentence records released. SASE required. Turnaround time varies. Fax notes: Will not fax out. Copy fee: $1.00 per page. Certification fee: $2.00. Fee payee: Division III. Business checks accepted. Prepayment is required.

Probate Court
102 E Wall St, Harrisonville, MO 64701; 816-380-8217; Fax: 816-380-8215. Hours: 8AM-4:30PM (CST). *Probate.*

Cedar County

Circuit Court
PO Box 665, Stockton, MO 65785; 417-276-6700; Fax: 417-276-5001. Hours: 8AM-4:30PM (CST). *Felony, Misdemeanor, Civil Actions Over $45,000.*
Civil Records: Access: Fax, mail, in person, online. Both court and visitors may perform in person searches. No search fee. Required to search: name, years to search. Civil cases indexed by defendant, plaintiff. Civil records on index cards since 1979, prior on docket books. Participates in the free state online court record system at http://casenet.osca.state.mo.us/casenet. online records go back to 9/20/1999. Online records include Probate Court.
Criminal Records: Access: Fax, mail, in person, online. Both court and visitors may perform in person searches. No search fee. Required to search: name, years to search. Criminal records on index cards since 1979, prior on docket books. Online access to criminal records is the same as civil.
General Information: No juvenile, mental, expunged, dismissed, or suspended imposition of sentence records released. Turnaround time varies. Fax notes: $1.00 per page. Copy fee: $1.00 per page. Certification fee: $3.00. Fee payee: Cedar County. Personal checks accepted. Prepayment is required.

Associate Circuit Court
PO Box 665, Stockton, MO 65785; 417-276-6700; Fax: 417-276-5001. Hours: 8AM-4:30PM (CST). *Misdemeanor, Civil Actions Under $45,000, Eviction, Small Claims, Probate.*
Civil Records: Access: Mail, in person, online. Both court and visitors may perform in person searches. No search fee. Required to search: name, years to search. Civil cases indexed by defendant, plaintiff. Civil records archived since 1830. Participates in the free state online court system at http://casenet.osca.state.mo.us/casenet.
Criminal Records: Access: Mail, in person. Only the court performs in person searches; visitors may not. No search fee. Required to search: name, years to search; also helpful: DOB. Criminal records archived since 1830.
General Information: No juvenile, mental, expunged, dismissed, or suspended imposition of sentence records released. SASE required. Turnaround time varies. Copy fee: $.25 per page. Certification fee: $1.50 plus $1.00

per page. Fee payee: Associate Circuit Court. Only cashiers checks and money orders accepted. Prepayment is required.

Chariton County

Circuit Court PO Box 112, Keytesville, MO 65261; 660-288-3602; Fax: 660-288-3763. Hours: 8:30AM-4:30PM (CST). *Felony, Misdemeanor, Civil Actions Over $25,000.*

Civil Records: Access: Fax, mail, in person. Both court and visitors may perform in person searches. Search fee: $4.00 per name. Required to search: name, years to search. Civil cases indexed by defendant, plaintiff. Civil records on index books since 1975, prior on docket books to 1827.
Criminal Records: Access: Fax, mail, in person. Both court and visitors may perform in person searches. Search fee: $4.00 per name. Required to search: name, years to search; also helpful: DOB, SSN. Criminal records on index books since 1975, prior on docket books to 1827.
General Information: No juvenile, mental, expunged, dismissed, or suspended imposition of sentence records released. SASE required. Turnaround time same day. Fax notes: Fee to fax results is $1.00 per page. Copy fee: $1.00 per page. Certification fee: $1.50. Fee payee: Chariton County Circuit Clerk. Personal checks accepted.

Associate Circuit Court 306 South Cherry, Keytesville, MO 65261; 660-288-3271; Fax: 660-288-1511. Hours: 8AM-4:30PM (CST). *Misdemeanor, Civil Actions Under $25,000, Eviction, Small Claims, Probate.*

Civil Records: Access: Phone, fax, mail, in person. Both court and visitors may perform in person searches. No search fee. Required to search: name, years to search. Civil cases indexed by defendant, plaintiff. Civil records indexed on cards by year from 1977.
Criminal Records: Access: Phone, fax, mail, in person. Both court and visitors may perform in person searches. No search fee. Required to search: name, years to search; also helpful: DOB, SSN. Criminal records indexed on cards by year from 1977.
General Information: No juvenile, mental, expunged, dismissed, or suspended imposition of sentence records released. SASE required. Turnaround time 1 week, phone turnaround time 2 days. Copy fee: $.25 per page. Certification fee: $1.50. Fee payee: Associate Circuit Court or Probate Court (depending on search). Personal checks accepted. Copy and certification fees may be billed.

Christian County

Circuit Court PO Box 278, Ozark, MO 65721; 417-581-6372; Fax: 417-581-0391. Hours: 8AM-4:30PM (CST). *Felony, Misdemeanor, Civil Actions Over $45,000.*

Civil Records: Access: Mail, in person. Both court and visitors may perform in person searches. Search fee: $6.00 per name. Required to search: name, years to search. Civil cases indexed by defendant, plaintiff. Civil records on computer since 9/97, pending cases indexed in card files. Old case card files back to 1979.
Criminal Records: Access: Mail, in person. Both court and visitors may perform in person searches. Search fee: $6.00 per name. Required to search: name, years to search. Criminal records on computer since 9/97, pending cases indexed in card files. Old case card files back to 1979.
General Information: No juvenile, mental, expunged, dismissed, or suspended imposition or execution of sentence records released. SASE required. Turnaround time 1 week. Copy fee: $.50 per page. Certification fee: $1.00. Fee payee: Christian County Circuit Clerk. Personal checks accepted. Prepayment is required.

Associate Circuit Court - Civil Division 1

110 W Elm St, Rm 203, Ozark, MO 65721; 417-581-2425. Hours: 8AM-4:30PM (CST). *Civil Actions Under $45,000, Eviction, Small Claims.*

Civil Records: Access: Phone, mail, in person. Both court and visitors may perform in person searches. No search fee. Required to search: name, years to search. Civil cases indexed by defendant. Civil records on computer since 07/91.
General Information: No juvenile, mental, expunged or dismissed records released. SASE required. Turnaround time 5 days, phone turnaround time immediate. Copy fee: $.25 per page. Certification fee: $1.50. Fee payee: Associate Division I. Personal checks accepted. Prepayment is required.

Associate Circuit Court - Criminal Division 2

110 W Elm St, Rm 105, Ozark, MO 65721; 417-581-4523; Fax: 417-581-1443. Hours: 8AM-4:30PM (CST). *Misdemeanor, Probate.*

Criminal Records: Access: Mail, fax, in person. Only the court performs in person searches; visitors may not. No search fee. Required to search: name, years to search. Criminal records on computer since 1984; prior on index cards. Will accept phone requests from attorneys and law enforcement officials.
General Information: No juvenile, mental, expunged or dismissed records released. SASE required. Turnaround time 5 days. Copy fee: $.30 per page. Certification fee: $1.50. Fee payee: Associate Division 2. Prepayment is required.

Clark County

Circuit Court 111 E Court, Kahoka, MO 63445; 660-727-3292; Fax: 660-727-1051. Hours: 8AM-4PM (CST). *Felony, Misdemeanor, Civil Actions Over $45,000.*

Civil Records: Access: Phone, fax, mail, in person. Both court and visitors may perform in person searches. No search fee. Required to search: name, years to search. Civil cases indexed by defendant, plaintiff. Civil records on books since 1991, prior archived since 1836.
Criminal Records: Access: Phone, fax, mail, in person. Both court and visitors may perform in person searches. No search fee. Required to search: name, years to search. Criminal records on books since 1991, prior archived since 1836.
General Information: Public access terminal is available. No juvenile, mental, expunged, dismissed, or suspended imposition of sentence records released. SASE required. Turnaround time 4 days. Fax notes: Fee to fax results is $1.00 per page. Copy fee: $.50 per page. Certification fee: $3.00. Fee payee: Clerk of Circuit Court. Personal checks accepted. Prepayment required.

Associate Circuit Court 113 W Court, Kahoka, MO 63445; 660-727-3628; Fax: 660-727-2544. Hours: 8AM-4PM (CST). *Misdemeanor, Civil Actions Under $45,000, Eviction, Small Claims, Probate.*

Civil Records: Access: Mail, fax, in person. Both the court and visitor may perform in person searches. No search fee. Required to search: name, years to search. Civil cases indexed by defendant, plaintiff. Civil records on index cards, archived since 1836.
Criminal Records: Access: Mail, fax, in person. Both the court and visitors may perform in person searches. No search fee. Required to search: name, years to search. Criminal records on computer since 1988, prior archived since 1836.
General Information: Public access terminal is available. No juvenile, mental, expunged, dismissed, or suspended imposition of sentence records released. SASE required. Turnaround time 1-10 days. Copy fee: $.25 per page. Certification fee: $1.50 plus $1.00 per add'l page. Fee payee: Associate Circuit Court. Personal checks accepted. Prepayment is required.

Clay County

Circuit Court PO Box 218, Liberty, MO 64069-0218; 816-792-7706; Fax: 816-792-7778. Hours: 8AM-5PM (CST). *Felony, Misdemeanor, Civil Actions Over $25,000.*

www.circuit7.net

Civil Records: Access: Fax, mail, in person, online. Both court and visitors may perform in person searches. No search fee. Required to search: name, years to search. Civil cases indexed by defendant, plaintiff. Civil records on computer since 1988; prior records on index. Online access to civil records on 7th Judicial Circuit database are available free at www.circuit7.net/pages/publicaccess/publicaccess.htm. Includes traffic.
Criminal Records: Access: In person, online. Visitors must perform in person searches for themselves. No search fee. Required to search: name, years to search, DOB. Criminal records on computer since 1988, prior on index cards. Online access to Circuit 7 records at www.circuit7.net/pages/publicaccess/publicaccess.htm.
General Information: Public access terminal is available. No juvenile, mental, expunged, dismissed, or suspended imposition of sentence records released. SASE required. Turnaround time 1-2 days. Copy fee: $.25 per page. Certification fee: $5.00. Fee payee: Clay County Circuit Clerk. Personal checks accepted.

Associate Circuit Court PO Box 218, Liberty, MO 64069-0218; 816-792-7706; Fax: 816-792-7778. Hours: 8AM-5PM (CST). *Misdemeanor, Civil Actions Under $25,000, Eviction, Small Claims, Probate.*

www.circuit7.net

Civil Records: Access: Mail, in person, online. Both court and visitors may perform in person searches. No search fee. Required to search: name, years to search. Civil cases indexed by defendant, plaintiff. Civil records on computer since 8/87, prior on microfilm. Online access to Circuit 7 records available free at www.circuit7.net/pages/publicaccess/publicaccess.htm.
Criminal Records: Access: Mail, in person, online. Both court and visitors may perform in person searches. No search fee. Required to search: name, years to search. Criminal records on computer since 8/87, prior on microfilm. Online access to Circuit 7 records at www.circuit7.net/pages/publicaccess/publicaccess.htm.
General Information: Public access terminal is available. No juvenile, mental, expunged, dismissed, or suspended imposition of sentence records released. SASE required. Turnaround time 7-10 days. Copy fee: $.25 per page. Certification fee: $5.00. Fee payee: Clay County Circuit Court. Personal checks accepted. Prepayment is required.

Clinton County

Circuit Court PO Box 275, Plattsburg, MO 64477; 816-539-3731; Fax: 816-539-3893. Hours: 8AM-5PM (CST). *Felony, Misdemeanor, Civil Actions Over $45,000.*

Civil Records: Access: In person only. Visitors must perform in person searches for themselves. No search fee. Required to search: name, years to search. Civil cases indexed by defendant, plaintiff. Civil records (Judgments) on computer from 1976, archived since 1833.
Criminal Records: Access: In person only. Visitors must perform in person searches for themselves. No search fee. Required to search: name, years to search. Criminal records (Judgments) on computer from 1976, archived since 1833.
General Information: Public access terminal is available. No juvenile, mental, expunged, dismissed, or suspended imposition of sentence records released. Copy fee: $1.00 per page. Certification fee: $1.00. Fee payee: Circuit Clerk. Personal checks accepted. Prepayment is required.

Associate Circuit Court PO Box 383, Plattsburg, MO 64477; 816-539-3755; Fax: 816-539-3439. Hours: 8AM-4:30PM (CST). *Misdemeanor, Civil Actions Under $45,000, Eviction, Small Claims, Probate.*

Civil Records: Access: Fax, mail, in person. Only the court performs in person searches; visitors may not. No search fee. Required to search: name, years to search. Civil cases indexed by defendant, plaintiff. Civil records on computer since 1992, prior on index cards since 1940s. Letterhead required for mail searches.

Criminal Records: Access: Fax, mail, in person. Only the court performs in person searches; visitors may not. No search fee. Required to search: name, years to search, DOB; also helpful - SSN. Criminal records on computer since 1992, prior on index cards since 1940s. Letterhead required for mail searches.

General Information: No juvenile, mental, expunged, dismissed, or suspended imposition of sentence records released. SASE required. Turnaround time 1 week. No copy fee. No personal checks accepted.

Cole County

Circuit Court PO Box 1870, Jefferson City, MO 65102-1870; 573-634-9151; Fax: 573-635-0796. 7:30AM-4:30PM (CST). *Felony, Misdemeanor, Civil Actions Over $25,000.*

Civil Records: Access: Fax, mail, in person, online. Both court and visitors may perform in person searches. No search fee. Required to search: name, years to search. Civil cases indexed by defendant, plaintiff. Civil records (pending) on computer, on books since 1820. Participates in the free state online court record system at http://casenet.osca.state.mo.us/casenet. Online records go back to 1/1980.

Criminal Records: Access: In person, online. Visitors must perform in person searches for themselves. No search fee. Required to search: name, years to search; also helpful: DOB, SSN. Criminal records on computer since 1989, prior on book since 1820. Participates in the free state online court record system at http://casenet.osca.state.mo.us/casenet. Online records go back to 1/1980.

General Information: No juvenile, mental, expunged, dismissed, or suspended imposition of sentence records released. Other access to criminal records: the court prefers that requesters go to the state highway patrol. SASE requested. Turnaround time 2-5 days. Fax notes: Fee to fax results is $1.00 per page. Copy fee: $.25 per page. Certification fee: $1.00. Fee payee: Cole County Circuit Clerk. Personal checks accepted.

Associate Circuit Court PO Box 503, Jefferson City, MO 65102; 573-634-9171; Fax: 573-635-5376. Hours: 7:30AM-4:30PM (CST). *Misdemeanor, Civil Actions Under $25,000, Eviction, Small Claims, Probate.*

Civil Records: Access: Fax, mail, in person, online. Only the court performs in person searches; visitors may not. No search fee. Required to search: name, years to search. Civil cases indexed by defendant, plaintiff. Civil records on cards for past 10 years. Participates in the free state online court record system at http://casenet.osca.state.mo.us/casenet. Online records go back to 1/1980. Probate online records go back to 6/2/1972.

Criminal Records: Access: Mail, in person, online. Only the court performs in person searches; visitors may not. No search fee. Required to search: name, years to search; also helpful: address, DOB, SSN. Criminal records on computer since 1990, prior on cards. Participates in the free state online court record system at http://casenet.osca.state.mo.us/casenet. Online records go back to 1/1980. This court prefers criminal record be searched through the State Highway Patrol Crim Records section, 573-526-6160.

General Information: No juvenile, mental, expunged, dismissed, or suspended imposition of sentence records released. SASE required. Turnaround time 1-2 days. Copy fee: $.25 per page. Certification fee: $1.00. Fee payee: Circuit Court Division III. Personal checks accepted. Prepayment is required.

Cooper County

Circuit Court 200 Main St, Rm 26, Boonville, MO 65233; 660-882-2232; Fax: 660-882-2043. Hours: 8:30AM-5:00PM (CST). *Felony, Misdemeanor, Civil Actions Over $25,000.*

Civil Records: Access: Phone, fax, mail, in person, online. Both court and visitors may perform in person searches. No search fee. Required to search: name, years to search. Civil cases indexed by defendant, plaintiff. Civil records on cards since 1975, case files from 1819 forward; on computer back to 2001. Access to civil records available free at http://casenet.osca.state.mo.us/casenet/. At the web site, select the judicial district, then search by name, case # or date. Online records go back to 4/2001.

Criminal Records: Access: Mail, in person, online. Both court and visitors may perform in person searches. No search fee. Required to search: name, years to search, DOB; also helpful: SSN. Criminal records on cards since 1975, case files from 1819 forward; on computer back to 2001. Online access to criminal records is the same as civil.

General Information: Public access terminal is available. No juvenile, mental, expunged, dismissed, or suspended imposition of sentence records released. SASE required. Turnaround time 1-2 days, phone-can tell you if record is available and cost. Copy fee: $1.00 per page. Certification fee: $1.50. Fee payee: Circuit Clerk or Recorder of Deeds. Personal checks accepted. Prepayment is required.

Associate Circuit Court 200 Main, Rm 31, Boonville, MO 65233; 660-882-5604; Fax: 660-882-8747. Hours: 8:30AM-5PM (CST). *Misdemeanor, Civil Actions Under $25,000, Eviction, Small Claims, Probate.*

Civil Records: Access: Mail, in person, online. No search fee. Required to search: name, years to search. Civil cases indexed by defendant, plaintiff. Civil records on index cards for 10 years. Access to civil records available free at http://casenet.osca.state.mo.us/casenet/. At the web site, select the judicial district, then search by name, case # or date. Online records go back to 4/2001.

Criminal Records: Access: Mail, in person, online. Only the court performs in person searches; visitors may not. No search fee. Required to search: name, years to search, DOB; also helpful: SSN. Criminal records on computer since mid-1990s, on index cards from 1980-1990. Online access to criminal records is the same as civil. Online criminal records go back 1/1990.

General Information: No juvenile, mental, expunged, dismissed, or suspended imposition of sentence records released. SASE required. Turnaround time 10 days. Copy fee: $1.00 per page. Certification fee: $1.50. Fee payee: Cooper County Associate Circuit Court. Prepayment is required.

Crawford County

Circuit Court PO Box 177, Steelville, MO 65565; 573-775-2866; Fax: 573-775-2452. Hours: 8AM-5PM (CST). *Felony, Misdemeanor, Civil Actions Over $25,000.*

Civil Records: Access: In person, online. Both court and visitors may perform in person searches. Search fee: $4.00 per name; court may not have time to perform searches. Required to search: name, years to search. Civil cases indexed by defendant, plaintiff. Civil records on computer from 03/02/92 for judgments only,

archived from 1800s, some records on index cards and books. Participates in the free state online Banner court record system at http://casenet.osca.state.mo.us/casenet.

Criminal Records: Access: Mail, in person, online. Both court and visitors may perform in person searches. Search fee: $4.00 per name; court may not have time to perform searches. Required to search: name, years to search, offense, date of offense. Criminal records on computer since 03/02/92, prior on cards. Online access to criminal court records is the same as civil.

General Information: Public access terminal is available. No juvenile, mental, expunged, dismissed, or suspended imposition of sentence records released. SASE required. Turnaround time 1-2 weeks. Copy fee: $.30 per page. Certification fee: $1.00. Fee payee: Crawford County Circuit Clerk. Personal checks accepted. Prepayment is required.

Associate Circuit Court PO Box B.C., Steelville, MO 65565; 573-775-2149; Fax: 573-775-4010. Hours: 8AM-5PM (CST). *Misdemeanor, Civil Actions Under $25,000, Eviction, Small Claims, Probate.*

Civil Records: Access: Phone, fax, mail, in person. Only the court performs in person searches; visitors may not. No search fee. Required to search: name, years to search. Civil cases indexed by defendant, plaintiff. Civil records kept since 1989, prior destroyed.

Criminal Records: Access: Mail, in person. Per judge's orders, court will not accept search requests or perform criminal record searches. No search fee. Required to search: name, years to search. Criminal records kept since 1989, prior destroyed. Court will refer search requests to State Hiway Patrol Criminal Records, POB 568, Jefferson Ctiy, MO 65102, 573-526-6153 ($5.00 per name fee).

General Information: No sealed records released. SASE required. Turnaround time 2 weeks. Fax notes: No fee to fax results. Copy fee: $.30 per page. Certification fee: $2.50. Fee payee: Associate Circuit Court. Personal checks accepted. Prepayment required.

Dade County

Circuit Court Courthouse, Greenfield, MO 65661; 417-637-2271; Fax: 417-637-5055. Hours: 8AM-4PM (CST). *Felony, Misdemeanor, Civil Actions Over $25,000.*

Civil Records: Access: Mail, in person, online. Only the court performs in person searches; visitors may not. No search fee. Required to search: name, years to search. Civil cases indexed by defendant, plaintiff. Civil records in index cards since 1982, prior on books to 1800's; on computer back to 2000. Participates in the free state online court record system at http://casenet.osca.state.mo.us/casenet. Online records go back to 9/20/1999. Online records include Probate Court.

Criminal Records: Access: Mail, in person, online. Only the court performs in person searches; visitors may not. No search fee. Required to search: name, years to search; also helpful-DOB, SSN, signed release. Criminal records in index cards since 1982, prior on book to 1800's; on computer back to 2000. Online access to criminal records is the same as civil.

General Information: No juvenile, mental, expunged, dismissed, or suspended imposition of sentence records released. SASE required. Turnaround time 2-3 days. Copy fee: $1.00 per page. Certification fee: $2.50. Fee payee: Dade County Circuit Clerk. Personal checks accepted. Prepayment is required.

Associate Circuit Court 300 W Water, Greenfield, MO 65661; 417-637-2741; Fax: 417-637-5055. Hours: 8AM-4PM (CST). *Misdemeanor, Civil Actions Under $25,000, Eviction, Small Claims, Probate.*

Civil Records: Access: Mail, fax, in person, online. Both court and visitors may perform in person searches. Search fee: $5.00. Required to search: name, years to search. Civil cases indexed by defendant, plaintiff. Civil records on index cards since 1943; on computer back to 2000. Participates in the free state online court record system at http://casenet.osca.state.mo.us/casenet.

Criminal Records: Access: Mail, fax, in person, online. Both court and visitors may perform in person searches. No search fee. Required to search: name, years to search, DOB; also helpful-SSN, signed release. Criminal records on index cards since 1943; on computer back to 2000. Online access to criminal records is the same as civil.

General Information: Public access terminal is available. No juvenile, mental, expunged, dismissed, or suspended imposition of sentence records released. SASE required. Turnaround time next day, phone turnaround time varies. Copy fee: $.25 per page. Certification fee: $2.50. Fee payee: Associate Circuit Court. Personal checks accepted. Prepayment required.

Dallas County

Circuit Court PO Box 373, Buffalo, MO 65622; 417-345-2243; Fax: 417-345-5539. Hours: 7:30AM-4PM (CST). *Felony, Misdemeanor, Civil Actions Over $25,000.*

www.positech.net/~dcourt

Civil Records: Access: Phone, fax, mail, in person, online. Both court and visitors may perform in person searches. No search fee. Required to search: name, years to search. Civil cases indexed by defendant, plaintiff. Civil records on computer since 1991, prior on book since 1951. Participates in the free state online court record system at http://casenet.osca.state.mo.us/casenet.

Criminal Records: Access: Phone, fax, mail, in person, online. Both court and visitors may perform in person searches. No search fee. Required to search: name, years to search; also helpful: DOB. Criminal records on computer since 1992, prior on book since 1951. Online access to criminal records is the same as civil.

General Information: Public access terminal is available. No juvenile, mental, expunged, dismissed, or suspended imposition of sentence records released. SASE required. Turnaround time 1-2 days. Fax notes: Fee to fax is $1.00 per page. Copy fee: $.25 per page. Certification fee: $1.00. Fee payee: Circuit Clerk. Personal checks accepted. Prepayment required.

Associate Circuit Court PO Box 1150, Buffalo, MO 65622; 417-345-7641; Fax: 417-345-5358. Hours: 8AM-4PM (CST). *Misdemeanor, Civil Actions Under $45,000, Eviction, Small Claims, Probate.*

www.positech.net/~dcourt

Civil Records: Access: Phone, mail, online, in person. Both court and visitors may perform in person searches. No search fee. Required to search: name, years to search. Civil cases indexed by defendant, plaintiff. Civil records on index cards since 1800s; computerized since 1990.

Criminal Records: Access: Phone, mail, online, in person. Both court and visitors may perform in person searches. No search fee. Required to search: name, years to search. Criminal records on computer since 1990, on index cards since 1800s.

General Information: No juvenile, mental, expunged, dismissed, or suspended imposition of sentence records released. SASE required. Turnaround time 1 day. Copy fee: $.25 per page. Fee payee: Associate Circuit Court. Only cashiers checks and money orders accepted. Prepayment required.

Daviess County

Circuit Court PO Box 337, Gallatin, MO 64640; 660-663-2932; Fax: 660-663-3376. Hours: 8AM-4:30PM (CST). *Felony, Misdemeanor, Civil Actions Over $45,000.*

Civil Records: Access: Phone, fax, mail, in person. Both court and visitors may perform in person searches. Search fee: $10.00 per name. Required to search: name, years to search. Civil cases indexed by defendant, plaintiff. Civil records on records books since 1839.

Criminal Records: Access: Phone, fax, mail, in person. Both court and visitors may perform in person searches. Search fee: $10.00 per name. Required to search: name, years to search, DOB. Criminal records on records books since 1839.

General Information: No juvenile, mental, expunged, dismissed, or suspended imposition of sentence records released. SASE required. Turnaround time 1 day, phone turnaround time immediate. Fax notes: $2.00 per page. Copy fee: $1.00 per page. Certification fee: $2.00. Fee payee: Daviess County Circuit Clerk. Business checks accepted. Prepayment is required.

Associate Division Circuit Court Courthouse, PO Box 233, Gallatin, MO 64640; 660-663-2532. Hours: 8AM-4:30PM (CST). *Misdemeanor, Civil Actions Under $45,000, Eviction, Small Claims, Probate.*

Civil Records: Access: Fax, mail, in person. Only the court may perform in person searches. No search fee. Required to search: name, years to search. Civil cases indexed by defendant, plaintiff. Civil records index cards since 9/84, prior on judgment books.

Criminal Records: Access: Mail, in person. Only the court may perform in person searches. No search fee. Required to search: name, years to search. Criminal records on index cards since 1979, prior on judgment books.

General Information: No juvenile, mental, expunged, dismissed, or suspended imposition of sentence records released. SASE required. Turnaround time 1-2 days. Copy fee: $1.00 per page. Certification fee: $1.50. Fee payee: Associate Division Court. Only cashiers checks and money orders accepted. Prepayment is required.

De Kalb County

Circuit Court PO Box 248, Maysville, MO 64469; 816-449-2602; Fax: 816-449-2440. Hours: 8:30AM-4:30PM (CST). *Felony, Civil Actions Over $45,000.*

Civil Records: Access: In person only. Visitors must perform in person searches for themselves. Search fee: No search fee. Required to search: name, years to search. Civil cases indexed by defendant, plaintiff. Civil records on index cards since 1970.

Criminal Records: Access: In person only. Visitors must perform in person searches for themselves. Search fee: No search fee. Required to search: name, years to search. Criminal records on index cards since 1970.

General Information: No juvenile or suspended imposition of sentence records released. Fax notes: Fee to fax results is $1.00 per page. Copy fee: $1.00 per page. Certification fee: $1.00. Fee payee: Clifton DeShon, Circuit Clerk. Personal checks accepted. Prepayment is required.

Associate Circuit Court PO Box 248, Maysville, MO 64469; 816-449-5400; Fax: 816-449-2440. Hours: 8:30AM-4:30PM (CST). *Misdemeanor, Civil Actions Under $45,000, Eviction, Small Claims, Probate.*

Civil Records: Access: Mail, in person. Only the court performs in person searches; visitors may not. No search fee. Required to search: name, years to search. Civil cases indexed by defendant, plaintiff. Civil records on index cards since 1960s.

Criminal Records: Access: Mail, in person. Only the court performs in person searches; visitors may not. No search fee. Required to search: name, years to search; DOB; also helpful-SSN, case number. Criminal records on index cards since 1980s.

General Information: No juvenile, mental, expunged, dismissed, or suspended imposition of sentence records released. SASE required. Turnaround time 5 days. Fax notes: Will not fax results. Copy fee: $1.00 per page. Certification fee: $2.50. Fee payee: Associate Circuit Court. Only cashiers checks and money orders accepted. Prepayment is required.

Dent County

Circuit Court 112 E 5th St, Salem, MO 65560; 573-729-3931; Fax: 573-729-9414. Hours: 8AM-4:30PM (CST). *Felony, Misdemeanor, Civil Actions Over $25,000.*

Civil Records: Access: Mail, fax, in person. Both court and visitors may perform in person searches. No search fee. Required to search: name, years to search. Civil cases indexed by defendant, plaintiff. Civil records on computer since 1993, on index cards since 1978.

Criminal Records: Access: Mail, fax, in person. Both court and visitors may perform in person searches. No search fee. Required to search: name, years to search. Criminal records on computer since 1993, on index cards since 1978.

General Information: Public access terminal is available. No juvenile, mental, expunged, dismissed, or suspended imposition of sentence records released. SASE required. Turnaround time 3-4 days. Copy fee: $.25 per page. Certification fee: $2.00. Fee payee: Dent County Circuit Clerk. Prepayment is required.

Associate Circuit Court 112 E 5th St, Salem, MO 65560; 573-729-3134; Fax: 573-729-5146. Hours: 8AM-4:30PM (CST). *Misdemeanor, Civil Actions Under $25,000, Eviction, Small Claims, Probate.*

Civil Records: Access: Mail, fax, in person. Both court and visitors may perform in person searches. No search fee. Required to search: name, years to search. Civil cases indexed by defendant, plaintiff. Civil records on computer since 1985, prior on index cards.

Criminal Records: Access: Mail, fax, in person. Both court and visitors may perform in person searches. No search fee. Required to search: name, years to search, DOB, signed release. Criminal records on computer since 1985, prior on index cards.

General Information: Public access terminal is available. No juvenile, mental, expunged, dismissed, or suspended imposition of sentence records released. SASE required. Turnaround time 2-3 days. Copy fee: $.25 per page. Certification fee: $2.00. Fee payee: Associate Circuit Court or Probate Court. Business checks accepted. Prepayment is required.

Douglas County

Circuit Court PO Box 249, Ava, MO 65608; 417-683-4713; Fax: 417-683-2794. Hours: 8AM-4:30PM (CST). *Felony, Misdemeanor, Civil Actions Over $25,000.*

Civil Records: Access: Phone, mail, in person. Visitors must perform in person searches for themselves. Search fee: $5.00 per name. Required to search: name, years to search. Civil cases indexed by defendant, plaintiff. Civil records on alpha cards since 1977.

Criminal Records: Access: Phone, mail, in person. Visitors must perform in person searches for themselves. Search fee: $5.00 per name. Required to search: name, years to search; also helpful: DOB, SSN. Criminal records on alpha cards since 1977.

General Information: Public access terminal is available. No juvenile, mental, expunged, dismissed, or suspended imposition of sentence records released. SASE required. Turnaround time 1 week. Copy fee:

$.25 per page. Certification fee: $2.50. Fee payee: Circuit Clerk. Personal checks accepted. Copy fees may be billed.

Associate Circuit Court PO Box 276, Ava, MO 65608; 417-683-2114; Fax: 417-683-3121. Hours: 8AM-4:30PM (CST). *Misdemeanor, Civil Actions Under $25,000, Eviction, Small Claims, Probate.*

Civil Records: Access: Phone, mail, in person. Both court and visitors may perform in person searches. No search fee. Required to search: name, years to search. Civil cases indexed by defendant, plaintiff. Civil records on index cards.

Criminal Records: Access: Phone, mail, in person. Both court and visitors may perform in person searches. No search fee. Required to search: name, years to search; also helpful: SSN. Criminal records on index cards.

General Information: No juvenile, mental, expunged, dismissed, or suspended imposition of sentence records released. SASE required. Turnaround time 2-3 days. Copy fee: $.25 per page. Certification fee: $1.50. Fee payee: Associate Circuit Court. Personal checks accepted. Prepayment is required.

Dunklin County

Circuit Court Division I PO Box 567, Kennett, MO 63857; 573-888-2456; Fax: 573-888-0319. Hours: 8:30AM-4:30PM (CST). *Felony, Misdemeanor, Civil Actions Over $25,000.*

www.osca.state.mo.us

Civil Records: Access: In person, online. Visitors must perform in person searches for themselves. No search fee. Required to search: name, years to search. Civil cases indexed by defendant, plaintiff. Civil records on index cards back to 1900; on computer back to 1990. Access to civil records available free at http://casenet.osca.state.mo.us/casenet/. At the web site, select the judicial district, then search by name, case number or date. Online records go back to 7/1/2001.

Criminal Records: Access: In person, online. Visitors must perform in person searches for themselves. No search fee. Required to search: name, years to search, DOB, SSN. Criminal records on computer back to 8/94. Online access to criminal records is the same as civil. Criminal records searches are referred to the MO State Hiway Patrol.

General Information: Public access terminal is available. No juvenile, mental, expunged or dismissed records released. Copy fee: $.50 per page. Certification fee: $2.00. Fee payee: Circuit Clerk. Personal checks accepted. Attorney's, courts and abstract companies.

Associate Circuit Court Courthouse Rm 103, Kennett, MO 63857; 573-888-3378; Probate phone: 573-888-3272; Fax: 573-888-0754. Hours: 8AM-4:30PM (CST). *Felony, Misdemeanor, Civil Actions Under $25,000, Eviction, Small Claims, Probate.*

Note: Probate address is Room #202.

Civil Records: Access: In person, online. Visitors must perform in person searches for themselves. No search fee. Required to search: name, years to search. Civil cases indexed by defendant, plaintiff. Civil records on index cards; on computer back to 2001. Access to civil records available free at http://casenet.osca.state.mo.us/casenet/. At the web site, select the judicial district, then search by name, case number or date. Online records go back to 7/1/2001.

Criminal Records: Access: Mail, in person, online. Visitors must perform in person searches for themselves. No search fee. Required to search: name, years to search, DOB. Criminal records on index cards back to 1979; on computer back to 1990. Online access to criminal records is the same as civil.

General Information: Public access terminal is available. No juvenile, mental, expunged, dismissed, or

suspended imposition of sentence records released. Turnaround time 1-2 days. Copy fee: $.50 per page. Certification fee: $2.50. Fee payee: Circuit Court Div 2. Business checks accepted. Prepayment is required.

Franklin County

Circuit Court 300 E Main St, Rm 301, Union, MO 63084; 636-583-6300. Hours: 8AM-4:30PM (CST). *Felony, Civil Actions Over $25,000.*

Civil Records: Access: Mail, online, in person. Both court and visitors may perform in person searches. Search fee: $2.00 per name. Required to search: name, years to search. Civil cases indexed by defendant, plaintiff. Civil records on computer back to 1995; others filed as originals. Participates in the free state online court record system at http://casenet.osca.state.mo.us/casenet. Online records go back to 1/1995.

Criminal Records: Access: Mail, online, in person. Both court and visitors may perform in person searches. Search fee: $2.00 per name. Required to search: name, years to search, DOB. Criminal records on computer back to 1995; others filed as originals. Participates in the free state online court record system at http://casenet.osca.state.mo.us/casenet. Online records go back to 1/1995.

General Information: Public access terminal is available. No juvenile, mental, expunged, dismissed, or suspended imposition of sentence records released. SASE required. Turnaround time 1-5 days. Copy fee: $1.00 per page or $.25 do-it-yourself. Certification fee: $1.00. Fee payee: Circuit Clerk. Personal checks accepted. Prepayment is required.

Associate Circuit Court PO Box 526, Union, MO 63084; 636-583-6326. Hours: 8AM-4:30PM (CST). *Misdemeanor, Civil Actions Under $25,000, Eviction, Small Claims, Probate.*

Civil Records: Access: Online, in person. Both court and visitors may perform in person searches. No search fee. Required to search: name, years to search. Civil cases indexed by defendant, plaintiff. Civil records on computer (limited), on index cards since 1983. Participates in the free state online court record system at http://casenet.osca.state.mo.us/casenet. Online records go back to 1/1995. Online probate court records go back to 10/14/1967.

Criminal Records: Access: Online, in person. Both court and visitors may perform in person searches. No search fee. Required to search: name, years to search. Criminal records on index cards since 1979. Participates in the free state online court record system at http://casenet.osca.state.mo.us/casenet. Online records go back to 1/1995.

General Information: No juvenile, mental, expunged, dismissed, or suspended imposition of sentence records released. Copy fee: $.05.

Gasconade County

Circuit Court 119 E 1st St, Rm 6, Hermann, MO 65041-1182; 573-486-2632; Fax: 573-486-5812. Hours: 8AM-4:30PM (CST). *Felony, Misdemeanor, Civil Actions Over $25,000.*

Civil Records: Access: Phone, fax, mail, in person, online. Both court and visitors may perform in person searches. No search fee. Required to search: name, years to search. Civil cases indexed by defendant, plaintiff. Civil records on index cards since 1976, prior on books stored in vault; on comptuer back to 9/2001. Participates in the free state online court record system at http://casenet.osca.state.mo.us/casenet. Online records go back to 7/31/2000.

Criminal Records: Access: Phone, fax, mail, in person, online. Only the court performs in person searches; visitors may not. No search fee. Required to search: name, years to search; also helpful: DOB, SSN.

Criminal records on index cards since 1976, prior on books stored in vault; on computer back to 9/2001. Participates in the free state online court record system at http://casenet.osca.state.mo.us/casenet. Online records go back to 7/31/2000.

General Information: Public access terminal is available. No juvenile, mental, expunged, dismissed, or suspended imposition of sentence records released. SASE required. Turnaround time 3-4 days. Fax notes: $2.00 for first page, $1.00 each add'l. Copy fee: $1.00 per page. Certification fee: $1.00. Fee payee: Gasconade Circuit Court. Personal checks accepted.

Associate Circuit Court 119 E. 1st St. Rm 3, Hermann, MO 65041; 573-486-2321; Fax: 573-486-3693. Hours: 8AM-4:30PM (CST). *Misdemeanor, Civil Actions Under $25,000, Eviction, Small Claims, Probate.*

Civil Records: Access: Fax, mail, in person, online. Only the court performs in person searches; visitors may not. No search fee. Required to search: name, years to search. Civil cases indexed by defendant, plaintiff. Civil records on computer since 1988, prior on index cards since 1979. Participates in the free state online court record system at http://casenet.osca.state.mo.us/casenet. Online records go back to 7/31/2000.

Criminal Records: Access: Fax, mail, in person, online. Only the court performs in person searches; visitors may not. No search fee. Required to search: name, years to search. Criminal records on computer since 1988, prior on index cards since 1979. Participates in the free state online court record system at http://casenet.osca.state.mo.us/casenet. Online records go back to 7/31/2000.

General Information: No juvenile, mental, expunged, dismissed, or suspended imposition of sentence records released. SASE required. Turnaround time varies. Copy fee: $1.00 per page. Certification fee: $2.50. Fee payee: Associate Circuit Court. Personal checks accepted. Will bill probate fees.

Gentry County

Circuit Court PO Box 27, Albany, MO 64402; 660-726-3618; Fax: 660-726-4102. Hours: 8AM-4:30PM (CST). *Felony, Misdemeanor, Civil Actions Over $25,000.*

Civil Records: Access: Mail, fax, in person. Both court and visitors may perform in person searches. No search fee. Required to search: name, years to search. Civil cases indexed by defendant, plaintiff. Civil records archived since 1885.

Criminal Records: Access: Mail, in person. Both court and visitors may perform in person searches. No search fee. Required to search: name, years to search; also helpful: DOB, SSN. Criminal records archived since 1885.

General Information: No juvenile, mental, expunged, dismissed, or suspended imposition of sentence records released. SASE required. Turnaround time 5 working days. Fax notes: Fee to fax results is $1.00 per page. Copy fee: $1.00 per page. Certification fee: $1.00. Fee payee: Circuit Clerk. Personal checks accepted. Prepayment is required.

Associate Circuit Court 200 W Clay St, Albany, MO 64402; 660-726-3411; Fax: 660-726-4102. Hours: 8AM-4:30PM (CST). *Misdemeanor, Civil Actions Under $25,000, Eviction, Small Claims, Probate.*

Civil Records: Access: In person, online. Visitors must perform in person searches for themselves. No search fee. Required to search: name, years to search. Civil cases indexed by defendant, plaintiff. Civil records on index cards.

Criminal Records: Access: In person only. Visitors must perform in person searches for themselves. No

search fee. Required to search: name, years to search. Criminal records on index cards.

General Information: No juvenile, mental, expunged, dismissed, or suspended imposition of sentence records released. Copy fee: $1.00 per page. Certification fee: $1.50. Fee payee: Associate Circuit Court. Personal checks accepted. Prepayment is required.

Greene County

Circuit Court 1010 Booneville, Springfield, MO 65802; 417-868-4074. Hours: 8AM-5AM (CST). *Felony, Civil Actions Over $25,000.*

www.greenecountymo.org

Civil Records: Access: Mail, in person, online. Both court and visitors may perform in person searches. Search fee: $5.00 per name. Required to search: name, years to search. Civil cases indexed by defendant, plaintiff. Civil records on computer back to 7/89, prior on index cards. Search online at www.greenecountymo.org/ccourt31/search.htm or visit the free state online court record system at http://casenet.osca.state.mo.us/casenet.

Criminal Records: Access: Mail, in person., online. Both court and visitors may perform in person searches. Search fee: $5.00 per name. Required to search: name, years to search; also helpful: address, DOB, SSN. Criminal records on computer back to 7/89, prior on index cards. Search free online at www.greenecountymo.org/ccourt31/search.htm or visit the free state online court record system at http://casenet.osca.state.mo.us/casenet.

General Information: Public access terminal is available. No juvenile, mental, expunged, sealed, dismissed or suspended imposition of sentence records released. SASE required. Turnaround time 1 week. Copy fee: $.20 per page. Certification fee: $5.00. Fee payee: Circuit Clerk. Personal checks accepted. Prepayment is required.

Associate Circuit Court 1010 Boonville, Springfield, MO 65802; 417-868-4110; Probate phone: 417-868-4027. Hours: 8AM-5PM (CST). *Misdemeanor, Civil Actions Under $25,000, Eviction, Small Claims, Probate.*

www.greenecountymo.org

Note: Probate is a separate court at the same address.

Civil Records: Access: Phone, mail, in person, online. Both court and visitors may perform in person searches. Search fee: $2.00 per name. Required to search: name, years to search. Civil cases indexed by defendant, plaintiff. Civil records on computer since mid-1989, prior on index cards. Search online at www.greenecountymo.org/ccourt31/search.htm or visit the free state online court record system at http://casenet.osca.state.mo.us/casenet.

Criminal Records: Access: Mail, in person, online. Both court and visitors may perform in person searches. Search fee: $2.00. Required to search: name, years to search; also helpful: SSN. Criminal records on computer since mid-1989, prior on index cards. Search at www.greenecountymo.org/ccourt31/search.htm or visit the free state online court record system at http://casenet.osca.state.mo.us/casenet.

General Information: Public access terminal is available. (Very limited.) No juvenile, mental, expunged, sealed, dismissed or suspended imposition of sentence records released. SASE required. Turnaround time 2 days; if certified, 1 week. Copy fee: $.10 per page. Fee payee: Associate Circuit Clerk. Business checks accepted. Prepayment is required.

Grundy County

Circuit Court Courthouse, 700 Main St, PO Box 196, Trenton, MO 64683; 660-359-6605; Fax: 660-359-6604. Hours: 8:30AM-4:30PM (CST). *Felony, Misdemeanor, Civil Actions Over $25,000.*

Civil Records: Access: In person, online. Visitors must perform in person searches. No search fee. Required to search: name, years to search. Civil cases indexed by defendant, plaintiff. Civil records archived since 1841; on computer back to 2000. Participates in the free state online court system at http://casenet.osca.state.mo.us/casenet. Online records go back to 9/97.

Criminal Records: Access: In person, online. Visitors must perform in person searches for themselves. No search fee. Required to search: name, years to search. Criminal records archived since 1841; on computer back to 2000. Online access to criminal records is the same as civil. Online records go back to 6/93.

General Information: Public access terminal is available. No juvenile, Title 4D, child support, mental, expunged, dismissed, or suspended imposition of sentence cases. Copy fee: $.25 per page. Certification fee: $2.00. Fee payee: Circuit Clerk. Personal checks accepted. Prepayment is required.

Associate Circuit Court PO Box 26, Trenton, MO 64683; 660-359-6606/6909. Hours: 8:30AM-4:30PM (CST). *Misdemeanor, Civil Actions Under $25,000, Eviction, Small Claims, Probate.*

Civil Records: Access: Mail, in person, online. Both court and visitors may perform in person searches. No search fee. Required to search: name, years to search. Civil cases indexed by defendant, plaintiff. Civil records on index cards, probate records archived. Participates in the free state online court record system at http://casenet.osca.state.mo.us/casenet. Online records go back to 3/29/2000.

Criminal Records: Access: Mail, in person, online. Both court and visitors may perform in person searches. No search fee. Required to search: name, years to search. Criminal records on index cards, probate records archived. Online access to criminal records is the same as civil.

General Information: No juvenile, mental, expunged, dismissed, or suspended imposition of sentence records released. SASE required. Turnaround time 1-2 days. Copy fee: $1.00 per page. Certification fee: $2.50 per document. Fee payee: Grundy County Circuit Court Division II. Business checks accepted. Prepayment is required.

Harrison County

Circuit Court PO Box 189, Bethany, MO 64424; 660-425-6425; Fax: 660-425-6390. Hours: 8AM-5PM (CST). *Felony, Misdemeanor, Civil Actions Over $25,000.*

Civil Records: Access: Mail, in person, online. Only the court performs in person searches; visitors may not. No search fee. Required to search: name, years to search. Civil cases indexed by defendant, plaintiff. Civil records on index cards since 1979, prior on index books. Participates in the free state online court record system at http://casenet.osca.state.mo.us/casenet. Online records go back to 1995.

Criminal Records: Access: Mail, in person, online. Only the court performs in person searches; visitors may not. No search fee. Required to search: name, years to search; also helpful: address, DOB, SSN. Criminal records on index cards since 1979, prior on index books. Online access to criminal records is the same as civil.

General Information: No juvenile, mental, expunged, dismissed, or suspended imposition of sentence records released. SASE required. Turnaround time varies. Copy fee: $.25 per page. Certification fee: $1.00. Fee payee:

Harrison County Circuit Court. Personal checks accepted. Prepayment is required.

Associate Circuit Court Box 189, Bethany, MO 64424; 660-425-6432; Fax: 660-425-6390. Hours: 8AM-4:30PM (CST). *Misdemeanor, Civil Actions Under $25,000, Eviction, Small Claims, Probate.*

Civil Records: Access: Mail, fax, in person, online. Both court and visitors may perform in person searches. No search fee. Required to search: name, years to search. Civil cases indexed by defendant, plaintiff. Civil records on index cards back to 1990 or archives. Participates in the free state online court record system at http://casenet.osca.state.mo.us/casenet. Court will perform searches only as time permits.

Criminal Records: Access: Mail, in person, online. Both court and visitors may perform in person searches. No search fee. Required to search: name, years to search. Criminal records on index cards back to 1990; on computer back to 2001. Participates in the free state online court record system at http://casenet.osca.state.mo.us/casenet. Court will perform searches only as time permits.

General Information: No juvenile, mental, expunged, dismissed, or suspended imposition of sentence records released. Turnaround time 7 days. Copy fee: $.25 per page. Certification fee: $1.00. Fee payee: Associate Circuit Court of Harrison County. Personal checks accepted. Prepayment is required.

Henry County

Circuit Court 100 W Franklin Rm 12, Clinton, MO 64735; 660-885-6963 X210; Fax: 660-885-8247. Hours: 8AM-4:30PM (CST). *Felony, Civil Actions Over $25,000.*

http://tacnet.missouri.org/~court27

Civil Records: Access: Mail, in person. Both court and visitors may perform in person searches. No search fee. Required to search: name, years to search. Civil cases indexed by defendant, plaintiff. Civil records on computer since 8/92, on index cards since 1979, archived since 1877. You can fax requests, but no results are faxed.

Criminal Records: Access: In person only. Only the court may perform in person searches. No search fee. Required to search: name, years to search. Criminal records on computer since 8/92, on index cards since 1979, archived since 1877. Criminal records searches can be directed to MO State Hwy Patrol, 573-526-6153.

General Information: Public access terminal is available. (Judgments only on public access terminal.) No juvenile, mental, expunged, dismissed, or suspended imposition of sentence records released. SASE required. Turnaround time 2 days. Copy fee: $.25 per page. There is a $2.50 fee for records copied from big books. Certification fee: $1.50. Fee payee: Henry County Circuit Clerk. Personal checks accepted. Copy fees may be billed.

Associate Circuit Court Courthouse, Clinton, MO 64735; 660-885-6963 X205/207; Fax: 660-885-5387. Hours: 8AM-4:30PM (CST). *Misdemeanor, Civil Actions Under $25,000, Eviction, Small Claims, Probate.*

Civil Records: Access: Mail, in person. Both court and visitors may perform in person searches. No search fee. Required to search: name, years to search. Civil cases indexed by defendant, plaintiff. Civil records on index cards since 1979, prior on judgment books.

Criminal Records: Access: Mail, in person. Both court and visitors may perform in person searches. No search fee. Required to search: name, years to search. Criminal records on index cards since 1979, prior on judgment books.

General Information: No juvenile, mental, expunged, dismissed, or suspended imposition of sentence records released. SASE required. Turnaround time 5 days.

Copy fee: $.25 per page. Certification fee: $1.50. Fee payee: Associate Circuit Court. Personal checks accepted.

Hickory County

Circuit Court PO Box 101, Hermitage, MO 65668; 417-745-6421; Fax: 417-745-6670. Hours: 8AM-4:30PM (CST). *Felony, Misdemeanor, Civil Actions Over $45,000.*

www.positech.net/~dcourt

Civil Records: Access: Mail, in person, online. Both court and visitors may perform in person searches. No search fee. Required to search: name, years to search. Civil cases indexed by defendant, plaintiff. Civil records on computer since 1992, prior on index books since 1976. Participates in the free state online court record system at http://casenet.osca.state.mo.us/casenet.

Criminal Records: Access: Mail, in person, online. Both court and visitors may perform in person searches. No search fee. Required to search: name, years to search, signed release. Criminal records on computer since 1992, prior on index books since 1976. Online access to criminal records is the same as civil.

General Information: No juvenile, mental, expunged, dismissed, or suspended imposition of sentence records released. SASE required. Turnaround time 1 week-10 days. Fax notes: Fee to fax results is 1.00 per page. Copy fee: $1.00 per page. Certification fee: $1.00. Fee payee: Hickory County Circuit Clerk. Personal checks accepted. Prepayment is required.

Associate Circuit Court PO Box 75, Hermitage, MO 65668; 417-745-6822; Fax: 417-745-6670. Hours: 8AM-Noon; 12:30PM-4:30PM (CST). *Misdemeanor, Civil Actions Under $45,000, Eviction, Small Claims, Probate.*

www.positech.net/~dcourt

Civil Records: Access: Mail, in person. Both court and visitors may perform in person searches. No search fee. Required to search: name, years to search. Civil cases indexed by defendant, plaintiff. Civil records on index cards since 1980.

Criminal Records: Access: Mail, in person. Both court and visitors may perform in person searches. No search fee. Required to search: name, years to search, DOB. Criminal records on index cards since 1980.

General Information: No juvenile, mental, expunged, dismissed, or suspended imposition of sentence records released. SASE required. Turnaround time 2-3 days. Copy fee: $.25.

Holt County

Circuit Court PO Box 318, Oregon, MO 64473; 660-446-3301; Fax: 660-446-3328. Hours: 8AM-4:30PM (CST). *Felony, Misdemeanor, Civil Actions Over $45,000.*

Civil Records: Access: Fax, mail, in person. Only the court performs in person searches; visitors may not. Search fee: $4.00. Required to search: name, years to search. Civil cases indexed by defendant, plaintiff. Civil records on books.

Criminal Records: Access: Fax, mail, in person. Only the court performs in person searches; visitors may not. Search fee: $4.00. Required to search: name, years to search. Criminal records on books.

General Information: No juvenile, mental, expunged, dismissed, or suspended imposition of sentence records released. SASE required. Turnaround time varies. Fax notes: $2.00 per document. Copy fee: $1.00 per page. Certification fee: $1.00. Fee payee: Recorder. Personal checks accepted. Prepayment is required.

Associate Circuit Court PO Box 173, Oregon, MO 64473; 660-446-3380. Hours: 8:30AM-4:30PM (CST). *Misdemeanor, Civil Actions Under $45,000, Eviction, Small Claims, Probate.*

Civil Records: Access: Mail, fax, in person. Court and visitors must perform in person searches. No search fee. Required to search: name, years to search. Civil cases indexed by defendant, plaintiff. Civil records on computer since 1991, prior on index cards since 1979.

Criminal Records: Access: Mail, fax, in person. Court and visitors must perform in person searches. No search fee. Required to search: name, years to search. Criminal records on computer since 1991, prior on index cards since 1979.

General Information: No juvenile, mental, expunged, dismissed, or suspended imposition of sentence records released. SASE required. Turnaround time varies. Copy fee: $.25 per page. Certification fee: $1.50. Fee payee: Associate Circuit Court. Personal checks accepted. Prepayment is required.

Howard County

Circuit Court 1 Courthouse Square, Fayette, MO 65248; 660-248-2194; Fax: 660-248-1075. Hours: 8:30AM-4:30PM (CST). *Felony, Misdemeanor, Civil Actions Over $30,000.*

Civil Records: Access: In person, online. Visitors must perform in person searches for themselves. No search fee. Required to search: name, years to search. Civil cases indexed by defendant, plaintiff. Civil records on index cards; computer records go back to the 1970's. Participates in the free state online court record system at http://casenet.osca.state.mo.us/casenet.

Criminal Records: Access: In person, online. Visitors must perform in person searches for themselves. No search fee. Required to search: name, years to search. Criminal records on index cards; computer records go back to the 1970's. Online access to criminal records is the same as civil.

General Information: Public access terminal is available. No juvenile, mental, expunged, dismissed, or suspended imposition of sentence records released. Copy fee: $.25 per page. Certification fee: $2.00. Fee payee: Circuit Clerk. Personal checks accepted. Prepayment is required.

Associate Circuit Court PO Box 370, Fayette, MO 65248; 660-248-3326; Fax: 660-248-1075. Hours: 8:30AM-4:30PM (CST). *Misdemeanor, Civil Actions Under $45,000, Eviction, Small Claims, Probate.*

Civil Records: Access: In person only. Visitors must perform in person searches for themselves. No search fee. Required to search: name, years to search. Civil cases indexed by defendant, plaintiff. Civil records go back to 1975.

Criminal Records: Access: In person only. Visitors must perform in person searches for themselves. No search fee. Required to search: name, years to search, DOB. Criminal records go back to 1975.

General Information: No juvenile, mental, expunged, dismissed, or suspended imposition of sentence records released. Copy fee: $.25 per page. Certification fee: $1.50. Fee payee: Associate Circuit Court. Personal checks accepted. Prepayment is required.

Howell County

Circuit Court PO Box 1011, West Plains, MO 65775; 417-256-3741; Fax: 417-256-4650. Hours: 8AM-5PM (CST). *Felony, Misdemeanor, Civil Actions Over $25,000.*

Civil Records: Access: Phone, fax, mail, in person, online. Both court and visitors may perform in person searches. No search fee. Required to search: name, years to search. Civil cases indexed by defendant, plaintiff. Civil records on index cards since 1977. Participates in the free state online court record system at http://casenet.osca.state.mo.us/casenet. Online records go back to 8/2000; pending cases back to 1990.

Criminal Records: Access: In person, online. Visitors must perform in person searches for themselves. No search fee. Required to search: name, years to search. Criminal records on index cards since 1977. Online access to criminal records is the same as civil. Written requests are referred to the State Highway Patrol.

General Information: No juvenile, mental, expunged, dismissed, or suspended imposition of sentence records released. SASE required. Turnaround time varies. Fax notes: $1.00 per page. Copy fee: $.10 per page. Certification fee: $1.50. Fee payee: Howell County Circuit Clerk. Personal checks accepted. Will bill fees to attorneys.

Associate Circuit Court 222 Courthouse, West Plains, MO 65775; 417-256-4050; Fax: 417-256-5826. Hours: 8AM-4:30PM (CST). *Misdemeanor, Civil Actions Under $45,000, Eviction, Small Claims, Probate.*

Civil Records: Access: Mail, in person, online. Both court and visitors may perform in person searches. No search fee. Required to search: name, years to search. Civil cases indexed by defendant, plaintiff. Civil records on index cards since 1/1/79, computerized since 2000. Participates in the free state online court record system at http://casenet.osca.state.mo.us/casenet. Online records go back to 1990.

Criminal Records: Access: Mail, in person, online. Both court and visitors may perform in person searches. No search fee. Required to search: name, years to search, DOB; also helpful: SSN. Criminal records on computer since early 1991, on index cards since 1/1/79, prior on books. Online access to criminal records is the same as civil.

General Information: Public access terminal is available. No juvenile, mental, expunged, dismissed, or suspended imposition of sentence records released. SASE required. Turnaround time ASAP. Copy fee: $.10 per page. Certification fee: $1.50. Fee payee: Associate/Probate Court. Only cashiers checks and money orders accepted. Prepayment is required.

Iron County

Circuit Court PO Box 24, Ironton, MO 63650; 573-546-2811; Fax: 573-546-2166. Hours: 8AM-4PM (CST). *Felony, Civil Actions Over $25,000.*

Civil Records: Access: In person only. Visitors must perform in person searches for themselves. No search fee. Required to search: name, years to search. Civil cases indexed by defendant, plaintiff. Civil records on index cards since 1976, prior on books.

Criminal Records: Access: In person only. Visitors must perform in person searches for themselves. No search fee. Required to search: name, years to search. Criminal records on index cards since 1976, prior on books to 1856.

General Information: Public access terminal is available. No juvenile, mental, expunged, dismissed, or suspended imposition of sentence records released. Copy fee: $1.00 per page. Certification fee: $2.00. Fee payee: Iron County Circuit Clerk. Personal checks accepted. Prepayment is required.

Associate Circuit Court PO Box 325, Ironton, MO 63650; 573-546-2511; Fax: 573-546-6006. Hours: 9AM-4PM (CST). *Misdemeanor, Civil Actions Under $25,000, Eviction, Small Claims, Probate.*

Civil Records: Access: Mail, in person. Both court and visitors may perform in person searches. No search fee. Required to search: name, years to search; also helpful: address. Civil cases indexed by defendant, plaintiff. Civil records on index cards since 1979, computerized from 1997.

Criminal Records: Access: Fax, mail, in person. Only the court performs in person searches; visitors may not. No search fee. Required to search: name, years to search, DOB; also helpful: address, signed release. Criminal records on index cards since 1979, computerized from 1997.

General Information: No juvenile, mental, expunged, dismissed, or suspended imposition of sentence records released. SASE required. Turnaround time 5 days. Copy fee: $.25 per page. Certification fee: $1.50 plus $1.00 per page. Fee payee: Associate Circuit Court. Personal checks accepted. Prepayment is required.

Jackson County

Circuit Court - Civil Division 415 E 12th, 3rd Fl, Kansas City, MO 64106; 816-881-3926; 881-3522; Probate phone: 816-881-3755; Fax: 816-881-3635. Hours: 8AM-5PM (CST). *Civil, Eviction, Small Claims, Probate.*

www.16thcircuit.org

Note: There is a combined computer system with the Independence civil court.

Civil Records: Access: Online, in person. Visitors must perform in person searches for themselves. No search fee. Required to search: name, years to search. Civil cases indexed by defendant, plaintiff. Civil records on computer since 1973, some records on microfiche and books, older records archived off-site. Participates in the free state online court record system at http://casenet.osca.state.mo.us/casenet. Jakcson Casenet records go back to 1/89. The Probate Court also participates in the Casenet system; probate records are also available at www.16thcircuit.org/publicaccess.asp.

General Information: Public access terminal is available. No juvenile, mental, expunged, dismissed, or suspended imposition of sentence records released. Copy fee: $.50 per page. Certification fee: $2.50. Fee payee: Court Administrator's Office. Business checks accepted. Prepayment is required.

Independence Circuit Court - Civil Annex 308 W Kansas #310, Independence, MO 64050; 816-881-4497; Probate phone: 816-881-4552; Fax: 816-881-4410. Hours: 8AM-5PM (CST). *Civil, Eviction, Small Claims, Probate.*

Note: Direct mail criminal record searches to suite #310; civil to suite #204. This court is on the same computer system as Kansas City for civil cases, but files maintained separately.

Civil Records: Access: Mail, online, in person. Both court and visitors may perform in person searches. No search fee. Required to search: name, years to search. Civil cases indexed by defendant, plaintiff. Civil records on computer since 1989. Participates in the free state online court record system at http://casenet.osca.state.mo.us/casenet. Online records go back to 1/89. Online access to probate records is available free at www.16thcircuit.org/publicaccess.asp. This includes private process servers, jury verdicts, criminal traffic, and criminal sureties. The court will not do background checks, except for attorneys. You must have case number if the court is to pull a record.

Criminal Records: Access: In person, mail. Only the court performs in person searches; visitors may not. No search fee. Required to search: name. The court will not do background checks, except for attorneys and government offices. Otherwise, requestor must have the case number to request file copies.

General Information: Public access terminal is available. No sealed records released. Turnaround time 1 day. Copy fee: $.50 per page. Certification fee: $2.50. Fee payee: District Court Clerk. Only cashiers checks and money orders accepted. Prepayment is required.

Circuit Court - Criminal Division 1315 Locust, 2nd Fl, Kansas City, MO 64106; 816-881-4350; Fax: 816-881-3420. Hours: 8AM-5PM (CST). *Felony, Misdemeanor.*

www.16thcircuit.org

Note: All background checks are sent to the Missouri Highway Patrol in Jefferson City. Court will only pull file copies if a case number is given.

Criminal Records: Access: In person, online. Only the court performs in person searches; visitors may not. No search fee. Required to search: name, years to search, DOB, signed release; also helpful: SSN. Criminal records on computer since 1968 for felonies, 1980 for misdemeanors. Participates in the free state online court record system at http://casenet.osca.state.mo.us/casenet. Jackson Casenet records go back to 1/89. Also, online access to criminal traffic dockets is available at www.16thcircuit.org/trafficdockets.asp. Also, search surety bonding agents at www.16thcircuit.org/suretyqualifications.asp.

General Information: No juvenile, mental, expunged, dismissed, or suspended imposition of sentence records released. Copy fee: $.50 per page. Certification fee: $3.00. Fee payee: Dept. of Civil or Criminal Records. Only cashiers checks and money orders accepted. Prepayment is required.

Jasper County

Circuit Court Courthouse, Rm 303, 302 S. Main St, Carthage, MO 64836; 417-358-0441; Fax: 417-358-0461. Hours: 8:00AM-5:00PM (CST). *Felony, Misdemeanor, Civil Actions Over $45,000.*

www.osca.state.mo.us/circuits/index.nsf

Civil Records: Access: Mail, in person, online. No search fee. Required to search: name, years to search. Civil cases indexed by defendant, plaintiff. Civil records on computer since 7/1/91, prior on cards since 1975. Participates in the free statewide Casenet court record system at http://casenet.osca.state.mo.us/casenet. Online records go back to 6/26/2000.

Criminal Records: Access: Mail, in person, online. Only the court performs in person searches; visitors may not. No search fee. Required to search: name, years to search. Criminal records on computer since 7/1/91, prior on cards since 1975. Online access to criminal records is the same as civil.

General Information: Public access terminal is available. No juvenile, mental, expunged, dismissed, or suspended imposition of sentence records released. SASE required. Turnaround time 1 week. Copy fee: $.25 per page. Certification fee: $1.50. Fee payee: Jasper County Circuit Clerk. Business checks accepted. Prepayment is required.

Joplin Circuit Court Courthouse, 3rd Fl, 601 S Pearl, Joplin, MO 64801; 417-625-4310; Fax: 417-625-7172. Hours: 8:00AM-5:00PM (CST). *Felony, Misdemeanor, Civil Actions Over $45,000.*

www.osca.state.mo.us/circuits/index.nsf

Civil Records: Access: Mail, fax, in person, online. Both court and visitors may perform in person searches. No search fee. Required to search: name, years to search. Civil cases indexed by defendant, plaintiff. Civil records on computer since 7/1/91, prior on cards since 1975. Participates in the free statewide Casenet court record system at http://casenet.osca.state.mo.us/casenet. Online records go back to 6/26/2000.

Criminal Records: Access: Mail, fax, in person, online. Both the court and visitors may perform in person searches. No search fee. Required to search: name, years to search. Criminal records on computer back to 1993, prior on cards back to 1975. Online access to criminal records is the same as civil.

General Information: Public access terminal is available. No juvenile, mental, expunged, dismissed, or suspended imposition of sentence records released. SASE required. Turnaround time 1 week. Copy fee: $.25 per page. Certification fee: $1.50. Fee payee: Jasper County Circuit Clerk. No checks accepted. Prepayment is required.

Carthage Associate Circuit Court Courthouse, Rm 304, 302 S. Main St, Carthage, MO 64836; 417-358-0450; Fax: 417-358-0460. Hours: 8:30AM-Noon, 1-4:30PM (CST). *Misdemeanor, Civil Actions Under $45,000, Eviction, Small Claims, Probate.*

Civil Records: Access: Fax, in person, online. Visitors must conduct in person searches for themselves. Search fee: Court does not perform civil searches. Required to search: name, years to search. Civil cases indexed by defendant, plaintiff. Civil records on computer back to 2000, prior on cards back to 1979. Participates in the free statewide Casenet record system at http://casenet.osca.state.mo.us/casenet. Online records go back to 6/26/2000. For mail or fax searches, court recommends Amer. Research at 417-358-6494.

Criminal Records: Access: In person, online. Visitors must conduct in person searches for themselves. Search fee: Court does not perform criminal searches. Required to search: name, years to search. Criminal records on computer back to 2000, prior on cards back to 1979. Online access to criminal records is the same as civil. For mail or fax searches, court recommends Amer. Research at 417-358-6494.

General Information: Public access terminal is available. No juvenile, mental, expunged, dismissed, or suspended imposition of sentence records released. Copy fee: $.25 per page. Certification fee: $1.50.

Joplin Associate Circuit Court Courthouse, 2nd Fl, 601 S Pearl, Joplin, MO 64801; 417-625-4316; Fax: 417-625-4340. Hours: 8AM-5PM (CST). *Misdemeanor, Civil Actions Under $45,000, Eviction, Small Claims, Probate.*

Civil Records: Access: Mail, fax, in person, online. Both court and visitors may perform in person searches. No search fee. Required to search: name, years to search. Civil cases indexed by defendant, plaintiff. Civil records on computer back to 1993, prior on cards back to mid-1970s. Participates in the free statewide Casenet court system at http://casenet.osca.state.mo.us/casenet. Online records go back to 6/26/2000.

Criminal Records: Access: Mail, fax, in person, online. Both court and visitors may perform in person searches. No search fee. Required to search: name, years to search. Criminal records on computer back to 1993, prior on cards back to mid-1970s. Online access to criminal records is the same as civil.

General Information: Public access terminal is available. No juvenile, mental, expunged, dismissed, or suspended imposition of sentence records released. SASE required. Turnaround time is 1-3 days. Fax notes: Will fax results, no fee. Copy fee: $.25 per page. Certification fee: $1.00.

Jefferson County

Circuit Court - Civil Division PO Box 100, Hillsboro, MO 63050; 636-797-5443; Fax: 636-797-5073. Hours: 8AM-5PM (CST). *Civil Actions Over $25,000.*

Civil Records: Access: Phone, fax, mail, in person. Both court and visitors may perform in person searches. No search fee. Required to search: name, years to search. Civil cases indexed by defendant, plaintiff. Civil records on computer since 10/90, prior on books since 1966.

General Information: Public access terminal is available. No juvenile, mental, expunged, dismissed, or suspended imposition of sentence records released. SASE required. Copy fee: $1.00 per page. Certification fee: $.50. Fee payee: Circuit Clerk. Business checks accepted. Prepayment is required.

Circuit Court - Criminal Division PO Box 100, Hillsboro, MO 63050; 636-797-5370; Fax: 636-797-5073. Hours: 8AM-4:30PM (CST). *Felony, Misdemeanor.*

Criminal Records: Access: Mail, fax, in person. Only the court performs in person searches; visitors may not. Search fee: $10.00 per name. Required to search: name, years to search, signed release, DOB or SSN. Criminal records on computer since 1989, on index cards 1976 to 1988, prior on books or microfilm.

General Information: No juvenile, mental, expunged, dismissed, or suspended imposition of sentence records released. SASE required. Turnaround time 1 week. Copy fee: $1.00 per page. Fee payee: Circuit Clerk. Business checks accepted.

Associate Circuit Court PO Box 100, Hillsboro, MO 63050; 636-797-5362; Probate phone: 636-797-5450; Fax: 636-797-5073. Hours: 8:00AM-5PM (CST). *Civil Under $25,000, Eviction, Small Claims, Probate.*

Civil Records: Access: Fax, mail, in person. No search fee. Required to search: name, years to search. Civil cases indexed by defendant, plaintiff. Civil records on computer since 1990, prior on books.

General Information: Public access terminal is available. No juvenile, mental, expunged, dismissed, or suspended imposition of sentence records released. SASE required. Turnaround time 3-5 days. Copy fee: $1.00 per page. Certification fee: $1.50. Fee payee: Circuit Clerk. Business checks accepted. Prepayment is required.

Johnson County

Circuit Court Courthouse, PO Box 436, Warrensburg, MO 64093; 660-747-6331; Fax: 660-747-7927. Hours: 8AM-4:30PM (CST). *Felony, Civil Actions Over $25,000.*

Civil Records: Access: In person only. Visitors must perform in person searches for themselves, except prior to 1976. Search fee: $10.00. Required to search: name, years to search. Civil cases indexed by defendant, plaintiff. Civil records on file since 1800s, microfilmed from 1950s to 1988.

Criminal Records: Access: In person only. Visitors must perform in person searches for themselves, except prior to 1976. Required to search: name, years to search, DOB, SSN. Criminal records on file since 1800s, microfilmed through 1988.

General Information: Public access terminal is available. No juvenile, adoptions, mental, expunged, dismissed, or suspended imposition of sentence records released. Copy fee: $.25 per page. Certification fee: $1.50. Fee payee: Circuit Clerk. Personal checks accepted.

Associate Circuit Court Johnson County Courthouse, 300 N Holden #304, Warrensburg, MO 64093; 660-747-2227. Hours: 8AM-4:30PM (CST). *Misdemeanor, Civil Actions Under $45,000, Eviction, Small Claims, Probate.*

Civil Records: Access: Mail, in person. Visitors must perform in person searches. No search fee. Required to search: name, years to search. Civil cases indexed by defendant, plaintiff. Civil records on computer since 1994, prior on index since 1979.

Criminal Records: Access: Mail, in person. Visitors must perform in person searches. No search fee. Required to search: name, years to search. Criminal records on computer since 1994, prior on index since 1979.

General Information: No juvenile, mental, expunged, dismissed, or suspended imposition of sentence records released. SASE required. Turnaround time varies. Copy fee: 1st 10 pages fee, $.25 per page thereafter. Fee payee: Associate Circuit Court. Personal checks accepted. Prepayment is required.

Knox County

Circuit Court PO Box 116, Edina, MO 63537; 660-397-2305; Fax: 660-397-3331. Hours: 8:30AM-4PM (CST). *Felony, Misdemeanor, Civil Actions Over $25,000.*

Civil Records: Access: Mail, in person. Both court and visitors may perform in person searches. No search fee.

Required to search: name, years to search. Civil cases indexed by defendant, plaintiff. Civil records on microfiche since 3/83, archived since 1845, no computerization.

Criminal Records: Access: Mail, in person. Both court and visitors may perform in person searches. No search fee. Required to search: name, years to search. Criminal records on microfiche since 3/83, archived since 1845, no computerization.

General Information: No juvenile, mental, expunged, dismissed, or suspended imposition of sentence records released. SASE not required. Turnaround time same day. Copy fee: $1.00 per page. Certification fee: $2.00. Fee payee: Circuit Court. Personal checks accepted. Prepayment is required.

Associate Circuit Court PO Box 126, Edina, MO 63537; 660-397-3146; Fax: 660-397-3331. Hours: 8:30AM-4PM (CST). *Misdemeanor, Civil Actions Under $25,000, Eviction, Small Claims, Probate.*

Civil Records: Access: Mail, in person. Both court and visitors may perform in person searches. No search fee. Required to search: name, years to search. Civil cases indexed by defendant, plaintiff. Civil records on computer since 1993, prior on index cards.

Criminal Records: Access: Mail, in person. Both court and visitors may perform in person searches. No search fee. Required to search: name, years to search; also helpful: DOB, SSN. Criminal records on computer since 1993, prior on index cards.

General Information: No juvenile, mental, expunged, dismissed, or suspended imposition of sentence records released. SASE required. Turnaround time 2-3 days. Copy fee: $.25 per page. Certification fee: $1.50. Fee payee: Associate Circuit Court. Personal checks accepted. Prepayment is required.

Laclede County

Circuit & Associate Court 200 N Adams St, Lebanon, MO 65536; 417-532-2471, 532-9196; Fax: 417-532-3683. Hours: 8AM-4PM (CST). *Felony, Misdemeanor, Civil. Eviction, Small Claims, Probate.*

Note: Now a consolidated court.

Civil Records: Access: Phone, fax, mail, in person. Both court and visitors may perform in person searches. No search fee. Required to search: name, years to search. Civil cases indexed by defendant, plaintiff. Civil records on cards since 1976, prior on books.

Criminal Records: Access: Phone, fax, mail, in person. Both court and visitors may perform in person searches. No search fee. Required to search: name, years to search; also helpful: SSN. Criminal records on cards since 1976, prior on books.

General Information: Public access terminal is available. No juvenile, mental, expunged, dismissed, or suspended imposition of sentence records released. SASE required. Turnaround time 1-2 days. Fax notes: $3.00 for first page, $1.00 each add'l. Copy fee: $.25 per page. Certification fee: $1.50. Fee payee: Laclede County Circuit Clerk. Personal checks accepted. Copy fees may be billed.

Lafayette County

Circuit Court PO Box 340, Lexington, MO 64067; 660-259-6101; Fax: 660-259-6148. Hours: 8AM-4:30PM (CST). *Felony, Misdemeanor, Civil Actions Over $25,000.*

Civil Records: Access: Mail, fax, in person. Only the court performs in person searches; visitors may not. No search fee. Required to search: name, years to search. Civil cases indexed by defendant, plaintiff. Civil records on books, archived since 1823; on computer back to 1987. All search requests must be in writing.

Criminal Records: Access: Mail, fax, in person. Only the court performs in person searches; visitors may not. No search fee. Required to search: name, years to

search; also helpful-case number. Criminal records on books, archived since 1823; on computer back to 1987.

General Information: No juvenile, mental, expunged, dismissed, or suspended imposition of sentence records released. SASE required. Turnaround time 5 days. Fax notes: Fee to fax results is $1.00 per page. Copy fee: $.25 per page. Certification fee: $2.50. Fee payee: Circuit Clerk. Personal checks accepted. Copy fees & attorney of record may be billed.

Associate Circuit Court - Division III PO Box 236, Lexington, MO 64067; 660-259-6151; Fax: 660-259-4997. Hours: 8AM-4:30PM (CST). *Misdemeanor, Civil Actions Under $25,000, Eviction, Small Claims, Probate.*

Note: Most civil action cases are directed to the Circuit Court.

Civil Records: Access: Mail, fax, n person. Only the court performs in person searches; visitors may not. No search fee. Required to search: name, years to search. Civil cases indexed by defendant, plaintiff. Civil records on index cards since 1985.

Criminal Records: Access: Mail, in person. Only the court performs in person searches; visitors may not. No search fee. Required to search: name, years to search, address, DOB, signed release. Criminal records on index cards since 1979.

General Information: No juvenile, mental, expunged, dismissed, or suspended imposition of sentence records released. SASE required. Turnaround time 1-2 days. No copy fee. Prepayment is required.

Lawrence County

Circuit Court One Courthouse Square #201, Mt Vernon, MO 65712; 417-466-2471. Hours: 8AM-5PM (CST). *Felony, Misdemeanor, Civil Actions Over $25,000.*

Civil Records: Access: Mail, in person. Both court and visitors may perform in person searches. Search fee: $5.00 per name. Required to search: name, years to search. Civil cases indexed by defendant, plaintiff. Civil records on computer back to 1991, prior archived since 1890.

Criminal Records: Access: Mail, in person. Both court and visitors may perform in person searches. Search fee: $5.00 per name. Required to search: name, years to search, DOB; also helpful: SSN. Criminal records on computer back to 1991, prior archived since 1890.

General Information: Public access terminal is available. No juvenile, mental, expunged, dismissed, or suspended imposition of sentence records released. SASE required. Turnaround time 1 week. Copy fee: $.25 per page. Certification fee: $2.00. Fee payee: Circuit Court. Business checks accepted. Prepayment is required.

Associate Circuit Court 1 Courthouse Sg #102, Mt Vernon, MO 65712; 417-466-2463. Hours: 8:30AM-5PM (CST). *Misdemeanor, Civil Actions Under $45,000, Eviction, Small Claims, Probate.*

Civil Records: Access: Mail, in person. Both court and visitors may perform in person searches. No search fee. Required to search: name, years to search. Civil cases indexed by defendant, plaintiff. Civil records on index cards since 1979, prior on books.

Criminal Records: Access: Mail, in person. Both court and visitors may perform in person searches. No search fee. Required to search: name, years to search; also helpful: DOB, SSN. Criminal records on index cards since 1979, prior on books.

General Information: No juvenile, mental, expunged, dismissed, or suspended imposition of sentence records released. SASE required. Turnaround time 2-3 days. Copy fee: $.35 per page. Fee payee: Associate Circuit Court. Personal checks accepted. Prepayment is required.

Lewis County

Circuit Court PO Box 97, Monticello, MO 63457; 573-767-5440; Fax: 573-767-5378. Hours: 8AM-Noon,1-4PM (CST). *Felony, Misdemeanor, Civil Actions Over $25,000.*

Civil Records: Access: In person only. Visitors must perform in person searches for themselves. No search fee. Required to search: name, years to search. Civil cases indexed by defendant, plaintiff. Civil records on computer back to 1976 (judgments) and index books, archived since 1830s.

Criminal Records: Access: In person only. Visitors must perform in person searches for themselves. No search fee. Required to search: name, years to search. Criminal records on computer and index books, archived since 1830s.

General Information: No juvenile, mental, expunged, dismissed, or suspended imposition of sentence records released. Certification fee: $2.50.

Associate Circuit Court PO Box 36, Monticello, MO 63457; 573-767-5352; Fax: 573-767-5342. Hours: 8AM-4:30PM (CST). *Misdemeanor, Civil Actions Under $25,000, Eviction, Small Claims, Probate.*

Civil Records: Access: Fax, mail, in person. Only the court performs in person searches; visitors may not. No search fee. Required to search: name, years to search. Civil cases indexed by defendant, plaintiff. Civil records on computer back to 1987; on books back to 1979.

Criminal Records: Access: Fax, mail, in person. Only the court performs in person searches; visitors may not. No search fee. Required to search: name, years to search; also helpful: DOB, SSN, signed release. Criminal records on computer back to 1986; on books back to 1980.

General Information: No juvenile, mental, expunged, dismissed, or suspended imposition of sentence records released. Turnaround time 1-2 days. Copy fee: $.10 per page. May bill fees to businesses and attorneys.

Lincoln County

Circuit Court 201 Main St, Troy, MO 63379; 636-528-6300. Hours: 8:00AM-4:30PM (CST). *Felony, Misdemeanor, Civil Actions Over $25,000.*

Civil Records: Access: In person only. Visitors must perform in person searches for themselves. No search fee. Required to search: name, years to search. Civil cases indexed by defendant, plaintiff. Civil records on computer since 8/92, prior on index cards since 1978.

Criminal Records: Access: In person only. Visitors must perform in person searches for themselves. No search fee. Required to search: name, years to search. Criminal records on computer since 8/92, prior on index cards since 1978.

General Information: Public access terminal is available. No juvenile, mental, expunged, dismissed, or suspended imposition of sentence records released. Copy fee: $.25 per page. Certification fee: $1.75. Fee payee: Lincoln County Circuit Clerk. Personal checks accepted. Prepayment is required.

Associate Circuit Court 201 Main St, Troy, MO 63379; 636-528-6300. Hours: 8AM-4:30PM (CST). *Misdemeanor, Civil Actions Under $25,000, Eviction, Small Claims, Probate.*

Civil Records: Access: Phone, in person, online. Visitors must perform in person searches for themselves. No search fee. Required to search: name, years to search. Civil cases indexed by defendant, plaintiff. Civil records on index cards, archived since 1820; computerized since. Scheduled to be on the free state online court record system at http://casenet.osca.state.mo.us/casenet in Fall, 2002.

Criminal Records: Access: Mail, in person, online. Only the court performs in person searches; visitors

may not. No search fee. Required to search: name, years to search, DOB. Criminal records on computer since 1991; on books or cards back to 1820s. Scheduled to be on the free state online court record system at http://casenet.osca.state.mo.us/casenet in Fall, 2002.

General Information: Public access terminal is available. No juvenile, mental, expunged or dismissed records released. SASE helpful. Turnaround time 1 week to 10 days, Probate up to 30 days. Copy fee: $.25 per page. Certification fee: $1.50 plus $.25 per page. Fee payee: Associate Circuit Court. Personal checks accepted. Prepayment is required.

Linn County

Linn County Circuit Court PO Box 84, Linneus, MO 64653-0084; 660-895-5212; Fax: 660-895-5277. Hours: 8AM-Noon,1-5PM (CST). *Felony, Misdemeanor, Civil Actions Over $25,000.*

Civil Records: Access: Fax, mail, in person. Only the court performs in person searches; visitors may not. No search fee. Required to search: name, years to search. Civil cases indexed by defendant, plaintiff. Civil records on books.

Criminal Records: Access: Fax, mail, in person. Only the court performs in person searches; visitors may not. No search fee. Required to search: name, years to search. Criminal records on books.

General Information: No juvenile, mental, expunged, dismissed, or suspended imposition of sentence records released. SASE required. Turnaround time 1 week, phone turnaround time 1-2 days. Fax notes: No fee to fax results. Copy fee: $.25 per page. Certification fee: $2.00. Fee payee: Linn County Circuit Court. Only cashiers checks and money orders accepted. Prepayment is required.

Consolidated Circuit Court Box 89, Linneus, MO 64653; 660-895-5212; Fax: 660-895-5277. Hours: 8AM-4:30PM (CST). *Misdemeanor, Civil Actions Under $25,000, Eviction, Small Claims, Probate.*

Civil Records: Access: Phone, mail, in person. Only the court performs in person searches; visitors may not. No search fee. Required to search: name, years to search. Civil cases indexed by defendant, plaintiff. Civil records on index cards since 1979.

Criminal Records: Access: Phone, mail, in person. Only the court performs in person searches; visitors may not. No search fee. Required to search: name, years to search. Criminal records on index cards since 1979.

General Information: No juvenile, mental, expunged, dismissed, or suspended imposition of sentence records released. SASE required. Copy fee: $1.00 per page. Certification fee: $1.50. Fee payee: Associate Circuit Court. Personal checks accepted.

Livingston County

Circuit Court 700 Webster St, Chillicothe, MO 64601; 660-646-1718; Fax: 660-646-2734. Hours: 8:00AM-5:ooPM (CST). *Felony, Misdemeanor, Civil Actions Over $25,000.*

Civil Records: Access: In person only. Visitors must perform in person searches for themselves. No search fee. Required to search: name, years to search. Civil cases indexed by defendant, plaintiff. Civil records on index cards since 1974, prior on record books.

Criminal Records: Access: In person only. Visitors must perform in person searches for themselves. No search fee. Required to search: name, years to search. Criminal records on index cards since 1974, prior on record books.

General Information: No juvenile, mental, expunged, dismissed, or suspended imposition of sentence records released. Copy fee: $.25 per page. Certification fee: $1.00. Fee payee: Livingston County Circuit Clerk. Personal checks accepted. Attorneys may bill copy fees.

Associate Circuit Court Livingston County Courthouse, #8, Chillicothe, MO 64601; 660-646-3103; Fax: 660-646-8014. Hours: Public hours: 8:30AM-4:30PM; Office hours: 8AM-5PM (CST). *Misdemeanor, Civil Actions Under $25,000, Eviction, Small Claims, Probate.*

Civil Records: Access: Phone, fax, mail, in person. Both court and visitors may perform in person searches. No search fee. Required to search: name, years to search; also helpful: address; Signed release required for closed records. Civil cases indexed by defendant, plaintiff. Civil records on index cards and record books since 1975, prior on record books.

Criminal Records: Access: Phone, fax, mail, in person. Both court and visitors may perform in person searches. No search fee. Required to search: name, years to search, DOB; Signed release required for closed records. Criminal records on index cards and record books since 1975, prior on record books.

General Information: No juvenile, mental, expunged, dismissed, or suspended imposition of sentence records released. SASE required. Turnaround time 5 days. Fax notes: Call for fax fee. Copy fee: $1.00 per page. Certification fee: $1.50. Fee payee: Associate Circuit Court. Personal checks accepted.

Macon County

Circuit Court PO Box 382, Macon, MO 63552; 660-385-4631; Fax: 660-385-4235. Hours: 8:30AM-4PM (CST). *Felony, Misdemeanor, Civil Actions Over $25,000.*

Civil Records: Access: Fax, mail, in person. Both court and visitors may perform in person searches. No search fee. Required to search: name, years to search. Civil cases indexed by defendant, plaintiff. Civil records on computer since 1/1/91, on index cards from 1976-1990, prior on books.

Criminal Records: Access: Fax, mail, in person. Both court and visitors may perform in person searches. Search fee: $1.00 per name. Required to search: name, years to search. Criminal records on computer since 1/1/91, on index cards from 1976-1990, prior on books.

General Information: No juvenile, mental, expunged, dismissed, or suspended imposition of sentence records released. SASE required. Turnaround time 2-5 days. Fax notes: $2.50 for first page, $.50 each add'l. Copy fee: $.25 per page. Certification fee: $3.00. Fee payee: Clerk of Circuit Court. Personal checks accepted. Prepayment is required.

Associate Circuit Court PO Box 491, Macon, MO 63552; 660-385-3531; Fax: 660-385-3132. Hours: 8AM-4:30PM (CST). *Misdemeanor, Civil Actions Under $25,000, Eviction, Small Claims, Probate.*

Civil Records: Access: Fax, mail, in person. Both court and visitors may perform in person searches. No search fee. Required to search: name, years to search. Civil cases indexed by defendant, plaintiff. Civil records on index cards and books; on computer back to 1992.

Criminal Records: Access: In person only. Visitors must perform in person searches for themselves. No search fee. Required to search: name, years to search, DOB. Criminal records on computer since 1992, prior on index cards back to 1989. Court will refer phone and mail requests to the State Police, 573-526-6153.

General Information: No juvenile, mental, expunged, dismissed, or suspended imposition of sentence records released. SASE required. Turnaround time 2 weeks. Copy fee: $1.00 per page. Certification fee: $1.50. Fee payee: Circuit Court Division II or Probate Court. Prepayment is required.

Madison County

Circuit Court PO Box 470, Fredericktown, MO 63645-0470; 573-783-2102; Fax: 573-783-2715. Hours: 8AM-5PM (CST). *Felony, Misdemeanor, Civil Actions Over $25,000.*

Civil Records: Access: In person. Visitors must perform in person searches. No search fee. Required to search: name, years to search. Civil cases indexed by defendant, plaintiff. Civil records on computer since 1991, prior on index cards from 1979-1991. Limit one name per mail request.

Criminal Records: Access: In person. Visitors must perform in person searches. No search fee. Required to search: name, years to search. Criminal records on computer since 1991, prior on index cards from 1979-1991.

General Information: Public access terminal is available. No juvenile, mental, expunged, dismissed, or suspended imposition of sentence records released. Copy fee: $1.00 per page. Certification fee: $2.00. Fee payee: Madison County Circuit Clerk. Personal checks accepted. Prepayment is required.

Associate Circuit Court PO Box 521, Fredericktown, MO 63645; 573-783-3105; Fax: 573-783-5920. Hours: 8AM-5PM (CST). *Misdemeanor, Civil Actions Under $25,000, Small Claims, Probate, Traffic.*

Civil Records: Access: Phone, fax, mail, in person. Both court and visitors may perform in person searches. No search fee. Required to search: name, years to search. Civil cases indexed by defendant, plaintiff. Civil records on index cards since 1979, prior on judgment books to 1960s; on computer back to 11/2000.

Criminal Records: Access: Phone, fax, mail, in person. Both court and visitors may perform in person searches. No search fee. Required to search: name, years to search; also helpful: DOB, SSN. Criminal records on index cards since 1979, prior on judgment books; on computer back to 11/2000.

General Information: No juvenile, mental, expunged, dismissed, or suspended imposition of sentence records released. SASE required. Turnaround time 1 week. Copy fee: $.25 per page. Certification fee: $2.50. Fee payee: Associate Circuit Court. Only cashiers checks and money orders accepted.

Maries County

Circuit Court PO Box 213, Vienna, MO 65582; 573-422-3338; Fax: 573-422-3976. Hours: 8AM-4PM (CST). *Felony, Misdemeanor, Civil Actions Over $25,000.*

Civil Records: Access: Fax, mail, in person. Both court and visitors may perform in person searches. No search fee. Required to search: name, years to search. Civil cases indexed by defendant, plaintiff. Civil records go back to 1940.

Criminal Records: Access: Fax, mail, in person. Both court and visitors may perform in person searches. No search fee. Required to search: name, years to search. Criminal records go back 10 1940.

General Information: No juvenile, mental, expunged, dismissed, or suspended imposition of sentence records released. Turnaround time 1-3 days. Fax notes: $.25 per page. Copy fee: $.25 per page. Certification fee: $1.50. Fee payee: Maries County Circuit Clerk. Personal checks accepted.

Associate Circuit Court PO Box 490, Vienna, MO 65582; 573-422-3303; Fax: 573-422-3100. Hours: 8AM-4PM (CST). *Misdemeanor, Civil Actions Under $25,000, Eviction, Small Claims, Probate.*

Note: Most civil cases are directed to the Circuit Court, regardless of limit.

Civil Records: Access: Mail, fax, in person. Both court and visitors may perform in person searches. No search

fee. Required to search: name, years to search. Civil cases indexed by defendant, plaintiff. Civil records on index cards since 1985, archived since 1855.

Criminal Records: Access: Mail, fax, in person. Only the court performs in person searches; visitors may not. No search fee. Required to search: name, years to search, DOB, signed release; also helpful-SSN. Criminal records on index cards since 1985, archived since 1855.

General Information: No juvenile, mental, expunged, dismissed, or suspended imposition of sentence records released. SASE required. Turnaround time 5 days. Copy fee: $.25 per page. Certification fee: $1.50. Fee payee: Sheriff of Maries County. Only cashiers checks and money orders accepted. Prepayment is required.

Marion County

Circuit Court PO Box 392, 100 S Main St, Palmyra, MO 63461; 573-769-2550; Fax: 573-769-6012. Hours: 8:30AM-5PM (CST). *Felony, Civil Actions Over $25,000.*

Civil Records: Access: In person only. Visitors must perform in person searches for themselves. No search fee. Required to search: name, years to search. Civil cases indexed by defendant, plaintiff. Civil records on index cards since 1977, prior on judgment books.

Criminal Records: Access: Fax, mail, in person. Both court and visitors may perform in person searches. No search fee. Required to search: name, years to search, DOB. Criminal records on index cards since 1977, prior on judgment books.

General Information: No juvenile, mental, expunged, dismissed, or suspended imposition of sentence records released. SASE required. Turnaround time 1-2 days. Fax notes: $1.00 per page. Copy fee: $1.00 per page. Certification fee: $2.00. Fee payee: Marion County Circuit Clerk of Division I. Business checks accepted. All fees may be billed.

Circuit Court (Twps of Miller & Mason only) 906 Broadway, Rm 105, Hannibal, MO 63401; 573-221-0198; Fax: 573-221-9328. Hours: 8AM-5PM (CST). *Felony, Misdemeanor, Civil Actions Over $25,000.*

Civil Records: Access: Fax, mail, in person. Both court and visitors may perform in person searches. Search fee: $.50 per name. Required to search: name, years to search. Civil cases indexed by defendant, plaintiff. Civil records on computer since 1991, prior on index cards.

Criminal Records: Access: Fax, mail, in person. Only the court performs in person searches; visitors may not. Search fee: $.50 per name. Required to search: name, years to search. Criminal records on computer.

General Information: No juvenile, mental, expunged, dismissed, or suspended imposition of sentence records released. SASE required. Turnaround time 1 week. Copy fee: $.50 per page. Certification fee: $5.00. Fee payee: Circuit Clerk District II. Personal checks accepted.

Hannibal Associate Circuit Court 906 Broadway, Hannibal, MO 63401; 573-221-0288; Fax: 573-221-0945. Hours: 8AM-5PM (CST). *Misdemeanor, Civil Actions Under $45,000, Eviction, Small Claims, Probate.*

Civil Records: Access: Mail, fax, in person. Only the court performs in person searches; visitors may not. No search fee. Required to search: name, years to search. Civil cases indexed by defendant, plaintiff. Civil records on index cards since 1979, prior on judgment books.

Criminal Records: Access: Mail, fax, in person. Only the court performs in person searches; visitors may not. No search fee. Required to search: name, years to search. Criminal records on computer since 3/93, on index cards since 1979, prior on judgment books.

General Information: No juvenile, mental, expunged, dismissed, or suspended imposition of sentence records

released. SASE required. Turnaround time 2 days. No copy fee.

Palmyra Associate Circuit Court PO Box 449, Palmyra, MO 63461; 573-769-2318; Fax: 573-769-4558. Hours: 8AM-Noon, 1-5PM (CST). *Misdemeanor, Civil Actions Under $45,000, Eviction, Small Claims, Probate.*

Civil Records: Access: Mail, in person. Only the court performs in person searches; visitors may not. No search fee. Required to search: name, years to search. Civil cases indexed by defendant, plaintiff. Civil records on index cards since 1979, prior on judgment books.

Criminal Records: Access: Mail, in person. Only the court performs in person searches; visitors may not. No search fee. Required to search: name, years to search; also helpful: DOB. Criminal records on computer since 1994, on index cards from 1979-1994, prior on judgment books.

General Information: No juvenile, mental, expunged, dismissed, or suspended imposition of sentence records released. SASE required. Turnaround time varies. Copy fee: $.50 per page. Fee payee: Circuit Court. Personal checks accepted.

McDonald County

Circuit & Associate Court PO Box 157, Pineville, MO 64856; 417-223-7515; Fax: 417-223-4125. Hours: 8AM-4:30PM (CST). *Felony, Misdemeanor, Civil, Small Claims, Probate.*

Civil Records: Access: Fax, mail, in person. Visitors must perform in person searches themselves. No search fee. Required to search: name, years to search. Civil cases indexed by defendant, plaintiff. Civil records on computer since 1999, on index cards since 1979, prior on index cards.

Criminal Records: Access: fax, mail, in person. Visitors must perform in person searches themselves. No search fee. Required to search: name, years to search; also helpful-charge. Criminal records on computer since 1999, on index cards since 1979, prior on index cards. Court will refer search requests to State Hiway Patrol Criminal Records, POB 568, Jefferson Ctiy, MO 65102, 573-526-6153 ($5.00 per name fee).

General Information: Public access terminal is available. No juvenile, mental, expunged, dismissed, paternity or suspended imposition of sentence records released. SASE required. Fax notes: Fee to fax results is $.25 per page. Copy fee: $.25 per page. Certification fee: $1.50. Fee payee: McDonald County Circuit Clerk. Business checks accepted. Prepayment is required.

Mercer County

Circuit Court Courthouse, 802 East Main, Princeton, MO 64673; 660-748-4335; Fax: 660-748-3180. Hours: 8:30AM-4:30PM (CST). *Felony, Misdemeanor, Civil Actions Over $45,000.*

Civil Records: Access: In person, online. Visitors must perform in person searches for themselves. No search fee. Required to search: name, years to search. Civil cases indexed by defendant, plaintiff. Civil records on computer since 1991, on index cards since 1977, prior on books. Participates in the free state online court record system at http://casenet.osca.state.mo.us/casenet. Online records go back to 3/29/2000.

Criminal Records: Access: In person, online. Visitors must perform in person searches for themselves. No search fee. Required to search: name, years to search, address, DOB, SSN, signed release. Criminal records on computer since 1991, on index cards since 1977, prior on books. Online access to criminal records is the same as civil.

General Information: No juvenile, mental, expunged, dismissed, or suspended imposition of sentence records released. Copy fee: $.25 per page. Certification fee: $1.00. Fee payee: Mercer County Circuit Clerk.

Personal checks not accepted if out of state, money orders preferred. Prepayment is required.

Associate Circuit Court Courthouse Rm 304, Carthage, MO 64836; 417-358-0450; Fax: 417-358-0460. Hours: 8:30AM-4:30PM (CST). *Misdemeanor, Civil Actions Under $45,000, Eviction, Small Claims, Probate.*

Civil Records: Access: Fax, in person, online. Both court and visitors may perform in person searches. No search fee. Required to search: name, years to search. Civil cases indexed by defendant, plaintiff. Civil records on computer since 2000, prior on index cards since 1979. Participates in the free state online court record system at http://casenet.osca.state.mo.us/casenet. Online records go back to 3/29/2000.

Criminal Records: Access: In person, online. Both court and visitors may perform in person searches. No search fee. Required to search: name, years to search. Criminal records on computer since 2000, prior on index cards since 1979. Online access to criminal records is the same as civil.

General Information: No juvenile, mental, expunged, dismissed, or suspended imposition of sentence records released. No copy fee.

Associate Circuit Court Courthouse, 802 E Main Street, Princeton, MO 64673; 660-748-4232; Fax: 660-748-4292. Hours: 8:30AM-4:30PM (CST). *Misdemeanor, Civil Actions Under $45,000, Eviction, Small Claims, Probate.*

Civil Records: Access: In person, online. Visitors must perform in person searches for themselves No search fee. Required to search: name, years to search. Civil cases indexed by defendant. Civil records on index. Participates in the free state online court record system at http://casenet.osca.state.mo.us/casenet. Online records go back to 3/2000.

Criminal Records: Access: In person, online. Visitors must perform in person searches for themselves No search fee. Required to search: name, years to search; also helpful: DOB, SSN. Criminal records on index. Online access to criminal records is the same as civil.

General Information: Public access terminal is available. No juvenile, mental, expunged, dismissed, or suspended imposition of sentence records released. Copy fee: $.25 per page. Certification fee: $1.50 plus $1.00 per page. Fee payee: Circuit Court Division II. Personal checks accepted. Prepayment is required.

Miller County

Circuit Court PO Box 11, Tuscumbia, MO 65082; 573-369-2303; Fax: 573-369-2910. Hours: 8AM-4:30PM (CST). *Felony, Misdemeanor, Civil Actions Over $25,000.*

Civil Records: Access: Phone, fax, mail, in person. Both court and visitors may perform in person searches. Search fee: $4.00 per name. Required to search: name, years to search. Civil cases indexed by defendant, plaintiff. Civil records on index cards since 1976, prior on books.

Criminal Records: Access: Phone, fax, mail, in person. Both court and visitors may perform in person searches. Search fee: $4.00 per name. Required to search: name, years to search. Criminal records on index cards since 1976, prior on books.

General Information: Public access terminal is available. No juvenile, mental, expunged, dismissed, or suspended imposition of sentence records released. SASE required. Turnaround time 1 week. Fax notes: No fee to fax results; other fees must be pre-paid. Will fax to local & 800 numbers only. Copy fee: $.50 per page. Certification fee: $2.00. Fee payee: Miller County Circuit Court. Personal checks accepted. Prepayment is required.

Associate Circuit Court Miller County Courthouse Annex, Tuscumbia, MO 65082; 573-369-2330. Hours: 8AM-4PM (CST). *Misdemeanor, Civil Actions Under $25,000, Eviction, Small Claims, Probate.*

Civil Records: Access: Mail, in person. Only the court performs in person searches; visitors may not. No search fee. Required to search: name, years to search. Civil cases indexed by defendant, plaintiff. Civil records on computer since 1/92, on microfiche since 1980, on cards since 1979, prior archived.

Criminal Records: Access: Mail, in person. Only the court performs in person searches; visitors may not. No search fee. Required to search: name, years to search. Criminal records on computer since 1979, on microfiche since 1980, prior archived.

General Information: No juvenile, mental, expunged, dismissed, or suspended imposition of sentence records released. SASE required. Turnaround time 1 week. Copy fee: $1.00 per page. Certification fee: $1.50. Fee payee: Associate Circuit Court. Only cashiers checks and money orders accepted. Prepayment is required.

Mississippi County

Circuit & Associate Court PO Box 369, Charleston, MO 63834; 573-683-2146; Fax: 573-683-7696. Hours: 8AM-5PM (CST). *Felony, Misdemeanor, Civil, Small Claims, Eviction, Probate.*

Note: The courts consolidated on July 1, 1999.

Civil Records: Access: Fax, mail, in person, online. Both court and visitors may perform in person searches. No search fee. Required to search: name, years to search. Civil cases indexed by defendant, plaintiff. Civil records in case files since 1976. Access to civil records available free at http://casenet.osca.state.mo.us/casenet/. At the web site, select the judicial district, then search by name, case # or date. Online records go back to 6/15/2001.

Criminal Records: Access: Fax, mail, in person, online. Both court and visitors may perform in person searches. No search fee. Required to search: name, years to search, DOB. Criminal records in case files since 1951. Online access to criminal records is the same as civil. A notarized, signed release by subject is necessary to obtain records of a dismissed case.

General Information: Public access terminal is available. No juvenile, mental, expunged, dismissed, or suspended imposition of sentence records released. SASE helpful. Turnaround time 1-2 days. Fax notes: No fee to fax results. Copy fee: $.25 per page. Certification fee: $.50. Fee payee: Circuit Clerk. Personal checks accepted. Copy fees may be billed.

Moniteau County

Circuit Court 200 E Main, California, MO 65018; 573-796-2071. Hours: 8AM-4:30PM (CST). *Felony, Misdemeanor, Civil Actions Over $25,000, Small Claims.*

Civil Records: Access: Mail, in person. Both court and visitors may perform in person searches. No search fee. Required to search: name, years to search; also helpful: case number. Civil cases indexed by defendant, plaintiff. Civil records on computer since 1992, prior on index cards and books.

Criminal Records: Access: Mail, in person. Both court and visitors may perform in person searches. No search fee. Required to search: name, years to search; also helpful: case number. Criminal records on computer since 1980, prior on index cards and books to 1845.

General Information: No juvenile, mental, expunged, dismissed, or suspended imposition of sentence records released. SASE required. Turnaround time 2-3 days. Fax notes: Fee to fax results is $1.00 per page. Copy fee: $.30 per page. Certification fee: $1.00. Fee payee: Montineau County Circuit Court. Personal checks accepted. Prepayment is required.

Associate Circuit Court 200 E Main, California, MO 65018; 573-796-2814. Hours: 8AM-4:30PM (CST). *Misdemeanor, Civil Actions Under $45,000, Eviction, Small Claims, Probate.*

Civil Records: Access: Phone, mail, in person. Both court and visitors may perform in person searches. No search fee. Required to search: name, years to search. Civil cases indexed by defendant, plaintiff. Civil records on index cards since 1979, prior on index books from 1948 to 1979, archived before.

Criminal Records: Access: Phone, mail, in person. Both court and visitors may perform in person searches. No search fee. Required to search: name, years to search. Criminal records on index cards since 1979, prior on index books from 1948 to 1979, archived before.

General Information: No juvenile, mental, expunged, dismissed, or suspended imposition of sentence records released. Turnaround time 1 week, phone turnaround time immediate. Copy fee: $.25 per page. Certification fee: $1.50 first page, $1.00 each additional. Personal checks accepted.

Monroe County

Circuit Court PO Box 227, Paris, MO 65275; 660-327-5204; Fax: 660-327-5781. Hours: 8AM-4:30PM (CST). *Felony, Misdemeanor, Civil Actions Over $45,000.*

Civil Records: Access: Mail, in person. Both court and visitors may perform in person searches. Search fee: $14.00 per name. Required to search: name, years to search. Civil cases indexed by defendant, plaintiff. Civil records on computer since 1996; index cards since 1979, prior on index books.

Criminal Records: Access: Mail, in person. Both court and visitors may perform in person searches. Search fee: $14.00 per name. Required to search: name, years to search, SSN, signed release. Criminal records on computer since 1996, on index cards from 1979 to 1990.

General Information: No juvenile, mental, expunged, dismissed, or suspended imposition of sentence records released. SASE required. Turnaround time 1 week. Fax notes: Fee to fax results is $1.00 per page. Copy fee: $1.00 per page. Certification fee: $2.00. Fee payee: Monroe County Circuit Court. Personal checks accepted. Prepayment is required.

Associate Circuit Court Courthouse, 300 N Main, Paris, MO 65275; 660-327-5220; Fax: 660-327-5781. Hours: 8AM-4:30PM (CST). *Misdemeanor, Civil Actions Under $45,000, Eviction, Small Claims, Probate.*

Civil Records: Access: Mail, in person. Both court and visitors may perform in person searches. Search fee: $3.00 per name. $4.00 if extensive search. Required to search: name, years to search. Civil cases indexed by defendant, plaintiff. Civil records on index cards since 1979, prior on books.

Criminal Records: Access: Mail, in person. Both court and visitors may perform in person searches. Search fee: $3.00 per name. $4.00 if extensive search. Required to search: name, years to search. Criminal records on index cards since 1979, prior on books.

General Information: No juvenile, mental, expunged, dismissed, or suspended imposition of sentence records released. SASE required. Turnaround time 2 weeks. Copy fee: $1.00 per page. Certification fee: $1.50 first page, $1.00 each additional. Fee payee: Associate Circuit Court. Personal checks accepted. Prepayment is required.

Montgomery County

Circuit Court 211 E 3rd, Montgomery City, MO 63361; 573-564-3341; Fax: 573-564-3914. Hours: 8AM-4:30PM (CST). *Felony, Misdemeanor, Civil Actions Over $25,000.*

Civil Records: Access: Online, in person. Both court and visitors may perform in person searches. No search fee. Required to search: name, years to search. Civil cases indexed by defendant, plaintiff. Civil records on computer since 1987 for judgments, on index cards since 1979, prior on books to 1864. Participates in the free state online court record system at http://casenet.osca.state.mo.us/casenet. Online records go back to 6/25/1997.

Criminal Records: Access: Online, in person. Both court and visitors may perform in person searches. No search fee. Required to search: name, years to search. Criminal records on computer since 1987 for judgments, on index cards since 1979, prior on books. Online access to criminal records is the same as civil. Online criminal records go back to 12/10/1996.

General Information: Public access terminal is available. (Judgments only.) No juvenile, mental, expunged, dismissed, or suspended imposition of sentence records released. Copy fee: $.25 per page. Certification fee: $1.00 plus $.25 per page. Fee payee: Montgomery County Circuit Court. Personal checks accepted. Prepayment is required.

Associate Circuit Court 211 E 3rd St, Montgomery City, MO 63361; 573-564-3348. Hours: 8:00AM-4:30PM (CST). *Misdemeanor, Civil Actions Under $25,000, Eviction, Small Claims, Probate.*

Civil Records: Access: Online, in person. Visitors must perform in person searches for themselves. No search fee. Required to search: name, years to search. Civil cases indexed by defendant, plaintiff. Civil records on computer back to 1976, prior on index cards. Participates in the free state online court record system at http://casenet.osca.state.mo.us/casenet. Online civil records go back to 6/25/1997.

Criminal Records: Access: Online, in person. Visitors must perform in person searches for themselves. No search fee. Required to search: name, years to search, DOB. Criminal records on computer back to 1976, prior on index cards. Online access to criminal records is the same as civil. Online criminal records go back to 8/29/1950.

General Information: Public access terminal is available. (Public terminal limited to judgments.) No juvenile, mental, expunged, dismissed, or suspended imposition of sentence records released. Copy fee: $.25 per page. Certification fee: $1.50 per page. Fee payee: Montgomery Circuit Clerk's Office. Personal checks accepted. Prepayment is required.

Morgan County

Circuit Court 211 E Newton, Versailles, MO 65084; 573-378-4413; Fax: 573-378-5356. Hours: 8AM-5PM (CST). *Felony, Civil Actions Over $25,000.*

Civil Records: Access: Phone, mail, in person. Both court and visitors may perform in person searches. No search fee. Required to search: name, years to search. Civil cases indexed by defendant, plaintiff. Civil records on computer since 1992, on index cards since 1979, prior archived since mid-1800s.

Criminal Records: Access: Phone, mail, in person. Both court and visitors may perform in person searches. No search fee. Required to search: name, years to search. Criminal records on computer since 1992, on index cards since 1979, prior archived since mid-1800s.

General Information: No juvenile, mental, expunged, dismissed, or suspended imposition of sentence records released. SASE required. Turnaround time 1 week, phone turnaround time immediate. Copy fee: $.25 per

page. Certification fee: $.50. Fee payee: Circuit Court. Personal checks accepted. Copy fees may be billed.

Associate Circuit Court 211 E Newton St, Versailles, MO 65084; 573-378-4235; Fax: 573-378-6847. Hours: 8:30AM-5PM (CST). *Misdemeanor, Civil Actions Under $25,000, Eviction, Small Claims, Probate.*

Civil Records: Access: Phone, mail, in person. Both court and visitors may perform in person searches. No search fee. Required to search: name, years to search. Civil cases indexed by defendant, plaintiff. Civil records on computer since 1991, prior on index.

Criminal Records: Access: Phone, mail, in person. Only the court performs in person searches; visitors may not. No search fee. Required to search: name, years to search; also helpful: address, DOB, SSN, singed release. Criminal records on computer since 1989, prior on index. Signed release required for some searches.

General Information: No juvenile, mental, expunged, dismissed, or suspended imposition of sentence records released. SASE required. Turnaround time 2-3 days. Copy fee: $1.00 per page. Certification fee: $1.50. Fee payee: Associate Circuit Court or Probate Court. Only cashiers checks and money orders accepted. Prepayment is required.

New Madrid County

Circuit Court County Courthouse, 450 Main Street, New Madrid, MO 63869; 573-748-2228. Hours: 8AM-4:30PM (CST). *Felony, Misdemeanor, Civil Actions Over $25,000.*

www.osca.state.mo.us

Civil Records: Access: Mail, in person, online. Both court and visitors may perform in person searches. No search fee. Required to search: name, years to search. Civil cases indexed by defendant, plaintiff. Civil records on Cott index since 1979, prior on books. Access to civil records available free at http://casenet.osca.state.mo.us/casenet/. At the web site, select the judicial district, then search by name, case # or date. Online records go back to 2/7/2001.

Criminal Records: Access: Mail, in person, online. Both court and visitors may perform in person searches. No search fee. Required to search: name, years to search. Criminal records on Cott index since 1979, prior on books. Online access to criminal records is the same as civil.

General Information: Public access terminal is available. No juvenile, mental, expunged, dismissed, or suspended imposition of sentence records released. SASE is required. Turnaround time 1 week. Copy fee: $1.00 per page. Certification fee: Certification fee is $5.00. Fee payee: Circuit Clerk. Personal checks not accepted. Prepayment is required.

Associate Circuit Court County Courthouse, New Madrid, MO 63869; 573-748-5556. Hours: 8AM-5PM (CST). *Misdemeanor, Civil Actions Under $25,000, Eviction, Small Claims, Probate.*

Civil Records: Access: Mail, in person, online. Only the court performs in person searches; visitors may not. No search fee. Required to search: name, years to search. Civil cases indexed by defendant, plaintiff. Probate records archived since 1803, records go back to 1980; computerized back to 1992. Access to civil records available http://casenet.osca.state.mo.us/casenet At the web site, select the judicial district, then search by name, case # or date. Online records go back to 2/7/2001.

Criminal Records: Access: Mail, in person, online. Only the court performs in person searches; visitors may not. No search fee. Required to search: name, years to search. Criminal records archived since 1947; records go back to 1980; computerized records back to 1992. Online access to criminal records is the same as civil.

General Information: Public access terminal is available. (Only Division 1 records are available on public access computer.) No juvenile, mental, expunged, dismissed, or suspended imposition of sentence records released. Turnaround time 1-2 weeks. No copy fee.

Newton County

Circuit Court PO Box 130, Neosho, MO 64850; 417-451-8257; Fax: 417-451-8298. Hours: 8:30AM-5PM (CST). *Felony, Misdemeanor, Civil Actions Over $25,000.*

Civil Records: Access: Fax, mail, in person. Only the court performs in person searches; visitors may not. No search fee. Required to search: name, years to search. Civil cases indexed by defendant, plaintiff. Civil records on computer since 1991, prior on index cards and books.

Criminal Records: Access: Fax, mail, in person. Only the court performs in person searches; visitors may not. No search fee. Required to search: name, years to search; also helpful: DOB, SSN. Criminal records on computer since 1991, prior on index cards and books.

General Information: No juvenile, mental, expunged, dismissed, or suspended imposition of sentence records released. SASE required. Turnaround time 1-2 days. Fax notes: $2.00 per page. Copy fee: $.25 per page. Fee payee: Newton County Circuit Clerk. Business checks accepted. Copy fees may be billed.

Associate Circuit Court PO Box 170, Neosho, MO 64850; 417-451-8212; Fax: 417-451-8272. Hours: 8AM-5PM (CST). *Misdemeanor, Civil Actions Under $25,000, Eviction, Small Claims, Probate.*

Civil Records: Access: Phone, mail, in person. Both court and visitors may perform in person searches. No search fee. Required to search: name, years to search. Civil cases indexed by defendant, plaintiff. Civil records on computer since 1989, prior on index cards.

Criminal Records: Access: Phone, mail, in person. Both court and visitors may perform in person searches. No search fee. Required to search: name, years to search, DOB. Criminal records on computer since 1989, prior on index cards.

General Information: No juvenile, mental, expunged, dismissed, or suspended imposition of sentence records released. SASE required. Turnaround time 1 week. Copy fee: $.25 per page. Certification fee: $1.00. Fee payee: Associate Circuit Court-Division II. Business checks accepted. Prepayment is required.

Nodaway County

Circuit Court PO Box 218, Maryville, MO 64468; 660-582-5431; Fax: 660-582-5499. Hours: 8AM-4:30PM (CST). *Felony, Misdemeanor, Civil Actions Over $25,000.*

Civil Records: Access: Phone, fax, mail, in person. Both court and visitors may perform in person searches. Search fee: $5.00 per name. Required to search: name, years to search. Civil cases indexed by defendant, plaintiff. Civil records on computer back to 5/91, archived since 1845.

Criminal Records: Access: Fax, mail, in person. Both court and visitors may perform in person searches. Search fee: $5.00 per name. Required to search: name, years to search, DOB, SSN, signed release. Criminal records on computer back to 5/91, archived since 1845.

General Information: Public access terminal is available. No juvenile, mental, expunged, dismissed, or suspended imposition of sentence records released. SASE required. Turnaround time same day. Fax notes: Fee to fax results is $1.00 per page. Copy fee: $1.00 per page. Certification fee: $1.00. Fee payee: Circuit Clerk. Personal checks accepted. Prepayment is required.

Associate Circuit Court Courthouse Annex, 303 N Market, Maryville, MO 64468; 660-582-2531;

Fax: 660-582-2047. Hours: 8AM-Noon; 12:30PM-4:30PM (CST). *Misdemeanor, Civil Actions Under $45,000, Eviction, Small Claims, Probate.*

Civil Records: Access: Mail, in person. Bothe the court and visitors may performs in person searches. Search fee: $5.00. Required to search: name, years to search. Civil cases indexed by defendant, plaintiff. Civil records on computer since 1981, archived since 1845.

Criminal Records: Access: Mail, in person. Both the court and visitors may perform in person searches. Search fee: $5.00. Required to search: name, years to search. Criminal records on computer since 1981, archived since 1845.

General Information: Public access terminal is available. No juvenile, mental, expunged, dismissed, or suspended imposition of sentence records released. SASE required. Turnaround time 2 days. Copy fee: $.50 per page. Certification fee: $1.50. Fee payee: Circuit Court Associate Division. Business checks accepted. Prepayment is required.

Oregon County

Circuit Court PO Box 406, Alton, MO 65606; 417-778-7460; Fax: 417-778-6641. Hours: 8AM-4PM (CST). *Felony, Misdemeanor, Civil Actions Over $45,000.*

Civil Records: Access: Phone, fax, mail, in person, online. Both court and visitors may perform in person searches. No search fee. Required to search: name, years to search; also helpful: address. Civil cases indexed by defendant, plaintiff. Civil records on books. Participates in the free state online court record system at http://casenet.osca.state.mo.us/casenet. Online records go back to 1991.

Criminal Records: Access: Phone, fax, mail, in person, online. Both court and visitors may perform in person searches. No search fee. Required to search: name, years to search; also helpful: DOB, SSN. Criminal records on books. Online access to criminal records is the same as civil.

General Information: No juvenile, mental, expunged, dismissed, or suspended imposition of sentence records released. SASE required. Turnaround time 1-2 days. Fax notes: $1.00 for first page, $.50 each add'l. Copy fee: $.50 per page. Certification fee: $2.00. Fee payee: Circuit Court. Personal checks accepted. Prepayment is required.

Associate Circuit Court PO Box 211, Alton, MO 65606; 417-778-7461; Fax: 417-778-6209. Hours: 8:00AM-4:00PM (CST). *Misdemeanor, Civil Actions Under $45,000, Eviction, Small Claims, Probate.*

Civil Records: Access: Mail, in person, online. Both court and visitors may perform in person searches. No search fee. Required to search: name, years to search. Civil cases indexed by defendant, plaintiff. Civil records on index cards, archived since 1850. Participates in the free state online court record system at http://casenet.osca.state.mo.us/casenet. Online records go back to 1991.

Criminal Records: Access: Mail, in person, online. Both court and visitors may perform in person searches. No search fee. Required to search: name, years to search. Criminal records on computer since 3/11/92, prior on files. Online access to criminal records is the same as civil.

General Information: Public access terminal is available. No juvenile, mental, expunged, dismissed, or suspended imposition of sentence records released. SASE not required. Turnaround time varies. Copy fee: $1.00 per page. Certification fee: $2.00. Fee payee: Associate Circuit Court. Business checks accepted. Prepayment is required.

Osage County

Circuit Court PO Box 825, Linn, MO 65051; 573-897-3114 573-897-2136 (Assoc Div). Hours: 8AM-4:30PM (CST). *Felony, Misdemeanor, Civil Actions Over $25,000.*

Civil Records: Access: Phone, mail, in person, online. Both court and visitors may perform in person searches. No search fee. Required to search: name, years to search. Civil cases indexed by defendant, plaintiff. Civil records on index cards and books. Participates in the free state online court record system at http://casenet.osca.state.mo.us/casenet. Online records go back to 6/20/1985.

Criminal Records: Access: Phone, mail, fax, in person, online. Both court and visitors may perform in person searches. No search fee. Required to search: name, years to search, DOB; also helpful: SSN. Criminal records on index cards and books, computerized since 1992. Participates in the free state online court record system at http://casenet.osca.state.mo.us/casenet. Online records go back to 8/26/1987.

General Information: Public access terminal is available. No juvenile, mental, expunged, dismissed, or suspended imposition of sentence records released. SASE required. Turnaround time ASAP. Fax notes: Fee to fax results is $1.00 per page. Copy fee: $.50 per page. $1.00 minimum. Certification fee: $2.00. Fee payee: Circuit Clerk. Personal checks accepted. Prepayment is required.

Associate Circuit Court PO Box 470, Linn, MO 65051; 573-897-2136; Fax: 573-897-4741. Hours: 8AM-4:30PM (CST). *Misdemeanor, Civil Actions Under $25,000, Eviction, Small Claims, Probate.*

Civil Records: Access: Phone, mail, in person, online. Both court and visitors may perform in person searches. No search fee. Required to search: name, years to search. Civil cases indexed by defendant, plaintiff. Civil records on computer back to 2000, prior on index cards. Participates in the free state online court record system at http://casenet.osca.state.mo.us/casenet. Online records go back to 7/14/1994. Online probate records go back to 9/18/2000.

Criminal Records: Access: Phone, mail, in person, online. Both court and visitors may perform in person searches. No search fee. Required to search: name, years to search; also helpful: DOB, SSN. Criminal records on computer back to 1995, prior on index cards. Participates in the free state online court record system at http://casenet.osca.state.mo.us/casenet. Online records go back to 5/30/1990. Also, traffic is available back to 7/4/1997.

General Information: Public access terminal is available. No juvenile, mental, expunged, dismissed, or suspended imposition of sentence records released. SASE not required. Turnaround time 2 weeks. Copy fee: $.25 per page. Certification fee: $2.00. Fee payee: Osage County Circuit Court-Associate Division. Personal checks accepted. Prepayment is required.

Ozark County

Circuit Court PO Box 36, Gainesville, MO 65655; 417-679-4232; Fax: 417-679-4554. Hours: 8AM-Noon, 12:30-4:30PM (CST). *Felony, Misdemeanor, Civil Actions Over $25,000.*

Civil Records: Access: Mail, in person. Only the court performs in person searches: visitors may not. No search fee. Required to search: name, years to search. Civil cases indexed by defendant, plaintiff. Civil records on index cards since 1979, archived since 1933.

Criminal Records: Access: Mail, in person. Only the court performs in person searches; visitors may not. No search fee. Required to search: name, years to search, DOB; also helpful: SSN. Criminal records on index cards since 1979, archived since 1933.

General Information: No juvenile, mental, expunged, dismissed, or suspended imposition of sentence records released. SASE requested. Turnaround time 10 days-2 weeks. Copy fee: $1.00 per page. Certification fee: $1.50. Fee payee: Ozark County Circuit Court. Personal checks accepted. Prepayment is required.

Associate Circuit Court PO Box 278, Gainesville, MO 65655; 417-679-4611; Fax: 417-679-2099. Hours: 8AM-4:30PM (CST). *Misdemeanor, Civil Actions Under $25,000, Eviction, Small Claims, Probate.*

Civil Records: Access: Fax, mail, in person. Only the court performs in person searches; visitors may not. No search fee. Required to search: name, years to search. Civil cases indexed by defendant, plaintiff. Civil records on case files.

Criminal Records: Access: Fax, mail, in person. Only the court performs in person searches; visitors may not. No search fee. Required to search: name, years to search, DOB, signed release; also helpful: SSN. Criminal records on computer since 1990.

General Information: No juvenile, mental, expunged, dismissed, or suspended imposition of sentence records released. SASE required. Turnaround time 2 weeks. Fax notes: $1.00 per page. Copy fee: $1.00 per page. Certification fee: $1.50. Fee payee: Associate Circuit Court. Personal checks accepted. Prepayment required.

Pemiscot County

Circuit Court County Courthouse, PO Box 34, Caruthersville, MO 63830; 573-333-0182. Hours: 7:30AM-4:30PM (CST). *Felony, Misdemeanor, Civil Actions Over $45,000.*

Civil Records: Access: In person, online. Visitors must perform in person searches for themselves. No search fee. Required to search: name, years to search. Civil cases indexed by defendant, plaintiff. Civil records on index cards since 1979, prior on books. Participates in the free state online court record system at http://casenet.osca.state.mo.us/casenet. Online records go back to 2/7/2001.

Criminal Records: Access: In person, online. Visitors must perform in person searches for themselves. No search fee. Required to search: name, years to search. Criminal records on index cards since 1979, prior on books. Online access to criminal records is the same as civil.

General Information: Public access terminal is available. No juvenile, mental, expunged, dismissed, or suspended imposition of sentence records released. Copy fee: $.25 per page. Fee payee: Pemiscot County Treasurer. Personal checks accepted.

Associate Circuit Court County Courthouse, PO Drawer 228, Caruthersville, MO 63830; 573-333-2784. Hours: 7:30AM-4:30PM (CST). *Misdemeanor, Civil Actions Under $45,000, Eviction, Small Claims, Probate.*

Civil Records: Access: Mail, in person, online. Both court and visitors may perform in person searches. No search fee. Required to search: name, years to search. Civil cases indexed by defendant, plaintiff. Civil records on computer back to 2000, index cards since 1979, prior on books. Participates in the free state online court record system at http://casenet.osca.state.mo.us/casenet. Online records go back to 2/7/2001.

Criminal Records: Access: Mail, in person. Both court and visitors may perform in person searches. No search fee. Required to search: name, years to search. Criminal records on computer since 5/90, on index cards from 1979-1990, prior on books. Online access to criminal records is the same as civil.

General Information: No juvenile, mental, expunged, dismissed, or suspended imposition of sentence records released. SASE required. Turnaround time varies. Copy fee: $1.00 per page. Fee payee: Pemiscot County Clerk.

Only cashiers checks and money orders accepted. Prepayment is required.

Perry County

Circuit Court 15 W Saint Maries St #2, Perryville, MO 63775-1399; 573-547-6581; Fax: 573-547-9323. Hours: 8AM-5PM (CST). *Felony, Misdemeanor, Civil Actions Over $25,000.*

Civil Records: Access: Fax, mail, in person, online. Visitors must perform in person searches for themselves. No search fee. Required to search: name, years to search. Civil cases indexed by defendant, plaintiff. Civil records on computer since 1994, prior on index cards. Access to civil records available free at http://casenet.osca.state.mo.us/casenet/. At the web site, select the judicial district, then search by name, case # or date. Online records go back to 7/1/2001.

Criminal Records: Access: Fax, mail, in person, online. Both court and visitors may perform in person searches. No search fee. Required to search: name, years to search. Criminal records on computer since 1993, prior on index cards. Online access to criminal records is the same as civil. Online public case records go back to 7/1/2001; judgments to 8/23/1993.

General Information: Public access terminal is available. No juvenile, mental, paternity (except final judgment), expunged, dismissed, or suspended imposition of sentence records released. SASE required. Turnaround time 3 days. Fax notes: No fee to fax results. Copy fee: $1.00 for first page, $.50 each add'l. Certification fee: $1.00. Fee payee: Perry County Circuit Clerk. Personal checks accepted. Prepayment is required.

Associate Circuit Court 15 W Saint Maries, #3, Perryville, MO 63775-1399; 573-547-7861; Fax: 573-547-9323. Hours: 8AM-5PM (CST). *Misdemeanor, Civil Actions Under $25,000, Eviction, Small Claims, Probate.*

Civil Records: Access: Mail, in person, online. Visitors must perform in person searches for themselves. No search fee. Required to search: name, years to search; also helpful: address. Civil cases indexed by defendant, plaintiff. Civil records on computer since 1994, prior on index cards. Access to civil records available free at http://casenet.osca.state.mo.us/casenet/. At the web site, select the judicial district, then search by name, case # or date. Online records go back to 7/1/2001.

Criminal Records: Access: Mail, in person, online. Visitors must perform in person searches for themselves. No search fee. Required to search: name, years to search, DOB; also helpful: address, SSN. Criminal records on computer since 1994, prior on index cards. Online access to criminal records is the same as civil. Online public case records go back to 7/1/2001.

General Information: Public access terminal is available. No juvenile, mental, expunged, dismissed, or suspended imposition of sentence records released. SASE required. Turnaround time varies. Copy fee: $.50 per page. Certification fee: $1.50 plus $1.00 per page. Fee payee: Circuit Court Division 6. Only cashiers checks and money orders accepted. Prepayment is required.

Pettis County

Circuit Court PO Box 804, Sedalia, MO 65302-0804; 660-826-0617; Fax: 660-826-4520. Hours: 8AM-5PM (CST). *Felony, Misdemeanor, Civil Actions Over $45,000.*

Note: Also see Associate Circuit Court for add'l civil actions over $45,000.

Civil Records: Access: Phone, fax, mail, in person, online. Both court and visitors may perform in person searches. No search fee. Required to search: name, years to search. Civil cases indexed by defendant,

plaintiff. Civil records on index books since 9/75, prior on judgment books. Access to civil records available free at http://casenet.osca.state.mo.us/casenet/. At the web site, select the judicial district, then search by name, case # or date. Online records go back to 4/2001.

Criminal Records: Access: Phone, fax, mail, in person, online. Both court and visitors may perform in person searches. No search fee. Required to search: name, years to search, DOB. Criminal records on computer since 1993, prior on index cards since 9/75. Online access to criminal records is the same as civil. Online criminal records go back to 1/1992.

General Information: Public access terminal is available. No juvenile, mental, expunged, dismissed, or suspended imposition of sentence records released. SASE required. Turnaround time 1-2 days. Fax notes: $2.50 for first page, $1.50 each add'l. Copy fee: $.15 per page. Certification fee: $1.50. Fee payee: Pettis County Circuit Clerk. Personal checks accepted.

Associate Circuit Court 415 S Ohio, Sedalia, MO 65301; 660-826-4699; Probate phone: 660-826-0368; Fax: 660-827-8637. Hours: 8:30AM-5PM (CST). *Misdemeanor, Civil Actions Under $45,000, Eviction, Small Claims, Probate.*

Note: Civil actions over $45,000 may also be filed here.

Civil Records: Access: Phone, fax, mail, in person, online. Both court and visitors may perform in person searches. No search fee. Required to search: name, years to search. Civil cases indexed by defendant, plaintiff. Civil records on index cards since 1975, prior on judgment books; on computer back to 4/2001. Access to civil records available free at http://casenet.osca.state.mo.us/casenet/. At the web site, select the judicial district, then search by name, case # or date. Online records go back to 4/2001.

Criminal Records: Access: Fax, mail, in person, online. Both court and visitors may perform in person searches. No search fee. Required to search: name, years to search, DOB, SSN; on some cases: signed release. Criminal records on computer back to 1993, on index cards from 1975-1993, prior on judgment books. Online access to criminal records is the same as civil. Online criminal records go back to 1/1993.

General Information: Public access terminal is available. No juvenile, mental, expunged, dismissed, or suspended imposition of sentence records released. SASE required. Turnaround time 1-2 weeks. Copy fee: $.15 per page. Certification fee: $1.50 per page. Fee payee: Circuit Court Division 6. Only cashiers checks and money orders accepted.

Phelps County

Circuit & Associate Court 200 N Main St, Rolla, MO 65401; 573-364-1891 X200; Fax: 573-364-1419. Hours: 8AM-5PM (CST). *Felony, Misdemeanor, Civil, Small Claims, Eviction, Probate.*

Civil Records: Access: Fax, mail, in person. Visitors must perform in person searches for themselves. No search fee. Required to search: name, years to search. Civil cases indexed by defendant, plaintiff. Civil records on computer since 1991; prior on books to 1957.

Criminal Records: Access: Fax, mail, in person. Visitors must perform in person searches for themselves. No search fee. Required to search: name, years to search. Criminal records on computer since 1991, prior on books to 1957.

General Information: Public access terminal is available. No juvenile, mental, expunged or dismissed records released. SASE required. Turnaround time 1 week. Fax notes: Fee to fax results is $1.00 per page. Copy fee: $.20 per page. Certification fee: $1.00. Fee payee: Circuit Clerk. Personal checks accepted. no out-of-state checks accepted. Copy fees may be billed.

Pike County

Circuit Court 115 W Main, Bowling Green, MO 63334; 573-324-3112. Hours: 8AM-4:30PM (CST). *Felony, Misdemeanor, Civil Actions Over $25,000.*

Civil Records: Access: Mail, in person. Both court and visitors may perform in person searches. No search fee. Required to search: name, years to search; also helpful: address. Civil cases indexed by defendant, plaintiff. Civil records on index cards since 1977, prior on books.

Criminal Records: Access: In person only. Visitors must perform in person searches for themselves. No search fee. Required to search: name, years to search; also helpful: DOB. Criminal records on index cards since 1977, prior on books. The Circuit Clerks will provide a from to mail requests to the State Patrol.

General Information: Public access terminal is available. No juvenile, mental, expunged, dismissed, or suspended imposition of sentence records released. SASE required. Turnaround time 1-2 days. Copy fee: $.25 per page. Certification fee: $1.00. Fee payee: Pike County Circuit Clerk. Personal checks accepted.

Associate Circuit Court 115 W Main, Bowling Green, MO 63334; 573-324-5582; Fax: 573-324-6297. Hours: 8AM-4:30PM (CST). *Misdemeanor, Civil Actions Under $25,000, Eviction, Small Claims, Probate.*

Civil Records: Access: Phone, mail, fax, in person. Both court and visitors may perform in person searches. No search fee. Required to search: name, years to search. Civil cases indexed by defendant, plaintiff. Civil records on index cards since 1979, archived since 1819.

Criminal Records: Access: Phone, mail, fax, in person. Only the court performs in person searches; visitors may not. No search fee. Required to search: name, years to search; also helpful: DOB. Criminal records on index cards since 1979, archived since 1819.

General Information: No juvenile, mental, expunged, dismissed records released. SASE required. Turnaround time 3-7 days. Copy fee: $.25 per page. Certification fee: $1.50. Fee payee: Associate Circuit or Probate Court. Business checks accepted. Prepayment is required.

Platte County

Circuit Court 415 Third Street #5, Platte City, MO 64079; 816-858-2232; Fax: 816-858-3392. Hours: 8AM-5PM (CST). *Felony, Misdemeanor, Civil Actions Over $25,000.*

Civil Records: Access: Mail, online, in person. Both court and visitors may perform in person searches. No search fee. Required to search: name, years to search. Civil cases indexed by defendant, plaintiff. Civil records on computer since 10/91. Participates in the free state online court record system at http://casenet.osca.state.mo.us/casenet.

Criminal Records: Access: Mail, online, in person. Both court and visitors may perform in person searches. No search fee. Required to search: name, years to search, DOB; also helpful: SSN. Criminal records on computer since 10/91. Online access to criminal records is the same as civil.

General Information: Public access terminal is available. No juvenile, mental, expunged, dismissed, or suspended imposition of sentence records released. SASE required. Turnaround time 2-3 days. Copy fee: $.25 per page. Certification fee: $1.00. Fee payee: Platte County Circuit Clerk. Only cashiers checks and money orders accepted. Prepayment is required.

Associate Circuit Court 415 Third Street #5, Platte City, MO 64079; 816-858-2232; Fax: 816-858-3392. Hours: 8AM-5PM (CST). *Misdemeanor, Civil Actions Under $25,000, Eviction, Small Claims.*

Civil Records: Access: Mail, online, in person. Both court and visitors may perform in person searches. No search fee. Required to search: name, years to search. Civil cases indexed by defendant, plaintiff. Civil records on computer since 11/91, prior on index cards. Participates in the free state online court record system at http://casenet.osca.state.mo.us/casenet.

Criminal Records: Access: Mail, online, in person. Both court and visitors may perform in person searches. No search fee. Required to search: name, years to search, DOB; also helpful: SSN. Criminal records on computer since 11/91, prior on index cards. Online access to criminal records is the same as civil.

General Information: Public access terminal is available. No juvenile, mental, expunged, dismissed, or suspended imposition of sentence records released. SASE required. Turnaround time 1-3 days. Copy fee: $.25 per page. Certification fee: $1.00. Fee payee: Circuit Clerk. Only cashiers checks and money orders accepted. Prepayment is required.

Probate Court 415 Third St, #95, Platte City, MO 64079; 816-858-2232 X3438; Fax: 816-858-3392. Hours: 8AM-5PM (CST). *Probate.*

Note: Can search by name or case number.

Polk County

Circuit Court 102 E Broadway, Rm 14, Bolivar, MO 65613; 417-326-4912; Fax: 417-326-4194. Hours: 8AM-5PM (CST). *Felony, Misdemeanor, Civil Actions Over $25,000.*

www.positech.net/~dcourt

Civil Records: Access: Fax, mail, in person, online. Both court and visitors may perform in person searches. Search fee: $5.00 per name. Required to search: name, years to search. Civil cases indexed by defendant, plaintiff. Civil records on computer since 1991, prior on card index since 1979. Participates in the free state online court record system at http://casenet.osca.state.mo.us/casenet.

Criminal Records: Access: Fax, mail, in person, online. Only the court performs in person searches; visitors may not. Search fee: $5.00 per name. Required to search: name, years to search. Criminal records on computer since 1991, prior on card index since 1979. Online access to criminal records is the same as civil.

General Information: Public access terminal is available. No juvenile, mental, expunged, dismissed, or suspended imposition of sentence records released. SASE required. Turnaround time 1 week. Fax notes: $3.00 for first page, $.25 each add'l. Copy fee: $.25 per page. Certification fee: $2.00. Fee payee: Circuit Clerk. Personal checks accepted.

Associate Circuit Court Courthouse, Rm 7, Bolivar, MO 65613; 417-326-4921; Fax: 417-326-5238. Hours: 8:00AM-5:00PM (CST). *Misdemeanor, Civil Actions Under $25,000, Eviction, Small Claims, Probate.*

www.positech.net/~dcourt

Civil Records: Access: Phone, fax, mail, in person, online. Only the court performs in person searches; visitors may not. No search fee. Required to search: name, years to search; also helpful: case number. Civil cases indexed by defendant, plaintiff. Civil records go back to 1980; on computer back to 1990. . Participates in the free state online court record system at http://casenet.osca.state.mo.us/casenet.

Criminal Records: Access: Phone, fax, mail, in person, online. Only the court performs in person searches; visitors may not. No search fee. Required to search: name, years to search; also helpful: case number, signed release. Criminal records go back to 1980; on computer back to 1990. . Participates in the free state online court record system at http://casenet.osca.state.mo.us/casenet.

General Information: No juvenile, mental, expunged, dismissed, or suspended imposition of sentence records

released. SASE required. Turnaround time 1 week. Fax notes: Will not fax results. Copy fee: $.25 per page. Certification fee: $1.50. Fee payee: Associate Circuit Court. Only cashiers checks and money orders accepted. Prepayment is required.

Pulaski County

Circuit & Associate Circuit Courts 301 Historic Rt 66 E, #202, Waynesville, MO 65583; 573-774-4755; Fax: 573-774-6967. Hours: 8AM-4:30PM (CST). *Felony, Misdemeanor, Civil, Eviction, Small Claims.*

Civil Records: Access: In person only. Visitors must perform in person searches for themselves. No search fee. Required to search: name, years to search; also helpful: address. Civil cases indexed by defendant, plaintiff. Civil records on computer since 1990, prior on books since 1903.

Criminal Records: Access: Fax, mail, in person. Both court and visitors may perform in person searches. No search fee. Required to search: name, years to search; also helpful: DOB, SSN. Criminal records on computer since 1990, prior on books since 1903.

General Information: Public access terminal is available. No juvenile, mental, paternity, expunged, dismissed, or suspended imposition of sentence records released. SASE requested. Turnaround time 1 day. Fax notes: No fee to fax results. Will only fax to 800 numbers. Copy fee: $.25 per page. Certification fee: $2.00. Fee payee: Circuit Clerk. Business checks accepted. Prepayment is required.

Probate Court 301 Historic 66 East, #316, Waynesville, MO 65583; 573-774-4784; Fax: 573-774-6673. *Probate.*

Putnam County

Circuit Court Courthouse Rm 202, Unionville, MO 63565; 660-947-2071; Fax: 660-947-2320. Hours: 8AM-12; 1PM-5PM (CST). *Felony, Misdemeanor, Civil Actions Over $45,000.*

Civil Records: Access: Mail, in person, online. Both court and visitors may perform in person searches. No search fee. Required to search: name, years to search. Civil cases indexed by defendant, plaintiff. Civil records on index cards since 1848; on computer since 03/00. Participates in the free state online court record system at http://casenet.osca.state.mo.us/casenet. Online records go back to 3/29/2000.

Criminal Records: Access: Mail, in person, online. Both court and visitors may perform in person searches. No search fee. Required to search: name, years to search. Criminal records on index cards since 11848; on computer since 03/00. Online access to criminal records is the same as civil.

General Information: Public access terminal is available. No juvenile, mental, expunged, dismissed, or suspended imposition of sentence records released. SASE required. Turnaround time same day. Fax notes: Fee to fax results is $1.00 for 1st page; $50 each add'l. Copy fee: $.25 per page. Certification fee: $1.00. Fee payee: Circuit Clerk. Business checks accepted. Prepayment is required.

Associate Circuit Court Courthouse Rm 101, Unionville, MO 63565; 660-947-2117; Fax: 660-947-7348. Hours: 9AM-5PM (CST). *Misdemeanor, Civil Actions Under $45,000, Eviction, Small Claims, Probate.*

Civil Records: Access: Mail, in person, online. Both court and visitors may perform in person searches. No search fee. Required to search: name, years to search. Civil cases indexed by defendant, plaintiff. Civil records on computer since 1994, prior on books. Participates in the free state online court record system at http://casenet.osca.state.mo.us/casenet. Online records go back to 3/29/2000.

Criminal Records: Access: Mail, in person, online. Only the court performs in person searches; visitors may not. No search fee. Required to search: name, years to search, DOB, SSN. Criminal records on computer since 1994, prior on books. Online access to criminal records is the same as civil.

General Information: No mental, expunged, dismissed, or suspended imposition of sentence records released. SASE required. Turnaround time 30-60 days. Copy fee: $1.00 per page. Certification fee: $1.50. Fee payee: Associate Circuit Court. Only cashiers checks and money orders accepted. Prepayment is required.

Ralls County

Circuit Court PO Box 444, New London, MO 63459; 573-985-5633. Hours: 8:30AM-4:30PM (CST). *Felony, Misdemeanor, Civil Actions Over $25,000.*

Civil Records: Access: Mail, in person. Only the court performs in person searches; visitors may not. No search fee. Required to search: name, years to search, DOB, SSN and signed release. Civil cases indexed by defendant, plaintiff. Civil records on index cards since 1976, prior on books.

Criminal Records: Access: Mail, in person. Only the court performs in person searches; visitors may not. No search fee. Required to search: name, years to search, signed release and SSN. Criminal records on index cards since 1976, prior on books.

General Information: No juvenile, mental, expunged, dismissed, or suspended imposition of sentence records released. SASE required. Turnaround time varies. Copy fee: $.25 per page. Certification fee: $1.00. Fee payee: Ralls County Circuit Clerk. Personal checks accepted. Prepayment is required.

Associate Circuit Court PO Box 466, New London, MO 63459; 573-985-5641; Fax: 573-985-3446. Hours: 8:00AM-4:30PM (CST). *Misdemeanor, Civil Actions Under $25,000, Eviction, Small Claims, Probate.*

Civil Records: Access: Phone, mail, fax, in person. Both court and visitors may perform in person searches. Search fee: $5.00 per name. Required to search: name, years to search. Civil cases indexed by defendant, plaintiff. Civil records on index cards since 1979, prior on record books.

Criminal Records: Access: Phone, mail, fax, in person. Both court and visitors may perform in person searches. Search fee: $5.00 per name. Required to search: name, years to search, signed release. Criminal records on index cards since 1979, prior on record books.

General Information: No juvenile, mental, expunged, dismissed, or suspended imposition of sentence records released. SASE required. Turnaround time 1-2 weeks, genealogy turnaround time varies. Copy fee: $.25 per page. Certification fee: $1.50. Fee payee: Associate Circuit Court. Personal checks accepted. Prepayment is required.

Randolph County

Circuit & Associate Court 223 N Williams, Moberly, MO 65270; 660-263-4474; Fax: 660-263-5966 Crim; 263-1007 civil. Hours: 8AM-4:30PM (CST). *Felony, Misdemeanor, Civil Actions, Eviction, Small Claims, Probate.*

Civil Records: Access: Fax, mail, in person, online. Both court and visitors may perform in person searches. No search fee. Required to search: name, years to search, address. Civil cases indexed by defendant, plaintiff. Civil records on index cards since 1975, prior on record books. Participates in the free state online court record system at http://casenet.osca.state.mo.us/casenet.

Criminal Records: Access: Fax, mail, in person, online. Both court and visitors may perform in person searches. No search fee. Required to search: name, years to search, address, DOB; also helpful: SSN. Criminal records on computer since 1994, prior on index books. Online access to criminal records is the same as civil.

General Information: Public access terminal is available. No juvenile, mental, expunged, dismissed, or suspended imposition of sentence records released. SASE required. Turnaround time 1 week. Fax notes: $4.00 per page. Copy fee: $.25 per page. Certification fee: $1.50. Fee payee: Randolph County Circuit Clerk. Personal checks accepted.

Ray County

Circuit Court PO Box 594, Richmond, MO 64085; 816-776-3377; Fax: 816-776-6016. Hours: 8AM-4PM (CST). *Felony, Misdemeanor, Civil Actions Over $25,000.*

www.osca.state.mo.us/circuits/index.nsf/County+/+Ray

Civil Records: Access: Phone, fax, mail, in person. Only the court performs in person searches; visitors may not. No search fee. Required to search: name, years to search. Civil cases indexed by defendant, plaintiff. Civil records on index cards since 1977, prior on judgment books.

Criminal Records: Access: Phone, fax, mail, in person. Only the court performs in person searches; visitors may not. No search fee. Required to search: name, years to search; also helpful: DOB, SSN. Criminal records on index cards since 1977, prior on judgment books.

General Information: No juvenile, mental, expunged, dismissed, or suspended imposition of sentence records released. SASE required. Turnaround time varies. Fax notes: Fee to fax results is $1.00 per page. Copy fee: $.25 per page. Certification fee: $1.50. Fee payee: Ray County Circuit Clerk. Business checks accepted. Prepayment is required.

Associate Circuit Court Ray County Courthouse, 100 W Main St, Richmond, MO 64085-1710; 816-776-2335; Fax: 816-776-2185. Hours: 8AM-4PM (CST). *Misdemeanor, Civil Actions Under $25,000, Eviction, Small Claims, Probate.*

Civil Records: Access: Fax, mail, in person. Only the court performs in person searches; visitors may not. No search fee. Required to search: name; also helpful: years to search. Civil cases indexed by defendant, plaintiff. Civil records on index cards since 1979, prior on books.

Criminal Records: Access: Fax, mail, in person. Only the court performs in person searches; visitors may not. No search fee. Required to search: name, DOB; also helpful: years to search, SSN. Criminal records on index cards since 1979, prior on books.

General Information: No juvenile, mental, expunged, dismissed, or suspended imposition of sentence records released. SASE required. Turnaround time varies. Fax notes: No fee to fax results. Copy fee: $.20 per page. Certification fee: $1.50. Fee payee: Associate Circuit Court. Business checks accepted. Prepayment required.

Reynolds County

Circuit Court PO Box 76, Centerville, MO 63633; 573-648-2494 X44; Fax: 573-648-2503. Hours: 8AM-4PM (CST). *Felony, Civil Actions Over $45,000.*

Civil Records: Access: Phone, mail, in person, online. Both court and visitors may perform in person searches. No search fee. Required to search: name, years to search. Civil cases indexed by defendant, plaintiff. Civil records on cards and books, archived since 1872. Access to civil records available free at http://casenet.osca.state.mo.us/casenet/. At the web site, select the judicial district, then search by name, case # or date.

Criminal Records: Access: Phone, mail, in person, online. Both court and visitors may perform in person searches. No search fee. Required to search: name,

years to search, DOB; also helpful: SSN, sex, signed release. Criminal records on cards and books, archived since 1872. Online access to criminal records is the same as civil.

General Information: Public access terminal is available. No juvenile, mental, expunged, dismissed, or suspended imposition of sentence records released. SASE required. Turnaround time 2 days. Fax notes: Fee to fax results is $2.00 per document plus $1.00 per page. Copy fee: $1.00 per page. Certification fee: $2.00. Fee payee: Randy L Cowin. Personal checks accepted. Prepayment is required.

Associate Circuit Court PO Box 39, Centerville, MO 63633; 573-648-2494 X41; Fax: 573-648-2296. Hours: 8AM-4PM (CST). *Misdemeanor, Civil Actions Under $45,000, Eviction, Small Claims, Probate.*

Civil Records: Access: Phone, mail, in person, online. Both court and visitors may perform in person searches. No search fee. Required to search: name, years to search. Civil cases indexed by defendant, plaintiff. Civil records on index cards and files (probate in books); on computer back to 2000. Participates in the free state online court record system at http://casenet.osca.state.mo.us/casenet.

Criminal Records: Access: Phone, mail, in person, online. Both court and visitors may perform in person searches. No search fee. Required to search: name, years to search. Criminal records on index cards and files back to early 1970's; on computer back to 2000. Online access to criminal records is the same as civil.

General Information: Public access terminal is available. No juvenile, mental, expunged, dismissed, or suspended imposition of sentence records released. SASE not required. Turnaround time 1 day, phone turnaround time same day. Copy fee: $1.00 per page. Certification fee: $2.00. Fee payee: Associate Circuit Court. Personal checks accepted.

Ripley County

Circuit Court Courthouse, Doniphan, MO 63935; 573-996-2818; Fax: 573-996-7826. Hours: 8AM-4PM (CST). *Felony, Misdemeanor, Civil Actions Over $25,000.*

Civil Records: Access: Phone, fax, mail, in person. Both court and visitors may perform in person searches. Search fee: $5.00 per name. Required to search: name, years to search. Civil cases indexed by defendant, plaintiff. Civil records on cards and books since 1976, archived since 1850s.

Criminal Records: Access: Fax, mail, in person. Both court and visitors may perform in person searches. Search fee: $5.00 per name. Required to search: name, years to search, DOB. Criminal records on cards and books since 1976, archived since 1850s.

General Information: No juvenile, mental, expunged, dismissed, or suspended imposition of sentence records released. SASE required. Turnaround time same day. Copy fee: $3.00 per page. Certification fee: $2.00 if done by in-person searcher, otherwise certification is included in the search fee. Fee payee: Circuit Clerk. Personal checks accepted. Prepayment is required.

Associate Circuit Court 100 Court Sq, Courthouse, Doniphan, MO 63935; 573-996-2013; Fax: 573-996-5014. Hours: 8AM-4PM (CST). *Misdemeanor, Civil Actions Under $25,000, Eviction, Small Claims, Probate.*

Civil Records: Access: Phone, fax, mail, in person. Both court and visitors may perform in person searches. No search fee. Required to search: name, years to search. Civil cases indexed by defendant, plaintiff. Civil records on index cards since 1984, prior on books.

Criminal Records: Access: Phone, mail, in person. Both court and visitors may perform in person searches. No search fee. Required to search: name, years to

search; also helpful: DOB, SSN. Criminal records on index cards since 1984, prior on books.

General Information: No juvenile, mental, expunged, dismissed, or suspended imposition of sentence records released. SASE required. Turnaround time 1 week. Copy fee: $.25 per page. Certification fee: $1.00. Fee payee: Circuit Court Division II. Only cashiers checks and money orders accepted.

Saline County

Circuit Court PO Box 597, Marshall, MO 65340; 660-886-2300. Hours: 8:00AM-4:30PM (CST). *Felony, Misdemeanor, Civil Actions Over $25,000.*

Civil Records: Access: Mail, in person, online. Both court and visitors may perform in person searches. No search fee. Required to search: name, years to search. Civil cases indexed by defendant, plaintiff. Civil records on index cards since 1974, prior on books since 1820. Records may be available free on state online court record system at http://casenet.osca.state.mo.us/casenet.

Criminal Records: Access: Mail, in person, online. Both court and visitors may perform in person searches. No search fee. Required to search: name, years to search. Criminal records on index cards since 1974, prior on books since 1820. Records may be available free on state online court record system at http://casenet.osca.state.mo.us/casenet. Criminal search requests are usually referred to the MO State Hwy Patrol, Jefferson City, 573-526-6153.

General Information: No juvenile, mental, expunged, dismissed, or suspended imposition of sentence records released. SASE required. Turnaround time 1 week. Copy fee: $.25 per page. Certification fee: $1.50. Fee payee: Saline County Circuit Court. Personal checks accepted. Copy fees may be billed.

Associate Circuit Court PO Box 751, Marshall, MO 65340; 660-886-6988; Fax: 660-886-2919. Hours: 8AM-4:30PM (CST). *Misdemeanor, Civil Actions Under $25,000, Eviction, Small Claims.*

Civil Records: Access: Phone, mail, in person. Only the court performs in person searches; visitors may not. No search fee. Required to search: name, years to search. Civil cases indexed by defendant, plaintiff. Civil records on index cards since 1979, prior on books.

Criminal Records: Access: Phone, mail, in person. Only the court performs in person searches; visitors may not. No search fee. Required to search: name, years to search. Criminal records on computer since 1993, prior on cards and books.

General Information: No juvenile, mental, expunged, dismissed, or suspended imposition of sentence records released. SASE required. Turnaround time 1-2 days. No copy fee.

Schuyler County

Circuit Court PO Box 186, Lancaster, MO 63548; 660-457-3784; Fax: 660-457-3016. Hours: 8AM-4PM (CST). *Felony, Misdemeanor, Civil Actions Over $45,000.*

Civil Records: Access: Mail, in person. Both court and visitors may perform in person searches. Search fee: $14.00 per name. Required to search: name, years to search. Civil cases indexed by defendant, plaintiff. Civil records on index cards & books.

Criminal Records: Access: Mail, in person. Both court and visitors may perform in person searches. Search fee: $14.00 per name. Required to search: name, years to search. Criminal records on index cards & books.

General Information: No juvenile, mental, expunged, dismissed, or suspended imposition of sentence records released. SASE required. Turnaround time 1-2 days. Fax notes: Fee to fax is $2.00 plus $1.00 each page. Copy fee: $1.00 per page. Certification fee: $1.00. Fee payee: Schuyler County Circuit Clerk. Personal checks accepted. Prepayment is required.

Associate Circuit Court Box 158, Lancaster, MO 63548; 660-457-3755; Fax: 660-457-3016. Hours: 8:00AM-4PM (CST). *Misdemeanor, Civil Actions Under $45,000, Eviction, Small Claims, Probate.*

Civil Records: Access: Mail, fax, in person. Both court and visitors may perform in person searches. Search fee: $5.00 per name. Required to search: name, years to search. Civil cases indexed by defendant, plaintiff. Civil records on index cards since 1976; computerized records go back to 1992.

Criminal Records: Access: Mail, fax, in person. Both court and visitors may perform in person searches. Search fee: $5.00 per name. Required to search: name, years to search, SSN, DOB. Criminal records on computer since 5/92, prior on index cards.

General Information: No juvenile, mental, expunged, dismissed, or suspended imposition of sentence records released. SASE required. Turnaround time 4 days. Copy fee: $1.00 per page. Certification fee: $1.50. Fee payee: Associate Circuit Court. Business checks accepted. Prepayment is required.

Scotland County

Circuit Court 117 S Market St #106, Memphis, MO 63555; 660-465-8605; Fax: 660-465-8673. Hours: 9AM-4PM (CST). *Felony, Misdemeanor, Civil Actions Over $25,000.*

Civil Records: Access: Mail, in person. Both court and visitors may perform in person searches. No search fee. Required to search: name, years to search. Civil cases indexed by defendant, plaintiff. Civil records on index cards since 1979, prior on books. Computerized records go back to 2001.

Criminal Records: Access: Mail, in person. Both court and visitors may perform in person searches. No search fee. Required to search: name, years to search, DOB, signed release; also helpful: address. Criminal records on index cards since 1979, prior on books. Computerized records go back to 9/2001.

General Information: No juvenile, mental, expunged, dismissed, or suspended imposition of sentence records released. SASE required. Turnaround time same day. Fax notes: Fax back fee $1.00 per page. Copy fee: $.25 per page. Certification fee: $2.00. Fee payee: Scotland County Circuit Clerk. Personal checks accepted. Prepayment is required.

Associate Circuit Court Courthouse, Rm 102, 117 S Market, Memphis, MO 63555; 660-465-2404; Fax: 660-465-8673. Hours: 8AM-4:30PM (CST). *Misdemeanor, Civil Actions Under $25,000, Eviction, Small Claims, Probate.*

Civil Records: Access: Phone, mail, fax, in person. Both court and visitors may perform in person searches. No search fee. Required to search: name, years to search. Civil cases indexed by defendant, plaintiff. Civil records on computer since 1986, prior on cards and books to 1841.

Criminal Records: Access: Phone, mail, in person. Both court and visitors may perform in person searches. No search fee. Required to search: name, years to search. Criminal records on computer since 1986, prior on cards and books to 1841.

General Information: No juvenile, mental, expunged, dismissed, or suspended imposition of sentence records released. SASE required. Turnaround time ASAP. Fax notes: Fee to fax results is 1.00 per page. Copy fee: $.25 per page. Certification fee: $1.50 plus $1.00 per page. Fee payee: Info provided on bill. Personal checks accepted.

Scott County

Circuit Court PO Box 277, Benton, MO 63736; 573-545-3596; Fax: 573-545-3597. Hours: 8:30AM-12, 1-5PM (CST). *Felony, Misdemeanor, Civil Actions Over $25,000.*

Civil Records: Access: In person, online. Visitors must perform in person searches for themselves. No search fee. Required to search: name, years to search. Civil cases indexed by defendant, plaintiff. Civil records on computer since 1991, prior on index cards and books. Access to civil records available free at http://casenet.osca.state.mo.us/casenet/. At the web site, select the judicial district, then search by name, case # or date. Online records go back to 6/15/2001.

Criminal Records: Access: Mail, fax, in person, online. Both court and visitors may perform in person searches. No search fee. Required to search: name, years to search, DOB, SSN. Criminal records on computer since 1991, prior on index cards and books. Online access to criminal records is the same as civil.

General Information: Public access terminal is available. No juvenile, mental, expunged, dismissed, or suspended imposition of sentence records released. SASE required. Turnaround time 2 days-1 week. Copy fee: $1.00 for first page, $.25 each add'l. Certification fee: $3.00. Fee payee: Pam Glastetter, Circuit Clerk. Personal checks accepted. Prepayment is required.

Associate Circuit Court PO Box 249, Benton, MO 63736; 573-545-3576; Fax: 573-545-4231. Hours: 8AM-5PM (CST). *Misdemeanor, Civil Actions Under $45,000, Eviction, Small Claims, Probate.*

Civil Records: Access: Phone, mail, in person, online. Both court and visitors may perform in person searches. No search fee. Required to search: name, years to search. Civil cases indexed by defendant, plaintiff. Civil records on index cards and books. Access to civil records available free at http://casenet.osca.state.mo.us/casenet. At the web site, select the judicial district, then search by name, case # or date. Online records go back to 6/15/2001.

Criminal Records: Access: Phone, mail, in person, online. Visitors must perform in person searches for themselves. No search fee. Required to search: name, years to search. Criminal records on index cards and books. Online access to criminal records is the same as civil.

General Information: No juvenile, mental, expunged, dismissed, or suspended imposition of sentence records released. SASE required. Turnaround time varies. No copy fee.

Shannon County

Circuit Court PO Box 148, Eminence, MO 65466; 573-226-3315; Fax: 573-226-5321. Hours: 8AM-4:30PM (CST). *Felony, Misdemeanor, Civil Actions Over $45,000.*

Civil Records: Access: Mail, in person, online. Both court and visitors may perform in person searches. No search fee. Required to search: name, years to search. Civil cases indexed by defendant, plaintiff. Civil records on index cards and books. Record index searchable on computer back to 1980. Participates in the free state online court record system at http://casenet.osca.state.mo.us/casenet. Online records go back to 1992.

Criminal Records: Access: Mail, in person, online. Both court and visitors may perform in person searches. No search fee. Required to search: name, years to search, offense. Criminal records on index cards and books. Record index searchable on computer back to 1980. Online access to criminal records is the same as civil.

General Information: Public access terminal is available. No juvenile, mental, expunged, dismissed, or suspended imposition of sentence records released.

SASE required. Turnaround time 1 week. Fax notes: Fee to fax results is $2.00 per page. Copy fee: $.25 per page. Certification fee: $2.00. Fee payee: Shannon County Circuit Clerk. Personal checks accepted. Prepayment is required.

Associate Circuit Court PO Box 845, Eminence, MO 65466-0845; 573-226-5515; Fax: 573-226-3239. Hours: 8AM-4:30PM (CST). *Misdemeanor, Civil Actions Under $45,000, Eviction, Small Claims, Probate.*

Civil Records: Access: Mail, fax, in person, online. Only the court performs in person searches; visitors may not. Search fee: $10.00 per name. Required to search: name, years to search. Civil cases indexed by defendant, plaintiff. Civil records on index cards since 1979, archived since 1881. Participates in the free state online court record system at http://casenet.osca.state.mo.us/casenet. Online records go back to 1992.

Criminal Records: Access: Mail, fax, in person, online. Only the court performs in person searches; visitors may not. Search fee: $10.00 per name. Required to search: name, years to search, DOB; also helpful: SSN. Criminal records on computer since 1992; prior on index cards to 1979. Online access to criminal records is the same as civil.

General Information: No juvenile, mental, expunged, dismissed, or suspended imposition of sentence records released. SASE required. Turnaround time 1 week. Fax notes: Fee to fax results in $3.00 per page. Copy fee: $.25 per page. Certification fee: $3.00. Fee payee: Associate Circuit Court. Personal checks accepted. Prepayment is required.

Shelby County

Circuit Court PO Box 176, Shelbyville, MO 63469; 573-633-2151; Fax: 573-633-1004. Hours: 8AM-4:30PM (CST). *Felony, Misdemeanor, Civil Actions Over $45,000.*

Civil Records: Access: Mail, fax, in person. Only the court may perform in person searches. No search fee. Required to search: name, years to search. Civil cases indexed by defendant, plaintiff. Civil records on index cards since 1975, prior on books since 1835.

Criminal Records: Access: Mail, fax, in person. Only the court may perform in person searches. No search fee. Required to search: name, years to search. Criminal records on index cards since 1975, prior on books since 1835.

General Information: No juvenile, mental, expunged, dismissed, or suspended imposition of sentence records released. SASE required. Turnaround time 1 day. Fax notes: Fee to fax results is $3.00 per document. Copy fee: $.25 per page. Certification fee: $2.00. Fee payee: Shelby County Circuit Clerk. Personal checks accepted. Prepayment is required.

Associate Circuit Court PO Box 206, Shelbyville, MO 63469; 573-633-2251; Fax: 573-633-2142. Hours: 8AM-4:30PM (CST). *Misdemeanor, Civil Actions Under $25,000, Eviction, Small Claims, Probate.*

Civil Records: Access: Fax, mail, in person. Both court and visitors may perform in person searches. No search fee. Required to search: name, years to search. Civil cases indexed by defendant, plaintiff. Civil records on index cards, archived from 1845 to 1950.

Criminal Records: Access: Phone, fax, mail, in person. Both court and visitors may perform in person searches. No search fee. Required to search: name, years to search, DOB. Criminal records on index cards, archived from 1845 to 1950.

General Information: No juvenile, mental, expunged, dismissed, or suspended imposition of sentence records released. SASE not required. Turnaround time 2 weeks. Fax notes: No fee to fax results. Copy fee: $.25 per page. Certification fee: $1.50. Fee payee: Probate Court or Associate Circuit Court. Personal checks accepted.

St. Charles County

Circuit Court 300 N 2nd St, St. Charles, MO 63301; 636-949-7900 X3098; Fax: 636-949-7390. Hours: 8:30AM-5PM (CST). *Felony, Misdemeanor, Civil Actions Over $25,000.*

Civil Records: Access: Mail, online, in person. Both court and visitors may perform in person searches. No search fee. Required to search: name, years to search. Civil cases indexed by defendant, plaintiff. Civil records on index cards since 1971, prior on books; judgment records (A-M) on computer since 1987. Participates in the free state online court record system at http://casenet.osca.state.mo.us/casenet. Online civil records go back to 1/1994. Clerk refers all record requests to the Sheriff or Highway Patrol.

Criminal Records: Access: Online, in person. Visitors must perform in person searches for themselves. No search fee. Required to search: name, years to search; also helpful: DOB. Criminal records on index cards since 1971, prior on books; judgment records (A-M) on computer since 1987. Online access to criminal records is the same as civil. Online criminal records go back to 10/1992.

General Information: Public access terminal is available. No juvenile, mental, expunged, dismissed, or suspended imposition of sentence records released. SASE required. Turnaround time varies. Copy fee: $.25 per page. Certification fee: $1.00. Fee payee: St. Charles Circuit Clerk. Personal checks accepted. Prepayment is required.

Associate Circuit Court 300 N 2nd, #436, St. Charles, MO 63301; 636-949-3043. Hours: 8:30AM-5:00PM (CST). *Civil Actions Under $25,000, Eviction, Small Claims, Probate.*

Civil Records: Access: Online, in person. Visitors must perform in person searches for themselves. No search fee. Required to search: name, years to search. Civil cases indexed by defendant, plaintiff. Civil records on computer since 1988 (judgments only), prior on index cards and books. Participates in the free state online court system at http://casenet.osca.state.mo.us/casenet. Online civil records go back to 1/1994.

General Information: SASE required. Turnaround time varies. Copy fee: $.25 per page. Fee payee: Associate Circuit Court. Only cashiers checks and money orders accepted. Prepayment is required.

St. Clair County

Circuit & Associate Circuit Courts PO Box 493, Osceola, MO 64776; 417-646-2226; Fax: 417-646-2401. Hours: 8AM-4:30PM (CST). *Felony, Misdemeanor, Civil, Eviction, Small Claims, Probate.*

Civil Records: Access: Mail, in person. Both court and visitors may perform in person searches. Search fee: $2.00 per name. Required to search: name, years to search. Civil cases indexed by defendant, plaintiff. Civil records on computer since 1991 for judgments, on index cards since 1980, prior records on index books.

Criminal Records: Access: Mail, in person. Both court and visitors may perform in person searches. Search fee: $2.00 per name. Required to search: name, years to search, DOB. Criminal records on computer since 1991, on index cards since 1980, prior records on index books.

General Information: No juvenile, mental, expunged, dismissed, or suspended imposition of sentence records released. SASE required. Turnaround time 1-2 days. No copy fee. Certification fee: $1.50. Fee payee: St Clair County Circuit Clerk. Personal checks accepted. Prepayment is required.

St. Francois County

Circuit Court - Division I & II 1 N Washington, Rm 303, Farmington, MO 63640; 573-756-4551; Fax: 573-756-3733. Hours: 8AM-5PM (CST). *Felony, Civil Actions Over $25,000.*

Civil Records: Access: Fax, mail, in person. Both court and visitors may perform in person searches. No search fee. Required to search: name, years to search. Civil cases indexed by defendant, plaintiff. Civil records on computer since 6/90, on microfiche since 1970, archived since 1821.

Criminal Records: Access: Fax, mail, in person. Both court and visitors may perform in person searches. No search fee. Required to search: name, years to search; also helpful: DOB, SSN. Criminal records on computer since 3/1/93.

General Information: Public access terminal is available. No juvenile, mental, expunged, dismissed, or suspended imposition of sentence records released. SASE required. Turnaround time 1-2 weeks. Copy fee: $.25 per page. Certification fee: $1.50. Fee payee: Clerk of Circuit Court. Business checks accepted.

Associate Circuit Court County Courthouse, 2nd Fl, 1 N. Washington, Rm 202, Farmington, MO 63640; 573-756-5755; Fax: 573-756-8173. Hours: 8AM-5PM (CST). *Misdemeanor, Civil Actions Under $25,000, Eviction, Small Claims, Probate.*

Civil Records: Access: Phone, mail, fax, in person. Only the court performs in person searches; visitors may not. No search fee. Required to search: name, years to search. Civil cases indexed by defendant, plaintiff. Civil records on index cards since 1979; on computer back to 1990.

Criminal Records: Access: Mail, fax, in person. Only the court performs in person searches; visitors may not. No search fee. Required to search: name, years to search. Criminal records on computer back to 1990; other records go back to 1980.

General Information: No juvenile, mental, expunged, dismissed, or suspended imposition of sentence records released. SASE not required. No copy fee. Business checks accepted.

St. Louis County

Circuit Court of St. Louis County 7900 Carondolet, Clayton, MO 63105-1766; 314-615-8029; Fax: 314-615-8739. Hours: 8AM-5PM (CST). *Felony, Misdemeanor, Civil.*

www.stlouisco.com/circuitcourt

Civil Records: Access: Phone, fax, mail, in person. Both court and visitors may perform in person searches. No search fee. Required to search: name, years to search; also helpful: address. Civil cases indexed by defendant, plaintiff. Civil records on computer back to 1990, prior on index cards. Permanent records on microfiche since 1978, earlier in books. Case files archived for 25 years.

Criminal Records: Access: Phone, fax, mail, in person. Both court and visitors may perform in person searches. No search fee. Required to search: name, years to search, DOB; also helpful: address, SSN. Criminal records on computer back to 1990; prior on index cards. Permanent records on microfiche since 1978, earlier in books. Case files archived for 25 years.

General Information: Public access terminal is available. No juvenile, paternity, mental, expunged, dismissed, or suspended imposition of sentence records released. SASE not required. Turnaround time up to 5 days. Copy fee: $.30 per page. Certification fee: $1.50 plus $.30 per page after first. Fee payee: Circuit Clerk. Personal checks accepted. Prepayment is required.

Associate Circuit - Civil Division 7900 Carondolet, Clayton, MO 63105; 314-615-8090; Probate phone: 314-615-2629; Fax: 314-615-2689.

Hours: 8AM-5PM (CST). *Civil Actions Under $25,000, Eviction, Small Claims, Probate.*

Note: Probate records are available free on the state online court record system at http://casenet.osca.state.mo.us/casenet.

Civil Records: Access: Phone, mail, in person. Both court and visitors may perform in person searches. No search fee. Required to search: name, years to search. Civil cases indexed by defendant, plaintiff. Civil records on computer since 1986, prior on cards.

General Information: Public access terminal is available. No juvenile, mental, expunged, dismissed, paternity, suspended imposition of sentence records released. SASE required. Turnaround time 1 week. Copy fee: $.30 per page. Certification fee: $1.50. Fee payee: Circuit Clerk-Civil Division. Personal checks accepted. Prepayment is required.

Associate Circuit Court - Criminal Division 7900 Carondolet Av, Clayton, MO 63105; 314-615-2675; Fax: 314-615-2689. *Misdemeanor.*

www.stlouisco.com/circuitcourt

Criminal Records: Access: Phone, mail, fax, in person. Both court and visitors may perform in person searches. No search fee. Required to search: name, years to search, DOB, offense, date of offense. Criminal records on computer back to 1990, prior on index cards. Permanent records on microfiche since 1978, earlier in books. Case files archived for 25 years.

General Information: Public access terminal is available. No juvenile, mental, expunged, dismissed, or suspended imposition of sentence records released. SASE required. Turnaround time varies. Copy fee: $.30 per page. Certification fee: $1.50. Fee payee: Circuit Clerk. Personal checks accepted. Prepayment required.

St. Louis City

Circuit & Associate Circuit Courts 10 N Tucker, Civil Courts Bldg, St Louis, MO 63101; 314-622-4405; Fax: 314-622-4537. Hours: 8:00AM-5:00PM (CST). *Civil, Eviction, Small Claims, Probate.*

Civil Records: Access: Mail, online, in person. No search fee. Required to search: name, years to search. Civil cases indexed by defendant, plaintiff. Civil records on computer since 1/80, on index cards since early 1800s. Remote access is through MoBar Net and is open only to attorneys. Call 314-535-1950 for information. Probate records are available free online at http://casenet.osca.state.mo.us/casenet. Online probate records go back to 5/31/2000.

General Information: Public access terminal is available. No sealed or confidential records released. SASE required. Turnaround time usually 1 week. Copy fee: $.20 per page. Certification fee: $3.50 for 1st page. Fee payee: City of St. Louis Circuit Clerk. Only cashiers checks and money orders accepted. Prepayment is required.

City of St Louis Circuit Court 1320 Market, St Louis, MO 63103; 314-622-4582; Fax: 314-622-3202. Hours: 8AM-5PM *Felony, Misdemeanor, Probate.*

Note: The Probate Court participates in the free state online court record system at http://casenet.osca.state.mo.us/casenet.

Criminal Records: Access: In person only. Both court and visitors may perform in person searches. No search fee. Required to search: name, years to search, DOB, signed release; also helpful: address, SSN. Criminal records on computer since 1990 for misdemeanor; since 1992 for felony.

General Information: No juvenile, mental, expunged, dismissed, or suspended imposition of sentence records released. SASE required. Copy fee: $.50 per page. Certification fee: $3.50. Fee payee: City of St. Louis Circuit Clerk. Business checks accepted. Prepayment is required.

Ste. Genevieve County

Circuit Court 55 S 3rd, Rm 23, Ste Genevieve, MO 63670; 573-883-2705; Fax: 573-883-9351. Hours: 8AM-5PM (CST). *Felony, Misdemeanor, Civil Actions Over $25,000.*

Civil Records: Access: In person only. Visitors must perform in person searches for themselves. No search fee. Required to search: name, years to search. Civil cases indexed by defendant, plaintiff. Civil records on books since early 1800s, recent civil records (1995) computerized.

Criminal Records: Access: In person only. Visitors must perform in person searches for themselves. No search fee. Required to search: name, years to search. Criminal Record indexes on books, not computerized.

General Information: Public access terminal is available. No juvenile, mental, expunged, paternity, dismissed, or suspended imposition of sentence records released. Copy fee: $1.00 per page. Certification fee: $1.50. Fee payee: St Genevieve County Circuit Clerk. Business checks accepted. Prepayment is required.

Associate Circuit Court 3rd and Market, Ste Genevieve, MO 63670; 573-883-2265; Fax: 573-883-9351. Hours: 8AM-5PM (CST). *Misdemeanor, Civil Actions Under $45,000, Eviction, Small Claims, Probate.*

Civil Records: Access: In person only. Visitors must perform in person searches for themselves. No search fee. Required to search: name, years to search. Civil cases indexed by defendant, plaintiff. Civil records on books.

Criminal Records: Access: In person only. Visitors must perform in person searches for themselves. No search fee. Required to search: name, years to search. Criminal records on books.

General Information: Public access terminal is available. No juvenile, mental, expunged, dismissed, or suspended imposition of sentence records released. Copy fee: $1.00 per page. Certification fee: $2.50. Only cashiers checks and money orders accepted.

Stoddard County

Circuit Court PO Box 30, Bloomfield, MO 63825; 573-568-4640; Fax: 573-568-2271. Hours: 8:30AM-4:30PM (CST). *Felony, Misdemeanor, Civil Actions Over $25,000.*

Civil Records: Access: Fax, mail, in person, online. Both court and visitors may perform in person searches. No search fee. Required to search: name, years to search. Civil cases indexed by defendant, plaintiff. Civil records on computer since 1991, prior on cards and books. Access to civil records available free at http://casenet.osca.state.mo.us/casenet/. At the web site, select the judicial district, then search by name, case # or date. Online records go back to 7/1/2001.

Criminal Records: Access: Mail, in person, online. Both court and visitors may perform in person searches. No search fee. Required to search: name, years to search; also helpful: DOB, SSN. Criminal records on computer since 1991, prior on cards and books. Online access to criminal records is the same as civil.

General Information: Public access terminal is available. No juvenile, mental, expunged, dismissed, or suspended imposition of sentence records released. SASE required. Turnaround time 1 day. Copy fee: $.10 per page. Certification fee: $1.50. Fee payee: Stoddard County Circuit Clerk. Personal checks accepted.

Division III & Probate PO Box 518, Bloomfield, MO 63825; 573-568-4640 ext 3; Fax: 573-568-3229. Hours: 7:30AM-4PM (CST). *Civil Actions Under $25,000, Eviction, Small Claims, Probate.*

Associate Circuit Court - Criminal Division II PO Box 218, Bloomfield, MO 63825;

573-568-4671; Fax: 573-568-2299. Hours: 8:30AM-4:30PM (CST). *Misdemeanor.*

Criminal Records: Access: In person, online. Visitors must perform in person searches for themselves. No search fee. Required to search: name, years to search, DOB, SSN, signed release. Criminal records on index cards, traffic on computer since 1996. Access to records is available free at http://casenet.osca.state.mo.us/casenet/. At the web site, select the judicial district, then search by name, case # or date. Online records go back to 7/1/2001.

General Information: Public access terminal is available. No juvenile, mental, expunged, dismissed, or suspended imposition of sentence records released. Copy fee: $.10. Certification fee: $1.50. Fee payee: Stoddard County. Personal checks accepted. Prepayment is required.

Stone County

Circuit Court PO Box 18, Galena, MO 65656; 417-357-6114; 417-357-6115 child support; Fax: 417-357-6163. Hours: 7:30AM-Noon; 12:30PM-4:00PM (CST). *Felony, Misdemeanor, Civil Actions Over $25,000.*

Civil Records: Access: Phone, fax, mail, in person. Both court and visitors may perform in person searches. No search fee. Required to search: name, years to search. Civil cases indexed by defendant, plaintiff. Civil records on cards and books, archived since 1852; computerized records since 1992.

Criminal Records: Access: Phone, fax, mail, in person. Both court and visitors may perform in person searches. No search fee. Required to search: name, years to search; also helpful: DOB, SSN. Criminal records on cards and books, archived since 1852; computerized records since 1992.

General Information: No juvenile, mental, expunged, dismissed, or suspended imposition of sentence records released. SASE required. Turnaround time 1 week. Fax notes: $3.00 per page. Copy fee: $.25 per page. Certification fee: $1.50. Fee payee: Circuit Court. Personal checks accepted.

Circuit Court - Division II & III PO Box 186, Galena, MO 65656; 417-357-6511; Fax: 417-357-6163. Hours: 7:30AM-4PM (CST). *Misdemeanor, Civil Actions, Eviction, Small Claims, Probate.*

Note: No collar limit on civil actions; prior to 2001, the civil action maximum limit was $25,000.

Civil Records: Access: Phone, fax, mail, in person. Both court and visitors may perform in person searches. No search fee. Required to search: name, years to search; also helpful: address. Civil cases indexed by defendant, plaintiff. Civil records go back to 1970.

Criminal Records: Access: Phone, fax, mail, in person. Both court and visitors may perform in person searches. No search fee. Required to search: name, years to search, DOB, SSN, signed release. Criminal records on computer back to 1990 and on microfiche.

General Information: No juvenile, mental, expunged, dismissed, or suspended imposition of sentence records released. SASE required. Turnaround time 2-3 weeks. Fax notes: $3.00 per page. Copy fee: $.25 per page. Certification fee: $2.50. Fee payee: Circuit Court Division II. Only cashiers checks and money orders accepted. Prepayment is required.

Sullivan County

Circuit & Associate Circuit Courts Courthouse, 109 N Main, Milan, MO 63556-1358; 660-265-4717 (Circ,); 660-265-3303 (Assoc. Circ); Fax: 660-265-5071. Hours: 9:00AM-4:30PM (CST). *Felony, Misdemeanor, Civil Actions, Eviction, Small Claims, Probate.*

Civil Records: Access: In person only. Visitors must perform in person searches for themselves. No search fee. Required to search: name, years to search. Civil

cases indexed by defendant, plaintiff. Civil records on index cards since 1979, prior on books.

Criminal Records: Access: In person only. Visitors must perform in person searches for themselves. No search fee. Required to search: name, years to search; also helpful: DOB, SSN. Criminal records on index cards since 1979, prior on books.

General Information: Public access terminal is available. No juvenile, mental, expunged, dismissed, or suspended imposition of sentence records released. Copy fee: $.25 per page. Certification fee: $1.50. Fee payee: Consolidated Circuit Court of Sullivan County. Personal checks accepted. Prepayment is required.

Taney County

Circuit Court PO Box 335, Forsyth, MO 65653; 417-546-7230; Fax: 417-546-6133. Hours: 8AM-5PM (CST). *Felony, Misdemeanor, Civil Actions Over $25,000.*

Civil Records: Access: Mail, in person. Both court and visitors may perform in person searches. Search fee: $4.00 per name. Required to search: name, years to search. Civil cases indexed by defendant, plaintiff. Civil records on computer since 1/95, prior on index cards and books since 1885.

Criminal Records: Access: Mail, in person. Both court and visitors may perform in person searches. Search fee: $4.00 per name. Required to search: name, years to search, DOB; also helpful: SSN. Criminal records on computer since 1/95, prior on index cards and books since 1885.

General Information: Public access terminal is available. No juvenile, mental, expunged, dismissed, or suspended imposition of sentence records released. SASE helpful. Copy fee: $.25 per page. Certification fee: $1.50. Fee payee: Circuit Clerk. Personal checks accepted. Prepayment is required.

Associate Circuit Court PO Box 129, Forsyth, MO 65653; 417-546-7212; Fax: 417-546-4513. Hours: 8AM-5PM (CST). *Misdemeanor, Civil Actions Under $25,000, Eviction, Small Claims, Probate.*

Civil Records: Access: Mail, in person. Only the court performs in person searches; visitors may not. Search fee: $4.00 per name. Required to search: name, years to search. Civil cases indexed by defendant, plaintiff. Civil records on computer since 1984, prior on cards and books.

Criminal Records: Access: Mail, in person. Only the court performs in person searches; visitors may not. Search fee: $4.00 per name. Required to search: name, years to search, DOB, SSN. Criminal records on computer since 1984, prior on cards and books.

General Information: No juvenile, mental, expunged, dismissed, or suspended imposition of sentence records released. SASE required. Turnaround time 2 days, more if busy. Copy fee: $.25 per page. Certification fee: $1.50. Fee payee: Associate Circuit Court. Personal checks accepted. Prepayment is required.

Texas County

Circuit Court 210 N Grand, Houston, MO 65483; 417-967-3742; Fax: 417-967-4220. Hours: 8:30-Noon; 12:30PM-4:30PM (CST). *Felony, Misdemeanor, Civil Actions Over $45,000.*

Civil Records: Access: In person only. Visitors must perform in person searches. No search fee. Required to search: name, years to search. Civil cases indexed by defendant, plaintiff. Civil records on index books since 1900s.

Criminal Records: Access: In person only. Visitors must perform in person searches. No search fee. Required to search: name, years to search. Criminal records on index books since 1900s.

General Information: No juvenile, mental, expunged, dismissed, or suspended imposition of sentence records released. Copy fee: $1.00 per page. Certification fee: $2.00. Fee payee: Texas County Circuit Clerk. Personal checks accepted. Prepayment is required.

Associate Circuit Court County Courthouse, 210 N Grand, #302, Houston, MO 65483; 417-967-3663; Fax: 417-967-4128. Hours: 8AM-noon; 1-5PM (CST). *Misdemeanor, Civil Actions Under $45,000, Eviction, Small Claims, Probate.*

Civil Records: Access: Phone, fax, mail, in person. Only the court performs in person searches; visitors may not. No search fee. Required to search: name, years to search. Civil cases indexed by defendant, plaintiff. Civil records on index cards since 1979, prior on cards and books.

Criminal Records: Access: Phone, fax, mail, in person. Only the court performs in person searches; visitors may not. No search fee. Required to search: name, years to search, SSN. Criminal records on index cards since 1979, prior on cards and books.

General Information: No juvenile, mental, expunged, dismissed, or suspended imposition of sentence records released. SASE required. Turnaround time 7-10 days, phone turnaround time immediate. Fax notes: $2.00 for first page, $.50 each add'l. Copy fee: $1.00 per page. Certification fee: $2.00. Fee payee: Associate Circuit Court. Business checks accepted.

Vernon County

Circuit Court Courthouse, 3rd Fl, Nevada, MO 64772; 417-448-2525; Fax: 417-448-2512. Hours: 8AM-4:30PM (CST). *Felony, Misdemeanor, Civil Actions Over $25,000.*

Civil Records: Access: Fax, mail, in person, online, email. Both court and visitors may perform in person searches. Search fee: $5.00 per name. Required to search: name, years to search. Civil cases indexed by defendant, plaintiff. Civil records go back to 1863; on computer back to 2000. Judgments only on index cards. Participates in the free state online court record system at http://casenet.osca.state.mo.us/casenet. Online records go back to 9/26/1999. Online records include probate court.

Criminal Records: Access: Fax, mail, in person, online. Both court and visitors may perform in person searches. Search fee: $5.00 per name. Required to search: name, years to search, DOB; also helpful: SSN. Criminal records go back to 1863; on computer back to 2000. Online access to criminal records is the same as civil.

General Information: Public access terminal is available. No juvenile, mental, expunged, dismissed, or suspended imposition of sentence records released. SASE required. Turnaround time varies. Fax notes: Will not fax results. Copy fee: $.20 per page. Certification fee: $1.50. Fee payee: Vernon County Circuit Clerk. Personal checks accepted. Prepayment is required.

Associate Circuit Court County Courthouse, Nevada, MO 64772; 417-448-2550; Fax: 417-448-2512. Hours: 8:30AM-4:30PM (CST). *Misdemeanor, Civil Actions Under $25,000, Eviction, Small Claims, Probate.*

Civil Records: Access: Fax, mail, in person, online. Both court and visitors may perform in person searches. Search fee: $5.00 per name. Required to search: name, years to search. Civil cases indexed by defendant, plaintiff. Civil records on computer since 1990, on index cards since 1979, prior on index books to 1863. Participates in the free state online court record system at http://casenet.osca.state.mo.us/casenet. Records go back to 9/2000.

Criminal Records: Access: Mail, in person, online. Both court and visitors may perform in person searches. Search fee: $5.00 per name. Required to search: name, years to search; also helpful: DOB, SSN. Criminal

records on computer since 1990, on index cards since 1979, prior on index books to 1863. Online access to criminal records is the same as civil.

General Information: Public access terminal is available. No juvenile, mental, expunged, dismissed, or suspended imposition of sentence records released. SASE required. Turnaround time 1-2 weeks. Fax notes: Will not fax results. Copy fee: $.20 per page. Certification fee: $1.50. Fee payee: Circuit Court. Personal checks accepted. Prepayment is required.

Warren County

Circuit Court 104 W Main, Warrenton, MO 63383; 636-456-3363; Fax: 636-456-2422. Hours: 8AM-4:30PM (CST). *Felony, Misdemeanor, Civil Actions Over $25,000.*

Civil Records: Access: Online, in person. Visitors must perform in person searches for themselves. No search fee. Required to search: name, years to search. Civil cases indexed by defendant, plaintiff. Civil records on index cards since 1976, prior on books. Participates in the free state online court record system at http://casenet.osca.state.mo.us/casenet. Online records go back to 9/20/1999.

Criminal Records: Access: Online, in person. Visitors must perform in person searches for themselves. No search fee. Required to search: name, years to search. Criminal records on index cards since 1976, prior on books. Online access to criminal records is the same as civil.

General Information: No juvenile, mental, expunged, dismissed, or suspended imposition of sentence records released. Copy fee: $.25 per page. Certification fee: $1.00. Fee payee: Warren County Circuit Clerk. Business checks accepted. Prepayment is required.

Associate Circuit Court Warren County Courthouse, 104 W Main, Warrenton, MO 63383; 636-456-3375; Fax: 636-456-2422. Hours: 8:30AM-4:30PM (CST). *Misdemeanor, Civil Actions Under $25,000, Eviction, Small Claims, Probate.*

http://casenet.osca.state.mo.us/casenet

Civil Records: Access: Phone, fax, online, mail, in person. Both court and visitors may perform in person searches. No search fee. Required to search: name, years to search. Civil cases indexed by defendant, plaintiff. Civil records on index cards since 1979, prior on books. Records may be available free on state online court system at http://casenet.osca.state.mo.us/casenet.

Criminal Records: Access: Phone, fax, mail, online, in person. Only the court performs in person searches; visitors may not. No search fee. Required to search: name, years to search; also helpful: DOB, SSN. Criminal records on computer since 2/92, on cards since 1979, prior on books. Online access to criminal records is the same as civil.

General Information: No juvenile, mental, expunged, dismissed, or suspended imposition of sentence records released. SASE not required. Turnaround time 1 week. Fax notes: $1.00 per page. Copy fee: $.25 per page. Certification fee: $1.50 plus $1.00 per page. Fee payee: Associate Circuit Clerk. Personal checks accepted. Prepayment is required.

Washington County

Circuit Court PO Box 216, Potosi, MO 63664; 573-438-4171; Fax: 573-438-7900. Hours: 8AM-5PM (CST). *Felony, Misdemeanor, Civil Actions Over $45,000.*

Civil Records: Access: Mail, in person. Both court and visitors may perform in person searches. No search fee. Required to search: name, years to search. Civil cases indexed by defendant, plaintiff. Civil records on index cards since 1976, prior on books.

Criminal Records: Access: Mail, in person. Both court and visitors may perform in person searches. No search

fee. Required to search: name, years to search. Criminal records on index cards since 1976, prior on books.

General Information: No juvenile, mental, expunged, dismissed, or suspended imposition of sentence records released. SASE required. Turnaround time 1-2 days. Copy fee: $.50 per page. Certification fee: $2.00. Fee payee: Washington County Circuit Clerk. Personal checks accepted. Prepayment is required.

Associate Circuit Court 102 N Missouri St, Potosi, MO 63664; 573-438-3691; Fax: 573-438-7900. Hours: 8AM-5PM (CST). *Misdemeanor, Civil Actions Under $45,000, Eviction, Small Claims, Probate.*

Civil Records: Access: Phone, fax, mail, in person. Only the court performs in person searches; visitors may not. No search fee. Required to search: name, years to search. Civil cases indexed by defendant, plaintiff. Civil records on index cards for 12 years, computerized since 1996, older records archived.

Criminal Records: Access: Phone, fax, mail, in person. Only the court performs in person searches; visitors may not. No search fee. Required to search: name, years to search; also helpful: DOB, SSN. Criminal records on index cards for 12 years, computerized since 1996, older records archived.

General Information: No juvenile, mental, expunged, dismissed, or suspended imposition of sentence records released. SASE required. Turnaround time 1 week. Copy fee: $.50 per page. Fee payee: Associate Circuit Clerk. Personal checks accepted. Prepayment is required.

Wayne County

Circuit Court PO Box 78, Greenville, MO 63944; 573-224-3014; Fax: 573-224-3015. 8:30AM-4:30PM *Felony, Misdemeanor, Civil Actions Over $45,000.*

Civil Records: Access: Mail, in person. Both court and visitors may perform in person searches. Search fee: $14.00 per name. Required to search: name, years to search. Civil cases indexed by defendant, plaintiff. Civil records on index cards since 1978, prior on books.

Criminal Records: Access: Mail, in person. Both court and visitors may perform in person searches. Search fee: $14.00 per name. Required to search: name, years to search; also helpful: DOB. Criminal records on index cards since 1978, prior on books.

General Information: No juvenile, mental, expunged, dismissed, or suspended imposition of sentence records released. SASE required. Turnaround time 1 week. Copy fee: $.25 per page. Certification fee: $2.00. Fee payee: Wayne County Circuit Clerk. Personal checks accepted. Prepayment is required.

Associate Circuit Court PO Box 47, Greenville, MO 63944; 573-224-3052; Fax: 573-224-3225. Hours: 8:30AM-4:30PM (CST). *Misdemeanor, Civil Actions Under $45,000, Eviction, Small Claims, Probate.*

Civil Records: Access: Phone, fax, mail, in person. Both court and visitors may perform in person searches. No search fee. Required to search: name, years to search. Civil cases indexed by defendant, plaintiff. Civil records on index cards since 1979; on computer back to 4/2001.

Criminal Records: Access: Phone, fax, mail, in person. Only the court performs in person searches; visitors may not. No search fee. Required to search: name, years to search, DOB; also helpful: SSN. Criminal records on computer since 1992, prior on index cards.

General Information: Public access terminal is available. (Access terminal is in Circuit Court office.) No juvenile, mental, expunged, dismissed, or suspended imposition of sentence records released. SASE required. Turnaround time 1 day. Fax notes: $.50 per page. Copy fee: $.25 per page. Certification fee: $1.50 per page. Fee payee: Associate Circuit Court. Personal checks accepted.

Webster County

Circuit Court PO Box 529, Marshfield, MO 65706; 417-859-2006; Fax: 417-468-3786. Hours: 8AM-5PM (CST). *Felony, Civil Actions Over $25,000.*

www.positech.net/~dcourt

Civil Records: Access: Fax, mail, in person, online. Both court and visitors may perform in person searches. No search fee. Required to search: name, years to search. Civil cases indexed by defendant, plaintiff. Civil records on computer since 1976 (judgment index). Participates in the free state online court record system at http://casenet.osca.state.mo.us/casenet.

Criminal Records: Access: Fax, mail, in person, online. Only the court performs in person searches; visitors may not. No search fee. Required to search: name, years to search, DOB. Criminal records on computer since 1976 (judgment index). Online access to criminal records is the same as civil.

General Information: Public access terminal is available. (Judgments only.) No juvenile, mental, expunged, dismissed, or suspended imposition of sentence records released. SASE required. Turnaround time 1 day. Fax notes: $2.00 per page. Copy fee: $.15 per page. Certification fee: $2.00. Fee payee: Webster County Circuit Clerk. Personal checks accepted.

Associate Circuit Court Courthouse, Marshfield, MO 65706; 417-859-2041; Fax: 417-859-6265. Hours: 8AM-5PM (CST). *Misdemeanor, Civil Actions Under $25,000, Eviction, Small Claims, Probate.*

www.positech.net/~dcourt

Civil Records: Access: Phone, fax, mail, in person, online. Only the court performs in person searches; visitors may not. No search fee. Required to search: name, years to search. Civil cases indexed by defendant, plaintiff. Civil records on computer since 1992; prior records on index cards since 1980 & on books. Access to civil records available free at http://casenet.osca.state.mo.us/casenet/. At the web site, select the judicial district, then search by name, case # or date.

Criminal Records: Access: Mail, in person, online. Only the court performs in person searches; visitors may not. No search fee. Required to search: name, years to search; also helpful: DOB, SSN. Criminal records on computer since 1992. Online access to criminal records is the same as civil.

General Information: No juvenile, mental, expunged, dismissed, or suspended imposition of sentence records released. SASE required. Turnaround time varies. Copy fee: $1.00 per page. Certification fee: $1.50. Fee payee: Associate Circuit Court. Only cashiers checks and money orders accepted. Prepayment is required.

Worth County

Circuit Court PO Box 340, Grant City, MO 64456; 660-564-2210; Fax: 660-564-2432. Hours: 8:30AM-4:30PM (CST). *Felony, Misdemeanor, Civil Actions Over $45,000.*

Civil Records: Access: Mail, in person. Both court and visitors may perform in person searches. No search fee. Required to search: name, years to search. Civil cases indexed by defendant, plaintiff. Civil records on computer since 1990, prior on index cards.

Criminal Records: Access: Mail, in person. Both court and visitors may perform in person searches. No search fee. Required to search: name, years to search. Criminal records on computer since 1990, prior on index cards.

General Information: Public access terminal is available. No juvenile, mental, expunged, dismissed, or suspended imposition of sentence records released. SASE required. Turnaround time same day. Copy fee: $.20 per page. Certification fee: $2.50. Fee payee: Worth County Circuit Clerk. Personal checks accepted. Prepayment is required.

Associate Circuit Court PO Box 428, Grant City, MO 64456; 660-564-2152; Fax: 660-564-2432. Hours: 9AM-4:30PM (CST). *Misdemeanor, Civil Actions Under $45,000, Eviction, Small Claims, Probate.*

Civil Records: Access: In person only. Visitors must perform in person searches for themselves. No search fee. Required to search: name, years to search. Civil cases indexed by defendant, plaintiff. Civil records on index cards since 1979, prior on index books.

Criminal Records: Access: Mail, in person. Both court and visitors may perform in person searches. No search fee. Required to search: name, years to search. Criminal records on index cards since 1979, prior on index books.

General Information: No juvenile, mental, expunged, dismissed, or suspended imposition of sentence records released. SASE required. Turnaround time varies. Copy fee: $1.00 per page. Certification fee: $2.50. Fee payee: Associate Circuit Court. Personal checks accepted. Prepayment is required.

Wright County

Circuit Court PO Box 39, Hartville, MO 65667; 417-741-7121; Fax: 417-741-7504. Hours: 8AM-4:30PM (CST). *Felony, Misdemeanor, Civil Actions Over $25,000.*

Civil Records: Access: Mail, in person. Both court and visitors may perform in person searches. No search fee. Required to search: name, years to search. Civil cases indexed by defendant, plaintiff. Civil records on index cards since 1979, prior on books.

Criminal Records: Access: Mail, in person. Both court and visitors may perform in person searches. No search fee. Required to search: name, years to search. Criminal records on index cards since 1979, prior on books.

General Information: No juvenile, mental, expunged, dismissed, or suspended imposition of sentence records released. SASE not required. Turnaround time 1 day. Copy fee: $.25 per page. Certification fee: $2.00. Fee payee: Wright County Circuit Clerk. Personal checks accepted. Prepayment is required.

Associate Circuit Court PO Box 58, Hartville, MO 65667; 417-741-6450; Fax: 417-741-7504. Hours: 8AM-4:30PM (CST). *Misdemeanor, Civil Actions Under $25,000, Eviction, Small Claims, Probate.*

Civil Records: Access: Phone, fax, mail, in person. Only the court performs in person searches; visitors may not. No search fee. Required to search: name, years to search. Civil cases indexed by defendant, plaintiff. Civil records on index cards since 1979, prior on books; on computer back to 1990.

Criminal Records: Access: Phone, fax, mail, in person. Only the court performs in person searches; visitors may not. No search fee. Required to search: name, years to search; also helpful: DOB, SSN. Criminal records on computer since 1989, prior on cards and books; on computer back to 1990.

General Information: No juvenile, mental, expunged, or dismissed records released. SASE required. Turnaround time 1 week. Fax notes: Fee to fax results is $1.00 per page. Copy fee: $.25 per page. Certification fee: $1.00. Fee payee: Associate Circuit Court. Only cashiers checks and money orders accepted.

Missouri Recording Offices

ORGANIZATION: 114 counties and one independent city, 115 recording offices. The recording officer is. Recorder of Deeds. The City of St. Louis has its own recording office. See the City/County Locator section at the end of this chapter for ZIP Codes that cover both the city and county of St. Louis. The entire state is in the Central Time Zone (CST).

REAL ESTATE RECORDS: A few counties will perform real estate searches. Copy and certification fees vary.

UCC RECORDS: Missouri was a dual filing state. Until 07/2001, financing statements were filed both at the state level and with the Recorder of Deeds, except for consumer goods, farm related and real estate related filings, which were filed only with the Recorder. Now only real estate relating filings are filed at the county level. Most all counties will perform UCC searches. Use search request form UCC-11. Search fees are usually $14.00 per debtor name without copies and $28.00 with copies. Copies usually cost $.50 per page.

TAX LIEN RECORDS: All federal and state tax liens are filed with the county Recorder of Deeds. They are usually indexed together. Some counties will perform tax lien searches. Search and copy fees vary widely.

OTHER LIENS: Mechanics, judgment, child support.

ONLINE ACCESS: A handful of counties offer online access. UCCs are available from the Secretary of State.

Adair County

Recorder of Deeds, Courthouse, 106 W. Washington St., Kirksville, MO 63501. Recorder of Deeds, R/E and UCC Recording 660-665-3890; Fax 660-785-3212. Will search UCC records. UCC search includes tax liens if requested. Will not search real estate records. **Other Phones:** Assessor 660-665-4423; Treasurer 660-665-6755; Appraiser/Auditor 660-665-4423; Elections 660-665-3350; Vital Records 660-665-8491.

Andrew County

Recorder of Deeds, P.O Box 208, Savannah, MO 64485. Recorder of Deeds, R/E and UCC Recording 816-324-4221; Fax 816-324-5667. Will search UCC records. This agency will not do a tax lien search. Will not search real estate records. **Other Phone Numbers:** Assessor 816-324-3023; Treasurer 816-324-3614; Elections 816-324-3624.

Atchison County

Recorder of Deeds, Box 280, Rock Port, MO 64482. 660-744-2707; Fax 660-744-5705. Will search UCC records. This agency will not do a tax lien search. Will not search real estate records. **Other Phone Numbers:** Assessor 660-744-2707; Treasurer 660-744-2800.

Audrain County

Recorder of Deeds, Room 105, Audrain County Courthouse, 101 N. Jefferson, Mexico, MO 65265. 573-473-5830; Fax 573-581-2380. Will search UCC records. UCC search includes tax liens if requested. Will not search real estate records. **Other Phone Numbers:** Assessor 573-473-5827.

Barry County

Recorder of Deeds, PO Box 340, Cassville, MO 65625. 417-847-2914; Fax 417-847-2914. Will search UCC records. Will not search real estate records. **Other Phones:** Assessor 417-847-4589.

Barton County

Recorder of Deeds, Courthouse, Room 107, 1004 Gulf, Lamar, MO 64759. Recorder of Deeds, R/E and UCC Recording 417-682-2110. Will search UCC records. This agency will not do a tax lien search. Will not search real estate records. **Other Phone Numbers:** Assessor 417-682-3553; Treasurer 417-682-5881; Elections 417-682-3529; Circuit Court 417-682-2444.

Bates County

Recorder of Deeds, Box 186, Butler, MO 64730. Recorder of Deeds, R/E and UCC Recording 660-679-3611. Will search UCC records. Will not search tax liens. Real estate record owner and mortgage searches available. **Other Phones:** Assessor 660-679-3157; Treasurer 660-679-3341; Elections 660-679-3371.

Benton County

Recorder of Deeds, PO Box 37, Warsaw, MO 65355. 660-438-5732; Fax 660-438-3652. Will search UCC records. Property transfer searches available. **Other Phone Numbers:** Assessor 660-438-5323; Treasurer 660-438-6313.

Bollinger County

Recorder of Deeds, Box 949, Marble Hill, MO 63764. 573-238-1900 R/E Recording: 573-238-1900 x7 UCC Recording: 573-238-1900 x7; Fax 573-238-2773. Will search UCC records. This agency will not do a tax lien search. Will not search real estate records.

Boone County

Recorder of Deeds, Boone County Gov't Center, 801 E. Walnut, Rm 132, Columbia, MO 65201-7728. Recorder of Deeds, R/E and UCC Recording 573-886-4345 UCC Recording: 573-886-4353; Fax 573-886-4359. www.showmeboone.com Will search UCC records. This agency will not do a tax lien search. Will not search real estate records. **Online Access:** Real Estate, Lien, Vital Statistic, UCC Records. Access to the County Recorder database is available free at www.showmeboone.com/recorder. **Other Phones:** Assessor 573-886-4270; Treasurer 573-886-4365; Appraiser/Auditor 573-886-4270; Elections 573-886-4295; Marriage License 573-886-4350.

Buchanan County

Recorder of Deeds, 411 Jules Sts, Courthouse, St. Joseph, MO 64501-1789. 816-271-1437; Fax 816-271-1582. Will Search UCC records. This agency will not do a tax lien search. Will not search real estate records. **Other Phone Numbers:** Assessor 816-271-1469; Treasurer 816-271-1432.

Butler County

Recorder of Deeds, 100 N. Main St, Courthouse, Poplar Bluff, MO 63901. Recorder of Deeds, R/E and UCC Recording 573-686-8086. Will search UCC records. Tax liens not included in UCC search. Will not search real estate records. **Other Phone Numbers:** Assessor 573-686-8084; Treasurer 573-686-8083; Appraiser/Auditor 573-686-8084; Elections 573-686-8050; Vital Records 573-686-8086.

Caldwell County

Recorder of Deeds, PO Box 86, Kingston, MO 64650. Recorder of Deeds, R/E and UCC Recording 816-586-3080; Fax 816-586-2705. Will search UCC records. This agency will not do a tax lien search. Will not search real estate records. **Other Phone Numbers:** Assessor 816-586-5261; Treasurer 816-586-2781; Elections 816-586-2571.

Callaway County

Recorder of Deeds, PO Box 406, Fulton, MO 65251. 573-642-0787; Fax 573-642-7929. Will search UCC records. This agency will not do a tax lien search. Will not search real estate records. **Other Phone Numbers:** Assessor 573-642-0766.

Camden County

Recorder of Deeds, 1 Court Circle, Camdenton, MO 65020. 573-346-4440 R/E Recording: 573-346-4440 x234 UCC Recording: 573-346-4440 x235; Fax 573-346-5422. Will search UCC records. This agency will not do a tax lien search. Will not search real estate records. **Other Phone Numbers:** Assessor 573-346-4440 x224-6; Treasurer 573-346-4440 x215-6.

Cape Girardeau County

Recorder of Deeds, PO Box 248, Jackson, MO 63755. 573-243-8123; Fax 573-204-2477. Will search UCC records. This agency will not do a tax lien search. Will not search real estate records. **Other Phone Numbers:** Assessor 573-243-2468; Treasurer 573-243-3720.

Carroll County

Recorder of Deeds, PO Box 245, Carrollton, MO 64633. 660-542-1466; Fax 660-542-1444.
Will search UCC records. UCC search includes tax liens if requested. Will not search real estate records. **Other Phone Numbers:** Assessor 660-542-2184; Treasurer 660-542-1977.

Carter County

Recorder of Deeds, PO Box 578, Van Buren, MO 63965. Recorder of Deeds, R/E and UCC Recording 573-323-4513; Fax 573-323-4885.
Will search UCC records. Tax liens not included in UCC search. Will not search real estate records. **Other Phone Numbers:** Assessor 573-323-4709; Treasurer 573-323-8271; Elections 573-323-4527.

Cass County

Recorder of Deeds, 102 E. Wall St, Cass County Court House, Harrisonville, MO 64701. Recorder of Deeds, R/E and UCC Recording 816-380-8117 UCC Recording: 816-380-8118; Fax 816-380-8165. www.casscounty.com/cassfr.htm
Will search UCC records. UCC search includes tax liens if requested. Will not search real estate records. **Online Access:** Real Estate, Lien Records. Access to county online records via modem requires a $250 monthly fee plus $.10 per minute after 90 minutes usage. Records date back to 1990. Images are viewable and can be printed, $1.00 each. Prepaid fax accounts available. For information, contact Sandy Gregory at 816-380-8117. **Other Phones:** Assessor 816-380-8117; Treasurer 816-380-8117; Elections 816-380-8102.

Cedar County

Recorder of Deeds, PO Box 665, Stockton, MO 65785. Recorder of Deeds, R/E and UCC Recording 417-276-6700 x246; Fax 417-276-5001.
Will search UCC records. This agency will not do a tax lien search. Will not search real estate records. **Other Phone Numbers:** Assessor 417-276-6700 X248; Treasurer 417-276-6700 X245; Elections 417-276-6700 X221.

Chariton County

Recorder of Deeds, PO Box 112, Keytesville, MO 65261. 660-288-3602; Fax 660-288-3763.
Will search UCC records. Will not search real estate records. **Other Phone Numbers:** Assessor 660-288-3873; Treasurer 660-288-3789.

Christian County

Recorder of Deeds, PO Box 278, Ozark, MO 65721. 417-581-6372; Fax 417-581-0391.
Will search UCC records. UCC search includes tax liens if requested. Will not search real estate records. **Other Phone Numbers:** Assessor 417-581-2440.

Clark County

Recorder of Deeds, 111 E. Court, Courthouse, Kahoka, MO 63445. Recorder of Deeds, R/E and UCC Recording 660-727-3292; Fax 660-727-1051.
Will search UCC records. This agency will not do a tax lien search. Will not search real estate records. **Other Phone Numbers:** Assessor 660-727-3023; Treasurer 660-727-3272; Elections 660-727-3283.

Clay County

Recorder of Deeds, PO Box 238, Liberty, MO 64069. Recorder of Deeds, R/E and UCC Recording 816-792-7641; http://recorder.co.clay.mo.us
Database from July 1, 1986 is on web site. Will search UCC records. Will not search real estate records. **Online Access:** Real Estate, Marriage, Military Discharge, UCC, Recording Records. Access to the recorder's database is available free at http://recorder.co.clay.mo.us/online_access.htm.
Overall index goes back to 1986; images back to 1998. UCCs are 1986-91 real estate only. **Other Phone Numbers:** Assessor 816-792-7664; Treasurer 816-792-7649 x284.

Clinton County

Recorder of Deeds, PO Box 275, Plattsburg, MO 64477. 816-539-3719; Fax 816-539-3893.
Will search UCC records. This agency will not do a tax lien search. Will not search real estate records. **Other Phone Numbers:** Assessor 816-539-3716; Treasurer 816-539-3724; Elections 816-539-3713.

Cole County

Recorder of Deeds, PO Box 353, Jefferson City, MO 65102. 573-634-9115.
Will search UCC records. Tax liens not included in UCC search. Real estate owner, mortgage, and property transfer searches available. **Other Phone Numbers:** Assessor 573-634-9135; Treasurer 573-634-9121.

Cooper County

Recorder of Deeds, 200 Main St, Courthouse - Room 26, Boonville, MO 65233-1276. 660-882-2232; Fax 660-882-2043.
Will search UCC records. UCC search includes tax liens if requested. Will not search real estate records. **Other Phone Numbers:** Assessor 660-882-2646.

Crawford County

Recorder of Deeds, PO Box 177, Steelville, MO 65565. Recorder of Deeds, R/E and UCC Recording 573-775-5048; Fax 573-775-3365.
Will search UCC records. Real estate record owner searches available. **Other Phone Numbers:** Assessor 573-775-2065; Treasurer 573-775-2899.

Dade County

Recorder of Deeds, Courthouse, Greenfield, MO 65661. 417-637-5373; Fax 417-637-5055.
Will search UCC records. This agency will not do a tax lien search. Will not search real estate records. **Other Phone Numbers:** Assessor 417-637-2224; Treasurer 417-637-2732.

Dallas County

Recorder of Deeds, PO Box 373, Buffalo, MO 65622. Recorder of Deeds, R/E and UCC Recording 417-345-2242; Fax 417-345-5539.
Will search UCC records. This agency will not do a tax lien search. Will not search real estate records. **Other Phone Numbers:** Assessor 417-345-8774; Treasurer 417-345-2020; Elections 417-345-2632.

Daviess County

Recorder of Deeds, PO Box 337, Gallatin, MO 64640. 660-663-2932; Fax 660-663-3376.
Will search UCC records. UCC search includes tax liens if requested. Will not search real estate records. **Other Phone Numbers:** Assessor 660-663-3300; Treasurer 660-663-2432.

De Kalb County

Recorder of Deeds, PO Box 248, Maysville, MO 64469-0248. Recorder of Deeds, R/E and UCC Recording 816-449-2602; Fax 816-449-2440.
Will search UCC records. UCC search includes tax liens if requested. Real estate record owner and mortgage searches available. **Other Phone Numbers:** Assessor 816-449-2212; Treasurer 816-449-5810.

Dent County

Recorder of Deeds, 112 E. 5th St, Salem, MO 65560-1444. 573-729-3931; Fax 573-729-9414.
Will search UCC records. UCC search includes tax liens if requested. Will not search real estate records.

Other Phone Numbers: Assessor 573-729-6010; Treasurer 573-729-8260.

Douglas County

Recorder of Deeds, PO Box 249, Ava, MO 65608. 417-683-4713; Fax 417-683-2794.
Will search UCC records. Tax liens not included in UCC search. Real estate owner, mortgage, and property transfer searches available. **Other Phone Numbers:** Assessor 417-683-2829; Treasurer 417-683-2183; Elections 417-683-4714.

Dunklin County

Recorder of Deeds, PO Box 389, Kennett, MO 63857. Recorder of Deeds, R/E and UCC Recording 573-888-3468.
Will search UCC records. This agency will not do a tax lien search. Will not search real estate records. **Other Phone Numbers:** Assessor 573-888-1409.

Franklin County

Recorder of Deeds, 300 E Main St #101, Union, MO 63084. Recorder of Deeds, R/E and UCC Recording 636-583-6367; Fax 636-583-7330.
Will search UCC records. This agency will not do a tax lien search. Will not search real estate records. **Other Phone Numbers:** Assessor 636-583-6346; Treasurer 636-583-6392.

Gasconade County

Recorder of Deeds, 119 E.1st St., Room 6, Hermann, MO 65041-1182. Recorder of Deeds, R/E and UCC Recording 573-486-2632; Fax 573-486-3693.
Will search UCC records. Tax liens not included in UCC search. Will not search real estate records. **Other Phone Numbers:** Assessor 573-486-3100; Treasurer 573-486-2411; Appraiser/Auditor 573-486-3100; Elections 573-486-5427.

Gentry County

Recorder of Deeds, PO Box 27, Albany, MO 64402. 660-726-3618; Fax 660-726-4102.
Will search UCC records. This agency will not do a tax lien search. Will not search real estate records. **Other Phone Numbers:** Assessor 660-726-5289.

Greene County

Recorder of Deeds, 940 Boonville, Room 100, Springfield, MO 65802. Recorder of Deeds, R/E and UCC Recording 417-868-4068; Fax 417-868-4807. www.greenecountymo.org
Will search UCC records. UCC search includes tax liens if requested. Will not search real estate records. **Online Access:** Divorce Records. Records for divorces that occurred 1837 to 1920 in Greene County are available free online at http://userdb.rootsweb.com/ivorces. **Other Phones:** Assessor 417-868-4101; Treasurer 417-868-4051; Elections 417-868-4055.

Grundy County

Recorder of Deeds, PO Box 196, Trenton, MO 64683. Recorder of Deeds, R/E and UCC Recording 660-359-5409; Fax 660-359-6604.
Will search UCC records. This agency will not do a tax lien search. Will not search real estate records. **Other Phone Numbers:** Assessor 660-359-2413; Treasurer 660-359-2171; Elections 660-359-6305.

Harrison County

Recorder of Deeds, PO Box 189, Bethany, MO 64424. Recorder of Deeds, R/E and UCC Recording 660-425-6425; Fax 660-425-3772.
This agency will not perform searches. **Other Phones:** Assessor 660-425-2313; Treasurer 660-425-6442.

Henry County

Recorder of Deeds, 100 W. Franklin #4, Courthouse, Clinton, MO 64735. 660-885-6963 R/E Recording: 660-885-6963 x233 UCC Recording: 660-885-6963 x233; Fax 660-885-2264.
Will search UCC records. This agency will not do a tax lien search. Will not search real estate records. **Other Phone Numbers:** Assessor 660-885-6963 x203; Treasurer 660-885-6963 x236.

Hickory County

Recorder of Deeds, PO Box 101, Hermitage, MO 65668. 417-745-6421; Fax 417-745-6670.
Will search UCC records. UCC search includes tax liens if requested. Will not search real estate records. **Other Phone Numbers:** Assessor 417-745-6346; Treasurer 417-745-6310; Appraiser/Auditor 417-745-6957; Elections 417-745-6450.

Holt County

Recorder of Deeds, PO Box 318, Oregon, MO 64473. Recorder of Deeds, R/E and UCC Recording 660-446-3301.
Will search UCC records. UCC search includes tax liens if requested. Will not search real estate records. **Other Phone Numbers:** Assessor 660-446-3329; Treasurer 660-446-3397; Elections 660-446-3303.

Howard County

Recorder of Deeds, 1 Courthouse Square, Fayette, MO 65248. Recorder of Deeds, R/E and UCC Recording 660-248-2194; Fax 660-248-1075.
Will search UCC records. UCC search includes tax liens if requested. Real estate owner, mortgage, and property transfer searches available. **Other Phones:** Assessor 660-248-3400; Treasurer 660-248-2196.

Howell County

Recorder of Deeds, PO Box 1011, West Plains, MO 65775. 417-256-3750.
Will search UCC records. Tax liens not included in UCC search. Will not search real estate records. **Other Phone Numbers:** Assessor 417-256-8284; Treasurer 417-256-4261.

Iron County

Recorder of Deeds, PO Box 24, Ironton, MO 63650. Recorder of Deeds, R/E and UCC Recording 573-546-2811; Fax 573-546-2166.
Will search UCC records. This agency will not do a tax lien search. Will not search real estate records. **Other Phone Numbers:** Assessor 573-546-7319; Treasurer 573-546-7611; Elections 573-546-2912; Vital Records 573-546-2811.

Jackson County (Kansas City)

Recorder of Deeds, 415 E. 12th St, Room 104, Kansas City, MO 64106. 816-881-3192 R/E Recording: 816-881-3048 UCC Recording: 816-881-3048; Fax 816-881-3719. www.co.jackson.mo.us
There is another office in Independence, which covers the western part of the county. However, it is not necessary to file there as the Kansas City office can search and record any UCC filings for the entire county. Will search UCC records. This agency will not do a tax lien search. Real estate record owner searches available. **Online Access:** Property, Tax Assessor, Recording, Marriages, Grantor/Grantee, Deed, Lien, Judgment, UCC Records. Records from the county tax assessor database are available free at www.jacksongov.org/Tax/Choice.asp. Search the recorder Grantor/Grantee database for fee at http://records.co.jackson.mo.us/search.asp?cabinet=opr. Search Kansas City land information for free at http://kivaweb.kcmo.org/kivanet/2/land/lookup/index.cfm?fa=dslladdr. Search the marriage records for free at http://records.co.jackson.mo.us/search.asp?cabinet=marriage. Search the UCC database for free at http://records.co.jackson.mo.us/search.asp?cabinet=ucc. **Other Phone Numbers:** Assessor 816-881-3187; Treasurer 816-881-3270; Appraiser/Auditor 816-881-3091; Elections 816-881-4820.

Jasper County

Recorder of Deeds, PO Box 387, Carthage, MO 64836-0387. 417-358-0432.
Will search UCC records. This agency will not do a tax lien search. Will not search real estate records. **Other Phone Numbers:** Assessor 417-358-0437; Treasurer 417-358-0448.

Jefferson County

Recorder of Deeds, PO Box 100, Hillsboro, MO 63050. Recorder of Deeds, R/E and UCC Recording 636-797-5414 UCC Recording: 636-797-5499; www.jeffcomo.org
Will search UCC records. This agency will not do a tax lien search. Will not search real estate records. **Other Phone Numbers:** Assessor 636-797-5466; Treasurer 636-797-5368; Appraiser/Auditor 636-797-5474; Elections 636-797-5486; Birth & Death Records 636-789-3372.

Johnson County

Recorder of Deeds, PO Box 32, Warrensburg, MO 64093. 660-747-6811.
Will search UCC records. This agency will not do a tax lien search. Will not search real estate records. **Other Phone Numbers:** Assessor 660-747-9822; Treasurer 660-747-7411.

Knox County

Recorder of Deeds, PO Box 116, Edina, MO 63537. 660-397-2305; Fax 660-397-3331.
Will search UCC records. This agency will not do a tax lien search. Will not search real estate records. **Other Phone Numbers:** Assessor 660-397-2423; Treasurer 660-397-3364.

Laclede County

Recorder of Deeds, 200 N Adams, 200 N. Adams, Lebanon, MO 65536-3046. Recorder of Deeds, R/E and UCC Recording 417-532-4011; Fax 417-532-3852. http://laclede.county.missouri.org/recorder/
Will search UCC records. UCC search includes tax liens if requested. Will not search real estate records. **Other Phone Numbers:** Assessor 417-532-7163; Treasurer 417-532-4741; Appraiser/Auditor 417-532-7163; Elections 417-532-5471; Vital Records 417-532-2134 (Birth); 4011 (Marriage); Collector 417-532-4301.

Lafayette County

Recorder of Deeds, PO Box 416, Lexington, MO 64067. 660-259-6178; Fax 660-259-2918.
Will search UCC records. This agency will not do a tax lien search. Will not search real estate records. **Other Phone Numbers:** Assessor 660-259-6158; Treasurer 660-259-3711.

Lawrence County

Recorder of Deeds, PO Box 449, Mount Vernon, MO 65712. 417-466-2670; Fax 417-466-4995.
Will search UCC records. This agency will not do a tax lien search. Will not search real estate records. **Other Phone Numbers:** Assessor 417-466-2831; Treasurer 417-466-2662.

Lewis County

Recorder of Deeds, PO Box 97, Monticello, MO 63457-0097. 573-767-5440; Fax 573-767-5378.
Will search UCC records. This agency will not do a tax lien search. Will not search real estate records. **Other Phone Numbers:** Assessor 573-767-5209.

Lincoln County

Recorder of Deeds, 201 Main St, Troy, MO 63379. 636-528-6300; Fax 636-528-2665.
Will search UCC records. Real estate record owner and mortgage searches available. **Other Phone Numbers:** Assessor 636-528-0320.

Linn County

Recorder of Deeds, PO Box 151, Linneus, MO 64653. 660-895-5216; Fax 660-895-5533.
Will search UCC records. UCC search includes tax liens if requested. Will not search real estate records. **Other Phone Numbers:** Assessor 660-895-5387; Treasurer 660-895-5410.

Livingston County

Recorder of Deeds, Courthouse, Suite 6, 700 Webster St., Chillicothe, MO 64601. Recorder of Deeds, R/E and UCC Recording 660-646-0166.
Will search UCC records. This agency will not do a tax lien search. Will not search real estate records. **Other Phone Numbers:** Assessor 660-646-2027; Treasurer 660-646-3076; Elections 660-646-2293.

Macon County

Recorder of Deeds, PO Box 382, Macon, MO 63552. Recorder of Deeds, R/E and UCC Recording 660-385-2732; Fax 660-385-4235.
Will search UCC records. This agency will not do a tax lien search. Will not search real estate records. **Other Phone Numbers:** Assessor 660-385-2416; Treasurer 660-385-2713.

Madison County

Recorder of Deeds, PO Box 470, Fredericktown, MO 63645-0470. 573-783-2102; Fax 573-783-2715.
Will search UCC records. This agency will not do a tax lien search. Will not search real estate records. **Other Phone Numbers:** Assessor 573-783-3325; Treasurer 573-783-3325.

Maries County

Recorder of Deeds, PO Box 213, Vienna, MO 65582. Recorder of Deeds, R/E and UCC Recording 573-422-3338; Fax 573-422-3269.
Will search UCC records. UCC search includes tax liens if requested. Will not search real estate records. **Other Phone Numbers:** Assessor 573-422-3540; Treasurer 573-422-3311; Elections 573-422-3388; Vital Records 573-422-3338; Collector 573-422-3343; Sheriff 573-422-3381;

Marion County

Recorder of Deeds, PO Box 392, Palmyra, MO 63461. 573-769-2550; Fax 573-769-6012.
Will search UCC records. This agency will not do a tax lien search. Will not search real estate records. **Other Phone Numbers:** Assessor 573-248-1514; Treasurer 573-769-2552; Elections 573-729-2549.

McDonald County

Recorder of Deeds, PO Box 157, Pineville, MO 64856. 417-223-7523; Fax 417-223-4125.
Will search UCC records. UCC search includes tax liens if requested. Will not search real estate records. **Other Phone Numbers:** Assessor 417-223-4361; Treasurer 417-223-4462.

Mercer County

Recorder of Deeds, Courthouse, Princeton, MO 64673. 660-748-4335; Fax 660-748-3180.
Will search UCC records. Tax liens not included in UCC search. Will not search real estate records. **Other Phone Numbers:** Assessor 660-748-3511; Treasurer 660-748-3435.

Miller County

Recorder of Deeds, PO Box 11, Tuscumbia, MO 65082. Recorder of Deeds, R/E and UCC Recording 573-369-2911; Fax 573-369-2910.
Will search UCC records. **Other Phone Numbers:** Assessor 573-369-2614; Treasurer 573-369-2214.

Mississippi County

County Recorder, PO Box 369, Charleston, MO 63834. 573-683-2146 R/E Recording: 573-683-2146 x226; Fax 573-683-7696.
Will search UCC records. **Other Phone Numbers:** Assessor 573-683-2146 x238; Treasurer 573-683-2146 x235; Elections 573-683-2146 x222.

Moniteau County

Circuit Clerk and Recorder, 200 E. Main St, California, MO 65018. 573-796-2071 R/E Recording: 573-796-4822 UCC Recording: 573-796-4822; Fax 573-796-2591.
Will search UCC records. Will not search real estate records. **Other Phone Numbers:** Assessor 573-796-4637; Treasurer 573-796-4608; Elections 573-796-4661; Vital Records 573-796-4671.

Monroe County

Recorder of Deeds, PO Box 227, Paris, MO 65275. 660-327-5204; Fax 660-327-5781.
Will search UCC records. Will not search real estate records. **Other Phone Numbers:** Assessor 660-327-5607; Treasurer 660-327-4711.

Montgomery County

Recorder of Deeds, 211 E. 3rd St, Montgomery City, MO 63361. Recorder of Deeds, R/E and UCC Recording 573-564-3157; Fax 573-564-3914.
Will search UCC records. **Other Phone Numbers:** Assessor 573-564-2445; Treasurer 573-564-2319; Elections 573-564-3357.

Morgan County

County Recorder, 100 Newton St, Courthouse, Versailles, MO 65084. County Recorder, R/E and UCC Recording 573-378-4029; Fax 573-378-6431.
Will search UCC records. Will not search real estate records. **Other Phone Numbers:** Assessor 573-378-5459; Treasurer 573-378-4404; Elections 573-378-5436.

New Madrid County

Recorder of Deeds, PO Box 217, New Madrid, MO 63869. 573-748-5146.
Will search UCC records. Tax liens not included in UCC search. Will not search real estate records. **Other Phone Numbers:** Assessor 573-748-2387.

Newton County

Recorder of Deeds, PO Box 130, Neosho, MO 64850-0130. 417-451-8224 R/E Recording: 417-451-8224 or 8225; Fax 417-451-8273.
Will search UCC records. Will not search real estate records. **Other Phone Numbers:** Assessor 417-451-8228; Treasurer 417-451-8226; Appraiser/Auditor 417-451-8227; Elections 417-451-8222; Health Dept (Birth & Death) 417-451-3743.

Nodaway County

Recorder of Deeds, 305 N. Main, Room 104, Maryville, MO 64468. 660-582-5711; Fax 660-582-5282.
Will search UCC records. Will not search real estate records. **Other Phone Numbers:** Assessor 660-582-3372.

Oregon County

Recorder of Deeds, PO Box 406, Alton, MO 65606. Recorder of Deeds, R/E and UCC Recording 417-778-7460; Fax 417-778-7206.
Will search UCC records. Will not search real estate records. **Other Phone Numbers:** Assessor 417-778-7471; Treasurer 417-778-6303; Elections 417-778-7475.

Osage County

Recorder of Deeds, PO Box 825, Linn, MO 65051-0825. Recorder of Deeds, R/E and UCC Recording 573-897-3114.
Will search UCC records. UCC search includes tax liens if requested. Will not search real estate records. **Other Phone Numbers:** Assessor 573-897-2217; Treasurer 573-897-3095; Elections 573-897-2139.

Ozark County

Circuit Clerk & Recorder, PO Box 36, Gainesville, MO 65655. Circuit Clerk & Recorder, R/E and UCC Recording 417-679-4232; Fax 417-679-4554.
Will search UCC records. Will not search tax liens. **Other Phone Numbers:** Assessor 417-679-4705; Treasurer 417-679-3553; Elections 417-679-3516.

Pemiscot County

Recorder of Deeds, Courthouse, 610 Ward Ave., Caruthersville, MO 63830. 573-333-2204.
Will search UCC records. UCC search includes tax liens if requested. Will not search real estate records. **Other Phone Numbers:** Assessor 573-333-1390; Treasurer 573-333-4171.

Perry County

Recorder of Deeds, 15 W. Ste. Marie St, Suite 1, Perryville, MO 63775. Recorder of Deeds, R/E and UCC Recording 573-547-1611; Fax 573-547-9323.
Will search UCC records. Will not search real estate records. **Other Phone Numbers:** Assessor 573-547-5211; Treasurer 573-547-4502; Elections 573-547-4242.

Pettis County

Recorder of Deeds, 415 S. Ohio, Sedalia, MO 65301. 660-826-1136; Fax 660-829-4479.
Will search UCC records. Will not search real estate records. **Other Phone Numbers:** Assessor 660-827-0023; Treasurer 660-827-0486; Elections 660-826-5395.

Phelps County

Recorder of Deeds, Courthouse, 200 N. Main, Rolla, MO 65401. 573-364-1891 R/E Recording: 573-364-1891 x210/211 UCC Recording: 573-364-1891 x210/211; Fax 573-364-1419.
Will search UCC records. Will not search real estate records. **Other Phone Numbers:** Assessor 573-364-1891 x140; Treasurer 573-364-1891 x130; Elections 573-364-1891 x100; Vital Records 573-364-1891 x490.

Pike County

Recorder of Deeds, 115 W. Main St, Bowling Green, MO 63334. 573-324-5567.
Will search UCC records. UCC search includes tax liens if requested. Will not search real estate records. **Other Phone Numbers:** Assessor 573-324-3261; Treasurer 573-324-2102; Appraiser/Auditor 573-528-5180; Elections 573-324-2412.

Platte County

Chief Deputy, 415 3rd St., Suite 70, Platte City, MO 64079. 816-858-3323 R/E Recording: 816-858-3326 UCC Recording: 816-858-3320; Fax 816-858-2379. www.co.platte.mo.us/recorder.html

Will search UCC records. Will not search real estate records. **Other Phone Numbers:** Assessor 816-858-3301; Treasurer 816-858-3318; Elections 816-858-4400.

Polk County

Recorder of Deeds, 102 E. Broadway, Courthouse, Bolivar, MO 65613-1502. Recorder of Deeds, R/E and UCC Recording 417-326-4924; Fax 417-326-6898.
Will search UCC records. Will not search real estate records. **Other Phone Numbers:** Assessor 417-326-4643; Treasurer 417-326-4913; Appraiser/Auditor 417-326-4346; Elections 417-326-4031; Vital Records 417-326-4031.

Pulaski County

Recorder of Deeds, 301 Historic Route 66, Courthouse Suite 202, Waynesville, MO 65583. 573-774-4760; Fax 573-774-6967.
Will search UCC records. This agency will not do a tax lien search. Will not search real estate records. **Other Phone Numbers:** Assessor 573-774-6609 x117; Treasurer 573-774-6609 x124.

Putnam County

Recorder of Deeds, Courthouse, Room 202, Unionville, MO 63565-1659. 660-947-2071; Fax 660-947-2320.
Will search UCC records. Will not search real estate records. **Other Phones:** Assessor 660-947-3900; Treasurer 660-947-2095; Elections 660-947-2674.

Ralls County

Recorder of Deeds, PO Box 444, New London, MO 63459-0444. 573-985-5631.
Will search UCC records. UCC search includes tax liens if requested. Will not search real estate records. **Other Phone Numbers:** Assessor 573-985-5671; Treasurer 573-985-7151.

Randolph County

Recorder of Deeds, 110 S. Main St., Courthouse, Huntsville, MO 65259. Recorder of Deeds, R/E and UCC Recording 660-277-4718; Fax 660-277-3246.
Will search UCC records. Will not search real estate records. **Other Phones:** Assessor 660-277-4716; Treasurer 660-277-4714; Elections 660-277-4717.

Ray County

Recorder of Deeds, PO Box 167, Richmond, MO 64085. 660-776-4500.
Will search UCC records. This agency will not do a tax lien search. Will not search real estate records. **Other Phone Numbers:** Assessor 660-776-2676; Treasurer 660-776-6140.

Reynolds County

Recorder of Deeds, PO Box 76, Centerville, MO 63633-0076. 573-648-2494; Fax 573-648-2296.
Will search UCC records. Will not search real estate records. **Other Phones:** Assessor 573-648-2494.

Ripley County

Recorder of Deeds, 100 Courthouse Square, Suite 3, Doniphan, MO 63935. 573-996-2818; Fax 573-966-5014.
Will search UCC records. Will not search real estate records. **Other Phones:** Assessor 573-996-7113.

Saline County

Recorder of Deeds, Courthouse, Room 206, Marshall, MO 65340. Recorder of Deeds, R/E and UCC Recording 660-886-2677; Fax 660-886-2603.
Will search UCC records. Will not search real estate records. **Other Phone Numbers:** Assessor 660-335-3111; Treasurer 660-886-3636.

Schuyler County

Recorder of Deeds, PO Box 186, Lancaster, MO 63548. 660-457-3784; Fax 660-457-3016.
Will search UCC records. **Other Phone Numbers:** Assessor 660-457-3211; Treasurer 660-457-3825.

Scotland County

Recorder of Deeds, 117 S. Market St., Ste 106, Memphis, MO 63555-1449. Recorder of Deeds, R/E and UCC Recording 660-465-8605; Fax 660-465-8673. Will search UCC records. UCC search includes tax liens if requested. Will not search real estate records. **Other Phone Numbers:** Assessor 660-465-2269; Treasurer 660-465-2529.

Scott County

Recorder of Deeds, PO Box 78, Benton, MO 63736. 573-545-3551.
Will search UCC records. UCC search includes tax liens if requested. Will not search real estate records. **Other Phone Numbers:** Assessor 573-545-3535; Treasurer 573-545-3543.

Shannon County

Recorder of Deeds, PO Box 148, Eminence, MO 65466. 573-226-3315; Fax 573-226-5321.
Will search UCC records. Will not search real estate records. **Other Phone Numbers:** Assessor 573-226-5539; Treasurer 573-226-3614.

Shelby County

Recorder of Deeds, PO Box 176, Shelbyville, MO 63469. Recorder of Deeds, R/E and UCC Recording 573-633-2151; Fax 573-633-1004.
Will search UCC records. Will not search real estate records. **Other Phone Numbers:** Assessor 573-633-2521; Treasurer 573-633-2574; Elections 573-633-2187.

St. Charles County

Recorder of Deeds, PO Box 99, St. Charles, MO 63302-0099. Recorder of Deeds, R/E and UCC Recording 636-949-7505 UCC Recording: 636-949-7508; Fax 636-949-7512. www.win.org
Will search UCC records. This agency will not do a tax lien search. Will not search real estate records. **Online Access:** Assessor Records. Records on the county Property Assessment database are available free online at www.win.org/library/library_office/assessment. No name searching; address, street or map ID only. **Other Phone Numbers:** Assessor 636-949-7425; Appraiser/Auditor 636-949-7431; Elections 636-949-7550; Vital Records 636-949-7558.

St. Clair County

Circuit Clerk / ex-officio, PO Box 493, Osceola, MO 64776-0493. 417-646-2226; Fax 417-646-2401.
Will search UCC records. Will not search real estate records. **Other Phone Numbers:** Assessor 417-646-2449; Treasurer 417-646-8068.

St. Francois County

Recorder of Deeds, Courthouse, Farmington, MO 63640. 573-756-2323.
Will search UCC records. This agency will not do a tax lien search. Real estate record owner searches available. **Other Phone Numbers:** Assessor 573-756-2509; Treasurer 573-756-3349.

St. Louis City

Recorder of Deeds, Tucker & Market Streets, City Hall Room 127, St. Louis, MO 63103. 314-622-4328; Fax 314-622-4175.
Will search UCC records. Will not search real estate records. **Other Phone Numbers:** Assessor 314-615-5124; Treasurer 314-622-2062.

St. Louis County

Recorder of Deeds, 41 S. Central Ave., 4th Floor, Clayton, MO 63105. Recorder of Deeds, R/E and UCC Recording 314-615-2500; Fax 314-615-4964.
Will search UCC records. Will not search real estate records. **Other Phone Numbers:** Assessor 314-615-4225; Vital Records 314-615-1684.

Ste. Genevieve County

Recorder of Deeds, 3rd St, Court House, Ste. Genevieve, MO 63670. 573-883-2706; Fax 573-883-5312.
Will search UCC records. Will not search real estate records. **Other Phone Numbers:** Assessor 573-883-2333.

Stoddard County

Recorder of Deeds, PO Box 217, Bloomfield, MO 63825-0217. Recorder of Deeds, R/E and UCC Recording 573-568-3444; Fax 573-568-2545.
Will search UCC records. Will not search real estate records. **Other Phone Numbers:** Assessor 573-568-3163; Treasurer 573-568-3327.

Stone County

Recorder of Deeds, PO Box 18, Galena, MO 65656. Recorder of Deeds, R/E and UCC Recording 417-357-6362; Fax 417-357-8131.
Will search UCC records. **Other Phone Numbers:** Assessor 417-357-6141; Treasurer 417-357-6131; Elections 417-357-6127.

Sullivan County

Recorder of Deeds, Courthouse, Milan, MO 63556. 660-265-3630; Fax 660-265-5071.
Will search UCC records. Will not search real estate records. **Other Phone Numbers:** Assessor 660-265-4474; Treasurer 660-265-4514.

Taney County

Recorder of Deeds, PO Box 335, Forsyth, MO 65653. Recorder of Deeds, R/E and UCC Recording 417-546-7234 UCC Recording: 417-546-7235.
Will search UCC records. Will search tax liens for $4.00 per name, copy fee $1.00 per page. Will not search real estate records. **Other Phone Numbers:** Assessor 417-546-4751; Treasurer 417-546-4584.

Texas County

Recorder of Deeds, 210 N. Grand, PO Box 237, Houston, MO 65483. 417-967-3742; Fax 417-967-4220.
Will search UCC records. Will not search real estate records. **Other Phone Numbers:** Assessor 417-967-4709; Treasurer 417-967-2589.

Vernon County

Recorder of Deeds, Courthouse, Nevada, MO 64772. Recorder of Deeds, R/E and UCC Recording 417-448-2520; Fax 417-448-2524.
Will search UCC records. This agency will not do a tax lien search. Will not search real estate records. **Other Phone Numbers:** Assessor 417-448-2530; Treasurer 417-448-2510; Elections 417-448-2500.

Warren County

Recorder of Deeds, 104 West Boone's Lick Rd., Warrenton, MO 63383. 636-456-9800.
Will search UCC records. This agency will not do a tax lien search. Will not search real estate records. **Other Phone Numbers:** Assessor 636-456-8885; Treasurer 636-456-3389.

Washington County

Recorder of Deeds, PO Box 216, Potosi, MO 63664-0216. Recorder of Deeds, R/E and UCC Recording 573-438-5023; Fax 573-438-7900.
Will search UCC records. Will not search real estate records. **Other Phone Numbers:** Assessor 573-438-4992; Treasurer 573-438-2031; Elections 573-438-4901.

Wayne County

Recorder of Deeds, PO Box 78, Greenville, MO 63944. 573-224-3041; Fax 573-224-3015.
Will search UCC records. Will not search real estate records. **Other Phone Numbers:** Assessor 573-224-3006; Treasurer 573-224-3011.

Webster County

Circuit Clerk & Recorder, PO Box 529, Marshfield, MO 65706. 417-468-2173; Fax 417-468-3786.
Will search UCC records. Will not search real estate records. **Other Phones:** Assessor 417-859-2169; Treasurer 417-859-2683; Elections 417-468-2224.

Worth County

Recorder of Deeds, Box 340, Grant City, MO 64456. 660-564-2210; Fax 660-564-2432.
Will search UCC records. **Other Phone Numbers:** Assessor 660-564-2153; Treasurer 660-564-2154.

Wright County

Deputy, PO Box 39, Hartville, MO 65667. Deputy, R/E and UCC Recording 417-741-7322; Fax 417-741-7504.
Will search UCC records. Will not search real estate records. **Other Phone Numbers:** Assessor 417-741-6400; Treasurer 417-741-7225; Elections 417-741-6661; Vital Records 573-751-6400.

Missouri County Locator

You will usually be able to find the city name in the City/County Cross Reference below. In that case, it is a simple matter to determine the county from the cross reference. However, only the official US Postal Service city names are included in this index. There are an additional 40,000 place names that people use in their addresses. Therefore, we have also included a ZIP/City Cross Reference immediately following the City/County Cross Reference.

If you know the ZIP Code but the city name does not appear in the City/County Cross Reference index, look up the ZIP Code in the ZIP/City Cross Reference, find the city name, then look up the city name in the City/County Cross Reference. For example, you want to know the county for an address of Menands, NY 12204. There is no "Menands" in the City/County Cross Reference. The ZIP/City Cross Reference shows that ZIP Codes 12201-12288 are for the city of Albany. Looking back in the City/County Cross Reference, Albany is in Albany County.

City/County Cross Reference

ADRIAN Bates
ADVANCE (63730) Stoddard(78), Cape Girardeau(16), Bollinger(5)
AGENCY Buchanan
ALBA Jasper
ALBANY Gentry
ALDRICH (65601) Polk(69), Dade(28), Cedar(1)
ALEXANDRIA Clark
ALLENDALE Worth
ALLENTON St. Louis
ALMA Lafayette
ALTAMONT Daviess
ALTENBURG (63732) Cape Girardeau(94), Perry(5)
ALTON Oregon
AMAZONIA Andrew
AMITY De Kalb
AMORET Bates
AMSTERDAM Bates
ANABEL Macon
ANDERSON McDonald
ANNADA Pike
ANNAPOLIS (63620) Iron(59), Madison(33), Reynolds(6)
ANNISTON Mississippi
APPLETON CITY (64724) St. Clair(94), Bates(5)
ARBELA (63432) Scotland(88), Clark(11)
ARBYRD Dunklin
ARCADIA (63621) Iron(67), Madison(32)
ARCHIE Cass
ARCOLA (65603) Dade(97), Cedar(2)
ARGYLE (65001) Maries(74), Osage(25)
ARMSTRONG (65230) Howard(95), Randolph(4)
ARNOLD Jefferson
ARROW ROCK Saline
ASBURY (64832) Barton(83), Jasper(16)
ASH GROVE (65604) Greene(65), Lawrence(32), Dade(2)
ASHBURN Pike
ASHLAND Boone
ATLANTA Macon
AUGUSTA St. Charles
AURORA (65605) Lawrence(91), Barry(8)
AUXVASSE (65231) Callaway(98), Audrain(1)
AVA (65608) Douglas(88), Taney(10)
AVALON Livingston
AVILLA Jasper
BAKERSFIELD (65609) Ozark(80), Howell(19)
BALLWIN St. Louis
BARING (63531) Knox(59), Scotland(40)
BARNARD Nodaway
BARNETT (65011) Morgan(94), Moniteau(5)
BARNHART Jefferson
BATES CITY (64011) Lafayette(92), Johnson(7)
BEAUFORT Franklin
BELGRADE Washington
BELL CITY (63735) Stoddard(91), Scott(8)
BELLE (65013) Maries(85), Osage(14)

BELLEVIEW (63623) Iron(96), Reynolds(3)
BELLFLOWER (63333) Montgomery(96), Lincoln(3)
BELTON Cass
BENDAVIS Texas
BENTON Scott
BENTON CITY Audrain
BERGER Franklin
BERNIE (63822) Stoddard(97), Dunklin(1)
BERTRAND (63823) Mississippi(91), Scott(8)
BETHANY Harrison
BETHEL Shelby
BEULAH (65436) Phelps(87), Texas(8), Pulaski(3)
BEVIER Macon
BILLINGS (65610) Christian(95), Lawrence(3)
BIRCH TREE (65438) Shannon(74), Oregon(25)
BISMARCK (63624) St. Francois(85), Washington(9), Iron(4)
BIXBY Iron
BLACK (63625) Reynolds(88), Iron(11)
BLACKBURN (65321) Saline(61), Lafayette(38)
BLACKWATER Cooper
BLACKWELL (63626) St. Francois(77), Washington(22)
BLAIRSTOWN Henry
BLAND (65014) Gasconade(82), Osage(10), Maries(7)
BLODGETT Scott
BLOOMFIELD Stoddard
BLOOMSDALE (63627) Ste. Genevieve(90), Jefferson(9)
BLUE EYE (65611) Stone(95), Taney(4)
BLUE SPRINGS Jackson
BLYTHEDALE Harrison
BOGARD Carroll
BOIS D ARC (65612) Greene(93), Lawrence(6)
BOLCKOW (64427) Andrew(83), Nodaway(16)
BOLIVAR Polk
BONNE TERRE (63628) St. Francois(96), Ste. Genevieve(2)
BONNOTS MILL Osage
BOONVILLE Cooper
BOSS (65440) Dent(58), Reynolds(32), Iron(9)
BOSWORTH Carroll
BOURBON (65441) Crawford(98), Washington(1)
BOWLING GREEN (63334) Pike(98), Lincoln(1)
BRADLEYVILLE (65614) Taney(90), Christian(9)
BRAGG CITY Pemiscot
BRAGGADOCIO Pemiscot
BRANDSVILLE Howell
BRANSON (65616) Taney(93), Stone(6)
BRASHEAR (63533) Adair(98), Knox(1)
BRAYMER (64624) Caldwell(79), Ray(12), Carroll(4), Livingston(3)

BRAZEAU Perry
BRECKENRIDGE (64625) Caldwell(82), Daviess(8), Livingston(8)
BRIAR Ripley
BRIDGETON St. Louis
BRIGHTON Polk
BRINKTOWN Maries
BRIXEY Ozark
BRONAUGH (64728) Vernon(72), Barton(27)
BROOKFIELD (64628) Linn(98), Chariton(1)
BROOKLINE STATION Greene
BROSELEY Butler
BROWNING (64630) Linn(65), Sullivan(34)
BROWNWOOD Stoddard
BRUMLEY Miller
BRUNER (65620) Christian(98), Douglas(1)
BRUNSWICK Chariton
BUCKLIN (64631) Linn(79), Macon(20)
BUCKNER Jackson
BUCYRUS Texas
BUFFALO (65622) Dallas(97), Polk(2)
BUNCETON Cooper
BUNKER (63629) Reynolds(66), Dent(25), Shannon(7)
BURFORDVILLE Cape Girardeau
BURLINGTON JUNCTION Nodaway
BUTLER Bates
BUTTERFIELD Barry
CABOOL (65689) Howell(72), Texas(25), Douglas(1)
CADET Washington
CAINSVILLE (64632) Harrison(69), Mercer(30)
CAIRO Randolph
CALEDONIA Washington
CALHOUN Henry
CALIFORNIA (65018) Moniteau(95), Cooper(4)
CALLAO Macon
CAMDEN Ray
CAMDEN POINT Platte
CAMDENTON Camden
CAMERON (64429) Clinton(70), De Kalb(27), Daviess(1)
CAMPBELL Dunklin
CANALOU New Madrid
CANTON (63435) Lewis(92), Clark(7)
CAPE FAIR (65624) Stone(95), Barry(3)
CAPE GIRARDEAU Cape Girardeau
CAPLINGER MILLS Cedar
CARDWELL Dunklin
CARL JUNCTION Jasper
CARROLLTON Carroll
CARTERVILLE Jasper
CARTHAGE Jasper
CARUTHERSVILLE Pemiscot
CASCADE Wayne
CASSVILLE Barry
CATAWISSA (63015) Franklin(76), Jefferson(23)
CATRON New Madrid
CAULFIELD (65626) Howell(68), Ozark(31)
CEDAR CITY Callaway

CEDAR HILL Jefferson
CEDARCREEK Taney
CENSUS BUREAU Boone
CENTER Ralls
CENTERTOWN (65023) Cole(88), Moniteau(11)
CENTERVIEW Johnson
CENTERVILLE Reynolds
CENTRALIA (65240) Boone(76), Audrain(21), Callaway(1)
CHADWICK (65629) Christian(98), Douglas(1)
CHAFFEE Scott
CHAMOIS Osage
CHARLESTON (63834) Mississippi(94), Scott(5)
CHERRYVILLE Crawford
CHESTERFIELD St. Louis
CHESTNUTRIDGE Christian
CHILHOWEE (64733) Johnson(70), Henry(24), Jackson(5)
CHILLICOTHE (64601) Livingston(98), Sullivan(1)
CHULA (64635) Livingston(79), Linn(10), Grundy(9)
CLARENCE (63437) Shelby(89), Macon(6), Monroe(4)
CLARK (65243) Boone(41), Audrain(30), Randolph(16), Howard(8)
CLARKSBURG (65025) Moniteau(51), Cooper(48)
CLARKSDALE De Kalb
CLARKSVILLE Pike
CLARKTON (63837) Dunklin(98), New Madrid(1)
CLEARMONT Nodaway
CLEVELAND Cass
CLEVER Christian
CLIFTON HILL (65244) Randolph(95), Chariton(4)
CLIMAX SPRINGS Camden
CLINTON (64735) Henry(98), Benton(1)
CLUBB Wayne
CLYDE Nodaway
COATSVILLE (63535) Schuyler(56), Putnam(43)
COFFEY (64636) Daviess(92), Harrison(7)
COLE CAMP (65325) Benton(93), Pettis(4), Morgan(1)
COLLINS St. Clair
COLUMBIA Boone
COMMERCE Scott
CONCEPTION Nodaway
CONCEPTION JUNCTION Nodaway
CONCORDIA (64020) Lafayette(90), Johnson(8), Saline(1)
CONRAN New Madrid
CONTEL CORPORATION St. Charles
CONWAY (65632) Laclede(52), Webster(29), Dallas(17)
COOK STATION (65449) Crawford(97), Phelps(2)
COOTER Pemiscot
CORDER Lafayette
CORNING Holt

COSBY Andrew
COTTLEVILLE St. Charles
COUCH Oregon
COWGILL (64637) Caldwell(78), Ray(21)
CRAIG Holt
CRANE (65633) Stone(93), Barry(6)
CREIGHTON (64739) Henry(77), Cass(22)
CROCKER (65452) Pulaski(95), Miller(4)
CROSS TIMBERS (65634) Hickory(94),
    Benton(4), Camden(1)
CRYSTAL CITY Jefferson
CUBA Crawford
CURRYVILLE Pike
DADEVILLE Dade
DAISY Cape Girardeau
DALTON Chariton
DARLINGTON Gentry
DAVISVILLE (65456) Crawford(98), Iron(1)
DAWN (64638) Livingston(84), Carroll(15)
DE KALB Buchanan
DE SOTO Jefferson
DE WITT Carroll
DEARBORN Platte
DEEPWATER (64740) Henry(70), St.
    Clair(29)
DEERFIELD Vernon
DEERING Pemiscot
DEFIANCE St. Charles
DELTA Cape Girardeau
DENVER (64441) Worth(51), Gentry(48)
DES ARC (63636) Iron(65), Madison(29),
    Wayne(4)
DEVILS ELBOW (65457) Pulaski(95),
    Phelps(4)
DEXTER Stoddard
DIAMOND (64840) Newton(97), Jasper(2)
DIGGINS Webster
DITTMER Jefferson
DIXON (65459) Pulaski(73), Maries(24),
    Miller(2)
DOE RUN St. Francois
DONIPHAN (63935) Ripley(97), Carter(1),
    Oregon(1)
DORA (65637) Ozark(63), Howell(23),
    Douglas(13)
DOVER Lafayette
DOWNING (63536) Schuyler(67),
    Scotland(32)
DREXEL (64742) Cass(88), Bates(11)
DRURY (65638) Douglas(89), Ozark(10)
DUDLEY Stoddard
DUENWEG Jasper
DUKE (65461) Phelps(95), Pulaski(4)
DUNNEGAN (65640) Polk(92), Cedar(7)
DURHAM (63438) Marion(65), Lewis(34)
DUTCHTOWN Cape Girardeau
DUTZOW Warren
EAGLE ROCK Barry
EAGLEVILLE Harrison
EARTH CITY St. Louis
EAST LYNNE Cass
EAST PRAIRIE Mississippi
EASTON Buchanan
EDGAR SPRINGS (65462) Phelps(97),
    Dent(2)
EDGERTON (64444) Platte(93),
    Buchanan(7)
EDINA Knox
EDWARDS (65326) Camden(60),
    Benton(38)
EL DORADO SPRINGS (64744)
    Cedar(90), Vernon(5), St. Clair(3)
ELDON (65026) Miller(95), Morgan(4)
ELDRIDGE Laclede
ELK CREEK Texas
ELKLAND (65644) Webster(58), Dallas(41)
ELLINGTON (63638) Reynolds(94),
    Shannon(3), Carter(1)
ELLSINORE (63937) Carter(83), Butler(15)
ELMER Macon
ELMO Nodaway
ELSBERRY (63343) Lincoln(96), Pike(3)

EMDEN (63439) Shelby(65), Marion(34)
EMINENCE Shannon
EMMA Lafayette
EOLIA (63344) Pike(59), Lincoln(40)
ESSEX Stoddard
ETHEL Macon
ETTERVILLE Miller
EUDORA Polk
EUGENE (65032) Cole(71), Miller(28)
EUNICE Texas
EUREKA (63025) St. Louis(65),
    Jefferson(34)
EVERTON (65646) Dade(61),
    Lawrence(38)
EWING (63440) Marion(46), Lewis(45),
    Shelby(7)
EXCELLO Macon
EXCELSIOR SPRINGS (64024) Clay(73),
    Ray(26)
EXETER (65647) Barry(77), Newton(20),
    McDonald(2)
FAGUS Butler
FAIR GROVE (65648) Greene(76),
    Dallas(13), Webster(9)
FAIR PLAY (65649) Polk(95), Cedar(4)
FAIRDEALING Ripley
FAIRFAX (64446) Atchison(94), Holt(5)
FAIRPORT De Kalb
FAIRVIEW (64842) Newton(97), Barry(2)
FALCON (65470) Wright(74), Laclede(24)
FARBER Audrain
FARLEY Platte
FARMINGTON (63640) St. Francois(98),
    Ste. Genevieve(1)
FARRAR Perry
FAUCETT Buchanan
FAYETTE Howard
FENTON St. Louis
FESTUS (63028) Jefferson(93), Ste.
    Genevieve(6)
FILLMORE Andrew
FISK Butler
FLEMINGTON (65650) Polk(52),
    Hickory(47)
FLETCHER (63030) Jefferson(79),
    Washington(20)
FLINTHILL St. Charles
FLORENCE Morgan
FLORISSANT St. Louis
FOLEY Lincoln
FORDLAND (65652) Webster(91),
    Christian(7), Douglas(1)
FOREST CITY Holt
FORISTELL (63348) St. Charles(65),
    Warren(30), Lincoln(3)
FORSYTH (65653) Taney(97), Christian(2)
FORT LEONARD WOOD Pulaski
FORTESCUE Holt
FORTUNA (65034) Morgan(62),
    Moniteau(37)
FOSTER Bates
FRANKFORD (63441) Pike(97), Ralls(2)
FRANKLIN Howard
FREDERICKTOWN (63645) Madison(97),
    Ste. Genevieve(2)
FREEBURG Osage
FREEMAN Cass
FREISTATT Lawrence
FREMONT (63941) Carter(63),
    Oregon(24), Ripley(12)
FRENCH VILLAGE (63036) St.
    Francois(76), Ste. Genevieve(23)
FRIEDHEIM Cape Girardeau
FROHNA Perry
FULTON Callaway
GAINESVILLE Ozark
GALENA (65656) Stone(77), Christian(22)
GALLATIN Daviess
GALT (64641) Grundy(79), Sullivan(20)
GARDEN CITY Cass
GARRISON (65657) Christian(98),
    Taney(1)

GASCONADE Gasconade
GATEWOOD Ripley
GENTRY Gentry
GERALD Franklin
GIBBS Adair
GIBSON Dunklin
GIDEON (63848) New Madrid(62),
    Pemiscot(37)
GILLIAM Saline
GILMAN CITY (64642) Harrison(75),
    Daviess(14), Grundy(10)
GIPSY Bollinger
GLASGOW (65254) Howard(95),
    Chariton(4)
GLENALLEN Bollinger
GLENCOE St. Louis
GLENWOOD Schuyler
GLOVER Iron
GOBLER (63849) Dunklin(63),
    Pemiscot(36)
GOLDEN Barry
GOLDEN CITY (64748) Barton(62),
    Jasper(21), Dade(15)
GOODMAN (64843) McDonald(63),
    Newton(36)
GOODSON Polk
GORDONVILLE Cape Girardeau
GORIN (63543) Scotland(96), Knox(2)
GOWER (64454) Buchanan(52),
    Clinton(47)
GRAFF Wright
GRAHAM (64455) Nodaway(94),
    Andrew(5)
GRAIN VALLEY Jackson
GRANBY Newton
GRANDIN (63943) Carter(79), Ripley(20)
GRANDVIEW Jackson
GRANGER Scotland
GRANT CITY (64456) Worth(98),
    Harrison(1)
GRASSY Bollinger
GRAVOIS MILLS (65037) Morgan(79),
    Camden(20)
GRAY SUMMIT Franklin
GRAYRIDGE Stoddard
GREEN CASTLE (63544) Sullivan(67),
    Adair(23), Putnam(9)
GREEN CITY Sullivan
GREEN RIDGE Pettis
GREENFIELD Dade
GREENTOP (63546) Adair(64),
    Schuyler(32), Scotland(3)
GREENVILLE Wayne
GREENWOOD (64034) Jackson(92),
    Cass(7)
GROVER St. Louis
GROVESPRING (65662) Wright(79),
    Laclede(19)
GRUBVILLE (63041) Franklin(78),
    Jefferson(21)
GUILFORD Nodaway
HALE (64643) Livingston(55), Carroll(44)
HALF WAY Polk
HALLSVILLE Boone
HALLTOWN Lawrence
HAMILTON (64644) Caldwell(84),
    Daviess(15)
HANNIBAL (63401) Marion(84), Ralls(15)
HARDENVILLE Ozark
HARDIN (64035) Ray(98), Carroll(1)
HARRIS (64645) Sullivan(85), Mercer(14)
HARRISBURG (65256) Boone(84),
    Howard(15)
HARRISONVILLE Cass
HARTSBURG (65039) Boone(91),
    Callaway(8)
HARTSHORN (65479) Texas(91),
    Shannon(8)
HARTVILLE Wright
HARVIELL (63945) Butler(98), Ripley(1)
HARWOOD Vernon
HATFIELD (64458) Harrison(96), Worth(3)

HAWK POINT (63349) Lincoln(96),
    Warren(3)
HAYTI Pemiscot
HAZELWOOD St. Louis
HELENA Andrew
HEMATITE Jefferson
HENLEY (65040) Cole(93), Miller(6)
HENRIETTA Ray
HERCULANEUM Jefferson
HERMANN Montgomery
HERMITAGE Hickory
HIGBEE (65257) Randolph(60),
    Howard(39)
HIGGINSVILLE Lafayette
HIGH HILL Montgomery
HIGH POINT Moniteau
HIGH RIDGE (63049) Jefferson(96), St.
    Louis(3)
HIGHLANDVILLE (65669) Christian(88),
    Stone(11)
HILLSBORO Jefferson
HIRAM Wayne
HOLCOMB (63852) Dunklin(98),
    Pemiscot(1)
HOLDEN Johnson
HOLLAND (63853) Pemiscot(92),
    Dunklin(7)
HOLLIDAY Monroe
HOLLISTER Taney
HOLT Clay
HOLTS SUMMIT Callaway
HOPKINS Nodaway
HORNERSVILLE Dunklin
HORTON Vernon
HOUSE SPRINGS Jefferson
HOUSTON Texas
HOUSTONIA (65333) Pettis(97), Saline(2)
HUGGINS Texas
HUGHESVILLE Pettis
HUMANSVILLE (65674) Polk(80),
    Cedar(14), Hickory(2), St. Clair(2)
HUME (64752) Bates(73), Vernon(26)
HUMPHREYS (64646) Sullivan(88),
    Linn(11)
HUNNEWELL (63443) Shelby(38),
    Monroe(32), Marion(29)
HUNTSVILLE Randolph
HURDLAND (63547) Knox(93), Adair(6)
HURLEY Stone
IBERIA Miller
IMPERIAL Jefferson
INDEPENDENCE Jackson
IONIA (65335) Pettis(82), Benton(17)
IRONDALE (63648) Washington(77), St.
    Francois(22)
IRONTON (63650) Iron(78), St.
    Francois(18), Madison(2)
ISABELLA Ozark
JACKSON Cape Girardeau
JACKSONVILLE (65260) Randolph(43),
    Macon(41), Monroe(15)
JADWIN Dent
JAMESON Daviess
JAMESPORT (64648) Daviess(97),
    Livingston(2)
JAMESTOWN (65046) Moniteau(91),
    Cooper(8)
JASPER (64755) Jasper(91), Barton(8)
JEFFERSON CITY Cole
JERICO SPRINGS (64756) Cedar(90),
    Dade(9)
JEROME Phelps
JONESBURG (63351) Montgomery(56),
    Warren(43)
JOPLIN (64804) Jasper(50), Newton(49)
KAHOKA Clark
KAISER (65047) Miller(98), Camden(1)
KANSAS CITY Jackson
KEARNEY Clay
KELSO Scott
KENNETT Dunklin
KEWANEE New Madrid

KEYTESVILLE Chariton
KIDDER (64649) Caldwell(73), Daviess(26)
KIMBERLING CITY Stone
KIMMSWICK Jefferson
KING CITY (64463) Gentry(94), De Kalb(3), Andrew(1)
KINGDOM CITY Callaway
KINGSTON Caldwell
KINGSVILLE (64061) Johnson(97), Jackson(2)
KIRBYVILLE Taney
KIRKSVILLE Adair
KISSEE MILLS Taney
KNOB LICK St. Francois
KNOB NOSTER (65336) Johnson(91), Pettis(8)
KNOX CITY (63446) Knox(93), Lewis(6)
KOELTZTOWN Osage
KOSHKONONG (65692) Oregon(51), Howell(48)
LA BELLE (63447) Lewis(93), Knox(6)
LA GRANGE Lewis
LA MONTE Pettis
LA PLATA (63549) Macon(95), Adair(4)
LA RUSSELL (64848) Lawrence(94), Jasper(6)
LABADIE Franklin
LACLEDE Linn
LADDONIA (63352) Audrain(93), Ralls(6)
LAKE OZARK (65049) Camden(70), Miller(29)
LAKE SAINT LOUIS St. Charles
LAKE SPRING Dent
LAMAR Barton
LAMPE Stone
LANAGAN McDonald
LANCASTER Schuyler
LAQUEY (65534) Pulaski(82), Laclede(17)
LAREDO (64652) Grundy(97), Sullivan(1)
LATHAM Moniteau
LATHROP (64465) Clinton(91), Caldwell(8)
LATOUR (64760) Johnson(50), Cass(49)
LAURIE Morgan
LAWSON (64062) Ray(65), Clay(17), Clinton(16)
LEADWOOD St. Francois
LEASBURG Crawford
LEBANON (65536) Laclede(98), Dallas(1)
LECOMA (65540) Dent(70), Phelps(29)
LEES SUMMIT Jackson
LEETON (64761) Johnson(92), Henry(7)
LENOX Dent
LENTNER (63450) Shelby(69), Monroe(30)
LEONARD (63451) Shelby(94), Knox(2), Macon(2)
LEOPOLD Bollinger
LESLIE Franklin
LESTERVILLE (63654) Reynolds(89), Iron(10)
LEVASY Jackson
LEWISTOWN Lewis
LEXINGTON Lafayette
LIBERAL Barton
LIBERTY Clay
LICKING Texas
LIGUORI Jefferson
LILBOURN (63862) Bollinger(77), New Madrid(22)
LINCOLN Benton
LINN Osage
LINN CREEK Camden
LINNEUS Linn
LIVONIA Putnam
LOCK SPRINGS Daviess
LOCKWOOD (65682) Dade(84), Lawrence(10), Barton(4)
LODI Wayne
LOHMAN Cole
LONE JACK (64070) Jackson(96), Johnson(3)
LONEDELL Franklin
LONG LANE Dallas

LOOSE CREEK Osage
LOUISBURG (65685) Dallas(97), Polk(2)
LOUISIANA Pike
LOWNDES Wayne
LOWRY CITY St. Clair
LUCERNE (64655) Putnam(98), Sullivan(1)
LUDLOW Livingston
LUEBBERING (63061) Franklin(96), Jefferson(3)
LURAY Clark
LYNCHBURG (65543) Laclede(89), Wright(9)
MACKS CREEK (65786) Camden(98), Dallas(1)
MACOMB (65702) Wright(72), Douglas(27)
MACON Macon
MADISON (65263) Monroe(98), Randolph(1)
MAITLAND Holt
MALDEN (63863) Dunklin(98), New Madrid(1)
MALTA BEND Saline
MANSFIELD (65704) Wright(95), Douglas(4)
MAPAVILLE Jefferson
MARBLE HILL (63764) Bollinger(92), Cape Girardeau(7)
MARCELINE (64658) Linn(82), Chariton(16)
MARIONVILLE (65705) Lawrence(81), Stone(18)
MARQUAND (63655) Madison(74), Bollinger(23), Wayne(1)
MARSHALL (65340) Saline(97), Pettis(2)
MARSHFIELD Webster
MARSTON New Madrid
MARTHASVILLE (63357) Warren(93), St. Charles(6)
MARTINSBURG (65264) Audrain(71), Callaway(25), Montgomery(2)
MARTINSVILLE Harrison
MARYLAND HEIGHTS St. Louis
MARYVILLE Nodaway
MATTHEWS New Madrid
MAYSVILLE De Kalb
MAYVIEW Lafayette
MAYWOOD (63454) Marion(88), Lewis(11)
MC BRIDE Perry
MC CLURG (65701) Taney(77), Douglas(22)
MC FALL (64657) Gentry(66), Harrison(25), Daviess(8)
MC GEE Wayne
MC GIRK Moniteau
MEADVILLE Linn
MEMPHIS Scotland
MENDON Chariton
MENFRO Perry
MERCER Mercer
META (65058) Maries(61), Miller(17), Osage(14), Cole(6)
METZ Vernon
MEXICO (65265) Audrain(98), Monroe(1)
MIAMI Saline
MID MISSOURI Boone
MIDDLE BROOK (63656) Iron(85), Reynolds(14)
MIDDLETOWN (63359) Pike(56), Montgomery(31), Lincoln(6), Audrain(4)
MILAN Sullivan
MILFORD Barton
MILL SPRING Wayne
MILLER Lawrence
MILLERSVILLE (63766) Cape Girardeau(88), Bollinger(11)
MILO Vernon
MINDENMINES Barton
MINERAL POINT Washington
MISSOURI CITY Clay
MISSOURI STATE LOTTERY COMM Cole
MOBERLY (65270) Randolph(98), Monroe(1)

MOKANE Callaway
MONETT (65708) Barry(58), Lawrence(41)
MONROE CITY (63456) Monroe(47), Marion(34), Ralls(18)
MONTGOMERY CITY (63361) Montgomery(80), Callaway(19)
MONTICELLO Lewis
MONTIER Shannon
MONTREAL Camden
MONTROSE (64770) Henry(91), Bates(7)
MOODY Howell
MOORESVILLE (64664) Livingston(98), Sullivan(1)
MORA (65345) Pettis(73), Morgan(13), Benton(12)
MOREHOUSE New Madrid
MORLEY Scott
MORRISON (65061) Gasconade(78), Osage(21)
MORRISVILLE Polk
MORSE MILL Jefferson
MOSBY Clay
MOSCOW MILLS Lincoln
MOUND CITY Holt
MOUNDVILLE Vernon
MOUNT MORIAH Harrison
MOUNT STERLING (65062) Gasconade(88), Osage(12)
MOUNT VERNON Lawrence
MOUNTAIN GROVE (65711) Wright(94), Douglas(4)
MOUNTAIN VIEW (65548) Howell(95), Shannon(3)
MYRTLE Oregon
NAPOLEON Lafayette
NAYLOR (63953) Ripley(96), Butler(3)
NECK CITY Jasper
NEELYVILLE (63954) Butler(96), Ripley(3)
NELSON (65347) Pettis(47), Saline(30), Cooper(22)
NEOSHO Newton
NEVADA Vernon
NEW BLOOMFIELD Callaway
NEW BOSTON (63557) Linn(70), Macon(27), Sullivan(1)
NEW CAMBRIA (63558) Macon(92), Chariton(7)
NEW FLORENCE (63363) Montgomery(89), Warren(10)
NEW FRANKLIN Howard
NEW HAMPTON (64471) Harrison(93), Gentry(6)
NEW HARTFORD Pike
NEW HAVEN (63068) Franklin(98), Gasconade(1)
NEW LONDON (63459) Ralls(93), Pike(6)
NEW MADRID New Madrid
NEW MELLE St. Charles
NEW OFFENBURG Ste. Genevieve
NEWARK Knox
NEWBURG Phelps
NEWTONIA Newton
NEWTOWN (64667) Sullivan(76), Mercer(15), Putnam(7)
NIANGUA (65713) Webster(89), Wright(10)
NIXA (65714) Christian(94), Stone(5)
NOBLE Ozark
NOEL McDonald
NORBORNE (64668) Carroll(82), Ray(17)
NORWOOD (65717) Wright(85), Douglas(14)
NOVELTY Knox
NOVINGER (63559) Adair(89), Putnam(10)
O FALLON St. Charles
OAK GROVE (64075) Jackson(88), Lafayette(11)
OAK RIDGE Cape Girardeau
ODESSA (64076) Lafayette(98), Johnson(1)
OLD APPLETON (63770) Cape Girardeau(68), Perry(31)
OLD MONROE Lincoln

OLDFIELD (65720) Christian(77), Douglas(22)
OLEAN Miller
OLNEY Lincoln
ORAN (63771) Scott(82), Stoddard(17)
OREGON Holt
ORONOGO (64855) Jasper(96), Barton(3)
ORRICK (64077) Ray(81), Clay(18)
OSAGE BEACH Camden
OSBORN (64474) De Kalb(97), Clinton(2)
OSCEOLA (64776) St. Clair(98), Benton(1)
OTTERVILLE (65348) Cooper(85), Morgan(10), Pettis(3)
OWENSVILLE (65066) Gasconade(93), Crawford(6)
OXLY Ripley
OZARK (65721) Christian(98), Greene(1)
PACIFIC (63069) Franklin(67), Jefferson(16), St. Louis(16)
PAINTON Stoddard
PALMYRA Marion
PARIS Monroe
PARK HILLS St. Francois
PARMA (63870) Stoddard(83), New Madrid(16)
PARNELL (64475) Nodaway(87), Worth(9), Gentry(2)
PASCOLA Pemiscot
PASSAIC Bates
PATTERSON Wayne
PATTON Bollinger
PATTONSBURG (64670) Daviess(76), De Kalb(19), Harrison(4)
PAYNESVILLE Pike
PEACE VALLEY (65788) Howell(95), Oregon(4)
PECULIAR Cass
PERKINS Scott
PERRY (63462) Ralls(79), Monroe(20)
PERRYVILLE Perry
PEVELY Jefferson
PHILADELPHIA (63463) Marion(97), Shelby(2)
PHILLIPSBURG (65722) Laclede(86), Dallas(13)
PICKERING Nodaway
PIEDMONT Wayne
PIERCE CITY (65723) Lawrence(89), Newton(6), Barry(3)
PILOT GROVE Cooper
PILOT KNOB Iron
PINEVILLE McDonald
PITTSBURG Hickory
PLATO (65552) Texas(97), Laclede(1)
PLATTE CITY Platte
PLATTSBURG Clinton
PLEASANT HILL (64080) Cass(96), Jackson(3)
PLEASANT HOPE (65725) Greene(77), Polk(22)
PLEVNA (63464) Knox(76), Marion(23)
POCAHONTAS Cape Girardeau
POINT LOOKOUT Taney
POLK (65727) Polk(89), Hickory(10)
POLLOCK (63560) Sullivan(91), Putnam(8)
POLO (64671) Caldwell(72), Ray(27)
POMONA Howell
PONCE DE LEON (65728) Christian(63), Stone(36)
PONTIAC Ozark
POPLAR BLUFF Butler
PORTAGE DES SIOUX St. Charles
PORTAGEVILLE (63873) New Madrid(85), Pemiscot(14)
PORTLAND Callaway
POTOSI Washington
POTTERSVILLE (65790) Howell(88), Ozark(11)
POWELL McDonald
POWERSITE Taney
POWERSVILLE (64672) Putnam(97), Mercer(2)

PRAIRIE HOME Cooper
PRESTON (65732) Hickory(94), Dallas(5)
PRINCETON Mercer
PROTEM Taney
PURCELL Jasper
PURDIN Linn
PURDY Barry
PUXICO (63960) Stoddard(96), Bollinger(3)
QUEEN CITY Schuyler
QUINCY (65735) Hickory(79), Benton(12), St. Clair(7)
QUITMAN Nodaway
QULIN Butler
RACINE Newton
RAVENWOOD (64479) Nodaway(95), Gentry(4)
RAYMONDVILLE Texas
RAYMORE Cass
RAYVILLE Ray
REA Andrew
REDFORD Reynolds
REEDS Jasper
REEDS SPRING (65737) Stone(98), Taney(1)
RENICK Randolph
REPUBLIC (65738) Greene(84), Christian(14)
REVERE Clark
REYNOLDS Reynolds
RHINELAND (65069) Montgomery(81), Callaway(18)
RICH HILL (64779) Bates(93), Vernon(6)
RICHARDS Vernon
RICHLAND (65556) Pulaski(60), Laclede(21), Camden(17)
RICHMOND Ray
RICHWOODS (63071) Washington(88), Jefferson(11)
RIDGEDALE Taney
RIDGEWAY Harrison
RISCO New Madrid
RIVES Dunklin
ROACH Camden
ROBERTSVILLE (63072) Franklin(96), Jefferson(3)
ROBY Texas
ROCHEPORT (65279) Boone(86), Howard(13)
ROCK PORT Atchison
ROCKAWAY BEACH Taney
ROCKBRIDGE Ozark
ROCKVILLE (64780) St. Clair(62), Bates(37)
ROCKY COMFORT (64861) McDonald(84), Newton(11), Barry(3)
ROCKY MOUNT (65072) Morgan(84), Miller(15)
ROGERSVILLE (65742) Webster(52), Greene(47)
ROLLA Phelps
ROMBAUER Butler
ROSCOE St. Clair
ROSEBUD (63091) Gasconade(81), Franklin(18)
ROSENDALE Andrew
ROTHVILLE Chariton
RUETER Taney
RUSH HILL Audrain
RUSHVILLE (64484) Buchanan(74), Platte(25)
RUSSELLVILLE (65074) Cole(76), Moniteau(22), Miller(1)
RUTLEDGE (63563) Scotland(55), Knox(44)
SAGINAW Newton
SAINT ALBANS Franklin
SAINT ANN St. Louis
SAINT CATHARINE Linn
SAINT CATHERINE Linn
SAINT CHARLES St. Charles

SAINT CLAIR Franklin
SAINT ELIZABETH Miller
SAINT JAMES (65559) Phelps(98), Maries(1)
SAINT JOSEPH Buchanan
SAINT LOUIS St. Louis City
SAINT MARY Ste. Genevieve
SAINT PATRICK Clark
SAINT PETERS St. Charles
SAINT ROBERT Pulaski
SAINT THOMAS (65076) Cole(97), Osage(2)
SAINTE GENEVIEVE Ste. Genevieve
SALEM (65560) Dent(98), Shannon(1)
SALISBURY (65281) Chariton(97), Howard(2)
SANTA FE Monroe
SARCOXIE (64862) Jasper(87), Lawrence(8), Newton(4)
SAVANNAH Andrew
SAVERTON Ralls
SCHELL CITY (64783) Vernon(79), St. Clair(20)
SCOTT CITY Scott
SEDALIA Pettis
SEDGEWICKVILLE (63781) Bollinger(77), Perry(20), Cape Girardeau(2)
SELIGMAN Barry
SENATH Dunklin
SENECA (64865) Newton(97), McDonald(2)
SEYMOUR (65746) Webster(98), Douglas(1)
SHELBINA (63468) Shelby(80), Monroe(19)
SHELBYVILLE Shelby
SHELDON (64784) Vernon(56), Jackson(21), Barton(20), Cedar(1)
SHELL KNOB (65747) Stone(58), Barry(41)
SHERIDAN (64486) Worth(55), Nodaway(44)
SHOOK Wayne
SIBLEY Jackson
SIKESTON (63801) Scott(95), New Madrid(4)
SILEX Lincoln
SILVA (63964) Wayne(85), Madison(14)
SKIDMORE (64487) Nodaway(93), Holt(6)
SLATER Saline
SMITHTON (65350) Pettis(94), Morgan(5)
SMITHVILLE (64089) Clay(98), Platte(1)
SOLO Texas
SOUTH FORK Howell
SOUTH GREENFIELD (65752) Dade(67), Lawrence(32)
SOUTH WEST CITY McDonald
SPARTA (65753) Christian(98), Douglas(1)
SPICKARD (64679) Grundy(90), Mercer(9)
SPOKANE (65754) Christian(84), Stone(15)
SPRINGFIELD Greene
SQUIRES (65755) Douglas(52), Ozark(47)
ST CATHARINE Linn
ST JOSEPH Buchanan
STANBERRY (64489) Gentry(93), Nodaway(6)
STANTON Franklin
STARK CITY Newton
STEEDMAN Callaway
STEELE (63877) Pemiscot(97), Dunklin(2)
STEELVILLE (65565) Crawford(98), Washington(1)
STEFFENVILLE (63470) Lewis(93), Shelby(6)
STELLA (64867) Newton(80), McDonald(20)
STET Carroll
STEWARTSVILLE (64490) De Kalb(56), Clinton(39), Buchanan(4)
STOCKTON (65785) Cedar(98), St. Clair(1)

STOTTS CITY Lawrence
STOUTLAND (65567) Laclede(61), Camden(38)
STOUTSVILLE Monroe
STOVER Morgan
STRAFFORD (65757) Greene(77), Webster(22)
STRASBURG Cass
STURDIVANT Bollinger
STURGEON (65284) Boone(95), Audrain(4)
SUCCESS Texas
SULLIVAN (63080) Franklin(81), Crawford(13), Washington(4)
SULPHUR SPRINGS Jefferson
SUMMERSVILLE (65571) Texas(84), Shannon(15)
SUMNER (64681) Chariton(84), Linn(15)
SUNRISE BEACH (65079) Camden(80), Morgan(19)
SWEDEBORG Pulaski
SWEET SPRINGS (65351) Saline(74), Pettis(23), Johnson(1)
SYRACUSE (65354) Morgan(89), Cooper(10)
TALLAPOOSA New Madrid
TANEYVILLE Taney
TARKIO Atchison
TAYLOR (63471) Marion(98), Lewis(1)
TEBBETTS Callaway
TECUMSEH Ozark
TERESITA Shannon
THAYER Oregon
THEODOSIA (65761) Ozark(75), Taney(25)
THOMPSON (65285) Audrain(98), Monroe(1)
THORNFIELD Ozark
TIFF Washington
TIFF CITY McDonald
TINA Carroll
TIPTON (65081) Moniteau(84), Cooper(14), Morgan(1)
TRELOAR Warren
TRENTON Grundy
TRIMBLE Clinton
TRIPLETT Chariton
TROY Lincoln
TRUXTON (63381) Lincoln(45), Warren(40), Montgomery(13)
TUNAS Dallas
TURNERS Greene
TURNEY Clinton
TUSCUMBIA Miller
UDALL Ozark
ULMAN Miller
UNION Franklin
UNION STAR De Kalb
UNIONTOWN Perry
UNIONVILLE (63565) Putnam(90), Sullivan(9)
URBANA (65767) Dallas(84), Hickory(13), Polk(1)
URICH (64788) Henry(83), Bates(16)
UTICA Livingston
VALLES MINES (63087) St. Francois(91), Jefferson(8)
VALLEY PARK St. Louis
VAN BUREN (63965) Carter(93), Reynolds(6)
VANDALIA (63382) Audrain(81), Ralls(10), Pike(8)
VANDUSER Scott
VANZANT Douglas
VERONA (65769) Lawrence(78), Barry(21)
VERSAILLES Morgan
VIBURNUM Iron
VICHY Maries
VIENNA Maries
VILLA RIDGE Franklin

VISTA St. Clair
VULCAN (63675) Iron(92), Washington(4), Reynolds(2)
WACO Jasper
WAKENDA Carroll
WALDRON Platte
WALKER Vernon
WALNUT GROVE Greene
WALNUT SHADE Taney
WAPPAPELLO (63966) Butler(67), Wayne(32)
WARDELL (63879) Pemiscot(98), New Madrid(1)
WARRENSBURG Johnson
WARRENTON (63383) Warren(97), Lincoln(2)
WARSAW (65355) Benton(98), Hickory(1)
WASHBURN (65772) Barry(85), McDonald(14)
WASHINGTON Franklin
WASOLA Ozark
WATSON Atchison
WAVERLY (64096) Lafayette(98), Saline(1)
WAYLAND Clark
WAYNESVILLE Pulaski
WEATHERBY (64497) De Kalb(69), Daviess(30)
WEAUBLEAU (65774) Hickory(89), St. Clair(10)
WEBB CITY Jasper
WELLINGTON Lafayette
WELLSVILLE (63384) Montgomery(89), Audrain(8), Callaway(1)
WENTWORTH (64873) Lawrence(66), Newton(33)
WENTZVILLE St. Charles
WESCO Crawford
WEST ALTON St. Charles
WEST PLAINS Howell
WESTBORO Atchison
WESTON Platte
WESTPHALIA Osage
WHEATLAND Hickory
WHEATON Barry
WHEELING (64688) Livingston(76), Linn(23)
WHITEMAN AIR FORCE BASE Johnson
WHITEOAK Dunklin
WHITESIDE Lincoln
WHITEWATER Cape Girardeau
WILLARD Greene
WILLIAMSBURG Callaway
WILLIAMSTOWN (63473) Lewis(56), Clark(43)
WILLIAMSVILLE (63967) Butler(60), Wayne(39)
WILLOW SPRINGS (65793) Howell(95), Texas(4)
WINDSOR (65360) Henry(56), Pettis(28), Johnson(10), Benton(5)
WINDYVILLE Dallas
WINFIELD Lincoln
WINIGAN (63566) Linn(80), Sullivan(19)
WINONA (65588) Shannon(93), Oregon(6)
WINSTON Daviess
WITTENBERG Perry
WOLF ISLAND Mississippi
WOOLDRIDGE (65287) Cooper(79), Moniteau(20)
WORTH (64499) Worth(75), Gentry(24)
WORTHINGTON Putnam
WRIGHT CITY (63390) Warren(90), Lincoln(9)
WYACONDA (63474) Clark(93), Scotland(5), Lewis(1)
WYATT Mississippi
YUKON Texas
ZALMA (63787) Bollinger(94), Wayne(5)
ZANONI Ozark

ZIP/City Cross Reference

63001-63001 ALLENTON	63361-63361 MONTGOMERY CITY	63547-63547 HURDLAND	63770-63770 OLD APPLETON
63005-63006 CHESTERFIELD	63362-63362 MOSCOW MILLS	63548-63548 LANCASTER	63771-63771 ORAN
63010-63010 ARNOLD	63363-63363 NEW FLORENCE	63549-63549 LA PLATA	63772-63772 PAINTON
63011-63011 BALLWIN	63364-63364 NEW HARTFORD	63551-63551 LIVONIA	63774-63774 PERKINS
63012-63012 BARNHART	63365-63365 NEW MELLE	63552-63552 MACON	63775-63775 PERRYVILLE
63013-63013 BEAUFORT	63366-63366 O FALLON	63555-63555 MEMPHIS	63776-63776 MC BRIDE
63014-63014 BERGER	63367-63367 LAKE SAINT LOUIS	63556-63556 MILAN	63779-63779 POCAHONTAS
63015-63015 CATAWISSA	63369-63369 OLD MONROE	63557-63557 NEW BOSTON	63780-63780 SCOTT CITY
63016-63016 CEDAR HILL	63370-63370 OLNEY	63558-63558 NEW CAMBRIA	63781-63781 SEDGEWICKVILLE
63017-63017 CHESTERFIELD	63371-63371 PAYNESVILLE	63559-63559 NOVINGER	63782-63782 STURDIVANT
63019-63019 CRYSTAL CITY	63373-63373 PORTAGE DES SIOUX	63560-63560 POLLOCK	63783-63783 UNIONTOWN
63020-63020 DE SOTO	63376-63376 SAINT PETERS	63561-63561 QUEEN CITY	63784-63784 VANDUSER
63021-63022 BALLWIN	63377-63377 SILEX	63563-63563 RUTLEDGE	63785-63785 WHITEWATER
63023-63023 DITTMER	63378-63378 TRELOAR	63565-63565 UNIONVILLE	63786-63786 WITTENBERG
63024-63024 BALLWIN	63379-63379 TROY	63566-63566 WINIGAN	63787-63787 ZALMA
63025-63025 EUREKA	63381-63381 TRUXTON	63567-63567 WORTHINGTON	63801-63801 SIKESTON
63026-63026 FENTON	63382-63382 VANDALIA	63601-63601 PARK HILLS	63820-63820 ANNISTON
63028-63028 FESTUS	63383-63383 WARRENTON	63620-63620 ANNAPOLIS	63821-63821 ARBYRD
63030-63030 FLETCHER	63384-63384 WELLSVILLE	63621-63621 ARCADIA	63822-63822 BERNIE
63031-63034 FLORISSANT	63385-63385 WENTZVILLE	63622-63622 BELGRADE	63823-63823 BERTRAND
63036-63036 FRENCH VILLAGE	63386-63386 WEST ALTON	63623-63623 BELLEVIEW	63824-63824 BLODGETT
63037-63037 GERALD	63387-63387 WHITESIDE	63624-63624 BISMARCK	63825-63825 BLOOMFIELD
63038-63038 GLENCOE	63388-63388 WILLIAMSBURG	63625-63625 BLACK	63826-63826 BRAGGADOCIO
63039-63039 GRAY SUMMIT	63389-63389 WINFIELD	63626-63626 BLACKWELL	63827-63827 BRAGG CITY
63040-63040 GROVER	63390-63390 WRIGHT CITY	63627-63627 BLOOMSDALE	63828-63828 CANALOU
63041-63041 GRUBVILLE	63394-63394 CONTEL CORPORATION	63628-63628 BONNE TERRE	63829-63829 CARDWELL
63042-63042 HAZELWOOD	63401-63401 HANNIBAL	63629-63629 BUNKER	63830-63830 CARUTHERSVILLE
63043-63043 MARYLAND HEIGHTS	63430-63430 ALEXANDRIA	63630-63630 CADET	63833-63833 CATRON
63044-63044 BRIDGETON	63431-63431 ANABEL	63631-63631 CALEDONIA	63834-63834 CHARLESTON
63045-63045 EARTH CITY	63432-63432 ARBELA	63632-63632 CASCADE	63837-63837 CLARKTON
63047-63047 HEMATITE	63433-63433 ASHBURN	63633-63633 CENTERVILLE	63838-63838 CONRAN
63048-63048 HERCULANEUM	63434-63434 BETHEL	63636-63636 DES ARC	63839-63839 COOTER
63049-63049 HIGH RIDGE	63435-63435 CANTON	63637-63637 DOE RUN	63840-63840 DEERING
63050-63050 HILLSBORO	63436-63436 CENTER	63638-63638 ELLINGTON	63841-63841 DEXTER
63051-63051 HOUSE SPRINGS	63437-63437 CLARENCE	63640-63640 FARMINGTON	63845-63845 EAST PRAIRIE
63052-63052 IMPERIAL	63438-63438 DURHAM	63644-63644 PARK HILLS	63846-63846 ESSEX
63053-63053 KIMMSWICK	63439-63439 EMDEN	63645-63645 FREDERICKTOWN	63847-63847 GIBSON
63055-63055 LABADIE	63440-63440 EWING	63646-63646 GLOVER	63848-63848 GIDEON
63056-63056 LESLIE	63441-63441 FRANKFORD	63648-63648 IRONDALE	63849-63849 GOBLER
63057-63057 LIGUORI	63442-63442 GRANGER	63650-63650 IRONTON	63850-63850 GRAYRIDGE
63060-63060 LONEDELL	63443-63443 HUNNEWELL	63651-63651 KNOB LICK	63851-63851 HAYTI
63061-63061 LUEBBERING	63445-63445 KAHOKA	63653-63653 LEADWOOD	63852-63852 HOLCOMB
63065-63065 MAPAVILLE	63446-63446 KNOX CITY	63654-63654 LESTERVILLE	63853-63853 HOLLAND
63066-63066 MORSE MILL	63447-63447 LA BELLE	63655-63655 MARQUAND	63855-63855 HORNERSVILLE
63068-63068 NEW HAVEN	63448-63448 LA GRANGE	63656-63656 MIDDLE BROOK	63857-63857 KENNETT
63069-63069 PACIFIC	63450-63450 LENTNER	63660-63660 MINERAL POINT	63860-63860 KEWANEE
63070-63070 PEVELY	63451-63451 LEONARD	63661-63661 NEW OFFENBURG	63862-63862 LILBOURN
63071-63071 RICHWOODS	63452-63452 LEWISTOWN	63662-63662 PATTON	63863-63863 MALDEN
63072-63072 ROBERTSVILLE	63453-63453 LURAY	63663-63663 PILOT KNOB	63866-63866 MARSTON
63073-63073 SAINT ALBANS	63454-63454 MAYWOOD	63664-63664 POTOSI	63867-63867 MATTHEWS
63074-63074 SAINT ANN	63456-63456 MONROE CITY	63665-63665 REDFORD	63868-63868 MOREHOUSE
63077-63077 SAINT CLAIR	63457-63457 MONTICELLO	63666-63666 REYNOLDS	63869-63869 NEW MADRID
63079-63079 STANTON	63458-63458 NEWARK	63670-63670 SAINTE GENEVIEVE	63870-63870 PARMA
63080-63080 SULLIVAN	63459-63459 NEW LONDON	63673-63673 SAINT MARY	63871-63871 PASCOLA
63083-63083 SULPHUR SPRINGS	63460-63460 NOVELTY	63674-63674 TIFF	63873-63873 PORTAGEVILLE
63084-63084 UNION	63461-63461 PALMYRA	63675-63675 VULCAN	63874-63874 RISCO
63087-63087 VALLES MINES	63462-63462 PERRY	63701-63705 CAPE GIRARDEAU	63875-63875 RIVES
63088-63088 VALLEY PARK	63463-63463 PHILADELPHIA	63730-63730 ADVANCE	63876-63876 SENATH
63089-63089 VILLA RIDGE	63464-63464 PLEVNA	63732-63732 ALTENBURG	63877-63877 STEELE
63090-63090 WASHINGTON	63465-63465 REVERE	63733-63733 ZALMA	63878-63878 TALLAPOOSA
63091-63091 ROSEBUD	63466-63466 SAINT PATRICK	63735-63735 BELL CITY	63879-63879 WARDELL
63099-63099 FENTON	63467-63467 SAVERTON	63736-63736 BENTON	63880-63880 WHITEOAK
63100-63199 SAINT LOUIS	63468-63468 SHELBINA	63737-63737 BRAZEAU	63881-63881 WOLF ISLAND
63301-63304 SAINT CHARLES	63469-63469 SHELBYVILLE	63738-63738 BROWNWOOD	63882-63882 WYATT
63330-63330 ANNADA	63470-63470 STEFFENVILLE	63739-63739 BURFORDVILLE	63901-63902 POPLAR BLUFF
63332-63332 AUGUSTA	63471-63471 TAYLOR	63740-63740 CHAFFEE	63931-63931 BRIAR
63333-63333 BELLFLOWER	63472-63472 WAYLAND	63742-63742 COMMERCE	63932-63932 BROSELEY
63334-63334 BOWLING GREEN	63473-63473 WILLIAMSTOWN	63743-63743 DAISY	63933-63933 CAMPBELL
63336-63336 CLARKSVILLE	63474-63474 WYACONDA	63744-63744 DELTA	63934-63934 CLUBB
63338-63338 COTTLEVILLE	63501-63501 KIRKSVILLE	63745-63745 DUTCHTOWN	63935-63935 DONIPHAN
63339-63339 CURRYVILLE	63530-63530 ATLANTA	63746-63746 FARRAR	63936-63936 DUDLEY
63341-63341 DEFIANCE	63531-63531 BARING	63747-63747 FRIEDHEIM	63937-63937 ELLSINORE
63342-63342 DUTZOW	63532-63532 BEVIER	63748-63748 FROHNA	63938-63938 FAGUS
63343-63343 ELSBERRY	63533-63533 BRASHEAR	63750-63750 GIPSY	63939-63939 FAIRDEALING
63344-63344 EOLIA	63534-63534 CALLAO	63751-63751 GLENALLEN	63940-63940 FISK
63345-63345 FARBER	63535-63535 COATSVILLE	63752-63752 GORDONVILLE	63941-63941 FREMONT
63346-63346 FLINTHILL	63536-63536 DOWNING	63753-63753 GRASSY	63942-63942 GATEWOOD
63347-63347 FOLEY	63537-63537 EDINA	63755-63755 JACKSON	63943-63943 GRANDIN
63348-63348 FORISTELL	63538-63538 ELMER	63758-63758 KELSO	63944-63944 GREENVILLE
63349-63349 HAWK POINT	63539-63539 ETHEL	63760-63760 LEOPOLD	63945-63945 HARVIELL
63350-63350 HIGH HILL	63540-63540 GIBBS	63763-63763 MC GEE	63947-63947 HIRAM
63351-63351 JONESBURG	63541-63541 GLENWOOD	63764-63764 MARBLE HILL	63950-63950 LODI
63352-63352 LADDONIA	63543-63543 GORIN	63765-63765 MENFRO	63951-63951 LOWNDES
63353-63353 LOUISIANA	63544-63544 GREEN CASTLE	63766-63766 MILLERSVILLE	63952-63952 MILL SPRING
63357-63357 MARTHASVILLE	63545-63545 GREEN CITY	63767-63767 MORLEY	63953-63953 NAYLOR
63359-63359 MIDDLETOWN	63546-63546 GREENTOP	63769-63769 OAK RIDGE	63954-63954 NEELYVILLE

63955-63955 OXLY	64442-64442 EAGLEVILLE	64658-64658 MARCELINE	64844-64844 GRANBY
63956-63956 PATTERSON	64443-64443 EASTON	64659-64659 MEADVILLE	64847-64847 LANAGAN
63957-63957 PIEDMONT	64444-64444 EDGERTON	64660-64660 MENDON	64848-64848 LA RUSSELL
63960-63960 PUXICO	64445-64445 ELMO	64661-64661 MERCER	64849-64849 NECK CITY
63961-63961 QULIN	64446-64446 FAIRFAX	64664-64664 MOORESVILLE	64850-64850 NEOSHO
63962-63962 ROMBAUER	64447-64447 FAIRPORT	64665-64665 MOUNT MORIAH	64853-64853 NEWTONIA
63963-63963 SHOOK	64448-64448 FAUCETT	64667-64667 NEWTOWN	64854-64854 NOEL
63964-63964 SILVA	64449-64449 FILLMORE	64668-64668 NORBORNE	64855-64855 ORONOGO
63965-63965 VAN BUREN	64451-64451 FOREST CITY	64670-64670 PATTONSBURG	64856-64856 PINEVILLE
63966-63966 WAPPAPELLO	64452-64452 FORTESCUE	64671-64671 POLO	64857-64857 PURCELL
63967-63967 WILLIAMSVILLE	64453-64453 GENTRY	64672-64672 POWERSVILLE	64858-64858 RACINE
64001-64001 ALMA	64454-64454 GOWER	64673-64673 PRINCETON	64859-64859 REEDS
64011-64011 BATES CITY	64455-64455 GRAHAM	64674-64674 PURDIN	64861-64861 ROCKY COMFORT
64012-64012 BELTON	64456-64456 GRANT CITY	64676-64676 ROTHVILLE	64862-64862 SARCOXIE
64013-64015 BLUE SPRINGS	64457-64457 GUILFORD	64677-64677 SAINT CATHERINE	64863-64863 SOUTH WEST CITY
64016-64016 BUCKNER	64458-64458 HATFIELD	64677-64677 SAINT CATHARINE	64864-64864 SAGINAW
64017-64017 CAMDEN	64459-64459 HELENA	64677-64677 ST CATHARINE	64865-64865 SENECA
64018-64018 CAMDEN POINT	64461-64461 HOPKINS	64679-64679 SPICKARD	64866-64866 STARK CITY
64019-64019 CENTERVIEW	64463-64463 KING CITY	64680-64680 STET	64867-64867 STELLA
64020-64020 CONCORDIA	64465-64465 LATHROP	64681-64681 SUMNER	64868-64868 TIFF CITY
64021-64021 CORDER	64466-64466 MAITLAND	64682-64682 TINA	64869-64869 WACO
64022-64022 DOVER	64467-64467 MARTINSVILLE	64683-64683 TRENTON	64870-64870 WEBB CITY
64024-64024 EXCELSIOR SPRINGS	64468-64468 MARYVILLE	64686-64686 UTICA	64873-64873 WENTWORTH
64028-64028 FARLEY	64469-64469 MAYSVILLE	64687-64687 WAKENDA	64874-64874 WHEATON
64029-64029 GRAIN VALLEY	64470-64470 MOUND CITY	64688-64688 WHEELING	64944-64999 KANSAS CITY
64030-64030 GRANDVIEW	64471-64471 NEW HAMPTON	64689-64689 WINSTON	65001-65001 ARGYLE
64034-64034 GREENWOOD	64473-64473 OREGON	64701-64701 HARRISONVILLE	65010-65010 ASHLAND
64035-64035 HARDIN	64474-64474 OSBORN	64720-64720 ADRIAN	65011-65011 BARNETT
64036-64036 HENRIETTA	64475-64475 PARNELL	64722-64722 AMORET	65013-65013 BELLE
64037-64037 HIGGINSVILLE	64476-64476 PICKERING	64723-64723 AMSTERDAM	65014-65014 BLAND
64040-64040 HOLDEN	64477-64477 PLATTSBURG	64724-64724 APPLETON CITY	65016-65016 BONNOTS MILL
64048-64048 HOLT	64478-64478 QUITMAN	64725-64725 ARCHIE	65017-65017 BRUMLEY
64050-64058 INDEPENDENCE	64479-64479 RAVENWOOD	64726-64726 BLAIRSTOWN	65018-65018 CALIFORNIA
64060-64060 KEARNEY	64480-64480 REA	64728-64728 BRONAUGH	65020-65020 CAMDENTON
64061-64061 KINGSVILLE	64481-64481 RIDGEWAY	64730-64730 BUTLER	65022-65022 CEDAR CITY
64062-64062 LAWSON	64482-64482 ROCK PORT	64733-64733 CHILHOWEE	65023-65023 CENTERTOWN
64063-64065 LEES SUMMIT	64483-64483 ROSENDALE	64734-64734 CLEVELAND	65024-65024 CHAMOIS
64066-64066 LEVASY	64484-64484 RUSHVILLE	64735-64735 CLINTON	65025-65025 CLARKSBURG
64067-64067 LEXINGTON	64485-64485 SAVANNAH	64738-64738 COLLINS	65026-65026 ELDON
64068-64069 LIBERTY	64486-64486 SHERIDAN	64739-64739 CREIGHTON	65031-65031 ETTERVILLE
64070-64070 LONE JACK	64487-64487 SKIDMORE	64740-64740 DEEPWATER	65032-65032 EUGENE
64071-64071 MAYVIEW	64489-64489 STANBERRY	64741-64741 DEERFIELD	65034-65034 FORTUNA
64072-64072 MISSOURI CITY	64490-64490 STEWARTSVILLE	64742-64742 DREXEL	65035-65035 FREEBURG
64073-64073 MOSBY	64491-64491 TARKIO	64743-64743 EAST LYNNE	65036-65036 GASCONADE
64074-64074 NAPOLEON	64492-64492 TRIMBLE	64744-64744 EL DORADO SPRINGS	65037-65037 GRAVOIS MILLS
64075-64075 OAK GROVE	64493-64493 TURNEY	64745-64745 FOSTER	65038-65038 LAURIE
64076-64076 ODESSA	64494-64494 UNION STAR	64746-64746 FREEMAN	65039-65039 HARTSBURG
64077-64077 ORRICK	64496-64496 WATSON	64747-64747 GARDEN CITY	65040-65040 HENLEY
64078-64078 PECULIAR	64497-64497 WEATHERBY	64748-64748 GOLDEN CITY	65041-65041 HERMANN
64079-64079 PLATTE CITY	64498-64498 WESTBORO	64750-64750 HARWOOD	65042-65042 HIGH POINT
64080-64080 PLEASANT HILL	64499-64499 WORTH	64751-64751 HORTON	65043-65043 HOLTS SUMMIT
64081-64082 LEES SUMMIT	64500-64500 SAINT JOSEPH	64752-64752 HUME	65046-65046 JAMESTOWN
64083-64083 RAYMORE	64500-64500 ST JOSEPH	64755-64755 JASPER	65047-65047 KAISER
64084-64084 RAYVILLE	64501-64508 SAINT JOSEPH	64756-64756 JERICO SPRINGS	65048-65048 KOELTZTOWN
64085-64085 RICHMOND	64601-64601 CHILLICOTHE	64759-64759 LAMAR	65049-65049 LAKE OZARK
64086-64086 LEES SUMMIT	64620-64620 ALTAMONT	64760-64760 LATOUR	65050-65050 LATHAM
64087-64087 LIBERTY	64621-64621 AVALON	64761-64761 LEETON	65051-65051 LINN
64088-64088 SIBLEY	64622-64622 BOGARD	64762-64762 LIBERAL	65052-65052 LINN CREEK
64089-64089 SMITHVILLE	64623-64623 BOSWORTH	64763-64763 LOWRY CITY	65053-65053 LOHMAN
64090-64090 STRASBURG	64624-64624 BRAYMER	64765-64765 METZ	65054-65054 LOOSE CREEK
64092-64092 WALDRON	64625-64625 BRECKENRIDGE	64766-64766 MILFORD	65055-65055 MC GIRK
64093-64093 WARRENSBURG	64628-64628 BROOKFIELD	64767-64767 MILO	65056-65056 HERMANN
64096-64096 WAVERLY	64630-64630 BROWNING	64769-64769 MINDENMINES	65058-65058 META
64097-64097 WELLINGTON	64631-64631 BUCKLIN	64770-64770 MONTROSE	65059-65059 MOKANE
64098-64098 WESTON	64632-64632 CAINSVILLE	64771-64771 MOUNDVILLE	65061-65061 MORRISON
64100-64199 KANSAS CITY	64633-64633 CARROLLTON	64772-64772 NEVADA	65062-65062 MOUNT STERLING
64401-64401 AGENCY	64635-64635 CHULA	64776-64776 OSCEOLA	65063-65063 NEW BLOOMFIELD
64402-64402 ALBANY	64636-64636 COFFEY	64777-64777 PASSAIC	65064-65064 OLEAN
64420-64420 ALLENDALE	64637-64637 COWGILL	64778-64778 RICHARDS	65065-65065 OSAGE BEACH
64421-64421 AMAZONIA	64638-64638 DAWN	64779-64779 RICH HILL	65066-65066 OWENSVILLE
64422-64422 AMITY	64639-64639 DE WITT	64780-64780 ROCKVILLE	65067-65067 PORTLAND
64423-64423 BARNARD	64640-64640 GALLATIN	64781-64781 ROSCOE	65068-65068 PRAIRIE HOME
64424-64424 BETHANY	64641-64641 GALT	64783-64783 SCHELL CITY	65069-65069 RHINELAND
64426-64426 BLYTHEDALE	64642-64642 GILMAN CITY	64784-64784 SHELDON	65072-65072 ROCKY MOUNT
64427-64427 BOLCKOW	64643-64643 HALE	64788-64788 URICH	65074-65074 RUSSELLVILLE
64428-64428 BURLINGTON JUNCTION	64644-64644 HAMILTON	64789-64789 VISTA	65075-65075 SAINT ELIZABETH
64429-64429 CAMERON	64645-64645 HARRIS	64790-64790 WALKER	65076-65076 SAINT THOMAS
64430-64430 CLARKSDALE	64646-64646 HUMPHREYS	64801-64804 JOPLIN	65077-65077 STEEDMAN
64431-64431 CLEARMONT	64647-64647 JAMESON	64830-64830 ALBA	65078-65078 STOVER
64432-64432 CLYDE	64648-64648 JAMESPORT	64831-64831 ANDERSON	65079-65079 SUNRISE BEACH
64433-64433 CONCEPTION	64649-64649 KIDDER	64832-64832 ASBURY	65080-65080 TEBBETTS
64434-64434 CONCEPTION JUNCTION	64650-64650 KINGSTON	64833-64833 AVILLA	65081-65081 TIPTON
64435-64435 CORNING	64651-64651 LACLEDE	64834-64834 CARL JUNCTION	65082-65082 TUSCUMBIA
64436-64436 COSBY	64652-64652 LAREDO	64835-64835 CARTERVILLE	65083-65083 ULMAN
64437-64437 CRAIG	64653-64653 LINNEUS	64836-64836 CARTHAGE	65084-65084 VERSAILLES
64438-64438 DARLINGTON	64654-64654 LOCK SPRINGS	64840-64840 DIAMOND	65085-65085 WESTPHALIA
64439-64439 DEARBORN	64655-64655 LUCERNE	64841-64841 DUENWEG	65101-65111 JEFFERSON CITY
64440-64440 DE KALB	64656-64656 LUDLOW	64842-64842 FAIRVIEW	65199-65199 MISSOURI STATE LOTTERY
64441-64441 DENVER	64657-64657 MC FALL	64843-64843 GOODMAN	COMM

Zip Range	City	Zip Range	City	Zip Range	City	Zip Range	City
65201-65218	COLUMBIA	65354-65354	SYRACUSE	65609-65609	BAKERSFIELD	65710-65710	MORRISVILLE
65230-65230	ARMSTRONG	65355-65355	WARSAW	65610-65610	BILLINGS	65711-65711	MOUNTAIN GROVE
65231-65231	AUXVASSE	65360-65360	WINDSOR	65611-65611	BLUE EYE	65712-65712	MOUNT VERNON
65232-65232	BENTON CITY	65401-65409	ROLLA	65612-65612	BOIS D ARC	65713-65713	NIANGUA
65233-65233	BOONVILLE	65433-65433	BENDAVIS	65613-65613	BOLIVAR	65714-65714	NIXA
65236-65236	BRUNSWICK	65436-65436	BEULAH	65614-65614	BRADLEYVILLE	65715-65715	NOBLE
65237-65237	BUNCETON	65438-65438	BIRCH TREE	65615-65616	BRANSON	65717-65717	NORWOOD
65239-65239	CAIRO	65439-65439	BIXBY	65617-65617	BRIGHTON	65720-65720	OLDFIELD
65240-65240	CENTRALIA	65440-65440	BOSS	65618-65618	BRIXEY	65721-65721	OZARK
65243-65243	CLARK	65441-65441	BOURBON	65619-65619	BROOKLINE STATION	65722-65722	PHILLIPSBURG
65244-65244	CLIFTON HILL	65443-65443	BRINKTOWN	65620-65620	BRUNER	65723-65723	PIERCE CITY
65246-65246	DALTON	65444-65444	BUCYRUS	65622-65622	BUFFALO	65724-65724	PITTSBURG
65247-65247	EXCELLO	65446-65446	CHERRYVILLE	65623-65623	BUTTERFIELD	65725-65725	PLEASANT HOPE
65248-65248	FAYETTE	65449-65449	COOK STATION	65624-65624	CAPE FAIR	65726-65726	POINT LOOKOUT
65250-65250	FRANKLIN	65452-65452	CROCKER	65625-65625	CASSVILLE	65727-65727	POLK
65251-65251	FULTON	65453-65453	CUBA	65626-65626	CAULFIELD	65728-65728	PONCE DE LEON
65254-65254	GLASGOW	65456-65456	DAVISVILLE	65627-65627	CEDARCREEK	65729-65729	PONTIAC
65255-65255	HALLSVILLE	65457-65457	DEVILS ELBOW	65629-65629	CHADWICK	65730-65730	POWELL
65256-65256	HARRISBURG	65459-65459	DIXON	65630-65630	CHESTNUTRIDGE	65731-65731	POWERSITE
65257-65257	HIGBEE	65461-65461	DUKE	65631-65631	CLEVER	65732-65732	PRESTON
65258-65258	HOLLIDAY	65462-65462	EDGAR SPRINGS	65632-65632	CONWAY	65733-65733	PROTEM
65259-65259	HUNTSVILLE	65463-65463	ELDRIDGE	65633-65633	CRANE	65734-65734	PURDY
65260-65260	JACKSONVILLE	65464-65464	ELK CREEK	65634-65634	CROSS TIMBERS	65735-65735	QUINCY
65261-65261	KEYTESVILLE	65466-65466	EMINENCE	65635-65635	DADEVILLE	65737-65737	REEDS SPRING
65262-65262	KINGDOM CITY	65468-65468	EUNICE	65636-65636	DIGGINS	65738-65738	REPUBLIC
65263-65263	MADISON	65470-65470	FALCON	65637-65637	DORA	65739-65739	RIDGEDALE
65264-65264	MARTINSBURG	65473-65473	FORT LEONARD WOOD	65638-65638	DRURY	65740-65740	ROCKAWAY BEACH
65265-65265	MEXICO	65479-65479	HARTSHORN	65640-65640	DUNNEGAN	65741-65741	ROCKBRIDGE
65270-65270	MOBERLY	65483-65483	HOUSTON	65641-65641	EAGLE ROCK	65742-65742	ROGERSVILLE
65274-65274	NEW FRANKLIN	65484-65484	HUGGINS	65644-65644	ELKLAND	65744-65744	RUETER
65275-65275	PARIS	65486-65486	IBERIA	65645-65645	EUDORA	65745-65745	SELIGMAN
65276-65276	PILOT GROVE	65501-65501	JADWIN	65646-65646	EVERTON	65746-65746	SEYMOUR
65278-65278	RENICK	65529-65529	JEROME	65647-65647	EXETER	65747-65747	SHELL KNOB
65279-65279	ROCHEPORT	65532-65532	LAKE SPRING	65648-65648	FAIR GROVE	65752-65752	SOUTH GREENFIELD
65280-65280	RUSH HILL	65534-65534	LAQUEY	65649-65649	FAIR PLAY	65753-65753	SPARTA
65281-65281	SALISBURY	65535-65535	LEASBURG	65650-65650	FLEMINGTON	65754-65754	SPOKANE
65282-65282	SANTA FE	65536-65536	LEBANON	65652-65652	FORDLAND	65755-65755	SQUIRES
65283-65283	STOUTSVILLE	65540-65540	LECOMA	65653-65653	FORSYTH	65756-65756	STOTTS CITY
65284-65284	STURGEON	65541-65541	LENOX	65654-65654	FREISTATT	65757-65757	STRAFFORD
65285-65285	THOMPSON	65542-65542	LICKING	65655-65655	GAINESVILLE	65758-65758	GAINESVILLE
65286-65286	TRIPLETT	65543-65543	LYNCHBURG	65656-65656	GALENA	65759-65759	TANEYVILLE
65287-65287	WOOLDRIDGE	65546-65546	MONTIER	65657-65657	GARRISON	65760-65760	TECUMSEH
65291-65291	CENSUS BUREAU	65548-65548	MOUNTAIN VIEW	65658-65658	GOLDEN	65761-65761	THEODOSIA
65299-65299	MID MISSOURI	65550-65550	NEWBURG	65659-65659	GOODSON	65762-65762	THORNFIELD
65299-65299	COLUMBIA	65552-65552	PLATO	65660-65660	GRAFF	65764-65764	TUNAS
65301-65302	SEDALIA	65555-65555	RAYMONDVILLE	65661-65661	GREENFIELD	65765-65765	TURNERS
65305-65305	WHITEMAN AIR FORCE BASE	65556-65556	RICHLAND	65662-65662	GROVESPRING	65766-65766	UDALL
65320-65320	ARROW ROCK	65557-65557	ROBY	65663-65663	HALF WAY	65767-65767	URBANA
65321-65321	BLACKBURN	65559-65559	SAINT JAMES	65664-65664	HALLTOWN	65768-65768	VANZANT
65322-65322	BLACKWATER	65560-65560	SALEM	65666-65666	HARDENVILLE	65769-65769	VERONA
65323-65323	CALHOUN	65564-65564	SOLO	65667-65667	HARTVILLE	65770-65770	WALNUT GROVE
65324-65324	CLIMAX SPRINGS	65565-65565	STEELVILLE	65668-65668	HERMITAGE	65771-65771	WALNUT SHADE
65325-65325	COLE CAMP	65566-65566	VIBURNUM	65669-65669	HIGHLANDVILLE	65772-65772	WASHBURN
65326-65326	EDWARDS	65567-65567	STOUTLAND	65672-65673	HOLLISTER	65773-65773	WASOLA
65327-65327	EMMA	65570-65570	SUCCESS	65674-65674	HUMANSVILLE	65774-65774	WEAUBLEAU
65329-65329	FLORENCE	65571-65571	SUMMERSVILLE	65675-65675	HURLEY	65775-65775	WEST PLAINS
65330-65330	GILLIAM	65572-65572	SWEDEBORG	65676-65676	ISABELLA	65776-65776	SOUTH FORK
65332-65332	GREEN RIDGE	65573-65573	TERESITA	65679-65679	KIRBYVILLE	65777-65777	MOODY
65333-65333	HOUSTONIA	65580-65580	VICHY	65680-65680	KISSEE MILLS	65778-65778	MYRTLE
65334-65334	HUGHESVILLE	65582-65582	VIENNA	65681-65681	LAMPE	65779-65779	WHEATLAND
65335-65335	IONIA	65583-65583	WAYNESVILLE	65682-65682	LOCKWOOD	65781-65781	WILLARD
65336-65336	KNOB NOSTER	65584-65584	SAINT ROBERT	65685-65685	LOUISBURG	65783-65783	WINDYVILLE
65337-65337	LA MONTE	65586-65586	WESCO	65686-65686	KIMBERLING CITY	65784-65784	ZANONI
65338-65338	LINCOLN	65588-65588	WINONA	65688-65688	BRANDSVILLE	65785-65785	STOCKTON
65339-65339	MALTA BEND	65589-65589	YUKON	65689-65689	CABOOL	65786-65786	MACKS CREEK
65340-65340	MARSHALL	65590-65590	LONG LANE	65690-65690	COUCH	65787-65787	ROACH
65344-65344	MIAMI	65591-65591	MONTREAL	65692-65692	KOSHKONONG	65788-65788	PEACE VALLEY
65345-65345	MORA	65601-65601	ALDRICH	65701-65701	MC CLURG	65789-65789	POMONA
65347-65347	NELSON	65603-65603	ARCOLA	65702-65702	MACOMB	65790-65790	POTTERSVILLE
65348-65348	OTTERVILLE	65604-65604	ASH GROVE	65704-65704	MANSFIELD	65791-65791	THAYER
65349-65349	SLATER	65605-65605	AURORA	65705-65705	MARIONVILLE	65793-65793	WILLOW SPRINGS
65350-65350	SMITHTON	65606-65606	ALTON	65706-65706	MARSHFIELD	65800-65899	SPRINGFIELD
65351-65351	SWEET SPRINGS	65607-65607	CAPLINGER MILLS	65707-65707	MILLER		
		65608-65608	AVA	65708-65708	MONETT		

Montana

General Help Numbers:

Governor's Office
PO Box 200801, State Capitol   406-444-3111
Helena, MT 59620-0801   Fax 406-444-5529
www.discoveringmontana.com/   8AM-5PM
gov2/css/default.asp

Attorney General's Office
PO Box 201401   406-444-2026
Helena, MT 59620   Fax 406-444-3549
www.doj.state.mt.us/ago/index.htm   8AM-5PM

State Court Administrator
PO Box 203002   406-444-2621
Helena, MT 59620-3002   Fax 406-444-0834
www.lawlibrary.state.mt.us   8AM-5PM

State Archives
Library/Archives Division   406-444-2694
PO Box 201201, 225 N Roberts St   Fax 406-444-2696
Helena, MT 59620-1201   8AM-5PM M-F;
www.his.state.mt.us   9AM-4:30PM
                      1st SA of each month

State Specifics:

Capital: Helena
                  Lewis and Clark County

Time Zone: MST

Number of Counties: 56

Population: 904,433

Web Site: www.discoveringmontana.com/css/default.asp

State Agencies

Criminal Records

Department of Justice, Criminal Records, PO Box 201403, Helena, MT 59620-1403; 406-444-3625, 406-444-0689 (Fax), 8AM-5PM.

www.doj.state.mt.us

Note: The state sexual offender list is available at http://svor2.doj.state.mt.us:8010/index.htm

Indexing & Storage: Records are available from 1950's on and are 100% computerized. It takes 1 week to 1 month before new records are available for inquiry. 85% of all arrests in database have final dispositions recorded.

Searching: Include the following in your request: name, date of birth, Social Security Number, any aliases. Place on request letterhead. Fingerprint searches are optional. 100% of records are fingerprint-supported. The following data is not released: Traffic offenses, unless felony driving under the influence of alcohol. All felonies and misdemeanors (except traffic violations) are released. Records without dispositions are released; the agency attempts to locate the disposition prior to public release.

Access by: mail, in person.

Fee & Payment: The fee is $5.00 per individual for a name check, or $8.00 per individual for a fingerprint check; $32.00 for a fingerprint check plus FBI fingerprint check, when required by statute for child care or schools. Account status to approved screening firms. Fee payee: Montana

Criminal Records Prepayment required. Personal checks accepted. No credit cards accepted.

Mail search: Turnaround time: 5-10 days. A self addressed stamped envelope is requested.

In person search: Turnaround time is usually immediate, unless there is a record or "hit."

Corporation Records
Limited Liability Company
Records
Fictitious Name
Limited Partnerships
Assumed Name
Trademarks/Servicemarks

Business Services Bureau, Secretary of State, PO Box 202801, Helena, MT 59620-2801 (Courier: State Capitol, Room 225, Helena, MT 59620); 406-444-3665, 406-444-3976 (Fax), 8AM-5PM.

http://sos.state.mt.us/css/index.asp

Indexing & Storage: Records are available from the 1860s. New records are available for inquiry immediately. Records are indexed on inhouse computer.

Searching: Include the following in your request: full name of business, specific records that you need copies of. In addition to the articles of incorporation, corporation records include the following information: Annual Reports, Officers, Directors, DBAs, Prior (merged) names, Inactive and Reserved names.

Access by: mail, phone, fax, in person, online.

Fee & Payment: There is no search fee, copies are $.50 each, certification is $2.00 per document. A computerized print-out is $1.00. Fee payee: Secretary of State. Prepayment required. Prepaid accounts may be established. Personal checks accepted. No credit cards accepted.

Mail search: Turnaround time: 2 weeks. A self addressed stamped envelope is requested.

Phone search: Limit of three requests per call.

Fax search: Fax requests are accepted for prepaid accounts at a cost of $3.00 for up to 10 pages and $.25 per additional page to fax back. Turnaround time is up to 10 business days.

In person search: Searching is available in person.

Online search: Visit http://app.discovering montana.com/bes/ for free searches of MT business entities.

Other access: Lists of the new corporations per month are available.

Expedited service: Expedited service is available for mail, phone and in person searches. Turnaround time: 1 day. Add $20.00 per search.

Uniform Commercial Code
Federal Tax Liens

Business Services Bureau, Secretary of State, Rm 260, PO Box 202801, Helena, MT 59620-2801 (Courier: State Capital, 2nd Fl, Helena, MT 59620); 406-444-3665, 406-444-3976 (Fax), 8AM-5PM.

http://sos.state.mt.us/css/index.asp

Indexing & Storage: Records are available from 1965, indexed on computer and on microfiche. Terminated or expired financing statements are not available with the exception of notices of federal tax liens. It takes one day before new records are available for inquiry.

Searching: Use search request form UCC-11. The search includes notice of federal tax liens on businesses and individuals. All state tax liens are filed at the county level. Include the following in your request: debtor exact name and any fictitious names.

Access by: mail, fax, in person, online.

Fee & Payment: The search fee is $7.00 per debtor name, copies are $.50 per page. Fee payee: Secretary of State. Prepayment required. The state will accept prepaid accounts. Personal checks accepted. No credit cards accepted.

Mail search: Turnaround time: 3 to 5 days. A self addressed stamped envelope is requested.

Fax search: Same fees and turnaround time apply.

In person search: Searching is available in person.

Online search: This web-based subscription service provides information about all active liens filed with the office. (It does not include lapsed and terminated liens.) To use the service, you need to establish a prepaid account with the Secretary of State's Office for a fee of $25 per month. Contact the Business Services Bureau, P.O. Box 202801, Helena MT 59620-2801, 406-444-3665 or visit the web site.

Other access: The agency offers farm bill filings lists on a monthly basis for $5.00 per product. A CD-Rom for Farm Products is available for $20.00.

Expedited service: Expedited service is available for fax searches. Turnaround time: 1 to 2 days. Add $20.00 per document.

State Tax Liens
Records not maintained by a state level agency.
Note: Records are at the county level.

Sales Tax Registrations
State does not impose sales tax.

Birth Certificates

Montana Department of Health, Vital Records, PO Box 4210, Helena, MT 59604 (Courier: 111 N Sanders, Rm 209, Helena, MT 59601); 406-444-4228 (Recording), 406-444-2685, 406-444-1803 (Fax), 8AM-5PM.

Indexing & Storage: Records are available from 1907 on. It takes 3 months before new records are available for inquiry.

Searching: Must be able to show direct and tangible interest of records. The decision if you can get copies of records will be up to the staff of the Vital Records department. Include the following in your request: full name, names of parents, mother's maiden name, date of birth, place of birth, relationship to person of record, reason for information request. Must include copy of guardianship papers, if you are guardian. All requesters must include photo ID and phone number.

Access by: mail, fax, in person.

Fee & Payment: A certified copy is $12.00 If you don't know the year add a search fee of $10.00 for first 5 years search, and $1.00 each add'l year. Add $5.00 for using a credit card. The search fee is per 5 years searched. Fee payee: Montana Vital Records. Prepayment required. Personal checks accepted. Credit cards accepted: MasterCard, Visa, AmEx, Discover.

Mail search: Turnaround time: 10 days. No self addressed stamped envelope is required. Search costs $10.00 for each name in request.

Fax search: Must use credit card for additional $5.50.

In person search: Search costs $10.00 for each name in request. Turnaround time same day.

Expedited service: Expedited service is available for mail and phone searches. Turnaround time: overnight delivery. Add $11.50 per package for Fed Ex return plus the $5.00 credit card fee, copy fee, and the $10.00 search fee if necessary.

Death Records

Montana Department of Health, Vital Records, PO Box 4210, Helena, MT 59604 (Courier: 111 N Sanders, Rm 209, Helena, MT 59601); 406-444-4228 (Recording), 406-444-2685, 406-444-1803 (Fax), 8AM-5PM.

Indexing & Storage: Records are available from 1907 on. It takes 3 months before new records are available for inquiry.

Searching: Records are open. Include the following in your request: full name, date of death, place of death, relationship to person of record, reason for information request. Requesters should include a copy of picture ID and phone number.

Access by: mail, fax, in person.

Fee & Payment: A certified copy is $12.00. If year not known, then add a search fee of $10.00 for 5 years serached and $1.00 each add'l year. Add $5.50 for using a credit card. Fee payee: Montana Vital Records. Prepayment required. Personal checks accepted. Credit cards accepted: MasterCard, Visa, AmEx, Discover.

Mail search: Turnaround time: 10 days.

Fax search: Must use credit card.

In person search: Turnaround time same day.

Expedited service: Expedited service is available for mail and phone searches. Turnaround time: overnight delivery. Add $11.50 per document for

Fed Ex return, plus the search, copy, and credit card fee.

Marriage Certificates
Divorce Records

Records not maintained by a state level agency.

Note: Marriage and divorce records are found at county of issue. The State is required by law to maintain an index of these records. The index is from 1943 to present. The State can direct you to the correct county for a fee of $10.00 per 5 years searched.

Workers' Compensation Records

Montana State Fund, PO Box 4759, Helena, MT 59604-4759 (Courier: 5 S. Last Chance Gulch, Helena, MT 59601); 406-444-6500, 406-444-7796 (Fax), 8AM-5PM.

www.montanastatefund.com

Indexing & Storage: Records are available from mid 1980's to 1995 on microfiche. Records 1996 forward are computerized.

Searching: Put request in writing, including reason for the request. They will determine whether the request is legitimate, unless you include a signed release form. Include the following in your request: claimant name, Social Security Number, date of accident, employer.

Access by: mail, fax, in person.

Fee & Payment: Copy fees are $.35 per page if from computer, $.50 per page if from microfiche. There is no search fee. Fee payee: Montana State Fund. Personal checks accepted. No credit cards accepted.

Mail search: Turnaround time: 7 days. No self addressed stamped envelope is required.

Fax search: Same criteria as mail searches.

In person search: One may request information in person.

Driver Records

Motor Vehicle Division, Driver's Services, PO Box 201430, Helena, MT 59620-1430 (Courier: Records Unit, 303 N Roberts, Room 262, Helena, MT 59620); 406-444-4590, 406-444-1631 (Fax), 8AM-5PM.

www.doj.state.mt.us

Note: Copies of tickets are available from the same address; requests must be in writing.

Indexing & Storage: Records are available for lifetime. For suspensions the time varies according to violation-90 days to indefinite and 6 years for an unsatisfied judgment. Note this is availability; records are stored indefinitely. It takes 5 to 10 days before new records are available for inquiry.

Searching: Anyone may order a driving record; however, personal information including address, SSN, photo, and medical information is not released. Opt out is not necessary. The driver's full name, DOB, and/or license number is required.

Access by: mail, in person, online.

Fee & Payment: The fee is $4.00 per three year record history and $10.00 for a certified history. Fee payee: Motor Vehicle Division. Prepayment

required. Billing or draw accounts available. Personal checks accepted. No credit cards accepted.

Mail search: Turnaround time: 3 days. Requests must be in writing, stating purpose and on letterhead. A self addressed stamped envelope is requested.

In person search: Up to 5 records may be requested in person for immediate delivery at this location.

Online search: Both interactive and batch delivery is offered. Fee is $6.00 per record. An Agreement for Driver's License Record Processing must be signed and a $50.00 annual fee is required. For more information, visit http://app.discoveringmontana.com/premium

Other access: Magnetic tape overnight batch retrieval is available for higher volume users.

Vehicle Ownership & Identification
Vessel Ownership & Registration

Department of Justice, Title and Registration Bureau, 1032 Buckskin Drive, Deer Lodge, MT 59722; 406-846-6000, 406-846-6039 (Fax), 8AM-5PM.

www.discoveringmontana.com

Note: Lien information appears on the title record.

Indexing & Storage: Records are available from 1976 to present on microfiche. Watercraft data is available from 1988. It takes 5 to 10 days before new records are available for inquiry.

Searching: Casual requesters may not obtain records without consent of the subject. DPPA requirements enforced. Items required for search could include full name, VIN, plate number, or title number.

Access by: mail, phone, fax, in person.

Fee & Payment: The fee is $6.00 per vehicle/vessel or name search. Fee payee: Title and Registration Bureau. Prepayment required. Personal checks accepted. No credit cards accepted.

Mail search: Turnaround time: 5 to 7 days. Requests must be in writing and signed; using letterhead or the state form is suggested. No self addressed stamped envelope is required.

Phone search: Phone-in accounts have to be pre-approved and must carry a "bank account" with the Bureau.

Fax search: Fee is $6.00 for the first page and a $1.00 for each additional page. Turnaround time is 5-7 days.

In person search: Searching is available in person.

Other access: Bulk or batch ordering of registration information is available on tape, disk, or paper. The user must fill out a specific form, which gives the user the capability of customization. For further information, contact the Registrar at address above.

Accident Reports

Montana Highway Patrol, Accident Records, 2550 Prospect Ave, Helena, MT 59620-1419; 406-444-3278, 406-444-4169 (Fax), 8AM-5PM.

Note: Digital images are available with previous year's data.

Indexing & Storage: Records are available for 10 years to present. Computer indexing since 1991. Digital images are available starting with the year 1995. It takes 10 to 14 days after the accident before new records are available for inquiry.

Searching: Records are only released to persons involved in accident, or an attorney involved in the case. Insurance representatives must have signed authority. Witness statements are only released with a signed authorization from the witness. Include the following in your request: location of accident, date of accident, full name.

Access by: mail, phone, in person.

Fee & Payment: The fee is $2.00 per report. Fee payee: Montana Highway Patrol. Prepayment required. Personal checks accepted. No credit cards accepted.

Mail search: Turnaround time: 3 to 4 working days. Requests must be submitted in writing following guidelines mentioned above. No self addressed stamped envelope is required.

Phone search: The agency will only release names over the phone of people involved in crash.

In person search: Records will be released if proper authorization is shown.

Other access: Statistics, but not reports, are available.

Legislation Records

State Legislature of Montana, State Capitol, Rm 110, PO Box 201706, Helena, MT 59620-1706; 406-444-3064, 406-444-3036 (Fax), 8AM-5PM.

www.leg.state.mt.us

Indexing & Storage: Records are available from 1983 to present, on computer since 1997 and on microfiche 1987 to 1997.

Searching: Include the following in your request: bill number, year.

Access by: mail, phone, in person, online.

Fee & Payment: Copy fee is $.15 per page. Fee payee: Montana Legislative Services Division. Personal checks accepted. No credit cards accepted.

Mail search: Turnaround time: variable. No self addressed stamped envelope is required. No fee for mail request.

Phone search: No fee for telephone request.

In person search: No fee for request. No cash will be accepted.

Online search: Information is available on the Internet. Committee minutes for 1999 forward are available on the Internet. Exhibits from 1999 forward are available on CD-ROM.

Other access: Current session bills and resolutions are available on CD-ROM for $150; other products include the Montana Code, House and Senate Journals, and Annotations, among others.

Voter Registration

Secretary of State, Election Records, PO Box 202801, Helena, MT 59620; 406-444-4732, 406-444-3976 (Fax), 8AM-5PM.

http://sos.state.mt.us

Note: Searching by state personnel depends on the voter file system workload.

Indexing & Storage: Records are available from 1998 (new centralized system). Counties will update the state database 3 times during a 2 year election cycle. Therefore, it is suggested to also search at the county level.

Searching: The following data is not released: Social Security Numbers.

Access by: mail, phone, fax, in person.

Fee & Payment: There are no fees at this time.

Mail search: Turnaround time: 2 to 4 days. No self addressed stamped envelope is required.

Phone search: Records are available by phone.

Fax search: Fax searching available.

In person search: Searching is available in person.

Other access: The state database can be purchased on disk or CD-ROM. Cost depends on sort parameters. For more information, contact Jelaine Graveley.

GED Certificates

Office of Public Instruction, GED Program, PO Box 202501, Helena, MT 59620-2501; 406-444-4438, 406-444-1373 (Fax), 7AM-4PM.

Indexing & Storage: It takes three weeks before new records are available for inquiry.

Searching: The agency will not issue duplicate diplomas. To search, submit the name, SSN and reason for request. The following are also helpful: a signed release, approximate year of test, date of birth, and city of test. Please include a self-addressed stamped envelope.

Access by: mail, phone, in person.

Fee & Payment: There is no fee for either a verification or transcript.

Mail search: Turnaround time 1 week. A self addressed stamped envelope is requested.

Phone search: Limited information is available by telephone.

In person search: No fee for request. Turnaround time same day.

Hunting License Information
Fishing License Information

Fish, Wildlife & Parks Department, Department of Fish & Wildlife, PO Box 200701, Helena, MT 59620-0701 (Courier: 1420 E 6th Ave, Helena, MT 59620); 406-444-2950, 406-444-4952 (Fax), 8AM-5PM.

http://fwp.state.mt.us

Indexing & Storage: Records are available from 1976 for the special resident and non-resident permits and the general permits go back for 5 years. Records are computerized for the current year, prior on microfiche. Records are indexed on inhouse computer, microfiche.

Searching: State law restricts distribution of license lists. The agency will only verify if a person has purchased a license. Include the following in your request: full name, date of birth, Social Security Number. The following data is not released: phone nor social security number

Access by: mail, phone, in person.

Fee & Payment: There is no search fee.

Mail search: Turnaround time: 1 week. A self addressed stamped envelope is requested.

Phone search: Records are available by phone.

In person search: Searching is available in person.

Montana State Licensing Agencies

Licenses Searchable Online

Acupuncturist #33 .... www.discoveringmontana.com/dli/bsd/license/bsd_boards/med_board/board_page.htm
Architect #5 .... www.discoveringmontana.com/dli/bsd/license/license.htm
Athletic Event/Event Timekeeper #3 ...... www.discoveringmontana.com/dli/bsd/license/license.htm
Audiologist #21 .... www.discoveringmontana.com/dli/bsd/license/license.htm
Barber/Barber Instructor #2 .... www.discoveringmontana.com/dli/bsd/license/BSD_boards/BAR_Board/Board_page.htm
Boxer/Boxing Professional #3 .... www.discoveringmontana.com/dli/bsd/license/license.htm
Boxing Manager/Promoter/Judge #3 ..... www.discoveringmontana.com/dli/bsd/license/license.htm
Cemetery #3 .... www.discoveringmontana.com/dli/bsd/license/license.htm
Chemical Dependency Counselor #19 ... www.discoveringmontana.com/dli/bsd/license/license.htm
Child Care Provider #26 .... http://vhsp.dphhs.state.mt.us/dph_r2.htm
Chiropractor #3 .... www.discoveringmontana.com/dli/bsd/license/license.htm
Clinical Social Worker #17 .... www.discoveringmontana.com/dli/bsd/license/license.htm
Construction Blaster #18 .... www.discoveringmontana.com/dli/bsd/license/license.htm
Contractor, Public #36 .... http://erd.dli.state.mt.us/WorkCompRegs/CRlist.pdf
Cosmetologist/Cosmetology Inst./School #2
.... www.discoveringmontana.com/dli/bsd/license/BSD_boards/COS_Board/Board_page.htm
Crematory/Crematory Operator/Technician #3
.... www.discoveringmontana.com/dli/bsd/license/license.htm
Day Care Center #26 .... http://vhsp.dphhs.state.mt.us/dph_r2.htm
Dental Hygienist #5 .... www.discoveringmontana.com/dli/bsd/license/license.htm
Dentist/Dental Assistant #5 .... www.discoveringmontana.com/dli/bsd/license/license.htm
Denturist #5 .... www.discoveringmontana.com/dli/bsd/license/license.htm
Drug Wholesaler #7 .... www.discoveringmontana.com/dli/bsd/license/license.htm
Drugs, Dangerous #7 .... www.discoveringmontana.com/dli/bsd/license/license.htm
Electrician #8 .... www.discoveringmontana.com/dli/ele
Electrologist #2 .... www.discoveringmontana.com/dli/bsd/license/BSD_boards/BAR_Board/Board_page.htm
Emergency Medical Technician #33 ...... www.discoveringmontana.com/dli/bsd/license/bsd_boards/med_board/board_page.htm
Engineer #10 .... www.discoveringmontana.com/dli/bsd/license/bsd_boards/pel_board/board_page.htm
Esthetician #2 .... www.discoveringmontana.com/dli/bsd/license/BSD_boards/BAR_Board/Board_page.htm
Firearms Instructor #9 .... www.discoveringmontana.com/dli/bsd/license/license.htm
Funeral Director #3 .... www.discoveringmontana.com/dli/bsd/license/license.htm
Hairstylist #21 .... www.discoveringmontana.com/dli/bsd/license/license.htm
Hearing Aid Dispenser #3 .... www.discoveringmontana.com/dli/bsd/license/license.htm
Insurance Adjuster #37 .... http://sao.state.mt.us/Database/findagent.htm
Insurance Producer #37 .... http://sao.state.mt.us/Database/findagent.htm
Land Surveyor #10 .... www.discoveringmontana.com/dli/bsd/license/bsd_boards/pel_board/board_page.htm
Landscape Architect #3 .... www.discoveringmontana.com/dli/bsd/license/license.htm
Manicurist #2 .... www.discoveringmontana.com/dli/bsd/license/BSD_boards/BAR_Board/Board_page.htm
Medical Doctor #33 .... www.discoveringmontana.com/dli/bsd/license/bsd_boards/med_board/board_page.htm
Midwife Nurse #32 .... www.discoveringmontana.com/dli/bsd/license/bsd_boards/nur_board/board_page.htm
Midwife, Direct Entry/Apprentice #1 ...... www.discoveringmontana.com/dli/ahc
Mortuary/Mortician #3 .... www.discoveringmontana.com/dli/bsd/license/license.htm
Naturopathic Physician #1 .... www.discoveringmontana.com/dli/ahc
Nurse Anesthetist #32 .... www.discoveringmontana.com/dli/bsd/license/bsd_boards/nur_board/board_page.htm
Nurse-RN/LPN #32 .... www.discoveringmontana.com/dli/bsd/license/bsd_boards/nur_board/board_page.htm
Nursing Professional #32 .... www.discoveringmontana.com/dli/bsd/license/bsd_boards/nur_board/board_page.htm
Nutritionist #33 .... www.discoveringmontana.com/dli/bsd/license/bsd_boards/med_board/board_page.htm
Occupational Therapist #21 .... www.discoveringmontana.com/dli/bsd/license/license.htm
Optometrist #7 .... www.odfinder.org/LicSearch.asp
Osteopathic Physician #33 .... www.discoveringmontana.com/dli/bsd/license/bsd_boards/med_board/board_page.htm
Outfitter #6 .... www.discoveringmontana.com/dli/bsd/license/license.htm
Pharmacist #7 .... www.discoveringmontana.com/dli/bsd/license/license.htm
Physical Therapist #17 .... www.discoveringmontana.com/dli/bsd/license/license.htm
Physician Assistant #33 .... www.discoveringmontana.com/dli/bsd/license/bsd_boards/med_board/board_page.htm
Plumber #8 .... www.discoveringmontana.com/dli/plu
Podiatrist #33 .... www.discoveringmontana.com/dli/bsd/license/bsd_boards/med_board/board_page.htm
Prescriptive Authority, Nurse #32 .... www.discoveringmontana.com/dli/bsd/license/bsd_boards/nur_board/board_page.htm

Private Investigator #9 .... www.discoveringmontana.com/dli/bsd/license/license.htm
Private Security Guard #9 .... www.discoveringmontana.com/dli/bsd/license/license.htm
Process Server #9 .... www.discoveringmontana.com/dli/bsd/license/license.htm
Property Manager #15 .... www.discoveringmontana.com/dli/bsd/license/bsd_boards/rre_board/board_page.htm
Psychologist #11 .... www.discoveringmontana.com/dli/bsd/license/license.htm
Public Accountant #12 .... http://app.discoveringmontana.com/bsdinq/index.html
Radiologic Technologist #21 .... www.discoveringmontana.com/dli/bsd/license/license.htm
Real Estate Appraiser #14 .... www.discoveringmontana.com/dli/bsd/license/license.htm
Real Estate Broker/Salesperson #15 ..... www.discoveringmontana.com/dli/bsd/license/bsd_boards/rre_board/board_page.htm
Referee #3 .... www.discoveringmontana.com/dli/bsd/license/license.htm
Respiratory Care Practitioner #21 .... www.discoveringmontana.com/dli/bsd/license/license.htm
Sanitarian #21 .... www.discoveringmontana.com/dli/bsd/license/license.htm
Security Alarm Installer #9 .... www.discoveringmontana.com/dli/bsd/license/license.htm
Security Company/Organization #9 .... www.discoveringmontana.com/dli/bsd/license/license.htm
Security Guard #21 .... www.discoveringmontana.com/dli/bsd/license/license.htm
Social Worker, LSW #17 .... www.discoveringmontana.com/dli/bsd/license/license.htm
Speech Pathologist #21 .... www.discoveringmontana.com/dli/bsd/license/license.htm
Surveyor, Land #10 .... www.discoveringmontana.com/dli/bsd/license/bsd_boards/pel_board/board_page.htm
Teacher #35 .... http://data.opi.state.mt.us/certification/
Timeshare Broker/Salesperson #15 .... www.discoveringmontana.com/dli/bsd/license/bsd_boards/rre_board/board_page.htm
Veterinarian #11 .... www.discoveringmontana.com/dli/bsd/license/license.htm
Wrestler #3 .... www.discoveringmontana.com/dli/bsd/license/license.htm

Licensing Quick Finder

Acupuncturist #33	406-841-2359
Adoption Agency #4	406-444-5916
Architect #5	406-841-2390
Asbestos Abatement Contractor/Spvr./Supplier #25	406-444-3490
Asbestos Abatement Inspector/Worker #25	406-444-3490
Asbestos Abatement Project Designer/Mgmt. Planner #25	406-444-3490
Athletic Event/Event Timekeeper #3	406-841-2393
Attorney #16	406-442-7660
Audiologist #21	406-444-3091
Barber/Barber Instructor #2	406-841-2333
Boxer/Boxing Professional #3	406-841-2393
Boxing Manager/Promoter/Judge #3	406-841-2393
Brand (Livestock) #29	406-444-2045
Brand Inspector #29	406-444-2045
Calcutta, Gaming #28	406-444-1971
Card Contractor/Card Tournament #28	406-444-1971
Card Dealer #28	406-444-1971
Card Table, Live #28	406-444-1971
Casino Night #28	406-444-1971
Cemetery #3	406-841-2393
Chemical Dependency Counselor #19	406-444-2827
Child Care Agency #4	406-444-1675
Child Care Provider #26	406-444-2012
Chiropractor #3	406-841-2393
Clinical Social Worker #17	406-841-2369
Construction Blaster #18	406-841-2351
Contractor, Public #36	406-444-7734
Cosmetologist/Cosmetology Instructor/School #2	406-841-2333
Crematory/Crematory Operator/Technician #3	406-841-2393
Day Care Center #26	406-444-2012
Dental Hygienist #5	406-841-2390
Dentist/Dental Assistant #5	406-841-2390
Denturist #5	406-841-2390
Dietitian #33	406-841-2359
Drug Wholesaler #7	406-841-2356
Drugs, Dangerous #7	406-841-2356
Electrician #8	406-841-2328
Electrologist #2	406-841-2333
Emergency Medical Technician #33	406-444-3895
Engineer #10	406-841-2367

Esthetician #2	406-841-2333
Firearms Instructor #9	406-841-2387
Foster Care Home/Program #4	406-444-1675
Funeral Director #3	406-841-2393
Fur/Hide Dealer #27	406-444-4558
Gambling Machine, Video/Electronic #28	406-444-1971
Gambling Operator #28	406-444-1971
Gaming Device Mfg./Dist. #28	406-444-1971
Group Home, Youth #30	406-444-6587
Hairstylist #21	406-444-4288
Hearing Aid Dispenser #3	406-841-2395
Horse Racing #22	406-444-4287
Insurance Adjuster #37	406-444-2040
Insurance Producer #37	406-444-2040
Jockey #22	406-444-4287
Land Surveyor #10	406-841-2367
Landscape Architect #3	406-841-2395
Livestock Dealer #29	406-444-2045
Living Trust Seller #38	406-444-2040
Lobbyist #43	406-444-2942
Lottery Retailer #23	406-444-5825
Manicurist #2	406-841-2333
Meat and Poultry #29	406-444-5202
Medical Doctor #33	406-841-2359
Midwife Nurse #32	406-441-2345
Midwife, Direct Entry/Apprentice #1	406-841-2394
Milk & Cream Weigher/Grader/Sampler/Tester #29	406-444-2875
Mortuary/Mortician #3	406-841-2393
Multi-level Marketing Company #38	406-444-2040
Naturopathic Physician #1	406-841-2394
Notary Public #13	406-444-5379
Nurse Anesthetist #32	406-441-2345
Nurse-RN/LPN #32	406-441-2345
Nurseryman #20	406-444-5400
Nursing Professional #32	406-441-2345
Nutritionist #33	406-841-2359
Occupational Therapist #21	406-444-3091
Optometrist #7	406-841-2395
Osteopathic Physician #33	406-841-2359
Outfitter #6	406-444-3738
Pesticide Applicator/Dealer #20	406-444-5400
Pharmacist #7	406-841-2356
Physical Therapist #17	406-841-2369

Physician Assistant #33	406-841-2359
Plumber #8	406-841-2328
Podiatrist #33	406-841-2359
Prescriptive Authority, Nurse #32	406-441-2345
Private Investigator #9	406-841-2387
Private Placement Offering #38	406-444-2040
Private Security Guard #9	406-841-2387
Process Server #9	406-841-2387
Property Manager #15	406-444-2961
Psychologist #11	406-841-2394
Public Accountant #12	406-841-2388
Radiologic Technologist #21	406-444-3091
Real Estate Appraiser #14	406-841-2386
Real Estate Broker/Salesperson #15	406-444-2961
Referee #3	406-841-2393
Respiratory Care Practitioner #21	406-444-3091
Sanitarian #21	406-444-3091
School Guidance Counselor #34	406-444-3150
School Librarian #34	406-444-3150
School Principal #34	406-444-3150
School Superintendent #34	406-444-3150
Securities Broker/Salesperson #38	406-444-2040
Security Alarm Installer #9	406-841-2387
Security Company/Organization #9	406-841-2387
Security Guard #21	406-444-4288
Septic Tank Cleaner #25	406-444-4400
Social Worker, LSW #17	406-841-2369
Speech Pathologist #21	406-444-3091
Surveyor, Land #10	406-841-2367
Taxidermist #27	406-444-4558
Teacher #35	406-444-3095
Telephone, Customer-Owned, Coin-Operated #38	406-444-2040
Timeshare Broker/Salesperson #15	406-444-2961
Underground Storage Tank Inspector #42	406-444-1420
Underground Storage Tank Installer/Remover #42	406-444-1420
Variable Annuities Seller #38	406-444-2040
Veterinarian #11	406-841-2394
Water & Sewage Plant Operator #25	406-444-4400
Weather Modifier #40	406-444-6601
Well Driller #40	406-444-6601
Wrestler #3	406-841-2393

Licensing Agency Information

#1 Board of Alternative Health Care, Division of Professional and Occupational Licensing, PO Box 200513 (301 S Park, 4th Fl), Helena, MT 59620-0513; 406-841-2394, Fax: 406-841-2305. www.discoveringmontana.com/dli/ahc Agency email: compolahc@state.mt.us. Search database at www.discoveringmontana.com/dli/ahc

#2 Board of Barbers & Cosmetologists, Division of Professional and Occupational Licensing, PO Box 200513 (301 S Park, 4th Fl), Helena, MT 59620-0513; 406-841-2333, Fax: 406-841-2305. www.discoveringmontana.com/dli/bsd/lisence/bus.index.htm. Agency email: compolbar@state.mt.us. Search database at www.discoveringmontana.com/dli/bsd/license/bus_licensing_boards.htm

#3 Board: Chiropractor, Funerary, Hearing, Landscape Architect, Athletic Events, Division of Professional and Occupational Licensing, PO Box 200513 (301 S Park, 4th Fl, #428), Helena, MT 59620-0513; 406-841-2393, Fax: 406-841-2305. www.discoveringmontana.com/dli/bsd Agency email: cheryls@state.mt.us. Search database at www.discoveringmontana.com/dli/bsd/license/license.htm

#4 Department of Public Health Human Services, Child & Family Services Division, PO Box 8005 (1400 Boadway), Helena, MT 59604; 406-444-5900, Fax: 406-444-5956. www.dphhs.mt.gov

#5 Board of Dentistry, Architects, Division of Professional and Occupational Licensing, PO Box 200513 (301 S Park), Helena, MT 59620-0513; 406-841-2390, Fax: 406-841-2305. www.discoveringmontana.com/dli/bsd Agency email: compolarch@state.mt.us. Search database at www.discoveringmontana.com/dli/bsd/license/license.htm

#6 Board of Outfitters, Division of Professional and Occupational Licensing, PO Box 200513 (301 S Park, 4th Fl), Helena, MT 59620-0513; 406-444-5983, Fax: 406-444-1667 Agency email: compolout@state.mt.us. Search database at www.discoveringmontana.com/dli/bsd/license/license.htm

#7 Board of Pharmacy & Optometry, Division of Professional and Occupational Licensing, PO Box 200513 (301 S Park, 4th Fl), Helena, MT 59620-0513; 406-841-2356, Fax: 406-841-2343. www.discoveringmontana.com/dli/bsd/license/bsd_boards/pha_board/board_page.htm. Agency email: dlibsdpha@state.mt.us. Search database at www.discoveringmontana.com/dli/bsd/license/license.htm

#8 Plumbing and Electrical Board, Division of Professional and Occupational Licensing, PO Box 200513 (301 S Park, 4th Fl), Helena, MT 59620-0513; 406-841-2328, Fax: 406-841-2309. Agency email: dlibsdele@state.mt.us. Search database at www.discoveringmontana.com/dli/bsd/license/license.htm

#9 Board of Private Security Patrol Officers & Invest., Division of Professional and Occupational Licensing, PO Box 200513 (301 S Park, 4th Fl), Helena, MT 59620-0513; 406-841-2387, 841-2304, Fax: 406-841-2305. Agency email: tersmith@state.mt.us.

Search database at www.discoveringmontana.com/dli/bsd/license/license.htm. Physical Therapy Board (406-841-2369) is separate, but at the same address. Physical Therapy Board email is dlibsdptp@state.mt.us.

#10 Board of Professional Engineers & Land Surveyors, Division of Professional and Occupational Licensing, PO Box 200513 (301 S Park, 4th Fl), Helena, MT 59620-0513; 406-841-2367, Fax: 406-841-2309. www.discoveringmontana.com/doa/aed/aeinfo.html. Agency email: compolpel@state.mt.us. Search database at www.discoveringmontana.com/dli/bsd/license/bsd_boards/pel_board/board_page.htm

#11 Veterinary Board, Board of Psychologists, PO Box 200513 (301 S Park, 4th Fl), Helena, MT 59620-0513; 406-841-2394, Fax: 406-841-2305. www.discoveringmontana.com/dli/bsd/license/license.htm. Agency email: compolpsy@state.mt.us. Search database at www.discoveringmontana.com/dli/bsd/license/license.htm

#12 Board of Public Accountants, 301 South Park (PO Box 200513), Helena, MT 59620-0513; 406-841-2388, Fax: 406-841-2309. www.discoveringmontana.com/dli/bsd/license/bsd_boards/pac_board/board_page.htm Agency email: compolpac@state.mt.us. Search database at http://app.discoveringmontana.com/bsdinq/index.html

#13 Notary Division, Secretary of State, PO Box 202801 (Rm 260), Helena, MT 59620; 406-444-5379, Fax: 406-444-3976. www.sos.state.mt.us/css/Notary/Contents.asp. Agency email: sosnotary@state.mt.us.

#14 Board of Real Estate Appraisers, PO Box 200513 (301 S Park Ave), Helena, MT 59620-0513; 406-841-2386, Fax: 406-841-2305. www.discoveringmontana.com/dli/bsd/license/bsd_boards/rea_board/board_page.htm Agency email: dlibsdrea@state.mt.us. Search database at www.discoveringmontana.com/dli/bsd/license/license.htm

#15 Board of Realty Regulation, Division of Professional and Occupational Licensing, PO Box 200513 (301 S. Park, 4th Fl), Helena, MT 59620-0513; 406-444-2961, Fax: 406-841-2323. www.discoveringmontana.com/dli/bsd/license/bsd_boards/rre_board/board_page.htm. Agency email: compolrre@state.mt.us. Search database www.discoveringmontana.com/dli/bsd/license/bsd_boards/rre_board/board_page.htm

#16 State Bar of Montana, PO Box 577 (7 W 6th Ave, #2B), Helena, MT 59624; 406-442-7660, Fax: 406-442-7763. www.montanabar.org Agency email: cwood@montanabar.org Use email cwood@montanabar.org to request to confirm an attorney's membership.

#17 Physical Therapy Board, Division of Professional & Occupational Licensing, PO Box 200513 (301 S Park), Helena, MT 59620-0513; 406-841-2369, Fax: 406-841-2305. Search database at www.discoveringmontana.com/dli/bsd/license/license.htm

#18 Construction Blasters, Division of Professional and Occupational Licensing, PO Box 200513 (301 S Park), Helena, MT 59620-0513; 406-841-2351, Fax: 406-841-2305. www.com.mt.gov/license/pol/licensing_boards.htm. Agency email: dlibsdbbc@state.mt.us. Search database at www.discoveringmontana.com/dli/bsd/license/license.htm

#19 Chemical Dependency Counselors Board, Division of Professional & Occupational Licensing, PO Box 200513 (301 S Park), Helena, MT 59620-0513; 406-841-2391, Fax: 406-841-2305. Search database at www.discoveringmontana.com/dli/bsd/license/license.htm

#20 Department of Agriculture, PO Box 200201, Helena, MT 59620; 406-444-5400, Fax: 406-444-7336.

#21 Department of Commerce, Licensing Boards, PO Box 200513 (301 South Park, 4th Fl), Helena, MT 59620-0513; 406-841-2300, Fax: 406-841-2305. www.discoveringmontana.com/dli/bsd/license/license.htm. Agency email: jokershisnik@state.mt.us.

#22 Department of Livestock, Board of Horse Racing, PO Box 200512 (1424 9th Av), Helena, MT 59620-0512; 406-444-4287, Fax: 406-444-4305. www.liv.state.mt.us/DOLORG/Horse Racing/index.htm

#23 Department of Commerce, Montana Lottery, 2525 N Montana Ave, Helena, MT 59601; 406-444-5825, Fax: 406-444-5830. www.montanalottery.com. Agency email: montanalottery@mail.com.

#25 Department of Environmental Quality, Permitting & Compliance Division, 1520 E 6th Ave, PO Box 200901, Helena, MT 59620-0901; 406-444-2544, Fax: 406-444-1374. www.deq.state.mt.us Agency email: ebenedict@state.mt.us.

#26 Department of Health & Human Services, Quality Assurance Division, PO Box 202953 (1400 Broadway, Helena), Helena, MT 59620; 406-444-2012, Fax: 406-444-1742. www.dphhs.state.mt.us/divisions/qad/qad.htm. Agency email: bfleming@state.mt.us.

#27 Department of Fish, Wildlife & Parks, Licensing/Data Bureau, 1420 E 6th Ave, Helena, MT 59620-0701; 406-444-4558, Fax: 406-444-4952. Agency email: bbeukelman@state.mt.us.

#28 Department of Justice, Gambling Control Division, 2550 Prospect Ave, Helena, MT 59620-1424; 406-444-1971, Fax: 406-444-9157. www.doj.mt.gov

#29 Department of Livestock, Brand Enforcement, Milk Control, PO Box 202001, Helena, MT 59620; 406-444-2045. www.liv.state.mt.us

#30 Department of Public Health Human Services, Research & Planning Bureau, 48 N Last Chance Gulch, Helena, MT 59620-4001; 406-444-6587, Fax: 406-444-5956. www.dphhs.mt.gov

#32 Board of Nursing, Division of Professional & Occupational Licensing, PO Box 200513 (301 S Park), Helena, MT 59620-0513; 406-441-2345, Fax: 406-841-2343.
www.discoveringmontana.com/dli/bsd/license/bsd _boards/nur_board/board_page.htm. Agency email: dlibsdnur@state.mt.us.
Search database at www.discoveringmontana.com/ dli/bsd/license/bsd_boards/nur_board/board_page. htm

#33 Board of Medical Examiners, PO Box 200513, Helena, MT 59620-0513; 406-444-4284, Fax: 406-841-2363.
Search database at www.discoveringmontana.com/ dli/bsd/license/bsd_boards/med_board/board_page .htm

#35 Certification Division, Office of Public Instruction, PO Box 1043, Helena, MT 59620-2501; 406-444-3095, Fax: 406-444-2893.
www.opi.state.mt.us
Search database at
http://data.opi.state.mt.us/certification

#36 Public Contractors Licensing, Department of Labor, PO Box 8011, Helena, MT 59604; 406-444-7734, Fax: 406-444-3465.
http://erd.dli.state.mt.us/WorkCompRegs/WCRccr eg.htm Search database at http://erd.dli.state.mt. us/WorkCompRegs/CRlist.pdf.

#37 Insurance Division, State Auditor's Office, 840 Helena Ave, Helena, MT 59601; 406-444-2040.
www.sao.state.mt.us
Search database at www.sao.state.mt.us

#38 Securities Division, State Auditor's Office, 840 Helena Ave, Helena, MT 59601; 406-444-2040, Fax: 406-444-5558.
www.discoveringmontana.com/sao/securities/secin tro.htm

#40 Dept. of Natural Resources & Conservation, Water Resources Division, PO Box 201601 (48 N Last Chance Gulch), Helena, MT 59620-1601; 406-444-6601, Fax: 406-444-0533.

#42 Department of Environmental Quality, Remediation Division, PO Box 200901, Helena, MT 59620-0901; 406-444-1420, Fax: 406-444-1901.
www.deq.state.mt.us/rem
Agency email: sburt@state.mt.us.

#43 Commissioner of Political Practices, Lobbyist Licensing, PO Box 202401 (1205 8th Ave), Helena, MT 59620; 406-444-2942, Fax: 406-444-1643.
http://www2.state.mt.us/cpp/css/default.asp.
Agency email: lvaughey@state.mt.us.

Montana Federal Courts

The following list indicates the district and division name for each county in the state. If the bankruptcy court location is different from the district court, then the location of the bankruptcy court appears in parentheses.

County/Court Cross Reference

County	Court	County	Court
Beaverhead	Butte	Meagher	Helena (Butte)
Big Horn	Billings (Butte)	Mineral	Missoula (Butte)
Blaine	Great Falls (Butte)	Missoula	Missoula (Butte)
Broadwater	Helena (Butte)	Musselshell	Billings (Butte)
Carbon	Billings (Butte)	Park	Billings (Butte)
Carter	Billings (Butte)	Petroleum	Billings (Butte)
Cascade	Great Falls (Butte)	Phillips	Billings (Butte)
Chouteau	Great Falls (Butte)	Pondera	Great Falls (Butte)
Custer	Billings (Butte)	Powder River	Billings (Butte)
Daniels	Billings (Butte)	Powell	Helena (Butte)
Dawson	Billings (Butte)	Prairie	Billings (Butte)
Deer Lodge	Butte	Ravalli	Missoula (Butte)
Fallon	Billings (Butte)	Richland	Billings (Butte)
Fergus	Great Falls (Butte)	Roosevelt	Billings (Butte)
Flathead	Missoula (Butte)	Rosebud	Billings (Butte)
Gallatin	Butte	Sanders	Missoula (Butte)
Garfield	Billings (Butte)	Sheridan	Billings (Butte)
Glacier	Great Falls (Butte)	Silver Bow	Butte
Golden Valley	Billings (Butte)	Stillwater	Billings (Butte)
Granite	Missoula (Butte)	Sweet Grass	Billings (Butte)
Hill	Great Falls (Butte)	Teton	Great Falls (Butte)
Jefferson	Helena (Butte)	Toole	Great Falls (Butte)
Judith Basin	Great Falls (Butte)	Treasure	Billings (Butte)
Lake	Missoula (Butte)	Valley	Billings (Butte)
Lewis and Clark	Helena (Butte)	Wheatland	Billings (Butte)
Liberty	Great Falls (Butte)	Wibaux	Billings (Butte)
Lincoln	Missoula (Butte)	Yellowstone	Billings (Butte)
Madison	Butte	Yellowstone Nat. Park (part)	Billings (Butte)
McCone	Billings (Butte)		

Standards for Federal Courts: The search fee is $20.00 per item (one party name or case number). Certification fee is $7.00 per document. Copy fee is $.50 per page. All fees standard unless noted in profile. Mail Search: always enclose a stamped self addressed envelope unless otherwise noted. Before releasing records, all courts require prepayment unless noted in profile.

Open records are located at the court unless otherwise noted. District courts index by defendant and plaintiff as well as by case number. Bankruptcy courts usually index by debtor and case number. While most courts now have their indexes on computer, many still maintain index card files as well.

The universal PACER sign-up number is 800-676-6856. Find PACER and the Party/Case Index on the Web at http://pacer.psc.uscourts.gov. PACER dial-up access is $.60 per minute. Also, courts offering internet access via RACER, PACER, Web-PACER or the new CM-ECF charge $.07 per page fee unless noted as free.

US District Court

District of Montana

Billings Division Clerk, Room 5405, Federal Bldg, 316 N 26th St, Billings, MT 59101 (Courier Address: Use mail address for courier delivery), 406-247-7000, Fax: 406-247-7008.

www.mtd.uscourts.gov

Counties: Big Horn, Carbon, Carter, Custer, Daniels, Dawson, Fallon, Garfield, Golden Valley, McCone, Musselshell, Park, Petroleum, Powder River, Prairie, Richland, Rosebud, Stillwater, Sweet Grass, Treasure, Wheatland,Wibaux, Yellowstone, Yellowstone National Park.

Indexing & Storage: Cases are indexed by defendant, plaintiff, and case number. New cases are available in the index 1 week after filing date. Open records are located at this court.

Fee & Payment Notes: The fee is $25.00 per item (one party name or case number). Payment may be made by money order, cashier check, personal check. Payee: Clerk, US District Court. You are allowed to make your own copies. These copies cost $.10 per page.

Phone Search: Only docket information is available by phone.

Fax Search: The fee is $15.00.

Mail Search: A stamped self addressed envelope is not required.

In Person Search: In person searching available.

PACER: Toll-free dial-up access: 800-305-5235. Local dial-up access: 406-452-9851. Case records are available back to 1992. Records are never purged. New records are available online after 5 days.

Butte Division Room 303, Federal Bldg, Butte, MT 59701 (Courier Address: Use mail address for courier delivery), 406-782-0432, Fax: 406-782-0537.

www.mtd.uscourts.gov

Counties: Beaverhead, Deer Lodge, Gallatin, Madison, Silver Bow.

Indexing & Storage: Cases are indexed by defendant, plaintiff, and case number. New cases are available in the index 1 week after filing date. Open records are located at this court.

Fee & Payment Notes: Payment may be made by money order, cashier check, personal check. Payee: Clerk, US District Court. You are allowed to make your own copies. These copies cost $.10 per page.

Phone Search: Searching not available by phone.

Fax Search: Will accept fax requests if search fee paid in advance.

Mail Search: A stamped self addressed envelope is not required.

In Person Search: In person searching available.

PACER: Toll-free dial-up access: 800-305-5235. Local dial-up access: 406-452-9851. Case records

are available back to 1992. Records are never purged. New records are available online after 5 days.

Great Falls Division Clerk, PO Box 2186, Great Falls, MT 59403 (Courier Address: 215 1st Ave N, Great Falls, MT 59401), 406-727-1922, Fax: 406-727-7648.

www.mtd.uscourts.gov

Counties: Blaine, Cascade, Chouteau, Daniels, Fergus, Glacier, Hill, Judith Basin, Liberty, Phillips, Pondera, Roosevelt, Sheridan, Teton, Toole, Valley.

Indexing & Storage: Cases are indexed by defendant, plaintiff, and case number. New cases are available in the index immediately after filing date. District wide searches are available for all information from this division.

Fee & Payment Notes: Payment may be made by money order, cashier check, personal check. Payee: Clerk, US District Court.

Phone Search: Only docket information available by case number.

In Person Search: In person searching available.

PACER: Toll-free dial-up access: 800-305-5235. Local dial-up access: 406-452-9851. Case records are available back to 1992. Records are never purged. New records are available online after 5 days.

Helena Division Federal Bldg, 301 S. Park Ave, Rm 542, Helena, MT 59626 (Courier Address: Room 542, 301 S Park Ave, Helena, MT 59626), 406-441-1355, Fax: 406-441-1357.

www.mtd.uscourts.gov

Counties: Broadwater, Jefferson, Lewis and Clark, Meagher, Powell.

Indexing & Storage: Cases are indexed by defendant, plaintiff, and case number. New cases are available in the index same day if possible after filing date. Cases filed in the Missoula division prior to January 1997 are held here.

Fee & Payment Notes: Payment may be made by money order, cashier check, personal check. Payee: Clerk, US District Court.

Phone Search: Information by phone is limited.

In Person Search: In person searching available.

PACER: Toll-free dial-up access: 800-305-5235. Local dial-up access: 406-452-9851. Case records are available back to 1992. Records are never purged. New records are available online after 5 days.

Missoula Division Russell Smith Courthouse, PO Box 8537, Missoula, MT 59807 (Courier Address: 201 E Broadway, Missoula, MT 59802), 406-542-7260, Fax: 406-542-7272.

www.mtd.uscourts.gov

Counties: Flathead, Granite, Lake, Lincoln, Mineral, Missoula, Ravalli, Sanders.

Indexing & Storage: Cases are indexed by defendant, plaintiff, and case number. New cases

are available in the index 1-2 days after filing date. Cases in this district originate here; after closing they are held here rather than being sent to a Federal Records Center.

Fee & Payment Notes: Payment may be made by money order, cashier check, personal check. Prepayment required except for attorneys. Court will fax results for a $5.00 fee. Payee: Clerk, US District Court.

Phone Search: Docket information is available by phone.

Mail Search: A stamped self addressed envelope is not required.

In Person Search: In person searching available.

PACER: Toll-free dial-up access: 800-305-5235. Local dial-up access: 406-452-9851. Case records are available back to 1992. Records are never purged. New records are available online after 5 days.

US Bankruptcy Court

District of Montana

Butte Division PO Box 689, Butte, MT 59703 (Courier Address: 303 Federal Bldg, 400 N Main St, Butte, MT 59703), 406-782-3354, Fax: 406-782-0537.

www.mtb.uscourts.gov

Counties: All counties in Montana.

Indexing & Storage: Cases are indexed by debtor as well as by case number. New cases are available in the index immediately after filing date. Open records are located at this court.

Fee & Payment Notes: Payment may be made by money order, cashier check, personal check. Debtor's checks are not accepted. Payee: Clerk, US Bankruptcy Court.

Phone Search: Only docket information is available by phone. An automated voice case information service (VCIS) is available. Call VCIS at 888-879-0071 or 406-782-1060.

Fax Search: Will accept fax searches. Will fax results at $1.00 per page.

Mail Search: A stamped self addressed envelope is not required.

In Person Search: In person searching available.

PACER: Toll-free dial-up access: 800-716-4305. Local dial-up access: 406-782-1051. Use of PC Anywhere v4.0 suggested. Case records are available back to 1986. New civil records are available online after 1 day. PACER is available online at http://pacer.mtb.uscourts.gov.

Electronic Filing: (Currently in the process of implementing CM/ECF.)

Other Online Access: Court does not participate in the U.S. party case index.

Montana County Courts

Court	Jurisdiction	No. of Courts	How Organized
District Courts*	General	56	22 Districts
Limited Jurisdiction Courts*	Limited	70	56 Counties
City Courts	Limited	83	
Municipal Court	Municipal	5	
Water Courts	Special		4 Divisions
Workers' Compensation Court	Special	1	

* Profiled in this Sourcebook.

CIVIL									
Court	Tort	Contract	Real Estate	Min. Claim	Max. Claim	Small Claims	Estate	Eviction	Domestic Relations
District Courts*	X	X	X	$5000-7000	No Max		X		X
Limited Jurisdiction Courts*	X	X	X	$0	$5000-7000	$3000		X	
City Courts	X	X	X	$0	$5000				
Municipal Court	X	X	X	$0	$5000	$3000			
Water Courts			X						
Workers' Comp. Court									

CRIMINAL					
Court	Felony	Misdemeanor	DWI/DUI	Preliminary Hearing	Juvenile
District Courts*	X			X	X
Limited Jurisdiction Courts*		X	X	X	
City Courts		X	X	X	
Municipal Court		X	X	X	
Water Courts					
Workers' Comp. Court					

ADMINISTRATION Court Administrator, Justice Building, 215 N Sanders, Room 315 (PO Box 203002), Helena, MT, 59620; 406-444-2621, Fax: 406-444-0834.

COURT STRUCTURE The District Courts have no maximum amount for civil judgment cases. Most District Courts handle civil over $7,000; there are exceptions that handle a civil minimum as low as $5,000. Limited Jurisdiction Courts, which are also known as Justice Courts, may handle civil actions up to $7,000. The Small Claims limit is $3000.

Many Montana Justices of the Peace maintain case record indexes on their personal PCs, which does speed the retrieval process.

ONLINE ACCESS There is no statewide internal or external online computer system available. A few individual county courts offer online access. Historical information of Supreme Courts decisions may be found online at www.state.mt.us/css/govt/state_agen cies.asp

Beaverhead County

District Court Beaverhead County Courthouse, 2 S Pacific St, Dillon, MT 59725; 406-683-3725; Fax: 406-683-3728. Hours: 8AM-5PM (MST). *Felony, Civil Actions Over $7,000, Eviction, Probate.*

Civil Records: Access: Fax, mail, in person. Both court and visitors may perform in person searches. Search fee: $.50 per name per year. Maximum fee-$25.00. Required to search: name, years to search. Civil cases indexed by defendant, plaintiff. Civil records in books back to 1870s; on computer since 1997. For fax, send fax copy of check for fee.

Criminal Records: Access: Fax, mail, in person. Both court and visitors may perform in person searches. Search fee: $.50 per name per year. Maximum fee-$25.00. Required to search: name, years to search. Criminal records in books back to 1870s; on computer since 1997. For fax, send fax copy of check for fee.

General Information: Public access terminal is available. No adoption, juvenile, sanity, paternity or dismissed criminal records released. SASE required. Turnaround time 1-2 days. Fax notes: $1.00 per page. Copy fee: $.50 per page. $.25 per page after first 5. Certification fee: $2.00. Fee payee: Clerk of Court. Personal checks not accepted. Prepayment is required.

Beaverhead County Justice Court PO Box 107, Lima, MT 59739; 406-276-3741. Hours: 3:30-6PM (MST). *Misdemeanor, Civil Actions Under $7,000, Eviction, Small Claims.*

Dillon Justice Court 2 S Pacific, Cluster #16, Dillon, MT 59725; 406-683-3755; Fax: 406-683-3778. Hours: 8AM-Noon (MST). *Misdemeanor, Civil Actions Under $7,000, Eviction, Small Claims.*

Big Horn County

District Court 121 West 3rd St, Room 221, PO Box 908, Hardin, MT 59034; 406-665-9750; Fax: 406-665-9755. Hours: 8AM-5PM (MST). *Felony, Civil Actions Over $7,000, Probate.*

Civil Records: Access: Phone, fax, mail, in person. Both court and visitors may perform in person searches. Search fee: $.50 per name per year. Maximum fee-$25.00. Required to search: name, years to search; also helpful: address. Civil cases indexed by defendant, plaintiff. Civil records in books and on microfilm back to 1913; on computer back to 1984.

Criminal Records: Access: Fax, mail, in person. Both court and visitors may perform in person searches. Search fee: $.50 per name per year. Maximum fee-$25.00. Required to search: name, years to search, DOB; also helpful: address, SSN. Criminal records in books and on microfilm back to 1913; on computer back to 1979. Court order required for confidential information.

General Information: Public access terminal is available. No adoption, sanity, pre-sentence, psychiatric evaluation, dependent & neglected, or confidential criminal justice records released. SASE required. Turnaround time same day. Fax notes: Fee to fax results is $1.00 per page. Copy fee: $.50 per page. $.25 per page after first 5. Certification fee: $2.00. Fee payee: Clerk of Court. No personal checks accepted. Prepayment is required. Will bill government agencies.

Limited Jurisdiction Court PO Box 908, Hardin, MT 59034; 406-665-9760; Fax: 406-665-9764. Hours: 8AM-5PM (MST). *Misdemeanor, Civil Actions Under $7,000, Eviction, Small Claims.*

Blaine County

District Court PO Box 969, Chinook, MT 59523; 406-357-3230; Fax: 406-357-2199. Hours: 8AM-5PM (MST). *Felony, Civil Actions Over $5,000, Eviction, Probate.*

Civil Records: Access: Fax, mail, in person. Both court and visitors may perform in person searches. Search fee: $.50 per name per year. Maximum fee-$25.00. Required to search: name, years to search. Civil cases indexed by defendant, plaintiff. Civil records in books from 1912; on computer back to 1995.

Criminal Records: Access: Fax, mail, in person. Both court and visitors may perform in person searches. Search fee: $.50 per name per year. Maximum fee-$25.00. Required to search: name, years to search, signed release. Criminal records in books from 1912; on computer back to 1995.

General Information: No adoption, juvenile or sanity records released. SASE required. Turnaround time same day. Fax notes: Fee to fax results is $1.00 per page. Copy fee: $.50 per page. $.25 per page after first 5. Certification fee: $2.00. Fee payee: Clerk of Court. Personal checks accepted. Prepayment is required.

Chinook Justice Court PO Box 1266, Chinook, MT 59523; 406-357-2335. Hours: 8AM-5PM M-F (MST). *Misdemeanor, Civil Actions Under $7,000, Eviction, Small Claims.*

Broadwater County

District Court 515 Broadway, Townsend, MT 59644; 406-266-9236; Fax: 406-266-4720. Hours: 8AM-Noon, 1-5PM (MST). *Felony, Civil Actions Over $7,000, Eviction, Probate.*

Civil Records: Access: Fax, mail, in person. Both court and visitors may perform in person searches. Search fee: $.50 per name per year. Maximum fee-$25.00. Required to search: name, years to search, DOB. Civil records on microfiche and archives back to 1897; on computer back to 1997.

Criminal Records: Access: Fax, mail, in person. Both court and visitors may perform in person searches. Search fee: $.50 per name per year. Maximum fee-$25.00. Required to search: name, years to search, DOB. Criminal records on microfiche and archives back to 1897; on computer back to 1997.

General Information: Public access terminal is available. No adoption, juvenile or sanity records released. SASE required. Turnaround time same day. Copy fee: $.50 per page. $.25 per page after first 5. Certification fee: $2.00. Fee payee: Clerk of Court. Personal checks accepted. Prepayment is required.

Limited Jurisdiction Court 515 Broadway, Townsend, MT 59644; 406-266-9231; Fax: 406-266-4720. Hours: 8AM-5PM (MST). *Misdemeanor, Civil Actions Under $7,000, Eviction, Small Claims.*

Carbon County

District Court PO Box 948, Red Lodge, MT 59068; 406-446-1225; Fax: 406-446-1911. Hours: 8AM-5PM (MST). *Felony, Civil Actions, Probate.*

Note: Also, this court holds youth, adoption and sanity records.

Civil Records: Access: Phone, fax, mail, in person. Both court and visitors may perform in person searches. Search fee: $.50 per name per year. Maximum fee-$25.00. Required to search: name, years to search. Civil cases indexed by defendant, plaintiff. Civil records on docket books from 1895; on computer back to 1997.

Criminal Records: Access: Fax, mail, in person. Only the court performs in person searches; visitors may not. Search fee: $.50 per name per year. Maximum fee-$25.00. Required to search: name, years to search.

Criminal records on docket books from 1895; on computer back to 1997.

General Information: No adoption, juvenile or sanity records released. SASE required. Turnaround time 1-2 days. Fax notes: $1.00 per page. Will fax to 800 numbers no charge. Copy fee: $.50 per page. $.25 per page after first 5. Certification fee: $2.00. Fee payee: Clerk of Court. Personal checks accepted. Prepayment is required.

Carbon County Justice Court PO Box 2, Red Lodge, MT 59068; 406-446-1440; Fax: 406-446-9175. Hours: 8AM-5PM (MST). *Misdemeanor, Civil Actions Under $7,000, Eviction, Small Claims.*

Joliet City Court PO Box 210, Joliet, MT 59041; 406-962-3133; Fax: 406-962-9803. Hours: 8AM-1PM on 1st, 2nd &3rd Wed of month (MST). *Misdemeanor, Civil Actions Under $7,000.*

Carter County

District Court PO Box 322, Ekalaka, MT 59324; 406-775-8714; Fax: 406-775-8730. Hours: 8AM-5PM (MST). *Felony, Civil Actions Over $5,000, Eviction, Probate.*

Civil Records: Access: Phone, fax, mail, in person. Both court and visitors may perform in person searches. Search fee: $.50 per name per year. Maximum fee-$25.00. Required to search: name, years to search. Civil cases indexed by defendant, plaintiff. Civil records in books from 1917; computerized back to 1996.

Criminal Records: Access: Phone, fax, mail, in person. Only the court performs in person searches; visitors may not. Search fee: $.50 per name per year. Maximum fee-$25.00. Required to search: name, years to search, signed release; also helpful: SSN. Criminal records in books from 1917; computerized back to 1996.

General Information: No adoption, juvenile or sanity records released. SASE required. Turnaround time 1-2 days, same to next day for phone requests. Fax notes: $1.00 per page. Copy fee: $.50 per page. $.25 per page after first 5. Certification fee: $2.00. Fee payee: Clerk of Court. Personal checks accepted. Prepayment is required.

Limited Jurisdiction Court PO Box 72, Ekalaka, MT 59324-0072; 406-775-8754; Fax: 406-775-8714. Hours: 8AM-5PM 1st,2nd,3rd Wed. of the month; 10AM-3:PM every 4th Wed. of the month (MST). *Misdemeanor, Civil Actions Under $7,000, Eviction, Small Claims.*

Note: 1st & 3rd Thurs of month here, 2nd & 4th Thurs of month in Alzada (406-775-8749)

Cascade County

District Court County Courthouse, 415 2nd Ave North, Great Falls, MT 59401; 406-454-6780. Hours: 8AM-5PM (MST). *Felony, Civil Actions Over $5,000, Probate.*

Civil Records: Access: Mail, in person. Both court and visitors may perform in person searches. Search fee: $.50 per name per year. Maximum fee-$25.00. Required to search: name, years to search. Civil cases indexed by defendant, plaintiff. Civil records on computer from 1987; on docket books to 1889.

Criminal Records: Access: Mail, in person. Both court and visitors may perform in person searches. Search fee: $.50 per name per year. Maximum fee-$25.00. Required to search: name, years to search, DOB, SSN. Criminal records on computer from 1987; on docket books to 1889.

General Information: Public access terminal is available. No adoption or sanity records released. SASE required. Turnaround time 1-2 days. Copy fee: $.50 per page. $.25 per page after first 5. Certification fee: $2.00.

Fee payee: Clerk of Court. Business checks accepted. Prepayment is required.

Cascade Justice Court Cascade County Courthouse, 415 2nd Ave N, Great Falls, MT 59401; 406-454-6870; Fax: 406-454-6877. Hours: 8AM-5PM (MST). *Misdemeanor, Civil Actions Under $7,000, Eviction, Small Claims.*

Chouteau County

District Court PO Box 459, Ft Benton, MT 59442; 406-622-5024; Fax: 406-622-3028. Hours: 8AM-5PM (MST). *Felony, Civil Actions Over $5,000, Eviction, Probate.*

Civil Records: Access: Fax, mail, in person. Both court and visitors may perform in person searches. Search fee: $.50 per name per year. Maximum fee-$25.00. Required to search: name, years to search. Civil cases indexed by defendant, plaintiff. Civil records on books from 1886; on computer back for 10 years.
Criminal Records: Access: Fax, mail, in person. Both court and visitors may perform in person searches. Search fee: $.50 per name per year. Maximum fee-$25.00. Required to search: name, years to search. Criminal records on books from 1886; on computer back for 10 years.
General Information: Public access terminal is available. No adoption, paternity, juvenile or sanity records released. SASE required. Turnaround time 1 day. Fax notes: $2.00 for first page, $1.00 each add'l. Copy fee: $.50 per page. $.25 per page after first 5. Certification fee: $2.00. Fee payee: Clerk of Court. Business checks accepted. Prepayment is required.

Big Sandy Justice Court PO Box 234, Big Sandy, MT 59520; 406-378-2203; Fax: 406-378-2378. Hours: 1-5PM Th (MST). *Misdemeanor, Civil Actions Under $7,000, Eviction, Small Claims.*

Note: Beginning 12/01/02, this court will be consolidated with the Fort Benton Court, records to be held in Fort Benton.

Ft Benton Justice Court PO Box 459, Ft Benton, MT 59442; 406-622-5502; Fax: 406-622-3815. Hours: 9AM-4PM M,T,W (MST). *Misdemeanor, Civil Actions Under $7,000, Eviction, Small Claims.*

Custer County

District Court 1010 Main, Miles City, MT 59301-3419; 406-874-3326; Fax: 406-874-3451. Hours: 8AM-5PM (MST). *Felony, Civil Actions Over $5,000, Eviction, Probate.*

Civil Records: Access: Phone, fax, mail, in person. Both court and visitors may perform in person searches. Search fee: $.50 per name per year. Maximum fee-$25.00. Required to search: name, years to search. Civil cases indexed by defendant, plaintiff. Civil records on computer back to 1990; also in books.
Criminal Records: Access: Mail, in person. Both court and visitors may perform in person searches. Search fee: $.50 per name per year. Maximum fee-$25.00. Required to search: name, years to search. Criminal records on computer back to 1990; also in books.
General Information: No dependent & neglected, juvenile or sanity records released. SASE required. Turnaround time 1-2 days. Copy fee: $.50 per page. $.25 per page after first 5. Certification fee: $2.00. Fee payee: Clerk of District Court. Personal checks accepted. Prepayment is required.

Limited Jurisdiction Court 1010 Main St, Miles City, MT 59301; 406-874-3408; Fax: 406-874-3452. Hours: 8AM-5PM (MST). *Misdemeanor, Civil Actions Under $7,000, Eviction, Small Claims.*

Note: Record search request must be in writing, fee is $25.00 per search.

Daniels County

District Court PO Box 67, Scobey, MT 59263; 406-487-2651. Hours: 8AM-5PM (MST). *Felony, Civil Actions Over $5,000, Eviction, Probate.*

Civil Records: Access: Phone, mail, in person. Only the court may perform in person searches, visitors my not. Search fee: $.50 per name per year. Maximum fee-$25.00. Required to search: name, years to search. Civil cases indexed by defendant, plaintiff. Civil records on books since 1920; on computer back to 1997.
Criminal Records: Access: Mail, in person. Only the court may perform in person searches, visitors my not. Search fee: $.50 per name per year. Maximum fee-$25.00. Required to search: name, years to search. Criminal records on books since 1920; on computer back to 1986.
General Information: No adoption, juvenile or sanity records released. SASE required. Turnaround time 1-2 days. Fax notes: Fee to fax results is $.50 per page. Copy fee: $.50 per document. Add $.25 per page after first 5. Certification fee: $2.00. Fee payee: Clerk of Court. Personal checks accepted. Prepayment is required.

Limited Jurisdiction Court Daniels County Courthouse, Scobey, MT 59263; 406-487-5432; Fax: 406-487-5432. Hours: 8AM-5PM (MST). *Misdemeanor, Civil Actions Under $7,000, Eviction, Small Claims.*

Dawson County

District Court 207 W Bell, Glendive, MT 59330; 406-377-3967; Fax: 406-377-7280. Hours: 8AM-5PM (MST). *Felony, Civil Actions Over $5,000, Eviction, Probate.*

Civil Records: Access: Mail, in person. Both court and visitors may perform in person searches. Search fee: $.50 per name per year. Maximum fee-$25.00. Required to search: name, years to search. Civil cases indexed by defendant, plaintiff. Civil records on computer from 1991, on card index prior.
Criminal Records: Access: Mail, in person. Only the court performs in person searches; visitors may not. Search fee: $.50 per name per year. Maximum fee-$25.00. Required to search: name, years to search, DOB, SSN. Criminal records on computer from 1991, on card index prior.
General Information: Public access terminal is available. No adoption, juvenile, sanity or expunged records released. SASE required. Turnaround time same day. Copy fee: $.50 per page. $.25 per page after first 5. Certification fee: $2.00. Fee payee: Justice Court. Only cashiers checks and money orders accepted. Prepayment is required.

Limited Jurisdiction Court 207 W Bell, Glendive, MT 59330; 406-377-5425; Fax: 406-377-2022. Hours: 8AM-5PM (MST). *Misdemeanor, Civil Actions Under $7,000, Eviction, Small Claims.*

Deer Lodge County

District Court 800 S Main, Anaconda, MT 59711; 406-563-4040; Fax: 406-563-4077. Hours: 8AM-5PM (MST). *Felony, Civil Actions Over $5,000, Eviction, Probate.*

Civil Records: Access: Phone, mail, in person. Both court and visitors may perform in person searches. Search fee: $.50 per name per year. Maximum fee-$25.00. Required to search: name, years to search. Civil cases indexed by defendant, plaintiff. Civil records in archives and index books; on computer back to 1996.
Criminal Records: Access: Mail, in person. Both court and visitors may perform in person searches. Search fee: $.50 per name per year. Maximum fee-$25.00. Required to search: name, years to search. Criminal

records in archives and index books; on computer back to 1996.
General Information: Public access terminal is available. No adoption, juvenile or sanity records released. SASE required. Turnaround time 2-3 days. Fax notes: Fee to fax results is $4.00 per document. Copy fee: $.50 per page. $.25 per page after first 5. Certification fee: $2.00. Fee payee: Clerk of Court. Personal checks accepted.

Limited Jurisdiction Court 800 S Main, Anaconda, MT 59711; 406-563-4025; Fax: 406-563-4028. Hours: 8AM-5PM (MST). *Misdemeanor, Civil Actions Under $7,000, Eviction, Small Claims.*

Fallon County

District Court PO Box 1521, Baker, MT 59313; 406-778-7114; Fax: 406-778-2815. Hours: 8AM-5PM (MST). *Felony, Civil Actions Over $5,000, Eviction, Probate.*

Civil Records: Access: Mail, in person. Both court and visitors may perform in person searches. Search fee: $.50 per name per year. Maximum fee-$25.00. Required to search: name, years to search, address. Civil cases indexed by defendant, plaintiff. Civil records in books.
Criminal Records: Access: Mail, in person. Both court and visitors may perform in person searches. Search fee: $.50 per name per year. Maximum fee-$25.00. Required to search: name, years to search. Criminal records in books.
General Information: Public access terminal is available. No confidential records released. SASE required. Turnaround time same day. Fax notes: Fee to fax results is $1.00 per page. Copy fee: $.50 per page. $.25 per page after first 5. Certification fee: $2.00. Fee payee: Clerk of Court. Personal checks accepted. Prepayment is required.

Justice Court Box 846, Baker, MT 59313; 406-778-7128; Fax: 406-778-2815. Hours: 11:00AM-4:00PM T,W,Th (MST). *Misdemeanor, Civil Actions Under $7,000, Eviction, Small Claims.*

Fergus County

District Court PO Box 1074 (712 W Main), Lewistown, MT 59457; 406-538-5026; Fax: 406-538-6076. Hours: 8AM-5PM (MST). *Felony, Civil Actions Over $7,000, Eviction, Probate.*

www.co.fergus.mt.us

Civil Records: Access: Phone, fax, mail, in person. Both court and visitors may perform in person searches. Search fee: $.50 per name per year. Maximum fee-$25.00. Required to search: name, years to search. Civil cases indexed by defendant, plaintiff. Civil records on computer back to 1997; prior on docket books, microfiche.
Criminal Records: Access: Phone, fax, mail, in person. Both court and visitors may perform in person searches. Search fee: $.50 per name per year. Maximum fee-$25.00. Required to search: name, years to search. Criminal records on computer back to 1997; prior on docket books, microfiche.
General Information: Public access terminal is available. No adoption, juvenile, sanity or expunged records released. SASE required. Turnaround time 1 day. Fax notes: Fee to fax results is $1.00 per page. Copy fee: $.50 per page. $.25 per page after first 5. Certification fee: $2.00. Fee payee: Clerk of Court. Personal checks accepted. Prepayment is required.

Limited Jurisdiction Court 121 8th Ave South, Lewistown, MT 59457; 406-538-5418; Fax: 406-538-3860. Hours: 9AM-4PM (MST). *Misdemeanor, Civil Actions Under $7,000, Eviction, Small Claims.*

Flathead County

District Court 800 S Main (920 S. Main, 3rd Fl), Kalispell, MT 59901; 406-758-5660. Hours: 8AM-5PM (MST). *Felony, Civil Actions Over $5,000, Probate.*

www.co.flathead.mt.us/clkcrt/index.html

Civil Records: Access: Mail, in person. Both court and visitors may perform in person searches. Search fee: $.50 per name per year. Maximum fee-$25.00. Required to search: name, years to search. Civil cases indexed by defendant, plaintiff. Civil records on computer since 1990; records go back to 1893.

Criminal Records: Access: Mail, in person. Only the court performs in person searches; visitors may not. Search fee: $.50 per name per year. Maximum fee-$25.00. Required to search: name, years to search. Criminal records on computer since 1990; records go back to 1893.

General Information: No adoption, dependent/neglected children or sanity records released. SASE required. Turnaround time 3 days. Fax notes: Fee to fax results is $.50 per page. Certification fee: $2.00. Fee payee: Clerk of Court. Personal checks accepted. Prepayment is required.

Limited Jurisdiction Court 800 S Main St, Kalispell, MT 59901; 406-758-5643; Fax: 406-758-5642. Hours: 8AM-5PM (MST). *Misdemeanor, Civil Actions Under $7,000, Eviction, Small Claims.*

www.co.flathead.mt.us/justice/index.html

Gallatin County

Clerk of District Court 615 S 16th, Rm 302, Bozeman, MT 59715; 406-582-2165; Fax: 406-582-2176. Hours: 8AM-5PM (MST). *Felony, Civil Actions Over $7,000, Probate.*

Civil Records: Access: Phone (with fee), mail, fax, in person. Both court and visitors may perform in person searches. Search fee: $.50 per name per year. Maximum fee-$25.00. Required to search: name, years to search. Civil cases indexed by defendant, plaintiff. Civil records on computer back to 1985; docket books back to 1860.

Criminal Records: Access: Mail, in person. Both court and visitors may perform in person searches. Search fee: $.50 per name per year. Maximum fee-$25.00. Required to search: name, years to search. Criminal records on computer back to 1985; docket books back to 1860.

General Information: Public access terminal is available. No adoption, juvenile or sanity records released. SASE required. Fax notes: Fee to fax results is $2.00 per page for the f1st page, $1.00 per page thereafter. Copy fee: $.50 per page. $.25 per page after first 5. Certification fee: $2.00. Fee payee: Clerk of Court. Personal checks accepted. Prepayment is required.

Belgrade Justice & City Court 91 E Central, Belgrade, MT 59714; 406-388-3774; Fax: 406-388-3779. Hours: 8AM-Noon M,W,F (MST). *Misdemeanor, Civil Actions Under $7,000, Eviction, Small Claims.*

Bozeman Justice Court 615 S 16th St, Bozeman, MT 59715; 406-582-2191; Fax: 406-582-2041. Hours: 8AM-5PM (MST). *Misdemeanor, Civil Actions Under $7,000, Eviction, Small Claims.*

Garfield County

District Court PO Box 8, Jordan, MT 59337; 406-557-6254; Fax: 406-557-2625. Hours: 8AM-5PM (MST). *Felony, Civil Actions Over $5,000, Eviction, Probate.*

Civil Records: Access: Phone, mail, in person. Both court and visitors may perform in person searches.

Search fee: $.50 per name per year. Maximum fee-$25.00. Required to search: name, years to search. Civil cases indexed by plaintiff. Civil records in books from early 1900s; computerized records go back to 1998. Some records lost due to fire in December, 1997.

Criminal Records: Access: Phone, mail, in person. Both court and visitors may perform in person searches. Search fee: $.50 per name per year. Maximum fee-$25.00. Required to search: name, years to search; also helpful: DOB. Criminal records in books from early 1900s, computerized records go back to 1998. Some records lost due to fire in December, 1997.

General Information: No adoption, juvenile or sanity records released. SASE required. Turnaround time 1 week. Copy fee: $.50 per page. $.25 per page after first 5. Certification fee: $2.00. Fee payee: Clerk of Court. Personal checks accepted. Prepayment is required.

Limited Jurisdiction Court PO Box 482, Jordan, MT 59337; 406-557-2733; Fax: 406-557-2735. Hours: 8AM-5PM Wed (MST). *Misdemeanor, Civil Actions Under $7,000, Eviction, Small Claims.*

Glacier County

District Court 512 E Main St, Cut Bank, MT 59427; 406-873-5063 X36; Fax: 406-873-5627. Hours: 8AM-5PM (MST). *Civil Actions, Probate.*

Civil Records: Access: Phone, fax, mail, in person, email. Both court and visitors may perform in person searches. Search fee: $.50 per name per year. Maximum fee-$25.00. Required to search: name, years to search. Civil cases indexed by defendant, plaintiff. Civil records in books from 1919; on computer since 1992. Email requests to dianderson@state.mt.us.

Criminal Records: Access: Fax, mail, in person. Both court and visitors may perform in person searches. Search fee: $.50 per name per year. Maximum fee-$25.00. Required to search: name, years to search, DOB, SSN. Criminal records in books from 1919; on computer since 1992. Written request required.

General Information: Public access terminal is available. No adoption, juvenile, sanity or paternity records released without court order. SASE required. Turnaround time usually same day, 2-3 hours for phone requests, depending on workload. Fax notes: Fee to fax results is $1.00 per page. Copy fee: $.50 per page. $.25 per page after first 5. Certification fee: $2.00. Fee payee: Clerk of District Court. Personal checks accepted. Prepayment is required.

Limited Jurisdiction Court 512 E Main St, Cut Bank, MT 59427; 406-873-5063 X39; Fax: 406-873-4218. Hours: 8AM-Noon, 1-5PM (MST). *Misdemeanor, Civil Actions Under $7,000, Eviction, Small Claims.*

Golden Valley County

District Court PO Box 10, Ryegate, MT 59074; 406-568-2231; Fax: 406-568-2598. Hours: 8AM-5PM (MST). *Felony, Civil Actions Over $5,000, Eviction, Probate.*

Civil Records: Access: Fax, mail, in person. Search fee: $.50 per name per year. Maximum fee-$25.00. Required to search: name, years to search, signed release. Civil cases indexed by defendant, plaintiff. Civil records on books back to 1923. Computerized records to 1997.

Criminal Records: Access: Fax, mail, in person. Only the court performs in person searches; visitors may not. Search fee: $.50 per name per year. Maximum fee-$25.00. Required to search: name, years to search, signed release. Criminal records on books to 1923. Computerized records go to 1997.

General Information: No adoption, juvenile or sanity records released. SASE required. Turnaround time 2-3 days. Fax notes: $1.00 per page; no fee to a toll-free number. Copy fee: $.50 per page. $.25 per page after

first 5. Certification fee: $2.00. Fee payee: Clerk of Court. Personal checks accepted. Prepayment is required.

Limited Jurisdiction Court PO Box 10, Ryegate, MT 59074; 406-568-2272; Fax: 406-568-2598. Hours: 10AM-2PM Tues (MST). *Misdemeanor, Civil Actions Under $7,000, Eviction, Small Claims.*

Granite County

District Court PO Box 399, Philipsburg, MT 59858-0399; 406-859-3712; Fax: 406-859-3817. Hours: 8AM-Noon, 1-5PM (MST). *Felony, Civil Actions Over $5,000, Eviction, Probate.*

Civil Records: Access: Phone, fax, mail, in person. Both court and visitors may perform in person searches. Search fee: $.50 per name per year. Maximum fee-$25.00. Required to search: name, years to search. Civil cases indexed by defendant, plaintiff. Civil records on docket books since 1893.

Criminal Records: Access: Phone, fax, mail, in person. Both court and visitors may perform in person searches. Search fee: $.50 per name per year. Maximum fee-$25.00. Required to search: name, years to search. Criminal records on docket books since 1893.

General Information: Public access terminal is available. No adoption, juvenile or sanity records released. SASE required. Turnaround time 1-4 days. Copy fee: $.50 per page. $.25 per page after first 5. Certification fee: $2.00. Fee payee: Clerk of Court. Personal checks accepted. Prepayment is required.

Drummond Justice Court #2 PO Box 159, Drummond, MT 59832; 406-288-3446; Fax: 406-288-3050. Hours: 9AM-4PM M,W,F (MST). *Misdemeanor, Civil Actions Under $7,000, Eviction, Small Claims.*

Philipsburg Justice Court PO Box 356, Philipsburg, MT 59858; 406-859-3006; Fax: 406-859-3817. Hours: 11AM-Noon, 1-5PM M,W,F (MST). *Misdemeanor, Civil Actions Under $7,000, Eviction, Small Claims.*

Hill County

District Court Hill County Courthouse, Havre, MT 59501; 406-265-5481 X224; Fax: 406-265-3693. Hours: 8AM-5PM (MST). *Felony, Civil Actions Over $5,000, Eviction, Probate.*

http://co.hill.mt.us

Civil Records: Access: Phone, fax, mail, in person. Both court and visitors may perform in person searches. Search fee: $.50 per name per year. Maximum fee-$25.00. Required to search: name, years to search. Civil cases indexed by defendant, plaintiff. Civil records on computer since 1985; prior records on docket books to 1912. Maiden name helpful in searching.

Criminal Records: Access: Fax, mail, in person. Both court and visitors may perform in person searches. Search fee: $.50 per name per year. Maximum fee-$25.00. Required to search: name, years to search; also helpful: maiden name. Criminal records on computer since 1988; prior records on docket books to 1912.

General Information: Public access terminal is available. No adoption, juvenile, paternity, sanity records released. SASE required. Turnaround time 2-3 days. Fax notes: $1.00 per page. Copy fee: $.50 per page. $.25 per page after first 5. Certification fee: $2.00. Fee payee: Clerk of Court. Business checks accepted. Prepayment is required.

Limited Jurisdiction Court Hill County Courthouse, Havre, MT 59501; 406-265-5481 X240; Fax: 406-262-9441. Hours: 8AM-4PM (MST). *Misdemeanor, Civil Actions Under $7,000, Eviction, Small Claims.*

http://co.hill.mt.us

Jefferson County

District Court PO Box H, Boulder, MT 59632; 406-225-4041 & 4042; Fax: 406-225-4044. Hours: 8AM-Noon, 1-5PM (MST). *Felony, Civil Actions Over $7,000, Eviction, Probate.*

Civil Records: Access: Mail, fax, in person. Both court and visitors may perform in person searches. Search fee: $.50 per name per year. Maximum fee-$25.00. Required to search: name, years to search. Civil cases indexed by defendant, plaintiff. Civil records on computer since 1993, on microfilm since 1925.

Criminal Records: Access: Mail, fax, in person. Both court and visitors may perform in person searches. Search fee: $.50 per name per year. Maximum fee-$25.00. Required to search: name, years to search. Criminal records on computer since 1992, on microfilm since 1925.

General Information: Public access terminal is available. Juvenile, sanity or adoption records not released. SASE required. Turnaround time same day. Fax notes: Fee to fax results is $1.00 per page. Copy fee: $.50 per page. $.25 per page after first 5. Certification fee: $2.00. Fee payee: Clerk of Court. Personal checks accepted. Prepayment is required.

Limited Jurisdiction Court PO Box H, Boulder, MT 59632; 406-225-4055. Hours: 8AM-5PM (MST). *Misdemeanor, Civil Actions Under $7,000, Eviction, Small Claims.*

Judith Basin County

District Court PO Box 307, Stanford, MT 59479; 406-566-2277 X113; Fax: 406-566-2211. Hours: 8AM-5PM (MST). *Felony, Civil Actions Over $5,000, Probate.*

Civil Records: Access: Phone, fax, mail, in person. Both court and visitors may perform in person searches. Search fee: $.50 per name per year. Maximum fee-$25.00. Required to search: name, years to search. Civil cases indexed by defendant, plaintiff. Civil records on books back to 1920; on computer back to 1996.

Criminal Records: Access: Phone, mail, in person. Both court and visitors may perform in person searches. Search fee: $.50 per name per year. Maximum fee-$25.00. Required to search: name, years to search, signed release. Criminal records on books back to 1920; on computer back to 1996.

General Information: No adoption, sanity records released. SASE required. Turnaround time 10 days. Copy fee: $.50 per page. $.25 per page after first 5. Certification fee: $2.00. Fee payee: Clerk of Court. Business checks accepted. Prepayment is required.

Hobson Justice Court PO Box 276, Hobson, MT 59452; 406-423-5503. Hours: 4:30-9:30PM M-Th (MST). *Misdemeanor, Civil Actions Under $7,000, Eviction, Small Claims.*

Stanford Justice Court PO Box 427, Stanford, MT 59479; 406-566-2277 X117. Hours: 8:00AM-5:00PM M-F (MST). *Misdemeanor, Civil Actions Under $7,000, Eviction, Small Claims.*

Lake County

District Court Clerk of District Court Office, 106 4th Ave E, Polson, MT 59860; 406-883-7254; Fax: 406-883-7343. Hours: 8AM-5PM (MST). *Felony, Civil Actions Over $7,000, Probate.*

Civil Records: Access: Phone, fax, mail, in person. Both court and visitors may perform in person searches. Search fee: $.50 per name per year. Maximum fee-$25.00. Required to search: name, years to search. Civil cases indexed by defendant, plaintiff. Civil records on books since 1923; on computer since 1990.

Criminal Records: Access: Phone, fax, mail, in person. Both court and visitors may perform in person

searches. Search fee: $.50 per name per year. Maximum fee-$25.00. Required to search: name, years to search, DOB, SSN. Criminal records on books since 1923; on computer since 1990.

General Information: Public access terminal is available. No adoption, juvenile, sanity or expunged records released. SASE required. Turnaround time 3 days; 2 hours for phone requests. Fax notes: $1.00 per page. Copy fee: $.50 per page. $.25 per page after first 5. Certification fee: $2.00. Fee payee: Clerk of Court. Business checks accepted. No credit cards. Prepayment is required.

Limited Jurisdiction Court 106 4th Ave E, Polson, MT 59860; 406-883-7258; Fax: 406-883-7343. Hours: 8AM-5PM (MST). *Misdemeanor, Civil Actions Under $7,000, Eviction, Small Claims.*

Lewis and Clark County

District Court 228 Broadway, PO Box 158, Helena, MT 59624; 406-447-8216; Fax: 406-447-8275. Hours: 8AM-5PM (MST). *Felony, Civil Actions Over $5,000, Eviction, Probate, Small Claims.*

www.co.lewis-clark.mt.us

Civil Records: Access: Fax, mail, online, in person. Both court and visitors may perform in person searches. Search fee: $.50 per name per year. Maximum fee-$25.00. Required to search: name, years to search. Civil cases indexed by defendant, plaintiff. Civil records on computer since 1990, microfilm prior to 01/90. Will accept e-mail record requests to ikallio@co.lewis-clark.mt.us.

Criminal Records: Access: Fax, mail, online, in person. Both court and visitors may perform in person searches. Search fee: $.50 per name per year. Maximum fee-$25.00. Required to search: name, years to search. Criminal records on computer since 1990, microfilm prior to 1/90. Will accept e-mail record requests to ikallio@co.lewis-clark.mt.us.

General Information: Public access terminal is available. No adoption, juvenile or sanity records released. SASE required. Turnaround time 2 days. Fax notes: Fee to fax results is $1.00 per page. Copy fee: $.50 per page. $.25 per page after first 5. Certification fee: $2.00. Fee payee: Clerk of Court. Personal checks accepted. Prepayment is required.

Limited Jurisdiction Court 228 Broadway, Helena, MT 59623; 406-447-8202; Fax: 406-447-8269. Hours: 8AM-Noon; 1PM-4PM (MST). *Misdemeanor, Civil Actions Under $7,000, Eviction, Small Claims.*

Liberty County

District Court PO Box 549, Chester, MT 59522; 406-759-5615; Fax: 406-759-5996. Hours: 8AM-5PM (MST). *Felony, Civil Actions Over $5,000, Eviction, Probate.*

Civil Records: Access: Phone, mail, in person. Only the court performs in person searches; visitors may not. Search fee: $.50 per name per year. Maximum fee-$25.00. Required to search: name, years to search, address. Civil cases indexed by defendant, plaintiff. Civil records on books since 1920.

Criminal Records: Access: Phone, mail, in person, fax. Both court and visitors may perform in person searches. Search fee: $.50 per name per year. Maximum fee-$25.00. Required to search: name, years to search, signed release. Criminal records on books since 1920.

General Information: No adoption, juvenile or sanity records released. SASE required. Turnaround time 2-3 days. Copy fee: $.50 per page. $.25 per page after first 5. Certification fee: $2.00. Fee payee: Clerk of Court. Personal checks accepted. Prepayment is required.

Limited Jurisdiction Court PO Box 170, Chester, MT 59522; 406-759-5172; Fax: 406-759-

5395. Hours: 9AM-5PM Tues (MST). *Misdemeanor, Civil Actions Under $7,000, Eviction, Small Claims.*

Lincoln County

District Court 512 California Ave, Libby, MT 59923; 406-293-7781; Fax: 406-293-9816. Hours: 8AM-5PM (MST). *Felony, Civil Actions Over $7,000, Eviction, Probate.*

Civil Records: Access: Mail, in person. Both court and visitors may perform in person searches. Search fee: $3.00 per name for ten year search; $.50 each add'l year with $25.00 maximum. Required to search: name, years to search. Civil cases indexed by defendant, plaintiff. Civil records on computer from 1991, prior on docket books.

Criminal Records: Access: Mail, in person. Both court and visitors may perform in person searches. Search fee: $3.00 per name. Fee is for 10 year search. Maximum fee $25.00. Required to search: name, years to search, DOB. Criminal records on computer from 1991, prior on docket books.

General Information: No adoption, juvenile or sanity records released. SASE required. Turnaround time 1 week. Copy fee: $.50 per page. $.25 per page after first 5. Certification fee: $2.00. Fee payee: Clerk of Court. Personal checks accepted. Prepayment is required.

Eureka Justice Court #2 PO Box 403, Eureka, MT 59917; 406-296-2622; Fax: 406-296-3829. Hours: 8AM-5M M-W (MST). *Misdemeanor, Civil Actions Under $7,000, Eviction, Small Claims.*

Libby Justice Court #1 418 Mineral Ave, Libby, MT 59923; 406-293-7781 X236, X259, X235; Fax: 406-293-5948. Hours: 8AM-5PM (MST). *Misdemeanor, Civil Actions Under $7,000, Eviction, Small Claims.*

Madison County

District Court PO Box 185, Virginia City, MT 59755; 406-843-4230; Fax: 406-843-5207. Hours: 8AM-5PM (MST). *Felony, Civil Actions Over $5,000, Eviction, Probate.*

Civil Records: Access: Phone, fax, mail, in person. Both court and visitors may perform in person searches. Search fee: $.50 per name per year. Maximum fee-$25.00. Required to search: name, years to search. Civil cases indexed by defendant, plaintiff. Civil records on books since 1864; on computer back to 1990.

Criminal Records: Access: Fax, mail, in person. Only the court performs in person searches; visitors may not. Search fee: $.50 per name per year. Maximum fee-$25.00. Required to search: name, years to search. Criminal records on books since 1864; on computer back to 1990.

General Information: Public access terminal is available. No adoption, juvenile or sanity records released. SASE required. Turnaround time 1 week. Fax notes: Fee to fax results is $4.00 1st page, $1.00 each add'l. Copy fee: $.50 per page. $.25 per page after first 5. Certification fee: $2.00. Fee payee: Clerk of Court. Personal checks accepted. Prepayment is required.

Limited Jurisdiction Court PO Box 277, Virginia City, MT 59755; 406-843-4237; Fax: 406-843-4219. Hours: 8AM-5PM (MST). *Misdemeanor, Civil Actions Under $7,000, Eviction, Small Claims.*

McCone County

District Court PO Box 199, Circle, MT 59215; 406-485-3410; Fax: 406-485-3410. Hours: 8AM-5PM (MST). *Felony, Civil Actions Over $5,000, Eviction, Probate.*

Civil Records: Access: Mail, in person. Only the court performs in person searches; visitors may not. Search fee: $.50 per name per year. Maximum fee-$25.00.

Required to search: name, years to search. Civil cases indexed by defendant, plaintiff. Civil records in books from 1919, computerized since 1996.

Criminal Records: Access: Mail, in person. Only the court performs in person searches; visitors may not. Search fee: $.50 per name per year. Maximum fee-$25.00. Required to search: name, years to search. Criminal records in books and microfilm since 1919, computerized since 1996.

General Information: No adoption, juvenile, sanity or mental health records released. SASE required. Turnaround time 1-2 days. Copy fee: $.50 per page. $.25 per page after first 5. Certification fee: $2.00. Fee payee: Clerk of Court. Personal checks accepted. Prepayment is required.

Limited Jurisdiction Court PO Box 192, Circle, MT 59215; 406-485-3548; Fax: 406-485-2689. Hours: 9AM-noon Tu & W (MST). *Misdemeanor, Civil Actions Under $7,000, Eviction, Small Claims.*

Meagher County

District Court PO Box 443, White Sulphur Springs, MT 59645; 406-547-3612 Ext110; Fax: 406-547-3836. Hours: 8AM-5PM (MST). *Felony, Civil Actions Over $5,000, Eviction, Probate.*

Civil Records: Access: Phone, mail, fax, in person. Both court and visitors may perform in person searches. Search fee: $.50 per name per year. Maximum fee-$25.00. Required to search: name, years to search. Civil cases indexed by defendant, plaintiff. Civil records on docket books or microfiche to 1900; on computer back to 1996.

Criminal Records: Access: Phone, mail, fax, in person. Both court and visitors may perform in person searches. Search fee: $.50 per name per year. Maximum fee-$25.00. Required to search: name, years to search, DOB. Criminal records on docket books or microfiche to 1900; on computer back to 1996.

General Information: No adoption, juvenile or sanity records released. SASE required. Turnaround time 3 days. Copy fee: $.50 per page. $.25 per page after first 5. Certification fee: $2.00. Fee payee: Clerk of Court. Personal checks accepted.

Limited Jurisdiction Court Justice Court, 15 W. Main St. (PO Box 698), White Sulphur Springs, MT 59645; 406-547-3954 X115; Fax: 406-547-3388, 547-3836. Hours: 8AM-5PM T-Th (MST). *Misdemeanor, Civil Actions Under $7,000, Eviction, Small Claims.*

Mineral County

District Court PO Box 129, Superior, MT 59872; 406-822-3538; Fax: 406-822-3579. Hours: 8AM-Noon,1-5PM (MST). *Felony, Civil Actions Over $5,000, Probate.*

Civil Records: Access: Phone, fax, mail, in person. Both court and visitors may perform in person searches. Search fee: $.50 per name per year. Maximum fee-$25.00. Required to search: name, years to search. Civil cases indexed by defendant, plaintiff. Civil records on docket books from 1914, on computer back to 1990.

Criminal Records: Access: Phone, fax, mail, in person. Only the court performs in person searches; visitors may not. Search fee: $.50 per name per year. Maximum fee-$25.00. Required to search: name, years to search. Criminal records on docket books from 1914, on computer back to 1990.

General Information: No adoption, sanity records released. SASE required. Turnaround time same day after payment received. Fax notes: Fee to fax results is $5.00 per document. Copy fee: $.50 per page. $.25 per page after first 5. Certification fee: $2.00. Fee payee: Clerk of Court. Personal checks accepted. Prepayment is required.

Limited Jurisdiction Court PO Box 658, Superior, MT 59872; 406-822-3550; Fax: 406-822-3579. Hours: 8AM-5PM (MST). *Misdemeanor, Civil Actions Under $7,000, Eviction, Small Claims.*

Missoula County

District Court 200 W Broadway, Missoula, MT 59802; 406-523-4780 X3523; Fax: 406-523-4899. Hours: 8AM-5PM (MST). *Felony, Civil Actions Over $5,000, Probate.*

Civil Records: Access: Fax, mail, in person. Both court and visitors may perform in person searches. Search fee: $.50 per name per year. Maximum fee-$25.00. Required to search: name, years to search. Civil cases indexed by defendant, plaintiff. Civil records on computer from 10/89, microfilm from 1970s, archived to late 1800s.

Criminal Records: Access: Fax, mail, in person. Both court and visitors may perform in person searches. Search fee: $.50 per name per year. Maximum fee-$25.00. Required to search: name, years to search. Criminal records on computer from 10/89, microfilm from 1970s, archived to late 1800s.

General Information: Public access terminal is available. No adoption, juvenile, sealed, expunged or pre-sentence psychiatric records released. SASE not required. Turnaround time up to 2 weeks. Fax notes: $2.00 per document. No fee if returning on toll free line. Copy fee: $.50 per page. $.25 per page after first 5. Certification fee: $2.00. Fee payee: Clerk of Court. Personal checks accepted. Credit cards accepted: Visa, MasterCard. Prepayment is required.

Limited Jurisdiction Court - Dept 1 200 W Broadway, Missoula County Courthouse, Missoula, MT 59802; 406-523-4871; Fax: 406-523-2835. Hours: 8AM-5PM (MST). *Misdemeanor, Civil Actions Under $7,000, Eviction, Small Claims.*
www.co.missoula.mt.us/jp1

Musselshell County

District Court 506 Main St, Roundup, MT 59072; 406-323-1413; Fax: 406-323-1710. Hours: 8AM-5PM (MST). *Felony, Civil Actions Over $5,000, Eviction, Probate.*

Civil Records: Access: Mail, in person. Both court and visitors may perform in person searches. Search fee: $.50 per name per year. Maximum fee-$25.00. Required to search: name, years to search. Civil cases indexed by defendant, plaintiff. Computerized records from 7/96, civil records on docket books from 1911.

Criminal Records: Access: Mail, in person. Both court and visitors may perform in person searches. Search fee: $.50 per name per year. Maximum fee-$25.00. Required to search: name, years to search. Criminal records on docket books from 1911.

General Information: No adoption, (some) juvenile or sanity records released. SASE required. Turnaround time 2-3 days. Copy fee: $.50 per page. $.25 per page after first 5. Certification fee: $2.00. Fee payee: Clerk of Court. Personal checks accepted. Prepayment is required.

Limited Jurisdiction Court PO Box 660, Roundup, MT 59072; 406-323-1078; Fax: 406-323-3452. Hours: 9AM-Noon (MST). *Misdemeanor, Civil Actions Under $7,000, Eviction, Small Claims.*

Park County

District Court PO Box 437, Livingston, MT 59047; 406-222-4125; Fax: 406-222-4128. Hours: 8AM-5PM (MST). *Felony, Civil Actions Over $7,000, Eviction, Probate.*

Civil Records: Access: Fax, mail, in person. Both court and visitors may perform in person searches. Search fee: $.50 per name per year. Maximum fee-$25.00.

Required to search: name, years to search. Civil cases indexed by defendant, plaintiff. Civil records on computer, microfiche, and docket books from 1889 to present.

Criminal Records: Access: Fax, mail, in person. Both court and visitors may perform in person searches. Search fee: $.50 per name per year. Maximum fee-$25.00. Required to search: name, years to search. Criminal records on computer, microfiche, and docket books from 1889 to present.

General Information: Public access terminal is available. No adoption, juvenile or sanity records released. SASE not required. Turnaround time 1-2 days for all requests. Copy fee: $.50 per page. $.25 per page after first 5. Certification fee: $2.00. Fee payee: Clerk of Court. Personal checks accepted. Prepayment is required.

Limited Jurisdiction Court 414 E Callender, Livingston, MT 59047; 406-222-4169/4170; Fax: 406-222-4103. Hours: 8AM-4:30PM (MST). *Misdemeanor, Civil Actions Under $7,000, Eviction, Small Claims.*

Petroleum County

District Court PO Box 226, Winnett, MT 59087; 406-429-5311; Fax: 406-429-6328. Hours: 8AM-5PM (MST). *Felony, Civil Actions Over $5,000, Eviction, Probate.*

Civil Records: Access: Phone, mail, in person. Both court and visitors may perform in person searches. Search fee: $.50 per name per year. Maximum fee-$25.00. Required to search: name, years to search. Civil cases indexed by defendant, plaintiff. Civil records on docket books from 1924.

Criminal Records: Access: Phone, mail, in person. Only the court performs in person searches; visitors may not. Search fee: $.50 per name per year. Maximum fee-$25.00. Required to search: name, years to search. Criminal records on docket books from 1924.

General Information: No adoption, juvenile or sanity records released. SASE required. Turnaround time 1 day. Copy fee: $.50 per page. $.25 per page after first 5. Certification fee: $2.00. Fee payee: Clerk of Court. Personal checks accepted. Prepayment is required.

Limited Jurisdiction Court PO Box 226, Winnett, MT 59087; 406-429-5311; Fax: 406-429-6328. Hours: 8AM-5PM M-F (MST). *Misdemeanor, Civil Actions Under $7,000, Eviction, Small Claims.*

Phillips County

District Court PO Box 530, Malta, MT 59538; 406-654-1023; Fax: 406-654-1023. Hours: 8AM-5PM (MST). *Felony, Civil Actions Over $5,000, Eviction, Probate.*

Civil Records: Access: Mail, in person. Only the court performs in person searches; visitors may not. Search fee: $.50 per name per year. Maximum fee-$25.00. Required to search: name, years to search; also helpful: address. Civil cases indexed by defendant, plaintiff. Civil records on computer back to 1997; books, microfilm back to 1915.

Criminal Records: Access: Mail, in person. Only the court performs in person searches; visitors may not. Search fee: $.50 per name per year. Maximum fee-$25.00. Required to search: name, years to search, signed release, DOB or SSN; also helpful: address. Criminal records on computer back to 1997; books, microfilm back to 1915.

General Information: No adoption, juvenile or sanity records released. SASE required. Turnaround time 1-2 days. Fax notes: There is a $5.00 fee to return by fax, unless a toll free line is used. Copy fee: $.50 per page. $.25 per page after first 5. Certification fee: $2.00. Fee payee: Clerk of Court. Personal checks accepted. Prepayment is required.

Limited Jurisdiction Court PO Box 1396, Malta, MT 59538; 406-654-1118; Fax: 406-654-1213. Hours: 10AM-4PM M-Th (MST). *Misdemeanor, Civil Actions Under $7,000, Eviction, Small Claims.*

Pondera County

District Court 20 Fourth Ave SW, Conrad, MT 59425; 406-271-4026; Fax: 406-271-4081. Hours: 8AM-5PM (MST). *Felony, Civil Actions Over $5,000, Eviction, Probate.*

Civil Records: Access: Fax, mail, in person. Both court and visitors may perform in person searches. Search fee: $.50 per name per year. Maximum fee-$25.00. Required to search: name, years to search. Civil cases indexed by defendant, plaintiff. Civil records on docket books from 1919; on computer back to 1995.
Criminal Records: Access: Fax, mail, in person. Both court and visitors may perform in person searches. Search fee: $.50 per name per year. Maximum fee-$25.00. Required to search: name, years to search. Criminal records on docket books from 1919; on computer back to 1995.
General Information: No adoption or sanity records released. SASE required. Turnaround time 2-3 days. Fax notes: Fax fee: $.50 1st 5 pages, $.25 each additional page. $1.00 for cover page. Copy fee: $.50 per page. $.25 per page after first 5. Certification fee: $2.00. Fee payee: Clerk of Court. Personal checks accepted. Prepayment is required.

Limited Jurisdiction Court 20 Fourth Ave SW, Conrad, MT 59425; 406-271-4030; Fax: 406-271-4070. Hours: 9AM-4PM (MST). *Misdemeanor, Civil Actions Under $7,000, Eviction, Small Claims.*

Powder River County

District Court PO Box 239, Broadus, MT 59317; 406-436-2320; Fax: 406-436-2325. Hours: 8AM-Noon, 1-5PM (MST). *Felony, Civil Actions Over $5,000, Probate.*

Civil Records: Access: Fax, mail, in person. Both court and visitors may perform in person searches. Search fee: $.50 per name per year. Maximum fee-$25.00. Required to search: name, years to search. Civil cases indexed by defendant, plaintiff. Civil records on computer since 1993, microfiche since 1974, and books since 1919.
Criminal Records: Access: Fax, mail, in person. Both court and visitors may perform in person searches. Search fee: $.50 per name per year. Maximum fee-$25.00. Required to search: name, years to search. Criminal records on computer since 1993, microfiche since 1974, and books since 1919.
General Information: Public access terminal is available. No adoption, juvenile, sanity, dismissed criminal records released. SASE required. Turnaround time same day if pre-paid. Fax notes: Fee to fax is $.50 per page. Copy fee: $.50 per page. $.25 per page after first 5. Certification fee: $2.00. Fee payee: Clerk of Court. Only cashiers checks and money orders accepted. Prepayment is required.

Limited Jurisdiction Court PO Box 488, Broadus, MT 59317; 406-436-2503; Fax: 406-436-2866. Hours: 9AM-3:30PM M-Th (MST). *Misdemeanor, Civil Actions Under $7,000, Eviction, Small Claims.*

Powell County

District Court 409 Missouri Ave, Deer Lodge, MT 59722; 406-846-3680 X234/235; Fax: 406-846-2784. Hours: 8AM-5PM (MST). *Felony, Civil Actions Over $5,000, Eviction, Probate.*

Civil Records: Access: Mail, in person. Both court and visitors may perform in person searches. Search fee: $.50 per name per year. Maximum fee-$25.00.

Required to search: name, years to search. Civil cases indexed by defendant, plaintiff. Civil records on docket books since turn of century, on computer since 1996.
Criminal Records: Access: Mail, in person. Both court and visitors may perform in person searches. Search fee: $.50 per name per year. Maximum fee-$25.00. Required to search: name, years to search, DOB, SSN. Criminal records on docket books since turn of century, on computer since 1996.
General Information: No adoption, juvenile or sanity records released. SASE required. Turnaround time 2-3 days, immediately over phone. Copy fee: $.50 per page. $.25 per page after first 5. Certification fee: $2.00. Fee payee: Clerk of Court. Personal checks accepted. Prepayment is required.

Limited Jurisdiction Court 409 Missouri, Powell County Courthouse, Deer Lodge, MT 59722; 406-846-3680. 8AM-5PM (MST). *Misdemeanor, Civil Actions Under $7,000, Eviction, Small Claims.*

Prairie County

District Court PO Box 125, Terry, MT 59349; 406-635-5575. Hours: 8AM-Noon; 1PM-5PM (MST). *Felony, Civil Actions Over $5,000, Eviction, Probate.*

Civil Records: Access: Mail, in person. Both court and visitors may perform in person searches. Search fee: $.50 per name per year. Maximum fee-$25.00. Required to search: name, years to search. Civil cases indexed by defendant, plaintiff. Civil records on books since 1915; computerized records go back to 1997.
Criminal Records: Access: Mail, in person. Both court and visitors may perform in person searches. Search fee: $.50 per name per year. Maximum fee-$25.00. Required to search: name, years to search, DOB, SSN. Criminal records on books since 1915; computerized records go back to 1997.
General Information: No adoption, juvenile or sanity records released. SASE required. Turnaround time 5 days. Copy fee: $.25 per page. Certification fee: $2.00. Fee payee: Clerk of Court. Personal checks accepted.

Limited Jurisdiction Court PO Box 40, Terry, MT 59349; 406-635-4466, 635-2100; Fax: 406-635-5580. Hours: 1-2PM (MST). *Misdemeanor, Civil Actions Under $7,000, Eviction, Small Claims.*

Ravalli County

District Court Ravalli County Courthouse, 205 Bedford #D, Hamilton, MT 59840; 406-375-6214; Fax: 406-375-6327. Hours: 8AM-5PM (MST). *Felony, Civil Actions Over $7,000, Probate.*

Civil Records: Access: Mail, in person. Both court and visitors may perform in person searches. Search fee: $.50 per name per year. Maximum fee-$25.00. Required to search: name, years to search. Civil cases indexed by defendant, plaintiff. Civil records on microfiche (1989), docket books (1914).
Criminal Records: Access: Mail, in person. Both court and visitors may perform in person searches. Search fee: $.50 per name per year. Maximum fee-$25.00. Required to search: name, years to search. Criminal records on microfiche (1989), docket books (1914).
General Information: Public access terminal is available. No adoption, juvenile, psychological, medical or expunged records released. SASE required. Turnaround time 4-5 days. Fax notes: $1.00 per page. Copy fee: $.50 per page. $.25 per page after first 5. Certification fee: $2.00. Fee payee: Clerk of Court. Personal checks accepted. Prepayment is required.

Limited Jurisdiction Court Courthouse Box 5023, Hamilton, MT 59840; 406-375-6252; Fax: 406-375-6383. Hours: 8AM-5PM (MST). *Misdemeanor, Civil Actions Under $7,000, Eviction, Small Claims.*

Richland County

District Court 201 W Main, Sidney, MT 59270; 406-433-1709; Fax: 406-433-6945. Hours: 8AM-5PM (MST). *Felony, Civil Actions Over $5,000, Eviction, Probate.*

Civil Records: Access: Phone, fax, mail, in person. Both court and visitors may perform in person searches. Search fee: $.50 per name per year. Maximum fee-$25.00. Required to search: name, years to search. Civil cases indexed by defendant, plaintiff. Civil records in books since 1914; on computer back to 1997.
Criminal Records: Access: Phone, fax, mail, in person. Both court and visitors may perform in person searches. Search fee: $.50 per name per year. Maximum fee-$25.00. Required to search: name, years to search. Criminal records in books since 1914; on computer back to 1997.
General Information: No adoption, juvenile, paternity, sanity, dismissed or expunged records released. SASE required. Turnaround time 1-3 days. Fax notes: $1.00 per page. Copy fee: $.50 per page. $.25 per page after first 5. Certification fee: $2.00. Fee payee: Clerk of Court. Personal checks accepted. Prepayment required.

Limited Jurisdiction Court 123 W Main, Sidney, MT 59270; 406-433-2815; Fax: 406-433-6885. Hours: 8AM-5PM (MST). *Misdemeanor, Civil Actions Under $7,000, Eviction, Small Claims.*

Roosevelt County

District Court County Courthouse, Wolf Point, MT 59201; 406-653-6266; Fax: 406-653-6203. Hours: 8AM-5PM (MST). *Felony, Civil Actions Over $5,000, Eviction, Probate.*

Civil Records: Access: Phone, fax, mail, in person. Only the court performs in person searches; visitors may not. Search fee: $.50 per name per year. Maximum fee-$25.00. Required to search: name, years to search. Civil cases indexed by defendant, plaintiff. Civil records on books and microfiche back to 1919, computerized back to 1996.
Criminal Records: Access: Fax, mail, in person. Only the court performs in person searches; visitors may not. Search fee: $.50 per name per year. Maximum fee-$25.00. Required to search: name, years to search; also helpful: DOB. Criminal records on books and microfiche back to 1919, computerized back to 1996.
General Information: No adoption, juvenile or sanity records released. SASE required. Turnaround time 2-3 days after receipt of payment. Fax notes: Fee to fax results is $3.00 per document. Copy fee: $.50 per page. $.25 per page after first 5. Certification fee: $2.00. Fee payee: Clerk of Court. Personal checks accepted. Prepayment is required.

Culbertson Justice Court Post #2 PO Box 421, Culbertson, MT 59218; 406-787-6607; Fax: 406-787-6607. Hours: 9AM-3PM M-Th (MST). *Misdemeanor, Civil Actions Under $7,000, Eviction, Small Claims.*

Wolf Point Justice Court Post #1 County Courthouse, 400 Second Ave. S., Wolf Point, MT 59201; 406-653-6261, 406-653-6258; Fax: 406-653-6203. Hours: 8AM-Noon M-F (MST). *Misdemeanor, Civil Actions Under $7,000, Eviction, Small Claims.*

Rosebud County

District Court PO Box 48, Forsyth, MT 59327; 406-356-7322; Fax: 406-356-7551. 8AM-5PM (MST). *Felony, Civil Actions Over $5,000, Eviction, Probate.*

Civil Records: Access: Fax, mail, in person. Only the court performs in person searches; visitors may not. Search fee: $.50 per name per year. Maximum fee-$25.00, written requests only. Required to search: name, years to search. Civil cases indexed by defendant, plaintiff. Civil records in books, on microfiche back to 1901; on computer back to 1996.

Criminal Records: Access: Mail, in person. Both court and visitors may perform in person searches. Search fee: $.50 per name per year. Maximum fee-$25.00, written requests only. Required to search: name, years to search, signed release. Criminal records in books, on microfiche back to 1901; on computer back to 1996.

General Information: Public access terminal is available. No adoption, juvenile, sanity or sealed records released. SASE required. Turnaround time 2 days. Fax notes: No fee to fax results. Copy fee: $.50 per page. $.25 per page after first 5. Certification fee: $2.00. Fee payee: Clerk of Court. Personal checks accepted. Prepayment is required.

Limited Jurisdiction Court #1 Rosebud County Courthouse, PO Box 504, Forsyth, MT 59327; 406-356-2638; Fax: 406-356-7551. Hours: 8AM-5PM (MST). *Misdemeanor, Civil Actions Under $7,000, Eviction, Small Claims.*

Limited Jurisdiction Court #2 PO Box 575, Colstrip, MT 59323; 406-748-2934; Fax: 406-748-4832. Hours: 8AM-5PM; Ashland 2nd & 4th Wed 1PM (MST). *Misdemeanor, Civil Actions Under $7,000, Eviction, Small Claims.*

Sanders County

District Court PO Box 519, Thompson Falls, MT 59873; 406-827-6962; Fax: 406-827-0094. Hours: 8AM-5PM (MST). *Felony, Civil Actions Over $5,000, Eviction, Probate.*

Civil Records: Access: Mail, in person. Both court and visitors may perform in person searches. Search fee: $.50 per name per year. Maximum fee-$25.00. Required to search: name, years to search. Civil cases indexed by defendant, plaintiff. Civil records on docket books since 1906, on computer since.

Criminal Records: Access: Mail, in person. Both court and visitors may perform in person searches. Search fee: $.50 per name per year. Maximum fee-$25.00. Required to search: name, years to search, DOB, SSN, signed release. Criminal records on docket books since 1906, on computer since.

General Information: Public access terminal is available. No adoption, juvenile, sanity or pre-sentence investigation records released. SASE required. Turnaround time 1-4 days. Copy fee: $.50 per page. $.25 per page after first 5. Certification fee: $2.00. Fee payee: Clerk of Court. Personal checks accepted. Prepayment is required.

Limited Jurisdiction Court PO Box 519, Thompson Falls, MT 59873; 406-827-6941; Fax: 406-827-0094. Hours: 8AM-5PM (MST). *Misdemeanor, Civil Actions Under $7,000, Eviction, Small Claims.*

Sheridan County

District Court 100 W Laurel, Plentywood, MT 59254; 406-765-3404; Fax: 406-765-2602. Hours: 8AM-Noon, 1-5PM (MST). *Felony, Civil Actions Over $5,000, Eviction, Probate.*

Civil Records: Access: Phone, mail, in person. Both court and visitors may perform in person searches. Search fee: $.50 per name per year. Maximum fee-$25.00. Required to search: name, years to search. Civil cases indexed by defendant, plaintiff. Civil records on docket books since 1913.

Criminal Records: Access: Phone, mail, in person. Both court and visitors may perform in person searches. Search fee: $.50 per name per year. Maximum fee-$25.00. Required to search: name, years to search. Criminal records on docket books since 1913.

General Information: No adoption, juvenile or sanity records released. SASE required. Turnaround time 1-2 days. Copy fee: $.50 per page. $.25 per page after first

5. Certification fee: $2.00. Fee payee: Clerk of District Court. Personal checks accepted. Prepayment required.

Justice Court 100 W Laurel, Plentywood, MT 59254; 406-765-2310; Fax: 406-765-3489. Hours: 8AM-5PM (MST). *Misdemeanor, Civil Actions Under $7,000, Eviction, Small Claims.*

Silver Bow County

District Court 155 W Granite St, Butte, MT 59701; 406-497-6350; Fax: 406-497-6358. Hours: 8AM-5PM (MST). *Felony, Civil Actions Over $5,000, Probate.*

Civil Records: Access: Fax, mail, in person. Both court and visitors may perform in person searches. Search fee: $.50 per name per year. Maximum fee-$25.00. Required to search: name, years to search. Civil cases indexed by defendant, plaintiff. Civil records in original files since 1970, on microfilm back to 1887; on computer back to 1996.

Criminal Records: Access: Fax, mail, in person. Both court and visitors may perform in person searches. Search fee: $.50 per name per year. Maximum fee-$25.00. Required to search: name, years to search. Criminal records in original files since 1970, on microfilm back to 1887; on computer back to 1995.

General Information: Public access terminal is available. No adoption, juvenile or sanity records released. SASE required. Turnaround time 1-3 days, will not do phone searches. Fax notes: Fee to fax results is $1.00 per page. Copy fee: $.50 per page. $.25 per page after first 5. Certification fee: $2.00. Fee payee: Clerk of Court. Personal checks accepted. Prepayment is required.

Limited Jurisdiction Court #1 & #2 155 W Granite St, Silver Bow County Courthouse, Butte, MT 59701; 406-497-6391/6392; Fax: 406-497-6468. Hours: 8AM-5PM (MST). *Misdemeanor, Civil Actions Under $7,000, Eviction, Small Claims.*

Note: There are two Justice Courts at this location. Both courts must be searched for records

Stillwater County

District Court PO Box 367, Columbus, MT 59019; 406-322-8030; Fax: 406-322-8048. Hours: 8AM-5PM (MST). *Felony, Civil Actions Over $5,000, Eviction, Probate.*

Civil Records: Access: Phone, mail, in person. Both court and visitors may perform in person searches. Search fee: $.50 per name per year. Maximum fee-$25.00. Required to search: name, years to search. Civil cases indexed by defendant, plaintiff. Civil records on docket books since 1913; on computer back to 1994.

Criminal Records: Access: Phone, mail, in person. Both court and visitors may perform in person searches. Search fee: $.50 per name per year. Maximum fee-$25.00. Required to search: name, years to search. Criminal records on docket books since 1913; on computer back to 1994.

General Information: No adoption, juvenile or sanity records released. SASE required. Turnaround time 1-2 days. Copy fee: $.50 per page. $.25 per page after first 5. Certification fee: $2.00. Fee payee: Clerk of Court. Personal checks accepted. Prepayment is required.

Limited Jurisdiction Court PO Box 77, Columbus, MT 59019; 406-322-8040; Fax: 406-322-8048. Hours: 9AM-5PM M-Th (MST). *Misdemeanor, Civil Actions Under $7,000, Eviction, Small Claims.*

Sweet Grass County

District Court PO Box 698, Big Timber, MT 59011; 406-932-5154; Fax: 406-932-5433. Hours: 8AM-Noon, 1-5PM (MST). *Felony, Civil Actions Over $5,000, Eviction, Probate.*

Civil Records: Access: Phone, mail, in person. Only the court performs in person searches; visitors may not. Search fee: $.50 per name per year. Maximum fee-$25.00. Required to search: name, years to search. Civil cases indexed by defendant, plaintiff. Civil records in books since 1895, on microfiche since 1972.

Criminal Records: Access: Phone, mail, in person. Only the court performs in person searches; visitors may not. Search fee: $.50 per name per year. Maximum fee-$25.00. Required to search: name, years to search. Criminal records in books since 1895, on microfiche since 1972.

General Information: No adoption, juvenile or sanity records released. SASE required. Turnaround time 1 day. Copy fee: $.50 per page. $.25 per page after first 5. Certification fee: $2.00. Fee payee: Clerk of Court. Personal checks accepted. Prepayment is required.

Limited Jurisdiction Court PO Box 1432, Big Timber, MT 59011; 406-932-5150; Fax: 406-932-5433. Hours: 8AM-5PM (MST). *Misdemeanor, Civil Actions Under $7,000, Eviction, Small Claims.*

Teton County

District Court PO Box 487, Choteau, MT 59422; 406-466-2909; Fax: 406-466-2138. Hours: 8AM-5PM (MST). *Felony, Civil Actions Over $5,000, Eviction, Probate.*

Civil Records: Access: Phone, fax, mail, in person. Only the court performs in person searches; visitors may not. Search fee: $.50 per name per year. Maximum fee-$25.00. Required to search: name, years to search. Civil cases indexed by defendant, plaintiff. Civil records on books from 1893; on computer back to 1995.

Criminal Records: Access: Phone, mail, in person. Only the court performs in person searches; visitors may not. Search fee: $.50 per name per year. Maximum fee-$25.00. Required to search: name, years to search. Criminal records on books from 1893; on computer back to 1995.

General Information: No adoption, juvenile or sanity records released. SASE required. Turnaround time 1 day. Fax notes: $1.00 per page. Copy fee: $.50 per page. $.25 per page after first 5. Certification fee: $2.00. Fee payee: Clerk of Court. Personal checks accepted. Prepayment is required.

Limited Jurisdiction Court PO Box 337, Choteau, MT 59422; 406-466-5611; Fax: 406-466-2138. Hours: 8AM-Noon (MST). *Misdemeanor, Civil Actions Under $7,000, Eviction, Small Claims.*

Toole County

District Court PO Box 850, Shelby, MT 59474; 406-434-2271; Fax: 406-434-7225. Hours: 8AM-5PM (MST). *Felony, Civil Actions Over $5,000, Eviction, Probate.*

Civil Records: Access: Phone, fax, mail, in person. Both court and visitors may perform in person searches. Search fee: $.50 per name per year. Maximum fee-$25.00. Required to search: name, years to search. Civil cases indexed by defendant, plaintiff. Civil records in books from 1914; on computer since 1997.

Criminal Records: Access: Phone, fax, mail, in person. Both court and visitors may perform in person searches. Search fee: $.50 per name per year. Maximum fee-$25.00. Required to search: name, years to search, DOB, SSN. Criminal records in books from 1914; on computer since 1997.

General Information: No adoption, juvenile or sanity records released. SASE is required. Turnaround time same day as request received. Fax notes: $.50 per page. Copy fee: $.50 per page. $.25 per page after first 5. Certification fee: $2.00 per document. Fee payee: Clerk of Court. Personal checks accepted. Prepayment is required.

Limited Jurisdiction Court PO Box 738, Shelby, MT 59474; 406-434-2651. Hours: 9:00AM-4:00PM T-F (MST). *Misdemeanor, Civil Actions Under $7,000, Eviction, Small Claims.*

Treasure County

District Court PO Box 392, Hysham, MT 59038; 406-342-5547; Fax: 406-342-5445. Hours: 8AM-5PM (MST). *Felony, Civil Actions Over $5,000, Eviction, Probate.*

Civil Records: Access: Fax, mail, in person. Both court and visitors may perform in person searches. Search fee: $.50 per name per year. Maximum fee-$25.00. Required to search: name, years to search; also helpful: address. Civil cases indexed by defendant, plaintiff. Civil records on books since 1919, on microfilm from 1985 to present; on computer back to 1996.

Criminal Records: Access: Fax, mail, in person. Both court and visitors may perform in person searches. Search fee: $.50 per name per year. Maximum fee-$25.00. Required to search: name, years to search, DOB; also helpful: address. Criminal records on books since 1919, on microfilm from 1985 to present; on computer back to 1996.

General Information: Public access terminal is available. No adoption or sanity records released. SASE required. Turnaround time 1 week. Fax notes: Fee to fax results to $1.50 per page. Copy fee: $.50 per page, $.25 per page after first 5. Certification fee: $2.00. Fee payee: Clerk of Court. Personal checks accepted. Prepayment is required.

Limited Jurisdiction Court PO Box 267, Hysham, MT 59038; 406-342-5532; Fax: 406-342-5532. Hours: 9AM-Noon (MST). *Misdemeanor, Civil Actions Under $7,000, Eviction, Small Claims.*

Valley County

District Court 501 Court Sq #4, Glasgow, MT 59230; 406-228-8221 X67/68; Fax: 406-228-9027/4601. Hours: 8AM-5PM (MST). *Felony, Civil Actions Over $5,000, Eviction, Probate.*

Civil Records: Access: Phone, fax, mail, in person. Only the court performs in person searches; visitors may not. Search fee: $.50 per name per year. Maximum fee-$25.00. Required to search: name, years to search. Civil cases indexed by defendant, plaintiff. Civil records in books since 1893; on computer back to 1996.

Criminal Records: Access: Fax, mail, in person. Only the court performs in person searches; visitors may not.

Search fee: $.50 per name per year. Maximum fee-$25.00. Required to search: name, years to search, signed release. Criminal records in books since 1893; on computer back to 1996.

General Information: No adoption, juvenile or sanity records released. SASE required. Turnaround time same day. Fax notes: Fee to fax results is $1.00 per page. Copy fee: $.50 per page. $.25 per page after first 5. Certification fee: $2.00. Fee payee: Clerk of Court. Business checks accepted. Prepayment is required.

Limited Jurisdiction Court 501 Court Sq #10, Glasgow, MT 59230; 406-228-8221 X71; Fax: 406-228-4601. Hours: 8AM-Noon (MST). *Misdemeanor, Civil Actions Under $7,000, Eviction, Small Claims.*

Wheatland County

District Court Box 227, Harlowton, MT 59036; 406-632-4893; Fax: 406-632-4873. Hours: 8AM-5PM (MST). *Felony, Civil Actions Over $5,000, Eviction, Probate.*

Civil Records: Access: Phone, fax, mail, in person. Only the court performs in person searches; visitors may not. Search fee: $.50 per name per year. Maximum fee-$25.00. Required to search: name, years to search. Civil cases indexed by defendant, plaintiff. Computerized records back to 1996, civil records on docket books since 1917, probate on microfiche from 1984.

Criminal Records: Access: Phone, mail, in person. Only the court performs in person searches; visitors may not. Search fee: $.50 per name per year. Maximum fee-$25.00. Required to search: name, years to search. Compterized records back to 1996, criminal records on docket books since 1917, probate on microfiche from 1984.

General Information: No adoption, juvenile or sanity records released. SASE required. Turnaround time 2-3 days. Copy fee: $.50 per page. $.25 per page after first 5. Certification fee: $2.00. Fee payee: Clerk of Court. Personal checks accepted. Prepayment is required.

Limited Jurisdiction Court PO Box 524, Harlowton, MT 59036; 406-632-4821; Fax: 406-632-5654. Hours: 10AM-1PM T,Th (MST). *Misdemeanor, Civil Actions Under $7,000, Eviction, Small Claims.*

Wibaux County

District Court PO Box 292, Wibaux, MT 59353; 406-796-2484; Fax: 406-796-2484. Hours: 8AM-5PM, Closed 12-1 (MST). *Felony, Civil Actions Over $5,000, Eviction, Probate.*

Civil Records: Access: Phone, fax, mail, in person. Both court and visitors may perform in person searches. Search fee: $.50 per name per year. Maximum fee-$25.00. Required to search: name, years to search. Civil

records on docket books since 1914, on computer since 01/97.

Criminal Records: Access: Phone, fax, mail, in person. Only the court performs in person searches; visitors may not. Search fee: $.50 per name per year. Maximum fee-$25.00. Required to search: name, years to search. Criminal records on docket books since 1914, on computer since 01/97.

General Information: No adoption, juvenile or sanity records released. SASE required. Turnaround time 1 week. Fax notes: $2.00 for first page, $.50 each add'l. Copy fee: $.50 per page. $.25 per page after first 5. Certification fee: $2.00. Fee payee: Clerk of Court. Personal checks accepted. Prepayment is required.

Limited Jurisdiction Court PO Box 199, Wibaux, MT 59353; 406-796-2484. Hours: 1-5PM M&W, 8AM-Noon F (MST). *Misdemeanor, Civil Actions Under $7,000, Eviction, Small Claims.*

Yellowstone County

District Court PO Box 35030 (217 N 27 St), Billings, MT 59107; Civil phone: 406-256-2851; Criminal phone: 406-256-2860; Probate phone: 406-256-2865; Fax: 406-256-2995. Hours: 8AM-5PM (MST). *Felony, Civil Actions Over $7,000, Probate.*

www.co.yellowstone.mt.us/clerk_court

Civil Records: Access: Mail, in person. Both court and visitors may perform in person searches. Search fee: $.50 per name per year. Maximum fee-$25.00. Required to search: name, years to search. Civil cases indexed by defendant, plaintiff. Civil records in books, on microfilm back to 1800s; on computer back to 1992.

Criminal Records: Access: Mail, in person. Both court and visitors may perform in person searches. Search fee: $.50 per name per year. Maximum fee-$25.00. Required to search: name, years to search. Criminal records in books, on microfilm back to 1800s; on comptuer back to 1990.

General Information: Public access terminal is available. No adoption, juvenile or sanity records released. SASE required. Turnaround time 1 day if record less than 10 years old. Copy fee: $.50 per page. $.25 per page after first 5. Certification fee: $2.00. Fee payee: Clerk of Court. Personal checks accepted. Prepayment is required.

Limited Jurisdiction Court PO Box 35032, Billings, MT 59107; 406-256-2895; Fax: 406-256-2898. Hours: 8AM-5PM (MST). *Misdemeanor, Civil Actions Under $7,000, Eviction, Small Claims.*

Montana Recording Offices

ORGANIZATION: 57 counties, 56 recording offices. The recording officer is County Clerk and Recorder (Clerk of District Court for state tax liens). Yellowstone National Park is considered a county, but is not included as a filing location. The entire state is in the Mountain Time Zone (MST).

REAL ESTATE RECORDS: Many Montana counties will perform real estate searches. Search and copy fees vary. Certification usually costs $2.00 per document.

UCC RECORDS: Financing statements are filed at the state level, except for real estate related collateral, which are filed with the Clerk and Recorder. However, prior to 07/2001, consumer goods collateral were also filed at the county and these older records can be searched there. All counties will perform UCC searches. Use search request form UCC-11. Search fees are usually $7.00 per debtor name. Copy fees vary.

TAX LIEN RECORDS: Federal tax liens on personal property of businesses are filed with the Secretary of State. Other federal tax liens are filed with the county Clerk and Recorder. State tax liens are filed with the Clerk of District Court. Usually tax liens on personal property filed with the Clerk and Recorder are in the same index with UCC financing statements. Most counties will perform tax lien searches, some as part of a UCC search and others for a separate fee, usually $7.00 per name. Copy fees vary.

OTHER LIENS: Mechanics, thresherman, judgment, lis pendens, construction, logger.

ONLINE ACCESS: Search for a for a Montana property owner by name and county on the Montana Cadastral Mapping Project GIS mapping database at http://gis.doa.state.mt.us

Beaverhead County

Clerk and Recorder, 2 South Pacific, Dillon, MT 59725-2799. Clerk and Recorder, R/E and UCC Recording 406-683-2642; Fax 406-683-5776.
Will search UCC records. UCC search includes federal tax liens if requested. Real estate owner, mortgage, and property transfer searches available. **Other Phone Numbers:** Assessor 406-683-5612; Treasurer 406-683-5821; Appraiser/Auditor 406-683-4000; Elections 406-683-2642; Vital Records 406-683-2642.

Big Horn County

Clerk and Recorder, PO Box 908, Hardin, MT 59034. 406-665-9730; Fax 406-665-9738.
Will search UCC records. Will search real estate records. **Other Phone Numbers:** Assessor 406-665-9710; Treasurer 406-665-9830.

Blaine County

Clerk and Recorder, PO Box 278, Chinook, MT 59523-0278. Clerk and Recorder, R/E and UCC Recording 406-357-3240; Fax 406-357-2199.
Will search UCC records. Will not search real estate records. **Other Phone Numbers:** Assessor 406-357-3210; Treasurer 406-357-3280; Appraiser/Auditor 406-357-3210; Elections 406-357-3240; Vital Records 406-357-3240.

Broadwater County

Clerk and Recorder, 515 Broadway, Townsend, MT 59644. Clerk and Recorder, R/E and UCC Recording 406-266-3443; Fax 406-266-3674.
Will search UCC records. **Other Phone Numbers:** Assessor 406-266-3430; Treasurer 406-266-3445; Appraiser/Auditor 406-266-3430; Elections 406-266-3443; Vital Records 406-266-3443.

Carbon County

Clerk and Recorder, PO Box 887, Red Lodge, MT 59068. Clerk and Recorder, R/E and UCC Recording 406-446-1220; Fax 406-446-2640.
Will search UCC records. Will not search real estate records. **Other Phone Numbers:** Assessor 406-466-1223; Treasurer 406-446-1221; Appraiser/Auditor 406-446-1224; Elections 406-446-1595; Vital Records 406-446-1220.

Carter County

Clerk and Recorder, PO Box 315, Ekalaka, MT 59324-0315. 406-775-8749; Fax 406-775-8750.
Will search UCC records. Will do a separate tax lien search- $7.00 per name. Add an Add'l $7 for a federal tax lien search. Will search real estate records. **Other Phone Numbers:** Assessor 406-775-8717; Treasurer 406-775-8735.

Cascade County

Clerk and Recorder, PO Box 2867, Great Falls, MT 59403-2867. 406-454-6800 R/E Recording: 406-454-6801 UCC Recording: 406-454-6801; Fax 406-454-6802. www.co.cascade.mt.us
Will search UCC records. **Other Phone Numbers:** Assessor 406-454-6744; Treasurer 406-454-6850; Appraiser/Auditor 406-454-7460; Elections 406-454-6803; Vital Records 406-454-6718.

Chouteau County

Clerk and Recorder, PO Box 459, Fort Benton, MT 59442-0459. 406-622-5151; Fax 406-622-3012.
Will search UCC records. UCC search includes federal tax liens if requested. Real estate owner, mortgage, and property transfer searches available. **Other Phone Numbers:** Assessor 406-622-5261; Treasurer 406-622-5032; Elections 406-622-5151; Vital Records 406-622-5151.

Custer County

Clerk and Recorder, 1010 Main St, Miles City, MT 59301-1010. 406-233-3343; Fax 406-233-3452.
Will search UCC records. Real estate record owner searches available. **Other Phone Numbers:** Assessor 406-232-1295; Treasurer 406-233-3427.

Daniels County

Clerk and Recorder, PO Box 247, Scobey, MT 59263. 406-487-5561.
Will search UCC records. UCC search includes federal tax liens if requested. Real estate record owner and mortgage searches available. **Other Phone Numbers:** Assessor 406-487-2791; Treasurer 406-487-2671.

Dawson County

Clerk and Recorder, 207 W. Bell, Glendive, MT 59330. Clerk and Recorder, R/E and UCC Recording 406-377-3058; Fax 406-377-2022.
Will search UCC records. **Other Phone Numbers:** Assessor 406-377-4256; Treasurer 406-377-3026; Appraiser/Auditor 406-377-4500; Elections 406-377-3058; Vital Records 406-377-3058.

Deer Lodge County

Clerk and Recorder, 800 S. Main St., Courthouse, Anaconda, MT 59711-2999. 406-563-4060 R/E Recording: 406-563-4061 UCC Recording: 406-563-4061; Fax 406-563-4001.
Will search UCC records. Will do limited real estate searches. **Other Phone Numbers:** Assessor 406-563-4045; Treasurer 406-563-4051; Appraiser/Auditor 406-563-4045; Elections 406-563-4060; Vital Records 406-563-4062.

Fallon County

Clerk and Recorder, PO Box 846, Baker, MT 59313-0846. Clerk and Recorder, R/E and UCC Recording 406-778-7106; Fax 406-778-3431.
Will search UCC records. **Other Phone Numbers:** Assessor 406-778-7172; Treasurer 406-778-7109; Appraiser/Auditor 406-778-7172; Elections 406-778-7106; Vital Records 406-778-7106.

Fergus County

Clerk and Recorder, 712 W. Main, Lewistown, MT 59457. 406-538-5242; Fax 406-538-9023.
Will search UCC records. UCC search includes tax liens if requested. Will not search real estate records. **Other Phone Numbers:** Treasurer 406-538-9220.

Flathead County

Clerk and Recorder, 800 S. Main, Courthouse, Kalispell, MT 59901-5400. 406-758-5532 R/E Recording: 406-758-5526 UCC Recording: 406-758-5526; Fax 406-758-5865. www.co.flathead.mt.us
Will search UCC records. UCC search includes federal tax liens if requested. Will not search real estate records. **Other Phone Numbers:** Assessor 406-758-5700; Treasurer 406-758-5680; Elections 406-758-5535; Vital Records 406-758-5526.

Gallatin County

Clerk and Recorder, 311 W. Main, Rm 204, Room 204, Bozeman, MT 59715. Clerk and Recorder, R/E and UCC Recording 406-582-3050; Fax 406-582-3037. Will search UCC records. UCC search does not include federal tax liens. Real estate record owner and mortgage searches available. **Other Phone Numbers:** Assessor 406-582-3400; Treasurer 406-582-3030; Appraiser/Auditor 406-582 3400; Elections 406-582-3060; Vital Records 406-582-3050.

Garfield County

Clerk and Recorder, PO Box 7, Jordan, MT 59337-0007. 406-557-2760; Fax 406-557-2625. Will search UCC records. **Other Phone Numbers:** Assessor 406-557-6164; Treasurer 406-557-2233; Appraiser/Auditor 406-557-2772; Elections 406-557-2760.

Glacier County

Deputy Clerk, 512 E. Main, Cut Bank, MT 59427. Deputy Clerk, R/E and UCC Recording 406-873-5063 x22; Fax 406-873-2125. Will search UCC records. Will not search real estate records. **Other Phone Numbers:** Assessor 406-873-5063 x43; Treasurer 406-873-5063 x31; Appraiser/Auditor 406-873-5063 x45; Elections 406-873-5063 x17; Vital Records 406-873-5063 x22.

Golden Valley County

Clerk and Recorder, PO Box 10, Ryegate, MT 59074. Clerk and Recorder, R/E and UCC Recording 406-568-2231; Fax 406-568-2598. Will search UCC records. Will not search real estate records. **Other Phone Numbers:** Assessor 406-586-2371; Treasurer 406-586-2342; Elections 406-568-2231; Vital Records 406-568-2231.

Granite County

Clerk and Recorder, PO Box 925, Philipsburg, MT 59858. Clerk and Recorder, R/E and UCC Recording 406-859-3771; Fax 406-859-3817. Will search UCC records. Will not search real estate records. **Other Phone Numbers:** Assessor 406-859-3521; Treasurer 406-859-3831; Elections 406-859-3771; Vital Records 406-859-3771.

Hill County

Clerk and Recorder, 315 4th St, Courthouse, Havre, MT 59501. 406-265-5481; Fax 406-265-2445. http://co.hill.mt.us Will search UCC records. UCC search includes federal tax liens if requested. Real estate record owner searches available. **Other Phone Numbers:** Assessor 406-265-5481 x210; Treasurer 406-265-5481 x257.

Jefferson County

Clerk and Recorder, PO Box H, Boulder, MT 59632. Clerk and Recorder, R/E and UCC Recording 406-225-4020; Fax 406-225-4149. http://co.jefferson.mt.us Will not search UCC records. **Other Phone Numbers:** Assessor 406-225-4001; Treasurer 406-225-4103; Appraiser/Auditor 406-225-4001; Elections 406-225-4018; Vital Records 406-225-4020.

Judith Basin County

Clerk and Recorder, PO Box 427, Stanford, MT 59479. Clerk and Recorder, R/E and UCC Recording 406-566-2277; Fax 406-566-2211. Will search UCC records. **Other Phone Numbers:** Assessor 406-566-2291; Treasurer 406-566-2277; Elections 406-566-2277; Vital Records 406-566-2277.

Lake County

Clerk and Recorder, 106 4th Ave East, Polson, MT 59860. 406-883-7210 R/E Recording: 406-883-7208; Fax 406-883-7283. www.lakecounty-mt.org Will search UCC records. UCC search includes federal tax liens if requested. Mortgage searches available. **Other Phone Numbers:** Assessor 406-883-7232; Treasurer 406-883-7224; Appraiser/Auditor 406-883-7227; Elections 406-883-7268; Vital Records 406-883-7208; Clerk of Court (tax liens) 406-883-7254.

Lewis and Clark County

Clerk and Recorder, PO Box 1721, Helena, MT 59624. Clerk and Recorder, R/E and UCC Recording 406-447-8337; Fax 406-457-8598. www.co.lewis-clark.mt.us Will search UCC records. UCC search includes federal tax liens if requested. Mortgage and property transfer searches available. **Online Access:** Real Estate, Lien, Recording Records. Currently the Records Department is in the processing of automating their recording and filing procedures. This automation will include document imaging. Available is the GIS map and parcel search at www.co.lewis-clark.mt.us/gis/atlas/index.html. **Other Phone Numbers:** Assessor 406-444-4000; Treasurer 406-447-8329; Elections 406-447-8338; Vital Records 406-447-8335.

Liberty County

Clerk and Recorder, PO Box 459, Chester, MT 59522-0459. Clerk and Recorder, R/E and UCC Recording 406-759-5365; Fax 406-759-5395. Will search UCC records. **Other Phone Numbers:** Treasurer 406-759-5455; Appraiser/Auditor 406-759-5126; Elections 406-759-5365; Vital Records 406-759-5365.

Lincoln County

Recorder, 512 California Ave, Libby, MT 59923. 406-293-7781 R/E Recording: 406-293-7781 x205 UCC Recording: 406-293-7781 x205; Fax 406-293-8577. Will search UCC records. Will not search real estate records. **Other Phone Numbers:** Assessor 406-293-7781 x213; Treasurer 406-293-7781; Appraiser/Auditor 406-293-7781 x219; Elections 406-293-7781 x283; Vital Records 406-293-7781 x205.

Madison County

Clerk and Recorder, PO Box 366, Virginia City, MT 59755. 406-843-4270. Will search UCC records. UCC search includes federal tax liens. Real estate record owner and property searches available. **Other Phone Numbers:** Assessor 406-843-5392; Treasurer 406-843-4212.

McCone County

Clerk and Recorder, PO Box 199, Circle, MT 59215-0199. Clerk and Recorder, R/E and UCC Recording 406-485-3505; Fax 406-485-2689. Will search UCC records. UCC search includes federal tax liens if requested. Real estate owner, mortgage, and property transfer searches available. **Other Phone Numbers:** Assessor 406-485-3565; Treasurer 406-485-3590; Appraiser/Auditor 406-485-3432; Elections 406-485-3505; Vital Records 406-485-3505.

Meagher County

Deputy Clerk & Recording, PO Box 309, White Sulphur Springs, MT 59645. Deputy Clerk & Recording, R/E and UCC Recording 406-547-3612; Fax 406-547-3388. Will search UCC records. **Other Phone Numbers:** Assessor 406-547-3653; Treasurer 406-547-3641; Appraiser/Auditor 406-547-3653; Elections 406-547-3612; Vital Records 406-547-3612.

Mineral County

Clerk and Recorder, PO Box 550, Superior, MT 59872-0550. 406-822-3520; Fax 406-822-3579. Will search UCC records. **Other Phone Numbers:** Assessor 406-822-3540; Treasurer 406-822-3530; Elections 406-822-3520; Vital Records 406-822-3520.

Missoula County

Clerk and Recorder, 200 W. Broadway, Missoula, MT 59802-4292. Clerk and Recorder, R/E and UCC Recording 406-523-4752; Fax 406-721-4043. www.co.missoula.mt.us Will search UCC records. Will not search real estate records. **Online Access:** Property, Assessor Records. Access to the county property information system is available free at www.co.missoula.mt.us/owner. No name searching at this time. **Other Phones:** Assessor 406-329-1400; Treasurer 406-523-4847; Appraiser/Auditor 406-329-1400; Elections 406-523-4751.

Musselshell County

Clerk and Recorder, 506 Main St, Courthouse, Roundup, MT 59072. Clerk and Recorder, R/E and UCC Recording 406-323-1104; Fax 406-323-3303. Will search UCC records. Will not search real estate records. **Other Phones:** Assessor 406-323-1513; Treasurer 406-323-2504; Appraiser/Auditor 406-323-1513; Elections 323-1104; Vital Records 323-1104.

Park County

Clerk and Recorder, PO Box 1037, Livingston, MT 59047. 406-222-4110; Fax 406-222-4199. Will search UCC records. UCC search does not include federal tax liens. Will not search real estate records. **Other Phone Numbers:** Assessor 406-222-6120 x227; Treasurer 406-222-6120 x252.

Petroleum County

Clerk and Recorder, PO Box 226, Winnett, MT 59087. 406-429-5311; Fax 406-429-6328. Will search UCC records. UCC search does not include federal tax liens. Mortgage searches available. **Other Phone Numbers:** Assessor 406-429-5531; Treasurer 406-429-5551.

Phillips County

Recorder, PO Box 360, Malta, MT 59538. 406-654-2423; Fax 406-654-2429. Will search UCC records. **Other Phone Numbers:** Assessor 406-654-2123; Treasurer 406-654-1742.

Pondera County

Clerk and Recorder, 20 4th Ave S.W., Conrad, MT 59425. 406-271-4000 R/E Recording: 406-271-4001; Fax 406-271-4070. http://ponderacountymontana.org Will search UCC records. **Other Phone Numbers:** Assessor 406-271-4015; Treasurer 406-271-4015; Appraiser/Auditor 406-271-4012.

Powder River County

Clerk and Recorder, PO Box 270, Broadus, MT 59317-0270. 406-436-2361; Fax 406-436-2151. Will search UCC records. UCC search does not include federal tax liens. Mortgage and property transfer searches available. **Other Phone Numbers:** Assessor 406-436-2407; Treasurer 406-436-2444.

Powell County

Clerk and Recorder, 409 Missouri Ave, Deer Lodge, MT 59722. 406-846-3680; Fax 406-846-2784. Will search UCC records. UCC search does not include federal tax liens. Mortgage and property transfer searches available. **Other Phone Numbers:** Assessor 406-846-3680 x230; Treasurer 406-846-3680 x226; Appraiser/Auditor 406-846-3680; Elections 406-846-3680 x223.

Prairie County

Clerk and Recorder, PO Box 125, Terry, MT 59349. 406-635-5575; Fax 406-635-5576.
Will search UCC records. **Other Phone Numbers:** Assessor 406-637-5560.

Ravalli County

Clerk and Recorder, Courthouse Box 5002, Hamilton, MT 59840. Clerk and Recorder, R/E and UCC Recording 406-375-6212; Fax 406-375-6326.
Will search UCC records. Will search real estate records. **Other Phone Numbers:** Assessor 406-375-6312; Treasurer 406-375-6300; Appraiser/Auditor 406-375-6312; Elections 406-375-6213; Vital Records 406-375-6212.

Richland County

Clerk and Recorder, 201 W. Main St, Sidney, MT 59270. 406-433-1708; Fax 406-433-3731.
Will search UCC records. **Other Phone Numbers:** Assessor 406-482-1203; Treasurer 406-433-1707; Appraiser/Auditor 406-433-2850; Elections 406-433-1708; Vital Records 406-433-1708.

Roosevelt County

Clerk and Recorder, 400 Second Ave South, Wolf Point, MT 59201. 406-653-6250; Fax 406-653-6289.
Will search UCC records. Will not search real estate records. **Other Phones:** Assessor 406-653-6256; Treasurer 406-653-6239; Appraiser/Auditor 406-653-6255.

Rosebud County

Clerk and Recorder, PO Box 47, Forsyth, MT 59327. 406-356-7318; Fax 406-356-7551.
Will search UCC records. **Other Phone Numbers:** Assessor 406-356-2516.

Sanders County

Clerk and Recorder, PO Box 519, Thompson Falls, MT 59873. Clerk and Recorder, R/E and UCC Recording 406-827-6922; Fax 406-827-4388.
Will search UCC records. **Other Phone Numbers:** Assessor 406-827-6922; Treasurer 406-827-6924; Appraiser/Auditor 406-827-6932; Elections 406-827-6922; Vital Records 406-827-6922.

Sheridan County

Clerk and Recorder, 100 W. Laurel Ave, Plentywood, MT 59254. Clerk and Recorder, R/E and UCC Recording 406-765-3403; Fax 406-765-2609. www.co.sheridan.mt.us
Will search UCC records. Will not search real estate records. **Other Phone Numbers:** Assessor 406-765-2291; Treasurer 406-765-3414; Appraiser/Auditor 406-765-2291; Elections 406-765-3403; Vital Records 406-765-3403.

Silver Bow County

Clerk and Recorder, 155 W Granite St #208, Butte, MT 59701. 406-723-8262; Fax 406-782-6637.
Will search UCC records. Will not search real estate records. **Other Phone Numbers:** Assessor 406-723-8262 x260; Treasurer 406-723-8262 x250.

Stillwater County

Clerk and Recorder, PO Box 149, Columbus, MT 59019. Clerk and Recorder, R/E and UCC Recording 406-322-8000; Fax 406-322-8007.
Will search UCC records. Mortgage searches available. **Other Phones:** Assessor 406-322-8015; Treasurer 406-322-8020; Appraiser/Auditor 406-322-8015; Elections 406-322-8000; Vital Records 406-322-8000.

Sweet Grass County

Clerk and Recorder, PO Box 888, Big Timber, MT 59011. Clerk and Recorder, R/E and UCC Recording 406-932-5152; Fax 406-932-5177.
Will search UCC records. Will not search real estate records. **Other Phones:** Assessor 406-932-5149; Treasurer 406-932-5151; Vital Records 406-932-5152.

Teton County

Clerk and Recorder, PO Box 610, Choteau, MT 59422. Clerk and Recorder, R/E and UCC Recording 406-466-2693; Fax 406-466-2138. www.tetoncomt.org
Will search UCC records. Will search real estate records. **Other Phone Numbers:** Assessor 406-466-2908; Treasurer 406-466-2694; Appraiser/Auditor 406-466-2908; Elections 406-466-2907; Vital Records 406-466-2693.

Toole County

Clerk and Recorder, 226 1st St South, Shelby, MT 59474. Clerk and Recorder, R/E and UCC Recording 406-434-2232; Fax 406-434-2467.
Will search UCC records. **Other Phone Numbers:** Assessor 406-434-2142; Treasurer 406-434-5501; Appraiser/Auditor 406-434-2142; Elections 406-434-2232; Vital Records 406-434-2232.

Treasure County

Clerk and Recorder, PO Box 392, Hysham, MT 59038. 406-342-5547; Fax 406-342-5445.
Will search UCC records. UCC search includes federal tax liens if requested. Real estate owner, mortgage, and property transfer searches available. **Other Phones:** Assessor 406-342-5540; Treasurer 406-342-5545.

Valley County

Clerk and Recorder, 501 Court Square, Box 2, Glasgow, MT 59230. 406-228-8221; Fax 406-228-9027.
Will search UCC records. **Other Phone Numbers:** Assessor 406-228-8221 x33; Treasurer 406-228-8221 x35.

Wheatland County

Clerk and Recorder, PO Box 1903, Harlowton, MT 59036. 406-632-4891; Fax 406-632-4880.
Will search UCC records. **Other Phone Numbers:** Assessor 406-632-4894; Treasurer 406-632-4892; Vital Records 406-632-4891.

Wibaux County

Clerk and Recorder, PO Box 199, Wibaux, MT 59353-0199. Clerk and Recorder, R/E and UCC Recording 406-796-2481; Fax 406-796-2625.
Will search UCC records. **Other Phone Numbers:** Assessor 406-795-2483; Treasurer 406-795-2482; Elections 406-796-2481; Vital Records 406-796-2481.

Yellowstone County

Clerk and Recorder, PO Box 35001, Billings, MT 59107. Clerk and Recorder, R/E and UCC Recording 406-256-2785; Fax 406-256-2736. www.co.yellowstone.mt.us/clerk
Will search UCC records. UCC search does not include federal tax liens. Property transfer searches available. **Online Access:** Assessor, Tax, Grantor/Grantee Records. Access to the county clerk & recorder records are available free online at www.co.yellowstone.mt.us/clerk. Also, access to the tax assessor records is available free at www.co.yellowstone.mt.us/gis. **Other Phone Numbers:** Assessor 406-896-4000; Treasurer 406-256-2785; Elections 406-256-2743; Vital Records 406-256-2788.

Montana County Locator

You will usually be able to find the city name in the City/County Cross Reference below. In that case, it is a simple matter to determine the county from the cross reference. However, only the official US Postal Service city names are included in this index. There are an additional 40,000 place names that people use in their addresses. Therefore, we have also included a ZIP/City Cross Reference immediately following the City/County Cross Reference.

If you know the ZIP Code but the city name does not appear in the City/County Cross Reference index, look up the ZIP Code in the ZIP/City Cross Reference, find the city name, then look up the city name in the City/County Cross Reference. For example, you want to know the county for an address of Menands, NY 12204. There is no "Menands" in the City/County Cross Reference. The ZIP/City Cross Reference shows that ZIP Codes 12201-12288 are for the city of Albany. Looking back in the City/County Cross Reference, Albany is in Albany County.

City/County Cross Reference

ABSAROKEE Stillwater
ACTON Yellowstone
ALBERTON (59820) Missoula(62), Mineral(37)
ALDER Madison
ALZADA Carter
ANACONDA (59711) Deer Lodge(90), Granite(5), Silver Bow(3)
ANGELA Rosebud
ANTELOPE Sheridan
ARLEE (59821) Lake(69), Missoula(27), Sanders(2)
ASHLAND Rosebud
AUGUSTA Lewis and Clark
AVON Powell
BABB Glacier
BAINVILLE Roosevelt
BAKER Fallon
BALLANTINE Yellowstone
BASIN Jefferson
BEARCREEK Carbon
BELFRY Carbon
BELGRADE Gallatin
BELT Cascade
BIDDLE Powder River
BIG ARM Lake
BIG SANDY Chouteau
BIG SKY Gallatin
BIG TIMBER Sweet Grass
BIGFORK (59911) Flathead(59), Lake(40)
BIGHORN Treasure
BILLINGS Yellowstone
BIRNEY Rosebud
BLACK EAGLE Cascade
BLOOMFIELD Dawson
BONNER Missoula
BOULDER Jefferson
BOX ELDER Hill
BOYD Carbon
BOYES Carter
BOZEMAN Gallatin
BRADY (59416) Chouteau(62), Pondera(36), Liberty(1)
BRIDGER Carbon
BROADUS Powder River
BROADVIEW (59015) Yellowstone(75), Stillwater(14), Musselshell(10)
BROCKTON Roosevelt
BROCKWAY (59214) McCone(85), Prairie(14)
BROWNING Glacier
BRUSETT Garfield
BUFFALO Fergus
BUSBY Big Horn
BUTTE Silver Bow
BYNUM Teton
CAMERON Madison
CANYON CREEK Lewis and Clark
CAPITOL Carter
CARDWELL (59721) Madison(54), Jefferson(45)
CARTER Chouteau
CASCADE Cascade

CAT CREEK Petroleum
CHARLO Lake
CHESTER Liberty
CHINOOK Blaine
CHOTEAU Teton
CIRCLE (59215) McCone(94), Dawson(5)
CLANCY Jefferson
CLINTON (59825) Missoula(82), Granite(17)
CLYDE PARK Park
COFFEE CREEK Fergus
COHAGEN Garfield
COLSTRIP Rosebud
COLUMBIA FALLS Flathead
COLUMBUS Stillwater
CONDON Missoula
CONNER Ravalli
CONRAD (59425) Pondera(97), Teton(1)
COOKE CITY Park
CORAM Flathead
CORVALLIS Ravalli
CORWIN SPRINGS Park
CRANE Richland
CROW AGENCY Big Horn
CULBERTSON Roosevelt
CUSTER Yellowstone
CUT BANK Glacier
DAGMAR (59219) Sheridan(98), Roosevelt(1)
DARBY Ravalli
DAYTON (59914) Flathead(72), Lake(27)
DE BORGIA Mineral
DECKER Big Horn
DEER LODGE (59722) Powell(96), Deer Lodge(3)
DELL Beaverhead
DENTON Fergus
DILLON Beaverhead
DIVIDE Silver Bow
DIXON Sanders
DODSON (59524) Phillips(77), Blaine(22)
DRUMMOND Granite
DUPUYER Pondera
DUTTON Teton
EAST GLACIER PARK Glacier
EAST HELENA (59635) Lewis and Clark(95), Jefferson(4)
EDGAR Carbon
EKALAKA Carter
ELLISTON Powell
ELMO Lake
EMIGRANT Park
ENNIS Madison
ESSEX Flathead
ETHRIDGE Toole
EUREKA Lincoln
FAIRFIELD Teton
FAIRVIEW Richland
FALLON Prairie
FISHTAIL Stillwater
FLAXVILLE Daniels
FLORENCE (59833) Ravalli(61), Missoula(38)

FLOWEREE (59440) Chouteau(70), Cascade(29)
FORESTGROVE Fergus
FORSYTH Rosebud
FORT BENTON Chouteau
FORT HARRISON Lewis and Clark
FORT PECK Valley
FORT SHAW (59443) Cascade(92), Teton(7)
FORTINE Lincoln
FOUR BUTTES Daniels
FRAZER Valley
FRENCHTOWN Missoula
FROID (59226) Roosevelt(84), Sheridan(15)
FROMBERG Carbon
GALATA (59444) Toole(75), Liberty(24)
GALLATIN GATEWAY Gallatin
GARDINER Park
GARNEILL Fergus
GARRISON Powell
GARRYOWEN Big Horn
GERALDINE Chouteau
GEYSER (59447) Judith Basin(96), Chouteau(3)
GILDFORD Hill
GLASGOW Valley
GLEN Beaverhead
GLENDIVE Dawson
GLENTANA Valley
GOLD CREEK Powell
GRANTSDALE Ravalli
GRASS RANGE Fergus
GREAT FALLS Cascade
GREENOUGH Missoula
GREYCLIFF Sweet Grass
HALL Granite
HAMILTON Ravalli
HAMMOND Carter
HARDIN Big Horn
HARLEM Blaine
HARLOWTON Wheatland
HARRISON Madison
HATHAWAY Rosebud
HAUGAN Mineral
HAVRE Hill
HAYS Blaine
HEART BUTTE Pondera
HELENA Lewis and Clark
HELMVILLE Powell
HERON Sanders
HIGHWOOD Chouteau
HILGER Fergus
HINGHAM Hill
HINSDALE Valley
HOBSON Judith Basin
HOGELAND Blaine
HOMESTEAD (59242) Sheridan(83), Roosevelt(16)
HOT SPRINGS (59845) Sanders(66), Flathead(24), Lake(9)
HUNGRY HORSE Flathead
HUNTLEY Yellowstone

HUSON Missoula
HYSHAM Treasure
INGOMAR Rosebud
INVERNESS (59530) Hill(93), Liberty(6)
ISMAY (59336) Custer(95), Prairie(4)
JACKSON Beaverhead
JEFFERSON CITY Jefferson
JOLIET Carbon
JOPLIN Liberty
JORDAN Garfield
JUDITH GAP Wheatland
KALISPELL Flathead
KEVIN Toole
KILA Flathead
KINSEY Custer
KREMLIN Hill
LAKE MC DONALD Flathead
LAKESIDE (59922) Flathead(70), Lake(29)
LAMBERT Richland
LAME DEER Rosebud
LARSLAN Valley
LAUREL (59044) Yellowstone(97), Carbon(2)
LAVINA Golden Valley
LEDGER (59456) Pondera(53), Liberty(46)
LEWISTOWN Fergus
LIBBY Lincoln
LIMA Beaverhead
LINCOLN (59639) Lewis and Clark(90), Powell(10)
LINDSAY (59339) Dawson(97), Prairie(2)
LIVINGSTON Park
LLOYD Blaine
LODGE GRASS Big Horn
LOLO Missoula
LOMA Chouteau
LONEPINE Sanders
LORING Phillips
LOTHAIR Liberty
LUTHER Carbon
MALMSTROM A F B Cascade
MALTA Phillips
MANHATTAN Gallatin
MARION Flathead
MARTIN CITY Flathead
MARTINSDALE Meagher
MARYSVILLE Lewis and Clark
MC ALLISTER Madison
MC CABE Roosevelt
MC LEOD (59052) Sweet Grass(80), Park(19)
MEDICINE LAKE Sheridan
MELROSE Silver Bow
MELSTONE Musselshell
MELVILLE Sweet Grass
MILDRED Prairie
MILES CITY Custer
MILL IRON Carter
MILLTOWN Missoula
MISSOULA Missoula
MOCCASIN Judith Basin
MOLT (59057) Yellowstone(68), Stillwater(31)

MONARCH Cascade
MOORE Fergus
MOSBY Garfield
MUSSELSHELL Musselshell
NASHUA Valley
NEIHART Cascade
NIARADA (59852) Sanders(85),
　Flathead(14)
NORRIS Madison
NOXON Sanders
NYE Stillwater
OILMONT Toole
OLIVE Powder River
OLNEY Flathead
OPHEIM Valley
OTTER (59062) Powder River(90),
　Rosebud(10)
OUTLOOK Sheridan
OVANDO Powell
PABLO Lake
PARADISE Sanders
PARK CITY Stillwater
PEERLESS Daniels
PENDROY Teton
PHILIPSBURG Granite
PINESDALE Ravalli
PLAINS Sanders
PLENTYWOOD Sheridan
PLEVNA Fallon
POLARIS Beaverhead
POLEBRIDGE Flathead
POLSON Lake
POMPEYS PILLAR Yellowstone
PONY Madison
POPLAR Roosevelt
POWDERVILLE Powder River
POWER (59468) Teton(84), Cascade(15)
PRAY Park
PROCTOR Lake

PRYOR Big Horn
RADERSBURG Broadwater
RAMSAY Silver Bow
RAPELJE Stillwater
RAVALLI Lake
RAYMOND Sheridan
RAYNESFORD Judith Basin
RED LODGE Carbon
REDSTONE Sheridan
REED POINT (59069) Stillwater(66), Sweet
　Grass(33)
REEDPOINT (59069) Stillwater(66), Sweet
　Grass(33)
RESERVE (59258) Sheridan(93),
　Roosevelt(6)
REXFORD Lincoln
RICHEY Dawson
RICHLAND Valley
RINGLING Meagher
ROBERTS Carbon
ROLLINS (59931) Flathead(89), Lake(10)
RONAN Lake
ROSCOE Carbon
ROSEBUD (59347) Rosebud(97),
　Custer(2)
ROUNDUP Musselshell
ROY Fergus
RUDYARD (59540) Hill(73), Chouteau(26)
RYEGATE (59074) Golden Valley(97),
　Stillwater(2)
SACO Phillips
SAINT IGNATIUS Lake
SAINT MARIE Valley
SAINT REGIS Mineral
SAINT XAVIER Big Horn
SALTESE Mineral
SAND COULEE Cascade
SAND SPRINGS Garfield
SANDERS Treasure

SANTA RITA Glacier
SAVAGE (59262) Richland(62),
　Dawson(37)
SCOBEY Daniels
SEELEY LAKE Missoula
SHAWMUT Wheatland
SHELBY Toole
SHEPHERD Yellowstone
SHERIDAN Madison
SIDNEY Richland
SILVER GATE Park
SILVER STAR Madison
SIMMS Cascade
SOMERS Flathead
SONNETTE Powder River
SPRINGDALE Park
STANFORD Judith Basin
STEVENSVILLE Ravalli
STOCKETT Cascade
STRYKER Lincoln
SULA Ravalli
SUMATRA Rosebud
SUN RIVER Cascade
SUNBURST Toole
SUPERIOR Mineral
SWEET GRASS Toole
SWEETGRASS Toole
TEIGEN Petroleum
TERRY Prairie
THOMPSON FALLS Sanders
THREE FORKS (59752) Gallatin(90),
　Broadwater(9)
TOSTON Broadwater
TOWNSEND Broadwater
TREGO Lincoln
TROUT CREEK Sanders
TROY Lincoln
TURNER Blaine
TWIN BRIDGES Madison

TWO DOT Wheatland
TWODOT Wheatland
ULM Cascade
VALIER Pondera
VANDALIA Valley
VAUGHN (59487) Cascade(88), Teton(11)
VICTOR Ravalli
VIDA McCone
VIRGINIA CITY Madison
VOLBORG Custer
WARM SPRINGS Deer Lodge
WARMSPRINGS Deer Lodge
WEST GLACIER Flathead
WEST YELLOWSTONE Gallatin
WESTBY Sheridan
WHITE SULPHUR SPRINGS Meagher
WHITEFISH Flathead
WHITEHALL (59759) Jefferson(80),
　Madison(18), Silver Bow(1)
WHITETAIL Daniels
WHITEWATER Phillips
WHITLASH Liberty
WIBAUX Wibaux
WILLARD Fallon
WILLOW CREEK Gallatin
WILSALL (59086) Park(79), Gallatin(19)
WINIFRED Fergus
WINNETT Petroleum
WINSTON Broadwater
WISDOM Beaverhead
WISE RIVER (59762) Beaverhead(53),
　Deer Lodge(46)
WOLF CREEK Lewis and Clark
WOLF POINT Roosevelt
WORDEN Yellowstone
WYOLA Big Horn
YELLOWTAIL Big Horn
ZORTMAN Phillips
ZURICH Blaine

ZIP/City Cross Reference

59001-59001 ABSAROKEE	59046-59046 LAVINA	59087-59087 WINNETT	59260-59260 RICHLAND
59002-59002 ACTON	59047-59047 LIVINGSTON	59088-59088 WORDEN	59261-59261 SACO
59003-59004 ASHLAND	59050-59050 LODGE GRASS	59089-59089 WYOLA	59262-59262 SAVAGE
59006-59006 BALLANTINE	59051-59051 LUTHER	59100-59117 BILLINGS	59263-59263 SCOBEY
59007-59007 BEARCREEK	59052-59052 MC LEOD	59201-59201 WOLF POINT	59270-59270 SIDNEY
59008-59008 BELFRY	59053-59053 MARTINSDALE	59211-59211 ANTELOPE	59273-59273 VANDALIA
59010-59010 BIGHORN	59054-59054 MELSTONE	59212-59212 BAINVILLE	59274-59274 VIDA
59011-59011 BIG TIMBER	59055-59055 MELVILLE	59213-59213 BROCKTON	59275-59275 WESTBY
59012-59012 BIRNEY	59057-59057 MOLT	59214-59214 BROCKWAY	59276-59276 WHITETAIL
59013-59013 BOYD	59058-59058 MOSBY	59215-59215 CIRCLE	59301-59301 MILES CITY
59014-59014 BRIDGER	59059-59059 MUSSELSHELL	59217-59217 CRANE	59311-59311 ALZADA
59015-59015 BROADVIEW	59061-59061 NYE	59218-59218 CULBERTSON	59312-59312 ANGELA
59016-59016 BUSBY	59062-59062 OTTER	59219-59219 DAGMAR	59313-59313 BAKER
59017-59017 CAT CREEK	59063-59063 PARK CITY	59221-59221 FAIRVIEW	59314-59314 BIDDLE
59018-59018 CLYDE PARK	59064-59064 POMPEYS PILLAR	59222-59222 FLAXVILLE	59315-59315 BLOOMFIELD
59019-59019 COLUMBUS	59065-59065 PRAY	59223-59223 FORT PECK	59316-59316 BOYES
59020-59020 COOKE CITY	59066-59066 PRYOR	59224-59224 FOUR BUTTES	59317-59317 BROADUS
59021-59021 CORWIN SPRINGS	59067-59067 RAPELJE	59225-59225 FRAZER	59318-59318 BRUSETT
59022-59022 CROW AGENCY	59068-59068 RED LODGE	59226-59226 FROID	59319-59319 CAPITOL
59024-59024 CUSTER	59069-59069 REEDPOINT	59230-59230 GLASGOW	59322-59322 COHAGEN
59025-59025 DECKER	59069-59069 REED POINT	59231-59231 SAINT MARIE	59323-59323 COLSTRIP
59026-59026 EDGAR	59070-59070 ROBERTS	59240-59240 GLENTANA	59324-59324 EKALAKA
59027-59027 EMIGRANT	59071-59071 ROSCOE	59241-59241 HINSDALE	59326-59326 FALLON
59028-59028 FISHTAIL	59072-59073 ROUNDUP	59242-59242 HOMESTEAD	59327-59327 FORSYTH
59029-59029 FROMBERG	59074-59074 RYEGATE	59243-59243 LAMBERT	59330-59330 GLENDIVE
59030-59030 GARDINER	59075-59075 SAINT XAVIER	59244-59244 LARSLAN	59332-59332 HAMMOND
59031-59031 GARRYOWEN	59076-59076 SANDERS	59245-59245 MC CABE	59333-59333 HATHAWAY
59032-59032 GRASS RANGE	59077-59077 SAND SPRINGS	59247-59247 MEDICINE LAKE	59336-59336 ISMAY
59033-59033 GREYCLIFF	59078-59078 SHAWMUT	59248-59248 NASHUA	59337-59337 JORDAN
59034-59034 HARDIN	59079-59079 SHEPHERD	59250-59250 OPHEIM	59338-59338 KINSEY
59035-59035 YELLOWTAIL	59080-59080 JOLIET	59252-59252 OUTLOOK	59339-59339 LINDSAY
59036-59036 HARLOWTON	59081-59081 SILVER GATE	59253-59253 PEERLESS	59341-59341 MILDRED
59037-59037 HUNTLEY	59082-59082 SPRINGDALE	59254-59254 PLENTYWOOD	59342-59342 MILL IRON
59038-59038 HYSHAM	59083-59083 SUMATRA	59255-59255 POPLAR	59343-59343 OLIVE
59039-59039 INGOMAR	59084-59084 TEIGEN	59256-59256 RAYMOND	59344-59344 PLEVNA
59041-59041 JOLIET	59085-59085 TWODOT	59257-59257 REDSTONE	59345-59345 POWDERVILLE
59043-59043 LAME DEER	59085-59085 TWO DOT	59258-59258 RESERVE	59347-59347 ROSEBUD
59044-59044 LAUREL	59086-59086 WILSALL	59259-59259 RICHEY	59348-59348 SONNETTE

59349-59349	TERRY
59351-59351	VOLBORG
59353-59353	WIBAUX
59354-59354	WILLARD
59401-59401	GREAT FALLS
59402-59402	MALMSTROM A F B
59403-59406	GREAT FALLS
59410-59410	AUGUSTA
59411-59411	BABB
59412-59412	BELT
59414-59414	BLACK EAGLE
59416-59416	BRADY
59417-59417	BROWNING
59418-59418	BUFFALO
59419-59419	BYNUM
59420-59420	CARTER
59421-59421	CASCADE
59422-59422	CHOTEAU
59424-59424	COFFEE CREEK
59425-59425	CONRAD
59427-59427	CUT BANK
59430-59430	DENTON
59432-59432	DUPUYER
59433-59433	DUTTON
59434-59434	EAST GLACIER PARK
59435-59435	ETHRIDGE
59436-59436	FAIRFIELD
59440-59440	FLOWEREE
59441-59441	FORESTGROVE
59442-59442	FORT BENTON
59443-59443	FORT SHAW
59444-59444	GALATA
59445-59445	GARNEILL
59446-59446	GERALDINE
59447-59447	GEYSER
59448-59448	HEART BUTTE
59450-59450	HIGHWOOD
59451-59451	HILGER
59452-59452	HOBSON
59453-59453	JUDITH GAP
59454-59454	KEVIN
59456-59456	LEDGER
59457-59457	LEWISTOWN
59460-59460	LOMA
59461-59461	LOTHAIR
59462-59462	MOCCASIN
59463-59463	MONARCH
59464-59464	MOORE
59465-59465	NEIHART
59466-59466	OILMONT
59467-59467	PENDROY
59468-59468	POWER
59469-59469	RAYNESFORD
59471-59471	ROY
59472-59472	SAND COULEE
59473-59473	SANTA RITA
59474-59474	SHELBY
59477-59477	SIMMS
59479-59479	STANFORD
59480-59480	STOCKETT
59482-59482	SUNBURST
59483-59483	SUN RIVER
59484-59484	SWEETGRASS
59484-59484	SWEET GRASS
59485-59485	ULM
59486-59486	VALIER
59487-59487	VAUGHN
59489-59489	WINIFRED
59501-59501	HAVRE
59520-59520	BIG SANDY
59521-59521	BOX ELDER
59522-59522	CHESTER
59523-59523	CHINOOK
59524-59524	DODSON
59525-59525	GILDFORD
59526-59526	HARLEM
59527-59527	HAYS
59528-59528	HINGHAM
59529-59529	HOGELAND
59530-59530	INVERNESS
59531-59531	JOPLIN
59532-59532	KREMLIN
59535-59535	LLOYD
59537-59537	LORING
59538-59538	MALTA
59540-59540	RUDYARD
59542-59542	TURNER
59544-59544	WHITEWATER
59545-59545	WHITLASH
59546-59546	ZORTMAN
59547-59547	ZURICH
59601-59626	HELENA
59631-59631	BASIN
59632-59632	BOULDER
59633-59633	CANYON CREEK
59634-59634	CLANCY
59635-59635	EAST HELENA
59636-59636	FORT HARRISON
59638-59638	JEFFERSON CITY
59639-59639	LINCOLN
59640-59640	MARYSVILLE
59641-59641	RADERSBURG
59642-59642	RINGLING
59643-59643	TOSTON
59644-59644	TOWNSEND
59645-59645	WHITE SULPHUR SPRINGS
59647-59647	WINSTON
59648-59648	WOLF CREEK
59701-59707	BUTTE
59710-59710	ALDER
59711-59711	ANACONDA
59713-59713	AVON
59714-59714	BELGRADE
59715-59715	BOZEMAN
59716-59716	BIG SKY
59717-59719	BOZEMAN
59720-59720	CAMERON
59721-59721	CARDWELL
59722-59722	DEER LODGE
59724-59724	DELL
59725-59725	DILLON
59727-59727	DIVIDE
59728-59728	ELLISTON
59729-59729	ENNIS
59730-59730	GALLATIN GATEWAY
59731-59731	GARRISON
59732-59732	GLEN
59733-59733	GOLD CREEK
59735-59735	HARRISON
59736-59736	JACKSON
59739-59739	LIMA
59740-59740	MC ALLISTER
59741-59741	MANHATTAN
59743-59743	MELROSE
59745-59745	NORRIS
59746-59746	POLARIS
59747-59747	PONY
59748-59748	RAMSAY
59749-59749	SHERIDAN
59750-59750	BUTTE
59751-59751	SILVER STAR
59752-59752	THREE FORKS
59754-59754	TWIN BRIDGES
59755-59755	VIRGINIA CITY
59756-59756	WARMSPRINGS
59756-59756	WARM SPRINGS
59758-59758	WEST YELLOWSTONE
59759-59759	WHITEHALL
59760-59760	WILLOW CREEK
59761-59761	WISDOM
59762-59762	WISE RIVER
59771-59773	BOZEMAN
59801-59812	MISSOULA
59820-59820	ALBERTON
59821-59821	ARLEE
59823-59823	BONNER
59824-59824	CHARLO
59825-59825	CLINTON
59826-59826	CONDON
59827-59827	CONNER
59828-59828	CORVALLIS
59829-59829	DARBY
59830-59830	DE BORGIA
59831-59831	DIXON
59832-59832	DRUMMOND
59833-59833	FLORENCE
59834-59834	FRENCHTOWN
59835-59835	GRANTSDALE
59836-59836	GREENOUGH
59837-59837	HALL
59840-59840	HAMILTON
59841-59841	PINESDALE
59842-59842	HAUGAN
59843-59843	HELMVILLE
59844-59844	HERON
59845-59845	HOT SPRINGS
59846-59846	HUSON
59847-59847	LOLO
59848-59848	LONEPINE
59851-59851	MILLTOWN
59852-59852	NIARADA
59853-59853	NOXON
59854-59854	OVANDO
59855-59855	PABLO
59856-59856	PARADISE
59858-59858	PHILIPSBURG
59859-59859	PLAINS
59860-59860	POLSON
59863-59863	RAVALLI
59864-59864	RONAN
59865-59865	SAINT IGNATIUS
59866-59866	SAINT REGIS
59867-59867	SALTESE
59868-59868	SEELEY LAKE
59870-59870	STEVENSVILLE
59871-59871	SULA
59872-59872	SUPERIOR
59873-59873	THOMPSON FALLS
59874-59874	TROUT CREEK
59875-59875	VICTOR
59901-59904	KALISPELL
59910-59910	BIG ARM
59911-59911	BIGFORK
59912-59912	COLUMBIA FALLS
59913-59913	CORAM
59914-59914	DAYTON
59915-59915	ELMO
59916-59916	ESSEX
59917-59917	EUREKA
59918-59918	FORTINE
59919-59919	HUNGRY HORSE
59920-59920	KILA
59921-59921	LAKE MC DONALD
59922-59922	LAKESIDE
59923-59923	LIBBY
59925-59925	MARION
59926-59926	MARTIN CITY
59927-59927	OLNEY
59928-59928	POLEBRIDGE
59929-59929	PROCTOR
59930-59930	REXFORD
59931-59931	ROLLINS
59932-59932	SOMERS
59933-59933	STRYKER
59934-59934	TREGO
59935-59935	TROY
59936-59936	WEST GLACIER
59937-59937	WHITEFISH

General Help Numbers:

Governor's Office
PO Box 94848
Lincoln, NE 68509-4848
http://gov.nol.org

402-471-2244
Fax 402-471-6031
8AM-5PM

Attorney General's Office
2115 State Capitol
Lincoln, NE 68509
www.ago.state.ne.us/

402-471-2682
Fax 402-471-3297
8AM-5PM

State Court Administrator
PO Box 98910
Lincoln, NE 68509-8910
http://court.nol.org/AOC

402-471-3730
Fax 402-471-2197
8AM-4:30PM

State Archives
Archives
PO Box 82554
Lincoln, NE 68501-2554

402-471-4771
Fax 402-471-8922
9:30AM-4:30PM M-F;
8-5 SA; 1:30PM-5PM SU

www.nebraskahistory.org

State Specifics:

Capital: Lincoln
                        Lancaster County

Time Zone: CST*
 * Nebraska's nineteen western-most counties are MST:

 They are: Arthur, Banner, Box Butte, Chase, Cherry, Cheyenne, Dawes, Deuel, Dundy, Garden, Grant, Hooker, Keith, Kimball, Morrill, Perkins, Scotts. Bluff, Sheridan, Sioux.

Number of Counties: 93

Population: 1,713,235

Web Site: www.state.ne.us

State Agencies

Criminal Records

Nebraska State Patrol, CID, PO Box 94907, Lincoln, NE 68509-4907 (Courier: 1500 Nebraska Highway 2, Lincoln, NE 68502); 402-479-4924, 402-471-4545, 8AM-4PM.

www.nebraska-state-patrol.org

Note: A Level 3 sexual offender registry search is available at www.nsp.state.ne.us/sor/find.cfm

Indexing & Storage: Records are available from 1937 to present. It takes 15 to 60 days before new records are available for inquiry. Records are indexed on inhouse computer, fingerprint cards. 64% of all arrests in database have final dispositions recorded.

Searching: Include the following in your request: full name, disposition, date of birth, Social Security Number, sex, race. Fingerprints required for certain state occupation checks; this includes an FBI fingerprint search. State keeps record of requesters and will inform the person of record if asked. 100% of records are fingerprint-supported. Felonies are required to be submitted this agency, though not all misdemeanors are. Agency will refer you to the proper county. The following data is not released: juvenile records. Records without dispositions are not released, except if an arrest without disposition is less than one year old.

Access by: mail, in person.

Fee & Payment: The search fee is $10.00 per name. A fingerprint search including FBI fingerprint check is $33.00. Fee payee: Nebraska State Patrol. Prepayment required. Personal checks accepted. No credit cards accepted.

Mail search: Turnaround time: 15 days. No self addressed stamped envelope is required.

In person search: They accept requests in person and turnaround is 15 minutes, but they will mail back the report if it is lengthy or incomplete (unless it is the requester's own report).

Corporation Records
Limited Liability Company Records
Limited Partnerships
Trade Names
Trademarks/Servicemarks

Secretary of State, Corporation Commission, 1305 State Capitol Bldg, Lincoln, NE 68509; 402-471-4079, 402-471-3666 (Fax), 8AM-5PM.

www.sos.state.ne.us/htm/corpmenu.htm

Indexing & Storage: Records are available from the beginning of state corporation filings. Records are indexed on microfilm, index cards.

Searching: Include the following in your request: full name of business. In addition to the articles of incorporation, corporation records include the following information: Reports, Officers, Directors, Prior (merged) names, Inactive and Reserved names and Occupation Tax records for the last 5 years.

Access by: mail, phone, fax, in person, online.

Fee & Payment: No search fee, copies are $1.00 per page. Fee payee: Secretary of State. They will send an invoice. Personal checks accepted. No credit cards accepted.

Mail search: Turnaround time: 2 days. No self addressed stamped envelope is required.

Phone search: Records are available by phone.

Fax search: Fax searching available.

In person search: Searching is available in person.

Online search: The state has designated Nebrask@ Online (800-747-8177) to facilitate online retrieval of records. Access is through both a dial-up system and the Internet; however an account and payment is required. The state Internet site has general information only.

Other access: Nebrask@ Online has the capability of offering database purchases.

Uniform Commercial Code
Federal Tax Liens
State Tax Liens

UCC Division, Secretary of State, PO Box 95104, Lincoln, NE 68509 (Courier: 1301 State Capitol Bldg, Lincoln, NE 68509); 402-471-4080, 402-471-4429 (Fax), 7:30AM-5PM.

www.sos.state.ne.us/htm/UCCmenu.htm

Note: Effective July 1, 1999, all federal and state tax liens are filed at this agency. Previously filed tax liens were filed at the county level. But, this agency has index of all tax liens. Actual hard copies must be secured at local level.

Indexing & Storage: Records are available from 1981 to present, on both computer and microfiche.

Searching: Use search request Nebraska version of the UCC-11 form. Include the following in your request: debtor name.

Access by: mail, fax, in person, online.

Fee & Payment: The search fee is $3.50 per debtor name. Copies are $.50 per page. Certification is an additional $4.00. Fee payee: Secretary of State. They will invoice fax requesters. Personal checks accepted. No credit cards accepted.

Mail search: Turnaround time: 1 day. A self addressed stamped envelope is requested.

Fax search: The fee is $5.00 per debtor. Use the Nebraska Search Form (UCC-11). Turnaround time is 4 hours or less.

In person search: Records are generally available with a short wait.

Online search: Access is outsourced to Nebrask@ Online at www.nol.org. The system is available 24 hours daily. There is an annual $50.00 fee but no further charges to view records. Call 800-747-8177 for more information.

Other access: Check with Nebrask@ Online for bulk purchase programs.

Sales Tax Registrations

Revenue Department, Taxpayer Assistance, PO Box 94818, Lincoln, NE 68509-4818 (Courier: 301 Centennial Mall South, Lincoln, NE 68509); 402-471-7729, 402-471-5990 (Fax), 8AM-5PM.

www.revenue.state.ne.us

Indexing & Storage: Records are available from 1967. Records are indexed on computer.

Searching: This office will confirm that a business is registered and supply requester will name, address and date of license. Include the following in your request: business name. They will also search by tax permit number or by federal tax ID.

Access by: mail, phone.

Mail search: A self addressed stamped envelope is requested. No fee for mail request.

Phone search: No fee for telephone request.

Birth Certificates

NE Health & Human Services System, Vital Statistics Section, PO Box 95065, Lincoln, NE 68509-5065 (Courier: 301 Centennial Mall S, 3rd Floor, Lincoln, NE 68509); 402-471-2871, 8AM-5PM.

www.hhs.state.ne.us/ced/cedindex.htm

Note: Records may also be ordered at regional offices in Omaha, Kearney, North Platte, and Scottsbluff.

Indexing & Storage: Records are available from 1904 to present. Records are indexed by Soundex code, year and county. Records are indexed by computer since 1912, and can be found on microfiche from 1912 to 1977.

Searching: Non-family members must have a signed release from person of record or immediate family member for investigative purposes. If the birth certificate is more than 50 years old, a release form is not required. Closed records are not released. Include the following in your request: full name, date of birth, place of birth, names of parents, mother's maiden name, relationship to person of record, reason for information request. If adopted, indicate so. Expedited services are only available from 9AM to 3PM. The following data is not released: original records of adoption or sealed records.

Access by: mail, phone, in person, online.

Fee & Payment: The fee is $8.00 per record. Fee payee: Vital Records. Prepayment required. Credit cards may only be used for expedited searches by calling in. The file search fee is non-refundable if no records are found. Personal checks accepted. Credit cards accepted: MasterCard, Visa, AmEx, Discover.

Mail search: Turnaround time: 2 to 3 weeks. If the agency receives the request by overnight mail, they will mail it back within 2 to 3 days. A self addressed stamped envelope is requested.

Phone search: See expedited service.

In person search: Turnaround time is 20 to 30 minutes.

Online search: Records may be ordered online from the Internet site.

Death Records

Health and Human Services System, Vital Statistics Section, PO Box 95065, Lincoln, NE 68509-5065 (Courier: 301 Centennial Mall S, 3rd Floor, Lincoln, NE 68509); 402-471-2871, 8AM-5PM.

www.hhs.state.ne.us/ced/cedindex.htm

Note: If a certificate is more than 50 years in the past, release form is not required.

Indexing & Storage: Records are available from 1904 to present. Records are on microfilm from 1956-1997.

Searching: Must have a signed release from immediate family member for investigative purposes. Include the following in your request: full name, date of death, place of death, relationship to person of record, reason for information request. Expedited services are available from 9AM to 3 PM.

Access by: mail, phone, in person.

Fee & Payment: The fee is $7.00 per record. Fee payee: Vital Records. Prepayment required. Credit cards may only be used for phone expedited service. The file search fee is non-refundable if no records are found. Personal checks accepted. Credit cards accepted: MasterCard, Visa, AmEx, Discover.

Mail search: Turnaround time: 2 to 3 weeks. If the agency receives a search request by overnight mail, they will mail the response within 2 to 3 days. A self addressed stamped envelope is requested.

Phone search: See expedited service.

In person search: Turnaround time is 20 to 30 minutes.

Marriage Certificates

Health and Human Services System, Vital Statistics Section, PO Box 95065, Lincoln, NE 68509-5065 (Courier: 301 Centennial Mall S, 3rd Floor, Lincoln, NE 68509); 402-471-2871, 8AM-5PM.

www.hhs.state.ne.us/ced/cedindex.htm

Note: If a certificate is more than 50 years old, a release is not required.

Indexing & Storage: Records are available from 1909 to present. Records are indexed by Soundex code, year and county and are on microfilm from 1956 to present. Records are indexed on microfiche.

Searching: Must have a signed release from persons of record or immediate family member for investigative purposes. Include the following in your request: names of husband and wife, date of marriage, place or county of marriage, relationship to person of record, reason for information request, wife's maiden name. Expedited service is only available from 9AM to 3PM.

Access by: mail, phone, in person.

Fee & Payment: The fee is $7.00 per record. Fee payee: Vital Records. Prepayment required. Credit cards may only be used for phone expedited service. The file search fee is non-refundable if no records are found. Personal checks accepted. Credit cards accepted: MasterCard, Visa, AmEx, Discover.

Mail search: Turnaround time: 2 to 3 weeks. If this agency receives a search request by overnight mail, they will mail a response within 2 to 3 days. A self addressed stamped envelope is requested.

Phone search: See expedited service.

In person search: Turnaround time is 30 minutes.

Divorce Records

Health and Human Services System, Vital Statistics Section, PO Box 95065, Lincoln, NE 68509-5065 (Courier: 301 Centennial Mall S, 3rd Floor, Lincoln, NE 68509); 402-471-2871, 8AM-5PM.

www.hhs.state.ne.us/ced/cedindex.htm

Note: If a certificate is more than 50 years, a release is not required.

Indexing & Storage: Records are available from 1909 to present. Records are indexed by Soundex code, year and county and are on microfilm from 1956 to present.

Searching: Must have a signed release from person of record or immediate family member for investigative purposes. Include the following in your request: names of husband and wife, date of divorce, relationship to person of record, reason for information request. Must also have county where divorce was granted. Expedited service is only available from 9AM to 3PM.

Access by: mail, phone, in person.

Fee & Payment: Fee is $7.00 per record. Fee payee: Vital Records. Prepayment required. Credit cards may only be used for phone expedited service. The file search fee is non-refundable if no records are found. Personal checks accepted. Credit cards accepted: MasterCard, Visa, AmEx, Discover.

Mail search: Turnaround time: 2 to 3 weeks. If this agency receives a request by overnight mail, they will mail a response within 2-3 days. A self addressed stamped envelope is requested.

Phone search: See expedited service.

In person search: Turnaround time is 20-30 minutes.

Workers' Compensation Records

Workers' Compensation Court, PO Box 98908, Lincoln, NE 68509-8908 (Courier: State Capitol, 13th Floor, Lincoln, NE 68509); 402-471-6468, 800-599-5155 (In-state), 402-471-2700 (Fax), 8AM-5PM.

www.nol.org/workcomp

Indexing & Storage: Records are available from 1972 on. It takes 2 days before new records are available for inquiry. Records are indexed on microfilm, printout sheets (SS# & name only), computer.

Searching: Must have a release form for medical records. All other records are public record. Include the following in your request: claimant name, Social Security Number, date of birth, date of accident, docket number. A date of injury is required for searches going back more than 10 years.

Access by: mail, in person, online.

Fee & Payment: A search is $5.00 per name for 5 years searched. If 10 years, then $10.00; if older than 1991, then $15.00. The first 20 pages of file copied are free, then the fee is $25 per page. Microfilm copies are $.50 per page. Fee payee: Workers' Compensation Court. Prepayment required. Personal checks accepted. No credit cards accepted.

Mail search: Turnaround time: 2 to 3 days. No self addressed stamped envelope is required.

In person search: Appointments are required.

Online search: Access to orders and decisions is available from the web site.

Driver Records

Department of Motor Vehicles, Driver & Vehicle Records Division, PO Box 94789, Lincoln, NE 68509-4789 (Courier: 301 Centennial Mall, S, Lincoln, NE 68509); 402-471-3918, 8AM-5PM.

www.nol.org/home/DMV

Note: It is suggested you obtain copies of tickets at the local courts.

Indexing & Storage: Records are available for 5 years for moving violations and suspensions; lifetime for DWIs. Accidents are reported on the record, but fault is not indicated. Surrendered licenses are purged one year after expiration date. It takes 30 days before new records are available for inquiry.

Searching: SSNs will not be released. The general public cannot get personal data. Only approved requesters receive the driver's address. The driver's full name and DOB or license number are needed for ordering. Occasional requesters with a permissible use should use the Application for Copy of Driving Record form.

Access by: mail, in person, online.

Fee & Payment: The fee is $3.00 per record. Fee payee: Department of Motor Vehicles. Prepayment required. Personal checks accepted. No credit cards accepted.

Mail search: Turnaround time: 24 hours. A self addressed stamped envelope is requested.

In person search: Walk-in requesters are not charged for a no record found.

Online search: Nebraska outsources all online and tape record requests through Nebrask@ Online (800-747-8177). The system is interactive and open 24 hours a day, 7 days a week. Fee is $3.00 per record. There is an annual fee of $50.00 and a $.40 per minute connect fee or $.12 if connected through the Internet.

Vehicle Ownership & Identification
Vessel Ownership

Department of Motor Vehicles, Driver & Vehicle Records Division, PO Box 94789, Lincoln, NE 68509-4789 (Courier: 301 Centennial Mall, S, Lincoln, NE 68509); 402-471-3918, 8AM-5PM.

www.nol.org/home/DMV

Indexing & Storage: Records are available from 1939. Boat ownership information is available from 1997. All motorized boats manufactured after 11/1/72 must be titled.

Searching: Only permissible use requesters receive full record data. The general public cannot obtain records, with or without obtain personal data, unless written consent of the subject is provided. Typical items required for search include; full name, VIN or plate number, and year and make.

Access by: mail, in person, online.

Fee & Payment: The fee is $1.00 per record. Lien information appears on the record. Fee payee: Department of Motor Vehicles. Prepayment required. Personal checks accepted. No credit cards accepted.

Mail search: Turnaround time: 7 to 10 days. A self addressed stamped envelope is requested.

In person search: Turnaround time is while you wait. "No record founds" are charged the full amount.

Online search: Electronic access is through Nebrask@ Online. There is a start-up fee and line charges are incurred in addition to the $1.00 per record fee. The system is open 24 hours a day, 7 days a week. Call 800-747-8177 for more information.

Other access: Bulk requesters must be authorized by state officials. Purpose of the request and subsequent usage are reviewed. For more information, call 402-471-3909.

Accident Reports

Department of Roads, Accident Records Bureau, Box 94669, Lincoln, NE 68509 (Courier: 1500 Nebraska Highway 2, Lincoln, NE 68502); 402-479-4645, 402-479-4325 (Fax), 8AM-5PM.

www.dor.state.ne.us

Indexing & Storage: Records are available from 1978 to 1994 on microfilm; however, fatal accidents are on microfilm since 1956. Records are computerized since 1988.

Searching: Individual driver's own reports are not released. Include the following in your request: full name, date of accident, county.

Access by: mail, phone, in person.

Fee & Payment: The fee is $6.00 per record. Fee payee: Accident Records Bureau. Prepayment required. Personal checks accepted. No credit cards accepted.

Mail search: Turnaround time: 1 week to 10 days. No self addressed stamped envelope is required.

Phone search: They will schedule requests by phone.

In person search: Searching is available in person.

Other access: Records can be purchased in bulk from the computer database (1988 to present).

Vessel Registration

Records not maintained by a state level agency.

Note: All boats must be registered. Records are found at the county recorder offices.

Legislation Records

Clerk of Legislature Office, PO Box 94604, Lincoln, NE 68509-4604 (Courier: State Capitol, 1445 K Street, Room 2018, Lincoln, NE 68509); 402-471-2271, 402-471-2126 (Fax), 8AM-5PM.

www.unicam.state.ne.us

Indexing & Storage: Records are available from 1961 to present (floor debate). They can pull histories on bills back to 1937.

Searching: Include the following in your request: bill number.

Access by: mail, phone, fax, in person, online.

Fee & Payment: There is no charge for a copy of a bill. A legislative history of a bill costs $.15 per page. Fee payee: State of Nebraska. Prepayment required. Personal checks accepted. No credit cards accepted.

Mail search: Turnaround time: 3 to 5 days. Bill number and year required to perform mail searches. No self addressed stamped envelope is required.

Phone search: You may call for information.

Fax search: Fee is $1.00 per page. Turnaround time is same day if possible or 1-2 days.

In person search: You may request information in person.

Online search: The web site features the state statutes, legislative bills for the present session and a legislative journal. You can search by bill number or subject.

Voter Registration

Access to Records is Restricted

Secretary of State, Election Divisions, PO Box 94608, Lincoln, NE 68509; 402-471-2554, 402-471-3237 (Fax), 8AM-5PM.

www.sos.state.ne.us/Elections/election.htm

Note: Individual look-ups must be done at the county level. The state has developed a new statewide system. Current law dictates that the database can only be sold for political purposes, and not for commercial purposes. A CD can be purchased for $500.

GED Certificates

NE Dept of Education, Adult Education, PO Box 94987, Lincoln, NE 68509 (Courier: 301 Centennial Mall S, Lincoln, NE 68509); 402-471-2475, 402-471-8127 (Fax).

Searching: To search, all of the following is required: a signed release, date of birth, all last names used, and Social Security Number. If known, the year and city of test are helpful.

Access by: mail, fax, in person.

Fee & Payment: There is no fee for verification. Copies of transcripts are $2.00. Fee payee: NE Dept of Education. Prepayment required. Money orders are accepted. Personal checks accepted. No credit cards accepted.

Mail search: Turnaround time: 1 to 2 days. No self addressed stamped envelope is required.

Fax search: Same criteria as mail searching.

In person search: Turnaround time is immediate in most instances.

Hunting License Information
Fishing License Information

Game & Parks Commission, PO Box 30370, Lincoln, NE 68503 (Courier: 2200 N 33rd St, Lincoln, NE 68503); 402-471-5455, 402-471-5528 (Fax), 8AM-5PM.

www.ngpc.state.ne.us/homepage.html

Indexing & Storage: Records are available from 1988 to present on microfiche for Big Game and current year for other hunting and fishing.

Searching: All information on the face of the license is public information, except for release of SSNs. Include the following in your request: date of birth, name. Date of application helpful.

Access by: mail, phone, in person.

Fee & Payment: There is no search fee.

Mail search: Turnaround time: 1 to 2 days. No self addressed stamped envelope is required.

Phone search: Records are available by phone, when personnel available.

In person search: Searching is available in person.

Nebraska State Licensing Agencies
Licenses Searchable Online

Alcohol/Drug Testing #30 ....www.hhs.state.ne.us/lis/lis.asp
Architect #2...www.ea.state.ne.us/search/arch.htm
Asbestos-related Occupation #30...............www.hhs.state.ne.us/lis/lis.asp
Assisted Living Facility #30.........................www.nlc.state.ne.us/docs/pilot/pubs/h.html
Athletic Trainer #30....................................www.hhs.state.ne.us/lis/lis.asp
Attorney #32 ....www.nebar.com/directory/dir.asp
Bank #31 ....www.ndbf.org/banks.htm
Barber School #1 ....www.barbers.state.ne.us/
Chiropractor #30...www.hhs.state.ne.us/lis/lis.asp
Collection Agency #26 ....www.nol.org/home/SOS/Collections/col-agn.htm
Cosmetology Salon/School #30...................www.hhs.state.ne.us/lis/lis.asp
Credit Union #31...www.ndbf.org/culist.htm
Debt Management Agency #26 ....www.nol.org/home/SOS/Collections/debtlist.htm
Delayed Deposit Service #31.......................www.ndbf.org/ddslist.htm
Dental Hygienist #30...................................www.hhs.state.ne.us/lis/lis.asp
Dentist #30 ....www.hhs.state.ne.us/lis/lis.asp
Developmentally Disabled Center #30..........www.nlc.state.ne.us/docs/pilot/pubs/h.html
Emergency Medical Care Facility/Clinic #30 ....www.hhs.state.ne.us/lis/lis.asp
Engineer #2 ....www.ea.state.ne.us/search
Environmental Health Specialist #30 ....www.hhs.state.ne.us/lis/lis.asp
Exterminator #18 ....www.kellysolutions.com/ne/
Funeral Establishment #30 ....www.hhs.state.ne.us/lis/lis.asp
Health Clinic #30...www.hhs.state.ne.us/lis/lis.asp
Hearing Aid Dispenser/Fitter #30................www.hhs.state.ne.us/lis/lis.asp
Home Health Agency #30 ....www.nlc.state.ne.us/docs/pilot/pubs/h.html
Hospice #30..www.nlc.state.ne.us/docs/pilot/pubs/h.html
Hospital #30..www.nlc.state.ne.us/docs/pilot/pubs/h.html
Insurance Company #14..............................www.nol.org/home/NDOI/company_search/index.html
Investigator, Plainclothes #26 ....www.nol.org/home/SOS/Privatedetectives/pilist.htm
Investment Advisor/Advisor Rep #11 ....www.nasdr.com/2001.asp
Landscape Architect #23 ....www.landarch.state.ne.us/registrants.pdf
Liquor Vendor #19 ....www.nol.org/home/NLCC/nlccsearch.html
Massage Therapy School #30 ....www.hhs.state.ne.us/lis/lis.asp
Mental Health Center #30 ....www.hhs.state.ne.us/lis/lis.asp
Nurse #30 ....www.hhs.state.ne.us/lis/lis.asp
Nursing Home #30.......................................www.hhs.state.ne.us/lis/lis.asp
Nutrition Therapy, Medical #30 ....www.hhs.state.ne.us/lis/lis.asp
Occupational Therapist #30.........................www.hhs.state.ne.us/lis/lis.asp
Optometrist #30..www.hhs.state.ne.us/lis/lis.asp
Pesticide Applicator/Dealer #18..................www.kellysolutions.com/ne/
Pharmacist #30...www.hhs.state.ne.us/lis/lis.asp
Pharmacy #30...www.hhs.state.ne.us/lis/lis.asp
Physical Therapist #30 ....www.hhs.state.ne.us/lis/lis.asp
Physician #30 ....www.hhs.state.ne.us/lis/lis.asp
Physician Assistant #30 ....www.hhs.state.ne.us/lis/lis.asp
Podiatrist #30...www.hhs.state.ne.us/lis/lis.asp
Polygraph Examiner, Private #26 ....www.nol.org/home/SOS/Polygraph/polypri.htm
Polygraph Examiner, Public #26 ....www.nol.org/home/SOS/Polygraph/polypub.htm
Polygraph/Voice Stress Examiner #26..........www.nol.org/home/SOS/Polygraph/voice.htm
Private Detective #26..................................www.nol.org/home/SOS/Privatedetectives/pdlist.htm
Psychologist #30...www.hhs.state.ne.us/lis/lis.asp
Public Accountant-CPA #5...........................www.nol.org/home/BPA/license/
Radiographer #30..www.hhs.state.ne.us/lis/lis.asp
Real Estate Appraiser #22 ....http://dbdec.nrc.state.ne.us/appraiser/docs/list.html
Respiratory Care #30...................................www.hhs.state.ne.us/lis/lis.asp
Securities Agent #11...................................www.nasdr.com/2001.asp
Securities Broker/Dealer #11 ....www.nasdr.com/2001.asp
Substance Abuse Treatment Center #30...............www.nlc.state.ne.us/docs/pilot/pubs/h.html
Surveyor, Land #3 ....www.sso.state.ne.us/bels/
Swimming Pool Operator #30 ....www.hhs.state.ne.us/lis/lis.asp
Veterinarian #30 ....www.hhs.state.ne.us/lis/lis.asp
Water Operator #30 ....www.hhs.state.ne.us/lis/lis.asp

Licensing Quick Finder

Abstractor #4	402-471-2383
Aerial Applicator #10	402-471-2371
Air Conditioning/Heating Contractor #12	
	402-441-7508
Alcohol/Drug Testing #30	402-471-2118
Amusement Ride Inspector #21	402-471-2031
Animal Technician #30	402-471-2118
Architect #2	402-471-2021
Asbestos-related Occupation #30	402-471-2299
Assisted Living Facility #30	402-471-4970
Athletic Trainer #30	402-471-2299
Attorney #32	402-471-7091
Auctioneer #6	402-441-7437
Bank #31	402-471-2171
Barber #1	402-471-2051
Barber School #1	402-471-2051
Boiler & Pressure Vessel Inspector #16	
	402-471-4721
Boxer #28	402-471-2009
Boxing Promoter #28	402-471-2009
Chauffeur #6	402-441-7437
Child Caring/Placing Agency #15	402-471-9138
Chiropractor #30	402-471-2299
Collection Agency #26	402-471-2555
Contractor #21	402-595-3189
Contractor, Building #12	402-441-6456
Contractor, General #12	402-471-5729
Cosmetology Salon/School #30	402-471-2115
Credit Union #31	402-471-2171
Debt Management Agency #26	402-471-2555
Delayed Deposit Service #31	402-471-2171
Dental Anesthesia Permit #30	402-471-2118
Dental Hygienist #30	402-471-2118
Dentist #30	402-471-2118
Developmentally Disabled Center #30	402-471-2115
Drug Distributor, Wholesale #30	402-471-2118
Drug Wholesale Facility #30	402-471-2115
Educational Interpreter Performance-Hearing Impaired #9	402-471-3593
Educational Media Specialist/Librarian #13	
	402-471-0739
Electrician #29	402-471-3550
Electrologist #15	402-471-2117
Elevator Inspector/Inspection Manager #21	
	402-471-8674
Embalmer #15	402-471-2115
Emergency Medical Care Facility/Clinic #30	
	402-471-2115

Employment Agency #21	402-471-2230
Engineer #2	402-471-2021
Environmental Health Specialist #30	402-471-2299
Esthetician #15	402-471-2117
Exterminator #18	402-471-2394
Farm Labor Contractor #21	402-471-2230
Fertilizer Professional/Business #18	402-471-2394
Fire Protection Sprinkler Contractor #12	
	402-441-6456
Foster/Group Home #15	402-471-9138
Funeral Director #15	402-471-2115
Funeral Establishment #30	402-471-2115
Health Clinic #30	402-471-2115
Hearing Aid Dispenser/Fitter #30	402-471-2299
Hearing Assessment (EIPA) #9	402-471-3593
Hearing Quality Assurance Screening Test #9	
	402-471-3593
Home Health Agency #30	402-471-2115
Hospice #30	402-471-2115
Hospital #30	402-471-2115
Insurance Agency/Agent/Broker/Producer #14	
	402-471-2201
Insurance Company #14	402-471-2201
Insurance Consultant #14	402-471-2201
Insurance Utilization Review Agent #14	402-471-2201
Interpreter for the Hearing Impaired (Nebraska Registry of Interpreters) #9	402-471-3593
Investigator, Plainclothes #26	402-471-2384
Investment Advisor/Advisor Rep. #11	402-471-3445
Jewelry Dealer, Secondhand #6	402-441-7437
Landscape Architect #23	402-471-2021
Law Enforcement Officer #20	308-385-6030
Liquor Vendor #19	402-471-2571
Lobbyist #8	402-471-2608
Local Anesthesia Certification #30	402-471-2118
Marriage & Family Therapist #15	402-471-9138
Massage Establishment #30	402-471-2115
Massage Therapy School #30	402-471-2115
Mental Health Center #30	402-471-2115
Notary Public #27	402-471-2558
Nurse #30	402-471-2115
Nursing Education Program #30	402-471-2115
Nursing Home #30	402-471-2115
Nursing Home Administrator #15	402-471-2115
Nutrition Therapy, Medical #30	402-471-2115
Occupational Therapist #30	402-471-2299
Optometrist #30	402-471-2118
Osteopathic Physician #30	402-471-2118

Pawnbroker #6	402-441-7437
Pesticide Applicator/Dealer #18	402-471-2394
Pharmacist #30	402-471-2118
Pharmacy #30	402-471-2115
Pharmacy, Mail Order #30	402-471-2115
Physical Therapist #30	402-471-2299
Physician #30	402-471-2118
Physician Assistant #30	402-471-2118
Plant Nursery/Nursery Professional #18	402-471-2394
Plumber Journeyman #7	402-466-5154
Podiatrist #30	402-471-2118
Polygraph Examiner, Private #26	402-471-4070
Polygraph Examiner, Public #26	402-471-4070
Polygraph/Voice Stress Examiner #26	402-471-4070
Preneed Seller #14	402-471-2201
Private Detective #26	402-471-2384
Psychologist #30	402-471-4905
Public Accountant-CPA #5	402-471-3595
Racing Event/Professional #24	402-471-4155
Radiographer #30	402-471-2118
Real Estate Appraiser #22	402-471-9015
Real Estate Broker #25	402-471-2004
Real Estate Salesperson #25	402-471-2004
Respiratory Care #30	402-471-2299
Sanitarian #17	402-471-0515
School Administrator/Supervisor #13	402-471-0739
School Nurse #13	402-471-0739
Securities Agent #11	402-471-3445
Securities Broker/Dealer #11	402-471-3445
Skin Care Salon #30	402-471-2115
Social Worker #15	402-471-9138
Speech-Language Pathologist/Audiologist #15	
	402-471-9138
Substance Abuse Treatment Ctr. #30	402-471-2115
Surplus Lines Seller #14	402-471-2201
Surveyor, Land #3	402-471-2566
Swimming Pool Operator #30	402-471-2299
Taxi Driver #6	402-441-7437
Teacher #13	402-471-0739
Veterinarian #30	402-471-2118
Veterinary Technician #15	402-471-2118
Water Operator #30	402-471-2299
Water Treatment Plant Operator #17	402-471-0515
Well Driller/Pump Installer #17	402-471-0515
Wrestler #28	402-471-2009
Wrestling/Boxing Matches #28	402-471-2009

Licensing Agency Information

#1 Board of Barber Examiners, 301 Centennial Mall S, 6th Fl, Lincoln, NE 68509-4723; 402-471-2051, Fax: 402-471-2052.
www.barbers.state.ne.us

#2 Board of Examiners for Engineers & Architects, PO Box 95165, 301 Centennial Mall S 6th Fl, Lincoln, NE 68509-4751; 402-471-2021, Fax: 402-471-0787.
www.ea.state.ne.us
Agency email: Admin@nol.org.
Search database at www.ea.state.ne.us

#3 Board of Examiners for Land Surveyors, 555 N Cotner Blvd, Lincoln, NE 68505; 402-471-2566, Fax: 402-471-3057.
www.sso.state.ne.us/bels/
Search database at www.sso.state.ne.us/bels

#4 Board of Examiners or Abstractors, 301 Centennial Mall S, Lincoln, NE 68509-4944; 402-471-2383.

#5 Board of Public Accountancy, PO Box 94725, Lincoln, NE 68509-4725; 402-471-3595, Fax: 402-471-4484.
www.nol.org/home/BPA
Agency email: nbpa01@nol.org.
Search database at
www.nol.org/home/BPA/license

#6 Applications & Permits, City Clerk's Office, 555 S 10th St, Lincoln, NE 68508; 402-441-7437, Fax: 402-441-8325.
http://interlinc.ci.lincoln.ne.us.

#7 City Codes Administration, 555 S 10th St, #203, Lincoln, NE 68508; 402-441-7785.

#8 Clerk of the Legislature, PO Box 94604, Lincoln, NE 68509-4604; 402-471-2608, Fax: 402-471-2126.
www.unicam.state.ne.us
Agency email: uio@unicam.state.ne.us.
Search database at www.unicam.state.ne.us

#9 Commission for the Deaf & Hard of Hearing, 4600 Valley Rd #420, Lincoln, NE 68510-4844; 402-471-3593, Fax: 402-471-3067.
www.nol.org/home/NCDHH
Agency email: lstaff@ncdhh.state.ne.us.

#10 Department of Aeronautics, 3431 Aviation Rd #150 (68524), Lincoln, NE 68501; 402-471-2371, Fax: 402-471-2906.
www.aero.state.ne.us
Agency email: sonis@mail.state.ne.us.

#11 Department of Banking & Finance, Bureau of Securities, PO Box 95006 (1200 "N" St, #311), Lincoln, NE 68509-5006; 402-471-3445.
www.ndbf.org/sec.htm
Search database at www.ndbf.org/actions.htm
The Orders and Actions search page includes state orders and cancelled or denied licenses. The NASD web search site is national.

#12 Department of Building & Safety, 555 S 10th St, Lincoln, NE 68508; 402-441-7791, Fax: 402-471-8214.
www.ci.lincoln.ne.us.

#13 Department of Education, Teacher Accreditation/Certification Division, 301 Centennial Mall S 6th Fl, Lincoln, NE 68509-4987; 402-471-0739, Fax: 402-471-9735.
www.nde.state.ne.us/TCERT/TCERT.html

#14 Department of Insurance, 941 O St #400, Lincoln, NE 68508-3639; 402-471-2201, Fax: 402-471-6559.
www.nol.org/home/NDOI
Agency email: consumer_affairs@doi.state.ne.us.

#15 Department of Health & Human Services, Credentialing & Licensing, PO Box 95044 (301 Centennial Mall S, 5th Fl), Lincoln, NE 68509; 402-471-9138, Fax: 402-471-9435.
www.hhs.state.ne.us/reg/regindex.htm

#16 Division of Safety & Labor Standards, Boiler Inspectors Section, PO Box 95024, Lincoln, NE 68509; 402-471-4721, Fax: 402-471-5039.
www.dol.state.ne.us/nwd/center.cfm?PRICAT=2&SUBCAT=2C
Agency email: dburns@dol.state.ne.us.

#17 Drinking Water & Environmental Sanitation Division, PO Box 95007 (301 Centennial Mall S), Lincoln, NE 68509; 402-471-2541, Fax: 402-471-6436.
www.hhs.state.ne.us

#18 Department of Agriculture, Bureau of Plant Industry, PO Box 94756 (301 Centennial Mall South), Lincoln, NE 68509; 402-471-2394, Fax: 402-471-6892.
www.kellysolutions.com/ne/
Search database at www.kellysolutions.com/ne

#19 Liquor Control Commission, 301 Centennial Mall S, 5th Fl, Lincoln, NE 68509-5046; 402-471-2571, Fax: 402-471-2814.
www.nol.org/home/NLCC
Agency email: nlcc01@nol.org.
Search database at
www.nol.org/home/NLCC/nlccsearch.html

#20 Crime Commission, 3600 N Academy Rd, Grand Island, NE 68801; 308-385-6030, Fax: 308-385-6032. www.nol.org/home/crimecom
Agency email: slamken@crimecom.state.ne.us.

#21 Department of Labor, State Capitol, #2300, Lincoln, NE 68509; 402-471-2230, Fax: 402-471-5039. www.dol.state.ne.us.
Agency email: ghirsh@dol.state.ne.us.

#22 Real Estate Appraiser Board, PO Box 94963, Lincoln, NE 68509-4963; 402-471-9015, Fax: 402-471-9017.
http://linux1.nrc.state.ne.us/appraiser
Agency email: mjhass@linux3.state.ne.us.
Search database at
http://dbdec.nrc.state.ne.us/appraiser/docs/list.html

#23 Board of Landscape Architects, PO Box 95165, Lincoln, NE 68509-5165; 402-471-2021, Fax: 402-471-0787.
www.landarch.state.ne.us
Agency email: landarch@nol.org.
Search database at
www.landarch.state.ne.us/registrants.pdf

#24 Racing Commission, 301 Centennial Mall S 4th Fl, Lincoln, NE 68509-5014; 402-471-4155, Fax: 402-471-2339.

#25 Real Estate Commission, 301 Centennial Mall S, 6th Fl, Lincoln, NE 68509-4667; 402-471-2004, Fax: 402-471-4492.
www.nol.org/home/NREC/index.htm
Agency email: infotech@nrec.state.ne.us.
Search database at http://nrec.nol.org/licenfodb

#26 Secretary of State, Business Services, State Capitol Rm 2300, PO Box 94608, Lincoln, NE 68509-4608; 402-471-2554, Fax: 402-471-3237.
www.nol.org/home/SOS
Agency email: sos04@nol.org.
Search database at
www.sos.state.ne.us/htm/businessmenu.htm

#27 Secretary of State, Notary Division, Rm 1301 State Capitol Bldg, Lincoln, NE 68509-5104; 402-471-2558, Fax: 402-471-4429.
www.nol.org/home/SOS/Notary/notary.htm

#28 Athletic Commission, 301 Centennial Mall S, 3rd Fl, Lincoln, NE 68509-4743; 402-471-2009, Fax: 402-471-3396.
www.athcomm.state.ne.us
Agency email: athcomm@mail.state.ne.us.

#29 Electrical Division, 800 S 13th St #109, Lincoln, NE 68509; 402-471-3550, Fax: 402-471-4297.

#30 NE Health & Human Svcs Regulation & Licensure, Credentialing Division, PO Box 94986, Lincoln, NE 68509-4986; 402-471-2115, Fax: 402-471-3577.
www.hhs.state.ne.us/crl/crlindex.htm. Agency email: marie.mcclatchey@hhss.state.ne.us.
Search database at www.hhs.state.ne.us/lis/lis.asp.
Boarding Homes do not need a license as of 1/1/2001. Domiciliary Facility and Residential Care Facility are now combined into Assisted Living Facility.

#31 Department of Banking and Finance, Financial Institutions Divison, PO Box 95006 (1200 "N" St. # 311), Lincoln, NE 68509-5006; 402-471-2171.
www.ndbf.org/fin.htm
Search database at www.ndbf.org/finsearch.htm

#32 Supreme Court, 635 S 14th PO Box 81809, Lincoln, NE 68501-1809; 402-471-3731, Fax: 402-475-7098.
www.nebar.com/index.htm.

Nebraska Federal Courts

The following list indicates the district and division name for each county in the state.

County/Court Cross Reference

County	Court		County	Court
Adams	Lincoln		Jefferson	Lincoln
Antelope	Lincoln		Johnson	Lincoln
Arthur	North Platte		Kearney	Lincoln
Banner	North Platte		Keith	North Platte
Blaine	North Platte		Keya Paha	North Platte
Boone	Lincoln		Kimball	North Platte
Box Butte	North Platte		Knox	Omaha
Boyd	Lincoln		Lancaster	Lincoln
Brown	North Platte		Lincoln	North Platte
Buffalo	Lincoln		Logan	North Platte
Burt	Omaha		Loup	North Platte
Butler	Lincoln		Madison	Lincoln
Cass	Lincoln		McPherson	North Platte
Cedar	Omaha		Merrick	Lincoln
Chase	North Platte		Morrill	North Platte
Cherry	North Platte		Nance	Lincoln
Cheyenne	North Platte		Nemaha	Lincoln
Clay	Lincoln		Nuckolls	Lincoln
Colfax	Lincoln		Otoe	Lincoln
Cuming	Omaha		Pawnee	Lincoln
Custer	North Platte		Perkins	North Platte
Dakota	Omaha		Phelps	Lincoln
Dawes	North Platte		Pierce	Omaha
Dawson	North Platte		Platte	Lincoln
Deuel	North Platte		Polk	Lincoln
Dixon	Omaha		Red Willow	North Platte
Dodge	Omaha		Richardson	Lincoln
Douglas	Omaha		Rock	North Platte
Dundy	North Platte		Saline	Lincoln
Fillmore	Lincoln		Sarpy	Omaha
Franklin	Lincoln		Saunders	Lincoln
Frontier	North Platte		Scotts. Bluff	North Platte
Furnas	North Platte		Seward	Lincoln
Gage	Lincoln		Sheridan	North Platte
Garden	North Platte		Sherman	Lincoln
Garfield	North Platte		Sioux	North Platte
Gosper	North Platte		Stanton	Omaha
Grant	North Platte		Thayer	Lincoln
Greeley	Lincoln		Thomas	North Platte
Hall	Lincoln		Thurston	Omaha
Hamilton	Lincoln		Valley	North Platte
Harlan	Lincoln		Washington	Omaha
Hayes	North Platte		Wayne	Omaha
Hitchcock	North Platte		Webster	Lincoln
Holt	Lincoln		Wheeler	Lincoln
Hooker	North Platte		York	Lincoln
Howard	Lincoln			

Standards for Federal Courts: The search fee is $20.00 per item (one party name or case number). Certification fee is $7.00 per document. Copy fee is $.50 per page. All fees standard unless noted in profile. Mail Search: always enclose a stamped self addressed envelope unless otherwise noted. Before releasing records, all courts require prepayment unless noted in profile.

Open records are located at the court unless otherwise noted. District courts index by defendant and plaintiff as well as by case number. Bankruptcy courts usually index by debtor and case number. While most courts now have their indexes on computer, many still maintain index card files as well.

The universal PACER sign-up number is 800-676-6856. Find PACER and the Party/Case Index on the Web at http://pacer.psc.uscourts.gov. PACER dial-up access is $.60 per minute. Also, courts offering internet access via RACER, PACER, Web-PACER or the new CM-ECF charge $.07 per page fee unless noted as free.

US District Court

District of Nebraska

Lincoln Division PO Box 83468, Lincoln, NE 68501 (Courier Address: 593 Federal Bldg, 100 Centennial Mall N, Lincoln, NE 68508), 402-437-5225, Fax: 402-437-5651.

www.ned.uscourts.gov

Counties: Nebraska cases may be filed in any of the three courts at the option of the attorney, except that filings in the North Platte Division must be during trial session.

Indexing & Storage: Cases are indexed by defendant, plaintiff, and case number. New cases are available in the index 1-2 days after filing date. Open records are located at this court.

Fee & Payment Notes: Payment may be made by money order, cashier check, personal check. Payee: Clerk, US District Court.

Phone Search: Only docket information available by telephone.

In Person Search: In person searching available.

PACER: Toll-free dial-up access: 800-252-9724. Local dial-up access: 402-661-7399. Case records are available back to late 1990. Records are purged every year. New records are available online after 2 days. PACER is available online at http://pacer.ned.uscourts.gov.

Electronic Filing: Information is available online at https://ecf.ned.uscourts.gov

North Platte Division c/o Lincoln Division, PO Box 83468, Lincoln, NE 68501 (Courier Address: 593 Federal Bldg, 100 Centennial Mall N, Lincoln, NE 68508), 402-437-5225, Fax: 402-437-5651.

www.ned.uscourts.gov

Counties: Nebraska cases may be filed in any of the three courts at the option of the attorney, except that filings in the North Platte Division must be during trial session. Some. Case records may be in the Omaha Division as well as the Lincoln Division.

Indexing & Storage: Cases are indexed by defendant, plaintiff, and case number. New cases are available in the index 1-2 days after filing date. Records can also be located at Omaha or Lincoln, depending on the judge assigned. Open records are located at the Lincoln Division.

Fee & Payment Notes: Payment may be made by money order, cashier check, personal check. Payee: Clerk, US District Court. You are allowed to make your own copies. These copies cost $.50 per page.

Phone Search: Searching not available by phone.

In Person Search: In person searching available.

PACER: Toll-free dial-up access: 800-252-9724. Local dial-up access: 402-661-7399. Case records are available back to late 1990. Records are purged every year. New records are available online after 2 days. PACER is available online at http://pacer.ned.uscourts.gov.

Electronic Filing: Information is available online at https://ecf.ned.uscourts.gov

Omaha Division 111 S 18th Plaza, Ste 1152, Omaha, NE 68102 (Courier Address: Use mail address for courier delivery), 402-661-7350, Fax: 402-661-7387.

www.ned.uscourts.gov

Counties: Nebraska cases may be filed in any of the three courts at the option of the attorney, except that filings in the North Platte Division must be during trial session.

Indexing & Storage: Cases are indexed by defendant, plaintiff, and case number. New cases are available in the index 1-2 days after filing date. Open records are located at this court.

Fee & Payment Notes: Payment may be made by money order, cashier check, personal check. Payee: Clerk, US District Court.

Phone Search: Searching not available by phone.

In Person Search: In person searching available.

PACER: Toll-free dial-up access: 800-252-9724. Local dial-up access: 402-661-7399. Case records are available back to late 1990. Records are purged every year. New records are available online after 2 days. PACER is available online at http://pacer.ned.uscourts.gov.

Electronic Filing: Information is available online at https://ecf.ned.uscourts.gov

US Bankruptcy Court

District of Nebraska

Lincoln Division 460 Federal Bldg, 100 Centennial Mall N, Lincoln, NE 68508 (Courier Address: Use mail address for courier delivery), 402-437-5100, Fax: 402-437-5454.

www.neb.uscourts.gov

Counties: Adams, Antelope, Boone, Boyd, Buffalo, Butler, Cass, Clay, Colfax, Fillmore, Franklin, Gage, Greeley, Hall, Hamilton, Harlan, Holt, Howard, Jefferson, Johnson, Kearney, Lancaster, Madison, Merrick, Nance, Nemaha, Nuckolls, Otoe, Pawnee, Phelps, Platte,Polk, Richardson, Saline, Saunders, Seward, Sherman, Thayer, Webster, Wheeler, York. Cases from the North Platte Division may also be assigned here.

Indexing & Storage: New cases are available in the index 1 day after filing date. All debtor names are indexed for files from 9/89 to the present. District wide searches are available from this division. This court maintains records for the main bankruptcy office in Omaha.

Fee & Payment Notes: Payment may be made by money order, cashier check, personal check. Debtor's checks are not accepted. Payee: Clerk, US Bankruptcy Court.

Phone Search: Only the debtor's name, case number, date filed, 341 information and date discharged and closed will be released. An automated voice case information service (VCIS) is available. Call VCIS at 800-829-0112 or 402-221-3757.

Mail Search: A stamped self addressed envelope is not required.

In Person Search: In person searching available.

PACER:. Case records are available back to September 1989. Records are purged every six months. New civil records are available online after 3 days. PACER is available online at http://pacer.neb.uscourts.gov.

Electronic Filing: Information is available online at https://ecf.neb.uscourts.gov

North Platte Division c/o Omaha Division, 111 S 18th Plaza, Ste 1125, Omaha, NE 68102 (Courier Address: Use mail address for courier delivery), 402-661-7444, Fax: 402-661-7492.

www.neb.uscourts.gov

Counties: Arthur, Banner, Blaine, Box Butte, Brown, Chase, Cherry, Cheyenne, Custer, Dawes, Dawson, Deuel, Dundy, Frontier, Furnas, Garden, Garfield, Gosper, Grant, Hayes, Hitchcock, Hooker, Keith, Keya Paha, Kimball, Lincoln, Logan, Loup, McPherson, Morrill,Perkins, Red Willow, Rock, Scotts Bluff, Sheridan, Sioux, Thomas, Valley. Cases may be randomly allocated to Omaha or Lincoln.

Indexing & Storage: New cases are available in the index 1 day after filing date. Open records are located at the Omaha Division. Case records may also be in the Lincoln Division (Lancaster County).

Fee & Payment Notes: Payment may be made by money order, cashier check. Business checks are not accepted. Personal checks are not accepted.

Phone Search: An automated voice case information service (VCIS) is available. Call VCIS at 800-829-0112 or 402-221-3757.

Mail Search: A stamped self addressed envelope is not required.

In Person Search: In person searching available.

PACER:. Case records are available back to September 1989. Records are purged every six months. New civil records are available online after 3 days. PACER is available online at http://pacer.neb.uscourts.gov.

Electronic Filing: Information is available online at https://ecf.neb.uscourts.gov

Omaha Division 111 S. 18th Plaza, Ste 1125, Omaha, NE 68102 (Courier Address: Use mail address for courier delivery), 402-661-7444, Fax: 402-661-7492.

www.neb.uscourts.gov

Counties: Burt, Cedar, Cuming, Dakota, Dixon, Dodge, Douglas, Knox, Pierce, Sarpy, Stanton, Thurston, Washington, Wayne.

Indexing & Storage: Cases are indexed by debtor and creditors as well as by case number. New cases are available in the index 24 hours after filing date. Open records are located at this court.

Fee & Payment Notes: Payment may be made by money order, cashier check, personal check. Payee: Clerk, US Bankruptcy Court.

Phone Search: Only docket information is available by phone. An automated voice case information service (VCIS) is available. Call VCIS at 800-829-0112 or 402-221-3757.

In Person Search: In person searching available.

PACER:. Case records are available back to September 1989. Records are purged every six months. New civil records are available online after 3 days. PACER is available online at http://pacer.neb.uscourts.gov.

Electronic Filing: Information is available online at https://ecf.neb.uscourts.gov

Nebraska County Courts

Court	Jurisdiction	No. of Courts	How Organized
District Courts*	General	93	12 Districts
County Courts*	Limited	93	11 Districts
Juvenile Courts	Special	3	3 Counties
Workers' Compensation Court	Special	1	

* Profiled in this Sourcebook.

Court	CIVIL								
	Tort	Contract	Real Estate	Min. Claim	Max. Claim	Small Claims	Estate	Eviction	Domestic Relations
District Courts*	X	X	X	$15,000	No Max				X
County Courts*	X	X	X	$0	$15,000	$1800	X	X	X
Juvenile Courts									
Workers' Compensation Court									

Court	CRIMINAL				
	Felony	Misdemeanor	DWI/DUI	Preliminary Hearing	Juvenile
District Courts*	X				
County Courts*		X	X	X	X
Juvenile Courts					X
Workers' Compensation Court					

ADMINISTRATION
Court Administrator, PO Box 98910, Lincoln, NE, 68509-8910; 402-471-2643, Fax: 402-471-2197. http://court.nol.org/AOC

COURT STRUCTURE
The District Court is the court of general jurisdiction. The minimum on civil judgment matters for District Courts is $15,000, however, the State raised the County Court limit on civil matters from $15,000 to $45,000 as of Sept. 1, 2001. As it is less expensive to file civil cases in County Court than in District Court, civil cases in the $15,000 to $45,000 range are more likely to be found in County Court, if after Sept. 1, 2001.

The number of judicial districts went from 21 to the current 12 in July 1992. County Courts have juvenile jurisdiction in all but 3 counties. Douglas, Lancaster, and Sarpy counties have separate Juvenile Courts.

ONLINE ACCESS
Online access to District and County courts is being tested and may offer statewide access to all 185 Nebraska District and County courts starting late in 2002. For more information, call John Cariotto at 402-471-2643. Currently, Douglas, Lancaster, and Sarpy county courts offer internet access with registration and password required.

ADDITIONAL INFORMATION
Most Nebraska courts require the public to do their own in-person searches and will not respond to written search requests. The State Attorney General has recommended that courts not perform searches because of the time involved and concerns over possible legal liability.

Adams County

County Court PO Box 95, Hastings, NE 68902-0095; 402-461-7143; Fax: 402-461-7144. Hours: 8AM-5PM (CST). *Misdemeanor, Civil Actions Under $45,000, Eviction, Small Claims, Probate.*

Civil Records: Access: In person only. Visitors must perform in person searches for themselves. No search fee. Required to search: name, years to search; also helpful: address. Civil cases indexed by defendant. Civil records on index cards and files from 1970s.

Criminal Records: Access: In person only. Visitors must perform in person searches for themselves. No search fee. Required to search: name, years to search; also helpful: DOB, SSN. Criminal records on index cards and files from 1970s.

General Information: Public access terminal is available. No adoption or juvenile records released. Copy fee: $.25 per page. Certification fee: $1.00. Fee payee: Adams County Court. Business checks accepted. Prepayment is required.

District Court PO Box 9, Hastings, NE 68902; 402-461-7264; Fax: 402-461-7269. Hours: 8:30AM-5PM (CST). *Felony, Civil Actions Over $15,000.*

Civil Records: Access: In person only. Visitors must perform in person searches for themselves. No search fee. Required to search: name, years to search. Civil cases indexed by defendant, plaintiff. Civil records on microfiche from 1800s, 5 yrs on index cards, on docket books from 1800s.

Criminal Records: Access: In person only. Visitors must perform in person searches for themselves. No search fee. Required to search: name, years to search. Criminal records on microfiche from 1800s, 5 yrs on index cards, on docket books from 1800s.

General Information: Public access terminal is available. No juvenile, search warrants or mental health records released. Copy fee: $.25 per page. Certification fee: $1.00.

Antelope County

District Court PO Box 45, Neligh, NE 68756; 402-887-4508; Fax: 402-887-4870. Hours: 8:30AM-5PM (CST). *Felony, Civil Actions Over $15,000.*

Civil Records: Access: In person only. Visitors must perform in person searches for themselves. No search fee. Required to search: name, years to search. Civil cases indexed by defendant, plaintiff. Civil records on index books from 1872, computerized since 1999.

Criminal Records: Access: In person only. Visitors must perform in person searches for themselves. No search fee. Required to search: name, years to search. Criminal records on index books from 1872, computerized since 1999.

General Information: Public access terminal is available. No juvenile, sealed, search warrants, or mental health record released. Copy fee: $.25 per page. Certification fee: $1.00. Fee payee: Clerk of District Court. Personal checks accepted.

Antelope County Court 501 Main, Neligh, NE 68756; 402-887-4650; Fax: 402-887-4160. Hours: 8:30AM-5PM (CST). *Misdemeanor, Civil Actions Under $45,000, Eviction, Small Claims, Probate.*

Civil Records: Access: In person only. Visitors must perform in person searches for themselves. No search fee. Required to search: name, years to search. Civil cases indexed by defendant, plaintiff. Civil records on computer from 1994, probate on microfiche from 1800s, civil and small claims indexed from 1983.

Criminal Records: Access: In person only. Visitors must perform in person searches for themselves. No search fee. Required to search: name, years to search, DOB, signed release; also helpful: SSN. Criminal index on computer from 1994, indexed from 1800s.

General Information: No adoption, or sealed records released. Copy fee: $.25 per page. Certification fee: $1.00 plus $.25 per page. Fee payee: Antelope County Court. Personal checks accepted. Prepayment required.

Arthur County

District & County Court PO Box 126, Arthur, NE 69121; 308-764-2203; Fax: 308-764-2216. Hours: 8AM-4PM (MST). *Felony, Misdemeanor, Civil, Eviction, Small Claims, Probate.*

Civil Records: Access: Phone, fax, mail, in person. Both court and visitors may perform in person searches. No search fee. Required to search: name, years to search. Civil cases indexed by defendant, plaintiff. Civil records on index books from 1987, on docket books from 1913.

Criminal Records: Access: Phone, fax, mail, in person. Both court and visitors may perform in person searches. No search fee. Required to search: name, years to search. Criminal records on index books from 1987, on docket books from 1913.

General Information: No search warrants, juvenile, adoption, mental health, or sealed records released. SASE required. Turnaround time 1-2 days. Fax notes: $1.00 per page. Incoming fax fee $.25. Copy fee: $.20 per page. Certification fee: $1.50 1st page; $.50 each add'l page. Fee payee: Arthur County Clerk. Personal checks accepted.

Banner County

District Court PO Box 67, Harrisburg, NE 69345; 308-436-5265; Fax: 308-436-4180. Hours: 8AM-5PM (MST). *Felony, Civil Actions Over $15,000.*

Civil Records: Access: Fax, mail, in person. Both court and visitors may perform in person searches. Search fee: $3.00 per name. Required to search: name, years to search; also helpful: address. Civil cases indexed by defendant, plaintiff. Civil records on docket books from 1800s.

Criminal Records: Access: Fax, mail, in person. Both court and visitors may perform in person searches. Search fee: $3.00 per name. Required to search: name, years to search, DOB; also helpful: address. Criminal records on docket books from 1800s.

General Information: No search warrants, mental health, or sealed records released. SASE required. Turnaround time 5-7 days. Fax notes: $1.00 per page. Copy fee: $.25 per page. Certification fee: $1.00. Fee payee: Banner County Clerk. Personal checks accepted. Prepayment is required.

Banner County Court PO Box 67, Harrisburg, NE 69345; 308-436-5268. Hours: 8AM-Noon, 1-5PM (MST). *Misdemeanor, Civil Actions Under $45,000, Eviction, Small Claims, Probate.*

Civil Records: Access: Mail, in person. Both court and visitors may perform in person searches. No search fee. Required to search: name, years to search. Civil cases indexed by defendant, plaintiff. Civil records on register of action cards from 1992, prior on docket books, on computer from 12/2000.

Criminal Records: Access: Mail, in person. Both court and visitors may perform in person searches. No search fee. Required to search: name, years to search, signed release; also helpful: address, DOB. Criminal records on register of action cards from 1992, prior on docket books, on computer from 6/2000.

General Information: No adoption, sealed records released. SASE required. Turnaround time 4 days from receipt. Fax notes: $3.00 for first page, $1.00 each add'l. Copy fee: $.25 per page. Certification fee: $1.00. Fee payee: Banner County Court. Personal checks accepted.

Blaine County

District Court Lincoln Ave, Box 136, Brewster, NE 68821; 308-547-2222; Fax: 308-547-2228. Hours: 8AM-4PM (CST). *Felony, Civil Actions Over $15,000.*
www.nol.org/home/DC8

Civil Records: Access: Fax, mail, in person. Only the court performs in person searches; visitors may not. Search fee: $1.00 per name. Required to search: name, years to search. Civil cases indexed by defendant, plaintiff. Civil records on index books from late 1800s.

Criminal Records: Access: Fax, mail, in person. Only the court performs in person searches; visitors may not. Search fee: $1.00 per name. Required to search: name, years to search, DOB. Criminal records on index books from late 1800s.

General Information: No search warrants, mental health, or sealed records released. SASE required. Turnaround time 1-2 days. Fax notes: $1.00 per page. Copy fee: $.25 per page. Certification fee: $1.50. Fee payee: Blaine County Clerk. Personal checks accepted. Prepayment is required.

Blaine County Court Lincoln Ave, Box 123, Brewster, NE 68821; 308-547-2225; Fax: 308-547-2228. Hours: 8AM-4PM (CST). *Misdemeanor, Civil Actions Under $45,000, Eviction, Small Claims, Probate.*

Civil Records: Access: Phone, fax, mail, in person. Only the court performs in person searches; visitors may not. No search fee. Required to search: name, years to search; also helpful: address. Civil cases indexed by defendant, plaintiff. Civil records on index books from 1960. on microfiche prior to 1960.

Criminal Records: Access: Phone, fax, mail, in person. Only the court performs in person searches; visitors may not. No search fee. Required to search: name, years to search; also helpful: address, DOB, SSN. Criminal records on index books from 1960. on microfiche prior to 1960.

General Information: No juvenile, adoption, or sealed records released. SASE required. Turnaround time 2 days. Fax notes: $1.00 per page. Copy fee: $.25 per page. Certification fee: $1.25. Fee payee: Blaine County Court. Personal checks accepted. Prepayment is required.

Boone County

District Court 222 Fourth St, Albion, NE 68620; 402-395-2057; Fax: 402-395-6592. Hours: 8:30AM-5PM (CST). *Felony, Civil Actions Over $45,000.*

Civil Records: Access: Phone, fax, mail, in person. Both court and visitors may perform in person searches. No search fee. Required to search: name, years to search. Civil cases indexed by defendant, plaintiff. Civil records in general index and dockets from 1800s, computerized records since 2001.

Criminal Records: Access: Phone, fax, mail, in person. Both court and visitors may perform in person searches. No search fee. Required to search: name, years to search; also helpful: DOB. Criminal records in general index and dockets from 1800s, computerized records since 2001.

General Information: No search warrants, mental health, or sealed records released. SASE required. Turnaround time 2-3 days. Fax notes: $3.00 for first page, $1.00 each add'l. Copy fee: $.25 per page. Certification fee: $1.00. Fee payee: Clerk of District Court. Personal checks accepted. Prepayment required.

Boone County Court 222 S 4th St, Albion, NE 68620; 402-395-6184; Fax: 402-395-6592. Hours: 8AM-5PM (CST). *Misdemeanor, Civil Actions Under $45,000, Eviction, Small Claims, Probate.*

Civil Records: Access: Fax, mail, in person. Both court and visitors may perform in person searches. No search fee. Required to search: name, years to search. Civil cases indexed by defendant, plaintiff. Civil records on general index and docket books from late 1800s; computerized back to 2000; probate on microfiche from 1970.

Criminal Records: Access: Fax, mail, in person. Both court and visitors may perform in person searches. No search fee. Required to search: name, years to search; also helpful: DOB. Criminal records on general index and docket books from late 1800s; computerized back to 2000; probate on microfiche from 1970.

General Information: Public access terminal is available. No adoption, or sealed records released. SASE required. Turnaround time 1-2 days. SASE required for large requests. Fax notes: No fee to fax results. Copy fee: $.25 per page. Certification fee: $1.00 + copy fee. Fee payee: Clerk of County Court. Personal checks accepted.

Box Butte County

District Court 515 Box Butte #300, Alliance, NE 69301; 308-762-6293; Fax: 308-762-5700. Hours: 9AM-4PM (MST). *Felony, Civil Actions Over $15,000.*

Civil Records: Access: In person only. Visitors must perform in person searches for themselves. No search fee. Required to search: name, years to search. Civil cases indexed by defendant, plaintiff. Civil records on general index and docket books from late 1800s.

Criminal Records: Access: In person only. Visitors must perform in person searches for themselves. No search fee. Required to search: name, years to search. Criminal records on general index and docket books from late 1800s.

General Information: No search warrants, mental health, or sealed records released. Copy fee: $.25 per page. Certification fee: $1.00.

Box Butte County Court PO Box 613, Alliance, NE 69301; 308-762-6800; Fax: 308-762-6802. Hours: 8:30AM-5PM (MST). *Misdemeanor, Civil Actions Under $45,000, Eviction, Small Claims, Probate.*

Civil Records: Access: In person. Both court and visitors may perform in person searches. No search fee. Required to search: name, years to search. Civil cases indexed by defendant, plaintiff. Civil records on microfiche for 10 years, on index cards to docket books from late 1800s; computerized records since 2000.

Criminal Records: Access: In person. Both court and visitors may perform in person searches. No search fee. Required to search: name, years to search, DOB. Criminal records on microfiche for 10 years, on index cards to docket books from late 1800s; computerized records since 2000.

General Information: Public access terminal is available. No juvenile, adoption, or sealed records released. Fax notes: No fee to fax results. Copy fee: $.25 per page. Certification fee: $1.00. Fee payee: Box Butte County Court. Personal checks accepted.

Boyd County

District Court PO Box 26, Butte, NE 68722; 402-775-2391; Fax: 402-775-2146. Hours: 8:15AM-Noon; 1-5PM (CST). *Felony, Civil Actions Over $15,000.*

Civil Records: Access: Mail, fax, in person. Both court and visitors may perform in person searches. Search fee: $3.00 per name. Required to search: name, years to search, address. Civil cases indexed by defendant, plaintiff. Civil records on general index and docket books from late 1800s.

Criminal Records: Access: Mail, fax, in person. Both court and visitors may perform in person searches. Search fee: $3.00 per name. Required to search: name, years to search, address. Criminal records on general index and docket books from late 1800s.

General Information: Public access terminal is available. No search warrants, mental health, or sealed

records released. SASE required. Turnaround time 3-4 days. Copy fee: $.25 per page. Certification fee: $1.50. Fee payee: Boyd County Clerk. Personal checks accepted. Prepayment is required.

Boyd County Court PO Box 396, Butte, NE 68722; 402-775-2211; Fax: 402-775-2146. Hours: 8AM-5PM W,Th (CST). *Misdemeanor, Civil Actions Under $45,000, Eviction, Small Claims, Probate.*

Civil Records: Access: In person only. Visitors must perform in person searches for themselves. No search fee. Required to search: name, years to search; also helpful: address. Civil cases indexed by defendant, plaintiff. Civil records on general index and docket books from late 1800s.

Criminal Records: Access: In person only. Visitors must perform in person searches for themselves. No search fee. Required to search: name, years to search; also helpful: address, DOB, SSN. Criminal records on general index and docket books from late 1800s.

General Information: No adoption, juvenile, or sealed records released. Copy fee: $.25 per page. Certification fee: $1.00. Fee payee: Boyd County Court. Personal checks accepted. Prepayment is required.

Brown County

District Court 148 W Fourth St, Ainsworth, NE 69210; 402-387-2705; Fax: 402-387-0918. Hours: 8AM-5PM (CST). *Felony, Civil Actions Over $15,000.*

Civil Records: Access: Phone, fax, mail, in person. Both court and visitors may perform in person searches. No search fee. Required to search: name, years to search; also helpful: address. Civil cases indexed by defendant, plaintiff. Civil records on general index and docket books from late 1886s; on computer back to 2000.

Criminal Records: Access: Fax, mail, in person. Both court and visitors may perform in person searches. No search fee. Required to search: name, years to search, signed release; also helpful: address, DOB, SSN. Criminal records on general index and docket books from late 1886; on computer back to 2000.

General Information: Public access terminal is available. No search warrants, mental health, or sealed records released. SASE required. Turnaround time 3-4 days. Fax notes: Fee to fax results is $3.00 per page. Copy fee: $.10 per page. Certification fee: $2.00. Fee payee: Clerk of District Court, Brown County. Personal checks accepted.

Brown County Court 148 W Fourth St, Ainsworth, NE 69210; 402-387-2864; Fax: 402-387-0918. Hours: 8AM-5PM (CST). *Misdemeanor, Civil Actions Under $45,000, Eviction, Small Claims, Probate.*

Civil Records: Access: Phone, fax, mail, in person. Only the court may perform in person searches. No search fee. Required to search: name, years to search. Civil cases indexed by defendant, plaintiff. Civil records in boxes in office since 1980; on computer since.

Criminal Records: Access: Phone, fax, mail, in person. Only the court may perform in person searches. No search fee. Required to search: name, years to search, DOB. Criminal records in boxes in office since 1979; on computer since.

General Information: No adoption, juvenile, or sealed records released. SASE required. Copy fee: $.25 per page. Certification fee: $1.00. Fee payee: Brown County Court. Personal checks accepted. Prepayment is required.

Buffalo County

District Court PO Box 520, Kearney, NE 68848; 308-236-1246; Fax: 308-233-3693. Hours: 8AM-5PM (CST). *Felony, Civil Actions Over $15,000.*

Civil Records: Access: Mail, in person. Both court and visitors may perform in person searches. No search fee.

Required to search: name, years to search; also helpful: address. Civil cases indexed by defendant, plaintiff. Civil records on computer from 1993, on microfiche through 1991, on books from 1800s.

Criminal Records: Access: In person only. Visitors must perform in person searches for themselves. No search fee. Required to search: name, years to search; also helpful: DOB, SSN. Criminal records on computer from 1993, on microfiche through 1991, on books from 1800s.

General Information: Public access terminal is available. No juvenile, mental health, search warrants or sealed records released. SASE required. Turnaround time 1 week. Copy fee: $.50 per page. Certification fee: $1.50. Fee payee: Clerk of District Court. Business checks accepted. Prepayment is required.

Buffalo County Court PO Box 520, Kearney, NE 68848; 308-236-1228; Fax: 308-236-1243. Hours: 8AM-5PM (CST). *Misdemeanor, Civil Actions Under $45,000, Eviction, Small Claims, Probate.*

Civil Records: Access: In person only. Visitors must perform in person searches for themselves. No search fee. Required to search: name, years to search. Civil cases indexed by defendant, plaintiff. Civil records on computer from 4/94, on microfiche, general index, and docket books from late 1800s.

Criminal Records: Access: In person only. Visitors must perform in person searches for themselves. No search fee. Required to search: name, years to search. Criminal records on computer from 4/94, on microfiche, general index, and docket books from late 1800s.

General Information: Public access terminal is available. No adoption, or sealed records released. Copy fee: $.25 per page. Certification fee: $1.00. Fee payee: County Court. Personal checks accepted. Prepayment is required.

Burt County

District Court 111 N 13th St, Tekamah, NE 68061; 402-374-2905; Fax: 402-374-2906. Hours: 8AM-4:30PM (CST). *Felony, Civil Actions Over $15,000.*

Civil Records: Access: Mail, in person. Both court and visitors may perform in person searches. No search fee. Required to search: name, years to search. Civil cases indexed by defendant, plaintiff. Civil records on books from 1800s.

Criminal Records: Access: Mail, in person. Both court and visitors may perform in person searches. No search fee. Required to search: name, years to search; also helpful: DOB, SSN. Criminal records on books from 1800s.

General Information: No mental health records released. SASE required. Copy fee: $.50 per page. Certification fee: $2.00. Fee payee: Clerk of District Court. Personal checks accepted.

Burt County Court 111 N 13th St, PO Box 87, Tekamah, NE 68061; 402-374-2950; Fax: 402-374-2951. Hours: 8AM-4:30PM (CST). *Misdemeanor, Civil Actions Under $45,000, Eviction, Small Claims, Probate.*

Civil Records: Access: In person only. Visitors must perform in person searches for themselves. No search fee. Required to search: name, years to search, address. Civil cases indexed by defendant, plaintiff. Civil records on index cards back to 1867, computerized back to 1998.

Criminal Records: Access: In person only. Visitors must perform in person searches for themselves. No search fee. Required to search: name, years to search, address, DOB, SSN, signed release. Criminal records on index cards back to 1867, computerized back to 1998.

General Information: No adoption records released. Copy fee: $.25 per page. Certification fee: $1.25. Fee payee: County Court. Personal checks accepted. Prepayment is required.

Butler County

District Court 451 5th St, David City, NE 68632-1666; 402-367-7460; Fax: 402-367-3249. Hours: 8:30AM-5PM (CST). *Felony, Civil Actions Over $15,000.*

Civil Records: Access: Phone, fax, mail, in person. Both court and visitors may perform in person searches. Search fee: $2.00 per name. Required to search: name, years to search. Civil cases indexed by defendant, plaintiff. Civil records on books.
Criminal Records: Access: Phone, fax, mail, in person. Both court and visitors may perform in person searches. Search fee: $2.00 per name. Required to search: name, years to search; also helpful: DOB, SSN. Criminal records on books.
General Information: No juvenile, mental health or protection order records released. SASE required. Turnaround time 1-2 days. Fax notes: No fee to fax results. Copy fee: $.10 per page. Certification fee: $1.50. Fee payee: District Court. Personal checks accepted.

Butler County Court 451 5th St, David City, NE 68632-1666; 402-367-7480; Fax: 402-367-3249. Hours: 8AM-Noon, 1-5PM (CST). *Misdemeanor, Civil Actions Under $45,000, Eviction, Small Claims, Probate.*

Civil Records: Access: In person only. Visitors must perform in person searches for themselves. No search fee. Required to search: name, years to search. Civil cases indexed by defendant, plaintiff. Civil records on computer since 1998, docket books from late 1800s, probate on microfiche. They can refer requestors to parties who perform searches at the court.
Criminal Records: Access: In person only. Visitors must perform in person searches for themselves. No search fee. Required to search: name, years to search; also helpful: DOB, SSN. Criminal records on computer since 1998, docket books from late 1800s, probate on microfiche. They can refer requestors to parties who perform searches at the court.
General Information: No adoption records released. Some juvenile requires signed release. Copy fee: $.25 per page. Certification fee: $1.00. Fee payee: Butler County Court. Personal checks accepted.

Cass County

District Court Cass County Courthouse, 346 Main Street, Plattsmouth, NE 68048; 402-296-9339; Fax: 402-296-9345. Hours: 8AM-5PM (CST). *Felony, Civil Actions Over $15,000.*

Civil Records: Access: In person only. Visitors must perform in person searches for themselves. No search fee. Required to search: name, years to search. Civil cases indexed by defendant, plaintiff. Civil records on index books from 1860s, index on computer since 09/97.
Criminal Records: Access: In person only. Visitors must perform in person searches for themselves. No search fee. Required to search: name, years to search. Criminal records on index books from 1860s, index on computer since 09/97.
General Information: Public access terminal is available. Copy fee: $.25 per page. Certification fee: $1.25. Fee payee: Clerk of District Court.

Cass County Court Cass County Courthouse, 346 Main St Rm 201, Plattsmouth, NE 68048; 402-296-9334. Hours: 8AM-5PM (CST). *Misdemeanor, Civil Actions Under $45,000, Eviction, Small Claims, Probate.*

Civil Records: Access: In person only. Visitors must perform in person searches for themselves. No search fee. Required to search: name, years to search. Civil

cases indexed by defendant, plaintiff. Civil records on index cards for 5 years then sent to Capital for storage; computerized records since 2000.
Criminal Records: Access: In person only. Visitors must perform in person searches for themselves. No search fee. Required to search: name, years to search. Criminal records on computer since 1/97.
General Information: Public access terminal is available. Copy fee: $.25 per page. Certification fee: $1.00. Fee payee: Cass County Court. No personal checks accepted. Prepayment is required.

Cedar County

District Court PO Box 796, Hartington, NE 68739-0796; 402-254-6957; Fax: 402-254-6954. Hours: 8AM-5PM (CST). *Felony, Civil Actions Over $45,000.*

Civil Records: Access: In person only. Visitors must perform in person searches for themselves. Search fee: No search fee. Required to search: name, years to search. Civil cases indexed by defendant, plaintiff. Civil records in books from 1890.
Criminal Records: Access: In person only. Visitors must perform in person searches for themselves. Search fee: No search fee. Required to search: name, years to search; also helpful: SSN. Criminal records in books from 1890.
General Information: No mental health records released. Copy fee: $.25 per page. Certification fee: $1.00. Fee payee: District Court. Prepayment is required.

Cedar County Court P O Box 695, Hartington, NE 68739; 402-254-7441; Fax: 402-254-6954. Hours: 8AM-5PM (CST). *Misdemeanor, Civil Actions Under $45,000, Eviction, Small Claims, Probate.*

Civil Records: Access: In person only. Visitors must perform in person searches for themselves. No search fee. Required to search: name, years to search. Civil cases indexed by defendant. Civil records on general index, docket books 15 years; some on microfiche.
Criminal Records: Access: In person only. Visitors must perform in person searches for themselves. Search fee: No search fee. Required to search: name, years to search, offense; also helpful: DOB. Criminal records on general index, docket books for 18 years, some on microfiche. Computerized records go back to 2000.
General Information: Public access terminal is available. No juvenile or judge sealed records released. Copy fee: $.25 per page. Certification fee: $1.00. Fee payee: Cedar County Court. Personal checks accepted. Prepayment is required.

Chase County

District Court PO Box 1299, Imperial, NE 69033; 308-882-5266; Fax: 308-882-5390. Hours: 8AM-4PM (MST). *Felony, Civil Actions Over $15,000.*

Civil Records: Access: Phone, fax, mail, in person. Both court and visitors may perform in person searches. Search fee: $5.00 per name. Required to search: name, years to search. Civil cases indexed by defendant, plaintiff. Civil records general index, docket books from early 1900s.
Criminal Records: Access: Phone, fax, mail, in person. Both court and visitors may perform in person searches. Search fee: $5.00 per name. Required to search: name, years to search; also helpful: DOB, SSN. Criminal records general index, docket books from early 1900s, computerized since 2000.
General Information: Public access terminal is available. No restrictions. SASE required. Turnaround time 5 days. Fax notes: $1.00 per page. Copy fee: $.25 per page. Certification fee: $1.50. Fee payee: Chase County Clerk. Personal checks accepted. Prepayment is required.

Chase County Court PO Box 1299, Imperial, NE 69033; 308-882-4690; Fax: 308-882-5679. Hours:

8:00AM-4:00PM (MST). *Misdemeanor, Civil Actions Under $45,000, Eviction, Small Claims, Probate.*

Civil Records: Access: Phone, mail, in person. No search fee. Required to search: name, years to search. Civil records on general index, docket books from 1910; prior incomplete. Some probate on microfiche.
Criminal Records: Access: Phone, mail, in person. Both court and visitors may perform in person searches. No search fee. Required to search: name, years to search, DOB. Criminal records on general index, docket books from 1910; prior incomplete. Some probate on microfiche.
General Information: Public access terminal is available. No adoption, juvenile. SASE required. Turnaround time 1 day. Copy fee: $.25 per page. Certification fee: $1.00. Fee payee: Chase County Court. Personal checks accepted. Prepayment required.

Cherry County

District Court 365 N Main St, Valentine, NE 69201; 402-376-1840; Fax: 402-376-3830. Hours: 8:30AM-4:30PM (MST). *Felony, Civil Actions Over $15,000.*

Civil Records: Access: In person only. Visitors must perform in person searches for themselves. No search fee. Required to search: name, years to search; also helpful: address. Civil cases indexed by defendant, plaintiff. Civil records on index books from late 1800s. Fax & mail access limited to partial search to confirm: if case was filed, case #, title & date of filing.
Criminal Records: Access: In person, mail, phone. Visitors must perform in person searches for themselves. No search fee. Required to search: name, years to search. Criminal records on index books from late 1800s; computerized records since 1999.
General Information: Public access terminal is available. No juvenile records released. Copy fee: $.25 per page. Certification fee: $1.00. Fee payee: Clerk of District Court. Personal checks accepted.

Cherry County Court 365 N Main St, Valentine, NE 69201; 402-376-2590; Fax: 402-376-5942. Hours: 8AM-5PM (CST). *Misdemeanor, Civil Actions Under $45,000, Eviction, Small Claims, Probate.*

Civil Records: Access: In person only. Visitors must perform in person searches for themselves. No search fee. Required to search: name, years to search. Civil cases indexed by defendant. Civil records on docket card file from 1986, general index prior from late 1800s.
Criminal Records: Access: In person only. Visitors must perform in person searches for themselves. No search fee. Required to search: name, years to search, DOB. Criminal records on docket card file from 1986, general index prior from late 1800s; on computer since 8/2000.
General Information: No adoption records released. Juvenile released only to parties involved. Copy fee: $.25 per page. Certification fee: $1.25. Fee payee: Cherry County Court. Personal checks accepted.

Cheyenne County

District Court PO Box 217, Sidney, NE 69162; 308-254-2814; Fax: 308-254-4293. Hours: 8AM-Noon,1-5PM (MST). *Felony, Civil Actions Over $15,000.*

Civil Records: Access: In person only. Visitors must perform in person searches for themselves. No search fee. Required to search: name, years to search. Civil cases indexed by defendant, plaintiff. Civil records on general index, docket books going back to late 1800s, on computer since 09/98.
Criminal Records: Access: In person only. Visitors must perform in person searches for themselves. No search fee. Required to search: name, years to search; also helpful: DOB, SSN. Criminal records on general

index, docket books going back to late 1800s, on computer since 09/98.

General Information: Public access terminal is available. No mental health or search warrants released. Copy fee: $.25 per page. Certification fee: $1.00. Fee payee: Clerk of District Court. Personal checks accepted. All fees can be billed to attorneys.

Cheyenne County Court 1000 10th Ave, Sidney, NE 69162; 308-254-2929; Fax: 308-254-4641 permission to use required. Hours: 8AM-5PM (MST). *Misdemeanor, Civil Actions Under $45,000, Eviction, Small Claims, Probate.*

Civil Records: Access: Mail, in person. Both court and visitors may perform in person searches. No search fee. Required to search: name, years to search. Civil cases indexed by defendant, plaintiff. Civil records on index books from late 1800s. Fax access requires special permission.

Criminal Records: Access: Mail, in person. Both court and visitors may perform in person searches. No search fee. Required to search: name, years to search; also helpful: DOB. Criminal records on index books from late 1800s; computerized records since 2000.

General Information: Public access terminal is available. No adoption, juvenile, confidential records released. SASE required. Turnaround time within 1 week. Copy fee: $.25 per page. Certification fee: $1.00. Fee payee: Cheyenne County Court. Personal checks accepted. Prepayment is required.

Clay County

District Court Clerk of The District Court, 111 W Fairfield St, Clay Center, NE 68933; 402-762-3595; Fax: 402-762-3604. Hours: 8:30AM-5PM (CST). *Felony, Civil Actions Over $15,000.*

Civil Records: Access: In person only. Visitors must perform in person searches for themselves. No search fee. Required to search: name; also helpful: years to search. Civil cases indexed by defendant, plaintiff. Civil records on index books from late 1800s, on microfiche from 1986, computerized since 1997.

Criminal Records: Access: In person only. Visitors must perform in person searches for themselves. No search fee. Required to search: name, DOB; also helpful: years to search, SSN. Criminal records on index books from late 1800s, on microfiche from 1986, computerized since 1997.

General Information: Public access terminal is available. No mental health records released. Copy fee: $.25 per page. Certification fee: $1.00. Fee payee: Clerk of District Court. Personal checks accepted.

Clay County Court 111 W Fairfield St, Clay Center, NE 68933; 402-762-3651; Fax: 402-762-3250. Hours: 8:30AM-5PM (CST). *Misdemeanor, Civil Actions Under $45,000, Eviction, Small Claims, Probate, Traffic.*

Civil Records: Access: In person only. Visitors must perform in person searches for themselves. No search fee. Required to search: name, years to search. Civil cases indexed by defendant. Civil records in index books from late 1800s, on computer from 4/2000.

Criminal Records: Access: In person only. Visitors must perform in person searches for themselves. No search fee. Required to search: name, years to search; also helpful: DOB, SSN. Criminal records in index books from late 1800s.

General Information: No adoption or juvenile records released. Copy fee: $.25 per page. Certification fee: $1.00. Fee payee: Clay County. Personal checks accepted.

Colfax County

District Court 411 E 11th St, PO Box 429, Schuyler, NE 68661; 402-352-8506; Fax: 402-352-2847. Hours: 8:30AM-5PM (CST). *Felony, Civil Actions Over $15,000.*

Civil Records: Access: In person only. Visitors must perform in person searches for themselves. No search fee. Required to search: name, years to search; also helpful: address. Civil cases indexed by defendant, plaintiff. Civil records on index books and general index from 1880.

Criminal Records: Access: In person only. Visitors must perform in person searches for themselves. No search fee. Required to search: name, years to search; also helpful: address, DOB, SSN. Criminal records on index books and general index from 1880.

General Information: Public access terminal is available. No juvenile or mental health records released. Copy fee: $.25 per page. Certification fee: $2.00. Fee payee: Clerk of District Court. Business checks accepted. Will take personal check if local. Prepayment is required.

Colfax County Court 411 E 11th St, Box 191, Schuyler, NE 68661; 402-352-8511; Fax: 402-352-8535. Hours: 8AM-5PM (CST). *Misdemeanor, Civil Actions Under $45,000, Eviction, Small Claims, Probate.*

Civil Records: Access: In person only. Visitors must perform in person searches for themselves. No search fee. Required to search: name, years to search. Civil cases indexed by defendant, plaintiff. Civil records on index books from 1880s; computerized records since 1996.

Criminal Records: Access: In person only. Visitors must perform in person searches for themselves. No search fee. Required to search: name, years to search; also helpful: DOB, SSN. Criminal records on index books from 1880s; computerized records since 1996.

General Information: Public access terminal is available. No juvenile records released. Copy fee: $.25 per page. Certification fee: $1.00. Fee payee: Colfax County Court. Personal checks accepted. Prepayment is required.

Cuming County

District Court 200 S Lincoln, Rm 200, West Point, NE 68788; 402-372-6004; Fax: 402-372-6017. Hours: 8:30AM-4:30PM (CST). *Felony, Civil Actions Over $15,000.*

Civil Records: Access: Mail, fax, in person. Both court and visitors may perform in person searches. Search fee: $10.00 (fax only). Required to search: name, years to search. Civil cases indexed by defendant, plaintiff. Civil records in books from 1939; on computer back to 2000.

Criminal Records: Access: Fax, in person. Both court and visitors may perform in person searches. Search fee: $10.00 (fax only). Required to search: name, years to search. Criminal records in books from 1939; on computer back to 2000.

General Information: Public access terminal is available. No mental health records released. Copy fee: $.25 per page. Certification fee: $1.00. No personal checks accepted.

Cuming County Court 200 S Lincoln, Rm 103, West Point, NE 68788; 402-372-6003; Fax: 402-372-6030. Hours: 8:30AM-4:30PM (CST). *Misdemeanor, Civil Actions Under $45,000, Eviction, Small Claims, Probate.*

Civil Records: Access: In person only. Visitors must perform in person searches for themselves. No search fee. Required to search: name, years to search. Civil cases indexed by defendant, plaintiff. Civil records on index cards, also on computer since April 2000.

Criminal Records: Access: In person only. Visitors must perform in person searches for themselves. No search fee. Required to search: name, years to search; also helpful: DOB, SSN. Criminal records on index cards, also on computer since April 2000.

General Information: Public access terminal is available. No mental health records released. Copy fee: $.25 per page. Certification fee: $1.00. Personal checks accepted. ID required for payment by check. Prepayment is required.

Custer County

District Court 431 S 10th Ave, Broken Bow, NE 68822; 308-872-2121; Fax: 308-872-5826. Hours: 9AM-5PM (CST). *Felony, Civil Actions Over $15,000.*

Civil Records: Access: Phone, fax, mail, in person. Both court and visitors may perform in person searches. No search fee. Required to search: name, years to search; also helpful: address. Civil cases indexed by defendant, plaintiff. Civil records on index books and docket books from late 1800s; on computer back to 4/1998.

Criminal Records: Access: Phone, fax, mail, in person. Both court and visitors may perform in person searches. No search fee. Required to search: name, years to search; also helpful: address, DOB, SSN. Criminal records on index books and docket books from late 1800s; on computer back to 4/1998.

General Information: Public access terminal is available. No search warrants, mental health, or sealed records released. SASE required. Turnaround time 3-4 days. Fax notes: Fee to fax results is $3.00 per page. Copy fee: $.25 per page. Certification fee: $1.25. Fee payee: Clerk of District Court. Business checks accepted. Prepayment is required.

Custer County Court 431 South 10th Ave, Broken Bow, NE 68822; 308-872-5761; Fax: 308-872-6052. Hours: 8AM-12 1-5PM (CST). *Misdemeanor, Civil Actions Under $45,000, Eviction, Small Claims, Probate.*

Civil Records: Access: In person only. Visitors must perform in person searches for themselves. No search fee. Required to search: name, years to search. Civil cases indexed by defendant, plaintiff. Civil records on computer back to 2000, on index books from 1988, probate from 1986, balance are archived.

Criminal Records: Access: In person only. Visitors must perform in person searches for themselves. No search fee. Required to search: name, years to search. Criminal records on computer back to 2000, index books from 1988, probate from 1986, balance are archived.

General Information: No adoption or juvenile records released. Copy fee: $.25 per page. Certification fee: $1.00. Fee payee: Custer County Court. Personal checks accepted. Prepayment is required.

Dakota County

District Court PO Box 66, Dakota City, NE 68731; 402-987-2114; Fax: 402-987-2117. Hours: 8AM-4:30PM (CST). *Felony, Civil Actions Over $15,000.*

Civil Records: Access: In person only. Visitors must perform in person searches for themselves. No search fee. Required to search: name, years to search. Civil cases indexed by defendant, plaintiff. Civil records on index books from 1985, prior records archived at NE State Historical Society, Lincoln, NE; computerized records since 1998.

Criminal Records: Access: In person only. Visitors must perform in person searches for themselves. No search fee. Required to search: name, years to search. Criminal records on index books from 1985, prior records archived at NE State Historical Society, Lincoln, NE; computerized records since 1998.

General Information: Public access terminal is available. No juvenile or mental health records released. Copy fee: $.25 per page. Certification fee: $1.00. Fee payee: Clerk of District Court. Personal checks accepted.

Dakota County Court PO Box 385, Dakota City, NE 68731; 402-987-2145; Fax: 402-987-2185. Hours: 8AM-4:30PM (CST). *Misdemeanor, Civil Actions Under $45,000, Eviction, Small Claims, Probate.*

Civil Records: Access: In person only. Visitors must perform in person searches for themselves. No search fee. Required to search: name, years to search. Civil cases indexed by defendant, plaintiff. Civil records on index books from late 1800s.
Criminal Records: Access: In person only. Visitors must perform in person searches for themselves. No search fee. Required to search: name, years to search. Criminal records on index books from late 1800s.
General Information: Public access terminal is available. No adoption or juvenile records released. Copy fee: $.25 per page. Certification fee: $1.00. Fee payee: Dakota County Court. Business checks accepted. Prepayment is required.

Dawes County

District Court PO Box 630, Chadron, NE 69337; 308-432-0109; Fax: 308-432-0110. Hours: 8:30AM-4:30PM (MST). *Felony, Civil Actions Over $15,000.*

Civil Records: Access: In person only. Visitors must perform in person searches for themselves. No search fee. Required to search: name, years to search. Civil cases indexed by defendant, plaintiff. Civil records on general index, docket books from 1886.
Criminal Records: Access: In person only. Visitors must perform in person searches for themselves. No search fee. Required to search: name, years to search. Criminal records on general index, docket books from 1886.
General Information: No mental health records released. Copy fee: $.25 per page. Certification fee: $1.00. Fee payee: Clerk of District Court. Personal checks accepted.

Dawes County Court PO Box 806, Chadron, NE 69337; 308-432-0116; Fax: 308-432-0118. Hours: 7:30AM-4:30PM (MST). *Misdemeanor, Civil Actions Under $45,000, Eviction, Small Claims, Probate.*

Civil Records: Access: In person only. Visitors must perform in person searches for themselves. No search fee. Required to search: name, years to search. Civil cases indexed by defendant, plaintiff. Civil records on case cards, case files kept since 1892; on computer back to 2001.
Criminal Records: Access: In person only. Visitors must perform in person searches for themselves. No search fee. Required to search: name, years to search, DOB; also helpful: address. Criminal records on case cards, case files kept since 1892; on computer back to 2000.
General Information: Public access terminal is available. No confidential records released. No copy fee. Certification fee: $1.00. Fee payee: Dawes County Court. Personal checks accepted. Prepayment required.

Dawson County

District Court PO Box 429, Lexington, NE 68850; 308-324-4261; Fax: 308-324-3374. Hours: 8AM-5PM (CST). *Felony, Civil Actions Over $15,000.*

Civil Records: Access: In person only. Visitors must perform in person searches for themselves. No search fee. Required to search: name, years to search. Civil cases indexed by defendant, plaintiff. Recent civil records on microfiche, some older records on microfilm, index books date to late 1800s.
Criminal Records: Access: In person only. Visitors must perform in person searches for themselves. No

search fee. Required to search: name, years to search. Recent records on microfiche, some older records on microfilm, index books date to late 1800s.
General Information: No juvenile or mental health records released. Copy fee: $.25 per page. Certification fee: $1.00. Fee payee: Clerk of District Court. Personal checks accepted. Prepayment is required.

Dawson County Court 700 N Washington St, Lexington, NE 68850; 308-324-5606; Fax: 308-324-5607. Hours: 8AM-5PM (CST). *Misdemeanor, Civil Actions Under $45,000, Eviction, Small Claims, Probate.*

Civil Records: Access: In person only. Visitors must perform in person searches for themselves. No search fee. Required to search: name, years to search; also helpful: address. Civil cases indexed by defendant, plaintiff. Civil records on books from late 1800s, docket books 15 years back; on computer since 1998.
Criminal Records: Access: In person only. Visitors must perform in person searches for themselves. No search fee. Required to search: name, years to search, offense, DOB; also helpful: address, SSN. Criminal records on books from late 1800s, docket books 15 years back; on computer since 1998.
General Information: No adoption or juvenile records released. Fax notes: Fee to fax is $3.00 plus $1.00 each add'l page. Copy fee: $.25 per page. Certification fee: $1.00. Fee payee: Dawson County Court. Personal checks accepted. Credit cards accepted: Visa, MasterCard. Prepayment is required.

Deuel County

District Court PO Box 327, Chappell, NE 69129; 308-874-3308; Fax: 308-874-3472. Hours: 8AM-4PM (MST). *Felony, Civil Actions Over $15,000.*

Civil Records: Access: Phone, fax, mail, in person. Both court and visitors may perform in person searches. No search fee. Required to search: name; also helpful: years to search. Civil cases indexed by defendant, plaintiff. Civil records on general index and docket books form late 1800s.
Criminal Records: Access: Phone, fax, mail, in person. Both court and visitors may perform in person searches. No search fee. Required to search: name; also helpful: years to search, DOB, SSN. Criminal records on general index and docket books form late 1800s.
General Information: No mental health or service discharge records released. SASE required. Turnaround time 1 week. Fax notes: No fee to fax results. Copy fee: $.25. Certification fee: $1.00 1st page, $.25 each add'l page. Fee payee: Clerk of District Court. Personal checks accepted. Prepayment is required.

Deuel County Court PO Box 514, Chappell, NE 69129; 308-874-2909; Fax: 308-874-3472. Hours: 8AM-4PM (MST). *Misdemeanor, Civil Actions Under $45,000, Eviction, Small Claims, Probate.*

Civil Records: Access: Mail, in person. Both court and visitors may perform in person searches. No search fee. Required to search: name, years to search. Civil cases indexed by defendant, plaintiff. Civil records on index cards.
Criminal Records: Access: Mail, in person. Both court and visitors may perform in person searches. No search fee. Required to search: name, years to search, DOB, signed release. Criminal records on index cards to 1992, computerized since 2001.
General Information: No juvenile records released. SASE required. Turnaround time 3-4 days. Copy fee: $.25 per page. Certification fee: $1.00 per page. Fee payee: Deuel County Court. No personal checks accepted. Prepayment is required.

Dixon County

District Court PO Box 395, Ponca, NE 68770; 402-755-2881; Fax: 402-755-2632. Hours: 8AM-Noon, 1-5PM (CST). *Felony, Civil Actions Over $15,000.*

Civil Records: Access: In person only. Visitors must perform in person searches for themselves. No search fee. Required to search: name, years to search. Civil cases indexed by defendant, plaintiff. Civil records on books from 1876; computerized records go back to 1999.
Criminal Records: Access: In person only. Visitors must perform in person searches for themselves. No search fee. Required to search: name, years to search, DOB. Criminal records on books from 1876; computerized records go back to 1999.
General Information: Public access terminal is available. No mental health records released. Copy fee: $.25 per page. Certification fee: $1.00. Fee payee: Clerk of District Court. Personal checks accepted. Will bill copy fees.

Dixon County Court PO Box 497, Ponca, NE 68770; 402-755-2355; Fax: 402-755-2632. Hours: 8AM-4:30PM (CST). *Misdemeanor, Civil Actions Under $45,000, Eviction, Small Claims, Probate.*

Civil Records: Access: In person only. Visitors must perform in person searches for themselves. No search fee. Required to search: name, years to search. Civil cases indexed by defendant, plaintiff. Civil records in files, cards from 1987, prior in dockets from 1876, computerized since 2000.
Criminal Records: Access: In person only. Visitors must perform in person searches for themselves. No search fee. Required to search: name, years to search, DOB. Criminal records in files, cards from 1987, prior in dockets from 1876, computerized since 2000.
General Information: Public access terminal is available. No adoption or juvenile records released. Copy fee: $.25 per page. Certification fee: $1.00. Fee payee: Dixon County Court. Personal checks accepted.

Dodge County

District Court PO Box 1237, Fremont, NE 68026; 402-727-2780; Fax: 402-727-2773. Hours: 8:30AM-4:30PM (CST). *Felony, Civil Actions Over $15,000.*

Civil Records: Access: In person only. Visitors must perform in person searches for themselves. No search fee. Required to search: name, years to search. Civil cases indexed by defendant, plaintiff. Civil records on general index, docket books from late 1800s; computerized records since 1997.
Criminal Records: Access: In person only. Visitors must perform in person searches for themselves. No search fee. Required to search: name, years to search. Criminal records on general index, docket books from late 1800s; computerized records since 1997.
General Information: Public access terminal is available. No mental health records released. Copy fee: $.25 per page. Certification fee: $1.50. Fee payee: District Court. Personal checks accepted. Prepayment is required.

Dodge County Court 428 N Broad St, Fremont, NE 68025; 402-727-2755; Fax: 402-727-2762. Hours: 8AM-5PM (CST). *Misdemeanor, Civil Actions Under $45,000, Eviction, Small Claims, Probate.*

Civil Records: Access: In person only. Visitors must perform in person searches for themselves. No search fee. Required to search: name, years to search. Civil cases indexed by defendant. Civil records on general index, docket books from early 1900s; on computer back to 1998. Probate on microfilm from early 1900s.
Criminal Records: Access: In person only. Visitors must perform in person searches for themselves. No search fee. Required to search: name, years to search; also helpful: DOB. Criminal records on general index,

docket books from early 1900s; on computer back to 1998.

General Information: Public access terminal is available. No adoption or juvenile records released. Fax notes: Fee to fax results is $3.00 for 1st page; $1.00 each add'l. Copy fee: $.25 per page. Certification fee: $1.00 per document plus $.25 per page. Fee payee: Dodge County Court. Prepayment is required.

Douglas County

District Court 1701 Farnam, Hall of Justice, Rm 300, Omaha, NE 68183; 402-444-7018. Hours: 8:30AM-4:30PM (CST). *Felony, Civil Actions Over $15,000.*

Civil Records: Access: Mail, in person. Both court and visitors may perform in person searches. No search fee. Required to search: name, years to search; also helpful: address. Civil cases indexed by defendant, plaintiff. Civil records on computer from 1980, on books back to late 1800s.

Criminal Records: Access: Mail, in person. Visitors must perform in person searches for themselves. No search fee. Required to search: name, years to search; also helpful: address, DOB, SSN. Criminal records on computer from 1980, on books back to late 1800s.

General Information: Public access terminal is available. No juvenile records released. SASE required. Turnaround time 1-2 days. Copy fee: $.50 per page. $1.00 minimum. Add $.50 postage fee. Certification fee: $3.50 for 1-5 pages, then $15.50 per page. Fee payee: Clerk of District Court. Personal checks accepted. Prepayment is required.

Douglas County Court 1819 Farnam, #F03, Omaha, NE 68183; Civil phone: 402-444-5425; Criminal phone: 402-444-5387. Hours: 8AM-4:30PM (CST). *Misdemeanor, Civil Actions Under $45,000, Eviction, Small Claims, Probate.*

www.co.douglas.ne.us

Civil Records: Access: Mail, online, in person. Visitors must perform in person searches for themselves. No search fee. Required to search: name, years to search. Civil cases indexed by defendant, plaintiff. Civil records on computer from 1987 (small claims), from 1983 (civil). Civil records are purged after about 20 years. Access to the Internet system requires registration and password. Call John at 402-471-3049 for more information. System can be searched by name or case number.

Criminal Records: Access: Mail, in person, online. Visitors must perform in person searches for themselves. No search fee. Required to search: name, years to search; also helpful: DOB. Criminal records on computer from 1987 (small claims), from 1983 (civil). Civil records are purged after about 20 years. Online access to criminal records is the same as civil.

General Information: Public access terminal is available. SASE required. Copy fee: $.25 per page. Certification fee: $1.00. Fee payee: Douglas County Court. Personal checks accepted. Prepayment required.

Dundy County

District Court PO Box 506, Benkelman, NE 69021; 308-423-2058. Hours: 8AM-5PM (MST). *Felony, Civil Actions Over $15,000.*

Civil Records: Access: Phone, mail, in person. Both court and visitors may perform in person searches. No search fee. Required to search: name, years to search; also helpful: address. Civil cases indexed by defendant, plaintiff. Civil records on index books from late 1800s.

Criminal Records: Access: Phone, mail, in person. Both court and visitors may perform in person searches. No search fee. Required to search: name, years to search; also helpful: address, DOB, SSN. Criminal records on index books from late 1800s.

General Information: No juvenile records released. SASE required. Turnaround time 1-2 days. Copy fee: $1.00 per page. Certification fee: $1.50. Fee payee: Clerk of District Court. Personal checks accepted. Prepayment is required.

Dundy County Court PO Box 377, Benkelman, NE 69021; 308-423-2374. Hours: 8AM-4:30PM (MST). *Misdemeanor, Civil Actions Under $45,000, Eviction, Small Claims, Probate.*

Civil Records: Access: Phone, mail, in person. Only the court performs in person searches; visitors may not. No search fee. Required to search: name, years to search. Civil cases indexed by defendant, plaintiff. Civil records on general index, docket books from late 1800s; some probate, civil on microfiche.

Criminal Records: Access: Phone, mail, in person, fax. Only the court performs in person searches; visitors may not. No search fee. Required to search: name, years to search, DOB, signed release; also helpful: address. Criminal records on general index, docket books from late 1800s, computerized since 2001; some probate, civil on microfiche.

General Information: No adoption or juvenile records released. SASE required. Turnaround time 3-4 days. Fax notes: $3.00 charge for first fax page, $1.00 each additional page. Copy fee: $.25 per page. Certification fee: $1.00 per document. Fee payee: Dundy County Court. Business checks accepted. Prepayment required.

Fillmore County

District Court PO Box 147, Geneva, NE 68361-0147; 402-759-3811; Fax: 402-759-4440. Hours: 8AM-Noon, 1-5PM (CST). *Felony, Civil Actions Over $15,000.*

Civil Records: Access: Phone, fax, mail, in person. Both court and visitors may perform in person searches. No search fee. Required to search: name, years to search. Civil cases indexed by defendant, plaintiff. Civil records on index books to late 1800s, last 10 years on microfiche.

Criminal Records: Access: Phone, fax, mail, in person. Both court and visitors may perform in person searches. No search fee. Required to search: name, years to search. Criminal records on index books to late 1800s, last 10 years on microfiche.

General Information: Public access terminal is available. No juvenile or mental health records released. SASE required. Turnaround time 1-5 days, 1 day for phone and FAX. Fax notes: $2.00 for first page, $1.00 each add'l. Copy fee: $.35 per page. Certification fee: $1.00. Fee payee: Clerk of District Court. Personal checks accepted. Will bill fax & copy fees.

Fillmore County Court PO Box 66, Geneva, NE 68361; 402-759-3514; Fax: 402-759-4440. Hours: 8AM-5PM (CST). *Misdemeanor, Civil Actions Under $45,000, Eviction, Small Claims, Probate.*

Civil Records: Access: Fax, mail, in person. Both court and visitors may perform in person searches. No search fee. Required to search: name, years to search. Civil cases indexed by defendant, plaintiff. Civil records on general index, docket books from late 1800s; probate on microfiche.

Criminal Records: Access: Fax, mail, in person. Both court and visitors may perform in person searches. No search fee. Required to search: name, years to search. Criminal records on general index, docket books from late 1800s; probate on microfiche.

General Information: No adoption or juvenile records released. SASE required. Turnaround time 7-8 days. Fax notes: $2.00 for first page, $1.00 each add'l. Copy fee: $.25 per page. Certification fee: $1.25. Fee payee: County Court. Personal checks accepted. Prepayment is required.

Franklin County

District Court PO Box 146, Franklin, NE 68939; 308-425-6202; Fax: 308-425-6093. Hours: 8:30AM-4:30PM (CST). *Felony, Civil Actions Over $15,000.*

Civil Records: Access: In person only. Visitors must perform in person searches for themselves. No search fee. Required to search: name, years to search. Civil cases indexed by defendant, plaintiff. Civil records on index books back to turn of century; on computer back to 2/2000.

Criminal Records: Access: In person only. Visitors must perform in person searches for themselves. No search fee. Required to search: name, years to search. Criminal records on index books back to turn of century; on computer back to 2/2000.

General Information: Public access terminal is available. No adoption or juvenile records released. Copy fee: $.25 per page. Certification fee: $1.00. Fee payee: Clerk of District Court or County Clerk. Personal checks accepted. Prepayment is required.

Franklin County Court PO Box 174, Franklin, NE 68939; 308-425-6288; Fax: 308-425-6289. Hours: 8:30AM-4:30PM M-F (CST). *Misdemeanor, Civil Actions Under $45,000, Eviction, Small Claims, Probate.*

Civil Records: Access: Mail, in person. Both court and visitors may perform in person searches. No search fee. Required to search: name, years to search. Civil cases indexed by defendant, plaintiff. Civil records on docket cards since 1988, prior on docket books.

Criminal Records: Access: Mail, in person. Both court and visitors may perform in person searches. No search fee. Required to search: name, years to search. Criminal records on docket cards since 1988, prior on docket books.

General Information: Public access terminal is available. No juvenile, adoption records released. SASE required. Turnaround time 2 days. Copy fee: $.25 per page. Certification fee: $1.00. Fee payee: Franklin County Court. Personal checks accepted.

Frontier County

District Court PO Box 40, Stockville, NE 69042; 308-367-8641; Fax: 308-367-8730. Hours: 9AM-4:30PM (CST). *Felony, Civil Actions Over $15,000.*

Civil Records: Access: Mail, in person. Both court and visitors may perform in person searches. No search fee. Required to search: name, years to search. Civil cases indexed by defendant, plaintiff. Civil records on general index, docket books from late 1800s; computerized records since 6/00.

Criminal Records: Access: Mail, in person. Both court and visitors may perform in person searches. No search fee. Required to search: name, years to search, DOB, signed release. Criminal records on general index, docket books from late 1800s; computerized records since 6/00.

General Information: Public access terminal is available. SASE required. Turnaround time 5 days. Copy fee: $.25 per page. Certification fee: $1.00. Fee payee: Clerk of District Court. Only cashiers checks and money orders accepted. Prepayment is required.

Frontier County Court PO Box 38, Stockville, NE 69042; 308-367-8629; Fax: 308-367-8730. Hours: 9AM-4:30PM (CST). *Misdemeanor, Civil Actions Under $45,000, Eviction, Small Claims, Probate.*

Civil Records: Access: Fax, mail, in person. Visitors must perform in person searches for themselves. No search fee. Required to search: name, years to search. Civil cases indexed by plaintiff. Civil records on general index, docket books from late 1800s; on computer back to 10/2000.

Criminal Records: Access: Fax, mail, in person. Visitors must perform in person searches for themselves. No search fee. Required to search: name, years to search, DOB; also helpful-signed release. Criminal records on general index, docket books from late 1800s; on computer back to 10/2000.

General Information: Public access terminal is available. No adoption or juvenile records released. SASE required. Turnaround time 5 days. Fax notes: Fee to fax results is $3.00 per page. Copy fee: $.25 per page. Certification fee: $1.00. Fee payee: County Court. Only cashiers checks and money orders accepted. Prepayment is required.

Furnas County

District Court PO Box 413, Beaver City, NE 68926; 308-268-4015; Fax: 308-268-3205. Hours: 10AM-Noon, 1-3PM (CST). *Felony, Civil Actions Over $15,000.*

Civil Records: Access: Mail, in person. Both court and visitors may perform in person searches. No search fee. Required to search: name, years to search. Civil cases indexed by defendant, plaintiff. Civil records in general index books and files from late 1800s.

Criminal Records: Access: Mail, in person. Both court and visitors may perform in person searches. No search fee. Required to search: name, years to search. Criminal records in general index books and files from late 1800s.

General Information: No mental health records released. SASE required. Turnaround time 3-4 days. Copy fee: $.25 per page. Certification fee: $1.00. Fee payee: Clerk of District Court. Personal checks accepted.

Furnas County Court 912 R St (PO Box 373), Beaver City, NE 68926; 308-268-4025. Hours: 8AM-4PM (CST). *Misdemeanor, Civil Actions Under $45,000, Eviction, Small Claims, Probate.*

Civil Records: Access: In person only. Visitors must perform in person searches for themselves. No search fee. Required to search: name, years to search. Civil cases indexed by defendant, plaintiff. Civil records on card system from 1984, docket books back to late 1800s.

Criminal Records: Access: In person only. Visitors must perform in person searches for themselves. No search fee. Required to search: name, years to search; also helpful: DOB. Criminal records on card system from 1984, docket books back to late 1800s.

General Information: No adoption, juvenile or sealed records released. Copy fee: $.25 per page. Certification fee: $1.00. Plus $.25 per page. Fee payee: County Court. Personal checks accepted.

Gage County

District Court PO Box 845, Beatrice, NE 68310; 402-223-1332; Fax: 402-223-1313. Hours: 8AM-5PM (CST). *Felony, Civil Actions Over $15,000.*

Civil Records: Access: Mail, fax, in person. Both court and visitors may perform in person searches. No search fee. Required to search: name, years to search. Civil cases indexed by defendant, plaintiff. Civil records on index books from late 1800s; on computer back to 1997.

Criminal Records: Access: Mail, fax, in person. Both court and visitors may perform in person searches. No search fee. Required to search: name, years to search, DOB. Criminal records on index books from late 1800s; on computer back to 1997.

General Information: Public access terminal is available. No juvenile or mental health records released. SASE required. Turnaround time up to 7-10 days. Copy fee: $.25 per page. Certification fee: $1.00. Fee payee: Clerk of District Court. Personal checks accepted. Prepayment is required.

Gage County Court PO Box 219, Beatrice, NE 68310; 402-223-1323. Hours: 8AM-5PM (CST).

Misdemeanor, Civil Actions Under $45,000, Eviction, Small Claims, Probate.

Civil Records: Access: Mail, in person. Both court and visitors may perform in person searches. No search fee. Required to search: name, years to search. Civil cases indexed by defendant, plaintiff. Civil records go back to 1987; on computer back to 1999. Probate records from 1860, probate on microfiche. Contact court before faxing.

Criminal Records: Access: Mail, in person. Both court and visitors may perform in person searches. No search fee. Required to search: name, years to search, DOB. Civil records go back to 1987; on computer back to 1996. Contact court before faxing.

General Information: Public access terminal is available. No adoption or juvenile records released. SASE required. Turnaround time 1-3 weeks. Copy fee: $.25 per page. Certification fee: $1.00. Fee payee: Gage County Court. Personal checks accepted. Prepayment is required.

Garden County

District Court PO Box 486, Oshkosh, NE 69154; 308-772-3924; Fax: 308-772-4143. Hours: 8AM-4PM (MST). *Felony, Civil Actions Over $15,000.*

Civil Records: Access: Fax, mail, in person. Both court and visitors may perform in person searches. No search fee. Required to search: name, years to search. Civil cases indexed by defendant, plaintiff. Civil records in files, docket books back to 1910; on computer back to 1998.

Criminal Records: Access: Fax, mail, in person. Both court and visitors may perform in person searches. No search fee. Required to search: name, years to search. Criminal records in files, docket books back to 1910; on computer back to 1998.

General Information: Public access terminal is available. No confidential records released. SASE required. Turnaround time same day. Fax notes: $2.00 for first page, $1.00 each add'l. Copy fee: $.50 per page. Certification fee: $5.00. Fee payee: Clerk of District Court. Personal checks accepted. Prepayment is required.

Garden County Court PO Box 465, Oshkosh, NE 69154; 308-772-3696. Hours: 8AM-4PM (MST). *Misdemeanor, Civil Actions Under $45,000, Eviction, Small Claims, Probate.*

Civil Records: Access: In person only. Visitors must perform in person searches for themselves. No search fee. Required to search: name, years to search. Civil cases indexed by defendant, plaintiff. Civil records on general index, docket books from 1910. Phone access limited to short searches.

Criminal Records: Access: In person only. Visitors must perform in person searches for themselves. No search fee. Required to search: name, years to search. Criminal records on general index, docket books from 1910.

General Information: No adoption or juvenile records released. Certification fee: $1.00. Fee payee: Garden County Court. Personal checks accepted. Prepayment is required.

Garfield County

District Court PO Box 218, Burwell, NE 68823; 308-346-4161. Hours: 9AM-5PM (CST). *Felony, Civil Actions Over $15,000.*

Civil Records: Access: Mail, in person. Both court and visitors may perform in person searches. Search fee: $5.00. Required to search: name, years to search; also helpful: address. Civil cases indexed by defendant, plaintiff. Civil records on index books from 1885.

Criminal Records: Access: Mail, in person. Both court and visitors may perform in person searches. Search fee: $5.00. Required to search: name, years to search;

---

also helpful: address, DOB, SSN. Criminal records on index books from 1885.

General Information: SASE required. Turnaround time 3-4 days. Copy fee: $.25 per page. Certification fee: $1.50. Fee payee: Clerk of District Court. Personal checks accepted. Prepayment is required.

Garfield County Court PO Box 431, Burwell, NE 68823; 308-346-4123; Fax: 308-346-5064. Hours: 9AM-4PM (CST). *Misdemeanor, Civil Actions Under $45,000, Eviction, Small Claims, Probate.*

Civil Records: Access: Mail, in person. Both court and visitors may perform in person searches. No search fee. Required to search: name, years to search. Civil cases indexed by defendant. Civil records on index books, from 1885 (probate), 25 years for civil; on computer back to 2000.

Criminal Records: Access: Mail, in person. Both court and visitors may perform in person searches. No search fee. Required to search: name, years to search. Criminal record keeping back for 25 years; on computer back to 2000.

General Information: No juvenile records released. SASE required. Turnaround time within 5 days. Fax notes: $3.00 for first page, $1.00 each add'l. Copy fee: $.25 per page. Certification fee: $1.00. Fee payee: County Court. Personal checks accepted. Prepayment is required.

Gosper County

District Court PO Box 136, Elwood, NE 68937; 308-785-2611. Hours: 8:30AM-4:30PM (CST). *Felony, Civil Actions Over $15,000.*

Civil Records: Access: In person only. Visitors must perform in person searches for themselves. No search fee. Required to search: name, years to search. Civil cases indexed by defendant, plaintiff. Civil records in general index books since late 1800s.

Criminal Records: Access: In person only. Visitors must perform in person searches for themselves. No search fee. Required to search: name, years to search; also helpful: DOB. Criminal records in general index books since late 1800s.

General Information: No juvenile records or search warrants released. Copy fee: $.25 per page. Certification fee: $1.00. Fee payee: Clerk of District Court. Personal checks accepted. Prepayment is required.

Gosper County Court PO Box 55, Elwood, NE 68937; 308-785-2531; Fax: 308-785-2300 (call before faxing). Hours: 8:30AM-4:30PM (CST). *Misdemeanor, Civil Actions Under $45,000, Eviction, Small Claims, Probate.*

Civil Records: Access: In person only. Visitors must perform in person searches for themselves. No search fee. Required to search: name, years to search. Civil cases indexed by defendant, plaintiff. Civil records on index cards, docket books kept for 10 years (civil), to late 1800s (probate). Mail access limited to short searches.

Criminal Records: Access: In person only. Visitors must perform in person searches for themselves. No search fee. Required to search: name, years to search, DOB. Criminal record keeping back for 10 years.

General Information: No adoption or juvenile records released. Copy fee: $.25 per page. Certification fee: $1.00. Fee payee: Gosper County Court. Personal checks accepted. Out of state checks not accepted. Prepayment is required.

Grant County

District Court PO Box 139, Hyannis, NE 69350; 308-458-2488; Fax: 308-458-2485. Hours: 8AM-4PM (MST). *Felony, Civil Actions Over $15,000.*

Civil Records: Access: Fax, mail, in person. Both court and visitors may perform in person searches. No search fee. Required to search: name, years to search. Civil cases indexed by defendant, plaintiff. Civil records on index books from 1888.

Criminal Records: Access: Fax, mail, in person. Both court and visitors may perform in person searches. No search fee. Required to search: name, years to search. Criminal records on index books from 1888.

General Information: No mental health records released. SASE required. Turnaround time 3-4 days. Fax notes: $.20 per page. Copy fee: $.20 per page. Certification fee: $1.50. Fee payee: Grant County Clerk. Personal checks accepted. Prepayment is required.

Grant County Court PO Box 97, Hyannis, NE 69350; 308-458-2433; Civil phone: 308-327-2692; Fax: 308-458-2283 (Sheriff). Hours: 8AM-4PM only on 2nd Tues of month (MST). *Misdemeanor, Civil Actions Under $45,000, Eviction, Small Claims, Probate.*

Note: This court will not do record searches by name etc., but will send and certify certify copies of specific records.

Civil Records: Access: In person. Visitors must perform in person searches for themselves. No search fee. Required to search: name, years to search; also helpful: address. Civil cases indexed by defendant, plaintiff. Civil records in files, docket books from 1888, computerized since 07/00.

Criminal Records: Access: In person. Visitors must perform in person searches for themselves. No search fee. Required to search: name, years to search, DOB; also helpful: address, SSN. Criminal records in files, docket books from 1888, computerized since 07/00.

General Information: No adoption records released. Limited phone searching immediate. Copy fee: $.20 per page. Certification fee: $1.50. Fee payee: Grant County Court. Personal checks accepted.

Greeley County

District Court PO Box 287, Greeley, NE 68842; 308-428-3625; Fax: 308-428-6500. Hours: 8AM-Noon; 1PM-4PM (CST). *Felony, Civil Actions Over $15,000.*

Civil Records: Access: Mail, in person. Only the court performs in person searches; visitors may not. No search fee. Required to search: name, years to search, address. Civil cases indexed by defendant, plaintiff. Civil records on general index books from late 1800s.

Criminal Records: Access: Mail, in person. Only the court performs in person searches; visitors may not. No search fee. Required to search: name, years to search, DOB, signed release. Criminal records on general index books from late 1800s.

General Information: No mental health records released. SASE required. Turnaround time 1 day. Copy fee: $.25 per page. Certification fee: $1.50. Fee payee: Clerk of District Court. Only cashiers checks and money orders accepted. Prepayment is required.

Greeley County Court PO Box 302, Greeley, NE 68842; 308-428-2705; Fax: 308-428-6500. Hours: 8AM-5PM (CST). *Misdemeanor, Civil Actions Under $45,000, Eviction, Small Claims, Probate.*

Civil Records: Access: In person only. Visitors must perform in person searches for themselves. No search fee. Required to search: name, years to search. Civil cases indexed by defendant, plaintiff. Civil records on index cards, kept from late 1800s, computerized since 5/00.

Criminal Records: Access: In person only. Visitors must perform in person searches for themselves. No search fee. Required to search: name, years to search. Criminal records on index cards, kept from late 1800s, computerized since 5/00.

General Information: Public access terminal is available. No adoption records released. Copy fee: $.25 per page. Certification fee: $1.00. Fee payee: County Court. Only cashiers checks and money orders accepted. Prepayment is required.

Hall County

District Court PO Box 1926, Grand Island, NE 68802; 308-385-5144; Fax: 308-385-5110. Hours: 8AM-5PM (CST). *Felony, Civil Actions Over $15,000.*

Civil Records: Access: Mail, in person. Both court and visitors may perform in person searches. No search fee. Required to search: name, years to search. Civil cases indexed by defendant, plaintiff. Many records on computer since 1985, some on microfilm, original index books back to late 1800s.

Criminal Records: Access: Mail, in person. Both court and visitors may perform in person searches. No search fee. Required to search: name, years to search. Many records on computer since 1985, some on microfilm, original index books back to late 1800s.

General Information: Public access terminal is available. No mental health records released. SASE required. Turnaround time 3-4 days. Copy fee: $.20 per page. Certification fee: $2.00. Fee payee: Clerk of District Court. Personal checks accepted. Prepayment is required.

Hall County Court 111 W 1st #1, Grand Island, NE 68801; 308-385-5135. Hours: 8AM-4:30PM (CST). *Misdemeanor, Civil Actions Under $45,000, Eviction, Small Claims, Probate.*

Civil Records: Access: In person only. Visitors must perform in person searches for themselves. No search fee. Required to search: name, years to search. Civil cases indexed by defendant. Civil records on index books, on computer after 1/24/00.

Criminal Records: Access: In person only. Visitors must perform in person searches for themselves. No search fee. Required to search: name, years to search, DOB. Criminal records on index books; on computer after 5/19/97.

General Information: Public access terminal is available. No confidential records released. Copy fee: $.25 per page. Certification fee: $1.00. Fee payee: County Court. Personal checks accepted. Prepayment is required.

Hamilton County

District Court PO Box 201, Aurora, NE 68818-0201; 402-694-3533; Fax: 402-694-2250. Hours: 8AM-5PM (CST). *Felony, Civil Actions Over $15,000.*

Civil Records: Access: In person only. Visitors must perform in person searches for themselves. No search fee. Required to search: name, years to search. Civil cases indexed by defendant, plaintiff. Civil records on index books and files from late 1800s.

Criminal Records: Access: In person only. Visitors must perform in person searches for themselves. No search fee. Required to search: name, years to search. Criminal records on index books and files from late 1800s.

General Information: No mental health board hearing records released. Copy fee: $.25 per page. Certification fee: $1.00. Fee payee: Clerk of District Court. Personal checks accepted. Prepayment is required.

Hamilton County Court PO Box 323, Aurora, NE 68818; 402-694-6188; Fax: 402-694-2250. *Misdemeanor, Civil Actions Under $45,000, Eviction, Small Claims, Probate.*

Civil Records: Access: In person only. Visitors must perform in person searches for themselves. No search fee. Required to search: name, years to search. Civil cases indexed by defendant, plaintiff. Civil records computerized since 1998, older on docket cards, probate on microfiche from late 1800s.

Criminal Records: Access: In person only. Visitors must perform in person searches for themselves. No search fee. Required to search: name, years to search. Computerized since 1997.

General Information: Public access terminal is available. No adoption records released. Copy fee: $.25 per page. Certification fee: $1.00. Fee payee: Hamilton County Court. Personal checks accepted. Credit cards accepted: Visa, MasterCard. Prepayment is required.

Harlan County

District Court PO Box 698, Alma, NE 68920; 308-928-2173; Fax: 308-928-2592. Hours: 8:30AM-4:30PM (CST). *Felony, Civil Actions Over $15,000.*

Civil Records: Access: Phone, mail, in person. Both court and visitors may perform in person searches. Search fee: $5.00 per name. Required to search: name, years to search. Civil cases indexed by defendant, plaintiff. Civil records on books and in files from late 1800s, on computer back to 3/2000.

Criminal Records: Access: Phone, mail, in person. Both court and visitors may perform in person searches. Search fee: $5.00 per name. Required to search: name, years to search. Criminal records on books and in files from late 1800s; on computer back to 3/2000.

General Information: Public access terminal is available. No juvenile records released. SASE not required. Turnaround time 1 day. Copy fee: $.25 per page. Certification fee: $1.00. Fee payee: Clerk of District Court. Personal checks accepted.

Harlan County Court PO Box 379, Alma, NE 68920; 308-928-2179; Fax: 308-928-2170. Hours: 8:30AM-4:30PM (CST). *Misdemeanor, Civil Actions Under $45,000, Eviction, Small Claims, Probate.*

Civil Records: Access: In person only. Visitors must perform in person searches for themselves. No search fee. Required to search: name, years to search; also helpful: address. Civil cases indexed by defendant. Civil records on index cards from 1900; computerized since 2000.

Criminal Records: Access: In person only. Visitors must perform in person searches for themselves. No search fee. Required to search: name, years to search; also helpful: address, DOB. Criminal records on index cards from 1900, computerized since 2000.

General Information: Public access terminal is available. (CD-ROM legal research only.) No adoption records released. Limited access to juvenile records. Copy fee: $.25 per page. Certification fee: $1.00. Fee payee: Harlan County Court. Business checks accepted. Prepayment is required. Payment is required at time of search.

Hayes County

District Court PO Box 370, Hayes Center, NE 69032; 308-286-3413; Fax: 308-286-3208. Hours: 8AM-4PM (CST). *Felony, Civil Actions Over $15,000.*

Civil Records: Access: Fax, mail, in person. Both court and visitors may perform in person searches. No search fee. Required to search: name; also helpful: years to search, address. Civil cases indexed by defendant, plaintiff. Civil records on index books back to late 1800s.

Criminal Records: Access: Fax, mail, in person. Both court and visitors may perform in person searches. No search fee. Required to search: name; also helpful: years to search, address, DOB, SSN. Criminal records on index books back to late 1800s.

General Information: No sealed records released. SASE required. Turnaround time 2 days. Copy fee: $.25 per page. Certification fee: $4.00. Fee payee: Clerk of District Court. Personal checks accepted. Prepayment is required.

Hayes County Court PO Box 370, Hayes Center, NE 69032; 308-286-3315. Hours: 9AM-Noon, 1-4PM Tuesday (Clerk's hours) (CST). *Misdemeanor, Civil Actions Under $45,000, Eviction, Small Claims, Probate.*

Civil Records: Access: Phone, mail, in person. Both court and visitors may perform in person searches. No search fee. Required to search: name, years to search. Civil cases indexed by defendant, plaintiff. Civil records on general index books and files back to late 1800s; on computer back to mid-2000.

Criminal Records: Access: Phone, mail, in person. Both court and visitors may perform in person searches. No search fee. Required to search: name, years to search, DOB. Criminal records on general index books and files back to late 1800s; on computer back to mid-2000.

General Information: No juvenile or adoption records released. SASE required. Turnaround time 1 week. Copy fee: $.25 per page. Certification fee: $1.00. Fee payee: County Court. Personal checks accepted. Prepayment is required.

Hitchcock County

District Court PO Box 248, Trenton, NE 69044; 308-334-5646; Fax: 308-334-5398. Hours: 8:30AM-4PM (CST). *Felony, Civil Actions Over $15,000.*

www.co.hitchcock.ne.us/court.html

Civil Records: Access: Phone, fax, mail, in person. Both court and visitors may perform in person searches. No search fee. Required to search: name, years to search. Civil cases indexed by defendant, plaintiff. Civil records on books from late 1800s; on computer back to 1999.

Criminal Records: Access: Phone, fax, mail, in person. Both court and visitors may perform in person searches. No search fee. Required to search: name, years to search. Criminal records on books from late 1800s; on computer back to 1999.

General Information: Public access terminal is available. No sealed records released. SASE required. Turnaround time 2 days. Fax notes: $3.00 for first page, $1.50 each add'l. Copy fee: $.25 per page. Certification fee: $1.00. Fee payee: Clerk of District Court. Personal checks accepted. Prepayment is required.

Hitchcock County Court PO Box 366, Trenton, NE 69044; 308-334-5383. Hours: 8:30AM-4PM (CST). *Misdemeanor, Civil Actions Under $45,000, Eviction, Small Claims, Probate.*

Civil Records: Access: Phone, mail, in person. Both court and visitors may perform in person searches. No search fee. Required to search: name, years to search. Civil cases indexed by defendant, plaintiff. Civil records on docket books, cards go back to 1960s; on computer back to 2000. Probate records go back to late 1800s.

Criminal Records: Access: Phone, mail, in person. Both court and visitors may perform in person searches. No search fee. Required to search: name, years to search, DOB. Criminal records go back to 1978 apx. on docket books, cards; on computer back to 2000.

General Information: No adoption or juvenile records released. SASE required. Turnaround time 2 weeks, limited phone searching same day. Copy fee: $.25 per page. Certification fee: $1.00. Fee payee: County Court. Personal checks accepted. Prepayment is required.

Holt County

District Court PO Box 755, O'Neill, NE 68763; 402-336-2840; Fax: 402-336-3601. Hours: 8AM-4:30PM (CST). *Felony, Civil Actions Over $15,000.*

Civil Records: Access: Phone, fax, mail, in person. Both court and visitors may perform in person searches. No search fee. Required to search: name, years to search; also helpful: address. Civil cases indexed by defendant, plaintiff. Civil records on docket books and general index books since late 1800, search last 15 years only.

Criminal Records: Access: Phone, fax, mail, in person. Both court and visitors may perform in person searches. No search fee. Required to search: name,

years to search, DOB. Criminal records on docket books and general index books archived since late 1800s, search last 15 years.

General Information: No juvenile or mental health records released. SASE required. Turnaround time 1 week or less. Fax notes: $3.00 for first page, $1.00 each add'l. Copy fee: $.25 per page. Certification fee: $1.00. Fee payee: Clerk of District Court. Personal checks accepted.

Holt County Court 204 N 4th St, O'Neill, NE 68763; 402-336-1662; Fax: 402-336-1663. Hours: 8AM-4:30PM (CST). *Misdemeanor, Civil Actions Under $45,000, Eviction, Small Claims, Probate.*

Civil Records: Access: In person only. Visitors must perform in person searches for themselves. No search fee. Required to search: name, years to search. Civil cases indexed by defendant. Civil records go back to 1980; on comptuer back to 2000; probate kept longer.

Criminal Records: Access: In person only. Visitors must perform in person searches for themselves. No search fee. Required to search: name, years to search, DOB. Criminal records go back to 1920, on computer back to 2000.

General Information: Public access terminal is available. No adoption records released. Copy fee: $.25 per page. Certification fee: $1.25. Fee payee: Holt County Court. Personal checks accepted. Prepayment is required.

Hooker County

District Court PO Box 184, Mullen, NE 69152; 308-546-2244; Fax: 308-546-2490. Hours: 8:30AM-Noon, 1-4:30PM (MST). *Felony, Civil Actions Over $15,000.*

Civil Records: Access: Phone, fax, mail, in person. Visitors must perform in person searches for themselves. No search fee. Required to search: name, years to search. Civil cases indexed by defendant, plaintiff. Civil records on index books since late 1800s.

Criminal Records: Access: Phone, fax, mail, in person. Visitors must perform in person searches for themselves. No search fee. Required to search: name, years to search. Criminal records on index books since late 1800s.

General Information: Public access terminal is available. No mental health records released. SASE required. Turnaround time 3-4 days. Fax notes: $2.00 for first page, $1.00 each add'l. Copy fee: $1.00 per page. Certification fee: $1.50. Fee payee: Clerk of District Court. Personal checks accepted. Prepayment is required.

Hooker County Court PO Box 184, Mullen, NE 69152; 308-546-2249; Fax: 308-546-2490 (Sheriff). Hours: 8:30AM-4:30PM (MST). *Misdemeanor, Civil Actions Under $45,000, Eviction, Small Claims, Probate.*

Civil Records: Access: Fax, mail, in person. Both court and visitors may perform in person searches. No search fee. Required to search: name, years to search. Civil cases indexed by defendant, plaintiff. Civil records on index cards and books from late 1800s.

Criminal Records: Access: Fax, mail, in person. Both court and visitors may perform in person searches. No search fee. Required to search: name, years to search; also helpful: DOB, SSN. Criminal records on index cards and books from late 1800s.

General Information: No adoption or juvenile records released. SASE required. Turnaround time 3-4 days. Fax notes: No fee to fax results. Copy fee: $.25 per page. Certification fee: $1.00. Fee payee: County Court. Business checks accepted. Prepayment is required.

Howard County

District Court PO Box 25, St Paul, NE 68873; 308-754-4343; Fax: 308-754-4125. Hours: 8AM-5PM (CST). *Felony, Civil Actions Over $15,000.*

Civil Records: Access: In person only. Both court and visitors may perform in person searches. No search fee. Required to search: name, years to search. Civil cases indexed by defendant, plaintiff. Civil records on microfiche from 1986, books prior.

Criminal Records: Access: In person only. Both court and visitors may perform in person searches. No search fee. Required to search: name, years to search, DOB. Criminal records on microfiche from 1986, books prior; on comptuer back to 9/1998.

General Information: Public access terminal is available. No pending case records released. Copy fee: $.25 per page. Certification fee: $5.00. Fee payee: Clerk of District Court. Personal checks accepted. Prepayment is required.

Howard County Court 612 Indian St #6, St Paul, NE 68873; 308-754-4192. Hours: 8AM-Noon; 1PM-5PM (CST). *Misdemeanor, Civil Actions Under $45,000, Eviction, Small Claims, Probate.*

Civil Records: Access: In person only. Visitors must perform in person searches for themselves. No search fee. Required to search: name, years to search. Civil cases indexed by defendant. Civil records on docket cards since 1982; computerized records since 2000.

Criminal Records: Access: In person only. Visitors must perform in person searches for themselves. No search fee. Required to search: name, years to search; also helpful: DOB. Criminal records on docket cards since 1982; computerized records since 2000.

General Information: Public access terminal is available. Copy fee: $.25 per page. Certification fee: $1.00. Fee payee: Howard County Court. Business checks accepted. Prepayment is required.

Jefferson County

District Court Jefferson County Courthouse, 411 Fourth Street, Fairbury, NE 68352; 402-729-2019; Fax: 402-729-6596. Hours: 9AM-5PM (CST). *Felony, Civil Actions Over $15,000.*

Civil Records: Access: Fax, mail, in person. Both court and visitors may perform in person searches. Search fee: No search fee. Required to search: name, years to search. Civil cases indexed by defendant, plaintiff. Civil records on index books from 1870s; on computer back to 1996.

Criminal Records: Access: In person only. Visitors must perform in person searches for themselves. Search fee: No search fee. Required to search: name, years to search, DOB. Criminal records on index books from 1870s; on computer back to 1996.

General Information: Public access terminal is available. No mental health records released. SASE required. Turnaround time 1-2 days. Fax notes: Fee to fax results is $2.00 per document. Copy fee: $.20 per page. Certification fee: $1.00. Fee payee: Clerk of District Court. Personal checks accepted. Prepayment is required.

Jefferson County Court 411 Fourth St, Fairbury, NE 68352; 402-729-2312. Hours: 8AM-Noon, 1-5PM (CST). *Misdemeanor, Civil Actions Under $45,000, Eviction, Small Claims, Probate.*

Civil Records: Access: Mail, in person. Both court and visitors may perform in person searches. No search fee. Required to search: name, years to search. Civil cases indexed by defendant, plaintiff. Civil records on cards from 1988, prior on docket books; computerized records from 10/1999.

Criminal Records: Access: Mail, in person. Both court and visitors may perform in person searches. No search fee. Required to search: name, years to search, DOB, signed release. Criminal records on cards from 1988, prior on docket books; computerized records from 9/1996.

General Information: Public access terminal is available. No adoption or sealed records released. SASE required. Turnaround time varies. Fax notes: Will not fax results. Copy fee: $.25 per page. Certification fee: $1.00. Fee payee: County Court. Personal checks accepted. Prepayment is required.

Johnson County

District Court PO Box 416, Tecumseh, NE 68450; 402-335-6301; Fax: 402-335-6311. Hours: 8AM-Noon, 1-4:30PM (CST). *Felony, Civil Actions Over $15,000.*

Civil Records: Access: In person only. Both court and visitors may perform in person searches. No search fee. Required to search: name, years to search. Civil cases indexed by defendant, plaintiff. Civil records on index and docket books from late 1800s, microfiche back 7 years.

Criminal Records: Access: In person only. Both court and visitors may perform in person searches. No search fee. Required to search: name, years to search. Criminal records on index and docket books from late 1800s, microfiche back 7 years.

General Information: Public access terminal is available. No juvenile records released. Fax notes: Fee to fax results is $2.00 per document. Copy fee: $.50 per page. Certification fee: $1.50. Fee payee: Clerk of District Court. Personal checks accepted. Prepayment is required.

Johnson County Court PO Box 285, Tecumseh, NE 68450; 402-335-6313; Fax: 402-335-6314. Hours: 8AM-4:30PM (CST). *Misdemeanor, Civil Actions Under $45,000, Eviction, Small Claims, Probate.*

Note: The court is in the process of computerizing their records.

Civil Records: Access: Mail, in person. Both court and visitors may perform in person searches. Search fee: cost of copies. Required to search: name, years to search; also helpful: address. Civil cases indexed by defendant, plaintiff. Civil records on index cards back 15 years, microfiche back to late 1800s for probate.

Criminal Records: Access: Mail, in person. Both court and visitors may perform in person searches. Search fee: cost of copies. Required to search: name, years to search, DOB, signed release; also helpful: address, SSN. Criminal records on index cards back 15 years.

General Information: No adoption or juvenile records released. Copy fee: $.25 per page. Certification fee: $1.00. Fee payee: County Court. Personal checks accepted. Prepayment is required.

Kearney County

District Court PO Box 208, Minden, NE 68959; 308-832-1742; Fax: 308-832-0636. Hours: 8:30AM-5PM (CST). *Felony, Civil Actions Over $15,000.*

Civil Records: Access: In person only. Visitors must perform in person searches for themselves. No search fee. Required to search: name, years to search. Civil cases indexed by defendant, plaintiff. All records on microfilm since 1800s; on computer back to 9/1998. Mail access available to attorneys only.

Criminal Records: Access: In person only. Visitors must perform in person searches for themselves. No search fee. Required to search: name, years to search. Criminal records on microfilm since 1800s; on computer back to 9/1998.

General Information: Public access terminal is available. (For records since 09/98.) No mental health records released. Copy fee: $.25 per page. Certification fee: $1.50. Fee payee: Clerk of District Court. Personal checks accepted. Prepayment is required.

Kearney County Court PO Box 377, Minden, NE 68959; 308-832-2719; Fax: 308-832-0636. Hours: 8:30AM-5PM (CST). *Misdemeanor, Civil Actions Under $45,000, Eviction, Small Claims, Probate.*

Civil Records: Access: In person only. Visitors must perform in person searches for themselves. No search fee. Required to search: name, years to search. Civil cases indexed by defendant. Civil records computerized since 10/99, rest on index cards, some probate on microfiche.

Criminal Records: Access: In person only. Visitors must perform in person searches for themselves. No search fee. Required to search: name, years to search. Criminal records computerized since 03/97.

General Information: Public access terminal is available. Copy fee: $.25 per page. Certification fee: $1.00. Fee payee: Kearney County Court. Personal checks accepted. Prepayment is required.

Keith County

District Court PO Box 686, Ogallala, NE 69153; 308-284-3849; Fax: 308-284-3978. Hours: 8AM-4PM (MST). *Felony, Civil Actions Over $15,000.*

Civil Records: Access: Fax, mail, in person. Both court and visitors may perform in person searches. No search fee. Required to search: name, years to search. Civil cases indexed by defendant, plaintiff. Civil records on index books from late 1800s; on computer back to 1975.

Criminal Records: Access: Fax, mail, in person. Both court and visitors may perform in person searches. No search fee. Required to search: name, years to search, DOB. Criminal records on index books from late 1800s; on computer back to 1975.

General Information: Public access terminal is available. No juvenile or mental health records released. SASE not required. Turnaround time 2-3 days. Fax notes: No fee to fax results. Fee is charged if long distance. Copy fee: $.25 per page. Certification fee: $1.00. Fee payee: Clerk of District Court. Personal checks accepted.

Keith County Court PO Box 358, Ogallala, NE 69153; 308-284-3693; Fax: 308-284-6825. Hours: 8AM-5PM (MST). *Misdemeanor, Civil Actions Under $45,000, Eviction, Small Claims, Probate.*

Civil Records: Access: In person only. Visitors must perform in person searches for themselves. No search fee. Required to search: name, years to search. Civil cases indexed by defendant, plaintiff. Civil records on index cards, files; computerized records since 1997.

Criminal Records: Access: In person only. Visitors must perform in person searches for themselves. No search fee. Required to search: name, years to search. Criminal records on index cards, files; computerized records since 1997.

General Information: Public access terminal is available. No adoption records released. Copy fee: $.25 per page. Certification fee: $1.25. Fee payee: County Court. Local checks only.

Keya Paha County

District Court PO Box 349, Springview, NE 68778; 402-497-3791; Fax: 402-497-3799. Hours: 8AM-5PM (CST). *Felony, Civil Actions Over $15,000.*

Civil Records: Access: Fax, mail, in person. Both court and visitors may perform in person searches. No search fee. Required to search: name, years to search. Civil cases indexed by defendant, plaintiff. Civil records on microfiche 7-9 years, on docket books since late 1800s.

Criminal Records: Access: Fax, mail, in person. Both court and visitors may perform in person searches. No search fee. Required to search: name, years to search. Computerized back to 2000, criminal records on microfiche 7-9 years, on docket books since late 1800s.

General Information: No confidential records released. SASE required. Turnaround time 3-4 days. Fax notes: $2.00 for first page, $1.00 each add'l. Copy fee: $.25 per page. Legal Size Copy Fee: $.30 per page. Certification fee: $4.00. Fee payee: Clerk of District Court. Personal checks accepted. Prepayment required.

Keya Paha County Court PO Box 275, Springview, NE 68778; 402-497-3021. Hours: 8AM-Noon M; 8AM-4:30PM Th,F (CST). *Misdemeanor, Civil Actions Under $45,000, Eviction, Small Claims, Probate.*

Civil Records: Access: In person only. Visitors must perform in person searches for themselves. No search fee. Required to search: name, years to search; also helpful: address. Civil cases indexed by defendant, plaintiff. Civil records in index books and files, many records on microfiche, back to late 1800s.

Criminal Records: Access: In person only. Visitors must perform in person searches for themselves. No search fee. Required to search: name, years to search; also helpful: address, DOB, SSN. Criminal records in index books and files, many records on microfiche, back to late 1800s.

General Information: No juvenile records released. Copy fee: $.25 per page. Certification fee: $1.25. Fee payee: County Clerk. Personal checks accepted.

Kimball County

District Court 114 E 3rd St, Kimball, NE 69145; 308-235-3591; Fax: 308-235-3654. Hours: 8AM-5PM M-Th, 8AM-4PM F (MST). *Felony, Civil Actions Over $15,000.*

Civil Records: Access: In person only. Visitors must perform in person searches for themselves. No search fee. Required to search: name, years to search. Civil cases indexed by defendant, plaintiff. Civil records on microfiche from 1960 forward, prior in books from early 1900s, computerized since 11/97.

Criminal Records: Access: In person only. Visitors must perform in person searches for themselves. No search fee. Required to search: name, years to search; also helpful: DOB. Criminal records on microfiche from 1960 forward, prior in books from early 1900s, computerized since 11/97.

General Information: Public access terminal is available. No mental health records released. Fax notes: Fee to fax results is $1.00 per page. Copy fee: $1.00 per page. Certification fee: $1.50. Fee payee: Clerk of District Court. Personal checks accepted. Prepayment is required.

Kimball County Court 114 E 3rd St, Kimball, NE 69145; 308-235-2831. Hours: 8AM-5PM (MST). *Misdemeanor, Civil Actions Under $45,000, Small Claims, Probate.*

Civil Records: Access: In person only. Visitors must perform in person searches for themselves. No search fee. Required to search: name, years to search. Civil cases indexed by defendant, plaintiff. Civil records on index cards and original files, also state computer.

Criminal Records: Access: In person only. Visitors must perform in person searches for themselves. No search fee. Required to search: name, years to search. Criminal records on index cards and original files.

General Information: Copy fee: The court reports that photocopying is not available. Certification fee: $1.25. Fee payee: County Court. Only cashiers checks and money orders accepted. Prepayment is required.

Knox County

District Court PO Box 126, Center, NE 68724; 402-288-4484; Fax: 402-288-4275. Hours: 8:30AM-4:30PM (CST). *Felony, Civil Actions Over $45,000.*

Civil Records: Access: In person only. Visitors must perform in person searches for themselves. No search fee. Required to search: name, years to search. Civil

cases indexed by defendant, plaintiff. Civil records on index books from 1874; on computer back to 9/1998.

Criminal Records: Access: In person only. Visitors must perform in person searches for themselves. No search fee. Required to search: name, years to search; also helpful: DOB. Criminal records on index books from 11874; on computer back 10 9/1998.

General Information: Public access terminal is available. No mental health records released. Copy fee: $.25 per page. Certification fee: $1.00. Fee payee: Clerk of District Court. Personal checks accepted.

Knox County Court PO Box 125, Center, NE 68724; 402-288-4277; Fax: 402-288-4275. Hours: 8:30AM-4:30PM (CST). *Misdemeanor, Civil Actions Under $45,000, Eviction, Small Claims, Probate.*

Civil Records: Access: In person only. Visitors must perform in person searches for themselves. No search fee. Required to search: name, years to search. Civil cases indexed by defendant, plaintiff. Civil records on index cards and general docket books from late 1800s; on computer from 10/2000.

Criminal Records: Access: In person only. Visitors must perform in person searches for themselves. No search fee. Required to search: name, years to search; also helpful: DOB. Criminal records on index cards and general docket books from late 1800s; on computer from 10/2000.

General Information: Public access terminal is available. No adoption records released. Fax notes: Fee to fax results is $1.00 per page. Copy fee: $.25 per page. Certification fee: $1.00. Fee payee: County Court. Personal checks accepted. Prepayment is required.

Lancaster County

District Court 575 S Tenth St, Lincoln, NE 68508-2810; 402-441-7328; Fax: 402-441-6190. Hours: 8AM-4:30PM (CST). *Felony, Civil Actions Over $15,000.*

www.ci.lincoln.ne.us/cnty/discrt/index.htm

Civil Records: Access: In person. Visitors may perform in person searches. No search fee. Required to search: name, years to search. Civil cases indexed by defendant, plaintiff. Civil records on computer from 1984, microfiche from 1900s, docket books from 1800s.

Criminal Records: Access: In person. Visitors may perform in person searches. No search fee. Required to search: name, years to search, DOB. Criminal records on computer from 1984, microfiche from 1900s, docket books from 1800s.

General Information: Public access terminal is available. No juvenile, mental health or grand jury records released. Copy fee: $.25 per page. Certification fee: $1.00. Fee payee: Clerk of District Court. Personal checks accepted. Prepayment is required.

Lancaster County Court 575 S 10th, Lincoln, NE 68508; 402-441-7291. Hours: 8AM-4:30PM (CST). *Misdemeanor, Civil Actions Under $45,000, Eviction, Small Claims, Probate.*

Civil Records: Access: In person, online. Visitors must perform in person searches for themselves. No search fee. Required to search: name, years to search. Civil cases indexed by defendant, plaintiff. Civil records on index books back to 1968, computerized since 11/98. Access to the Internet system requires registration and password. Call John at 402-471-3049 for more information. System can be searched by name or case number.

Criminal Records: Access: In person, online. Visitors must perform in person searches for themselves. No search fee. Required to search: name, years to search; also helpful: DOB. Criminal records on computer since 2/95; prior records are available if the case number is known. Online access to criminal records is the same as civil.

General Information: Public access terminal is available. (Criminal only.) No adoption records released. Copy fee: $.25 per page. Certification fee: $1.00. Fee payee: County Court. Personal checks accepted. Credit cards accepted: Visa, MasterCard. $3.00 service charge. Prepayment is required.

Lincoln County

District Court (301 N Jeffers Third Floor), PO Box 1616, North Platte, NE 69103-1616; 308-534-4350 X301 & X303. Hours: 8AM-5PM (CST). *Felony, Civil Actions Over $15,000.*

Civil Records: Access: In person only. Visitors must perform in person searches for themselves. No search fee. Required to search: name, years to search. Civil cases indexed by defendant, plaintiff. Civil records on computer back to 5/1997; books from 1866.

Criminal Records: Access: In person only. Visitors must perform in person searches for themselves. No search fee. Required to search: name, years to search. Criminal records on computer back to 5/1997; books from 1866.

General Information: Public access terminal is available. No sealed, court ordered or mental health records released. Copy fee: $.25 per page. Certification fee: $1.00. Fee payee: Clerk of District Court. Personal checks accepted. Prepayment is required.

Lincoln County Court PO Box 519, North Platte, NE 69103; 308-534-4350; Fax: 308-534-6468. Hours: 8AM-5PM (CST). *Misdemeanor, Civil Actions Under $45,000, Eviction, Small Claims, Probate.*

Civil Records: Access: In person only. Visitors must perform in person searches for themselves. No search fee. Required to search: name, years to search. Civil cases indexed by defendant, plaintiff. Civil records kept on index books back 20-25 years.

Criminal Records: Access: In person only. Visitors must perform in person searches for themselves. No search fee. Required to search: name, years to search, DOB. Criminal records on computer since 04/97; prior on books back 20 years.

General Information: Public access terminal is available. No adoption records released. Copy fee: $.25 per page. Certification fee: $1.00. Fee payee: County Court. Personal checks accepted. Credit cards accepted: Visa, MasterCard, Discover. $3.00 service charge. Prepayment is required.

Logan County

District Court PO Box 8, Stapleton, NE 69163; 308-636-2311. Hours: 8:30AM-Noon; 1PM-4:30PM M-TH; 8:30AM-Noon; 1PM-4PM F (CST). *Felony, Civil Actions Over $15,000.*

Civil Records: Access: Mail, in person. Both court and visitors may perform in person searches. No search fee. Required to search: name, years to search. Civil cases indexed by defendant, plaintiff. Civil records on docket books; computerized records since 2000.

Criminal Records: Access: Mail, in person. Both court and visitors may perform in person searches. No search fee. Required to search: name, years to search. Criminal records on docket books; computerized records since 2000.

General Information: Turnaround time same day. Copy fee: $.50 per page. Certification fee: $1.00. Fee payee: Clerk of the District Court. Personal checks accepted. Prepayment is required.

Logan County Court PO Box 8, Stapleton, NE 69163; 308-636-2677. Hours: 8AM-Noon, 1-4:30PM M-Th; 8:30AM-Noon, 1-4PM F (CST). *Misdemeanor, Civil Actions Under $45,000, Eviction, Small Claims, Probate.*

Civil Records: Access: Fax, mail, in person. Both court and visitors may perform in person searches. No search fee. Required to search: name, years to search; also

helpful: address. Civil cases indexed by defendant, plaintiff. Civil records on docket books since 1837.

Criminal Records: Access: Fax, mail, in person. Both court and visitors may perform in person searches. No search fee. Required to search: name, years to search, signed release; also helpful: DOB. Criminal records on docket books since 1837.

General Information: Adoption and juvenile records are not released. SASE required. Turnaround time 3-4 days. Fax notes: Fee to fax results is $3.00 1st page, $1.00 each add'l. Copy fee: $.25 per page. Certification fee: $1.00. Fee payee: County Court. Personal checks accepted. Prepayment is required.

Loup County

District Court PO Box 146, Taylor, NE 68879; 308-942-6035; Fax: 308-942-6015. Hours: 8:30AM-4:30PM M-Th, 8:30AM-Noon F (CST). *Felony, Civil Actions Over $15,000.*

Civil Records: Access: In person only. Visitors must perform in person searches for themselves. No search fee. Required to search: name, years to search. Civil cases indexed by defendant, plaintiff. Civil records in index books from late 1800s.

Criminal Records: Access: In person only. Visitors must perform in person searches for themselves. No search fee. Required to search: name, years to search; also helpful: address, DOB, SSN. Criminal records in index books from late 1800s.

General Information: No juvenile or adoption records released. Fax notes: Fee to fax results is $3.00 1st page; $1.00 each add'l. Copy fee: $.25 per page. Certification fee: $1.00. Fee payee: Clerk of District Court. Personal checks accepted. Prepayment is required.

Loup County Court PO Box 146, Taylor, NE 68879; 308-942-6035; Fax: 308-942-6015. Hours: 8:30AM-4:30PM M-Th, 8:30AM-Noon F (CST). *Misdemeanor, Civil Actions Under $45,000, Eviction, Small Claims, Probate.*

Civil Records: Access: In person only. Visitors must perform in person searches for themselves. No search fee. Required to search: name, years to search. Civil cases indexed by defendant, plaintiff. Civil records on index books since late 1800s. Some records have been filmed and forwarded to state archives.

Criminal Records: Access: In person only. Visitors must perform in person searches for themselves. No search fee. Required to search: name, years to search. Criminal records on index books since late 1800s. Some records have been filmed and forwarded to state archives.

General Information: Fax notes: Fee to fax results is $3.00 1st page; $1.00 each add'l. Copy fee: $.25 per page. Certification fee: $1.00. Fee payee: County Court. Personal checks accepted. Prepayment is required.

Madison County

District Court PO Box 249, Madison, NE 68748; 402-454-3311 X140; Fax: 402-454-6528. Hours: 8AM-5PM (CST). *Felony, Civil Actions Over $15,000.*

Civil Records: Access: In person only. Visitors must perform in person searches for themselves. No search fee. Required to search: name, years to search. Civil cases indexed by defendant, plaintiff. Civil records on microfiche from late 1970s, prior on docket books from 1800s; computerized records go back to 1987.

Criminal Records: Access: In person only. Visitors must perform in person searches for themselves. No search fee. Required to search: name, years to search. Criminal records on microfiche from late 1970s, prior on docket books from 1800s; computerized records go back to 1987.

General Information: Public access terminal is available. No mental health records released. Copy fee:

$.25 per page. Certification fee: $1.50. Fee payee: Clerk of District Court. Personal checks accepted.

Madison County Court PO Box 230, Madison, NE 68748; 402-454-3311 X73; Fax: 402-454-3438. Hours: 8:30AM-5PM (CST). *Misdemeanor, Civil Actions Under $45,000, Eviction, Small Claims, Probate.*

Civil Records: Access: Mail, in person. Visitors must perform in person searches for themselves. No search fee. Required to search: name, years to search. Civil cases indexed by defendant, plaintiff. Civil records on computer since 1986, prior on docket book, cards.

Criminal Records: Access: Mail, in person. Visitors must perform in person searches for themselves. No search fee. Required to search: name, years to search, DOB. Criminal records on computer from 1986.

General Information: Public access terminal is available. No adoption records released. Copy fee: $.25 per page. Certification fee: $1.00. Fee payee: Madison County Court. Personal checks accepted. Prepayment is required.

McPherson County

District Court PO Box 122, Tryon, NE 69167; 308-587-2363; Fax: 308-587-2363 (Call first). Hours: 8:30AM-4:30PM (CST). *Felony, Civil Actions Over $15,000.*

Civil Records: Access: Fax, mail, in person. Both court and visitors may perform in person searches. No search fee. Required to search: name, years to search; also helpful: address. Civil cases indexed by defendant, plaintiff. Civil records on index books since late 1800s.

Criminal Records: Access: Fax, mail, in person. Both court and visitors may perform in person searches. No search fee. Required to search: name, years to search; also helpful: address, DOB, SSN. Criminal records on index books since late 1800s.

General Information: No adoption records released. SASE required. Turnaround time 3-4 days. Fax notes: $2.00 for first page, $1.00 each add'l. Copy fee: $.50 per page. Certification fee: $1.50. Fee payee: Clerk of District Court. Business checks accepted. Prepayment is required.

McPherson County Court PO Box 122, Tryon, NE 69167; 308-587-2363; Fax: 308-587-2363 (Call first). Hours: 8:30AM-Noon, 1-4:30PM (CST). *Misdemeanor, Civil Actions Under $45,000, Eviction, Small Claims, Probate.*

Civil Records: Access: Fax, mail, in person. Both court and visitors may perform in person searches. No search fee. Required to search: name, years to search; also helpful: address. Civil cases indexed by defendant, plaintiff. Civil records computerized since 06/99, rest on index cards, are not computerized.

Criminal Records: Access: Fax, mail, in person. Both court and visitors may perform in person searches. No search fee. Required to search: name, years to search, signed release; also helpful: address, DOB. Criminal records computerized since 08/98.

General Information: Adoption and juvenile records are not released. SASE required. Turnaround time 3-4 days. Fax notes: Fee to fax results is $3.00 1st page, $1.00 each add'l. Copy fee: $.25 per page. Certification fee: $1.00. Fee payee: County Court. Personal checks accepted. Prepayment is required.

Merrick County

District Court PO Box 27, Central City, NE 68826; 308-946-2461; Fax: 308-946-3692. Hours: 8AM-5PM (CST). *Felony, Civil Actions Over $15,000.*

Civil Records: Access: In person only. Visitors must perform in person searches for themselves. No search fee. Required to search: name, years to search. Civil cases indexed by defendant, plaintiff. Civil records on index books from 1860; on computer back to 1994.

Criminal Records: Access: In person only. Visitors must perform in person searches for themselves. No search fee. Required to search: name, years to search, signed release. Criminal records on index books from 1860; on computer back to 1994.

General Information: Public access terminal is available. No probation or mental health records released. Copy fee: $.25 per page. Certification fee: $1.00. Fee payee: Clerk of District Court. Personal checks accepted.

Merrick County Court County Courthouse, PO Box 27, Central City, NE 68826; 308-946-2812. Hours: 8AM-5PM (CST). *Misdemeanor, Civil Actions Under $45,000, Eviction, Small Claims, Probate.*

Civil Records: Access: In person only. Visitors must perform in person searches for themselves. No search fee. Required to search: name, years to search. Civil cases indexed by defendant, plaintiff. Civil records on index books from 1860; on computer back to 1994.

Criminal Records: Access: In person only. Visitors must perform in person searches for themselves. No search fee. Required to search: name, years to search, DOB. Criminal records on index books from 1860; on computer back to 1994.

General Information: Public access terminal is available. No financial affidavits or sealed records released. Copy fee: $.25 per page. Certification fee: $1.00. Fee payee: County Court. Personal checks accepted. Prepayment is required.

Morrill County

District Court PO Box 824, Bridgeport, NE 69336; 308-262-1261; Fax: 308-262-1799. Hours: 8AM-Noon, 1-4:30PM (MST). *Felony, Civil Actions Over $15,000.*

Civil Records: Access: In person only. Visitors must perform in person searches for themselves. Search fee: No search fee. Required to search: name, years to search. Civil cases indexed by defendant, plaintiff. Computerized records back to 11/97; civil records on microfilm, books dating back to late 1800s.

Criminal Records: Access: In person. Visitors must perform in person searches for themselves. Search fee: No search fee. Required to search: name, years to search. Criminal records on microfilm, books dating back to late 1800s.

General Information: Public access terminal is available. No mental health records released. Certification fee: $1.00. Fee payee: Clerk of District Court. Prepayment is required.

Morrill County Court PO Box 418, Bridgeport, NE 69336; 308-262-0812. Hours: 8AM-4:30PM (MST). *Misdemeanor, Civil Actions Under $45,000, Eviction, Small Claims, Probate.*

Civil Records: Access: In person only. Visitors must perform in person searches for themselves. No search fee. Required to search: name, years to search. Civil cases indexed by defendant, plaintiff. Civil records on index books to 1908; probate on microfiche.

Criminal Records: Access: In person only. Visitors must perform in person searches for themselves. No search fee. Required to search: name, years to search. Criminal records on index books to 1908; probate on microfiche.

General Information: No adoption records released. No copy fee. Certification fee: $1.00. Fee payee: County Court. Personal checks accepted. Prepayment is required.

Nance County

District Court PO Box 338, Fullerton, NE 68638; 308-536-2365; Fax: 308-536-2742. Hours: 8AM-5PM (CST). *Felony, Civil Actions Over $15,000.*

Civil Records: Access: Phone, fax, mail, in person. Both court and visitors may perform in person searches. No search fee. Required to search: name, years to

search; also helpful: address. Civil cases indexed by defendant, plaintiff. Civil records on index books from late 1800s.

Criminal Records: Access: Phone, fax, mail, in person. Both court and visitors may perform in person searches. No search fee. Required to search: name, years to search; also helpful: address, DOB, SSN. Criminal records on index books from late 1800s.

General Information: No mental health records released. SASE required. Turnaround time 2 days. Fax notes: $1.00 per page plus copy fees. Copy fee: $.25 per page. Certification fee: $1.00. Fee payee: Clerk of District Court. Personal checks accepted. Prepayment is required.

Nance County Court PO Box 837, Fullerton, NE 68638; 308-536-2675; Fax: 308-536-2742. Hours: 8AM-5PM (CST). *Misdemeanor, Civil Actions Under $45,000, Eviction, Small Claims, Probate.*

Civil Records: Access: Mail, in person. Both court and visitors may perform in person searches. No search fee. Required to search: name, years to search; also helpful: address. Civil cases indexed by defendant, plaintiff. Civil records on index cards since late 1800s, computerized since 01/01, probate on microfilm.

Criminal Records: Access: Mail, in person. Both court and visitors may perform in person searches. No search fee. Required to search: name, years to search; also helpful: address, DOB. Criminal records on index cards since late 1800s, computerized since 01/01, probate on microfilm.

General Information: Public access terminal is available. No juvenile, psychological reports or adoption records released. SASE required. Turnaround time 1-2 days. Copy fee: $.25 per page. Certification fee: $1.00. Fee payee: County Court. Personal checks accepted. Prepayment is required.

Nemaha County

District Court 1824 N St, Auburn, NE 68305; 402-274-3616; Fax: 402-274-4478. Hours: 8AM-5PM (CST). *Felony, Civil Actions Over $15,000.*

Civil Records: Access: In person, mail. Both court and visitors may perform in person searches. Court will search on a time available basis No search fee. Required to search: name, years to search; also helpful: address. Civil cases indexed by defendant, plaintiff. Civil records on general index and docket books since the late 1800s; computerized records go back to 1998.

Criminal Records: Access: In person, mail. Both court and visitors may perform in person searches. Court will search on a time available basis. No search fee. Required to search: name, years to search; also helpful: address, DOB, SSN. Criminal records on general index and docket books since1950; computerized records go back to 1998.

General Information: Public access terminal is available. No mental, juvenile records released. Copy fee: $.25 per page. Certification fee: $1.00. Fee payee: Clerk of District Court. Personal checks accepted. Prepayment is required.

Nemaha County Court 1824 N St, Auburn, NE 68305; 402-274-3008; Fax: 402-274-4605. Hours: 8AM-Noon, 1-5PM (CST). *Misdemeanor, Civil Actions Under $45,000, Eviction, Small Claims, Probate.*

Note: This court also handles adoption, juvenile, and preliminary felony hearings.

Civil Records: Access: In person only. Visitors must perform in person searches for themselves. No search fee. Required to search: name, years to search. Civil cases indexed by defendant, plaintiff. Civil records on index books since late 1800s, computerized records go back to 4/2000.

Criminal Records: Access: In person only. Visitors must perform in person searches for themselves. No

search fee. Required to search: name, years to search; also helpful: DOB, SSN. Criminal records on index books since late 1800s, computerized records go back to 4/2000.

General Information: No adoption records released. Copy fee: $.25 per page. Certification fee: $1.00. Fee payee: Clerk of County Court. Personal checks accepted.

Nuckolls County

District Court PO Box 362, Nelson, NE 68961; 402-225-4341; Fax: 402-225-2373. Hours: 8:30AM-4:30PM (CST). *Felony, Civil Actions Over $15,000.*

Civil Records: Access: In person only. Visitors must perform in person searches for themselves. No search fee. Required to search: name, years to search. Civil cases indexed by defendant, plaintiff. Civil records on index books since late 1800s, computerized since 2000. Search services not available to employment agencies.

Criminal Records: Access: In person. Visitors must perform in person searches for themselves. No search fee. Required to search: name, years to search. Criminal records on index books since late 1800s, computerized since 2000.

General Information: Public access terminal is available. Copy fee: $.25 per page. Certification fee: $1.00. Fee payee: Clerk of District Court. Personal checks accepted. Prepayment is required.

Nuckolls County Court PO Box 372, Nelson, NE 68961; 402-225-2371; Fax: 402-225-2373. Hours: 8AM-4:30PM (CST). *Misdemeanor, Civil Actions Under $45,000, Eviction, Small Claims, Probate.*

Civil Records: Access: In person only. Visitors must perform in person searches for themselves. No search fee. Required to search: name, years to search. Civil cases indexed by defendant, plaintiff. Civil records on index cards, probate on microfilm. Mail access limited to short searches.

Criminal Records: Access: In person only. Visitors must perform in person searches for themselves. No search fee. Required to search: name, years to search. Criminal records on index cards, probate on microfilm.

General Information: No adoption or juvenile records released. Copy fee: $.25 per page. Certification fee: $1.00. Fee payee: County Court. Personal checks accepted. Prepayment is required.

Otoe County

District Court 1021 Central Ave, Rm 209, PO Box 726, Nebraska City, NE 68410; 402-873-9550. Hours: 8AM-Noon, 1-5PM (CST). *Felony, Civil Actions Over $15,000.*

Civil Records: Access: In person only. Visitors must perform in person searches for themselves. No search fee. Required to search: name, years to search, address. Civil cases indexed by defendant, plaintiff. Civil records on index books from late 1800s, computerized from 08/97.

Criminal Records: Access: In person only. Visitors must perform in person searches for themselves. No search fee. Required to search: name, years to search. Criminal records on index books from late 1800s, computerized from 08/97.

General Information: Public access terminal is available. Copy fee: $1.00 per page. Certification fee: $1.00. Fee payee: Clerk of District Court. Personal checks accepted. Prepayment is required.

Otoe County Court 1021 Central Ave, Rm 109, PO Box 487, Nebraska City, NE 68410-0487; 402-873-9575; Fax: 402-873-9030. Hours: 8AM-5PM (CST). *Misdemeanor, Civil Actions Under $45,000, Eviction, Small Claims, Probate.*

Civil Records: Access: Phone, fax, mail, in person. Only the court performs in person searches; visitors may not. No search fee. Required to search: name, years

to search. Civil cases indexed by defendant, plaintiff. Civil records go back to 1986; computerized records go to 1999.

Criminal Records: Access: Fax, mail, in person. Both the court and visitors may perform in person searches No search fee. Required to search: name, offense; also helpful: years to search, address, DOB. Criminal records go back to 1981; computerized since 1977.

General Information: Public access terminal is available. (Public access is thru the District Court terminal) No adoption records released without court order; juvenile records only released with signed release statement. SASE required. Turnaround time 2-3 days. Fax notes: $1.00 per page. Copy fee: $.25 per page. Certification fee: $1.00. Fee payee: County Court. Personal checks accepted. Prepayment is required.

Pawnee County

District Court PO Box 431, Pawnee City, NE 68420; 402-852-2963. Hours: 8AM-4PM (CST). *Felony, Civil Actions Over $15,000.*

Civil Records: Access: Phone, mail, in person. Both court and visitors may perform in person searches. Search fee: $3.00 per name. Required to search: name, years to search. Civil cases indexed by defendant, plaintiff. Civil records on index books since late 1800s.

Criminal Records: Access: Phone, mail, in person. Both court and visitors may perform in person searches. Search fee: $3.00 per name. Required to search: name, years to search. Criminal records on index books since late 1800s.

General Information: No mental health records released. SASE required. Turnaround time 2 weeks, limited phone searches immediate. Copy fee: $.50 per page. Certification fee: $1.00. Fee payee: Clerk of District Court. Personal checks accepted.

Pawnee County Court PO Box 471, Pawnee City, NE 68420; 402-852-2388; Fax: 402-852-2388. Hours: 8AM-4:30PM (CST). *Misdemeanor, Civil Actions Under $45,000, Eviction, Small Claims, Probate.*

Note: Probate requests are accepted by mail.

Civil Records: Access: In person only. Visitors must perform in person searches for themselves. No search fee. Required to search: name, years to search; also helpful: address. Civil cases indexed by defendant, plaintiff. Civil records indexed on computer since late 1980s and books back to late 1800s.

Criminal Records: Access: In person only. Visitors must perform in person searches for themselves. No search fee. Required to search: name, years to search, DOB; also helpful: SSN. Criminal records indexed on computer since late 1980s and books back to late 1800s.

General Information: Public access terminal is available. No adoption records released. Copy fee: $.25 per page. Certification fee: $1.00. Fee payee: County Court. Personal checks accepted. Prepayment required.

Perkins County

District Court PO Box 156, Grant, NE 69140; 308-352-4643; Fax: 308-352-2455. Hours: 8AM-4PM (MST). *Felony, Civil Actions Over $15,000.*

Civil Records: Access: Fax, mail, in person. Both court and visitors may perform in person searches. No search fee. Required to search: name, years to search. Civil cases indexed by defendant, plaintiff. Civil records on index books since late 1800s.

Criminal Records: Access: Fax, mail, in person. Both court and visitors may perform in person searches. No search fee. Required to search: name, years to search. Criminal records on index books since late 1800s.

General Information: All records public. SASE required. Turnaround time is 2-4 days. Fax notes: $3.00 per document. add'l fees if over 10 pages. Copy fee: $.50 per page. Certification fee: $1.50. Fee payee: Clerk

of District Court. Personal checks accepted. All fees may billed.

Perkins County Court PO Box 222, Grant, NE 69140; 308-352-4415; Fax: 308-352-2455. Hours: 8AM-4PM (MST). *Misdemeanor, Civil Actions Under $45,000, Eviction, Small Claims, Probate.*

Civil Records: Access: Phone, fax, mail, in person. Both court and visitors may perform in person searches. No search fee. Required to search: name, years to search. Civil cases indexed by defendant, plaintiff. Civil records on index cards from 1987, prior on books; probate on microfilm & hard copy.

Criminal Records: Access: Phone, fax, mail, in person. Both court and visitors may perform in person searches. No search fee. Required to search: name, years to search; also helpful: DOB, SSN. Criminal records on index cards from 1987, prior on books; probate on microfilm & hard copy.

General Information: No sealed records released. SASE required. Turnaround time 3-4 days. Copy fee: $.25 per page. Certification fee: $1.00. Fee payee: Perkins County Court. Personal checks accepted. Prepayment is required.

Phelps County

District Court PO Box 462, Holdrege, NE 68949; 308-995-2281. Hours: 9AM-5PM (CST). *Felony, Civil Actions Over $45,000.*

Civil Records: Access: In person only. Visitors must perform in person searches for themselves. Search fee: No search fee. Required to search: name, years to search. Civil cases indexed by defendant, plaintiff. Civil records on computer from 3/1998, on books back to 1885.

Criminal Records: Access: In person only. Visitors must perform in person searches for themselves. No search fee. Required to search: name, years to search; also helpful: DOB. Criminal records on computer from 3/1998, on books prior back to 1885.

General Information: Public access terminal is available. No mental health, sealed records released. Copy fee: $.25 per page. Certification fee: $1.00. Fee payee: Clerk of District Court. Personal checks accepted.

Phelps County Court PO Box 255, Holdrege, NE 68949; 308-995-6561; Fax: 308-995-6562. Hours: 8AM-5PM (CST). *Misdemeanor, Civil Actions Under $45,000, Eviction, Small Claims, Probate.*

Civil Records: Access: In person only. Visitors must perform in person searches for themselves. No search fee. Required to search: name, years to search. Civil cases indexed by defendant, plaintiff. Civil records computerized since 1999, on index cards going back to late 1970s; probate on microfiche to late 1800s.

Criminal Records: Access: In person only. Visitors must perform in person searches for themselves. No search fee. Required to search: name, years to search, DOB, signed release. Criminal records computerized since 1998, in files to 1987.

General Information: Public access terminal is available. No adoption records released. Copy fee: $.25 per page. Certification fee: $1.25. Fee payee: County Court. Personal checks accepted. Prepayment required.

Pierce County

District Court 111 W Court St, Rm 12, Pierce, NE 68767; 402-329-4335; Fax: 402-329-6412. Hours: 8:30 AM-4:30PM (CST). *Felony, Civil Actions Over $15,000.*

Civil Records: Access: In person only. Visitors must perform in person searches for themselves. No search fee. Required to search: name, years to search. Civil cases indexed by defendant, plaintiff. Civil records on index books from 1870s; on computer back to 3/1999.

Criminal Records: Access: In person only. Visitors must perform in person searches for themselves. No search fee. Required to search: name, years to search; also helpful: address, DOB, SSN. Criminal records on index books from 1870s; on computer back to 3/1999.
General Information: Public access terminal is available. No mental health records released. Copy fee: $.25 per page. Certification fee: $1.00. Fee payee: Clerk of District Court. Personal checks accepted.

Pierce County Court 111 W Court St, Rm 11, Pierce, NE 68767; 402-329-6245; Fax: 402-329-6412. Hours: 8:30AM-4:30PM (CST). *Misdemeanor, Civil Actions Under $45,000, Eviction, Small Claims, Probate.*
Civil Records: Access: In person only. Visitors must perform in person searches for themselves. No search fee. Required to search: name, years to search. Civil cases indexed by defendant, plaintiff. Civil records on index books back about 15 years.
Criminal Records: Access: In person only. Visitors must perform in person searches for themselves. No search fee. Required to search: name, years to search. Criminal records on index books back about 15 years.
General Information: Public access terminal is available. No adoption records released. Copy fee: $.25 per page. Certification fee: $1.00. Fee payee: County Court. Personal checks accepted. Prepayment required.

Platte County

District Court PO Box 1188, Columbus, NE 68602-1188; 402-563-4906; Fax: 402-562-6718. Hours: 8:30AM-5PM (CST). *Felony, Civil Actions Over $15,000.*
Civil Records: Access: In person only. Visitors must perform in person searches for themselves. No search fee. Required to search: name, years to search. Civil cases indexed by defendant, plaintiff. Civil records go back to 1800, civil records filed as hard copies; also on computer after 8/1/97.
Criminal Records: Access: In person only. Visitors must perform in person searches for themselves. No search fee. Required to search: name, years to search, DOB. Criminal records go back to 1880's, criminal records filed as hard copies; also on computer after 8/1/97.
General Information: Public access terminal is available. No juvenile or sealed records released. Copy fee: $.25 per page. Certification fee: $1.00. Fee payee: District Court. Only cashiers checks and money orders accepted.

Platte County Court PO Box 538, Columbus, NE 68602-0538; 402-563-4905; Fax: 402-562-8158. Hours: 8AM-5PM (CST). *Misdemeanor, Civil Actions Under $45,000, Eviction, Small Claims, Probate.*
Civil Records: Access: In person only. Visitors must perform in person searches for themselves. No search fee. Required to search: name, years to search. Civil cases indexed by defendant, plaintiff. Civil records on index books from 1980; on computer back to 1996.
Criminal Records: Access: In person only. Visitors must perform in person searches for themselves. No search fee. Required to search: name, years to search, DOB. Criminal records on index books from 1980; on computer back to 1996.
General Information: Public access terminal is available. No adoption records released. Copy fee: $.25 per page. Certification fee: $1.00 for seal. Fee payee: Platte County Court. Personal checks accepted. Prepayment required.

Polk County

District Court PO Box 447, Osceola, NE 68651; 402-747-3487; Fax: 402-747-8299. Hours: 8AM-Noon,1-5PM (CST). *Felony, Civil Actions Over $15,000.*
Civil Records: Access: In person only. Visitors must perform in person searches for themselves. No search fee. Required to search: name, years to search. Civil cases indexed by defendant, plaintiff. Civil records on index books from 1871.
Criminal Records: Access: In person only. Visitors must perform in person searches for themselves. No search fee. Required to search: name, years to search, DOB, signed release. Criminal records on index books from 1871.
General Information: Public access terminal is available. Copy fee: $.25 per page. Certification fee: $1.00. Fee payee: Clerk of District Court. Personal checks accepted. Prepayment is required.

Polk County Court PO Box 506, Osceola, NE 68651; 402-747-5371; Fax: 402-747-2656. Hours: 8AM-5PM (CST). *Misdemeanor, Civil Actions Under $45,000, Eviction, Small Claims, Probate.*
Civil Records: Access: In person only. Visitors must perform in person searches for themselves. No search fee. Required to search: name, years to search. Civil cases indexed by defendant, plaintiff. Civil records on index cards back to late 1970s; probate records back to late 1800s.
Criminal Records: Access: In person only. Visitors must perform in person searches for themselves. No search fee. Required to search: name, years to search, DOB. Criminal records on index cards back to late 1970s; on computer back to 8/2000.
General Information: Public access terminal is available. No adoption, juvenile records released. Copy fee: $.25 per page. Certification fee: $1.00 each. Fee payee: County Court. Personal checks accepted. Prepayment is required.

Red Willow County

District Court 520 Norris Ave (PO Box 847), McCook, NE 69001; 308-345-4583; Fax: 308-345-7907. Hours: 8AM-4PM (CST). *Felony, Civil Actions Over $15,000.*
Civil Records: Access: Fax, mail, in person, email. Both court and visitors may perform in person searches. No search fee. Required to search: name, years to search. Civil cases indexed by defendant, plaintiff. Civil records on index books since 1871, on microfiche since mid 1980s, computerized since 1998.
Criminal Records: Access: Fax, mail, in person., email. Both court and visitors may perform in person searches. No search fee. Required to search: name, years to search. Criminal records on index books since 1871, on microfiche since mid 1980s, computerized since 1998.
General Information: Public access terminal is available. SASE required. Turnaround time 2-4 days. Fax notes: $3.00 for first page, $1.00 each add'l. Copy fee: $.50 per page. Certification fee: $1.00. Fee payee: Clerk of District Court. Personal checks accepted. Prepayment is required.

Red Willow County Court 502 Norris Ave (PO Box 199), McCook, NE 69001; 308-345-1904; Fax: 308-345-1503. Hours: 8AM-4PM (CST). *Misdemeanor, Civil Actions Under $45,000, Eviction, Small Claims, Probate.*
Civil Records: Access: Mail, fax, in person. Both court and visitors may perform in person searches. No search fee. Required to search: name, years to search. Civil cases indexed by defendant, plaintiff. Civil records on case files and docket cards since 1984, probate on microfilm since 1977; on computer back to 1998.

Criminal Records: Access: Mail, fax, in person. Both court and visitors may perform in person searches. No search fee. Required to search: name, years to search, DOB. Criminal records on books since 1984; on computer back to 1998.
General Information: No adoption, juvenile, convictions set aside on misdemeanor offense, sealed records released. SASE required. Turnaround time 2 days. Fax notes: Fee to fax results is $3.00 per document. Copy fee: $.25 per page. Certification fee: $1.00. Fee payee: County Court. Personal checks accepted.

Richardson County

District Court 1700 Stone St, Falls City, NE 68355; 402-245-2023; Fax: 402-245-3725. Hours: 8:30AM-5PM (CST). *Felony, Civil Actions Over $15,000.*
Civil Records: Access: In person only. Visitors must perform in person searches for themselves. No search fee. Required to search: name, years to search. Civil cases indexed by defendant, plaintiff. Civil records on microfiche and at state archives to 1930; on computer back to 1998.
Criminal Records: Access: In person only. Visitors must perform in person searches for themselves. No search fee. Required to search: name, years to search, DOB, signed release. Criminal records on microfiche and at state archives to 1930; on computer back to 1998.
General Information: Public access terminal is available. No sealed records released. Copy fee: $.25 per page. Certification fee: $1.00. Fee payee: Clerk of District Court. Personal checks accepted. Prepayment is required.

Richardson County Court 1700 Stone St Room 205, Falls City, NE 68355; 402-245-2812; Fax: 402-245-3352. Hours: 8AM-5PM (CST). *Misdemeanor, Civil Actions Under $45,000, Eviction, Small Claims, Probate.*
Civil Records: Access: In person only. Visitors must perform in person searches for themselves. No search fee. Required to search: name, years to search. Civil cases indexed by defendant, plaintiff. Civil records on index cards back to 1970s.
Criminal Records: Access: In person only. Visitors must perform in person searches for themselves. No search fee. Required to search: name, years to search; also helpful: DOB. Criminal records on index cards back to 1970s.
General Information: Public access terminal is available. No adoption records released. Copy fee: $.25 per page. Certification fee: $1.00. Fee payee: County Court. Only cashiers checks and money orders accepted. Prepayment is required.

Rock County

District Court PO Box 367, Bassett, NE 68714; 402-684-3933; Fax: 402-684-2741. Hours: 9AM-5PM (CST). *Felony, Civil Actions Over $15,000.*
Civil Records: Access: Phone, fax, mail, in person. Both court and visitors may perform in person searches. No search fee. Required to search: name, years to search. Civil cases indexed by defendant, plaintiff. Civil records on index books since 1800s.
Criminal Records: Access: Phone, fax, mail, in person. Both court and visitors may perform in person searches. No search fee. Required to search: name, years to search, DOB. Criminal records on index books since 1800s.
General Information: No juvenile or sealed records released. SASE required. Turnaround time 1-2 days. Copy fee: $.25 per page. Certification fee: $1.50. Fee payee: Clerk of District Court. Personal checks accepted. Prepayment is required.

Rock County Court PO Box 249, Bassett, NE 68714; 402-684-3601; Fax: 402-684-2741. Hours:

8AM-5PM (CST). *Misdemeanor, Civil Actions Under $45,000, Eviction, Small Claims, Probate.*

Civil Records: Access: In person only. Visitors must perform in person searches for themselves. No search fee. Required to search: name, years to search. Civil cases indexed by defendant, plaintiff. Civil records on index books from 1800s, index cards from 1985; on computer back to 8/2000.

Criminal Records: Access: In person only. Visitors must perform in person searches for themselves. No search fee. Required to search: name, years to search, DOB. Criminal records on index books from 1800s, index cards from 1985; on computer back to 8/2000.

General Information: Public access terminal is available. Fax notes: Fee to fax results is $3.00 plus $1.00 per page. Copy fee: $.25 per page. Certification fee: $1.00. Fee payee: County Court. Personal checks accepted. Prepayment is required.

Saline County

District Court 215 S Court St, Wilber, NE 68465; 402-821-2823; Fax: 402-821-2132. Hours: 8AM-Noon, 1-5PM (CST). *Felony, Civil Actions Over $15,000.*

Civil Records: Access: In person only. Visitors must perform in person searches for themselves. No search fee. Required to search: name, years to search. Civil cases indexed by defendant, plaintiff. Civil records being entered on computer beginning 8/94, index in dockets books from 1800s.

Criminal Records: Access: In person only. Visitors must perform in person searches for themselves. No search fee. Required to search: name, years to search; also helpful: DOB. Criminal records being entered on computer beginning 8/94, index in dockets books from 1800s.

General Information: Public access terminal is available. No sealed or mental health records released. Copy fee: $.25 per page. Certification fee: $1.00. Fee payee: Clerk of District Court. Personal checks accepted. Prepayment is required.

Saline County Court PO Box 865, Wilber, NE 68465; 402-821-2131; Fax: 402-821-2132. Hours: 8AM-Noon; 1PM-5PM (CST). *Misdemeanor, Civil Actions Under $45,000, Eviction, Small Claims, Probate.*

Civil Records: Access: Fax, mail, in person. Both court and visitors may perform in person searches. No search fee. Required to search: name, years to search. Civil cases indexed by defendant, plaintiff. Civil records on index books from 1860s; computerized records since 1994.

Criminal Records: Access: Fax, mail, in person. Both court and visitors may perform in person searches. No search fee. Required to search: name, years to search. Criminal records on index books from 1860s; computerized records since 1994.

General Information: Public access terminal is available. (Available in District Court.) No juvenile or sealed records released. SASE required. Turnaround time 2-3 days. Fax notes: No fee to fax results. Copy fee: $.25 per page. Certification fee: $1.25. Fee payee: County Court. Personal checks accepted. Prepayment is required.

Sarpy County

District Court 1210 Golden Gate Dr, Ste 3141, Papillion, NE 68046; 402-593-2267; Fax: 402-593-4403. Hours: 8AM-4:45PM (CST). *Felony, Civil Actions Over $15,000.*

Civil Records: Access: Phone, mail, in person. Both court and visitors may perform in person searches. No search fee. Required to search: name, years to search. Civil cases indexed by defendant, plaintiff. Civil records on computer from 1979 forward, on books prior.

Criminal Records: Access: Phone, mail, in person. Both court and visitors may perform in person searches. No search fee. Required to search: name, years to search. Criminal records on computer from 1979 forward, on books prior. For phone requests, will only verify from computer index.

General Information: Public access terminal is available. No mental health or search warrant records released. SASE required. Turnaround time 1-2 days. Copy fee: $.75 for first page, $.25 each add'l. Certification fee: $1.00. Fee payee: Clerk of District Court. Only cashiers checks and money orders accepted. Prepayment is required.

Sarpy County Court 1210 Golden Gate Dr, Ste 3142, Papillion, NE 68046; 402-593-2246. Hours: 8AM-4:45PM (CST). *Misdemeanor, Civil Actions Under $45,000, Eviction, Small Claims, Probate.*

Civil Records: Access: In person, online. Visitors must perform in person searches for themselves. No search fee. Required to search: name, years to search. Civil cases indexed by defendant, plaintiff. Civil records on computer since 08/97; prior records on docket books and cards from 1800s. Access to the Internet system requires registration and password. Call John at 402-471-3049 for more information. System can be searched by name or case number.

Criminal Records: Access: In person, online. Visitors must perform in person searches for themselves. No search fee. Required to search: name, years to search, DOB. Criminal records on computer since 08/97; prior records on docket books and cards from 1800s. Online access to criminal records is the same as civil.

General Information: Public access terminal is available. No adoption records released. Copy fee: $.25 per page. Certification fee: $1.00. Fee payee: County Court. Personal checks accepted.

Saunders County

District Court County Courthouse, 433 N Chestnut, Wahoo, NE 68066; 402-443-8113; Fax: 402-443-8170. Hours: 8AM-5PM (CST). *Felony, Civil Actions Over $15,000.*

Civil Records: Access: In person only. Visitors must perform in person searches for themselves. No search fee. Required to search: name, years to search. Civil cases indexed by defendant, plaintiff. Civil records on index books to late 1800s; on computer back to 1998.

Criminal Records: Access: In person only. Visitors must perform in person searches for themselves. No search fee. Required to search: name, years to search; also helpful: DOB, SSN. Criminal records on index books to late 1800s; on computer back to 1998.

General Information: Public access terminal is available. No mental health records released. Copy fee: $.25 per page. Certification fee: $1.00. Fee payee: Clerk of District Court. Personal checks accepted.

Saunders County Court 433 N Chestnut, Wahoo, NE 68066; 402-443-8119; Fax: 402-443-5010. Hours: 8AM-5PM (CST). *Misdemeanor, Civil Actions Under $45,000, Eviction, Small Claims, Probate.*

Civil Records: Access: In person only. Visitors must perform in person searches for themselves. No search fee. Required to search: name, years to search. Civil cases indexed by defendant, plaintiff. Civil records on index books.

Criminal Records: Access: In person only. Visitors must perform in person searches for themselves. No search fee. Required to search: name, years to search. Criminal records on index books.

General Information: No adoption or sealed records released. Copy fee: $.25 per page. Certification fee: $1.00. Fee payee: County Court. Personal checks accepted. Prepayment is required.

Scotts Bluff County

District Court 1725 10th St, PO Box 47, Gering, NE 69341-0047; 308-436-6641; Fax: 308-436-6759. Hours: 8AM-4:30PM (MST). *Felony, Civil Actions Over $15,000.*

Civil Records: Access: In person only. Visitors must perform in person searches for themselves. No search fee. Required to search: name, years to search. Civil cases indexed by defendant, plaintiff. Civil records on index books to 1800s; on computer back to 1997.

Criminal Records: Access: In person only. Both court and visitors may perform in person searches. No search fee. Criminal records on index books to 1800s; on computer back to 1997.

General Information: Public access terminal is available. No juvenile or mental health records released. Copy fee: $.50 per page. Certification fee: $1.00. Fee payee: Clerk of District Court. Business checks accepted. Prepayment is required.

Scotts Bluff County Court 1725 10th St, Gering, NE 69341; 308-436-6648. Hours: 8AM-5PM (MST). *Misdemeanor, Civil Actions Under $45,000, Eviction, Small Claims, Probate.*

Civil Records: Access: In person only. Visitors must perform in person searches for themselves. No search fee. Required to search: name, years to search. Civil cases indexed by defendant, plaintiff. Civil records computerized since 2000.

Criminal Records: Access: In person only. Visitors must perform in person searches for themselves. No search fee. Required to search: name, years to search, DOB. Criminal records computerized since 2000.

General Information: Public access terminal is available. No adoption records released. Copy fee: $.25 per page. Certification fee: $1.00. Fee payee: County Court. Personal checks accepted. Prepayment is required.

Seward County

District Court PO Box 36, Seward, NE 68434; 402-643-4895. Hours: 8AM-5PM (CST). *Felony, Civil Actions Over $15,000.*

Civil Records: Access: In person only. Visitors must perform in person searches for themselves. No search fee. Required to search: name, years to search. Civil cases indexed by defendant, plaintiff. Civil records on index books since late 1800s; computerized since 6/98.

Criminal Records: Access: In person only. Visitors must perform in person searches for themselves. No search fee. Required to search: name, years to search. Criminal records on index books since late 1800s; computerized since 6/98.

General Information: Personal checks not accepted.

Seward County Court PO Box 37, Seward, NE 68434; 402-643-3341; Fax: 402-643-2950. Hours: 8AM-5PM (CST). *Misdemeanor, Civil Actions Under $45,000, Eviction, Small Claims, Probate.*

Civil Records: Access: Mail, in person. Both court and visitors may perform in person searches. No search fee. Required to search: name, years to search. Civil cases indexed by defendant, plaintiff. Civil records on index books, cards back to 1975, computerized back to 1997.

Criminal Records: Access: In person only. Both court and visitors may perform in person searches. No search fee. Required to search: name, years to search. Criminal records on index books, cards back to 1950.

General Information: No adoption, juvenile or sealed records released. Copy fee: $.25 per page. Certification fee: $1.00. Fee payee: County Court. Personal checks accepted. Prepayment is required.

Sheridan County

District Court PO Box 581, Rushville, NE 69360; 308-327-2123; Fax: 308-327-2689. Hours: 8:30AM-4:30PM (MST). *Felony, Civil Actions Over $10,000.*

Civil Records: Access: Mail, fax, in person. Both court and visitors may perform in person searches. Search fee: $5.00 per name. Required to search: name, years to search. Civil cases indexed by defendant, plaintiff. Civil records on index and docket books since 1800s, computerized since 1998.

Criminal Records: Access: Mail, fax, in person. Both court and visitors may perform in person searches. Search fee: $5.00 per name. Required to search: name, years to search, signed release; also helpful: DOB. Criminal records on index and docket books since 1800s, computerized since 1998.

General Information: Public access terminal is available. No mental health, grand jury records released. SASE required. Turnaround time 1-2 days. Copy fee: $.25 per page. Certification fee: $1.00. Fee payee: Clerk of District Court. Personal checks accepted.

Sheridan County Court PO Box 430, Rushville, NE 69360; 308-327-2692; Fax: 308-327-2936. Hours: 8AM-4:30PM (MST). *Misdemeanor, Civil Actions Under $45,000, Eviction, Small Claims, Probate.*

Civil Records: Access: In person only. Visitors must perform in person searches for themselves. No search fee. Required to search: name, years to search. Civil cases indexed by defendant, plaintiff. Civil records on index books, on microfiche from 1920 forward; on computer back to 6/2000.

Criminal Records: Access: Fax, mail, in person. Visitors must perform in person searches for themselves. No search fee. Required to search: name, years to search. Criminal records on index books, on microfiche from 1920 forward; on computer back to 6/2000.

General Information: Public access terminal is available. No adoption or confidential records released. SASE required. Turnaround time 1-2 days. Fax notes: No fee to fax results. Faxing available to 800 numbers only. Copy fee: $.25 per page. Certification fee: $1.00. Fee payee: Sheridan County Court. Personal checks accepted. Prepayment is required.

Sherman County

District Court 630 O St, PO Box 456, Loup City, NE 68853; 308-745-1513; Fax: 308-745-1820. Hours: 8:30AM-4:30PM (CST). *Felony, Civil Actions Over $15,000.*

Civil Records: Access: Mail, in person. Both court and visitors may perform in person searches. Search fee: $10.00 per name. Required to search: name, years to search. Civil cases indexed by defendant, plaintiff. Civil records on index and docket books since late 1800s; on computer back to 4/2000.

Criminal Records: Access: Mail, in person. Both court and visitors may perform in person searches. Search fee: $10.00 per name. Required to search: name, years to search. Criminal records on index and docket books since late 1800s; on computer back to 4/2000.

General Information: Public access terminal is available. No mental health records released. SASE required. Turnaround time 1-2 days. Copy fee: $.50 per page. Certification fee: $1.50. Fee payee: Clerk of District Court. Personal checks accepted.

Sherman County Court 630 O St, PO Box 55, Loup City, NE 68853; 308-745-1513 x102; Fax: 308-745-1510. Hours: 8:30AM-4:30PM (CST). *Misdemeanor, Civil Actions Under $45,000, Eviction, Small Claims, Probate.*

Civil Records: Access: Fax, mail, in person. Both court and visitors may perform in person searches. No search fee. Required to search: name, years to search. Civil

cases indexed by defendant, plaintiff. Civil records on index books from late 1800s; on computer back to 5/2000 in DC office. Newer names indexed by defendant only.

Criminal Records: Access: Fax, mail, in person. Both court and visitors may perform in person searches. No search fee. Required to search: name, years to search, DOB. Criminal records on index books from late 1800s; on computer back to 5/2000. Newer names indexed by defendant only.

General Information: Public access terminal is available. (Terminal located in District Court Office) No adoption records released. SASE required. Turnaround time 1-2 weeks. Fax notes: Fee to fax results is $3.00 1st page; $1.00 each add'l. No copy fee. Certification fee: $1.00. Fee payee: Sherman County Court. Business checks accepted. Prepayment required.

Sioux County

District Court PO Box 158, Harrison, NE 69346; 308-668-2443; Fax: 308-668-2443. Hours: 8AM-4;30PM (MST). *Felony, Civil Actions Over $15,000.*

Civil Records: Access: Mail, in person. Both court and visitors may perform in person searches. No search fee. Required to search: name, years to search. Civil cases indexed by defendant, plaintiff. Civil records in index and docket books since 1800s; computerized records since 1992.

Criminal Records: Access: Mail, in person. Both court and visitors may perform in person searches. No search fee. Required to search: name, years to search; also helpful: DOB, SSN. Criminal records in index and docket books since 1800s; computerized records since 1992.

General Information: Public access terminal is available. No adoption or sealed records released. SASE required. Turnaround time 3-4 days. Copy fee: $.25 per page. Certification fee: $1.00 per page. Fee payee: Clerk of District Court. Personal checks accepted. Prepayment is required.

Sioux County Court PO Box 158, Harrison, NE 69346; 308-668-2443; Fax: same. Hours: 8AM-4:30 (MST). *Misdemeanor, Civil Actions Under $45,000, Eviction, Small Claims, Probate.*

Civil Records: Access: Phone, fax, mail, in person. Both court and visitors may perform in person searches. No search fee. Required to search: name, years to search. Civil cases indexed by defendant, plaintiff. Civil records on index books from late 1800s. Prefer to take phone requests. Very few civil cases handled each year.

Criminal Records: Access: Phone, fax, mail, in person. Both court and visitors may perform in person searches. No search fee. Required to search: name, years to search. Criminal records on index books from late 1800s.

General Information: Public access terminal is available. No sealed, expunged, or adoption records released. SASE required. Turnaround time 3-4 days. Copy fee: $.25 per page. Certification fee: $1.00. Fee payee: County Court. Personal checks accepted. Prepayment is required.

Stanton County

District Court PO Box 347, Stanton, NE 68779; 402-439-2222; Fax: 402-439-2200. Hours: 8:30AM-4:30PM (CST). *Felony, Civil Actions Over $15,000.*

Civil Records: Access: Fax, mail, in person. Both court and visitors may perform in person searches. Search fee: $1.00 per name. Required to search: name, years to search. Civil cases indexed by defendant, plaintiff. Civil records on books from 1867, on computer from December 1999.

Criminal Records: Access: Fax, mail, in person. Both court and visitors may perform in person searches. Search fee: $1.00 per name. Required to search: name,

years to search; also helpful: address, DOB, SSN. Criminal records on books from 1867, on computer from December 1999.

General Information: Public access terminal is available. No juvenile records released. SASE required. Turnaround time 1-2 days, limited phone data immediately. Fax notes: $2.50 for first page, $1.00 each add'l. Copy fee: $.50 per page. Certification fee: $1.50 per page. Fee payee: Clerk of District Court. Personal checks accepted. Prepayment is required.

Stanton County Court 804 Ivy St, PO Box 536, Stanton, NE 68779; 402-439-2221; Fax: 402-439-2229. Hours: 8:30AM-4:30PM (CST). *Misdemeanor, Civil Actions Under $45,000, Eviction, Small Claims, Probate.*

Civil Records: Access: In person only. Visitors must perform in person searches for themselves. No search fee. Required to search: name, years to search. Civil cases indexed by defendant, plaintiff. Civil records on docket cards and books back to 1950s; criminal records go back to 1999, probate on microfilm.

Criminal Records: Access: In person only. Visitors must perform in person searches for themselves. No search fee. Required to search: name, years to search, DOB. Criminal records on docket cards and books back to 1900s; criminal records computerized back to 1999, probate on microfilm.

General Information: Public access terminal is available. No adoption records released. Copy fee: $.25 per page. Certification fee: $1.00. Fee payee: Stanton County. Personal checks accepted. Prepayment is required.

Thayer County

District Court PO Box 297, Hebron, NE 68370; 402-768-6116; Fax: 402-768-7232. Hours: 8AM-Noon, 1:00PM-4:30PM (CST). *Felony, Civil Actions Over $15,000.*

Civil Records: Access: In person only. Visitors must perform in person searches for themselves. No search fee. Required to search: name, years to search. Civil cases indexed by defendant, plaintiff. Civil records on books from 1900s; computerized records go back 6/2000.

Criminal Records: Access: Fax, mail, in person. Visitors must perform in person searches for themselves. No search fee. Required to search: name, years to search. Criminal records on books from 190; computerized records go back 6/2000.

General Information: Public access terminal is available. No mental health or sealed records released. SASE required. Turnaround time 5 days. Copy fee: $.25 per page. Certification fee: $1.00. Fee payee: Thayer Co. Treasurer. Personal checks accepted.

Thayer County Court PO Box 94, Hebron, NE 68370; 402-768-6325; Fax: 402-768-7232. Hours: 8AM-5PM (CST). *Misdemeanor, Civil Actions Under $45,000, Eviction, Small Claims, Probate.*

Civil Records: Access: Mail, in person. Both court and visitors may perform in person searches. No search fee. Required to search: name, years to search, address. Civil cases indexed by defendant, plaintiff. Civil records on docket cards from 1871; probate on microfiche.

Criminal Records: Access: Mail, in person. Both court and visitors may perform in person searches. No search fee. Required to search: name, years to search, DOB. Criminal records on docket cards from 1871; probate on microfiche.

General Information: No adoption or juvenile records released. SASE required. Turnaround time within 2 weeks. Copy fee: $.25 per page. Certification fee: $1.00. Fee payee: County Court. Prepayment is required.

Thomas County

District Court PO Box 226, Thedford, NE 69166; 308-645-2261; Fax: 308-645-2623. Hours: 8AM-Noon,1-4PM (CST). *Felony, Civil Actions Over $15,000.*

Civil Records: Access: Mail, fax, in person. Both court and visitors may perform in person searches. Search fee: $3.00 per name. Required to search: name, years to search. Civil cases indexed by defendant, plaintiff. Civil records indexed in books and in case files since 1800s; on computer back to 6/2000.

Criminal Records: Access: Fax, mail, in person. Both court and visitors may perform in person searches. Search fee: $3.00 per name. Required to search: name, years to search, DOB; also helpful- SSN, signed release. Criminal records indexed in books and in case files since 1800s; on computer back to 6/2000.

General Information: No sealed or juvenile records released. SASE required. Turnaround time 2 days. Fax notes: Fee to fax results is $1.00 per document and $.25 per page. Copy fee: $.25 per page. Certification fee: $4.00. Fee payee: Clerk of District Court. Personal checks accepted.

Thomas County Court PO Box 233, Thedford, NE 69166; 308-645-2266; Fax: 308-645-2623. Hours: 8AM-Noon, 1-4PM (CST). *Misdemeanor, Civil Actions Under $45,000, Eviction, Small Claims, Probate.*

Civil Records: Access: Phone, fax, mail, in person. Both court and visitors may perform in person searches. No search fee. Required to search: name, years to search. Civil cases indexed by defendant, plaintiff. Civil records on index cards and books from late 1800s.

Criminal Records: Access: Fax, mail, in person. Both court and visitors may perform in person searches. No search fee. Required to search: name, years to search, DOB, signed release. Criminal records on index cards and books from late 1800s.

General Information: No adoption or juvenile records released. SASE required. Turnaround time 2 days. Copy fee: $.25 per page. Certification fee: $1.00. Fee payee: County Court. Personal checks accepted. Prepayment is required.

Thurston County

District Court PO Box 216, Pender, NE 68047; 402-385-3318; Fax: 402-385-2762. Hours: 8:30AM-5PM (CST). *Felony, Civil Actions Over $15,000.*

Civil Records: Access: In person only. Visitors must perform in person searches for themselves. No search fee. Required to search: name, years to search. Civil cases indexed by defendant, plaintiff. Civil records on index books from late 1800s; on computer back to 1998.

Criminal Records: Access: In person only. Visitors must perform in person searches for themselves. No search fee. Required to search: name, years to search. Criminal records on index books from late 1800s; on computer back to 1998.

General Information: Public access terminal is available. No mental health records released. Fax notes: Fee to fax results is $.25 per page. Copy fee: $.25 per page. Certification fee: $1.00. Fee payee: Clerk of District Court. No personal checks accepted. Prepayment is required.

Thurston County Court County Courthouse, PO Box 129, Pender, NE 68047; 402-385-3136; Fax: 402-385-3143. Hours: 8:30AM-Noon,1-5PM (CST). *Misdemeanor, Civil Actions Under $45,000, Eviction, Small Claims, Probate.*

Civil Records: Access: In person only. Visitors must perform in person searches for themselves. No search fee. Required to search: name, years to search. Civil cases indexed by defendant, plaintiff. Civil records on

books; probate on microfiche since 1800s; on computer back to 1/2000.

Criminal Records: Access: In person only. Visitors must perform in person searches for themselves. No search fee. Required to search: name, years to search. Criminal records on books per state requirement; on computer back to 1/2000.

General Information: Public access terminal is available. No adoption or juvenile records released. Fax notes: Fee to fax results is $3.00 per document. Copy fee: $.25 per page. Certification fee: $1.00. Fee payee: County Court. Personal checks accepted. Out of state personal checks not accepted.

Valley County

District Court 125 S 15th St, Ord, NE 68862; 308-728-3700; Fax: 308-728-7725. Hours: 8AM-5PM (CST). *Felony, Civil Actions Over $15,000.*

Civil Records: Access: Phone, fax, mail, in person. Both court and visitors may perform in person searches. Search fee: $5.00 per name. Required to search: name, years to search. Civil cases indexed by defendant, plaintiff. Civil records in general index books since late 1800s.

Criminal Records: Access: Fax, mail, in person. Both court and visitors may perform in person searches. Search fee: $5.00 per name. Required to search: name, years to search; also helpful: DOB, SSN. Criminal records in general index books since late 1800s; on computer back to 3/2000. All requests must be in writing.

General Information: Public access terminal is available. SASE required. Turnaround time 3-5 days. Fax notes: Will fax back to a toll-free number. Copy fee: $.10 per page. $.15 per page for legal size copy. Certification fee: $1.00. Fee payee: Valley County Clerk. Personal checks accepted. Prepayment is required.

Valley County Court 125 S 15th St, Ord, NE 68862; 308-728-3831; Fax: 308-728-7725. Hours: 8AM-5PM (CST). *Misdemeanor, Civil Actions Under $45,000, Eviction, Small Claims, Probate.*

Civil Records: Access: Phone, fax, mail, in person. Both court and visitors may perform in person searches. No search fee. Required to search: name, years to search. Civil cases indexed by defendant, plaintiff. Civil records on books and in files since 1890s; probate on microfiche.

Criminal Records: Access: Phone, fax, mail, in person. Both court and visitors may perform in person searches. No search fee. Required to search: name, years to search. Criminal records on books and in files since 1890s; probate on microfiche.

General Information: No adoption records released. SASE required. Turnaround time 1 week. Fax notes: $3.00 for first page, $1.00 each add'l. Copy fee: $.25 per page. Certification fee: $1.25. Fee payee: Valley County Court. Personal checks accepted.

Washington County

District Court PO Box 431, Blair, NE 68008; 402-426-6899; Fax: 402-426-6898. Hours: 8AM-Noon; 1PM-4:30PM (CST). *Felony, Civil Actions Over $15,000.*

Civil Records: Access: In person only. Visitors must perform in person searches for themselves. No search fee. Required to search: name, years to search. Civil cases indexed by defendant, plaintiff. Civil records on index books and in files since 1930s; computerized records since 1997, prior sent to capitol.

Criminal Records: Access: In person only. Visitors must perform in person searches for themselves. No search fee. Required to search: name, years to search, DOB. Criminal records on index books and in files

since 1930s; computerized records since 1997, prior sent to capitol.

General Information: Public access terminal is available. No juvenile, mental health records released. Copy fee: $.25 per page. Certification fee: $1.00. Fee payee: Clerk of District Court. Personal checks accepted. Prepayment is required.

Washington County Court 1555 Colfax St, Blair, NE 68008; 402-426-6833; Fax: 402-426-6840. Hours: 8AM-4:30PM (CST). *Misdemeanor, Civil Actions Under $45,000, Eviction, Small Claims, Probate.*

Civil Records: Access: In person only. Visitors must perform in person searches for themselves. No search fee. Required to search: name, years to search. Civil cases indexed by defendant, plaintiff. Civil records on index books, cards; probate on microfilm since 1867; on computer back to 1997.

Criminal Records: Access: In person only. Visitors must perform in person searches for themselves. No search fee. Required to search: name, years to search, DOB, SSN. Criminal records on index books, cards; probate on microfilm since 1867; on computer back to 1997.

General Information: Public access terminal is available. No adoption records released. Copy fee: $.25 per page. Certification fee: $1.25. Fee payee: Washington County Court. Personal checks accepted. Prepayment is required.

Wayne County

District Court 510 Pearl St, Wayne, NE 68787; 402-375-2260. Hours: 8:30AM-5PM (CST). *Felony, Civil Actions Over $15,000.*

Civil Records: Access: In person only. Visitors must perform in person searches for themselves. No search fee. Required to search: name, years to search. Civil cases indexed by defendant, plaintiff. Civil records on index books from late 1800s, computerized since 03/99.

Criminal Records: Access: In person only. Visitors must perform in person searches for themselves. No search fee. Required to search: name, years to search. Criminal records on index books from late 1800s, computerized since 03/99.

General Information: No mental health records released. Copy fee: $.25 per page. $1.00 minimum. Certification fee: $1.00. Fee payee: Clerk of District Court. Only cashiers checks and money orders accepted. Prepayment is required.

Wayne County Court 510 Pearl St, Wayne, NE 68787; 402-375-1622; Fax: 402-375-1622. Hours: 8:30AM-5PM (CST). *Misdemeanor, Civil Actions Under $45,000, Eviction, Small Claims, Probate.*

Civil Records: Access: In person only. Visitors must perform in person searches for themselves. No search fee. Required to search: name, years to search. Civil cases indexed by defendant, plaintiff. Civil records on index books, cards from late 1800s.

Criminal Records: Access: In person only. Visitors must perform in person searches for themselves. No search fee. Required to search: name, years to search. Criminal records on index books, cards from late 1800s.

General Information: No adoption records released. Copy fee: $.25 per page. Certification fee: $1.00. Fee payee: County Court. Personal checks accepted. Prepayment is required.

Webster County

District Court 621 N Cedar, Red Cloud, NE 68970; 402-746-2716; Fax: 402-746-2710. Hours: 8:30AM-4:30PM (CST). *Felony, Civil Actions Over $15,000.*

Civil Records: Access: In person only. Visitors must perform in person searches for themselves. No search fee. Required to search: name, years to search. Civil

cases indexed by defendant, plaintiff. Civil records indexed on microfiche; in files back to 1800s.

Criminal Records: Access: In person. Visitors must perform in person searches for themselves. No search fee. Required to search: name, years to search; also helpful: address, DOB, SSN. Criminal records indexed on microfiche; in files back to 1800s.

General Information: No mental health records released. Copy fee: $1.00 per page if by court. Certification fee: $1.50. Fee payee: Clerk of District Court. Personal checks accepted. Prepayment required.

Webster County Court 621 N Cedar, Red Cloud, NE 68970; 402-746-2777; Fax: 402-746-2771. Hours: 8:30AM-4:30PM (CST). *Misdemeanor, Civil Actions Under $45,000, Eviction, Small Claims, Probate.*

Civil Records: Access: In person only. Visitors must perform in person searches for themselves. No search fee. Required to search: name, years to search; also helpful: address. Civil cases indexed by defendant. Civil records on index cards and books; probate on microfiche since late 1930.

Criminal Records: Access: In person only. Visitors must perform in person searches for themselves. No search fee. Required to search: name, years to search, DOB, SSN. Criminal records on index cards and books; probate on microfiche since late 1930.

General Information: No adoption or juvenile records released. Copy fee: $.25 per page. Sales tax is added to the fee. Certification fee: $1.00. Fee payee: County Court. Business checks accepted. Prepayment required.

Wheeler County

District Court PO Box 127, Bartlett, NE 68622; 308-654-3235; Fax: 308-654-3442. Hours: 9AM-Noon, 1-5PM (CST). *Felony, Civil Actions Over $15,000.*

Civil Records: Access: In person only. Visitors must perform in person searches for themselves. No search fee. Required to search: name, years to search. Civil cases indexed by defendant, plaintiff. Civil records on index books from late 1800s. Mail access limited to short searches.

Criminal Records: Access: In person only. Visitors must perform in person searches for themselves. No search fee. Required to search: name, years to search. Criminal records on index books from late 1800s.

General Information: No juvenile or adoption records released. Copy fee: $.15 per page. Certification fee: $7.00. Fee payee: Clerk of District Court. Personal checks accepted.

Wheeler County Court PO Box 127, Bartlett, NE 68622; 308-654-3376; Fax: 308-654-3442. Hours: 9AM-4PM (CST). *Misdemeanor, Civil Actions Under $45,000, Eviction, Small Claims, Probate.*

Civil Records: Access: Mail, in person. Only the court performs in person searches; visitors may not. No search fee. Required to search: name, years to search. Civil cases indexed by defendant, plaintiff. Civil records on index books from late 1800s.

Criminal Records: Access: Mail, in person. Visitors must perform in person searches for themselves. No search fee. Required to search: name, years to search. Criminal records on index books from late 1800s.

General Information: No adoption records released. SASE required. Turnaround time 1-2 weeks. Copy fee: $.25 per page. Certification fee: $1.00. Fee payee: County Court. Personal checks accepted.

York County

District Court 510 Lincoln Ave, York, NE 68467; 402-362-4038; Fax: 402-362-2577. Hours: 8:30AM-5PM (CST). *Felony, Civil Actions Over $15,000.*

Note: The SSN does not show up in the computer index, but will show in the case files.

Civil Records: Access: In person only. Visitors must perform in person searches for themselves. No search fee. Required to search: name, years to search. Civil cases indexed by defendant, plaintiff. Civil records on index books and in files from 1875, computerized go back to 1998.

Criminal Records: Access: In person only. Visitors must perform in person searches for themselves. No search fee. Required to search: name, years to search. Criminal records on index books and in files from 1875, computerized records go back to 1998.

General Information: Public access terminal is available. Copy fee: $.25 per page. Certification fee: $1.00. Fee payee: Clerk of District Court. Personal checks accepted. Prepayment is required.

York County Court 510 Lincoln Ave, York, NE 68467; 402-362-4925; Fax: 402-362-2577. Hours: 8AM-5PM (CST). *Misdemeanor, Civil Actions Under $45,000, Eviction, Small Claims, Probate.*

Civil Records: Access: In person only. Visitors must perform in person searches for themselves. No search fee. Required to search: name, years to search. Civil cases indexed by defendant, plaintiff. Civil records on docket cards, files from 1875.

Criminal Records: Access: In person only. Visitors must perform in person searches for themselves. No search fee. Required to search: name, years to search. Criminal records on docket cards, files from 1875.

General Information: Public access terminal is available. No adoption or sealed records released. Copy fee: $.25 per page. Certification fee: $1.00. Fee payee: York County Court. Personal checks accepted. Credit cards accepted: Visa, MasterCard. $3.00 service charge.

Nebraska Recording Offices

ORGANIZATION: 93 counties, 109 recording offices. The recording officers are County Clerk (UCC and some state tax liens) and Register of Deeds (real estate and most tax liens). Most counties have a combined Clerk/Register office, which are designated "County Clerk" in this section. Sixteen counties have separate offices for County Clerk and for Register of Deeds - Adams, Cass, Dakota, Dawson, Dodge, Douglas, Gage, Hall, Lancaster, Lincoln, Madison, Otoe, Platte, Sarpy, Saunders, and Scotts. Bluff. In combined offices, the Register of Deeds is frequently a different person from the County Clerk. 74 counties are in the Central Time Zone (CST) and 19 are in the Mountain Time Zone (MST).

REAL ESTATE RECORDS: Some Nebraska counties will perform real estate searches, including owner of record from the legal description of the property. Address search requests and make checks payable to the Register of Deeds, not the County Clerk. Fees vary.

UCC RECORDS: Financing statements are filed at the state level, and real estate related collateral are filed with the County Clerk. Previously, financing statements could be filed at any county. All non-real estate UCC filings are entered into a statewide database that is accessible from any county office. All but a few counties will perform UCC searches. Use search request form UCC-11. The UCC statute allows for telephone searching. Search fees are usually $4.00 per debtor name. Copy fees vary.

TAX LIEN RECORDS: All federal and some state tax liens are filed with the County Register of Deeds. Some state tax liens on personal property are filed with the County Clerk. Most counties will perform tax lien searches, some as part of a UCC search, and others for a separate fee, usually $3.50 per name in each index. Copy fees vary.

OTHER LIENS: Mechanics, artisans, judgment, motor vehicle, agricultural.

ONLINE ACCESS: Nebrask@online offers online access to Secretary of State's UCC database; registration and a usage fee is required. For information, visit www.nol.org/subinfo.html. The state treasurer's unclaimed proeprty database is searchable free at www.treasurer.state.ne.us/ie/uphome.asp

Adams County Clerk

County Clerk, PO Box 2067, Hastings, NE 68902. 402-461-7107 R/E Recording: 402-461-7148 UCC Recording: 402-461-7148; Fax 402-461-7185.
Will not search UCC records. See Register of Deeds for real estate records. **Other Phones:** Assessor 402-461-7116; Treasurer 402-461-7120; Appraiser/Auditor 402-461-7116; Elections 402-461-7107.

Adams County Register of Deeds

County Clerk, PO Box 203, Hastings, NE 68902. County Clerk, R/E and UCC Recording 402-461-7148; Fax 402-461-7154. www.adamscounty.org
Will search UCC records. Will not search real estate records. **Other Phones:** Assessor 402-461-7116; Treasurer 402-461-7120; Elections 402-461-7165.

Antelope County

County Clerk, 501 Main St., Neligh, NE 68756. 402-887-4410; Fax 402-887-4719.
Will search UCC records. **Other Phone Numbers:** Assessor 402-887-4515; Treasurer 402-887-4247.

Arthur County

County Clerk, Box 126, Arthur, NE 69121-0126. 308-764-2203; Fax 308-764-2216.
Will search UCC records.
Other Phone Numbers: Assessor 308-764-2203.

Banner County

County Clerk, PO Box 67, Harrisburg, NE 69345-0067. 308-436-5265; Fax 308-436-4180.
Will search UCC records. UCC search includes tax liens if requested. Will not search real estate records. **Other Phone Numbers:** Assessor 308-436-5265; Treasurer 308-436-5260.

Blaine County

County Clerk, PO Box 136, Brewster, NE 68821. County Clerk, R/E and UCC Recording 308-547-2222; Fax 308-547-2228.
Will search UCC records. **Other Phone Numbers:** Assessor 308-541-2222; Treasurer 308-547-2223; Elections 308-547-2222.

Boone County

County Clerk, 222 S. 4th St, Albion, NE 68620-1247. County Clerk, R/E and UCC Recording 402-395-2055 UCC Recording: 402-471-4080; Fax 402-395-6592. www.co.boone.ne.us
Will search UCC records. Will not search real estate records. **Other Phone Numbers:** Assessor 402-395-2045; Treasurer 402-395-2513; Elections 402-395-2055; Vital Records 402-395-2055 or 402-471-2871.

Box Butte County

Box Butte County Clerk, Box 678, Alliance, NE 69301-0678. Box Butte County Clerk, R/E and UCC Recording 308-762-6565 UCC Recording: 402-471-4080 (Sec of State); Fax 308-762-2867.
The recording officers are County Clerk (state tax liens) Register of Deeds (real estate and most tax liens). Will search UCC records. Will not search real estate records. **Other Phone Numbers:** Assessor 308-762-6101; Treasurer 308-762-6975; Elections 308-762-6565; Vital Records 402-471-2871.

Boyd County

County Clerk, PO Box 26, Butte, NE 68722. 402-775-2391; Fax 402-775-2146.
Will search UCC records. **Other Phone Numbers:** Assessor 402-775-2311; Treasurer 402-775-2581.

Brown County

Brown County Clerk, Courthouse, 148 W. 4th St., Ainsworth, NE 69210. 402-387-2705; Fax 402-387-0918.
Will search UCC records. **Other Phone Numbers:** Assessor 402-387-1621; Treasurer 402-387-2650; Elections 402-387-2705; Secretary of State (UCC) 402-471-2554.

Buffalo County

Register of Deeds, PO Box 1270, Kearney, NE 68848-1270. Register of Deeds, R/E and UCC Recording 308-236-1239 UCC Recording: 402-471-2558; Fax 308-236-1291.
Will search UCC records. Will not search real estate records. **Other Phone Numbers:** Assessor 308-236-1205; Treasurer 308-236-1250; Elections 308-236-1233; Vital Records 402-471-2871.

Burt County

County Clerk, PO Box 87, Tekamah, NE 68061. 402-374-2955; Fax 402-374-2956.
Will search UCC records. Will not search real estate records. **Other Phones:** Assessor 402-374-2926; Treasurer 402-374-2911; Elections 402-374-2955.

Butler County

Deputy Clerk, PO Box 289, David City, NE 68632-0289. 402-367-7430 R/E Recording: 402-367-7431 UCC Recording: 402-471-4080; Fax 402-367-3329.
Will search UCC records. Will not search real estate records. **Other Phone Numbers:** Assessor 402-367-7420; Treasurer 402-367-7450; Elections 402-367-7430; Vital Records 402-471-2871.

Cass County Clerk

County Clerk, Courthouse, Room 202, 346 Main St., Plattsmouth, NE 68048-1964. 402-296-9300; Fax 402-296-9327.

Will search UCC records. This agency will not do a tax lien search. See Register of Deeds for real estate records. **Other Phone Numbers:** Assessor 402-296-9310.

Cass County Register of Deeds

County Clerk, County Courthouse, 346 Main St., Plattsmouth, NE 68048-1964. 402-296-9330; Fax 402-296-9331. www.cassne.org

Will search UCC records. Will search real estate records for one legal description. **Other Phone Numbers:** Assessor 402-296-9310; Treasurer 402-296-9320; Appraiser/Auditor 402-296-9310; Elections 402-296-9306.

Cedar County

County Clerk, PO Box 47, Hartington, NE 68739. County Clerk, R/E and UCC Recording 402-254-7411 UCC Recording: 402-471-2554; Fax 402-254-7410.

Will search UCC records. Will not search real estate records. **Other Phone Numbers:** Assessor 402-254-7431; Treasurer 402-254-7421; Elections 402-254-7411; Vital Records 402-254-7411.

Chase County

County Clerk, Box 1299, Imperial, NE 69033-1299. 308-882-5266; Fax 308-882-5390.

Will search UCC records. **Other Phone Numbers:** Assessor 308-882-5207; Treasurer 308-882-4756.

Cherry County

County Clerk, Box 120, Valentine, NE 69201-0120. County Clerk, R/E and UCC Recording 402-376-2771; Fax 402-376-3095.

Will search UCC records. Will not search real estate records. **Other Phone Numbers:** Assessor 402-376-1630; Treasurer 402-376-1580; Elections 402-376-2771; Vital Records 402-471-2871.

Cheyenne County

County Clerk, PO Box 217, Sidney, NE 69162-0217. 308-254-2141; Fax 308-254-4293. www.co.cheyenne.ne.us

Will search UCC records. Will not search real estate records. **Other Phone Numbers:** Assessor 308-254-2633; Treasurer 308-254-2733.

Clay County

County Clerk, 111 W. Fairfield St, Clay Center, NE 68933-1499. 402-762-3463; Fax 402-762-3250.

Will search UCC records. Will not search real estate records. **Other Phone Numbers:** Assessor 402-762-3792; Treasurer 402-762-3505.

Colfax County

County Clerk, 411 E. 11th St, Schuyler, NE 68661. 402-352-8504; Fax 402-352-8515. www.state.ne.us/colfax/

Will search UCC records. This agency will not do a tax lien search. Real estate record owner and mortgage searches available. **Other Phone Numbers:** Assessor 402-352-8500; Treasurer 402-352-2105.

Cuming County

County Clerk, Box 290, West Point, NE 68788. County Clerk, R/E and UCC Recording 402-372-6002; Fax 402-372-6013. www.co.cuming.ne.us

Will search UCC records. Will not search real estate records. **Other Phone Numbers:** Assessor 402-372-6000; Treasurer 402-372-6011; Elections 402-372-6002.

Custer County

County Clerk, 431 S. 10th, Broken Bow, NE 68822. 308-872-5701.

Will search UCC records. Tax liens not included in UCC search. Real estate record owner searches available. **Other Phone Numbers:** Assessor 308-872-2981; Treasurer 308-872-2921.

Dakota County Clerk

Register of Deeds, PO Box 39, Dakota City, NE 68731-0039. Register of Deeds, R/E and UCC Recording 402-987-2166 UCC Recording: 402-987-2126; Fax 402-494-9228. www.sscdc.net/county

Will search county level UCC records. See Register of Deeds for real estate records. **Other Phone Numbers:** Assessor 402-987-0264; Treasurer 402-987-2131; Elections 402-987-2126; Vital Records 402-471-2871.

Dakota County Register of Deeds

County Register of Deeds, PO Box 511, Dakota City, NE 68731. 402-987-2166.

Will search UCC records, but only real estate related UCC filed here. This agency will not do a tax lien search. Will not search real estate records. **Other Phone Numbers:** Assessor 402-987-0264; Treasurer 402-987-2131.

Dawes County

County Clerk, 451 Main St, Courthouse, Chadron, NE 69337-2698. County Clerk, R/E and UCC Recording 308-432-0100; Fax 308-432-5179.

Will search UCC records. Tax liens not included in UCC search. Will not search real estate records. **Other Phone Numbers:** Assessor 308-432-0103; Treasurer 308-432-0105; Elections 308-432-0100.

Dawson County Clerk

County Clerk, PO Box 370, Lexington, NE 68850-0370. 308-324-2127 R/E Recording: 308-324-4271; Fax 308-324-6106.

Will search UCC records. See Register of Deeds for real estate records. **Other Phone Numbers:** Assessor 308-324-3471; Treasurer 308-324-3241; Appraiser/Auditor 308-324-3471; Elections 308-324-6106; Vital Records 308-324-2127.

Dawson County Register of Deeds

County Register of Deeds, County Courthouse, 700 N. Washington, Lexington, NE 68850. 308-324-4271.

Will search UCC records, but only real estate related UCC filed here. This agency will not do a tax lien search. Will not search real estate records. **Other Phone Numbers:** Assessor 308-324-3471; Treasurer 308-324-3241.

Deuel County

County Clerk, PO Box 327, Chappell, NE 69129. 308-874-3308; Fax 308-874-3472.

Will search UCC records. **Other Phone Numbers:** Assessor 308-874-2608; Treasurer 308-874-3307.

Dixon County

County Clerk, Box 546, Ponca, NE 68770-0546. 402-755-2208; Fax 402-755-4276.

Will search UCC records. UCC search includes tax liens if requested. Will not search real estate records. **Other Phone Numbers:** Assessor 402-755-2626; Treasurer 402-755-2701.

Dodge County Clerk

County Clerk, 435 North Park, Courthouse - Room 102, Fremont, NE 68025-4967. 402-727-2767 R/E Recording: 402-727-2735 UCC Recording: 402-471-4080; Fax 402-727-2764.

Will search UCC records. See Register of Deeds for real estate records. **Other Phone Numbers:** Assessor 402-727-3911; Treasurer 402-727-2750; Appraiser/Auditor 402-727-3911; Elections 402-727-2767; Vital Records 402-471-2871; UCC Searches-County Level 402-727-2767.

Dodge County Register of Deeds

County Register of Deeds, 435 North Park, Room 201, Fremont, NE 68025. 402-727-2735; Fax 402-727-2734. www.registerofdeeds.com

Will search UCC records, but only real estate related UCC filed here. This agency will not do a tax lien search. Will not search real estate records. **Online Access:** Real Estate Records. Access to Register of Deeds mortgages database is available at the web site. Registration is required. The site is under development. **Other Phone Numbers:** Assessor 402-727-3911; Treasurer 402-727-2750.

Douglas County Clerk

County Clerk, 1819 Farnam St., Room H08, Omaha, NE 68183-0008. 402-444-6744; Fax 402-444-6456.

Will search UCC records. See Register of Deeds for real estate records. **Online Access:** Assessor Records. Property tax records on the county assessor database are available free online at www.co.douglas.ne.us/ dept.assessor/framevalinfo.htm. There is no name searching. **Other Phone Numbers:** Assessor 402-444-7060.

Douglas County Register of Deeds

County Clerk, 1819 Farnam, Room H09, Omaha, NE 68183. 402-444-7194; Fax 402-444-6693.

Will search UCC records. Will not search real estate records. **Other Phone Numbers:** Assessor 402-444-7060; Treasurer 402-444-7272.

Dundy County

County Clerk, PO Box 506, Benkelman, NE 69021-0506. 308-423-2058.

Will search UCC records. UCC search includes tax liens. Will not search real estate records. **Other Phone Numbers:** Assessor 308-423-2821; Treasurer 308-423-2346.

Fillmore County

Register of Deeds, PO Box 307, Geneva, NE 68361-0307. 402-759-4931; Fax 402-759-4307. www.fillmorecounty.org/government/gov1.html

The recording officers are County Clerk (Federal and state tax liens) and Register of Deeds (real estate and most tax liens). Will not search UCC records, but will search tax liens. Will search tax liens-$3.50 per name. **Other Phone Numbers:** Assessor 402-759-3613; Treasurer 402-759-3812; Elections 402-759-4931.

Franklin County

County Clerk, PO Box 146, Franklin, NE 68939. 308-425-6202; Fax 308-425-6289.

Will search UCC records. Will not search real estate records. **Other Phone Numbers:** Assessor 308-425-6229; Treasurer 308-425-6265.

Frontier County

County Clerk, PO Box 40, Stockville, NE 69042--004. 308-367-8641; Fax 308-367-8730.

Will search UCC records. UCC search includes tax liens if requested. Real estate owner, mortgage, and property transfer searches available. **Other Phone Numbers:** Assessor 308-367-8637; Treasurer 308-367-8631; Appraiser/Auditor 308-367-8637; Elections 308-367-8641.

Furnas County

County Clerk, PO Box 387, Beaver City, NE 68926. 308-268-4145.
Will search UCC records. This agency will not do a tax lien search. Will not search real estate records. **Other Phone Numbers:** Assessor 308-268-3145; Treasurer 308-268-2195.

Gage County Clerk

County Clerk, PO Box 429, Beatrice, NE 68310-0429. 402-223-1300 R/E Recording: 402-223-1361; Fax 402-223-1371. www.nol.org/gage/
Will search UCC records. See Register of Deeds for real estate records. **Other Phone Numbers:** Assessor 402-223-1308; Treasurer 402-223-1315; Appraiser/Auditor 402-223-1308; Elections 402-223-1300; Vital Records 402-223-1300.

Gage County Register of Deeds

County Register of Deeds, PO Box 337, Beatrice, NE 68310. 402-223-1361.
Will search UCC records, but only real estate related UCC filed here. This agency will not do a tax lien search. Will not search real estate records. **Other Phone Numbers:** Assessor 402-223-1308; Treasurer 402-223-1315.

Garden County

County Clerk, PO Box 486, Oshkosh, NE 69154. County Clerk, R/E and UCC Recording 308-772-3924; Fax 308-772-4143.
Will search UCC records. Will not search real estate records. **Other Phone Numbers:** Assessor 308-772-4464; Treasurer 308-772-3622.

Garfield County

County Clerk, Box 218, Burwell, NE 68823. 308-346-4161.
Will search UCC records. Tax liens not included in UCC search. Will not search real estate records. **Other Phone Numbers:** Assessor 308-346-4045; Treasurer 308-346-4125.

Gosper County

County Clerk, PO Box 136, Elwood, NE 68937-0136. County Clerk, R/E and UCC Recording 308-785-2611; Fax 308-785-2300.
Will search UCC records. UCC search includes tax liens if requested. Will not search real estate records. **Other Phone Numbers:** Assessor 308-785-2250; Treasurer 308-785-2450; Appraiser/Auditor 308-785-2250; Elections 308-785-2611; Vital Records 308-785-2611.

Grant County

County Clerk, PO Box 139, Hyannis, NE 69350-0139. 308-458-2488; Fax 308-458-2485.
Will search UCC records. **Other Phone Numbers:** Assessor 308-458-2488; Treasurer 308-458-2422; Appraiser/Auditor 308-762-2474; Elections 308-458-2488; Marriages 308-458-2488.

Greeley County

County Clerk, PO Box 287, Greeley, NE 68842. 308-428-3625; Fax 308-428-6500.
Will search UCC records. Will not search real estate records. **Other Phone Numbers:** Assessor 308-428-5310; Treasurer 308-428-3535.

Hall County Clerk

County Clerk, PO Box 1692, Grand Island, NE 68802-1692. 308-385-5080; Fax 308-385-5094.
Will search UCC records. See Register of Deeds for real estate records. **Other Phone Numbers:** Assessor 308-385-5050.

Hall County Register of Deeds

County Register of Deeds, PO Box 1692, Grand Island, NE 68802-1692. County Register of Deeds, R/E and UCC Recording 308-385-5040; www.grand-island.com
Will search UCC records, but only real estate related UCC filed here. This agency will not do a tax lien search. Will not search real estate records. **Other Phone Numbers:** Assessor 308-385-5050; Treasurer 308-385-5025.

Hamilton County

County Clerk, Register of Deeds, Courthouse, 1111 13th St. - Suite 1, Aurora, NE 68818-2017. County Clerk, Register of Deeds, R/E and UCC Recording 402-694-3443 UCC Recording: 402-471-2554; Fax 402-694-2396. www.co.hamilton.ne.us
Will search UCC records. Will not search real estate records. **Other Phone Numbers:** Assessor 402-694-2757; Treasurer 402-694-2291; Elections 402-694-3443; Vital Records 402-471-2871.

Harlan County

County Clerk, PO Box 698, Alma, NE 68920-0698. 308-928-2173; Fax 308-928-2592.
This agency will not search real estate or UCC records. **Other Phone Numbers:** Assessor 308-928-2177; Treasurer 308-928-2171.

Hayes County

County Clerk, PO Box 370, Hayes Center, NE 69032-0370. 308-286-3413; Fax 308-286-3208.
Will search UCC records. This agency will not do a tax lien search. Will not search real estate records. **Other Phone Numbers:** Assessor 308-286-3399; Treasurer 308-286-3214.

Hitchcock County

County Clerk, PO Box 248, Trenton, NE 69044. County Clerk, R/E and UCC Recording 308-334-5646; Fax 308-334-5398. www.co.hitchcock.ne.us
Will search UCC records. Will search real estate records. **Other Phone Numbers:** Assessor 308-334-5219; Treasurer 308-334-5544; Appraiser/Auditor 308-334-5219; Elections 308-334-5646.

Holt County

County Clerk, PO Box 329, O'Neill, NE 68763-0329. 402-336-2250; Fax 402-336-1762.
Will search UCC records. Will not search real estate records. **Other Phone Numbers:** Assessor 402-336-1624; Treasurer 402-336-1291.

Hooker County

County Clerk, PO Box 184, Mullen, NE 69152. County Clerk, R/E and UCC Recording 308-546-2244; Fax 308-546-2490.
Will search UCC records. UCC search includes tax liens if requested. Real estate owner, mortgage, and property transfer searches available. **Other Phone Numbers:** Assessor 308-546-2244; Treasurer 308-546-2245; Elections 308-546-2244.

Howard County

County Clerk, PO Box 25, St. Paul, NE 68873. 308-754-4343; Fax 308-754-4725.
Will search UCC records. UCC search includes tax liens if requested. Will not search real estate records. **Other Phone Numbers:** Assessor 308-754-4261; Treasurer 308-754-4852; Elections 308-754-4343.

Jefferson County

County Clerk, 411 4th, Courthouse, Fairbury, NE 68352-1619. County Clerk, R/E and UCC Recording 402-729-5201 UCC Recording: 402-471-2554; Fax 402-729-2016.

The recording officers are County Clerk (some state tax liens) and Register of Deeds (real estate and most tax liens). Will search UCC records. Will search real estate records. **Other Phone Numbers:** Assessor 402-729-3103; Treasurer 402-729-2411; Elections 402-729-2323; Vital Records 402-471-2872.

Johnson County

County Clerk, PO Box 416, Tecumseh, NE 68450. County Clerk, R/E and UCC Recording 402-335-6300; Fax 402-335-6311.
Will search UCC records. UCC search includes tax liens. Will not search real estate records. **Other Phone Numbers:** Assessor 402-335-3845; Treasurer 402-335-6310; Elections 402-335-6300.

Kearney County

County Clerk, PO Box 339, Minden, NE 68959-0339. 308-832-2723; Fax 308-832-1748.
Will search UCC records. **Other Phone Numbers:** Assessor 308-832-2625; Treasurer 308-832-2730.

Keith County

County Clerk, PO Box 149, Ogallala, NE 69153. 308-284-4726; Fax 308-284-6277.
Will search UCC records. Will not search real estate records. **Other Phone Numbers:** Assessor 308-284-8040; Treasurer 308-284-3231.

Keya Paha County

County Clerk, PO Box 349, Springview, NE 68778. 402-497-3791; Fax 402-497-3799.
Will search UCC records. UCC search includes tax liens. Will not search real estate records. **Other Phone Numbers:** Assessor 402-497-3791; Treasurer 402-497-3891.

Kimball County

County Clerk, 114 E. Third St, Kimball, NE 69145-1296. 308-235-2241; Fax 308-235-3654.
Will search UCC records. Will not search real estate records. **Other Phones:** Assessor 308-235-2362; Treasurer 308-235-2242; Elections 308-235-2241.

Knox County Clerk

County Clerk, PO Box 166, Center, NE 68724-0166. County Clerk, R/E and UCC Recording 402-288-4424 UCC Recording: 402-288-4282; Fax 402-288-4424. www.co.knox.ne.us
Will search UCC records. Will not search real estate records. **Other Phone Numbers:** Assessor 402-288-4255; Treasurer 402-288-4491.

Lancaster County Clerk

County Clerk, 555 S. 10th St, County-City Building, Lincoln, NE 68508-2867. 402-441-7482 R/E Recording: 402-441-7577; Fax 402-441-8728. http://interlinc.ci.lincoln.ne.us
Will search UCC records. This agency will do a state tax lien search only. See Register of Deeds for real estate records. **Online Access:** Assessor, Recording, Grantor/Grantee, Deed, Judgment, Dog Tag, Treasurer, Marriage, Accident, Parking Ticket, Building Permit Records. Records on the county Assessor Property Information Search database are available free at www.dcassessor.org/valuation.html. Search parking tickets at www.ci.lincoln.ne.us/city/finance/treas/tickets.htm. Also, search the register of deeds Grantor/Grantee index for free at www.ci.lincoln.ne.us/cnty/deeds/deeds.htm. Search City of Lincoln accident reports at www.ci.lincoln.ne.us/city/police/stats/acc.htm. Also, search treasurer' property information at www.ci.lincoln.ne.us/cnty/treas/property.htm. Search dog tag registrations at www.ci.lincoln.ne.us/city/health/animal/acttag.htm. Search marriages at www.ci.lincoln.ne.us/cnty/clerk/marrsrch.htm. **Other**

Phone Numbers: Assessor 402-441-7463; Treasurer 402-441-7425; Appraiser/Auditor 402-441-7463; Elections 402-441-7311; Vital Records 402-471-2872.

Lancaster County Register of Deeds

Register of Deeds, 555 S. 10th St, Lincoln, NE 68508. 402-441-7577; Fax 402-441-7012. www.ci.lincoln.ne.us/cnty/co_agenc.htm
Will search UCC records. Will search real estate records. **Online Access:** Real Estate, Lien, Grantor/Grantee, Assessor, Treasurer Records. Access to the county online deeds search is available free at www.ci.lincoln.ne.us/cnty/deeds/deeds.htm. Also, access to the assessor database is available at www.ci.lincoln.ne.us/cnty/assess/property.htm. Treasurer information is also here. Also, search property information free on the map server site at http://ims.ci.lincoln.ne.us/isa/parcel. **Other Phone Numbers:** Assessor 402-441-7643; Treasurer 402-441-7425; Vital Records 402-441-2871.

Lincoln County Clerk

County Clerk, Courthouse, Room 101, 301 N. Jeffers, North Platte, NE 69101. 308-534-4350.
Will search UCC records. UCC search includes state tax liens. See Register of Deeds for real estate records. **Other Phone Numbers:** Assessor 308-534-4350.

Lincoln County Register of Deeds

County Clerk, 301 N. Jeffers, Room 103, North Platte, NE 69101-3931. 308-534-4350 R/E Recording: 308-534-4350 X 192 UCC Recording: 308-534-4350 X 192; Fax 308-534-5287.
Will search UCC records. Will not search real estate records. **Other Phone Numbers:** Assessor 308-534-4350; Treasurer 308-534-4350.

Logan County

County Clerk, PO Box 8, Stapleton, NE 69163. 308-636-2311.
Will search UCC records. UCC search includes tax liens if requested. Will not search real estate records. **Other Phone Numbers:** Assessor 308-636-2311; Treasurer 308-636-2441.

Loup County

County Clerk, PO Box 187, Taylor, NE 68879-0187. 308-942-3135; Fax 308-942-6015.
Will search UCC records. UCC search includes tax liens if requested. Will not search real estate records. **Other Phone Numbers:** Assessor 308-942-3135; Treasurer 308-942-3115.

Madison County Clerk

County Clerk, PO Box 290, Madison, NE 68748-0290. 402-454-3311 x137 R/E Recording: 402-454-3311 x124 UCC Recording: 402-454-3311 x136; Fax 402-454-6682.
Will search UCC records. See Register of Deeds for real estate records. **Other Phone Numbers:** Assessor 402-454-3311 x178; Treasurer 402-454-3311 x133; Appraiser/Auditor 402-454-3311; Elections 402-454-3311 x136; Vital Records 402-471-2871.

Madison County Register of Deeds

County Register of Deeds, PO Box 229, Madison, NE 68748. 402-454-3311 R/E Recording: 402-454-3311 x124 UCC Recording: 402-454-3311 x124; Fax 402-454-6682.
Will search UCC records, but only real estate related UCC filed here. This agency will not do a tax lien search. Will not search real estate records. **Other Phone Numbers:** Assessor 402-454-3311 x178; Treasurer

402-454-3311 x133; Elections 402-454-3311 x136; Vital Records 402-471-2871.

McPherson County

County Clerk, PO Box 122, Tryon, NE 69167-0122. 308-587-2363; Fax 308-587-2363.
Will search UCC records. Will not search real estate records. **Other Phone Numbers:** Assessor 308-587-2363; Treasurer 308-587-2363.

Merrick County

County Clerk, PO Box 27, Central City, NE 68826. 308-946-2881; Fax 308-946-2332.
Will search pre-1999 UCC records. UCC search does not include tax liens. Will not search real estate records. **Other Phone Numbers:** Assessor 308-946-2443; Treasurer 308-946-2171; Elections 308-946-2881.

Morrill County

County Clerk, PO Box 610, Bridgeport, NE 69336. County Clerk, R/E and UCC Recording 308-262-0860; Fax 308-262-1469.
Will search UCC records. Will not search real estate records. **Other Phones:** Assessor 308-262-1534; Treasurer 308-262-1177; Elections 308-262-0860.

Nance County

County Clerk, PO Box 338, Fullerton, NE 68638. 308-536-2331; Fax 308-536-2742.
Will search UCC records. Will not search real estate records. **Other Phones:** Assessor 308-536-2653; Treasurer 308-536-2165; Elections 308-536-2331.

Nemaha County

County Clerk, 1824 N St, Courthouse, Auburn, NE 68305-2399. County Clerk, R/E and UCC Recording 402-274-4213; Fax 402-274-4389.
Will search UCC records. UCC search includes tax liens. Will not search real estate records. **Other Phone Numbers:** Assessor 402-274-3820; Treasurer 402-274-3319.

Nuckolls County

County Clerk, PO Box 366, Nelson, NE 68961-0366. County Clerk, R/E and UCC Recording 402-225-4361; Fax 402-225-4301.
Will search UCC records. **Other Phone Numbers:** Assessor 402-225-2401; Treasurer 402-225-4351; Elections 402-225-4361.

Otoe County Clerk

Register of Deeds, PO Box 249, Nebraska City, NE 68410-0249. 402-873-9505 R/E Recording: 402-873-9530; Fax 402-873-9506. www.co.otoe.ne.us/deeds.html
Will search UCC records. See Register of Deeds for real estate records. **Other Phones:** Assessor 402-873-9520; Treasurer 402-873-9510; Appraiser/Auditor 402-873-9522; Elections 402-873-9505; Vital Records 402-471-2872.

Otoe County Register of Deeds

County Register of Deeds, 1021 Central Ave., Room 203, Nebraska City, NE 68410. 402-873-9530; Fax 402-873-6130.
Will search UCC records, but only real estate related UCC filed here. This agency will not do a tax lien search. Will not search real estate records. **Other Phone Numbers:** Assessor 402-873-9520; Treasurer 402-873-3589.

Pawnee County

County Clerk, PO Box 431, Pawnee City, NE 68420. 402-852-2962; Fax 402-852-2963.
Will search UCC records. UCC search includes tax liens if requested. Real estate record owner and

mortgage searches available. **Other Phone Numbers:** Assessor 402-852-2292; Treasurer 402-852-2380.

Perkins County

County Clerk, PO Box 156, Grant, NE 69140-0156. County Clerk, R/E and UCC Recording 308-352-4643; Fax 308-352-2455.
Will search UCC records. Will not search real estate records. **Other Phones:** Assessor 308-352-4938; Treasurer 308-352-4542; Elections 308-352-4643.

Phelps County

County Clerk, PO Box 404, Holdrege, NE 68949-0404. 308-995-4469; Fax 308-995-4368.
Will search UCC records. Will search real estate records only from legal description. **Other Phones:** Assessor 308-995-4061; Treasurer 308-995-6115.

Pierce County

County Clerk, 111 W. Court, Courthouse - Room 1, Pierce, NE 68767-1224. 402-329-4225; Fax 402-329-6439.
Will search UCC records. UCC search includes tax liens. Will not search real estate records. **Other Phone:** Assessor 402-329-4215; Treasurer 402-329-6335.

Platte County Clerk

County Clerk, 2610 14th St, Columbus, NE 68601. 402-563-4904 R/E Recording: 402-563-4911; Fax 402-564-4614.
Will search UCC records. See Register of Deeds for real estate records. **Other Phone Numbers:** Assessor 402-563-4902; Treasurer 402-563-4913; Elections 402-563-4908.

Platte County Register of Deeds

County Register of Deeds, 2610 14th St, Columbus, NE 68601. 402-563-4911.
Will search UCC records, but only real estate related UCC filed here. This agency will not do a tax lien search. Will not search real estate records. **Other Phone Numbers:** Assessor 402-563-4902; Treasurer 402-563-4913.

Polk County

County Clerk, PO Box 276, Osceola, NE 68651-0276. 402-747-5431; Fax 402-747-2656.
Will search UCC records. UCC search includes tax liens if requested. Will not search real estate records. **Other Phone Numbers:** Assessor 402-747-4491; Treasurer 402-747-5441; Vital Records 402-471-2871.

Red Willow County

County Clerk, 502 Norris Ave, McCook, NE 69001. County Clerk, R/E and UCC Recording 308-345-1552 UCC Recording: (State Office 402-471-4080); Fax 308-345-7307.
Will search UCC records. UCC search includes tax liens if requested. Will not search real estate records. **Other Phone Numbers:** Assessor 308-345-4388; Treasurer 308-345-6515; Elections 308-345-1552; Vital Records State Office 402-471-2306).

Richardson County

County Clerk, Courthouse, 1700 Stone, Falls City, NE 68355. 402-245-2911; Fax 402-245-3725.
Will search UCC records. Will not search real estate records. **Other Phone Numbers:** Assessor 402-245-4012; Treasurer 402-245-3511.

Rock County

County Clerk, PO Box 367, Bassett, NE 68714. 402-684-3933.
Will search UCC records. UCC search includes tax liens. Will not search real estate records. **Other Phone Numbers:** Assessor 402-684-3831; Treasurer 402-684-3515.

Saline County

Real Estate-County Clerek, PO Box 865, Wilber, NE 68465. Real Estate-County Clerek, R/E and UCC Recording 402-821-2374 UCC Recording: 402-471-4080 (filed at State level); Fax 402-821-3381.
Will search UCC records. Will not search real estate records. **Other Phone Numbers:** Assessor 402-821-2588; Treasurer 402-821-2375; Elections 402-821-2374; Vital Records 402-471-2872 (State Bureau of Vital Statistics).

Sarpy County Clerk

County Clerk, 1210 Golden Gate Drive, Suite 1118, Papillion, NE 68046-2895. 402-593-2114; Fax 402-593-4360. www.sarpy.com
Will not search UCC records. See Register of Deeds for real estate records. **Online Access:** Real Estate Records. Records on the county Property Lookup database are available free online at www.sarpy.com/boe/capslookup.htm. **Other Phone Numbers:** Assessor 402-593-2121.

Sarpy County Register of Deeds

County Clerk, 1210 Golden Gate Drive #1109, Papillion, NE 68046. 402-593-2186; Fax 402-593-2338.
Will search UCC records. Will not search real estate records. **Other Phone Numbers:** Assessor 402-593-2121; Treasurer 402-436-6621.

Saunders County Clerk

County Clerk, PO Box 61, Wahoo, NE 68066-0187. 402-443-8101; Fax 402-443-5010.
Will search UCC records. UCC search includes state tax liens. See Register of Deeds for real estate records. **Other Phone Numbers:** Assessor 402-443-5700.

Saunders County Register of Deeds

Register of Deeds, PO Box 184, Wahoo, NE 68066. Register of Deeds, R/E and UCC Recording 402-443-8111; Fax 402-443-5010.
Will search UCC records. Will not search real estate records. **Other Phone Numbers:** Assessor 402-443-5700; Treasurer 402-443-8129; Appraiser/Auditor 402-443-5702; Elections 402-443-8100.

Scotts Bluff County Clerk

County Clerk, 1825 10th St, Administration Office Building, Gering, NE 69341. 308-436-6601; Fax 308-436-3178.
Will search UCC records. UCC search includes state tax liens. See Register of Deeds for real estate records. **Other Phone Numbers:** Assessor 308-436-6627.

Scotts Bluff County Register of Deeds

County Register of Deeds, 1825 10th St, Administration Office Building, Gering, NE 69341. County Register of Deeds, R/E and UCC Recording 308-436-6607; Fax 308-436-6609.
Will search UCC records, but only real estate related UCC filed here. This agency will not do a tax lien search. Will not search real estate records. **Other Phone Numbers:** Assessor 308-436-6627; Treasurer 308-436-6621.

Seward County

County Clerk, PO Box 190, Seward, NE 68434-0190. 402-643-2883; Fax 402-643-9243. http://connectseward.org/www/docs/cgov
Will search UCC records. Will not search real estate records. **Other Phone Numbers:** Assessor 402-643-3311; Treasurer 402-643-4574; Elections 402-643-2883; Land or Marriage records 402-643-2883.

Sheridan County

County Clerk, PO Box 39, Rushville, NE 69360. County Clerk, R/E and UCC Recording 308-327-2633. Will search UCC records. UCC search includes tax liens if requested. Will not search real estate records. **Other Phone Numbers:** Assessor 308-327-2113; Treasurer 308-327-2362.

Sherman County

County Clerk, PO Box 456, Loup City, NE 68853-0456. 308-745-1513; Fax 308-745-1820.
Will search UCC records. **Other Phone Numbers:** Assessor 308-745-0113; Treasurer 308-745-1513.

Sioux County

County Clerk, PO Box 158, Harrison, NE 69346. 308-668-2443; Fax 308-668-2443.
Will search UCC records. Will not search real estate records. **Other Phone Numbers:** Assessor 308-668-2443; Treasurer 308-668-2422.

Stanton County

Register of Deeds, PO Box 347, Stanton, NE 68779-0347. Register of Deeds, R/E and UCC Recording 402-439-2222; Fax 402-439-2200.
Will search UCC records. Will not search real estate records. **Other Phone Numbers:** Assessor 402-439-2210; Treasurer 402-439-2223; Elections 402-439-2222.

Thayer County

County Clerk, PO Box 208, Hebron, NE 68370. 402-768-6126.
Will search UCC records. UCC search includes tax liens if requested. Real estate owner, mortgage, and property transfer searches available. **Other Phone Numbers:** Assessor 402-768-6417; Treasurer 402-768-6227.

Thomas County

County Clerk, PO Box 226, Thedford, NE 69166-0226. 308-645-2261; Fax 308-645-2623.
Will search UCC records. UCC search includes tax liens if requested. Will not search real estate records. **Other Phone Numbers:** Assessor 308-645-2261; Treasurer 308-645-2262.

Thurston County

County Clerk, PO Box G, Pender, NE 68047. 402-385-2343; Fax 402-385-3544.
Will search UCC records. Will not search real estate records. **Other Phones:** Assessor 402-385-2251; Treasurer 402-385-3058; Elections 402-385-2343.

Valley County

County Clerk, 125 S. 15th, Ord, NE 68862-1499. 308-728-3700.
Will Search UCC records. UCC search includes tax liens. Will not search real estate records. **Other Phone Numbers:** Assessor 308-728-5081; Treasurer 308-728-5606.

Washington County

County Clerk, PO Box 466, Blair, NE 68008. 402-426-6822; Fax 402-426-6825.
Will search UCC records. **Other Phone Numbers:** Assessor 402-426-6800; Treasurer 402-426-6888.

Wayne County

County Clerk, PO Box 248, Wayne, NE 68787-0248. 402-375-2288; Fax 402-375-2288.
Will search UCC records. This agency will not do a tax lien search. Will not search real estate records. **Other Phone Numbers:** Assessor 402-375-1979; Treasurer 402-375-3885; Elections 402-375-2288.

Webster County

County Clerk, Webster County Clerk PO Box 250, Red Cloud, NE 68970. 402-746-2716; Fax 402-746-2710.
Will search UCC records. **Other Phone Numbers:** Assessor 402-746-2717; Treasurer 402-746-2877; Elections 402-746-2716.

Wheeler County

County Clerk, PO Box 127, Bartlett, NE 68622. 308-654-3235; Fax 308-654-3442.
Will search UCC records. Will not search real estate records. **Other Phone Numbers:** Assessor 308-654-3235; Treasurer 308-654-3236.

York County

County Clerk, Courthouse, 510 Lincoln Ave., York, NE 68467. 402-362-7759; Fax 402-362-2651.
Will search UCC records. Will not search real estate records. **Other Phone Numbers:** Assessor 402-362-4926; Treasurer 402-362-4949.

Nebraska County Locator

You will usually be able to find the city name in the City/County Cross Reference below. In that case, it is a simple matter to determine the county from the cross reference. However, only the official US Postal Service city names are included in this index. There are an additional 40,000 place names that people use in their addresses. Therefore, we have also included a ZIP/City Cross Reference immediately following the City/County Cross Reference.

If you know the ZIP Code but the city name does not appear in the City/County Cross Reference index, look up the ZIP Code in the ZIP/City Cross Reference, find the city name, then look up the city name in the City/County Cross Reference. For example, you want to know the county for an address of Menands, NY 12204. There is no "Menands" in the City/County Cross Reference. The ZIP/City Cross Reference shows that ZIP Codes 12201-12288 are for the city of Albany. Looking back in the City/County Cross Reference, Albany is in Albany County.

City/County Cross Reference

ABIE Butler
ADAMS (68301) Gage(73), Lancaster(22), Otoe(3)
AINSWORTH Brown
ALBION Boone
ALDA Hall
ALEXANDRIA (68303) Thayer(97), Jefferson(2)
ALLEN Dixon
ALLIANCE (69301) Box Butte(97), Sioux(1)
ALMA Harlan
ALVO Cass
AMELIA Holt
AMES Dodge
AMHERST Buffalo
ANGORA Morrill
ANSELMO (68813) Custer(83), Blaine(9), Loup(6)
ANSLEY Custer
ARAPAHOE (68922) Furnas(80), Gosper(19)
ARCADIA (68815) Valley(64), Custer(18), Sherman(16)
ARCHER Merrick
ARLINGTON Washington
ARNOLD (69120) Custer(70), Lincoln(18), Logan(10)
ARTHUR Arthur
ASHBY (69333) Grant(89), Garden(10)
ASHLAND (68003) Saunders(76), Cass(23)
ASHTON (68817) Sherman(91), Howard(8)
ATKINSON Holt
ATLANTA Phelps
AUBURN Nemaha
AURORA (68818) Hamilton(98), Clay(1)
AVOCA (68307) Cass(85), Otoe(14)
AXTELL (68924) Kearney(93), Phelps(6)
AYR Adams
BANCROFT Cuming
BARNESTON Gage
BARTLETT Wheeler
BARTLEY Red Willow
BASSETT (68714) Rock(97), Brown(2)
BATTLE CREEK Madison
BAYARD (69334) Morrill(63), Scotts Bluff(34), Banner(1)
BEATRICE Gage
BEAVER CITY Furnas
BEAVER CROSSING (68313) Seward(98), York(1)
BEE (68314) Seward(88), Butler(11)
BEEMER Cuming
BELDEN Cedar
BELGRADE (68623) Nance(94), Boone(5)
BELLEVUE (68147) Sarpy(97), Douglas(2)
BELLWOOD Butler
BELVIDERE Thayer
BENEDICT (68316) York(95), Polk(4)
BENKELMAN Dundy
BENNET (68317) Lancaster(94), Otoe(5)
BENNINGTON (68007) Douglas(90), Washington(9)
BERTRAND (68927) Phelps(77), Gosper(22)
BERWYN Custer

BIG SPRINGS (69122) Deuel(82), Keith(8), Perkins(5), Garden(3)
BINGHAM (69335) Garden(73), Sheridan(26)
BLADEN (68928) Webster(79), Adams(20)
BLAIR Washington
BLOOMFIELD Knox
BLOOMINGTON Franklin
BLUE HILL (68930) Webster(80), Adams(19)
BLUE SPRINGS Gage
BOELUS Howard
BOONE Boone
BOYS TOWN Douglas
BRADSHAW (68319) York(95), Hamilton(4)
BRADY Lincoln
BRAINARD (68626) Butler(98), Saunders(1)
BREWSTER Blaine
BRIDGEPORT (69336) Morrill(97), Banner(2)
BRISTOW Boyd
BROADWATER Morrill
BROCK Nemaha
BROKEN BOW Custer
BROWNVILLE Nemaha
BRULE (69127) Keith(98), Perkins(1)
BRUNING (68322) Thayer(59), Fillmore(40)
BRUNO (68014) Butler(85), Saunders(14)
BRUNSWICK Antelope
BURCHARD (68323) Pawnee(98), Gage(1)
BURR (68324) Otoe(98), Johnson(1)
BURWELL (68823) Garfield(66), Loup(17), Valley(10), Rock(3)
BUSHNELL Kimball
BUTTE Boyd
BYRON Thayer
CAIRO (68824) Hall(96), Howard(3)
CALLAWAY Custer
CAMBRIDGE (69022) Furnas(74), Frontier(15), Red Willow(7), Gosper(2)
CAMPBELL (68932) Franklin(57), Adams(18), Kearney(14), Webster(9)
CARLETON (68326) Thayer(98), Fillmore(1)
CARROLL Wayne
CEDAR BLUFFS Saunders
CEDAR CREEK Cass
CEDAR RAPIDS (68627) Boone(90), Nance(7), Greeley(1)
CENTER Knox
CENTRAL CITY Merrick
CERESCO (68017) Saunders(62), Lancaster(37)
CHADRON Dawes
CHAMBERS (68725) Holt(96), Wheeler(2), Garfield(1)
CHAMPION Chase
CHAPMAN Merrick
CHAPPELL (69129) Deuel(90), Garden(9)
CHESTER Thayer
CLARKS (68628) Merrick(82), Hamilton(9), Polk(7)
CLARKSON (68629) Colfax(73), Stanton(26)

CLATONIA Gage
CLAY CENTER Clay
CLEARWATER (68726) Antelope(94), Holt(5)
CODY Cherry
COLERIDGE Cedar
COLON Saunders
COLUMBUS Platte
COMSTOCK (68828) Custer(67), Valley(32)
CONCORD Dixon
COOK (68329) Otoe(51), Johnson(47)
CORDOVA Seward
CORNLEA Platte
CORTLAND Gage
COTESFIELD (68829) Howard(89), Greeley(10)
COZAD Dawson
CRAB ORCHARD (68332) Johnson(91), Gage(8)
CRAIG (68019) Burt(96), Washington(2), Dodge(1)
CRAWFORD Dawes
CREIGHTON (68729) Knox(89), Antelope(10)
CRESTON (68631) Platte(89), Stanton(10)
CRETE (68333) Saline(92), Lancaster(7)
CROFTON (68730) Knox(55), Cedar(44)
CROOKSTON Cherry
CULBERTSON (69024) Hitchcock(86), Hayes(6), Red Willow(6)
CURTIS (69025) Frontier(79), Lincoln(19)
DAKOTA CITY Dakota
DALTON Cheyenne
DANBURY Red Willow
DANNEBROG Howard
DAVENPORT (68335) Thayer(66), Nuckolls(23), Fillmore(8)
DAVEY Lancaster
DAVID CITY Butler
DAWSON Richardson
DAYKIN (68338) Jefferson(93), Saline(6)
DE WITT (68341) Saline(58), Gage(41)
DECATUR Burt
DENTON (68339) Lancaster(68), Seward(29), Saline(1)
DESHLER Thayer
DEWEESE (68934) Clay(72), Nuckolls(27)
DICKENS Lincoln
DILLER (68342) Jefferson(77), Gage(22)
DIX (69133) Kimball(98), Cheyenne(1)
DIXON (68732) Dixon(98), Cedar(1)
DODGE (68633) Dodge(72), Cuming(22), Colfax(5)
DONIPHAN (68832) Hall(74), Hamilton(25)
DORCHESTER (68343) Saline(88), Seward(11)
DOUGLAS Otoe
DU BOIS (68345) Pawnee(75), Richardson(24)
DUNBAR Otoe
DUNCAN Platte
DUNNING (68833) Blaine(79), Logan(13), Custer(6)
DWIGHT Butler

EAGLE (68347) Cass(71), Otoe(27)
EDDYVILLE (68834) Dawson(83), Custer(16)
EDGAR (68935) Clay(82), Nuckolls(17)
EDISON (68936) Furnas(74), Gosper(14), Greeley(11)
ELBA (68835) Howard(96), Greeley(3)
ELGIN (68636) Antelope(97), Wheeler(1)
ELK CREEK (68348) Johnson(78), Nemaha(12), Pawnee(9)
ELKHORN Douglas
ELLSWORTH Sheridan
ELM CREEK (68836) Buffalo(73), Phelps(16), Dawson(9)
ELMWOOD Cass
ELSIE (69134) Perkins(88), Chase(11)
ELSMERE (69135) Cherry(52), Brown(47)
ELWOOD (68937) Gosper(84), Dawson(15)
ELYRIA Valley
EMERSON (68733) Dakota(47), Dixon(32), Thurston(19)
EMMET Holt
ENDERS (69027) Chase(96), Dundy(3)
ENDICOTT Jefferson
ERICSON (68637) Wheeler(79), Garfield(20)
EUSTIS (69028) Frontier(64), Dawson(26), Gosper(9)
EWING (68735) Holt(73), Antelope(16), Wheeler(10)
EXETER (68351) Fillmore(81), York(18)
FAIRBURY Jefferson
FAIRFIELD Clay
FAIRMONT (68354) Fillmore(90), York(9)
FALLS CITY Richardson
FARNAM (69029) Dawson(83), Lincoln(16)
FARWELL Howard
FILLEY (68357) Gage(98), Johnson(1)
FIRTH (68358) Lancaster(67), Gage(32)
FORDYCE Cedar
FORT CALHOUN Washington
FOSTER Pierce
FRANKLIN Franklin
FREMONT Dodge
FRIEND (68359) Saline(95), Seward(4)
FULLERTON (68638) Nance(97), Merrick(2)
FUNK Phelps
GARLAND Seward
GENEVA Fillmore
GENOA (68640) Nance(62), Platte(35), Merrick(1)
GERING Scotts Bluff
GIBBON (68840) Buffalo(94), Kearney(5)
GILEAD Thayer
GILTNER Hamilton
GLENVIL (68941) Clay(55), Adams(44)
GOEHNER Seward
GORDON (69343) Sheridan(93), Cherry(6)
GOTHENBURG (69138) Dawson(93), Lincoln(4), Custer(2)
GRAFTON (68365) Fillmore(96), York(3)
GRAND ISLAND Hall
GRANT Perkins

GREELEY Greeley
GREENWOOD (68366) Cass(95), Lancaster(2), Saunders(1)
GRESHAM (68367) York(54), Seward(24), Polk(20), Butler(1)
GRETNA Sarpy
GUIDE ROCK (68942) Webster(80), Nuckolls(19)
GURLEY Cheyenne
HADAR Pierce
HAIGLER (69030) Dundy(89), Chase(10)
HALLAM (68368) Lancaster(93), Gage(6)
HALSEY Thomas
HAMLET Hayes
HAMPTON (68843) Hamilton(94), York(5)
HARDY Nuckolls
HARRISBURG Banner
HARRISON Sioux
HARTINGTON Cedar
HARVARD (68944) Hamilton(51), Clay(48)
HASTINGS Adams
HAY SPRINGS (69347) Sheridan(65), Dawes(34)
HAYES CENTER Hayes
HAZARD Sherman
HEARTWELL Kearney
HEBRON Thayer
HEMINGFORD (69348) Box Butte(66), Dawes(33)
HENDERSON (68371) York(73), Hamilton(26)
HENDLEY Furnas
HENRY (69349) Scotts Bluff(84), Sioux(15)
HERMAN (68029) Washington(90), Burt(9)
HERSHEY Lincoln
HICKMAN Lancaster
HILDRETH (68947) Franklin(78), Kearney(21)
HOLBROOK (68948) Furnas(71), Gosper(24), Frontier(3)
HOLDREGE (68949) Phelps(98), Harlan(1)
HOLMESVILLE Gage
HOLSTEIN Adams
HOMER Dakota
HOOPER (68031) Dodge(92), Washington(6), Cuming(1)
HORDVILLE Hamilton
HOSKINS (68740) Wayne(89), Stanton(10)
HOWELLS (68641) Colfax(47), Cuming(32), Stanton(20)
HUBBARD Dakota
HUBBELL Thayer
HUMBOLDT (68376) Richardson(90), Nemaha(7), Pawnee(2)
HUMPHREY (68642) Platte(89), Madison(10)
HUNTLEY Harlan
HYANNIS Grant
IMPERIAL (69033) Chase(97), Perkins(2)
INAVALE Webster
INDIANOLA (69034) Red Willow(89), Frontier(10)
INLAND Clay
INMAN Holt
ITHACA Saunders
JACKSON Dakota
JANSEN Jefferson
JOHNSON (68378) Nemaha(86), Johnson(7), Otoe(6)
JOHNSTOWN (69214) Brown(98), Cherry(1)
JULIAN Nemaha
JUNIATA Adams
KEARNEY Buffalo
KENESAW (68956) Adams(80), Buffalo(11), Hall(7)
KENNARD Washington
KEYSTONE (69144) Keith(97), Arthur(2)
KILGORE Cherry
KIMBALL (69145) Kimball(96), Banner(3)
LAKESIDE Sheridan
LAMAR Chase

LAUREL (68745) Cedar(94), Wayne(3), Dixon(1)
LAVISTA (68128) Sarpy(98), Douglas(1)
LAWRENCE (68957) Nuckolls(58), Webster(33), Adams(7)
LEBANON Red Willow
LEIGH (68643) Colfax(42), Platte(36), Stanton(20)
LEMOYNE (69146) Keith(95), Arthur(4)
LESHARA Saunders
LEWELLEN (69147) Keith(62), Garden(37)
LEWISTON Pawnee
LEXINGTON Dawson
LIBERTY (68381) Gage(88), Pawnee(11)
LINCOLN Lancaster
LINDSAY (68644) Platte(82), Madison(17)
LINWOOD (68036) Butler(89), Saunders(10)
LISCO (69148) Garden(86), Morrill(13)
LITCHFIELD (68852) Sherman(90), Custer(9)
LODGEPOLE (69149) Cheyenne(84), Garden(15)
LONG PINE Brown
LOOMIS Phelps
LORTON Otoe
LOUISVILLE Cass
LOUP CITY Sherman
LYMAN Scotts Bluff
LYNCH (68746) Boyd(82), Holt(17)
LYONS (68038) Burt(93), Cuming(6)
MACY Thurston
MADISON (68748) Madison(97), Stanton(1)
MADRID Perkins
MAGNET Cedar
MALCOLM Lancaster
MALMO Saunders
MANLEY Cass
MARQUETTE Hamilton
MARSLAND Dawes
MARTELL Lancaster
MASKELL Dixon
MASON CITY Custer
MAX Dundy
MAXWELL Lincoln
MAYWOOD (69038) Frontier(82), Lincoln(17)
MC COOK (69001) Red Willow(97), Frontier(1)
MC COOL JUNCTION (68401) York(98), Fillmore(1)
MCGREW Scotts Bluff
MCLEAN (68747) Pierce(98), Cedar(1)
MEAD Saunders
MEADOW GROVE (68752) Madison(92), Pierce(7)
MELBETA Scotts Bluff
MEMPHIS Saunders
MERNA Custer
MERRIMAN Cherry
MILFORD (68405) Seward(98), Saline(1)
MILLER (68858) Buffalo(97), Custer(2)
MILLIGAN (68406) Fillmore(82), Saline(17)
MILLS Keya Paha
MINATARE Scotts Bluff
MINDEN Kearney
MITCHELL (69357) Scotts Bluff(95), Sioux(4)
MONROE Platte
MOOREFIELD (69039) Frontier(63), Lincoln(36)
MORRILL (69358) Scotts Bluff(83), Sioux(16)
MORSE BLUFF Saunders
MULLEN Hooker
MURDOCK Cass
MURRAY Cass
NAPER Boyd
NAPONEE (68960) Franklin(75), Harlan(20), Webster(4)
NEBRASKA CITY Otoe

NEHAWKA (68413) Cass(97), Otoe(2)
NELIGH Antelope
NELSON Nuckolls
NEMAHA Nemaha
NENZEL Cherry
NEWCASTLE (68757) Dixon(98), Cedar(1)
NEWMAN GROVE (68758) Madison(67), Platte(25), Boone(7)
NEWPORT (68759) Rock(67), Keya Paha(32)
NICKERSON (68044) Washington(55), Dodge(44)
NIOBRARA Knox
NORFOLK Madison
NORMAN Kearney
NORTH BEND Dodge
NORTH LOUP (68859) Valley(95), Greeley(3), Sherman(1)
NORTH PLATTE Lincoln
OAK (68964) Nuckolls(94), Thayer(5)
OAKDALE Antelope
OAKLAND (68045) Burt(95), Cuming(4)
OBERT Cedar
OCONTO (68860) Custer(94), Dawson(5)
OCTAVIA Butler
ODELL Gage
ODESSA Buffalo
OFFUTT A F B Sarpy
OGALLALA Keith
OHIOWA (68416) Fillmore(95), Thayer(4)
OMAHA Douglas
ONEILL Holt
ONG (68452) Clay(82), Fillmore(17)
ORCHARD (68764) Antelope(61), Knox(33), Holt(5)
ORD Valley
ORLEANS Harlan
OSCEOLA Polk
OSHKOSH Garden
OSMOND Pierce
OTOE Otoe
OVERTON (68863) Dawson(88), Phelps(11)
OXFORD (68967) Furnas(60), Harlan(39)
PAGE Holt
PALISADE (69040) Hitchcock(61), Hayes(38)
PALMER (68864) Merrick(77), Nance(21)
PALMYRA (68418) Otoe(96), Cass(3)
PANAMA Lancaster
PAPILLION Sarpy
PARKS Dundy
PAWNEE CITY Pawnee
PAXTON Keith
PENDER (68047) Thurston(63), Cuming(26), Wayne(9)
PERU (68421) Nemaha(90), Otoe(9)
PETERSBURG (68652) Boone(93), Antelope(6)
PHILLIPS Hamilton
PICKRELL Gage
PIERCE Pierce
PILGER (68768) Stanton(88), Cuming(7), Wayne(4)
PLAINVIEW (68769) Pierce(78), Antelope(12), Knox(8)
PLATTE CENTER Platte
PLATTSMOUTH Cass
PLEASANT DALE (68423) Seward(80), Lancaster(18), Saline(1)
PLEASANTON (68866) Buffalo(98), Custer(1)
PLYMOUTH (68424) Jefferson(98), Gage(1)
POLK (68654) Polk(56), York(27), Hamilton(16)
PONCA (68770) Dixon(56), Dakota(43)
POTTER (69156) Cheyenne(81), Banner(12), Kimball(5)
PRAGUE Saunders
PRIMROSE (68655) Boone(93), Greeley(6)
PROSSER Adams

PURDUM (69157) Blaine(47), Cherry(34), Thomas(13), Brown(4)
RAGAN Harlan
RANDOLPH (68771) Cedar(61), Wayne(20), Pierce(17)
RAVENNA (68869) Buffalo(94), Sherman(5)
RAYMOND (68428) Lancaster(98), Seward(1)
RED CLOUD Webster
REPUBLICAN CITY Harlan
REYNOLDS Thayer
RICHFIELD Sarpy
RISING CITY (68658) Butler(96), Polk(3)
RIVERDALE Buffalo
RIVERTON Franklin
ROCA Lancaster
ROCKVILLE Sherman
ROGERS Colfax
ROSALIE (68055) Thurston(84), Cuming(15)
ROSE (68772) Rock(90), Loup(9)
ROSELAND Adams
ROYAL (68773) Antelope(96), Brown(3)
RULO Richardson
RUSHVILLE Sheridan
RUSKIN (68974) Nuckolls(87), Thayer(12)
SAINT EDWARD (68660) Boone(53), Platte(39), Nance(6)
SAINT HELENA Cedar
SAINT LIBORY (68872) Howard(82), Merrick(17)
SAINT MARY Johnson
SAINT PAUL Howard
SALEM Richardson
SARGENT (68874) Custer(95), Loup(2), Hall(1)
SARONVILLE (68975) Fillmore(55), Clay(44)
SCHUYLER Colfax
SCOTIA (68875) Greeley(96), Howard(3)
SCOTTSBLUFF Scotts Bluff
SCRIBNER Dodge
SENECA (69161) Thomas(62), Cherry(37)
SEWARD Seward
SHELBY (68662) Polk(94), Butler(5)
SHELTON (68876) Buffalo(85), Hall(14)
SHICKLEY (68436) Fillmore(98), Clay(1)
SHUBERT (68437) Richardson(87), Nemaha(12)
SIDNEY Cheyenne
SILVER CREEK (68663) Merrick(50), Polk(26), Nance(22), Platte(1)
SMITHFIELD Gosper
SNYDER Dodge
SOUTH BEND Cass
SOUTH SIOUX CITY Dakota
SPALDING (68665) Greeley(76), Wheeler(23)
SPARKS Cherry
SPENCER (68777) Boyd(85), Holt(14)
SPRAGUE Lancaster
SPRINGFIELD Sarpy
SPRINGVIEW Keya Paha
ST COLUMBANS Sarpy
ST MARY Johnson
STAMFORD (68977) Harlan(68), Furnas(31)
STANTON Stanton
STAPLEHURST Seward
STAPLETON (69163) Logan(66), Lincoln(33)
STEELE CITY Jefferson
STEINAUER (68441) Pawnee(98), Johnson(2)
STELLA (68442) Richardson(80), Nemaha(19)
STERLING (68443) Johnson(93), Otoe(6)
STOCKVILLE Frontier
STRANG Fillmore
STRATTON (69043) Hitchcock(95), Dundy(4)

STROMSBURG (68666) Polk(96), York(3)
STUART Holt
SUMNER (68878) Dawson(94), Custer(5)
SUPERIOR Nuckolls
SURPRISE Butler
SUTHERLAND (69165) Lincoln(82), Arthur(8), Keith(5), McPherson(4)
SUTTON (68979) Clay(84), Fillmore(9), Hamilton(4)
SWANTON Saline
SYRACUSE Otoe
TABLE ROCK (68447) Pawnee(95), Johnson(2), Nemaha(2)
TALMAGE (68448) Otoe(84), Nemaha(9), Johnson(6)
TAYLOR Loup
TECUMSEH Johnson
TEKAMAH Burt
THEDFORD Thomas
THURSTON Thurston
TILDEN (68781) Madison(65), Antelope(29), Pierce(4), Boone(1)
TOBIAS (68453) Saline(84), Fillmore(9), Jefferson(4), Thayer(1)

TRENTON Hitchcock
TRUMBULL (68980) Clay(68), Adams(30), Hamilton(1)
TRYON McPherson
UEHLING Dodge
ULYSSES (68669) Butler(86), Seward(13)
UNADILLA (68454) Otoe(98), Cass(1)
UNION (68455) Cass(98), Otoe(1)
UPLAND (68981) Franklin(84), Kearney(15)
UTICA Seward
VALENTINE (69201) Cherry(98), Merrick(1)
VALLEY Douglas
VALPARAISO (68065) Saunders(54), Lancaster(37), Seward(6), Butler(1)
VENANGO (69168) Perkins(66), Chase(33)
VERDIGRE Knox
VERDON Richardson
VIRGINIA (68458) Gage(91), Pawnee(6), Johnson(2)
WACO (68460) York(98), Seward(1)
WAHOO Saunders
WAKEFIELD (68784) Dixon(60), Wayne(38)

WALLACE (69169) Lincoln(80), Perkins(16), Hayes(2)
WALTHILL Thurston
WALTON (68461) Lancaster(97), Cass(1)
WASHINGTON Washington
WATERBURY (68785) Dixon(77), Dakota(22)
WATERLOO (68069) Douglas(96), Sarpy(3)
WAUNETA (69045) Chase(77), Dundy(19), Hitchcock(3)
WAUSA (68786) Knox(90), Cedar(5), Pierce(4)
WAVERLY (68462) Lancaster(98), Cass(2)
WAYNE (68787) Wayne(98), Dixon(1)
WEEPING WATER Cass
WEISSERT Custer
WELLFLEET Lincoln
WEST POINT Cuming
WESTERN (68464) Saline(97), Jefferson(2)
WESTERVILLE Custer
WESTON Saunders
WHITECLAY Sheridan

WHITMAN Grant
WHITNEY Dawes
WILBER (68465) Saline(92), Gage(6), Lancaster(1)
WILCOX (68982) Harlan(31), Kearney(30), Franklin(23), Phelps(15)
WILLOW ISLAND Dawson
WILSONVILLE (69046) Furnas(92), Red Willow(7)
WINNEBAGO Thurston
WINNETOON Knox
WINSIDE Wayne
WINSLOW Dodge
WISNER (68791) Cuming(93), Wayne(5)
WOLBACH (68882) Greeley(51), Howard(38), Nance(7), Boone(2)
WOOD LAKE Cherry
WOOD RIVER Hall
WYMORE Gage
WYNOT Cedar
YORK York
YUTAN Saunders

ZIP/City Cross Reference

ZIP	City
68001-68001	ABIE
68002-68002	ARLINGTON
68003-68003	ASHLAND
68004-68004	BANCROFT
68005-68005	BELLEVUE
68007-68007	BENNINGTON
68008-68009	BLAIR
68010-68010	BOYS TOWN
68014-68014	BRUNO
68015-68015	CEDAR BLUFFS
68016-68016	CEDAR CREEK
68017-68017	CERESCO
68018-68018	COLON
68019-68019	CRAIG
68020-68020	DECATUR
68022-68022	ELKHORN
68023-68023	FORT CALHOUN
68025-68026	FREMONT
68028-68028	GRETNA
68029-68029	HERMAN
68030-68030	HOMER
68031-68031	HOOPER
68033-68033	ITHACA
68034-68034	KENNARD
68035-68035	LESHARA
68036-68036	LINWOOD
68037-68037	LOUISVILLE
68038-68038	LYONS
68039-68039	MACY
68040-68040	MALMO
68041-68041	MEAD
68042-68042	MEMPHIS
68044-68044	NICKERSON
68045-68045	OAKLAND
68046-68046	PAPILLION
68047-68047	PENDER
68048-68048	PLATTSMOUTH
68050-68050	PRAGUE
68054-68054	RICHFIELD
68055-68055	ROSALIE
68056-68056	ST COLUMBANS
68057-68057	SCRIBNER
68058-68058	SOUTH BEND
68059-68059	SPRINGFIELD
68061-68061	TEKAMAH
68062-68062	THURSTON
68063-68063	UEHLING
68064-68064	VALLEY
68065-68065	VALPARAISO
68066-68066	WAHOO
68067-68067	WALTHILL
68068-68068	WASHINGTON
68069-68069	WATERLOO
68070-68070	WESTON
68071-68071	WINNEBAGO
68072-68072	WINSLOW
68073-68073	YUTAN
68100-68112	OMAHA
68113-68113	OFFUTT A F B
68114-68122	OMAHA
68123-68123	BELLEVUE
68124-68127	OMAHA
68128-68128	LAVISTA
68130-68132	OMAHA
68133-68133	PAPILLION
68134-68145	OMAHA
68147-68147	BELLEVUE
68152-68198	OMAHA
68301-68301	ADAMS
68303-68303	ALEXANDRIA
68304-68304	ALVO
68305-68305	AUBURN
68307-68307	AVOCA
68309-68309	BARNESTON
68310-68310	BEATRICE
68313-68313	BEAVER CROSSING
68314-68314	BEE
68315-68315	BELVIDERE
68316-68316	BENEDICT
68317-68317	BENNET
68318-68318	BLUE SPRINGS
68319-68319	BRADSHAW
68320-68320	BROCK
68321-68321	BROWNVILLE
68322-68322	BRUNING
68323-68323	BURCHARD
68324-68324	BURR
68325-68325	BYRON
68326-68326	CARLETON
68327-68327	CHESTER
68328-68328	CLATONIA
68329-68329	COOK
68330-68330	CORDOVA
68331-68331	CORTLAND
68332-68332	CRAB ORCHARD
68333-68333	CRETE
68335-68335	DAVENPORT
68336-68336	DAVEY
68337-68337	DAWSON
68338-68338	DAYKIN
68339-68339	DENTON
68340-68340	DESHLER
68341-68341	DE WITT
68342-68342	DILLER
68343-68343	DORCHESTER
68344-68344	DOUGLAS
68345-68345	DU BOIS
68346-68346	DUNBAR
68347-68347	EAGLE
68348-68348	ELK CREEK
68349-68349	ELMWOOD
68350-68350	ENDICOTT
68351-68351	EXETER
68352-68352	FAIRBURY
68354-68354	FAIRMONT
68355-68355	FALLS CITY
68357-68357	FILLEY
68358-68358	FIRTH
68359-68359	FRIEND
68360-68360	GARLAND
68361-68361	GENEVA
68362-68362	GILEAD
68364-68364	GOEHNER
68365-68365	GRAFTON
68366-68366	GREENWOOD
68367-68367	GRESHAM
68368-68368	HALLAM
68370-68370	HEBRON
68371-68371	HENDERSON
68372-68372	HICKMAN
68374-68374	HOLMESVILLE
68375-68375	HUBBELL
68376-68376	HUMBOLDT
68377-68377	JANSEN
68378-68378	JOHNSON
68379-68379	JULIAN
68380-68380	LEWISTON
68381-68381	LIBERTY
68382-68382	LORTON
68401-68401	MC COOL JUNCTION
68402-68402	MALCOLM
68403-68403	MANLEY
68404-68404	MARTELL
68405-68405	MILFORD
68406-68406	MILLIGAN
68407-68407	MURDOCK
68409-68409	MURRAY
68410-68410	NEBRASKA CITY
68413-68413	NEHAWKA
68414-68414	NEMAHA
68415-68415	ODELL
68416-68416	OHIOWA
68417-68417	OTOE
68418-68418	PALMYRA
68419-68419	PANAMA
68420-68420	PAWNEE CITY
68421-68421	PERU
68422-68422	PICKRELL
68423-68423	PLEASANT DALE
68424-68424	PLYMOUTH
68428-68428	RAYMOND
68429-68429	REYNOLDS
68430-68430	ROCA
68431-68431	RULO
68432-68432	SAINT MARY
68432-68432	ST MARY
68433-68433	SALEM
68434-68434	SEWARD
68436-68436	SHICKLEY
68437-68437	SHUBERT
68438-68438	SPRAGUE
68439-68439	STAPLEHURST
68440-68440	STEELE CITY
68441-68441	STEINAUER
68442-68442	STELLA
68443-68443	STERLING
68444-68444	STRANG
68445-68445	SWANTON
68446-68446	SYRACUSE
68447-68447	TABLE ROCK
68448-68448	TALMAGE
68450-68450	TECUMSEH
68452-68452	ONG
68453-68453	TOBIAS
68454-68454	UNADILLA
68455-68455	UNION
68456-68456	UTICA
68457-68457	VERDON
68458-68458	VIRGINIA
68460-68460	WACO
68461-68461	WALTON
68462-68462	WAVERLY
68463-68463	WEEPING WATER
68464-68464	WESTERN
68465-68465	WILBER
68466-68466	WYMORE
68467-68467	YORK
68500-68588	LINCOLN
68601-68602	COLUMBUS
68620-68620	ALBION
68621-68621	AMES
68622-68622	BARTLETT
68623-68623	BELGRADE
68624-68624	BELLWOOD
68625-68625	BOONE
68626-68626	BRAINARD
68627-68627	CEDAR RAPIDS
68628-68628	CLARKS
68629-68629	CLARKSON
68630-68630	CORNLEA
68631-68631	CRESTON
68632-68632	DAVID CITY
68633-68633	DODGE
68634-68634	DUNCAN
68635-68635	DWIGHT
68636-68636	ELGIN
68637-68637	ERICSON
68638-68638	FULLERTON
68640-68640	GENOA
68641-68641	HOWELLS
68642-68642	HUMPHREY
68643-68643	LEIGH
68644-68644	LINDSAY
68647-68647	MONROE
68648-68648	MORSE BLUFF
68649-68649	NORTH BEND
68650-68650	OCTAVIA
68651-68651	OSCEOLA
68652-68652	PETERSBURG
68653-68653	PLATTE CENTER
68654-68654	POLK
68655-68655	PRIMROSE
68658-68658	RISING CITY
68659-68659	ROGERS
68660-68660	SAINT EDWARD
68661-68661	SCHUYLER

68662-68662 SHELBY	68790-68790 WINSIDE	68933-68933 CLAY CENTER
68663-68663 SILVER CREEK	68791-68791 WISNER	68934-68934 DEWEESE
68664-68664 SNYDER	68792-68792 WYNOT	68935-68935 EDGAR
68665-68665 SPALDING	68801-68803 GRAND ISLAND	68936-68936 EDISON
68666-68666 STROMSBURG	68810-68810 ALDA	68937-68937 ELWOOD
68667-68667 SURPRISE	68812-68812 AMHERST	68938-68938 FAIRFIELD
68669-68669 ULYSSES	68813-68813 ANSELMO	68939-68939 FRANKLIN
68701-68702 NORFOLK	68814-68814 ANSLEY	68940-68940 FUNK
68710-68710 ALLEN	68815-68815 ARCADIA	68941-68941 GLENVIL
68711-68711 AMELIA	68816-68816 ARCHER	68942-68942 GUIDE ROCK
68713-68713 ATKINSON	68817-68817 ASHTON	68943-68943 HARDY
68714-68714 BASSETT	68818-68818 AURORA	68944-68944 HARVARD
68715-68715 BATTLE CREEK	68819-68819 BERWYN	68945-68945 HEARTWELL
68716-68716 BEEMER	68820-68820 BOELUS	68946-68946 HENDLEY
68717-68717 BELDEN	68821-68821 BREWSTER	68947-68947 HILDRETH
68718-68718 BLOOMFIELD	68822-68822 BROKEN BOW	68948-68948 HOLBROOK
68719-68719 BRISTOW	68823-68823 BURWELL	68949-68949 HOLDREGE
68720-68720 BRUNSWICK	68824-68824 CAIRO	68950-68950 HOLSTEIN
68722-68722 BUTTE	68825-68825 CALLAWAY	68951-68951 HUNTLEY
68723-68723 CARROLL	68826-68826 CENTRAL CITY	68952-68952 INAVALE
68724-68724 CENTER	68827-68827 CHAPMAN	68954-68954 INLAND
68725-68725 CHAMBERS	68828-68828 COMSTOCK	68955-68955 JUNIATA
68726-68726 CLEARWATER	68829-68829 COTESFIELD	68956-68956 KENESAW
68727-68727 COLERIDGE	68831-68831 DANNEBROG	68957-68957 LAWRENCE
68728-68728 CONCORD	68832-68832 DONIPHAN	68958-68958 LOOMIS
68729-68729 CREIGHTON	68833-68833 DUNNING	68959-68959 MINDEN
68730-68730 CROFTON	68834-68834 EDDYVILLE	68960-68960 NAPONEE
68731-68731 DAKOTA CITY	68835-68835 ELBA	68961-68961 NELSON
68732-68732 DIXON	68836-68836 ELM CREEK	68963-68963 NORMAN
68733-68733 EMERSON	68837-68837 ELYRIA	68964-68964 OAK
68734-68734 EMMET	68838-68838 FARWELL	68966-68966 ORLEANS
68735-68735 EWING	68840-68840 GIBBON	68967-68967 OXFORD
68736-68736 FORDYCE	68841-68841 GILTNER	68969-68969 RAGAN
68737-68737 FOSTER	68842-68842 GREELEY	68970-68970 RED CLOUD
68738-68738 HADAR	68843-68843 HAMPTON	68971-68971 REPUBLICAN CITY
68739-68739 HARTINGTON	68844-68844 HAZARD	68972-68972 RIVERTON
68740-68740 HOSKINS	68845-68845 KEARNEY	68973-68973 ROSELAND
68741-68741 HUBBARD	68846-68846 HORDVILLE	68974-68974 RUSKIN
68742-68742 INMAN	68847-68849 KEARNEY	68975-68975 SARONVILLE
68743-68743 JACKSON	68850-68850 LEXINGTON	68976-68976 SMITHFIELD
68745-68745 LAUREL	68852-68852 LITCHFIELD	68977-68977 STAMFORD
68746-68746 LYNCH	68853-68853 LOUP CITY	68978-68978 SUPERIOR
68747-68747 MCLEAN	68854-68854 MARQUETTE	68979-68979 SUTTON
68748-68748 MADISON	68855-68855 MASON CITY	68980-68980 TRUMBULL
68749-68749 MAGNET	68856-68856 MERNA	68981-68981 UPLAND
68751-68751 MASKELL	68858-68858 MILLER	68982-68982 WILCOX
68752-68752 MEADOW GROVE	68859-68859 NORTH LOUP	69001-69001 MC COOK
68753-68753 MILLS	68860-68860 OCONTO	69020-69020 BARTLEY
68755-68755 NAPER	68861-68861 ODESSA	69021-69021 BENKELMAN
68756-68756 NELIGH	68862-68862 ORD	69022-69022 CAMBRIDGE
68757-68757 NEWCASTLE	68863-68863 OVERTON	69023-69023 CHAMPION
68758-68758 NEWMAN GROVE	68864-68864 PALMER	69024-69024 CULBERTSON
68759-68759 NEWPORT	68865-68865 PHILLIPS	69025-69025 CURTIS
68760-68760 NIOBRARA	68866-68866 PLEASANTON	69026-69026 DANBURY
68761-68761 OAKDALE	68868-68868 PROSSER	69027-69027 ENDERS
68762-68762 OBERT	68869-68869 RAVENNA	69028-69028 EUSTIS
68763-68763 ONEILL	68870-68870 RIVERDALE	69029-69029 FARNAM
68764-68764 ORCHARD	68871-68871 ROCKVILLE	69030-69030 HAIGLER
68765-68765 OSMOND	68872-68872 SAINT LIBORY	69031-69031 HAMLET
68766-68766 PAGE	68873-68873 SAINT PAUL	69032-69032 HAYES CENTER
68767-68767 PIERCE	68874-68874 SARGENT	69033-69033 IMPERIAL
68768-68768 PILGER	68875-68875 SCOTIA	69034-69034 INDIANOLA
68769-68769 PLAINVIEW	68876-68876 SHELTON	69035-69035 LAMAR
68770-68770 PONCA	68878-68878 SUMNER	69036-69036 LEBANON
68771-68771 RANDOLPH	68879-68879 TAYLOR	69037-69037 MAX
68772-68772 ROSE	68880-68880 WEISSERT	69038-69038 MAYWOOD
68773-68773 ROYAL	68881-68881 WESTERVILLE	69039-69039 MOOREFIELD
68774-68774 SAINT HELENA	68882-68882 WOLBACH	69040-69040 PALISADE
68776-68776 SOUTH SIOUX CITY	68883-68883 WOOD RIVER	69041-69041 PARKS
68777-68777 SPENCER	68901-68902 HASTINGS	69042-69042 STOCKVILLE
68778-68778 SPRINGVIEW	68920-68920 ALMA	69043-69043 STRATTON
68779-68779 STANTON	68922-68922 ARAPAHOE	69044-69044 TRENTON
68780-68780 STUART	68923-68923 ATLANTA	69045-69045 WAUNETA
68781-68781 TILDEN	68924-68924 AXTELL	69046-69046 WILSONVILLE
68783-68783 VERDIGRE	68925-68925 AYR	69101-69103 NORTH PLATTE
68784-68784 WAKEFIELD	68926-68926 BEAVER CITY	69120-69120 ARNOLD
68785-68785 WATERBURY	68927-68927 BERTRAND	69121-69121 ARTHUR
68786-68786 WAUSA	68928-68928 BLADEN	69122-69122 BIG SPRINGS
68787-68787 WAYNE	68929-68929 BLOOMINGTON	69123-69123 BRADY
68788-68788 WEST POINT	68930-68930 BLUE HILL	69125-69125 BROADWATER
68789-68789 WINNETOON	68932-68932 CAMPBELL	69127-69127 BRULE

69128-69128 BUSHNELL
69129-69129 CHAPPELL
69130-69130 COZAD
69131-69131 DALTON
69132-69132 DICKENS
69133-69133 DIX
69134-69134 ELSIE
69135-69135 ELSMERE
69138-69138 GOTHENBURG
69140-69140 GRANT
69141-69141 GURLEY
69142-69142 HALSEY
69143-69143 HERSHEY
69144-69144 KEYSTONE
69145-69145 KIMBALL
69146-69146 LEMOYNE
69147-69147 LEWELLEN
69148-69148 LISCO
69149-69149 LODGEPOLE
69150-69150 MADRID
69151-69151 MAXWELL
69152-69152 MULLEN
69153-69153 OGALLALA
69154-69154 OSHKOSH
69155-69155 PAXTON
69156-69156 POTTER
69157-69157 PURDUM
69160-69160 SIDNEY
69161-69161 SENECA
69162-69162 SIDNEY
69163-69163 STAPLETON
69165-69165 SUTHERLAND
69166-69166 THEDFORD
69167-69167 TRYON
69168-69168 VENANGO
69169-69169 WALLACE
69170-69170 WELLFLEET
69171-69171 WILLOW ISLAND
69190-69190 OSHKOSH
69201-69201 VALENTINE
69210-69210 AINSWORTH
69211-69211 CODY
69212-69212 CROOKSTON
69214-69214 JOHNSTOWN
69216-69216 KILGORE
69217-69217 LONG PINE
69218-69218 MERRIMAN
69219-69219 NENZEL
69220-69220 SPARKS
69221-69221 WOOD LAKE
69301-69301 ALLIANCE
69331-69331 ANGORA
69333-69333 ASHBY
69334-69334 BAYARD
69335-69335 BINGHAM
69336-69336 BRIDGEPORT
69337-69337 CHADRON
69339-69339 CRAWFORD
69340-69340 ELLSWORTH
69341-69341 GERING
69343-69343 GORDON
69345-69345 HARRISBURG
69346-69346 HARRISON
69347-69347 HAY SPRINGS
69348-69348 HEMINGFORD
69349-69349 HENRY
69350-69350 HYANNIS
69351-69351 LAKESIDE
69352-69352 LYMAN
69353-69353 MCGREW
69354-69354 MARSLAND
69355-69355 MELBETA
69356-69356 MINATARE
69357-69357 MITCHELL
69358-69358 MORRILL
69360-69360 RUSHVILLE
69361-69363 SCOTTSBLUFF
69365-69365 WHITECLAY
69366-69366 WHITMAN
69367-69367 WHITNEY

Nevada

General Help Numbers:

Governor's Office
Capitol Building   775-684-5670
Carson City, NV 89701   Fax 775-684-5683
http://gov.state.nv.us   8AM-5PM

Attorney General's Office
100 N Carson St   775-684-1100
Carson City, NV 89710   Fax 775-684-1108
http://ag.state.nv.us   8AM-5PM

State Court Administrator
Administrative Office of the Courts   775-684-1700
201 S Carson St, #250   Fax 775-684-1723
Carson City, NV 89701-4702   8AM-5PM
http://silver.state.nv.us/elec_judicial.htm

State Archives
100 N Stewart St   775-684-3360
Carson City, NV 89701-4285   Fax 775-684-3330
http://dmla.clan.lib.nv.us/docs/nsla   8AM-5PM M-F

State Specifics:

Capital:	Carson City
	Carson City County
Time Zone:	PST
Number of Counties:	17
Number of Filing Locations:	17
Population:	2,106,074
Web Site:	http://silver.state.nv.us/

State Agencies

Criminal Records

Nevada Highway Patrol, Record & ID Services, 808 W Nye Lane, Carson City, NV 89703; 775-687-1600, 775-687-1843 (Fax), 8AM-5PM.

www.nvrepository.state.nv.us

Note: A sex offender registry is not available online to the public; make phone or mail requests with name, DOB, DR or SSN# to the agency; responses take one week, fee is $8.00.

Indexing & Storage: Records are available from 1987 and are on computer. Records are indexed on on computer. Records are normally destroyed after (records maintained indefinitely, unless purged due to court order). 40% of all arrests in database have final dispositions recorded, approximately 25% for those arrests within last 5 years.

Searching: This repository maintains all "fingerprintable charges," meaning, essentially, all felony records and misdemeanor offenses including DUI and domestic violence. Sex offender records go back to 1998; will only release where, when and what of conviction. Include the following in your request: set of fingerprints, signed release, full name. DOB, SS#, sex and race are helpful. The following data is not released: sealed records or juvenile records. Records without dispositions are not released, unless an approved waiver is submitted.

Access by: mail, in person.

Fee & Payment: The fingerprint search fee is $15.00 per individual. If the search requires an FBI fingerprint check (for record checks on occupations concerning children or the elderly, per state stutute), the fee is $39.00. Fee payee: Nevada Highway Patrol. Prepayment required. Cash, money order or cashier's check required. No credit cards or personal checks accepted.

Mail search: Turnaround time: 15 working days. No self addressed stamped envelope is required.

In person search: Records are still returned by mail.

Corporation Records
Limited Partnerships
Limited Liability Company
  Records
Limited Partnership Records

Secretary of State, Records, 101 N Carson, #3, Carson City, NV 89701-4786; 775-684-5708, 702-486-2880 (Las Vegas Ofc.:), 702-486-2888 (Las Vegas Ofc fax:), 775-684-5725 (Fax), 8AM-5PM.

www.sos.state.nv.us

Note: File are here, but records can also be looked up on computer at the Las Vegas office (555 E Washington Ave., #2900, Las Vegas, NV 89101). To get forms, use their Document-on-Demand System 800-583-9486.

Indexing & Storage: Records are available since inception of laws. Old, inactive records are purged from computer and archived. New records are available for inquiry immediately. Records are indexed on microfiche, inhouse computer.

Searching: Fax searching is available only for state government agencies. Include the following in your request: full name of business, corporation file number. In addition to the articles of incorporation, corporation records include the following information: Annual Lists of Officers & Directors, Prior (merged) names, Inactive and Reserved names, and Resident Agent names.

Access by: mail, phone, in person, online.

Fee & Payment: The search fee is $20.00, and $40.00 for LLCs. The certification fee is $20.00. Copy fees are $1.00 per page. There are set fees for certain specific documents that range from $10.00 to $25.00. Fee payee: Secretary of State. Prepayment required. Personal checks accepted. Credit cards accepted: MasterCard, Visa.

Mail search: Turnaround time: 1 to 2 weeks. No self addressed stamped envelope is required.

Phone search: Staff will give status for corporations and partnerships, corporate officer names, and trademark information.

In person search: Information requests are available.

Online search: Online access is offered on the Internet site for no charge. You can search by corporate name, resident agent, corporate officers, or by file number.

Expedited service: Expedited service is available for mail, phone and in person searches. There is a $25.00 fee for overnight service of copies if 1 to 10 pages, and $50.00 if over 10 pages.

Assumed Name
Fictitious Name

Records not maintained by a state level agency.

Note: Records are at the county level.

Trademarks/Servicemarks

Secretary of State, Corporate Expedite Office, 555 E. Washington Ave., #2900, Las Vegas, NV 89101, 702-486-2885, 702-486-2888 (Fax), 8AM-5PM.

www.sos.state.nv.us

Note: Trademark files are kept here; however, they are on the same computer system as the Carson City office. They can do all of the same searches on corporate records as Carson City, except for making copies of actual documents in files.

Indexing & Storage: Records are available since inception.

Searching: The same search requirements apply here as in Carson City.

Access by: mail, phone, fax, in person.

Fee & Payment: Certified copies of trademarks are $10.00. Fee payee: NV Secretary of State. Prepayment required. Personal checks accepted. No credit cards accepted.

Mail search: Turnaround time: 1 to 2 weeks.

Phone search: Limited information is offered over the phone.

Fax search: Turnaround time is 1-2 weeks. Add $1.00 per page.

In person: Searching is available in person.

Uniform Commercial Code
Federal Tax Liens
State Tax Liens

UCC Division, Secretary of State, 200 N Carson St, Carson City, NV 89701-4069; 775-684-5708, 775-684-5630 (Fax), 8AM-5PM.

www.sos.state.nv.us

Note: Federal tax lien search must be requested separately and only contain data on businesses. Tax liens on individuals are filed at the county level. There is no state income tax, thus no recorded state tax liens.

Indexing & Storage: Records are available from 1967 on both computer and microfilm.

Searching: Use search request form UCC-11. Include the following in your request: debtor name.

Access by: mail, in person, online.

Fee & Payment: The fee for written request to search a debtor name is $20.00. Copies cost $1.00 per page. Fee payee: Secretary of State. Prepayment required. Personal checks accepted. Credit cards accepted: MasterCard, Visa.

Mail search: Turnaround time: 3 to 5 days. A self addressed stamped envelope is requested.

In person search: You may request information in person.

Online search: This is a PC dial-up system. The fee is $24.50 per hour or $10.75 per hour on an 800 number for unlimited access. There is a $50.00 minimum deposit. The system is up from 7 AM to 5 PM. Call 775-684-5704 and ask for Tom Horgan.

Expedited service: Expedited service is available for mail and fax request searches. Searches will not be returned by fax. Turnaround time: 1 day. Add $50.00 per entity name.

Sales Tax Registrations

State does not impose sales tax.

Birth Certificates

Nevada Department of Health, Office of Vital Statistics, 505 E King St, Rm 102, Carson City, NV 89701-4749; 775-684-4242, 775-684-4280 (Message Phone), 775-684-4156 (Fax), 8AM-4PM.

Indexing & Storage: Records are available from 1911 to present. It takes 30 days of filing before new records are available for inquiry. Records are indexed on microfiche, index cards, inhouse computer, hard copy.

Searching: Birth and death records are considered confidential and not open to the general public. Include the following in your request: full name, names of parents, mother's maiden name, date of birth, place of birth, relationship to person of record, reason for information request. Parents' names are a must to get record.

Access by: mail, phone, fax, in person.

Fee & Payment: The fee for a verification only is $8.00. For a certified copy the fee is $11.00. If you wish to purchase using a credit card, there is an additional $5.50 fee. Fee payee: Office of Vital Statistics. Prepayment required. Personal checks accepted. Credit cards accepted: MasterCard, Visa, AmEx, Discover.

Mail search: Turnaround time: 2 to 3 days. No self addressed stamped envelope is required.

Phone search: You must use a credit card.

Fax search: You must use a credit card.

In person search: Turnaround time 20 minutes.

Expedited service: Expedited service is available for mail, phone and fax searches. The overnight fee is $16.00. Use of credit card required.

Death Records

Nevada Department of Health, Office of Vital Statistics, 505 E King St, Rm 102, Carson City, NV 89701-4749; 775-684-4242, 775-684-4280 (Message Phone), 775-684-4156 (Fax), 8AM-4PM.

Indexing & Storage: Records are available from 1911 on. It takes 30 days of filing before new records are available for inquiry. Records are indexed on microfiche, index cards, inhouse computer, hard copy.

Searching: Records are considered confidential, need to state relationship. However, a verification printout with name, date, and location is available to the public. Include the following in your request: full name, date of death, place of death, relationship to person of record, reason for information request.

Access by: mail, phone, fax, in person.

Fee & Payment: The fee for a verification only is $8.00. A certified copy is $8.00. There is an additional $5.50 fee if using a credit card. Fee payee: Office of Vital Statistics. Prepayment required. Personal checks accepted. Credit cards accepted: MasterCard, Visa, AmEx, Discover.

Mail search: Turnaround time: 5 to 10 working days. No self addressed stamped envelope is required.

Phone search: Use of credit card required.

Fax search: Same search criteria.

In person search: Turnaround time is 20 minutes.

Expedited service: Expedited service is available for mail, phone and fax searches. Records are sent overnight at expense of requester, usually $16.00. A credit card is required.

Marriage Certificates
Divorce Records

Access to Records is Restricted

Nevada Department of Health, Office of Vital Statistics, 505 E King St, Rm 102, Carson City, NV 89701-4749; 775-684-4481.

Note: Marriage and Divorce records are found at county of issue. However, the agency has an index and will relate the county and date of the event. The fee is $8.00. Call 775-684-4242.

Workers' Compensation Records

Employers Insurance Co of NV, Workers Compensation Records, 2550 Paseo Verde Parkway, Henderson, NV 89074-7117; 888-682-6671, 702-671-7674 (Fax), 8AM-5PM.

www.employersinsco.com

Note: Effective 1/1/00, State of Nevada privatized the business of workers' compensation insurance. The state agency formally named State Industrial Insurance System became a private company. This company holds the records from the state agency.

Indexing & Storage: Records are available from 1940's on. It takes 1 week before new records are available for inquiry. Records are indexed on microfilm, inhouse computer, file folders.

Searching: Must have a signed release form from claimant and you must specify what you want from the file. Older records are kept on microfilm, the records on the in-house computer are for general information only. Include the following in your request: claimant name, Social Security Number, claim number, date of accident. This office is the phone service center. There are also hard copy records iat the Reno office. 9790 Gateway Dr #100, Reno NV 89521. Their fax # is 775-886-1797.

Access by: mail, fax, in person.

Fee & Payment: Fee is $.20 per page if copies are over 20 pages. Fee payee: Employers Insurance Co of NV. Personal checks accepted. No credit cards accepted.

Mail search: Turnaround time: 30 days. A self addressed stamped envelope is requested.

Fax search: Fax requests are accepted.

In person search: By going in person, you will only reduce the mail time.

Driver Records

Department of Motor Vehicles, Records Section, 555 Wright Way, Carson City, NV 89711-0250; 775-684-4590, 800-992-7945 (In-state), 8AM-5PM.

www.dmvstat.com

Note: Copies of citations may be obtained at the same address. There is no fee when requesting your own citation, otherwise the fee is $8.00.

Indexing & Storage: Records are available for 3 years. Non-moving violations are not listed on the driving record for non-CDL drivers. Nevada complies with the Driver's Privacy Protection Act, so personal information is available only to specific users. Records are computer indexed since 1980.

Searching: Authorized users may establish an account by completing the appropriate application. Call 775-684-4590 to request an application. Casual requesters without written consent of subject receive records without personal information. The driver's license number, or name and DOB are needed for a request. The SSN is helpful for searching, but will not be released on the record. Accidents do not appear on the record.

Access by: mail, phone.

Fee & Payment: The fee is $5.00 per record. Fee payee: Nevada Department of Motor Vehicles. Prepayment required. Personal checks accepted. No credit cards accepted.

Mail search: Turnaround time: 10 days. Your request must be on department approved forms. No self addressed stamped envelope is required.

Phone search: Phone-in requesters must be pre-approved, are assigned a five-digit account number and can request up to five records at one time over the phone. Call 775-684-4590 for more information. There is an in-state toll free line at 800-992-7945.

Other access: Overnight magnetic tape requesting is available for high volume users.

Vehicle Ownership
Vehicle Identification

Department of Motor Vehicles, Motor Vehicle Record Section, 555 Wright Way, Carson City, NV 89711-0250; 775-684-4590, 775-684-4740 (Fax), 8AM-5PM.

www.dmvstat.com

Indexing & Storage: Records are available for the present on computer and on microfilm back to 1980.

Searching: Social Security Numbers, withdrawal action, accidents, and information connected to a license plate are not released to the general public. Nevada complies with DPPA and restricts access of records with personal information to permissible users. Requesters must show a legal right to the information or provide written consent or records are released with no perosnal data.

Access by: mail, phone.

Fee & Payment: The cost is $5.00 per record. Fee payee: Nevada Department of Motor Vehicles. Prepayment required. Personal checks accepted. No credit cards accepted.

Mail search: Turnaround time: 10 days. Be sure to give as much specific information as possible. Your request must be on department-approved

forms. No self addressed stamped envelope is required.

Phone search: Phone-in requesters must be pre-approved, are assigned a five-digit account number and can request up to five records at one time over the phone. Call 775-684-4590 for more information. There is an in-state toll free line at 800-992-7945.

Other access: Database is available for sale to permissible users under DPPA at costs varying from $500 to $2,500.

Accident Reports

Department of Motor Vehicles, Highway Patrol Division, 555 Wright Way, Carson City, NV 89711; 775-684-4870, 775-684-4879 (Fax), 8AM-5PM.

http://ps.state.nv.us/index.htm

Indexing & Storage: Records are available only for those records at least three years old. Records are indexed on inhouse computer.

Searching: Requests must be in writing. Include the following in your request: full name, date of accident, location of accident, report number. For accidents 4 years old or less, the reports will be found at a regional office (Las Vegas 702-486-4100; Reno 775-688-2500; or Elko 775-738-8035) associated with where the accidents occurred. Same fees apply.

Access by: mail, fax, in person.

Fee & Payment: The fee is $3.50 per report, and report(s) will not be mailed until payment has been received. Fee payee: Nevada Highway Patrol. Prepayment required. Personal checks accepted. No credit cards accepted.

Mail search: Turnaround time: 3 days. The turnaround time for the Las Vegas office is often 4 to 6 weeks. A self addressed stamped envelope is requested.

Fax search: Fax searching available.

In person search: Turnaround time is immediate if the record is on file.

Vessel Ownership
Vessel Registration

Division of Wildlife Headquarters, Boat Registration, 1100 Valley Rd, Reno, NV 89512-2815; 775-688-1983, 8AM-5PM M-F.

http://nevadadivisionofwildlife.org

Indexing & Storage: Records are available from 1972 to the present and are indexed on computer. All boats must be registered.

Searching: To search, one of the following is required: hull ID #, boat #, or name. The following data is not released: Social Security Numbers.

Access by: mail, in person.

Fee & Payment: The fee is $5.00 per boat or person, which includes 1 computer print-out. Photocopies cost $.50 per page. Fee payee: NDOW. Prepayment required. Cash is accepted from in person searchers only. No credit cards accepted.

Mail search: Turnaround time: 4 days. No self addressed stamped envelope is required.

In person search: Turnaround time can be immediate if search is not lengthy.

Other access: Information is available on magnetic tape, labels, and printed lists. Fees depend on media type, can be up to $750.

Legislation Records

Nevada Legislature, 401 S Carson St, Carson City, NV 89701-4747; 775-684-6827 (Bill Status Only), 775-684-6800 (Main Number), 775-684-6835 (Publications), 775-684-6600 (Fax), 8AM-5PM.

www.leg.state.nv.us

Note: If you want to order copies, call the publications number.

Indexing & Storage: Records are available from 1915 to present. Records are computer indexed from 1985 to present, and on microfiche from 1967 to present.

Searching: Include the following in your request: bill number, year.

Access by: mail, phone, fax, in person, online.

Fee & Payment: No charge for one or two bills. If you request more than two, the fee varies by page numbers requested, You may request any search by mail or telephone. The agency will determine fee, but will not release copies until paid. Fee payee: Legislative Council Bureau. Prepayment required. Personal checks accepted. Credit cards accepted: MasterCard, Visa.

Mail search: Turnaround time: 1 to 2 days. Information requests are available. No self addressed stamped envelope is required.

Phone search: You may request bills by phone.

Fax search: Turnaround time is generally in 1 to 2 days.

In person search: You may request bills in person.

Online search: Bills and bill status information is available via this agency's web site. Legislative bills, hearings, journals are searchable online for years 1997, 1999, and 2001.

Expedited service: Expedited service is available for mail and phone searches. You must provide an account number with a shipper.

Voter Registration

Records not maintained by a state level agency.

Note: Records are open to the public at the county level. All data is released except for SSNs.

GED Certificates

Department of Education, State GED Administrator, 700 E 5th Street, Carson City, NV 89701; 775-687-9104, 775-687-9114 (Fax), 8AM-5PM.

www.nde.state.nv.us

Indexing & Storage: Records are available from 1954 to present, for GED. This agencies also holds many other education-based records including military, federal prison, etc.

Searching: Include the following in your request: name used when tested, signed release, date of birth, Social Security Number. There is a possibility that this office may not have the tests results, so it is important to also submit the location and year of the test. They will fax back.

Access by: mail, fax, in person.

Fee & Payment: There is no fee.

Mail search: Turnaround time: 7 to 10 days.

Fax search: Same criteria as mail searching.

In person search: Searching is available in person.

Hunting License Information
Fishing License Information

Division of Wildlife, 1100 Valley Rd, Reno, NV 89512-2817; 775-688-1500, 775-688-1509 (Fax), 8AM-5PM.

www.nevadadivisionofwildlife.org

Indexing & Storage: Records are available from 1976 to present on microfiche.

Searching: Include the following in your request: full name, date of birth, Social Security Number. The following data is not released: Social Security Numbers or telephone numbers.

Access by: mail.

Fee & Payment: The fee is $5.00 per name per year searched. Fee payee: NDOW Prepayment required with guaranteed funds. No credit cards accepted.

Mail search: Turnaround time: 3 to 4 working days. No self addressed stamped envelope is required.

Other access: The Division offers mailing lists, labels, magnetic tapes of hunting and fishing license holders for fees ranging from $150 to $365.

Nevada State Licensing Agencies

Licenses Searchable Online

Ambulatory Surgery Centers (Pharm) #16.............http://glsuitewww.glsuite.com/NVBoPWeb/Consumers/default.asp
Architect #2...http://nsbaidrd.state.nv.us
Carpentry Contractor #46 ....http://nscb.tecxprs.com
Chiropractor #3...www.state.nv.us/chirobd/home.htm
Dental Hygienist #4...www.nvdentalboard.org/databaseRDH.html
Dentist #4 ....www.nvdentalboard.org/databaseDDS.html
Drug Wholesalers/Distributor/Mfg #16 ....http://glsuitewww.glsuite.com/NVBoPWeb/Consumers/default.asp
Engineer #19 ....http://boe.state.nv.us/ROST_HOME.HTM
Euthanasia Technicians (Animal) #16 ....http://glsuitewww.glsuite.com/NVBoPWeb/Consumers/default.asp
Floor & Carpet Layer #46....................................http://nscb.tecxprs.com
GCB Most-Wanted & Banned List #36 ....http://gaming.state.nv.us/wanted_main.htm
Glazier Contractor #46..http://nscb.tecxprs.com
Guard Dog Handler #39..http://ag.state.nv.us/pilb/020802pilb.pdf
Heating & Air Conditioning Mechanic #46............http://nscb.tecxprs.com
Hospital Pharmacy, Institutional #16....................http://glsuitewww.glsuite.com/NVBoPWeb/Consumers/default.asp
Insulation Installer Contractor #46 ....http://nscb.tecxprs.com
Interior Designer #2 ....http://nsbaidrd.state.nv.us
Lobbyist #27 ....www.leg.state.nv.us/lobbyistdb/index.cfm
Medical Devices, Equipment & Gases #16............http://glsuitewww.glsuite.com/NVBoPWeb/Consumers/default.asp
Narcotic Treatment Center #16.............................http://glsuitewww.glsuite.com/NVBoPWeb/Consumers/default.asp
Nurse, Advanced Practitioner #16 ....http://glsuitewww.glsuite.com/NVBoPWeb/Consumers/default.asp
Optometrist #0 ....www.odfinder.org/LicSearch.asp
Painter #46 ....http://nscb.tecxprs.com
Painter/Paper Hanger #46 ....http://nscb.tecxprs.com
Patrol Company/Man, Private #39 ....http://ag.state.nv.us/pilb/020802pilb.pdf
Pharmacist/Pharmaceutical Technician #16 ....http://glsuitewww.glsuite.com/NVBoPWeb/Consumers/default.asp
Pharmacy #16..http://glsuitewww.glsuite.com/NVBoPWeb/Consumers/default.asp
Pharmacy Practitioner #16...................................http://glsuitewww.glsuite.com/NVBoPWeb/Consumers/default.asp
Physician Assistant (Pharm) #16 ....http://glsuitewww.glsuite.com/NVBoPWeb/Consumers/default.asp
Plasterer/Drywall Installer #46 ....http://nscb.tecxprs.com
Plumber #46 ....http://nscb.tecxprs.com
Polygraph Examiner #39......................................http://ag.state.nv.us/pilb/020802pilb.pdf
Prison (correctional - Pharmacy) #16...................http://glsuitewww.glsuite.com/NVBoPWeb/Consumers/default.asp
Private Investigator #39 ....http://ag.state.nv.us/pilb/020802pilb.pdf
Process Server #39 ....http://ag.state.nv.us/pilb/020802pilb.pdf
Repossessor #39 ....http://ag.state.nv.us/pilb/020802pilb.pdf
Residential Designer #2.......................................http://nsbaidrd.state.nv.us
Roofer #46 ....http://nscb.tecxprs.com
Surveyor, Land #19 ....http://boe.state.nv.us/ROST_HOME.HTM
Water Well Driller #30..http://ndwr.state.nv.us/Engineering/welldrill.htm
Well Driller/Monitor #30 ....http://ndwr.state.nv.us/Engineering/welldrill.htm

Licensing Quick Finder

Acupuncturist #14 702-486-7280
Adult Day Care #22 775-687-4475
Adult Group Care #22.........................775-687-4475
Aesthetician #38 702-486-6542
Alcohol & Drug Abuse Center #22 775-687-4475
Alcohol & Drug Abuse Counselor #22..775-687-4475
Ambulance Attendant #22 775-687-4475
Ambulance Permit #22 775-687-4475
Ambulatory Surgery Centers (Pharm) #16
....775-850-1440
Animal Technician #21 775-688-1788
Announcer, Athletic Event (Ring) #35 ..702-486-2575
Appraiser (MVD) #24..........................702-486-4009
Architect #2..702-486-7300
Athletic Promoter (Professional & Amateur) #35
....702-486-2575
Attorney #44 702-382-2200
Audiologist #31 775-857-3500

Auditor #1...775-786-0231
Barber #45..702-456-4769
Blood Gas Technician/Technologist #22
....775-687-4475
Boxer #35 702-486-2575
Bus Driver #25....................................775-684-4590
Carpentry Contractor #46...................702-486-1100
Casino General Manager #36 775-684-7770
Cemetery #7 702-646-6860
Chiropractor #3...................................775-688-1919
Claims Adjuster #24............................702-486-4009
Clinical Laboratory Technologist #22...775-687-4475
Coach Dealer, Commercial #34 702-486-4590
Cosmetologist #38..............................702-486-6542
Court Reporter, Certified #23 702-384-1663
Crematorium #7..................................702-646-6860
Dental Hygienist #4 702-486-7044
Dentist #4 702-486-7044

Director (Medical Laboratory) #22 775-687-4475
Driller, Rotary #29 775-687-3861
Drug Wholesalers/Distributor/Mfg #16 . 775-850-1440
Electrologist #38.................................702-486-6542
Embalmer #7.......................................702-646-6860
Emergency Care Center, Independent #22
....775-687-4475
Emergency Medical Technician #22.....775-687-4475
Engineer #19 775-688-1231
Environmental Health Specialist #42 ...775-328-2422
ESRD #22 775-687-4475
Euthanasia Technician #21.................775-688-1788
Euthanasia Technicians (Animal) #16 . 775-850-1440
Exempt Laboratory #22.......................775-687-4475
Financial Advisor (Investment Advisor) #40
....702-486-2440
First Responder EMT #22...................775-687-4475
Fishing Guide #26 775-688-1541

Floor & Carpet Layer #46 702-486-1100	Manicurist #38 702-486-6542	Physician Assistant (Pharm) #16 775-850-1440
Funeral Director #7.........................702-646-6860	Marriage & Family Therapist #32.........702-486-7388	Plasterer/Drywall Installer #46 702-486-1100
Fur Dealer #26 775-688-1541	Medical Devices, Equipment & Gases #16	Plumber #46...................................702-486-1100
Gaming #36 775-684-7770	775-850-1440	Podiatrist #18 775-829-8066
Gaming Device Mfg./Dist. #36...........775-684-7770	Medical Doctor #11..........................775-688-2559	Polygraph Examiner #39....................775-687-3223
Gaming License Company #36...........775-684-7770	Medical Technician #22.....................775-687-4475	Prison (correctional - Pharm) #16 775-850-1440
GCB Most-Wanted & Banned List #36..775-684-7770	Mobile Home Dealer/Limited Dealer #34	Private Investigator #39 775-687-3223
Glazier Contractor #46.....................702-486-1100	702-486-4590	Process Server #39..........................775-687-3223
Groundskeeper/Gardener #28 .....775-688-1182x243	Mobile Home Installer/Mfg. #34 702-486-4590	Psychologist #20 775-688-1268
Guard Dog Handler #39 775-687-3223	Mobile Home Salesman #34 702-486-4590	Public Accountant-CPA #1 775-786-0231
Hair Stylist (Designer) #38................702-486-6542	Mobile Home Serviceman/Limited Serviceman #34	Racing #37 775-684-7900
Health Clinic, Rural #22....................775-687-4475	702-486-4590	Real Estate Broker #50 702-486-4033
Hearing Aid Specialist #8 702-571-9000	Mobile/Manufactured Home Rebuilder #34	Real Estate Salesperson #50 702-486-4033
Heating & Air Conditioning Mechanic #46	702-486-4590	Referee/Judge/Timekeeper #35 702-486-2575
....702-486-1100	Mobile/Manufactured Home RME #34 ..702-486-4590	Rehabilitation Service #22 775-687-4475
Histotechnologist #22.......................775-687-4475	Narcotic Treatment Center #16 775-850-1440	Repossessor #39 775-687-3223
Histologic Technician #22..................775-687-4475	Notary Public #41 775-684-5749	Residential Designer #2.....................702-486-7300
Home Health Agency #22...................775-687-4475	Nurse, Advanced Practitioner #16 775-850-1440	Roofer #46......................................702-486-1100
Homeopathic Physician/Assistant #9 ...702-451-3332	Nursing Care (Skilled) Facility #22........775-687-4475	Sanitarian, Public #42 775-328-2418
Homeopathic Practitioner, Advanced #9	Nursing Facility #22..........................775-687-4475	School Administrator #47 702-486-6458
....702-451-3332	Nursing Home Administrator #49 702-486-5445	School Counselor #47 702-486-6458
Hospice #22....................................775-687-4475	Nursing Pool Operator #22.................775-687-4475	School Librarian #47 702-486-6458
Hospital #22....................................775-687-4475	Occupational Therapist/Assistant #12...775-857-1700	School Program Administrator #47 702-486-6458
Hospital Pharmacy, Institutional #16....775-850-1440	Optician #5 775-853-1421	Scientific Collection Permit #26 775-688-1541
IC Emergency Center #22...................775-687-4475	Optician Apprentice #5 775-853-1421	Securities Branch Office #40 702-486-2440
Insulation Installer Contractor #46........702-486-1100	Optometrist #0.................................775-883-8367	Securities Broker/Dealer #40 702-486-2440
Insurance Agent #24 ....,.........702-486-4009	Osteopathic Physician #15.................702-732-2147	Securities Registration #40 702-486-2440
Interior Designer #2..........................702-486-7300	Osteopathic Physician Assistant #15...702-732-2147	Securities Sales Representative #40...702-486-2440
Intermediate Care Facility for the Mentally Retarded	Painter #46.....................................702-486-1100	Slot Route Operator #36 775-684-7770
#22..775-687-4475	Painter/Paper Hanger #46...................702-486-1100	Social Worker #6..............................702-688-2555
Intermedical Care Facility #22.............775-687-4475	Pathologist Assistant #22...................775-687-4475	Speech Pathologist/Audiologist #31 775-857-3500
Investment Advisor #40 702-486-2440	Patrol Company/Man, Private #39 775-687-3223	Supervisory Medical Technology, General #22
Kickboxer #35 702-486-2575	Pest Control Applicator/Company #28	775-687-4475
Laboratory Assist./Blood Gas Assist. #22	....775-688-1182x252	Surgical Center, Ambulatory #22.........775-687-4475
....775-687-4475	Pesticide, Restricted Use #28 ......775-688-1182x251	Surveyor, Land #19...........................775-688-1231
Laboratory Certification #22 775-687-4475	Pharmacist/Pharmaceutical Technician #16	Taxi Driver #48................................702-486-6532
Laboratory Office Assistant #22 775-687-4475	775-850-1440	Teacher #47 702-486-6458
Laboratory, Medical #22 775-687-4475	Pharmacy #16 775-850-1440	Veterinarian #21...............................775-688-1788
Landscape Architect #10 775-626-0604	Pharmacy Practitioner #16 775-850-1440	Veterinary Facility #21.......................775-688-1788
Lobbyist #27 775-684-6800	Physical Therapist #17 702-876-5535	Water Well Driller #30 775-687-3861
LPG-Liquefied Petroleum Dist./Technician #33	Physical Therapist Assistant #17 702-876-5535	Well Driller/Monitor #30.....................775-687-3861
....775-687-4890	Physician Assistant #11 775-688-2559	Wrestler #35....................................702-486-2575

Licensing Agency Information

#1 Board of Accountancy, 200 S Virginia St, #670, Reno, NV 89501; 775-786-0231, Fax: 775-786-0234.
www.state.nv.us/accountancy
Agency email: nvpabd@govmail.state.nv.us.

#2 Interior & Residential Design, Board of Architecture, 2080 E Flamingo Rd, #225, Las Vegas, NV 89119; 702-486-7300, Fax: 702-486-7304.
http://nsbaidrd.state.nv.us
Agency email: nsbaidrd@govmail.state.nv.us.
Search database at http://nsbaidrd.state.nv.us

#3 Board of Chiropractic Examiners, 4600 Kietzke Ln, M, #245, Reno, NV 89502; 775-688-1919, Fax: 775-688-1920.
www.state.nv.us/chirobd/home.htm
Agency email: chirobd@govmail.state.nv.us.
Search database at www.state.nv.us/chirobd/home.htm. Data is presented in a PDF format; click on "Licensed Chiropractic Physicians."

#4 Board of Dental Examiners, 2295 Renaissance Dr, #B, Las Vegas, NV 89119-6171; 800-337-3926 or 702-486-7044, Fax: 702-486-7046.
www.nvdentalboard.org
Agency email: nsbde@govmail.state.nv.us.
Search database at
www.nvdentalboard.org/DatabaseIndex.html

#5 Board of Dispensing Opticians, PO Box 19625, Reno, NV 89511; 775-853-1421, Fax: 775-853-1408.
http://nvbdo.state.nv.us. Agency email: nvbdo@govmail.state.nv.us. Complete list is available by mail from the board for a minimal fee.

#6 Board of Examiners for Social Workers, 4600 Kietzke Ln, Bldg C, Rm 121, Reno, NV 89502; 775-688-2555, Fax: 775-688-2557.
http://socwork.state.nv.us

#7 Board of Funeral Directors & Embalmers, 4894 Lone Mt Rd PMB186, Las Vegas, NV 89130; 702-646-6860, Fax: 702-648-5858.
http://funeral.state.nv.us

#8 Board of Hearing Aid Specialists, PO Box 190, Carson City, NV 89702; 702-571-9000.
www.state.nv.us/boards/hearing
Agency email: Lloyddr@earthlink.net.

#9 Board of Homeopathic Medical Examiners, 4475 S Pecos Rd, Las Vegas, NV 89121; 702-451-3332, Fax: 702-451-3332.
www.nvbhme.com

#10 Board of Landscape Architecture, PO Box 51780, Sparks, NV 89435; 775-688-1316, Fax: 775-688-1317.

http://nsbla.state.nv.us. Agency email: nsbla@govmail.state.nv.u. Complete list is available for $5.00 from the Board.

#11 Board of Medical Examiners, 1105 Terminal Way, #301, Reno, NV 89510; 775-688-2559, Fax: 775-688-2321.
www.state.nv.us/medical
Agency email: nsbme@govmail.state.nv.us.

#12 Board of Occupational Therapy, PO Box 70220, Reno, NV 89570-0220; 775-857-1700, Fax: 775-857-2121.
www.nvot.org
Agency email: occtherapy@gbis.com.

#14 Board of Oriental Medicine, 900 E Karen, Ste. B203, Las Vegas, NV 89109; 702-486-7280.
www.oriental_medicine.state.nv.us

#15 Board of Osteopathic Medicine, 2860 E Flamingo, #G, Las Vegas, NV 89121; 702-732-2147, Fax: 702-732-2079.
www.osteo.state.nv.us
Agency email: osteo@govmail.state.nv.us.

#16 Board of Pharmacy, 555 Double Eagle Ct #1100, Reno, NV 89511-8991; 775-850-1440, 800-364-2081, Fax: 775-850-1444.
http://glsuitewww.glsuite.com/nvbopweb/
Search database at http://glsuitewww.glsuite.com/NVBoPWeb/Consumers/default.asp

#17 Board of Physical Therapy Examiners, 3150 W Sahara Ave #B-13, Las Vegas, NV 89102; 702-876-5535, Fax: 702-876-2097.
http://ptherapy.state.nv.us
Agency email: nsbpte@govmail.state.nv.us.

#18 Board of Podiatry, PO Box 12215, Reno, NV 89510-2215; 775-789-2605, Fax: 775-829-8069.
http://podiatry.state.nv.us/.

#19 Board of Professional Engineers & Land Surveyors, 1755 E Plumb Ln, #135, Reno, NV 89502; 775-688-1231, Fax: 775-688-2991.
http://boe.state.nv.us
Agency email: jrobins@natinfo.net.
Search database at
http://boe.state.nv.us/ROST_HOME.HTM

#20 Board of Psychological Examiners, PO Box 2286 (275 Hill St, #246), Reno, NV 89505-2286; 775-688-1268, Fax: 775-688-1272. Agency email: nbop@govmail.state.nv.us.

#21 Board of Veterinary Medical Examiners, 4600 Kietzke, Bldg O, #265, Reno, NV 89502; 775-688-1788, Fax: 775-688-1808.
www.state.nv.us/vet
Agency email: vetbbdinfo@govmail.state.nv.us.

#22 Bureau of Licensure & Certification, Medical Laboratory Services, 1550 College Parkway #158, Carson City, NV 89710; 775-687-4475, Fax: 775-687-6588.

#23 Certified Court Reporters Board, 3355 Spring Mountain Rd #2, Las Vegas, NV 89102-8631; 702-384-1663, Fax: 702-876-9249.

#24 Department of Business & Industry, Insurance Division, 2501 E Sahara Ave, #302, Las Vegas, NV 89104; 702-486-4009, Fax: 702-486-4007.
www.doi.state.nv.us

#25 Department of Motor Vehicles & Public Safety, Records Section, 555 Wright Way, Carson City, NV 89711-0250; 775-684-4590, Fax: 775-684-4740.
http://nevadadmv.state.nv.us
Agency email: jfogliani@dmv.state.nv.us.

#26 Wildlife Commission, Law Enforcement, 1100 Valley Rd, Reno, NV 89520; 775-688-1530, Fax: 775-688-1551.
www.nevadadivisionofwildlife.org/nwc/index.htm
Agency email: jcfishcomish@worldnet.att.net.

#27 Director of Legislative Counsel Bureau, 401 S Carson, Carson City, NV 89701-4747; 775-684-6800, Fax: 775-684-6600.
www.leg.state.nv.us/lcb/admin/lobbyist.htm
Agency email: weise@icb.state.nv.us.
Search database at
www.leg.state.nv.us/lobbyistdb/index.cfm

#28 Department of Agriculture, Pest Control Licensing Division, 350 Capitol Hill, Reno, NV 89502-2923; 775-688-1180, Fax: 775-688-1178.
http://agri.state.nv.us/PCOs/

#29 Division of Water Resources, 123 W Nye Lane, #246, Carson City, NV 89706; 775-687-4380, Fax: 775-687-6972.
http://ndwr.state.nv.us

#30 Division of Water Resources, Well Drillers' Advisory Board, 123 W Nye Ln, Capitol Complex Rm 246, Carson City, NV 89706-0818; 775-687-3861, Fax: 775-687-1393.
http://ndwr.state.nv.us
Search database at
http://ndwr.state.nv.us/Engineering/welldrill.htm

#31 Examiners for Audiology & Speech Pathology, Speech Pathology & Audiology Board, Redfield Bldg #152, Reno, NV 89557; 775-784-4887, Fax: 775-857-2121.
http://speech_pathology.state.nv.us

#32 Board of Examiners of Marriage & Family Therapists, PO Box 72758, Las Vegas, NV 89170; 702-486-7388, Fax: 702-434-7181. Agency email: nvmftbd@aol.com.

#33 Liquefied Petroleum Gas Regulation Board, PO Box 338 (106 E Adams, Rm 216), Carson City, NV 89702; 775-687-4890, Fax: 775-687-3956.
www.state.nv.us/lpg

#34 Attn: Gisele Jordan, Licensing Officer, Manufactured Housing Division, 2501 E Sahara Ave, #205, Las Vegas, NV 89104; 702-486-4590, Fax: 702-486-4309.
www.mnd.state.nv.us
Agency email: mhlicens@mnd.state.nv.us.

#35 Athletic Commission, 555 E Washington St #1500, Las Vegas, NV 89101; 702-486-2575, Fax: 702-486-2577.
www.state.nv.us/b&i/ac
Agency email: boxing@govmail.state.nv.us.

#36 Tax & License Division, Gaming Control Board, 1919 E College Pky (PO Box 8003, 89702-8003), Carson City, NV 89706; 775-684-7770.
http://gaming.state.nv.us

#37 Gaming Control Board, Enforcement Division, 1919 E College Pky, Carson City, NV 89706; 775-684-7900.
http://gaming.state.nv.us

#38 Board of Cosmetology, 1785 E Sahara Ave, #255, Las Vegas, NV 89104; 702-486-6542, Fax: 702-369-8064. Agency email: nvcosmbd@govmail.state.nv.us.

#39 Office of the Attorney General, Private Investigators Licensing Board, 3476 Executive Pointe Way #14, Carson City, NV 89706; 775-687-3223, Fax: 775-687-3226.
http://ag.state.nv.us/pilb/home.htm
Agency email: pilbinfo@aq.state.nv.us
Lists only those who want to be listed.

#40 Office of the Secretary of State, Securities Division, 555 E Washington Av #5200, Las Vegas, NV 89101; 702-486-2440, Fax: 702-486-2452.
www.sos.state.nv.us/securities

#41 Office of the Secretary of State, Notary Division, 101 N Carson St, Carson City, NV 89710-4786; 775-684-5708, Fax: 775-684-5725.
http://sos.state.nv.us/notary
Agency email: nvnotary@govmail.state.nv.us.

#42 Environmental Health Services, c/o Washoe County District Health Department, PO Box 1130 (1001 E 9th St), Reno, NV 89520; 775-328-2434, Fax: 775-328-6176.

#44 State Bar of Nevada, 600 E Charleston Blvd, Las Vegas, NV 89104; 702-382-2200, Fax: 702-385-2878.
www.nvbar.org. Agency email: pamik@nvbar.org.

#45 Barbers' Health & Sanitation Board, 4710 E Flamingo Rd, Las Vegas, NV 89121; 702-456-4769 LV (775-688-1988 Reno), Fax: 702-456-1948.
http://barber.state.nv.us

#46 Contractors' Board, 9670 Gateway Dr #100, Reno, NV 89521; 702-486-1100 LV (775-688-1141 Reno), Fax: 702-486-1190 LV (775-688-1271 Reno).
http://nscb.state.nv.us
Agency email: cntractr@govmail.state.nv.us.
Search database at http://nscb.tecxprs.com

#47 Department of Education, Teacher Licensure, 1820 E Sahara, #205, Las Vegas, NV 89104; 702-486-6458, Fax: 702-687-9101.
www.nde.state.nv.us/licensure/index.html
Agency email: license@nsn.k12.nv.us.

#48 Taxicab Authority, 1785 E Sahara Ave #200, Las Vegas, NV 89104; 702-486-6532, Fax: 702-486-7350.
www.state.nv.us/b&i/ta
Agency email: ranselmo@govmail.state.nv.us.

#49 Board of Examiners for Long Term Care Administrators, 3157 N Rainbow Blvd, PMB 313, Las Vegas, NV 89108; 702-486-5445.

#50 Department of Business & Industry, Real Estate Division, 2501 E Sahara Ave, Las Vegas, NV 89158; 702-486-4033, Fax: 702-486-4275.
www.red.state.nv.us
Agency email: realest@govmail.state.nv.us.

Nevada Federal Courts

The following list indicates the district and division name for each county in the state. If the bankruptcy court location is different from the district court, then the location of the bankruptcy court appears in parentheses.

County/Court Cross Reference

Carson City .... Reno	Lincoln .... Las Vegas
Churchill .... Reno	Lyon .... Reno
Clark .... Las Vegas	Mineral .... Reno
Douglas .... Reno	Nye .... Las Vegas
Elko .... Reno	Pershing .... Reno
Esmeralda .... Las Vegas	Storey .... Reno
Eureka .... Reno	Washoe .... Reno
Humboldt .... Reno	White Pine .... Reno
Lander .... Reno	

Standards for Federal Courts: The search fee is $20.00 per item (one party name or case number). Certification fee is $7.00 per document. Copy fee is $.50 per page. All fees standard unless noted in profile. Mail Search: always enclose a stamped self addressed envelope unless otherwise noted. Before releasing records, all courts require prepayment unless noted in profile. Open records are located at the court unless otherwise noted. District courts index by defendant and plaintiff as well as by case number. Bankruptcy courts usually index by debtor and case number. While most courts now have their indexes on computer, many still maintain index card files as well. The universal PACER sign-up number is 800-676-6856. Find PACER and the Party/Case Index on the Web at http://pacer.psc.uscourts.gov. PACER dial-up access is $.60 per minute. Also, courts offering internet access via RACER, PACER, Web-PACER or the new CM-ECF charge $.07 per page fee unless noted as free.

US District Court

District of Nevada

Las Vegas Division Room 4425, 300 Las Vegas Blvd S, Las Vegas, NV 89101 (Use mail address for courier delivery), 702-464-5400.

www.nvd.uscourts.gov

Counties: Clark, Esmeralda, Lincoln, Nye.

Indexing & Storage: Cases are indexed by defendant, plaintiff, and case number. New cases are available in the index 2 weeks after filing date. Open records are located at this court.

Fee & Payment Notes: Payment may be made by money order, cashier check, personal check. Payee: Clerk, US District Court.

Phone Search: Only docket information available by phone.

Mail Search: A SASE is not required.

In Person Search: In person searching available.

PACER: Access fee is. Document images are available online. PACER is available online at https://pacer.psc.uscourts.gov/cgi-bin/login/login .pl?court_id=nvdc. Document images available.

Reno Division Room 301, 400 S Virginia St, Reno, NV 89501 (Use mail address for courier delivery), 775-686-5800, Fax: 702-686-5851.

www.nvd.uscourts.gov

Counties: Carson City, Churchill, Douglas, Elko, Eureka, Humboldt, Lander, Lyon, Mineral, Pershing, Storey, Washoe, White Pine.

Indexing & Storage: Cases are indexed by defendant, plaintiff, and case number. New cases are available in the index 1-2 days after filing date. Records are also indexed on microfiche. Open records are located at this court.

Fee & Payment Notes: Payment may be made by money order, cashier check, personal check. Payee: Clerk, US District Court.

Phone Search: Only docket information available by phone.

Fax Search: The cost for a fax search is $15.00 per name to be certified. Will fax results for $.50 per page prepaid.

Mail Search: A stamped self addressed envelope is not required.

In Person Search: In person searching available.

PACER: Access fee is. Document images available. PACER is available online at https://pacer.psc.uscourts.gov/cgi-bin/login/login. pl?court_id=nvdc. Document images available.

US Bankruptcy Court

District of Nevada

Las Vegas Division 8th Floor, Suite 8112, Lloyd D. George Federal Bldg, 333 Las Vegas Boulevard South, Las Vegas, NV 89101 (Courier Address: Clerk's Office, 1st Fl, Lloyd D. George Federal Bldg, 333 Las Vegas Boulevard South, Las Vegas, NV 89101), 702-388-6257.

www.nvb.uscourts.gov

Counties: Clark, Esmeralda, Lincoln, Nye.

Indexing & Storage: Cases are indexed by debtor as well as by case number. New cases are available in the index 24 hours after filing date. Open records are located at this court.

Fee & Payment Notes: Payment may be made by money order, cashier check, personal check. Debtor's checks are not accepted. Payee: Clerk, US Bankruptcy Court. You are allowed to make your own copies. These copies cost $.25 per page.

Phone Search: An automated voice case information service (VCIS) is available. Call VCIS at 800-314-3436 or 702-388-6708.

In Person Search: In person searching available.

PACER: Access fee is. Case records are available back to September 1993. Records are purged every 16 months. New civil records are available online after 1 day. PACER is available online at http://pacer.nvb.uscourts.gov. Any cases filed as of 8/1/2002 are found on PACER only.

Electronic Filing: Information is available online at https://ecf.nvb.uscourts.gov

Other Online Access: Search records online using RACER. Currently the system, which is being phased out, is free and requires free registration. Access RACER via the court main web site, above. Allows acces to cases from 1998 through 7/31/2002.

Reno Division Room 1109, 300 Booth St, Reno, NV 89509 (Use mail address for courier delivery), 775-784-5559.

www.nvb.uscourts.gov

Counties: Carson City, Churchill, Douglas, Elko, Eureka, Humboldt, Lander, Lyon, Mineral, Pershing, Storey, Washoe, White Pine.

Indexing & Storage: Cases are indexed by debtor as well as by case number. New cases are available in the index 24 hours after filing date. Open records are located at this court.

Fee & Payment Notes: Payment may be made by money order, cashier check, personal check. Debtor's checks are not accepted. Payee: Clerk, US Bankruptcy Court.

Phone Search: An automated voice case information service (VCIS) is available. Call VCIS at 800-314-3436 or 702-388-6708.

In Person Search: In person searching available.

PACER: Access fee is. Case records are available back to September 1993. Records are purged every 16 months. New civil records are available online after 1 day. PACER is available online at http://pacer.nvb.uscourts.gov. Any cases filed as of 8/1/2002 are found on PACER only.

Electronic Filing: Information is available online at https://ecf.nvb.uscourts.gov

Other Online Access: Search records online using RACER. Currently the system, which is being phased out, is free and requires free registration. Access RACER via the court main web site, above. Allows acces to cases from 1998 through 7/31/2002.

Nevada County Courts

Court	Jurisdiction	No. of Courts	How Organized
District Courts*	General	17	9 Districts
Justice Courts*	Limited	45	56 Townships
Municipal Courts	Municipal	19	19 Incorporated Cities/Towns

* Profiled in this Sourcebook.

Court	CIVIL								
	Tort	Contract	Real Estate	Min. Claim	Max. Claim	Small Claims	Estate	Eviction	Domestic Relations
District Courts*	X	X	X	$7500	No Max		X		X
Justice Courts*	X	X	X	$0	$7500	$3500		X	
Municipal Courts	X	X	X	$0	$3500	$3500			

Court	CRIMINAL				
	Felony	Misdemeanor	DWI/DUI	Preliminary Hearing	Juvenile
District Courts*	X	X	X		X
Justice Courts*		X	X	X	
Municipal Courts					

ADMINISTRATION Supreme Court of Nevada, Administrative Office of the Courts, Capitol Complex, 201 S Carson Street, Carson City, Nevada, 89701; 775-684-1700, Fax: 775-684-1723. http://nvcourtaoc.state.nv.us

COURT STRUCTURE There are 17 District Courts within 9 judicial districts. The 45 Justice Courts are named for the township of jurisdiction. Note that, due to their small populations, some townships no longer have Justice Courts. Probate is handled by the District Courts.

ONLINE ACCESS Some Nevada Courts have internal online computer systems, but only Clark County has online access available to the public. A statewide court automation system is being implemented. The Supreme Court web site gives access to opinions.

ADDITIONAL INFORMATION Many Nevada Justice Courts are small and have very few records. Their hours of operation vary widely and contact is difficult. It is recommended that requesters call ahead for information prior to submitting a written request or attempting an in-person retrieval.

Carson City

1st Judicial District Court 885 E Musser St #3031, Carson City, NV 89701-4775; 775-887-2082; Fax: 775-887-2177. Hours: 9AM-5PM (PST). *Felony, Gross Misdemeanor, Civil Actions Over $7,500, Probate.*

Note: The Justice Courts retain records for minor misdemeanors.

Civil Records: Access: Mail, in person. Only the court performs in person searches; visitors may not. Search fee: $1.00 per name per year. Required to search: name, years to search. Civil cases indexed by defendant, plaintiff. Civil records on computer from 1987, on microfiche and archives from 1861.
Criminal Records: Access: Mail, in person. Only the court performs in person searches; visitors may not. Search fee: $1.00 per name per year. Required to search: name, years to search. Criminal records on computer from 1987, on microfiche and archives from 1861.
General Information: No sealed or juvenile records released. SASE required. Turnaround time 2-7 days.

Copy fee: $1.00 per page. Certification fee: $5.00. Fee payee: Carson City. Personal checks accepted. Personal check accepted with check guarantee card only. Prepayment is required.

Justice & Municipal Court 885 E Musser St #2007, Carson City, NV 89701-4775; 775-887-2121; Fax: 775-887-2297. Hours: 8:30AM-5PM (PST). *Misdemeanor, Civil Actions Under $7,500, Eviction, Small Claims.*

Civil Records: Access: Mail, in person. Only the court performs in person searches; visitors may not. Search fee: $1.00 per name per year. Required to search: name, years to search. Criminal records on computer alpha index from 1991.
Criminal Records: Access: Mail, in person. Only the court performs in person searches; visitors may not. Search fee: $1.00 per name per year. Required to search: name, years to search. Criminal records on computer alpha index from 1991.
General Information: No sealed, sexual victims, juvenile records released. SASE required. Turnaround time 1 week. Copy fee: $1.00 per page. Certification

fee: $3.00. Fee payee: Carson City. Personal checks accepted. Prepayment is required.

Churchill County

3rd Judicial District Court 73 N Maine St, Ste B, Fallon, NV 89406; 775-423-6080; Fax: 775-423-8578. Hours: 8AM-Noon, 1-5PM (PST). *Felony, Gross Misdemeanor, Civil Actions Over $7,500, Probate.*

Civil Records: Access: Fax, mail, in person. Only the court performs in person searches; visitors may not. Search fee: $1.00 per name per year. Required to search: name, years to search. Civil cases indexed by defendant, plaintiff. Civil records on computer from 1990, prior on books, microfiche.
Criminal Records: Access: Fax, mail, in person. Only the court performs in person searches; visitors may not. Search fee: $1.00 per name per year. Required to search: name, years to search, DOB; also helpful: SSN. Criminal records on computer from 1990, prior on books, microfiche.
General Information: No juvenile, adoption or sealed records released. SASE required. Turnaround time 1-2 day. Fax notes: No fee to fax results. local or toll free

numbers only. Copy fee: $1.00 per page. Certification fee: $5.00. Fee payee: Office of Court Clerk. Personal checks accepted. Prepayment is required.

Justice Court 71 N Maine St, Fallon, NV 89406; 775-423-2845; Fax: 775-423-0472. Hours: 8AM-5PM (PST). *Misdemeanor, Civil Actions Under $7,500, Eviction, Small Claims.*

Civil Records: Access: Mail, fax, in person. Both court and visitors may perform in person searches. Search fee: $1.00 per name per year. Required to search: name, years to search. Civil cases indexed by defendant, plaintiff. Civil records on computer from 1987, prior on microfiche back to 1980.

Criminal Records: Access: Mail, fax, in person. Both court and visitors may perform in person searches. Search fee: $1.00 per name per year. Required to search: name, years to search, DOB. Criminal records on computer from 1987, prior on microfiche back to 1980.

General Information: No sealed records released. SASE not required. Turnaround time 1 day. Copy fee: $.30 per page. Certification fee: $3.00. Fee payee: Justice Court. Personal checks accepted. Credit cards accepted: Visa, MasterCard. Prepayment is required.

Clark County

8th Judicial District Court 200 S 3rd (PO Box 551601), Las Vegas, NV 89155; 702-455-3156; Fax: 702-455-4929. Hours: 8AM-5PM (PST). *Felony, Gross Misdemeanor, Civil Actions Over $7,500, Probate.*

www.co.clark.nv.us/district_court/courthome.htm

Civil Records: Access: Mail, online, in person. Visitors must perform in person searches for themselves. Search fee: $1.00 per name per year. Fee is per case type. Required to search: name, years to search. Civil cases indexed by defendant, plaintiff. Civil records on computer back to 11/90, prior records on microfilm to 1909. Records from the court available free online at http://courtgate.coca.co.clark.nv.us:8490. Search by case number or party name. Probate also available.

Criminal Records: Access: Mail, online, in person. Visitors must perform in person searches for themselves. Search fee: $1.00 per name per year. Fee is per case type. Required to search: name, years to search. Criminal records on computer back to 11/90, prior records on microfilm to 1909. Online access to criminal records is the same as civil.

General Information: Public access terminal is available. No sealed records released. SASE required. Turnaround time 10 working days. Copy fee: $1.00 per page. Certification fee: $3.00. Fee payee: County Clerk's Office. Personal checks accepted. Prepayment is required.

Boulder Township Justice Court 505 Avenue G, Boulder City, NV 89005; 702-455-8000; Fax: 702-455-8003. Hours: 8AM-4PM M-TH (PST). *Misdemeanor, Civil Actions Under $7,500, Eviction, Small Claims.*

Civil Records: Access: Fax, mail, in person. Both court and visitors may perform in person searches. Search fee: $1.00 per name per year. Required to search: name, years to search; also helpful: address. Civil cases indexed by defendant. Civil records on microfiche varies depending on subject.

Criminal Records: Access: Fax, mail, in person. Only the court performs in person searches; visitors may not. Search fee: $1.00 per name per year. Required to search: name, years to search, DOB, date of offense; also helpful: SSN. Criminal records on microfiche varies depending on subject.

General Information: No financial records released. SASE required. Turnaround time 1 week. Copy fee: $.30 per page. Certification fee: $3.00. Fee payee:

Justice Court. Personal checks accepted. Prepayment is required.

Bunkerville Justice Court 190 W Virgin St, Bunkerville, NV 89007; 702-346-5711; Fax: 702-346-7212. Hours: 7AM-5PM M-Th (PST). *Misdemeanor, Civil Actions Under $7,500, Eviction, Small Claims.*

Civil Records: Access: Mail, in person. Only the court performs in person searches; visitors may not. Search fee: $1.00 per name per year. Required to search: name, years to search. Civil cases indexed by plaintiff. Civil records (citations) on computer from 1991, on docket books.

Criminal Records: Access: Mail, in person. Only the court performs in person searches; visitors may not. Search fee: $1.00 per name per year. Required to search: name, years to search, DOB; also helpful: SSN. Criminal records (citations) on computer from 1991, on docket books.

General Information: No sealed or confidential records released. SASE required. Turnaround time 2 weeks. Copy fee: $.30 per page. Certification fee: $3.00. Fee payee: Bunkerville Justice Court. Only cashiers checks and money orders accepted. Prepayment is required.

Goodsprings Township Jean Justice Court 1 Main St (PO Box 19155), Jean, NV 89019; 702-874-1405; Fax: 702-874-1612. Hours: 7AM-5PM M-Th (PST). *Misdemeanor, Civil Actions Under $7,500, Eviction, Small Claims.*

Civil Records: Access: Phone, fax, mail, in person. Only the court performs in person searches; visitors may not. Search fee: $1.00 per name per year. Required to search: name, years to search. Civil cases indexed by defendant, plaintiff. Civil records on computer for 6 months, file reports from 1990.

Criminal Records: Access: Phone, fax, mail, in person. Only the court performs in person searches; visitors may not. Search fee: $1.00 per name per year. Required to search: name, years to search, DOB; also helpful: SSN. Criminal records on computer for 6 months, file reports from 1990.

General Information: No sealed records released. SASE required. Turnaround time within 2-3 days. Copy fee: $.25 per page. Certification fee: $2.00. Fee payee: Jean Justice Court. Business checks accepted.

Henderson Township Justice 243 Water St, Henderson, NV 89015; 702-455-7951; Fax: 702-455-7935. Hours: 7AM-6PM M-Th (PST). *Misdemeanor, Civil Actions Under $7,500, Eviction, Small Claims.*

www.co.clark.nv.us/district_court/courthome.htm

Civil Records: Access: Mail, in person. Only the court performs in person searches; visitors may not. Search fee: $1.00 per name per year. Required to search: name, years to search. Civil cases indexed by defendant. Civil records on index cards and docket books. Evictions kept for 2 years; civil and small claims for 6 years.

Criminal Records: Access: Mail, in person. Only the court performs in person searches; visitors may not. Search fee: $1.00 per name per year. Required to search: name, years to search, DOB; also helpful: SSN. Criminal records on index cards and docket books. Evictions kept for 2 years; civil and small claims for 6 years.

General Information: SASE required. Turnaround time 2 weeks. Fax notes: Fee to fax results is $.30 per page. Copy fee: $.30 per page. Certification fee: $3.00. Fee payee: Henderson Justice Court. Personal checks accepted. Prepayment is required.

Las Vegas Township Justice PO Box 552511 (200 S 3rd, 2nd Fl), Las Vegas, NV 89155-2511; 702-455-4435; Fax: 702-455-4529. Hours: 8AM-5PM (PST). *Misdemeanor, Civil Actions Under $7,500, Eviction, Small Claims.*

www.co.clark.nv.us/justicecourt_lv/welcome.htm

Note: Calendars are available online at the web site.

Civil Records: Access: Phone, fax, mail, in person. Both court and visitors may perform in person searches. Search fee: $1.00 per name per year. Required to search: name, years to search. Civil cases indexed by defendant, plaintiff. Civil records go back 8 years.

Criminal Records: Access: Phone, fax, mail, in person. Only the court performs in person searches; visitors may not. Search fee: $1.00 per name per year. Required to search: name, years to search, DOB; also helpful: SSN. Criminal records go back 10 years.

General Information: No sealed, confidential or judge's notes records released. SASE required. Turnaround time 2 weeks. Copy fee: $.30 per page. Certification fee: $3.00. Fee payee: Justice Court, Las Vegas Township. Personal checks accepted. Prepayment is required.

Laughlin Township Justice Court 101 Civic Way #2, Laughlin, NV 89029; 702-298-4622; Fax: 702-298-7508. Hours: 8AM-5PM (T-Fri) (PST). *Misdemeanor, Civil Actions Under $7,000, Eviction, Small Claims.*

Civil Records: Access: Fax, mail, in person. Search fee: $1.00 per name per year. Required to search: name, years to search. Civil cases indexed by defendant, plaintiff. Civil records on docket book by name and case number.

Criminal Records: Access: Fax, mail, in person. Only the court performs in person searches; visitors may not. Search fee: $1.00 per name per year. Required to search: name, years to search, DOB. Criminal records on computer from 1990, prior in files and must be cross referenced.

General Information: No sealed records released. SASE required. Turnaround time 2 weeks. Copy fee: $.30 per page. Certification fee: $3.00. Fee payee: Laughlin Justice Court. Personal checks accepted. Prepayment is required.

Mesquite Township Justice Court PO Box 1209 (51 E 1st North), Mesquite, NV 89024; 702-346-5298; Fax: 702-346-7319. Hours: 7AM-4PM (PST). *Felony, Misdemeanor, Civil Actions Under $7,500, Eviction, Small Claims.*

Civil Records: Access: Fax, mail, in person. Only the court performs in person searches; visitors may not. Search fee: $1.00 per name per year. Required to search: name, years to search. Civil cases indexed by defendant. Criminal records go back to 1989; on computer back to 1996.

Criminal Records: Access: Phone, fax, mail, in person. Only the court performs in person searches; visitors may not. Search fee: $1.00 per name per year. Required to search: name, years to search, DOB; also helpful: SSN. Criminal records go back to 1989; on computer back to 1996.

General Information: No sealed records released. SASE not required. Turnaround time approx 1-2 weeks. Copy fee: $.30 per page. Certification fee: $3.00. Fee payee: Mesquite Justice Court. Only cashiers checks and money orders accepted. Prepayment is required.

Moapa Township Justice Court 1340 E Com Hwy, PO Box 280, Moapa, NV 89025; 702-864-2333; Fax: 702-864-2585. Hours: 8AM-5PM M-Th (PST). *Misdemeanor, Civil Actions Under $7,500, Eviction, Small Claims.*

Civil Records: Access: Fax, mail, in person. Only the court performs in person searches; visitors may not. Search fee: $1.00 per name per year. Required to search: name, years to search. Civil cases indexed by defendant, plaintiff. Civil records on computer from 10/90, prior records on index cards and docket books. Archives flooded in 1980s.

Criminal Records: Access: Fax, mail, in person. Only the court performs in person searches; visitors may not. Search fee: $1.00 per name per year. Required to search: name, years to search; also helpful: DOB, SSN. Criminal records on computer from 10/90, prior records on index cards and docket books. Archives flooded in 1980s.

General Information: No sealed records released. SASE required. Turnaround time 1-5 days. Fax notes: No fee to fax results. Copy fee: $.25 per page. Certification fee: $3.00. Fee payee: Moapa Township Justice Court. Personal checks accepted. Prepayment is required.

Moapa Valley Township Justice Court
320 N Moapa Valley Blvd, PO Box 337, Overton, NV 89040; 702-397-2840; Fax: 702-397-2842. Hours: 6:30AM-4:30PM M-Th (PST). *Misdemeanor, Civil Actions Under $7,500, Eviction, Small Claims.*

Civil Records: Access: Mail, in person. Only the court performs in person searches; visitors may not. Search fee: $1.00 per name per year. Required to search: name, years to search. Civil cases indexed by defendant, plaintiff. Civil records on computer from 1991, prior on docket books.

Criminal Records: Access: Mail, in person. Only the court performs in person searches; visitors may not. Search fee: $1.00 per name per year. Required to search: name, years to search, DOB; also helpful: SSN. Criminal records on computer from 1991, prior on docket books.

General Information: No sealed records released. SASE required. Turnaround time approx 1-2 weeks. Copy fee: $.30 per page. Certification fee: $3.00. Fee payee: Moapa Valley Justice Court. Personal checks accepted. Prepayment is required.

North Las Vegas Township Justice
2428 N Martin L King Blvd, N Las Vegas, NV 89032-3700; 702-455-7802; Civil phone: 702-455-7801; Fax: 702-455-7831. Hours: 7AM-5:45PM (PST). *Misdemeanor, Civil Actions Under $7,500, Eviction, Small Claims.*

Note: Judge must approve all search requests.

Civil Records: Access: Phone, in person. Visitors must perform in person searches for themselves. No search fee. Required to search: name, years to search. Civil cases indexed by defendant, plaintiff. Civil records on docket books, microfilm.

Criminal Records: Access: Phone, mail, in person. Only the court performs in person searches; visitors may not. Search fee: $1.00 per name per year. Required to search: name, years to search, DOB, SSN. Criminal records on docket books, microfilm.

General Information: SASE required. Turnaround time 1-10 days. Copy fee: $.30 per page. Certification fee: $3.00. Fee payee: Clark County Justice Court. Personal checks accepted. Personal check accepted with bank card. Prepayment is required.

Searchlight Township Justice
PO Box 815, Searchlight, NV 89046; 702-297-1252; Fax: 702-297-1022. Hours: 7AM-5:30PM M-Th (PST). *Misdemeanor, Civil Actions Under $7,500, Eviction, Small Claims.*

Civil Records: Access: Fax, mail, in person. Only the court performs in person searches; visitors may not. Search fee: $1.00 per name per year. Required to search: name, years to search. Civil cases indexed by defendant, plaintiff. Civil records on computer from 1988, prior to 1988 filed by case number.

Criminal Records: Access: Fax, mail, in person. Only the court performs in person searches; visitors may not. Search fee: $1.00 per name per year. Required to search: name, years to search, DOB; also helpful: SSN. Criminal records on computer from 1988, prior to 1988 filed by case number.

General Information: No sealed records released. SASE required. Turnaround time 1-2 weeks. Copy fee: $1.00 per page. Certification fee: $2.00. Fee payee: Searchlight Justice Court. Personal checks accepted. Prepayment is required.

Douglas County

9th Judicial District Court
Box 218, Minden, NV 89423; 775-782-9820; Fax: 775-782-9954. Hours: 8AM-5PM (PST). *Felony, Civil Actions Over $7,500, Probate.*

http://cltr.co.douglas.nv.us/CourtClerk/courtideas/courtclerkhome.htm

Note: Misdemeanors are handled by the East Fork Justice Court.

Civil Records: Access: Mail, fax, in person. Only the court performs in person searches; visitors may not. Search fee: $1.00 per name per year. Required to search: name, years to search. Civil cases indexed by defendant, plaintiff. Civil records on index cards from 1962, docket books prior to 1962, archived from mid-1850s. On computer back to 1996.

Criminal Records: Access: Mail, in person. Only the court performs in person searches; visitors may not. Search fee: $1.00 per name per year. Required to search: name, years to search, DOB. Criminal records on index cards from 1962, docket books prior to 1962, archived from mid-1850s. On computer back to 1996.

General Information: No sealed records released. SASE required. Turnaround time 1 week. Copy fee: $1.00 per page. Certification fee: $3.00. Fee payee: Douglas County Court Clerk. Business checks accepted. Prepayment is required.

East Fork Justice Court
PO Box 218, Minden, NV 89423; 775-782-9955; Fax: 775-782-9947. Hours: 8AM-5PM (PST). *Misdemeanor, Civil Actions Under $7,500, Eviction, Small Claims.*

Civil Records: Access: Mail, in person. Only the court performs in person searches; visitors may not. Search fee: $1.00 per name per year. Required to search: name, years to search, DOB or SSN. Civil cases indexed by defendant, plaintiff. Computerized records from 1996.

Criminal Records: Access: Mail, in person. Only the court performs in person searches; visitors may not. Search fee: $1.00 per name per year. Required to search: name, years to search, DOB or SSN. Computerized records from 1996.

General Information: No sealed records released. SASE required. Turnaround time 2-4 days. Copy fee: $.30 per page. Certification fee: $3.00. Fee payee: East Fork Justice Court. Only local personal or business checks accepted. Prepayment is required.

Tahoe Justice Court
PO Box 7169, Stateline, NV 89449; 775-586-7200; Fax: 775-588-7203. Hours: 9AM-5PM (PST). *Misdemeanor, Civil Actions Under $7,500, Eviction, Small Claims.*

Civil Records: Access: Phone, mail, in person. Only the court performs in person searches; visitors may not. Search fee: $1.00 per name per year. Required to search: name, years to search. Civil cases indexed by defendant, plaintiff. Civil records on index cards from 1985-1995; 1995-present on computer. Prior to 1/1/81 some records in docket books, some on microfilm.

Criminal Records: Access: Phone, mail, in person. Only the court performs in person searches; visitors may not. Search fee: $1.00 per name per year. Required to search: name, years to search, DOB. Criminal records prior to 1/1/81 some records in docket books, some on micro film.

General Information: No sealed records released. SASE required. Turnaround time 2 weeks. Copy fee: $.30 per page. Certification fee: $3.00 per page. Fee payee: Tahoe Justice Court. Credit cards accepted: Visa, MasterCard. Prepayment is required.

Elko County

4th Judicial District Court
571 Idaho St, 3rd Flr, Elko, NV 89801; 775-753-4600; Fax: 775-753-4610. Hours: 9AM-5PM (PST). *Felony, Gross Misdemeanor, Civil Actions Over $7,500, Probate.*

Civil Records: Access: Phone, mail, in person, email. Both court and visitors may perform in person searches. Search fee: $1.00 per name per year. Fee is for years prior to 10/01/91. Required to search: name, years to search. Civil cases indexed by defendant, plaintiff. Civil records on computer back to 1970; prior on microfilm.

Criminal Records: Access: Phone, mail, in person. Both court and visitors may perform in person searches. Search fee: $1.00 per name per year. Fee is for years prior to 1980. Required to search: name, years to search. Criminal records on computer back to 1970; prior primarily on microfilm (including probate).

General Information: Public access terminal is available. No sealed records released. SASE required. Turnaround time 1 day. Fax notes: Fee to fax results is $1.00 per page. Copy fee: $1.00 per page. Certification fee: $3.00 if court prepares copies, $5.00 if you prepare copies. Fee payee: Elko County Clerk. Personal checks accepted. Visa/MC accepted. Prepayment is required.

Carlin Justice Court
PO Box 789, Carlin, NV 89822; 775-754-6321; Fax: 775-754-6893. Hours: 8AM-5PM (PST). *Misdemeanor, Civil Actions Under $7,500, Eviction, Small Claims.*

Civil Records: Access: Mail, in person. Both court and visitors may perform in person searches. Search fee: $1.00 per name per year. Required to search: name, years to search. Civil cases indexed by defendant, plaintiff. Civil records on computer starting in 1994, prior are in books.

Criminal Records: Access: Mail, in person. Only the court performs in person searches; visitors may not. Search fee: $1.00 per name per year. Required to search: name, years to search, DOB, SSN. Criminal records on computer starting in 1994, prior are in books.

General Information: SASE required. Turnaround time 1 week. Copy fee: $.30 per page. Certification fee: $3.00. Fee payee: Carlin Court. Personal checks accepted. Prepayment is required.

Eastline Justice Court
PO Box 2300, West Wendover, NV 89883; 775-664-2305; Fax: 775-664-2979. Hours: 9AM-4PM (PST). *Misdemeanor, Civil Actions Under $7,500, Eviction, Small Claims.*

Civil Records: Access: Mail, in person. Only the court performs in person searches; visitors may not. Search fee: $7.00 per name per year. Required to search: name, years to search. Civil cases indexed by defendant. Civil records on computer from 1992, prior on index, docket book.

Criminal Records: Access: Mail, in person. Only the court performs in person searches; visitors may not. Search fee: $1.00 per name per year. Required to search: name, years to search; also helpful: DOB. Criminal records on computer from 1992, prior on index, docket book.

General Information: No open case records released. SASE required. Turnaround time 1 week. Copy fee: $.30 per page. Certification fee: $3.00. Fee payee: Eastline Justice Court. Only cashiers checks and money orders accepted. Prepayment is required.

Elko Justice Court
PO Box 176, Elko, NV 89803; 775-738-8403; Fax: 775-738-8416. Hours: 9AM-Noon, 1-5PM (PST). *Misdemeanor, Civil Actions Under $7,500, Eviction, Small Claims.*

Note: There is a small Justice Court located in Tecoma Township at PO Box 8, Montello, NV 89830, 775-776-2544.

Civil Records: Access: Fax, mail, in person. Both court and visitors may perform in person searches. Search fee: $1.00 per name per year. Fee is per court. Required to search: name, years to search. Civil cases indexed by defendant, plaintiff. Civil records on computer after 1994, on docket books after 1970s, prior in county archives.

Criminal Records: Access: Mail, in person. Both court and visitors may perform in person searches. Search fee: $1.00 per name per year. Fee is per court. Required to search: name, years to search; DOB or SSN also required. Criminal records on computer after 1994, on docket books after 1970s, prior in county archives.

General Information: No confidential evaluations or sealed records released. SASE required. Turnaround time 7-10 days. Copy fee: $.30 per page. Certification fee: $3.00. Fee payee: Elko Justice Court. Personal checks accepted. Prepayment is required.

Jackpot Justice Court PO Box 229, Jackpot, NV 89825; 775-755-2456; Fax: 775-755-2727. Hours: 9AM-Noon, 1-5PM (PST). *Misdemeanor, Civil Actions Under $7,500, Eviction, Small Claims.*

Civil Records: Access: Mail, in person. Only the court performs in person searches; visitors may not. Search fee: $1.00 per name per year. Required to search: name, years to search. Civil cases indexed by defendant. Civil records on docket books per year since 1978; on computer back to 1995.

Criminal Records: Access: Fax, mail, in person. Only the court performs in person searches; visitors may not. Search fee: $1.00 per name per year. Required to search: name, years to search, DOB. Criminal records on docket books per year since 1978; on computer back to 1995.

General Information: SASE required. Turnaround time 1 week. Fax notes: No fee to fax results. Copy fee: $.25 per page. Certification fee: $3.00. Fee payee: Jackpot Justice Court. Business checks accepted.

Jarbidge Justice Court PO Box 26001, Jarbidge, NV 89826-2001; 775-488-2331. *Misdemeanor, Civil Actions Under $7,500, Eviction, Small Claims.*

Note: This is "unincorporated ghost town." No criminal or civil cases in more than 20 years. Mostly marriages, fish and game violations. Only 40 year round residents here.

Civil Records: Access: In person only. Visitors must perform in person searches for themselves. No search fee. Required to search: name, years to search.

Criminal Records: Access: In person only. Visitors must perform in person searches for themselves. No search fee. Required to search: name, years to search.

Mountain City Justice Court PO Box 116, Mountain City, NV 89831; 775-763-6699. *Misdemeanor, Civil Actions Under $7,500, Eviction, Small Claims.*

Note: New records held in Elko Justice Court, 775-738-8403; older records may soon be transferred also. Limited cases heard here. Phone listed is Elko clerk. Only 49 people living here.

Civil Records: Access: Mail, in person. Both court and visitors may perform in person searches. No search fee. Required to search: name, years to search. Civil cases indexed by defendant.

Criminal Records: Access: Mail, in person. Both court and visitors may perform in person searches. No search fee. Required to search: name, years to search, DOB.

General Information: SASE required. Copy fee: $.25 per page. Certification fee: $3.00.

Wells Justice Municipal Court PO Box 297, Wells, NV 89835; 775-752-3726; Fax: 775-752-3363. Hours: 9AM-Noon,1-5PM (PST). *Misdemeanor, Civil Actions Under $7,500, Eviction, Small Claims.*

Civil Records: Access: Mail, in person. Only the court performs in person searches; visitors may not. Search

fee: $1.00 per name per year. Required to search: name, years to search. Civil cases indexed by defendant, plaintiff. Civil records on computer after 1989, prior on docket books. In person access may require fee for clerical assistance.

Criminal Records: Access: Mail, in person. Only the court performs in person searches; visitors may not. Search fee: $1.00 per name per year. Required to search: name, years to search; also DOB or SSN. Criminal records on computer from 1989, prior on docket books. Same as civil.

General Information: No pending, confidential records released. SASE required. Turnaround time 2 weeks. Copy fee: $.30 per page. Certification fee: $3.00. Fee payee: Wells Justice Court. Personal checks accepted. Prepayment is required.

Esmeralda County

5th Judicial District Court PO Box 547, Goldfield, NV 89013; 775-485-6367; Fax: 775-485-6376. Hours: 8AM-5PM (PST). *Felony, Gross Misdemeanor, Civil Actions Over $7,500, Probate.*

Civil Records: Access: Fax, mail, in person. Both court and visitors may perform in person searches. Search fee: $1.00 per name per year. Required to search: name, years to search. Civil cases indexed by defendant, plaintiff. Civil records on docket books from 1800s.

Criminal Records: Access: Fax, mail, in person. Both court and visitors may perform in person searches. No search fee. Required to search: name, years to search. Criminal records on docket books from 1800s.

General Information: No juvenile or pre-sentence records released. SASE required. Turnaround time 2 weeks. Fax notes: Fee to fax results is $1.00 per page. Copy fee: $1.00 per page. Certification fee: $3.00. Fee payee: Esmeralda County Clerk. Personal checks accepted. Credit cards accepted: Visa and MasterCard. Prepayment is required.

Esmeralda Justice Court PO Box 370, Goldfield, NV 89013; 775-485-6359; Fax: 775-485-3462. Hours: 8AM-5PM (PST). *Misdemeanor, Civil Actions Under $7,500, Eviction, Small Claims.*

Civil Records: Access: Phone, fax, mail, in person. Only the court performs in person searches; visitors may not. Search fee: $1.00 per name per year. Required to search: name, years to search. Civil cases indexed by plaintiff. Civil records on docket books for 6 years.

Criminal Records: Access: Phone, fax, mail, in person. Only the court performs in person searches; visitors may not. Search fee: $1.00 per name per year. Required to search: name, years to search. Criminal records on docket books for 6 years.

General Information: No sealed records released. SASE required. Turnaround time 1 day. Fax notes: $1.00 per page. Copy fee: $.30 per page. Certification fee: $3.00. Fee payee: Justice Court. Only cashiers checks and money orders accepted. Prepayment is required.

Eureka County

7th Judicial District Court PO Box 677, Eureka, NV 89316; 775-237-5262; Fax: 775-237-6015. Hours: 8AM-Noon, 1-5PM (PST). *Felony, Gross Misdemeanor, Civil Actions Over $7,500, Probate.*

Civil Records: Access: Phone, fax, mail, in person. Both court and visitors may perform in person searches. Search fee: $1.00 per name per year. Required to search: name, years to search. Civil cases indexed by defendant, plaintiff. Civil records archived from 1873. Public can search docket books.

Criminal Records: Access: Phone, fax, mail, in person. Both court and visitors may perform in person searches. Search fee: $1.00 per name per year. Required to search: name, years to search. Criminal records archived from 1873. Public can search docket books.

General Information: No juvenile, sealed records released. SASE required. Turnaround time 1 day. Copy fee: $1.00 per page. Certification fee: $3.00. Fee payee: Eureka County Clerk. Personal checks accepted. Prepayment is required.

Beowawe Justice Court PO Box 211338, Crescent Valley, NV 89821; 775-468-0244; Fax: 775-468-0323. Hours: 8AM-Noon, 1-5PM (PST). *Misdemeanor, Civil Actions Under $7,500, Eviction, Small Claims.*

Civil Records: Access: Mail, in person. Only the court performs in person searches; visitors may not. Search fee: $1.00 per name per year. Required to search: name, years to search. Civil cases indexed by plaintiff. Civil records go back to 2/1994; computerized records go back to 1997.

Criminal Records: Access: Mail, in person. Only the court performs in person searches; visitors may not. Search fee: $1.00 per name per year. Required to search: name, years to search. Criminal records go back to 11/1993; computerized records go back to 1997.

General Information: SASE required. Copy fee: $.30 per page. Certification fee: $3.00. Fee payee: Beowawe Justice Court. Only cashiers checks and money orders accepted. Prepayment is required.

Eureka Justice Court PO Box 496, Eureka, NV 89316; 775-237-5540; Fax: 775-237-6016. Hours: 8AM-Noon,1-5PM (PST). *Misdemeanor, Civil Actions Under $7,500, Eviction, Small Claims.*

Civil Records: Access: Phone, mail, in person. Only the court performs in person searches; visitors may not. No search fee. Required to search: name, years to search. Civil cases indexed by defendant, plaintiff. Civil records on computer since 1995; on docket books, archived from 1940.

Criminal Records: Access: Phone, mail, in person. Only the court performs in person searches; visitors may not. No search fee. Required to search: name, years to search. Criminal records on computer since 1995; on docket books, archived from 1940.

General Information: SASE required. Turnaround time 2 days. Copy fee: $.50 per page. Certification fee: $3.00. Fee payee: Eureka Justice Court. Only cashiers checks and money orders accepted. Prepayment is required.

Humboldt County

6th Judicial District Court 50 W Fifth St, Winnemucca, NV 89445; 775-623-6343; Fax: 775-623-6309. Hours: 8AM-5PM (PST). *Felony, Gross Misdemeanor, Civil Actions Over $7,500, Probate.*

Civil Records: Access: Phone, fax, mail, in person. Both court and visitors may perform in person searches. Search fee: $1.00 per name per year. Required to search: name, years to search. Civil cases indexed by defendant, plaintiff. Civil records on computer from 1984, on microfiche from 1900.

Criminal Records: Access: Phone, fax, mail, in person. Both court and visitors may perform in person searches. Search fee: $1.00 per name per year. Required to search: name, years to search. Criminal records on computer from 1984, on microfiche from 1900.

General Information: Public access terminal is available. No adoption, sealed records released. SASE required. Turnaround time 1 day, immediate if on computer and requested by phone. Copy fee: $1.00 per page. Certification fee: $3.00. Fee payee: Humboldt County Clerk. Personal checks accepted. Prepayment is required.

Union Justice Court PO Box 1218, Winnemucca, NV 89446; 775-623-6377; Fax: 775-623-6439. Hours: 7AM-5PM (PST). *Misdemeanor, Civil Actions Under $7,500, Eviction, Small Claims.*
www.humboldt-county-nv.net/justice

Civil Records: Access: Fax, mail, in person. Only the court performs in person searches; visitors may not. Search fee: $1.00 per name per year; minimum of $7.00. Required to search: name, years to search; also helpful: address. Civil cases indexed by defendant, plaintiff. Civil records on computer from 1988, prior on docket books.

Criminal Records: Access: Fax, mail, in person. Only the court performs in person searches; visitors may not. Search fee: $1.00 per name per year; minimum of $7.00. Required to search: name, years to search, DOB; also helpful: address, SSN. Criminal records on computer from 1988.

General Information: SASE required. Turnaround time 1-2 days. Fax notes: No fee to fax results. Certification fee: $3.00. Fee payee: Justice Court. Personal checks accepted. Prepayment is required.

Lander County

6th Judicial District Court 315 S Humboldt, Battle Mountain, NV 89820; 775-635-5738; Fax: 775-635-5761. Hours: 8AM-5PM (PST). *Felony, Gross Misdemeanor, Civil Actions Over $7,500, Probate.*

Civil Records: Access: Phone, fax, mail, in person. Only the court performs in person searches; visitors may not. No search fee. Required to search: name, years to search. Civil cases indexed by defendant, plaintiff. Civil records on computer from 1990, on index from 1986-1990, on microfiche until 1985, prior records on docket books.

Criminal Records: Access: Phone, fax, mail, in person. Only the court performs in person searches; visitors may not. No search fee. Required to search: name, years to search. Criminal records on computer from 1990, on index from 1986-1990, on microfiche until 1985, prior records on docket books.

General Information: No juvenile, sealed records released. SASE required. Turnaround time 7 days. Fax notes: Fee to fax results is $1.00 per page. Copy fee: $1.00 per page. Certification fee: $5.00. Fee payee: Lander County Clerk. Personal checks accepted.

Argenta Justice Court 315 S Humboldt, Battle Mountain, NV 89820; 775-635-5151; Fax: 775-635-0604. Hours: 8AM-5PM (PST). *Misdemeanor, Civil Actions Under $7,500, Eviction, Small Claims.*

Civil Records: Access: Phone, fax, mail, in person. Only the court performs in person searches; visitors may not. Search fee: $1.00 per name per year. Required to search: name, years to search. Civil cases indexed by defendant, plaintiff. Civil records on computer from 1988, prior on docket books.

Criminal Records: Access: Phone, fax, mail, in person. Only the court performs in person searches; visitors may not. Search fee: $1.00 per name per year. Required to search: name, years to search; also helpful: DOB, SSN. Criminal records on computer from 1988, prior on docket books.

General Information: No unserved search warrant records released. SASE required. Turnaround time 1 day. Fax notes: $1.00 per page. Copy fee: $.50 per page. Certification fee: $3.00 per page. Fee payee: Argenta Justice Court. Only cashiers checks and money orders accepted.

Austin Justice Court PO Box 100, Austin, NV 89310; 775-964-2380; Fax: 775-964-2327. Hours: 8AM-5PM M, 8AM-Noon T-Th (PST). *Misdemeanor, Civil Actions Under $7,500, Eviction, Small Claims.*

Note: No fees for requests from government agencies.

Civil Records: Access: Phone, mail, fax, in person. Only the court performs in person searches; visitors may not. No search fee. Required to search: name, years to search. Civil cases indexed by plaintiff and defendant. Civil records on docket books.

Criminal Records: Access: Phone, mail, fax, in person. Only the court performs in person searches;

visitors may not. No search fee. Required to search: name, years to search. Criminal records on computer from 1988.

General Information: SASE required. Turnaround time 1 week. Copy fee: $.25 per page. Fee payee: Austin Justice Court. Prepayment is required.

Lincoln County

7th Judicial District Court PO Box 90, Pioche, NV 89043; 775-962-5390; Fax: 702-962-5180. Hours: 9AM-5PM (PST). *Felony, Gross Misdemeanor, Civil Actions Over $7,500, Probate.*

Civil Records: Access: Mail, in person. Both court and visitors may perform in person searches. Search fee: $1.00 per name per year. Required to search: name, years to search. Civil cases indexed by defendant, plaintiff. Civil records on docket books from 1876. Records are computerized since 2001.

Criminal Records: Access: Mail, in person. Both court and visitors may perform in person searches. Search fee: $1.00 per name per year. Required to search: name, years to search. Criminal records on docket books from 1876. Records are computerized since 2001.

General Information: No juvenile, sealed records released. SASE not required. Turnaround time 2-3 days. Fax notes: Fee to fax results is $1.00 per page. Copy fee: $1.00 per page. Certification fee: $5.00. Fee payee: Lincoln County Clerk. Personal checks accepted. Prepayment is required.

Meadow Valley Justice Court PO Box 36, Pioche, NV 89043; 775-962-5140; Fax: 775-962-5559. Hours: 9AM-5PM (PST). *Misdemeanor, Civil Actions Under $7,500, Eviction, Small Claims.*

Civil Records: Access: Phone, fax, mail, in person. Only the court performs in person searches; visitors may not. Search fee: $1.00 per name per year. Required to search: name, years to search. Civil cases indexed by defendant, plaintiff. Civil records archived from 1982 on docket books; on computer back to 2000.

Criminal Records: Access: Phone, fax, mail, in person. Only the court performs in person searches; visitors may not. Search fee: $1.00 per name per year. Required to search: name, years to search. Criminal records are all originals; they go back to 1982; on computer back to 2000.

General Information: Juvenile records are not released. SASE required. Turnaround time 1-5 days. Fax notes: $3.00 for first page, $1.00 each add'l. Copy fee: $1.00 per page. Fee payee: Meadow Valley Justice Court. Personal checks accepted. Prepayment is required.

Pahranagat Valley Justice Court PO Box 449, Alamo, NV 89001; 775-725-3357; Fax: 775-725-3566. Hours: 9AM-5PM (PST). *Misdemeanor, Civil Actions Under $7,500, Eviction, Small Claims.*

Civil Records: Access: Fax, mail, in person. Only the court performs in person searches; visitors may not. No search fee. Required to search: name, years to search. Civil cases indexed by defendant. Civil records on docket books to 1980; on computer back to 1997.

Criminal Records: Access: Fax, mail, in person. Only the court performs in person searches; visitors may not. No search fee. Required to search: name, years to search, DOB; also helpful: SSN, signed release. Criminal records on docket books to 1980; on computer back to 1997.

General Information: No personal notes released. SASE required. Turnaround time 1-3 days. Fax notes: No fee to fax results. Copy fee: $.25 per page. Certification fee: $2.00 per page. Fee payee: Pahranagat Valley Justice Court. Personal checks accepted. Prepayment is required.

Lyon County

3rd Judicial District Court 27 S Main St (PO box 816), Yerington, NV 89447; 775-463-6503; Fax: 775-463-6575. Hours: 8AM-5PM (PST). *Felony, Gross Misdemeanor, Civil Actions Over $7,500, Probate.*

Civil Records: Access: Phone, mail, in person. Only the court performs in person searches; visitors may not. Search fee: $1.00 per name per year. Required to search: name, years to search. Civil cases indexed by defendant, plaintiff. Civil records on computer back to 1989.

Criminal Records: Access: Phone, mail, in person. Only the court performs in person searches; visitors may not. Search fee: $1.00 per name per year. Required to search: name, years to search. Criminal records on computer back to 1985.

General Information: No adoption, juvenile or sealed records released. SASE required. Turnaround time 1 week for mail requests, immediate for phone requests if on computer. Copy fee: $.25 per page. Certification fee: $3.00. Fee payee: Lyon County Clerk. Personal checks accepted. Prepayment is required.

Dayton Township Justice Court 235 Main St, Dayton, NV 89403; 775-246-6233; Fax: 775-246-6203. Hours: 8AM-5PM (PST). *Misdemeanor, Civil Actions Under $7,500, Eviction, Small Claims.*

Civil Records: Access: Phone, fax, mail, in person. Only the court performs in person searches; visitors may not. Search fee: $1.00 per name per year. Required to search: name, years to search. Civil cases indexed by defendant, plaintiff. Civil records on computer from 1991, on docket books by year.

Criminal Records: Access: Phone, fax, mail, in person. Only the court performs in person searches; visitors may not. Search fee: $1.00 per name per year. Required to search: name, years to search. Criminal records on computer from 1991, prior on docket books by year.

General Information: No sealed records released. SASE required. Turnaround time within 1 week. Copy fee: $.30 per page. Certification fee: $3.00. Fee payee: Dayton Township Justice Court. Personal checks accepted. Prepayment is required.

Fernley Justice Court 565 E Main St, Fernley, NV 89408; 775-575-3355; Fax: 775-575-3359. Hours: 8AM-5PM (PST). *Misdemeanor, Civil Actions Under $7,500, Eviction, Small Claims.*

Civil Records: Access: Phone, mail, in person. Only the court performs in person searches; visitors may not. Search fee: $1.00 per name per year. Required to search: name, years to search. Civil cases indexed by defendant, plaintiff. Civil records on computer from 1992, prior on docket books.

Criminal Records: Access: Phone, mail, in person. Only the court performs in person searches; visitors may not. Search fee: $1.00 per name per year. Required to search: name, years to search; also helpful: SSN. Criminal records on computer from 1992, prior on docket books.

General Information: No police reports or sealed records released. SASE required. Turnaround time 1 week. Copy fee: $.30 per page. Certification fee: $2.00. Fee payee: Fernley Justice Court. Personal checks accepted. Out of state checks not accepted. Prepayment is required.

Mason Valley Justice Court 30 Nevin Way, Yerington, NV 89447; 775-463-6639; Fax: 775-463-6610. Hours: 8AM-5PM (PST). *Misdemeanor, Civil Actions Under $7,500, Eviction, Small Claims.*

Civil Records: Access: Phone, mail, in person. Only the court performs in person searches; visitors may not. Search fee: $1.00 per name per year. Required to search: name, years to search. Civil cases indexed by defendant, plaintiff. Civil records on computer from 1988, archives from 1900s.

Criminal Records: Access: Phone, mail, in person. Only the court performs in person searches; visitors may not. Search fee: $1.00 per name per year. Required to search: name, years to search; also helpful: DOB, SSN. Criminal records on computer from 1988, archives from 1900s.

General Information: No police, sheriff reports released. SASE required. Turnaround time 3 days, immediate for phone requests. Copy fee: $.25 per page. Certification fee: $3.00. Fee payee: Mason Valley Justice Court. Personal checks accepted. Prepayment is required.

Smith Valley Justice Court PO Box 141, Smith, NV 89430; 775-465-2313; Fax: 775-465-2153. Hours: 8AM-Noon Tues & Fri or by appointment (PST). *Misdemeanor, Civil Actions Under $7500.00, Eviction, Small Claims.*

Civil Records: Access: Phone, fax, mail, in person. Only the court performs in person searches; visitors may not. No search fee. Required to search: name, years to search; also helpful: address. Civil cases indexed by defendant, plaintiff. Criminal records on computer from 1994. Overall records go back to 1992.

Criminal Records: Access: Phone, mail, in person. Only the court performs in person searches; visitors may not. No search fee. Required to search: name, years to search; also helpful: address, DOB, SSN. Criminal records on computer from 1994. Overall records go back to 1992.

General Information: SASE required. Turnaround time 1-2 weeks. Fax notes: Fax back $3.00 per page. Copy fee: $.30 per page. Certification fee: $5.00. Fee payee: Smith Valley Justice Court. Personal checks accepted. Prepayment is required.

Mineral County

5th Judicial District Court PO Box 1450, Hawthorne, NV 89415; 775-945-2446; Fax: 775-945-0706. Hours: 8AM-5PM (PST). *Felony, Gross Misdemeanor, Civil Actions Over $7,500, Probate.*

Civil Records: Access: Phone, fax, mail, in person. Both court and visitors may perform in person searches. Search fee: $1.00 per name per year. Required to search: name, years to search. Civil cases indexed by defendant, plaintiff. Civil records go back to 1911; computerized records since 1993.

Criminal Records: Access: Phone, fax, mail, in person. Both court and visitors may perform in person searches. Search fee: $1.00 per name per year. Required to search: name, years to search. Criminal records go back to 1911; computerized records since 1993.

General Information: No juvenile records released. SASE required. Turnaround time 1 day. Fax notes: $1.50 per page. Copy fee: $1.00 per page. Certification fee: $3.00. Fee payee: Mineral County Clerk. Personal checks accepted. Prepayment is required.

Hawthorne Justice Court PO Box 1660, Hawthorne, NV 89415; 775-945-3859; Fax: 775-945-0700. Hours: 8AM-5PM (PST). *Misdemeanor, Civil Actions Under $7,500, Eviction, Small Claims.*

Note: This court holds records from Schurz Justice Court.

Civil Records: Access: Phone, mail, in person. Both court and visitors may perform in person searches. No search fee. Required to search: name, years to search. Civil cases indexed by defendant. Civil records on computer from 1994, prior on docket books.

Criminal Records: Access: Phone, mail, in person. Both court and visitors may perform in person searches. No search fee. Required to search: name, years to search. Criminal records on computer from 1992.

General Information: No pending case or sealed records released. SASE required. Turnaround time 1-5 days. Copy fee: $.25 per page. Legal Size Copy Fee: $1.00 per page. Fee payee: Hawthorne Justice Court. Personal checks accepted.

Mina Justice Court PO Box 415, Mina, NV 89422; 775-573-2547; Fax: 775-573-2663. Hours: 9AM-1PM Tues-Fri. (PST). *Misdemeanor, Civil Actions Under $7,500, Eviction, Small Claims.*

Civil Records: Access: Phone, mail, in person. Only the court performs in person searches; visitors may not. No search fee. Required to search: name, years to search. Civil cases indexed by plaintiff. Civil records on docket books to 1936.

Criminal Records: Access: Phone, mail, in person. Only the court performs in person searches; visitors may not. No search fee. Required to search: name, years to search; also helpful DOB, SSN. Criminal records on docket books to 1936.

General Information: No sealed records released. SASE required. Turnaround time 1 day. Copy fee: $.50 for first page, $.25 each add'l. Fee payee: Mina Justice Court. Personal checks accepted. Prepayment is required.

Schurz Justice Court c/o Hawthorne Justice Ct, PO Box 1660, Hawthorne, NV 89415.

Note: Schurz court closed 1/1/2001; records now housed at Hawthorne Justice Court (see above.)

Nye County

5th Judicial District Court PO Box 1031, Tonopah, NV 89049; 775-482-8131; Fax: 775-482-8133. Hours: 8AM-5PM (PST), *Felony, Gross Misdemeanor, Civil Actions Over $7,500, Probate.*

Civil Records: Access: Phone, fax, mail, in person. Search fee: $1.00 per name per year. Required to search: name, years to search. Civil records on computer from 1991, on docket books from 1800s, many are microfilmed.

Criminal Records: Access: Phone, fax, mail, in person. Only the court performs in person searches; visitors may not. Search fee: $1.00 per name per year. Required to search: name, years to search. Criminal records on computer from 1991, on docket books from 1800s, many are microfilmed.

General Information: No adoptions or juvenile records released. SASE required. Turnaround time 1 day. Fax notes: $2.00 for first page, $1.00 each add'l. Copy fee: $1.00 per page. Certification fee: $3.00. Fee payee: Nye County Clerk. Business checks accepted. In-state personal checks accepted. Prepayment is required. Payment required if more than $15.00.

Beatty Justice Court PO Box 805, Beatty, NV 89003; 775-553-2951; Fax: 775-553-2136. Hours: 8AM-5PM (PST). *Misdemeanor, Civil Actions Up to $7,500, Eviction, Small Claims.*

Civil Records: Access: Phone, mail, in person. Only the court performs in person searches; visitors may not. Search fee: $1.00 per name per year. Computer printouts on all civil actions (no way to segregate small claims or evictions) is $.50 per page. Required to search: name, years to search. Civil cases indexed by defendant, plaintiff. Civil records on computer from 1991, archived from 1950s, some on docket books.

Criminal Records: Access: Phone, mail, in person. Only the court performs in person searches; visitors may not. Search fee: $1.00 per name per year. Required to search: name, years to search, DOB. Criminal records on computer from 1989.

General Information: No sealed, confidential records released. SASE required. Turnaround time 1 week for mail requests, same day for phone requests when possible. Copy fee: $.30 per page. Certification fee:

$3.00. Fee payee: Beatty Justice Court. Personal checks accepted. Prepayment is required.

Gabbs Justice Court PO Box 1151, Tonopah, NV 89049. Hours: 9AM-4PM M-Th (PST). *Misdemeanor, Civil Actions Under $7,500, Eviction, Small Claims.*

Note: This court is closed; any records are now at Tonopah (address above), 775-482-8155.

Civil Records: Access: Phone, mail, in person. Only the court performs in person searches; visitors may not. Search fee: $1.00 per name per year. Required to search: name, years to search. Civil cases indexed by plaintiff. Civil records on computer from 1993, archived from 1950s, some on docket books.

Criminal Records: Access: Phone, mail, in person. Only the court performs in person searches; visitors may not. Search fee: $1.00 per name per year. Required to search: name, years to search, DOB, offense, date of offense; also helpful: SSN. Criminal records on computer from 1993, archived from 1950s, some on docket books.

General Information: No juvenile records released. SASE required. Turnaround time same day. Copy fee: $1.00 per page. Fee payee: Gabbs Justice Court. Personal checks accepted.

Tonopah Justice Court PO Box 1151, Tonopah, NV 89049; 775-482-8155. Hours: 8AM-Noon, 1-5PM (PST). *Misdemeanor, Civil Actions Under $7,500, Eviction, Small Claims.*

Civil Records: Access: Phone, mail, in person. Only the court performs in person searches; visitors may not. Search fee: $1.00 per name per year. Required to search: name, years to search. Civil cases indexed by plaintiff. Civil records on computer from 1992, on archives from 1950s, some on docket books.

Criminal Records: Access: Phone, mail, in person. Only the court performs in person searches; visitors may not. Search fee: $1.00 per name per year. Required to search: name, years to search, offense, date of offense; also helpful: DOB, SSN. Criminal records on computer from 1992, on docket books from 1943.

General Information: SASE required. Turnaround time 1-2 weeks. Copy fee: $.30 per page. Certification fee: $3.00 per certification. Fee payee: Tonopah Justice Court. Business checks accepted.

Pershing County

6th Judicial District Court PO Box 820, Lovelock, NV 89419; 775-273-2410; Fax: 775-273-2434. Hours: 9AM-5PM (PST). *Felony, Civil Actions Over $7,500, Probate.*

Note: Misdemeanors are handled by the Lake Justice Court.

Civil Records: Access: Phone, fax, mail, in person. Only the court performs in person searches; visitors may not. Search fee: $1.00 per name per year. Required to search: name, years to search. Civil cases indexed by defendant, plaintiff. Civil records on computer from 1992, microfilmed from 1919-1938, books from 1919.

Criminal Records: Access: Phone, fax, mail, in person. Only the court performs in person searches; visitors may not. Search fee: $1.00 per name per year. Required to search: name, years to search. Criminal records on computer from 1992, microfilmed from 1919-1938, books from 1919.

General Information: No adoption, juvenile or sealed records released. SASE required. Turnaround time 1-3 days. Fax notes: No fee to fax results. Copy fee: $1.00 per page. Certification fee: $3.00. Fee payee: Pershing County Clerk. Personal checks accepted. Prepayment is required.

Lake Township Justice Court PO Box 8, Lovelock, NV 89419; 775-273-2753; Fax: 775-273-

0416. Hours: 8AM-5PM (PST). *Misdemeanor, Civil Actions Under $7,500, Eviction, Small Claims.*

Civil Records: Access: Phone, mail, in person. Visitors must perform in person searches for themselves. Search fee: $1.00 per name per year. Required to search: name, years to search; also helpful: address. Civil cases indexed by defendant, plaintiff. Civil records on computer from 1988, on docket books prior.

Criminal Records: Access: Phone, mail, in person. Visitors must perform in person searches for themselves. Search fee: $1.00 per name per year. Required to search: name, years to search; also helpful: DOB. Criminal records on computer from 1988, on docket books prior.

General Information: Public access terminal is available. No sealed, driver's history or highway patrol records released. SASE required. Turnaround time 2 days, 30 minutes for phone requests for records prior to 1988. Copy fee: $.25 per page. Certification fee: $3.00. Fee payee: Lake Township Justice Court. Personal checks accepted. For payment by check proof of ID required.

Storey County

1st Judicial District Court PO Drawer D, Virginia City, NV 89440; 775-847-0969; Fax: 775-847-0921. Hours: 9AM-5PM (PST). *Felony, Gross Misdemeanor, Civil Actions Over $7,500, Probate.*

Civil Records: Access: Phone, mail, fax, in person. Both court and visitors may perform in person searches. Search fee: $1.00 per name per year. Required to search: name, years to search. Civil cases indexed by defendant, plaintiff. Civil records on computer since 1992; prior years on books. Search by phone only if paid in advance.

Criminal Records: Access: Phone, mail, fax, in person. Both court and visitors may perform in person searches. Search fee: $1.00 per name per year. Required to search: name, years to search, signed release; also helpful: DOB, SSN. Criminal records on computer since 1992; prior years on books. Search by phone only if pre-paid.

General Information: No juvenile or sealed records released. SASE required. Turnaround time 1 week, 5 minutes for phone requests when possible. Copy fee: $1.00 per page. Certification fee: $5.00. Fee payee: Storey County Clerk. Personal checks accepted. Prepayment is required.

Virginia City Justice Court PO Box 674, Virginia City, NV 89440; 775-847-0962; Fax: 775-847-0915. Hours: 9AM-5PM (PST). *Misdemeanor, Civil Actions Under $7,500, Eviction, Small Claims.*

Civil Records: Access: Phone, mail, in person. Only the court performs in person searches; visitors may not. Search fee: $1.00 per name per year. Required to search: name, years to search. Civil cases indexed by defendant, plaintiff. Civil records retained for 7 years, some on docket books.

Criminal Records: Access: Phone, mail, in person. Both court and visitors may perform in person searches. Search fee: $1.00 per name per year. Required to

search: name, years to search, DOB; also helpful: SSN. Criminal records on computer since 1988.

General Information: SASE required. Turnaround time 1 week. Copy fee: $.25 per page. Certification fee: $3.00. Fee payee: Justice Court. Personal checks accepted. Prepayment is required.

Washoe County

2nd Judicial District Court PO Box 30083, Reno, NV 89520; 775-328-3110; Fax: 775-328-3515. Hours: 8AM-5PM (PST). *Felony, Gross Misdemeanor, Civil Actions Over $7,500, Probate.*

Civil Records: Access: Phone, mail, fax, in person. Both court and visitors may perform in person searches. Search fee: $1.00 per name per year. Required to search: name, years to search. Civil cases indexed by defendant, plaintiff. Civil records on computer back to 1984, microfiche from 1983, archives from 1920. Phone access limited to computer records.

Criminal Records: Access: Phone, Mail, fax, in person. Both court and visitors may perform in person searches. Search fee: $1.00 per name per year. Required to search: name, years to search. Criminal records on computer back to 1984, microfiche from 1983, archives from 1920. Phone access limited to computer records.

General Information: No sealed or juvenile records released. SASE required. Turnaround time 2 weeks. Copy fee: $1.00 per page. Certification fee: $6.00. Fee payee: Washoe County Clerk. Business checks accepted. Prepayment is required.

Reno Justice Court PO Box 30083, Reno, NV 89520; 775-325-6501; Criminal phone: 775-325-6500; Fax: 775-325-6510. Hours: 8AM-5PM (PST). *Misdemeanor, Civil Actions Under $7,500, Eviction, Small Claims.*

Civil Records: Access: Mail, in person. Both court and visitors may perform in person searches. Search fee: $1.00 per name per year. Required to search: name, years to search. Civil cases indexed by defendant. Civil records archived from 1982, on docket book; computerized records since 1980. For mail access call first. Court will send form to be filled out & returned with payment.

Criminal Records: Access: Mail, in person. Only the court performs in person searches; visitors may not. Search fee: $1.00 per name per year. Required to search: name, years to search; also helpful: DOB, SSN, aliases. Criminal records archived from 1982, on docket books; computerized records since 1980. Same as civil.

General Information: No sealed records released. SASE required. Turnaround time 2-5 days. Copy fee: $.30 per page. Certification fee: $3.00 per page. Fee payee: Reno Justice Court. Only cashiers checks and money orders accepted.

Sparks Justice Court 630 Greenbrae Dr, Sparks, NV 89431; 775-352-3000. Hours: 8AM-5PM (PST). *Misdemeanor, Civil Actions Under $7,500, Eviction, Small Claims.*

Civil Records: Access: Phone, mail, in person. Both court and visitors may perform in person searches.

Search fee: $1.00 per name per year. Required to search: name, years to search. Civil cases indexed by defendant, plaintiff. Civil records on computer last 11 years, prior in books and on cards.

Criminal Records: Access: Phone, mail, in person. Both court and visitors may perform in person searches. Search fee: $1.00 per name per year. Required to search: name, years to search; also helpful: DOB, SSN. Criminal records on computer last 6 years, prior in books and on cards.

General Information: Public access terminal is available. Turnaround time 1-3 days. Fax notes: Will fax results if prepayment received. Copy fee: $.30 per document. Certification fee: $3.00. Fee payee: Justice Court. Personal checks accepted. For payment by check guarantee card required. Prepayment is required.

White Pine County

Ely Justice Court 801 Clark St #6, Ely, NV 89301; 775-289-2678; Fax: 775-289-3392. Hours: 9AM-5PM (PST). *Misdemeanor, Civil Actions Under $7,500, Eviction, Small Claims.*

Civil Records: Access: Phone, fax, mail, in person. Only the court performs in person searches; visitors may not. Search fee: $1.00 per name per year. Required to search: name, years to search. Civil cases indexed by defendant, plaintiff. Civil records on computer from 1988, archived from 1899.

Criminal Records: Access: Phone, fax, mail, in person. Only the court performs in person searches; visitors may not. Search fee: $1.00 per name per year. Required to search: name, years to search; also helpful: DOB, SSN. Criminal records on computer from 1988, archived from 1899.

General Information: No sealed records released. SASE required. Turnaround time 1-5 days. Copy fee: $.30 per page. Certification fee: $3.00. Fee payee: Ely Justice Court. Only cashiers checks and money orders accepted. Prepayment is required.

Lund Justice Court PO Box 87, Lund, NV 89317; 775-238-5400; Fax: 775-238-5400. Hours: 10AM-2:30PM M,W,F (PST). *Misdemeanor, Civil Actions Under $7,500, Eviction, Small Claims.*

Civil Records: Access: Mail, in person. Only the court performs in person searches; visitors may not. Search fee: $1.00 per name per year. Required to search: name, years to search. Civil records only kept in files, archives from 1899.

Criminal Records: Access: Mail, in person. Only the court performs in person searches; visitors may not. Search fee: $1.00 per name per year. Required to search: name, years to search, DOB; also helpful: SSN. Criminal records only kept in files, archives from 1899.

General Information: SASE required. Turnaround time 1 day. Copy fee: $.25 per page. Certification fee: $2.00. Fee payee: Lund Justice Court. Personal checks accepted. Prepayment is required.

Nevada Recording Offices

ORGANIZATION: 16 counties and one independent city, 17 recording offices. The recording officer is County Recorder. Carson City has a separate filing office. The entire state is in the Pacific Time Zone (PST).

REAL ESTATE RECORDS: Most counties will not provide real estate searches. Copies cost $1.00 per page and certification fees are usually $4.00 per document.

UCC RECORDS: Financing statements are filed at the state level, except for real estate related collateral, which are filed with the County Recorder. However, prior to 07/2001, consumer goods and farm collateral were also filed at the County Recorder and these older records can be searched there. All recording offices will perform UCC searches. Search fees are $15.00 per debtor name using the approved UCC-3 request form and $20.00 using a non-standard form. Copies cost $1.00 per page.

TAX LIEN RECORDS: Federal tax liens on personal property of businesses are filed with the Secretary of State. Federal tax liens on personal property of individuals are filed with the County Recorder. Although not called state tax liens, employment withholding judgments have the same effect and are filed with the County Recorder. Most counties will provide tax lien searches for a fee of $15.00 per name - $20.00 if the standard UCC request form is not used.

OTHER LIENS: Mechanics

ONLINE ACCESS: Clark County has many searchable databases online. A private company, GoverNet, offers online access to Assessor, Treasurer, Recorder and other county databases. Registration is required, sliding monthly and per-hit fees apply. Counties online are Churchill, Clark, Elko, Esmeralda, Eureka, Humboldt, Lander, Lyon, Mineral, Nye, Pershing, Storey, Washoe, and White Pine. System includes access to Secretary of State's Corporation, Partnership, UCC, Fictitious Name, and Federal Tax Lien records. For more information, visit www.governet.net/SurfNV/ or call 208-522-1225.

Carson City

City Recorder, 885 E. Musser St., Ste 1028, Carson City, NV 89701-4775. City Recorder, R/E and UCC Recording 775-887-2260 UCC Recording: 775-887-2260 city level or 775-687-4280 St level; Fax 775-887-2146.
Will search UCC records. UCC search includes federal tax liens if requested. Will not search real estate records. **Online Access:** Assessor, Recorder, Treasurer Records. Access is available on goverNet (www.governet.net/surfnv) 208-522-1225; requires registration and fees; see beginning of this section. **Other Phone Numbers:** Assessor 775-887-2130; Treasurer 775-887-2092; Elections 775-887-2087; Vital Records 775-684-4242.

Churchill County

County Recorder, 155 N. Taylor, Suite 131, Fallon, NV 89406-2748. County Recorder, R/E and UCC Recording 775-423-6001; Fax 775-423-8933. www.churchillcounty.org
Will search UCC records. UCC search includes federal tax liens if requested. Will not search real estate records. **Online Access:** Assessor, Treasurer, Recording Records. Access is available on goverNet (www.governet.net/surfnv) 208-522-1225; requires registration and fees; see beginning of this section. **Other Phone Numbers:** Assessor 775-423-6584; Treasurer 775-423-6028; Appraiser/Auditor 775-423-6584; Elections 775-423-6028; Vital Records 775-684-4280.

Clark County

County Recorder, PO Box 551510, Las Vegas, NV 89155-1510. 702-455-4336 R/E Recording: 702-455-6566; Fax 702-455-5644. www.co.clark.nv.us/recorder/recindex.htm
Will search UCC records. Will not search real estate records. **Online Access:** Real Estate, Lien, Deed, UCC, Vital Statistic, Marriage, Property Assessor, Fictitious Name, Business License Records. Property records, assessor maps, manufactured housing and road documents on the county Assessor database are available free online at www.co.clark.nv.us/assessor/Disclaim.htm. Marriage records available at www.co.clark.nv.us/recorder/mar_srch.htm. Search property owners at the GIS site at http://gisgate.co.clark.nv.us:8487/openweb. Search business licenses at http://sandgate.co.clark.nv.us:8498/businessLicense/blindex.htm. Recorder's real estate, UCC and Vital records are available online at www.co.clark.nv.us/recorder/recindex.htm. UCCs go back to 1986; liens to '84. Search county fictitious names at http://sandgate.co.clark.nv.us:8498/clarkcounty/clerk/clerkSearch.html. **Other Phone Numbers:** Assessor 702-455-3891; Treasurer 702-455-4323.

Douglas County

County Recorder, PO Box 218, Minden, NV 89423. 775-782-9025 R/E Recording: 775-782-9027; Fax 775-783-6413. http://recorder.co.douglas.nv.us
Will search UCC records. Will not search real estate records. **Online Access:** Assessor, Real Estate, Property Tax Records. Property records on the Assessor's database are available free at www.co.douglas.nv.us/databases/assessors. Also, the clerk/treasurer propety tax database is available free at www.co.douglas.nv.us/databases/treasurers. **Other Phone Numbers:** Assessor 775-782-9830; Treasurer 775-782-9022; Vital Records 775-782-9027.

Elko County

County Recorder, 571 Idaho St., Room 103, Elko, NV 89801-3770. County Recorder, R/E and UCC Recording 775-738-6526; Fax 775-738-3299. www.governet.net/nv/co/elk/dir.cfm
Will search UCC records. Will not search real estate records. **Online Access:** Assessor, Treasurer, Recording Records. Access is available on goverNet (www.governet.net/surfnv) 208-522-1225; requires registration and fees; see beginning of this section. **Other Phone Numbers:** Assessor 775-738-3088; Treasurer 775-738-5694; Elections 775-738-4600; Marriages 775-738-6526.

Esmeralda County

County Recorder, PO Box 458, Goldfield, NV 89013. 775-485-6337; Fax 775-485-3524.
Will search UCC records. **Online Access:** Assessor, Treasurer, Recording Records. Access is available on goverNet (www.governet.net/surfnv) 208-522-1225; requires registration and fees; see beginning of this section. **Other Phone Numbers:** Assessor 775-485-6380; Treasurer 775-485-6367.

Eureka County

County Recorder, PO Box 556, Eureka, NV 89316. County Recorder, R/E and UCC Recording 775-237-5263; Fax 775-237-5614.
Will search UCC records. Will not search real estate records. **Online Access:** Assessor, Treasurer, Recorder Records. Access is available on goverNet (www.governet.net/surfnv) 208-522-1225; requires registration and fees; see beginning of this section. **Other Phone Numbers:** Assessor 775-237-5270; Treasurer 775-237-5262; Appraiser/Auditor 775-237-5270; Elections 775-237-5262.

Humboldt County

County Recorder, 25 W. 4th St, Winnemucca, NV 89445. County Recorder, R/E and UCC Recording 775-623-6414 UCC Recording: 775-623-6412; Fax 775-623-6337. www.humboldt-county-nv.net
Will search UCC records. UCC search does not include federal tax liens. Will not search real estate records. **Online Access:** Assessor, Recorder, Treasurer Records. Access is available on goverNet (www.governet.net/surfnv) 208-522-1225; requires registration and fees; see beginning of this section. **Other Phone Numbers:** Assessor 775-623-6310; Treasurer 775-623-6444; Appraiser/Auditor 775-623-6310; Elections 775-623-6343; Vital Records 775-623-6412; 775-623-6414.

Lander County

County Recorder, 315 S. Humboldt, Battle Mountain, NV 89820. County Recorder, R/E and UCC Recording 775-635-5173; Fax 775-635-8272.
Will search UCC records. Federal tax liens not included in UCC search. Will not search real estate records. **Online Access:** Assessor, Recorder Records. Access is available on goverNet (www.governet.net/surfnv) 208-522-1225; requires registration and fees; see beginning of this section. **Other Phone Numbers:** Assessor 775-635-2610; Treasurer 775-635-5127.

Lincoln County

County Recorder, PO Box 218, Pioche, NV 89043. 775-962-5495; Fax 775-962-5180.
Will search UCC records. Will not search real estate records. **Other Phone Numbers:** Assessor 775-962-5890; Treasurer 775-962-5805.

Lyon County

County Recorder, PO Box 927, Yerington, NV 89447-0927. County Recorder, R/E and UCC Recording 775-463-6581; Fax 775-463-6585.
Will search UCC records. Will not search real estate records. **Online Access:** Assessor, Recorder, Treasurer Records. Access is available on goverNet (www.governet.net/surfnv) 208-522-1225; requires registration and fees; see beginning of this section. **Other Phones:** Assessor 775-463-6524; Treasurer 775-463-6502; Appraiser/Auditor 775-463-6524; Elections 775-463-6502; Vital Records 775-463-6581.

Mineral County

County Recorder, PO Box 1447, Hawthorne, NV 89415-1447. 775-945-3676; Fax 775-945-1749.
Will search UCC records. Will not search real estate records. **Online Access:** Assessor, Treasurer, Recording Records. Access is available on goverNet (www.governet.net/surfnv) 208-522-1225; requires registration and fees; see beginning of this section. **Other Phone Numbers:** Assessor 775-945-3684; Treasurer 775-945-2446.

Nye County

County Recorder, PO Box 1111, Tonopah, NV 89049-1111. 775-482-8116 R/E Recording: 775-482-8118; Fax 775-482-8111.
Will search UCC records. Will not search real estate records. **Online Access:** Assessor, Treasurer, Recording Records. Access is available on goverNet (www.governet.net/surfnv) 208-522-1225; requires registration and fees; see beginning of this section. **Other Phone Numbers:** Assessor 775-482-8174; Treasurer 775-482-8194.

Pershing County

County Recorder, PO Box 736, Lovelock, NV 89419-0736. County Recorder, R/E and UCC Recording 775-273-2408; Fax 775-273-1039.
Will search UCC records. UCC search does not include federal tax liens. Will not search real estate records. **Online Access:** Assessor, Treasurer, Recording Records. Access is available on goverNet (www.governet.net/surfnv) 208-522-1225; requires registration and fees; see beginning of this section. **Other Phone Numbers:** Assessor 775-273-2369; Treasurer 775-273-2208.

Storey County

County Recorder, PO Box 493, Virginia City, NV 89440. 775-847-0967; Fax 775-847-1009.
Will search UCC records. UCC search does not include federal tax liens. Will not search real estate records. **Online Access:** Assessor, Treasurer, Recording Records. Access is available on goverNet (www.governet.net/surfnv) 208-522-1225; requires registration and fees; see beginning of this section. **Other Phone Numbers:** Assessor 775-847-0961; Treasurer 775-847-0969; Elections 775-847-0969.

Washoe County

County Recorder, PO Box 11130, Reno, NV 89520-0027. 775-328-3661 R/E Recording: 775-328-2230.
Will search UCC records. UCC search does not include federal tax liens. Will not search real estate records. **Online Access:** Assessor, Treasurer, Recording Records. Access is available on goverNet (www.governet.net/surfnv) 208-522-1225; requires registration and fees; see beginning of this section. **Other Phone Numbers:** Assessor 775-328-2277; Treasurer 775-328-2510.

White Pine County

County Recorder, PO Box 68, Ely, NV 89301. County Recorder, R/E and UCC Recording 775-289-4567; Fax 775-289-1541.
Will search UCC records. Will not search real estate records. **Online Access:** Assessor, Recorder Records. Access is available on goverNet (www.governet.net/surfnv) 208-522-1225; requires registration and fees; see beginning of this section. **Other Phone Numbers:** Assessor 775-289-3016; Treasurer 775-289-4783.

Nevada County Locator

You will usually be able to find the city name in the City/County Cross Reference below. In that case, it is a simple matter to determine the county from the cross reference. However, only the official US Postal Service city names are included in this index. There are an additional 40,000 place names that people use in their addresses. Therefore, we have also included a ZIP/City Cross Reference immediately following the City/County Cross Reference.

If you know the ZIP Code but the city name does not appear in the City/County Cross Reference index, look up the ZIP Code in the ZIP/City Cross Reference, find the city name, then look up the city name in the City/County Cross Reference. For example, you want to know the county for an address of Menands, NY 12204. There is no "Menands" in the City/County Cross Reference. The ZIP/City Cross Reference shows that ZIP Codes 12201-12288 are for the city of Albany. Looking back in the City/County Cross Reference, Albany is in Albany County.

City/County Cross Reference

ALAMO Lincoln
AMARGOSA VALLEY Nye
AUSTIN Lander
BAKER White Pine
BATTLE MOUNTAIN Lander
BEATTY Nye
BLUE DIAMOND Clark
BOULDER CITY Clark
BUNKERVILLE Clark
CAL NEV ARI Clark
CALIENTE Lincoln
CARLIN Elko
CARSON CITY Carson City
CRESCENT VALLEY Eureka
CRYSTAL BAY Washoe
DAYTON (89403) Lyon(86), Storey(13)
DEETH Elko
DENIO Humboldt
DUCKWATER White Pine
DYER Esmeralda
EAST ELY White Pine
ELKO Elko
ELY White Pine
EMPIRE Washoe
EUREKA Eureka

FALLON Churchill
FERNLEY (89408) Lyon(96), Churchill(3)
GABBS Nye
GARDNERVILLE Douglas
GENOA Douglas
GERLACH Washoe
GLENBROOK Douglas
GOLCONDA Humboldt
GOLDFIELD Esmeralda
HALLECK Elko
HAWTHORNE Mineral
HENDERSON Clark
HIKO Lincoln
IMLAY Pershing
INCLINE VILLAGE Washoe
INDIAN SPRINGS Clark
JACKPOT Elko
JARBIDGE Elko
JEAN Clark
LAMOILLE Elko
LAS VEGAS Clark
LAUGHLIN Clark
LOGANDALE Clark
LOVELOCK Pershing
LUND White Pine

LUNING Mineral
MANHATTAN Nye
MC DERMITT Humboldt
MC GILL White Pine
MERCURY Nye
MESQUITE Clark
MINA Mineral
MINDEN Douglas
MOAPA Clark
MONTELLO Elko
MOUNTAIN CITY Elko
NELLIS AFB Clark
NIXON Washoe
NORTH LAS VEGAS Clark
OROVADA Humboldt
OVERTON Clark
OWYHEE Elko
PAHRUMP Nye
PANACA Lincoln
PARADISE VALLEY Humboldt
PIOCHE Lincoln
RENO Washoe
ROUND MOUNTAIN Nye
RUBY VALLEY Elko
RUTH White Pine

SCHURZ Mineral
SEARCHLIGHT Clark
SILVER CITY Lyon
SILVER SPRINGS Lyon
SILVERPEAK Esmeralda
SMITH Lyon
SPARKS Washoe
SPRING CREEK Elko
STATELINE Douglas
SUN VALLEY Washoe
THE LAKES Clark
TONOPAH Nye
TUSCARORA Elko
VALMY Humboldt
VERDI Washoe
VIRGINIA CITY Storey
WADSWORTH Washoe
WASHOE VALLEY Washoe
WELLINGTON Lyon
WELLS Elko
WEST WENDOVER Elko
WINNEMUCCA Humboldt
YERINGTON Lyon
ZEPHYR COVE Douglas

ZIP/City Cross Reference

88901-88901 THE LAKES
88902-88904 LAS VEGAS
88905-88905 THE LAKES
89001-89001 ALAMO
89003-89003 BEATTY
89004-89004 BLUE DIAMOND
89005-89006 BOULDER CITY
89007-89007 BUNKERVILLE
89008-89008 CALIENTE
89009-89009 HENDERSON
89010-89010 DYER
89011-89012 HENDERSON
89013-89013 GOLDFIELD
89014-89016 HENDERSON
89017-89017 HIKO
89018-89018 INDIAN SPRINGS
89019-89019 JEAN
89020-89020 AMARGOSA VALLEY
89021-89021 LOGANDALE
89022-89022 MANHATTAN
89023-89023 MERCURY
89024-89024 MESQUITE
89025-89025 MOAPA
89026-89026 JEAN
89027-89027 MESQUITE
89028-89029 LAUGHLIN
89030-89036 NORTH LAS VEGAS
89039-89039 CAL NEV ARI
89040-89040 OVERTON
89041-89041 PAHRUMP

89042-89042 PANACA
89043-89043 PIOCHE
89045-89045 ROUND MOUNTAIN
89046-89046 SEARCHLIGHT
89047-89047 SILVERPEAK
89048-89048 PAHRUMP
89049-89049 TONOPAH
89052-89053 HENDERSON
89060-89061 PAHRUMP
89070-89070 INDIAN SPRINGS
89074-89077 HENDERSON
89084-89086 NORTH LAS VEGAS
89101-89162 LAS VEGAS
89163-89163 THE LAKES
89164-89185 LAS VEGAS
89191-89191 NELLIS AFB
89193-89199 LAS VEGAS
89301-89301 ELY
89310-89310 AUSTIN
89311-89311 BAKER
89314-89314 DUCKWATER
89315-89315 EAST ELY
89315-89315 ELY
89316-89316 EUREKA
89317-89317 LUND
89318-89318 MC GILL
89319-89319 RUTH
89402-89402 CRYSTAL BAY
89403-89403 DAYTON
89404-89404 DENIO

89405-89405 EMPIRE
89406-89407 FALLON
89408-89408 FERNLEY
89409-89409 GABBS
89410-89410 GARDNERVILLE
89411-89411 GENOA
89412-89412 GERLACH
89413-89413 GLENBROOK
89414-89414 GOLCONDA
89415-89416 HAWTHORNE
89418-89418 IMLAY
89419-89419 LOVELOCK
89420-89420 LUNING
89421-89421 MC DERMITT
89422-89422 MINA
89423-89423 MINDEN
89424-89424 NIXON
89425-89425 OROVADA
89426-89426 PARADISE VALLEY
89427-89427 SCHURZ
89428-89428 SILVER CITY
89429-89429 SILVER SPRINGS
89430-89430 SMITH
89431-89432 SPARKS
89433-89433 SUN VALLEY
89434-89436 SPARKS
89438-89438 VALMY
89439-89439 VERDI
89440-89440 VIRGINIA CITY
89442-89442 WADSWORTH

89444-89444 WELLINGTON
89445-89446 WINNEMUCCA
89447-89447 YERINGTON
89448-89448 ZEPHYR COVE
89449-89449 STATELINE
89450-89452 INCLINE VILLAGE
89496-89496 FALLON
89500-89599 RENO
89701-89703 CARSON CITY
89704-89704 WASHOE VALLEY
89705-89721 CARSON CITY
89801-89803 ELKO
89815-89815 SPRING CREEK
89820-89820 BATTLE MOUNTAIN
89821-89821 CRESCENT VALLEY
89822-89822 CARLIN
89823-89823 DEETH
89824-89824 HALLECK
89825-89825 JACKPOT
89826-89826 JARBIDGE
89828-89828 LAMOILLE
89830-89830 MONTELLO
89831-89831 MOUNTAIN CITY
89832-89832 OWYHEE
89833-89833 RUBY VALLEY
89834-89834 TUSCARORA
89835-89835 WELLS
89883-89883 WEST WENDOVER

New Hampshire

General Help Numbers:

Governor's Office

State House
107 N Main St, Rm 204
Concord, NH 03301-4990
www.state.nh.us/governor/index.html

603-271-2121
Fax 603-271-5686
8AM-5PM

Attorney General's Office

33 Capitol St
Concord, NH 03301-6397
http://webster.state.nh.us/nhdoj

603-271-3658
Fax 603-271-2110
8AM-5PM

State Court Administrator

2 Noble Dr
Concord, NH 03301-6160
www.state.nh.us/courts/aoc.htm

603-271-2521
Fax 603-271-3977
8AM-5PM

State Archives

Division of Records Management
& Archives
71 S Fruit St
Concord, NH 03301
http://webster.state.nh.us/state

603-271-2236

Fax 603-271-2272
8AM-4:30PM

State Specifics:

Capital:

Concord
Merrimack County

Time Zone:

EST

Number of Counties:

10

Population:

1,259,181

Web Site:

www.state.nh.us

State Agencies

Criminal Records

State Police Headquarters, Criminal Records, James H. Hayes Bldg, 10 Hazen Dr, Concord, NH 03305; 603-271-2538, 603-271-2339 (Fax), 8:15AM-4:15PM.

www.state.nh.us/safety/nhsp/cr.html

Note: Sex offender data is currently not available online; list can be accessed through local sheriffs' offices.

Indexing & Storage: Records are available from circa 1900. It takes 1 day before new records are

available for inquiry. 80% of all arrests in database have final dispositions recorded, 90% for those arrests within last 5 years.

Searching: Requester must have "authorization in writing, duly signed and notarized, explicitly allowing the requester to receive such information." Also specify exactly what information is needed. Statutorily-required fingerprint searches include FBI check. Include the following in your request: notarized release, full name, date of birth, any aliases, sex, race. Fingerprint searches are required for certain

occupations (teachers) per state statute. 75% of the records are fingerprint supported. Records without convictions are not released.

Access by: mail, in person.

Fee & Payment: The search fee is $10.00 per name. When required, FBI fingerprint searches are an additional $24.00 Fee payee: NH State Police. Prepayment required. Personal checks accepted. No credit cards accepted.

Mail search: Turnaround time: 1 week. A self addressed envelope is requested.

In person search: In person requests are processed immediately.

Corporation Records
Limited Partnership Records
Limited Liability Company Records
Trademarks/Servicemarks
Trade Names
Limited Liability Partnerships
Not For Profit Entities

Secretary of State, Corporation Division, State House, Room 204, Concord, NH 03301; 603-271-3246, 603-271-3244, 603-271-3247 (Fax), 8AM-4:30PM.

www.state.nh.us/sos/corporate/index.htm

Indexing & Storage: Records are available from inception of the laws. Older records and inactive records are stored at the State Archives. Records also include foreign partnerships, investment trusts and cooperatives. New records are available for inquiry immediately. Records are indexed on inhouse computer.

Searching: Include the following in your request: full name of business, specific records that you need copies of. In addition to the articles of incorporation, corporation records include the following information: Annual Reports, Officers, Directors, Prior (merged) names, Inactive and Reserved names.

Access by: mail, phone, fax, in person.

Fee & Payment: There is no charge for 20 pages or less. If more than 20 pages, the charge is $.50 per page for every page. Certification is $5.00 plus $1.00 per page. Note that they do not print computer screens, but take copies straight from files. Fee payee: Secretary of State. They will invoice for copy fees, but you must pay in advance for certificates of good standing. Fax accounts may be billed monthly. Personal checks accepted. No credit cards accepted.

Mail search: Turnaround time: 1 to 2 days. A self addressed stamped envelope is requested.

Phone search: No fee for telephone request. An information line, 603-271-3246, is open from 8 to 12 and 1 to 4. You can obtain name, address, incorporation date, and registered agent, check name availability, and request document copies.

Fax search: Fax requests are considered expedited service. Requests received by 2PM will be completed same business day. Fee is $10.00 per request, two may be faxed per call.

In person search: You may request information in person, the agency does the copying.

Other access: Corporation or trade name monthly hard copies are $20.00 each or $180.00 for a 1 year subscription. A list of new registrations is $350.00 per 6 months.

Uniform Commercial Code
Federal Tax Liens
State Tax Liens

UCC Division, Secretary of State, 25 Capitol St, State House Annex, 3rd Floor, Concord, NH 03301; 603-271-3276, 9AM-3:30PM (searches).

www.state.nh.us/sos/ucc/index.htm

Indexing & Storage: Records are available for active filings only.

Searching: Use search request form UCC-11. In general, tax liens on businesses are filed here and on individuals at the town/county level. It is suggested to search both places. Include the following in your request: debtor name.

Access by: mail, in person.

Fee & Payment: Fees is $10.00 per name, copies $1.00 per page. Fee payee: Secretary of State. Prepayment required. Search requests and filings must be prepaid, they will invoice for copies. Personal checks accepted. No credit cards accepted.

Mail search: Turnaround time: 2 weeks. A self addressed stamped envelope is requested.

In person search: You may request information in person.

Sales Tax Registrations
State does not impose sales tax.

Birth Certificates

Office of Community and Public Health, Bureau of Vital Records, 6 Hazen Dr, Concord, NH 03301-6527; 603-271-4650, 603-271-4654 (Recording), 800-852-3345 x4651 (In-state), 603-271-3447 (Fax), 8:30AM-4PM.

www.dhhs.state.nh.us/

Note: For genealogical purposes, birth records prior to 1901 may be released without restriction.

Indexing & Storage: Records are available from 1640 to present. Records are on computer since 1990, indexed since 1948. Records are indexed on microfiche, index cards, computer.

Searching: Must have a signed release from person of record or immediate family member or show proof of "tangible interest." Order forms are available at the web site. Include the following in your request: full name, names of parents, mother's maiden name, date of birth, place of birth, relationship to person of record, reason for information request.

Access by: mail, phone, in person.

Fee & Payment: The search fee is $12.00 per record and $8.00 for each additional copy of the same record. Fee payee: Treasurer of State of New Hampshire. Prepayment required. Credit cards accepted for expedited service only. Personal checks accepted. Credit cards accepted: MasterCard, Visa, AmEx, Discover.

Mail search: Turnaround time: 3 to 5 days. A self addressed stamped envelope is requested.

Phone search: Must use credit card for additional $6.00 fee.

In person search: Turnaround time while you wait.

Expedited service: Expedited service is available for mail and phone searches. Turnaround time:

overnight delivery. Add $12.50 per package. Add regular fees and credit card fee.

Death Records

Office of Community and Public Health, Bureau of Vital Records, 6 Hazen Dr, Concord, NH 03301-6527; 603-271-4650, 603-271-4654 (Recording), 800-852-3345 x4651 (In-state), 603-271-3447 (Fax), 8:30AM-4PM.

www.dhhs.state.nh.us

Note: For genealogical purposes, death records prior to 1938 may be released without restriction.

Indexing & Storage: Records are available from 1640 to present. Records are computerized since 1990, indexed on computer since 1948. Records are indexed on microfiche, index cards, computer.

Searching: Must have a signed release form from immediate family member. Include the following in your request: full name, date of death, place of death, parents' names, relationship to person of record, reason for information request. The following data is not released: cause of death.

Access by: mail, phone, in person.

Fee & Payment: The search fee is $12.00 per record, additional copies are $8.00 each. Fee payee: Treasurer of State of New Hampshire. Prepayment required. Credit cards accepted for expedited service only. Personal checks accepted. Credit cards accepted: MasterCard, Visa, AmEx, Discover.

Mail search: Turnaround time: 3 to 5 days. A self addressed stamped envelope is requested.

Phone search: Must use a credit card for an additional $6.00 fee.

In person search: Turnaround time while you wait.

Expedited service: Expedited service is available for mail and phone searches. Turnaround time: overnight delivery. Add $12.50 per package. Add regular fees and credit card fee.

Marriage Certificates

Office of Community and Public Health, Bureau of Vital Records & Health Statistics, 6 Hazen Dr, Concord, NH 03301-6527; 603-271-4650, 603-271-4654 (Recording), 800-852-3345 x4651 (In-state), 603-271-3447 (Fax), 8:30AM-4PM.

www.dhhs.state.nh.us

Note: For genealogical purposes, marriage records prior to 1938 may be released without restriction.

Indexing & Storage: Records are available from 1640 to present. Records are computerized from 1990, indexed on computer since 1948. Records are indexed on microfiche, index cards.

Searching: Must have a signed release form from persons of record or immediate family member. Include the following in your request: names of husband and wife, date of marriage, place or county of marriage, relationship to person of record, reason for information request, wife's maiden name.

Access by: mail, phone, in person.

Fee & Payment: The search fee is $12.00 per record, each additional copy is $8.00. Fee payee: Treasurer of State of New Hampshire. Prepayment required. Credit cards accepted for expedited service only. Personal checks accepted. Credit cards accepted: MasterCard, Visa, AmEx, Discover.

Mail search: Turnaround time: 3 to 5 days. A self addressed stamped envelope is requested.

Phone search: Must use a credit card for an additional $6.00 fee.

In person search: Turnaround time while you wait.

Expedited service: Expedited service is available for mail and phone searches. Turnaround time: overnight delivery. Add $13.00 per package. Add regular search fee and credit card fee.

Divorce Records

Office of Community and Public Health, Bureau of Vital Records, 6 Hazen Dr, Concord, NH 03301-6527; 603-271-4650, 603-271-4654 (Recording), 800-852-3345 x4651 (In-state), 603-271-3447 (Fax), 8:30AM-4PM.

www.dhhs.state.nh.us

Note: For genealogical purposes, divorce records prior to 1938 may be released without restriction.

Indexing & Storage: Records are available from 1640 to present. Records are computerized since 1990, indexed on computer since 1948. Records are indexed on microfiche, index cards.

Searching: Must have a signed release from person of record or immediate family member. Include the following in your request: names of husband and wife, date of divorce, year divorce case began, city or town, case number (if known), relationship to person of record, reason for information request.

Access by: mail, phone, in person.

Fee & Payment: The search fee is $12.00 per record, additional copies are $8.00 each. Fee payee: Treasurer of State of New Hampshire. Prepayment required. Credit cards accepted for expedited service only. Personal checks accepted. Credit cards accepted: MasterCard, Visa, AmEx, Discover.

Mail search: Turnaround time: 3 to 5 days. A self addressed stamped envelope is requested.

Phone search: Must use a credit card for an additional $6.00 fee.

In person search: Turnaround time while you wait.

Expedited service: Expedited service is available for mail and phone searches. Turnaround time: overnight delivery. Add $13.00 per package. Add search fee and credit card fee.

Workers' Compensation Records

Labor Department, Workers Compensation Division, 95 Pleasant St, Concord, NH 03301; 603-271-3174, 603-271-6149 (Fax), 8AM-4:30PM.

Indexing & Storage: Records are available from 1990 to present. Records prior to 1990 are kept at the State Archives. However, one must go through this office for records. It takes 1-2 weeks before new records are available for inquiry. Records are indexed on microfilm.

Searching: Must have an authorized release from claimant. Include the following in your request: claimant name, Social Security Number, date of accident, place of employment at time of accident.

Access by: mail, fax.

Fee & Payment: There is no search fee, copy fee is $.35 per page. Fee payee: Labor Department. Prepayment required. Personal checks accepted. No credit cards accepted.

Mail search: Turnaround time: 2 to 3 weeks. A self addressed stamped envelope is requested.

Fax search: Allow 1 week turnaround time.

Driver Records

Department of Motor Vehicles, Driving Records, 10 Hazen Dr, Concord, NH 03305; 603-271-2322, 8:15AM-4:15PM.

http://webster.state.nh.us/dmv

Note: New Hampshire recommends going to the local courts for copies of tickets or to state Financial Responsibility agency.

Indexing & Storage: Records are available for 5 years for moving violations and 7 for DWIs. Surrendered license information remains on the system at least 5 years after the expiration date. The driver's address is on manually processed records, but not on tape records. It takes 2 to 3 weeks normally before new records are available for inquiry.

Searching: Use of DSMV Form 505 is recommended. Frequent requesters should establish an account with the state. Include the following in your request: full name, date of birth. Casual (non-permissible use) requesters are required submit the subject's notarized signature on the Form 505. The license number is not required for a search, but is suggested.

Access by: mail, in person, online.

Fee & Payment: Records are $7.00. If you wish the record certified records the fee is $10.00. Fee payee: Department of Safety. Prepayment required. Personal checks accepted. No credit cards accepted.

Mail search: Turnaround time: 2 days. Mail-in requests must include requester's name and address. A self addressed stamped envelope is requested.

In person search: Three requests can be processed while you wait.

Online search: Online access is offered for approved commercial accounts. The system is open 22 hours a day. Searches are by license number or by name and DOB. Fee is $7.00 per record. For more information, call the Diretcor's Office.

Other access: Overnight magnetic tape access is available for higher volume users. Minimum order is 50 requests.

Vehicle Identification

Department of Safety, Bureau of Titles, 10 Hazen Dr, Concord, NH 03305; 603-271-3111 (Bureau of Title), 8:15AM-4:15PM.

www.state.nh.us/dmv

Indexing & Storage: Records are available 11 years to present. It takes 2 weeks before new records are available for inquiry.

Searching: The state will only release to requesters authorized by statute or to casual requesters with a signed release form subject.

Access by: mail, in person.

Fee & Payment: The fee is $20.00 for a title and lien history and $5.00 for a registration listing. Fee payee: Department of Safety. Prepayment

required. Personal checks accepted. No credit cards accepted.

Mail search: Turnaround time: 4 to 5 days. A self addressed stamped envelope is requested.

In person search: Turnaround time while you wait, depending on workload of personnel.

Vehicle Ownership Vessel Registration

Department of Safety, Boat Desk, 10 Hazen Dr, Concord, NH 03305; 603-271-2333, 8:15AM-4:15PM.

Indexing & Storage: Records are available for current registration records only. All motorized boats and all sailboats over 14 ft must be registered. (Boats are not titled and liens on boats are found at the Secretary of State - 603-271-3242.

Searching: Records are restricted to those authorized by statute. Authorization is stricter than the DPPA requirements. Include the following in your request: owner's name, plate number or VIN is required to search.

Access by: mail, in person.

Fee & Payment: The fee is $5.00 per record. Fee payee: State of New Hampshire. Personal checks accepted. No credit cards accepted.

Mail search: Turnaround time: 3 to 5 days.

In person search: Turnaround time is immediate.

Accident Reports

Department of Safety, Accident Reproduction Section, 10 Hazen Dr, Concord, NH 03305; 603-271-2128, 8:15AM-4:15PM.

Indexing & Storage: Records are available for 5 years. Records are indexed on computer. It takes 3 to 4 weeks before new records are available for inquiry.

Searching: Access is not open to the public due to Privacy Act, Chapter 295,260:14. This requires by law a notarized DSMV 505 Form to be filled out by the subject involved or by an insurance representative licensed to write auto policies in this state. Include the following in your request: full name, date of birth, date of accident, location of accident. It is suggested to include both operators' names in the request.

Access by: mail.

Fee & Payment: The fee is $1.00 per page. There is no charge for a "no record found." Requesters are notified of the fee for reports after the report has become available. Fee payee: Department of Safety. Prepayment required. Personal checks and credit cards accepted.

Mail search: Turnaround time: 3 to 4 weeks. A self addressed stamped envelope is requested.

Legislation Records

New Hampshire State Library, 20 Part St, Concord, NH 03301; 603-271-2239, 603-271-2205 (Fax), 8AM-4:30PM.

http://gencourt.state.nh.us/ie

Note: Visit http://webster.state.nh.us/nhsl/ for the state statutes.

Indexing & Storage: Records are available from 1989 to present on computer. There are also bound House and Senate Journals from 1800's to present.

Searching: Bill number or key word required to search.

Access by: mail, phone, fax, in person, online.

Fee & Payment: There is no search fee, but there is a copy fee of $.20 per page, minimum $1.00. Fee payee: New Hampshire State Library. Personal checks accepted. No credit cards accepted.

Mail search: Turnaround time: 1 day. No self addressed stamped envelope is required.

Phone search: Will invoice.

Fax search: Fax charge is $.35 per page, minimum $1.00.

In person search: Searching is available in person.

Online search: Information can be viewed from the web site.

Voter Registration

Records not maintained by a state level agency.

Note: All records are kept by Town Clerks. Records are open.

GED Certificates

Department of Education, GED Testing, 101 Pleasant Street, Concord, NH 03301; 603-271-6699, 603-271-3454 (Fax), 7:30AM-4PM.

www.ed.state.nh.us

Indexing & Storage: Records are indexed on microfiche.

Searching: Include the following in your request: Social Security Number, date of birth, year of issue, name at the time. The date is needed since records are filed by year. For a copy of a transcript, include a signed release.

Access by: mail.

Fee & Payment: The fee is $5.00 for a transcript, there is no fee for a verification. Fee payee: State of New Hampshire. Prepayment required. No credit cards accepted.

Mail search: Turnaround time: 1 week. No self addressed stamped envelope is required.

Hunting License Information
Fishing License Information

Fish & Game Department, Licensing Department, Two Hazen Dr, Concord, NH 03301; 603-271-3421, 603-271-5829 (Fax), 8AM-4:30PM.

www.wildlife.state.nh.us

Indexing & Storage: Records are available for 3 years back to present. Records are indexed on computer. Records are indexed on inhouse computer.

Searching: Requests must be in writing using their form. Include the following in your request: full name, date of birth. The following data is not released: financial information.

Access by: mail, in person.

Fee & Payment: There may be a charge of $.10 per page. Fee payee: NH Fish & Game. Personal checks accepted.

Mail search: Turnaround time: 2 -3 days. Request must be in writing with payment in advance. A self addressed stamped envelope is required.

In person search: Written request is require with payment in advance.

Other access: Mailing labels are available at a cost of $25.00 plus $.10 per label.

New Hampshire State Licensing Agencies

Licenses Searchable Online

Architect #34...www.state.nh.us/jtboard/arlist.htm
Bank #1 ....http://webster.state.nh.us/banking/banking.html
Credit Union #1 ....http://webster.state.nh.us/banking/banking.html
Engineer #34 ....www.state.nh.us/jtboard/pe.htm
Forester #34 ....www.state.nh.us/jtboard/forlist.htm
Lobbyist #42 ....http://webster.state.nh.us/sos/lobbyist information.htm
Marital Mediator #36 ....www.state.nh.us/marital/mediators.html
Natural Scientist #34.......................................www.state.nh.us/jtboard/ns.htm
Nurse, LPN/Practical/Advanced #18...........www.nh.inthe.org/
Nursing Assistant #18....................................www.nh.inthe.org/
Optometrist #23 ....www.odfinder.org/LicSearch.asp
Pharmacist #27 ....www.state.nh.us/pharmacy/database.html
Pharmacy #27..www.state.nh.us/pharmacy/database.html
Real Estate Appraiser #31 ....www.asc.gov/content/category1/appr_by_state.asp
Surveyor, Land #34 ....www.state.nh.us/jtboard/lsis.htm

Licensing Quick Finder

Accessibility Lift Mechanic #28.............603-271-2585	Energy Facility Site #8.........................603-271-3503	Pastoral Psychotherapist #26 603-271-6762
Acupuncturist #10....................................603-335-1425	Engineer #34...603-271-2219	Pesticide Dealer/Seller #6......................603-271-3550
Alcohol/Drug Counselor #41.................603-271-6112	Esthetician #4 603-271-3608	Pesticide Disposal/Labeling #6.............603-271-3550
Ambulance Attendant #22.....................603-271-7048	Explosive Storage License #39.............603-271-3575	Pesticide User #6....................................603-271-3550
Ambulance Service #22.........................603-271-7048	Explosives Competency License #39 ..603-271-3575	Pharmacist #27.......................................603-271-2350
Architect #34..603-271-2219	Fire Inspector #38..................................603-271-2661	Pharmacy #27...603-271-2350
Asbestos Abatement Worker #46.........603-271-4609	Firefighter #38..603-271-2661	Pharmacy Technician #27.......................603-271-2350
Athletic Trainer #45...............................603-271-8389	Fireworks Competency License #39....603-271-3575	Physical Therapist #45............................603-271-8389
Attorney #43...603-271-2646	Forester #34..603-271-2219	Physical Therapist Assistant #45.........603-271-8389
Auctioneer #3...603-271-3242	Foster Family Home #10 800-852-3345	Physician #19..603-271-1203
Audiologist #47 603-271-4501	Funeral Director #17...............................603-271-4648	Physician Assistant #19.........................603-271-1203
Bail Bondsman #50................................603-271-1463	Hearing Aid Dispenser/Fitter #25.........603-271-5127	Podiatrist #19..603-271-1203
Bail Recovery Agent #50 603-271-1463	Horse Trainer #48...................................603-271-2158	Plumber #9..603-271-3267
Bank #1...603-271-3561	Insurance Adjuster #33..........................603-271-2261	Police Officer/Detective #49..................603-271-2133
Bank Holding Company #1....................603-271-3561	Insurance Advisor/Consultant #33 ...603-271-2261	Private Detective #39..............................603-271-3575
Bank, Cooperative #1............................603-271-3561	Insurance Agent/Broker #33..................603-271-2261	Psychologist #26....................................603-271-6762
Barber #4..603-271-3608	Insurance Company #33.........................603-271-2261	Public Accountant-CPA #2.....................603-271-3286
Bingo/Lottery Operation #44.................603-271-3391	Investment Advisor #50..........................603-271-1463	Public Health Clinic #27 603-271-2350
Boiler Inspector #28..............................603-271-2585	Itinerant Vendor #30...............................603-271-3242	Pump Installer #40 603-271-3503
Boxing/Wrestling Contestant #30.........603-271-3242	Leadworker #46.......................................603-271-4609	Real Estate Appraiser #31 603-271-6186
Boxing/Wrestling Manager/Promoter #30	Liquor License #35..................................603-271-3755	Real Estate Broker #32 603-271-2701
....603-271-3242	Loan Company, Small #1........................603-271-3561	Real Estate Firm #32..............................603-271-2701
Boxing/Wrestling Referee/Second/Timekeeper #30	Loan Production Office #1 603-271-3561	Real Estate Salesperson #32 603-271-2701
....603-271-3242	Lobbyist #30 603-271-3242	Residential Care Facility, Children #21. 603-271-4624
Canadian Broker/Dealer #50................603-271-1463	Lobbyist #42 603-271-3242	Respiratory Care Practitioner #20........603-271-1203
Cash Dispensing Machine, Non-bank #1	Manicurist #4...603-271-3608	Respiratory Care Practitioner #45........603-271-8389
....603-271-3561	Marital Mediator #36...............................603-271-6593	Savings Bank #1 603-271-3561
Child Care Facility #21.........................603-271-4624	Marriage & Family Therapist #26..........603-271-6762	School Administrator #7..........................603-271-3871
Child Placing Agency #10.....................800-852-3345	Mental Health Counselor, Clinical #26..603-271-6762	Securities Broker/Dealer/Agent #50......603-271-1463
Chiropractor #14....................................603-271-4560	Midwife #24...603-271-4667	Securities Salesperson #50...................603-271-1463
Concealed Weapons License, Non-Resident #39	Mortgage (1st) Banker, Non-Depository #1	Security Guard #39 603-271-3575
....603-271-3575	603-271-3561	Shorthand Reporter #37..........................603-271-2030
Corrections Officer #49.........................603-271-2133	Mortgage (1st) Broker #1 603-271-3561	Social Worker #25...................................603-271-6762
Cosmetologist #4...................................603-271-3608	Mortgage (2nd) Home Loan Lender #1. 603-271-3561	Social Worker, Clinical #26 603-271-6762
Court Reporter #37................................603-271-2030	Mortgage Servicer #1.............................603-271-3561	Speech Language Pathology #45..........603-271-8389
Credit Union #1......................................603-271-3561	Motor Vehicle Retail Seller #1 603-271-3561	Speech-Language Pathologist #10........603-271-1203
Debt Adjuster #1....................................603-271-3561	Motor Vehicle Sales Finance Company #1	Surveyor, Land #34................................603-271-2219
Dental Hygienist #15.............................603-271-4561	603-271-3561	Tattoo Establishment/Practitioner #13.. 603-271-4594
Dentist #15...603-271-4561	Natural Scientist #34 603-271-2219	Teacher #7 603-271-3871
Dog Trainer #48.....................................603-271-2158	Naturopath #10..603-271-5127	Tobacco Law Enforcement #35 603-271-3755
Drug Wholesaler/Manufacturer #27.....603-271-2350	Notary Public #42....................................603-271-3242	Trust Company #1...................................603-271-3561
Electrician, Master/Journeyman/Apprentice #29	Nurse, LPN/Practical/Advanced #18....603-271-2323	Veterinary Medicine #5 603-271-3706
....603-271-3748	Nursing Assistant #18............................603-271-2323	Vocational Rehabilitation Provider #28. 603-271-3328
Electrologist #12....................................603-271-5127	Nursing Home Administrator #16...........603-271-6936	Waste Water Treatment Plant Operator #40
Elevator Inspector #28..........................603-271-2585	Occupational Therapist #45...................603-271-8389	603-271-3503
Elevator Mechanic #28.........................603-271-2585	Occupational Therapy Assistant #45 ...603-271-8389	Water Distribution System Operator #40
Embalmer #17 603-271-4648	Ophthalmic Dispenser #10 603-271-5127	603-271-3503
Energy Facility Construction #8...........603-271-3503	Optometrist #23......................................603-271-2428	Water Well Contractor #40....................603-271-3503

Licensing Agency Information

#1 Banking Department, 56 Old Suncook Rd, Concord, NH 03301-5127; 603-271-3561, Fax: 603-271-1090.
http://webster.state.nh.us/banking/

#2 Department of State, Board of Accountancy, 57 Regional Dr, Concord, NH 03301-8506; 603-271-3286, Fax: 603-271-2856.
www.state.nh.us/accountancy/index.html
Agency email: lcollier@boa.state.nh.us.

#3 Secretary of State, Board of Auctioneers, 107 N Main St, State House Rm 204, Concord, NH 03301; 603-271-3242, Fax: 603-271-6316.
www.webster.state.nh.us/soso

#4 Board of Barbering, Cosmetology & Esthetics, 2 Industrial Park Dr, Concord, NH 03301; 603-271-3608, Fax: 603-271-8889.
http://webster.state.nh.us/cosmet/

#5 Board of Veterinary Medicine, PO Box 2042 (25 Capitol St), Concord, NH 03302-2042; 603-271-3706, Fax: 604-271-1109.
www.state.nh.us/veterinary/index.html
Agency email: pduncklee@agr.state.nh.us.

#6 Department of Agriculture, 25 Capitol St 2nd Fl, Concord, NH 03301-2042; 603-271-3551, Fax: 603-271-1109.
www.state.nh.us/agric/peco.html

#7 Department of Education, Division of Educational Improvement, 101 Pleansant St, State Office Park S, Concord, NH 03301-3860; 603-271-3494, Fax: 603-271-4134.
www.ed.state.nh.us
Agency email: kcafiero@ed.state.nh.us.

#8 Department of Environmental Services, 6 Hazen Dr. POB 95, Concord, NH 03301; 603-271-3503, Fax: 603-271-8013.
www.des.state.nh.us

#9 Plumbing Licensing Board, PO Box 1386, Concord, NH 03302-1386; 603-271-3267, Fax: 603-271-6656.
http://webster.state.nh.us/plumbing
Agency email: info@plumbing.state.nh.

#10 Department of Health & Human Services, 129 Pleasant, Concord, NH 03301; 800-852-3345, Fax: 603-271-4729.
www.dhhs.state.nh.us/Index.nsf?Open
Agency email: lmeffert@dhhs.state.nh.us.

#12 Department of Health & Human Services, Advisory Board of Electrologists, 129 Pleasant, Concord, NH 03301; 603-271-5127, Fax: 603-271-3745.
www.dhhs.state/nh.us/index.nsf?Open

#13 Department of Health & Human Services, Advisory Board of Massage Practitioners, 129 Pleasant, Concord, NH 03301; 603-271-4594, Fax: 603-271-4968.
www.dhhs.state.nh.us/index.nsf?Open

#14 Department of Health & Human Services, Board of Chiropractic Examiners, 125 Pleasant, Concord, NH 03301; 603-271-4560, Fax: 603-271-3745.
www.dhhs.state.nh.us/index.nsf?Open

#15 Department of Health & Human Services, Board of Dental Examiners, 2 Industrial Park Dr, Concord, NH 03301-8520; 603-271-4561, Fax: 603-271-6702.
http://webster.state.nh.us/dental
Agency email: pthomson@nhsa.state.nh.us.

#16 Department of Health & Human Services, Board of Examiners of Nursing Home Administrators, 2 Industrial Park Dr #8, Concord, NH 03301; 603-271-4728, Fax: 603-271-6702.

#17 Department of Health & Human Services, Board of Funeral Directors & Embalmers, 6 Hazen Dr, Concord, NH 03301-6507; 603-271-4648, Fax: 603-271-3447.
http://webster.state.nh.us/funeral
Agency email: funeralbd@dhhs.state.nh.us.

#18 Department of Health & Human Services, Board of Nursing, PO Box 3898, 78 Regional Dr, Bldg B, Concord, NH 03302-3898; 603-271-2323, Fax: 603-271-6282.
www.state.nh.us/nursing/nursing/htm
Agency email: sgoodness@nhbon.org.
Search database at www.nh.inthe.org

#19 Department of Health & Human Services, 2 Industrial Park Dr #8, Concord, NH 03301; 603-271-1203, Fax: 603-271-6702.
www.state.nh.us/podiatry/index.html.

#20 Department of Health & Human Services, Board of Allied Health Professionals, 2 Industrial Park Dr, Concord, NH 03301; 603-271-1203, Fax: 603-271-6702.
www.dhhs.state.nh.us/index.nsf?Open

#21 Department of Health & Human Services, Bureau of Child Care Licensing, 129 Pleasant St, Brown Bldg, Concord, NH 03301-3857; 603-271-4624, Fax: 603-271-4782.
www.dhhs.state.nh.us/DHHS/BCCL/default.htm

#22 Department of Safety, Division of Emergency Medical Services, 10 Hazen Dr, Concord, NH 03305-0003; 603-271-4568, Fax: 603-271-4567.
http://webster.state.nh.us/safety/ems
Agency email: tfortier@nhems.mv.com.

#23 Department of Health & Human Services, Board of Registration in Optometry, 2 Industrial Park Dr. # 8, Concord, NH 03301; 603-271-2428, Fax: 603-271-6702.
http://webster.state.nh.us/optometry/
Search database at www.odfinder.org/LicSearch.asp

#24 Department of Health & Human Services, Committee for the Practice of Lay-Midwifery, 129 Pleasant, Concord, NH 03301; 603-271-4667, Fax: 603-271-3827.
www.dhhs.state.nh.us/index.nsf?Open

#25 Department of Health & Human Services, Council on the Sale & Fitting of Hearing Aids, 129 Pleasant, Concord, NH 03301; 603-271-4816, Fax: 603-271-4141.
www.dhhs.state.nh.us/index.nsf?Open

#26 Board of Mental Health Practices, 49 Donovan St, Concord, NH 03301; 603-271-6762, Fax: 603-271-3950.
http://webster.state.nh.us/mhpb

#27 Department of Health & Human Services, Board of Pharmacy, 57 Regional Dr, Concord, NH 03301-8518; 603-271-2350, Fax: 603-271-2856.
www.state.nh.us/pharmacy. Agency email: nhpharmacy@nhsa.state.nh.us.
Search database at
www.state.nh.us/pharmacy/database.html

#28 Department of Labor, 95 Pleasant St, State Office Park S, Concord, NH 03301-3836; 603-271-3176, Fax: 603-271-2668.
www.state.nh.us/dol/index.htm

#29 Electricians' Licensing Board, 2 Industrial Park Dr (PO Box 646, 03302-0646), Concord, NH 03302-0646; 603-271-3748, Fax: 603-271-2257.
http://webster.state.nh.us/electrician
Agency email: inspector@elecboard.state.nh.us.

#30 Department of State, Boxing & Wrestling Commission, 107 N Main #204, Concord, NH 03301; 603-271-3242.
www.state.nh.us/sos

#31 Real Estate Appraiser Board, 25 Capitol St, Rm 426, Concord, NH 03301-6312; 603-271-6186, Fax: 603-271-6513.
http://webster.state.nh.us/nhreab
Agency email: nhreab@state.nh.us.

#32 Department of State, Real Estate Commission, 25 Capitol St Rm 437, Concord, NH 03301; 603-271-2701, Fax: 603-271-1039.
www.state.nh.us/nhrec/license.html

#33 Insurance Department, Division of Licensing, 56 Old Suncook Rd, Concord, NH 03301-7131; 603-271-2261, Fax: 603-271-1406.
http://webster.state.nh.us/insurance
Agency email: Requests@ins.state.nh.us.

#34 Joint Board of Licensure & Certification, 57 Regional Dr, Concord, NH 03301; 603-271-2219, Fax: 603-271-6990.
www.state.nh.us/jtboard/home.htm
Agency email: llavertu@nhsa.state.nh.us.
Search database at
www.state.nh.us/jtboard/home.htm

#35 Licensing & Enforcement, Liquor Commission, 10 Commercial St, Concord, NH 03301; 603-271-3755, Fax: 603-271-3758.
www.state.nh.us/liquor/index.html

#36 c/o Judicial Council, Marital Mediator Certification Board, 25 Capitol St Rm 424, Concord, NH 03301; 603-224-6593, Fax: 603-224-8388.
http://webster.state.nh.us/marital/
Search database at
www.state.nh.us/marital/mediators.html

#37 Superior Court Center, 17 Chenell Dr #1, Concord, NH 03301; 603-271-2030, Fax: 603-271-2033.

#38 Department of Safety, Division of Fire Standards & Training, 10 Hazen Dr, Concord, NH 03305-0002; 603-271-2661, Fax: 603-271-1091.
www.state.nh.us/safety/fst/index.html. Agency email: fireacademy@safety.state.nh.us.

#39 State Police, Permits and License Unit, 10 Hazen Dr, Concord, NH 03305; 603-271-3575.
www.state.nh.us/nhsp

#40 Department of Environmental Services, Water Division, 6 Hazen Dr PO Box 95, Concord, NH 03302-0095; 603-271-3503, Fax: 603-271-2867. www.des.state.nh.us
Agency email: pip@des.state.nh.us.

#41 Office of Alcohol & Drug Abuse Prevention, 105 Pleasant St, Concord, NH 03301; 603-271-6112, Fax: 603-271-6116.

#42 Office of Secretary of State, 107 N Main St, State House Rm 204, Concord, NH 03301-4989; 603-271-3242, Fax: 603-271-6316.
http://webster.state.nh.us/sos

#43 Supreme Court, 1 Noble Dr, Concord, NH 03301; 603-271-2646, Fax: 603-271-6630.
www.state.nh.us/sos/electionsnew.htm

#44 Bingo/Lucky 7 Division, Sweepstakes Commission, 14 Integra Dr, Concord, NH 03301-1208; 603-271-3391, Fax: 603-271-1160.
www.state.nh.us/lottery/nhlotto.htm

#45 Office of Allied Health Professions, 2 Industrial Park Dr, Concord, NH 03301-8520; 603-271-8389.

#46 Department of Health & Human Svcs, Bureau of Health Risk Assessment, 6 Hazen Dr, Concord, NH 03301-6527; 603-271-4609, Fax: 603-271-2667.

#47 Board of Hearing Care Providers, Division of Public Health Services, 6 Hazen Dr, Concord, NH 03301; 603-271-4501.
www.state.nh.us/nhdoj/comsumer/lip.html

#48 Pari-Mutuel Commission, 244 N Main St 3rd Fl, Concord, NH 03301; 603-271-2158, Fax: 603-271-3381.
http://webster.state.nh.us/nhpmc/

#49 Police Standards & Training Council, 17 Institution Dr, Concord, NH 03301-7413; 603-271-2133.

#50 Department of State, Bureau of Securities Regulation, State House Rm 204, Concord, NH 03301; 603-271-1463, Fax: 603-271-7933.
www.state.nh.us/sos/securities/

New Hampshire Federal Courts

The following list indicates the district and division name for each county in the state. If the bankruptcy court location is different from the district court, then the location of the bankruptcy court appears in parentheses.

County/Court Cross Reference

Belknap ....Concord (Manchester)	Hillsborough ....Concord (Manchester)
Carroll ....Concord (Manchester)	Merrimack ....Concord (Manchester)
Cheshire ....Concord (Manchester)	Rockingham ....Concord (Manchester)
Coos ....Concord (Manchester)	Strafford ....Concord (Manchester)
Grafton ....Concord (Manchester)	Sullivan ....Concord (Manchester)

US District Court

District of New Hampshire

Concord Division Warren B Rudman Courthouse, 55 Pleasant St, #110, Concord, NH 03301 (Courier Address: Use mail address for courier delivery), 603-225-1423.

www.nhd.uscourts.gov

Counties: Belknap, Carroll, Cheshire, Coos, Grafton, Hillsborough, Merrimack, Rockingham, Strafford, Sullivan.

Indexing & Storage: Cases are indexed by defendant, plaintiff, and case number. New cases are available in the index 24 hours after filing date. Open records are located at this court.

Fee & Payment Notes: Payment may be made by money order, cashier check, business check. Personal checks are not accepted. Payee: Clerk, US District Court. You are allowed to make your own copies. These copies cost $.10 per page. Public copiers are available.

Phone Search: Only docket information is available by phone.

Mail Search: A stamped self addressed envelope is not required.

In Person Search: In person searching available.

PACER:. Case records are available back to 1980. Records are purged every two years. New records are available online after 1 day. PACER is available online at http://pacer.nhd.uscourts.gov.

US Bankruptcy Court

District of New Hampshire

Manchester Division Room 404, 275 Chestnut St, Manchester, NH 03101 (Courier Address: Use mail address for courier delivery), 603-222-2600, Fax: 603-666-7408.

www.nhb.uscourts.gov

Counties: Belknap, Carroll, Cheshire, Coos, Grafton, Hillsborough, Merrimack, Rockingham, Strafford, Sullivan.

Indexing & Storage: Cases are indexed by debtor as well as by case number. New cases are available in the index 24 hours after filing date. Open records are located at this court.

Fee & Payment Notes: Payment may be made by money order, cashier check, personal check, Visa or Mastercard. Debtor checks are not accepted. Payee: Clerk, US Bankruptcy Court. You are allowed to make your own copies. These copies cost $.25 per page.

Phone Search: Only the case number, name, trustee, attorney for the debtor and deadlines will be released. An automated voice case information service (VCIS) is available. Call VCIS at 800-851-8954 or 603-666-7424.

Mail Search: A stamped self addressed envelope is not required.

In Person Search: In person searching available.

PACER:. Case records are available back to 1989. Records are purged every six months. New civil records are available online after 2 days. PACER is available online at http://pacer.nhb.uscourts.gov.

Electronic Filing: Information is available online at https://ecf.nhb.uscourts.gov

Standards for Federal Courts: The search fee is $20.00 per item (one party name or case number). Certification fee is $7.00 per document. Copy fee is $.50 per page. All fees standard unless noted in profile. Mail Search: always enclose a stamped self addressed envelope unless otherwise noted. Before releasing records, all courts require prepayment unless noted in profile.

Open records are located at the court unless otherwise noted. District courts index by defendant and plaintiff as well as by case number. Bankruptcy courts usually index by debtor and case number. While most courts now have their indexes on computer, many still maintain index card files as well.

The universal PACER sign-up number is 800-676-6856. Find PACER and the Party/Case Index on the Web at http://pacer.psc.uscourts.gov. PACER dial-up access is $.60 per minute. Also, courts offering internet access via RACER, PACER, Web-PACER or the new CM-ECF charge $.07 per page fee unless noted as free.

New Hampshire County Courts

Court	Jurisdiction	No. of Courts	How Organized
Superior Courts*	General	11	10 Counties
District Courts*	Limited	37	40 Districts
Probate Courts*	Probate	10	10 Counties
Family Court	Special	8	

* Profiled in this Sourcebook.

Court	CIVIL								
	Tort	Contract	Real Estate	Min. Claim	Max. Claim	Small Claims	Estate	Eviction	Domestic Relations
Circuit Courts*	X	X	X	$1500	No Max				X
District Courts*	X	X	X	$0	$25,000	$5000		X	X
Probate Courts*							X		X
Family Courts									X

Court	CRIMINAL				
	Felony	Misdemeanor	DWI/DUI	Preliminary Hearing	Juvenile
Circuit Courts*	X				
District Courts*		X	X	X	X
Probate Courts*					
Family Courts					X

ADMINISTRATION Administrative Office of the Courts, Supreme Court Bldg, Noble Dr, Concord, NH, 03301; 603-271-2521, Fax: 603-271-3977. www.state.nh.us/courts/home.htm

COURT STRUCTURE The Superior Court is the court of General Jurisdiction. Felony cases include Class A misdemeanors.

The District Court upper civil limit was increased to $25,000 from $10,000 on 1/1/93. Filing a civil case in the monetary "overlap" area between the Superior Court minimum and the District Court maximum is at the discretion of the filer.

The municipal courts have been closed as the judges retire. The caseload and records are absorbed by the nearest District Court.

ONLINE ACCESS There is no remote online computer access available.

ADDITIONAL INFORMATION A statutory search fee has been implemented in the District Courts, as follows:

Computer search - $10.00 for up to 10 names in one request; $25.00 for 10 or more names in one request; $25.00 per hour for search time beyond one hour.

Manual search - $25.00 per hour.

If the search requires both types, the fee is the total for each.

📖📖📖📖📖📖📖

Belknap County

Superior Court 64 Court St, Laconia, NH 03246; 603-524-3570. Hours: 8AM-4:30PM (EST). *Felony, Civil Actions Over $1,500.*

Civil Records: Access: Phone, mail, in person. Only the court performs in person searches; visitors may not. No search fee. Required to search: name, years to search. Civil cases indexed by defendant, plaintiff. Civil records on computer from 1/80, index cards from 1900, docket books from 1840.

Criminal Records: Access: Phone, mail, in person. Only the court performs in person searches; visitors may not. No search fee. Required to search: name, years to search; also helpful: DOB, SSN. Criminal records on computer from 1/80, index cards from 1900, docket books from 1840.

General Information: No adoptions, sealed, juvenile, mental health, expunged, or dismissed records released. SASE not required. Turnaround time 1 week. Copy fee: $.50 per page. Certification fee: $5.00. Fee payee: Belknap County Superior Court. Business checks accepted. Prepayment is required.

Laconia District Court 26 Academy St, PO Box 1010, Laconia, NH 03247; 603-524-4128. Hours: 8AM-4PM (EST). *Misdemeanor, Civil Actions Under $25,000, Eviction, Small Claims.*

Note: Adoptions handled by probate court. Includes City of Laconia and the towns of Meredith, New Hampton, Gilford, Belmont, Alton, Gilmanton, Center Harbor, and Barnstead.

Civil Records: Access: Mail, in person. Only the court performs in person searches; visitors may not. Search fee: $25.00 for records before 5/2/92; $10.00 after 5/92. Required to search: name, years to search. Civil cases indexed by defendant, plaintiff. Civil records on computer from 5/92, index cards from 7/64.

Criminal Records: Access: Mail, in person. Only the court performs in person searches; visitors may not. Search fee: $25.00 for records before 5/2/92; $10.00 after 5/92. Required to search: name, years to search, DOB. Criminal records on computer from 1992, index cards from 7/64.

General Information: No sealed, juvenile, mental health, expunged or dismissed records released. SASE required. Turnaround time 2 weeks. Copy fee: $.50 per page. Certification fee: $5.00. Fee payee: Laconia District Court. Personal checks accepted. Prepayment is required.

Probate Court 64 Court St, PO Box 1343, Laconia, NH 03247-1343; 603-524-0903. Hours: 8AM-4PM (EST). *Probate.*

Carroll County

Superior Court PO Box 433, Ossipee, NH 03864; 603-539-2201. Hours: 8AM-4:30PM (EST). *Felony, Civil Actions Over $1,500.*

Civil Records: Access: Mail, in person. Only the court performs in person searches; visitors may not. No search fee. Required to search: name, years to search. Civil cases indexed by defendant, plaintiff. Civil records on index cards from 1960, index books from 1840.

Criminal Records: Access: Mail, in person. Only the court performs in person searches; visitors may not. No search fee. Required to search: name, years to search; also helpful: DOB, SSN. Criminal records on index cards from 1960, index books from 1840.

General Information: No adoptions, sealed, juvenile, mental health, expunged or dismissed records released. SASE required. Turnaround time same day. Copy fee: $.50 per page. Certification fee: $5.00. Fee payee: Carroll County. Personal checks accepted. Prepayment is required.

Northern Carroll County District Court PO Box 940, Conway, NH 03818; 603-356-7710. Hours: 8:30AM-4:30PM (EST). *Misdemeanor, Civil Actions Under $25,000, Eviction, Small Claims.*

Note: Note: Includes Towns of Conway, Bartlett, Jackson, Eaton, Chatham, Hart's Location, Albany, Madison and the unincorporated places of Hale's Location, Cutt's Grant, Hadley's Purchase, and portions of Livermore and Waterville.

Civil Records: Access: Phone, mail, in person. Both court and visitors may perform in person searches. Search fee: $25.00 before 10/01/92; $10.00 after 10/01/92. Required to search: name, years to search. Civil cases indexed by defendant, plaintiff. Civil records on computer from 1993, on index cards from 1980, on index books from 1954.

Criminal Records: Access: Phone, mail, in person. Both court and visitors may perform in person searches. Search fee: $10.00 per name. Required to search: name, years to search; also helpful: DOB, SSN. Criminal records on computer from 1993, on index cards from 1980, on index books from 1954.

General Information: No adoptions, sealed, juvenile, mental health, expunged or dismissed records released. SASE required. Turnaround time 1 week. Copy fee: $.50 per page. Certification fee: $5.00 per page. Fee payee: District Court for Northern Carroll County. Personal checks accepted. Prepayment is required.

Southern Carroll County District Court PO Box 421, Ossipee, NH 03864; 603-539-4561. Hours: 8AM-4PM (EST). *Misdemeanor, Civil Actions Under $25,000, Eviction, Small Claims.*

Note: The former Wolfeboro District Court has been combined with this court. Includes Towns of Ossipee, Tamworth, Freedom, Effingham, Wakefield, Wolfeboro, Brookfield, Tuftonboro, Moultonborough, and Sandwich.

Civil Records: Access: Mail, in person. Only the court performs in person searches; visitors may not. Search fee: $10.00. Required to search: name, years to search. Civil cases indexed by defendant, plaintiff. Civil records on computer from 1992, on index cards from 1989.

Criminal Records: Access: Mail, in person. Only the court performs in person searches; visitors may not. Search fee: $10.00. Required to search: name, years to search; also helpful: DOB, SSN. Criminal records on computer from 1992, on index cards from 1989.

General Information: No sealed, juvenile, mental health, expunged or dismissed records released. SASE required. Turnaround time 2-3 days. Copy fee: $.50 per page. Certification fee: $5.00. Fee payee: South Carroll County District Court. Only cashiers checks and money orders accepted. Prepayment is required.

Probate Court PO Box 419, Ossipee, NH 03864; 603-539-4123; Fax: 603-539-4761. Hours: 8:30AM-4:30PM (EST). *Probate.*

Cheshire County

Superior Court 12 Court St, Keene, NH 03431; 603-352-6902. Hours: 8AM-4PM (EST). *Felony, Civil Actions Over $1,500.*

Civil Records: Access: Mail, in person. Only the court performs in person searches; visitors may not. No search fee. Required to search: name, years to search. Civil cases indexed by defendant, plaintiff. Civil records on computer from 1992, on index cards from 1920; records prior to 1918 difficult to access; organized 1769.

Criminal Records: Access: Mail, in person. Only the court performs in person searches; visitors may not. No search fee. Required to search: name, years to search, DOB. Criminal records on computer from 1990, criminal records go back to 1900.

General Information: No adoptions, sealed, juvenile, mental health, expunged or dismissed records released. SASE required. Turnaround time 2 weeks. Copy fee: $.50 per page. Certification fee: $5.00. Fee payee: Clerk of Superior Court. Personal checks accepted. Prepayment is required.

Jaffrey-Peterborough District Court 7 Knight St, PO Box 39, Jaffrey, NH 03452-0039; 603-532-8698. Hours: 8AM-4PM (EST). *Misdemeanor, Civil Actions Under $25,000, Eviction, Small Claims.*

Note: Includes towns of Peterborough, Hancock, Greenville, Greenfield, New Ipswich, Temple, Sharon, Jaffrey, Dublin, Fitzwilliam, and Rindge.

Civil Records: Access: Mail, in person. Only the court performs in person searches; visitors may not. Search fee: $35.00 per name. Required to search: name, years to search. Civil cases indexed by defendant, plaintiff. Civil records on computer back to 1993, on index cards from 1980, index books in back room.

Criminal Records: Access: Mail, in person. Only the court performs in person searches; visitors may not. Search fee: $35.00 per name. Required to search: name, years to search, DOB; also helpful: SSN. Criminal records on computer back to 4/1993, on index cards from 1980, index books in back room.

General Information: No sealed, juvenile, mental health records released. SASE required. Turnaround time 3-4 weeks. Copy fee: $.50 per page. Certification fee: $5.00. Fee payee: Jaffrey-Peterborough District Court. Personal checks accepted. Prepayment is required.

Keene District Court PO Box 364, Keene, NH 03431; 603-352-2559. Hours: 8AM-4PM (EST). *Misdemeanor, Civil Actions Under $25,000, Eviction, Small Claims.*

Note: Includes city of Keene and the towns of Stoddard, Westmoreland, Surry, Gilsum, Sullivan, Nelson, Roxbury, Marlow, Swanzey, Marlborough, Winchester, Richmond, Hinsdale, Harrisville, Walpole, Alstead, Troy, and Chesterfield.

Civil Records: Access: Mail, in person. Only the court performs in person searches; visitors may not. Search fee: $10.00 electronic search (1992 to present), $25.00 if previous. Required to search: name, years to search. Civil cases indexed by defendant, plaintiff. Civil records on computer from 7/92, on index cards from 1980, docket books from 1968 to 1979.

Criminal Records: Access: Mail, in person. Only the court performs in person searches; visitors may not. Search fee: $10.00 computer search (1992 forward), $25.00 for previous years. Required to search: name, years to search; also helpful: DOB, SSN. Criminal records on computer from 7/92, on index cards from 1980, docket books from 1968 to 1979.

General Information: No sealed, juvenile, mental health or expunged records released. SASE required. Turnaround time 5-10 days. Fax notes: Will not use fax to send or receive requests for information. Copy fee: $.50 per page. There is no copy fee is document is certified. Certification fee: $5.00. Fee payee: Keene District Court. Personal checks accepted. Prepayment is required.

Probate Court 12 Court St, Keene, NH 03431; 603-357-7786. Hours: 8AM-4:30PM (EST). *Probate.*

Coos County

Superior Court 55 School St #301, Lancaster, NH 03584; 603-788-4900. Hours: 8AM-4:15PM (EST). *Felony, Civil Actions Over $1,500.*

Civil Records: Access: Mail, in person. Only the court performs in person searches; visitors may not. No search fee. Required to search: name, years to search. Civil cases indexed by defendant, plaintiff. Civil records on computer from 1994, on index cards from 1960, index books from 1887; courthouse burned in 1887, prior records lost (organized 1803).

Criminal Records: Access: Mail, in person. Only the court performs in person searches; visitors may not. No search fee. Required to search: name, years to search, DOB. Criminal records on computer from 1992; prior records on index cards from 1960, index books from 1887.

General Information: No adoptions, sealed, juvenile, mental health, expunged or dismissed records released. SASE required. Turnaround time 2-3 days. Copy fee: $.50 per page. Certification fee: $5.00. Fee payee: Coos Superior Court. Personal checks accepted. Prepayment is required.

Berlin District Court 220 Main St, Berlin, NH 03570; 603-752-3160. Hours: 8AM-4PM (EST). *Misdemeanor, Civil Actions Under $25,000, Eviction, Small Claims.*

Note: Includes towns of Berlin, Dummer, and Milan and the unincorporated places of Cambridge and Success.

Civil Records: Access: Mail, in person. Only the court performs in person searches; visitors may not. Search fee: $25.00 per name before 1993; $10.00 per name after 1993. Required to search: name, years to search. Civil cases indexed by defendant, plaintiff. Computerized records from 1993, civil records on index cards from 1980, index books from 1970, prior to 1970 archived in basement.

Criminal Records: Access: Mail, in person. Only the court performs in person searches; visitors may not. Search fee: $25.00 per name before 1993; $10.00 per name after 1993. Required to search: name, years to search, DOB, SSN. Criminal records on index cards from 1980, index books from 1970, prior to 1970 archived in basement.

General Information: No sealed, juvenile, mental health, expunged or dismissed records released. SASE required. Turnaround time 1-2 weeks. Copy fee: $.50 per page. Certification fee: $5.00. Fee payee: Berlin District Court. Personal checks accepted. Credit cards accepted. Prepayment is required.

Colebrook District Court PO Box 5 - 10 Bridge St, Colebrook, NH 03576; 603-237-4229. Hours: 8AM-Noon,1-4PM (EST). *Misdemeanor, Civil Actions Under $25,000, Eviction, Small Claims.*

Note: Includes towns of Colebrook, Pittsburg, Clarksville, Wentworth's Location, Errol, Millsfield, Columbia, Stewartstown, Stratford, and unincorporated areas of Dix's Grant, Atkinson & Gilmanton Academy Grant, Second College, Grant, Dixville, Erving's Location, and Odell.

Civil Records: Access: Mail, in person. Only the court performs in person searches; visitors may not. Search fee: $10.00 for computer search 93 to present. $25.00 for manual search, prior to 93. Required to search: name, years to search. Civil cases indexed by defendant, plaintiff. Civil records on index cards from 1979, index books from 1964.

Criminal Records: Access: Mail, in person. Only the court performs in person searches; visitors may not. Search fee: $10.00 for computer search. $25.00 for manual search. Required to search: name, years to search, DOB. Criminal records on index cards from 1979, index books from 1964.

General Information: No sealed, juvenile, mental health or expunged records released. SASE required. Turnaround time same day. Copy fee: $.50 per page. Certification fee: $5.00 per page. Fee payee: Colebrook District Court. Personal checks accepted. Prepayment is required.

Gorham District Court PO Box 176, Gorham, NH 03581; 603-466-2454. Hours: 8AM-4PM (EST). *Misdemeanor, Civil Actions Under $25,000, Eviction, Small Claims.*

Note: Includes towns of Gorham, Shelburne, and Randolph and the unincorporated places of Bean's Purchase, Martin's Location, Green's Grant, Pinkham's Grant, Sargent's Purchase, Thompson & Meserve's Purchase and Low & Burbank's Grant.

Civil Records: Access: Mail, in person. Only the court performs in person searches; visitors may not. Search fee: $25.00 per hour. Electronic searches are $10 for less than 10 names, $25 for 10-25 names, then the hourly kicks in. Required to search: name, years to search. Civil cases indexed by defendant, plaintiff. Civil records on computer from 1993, on index cards from 1980, index books from 1964.

Criminal Records: Access: Mail, in person. Only the court performs in person searches; visitors may not. Search fee: Same fees as civil. Required to search: name, years to search, DOB. Criminal records on computer from 1993, on index cards from 1980, index books from 1964.

General Information: No adoptions, sealed, juvenile, mental health, expunged or dismissed records released. SASE required. Turnaround time 3-4 days. Copy fee: $.50 per page. Certification fee: $10.00. Fee payee: Gorham District Court. Personal checks accepted. Prepayment is required.

Lancaster District Court 55 School St, #201, Lancaster, NH 03584; 603-788-4485. Hours: 8:30AM-4PM (EST). *Misdemeanor, Civil Actions Under $25,000, Eviction, Small Claims.*

Note: Includes city of Laconia and the towns of Meredith, New Hampton, Gilford, Belmont, Alton, Gilmanton, Center Harbor, and Barnstead.

Civil Records: Access: Mail, in person. Only the court performs in person searches; visitors may not. Search fee: $25.00. Required to search: name, years to search; also helpful: address. Civil cases indexed by defendant, plaintiff. Civil records on index cards from 1981, index books for public review only, computerized since 1993.

Criminal Records: Access: Mail, in person. Only the court performs in person searches; visitors may not.

Search fee: Fee is based on type of search, and is normally $10.00 per request. See state introduction. Required to search: name, years to search, DOB; also helpful: address. Criminal records on index cards from 198o, index books for public review only, computerized since 1993.

General Information: No adoptions, sealed, juvenile, mental health, expunged or dismissed records released. SASE required. Turnaround time 1 week. Copy fee: $.50 per page. Certification fee: $5.00 per page. Fee payee: Lancaster District Court. Personal checks accepted. Prepayment is required.

Probate Court 55 School St #104, Lancaster, NH 03584; 603-788-2001. 8AM-4PM (EST). *Probate.*

Grafton County

Superior Court RR1 Box 65, North Haverhill, NH 03774; 603-787-6961. Hours: 8AM-4:30PM (EST). *Felony, Civil Actions Over $1,500.*

Civil Records: Access: Mail, in person. Only the court performs in person searches; visitors may not. No search fee. Required to search: name, years to search. Civil cases indexed by defendant, plaintiff. Civil records on index cards from 1900, index books from 1950. All prior records are found at the Archives in Concord.

Criminal Records: Access: Mail, in person. Only the court performs in person searches; visitors may not. No search fee. Required to search: name, years to search; also helpful: DOB, SSN. Criminal records on index cards from 1900, index books from 1950. All prior records are found at the Archives in Concord.

General Information: No sealed records released. SASE required. Turnaround time 10 days. Copy fee: $.50 per page. Certification fee: $5.00 plus $.50 per add'l page. Fee payee: Grafton County Superior Court. Personal checks accepted. Prepayment is required.

Haverhill District Court Grafton County Courthouse, 3785 Dartmouth College Highway - Box 10, North Haverhill, NH 03774; 603-787-6626. Hours: 8:00AM-4:30PM (EST). *Misdemeanor, Civil Actions Under $25,000, Eviction, Small Claims.*

Note: Includes towns of Haverhill, Bath, Landaff, Benton, Piermont, and Warren.

Civil Records: Access: Mail, in person. Only the court performs in person searches; visitors may not. Search fee: Electronic records search fee is $10.00 per name (less than 10 names); 10 or more names are $25.00 each search. Manual search fee is $25.00 per hour. Required to search: name, years to search. Civil cases indexed by defendant, plaintiff. Civil records on computer from 1993, on index cards from 1980, index books from 1950s.

Criminal Records: Access: Mail, in person. Only the court performs in person searches; visitors may not. Search fee: Same fees as civil. Required to search: name, years to search, DOB. Criminal records on computer from 1993, on index cards from 1980, index books from 1950s.

General Information: No adoptions, sealed, juvenile, mental health, expunged or dismissed records released. SASE required. Turnaround time 1-2 days. Copy fee: $.50 per page. Certification fee: $5.00. Fee payee: Haverhill District Court. Personal checks accepted. Prepayment is required.

Lebanon District Court 38 Centerra Parkway, Lebanon, NH 03766; 603-643-3555. Hours: 8AM-4PM (EST). *Misdemeanor, Civil Actions Under $25,000, Eviction, Small Claims.*

Note: Includes towns of Lebanon, Enfield, Canaan, Grafton, Orange, Hanover, Orford, and Lyme.

Civil Records: Access: Mail, in person. Only the court performs in person searches; visitors may not. Search fee: $10.00 for computer search (1993-present); $25 for

index search (prior to 1993). Required to search: name, years to search. Civil cases indexed by defendant, plaintiff. Civil records on computer from 1993, on index cards from 1986, index books from 1960s.

Criminal Records: Access: Mail, in person. Only the court performs in person searches; visitors may not. Search fee: $10.00 for computer search (1993-present); $25 for index search (prior to 1993). Required to search: name, years to search, DOB. Criminal records on computer from 1993, on index cards from 1986, index books from 1960s.

General Information: No sealed, juvenile, mental health or expunged records released. SASE required. Turnaround time 5 days. Copy fee: $.50 per page. Certification fee: $1.00. Fee payee: Lebanon District Court. Personal checks accepted. Prepayment required.

Littleton District Court 134 Main St, Littleton, NH 03561; 603-444-7750. Hours: 8AM-4PM (EST). *Misdemeanor, Civil Actions Under $25,000, Eviction, Small Claims.*

Note: Includes towns of Littleton, Monroe, Lyman, Lisbon, Franconia, Bethlehem, Sugar Hill, and Easton.

Civil Records: Access: Mail, in person. Only the court performs in person searches; visitors may not. Search fee: $10.00 per name. Required to search: name, years to search. Civil cases indexed by defendant, plaintiff. Civil records on computer from 1993, index cards from 1985, index books from 1950.

Criminal Records: Access: Mail, in person. Only the court performs in person searches; visitors may not. Search fee: $10.00 per name. Required to search: name, years to search; also helpful: DOB, SSN. Criminal records on computer from 1993, index cards from 1985, index books from 1950.

General Information: No adoptions, sealed, juvenile, mental health, domestic violence, expunged or dismissed records released. SASE required. Turnaround time 3 weeks. Copy fee: $.50 per page. Certification fee: $5.00. Fee payee: Littleton District Court. Personal checks accepted. Prepayment is required.

Plymouth District Court 26 Green St, Plymouth, NH 03264; 603-536-3326. Hours: 8AM-4PM (EST). *Misdemeanor, Civil Actions Under $25,000, Eviction, Small Claims.*

Note: Includes towns of Plymouth, Bristol, Dorchester, Groton, Wentworth, Rumney, Ellsworth, Thornton, Campton, Ashland, Hebron, Holderness, Bridgewater, Alexandria, Lincoln, Woodstock, and portions of Livermore and Waterville.

Civil Records: Access: Mail, in person. Only the court performs in person searches; visitors may not. Search fee: $10.00 per name. If a complete search (from 1981) is required, fee is $25.00. Required to search: name, years to search. Civil cases indexed by defendant, plaintiff. Civil records on computer from 1991, index cards from 1981. Request for an appointment must be made two weeks prior to in person searching.

Criminal Records: Access: Mail, in person. Only the court performs in person searches; visitors may not. Search fee: $10.00 per name. same fees as civil. Required to search: name, years to search; also helpful: DOB, SSN. Criminal records on computer from 1991, index cards from 1981. Request for an appointment must be made two weeks prior to in person searching.

General Information: No sealed, mental health, expunged or dismissed records released. SASE required. Turnaround time one week. Copy fee: $.50 per page. Certification fee: $5.00. Fee payee: Plymouth District Court. Personal checks accepted. Prepayment is required.

Probate Court 3785 Dartmouth College Hwy, Box 3, North Haverhill, NH 03774-9700; 603-787-6931. Hours: 8AM-4PM (EST). *Probate.*

Hillsborough County

Superior Court - North District 300 Chestnut St Rm 127, Manchester, NH 03101; 603-424-9951. Hours: 8AM-4PM (EST). *Felony, Civil Actions Over $1,500.*

Civil Records: Access: Mail, in person. Only the court performs in person searches; visitors may not. No search fee. Required to search: name, years to search. Civil cases indexed by defendant, plaintiff. Civil records on computer from 5/85, index cards from 1980s, index books from 1900s; organized 1769.
Criminal Records: Access: Mail, in person. Only the court performs in person searches; visitors may not. No search fee. Required to search: name, years to search, DOB. Criminal records on computer from 5/85, index cards from 1980s, index books from 1900s; organized 1769.
General Information: No sealed, juvenile, mental health records released. SASE required. Turnaround time 3 days. Copy fee: $.50 per page. Certification fee: $5.00. Fee payee: Hillsborough Superior Court-Northern District. Personal checks accepted.

Superior Court - Southern District 30 Spring St, Nashua, NH 03061; 603-883-6461. Hours: 8AM-4PM (EST). *Felony, Civil Actions Over $1,500.*

Civil Records: Access: Mail, in person. Only the court performs in person searches; visitors may not. No search fee. Required to search: name, years to search. Civil cases indexed by defendant, plaintiff. Civil records on computer back to 3/92; overall records go back to 1992.
Criminal Records: Access: Mail, in person. Only the court performs in person searches; visitors may not. No search fee. Required to search: name, years to search; also helpful: DOB. Criminal records on computer back to 3/92; overall records go back to 1992.
General Information: No sealed, juvenile or annulled records released. Turnaround time 2-3 days. Copy fee: $.50 per page. Certification fee: $5.00. Fee payee: Superior Court. Personal checks accepted. Prepayment is required.

Goffstown District Court PO Box 129, Goffstown, NH 03045; 603-497-2597. Hours: 8AM-4PM (EST). *Misdemeanor, Civil Actions Under $25,000, Eviction, Small Claims.*

Note: Includes towns of Goffstown, Weare, New Boston, and Francestown.

Civil Records: Access: Mail, in person. Only the court performs in person searches; visitors may not. Search fee: $10.00 fee for electronic search up to 10 names, $25.00 for 10+ names. Manual search is $25.00 per name. Required to search: name, years to search. Civil cases indexed by defendant, plaintiff. Civil records on computer from 3/92, kept in files prior.
Criminal Records: Access: Mail, in person. Only the court performs in person searches; visitors may not. Search fee: Same fees as civil. Required to search: name, years to search, DOB; also helpful: SSN. Criminal records on computer from 3/92, kept in files prior.
General Information: No sealed, juvenile, mental health, expunged or dismissed records released. SASE required. Turnaround time 2 weeks. Copy fee: $.50 per page. Certification fee: $5.00. Fee payee: Goffstown District Court. Personal checks accepted. Prepayment is required.

Hillsborough District Court PO Box 763, Hillsborough, NH 03244; 603-464-5811. Hours: 8AM-4PM (EST). *Misdemeanor, Civil Actions Under $25,000, Eviction, Small Claims.*

Note: Includes towns of Hillsborough, Deering, Windsor, Antrim, and Bennington.

Civil Records: Access: Mail, in person. Both court and visitors may perform in person searches. Search fee: Research fees will vary, call first. Required to search: name, years to search. Civil cases indexed by defendant, plaintiff. Civil records on computer from 1992, on index cards from 1980, index books from 1960. Appointment required for in person searching.
Criminal Records: Access: Mail, in person. Both court and visitors may perform in person searches. Search fee: Research fees will vary, call first. Required to search: name, years to search, DOB; also helpful: SSN. Criminal records on computer from 1992, on index cards from 1980, index books from 1960.
General Information: No adoptions, sealed, juvenile, mental health, expunged or dismissed records released. SASE required. Turnaround time 1 week. Copy fee: $.50 per page. Certification fee: $5.00. Fee payee: Hillsborough District Court. Personal checks accepted. Prepayment is required.

Manchester District Court PO Box 456, Manchester, NH 03105; 603-624-6510. Hours: 8AM-4PM (EST). *Misdemeanor, Civil Actions Under $25,000, Eviction, Small Claims.*

Note: Includes city of Manchester.

Civil Records: Access: Mail, in person. Only the court performs in person searches; visitors may not. Search fee: $10.00 per request up to 10 names or $25.00 per request over 10. Manual searches $25.00 per hour. Required to search: name, years to search, DOB; also helpful: address. Civil cases indexed by defendant, plaintiff. Civil records on computer from 6/92, on index cards from 1960.
Criminal Records: Access: Mail, in person. Only the court performs in person searches; visitors may not. Search fee: $10.00 per request up to 10 names or $25.00 per request over 10. Manual searches $25.00 per hour. Required to search: name, years to search, DOB; also helpful: address. Criminal records on computer from 6/92, on index cards from 1960.
General Information: No adoptions, sealed, juvenile, mental health, expunged or dismissed records released. SASE required. Turnaround time 2 weeks. Copy fee: $.50 per page. Certification fee: $1.00. Fee payee: Manchester District Court. Personal checks accepted.

Merrimack District Court PO Box 324, Merrimack, NH 03054-0324; 603-424-9916. Hours: 8AM-4PM (EST). *Misdemeanor, Civil Actions Under $25,000, Eviction, Small Claims.*

Note: Includes towns of Merrimack, Litchfield, and Bedford.

Civil Records: Access: Mail, in person. Only the court performs in person searches; visitors may not. Search fee: $25 per hour for manual searches. For electronic, $10 for up to first 9 names or $25 for first 25 names, then hour rate. Required to search: name, years to search. Civil cases indexed by defendant, plaintiff. Civil records on computer from 7/92, on index cards from 1972, index books in archives at Concord.
Criminal Records: Access: Mail, in person. Both court and visitors may perform in person searches. Search fee: Same fees as civil. Required to search: name, years to search; also helpful: DOB. Criminal records on computer from 7/92, on index cards from 1972, index books in archives at Concord.
General Information: No adoptions, sealed, juvenile, mental health, expunged or dismissed records released. SASE required. Turnaround time 1-2 days. Copy fee: $.50 per page. Certification fee: $5.00. Fee payee: Merrimack District Court. Personal checks accepted. Prepayment is required.

Milford District Court 180 Elm St, Milford, NH 03055-4735; 603-673-2900. Hours: 8AM-4PM (EST).

Misdemeanor, Civil Actions Under $25,000, Eviction, Small Claims.

Note: Includes towns of Milford, Brookline, Amherst, Mason, Wilton, Lyndeborough, and Mont Vernon.

Civil Records: Access: Mail, in person. Only the court performs in person searches; visitors may not. Search fee: Searching via computer is $10.00 per name; lengthy manual searching is $25.00 per hour. Required to search: name, years to search. Civil cases indexed by defendant, plaintiff. Civil records on computer from 08/92, on index cards from 1950s, prior records may or may not be at old courthouse.
Criminal Records: Access: Mail, in person. Only the court performs in person searches; visitors may not. Search fee: Same as Civil. Required to search: name, years to search; also helpful: DOB, SSN. Criminal records on computer from 08/92, on index cards from 1950s, prior records may or may not be at old courthouse.
General Information: No adoptions, sealed, juvenile, mental health, expunged or dismissed records released. SASE required. Turnaround time 10 days. Copy fee: $.50 per page. Certification fee: $5.00. Fee payee: Milford District Court. Personal checks accepted. Prepayment is required.

Nashua District Court Walnut St Oval, Nashua, NH 03060; 603-880-3333. Hours: 8AM-4PM (EST). *Misdemeanor, Civil Actions Under $25,000, Eviction, Small Claims.*

Note: Includes city of Nashua and the towns of Hudson and Hollis.

Civil Records: Access: Mail, in person. Only the court performs in person searches; visitors may not. Search fee: $25.00 for records prior to 08/92; after are $10.00. Required to search: name, years to search. Civil cases indexed by defendant, plaintiff. Civil records on computer from 1993, index cards from 1982. All requests must be in writing.
Criminal Records: Access: Mail, in person. Only the court performs in person searches; visitors may not. Search fee: Same fees as civil. Required to search: name, years to search; also helpful: DOB, SSN. Criminal records on computer from August 1992, index cards from 1982. All requests must be in writing.
General Information: No adoptions, sealed, juvenile, mental health, expunged records released. SASE required. Turnaround time 10 days. Copy fee: $.50 per page. Certification fee: $5.00. Fee payee: Nashua District Court. Personal checks accepted. Prepayment is required.

Probate Court PO Box P, Nashua, NH 03061-6015; 603-882-1231; Fax: 603-882-1620. Hours: 8AM-4PM (EST). *Probate.*

Merrimack County

Superior Court PO Box 2880, Concord, NH 03302-2880; 603-225-5501. Hours: 8:30AM-4PM (EST). *Felony, Civil Actions Over $1,500.*

Civil Records: Access: Mail, in person. Only the court performs in person searches; visitors may not. No search fee. Required to search: name, years to search. Civil cases indexed by defendant, plaintiff. Civil records on computer from 1983, index cards from 1950, index books from 1800s; organized 1823.
Criminal Records: Access: Phone, mail, in person. Only the court performs in person searches; visitors may not. No search fee. Required to search: name, years to search, DOB; also helpful: SSN. Criminal records on computer since 1984.
General Information: No adoptions, sealed, juvenile, mental health, expunged or dismissed records released. SASE required. Turnaround time 2-3 days. Copy fee: $.50 per page. Certification fee: $5.00. Fee payee:

Merrimack Superior Court. Personal checks accepted. Prepayment is required.

Concord District Court 32 Clinton St, PO Box 3420, Concord, NH 03302-3420; 603-271-6400. Hours: 8AM-4PM (EST). *Misdemeanor, Civil Actions Under $25,000, Eviction, Small Claims.*

Note: The former Pittsfield District Court has been combined with this court. Includes city of Concord, and the towns of Loudon, Canterbury, Dunbarton, Bow, Hopkinton, Pittsfield, Chichester, and Epsom.

Civil Records: Access: Mail, in person. Only the court performs in person searches; visitors may not. Search fee: $10 for less than 10 electronic searches or $25 per hour. Required to search: name, years to search. Civil cases indexed by defendant, plaintiff. Civil records on computer from 1989, index cards from 1978, docket books from 1800.

Criminal Records: Access: Mail, in person. Only the court performs in person searches; visitors may not. Search fee: $10 for less than 10 electronic searches or $25 per hour. Required to search: name, years to search, DOB. Criminal records on computer from 1989, index cards from 1978, docket books from 1800.

General Information: No sealed, juvenile, mental health, expunged or dismissed records released. SASE required. Turnaround time 10 days. Copy fee: $.50 per page. Certification fee: $5.00. Fee payee: Concord District Court. Personal checks accepted. Prepayment is required.

Franklin District Court 7 Hancock Terrace, Franklin, NH 03235; 603-934-3290. Hours: 8AM-4PM (EST). *Misdemeanor, Civil Actions Under $25,000, Eviction, Small Claims.*

Note: Includes city of Franklin and the towns of Northfield, Danbury, Andover, Boscawen, Salisbury, Hill, Webster, Sanbornton, and Tilton.

Civil Records: Access: Mail, in person. Only the court performs in person searches; visitors may not. Search fee: $10.00 per name. Required to search: name, years to search. Civil cases indexed by plaintiff. Civil records on computer from 1/91, index cards from 1/80, index books from 1960s.

Criminal Records: Access: Mail, in person. Only the court performs in person searches; visitors may not. Search fee: $10.00 per name. Required to search: name, years to search; also helpful: DOB, SSN. Criminal records on computer from 1/91, index cards from 1/80, index books from 1960s.

General Information: No adoptions, sealed, juvenile, mental health, expunged or dismissed records released. SASE required. Turnaround time 2-3 days. No copy fee. Certification fee: $5.00 per document. Fee payee: Franklin District Court. Personal checks accepted. Prepayment is required.

Henniker District Court 2 Depot St, Henniker, NH 03242; 603-428-3214. Hours: 8AM-4PM (EST). *Misdemeanor, Civil Actions Under $25,000, Eviction, Small Claims.*

Note: Includes towns of Henniker, Warner, and Bradford.

Civil Records: Access: Mail, in person. Only the court performs in person searches; visitors may not. Search fee: Searching via computer is $10.00 per name; lengthy manual searching is $25.00 per hour. Required to search: name, years to search. Civil cases indexed by defendant, plaintiff. Civil records on index cards from 1988, index books from 1960s; on computer back to 1989.

Criminal Records: Access: Mail, in person. Only the court performs in person searches; visitors may not. Search fee: Same as Civil. Required to search: name, years to search, DOB; also helpful: SSN. Criminal

records on index cards from 1988, index books from 1960s; on computer back to 1989.

General Information: No adoptions, sealed, juvenile, mental health, expunged or dismissed records released. SASE required. Turnaround time can take as long as 6 weeks. Copy fee: $.50 per page. Certification fee: $5.00. Fee payee: Henniker District Court. Personal checks accepted. Prepayment is required.

Hooksett District Court 101 Merrimack, Hooksett, NH 03106; 603-485-9901. Hours: 8AM-4PM (EST). *Misdemeanor, Civil Actions Under $25,000, Eviction, Small Claims.*

Note: Includes towns of Allenstown, Pembroke, and Hooksett.

Civil Records: Access: Mail, in person. Only the court performs in person searches; visitors may not. Search fee: Fee for electronic searching is $10.00 per name if less than 10 names submitted; 10 or more names are $25.00 each. Manual research is charged at $25.00 per hour. Browse screens are $.50 per page (bilk case info). Required to search: name, years to search. Civil cases indexed by defendant, plaintiff. Civil records on computer from 1993, on index cards from 1980, index books from 1975. All requests must be in writing.

Criminal Records: Access: Mail, in person. Only the court performs in person searches; visitors may not. Search fee: Same fees as civil. Required to search: name, years to search; also helpful: DOB, SSN. Criminal records on computer from 1993, on index cards from 1980, index books from 1975.

General Information: No sealed, juvenile, mental health, expunged or dismissed records released. SASE required. Turnaround time 1-2 months. Copy fee: $.50 per page. Certification fee: $5.00. Fee payee: Hooksett District Court. Personal checks accepted. Prepayment is required.

New London District Court PO Box 1966, New London, NH 03257; 603-526-6519. Hours: 8:30AM-4PM (EST). *Misdemeanor, Civil Actions Under $25,000, Eviction, Small Claims.*

Note: Includes towns of New London, Wilmot, Newbury, and Sutton.

Civil Records: Access: Mail, in person. Only the court performs in person searches; visitors may not. Search fee: $10.00 for 1-10 names; 11-24 names is $25.00; 25+ names is $25.00 per hour. Required to search: name, years to search. Civil cases indexed by defendant, plaintiff. Civil records on computer from 1993, on index cards from 1980, index books from 1800s. An appointment is necessary before performing an in person search.

Criminal Records: Access: Mail, in person. Only the court performs in person searches; visitors may not. Search fee: Same fees as civil. Required to search: name, years to search; also helpful: DOB, SSN. Criminal records on computer from 1993, on index cards from 1980, index books from 1800s. An appointment is necessary before performing an in person search.

General Information: No adoptions, sealed, juvenile, mental health, expunged or dismissed records released. SASE required. Turnaround time 1-2 days. Copy fee: $.50 per page. Certification fee: $1.00. Fee payee: New London District Court. Personal checks accepted. Prepayment is required.

Probate Court 163 N Main St, Concord, NH 03301; 603-224-9589. 8AM-4:30PM (EST). *Probate.*

Rockingham County

Superior Court PO Box 1258, Kingston, NH 03848-1258; 603-642-5256. Hours: 8AM-4PM (EST). *Felony, Civil Actions Over $1,500.*

Civil Records: Access: In person only. Only the court performs in person searches; visitors may not. No search fee. Required to search: name, years to search. Civil cases indexed by defendant, plaintiff. Civil records on computer from 1988, index cards from 1920, organized 1769.

Criminal Records: Access: In person only. Only the court performs in person searches; visitors may not. No search fee. Required to search: name, years to search; also helpful: DOB. Criminal records on computer from 1988, index cards from 1920, organized 1769.

General Information: No sealed, juvenile, mental health, expunged, annulled records released. Copy fee: $.50 if court makes the copy, $.25 if visitor makes the copy. Certification fee: $5.00. Fee payee: Clerk Superior Court. Personal checks accepted. Prepayment is required.

Auburn District Court 5 Priscilla Lane, Auburn, NH 03032; Civil phone: 603-624-2265; Criminal phone: 603-624-2084. Hours: 8AM-4PM (EST). *Misdemeanor, Civil Actions Under $25,000, Eviction, Small Claims.*

Note: Includes towns of Auburn, Candia, Deerfield, Northwood, Nottingham, and Raymond.

Civil Records: Access: Mail, in person. Only the court performs in person searches; visitors may not. Search fee: $25.00 per hour. Required to search: name, years to search; also helpful: address. Civil cases indexed by defendant, plaintiff. Civil records on computer from 5/92, index cards from 1980, index books from 1968.

Criminal Records: Access: Mail, in person. Only the court performs in person searches; visitors may not. Search fee: $25.00 per hour. Required to search: name, years to search, DOB, signed release. Criminal records on computer from 5/92, index cards from 1980, index books from 1968.

General Information: No adoptions, sealed, juvenile, mental health, expunged or dismissed records released. SASE required. Turnaround time 3 days. Copy fee: $.50 per page. Certification fee: $5.00. Fee payee: Auburn District Court. Personal checks accepted. Prepayment is required.

Derry District Court 10 Manning St, Derry, NH 03038; 603-434-4676. Hours: 8AM-4PM (EST). *Misdemeanor, Civil Actions Under $25,000, Eviction, Small Claims.*

Note: Includes towns of Derry, Londonderry, Chester, and Sandown.

Civil Records: Access: Phone, mail, in person. Only the court performs in person searches; visitors may not. Search fee: $10.00 fee applies for all computer searches for up to 10 names. If searching over 10 names in the computer, the fee is $25.00. For lengthy computer searches, the fee is $25.00 per hour. All index book searches are $25.00 per hour. Required to search: name, years to search. Civil cases indexed by defendant, plaintiff. Civil records on computer from 10/92, on index cards prior.

Criminal Records: Access: Phone, mail, in person. Only the court performs in person searches; visitors may not. Search fee: Same fees as civil. Required to search: name, years to search; also helpful: DOB, SSN. Criminal records on computer from 10/92, on index cards prior.

General Information: No adoptions, sealed, juvenile, mental health, expunged, dismissed or annulment records released. SASE required. Turnaround time 1 week. Copy fee: $.50 per page. Certification fee: $5.00.

Fee payee: Derry District Court. Personal checks accepted. Prepayment is required.

Exeter District Court PO Box 394, Exeter, NH 03833; 603-772-2931. Hours: 8AM-4PM (EST). *Misdemeanor, Civil Actions Under $25,000, Eviction, Small Claims.*

Note: Includes towns of Exeter, Newmarket, Stratham, Newfields, Fremont, East Kingston, Kensington, Epping, and Brentwood.

Civil Records: Access: Mail, in person. Only the court performs in person searches; visitors may not. Search fee: $10.00. Required to search: name, years to search; also helpful: address. Civil cases indexed by defendant, plaintiff. Civil records on computer back to 1991.
Criminal Records: Access: Mail, in person. Both court and visitors may perform in person searches. Search fee: $10.00. Required to search: name, years to search, DOB. Criminal records on computer back to 1991.
General Information: No adoptions, sealed, juvenile, mental health, expunged or dismissed records released. SASE required. Turnaround time 3 days. Copy fee: $.50 per page. Certification fee: $5.00. Fee payee: Exeter District Court. Personal checks accepted. Prepayment is required.

Hampton District Court PO Box 10, Hampton, NH 03843-0010; 603-926-8117. Hours: 8AM-4PM (EST). *Misdemeanor, Civil Actions Under $25,000, Eviction, Small Claims.*

Note: Includes towns of Hampton, Hampton Falls, North Hampton, South Hampton, and Seabrook.

Civil Records: Access: Mail, in person. Only the court performs in person searches; visitors may not. Search fee: $10.00 fee applies for all computer searches for up to 10 names. If searching over 10 names in the computer, the fee is $25.00. For lengthy computer searches, the fee is $25.00 per hour. All index book searches are $25.00 per hour. Required to search: name, years to search. Civil cases indexed by defendant. Civil records on computer from 4/91, index cards from 1979, index books from 1900s.
Criminal Records: Access: Mail, in person. Only the court performs in person searches; visitors may not. Search fee: Same fees as civil. Required to search: name, years to search; also helpful: DOB, SSN. Criminal records on computer from 4/91, index cards from 1979, index books from 1900s.
General Information: No adoptions, sealed, juvenile, mental health, expunged or dismissed records released. SASE required. Turnaround time 1 week. No copy fee. Certification fee: $5.00. Fee payee: Hampton District Court. Personal checks accepted. Prepayment required.

Plaistow District Court 14 Elm Street (PO Box 129), Plaistow, NH 03865; 603-382-4651; Fax: 603-382-4952. Hours: 8AM-4PM (EST). *Misdemeanor, Civil Actions Under $25,000, Eviction, Small Claims.*

Note: Includes towns of Plaistow, Hampstead, Kingston, Newton, Atkinson, and Danville.

Civil Records: Access: Mail, in person. Only the court performs in person searches; visitors may not. Search fee: $10.00 1-9 names; $25.00 10 or more names. $25.00 per hour manual search fee. Required to search: name, years to search. Civil cases indexed by defendant, plaintiff. Civil records on computer from 7/91, index cards from 1980, index books from 1960s.
Criminal Records: Access: Mail, in person. Only the court performs in person searches; visitors may not. Search fee: $10.00 1-9 names; $25.00 10 or more names. $25.00 per hour manual search fee. Required to search: name, years to search, DOB. Criminal records on computer from 7/91, index cards from 1980, index books from 1960s.
General Information: No adoptions, sealed, juvenile, mental health, expunged or dismissed records released.

SASE required. Turnaround time 2-3 days. Copy fee: $.50 per page. Certification fee: $5.00. Fee payee: Plaistow District Court. Personal checks accepted. Prepayment is required.

Portsmouth District Court 111 Parrott Ave, Portsmouth, NH 03801; 603-431-2192. Hours: 8AM-4PM (EST). *Misdemeanor, Civil Actions Under $25,000, Eviction, Small Claims.*

Note: Includes city of Portsmouth and the towns of Newington, Greenland, Rye, and New Castle.

Civil Records: Access: Mail, in person. Only the court performs in person searches; visitors may not. Search fee: $10.00 if computerized search (after 1992), otherwise $35.00. Required to search: name, years to search. Civil cases indexed by defendant, plaintiff. Civil records on computer from 04/92, docket cards from 1980, index books from 1960s.
Criminal Records: Access: Mail, in person. Only the court performs in person searches; visitors may not. Search fee: Same fees as civil. Required to search: name, years to search; also helpful: DOB, SSN. Criminal records on computer from 04/92, docket cards from 1980, index books from 1960s.
General Information: No adoptions, sealed, juvenile, mental health, expunged or dismissed records released. SASE required. Turnaround time 2-3 days. Copy fee: $.50 per page. Certification fee: $1.00 per page (included in search fee). Fee payee: Portsmouth District Court. Personal checks accepted. Prepayment is required.

Salem District Court 35 Geremonty Dr, Salem, NH 03079; 603-893-4483. Hours: 8AM-4PM (EST). *Misdemeanor, Civil Actions Under $25,000, Eviction, Small Claims.*

Towns of Salem, Windham, and Pelham.

Civil Records: Access: Mail, in person. Search fee: Fee varies based on number of names per request. Required to search: name, years to search. Civil cases indexed by defendant, plaintiff. Civil records on computer from 4/92, docket cards from 1980, docket books from 1950. An appointment is necessary before performing an in person search.
Criminal Records: Access: Mail, in person. Only the court performs in person searches; visitors may not. Search fee: Fee varies based on number of names per request. Required to search: name, years to search, DOB. Criminal records on computer from 4/92, docket cards from 1980, docket books from 1950.
General Information: No adoptions, sealed, juvenile, mental health, expunged or dismissed records released. SASE required. Turnaround time 2-3 week. Copy fee: $.50 per page. Certification fee: $5.00. Fee payee: Salem District Court. Personal checks accepted. Prepayment is required.

Probate Court PO Box 789, Kingston, NH 03848; 603-642-7117. Hours: 8AM-4PM (EST). *Probate.*

Strafford County

Superior Court PO Box 799, Dover, NH 03821-0799; 603-742-3065. Hours: 8:30AM-4PM (EST). *Felony, Civil Actions Over $1,500.*

Civil Records: Access: Mail, in person. Only the court performs in person searches; visitors may not. No search fee. Required to search: name, years to search. Civil cases indexed by defendant, plaintiff. Civil records on computer from 3/89, index cards from 1970, index books from 1900s, organized 1769.
Criminal Records: Access: Mail, in person. Only the court performs in person searches; visitors may not. No search fee. Required to search: name, years to search; also helpful: DOB, SSN. Criminal records on computer from 3/89, index cards from 1970, index books from 1900s, organized 1769.

General Information: No sealed, juvenile, mental health, expunged or dismissed records released. SASE required. Turnaround time 1 week. Copy fee: $.50 per page. Certification fee: $5.00. Fee payee: Superior Court Clerk. Personal checks accepted. Prepayment is required.

Dover District Court 25 St Thomas St, Dover, NH 03820; 603-742-7202. Hours: 8AM-4PM (EST). *Misdemeanor, Civil Actions Under $20,000, Eviction, Small Claims.*

Note: Includes city of Dover.

Civil Records: Access: Mail, in person. Only the court performs in person searches; visitors may not. Search fee: $10.00 per name. Required to search: name, years to search. Civil cases indexed by defendant, plaintiff. Civil records on computer from 1993, on index cards from 1980, index books from 1970.
Criminal Records: Access: Mail, in person. Only the court performs in person searches; visitors may not. Search fee: $10.00 per name. Required to search: name, years to search, DOB. Criminal records on computer from 1993, on index cards from 1980, index books from 1970.
General Information: No adoptions, sealed, juvenile, mental health, expunged or dismissed records released. SASE required. Turnaround time 1-2 days. Copy fee: $.50 per page. Certification fee: $5.00. Fee payee: Dover District Court. Personal checks accepted. Prepayment is required.

Durham District Court 1 Main Street, Durham, NH 03824; 603-868-2323. Hours: 8:30AM-4PM (EST). *Misdemeanor, Civil Actions Under $25,000, Eviction, Small Claims.*

Note: Includes towns of Durham, Lee, and Madbury.

Civil Records: Access: Mail, in person. Only the court performs in person searches; visitors may not. Search fee: Searching via computer is $10.00 per name; lengthy manual searching is $25.00 per hour. Required to search: name, years to search. Civil cases indexed by defendant, plaintiff. Civil records on computer fback to 1990; index cards from 1980, index books from 1945.
Criminal Records: Access: Mail, in person. Only the court performs in person searches; visitors may not. Search fee: Same as Civil. Required to search: name, years to search, DOB; also helpful: SSN. Criminal records on computer back to 1990; index cards from 1980, index books from 1948.
General Information: No adoptions, sealed, juvenile, mental health, expunged or dismissed records released. SASE required. Turnaround time 4 days. Copy fee: $.50 per page. Certification fee: $5.00. Fee payee: Durham District Court. Personal checks accepted. Prepayment is required.

Rochester District Court 76 N Main St, Rochester, NH 03867; 603-332-3516. Hours: 8AM-4PM (EST). *Misdemeanor, Civil Actions Under $25,000, Eviction, Small Claims.*

Note: Includes city of Rochester and the towns of Barrington, Milton, New Durham, Farmington, Strafford, and Middleton.

Civil Records: Access: Mail, in person. Only the court performs in person searches; visitors may not. Search fee: If on computer, $10 for up to 10 names, $25.00 if over 10 names. If manual, then 25.00. Required to search: name, years to search; also helpful DOB. Civil cases indexed by defendant, plaintiff. Civil records on computer from 1989, index cards from 7/80, index books from 1960s.
Criminal Records: Access: Mail, in person. Only the court performs in person searches; visitors may not. Search fee: Same fees as civil. Required to search: name, years to search; also helpful: DOB. Criminal

records on computer from 1989, index cards from 7/80, index books from 1960s.

General Information: No sealed, juvenile, mental health, expunged records released. SASE required. Turnaround time 1 week. Copy fee: $.50 per page. Certification fee: $5.00 per page. Fee payee: Rochester District Court. Personal checks accepted. Prepayment is required.

Somersworth District Court 2 Pleasant St, Somersworth, NH 03878-2543; 603-692-5967; Fax: 603-692-5752. Hours: 8AM-4PM (EST). *Misdemeanor, Civil Actions Under $25,000, Eviction, Small Claims.*

Note: The first 3 Tuesdays of the month the court is open until 8:30PM. Includes City of Somersworth and town of Rollinsford.

Civil Records: Access: Phone, mail, in person. Only the court performs in person searches; visitors may not. Search fee: Fee is based on type of search. See state introduction. Required to search: name, years to search. Civil cases indexed by defendant, plaintiff. Civil records on computer from 1991, on index cards from 1981, index books from 1960s.

Criminal Records: Access: Phone, mail, in person. Only the court performs in person searches; visitors may not. Search fee: Fee is based on type of search. See state introduction. Required to search: name, years to search, DOB. Criminal records on computer from 1991, on index cards from 1981, index books from 1960s.

General Information: No adoptions, sealed, juvenile, mental health, expunged or dismissed records released. SASE required. Turnaround time 7-10 days. Copy fee: $.50 per page. No fee for computer printouts. Certification fee: $5.00. Fee payee: Somersworth District Court. Personal checks accepted. Credit cards accepted. Prepayment is required.

Probate Court PO Box 799, Dover, NH 03821-0799; 603-742-2550. 8AM-4:30PM (EST). *Probate.*

www.state.nh.us/courts/probate.htm

Sullivan County

Superior Court 22 Main St, Newport, NH 03773; 603-863-3450. Hours: 8AM-4:30PM (EST). *Felony, Civil Actions Over $1,500.*

Civil Records: Access: Mail, in person. Only the court performs in person searches; visitors may not. No search fee. Required to search: name, years to search. Civil cases indexed by defendant, plaintiff. Civil records on computer from 1992, on index cards from 1980s, index books from 1800s.

Criminal Records: Access: Mail, in person. Only the court performs in person searches; visitors may not. No search fee. Required to search: name, years to search, DOB. Criminal records on computer from 1992, on index cards from 1980s, index books from 1800s.

General Information: No adoptions, sealed, juvenile, mental health, expunged or dismissed records released. SASE required. Turnaround time 1 week. Copy fee: $.50 per page. Certification fee: $5.00. Fee payee: Sullivan County Superior Court. Personal checks accepted. Prepayment is required.

Claremont District Court PO Box 313, Claremont, NH 03743; 603-542-6064. Hours: 8AM-4PM (EST). *Misdemeanor, Civil Actions Under $25,000, Eviction, Small Claims.*

Note: Includes city of Claremont and the towns of Cornish, Unity, Charlestown, Acworth, Langdon, and Plainfield.

Civil Records: Access: Phone, mail, in person. Only the court performs in person searches; visitors may not. Search fee: $10.00 1992 to present. $35.00 prior to 1992. Required to search: name, years to search, DOB. Civil cases indexed by defendant, plaintiff. Civil records on computer from 10/92, on index cards from 1980, index books from 1960.

Criminal Records: Access: Phone, mail, in person. Only the court performs in person searches; visitors may not. Search fee: $10.00 1992 to present. $35.00

prior to 1992. Required to search: name, years to search, DOB. Criminal records on computer from 10/92, on index cards from 1980, index books from 1960.

General Information: No adoptions, sealed, juvenile, mental health, expunged or dismissed records released. SASE required. Turnaround time 1 week. Copy fee: $.50 per page. Certification fee: $5.00. Fee payee: Claremont District Court. Personal checks accepted. Prepayment is required.

Newport District Court PO Box 581, Newport, NH 03773; 603-863-1832. Hours: 8AM-4PM (EST). *Misdemeanor, Civil Actions Under $25,000, Eviction, Small Claims.*

Note: Includes towns of Newport, Grantham, Croydon, Springfield, Sunapee, Goshen, Lempster, and Washington.

Civil Records: Access: Phone, mail, in person. Only the court performs in person searches; visitors may not. Search fee: $25.00 per hour. Required to search: name, years to search. Civil cases indexed by defendant, plaintiff. Civil records on computer from 1993, on index cards from 1980, index books from 1960s.

Criminal Records: Access: Phone, mail, in person. Only the court performs in person searches; visitors may not. Search fee: $25.00 per hour. Required to search: name, years to search, DOB. Criminal records on computer from 1993, on index cards from 1980, index books from 1960s.

General Information: No adoptions, sealed, juvenile, mental health, expunged or dismissed records released. SASE required. Turnaround time 2-3 days. Copy fee: $.50 per page. Certification fee: $1.00. Fee payee: Newport District Court. Personal checks accepted. Prepayment is required.

Probate Court PO Box 417, Newport, NH 03773; 603-863-3150. Hours: 8AM-4PM (EST). *Probate.*

New Hampshire Recording Offices

ORGANIZATION: 238 cities/towns and 10 counties, 10 recording offices and 242 UCC filing offices. The recording officers are Town/City Clerk (UCC) and Register of Deeds (real estate only). Each town/city profile indicates the county in which the town/city is located. Be careful to distinguish the following names that are identical for both a town/city and a county - Grafton, Hillsborough, Merrimack, Strafford, and Sullivan. Many towns are so small that their mailing addresses are within another town. The following unincorporated towns do not have a Town Clerk, so all liens are located at the corresponding county: Cambridge (Coos), Dicksville (Coos), Green's Grant (Coos), Hale's Location (Carroll), Millsfield (Coos), and Wentworth's Location (Coos). The entire state is in the Eastern Time Zone (EST).

REAL ESTATE RECORDS: Real estate transactions are recorded at the county level, and property taxes are handled at the town/city level. Local town real estate ownership and assessment records are usually located at the Selectman's Office. Each town/city profile indicates the county in which the town/city is located. Most counties will not perform real estate searches. Copy fees vary. Certification fees generally are $2.00 per document.

UCC RECORDS: This was a dual filing state until Revised Article 9. Previously, financing statements were filed at the state level and with the Town/City Clerk, except for consumer goods and farm related collateral, which were filed only with the Town/City Clerk, and real estate related collateral, which was and still is filed with the county Register of Deeds. Most recording offices will perform UCC searches. Use search request form UCC-11. Search fees are usually $5.00 per debtor name using the standard UCC-11 request form and $7.00 using a non-standard form. Copy fees are usually $.75 per page.

TAX LIEN RECORDS: Federal and state tax liens on personal property of businesses are filed with the Secretary of State. Other federal and state tax liens on personal property are filed with the Town/City Clerk. Federal and state tax liens on real property are filed with the county Register of Deeds. There is wide variation in indexing and searching practices among the recording offices. Where a search fee of $7.00 is indicated, it refers to a non-standard request form such as a letter.

OTHER LIENS: Condominium, town tax, mechanics, welfare.

ONLINE ACCESS: The New Hampshire Counties Registry of Deeds web site allows free searching of real estate related records for Belknap, Cheshire, Hillsborough and Strafford counties at www.nhdeeds.com. Also, a private vendor has placed on the Internet the assessor records from a number of towns. Visit http://data.visionappraisal.com

Acworth Town

Town Clerk, PO Box 193, Town Clerk, Acworth, NH 03601. 603-835-6879.
Will search UCC records prior to 7/2001 and current liens only. This agency will not do a tax lien search. Real estate records located in Sullivan County.

Albany Town

Town Clerk, 19728 NH Route 16, Conway, NH 03818. 603-447-2877; Fax 603-447-2877.
Will search UCC records prior to 7/2001 and current liens only. Real estate records located in Carroll County. **Other Phone Numbers:** Assessor 603-586-4402.

Alexandria Town

Town Clerk, 44 Perkins Hill Road, Alexandria, NH 03222. 603-744-3288 R/E Recording: 603-787-6921; Fax 603-744-1079.
Will search UCC records. This agency will not do a tax lien search. Real estate records located in Grafton County. **Other Phone Numbers:** Assessor 603-744-3220.

Allenstown Town

Town Clerk, 16 School St, Allenstown, NH 03275. Town Clerk, R/E and UCC Recording 603-485-4276; Fax 603-485-8669. www.allenstown.org
Will search UCC records prior to 7/2001 and current liens only. Real estate records located in Merrimack County. **Other Phone Numbers:** Assessor 603-485-4276; Treasurer 603-485-4276; Elections 603-485-4276; Vital Records 603-485-4276.

Alstead Town

Town Clerk, Box 65, Alstead, NH 03602. 603-835-2242; Fax 603-835-2986.
Will search UCC records prior to 7/2001 and current liens only. Real estate records located in Cheshire County.

Alton Town

Town Clerk, Box 637, Alton, NH 03809. 603-875-2101 R/E Recording: 603-875-5095; Fax 603-875-3894.
Will search UCC records prior to 7/2001 and current liens only. Real estate records located in Belknap County. **Other Phones:** Assessor 603-875-2162; Treasurer 603-875-2161; Appraiser/Auditor 603-875-5095; Elections 875-2101; Vital Records 875-2101.

Amherst Town

Town Clerk, PO Box 960, Amherst, NH 03031. 603-673-6041 UCC Recording: 603-673-6041 x207; Fax 603-673-6794.
Will search UCC records prior to 7/2001 and current liens only. This agency will not do a tax lien search. Real estate records located in Hillsborough County. **Other Phone Numbers:** Assessor 603-673-6041; Treasurer 603-673-6041.

Andover Town

Town Clerk, PO Box 61, Andover, NH 03216. 603-735-5332; Fax 603-735-6975.
Will search UCC records. Real estate records located in Merrimack County. **Other Phone Numbers:** Assessor 603-735-5332; Treasurer 603-735-5516; Vital Records 603-735-5332.

Antrim Town

Town Clerk, PO Box 517, Antrim, NH 03440. 603-588-6785; Fax 603-588-2969.
Will search UCC records prior to 7/2001 and current liens only. Real estate records located in Hillsborough County.

Ashland Town

Town Clerk, PO Box 517, Ashland, NH 03217. 603-968-4432; Fax 603-968-3776.
Will search UCC records prior to 7/2001 and current liens only. Real estate records located in Grafton County.

Atkinson Town

Town Clerk, 21 Academy Ave, Town Hall, Atkinson, NH 03811-2204. 603-362-4920; Fax 603-362-5305.
Will search UCC records prior to 7/2001 and current liens only. This agency will not do a tax lien search. Real estate records located in Rockingham County.

Auburn Town

Town Clerk, PO Box 309, Auburn, NH 03032-0309. 603-483-2281 UCC Recording: 603-483-2281 x1; Fax 603-483-0518.
Will search UCC records prior to 7/2001 and current liens only. Real estate records located in Rockingham County. **Other Phones:** Assessor 603-483-5052.

Barnstead Town

Town Clerk, PO Box 11, Center Barnstead, NH 03225. 603-269-4631; Fax 603-269-4072.
Will search UCC records prior to 7/2001 and current liens only. Real estate records located in Belknap

County. **Other Phone Numbers:** Assessor 603-269-4071; Treasurer 603-269-4071; Elections 603-269-4631; Vital Records 603-269-4631.

Barrington Town

Town Clerk, 41 Province Lane, Barrington, NH 03825. 603-664-5476; Fax 603-664-5179.
Will search UCC records prior to 7/2001 and current liens only. Real estate records located at Strafford County. **Other Phone Numbers:** Assessor 603-664-9007; Elections 603-664-5476; Vital Records 603-664-5476; Tax Collector 603-664-2230.

Bartlett Town

Town Clerk, RFD 1 Box 50, Intervale, NH 03845. 603-356-2300 R/E Recording: 603-356-2950.
Will search UCC records. This agency will not do a tax lien search. Real estate records located in Carroll County. **Other Phone Numbers:** Assessor 603-356-2950; Treasurer 603-356-2950; Elections 603-356-2300; Vital Records 603-356-2300.

Bath Town

Town Clerk, PO Box 165, Bath, NH 03740. 603-747-2454; Fax 603-747-0497.
Will not search UCC records. This agency will not do a tax lien search. Real estate records located in Grafton County. **Other Phones:** Treasurer 603-747-2454.

Bedford Town

Town Clerk, 24 N. Amherst Road, Bedford, NH 03110. 603-472-3550;   Fax   603-472-4573. www.ci.bedford.nh.us
Will search UCC records prior to 7/2001 and current liens only. Real estate records located in Hillsborough County. **Other Phone Numbers:** Assessor 603-472-8104; Vital Records 603-472-3550.

Belknap County

Register of Deeds, PO Box 1343, Laconia, NH 03247-1343. Register of Deeds, R/E and UCC Recording 603-527-5420; Fax 603-527-5429.
Will search UCC records prior to 7/2001 and current liens only. Will not search real estate records. **Online Access:** Real Estate, Deed, Mortgage, Lien Records. Access to county register of deeds data is available free at   www.nhdeeds.com/belk/web/agree5.htm.   Online records go back to 1960.

Belmont Town

Town Clerk, PO Box 310, Belmont, NH 03220. 603-267-8302; Fax 603-267-8305.
Will search UCC records prior to 7/2001 and current liens only. Real estate records located at Belknap County. **Other Phone Numbers:** Assessor 603-267-8300; Treasurer 603-267-8300; Appraiser/Auditor 603-267-8300; Elections 603-267-8302; Vital Records 603-267-8303.

Bennington Town

Town Clerk, 7 School St, #101, Bennington, NH 03442. 603-588-2189; Fax 603-588-8005.
Will search UCC records prior to 7/2001 and current liens only. Real estate records located in Hillsborough County. **Other Phone Numbers:** Assessor 603-588-2189.

Benton Town

Town Clerk, 30 Ingerson Rd., Benton, NH 03785. 603-787-6541 R/E Recording: 603-787-6053; Fax 603-787-6883.
Will search UCC records prior to 7/2001 and current liens only. Real estate records located in Grafton County. **Other Phone Numbers:** Assessor 603-787-6053; Treasurer 603-787-6004; Appraiser/Auditor 603-787-6053; Elections 603-787-2129; Vital Records 603-787-6541.

Berlin City

City Clerk, 168 Main St, City Hall, Berlin, NH 03570. 603-752-2340; Fax 603-752-8586.
Will search UCC records prior to 7/2001 and current liens only. Real estate records located in Coos County. **Other Phone Numbers:** Assessor 603-752-5245; Treasurer 603-752-1610.

Bethlehem Town

Town Clerk, PO Box 189, Bethlehem, NH 03574. 603-869-2293; Fax 603-869-2280.
Will search UCC records prior to 7/2001 and current liens only. UCC search includes federal tax liens if requested. Real estate records located in Grafton County. **Other Phones:** Assessor 603-869-3351.

Boscawen Town

Town Clerk, 17 High St, Boscawen, NH 03303. 603-796-2426; Fax 603-796-2316.
Will search UCC records prior to 7/2001 and current liens only. Real estate records located in Merrimack County. **Other Phone Numbers:** Assessor 603-796-2426; Treasurer 603-796-2343.

Bow Town

Town Clerk, 10 Grandview Road, Bow, NH 03304-3410. 603-225-2683.
Will search UCC records prior to 7/2001 and current liens only. This agency will not do a tax lien search. Real estate records located in Merrimack County. **Other Phone Numbers:** Assessor 603-228-1189.

Bradford Town

Town Clerk/Tax Collector, PO Box 607, Bradford, NH 03221-0607. 603-938-2288; Fax 603-938-5900.
Will search UCC records prior to 7/2001 and current liens only. Real estate records located in Merrimack County. **Other Phones:** Assessor 603-938-5900.

Brentwood Town

Town Clerk, 1 Dalton Road, Brentwood, NH 03833. 603-642-6400 x14; Fax 603-642-6310.
Will search UCC records prior to 7/2001 and current liens only. This agency will not do a tax lien search. Real estate records located in Rockingham County. **Other Phone Numbers:** Assessor 603-642-6400 x10; Treasurer 603-642-6400 x19; Elections 603-642-6400 x14; Vital Records 603-642-6400 x14.

Bridgewater Town

Town Clerk, PO Box 419, Plymouth, NH 03264. 603-968-7911; Fax 603-968-3506.
Will search UCC records prior to 7/2001 and current liens only. This agency will not do a tax lien search. Real estate records located in Grafton County. **Online Access:** Property Assessor Records. Search the town assessor database at http://data.visionappraisal.com/BridgewaterNH. Free registration required.

Bristol Town

Town Clerk, 230 Lake St, Suite A, Bristol, NH 03222-1120. 603-744-8478; Fax 603-744-2521.
Will search UCC records prior to 7/2001 and current liens only. Real estate records located in Grafton County. **Other Phone Numbers:** Assessor 603-744-3354; Appraiser/Auditor 603-744-3354.

Brookfield Town

Town Clerk, PO Box 756, Sanbornville, NH 03872. 603-522-3231; Fax 603-522-6245.
Will search UCC records prior to 7/2001 and current liens only. UCC search includes tax liens if requested. Real estate records located in Carroll County. **Other Phone Numbers:** Assessor 603-522-6018; Treasurer 603-522-6756; Appraiser/Auditor 603-522-6018.

Brookline Town

Town Clerk, PO Box 336, Brookline, NH 03033. 603-673-8933 UCC Recording: 603-673-8855 X218; Fax 603-673-8136. www.brookline.nh.us
Will search UCC records prior to 7/2001 and current liens only. UCC search includes tax liens. Real estate records located in Hillsborough County. **Other Phone Numbers:** Assessor 603-673-8855 X216; Elections 603-673-8855 X218; Vital Records 603-673-8855 X218.

Campton Town

Town Clerk, PO Box 127, Campton, NH 03223. 603-726-3223 UCC Recording: 603-726-3223 x102; Fax 603-726-9817.
Will not search UCC records. Real estate records located in Grafton County. **Other Phone Numbers:** Assessor 603-726-3223.

Canaan Town

Town Clerk, PO Box 38, Canaan, NH 03741-0038. 603-523-7106; Fax 603-523-4526.
Will search UCC records prior to 7/2001 and current liens only. Real estate records located in Grafton County. **Other Phone Numbers:** Appraiser/Auditor 603-523-4501.

Candia Town

Town Clerk, 74 High St, Candia, NH 03034-2713. 603-483-5573 R/E Recording: 603-483-8101; Fax 603-483-0252.
Will search UCC records prior to 7/2001 and current liens only. Real estate records located in Rockingham County. **Other Phone Numbers:** Assessor 603-483-8101; Appraiser/Auditor 603-483-8101; Elections 603-483-5573; Vital Records 603-483-5573.

Canterbury Town

Town Clerk, PO Box 500, Canterbury, NH 03224. 603-783-9955; Fax 603-783-9955.
Will search UCC records prior to 7/2001 and current liens only. UCC search includes tax liens. Real estate records located in Merrimack County.

Carroll County

Register of Deeds, PO Box 163, Ossipee, NH 03864-0163. 603-539-4872; Fax 603-539-5239.
This agency will not search real estate or UCC records.

Carroll Town

Town Clerk, PO Box 88, Twin Mountain, NH 03595-0088. 603-846-5494; Fax 603-846-5713.
Will search UCC records prior to 7/2001 and current liens only. Real estate records located in Carroll County. **Other Phone Numbers:** Assessor 603-846-5754.

Center Harbor Town

Town Clerk, PO Box 140, Center Harbor, NH 03226. 603-253-4561; Fax 603-253-8420.
Will search UCC records prior to 7/2001 and current liens only. Real estate records located in Belknap County.

Charlestown Town

Town Clerk, PO Box 834, Charlestown, NH 03603. 603-826-5821.
Will search UCC records prior to 7/2001 and current liens only. UCC search includes tax liens if requested. Real estate records located in Sullivan County. **Other Phone Numbers:** Assessor 603-826-4400.

Chatham Town

Town Clerk, 1717 Main Road, Chatham, NH 03813. 603-694-2043.
Will search UCC records prior to 7/2001 and current liens only. This agency will not do a tax lien search.

Real estate records located in Carroll County. **Other Phone Numbers:** Treasurer 603-694-2321; Elections 603-694-2043; Vital Records 603-694-2043.

Cheshire County

Registry of Deeds, PO Box 584, Keene, NH 03431. 603-352-0403; Fax 603-352-7678. www.nhdeeds.com This agency will not search real estate or UCC records. **Online Access:** Real Estate, Deed, Mortgage, Lien Records. Access to county register of deeds data is available free at www.nhdeeds.com/chsr/web/agree2.htm. Online records go back to 1980.

Chester Town

Town Clerk, PO Box 275, Chester, NH 03036. 603-887-3636.
Will search UCC records prior to 7/2001 and current liens only. UCC search includes tax liens if requested. Real estate records located in Rockingham County. **Other Phone Numbers:** Assessor 603-887-4045; Elections 603-887-4344.

Chesterfield Town

Town Clerk, PO Box 64, Chesterfield, NH 03443-0064. 603-363-8071 R/E Recording: 603-363-4624; Fax 603-363-8047. www.nhchesterfield.com
Will search UCC records prior to 7/2001 and current liens only. UCC search includes tax liens if requested. Real estate records located in Cheshire County. **Other Phone Numbers:** Assessor 603-363-4624; Treasurer 603-363-4624; Appraiser/Auditor 603-363-4624; Elections 603-363-8071; Vital Records 603-363-8071.

Chichester Town

Town Clerk, 54 Main St., Chichester, NH 03234. 603-798-5808 R/E Recording: 603-798-5350; Fax 603-798-3170.
Will search UCC records prior to 7/2001 and current liens only. Real estate records located in Merrimack County. **Other Phone Numbers:** Assessor 603-798-5350; Appraiser/Auditor 603-798-5350; Elections 603-798-5808; Vital Records 603-798-5808.

Claremont City

City Clerk, City Hall - Finance Office, 58 Tremont Square, Claremont, NH 03743. 603-542-7001 UCC Recording: 603-542-7003; Fax 603-542-7014. www.claremontnh.com
Will search UCC records prior to 7/2001 and current liens only. Real estate records located in Sullivan County. **Other Phone Numbers:** Assessor 603-542-7008; Treasurer 603-542-7000; Elections 603-542-7003; Vital Records 603-542-7003.

Clarksville Town

Town Clerk, 408 NH Route 145, Clarksville, NH 03592. Town Clerk, R/E and UCC Recording 603-246-7751; Fax 603-246-3480.
The County Register of Deeds records real estate transactions, and the City Clerk records UCC filings. Will search UCC records prior to 7/2001 and current liens only. UCC search includes tax liens if requested. Real estate records located in Coos County. **Other Phone Numbers:** Assessor 603-417-2297; Treasurer 603-246-8896; Appraiser/Auditor 800-417-2297; Elections 603-246-7751; Vital Records 603-246-7751.

Colebrook Town

Assessor, 10 Bridge St, Colebrook, NH 03576. 603-237-5200 R/E Recording: 603-237-4070; Fax 603-237-9852.
Will search UCC records prior to 7/2001 and current liens only. Real estate records located in Coos County. **Other Phone Numbers:** Assessor 603-237-4070; Treasurer 603-237-4142; Appraiser/Auditor 603-237-4142; Elections 603-237-5200; Vital Records 603-237-5200.

Columbia Town

Town Clerk, PO Box 157, Colebrook, NH 03576. 603-237-5255; Fax 603-237-8270.
Will search UCC records prior to 7/2001 and current liens only. Real estate records located in Coos County.

Concord City

City Clerk, 41 Green St, Room 2, Concord, NH 03301-4255. 603-225-8500; Fax 603-228-2724.
Will search UCC records prior to 7/2001 and current liens only. Real estate records located in Merrimack County. **Online Access:** Assessor Records. Records on the city assessor database are available free online at http://data.visionappraisal.com/ConcordNH. Registration is required to view full data. **Other Phone Numbers:** Assessor 603-225-8550.

Conway Town

Town Clerk, 1634 E Main St, Center Conway, NH 03813. 603-447-3822; Fax 603-447-1348. Hours: 9AM-5PM (EST)
Will search UCC records prior to 7/2001 and current liens only. Fed. tax lien search included in UCC search. Real estate records located in Carroll County. **Other Phone Numbers:** Assessor 603-447-3811.

Coos County

Register of Deeds, Coos County Courthouse, 55 School St, Suite 103, Lancaster, NH 03584. Register of Deeds, R/E and UCC Recording 603-788-2392; Fax 603-788-4291.
The County Register of Deeds records real estate and Real Estate/UCC transactions, and the Town/City Clerk records UCC filings. Will search UCC records prior to 7/2001 and current liens only. This agency will not do a tax lien search. Will not search real estate records.

Cornish Town

Town Clerk, PO Box 183, Cornish Flat, NH 03746. 603-675-5207; Fax 603-675-5605.
Will search UCC records prior to 7/2001 and current liens only. Real estate records located in Sullivan County.

Croydon Town

Town Clerk, 879 NHRT10, Newport, NH 03773. 603-863-7830; Fax 603-863-2601.
Will search UCC records prior to 7/2001 and current liens only. This agency will not do a tax lien search. Real estate records located in Sullivan County. **Other Phone Numbers:** Assessor 603-863-7830.

Dalton Town

Town Clerk, 741 Dalton Rd, Dalton, NH 03598. 603-837-2096; Fax 603-837-9642.
Will search UCC records prior to 7/2001 and current liens only. Real estate records located in Coos County. **Other Phone Numbers:** Treasurer 603-837-9802.

Danbury Town

Town Clerk, 23 High St., Danbury, NH 03230. 603-768-5448; Fax 603-768-3313.
Will search UCC records prior to 7/2001 and current liens only. This agency will not do a tax lien search. Real estate records located in Merrimack County. **Other Phone Numbers:** Assessor 603-768-3313.

Danville Town

Town Clerk, PO Box 11, Danville, NH 03819. 603-382-8253; Fax 603-382-3363.
Will search UCC records prior to 7/2001 and current liens only. Real estate records located in Rockingham County.

Deerfield Town

Town Clerk, PO Box 159, Deerfield, NH 03037. 603-463-8811; Fax 603-463-2820.
Will search UCC records prior to 7/2001 and current liens only. Real estate records located in Rockingham County. **Other Phone Numbers:** Assessor 603-463-8811; Treasurer 603-463-8811; Appraiser/Auditor 603-463-8811; Elections 603-463-8811; Vital Records 603-463-8811.

Deering Town

Town Clerk, 762 Deering Center Rd., Deering, NH 03244. 603-464-6557; Fax 603-464-3804. www.deering.nh.us
Will search UCC records prior to 7/2001 and current liens only. Real estate records located in Hillsborough County.

Derry Town

Town Clerk, 48 E. Broadway, Derry, NH 03038. 603-432-6105; Fax 603-432-6131. www.derry.nh.us
Will search UCC records prior to 7/2001 and current liens only. Real estate records located in Rockingham County. **Online Access:** Assessor, Property, Sales Records. Records of Derry assessed values are available free at www.derry.nh.us/assessor/default.htm. Lists are by address; names are provided. **Other Phone Numbers:** Assessor 603-432-6104.

Dorchester Town

Town Clerk, 368 N Dorchester Rd, Dorecester, NH 03266. 603-786-9076 UCC Recording: 603-786-9476.
Will search UCC records prior to 7/2001 and current liens only. UCC search includes tax liens. Real estate records located in Grafton County. **Other Phones:** Assessor 603-523-7658; Treasurer 603-523-9658; Elections 603-786-9076; Vital Records 603-786-9076.

Dover City

City Clerk, 288 Central Ave, City Hall, Dover, NH 03820. 603-743-6021; Fax 603-516-6666. www.ci.dover.nh.us
Will search UCC records prior to 7/2001 and current liens only. Real estate records located in Strafford County. **Other Phone Numbers:** Assessor 603-743-6014; Treasurer 603-743-6030; Elections 603-743-6021; Vital Records 603-743-6021.

Dublin Town

Town Clerk, Box 62, Dublin, NH 03444. 603-563-8859; Fax 603-563-9221.
Will not search UCC records. Separate federal tax lien search available. Real estate records located in Cheshire County. **Other Phone Numbers:** Assessor 603-563-8544.

Dummer Town

Town Clerk, 1420 East Side River Rd., Dummer, NH 03588. 603-449-3408; Fax 603-449-3349.
Will search UCC records prior to 7/2001 and current liens only. This agency will not do a tax lien search. Real estate records located in Coos County. **Other Phone Numbers:** Treasurer 603-449-3417; Elections 603-449-3442; Vital Records 603-449-3408.

Dunbarton Town

Town Clerk, 1011 School St., Dunbarton, NH 03045. 603-774-3547; Fax 603-774-5541.
Will search UCC records prior to 7/2001 and current liens only. Real estate records located in Merrimack County. **Other Phone Numbers:** Assessor 603-774-3547.

Durham Town

Town Clerk/Tax Collector, 15 Newmarket Road, Town Hall, Durham, NH 03824-2898. 603-868-5577; Fax

603-868-8033.
www.ci.durham.nh.us/DEPARTMENTS/town_clerk/clerk.html
Will search UCC records prior to 7/2001 and current liens only. Real estate records located in Strafford County. **Other Phone Numbers:** Assessor 603-868-8065; Treasurer 603-868-8043.

East Kingston Town

Town Clerk, PO Box 249, East Kingston, NH 03827-0249. Town Clerk, R/E and UCC Recording 603-642-8794; Fax 603-642-8406.
Will search UCC records prior to 7/2001 and current liens only. Real estate records located in Rockingham County. **Other Phones:** Assessor 603-642-8406; Treasurer 603-642-8406; Appraiser/Auditor 603-642-8406; Elections 642-8794; Vital Records 642-8794.

Easton Town

Town Clerk, 381 Easton Valley Road, Easton, NH 03580. 603-823-5293; Fax 603-823-7780.
Will search UCC records prior to 7/2001 and current liens only. This agency will not do a tax lien search. Real estate records located in Grafton County.

Eaton Town

Town Clerk, Box 118, Eaton Center, NH 03832. 603-447-2840; Fax 603-447-2560.
Will search UCC records prior to 7/2001 and current liens only. Real estate records located in Carroll County.

Effingham Town

Town Clerk, PO Box 48, South Effingham, NH 03882. 603-539-7551; Fax 603-539-7799.
Will search UCC records prior to 7/2001 and current liens only. Real estate records located in Carroll County.

Ellsworth Town

Town Clerk, Ellsworth Pond Road, RR 1, Box 852, Plymouth, NH 03264-9608. 603-536-1732; Fax 603-536-0036.
Will search UCC records prior to 7/2001 and current liens only. This agency will not do a tax lien search. Real estate records located in Grafton County. **Other Phone Numbers:** Treasurer 603-726-8668.

Enfield Town

Town Clerk, PO Box 373, Enfield, NH 03748-0373. 603-632-5001; Fax 603-632-5182. www.enfield.nh.us
Will search UCC records prior to 7/2001 and current liens only. This agency will not do a tax lien search. Real estate records located in Grafton County. **Other Phone Numbers:** Assessor 603-632-4201.

Epping Town

Town Clerk, 157 Main St, Epping, NH 03042. 603-679-8288; Fax 603-679-3302.
Will search UCC records prior to 7/2001 and current liens only. Real estate records located in Rockingham County.

Epsom Town

Town Clerk, PO Box 10, Epsom, NH 03234. 603-736-4825; Fax 603-736-8539.
Will search UCC records prior to 7/2001 and current liens only. Real estate records located in Merrimack County. **Other Phones:** Appraiser/Auditor 736-9002.

Errol Town

Town Clerk, PO Box 100, Errol, NH 03579. 603-482-3351; Fax 603-482-3804.
Will search UCC records prior to 7/2001 and current liens only. Real estate records located in Coos County. **Other Phone Numbers:** Assessor 603-482-3351; Treasurer 603-482-3351.

Exeter Town

Town Clerk, 10 Front St, Exeter, NH 03833-2792. 603-778-0591; Fax 603-772-4709. www.exeternh.org/tnclk/index.html
Will search UCC records prior to 7/2001 and current liens only. Real estate records located in Rockingham County. **Other Phone Numbers:** Assessor 603-778-0591.

Farmington Town

Town Clerk, Main St, Town Hall, Farmington, NH 03835. 603-755-3657; Fax 603-755-9128.
Will search UCC records prior to 7/2001 and current liens only. Real estate records located in Strafford County. **Other Phone Numbers:** Assessor 603-755-2208; Treasurer 603-755-3657; Elections 603-755-3657; Vital Records 603-755-3657.

Fitzwilliam Town

Town Clerk, PO Box 504, Fitzwilliam, NH 03447-0504. 603-585-7791; Fax 603-585-7744.
Will search UCC records prior to 7/2001 and current liens only. Real estate records located in Cheshire County.

Francestown Town

Town Clerk, PO Box 67, Francestown, NH 03043-0067. 603-547-6251; Fax 603-547-2818. Will search UCC records prior to 7/2001 and current liens only. Real estate records located in Hillsborough County.

Franconia Town

Town Clerk, PO Box 900, Franconia, NH 03580. 603-823-5237; Fax 603-823-5581.
Will search UCC records prior to 7/2001 and current liens only. UCC search includes tax liens if requested. Real estate records located in Grafton County.

Franklin City

City Clerk, 316 Central St, Franklin, NH 03235. 603-934-3109.
Will search UCC records prior to 7/2001 and current liens only. This agency will not do a tax lien search. Real estate records located in Merrimack County. **Other Phone Numbers:** Assessor 603-934-5449.

Freedom Town

Town Clerk, PO Box 457, Freedom, NH 03836. 603-539-6323 R/E Recording: 603-539-4872; Fax 603-539-8270.
Will search UCC records prior to 7/2001 and current liens only. Real estate records located in Carroll County. **Other Phone Numbers:** Assessor 603-539-6323; Treasurer 603-539-6323.

Fremont Town

Town Clerk, PO Box 120, Fremont, NH 03044. Town Clerk, R/E and UCC Recording 603-895-2226; Fax 603-895-3149.
Will search UCC records prior to 7/2001 and current liens only. Real estate records located in Rockingham County. **Other Phone Numbers:** Assessor 603-895-2226; Treasurer 603-895-6936; Elections 603-895-2226; Vital Records 603-895-2226.

Gilford Town

Town Clerk, 47 Cherry Valley Road, Town Hall, Gilford, NH 03246. 603-524-3286; Fax 603-528-1183.
Will search UCC records prior to 7/2001 and current liens only. Real estate records located in Belknap County. **Other Phones:** Assessor 603-524-3293.

Gilmanton Town

Town Clerk, PO Box 550, Gilmanton, NH 03237-0550. 603-267-6726; Fax 603-267-6701.

Will search UCC records prior to 7/2001 and current liens only. Real estate records located in Belknap County.

Gilsum Town

Town Clerk, PO Box 36, Gilsum, NH 03448. 603-357-0320; Fax 603-352-0845.
Will not search UCC records. Real estate records located in Cheshire County. **Other Phone Numbers:** Assessor 603-357-0320.

Goffstown Town

Town Clerk, 16 Main St, Goffstown, NH 03045. 603-497-3613 R/E Recording: 603-497-3611; Fax 603-497-8993. www.ci.goffstown.nh.us
Will search UCC records prior to 7/2001 and current liens only. Real estate records located in Hillsborough County. **Other Phone Numbers:** Assessor 603-497-3611; Treasurer 603-497-3615; Elections 603-497-3613; Vital Records 603-497-3617.

Gorham Town

Town Clerk, 20 Park St, Gorham, NH 03581-1694. 603-466-2744; Fax 603-466-3100. www.gorhamnh.org
Will search UCC records prior to 7/2001 and current liens only. Real estate records located in Coos County. **Other Phone Numbers:** Assessor 603-466-3322; Vital Records 603-466-2744.

Goshen Town

Town Clerk, PO Box 58, Goshen, NH 03752. 603-863-5655; Fax 603-863-6139.
Will search UCC records prior to 7/2001 and current liens only. This agency will not do a tax lien search. Real estate records located in Sullivan County. **Other Phone Numbers:** Assessor 603-863-5080.

Grafton County

Registry of Deeds, 3785 Dartmouth College Hwy, Box 2, North Haverhill, NH 03774-9700. Registry of Deeds, R/E and UCC Recording 603-787-6921; Fax 603-787-2363.
This agency will not search real estate or UCC records. **Online Access:** Real Estate, Lien Records. Access to the County dial-up service requires a $100 set up fee and $40 per month access fee. Two years of data are kept on system; prior years on CD. Lending agency information is available. A fax-back service is available in-state only. For further information, call 603-787-6921. **Other Phone Numbers:** Treasurer 603-787-6941; Elections 603-787-6941.

Grafton Town

Town Clerk, PO Box 297, Grafton, NH 03240. 603-523-7270 R/E Recording: 603-523-7700; Fax 603-523-4397.
Will search UCC records prior to 7/2001 and current liens only. Real estate records located in Grafton County. **Other Phone Numbers:** Treasurer 603-523-7700; Appraiser/Auditor 603-523-7700; Elections 603-523-7270; Vital Records 603-523-7270.

Grantham Town

Town Clerk, PO Box 135, Grantham, NH 03753-0135. 603-863-5608; Fax 603-863-4499.
Will search UCC records prior to 7/2001 and current liens only. This agency will not do a tax lien search. Real estate records located in Sullivan County. **Other Phone Numbers:** Assessor 603-863-5608; Treasurer 603-863-5608.

Greenfield Town

Town Clerk, PO Box 256, Greenfield, NH 03047. 603-547-2782; Fax 603-547-3004. http://greenfieldnh.org
Will search UCC records prior to 7/2001 and current liens only. Real estate records located in Hillsborough County.

Greenland Town

Town Clerk, PO Box 100, Greenland, NH 03840-0100. Town Clerk, R/E and UCC Recording 603-431-7111; Fax 603-430-3761.

Will search UCC records prior to 7/2001 and current liens only. Real estate records located in Rockingham County. **Online Access:** Assessor, Property Records. Access is via a private company at http://data.visionappraisal.com/GreenlandNH. Free registration is required to view full data. **Other Phone Numbers:** Assessor 603-431-7111; Treasurer 603-431-7111; Appraiser/Auditor 603-431-7111; Elections 603-431-7111; Vital Records 603-431-7111.

Greenville Town

Town Clerk, PO Box 354, Greenville, NH 03048-0354. 603-878-4155; Fax 603-878-4645.

Will search UCC records prior to 7/2001 and current liens only. Real estate records located in Hillsborough County. **Other Phones:** Assessor 603-878-2084.

Groton Town

Town Clerk, 63-1 N. Groton Rd, Groton, NH 03241. 603-744-8849.

Will search UCC records prior to 7/2001 and current liens only. This agency will not do a tax lien search. Real estate records located in Grafton County.

Hampstead Town

Town Clerk, PO Box 298, Hampstead, NH 03841. 603-329-4100; Fax 603-329-7174.

Will search UCC records prior to 7/2001 and current liens only. Real estate records located in Rockingham County.

Hampton Falls Town

Town Clerk, 1 Drinkwater Road, Town Hall, Hampton Falls, NH 03844. 603-926-4618 R/E Recording: 603-929-0828; Fax 603-926-1848.

Will search UCC records prior to 7/2001 and current liens only. Real estate records located in Rockingham County. **Other Phone Numbers:** Assessor 603-929-0828; Treasurer 603-929-3613; Elections 603-926-4618; Vital Records 603-926-4618; Town Hall 603-926-7101.

Hampton Town

Town Clerk, 100 Winnacunnet Road, Hampton, NH 03842. 603-926-0406; Fax 603-929-5917.

Will search UCC records prior to 7/2001 and current liens only. Real estate records located in Rockingham County. **Other Phone Numbers:** Assessor 603-929-5923; Elections 603-926-0406; Vital Records 603-926-0406.

Hancock Town

Town Clerk, PO Box 6, Hancock, NH 03449. 603-525-4441; Fax 603-525-9327.

Will search UCC records prior to 7/2001 and current liens only. Real estate records located in Hillsborough County. **Other Phone Numbers:** Assessor 603-525-4441; Treasurer 603-525-4441.

Hanover Town

Town Clerk, PO Box 483, Hanover, NH 03755-0483. 603-643-4123; Fax 603-643-1720.

Will search UCC records prior to 7/2001 and current liens only. Real estate records located in Grafton County. **Other Phone Numbers:** Assessor 603-643-0703; Treasurer 603-643-4123.

Harrisville Town

Town Clerk, PO Box 284, Harrisville, NH 03450. 603-827-5546; Fax 603-827-2917.

Will search UCC records prior to 7/2001 and current liens only. Real estate records located in Cheshire County.

Hart's Location Town

Town Clerk, 5 Forest Rd, Hart's Location, NH 03812. 603-374-2436.

Will search UCC records prior to 7/2001 and current liens only. UCC search includes tax liens if requested. Real estate records located in Carroll County.

Haverhill Town

Town Clerk, 2975 Dartmouth College Hwy, N. Haverhill, NH 03774. 603-787-6200 R/E Recording: 603-787-6444; Fax 603-787-2226.

Will search UCC records prior to 7/2001 and current liens only. Real estate records located in Grafton County. **Other Phone Numbers:** Assessor 603-787-6444; Treasurer 603-747-2735.

Hebron Town

Town Clerk, HC 58, Box 286, East Hebron, NH 03232. 603-744-7999; Fax 603-744-7999.

Will search UCC records prior to 7/2001 and current liens only. This agency will not do a tax lien search. Real estate records located in Grafton County.

Henniker Town

Town Clerk, 2 Depot Hill Road, Henniker, NH 03242. Town Clerk, R/E and UCC Recording 603-428-3240; Fax 603-428-4366.

Will search UCC records prior to 7/2001 and current liens only. Real estate records located in Merrimack County. **Other Phone Numbers:** Assessor 603-428-3221; Elections 603-428-3240; Vital Records 603-428-3240.

Hill Town

Town Clerk, PO Box 251, Hill, NH 03243. 603-934-3951; Fax 603-934-1094.

Will search UCC records prior to 7/2001 and current liens only. Real estate records located in Merrimack County.

Hillsborough County

Register of Deeds, PO Box 370, Nashua, NH 03061-0370. 603-882-6933; Fax 603-594-4137.

Will search UCC records prior to 7/2001 and current liens only. Will not search real estate records. **Online Access:** Real Estate, Deed, Mortgage, Lien Records. Access to county register of deeds data is available free at www.nhdeeds.com/hils/web/argthc.htm. Online records go back to 1966.

Hillsborough Town

Town Clerk, PO Box 1699, Hillsborough, NH 03244. 603-464-5571; Fax 603-464-4270.

Will search UCC records prior to 7/2001 and current liens only. Real estate records located in Hillsborough County. **Other Phone Numbers:** Assessor 603-464-3877.

Hinsdale Town

Town Clerk, PO Box 31, Hinsdale, NH 03451. 603-336-5719.

Will search UCC records prior to 7/2001 and current liens only. This agency will not do a tax lien search. Real estate records located in Cheshire County.

Holderness Town

Town Clerk, PO Box 203, Holderness, NH 03245. 603-968-7536; Fax 603-968-9954.

Will search UCC records prior to 7/2001 and current liens only. Real estate records located in Grafton County.

Hollis Town

Town Clerk, 7 Monument Square, Hollis, NH 03049-6568. 603-465-2064; Fax 603-465-2964.

Will search UCC records prior to 7/2001 and current liens only. Real estate records located in Hillsborough County. **Online Access:** Property Assessor Records. Search the town assessor database at http://data.visionappraisal.com/HollisNH. Free registration required.

Hooksett Town

Town Clerk, 16 N. Main St, Hooksett, NH 03106. 603-485-9534; Fax 603-485-4423.

Will search UCC records prior to 7/2001 and current liens only. Real estate records located in Merrimack County. **Other Phone Numbers:** Assessor 603-268-0003.

Hopkinton Town

Town Clerk, PO Box 446, Contoocook, NH 03229-0446. 603-746-3180; Fax 603-746-4011. www.hopkintonnh.org

Will search UCC records prior to 7/2001 and current liens only. Real estate records located in Merrimack County. **Other Phone Numbers:** Assessor 603-746-3170; Treasurer 603-746-3180.

Hudson Town

Town Clerk, 12 School St, Hudson, NH 03051-4294. 603-886-6003.

Will search UCC records prior to 7/2001 and current liens only. UCC search includes tax liens if requested. Real estate records located in Hillsborough County. **Other Phone Numbers:** Assessor 603-886-6024; Treasurer 603-886-6000.

Jackson Town

Town Clerk, PO Box 336, Jackson, NH 03846-0336. 603-383-6248; Fax 603-383-6980.

Will search UCC records prior to 7/2001 and current liens only. Real estate records located in Carroll County. **Other Phone Numbers:** Assessor 603-383-4223.

Jaffrey Town

Town Clerk, 10 Goodnow St., Jaffrey, NH 03452. 603-532-7861; Fax 603-532-7862.

Will search UCC records prior to 7/2001 and current liens only. Real estate records located in Cheshire County. **Other Phone Numbers:** Assessor 603-532-7445; Treasurer 603-532-7445.

Jefferson Town

Town Clerk, RFD #1 Box 162A, Jefferson, NH 03583. 603-586-4553; Fax 603-586-4553.

Will search UCC records prior to 7/2001 and current liens only. Real estate records located in Coos County. **Other Phone Numbers:** Assessor 603-586-4553; Treasurer 603-586-4400; Appraiser/Auditor 603-586-4553; Elections 603-586-4553.

Keene City

City Clerk, 3 Washington St, Keene, NH 03431. 603-352-0133; Fax 603-357-9884.

Will search UCC records prior to 7/2001 and current liens only. Real estate records located in Cheshire County. **Other Phone Numbers:** Assessor 603-352-2125; Treasurer 603-357-9801.

Kensington Town

Town Clerk, Town Hall, 95 Amesbury Rd., Rte 150, Kensington, NH 03833. Town Clerk, R/E and UCC Recording 603-772-5423; Fax 603-772-6841. http://town.kensington.nh.us

Will search UCC records prior to 7/2001 and current liens only. Real estate records located in Rockingham County. **Other Phone Numbers:** Assessor 603-436-

5916; Treasurer 603-772-5423; Elections 603-772-5423; Vital Records 603-772-5423.

Kingston Town

Town Clerk, PO Box 657, Kingston, NH 03848-0657. 603-642-3112; Fax 603-642-3204.
Will search UCC records prior to 7/2001 and current liens only. Real estate records located in Rockingham County. **Other Phone Numbers:** Assessor 603-642-3342; Treasurer 603-643-8195.

Laconia City

City Clerk, PO Box 489, Laconia, NH 03247. 603-527-1265 R/E Recording: 603-527-5420; Fax 603-524-1766. http://data.visionappraisal.com/LaconiaNH
Will search UCC records prior to 7/2001 and current liens only. Real estate records located in Belknap County. **Online Access:** Assessor Records. Property records on the Town assessor database are available online at http://data.visionappraisal.com/LaconiaNH. Free registration is required for full access. **Other Phone Numbers:** Assessor 603-527-1268; Treasurer 603-524-3877; Elections 603-527-1265; Vital Records 603-527-1265; Tax Office 603-527-1269.

Lancaster Town

Town Clerk, 25 Main St, Lancaster, NH 03584. 603-788-2306; Fax 603-788-2114.
Will search UCC records prior to 7/2001 and current liens only. Real estate records located in Coos County. **Other Phone Numbers:** Assessor 603-788-3391; Treasurer 603-788-3391.

Landaff Town

Town Clerk, PO Box 125, Landaff, NH 03585. 603-838-6220; Fax 603-838-6220.
Will search UCC records prior to 7/2001 and current liens only. UCC search includes tax liens. Real estate records located in Grafton County. **Other Phones:** Assessor 207-778-3881; Treasurer 603-835-2907.

Langdon Town

Town Clerk, 5 Walker Hill Rd, Langdon Town Hall, Langdon, NH 03602. 603-835-2389; Fax 603-835-2389.
Will search UCC records prior to 7/2001 and current liens only. UCC search includes tax liens. Real estate records located in Sullivan County.

Lebanon City

City Clerk, 51 N. Park St, Lebanon, NH 03766. 603-448-3054; Fax 603-448-4891. www.lebcity.com
Will search UCC records prior to 7/2001 and current liens only. Real estate records located in Grafton County. **Online Access:** Assessor Records. Records from the city assessor database are available free online at http://data.visionappraisal.com/LEBANONNH. Free registration is required to view full data. **Other Phone Numbers:** Assessor 603-448-1499; Elections 603-448-3054; Vital Records 603-448-3054.

Lee Town

Town Clerk, 7 Mast Road, Town Hall, Lee, NH 03824. 603-659-2964; Fax 603-659-7202.
Will search UCC records prior to 7/2001 and current liens only. Real estate records located in Strafford County. **Other Phone Numbers:** Assessor 603-659-5414; Treasurer 603-659-5414; Appraiser/Auditor 603-659-5414; Elections 603-659-2964; Vital Records 603-659-2964.

Lempster Town

Town Clerk, PO Box 33, East Lempster, NH 03605-0033. 603-863-3213; Fax 603-863-8105.
Will search UCC records prior to 7/2001 and current liens only. Real estate records located in Sullivan County. **Other Phones:** Treasurer 603-863-3213.

Lincoln Town

Town Clerk, PO Box 25, Lincoln, NH 03251. 603-745-8971; Fax 603-745-6743.
Will search UCC records prior to 7/2001 and current liens only. UCC search includes tax liens if requested. Real estate records located in Grafton County. **Other Phone Numbers:** Assessor 603-745-2757; Treasurer 603-745-8971.

Lisbon Town

Town Clerk, 21 School St, Lisbon, NH 03585. 603-838-2862; Fax 603-838-6790.
Will search UCC records prior to 7/2001 and current liens only. Real estate records located in Grafton County. **Other Phone Numbers:** Assessor 603-838-6377.

Litchfield Town

Town Clerk, 2 Liberty Way, Suite 3, Litchfield, NH 03052. 603-424-4045 R/E Recording: 603-882-6933.
Will search UCC records prior to 7/2001 and current liens only. This agency will not do a tax lien search. Real estate records located in Hillsborough County. **Other Phone Numbers:** Assessor 603-424-4046; Vital Records 603-424-4045.

Littleton Town

Town Clerk, 125 Main St #200, Littleton, NH 03561. 603-444-3995 x40 UCC Recording: 603-444-3995; Fax 603-444-1715.
Will search UCC records prior to 7/2001 and current liens only. Real estate records located in Grafton County. **Other Phone Numbers:** Assessor 603-444-3995 x16.

Londonderry Town

Town Clerk, 50 Nashua Rd., Suite 100, Londonderry, NH 03053. 603-432-1100 x133 R/E Recording: 603-432-1100 x135 UCC Recording: 603-432-1100 x118; Fax 603-432-1142. www.londonderry.org
Will search UCC records prior to 7/2001 and current liens only. Real estate records located in Rockingham County. **Other Phone Numbers:** Assessor 603-432-1120; Treasurer 603-432-1126; Appraiser/Auditor 603-432-1100 x119; Elections 603-432-1100 x114; Vital Records 603-432-1100 x118.

Loudon Town

Town Clerk, PO Box 7837, Loudon, NH 03301. 603-798-4542 R/E Recording: 603-798-4541; Fax 603-798-4546.
Will search UCC records prior to 7/2001 and current liens only. Real estate records located in Merrimack County. **Other Phone Numbers:** Assessor 603-798-4541; Treasurer 603-798-4541; Elections 603-798-4542; Vital Records 603-798-4542.

Lyman Town

Town Clerk, 65 Parker Hill Rd, Lyman, NH 03585. 603-838-6113; Fax 603-838-6818.
Will search UCC records prior to 7/2001 and current liens only. Real estate records located in Grafton County. **Other Phone Numbers:** Assessor 603-838-5900; Treasurer 603-838-6689.

Lyme Town

Town Clerk, PO Box 342, Lyme, NH 03768. 603-795-2535 R/E Recording: 603-795-4639 (Selectmen's office); Fax 603-795-4637.
Will search UCC records. This agency will not do a tax lien search. Real estate records located in Grafton County. **Other Phone Numbers:** Assessor 603-795-4639 (Selectmen's office); Treasurer 603-795-4639 (Selectmen's office); Elections 603-795-2535; Vital Records 603-795-2535.

Lyndeborough Town

Town Clerk, PO Box 164, Lyndeborough, NH 03082. 603-654-9653; Fax 603-654-5777.
Will search UCC records prior to 7/2001 and current liens only. UCC search includes tax liens if requested. Real estate records located in Hillsborough County. **Other Phone Numbers:** Assessor 603-654-5955.

Madbury Town

Town Clerk, 13 Town Hall Road, Madbury, NH 03820-9510. 603-742-5131; Fax 603-742-2505.
Will search UCC records prior to 7/2001 and current liens only. Real estate records located in Strafford County. **Other Phones:** Assessor 603-742-5131.

Madison Town

Town Clerk, PO Box 248, Madison, NH 03849. 603-367-9931 R/E Recording: 603-538-4872 UCC Recording: 603-367-3276; Fax 603-367-4547.
Will search UCC records prior to 7/2001 and current liens only. Real estate records located in Carroll County. **Other Phone Numbers:** Assessor 603-367-4332; Treasurer 603-367-4332; Elections 603-367-9931; Vital Records 603-367-9931.

Manchester City

City Clerk, One City Hall Plaza, Manchester, NH 03101. 603-624-6455 R/E Recording: 603-624-6520; Fax 603-624-6481.
Will search UCC records prior to 7/2001 and current liens only. UCC search includes tax liens. Real estate records located in Hillsborough County. **Other Phone Numbers:** Assessor 603-624-6520; Treasurer 603-624-6460; Elections 603-624-6455; Vital Records 603-624-6455.

Marlborough Town

Town Clerk, PO Box 487, Marlborough, NH 03455-0487. 603-876-4529 R/E Recording: 603-876-3751; Fax 603-876-3313.
Will search UCC records prior to 7/2001 and current liens only. Real estate records located in Cheshire County. **Other Phone Numbers:** Assessor 603-876-4529; Treasurer 603-876-3842; Appraiser/Auditor 603-876-3751; Elections 603-876-4529; Vital Records 603-876-4703.

Marlow Town

Tax Collector, PO Box 184, Marlow, NH 03456. 603-446-2245; Fax 603-446-3806. www.marlow-nh.com/
Will search UCC records prior to 7/2001 and current liens only. Real estate records located in Cheshire County. **Other Phones:** Treasurer 603-446-2245; Elections 603-446-2245; Vital Records 603-446-2245.

Mason Town

Town Clerk, 16 Darling Hill Rd., Mason, NH 03048-4717. Town Clerk, R/E and UCC Recording 603-878-2070; Fax 603-878-6146.
Will search UCC records prior to 7/2001 and current liens only. Real estate records located in Hillsborough County. **Other Phone Numbers:** Assessor 603-878-2070; Treasurer 603-878-2098; Appraiser/Auditor 603-878-2070; Elections 603-878-3801; Vital Records 603-878-2070.

Meredith Town

Town Clerk, 41 Main St, Meredith, NH 03253-9704. 603-279-4538; Fax 603-279-1042.
Will search UCC records prior to 7/2001 and current liens only. Real estate records located in Belknap County.

Merrimack County

Register of Deeds, PO Box 248, Concord, NH 03302-0248. 603-228-0101; Fax 603-226-0868. www.nhdeeds.com
Will not search any records. Will not search real estate records. **Online Access:** Real Estate Records. Records on the county Registry of Deeds database are available free online at www.nhdeeds.com. **Other Phone Numbers:** Vital Records 603-271-4650 (State).

Merrimack Town

Town Clerk, PO Box 27, Merrimack, NH 03054. 603-424-3651; www.ci.merrimack.nh.us
Will search UCC records prior to 7/2001 and current liens only. UCC search includes tax liens if requested. Real estate records located in Hillsborough County. **Other Phone Numbers:** Assessor 603-424-5136; Treasurer 603-424-3531.

Middleton Town

Town Clerk, Middleton Town Offices, 182 Kings Highway, Middleton, NH 03887. 603-473-2576; Fax 603-473-2577.
Will search UCC records prior to 7/2001 and current liens only. Real estate records located in Strafford County. **Other Phone Numbers:** Assessor 603-473-2261; Treasurer 603-473-2134.

Milan Town

Town Clerk, PO Box 158, Milan, NH 03588. 603-449-3461; Fax 603-449-2142.
Will search UCC records prior to 7/2001 and current liens only. Real estate records located in Coos County.

Milford Town

Town Clerk, 1 Union Square, Milford, NH 03055. 603-673-3403; Fax 603-673-2273.
Will search UCC records. Real estate records located in Hillsborough County. **Other Phone Numbers:** Assessor 603-672-0525; Treasurer 603-672-1061; Elections 603-673-3403; Vital Records 603-673-3403.

Milton Town

Town Clerk, PO Box 180, Milton, NH 03851-0180. 603-652-9414; Fax 603-652-4120. www.miltonnh-us.com
Will search UCC records prior to 7/2001 and current liens only. Real estate records located in Strafford County. **Other Phones:** Assessor 603-652-4501; Treasurer 603-652-4501; Elections 603-652-9414.

Monroe Town

Treasurer, PO Box 63, Monroe, NH 03771-0063. 603-638-2644; Fax 603-638-2021.
Will search UCC records. Real estate records located in Grafton County. **Other Phones:** Assessor 603-638-2644; Treasurer 603-638-2644; Appraiser/Auditor 603-638-2644; Vital Records 603-638-2644.

Mont Vernon Town

Town Clerk, Box 444, Mont Vernon, NH 03057. 603-673-9126; Fax 603-672-9021.
Will search UCC records prior to 7/2001 and current liens only. This agency will not do a tax lien search. Real estate records located in Hillsborough County. **Other Phone Numbers:** Assessor 603-673-9126.

Moultonborough Town

Town Clerk, PO Box 15, Moultonborough, NH 03254. Town Clerk, R/E and UCC Recording 603-476-2347; Fax 603-476-5835.
Will search UCC records. Real estate records located in Carroll County. **Other Phone Numbers:** Assessor 603-476-2347; Treasurer 603-476-2347; Appraiser/Auditor 603-476-2347; Elections 603-476-2347; Vital Records 603-476-2347.

Nashua City

City Clerk, 229 Main St, Nashua, NH 03061-2019. 603-589-3010.
Will search UCC records prior to 7/2001 and current liens only. Real estate records located in Hillsborough County. **Online Access:** Property Assessor Records. Search the City Assessor database for free at www.ci.nashua.nh.us/defaulto.asp?url=/welcome.asp. **Other Phone Numbers:** Assessor 603-594-3040.

Nelson Town

Town Clerk, HCR 33 Box 660, Nelson, NH 03457. 603-847-9043 R/E Recording: 603-847-0047; Fax 603-847-9043.
Will search UCC records prior to 7/2001 and current liens only. Real estate records located in Cheshire County. **Other Phone Numbers:** Assessor 603-847-9043; Treasurer 603-847-9043; Appraiser/Auditor 603-847-0047; Elections 603-847-9043; Vital Records 603-847-9043.

New Boston Town

Town Clerk, PO Box 250, New Boston, NH 03070-0250. 603-487-5571; Fax 603-487-2975. www.new-boston.nh.us
Will search UCC records prior to 7/2001 and current liens only. This agency will not do a tax lien search. Real estate records located in Hillsborough County. **Other Phone Numbers:** Assessor 603-487-5504; Treasurer 603-487-5504; Elections 603-487-5571; Vital Records 603-487-5571.

New Castle Town

Town Clerk, PO Box 367, New Castle, NH 03854-0367. Town Clerk, R/E and UCC Recording 603-431-6710; Fax 603-433-6198.
Will search UCC records prior to 7/2001 and current liens only. Real estate records located in Rockingham County. **Other Phones:** Assessor 603-431-6710; Treasurer 603-431-6710; Appraiser 603-431-6710; Elections 603-431-6710; Vital Records 603-431-6710.

New Durham Town

Town Clerk, PO Box 207, New Durham, NH 03855. 603-859-2091; Fax 603-859-6644.
Will search UCC records prior to 7/2001 and current liens only. Real estate records located in Strafford County.

New Hampton Town

Town Clerk, PO Box 538, New Hampton, NH 03256. 603-744-8454; Fax 603-744-5106. www.new-hampton.nh.us
Will search UCC records prior to 7/2001 and current liens only. Real estate records located in Belknap County. **Other Phone Numbers:** Elections 603-744-8454; Vital Records 603-744-8454.

New Ipswich Town

Town Clerk, 661 Turnpike Rd., New Ipswich, NH 03071. 603-878-3567; Fax 603-878-3855.
Will search UCC records prior to 7/2001 and current liens only. Real estate records located in Hillsborough County. **Other Phone Numbers:** Assessor 603-878-2772; Treasurer 603-878-2772.

New London Town

Town Clerk, PO Box 314, New London, NH 03257-0314. 603-526-4046; Fax 603-526-9494.
Will search UCC records prior to 7/2001 and current liens only. Real estate records located in Merrimack County. **Online Access:** Property Appraiser Records. Search the town assessor database at http://data.visionappraisal.com/HollisNH. Free registration required. **Other Phone Numbers:** Assessor 603-526-4821; Treasurer 603-526-4821; Elections 603-526-4046; Vital Records 603-526-4046.

Newbury Town

Town Clerk, PO Box 253, Newbury, NH 03255. 603-763-5326.
Will search UCC records prior to 7/2001 and current liens only. This agency will not do a tax lien search. Real estate records located in Merrimack County. **Other Phone Numbers:** Assessor 603-763-4940; Treasurer 603-763-4940.

Newfields Town

Town Clerk, PO Box 300, Newfields, NH 03856-0300. Town Clerk, R/E and UCC Recording 603-772-5070; Fax 603-772-9004.
Will search UCC records prior to 7/2001 and current liens only. Real estate records located in Rockingham County. **Other Phone Numbers:** Assessor 603-772-7047; Treasurer 603-772-7199; Elections 603-772-5070; Vital Records 603-772-5070.

Newington Town

Town Clerk, 205 Nimble Hill Road, Town Offices, Newington, NH 03801. 603-436-7640; Fax 603-436-7188.
Will search UCC records prior to 7/2001 and current liens only. Real estate records located in Rockingham County. **Other Phones:** Assessor 603-436-7640.

Newmarket Town

Town Clerk, 186 Main St, Town Hall, Newmarket, NH 03857. 603-659-3073; Fax 603-659-3441. www.visionappraisal.com
Will search UCC records prior to 7/2001 and current liens only. Real estate records located in Rockingham County. **Online Access:** Assessor, Property Records. Access is via a private company at http://data.visionappraisal.com/NewMarketNH. You may apply for a free registered user ID (more data) or search anonymously (less data, no name searching). **Other Phone Numbers:** Assessor 603-659-3073.

Newport Town

Town Clerk, 15 Sunapee St, Newport, NH 03773. 603-863-2224 R/E Recording: 603-863-6407; Fax 603-863-8008.
Will search UCC records prior to 7/2001 and current liens only. Real estate records located in Sullivan County. **Other Phone Numbers:** Assessor 603-863-6407; Treasurer 603-863-3000; Appraiser/Auditor 603-863-6407; Elections 603-863-2224; Vital Records 603-863-2224.

Newton Town

Tax Collector, Box 375, Newton, NH 03858-0375. Tax Collector, R/E and UCC Recording 603-382-4096; Fax 603-382-9140.
Will search UCC records prior to 7/2001 and current liens only. Real estate records located in Rockingham County. **Other Phone Numbers:** Assessor 603-382-4405; Treasurer 603-382-4405; Appraiser/Auditor 603-382-4405; Elections 603-382-4096; Vital Records 603-382-4096.

North Hampton Town

Town Clerk, PO Box 141, North Hampton, NH 03862-0141. 603-964-6029 R/E Recording: 603-964-8087; Fax 603-964-1514. www.north-hampton-nh.com
Will search UCC records prior to 7/2001 and current liens only. Real estate records located in Rockingham County. **Other Phone Numbers:** Assessor 603-964-8087; Treasurer 603-964-8087; Elections 603-964-6029; Vital Records 603-964-6029.

Northfield Town

Town Clerk, 21 Summer St, Northfield, NH 03276. 603-286-4482; Fax 603-286-3328.
Will search UCC records. Real estate records located in Merrimack County. **Other Phone Numbers:** Assessor 603-286-7039; Elections 603-286-4482; Vital Records 603-286-4482.

Northumberland Town

Town Clerk, 2 State St, Groveton, NH 03582. 603-636-1451 UCC Recording: 603-636-1450; Fax 603-636-1450.
Will search UCC records prior to 7/2001 and current liens only. Real estate records located in Coos County. **Other Phones:** Assessor 603-636-1450; Appraiser/ Auditor 603-636-1450; Elections 603-636-1450.

Northwood Town

Town Clerk, PO Box 314, Northwood, NH 03261-0314. 603-942-5422; Fax 603-942-9107.
Will search UCC records. Real estate records located in Rockingham County. **Other Phone Numbers:** Assessor 603-942-5586; Vital Records 603-942-5422.

Nottingham Town

Town Clerk, PO Box 114, Nottingham, NH 03290. 603-679-1630; Fax 603-679-1013.
Will search UCC records prior to 7/2001 and current liens only. UCC search includes tax liens. Real estate records located in Rockingham County. **Other Phone Numbers:** Assessor 603-679-5022.

Orford Town

Town Clerk, Clerk's Office, RR 1 Box 243, Orford, NH 03777. 603-353-4404.
Will not search UCC records. UCC search includes tax liens if requested. Real estate records located in Grafton County. **Other Phones:** Assessor 603-353-4404.

Ossipee Town

Town Clerk, PO Box 67, Center Ossipee, NH 03814. 603-539-2008 R/E Recording: 603-539-4872; Fax 603-539-4183.
Will search UCC records prior to 7/2001 and current liens only. Real estate records located in Carroll County. **Other Phone Numbers:** Assessor 603-539-4181; Treasurer 603-539-4181; Elections 603-539-2008; Vital Records 603-539-2008.

Pelham Town

Town Clerk, 6 Main St, Town Hall, Pelham, NH 03076. 603-635-2040; Fax 603-635-6954.
Will search UCC records prior to 7/2001 and current liens only. Real estate records located in Hillsborough County **Other Phones:** Assessor 603-635-3317.

Pembroke Town

Town Clerk, 311 Pembroke St, Pembroke, NH 03275. 603-485-4747; Fax 603-485-3967.
Will search UCC records prior to 7/2001 and current liens only. Real estate records located in Merrimack County. **Other Phones:** Assessor 603-485-4747.

Peterborough Town

Tax Collector, 1 Grove St, Peterborough, NH 03458. 603-924-8010 R/E Recording: 603-924-8020; Fax 603-924-8001. www.townofpeterborough.com
Will search UCC records prior to 7/2001 and current liens only. Real estate records located in Hillsborough County. **Other Phone Numbers:** Assessor 603-924-8000; Treasurer 603-924-7155; Elections 603-924-8010; Vital Records 603-924-8010.

Piermont Town

Town Clerk, PO Box 27, Piermont, NH 03779. 603-272-4840; Fax 603-272-4947.
Will search UCC records prior to 7/2001 and current liens only. Real estate records located in Grafton County.

Pittsburg Town

Town Clerk, RD 1, Box 581, Pittsburg, NH 03592. 603-538-6699 R/E Recording: 603-538-6697; Fax 603-538-6697.
Will search UCC records prior to 7/2001 and current liens only. Real estate records located in Coos County. **Other Phone Numbers:** Assessor 603-538-6697; Treasurer 603-538-6697; Elections 603-538-6699; Vital Records 603-538-6699.

Pittsfield Town

Town Clerk, Box 98, Pittsfield, NH 03263-0098. 603-435-6773; Fax 603-435-7922. www.pittsfield-nh.com
Will search UCC records prior to 7/2001 and current liens only. Real estate records located in Merrimack County. **Other Phones:** Assessor 603-435-6773.

Plainfield Town

Town Clerk, Town Clerk's Office, Box 380, Meriden, NH 03770. 603-469-3201; Fax 603-469-3642.
Will search UCC records prior to 7/2001 and current liens only. Real estate records located in Sullivan County. **Other Phones:** Assessor 603-469-3201; Elections 603-469-3201; Vital Records 603-469-3201.

Plaistow Town

Town Clerk, 145 Main St, Town Hall, Suite 2, Plaistow, NH 03865. 603-382-8129; Fax 603-382-7183.
Will search UCC records prior to 7/2001 and current liens only. Real estate records located in Rockingham County. **Other Phone Numbers:** Assessor 603-382-8469; Treasurer 603-382-8469.

Plymouth Town

Town Clerk, 6 PO Square, Town Hall, Plymouth, NH 03264. 603-536-1732; Fax 603-536-0036.
Will search UCC records prior to 7/2001 and current liens only. Real estate records located in Grafton County. **Other Phones:** Assessor 603-536-1731.

Portsmouth City

City Clerk, PO Box 628, Portsmouth, NH 03802-0628. 603-431-2000; Fax 603-427-1526.
Will search UCC records prior to 7/2001 and current liens only. Real estate records located in Rockingham County. **Online Access:** Assessor Records. Records from the Portsmouth Assessed Property Values database are available free online at www.portsmouthnh.com/realestate/index.html. **Other Phone Numbers:** Assessor 603-431-2000 x212; Treasurer 603-431-2000 x221.

Randolph Town

Town Clerk, RD 1, Town Hall, Randolph, NH 03570. 603-466-5771; Fax 603-466-9856.
Will search UCC records prior to 7/2001 and current liens only. This agency will not do a tax lien search. Real estate records located in Coos County.

Raymond Town

Town Clerk, Epping St, Town Office Building, Raymond, NH 03077. 603-895-4735 X110 R/E Recording: 603-895-4735 UCC Recording: 603-895-4735; Fax 603-895-0903.
Will search UCC records prior to 7/2001 and current liens only. Real estate records located in Rockingham County. **Online Access:** Assessor Records. Free access via a private company to the Town assessor database is available online at http://data.visionappraisal.com/ RaymondNH. Free registration is required to view full data. **Other Phone Numbers:** Assessor 603-895-4735;

Treasurer 603-895-4735; Elections 603-895-4735; Vital Records 603-895-4735.

Richmond Town

Town Clerk, 105 Old Homestead Hwy., Richmond, NH 03470. 603-239-6202.
Will search UCC records prior to 7/2001 and current liens only. Tax liens not included in UCC search. Real estate records located in Cheshire County. **Other Phone Numbers:** Assessor 603-239-4202; Elections 603-239-6202; Vital Records 603-239-6202.

Rindge Town

Town Clerk, PO Box 11, Rindge, NH 03461. Town Clerk, R/E and UCC Recording 603-899-3354; Fax 603-899-2101.
See Town Tax Collector for property tax liens. Will search UCC records prior to 7/2001 and current liens only. Separate federal and state tax lien search costs same as UCC search. Real estate records and property tax liens are found at the town tax collector. **Other Phone Numbers:** Assessor 603-899-5181; Treasurer 603-899-5579; Elections 603-899-5539; Vital Records 603-899-3354.

Rochester City

City Clerk, 31 Wakefield St, City Hall, Rochester, NH 03867-1917. 603-332-2130; Fax 603-335-7565.
Will search UCC records. Real estate records located in Strafford County. **Other Phone Numbers:** Assessor 603-332-5109; Treasurer 603-335-7502; Appraiser/ Auditor 603-332-5109; Elections 603-332-2130; Vital Records 603-332-2130.

Rockingham County

Register of Deeds, PO Box 896, Kingston, NH 03848. 603-642-5526; Fax 603-642-8548.
For Assessor data, you must contact the Tax Assessor for each town within the county. Will search UCC records prior to 7/2001 and current liens only. Will not search real estate records. **Online Access:** Most Wanted Records. The sheriff's most wanted list is available free at www.co.rockingham.nh.us/sheriff/warrants.htm.

Rollinsford Town

Town Clerk, PO Box 309, Rollinsford, NH 03869. 603-742-2510; Fax 603-740-0254.
Will search UCC records prior to 7/2001 and current liens only. Real estate records located in Strafford County.

Roxbury Town

Town Clerk, 404 Branch Rd., Roxbury, NH 03431. 603-352-4903.
Will search UCC records prior to 7/2001 and current liens only. This agency will not do a tax lien search. Real estate records located in Cheshire County.

Rumney Town

Town Clerk, PO Box 275, 79 Depot St, Rumney, NH 03266. 603-786-2237; Fax 603-786-2237.
Will search UCC records prior to 7/2001 and current liens only. Real estate records located in Grafton County. **Other Phones:** Assessor 603-786-9511.

Rye Town

Town Clerk, 10 Central Road, Rye, NH 03870. 603-964-8562; Fax 603-964-4132.
Will search UCC records prior to 7/2001 and current liens only. Real estate records located in Rockingham County. **Online Access:** Assessor, Property Records. Access is via a private company at http://data.visionappraisal.com/RyeNH. Free registration is required to view full data. **Other Phone Numbers:** Assessor 603-964-5523.

Salem Town

Town Clerk, 33 Geremonty Drive, Municipal Building, Salem, NH 03079-3390. 603-890-2110 UCC Recording: 603-890-2116; Fax 603-898-1223. www.ci.salem.nh.us
Will search UCC records prior to 7/2001 and current liens only. UCC search includes tax liens. Real estate records located in Rockingham County. **Online Access:** Assessor, Property Records. Records from the Town database are available free online at http://data.visionappraisal.com/SalemNH. Registration is required, no charge. **Other Phone Numbers:** Assessor 603-893-5731.

Salisbury Town

Town Clerk, RFD Box 180, Franklin Rd., Salisbury, NH 03268-0180. Town Clerk, R/E and UCC Recording 603-648-2473; Fax 603-648-6658.
Will search UCC records prior to 7/2001 and current liens only. Real estate records located in Merrimack County. **Other Phone Numbers:** Assessor 603-648-2473; Treasurer 603-648-2473; Appraiser/Auditor 603-648-2473; Elections 603-648-2473; Vital Records 603-648-2473.

Sanbornton Town

Town Clerk, PO Box 124, Sanbornton, NH 03269. 603-286-4034; Fax 603-286-9544.
Will search UCC records prior to 7/2001 and current liens only. Real estate records located in Belknap County. **Other Phone Numbers:** Assessor 603-286-8303.

Sandown Town

Town Clerk, 320 Main St, Town Hall, Sandown, NH 03873-2627. 603-887-4870 R/E Recording: 603-887-3646; Fax 603-887-5163.
Will search UCC records prior to 7/2001 and current liens only. Real estate records located in Rockingham County. **Other Phone Numbers:** Assessor 603-887-3646; Treasurer 603-887-3646; Elections 603-887-4870; Vital Records 603-887-4870.

Sandwich Town

Town Clerk, PO Box 194, Center Sandwich, NH 03227. 603-284-7113; Fax 603-284-6819.
Will search UCC records prior to 7/2001 and current liens only. Real estate records located in Carroll County.

Seabrook Town

Town Clerk, PO Box 476, Seabrook, NH 03874. 603-474-3152; Fax 603-474-8007.
Will search UCC records prior to 7/2001 and current liens only. UCC search includes tax liens if requested. Real estate records located in Rockingham County. **Other Phone Numbers:** Assessor 603-474-2966.

Sharon Town

Town Clerk, 423 Route 123, Sharon, NH 03458. 603-924-9250; Fax 603-924-9250.
Will search UCC records prior to 7/2001 and current liens only. This agency will not do a tax lien search. Real estate records located in Hillsborough County. **Other Phone Numbers:** Assessor 603-924-9250.

Shelburne Town

Town Clerk, 881 N. Road, Philbrook Farm Inn, Shelburne, NH 03581. 603-466-3831.
Will search UCC records prior to 7/2001 and current liens only. This agency will not do a tax lien search. Real estate records located in Coos County. **Other Phone Numbers:** Assessor 603-466-3926.

Somersworth City

City Clerk, 1 Government Way, Somersworth, NH 03878-9574. 603-692-4262 UCC Recording: 603-692-9511/9512; Fax 603-692-7338.
Will search UCC records prior to 7/2001 and current liens only. Real estate records located in Strafford County. **Other Phone Numbers:** Assessor 603-692-9520/9518.

South Hampton Town

Town Clerk, 3 Hilldale Ave., South Hampton, NH 03827. 603-394-7696.
Will search UCC records prior to 7/2001 and current liens only. This agency will not do a tax lien search. Real estate records located in Rockingham County.

Springfield Town

Town Clerk, PO Box 22, Springfield, NH 03284. 603-763-4805; Fax 603-763-3336.
Will search UCC records prior to 7/2001 and current liens only. Real estate records located in Sullivan County. **Other Phones:** Assessor 603-763-4805.

Stark Town

Town Clerk, 1189 Stark Hwy., Groveton, NH 03582. Town Clerk, R/E and UCC Recording 603-636-2118; Fax 603-636-6199.
Will search UCC records prior to 7/2001 and current liens only. This agency will not do a tax lien search. Real estate records located in Coos County. **Other Phone Numbers:** Assessor 603-636-2118; Treasurer 603-636-2118; Appraiser/Auditor 603-636-2118; Elections 603-636-2118; Vital Records 603-636-2118.

Stewartstown Town

Town Clerk, PO Box 35, West Stewartstown, NH 03597-0035. 603-246-3329; Fax 603-246-3329.
Will search UCC records prior to 7/2001 and current liens only. UCC search includes tax liens if requested. Real estate records located in Coos County. **Other Phone Numbers:** Assessor 603-246-3329.

Stoddard Town

Town Clerk, 2175 Route 9, Stoddard, NH 03464. 603-446-2203 R/E Recording: 603-847-3029; Fax 603-446-2203.
Will search UCC records prior to 7/2001 and current liens only. Real estate records located in Cheshire County. **Other Phone Numbers:** Assessor 603-446-3326; Treasurer 603-446-3442; Appraiser/Auditor 603-446-3326; Elections 603-446-3326; Vital Records 603-446-2203.

Strafford County

Register of Deeds, PO Box 799, Dover, NH 03820. 603-742-1741; Fax 603-749-5130.
Will search UCC records prior to 7/2001 and current liens only. Will not search real estate records. **Online Access:** Real Estate, Deed, Mortgage, Lien Records. Access to county register of deeds data is available free at www.nhdeeds.com/stfd/web/agree3.htm. Online records go back to 1970. **Other Phone Numbers:** Assessor 603-743-6014; Treasurer 603-742-1458.

Strafford Town

Town Clerk, PO Box 169, Strafford, NH 03884-0169. 603-664-2192; Fax 603-664-7276.
Will search UCC records prior to 7/2001 and current liens only. Real estate records located in Strafford County.

Stratford Town

Town Clerk, PO Box 366, North Stratford, NH 03590. 603-922-5598; Fax 603-922-5533.
Will search UCC records prior to 7/2001 and current liens only. Real estate records located in Coos County.

Stratham Town

Town Clerk, 10 Bunker Hill Ave, Stratham, NH 03885. 603-772-4741; Fax 603-775-0517. www.strathamnh.org
Will search UCC records prior to 7/2001 and current liens only. Real estate records located in Rockingham County. **Other Phone Numbers:** Assessor 603-772-4741.

Sugar Hill Town

Town Clerk, Box 574, Sugar Hill, NH 03585. 603-823-8516; Fax 603-823-8446.
Will search UCC records prior to 7/2001 and current liens only. Real estate records located in Grafton County.

Sullivan County

Register of Deeds, PO Box 448, Newport, NH 03773. Register of Deeds, R/E and UCC Recording 603-863-2110; Fax 603-863-0013.
Will search UCC records prior to 7/2001 and current liens only. Will not search real estate records. **Other Phone Numbers:** Assessor 603-863-2110; Treasurer 603-863-2110.

Sullivan Town

Town Clerk, 522 South Rd, Sullivan, NH 03445. 603-352-1495 R/E Recording: 603-352-0403.
Will search UCC records prior to 7/2001 and current liens only. This agency will not do a tax lien search. Real estate records located in Cheshire County. **Other Phone Numbers:** Assessor 603-847-9720; Treasurer 603-847-2340.

Sunapee Town

Town Clerk, PO Box 303, Sunapee, NH 03782-0303. 603-763-2449; Fax 603-763-4608.
Will search UCC records prior to 7/2001 and current liens only. This agency will not do a tax lien search. Real estate records located in Sullivan County. **Other Phone Numbers:** Assessor 603-763-2212; Vital Records 603-763-2212.

Surry Town

Tax Collector, 1 Village Rd., Surry, NH 03431. 603-352-3075; Fax 603-357-4890.
Will search UCC records prior to 7/2001 and current liens only. Real estate records located in Cheshire County.

Sutton Town

Town Clerk, PO Box 554, South Sutton, NH 03273. 603-927-4575; Fax 603-927-4631.
Will not search UCC records. Real estate records located in Merrimack County. **Other Phone Numbers:** Assessor 603-927-4416.

Swanzey Town

Town Clerk, PO Box 10009, Swanzey, NH 03446. 603-352-7411; Fax 603-352-6250.
Will search UCC records prior to 7/2001 and current liens only. Real estate records located in Cheshire County. **Other Phones:** Assessor 603-352-7411.

Tamworth Town

Town Clerk, PO Box 279, Tamworth, NH 03886. 603-323-7971; Fax 603-323-2347.
Will search UCC records prior to 7/2001 and current liens only. UCC search includes tax liens if requested. Real estate records located in Carroll County. **Other Phone Numbers:** Assessor 603-323-7525.

Temple Town

Town Clerk, Box 69, Temple, NH 03084. 603-878-3873; Fax 603-878-5067.
Will search UCC records prior to 7/2001 and current liens only. Real estate records located in Hillsborough County. **Other Phone Numbers:** Assessor 603-878-2536; Treasurer 603-878-3873.

Thornton Town

Town Clerk, 16 Merrill Access Rd, Thornton, NH 03223. 603-726-4232; Fax 603-726-2078.
Will not search UCC records. Real estate records located in Grafton County. **Other Phone Numbers:** Assessor 603-726-3223; Treasurer 603-764-9450.

Tilton Town

Town Clerk, 257 Main St, Tilton, NH 03276-1207. 603-286-4425; Fax 603-286-3519. www.ci.tilton.nh.us
Will search UCC records prior to 7/2001 and current liens only. Real estate records located in Belknap County. **Other Phone Numbers:** Assessor 603-286-4521; Treasurer 603-286-4521; Appraiser/Auditor 603-286-4521; Elections 603-286-4425; Vital Records 603-286-4425; Land Use 603-286-7817.

Troy Town

Town Clerk, PO Box 249, Troy, NH 03465-0249. 603-242-3845; Fax 603-242-3430. www.town.troy.nh.us
Will search UCC records prior to 7/2001 and current liens only. This agency will not do a tax lien search. Real estate records located in Cheshire County. **Other Phone Numbers:** Assessor 603-242-7722; Vital Records 603-242-3845.

Tuftonboro Town

Town Clerk, PO Box 98, Center Tuftonboro, NH 03816. 603-569-4539; Fax 603-569-4328.
Will search UCC records prior to 7/2001 and current liens only. Real estate records located in Carroll County. **Other Phone Numbers:** Assessor 603-569-4539.

Unity Town

Town Clerk, HCR 66, Box 176A, Newport, NH 03773. 603-542-9665; Fax 603-542-9736.
Will search UCC records prior to 7/2001 and current liens only. Real estate records located in Sullivan County. **Other Phones:** Assessor 603-542-9665.

Wakefield Town

Town Clerk, 2 High St., Sanbornville, NH 03872. 603-522-6205 x306 R/E Recording: 603-539-4872; Fax 603-522-6794.
Will search UCC records prior to 7/2001 and current liens only. Real estate records located in Carroll County. **Other Phone Numbers:** Assessor 603-522-6205; Appraiser/Auditor 603-522-6205 x300; Elections 603-522-6205 x306; Vital Records 603-522-6205.

Walpole Town

Town Clerk, PO Box 756, Walpole, NH 03608. 603-756-3514; Fax 603-756-4153.
Drewsville and North Walpole are in the Town of Walpole. Will search UCC records prior to 7/2001 and current liens only. This agency will not do a tax lien search. Real estate records located in Cheshire County. **Other Phone Numbers:** Assessor 603-756-3672.

Warner Town

Town Clerk, PO Box 265, Warner, NH 03278-0265. 603-456-3362 R/E Recording: 603-228-0101; Fax 603-456-3647. www.warner.nh.us/departments.htm
Will search UCC records prior to 7/2001 and current liens only. Real estate records located in Merrimack County. **Other Phone Numbers:** Assessor 603-456-2298; Treasurer 603-456-2298; Appraiser/Auditor 603-456-2298; Elections 603-456-3362; Vital Records 603-456-3362.

Warren Town

Town Clerk, Rte. 25, RR 1 Box 2008, Warren, NH 03279. 603-764-9463; Fax 603-764-9315.
Will search UCC records prior to 7/2001 and current liens only. Real estate records located in Grafton County. **Other Phone Numbers:** Assessor 603-764-5780.

Washington Town

Town Clerk, PO Box 109, Washington, NH 03280-0109. 603-495-3667; Fax 603-495-3299.
Will search UCC records prior to 7/2001 and current liens only. Real estate records located in Sullivan County. **Other Phone Numbers:** Assessor 603-495-3074; Treasurer 603-495-3667.

Waterville Valley Town

Town Clerk, Box 500, Waterville Valley, NH 03215. 603-236-4730; Fax 603-236-2056.
Will search UCC records prior to 7/2001 and current liens only. This agency will not do a tax lien search. Real estate records located in Grafton County. **Other Phone Numbers:** Assessor 603-236-4730.

Weare Town

Town Clerk, PO Box 190, Weare, NH 03281-0190. 603-529-7575; Fax 603-529-4554. www.town.weare.nh.us
Will search UCC records prior to 7/2001 and current liens only. Real estate records located in Hillsborough County. **Other Phone Numbers:** Assessor 603-629-1515; Elections 603-529-7575; Vital Records 603-529-7575.

Webster Town

Town Clerk, 945 Battle St., Rte 127, Webster, NH 03303. 603-648-2538; Fax 603-648-2448.
Will search UCC records. This agency will not do a tax lien search. Real estate records located in Merrimack County.

Wentworth Town

Town Clerk, PO Box 2, Wentworth, NH 03282. 603-764-5244; Fax 603-764-9362.
Will search UCC records prior to 7/2001 and current liens only. Real estate records located in Grafton County.

Westmoreland Town

Town Clerk, 108 Pierce Lane, Westmoreland, NH 03467. 603-399-4471.
Will search UCC records prior to 7/2001 and current liens only. This agency will not do a tax lien search. Real estate records located in Cheshire County. **Other**

Phone Numbers: Assessor 603-399-4471; Treasurer 603-399-4471.

Whitefield Town

Town Clerk, 7 Jefferson Road, Whitefield, NH 03598. 603-837-9871; Fax 603-837-3148.
Will search UCC records prior to 7/2001 and current liens only. Real estate records located in Grafton County. **Other Phone Numbers:** Assessor 603-837-2551; Treasurer 603-837-2551.

Wilmot Town

Town Clerk, PO Box 94, Wilmot, NH 03287. 603-526-9639; Fax 603-526-2523.
Will search UCC records prior to 7/2001 and current liens only. Real estate records located in Merrimack County. **Other Phone Numbers:** Assessor 603-526-4802.

Wilton Town

Town Clerk, PO Box 83, Wilton, NH 03086. 603-654-9451; Fax 603-654-6663.
Will search UCC records prior to 7/2001 and current liens only. Real estate records located in Hillsborough County. **Other Phone Numbers:** Assessor 603-654-9451.

Winchester Town

Town Clerk, 1 Richmond Rd, Winchester, NH 03470. 603-239-6233; Fax 603-239-4710.
Clerk will only give out book and page number over the phone. Visitors must perform tax lien searches for themselves. Real estate records located in Cheshire County **Other Phones:** Assessor 603-239-4951.

Windham Town

Town Clerk, 3 N. Lowell Road, PO Box 120, Windham, NH 03087. 603-434-5075; Fax 603-425-6582.
Will search UCC records prior to 7/2001 and current liens only. Real estate records located in Rockingham County. **Other Phone Numbers:** Assessor 603-434-7530; Treasurer 603-432-7732.

Windsor Town

Town Clerk, 14 White Pond Rd, Windsor, NH 03244. 603-478-3292; Fax 603-478-3213.
Will not search UCC records. Real estate records located in Hillsborough County.

Wolfeboro Town

Town Clerk, Box 1207, Wolfeboro, NH 03894. 603-569-5328; Fax 603-569-8167.
Will search UCC records prior to 7/2001 and current liens only. Real estate records located in Carroll County. **Other Phone Numbers:** Assessor 603-569-8152; Appraiser/Auditor 603-569-8152; Elections 603-569-5328; Vital Records 603-569-5328.

Woodstock Town

Town Clerk, Box 156, North Woodstock, NH 03262. 603-745-8752; Fax 603-745-2393.
Will search UCC records prior to 7/2001 and current liens only. Real estate records located in Grafton County. **Other Phone Numbers:** Assessor 603-745-8752; Treasurer 603-745-9085.

New Hampshire County Locator

You will usually be able to find the city name in the City/County Cross Reference below. In that case, it is a simple matter to determine the county from the cross reference. However, only the official US Postal Service city names are included in this index. There are an additional 40,000 place names that people use in their addresses. Therefore, we have also included a ZIP/City Cross Reference immediately following the City/County Cross Reference.

If you know the ZIP Code but the city name does not appear in the City/County Cross Reference index, look up the ZIP Code in the ZIP/City Cross Reference, find the city name, then look up the city name in the City/County Cross Reference. For example, you want to know the county for an address of Menands, NY 12204. There is no "Menands" in the City/County Cross Reference. The ZIP/City Cross Reference shows that ZIP Codes 12201-12288 are for the city of Albany. Looking back in the City/County Cross Reference, Albany is in Albany County.

City/County Cross Reference

ACWORTH Sullivan
ALSTEAD Cheshire
ALTON Belknap
ALTON BAY Belknap
AMHERST Hillsborough
ANDOVER Merrimack
ANTRIM Hillsborough
ASHLAND Grafton
ASHUELOT Cheshire
ATKINSON Rockingham
AUBURN Rockingham
BARNSTEAD Belknap
BARRINGTON Strafford
BARTLETT Carroll
BATH Grafton
BEDFORD Hillsborough
BELMONT Belknap
BENNINGTON Hillsborough
BERLIN Coos
BETHLEHEM Grafton
BOW Merrimack
BRADFORD Merrimack
BRETTON WOODS Coos
BRISTOL Grafton
BROOKLINE Hillsborough
CAMPTON Grafton
CANAAN Grafton
CANDIA Rockingham
CANTERBURY Merrimack
CENTER BARNSTEAD Belknap
CENTER CONWAY Carroll
CENTER HARBOR Belknap
CENTER OSSIPEE Carroll
CENTER SANDWICH Carroll
CENTER STRAFFORD Strafford
CENTER TUFTONBORO Carroll
CHARLESTOWN Sullivan
CHESTER Rockingham
CHESTERFIELD Cheshire
CHICHESTER Merrimack
CHOCORUA Carroll
CLAREMONT Sullivan
COLEBROOK Coos
CONCORD Merrimack
CONTOOCOOK Merrimack
CONWAY Carroll
CORNISH Sullivan
CORNISH FLAT Sullivan
DANBURY Merrimack
DANVILLE Rockingham
DEERFIELD Rockingham
DERRY Rockingham
DOVER Strafford
DREWSVILLE Cheshire
DUBLIN Cheshire
DUNBARTON Merrimack
DURHAM Strafford
EAST ANDOVER Merrimack
EAST CANDIA Rockingham
EAST DERRY Rockingham
EAST HAMPSTEAD Rockingham
EAST HEBRON Grafton
EAST KINGSTON Rockingham
EAST WAKEFIELD Carroll

EATON CENTER Carroll
ELKINS Merrimack
ENFIELD (03748) Grafton(96), Sullivan(3)
ENFIELD CENTER Grafton
EPPING Rockingham
EPSOM Merrimack
ERROL Coos
ETNA Grafton
EXETER Rockingham
FARMINGTON Strafford
FITZWILLIAM Cheshire
FRANCESTOWN Hillsborough
FRANCONIA Grafton
FRANKLIN Merrimack
FREEDOM Carroll
FREMONT Rockingham
GEORGES MILLS Sullivan
GILFORD Belknap
GILMANTON Belknap
GILMANTON IRON WORKS Belknap
GILSUM Cheshire
GLEN Carroll
GLENCLIFF Grafton
GOFFSTOWN Hillsborough
GORHAM Coos
GOSHEN Sullivan
GRAFTON Grafton
GRANTHAM Sullivan
GREENFIELD Hillsborough
GREENLAND Rockingham
GREENVILLE Hillsborough
GROVETON Coos
GUILD Sullivan
HAMPSTEAD Rockingham
HAMPTON Rockingham
HAMPTON FALLS Rockingham
HANCOCK Hillsborough
HANOVER Grafton
HARRISVILLE Cheshire
HAVERHILL Grafton
HEBRON Grafton
HENNIKER (03242) Merrimack(98),
   Hillsborough(1)
HILL Merrimack
HILLSBORO (03244) Hillsborough(98),
   Sullivan(1)
HINSDALE Cheshire
HOLDERNESS Grafton
HOLLIS Hillsborough
HOOKSETT Merrimack
HUDSON Hillsborough
INTERVALE Carroll
JACKSON Carroll
JAFFREY Cheshire
JEFFERSON Coos
KEARSARGE Carroll
KEENE Cheshire
KINGSTON Rockingham
LACONIA Belknap
LANCASTER Coos
LEBANON Grafton
LEMPSTER Sullivan
LINCOLN Grafton
LISBON Grafton

LITCHFIELD Hillsborough
LITTLETON Grafton
LOCHMERE Belknap
LONDONDERRY Rockingham
LOUDON Merrimack
LYME Grafton
LYME CENTER Grafton
LYNDEBOROUGH Hillsborough
MADISON Carroll
MANCHESTER Hillsborough
MARLBOROUGH Cheshire
MARLOW Cheshire
MEADOWS Coos
MELVIN VILLAGE Carroll
MEREDITH Belknap
MERIDEN Sullivan
MERRIMACK Hillsborough
MILAN Coos
MILFORD Hillsborough
MILTON Strafford
MILTON MILLS Strafford
MIRROR LAKE Carroll
MONROE Grafton
MONT VERNON Hillsborough
MOULTONBOROUGH Carroll
MOUNT SUNAPEE Merrimack
MOUNT WASHINGTON Coos
MUNSONVILLE Cheshire
NASHUA Hillsborough
NEW BOSTON Hillsborough
NEW CASTLE Rockingham
NEW DURHAM Strafford
NEW HAMPTON Belknap
NEW IPSWICH Hillsborough
NEW LONDON (03257) Merrimack(97),
   Sullivan(2)
NEWBURY Merrimack
NEWFIELDS Rockingham
NEWMARKET Rockingham
NEWPORT Sullivan
NEWTON Rockingham
NEWTON JUNCTION Rockingham
NORTH CONWAY Carroll
NORTH HAMPTON Rockingham
NORTH HAVERHILL Grafton
NORTH SALEM Rockingham
NORTH SANDWICH Carroll
NORTH STRATFORD Coos
NORTH SUTTON Merrimack
NORTH WALPOLE Cheshire
NORTH WOODSTOCK Grafton
NORTHWOOD Rockingham
NOTTINGHAM Rockingham
ORFORD Grafton
OSSIPEE Carroll
PELHAM Hillsborough
PETERBOROUGH Hillsborough
PIERMONT Grafton
PIKE Grafton
PITTSBURG Coos
PITTSFIELD Merrimack
PLAINFIELD Sullivan
PLAISTOW Rockingham
PLYMOUTH Grafton

PORTSMOUTH Rockingham
RAYMOND Rockingham
RINDGE Cheshire
ROCHESTER Strafford
ROLLINSFORD Strafford
RUMNEY Grafton
RYE Rockingham
RYE BEACH Rockingham
SALEM Rockingham
SALISBURY Merrimack
SANBORNTON Belknap
SANBORNVILLE Carroll
SANDOWN Rockingham
SEABROOK Rockingham
SILVER LAKE Carroll
SOMERSWORTH Strafford
SOUTH ACWORTH Sullivan
SOUTH EFFINGHAM Carroll
SOUTH NEWBURY Merrimack
SOUTH SUTTON Merrimack
SOUTH TAMWORTH Carroll
SPOFFORD Cheshire
SPRINGFIELD Sullivan
STINSON LAKE Grafton
STODDARD Cheshire
STRAFFORD Strafford
STRATHAM Rockingham
SULLIVAN Cheshire
SUNAPEE Sullivan
SUNCOOK Merrimack
SWANZEY Cheshire
TAMWORTH Carroll
TEMPLE Hillsborough
TILTON Belknap
TROY Cheshire
TWIN MOUNTAIN Coos
UNION (03887) Strafford(76), Carroll(23)
WALPOLE Cheshire
WARNER Merrimack
WARREN Grafton
WASHINGTON Sullivan
WATERVILLE VALLEY Grafton
WEARE Hillsborough
WENTWORTH Grafton
WEST CHESTERFIELD Cheshire
WEST LEBANON Grafton
WEST NOTTINGHAM Rockingham
WEST OSSIPEE Carroll
WEST PETERBOROUGH Hillsborough
WEST STEWARTSTOWN Coos
WEST SWANZEY Cheshire
WESTMORELAND Cheshire
WHITEFIELD Coos
WILMOT Merrimack
WILTON Hillsborough
WINCHESTER Cheshire
WINDHAM Rockingham
WINNISQUAM Belknap
WOLFEBORO Carroll
WOLFEBORO FALLS Carroll
WONALANCET Carroll
WOODSTOCK Grafton
WOODSVILLE Grafton

ZIP/City Cross Reference

ZIP	City	ZIP	City	ZIP	City	ZIP	City
00210-00215	PORTSMOUTH	03245-03245	HOLDERNESS	03467-03467	WESTMORELAND	03811-03811	ATKINSON
03031-03031	AMHERST	03246-03247	LACONIA	03468-03468	WEST PETERBOROUGH	03812-03812	BARTLETT
03032-03032	AUBURN	03249-03249	GILFORD	03469-03469	WEST SWANZEY	03813-03813	CENTER CONWAY
03033-03033	BROOKLINE	03251-03251	LINCOLN	03470-03470	WINCHESTER	03814-03814	CENTER OSSIPEE
03034-03034	CANDIA	03252-03252	LOCHMERE	03561-03561	LITTLETON	03815-03815	CENTER STRAFFORD
03036-03036	CHESTER	03253-03253	MEREDITH	03570-03570	BERLIN	03816-03816	CENTER TUFTONBORO
03037-03037	DEERFIELD	03254-03254	MOULTONBOROUGH	03574-03574	BETHLEHEM	03817-03817	CHOCORUA
03038-03038	DERRY	03255-03255	NEWBURY	03575-03575	BRETTON WOODS	03818-03818	CONWAY
03040-03040	EAST CANDIA	03256-03256	NEW HAMPTON	03576-03576	COLEBROOK	03819-03819	DANVILLE
03041-03041	EAST DERRY	03257-03257	NEW LONDON	03579-03579	ERROL	03820-03822	DOVER
03042-03042	EPPING	03258-03258	CHICHESTER	03580-03580	FRANCONIA	03824-03824	DURHAM
03043-03043	FRANCESTOWN	03259-03259	NORTH SANDWICH	03581-03581	GORHAM	03825-03825	BARRINGTON
03044-03044	FREMONT	03260-03260	NORTH SUTTON	03582-03582	GROVETON	03826-03826	EAST HAMPSTEAD
03045-03045	GOFFSTOWN	03261-03261	NORTHWOOD	03583-03583	JEFFERSON	03827-03827	EAST KINGSTON
03046-03046	DUNBARTON	03262-03262	NORTH WOODSTOCK	03584-03584	LANCASTER	03830-03830	EAST WAKEFIELD
03047-03047	GREENFIELD	03263-03263	PITTSFIELD	03585-03585	LISBON	03832-03832	EATON CENTER
03048-03048	GREENVILLE	03264-03264	PLYMOUTH	03587-03587	MEADOWS	03833-03833	EXETER
03049-03049	HOLLIS	03265-03265	ANDOVER	03588-03588	MILAN	03835-03835	FARMINGTON
03051-03051	HUDSON	03266-03266	RUMNEY	03589-03589	MOUNT WASHINGTON	03836-03836	FREEDOM
03052-03052	LITCHFIELD	03268-03268	SALISBURY	03590-03590	NORTH STRATFORD	03837-03837	GILMANTON IRON WORKS
03053-03053	LONDONDERRY	03269-03269	SANBORNTON	03592-03592	PITTSBURG	03838-03838	GLEN
03054-03054	MERRIMACK	03272-03272	SOUTH NEWBURY	03595-03595	TWIN MOUNTAIN	03839-03839	ROCHESTER
03055-03055	MILFORD	03273-03273	SOUTH SUTTON	03597-03597	WEST STEWARTSTOWN	03840-03840	GREENLAND
03057-03057	MONT VERNON	03274-03274	STINSON LAKE	03598-03598	WHITEFIELD	03841-03841	HAMPSTEAD
03060-03064	NASHUA	03275-03275	SUNCOOK	03601-03601	ACWORTH	03842-03843	HAMPTON
03070-03070	NEW BOSTON	03276-03276	TILTON	03602-03602	ALSTEAD	03844-03844	HAMPTON FALLS
03071-03071	NEW IPSWICH	03278-03278	WARNER	03603-03603	CHARLESTOWN	03845-03845	INTERVALE
03073-03073	NORTH SALEM	03279-03279	WARREN	03604-03604	DREWSVILLE	03846-03846	JACKSON
03076-03076	PELHAM	03280-03280	WASHINGTON	03605-03606	LEMPSTER	03847-03847	KEARSARGE
03077-03077	RAYMOND	03281-03281	WEARE	03607-03607	SOUTH ACWORTH	03848-03848	KINGSTON
03079-03079	SALEM	03282-03282	WENTWORTH	03608-03608	WALPOLE	03849-03849	MADISON
03082-03082	LYNDEBOROUGH	03284-03284	SPRINGFIELD	03609-03609	NORTH WALPOLE	03850-03850	MELVIN VILLAGE
03084-03084	TEMPLE	03285-03285	CAMPTON	03740-03740	BATH	03851-03851	MILTON
03086-03086	WILTON	03287-03287	WILMOT	03741-03741	CANAAN	03852-03852	MILTON MILLS
03087-03087	WINDHAM	03289-03289	WINNISQUAM	03743-03743	CLAREMONT	03853-03853	MIRROR LAKE
03100-03105	MANCHESTER	03290-03290	NOTTINGHAM	03745-03745	CORNISH	03854-03854	NEW CASTLE
03106-03106	HOOKSETT	03291-03291	WEST NOTTINGHAM	03746-03746	CORNISH FLAT	03855-03855	NEW DURHAM
03107-03109	MANCHESTER	03293-03293	WOODSTOCK	03748-03748	ENFIELD	03856-03856	NEWFIELDS
03110-03110	BEDFORD	03298-03299	TILTON	03749-03749	ENFIELD CENTER	03857-03857	NEWMARKET
03111-03111	MANCHESTER	03300-03303	CONCORD	03750-03750	ETNA	03858-03858	NEWTON
03215-03215	WATERVILLE VALLEY	03304-03304	BOW	03751-03751	GEORGES MILLS	03859-03859	NEWTON JUNCTION
03216-03216	ANDOVER	03305-03306	CONCORD	03752-03752	GOSHEN	03860-03860	NORTH CONWAY
03217-03217	ASHLAND	03307-03307	LOUDON	03753-03753	GRANTHAM	03862-03862	NORTH HAMPTON
03218-03218	BARNSTEAD	03431-03435	KEENE	03754-03754	GUILD	03864-03864	OSSIPEE
03220-03220	BELMONT	03440-03440	ANTRIM	03755-03755	HANOVER	03865-03865	PLAISTOW
03221-03221	BRADFORD	03441-03441	ASHUELOT	03756-03756	LEBANON	03866-03868	ROCHESTER
03222-03222	BRISTOL	03442-03442	BENNINGTON	03765-03765	HAVERHILL	03869-03869	ROLLINSFORD
03223-03223	CAMPTON	03443-03443	CHESTERFIELD	03766-03766	LEBANON	03870-03870	RYE
03224-03224	CANTERBURY	03444-03444	DUBLIN	03768-03768	LYME	03871-03871	RYE BEACH
03225-03225	CENTER BARNSTEAD	03445-03445	SULLIVAN	03769-03769	LYME CENTER	03872-03872	SANBORNVILLE
03226-03226	CENTER HARBOR	03446-03446	SWANZEY	03770-03770	MERIDEN	03873-03873	SANDOWN
03227-03227	CENTER SANDWICH	03447-03447	FITZWILLIAM	03771-03771	MONROE	03874-03874	SEABROOK
03229-03229	CONTOOCOOK	03448-03448	GILSUM	03772-03772	MOUNT SUNAPEE	03875-03875	SILVER LAKE
03230-03230	DANBURY	03449-03449	HANCOCK	03773-03773	NEWPORT	03878-03878	SOMERSWORTH
03231-03231	EAST ANDOVER	03450-03450	HARRISVILLE	03774-03774	NORTH HAVERHILL	03882-03882	SOUTH EFFINGHAM
03232-03232	EAST HEBRON	03451-03451	HINSDALE	03777-03777	ORFORD	03883-03883	SOUTH TAMWORTH
03233-03233	ELKINS	03452-03452	JAFFREY	03779-03779	PIERMONT	03884-03884	STRAFFORD
03234-03234	EPSOM	03455-03455	MARLBOROUGH	03780-03780	PIKE	03885-03885	STRATHAM
03235-03235	FRANKLIN	03456-03456	MARLOW	03781-03781	PLAINFIELD	03886-03886	TAMWORTH
03237-03237	GILMANTON	03457-03457	MUNSONVILLE	03782-03782	SUNAPEE	03887-03887	UNION
03238-03238	GLENCLIFF	03458-03460	PETERBOROUGH	03784-03784	WEST LEBANON	03890-03890	WEST OSSIPEE
03240-03240	GRAFTON	03461-03461	RINDGE	03785-03785	WOODSVILLE	03894-03894	WOLFEBORO
03241-03241	HEBRON	03462-03462	SPOFFORD	03801-03804	PORTSMOUTH	03896-03896	WOLFEBORO FALLS
03242-03242	HENNIKER	03464-03464	STODDARD	03805-03805	ROLLINSFORD	03897-03897	WONALANCET
03243-03243	HILL	03465-03465	TROY	03809-03809	ALTON		
03244-03244	HILLSBORO	03466-03466	WEST CHESTERFIELD	03810-03810	ALTON BAY		

New Jersey

General Help Numbers:

Governor's Office
PO Box 001, 125 W State St
Trenton, NJ 08625-0001
www.state.nj.us/governor

609-292-6000
Fax 609-292-3454
8:30AM-4:30PM

Attorney General's Office
Law & Public Safety Department
PO Box 080, 25 Market St
Trenton, NJ 08625-0080
www.state.nj.us/lps

609-292-8740
Fax 609-292-3508
8:30AM-5PM

State Court Administrator
RJH Justice Complex
PO Box 037, Courts Bldg, 7th Floor
Trenton, NJ 08625
www.judiciary.state.nj.us/admin.htm

609-984-0275
Fax 609-984-6968
8:30AM-4:30PM

State Archives
PO Box 307, 225 W. State Street, L2
Trenton, NJ 08625-0307
www.state.nj.us/state/darm/index.html

609-292-6260
Fax 609-396-2454

8:30AM-4:30PM TU-F

State Specifics:

Capital:	Trenton
	Mercer County
Time Zone:	EST
Number of Counties:	21
Population:	8,484,431
Web Site:	www.state.nj.us

State Agencies

Criminal Records

Division of State Police, Records and Identification Section, PO Box 7068, West Trenton, NJ 08628-0068; 609-882-2000 x2878, 609-530-5780 (Fax), 9AM-5PM.

www.state.nj.us/njsp

Note: Sexual offender data is available at www.njsp.org/info/reg_sexoffend.html

Indexing & Storage: It takes 1 to 5 days before new records are available for inquiry. Records are indexed on inhouse computer. 85% of all arrests in

database have final dispositions recorded, 95% for those arrests within last 5 years.

Searching: Criminal records are not open to the public, but can be obtained by employers, volunteer organizations, private investigators, screening firms, attorney firms, and the subject. Include the following in your request: date of birth, Social Security Number. A set of fingerprints is optional. The name must match exactly. All requesters, except attorney firms, must submit Form 212 B which must be signed by the subject. Attorney firms require a subpoena. 100%

of the records are fingerprint supported. The following data is not released: Juvenile records are restricted. Dismissals, acquittals, not-guilty verdicts are also excluded to the general public. All records are released, including those without dispositions.

Access by: mail, in person.

Fee & Payment: The fee is $15.00 for a name check and $25.00 for a full check with fingerprints. Will not do FBI fingerprint checks. Fee payee: Division of State Police-SBI.

Prepayment required. No personal checks or credit cards accepted.

Mail search: Turnaround time: 5 to 10 working days.

In person search: Walk-in requests do not receive priority; they are treated as mail requests. Results are mailed.

Corporation Records
Limited Liability Company Records
Fictitious Name
Limited Partnerships

Division of Revenue, Business Support Services Bureau, PO 308, Trenton, NJ 08625 (Courier: 225 W State St, 3rd Fl, Trenton, NJ 08608); 609-292-9292, 8:30AM-5:00PM.

www.state.nj.us/njbgs

Indexing & Storage: Records are available from inception of laws. New records are available for inquiry immediately. Records are indexed on inhouse computer.

Searching: Include the following in your request: full name of business. In addition to the articles of incorporation, corporation records include the following information: Annual Reports, Officers, Directors, Prior (merged) names, Inactive and Reserved names. Assumed names are located at the county level.

Access by: mail, phone, fax, in person, online.

Fee & Payment: A status report is $5.00. Copies are $1.00 per page (except LLC, then $10.00 first and $2.00 each additional). There is a $25.00 ($15.00 if non-profit) fee to certify a document. A Good Standing is $25.00. Fee payee: Treasurer, State of NJ. Prepayment required. Ongoing requesters may set up a pre-paid account. Call 609-633-8255 for more information. Personal checks accepted. Credit cards accepted: MasterCard, Visa, Discover, AMEX

Mail search: Turnaround time: 2 to 3 weeks.

Phone search: This is considered expedited service.

Fax search: This is considered expedited service.

In person search: You can look at 3 records per day for no fee. Copies can be provided. The turnaround time is over 1 week.

Online search: Records are available from the New Jersey Business Gateway Service (NJBGS) web site at www.state.nj.us/njbgs. There is no fee to browse the site to locate a name; however fees are involved for copies or status reports.

Expedited service: Expedited service is available for phone, fax, and in person searches. Turnaround time: 8.5 business hours. Add $10.00 per search. Records may be picked up the next day.

Trademarks/Servicemarks

Department of Treasury, Trademark Division, PO Box 453, Trenton, NJ 08625-0453 (Courier: 225 W State St, 3rd Floor, Trenton, NJ 08608); 609-633-8259, 8:30AM-5PM.

www.state.nj.us/njbgs/services.html

Indexing & Storage: Records are available from the inception of the Division. It takes less than 1 day before new records are available for inquiry. Records are indexed on computer.

Searching: Include the following in your request: trademark/servicemark name, name of owner, date of application. Information returned includes name and address of owner and date of filing.

Access by: mail, in person.

Fee & Payment: Search fee is $25.00 for up to 3 names (for name availability). Copies are $1.00 per page. A status is $5.00 per name searched. Fee payee: NJ State Treasurer. Prepayment required. Personal checks and credit cards are accepted.

Mail search: Turnaround time: 1 week. A self addressed stamped envelope is appreciated.

In person search: You can take the request in person, but they return the records by mail unless expedited service is requested.

In person search: Search the trademark/service-marks and trade names list for free at www.accessnet.state.nj.us/businesslistsearch.asp.

Uniform Commercial Code

UCC Section, Secretary of State, PO 303, Trenton, NJ 08625 (Courier: 225 West State St, Trenton, NJ 08608); 609-292-9292, 8AM-5PM.

www.state.nj.us/njbgs

Indexing & Storage: Records are indexed on inhouse computer.

Searching: Use search request form UCC-11. Federal tax liens are filed at the county level. State tax liens follow two rules: certificates of debt are filed in Superior Court at Trenton; a warrant of execution is filed at the county level. Include the following in your request: debtor name, address.

Access by: mail, fax, in person, online.

Fee & Payment: The fee is $25.00 for a search certificate per debtor name, $25.00 for certification of any document, copies are $1.00 per page. Fee payee: Secretary of State. Prepayment required. Regular requesters can set up a pre-paid account, call 609-530-6424. Personal checks accepted. Credit cards accepted: MasterCard, Visa.

Mail search: Turnaround time: 2 weeks. A self addressed stamped envelope is requested.

Fax search: You can order using a credit card; however, results will be mailed or available for pickup by a courier.

In person search: Information is mailed, unless you pay the $15.00 expedite fee for 24 hour service.

Online search: Go to www.accessnet.state.nj.us/home.asp to find a business entity, UCC debtor, or other business name without accruing a service charge with the Division of Revenue. However, if you wish to receive status reports or other information services, you will need to pay the applicable statutory fee.

Federal Tax Liens
State Tax Liens
Records not maintained by a state level agency.

Note: Federal tax liens are filed with the county clerk or register of deeds. All state "docket judgment" liens are filed at the Superior Court in Trenton. "Certificates of Debt" are filed at the respective county superior court.

Sales Tax Registrations
Access to Records is Restricted

State of New Jersey, Division of Taxation - Taxpayer Services, PO Box 281, Trenton, NJ 08695; 609-292-6400, 609-777-4319, 609-292-5995, 609-826-4339 (Fax), 8:30AM-4:30PM.

www.state.nj.us/treasury/taxation

Note: Sales tax information is considered confidential. The only way to verify if an entity has a license is to ask to look at the certificate at the place of business, per Ed Scheingold, Chief of Customer Services Branch.

Birth Certificates

Department of Health, Bureau of Vital Statistics, PO Box 370, Trenton, NJ 08625-0370 (Courier: S Warren St, Room 504, Health & Agriculture Building, Trenton, NJ 08625); 609-292-4087, 609-633-2860 (Credit Card Requests), 609-392-4292 (Fax), 9AM-5PM.

www.state.nj.us/health/vital/vital.htm

Indexing & Storage: Records are available from 1878 to present. New records are available for inquiry immediately. Records are indexed on microfiche.

Searching: The general public is denied access to records. You must include the county in your request if it is regarding events before 1903. Include the following in your request: full name, names of parents, mother's maiden name, date of birth, place of birth.

Access by: mail, phone, fax, in person.

Fee & Payment: The fee is $4.00 per record. Add $2.00 per copy for additional copies. Add $1.00 per year for each additional year searched. The fee for using a credit card is $8.95. Fee payee: New Jersey Department of Health & Senior Services. Prepayment required. Personal checks accepted. Credit cards accepted: MasterCard, Visa, AmEx, Discover.

Mail search: Turnaround time: 3 to 4 weeks. No self addressed stamped envelope is required.

Phone search: Must use a credit card. The hours are 8AM to 3PM.

Fax search: Same criteria as phone searching.

In person search: Turnaround time 2 hours.

Expedited service: Expedited service is available for fax searches. Turnaround time: 2 to 3 days. Add fee of overnight carrier ($14.75) if used, plus credit card fee. Federal Express 5-7 day service available.

Death Records

Department of Health, Bureau of Vital Statistics, PO Box 370, Trenton, NJ 08625-0370 (Courier: S Warren St, Room 504, Health & Agriculture Building, Trenton, NJ 08625); 609-292-4087, 609-633-2860 (Credit Card Requests), 609-392-4292 (Fax), 9AM-4PM.

www.state.nj.us/health/vital/vital.htm

Indexing & Storage: Records are available from 1878 to present. It takes the 10th of the following month before new records are available for inquiry. Records are indexed on microfiche.

Searching: Cause of death, unless immediate family, is not released. Only those with a legal interest may obtain a record. Include the following in your request: full name, date of death, place of death, Social Security Number.

Access by: mail, phone, fax, in person.

Fee & Payment: The fee is $4.00 per record. Add $2.00 per copy for additional copies. Add $1.00 per year for each additional year searched. Add $8.95 if credit card is used. Fee payee: NJ Department of Health and Senior Services. Prepayment required. Personal checks accepted. Credit cards accepted: MasterCard, Visa, AmEx, Discover.

Mail search: Turnaround time: 1 month. No self addressed stamped envelope is required.

Phone search: Must use a credit card.

Fax search: Same criteria as phone, turnaround time is 10-15 days.

In person search: Turnaround time 2 hours.

Expedited service: Expedited service is available for mail, phone and fax searches. Turnaround time: 2 to 3 days. Add carrier fee of $14.75 plus the $8.95 credit card fee. Federal Express 5-7 day service available.

Marriage Certificates

Department of Health, Bureau of Vital Statistics, PO Box 370, Trenton, NJ 08625-0370 (Courier: S Warren St, Room 504, Health & Agriculture Building, Trenton, NJ 08625); 609-292-4087, 609-633-2860 (Credit Card Requests), 609-392-4292 (Fax), 8:45AM-5PM.

www.state.nj.us/health/vital/vital.htm

Indexing & Storage: Records are available from 1878 to present. New records are available for inquiry immediately. Records are indexed on microfiche.

Searching: The general public is denied access to the records. You must include the county in your request if it is regarding events before 1903. Include the following in your request: names of husband and wife, date of marriage, place or county of marriage.

Access by: mail, phone, fax, in person.

Fee & Payment: The fee is $4.00 per record. Add $2.00 per copy for additional copies. Add $1.00 per year for each additional year searched. The fee to use a credit card is $8.95. Fee payee: New Jersey Department of Health. Prepayment required. Personal checks accepted. Credit cards accepted: MasterCard, Visa, AmEx, Discover.

Mail search: Turnaround time: 3 to 4 weeks. No self addressed stamped envelope is required.

Phone search: Must use a credit card. The hours are from 8AM to 3PM.

Fax search: Same criteria as phone searches.

In person search: Turnaround time 2 hours.

Expedited service: Expedited service is available for fax searches. Turnaround time: 2 to 3 days. Add $14.75 carrier fees for overnight shipping and the $8.95 credit card fee. Federal Express 5-7 day service available.

Divorce Records

Clerk of Superior Court, Records Center, PO Box 967, Trenton, NJ 08625-0967 (Courier: Corner of Jerser & Tremont Streets, Building #2, Trenton, NJ 08625); 609-777-0092, 609-777-0094 (Fax), 8:30AM-4PM.

Indexing & Storage: Records are available until 9/89. Records after 1989 must be obtained from the Family Division Court in county of occurrence.

Searching: Also provide married name, unless maiden name was used during the marriage. Information on cases that are impounded is not released. Include the following in your request: names of husband and wife, date of divorce, year divorce case began, docket number (if known). No copies are made and no records are retrieved after 3:30PM. The following data is not released: adoption, impound cases.

Access by: mail, fax, in person.

Fee & Payment: There is no search fee, but there is a $10.00 certification fee. Fee payee: Clerk of Superior Court. Prepayment required. If you are not sure how many pages the results or your request will be, you may send a blank check with "Not to exceed $25.00" written in the memo. Personal checks accepted. No credit cards accepted.

Mail search: Turnaround time: 2 to 3 weeks. Mail is the preferred request method. A self addressed stamped envelope is requested.

Fax search: Requesters must be pre-approved to fax, and only written information is faxed back. Attorneys with charge accounts with the Superior Court can receive copies, without the seal of the court, via fax.

In person search: Turnaround time: while you wait. The Clerk's Office recommends that you not come to the office in person except for emergency requests.

Workers' Compensation Records

Labor Department, Division of Workers Compensation, John Fitch Plaza, PO Box 381, Trenton, NJ 08625 (Courier: Labor Building, 6th Floor, John Fitch Plaza, Trenton, NJ 08625); 609-292-6026, 609-984-3924 (Fax), 8:30AM-4:30PM.

www.state.nj.us/labor/wc/Default.htm

Indexing & Storage: Records are available for 45 years, then are purged. New records are available for inquiry immediately. Records are indexed on inhouse computer.

Searching: First report of injury-accident is not available to the public. All other records are subject to NJSA 34:15-128 which prohibits the copying of records for resale. Use WC-147 if you want copies of a case. Include the following in your request: claimant name, Social Security Number, date of accident.

Access by: mail, in person.

Fee & Payment: There is no search fee. The copy fee is $.75 each for first 10 pages; $.50 each for next 10; and $.25 per page over 20. Fee payee:

Division of Workers' Compensation. Prepayment required. Personal checks accepted. No credit cards accepted.

Mail search: Turnaround time: 4 to 6 weeks. If request is just to know if the person has a claim, the turnaround time is same day. A self addressed stamped envelope is requested.

In person search: Turnaround time is same day.

Driver Records

Motor Vehicle Services, Driver History Abstract Unit, PO Box 142, Trenton, NJ 08666; 609-292-6500 (Forms request), 888-486-3339 (In-state only), 609-292-7500 (Suspensions), 8AM-5PM.

www.state.nj.us/mvs

Note: Copies of tickets are not kept on file and must be obtained from the municipal courts.

Indexing & Storage: Records are available for five years for the public (complete history for attorneys). Non-moving violations are not reported on the record. Accidents are reported, but fault is not shown. The driver's address is provided on the record. It takes 3 days to 2 weeks normally before new records are available for inquiry.

Searching: Access of driving records is strict, release to casual requesters is prohibited unless Form ISM/DO-21A contains notarized authority from subject. Permissible use requesters should use Form ISM-21. The driver's license number should be submitted with all requests. The full name, DOB, sex, and eye color are also helpful. The following data is not released: Social Security Numbers or medical records.

Access by: mail, in person, online.

Fee & Payment: The current fee is $10.00 for certified mail-in or walk-in requests, and $8.00 for other media including magnetic tape, control cards (100 minimum purchase), and online access. Fee payee: Motor Vehicle Services. Prepayment required. Personal checks accepted. No credit cards accepted.

Mail search: Turnaround time: 2 weeks. A self addressed stamped envelope is requested.

In person search: Driving records can obtained at any one of the four Regional Service Centers - Deptford, Wayne, Eatontown, and Trenton.

Online search: Fee is $10.00 per record. Access is limited to insurance, bus and trucking companies, parking authorities, and approved vendors. There is a minimum of 100 requests per quarter. For more information, call 609-984-7771.

Other access: High volume requesters can use the magnetic tape method to obtain overnight records (minimum 500 requests) or purchase control cards at (100 purchased at a time, used whenever).

Vehicle Ownership & Identification
Vessel Ownership & Registration

Motor Vehicle Services, Certified Information Unit, PO Box 146, Trenton, NJ 08666; 609-292-6500, 888-486-3339 (In-state), 8AM-5PM.

www.state.nj.us/mvs

Note: Lien records must be ordered from Special Titles at Motor Vehicle Services, CN-017 (Zip is 08666-0017). Lien records are on the complete title history, or can be purchased at $5.00 for each lien history search.

Indexing & Storage: Records are available from 1986 for most records. All boats 12 ft and over must be titled and registered. All motorized boats and all sailboats over 12 ft must be registered. Also, this agency maintains records on mobile homes. It takes 3 days to 3 weeks normally before new records are available for inquiry.

Searching: SSNs and medical information are not currently released and more restrictions are forthcoming. Casual requesters cannot obtain records. A special request form is required for most searches as follows: ISM/DO-22A for title search, ISM/DO-22 for lien search, ISM/DO-11 for vehicle registration application search.

Access by: mail, online.

Fee & Payment: The fee is $8.00 per record non-certified and $10.00 certified and take 1-2 weeks to process. A lien history search is $5.00 for each lien. A complete title history costs $10.50 and can take as long as 12 weeks to obtain. Fee payee: Motor Vehicle Services. Prepayment required. Personal checks accepted. No credit cards accepted.

Mail search: Requests must be submitted on Form ISM/DO-11A for registration requests and on Form ISM/DO-22A for title record requests. A self addressed stamped envelope is requested.

Online search: Limited online access is available for insurance companies, bus and trucking companies, highway/parking authorities, and approved vendors for these businesses. Participation requires a minimum of 100 requests per calendar quarter at $4.00 per request. Call 609-684-7771 for more information.

Other access: Electronic file transfer is available for volume users at $4.00 per record. There is no program for massive/customized bulk look-ups. Each request is looked at on an individual basis.

Records are not sold for commercial or political reasons.

Accident Reports

New Jersey State Police, Criminal Justice Records Section, PO Box 7068, West Trenton, NJ 08628-0068; 609-882-2000 x2234, 8AM-5PM.

www.njsp.org

Indexing & Storage: Records are available for 7 years. Records are computer indexed. It takes 3 to 4 weeks before new records are available for inquiry.

Searching: Fatal accident information is not available until it has been released from the County Prosecutor. Include the following in your request: location of accident, date of accident, driver's full name.

Access by: mail.

Fee & Payment: Fees: $10.00 for first 3 pages and $2.00 for each additional page with a maximum fee of $16.00. Fee payee: New Jersey State Police Department. Prepayment required. Personal checks accepted. No credit cards accepted.

Mail search: Turnaround time: 3 weeks. A self addressed stamped envelope is requested.

Legislation Records

New Jersey State Legislature, State House Annex, PO Box 068, Room B01, Trenton, NJ 08625-0068; 609-292-4840 (Bill Status Only), 609-292-6395 (Copy Room), 800-792-8630 (In State Only), 609-777-2440 (Fax), 8:30AM-5PM.

www.njleg.state.nj.us

Note: Older bills may be found at the State Law Library.

Indexing & Storage: Records are available from 1988 to present. New records are available for inquiry immediately.

Searching: Include the following in your request: bill number and/or sponsor.

Access by: mail, phone, fax, in person, online.

Fee & Payment: There is no search fee.

Mail search: Turnaround time: same day. For mail searches, provide bill number with the year or sponsor with accurate bill description. No self addressed stamped envelope is required.

Phone search: Certain records are available by phone.

Fax search: Fax searching available.

In person search: For in person searches, please provide bill number with year or sponsor with accurate bill description.

Online search: The web site is a good source of information about bills. All statutes are online, also.

Voter Registration
Access to Records is Restricted

Dept of Law and Public Safety, Division of Elections, PO Box 304, Trenton, NJ 08625; 609-292-3760, 609-777-1280 (Fax), 8:30AM-5PM.

www.state.nj.us/lps/services_elec.htm

Note: The Commissioner of Registration maintains these records, but they can only be accessed at the county level. While these county agencies may permit individual look-ups, records in mass may only be purchased for political purposes.

GED Certificates

GED Testing Program, Dept. of Education - Bureau Adult Ed. & Literacy, PO Box 500, Trenton, NJ 08625-0500; 609-777-0577.

www.state.nj.us/njded/students/ged

Searching: GED Information Request Form is required and can be obtained by calling 609-777-0577. To search, all of the following is required: a signed release, name, date/year of test, Social Security Number, and city of test. Records are not maintained for persons tested at federal correctional institutions.

Access by: mail.

Fee & Payment: The fee is $5.00 for a verification or a copy of the transcript. Fee payee: Commissioner of Education. Prepayment required. Money orders and business checks are accepted. No credit cards accepted.

Mail search: Turnaround time can take as long as 4 weeks.

Hunting License Information
Fishing License Information
Records not maintained by a state level agency.

Note: They do not have a central database. You must contact the vendor where the license was purchased.

New Jersey State Licensing Agencies

Licenses Searchable Online

Acupuncturist #1	www.state.nj.us/lps/ca/bme/acupdir.htm
Alcohol/Drug Counselor #13	www.state.nj.us/lps/ca/marriage/pcdir.htm
Appraiser, General/Residential #23	www.state.nj.us/lps/ca/real/realdir.htm
Architect #6	www.state.nj.us/lps/ca/arch/archdir.htm
Audiologist #7	www.state.nj.us/lps/ca/aud/auddir.htm
Barber #9	www.state.nj.us/lps/ca/cosmetology/bardir.htm
Beautician #9	www.state.nj.us/lps/ca/cosmetology/beautdir.htm
Cemetery Salesperson #46	www.state.nj.us/lps/ca/cemetery/cemdir.htm
Charities #61	www.state.nj.us/lps/ca/charfrm.htm
Chiropractor #8	www.state.nj.us/lps/ca/chiro/chirofrm.htm
Cosmetologist/Hairstylist #9	www.state.nj.us/lps/ca/cosmetology/cosmodir.htm
Counselor, Social Work #25	www.state.nj.us/lps/ca/social/socdir.htm
Court Reporter #24	www.state.nj.us/lps/ca/short/shortdir.htm
Dentist #10	www.state.nj.us/lps/ca/dentistry/dentdir.htm
Electrical Contractor #11	www.state.nj.us/lps/ca/electric/elecdir.htm
Embalmer #15	www.state.nj.us/lps/ca/mort/mortdir.htm
Engineer #20	www.state.nj.us/lps/ca/pels/engdir.htm
Funeral Practitioner #15	www.state.nj.us/lps/ca/mort/mortdir.htm
Hearing Aid Dispenser/Fitter #44	www.state.nj.us/lps/ca/hear/heardir.htm
Home Health Aide #16	www.state.nj.us/lps/ca/medical.htm#nur6
Lab Director, Bio-Analytical #14	www.state.nj.us/lps/ca/bme/labdir.htm
Landscape Architect #6	www.state.nj.us/lps/ca/arch/landdir.htm
Manicurist/Manicure Shop #9	www.state.nj.us/lps/ca/cosmetology/mandir.htm
Marriage & Family Counselor, Professional #13	www.state.nj.us/lps/ca/marriage/pcdir.htm
Marriage & Family Therapist #25	www.state.nj.us/lps/ca/marriage/pcdir.htm
Marriage Counselor #13	www.state.nj.us/lps/ca/marriage/pcdir.htm
Midwife #14	www.state.nj.us/lps/ca/bme/middir.htm
Mortician #15	www.state.nj.us/lps/ca/mort/mortdir.htm
Nurse, Advance Practice #16	www.state.nj.us/lps/ca/medical.htm#nur6
Nurse-LPN #16	www.state.nj.us/lps/ca/medical.htm#nur6
Nurse-RN #16	www.state.nj.us/lps/ca/medical.htm#nur6
Occupational Therapy Asst #60	www.state.nj.us/lps/ca/occup/otadir.htm
Occupational Therapist #60	www.state.nj.us/lps/ca/occup/otdir.htm
Opthalmic Dispenser/Technician #51	www.state.nj.us/lps/ca/ophth/tddir.htm
Optician/Optician Technician #51	www.state.nj.us/lps/ca/ophth/ttdir.htm
Optometrist #17	www.state.nj.us/lps/ca/optometry/optdir.htm
Pharmacist #18	www.state.nj.us/lps/ca/pharm/pharmdir.htm
Physical Therapist #19	www.state.nj.us/lps/ca/pt/ptdir.htm
Physical Therapist Assistant #19	www.state.nj.us/lps/ca/pt/ptdir.htm
Physician #14	www.state.nj.us/lps/ca/bme/docdir.htm
Planner, Professional #21	www.state.nj.us/lps/ca/plan/plandir.htm
Plumber/Master Plumber #12	www.state.nj.us/lps/ca/plumber/plumdir.htm
Podiatrist #14	www.state.nj.us/lps/ca/bme/poddir.htm
Psychologist #22	www.state.nj.us/lps/ca/psy/psydir.htm
Public Accountant-CPA #5	www.state.nj.us/lps/ca/accountancy/accdir.htm
Real Estate Appraiser/Apprentice #23	www.state.nj.us/lps/ca/real/realdir.htm
Real Estate School/ Instructor #48	www.state.nj.us/dobi/recskool.htm
Respiratory Therapist #54	www.state.nj.us/lps/ca/respcare/respdir.htm
Shorthand Reporter #24	www.state.nj.us/lps/ca/short/shortdir.htm
Skin Care Specialist #9	www.state.nj.us/lps/ca/cosmetology/skindir.htm
Social Worker #25	www.state.nj.us/lps/ca/social/socdir.htm
Speech-Language Pathologist #7	www.state.nj.us/lps/ca/aud/auddir.htm
Surveyor, Land #20	www.state.nj.us/lps/ca/pels/engdir.htm
Tree Expert #55	www.state.nj.us/dep/forestry/community/cte.html
Veterinarian #26	www.state.nj.us/lps/ca/vetmed/vetdir.htm

Licensing Quick Finder

Accountant, Municipal #5	973-504-6380
Acupuncturist #1	973-273-8090
Alcohol/Drug Counselor #13	973-504-6069
Animal Control Officer #59	609-588-3121
Appraiser, General/Residential #23	973-504-6480
Architect #6	973-504-6385
Asbestos Employee/Employer #33	609-633-3760
Asbestos Permit #33	609-633-3760
Athletic Booking Agency #40	973-504-6370
Attorney #49	609-984-7783
Audiologist #7	973-504-6390
Automobile Dealer #42	609-292-4517
Barber #9	973-504-6400
Barber Shop #9	973-504-6400
Beautician #9	973-504-6400
Boiler Operator #34	609-984-3001
Boxer #53	609-292-0317
Boxing Manager #28	609-292-0317
Building Inspector #45	609-984-7834
Career Counselor #40	973-504-6367
Casino #28	609-441-3555
Casino Employee #28	609-441-3015
Cemetery #46	973-504-6553
Cemetery Salesperson #46	973-504-6553
Charities #61	973-504-6215
Check Casher/Seller #38	609-292-5340
Chiropractor #8	973-504-6395
Club/Cabaret #37	609-984-3231
Computer Job-Matching Service #40	973-504-6370
Construction Code Official #45	609-984-7834
Cosmetologist/Hairstylist #9	973-504-6400
Counselor, Social Work #25	973-504-6495
Court Reporter #24	973-273-8090
Crane Operator #34	609-984-3001
Dental Assistant, Ltd/Registered #10	973-504-6405
Dental Hygienist #10	973-504-6405
Dentist #10	973-504-6405
Educational Media Specialist/Librarian #29	609-292-0739
Electrical Contractor #11	973-504-6410
Elevator Inspector #45	609-984-7834
Embalmer #15	973-273-8090
Emergency Medical Service Provider #32	609-633-7777
Emergency Medical Technician #32	609-633-7777
Employment Agency #40	973-504-6367
Engineer #20	973-504-6460
Fire Protection Inspector #45	609-984-7834
Firefighter #58	609-633-6117

Funeral Practitioner #15	973-273-8090
Health Care Service Agency #40	973-504-6367
Health Spa #40	973-504-6370
Hearing Aid Dispenser/Fitter #44	973-504-6331
Home Health Aide #16	973-504-6586
Home Repair Contractor/Seller #39	609-292-3420
Hotel/Motel #37	609-984-3231
Implant Inspector #45	609-984-7834
Insurance Agent #41	609-292-5360
Insurance Public Adjuster #41	609-292-5360
Investment Advisor #27	201-504-6200
Job Listing Service #40	973-504-6370
Lab Director, Bio-Analytical #14	609-292-4843
Landscape Architect #6	973-504-6385
Lender, Consumer #39	609-292-5340
Librarian #29	609-292-2070
Liquor Control #37	609-984-3231
Liquor Distribution, Plenary Retail/Limited Retail #37	609-984-3231
Liquor Rectifier/Blender #37	609-984-3231
Liquor Retail, Plenary/Seasonal #37	609-984-3231
Liquor Sales, Retail/Limited/Plenary #37	609-984-3231
Liquor Transit, Plenary Retail #37	609-984-3231
Liquor Wholesale, Limited/Plenary #37	609-984-3231
Lobbyist #43	609-292-8700
Manicurist/Manicure Shop #9	973-504-6400
Marriage & Family Counselor, Professional #13	973-504-6082
Marriage & Family Therapist #25	973-504-6495
Marriage Counselor #13	973-504-6415
Midwife #14	609-292-4843
Modeling & Talent Agency #40	973-504-6367
Mortgage (2nd) Lender #39	609-292-5340
Mortgage Banker/Broker #27	201-504-6200
Mortician #15	973-273-8090
Mover/Warehouseman #2	973-504-6512
Notary Public #36	609-292-9292
Nurse, Advance Practice #16	973-504-6586
Nurse-LPN #16	973-504-6586
Nurse-RN #16	973-504-6586
Occupational Therapist #60	973-504-6570
Occupational Therapy Asst. #60	973-504-6570
Optician/Optician Technician #51	973-504-6435
Optometrist #17	973-504-6440
Orthodontic Assistant, Ltd/ Registered #10	973-504-6405
Orthopedist #14	609-292-4843
Orthotist/Prosthetist #52	973-504-6445

Paramedic #32	609-633-7777
Pesticide Applicator/Operator #31	609-530-4070
Pesticide Dealer #31	609-530-4070
Pharmacist #18	973-504-6450
Pharmacy #18	973-504-6450
Physical Therapist #19	973-504-6455
Physical Therapist Assistant #19	973-504-6455
Physician #14	609-292-4843
Planner, Professional #21	973-504-6465
Plumber/Master Plumber #12	973-504-6420
Podiatrist #14	609-292-4843
Private Detective #56	609-882-2000 X2680
Psychologist #22	973-504-6470
Public Accountant-CPA #5	973-504-6380
Pump Installer #30	609-777-1007
Race Horse #47	609-292-0613
Race Horse Owner/Trainer #47	609-292-0613
Real Estate Agent/Broker #48	609-292-8280
Real Estate Appraiser/Apprentice #23	973-504-6480
Real Estate Salesperson #48	609-292-8280
Real Estate School/ Instructor #48	609-292-8280
Refrigeration Technician #34	609-984-3001
Respiratory Therapist #54	973-504-6485
Resume Service #40	973-504-6370
School Accountant #5	973-504-6380
School Counselor #29	609-292-0739
School Principal/Admin./Supvr. #29	609-292-0739
School, Accredited #29	609-292-0739
Securities Agent #27	201-504-6200
Securities Broker/Dealer #27	201-504-6200
Securities Issuer #27	201-504-6200
Shorthand Reporter #24	973-273-8090
Skin Care Specialist #9	973-504-6400
Social Worker #25	973-504-6495
Speech-Language Pathologist #7	973-504-6390
Stable Mate #47	609-292-0613
Student Personnel Svc Director #29	609-292-0739
Surveyor, Land #20	973-504-6460
Teacher #29	609-292-0739
Temporary Health Agency #40	973-504-6370
Theater #37	609-984-3231
Ticket Reseller #40	973-504-6370
Tree Expert #55	609-292-2532
Veterinarian #26	973-504-6500
Waste Water System Operator #30	609-777-1007
Weighmaster #35	732-815-4845
Weights & Measures Mechanic #35	732-815-4845
Well Driller #30	609-777-1007
Wine Wholesaler/Winery #37	609-984-3231

Licensing Agency Information

#1 Board of Medical Examiners, Acupuncture Examining Board, PO Box 183, Trenton, NJ 08625-0183; 609-826-7100.
Search database at
www.state.nj.us/lps/ca/bme/acupdir.htm

#2 Office of Consumer Protection, Regulated Business Section, 124 Halsey St, Newark, NJ 07101; 973-504-6442, Fax: 973-648-2807.
www.state.nj.us/lps/ca. Agency email: askconsumeraffairs@smtp.lps.state.nj.us.

#5 Board of Accountancy, PO Box 45000, Newark, NJ 07101; 973-504-6380, Fax: 973-648-2855.
www.state.nj.us/lps/ca/nonmed.htm#acc1
Search database at
www.state.nj.us/lps/ca/accountancy/accdir.htm

#6 Board of Architects, Division of Consumer Affairs, 124 Halsey St, Newark, NJ 07102; 973-504-6385, Fax: 973-504-6458.
www.state.nj.us/lps/ca
Search database at
www.state.nj.us/lps/ca/director.htm

#7 Board of Audiology & Speech Language Pathology, 124 Halsey St (07102), Newark, NJ 07101; 973-504-6390, Fax: 973-648-3355.
Search database at
www.state.nj.us/lps/ca/aud/auddir.htm

#8 Board of Chiropractic Examiners, Division of Consumer Affairs, 124 Halsey St, Newark, NJ 07102; 973-504-6395, Fax: 973-648-3538.
www.state.nj.us/lps/ca
Agency email: lpyqidr@oag.lps.state.nj.us.
Search database at
www.state.nj.us/lps/ca/director.htm

#9 Board of Cosmetology & Hairstyling, PO Box 45003, Newark, NJ 07101; 973-504-6400, Fax: 973-648-3536.
Search database at
www.state.nj.us/lps/ca/director.htm

#10 Board of Dentistry, PO Box 45005, 124 Halsey St (07102), Newark, NJ 07101; 973-504-6405, Fax: 973-273-8075.
www.state.nj.us/lps/ca/dentistry
Search database at
www.state.nj.us/lps/ca/director.htm. There is an automated license verification line (need license number) 973-273-8090 with fax back capability for written verifications.

#11 Board of Examiners of Electrical Contractors, Division of Consumer Affairs, 124 Halsey St (07102), Newark, NJ 07101; 973-504-6410, Fax: 973-648-3355.
www.state.nj.us/lps/ca/boards/list1.htm. Agency email: AskConsumerAffairs@oag.lps.state.nj.us.
Search database at
www.state.nj.us/lps/ca/electric/elecdir.htm

#12 Board of Examiners of Master Plumbers, PO Box 45008 (124 Halsey St, 07102), Newark, NJ 07101; 973-504-6420.
www.state.nj.us/lps/ca/home.htm
Search database at
www.state.nj.us/lps/ca/plumber/plumdir.htm

#13 Board of Marriage & Family Therapy Examiners, 124 Halsey St (07102), 6th Fl, Newark, NJ 07101; 973-594-6415, Fax: 973-648-3536.

www.state.nj.us/lps/ca/boards.htm
Search database at
www.state.nj.us/lps/ca/marriage/pcdir.htm

#14 Board of Medical Examiners, PO Box 183, Trenton, NJ 08625-0183; 609-292-4843, Fax: 609-984-3950.
www.state.nj.us./lps/ca/medical.htm
Search database at
www.state.nj.us/lps/ca/director.htm

#15 Board of Mortuary Science, Division of Consumer Affairs, 124 Halsey St, Newark, NJ 07102; 973-504-6425, Fax: 973-648-3636.
www.state.nj.us/lps/ca
Agency email: lpywidr@oag.lps.state.nj.us.
Search database at
www.state.nj.us/lps/ca/mort/mortdir.htm

#16 Board of Nursing, 124 Halsey St (07102), Newark, NJ 07101; 973-504-6586, Fax: 973-648-3481.
www.state.nj.us/lps/ca/home.htm. Agency email: AskConsumerAffairs@oag.lps.state.nj.us.
Search database at
www.state.nj.us/lps/ca/medical.htm#nur6

#17 Board of Optometrists, Division of Consumer Affairs, 124 Halsey St (07102), Newark, NJ 07101; 973-504-6440, Fax: 973-645-3536.
www.state.nj.us/lps/ca/optometry/optdir.htm
Search database at
www.state.nj.us/lps/ca/optometry/optdir.htm

#18 Board of Pharmacy, PO Box 45013 (124 Halsey St, 07102), Newark, NJ 07101; 973-504-6450, Fax: 973-648-3355.
www.state.nj.us/lps/ca/medical.htm#pharm11
Search database at
www.state.nj.us/lps/ca/pharm/pharmdir.htm

#19 Board of Physical Therapists, 124 Halsey St, Newark, NJ 07101; 973-504-6455, Fax: 973-648-3536.
Search database at
www.state.nj.us/lps/ca/pt/ptdir.htm

#20 Board of Professional Engineers & Land Surveyors, 124 Halsey St (07102), Newark, NJ 07101; 973-504-6460, Fax: 973-648-3536.
www.state.nj.us/lps/ca/nonmed.htm
Search database at
www.state.nj.us/lps/ca/pels/engdir.htm

#21 Board of Professional Planners, PO Box 45016 (124 Halsey St, 07102), Newark, NJ 07101; 973-504-6465, Fax: 973-648-3536.
www.state.nj.us/lps/ca/plan/planner.htm
Search database at
www.state.nj.us/lps/ca/plan/plandir.htm

#22 Board of Psychological Examiners, Division of Consumer Affairs, 124 Halsey St, Newark, NJ 07102; 973-504-6470.
www.state.nj.us/lps/ca
Search database at
www.state.nj.us/lps/ca/psy/psydir.htm

#23 Board of Real Estate Appraisers, Division of Consumer Affairs, PO Box 45032 (124 Halsey St, 07102), Newark, NJ 07101; 973-504-6480, Fax: 973-648-3536.
www.state.nj.us/lps/ca
Search database at
www.state.nj.us/lps/ca/real/realdir.htm

#24 Board of Shorthand Reporting, Po Box 45019, Newark, NJ 07101; 973-504-6490, Fax: 973-648-3536.
www.state.nj.us/lps/ca/nonmed.htm#short12
Search database at
www.state.nj.us/lps/ca/short/shortdir.htm

#25 Board of Social Work Examiners, PO Box 45033, Newark, NJ 07101; 973-504-6495, Fax: 973-648-3536.
www.state.nj.us/lps/ca/medical.htm#sw15
Search database at
www.state.nj.us/lps/ca/director.htm. A license verification telephone service is available at 973-273-8090.

#26 Board of Veterinary Medical Examiners, PO Box 45033, Newark, NJ 07101; 973-504-6500, Fax: 973-648-3355.
www.state.nj.us/lps/ca/medical.htm
Agency email: romanod@smtd.lps.state.nj.us.
Search database at
www.state.nj.us/lps/ca/vetmed/vetdir.htm

#27 Bureau of Securities, PO Box 47029, 153 Halsey St 6th Fl, Newark, NJ 07101; 973-504-3600, Fax: 973-504-3601.
www.state.nj.us/lps/ca/bos.htm

#28 Casino Control Commission, Tennessee Ave & Boardwalk, Arcade Bldg, Atlantic City, NJ 08401; 609-441-3000, Fax: 609-441-3752.
www.state.nj.us/casinos

#29 Department of Education, Board of Examiners, PO Box 500, 100 Riverview Plaza, Trenton, NJ 08625-0500; 609-292-2045, Fax: 609-292-3768.

#30 Department of Environmental Protection, PO Box 402 (401 E State St, CN-402), Trenton, NJ 08625; 609-292-8046, Fax: 609-633-3727.
www.state.nj.us/dep/index.htm.

#31 Department of Environmental Protection, Pesticide Control Program, PO Box 411, Trenton, NJ 08625-0411; 609-530-4070, Fax: 609-984-6555.
www.state.nj.us/dep/enforcement/pcp
Agency email: askDEP@dep.state.nj.us.

#32 Office of Emergency Medical Svcs, Department of Health, 50 E State St 6th Fl (PO Box 360), Trenton, NJ 08625; 609-633-7777, Fax: 609-633-7954.
www.state.nj.us/health/ems/index.html
Agency email: ems@doh.state.ny.us
Only disciplinary actions, fines, and enforcement actions are available online.

#33 Bureau of Code Svcs, Asbestos Contractor Program, Department of Community Affairs, PO Box 816, 101 S Broad St 4th Fl, Trenton, NJ 08625-0816; 609-633-3760, Fax: 609-984-7952.

#34 Bureau of Boiler & Pressure Vessel Compliance, Division of Community Affairs, PO Box 814 (101 South Broad St), Trenton, NJ 08625-0814; 609-984-3001, Fax: 609-984-1577.

#35 Department of Law & Public Safety, Office of Weights & Measures, 1261 Route 1 & 9 South, Avanel, NJ 07001; 732-815-4845, Fax: 732-382-5298.
www.state.nj.us/lps/index.html.

#36 Department of Treasury, Division of Revenue, Notary Section, PO Box 452, West Trenton, NJ 08625; 609-292-9292, Fax: 609-984-6681. www.state.nj.us/treasury/revenue/dcr/programs/notary.html.

#37 Division of Alcoholic Beverage Control, 140 E Front St, CN087, Trenton, NJ 08625-0087; 609-984-3230, Fax: 609-633-6078. www.state.nj.us/lps/abc/licbur.htm

#38 Division of Banking, Consumer Credit Bureau, 20 W State St CN-040, Trenton, NJ 08625; 609-292-5340, Fax: 609-292-5461. www.nail.org/nj/NJHOME.PG.html

#39 Division of Banking, Office of Consumer Finance, 20 W State St CN-040, Trenton, NJ 08625; 609-292-5340, Fax: 609-292-5461. www.nail.org/nj/NJHOME.PG.html

#40 Regulated Business Section, Division of Consumer Affairs, PO Box 45028 (124 Halsey St), Newark, NJ 07101; 973-504-6370, Fax: 973-648-2807. www.state.nj.us/lps/ca

#41 Division of Insurance, License Processing, PO Box 327 (20 W. State St), Trenton, NJ 08625-0327; 609-292-5360, Fax: 609-984-5263. www.njdobi.org

#42 Division of Motor Vehicles, Dealer Licensing Section, 225 E State St, Trenton, NJ 08666; 609-292-4517, Fax: 609-292-5153. www.state.nj.us/mvs

#43 Election Law Enforcement Commission, PO Box 185, CN-185 (28 W State St), Trenton, NJ 08625-0185; 609-292-8700, Fax: 609-633-9854. www.elec.state.nj.us

#44 Hearing Aid Dispensers Examining Committee, PO Box 45038, Newark, NJ 07101; 973-504-6331, Fax: 973-648-3355. www.state.nj.us/lps/ca/medical.htm
Search database at www.state.nj.us/lps/ca/hear/heardir.htm.

#45 Department of Community Affairs, Bureau of Code Services, Attn: Licensing Unit, CN-816, Trenton, NJ 08625-0816; 609-984-7834, Fax: 609-984-7952. www.state.nj.us/dca/codes/

#46 Cemetery Board, PO Box 45036, Newark, NJ 07101; 973-504-6553, Fax: 973-648-3536. www.state.nj.us/lps/ca/nonmed.htm
Search database at www.state.nj.us/lps/ca/director.htm

#47 Racing Commission, POB 088 (140 Front St), Trenton, NJ 08625-0080; 609-292-0613, Fax: 609-599-1785.

#48 Department of Banking & Insurance, Real Estate Commission, 399 Washington St 5th Fl, Trenton, NJ 08625-0328; 609-292-8280, Fax: 609-292-0944. www.state.nj.us/dobi/remnu.htm. Agency email: realestate@dobi.state.nj.us.

#49 State Bar Association, Board of Bar Exams, PO Box 973 (25 Market St, 8th Fl), Trenton, NJ 08625; 609-984-7783, Fax: 609-984-6859. www.judiciary.state.nj.us

#51 Ophthalmic Dispensers & Ophthalmic Technicians Board, Division of Consumer Affairs, 124 Halsey St, Newark, NJ 07102; 973-504-6435, Fax: 973-648-3355.
Search database at www.state.nj.us/lps/ca/director.htm

#52 Orthotics & Prosthetics Board of Examiners, Division of Consumer Affairs, PO Box 45034 (124 Halsey St., Newark, NJ 07112; 973-504-6445, Fax: 973-648-3536. www.state.nj.us/lps/ca

#53 Athletic Control Board, 140 E Front St, CN-180, Trenton, NJ 08625-0180; 609-292-0317, Fax: 609-292-3756.

#54 Board of Respiratory Care, 122 Halsey St, Newark, NJ 07101; 973-504-6485, Fax: 973-648-3355.
www.state.nj.us/lps/ca/home.htm
Search database at www.state.nj.us/lps/ca/respcare/respdir.htm

#55 Forestry Service, 501 E State St CN-404, Trenton, NJ 08625-0404; 609-292-2532, Fax: 609-984-0378.
www.state.nj.us/dep/forestry/community/home.htm
Search database at www.state.nj.us/dep/forestry/community/cte.html

#56 State Police Department, Private Detective Division, River Rd, Trenton, NJ 08628; 609-882-2000 x2680, Fax: 609-637-9583. www.njsp.org/about/srb.html

#58 Department of Community Affairs, Division of Fire Safety, PO Box 809, Trenton, NJ 08625-0809; 609-633-6117, Fax: 609-633-6744.

#59 Department of Health & Senior Svcs, Infectious & Zoonotic Program, PO Box 369, Trenton, NJ 08625-0369; 609-588-3121, Fax: 609-588-3894. www.state.nj.us

#60 Occupational Therapy Advisory Council, Division of Consumer Affairs, PO Box 45037 (124 Halsey St), Newark, NJ 07101; 973-504-6570. www.state.nj.us/lps/ca/medical.htm#occ7. Agency email: lpyqidr@oag.lps.state.nj.us. Search database at www.state.nj.us/lps/ca/director.htm

#61 Charities Registration Section, Division of Consumer Affairs, PO Box 45021 (124 Halsey St), Newark, NJ 07101; 973-504-6215. www.state.nj.us/lps/ca
Search database at www.state.nj.us/lps/ca/charfrm.htm

New Jersey Federal Courts

The following list indicates the district and division name for each county in the state. If the bankruptcy court location is different from the district court, then the location of the bankruptcy court appears in parentheses.

County/Court Cross Reference

Atlantic	Camden	Middlesex	Newark (Trenton)
Bergen	Newark	Monmouth	Newark (Trenton)
Burlington	Camden	Morris	Newark
Camden	Camden	Ocean	Trenton
Cape May	Camden	Passaic	Newark
Cumberland	Camden	Salem	Camden
Essex	Newark	Somerset	Trenton
Gloucester	Camden	Sussex	Newark
Hudson	Newark	Union	Newark
Hunterdon	Trenton	Warren	Trenton
Mercer	Trenton		

Standards for Federal Courts: The search fee is $20.00 per item (one party name or case number). Certification fee is $7.00 per document. Copy fee is $.50 per page. All fees standard unless noted in profile. Mail Search: always enclose a stamped self addressed envelope unless otherwise noted. Before releasing records, all courts require prepayment unless noted in profile.

Open records are located at the court unless otherwise noted. District courts index by defendant and plaintiff as well as by case number. Bankruptcy courts usually index by debtor and case number. While most courts now have their indexes on computer, many still maintain index card files as well.

The universal PACER sign-up number is 800-676-6856. Find PACER and the Party/Case Index on the Web at http://pacer.psc.uscourts.gov. PACER dial-up access is $.60 per minute. Also, courts offering internet access via RACER, PACER, Web-PACER or the new CM-ECF charge $.07 per page fee unless noted as free.

US District Court

District of New Jersey

Camden Division Clerk, PO Box 2797, Camden, NJ 08101 (Courier Address: Room 1050, 4th & Cooper Sts, Camden, NJ 08101), 856-757-5021, Fax: 856-757-5370.

http://pacer.njd.uscourts.gov

Counties: Atlantic, Burlington, Camden, Cape May, Cumberland, Gloucester, Salem.

Indexing & Storage: Cases are indexed by defendant, plaintiff, and case number. New cases are available in the index 1-2 days after filing date. Records are also indexed on microfiche. District wide searches are available for all information from this court.

Fee & Payment Notes: Payment may be made by money order, cashier check, personal check. Payee: Clerk, US District Court.

Phone Search: Only docket information is available by phone.

In Person Search: In person searching available.

PACER: Toll-free dial-up access: 888-297-9938. Local dial-up access: 609-989-0590. Case records are available back to May 1991. Records are never purged. New records are available online after 1 day. PACER is available online at http://pacer.njd.uscourts.gov.

Opinions Online: Court opinions available online at http://lawlibrary.rutgers.edu/fed/search.html

Newark Division ML King, Jr Federal Bldg. & US Courthouse, 50 Walnut St, Room 4015, Newark, NJ 07101 (Courier Address: Use mail address for courier delivery), 973-645-3730.

http://pacer.njd.uscourts.gov

Counties: Bergen, Essex, Hudson, Middlesex, Monmouth, Morris, Passaic, Sussex, Union. Monmouth County was transferred from Trenton Division in late 1997; closed cases remain in Trenton.

Indexing & Storage: Cases are indexed by defendant, plaintiff, and case number. New cases are available in the index 1-3 days after filing date. Open records are located at this court.

Fee & Payment Notes: Payment may be made by money order, cashier check, business check. Personal checks are not accepted. Payee: Clerk, US District Court.

Phone Search: Only docket information available by telephone.

In Person Search: In person searching available.

PACER: Toll-free dial-up access: 888-297-9938. Local dial-up access: 609-989-0590. Case records are available back to May 1991. Records are never purged. New records are available online after 1 day. PACER is available online at http://pacer.njd.uscourts.gov.

Opinions Online: Court opinions available online at http://lawlibrary.rutgers.edu/fed/search.html

Trenton Division Clerk, US District Court, Room 2020, 402 E State St, Trenton, NJ 08608 (Courier Address: Use mail address for courier delivery), 609-989-2065.

http://pacer.njd.uscourts.gov

Counties: Hunterdon, Mercer, Ocean, Somerset, Warren. Monmouth County was transferred to Newark and Camden Division in late 1997; closed Monmouth cases remain in Trenton.

Indexing & Storage: Cases are indexed by defendant, plaintiff, and case number. New cases are available in the index several days after filing date. Records are also indexed on microfiche. District wide searches are available for information from 1920 from this district. This court also maintained closed files for the Newark division until 1997.

Fee & Payment Notes: Payment may be made by money order, cashier check, personal check. Payee: Clerk, US District Court.

Phone Search: Only docket information available by phone.

Mail Search: A stamped self addressed envelope is not required.

In Person Search: In person searching available.

PACER: Toll-free dial-up access: 888-297-9938. Local dial-up access: 609-989-0590. Case records are available back to May 1991. Records are never purged. New records are available online after 1 day. PACER is available online at http://pacer.njd.uscourts.gov.

Opinions Online: Court opinions available online at http://lawlibrary.rutgers.edu/fed/search.html

US Bankruptcy Court

District of New Jersey

Camden Division PO Box 2067, Camden, NJ 08101 (Courier Address: 401 Market St, 2nd Floor, Camden, NJ 08101), 856-757-5485.

www.njb.uscourts.gov

Counties: Atlantic, Burlington (partial), Camden, Cape May, Cumberland, Gloucester, Salem.

Indexing & Storage: Cases are indexed by debtor as well as by case number. New cases are available in the index immediately after filing date. Open records are located at this court.

Fee & Payment Notes: Payment may be made by money order, cashier check, business check. Personal checks are not accepted. Payee: Clerk, US Bankruptcy Court.

Phone Search: Only docket information available by phone. An automated voice case information service (VCIS) is available. Call VCIS at 877-239-2547 or 973-645-6044.

In Person Search: In person searching available.

PACER: Document images available. Case records are available back to 1991. Records are purged every 6 months. New civil records are available online after 1 day. PACER is available online at http://pacer.njb.uscourts.gov. Document images available.

Electronic Filing: Information is available online at https://ecf.njb.uscourts.gov

Other Online Access: Search records on RACER at http://racer.njb.uscourts.gov.

Newark Division PO Box 1352, Newark, NJ 07101 (Courier Address: ML King Jr Federal Bldg, 50 Walnut St, 3rd Fl, Newark, NJ 07102), 973-645-4764.

www.njb.uscourts.gov

Counties: Bergen, Essex, Hudson, Morris, Passaic, Sussex. Also Elizabeth, Springfield and Hillside townships in Union County.

Indexing & Storage: Cases are indexed by debtor as well as by case number. New cases are available in the index immediately after filing date. Open records are located at this court.

Fee & Payment Notes: Payment may be made by money order, cashier check, business check. Personal checks are not accepted. Payee: Clerk, US Bankruptcy Court.

Phone Search: An automated voice case information service (VCIS) is available. Call VCIS at 877-239-2547 or 973-645-6044.

In Person Search: In person searching available.

PACER: Case records are available back to 1991. Records are purged every 6 months. New civil records are available online after 1 day. PACER is available online at http://pacer.njb.uscourts.gov. Document images available.

Electronic Filing: Information is available online at https://ecf.njb.uscourts.gov

Other Online Access: Search records on RACER at http://racer.njb.uscourts.gov.

Trenton Division Clerk of Court, 402 E State St, 1st Fl, Trenton, NJ 08608 (Courier Address: Use mail address for courier delivery), 609-989-2128.

www.njb.uscourts.gov

Counties: Burlington (partial), Hunterdon, Mercer, Middlesex, Monmouth, Ocean, Somerset, Warren, Union except the townships of Elizabeth, Hillside and Springfield.

Indexing & Storage: Cases are indexed by debtor as well as by case number. New cases are available in the index immediately after filing date. Open records are located at this court.

Fee & Payment Notes: Payment may be made by money order, cashier check, business check. Personal checks are not accepted. Payee: Clerk, US Bankruptcy Court.

Phone Search: An automated voice case information service (VCIS) is available. Call VCIS at 877-239-2547 or 973-645-6044.

In Person Search: In person searching available.

PACER: Case records are available back to 1991. Records are purged every 6 months. New civil records are available online after 1 day. PACER is available online at http://pacer.njb.uscourts.gov. Document images available.

Electronic Filing: Information is available online at https://ecf.njb.uscourts.gov

Other Online Access: Search records on RACER at http://racer.njb.uscourts.gov.

New Jersey County Courts

Court	Jurisdiction	No. of Courts	How Organized
Superior Courts*	General	21	21 Counties/15 Vicinages
Special Civil Part*	Limited	21	21 Counties
Municipal Courts	Municipal	535	
Tax Court	Special	1	

* Profiled in this Sourcebook.

Court	CIVIL								
	Tort	Contract	Real Estate	Min. Claim	Max. Claim	Small Claims	Estate	Eviction	Domestic Relations
Superior Courts*	X	X	X	$10,000	No Max		X		X
Special Civil Part*	X	X	X	$0	$10,000	$2000		X	
Municipal Courts									
Tax Court									

Court	CRIMINAL				
	Felony	Misdemeanor	DWI/DUI	Preliminary Hearing	Juvenile
Superior Courts*	X				X
Special Civil Part*					
Municipal Courts		X	X		
Tax Court					

ADMINISTRATION

Administrative Office of the Courts, RJH Justice Complex, Courts Bldg 7th Floor, CN 037, Trenton, NJ, 08625; 609-984-0275, Fax: 609-984-6968. www.judiciary.state.nj.us

COURT STRUCTURE

Each Superior Court has 2 divisions; one for the Civil Division and another for the Criminal Division. Search requests should be addressed separately to each division.

The Special Civil Part of the Superior Court acts like a division of the court, and handles only the smaller civil claims. The small claims limit is $2,000. The Superior Court designation refers to the court where criminal cases and civil claims over $10,000 are heard. Probate is handled by Surrogates.

ONLINE ACCESS

Online computer access is available through the ACMS, AMIS, and FACTS systems.

- ACMS (Automated Case Management System) contains data on all active civil cases statewide from the Law Division-Civil Part, Chancery Division-Equity Part, the Special Civil Part statewide, and the Appellate Division.

- AMIS (Archival Management Information System) contains closed case information.

- FACTS (Family Automated Case Tracking System) contains information on dissolutions from all counties.

The fee is $1.00 per minute of use. For further information and/or an Inquiry System Guidebook containing hardware and software requirements and an enrollment form, write to: Superior Court Clerk's Office, Electronic Access Program, 25 Market St, CN971, Trenton NJ 08625, FAX 609-292-6564, or call 609-292-4987.

The Judiciary's civil motion calendar is searchable online at the web site above. The database includes all Superior Court Motion Calendars for the Civil Division (Law-Civil Part, Special Civil Part and Chancery-General Equity), and proceeding information for a six-week period (two weeks prior to the current date and four weeks following the current date).

ADDITIONAL INFORMATION

Effective 1/1/95, all court employees became state employees and each section is responsible for its own fees. Note that Cape May County offices are located in the city of Cape May Court House, and not in the city of Cape May.

Atlantic County

Superior Court - Criminal Division Criminal Courthouse, 5909 Main St, Mays Landing, NJ 08330; 609-625-7000; Fax: 609-645-5875. Hours: 8:30AM-4:30PM (EST). *Felony.*

www.judiciary.state.nj.us/atlantic/index.htm

Criminal Records: Access: Mail, fax, in person. Both court and visitors may perform in person searches. No search fee. Required to search: name, years to search, DOB; also helpful: SSN. Criminal records on computer from 1985, prior on docket books and index cards back to 1940.

General Information: Public access terminal is available. No sealed, expunged, judges notes, PSI's, or mental illness records released. SASE required. Copy fee: $.75 per page. Certification fee: $5.00. Fee payee: Treasurer-State of New Jersey. No personal checks accepted. Prepayment is required.

Superior Court - Civil Division 5905 Main St, Mays Landing, NJ 08330; 609-625-7000 X3370; Fax: 609-645-5875. Hours: 8:30AM-4:30PM (EST). *Civil Actions Over $10,000, Probate.*

www.judiciary.state.nj.us/atlantic/index.htm

Civil Records: Access: Mail, online, in person. No search fee. Required to search: name, years to search. Civil cases indexed by defendant, plaintiff. Civil records on computer from 9/84, on dockets from 1960, prior to 1960 archived. Prior to 1960 records are for public review only (in large books, difficult to find records). Participates in the court records statewide Electronic Access Program; for signup, information and booklet call 609-292-4987.

General Information: No sealed, expunged, judges notes, PSI's, or mental illness records released. SASE required. Turnaround time 1 day. Copy fee: $.75 per page 1st 1-10 pages; $.50 per page 11-20 pages; $.25 per page 20 plus pages. Fee payee: Treasurer-State of New Jersey. No personal checks accepted. Prepayment is required.

Superior Court Special Civil Part 1201 Bacharach Blvd., Atlantic City, NJ 08401; 609-345-6700 X3376; Fax: 609-343-2326. Hours: 8:30AM-4:30PM (EST). *Civil Actions Under $10,000, Eviction, Small Claims.*

www.judiciary.state.nj.us/atlantic/index.htm

Civil Records: Access: Mail, online, in person. Both court and visitors may perform in person searches. No search fee. Required to search: name, years to search. Civil cases indexed by defendant, plaintiff. Civil records on computer from 1985 (some from 1987), prior on index books. In order to review index books, call in advance for an appointment. Participates in the court records statewide Electronic Access Program; for signup, information and booklet call 609-292-4987.

General Information: Public access terminal is available. No adoption, sealed, juvenile, expunged, dismissed, or mental health records released. SASE required. Turnaround time 1 week. Copy fee: $.75 per page. Certification fee: $5.00. Fee payee: Clerk, Special Civil Part. Personal checks accepted. Prepayment is required.

Bergen County

Superior Court - Criminal Division 10 Main St, Rm 134, Justice Center, Hackensack, NJ 07601; 201-336-7053; Fax: 201-342-9083. Hours: 8:30AM-4:30PM (EST). *Felony.*

www.judiciary.state.nj.us/bergen/index.htm

Criminal Records: Access: Fax, mail, in person. Both court and visitors may perform in person searches. Search fee: $2.00 per name. Required to search: name, years to search, SSN, DOB, signed release; also helpful: address, DOB. Criminal records on computer from 1973.

General Information: No sealed, expunged, dismissed, judges notes, PSI's, or discovery packets records released. SASE required. Turnaround time 1 week. Copy fee: $.25. No charge for single copy of criminal record. Certification fee: $5.00. Fee payee: Bergen County Clerk. Personal checks accepted. Prepayment is required.

Superior Court - Civil Division 10 Main St. Rm 119, Justice Center, Hackensack, NJ 07601; 201-646-2783/3011; Fax: 201-752-4031. Hours: 8:30AM-4:30PM (EST). *Civil Actions Over $10,000, Probate.*

www.judiciary.state.nj.us/bergen/index.htm

Civil Records: Access: Mail, online, in person. Only the court performs in person searches; visitors may not. No search fee. Required to search: name, years to search. Civil cases indexed by defendant, plaintiff. Civil records on computer for 2-5 years, on dockets from 1900s. Participates in the court records statewide Electronic Access Program; for signup, information and booklet call 609-292-4987.

General Information: No sealed, expunged, dismissed, judges notes, PSI's, or discovery packets records released. SASE required. Turnaround time 1 week. Copy fee: $.50 per page. Certification fee: $5.00. Fee payee: Bergen County Clerk. Personal checks accepted. Prepayment is required.

Superior Court Special Civil Part 10 Main St. Rm 430, Justice Center, Hackensack, NJ 07601; 201-646-2289/2243. Hours: 8:30AM-5PM (EST). *Civil Actions Under $10,000, Eviction, Small Claims.*

www.judiciary.state.nj.us/bergen/index.htm

Civil Records: Access: Mail, online, in person, phone. Both court and visitors may perform in person searches. No search fee. Required to search: name, years to search. Civil cases indexed by defendant, plaintiff. Civil records on computer from 1990, prior on index cards. Participates in the court records statewide Electronic Access Program; for signup, information and booklet call 609-292-4987.

General Information: No adoption, sealed, juvenile, expunged, dismissed, or mental illness records released. SASE required. Turnaround time varies from 2 days-3 weeks. Copy fee: $.50 per page. Certification fee: $5.00. Fee payee: Bergen County Special Civil Part. Personal checks accepted. Prepayment is required.

Burlington County

Superior Court - Criminal Division 49 Rancocas Rd, Mount Holly, NJ 08060; 609-518-2568. Hours: 8AM-5PM (EST). *Felony.*

www.judiciary.state.nj.us/burlington/index.htm

Criminal Records: Access: Mail, in person. Both court and visitors may perform in person searches. Search fee: $5.00 per name. Required to search: name, years to search; also helpful: DOB, SSN. Criminal records on computer from 1986, on docket books from 1954.

General Information: No sealed, expunged, judges notes, PSI's, or discovery packets released. SASE required. Turnaround time 10 days. Copy fee: $.75 per page for first ten pages; $.50 per page next ten; each add'l page $.25. Certification fee: $5.00. Fee payee: State of New Jersey. Personal checks accepted. Prepayment is required.

Superior Court - Civil Division 49 Rancocas Rd, Mount Holly, NJ 08060; 609-518-2622. Hours: 8AM-5PM (EST). *Civil Actions Over $10,000, Probate.*

www.judiciary.state.nj.us/burlington/index.htm

Civil Records: Access: Mail, online, in person. Both court and visitors may perform in person searches. No search fee. Required to search: name, years to search.

Civil cases indexed by defendant, plaintiff. Local judgment records on computer since 1989, all others from 1954 to present. Participates in the court records statewide Electronic Access Program; for signup, information and booklet call 609-292-4987.

General Information: Public access terminal is available. No sealed, expunged, judges notes, PSI's, or discovery packets released. SASE required. Turnaround time 10 days. Copy fee: $.75 per page for first ten, $.50 per page for next ten pages, and $.25 per page thereafter. Certification fee: $5.00. Fee payee: State of New Jersey. Personal checks accepted. Prepayment is required.

Superior Court Special Civil Part 49 Rancocas Rd., Mount Holly, NJ 08060; 609-518-2865; Fax: 609-518-2872. Hours: 8AM-5PM (EST). *Civil Actions Under $10,000, Eviction, Small Claims.*

www.judiciary.state.nj.us/burlington/index.htm

Civil Records: Access: Phone, fax, mail, in person. Both court and visitors may perform in person searches. No search fee. Required to search: name, years to search. Civil cases indexed by defendant, plaintiff. Civil records on computer from 1995, microfilm from 1984, prior on index books by docket number. Participates in the court records statewide Electronic Access Program; for signup, information and booklet call 609-292-4987.

General Information: Public access terminal is available. This court does not handle criminal matters in the Special Civil Part. Turnaround time 1-2 weeks. Fax notes: No fee to fax results. Copy fee: $.75 per page. Fee is for first 10 pages; $.50 per page next 10; each add'l $.25. Certification fee: $5.00. Fee payee: State of New Jersey. Personal checks accepted.

Camden County

Superior Court - Criminal Division Hall of Justice, 101 S 5th St, Camden, NJ 08103; 856-225-7452. Hours: 8AM-4PM (EST). *Felony.*

www.judiciary.state.nj.us/camden/index.htm

Criminal Records: Access: Mail, in person. Both court and visitors may perform in person searches. Search fee: $7.00 per name. Required to search: name, years to search, DOB, SSN. Criminal records on computer from 1986, on docket books from 1970.

General Information: Public access terminal is available. No sealed, expunged, dismissed, judges notes, PSI's or discovery packets records released. SASE required. Turnaround time 3 days. No copy fee. Fee payee: Clerk of Superior Court. Business checks accepted. Prepayment is required.

Superior Court - Civil Division Hall of Justice, 101 S 5th St, Camden, NJ 08103; 856-225-7494. Hours: 8AM-4PM (EST). *Civil Actions Over $10,000, Probate.*

www.judiciary.state.nj.us/camden/index.htm

Civil Records: Access: Mail, online, in person. Only the court performs in person searches; visitors may not. No search fee. Required to search: name, years to search. Civil cases indexed by defendant, plaintiff. Civil records on computer from 1987. Participates in the court records statewide Electronic Access Program; for signup, information and booklet call 609-292-4987.

General Information: No sealed, dismissed, judges notes, or discovery packets records released. SASE required. Turnaround time 3 days. Copy fee: $.75 per page. Fee is for first 10 pages; $.50 per page next 10; each add'l $.25. Certification fee: $5.00. Fee payee: Clerk of Superior Court. Personal checks accepted. Prepayment is required.

Superior Court Special Civil Part Hall of Justice Complex, 101 S. 5th St., Camden, NJ 08103; 856-225-7433. Hours: 8:30AM-4:30PM (EST). *Civil Actions Under $10,000, Eviction, Small Claims.*

www.judiciary.state.nj.us/camden/index.htm

Civil Records: Access: Mail, online, in person. Both court and visitors may perform in person searches. No search fee. Required to search: name, years to search. Civil cases indexed by defendant, plaintiff. Civil records on computer from 1988. Prior records on docket books. In person access is limited to one name. Participates in the court records statewide Electronic Access Program; for signup, information & booklet call 609-292-4987, or contact Admin Office of Court, Hughes Justice Complex, PO Box 981, Trenton, NJ 08625.

General Information: No adoption, sealed, juvenile, expunged, restricted, or mental health records released. Turnaround time varies. Copy fee: $.75 per page for the first ten, $.50 per page for the next ten, and $.25 per page thereafter. Certification fee: $5.00. Fee payee: Clerk Special Civil Part. Personal checks accepted. Prepayment is required.

Cape May County

Superior Court - Criminal Division 9 N Main St, Superior Court, Cape May Court House, NJ 08210; 609-463-6550; Fax: 609-463-6458. Hours: 8:30AM-4:30PM (EST). *Felony.*

www.judiciary.state.nj.us/atlantic/index.htm

Criminal Records: Access: In person only. Visitors must perform in person searches for themselves. No search fee. Required to search: name, years to search, DOB; also helpful: SSN. Criminal records on computer from 1985; on index books back to 1950.

General Information: No sealed, expunged, dismissed, judges notes, PSI's, or discovery packets records released. Copy fee: $.75 per page. Certification fee: $5.00. Fee payee: State of New Jersey. Personal checks accepted. Prepayment is required.

Superior Court Civil/Equity Division-Law, DN-203, 9 N Main St, Cape May Court House, NJ 08210; 609-463-6506; Fax: 609-463-6465. Hours: 8:30AM-4:30PM (EST). *Civil Actions Over $10,000, Probate.*

www.judiciary.state.nj.us/atlantic/index.htm

Civil Records: Access: Mail, online, in person. Both court and visitors may perform in person searches. Search fee: No search fee. Required to search: name, years to search. Civil cases indexed by defendant, plaintiff. Civil records on computer from 04/91, on index books and archived from 1900s. Participates in the court records statewide Electronic Access Program; for signup, information and booklet call 609-292-4987. A fee is charged for online access.

General Information: Public access terminal is available. No sealed records released. SASE required. Turnaround time 1 week. Copy fee: pgs 1-10, $.75 per pg; pgs 11-20, $.50 per pg; over 20 pgs $.25 per pg. Certification fee: First copy free; $5.00 1st 5 pgs; $.75 per pg each add'l pg. $5.00 minimum charge. Fee payee: Clerk of Superior Court. Personal checks accepted. Prepayment is required.

Superior Court Special Civil Part, DN-203, 9 N. Main St, Cape May Court House, NJ 08210; 609-463-6502; Fax: 609-463-6465. Hours: 8:30AM-4:30PM (EST). *Civil Actions Under $10,000, Eviction, Small Claims.*

www.judiciary.state.nj.us/atlantic/index.htm

Civil Records: Access: Mail, online, in person. Both court and visitors may perform in person searches. No search fee. Required to search: name, years to search; also helpful: address. Civil cases indexed by defendant, plaintiff. Civil records on computer from 4/1991, on index from 1973. Participates in the court records statewide Electronic Access Program; for signup, information and booklet call 609-292-4987. A fee is charged for remote online access.

General Information: Public access terminal is available. No sealed records released. SASE required.

Turnaround time 1 week. Copy fee: $.75 per page for the first ten pages, $.50 per page for the next ten, and $.25 per page thereafter. Certification fee: none if a party to the action; $5.00 if not. Fee payee: Clerk of the Special Civil Part. Personal checks accepted. Prepayment is required.

Cumberland County

Superior Court - Criminal Division PO Box 757, Bridgeton, NJ 08302; 856-453-4300; Fax: 856-451-7152. Hours: 8:30AM-4:30PM (EST). *Felony.*

www.judiciary.state.nj.us/gloucester/cum/index.htm

Criminal Records: Access: Mail, in person. Both the court and visitors may perform in person searches. Search fee: $4.00 per name. Required to search: name, years to search, DOB, SSN, signed release; also helpful: address. Criminal records on computer from 1986, on index from 1900.

General Information: No sealed, expunged, dismissed, judges notes, PSI's, or discovery packets records released. SASE Required. Turnaround time 1 week. Copy fee: $.25 per page. Certification fee: $5.00. Fee payee: State of New Jersey, Misc Fund. Personal checks accepted. Prepayment is required.

Superior Court - Civil Division PO Box 757, Bridgeton, NJ 08302; 856-453-4300; Fax: 856-451-7152. Hours: 8:30AM-4:30PM (EST). *Civil Actions Over $10,000, Probate.*

www.judiciary.state.nj.us/gloucester/cum/index.htm

Civil Records: Access: Mail, online, in person. Search fee: $4.00 per name. Required to search: name, years to search. Civil records on computer from 1986, on index from 1900. Participates in the court records statewide Electronic Access Program; for signup, information and booklet call 609-292-4987.

General Information: Public access terminal is available. No sealed, expunged, dismissed, judges notes, PSI's, or discovery packets records released. SASE Required. Turnaround time 1 week. Copy fee: $.25 per page. Certification fee: $5.00. Fee payee: State of New Jersey, Misc Fund. Personal checks accepted. Prepayment is required.

Superior Court Special Civil Part PO Box 10, Bridgeton, NJ 08302; 856-453-4350. Hours: 8:30AM-4:30PM (EST). *Civil Actions Under $10,000, Eviction, Small Claims.*

www.judiciary.state.nj.us/gloucester/cum/index.htm

Civil Records: Access: Phone, mail, online, in person. Only the court performs in person searches; visitors may not. No search fee. Required to search: name, years to search. Civil cases indexed by defendant, plaintiff. Civil records on computer from 12/89, on docket books from 1949 to 11/89. Participates in the court records statewide Electronic Access Program; for signup, information and booklet call 609-292-4987. Phone access is limited to 1 or 2 searches.

General Information: No adoption, sealed, juvenile, expunged, dismissed, or mental illness records released. SASE requested. Turnaround time 1 week. Copy fee: $.75 per page for the first ten, $.50 per page for the next ten, and $.25 per page thereafter. Fee payee: Clerk, Special Civil Part. Personal checks accepted. Prepayment is required.

Essex County

Superior Court - Criminal Division 50 W Market St, Rm 610, Essex County Court Bldg, Newark, NJ 07102-1681; 973-693-5700. Hours: 8:30AM-4:30PM (EST). *Felony.*

www.judiciary.state.nj.us/essex/index.htm

Criminal Records: Access: Fax, mail, in person. Only the court performs in person searches; visitors may not. Search fee: $3.00 per name. Required to search: name,

years to search, DOB, SSN, signed release. Criminal records on computer from 1985.

General Information: No sealed, expunged, dismissed, judges notes, PSI's, or discovery packets records released. SASE required. Turnaround time 1 week. Copy fee: $.25 per page. Certification fee: $5.00. Fee payee: State of New Jersey Judiciary. Business checks accepted. Prepayment is required.

Superior Court - Civil Division 465 Dr. Martin Luther King Blvd, Newark, NJ 07102-1681; 973-693-6460. Hours: 8:30AM-4:30PM (EST). *Civil Actions Over $10,000, Probate.*

www.judiciary.state.nj.us/essex/index.htm

Civil Records: Access: Online, in person. Only the court performs in person searches; visitors may not. No search fee. Required to search: name, years to search. Civil cases indexed by defendant, plaintiff. Civil records on computer from 1984, on index from 1930. Participates in the court records statewide Electronic Access Program; for signup, information and booklet call 609-292-4987.

General Information: No sealed, expunged, dismissed, judges notes, PSI's, or discovery packets records released. SASE required. Turnaround time 1 week. Fax notes: $3.00 per page. Copy fee: $.75 per page. Certification fee: $5.00. Fee payee: State of New Jersey Judiciary. Business checks accepted. Prepayment is required.

Superior Court Special Civil Part 465 Martin Luther King Blvd, Newark, NJ 07102; 973-693-6494; 693-6458 (general info); Fax: 973-621-5914. Hours: 8:30AM-4:30PM (EST). *Civil Actions Under $10,000, Eviction, Small Claims.*

www.judiciary.state.nj.us/essex/index.htm

Civil Records: Access: Mail, online, in person. Both court and visitors may perform in person searches. No search fee. Required to search: name, years to search. Civil cases indexed by defendant, plaintiff. Civil records on computer from 1986 and archived back to 1982. Participates in the court records statewide Electronic Access Program; for signup, information and booklet call 609-292-4987.

General Information: No adoption, sealed, juvenile, expunged, dismissed, or mental illness records released. SASE required. Turnaround time 7-10 days. Fax notes: Fee to fax results is $.75 per page. Fee payee: Essex County Special Civil Part. Personal checks accepted. Prepayment is required.

Gloucester County

Superior Court - Criminal Division PO Box 187 (1 N Broad St), Woodbury, NJ 08096; 856-853-3531. Hours: 8:30AM-4:30 PM (EST). *Felony.*

www.judiciary.state.nj.us/gloucester/glo/index.htm

Criminal Records: Access: Mail, in person. Visitors must perform in person searches for themselves. Search fee: $4.00 per name. Required to search: name, years to search, DOB, SSN, signed release. Criminal records on computer from 1982, on index from 1955.

General Information: No sealed, expunged, dismissed, judges notes, PSI's, or discovery packets records released. SASE required. Turnaround time 1-3 days. Copy fee: $1.00 per page. Certification fee: $1.50. Fee payee: State of New Jersey, Miscellaneous. Personal checks accepted. Prepayment is required.

Superior Court - Civil Division 1 North Broad St, Woodbury, NJ 08096; 856-853-3250. Hours: 8:30AM-4:30 PM (EST). *Civil Actions Over $10,000, Probate.*

www.judiciary.state.nj.us/gloucester/glo/index.htm

Civil Records: Access: Mail, online, in person. Only the court performs in person searches; visitors may not. No search fee. Required to search: name, years to search. Civil cases indexed by defendant, plaintiff. Civil records on computer from 1988, prior records on county books. Participates in the court records statewide Electronic Access Program; for signup, information and booklet call 609-292-4987.

General Information: No sealed, expunged, dismissed, judges notes, PSI's, or discovery packets records released. SASE required. Turnaround time 1-2 days. Copy fee: $1.00 per page. Certification fee: $1.50. Fee payee: State of New Jersey. Personal checks accepted. Prepayment is required.

Superior Court Special Civil Part
Old Courthouse, 1 N Broad St., Woodbury, NJ 08096; 856-853-3392; Fax: 856-853-3416. Hours: 8:30AM-4:30PM (EST). *Civil Actions Under $10,000, Eviction, Small Claims.*

www.judiciary.state.nj.us/gloucester/glo/index.htm

Civil Records: Access: Mail, online, in person. No search fee. Required to search: name, years to search, address. Civil cases indexed by defendant, plaintiff. Civil records on computer from 08/89, on index books from 1900. Participates in the court records statewide Electronic Access Program; for signup, information and booklet call 609-292-4987.

General Information: SASE required. Copy fee: $.75 per page. Fee is for less after 10 pages. Fee payee: Clerk, Special Civil Part. Personal checks accepted. Prepayment is required.

Hudson County

Superior Court - Criminal Division
595 Newark Ave, Jersey City, NJ 07306; 201-795-6704. Hours: 8:30AM-4:30PM (EST). *Felony.*

www.judiciary.state.nj.us/hudson/index.htm

Criminal Records: Access: Mail, in person. Both court and visitors may perform in person searches. No search fee. Required to search: name, years to search, DOB, SSN. Criminal records on computer from 1985, on index books from 1900.

General Information: Public access terminal is available. No sealed, expunged, dismissed, judges notes, PSI's, or discovery packets records released. Turnaround time 1 week. Copy fee: $.75 per page for the first ten pages, $.50 per page for the next ten pages, and $.25 per page thereafter. Certification fee: $5.00. An uncertified copy of a judgment of conviction is $1.50. Fee payee: Treasurer, State of New Jersey. Personal checks accepted. Prepayment is required.

Superior Court - Civil Division
583 Newark Ave, Jersey City, NJ 07306; 201-795-6723; 201-217-5163 (Records Rm). Hours: 8:30AM-4:30PM (EST). *Civil Actions Over $10,000, Probate.*

www.judiciary.state.nj.us/hudson/index.htm

Civil Records: Access: Mail, online, in person. Both court and visitors may perform in person searches. No search fee. Required to search: name, years to search. Civil cases indexed by defendant, plaintiff. Civil records on computer for three years, on index books from 1900. Mail access is limited to one name. Participates in the court records statewide Electronic Access Program; for signup, information and booklet call 609-292-4987.

General Information: No sealed, expunged, dismissed, judges notes, PSI's, or discovery packets records released. Turnaround time 1 week. Copy fee: $.35 per page. Certification fee: $5.00. Fee payee: Clerk of Superior Court. Personal checks accepted. Prepayment is required.

Superior Court Special Civil Part
595 Newark Ave, Jersey City, NJ 07306; 201-795-6056. Hours: 8:30AM-4:30PM (EST). *Civil Actions Under $10,000, Eviction, Small Claims.*

www.judiciary.state.nj.us/hudson/index.htm

Civil Records: Access: Online, in person. Visitors must perform in person searches for themselves. No search fee. Required to search: name, years to search, address. Civil cases indexed by defendant, plaintiff. Civil records on index cards from 1993, prior on docket books. Participates in the court records statewide Electronic Access Program; for signup, information and booklet call 609-292-4987.

General Information: No adoptions, sealed, juvenile, expunged, dismissed, or mental illness released. Copy fee: $.75 1-10 pages, $.50 11-20 pages; $.25 20 plus pages. Certification fee: $5.00. Fee payee: Clerk, Special Civil Part. Personal checks accepted. Prepayment is required.

Hunterdon County

Superior Court - Criminal Division
65 Park Ave, Flemington, NJ 08822; 908-806-4338; Fax: 908-806-4378. Hours: 8:30AM-4:30PM (EST). *Felony.*

www.judiciary.state.nj.us/somerset/index.htm

Criminal Records: Access: Fax, mail, in person. Visitors must perform in person searches for themselves. Search fee: $6.00 per name. Required to search: name, years to search, DOB; also helpful: SSN. Criminal records on computer from 1987, prior on index books.

General Information: Public access terminal is available. No sealed, expunged, dismissed, judges notes, PSI's, or discovery packets records released. SASE required. Turnaround time 1 week. Fax notes: Will fax results, no charge. Copy fee: $1.50 per page. Certification fee: $3.00. Fee payee: State of New Jersey. Personal checks accepted. Prepayment is required.

Superior Court - Civil Division
Hunterdon County Justice Center, 65 Park Ave, Flemington, NJ 08822; 908-806-5123. Hours: 8:30AM-4:30PM (EST). *Civil Actions.*

www.judiciary.state.nj.us/somerset/index.htm

Civil Records: Access: Mail, online, in person, phone. Both court and visitors may perform in person searches. No search fee. Required to search: name, years to search. Civil cases indexed by defendant, plaintiff. Civil records on computer since 1990, on index from 1950. Participates in the court records statewide Electronic Access Program; for signup, information and booklet call 609-292-4987.

General Information: Public access terminal is available. (Public Access Terminal for Civil only) No sealed, expunged, dismissed, judges notes, PSI's, or discovery packets records released. SASE required. Turnaround time 1-2 weeks. Copy fee: $.75 per page 1st 10; $.50 for 2nd 10; $.25 each add'l. Certification fee: $5.00. Fee payee: State of New Jersey Judiciary. Personal checks accepted. Prepayment is required.

Superior Court Special Civil Part
Hunterdon County Justice Center, 65 Park Ave, 2nd Floor, Flemington, NJ 08822; 908-806-5123. Hours: 8:30AM-4:30PM (EST). *Civil Actions Under $10,000, Eviction, Small Claims.*

www.judiciary.state.nj.us/somerset/index.htm

Civil Records: Access: Phone, mail, online, in person. Both the court and visitors may perform in person searches; court limits itself to one name search. No search fee. Required to search: name, years to search. Civil cases indexed by defendant, plaintiff. Civil records on computer from 1991, on index books from 1900. Participates in the court records statewide Electronic Access Program; for signup, information and booklet call 609-292-4987.

General Information: Public access terminal is available for Civil Only. No protective order files records released. SASE required. Turnaround time 1-2 weeks. Copy fee: $.75 per page for the first ten, $.50 per page for the next ten, and $.25 per page thereafter.

Certification fee: $5.00. Fee payee: Superior Court of New Jersey. Personal checks accepted. Prepayment is required.

Mercer County

Superior Court - Criminal Division
209 S. Broad, PO Box 8068, Trenton, NJ 08650-0068; 609-989-6462; Fax: 609-989-6975. Hours: 8:30AM-4:30PM; Search Hours: 9AM-3:30PM (EST). *Felony.*

www.judiciary.state.nj.us/mercer/index.htm

Criminal Records: Access: In person only. Visitors must perform in person searches for themselves. No search fee. Required to search: name, years to search, DOB, SSN. Criminal records on computer from 1985, on docket books from 1900s.

General Information: No sealed, expunged, judges notes, PSI's, or discovery packets records released. SASE required for Civil. Turnaround time up to 2 weeks. Copy fee: $.75 per page. $5.00 minimum. Fee less after 10 pages. Certification fee: $5.00. Fee payee: Clerk of Superior Court. Personal checks accepted. Prepayment is required.

Superior Court - Civil Division
175 S Broad, PO Box 8068, Trenton, NJ 08650-0068; 609-989-6450; Fax: 609-278-5761. Hours: 8:30AM-4:30PM (EST). *Civil Actions Over $10,000, Probate.*

www.judiciary.state.nj.us/mercer/index.htm

Civil Records: Access: Fax, mail, online, in person. Only the court performs in person searches; visitors may not. No search fee. Required to search: name, years to search. Civil cases indexed by defendant, plaintiff. Civil records on computer since 1995, archived from 1972, on microfiche from 1965, prior indexed from 1894. Participates in the court records statewide Electronic Access Program; for signup, information and booklet call 609-292-4987.

General Information: No sealed, expunged, dismissed, judges notes, PSI's, or discovery packets records released. SASE required for Civil. Turnaround time up to 2 weeks. Copy fee: $.75 1-10 pages; $.50 11-20 pages; $.25 20 plus pages. Certification fee: $5.00. Fee payee: Clerk of Superior Court. Personal checks accepted. Prepayment is required.

Superior Court Special Civil Part
Box 8068, Trenton, NJ 08650; 609-989-6206; Fax: 609-278-2721. Hours: 8:30AM-4:30PM (EST). *Civil Actions Under $10,000, Eviction, Small Claims.*

www.judiciary.state.nj.us/mercer/index.htm

Civil Records: Access: Mail, online, in person. Visitors must perform in person searches for themselves. No search fee. Required to search: name, years to search. Civil cases indexed by defendant, plaintiff. Civil records on computer from 1989, on index from 1984. Participates in the court records statewide Electronic Access Program; for signup, information and booklet call 609-292-4987.

General Information: Public access terminal is available. No adoptions, sealed, juvenile, expunged, dismissed, or mental illness records released. Turnaround time 1 week. Copy fee: $.75 per page for the first ten pages, $.50 per page for the next ten, and $.25 per page thereafter. Fee payee: State of New Jersey. Only cashiers checks and money orders accepted.

Middlesex County

Superior Court - Criminal Division
PO Box 2673 (1 JFK Sq), New Brunswick, NJ 08903; 732-981-3128. Hours: 8:30AM-4:30PM (EST). *Felony.*

www.judiciary.state.nj.us/middlesex/index.htm

Criminal Records: Access: Mail, in person. Both court and visitors may perform in person searches. Court will only search if provided with arrest date, summons, complaint or indictment number. Search fee: $4.00 per name. Required to search: name, years to search, DOB; also helpful: SSN, singed release. Criminal records on computer from 1981, prior on index books back to 1956.

General Information: No sealed, expunged, dismissed, judges notes, PSI's, on discovery packets records released. SASE required. Turnaround time up to 2 weeks. Copy fee: $.75 per page first 10, $.50 each next 10, then $.25 per page. Certification fee: $5.00 per document. Fee payee: State of New Jersey Judiciary. No personal checks accepted. Prepayment is required.

Superior Court - Civil Division PO Box 2633 (1 JFK Sq), New Brunswick, NJ 08903; 732-981-2464. Hours: 8:30AM-4:30PM (EST). *Civil Actions Over $10,000, Probate.*

www.judiciary.state.nj.us/middlesex/index.htm

Civil Records: Access: Mail, online, in person. Search fee: No search fee. Required to search: name, years to search, ic opies needed place request in writing. Civil cases indexed by defendant, plaintiff. Civil records on computer from 1992, on docket books from 1940. Participates in the court records statewide Electronic Access Program; for signup, information and booklet call 609-292-4987.

General Information: Public access terminal is available. No sealed, expunged, dismissed, judges notes, PSI's, on discovery packets records released. SASE required. Turnaround time up to 3 weeks. Certification fee: $5.00. Fee payee: State of New Jersey, Clerk of Superior Court. Personal checks accepted. Prepayment is required.

Superior Court Special Civil Part PO Box 2633 (1 JKF Sq), New Brunswick, NJ 08903; 732-981-3300. Hours: 8:30AM-4:30PM (EST). *Civil Actions Under $10,000, Eviction, Small Claims.*

www.judiciary.state.nj.us/middlesex/index.htm

Civil Records: Access: Mail, online, in person. Both court and visitors may perform in person searches. No search fee. Required to search: name, years to search. Civil cases indexed by defendant, plaintiff. Civil records on computer from 1985, on docket books from 1960. Participates in the court records statewide Electronic Access Program; for signup, information and booklet call 609-292-4987.

General Information: Public access terminal is available. No adoption, sealed, juvenile, expunged, dismissed, or mental health records released. Turnaround time 30 days. Copy fee: 1st page $1.00; 2-10 pages $.75; 11-20 pages $.50; 20 plus $.25. Certification fee: $5.00. Fee payee: Middlesex Special Civil Part. Personal checks accepted. Prepayment is required.

Monmouth County

Superior Court - Criminal Division 71 Monument Park, Rm 149, PO Box 1271, Freehold, NJ 07728-1271; 732-431-7880; Fax: 732-866-3565. Hours: 8:30AM-4:30PM (EST). *Felony.*

www.judiciary.state.nj.us/monmouth/index.htm

Criminal Records: Access: In person only. Visitors must perform in person searches for themselves. No search fee. Required to search: name, years to search. Criminal records on computer back to 1990, on index books from 1956.

General Information: Public access terminal is available. (Information on civil cases only.) No sealed, expunged, dismissed, judges notes, PSI's, or discovery packets records released. Copy fee: $.75 per page. Fee is for first 10 pages; $.50 per page next 10; each add'l $.25. Certification fee: $5.00. Fee payee: State of New Jersey. Personal checks accepted. ID required for payment by personal check. Prepayment is required.

Superior Court - Civil Division PO Box 1255 (71 Monument Pk), Freehold, NJ 07728-1255; 732-

431-8783. Hours: 8:30AM-4:30PM (EST). *Civil Actions Over $10,000, Probate.*

www.judiciary.state.nj.us/monmouth/index.htm

Civil Records: Access: Mail, online, in person. Visitors must perform in person searches for themselves. No search fee. Required to search: name, years to search. Civil cases indexed by defendant, plaintiff. Civil records on computer from 1990, on index books from 1956. Participates in the court records statewide Electronic Access Program; for signup, information and booklet call 609-292-4987.

General Information: Public access terminal is available. (Information on civil cases only.) No sealed, expunged, dismissed, judges notes, PSI's, or discovery packets records released. Copy fee: $.25. Certification fee: $5.00. Fee payee: Clerk of Superior Court. Personal checks accepted. Prepayment is required.

Superior Court Special Civil Part Courthouse, 71 Monument Pk., PO Box 1270, Freehold, NJ 07728; 732-577-6749. Hours: 8:30AM-4:30PM (EST). *Civil Actions Under $10,000, Eviction, Small Claims.*

www.judiciary.state.nj.us/monmouth/index.htm

Civil Records: Access: Mail, online, in person. Both court and visitors may perform in person searches. No search fee. Required to search: name, years to search. Civil cases indexed by defendant, plaintiff. Civil records on computer from 1996, on index books from 1985, prior in archives. Participates in the court records statewide Electronic Access Program; for signup, information and booklet call 609-292-4987.

General Information: Public access terminal is available. SASE required. Turnaround time 1 day to weeks; longer if archived. Copy fee: $.75 per page. Fee is for first 10 pages; $.50 per page next 10; each add'l $.25. Certification fee: $5.00. Fee payee: Monmouth Special Civil Part. Personal checks accepted. Prepayment is required.

Morris County

Superior Court - Criminal Division PO Box 910 (Washington St), Morristown, NJ 07960-0910; 973-656-4115; Fax: 973-656-4123. Hours: 8:30AM-4:30PM (EST). *Felony.*

www.judiciary.state.nj.us/morris/index.htm

Criminal Records: Access: Fax, mail, in person. Both court and visitors may perform in person searches. No search fee. Required to search: name, years to search, DOB, SSN, signed release. Criminal records on computer from 1984, on index books from 1966.

General Information: No sealed, expunged, dismissed, judges notes, PSI's, or discovery packets records released. SASE required. Turnaround time 1 week. Copy fee: $.75 per page. Fee is for first 10 pages; $.50 per page next 10; each add'l $.25. Certification fee: $5.00. Fee payee: State of New Jersey. Personal checks accepted. Prepayment is required.

Superior Court - Civil Division PO Box 910 (Washington St), Morristown, NJ 07963-0910; 973-656-4115; Fax: 973-656-4123. Hours: 8:30AM-4:30PM (EST). *Civil Actions Over $10,000, Probate.*

www.judiciary.state.nj.us/morris/index.htm

Civil Records: Access: Online, in person. Visitors must perform in person searches for themselves. No search fee. Required to search: name, years to search; also helpful: address. Civil cases indexed by defendant, plaintiff. Civil records on computer from 1984, on index books from 1966. Participates in the court records statewide Electronic Access Program; for signup, information and booklet call 609-292-4987.

General Information: Public access terminal is available. No sealed, expunged, dismissed, judges notes, PSI's, or discovery packets records released. Copy fee: $.25 per page. Certification fee: $5.00. Fee

payee: State of New Jersey. Personal checks accepted. Prepayment is required.

Superior Court Special Civil Part PO Box 910 (Court St), Morristown, NJ 07963-0910; 973-656-4125. Hours: 8:30AM-4:30PM (EST). *Civil Actions Under $10,000, Eviction, Small Claims.*

www.judiciary.state.nj.us/morris/index.htm

Civil Records: Access: Mail, online, in person. Visitors must perform in person searches for themselves. No search fee. Required to search: name, years to search. Civil cases indexed by defendant, plaintiff. Civil records on computer from 8/1988, on index books from 1979. Participates in the court records statewide Electronic Access Program; for signup, information and booklet call 609-292-4987.

General Information: Public access terminal is available. No adoptions, sealed, juvenile, expunged, dismissed, or mental illness records released. Turnaround time 1 week. Fax notes: Will not fax results. Copy fee: $.75 per page for first 10, $.50 per page for next 10, and $.25 per page thereafter. Public copier is $.25 per copy. Certification fee: $5.00. Fee payee: State of New Jersey. Personal checks accepted.

Ocean County

Superior Court - Criminal Division PO Box 2191 (100 Washington St), Justice Complex, Rm 220, Toms River, NJ 08754-2191; 732-929-2009. Hours: 8:30AM-4:30PM (EST). *Felony.*

www.judiciary.state.nj.us/ocean/index.htm

Criminal Records: Access: Mail, in person. Both court and visitors may perform in person searches. Search fee: $3.00 per name if court performs search. Required to search: name, years to search; also helpful: address, DOB, SSN. Criminal records on computer from 1990, on index books from 1920.

General Information: Public access terminal is available. (Allows you to search statewide.) No sealed, expunged, judges notes, PSI's, or discovery packets records released. Turnaround time 1 week. Copy fee: $.75 per page, 11-20 pages $.50 per page, over 20 pages $.25 per page. Certification fee: $5.00. Fee payee: NJ State Treasurer. Personal checks accepted. Prepayment is required.

Superior Court - Civil Division 118 Washington #121, Toms River, NJ 08754; 732-929-2035. Hours: 8:30AM-4:30PM (EST). *Civil Actions Over $10,000, Probate.*

www.judiciary.state.nj.us/ocean/index.htm

Civil Records: Access: Online, in person. Visitors must perform in person searches. No search fee. Required to search: name, years to search. Civil cases indexed by defendant, plaintiff. Civil records on computer from 1989, on index books from 1920. Participates in the court records statewide Electronic Access Program; for signup, information and booklet call 609-292-4987.

General Information: Public access terminal is available. (Public Access Terminal is located at 201 Courthouse Lane) Turnaround time 1 week. Copy fee: $.25.. Fee payee: Superior Court Clerk. Personal checks accepted. Prepayment is required.

Superior Court Special Civil Part Box 2191 (100 Washington St), Toms River, NJ 08754; 732-929-2016; Fax: 732-506-5398. Hours: 8:30AM-4:30PM (EST). *Civil Actions Under $10,000, Eviction, Small Claims.*

www.judiciary.state.nj.us/ocean/index.htm

Civil Records: Access: Online, in person. Both court and visitors may perform in person searches. No search fee. Required to search: name, years to search. Civil cases indexed by defendant, plaintiff. Civil records on computer from 1985, on index books from 1972, on microfilm prior. Participates in the court records statewide Electronic Access Program; for signup, information and booklet call 609-292-4987.

General Information: No adoptions, sealed, juvenile, expunged, dismissed, or mental illness records released. Turnaround time 1-2 days. Copy fee: $.25. Certification fee: $5.00. Fee payee: Ocean County Special Civil Part. Personal checks accepted.

Passaic County

Superior Court - Criminal Division 77 Hamilton St., Paterson, NJ 07505-2108; 973-247-8403; Fax: 973-247-8401. 8:30AM-4:30PM (EST). *Felony.*

www.judiciary.state.nj.us/passaic/index.htm

Criminal Records: Access: Mail, in person. Both court and visitors may perform in person searches. Search fee: $5.00 per name. Required to search: name, years to search, DOB, SSN; also helpful: address. Criminal records on computer from 1986, on microfiche prior.

General Information: Public access terminal is available. (Only criminal information can be accessed.) No sealed, expunged, dismissed, judges notes, PSI's, or discovery packets records released. Turnaround time 3-4 days. Copy fee: $.75 per page for the first 10 pages, $.50 per page for the second set of 10 pages, and $.25 per page thereafter. Certification fee: $5.00. Fee payee: Superior Court of New Jersey. Personal checks accepted. Prepayment is required.

Superior Court - Civil Division 77 Hamilton St. 3rd Fl, Paterson, NJ 07505-2108; 973-247-8215. Hours: 8:30AM-4:30PM (EST). *Civil Actions Over $10,000, Probate.*

www.judiciary.state.nj.us/passaic/index.htm

Civil Records: Access: Phone, mail, online, in person. Both court and visitors may perform in person searches. No search fee. Required to search: name, years to search. Civil cases indexed by defendant, plaintiff. Civil records on computer from 1986, on index books from 1979. Participates in the court records statewide Electronic Access Program; for signup, information and booklet call 609-292-4987. Phone access limited to short searches.

General Information: No sealed, expunged, dismissed, judges notes, PSI's, or discovery packets records released. Turnaround time up to 1 week. Copy fee: $.25 per page. Certification fee: $5.00. Fee payee: State of New Jersey or Clerk of Superior Court. Personal checks accepted. Prepayment is required.

Superior Court Special Civil Part 71 Hamilton St., Paterson, NJ 07505; 973-247-8238. Hours: 8:30AM-4:30PM (EST). *Civil Actions Under $10,000, Eviction, Small Claims.*

www.judiciary.state.nj.us/passaic/index.htm

Civil Records: Access: Mail, online, in person. Both court and visitors may perform in person searches. No search fee. Required to search: name, years to search. Civil cases indexed by defendant, plaintiff. Civil records on computer from 1993, on index from 1980, prior archived. Include phone # with written requests. Participates in the court records statewide Electronic Access Program; for signup, information and booklet call 609-292-4987.

General Information: Public access terminal is available. No adoptions, sealed, juvenile, expunged, dismissed, or mental illness records released. Turnaround time 2-3 days. Copy fee: $.75 per page. Fee is for first 10 pages; $.50 per page next 10; each add'l $.25. Fee payee: Passaic County Special Civil Part. Personal checks accepted. Prepayment is required.

Salem County

Superior Court - Criminal Division PO Box 78 (92 Market St), Salem, NJ 08079-1913; 856-935-7510. Hours: 8:30AM-4:30PM (EST). *Felony.*

www.judiciary.state.nj.us/gloucester/sal/index.htm

Criminal Records: Access: Mail, in person. Both court and visitors may perform in person searches. Search fee: $4.00 per name. Required to search: name, years to search, DOB, SSN. Criminal records on computer back to 1989; indexed from 1957.

General Information: No sealed, expunged, dismissed, judges notes, PSI's, or discovery packets records released. SASE required. Turnaround time 3-4 days. Copy fee: $.25 per page. Certification fee: $5.00. Fee payee: State of New Jersey. Personal checks accepted. Prepayment is required.

Superior Court - Civil Division PO Box 29 (92 Market St), Salem, NJ 08079-1913; 856-935-7510 X8210; Probate phone: 856-935-7510 X8322; Fax: 856-935-6551. Hours: 8:30AM-4:30PM (EST). *Civil Actions Over $10,000, Probate.*

www.judiciary.state.nj.us/gloucester/sal/index.htm

Note: Probate located at 92 Market Street in Salem

Civil Records: Access: Phone, fax, mail, online, in person. Only the court performs in person searches; visitors may not. No search fee. Required to search: name, years to search. Civil cases indexed by defendant, plaintiff. Civil records on computer from 1987, indexed from 1953. Participates in the court records statewide Electronic Access Program; for signup, information and booklet call 609-292-4987.

General Information: No sealed, expunged, dismissed, judges notes, PSI's, or discovery packets records released. SASE required. Turnaround time 1-2 days. Copy fee: $.25 per page. Certification fee: $5.00. Fee payee: Special Civil Part. Personal checks accepted. Prepayment is required.

Superior Court Special Civil Part PO Box 29 (92 Market St), Salem, NJ 08079; 856-935-7510 x8214; Fax: 856-935-6551. Hours: 8:30AM-4:30PM (EST). *Civil Actions Under $10,000, Eviction, Small Claims.*

www.judiciary.state.nj.us/gloucester/sal/index.htm

Civil Records: Access: Phone, fax, mail, online, in person. Only the court performs in person searches; visitors may not. No search fee. Required to search: name, years to search. Civil cases indexed by defendant, plaintiff. Civil records on computer from 1990, on index from 1953. Participates in the court records statewide Electronic Access Program; for signup, information and booklet call 609-292-4987.

General Information: No adoptions, sealed, juvenile, expunged, dismissed, or mental illness records released. Turnaround time 1-2 days. Copy fee: $25 per page. Certification fee: $5.00. Fee payee: Special Civil Part. Personal checks accepted. Prepayment is required.

Somerset County

Superior Court - Criminal Division PO Box 3000 (20 North Bridge St, 2nd Fl), Somerville, NJ 08876-1262; 908-231-7600. Hours: 8:30AM-4:30PM (EST). *Felony.*

www.judiciary.state.nj.us/somerset/index.htm

Criminal Records: Access: Phone, fax, mail, in person. Both court and visitors may perform in person searches. Search fee: $6.00 per name. Required to search: name, years to search, DOB; also helpful: SSN. Criminal records on computer back to 1981, prior on index books. Public access terminal does not include criminal records.

General Information: No sealed, expunged, judges notes, PSI's, or discovery packets records released.

SASE required. Turnaround time 1-2 days. Copy fee: $1.50 per page. Certification fee: $3.00 plus $1.50 per page. Fee payee: State of New Jersey. Personal checks accepted. Prepayment is required.

Superior Court - Civil Division Somerset Cty Courthouse, Civil Division, PO Box 3000 (Bridge & Main St), Somerville, NJ 08876-1262; 908-231-7054. Hours: 8:30AM-4:30PM (EST). *Civil Actions, Probate.*

www.judiciary.state.nj.us/somerset/index.htm

Civil Records: Access: Phone, mail, online, in person. Both court and visitors may perform in person searches. No search fee. Required to search: name; also helpful: years to search. Civil cases indexed by defendant, plaintiff. Civil records on computer from 1990. Participates in the court records statewide Electronic Access Program; for signup, information and booklet call 609-292-4987. Civil cases are archived 18 months after their last activity.

General Information: Public access terminal is available. No sealed, expunged, dismissed, judges notes, PSI's, or discovery packets records released. SASE required. Turnaround time 1-2 days. Copy fee: $.75 per page. Fee after 1st 10 pages $.50 per pg up to 20pgs, then $.25 per pg. Certification fee: $5.00 per page. Fee payee: Superior Court of NJ. Personal checks accepted. Prepayment is required.

Superior Court Special Civil Part Somerset County Courthouse, Bridge and Main St, PO Box 3000, Somerville, NJ 08876-1262; 908-231-7014/7015. Hours: 8:30AM-4:30PM (EST). *Civil Actions Under $10,000, Eviction, Small Claims.*

www.judiciary.state.nj.us/somerset/index.htm

Civil Records: Access: Mail, online, in person. Both court and visitors may perform in person searches. No search fee. Required to search: name, years to search. Civil cases indexed by defendant, plaintiff. Civil records on computer from 1990, prior on index books. In person access requires an appointment. Participates in the court records statewide Electronic Access Program; for signup, information and booklet call 609-292-4987.

General Information: Public access terminal is available. (By appointment/For public at counter. Book help available only.) No adoptions, sealed, juvenile, expunged, dismissed, or mental illness records released. SASE required. Turnaround time varies, may be lengthy. Copy fee: $.75 per page for the first ten, $.50 per page for the next ten, and $.25 per page thereafter. Fee payee: Superior Court of New Jersey. Personal checks accepted. Prepayment is required.

Sussex County

Superior Court - Criminal Division 43-47 High St, Sussex Judicial Center, Newton, NJ 07860; 973-579-0696. 8:30AM-4:30PM (EST). *Felony.*

www.judiciary.state.nj.us/morris/index.htm

Criminal Records: Access: In person only. Visitors must perform in person searches for themselves. No search fee. Required to search: name, years to search, DOB, signed release; also helpful: SSN. Criminal records on computer from 1986, on docket books to 1950s.

General Information: Public access terminal is available. No sealed, expunged, dismissed, judges notes, PSI's, or discovery packets records released. Turnaround time up to 1 week. Copy fee: $.75 per page. Fee is for first 10 pages; $.50 per page next 10; each add'l $.25. Certification fee: $5.00. Fee payee: State of New Jersey Judiciary. Only cashiers checks and money orders accepted. Prepayment is required.

Superior Court - Civil Division 43-47 High St, Sussex Judicial Center, Newton, NJ 07860; 973-579-0914/0915. Hours: 8:30AM-4:30PM (EST). *Civil Actions Over $10,000, Probate.*

www.judiciary.state.nj.us/morris/index.htm

Civil Records: Access: Phone, mail, online, in person. Only the court performs in person searches; visitors may not. No search fee. Required to search: name, years to search. Civil cases indexed by defendant, plaintiff. Civil records on computer from 1989, on microfiche by plaintiff prior to 1989, closed cases archived yearly and sent to Trenton. Participates in the court records statewide Electronic Access Program; for signup, information and booklet call 609-292-4987.

General Information: No sealed, expunged, dismissed, judges notes, PSI's, or discovery packets records released. Turnaround time 1 week. Copy fee: $.75 per page for the first ten pages, $.50 per page for the next ten, and $.25 per page thereafter. Certification fee: $5.00. Fee payee: Clerk of Superior Court. Personal checks accepted. Prepayment is required.

Superior Court Special Civil Part 43-47 High St., Newton, NJ 07860; 973-579-0918. Hours: 8:30AM-4:30PM (EST). *Civil Actions Under $10,000, Eviction, Small Claims.*

www.judiciary.state.nj.us/morris/index.htm

Civil Records: Access: Phone, mail, online, in person. Both court and visitors may perform in person searches. No search fee. Required to search: name, years to search. Civil cases indexed by defendant, plaintiff. Civil records on computer from mid 1989, on index books from 1940. Participates in the court records statewide Electronic Access Program; for signup, information and booklet call 609-292-4987.

General Information: No adoptions, sealed, juvenile, expunged, dismissed, or mental illness records released. Turnaround time up to 2 weeks. Copy fee: $.75 per page for first 10 pages; $.50 per page next 10; each add'l $.25. Certification fee: $5.00. Fee payee: State of New Jersey Judiciary. Personal checks accepted. Prepayment is required.

Union County

Superior Court - Criminal Division County Courthouse - New Annex, Rm 201, Elizabeth, NJ 07207; 908-659-3376; Fax: 908-659-3391. Hours: 8:30AM-4:30PM (EST). *Felony.*

www.judiciary.state.nj.us/union/index.htm

Criminal Records: Access: In person only. Visitors must perform in person searches for themselves. No search fee. Required to search: name, years to search; also helpful: DOB, SSN. Criminal records on computer from 1985 updated monthly, prior on index books from 1960. In person access available 9AM-3:30PM.

General Information: No sealed, expunged, dismissed, judges notes, PSI's, or discovery packets records released. Turnaround time is a minimum of 5 business days. Copy fee: $.75 per page. Fee is for first 10 pages; $.50 per page next 10; each add'l $.25.

Certification fee: $5.00. Fee payee: State of New Jersey Judiciary. Business checks accepted. Prepayment is required.

Superior Court - Civil Division 2 Broad St, Elizabeth, NJ 07207; 908-659-4176; Fax: 908-659-4185. Hours: 8:30AM-4:30PM (EST). *Civil Actions Over $10,000.*

www.judiciary.state.nj.us/union/index.htm

Civil Records: Access: Phone, mail, online, in person. Visitors must perform in person searches for themselves. No search fee. Required to search: name, years to search. Civil cases indexed by defendant, plaintiff. Civil records on computer from 1988, prior records archived in Trenton NJ. Participates in the court records statewide Electronic Access Program; for signup, information and booklet call 609-292-4987.

General Information: Public access terminal is available. No sealed, expunged, dismissed, judges notes, PSI's, or discovery packets records released. Turnaround time varies. Copy fee: $.75 per page for the first ten pages, $.50 per page for the next ten, and $.25 per page thereafter. Certification fee: $5.00. Fee payee: Clerk of Superior Court. Personal checks accepted. Prepayment is required.

Superior Court Special Civil Part 2 Broad St, Elizabeth, NJ 07207; 908-659-3637/8. Hours: 8:30AM-4:30PM (EST). *Civil Actions Under $10,000, Eviction, Small Claims.*

www.judiciary.state.nj.us/union/index.htm

Civil Records: Access: Phone, mail, online, in person. Both court and visitors may perform in person searches. No search fee. Required to search: name, years to search. Civil cases indexed by defendant, plaintiff. Civil records on computer from 1993, on index books 1965, prior archived. Phone access limited to info after 11/93. Participates in the court records statewide Electronic Access Program; for signup, information and booklet call 609-292-4987.

General Information: No adoptions, sealed, juvenile, expunged, dismissed, or mental illness records released. Turnaround time varies. Copy fee: $.75 per page. Fee is for first 10 pages; $.50 per page next 10; each add'l $.25. Fee payee: Special Civil Part. Personal checks accepted. Prepayment is required.

Warren County

Warren County Superior Court Criminal Case Management Division, PO Box 900, Belvidere, NJ 07823; 908-475-6990; Fax: 908-475-6982. Hours: 8:30AM-4:30PM (EST). *Felony.*

www.judiciary.state.nj.us/somerset/index.htm

Criminal Records: Access: Phone, mail, fax, in person. Only the court performs in person searches; visitors may not. Search fee: $6.00 per name. Required

to search: name, years to search, DOB; also helpful: SSN, signed release. Criminal records on computer back 10 years; prior on index cards to 1927.

General Information: No sealed, expunged, dismissed, judges notes, PSI's, or discovery packets records released. Turnaround time 2 days. Copy fee: $1.50 per page. Certification fee: $3.00. Fee payee: State of New Jersey Judiciary. Personal checks accepted. Prepayment is required.

Superior Court - Civil Division PO Box 900 (314 2nd St), Belvidere, NJ 07823; 908-475-6140. Hours: 8:30AM-4:30PM (EST). *Civil Actions Over $10,000, Probate.*

www.judiciary.state.nj.us/somerset/index.htm

Civil Records: Access: Mail, online, in person. Only the court performs in person searches; visitors may not. No search fee for 1 search. Required to search: name, years to search. Civil cases indexed by defendant, plaintiff. Civil records on computer from 1990, prior on index cards. Participates in the court records statewide Electronic Access Program; for signup, information and booklet call 609-292-4987.

General Information: No sealed, expunged, dismissed, judges notes, PSI's, or discovery packets records released. Turnaround time 2 days. Copy fee: $.75 fee per page for first 10 pages; $.50 per page next 10; each add'l $.10. Certification fee: Certification is free for 1st page, next 5 pgs $5.00; each add'l pg $.75. Fee payee: Superior Court of New Jersey. Personal checks accepted. Prepayment is required.

Superior Court Special Civil Part PO Box 900 (314 2nd St), Belvidere, NJ 07823; 908-475-6140. Hours: 8:30AM-4:30PM (EST). *Civil Actions Under $10,000, Eviction, Small Claims.*

www.judiciary.state.nj.us/somerset/index.htm

Civil Records: Access: Mail, online, in person. Only the court performs in person searches; visitors may not. No search fee for 1 search. Required to search: name, years to search. Civil cases indexed by defendant, plaintiff. Civil records on computer from 10/91, prior on index books from 1951. In person access requires an appointment. Participates in the court records statewide Electronic Access Program; for signup, information and booklet call 609-292-4987.

General Information: No adoptions, sealed, juvenile, expunged, dismissed, or mental illness records released. SASE required. Turnaround time 2-3 days. Copy fee: $.75 per page for the first ten pages, $.50 per page for the second ten pages, and $.25 per page thereafter. Fee payee: Superior Court of New Jersey. Personal checks accepted. Prepayment is required.

New Jersey Recording Offices

ORGANIZATION: 21 counties, 21 recording offices. The recording officer title varies depending upon the county. It is either Register of Deeds or County Clerk. The Clerk of Circuit Court records the equivalent of some state's tax liens. The entire state is in the Eastern Time Zone (EST).

REAL ESTATE RECORDS: No counties will provide real estate searches. Copy and certification fees vary. Assessment and tax offices are at the municipal level.

UCC RECORDS: Financing statements are filed at the state level, except for real estate related collateral, which are filed with the County Clerk. However, prior to 07/2001, consumer goods and farm collateral were also filed at the County Clerk and these older records can be searched there. About half of the recording offices will perform UCC searches. Use search request form UCC-11. Search fees are usually $25.00 per debtor name and copy fees vary.

TAX LIEN RECORDS: All federal tax liens are filed with the County Clerk/Register of Deeds and are indexed separately from all other liens. State tax liens comprise two categories - certificates of debt are filed with the Clerk of Superior Court (some, called docketed judgments are filed specifically with the Trenton court), and warrants of execution are filed with the County Clerk/Register of Deeds. Few counties will provide tax lien searches. Refer to the County Court section for information about New Jersey Superior Courts.

OTHER LIENS: Judgment, mechanics, bail bond.

ONLINE ACCESS: A statewide database of property tax records can be accessed at http://taxrecords.com

Atlantic County

County Clerk, 5901 Main St, Courthouse-CN 2005, Mays Landing, NJ 08330-1797. 609-625-4011; Fax 609-625-4738. www.atlanticcountyclerk.org
Will search UCC records. Will not search real estate records. **Online Access:** Real Estate Records. Property records for communities along the Jersey Shore in Atlantic county are available free online at www.philly.com/packages/njshore/lookup.htm. Site is sponsored by the Philadelphia Inquirer. Search by clicking on community name, then search by owner name, owner's city/state, address, or property value range.

Bergen County

County Clerk, Justice Center Room 214, 10 Main St., Hackensack, NJ 07601-7000. 201-646-2291.
Will search UCC records. Tax liens not included in UCC search. Will not search real estate records. **Other Phone Numbers:** Assessor 201-646-3185; Treasurer 201-646-3237.

Burlington County

County Clerk, PO Box 6000, Mount Holly, NJ 08060. 609-265-5182; Fax 609-265-0696.
Will search UCC records. Will not search real estate records. **Other Phones:** Assessor 609-265-5056.

Camden County

County Clerk, Courthouse Room 102, 520 Market St, Camden, NJ 08102-1375. County Clerk, R/E and UCC Recording 856-225-5300; Fax 856-225-7100.
Will search UCC records. This agency will not do a tax lien search. Computer index available for all transactions after August 1988

Cape May County

County Clerk, PO Box 5000, Cape May Court House, NJ 08210-5000. County Clerk, R/E and UCC Recording 609-465-1010; Fax 609-465-8625. www.co.cape-may.nj.us
Will not search UCC records or tax liens. Will not search real estate records. **Online Access:** Real Estate, Recording Records. Property records for Cape May county are available to view free online at http://209.201.24.238/ALIS/WW400R.PGM. To print and have full access to documents, registration and login is required. Online documents go back to 1996, images to 2000. **Other Phone Numbers:** Elections 609-465-1013; Vital Records 609-465-1023.

Cumberland County

County Clerk, PO Box 716, Bridgeton, NJ 08302. 856-453-4864; Fax 856-455-1410.
Will search UCC records. Will not search real estate records. **Other Phone Numbers:** Assessor 856-451-6699; Elections 856-453-4850.

Essex County

County Register of Deeds, 465 Martin Luther King Boulevard, Hall of Records, Room 130, Newark, NJ 07102. 973-621-4960 R/E Recording: 973-621-4960 x228 UCC Recording: 973-621-4960 x225; Fax 973-621-6114. www.essexregister.com
Will search UCC records. This agency will not do a tax lien search. Will not search real estate records. **Other Phone Numbers:** Assessor 973-673-2344; Treasurer 973-621-4997.

Gloucester County

County Clerk, PO Box 129, Woodbury, NJ 08096-0129. County Clerk, R/E and UCC Recording 856-853-3230; Fax 856-853-3327. www.co.gloucester.nj.us
Will search UCC records. This agency will not do a tax lien search. Will not search real estate records. **Online Access:** Real Estate, Recording Records. County Recorder records are accessible through a private online service at www.landaccess.com; Fees and registration are required. **Other Phone Numbers:** Assessor 856-384-6945; Treasurer 856-853-3353; Elections 856-853-3243; Tax Collector 856-853-6945.

Hudson County

County Clerk, 595 Newark Ave, Room 105, Jersey City, NJ 07306. 201-795-6571; Fax 201-795-5179.
Will search UCC records. Will not search real estate records.

Hunterdon County

County Clerk, 71 Main St, Hall of Records, Flemington, NJ 08822. 908-788-1221; Fax 908-782-4068.
Will search UCC records. Will not search real estate records. **Other Phones:** Assessor 908-788-1173.

Mercer County

County Clerk, 209 S. Broad St, Courthouse, Room 100, Trenton, NJ 08650. 609-989-6466 R/E Recording: 609-989-6487 UCC Recording: 609-989-6487; Fax 609-989-1111. www.mercercounty.org
Will not search real estate records. **Other Phones:** Assessor 609-989-6704; Treasurer 609-989-6694; Elections 609-989-6495; Vital Records 609-292-4087.

Middlesex County

County Clerk, PO Box 1110, New Brunswick, NJ 08903. 732-745-3204.
Will search UCC records. This agency will not do a tax lien search. Will not search real estate records. **Other Phone Numbers:** Assessor 732-745-3000; Treasurer 732-754-3482.

Monmouth County

County Clerk, Market Yard, PO Box 1251, Freehold, NJ 07728. 732-431-7324 R/E Recording: 832-431-7321 UCC Recording: 832-431-7321; www.co.monmouth.nj.us
Will search UCC records. This agency will not do a tax lien search. Will not search real estate records. **Online Access:** Real Estate, Deed, Mortgage Records. Access to the county clerk database is available free at http://tax0.co.monmouth.nj.us/monmouthnew/monmouth/search.asp. Records from 10/1/96 to present. **Other Phone Numbers:** Assessor 732-431-7404; Treasurer 732-431-7391; Appraiser/Auditor 732-431-7404; Elections 732-431-7780.

Morris County

County Clerk, PO Box 315, Morristown, NJ 07963-0315. 973-285-6135; Fax 973-285-5231.
This agency will not search real estate or UCC records.

Ocean County

County Clerk, PO Box 2191, Toms River, NJ 08754. 732-929-2110; Fax 732-349-4336. www.oceancountyclerk.com
Will search UCC records. This agency will not do a tax lien search. Will not search real estate records. **Online Access:** Property Tax, Real Estate Records. Land records on the County Clerk database are available free online at www.oceancountyclerk.com/search.htm. Search by parties, document or instrument type, or township. Tax records for Ocean county are also available on the taxrecords.com web site at http://oc.taxrecords.com. Search by name, address or property description.

Passaic County

County Clerk.Registry Division, 77 Hamilton St, Courthouse, Paterson, NJ 07505. 973-881-4777.
This agency will not perform searches.

Salem County

County Clerk, 92 Market St, Salem, NJ 08079-1911. 856-935-7510 x8218; Fax 856-935-8882.
Will search UCC records. Will not search real estate records. **Other Phone Numbers:** Assessor 856-935-9231; Treasurer 856-935--9036.

Somerset County

County Clerk, PO Box 3000, Somerville, NJ 08876. County Clerk, R/E and UCC Recording 908-231-7006; Fax 908-253-8853. www.co.somerset.nj.us
This agency will not perform searches. **Online Access:** Property, Recording Records. Access to the County Clerk's recordings database is available free at http://209.92.88.21. Registration required, or enter as "Guest." Index available back to 1/93; images back to 6/11/01. **Other Phone Numbers:** Treasurer 908-231-7000 x7631.

Sussex County

County Clerk, 4 Park Place, Hall of Records, Newton, NJ 07860-1795. County Clerk, R/E and UCC Recording 973-579-0900; Fax 973-383-7493. www.sussexcountyclerk.com
This agency will not search real estate or UCC records. **Other Phone Numbers:** Assessor 973-579-0970; Treasurer 973-579-0330; Elections 973-579-0950.

Union County

County Clerk, 2 Broad St, Courthouse, Room 115, Elizabeth, NJ 07207. County Clerk, R/E and UCC Recording 908-527-4787 UCC Recording: 908-527-4794; Fax 908-558-2589. www.unioncountynj.org/constit/clerk/record.html
Will search UCC records. This agency will not do a tax lien search. Will not search real estate records. **Other Phone Numbers:** Elections 908-527-4996.

Warren County

County Clerk, 413 Second St, Courthouse, Belvidere, NJ 07823-1500. County Clerk, R/E and UCC Recording 908-475-6211.
This agency will not perform searches.
Other Phone Numbers: Elections 908-475-6211.

New Jersey County Locator

You will usually be able to find the city name in the City/County Cross Reference below. In that case, it is a simple matter to determine the county from the cross reference. However, only the official US Postal Service city names are included in this index. There are an additional 40,000 place names that people use in their addresses. Therefore, we have also included a ZIP/City Cross Reference immediately following the City/County Cross Reference.

If you know the ZIP Code but the city name does not appear in the City/County Cross Reference index, look up the ZIP Code in the ZIP/City Cross Reference, find the city name, then look up the city name in the City/County Cross Reference. For example, you want to know the county for an address of Menands, NY 12204. There is no "Menands" in the City/County Cross Reference. The ZIP/City Cross Reference shows that ZIP Codes 12201-12288 are for the city of Albany. Looking back in the City/County Cross Reference, Albany is in Albany County.

City/County Cross Reference

ABSECON Atlantic
ADELPHIA Monmouth
ALLAMUCHY Warren
ALLENDALE Bergen
ALLENHURST Monmouth
ALLENTOWN (08501) Monmouth(72), Mercer(14), Burlington(13)
ALLENWOOD Monmouth
ALLOWAY Salem
ALPINE Bergen
ANDOVER Sussex
ANNANDALE Hunterdon
ASBURY (08802) Hunterdon(67), Warren(32)
ASBURY PARK Monmouth
ATCO (08004) Camden(94), Burlington(5)
ATLANTIC CITY Atlantic
ATLANTIC HIGHLANDS Monmouth
AUDUBON Camden
AUGUSTA Sussex
AVALON Cape May
AVENEL Middlesex
AVON BY THE SEA Monmouth
BAPTISTOWN Hunterdon
BARNEGAT Ocean
BARNEGAT LIGHT Ocean
BARRINGTON Camden
BASKING RIDGE Somerset
BAYONNE Hudson
BAYVILLE Ocean
BEACH HAVEN Ocean
BEACHWOOD Ocean
BEDMINSTER Somerset
BELFORD Monmouth
BELLE MEAD Somerset
BELLEVILLE Essex
BELLMAWR Camden
BELMAR Monmouth
BELVIDERE Warren
BERGENFIELD Bergen
BERKELEY HEIGHTS Union
BERLIN Camden
BERNARDSVILLE Somerset
BEVERLY Burlington
BIRMINGHAM Burlington
BLACKWOOD (08012) Camden(55), Gloucester(44)
BLAIRSTOWN Warren
BLAWENBURG Somerset
BLOOMFIELD Essex
BLOOMINGDALE Passaic
BLOOMSBURY (08804) Hunterdon(61), Warren(38)
BOGOTA Bergen
BOONTON Morris
BORDENTOWN Burlington
BOUND BROOK Somerset
BRADLEY BEACH Monmouth
BRANCHVILLE Sussex
BRICK Ocean
BRIDGEPORT Gloucester
BRIDGETON (08302) Cumberland(93), Salem(6)
BRIDGEWATER Somerset
BRIELLE Monmouth
BRIGANTINE Atlantic

BROADWAY Warren
BROOKSIDE Morris
BROWNS MILLS Burlington
BUDD LAKE Morris
BUENA Atlantic
BURLINGTON Burlington
BUTLER Morris
BUTTZVILLE Warren
CALDWELL Essex
CALIFON (07830) Hunterdon(87), Morris(12)
CAMDEN Camden
CAPE MAY Cape May
CAPE MAY COURT HOUSE Cape May
CAPE MAY POINT Cape May
CARLSTADT Bergen
CARTERET Middlesex
CEDAR BROOK Camden
CEDAR GROVE Essex
CEDAR KNOLLS Morris
CEDARVILLE Cumberland
CHANGEWATER Warren
CHATHAM Morris
CHATSWORTH Burlington
CHERRY HILL Camden
CHESTER Morris
CLARK Union
CLARKSBORO Gloucester
CLARKSBURG Monmouth
CLAYTON Gloucester
CLEMENTON Camden
CLIFFSIDE PARK Bergen
CLIFFWOOD Monmouth
CLIFTON Passaic
CLINTON Hunterdon
CLOSTER Bergen
COLLINGSWOOD Camden
COLOGNE Atlantic
COLONIA Middlesex
COLTS NECK Monmouth
COLUMBIA Warren
COLUMBUS Burlington
COOKSTOWN Burlington
CRANBURY Middlesex
CRANFORD Union
CREAM RIDGE (08514) Monmouth(70), Ocean(29)
CREAMRIDGE (08514) Monmouth(70), Ocean(29)
CRESSKILL Bergen
CROSSWICKS Burlington
DAYTON Middlesex
DEAL Monmouth
DEEPWATER Salem
DEERFIELD STREET Cumberland
DELAWARE Warren
DELMONT Cumberland
DEMAREST Bergen
DENNISVILLE Cape May
DENVILLE Morris
DIVIDING CREEK Cumberland
DORCHESTER Cumberland
DOROTHY Atlantic
DOVER Morris
DUMONT Bergen

DUNELLEN (08812) Somerset(51), Middlesex(47)
EAST BRUNSWICK Middlesex
EAST HANOVER Morris
EAST ORANGE Essex
EAST RUTHERFORD Bergen
EATONTOWN Monmouth
EDGEWATER Bergen
EDISON Middlesex
EGG HARBOR CITY (08215) Atlantic(95), Burlington(4)
EGG HARBOR TOWNSHIP Atlantic
ELIZABETH Union
ELMER Salem
ELMWOOD PARK Bergen
ELWOOD Atlantic
EMERSON Bergen
ENGLEWOOD Bergen
ENGLEWOOD CLIFFS Bergen
ENGLISHTOWN Monmouth
ESSEX FELLS Essex
ESTELL MANOR Atlantic
EWAN Gloucester
FAIR HAVEN Monmouth
FAIR LAWN Bergen
FAIRFIELD Essex
FAIRTON Cumberland
FAIRVIEW Bergen
FANWOOD Union
FAR HILLS (07931) Somerset(81), Morris(18)
FARMINGDALE Monmouth
FLAGTOWN Somerset
FLANDERS Morris
FLEMINGTON Hunterdon
FLORENCE Burlington
FLORHAM PARK Morris
FORDS Middlesex
FORKED RIVER Ocean
FORT LEE Bergen
FORT MONMOUTH Monmouth
FORTESCUE Cumberland
FRANKLIN Sussex
FRANKLIN LAKES Bergen
FRANKLIN PARK Somerset
FRANKLINVILLE Gloucester
FREEHOLD Monmouth
FRENCHTOWN Hunterdon
GARFIELD Bergen
GARWOOD Union
GIBBSBORO Camden
GIBBSTOWN Gloucester
GILLETTE Morris
GLADSTONE Somerset
GLASSBORO Gloucester
GLASSER Sussex
GLEN GARDNER Hunterdon
GLEN RIDGE Essex
GLEN ROCK Bergen
GLENDORA Camden
GLENWOOD Sussex
GLOUCESTER CITY Camden
GOSHEN Cape May
GREAT MEADOWS Warren
GREEN CREEK Cape May
GREEN VILLAGE Morris

GREENDELL Sussex
GREENWICH Cumberland
GRENLOCH Gloucester
HACKENSACK Bergen
HACKETTSTOWN (07840) Warren(77), Morris(22)
HADDON HEIGHTS Camden
HADDONFIELD Camden
HAINESPORT Burlington
HALEDON Passaic
HAMBURG Sussex
HAMMONTON (08037) Atlantic(81), Camden(18)
HAMPTON Hunterdon
HANCOCKS BRIDGE Salem
HARRINGTON PARK Bergen
HARRISON Hudson
HARRISONVILLE Gloucester
HASBROUCK HEIGHTS Bergen
HASKELL Passaic
HAWORTH Bergen
HAWTHORNE Passaic
HAZLET Monmouth
HEISLERVILLE Cumberland
HELMETTA Middlesex
HEWITT (07421) Passaic(98), Sussex(1)
HIBERNIA Morris
HIGH BRIDGE Hunterdon
HIGHLAND LAKES Sussex
HIGHLAND PARK Middlesex
HIGHLANDS Monmouth
HIGHTSTOWN Mercer
HILLSBOROUGH Somerset
HILLSDALE Bergen
HILLSIDE Union
HO HO KUS Bergen
HOBOKEN Hudson
HOLMDEL Monmouth
HOPATCONG Sussex
HOPE Warren
HOPEWELL (08525) Mercer(92), Hunterdon(7)
HOWELL Monmouth
IMLAYSTOWN Monmouth
IRONIA Morris
IRVINGTON Essex
ISELIN Middlesex
ISLAND HEIGHTS Ocean
JACKSON Ocean
JAMESBURG Middlesex
JERSEY CITY Hudson
JOBSTOWN Burlington
JOHNSONBURG Warren
JULIUSTOWN Burlington
KEANSBURG Monmouth
KEARNY Hudson
KEASBEY Middlesex
KENDALL PARK Middlesex
KENILWORTH Union
KENVIL Morris
KEYPORT (07735) Monmouth(92), Middlesex(7)
KINGSTON Somerset
KIRKWOOD VOORHEES Camden
LAFAYETTE Sussex
LAKE HIAWATHA Morris

LAKE HOPATCONG Morris
LAKEHURST Ocean
LAKEWOOD Ocean
LAMBERTVILLE (08530) Hunterdon(95), Mercer(4)
LANDING Morris
LANDISVILLE Atlantic
LANOKA HARBOR Ocean
LAVALLETTE Ocean
LAWNSIDE Camden
LAYTON Sussex
LEBANON Hunterdon
LEDGEWOOD Morris
LEEDS POINT Atlantic
LEESBURG Cumberland
LEONARDO Monmouth
LEONIA Bergen
LIBERTY CORNER Somerset
LINCOLN PARK Morris
LINCROFT Monmouth
LINDEN Union
LINWOOD Atlantic
LITTLE FALLS Passaic
LITTLE FERRY Bergen
LITTLE SILVER Monmouth
LITTLE YORK Hunterdon
LIVINGSTON Essex
LODI Bergen
LONG BRANCH Monmouth
LONG VALLEY Morris
LONGPORT Atlantic
LUMBERTON Burlington
LYNDHURST Bergen
LYONS Somerset
MADISON Morris
MAGNOLIA Camden
MAHWAH Bergen
MALAGA Gloucester
MANAHAWKIN Ocean
MANASQUAN Monmouth
MANTOLOKING Ocean
MANTUA Gloucester
MANVILLE Somerset
MAPLE SHADE Burlington
MAPLEWOOD Essex
MARGATE CITY Atlantic
MARLBORO Monmouth
MARLTON Burlington
MARMORA Cape May
MARTINSVILLE Somerset
MATAWAN (07747) Monmouth(79), Middlesex(20)
MAURICETOWN Cumberland
MAYS LANDING Atlantic
MAYWOOD Bergen
MC AFEE Sussex
MEDFORD Burlington
MENDHAM Morris
MERCHANTVILLE Camden
METUCHEN Middlesex
MICKLETON Gloucester
MIDDLESEX Middlesex
MIDDLETOWN Monmouth
MIDDLEVILLE Sussex
MIDLAND PARK Bergen
MILFORD Hunterdon
MILLBURN Essex
MILLINGTON Morris
MILLTOWN Middlesex
MILLVILLE Cumberland
MILMAY Atlantic
MINE HILL Morris
MINOTOLA Atlantic
MIZPAH Atlantic
MONMOUTH BEACH Monmouth
MONMOUTH JUNCTION Middlesex
MONROE TOWNSHIP Middlesex
MONROEVILLE (08343) Gloucester(58), Salem(41)
MONTAGUE (07827) Sussex(97), Morris(2)
MONTCLAIR (07043) Essex(96), Passaic(3)

MONTVALE Bergen
MONTVILLE Morris
MOONACHIE Bergen
MOORESTOWN Burlington
MORGANVILLE Monmouth
MORRIS PLAINS Morris
MORRISTOWN Morris
MOUNT ARLINGTON Morris
MOUNT EPHRAIM Camden
MOUNT FREEDOM Morris
MOUNT HOLLY Burlington
MOUNT LAUREL Burlington
MOUNT ROYAL Gloucester
MOUNT TABOR Morris
MOUNTAIN LAKES Morris
MOUNTAINSIDE Union
MULLICA HILL Gloucester
MUSICAL HERITAGE Monmouth
NATIONAL PARK Gloucester
NAVESINK Monmouth
NEPTUNE Monmouth
NESHANIC STATION (08853) Somerset(97), Hunterdon(2)
NETCONG Morris
NEW BRUNSWICK Middlesex
NEW EGYPT Ocean
NEW GRETNA Burlington
NEW LISBON Burlington
NEW MILFORD Bergen
NEW PROVIDENCE Union
NEW VERNON Morris
NEWARK Essex
NEWFIELD (08344) Gloucester(68), Cumberland(24), Salem(4), Atlantic(2)
NEWFOUNDLAND Passaic
NEWPORT Cumberland
NEWTON Sussex
NEWTONVILLE Atlantic
NORMA Salem
NORMANDY BEACH Ocean
NORTH ARLINGTON Bergen
NORTH BERGEN Hudson
NORTH BRUNSWICK Middlesex
NORTHFIELD Atlantic
NORTHVALE Bergen
NORWOOD Bergen
NUTLEY Essex
OAK RIDGE (07438) Passaic(78), Morris(21)
OAKHURST Monmouth
OAKLAND Bergen
OAKLYN Camden
OCEAN CITY Cape May
OCEAN GATE Ocean
OCEAN GROVE Monmouth
OCEAN VIEW Cape May
OCEANPORT Monmouth
OCEANVILLE Atlantic
OGDENSBURG Sussex
OLD BRIDGE Middlesex
OLDWICK Hunterdon
ORADELL Bergen
ORANGE Essex
OSGLI Essex
OXFORD Warren
PALISADES PARK Bergen
PALMYRA Burlington
PARAMUS Bergen
PARK RIDGE Bergen
PARLIN Middlesex
PARSIPPANY Morris
PASSAIC Passaic
PATERSON Passaic
PAULSBORO Gloucester
PEAPACK Somerset
PEDRICKTOWN Salem
PEMBERTON Burlington
PENNINGTON Mercer
PENNS GROVE Salem
PENNSAUKEN Camden
PENNSVILLE Salem
PEQUANNOCK Morris

PERRINEVILLE (08535) Monmouth(86), Ocean(13)
PERTH AMBOY Middlesex
PHILLIPSBURG Warren
PICATINNY ARSENAL Morris
PINE BEACH Ocean
PINE BROOK Morris
PISCATAWAY Middlesex
PITMAN Gloucester
PITTSTOWN Hunterdon
PLAINFIELD (07063) Union(72), Somerset(27)
PLAINSBORO Middlesex
PLEASANTVILLE Atlantic
PLUCKEMIN Somerset
POINT PLEASANT BEACH Ocean
POMONA Atlantic
POMPTON LAKES Passaic
POMPTON PLAINS Passaic
PORT ELIZABETH Cumberland
PORT MONMOUTH Monmouth
PORT MURRAY Warren
PORT NORRIS Cumberland
PORT READING Middlesex
PORT REPUBLIC Atlantic
POTTERSVILLE Hunterdon
PRINCETON Mercer
PRINCETON JUNCTION Mercer
QUAKERTOWN Hunterdon
QUINTON Salem
RAHWAY Union
RAMSEY Bergen
RANCOCAS Burlington
RANDOLPH Morris
RARITAN Somerset
READINGTON Hunterdon
RED BANK Monmouth
RICHLAND Atlantic
RICHWOOD Gloucester
RIDGEFIELD Bergen
RIDGEFIELD PARK Bergen
RIDGEWOOD Bergen
RINGOES Hunterdon
RINGWOOD Passaic
RIO GRANDE Cape May
RIVER EDGE Bergen
RIVERDALE Morris
RIVERSIDE Burlington
RIVERTON Burlington
ROCHELLE PARK Bergen
ROCKAWAY Morris
ROCKY HILL Somerset
ROEBLING Burlington
ROOSEVELT Monmouth
ROSELAND Essex
ROSELLE Union
ROSELLE PARK Union
ROSEMONT Hunterdon
ROSENHAYN Cumberland
RUMSON Monmouth
RUNNEMEDE Camden
RUTHERFORD Bergen
SADDLE BROOK Bergen
SADDLE RIVER Bergen
SALEM Salem
SAYREVILLE Middlesex
SCHOOLEYS MOUNTAIN Morris
SCOTCH PLAINS Union
SEA GIRT Monmouth
SEA ISLE CITY Cape May
SEASIDE HEIGHTS Ocean
SEASIDE PARK Ocean
SECAUCUS Hudson
SERGEANTSVILLE Hunterdon
SEWAREN Middlesex
SEWELL Gloucester
SHILOH Cumberland
SHORT HILLS Essex
SHREWSBURY Monmouth
SICKLERVILLE (08081) Camden(96), Gloucester(3)

SKILLMAN (08558) Somerset(98), Mercer(1)
SOMERDALE Camden
SOMERS POINT Atlantic
SOMERSET Somerset
SOMERVILLE (08876) Somerset(98), Hunterdon(1)
SOUTH AMBOY Middlesex
SOUTH BOUND BROOK Somerset
SOUTH DENNIS Cape May
SOUTH HACKENSACK Bergen
SOUTH ORANGE Essex
SOUTH PLAINFIELD Middlesex
SOUTH RIVER Middlesex
SOUTH SEAVILLE Cape May
SPARTA Sussex
SPOTSWOOD Middlesex
SPRING LAKE Monmouth
SPRINGFIELD Union
STANHOPE Sussex
STANTON Hunterdon
STEWARTSVILLE Warren
STILLWATER Sussex
STIRLING Morris
STOCKHOLM (07460) Sussex(96), Morris(2)
STOCKTON Hunterdon
STONE HARBOR Cape May
STRATFORD Camden
STRATHMERE Cape May
SUCCASUNNA Morris
SUMMIT Union
SUSSEX Sussex
SWARTSWOOD Sussex
SWEDESBORO Gloucester
TEANECK Bergen
TENAFLY Bergen
TENNENT Monmouth
TETERBORO Bergen
THOROFARE Gloucester
THREE BRIDGES Hunterdon
TITUSVILLE Mercer
TOMS RIVER Ocean
TOTOWA Passaic
TOWACO Morris
TOWNSHIP OF WASHINGTON Bergen
TRANQUILITY Sussex
TRENTON Mercer
TUCKAHOE Cape May
TUCKERTON (08087) Ocean(94), Burlington(5)
UNION Union
UNION CITY Hudson
VAUXHALL Union
VENTNOR CITY Atlantic
VERNON Sussex
VERONA Essex
VIENNA Warren
VILLAS Cape May
VINCENTOWN Burlington
VINELAND Cumberland
VOORHEES Camden
WALDWICK Bergen
WALLINGTON Bergen
WALLPACK CENTER Sussex
WANAQUE Passaic
WARETOWN Ocean
WARREN Somerset
WASHINGTON Warren
WATCHUNG Somerset
WATERFORD WORKS Camden
WAYNE Passaic
WEEHAWKEN Hudson
WENONAH Gloucester
WEST BERLIN Camden
WEST CREEK Ocean
WEST LONG BRANCH Monmouth
WEST MILFORD Passaic
WEST NEW YORK Hudson
WEST ORANGE Essex
WESTFIELD Union
WESTVILLE Gloucester

WESTWOOD Bergen
WHARTON Morris
WHIPPANY Morris
WHITEHOUSE Hunterdon
WHITEHOUSE STATION Hunterdon
WHITESBORO Cape May
WHITING Ocean

WICKATUNK Monmouth
WILDWOOD Cape May
WILLIAMSTOWN (08094) Gloucester(90), Atlantic(9)
WILLINGBORO Burlington
WINDSOR Mercer
WINSLOW Camden

WOOD RIDGE Bergen
WOODBINE (08270) Cape May(89), Atlantic(10)
WOODBRIDGE Middlesex
WOODBURY Gloucester
WOODBURY HEIGHTS Gloucester
WOODCLIFF LAKE Bergen

WOODSTOWN Salem
WRIGHTSTOWN Burlington
WYCKOFF Bergen
ZAREPHATH Somerset

ZIP/City Cross Reference

07001-07001 AVENEL	07097-07097 JERSEY CITY	07626-07626 CRESSKILL	07760-07760 RUMSON
07002-07002 BAYONNE	07098-07098 AVENEL	07627-07627 DEMAREST	07762-07762 SPRING LAKE
07003-07003 BLOOMFIELD	07099-07099 KEARNY	07628-07628 DUMONT	07763-07763 TENNENT
07004-07004 FAIRFIELD	07100-07108 NEWARK	07630-07630 EMERSON	07764-07764 WEST LONG BRANCH
07005-07005 BOONTON	07109-07109 BELLEVILLE	07631-07631 ENGLEWOOD	07765-07765 WICKATUNK
07006-07007 CALDWELL	07110-07110 NUTLEY	07632-07632 ENGLEWOOD CLIFFS	07777-07777 HOLMDEL
07008-07008 CARTERET	07111-07111 IRVINGTON	07640-07640 HARRINGTON PARK	07799-07799 EATONTOWN
07009-07009 CEDAR GROVE	07112-07187 NEWARK	07641-07641 HAWORTH	07801-07802 DOVER
07010-07010 CLIFFSIDE PARK	07187-07187 OSGLI	07642-07642 HILLSDALE	07803-07803 MINE HILL
07011-07015 CLIFTON	07188-07199 NEWARK	07643-07643 LITTLE FERRY	07806-07806 PICATINNY ARSENAL
07016-07016 CRANFORD	07200-07202 ELIZABETH	07644-07644 LODI	07820-07820 ALLAMUCHY
07017-07019 EAST ORANGE	07203-07203 ROSELLE	07645-07645 MONTVALE	07821-07821 ANDOVER
07020-07020 EDGEWATER	07204-07204 ROSELLE PARK	07646-07646 NEW MILFORD	07822-07822 AUGUSTA
07021-07021 ESSEX FELLS	07205-07205 HILLSIDE	07647-07647 NORTHVALE	07823-07823 BELVIDERE
07022-07022 FAIRVIEW	07206-07216 ELIZABETH	07648-07648 NORWOOD	07825-07825 BLAIRSTOWN
07023-07023 FANWOOD	07300-07399 JERSEY CITY	07649-07649 ORADELL	07826-07826 BRANCHVILLE
07024-07024 FORT LEE	07401-07401 ALLENDALE	07650-07650 PALISADES PARK	07827-07827 MONTAGUE
07026-07026 GARFIELD	07403-07403 BLOOMINGDALE	07652-07653 PARAMUS	07828-07828 BUDD LAKE
07027-07027 GARWOOD	07405-07405 BUTLER	07656-07656 PARK RIDGE	07829-07829 BUTTZVILLE
07028-07028 GLEN RIDGE	07407-07407 ELMWOOD PARK	07657-07657 RIDGEFIELD	07830-07830 CALIFON
07029-07029 HARRISON	07410-07410 FAIR LAWN	07660-07660 RIDGEFIELD PARK	07831-07831 CHANGEWATER
07030-07030 HOBOKEN	07416-07416 FRANKLIN	07661-07661 RIVER EDGE	07832-07832 COLUMBIA
07031-07031 NORTH ARLINGTON	07417-07417 FRANKLIN LAKES	07662-07662 ROCHELLE PARK	07833-07833 DELAWARE
07032-07032 KEARNY	07418-07418 GLENWOOD	07663-07663 SADDLE BROOK	07834-07834 DENVILLE
07033-07033 KENILWORTH	07419-07419 HAMBURG	07666-07666 TEANECK	07836-07836 FLANDERS
07034-07034 LAKE HIAWATHA	07420-07420 HASKELL	07670-07670 TENAFLY	07837-07837 GLASSER
07035-07035 LINCOLN PARK	07421-07421 HEWITT	07675-07675 WESTWOOD	07838-07838 GREAT MEADOWS
07036-07036 LINDEN	07422-07422 HIGHLAND LAKES	07676-07676 TWSP OF WASHINGTON	07839-07839 GREENDELL
07039-07039 LIVINGSTON	07423-07423 HO HO KUS	07677-07677 WOODCLIFF LAKE	07840-07840 HACKETTSTOWN
07040-07040 MAPLEWOOD	07424-07424 LITTLE FALLS	07688-07688 TEANECK	07842-07842 HIBERNIA
07041-07041 MILLBURN	07428-07428 MC AFEE	07701-07701 RED BANK	07843-07843 HOPATCONG
07042-07043 MONTCLAIR	07430-07430 MAHWAH	07702-07702 SHREWSBURY	07844-07844 HOPE
07044-07044 VERONA	07432-07432 MIDLAND PARK	07703-07703 FORT MONMOUTH	07845-07845 IRONIA
07045-07045 MONTVILLE	07435-07435 NEWFOUNDLAND	07704-07704 FAIR HAVEN	07846-07846 JOHNSONBURG
07046-07046 MOUNTAIN LAKES	07436-07436 OAKLAND	07709-07709 ALLENHURST	07847-07847 KENVIL
07047-07047 NORTH BERGEN	07438-07438 OAK RIDGE	07710-07710 ADELPHIA	07848-07848 LAFAYETTE
07050-07051 ORANGE	07439-07439 OGDENSBURG	07711-07711 ALLENHURST	07849-07849 LAKE HOPATCONG
07052-07052 WEST ORANGE	07440-07440 PEQUANNOCK	07712-07712 ASBURY PARK	07850-07850 LANDING
07054-07054 PARSIPPANY	07442-07442 POMPTON LAKES	07713-07713 MUSICAL HERITAGE	07851-07851 LAYTON
07055-07055 PASSAIC	07444-07444 POMPTON PLAINS	07715-07715 BELMAR	07852-07852 LEDGEWOOD
07057-07057 WALLINGTON	07446-07446 RAMSEY	07716-07716 ATLANTIC HIGHLANDS	07853-07853 LONG VALLEY
07058-07058 PINE BROOK	07450-07451 RIDGEWOOD	07717-07717 AVON BY THE SEA	07855-07855 MIDDLEVILLE
07059-07059 WARREN	07452-07452 GLEN ROCK	07718-07718 BELFORD	07856-07856 MOUNT ARLINGTON
07060-07063 PLAINFIELD	07456-07456 RINGWOOD	07719-07719 BELMAR	07857-07857 NETCONG
07064-07064 PORT READING	07457-07457 RIVERDALE	07720-07720 BRADLEY BEACH	07860-07860 NEWTON
07065-07065 RAHWAY	07458-07458 SADDLE RIVER	07721-07721 CLIFFWOOD	07863-07863 OXFORD
07066-07066 CLARK	07460-07460 STOCKHOLM	07722-07722 COLTS NECK	07865-07865 PORT MURRAY
07067-07067 COLONIA	07461-07461 SUSSEX	07723-07723 DEAL	07866-07866 ROCKAWAY
07068-07068 ROSELAND	07462-07462 VERNON	07724-07724 EATONTOWN	07869-07869 RANDOLPH
07069-07069 WATCHUNG	07463-07463 WALDWICK	07726-07726 ENGLISHTOWN	07870-07870 SCHOOLEYS MOUNTAIN
07070-07070 RUTHERFORD	07465-07465 WANAQUE	07727-07727 FARMINGDALE	07871-07871 SPARTA
07071-07071 LYNDHURST	07470-07477 WAYNE	07728-07728 FREEHOLD	07874-07874 STANHOPE
07072-07072 CARLSTADT	07480-07480 WEST MILFORD	07730-07730 HAZLET	07875-07875 STILLWATER
07073-07073 EAST RUTHERFORD	07481-07481 WYCKOFF	07731-07731 HOWELL	07876-07876 SUCCASUNNA
07074-07074 MOONACHIE	07495-07498 MAHWAH	07732-07732 HIGHLANDS	07877-07877 SWARTSWOOD
07075-07075 WOOD RIDGE	07501-07505 PATERSON	07733-07733 HOLMDEL	07878-07878 MOUNT TABOR
07076-07076 SCOTCH PLAINS	07506-07507 HAWTHORNE	07734-07734 KEANSBURG	07879-07879 TRANQUILITY
07077-07077 SEWAREN	07508-07508 HALEDON	07735-07735 KEYPORT	07880-07880 VIENNA
07078-07078 SHORT HILLS	07509-07510 PATERSON	07737-07737 LEONARDO	07881-07881 WALLPACK CENTER
07079-07079 SOUTH ORANGE	07511-07512 TOTOWA	07738-07738 LINCROFT	07882-07882 WASHINGTON
07080-07080 SOUTH PLAINFIELD	07513-07533 PATERSON	07739-07739 LITTLE SILVER	07885-07885 WHARTON
07081-07081 SPRINGFIELD	07538-07538 HALEDON	07740-07740 LONG BRANCH	07890-07890 BRANCHVILLE
07082-07082 TOWACO	07543-07544 PATERSON	07746-07746 MARLBORO	07901-07902 SUMMIT
07083-07083 UNION	07601-07602 HACKENSACK	07747-07747 MATAWAN	07920-07920 BASKING RIDGE
07086-07086 WEEHAWKEN	07603-07603 BOGOTA	07748-07748 MIDDLETOWN	07921-07921 BEDMINSTER
07087-07087 UNION CITY	07604-07604 HASBROUCK HEIGHTS	07750-07750 MONMOUTH BEACH	07922-07922 BERKELEY HEIGHTS
07088-07088 VAUXHALL	07605-07605 LEONIA	07751-07751 MORGANVILLE	07924-07924 BERNARDSVILLE
07090-07091 WESTFIELD	07606-07606 SOUTH HACKENSACK	07752-07752 NAVESINK	07926-07926 BROOKSIDE
07092-07092 MOUNTAINSIDE	07607-07607 MAYWOOD	07753-07754 NEPTUNE	07927-07927 CEDAR KNOLLS
07093-07093 WEST NEW YORK	07608-07608 TETERBORO	07755-07755 OAKHURST	07928-07928 CHATHAM
07094-07094 SECAUCUS	07620-07620 ALPINE	07756-07756 OCEAN GROVE	07930-07930 CHESTER
07095-07095 WOODBRIDGE	07621-07621 BERGENFIELD	07757-07757 OCEANPORT	07931-07931 FAR HILLS
07096-07096 SECAUCUS	07624-07624 CLOSTER	07758-07758 PORT MONMOUTH	07932-07932 FLORHAM PARK

ZIP Range	Place	ZIP Range	Place	ZIP Range	Place	ZIP Range	Place
07933-07933	GILLETTE	08071-08071	PITMAN	08320-08320	FAIRTON	08739-08739	NORMANDY BEACH
07934-07934	GLADSTONE	08072-08072	QUINTON	08321-08321	FORTESCUE	08740-08740	OCEAN GATE
07935-07935	GREEN VILLAGE	08073-08073	RANCOCAS	08322-08322	FRANKLINVILLE	08741-08741	PINE BEACH
07936-07936	EAST HANOVER	08074-08074	RICHWOOD	08323-08323	GREENWICH	08742-08742	POINT PLEASANT BEACH
07938-07938	LIBERTY CORNER	08075-08075	RIVERSIDE	08324-08324	HEISLERVILLE	08750-08750	SEA GIRT
07939-07939	LYONS	08076-08077	RIVERTON	08326-08326	LANDISVILLE	08751-08751	SEASIDE HEIGHTS
07940-07940	MADISON	08078-08078	RUNNEMEDE	08327-08327	LEESBURG	08752-08752	SEASIDE PARK
07945-07945	MENDHAM	08079-08079	SALEM	08328-08328	MALAGA	08753-08757	TOMS RIVER
07946-07946	MILLINGTON	08080-08080	SEWELL	08329-08329	MAURICETOWN	08758-08758	WARETOWN
07950-07950	MORRIS PLAINS	08081-08081	SICKLERVILLE	08330-08330	MAYS LANDING	08759-08759	WHITING
07960-07963	MORRISTOWN	08083-08083	SOMERDALE	08332-08332	MILLVILLE	08801-08801	ANNANDALE
07970-07970	MOUNT FREEDOM	08084-08084	STRATFORD	08340-08340	MILMAY	08802-08802	ASBURY
07974-07974	NEW PROVIDENCE	08085-08085	SWEDESBORO	08341-08341	MINOTOLA	08803-08803	BAPTISTOWN
07976-07976	NEW VERNON	08086-08086	THOROFARE	08342-08342	MIZPAH	08804-08804	BLOOMSBURY
07977-07977	PEAPACK	08087-08087	TUCKERTON	08343-08343	MONROEVILLE	08805-08805	BOUND BROOK
07978-07978	PLUCKEMIN	08088-08088	VINCENTOWN	08344-08344	NEWFIELD	08807-08807	BRIDGEWATER
07979-07979	POTTERSVILLE	08089-08089	WATERFORD WORKS	08345-08345	NEWPORT	08808-08808	BROADWAY
07980-07980	STIRLING	08090-08090	WENONAH	08346-08346	NEWTONVILLE	08809-08809	CLINTON
07981-07999	WHIPPANY	08091-08091	WEST BERLIN	08347-08347	NORMA	08810-08810	DAYTON
08001-08001	ALLOWAY	08092-08092	WEST CREEK	08348-08348	PORT ELIZABETH	08812-08812	DUNELLEN
08002-08003	CHERRY HILL	08093-08093	WESTVILLE	08349-08349	PORT NORRIS	08816-08816	EAST BRUNSWICK
08004-08004	ATCO	08094-08094	WILLIAMSTOWN	08350-08350	RICHLAND	08817-08820	EDISON
08005-08005	BARNEGAT	08095-08095	WINSLOW	08352-08352	ROSENHAYN	08821-08821	FLAGTOWN
08006-08006	BARNEGAT LIGHT	08096-08096	WOODBURY	08353-08353	SHILOH	08822-08822	FLEMINGTON
08007-08007	BARRINGTON	08097-08097	WOODBURY HEIGHTS	08358-08358	CHERRY HILL	08823-08823	FRANKLIN PARK
08008-08008	BEACH HAVEN	08098-08098	WOODSTOWN	08360-08362	VINELAND	08824-08824	KENDALL PARK
08009-08009	BERLIN	08099-08099	BELLMAWR	08370-08370	RIVERSIDE	08825-08825	FRENCHTOWN
08010-08010	BEVERLY	08100-08105	CAMDEN	08400-08401	ATLANTIC CITY	08826-08826	GLEN GARDNER
08011-08011	BIRMINGHAM	08106-08106	AUDUBON	08402-08402	MARGATE CITY	08827-08827	HAMPTON
08012-08012	BLACKWOOD	08107-08107	OAKLYN	08403-08403	LONGPORT	08828-08828	HELMETTA
08014-08014	BRIDGEPORT	08108-08108	COLLINGSWOOD	08404-08405	ATLANTIC CITY	08829-08829	HIGH BRIDGE
08015-08015	BROWNS MILLS	08109-08109	MERCHANTVILLE	08406-08406	VENTNOR CITY	08830-08830	ISELIN
08016-08016	BURLINGTON	08110-08110	PENNSAUKEN	08411-08411	ATLANTIC CITY	08831-08831	JAMESBURG
08018-08018	CEDAR BROOK	08201-08201	ABSECON	08501-08501	ALLENTOWN	08831-08831	MONROE TOWNSHIP
08019-08019	CHATSWORTH	08202-08202	AVALON	08502-08502	BELLE MEAD	08832-08832	KEASBEY
08020-08020	CLARKSBORO	08203-08203	BRIGANTINE	08504-08504	BLAWENBURG	08833-08833	LEBANON
08021-08021	CLEMENTON	08204-08204	CAPE MAY	08505-08505	BORDENTOWN	08834-08834	LITTLE YORK
08022-08022	COLUMBUS	08205-08205	ABSECON	08510-08510	CLARKSBURG	08835-08835	MANVILLE
08023-08023	DEEPWATER	08210-08210	CAPE MAY COURT HOUSE	08511-08511	COOKSTOWN	08836-08836	MARTINSVILLE
08025-08025	EWAN	08212-08212	CAPE MAY POINT	08512-08512	CRANBURY	08837-08837	EDISON
08026-08026	GIBBSBORO	08213-08213	COLOGNE	08514-08514	CREAMRIDGE	08840-08840	METUCHEN
08027-08027	GIBBSTOWN	08214-08214	DENNISVILLE	08514-08514	CREAM RIDGE	08844-08844	HILLSBOROUGH
08028-08028	GLASSBORO	08215-08215	EGG HARBOR CITY	08515-08515	CROSSWICKS	08846-08846	MIDDLESEX
08029-08029	GLENDORA	08217-08217	ELWOOD	08518-08518	FLORENCE	08848-08848	MILFORD
08030-08030	GLOUCESTER CITY	08218-08218	GOSHEN	08520-08520	HIGHTSTOWN	08850-08850	MILLTOWN
08031-08031	BELLMAWR	08219-08219	GREEN CREEK	08525-08525	HOPEWELL	08852-08852	MONMOUTH JUNCTION
08032-08032	GRENLOCH	08220-08220	LEEDS POINT	08526-08526	IMLAYSTOWN	08853-08853	NESHANIC STATION
08033-08033	HADDONFIELD	08221-08222	LINWOOD	08527-08527	JACKSON	08854-08855	PISCATAWAY
08034-08034	CHERRY HILL	08223-08223	MARMORA	08528-08528	KINGSTON	08857-08857	OLD BRIDGE
08035-08035	HADDON HEIGHTS	08224-08224	NEW GRETNA	08530-08530	LAMBERTVILLE	08858-08858	OLDWICK
08036-08036	HAINESPORT	08225-08225	NORTHFIELD	08533-08533	NEW EGYPT	08859-08859	PARLIN
08037-08037	HAMMONTON	08226-08226	OCEAN CITY	08534-08534	PENNINGTON	08861-08862	PERTH AMBOY
08038-08038	HANCOCKS BRIDGE	08227-08227	LINWOOD	08535-08535	PERRINEVILLE	08863-08863	FORDS
08039-08039	HARRISONVILLE	08230-08230	OCEAN VIEW	08536-08536	PLAINSBORO	08865-08865	PHILLIPSBURG
08040-08040	KIRKWOOD VOORHEES	08231-08231	OCEANVILLE	08540-08544	PRINCETON	08867-08867	PITTSTOWN
08041-08041	JOBSTOWN	08232-08233	PLEASANTVILLE	08550-08550	PRINCETON JUNCTION	08868-08868	QUAKERTOWN
08042-08042	JULIUSTOWN	08234-08234	EGG HARBOR TOWNSHIP	08551-08551	RINGOES	08869-08869	RARITAN
08043-08043	VOORHEES	08240-08240	POMONA	08553-08553	ROCKY HILL	08870-08870	READINGTON
08045-08045	LAWNSIDE	08241-08241	PORT REPUBLIC	08554-08554	ROEBLING	08871-08872	SAYREVILLE
08046-08046	WILLINGBORO	08242-08242	RIO GRANDE	08555-08555	ROOSEVELT	08873-08875	SOMERSET
08048-08048	LUMBERTON	08243-08243	SEA ISLE CITY	08556-08556	ROSEMONT	08876-08876	SOMERVILLE
08049-08049	MAGNOLIA	08244-08244	SOMERS POINT	08557-08557	SERGEANTSVILLE	08877-08877	SOUTH RIVER
08050-08050	MANAHAWKIN	08245-08245	SOUTH DENNIS	08558-08558	SKILLMAN	08878-08879	SOUTH AMBOY
08051-08051	MANTUA	08246-08246	SOUTH SEAVILLE	08559-08559	STOCKTON	08880-08880	SOUTH BOUND BROOK
08052-08052	MAPLE SHADE	08247-08247	STONE HARBOR	08560-08560	TITUSVILLE	08882-08882	SOUTH RIVER
08053-08053	MARLTON	08248-08248	STRATHMERE	08561-08561	WINDSOR	08884-08884	SPOTSWOOD
08054-08054	MOUNT LAUREL	08250-08250	TUCKAHOE	08562-08562	WRIGHTSTOWN	08885-08885	STANTON
08055-08055	MEDFORD	08251-08251	VILLAS	08570-08570	CRANBURY	08886-08886	STEWARTSVILLE
08056-08056	MICKLETON	08252-08252	WHITESBORO	08600-08695	TRENTON	08887-08887	THREE BRIDGES
08057-08057	MOORESTOWN	08260-08260	WILDWOOD	08701-08701	LAKEWOOD	08888-08888	WHITEHOUSE
08059-08059	MOUNT EPHRAIM	08270-08270	WOODBINE	08720-08720	ALLENWOOD	08889-08889	WHITEHOUSE STATION
08060-08060	MOUNT HOLLY	08302-08302	BRIDGETON	08721-08721	BAYVILLE	08890-08890	ZAREPHATH
08061-08061	MOUNT ROYAL	08310-08310	BUENA	08722-08722	BEACHWOOD	08896-08896	RARITAN
08062-08062	MULLICA HILL	08311-08311	CEDARVILLE	08723-08724	BRICK	08899-08899	EDISON
08063-08063	NATIONAL PARK	08312-08312	CLAYTON	08730-08730	BRIELLE	08901-08901	NEW BRUNSWICK
08064-08064	NEW LISBON	08313-08313	DEERFIELD STREET	08731-08731	FORKED RIVER	08902-08902	NORTH BRUNSWICK
08065-08065	PALMYRA	08314-08314	DELMONT	08732-08732	ISLAND HEIGHTS	08903-08903	NEW BRUNSWICK
08066-08066	PAULSBORO	08315-08315	DIVIDING CREEK	08733-08733	LAKEHURST	08904-08904	HIGHLAND PARK
08067-08067	PEDRICKTOWN	08316-08316	DORCHESTER	08734-08734	LANOKA HARBOR	08905-08989	NEW BRUNSWICK
08068-08068	PEMBERTON	08317-08317	DOROTHY	08735-08735	LAVALLETTE		
08069-08069	PENNS GROVE	08318-08318	ELMER	08736-08736	MANASQUAN		
08070-08070	PENNSVILLE	08319-08319	ESTELL MANOR	08738-08738	MANTOLOKING		

New Mexico

General Help Numbers:

Governor's Office
State Capitol, Room 400
Santa Fe, NM 87503
www.governor.state.nm.us

505-827-3000
Fax 505-827-3026
8AM-5PM

Attorney General's Office
PO Drawer 1508
Santa Fe, NM 87504-1508
www.ago.state.nm.us

505-827-6000
Fax 505-827-5826
8AM-5PM

State Court Administrator
237 Don Gaspar, Rm 25
Santa Fe, NM 87501
www.nmcourts.com/aoc.htm

505-827-4800
Fax 505-827-4246
8AM-5PM

State Archives
1205 Camino Carlos Rey
Santa Fe, NM 87505
www.nmcpr.state.nm.us/

505-476-7908
Fax 505-476-7909
8AM-5PM

State Specifics:

Capital: Santa Fe
Santa Fe County

Time Zone: MST

Number of Counties: 33

Population: 1,829,146

Web Site: www.state.nm.us

State Agencies

Criminal Records

Department of Public Safety, Records Bureau, PO Box 1628, Santa Fe, NM 87504-1628 (Courier: 4491 Cerrillos Rd, Santa Fe, NM 87504); 505-827-9181, 505-827-3388 (Fax), 8AM-5PM.

www.dps.nm.org

Note: The state sexual offender list is available at www.nmsexoffender.dps.state.nm.us

Indexing & Storage: Records are available from 1935 on. It takes 2 to 4 weeks before new records are available for inquiry. Records are indexed on inhouse computer (93%); historical paper records are added to computer once requested. Records are normally destroyed after 99 years. 33% of all arrests in database have final dispositions recorded, 35% for those arrests within last 5 years.

Searching: Must have a state notarized signed release from person of record authorizing the State of New Mexico to release records to requester. Except for law enforcement officials, specify which records you want. Include the following in your request: date of birth, Social Security Number, full name. Fingerprint search requests are not available except for checks for childern or elderly-related occupations mandated by state statute. The state's records are 100% fingerprint-supported. All records are released, including those without dispositions.

Access by: mail, in person.

Fee & Payment: The fee is $7.00 per individual. Fee payee: Department of Public Safety. Prepayment required. Must use cashiers check or money order. No credit cards accepted.

Mail search: Turnaround time: 1 to 2 weeks. Turnaround time is for "no record found." If records exist, turnaround time may be 3 to 4 weeks. A self addressed stamped envelope is requested.

In person search: If records are found, they may be available in 5 to 7 working days.

Corporation Records
Limited Liability Company Records

New Mexico Public Regulation Commission, Corporations Bureau, PO Box 1269, Santa Fe, NM 87504-1269 (Courier: 1120 Paseo de Peralta, Pera Bldg 4th Fl, Rm 413, Santa Fe, NM 87501); 505-827-4502 (Main Number), 800-947-4722 (In-state Only), 505-827-4510 (Good Standing), 505-827-4513 (Copy Request), 505-827-4387 (Fax), 8AM-12:00: 1PM-5PM.

www.nmprc.state.nm.us/corporation.htm

Note: For Charter Requirement Information call 505-827-4511.

Indexing & Storage: Records are available for all entities. Records are indexed on microfilm.

Searching: Include the following in your request: full name of business. In addition to the articles of incorporation, corporation records include the following information: Annual Reports, Officers, Directors, Prior (merged) names, Inactive, Registered and Reserved names. The following data is not released: financial information.

Access by: mail, phone, fax, in person, online.

Fee & Payment: There is no charge for a computer printout. Copies are $1.00 per page with minimum fee of $10.00 for for-profit companies or domestic LLCs and $5.00 for non-profit companies. Certification fee is $25.00, except for non-profits which is $10.00. Fee payee: Public Regulation Commission. Payment is due in 10 days. Personal checks accepted. No credit cards accepted.

Mail search: Turnaround time: 2 days. A self addressed stamped envelope is requested.

Phone search: Limited information is given over the phone.

Fax search: Information can be requested by fax, but is returned by mail in 3-5 days.

In person search: Call is to schedule viewing time for microfilm.

Online search: There is no charge to view records at the Internet site, www.nmprc.state.nm.us/ftq.htm. Records can be searched by company name or by director name.

Other access: The state makes the database available on electronic format using a 3480 tape cartridge. .

Trademarks/Servicemarks
Trade Names

Secretary of State, Trademarks Division, State Capitol North, Santa Fe, NM 87503; 505-827-3600, 505-827-3611 (Fax), 8AM-5PM.

www.sos.state.nm.us

Note: Effective July 1, 1997, New Mexico no longer registers trade names. However, the agency will do searches for records on file.

Indexing & Storage: Records are available from 1980 to present. It takes 1 to 2 days before new records are available for inquiry. Records are indexed on inhouse computer.

Searching: Include the following in your request: trademark/servicemark name. Include your full name, address and telephone number.

Access by: mail, phone, fax, in person.

Fee & Payment: Prepayment required. Fee payee: Secretary of State. Personal checks accepted.

Mail search: Turnaround time: 2 to 3 days. No self addressed stamped envelope is required. No fee for mail request.

Phone search: They will do a computer search and will give you the information over the phone for no fee.

Fax search: There is no fee. Turnaround time: 24 hours.

In person search: No fee for request. Turnaround time is usually immediate.

Other access: Monthly listings are available at $.10 per trademark/service mark record.

Uniform Commercial Code

UCC Division, Secretary of State, State Capitol North, Santa Fe, NM 87503; 505-827-3610, 505-827-3611 (Fax), 8AM-5PM.

www.sos.state.nm.us/ucc/ucchome.htm

Note: This agency will not conduct in-person searches. You must come in yourself, hire a local search company, or conduct your search at the agency web site.

Indexing & Storage: Records are available from 1965. It takes 24 hours before new records are available for inquiry.

Searching: Please note that all tax liens are filed at the county level. The system does not give information on collateral.

Access by: in person, online.

Fee & Payment: Copies are S1.00 per page plus $3.00 if certification requested. Fee payee: Secretary of State. Prepayment required. Personal checks accepted. No credit cards accepted. No self addressed stamped envelope is required.

In person search: You may use their in-house computer by appointment only. Call 505-827-3614. You may view documents for free.

Online search: The web site permits searches and provides a form to use to order copies of filings. You can also request records via e-mail.

Federal Tax Liens
State Tax Liens

Records not maintained by a state level agency.

Note: Records are filed with the Clerk at the county level.

Sales Tax Registrations

Taxation & Revenue Department, Tax Administrative Services Division, PO Box 630, Santa Fe, NM 87504-0630 (Courier: Montoya Bldg, 1100 S St Francis Drive, Santa Fe, NM 87501); 505-827-0825, 505-827-0614 (Fax), 8AM-5PM.

www.state.nm.us/tax

Indexing & Storage: Records are available from 1988.

Searching: This agency will only confirm that a business is registered and active. They will provide no other information. The business name is required, the permit number and federal ID are optional.

Access by: mail, phone, in person.

Fee & Payment: There is no search fee, copies are $.05 per page

Mail search: Turnaround time: 6 to 12 weeks. A self addressed stamped envelope is requested.

Phone search: Records are available by phone.

In person search: Searching is available in person.

Birth Certificates

Department of Health, Bureau of Vital Records, PO Box 26111, Santa Fe, NM 87502 (Courier: 1105 South St Francis Dr, Santa Fe, NM 87502); 505-827-0121, 505-827-2338 (Information), 505-984-1048 (Fax), 8AM-5:00PM (Counter Service: 9AM-4PM).

www.health.state.nm.us

Note: All requesters must sign and date the request. It is a felony to obtain a record fraudulently.

Indexing & Storage: Records are available from 1920 on. New records are available for inquiry immediately. Records are indexed on microfiche, inhouse computer.

Searching: Records available only to immediate family members or those demonstrating legal tangible interest in the desired record. Sealed records (e.g. adoptions and paternity) are unavailable. Include the following in your request: full name, names of parents, mother's maiden name, date of birth, place of birth, relationship to person of record, reason for information request. Signature of requester and physical & mailing addresses are required.

Access by: mail, phone, fax, in person.

Fee & Payment: The search fee is $10.00 per record. There is an additional $10.00 fee if you order by phone or by fax for use of a credit card. Fee payee: NM Vital Records. Prepayment required. Personal checks accepted. Credit cards accepted: MasterCard, Visa, AmEx, Discover.

Mail search: Turnaround time: 3 weeks. No self addressed stamped envelope is required.

Phone search: Records are available by phone.

Fax search: Same criteria as phone searches.

In person search: Turnaround time is usually less than 1/2 hour.

Expedited service: Expedited service is available for phone searches. Turnaround time: 24 hours. Use of credit card required for additional fee and add fee for delivery service. (Call for fees.)

Death Records

Department of Health, Bureau of Vital Records, PO Box 26111, Santa Fe, NM 87502 (Courier: 1105 South St Francis Dr, Santa Fe, NM 87502); 505-827-0121, 505827-2338 (Information), 505-984-1048 (Fax), 8AM-5PM (Counter Service: 9AM-4PM).

www.health.state.nm.us

Indexing & Storage: Records are available from 1920 to present. New records are available for inquiry immediately. Records are indexed on microfiche, inhouse computer.

Searching: Only immediate family member or a person with tangible interest can receive record. Include the following in your request: full name, date of death, place of death, Social Security

Number, relationship to person of record, reason for information request. Age at death and name of mortuary must also be included for search.

Access by: mail, phone, fax, in person.

Fee & Payment: The fee is $5.00 per record. An additional fee may be charged if required information is not submitted. Use of credit card is an additional $10.00. Fee payee: NM Vital Records. Prepayment required. Credit cards are only used for phone and fax ordering. Personal checks accepted. Credit cards accepted: MasterCard, Visa, AmEx, Discover.

Mail search: Turnaround time: 3 to 4 weeks. No self addressed stamped envelope is required.

Phone search: You must use a credit card.

Fax search: Same criteria as phone searches.

In person search: Turnaround time is usually 1 hour or less.

Expedited service: Expedited service is available for mail, phone and fax searches. Turnaround time: 24 hours. Use of credit card required. Delivery fee is $13.25 minimum.

Marriage Certificates
Divorce Records

Records not maintained by a state level agency.

Note: Marriage and Divorce records are found at county of issue.

Workers' Compensation Records

Access to Records is Restricted

Workers Compensation Administration, PO Box 27198, Albuquerque, NM 87125-7198 (Courier: 2410 Centre Ave, SE, Albuquerque, NM 87106); 505-841-6000, 800-255-7965 (In-State Toll Free), 505-841-6060 (Fax), 8AM-5PM.

www.state.nm.us/wca

Note: The subject must write the agency, provide proof of ID with a driver's license, and request the record, and pay a copy fee of $.25 per page. Most records are confidential but access is permitted for all parties to a case and other cases involving the same worker; positive ID is required.

Driver Records

Motor Vehicle Division, Driver Services Bureau, PO Box 1028, Santa Fe, NM 87504-1028 (Courier: Joseph M. Montoya Bldg, 1100 S St. Francis Dr, 2nd Floor, Santa Fe, NM 87504); 505-827-2234, 505-827-2267 (Fax), 8AM-5PM.

www.state.nm.us/tax/mvd

Note: Copies of tickets may be obtained from the same address. There is no fee.

Indexing & Storage: Records are available for 3 years for moving violations; 25 years DWIs. Accidents are not reported on the record and neither are violations less than 10 mph over the limit in 55 or 65 zones. The driver's address is included on the record. It takes 30 to 40 days before new records are available for inquiry.

Searching: The law lists 9 permissible user groups and permits release of records with written consent. Purchasers may not use the information for direct mail solicitation or resell the reports after

usage. The full name, DOB and either the license number or Social Security Number is required when ordering. The following data is not released: Social Security Numbers, addresses or date of birth.

Access by: mail, in person, online.

Fee & Payment: There is no fee for mail or walk-in requests. Fee payee: Motor Vehicle Division. Prepayment required. Personal checks accepted. No credit cards accepted.

Mail search: Turnaround time: 3 to 5 days. No fee for manual search. A self addressed stamped envelope is requested.

In person search: No fee for manual search. Up to 2 requests can be processed while you wait, the rest must be in writing and left overnight.

Online search: Records are avilable, for authorized users, from the state's designated vendors - Oso Grande (505-345-655) and Samba (888-94-samba). Subscription fees are $2.50 per record for interactive, $1.50 per record for batch, plus a $.25 per minute network fee. The system is open 24 hours a day, batch requesters must wait 24 hours.

Vehicle Ownership & Identification
Vessel Ownership & Registration

Motor Vehicle Division, Vehicle Services Bureau, PO Box 1028, Santa Fe, NM 87504-1028 (Courier: Joseph M. Montoya Bldg, 1100 S St. Francis Dr, 2nd Floor, Santa Fe, NM 87504); 505-827-4636, 505-827-1004, 505-827-0395 (Fax), 8AM-5PM.

www.state.nm.us/tax/mvd

Indexing & Storage: Records are available for a minimum of 3 years on boats and 6 years on vehicles. All motorized boats, sailboats, and jet skis must be both titled and registered if over 10 ft, and only registered if 10 ft or less. It takes 30 days before new records are available for inquiry.

Searching: Authorized requesters are restricted to 9 user groups and must sign a contract that states purpose of request and subsequent use. Requesters may not use ownership and vehicle information to create a resalable database. The following data is not released: addresses, Social Security Numbers or date of birth.

Access by: mail, in person, online.

Fee & Payment: There are no fees for mail or in person requests. A vehicle history search (microfilm) goes back 6 years. Fee payee: Department of Motor Vehicles. Prepayment required. Personal checks accepted. No credit cards accepted.

Mail search: Turnaround time: 3 to 4 weeks. A self addressed stamped envelope is requested.

In person search: Up to ten requests will be processed while you wait.

Online search: Records are available, for authorized users, from the state's designated vendors - Oso Grande (505-345-6555) and Samba (888-94-samba).

Other access: Bulk requests for vehicle or ownership information must be approved by the Director's office. Once a sale is made, further resale is prohibited.

Accident Reports

Department of Public Safety, Records, PO Box 1628, Santa Fe, NM 87504-1628 (Courier: New Mexico State Police Complex, 4491 Cerrillos Rd, Santa Fe, NM 87504); 505-827-9181, 505-827-9189 (Fax), 8AM-5PM.

www.dps.nm.org

Indexing & Storage: Records are available 1 year to present in-house (on computer) and up to 10 years archived (25 years for fatalities). It takes 15 days before new records are available for inquiry.

Searching: Arrest information is not released. Include the following in your request: full name, date of accident, county, location of accident.

Access by: mail, phone, in person, online.

Fee & Payment: The fee is $1.00 per page. There is no fee for a no record found. There is no fee charged for persons directly involved in the accident. Fee payee: Department of Public Safety. Prepayment required. Personal checks accepted. No credit cards accepted.

Mail search: Turnaround time: 2 weeks. A self addressed stamped envelope is requested.

Phone search: No fee for telephone request.

In person search: Turnaround time is immediate if incident one year or less old.

Online search: Reports are available online at https://www.nmaccidentreports.com. The officer's diagram and narrative is included. There is a $1.00 fee. Credit cards are accepted.

Legislation Records

Legislative Council Service, State Capitol Bldg, Room 411, Santa Fe, NM 87501; 505-986-4600, 505-986-4350 (Bill Room During Session Only), 505-986-4610 (Fax), 8AM-5PM.

http://legis.state.nm.us

Note: Signed laws of the current year can be obtained from the Secretary of State's Office at 505-827-3600. Searchers are encouraged to use the web.

Indexing & Storage: Records are available for current back five years, online. The current session meets starting the third Tuesday in January. Sessions are 60 days in odd-numbered years and 30 days in even-numbered years.

Searching: Submit bill number or topic to search. Records on computer.

Access by: mail, phone, in person, online.

Fee & Payment: Depending on the extent of the search, the agency may charge for copies. There is no search fee. Fee payee: New Mexico State Legislature. Personal checks accepted. No credit cards accepted.

Mail search: Turnaround time: variable.

Phone search: Limited searching is available during session.

In person search: You may request bills in person.

Online search: The Internet site is a complete source of information about bills and legislators. There are also links to other NM state agencies and NM statutes.

Other access: Subscription purchase for the complete file of current session is available. However, you must request your subscription by mid-session.

Voter Registration

Access to Records is Restricted

Secretary of State, Bureau of Elections, State Capitol Annex, Ste 300, Santa Fe, NM 87503; 505-827-3620, 505-827-4954 (Fax), 8AM-5PM.

www.sos.state.nm.us/ELECTNET.HTM

Note: Individual look-ups must be done at the county level. This agency will sell its database, but for restricted purposes only (not for commercial purposes).

GED Certificates

Department of Education, GED Testing Program, 300 Don Gaspar, Rm 122, Santa Fe, NM 87501-2786; 505-827-6702, 505-827-6616 (Fax), 8AM-5PM.

http://sde.state.nm.us

Indexing & Storage: Records are available from 1942 to present It takes 45 days before new records are available for inquiry.

Searching: The SSN, DOB, and year of test are needed for a verification. A signed release is needed for a copy of a transcript.

Access by: mail, fax, in person.

Fee & Payment: There are no fees.

Mail search: Turnaround time: 2 weeks. No self addressed stamped envelope is required.

Fax search: Same criteria as mail searching.

In person search: Searching is available in person.

Hunting License Information
Fishing License Information

NM Dept of Game & Fish, PO Box 25112, Santa Fe, NM 87504 (Courier: Villagra Bldg, 408 Galisto St, Santa Fe, NM 87501); 505-827-7911, 800-862-9310, 505-827-7915 (Fax), 8AM-12PM; 1PM-5PM.

www.gmfsh.state.nm.us

Indexing & Storage: Records are available for last season only. Records are indexed on hard copy.

Searching: Include the following in your request: name.

Access by: in person, mail.

Fee & Payment: Fee is $60 per hour plus $.25 per copy. Fee payee: NM Dept of Fish & Game. Records are available by mail.

Mail search: Turnaround time: 1 to 2 weeks. No self addressed stamped envelope is required.

In person search: You may do the search yourself for no fee.

New Mexico State Licensing Agencies

Licenses Searchable Online

Acupuncturist #26 .... www.rld.state.nm.us/b&c/acupuncture/licensee_search.asp
Alcohol Server #14 .... www.rld.state.nm.us/agd/licensee_search_servers.asp
Architect #17 .... www.nmbea.org/People/Aroster.htm
Art Therapist #57 .... www.rld.state.nm.us/b&c/counseling/licensee_search.asp
Athletic Trainer #1 .... www.rld.state.nm.us/b&c/athtrn/licensee_search.asp
Attorney #20 .... http:www.nmbar.org/cgi-bin/QQQ/search.pl
Audiologist #11 .... www.rld.state.nm.us/b&c/speech/licensee_search.asp
Bank #51 .... www.rld.state.nm.us/fid/licensee_search_index.htm
Barber #2 .... www.rld.state.nm.us/b&c/barbcosmo/licensee_search.asp
Barber Shop/School #2 .... www.rld.state.nm.us/b&c/barbcosmo/licensee_search.asp
Boiler Operator Journeyman #33 .... www.contractorsnm.com/searchlic.html
Chiropractor #3 .... www.rld.state.nm.us/b&c/chiro/licensee_search.asp
Clinical Nurse Specialist #19 .... www.state.nm.us/nursing/lookup.html
Collection Agency #51 .... www.rld.state.nm.us/fid/licensee_search_index.htm
Collection Agency Manager #51 .... www.rld.state.nm.us/fid/licensee_search_index.htm
Consumer Credit Grantor #51 .... www.rld.state.nm.us/fid/licensee_search_index.htm
Consumer Loan Company #51 .... www.rld.state.nm.us/fid/licensee_search_index.htm
Contractor #13 .... www.contractorsnm.com/searchlic.html
Cosmetologist #2 .... www.rld.state.nm.us/b&c/barbcosmo/licensee_search.asp
Cosmetology Shop/School #2 .... www.rld.state.nm.us/b&c/barbcosmo/licensee_search.asp
Credit Union #51 .... www.rld.state.nm.us/fid/licensee_search_index.htm
Crematory #12 .... www.rld.state.nm.us/b&c/thanato/licensee_search_facilities.asp
Dental Assistant #4 .... www.rld.state.nm.us/b&c/dental/
Dental Hygienist #4 .... www.rld.state.nm.us/b&c/dental/
Dentist #4 .... www.rld.state.nm.us/b&c/dental/
Direct Disposer (Funerary) #12 .... www.rld.state.nm.us/b&c/thanato/licensee_search_index.asp
Doctor of Oriental Medicine #26 .... www.rld.state.nm.us/b&c/acupuncture/licensee_search.asp
Electrologist #2 .... www.rld.state.nm.us/b&c/barbcosmo/licensee_search.asp
Electrophysician #2 .... www.rld.state.nm.us/b&c/barbcosmo/licensee_search.asp
Endowed/Perpetual Care Cemetery #51 .... www.rld.state.nm.us/fid/licensee_search_endowed_care.asp
Engineer #44 .... www.state.nm.us/pepsboard/roster.htm
Escrow Company #51 .... www.rld.state.nm.us/fid/licensee_search_index.htm
Esthetician #2 .... www.rld.state.nm.us/b&c/barbcosmo/licensee_search.asp
Funeral Director/Practitioner #12 .... www.rld.state.nm.us/b&c/thanato/licensee_search_fsp.asp
Funeral Home #12 .... www.rld.state.nm.us/b&c/thanato/licensee_search_facilities.asp
Funeral Service Intern #12 .... www.rld.state.nm.us/b&c/thanato/licensee_search_index.asp
Hearing Aid Specialist #11 .... www.rld.state.nm.us/b&c/speech/licensee_search.asp
Hemodialysis Technician #19 .... www.state.nm.us/nursing/lookup.html
Journeyman #13 .... www.contractorsnm.com/searchlic.html
Landscape Architect #18 .... www.rld.state.nm.us/b&c/landscape/licensee_search.asp
Lobbyist #32 .... http://web.state.nm.us/LOBBY/LOB.htm
LPG-Liquefied Petroleum Gas Licensing #13 ...... www.contractorsnm.com/searchlic.html
Manicurist #2 .... www.rld.state.nm.us/b&c/barbcosmo/licensee_search.asp
Marriage & Family Therapist #57 .... www.rld.state.nm.us/b&c/counseling/licensee_search.asp
Massage Instructor/Practitioner/School #5 .... www.rld.state.nm.us/b&c/massage/licensee_search.asp
Massage Therapist #5 .... www.rld.state.nm.us/b&c/massage/licensee_search.asp
Medical Doctor #36 .... www.docboard.org/nm/
Medication Aide #19 .... www.state.nm.us/nursing/lookup.html
Mental Health Counselor #57 .... www.rld.state.nm.us/b&c/counseling/licensee_search.asp
Money Order Agent/Exempt Agent #51 .... www.rld.state.nm.us/fid/licensee_search_index.htm
Money Order Company #51 .... www.rld.state.nm.us/fid/licensee_search_index.htm
Mortgage Company/Loan Broker/Branch #51 ...... www.rld.state.nm.us/fid/licensee_search_index.htm
Motor Vehicle Sales Finance Company #51 .... www.rld.state.nm.us/fid/licensee_search_index.htm
Nurse #19 .... www.state.nm.us/nursing/lookup.html
Nurse Anesthetist #19 .... www.state.nm.us/nursing/lookup.html
Nurse-LPN #19 .... www.state.nm.us/nursing/lookup.html
Nurse-RN #19 .... www.state.nm.us/nursing/lookup.html
Nursing Home Administrator #6 .... www.rld.state.nm.us/b&c/nhab/licensee_search.asp
Occupational Therapist #27 .... www.rld.state.nm.us/b&c/otb/licensee_search.asp
Occupational Therapist Assistant #27 .... www.rld.state.nm.us/b&c/otb/licensee_search.asp
Optometrist #40 .... www.rld.state.nm.us/b&c/optometry/licensee_search.asp
Osteopathic Physician #7 .... www.rld.state.nm.us/b&c/osteo/licensee_search.asp

Physical Therapist #28	www.rld.state.nm.us/b&c/ptb/licensee_search.asp
Physical Therapist Assistant #28	www.rld.state.nm.us/b&c/ptb/licensee_search.asp
Physician Assistant #36	www.docboard.org/nm/
Podiatrist #42	www.rld.state.nm.us/b&c/podiatry/licensee_search.asp
Psychologist #37	www.rld.state.nm.us/b&c/rcb/licensee_search.asp
Public Accountant-CPA #35	www.rld.state.nm.us/b&c/accountancy/licensee_search.asp
Real Estate Agent/Salesperson #46	www.rld.state.nm.us/b&c/rec/licensee_search.asp
Real Estate Appraiser #49	www.rld.state.nm.us/b&c/reappraisers/licensee_search.asp
Real Estate Broker #46	www.rld.state.nm.us/b&c/rec/licensee_search.asp
Respiratory Care Therapist #56	www.rld.state.nm.us/b&c/rcb/licensee_search.asp
Savings & Loan #51	www.rld.state.nm.us/fid/licensee_search_index.htm
Small Loan Company #51	www.rld.state.nm.us/fid/licensee_search_index.htm
Speech-Language Pathologist #11	www.rld.state.nm.us/b&c/speech/licensee_search.asp
Substance Abuse Counselor/Intern #57	www.rld.state.nm.us/b&c/counseling/licensee_search.asp
Surveyor, Land #44	www.state.nm.us/pepsboard/roster.htm
Trust Company #51	www.rld.state.nm.us/fid/licensee_search_index.htm

Licensing Quick Finder

Acupuncturist #26	505-476-7081
Alcohol Server #14	505-827-7066
Animal Pregnancy Diagnosis #55	505-841-9112
Announcer, Athletic Event (Ring) #39	505-827-7172
Architect #17	505-827-6375
Art Therapist #57	505-476-7102
Artificial Inseminator #55	505-841-9112
Athletic Promoter/Matchmaker #39	505-827-7172
Athletic Trainer #1	505-476-7098
Attorney #20	505-271-9706
Audiologist #11	505-476-7098
Bank #51	505-827-7100
Barber #2	505-476-7110
Barber Shop/School #2	505-476-7110
Bingo/Raffles, Non-profit #14	505-827-7066
Boiler Operator Journeyman #33	505-452-8311
Booking Agent #39	505-827-7172
Boxer #39	505-827-7172
Boxer Manager #39	505-827-7172
Boxing Judge/Timekeeper #39	505-827-7172
Chiropractor #3	505-827-7120
Clinical Nurse Specialist #19	505-841-8340
Collection Agency #51	505-827-7100
Collection Agency Manager #51	505-827-7100
Consumer Credit Grantor #51	505-827-7100
Consumer Loan Company #51	505-827-7100
Contractor #13	505-827-7030
Cosmetologist #2	505-476-7110
Cosmetology Shop/School #2	505-476-7110
Credit Union #51	505-827-7100
Crematory #12	505-476-7090
Dental Assistant #4	505-476-7125
Dental Hygienist #4	505-476-7125
Dentist #4	505-476-7125
Dietitian/Nutritionist #8	505-476-7053
Direct Disposer (Funerary) #12	505-476-7090
Electrologist #2	505-827-7550
Electrophysician #2	505-476-7110
Emergency Medical Technician #22	505-476-7000
Endowed/Perpetual Care Cemetery #51	505-827-7100
Engineer #44	505-827-7561
Escrow Company #51	505-827-7100
Esthetician #2	505-476-7110
Fireworks Distributor Class C or B #54	505-827-3761
Fireworks Manufacturer 1.4G #54	505-827-3761
Fireworks Vendor (Retail, Wholesale) #54	505-827-3761
Funeral Director/Practitioner #12	505-476-7090

Funeral Home #12	505-476-7090
Funeral Service Intern #12	505-476-7090
Gambling, Non-Profit #14	505-827-7066
Hearing Aid Specialist #11	505-476-7098
Hemodialysis Technician #19	505-841-8340
Insurance Agent #23	505-827-4349
Interior Designer #25	505-476-7078
Investment Advisor/Representative #32	505-827-7140
Journeyman #13	505-827-7030
Landscape Architect #18	505-476-7078
Liquor Distributor #14	505-827-7066
Lobbyist #32	505-827-7140
LPG-Liquefied Petroleum Gas Licensing #13	505-827-7030
Manicurist #2	505-476-7110
Manufactured Housing Dealer/Broker #52	505-827-7070
Manufactured Housing Installer/Repairman #52	505-827-7070
Manufactured Housing Manufacturer #52	505-827-7070
Manufactured Housing Salesperson #52	505-827-7070
Marriage & Family Therapist #57	505-476-7102
Massage Instructor/Practitioner/School #5	505-476-7090
Massage Therapist #5	505-476-7090
Medical Doctor #36	505-827-6784
Medical Researcher #41	505-841-9102
Medical Wholesale Company #41	505-841-9102
Medication Aide #19	505-841-8340
Mental Health Counselor #57	505-476-7102
Midwife #34	505-476-8908
Midwife (CNM) #34	505-476-8908
Money Order Agent/Exempt Agent #51	505-827-7100
Money Order Company #51	505-827-7100
Mortgage Company/Loan Broker/Branch #51	505-827-7100
Motor Vehicle Sales Finance Company #51	505-827-7100
Notary Public #53	505-827-3605
Nuclear Medicine Technologist #38	505-827-2855
Nurse #19	505-841-8340
Nurse Anesthetist #19	505-841-8340
Nurse-LPN #19	505-841-8340
Nurse-RN #19	505-841-8340
Nursing Home Administrator #6	505-827-7121
Occupational Therapist #27	505-476-7085

Occupational Therapist Assistant #27	505-476-7085
Optometrist #40	505-827-7121
Osteopathic Physician #7	505-476-7120
Osteopathic Physician Assistant #7	505-476-7120
Patrol Operator, Private #43	505-476-7080
Pest Management Consultant #21	505-646-2133
Pesticide Applicator/Operator #21	505-646-2133
Pesticide Dealer #21	505-646-2133
Pharmacist #41	505-841-9102
Pharmacy, Non-Residential #41	505-841-9102
Physical Therapist #28	505-476-7085
Physical Therapist Assistant #28	505-476-7085
Physician #41	505-841-9102
Physician Assistant #36	505-827-6784
Podiatrist #42	505-827-7120
Polygraph Examiner #43	505-476-7080
Private Investigator #9	505-827-7080
Psychologist #37	505-476-7077
Psychologist Associate #37	505-476-7077
Public Accountant-CPA #35	505-841-9108
Racing #41	505-841-6400
Radiation Therapy Technologist #38	505-827-2855
Radiologic Technologist #38	505-827-2855
Real Estate Agent/Salesperson #46	505-841-9120
Real Estate Appraiser #49	505-476-7096
Real Estate Broker #46	505-841-9120
Referee #39	505-827-7172
Respiratory Care Therapist #56	505-476-7121
Savings & Loan #51	505-827-7100
School Administrator #24	505-827-6587
School Counselor #24	505-827-6587
Securities Broker/Dealer #32	505-827-7140
Securities Division Agent #32	505-827-7140
Securities Sales Representative #32	505-827-7140
Security Guard #43	505-476-7080
Shorthand Reporter #16	505-841-6740
Small Loan Company #51	505-827-7100
Social Worker (LBSW) (LI) (LM) #10	505-476-7100
Social Worker, Provisional #10	505-476-7100
Speech-Language Pathologist #11	505-476-7098
Substance Abuse Counselor/Intern #57	505-476-7102
Surveyor, Land #44	505-827-7561
Teacher #24	505-827-6587
Trust Company #51	505-827-7100
Veterinarian/Veterinary Technician #55	505-841-9112
Veterinary Facility #55	505-841-9112
Waste Water System Operator #38	505-827-2836
Wrestler #39	505-827-7172

Licensing Agency Information

#1 Regulation & Licensing Dept., Athletic Trainers Board, POB 2055 (2055 S Pacheco St #300), Santa Fe, NM 87505; 505-476-7098. www.rld.state.nm.us/b&c/athtrn/index.htm. Agency email: AthleticTrainerBoard@state.nm.us. Search database at www.rld.state.nm.us/b&c/ athtrn/licensee_search.asp

#2 Regulation & Licensing Dept., Board of Barbers & Cosmetologists, 2055 S Pacheco St #400, Santa Fe, NM 87504; 505-476-7110, Fax: 505-476-7118. www.rld.state.nm.us/b&c/barber_and_cosmetologi st_board.htm Search database at www.rld.state.nm.us/b&c/barb cosmo/licensee_search.asp

#3 Regulation & Licensing Dept., Board of Chiropractic Examiners, PO Box 25101 (2055 S Pacheco St #400), Santa Fe, NM 87504; 505-476-7120, Fax: 505-476-7095. www.rld.state.nm.us/b&c/chiro/index.htm. Agency email: ChiroBoard@state.nm.us. Search database at www.rld.state.nm.us/b&c/ chiro/licensee_search.asp

#4 Regulation & Licensing Dept., Board of Dental Health Care, 2055 S Pacheco St #400, Santa Fe, NM 87504; 505-476-7125, Fax: 505-476-7095. www.rld.state.nm.us/b&c/dental/index.htm. Agency email: Cynthia.Salazar@state.nm.us. Search database at www.rld.state.nm.us/b&c/dental

#5 Regulation & Licensing Dept., Massage Therapy Board, 2055 S Pacheco St #400, Santa Fe, NM 87504; 505-476-7090, Fax: 505-476-7095. www.rld.state.nm.us/b&c/massage/index.htm. Agency email: MassageBoard@state.nm.us. Search database at www.rld.state.nm.us/b&c/ massage/licensee_search.asp

#6 Regulation & Licensing Dept., Nursing Home Administrators Board, 2055 S Pacheco St #400, Santa Fe, NM 87504; 505-476-7121, Fax: 505-827-7095. www.rld.state.nm.us/b&c/nhab/index.htm. Agency email: NursingHomeAdminBd@state.nm.us. Search database at www.rld.state.nm.us/b&c/ nhab/licensee_search.asp

#7 Regulation & Licensing Dept., Board of Osteopathic Medical Examiners, 2055 S Pacheco St #400 (PO Box 25101), Santa Fe, NM 87504; 505-476-7120, Fax: 505-476-7095. www.rld.state.nm.us/b&c/osteo/index.htm. Agency email: OsteoBoard@state.nm.us. Search database at www.rld.state.nm.us/b&c/ osteo/licensee_search.asp

#8 Regulation & Licensing Dept., Nutrition & Dietetics Practice Board, 2055 S Pacheco #400, Santa Fe, NM 87504; 505-476-7053, Fax: 505-476-7094. Agency email: NutritionDieteticsBd@state.nm.us.

#9 Regulation & Licensing Dept., Private Investigators Board, 2055 S Pacheco St #400, Santa Fe, NM 87501; 505-476-7080. www.rld.state.nm.us/b&c/private_investigators_bo ard.htm

#10 Regulation & Licensing Dept., Social Work Examiners Board, 2055 S Pacheco St #300, Santa Fe, NM 87504; 505-476-7100, Fax: 505-827-7548. www.rld.state.nm.us/b&c/social_work_examiners _board.htm Agency email: SocialWorkBoard@state.nm.us.

#11 Regulation & Licensing Dept., Speech, Language, Audiology, & Hearing Aid Board, 2055 S Pacheco St #300, Santa Fe, NM 87504; 505-476-7100, Fax: 505-476-7094. www.rld.state.nm.us/b&c/speech/index.htm. Agency email: Speech/Hearing@state.nm.us. Search database at www.rld.state.nm.us/b&c/ speech/licensee_search.asp

#12 Regulation & Licensing Dept., Thanatopractice Board, 2055 S Pacheco St #400, Santa Fe, NM 87504; 505-476-7090, Fax: 505-476-7095. www.rld.state.nm.us/b&c/thanato Agency email: FuneralBoard@state.nm.us. Search database at www.rld.state.nm.us/b&c/ thanato/licensee_search_index.asp

#13 Regulation & Licensing Dept., Construction Industries Division, 725 St. Michaels Dr, Sante Fe, NM 87505; 505-827-7030, Fax: 505-765-5670. http://rld.state.nm.us/cid Agency email: rldcide@state.nm.us. Search database at www.contractorsnm.com/searchlic.html

#14 Regulation & Licensing Dept., Alcohol & Gaming Division, 725 St. Michaels Dr, Santa Fe, NM 87505-7605; 505-827-7066, Fax: 505-827-7168. www.rld.state.nm.us/agd/index.htm Agency email: agd@state.nm.us.

#16 Board Governing Recording of Judicial Proceedings, PO Box 25883, Albuquerque, NM 87125; 505-797-6000, Fax: 505-843-8765.

#17 Board of Examiners for Architects, PO Box 509, Santa Fe, NM 87504; 505-827-6375, Fax: 505-827-6373. www.nmbea.org Search database at www.nmbea.org/People/ Aroster.htm

#18 Board of Landscape Architects, 2055 S Pacheco St #400, Santa Fe, NM 87504; 505-476-7078, Fax: 505-476-7087. www.rld.state.nm.us/b&c/landscape/index.htm. Agency email: LandscapeArchitects@state.nm.us. Search database at www.rld.state.nm.us/b&c/ landscape/licensee_search.asp

#19 Board of Nursing, 4206-A Lousiana Blvd NE, Albuquerque, NM 87109; 505-841-8340, Fax: 505-841-8347. www.state.nm.us/nursing Search database at www.state.nm.us/nursing/lookup.html

#20 Board of Bar Examiners, 9420 Indian School NE, Albuquerque, NM 87112; 505-271-9706, Fax: 505-271-9768. www.nmbar.org Search database at http:www.nmbar.org/cgi-bin/QQQ/search.pl

#21 Department of Agriculture, Pesticide Management Bureau, MSC 3AQ, PO Box 30005, Las Cruces, NM 88003-8005; 505-646-2133, Fax: 505-646-5977. http://nmdaweb.nmsu.edu/AES/PEST/tconlic.htm. Agency email: webmastr@nmsu.edu.

#22 Department of Health, Injury Prevention & EMS Bureau, PO Box 26110 (1190 S St. Francis Dr, Santa Fe, NM 87502; 505-476-7000, Fax: 505-476-7010. www.health.state.nm.us/website.nsf/ frames?ReadForm

#23 Department of Insurance, Insurance Licensing Division, PO Drawer 1269 (Old Santa Fe Trail Bldg, 4th Fl), Santa Fe, NM 87501; 505-827-4349, Fax: 505-827-4734. www.nmprc.state.nu.us

#24 Education Department, Professional Licensure, 300 Don Gaspar, Education Bldg, Santa Fe, NM 87501-2786; 505-827-6587, Fax: 505-827-6696. www.sde.state.nm.us

#25 Regulation & Licensing Dept., Board of Interior Design, 2055 S Pacheco St #400, Santa Fe, NM 87504; 505-476-7078, Fax: 505-827-7087. www.rld.state.nm.us/b&c/interior_design_board.ht m. Agency email: InteriorDesignBd@state.nm.us.

#26 Regulation & Licensing Dept., Acupuncture & Oriental Medicine Board, 2055 S Pacheco St #400, Santa Fe, NM 87504; 505-476-7081, Fax: 505-476-7095. www.rld.state.nm.us/b&c/acupuncture/index.htm. Agency email: AccOrMedBoard@state.nm.us. Search database at www.rld.state.nm.us/b&c/acupuncture/licensee_se arch.asp

#27 Regulation & Licensing Dept., Occupational Therapy Board, 2055 S Pacheco St #400, Santa Fe, NM 87504; 505-476-7085, Fax: 505-476-7086. www.rld.state.nm.us/b&c/otb/index.htm. Agency email: OccupationalTherapy@state.nm.us. Search database at www.rld.state.nm.us/b&c/otb/ licensee_search.asp

#28 Regulation & Licensing Dept., Physical Therapy Board, 2055 S Pacheco St #400, Santa Fe, NM 87505; 505-476-7085, Fax: 505-476-7095. www.rld.state.nm.us/b&c/ptb/index.htm. Agency email: PhysicalThearpy@state.nm.us. Search database at www.rld.state.nm.us/b&c/ ptb/licensee_search.asp

#32 Securities Division, Regulation and Licensing Dept., 725 St Michaels Dr., Santa Fe, NM 87505; 505-827-7140, Fax: 505-984-0617. www.rld.state.nm.us/sec/index.htm Agency email: rldsd@state.nm.us.

#33 Boiler Operator Journeyman Licensing Board, c/o Contractor Licensing Services, 3211 Coors Blvd SW #D4, Albuquerque, NM 87121; 505-452-8311, Fax: 505-452-8310. www.contractorsnm.com Search database at www.contractorsnm.com/ searchlic.html

#34 Maternal Health Program, Family Health Bureau, PO Box 26110, Santa Fe, NM 87502; 505-476-8908.

#35 Regulation & Licensing Dept., Board of Accountancy, 1650 University Blvd, #400A, Albuquerque, NM 87102; 505-841-9108, Fax: 505-841-9101.
www.rld.state.nm.us/b&c/accountancy. Agency email: publicaccountancyboard@state.nm.us.
Search database at www.rld.state.nm.us/b&c/accountancy/licensee_search.asp

#36 Board of Medical Examiners, 491 Old Sante Fe Trail, Lamy Bldg, 2nd Fl, Santa Fe, NM 87501; 505-827-5022, Fax: 505-827-7377.
www.state.nm.us/nmbme/
Search database at www.docboard.org/nm

#37 Regulation & Licensing Dept., Board of Psychologist Examiners, 2055 S Pacheco St #400, Santa Fe, NM 87504; 505-476-7077, Fax: 505-827-7017.
www.rld.state.nm.us/b&c/psychology. Agency email: psychologistexaminers@state.nm.us.
Search database at www.rld.state.nm.us/b&c/rcb/licensee_search.asp

#38 Environment Department, Licensing & Registration Section, 1190 Saint Francis Dr, Santa Fe, NM 87502; 505-827-2855.
www.nmenv.state.nm.us.

#39 Regulation & Licensing Dept., Athletic Commission, PO Box 25101, Santa Fe, NM 87504; 505-827-7124, Fax: 505-827-7095.
www.state.nm.us/cgi-bin/intcrccpt.pl?/rld/b&c/athletic%20commission.htm
Agency email: henrietta.leos@state.nm.us.

#40 Regulation & Licensing Dept., Board of Examiners in Optometry, 2055 S Pacheco St #400, Santa Fe, NM 87504; 505-476-7121, Fax: 505-476-7095.
www.rld.state.nm.us/b&c/optometry/index.htm. Agency email: optometrybd@state.nm.us.
Search database at www.rld.state.nm.us/b&c/optometry/licensee_search.asp

#41 Regulation & Licensing Dept., Pharmacy Board, 1650 University Blvd, Ste. 400B, Albuquerque, NM 87102; 505-841-9102, Fax: 505-841-9113.
www.state.nm.us/pharmacy. Agency email: NMBOP@nm-us.campuscwix.net.

#42 Regulation & Licensing Dept., Podiatry Board, 2055 S Pacheco St #300, Santa Fe, NM 87504; 505-476-7096, Fax: 505-827-7095.
www.rld.state.nm.us/b&c/podiatry_board.htm. Agency email: PodiatryBoard@state.nm.us.
Search database at www.rld.state.nm.us/b&c/podiatry/licensee_search.asp

#43 Regulation & Licensing Dept., Private Investigators & Polygraph Board, 2055 S Pacheco St #400, Santa Fe, NM 87504; 505-476-7080, Fax: 505-476-7095.
www.rld.state.nm.us/b&c/pipolygraph/index.htm. Agency email: PIPolygraphBd@state.nm.us.

#44 Professional Engineers & Surveyors Board, 1010 Marquez Pl, Santa Fe, NM 87501; 505-827-7561, Fax: 505-827-7566.
www.state.nm.us/pepsboard
Search database at www.state.nm.us/pepsboard/roster.htm

#45 Racing Commission, 300 San Mateo Blvd NE, #110, Albuquerque, NM 87198; 505-841-6400, Fax: 505-841-6400.
www.nmprc.state.nm.us
Agency email: nmrc@state.nm.us.

#46 Regulation & Licensing Dept., Real Estate Commission, 1650 University Blvd, #490, Albuquerque, NM 87102; 505-841-9120, Fax: 505-276-0725.
www.state.nm.us/nmrec
Agency email: NMREC@state.nm.us.
Search database at www.rld.state.nm.us/b&c/rec/licensee_search.asp

#49 Regulation & Licensing Dept., Real Estate Appraisers Board, 2055 S Pacheco St #300, Santa Fe, NM 87504; 505-476-7096, Fax: 505-827-7096.
www.rld.state.nm.us/b&c/real_estate_appraisers_board.htm
Agency email: AppraiserBoard@state.nm.us.

Search database at www.rld.state.nm.us/b&c/reappraisers/licensee_search.asp

#51 Regulation & Licensing Dept., Financial Institutions Division, 725 St. Michaels Drive, Santa Fe, NM 87501; 505-827-7100, Fax: 505-827-7107.
www.rld.state.nm.us/fid/index.htm. Agency email: rldfid@state.nm.us.
Search database at www.rld.state.nm.us/fid/licensee_search_index.htm

#52 Regulation & Licensing Dept., Manufactured Housing Division, 725 St Michaels Dr, Santa Fe, NM 87501; 505-827-7070, Fax: 505-827-7074.
www.rld.state.nm.us/mhd/index.htm
Agency email: MHD@state.nm.us.

#53 Secretary of State, Notary Public, State Capitol North, Santa Fe, NM 87503; 505-827-3600, Fax: 505-827-3611.
www.sos.state.nm.us

#54 State Fire Marshal, Public Regulation Commission, PO Drawer 1269, Santa Fe, NM 87504; 505-827-3761, Fax: 505-827-3778.

#55 Veterinary Medicine Board, 1650 University Blvd NE, #400C, Albuquerque, NM 87102; 505-841-9112, Fax: 505-841-9113.
www.state.nm.us/vetbd

#56 Regulation & Licensing Dept., Repiratory Care Advisory Board, 2055 S Pacheco St #400, Santa Fe, NM 87504; 505-476-7121, Fax: 505-476-7095.
www.rld.state.nm.us/b&c/rcb/index.htm. Agency email: respiratorycarebd@state.mt.us.
Search database at www.rld.state.nm.us/b&c/rcb/licensee_search.asp

#57 Regulation & Licensing Dept., Counseling & Therapy Practice Board, 2055 S Pacheco St #300, Sante Fe, NM 87504; 505-476-7102, Fax: 505-476-7148.
www.rld.state.nm.us/b&c/counseling/index.htm. Agency email: CounselingBoard@state.nm.us.
Search database at www.rld.state.nm.us/b&c/counseling/licensee_search.asp

New Mexico Federal Courts

The following list indicates the district and division name for each county in the state.

County/Court Cross Reference

Bernalillo	Albuquerque	McKinley	Albuquerque
Catron	Albuquerque	Mora	Albuquerque
Chaves	Albuquerque	Otero	Albuquerque
Cibola	Albuquerque	Quay	Albuquerque
Colfax	Albuquerque	Rio Arriba	Albuquerque
Curry	Albuquerque	Roosevelt	Albuquerque
De Baca	Albuquerque	San Juan	Albuquerque
Dona Ana	Albuquerque	San Miguel	Albuquerque
Eddy	Albuquerque	Sandoval	Albuquerque
Grant	Albuquerque	Santa Fe	Albuquerque
Guadalupe	Albuquerque	Sierra	Albuquerque
Harding	Albuquerque	Socorro	Albuquerque
Hidalgo	Albuquerque	Taos	Albuquerque
Lea	Albuquerque	Torrance	Albuquerque
Lincoln	Albuquerque	Union	Albuquerque
Los Alamos	Albuquerque	Valencia	Albuquerque
Luna	Albuquerque		

US District Court

District of New Mexico

Albuquerque Division 333 Lomas Blvd NW #270, Albuquerque, NM 87102-2274 (Courier Address: Use mail address for courier delivery), 505-348-2000, Fax: 505-348-2028.

www.nmcourt.fed.us/dcdocs

Counties: All counties in New Mexico. Cases may be assigned to any of its three divisions.

Indexing & Storage: Cases are indexed by defendant, plaintiff, and case number. New cases are available in the index 2 days after filing date. Inquirer's phone number and the years to search are required to search for a record. Records from 1990 to the present can be searched by the plaintiff's name. Prior records can be searched by defendant or case number. Open records are located at this court.

Fee & Payment Notes: Payment may be made by money order, cashier check, personal check. Copies are made through a copy service only. They charge $.15 per page. Payee: Clerk, US District Court. Copy fee: $.35 per page.

Phone Search: Only docket information available by phone.

Mail Search: A stamped self addressed envelope is not required.

In Person Search: In person searching available.

PACER: Sign-up number is. Access fee is. Case records are available back to 1990. Records are purged every six months. New records are available online after 2 weeks.

Electronic Filing: This utilizes ACE (Advanced Court Engin.), and not the US Courts standard CM/ECF system. Information is available online at www.nmcourt.fed.us/dcdocs (Click on Electronic Filing)

Other Online Access: Email alerts for cases or names you select are available; must use your ACE user name and password to set up.

US Bankruptcy Court

District of New Mexico

Albuquerque Division PO Box 546, Albuquerque, NM 87103-0546 (Courier Address: 3rd Floor, Room 316, 421 Gold Ave SW, Albuquerque, NM 87102), 505-348-2500, Fax: 505-348-2473.

www.nmcourt.fed.us/bkdocs

Counties: All counties in New Mexico.

Indexing & Storage: Cases are indexed by debtor as well as by case number. New cases are available in the index 24 hours after filing date. Card indexes are maintained on cases filed prior to May 26, 1987. Cases filed after that date are indexed in the computer. Open records are located at this court.

Fee & Payment Notes: Payment may be made by money order, cashier check, personal check, Visa or Mastercard. Debtor's checks are not accepted. Payee: Clerk, US Bankruptcy Court.

Phone Search: Index, docket and claim information will be released over the phone. An automated voice case information service (VCIS) is available. Call VCIS at 888-435-7822 or 505-248-6536.

Fax Search: The fee is $15.00 and must be prepaid.

Mail Search: Fee will be charged only when a case file search is required. Always enclose a stamped self addressed envelope.

In Person Search: In person searching available.

PACER: Toll-free dial-up access: 888-821-8813. Local dial-up access: 505-348-2496. Case records are available back to July 1, 1991. New civil records are available online after 1 day.

Electronic Filing: (Currently in the process of implementing CM/ECF.)

Standards for Federal Courts: The search fee is $20.00 per item (one party name or case number). Certification fee is $7.00 per document. Copy fee is $.50 per page. All fees standard unless noted in profile. Mail Search: always enclose a stamped self addressed envelope unless otherwise noted. Before releasing records, all courts require prepayment unless noted in profile.

Open records are located at the court unless otherwise noted. District courts index by defendant and plaintiff as well as by case number. Bankruptcy courts usually index by debtor and case number. While most courts now have their indexes on computer, many still maintain index card files as well.

The universal PACER sign-up number is 800-676-6856. Find PACER and the Party/Case Index on the Web at http://pacer.psc.uscourts.gov. PACER dial-up access is $.60 per minute. Also, courts offering internet access via RACER, PACER, Web-PACER or the new CM-ECF charge $.07 per page fee unless noted as free.

New Mexico County Courts

Court	Jurisdiction	No. of Courts	How Organized
District Courts*	General	30	13 Districts
Magistrate Courts*	Limited	48	32 Magistrate Districts
Metropolitan Court of Bernalillo County*	Municipal	1	
Municipal Courts	Municipal	82	
Probate Courts	Probate	30	33 Counties

* Profiled in this Sourcebook.

Court	CIVIL								
	Tort	Contract	Real Estate	Min. Claim	Max. Claim	Small Claims	Estate	Eviction	Domestic Relations
District Courts*	X	X	X	$0	No Max		X		X
Magistrate Courts*	X	X	X	$0	$7500	$5000		X	
Metropolitan Court of Bernalillo County*	X	X	X	$0	$5000	$5000			
Municipal Courts									
Probate Courts*							X		

Court	CRIMINAL				
	Felony	Misdemeanor	DWI/DUI	Preliminary Hearing	Juvenile
District Courts*	X				X
Magistrate Courts*		X	X	X	
Metropolitan Court of Bernalillo County*		X	X	X	
Municipal Courts					
Probate Courts*					

ADMINISTRATION

Administrative Office of the Courts, Supreme Court Building Room 25, Santa Fe, NM, 87503; 505-827-4800, Fax: 505-827-7549. www.nmcourts.com/aoc.htm

COURT STRUCTURE

The 30 District Courts in 13 districts are the courts of general jurisdiction. Starting July 1, 2001, the Magistrate Courts will handle civil cases up to $10,000. Previously, the Magistrate Court limit was $7,500. The Bernalillo Metropolitan Court has jurisdiction in cases up to $5000.

ONLINE ACCESS

The www.nmcourts.com web site offers free access to District and Magistrate Court case information. In general, records are available from June 1997 forward.

Also, a commercial online service is available for the Metropolitan Court of Bernalillo County. There is a $35.00 set up fee, a connect time fee based on usage. The system is available 24 hours a day. Call 505-345-6555 for more information.

ADDITIONAL INFORMATION

There are some "shared" courts in New Mexico, with one county handling cases arising in another. Records are held at the location(s) indicated in the text.

All magistrate courts and the Bernalillo Metropolitan Court have public access terminals to access civil records only.

PROBATE COURTS

County Clerks handle "informal" (uncontested) probate cases, and the District Courts handle "formal" (contested) probate cases.

Bernalillo County

2nd Judicial District Court PO Box 488, Albuquerque, NM 87103; 505-841-7425 (Administration); Civil phone: 505-841-7451; Criminal phone: 505-841-7542; Probate phone: 505-841-6787; Fax: 505-841-7446. Hours: 8AM-5PM (MST). *Felony, Civil.*

www.cabq.gov/cjnet/dst2alb

Civil Records: Access: Mail, online, in person. Both court and visitors may perform in person searches. Search fee: $1.50 per name. Required to search: name, years to search. Civil cases indexed by defendant, plaintiff. Civil records on computer from 1984, prior on docket books/microfiche. Online access is available free at www.nmcourts.com/disclaim.html. Most data goes back to 6/1997.

Criminal Records: Access: Mail, online, in person. Both court and visitors may perform in person searches. Search fee: $1.50 per name. Required to search: name, years to search; also helpful: DOB, SSN. Criminal records on computer from 1979, prior on docket books/microfiche. Online access to criminal records is available free at www.nmcourts.com/disclaim.html. Most data goes back to 6/1997.

General Information: No sequestered or juvenile records released. SASE required. Turnaround time up to 10 days. Copy fee: $.35 per page. Certification fee: $1.50. Fee payee: Clerk of the Court. Only cashiers checks and money orders accepted. Prepayment is required.

Metropolitan Court 401 Roma NW, Albuquerque, NM 87102; 505-841-8151/841-8160; Fax: 505-222-4800. Hours: 8AM-5PM (MST). *Misdemeanor, Civil Actions Under $10,000, Eviction, Small Claims.*

www.metrocourt.state.nm.us

Civil Records: Access: Phone, fax, mail, online, in person. Both court and visitors may perform in person searches. No search fee. Required to search: name, years to search. Civil cases indexed by defendant, plaintiff. Civil records on computer from 1987. Max. 5 years back except uncollected judgments which stay open 14 years from date of judgment. Access Metropolitan court civil records online at www.technet.nm.net/newmenu/new-mexico-courts.htm. There is set up fee plus a per minute charge based on usage. For information or to obtain an account call 505-345-6555. Also, Metro Court dockets are available free at www.metrocourt.state.nm.us/ docket_help.htm.

Criminal Records: Access: Phone, fax, mail, online, in person. Both court and visitors may perform in person searches. No search fee. Required to search: name, SSN; also helpful: DOB. Criminal records on computer from 1983. Online access to criminal records is available free at http://164.64.140.222/metro1/ website.nsf/frames?readform. Also, online access to Metro Court criminal dockets is available free at www.metrocourt.state.nm.us/docket_help.htm.

General Information: Public access terminal is available. (Only civil records are available.) No pre-sentence reports, psychological evaluations, confidential records released. SASE required. Turnaround time 5-10 days. Copy fee: $.50 per page. Computer printouts are $1.00 per page. Certification fee: $1.50. Fee payee: Metro Court. Personal checks accepted. Credit cards accepted: Visa, MC. Prepayment is required.

County Clerk #1 Civic Plaza NW, 6th Fl, Albuquerque, NM 87102; 505-768-4247. Hours: 8AM-4:30PM (MST). *Probate.*

Catron County

7th Judicial District Court PO Drawer 1129, Socorro, NM 87801; 505-835-0050; Fax: 505-838-5217. Hours: 8AM-4PM (MST). *Felony, Civil.*

Note: This court is also responsible for Socorro County.

Civil Records: Access: Phone, fax, mail, online, in person. Both court and visitors may perform in person searches. No search fee. Required to search: name, years to search. Civil cases indexed by defendant, plaintiff. Civil records on microfiche and hard copies from 1925; on computer back to 1997. Access to court records from 1997 forward is available free online at www.nmcourts.com/disclaim.html.

Criminal Records: Access: Phone, fax, mail, online, in person. Both court and visitors may perform in person searches. No search fee. Required to search: name, years to search, DOB; also helpful-SSN, signed release. Criminal records on microfiche and hard copies from 1925; on computer back to 1997. Online access to criminal records is available free at www.nmcourts.com/disclaim.html.

General Information: Public access terminal is available. No sequestered records released. SASE required. Turnaround time 1 day. Copy fee: $.35 per page. Certification fee: $2.50. Fee payee: District Court Clerk. Business checks accepted. Prepayment is required.

Quemado Magistrate Court PO Box 283, Quemado, NM 87829; 505-773-4604; Fax: 505-773-4688. Hours: 8AM-5PM (MST). *Misdemeanor, Civil Actions Under $10,000, Eviction, Small Claims.*

Reserve Magistrate Court PO Box 447, Reserve, NM 87830; 505-533-6474; Fax: 505-533-6623. Hours: 8AM-5PM (MST). *Misdemeanor, Civil Actions Under $10,000, Eviction, Small Claims.*

County Clerk PO Box I, Socorro, NM 87801; 505-835-0423. Hours: 8AM-5PM (MST). *Probate.*

Chaves County

5th Judicial District Court Box 1776, Roswell, NM 88202; 505-622-2212; Fax: 505-624-9510. Hours: 8AM-Noon,1-5PM (MST). *Felony, Civil.*

www.fifthdistrictcourt.com

Civil Records: Access: Online, in person. Visitors must perform in person searches for themselves. No search fee. Required to search: name, years to search. Civil cases indexed by defendant, plaintiff. Civil records on computer from 1996, on microfiche and archived from 1891. Access to court records from 1997 forward is available free online at www.nmcourts.com/ disclaim.html.

Criminal Records: Access: Online, in person. Visitors must perform in person searches for themselves. No search fee. Required to search: name, years to search, DOB, aliases. Criminal records on computer from 1996, on microfiche and archived from 1891. Online access to criminal records is available free at www.nmcourts.com/disclaim.html.

General Information: Public access terminal is available. No sequestered records released. Copy fee: $.35 per page. Certification fee: $1.50. Fee payee: District Court Clerk. Only cashiers checks and money orders accepted. Prepayment is required.

Magistrate Court 200 E 4th St, Roswell, NM 88201; 505-624-6088; Fax: 505-624-6092. Hours: 8AM-4PM M, T, TH, F; 9AM-4PM W (MST). *Misdemeanor, Civil Actions Under $10,000, Eviction, Small Claims.*

www.nmcourts.com

County Clerk Box 820, Roswell, NM 88201; 505-624-6614; Fax: 505-624-6523. Hours: 7AM-5PM (MST). *Probate.*

Cibola County

13th Judicial District Court Box 758, Grants, NM 87020; 505-287-8831; Fax: 505-285-5755. Hours: 8AM-5PM (MST). *Felony, Civil, Probate.*

Civil Records: Access: Fax, mail, online, in person. Both court and visitors may perform in person searches. Search fee: $5.00 for 2 names; 3-10 for 10 names; $20.00 over 20 names. Required to search: name, years to search. Civil cases indexed by defendant, plaintiff. Civil records on microfiche from 1981; prior to 1981 belong to Valencia County. Access to court records from 1997 forward is available free online at www.nmcourts.com/disclaim.html.

Criminal Records: Access: Fax, mail, online, in person. Search fee: $5.00 per name. Required to search: name, years to search. Criminal records on microfiche from 1981; prior to 1981 belong to Valencia County. Online access to criminal records is available free at www.nmcourts.com/disclaim.html.

General Information: Public access terminal is available. No sequestered records released. Turnaround time 2-3 days. Fax notes: Will fax results: $2.50 in-state; $5.00 out-of-state unless toll-free # is provided. Copy fee: $.35 per page. Certification fee: $1.50. Fee payee: District Court Clerk. Business checks accepted. Prepayment is required.

Magistrate Court 515 W High, PO Box 130, Grants, NM 87020; 505-285-4605. Hours: 8AM-4PM (MST). *Misdemeanor, Civil Actions Under $10,000, Eviction, Small Claims.*

County Clerk 515 W. High St, PO Box 190, Grants, NM 87020; 505-285-2535; Fax: 505-285-2562. Hours: 8AM-5PM (MST). *Probate.*

Colfax County

8th Judicial District Court Box 160, Raton, NM 87740; 505-445-5585; Fax: 505-445-2626. Hours: 8AM-4PM (MST). *Felony, Civil.*

Civil Records: Access: Phone, mail, online, in person. Both court and visitors may perform in person searches. No search fee. Required to search: name, years to search. Civil cases indexed by defendant, plaintiff. Civil records archived from 1912. Access to court records from 1997 forward is available free online at www.nmcourts.com/disclaim.html.

Criminal Records: Access: Phone, mail, online, in person. Both court and visitors may perform in person searches. No search fee. Required to search: name, years to search; also helpful: DOB, SSN. Criminal records archived from 1912; computerized records go back to 1996/97. Online access to criminal records is available free at www.nmcourts.com/disclaim.html.

General Information: Public access terminal is available. No adoption, mental, guardianship, children's cases (neglect & child in need of supervision) records released. SASE required. Turnaround time 1 week. Fax notes: Fee to fax results is $2.00 per page. Copy fee: $.35 per page. Certification fee: $1.50. Fee payee: District Court. Business checks accepted.

Cimarron Magistrate Court PO Drawer 367, Highway 21, Cimarron, NM 87714; 505-376-2634. *Misdemeanor, Civil Actions Under $10,000, Eviction, Small Claims.*

Raton Magistrate Court PO Box 68, Raton, NM 87740; 505-445-2220; Fax: 505-445-8966. Hours: 8AM-5PM (MST). *Misdemeanor, Civil Actions Under $10,000, Eviction, Small Claims.*

Springer Magistrate Court 300 Colbert Ave. PO Box 760, Springer, NM 87747; 505-483-2417; Fax: 505-483-0127. Hours: 8AM-Noon, 1-5PM (MST). *Misdemeanor, Civil Actions Under $10,000, Eviction, Small Claims.*

County Clerk PO Box 159, Raton, NM 87740; 505-445-5551; Fax: 505-445-4031. Hours: 8AM-5PM (MST). *Probate.*

Curry County

9th Judicial District Court Curry County Courthouse, 700 N Main, #11, Clovis, NM 88101; 505-762-9148; Fax: 505-763-5160. Hours: 8AM-4PM (MST). *Felony, Civil.*

Civil Records: Access: Online, in person. Visitors must perform in person searches for themselves. No search fee. Required to search: name, years to search, address. Civil cases indexed by defendant, plaintiff. Civil records on computer from 1986, on microfiche and archived from 1910. Access to court records from 1997 forward is available free online at www.nmcourts.com/disclaim.html.
Criminal Records: Access: Online, in person. Visitors must perform in person searches for themselves. No search fee. Required to search: name, years to search; also helpful: SSN. Criminal records on computer from 1986, on microfiche and archived from 1910. Online access to criminal records is available free at www.nmcourts.com/disclaim.html.
General Information: No adoptions, insanity, sequestered, neglect or abuse released. Copy fee: $.35 per page. Certification fee: $1.50. Fee payee: 9th Judicial District Court. Only cashiers checks and money orders accepted. Prepayment is required.

Magistrate Court 900 Main St, Clovis, NM 88101; 505-762-3766; Fax: 505-769-1437. Hours: 8AM-4PM (MST). *Misdemeanor, Civil Actions Under $10,000, Eviction, Small Claims.*

De Baca County

10th Judicial District Court Box 910, Ft. Sumner, NM 88119; 505-355-2896; Fax: 505-355-2899. Hours: 8AM-4:30PM (MST). *Felony, Civil.*

Civil Records: Access: Phone, mail, online, in person. Only the court performs in person searches; visitors may not. No search fee. Required to search: name, years to search. Civil cases indexed by defendant, plaintiff. Civil records on index cards and docket books archived from 1917; on computer since 1997. Access to court records from 1997 forward is available free online at www.nmcourts.com/disclaim.html.
Criminal Records: Access: Phone, mail, online, in person. Only the court performs in person searches; visitors may not. No search fee. Required to search: name, years to search. Criminal records on index cards and docket books archived from 1917; on computer since 1997. Online access to criminal records is available free at www.nmcourts.com/disclaim.html.
General Information: No mental, adoptions, or juvenile released. SASE required. Turnaround time 2 days. Fax notes: Fee to fax results is $1.00 per page. Copy fee: $.35 per page. Certification fee: $1.50. Fee payee: District Court. Only cashiers checks and money orders accepted. Prepayment is required.

Magistrate Court Box 24, Ft Sumner, NM 88119; 505-355-7371; Fax: 505-355-7149. Hours: 8AM-5PM (MST). *Misdemeanor, Civil Actions Under $10,000, Eviction, Small Claims.*

County Clerk 514 Ave C, PO Box 347, Ft. Sumner, NM 88119; 505-355-2601; Fax: 505-355-2441. Hours: 8AM-Noon, 1-4:30PM (MST). *Probate.*

Dona Ana County

3rd Judicial District Court 201 W Picacho, #A, Las Cruces, NM 88005; 505-523-8200; Fax: 505-523-8290. Hours: 8AM-Noon, 1-5PM (MST). *Felony, Civil.*

Civil Records: Access: Mail, online, in person. Both court and visitors may perform in person searches. Search fee: $1.50 per name. Required to search: name, years to search. Civil cases indexed by defendant, plaintiff. Civil records on computer from 1986, on microfiche and archived from 1912. Access to court records from 1997 forward is available free online at www.nmcourts.com/disclaim.html.
Criminal Records: Access: Mail, online, in person. Both court and visitors may perform in person searches. Search fee: $1.50 per name. Required to search: name, years to search; also helpful: DOB, SSN. Criminal records on computer from 1986, on microfiche and archived from 1912. Online access to criminal records is available free at www.nmcourts.com/disclaim.html.
General Information: Public access terminal is available. No adoption, mental health, or juvenile released. SASE required. Turnaround time 2-3 days. Copy fee: $.35 per page. Certification fee: $1.50. Fee payee: 3rd Judicial District. Only cashiers checks and money orders accepted. Prepayment is required.

Anthony Magistrate Court PO Box 1259, Anthony, NM 88021; 505-233-3147. Hours: 8AM-Noon, 1-5PM (MST). *Misdemeanor, Civil Actions Under $10,000, Eviction, Small Claims.*

Las Cruces Magistrate Court 151 N Church, Las Cruces, NM 88001; 505-524-2814; Fax: 505-525-2951. Hours: 8AM-4PM (MST). *Misdemeanor, Civil Actions Under $10,000, Eviction, Small Claims.*

County Clerk c/o Third Judicial District, 201 W Picacho #A, Los Cruces, NM 88005; 505-523-8200; Fax: 505-523-8290. 8AM-5PM (MST). *Probate.*

Eddy County

5th Judicial District Court 102 N Canal St #240, Carlsbad, NM 88220; 505-885-4740; Fax: 505-887-7095. Hours: 8AM-Noon, 1-5PM (MST). *Felony, Civil.*

www.fifthdistrictcourt.com

Civil Records: Access: Phone, mail, fax, online, in person, online. Both court and visitors may perform in person searches. No search fee. Required to search: name, years to search. Civil cases indexed by defendant. Civil records on computer from 1986, microfiche from 1891. Access to court records from 1997 forward is free online at www.nmcourts.com/disclaim.html, or via the court web site above.
Criminal Records: Access: Phone, mail, online, in person. Only the court performs in person searches. No search fee. Required to search: name, years to search. Criminal records on computer from 1986, microfiche from 1900s. Online access to criminal records is available free at www.nmcourts.com/disclaim.html.
General Information: Public access terminal is available. No adoption, SS case w/children, or guardianship released. SASE required. Turnaround time 1 day. Copy fee: $.35 per page. Certification fee: $1.50. Fee payee: District Court Clerk. Only cashiers checks and money orders accepted. Law firm checks only. Prepayment is required.

Artesia Magistrate Court 611 Mahone Dr Ste A, Artesia, NM 88210; 505-746-2481; Fax: 505-746-6763. Hours: 8AM-4PM (MST). *Misdemeanor, Civil Actions Under $10,000, Eviction, Small Claims.*

www.nmcourts.com

Note: This court also handles preliminary felonies, traffic, and DUI cases.

Carlsbad Magistrate Court 1949 S Canal St, Carlsbad, NM 88220; 505-885-3218; Fax: 505-887-3460. Hours: 8AM-4PM (MST). *Felony, Misdemeanor, Civil Actions Under $10,000, Eviction, Small Claims.*

County Clerk Eddy County Probate Judge, Rm 100, PO Box 850, Carlsbad, NM 88221; 505-885-4008; Fax: 505-887-1039. Hours: 8AM-5PM (MST). *Probate.*

Grant County

6th Judicial District Court Box 2339, Silver City, NM 88062; 505-538-3250; Fax: 505-588-5439. Hours: 8AM-5PM (MST). *Felony, Civil.*

Civil Records: Access: Fax, mail, online, in person. Both court and visitors may perform in person searches. Search fee: $3.00 per name. Required to search: name, years to search. Civil cases indexed by defendant, plaintiff. Civil records on microfiche from 1912-1977, on books from 1977; on computer back to 1996. Access to court records from 1997 forward is available free online at www.nmcourts.com/disclaim.html.
Criminal Records: Access: Fax, mail, online, in person. Both court and visitors may perform in person searches. Search fee: $3.00 per name. Required to search: name, years to search. Criminal records on microfiche from 1912-1977, on books from 1977; on computer back to 1996. Online access to criminal records is available free at www.nmcourts.com/disclaim.html.
General Information: Public access terminal is available. No adoptions or abuse records released. SASE required. Turnaround time 1 day. Fax notes: Fee to fax results is $2.50 per page. Copy fee: $.35 per page. Certification fee: $1.50. Fee payee: District Court Clerk. Only cashiers checks and money orders accepted. Prepayment is required.

Bayard Magistrate Court PO Box 125, Bayard, NM 88023; 505-537-3402; Fax: 505-537-7365. Hours: 8AM-5PM (MST). *Misdemeanor, Civil Actions Under $10,000, Eviction, Small Claims.*

Silver City Magistrate Court 1620 E Pine St, Silver City, NM 88061; 505-538-3811; Fax: 505-538-8079. Hours: 8AM-5PM; Public hours 9AM-4PM (MST). *Misdemeanor, Civil Actions Under $10,000, Eviction, Small Claims.*

www.nmcourts.com

County Clerk Box 898, Silver City, NM 88061; 505-574-0042; Fax: 505-574-0076. Hours: 8AM-5PM (MST). *Probate.*

Note: Access to court records from 1997 forward is available free online at www.nmcourts.com/disclaim.html.

Guadalupe County

4th Judicial District Court 420 Parker Ave #5, Guadalupe County Courthouse, Santa Rosa, NM 88435; 505-472-3888; Fax: 505-472-3888. Hours: 8AM-Noon; 1PM-5PM (MST). *Felony, Civil.*

Civil Records: Access: Online, in person. Visitors must perform in person searches for themselves. No search fee. Required to search: name, years to search. Civil cases indexed by defendant, plaintiff. Civil records on docket books from 1912. Access to court records from

1997 forward is available free online at www.nmcourts.com/disclaim.html.

Criminal Records: Access: Online, in person. Visitors must perform in person searches for themselves. No search fee. Required to search: name, years to search, DOB; also helpful: SSN. Criminal records on docket books from 1912. Online access to criminal records is available free at www.nmcourts.com/disclaim.html.

General Information: Public access terminal is available. No adoption, insanity, juvenile, guardianship records released. Copy fee: $.35 per page. Certification fee: $1.50. Fee payee: District Court Clerk Office. Only cashiers checks and money orders accepted.

Santa Rosa Magistrate Court 603 Parker Ave, Santa Rosa, NM 88435; 505-472-3237. Hours: 8AM-Noon, 1-5PM (MST). *Misdemeanor, Civil Actions Under $10,000, Eviction, Small Claims.*

Vaughn Magistrate Court c/o Santa Rosa Justice Court, 602 Parker Av, Santa Rosa, NM 88435; 505-584-2345. Hours: 8AM-4PM (MST). *Misdemeanor, Civil Actions Under $10,000, Eviction, Small Claims.*

Note: The Vaugh court is only open the 2nd Wednesday of the month. It is located at 8th & Calle De Carill, Vaughn, NM 88353. Most records are at Santa Rosa (phone # given here).

County Clerk 420 Parker Ave, Courthouse, Santa Rosa, NM 88435; 505-472-3791; Fax: 505-472-3735. Hours: 8AM-5PM (MST). *Probate.*

Harding County

10th Judicial District Court Box 1002, Mosquero, NM 87733; 505-673-2252; Fax: 505-673-2252. Hours: 9AM-3PM M-W,F (MST). *Felony, Civil.*

Civil Records: Access: Phone, fax, mail, online, in person. No search fee. Required to search: name; also helpful: years to search. Civil cases indexed by defendant, plaintiff. Civil records on books from 1927. Computerized records go back to 1997. Access to court records from 1997 forward is available free online at www.nmcourts.com/disclaim.html.

Criminal Records: Access: Phone, fax, mail, online, in person. Visitors must perform in person searches for themselves. No search fee. Required to search: name, DOB, SSN; also helpful: years to search. Criminal records on books from 1927. Computerized records go back to 1997. Online access to criminal records is available free at www.nmcourts.com/disclaim.html.

General Information: No adoption records released. SASE required. Turnaround time 1 week. Fax notes: $1.00 per page. Copy fee: $.35 per page. Certification fee: $1.50. Fee payee: District Court Clerk. Business checks accepted. Prepayment is required.

Magistrate Court Box 9, Roy, NM 87743; 505-485-2549; Fax: 505-485-2407. Hours: 8AM-4:30PM (MST). *Misdemeanor, Civil Actions Under $10,000, Eviction, Small Claims.*

County Clerk County Clerk, Box 1002, Mosquero, NM 87733; 505-673-2301; Fax: 505-673-2922. Hours: 8AM-5PM (MST). *Probate.*

Hidalgo County

6th Judicial District Court PO Box 608, Lordsburg, NM 88045; 505-542-3411; Fax: 505-542-3481. 8AM-Noon, 1-5PM (MST). *Felony, Civil.*

Civil Records: Access: Phone, fax, mail, online, in person. Only the court performs in person searches; visitors may not. No search fee. Required to search: name, years to search. Civil cases indexed by defendant, plaintiff. Civil records on microfiche and archived from 1920. Access to court records from 1997 forward is

available free online at www.nmcourts.com/disclaim.html.

Criminal Records: Access: Phone, fax, mail, online, in person. Only the court performs in person searches; visitors may not. No search fee. Required to search: name, years to search; also helpful: alias. Criminal records on microfiche and archived from 1920. Online access to criminal records is available free at www.nmcourts.com/disclaim.html.

General Information: No juvenile or adoption records released. SASE required. Turnaround time 3-5 days. Fax notes: Fee to fax results is $5.00 per document; will only fax back results to toll-free numbers. Copy fee: $.35 per page. Certification fee: $1.50. Fee payee: District Court Clerk. Business checks accepted. No personal checks. Prepayment is required.

Magistrate Court 420 Wabash Ave, Lordsburg, NM 88045; 505-542-3582. Hours: 8AM-5PM (MST). *Misdemeanor, Civil Actions Under $10,000, Eviction, Small Claims.*

www.nmcourts.com

County Clerk 300 S Shakespeare, Lordsburg, NM 88045; 505-542-9213; Fax: 505-542-3193. Hours: 9AM-Noon (MST). *Probate.*

Lea County

5th Judicial District Court 100 N. Main, #6C, Lovington, NM 88260; 505-396-8571; Fax: 505-396-2428. Hours: 8AM-5PM (MST). *Felony, Civil.*

www.fifthdistrictcourt.com

Civil Records: Access: Fax, mail, online, in person. Both court and visitors may perform in person searches. No search fee. Required to search: name, years to search. Civil cases indexed by defendant, plaintiff. Civil records on computer from 1990, on microfiche from 1912. Access to court records from 1997 forward is available free online at www.nmcourts.com/disclaim.html. Court refers search requests to a private researcher.

Criminal Records: Access: Fax, mail, online, in person. Both court and visitors may perform in person searches. No search fee. Required to search: name, years to search. Criminal records on computer from 1997, on microfiche from 1912. Online access to criminal records is available free at www.nmcourts.com/disclaim.html. Court refers searches to a private researcher.

General Information: Public access terminal is available. No adoptions, mental, abuse records released. SASE required. Turnaround time 1-3 days. Copy fee: $.35 per page. Certification fee: $1.50. Fee payee: District Court Clerk. Only cashiers checks and money orders accepted. Prepayment is required.

Eunice Magistrate Court PO Box 240, Eunice, NM 88231; 505-394-3368; Fax: 505-394-3335. *Misdemeanor, Civil Actions Under $10,000, Eviction, Small Claims.*

Hobbs Magistrate Court 2110 N Alto Dr, Hobbs, NM 88240-3455; 505-397-3621; Fax: 505-393-9121. Hours: 8AM-4PM (MST). *Misdemeanor, Civil Actions Under $10,000, Eviction, Small Claims.*

www.nmcourts.com

Lovington Magistrate Court 100 W Central, #D, Lovington, NM 88260; 505-396-6677; Fax: 505-396-6163. Hours: 8AM-4PM (MST). *Misdemeanor, Civil Actions Under $10,000, Eviction, Small Claims.*

www.nmcourts.com

Tatum Magistrate Court PO Box 918, Tatum, NM 88267; 505-398-5300; Fax: 505-398-5310. Hours: 8AM-4PM (MST). *Misdemeanor, Civil Actions Under $10,000, Eviction, Small Claims.*

County Clerk Box 1507, Lovington, NM 88260; 505-396-8531; Fax: 505-396-3293. Hours: 8AM-5PM (MST). *Probate.*

www.leacounty-nm.org

Lincoln County

12th Judicial District Court Box 725, Carrizozo, NM 88301; 505-648-2432; Fax: 505-648-2581. Hours: 8AM-5PM (MST). *Felony, Civil.*

www.12thdistrict.com

Civil Records: Access: Online, mail, n person. Visitors must perform in person searches for themselves. No search fee. Required to search: name, years to search. Civil cases indexed by defendant, plaintiff. Civil records on computer from 1991, docket books from 1960, microfiche to 1960. Access to court records from 1997 forward is available free online at www.nmcourts.com/disclaim.html.

Criminal Records: Access: Online, in person. Visitors must perform in person searches for themselves. No search fee. Required to search: name, years to search. Criminal records on computer from 1991, docket books from 1960, microfiche to 1960. Online access to criminal records is available free at www.nmcourts.com/disclaim.html. The court will refer all search requests to a private researcher.

General Information: No juvenile, adoption, or mental records released. Copy fee: $.35 per page. Certification fee: $1.50. Fee payee: District Court Clerk. Business checks accepted. Prepayment is required.

Ruidoso Magistrate Court 301 W Highway 70 #2, Ruidoso, NM 88345; 505-378-7022; Fax: 505-378-8508. Hours: 8AM-4PM (MST). *Misdemeanor, Civil Actions Under $10,000, Eviction, Small Claims.*

County Clerk PO Box 338, Carrizozo, NM 88301; 505-648-2394; Fax: 505-648-2576. Hours: 8AM-5PM (MST). *Probate.*

Note: This court will do searches

Los Alamos County

1st Judicial District Court c/o Santa Fe 1st District Court, PO Box 2268, Santa Fe, NM 87504.

http://firstdistrictcourt.com

Note: All civil and criminal cases handled by Santa Fe District Court

Magistrate Court 1319 Trinity Dr, Los Alamos, NM 87544; 505-662-2727; Fax: 505-661-6258. Hours: 8AM-4PM (MST). *Misdemeanor, Civil Actions Under $10,000, Eviction, Small Claims.*

County Clerk-Probate PO Box 30, Los Alamos, NM 87544; 505-662-8010; Fax: 505-662-8008. Hours: 8AM-5PM (MST). *Probate.*

Luna County

6th Judicial District Court Luna County Courthouse Room 40, Deming, NM 88030; 505-546-9611; Fax: 505-546-0971. Hours: 8AM-4PM (MST). *Felony, Civil.*

www.nmcourts.com

Civil Records: Access: Mail, online, in person. Both court and visitors may perform in person searches. Search fee: $5.00 per name. Required to search: name, years to search. Civil cases indexed by defendant, plaintiff. Civil records on microfiche from 1911; on computer back to 1997. Access to court records from 1997 forward is available free online at www.nmcourts.com/disclaim.html.

Criminal Records: Access: Mail, online, in person. Both court and visitors may perform in person searches. Search fee: $5.00 per name. Required to search: name, years to search. Criminal records on microfiche from

1911; on computer back to 1997. Online access to criminal records is available free at www.nmcourts.com/disclaim.html.

General Information: Public access terminal is available. No adoptions, mental, sequestered or juvenile records released. SASE required. Turnaround time 5 days. Fax notes: Fee to fax results is $.35 per page. Copy fee: $.35 per page. Certification fee: $1.50. Only cashiers checks and money orders accepted. Prepayment is required.

Magistrate Court 912 S Silver St, Deming, NM 88030; 505-546-9321; Fax: 505-546-4896. Hours: 8AM-Noon, 1-5PM (MST). *Misdemeanor, Civil Actions Under $10,000, Eviction, Small Claims.*

www.nmcourts.com

County Clerk PO Box 1838, Deming, NM 88031; 505-546-0491; Fax: 505-546-4708. Hours: 8AM-5PM (MST). *Probate.*

Note: There can be some probate cases (those in dispute) at the District Court level.

McKinley County

11th Judicial District Court 201 W. Hill, Room 4, Gallup, NM 87301; 505-863-6816; Fax: 505-722-9172. Hours: 8AM-Noon, 1-5PM (MST). *Felony, Civil.*

Civil Records: Access: Phone, mail, online, in person. Both court and visitors may perform in person searches. No search fee. Required to search: name, years to search. Civil cases indexed by defendant, plaintiff. Civil records on computer from 1989, on microfiche from 1923. Access to court records from 1997 forward is free online at www.nmcourts.com/disclaim.html. One name only by phone.

Criminal Records: Access: Phone, mail, online, in person. Both court and visitors may perform in person searches. No search fee. Required to search: name, years to search, DOB; also helpful: SSN. Criminal records on computer from 1989, on microfiche from 1923. Online access to criminal records is available free at www.nmcourts.com/disclaim.html. Will search one name only by phone.

General Information: Public access terminal is available. No adoption or juvenile records released. SASE required. Turnaround time 3-5 days. Fax notes: Fee to fax results is $5.00 per call. Copy fee: $.35 per page. Certification fee: $1.50. Fee payee: McKinley County District Court. No personal checks accepted. Prepayment is required.

Magistrate Court 285 S Boardman Dr, Gallup, NM 87301; 505-722-6636; Fax: 505-863-3510. Hours: 8AM-4PM (MST). *Misdemeanor, Civil Actions Under $10,000, Eviction, Small Claims.*

Note: Felony preliminary hearings.

County Clerk PO Box 1268, Gallup, NM 87305; 505-863-6866; Fax: 505-863-1419. Hours: 8AM-5PM (MST). *Probate.*

Mora County

4th Judicial District Court PO Box 1540, Las Vegas, NM 87701; 505-425-7281; Fax: 505-425-6307. Hours: 8AM-Noon, 1-5PM (MST). *Felony, Civil.*

Civil Records: Access: Online, in person. Both the court and visitor may perform in person searches No search fee. Required to search: name, years to search. Civil cases indexed by defendant, plaintiff. Civil records on microfiche from 1912, archived before 1912. Access to court records from 1997 forward is available free online at www.nmcourts.com/disclaim.html.

Criminal Records: Access: Online, in person. Both the court and visitor may perform in person searches No search fee. Required to search: name, years to search.

Criminal records on microfiche from 1912, archived before 1912. Online access to criminal records is available free at www.nmcourts.com/disclaim.html.

General Information: No adoptions, insanity, or juvenile records released. Copy fee: $.35 per page. Certification fee: $1.50. Fee payee: 4th Judicial District Court. Only cashiers checks and money orders accepted. Prepayment is required.

Magistrate Court 1927 7th Street, Las Vegas, NM 87701-4957; 505-425-5204. Hours: 8AM-4PM (closed for lunch) (MST). *Misdemeanor, Civil Actions Under $10,000, Eviction, Small Claims.*

Probate Court PO Box 360, Mora, NM 87732; 505-387-5014. Hours: 8AM-5PM (MST). *Probate.*

Otero County

12th Judicial District Court 1000 New York Ave, Rm 209, Alamogordo, NM 88310-6940; 505-437-7310; Fax: 505-434-8886. Hours: 8AM-5PM (MST). *Felony, Civil.*

www.12thdistrict.com

Civil Records: Access: Online, in person. Visitors must perform in person searches for themselves. No search fee. Required to search: name, years to search. Civil cases indexed by defendant, plaintiff. Civil records on computer from 1991, on microfiche from 1926. Access to court records from 1997 forward is available free online at www.nmcourts.com/disclaim.html. Also, current court dockets are available at the court web site. Phone & mail access limited to 5 names each.

Criminal Records: Access: Online, in person. Visitors must perform in person searches for themselves. No search fee. Required to search: name, years to search. Criminal records on computer from 1991, on microfiche from 1926. Online access to criminal records is available free at www.nmcourts.com/disclaim.html. Phone & mail access limited to 5 names each. Only court performs searches prior to March 1986.

General Information: Public access terminal is available. No sealed, adoption records released. Copy fee: $.35 per page. Certification fee: $1.50. Fee payee: District Court. Only cashiers checks and money orders accepted. Prepayment is required.

Magistrate Court 263 Robert H Bradley Dr, Alamogordo, NM 88310-8288; 505-437-9000 x256; Fax: 505-439-1365. Hours: 8AM-4PM (MST). *Misdemeanor, Civil Actions Under $10,000, Eviction, Small Claims.*

County Clerk 1000 New York Ave, Rm 108, Alamogordo, NM 88310-6932; 505-437-4942; Fax: 505-443-2922. Hours: 7:30AM-6PM (MST). *Probate.*

Quay County

10th Judicial District Court Box 1067, Tucumcari, NM 88401; 505-461-2764; Fax: 505-461-4498. Hours: 8AM-5PM (MST). *Felony, Civil.*

Note: May change to new area code 575 late in 2001.

Civil Records: Access: Phone, fax, mail, online, in person. Both court and visitors may perform in person searches. No search fee. Required to search: name, years to search. Civil cases indexed by defendant, plaintiff. Civil records on hard copy file from 1995 to present, microfiche 1912 to 1994, archived from 1911, on computer back to 1997. Access to court records from 1997 forward is available free online at www.nmcourts.com/disclaim.html.

Criminal Records: Access: Phone, fax, mail, online, in person. Both court and visitors may perform in person searches. No search fee. Required to search: name; also helpful: years to search, DOB, SSN. Criminal records on hard copy file from 1995 to present, microfiche 1912 to 1994, archived from 1911, on computer back to

1997. Online access to criminal records is available free at www.nmcourts.com/disclaim.html.

General Information: Public access terminal is available. No adoptions, juvenile, insanity records released. SASE required. Turnaround time same day. Fax notes: $2.00 for first page, $1.00 each add'l. Copy fee: $.35 per page. Certification fee: $1.50. Fee payee: District Court Clerk. Only cashiers checks and money orders accepted.

Tucumcari Magistrate Court PO Box 1301, Tucumcari, NM 88401; 505-461-1700; Fax: 505-461-4522. Hours: 8AM-4PM (MST). *Misdemeanor, Civil Actions Under $10,000, Eviction, Small Claims.*

Note: San Jon Magistrate Court (closed) records are found here.

County Clerk 300 S Third St, PO Box 1225, Tucumcari, NM 88401; 505-461-0510; Fax: 505-461-0513. Hours: 8AM-5PM (MST). *Probate.*

Rio Arriba County

1st Judicial District Court c/o Santa Fe 1st District Court, PO Box 2268, Santa Fe, NM 87504.

http://firstdistrictcourt.com

Note: All civil and criminal cases handled by Santa Fe District Court

Rio Arriba Magistrate Court - Division 1 PO Box 538, Chama, NM 87520; 505-756-2278. Hours: 8AM-Noon, 1-5PM (MST). *Misdemeanor, Civil Actions Under $10,000, Eviction, Small Claims.*

Rio Arriba Magistrate Court - Division 2 410 Paseo de Onate, Espanola, NM 87532; 505-753-2532; Fax: 505753-4802. Hours: 8AM-4PM (MST). *Misdemeanor, Civil Actions Under $10,000, Eviction, Small Claims.*

County Clerk PO Box 158, Tierra Amarilla, NM 87575; 505-588-7724; Fax: 505-588-7418. Hours: 8AM-5PM (MST). *Probate.*

Roosevelt County

9th Judicial District Court 109 West 1st St, #207, Portales, NM 88130; 505-356-4463; Fax: 505-359-2140. Hours: 8AM-4PM (MST). *Felony, Civil.*

Civil Records: Access: Online, in person. Visitors must perform in person searches for themselves. No search fee. Required to search: name, years to search. Civil cases indexed by defendant, plaintiff. Civil records on microfiche from 1912, archived before 1912. Access to court records from 1997 forward is available free online at www.nmcourts.com/disclaim.html.

Criminal Records: Access: Online, in person. Visitors must perform in person searches for themselves. No search fee. Required to search: name, years to search. Criminal records on microfiche from 1912, archived before 1912. Online access to criminal records is available free at www.nmcourts.com/disclaim.html.

General Information: No adoption, guardianship, insanity records released. Copy fee: $.35 per page. Certification fee: $1.50. Fee payee: 9th Judicial District Court. Only cashiers checks and money orders accepted. Prepayment is required.

Magistrate Court 42427 US Hwy 70, Portales, NM 88130; 505-356-8569; Fax: 505-359-6883. Hours: 8AM-4PM (MST). *Misdemeanor, Civil Actions Under $10,000, Eviction, Small Claims.*

www.nmcourts.com

County Clerk Roosevelt County Courthouse, 109 W First, Portales, NM 88130; 505-356-8562; Fax: 505-356-3560. Hours: 8AM-5PM (MST). *Probate.*

San Juan County

11th Judicial District Court 103 S. Oliver, Aztec, NM 87410; 505-334-6151; Fax: 505-334-1940. Hours: 8AM-Noon, 1-5PM (MST). *Felony, Civil.*

Civil Records: Access: Online, in person. Visitors must perform in person searches for themselves. No search fee. Required to search: name, years to search; also helpful: address. Civil cases indexed by defendant, plaintiff. Civil records on computer from 1986, on microfiche from 1925, on cards from 1912. Access to court records from 1997 forward is available free online at www.nmcourts.com/disclaim.html.
Criminal Records: Access: Online, in person. Both the court (if after 1986) and visitors may perform in person searches. No search fee. Required to search: name, years to search, DOB; also helpful: address, SSN. Criminal records on computer from 1986, on microfiche from 1925, on cards from 1912. Online access to criminal records is available free at www.nmcourts.com/disclaim.html.
General Information: Public access terminal is available. No adoptions, insanity, sealed, expunged records released. Copy fee: $.35 per page. Certification fee: $1.50 per page. Fee payee: Eleventh District Court. No personal or out-of-state checks accepted. Prepayment is required.

Aztec Magistrate Court 200 Gossett, Aztec, NM 87410; 505-334-9479; Fax: 505-334-2178. Hours: 8AM-Noon, 1-5PM (MST). *Misdemeanor, Civil Actions Under $10,000, Eviction, Small Claims.*

Farmington Magistrate Court 950 W Apache St, Farmington, NM 87401; 505-326-4338; Fax: 505-325-2618. Hours: 8AM-4PM (MST). *Misdemeanor, Civil Actions Under $10,000, Eviction, Small Claims.*
www.nmcourts.com

County Clerk PO Box 550, Aztec, NM 87410; 505-334-9471; Fax: 505-334-3635. Hours: 7AM-5:30PM (MST). *Probate.*

San Miguel County

4th Judicial District Court PO Box 1540, Las Vegas, NM 87701; 505-425-7281; Fax: 505-454-8611. 8AM-Noon, 1-5PM (MST). *Felony, Civil, Probate.*

Note: Also handles cases for Mora County.

Civil Records: Access: Phone, mail, online, in person, fax. Visitors must perform in person searches for themselves. No search fee. Required to search: name, years to search. Civil cases indexed by defendant, plaintiff. Civil records on microfiche from 1912, archived before 1912. Access to court records from 1997 forward is available free online at www.nmcourts.com/disclaim.html.
Criminal Records: Access: Online, in person. Visitors must perform in person searches for themselves. No search fee. Required to search: name, years to search. Criminal records on microfiche from 1912, archived before 1912. Online access to criminal records is available free at www.nmcourts.com/disclaim.html.
General Information: No adoptions, insanity, juvenile records released. SASE required. Turnaround time 2 days. Copy fee: $.35 per page. Certification fee: $1.50. Fee payee: 4th Judicial District Court Clerk. Only cashiers checks and money orders accepted.

Magistrate Court 1927 7th St, Las Vegas, NM 87701-4957; 505-425-5204; Fax: 505-425-0422. Hours: 8AM-4PM (MST). *Misdemeanor, Civil Actions Under $10,000, Eviction, Small Claims.*

County Clerk San Miguel County Clerk, 500 W. National Av, Las Vegas, NM 87701; 505-425-9331; Fax: 505-454-7199. Hours: 8AM-Noon, 1-5PM (MST). *Probate.*

Sandoval County

13th Judicial District Court 100 Avenida De Justicia, Bernalillo, NM 87004; 505-867-2376. Hours: 8AM-Noon, 1-5PM (MST). *Felony, Civil.*

Civil Records: Access: Fax, mail, online, in person. Both court and visitors may perform in person searches. Search fee: $5.00 search fee. Required to search: name, years to search. Civil cases indexed by defendant, plaintiff. Civil records indexed on computer back to 11/96; prior on microfiche. Access to court records from 1997 forward is available free online at www.nmcourts.com/disclaim.html.
Criminal Records: Access: Fax, mail, online, in person. Both court and visitors may perform in person searches. Search fee: $5.00 per name. Required to search: name, years to search. Criminal records on computer back to 11/96. Online access to criminal records is available free at www.nmcourts.com/disclaim.html.
General Information: Public access terminal is available. No sequestered, juvenile, probate or guardianship records released. Turnaround time 2-3 days. Fax notes: Fee to fax results is $2.50 per page. Out of state $5.00 per page. Copy fee: $.35 per page. Microfilm copies $.50 per page (1991 and prior). Certification fee: $1.50. Fee payee: 13th Judicial District Court. Business checks accepted.

Bernalillo Magistrate Court PO Box 818, Bernalillo, NM 87004; 505-867-5202 X2-6; Fax: 505-867-0970. Hours: 8AM-4PM (MST). *Misdemeanor, Civil Actions Under $10,000, Eviction, Small Claims.*

Cuba Magistrate Court 6354 US 550, Cuba, NM 87013; 505-289-3519; Fax: 505-289-3013. Hours: 8AM-Noon, 1-5PM (MST). *Misdemeanor, Civil Actions Under $10,000, Eviction, Small Claims.*

County Clerk PO Box 40, Bernalillo, NM 87004; 505-867-7572; Fax: 505-771-8610. Hours: 8AM-5PM (MST). *Probate.*

Santa Fe County

First Judicial District Court Box 2268, Santa Fe, NM 87504; 505-476-0189; Fax: 505-827-5055. Hours: 8AM-4PM (MST). *Felony, Civil.*

http://firstdistrictcourt.com

Note: Because this court also handles the counties of Los Alamos and Rio Arriba, you must indicate which county you are searching.

Civil Records: Access: Phone, mail, online, in person. Both court and visitors may perform in person searches. Search fee: $10.00 minimum if more than 5 names requested or to search docket books. Required to search: name, years to search. Civil cases indexed by defendant, plaintiff. Civil records on computer from 1984, older records on docket books. Access to court records from 1997 forward is available free online at www.nmcourts.com/disclaim.html.
General Information: Public access terminal is available. No adoption, juvenile, mental or abuse records released. SASE required. Turnaround time 2 days. Copy fee: $.35 per page. Certification fee: $1.50. Fee payee: District Court. Business checks accepted. Prepayment is required.

Magistrate Court 2056 Galisteo St, Santa Fe, NM 87505; 505-476-0189, 505-984-9914; Fax: 505-986-5866. Hours: 8AM-4PM (MST). *Misdemeanor, Civil Actions Under $10,000, Eviction, Small Claims.*

Note: Also, the clerk for the Pojoaque Magistrate Court may be contacted here.

Pojoaque Magistrate Court 2052 Galisteo St, Santa Fe, NM 87505; 505-455-7938; Fax: 505-455-3053. Hours: 8AM-Noon,1-5PM (MST).

Misdemeanor, Civil Actions Under $10,000, Eviction, Small Claims.

Note: The Court In Pojoaque is often closed; the clerk can be contacted at the Santa Fe Magistrate Court, 505-476-0189 (address above).

County Clerk Box 276, Santa Fe, NM 87504; 505-986-6279; Fax: 505-986-6362. Hours: 8AM-5PM (MST). *Probate.*

Sierra County

7th Judicial District Court PO Box 3009, Truth or Consequences, NM 87901; 505-894-7167; Fax: 505-894-7168. Hours: 8AM-4PM (MST). *Felony, Civil.*

Civil Records: Access: Fax, mail, online, in person. Both court and visitors may perform in person searches. No search fee. Required to search: name, years to search, address. Civil cases indexed by defendant, plaintiff. Civil records on microfiche from 1920, archived before 1920. Access to court records from 1997 forward is available free online at www.nmcourts.com/disclaim.html.
Criminal Records: Access: Fax, mail, online, in person. Both court and visitors may perform in person searches. No search fee. Required to search: name, years to search, address, SSN. Criminal records on microfiche from 1920, archived before 1920. Online access to criminal records is available free at www.nmcourts.com/disclaim.html.
General Information: Public access terminal is available. No adoptions, insanity, juvenile, guardianship records released. SASE required. Turnaround time 2 days. Copy fee: $.35 per page. Certification fee: $1.50. Fee payee: Sierra County District Court. Only cashiers checks and money orders accepted. Prepayment is required.

Magistrate Court 155 W Barton, Truth or Consequences, NM 87901; 505-894-3051; Fax: 505-894-0476. Hours: 8AM-4PM (MST). *Misdemeanor, Civil Actions Under $10,000, Eviction, Small Claims.*

County Clerk 311 Date St., (Probate Records), Truth or Consequences, NM 87901; 505-894-2840; Probate phone: 505-894-4416; Fax: 505-894-2516. Hours: 8AM-5PM (MST). *Probate.*

Socorro County

7th Judicial District Court c/o Catron County District Court, PO Drawer 1129, Socorro, NM 87801.
Note: All civil and criminal cases are handled by Catron County District Court.

Magistrate Court 404 Park St, Socorro, NM 87801; 505-835-2500. Hours: 8AM-Noon, 1-5PM (MST). *Misdemeanor, Civil Actions Under $10,000, Eviction, Small Claims.*

County Clerk 200 Church St, Socorro, NM 87801; 505-835-0423; Fax: 505-835-1043. Hours: 8AM-5PM (MST). *Probate.*

Taos County

8th Judicial District Court 105 Albright St Ste H, Taos, NM 87571; 505-758-3173; Fax: 505-751-1281. Hours: 8AM-4PM (MST). *Felony, Civil.*

Civil Records: Access: In person, online. Visitors must perform in person searches for themselves. No search fee. Required to search: name, years to search. Civil cases indexed by defendant, plaintiff. Civil records on computer since 1993, books since 1912, microfiche from 1912-1980. Access to court records from 1993 forward is available free online at www.nmcourts.com/disclaim.html.
Criminal Records: Access: In person, online. Visitors must perform in person searches for themselves. No search fee. Required to search: name, years to search,

DOB; also helpful: signed release, SSN. Criminal records on computer since 1993, books since 1912, microfiche from 1912-1950. Online access to criminal records is available free at www.nmcourts.com/disclaim.html.

General Information: No adoption, juvenile, abuse or sequestered case records released. Copy fee: $.35 per page. Certification fee: $1.50. Fee payee: District Court. Only cashiers checks and money orders accepted. Prepayment is required.

Questa Magistrate Court PO Box 586, Questa, NM 87556; 505-586-0761; Fax: 505-586-0428. Hours: 8AM-Noon,1-5PM (MST). *Misdemeanor, Civil Actions Under $10,000, Eviction, Small Claims.*

Taos Magistrate Court 920 Salazar Rd #B, Taos, NM 87571; 505-758-4030; Fax: 505-751-0983. Hours: 8AM-4PM (MST). *Misdemeanor, Civil Actions Under $10,000, Eviction, Small Claims.*

County Clerk 105 Albright, #D, Taos, NM 87551; 505-758-8266; Fax: 505-751-3391. Hours: 8AM-5PM (MST). *Probate.*

Torrance County

7th Judicial District Court County Courthouse, PO Box 78, Estancia, NM 87016; 505-384-2974; Fax: 505-384-2229. 8AM-4PM (MST). *Felony, Civil.*

www.nmcourts.com

Civil Records: Access: Mail, online, in person. Both court and visitors may perform in person searches. No search fee. Required to search: name, years to search. Civil cases indexed by defendant, plaintiff. Civil records on hard copy until filmed, microfiche from 1912; on computer back to 1997. Access to court records from 1997 forward is available free online at www.nmcourts.com/disclaim.html.

Criminal Records: Access: Mail, online, in person. Only the court performs in person searches; visitors may not. No search fee. Required to search: name, years to search; also helpful: SSN, DOB. Criminal records on hard copy until filmed, microfiche from 1912; on computer back to 1997. Online access to criminal records is available free at www.nmcourts.com/disclaim.html.

General Information: Public access terminal is available. No juvenile, neglect, adoption, mental health records released. SASE required. Turnaround time 1

day. Copy fee: $.35 per page. Certification fee: $1.50. Fee payee: Seventh Judicial District Court. Only cashiers checks and money orders accepted. Prepayment is required.

Moriarty Magistrate Court PO Box 2027, Moriarty, NM 87035; 505-832-4476; Fax: 505-832-1563. Hours: 8AM-4PM (MST). *Misdemeanor, Civil Actions Under $10,000, Eviction, Small Claims.*

County Clerk PO Box 48, Estancia, NM 87016; 505-384-2221/1226; Fax: 505-384-4080. Hours: 8AM-Noon, 1-5PM (MST). *Probate.*

Union County

8th Judicial District Court Box 310, Clayton, NM 88415; 505-374-9577; Fax: 505-374-2089. Hours: 8AM-Noon, 1-5PM (MST). *Felony, Civil.*

Civil Records: Access: Mail, online, in person. Both court and visitors may perform in person searches. No search fee. Required to search: name, years to search. Civil cases indexed by defendant, plaintiff. Civil records on cards from 1981. Computerized records go to 1997. Access to court records from 1997 forward is available free online at www.nmcourts.com/disclaim.html.

Criminal Records: Access: Mail, online, in person. Both court and visitors may perform in person searches. No search fee. Required to search: name, years to search. Criminal records on docket sheets from 1981. Computerized records go to 1997. Online access to criminal records is available free at www.nmcourts.com/disclaim.html.

General Information: Public access terminal is available. No adoption, juvenile records released. SASE required. Turnaround time 1-2 days. Fax notes: Fax back $.35 per page. Copy fee: $.35 per page. Certification fee: $3.00. Fee payee: Clerk of District Court. Only cashiers checks and money orders accepted. Prepayment is required.

Magistrate Court 836 Main Street, Clayton, NM 88415; 505-374-9472; Fax: 505-374-9368. Hours: 8AM-Noon, 1-5PM (MST). *Misdemeanor, Civil Actions Under $10,000, Eviction, Small Claims.*

Note: The court also hanles preliminary felony hearings.

County Clerk PO Box 430, Clayton, NM 88415; 505-374-9491; Fax: 505-374-2763. Hours: 9AM-Noon, 1-5PM (MST). *Probate.*

Valencia County

13th Judicial District Court Box 1089, Los Lunas, NM 87031; 505-865-4291; Fax: 505-865-8801. Hours: 8AM-5PM (MST). *Felony, Civil.*

www.co.valencia.nm.us

Civil Records: Access: Fax, mail, online, in person. Both court and visitors may perform in person searches. Search fee: $5.00 for up to 2 names, $10.00 for 3-10 names. Required to search: name, years to search. Civil cases indexed by defendant, plaintiff. Civil records on microfiche from 1915. Access to court records from 1997 forward is available free online at www.nmcourts.com/disclaim.html.

Criminal Records: Access: Mail, online, in person. Both court and visitors may perform in person searches. Search fee: $5.00 fee for 2 names, $10.00 for 3-10 names. Required to search: name, years to search. Criminal records on microfiche from 1915. Online access to criminal records is available free at www.nmcourts.com/disclaim.html.

General Information: Public access terminal is available. No adoptions or juvenile records released. SASE required. Turnaround time 2 days. Fax notes: Fax fees: $2.50 in-state; $5.00 out-of-state. Copy fee: $.35 per page. Certification fee: $1.50. Fee payee: 13th Judicial District Court. Only cashiers checks and money orders accepted.

Belen Magistrate Court 909 W Castillo, Belen, NM 87002; 505-864-7509; Fax: 505-864-9532. Hours: 8AM-4PM (MST). *Misdemeanor, Civil Actions Under $10,000, Eviction, Small Claims.*

Los Lunas Magistrate Court 1206 Main St, Los Lunas, NM 87031; 505-865-4637. Hours: 8AM-4PM (MST). *Misdemeanor, Civil Actions Under $10,000, Eviction, Small Claims.*

County Clerk PO Box 969, Los Lunas, NM 87031; 505-866-2073; Fax: 505-866-2023. Hours: 8AM-4:30PM (MST). *Probate.*

www.co.valencia.nm.us/Clerk.htm

New Mexico Recording Offices

ORGANIZATION: 33 counties, 33 recording offices. The recording officer is County Clerk. Most counties maintain a grantor/grantee index and a miscellaneous index. The entire state is in the Mountain Time Zone (MST).

REAL ESTATE RECORDS: Most counties will not perform real estate searches. Copy and certification fees vary.

UCC RECORDS: Financing statements are filed at the state level, except for real estate related collateral, which are filed with the County Clerk. However, prior to 07/2001, consumer goods and farm collateral were also filed at the County Clerk and these older records can be searched there. Only a few recording offices will perform UCC searches. Use search request form UCC-11. Search and copy fees vary, but search fee is usually $5.00.

TAX LIEN RECORDS: All federal and state tax liens are filed with the County Clerk. Most counties will not provide tax lien searches.

OTHER LIENS: Judgment, mechanics, lis pendens, contractors, hospital.

ONLINE ACCESS: Several counties offer online access, but there is no statewide system.

Bernalillo County

County Clerk, PO Box 542, Albuquerque, NM 87103-0542. 505-768-4059 R/E Recording: 505-768-4268 UCC Recording: 505-768-4268; Fax 505-768-4190. www.berncotreasurer.com
Will search UCC records. Tax liens not included in UCC search. Real estate record owner and mortgage searches available. **Online Access:** Real Estate, Property Assessor Records. Records on the county treasurer tax bill page are available free online at www.berncotreasurer.com/ProcessSearch.asp?cmd=NewSearch. No name searching. Also, search via the assessor records at www.bernco-assessor.com. Also, search property information via the GIS-mapping site at http://outside.bernco.gov/website/blcas31/viewer.htm. Also, the recorders data and Grantor/Grantee index is available at http://cyclops.bernco.gov/splash.jsp. Free registration and password required. For information call 505-768-4090. **Other Phones:** Assessor 505-768-4040.

Catron County

County Clerk, PO Box 197, Reserve, NM 87830-0197. County Clerk, R/E and UCC Recording 505-533-6400; Fax 505-533-6400.
This agency will not perform searches. **Other Phone Numbers:** Assessor 505-533-6577; Treasurer 505-533-6384; Elections 505-533-6400.

Chaves County

County Clerk, Box 580, Roswell, NM 88202-0580. County Clerk, R/E and UCC Recording 505-624-6614; Fax 505-624-6523.
This agency will not perform searches. **Other Phone Numbers:** Assessor 505-624-6603; Treasurer 505-624-6618; Appraiser/Auditor 505-624-6603; Elections 505-624-6614; Vital Records 505-827-0121.

Cibola County

County Clerk, PO Box 190, Grants, NM 87020. 505-287-9431 R/E Recording: 505-285-2539 UCC Recording: 505-285-2539; Fax 505-285-2562.
This agency will not search real estate or UCC records. **Other Phone Numbers:** Assessor 505-285-2527; Treasurer 505-285-2520; Elections 505-285-2540.

Colfax County

County Clerk, PO Box 159, Raton, NM 87740-0159. County Clerk, R/E and UCC Recording 505-445-5551; Fax 505-445-4031.
This agency will not search real estate or UCC records. **Other Phone Numbers:** Assessor 505-445-2341; Treasurer 505-445-3171; Elections 505-445-5551; Vital Records 505-445-5551.

Curry County

County Clerk, PO Box 1168, Clovis, NM 88102-1168. County Clerk, R/E and UCC Recording 505-763-5591; Fax 505-763-4232. www.currycounty.org/clerk's.html
Will not search UCC records or tax liens. Will not search real estate records. **Other Phone Numbers:** Assessor 505-763-5731; Treasurer 505-763-3931; Appraiser/Auditor 505-763-5731; Elections 505-763-5591; Vital Records 505-827-0121.

De Baca County

County Clerk, PO Box 347, Fort Sumner, NM 88119. 505-355-2601; Fax 505-355-2441.
Will search UCC records. Will not search real estate records. **Other Phone Numbers:** Assessor 505-355-7448; Treasurer 505-355-7395; Elections 505-355-2601.

Dona Ana County

County Clerk, 251 W. Amador, Room 103, Las Cruces, NM 88005-2893. 505-647-7421 R/E Recording: 505-647-7420; Fax 505-647-7464. www.co.dona-ana.nm.us
This agency will not search real estate or UCC records. **Online Access:** Assessor, Real Estate, Personal Property, Voter Registration Records. Records on the Real Property database are available free online at www.co.dona-ana.nm.us/assr/search.html. Also, search the voter registration rolls for free at www.co.dona-ana.nm.us/boe/voter.html. **Other Phone Numbers:** Assessor 505-647-7400; Treasurer 505-647-7433; Appraiser/Auditor 505-647-7400; Elections 505-647-7466.

Eddy County

County Clerk, 101 W. Greene St., Room 312, Carlsbad, NM 88220. County Clerk, R/E and UCC Recording 505-885-3383; Fax 505-234-1793.
Will search UCC records. Will not search real estate records. **Other Phone Numbers:** Assessor 505-885-3813; Treasurer 505-885-9313; Appraiser/Auditor 505-885-3813; Elections 505-885-3383; Vital Records 505-827-0121.

Grant County

County Clerk, PO Box 898, Silver City, NM 88062. 505-538-2979 R/E Recording: 505-574-0042 UCC Recording: 505-574-0042; Fax 505-538-8926.
Will not search UCC records. **Other Phone Numbers:** Assessor 505-574-0030; Treasurer 505-574-0055; Appraiser/Auditor 505-574-0030; Elections 505-574-0042; Vital Records 505-574-0042.

Guadalupe County

County Clerk, 420 Parker Ave, Courthouse-Suite 1, Santa Rosa, NM 88435. 505-472-3791; Fax 505-472-3735.
Will search UCC records. **Other Phone Numbers:** Assessor 505-472-3738; Treasurer 505-472-3133; Elections 505-472-3741; Vital Records 505-472-3211.

Harding County

County Clerk, PO Box 1002, Mosquero, NM 87733-1002. County Clerk, R/E and UCC Recording 505-673-2301; Fax 505-673-2922.
This agency will not perform searches. **Other Phone Numbers:** Assessor 505-673-2926; Treasurer 505-673-2928; Appraiser/Auditor 505-673-2926; Elections 505-673-2301.

Hidalgo County

County Clerk, 300 Shakespeare St, Lordsburg, NM 88045. 505-542-9213.
Will search UCC records. This agency will not do a tax lien search. Will not search real estate records. **Other Phone Numbers:** Assessor 505-542-3433; Treasurer 505-542-9313.

Lea County

County Clerk, PO Box 1507, Lovington, NM 88260. County Clerk, R/E and UCC Recording 505-396-8531; Fax 505-396-3293. www.leacounty-nm.org
Will search UCC records. Will not search real estate records. **Other Phone Numbers:** Assessor 505-396-8527; Elections 505-396-8531.

Lincoln County

County Clerk, PO Box 338, Carrizozo, NM 88301. County Clerk, R/E and UCC Recording 505-648-2394; Fax 505-648-2576.
This agency will not search real estate or UCC records. **Other Phone Numbers:** Assessor 505-648-2306; Treasurer 505-648-2397; Appraiser/Auditor 505-648-2306; Elections 505-648-2331; Vital Records 505-648-2394; Manager 505-648-2385.

Los Alamos County

County Clerk, PO Box 30, Los Alamos, NM 87544. County Clerk, R/E and UCC Recording 505-662-8010; www.lac.losalamos.nm.us
This agency will not perform searches. **Other Phone Numbers:** Assessor 505-662-8030; Treasurer 505-662-8070; Elections 505-662-8011; Vital Records 505-827-2338.

Luna County

County Clerk, PO Box 1838, Deming, NM 88031-1838. County Clerk, R/E and UCC Recording 505-546-0491; Fax 505-546-4708.
Will search UCC records. **Other Phone Numbers:** Assessor 505-546-0404; Treasurer 505-546-0401; Elections 505-546-0491; Vital Records 505-827-0121 (Santa Fe, NM).

McKinley County

County Clerk, PO Box 1268, Gallup, NM 87301. County Clerk, R/E and UCC Recording 505-863-6866; Fax 505-863-1419.
Will not search UCC records. This agency will not do a tax lien search. Real estate owner, mortgage, and property transfer searches available. **Other Phone Numbers:** Assessor 505-863-3032; Treasurer 505-722-4459; Appraiser/Auditor 505-863-3032; Elections 505-722-4469; Vital Records 505-821-0121.

Mora County

County Clerk, PO Box 360, Mora, NM 87732-0360. 505-387-2448; Fax 505-387-9023.
Will search UCC records. **Other Phone Numbers:** Assessor 505-387-5029; Treasurer 505-387-2756; Elections 505-387-2448.

Otero County

County Clerk, 1000 New York Ave, Room 108, Alamogordo, NM 88310-6932. County Clerk, R/E and UCC Recording 505-437-4942; Fax 505-443-2922.
Will search UCC records. This agency will not do a tax lien search. Will not search real estate records. **Other Phone Numbers:** Assessor 505-437-5310; Treasurer 505-437-2030; Elections 505-437-4942.

Quay County

County Clerk, PO Box 1225, Tucumcari, NM 88401-1225. County Clerk, R/E and UCC Recording 505-461-0510; Fax 505-461-0513.
Will search UCC records. **Other Phone Numbers:** Assessor 505-461-1760; Treasurer 505-461-0470; Appraiser/Auditor 505-461-1760; Elections 505-461-0510; Vital Records 505-827-2338.

Rio Arriba County

County Clerk, PO Box 158, Tierra Amarilla, NM 87575. 505-588-7724.
Will search UCC records. This agency will not do a tax lien search. Will not search real estate records. **Other Phone Numbers:** Assessor 505-588-7726; Treasurer 505-588-7727.

Roosevelt County

County Clerk, 101 W. First, Portales, NM 88130. 505-356-8562; Fax 505-356-8562.
This agency will not search real estate or UCC records. **Other Phone Numbers:** Assessor 505-356-6971; Treasurer 505-356-4081.

San Juan County

County Clerk and Recorder, PO Box 550, Aztec, NM 87410. County Clerk and Recorder, R/E and UCC Recording 505-334-9471; Fax 505-334-3635. www.co.san-juan.nm.us
This agency will not search real estate or UCC records. **Online Access:** Real Estate, Assessor Records. Access to county real estate tax data is available free at www.co.san-juan.nm.us/Empire/CountyTax.htm.
Other Phone Numbers: Assessor 505-334-6157; Treasurer 505-334-9421; Appraiser/Auditor 505-334-6157; Elections 505-334-9471.

San Miguel County

County Clerk, Courthouse, Las Vegas, NM 87701. County Clerk, R/E and UCC Recording 505-425-9331; Fax 505-425-7019.
Will search UCC records. Will not search real estate records. **Other Phone Numbers:** Assessor 505-454-4980; Treasurer 505-425-9376; Elections 505-425-9331; Vital Records 505-425-9368.

Sandoval County

County Clerk, PO Box 40, Bernalillo, NM 87004. County Clerk, R/E and UCC Recording 505-867-7572; Fax 505-771-8610.
Will search UCC records. Will not search real estate records. **Other Phone Numbers:** Assessor 505-867-2355; Treasurer 505-867-2945; Appraiser/Auditor 505-867-7503; Elections 505-867-7577; Vital Records 505-841-4185.

Santa Fe County

County Clerk, PO Box 1985, Santa Fe, NM 87504-1985. 505-986-6280; Fax 505-995-2767.
Will search UCC records. **Other Phone Numbers:** Assessor 505-986-6308; Treasurer 505-986-6253.

Sierra County

County Clerk, 100 Date St, Truth or Consequences, NM 87901. County Clerk, R/E and UCC Recording 505-894-2840; Fax 505-894-2516.
Will search UCC records. This agency will not do a tax lien search. Will not search real estate records. **Other Phone Numbers:** Assessor 505-894-2589; Treasurer

505-894-3524; Elections 505-894-2840; Vital Records 505-827-2338.

Socorro County

County Clerk, PO Box I, Socorro, NM 87801. 505-835-3263 R/E Recording: 505-835-0423 UCC Recording: 505-835-0589; Fax 505-835-1043.
Will search UCC records. Will not search real estate records. **Other Phone Numbers:** Assessor 505-835-0714; Treasurer 505-835-1701; Appraiser/Auditor 505-835-0714; Elections 505-835-0423; Vital Records 505-835-0423.

Taos County

County Clerk, 105 Albright St, Suite D, Taos, NM 87571-. County Clerk, R/E and UCC Recording 505-751-8654; Fax 505-751-8637.
Will search UCC records. Will not search real estate records. **Other Phone Numbers:** Assessor 505-751-8651; Treasurer 505-751-8672; Appraiser/Auditor 505-751-8554; Elections 505-751-8657.

Torrance County

County Clerk, PO Box 48, Estancia, NM 87016. 505-384-2221; Fax 505-384-4080.
This agency will not search real estate or UCC records. **Other Phone Numbers:** Assessor 505-384-2331; Treasurer 505-384-2241.

Union County

County Clerk, PO Box 430, Clayton, NM 88415. County Clerk, R/E and UCC Recording 505-374-9491; Fax 505-374-2763.
Will search UCC records. Will not search real estate records. **Other Phone Numbers:** Assessor 505-374-9441; Treasurer 505-374-2331; Appraiser/Auditor 505-374-9441; Elections 505-374-9491.

Valencia County

County Clerk, PO Box 969, Los Lunas, NM 87031. County Clerk, R/E and UCC Recording 505-866-2073; Fax 505-866-2023.
Will search UCC records. **Other Phone Numbers:** Assessor 505-866-2065; Treasurer 505-866-2090; Elections 505-866-2080; Vital Records 505-841-4100.

New Mexico County Locator

You will usually be able to find the city name in the City/County Cross Reference below. In that case, it is a simple matter to determine the county from the cross reference. However, only the official US Postal Service city names are included in this index. There are an additional 40,000 place names that people use in their addresses. Therefore, we have also included a ZIP/City Cross Reference immediately following the City/County Cross Reference.

If you know the ZIP Code but the city name does not appear in the City/County Cross Reference index, look up the ZIP Code in the ZIP/City Cross Reference, find the city name, then look up the city name in the City/County Cross Reference. For example, you want to know the county for an address of Menands, NY 12204. There is no "Menands" in the City/County Cross Reference. The ZIP/City Cross Reference shows that ZIP Codes 12201-12288 are for the city of Albany. Looking back in the City/County Cross Reference, Albany is in Albany County.

City/County Cross Reference

ABIQUIU Rio Arriba
ALAMOGORDO Otero
ALBUQUERQUE Bernalillo
ALCALDE Rio Arriba
ALGODONES Sandoval
ALTO Lincoln
AMALIA Taos
AMISTAD Union
ANGEL FIRE Colfax
ANIMAS Hidalgo
ANTHONY (88021) Dona Ana(89), Otero(10)
ANTON CHICO Guadalupe
ARAGON Catron
ARENAS VALLEY Grant
ARREY Sierra
ARROYO HONDO Taos
ARROYO SECO Taos
ARTESIA Eddy
AZTEC San Juan
BARD Quay
BAYARD Grant
BELEN Valencia
BELL RANCH San Miguel
BELLVIEW Curry
BENT Otero
BERINO Dona Ana
BERNALILLO Sandoval
BINGHAM Socorro
BLANCO San Juan
BLOOMFIELD San Juan
BLUEWATER Cibola
BOSQUE (87006) Socorro(83), Valencia(16)
BOSQUE FARMS (87068) Bernalillo(97), Valencia(2)
BRIMHALL McKinley
BROADVIEW (88112) Curry(87), Quay(12)
BUCKHORN Grant
BUENA VISTA Mora
BUEYEROS Harding
CABALLO Sierra
CANJILON Rio Arriba
CANNON AFB Curry
CANONES Rio Arriba
CAPITAN Lincoln
CAPROCK Lea
CAPULIN Union
CARLSBAD Eddy
CARRIZOZO (88301) Lincoln(80), Torrance(20)
CARSON Taos
CASA BLANCA Cibola
CAUSEY Roosevelt
CEBOLLA Rio Arriba
CEDAR CREST Bernalillo
CEDARVALE Torrance
CERRILLOS Santa Fe
CERRO Taos
CHACON Mora
CHAMA Rio Arriba
CHAMBERINO Dona Ana

CHAMISAL Taos
CHIMAYO Rio Arriba
CHURCH ROCK McKinley
CIMARRON Colfax
CLAUNCH Socorro
CLAYTON Union
CLEVELAND Mora
CLIFF Grant
CLINES CORNERS Torrance
CLOUDCROFT Otero
CLOVIS Curry
COCHITI LAKE Sandoval
COCHITI PUEBLO Sandoval
COLUMBUS Luna
CONCHAS DAM San Miguel
CONTINENTAL DIVIDE McKinley
CORDOVA Rio Arriba
CORONA Lincoln
CORRALES Sandoval
COSTILLA Taos
COUNSELOR Sandoval
COYOTE Rio Arriba
CROSSROADS Lea
CROWNPOINT McKinley
CUBA Sandoval
CUBERO Cibola
CUCHILLO Sierra
CUERVO Guadalupe
DATIL Catron
DEMING Luna
DERRY Sierra
DES MOINES Union
DEXTER Chaves
DIXON Rio Arriba
DONA ANA Dona Ana
DORA Roosevelt
DULCE Rio Arriba
DURAN Torrance
EAGLE NEST Colfax
EDGEWOOD Santa Fe
EL PRADO Taos
EL RITO Rio Arriba
ELEPHANT BUTTE Sierra
ELIDA (88116) Roosevelt(95), Chaves(4)
EMBUDO Rio Arriba
ENCINO Torrance
ESPANOLA Rio Arriba
ESTANCIA Torrance
EUNICE Lea
FAIRACRES Dona Ana
FARMINGTON San Juan
FAYWOOD Grant
FENCE LAKE Cibola
FLORA VISTA San Juan
FLOYD (88118) Roosevelt(94), Curry(5)
FLYING H Chaves
FOLSOM Union
FORT BAYARD Grant
FORT STANTON Lincoln
FORT SUMNER De Baca
FORT WINGATE McKinley
FRUITLAND San Juan

GALLINA Rio Arriba
GALLUP San Juan
GAMERCO McKinley
GARFIELD Dona Ana
GARITA San Miguel
GILA Grant
GLADSTONE Union
GLENCOE Lincoln
GLENRIO Quay
GLENWOOD Catron
GLORIETA Santa Fe
GONZALES RANCH San Miguel
GRADY (88120) Quay(80), Curry(19)
GRANTS Cibola
GRENVILLE Union
GUADALUPITA Mora
HACHITA Grant
HAGERMAN Chaves
HANOVER Grant
HATCH Dona Ana
HERNANDEZ Rio Arriba
HIGH ROLLS MOUNTAIN PARK Otero
HILLSBORO Sierra
HOBBS Lea
HOLLOMAN AIR FORCE BASE Otero
HOLMAN Mora
HONDO Lincoln
HOPE (88250) Chaves(60), Eddy(39)
HOUSE Quay
HURLEY Grant
ILFELD San Miguel
ISLETA Bernalillo
JAL Lea
JAMESTOWN McKinley
JARALES Valencia
JEMEZ PUEBLO Sandoval
JEMEZ SPRINGS Sandoval
KENNA Roosevelt
KIRTLAND San Juan
KIRTLAND AFB Bernalillo
LA JARA Sandoval
LA JOYA Socorro
LA LOMA Guadalupe
LA LUZ Otero
LA MADERA Rio Arriba
LA MESA Dona Ana
LA PLATA San Juan
LAGUNA Cibola
LAKE ARTHUR (88253) Chaves(97), Eddy(2)
LAKEWOOD Eddy
LAMY Santa Fe
LAS CRUCES Dona Ana
LAS TABLAS Rio Arriba
LAS VEGAS San Miguel
LEDOUX Mora
LEMITAR Socorro
LINCOLN Lincoln
LINDRITH Rio Arriba
LINGO Roosevelt
LLANO Taos
LOCO HILLS Eddy

LOGAN Quay
LORDSBURG Hidalgo
LOS ALAMOS Los Alamos
LOS LUNAS Valencia
LOS OJOS Rio Arriba
LOVING Eddy
LOVINGTON Lea
LUMBERTON Rio Arriba
LUNA Catron
MAGDALENA Socorro
MALAGA Eddy
MALJAMAR Lea
MAXWELL Colfax
MAYHILL (88339) Otero(79), Chaves(20)
MC ALISTER Quay
MC DONALD Lea
MC INTOSH Torrance
MEDANALES Rio Arriba
MELROSE (88124) Curry(80), Quay(12), Roosevelt(6)
MENTMORE McKinley
MESCALERO Otero
MESILLA Dona Ana
MESILLA PARK Dona Ana
MESQUITE Dona Ana
MEXICAN SPRINGS McKinley
MIAMI Colfax
MILAN Cibola
MILLS Harding
MILNESAND Roosevelt
MIMBRES Grant
MONTEZUMA San Miguel
MONTICELLO Sierra
MONUMENT Lea
MORA Mora
MORIARTY Torrance
MOSQUERO Harding
MOUNT DORA Union
MOUNTAINAIR Torrance
MULE CREEK Grant
NAGEEZI San Juan
NARA VISA Quay
NAVAJO (87328) McKinley(85), San Juan(14)
NAVAJO DAM San Juan
NEW LAGUNA Cibola
NEWCOMB San Juan
NEWKIRK Guadalupe
NOGAL Lincoln
OCATE Mora
OIL CENTER Lea
OJO CALIENTE Taos
OJO FELIZ Mora
OJO SARCO Rio Arriba
ORGAN Dona Ana
OROGRANDE Otero
PAGUATE Cibola
PECOS San Miguel
PENA BLANCA Sandoval
PENASCO Taos
PEP Roosevelt
PERALTA Valencia

PETACA Rio Arriba
PICACHO Lincoln
PIE TOWN Catron
PINEHILL Cibola
PINON (88344) Chaves(85), Otero(14)
PINOS ALTOS Grant
PLACITAS Sandoval
PLAYAS Hidalgo
POLVADERA Socorro
PONDEROSA Sandoval
PORTALES Roosevelt
PREWITT McKinley
PUEBLO OF ACOMA Valencia
QUAY Quay
QUEMADO Catron
QUESTA Taos
RADIUM SPRINGS Dona Ana
RAINSVILLE Mora
RAMAH (87321) McKinley(52), Cibola(47)
RANCHOS DE TAOS Taos
RATON Colfax
RED RIVER Taos
REDROCK Grant
REGINA Sandoval
REHOBOTH McKinley
RESERVE Catron
RIBERA San Miguel
RINCON Dona Ana
RIO RANCHO Bernalillo
ROCIADA (87742) Mora(70), San
   Miguel(30)
RODARTE Taos
RODEO Hidalgo
ROGERS Roosevelt

ROSWELL Chaves
ROWE San Miguel
ROY Harding
RUIDOSO Lincoln
RUIDOSO DOWNS Lincoln
RUTHERON Rio Arriba
SACRAMENTO Otero
SAINT VRAIN Curry
SALEM Dona Ana
SAN ACACIA Socorro
SAN ANTONIO Socorro
SAN CRISTOBAL Taos
SAN FIDEL Cibola
SAN JON Quay
SAN JOSE San Miguel
SAN JUAN PUEBLO Rio Arriba
SAN MATEO Cibola
SAN MIGUEL Dona Ana
SAN PATRICIO Lincoln
SAN RAFAEL Cibola
SAN YSIDRO Sandoval
SANDIA PARK (87047) Santa Fe(51),
   Bernalillo(48)
SANOSTEE San Juan
SANTA CLARA Grant
SANTA CRUZ Santa Fe
SANTA FE Santa Fe
SANTA ROSA Guadalupe
SANTA TERESA Dona Ana
SANTO DOMINGO PUEBLO Sandoval
SAPELLO San Miguel
SEBOYETA Cibola
SEDAN Union
SENA San Miguel

SENECA Union
SERAFINA San Miguel
SHEEP SPRINGS San Juan
SHIPROCK San Juan
SILVER CITY Grant
SMITH LAKE McKinley
SOCORRO Socorro
SOLANO Harding
SPRINGER Colfax
STANLEY Santa Fe
STEAD Union
SUNLAND PARK Dona Ana
SUNSPOT Otero
TAIBAN (88134) De Baca(71),
   Roosevelt(20), Quay(8)
TAJIQUE Torrance
TAOS Taos
TAOS SKI VALLEY Taos
TATUM Lea
TERERRO San Miguel
TESUQUE Santa Fe
TEXICO Curry
THOREAU McKinley
TIERRA AMARILLA Rio Arriba
TIJERAS Bernalillo
TIMBERON Otero
TINNIE Lincoln
TOHATCHI McKinley
TOME Valencia
TORREON Torrance
TRAMPAS Taos
TREMENTINA San Miguel
TRES PIEDRAS Taos
TRUCHAS Rio Arriba

TRUTH OR CONSEQUENCES Sierra
TUCUMCARI Quay
TULAROSA Otero
TYRONE Grant
UTE PARK Colfax
VADITO Taos
VADO Dona Ana
VALDEZ Taos
VALLECITOS Rio Arriba
VALMORA Mora
VANADIUM Grant
VANDERWAGEN McKinley
VAUGHN Guadalupe
VEGUITA Socorro
VELARDE Rio Arriba
VILLANUEVA San Miguel
WAGON MOUND Mora
WATERFLOW San Juan
WATROUS Mora
WEED Otero
WHITE SANDS MISSILE RANGE Dona
   Ana
WHITES CITY Eddy
WILLARD Torrance
WILLIAMSBURG Sierra
WINSTON Sierra
YATAHEY McKinley
YESO De Baca
YOUNGSVILLE Rio Arriba
ZUNI McKinley

ZIP/City Cross Reference

87001-87001   ALGODONES
87002-87002   BELEN
87004-87004   BERNALILLO
87005-87005   BLUEWATER
87006-87006   BOSQUE
87007-87007   CASA BLANCA
87008-87008   CEDAR CREST
87009-87009   CEDARVALE
87010-87010   CERRILLOS
87011-87011   CLAUNCH
87012-87012   COYOTE
87013-87013   CUBA
87014-87014   CUBERO
87015-87015   EDGEWOOD
87016-87016   ESTANCIA
87017-87017   GALLINA
87018-87018   COUNSELOR
87020-87020   GRANTS
87021-87021   MILAN
87022-87022   ISLETA
87023-87023   JARALES
87024-87024   JEMEZ PUEBLO
87025-87025   JEMEZ SPRINGS
87026-87026   LAGUNA
87027-87027   LA JARA
87028-87028   LA JOYA
87029-87029   LINDRITH
87031-87031   LOS LUNAS
87032-87032   MC INTOSH
87034-87034   PUEBLO OF ACOMA
87035-87035   MORIARTY
87036-87036   MOUNTAINAIR
87037-87037   NAGEEZI
87038-87038   NEW LAGUNA
87040-87040   PAGUATE
87041-87041   PENA BLANCA
87042-87042   PERALTA
87043-87043   PLACITAS
87044-87044   PONDEROSA
87045-87045   PREWITT
87046-87046   REGINA
87047-87047   SANDIA PARK
87048-87048   CORRALES

87049-87049   SAN FIDEL
87050-87050   SAN MATEO
87051-87051   SAN RAFAEL
87052-87052   SANTO DOMINGO PUEBLO
87053-87053   SAN YSIDRO
87055-87055   SEBOYETA
87056-87056   STANLEY
87057-87057   TAJIQUE
87059-87059   TIJERAS
87060-87060   TOME
87061-87061   TORREON
87062-87062   VEGUITA
87063-87063   WILLARD
87064-87064   YOUNGSVILLE
87068-87068   BOSQUE FARMS
87070-87070   CLINES CORNERS
87072-87072   COCHITI PUEBLO
87083-87083   COCHITI LAKE
87100-87116   ALBUQUERQUE
87117-87117   KIRTLAND AFB
87118-87123   ALBUQUERQUE
87124-87124   RIO RANCHO
87125-87158   ALBUQUERQUE
87174-87174   RIO RANCHO
87176-87201   ALBUQUERQUE
87300-87305   GALLUP
87310-87310   BRIMHALL
87311-87311   CHURCH ROCK
87312-87312   CONTINENTAL DIVIDE
87313-87313   CROWNPOINT
87315-87315   FENCE LAKE
87316-87316   FORT WINGATE
87317-87317   GAMERCO
87319-87319   MENTMORE
87320-87320   MEXICAN SPRINGS
87321-87321   RAMAH
87322-87322   REHOBOTH
87323-87323   THOREAU
87324-87324   GALLUP
87325-87325   TOHATCHI
87326-87326   VANDERWAGEN
87327-87327   ZUNI
87328-87328   NAVAJO

87347-87347   JAMESTOWN
87357-87357   PINEHILL
87364-87364   SHEEP SPRINGS
87365-87365   SMITH LAKE
87375-87375   YATAHEY
87401-87402   FARMINGTON
87410-87410   AZTEC
87412-87412   BLANCO
87413-87413   BLOOMFIELD
87415-87415   FLORA VISTA
87416-87416   FRUITLAND
87417-87417   KIRTLAND
87418-87418   LA PLATA
87419-87419   NAVAJO DAM
87420-87420   SHIPROCK
87421-87421   WATERFLOW
87455-87455   NEWCOMB
87461-87461   SANOSTEE
87499-87499   FARMINGTON
87500-87509   SANTA FE
87510-87510   ABIQUIU
87511-87511   ALCALDE
87512-87512   AMALIA
87513-87513   ARROYO HONDO
87514-87514   ARROYO SECO
87515-87515   CANJILON
87516-87516   CANONES
87517-87517   CARSON
87518-87518   CEBOLLA
87519-87519   CERRO
87520-87520   CHAMA
87521-87521   CHAMISAL
87522-87522   CHIMAYO
87523-87523   CORDOVA
87524-87524   COSTILLA
87525-87525   TAOS SKI VALLEY
87527-87527   DIXON
87528-87528   DULCE
87529-87529   EL PRADO
87530-87530   EL RITO
87531-87531   EMBUDO
87532-87533   ESPANOLA
87535-87535   GLORIETA

87536-87536   GONZALES RANCH
87537-87537   HERNANDEZ
87538-87538   ILFELD
87539-87539   LA MADERA
87540-87540   LAMY
87541-87541   LAS TABLAS
87543-87543   LLANO
87544-87545   LOS ALAMOS
87547-87547   LUMBERTON
87548-87548   MEDANALES
87549-87549   OJO CALIENTE
87550-87550   OJO SARCO
87551-87551   LOS OJOS
87552-87552   PECOS
87553-87553   PENASCO
87554-87554   PETACA
87556-87556   QUESTA
87557-87557   RANCHOS DE TAOS
87558-87558   RED RIVER
87560-87560   RIBERA
87561-87561   RODARTE
87562-87562   ROWE
87563-87563   RUTHERON
87564-87564   SAN CRISTOBAL
87565-87565   SAN JOSE
87566-87566   SAN JUAN PUEBLO
87567-87567   SANTA CRUZ
87568-87568   SENA
87569-87569   SERAFINA
87571-87571   TAOS
87573-87573   TERERRO
87574-87574   TESUQUE
87575-87575   TIERRA AMARILLA
87576-87576   TRAMPAS
87577-87577   TRES PIEDRAS
87578-87578   TRUCHAS
87579-87579   VADITO
87580-87580   VALDEZ
87581-87581   VALLECITOS
87582-87582   VELARDE
87583-87583   VILLANUEVA
87592-87594   SANTA FE
87701-87701   LAS VEGAS

87710-87710 ANGEL FIRE	87941-87941 SALEM	88114-88114 CROSSROADS	88330-88330 HOLLOMAN AIR FORCE
87711-87711 ANTON CHICO	87942-87942 WILLIAMSBURG	88115-88115 DORA	BASE
87712-87712 BUENA VISTA	87943-87943 WINSTON	88116-88116 ELIDA	88336-88336 HONDO
87713-87713 CHACON	88000-88001 LAS CRUCES	88118-88118 FLOYD	88337-88337 LA LUZ
87714-87714 CIMARRON	88002-88002 WHITE SANDS MISSILE	88119-88119 FORT SUMNER	88338-88338 LINCOLN
87715-87715 CLEVELAND	RANGE	88120-88120 GRADY	88339-88339 MAYHILL
87718-87718 EAGLE NEST	88003-88006 LAS CRUCES	88121-88121 HOUSE	88340-88340 MESCALERO
87722-87722 GUADALUPITA	88008-88008 SANTA TERESA	88122-88122 KENNA	88341-88341 NOGAL
87723-87723 HOLMAN	88009-88009 PLAYAS	88123-88123 LINGO	88342-88342 OROGRANDE
87724-87724 LA LOMA	88011-88012 LAS CRUCES	88124-88124 MELROSE	88343-88343 PICACHO
87725-87725 LEDOUX	88020-88020 ANIMAS	88125-88125 MILNESAND	88344-88344 PINON
87728-87728 MAXWELL	88021-88021 ANTHONY	88126-88126 PEP	88345-88345 RUIDOSO
87729-87729 MIAMI	88022-88022 ARENAS VALLEY	88130-88130 PORTALES	88346-88346 RUIDOSO DOWNS
87730-87730 MILLS	88023-88023 BAYARD	88132-88132 ROGERS	88347-88347 SACRAMENTO
87731-87731 MONTEZUMA	88024-88024 BERINO	88133-88133 SAINT VRAIN	88348-88348 SAN PATRICIO
87732-87732 MORA	88025-88025 BUCKHORN	88134-88134 TAIBAN	88349-88349 SUNSPOT
87733-87733 MOSQUERO	88026-88026 SANTA CLARA	88135-88135 TEXICO	88350-88350 TIMBERON
87734-87734 OCATE	88027-88027 CHAMBERINO	88136-88136 YESO	88351-88351 TINNIE
87735-87735 OJO FELIZ	88028-88028 CLIFF	88201-88203 ROSWELL	88352-88352 TULAROSA
87736-87736 RAINSVILLE	88029-88029 COLUMBUS	88210-88211 ARTESIA	88353-88353 VAUGHN
87740-87740 RATON	88030-88031 DEMING	88213-88213 CAPROCK	88354-88354 WEED
87742-87742 ROCIADA	88032-88032 DONA ANA	88220-88221 CARLSBAD	88355-88355 RUIDOSO
87743-87743 ROY	88033-88033 FAIRACRES	88230-88230 DEXTER	88401-88401 TUCUMCARI
87745-87745 SAPELLO	88034-88034 FAYWOOD	88231-88231 EUNICE	88410-88410 AMISTAD
87746-87746 SOLANO	88036-88036 FORT BAYARD	88232-88232 HAGERMAN	88411-88411 BARD
87747-87747 SPRINGER	88038-88038 GILA	88240-88244 HOBBS	88412-88412 BUEYEROS
87749-87749 UTE PARK	88039-88039 GLENWOOD	88250-88250 HOPE	88414-88414 CAPULIN
87750-87750 VALMORA	88040-88040 HACHITA	88252-88252 JAL	88415-88415 CLAYTON
87752-87752 WAGON MOUND	88041-88041 HANOVER	88253-88253 LAKE ARTHUR	88416-88416 CONCHAS DAM
87753-87753 WATROUS	88042-88042 HILLSBORO	88254-88254 LAKEWOOD	88417-88417 CUERVO
87801-87801 SOCORRO	88043-88043 HURLEY	88255-88255 LOCO HILLS	88418-88418 DES MOINES
87815-87815 BINGHAM	88044-88044 LA MESA	88256-88256 LOVING	88419-88419 FOLSOM
87820-87820 ARAGON	88045-88045 LORDSBURG	88260-88260 LOVINGTON	88421-88421 GARITA
87821-87821 DATIL	88046-88046 MESILLA	88262-88262 MC DONALD	88422-88422 GLADSTONE
87823-87823 LEMITAR	88047-88047 MESILLA PARK	88263-88263 MALAGA	88423-88423 GLENRIO
87824-87824 LUNA	88048-88048 MESQUITE	88264-88264 MALJAMAR	88424-88424 GRENVILLE
87825-87825 MAGDALENA	88049-88049 MIMBRES	88265-88265 MONUMENT	88426-88426 LOGAN
87827-87827 PIE TOWN	88051-88051 MULE CREEK	88266-88266 OIL CENTER	88427-88427 MC ALISTER
87828-87828 POLVADERA	88052-88052 ORGAN	88267-88267 TATUM	88429-88429 MOUNT DORA
87829-87829 QUEMADO	88053-88053 PINOS ALTOS	88268-88268 WHITES CITY	88430-88430 NARA VISA
87830-87830 RESERVE	88054-88054 RADIUM SPRINGS	88301-88301 CARRIZOZO	88431-88431 NEWKIRK
87831-87831 SAN ACACIA	88055-88055 REDROCK	88310-88311 ALAMOGORDO	88432-88432 SANTA ROSA
87832-87832 SAN ANTONIO	88056-88056 RODEO	88312-88312 ALTO	88433-88433 QUAY
87901-87901 TRUTH OR	88058-88058 SAN MIGUEL	88314-88314 BENT	88434-88434 SAN JON
CONSEQUENCES	88061-88062 SILVER CITY	88316-88316 CAPITAN	88435-88435 SANTA ROSA
87930-87930 ARREY	88063-88063 SUNLAND PARK	88317-88317 CLOUDCROFT	88436-88436 SEDAN
87931-87931 CABALLO	88065-88065 TYRONE	88318-88318 CORONA	88437-88437 SENECA
87932-87932 CUCHILLO	88072-88072 VADO	88319-88319 DURAN	88438-88438 STEAD
87933-87933 DERRY	88073-88073 VANADIUM	88321-88321 ENCINO	88439-88439 TREMENTINA
87935-87935 ELEPHANT BUTTE	88101-88102 CLOVIS	88322-88322 FLYING H	88441-88441 BELL RANCH
87936-87936 GARFIELD	88103-88103 CANNON AFB	88323-88323 FORT STANTON	
87937-87937 HATCH	88111-88111 BELLVIEW	88324-88324 GLENCOE	
87939-87939 MONTICELLO	88112-88112 BROADVIEW	88325-88325 HIGH ROLLS MOUNTAIN	
87940-87940 RINCON	88113-88113 CAUSEY	PARK	

New York

General Help Numbers:

Governor's Office
Executive Chamber, State Capitol   518-474-8390
Albany, NY 12224
www.state.ny.us/governor   9AM-5PM

Attorney General's Office
State Capitol   518-474-7330
Albany, NY 12224-0341   Fax 518-473-9909
www.oag.state.ny.us   9AM-5:30PM

State Court Administrator
Empire State Plaza   518-473-1196
Agency Bldg #4, Suite 2001   Fax 518-473-6860
Albany, NY 12223   9AM-5PM
www.courts.state.ny.us

State Court Administrator-NYC
New York City Office   212-428-2100
25 Beaver St   Fax 212-428-2190
New York, NY 10004   9AM-5PM
www.courts.state.ny.us

State Specifics:

Capital: Albany
    Albany County

Time Zone: EST

Number of Counties: 62

Population: 19,011,378

Web Site: www.state.ny.us

State Archives
Empire State Plaza   518-474-8955
Cultural Education Center Rm 11D40   Fax 518-473-9985
Albany, NY 12230   9AM-5PM
www.sara.nysed.gov

State Agencies

Criminal Records

Access to Records is Restricted

Division of Criminal Justice Services, 4 Tower Place, Albany, NY 12203; 518-457-6043, 518-457-6550 (Fax), 8AM-5PM.

www.criminaljustice.state.ny.us

Note: Records are only released pursuant to court order, subpoena, to entities authorized by statute, or to person of record. 99% of records are fingerprint supported. The public must search at the county court level. The sex offender registry Level 3 can be searched at www.criminaljustice.state.ny.us/nsor/index.htm.

Corporation Records
Limited Partnership Records
Limited Liability Company Records
Limited Liability Partnerships

Division of Corporations, Department of State, 41 State St, Albany, NY 12231; 518-473-2492 (General Information), 900-835-2677 (Corporate Searches), 518-474-1418 (Fax), 8AM-4:30PM.

www.dos.state.ny.us

Note: Information available includes date of incorporation, subsequent filings, status, principle business location, registered agent, service of process address, number and type of stock shares entitled to issue, and biennial statements w/addresses.

Indexing & Storage: Records are available from inception. Information on active entities is automated. Records on entities inactive prior to 1978 are not automated and require additional research. New records are available for inquiry immediately.

Searching: All data is considered public information. Include the following in your request: full name of business.

Access by: mail, phone, in person, online.

Fee & Payment: There is no fee for basic information up to 5 names. Over 5 names, the fee is $5.00 per name. For documents, the certification fee is $10.00, $25.00 if SOS seal is required. The fee is $5.00 for every name availability checked. Fee payee: New York Department of State. Payments must be by check, money order, credit card or drawdown account.

Mail search: Turnaround time: 1 week. A self addressed stamped envelope is requested.

Phone search: Call 1-900-TEL-CORP. You may search up to 5 names per call for a flat rate charge of $4.00 per call.

In person search: The general public may obtain copies of documents and certificates under seal while they wait ONLY if expedited fees are paid.

Expedited service: Expedited service is available for mail, phone and in person searches. Turnaround time: 24 hours. Fees are $150 for 2-hour service; $75 for same day service and $25 for 24-hour service.

Online search: A commercial account can be set up for direct access. Fee is $.75 per transaction through a drawdown account. There is an extensive amount of information available including historical information. Also, the Division's corporate and business entity database may be accessed via the Internet without charge. Historical information is not available, nor is it real time. The Internet files are updated weekly. The web has not for profit corporations, limited partnerships, limited liability companies and limited liability partnerships as well.

Other access: You may submit an e-mail search request at corporations@dos.state.ny.us.

Trademarks/Servicemarks

Department of State, Miscellaneous Records, 41 State St, Albany, NY 12231; 518-474-4770, 518-473-0730 (Fax), 8:30AM-4:30PM.

http://dos.state.ny.us

Indexing & Storage: Records are available for past 10 years. It takes 1 to 2 weeks before new records are available for inquiry.

Searching: Searches are only done on registered marks, not on pending marks. You need to provide written description of design or features of the mark.

Access by: mail, phone, fax, in person.

Fee & Payment: The first two requests by mail, fax, or phone are free. Additional requests cost $5.00 per search. Fee payee: New York Department of State. Prepayment required. Payments of more than $500.00 must be certified check or money order; personal checks accepted for amounts less than $500.00 Personal checks accepted. No credit cards accepted.

Mail search: Turnaround time: 2 to 3 days. A self addressed stamped envelope is requested.

Phone search: Limited verification information is available.

Fax search: Turnaround time is 2-3 days. There is a $.50 fee per page to return results by fax.

In person search: No fee for request. You can request 1 search in person.

Other access: New marks can be photocopied and sent out on a regular monthly basis. Fees are determined by numbers of marks.

Uniform Commercial Code
Federal Tax Liens
State Tax Liens

UCC Division, Department of State, 41 State Street, Albany, NY 12231; 518-474-4763, 518-474-5418, 518-474-4478 (Fax), 8AM-4:30PM.

www.dos.state.ny.us/corp/uccfaq.html

Indexing & Storage: Records are available from 1964. Records are computerized from 1/96. Records are indexed on computer, microfilm.

Searching: Use search request form UCC-11. Federal tax liens on businesses will be included. Lists of state tax liens (warrants) are available, but must be searched separately on premises. Federal tax liens on individuals are filed at the county level. Include the following in your request: debtor name. It is suggested for written requests that the form be 5" x 8" or use a UCC-11.

Access by: mail, in person.

Fee & Payment: UCC search is $7.00 per debtor name, one name per form. Individual debtor names should list addresses. The copy fee is $1.50 per page. You can search state tax liens, in person, at no charge. Fee payee: Department of State. Prepayment required. All checks over $500.00 must be certified. No credit cards accepted.

Mail search: Turnaround time: 2 days. No self addressed stamped envelope is required.

In person search: You may request information in person.

Other access: The state offers its database for sale on microfilm.

Sales Tax Registrations

Sales Tax Registration Bureau, WA Harriman Campus, Building 8, Rm 408, Albany, NY 12227; 518-457-0572, 800-CALLTAX, 518-457-0453 (Fax), 7AM-5PM.

Indexing & Storage: Records are available for current records only. Records are computerized since 1970.

Searching: This agency will confirm that a business is registered and release the legal name. Include the following in your request: business name. They will also search by tax permit number or federal tax number.

Access by: mail, phone, fax, in person.

Mail search: Turnaround time: 2 to 3 weeks. A self addressed stamped envelope is requested. No fee for mail request.

Phone search: No fee for telephone request.

Fax search: Fax searching available.

In person search: No fee for request.

Birth Certificates

Vital Records Section, Certification Unit, PO Box 2602, Albany, NY 12220-2602; 518-474-3038, 518-474-3077, 877-854-4481 (Searching), 877-854-4607 (Fax), 8:30AM-4:30PM.

www.health.state.ny.us

Note: For records from New York City information, see that profile. Records may be ordered online from web site via Vitalchek.

Indexing & Storage: Records are available from 1881 on. New records are available for inquiry immediately. Records are indexed on microfiche, inhouse computer.

Searching: May only obtain your own or a dependent child's records, without notarized release. They will not return records to a PO Box or an "in care of." Include the following in your request: full name, names of parents, mother's maiden name, date of birth, place of birth, relationship to person of record, reason for information request. Requester must show or include valid identification.

Access by: mail, phone, fax, in person.

Fee & Payment: The fee is $15.00 per name per record for a 3-year search. Fee payee: New York State Department of Health. Prepayment required. Personal checks accepted. Credit cards accepted: MasterCard, Visa, AmEx, Discover.

Mail search: Turnaround time: 2 to 3 months. Turnaround time will be 2 weeks if you send your request by Express Mail. A self addressed stamped envelope is requested.

Phone search: Use of a credit card is required, there is an additional $8.95 fee. Turnaround time is 1 week.

Fax search: Same criteria as phone searches.

In person: Results are still returned by mail.

Expedited service: Expedited service is available for mail, phone and fax searches. Add $8.95 for use of credit card and $11.00 for express delivery.

Death Records

Vital Records Section, Certification Unit, 733 Broadway, Albany, NY 12207 (Courier: PO Box 2602, Albany, NY 12220-2602); 518-474-3038, 518-474-3077, 518-474-9168 (Fax), 8:30AM-4:30PM.

www.health.state.ny.us

Note: For New York City, see the separate entry. Records may be ordered online from web site via Vitalchek.

Indexing & Storage: Records are available from 1880 on. New records are available for inquiry immediately. Records are indexed on microfiche, inhouse computer.

Searching: You must show cause why record is needed on letterhead, if not member of the immediate family. Include the following in your request: full name, date of death, place of death, relationship to person of record, reason for information request, and telephone number.

Access by: mail, in person.

Fee & Payment: The fee is $15.00 per record. Use of credit card adds $8.95. Fee payee: New York State Department of Health. Prepayment required. Personal checks accepted. Credit cards accepted: MasterCard, Visa, AmEx, Discover.

Mail search: Turnaround time: 2 to 3 months. If request is sent by express mail, turnaround time shortened to 2 weeks. A self addressed stamped envelope is requested.

In person search: Turnaround time shortened by mail time only.

Expedited service: Expedited service is available for mail, phone and fax searches. Use of credit card is required, add $10.50 for overnight delivery.

Marriage Certificates

Vital Records Section, Certification Unit, 733 Broadway, Albany, NY 12207 (Courier: PO Box 2602, Albany, NY 12220-2602); 518-474-3038, 518-474-3077, 8:30AM-4:30PM.

www.health.state.ny.us

Note: For New York City information, see the separate entry. Records may be ordered online from web site via Vitalchek.

Indexing & Storage: Records are available from 1881 on. New records are available for inquiry immediately. Records are indexed on microfiche, inhouse computer.

Searching: Must have a notarized release form from persons of record or immediate family member for investigative purposes. Include the following in your request: names of husband and wife, date of marriage, place or county of marriage, relationship to person of record, reason for information request, wife's maiden name.

Access by: mail, in person.

Fee & Payment: The fee is $5.00 per record (for 1-3 years, additional years cost more). Also, there is a $8.95 fee to use a credit card. Fee payee: New York State Department of Health. Prepayment required. Personal checks accepted. Credit cards accepted: MasterCard, Visa, AmEx, Discover.

Mail search: Turnaround time: 2 to 3 months. Turnaround time is 2 weeks if request is sent by overnight express mail. A self addressed stamped envelope is requested.

In person search: Turnaround time shortened by mail time only.

Expedited service: Expedited service is available for mail, phone and fax searches. Add credit card fee and express delivery fee ($10.50).

Divorce Records

Vital Records Section, Certification Unit, 733 Broadway, Albany, NY 12207 (Courier: PO Box 2602, Albany, NY 12220-2602); 518-474-3038, 518-474-3077, 8:30AM-4:30PM.

www.health.state.ny.us

Note: For New York City information, see the separate entry.

Indexing & Storage: Records are available from 1963 on. New records are available for inquiry immediately. Records are indexed on microfiche, inhouse computer.

Searching: If you are not a party to the divorce you must have a court order to obtain records or show legal cause. Include the following in your request: names of husband and wife, date of divorce, place of divorce, relationship to person of record, reason for information request, and your telepphone number.

Access by: mail, in person.

Fee & Payment: The fee is $15.00 for searching 1994 to present; $25.00 for 1975-1994; $35 for search from 1963-1994. Add $8.95 for use of credit card. Fee payee: New York State

Department of Health. Prepayment required. Personal checks accepted. Credit cards accepted: MasterCard, Visa, AmEx, Discover.

Mail search: Turnaround time: 2 to 3 months. A self addressed stamped envelope is requested.

In person search: Turnaround time shortened by mail time only.

Expedited service: Expedited service is available for mail, phone and fax searches. Plus $8.95 for using a credit card and $10.50 for express delivery.

Birth Certificate-NYC
Death Records-NYC

Department of Health, Bureau of Vital Records, 125 Worth St, Rm 133, New York, NY 10013; 212-788-4520, 212-442-1999, 212-962-6105 (Fax), 9AM-4PM.

www.nyc.gov/html/doh

Note: Records may be ordered online from web site via Vitalchek.

Indexing & Storage: Records are available from 1910 to present for birth and from 1949 forward for death. For prior records, call Municipal Archives at 212-788-8580. It takes 2 months before new records are available for inquiry. Records are indexed on microfiche, inhouse computer.

Searching: Must have a notarized signed release from immediate family member. Include a copy of your photo ID. Include the following in your request: full name, date of birth, date of death, place of birth, place of death, reason for information request, name of the hospital. Parents' names are also required, mother's maiden name for birth.

Access by: mail, phone, fax, in person.

Fee & Payment: The fee is $15.00 per record plus $5.50 if using a credit card. Only those parties appearing on the birth record may order via a credit card. All other parties must order by mail or in-person and show cause or reason for the request. Fee payee: Department of Health. Prepayment required. Personal checks accepted. Credit cards accepted: MasterCard, Visa, AmEx, Discover.

Mail search: Allow 3-4 weeks for a birth record and 8-10 weeks for a death record. A self addressed stamped envelope is requested.

Phone search: Birth only. Use of credit card is required. Turnaround time is 5-7 days.

Fax search: Same criteria as phone searching.

In person search: Turnaround time is usually while you wait.

Expedited service: Expedited service is available for fax searches. Turnaround time: 1 to 2 days. Add $11.00 for delivery service. The $15.00 search fee and $5.00 credit card fee must also be included.

Marriage Certificate-NYC

City Clerk's Office, Department of Records & Information Services, 1 Centre Street, Rm 252, New York, NY 10007; 212-669-8898, 8AM-4PM M-F.

Note: Records from 1866-1929 can be obtained from the Municipal Archives at 212-788-8580. Records from 1995 forward can be obtained from

the City Clerk's Borough Office. Call this office for further information.

Indexing & Storage: Records are available from 1930 to present.

Searching: Current records are not public information and are only available to the parties involved or their authorization or to legal representatives for litigation purposes.

Access by: mail, in person.

Fee & Payment: Search fee of $15.00 includes certification. Each additional year searched is add'l $1.00. Additional copies same search are $10.00 each. Fee payee: City Clerk. Prepayment required. No personal checks accepted, except attorneys.

Mail search: Turnaround time: 6-8 weeks.

In person: Searching is available in person.

Divorce Records-NYC

New York County Clerk's Office, Division of Old Records, 60 Centre Street, Rm 141B, New York City, NY 10007; 212-374-4376, 9AM-3PM, M-F.

Note: Records of divorces from 1979 to 1991 can be found at 31 Chambers St, Room 703. This is open Tuesdays and Thursdays from 9-1 and 2-5. Call for specific details.

Indexing & Storage: Records are available from 1955 to 1970 on index cards, computerized since 1971.

Searching: Manhattan records are limited by statute to parties or attorneys of record or with notarized authorization from party involved.

Access by: mail, in person.

Fee & Payment: Fee is $8.00 for the search and a certified copy. Fee payee: New York County Clerk. Prepayment required. On site requests require cash; mail requests require postal money order or certified check. No credit cards accepted.

Mail search: Turnaround time: 2 weeks.

In person search: You may make copies at $.25 per page. Go to basement, either room 103 or room 141 and bring identification.

Workers' Compensation Records

NY Workers' Compensation Board, Director of Claims Office, 250 J Street, 9th Fl, Brooklyn, NY 11201; 718-222-5100, 718-222-2391 (Fax), 9AM-5PM.

www.wcb.state.ny.us

Note: File copies of records are not released for employment purposes, even with a signed release.

Indexing & Storage: Records are available for up to 18 years after the case is closed. Older records are destroyed. New records are available for inquiry immediately. Records are indexed on inhouse computer.

Searching: Must have a notarized release from claimant naming requesting party and stating the purpose for which information is going to be used to access case files. Include the following in your request: claimant name, Social Security Number, claim number, date of accident.

Access by: mail, in person.

Fee & Payment: There is a $10.00 "mailing and handling fee" but no search fee. Copies are $.25 each. Fee payee: Workers' Compensation Board.

Prepayment required. Personal checks accepted. No credit cards accepted.

Mail search: Turnaround time: 2 weeks. No self addressed stamped envelope is required.

In person search: Turnaround time is while you wait.

Driver Records

Department of Motor Vehicles, MV-15 Processing, 6 Empire State Plaza, Room 430, Albany, NY 12228; 518-473-5595, 800-225-5368 (In-state), 8AM-5PM.

www.nydmv.state.ny.us

Note: Copies of tickets may be purchased from the same address for a fee of $6.00 per ticket.

Indexing & Storage: Records are available for 3 years in addition to the current year for moving violations, 10 years for DWIs, and indefinitely for open (4 years for closed) suspensions. Most non-moving violations are not shown on record. It takes a few days after conviction before new records are available for inquiry. Records are normally destroyed after 5 years from expiration.

Searching: New York restricts the release of personal information on driving records to casual requesters. However, they will provide a "masked" abstract that contains no personal information. This record is only available from the DMV Albany Central Office. The driver's license number (ID#), name, and DOB are required when ordering a record. Use Form MV-15.

Access by: mail, phone, in person, online.

Fee & Payment: The fee is $5.00 per record search, $4.00 if online or by tape. Fee payee: Department of Motor Vehicles. Prepayment required. Escrow accounts can be set up for high volume users. Personal checks accepted. No credit cards accepted.

Mail search: Turnaround time: 4 to 6 weeks. Form MV-15 is required when ordering. A self addressed stamped envelope is requested.

Phone search: Only drivers wishing to obtain their own record may call. The DL# or name, DOB and sex are required when ordered. Payment by a credit card is required and an additional $5.00 is charged.

In person search: Records can be ordered from most any county-operated motor vehicle office and at the state offices in Albany. A photo ID of the requester and use of Form MV-15C is required.

Online search: NY has implemented a "Dial-In Inquiry" system which enables customers to obtain data online 24 hours a day. The DL# or name, DOB and sex are required to retrieve. If the DOB and sex are not entered, the system defaults to a limited group of 5 records. The fee is $5.00 per record. For more information, call 518-474-4293.

Other access: The state offers a program to employers whereby the state will notify the employers when an event is posted to an employee's record. To find out about the "LENS" program, call 518-486-4480.

Vehicle Ownership & Identification
Vessel Ownership & Registration

Department of Motor Vehicles, Customer Service Center, 6 Empire State Plaza, Room 430, Albany, NY 12228; 518-474-0710, 518-474-8510, 8AM-5PM.

www.nydmv.state.ny.us

Indexing & Storage: Records are available for a minimum of 4 years on computer. All motorized vessels must be registered. Titles on boats are issued for model year 1987 and newer, if boat is at least 14 ft long. New records are available for inquiry immediately.

Searching: Generally, vehicle and ownership information is available. However, accessed is restricted in adherence to the Drivers' Privacy Protection Act and casual requesters cannot obtain records. Use of Form MV-15 required. The form is downloadable from the web site.

Access by: mail, in person, online.

Fee & Payment: Mail requests are $5.00 per record, online inquiries are $4.00 per record. Fee payee: Commissioner of Motor Vehicles. Prepayment required. For information regarding deposit accounts, call 518-474-4293. Personal checks accepted. No credit cards accepted.

Mail search: Turnaround time: 2 to 4 weeks. Include copy of requester's ID. Mail to MV-15 Form Processing for fastest turnaround time. A self addressed stamped envelope is requested.

In person search: Results are returned by mail.

Online search: New York offers plate, VIN and ownership data through the same network discussed in the Driving Records Section. The system is interactive and open 24 hours a day. The fee is $5.00 per record. Call 518-474-4293 for more information.

Accident Reports

DMV Certified Document Center, Accident Report Section, 6 Empire State Plaza, Swan St Bldg, Albany, NY 12228; 518-474-0710, 8AM-4:30PM.

www.nysdmv.com

Indexing & Storage: Records are available for 4 years to present. It takes 120 days after date of accident before new records are available for inquiry. Records are indexed on inhouse computer.

Searching: Records are open to the public, but request must be in writing. Use of Form MV-198C is suggested. Release of records is restricted based on the Drivers' Privacy Protection Act. Include the following in your request: date of accident, location of accident, full name. Provide driver's address, if known.

Access by: mail, in person.

Fee & Payment: Fees: $5.00 per search and $15.00 per accident report. Express mail is given priority. Fee payee: Commissioner of Motor Vehicle. Prepayment required. Personal checks accepted. No credit cards accepted.

Mail search: Turnaround time: 4 to 6 weeks. No self addressed stamped envelope is required.

In person search: Turnaround time is next day pickup.

Legislation Records

NY Senate Document Room, State Capitol, State Street Rm 317, Albany, NY 12247, 518-455-2312 (Senate Document Room), 518-455-3216, 9AM-5PM.

www.senate.state.ny.us

Note: Prior session bills may be found at the State Library, 518-474-5355.

Indexing & Storage: Records are available for current session and back to 1995. Records are indexed on computer.

Searching: Include the following in your request: bill number. The law section number or description can be helpful.

Access by: mail, phone, in person, online.

Fee & Payment: There is no search fee.

Mail search: Turnaround time: same day. No self addressed stamped envelope is required.

Phone search: Records are available by phone.

In person search: research materials are available if bill number is not known.

Online search: Both the Senate - www.senate.state.ny.us - and the Assembly - www.assembly.state.ny.us - have web sites to search for a bill or specific bill text. A much more complete system is the LRS online system. This offers complete state statutes, agency rules and regulations, bill text, bill status, summaries, and more. For more information, call Barbara Lett at 800-356-6566.

Voter Registration

Records not maintained by a state level agency.

Note: Records may only be viewed or purchased at the county level. Purchases are restricted for political purposes only.

GED Certificates

NY State Education Dept, GED Testing, PO Box 7348, Albany, NY 12224-0348; 518-474-5906, 518-474-3041 (Fax), 10AM-12PM, 1-3PM M-F.

www.emsc.nysed.gov/workforce/ged

Searching: To search, all of the following is required: full name, SSN, and date of birth. If the subject was tested prior to 1985, include the address, year of test, and location.

Access by: mail, phone.

Fee & Payment: There is no fee for verification. Copies of transcripts are $4.00 each. Copies of diplomas are $10.00 each. Fee payee: NY State Education Dept. Prepayment required. Money orders are accepted. No credit cards accepted.

Mail search: Turnaround time is 3 to 4 weeks. No self addressed stamped envelope is required.

Phone search: Automated phone verifications can be accomplished for records that are from 1985 to the present.

Hunting License Information
Fishing License Information

Records not maintained by a state level agency.

Note: They do not have a central database. Only vendors have the names and addresses.

New York State Licensing Agencies

Licenses Searchable Online

Accountant, CPA/Public #19.....................................www.op.nysed.gov/opsearches.htm#nme
Acupuncturist/Acupuncturist Assistant #19.............www.op.nysed.gov/opsearches.htm#nme
Apartment Information Vendor #10.........................http://wdb.dos.state.ny.us/lcns_public/lcns_wdb.status_check_lcns.show
Apartment Sharing Manager #10.............................http://wdb.dos.state.ny.us/lcns_public/lcns_wdb.status_check_lcns.show
Appearance Enhancement Business #10................http://wdb.dos.state.ny.us/lcns_public/lcns_wdb.status_check_lcns.show
Architect #19..www.op.nysed.gov/opsearches.htm#nme
Armored Car/Car Carrier #10...................................http://wdb.dos.state.ny.us/lcns_public/lcns_wdb.status_check_lcns.show
Athletic Trainer #19...www.op.nysed.gov/opsearches.htm#nme
Attorney #18 ....www.courts.state.ny.us/webdb/wdbcgi.exe/apps/INTERNETDB.attyreghome.show
Audiologist #19 ....www.op.nysed.gov/opsearches.htm#nme
Bail Enforcement Agent #10 ....http://wdb.dos.state.ny.us/lcns_public/lcns_wdb.status_check_lcns.show
Barber #10..http://wdb.dos.state.ny.us/lcns_public/lcns_wdb.status_check_lcns.show
Chiropractor #19...www.op.nysed.gov/opsearches.htm#nme
Court Reporter #19...www.op.nysed.gov/opsearches.htm#nme
Dental Hygienist #19..www.op.nysed.gov/opsearches.htm#nme
Dentist/Dental Assistant #19.....................................www.op.nysed.gov/opsearches.htm#nme
Dietitian #19...www.op.nysed.gov/opsearches.htm#nme
Dispatch Facility (Alarm/Security/Fire) #10 ....http://wdb.dos.state.ny.us/lcns_public/lcns_wdb.status_check_lcns.show
Engineer #19 ....www.op.nysed.gov/opsearches.htm#nme
Guard Dog Agency #10 ....http://wdb.dos.state.ny.us/lcns_public/lcns_wdb.status_check_lcns.show
Guard/Patrol Agency #10...http://wdb.dos.state.ny.us/lcns_public/lcns_wdb.status_check_lcns.show
Hearing Aid Dealer #10...http://wdb.dos.state.ny.us/lcns_public/lcns_wdb.status_check_lcns.show
HMO #12 ....www.ins.state.ny.us/tocol4.htm
Insurance Company #12...www.ins.state.ny.us/tocol4.htm
Interior Designer #19 ....www.op.nysed.gov/opsearches.htm#nme
Landscape Architect #19 ....www.op.nysed.gov/opsearches.htm#nme
Lobbyist #16 ....www.nylobby.state.ny.us/lobbysearch.html
Massage Therapist #19 ....www.op.nysed.gov/opsearches.htm#nme
Medical Doctor #19..www.op.nysed.gov/opsearches.htm#nme
Midwife #19..www.op.nysed.gov/opsearches.htm#nme
Notary Public #10 ....http://wdb.dos.state.ny.us/lcns_public/lcns_wdb.status_check_lcns.show
Nurse #19 ....www.op.nysed.gov/opsearches.htm#nme
Nurse-LPN #19 ....www.op.nysed.gov/opsearches.htm#nme
Nurse-RPN #19 ....www.op.nysed.gov/opsearches.htm#nme
Nutritionist #19...www.op.nysed.gov/opsearches.htm#nme
Occupational Therapist/Assistant #19 ....www.op.nysed.gov/opsearches.htm#nme
Ophthalmic Dispenser #19...www.op.nysed.gov/opsearches.htm#nme
Optometrist #19 ....www.op.nysed.gov/opsearches.htm#nme
Pharmacist #19..www.op.nysed.gov/opsearches.htm#nme
Physical Therapist/Assistant #19 ....www.op.nysed.gov/opsearches.htm#nme
Physician #19 ....www.op.nysed.gov/opsearches.htm#nme
Physician Assistant #19 ....www.op.nysed.gov/opsearches.htm#nme
Physicians' Specialist Assistant #19 ....www.op.nysed.gov/opsearches.htm#nme
Podiatrist #19 ....www.op.nysed.gov/opsearches.htm#nme
Private Investigator #10 ....http://wdb.dos.state.ny.us/lcns_public/lcns_wdb.status_check_lcns.show
Psychiatrist #19 ....www.nyspsych.org
Psychologist #19..www.op.nysed.gov/opsearches.htm#nme
Public Accountant-CPA #19.......................................www.op.nysed.gov/opsearches.htm#nme
Radiologic Technology School #14 ....www.health.state.ny.us/nysdoh/radtech/schlist2.htm
Radon Testing Lab #14 ....www.wadsworth.org/labcert/elap/radon.html
Real Estate Sales/Broker/Appraiser #10.................http://wdb.dos.state.ny.us/lcns_public/lcns_wdb.status_check_lcns.show
Respiratory Therapist/Therapy Technician #19 ......www.op.nysed.gov/opsearches.htm#nme
Security & Fire Alarm Installer #10 ....http://wdb.dos.state.ny.us/lcns_public/lcns_wdb.status_check_lcns.show
Security Guard #10...http://wdb.dos.state.ny.us/lcns_public/lcns_wdb.status_check_lcns.show
Social Worker #19 ....www.op.nysed.gov/opsearches.htm#nme
Speech Pathologist/Audiologist #19 ....www.op.nysed.gov/opsearches.htm#nme
Surveyor, Land #19 ....www.op.nysed.gov/opsearches.htm#nme
Teacher #17 ....www.highered.nysed.gov/tcert/respublic/ocvs.htm
Telemarketer Business #10 ....http://wdb.dos.state.ny.us/lcns_public/lcns_wdb.status_check_lcns.show
Veterinarian/Veterinary Technician #19.................www.op.nysed.gov/opsearches.htm#nme

Licensing Quick Finder

Accountant, CPA/Public #19 518-474-3817	Guard/Patrol Agency #10 518-474-4429	Physician Assistant #19 518-474-3817
Acupuncturist/Acupuncturist Assistant #19 518-474-3817	Guide #3 518-457-9311	Physicians' Specialist Assistant #19 518-474-3817
Apartment Information Vendor #10 518-474-4429	Hair Styling, Natural #10 518-474-4429	Podiatrist #19 518-474-3817
Apartment Manager/Vendor/Agent #10. 518-474-4429	Health Club #10 518-474-4429	Private Investigator #10 518-474-4429
Apartment Sharing Manager #10 518-474-4429	Hearing Aid Dealer #10 518-474-4429	Psychiatrist #19 518-474-3817
Appearance Enhancement Business #10 518-474-4429	Hiking Guide #3 518-457-9311	Psychologist #19 518-474-3817
Architect #19 518-474-3817	HMO #12 518-474-6630	Public Accountant-CPA #19 518-474-3817
Armored Car/Car Carrier #10 518-474-4429	Hunting Guide #3 518-457-9311	Racetrack #15 .... 518-453-8460 X2
Athletic Trainer #19 518-474-3817	Insurance Agent/Consultant/Broker #12 518-474-6630	Racing #15 .... 518-453-8460 X2
Attorney #18 212-428-2800	Insurance Appraiser #12 518-474-6630	Radiation Therapy Technologist #14 ... 518-402-7580
Audiologist #19 518-474-3817	Insurance Company #12 518-474-6630	Radiologic Technologist #14 518-402-7580
Bail Bond Agent #12 518-474-6630	Interior Designer #19 518-474-3817	Radiologic Technology School #14 518-402-7580
Bail Enforcement Agent #10 518-474-4429	Investment Advisor #1 212-416-8222	Radon Testing Lab #14 518-402-7580
Barber #10 518-474-4429	Landscape Architect #19 518-474-3817	Rafting Guide, Whitewater #3 518-457-9311
Blaster #9 518-457-2735	Lobbyist #16 518-474-7126	Real Estate Salesperson/Broker/Appraiser #10 518-474-4429
Casino Employee #15 .... 518-453-8460 X2	Massage Therapist #19 518-474-3817	
Charitable Gaming #15 .... 518-453-8460 X2	Medical Doctor #19 518-474-3817	Respiratory Therapist/Therapy Technician #19 518-474-3817
Chiropractor #19 518-474-3817	Midwife #19 518-474-3817	
Collection Agency #11 702-687-4259	Nail Technology #10 518-474-4429	School Administrator/Supervisor #17... 518-474-3901
Commercial Applicator #2 518-402-8748	Notary Public #10 518-474-4429	School Counselor #17 518-474-3901
Cosmetologist #10 518-474-4429	Nurse #19 518-474-3817	School Media Specialist #17 518-474-3901
Court Reporter #19 518-474-3817	Nurse-LPN #19 518-474-3817	Securities Broker/Dealer #1 212-416-8222
Dental Hygienist #19 518-474-3817	Nurse-RPN #19 518-474-3817	Securities Salesperson #1 212-416-8222
Dentist/Dental Assistant #19 518-474-3817	Nurses' Aide #5 518-474-3817	Security & Fire Alarm Installer #10 518-474-4429
Dietitian #19 518-474-3817	Nursing Home Administrator #5 518-474-3817	Security Guard #10 518-474-4429
Dispatch Facility (Alarm/Security/Fire) #10 518-474-4429	Nutritionist #19 518-474-3817	Short Hand Reporter #19 518-474-3817
	Occupational Therapist/Assistant #19... 518-474-3817	Social Worker #19 518-474-3817
Emergency Medical Technician-Paramedic #7 518-402-0996	Off-Track Betting #15 .... 518-453-8460 X2	Speech Pathologist/Audiologist #19 ... 518-474-3817
	Ophthalmic Dispenser #19 518-474-3817	Surveyor, Land #19 518-474-3817
Engineer #19 518-474-3817	Optometrist #19 518-474-3817	Teacher #17 518-474-3901
Esthetics Specialist #10 518-474-4429	Pesticide Applicator #2 518-402-8748	Telemarketer Business #10 518-474-4429
Fishing Guide #3 518-457-9311	Pesticide Distributor #2 518-402-8748	Theatrical Syndication #1 212-416-8222
Franchise Sales #1 212-416-8222	Pesticide Distributor, Restricted #2 518-402-8748	Upholster & Bedding Industry #10 518-474-4429
Funeral Home/Director #6 518-402-0785	Pet Cemetery #10 518-474-4429	Veterinarian/Veterinary Technician #19 518-474-3817
Games of Chance Registration #10 518-474-4429	Pharmacist #19 518-474-3817	Water Treatment Plant Operator #13... 518-458-6755
Guard Dog Agency #10 518-474-4429	Physical Therapist/Assistant #19 518-474-3817	
	Physician #19 518-474-3817	

Licensing Agency Information

#1 Bureau of Investor Protection & Securities, 120 Broadway, 23rd Floor, New York, NY 10271; 212-416-8222, Fax: 212-416-8816.
www.oag.state.ny.us

#2 Department of Environmental Conservation, Bureau of Pesticide & Radiation, 625 Broadway, Albany, NY 12233-7254; 518-402-8748, Fax: 518-485-8366.
www.dec.state.ny.us

#3 Department of Environmental Conservation, Division of Forest Protection & Fire Mgmt., 50 Wolf Rd Rm 440C, Albany, NY 12233-2560; 518-457-5740, Fax: 518-485-8458.
www.dec.state.ny.us/website/protection/rangers/fr guid6.html
Agency email: dpaeweb@gw.dec.state.ny.us.

#5 Board of Examiners of Nursing Home Administrators, Bureau of Proffessional Credentialling, 161 Delaware Av, Delmar, NY 10254; 518-478-1060.

#6 Department of Health, Bureau of Funeral Directing, 433 River St #303, Troy, NY 12180-2299; 518-402-0785, Fax: 518-402-0784.

#7 Department of Health, Emergency Medical Services, 433 River St, #303, Troy, NY 12180; 518-402-0996, Fax: 518-402-0985.
www.health.state.ny.us/nysdoh/ems/main.htm

#10 Department of State, Division of Licensing Services, 84 Holland Ave, Albany, NY 12208-3490; 518-474-4429, Fax: 518-473-6648.
www.dos.state.ny.us/lcns/licensing.html
Agency email: info@dos.state.ny.us.
Search database at
http://wdb.dos.state.ny.us/lcns_public/lcns_wdb.st atus_check_lcns.show

#12 Insurance Department, Licensing Bureau Agency, Empire State Plaza, Bldg 1, Albany, NY 12257; 518-474-6630.
www.ins.state.ny.us

#13 Department of Health, Bureau of Public Water Supply Protection, 150 Broadway #8, Albany, NY 12204-2719; 518-458-6731, Fax: 518-458-6732.
www.health.state.ny.us

#14 Department of Health, Bureau of Environmental Radiation Protection, Flanigan Sq, Room 530, 547 River St, Troy, NY 12180-2216; 518-402-7580, Fax: 518-402-7575.
www.health.state.ny.us/nysdoh/radtech/radtech.htm.
Agency email: berp@health.state.ny.us.
Search database at
www.health.state.ny.us/nysdoh/radtech/radtech.htm

#15 Racing & Wagering Board, 1 Watervliet Av Extension #2, Albany, NY 12206; 518-453-8460 x2, Fax: 518-453-8492.
www.racing.state.ny.us

#16 Temporary Commission on Lobbying, Agency Bldg #2, 17th Fl, Albany, NY 12223-1254; 518-474-7126, Fax: 518-473-6492.
www.nylobby.state.ny.us
Agency email: lobcom@emi.com.
Search database at
www.nylobby.state.ny.us/lobbysearch.html

#17, 5N Education Bldg, Albany, NY 12234; 518-474-3901, Fax: 518-473-0271.
www.highered.nysed.gov/tcert.
Search database at
www.highered.nysed.gov/tcert/respublic/ocvs.htm

#18 Unified Court System, Attorney Registration Unit, PO Box 2806, Church Street Station, New York, NY 10008; 212-428-2800, Fax: 212-428-2804.
www.courts.state.ny.us
Agency email: relias@courts.state.ny.us
Search database at
www.courts.state.ny.us/webdb/wdbcgi.exe/apps/I NTERNETDB.attyreghome.show

#19 Education Department, Office of the Professions, State Education Bldg, 2nd Fl, 89 Washington Ave, Albany, NY 12234; 518-474-3817 attendant available 9-11:45AM and 12:45-4:30PM ESTTDD 518-473-1426.
www.op.nysed.gov
Agency email: op4info@mail.nysed.gov.
Search database at
www.op.nysed.gov/opsearches.htm#nme

New York Federal Courts

The following list indicates the district and division name for each county in the state. If the bankruptcy court location is different from the district court, then the location of the bankruptcy court appears in parentheses.

County/Court Cross Reference

County	District	Location
Albany	Northern	Albany
Allegany	Western	Buffalo
Bronx	Southern	New York City
Broome	Northern	Binghamton (Utica)
Cattaraugus	Western	Buffalo
Cayuga	Northern	Syracuse (Utica)
Chautauqua	Western	Buffalo
Chemung	Western	Rochester
Chenango	Northern	Binghamton (Utica)
Clinton	Northern	Albany
Columbia	Northern (Southern)	Albany (Poughkeepsie)
Cortland	Northern	Syracuse (Utica)
Delaware	Northern	Binghamton (Utica)
Dutchess	Southern	White Plains (Poughkeepsie)
Erie	Western	Buffalo
Essex	Northern	Albany
Franklin	Northern	Binghamton (Albany)
Fulton	Northern	Syracuse (Albany)
Genesee	Western	Buffalo
Greene	Northern (Southern)	Albany (Poughkeepsie)
Hamilton	Northern	Syracuse (Utica)
Herkimer	Northern	Syracuse (Utica)
Jefferson	Northern	Binghamton (Albany)
Kings	Eastern	Brooklyn
Lewis	Northern	Binghamton (Utica)
Livingston	Western	Rochester
Madison	Northern	Syracuse (Utica)
Monroe	Western	Rochester
Montgomery	Northern	Syracuse (Albany)
Nassau	Eastern	Brooklyn (Westbury)
New York	Southern	New York City
Niagara	Western	Buffalo
Oneida	Northern	Utica
Onondaga	Northern	Syracuse (Utica)
Ontario	Western	Rochester
Orange	Southern	White Plains (Poughkeepsie)
Orleans	Western	Buffalo
Oswego	Northern	Syracuse (Utica)
Otsego	Northern	Binghamton (Utica)
Putnam	Southern	White Plains (Poughkeepsie)
Queens	Eastern	Brooklyn
Rensselaer	Northern	Albany
Richmond	Eastern	Brooklyn
Rockland	Southern	White Plains
Saratoga	Northern	Albany
Schenectady	Northern	Albany
Schoharie	Northern	Albany
Schuyler	Western	Rochester
Seneca	Western	Rochester
St. Lawrence	Northern	Binghamton (Albany)
Steuben	Western	Rochester
Suffolk	Eastern	Central Islip
Sullivan	Southern	White Plains (Poughkeepsie)
Tioga	Northern	Binghamton (Utica)
Tompkins	Northern	Syracuse (Utica)
Ulster	Northern (Southern)	Albany (Poughkeepsie)
Warren	Northern	Albany
Washington	Northern	Albany
Wayne	Western	Rochester
Westchester	Southern	White Plains
Wyoming	Western	Buffalo
Yates	Western	Rochester

Standards for Federal Courts: The search fee is $20.00 per item (one party name or case number). Certification fee is $7.00 per document. Copy fee is $.50 per page. All fees standard unless noted in profile. Mail Search: always enclose a stamped self addressed envelope unless otherwise noted. Before releasing records, all courts require prepayment unless noted in profile. Open records are located at the court unless otherwise noted. District courts index by defendant and plaintiff as well as by case number. Bankruptcy courts usually index by debtor and case number. While most courts now have their indexes on computer, many still maintain index card files as well.

The universal PACER sign-up number is 800-676-6856. Find PACER and the Party/Case Index on the Web at http://pacer.psc.uscourts.gov. PACER dial-up access is $.60 per minute. Also, courts offering internet access via RACER, PACER, Web-PACER or the new CM-ECF charge $.07 per page fee unless noted as free.

US District Court

Eastern District of New York

Brooklyn Division Brooklyn Courthouse, 225 Cadman Plaza E, Room 130, Brooklyn, NY 11201 (Courier Address: Use mail address for courier delivery), 718-260-2600.

www.nyed.uscourts.gov

Counties: Kings, Queens, Richmond. Cases from Nassau and Suffolk may also be heard here.

Indexing & Storage: Cases are indexed by defendant, plaintiff, and case number. New cases are available in the index 2 days after filing date. Open records are located at this court.

Fee & Payment Notes: Payment may be made by money order, cashier check, personal check. Payee: Clerk, US District Court. You are allowed to make your own copies. These copies cost $.25 per page.

Phone Search: Searching not available by phone.

Mail Search: A stamped self addressed envelope is not required.

In Person Search: In person searching available.

PACER: Toll-free dial-up access: 888-331-4965. Local dial-up access: 718-250-4420. Case records are available back to January 1, 1990. Records are never purged. New records are available online after 1 day. PACER is available online at http://pacer.nyed.uscourts.gov.

Electronic Filing: Only law firms and practitioners may file cases electronically. Anyone can search online. Information is available online at https://ecf.nyed.uscourts.gov

Central Islip Division 100 Federal Plaza, Central Islip, NY 17722-4438 (Use mail address for courier delivery), 613-712-6000.

www.nyed.uscourts.gov

Counties: Nassau, Suffolk.

Indexing & Storage: Cases are indexed by defendant, plaintiff, and case number. New cases are available in the index 2 days after filing date. Indexes and files are available here from 1987 on. Open records are located at this court.

Fee & Payment Notes: Payment may be made by money order, cashier check, personal check. Payee: Clerk, US District Court. You are allowed to make your own copies. These copies cost $.25 per page.

Phone Search: Some limited docket information is available by phone.

Fax Search: Fax requests may only be made for a few names at most. Regular fees apply to fax requests.

In Person Search: In person searching available.

PACER: Toll-free dial-up access: 888-331-4965. Local dial-up access: 718-250-4420. Case records are available back to January 1, 1990. Records are never purged. New records are available online after 1 day. PACER is available online at http://pacer.nyed.uscourts.gov.

Electronic Filing: Only law firms and practitioners may file cases electronically. Anyone can search online. Information is available online at https://ecf.nyed.uscourts.gov

US Bankruptcy Court

Eastern District of New York

Brooklyn Division 75 Clinton St, Brooklyn, NY 11201 (Courier Address: Use mail address for courier delivery), 718-330-2188.

www.nyeb.uscourts.gov

Counties: Kings, Queens, Richmond. Kings and Queens County Chapter 11 cases may also be assigned to Westbury. Other Queens County cases may be assigned to Westbury Division. Nassau County Chapter 11 cases may be assigned here.

Indexing & Storage: Cases are indexed by debtor as well as by case number. New cases are available in the index 1 day after filing date. Older cases are indexed on microfiche. Open records are located at this court.

Fee & Payment Notes: Payment may be made by money order, cashier check, business check. Personal checks are not accepted. Payee: Clerk, US Bankruptcy Court. You are allowed to make your own copies. These copies cost $.10 per page.

Phone Search: Only docket information is available by phone. An automated voice case information service (VCIS) is available. Call VCIS at 800-252-2537 or 718-852-5726.

Mail Search: A stamped self addressed envelope is not required.

In Person Search: In person searching available.

PACER: Toll-free dial-up access: 800-263-7790. Local dial-up access: 718-488-7012, 718-488-7013. Case records are available back to 1991. Records are purged every year. New civil records are available online after 3 days. PACER is available online at http://pacer.nyeb.uscourts.gov.

Electronic Filing: Information is available online at https://ecf.nyeb.uscourts.gov

Central Islip Division Long Island Federal Courthouse, 290 Federal Plaza, 2nd Fl, Central Islip, NY 11722 (Courier Address: Use mail address for courier delivery), 631-712-6200.

www.nyeb.uscourts.gov

Counties: Suffolk, Nassau.

Indexing & Storage: Cases are indexed by debtor as well as by case number. New cases are available in the index 1-2 days after filing date. Open records are located at this court.

Fee & Payment Notes: Payment may be made by money order, cashier check, personal check. Debtor's checks are not accepted. Enclose a FedEx package for expedited service. Payee: Clerk, US Bankruptcy Court. You are allowed to make your own copies. These copies cost $.10 per page.

Phone Search: Basic docket information only available by phone. An automated voice case information service (VCIS) is available. Call VCIS at 800-252-2537 or 718-852-5726.

Mail Search: A stamped self addressed envelope is not required.

In Person Search: In person searching available.

PACER: Toll-free dial-up access: 800-263-7790. Local dial-up access: 718-488-7012, 718-488-7013. Case records are available back to 1991. Records are purged every year. New civil records are available online after 3 days. PACER is available online at http://pacer.nyeb.uscourts.gov.

Electronic Filing: Information is available online at https://ecf.nyeb.uscourts.gov

US District Court

Northern District of New York

Albany Division 445 Broadway, Room 222, James T Foley Courthouse, Albany, NY 12207-2924 (Courier Address: Use mail address for courier delivery), 518-257-1800.

www.nynd.uscourts.gov

Counties: Albany, Clinton, Columbia, Essex, Greene, Rensselaer, Saratoga, Schenectady, Schoharie, Ulster, Warren, Washington.

Indexing & Storage: Cases are indexed by defendant, plaintiff, and case number. New cases are available in the index 1 day after filing date. Case indexes are available on computer terminal in any of the divisions in the Northern District. Open records are located at this court.

Fee & Payment Notes: Payment may be made by money order, cashier check, personal check. Payee: Clerk, US District Court.

Phone Search: Searching not available by phone.

Mail Search: A stamped self addressed envelope is not required.

In Person Search: In person searching available.

PACER: Toll-free dial-up access: 800-480-7525. Local dial-up access: 315-234-8663. Case records are available back to June 1991. New records are available online after 2 days.

Binghamton Division 15 Henry St, Binghamton, NY 13901 (Courier Address: Use mail address for courier delivery), 607-773-2893.

www.nynd.uscourts.gov

Counties: Broome, Chenango, Delaware, Franklin, Jefferson, Lewis, Otsego, St. Lawrence, Tioga.

Indexing & Storage: Cases are indexed by defendant, plaintiff, and case number. New cases are available in the index 1 day after filing date. Open records are located at this court.

Fee & Payment Notes: Payment may be made by money order, cashier check, personal check. Payee: Clerk, US District Court.

Phone Search: Searching not available by phone. Only docket information is available by phone.

In Person Search: In person searching available.

PACER: Toll-free dial-up access: 800-480-7525. Local dial-up access: 315-234-8663. Case records are available back to June 1991. New records are available online after 2 days.

Syracuse Division PO Box 7367, Syracuse, NY 13261-7367 (Courier Address: 100 S Clinton St, Syracuse, NY 13261-7367), 315-234-8500.

www.nynd.uscourts.gov

Counties: Cayuga, Cortland, Fulton, Hamilton, Herkimer, Madison, Montgomery, Onondaga, Oswego, Tompkins.

Indexing & Storage: Cases are indexed by defendant, plaintiff, and case number. New cases are available in the index 1 day after filing date. Open records are located at this court.

Fee & Payment Notes: Payment may be made by money order, cashier check, personal check. Credit cards acepted in person only. Payee: Clerk, US District Court.

Phone Search: Searching not available by phone. Only docket information is available by phone.

In Person Search: In person searching available.

PACER: Toll-free dial-up access: 800-480-7525. Local dial-up access: 315-234-8663. Case records are available back to June 1991. New records are available online after 2 days.

Utica Division Alexander Pirnie Bldg, 10 Broad St, Utica, NY 13501 (Courier Address: Use mail address for courier delivery), 315-793-8151.

www.nynd.uscourts.gov

Counties: Oneida.

Indexing & Storage: Cases are indexed by defendant, plaintiff, and case number. New cases are available in the index 1 day after filing date. Indexes are on computer starting in 1991 and on cards prior to that. Closed. Case records from the other three Northern district courts were assembled here before going to the New York Federal Records Center. Starting in 1995, Albany and Binghamton and Syracuse are no longer sending their records to Utica.

Fee & Payment Notes: Payment may be made by money order, cashier check, business check. Personal checks are not accepted. Payee: Clerk, US District Court.

Phone Search: Information from the computer for 1991 forward is available by phone.

Mail Search: A stamped self addressed envelope is not required.

In Person Search: In person searching available.

PACER: Toll-free dial-up access: 800-480-7525. Local dial-up access: 315-234-8663. Case records are available back to June 1991. New records are available online after 2 days.

US Bankruptcy Court

Northern District of New York

Albany Division James T Foley Courthouse, 445 Broadway #330, Albany, NY 12207 (Courier Address: Use mail address for courier delivery), 518-257-1661.

www.nynb.uscourts.gov

Counties: Albany, Clinton, Essex, Franklin, Fulton, Jefferson, Montgomery, Rensselaer, Saratoga, Schenectady, Schoharie, St. Lawrence, Warren, Washington.

Indexing & Storage: Cases are indexed by debtor as well as by case number. New cases are available in the index 48 hours after filing date. As of January 1, 1995, Jefferson and St. Lawrence Counties moved to Albany Division from Utica, while Broome, Chenango, Delaware, Otsego, Tioga and Tompkins Counties moved to Utica Division from Albany.

Fee & Payment Notes: Payment may be made by money order, cashier check. Business checks are not accepted, Visa or Mastercard. Personal checks are not accepted. Credit cards are only accepted from in-person searchers. Payee: Clerk, US Bankruptcy Court. Copy fee: $.25 per page.

Phone Search: Only docket information is available by phone. An automated voice case information service (VCIS) is available. Call VCIS at 800-206-1952.

Mail Search: If a case number is not known, the turnaround time may be as long as 5 days after the request is received. Always enclose a stamped self addressed envelope.

In Person Search: In person searching available.

PACER: Toll-free dial-up access: 800-390-8432. Local dial-up access: 518-257-1669. Case records are available back to 1992. New civil records are available online after 48 hours. PACER is available online at http://pacer.nynb.uscourts.gov.

Electronic Filing: (Currently in the process of implementing CM/ECF.)

Utica Division Room 230, 10 Broad St, Utica, NY 13501 (Courier Address: Use mail address for courier delivery), 315-793-8101, Fax: 315-793-8128.

www.nynb.uscourts.gov

Counties: Broome, Cayuga, Chenango, Cortland, Delaware, Hamilton, Herkimer, Lewis, Madison, Oneida, Onondaga, Otsego, Oswego, Tioga, Tompkins.

Indexing & Storage: Cases are indexed by debtor as well as by case number. New cases are available in the index 24 hours after filing date. As of January 1, 1995, Jefferson and St. Lawrence Counties moved to Albany Division from Utica, while Broome, Chenango, Delaware, Otsego, Tioga and Tompkins Counties moved to Utica Division from Albany.

Fee & Payment Notes: Payment may be made by money order, cashier check, personal check. Debtor's checks are not accepted. Payee: Clerk, US Bankruptcy Court.

Phone Search: Only docket information is available by phone. An automated voice case information service (VCIS) is available. Call VCIS at 800-206-1952.

Mail Search: A stamped self addressed envelope is not required.

In Person Search: In person searching available.

PACER: Toll-free dial-up access: 800-390-8432. Local dial-up access: 518-257-1669. Case records are available back to 1992. New civil records are available online after 48 hours. PACER is available online at http://pacer.nynb.uscourts.gov.

Electronic Filing: (Currently in the process of implementing CM/ECF.)

US District Court

Southern District of New York

New York City Division 500 Pearl St, New York, NY 10007 (Courier Address: Use mail address for courier delivery), 212-805-0136.

www.nysd.uscourts.gov

Counties: Bronx, New York. Some cases from the counties in the White Plains Division are also assigned to the New York Division.

Indexing & Storage: Cases are indexed by defendant, plaintiff, and case number. New cases are available in the index 2 days after filing date. Open records are located at this court.

Fee & Payment Notes: Payment may be made by money order, cashier check. Business checks are not accepted. Personal checks are not accepted. Payee: Clerk of Court, S.D.N.Y. You are allowed to make your own copies. These copies cost - current fee is not known - per page.

Phone Search: Searching not available by phone. Only docket information is available by phone.

In Person Search: In person searching available.

PACER: Local dial-up access: 212-805-6373. Case records are available back to early 1990. Records are purged every six months. New records are available online after 1 day.

Electronic Filing: (Currently in the process of implementing CM/ECF.)

Opinions Online: Selected rulings are searchable online using CourtWeb. To download and view copies of rulings you must have Adobe Acrobat Reader. Court opinions are available online at www.nysd.uscourts.gov/courtweb

White Plains Division 300 Quarropas St, White Plains, NY 10601 (Courier Address: Use mail address for courier delivery), 914-390-4000.

www.nysd.uscourts.gov

Counties: Dutchess, Orange, Putnam, Rockland, Sullivan, Westchester. Some cases may be assigned to New York Division.

Indexing & Storage: Cases are indexed by defendant, plaintiff, and case number. New cases are available in the index 2 days after filing date. Indexes have been automated since 1983. Open records are located at this court.

Fee & Payment Notes: Payment may be made by money order, cashier check. Business checks are not accepted. Personal checks are not accepted. Attorney checks are accepted. Payee: Clerk of Court, S.D.N.Y. You are allowed to make your own copies. These copies cost $.15 per page.

Phone Search: Searching not available by phone.

In Person Search: In person searching available.

PACER: Local dial-up access: 212-805-6373. Case records are available back to early 1990. Records are purged every six months. New records are available online after 1 day.

Electronic Filing: (Currently in the process of implementing CM/ECF.)

Opinions Online: Selected rulings are searchable online using CourtWeb. To download and view copies of rulings you must have Adobe Acrobat Reader. Court opinions are available online at www.nysd.uscourts.gov/courtweb

US Bankruptcy Court

Southern District of New York

New York Division Room 534, 1 Bowling Green, New York, NY 10004-1408 (Courier Address: Use mail address for courier delivery), 212-668-2870.

www.nysb.uscourts.gov

Counties: Bronx, New York.

Indexing & Storage: Cases are indexed by debtor as well as by case number. New cases are available in the index 1-3 days after filing date. Open records are located at this court.

Fee & Payment Notes: Payment may be made by money order, cashier check, business check. Personal checks are not accepted. Payee: Clerk, US Bankruptcy Court. You are allowed to make your own copies. These copies cost $.25 per page.

Phone Search: Over the phone, this court will only provide whether a case is pending. A copy service is available at 212-480-0737 if you have the case number. An automated voice case information service (VCIS) is available. Call VCIS at 212-668-2772.

Mail Search: A stamped self addressed envelope is not required.

In Person Search: In person searching available.

PACER: Local dial-up access: 212-668-2896, 212-668-2897, 212-668-2898. Case records are available back to June 1991. Records are purged every six months. New civil records are available online after 2 days. PACER is available online at https://ecf.nysb.uscourts.gov/cgi-bin/login.pl

Electronic Filing: Information is available online at http://ecf.nysb.uscourts.gov

Poughkeepsie Division 176 Church St, Poughkeepsie, NY 12601 (Courier Address: Use mail address for courier delivery), 845-452-4200, Fax: 845-452-8375.

www.nysb.uscourts.gov

Counties: Columbia, Dutchess, Greene, Orange, Putnam, Sullivan, Ulster.

Indexing & Storage: Cases are indexed by debtor as well as by case number. New cases are available in the index 1-3 days after filing date. Open records are located at this court.

Fee & Payment Notes: Payment may be made by money order, cashier check, business check. Personal checks are not accepted. Payee: Clerk, US Bankruptcy Court. You are allowed to make your own copies. These copies cost $.15 per page.

Phone Search: Over the phone, this court will only reveal whether the case is pending. An automated voice case information service (VCIS) is available. Call VCIS at 212-668-2772.

Mail Search: A stamped self addressed envelope is not required.

In Person Search: In person searching available.

PACER: Local dial-up access: 212-668-2896, 212-668-2897, 212-668-2898. Case records are available back to June 1991. Records are purged every six months. New civil records are available online after 2 days. PACER is available online at https://ecf.nysb.uscourts.gov/cgi-bin/login.pl

Electronic Filing: Information is available online at http://ecf.nysb.uscourts.gov

White Plains Division 300 Quarropas St, White Plains, NY 10601 (Courier Address: Use mail address for courier delivery), 914-390-4060.

www.nysb.uscourts.gov

Counties: Rockland, Westchester.

Indexing & Storage: Cases are indexed by debtor as well as by case number. New cases are available in the index 1-3 days after filing date. Records are also indexed on microfiche. District wide searches are available for cases from 1991 from this court.

Fee & Payment Notes: Payment may be made by money order, business check. Personal checks are not accepted. Checks and credit cards are not accepted from debtors. Payee: Clerk, US Bankruptcy Court. You are allowed to make your own copies. These copies cost $.15 per page. Visa and MasterCard are only accepted for in person searches.

Phone Search: Over the phone, this court will only reveal whether the case is pending. An automated voice case information service (VCIS) is available. Call VCIS at 212-668-2772.

In Person Search: In person searching available.

PACER: Local dial-up access: 212-668-2896, 212-668-2897, 212-668-2898. Case records are available back to June 1991. Records are purged every six months. New civil records are available online after 2 days. PACER is available online at https://ecf.nysb.uscourts.gov/cgi-bin/login.pl

Electronic Filing: Information is available online at http://ecf.nysb.uscourts.gov

US District Court
Western District of New York

Buffalo Division Room 304, 68 Court St, Buffalo, NY 14202 (Courier Address: Use mail address for courier delivery), 716-551-4211, Fax: 716-551-4850.

www.nywd.uscourts.gov

Counties: Allegany, Cattaraugus, Chautauqua, Erie, Genesee, Niagara, Orleans, Wyoming. Prior to 1982, this division included what is now the Rochester Division.

Indexing & Storage: Cases are indexed by defendant, plaintiff, and case number. New cases are available in the index 2 days after filing date. Open records are located at this court.

Fee & Payment Notes: Payment may be made by money order, cashier check, personal check. Payee: Clerk, US District Court.

Phone Search: Searching not available by phone.

Mail Search: A stamped self addressed envelope is not required.

In Person Search: In person searching available.

PACER:. Case records are available back to 1992. Records are never purged. New civil records are available online after 1 day. New criminal records are available online after 2 days. PACER is available online at http://pacer.nywd.uscourts.gov.

Rochester Division Room 2120, 100 State St, Rochester, NY 14614 (Courier Address: Use mail address for courier delivery), 585-263-6263, Fax: 585-263-3178.

www.nywd.uscourts.gov

Counties: Chemung, Livingston, Monroe, Ontario, Schuyler, Seneca, Steuben, Wayne, Yates.

Indexing & Storage: Cases are indexed by defendant, plaintiff, and case number. New cases are available in the index 1 day after filing date. This division was established in 1981. Cases closed from 1996 to present are also held here. Earlier. Case records and indexes are held in the Buffalo Division (Erie County).

Fee & Payment Notes: Payment may be made by money order, cashier check, personal check. Payee: Clerk, US District Court.

Phone Search: Simple docket information available by phone.

Fax Search: Fees for fax requests depend on the nature of the search. Call for more information. Will fax results. Call for instructions.

Mail Search: Mail searches including years prior to 1982 will be forwarded to the Buffalo Division. A stamped self addressed envelope is not required.

In Person Search: In person searching available.

PACER:. Case records are available back to 1992. Records are never purged. New civil records are available online after 1 day. New criminal records are available online after 2 days. PACER is available online at http://pacer.nywd.uscourts.gov.

US Bankruptcy Court
Western District of New York

Buffalo Division Olympic Towers, 300 Pearl St #250, Buffalo, NY 14202-2501 (Courier Address: Use mail address for courier delivery), 716-551-4130.

www.nywb.uscourts.gov

Counties: Allegany, Cattaraugus, Chautauqua, Erie, Genesee, Niagara, Orleans, Wyoming.

Indexing & Storage: Cases are indexed by debtor as well as by case number. New cases are available in the index 24 hours after filing date. Open records are located at this court.

Fee & Payment Notes: Payment may be made by money order, cashier check, business check. Personal checks are not accepted. Payee: Clerk, US Bankruptcy Court.

Phone Search: Only docket information is available by phone. An automated voice case information service (VCIS) is available. Call VCIS at 800-776-9578 or 716-551-5311.

In Person Search: In person searching available.

PACER: Toll-free dial-up access: 800-450-8052. Local dial-up access: 716-551-3152. Case records are available back to August 1987. Records are never purged. New civil records are available online after 1 day. PACER is available online at http://pacer.nywb.uscourts.gov.

Electronic Filing: (Currently in the process of implementing CM/ECF.)

Rochester Division Room 1220, 100 State St, Rochester, NY 14614 (Courier Address: Use mail address for courier delivery), 585-263-3148.

www.nywb.uscourts.gov

Counties: Chemung, Livingston, Monroe, Ontario, Schuyler, Seneca, Steuben, Wayne, Yates.

Indexing & Storage: Cases are indexed by debtor as well as by case number. New cases are available in the index 24 hours after filing date. Records are also indexed on microfiche. District wide searches are available for information from August 1, 1987 from this division.

Fee & Payment Notes: Payment may be made by money order, cashier check, business check. Personal checks are not accepted. The SASE should be large enough to hold all copies and have sufficient postage to send them. Payee: Clerk, US Bankruptcy Court.

Phone Search: Only docket information is available by phone. An automated voice case information service (VCIS) is available. Call VCIS at 800-776-9578 or 716-551-5311.

In Person Search: In person searching available.

PACER: Toll-free dial-up access: 800-450-8052. Local dial-up access: 716-551-3152. Case records are available back to August 1987. Records are never purged. New civil records are available online after 1 day. PACER is available online at http://pacer.nywb.uscourts.gov.

Electronic Filing: (Currently in the process of implementing CM/ECF.)

New York County Courts

Court	Jurisdiction	No. of Courts	How Organized
Supreme Courts*	General	11	12 Districts
County Courts*	General	2	57 Counties
Combined Courts*	General	57	
City Courts*	Limited	61	61 Cities (outside of NYC)
District Courts*	Limited	10	Nassau, Suffolk Counties
Civil /Criminal Courts of the City of New York*	Municipal	6	Boroughs
Town and Village Justice Courts	Municipal	2173	
Surrogates' Courts*	Probate	62	62 Counties and Boroughs
Court of Claims	Limited	1	
Family Courts	Special	62	62 Counties and Boroughs

* Profiled in this Sourcebook.

CIVIL									
Court	Tort	Contract	Real Estate	Min. Claim	Max. Claim	Small Claims	Estate	Eviction	Domestic Relations
Supreme Courts*	X	X	X	$25,000	No Max				X
County Courts*	X	X	X	$0	$25,000				
City Courts*	X	X	X	$0	$15,000	$3000		X	
District Courts*	X	X	X	$0	$15,000	$3000		X	
Civil /Criminal Courts of the City of New York*	X	X	X	$0	$25,000	$3000		X	
Town and Village Justice Courts	X	X	X	$0	$3000	$3000			
Surrogates' Courts*							X		X
Court of Claims	X	X	X	$0	No Max				
Family Courts									X

CRIMINAL					
Court	Felony	Misdemeanor	DWI/DUI	Preliminary Hearing	Juvenile
Supreme Courts*	X				
County Courts*				X	
City Courts*	X	X	X	X	
District Courts*		X	X	X	
Civil /Criminal Courts of the City of New York*		X	X	X	
Town and Village Justice Courts		X	X	X	
Surrogates' Courts*					
Court of Claims					
Family Courts					X

ADMINISTRATION   Office of Court Administration, Empire State Plaza, Agency Plaza #4, Suite 2001, Albany, NY, 12223; 518-473-1196, Fax: 518-473-6860. www.courts.state.ny.us

COURT STRUCTURE   New York State has two sites for Administration; in addition to the Albany address above, there is a New York City office at this address: Office of Administration, 25 Beaver St, New York NY 10004, and telephone: 212-428-2100.

"Supreme Courts" are the highest trial courts in the state, equivalent to Circuit or District Courts in other states; they are not appeals courts. Many New York City courts are indexed by plaintiff only.

Records for Supreme and County Courts are maintained by County Clerks. In most counties, the address for the clerk is the same as the court. Exceptions are noted in the court profiles.

In at least 20 New York Counties, Misdemeanor records are only available at city, town or village courts. This is also true of small claims and eviction records. Town and Village Courts are be listed at the end of each county section.

CRIMINAL COURTS   The New York State Office of Court Administration-OCA (address below) will perform an electronic search for criminal history information from a database of criminal case records from the boroughs and counties of Bronx, Dutchess, Erie, Kings, Nassau, New York, Orange, Putnam, Queens, Richmond, Rockland, Suffolk and Westchester. The request must include complete name and date of birth, and, for mail requests, be accompanied by two (2) self addressed stamped return envelopes. The fee, payable by check, is $16.00 per name per county. Mail and in person requests go to

> Office of Court Administration (OCA)
> Criminal History Search
> 25 Beaver St, 8th Floor
> New York, NY 10004

You may obtain copies of any case dispositions found from the applicable county court.

ONLINE ACCESS   Civil Supreme Court case information is available for all 62 New York counties through the court system's web site - http://e.courts.state.ny.us. More limited case information for housing courts and criminal courts, and a directory of all New York State attorneys is also available at that site. There is no charge for this information. The information is also available at all courts.

Also, you may search for future court dates for defendants in these 21 criminal courts: Bronx Criminal Court, Bronx Supreme Court, Dutchess County Court, Buffalo City Court, Erie County Court, Kings Criminal Court, Kings Supreme Court, Nassau County Court, Nassau District Court, New York Criminal Court, New York Supreme Court, Orange County Court, Putnam County, Queens Criminal Court, Queens Supreme Court, Richmond Criminal Court, Richmond Supreme Court, Rockland County Court, Suffolk County Court, Suffolk District Court, Westchester County Court.

ADDITIONAL INFORMATION   Supreme and County Court records are generally maintained in the County Clerk's Office, which outside of New York City may index civil cases by defendant, whereas the court itself maintains only a plaintiff index.

Fees for Supreme and County Courts are generally as follows: $5.00 per 2 year search per name for a manual search, and $16.00 per name for a computer or OCA search; $.50 per page (minimum $1.00) for copies; and $4.00 for certification. City Courts charge $5.00 for certification. Some New York State courts and county clerks accept credit cards. Some online transactions involve the use of a credit card.

📖 📖 📖 📖 📖 📖 📖

Albany County

Supreme & County Court Courthouse Rm 128, 16 Eagle St, Albany, NY 12207; 518-487-5118; Fax: 518-487-5099. Hours: 9AM-5PM (EST). *Felony, Civil.* www.albanycounty.com/clerk

Civil Records: Access: Mail, in person. Both court and visitors may perform in person searches. Search fee: $5.00 per name. Fee is for each two years requested. Required to search: name, years to search. Civil cases indexed by defendant, plaintiff. Civil records on computer from 1981, prior in books.

Criminal Records: Access: Mail, in person. Both court and visitors may perform in person searches. Search fee: $5.00 per name. Fee is per two years requested. Required to search: name, years to search, DOB.

Criminal records on computer from 1981, prior in books. Search requests must be in writing.

General Information: Public access terminal is available. No sealed, expunged, adoption, sex offense, juvenile, mental health or divorce records released. SASE appreciated. Turnaround time 1-3 days. Copy fee: $.50 per page. Certification fee: $4.00. Fee payee: County Clerk. Personal checks accepted. Prepayment is required.

Albany City Court - Civil Part City Hall Rm 209, Albany, NY 12207; 518-434-5115; Fax: 518-434-5034. Hours: 8:30AM-5PM (EST). *Civil Actions Under $15,000, Eviction, Small Claims.*

Civil Records: Access: Mail, in person. Only the court performs in person searches; visitors may not. Search fee: $16.00 per name. Required to search: name, years

to search. Civil cases indexed by plaintiff. Civil records on computer from 1993, records go back 25 years.

General Information: No code enforcement records released. SASE required. Turnaround time varies. Copy fee: $1.00 for first page, $.50 each add'l. Certification fee: $5.00. Fee payee: Albany City Court. Business checks accepted.

Albany City Court - Misdemeanors Morton & Broad St, Albany, NY 12202; 518-462-6714; Fax: 518-447-8778. Hours: 8AM-4PM (EST). *Misdemeanor.*

Criminal Records: Access: Phone, mail, in person. Only the court performs in person searches; visitors may not. Search fee: $5.00 per name. Required to search: name, years to search, DOB, SSN, signed release. Criminal records on computer since mid-'93, on index cards prior.

General Information: No sealed, expunged, adoption, sex offense, juvenile, or mental health records released without a signed release from the party. SASE required. Turnaround time 5 Days. Copy fee: $.50 per page. Certification fee: $4.00. Fee payee: Albany City Court Criminal Part. Business checks accepted. Prepayment is required.

Cohoes City Court 97 Mohawk St, PO Box 678, Cohoes, NY 12047-0678; Civil phone: 518-233-2133; Criminal phone: 518-233-2134. Hours: 8AM-4PM (EST). *Misdemeanor, Civil Actions Under $15,000, Eviction, Small Claims.*

Civil Records: Access: Mail, in person. Only the court performs in person searches; visitors may not. Search fee: $16.00 per name. Required to search: name, years to search. Civil cases indexed by defendant, plaintiff. Civil records on computer from 1/95, prior in books, on cards.

Criminal Records: Access: Mail, in person. Only the court performs in person searches; visitors may not. Search fee: $16.00 per name by computer; $5 per name plus $5 for each consecutive 2 year period searched manually. Required to search: name, years to search, DOB; also helpful: SSN. Criminal records on computer from 1/95, prior in books, on cards.

General Information: No sealed or expunged records released. SASE required. Turnaround time 2 weeks. Copy fee: $.25 per page. Certification fee: $5.00. Fee payee: City Court. Only cashiers checks and money orders accepted. Prepayment is required.

Watervliet City Court 2 Fifteenth St, Watervliet, NY 12189; 518-270-3803; Fax: 518-270-3812. Hours: 8AM-3PM (EST). *Misdemeanor, Civil Actions Under $15,000, Eviction, Small Claims.*

Civil Records: Access: Phone, fax, mail, in person. Only the court performs in person searches; visitors may not. Search fee: $5.00 per name. Required to search: name, years to search. Civil cases indexed by plaintiff. Civil records on computer from 1991, prior on index cards back to 1975.

Criminal Records: Access: Mail, in person. Only the court performs in person searches; visitors may not. Search fee: $5.00 per name. Required to search: name, years to search, DOB. Criminal records on computer from 1991, prior on index cards back to 1975.

General Information: SASE required. Turnaround time 1-2 weeks. Fax notes: Fee to fax results is $5.00 per document. Copy fee: $5.00 per page. Certification fee: $5.00. Fee payee: City Court. Business checks accepted. Prepayment is required.

Surrogate Court Courthouse, 16 Eagle St, Albany, NY 12207; 518-487-5393. Hours: 9AM-5PM (EST). *Probate.*

Note: Search fee is $25.00 for up to 25 year search, $70 over

Town/Village Courts *Misdemeanor, Civil Actions Under $3,000, Small Claims:* Menands Village, 518-434-3992; New Scotland Town, 518-475-0493; Bethlehem Town, 518-439-8717; Guilderland Town, 518-356-1980; Rensselaerville Town, 518-239-4225; Voorheesville Village, 518-765-5524; Ravena Village, 518-756-2313; Knox Town, 518-872-2551; Westerlo Town, 518-797-3239; Berne Town, 518-872-1448; Altamont Village, 518-861-8554; Colonie Town, 518-783-2714; Green Island Town, 518-273-0661; Coeymans Town, 518-756-8480.

Allegany County

Supreme & County Court 7 Court Street, Belmont, NY 14813; 585-268-5813; Fax: 585-268-7090. Hours: 9AM-5PM; 8:30AM-4PM June,July,August (EST). *Felony, Civil.*

Note: Misdemeanor records are maintained by city, town and village courts.

Civil Records: Access: Phone, mail, in person. Only the court performs in person searches; visitors may not. No search fee. Required to search: name, years to search. Civil cases indexed by defendant. Civil records with the County Court books, all in books, no computer.

Criminal Records: Access: Fax, mail, in person. Only the court performs in person searches; visitors may not. Search fee: $5.00 for each 2 year period. Required to search: name, years to search, DOB. Criminal records with the Supreme Court, no computer, all in books.

General Information: No youth offender or sealed records released. SASE required. Turnaround time 7-10 days. Fax notes: No fee to fax results. Will fax to toll free numbers only. Copy fee: $1.00 per page. Fee payee: Joseph Presutti, County Clerk. Personal checks accepted. Prepayment is required.

Surrogate Court Courthouse, 7 Court St, Belmont, NY 14813; 585-268-5815; Fax: 585-268-7090. Hours: 9AM-5PM Sept-May; 8:30AM-4PM June-Aug (EST). *Probate.*

Town/Village Courts *Misdemeanor, Civil Actions Under $3,000, Small Claims:* Wellsville Village, 585-593-5609; Burns Town, 607-545-8998; Rushford Town, 585-437-2206; Cuba Town, 585-968-1690; Caneadea Town, 585-365-8240; Bolivar Village, 585-928-2234; Scio Town, 585-593-5777; West Almond Town, 607-276-6680; Wellsville Town, 585-593-1750; Independence Town; Centerville Town, 585-567-8425; Alfred Town, 607-587-8524; Alfred Village, 607-587-9142; Almond Town, 607-276-6665; Allen Town; Alma Town, 585-593-4021; Clarksville Town; Angelica Village Court; New Hudson Town, 585-968-3288; Canaseraga Village, 607-545-0963; Angelica Town, 585-466-7928; Andover Village, 607-478-8455; Belfast Town, 585-365-2623; Andover Town, 607-478-8446; Friendship Town, 585-973-7566; Belmont Village, 585-268-5305; Wirt Town, 585-928-2130; Bolivar Town, 585-928-1860; Genesee Town, 585-928-1384; Amity Town, 585-268-5305; Richburg Village Court; Granger Town, 585-567-4575; Willing Town.

Bronx County

Supreme Court - Civil Division 851 Grand Concourse, Bronx, NY 10451; 718-590-3603; Fax: 718-590-8122. Hours: 9AM-5PM (EST). *Civil Actions Over $25,000.*

Civil Records: Access: In person. Both court and visitors may perform in person searches. No search fee. Required to search: name, years to search. Civil cases indexed by defendant, plaintiff. Civil records on computer since 1998; prior records on microfilm.

General Information: Public access terminal is available. No marriage or divorce records released. SASE required. Turnaround time 7-10 days. Copy fee: $.75 per page. Certification fee: $5.00 per document. Fee payee: Bronx County Clerk. Only cashiers checks and money orders accepted. Prepayment is required.

Supreme Court - Criminal Division 851 Grand Concourse, Rm 123, Bronx, NY 10451; 718-590-3803. Hours: 9AM-5PM (EST). *Felony.*

Criminal Records: Access: Mail, in person. Only the court performs in person searches; visitors may not. Search fee: $16.00 per name. Fee is per county searched. Required to search: name, years to search, DOB. Criminal records on computer back to 1977, prior on microfiche.

General Information: No sealed, expunged, juvenile or sex offense records released. SASE required. Copy fee: $.75 per page. Certification fee: $10.00. Fee payee: Bronx County Clerk. Only cashiers checks and money orders accepted. Prepayment is required.

Civil Court of the City of New York - Bronx Branch 851 Grand Concourse, Bronx, NY 10451; 718-590-3601. Hours: 9AM-5PM (EST). *Civil Actions Under $25,000, Eviction, Small Claims.*

Civil Records: Access: In person only. Visitors must perform in person searches for themselves. No search fee. Required to search: name, years to search. Civil cases indexed by defendant, plaintiff. Civil records in books, on file cards.records go back to the 1970's; computerized records since 1998. Records archived after five years, requiring 3-5 days to requisition.

General Information: Public access terminal is available. Copy fee: $.25 per page. Certification fee: $5.00. Fee payee: County Clerk. Business checks accepted.

Supreme Court - Criminal Div. - Misdemeanors Central Clerk's Office, 215 W 161st St, Bronx, NY 10451; 718-590-2853. Hours: 9AM-5PM (EST). *Misdemeanor.*

Criminal Records: Access: Mail, in person. Only the court performs in person searches; visitors may not. Search fee: None reported. Required to search: name, years to search, DOB. Some criminal records on computer back to 1976, prior on microfiche.

General Information: No sealed, expunged, juvenile or sex offense records released. SASE required. Certification fee: $5.00. Fee payee: Bronx Central Clerk's Office. Only cashiers checks and money orders accepted. Prepayment is required.

Surrogate Court 851 Grand Concourse, Bronx, NY 10451; 718-590-4515; Fax: 718-537-5158. Hours: 9AM-5PM (EST). *Probate.*

Broome County

Supreme & County Court PO Box 2062, Broome County Clerk, County Office Bldg, Binghamton, NY 13902; 607-778-2451; Fax: 607-778-2243. Hours: 8AM-5PM; 7:30AM-4PM June-August (EST). *Felony, Civil.*

Civil Records: Access: Fax, mail, in person. Both court and visitors may perform in person searches. Search fee: $5.00 per name. Fee is per 2 years searched, 10 years maximum. Required to search: name, years to search. Civil cases indexed by defendant, plaintiff. Civil records on computer from 1985, prior in books.

Criminal Records: Access: Fax, mail, in person. Both court and visitors may perform in person searches. Search fee: $5.00 per name. Fee is per 2 years searched, 10 year maximum. Required to search: name, years to search, DOB. Criminal records on computer from 1985, prior in books.

General Information: Public access terminal is available. No sealed or youthful offender records released. SASE required. Turnaround time 3-5 days. Fax notes: $1.00 per page. Copy fee: $.50 per page. $1.00 minimum. Certification fee: $4.00. Fee payee: Brome County Clerk. Personal checks accepted. No personal checks over $1000.00. Prepayment is required.

Binghamton City Court Governmental Plaza, Binghamton, NY 13901; 607-772-7006; Fax: 607-772-7041. Hours: 9AM-5PM (EST). *Misdemeanor, Civil Actions Under $15,000, Eviction, Small Claims.*

Civil Records: Access: Phone, mail, in person. Both court and visitors may perform in person searches. No search fee. Required to search: name, years to yearch. Civil cases indexed by defendant. Civil records on computer from 1990, prior in books, index cards. In person searching only for 04/21/99 forward.

Criminal Records: Access: Mail, in person. Only the court performs in person searches; visitors may not. Search fee: $5.00 fee per each 2 years for a manual search prior to 1990; electronic search $16.00 (pending or disposed) 1990 to present. Required to search: name, years to search, DOB. Criminal records on computer from 1990.

General Information: Public access terminal is available. (Only civil records since 1996 are available.) No sealed records released. SASE required. Turnaround time 1-2 weeks. Copy fee: $.50 per page. $1.00 minimum. Certification fee: $5.00. per certificate. Fee payee: Binghamton City Court. Only cashiers checks and money orders accepted. Prepayment is required.

Surrogate Court Courthouse, 92 Court St, Rm 109, Binghamton, NY 13901; 607-778-2111; Fax: 607-778-2308. Hours: 9AM-5PM (EST). *Probate.*

Note: $25 search fee.

Town/Village Courts *Misdemeanor, Civil Actions Under $3,000, Small Claims:* Dickinson Town, 607-723-9403; Fenton Town, 607-648-4801; Triangle Town, 607-692-4332; Windsor Town, 607-655-1973; Union Town, 607-754-2102; Johnson City Village, 607-798-0002; Endicott Village, 607-757-2483; Conklin Town, 607-775-5244; Colesville Town, 607-693-1172; Barker Town, 607-648-6961; Chenango Town, 607-722-4191; Maine Town, 607-862-3427; Binghampton Town, 607-772-0357; Kirkwood Town, 607-775-2653; Nanticoke Town, 607-692-4041; Deposit Village, 607-467-4240; Vestal Town, 607-748-1514; Sanford Town, 607-467-3157; Lisle Town, 607-849-6969

Cattaraugus County

Supreme & County Court 303 Court St, Little Valley, NY 14755; 716-938-9111; Fax: 716-938-6413. Hours: 9AM-5PM (EST). *Felony, Civil.*

Note: Misdemeanor records are maintained by city, town and village courts.

Civil Records: Access: Mail, in person. Both court and visitors may perform in person searches. Search fee: $5.00 per name. Fee is per 2 years searched. Required to search: name, years to search. Civil cases indexed by defendant, plaintiff. Civil records on computer from 1989, prior in books, index cards from 1900.

Criminal Records: Access: Phone, mail, in person. Both court and visitors may perform in person searches. Search fee: $5.00 per name. Fee is per 2 years searched. Required to search: name, years to search, DOB. Criminal records on computer from 1989, prior in books, index cards from 1900.

General Information: No sealed or youthful offender records released. SASE not required. Turnaround time 2-3 days. Copy fee: $1.00 per page. Certification fee: $4.00. Fee payee: County Clerk. Business checks accepted. Prepayment is required.

Olean City Court PO Box 631, Olean, NY 14760; 716-376-5620; Fax: 716-376-5623. Hours: 8:30AM-5PM (EST). *Misdemeanor, Civil Actions Under $15,000, Eviction, Small Claims.*

Civil Records: Access: Phone, mail. Only the court performs in person searches; visitors may not. Search fee: $5.00 per name. Required to search: name, years to search. Civil cases indexed by defendant. Civil records on docket books.

Criminal Records: Access: Phone, mail. Only the court performs in person searches; visitors may not. Search fee: $5.00 per name. Required to search: name, years to search, DOB, signed release. Criminal records on computer from 1990, prior in books.

General Information: No sealed or youthful offender records released. SASE required. Turnaround time 2 days. Copy fee: $.25 per page. Certification fee: $5.00.

Fee payee: City Court. Business checks accepted. Prepayment is required.

Salamanca City Court Municipal Center, 225 Wildwood, Salamanca, NY 14779; 716-945-4153. Hours: 8AM-4PM (EST). *Misdemeanor, Civil Actions Under $15,000, Eviction, Small Claims.*

Civil Records: Access: Mail, in person. Only the court performs in person searches; visitors may not. Search fee: $16.00 per name. Required to search: name, years to search. Civil cases indexed by defendant. Civil records on dockets from 1930s; on computer back to 1995.

Criminal Records: Access: Mail, in person. Only the court performs in person searches; visitors may not. Search fee: $16.00 per name. Required to search: name, years to search, DOB, SSN. Criminal records on dockets from 1930s; on computer back to 1995.

General Information: No sealed records released. SASE required. Turnaround time 1-2 weeks. Certification fee: $5.00. Fee payee: Salamanca City Court. No personal checks accepted. Prepayment is required.

Surrogate Court 303 Court St, Little Valley, NY 14755; 716-938-9111 X2327; Fax: 716-938-6983. Hours: 9AM-5PM (EST). *Probate.*

Note: Public can search, but if court has to search there is a fee.

Town/Village Courts *Misdemeanor, Civil Actions Under $3,000, Small Claims:* Farmersville Town, 716-676-3030; Little Valley Town; Humphrey Town; Conewango Town, 716-358-6386; South Dayton Village, 716-988-3833; Machias Town, 716-353-8207; South Valley Town, 716-354-5854; Ellicottville Town, 716-699-2240; Ashford Town; Mansfield Town; Carrollton Town, 716-925-8508; Ischua Town, 716-557-2236; Lyndon Town, 716-676-9928; Randolph Town, 716-358-2591; Dayton Town, 716-532-3758; Perrysburg Town, 716-532-4090; Persia Town, 716-532-4042; Great Valley Town, 716-945-4200; Coldspring Town, 716-354-5752; Red House Town; Napoli Town, 716-938-9418; Salamanca Town; Allegany Town, 716-373-3670; East Otto Town; Olean Town, 716-373-0582; New Albion Town, 716-257-3661; Portville Town, 716-933-6658; Portville Village, 716-933-8407; Freedom Town, 716-492-0961; Otto Town, 716-257-3111; Fraklinville Town, 716-676-3077; Allegany Village, 716-373-1460; Cattaraugus Village, 716-257-3661; Ellicottville Village, 716-699-4636; Yorkshire Town, 716-492-1640; Hinsdale Town.

Cayuga County

Supreme & County Court 160 Genesee St, Auburn, NY 13021-3424; 315-253-1271; Fax: 315-253-1586. Hours: 9AM-5PM Sept-June; 8AM-4PM July-Aug (EST). *Felony, Misdemeanor, Civil.*

Note: The court is located at 154 Genesee Street.

Civil Records: Access: Mail, in person. Both court and visitors may perform in person searches. Search fee: $5.00 per name. Required to search: name, years to search. Civil cases indexed by defendant, plaintiff. Civil records on computer from 1986, prior in books.

Criminal Records: Access: Mail, in person. Both court and visitors may perform in person searches. Search fee: $16.00 per name. Required to search: name, years to search, DOB. Criminal records names are computerized since 1930.

General Information: Public access terminal is available. No sealed records released. SASE required. Turnaround time 1 day. Copy fee: $.50 per page. Certification fee: $4.00 plus $.50 per page after first 8. Fee payee: County Clerk. Personal checks accepted. Prepayment is required.

Auburn City Court 153 Genesee St, Auburn, NY 13021-3434; 315-253-1570; Fax: 315-253-1085.

Hours: 8AM-4PM (EST). *Misdemeanor, Civil Actions Under $15,000, Eviction, Small Claims.*

Civil Records: Access: Mail, in person. Only the court performs in person searches; visitors may not. Search fee: Electronic search is $16.00, extra years are $5.00. Required to search: name, years to search. Civil cases indexed by defendant. Civil records on computer from 1986.

Criminal Records: Access: Mail, in person. Only the court performs in person searches; visitors may not. Search fee: Electronic search is $16.00, extra years are $5.00 per 2 years. Required to search: name, years to search, DOB. Criminal records on computer from 1986.

General Information: No sealed, expunged, adoption, sex offense, juvenile or mental health records released. SASE required. Turnaround time 3 days. Certification fee: $5.00. Fee payee: City Court. Only money orders accepted. Prepayment is required.

Surrogate Court Courthouse, 152 Genesee St, Auburn, NY 13021-3471; 315-255-4316; Fax: 315-255-4322. Hours: 8:30AM-4:30PM; Summer hours 8AM-4:00PM (EST). *Probate.*

www.courts.state.ny.us/www/jd7/cayuga_surrogate.htm

Town/Village Courts *Misdemeanor, Civil Actions Under $3,000, Small Claims:* Owasco Town, 315-253-9021; Fleming Town, 315-252-8988; Brutus Town, 315-834-6618; Sterling Town, 315-865-5087; Genoa Town; Locke Town, 315-497-1932; Summerhill Town; Conquest Town, 315-776-5288; Throop Town, 315-252-7373; Ledyard Town, 315-364-8169; Port Byron Village Court; Victory Town, 315-626-6817; Sempronius Town, 315-497-0549; Montezuma Town, 315-776-8822; Moravia Town, 315-497-1972; Springport Town; Sennett Town, 315-253-7748; Meridian Village, 315-626-6230; Weedsport Village, 315-834-6634; Niles Town, 315-497-0066; Ira Town, 315-626-2154; Mentz Town, 315-776-8692; Moravia Village, 315-497-1820; Cato Town, 315-626-6230; Venice Town, 315-364-8936; Cato Village, 315-626-2397; Aurelius Town, 315-255-0065; Scipio Town, 315-364-7754.

Chautauqua County

Supreme & County Court - Civil PO Box 170, Mayville, NY 14757; 716-753-4331. Hours: 9AM-5PM/Summer 8:30AM-4:30PM (EST). *Civil.*

Civil Records: Access: Mail, in person. Only the court performs in person searches; visitors may not. No search fee. Required to search: name, years to search. Civil cases indexed by plaintiff. Civil records in docket books or cards; on computer back to 8/1/1997.

General Information: No sealed records released. SASE required. Turnaround time 1-2 days. Copy fee: $4.00. Add $1.00 per page after first 4. Fee payee: Chautauqua County Clerk. Personal checks accepted. Prepayment is required.

Supreme & County Court - Criminal Courthouse, PO Box 292, Mayville, NY 14757; 716-753-4266; Fax: 716-753-4993. Hours: 9AM-5PM/Summer 8:30AM-4:30PM (EST). *Felony.*

Note: Misdemeanor records are maintained by city, town and village courts.

Criminal Records: Access: Mail, in person. Only the court performs in person searches; visitors may not. Search fee: $16.00 per name. Also, a Certificate of Conviction can be ordered for $5.00. Required to search: name, years to search, DOB, signed release. Criminal records on computer from 1/1987. Be advised that all requests without a DOB will be returned.

General Information: No sealed records released. SASE required. Turnaround time 1-2 days. Copy fee: $4.00. Add $1.00 per page after first 4. Fee payee: County Clerk. Prepayment is required.

Dunkirk City Court City Hall, 342 Central Ave, Dunkirk, NY 14048; 716-366-2055; Fax: 716-366-3622. Hours: 9AM-5PM (EST). *Misdemeanor, Civil Actions Under $15,000, Eviction, Small Claims.*

Civil Records: Access: Mail, fax, in person. Only the court performs in person searches; visitors may not. Search fee: $16.00 per name. Required to search: name, years to search. Civil cases indexed by defendant. Civil records on computer back to 1990, prior in books.

Criminal Records: Access: Mail, fax, in person. Only the court performs in person searches; visitors may not. Search fee: $16.00 per name. Required to search: name, years to search, DOB. Criminal records on computer back to 1990, prior in books.

General Information: No sealed, expunged, adoption, sex offense, juvenile or mental health records released. SASE required. Turnaround time 1 week. Copy fee: $.50 per page. Certification fee: $5.00. Fee payee: Dunkirk City Court. Only cashiers checks and money orders accepted. Prepayment is required.

Jamestown City Court City Hall, Jamestown, NY 14701; 716-483-7561/7562; Fax: 716-483-7519. Hours: 9AM-5PM (EST). *Misdemeanor, Civil Actions Under $15,000, Eviction, Small Claims.*

Civil Records: Access: Fax, mail, in person. Both court and visitors may perform in person searches. No search fee. Required to search: name, years to search. Civil cases indexed by defendant. Civil records on computer back to 1989, prior in books.

Criminal Records: Access: Fax, mail, in person. Only the court performs in person searches; visitors may not. Search fee: $5.00 per name. Fee is for 2 year search, or $16.00 for automated search. Required to search: name, years to search, DOB, signed release; also helpful: address, SSN. Criminal records on computer back to 1989, prior in books to 1965.

General Information: No sealed records released. SASE required. Turnaround time 1 week. Copy fee: $1.00 per page. Certification fee: $5.00. Fee payee: City Court. Business checks accepted. Prepayment is required.

Surrogate's Court Gerace Office Bldg (3 N. Erie St), PO Box C, Mayville, NY 14757; 716-753-4339; Fax: 716-753-4600. Hours: 9AM-5PM (EST). *Probate.*

Town/Village Courts *Misdemeanor, Civil Actions Under $3,000, Small Claims:* Silver Creek Village, 716-934-3558; Portland Town, 716-792-4111; Sherman Town, 716-761-6770; Sheridan Town, 716-672-2600; Mina Town, 716-769-7555; Pomfret Town, 716-672-6867; Ellery Town, 716-386-2521; Stockton Town, 716-595-2259; Poland Town, 716-267-2912; Ripley Town, 716-736-7575; North Harmony Town, 716-789-3445; Busti Town, 716-763-4695; Arkwright Town, 716-679-4445; Clymer Town, 716-355-6331; Dunkirk Town, 716-366-3945; Ellicott Town, 716-665-5319; Brocton Village Court; Ellington Town, 716-287-2026; Hanover Town, 716-934-4770; Kiantone Town, 716-488-0383; Gerry Town, 716-985-5323; Cherry Creek Town, 716-296-5721; French Creek Town, 716-355-8801; Chautauqua Town, 716-753-5245; Harmony Town; Charlotte Town; Carroll Town, 716-569-5365; Westfield Town, 716-326-3211; Westfield Village, 716-326-4961; Villenova Town, 716-988-3678; Fredonia Village, 716-679-2312.

Chemung County

Supreme & County Court - Civil 210 Lake St, Elmira, NY 14901; 607-737-2920; Fax: 607-737-2897. Hours: 8:30AM-4:30PM (EST). *Civil.*

www.chemungcounty.com

Civil Records: Access: Mail, fax, in person. Both court and visitors may perform in person searches. Search fee: $5.00 per name. Fee is per 2 years searched. Required to search: name, years to search. Civil cases

indexed by defendant, plaintiff. Civil records on computer from 1994, prior in books to 1800s.

General Information: Public access terminal is available. (For land records only from 1991 forward.) No sealed, divorce or adoption records released. SASE required. Turnaround time 4-6 weeks. Copy fee: $.50 per page. $1.00 minimum. Certification fee: $4.00 plus $1.00 per page after first 4. Fee payee: County Clerk. Personal checks accepted. Prepayment is required.

Supreme & County Court - Criminal PO Box 588, Elmira, NY 14902-0588; 607-737-2844. Hours: 8:30AM-4:30PM (EST). *Felony.*

Criminal Records: Access: Mail, in person. Only the court performs in person searches; visitors may not. Search fee: $5.00 for every 2 years searched or $20.00 for a seven year search. Searches with both maiden and married names are considered two searches. Required to search: name, years to search, DOB, SSN. Criminal records in docket books back to 1979.

General Information: No sealed, divorce or adoption records released. SASE required. Turnaround time 4-6 weeks. Copy fee: $.50 per page. Certification fee: $5.00. Fee payee: County Clerk. Personal checks accepted. Prepayment is required.

Elmira City Court 317 E Church St, Elmira, NY 14901-2790; 607-737-5681; Fax: 607-737-5820. Hours: 8AM-4PM (EST). *Misdemeanor, Civil Actions Under $15,000, Eviction, Small Claims.*

http://courts.state.ny.us/6jd/web/countymaps/chemung/city/default.html

Civil Records: Access: Mail, in person. Both court and visitors may perform in person searches. Search fee: $16.00 per name. Required to search: name, years to search. Civil cases indexed by defendant. Civil records on computer back to 1997; prior records on index cards.

Criminal Records: Access: Mail, in person. Only the court performs in person searches; visitors may not. Search fee: $16.00 per name; if 1987 to present;, fee is $5.00 per name per 2 years. Required to search: name, years to search, DOB, signed release; also helpful: SSN. Criminal records on computer back to 1987; prior on books.

General Information: Public access terminal is available. (Only civil records are available.) No sealed records released. SASE required. Turnaround time 3-5 days. Copy fee: $.50 per page; $1.00 minimum. Certification fee: $5.00. Fee payee: Elmira City Court. Personal checks accepted. Prepayment is required.

Surrogate Court 224 Lake St, Elmira, NY 14901; 607-737-2946/2819; Fax: 607-737-2874. Hours: 9AM-5PM (EST). *Probate.*

Town/Village Courts *Misdemeanor, Civil Actions Under $3,000, Small Claims:* Chemung Town, 607-529-3322; Catlin Town, 607-739-5598; Horseheads Village, 607-739-0158; Baldwin Town; Van Etten Town, 607-589-4435; Erin Town, 607-739-8681; Elmira Town, 607-734-5971; Big Flats Town, 607-562-3516; Ashland Town, 607-732-0723; Wellsburg Village, 607-733-8211; Elmira Heights Village, 607-734-9693; Horseheads Town, 607-739-2113; Veteran Town, 607-739-1476; Southport Town, 607-734-1548; Millport Village.

Chenango County

Supreme & County Court County Office Bldg, Norwich, NY 13815-1676; 607-337-1450. Hours: 8:30AM-5PM (EST). *Felony, Civil.*

Civil Records: Access: Mail, in person. Both court and visitors may perform in person searches. Search fee: $5.00 per name. Fee is per 2 years searched. Required to search: name, years to search. Civil cases indexed by defendant, plaintiff. Civil records on computer from 1994, prior in books since 1880.

Criminal Records: Access: Mail, in person. Both court and visitors may perform in person searches. Search fee: $5.00 per name. Fee is per 2 years searched. Required to search: name, years to search, DOB. Criminal records in docket books.

General Information: No sealed, expunged, adoption, sex offense, juvenile or mental health records released. SASE required. Turnaround time 1 week. Copy fee: $.50 per page. $1.00 minimum. Certification fee: Certification fee is $1.00 per pg, $4.00 minimum. Fee payee: County Clerk. Personal checks accepted. Prepayment is required.

Norwich City Court 1 Court Plaza, Norwich, NY 13815; 607-334-1224; Fax: 607-334-8494. Hours: 8:30AM-4:30PM (EST). *Misdemeanor, Civil Actions Under $15,000, Eviction, Small Claims.*

Civil Records: Access: Fax, mail, in person. Both court and visitors may perform in person searches. Search fee: $16.00 per name. Required to search: name, years to search. Civil cases indexed by defendant. Civil records on computer from 1990, prior in books.

Criminal Records: Access: Fax, mail, in person. Both court and visitors may perform in person searches. Search fee: $16.00 per name 1990-present; $5.00 if prior to 1990. Required to search: name, years to search, DOB, signed release. Criminal records on computer from 1990, prior in books.

General Information: No sealed, expunged, adoption, sex offense, juvenile or mental health records released. SASE required. Turnaround time 1 week. Certification fee: $5.00. Fee payee: City Court. Business checks accepted. Prepayment is required.

Surrogate Court County Office Bldg, 5 Court St, Norwich, NY 13815; 607-337-1822/1827; Fax: 607-337-1834. Hours: 9AM-Noon, 1-5PM (EST). *Probate.*

Town/Village Courts *Misdemeanor, Civil Actions Under $3,000, Small Claims:* Smithville Town, 607-656-7969; Bainbridge Village, 607-967-7465; Pitcher Town; Coventry Town, 607-656-8602; Pharsalia Town, 607-647-5203; New Berlin Village, 607-847-6249; Bainbridge Town, 607-967-7465; Earlville Village, 315-691-6020; Otselic Town, 315-653-7201; Norwich Town, 607-334-6359; Guilford Town, 607-895-6818; North Norwich Town, 607-334-9224; Sherburne Village, 607-674-4827; Oxford Village, 607-843-9772; Greene Town, 607-656-4333; New Berlin Town, 607-847-8909; Smyrna Town; Sherburne Town, 607-674-4827; Columbus Town; Sherburne Village, 607-674-4827; Greene Village Court; Oxford Town, 607-843-9772; German Town; Lincklaen Town, 315-852-6128; Afton Village Court; Plymouth Town; Preston Town, 607-336-1013; Afton Town.

Clinton County

Supreme & County Court County Government Center, 137 Margaret St, Plattsburgh, NY 12901; 518-565-4715; Fax: 518-565-4708. Hours: 9AM-5PM (EST). *Felony, Civil.*

www.courts.state.ny.us

Civil Records: Access: In person only. Visitors must perform in person searches for themselves. No search fee. Required to search: name, years to search. Civil cases indexed by defendant. Civil records in docket books. Online access to current and pending civil cases is available free at http://e.courts.state.ny.us/descCaseSearch.html.

Criminal Records: Access: Mail, in person. Both court and visitors may perform in person searches. Search fee: $16.00 per name. Required to search: name, years to search, DOB. Criminal records on computer from 1986, prior in docket books from 1961.

General Information: No sealed or sex case records released. SASE required. Turnaround time 3-4 days. Copy fee: $.50 per page. Certification fee: Certification

$4.00 up to 4 pages, then $1.00 per additional page. Fee payee: County Clerk. Personal checks accepted. Prepayment is required.

Plattsburg City Court 41 City Hall Pl, Plattsburgh, NY 12901; 518-563-7870; Fax: 518-563-3124. Hours: 8AM-4PM (EST). *Misdemeanor, Civil Actions Under $15,000, Eviction, Small Claims.*

Civil Records: Access: Mail, in person. Only the court performs in person searches; visitors may not. Search fee: $16.00 for computerized search. Required to search: name, years to search. Civil cases indexed by defendant. Civil records on computer back to 1986, prior in books.

Criminal Records: Access: Mail, in person. Only the court performs in person searches; visitors may not. Search fee: $16.00 per name. Required to search: name, years to search, DOB, signed release. Criminal records on computer back to 1986, prior in books.

General Information: No sealed records released. SASE required. Turnaround time same day. Copy fee: $1.00 per page. Certification fee: $5.00. Fee payee: City Court. Only cashiers checks and money orders accepted. Prepayment is required.

Surrogate Court 137 Margaret St, #315, Plattsburgh, NY 12901-2933; 518-565-4630; Fax: 518-565-4769. Hours: 9AM-5PM (EST). *Probate.*

Town/Village Courts *Misdemeanor, Civil Actions Under $3,000, Small Claims:* Plattsburgh Town, 518-563-8100; Saranac Town, 518-293-6666; Champlain Village Court; Dannemora Village, 518-492-7000; Black Brook Town, 518-647-5412; Beekmantown Town, 518-563-9930; AuSable Town, 518-834-9052; Peru Town, 518-643-2745; Dannemora Town, 518-492-7541; Champlain Town, 518-298-2043; Ellenburg Town, 518-594-7708; Chazy Town, 518-846-8600; Clinton Town, 518-497-6133; Altona Town; Mooers Town; Schuyler Falls Town, 518-563-1129; Rouses Point Village, 518-297-6648.

Columbia County

Supreme & County Court 560 Warren Street, Hudson, NY 12534; 518-828-3339; Fax: 518-828-5299. Hours: 9AM-5PM (EST). *Felony, Civil.*

Note: Supreme and County courts are actually located at 401 Union in Hudson, but records for both courts are located at the County Clerk's Office as listed above.

Civil Records: Access: Mail, in person. Both court and visitors may perform in person searches. Search fee: $5.00 per name. Fee is per 2 years searched. Required to search: name, years to search. Civil cases indexed by defendant. Civil records on computer from 1993, prior on cards to 1985.

Criminal Records: Access: Mail, in person. Both court and visitors may perform in person searches. Search fee: $5.00 per name. Required to search: name, years to search, DOB. Criminal records on computer from 1993, prior on cards to 1985.

General Information: Public access terminal is available. No sealed records released. SASE required. Turnaround time 1 week. Copy fee: $.25 per page. Certification fee: $4.00. Fee payee: County Clerk. Personal checks accepted. Prepayment is required.

Hudson City Court 429 Warren St, Hudson, NY 12534; 518-828-3100; Fax: 518-828-3628. Hours: 8AM-3:45PM (EST). *Misdemeanor, Civil Actions Under $15,000, Eviction, Small Claims.*

Civil Records: Access: Fax, mail, in person. Only the court performs in person searches; visitors may not. Search fee: $16.00 per name. Required to search: name, years to search; also helpful: address. Civil cases indexed by defendant, plaintiff. Civil records on computer from 1991, prior in books.

Criminal Records: Access: Fax, mail, in person. Only the court performs in person searches; visitors may not.

Search fee: $16.00 per name for 10 year search. Required to search: name, years to search, DOB. Criminal records on computer from 1991, prior in books.

General Information: No sealed, expunged, adoption, sex offense, juvenile or mental health records released. SASE required. Turnaround time 1 week. Copy fee: $.50 per page. Certification fee: $5.00. Fee payee: Hudson City Court. Business checks accepted. Prepayment is required.

Surrogate Court Courthouse, 401 Union St, Hudson, NY 12534; 518-828-0414; Fax: 518-828-1603. Hours: 9AM-5PM (EST). *Probate.*

Town/Village Courts *Misdemeanor, Civil Actions Under $3,000, Small Claims:* New Lebanon Town, 518-794-9456; Stuyvesant Town; Stockport Town, 518-828-9389; Chatham Town; Claverack Town, 518-672-4468; Hillsdale Town, 518-325-5073; Chatham Village, 518-392-9476; Ancram Town, 518-329-6512; Valatie Village, 518-758-9838; Canaan Town, 518-781-4455; Ghent Town, 518-392-4644; Philmont Village, 518-672-7032; Taghkanic Town, 518-329-3030; Germantown Town, 518-537-6687; Greenport Town, 518-828-4656; Clermont Town, 518-537-6868; Austerlitz Town, 518-392-3260; Gallatin Town, 518-329-3030; Livingston Town, 518-851-7201; Kinderhook Town, 518-784-2506; Kinderhook Village Court; Copake Town, 518-329-1234.

Cortland County

Supreme & County Court 46 Greenbush St, Ste 301, Cortland, NY 13045; Civil phone: 607-753-5021; Criminal phone: 607-753-5010; Fax: 607-756-3409. Hours: 9AM-5PM (EST). *Felony, Civil.*

Civil Records: Access: Mail, in person. Both court and visitors may perform in person searches. Search fee: $5.00 per name. per 2 year search. Required to search: name, years to search. Civil cases indexed by defendant, plaintiff. Civil records on computer from 5/94, prior in books.

Criminal Records: Access: Mail, in person. Only the court performs in person searches; visitors may not. Search fee: $5.00 per name. Per 2 year search. Required to search: name, years to search, DOB. Criminal records on computer from 1986, prior in books.

General Information: No sealed or youthful offender records released. SASE required. Turnaround time 1 day. Copy fee: $.50 per page. Certification fee: $1.00. Minimum $4.00. Fee payee: County Clerk. Personal checks accepted. Prepayment is required.

Cortland City Court 25 Court St, Cortland, NY 13045; 607-753-1811; Fax: 607-753-9932. Hours: 8:30AM-4:30PM (EST). *Misdemeanor, Civil Actions Under $15,000, Eviction, Small Claims.*

Civil Records: Access: Mail, in person. Only the court performs in person searches; visitors may not. Search fee: $5.00 per name per 2 years prior to 1991. Required to search: name, years to search. Civil cases indexed by defendant. Civil records on computer from 1991, prior in books.

Criminal Records: Access: Mail, in person. Only the court performs in person searches; visitors may not. Search fee: $5.00 per name per 2 years. $16.00 for electronic search. Required to search: name, years to search, DOB. Criminal records on computer from 1991, prior in books.

General Information: No sealed records released. SASE required. Turnaround time 10 days. Copy fee: $.50 per page. Certification fee: $5.00. Fee payee: City Court. Only cashiers checks and money orders accepted. Prepayment is required.

Surrogate Court 46 Greenbush St, Ste 301, Cortland, NY 13045; 607-753-5355; Fax: 607-756-3409. Hours: 9AM-5PM (EST). *Probate.*

www.courts.state.ny.us/6jd/web/countymaps/cortland/mb

Town/Village Courts *Misdemeanor, Civil Actions Under $3,000, Small Claims:* Cuyler Town; Taylor Town, 607-863-3716; Preble Town, 607-749-2377; Truxton Town, 607-842-6291; Lapeer Town, 607-849-3808; Freetown Town, 607-849-6372; Virgil Town, 607-835-6587; Solon Town; Cortlandville Town, 607-756-2352; Cincinnatus Town, 607-863-4220; Marathon Village, 607-849-6966; Marathon Town; Homer Village, 607-749-2326; Homer Town, 607-749-2326; Willet Town, 607-863-3265; Scott Town, 607-749-2902; Harford Town.

Delaware County

Supreme & County Court 3 Court St, Delhi, NY 13753; 607-746-2131; Fax: 607-746-3253. Hours: 9AM-5PM (EST). *Felony, Civil.*

Note: Misdemeanor records are maintained by city, town and village courts.

Civil Records: Access: Mail, in person. Both court and visitors may perform in person searches. Search fee: $5.00 per name. Required to search: name, years to search. Civil cases indexed by defendant, plaintiff. Civil records in books.

Criminal Records: Access: Mail, in person. Both court and visitors may perform in person searches. Search fee: $5.00 per name. Required to search: name, years to search, DOB. Criminal records in books.

General Information: No sealed records released. SASE required. Turnaround time 2 days. Copy fee: $.50 per page. Certification fee: Certification $4.00 for up to 4 pages, then $1.00 per page. Fee payee: County Clerk. Personal checks accepted. Prepayment required.

Surrogate Court 3 Court St, Delhi, NY 13753; 607-746-2126; Fax: 607-746-3253. *Probate.*

Town/Village Courts *Misdemeanor, Civil Actions Under $3,000, Small Claims:* Davenport Town; Delhi Town, 607-746-7278; Colchester Town, 845-498-5575; Delhi Village, 607-746-7161; Deposit Town, 607-467-3208; Roxbury Town, 607-588-7507; Fleischmanns Village, 845-254-5514; Hancock Town, 607-637-3651; Walton Village Court; Sidney Village, 845-561-2307; Sidney Town, 845-561-2309; Middletown Town, 845-586-2575; Harpersfield Town, 607-652-5060; Meredith Town, 607-746-2341; Masonville Town; Walton Town, 607-865-5182; Hancock Village, 607-637-5341; Stamford Town, 607-538-9421; Stamford Village, 607-652-6671; Tompkins Town, 607-865-4979; Bovina Town; Andes Town, 845-676-3550; Kortright Town; Hamden Town, 607-746-6660.

Dutchess County

Supreme & County Court 22 Market St, Poughkeepsie, NY 12601-3203; 845-486-2125. Hours: 9AM-5PM (EST). *Felony, Civil.*

www.dutchessny.gov/dcclerk.htm

Civil Records: Access: In person only. Visitors must perform in person searches for themselves. No search fee. Required to search: name, years to search. Civil cases indexed by defendant, plaintiff. Civil records in books back to 1847; on computer back to 1986.

Criminal Records: Access: Mail, in person. Both court and visitors may perform in person searches. Search fee: $5.00 per name. Fee is per 2 years or part thereof (convictions only). Prepayment required. Required to search: name, years to search, aliases. Criminal records go back to 1847; on computer back to 1987. They will only create a certificate if their staff performs the search.

General Information: Public access terminal is available. No sealed or youthful offender records released. SASE required. Turnaround time 2 weeks. Copy fee: $5.00 per document. Certification fee: $4.00 plus $.50 per page after first 8 in person. $6.00 per document by mail. $5.00 for assumed name, if in person. Fee payee: Dutchess County Clerk. Personal checks accepted. Prepayment is required.

Beacon City Court One Municipal Plaza, #2, Beacon, NY 12508; 845-838-5030; Fax: 845-838-5041. Hours: 8AM-4PM (EST). *Misdemeanor, Civil Actions Under $15,000, Eviction, Small Claims.*

Civil Records: Access: Mail, in person. Court only performs searches. Search fee: $16.00 per name. Required to search: name, date of birth, address, years to search. Civil cases indexed by defendant, plaintiff. Civil records on computer from 1996, prior in books and cards.

Criminal Records: Access: Mail, in person. Only the court performs in person searches; visitors may not. Search fee: $16.00 per name. Required to search: name, years to search, DOB, SSN, signed release. Criminal records computerized since 1990.

General Information: No sealed or youthful offender records released. SASE required. Turnaround time 7-10 days. Copy fee: $1.00 first page, $.50 every page thereafter. Certification fee: $5.00. Fee payee: City Court of Beacon. Only cashiers checks and money orders accepted. Prepayment is required.

Poughkeepsie City Court Civic Center Plaza, PO Box 300, Poughkeepsie, NY 12602; 845-451-4091; Fax: 845-485-6795. Hours: 8AM-4PM (EST). *Misdemeanor, Civil Actions Under $15,000, Eviction, Small Claims.*

Civil Records: Access: Mail, in person. Both court and visitors may perform in person searches. Search fee: $16.00 per name. $5.00 for certificate of disposition. Required to search: name, years to search. Civil cases indexed by defendant. Civil records on computer from 1993.

Criminal Records: Access: Mail, in person. Both court and visitors may perform in person searches. Search fee: $16.00 per name. $5.00 per certified disposition. Required to search: name, years to search, DOB, signed release. Criminal records on computer from 1990.

General Information: No sealed, expunged, adoption, sex offense, juvenile or mental health records released. SASE required. Turnaround time 1 week. Copy fee: $.50 per page. Certification fee: $5.00. Fee payee: Poughkeepsie City Court. Only cashiers checks and money orders accepted. Prepayment is required.

Surrogate Court 10 Market St, Poughkeepsie, NY 12601; 845-486-2235; Fax: 845-486-2234. Hours: 9AM-5PM (EST). *Probate.*

Town/Village Courts *Misdemeanor, Civil Actions Under $3,000, Small Claims:* Beekman Town, 845-724-5581; Pine Plains Town, 518-398-7194; Milan Town, 914-758-6960; LaGrange Town, 845-452-1837; Pleasant Valley Town, 845-635-2856; Red Hook Town, 845-758-5851; Rhinebeck Town, 845-876-7303; Stanford Town, 845-868-2269; Red Hook Village, 845-758-4113; Poughkeepsie Town, 845-485-3695; Amenia Town, 845-373-7017; Dover Town; Union Vale Town, 845-724-5600; Rhinebeck Village, 845-876-4119; Pawling Village, 845-855-5602; North East Town, 518-789-3080; Millbrook Village, 845-677-8277; Wappinger Town, 845-297-6070; East Fishkill Town, 845-226-4229; Wappingers Falls Village, 845-297-6777; Washington Town, 845-677-6366; Hyde Park Town, 845-229-2606; Tivoli Village, 845-757-2021; Clinton Town, 845-266-5988; Fishkill Village, 914-879-2103; Fishkill Town, 845-831-7800; Pawling Town, 845-855-3516.

Erie County

Supreme & County Court 25 Delaware Ave, Buffalo, NY 14202; Civil phone: 716-858-7766; Criminal phone: 716-858-7877; Fax: 716-858-6550. Hours: 9AM-5PM (EST). *Felony, Civil.*

www.erie.gov

Civil Records: Access: Mail, in person, online. Both court and visitors may perform in person searches. Search fee: $5.00 per name. Fee is per 2 years searched. Required to search: name, years to search. Civil cases indexed by defendant. Civil records on computer from 1994, prior in books back to 1900's. Online access to the county clerk's database of civil matters is available free at http://ecclerk.erie.gov. Records go back to 2/1994.

Criminal Records: Access: Mail, in person. Both court and visitors may perform in person searches. Search fee: $5.00 per name. Fee is per 2 years searched. Required to search: name, years to search, DOB. Criminal records in books back to 1900's.

General Information: Public access terminal is available. (Public access terminal for civil in person searches.) No sealed records released. SASE required. Turnaround time 3-4 days. Copy fee: $1.00 per page. Certification fee: $4.00. Fee payee: County Clerk. Personal checks accepted. Prepayment is required.

Buffalo City Court 50 Delaware Ave, Buffalo, NY 14202; 716-847-8200; Fax: 716-847-8257. Hours: 9AM-5PM (EST). *Misdemeanor, Civil Actions Under $15,000, Eviction, Small Claims.*

Civil Records: Access: Mail, fax, in person. Both court and visitors may perform in person searches. Search fee: $5.00 per name. Required to search: name, years to search. Civil cases indexed by defendant, plaintiff. Criminal records on computer back to 1983, prior in books back to 1974.

Criminal Records: Access: In person only. Only the court performs in person searches; visitors may not. Search fee: $5.00 per disposition. Required to search: name, DOB, date of offense. Criminal records on computer back to 1983, prior in books back to 1974. Will perform a disposition search. No general searches are done; searches are directed to OCA in NYC.

General Information: No sealed or youthful offender records released. SASE required. Turnaround time 3 days. Copy fee: $1.00 per page. Certification fee: $5.00. Fee payee: City Court. Business checks accepted. Prepayment is required.

Lackawanna City Court 714 Ridge Rd, Rm 225, Lackawanna, NY 14218; 716-827-6486; Fax: 716-825-1874. Hours: 8:30AM-4:30PM (EST). *Misdemeanor, Civil Actions Under $15,000, Eviction, Small Claims.*

Civil Records: Access: Mail, in person. Only the court may perform in person searches. Search fee: $16.00 per name. Required to search: name; also helpful: years to search. Civil cases indexed by defendant. Civil records on computer from 1994, prior on docket books. Mail access available to government agencies only.

Criminal Records: Access: Mail, in person. Only the court performs in person searches; visitors may not. Search fee: $16.00 per name. Required to search: name; also helpful: years to search, DOB. Criminal records on computer from 1994, prior on docket books. Mail access available to government agencies only.

General Information: No sealed or youthful offender records released. SASE required. Turnaround time 2-3 days. Copy fee: $1.00 per page. Certification fee: $5.00. Fee payee: City Court. Only cashiers checks and money orders accepted. Prepayment is required.

Tonawanda City Court 200 Niagara St, Tonawanda, NY 14150; 716-693-3484; Fax: 716-693-1612. Hours: 9AM-4PM (EST). *Misdemeanor, Civil*

Actions Under $15,000, Eviction, Small Claims, Criminal.

Civil Records: Access: Mail, in person. Only the court performs in person searches; visitors may not. Search fee: $5.00 per name. Required to search: name, years to search. Civil cases indexed by defendant, plaintiff. Civil records on computer since 1997, prior on index cards, in books.

Criminal Records: Access: Mail, in person. Only the court performs in person searches; visitors may not. Search fee: $16.00 per name. Required to search: name, years to search, DOB, signed release. Criminal records on computer since 19867, prior on index cards, in books.

General Information: No sealed records released. SASE not required. Turnaround time 3-5 days. Copy fee: $1.00 per page. Certification fee: $5.00. Fee payee: City Court of Tonawanda. Business checks accepted. Prepayment is required.

Surrogate Court 92 Franklin St, Buffalo, NY 14202; 716-854-7867; Fax: 716-853-3741. Hours: 9AM-5PM (EST). *Probate.*

Town/Village Courts *Misdemeanor, Civil Actions Under $3,000, Small Claims:* Brant Town, 716-549-0300; Hamburg Town, 716-649-6111; East Aurora Village, 716-652-5275; Lancaster Town, 716-683-1814; Lancaster Village, 716-683-6780; Elma Town, 716-652-1855; Orchard Park Town, 716-662-6415; Depew Village, 716-683-0978; Hamburg Village, 716-649-7204; Orchard Park Village, 716-662-6415; Clarence Town, 716-741-2802; North Collins Town, 716-337-3712; Marilla Town, 716-652-5350; Kenmore Village Court; Evans Town, 716-549-3707; Farnham Village Court; Holland Town, 716-457-3022; Grand Island Town, 716-773-9650; Cheektowaga Town, 716-686-3437; Newstead Town, 716-542-4575; Eden Town, 716-992-3559; Boston Town, 716-941-6115; Blasdell Village, 716-822-7118; West Seneca Town, 716-674-5600; Amherst Town, 716-689-4200; Angola Village Court; Concord Town, 716-592-9898; Wales Town, 716-652-3320; Collins Town, 716-532-4887; Colden Town, 716-941-5012; Tonawanda Town, 716-876-5536; Sardinia Town, 716-496-8900; Alden Town, 716-937-3411; Williamsville Village, 716-632-0450; Akron Village, 716-542-9636; Alden Village, 716-937-9057; Aurora Town, 716-652-5275.

Essex County

Supreme & County Courts Essex County Government Center, Court St, PO Box 217, Elizabethtown, NY 12932; Civil phone: 518-873-3600; Criminal phone: 518-873-3370; Fax: 518-873-3376. Hours: 8:30AM-5PM (EST). *Felony, Civil.*

Note: Misdemeanor records are maintained by city, town and village courts.

Civil Records: Access: Mail, in person. Both court and visitors may perform in person searches. No search fee. Required to search: name, years to search. Civil cases indexed by defendant, plaintiff. Civil records on computer from 11/93, prior in books.

Criminal Records: Access: Mail, in person. Both court and visitors may perform in person searches. Search fee: Two types of searches available-manual since 1956 at $5.00 per name per each two years, and computer at $16.00 per name. Call for copy of special form to compute fee and submit with payment. Required to search: name, years to search, DOB. Criminal records on computer from 1950s, prior in books.

General Information: No sealed or youthful offender records released. SASE required. Turnaround time same day. Copy fee: $.50 per page. Certification fee: $1.00. Minimum $4.00. Fee payee: Essex County Clerk. Personal checks accepted. Prepayment required.

Surrogate Court 100 Court St, PO Box 505, Elizabethtown, NY 12932; 518-873-3384. Hours: 9AM-5PM (EST). *Probate.*

www.courts.state.ny.us

Town/Village Courts *Misdemeanor, Civil Actions Under $3,000, Small Claims:* North Elba Town, 518-523-9516; Lewis Town, 518-873-6777; Chesterfield Town, 518-834-9211; St Armand Town; Elizabethtown Town, 518-873-6555; Minerva Town, 518-251-2869; Moriah Town; Ticonderoga Town, 518-585-7141; Newcomb Town, 518-582-2010; Schroon Town, 518-532-0659; Crown Point Town, 518-597-4144; North Hudson Town; Westport Town, 518-962-4882; Lake Placid Village, 518-523-2004; Keene Town, 518-576-4444; Essex Town, 518-963-4287; Jay Town; Wilmington Town, 518-946-2105; Willsboro Town, 518-963-8933.

Franklin County

Supreme & County Court 355 West Main St, Malone, NY 12953-1817; 518-481-1681; Criminal phone: 518-481-1749. Hours: 9AM-5PM (EST). *Felony, Civil.*

Civil Records: Access: In person. Visitors may perform in person searches. No search fee. Required to search: name, years to search. Civil cases indexed by defendant. Civil records on computer from 1990, prior in file folders in Clerk's office.

Criminal Records: Access: Mail, in person. Both court and visitors may perform in person searches. Search fee: $5.00 per name per year. Fee is per 2 years. Computer search by court: $16.00. Required to search: name, years to search, DOB. Criminal records on computer from 1962.

General Information: Public access terminal is available. (Terminal is for criminal records only.) No sealed or youthful offender records released. SASE required. Turnaround time 1 week. Copy fee: $.50 per page. Certification fee: $1.00 per page, 4 page minimum. Fee payee: County Clerk. Personal checks accepted.

Surrogate Court 355 W Main St, Malone, NY 12953-1817; 518-481-1736 & 1737; Fax: 518-483-7583. Hours: 8AM-5PM (EST). *Probate.*

Town/Village Courts *Misdemeanor, Civil Actions Under $3,000, Small Claims:* Bombay Town, 518-358-9939; Franklin Town; Santa Clara Town, 518-891-1919; Brandon Town; Saranac Lake Village, 518-891-4423; Fort Covington Town; Chateaugay Town, 518-497-6931; Westville Town, 518-358-4180; Tupper Lake Village, 518-359-9161; Harrietstown Town, 518-891-4500; Malone Village, 518-483-5210; Waverly Town, 518-856-9482; Moira Town, 518-529-6080; Altamont Town, 518-359-9278; Burke Town, 518-483-5497; Malone Town, 518-481-6634; Constable Town, 518-481-6113; Duane Town, 518-483-0386; Brighton Town, 518-327-3202; Dickinson Town, 518-856-9339; Bangor Town; Bellmont Town.

Fulton County

Supreme & County Court 223 West Main St, County Bldg, Johnstown, NY 12095; 518-736-5539; Fax: 518-762-5078. Hours: 9AM-5PM (EST). *Felony, Civil.*

Civil Records: Access: Phone, mail, fax, in person. Both court and visitors may perform in person searches. Search fee: $16.00 per name. Fee is $5.00 for in person searching, if record found. Required to search: name, years to search. Civil cases indexed by defendant, plaintiff. Civil records computerized since 1994.

Criminal Records: Access: Phone, mail, fax, in person. Only the court performs in person searches; visitors may not. Search fee: $16.00 per name. Fee is $5.00 for in person searching, if record is found.

Required to search: name, years to search, DOB. Criminal records in file folders since 1915, computerized since 1977.

General Information: No sealed, expunged, adoption, sex offense, juvenile or mental health records released. SASE required. Turnaround time 1 week. Copy fee: $1.00 per page. $.50 per page self service. Certification fee: $4.00. Fee payee: County Clerk. Business checks accepted. Prepayment is required.

Gloversville City Court City Hall, Frontage Rd, Gloversville, NY 12078; 518-773-4527; Fax: 518-773-4599. Hours: 8AM-4PM (EST). *Misdemeanor, Civil Actions Under $15,000, Eviction, Small Claims.*

Civil Records: Access: Mail, in person. Only the court performs in person searches; visitors may not. Search fee: $16.00 per name. Required to search: name, years to search. Civil cases indexed by plaintiff. Civil records in books; on computer since.

Criminal Records: Access: Mail, in person. Only the court performs in person searches; visitors may not. Search fee: $16.00 per name. Required to search: name, years to search, DOB. Criminal records in books, on computer since.

General Information: No sealed, youthful offender records released. SASE required. Turnaround time 2 weeks. Copy fee: $.50. There is a $1.00 minimum. Certification fee: $5.00. Fee payee: Gloversville City Court. Only cashiers checks and money orders accepted. Prepayment is required.

Johnstown City Court 2753 State Highway 89A, PO Box 88, Johnstown, NY 12095; 518-762-7070; Fax: 518-762-2720. Hours: 8AM-4PM (EST). *Misdemeanor, Civil Actions Under $15,000, Eviction, Small Claims.*

Civil Records: Access: Mail, in person. Only the court performs in person searches; visitors may not. Search fee: $16.00 per name. Required to search: name, years to search. Civil cases indexed by plaintiff. Civil records in file folders, computerized since 1995.

Criminal Records: Access: Mail, in person. Only the court performs in person searches; visitors may not. Search fee: $16.00 per name. Required to search: name, years to search, DOB. Criminal records on computer from 1990.

General Information: No sealed or youthful offender records released. SASE required. Turnaround time 1 month. Copy fee: $.50 per page, $1.00 minimum. Certification fee: $5.00. Fee payee: City Court. Only cashiers checks and money orders accepted. Prepayment is required.

Surrogate Court 223 West Main St, Johnstown, NY 12095; 518-763-5685; Fax: 518-762-6372. Hours: 9AM-5PM (8AM-4PM July-August) (EST). *Probate.*

Town/Village Courts *Misdemeanor, Civil Actions Under $3,000, Small Claims:* Caroga Town, 518-835-4211; Oppenheim Town, 518-568-7503; Broadalbin Village, 518-883-3353; Mayfield Town, 518-661-5225; Bleeker Town, 518-725-3684; Broadalbin Town, 518-883-5131; Stratford Town, 315-429-8612; Ephratah Town, 518-568-7560; Perth Town, 518-843-6977; Northampton Town, 518-863-4875; Johnstown Town, 518-762-7070.

Genesee County

Supreme & County Court PO Box 379 (15 Main St), Batavia, NY 14021-0379; 585-344-2550 X2243; Civil phone: x2310 for court info; Fax: 585-344-8521. Hours: 8:30AM-5PM (EST). *Felony, Civil.*

Note: 2002 Area Code will be 585. All records maintained at County Clerk's office, PO Box 379, Batavia, NY 14021.

Civil Records: Access: Mail, in person. Both court and visitors may perform in person searches. Search fee: $5.00 per five year period. Required to search: name,

years to search; also helpful: address. Civil cases indexed by defendant, plaintiff; indexed by defendant only prior to 1995. Civil records in books from 1802; on computer back to 1995.

Criminal Records: Access: Fax, mail, in person. Both court and visitors may perform in person searches. Search fee: $5.00 per five year period, $15.00 seven-ten years, $20.00 eleven-twenty years. Required to search: name, years to search, DOB; also helpful: SSN. Criminal records in books from 1802; on computer back to 1995.

General Information: Public access terminal is available. No sealed, expunged, adoption, sex offense, juvenile or mental health records released. SASE required. Turnaround time 1-3 days. Fax notes: Fee to fax results is $5.00 per document; no charge if to a toll free number. Copy fee: $1.00 for first page, $.50 each add'l. Certification fee: $4.00 plus $.50 per page in excess of 8 pages. Fee payee: County Clerk. Personal checks accepted. Prepayment is required.

Batavia City Court Genesee County Courts Facility, 1 W Main St, Batavia, NY 14020; 585-344-2550 X2416, 2417, 2418; Fax: 585-344-8556. Hours: 9AM-5PM (EST). *Misdemeanor, Civil Actions Under $15,000, Eviction, Small Claims.*

Civil Records: Access: Fax, mail, in person. Both court and visitors may perform in person searches. Search fee: $5.00 per name. Required to search: name, years to search. Civil cases indexed by plaintiff. Civil records on computer from 1990, in books from 1957.

Criminal Records: Access: Fax, mail, in person. Only the court performs in person searches; visitors may not. Search fee: $16.00 per name. Required to search: name, years to search, DOB. Criminal records on computer from 1993, in books from 1947.

General Information: No sealed, expunged, sex offense or mental health records released. SASE required. Turnaround time 1-3 days. Copy fee: $.50 per page. Certification fee: $5.00. Fee payee: City Court. Only cashiers checks and money orders accepted. Prepayment is required.

Surrogate Court 1 West Main St, Batavia, NY 14020; 585-344-2550 ext 2237; Fax: 585-344-8517. Hours: 9AM-5PM (EST). *Probate.*

Note: $25.00 search fee

Town/Village Courts *Misdemeanor, Civil Actions Under $3,000, Small Claims:* Darien Town, 585-547-2274; Oakfield Town, 585-948-5835; Bethany Town, 585-343-3325; Elba Town, 585-757-9200; Alabama Town; Oakfield Village, 585-948-9588; Bergen Town, 585-494-1121; Corfu Village, 585-599-3327; Stafford Town, 585-344-4020; LeRoy Town, 585-768-6910; Pembroke Town, 585-591-4892; Batavia Town, 585-343-1729; Byron Town, 585-548-7123; Alexander Town, 585-591-0908; Pavilion Town, 585-584-3850.

Greene County

Supreme & County Court Courthouse, 320 Main St, Catskill, NY 12414; 518-943-2230; Fax: 518-943-7763. Hours: 9AM-5PM (EST). *Felony, Misdemeanor, Civil.*

Civil Records: Access: Phone, fax, mail, in person. Both court and visitors may perform in person searches. No search fee. Required to search: name, years to search. Civil cases indexed by defendant, plaintiff. Civil records in file folder, computerized since 06/13/97.

Criminal Records: Access: Fax, mail, in person. Only the court performs in person searches; visitors may not. Search fee: $17.50 per name. Required to search: name, years to search, DOB. Criminal records on index cards. Address requests to the County Clerk's office.

General Information: Public access terminal is available. No sealed or youthful offender records released. SASE required. Turnaround time 1 week. Fax notes: $1.00 per document. Copy fee: $1.00 per page. Certification fee: $5.00. Fee payee: County Clerk. Personal checks accepted. Prepayment is required.

Surrogate Court Courthouse, 320 Main St, Catskill, NY 12414; 518-943-2484; Fax: 518-943-4372. Hours: 9AM-5PM (EST). *Probate.*

Town/Village Courts *Misdemeanor, Civil Actions Under $3,000, Small Claims:* Windham Town, 518-734-3431; Durham Town, 518-239-6122; Coxsackie Village, 518-731-2225; New Baltimore Town, 518-756-2079; Coxsackie Town, 518-731-6934; Greenville Town, 518-966-4873; Halcott Town, 518-254-5132; Hunter Village, 518-263-4288; Athens Town, 518-945-3360; Catskill Village, 518-943-9544; Prattsville Town, 518-299-3125; Lexington Town, 518-989-6303; Tannersville Village, 518-589-7168; Catskill Town, 518-943-2142; Hunter Town, 518-589-6150; Athens Village Court; Cairo Town, 518-622-3388; Ashland Town, 518-734-3636; Jewett Town.

Hamilton County

Supreme & County Court Hamilton County Clerk, PO Box 204, Route 8, Lake Pleasant, NY 12108; 518-548-7111. Hours: 8:30AM-4:30PM (EST). *Felony, Civil.*

Note: Misdemeanor records are maintained by city, town and village courts.

Civil Records: Access: Mail, fax, phone, in person. Both court and visitors may perform in person searches. No search fee. Required to search: name, years to search. Civil cases indexed by defendant. Civil records in books, records go back to 1850's.

Criminal Records: Access: Mail, in person. Only the court performs in person searches; visitors may not. Search fee: $5.00 per name. Fee is per two years searched. Required to search: name, years to search, DOB. Criminal records go back to 1878; no computerized records. Request must be in writing.

General Information: No sealed or youthful offender records released. SASE not required. Turnaround time 2-3 days. Fax notes: Fee to fax results is $1.00 per document. Copy fee: $.50 per page. $1.00 minimum. Certification fee: $1.00 per page; $4.00 minimum. Fee payee: Hamilton County Clerk. Personal checks accepted. Prepayment is required.

Surrogate Court Hamilton County Ofc. Bldg, White Birch Lane, Indian Lake, NY 12842; 518-648-5411; Fax: 518-648-6286. Hours: 8:30AM-4:30PM (EST). *Probate.*

Note: Mail address to PO Box 780.

Town/Village Courts *Misdemeanor, Civil Actions Under $3,000, Small Claims:* Lake Pleasant Town, 518-548-3625; Long Lake Town; Benson Town, 518-863-8510; Inlet Town, 315-357-6121; Arietta Town, 518-548-6203; Hope Town, 518-924-2662; Wells Town, 518-924-9285; Hamilton Village, 315-824-3508; Morehouse Town; Indian Lake Town, 518-648-6226.

Herkimer County

Supreme & County Court 301 N Washington Street, Herkimer County Office Bldg, Herkimer, NY 13350-1993; 315-867-1209; Fax: 315-866-1802. Hours: 9AM-5PM Sept-May; 8:30AM-4PM June-Aug (EST). *Felony, Civil.*

Note: Misdemeanor records are maintained by city, town and village courts.

Civil Records: Access: Phone, mail, in person. Only the court performs in person searches; visitors may not. Search fee: $5.00 per name. Search is per 2 year period. Required to search: name, years to search. Civil cases indexed by defendant, plaintiff. Civil records on index books since 1800s.

Criminal Records: Access: Phone, mail, in person. Only the court performs in person searches; visitors may not. Search fee: $16.00 per name. Required to search: name, years to search, DOB. Criminal records on index books since 1800s.

General Information: No sealed, expunged, adoption, sex offense, juvenile or mental health records released. SASE required. Turnaround time varies. Copy fee: $1.00 for first page, $.50 each add'l. Certification fee: $1.00 per page, $4.00 minimum. Fee payee: County Clerk. Personal checks accepted. Prepayment required.

Little Falls City Court 659 E Main St, Little Falls, NY 13365; 315-823-1690; Fax: 315-823-1623. Hours: 8:30AM-4:30PM (EST). *Misdemeanor, Civil Actions Under $15,000, Eviction, Small Claims.*

Civil Records: Access: Mail, fax, in person. Only the court performs in person searches; visitors may not. Search fee: $5.00 per name. Required to search: name, years to search. Civil cases indexed by defendant. Civil records go back to 1973; on computer back to 4/02.

Criminal Records: Access: Mail, in person. Only the court performs in person searches; visitors may not. Search fee: $5.00 per name. Required to search: name, years to search, DOB, signed release. Criminal records go back to 1948; on computer back to 4/02.

General Information: No sealed, expunged, adoption, sex offense, juvenile or mental health records released. SASE required. Turnaround time 1 week. Copy fee: $.50 per page; minimum $1.00. Certification fee: $5.00. Fee payee: City Court. Only cashiers checks and money orders accepted. Prepayment is required.

Surrogate Court 301 N Washington St #5548, Herkimer, NY 13350; 315-867-1170. Hours: 9AM-5PM Sept-May; 8:30AM-4PM June-Aug (EST). *Probate.*

Town/Village Courts *Misdemeanor, Civil Actions Under $3,000, Small Claims:* Ilion Village, 315-894-4175; Litchfield Town; Newport Town; Newport Village, 315-845-8938; Schuyler Town, 315-733-1093; Webb Town, 315-369-3321; German Flatts Town, 315-866-3571; Winfield Town, 315-822-4555; Frankfort Town, 315-895-7267; Salisbury Town, 315-429-8581; Little Falls Town, 315-823-3390; Herkimer Village, 315-866-0604; Mohawk Village, 315-866-4312; Manheim Town, 315-429-9631; Columbia Town, 315-866-1309; Fairfield Town, 315-891-7645; Russia Town, 315-826-3432; Ohio Town, 315-826-7912; Herkimer Town, 315-866-1280; Warren Town; Cold Brook Village, 315-826-3772; Norway Town, 315-845-8272; Poland Village, 315-826-3422; Frankfort Village, 315-894-8513; Danube Town; Stark Town, 315-858-2091; Middleville Village.

Jefferson County

Supreme & County Court Jefferson County Clerk's Office-Court Records, 175 Arsenal St, County Building, Watertown, NY 13601-3783; 315-785-3200; Fax: 315-785-5145. Hours: 9AM-5PM Sept-June; 8:30AM-4PM July-Aug (EST). *Felony, Civil.*

www.sunyjefferson.edu/jc

Civil Records: Access: In person only. Visitors must perform in person searches for themselves. No search fee. Required to search: name, years to search. Civil cases indexed by defendant, plaintiff. Civil records on computer back to 1/1992; prior in books from 1805 by first defendant name only.

Criminal Records: Access: Mail, in person. Both court and visitors may perform in person searches. Search fee: $5.00 per name. Fee is per 2 years searched. Required to search: name, years to search; also helpful: DOB, signed release. Criminal records on computer back to 1/1992; prior in books from 1805 by first defendant name only.

General Information: Public access terminal is available. No sealed, expunged, adoption, sex offense, juvenile or mental health records. SASE required. Turnaround time 1 week. Copy fee: $.50 per page. The minimum copy fee is $1.00. Certification fee: $4.00. Plus $1.00 per page. Fee payee: County Clerk of Jefferson County. Personal checks accepted. Prepayment is required.

Watertown City Court Municipal Bldg, 245 Washington St, Watertown, NY 13601; 315-785-7785; Fax: 315-785-7818. Hours: 9AM-5PM (EST). *Misdemeanor, Civil Actions Under $15,000, Eviction, Small Claims.*

Civil Records: Access: Mail, in person. Only the court performs in person searches; visitors may not. Search fee: $5.00 per name. Fee is per name & docket. Required to search: name, years to search. Civil cases indexed by defendant. Civil records in docket books.

Criminal Records: Access: Mail, in person. Only the court performs in person searches; visitors may not. Search fee: $16.00 per name. Required to search: name, years to search, DOB. Criminal records in docket books.

General Information: No sealed records released. SASE required. Turnaround time same day. Copy fee: $.50 per page. Certification fee: $5.00. Fee payee: City Court. Only cashiers checks and money orders accepted. Prepayment is required.

Surrogate Court County Office Bldg, 7th Flr, 175 Arsenal St, Watertown, NY 13601-2562; 315-785-3019; Fax: 315-785-5194. Hours: 9AM-5PM Sept-May; 8:30AM-4PM June-Aug (EST). *Probate.*

Town/Village Courts *Misdemeanor, Civil Actions Under $3,000, Small Claims:* Lyme Town, 315-649-2791; Clayton Town; Orleans Town, 315-482-9210; Champion Town, 315-788-1912; Alexandria Bay Village, 315-482-4786; West Carthage Village, 315-493-6345; Ellisburg Town, 315-846-5116; Adams Village Court; Alexandria Town, 315-482-9519; Clayton Village, 315-686-2427; Pamelia Town, 315-785-9794; Dexter Village Court; Sackets Harbor Village, 315-646-3548; Evans Mills Village, 315-629-4052; Henderson Town, 315-938-5614; Cape Vincent Town, 315-654-2471; Worth Town; Brownville Town, 315-788-7889; Carthage Village, 315-493-2890; Brownville Village, 315-782-7650; Watertown Town; Hounsfield Town, 315-646-2030; Rutland Town, 315-688-4249; Antwerp Town, 315-659-2432; Adams Town, 315-583-5085; Wilna Town, 315-493-2771; Glen Park Village, 315-788-7889; LeRay Town, 315-629-4052; Rodman Town, 315-232-4029; Philadelphia Town, 315-642-3421; Philadelphia Village, 315-642-3452; Theresa Town, 315-628-5758; Chaumont Village Court; Lorraine Town, 315-232-2548.

Kings County

Supreme Court - Civil Division 360 Adams St, Brooklyn, NY 11201; 718-643-5894; Fax: 718-643-8187. Hours: 9AM-5PM (EST). *Civil Actions Over $25,000.*

www.courts.state.ny.us/courtguides/Guide_24.pdf

Civil Records: Access: In person only. Visitors must perform in person searches for themselves. No search fee. Required to search: name, years to search; also helpful-index number. Civil cases indexed by defendant. Civil records on computer back to 1993; in books, on microfiche back to 1900's. Picture ID required.

General Information: Public access terminal is available. No sealed, expunged, adoption, sex offense, juvenile or mental health records released. Copy fee: $.75 per page. Certification fee: $8.00. Fee payee: County Clerk. Only cashiers checks and money orders accepted. Prepayment is required.

Supreme Court - Criminal 120 Schermerhorn St, Brooklyn, NY 11210; 718-428-2810; Fax: 718-643-7733. Hours: 9:30AM-4:30PM (EST). *Felony, Misdemeanor.*

www.courts.state.ny.us/courtguides/Guide_24.pdf

Criminal Records: Access: In person only. Only the court performs in person searches; visitors may not. Search fee: $16.00 per name. Fee is per county. Required to search: name, DOB, signed release. Criminal records on computer from 1976, prior on index. Criminal record searches are done at 25 Beaver St., 212-428-2810.

General Information: No sealed, sex offense or youthful offender records released. SASE required. Turnaround time 1-3 days. Copy fee: Included in search fee. Certification fee: Included in search fee. Fee payee: Office of Court Administration. Personal checks accepted and money orders. Prepayment is required.

Civil Court of the City of New York - Kings Branch 141 Livingston St, Brooklyn, NY 11201; 718-643-5069/643-8133 Clerk. Hours: 9AM-5PM (EST). *Civil Actions Under $25,000, Eviction, Small Claims.*

www.courts.state.ny.us/courtguides/Guide_24.pdf

Civil Records: Access: In person only. Visitors must perform in person searches for themselves. No search fee. Required to search: name, years to search. Civil cases indexed by plaintiff. Civil records on computer from 1987 for small claims, 1990 for tenant/landlord, and from January 1998 for civil.

General Information: Public access terminal is available. (Landlord & Tenant, civil, and small claims since 1998.) All records public. Copy fee: $.15 public copying machine fee. Certification fee: $5.00. Fee payee: NYC Civil Court. Only cashiers checks and money orders accepted. Prepayment is required.

Surrogate Court 2 Johnson St, Brooklyn, NY 11201; 718-643-5262. 9AM-5PM (EST). *Probate.*

www.courts.state.ny.us/courtguides/Guide_24.pdf

Lewis County

Supreme & County Court Courthouse, PO Box 232, Lowville, NY 13367; 315-376-5333; Fax: 315-376-3768. 8:30AM-4:30PM (EST). *Felony, Civil.*

Note: Misdemeanor records are maintained by city, town and village courts.

Civil Records: Access: Mail, in person. Both court and visitors may perform in person searches. Search fee: $10.00 per name. Required to search: name, years to search. Civil cases indexed by defendant. Civil records on index cards from 1935.

Criminal Records: Access: Mail, in person. Both court and visitors may perform in person searches. Search fee: $10.00 per name. Required to search: name, years to search. Criminal records on index cards from 1935.

General Information: No sealed, youthful offender or sex abuse case records released. SASE required. Turnaround time 2 days. Copy fee: $.50 per page. Certification fee: $4.00. Fee payee: County Clerk. Personal checks accepted. Prepayment is required.

Lyons Falls Village Court 4300 Cherry St, Lyons Falls, NY 13368; 315-348-8971. *Misdemeanor, Civil Actions Under $3,000, Small Claims.*

Surrogate Court Courthouse, 7660 State St, Lowville, NY 13367; 315-376-5344; Fax: 315-376-4145. Hours: 8:30AM-4:30PM (EST). *Probate.*

Note: Fee is $25 for under 25 years to $70 for over 70 years

Town/Village Courts *Misdemeanor, Civil Actions Under $3,000, Small Claims:* Lyonsdale Town; Lewis Town; Turin Town, 315-348-6403; Denmark Town; Watson Town, 315-376-3866; Pinckney Town;

Lowville Village Court; Lowville Town, 315-376-8070; Diana Town, 315-543-2628; New Bremen Town, 315-376-3752; Leyden Town, 315-348-6215; Osceola Town, 315-599-8869; Port Leyden Village, 315-348-6215; Martinsburg Town, 315-376-2299; Croghan Town, 315-346-1212; West Turin Town, 315-348-8971; Greig Town.

Livingston County

Supreme & County Court 6 Court St, Rm 201, Geneseo, NY 14454; 585-243-7010. Hours: 8:30AM-4:30PM Oct-May; 8AM-4PM June-Sept (EST). *Felony, Civil.*

Note: Misdemeanor records are maintained by city, town and village courts.

Civil Records: Access: Mail, in person. Both court and visitors may perform in person searches. Search fee: $2.50 per name per year. Required to search: name, years to search. Civil cases indexed by defendant, plaintiff. Civil records on computer since 1996. Plaintiff index available only on computer searches.

Criminal Records: Access: Mail, in person. Both court and visitors may perform in person searches. Search fee: $2.50 per name per year. Required to search: name, years to search. Criminal records on computer since 1996. Plaintiff index available only on computer searches.

General Information: Public access terminal is available. No sealed or youthful offender records released. SASE required. Turnaround time same day. Copy fee: $.50 per page. Certification fee: $4.00 plus $.50 per page after first 4. Fee payee: County Clerk. Personal checks accepted and money orders. Prepayment is required.

Surrogate Court 2 Court St, Geneseo, NY 14454; 585-243-7095; Fax: 585-243-7583. Hours: 9AM-5PM (EST). *Probate.*

Town/Village Courts *Misdemeanor, Civil Actions Under $3,000, Small Claims:* Groveland Town, 585-243-3782; Avon Village, 585-226-3660; Springwater Town, 585-669-2635; Avon Town, 585-226-2130; Leicester Town, 585-382-9419; North Dansville Town, 585-335-1460; Geneseo Town, 585-243-4530; Lima Town, 585-582-1011; Portage Town; West Sparta Town, 585-335-2443; Caledonia Town, 585-538-4927; York Town, 585-243-0666; Ossian Town, 585-335-8040; Geneseo Village, 585-243-4530; Sparta Town; Nunda Town, 585-468-2215; Nunda Village, 585-468-5739; Mount Morris Village, 585-658-3249; Dansville Village, 585-335-2460; Conesus Town, 585-346-3130; Caledonia Village, 585-538-4800; Mount Morris Town, 585-658-2333; Livonia Town, 585-346-3710.

Madison County

Supreme & County Court County Office Bldg, PO Box 668, Wampsville, NY 13163; 315-366-2261; Fax: 315-366-2615. 9AM-5PM (EST). *Felony, Civil.*

Note: Misdemeanor records are maintained by city, town and village courts.

Civil Records: Access: Mail, in person. Both court and visitors may perform in person searches. Search fee: $5.00 per name. Fee is per 5 years searched. Required to search: name, years to search. Civil cases indexed by defendant. Judgment records on computer from 1997, prior in books.

Criminal Records: Access: Mail, in person. Both court and visitors may perform in person searches. Search fee: $5.00 per name. Per 5 years. Required to search: name, years to search, DOB. Criminal records on computer to 1989, previous years in books.

General Information: No sealed, expunged, adoption, sex offense, juvenile or mental health records released. SASE required. Turnaround time 2 days. Copy fee:

$1.00 for first page, $.50 each add'l. Certification fee: $1.00. Minimum $4.00. Fee payee: County Clerk. Personal checks accepted. Prepayment is required.

Oneida City Court 109 N Main St, Oneida, NY 13421; 315-363-1310; Fax: 315-363-3230. Hours: 8:30AM-4:30PM (EST). *Misdemeanor, Civil Actions Under $15,000, Eviction, Small Claims.*

Civil Records: Access: Mail, in person. Only the court performs in person searches; visitors may not. Search fee: $5.00 per name. Fee is for search prior to 1990, other years $16.00 per name. Required to search: name, years to search. Civil cases indexed by plaintiff. Civil records on computer from 1990, prior in books back to 1950s.

Criminal Records: Access: Mail, in person. Only the court performs in person searches; visitors may not. Search fee: $16 fee is for 1989 forward; searches prior to 1989 are $5.00 per name, per 2 years. Required to search: name, years to search, DOB. Criminal records on computer back to 1989; prior in books back to 1950s.

General Information: No sealed, expunged, sex offense, mental health or youthful offender records released. SASE required. Turnaround time 1-2 days. Copy fee: $.50 per page. Certification fee: $5.00. Fee payee: City Court. Personal checks accepted. Prepayment is required.

Surrogate Court County Courthouse, North Court st, Wampsville, NY 13163; 315-366-2392; Fax: 315-366-2539. Hours: 9AM-5PM (EST). *Probate.*

Town/Village Courts *Misdemeanor, Civil Actions Under $3,000, Small Claims:* Lenox Town; Georgetown Town, 315-837-4795; Lebanon Town, 315-837-4835; Chittenango Village Court; Wampsville Village, 315-363-5810; DeRuyter Village, 315-852-9650; Smithfield Town; Lincoln Town, 315-697-7018; Hamilton Town, 315-824-3508; Sullivan Town, 315-687-3347; Stockbridge Town, 315-495-3333; Brookfield Town; Morrisville Village, 315-684-9111; Nelson Town, 315-655-8582; Canastota Village, 315-697-9410; Cazenovia Village, 315-655-4011; Cazenovia Town; Fenner Town, 315-655-2705; Madison Town, 315-893-7544; Madison Village Court; Eaton Town, 315-684-9111.

Monroe County

Supreme & County Court County Office Bldg, County Clerk's Office, 39 Main Street West, Rochester, NY 14614; 585-428-5151; Fax: 716-428-4698. Hours: 9AM-5PM (EST). *Felony, Civil.*

www.clerk.co.monroe.ny.us

Civil Records: Access: Fax, mail, online, in person. Both court and visitors may perform in person searches. Search fee: $5.00 per name. Fee is per 2 years searched. Required to search: name, years to search. Civil cases indexed by defendant. Civil records on computer since 6/93, prior in books. Online access to felony, civil, and divorce records available free online at www.clerk.co.monroe.ny.us. Records go back to 6/1993, although earlier film images are being added. Also, access to the remote online system requires $.50 per minute usage. Fax back available for $.50 per page. Call Tom Fiorilli 716-428-5151 for more information.

Criminal Records: Access: Fax, mail, online, in person. Both court and visitors may perform in person searches. Search fee: $5.00 per name. Fee is per 2 years searched. Required to search: name, years to search, DOB. Criminal records on computer since 6/93, prior in books. Online access to criminal records is the same as civil.

General Information: Public access terminal is available. No sealed, divorce records, confidential files released. SASE required. Turnaround time 2 weeks. Copy fee: $.50 per page. $1.00 minimum. Call Tom

Fiorilli for more information. Certification fee: $4.00 plus $1.00 per page after first 4. Fee payee: County Clerk. Personal checks accepted. Prepayment is required.

Rochester City Court
Hall of Justice, Rochester, NY 14614; Civil phone: 585-428-2444; Criminal phone: 585-428-2447; Fax: 585-428-2588 (Civil) 428-2732 (Criminal). Hours: 9AM-5PM (EST). *Misdemeanor, Civil Actions Under $15,000, Eviction, Small Claims.*

Civil Records: Access: Phone, fax, mail, in person. Both court and visitors may perform in person searches. Search fee: $16.00 per name. Required to search: name, years to search. Civil cases indexed by defendant, plaintiff. Civil records on computer from 1983, prior in books from 1973.

Criminal Records: Access: Phone, fax, mail, in person. Both court and visitors may perform in person searches. Search fee: $16.00 per name. Required to search: name, years to search, DOB, SSN, signed release. Criminal records on computer since 1986, prior on books from 1973. Certificate of disposition $5.00.

General Information: Public access terminal is available. No sealed, expunged, probation reports, adoption, sex offense, juvenile or mental health records released. SASE required. Turnaround time 1 week. Copy fee: $1.00 per page. Certification fee: $5.00. Only cashiers checks and money orders accepted. Prepayment is required.

Surrogate Court
Hall of Justice, Rm 541, 99 Exchange Blvd, Rochester, NY 14614; 585-428-5200; Fax: 528-428-2650. Hours: 9AM-4PM (EST). *Probate.*

Town/Village Courts
Misdemeanor, Civil Actions Under $3,000, Small Claims: Parma Town, 585-392-9470; Penfield Town, 585-377-8623; Pittsford Town, 585-248-6238; Sweden Town, 585-637-9157; Perinton Town, 585-377-3388; Rush Town, 585-533-1130; Irondequoit Town, 585-336-6040; Brighton Town, 585-473-8849; Hamlin Town, 585-964-8641; East Rochester Town, 585-385-2576; Chili Town, 585-889-1999; Greece Town, 585-227-3155; Ogden Town, 585-352-3498; Henrietta Town, 585-359-2640; Riga Town; Clarkson Town, 585-637-1134; Gates Town, 585-247-6106; Mendon Town, 585-624-6064; Webster Town, 585-872-1000; Honeoye Falls Village, 585-624-1711; Wheatland Town, 585-889-3074; Fairport Village, 585-223-0316.

Montgomery County

Supreme & County Court
Montgomery County Office Bldg, PO Box 1500, Fonda, NY 12068; Civil phone: 518-853-8113; Criminal phone: 518-853-4516; Fax: 518-853-3596 (Criminal). Hours: 9AM-5PM; 8:30AM-4PM (civil) (EST). *Felony, Misdemeanor, Civil.*

Note: Court keeps record of its own Misdemeanor cases only; also search city, town and village courts.

Civil Records: Access: Mail, in person. Both court and visitors may perform in person searches. Search fee: $5.00 per name. Fee is per 2 years searched. Required to search: name, years to search, address. Civil cases indexed by defendant, plaintiff. Civil records in books and on index cards back to 1965; on computer back to 1992. Public access terminal available for Civil records.

Criminal Records: Access: Mail, in person. Both court and visitors may perform in person searches. Search fee: $16.00 per name. Required to search: name, years to search, DOB; also helpful-SSN. Criminal records on computer back to 1992; file index back to 1965. Public access terminal not available for Criminal records.

General Information: No sealed or youthful offender records released. SASE required. Turnaround time 1 week. Copy fee: $1.00 per page. Certification fee: $4.00

plus $1.00 per page after first. Fee payee: County Clerk. Personal checks accepted. Prepayment is required.

Amsterdam City Court
Public Safety Bldg, Rm 208, One Guy Park Ave Ext, Amsterdam, NY 12010; 518-842-9510; Fax: 518-843-8474. Hours: 8AM-4PM (EST). *Misdemeanor, Civil Actions Under $15,000, Eviction, Small Claims.*

Civil Records: Access: Mail, in person. Only the court performs in person searches; visitors may not. Search fee: $16.00 per name. Required to search: name, years to search. Civil cases indexed by defendant. Civil records on computer since 1995, on index cards.

Criminal Records: Access: Mail, in person. Only the court performs in person searches; visitors may not. Search fee: $16.00 per name. Required to search: name, years to search, DOB. Criminal records on computer from 11/93, prior on index cards.

General Information: No sealed, expunged, adoption, sex offense, juvenile or mental health records released. Turnaround time 1 week. Copy fee: $.25 per page. Certification fee: $10.00. Fee payee: City Court. Only cashiers checks and money orders accepted. Prepayment is required.

Surrogate Court
58 Broadway, Fonda, NY 12068; 518-853-8108; Fax: 518-853-8230. Hours: 9AM-5PM (EST). *Probate.*

Note: Court also handles administration of estates, guardianships and adoptions.

Town/Village Courts
Misdemeanor, Civil Actions Under $3,000, Small Claims: Glen Town, 518-853-4825; Amsterdam Town, 518-842-7961; Charleston Town, 518-922-6771; Florida Town, 518-843-6468; Mohawk Town, 518-853-3031; Canajoharie Village, 518-673-5116; Palatine Town, Minden Town, 518-568-2728; Canajoharie Town, 518-673-3013; St Johnsville Village, 518-568-2226; St Johnsville Town, 518-568-2662.

Nassau County

Supreme Court
Supreme Court Bldg, Supreme Court Dr, Mineola, NY 11501; 516-571-1660; Civil phone: 516-571-2906. Hours: 9AM-5PM (EST). *Civil Actions Over $15,000.*

Note: All records are maintained at the County Clerk's Office, 240 Old County Rd, Mineola, NY, 11501, 516-571-2664/2272.

Civil Records: Access: Mail, in person. Both court and visitors may perform in person searches. Search fee: $5.00 per name. Fee is for archived cases only. Required to search: name, years to search. Civil cases indexed by defendant, plaintiff. Civil records on computer from 1992, prior in books.

General Information: Public access terminal is available. No sealed, expunged, adoption, sex offense, juvenile or mental health records released. SASE required. Turnaround time 3 weeks for cases prior to 1996. Copy fee: $.25 per page. Certification fee: $4.00. Includes up to 4 pages, then $1.00 per page additional. Includes copy fees. Fee payee: Nassau County Clerk's Office. Personal checks accepted. Prepayment is required.

County Court
262 Old Country Rd, Mineola, NY 11501; 516-571-2800; Fax: 516-571-2160. Hours: 9AM-5PM (EST). *Felony.*

Criminal Records: Access: Mail, in person. Only the court performs in person searches; visitors may not. Search fee: $16.00 per name. Searches 1982-present done at OCA. Required to search: name, years to search, DOB. Criminal records on computer from 1982, prior in archives or on microfilm.

General Information: No sealed, expunged, sex offense, juvenile, or mental health records released. Turnaround time 3 weeks. Copy fee: $.50 per page.

$1.00 minimum. Certification fee: $5.00. Fee payee: Clerk of Court. Only cashiers checks and money orders accepted. Prepayment is required.

District Court - 1st & 2nd Districts
99 Main St, Hempstead, NY 11550; 516-572-2355. Hours: 9AM-5PM (EST). *Misdemeanor, Civil Actions Under $15,000, Eviction, Small Claims.*

Note: Records for 2nd District are separate prior to 1980. 1st District handles Misdemeanor case records.

Civil Records: Access: Mail, in person. Both court and visitors may perform in person searches. Search fee: $16.00 per name. Required to search: name, years to search. Civil cases indexed by defendant, plaintiff. Civil records on computer back to 1980, prior in books back to 1960.

Criminal Records: Access: Mail, in person. Both court and visitors may perform in person searches. Search fee: $16.00 per name. Required to search: name, years to search; also helpful DOB. Criminal records on computer back to 1980, prior in books back to 1960.

General Information: No sealed records released. SASE required. Turnaround time 5-10 days. Copy fee: $1.00. Add $.50 per page after 2. Certification fee: $5.00. Fee payee: Clerk of Court. Only cashiers checks and money orders accepted. Prepayment is required.

District Court - 3rd District
435 Middle Neck, Great Neck, NY 11023; 516-571-8400/8402; Fax: 516-571-8403. Hours: 9AM-5PM (EST). *Civil Actions Under $15,000, Eviction, Small Claims.*

Civil Records: Access: Mail, in person. Only the court performs in person searches; visitors may not. Search fee: $16.00 per name. Required to search: name, years to search. Civil cases indexed by defendant, plaintiff. Civil records on computer from 1989, prior in books.

General Information: No sealed, expunged, adoption, sex offense, juvenile or mental health records released. SASE required. Turnaround time 1 week. Copy fee: $1.00 for first page, $.50 each add'l. Certification fee: $5.00. Fee payee: Clerk of Court. Only cashiers checks and money orders accepted. Prepayment is required.

District Court - 4th District
87 Bethpage Rd, Hicksville, NY 11801; 516-571-7090. Hours: 9AM-5PM (EST). *Civil Actions Under $15,000, Eviction, Small Claims.*

Civil Records: Access: Phone, mail, in person. Only the court performs in person searches; visitors may not. Search fee: $16.00 per name. Required to search: name, years to search. Civil cases indexed by defendant. Civil records on computer back to 1990; prior in books.

General Information: SASE required. Turnaround time 1 week. Copy fee: $1.00. Add $.50 per page after first 2. Certification fee: $5.00. Fee payee: Clerk of District Court. Only cashiers checks and money orders accepted. Prepayment is required.

Glen Cove City Court
13 Glen St, Glen Cove, NY 11542-2704; 516-676-0109; Fax: 516-676-1570. Hours: 9AM-5PM (EST). *Misdemeanor, Civil Actions Under $15,000, Eviction, Small Claims.*

Civil Records: Access: Mail, fax, in person. Only the court performs in person searches; visitors may not. Search fee: $16.00 per name. Required to search: name, years to search. Civil records go back to 1970; on computer back to 1996.

Criminal Records: Access: Mail, fax, in person. Only the court performs in person searches; visitors may not. Search fee: $16.00 per name. Required to search: name, years to search, DOB, signed release. Criminal records go back to 1966; on computer back to 1996.

General Information: No sealed, expunged, adoption, sex offense, juvenile or mental health records released. SASE required. Turnaround time 3-5 days. Copy fee: Varies. Certification fee: $5.00. Fee payee: Glen Cove City Court. Only cashiers checks and money orders accepted. Prepayment is required.

Long Beach City Court 1 West Chester St, Long Beach, NY 11561; 516-431-1000; Fax: 516-889-3511. Hours: 9AM-5PM (EST). *Misdemeanor, Civil Actions Under $15,000, Eviction, Small Claims.*

Civil Records: Access: Mail, in person. Only the court performs in person searches; visitors may not. Search fee: $16.00. Required to search: name, years to search. Computerized records since 1997.

Criminal Records: Access: Mail, in person. Only the court performs in person searches; visitors may not. Search fee: $16.00 per name. Required to search: name, years to search, DOB. Criminal records on computer from 1977.

General Information: No sealed, expunged, adoption, sex offense, juvenile or mental health records released. Copy fee: $1.00 for first page, $.50 each add'l. Certification fee: $5.00. Fee payee: City Court of Long Beach. Only cashiers checks and money orders accepted. Prepayment is required.

Surrogate Court 262 Old Country Rd, Mineola, NY 11501; 516-571-2082; Fax: 516-571-3864. Hours: 9AM-5PM (EST). *Probate.*

Town/Village Courts *Misdemeanor, Civil Actions Under $3,000, Small Claims:* Floral Park Village, 516-326-6325; Kings Point Village, 516-482-7872; Thomaston Village Court; Roslyn Harbor Village, 516-621-0368; Old Westbury Village, 516-626-0800; Kensington Village, 516-482-4409; Roslyn Estates Village, 516-621-3541; Great Neck Village, 516-487-0775; Upper Brookville Village, 516-676-5619; Flower Hill Village Court; Plandome Manor Village Court; Lattington Village, 516-922-0767; Laurel Hollow Village, 516-692-8826; Lake Success Village, 516-482-7430; Plandome Heights Village, 516-365-0501; North Hills Village Court; Old Brookville Village Court; East Hills Village, 516-621-4251; Plandome Village Court; Rockville Centre Village, 516-678-9233; Williston Park Village, 516-248-5150; Bayville Village, 516-628-1410; Great Neck Estates Village, 516-482-6430; Great Neck Plaza Village, 516-482-4500; Lawrence Village, 516-239-9166; Sands Point Village, 516-883-3100; Sea Cliff Village, 516-671-0328; Freeport Village, 516-378-8687; Garden City Village, 516-742-5800; Bellerose Village, 516-358-2962; Malverne Village Court; Stewart Manor Village, 516-352-6240; Hempstead Village, 516-489-3400; Mill Neck Village, 516-922-6722; Cedarhurst Village, 516-295-5522; Centre Island Village, 516-922-0606; Manorhaven Village Court; South Floral Park Village, 516-353-8047; Cove Neck Village, 516-624-9600; Russell Gardens Village Court; Woodsburgh Village Court; Matinecock Village, 516-922-8198; Oyster Bay Cove Village, 516-681-9271; Sadd'le Rock Village Court; Roslyn Village, 516-621-1961; New Hyde Park Village, 516-354-6330; Farmingdale Village, 516-293-2292; East Rockaway Village Court; Mineola Village, 516-746-0754; Massapequa Park Village Court; Valley Stream Village Court; Westbury Village, 516-334-1700; Muttontown Village, 516-364-2240; Lynbrook Village, 516-599-0416; Munsey Park Village, 516-365-7790; Brookville Village, 516-922-2983; Atlantic Beach Village, 516-371-4552.

New York County

Supreme Court - Civil Division County Clerk, 60 Centre St, Room 103, New York City, NY 10007; 212-374-4704/374-8339. Hours: 9AM-3PM (EST). *Civil Actions.*

Civil Records: Access: Mail, in person. Both court and visitors may perform in person searches. Search fee: $5.00 per name. Fee is per 2 years searched. Required to search: name, years to search. Civil cases indexed by defendant, plaintiff. Civil records on computer from 1993, prior in books.

General Information: SASE required. Turnaround time 1 month. Certification fee: $8.00 per document. Fee payee: County Clerk. Only cashiers checks and money orders accepted. Prepayment is required.

Supreme Court - Criminal Division 100 Centre St, Room 1000, New York, NY 10013; 212-374-4984. Hours: 9AM-5PM (EST). *Felony, Misdemeanor.*

Criminal Records: Access: In person only. Visitors must perform in person searches for themselves. Search fee: If written to OAS $16.00 for their electronic search, or $5.00 for a 5 year manual search. Required to search: name, years to search, DOB. Criminal records on computer from 1977, prior records archived. Written requests must be directed to OAS, Criminal History Searches, Ofc. Court Admin., 25 Beaver St. NY, NY.

General Information: No sealed, expunged, adoption, sex offense, juvenile or mental health records released. SASE required. Turnaround time 1-2 days. Fax notes: Will not fax results. Copy fee: $.15 per page self-serve. Certification fee: $8.00 per document; $10.00 for certificate of disposition. Fee payee: Office of Court Administration. No personal checks accepted. Prepayment is required.

Civil Court of the City of New York 111 Centre St, New York, NY 10013; 212-374-7915; Fax: 212-374-5709. Hours: 9AM-5PM (EST). *Civil Actions Under $25,000, Eviction, Small Claims.*

Civil Records: Access: Mail, in person, phone. Visitors must perform in person searches for themselves. No search fee. Required to search: name, years to search; also helpful: address. Civil cases indexed by plaintiff; computerized records since 1994. Landlord/Tenant records on computer from 1984, civil from 1994, prior in books. Records are archived after 3 years; search by defendant available only from 6/94 on.

General Information: Public access terminal is available. (Available for cases since 1994.) no sealed records released. SASE required. No copy fee. Certification fee: $5.00. Fee payee: Clerk of Civil Court. Only cashiers checks and money orders accepted. Attorney's and certified checks accepted. Prepayment is required.

Surrogate Court 31 Chambers St, New York City, NY 10007; 212-374-8233. Hours: 9AM-5PM (EST). *Probate.*

Niagara County

Supreme Court 775 3rd St, Niagara Falls, NY 14302; 716-278-1800; Fax: 716-278-1809. Hours: 9AM-5PM (EST). *Felony, Civil Actions Over $25,000.*

Note: All records are maintained at County Clerk's Office, 75 Hawley St, Lockport, NY 14094 (716-439-7030).

Civil Records: Access: Mail, in person. Both court and visitors may perform in person searches. No search fee. Required to search: name, years to search. Civil cases indexed by defendant. Civil records in index books back to 1950, computerized since 1997.

Criminal Records: Access: Mail, in person. Only the court performs in person searches; visitors may not.

Search fee: $5.00 per name. per every 2 years searched. Required to search: name, years to search, DOB. Criminal records in index books back to 1950, computerized since 1997.

General Information: No sealed or youthful offender records released. SASE not required. Turnaround time 3 days. Copy fee: $1.00 per page. Certification fee: $4.00. Fee payee: County Clerk. Personal checks accepted. Prepayment is required.

County Court Courthouse, 175 Hawley St, Lockport, NY 14094; 716-439-7022; Fax: 716-439-4023. Hours: 9AM-5PM (EST). *Felony, Civil Actions Under $25,000.*

Civil Records: Access: Fax, mail, in person. Only the court performs in person searches; visitors may not. Search fee: $5.00 per name. Fee is per two years searched. Required to search: name, years to search. Civil cases indexed by defendant, plaintiff. Civil records on computer since 1/96; prior records in books.

Criminal Records: Access: Fax, mail, in person. Both court and visitors may perform in person searches. Search fee: $5.00 per name. Fee is per two years searched. Required to search: name, years to search, DOB. Criminal records on computer since 1/96; prior records in books.

General Information: Public access terminal is available. (Only civil records are available.) No sealed, youthful offender or sex abuse case records released. SASE required. Turnaround time 1 day. Fax notes: $1.00 per page. Copy fee: $1.00 per page. Certification fee: $4.00. Fee payee: County Clerk. Business checks accepted. Prepayment is required.

Lockport City Court Municipal Bldg, One Locks Plaza, Lockport, NY 14094; Civil phone: 716-439-6660; Criminal phone: 716-439-6671; Fax: 716-439-6684. Hours: 8AM-4:30PM (EST). *Misdemeanor, Civil Actions Under $15,000, Eviction, Small Claims.*

Civil Records: Access: Phone, fax, mail, in person. Both court and visitors may perform in person searches. Search fee: $16.00 per name. Required to search: name, years to search. Civil cases indexed by defendant. Civil records on computer from 1988, prior in books from 1900s.

Criminal Records: Access: Phone, fax, mail, in person. Both court and visitors may perform in person searches. Search fee: $16.00 per name. Required to search: name, years to search, DOB. Criminal records in books from 1977 forward; computerized since 1998.

General Information: No sealed, expunged, adoption, sex offense, juvenile or mental health records released. SASE required. Turnaround time 1 week. Copy fee: $1.00 per page. Certification fee: $5.00. Fee payee: City Court of Lockport. Only cashiers checks and money orders accepted. Prepayment is required.

Niagara Falls City Court PO Box 1586, Niagara Falls, NY 14302-2725; Civil phone: 716-278-9860; Criminal phone: 716-278-9800; Fax: 716-278-9809. Hours: 8:30AM-4:30PM (EST). *Misdemeanor, Civil Actions Under $15,000, Eviction, Small Claims.*

Civil Records: Access: Mail, in person. Both court and visitors may perform in person searches. Search fee: $5.00 per name for 2 years; computer search is $16.00. Required to search: name, years to search. Civil cases indexed by defendant. Civil records on microfilm from 1985, in books since 1970.

Criminal Records: Access: Mail, in person. Both court and visitors may perform in person searches. Search fee: $5.00 per name for 2 years; computer search is $16.00. Required to search: name, years to search, DOB. Criminal records in books from 1970.

General Information: No sealed, expunged, adoption, sex offense, juvenile or mental health records released. SASE required. Turnaround time 7-10 working days. Copy fee: $1.00 per page. Certification fee: Certificate of Disposition is $5.00. Fee payee: City Court of

Niagara Falls. Cash or money order only. No checks accepted. Prepayment is required.

North Tonawanda City Court
City Hall, North Tonawanda, NY 14120-5446; 716-693-1010; Fax: 716-743-1754. Hours: 8AM-5PM (EST). *Misdemeanor, Civil Actions Under $15,000, Eviction, Small Claims.*

Civil Records: Access: Mail, in person. Only the court performs in person searches; visitors may not. Search fee: $16.00 for an electronic search plus $5.00 per name to certify. Required to search: name, years to search. Civil cases indexed by defendant. Civil records on computer from 1993, prior in books.

Criminal Records: Access: Mail, in person. Only the court performs in person searches; visitors may not. Search fee: Fees same as civil. Required to search: name, years to search, DOB, signed release. Criminal records on computer from 1986, prior in books.

General Information: No sealed, expunged, adoption, sex offense, juvenile or mental health records released. SASE requested. Turnaround time 2 days. Copy fee: $1.00 per page. Certification fee: $5.00. Fee payee: City Court. Only cashiers checks and money orders accepted. Prepayment is required.

Surrogate Court
Niagara County Courthouse, 175 Hawley St, Lockport, NY 14094; 716-439-7130; Fax: 716-439-7157. Hours: 9AM-5PM (EST). *Probate.*

Town/Village Courts
Misdemeanor, Civil Actions Under $3,000, Small Claims: Hartland Town, 716-735-7239; Wilson Town, 716-751-0549; Wheatfield Town, 716-694-6793; Porter Town, 716-745-7036; Lewiston Town, 716-754-8213; Niagara Town, 716-297-2150; Cambria Town, 716-433-7664; Newfane Town, 716-778-9292; Lockport Town, 716-439-9528; Barker Village, 716-795-9193; Royalton Town, 716-772-2588; Pendleton Town, 716-625-8833; Somerset Town, 716-795-9193.

Oneida County

Supreme & County Court
800 Park Ave, Utica, NY 13501; 315-798-5790. Hours: 9AM-5PM (EST). *Felony, Civil.*

Civil Records: Access: Mail, in person. Both court and visitors may perform in person searches. Search fee: $5.00 per name. Fee is for 2 year search. Required to search: name, years to search. Civil cases indexed by defendant, plaintiff. Civil records on computer from 1992, prior in books by plaintiff only.

Criminal Records: Access: Mail, in person. Both court and visitors may perform in person searches. Search fee: $5.00 per name. Fee is for 2 year search. Required to search: name, years to search, SSN, signed release. Criminal records on computer from 1992, prior in books by plaintiff only.

General Information: Public access terminal is available. No sealed, expunged, adoption, sex offense, juvenile or mental health records released. SASE required. Turnaround time 1 week. Copy fee: $1.00 per page. Certification fee: $4.00. Fee payee: County Clerk. Personal checks accepted. Prepayment is required.

Rome City Court
100 W Court St, Rome, NY 13440; 315-337-6440; Fax: 315-338-0343. Hours: 9AM-5PM (EST). *Misdemeanor, Civil Actions Under $15,000, Eviction, Small Claims.*

Civil Records: Access: Mail, in person. Only the court performs in person searches; visitors may not. Search fee: $5.00 per name. Required to search: name, years to search. Civil cases indexed by defendant, plaintiff. Civil records in books and some on computer.

Criminal Records: Access: Mail, in person. Only the court performs in person searches; visitors may not. Search fee: $16.00 for electronic automated search or $5.00 for manual search per 2 years. Required to search: name, years to search, DOB. Most records are computerized.

General Information: No sealed or youthful offender records released. SASE required. Turnaround time 5-7 days. Copy fee: $.50 per page. $1.00 minimum. Certification fee: $5.00. Fee payee: Rome City Court. Only cashiers checks and money orders accepted. Prepayment is required.

Sherrill City Court
373 Sherrill Rd, Sherrill, NY 13461; 315-363-0996; Fax: 315-363-1176. Hours: 8AM-4PM (EST). *Misdemeanor, Civil Actions Under $15,000, Eviction, Small Claims.*

Civil Records: Access: Mail, in person. Only the court performs in person searches; visitors may not. Search fee: $5.00 per name. Required to search: name, years to search. Civil cases indexed by defendant, plaintiff. Civil records in books since 1800s.

Criminal Records: Access: Mail, in person. Only the court performs in person searches; visitors may not. Search fee: $5.00 per name. Required to search: name, years to search; also helpful: DOB. Criminal records in books since 1800s.

General Information: No sealed, expunged, adoption, sex offense, juvenile or mental health records released. SASE required. Turnaround time 1-2 days. Copy fee: $.50 per page. Certification fee: $5.00. Fee payee: Sherrill City Court. Personal checks accepted. Prepayment is required.

Steuben Town Court
9458 Soule Rd, Remsen, NY 13438. *Misdemeanor, Civil Actions Under $3,000, Small Claims.*

Utica City Court
411 Oriskany St West, Utica, NY 13502; Civil phone: 315-724-8157; Criminal phone: 315-724-8227; Fax: 315-724-0762 (criminal)/792-8038 (civil). Hours: 8:30AM-4:30PM (EST). *Misdemeanor, Civil Actions Under $15,000, Eviction, Small Claims.*

Civil Records: Access: Mail, in person. Both court and visitors may perform in person searches. Search fee: $5.00 per name. Required to search: name, years to search, address. Civil cases indexed by defendant. Civil records in books from 1900s, computerized records back to 1980's.

Criminal Records: Access: Mail, in person. Only the court performs in person searches; visitors may not. Search fee: Computer criminal history search $16.00, manual 2 year search is $5.00. Required to search: name, years to search, address, DOB, signed release. Criminal records in books from 1900s, computerized records back to 1980's.

General Information: No sealed, expunged, adoption, sex offense, juvenile or mental health records released. SASE required. Turnaround time 1-2 days. Copy fee: $.50 per page. $1.00 minimum. Certification fee: $5.00. Fee payee: City Court of Utica. Only cashiers checks and money orders accepted. Prepayment is required.

Surrogate Court
Oneida County Office Bldg - 8th Floor, 800 Park Ave, Utica, NY 13501; 315-797-9320. Hours: 9AM-5PM Sept-May; 8:30AM-4PM June-Aug (EST). *Probate.*

Town/Village Courts
Misdemeanor, Civil Actions Under $3,000, Small Claims: Florence Town; Boonville Town, 315-942-3416; Marcy Town; Vernon Village, 315-829-2691; Ava Town, 315-942-6542; Whitestown Town, 315-736-1251; Whitesboro Village, 315-736-4353; Bridgewater Town, 315-822-6808; Vienna Town, 315-245-2191; Remsen Village Court; New York Mills Village, 315-736-7811; Verona Town, 315-363-4394; Marshall Town, 315-841-8515; New Hartford Village, 315-732-5924; Westmoreland Town, 315-853-4333; New Hartford Town, 315-732-5924; Western Town, 315-827-4928; Clinton Village Court; Augusta Town, 315-843-4811; Camden Town, 315-245-0817; Waterville Village, 315-841-8007; Deerfield Town, 315-724-0605; Remsen Town, 315-831-5330; Lee Town, 315-336-1585; Kirkland Town, 315-853-5082; Orinsky Village, 315-736-3512; Annsville

Town, 315-336-1295; Sylvan Beach Village, 315-762-4240; Boonville Village, 315-942-3438; Floyd Town, 315-865-4256; Forestport Town, 315-392-2801; Paris Town, 315-839-5400; Trenton Town, 315-896-4510; Vernon Town, 315-829-3211; Sangerfield Town, 315-841-8631.

Onondaga County

Supreme & County Court
401 Montgomery St Room 200, Syracuse, NY 13202; 315-435-2226. Hours: 8AM-5PM (EST). *Felony, Civil.*

Civil Records: Access: Mail, in person. Both court and visitors may perform in person searches. Search fee: $5.00 per name. Fee is per name & per 2 years searched. Required to search: name, years to search. Civil cases indexed by defendant, plaintiff. Civil records on computer from 1989, prior in books.

Criminal Records: Access: Mail, in person. Both court and visitors may perform in person searches. Search fee: $5.00 per name. Fee is per 2 years searched. Required to search: name, years to search; also helpful: DOB. Criminal records computerized from 1990, prior in books.

General Information: Public access terminal is available. No sealed, divorce, judgment or sexual abuse records released. SASE required. Turnaround time 2-3 days. Copy fee: $.50 per page. $1.00 minimum. Certification fee: Fee is $1.00 per page with a $4.00 minimum. Fee payee: County Clerk. Personal checks accepted. $60.00 limit for personal checks. Prepayment is required.

Syracuse City Court
511 State St, Syracuse, NY 13202-2179; Civil phone: 315-477-2782; Criminal phone: 315-477-2760; Fax: 315-426-8454 Civil; 472-2963 Criminal. Hours: 9AM-4PM (EST). *Misdemeanor, Civil Actions Under $15,000, Eviction, Small Claims.*

Note: Criminal records are in Room 115, Civil in Room 107. Small claims (Rm 107) phone is 315-477-2784; their fax is 315-426-8454.

Civil Records: Access: Phone, fax, mail, in person. Both court and visitors may perform in person searches. Search fee: $16.00 per name. Required to search: name, years to search; also helpful: address. Civil cases indexed by defendant, plaintiff. Civil records on computer from 1993, from 1980-94 on fiche or microfilm.

Criminal Records: Access: Phone, fax, mail, in person. Both court and visitors may perform in person searches. Search fee: 1995-present is $16.00 per name. 1989-present is $31.00; $5.00 per name per 2 years. Fee is for certificate of conviction or of disposition. Required to search: name, years to search, DOB; also helpful: offense. Criminal records from 1960 to present are on either computer, dockets or manual books. Fee for search from 1993-present is $21.00; search from 1991-present is $26.00.

General Information: No sealed, expunged, adoption, sex offense, juvenile or mental health records released. SASE required. Turnaround time 1-2 weeks. Copy fee: $.50 per page. $1.00 minimum. Certification fee: $5.00 cert fee is for civil only; criminal records are certified as part of search fee. Fee payee: Syracuse City Court. Only cashiers checks and money orders accepted. Attorney checks only. Prepayment is required.

Surrogate Court
Onondaga Courthouse, Rm 209, 401 Montgomery St, Syracuse, NY 13202; 315-671-2100; Fax: 315-671-1162. Hours: 9AM-5PM (EST). *Probate.*

Town/Village Courts
Misdemeanor, Civil Actions Under $3,000, Small Claims: Geddes Town, 315-468-3613; Baldwinsville Village, 315-635-6355; East Syracuse Village, 315-437-6456; LaFayette Town, 315-677-9350; Spafford Town; Cicero Town, 315-

699-8478; Skaneateles Town, 315-685-5880; Fayetteville Village, 315-637-8070; Minoa Village, 315-656-2203; Marcellus Town, 315-673-1773; Tully Town, 315-696-5884; Otisco Town; Elbridge Town, 315-689-7380; Liverpool Village, 315-457-5379; North Syracuse Village, 315-458-4695; Lysander Town, 315-638-1308; Van Buren Town, 315-635-3523; Pompey Town, 315-682-9877; Jordan Village, 315-689-7350; Solvay Village, 315-468-1608; DeWitt Town, 315-446-9180; Onondaga Town, 315-469-1674; Clay Town, 315-652-3800; Manlius Town, 315-637-3251; Fabius Town, 315-696-8725; Manlius Village, 315-682-7245; Camillus Town, 315-487-7066; Salina Town, 315-457-5379.

Ontario County

Supreme & County Court 27 N Main St, Rm 130, Canandaigua, NY 14424-1447; 585-396-4239; Fax: 585-396-4576. Hours: 9AM-5PM (EST). *Felony, Civil.*

Note: Records are maintained at County Clerk's office, 20 Ontario, Municipal Bldg, NY 14424, 716-396-4205.

Civil Records: Access: Phone, fax, mail, in person. Only the court performs in person searches; visitors may not. Search fee: $5.00. Required to search: name, years to search. Civil cases indexed by defendant, plaintiff. Civil records on computer from 1992, records go back to 1887.

Criminal Records: Access: Phone, fax, mail, in person. Only the court performs in person searches; visitors may not. Search fee: $5.00. Required to search: name, years to search, DOB. Criminal records on computer from 1990, records go back to 1919.

General Information: No sealed, youthful offender, sex abuse, sex crime, marriage or incompetence records released. SASE required. Turnaround time 1 week. Copy fee: $.50 per page. Certification fee: $4.00. Fee payee: County Clerk. Personal checks accepted. Prepayment is required.

Canandaigua City Court 2 N Main St, Canandaigua, NY 14424-1448; 585-396-5011; Fax: 585-396-5012. Hours: 8AM-4PM (EST). *Misdemeanor, Civil Actions Under $15,000, Eviction, Small Claims.*

Civil Records: Access: Mail, in person. Only the court performs in person searches; visitors may not. Search fee: $5.00 per two years searched. Required to search: name, years to search. Civil cases indexed by defendant, plaintiff. Civil records on computer from 1986, prior in books from 1960.

Criminal Records: Access: Mail, in person. Only the court performs in person searches; visitors may not. Search fee: $5.00 per two years searched. Required to search: name, years to search, DOB. Criminal records on computer from 1986, prior in books from 1960.

General Information: No sealed, expunged, adoption, sex offense, juvenile or mental health records released. SASE required. Turnaround time 1 week. Copy fee: $.50 per page. Fee payee: Canandaigua City Court. Only cashiers checks and money orders accepted. Prepayment is required.

Geneva City Court 255 Exchange Street, Geneva, NY 14456; 315-789-6560; Fax: 315-781-2802. Hours: 8AM-4PM (EST). *Misdemeanor, Civil Actions Under $15,000, Eviction, Small Claims.*

Civil Records: Access: Phone, mail, in person. Only the court performs in person searches; visitors may not. No search fee. Required to search: name, years to search. Civil cases indexed by plaintiff. Civil records on computer from 1992, prior in books.

Criminal Records: Access: Mail, in person. Only the court performs in person searches; visitors may not. Search fee: $16.00 and $5.00 fee for a certificate of conviction. Required to search: name, years to search,

DOB. Criminal records on computer from 1992, prior in books.

General Information: No youthful offender records released. SASE required. Turnaround time 1 month. Copy fee: $1.00 per page. Certification fee: $5.00. Fee payee: City Court. Only cashiers checks and money orders accepted. Prepayment is required.

Surrogate Court 27 N Main St, Canandaigua, NY 14424-1447; 585-396-4055. Hours: 9AM-5PM (EST). *Probate.*

Town/Village Courts *Misdemeanor, Civil Actions Under $3,000, Small Claims:* Geneva Town, 315-789-3922; Naples Town, 585-374-2500; Bristol Town, 585-229-2400; West Bloomfield Town, 585-624-2914; Seneca Town, 585-526-4780; Shortsville Village, 585-289-3010; East Bloomfield Town, 585-657-7248; Clifton Springs Village, 315-462-3048; Phelps Town, 315-548-2090; Gorham Town, 585-526-6298; Richmond Town; Canadice Town, 585-367-2560; Victor Town, 585-924-5262; Canandaigua Town, 585-394-9040; South Bristol Town, 585-374-6341; Hopewell Town, 585-394-0036; Manchester Town, 585-289-6846; Farmington Town, 315-986-4774.

Orange County

Supreme & County Court 255 Main St, Goshen, NY 10924; 845-291-2690; Civil phone: 845-291-3076; Criminal phone: 845-291-3083; Fax: 845-291-2595. Hours: 9AM-5PM (EST). *Felony, Civil.*

Note: Misdemeanor records are maintained by city, town and village courts.

Civil Records: Access: Mail, in person. Both court and visitors may perform in person searches. Search fee: $2.50 per name; $5.00 per 2 years. Required to search: name, years to search. Civil cases indexed by defendant, plaintiff. Civil records on computer from 1993; prior indexed only by plaintiff.

Criminal Records: Access: Mail, in person. Both court and visitors may perform in person searches. Search fee: $2.50 per name; $5.00 per 2 years. Required to search: name, years to search, DOB. Criminal records on computer since 1993; prior on index Rolodex cards.

General Information: Public access terminal is available. No sealed records released. SASE required. Turnaround time 2 weeks. Copy fee: $.50 per page. Minimum $1.00. Certification fee: $1.00 per page, $4.00 minimum. Fee payee: County Clerk. Business checks accepted. Prepayment is required.

Middletown City Court 2 James St, Middletown, NY 10940; 845-346-4050; Fax: 845-343-5737. Hours: 8AM-4PM (EST). *Misdemeanor, Civil Actions Under $15,000, Eviction, Small Claims.*

Civil Records: Access: Mail, in person. Only the court performs in person searches; visitors may not. Search fee: $16.00 per name. Prior to 1986 is $5.00 per name per 2 year search. Required to search: name, years to search. Civil cases indexed by defendant, plaintiff. Civil records on computer from 1986, prior on cards.

Criminal Records: Access: Mail, in person. Only the court performs in person searches; visitors may not. Search fee: $16.00 per name. Prior to 1986 $5.00 per name per 2 year search. Required to search: name, years to search, DOB; also helpful: SSN, date of offense. Criminal records on computer from 1986, prior on cards.

General Information: No sealed or youthful offender records released. SASE required. Turnaround time 2-3 weeks. Copy fee: $.50 per page. $1.00 minimum. Certification fee: $5.00. Fee payee: City Court of Middletown. Only cashiers checks and money orders accepted. Prepayment is required.

Newburgh City Court 57 Broadway, Newburgh, NY 12550; 845-565-3208. Hours: 8AM-4PM (EST).

Misdemeanor, Civil Actions Up to $15,000, Eviction, Small Claims.

Civil Records: Access: Mail, in person. Only the court performs in person searches; visitors may not. Search fee: $5.00 per name. $16.00 for computer search. Required to search: name, years to search. Civil cases indexed by defendant. Civil records on computer from 1997, prior in books or on cards.

Criminal Records: Access: Mail, in person. Only the court performs in person searches; visitors may not. Search fee: $5.00 per name. $16.00 for computer search. Required to search: name, years to search, DOB. Criminal records on computer from 1986.

General Information: No sealed, youthful offender or sex abuse victim records released. SASE required. Turnaround time 3-5 days. Copy fee: $.50 per page. Certification fee: $5.00. Fee payee: Newburgh City Court. Only cashiers checks and money orders accepted. Prepayment is required.

Port Jervis City Court 14-18 Hammond St, Port Jervis, NY 12771-2495; 845-858-4034; Fax: 845-856-2767. Hours: 9AM-5PM (EST). *Misdemeanor, Civil Actions Under $15,000, Eviction, Small Claims.*

Civil Records: Access: Mail, in person. Both court and visitors may perform in person searches. Search fee: $16.00 per name. Fee is computer search. Required to search: name, years to search. Civil cases indexed by defendant. Civil records on dockets from 1974, computerized since 1996.

Criminal Records: Access: Mail, in person. Both court and visitors may perform in person searches. Search fee: $16.00 per name. A certified disposition or conviction is $5.00. Required to search: name, years to search, DOB. Criminal records on dockets from 1976, computerized since 1996.

General Information: No sealed, expunged, adoption, sex offense, juvenile or mental health records released. SASE required. Turnaround time 1 week. Copy fee: $1.00 for first page, $.50 each add'l. Certification fee: $5.00. Fee payee: City Court. Only cashiers checks and money orders accepted. Prepayment is required.

Surrogate Court 30 Park Place, Surrogate's Courthouse, Goshen, NY 10924; 845-291-2193; Fax: 845-291-2196. Hours: 9AM-5PM; Vault closes at 4PM (EST). *Probate.*

Town/Village Courts *Misdemeanor, Civil Actions Under $3,000, Small Claims:* Warwick Town, 845-986-1128; Maybrook Village, 845-427-2717; Florida Village, 845-651-4940; Tuxedo Park Village, 845-351-4745; Cornwall Town, 845-534-8717; Unionville Village Court; New Windsor Town, 845-563-4682; Warwick Village, 845-986-7044; Greenville Town, 845-856-5064/8890; Wallkill Town, 845-692-5811; Hamptonburgh Town, 845-427-5432; Goshen Village, 845-294-5826; Goshen Town, 845-294-6477; Greenwood Lake Village, 845-477-9218; Newburgh Town, 845-564-0960; Walden Village, 845-778-1632; Crawford Town, 845-744-1435; Blooming Grove Town, 845-496-7631; Minisink Town, 845-726-3700; Wawayanda Town, 845-355-1313; Highlands Town, 845-446-8666; Monroe Town, 845-783-9733; Montgomery Town, 845-457-2620; Montgomery Village, 845-457-9037; Chester Village, 845-469-2388; Tuxedo Town, 845-351-5655; Chester Town, 845-469-9541; Deerpark Town, 845-856-2928; Harriman Village, 845-782-6143; Mount Hope Town, 845-386-5303; Woodbury Town, 845-928-2311; Washingtonville Village, 914-419-9797; Otisville Village, 845-386-1004.

Orleans County

Supreme & County Court Courthouse, Albion, NY 14411-9998; 585-589-5458; Criminal phone: 585-589-5489; Fax: 585-589-0632. Hours: 9AM-5PM (EST). *Felony, Civil.*

Note: Misdemeaner, Evictions and Small Claims are at Town and Village courts.

Civil Records: Access: Mail, in person. Both court and visitors may perform in person searches. Search fee: $5.00 per name. Fee is for 2 year search. Required to search: name, years to search. Civil cases indexed by defendant. Civil records in books to 1940s; on computer back to 1993.

Criminal Records: Access: Mail, in person. Only the court performs in person searches; visitors may not. Search fee: $5.00 per name. Required to search: name, years to search, DOB. Criminal records in books to 1940s; on computer back to 1993.

General Information: No sealed or divorce records released. SASE required. Turnaround time 1 week. Copy fee: $1.00 per page. Certification fee: $4.00 plus $1.00 per page after first 4. Fee payee: County Clerk. Personal checks accepted. Prepayment is required.

Surrogate Court 3 S Main St, Albion, NY 14411; 585-589-4457; Fax: 585-589-0632. Hours: 9AM-5PM (EST). *Probate.*

Town/Village Courts *Misdemeanor, Civil Actions Under $3,000, Small Claims:* Barre Town, 585-589-5100; Carlton Town, 585-682-3356; Murray Town, 585-638-6727; Shelby Town, 585-798-3120; Yates Town, 585-765-9603; Albion Village, 585-589-2335; Ridgeway Town, 585-798-0730; Albion Town, 585-589-7048; Clarendon Town, 585-638-6371; Medina Village, 585-798-4875; Kendall Town, 585-659-8540; Gaines Town, 585-589-4525.

Oswego County

Supreme & County Court 46 E Bridge St, Oswego, NY 13126; 315-349-3277, 315-349-8616 (Clk); Fax: 315-349-8513. Hours: 9AM-5PM (EST). *Felony, Civil.*

Civil Records: Access: Mail, in person. Both court and visitors may perform in person searches. Search fee: $5.00 per name. Required to search: name, years to search. Civil cases indexed by defendant and plaintiff. Civil records on computer from 1/90, prior in books from 1926.

Criminal Records: Access: Mail, in person. Only the court performs in person searches; visitors may not. Search fee: $5.00 per name. Required to search: name, years to search, DOB, signed release. Criminal records on computer from 1973; prior in docket books from 1950.

General Information: Public access terminal is available. (The Public access terminal is only for civil records.) No sealed, youthful offender or divorce records released. SASE required. Turnaround time 2-3 days. Copy fee: $.50 per page. Certification fee: $4.00. Fee payee: County Clerk. Personal checks accepted. Prepayment is required.

Fulton City Court 141 S 1st St, Fulton, NY 13069; 315-593-8400; Fax: 315-592-3415. Hours: 8:30AM-4:30PMSummer 8:30AM-4PM (EST). *Misdemeanor, Civil Actions Under $15,000, Eviction, Small Claims.*

Civil Records: Access: Mail, in person. Only the court performs in person searches; visitors may not. No search fee. Required to search: name, years to search. Civil cases indexed by defendant. Civil records on dockets from 1991; computerized records since 1998.

Criminal Records: Access: Mail, in person. Only the court performs in person searches; visitors may not. Search fee: $16.00 per name. Fee is for computer search. $5.00 for manual search per 2 years searched.

Required to search: name, years to search, DOB. Criminal records go back to 1918, computerized records since 1997, criminal records on dockets from 1987.

General Information: No sealed, expunged, adoption, sex offense, juvenile or mental health records released. SASE not required. Turnaround time 1 week. Copy fee: $.50 per page. Certification fee: $5.00. Fee payee: Fulton City Court. Only cashiers checks and money orders accepted. Prepayment is required.

Oswego City Court Conway Municipal Building, 20 West Oneida St, Oswego, NY 13126; 315-343-0415; Fax: 315-343-0531. Hours: 8:30AM-5PM (EST). *Misdemeanor, Civil Actions Under $15,000, Eviction, Small Claims.*

Civil Records: Access: Mail, in person. Only the court performs in person searches; visitors may not. No search fee. Required to search: name, years to search. Civil cases indexed by defendant. Civil records on computer from 1987, prior in books.

Criminal Records: Access: Mail, in person. Only the court performs in person searches; visitors may not. No search fee. Required to search: name, years to search, DOB. Criminal records on computer from 1987, prior in books.

General Information: No sealed or youthful offender records released. SASE required. Turnaround time 3-4 days. Copy fee: $.50 per page. Certification fee: $5.00 plus $.50 per page after first. Fee payee: Oswego City Court. Only cashiers checks and money orders accepted. Prepayment is required.

Surrogate Court Courthouse, 25 E Oneida St, Oswego, NY 13126; 315-349-3295. Hours: 9AM-5PM Sept-May; 8:30AM-3:30 PM June-Aug (EST). *Probate.*

Town/Village Courts *Misdemeanor, Civil Actions Under $3,000, Small Claims:* Palermo Town, 315-593-2333; Sandy Creek Town, 315-387-5456; Pulaski Village, 315-298-2526; Orwell Town, 315-298-5563; Oswego Town, 315-343-7249; Boylston Town; Parish Town, 315-625-7362; Granby Town, 315-598-2958; Amboy Town, 315-964-1165; Constantia Town, 315-623-7713; Redfield Town, 315-599-7786; Cleveland Village, 315-675-8611; West Monroe Town, 315-668-8314; Mexico Town, 315-963-3785; New Haven Town, 315-963-3900; Scriba Town, 315-343-3250; Albion Town, 315-298-6325; Volney Town, 315-598-7082; Hannibal Town, 315-564-6037; Williamstown Town; Minetto Town, 315-343-2393; Richland Town, 315-298-5174; Schroeppel Town, 315-695-6177; Hastings Town, 315-676-4317.

Otsego County

Supreme & County Court 197 Main St, Cooperstown, NY 13326; 607-547-4364; Fax: 607-547-7567. Hours: 9AM-5PM (EST). *Felony, Criminal, Civil.*

Note: Misdemeanor records are maintained by city, town and village courts.

Civil Records: Access: Mail, in person. Both court and visitors may perform in person searches. Search fee: $5.00 per name. Required to search: name, years to search. Civil cases indexed by defendant. Civil records on computer back to 1997; prior in books.

Criminal Records: Access: Mail, in person. Both court and visitors may perform in person searches. Search fee: $5.00 per name. Required to search: name, years to search, address, DOB. Criminal records on computer back to 1997; prior in books.

General Information: Public access terminal is available. No sealed, expunged, adoption, sex offense, juvenile or mental health records released. SASE required. Turnaround time 1-2 days. Copy fee: $1.00 per page. Certification fee: $4.00. Fee payee: County

Clerk. Business checks accepted. Prepayment is required.

Oneonta City Court 81 Main St, Oneonta, NY 13820; 607-432-4480; Fax: 607-432-2328. Hours: 8AM-4PM (EST). *Misdemeanor, Civil Actions Under $15,000, Eviction, Small Claims.*

Civil Records: Access: Mail, in person. Only the court performs in person searches; visitors may not. Search fee: $16.00 per name for 10 years. Additional is $5.00 per 2 years searched. Required to search: name, years to search. Civil cases indexed by defendant. Civil records on computer from 1987, prior in books.

Criminal Records: Access: Mail, in person. Only the court performs in person searches; visitors may not. Search fee: $16.00 per name for 10 years. Additional is $5.00 per 2 years searched. Required to search: name, years to search, DOB. Criminal records on computer from 1987, prior in books.

General Information: No sealed or youthful offender records released. SASE required. Turnaround time 1 day. Copy fee: $.50 per page. $1.00 minimum. Certification fee: $5.00. Fee payee: Oneonta City Court. Only cashiers checks and money orders accepted. Prefer certified funds. Prepayment is required.

Surrogate Court Surrogate's Office, 197 Main St, Cooperstown, NY 13326; 607-547-4338; Fax: 607-547-7566. Hours: 9AM-5PM (EST). *Probate.*

Town/Village Courts *Misdemeanor, Civil Actions Under $3,000, Small Claims:* Cherry Valley Village, 607-264-3791; Morris Village, 607-263-5944; Otego Town, 607-988-2698; Cherry Valley Town, 607-264-8491; Otsego Town, 607-547-5689; Worcester Town, 607-397-8182; Unadilla Town, 607-369-7458; Edmeston Town, 607-965-9823; Hartwick Town, 607-293-6614; Roseboom Town, 607-264-3293; Plainfield Town; Milford Town, 607-286-7773; Laurens Village Court; Laurens Town, 607-433-2816; Middlefield Town, 607-547-8800; Pittsfield Town, 607-847-6524; Morris Town, 607-263-5944; Cooperstown Village, 607-547-9597; Burlington Town; Decatur Town, 607-397-9116; Richfield Springs Village Court; Springfield Town, 315-858-1508; Exeter Town, 315-858-0937; New Lisbon Town, 607-965-8627; Richfield Town, 315-858-2830; Oneonta Town, 607-432-0124; Maryland Town, 607-738-9495; Westford Town, 607-397-9210; Butternuts Town, 607-783-2758.

Putnam County

Supreme & County Court 40 Gleneida Ave, Carmel, NY 10512; 845-225-3641 X307; Fax: 845-228-0231. Hours: 9AM-5PM (EST). *Felony, Civil.*

Civil Records: Access: Mail, in person. Both court and visitors may perform in person searches. Search fee: $5.00 per name. Fee is per 2 years searched. Required to search: name, years to search. Civil cases indexed by defendant, plaintiff. Civil records on computer from 4/93, prior in books.

Criminal Records: Access: Mail, in person. Both court and visitors may perform in person searches. Search fee: $5.00 per name. Fee is per 2 years searched. Required to search: name, years to search, DOB. Criminal records computerized since 1983.

General Information: Public access terminal is available. No sealed or youthful offender records released. SASE required. Turnaround time 2 days. Copy fee: $1.00 per page. Certification fee: $4.00. Fee payee: County Clerk. Personal checks accepted. Prepayment is required.

Surrogate Court 44 Gleneida Ave, Carmel, NY 10512; 845-225-3641 X295; Fax: 845-228-5761. Hours: 9AM-5PM (EST). *Probate.*

Town/Village Courts *Misdemeanor, Civil Actions Under $3,000, Small Claims:* Cold Spring Village, 845-265-9070; Southeast Town, 845-279-8939; Kent

Town, 845-225-1606; Philipstown Town, 845-265-2951; Nelsonville Village Court; Brewster Village, 845-279-4020; Putnam Valley Town, 845-526-3050; Carmel Town, 845-628-1500; Patterson Town, 845-878-6500.

Queens County

Supreme Court - Civil Division 88-11 Sutphin Blvd #106, Jamaica, NY 11435; 718-520-3136; Fax: 718-520-4731. Hours: 9AM-5PM, no cashier transactions after 4:45PM (EST). *Civil Actions Over $25,000.*

Civil Records: Access: Mail, in person. Both court and visitors may perform in person searches. Search fee: $10.00 per name. Fee is for first two years. Add $5.00 per additional 2 years. Required to search: name, years to search, address. Civil cases indexed by plaintiff. Civil records on computer from 1992, prior in books.
General Information: No marriage or incompetence records released. Identification required to review confidential matrimonial case records. SASE required. Turnaround time 1 week. Copy fee: $4.00 per document. Certification fee: $8.00. Fee payee: County Clerk. Only cashiers checks and money orders accepted. Prepayment is required.

Supreme Court - Criminal Division 125-01 Queens Blvd, Kew Gardens, NY 11415; 718-520-3494. Hours: 9:30AM-4:30PM (EST). *Felony, Misdemeanor.*

Criminal Records: Access: Mail, in person. Only the court performs in person searches; visitors may not. Search fee: $16.00 per name. Required to search: name, years to search, SSN, signed release. Criminal records on computer from 1990, prior in books. Searches done at OCA.
General Information: No sealed or youthful offender records released. SASE required. Turnaround time 1-2 days. Copy fee: $.15 per page. Certification fee: $4.00. Based on $1.00 per page with 4 page minimum. Fee payee: County Clerk. Personal checks accepted. Prepayment is required.

Civil Court of the City of New York - Queens Branch 89-17 Sutphin Blvd, Jamaica, NY 11435; 718-262-7100. Hours: 9AM-5PM (EST). *Civil Actions Under $25,000, Eviction, Small Claims.*

Civil Records: Access: In person only. Visitors must perform in person searches for themselves. No search fee. Required to search: name, years to search. Civil cases indexed by plaintiff. Civil records on computer from 1996, prior in books.
General Information: Public access terminal is available. (Civil only.) No sealed, youthful offender or sex victim records released. SASE required. Turnaround time 3-5 days; 7-10 for older records. Copy fee: $.25 per page. Certification fee: $5.00. Fee payee: Civil Court. Only cashiers checks and money orders accepted. Prepayment is required.

Surrogate Court 88-11 Sutphin Blvd, Jamaica, NY 11435; 718-520-3132. Hours: 9AM-5PM (EST). *Probate.*

Rensselaer County

Supreme & County Court 105 3rd Street, Troy, NY 12180; 518-270-4080; Fax: 518-271-7998. Hours: 9AM-5PM (EST). *Felony, Civil.*

www.rensco.com

Civil Records: Access: Mail, in person. Visitors must perform in person searches for themselves. No search fee. Required to search: name, years to search. Civil cases indexed by plaintiff pre-1996; by defendant & plaintiff after 1996. Civil records on computer back to 1990s; prior in books to 1970s.

Criminal Records: Access: Mail, in person. Only the court performs in person searches; visitors may not. Search fee: $5.00 per name. Fee is per 2 years searched. Required to search: name, years to search, DOB. Criminal records on computer back to 1986; prior in books to 1976.
General Information: No sealed, open/pending cases, youthful offender records released. SASE required. Turnaround time 1 week. Copy fee: $1.00 per page. Certification fee: $4.00 plus $.50 per page after first 8. Fee payee: County Clerk. Personal checks accepted. Prepayment is required.

Rensselaer City Court City Hall, Rensselaer, NY 12144; 518-462-6751; Fax: 518-462-3307. Hours: 8AM-3:30PM (EST). *Misdemeanor, Civil Actions Under $15,000, Eviction, Small Claims.*

Civil Records: Access: Mail, in person. Both court and visitors may perform in person searches. Search fee: $5.00. Required to search: name, years to search. Civil cases indexed by defendant. Civil records in books back 10 years; on computer back 2 years.
Criminal Records: Access: Mail, in person. Both court and visitors may perform in person searches. Search fee: $5.00 per name. Required to search: name, years to search, DOB, signed release. Criminal records in books go back 10 years; on computer back 2 years. Court will only confirm convictions.
General Information: No sealed, expunged, adoption, sex offense, juvenile or mental health records released. Copy fee: $.50 per page. Certification fee: $5.00. Fee payee: Rensselaer City Court. Only cashiers checks and money orders accepted. Prepayment is required.

Troy City Court 51 State St, 2nd Fl, Troy, NY 12180; 518-271-1602; Fax: 518-274-2816. Hours: 9AM-3:30PM (EST). *Misdemeanor.*

Criminal Records: Access: Mail, in person. Only the court performs in person searches; visitors may not. Search fee: $16.00 per name. Required to search: name, years to search, DOB, aliases, offense. Criminal records on computer from 1989, prior in books.
General Information: No sealed records released. SASE required. Turnaround time 1 week. No copy fee. Certification fee: $5.00. Fee payee: City Court. Personal checks accepted.

Surrogate Court County Courthouse, 72 Second St, Troy, NY 12180; 518-270-3724. Hours: 9AM-5PM (EST). *Probate.*

Town/Village Courts *Misdemeanor, Civil Actions Under $3,000, Small Claims:* East Greenbush Town, 518-477-5412; Petersburg Town, 518-658-3777; Nassau Village, 518-766-3044; Berlin Town, 518-650-2020; Poestenkill Town, 518-283-5100; Brunswick Town, 518-279-3461; Sand Lake Town, 518-674-3033; Schaghticoke Town, 518-753-6915; Schodack Town, 518-477-9390; Pittstown Town; North Greenbush Town; Stephentown Town, 518-733-5636; Castleton-on-Hudson Village, 518-732-2211; Hoosick Town, 518-686-4571; Hoosick Falls Village, 518-686-7900; Nassau Town, 518-766-2813; Grafton Town, 518-279-3565.

Richmond County

Supreme Court - Civil Division 130 Stuyvesant Pl, Staten Island, NY 10301; 718-390-5389 Court Desk; Civil phone: 718-390-5352. Hours: 9AM-5PM (EST). *Civil Actions Over $25,000.*

Civil Records: Access: In person only. Visitors must perform in person searches for themselves. No search fee. Required to search: name, years to search. Civil cases indexed by plaintiff. Civil records go back to 1990; on computer back to 1993.
General Information: Public access terminal is available. No matrimonial records released. Fax notes: Will not fax results. Copy fee: $.25. Certification fee:

$8.00. Fee payee: Richmond County Clerk. Only cashiers checks and money orders accepted. Prepayment is required.

Supreme Court - Criminal Division 18 Richmond Terrace, Rm 110, Staten Island, NY 10301; 718-390-5280. Hours: 9AM-5PM, Closed 1-2PM (EST). *Felony, Misdemeanor.*

Criminal Records: Access: Mail, in person. Visitors must perform in person searches for themselves. Court will search for verified (known) cases only and will certify dispositions. Search fee: None, but court does not perform name only searches. Electronic searches referred to 202-428-2940, $16.00 per county payable to NY State Of. of Court Admin. Required to search: name, years to search, DOB. A notarized signed release is required for access to sealed records. Criminal records on computer back to 1975, prior archived bacl tp 1960.
General Information: No sealed or youthful offender records released unless to subject. SASE required. Turnaround time 1-2 days. Copy fee: $.50 per page. Certification fee: $10.00. Fee payee: If this court performs the search, make check payable to County Clerk Richmond County. Only cashiers checks and money orders accepted. Prepayment is required.

Civil Court of the City of New York - Richmond Branch 927 Castleton Ave, Staten Island, NY 10310; 718-390-5417-5419. Hours: 9AM-4:30PM (EST). *Civil Actions Under $25,000, Eviction, Small Claims.*

Civil Records: Access: Mail, in person. Both court and visitors may perform in person searches. No search fee. Required to search: name. Civil cases indexed by plaintiff. Civil records on computer since 1999; prior on books.
General Information: Public access terminal is available. No sealed records released. SASE required. Turnaround time 3-5 days. Copy fee: No search fee. Certification fee: $5.00. Fee payee: Clerk Civil Court. Only cashiers checks and money orders accepted. Prepayment is required.

Surrogate Court 18 Richmond Terrace, Rm 201, Staten Island, NY 10301; 718-390-5400. Hours: 9AM-5PM (EST). *Probate.*

Rockland County

Supreme & County Court 1 S Main St #100, New City, NY 10956; 845-638-5070; Fax: 845-638-5647. Hours: 7AM-6PM (EST). *Felony, Civil.*

www.rocklandcountyclerk.com

Note: Court may have a misdemeanor record if you provide the index number. Misdemeanor records are maintained by city, town and village courts.

Civil Records: Access: Mail, online, in person. Both court and visitors may perform in person searches. Search fee: $5.00 per name. Fee is per each 2 years searched. Required to search: name, years to search. Civil cases indexed by defendant, plaintiff. Civil records on computer from 1982. Online access is the county clerk's court records index is available free at www.rocklandcountyclerk.com/court_records.html. Includes civil judgments, real estate records, tax warrants. Call Paul Pipearto at 845-638-5221 for more information.
Criminal Records: Access: Mail, online, in person. Both court and visitors may perform in person searches. Search fee: $5.00 per name. Fee is per each 2 years searched. Required to search: name, years to search. Criminal records on computer from 1982. Online access is the county clerk's court records index is available free at www.rocklandcountyclerk.com/court_records.html. Includes criminal index back to 1982.
General Information: Public access terminal is available. No retention records released. SASE

required. Turnaround time 10 days. Fax notes: Fee to fax results is $1.00 per page. Copy fee: $1.00 per page. Certification fee: $4.00. Fee payee: County Clerk. Personal checks accepted. Prepayment is required.

Surrogate Court 18 New Hempstead Rd, New City, NY 10956; 845-638-5330; Fax: 845-638-5632. Hours: 9AM-5PM (EST). *Probate.*

Town/Village Courts *Misdemeanor, Civil Actions Under $3,000, Small Claims:* Orangetown Town, 845-359-5100; New Hempstead Village, 845-354-8101; Chestnut Ridge Village, 845-425-3108; Clarkstown Town, 845-639-2165; Ramapo Town, 845-357-5100; Spring Valley Village, 845-352-1100; Piermont Village, 845-359-0345; Sloatsburg Village, 845-753-2727; South Nyack Village, 845-358-5078; New Square Village Court; Grand View-on-Hudson Village, 845-358-2919; Suffern Village, 845-357-6424; Wesley Hills Village, 845-354-0404; Haverstraw Town, 845-354-7800; Upper Nyack Village, 845-358-0084; Stony Point, 845-786-2506; Haverstraw Village, 914-490-0303; Hillburn Village, 845-357-2036; Nyack Village, 845-358-4464; West Haverstraw Village.

Saratoga County

Supreme & County Court 40 McMaster St, Ballston Spa, NY 12020; 518-885-2213 X4420; Fax: 518-884-4726. Hours: 9AM-5PM (EST). *Felony, Civil.*

Note: Misdemeanor records are maintained by city, town and village courts.

Civil Records: Access: Mail, in person. Both court and visitors may perform in person searches. Search fee: $5.00 per name. Fee is per 2 years searched. Required to search: name, years to search; also helpful: address. Civil cases indexed by defendant, plaintiff. Civil records on computer from 03/88, prior in books.
Criminal Records: Access: Mail, in person. Both court and visitors may perform in person searches. Search fee: $16.00 per name. Required to search: name, years to search, DOB; also helpful: address. Criminal records not computerized here, on books.
General Information: Public access terminal is available. No youthful offender or divorce records released. SASE required. Turnaround time 3-4 days. Copy fee: $1.00 per page. Certification fee: $4.00 for 1st-4pages, $1.00 each additional page. Fee payee: County Clerk. Personal checks accepted. Prepayment is required.

Mechanicville City Court 36 N Main St, Mechanicville, NY 12118; 518-664-9876; Fax: 518-664-8606. Hours: 8AM-4PM (EST). *Misdemeanor, Civil Actions Under $15,000, Eviction, Small Claims.*

Civil Records: Access: Mail, in person. Both court and visitors may perform in person searches. Search fee: $16.00 per name. Required to search: name, years to search. Civil cases indexed by defendant. Civil records on computer since 1/94; records go back to 1900.
Criminal Records: Access: Mail, in person. Only the court performs in person searches; visitors may not. Search fee: Manual search: $5.00 per 2 year period. Computer search: $16.00 per name. Required to search: name, years to search, DOB. Criminal records on computer from 9/93; records go back to 1900.
General Information: No sealed, expunged, adoption, sex offense, juvenile or mental health records released. SASE required. Turnaround time 1 day. Copy fee: $.50 per page; $1.00 minimum. Certification fee: $5.00. Fee payee: City Court. Personal checks accepted. Prepayment is required.

Saratoga Springs City Court City Hall, 474 Broadway, Saratoga Springs, NY 12866; 518-581-1797. Hours: 9AM-4:30PM (EST). *Misdemeanor, Civil Actions Under $15,000, Eviction, Small Claims.*

Civil Records: Access: Mail, in person. Only the court performs in person searches; visitors may not. Search

fee: $5.00 per name per 2 years or $16.00 computer search back to 10/94. Required to search: name, years to search. Civil cases indexed by defendant. Civil records on computer back to 10/94; prior records on index cards.
Criminal Records: Access: Mail, in person. Only the court performs in person searches; visitors may not. Search fee: $16.00 per name. For search prior to 1994 fee is $5.00 per 2 years searched. Required to search: name, years to search, DOB, notarized release. Criminal records on computer back to 08/93.
General Information: Sealed files not released. SASE required. Turnaround time 5-10 days. Certification fee: $5.00. Fee payee: City Court. Only cashiers checks and money orders accepted. Prepayment is required.

Surrogate Court 30 McMaster St, Bldg 3, Ballston Spa, NY 12020; 518-884-4722. Hours: 9AM-5PM (EST). *Probate.*

Town/Village Courts *Misdemeanor, Civil Actions Under $3,000, Small Claims:* Day Town, 518-696-3789; Ballston Town, 518-885-8559; Galway Village, 518-882-6070; Milton Town, 518-885-9267; Clifton Park Town, 518-371-6668; Ballston Spa Village Court; Edinburg Town, 518-863-2034; Galway Town, 518-882-6070; Moreau Town, 518-793-3188; Waterford Town, 518-237-6788; Providence Town; Hadley Town, 518-696-4379; Stillwater Village, 518-664-5392; Saratoga Town, 518-695-3644; Stillwater Town; Greenfield Town, 518-893-7432; Wilton Town, 518-587-1980; Northumberland Town, 518-792-9179; Halfmoon Town, 518-371-1592; Malta Town, 518-899-2687; Corinth Town, 518-654-6991; Charlton Town, 518-384-0152

Schenectady County

Supreme & County Court 612 State St, Schenectady, NY 12305; 518-388-4322; Fax: 518-388-4520. Hours: 9AM-5PM (EST). *Felony, Civil.*

Civil Records: Access: Mail, in person. Both court and visitors may perform in person searches. Search fee: $5.00 per name. Fee is per 2 years searched. Required to search: name, years to search. Civil cases indexed by plaintiff. Civil records on computer from 1989, prior on index cards.
Criminal Records: Access: Mail, in person. Both court and visitors may perform in person searches. Search fee: Automated computer search $16.00 per name. Required to search: name, years to search, DOB. Criminal records on computer from 1989, prior in index books. Notarized, signed release required to access sealed records.
General Information: No sealed, youthful offenders, infant compromise or divorce records released. SASE required. Turnaround time 4 days. Copy fee: $.50 per page. Certification fee: $5.00. Fee payee: County Clerk. Personal checks accepted. Prepayment is required.

Schenectady City Court Jay St, City Hall #215, Schenectady, NY 12305; Civil phone: 518-382-5077; Criminal phone: 518-382-5239; Fax: 518-382-5080/5241. Hours: 8AM-4PM (EST). *Misdemeanor, Civil Actions Under $15,000, Eviction, Small Claims.*

Civil Records: Access: Mail, in person. Only the court performs in person searches; visitors may not. Search fee: $16.00 per name. Required to search: name, years to search. Civil cases indexed by defendant. Civil records on computer from 1981, prior in books.
Criminal Records: Access: Fax, mail, in person. Only the court performs in person searches; visitors may not. Search fee: $16.00 per name. Required to search: name, years to search, DOB, signed release. Criminal records on computer from 1981, prior in books.
General Information: No sealed or youthful offender records released. SASE required. Turnaround time 2 weeks. Copy fee: $.50 per page. Certification fee: $5.00.

Fee payee: City Court. Only cashiers checks and money orders accepted. Prepayment is required.

Surrogate Court 612 State St, Judicial Building, Schenectady, NY 12305; 518-388-4293; Fax: 518-377-6378. Hours: 9AM-5PM (EST). *Probate.*

Town/Village Courts *Misdemeanor, Civil Actions Under $3,000, Small Claims:* Scotia Village, 518-374-2099; Rotterdam Town, 518-356-2038; Princetown Town, 518-864-5256; Glenville Town, 518-382-3851; Niskayuna Town, 518-386-4560; Duanesburg Town, 518-895-8922.

Schoharie County

Supreme & County Court PO Box 549, Schoharie, NY 12157; 518-295-8316; Fax: 518-295-8338. Hours: 8:30AM-5PM (EST). *Felony, Civil, Misdemeanor, Eviction, Small Claims.*

Civil Records: Access: Fax, mail, in person. Both court and visitors may perform in person searches. Search fee: $5.00 per name. Fee is per 2 years searched. Required to search: name, years to search. Civil cases indexed by defendant, plaintiff. Civil records on computer from 1994, prior in books.
Criminal Records: Access: Fax, mail, in person. Both court and visitors may perform in person searches. Search fee: $5.00 per name. Fee is per 2 years searched. Required to search: name, years to search, DOB or SSN. Criminal records in books back to 1930; on computer back to 1994.
General Information: Public access terminal is available. No sealed criminal or divorce records released. SASE required. Turnaround time same day. Fax notes: Fee to fax results is $1.00 per page unless provided toll-free #. Copy fee: $.50 per page. Certification fee: $4.00. Fee payee: County Clerk. Personal checks accepted. Prepayment is required.

Surrogate Court Courthouse, 300 Main St, Schoharie, NY 12157; 518-295-8387. Hours: 9AM-5PM (EST). *Probate.*

Town/Village Courts *Misdemeanor, Civil Actions Under $3,000, Small Claims:* Blenheim Town, 518-827-6157; Richmondville Town, 518-294-2851; Schoharie Town; Schoharie Village Court; Sharon Town, 518-284-3419; Cobleskill Town, 518-234-7886; Summit Town; Conesville Town, 607-588-7211; Wright Town, 518-872-1931; Cobleskill Village, 518-234-9886; Seward Town; Gilboa Town, 607-588-7526; Esperance Town, 518-875-6109; Jefferson Town, 607-652-2109; Carlisle Town, 518-868-4167; Middleburgh Town, 518-827-5100; Middleburgh Village, 518-827-5143; Broome Town, 518-827-5074; Fulton Town, 518-827-6300.

Schuyler County

Supreme & County Court Courthouse, 105 Ninth St, Unit #35, Watkins Glen, NY 14891; Civil phone: 607-535-8133; Criminal phone: 607-535-7760; Fax: 607-535-4198. Hours: 9AM-5PM (EST). *Felony, Civil.*

Note: Misdemeanor, Eviction, Small Claims cases are heard at Town and Village Courts.

Civil Records: Access: Mail, in person. Both court and visitors may perform in person searches. Search fee: $5.00 per name. Required to search: name, years to search. Civil cases indexed by defendant. Civil records are indexed in books; on computer back to 1987.
Criminal Records: Access: Mail, in person. Only the court performs in person searches; visitors may not. Search fee: $5.00 per name. Required to search: name, years to search, DOB. Criminal records are indexed in books; on computer back to 1987.
General Information: No sealed or youthful offender records released. SASE required. Turnaround time 2-3 days. Copy fee: $.50 per page. Certification fee: $4.00.

Fee payee: County Clerk. Personal checks accepted. Prepayment is required.

Surrogate Court County Courthouse, 105 Ninth St, Watkins Glen, NY 14891; 607-535-7144; Fax: 607-535-4918. Hours: 9AM-5PM (EST). *Probate.*

Town/Village Courts *Misdemeanor, Civil Actions Under $3,000, Small Claims:* Montour Falls Village, 607-535-7362; Dix Town, 607-535-7973; Tyrone Town; Watkins Glen Village, 607-535-9717; Hector Town, 607-546-5286; Odessa Village Court; Montour Town, 607-535-7362; Orange Town; Reading Town; Catharine Town; Cayuta Town.

Seneca County

Supreme & County Court 1 DiPronio Dr, Waterloo, NY 13165-1396; 315-539-1771; Fax: 315-539-3789. Hours: 8:30AM-5PM (EST). *Felony, Civil.*

Note: Misdemeanor records are maintained by city, town and village courts.

Civil Records: Access: Fax, mail, in person. Both court and visitors may perform in person searches. Search fee: $10.00 per name. Required to search: name, years to search. Civil cases indexed by defendant. Civil records on computer since March 1, 1997; prior records in books.

Criminal Records: Access: Fax, mail, in person. Both court and visitors may perform in person searches. Search fee: $10.00 per name. Required to search: name, years to search, signed release. Criminal records on computer since March 1, 1997; prior records in books.

General Information: Public access terminal is available. No divorce records released. SASE required. Turnaround time 1 week. No copy fee. Certification fee: $4.00. Fee payee: Seneca County Clerk. Personal checks accepted. Prepayment is required.

Surrogate Court 48 W Williams St, Waterloo, NY 13165; 315-539-7531; Fax: 315-539-3267. Hours: 9AM-5PM (EST). *Probate.*

Town/Village Courts *Misdemeanor, Civil Actions Under $3,000, Small Claims:* Waterloo Town, 315-539-3213; Covert Town, 607-387-6802; Junius Town; Seneca Falls Village, 315-568-2343; Seneca Falls Town; Waterloo Village, 315-539-2512; Varick Town; Fayette Town; Ovid Town, 607-869-5560; Lodi Town; Tyre Town; Romulus Town, 607-869-9650.

St. Lawrence County

Supreme & County Court 48 Court St, Canton, NY 13617-1169; 315-379-2237; Fax: 315-379-2302. Hours: 8:30AM-4:30PM (Thurs. til 7PM) (EST). *Felony, Civil.*

Note: Misdemeanor records are maintained by city, town and village courts.

Civil Records: Access: Fax, mail, in person. Both court and visitors may perform in person searches. Search fee: $5.00 per name. Required to search: name, years to search. Civil cases indexed by defendant, plaintiff. Civil records on computer since 1990, prior in books.

Criminal Records: Access: Fax, mail, in person. Both court and visitors may perform in person searches. Search fee: $5.00 per name. Required to search: name, years to search, DOB. Criminal records on computer since 1985, prior in books.

General Information: Public access terminal is available. No sealed or divorce records released. SASE required. Turnaround time 2-3 days. Fax notes: $4.00 per document. No fee for 800 numbers. Copy fee: $.50 per page. Certification fee: $4.00. Fee payee: County Clerk. Personal checks accepted.

Ogdensburg City Court 330 Ford St, Ogdensburg, NY 13669; 315-393-3941; Fax: 315-393-

6839. Hours: 8AM-4PM (EST). *Misdemeanor, Civil Actions Under $15,000, Eviction, Small Claims.*

Civil Records: Access: Mail, in person. Only the court performs in person searches; visitors may not. No search fee. Required to search: name, years to search. Civil cases indexed by defendant. Civil records on computer since 1995; prior records in books.

Criminal Records: Access: Mail, in person. Only the court performs in person searches; visitors may not. Search fee: $16.00 for computer search, manual search is $5.00 for every 2 years. Required to search: name, years to search, DOB. Criminal records on computer from 1994.

General Information: No youthful offender records released. SASE required. Turnaround time 1 week. Certification fee: $5.00. Fee payee: City Court. Business checks accepted. Prepayment is required.

Surrogate Court 48 Court St, Surrogate Bldg, Canton, NY 13617; 315-379-2217/9427. Hours: 9AM-5PM Sept-June; 8AM-4PM July-Aug (EST). *Probate.*

Town/Village Courts *Misdemeanor, Civil Actions Under $3,000, Small Claims:* Canton Village, 315-379-9844; Waddington Town, 315-388-5629; Canton Town, 315-379-9844; Clare Town, 315-386-1970; Colton Town; Stockholm Town, 315-389-5171; Hopkinton Town, 315-328-4187; Hermon Town, 315-397-3606; Lawrence Town, 315-389-4487; DePeyster Town, 315-344-7259; Fowler Town, 315-287-0045; Parishville Town, 315-265-2131; Piercefield Town, 518-359-9660; Brasher Town, 315-769-5374; Pierrepont Town, 315-386-8311; Pitcairn Town, 315-543-2111; Norfolk Town, 315-384-4721; Morristown Town, 315-375-6510; Potsdam Town, 315-265-4318; Potsdam Village, 315-265-5890; Edwards Town, 315-562-8113; Clifton Town, 315-848-2915; Massena Village, 315-769-5431; Hammond Town, 315-324-5321; DeKalb Town; Rossie Town; Massena Town, 315-769-5431; Madrid Town, 315-322-5760; Macomb Town; Russell Town, 315-347-2162; Lisbon Town, 315-393-0489; Louisville Town, 315-764-1424; Fine Town; Gouverneur Town, 315-287-4623; Gouverneur Village, 315-287-0850; Oswegatchie Town, 315-344-2400.

Steuben County

Supreme & County Court 3 E Pulteney Square - County Clerk, Bath, NY 14810; 607-776-9631 x3210; Fax: 607-776-7158. Hours: 9AM-5PM (EST). *Felony, Civil.*

Note: Direct record requests to County Clerk.

Civil Records: Access: Fax, mail, in person. Both court and visitors may perform in person searches. Search fee: $10.00 per name. Required to search: name, years to search. Civil cases indexed by defendant. Civil records on computer from 1984, in book from 1931, prior archived.

Criminal Records: Access: Fax, mail, in person. Only the court performs in person searches; visitors may not. Search fee: $10.00 per name. Required to search: name, years to search, DOB, SSN, signed release. Criminal records on computer from 1984, in book from 1931, prior archived.

General Information: No sealed, expunged, adoption, sex offense, juvenile or mental health records released. SASE required. Turnaround time 1 day. Copy fee: $.50 per page. Certification fee: $4.00. Fee payee: County Clerk. Personal checks accepted. Prepayment is required.

Corning City Court 12 Civic Center Plaza, Corning, NY 14830-2884; 607-936-4111; Fax: 607-936-0519. Hours: 8AM-4PM (EST). *Misdemeanor, Civil Actions Under $15,000, Eviction, Small Claims.*

Civil Records: Access: Mail, in person. Only the court performs in person searches; visitors may not. Search

fee: $16.00 for 7 year search. Required to search: name, years to search. Civil cases indexed by defendant. Civil records on computer from 1986, prior in books. Request must be in writing.

Criminal Records: Access: Mail, in person. Only the court performs in person searches; visitors may not. Search fee: $16.00 per 7 year search. Required to search: name, years to search, DOB; also helpful: date of offense. Criminal records on computer from 1986, prior in books. Request must be in writing.

General Information: No sealed or youthful offender records released. SASE required. Turnaround time 1 week. Copy fee: $5.00 per document. Certification fee: $5.00. Fee payee: Corning City Court. Prepayment is required.

Hornell City Court PO Box 627 (82 Main St.), Hornell, NY 14843-0627; 607-324-7531; Fax: 607-324-6325. Hours: 8AM-3:30PM (EST). *Misdemeanor, Civil Actions Under $15,000, Eviction, Small Claims.*

Civil Records: Access: Fax, mail, in person. Only the court performs in person searches; visitors may not. Search fee: $16.00 for 6-year search. Required to search: name, years to search. Civil cases indexed by defendant, plaintiff. Civil records on computer from 1985, prior in books, folders and index cards go back 25 years.

Criminal Records: Access: Fax, mail, in person. Only the court performs in person searches; visitors may not. Search fee: $16.00 for 6-year search. Required to search: name, years to search, DOB; also helpful: SSN. Criminal records on computer from 1985, records go back 25 years.

General Information: No sealed or sexual offense records released. SASE required. Turnaround time 2 days. Copy fee: $.50 per page. Certification fee: $5.00. Fee payee: Hornell City Court. Only cashiers checks and money orders accepted. Prepayment is required.

Surrogate Court 3 E Pulteney Square, Bath, NY 14810-1598; 607-776-7126; Fax: 607-776-4987. Hours: 9AM-5PM (EST). *Probate.*

Town/Village Courts *Misdemeanor, Civil Actions Under $3,000, Small Claims:* Addison Town, 607-359-3615; Caton Town, 607-524-6303; Arkport Village, 607-295-8207; Canisteo Village, 607-698-4378; Canisteo Town; Cameron Town; Avoca Town, 607-566-2093; Avoca Village, 607-566-2093; Bath Town, 607-776-3192; Bath Village, 607-776-4666; Bradford Town, 607-583-4270; Campbell Town, 607-527-8244; Prattsburgh Town, 607-522-3761; Tuscarora Town, 607-359-2360; Troupsburg Town, 607-525-6403; Erwin Town, 607-936-3122; Thurston Town, 607-776-9448; Fremont Town, 607-324-7786; Rathbone Town; Urbana Town, 607-569-3369; Pulteney Town, 607-868-3913; Greenwood Town, 607-225-4558; Hartsville Town, 607-698-2672; Hornby Town, 607-962-0683; Hornellsville Town, 607-295-7768; Howard Town, 607-566-2554; Jasper Town, 607-792-3338; Cohocton Town, 607-384-5252; Lindley Town, 607-523-8816; Hammondsport Village Court; Wayland Village, 585-728-5156; Dansville Town, 607-295-7223; West Union Town; Cohocton Village Court; Wayland Town, 585-728-5660; Corning Town, 607-936-9062; Wayne Town, 607-292-3450; Woodhull Town, 607-458-5178; Wheeler Town.

Suffolk County

Supreme & County Court 310 Centre Dr, Attn: Court Actions, Riverhead, NY 11901; 631-852-3793. Hours: 9AM-5PM (EST). *Felony, Civil.*

www.co.suffolk.ny.us/clerk

Civil Records: Access: Mail, in person. Both court and visitors may perform in person searches. Search fee: $5.00 per name. Fee is per 2 years searched. Required to search: name, years to search. Civil cases indexed by defendant, plaintiff. Civil records on computer back to 04/84; prior in books.

Criminal Records: Access: Mail, in person. Both court and visitors may perform in person searches. Search fee: $5.00 per name. Fee is per 2 years searched prior to 1985; $16.00 for 1985 to present. Required to search: name, years to search, DOB. Criminal records on computer back to 1984.

General Information: Public access terminal is available. No sealed or divorce records released. SASE required. Turnaround time 7-10 days. Fax notes: Will not fax results. Copy fee: $1.00 per page. Certification fee: $.50 per page, $4.00 minimum. Fee payee: County Clerk. Personal checks accepted. Prepayment is required.

Suffolk District Court - Criminal 400 Carleton Ave, Central Islip, NY 11722; 631-853-7500 (All District Courts). Hours: 9AM-5PM (EST). *Misdemeanor.*

Civil Records: Access: Mail, in person. Both court and visitors may perform in person searches. Search fee: $16.00 per name. Required to search: name, years to search. Civil cases indexed by plaintiff. Civil records on computer back to 1989, prior in books back to 1969.

Criminal Records: Access: Mail, in person. Only the court may perform in person searches, visitors may not. Search fee: $16.00 per name. Required to search: name, years to search, DOB (signed release required if records are sealed). Criminal records on computer back to 1983, prior in books back to 1964.

General Information: Public access terminal is available. No sealed or youthful offender records released. SASE required. Turnaround time 3-5 days. Copy fee: $1.00 per page. Certification fee: $5.00. Fee payee: District Court Clerk. Only cashiers checks and money orders accepted. Prepayment is required.

2nd District Court 375 Cormac Rd, Deer Park, NY 11702; 631-854-1950. Hours: 9AM-Noon, 1-4:30PM (EST). *Misdemeanor, Civil Actions Under $15,000, Eviction, Small Claims.*

Civil Records: Access: Mail, in person. Only the court performs in person searches; visitors may not. Search fee: $16.00 per name. Required to search: name, years to search. Civil cases indexed by plaintiff. Civil records on computer from 1989, prior in books, on cards.

Criminal Records: Access: Mail, in person. Only the court performs in person searches; visitors may not. Search fee: $16.00 per name. Required to search: name, years to search, DOB, SSN, signed release. Criminal records on computer from 1989, prior in books, on cards.

General Information: No sealed or youthful offender records released. SASE required. Turnaround time 1 week. Copy fee: $.50 per page. Certification fee: $10.00 per document. Fee payee: County Clerk. Only cashiers checks and money orders accepted. Prepayment is required.

3rd District Court 1850 New York Ave, Huntington Station, NY 11746; 631-854-4545. Hours: 9AM-4:30PM (EST). *Misdemeanor, Civil Actions Under $15,000, Eviction, Small Claims.*

Civil Records: Access: Mail, in person. Only the court performs in person searches; visitors may not. Search fee: $16.00 per name. Required to search: name, years

to search. Civil cases indexed by defendant. Civil records on computer from 1988, prior in books, on microfilm.

Criminal Records: Access: Mail, in person. Only the court performs in person searches; visitors may not. Search fee: $16.00 per name. Required to search: name, years to search, DOB, SSN, signed release. Criminal records on computer from 1988, prior in books, on microfilm.

General Information: No sealed records released. SASE required. Turnaround time 2 weeks. Certification fee: Included in search fee. Fee payee: Clerk of the Court. Business checks accepted. Attorney checks accepted. Prepayment is required.

4th District Court North County Complex Bldg C158, Hauppauge, NY 11787; Civil phone: 631-853-5400; Criminal phone: 631-853-5357. Hours: 9AM-5PM (EST). *Misdemeanor, Civil Actions Under $15,000, Eviction, Small Claims.*

Civil Records: Access: Mail, in person. Only the court performs in person searches; visitors may not. Search fee: $16.00 per name. Required to search: name, years to search. Civil cases indexed by defendant, plaintiff. Civil records on computer from 1987, prior in books.

Criminal Records: Access: Mail, in person. Only the court performs in person searches; visitors may not. Search fee: $16.00 per name. Required to search: name, years to search, DOB. Criminal records on computer from 1987, prior in books. Criminal searches limited to township searches. All others must be done at 1st District Court, 631-853-4530; 400 Carleton Ave, Central Islip, NY 11722.

General Information: No sealed records released. SASE required. Turnaround time 1-2 weeks. Copy fee: $.50 per page. Certification fee: $5.00. Fee payee: Clerk of Court. Only cashiers checks and money orders accepted. Prepayment is required.

6th District Court 150 W Main St, Patchogue, NY 11772; 631-854-1440. Hours: 9AM-5PM (EST). *Misdemeanor, Civil Actions Under $15,000, Eviction, Small Claims.*

Note: Criminal searches must be done at the Central Islip District Court, 631-853-7500.

Civil Records: Access: Mail, in person. Only the court performs in person searches; visitors may not. Search fee: $16.00 per name. Required to search: name, years to search. Civil records on computer from 1989, prior on microfilm.

Criminal Records: Access: Mail, in person. Only the court performs in person searches; visitors may not. Search fee: $16.00 per name. Required to search: name, years to search. Criminal records on computer from 1989, prior on microfilm. Criminal searches must be done at the Central Islip District Court, 631-853-7500.

General Information: No sealed or youthful offender records released. SASE required. Copy fee: $1.00 for first page, $.50 each add'l. Certification fee: $5.00. Fee payee: Clerk of Court. Only cashiers checks and money orders accepted. Prepayment is required.

Suffolk District Courts 1 & 5 - Civil 3105-1 Veterans Memorial Hwy, Ronkonkoma, NY 11779-7614; 631-854-9676 (1st); 9673 (5th). Hours: 9AM-5PM (EST). *Civil Actions Under $15,000, Eviction, Small Claims.*

Civil Records: Access: Mail, in person. Only the court performs in person searches; visitors may not. Search fee: $16.00 per name. Required to search: name, years to search. Civil cases indexed by defendant. Civil records on computer back to 1989, prior in books back to 1969.

General Information: No sealed or youthful offender records released. SASE required. Turnaround time 2 weeks. Copy fee: $1.00 for first page, $.50 each add'l. Certification fee: $5.00. Fee payee: Clerk of the Court.

Only cashiers checks and money orders accepted. Prepayment is required.

Surrogate Court 320 Centre Dr, Riverhead, NY 11901; 631-852-1745; Fax: 631-852-1777. Hours: 9AM-5PM (EST). *Probate.*

Town/Village Courts *Misdemeanor, Civil Actions Under $3,000, Small Claims:* Hewlett Bay Park Village Court; Poquott Village Court; Port Jefferson Village, 631-473-8287; East Hampton Town, 631-324-4134; Belle Terre Village, 631-928-5785; Westhampton Beach Village Court; Quogue Village, 631-653-4498; Bellport Village, 516-475-2753; Patchogue Village, 631-475-2753; Old Field Village, 631-941-9412; Islandia Village, 631-348-0470; Ocean Beach Village, 631-583-5940; Northport Village, 631-261-7500; Lindenhurst Village, 631-957-7509; Brightwaters Village, 631-665-1281; Lake Grove Village, 631-585-2008; Lloyd Harbor Village Court; Huntington Bay Village Court; Shoreham Village Justice; Asharoken Village, 631-261-8677; Amityville Village, 631-691-3303; Village of the Branch Court; Riverhead Town, 631-727-3200; Greenport Village, 631-477-0853; Harbor Village, 631-584-5550; Saltaire Village, 631-583-5566; Babylon Village Court; Shelter Island Town, 631-749-8989; Southold Town, 631-765-1852; Nissequogue Village, 631-862-8576; Southampton Town, 631-283-6000.

Sullivan County

Supreme & County Court County Courthouse, 414 Broadway, Monticello, NY 12701; 845-794-4066. Hours: 9AM-5PM (EST). *Felony, Civil, Misdemeanor.*

Note: Civil records maintained at County Clerk's office, Sullivan Gov't Center, 100 North St, Monticello, NY 12701. Small claims and evictions are handled by town & village justice courts.

Civil Records: Access: Phone, mail, in person. Both court and visitors may perform in person searches. Search fee: $16.00 per name for 10 years with additional $5.00 for every 2 years prior. Required to search: name, years to search. Civil cases indexed by plaintiff. Civil records on computer from 1990, prior in books from 1800s.

Criminal Records: Access: Mail, in person. Only the court performs in person searches; visitors may not. Search fee: $16.00 per name. Required to search: name, years to search, DOB. Criminal records go back to 1967; on computer back to 1988.

General Information: Public access terminal is available. (Terminal available for civil records only.) No sealed, expunged, adoption, sex offense, juvenile or mental health records released. SASE not required. Turnaround time 1-2 weeks. Copy fee: $.50 per page. Certification fee: $4.00. Fee payee: County Clerk for civil; to Court Clerk for criminal. Personal checks accepted. Prepayment is required.

Surrogate Court County Government Center, 100 North St, Monticello, NY 12701; 845-794-3000 X3450/3451; Fax: 845-794-0310. Hours: 9AM-5PM (EST). *Probate.*

Town/Village Courts *Misdemeanor, Civil Actions Under $3,000, Small Claims:* Callicoon Town, 845-482-5390; Lumberland Town, 845-858-8548; Thompson Town, 845-794-7130; Fallsburg Town, 845-434-4574; Mamakating Town, 845-888-4712; Monticello Village Court; Neversink Town, 845-985-7685; Jeffersonville Village, 845-482-4275; Forestburgh Town, 845-794-0679; Fremont Town; Woodridge Village, 845-434-7444; Bloomingburg Village Court; Bethel Town, 845-583-7420; Highland Town, 845-557-8132; Tusten Town, 845-252-3310; Cochecton Town; Rockland Town, 845-439-3464; Delaware Town, 845-887-5250; Liberty Village, 845-292-0290;

Liberty Town, 845-292-6980; Wurtsboro Village, 845-888-4712.

Tioga County

Supreme & County Court PO Box 307, Owego, NY 13827; 607-687-0544; Fax: 607-687-3240. Hours: 9AM-5PM (EST). *Felony, Civil, Misdemeanor, Eviction, Small Claims.*

Civil Records: Access: In person only. Visitors must perform in person searches for themselves. No search fee. Required to search: name, years to search. Civil cases indexed by defendant. Civil records in books. Visitor can search in County Clerk's Office.

Criminal Records: Access: Mail, in person. Both court and visitors may perform in person searches. Search fee: $5.00 per name. No fee for in person searches. Required to search: name, years to search, DOB. Criminal records in books since 1984.

General Information: No sealed, expunged, adoption, sex offense, juvenile or mental health records released. SASE required. Turnaround time varies. Copy fee: $.50 per page. Certification fee: $4.00. Fee payee: County Clerk. Personal checks accepted.

Surrogate Court County Court Annex Bldg, 20 Court St, Owego, NY 13827; 607-687-1303. Hours: 9AM-5PM (EST). *Probate.*

Town/Village Courts *Misdemeanor, Civil Actions Under $3,000, Small Claims:* Newark Valley Town, 607-642-8746; Waverly Village, 607-565-4771; Tioga Town, 607-687-9577; Nichols Town, 607-699-3981; Spencer Village, 607-589-4310; Spencer Town; Owego Village Court; Berkshire Town, 607-657-2705; Richford Town; Barton Town, 607-565-8609; Owego Town, 607-687-2822; Candor Town, 607-659-3175; Candor Village, 607-659-3175.

Tompkins County

Supreme & County Court 320 N Tioga St, Ithaca, NY 14850; 607-274-5431; Fax: 607-274-5445. Hours: 9AM-5PM (EST). *Felony, Civil.*

Civil Records: Access: Fax, mail, in person. Both court and visitors may perform in person searches. Search fee: $5.00 per name. Fee is per 2 years searched. Required to search: name, years to search. Civil cases indexed by defendant, plaintiff. Civil records in books. Fax requests must be pre-paid.

Criminal Records: Access: Fax, mail, in person. Only the court performs in person searches; visitors may not. Search fee: $5.00 per name. Fee is per 2 years searched. Required to search: name, years to search, signed release; also helpful: DOB, SSN. Criminal records in books. Fax requests must be pre-paid.

General Information: No sealed, expunged, adoption, sex offense, juvenile or mental health records released. SASE required. Turnaround time 1-2 days. Copy fee: $1.00 for first page, $.50 each add'l. Certification fee: $4.00. Fee payee: County Clerk. Personal checks accepted. Prepayment is required.

Ithaca City Court 118 E Clinton St, Ithaca, NY 14850; 607-273-2263. Hours: 8AM-4PM (EST). *Misdemeanor, Civil Actions Under $15,000, Eviction, Small Claims.*

www.courts.state.ny.us/ithaca/city

Civil Records: Access: Mail, in person. Only the court performs in person searches; visitors may not. Search fee: $16.00 per name. For records prior to 1996, fee is $5.00 per each 2 year period searched. Required to search: name, years to search. Civil cases indexed by defendant. Civil records on computer since 1996; prior records in books.

Criminal Records: Access: Mail, in person. Only the court performs in person searches; visitors may not. Search fee: $16.00 per name. For records prior to 1990, fee is $5.00 per each 2 year period searched. Required

to search: name, years to search, DOB. Criminal records on computer from 1990, prior in books.

General Information: No sealed, youthful offender records released. SASE required. Turnaround time 1 week. Copy fee: $.50 per page. $1.00 minimum. Certification fee: $5.00. Fee payee: City Court. Only cashiers checks and money orders accepted. Prepayment is required.

Surrogate Court 320 N Tioga St, Ithaca, NY 14850; 607-277-0622; Fax: 607-256-2572. Hours: 9AM-5PM (EST). *Probate.*

Town/Village Courts *Misdemeanor, Civil Actions Under $3,000, Small Claims:* Groton Village, 607-898-3711; Danby Town, 607-277-4788; Dryden Town, 607-844-8621; Ulysses Town, 607-387-5411; Enfield Town, 607-272-6490; Freeville Village, 607-844-8470; Groton Town, 607-898-5273; Cayuga Heights Village, 607-257-3944; Caroline Town, 607-539-7796; Ithaca Town, 607-273-1721; Newfield Town, 607-564-9571; Lansing Town, 607-533-4776.

Ulster County

Supreme & County Court PO Box 1800, Kingston, NY 12401; 845-340-3288; Fax: 845-340-3299. Hours: 9AM-5PM (EST). *Felony, Civil.*

Civil Records: Access: Phone, mail, online, in person. Both court and visitors may perform in person searches. Search fee: $5.00 per name. Fee is per name & per 2 years searched. Required to search: name, years to search. Civil cases indexed by defendant, plaintiff. Civil records on computer from 1987, in books from 1920s, prior archived. Access to the remote online system requires minimum $33.33 per month fee (over 2500 transactions is $44.50), 12 months required to signup. Search by name or case number. Call Valerie Harris 845-334-5367 for more information.

Criminal Records: Access: Phone, mail, online, in person. Both court and visitors may perform in person searches. Search fee: $5.00 per name. Fee is per 2 years searched. Required to search: name, years to search. Criminal records on computer from 1987, in books from 1920s, prior archived. Online access to criminal records is the same as civil.

General Information: Public access terminal is available. No sealed, expunged, adoption, sex offense, juvenile or mental health records released. SASE not required. Turnaround time 5 days. Copy fee: $.50 per page. Certification fee: $4.00. Fee payee: County Clerk. Personal checks accepted. Prepayment is required.

Kingston City Court 25 Kiersted Ave, Kingston, NY 12401; 845-338-2974. Hours: 8AM-4PM (EST). *Misdemeanor, Civil Actions Under $15,000, Eviction, Small Claims.*

Note: They are located at 25 Kiersted until Fall, 2002.

Civil Records: Access: Mail, in person. Only the court performs in person searches; visitors may not. Search fee: $5.00 per name. Fee is per case. Required to search: name, years to search. Civil cases indexed by plaintiff. Civil records on computer from 1995. Overall records go back to 1983. Request must be in writing.

Criminal Records: Access: Mail, in person. Only the court performs in person searches; visitors may not. Search fee: $5.00 per name. Fee is per 2 years searched. Required to search: name, years to search; also helpful: DOB. Criminal records on computer from 1995. Overall records go back to 1983. Request must be in writing.

General Information: No sealed or youthful offender records released. SASE required. Turnaround time 2 weeks. Copy fee: $1.00 per page. Certification fee: $5.00. Fee payee: City Court. Personal checks accepted. Prepayment is required.

Surrogate Court PO Box 1800, Kingston, NY 12402; 845-340-3348; Fax: 845-340-3352. Hours: 9AM-5PM (EST). *Probate.*

Town/Village Courts *Misdemeanor, Civil Actions Under $3,000, Small Claims:* Wawarsing Town, 845-647-4770; Olive Town, 845-657-2912; Saugerties Town, 845-246-9989; Lloyd Town, 845-691-7544; Esopus Town, 845-331-5776; Ellenville Village, 845-647-5107; Gardiner Town, 845-255-9675; Saugerties Village, 845-246-4979; Rosendale Town, 845-658-3686; New Paltz Town, 845-255-0043; Ulster Town, 845-382-1737; Plattekill Town, 845-883-5805; Marlborough Town, 845-795-2256; Woodstock Town, 845-679-6345; Shawangunk Town, 845-895-2111; Rochester Town, 845-626-2522; Marbletown Town, 845-687-4324; Hurley Town; Shandaken Town, 845-688-5005; Hardenburgh Town; Kingston Town, 845-336-8853; Denning Town, 845-985-2411.

Warren County

Supreme & County Court - Civil Rt US 9, Lake George, NY 12845; 518-761-6426; Fax: 518-761-6253. Hours: 9AM-5PM (EST). *Civil.*

Civil Records: Access: Phone, mail, in person. Both court and visitors may perform in person searches. Search fee: $5.00 for each two years. Computer search back to 1989 is $16.00. Required to search: name, years to search. Civil cases indexed by plaintiff. Civil records on computer from 1986, prior on index from 1813.

General Information: No adoption, juvenile or mental health records released. SASE required. Turnaround time same day. Copy fee: $.50 per page. Certification fee: $4.00. Fee payee: Warren County Clerk. Personal checks accepted. Prepayment is required.

Supreme & County Court - Criminal Rt US 9, Lake George, NY 12845; 518-761-6430/6431; Fax: 518-761-6253. Hours: 9AM-5PM (EST). *Felony.*

Note: Misdemeanor records are maintained by city, town and village courts.

Criminal Records: Access: Fax, mail, in person. Both court and visitors may perform in person searches. Search fee: $5.00 per 2 year search per name, information starts with 1929. Computer search: $16.00 per name, information starts with 1989. Required to search: name, years to search, DOB, SSN, signed release. Criminal records on computer from 1986, prior on index from 1929.

General Information: No adoption, juvenile or mental health records released. SASE required. Turnaround time same day. Copy fee: $.50 per page. Certification fee: $4.00. Fee payee: Warren County Clerk. Personal checks accepted. Prepayment is required.

Glens Falls City Court 42 Ridge St, Glens Falls, NY 12801; 518-798-4714; Fax: 518-798-0137. Hours: 8:30AM-4:30PM (EST). *Misdemeanor, Civil Actions Under $15,000, Eviction, Small Claims.*

Civil Records: Access: Mail, in person. Only the court performs in person searches; visitors may not. Search fee: $16.00 per name. Fee is for computer search. No fee for manual search. Required to search: name, years to search. Civil cases indexed by defendant, plaintiff. Civil records go back to 1975; on computer from 1987, prior on microfilm.

Criminal Records: Access: Mail, in person. Only the court performs in person searches; visitors may not. Search fee: $16.00 per name. Fee prior to 1988 is $5.00 for each consecutive 2 yr search. Required to search: name, years to search, DOB; also helpful: SSN. Criminal records go back to the late 1960's; on computer from 1990, prior on microfilm.

General Information: No sealed records released. SASE required. Turnaround time 1 week. Copy fee: $.50 per page. There is a $1.00 minimum. Certification fee: $5.00. Fee payee: City Court. Only cashiers checks and money orders accepted. Prepayment is required.

Surrogate Court 1340 State Route 9, County Municipal Ctr, Lake George, NY 12845; 518-761-6514; Fax: 518-761-6465. Hours: 9AM-5PM (EST). *Probate.*

Town/Village Courts *Misdemeanor, Civil Actions Under $3,000, Small Claims:* Warrensburg Town, 518-623-9776; Chester Town, 518-494-3133; Bolton Town, 518-644-2202; Horicon Town, 518-494-7958; Johnsburg Town, 518-251-3011; Lake Luzerne Town, 518-696-2711; Hague Town, 518-543-6161; Thurman Town, 518-623-9649; Lake George Town, 518-668-5420; Stony Creek Town, 518-696-3575; Queensbury Town, 518-745-5571.

Washington County

Supreme & County Court 383 Broadway, Fort Edward, NY 12828; Civil phone: 518-746-2170; Criminal phone: 518-746-2521. Hours: 8:30AM-4:30PM (EST). *Felony, Civil.*

Note: Misdemeanor records are maintained by city, town and village courts.

Civil Records: Access: In person only. Visitors must perform in person searches for themselves. No search fee. Required to search: name, years to search. Civil cases indexed by defendant. Civil records on books from 1800s.
Criminal Records: Access: Mail, in person. Both court and visitors may perform in person searches. Search fee: $16.00 per name. Required to search: name, years to search. Criminal records on books from 1800s.
General Information: No sealed or youthful offender records released. SASE required. Turnaround time 1-2 days. Copy fee: $1.00 per page. Certification fee: $4.00. Fee payee: County Clerk. Business checks accepted. Prepayment is required.

Surrogate Court 383 Broadway, Fort Edward, NY 12828; 518-746-2546; Fax: 518-746-2547. Hours: 8:30AM-4:30PM (EST). *Probate.*

Town/Village Courts *Misdemeanor, Civil Actions Under $3,000, Small Claims:* Hebron Town, 518-854-9300; Granville Town, 518-642-1500; Salem Village, 518-854-9215; Hartford Town, 518-632-5255; Salem Town, 518-854-9215; Greenwich Village Court; Hampton Town, 518-282-9830; Putnam Town, 518-547-8317; Cambridge Town, 518-677-8936; Granville Village, 518-642-9386; Easton Town, 518-692-2678; Whitehall Village, 518-499-0772; Whitehall Town, 518-499-0772; White Creek Town, 518-677-8545; Dresden Town, 518-499-2040; Fort Edward Village, 518-747-6563; Kingsbury Town, 518-747-9436; Jackson Town; Fort Ann Town, 518-639-8929; Argyle Town, 518-638-8681; Greenwich Town; Cambridge Village, 518-677-2414; Fort Edward Town, 518-747-4023; Hudson Falls Village, 518-747-3292.

Wayne County

Supreme & County Court 9 Pearl St, PO Box 608, Lyons, NY 14489-0608; 315-946-7470; Fax: 315-946-5978. Hours: 9AM-5PM (EST). *Felony, Civil, Eviction, Small Claims.*

Civil Records: Access: Phone, fax, mail, in person, email. Both court and visitors may perform in person searches. Search fee: $5.00 per name per every 2 years. Required to search: name, years to search. Civil cases indexed by defendant, plaintiff. Civil records on computer back to 1985, prior in books.
Criminal Records: Access: Fax, mail, in person. Both court and visitors may perform in person searches. Search fee: $5.00 per name uncertified back to 1979. $5.00 per name for every 2 years certified search. Required to search: name, years to search, DOB; also

helpful: gender. Criminal records on computer back to 1979.
General Information: Public access terminal is available. No matrimonial records released. SASE requested. Turnaround time 5-7 days. Fax notes: Fees to fax results: long distance within Wayne County $2.00 1st page, $1.00 each additional page; long distance outside Wayne County $3.00 1st page, $1.00 each additional page; no fax charge for 800 number. Copy fee: $.50 per page. $1.00 minimum. Certification fee: $4.00 plus $1.00 per page after first 4. Fee payee: County Clerk. Personal checks accepted. Prepayment is required.

Surrogate Court 54 Broad St #106, Hall of Justice, Lyons, NY 14489; 315-946-5430; Fax: 315-946-5433. Hours: 9AM-4PM (EST). *Probate.*

Town/Village Courts *Misdemeanor, Civil Actions Under $3,000, Small Claims:* Rose Town, 315-587-4418; Clyde Village, 315-923-9375; Wolcott Village, 315-594-9501; Wolcott Town, 315-594-8257; Williamson Town, 315-589-8250; Macedon Village Court; Walworth Town; Galen Town, 315-923-9375; Savannah Town, 315-365-2811; Sodus Point Village, 315-483-6217; Arcadia Town, 315-331-2744; Sodus Town, 315-483-6807; Huron Town, 315-594-8074; Butler Town, 315-594-2719; Macedon Town, 315-986-9108; Palmyra Town, 315-597-5431; Ontario Town, 315-524-6511; Palmyra Village, 315-597-6757; Lyons Village, 315-946-4565; Newark Village, 315-331-7666; Lyons Town, 315-946-4565.

Westchester County

Supreme & County Court 110 Dr Martin L King Blvd, White Plains, NY 10601; 914-995-3070; Fax: 914-995-3172. Hours: 8AM-5:45PM (EST). *Felony, Civil, Misdemeanor, Eviction, Small Claims.*

www.westchesterclerk.com

Civil Records: Access: Mail, in person. Both court and visitors may perform in person searches. Search fee: $5.00 per name. Fee is per 2 years searched. Required to search: name, years to search. Civil cases indexed by defendant, plaintiff. Civil records on computer from 1986, prior in books from 1847.
Criminal Records: Access: Mail, in person. Both court and visitors may perform in person searches. Search fee: $5.00 per name. Fee is per 2 years searched. Required to search: name, years to search. Criminal records on computer from 1986, prior in books from 1847.
General Information: Public access terminal is available. No sealed, expunged, adoption, sex offense, juvenile or mental health records released. SASE required. Turnaround time 1 week. Included in search fee Certification fee: $4.00. The fee covers up to 8 pages, each add'l page is $.50. Fee payee: County Clerk. Personal checks accepted. Prepayment is required.

Mt Vernon City Court Municipal Bldg, Roosevelt Square, Mt Vernon, NY 10550-2019; 914-665-2400; Fax: 914-699-1230. Hours: 8:30AM-4:30PM (EST). *Misdemeanor, Civil Actions Under $15,000, Eviction, Small Claims.*

www.courts.state.ny.us

Civil Records: Access: Mail, in person. Only the court performs in person searches; visitors may not. Search fee: $16.00 per name. Required to search: name, years to search; also helpful: address. Civil cases indexed by defendant, plaintiff. Civil records on computer since 1986, prior in books.
Criminal Records: Access: Mail, in person. Only the court performs in person searches; visitors may not. Search fee: $16.00 per name. Required to search: name, years to search; also helpful: DOB. Criminal records on computer since 1986, prior in books.

General Information: No sealed records released. SASE required. Turnaround time 2 weeks. Copy fee: $1.00 per page. Certification fee: $5.00. Fee payee: City Court. Only cashiers checks and money orders accepted. Prepayment is required.

Peekskill City Court 2 Nelson Ave, Peekskill, NY 10566; 914-737-3405. Hours: 9AM-5PM (EST). *Misdemeanor, Civil Actions Under $15,000, Eviction, Small Claims.*

Civil Records: Access: Mail, in person. Only the court performs in person searches; visitors may not. Search fee: $5.00 per name per 2-years searched. Required to search: name, years to search. Civil cases indexed by plaintiff. Civil records on computer back to 1994, prior in books. Request must be in writing.
Criminal Records: Access: Mail, in person. Only the court performs in person searches; visitors may not. Search fee: $16.00 per name. Required to search: name, years to search, DOB, signed release. Criminal records on computer back to 1990, prior on cards. Request must be in writing.
General Information: No sealed records released. SASE required. Turnaround time 3-5 days. Copy fee: $.50 per page, $1.00 minimum. Certification fee: $5.00. Fee payee: Peekskill City Court. Only cash, cashiers checks and money orders accepted. Prepayment is required.

Rye City Court 21 McCullough Place, Rye, NY 10580; 914-967-1599; Fax: 914-967-3308. Hours: 8:30AM-4:30PM (EST). *Misdemeanor, Civil Actions Under $15,000, Eviction, Small Claims.*

Civil Records: Access: Mail, in person. Only the court performs in person searches; visitors may not. Search fee: $5.00 per name. Required to search: name, years to search. Civil cases indexed by plaintiff. Civil records on computer from 1994, prior on index cards.
Criminal Records: Access: Mail, in person. Only the court performs in person searches; visitors may not. Search fee: $21.00 per name. Required to search: name, years to search, DOB. Criminal records on computer from 1986.
General Information: No sealed records released. SASE required. Turnaround time 1 month. Copy fee: $.50 per page. Certification fee: $5.00. Fee payee: City Court. Only cashiers checks and money orders accepted. Prepayment is required.

White Plains City Court 77 S Lexington Ave, White Plains, NY 10601; Civil phone: 914-422-6050; Criminal phone: 914-422-6075; Fax: 914-422-6058. Hours: 8:30AM-4:30PM (EST). *Misdemeanor, Civil Actions Under $15,000, Eviction, Small Claims.*

Civil Records: Access: Mail, fax, in person. Only the court performs in person searches; visitors may not. Search fee: $5.00 per name; $21.00 for known case files (this adds $16.00 for printout and certification). Required to search: name, years to search. Civil cases indexed by defendant. Civil records on docket cards and computer.
Criminal Records: Access: Mail, fax, in person. Only the court performs in person searches; visitors may not. Search fee: $5.00 per name; $21.00 for known case files (this adds $16.00 for printout and certification). Required to search: name, years to search, DOB. Criminal records on computer from 1988, prior on cards.
General Information: No sealed, youthful offender or sex case records released. SASE required. Turnaround time 5-10 days. Fax notes: Will fax results no fee, if prepaid. Copy fee: $.25 per page. Certification fee: Included in search fee for a found case file. Fee payee: City Court. Only cashiers checks and money orders accepted. Prepayment is required.

Yonkers City Court 100 S Broadway, Yonkers, NY 10701; 914-377-6352; Fax: 914-377-6395. Hours: 9AM-3:30PM (EST). *Misdemeanor, Civil Actions Under $15,000, Eviction, Small Claims.*

Civil Records: Access: Mail, in person. Only the court performs in person searches; visitors may not. Search fee: $16.00 per name. Required to search: name, years to search. Civil cases indexed by plaintiff. Civil records on computer since 01/95.

Criminal Records: Access: Mail, in person. Only the court performs in person searches; visitors may not. Search fee: $16.00 per name. Required to search: name, years to search, DOB, signed release; also helpful: date of offense. Criminal records on computer since 1993; prior records on index cards.

General Information: No sealed records released. SASE not required. Turnaround time 2-3 weeks. Copy fee: No search fee. Certification fee: $5.00 per document. Fee payee: City Court. Only cashiers checks and money orders accepted. Prepayment is required.

Surrogate Court 140 Grand St, 8th Floor, White Plains, NY 10601; 914-995-3712; Fax: 914-995-3728. Hours: 9AM-5PM (EST). *Probate.*

Town/Village Courts *Misdemeanor, Civil Actions Under $3,000, Small Claims:* Greenburgh Town, 914-682-5377; Elmsford Village, 914-592-8949; Tuckahoe Village, 914-961-4787; North Castle Town, 914-273-8627; North Salem Town, 914-669-9691; Irvington Village, 914-591-9505; Tarrytown Village, 914-631-5115; Ardsley Village, 914-693-1703; Ossining Town, 914-762-8562; North Tarrytown Village, 914-631-2783; Eastchester Town, 914-771-3354; New Castle Town, 914-238-4771; Bronxville Village, 914-337-2454; Mount Pleasant Town, 914-742-2354; Dobbs Ferry Village, 914-693-6161; Mount Kisco Town, 914-241-0500; Larchmont Village, 914-834-1826; Cronton-on-Hudson Village, 914-271-6266; Buchanan Village, 914-737-1033; Mamaroneck Village, 914-777-7710; Mamaroneck Town, 914-381-7875; Cortlandt Town, 914-734-1090; Yorktown Town, 914-962-6216; Rye Town, 914-939-3305; Scarsdale Town; Scarsdale Village, 914-723-5734; Pleasantville Village, 914-769-2027; Port Chester Village Court; Ossining Village, 914-941-3067; Hastings-on-Hudson Village, 914-478-3403; Pelham Town, 914-738-2205; Somers Town, 914-277-8225; Pound Ridge Town, 914-764-5511; Harrison Town, 914-835-2000; Bedford Town, 914-666-6965; Lewisboro Town, 914-763-5417; Briarcliff Manor Village, 914-941-4800.

Wyoming County

Supreme & County Court 147 N Main St, Warsaw, NY 14569; 585-786-2253; 585-8810-County Clerk; Fax: 585-786-2818. Hours: 9AM-5PM (EST). *Felony, Civil, Small Claims over $3,000.*

Note: All records maintained at County Clerk's office.

Civil Records: Access: Phone, fax, mail, in person. Only the court performs in person searches; visitors may not. Search fee: $5.00 per name. Required to search: name, years to search. Civil cases indexed by defendant. Civil records on computer back to 2/14/2001; prior on books.

Criminal Records: Access: Phone, fax, mail, in person. Only the court performs in person searches; visitors may not. Search fee: $5.00 per name. Required to search: name, years to search, DOB. Criminal records in books.

General Information: No sealed, divorce or sexual abuse records released. SASE required. Turnaround time 2-3 days. Fax notes: $.50 per page. Copy fee: $.50 per page. Certification fee: $4.00. Fee payee: County Clerk. Personal checks accepted. Prepayment is required.

Surrogate Court 147 N Main St, Warsaw, NY 14569; 585-786-3148; Fax: 585-786-3800. Hours: 9AM-5PM (EST). *Probate.*

Town/Village Courts *Misdemeanor, Civil Actions Under $3,000, Small Claims:* Middlebury Town, 585-495-6300; Eagle Town, 585-322-7667; Bennington Town, 585-591-2157; Covington Town, 585-584-3565; Warsaw Village, 585-786-3361; Warsaw Town, 585-786-3361; Arcade Town, 585-492-1340; Pike Town, 585-493-5140; Wethersfield Town; Attica Town; Java Town, 585-457-3022; Perry Town, 585-237-2216; Sheldon Town, 585-535-7644; Genesee Falls Town; Castile Town, 585-493-5875; Gainesville Town; Orangeville Town, 585-786-2883; Attica Village, 585-591-0881; Arcade Village, 585-492-4479; Perry Village, 585-237-2216; Silver Springs Village, 585-493-2500.

Yates County

Supreme & County Court 416 Liberty St #1107, Penn Yan, NY 14527-1122; 315-536-5120; Fax: 315-536-5545. Hours: 9AM-5PM (EST). *Felony, Civil, Misdemeanor, Eviction, Small Claims.*

Civil Records: Access: Phone, mail, fax, in person. Both court and visitors may perform in person searches. Search fee: $10.00 per name. Required to search: name, years to search. Civil cases indexed by defendant, plaintiff. Civil records on computer back to 9/1987, prior in books.

Criminal Records: Access: Mail, fax, in person. Both court and visitors may perform in person searches. Search fee: $10.00 per name. Required to search: name, years to search. Criminal records on book index; not computerized.

General Information: Public access terminal is available. No divorce records outside parties involved, sealed records released. SASE required. Turnaround time 2-3 days. Fax notes: Will not fax results. Copy fee: $.50 per page, $1.00 minimum. Certification fee: $1.00 per page. Fee payee: Yates County Clerk. Personal checks accepted. Prepayment is required.

Surrogate Court 415 Liberty St, Penn Yan, NY 14527; 315-536-5130; Fax: 315-536-5190. Hours: 9AM-5PM (EST). *Probate.*

Town/Village Courts *Misdemeanor, Civil Actions Under $3,000, Small Claims:* Starkey Town; Barrington Town; Rushville Village Court; Middlesex Town, 585-554-3607; Jerusalem Town; Italy Town; Potter Town, 585-554-6758; Torrey Town; Penn Yan Village, 315-536-7243; Benton Town, 315-536-2320; Dundee Village, 607-243-5551; Milo Town, 315-536-8911.

New York Recording Offices

ORGANIZATION: 62 counties, 62 recording offices. The recording officers are County Clerk (New York City Register in the counties of Bronx, Kings, New York, and Queens). The entire state is in the Eastern Time Zone (EST).

REAL ESTATE RECORDS: Some counties will perform real estate searches. Certified copy fees are usually $1.00 per page with a $4.00 minimum. Tax records are located at the Treasurer's Office.

UCC RECORDS: This was a dual filing state. Financing statements werefiled both at the state level and with the County Clerk, except for consumer goods, cooperatives (as in cooperative apartments), farm related and real estate related collateral, which were filed only with the County Clerk. Effective 07/2001, only real estate related collateral is filed at the county, but searches may still be done on all the records prior to 07/2001. All counties will perform UCC searches. Use search request form UCC-11. Search fees are usually $7.00 per debtor name using the approved UCC-11 request form and sometimes $12.00 using a non-New York form. Copies usually cost $1.50 per page.

TAX LIEN RECORDS: Federal tax liens on personal property of businesses are filed with the Secretary of State. Other federal tax liens are filed with the County Clerk. State tax liens are filed with the County Clerk, with a master list - called state tax warrants - available at the Secretary of State's office. Federal tax liens are usually indexed with UCC Records. State tax liens are usually indexed with other miscellaneous liens and judgments. Some counties include federal tax liens as part of a UCC search, and others will search tax liens for a separate fee. Search fees and copy fees vary.

OTHER LIENS: Judgment, mechanics, welfare, hospital, matrimonial, wage assignment, lis pendens.

ONLINE ACCESS: There are a handful of counties and towns offering free Internet access to assessor records, and the number is growing.

Albany County

County Clerk, County Courthouse, Room 128, Albany, NY 12207. County Clerk, R/E and UCC Recording 518-487-5120; Fax 518-487-5099. www.albanycounty.com/departments
Will search UCC records. **Online Access:** Naturalization Records. Access to the clerk's naturalization records from 1821-1991 are available free online at www.albanycounty.com/online/online.asp. Records are being added by volunteers. **Other Phone Numbers:** Assessor 518-487-5350; Treasurer 518-447-7070; Elections-487-5060; Vital Records 434-5045.

Allegany County

County Clerk, 7 Court St., 7 Court St., Belmont, NY 14813-0087. 585-268-9270; Fax 585-268-9659. www.alleganyco.com
Will search UCC records. UCC-11 search includes federal tax liens if requested. Will not search real estate records. **Other Phone Numbers:** Assessor 585-268-9381; Treasurer 585-268-9282.

Bronx County

City Register, 1932 Arthur Ave, Bronx, NY 10457. 718-579-6827.
Will search UCC records. Federal tax lien search included in the UCC search. Will not search real estate records. **Online Access:** Real Estate, Lien, Deed, UCC, Tax Assessor Records. Two sources are available. Access to Bronx County online records - including Boroughs of Brooklyn, Queens, Staten Island, Bronx, Manhattan - requires a $250 monthly fee and $5 per transaction fee. Records are kept 3-6 years. For information, contact Richard Reskin at 718-935-6523. Also, they offer daily downloads are available for borough-wide transactions of UCCs, Fed Liens, deeds, real estate. Also, property assessment rolls from NYC's Dept. of Finance are available free online at www.ci.nyc.ny.us/html/dof/html/asmt.html. Search by borough, block and lot number. Tax reports are also available, with enrollment required. **Other Phone Numbers:** Assessor 718-579-6879.

Broome County

County Clerk, PO Box 2062, Binghamton, NY 13902-2062. 607-778-2451; Fax 607-778-2243.
Will search UCC records. **Other Phone Numbers:** Assessor 607-778-2169; Treasurer 607-778-2161.

Cattaraugus County

County Clerk, 303 Court St, Little Valley, NY 14755. County Clerk, R/E and UCC Recording 716-938-9111; Fax 716-938-6009.
Will search UCC records. Will not search real estate records. **Online Access:** Real Estate, Tax Assessor Records. Records on the City of Olean assessor database are available free online at www.cityofolean.com/Assessor/main.htm. **Other Phone Numbers:** Assessor 716-938-9111; Treasurer 716-938-9111.

Cayuga County

County Clerk, 160 Genesee St, Auburn, NY 13021. County Clerk, R/E and UCC Recording 315-253-1271; Fax 315-253-1653.
Will search UCC records. Will not search real estate records. **Other Phone Numbers:** Assessor 315-253-1270; Treasurer 315-253-1211; Elections 315-253-1285; Vital Records 315-255-4100.

Chautauqua County

County Clerk, PO Box 170, Mayville, NY 14757-0170. 716-753-4980; Fax 716-753-4310.
Will search UCC records. Will not search real estate records. **Other Phone Numbers:** Assessor 716-661-7223.

Chemung County

County Clerk, PO Box 588, Elmira, NY 14902-0588. 607-737-2920; Fax 607-737-2897. www.chemungcounty.com
Will search UCC records. Will not search real estate records. **Other Phone Numbers:** Assessor 607-737-2988; Treasurer 607-737-2927; Elections 607-737-5475; Vital Records 607-737-2018.

Chenango County

County Clerk, 5 Court St, Norwich, NY 13815. 607-337-1452. Will search UCC records. UCC search includes Federal (only) tax liens. Will not search real estate records. **Other Phone Numbers:** Assessor 607-337-1490; Treasurer 607-337-1414.

Clinton County

County Clerk, 137 Margaret St, Government Center, Plattsburgh, NY 12901-2974. County Clerk, R/E and UCC Recording 518-565-4700 UCC Recording: 518-565-4846; Fax 518-565-4718. www.co.clinton.ny.us/Departments/CC/CCHome.htm
Will search UCC records. UCC search includes tax liens if requested. Will not search real estate records. **Other Phone Numbers:** Assessor 518-565-4760; Treasurer 518-565-4730.

Columbia County

County Clerk, 560 Warren St., Hudson, NY 12534. County Clerk, R/E and UCC Recording 518-828-3339; Fax 518-828-5299.
Will search UCC records. Will not search real estate records. **Other Phones:** Assessor 518-828-7334; Treasurer 518-828-0513; Elections 518-828-3115.

Cortland County

County Clerk, 46 Greenbush St Suite 101, 46 Greenbush St., Cortland, NY 13045-3702. 607-753-5021 R/E Recording: 607-758-5021 UCC Recording: 607-758-5021; Fax 607-758-5500. http://www2.cortland-co.org
Will search UCC records. Will search real estate records. **Other Phone Numbers:** Assessor 607-753-5040 (Real Property); Treasurer 607-753-5070; Elections 607-753-5032; Vital Records 607-756-6521.

Delaware County

County Clerk, PO Box 426, Delhi, NY 13753. County Clerk, R/E and UCC Recording 607-746-2123; Fax 607-746-6924.

Will search UCC records. Will not search real estate records. **Other Phones:** Assessor 607-746-3747; Treasurer 607-746-2121; Elections 607-746-2315.

Dutchess County

County Clerk, 22 Market St, Poughkeepsie, NY 12601. County Clerk, R/E and UCC Recording 845-486-2120 UCC Recording: 845-486-2125; Fax 845-486-2138. www.dutchessny.gov
Will search UCC records. This agency will not do a tax lien search. Will not search real estate records. **Other Phone Numbers:** Assessor 845-431-2140; Treasurer 845-431-2025; Elections 845-486-2480.

Erie County

County Clerk, 25 Delaware Ave, County Hall, Buffalo, NY 14202. 716-858-6724; Fax 716-858-6550. http://ecclerk.erie.gov
Will search UCC records. Will search state tax liens. Search per debtor name- $5.00 per 2 years. Will search federal tax liens- $7.00 per 2 years. Will search real estate records. **Online Access:** Recording, Deed, Mortgage, Judgment Records. Access to the county clerk's data is available free at http://ecclerk.erie.gov. Records go back to 2/1994. **Other Phone Numbers:** Assessor 716-858-8322; Treasurer 716-858-3236.

Essex County

County Clerk, PO Box 247, Elizabethtown, NY 12932. County Clerk, R/E and UCC Recording 518-873-3600; Fax 518-873-3548.
Will search UCC records. UCC search includes tax liens if requested. Real estate owner, mortgage, and property transfer searches available. **Other Phone Numbers:** Assessor 518-873-3390; Treasurer 518-873-3310; Elections 518-873-3474.

Franklin County

County Clerk, PO Box 70, Malone, NY 12953. County Clerk, R/E and UCC Recording 518-481-1681; Fax 518-483-9143.
Will search UCC records. Will not search real estate records. **Other Phone Numbers:** Assessor 518-481-1502; Treasurer 518-481-1516; Elections 518-481-1662; Vital Records 518-481-1671.

Fulton County

Clerk, PO Box 485, Johnstown, NY 12095. Clerk, R/E and UCC Recording 518-736-5555; Fax 518-762-3839. Will search UCC records. Will not search real estate records. **Other Phone Numbers:** Assessor 518-736-5510; Treasurer 518-736-5580; Elections 518-736-5526.

Genesee County

County Clerk, PO Box 379, Batavia, NY 14021-0379. 585-344-2550 x2245 R/E Recording: 585-344-2550 x2242 UCC Recording: 585-344-2550 x2243; Fax 585-344-8521. www.co.genesee.ny.us
Will search UCC records. Will not search real estate records. **Other Phone Numbers:** Assessor 585-344-2550 x2219; Treasurer 585-344-2550 x2210; Elections 585-344-2550 x2206.

Greene County

County Clerk, PO Box 446, Catskill, NY 12414. 518-943-2050; Fax 518-943-2146.
Will search UCC records. This agency will not do a tax lien search. Will not search real estate records. **Other Phone Numbers:** Assessor 518-943-6977; Treasurer 518-943-4152.

Hamilton County

County Clerk, PO Box 204, Rte. 8, Lake Pleasant, NY 12108. County Clerk, R/E and UCC Recording 518-548-7111; Fax 518-548-9740.

Will search UCC records. This agency will not do a tax lien search. Will not search real estate records. **Other Phone Numbers:** Assessor 518-548-5531; Treasurer 518-548-7911.

Herkimer County

County Clerk, 109 Mary St, Suite 1111, Herkimer, NY 13350. 315-867-1137; Fax 315-867-1349.
Will search UCC records. Will not search real estate records. **Other Phone Numbers:** Treasurer 315-867-1153; Elections 315-867-1102.

Jefferson County

County Clerk, 175 Arsenal St, Watertown, NY 13601-2555. County Clerk, R/E and UCC Recording 315-785-3081; Fax 315-785-5048.
Will search UCC records. **Other Phone Numbers:** Assessor 315-785-3074; Treasurer 315-785-3055; Elections 315-785-5119.

Kings County

County Clerk, Municipal Building, 1st Floor, Room 2, 210 Joralemon St, Brooklyn, NY 11201. 718-802-3589; Fax 718-802-3745.
Will search UCC records. Will not search real estate records. **Online Access:** Real Estate, Lien, Tax Assessor Records. Two sources exist: the fee service supports the Boroughs of Brooklyn, Queens, Staten Island, Bronx, and Manhattan. There is a $250 monthly fee and a $5.00 fee per transaction. Records are kept 2-5 years. Search by name, grantor/grantee, and address. For information, contact Richard Reskin at 718-935-6523. Also, property assessment rolls from NYC's Dept. of Finance are available free online at www.ci.nyc.ny.us/html/dof/html/asmt.html. Search by borough, block and lot number. Tax reports are also available, with enrollment required. **Other Phone Numbers:** Assessor 718-802-3560; Treasurer 718-669-2746.

Lewis County

County Clerk, PO Box 232, Lowville, NY 13367-0232. County Clerk, R/E and UCC Recording 315-376-5333; Fax 315-376-3768.
Will search UCC records. UCC search includes federal tax liens. Will not search real estate records. **Other Phone Numbers:** Assessor 315-376-5356; Treasurer 315-376-5326; Elections 315-376-5329.

Livingston County

County Clerk, Government Center, 6 Court St., Room 201, Geneseo, NY 14454-1043. 585-243-7010.
Will search UCC records. This agency will not do a tax lien search. Will not search real estate records. **Other Phone Numbers:** Assessor 585-243-7192; Treasurer 585-243-7050.

Madison County

County Clerk, PO Box 668, Wampsville, NY 13163. County Clerk, R/E and UCC Recording 315-366-2261 UCC Recording: 315-366-2262; Fax 315-366-2615.
Will search UCC records. **Other Phone Numbers:** Assessor 315-366-2346; Treasurer 315-366-2371; Elections 315-366-2371.

Monroe County

County Clerk, 39 W. Main St, Rochester, NY 14614. County Clerk, R/E and UCC Recording 585-428-5151; Fax 585-428-5447. www.co.monroe.ny.us
Will search UCC records. **Online Access:** Land, Judgment, UCC, Lien, Court Records. Access to the county clerk database are available online at www.clerk.co.monroe.ny.us. Includes mortgages, deeds, court records; free registration. Land records back to 1984. Liens, judgments, UCCS back to 5/1989. Court records - civil, felony, divorce - back to June, 1993. Earlier microfilm images are being added as time

permits. **Other Phone Numbers:** Assessor 585-428-5290; Treasurer 585-428-5290; Elections 585-428-4550; Vital Records 585-274-6141.

Montgomery County

County Clerk, PO Box 1500, Fonda, NY 12068-1500. 518-853-8115 R/E Recording: 518-853-8111.
Will search UCC records. UCC search includes only federal tax liens if requested. Will search real estate records if in writing. **Other Phone Numbers:** Assessor 518-853-3996; Treasurer 518-853-8175.

Nassau County

County Clerk, 240 Old Country Road, Mineola, NY 11501. 516-571-2667; Fax 516-742-4099.
Will search UCC records. **Other Phone Numbers:** Assessor 516-571-2490; Treasurer 516-571-5021.

New York County

City Register, 66 John St, Room 202, New York, NY 10007. 212-361-7550.
Will search UCC records. This agency will not do a tax lien search. Will not search real estate records. **Online Access:** Real Estate, Lien, Tax Assessor Records. Several sources available. Access to NY County online records - including Boroughs of Brooklyn, Queens, Staten Is, Bronx, Manhattan - requires $250 monthly and $5 per transaction. Records are kept 2-5 years. Call Richard Reskin at 718-935-6523. Also, property assessment rolls from NYC's Dept. of Finance are available free online at www.ci.nyc.ny.us/html/dof/html/asmt.html. Search by borough, block and lot number. Tax reports are also available, with enrollment required. Also, online access to assessor's property db is available free at http://nycserv.nyc.gov/nycproperty/nynav/jsp/selectbbl.jsp. Search by address of property description. **Other Phone Numbers:** Assessor 212-669-2387; Treasurer 212-669-3913.

Niagara County

County Clerk, PO Box 461, Lockport, NY 14095. County Clerk, R/E and UCC Recording 716-439-7022 UCC Recording: 716-439-7030; Fax 716-439-7066.
Will search UCC records. UCC search includes tax liens if requested. Real estate record owner and mortgage searches available. **Other Phone Numbers:** Assessor 716-439-7077; Treasurer 716-439-7007; Elections 716-438-4040; Vital Records 716-439-6676.

Oneida County

County Clerk, 800 Park Ave, Utica, NY 13501. 315-798-5792; Fax 315-798-6440. www.oneidacounty.org/index1.htm
Will search UCC records. UCC search includes only federal tax liens if requested. Real estate record owner and mortgage searches available. **Other Phones:** Assessor 315-798-5750; Treasurer 315-798-5750; Elections 315-798-5763; Vital Records 315-798-5833.

Onondaga County

County Clerk, 401 Montgomery St., Room 200, Syracuse, NY 13202. 315-435-8200; Fax 315-435-3455.
Will search UCC records. **Other Phone Numbers:** Treasurer 315-435-2426.

Ontario County

County Clerk, Ontario County Municipal Bldg., 20 Ontario St., Canandaigua, NY 14424. County Clerk, R/E and UCC Recording 585-396-4200; Fax 585-393-2951. www.co.ontario.ny.us
Will search UCC records. **Other Phone Numbers:** Assessor 585-396-4396; Treasurer 585-396-4432; Elections 585-396-4005.

Orange County

County Clerk, 255-275 Main St, Goshen, NY 10924. 845-291-2690 R/E Recording: 845-291-3062 UCC Recording: 845-291-3062; Fax 845-291-2691. www.co.orange.ny.us
Will search UCC records. UCC search includes tax liens if requested. Real estate owner, mortgage, and property transfer searches available. **Other Phone Numbers:** Assessor 845-291-2480; Treasurer 845-291-2485; Elections 845-291-2444.

Orleans County

County Clerk, 3 S. Main St, Courthouse Square, Albion, NY 14411-1498. County Clerk, R/E and UCC Recording 585-589-5334; Fax 585-589-0181.
Will search UCC records. **Other Phone Numbers:** Assessor 585-589-5400; Treasurer 585-589-5353; Elections 585-589-7004.

Oswego County

County Clerk, 46 E. Bridge St, Oswego, NY 13126. 315-349-8385; Fax 315-343-8383.
Will search UCC records. **Other Phone Numbers:** Assessor 315-349-8315; Treasurer 315-349-8393.

Otsego County

County Clerk, PO Box 710, Cooperstown, NY 13326-0710. 607-547-4278; Fax 607-547-7544.
Will search UCC records. Will not search real estate records. **Other Phones:** Assessor 607-547-4222.

Putnam County

County Clerk, 40 Gleneida Ave., Carmel, NY 10512. 845-225-3641 R/E Recording: 845-225-3641 x304, x305 UCC Recording: 845-225-3641 x309; Fax 845-228-0231. www.putnamcountyny.com
Will search UCC records. UCC search includes tax liens if requested. Real estate record owner and mortgage searches available. **Online Access:** Land, Court, Judgment Records. County Recorder records are accessible through a private online service at www.landaccess.com; Fees and registration are required. **Other Phone Numbers:** Assessor 845-225-3641 x310; Treasurer 845-225-3641 x321; Elections 845-278-6970.

Queens County

City Register, 144-06 94th Ave., Jamaica, NY 11435. 718-298-7000.
Will search UCC records. This agency will not do a tax lien search. Will not search real estate records. **Online Access:** Real Estate, Lien, Tax Assessor Records. Two sources are available. Access to Queens County online records - including Boroughs of Brooklyn, Queens, Staten Island, Bronx, Manhattan - requires a $250 monthly fee and $5 per transaction fee. Records are kept 2-5 years. For information, contact Richard Reskin at 718-935-6523. Also, property assessment rolls from NYC's Dept. of Finance are available free online at www.ci.nyc.ny.us/html/dof/html/asmt.html. Search by borough, block and lot number. Tax reports are also available, with enrollment required. **Other Phone Numbers:** Assessor 718-658-4626.

Rensselaer County

County Clerk, Courthouse, Congress & 2nd St, Troy, NY 12180. 518-270-4080.
Will search UCC records. This agency will not do a tax lien search. Will search deeds and mortgages with name and year. **Other Phone Numbers:** Assessor 518-270-2751; Treasurer 518-270-2751.

Richmond County

County Clerk, 130 Stuyvesant Pl, Staten Island, NY 10301. 718-390-5386 R/E Recording: 718-390-5387 UCC Recording: 719-390-5386.

Will search UCC records. This agency will not do a tax lien search. Will not search real estate records. **Online Access:** Real Estate, Lien, Tax Assessor Records. Two sources are available. Access to Richmond-Staten Is. online records - including Boroughs of Brooklyn, Queens, Staten Island, Bronx, Manhattan - requires a $250 monthly fee and $5 per transaction fee. Records are kept 2-5 years. For further information, contact Richard Reskin at 718-935-6523. Property assessment rolls from NYC's Dept. of Finance are available free online at www.ci.nyc.ny.us/html/dof/html/asmt.html. Search by borough, block and lot number. Tax reports are also available, with enrollment required. **Other Phone Numbers:** Assessor 718-390-5292.

Rockland County

County Clerk, 1 S. Main St #100, New City, NY 10956. 845-638-5070 R/E Recording: 845-638-5069 UCC Recording: 845-638-5354; Fax 845-638-5647. www.rocklandcountyclerk.com
Will search UCC records. Tax liens not included in UCC search. Real estate owner, mortgage, and property transfer searches available. **Online Access:** Real Estate, Lien, Deed, Court Records. Access is the county clerk's records index is available free at www.rocklandcountyclerk.com/court_records.html. Includes criminal records back to 1982, civil judgments, real estate records, tax warrants. Images back to 6/96 are viewable, and more are being added. Call Paul Pipearto at 845-638-5221 for more information. **Other Phones:** Assessor 845-638-5131; Elections 845-638-5712.

Saratoga County

County Clerk, 40 McMaster St, Ballston Spa, NY 12020. 518-885-2213; Fax 518-884-4726.
Will search UCC records. UCC search includes tax liens if requested. Real estate record owner and mortgage searches available. **Other Phone Numbers:** Assessor 518-885-5381 x455; Treasurer 518-885-5381 x281.

Schenectady County

County Clerk, 620 State St, Schenectady, NY 12305-2114. 518-388-4220; Fax 518-388-4224. www.scpl.org
Will search UCC records. **Online Access:** Real Estate, Tax Assessor Records. Records for approximately 2/5 of the county property assessments are available free online on the library database at www.scpl.org/assessments. **Other Phone Numbers:** Assessor 518-388-4247; Treasurer 518-388-4262.

Schoharie County

County Clerk, PO Box 549, Schoharie, NY 12157. County Clerk, R/E and UCC Recording 518-295-8316; Fax 518-295-8338.
Will search UCC records. Will not search real estate records. **Other Phone Numbers:** Assessor 518-295-7141; Treasurer 518-295-8386.

Schuyler County

County Clerk, 105 Ninth St Unit 8, County Office Building, Watkins Glen, NY 14891. 607-535-8133.
Will search UCC records. This agency will not do a tax lien search. Will not search real estate records. **Other Phone Numbers:** Assessor 607-535-8118; Treasurer 607-535-8181.

Seneca County

County Clerk, 1 DiPronio Drive, Waterloo, NY 13165. 315-539-1771 R/E Recording: 315-539-1770 UCC Recording: 315-539-1772; Fax 315-539-3789.
Will search UCC records. Will not search real estate records. **Other Phone Numbers:** Assessor 315-539-1720; Treasurer 315-539-1738; Appraiser/Auditor 315-539-1718; Elections 315-539-1762.

St. Lawrence County

County Clerk, 48 Court St, Canton, NY 13617-1198. County Clerk, R/E and UCC Recording 315-379-2237; Fax 315-379-2302. www.co.st-lawrence.ny.us/CoTOC2.htm
Will search UCC records. This agency will not do a tax lien search. Will not search real estate records. **Other Phone Numbers:** Assessor 315-379-2272; Treasurer 315-379-2234; Appraiser/Auditor 315-379-2272; Elections 315-379-2202.

Steuben County

County Clerk, 3 E. Pulteney Square, County Office Building, Bath, NY 14810. County Clerk, R/E and UCC Recording 607-776-9631 x3203 UCC Recording: 607-776-9631; Fax 607-776-7158. www.steubencony.org
Will search UCC records. **Online Access:** Tax Assessor Records. Search Town of Erwin Real Property Assessment Roll free online at www.pennynet.org/erwin/er95tax.htm. **Other Phones:** Assessor 607-324-3074; Treasurer 607-324-7421.

Suffolk County

Clerk's Office, 310 Center Drive, Riverhead, NY 11901-3392. 631-852-2038 R/E Recording: 631-852-2043; Fax 631-852-2004.
Will search UCC records. Will not search real estate records. **Other Phone Numbers:** Assessor 631-852-1551; Treasurer 631-852-1500.

Sullivan County

County Clerk, PO Box 5012, Monticello, NY 12701. 845-794-3000 x3152.
Will search UCC records. This agency will not do a tax lien search. Will not search real estate records. **Other Phone Numbers:** Assessor 845-794-3000 x5014; Treasurer 845-794-3000.

Tioga County

County Clerk, PO Box 307, Owego, NY 13827. County Clerk, R/E and UCC Recording 607-687-8660; Fax 607-687-4612.
Will search UCC records. Will not search real estate records. **Other Phones:** Assessor 607-687-8661; Treasurer 607-687-8670; Elections 607-687-8261.

Tompkins County

County Clerk, 320 N. Tioga St, Ithaca, NY 14850-4284. 607-274-5432 R/E Recording: 607-274-5431 UCC Recording: 607-274-5431; Fax 607-274-5445. www.tompkins-co.org
Will search UCC records. UCC search includes federal tax liens. Real estate owner, mortgage, and property transfer searches available. **Online Access:** Real Estate, Assessor Records. Access to property records on the ImageMate system at www.tompkins-co.org/assessment/online.html has two levels: basic free and a registration/password fee-based full system. There is no name searching on the free version. The fee service is $20 monthly or $200 per year. For information and registration for the latter, email assessment@tompkins-co.org. **Other Phone Numbers:** Assessor 607-274-5517; Treasurer 607-274-5545; Elections 607-274-5522; Vital Records 607-274-642.

Ulster County

County Clerk, PO Box 1800, Kingston, NY 12402-0800. County Clerk, R/E and UCC Recording 845-340-3288; Fax 845-340-3299. www.co.ulster.ny.us
Will search UCC records. Tax liens not included in UCC search. Real estate owner, mortgage, and property transfer searches available. **Online Access:** Real Estate, Lien, Property Tax, Voter Registration, Court Records. Two sources exist. Access to county online records requires a $33.33 (under 25 transactions) or $44.55

monthly fee; 12 month agreement required. Land Records date back to 1984. Includes county court records back to 7/1987. Lending agency information is available. For information, contact Valerie Harris at 845-334-5367. Also, the Ulster County Parcel Viewer at www.maphost.com/ulster provides free access to tax parcel information. Search by GIS map, parcel ID number, street name, or other criteria. **Other Phone Numbers:** Assessor 845-340-3431; Treasurer 845-340-3431; Elections 845-340-5470.

Warren County

County Clerk, Municipal Center, 1340 State Route 9, Lake George, NY 12845. 518-761-6426; Fax 518-761-6551.

Will search UCC records. Will not search real estate records. **Other Phone Numbers:** Assessor 518-761-6465.

Washington County

County Clerk, 383 Broadway, Bldg A, Fort Edward, NY 12828. County Clerk, R/E and UCC Recording 518-746-2170; Fax 518-746-2166.

Will search UCC records. This agency will not do a tax lien search. Will not search real estate records. **Other Phone Numbers:** Assessor 518-746-2130 (Real Property Tax); Treasurer 518-746-2220; Elections 518-746-2180.

Wayne County

County Clerk, PO Box 608, Lyons, NY 14489-0608. County Clerk, R/E and UCC Recording 315-946-7470; Fax 315-946-5978. www.co.wayne.ny.us

Will search UCC records. **Other Phone Numbers:** Assessor 315-946-5916; Treasurer 315-946-7443; Elections 315-946-7400.

Westchester County

County Clerk, 110 Dr. Martin Luther King Jr. Blvd., White Plains, NY 10601. 914-995-3098; Fax 914-995-3172.

Will search UCC records. Will not search real estate records. **Other Phone Numbers:** Assessor 914-422-1223.

Wyoming County

County Clerk, 143 N Main St, Suite 104, Warsaw, NY 14569. County Clerk, R/E and UCC Recording 585-786-8810; Fax 585-786-3703.

Will search UCC records. Tax liens not included in UCC search. Real estate owner, mortgage, and property transfer searches available. **Online Access:** Real Estate, Recording Records. County Recorder records are accessible through a private online service at www.landaccess.com; Fees and registration are required. **Other Phone Numbers:** Assessor 585-786-8828; Treasurer 585-786-8812; Elections 585-786-8931.

Yates County

County Clerk, 110 Court St, Penn Yan, NY 14527. County Clerk, R/E and UCC Recording 315-536-5120; Fax 315-536-5545.

Will search UCC records. Will not search real estate records. **Other Phone Numbers:** Assessor 315-536-5165; Treasurer 315-536-5192; Elections 315-536-5135.

New York County Locator

You will usually be able to find the city name in the City/County Cross Reference below. In that case, it is a simple matter to determine the county from the cross reference. However, only the official US Postal Service city names are included in this index. There are an additional 40,000 place names that people use in their addresses. Therefore, we have also included a ZIP/City Cross Reference immediately following the City/County Cross Reference.

If you know the ZIP Code but the city name does not appear in the City/County Cross Reference index, look up the ZIP Code in the ZIP/City Cross Reference, find the city name, then look up the city name in the City/County Cross Reference. For example, you want to know the county for an address of Menands, NY 12204. There is no "Menands" in the City/County Cross Reference. The ZIP/City Cross Reference shows that ZIP Codes 12201-12288 are for the city of Albany. Looking back in the City/County Cross Reference, Albany is in Albany County.

City/County Cross Reference

ACCORD Ulster
ACRA Greene
ADAMS Jefferson
ADAMS BASIN Monroe
ADAMS CENTER Jefferson
ADDISON Steuben
ADIRONDACK Warren
AFTON (13730) Chenango(94), Broome(5)
AKRON (14001) Erie(92), Niagara(4), Genesee(3)
ALABAMA Genesee
ALBANY Albany
ALBERTSON Nassau
ALBION Orleans
ALCOVE Albany
ALDEN (14004) Erie(92), Wyoming(5), Genesee(1)
ALDER CREEK Oneida
ALEXANDER Genesee
ALEXANDRIA BAY Jefferson
ALFRED Allegany
ALFRED STATION (14803) Allegany(89), Steuben(10)
ALLEGANY Cattaraugus
ALLENTOWN Allegany
ALMA Allegany
ALMOND Allegany
ALPINE Schuyler
ALPLAUS Schenectady
ALTAMONT Albany
ALTMAR Oswego
ALTON Wayne
ALTONA Clinton
AMAGANSETT Suffolk
AMAWALK Westchester
AMENIA Dutchess
AMITYVILLE Suffolk
AMSTERDAM (12010) Montgomery(96), Schenectady(3)
ANCRAM Columbia
ANCRAMDALE Columbia
ANDES Delaware
ANDOVER (14806) Allegany(85), Steuben(14)
ANGELICA Allegany
ANGOLA Erie
ANNANDALE ON HUDSON Dutchess
ANTWERP Jefferson
APALACHIN Tioga
APPLETON Niagara
APULIA STATION Onondaga
AQUEBOGUE Suffolk
ARCADE (14009) Wyoming(90), Cattaraugus(8)
ARDEN Orange
ARDSLEY Westchester
ARDSLEY ON HUDSON Westchester
ARGYLE Washington
ARKPORT (14807) Steuben(79), Allegany(20)
ARKVILLE (12406) Delaware(89), Ulster(10)
ARMONK Westchester

ASHLAND Greene
ASHVILLE Chautauqua
ATHENS Greene
ATHOL Warren
ATHOL SPRINGS Erie
ATLANTA Steuben
ATLANTIC BEACH Nassau
ATTICA (14011) Wyoming(91), Genesee(8)
AU SABLE FORKS (12912) Clinton(98), Essex(1)
AUBURN Cayuga
AURIESVILLE Montgomery
AURORA Cayuga
AUSTERLITZ Columbia
AVA Oneida
AVERILL PARK Rensselaer
AVOCA Steuben
AVON Livingston
BABYLON Suffolk
BAINBRIDGE (13733) Chenango(96), Delaware(2)
BAKERS MILLS Warren
BALDWIN Nassau
BALDWIN PLACE (10505) Westchester(71), Putnam(28)
BALDWINSVILLE Onondaga
BALLSTON LAKE Saratoga
BALLSTON SPA Saratoga
BALMAT St. Lawrence
BANGALL Dutchess
BANGOR Franklin
BARKER (14012) Niagara(95), Orleans(4)
BARNEVELD Oneida
BARRYTOWN Dutchess
BARRYVILLE Sullivan
BARTON Tioga
BASOM Genesee
BATAVIA Genesee
BATH Steuben
BAY SHORE Suffolk
BAYPORT Suffolk
BAYSIDE Queens
BAYVILLE Nassau
BEACON Dutchess
BEAR MOUNTAIN Rockland
BEARSVILLE Ulster
BEAVER DAMS (14812) Schuyler(45), Chemung(32), Steuben(21)
BEAVER FALLS Lewis
BEDFORD Westchester
BEDFORD HILLS Westchester
BELFAST Allegany
BELLEVILLE Jefferson
BELLMORE Nassau
BELLONA Yates
BELLPORT Suffolk
BELLVALE Orange
BELMONT Allegany
BEMUS POINT Chautauqua
BERGEN (14416) Genesee(90), Monroe(9)
BERKSHIRE (13736) Tioga(94), Broome(4), Tompkins(1)
BERLIN Rensselaer

BERNE (12023) Albany(92), Schoharie(7)
BERNHARDS BAY Oswego
BETHEL Sullivan
BETHPAGE Nassau
BIBLE SCHOOL PARK Broome
BIG FLATS (14814) Chemung(84), Steuben(15)
BIG INDIAN Ulster
BILLINGS Dutchess
BINGHAMTON Broome
BLACK CREEK Allegany
BLACK RIVER Jefferson
BLAUVELT Rockland
BLISS (14024) Wyoming(92), Allegany(7)
BLODGETT MILLS Cortland
BLOOMFIELD Ontario
BLOOMING GROVE Orange
BLOOMINGBURG (12721) Sullivan(92), Orange(7)
BLOOMINGDALE (12913) Essex(70), Franklin(30)
BLOOMINGTON Ulster
BLOOMVILLE Delaware
BLOSSVALE Oneida
BLUE MOUNTAIN LAKE Hamilton
BLUE POINT Suffolk
BOHEMIA Suffolk
BOICEVILLE Ulster
BOLIVAR Allegany
BOLTON LANDING Warren
BOMBAY Franklin
BOONVILLE (13309) Oneida(94), Lewis(5)
BOSTON Erie
BOUCKVILLE Madison
BOUQUET Essex
BOVINA CENTER Delaware
BOWMANSVILLE Erie
BRADFORD (14815) Schuyler(64), Steuben(36)
BRAINARD Rensselaer
BRAINARDSVILLE Franklin
BRANCHPORT (14418) Yates(89), Steuben(10)
BRANT Erie
BRANT LAKE Warren
BRANTINGHAM Lewis
BRASHER FALLS St. Lawrence
BREESPORT Chemung
BRENTWOOD Suffolk
BREWERTON Onondaga
BREWSTER (10509) Putnam(98), Westchester(1)
BRIARCLIFF MANOR Westchester
BRIDGEHAMPTON Suffolk
BRIDGEPORT (13030) Onondaga(79), Madison(20)
BRIDGEWATER Oneida
BRIER HILL St. Lawrence
BRIGHTWATERS Suffolk
BROADALBIN Fulton
BROCKPORT Monroe
BROCTON Chautauqua
BRONX Bronx

BRONXVILLE Westchester
BROOKFIELD Madison
BROOKHAVEN Suffolk
BROOKLYN Kings
BROOKTONDALE (14817) Tompkins(94), Tioga(5)
BROOKVIEW Rensselaer
BROWNVILLE Jefferson
BRUSHTON Franklin
BUCHANAN Westchester
BUFFALO Erie
BULLVILLE Orange
BURDETT Schuyler
BURKE Franklin
BURLINGHAM Sullivan
BURLINGTON FLATS Otsego
BURNT HILLS (12027) Saratoga(84), Schenectady(15)
BURT Niagara
BUSKIRK Rensselaer
BYRON (14422) Genesee(97), Orleans(2)
CADYVILLE Clinton
CAIRO Greene
CALCIUM Jefferson
CALEDONIA (14423) Livingston(98), Monroe(1)
CALLICOON Sullivan
CALLICOON CENTER Sullivan
CALVERTON Suffolk
CAMBRIDGE Washington
CAMDEN Oneida
CAMERON Steuben
CAMERON MILLS Steuben
CAMILLUS Onondaga
CAMPBELL Steuben
CAMPBELL HALL Orange
CANAAN Columbia
CANAJOHARIE Montgomery
CANANDAIGUA Ontario
CANASERAGA (14822) Allegany(88), Livingston(11)
CANASTOTA Madison
CANDOR Tioga
CANEADEA Allegany
CANISTEO Steuben
CANTON St. Lawrence
CAPE VINCENT Jefferson
CARLE PLACE Nassau
CARLISLE Schoharie
CARMEL Putnam
CAROGA LAKE Fulton
CARTHAGE (13619) Jefferson(91), Lewis(8)
CASSADAGA Chautauqua
CASSVILLE Oneida
CASTILE Wyoming
CASTLE CREEK Broome
CASTLE POINT Dutchess
CASTLETON ON HUDSON Rensselaer
CASTORLAND Lewis
CATO (13033) Cayuga(96), Onondaga(3)
CATSKILL Greene
CATTARAUGUS Cattaraugus

CAYUGA Cayuga
CAYUTA (14824) Schuyler(71), Chemung(28)
CAZENOVIA (13035) Madison(96), Onondaga(3)
CEDARHURST Nassau
CELORON Chautauqua
CEMENTON Greene
CENTER MORICHES Suffolk
CENTEREACH Suffolk
CENTERPORT Suffolk
CENTERVILLE Allegany
CENTRAL BRIDGE Schoharie
CENTRAL ISLIP Suffolk
CENTRAL SQUARE Oswego
CENTRAL VALLEY Orange
CERES Allegany
CHADWICKS Oneida
CHAFFEE (14030) Erie(76), Cattaraugus(17), Wyoming(6)
CHAMPLAIN Clinton
CHAPPAQUA Westchester
CHARLOTTEVILLE (12036) Schoharie(90), Otsego(9)
CHASE MILLS St. Lawrence
CHATEAUGAY Franklin
CHATHAM Columbia
CHAUMONT Jefferson
CHAUTAUQUA Chautauqua
CHAZY Clinton
CHELSEA Dutchess
CHEMUNG Chemung
CHENANGO BRIDGE Broome
CHENANGO FORKS (13746) Broome(74), Chenango(25)
CHERRY CREEK Chautauqua
CHERRY PLAIN Rensselaer
CHERRY VALLEY Otsego
CHESTER Orange
CHESTERTOWN Warren
CHICHESTER Ulster
CHILDWOLD St. Lawrence
CHIPPEWA BAY St. Lawrence
CHITTENANGO Madison
CHURCHVILLE Monroe
CHURUBUSCO Clinton
CICERO Onondaga
CINCINNATUS Cortland
CIRCLEVILLE Orange
CLARENCE Erie
CLARENCE CENTER (14032) Erie(98), Niagara(1)
CLARENDON Orleans
CLARK MILLS Oneida
CLARKSON Monroe
CLARKSVILLE Albany
CLARYVILLE (12725) Sullivan(57), Ulster(42)
CLAVERACK Columbia
CLAY Onondaga
CLAYTON Jefferson
CLAYVILLE (13322) Herkimer(78), Oneida(21)
CLEMONS Washington
CLEVELAND Oswego
CLEVERDALE Warren
CLIFTON PARK Saratoga
CLIFTON SPRINGS Ontario
CLIMAX Greene
CLINTON Oneida
CLINTON CORNERS Dutchess
CLINTONDALE Ulster
CLOCKVILLE Madison
CLYDE (14433) Wayne(94), Seneca(5)
CLYMER Chautauqua
COBLESKILL Schoharie
COCHECTON Sullivan
COCHECTON CENTER Sullivan
COEYMANS Albany
COEYMANS HOLLOW (12046) Albany(89), Greene(10)
COHOCTON Steuben

COHOES Albany
COLD BROOK Herkimer
COLD SPRING Putnam
COLD SPRING HARBOR Suffolk
COLDEN Erie
COLLIERSVILLE Otsego
COLLINS Erie
COLLINS CENTER Erie
COLTON St. Lawrence
COLUMBIAVILLE Columbia
COMMACK Suffolk
COMSTOCK Washington
CONESUS Livingston
CONEWANGO VALLEY (14726) Cattaraugus(90), Chautauqua(10)
CONGERS Rockland
CONKLIN Broome
CONNELLY Ulster
CONSTABLE Franklin
CONSTABLEVILLE Lewis
CONSTANTIA Oswego
COOPERS PLAINS Steuben
COOPERSTOWN Otsego
COPAKE Columbia
COPAKE FALLS Columbia
COPENHAGEN (13626) Lewis(90), Jefferson(9)
COPIAGUE Suffolk
CORAM Suffolk
CORBETTSVILLE Broome
CORFU (14036) Genesee(97), Erie(2)
CORINTH Saratoga
CORNING Steuben
CORNWALL Orange
CORNWALL ON HUDSON Orange
CORNWALLVILLE Greene
CORTLAND (13045) Cortland(91), Cayuga(6), Tompkins(1)
CORTLANDT MANOR Westchester
COSSAYUNA Washington
COTTEKILL Ulster
COWLESVILLE (14037) Wyoming(76), Erie(23)
COXSACKIE Greene
CRAGSMOOR Ulster
CRANBERRY LAKE St. Lawrence
CRARYVILLE Columbia
CRITTENDEN Erie
CROGHAN Lewis
CROMPOND Westchester
CROPSEYVILLE Rensselaer
CROSS RIVER Westchester
CROTON FALLS Westchester
CROTON ON HUDSON Westchester
CROWN POINT Essex
CUBA (14727) Allegany(80), Cattaraugus(19)
CUDDEBACKVILLE Orange
CUTCHOGUE Suffolk
CUYLER (13050) Cortland(95), Onondaga(4)
DALE Wyoming
DALTON (14836) Livingston(58), Allegany(41)
DANNEMORA Clinton
DANSVILLE (14437) Livingston(91), Steuben(8)
DARIEN CENTER (14040) Genesee(87), Wyoming(12)
DAVENPORT Delaware
DAVENPORT CENTER Delaware
DAYTON Cattaraugus
DE KALB JUNCTION St. Lawrence
DE LANCEY Delaware
DE PEYSTER St. Lawrence
DE RUYTER (13052) Madison(86), Chenango(12), Onondaga(1)
DEANSBORO Oneida
DEER PARK Suffolk
DEER RIVER Lewis
DEFERIET Jefferson

DELANSON (12053) Schenectady(81), Albany(14), Schoharie(3)
DELEVAN Cattaraugus
DELHI Delaware
DELMAR Albany
DENMARK Lewis
DENVER Delaware
DEPAUVILLE Jefferson
DEPEW Erie
DEPOSIT (13754) Broome(62), Delaware(37)
DERBY Erie
DEWITTVILLE Chautauqua
DEXTER Jefferson
DIAMOND POINT Warren
DICKINSON CENTER Franklin
DOBBS FERRY Westchester
DOLGEVILLE (13329) Herkimer(95), Fulton(4)
DORMANSVILLE Albany
DOVER PLAINS Dutchess
DOWNSVILLE Delaware
DRESDEN Yates
DRYDEN (13053) Tompkins(83), Cortland(16)
DUANESBURG Schenectady
DUNDEE (14837) Yates(75), Schuyler(21), Steuben(2)
DUNKIRK Chautauqua
DURHAM Greene
DURHAMVILLE Oneida
EAGLE BAY Herkimer
EAGLE BRIDGE (12057) Rensselaer(80), Washington(19)
EAGLE HARBOR Orleans
EARLTON Greene
EARLVILLE (13332) Chenango(78), Madison(21)
EAST AMHERST Erie
EAST AURORA Erie
EAST BERNE Albany
EAST BETHANY (14054) Genesee(90), Wyoming(9)
EAST BLOOMFIELD Ontario
EAST BRANCH Delaware
EAST CHATHAM Columbia
EAST CONCORD Erie
EAST DURHAM Greene
EAST FREETOWN Cortland
EAST GREENBUSH Rensselaer
EAST GREENWICH Washington
EAST HAMPTON Suffolk
EAST HOMER Cortland
EAST ISLIP Suffolk
EAST JEWETT Greene
EAST MARION Suffolk
EAST MEADOW Nassau
EAST MEREDITH Delaware
EAST MORICHES Suffolk
EAST NASSAU (12062) Columbia(87), Rensselaer(12)
EAST NORTHPORT Suffolk
EAST NORWICH Nassau
EAST OTTO Cattaraugus
EAST PALMYRA Wayne
EAST PEMBROKE Genesee
EAST PHARSALIA Chenango
EAST QUOGUE Suffolk
EAST RANDOLPH Cattaraugus
EAST ROCHESTER Monroe
EAST ROCKAWAY Nassau
EAST SCHODACK Rensselaer
EAST SETAUKET Suffolk
EAST SPRINGFIELD Otsego
EAST SYRACUSE Onondaga
EAST WILLIAMSON Wayne
EAST WORCESTER Otsego
EASTCHESTER Westchester
EASTPORT Suffolk
EATON Madison
EDEN Erie

EDMESTON Otsego
EDWARDS St. Lawrence
ELBA (14058) Genesee(95), Orleans(4)
ELBRIDGE Onondaga
ELDRED Sullivan
ELIZABETHTOWN Essex
ELIZAVILLE Columbia
ELKA PARK Greene
ELLENBURG Clinton
ELLENBURG CENTER Clinton
ELLENBURG DEPOT Clinton
ELLENVILLE Ulster
ELLICOTTVILLE Cattaraugus
ELLINGTON Chautauqua
ELLISBURG Jefferson
ELMA Erie
ELMHURST Queens
ELMIRA Chemung
ELMONT Nassau
ELMSFORD Westchester
ENDICOTT Broome
ENDWELL Broome
ERIEVILLE Madison
ERIN Chemung
ESOPUS Ulster
ESPERANCE (12066) Montgomery(93), Schoharie(6)
ESSEX Essex
ETNA Tompkins
EVANS MILLS Jefferson
FABIUS Onondaga
FAIR HAVEN (13064) Oswego(94), Onondaga(5)
FAIRFIELD Herkimer
FAIRPORT Monroe
FALCONER Chautauqua
FALLSBURG Sullivan
FANCHER Orleans
FAR ROCKAWAY Queens
FARMERSVILLE STATION (14060) Allegany(55), Cattaraugus(44)
FARMINGDALE Nassau
FARMINGTON Ontario
FARMINGVILLE Suffolk
FARNHAM Erie
FAYETTE Seneca
FAYETTEVILLE Onondaga
FELTS MILLS Jefferson
FERNDALE Sullivan
FEURA BUSH Albany
FILLMORE Allegany
FINDLEY LAKE Chautauqua
FINE St. Lawrence
FISHERS Ontario
FISHERS ISLAND Suffolk
FISHERS LANDING Jefferson
FISHKILL Dutchess
FISHS EDDY Delaware
FLEISCHMANNS (12430) Greene(56), Delaware(43)
FLORAL PARK Queens
FLORIDA Orange
FLUSHING Queens
FLY CREEK Otsego
FONDA (12068) Montgomery(98), Fulton(1)
FORESTBURGH Sullivan
FORESTPORT (13338) Oneida(97), Herkimer(2)
FORESTVILLE Chautauqua
FORT ANN Washington
FORT COVINGTON Franklin
FORT DRUM Jefferson
FORT EDWARD (12828) Washington(56), Saratoga(43)
FORT HUNTER Montgomery
FORT JACKSON St. Lawrence
FORT JOHNSON Montgomery
FORT MONTGOMERY Orange
FORT PLAIN (13339) Montgomery(73), Herkimer(16), Fulton(10)
FRANKFORT Herkimer
FRANKLIN Delaware

FRANKLIN SPRINGS Oneida
FRANKLIN SQUARE Nassau
FRANKLINVILLE (14737) Cattaraugus(98),
   Allegany(1)
FREDONIA Chautauqua
FREEDOM (14065) Cattaraugus(53),
   Allegany(46)
FREEHOLD Greene
FREEPORT Nassau
FREEVILLE Tompkins
FREMONT CENTER Sullivan
FREWSBURG (14738) Chautauqua(90),
   Cattaraugus(9)
FRIENDSHIP Allegany
FULTON Oswego
FULTONHAM Schoharie
FULTONVILLE Montgomery
GABRIELS Franklin
GAINESVILLE Wyoming
GALLUPVILLE Schoharie
GALWAY Saratoga
GANSEVOORT Saratoga
GARDEN CITY Nassau
GARDINER Ulster
GARNERVILLE Rockland
GARRATTSVILLE Otsego
GARRISON Putnam
GASPORT Niagara
GENESEO Livingston
GENEVA (14456) Ontario(92), Seneca(6)
GENOA Cayuga
GEORGETOWN Chenango
GERMANTOWN Columbia
GERRY Chautauqua
GETZVILLE Erie
GHENT Columbia
GILBERTSVILLE Otsego
GILBOA Schoharie
GLASCO Ulster
GLEN AUBREY Broome
GLEN COVE Nassau
GLEN HEAD Nassau
GLEN OAKS Queens
GLEN SPEY Sullivan
GLEN WILD Sullivan
GLENFIELD Lewis
GLENFORD Ulster
GLENHAM Dutchess
GLENMONT Albany
GLENS FALLS Warren
GLENWOOD Erie
GLENWOOD LANDING Nassau
GLOVERSVILLE Fulton
GODEFFROY Orange
GOLDENS BRIDGE Westchester
GORHAM Ontario
GOSHEN Orange
GOUVERNEUR St. Lawrence
GOWANDA (14070) Cattaraugus(58),
   Erie(41)
GRAFTON Rensselaer
GRAHAMSVILLE (12740) Sullivan(89),
   Ulster(10)
GRAND GORGE Delaware
GRAND ISLAND Erie
GRANITE SPRINGS Westchester
GRANVILLE Washington
GREAT BEND Jefferson
GREAT NECK Nassau
GREAT RIVER Suffolk
GREAT VALLEY Cattaraugus
GREENE (13778) Chenango(67),
   Broome(32)
GREENFIELD CENTER Saratoga
GREENFIELD PARK Ulster
GREENHURST Chautauqua
GREENLAWN Suffolk
GREENPORT Suffolk
GREENVALE Nassau
GREENVILLE (12083) Greene(96),
   Albany(3)
GREENWICH Washington

GREENWOOD Steuben
GREENWOOD LAKE Orange
GREIG Lewis
GROTON (13073) Tompkins(98),
   Cayuga(1)
GROVELAND Livingston
GUILDERLAND Albany
GUILDERLAND CENTER Albany
GUILFORD Chenango
HADLEY Saratoga
HAGAMAN Montgomery
HAGUE Warren
HAILESBORO St. Lawrence
HAINES FALLS Greene
HALCOTTSVILLE Delaware
HALL Ontario
HAMBURG Erie
HAMDEN Delaware
HAMILTON Madison
HAMLIN (14464) Monroe(97), Orleans(2)
HAMMOND St. Lawrence
HAMMONDSPORT (14840) Steuben(97),
   Schuyler(2)
HAMPTON Washington
HAMPTON BAYS Suffolk
HANCOCK Delaware
HANKINS Sullivan
HANNACROIX (12087) Greene(98),
   Albany(1)
HANNAWA FALLS St. Lawrence
HANNIBAL Oswego
HARFORD Cortland
HARPERSFIELD Delaware
HARPURSVILLE (13787) Broome(96),
   Chenango(3)
HARRIMAN Orange
HARRIS Sullivan
HARRISON Westchester
HARRISVILLE (13648) St. Lawrence(63),
   Lewis(36)
HARTFORD Washington
HARTSDALE Westchester
HARTWICK Otsego
HARTWICK SEMINARY Otsego
HASTINGS Oswego
HASTINGS ON HUDSON Westchester
HAUPPAUGE Suffolk
HAVERSTRAW Rockland
HAWTHORNE Westchester
HECTOR Schuyler
HELENA St. Lawrence
HELMUTH Erie
HEMLOCK (14466) Ontario(57),
   Livingston(42)
HEMPSTEAD Nassau
HENDERSON Jefferson
HENDERSON HARBOR Jefferson
HENRIETTA Monroe
HENSONVILLE Greene
HERKIMER Herkimer
HERMON St. Lawrence
HEUVELTON St. Lawrence
HEWLETT Nassau
HICKSVILLE Nassau
HIGH FALLS Ulster
HIGHLAND Ulster
HIGHLAND FALLS Orange
HIGHLAND LAKE Sullivan
HIGHLAND MILLS Orange
HIGHMOUNT Ulster
HILLBURN Rockland
HILLSDALE Columbia
HILTON Monroe
HIMROD Yates
HINCKLEY Oneida
HINSDALE Cattaraugus
HOBART Delaware
HOFFMEISTER Hamilton
HOGANSBURG Franklin
HOLBROOK Suffolk
HOLLAND Erie
HOLLAND PATENT Oneida

HOLLEY (14470) Orleans(97), Monroe(2)
HOLLOWVILLE Columbia
HOLMES (12531) Dutchess(82),
   Putnam(17)
HOLTSVILLE Suffolk
HOMER Cortland
HONEOYE Ontario
HONEOYE FALLS (14472) Monroe(90),
   Livingston(6), Ontario(2)
HOOSICK Rensselaer
HOOSICK FALLS Rensselaer
HOPEWELL JUNCTION (12533)
   Dutchess(98), Putnam(1)
HOPKINTON St. Lawrence
HORNELL Steuben
HORSEHEADS Chemung
HORTONVILLE Sullivan
HOUGHTON Allegany
HOWELLS Orange
HOWES CAVE Schoharie
HUBBARDSVILLE Madison
HUDSON Columbia
HUDSON FALLS Washington
HUGHSONVILLE Dutchess
HUGUENOT Orange
HULETTS LANDING Washington
HUME Allegany
HUNT (14846) Livingston(76), Allegany(23)
HUNTER Greene
HUNTINGTON Suffolk
HUNTINGTON STATION Suffolk
HURLEY Ulster
HURLEYVILLE Sullivan
HYDE PARK Dutchess
ILION Herkimer
INDIAN LAKE Hamilton
INDUSTRY Monroe
INLET Hamilton
INTERLAKEN Seneca
INWOOD Queens
IONIA (14475) Ontario(91), Monroe(8)
IRVING (14081) Chautauqua(52), Erie(45),
   Cattaraugus(2)
IRVINGTON Westchester
ISLAND PARK Nassau
ISLANDIA Suffolk
ISLIP Suffolk
ISLIP TERRACE Suffolk
ITHACA Tompkins
JACKSONVILLE Tompkins
JAMAICA Queens
JAMESPORT Suffolk
JAMESTOWN Chautauqua
JAMESVILLE Onondaga
JASPER Steuben
JAVA CENTER Wyoming
JAVA VILLAGE Wyoming
JAY Essex
JEFFERSON (12093) Schoharie(63),
   Delaware(36)
JEFFERSON VALLEY Westchester
JEFFERSONVILLE Sullivan
JERICHO Nassau
JEWETT Greene
JOHNSBURG Warren
JOHNSON Orange
JOHNSON CITY Broome
JOHNSONVILLE Rensselaer
JOHNSTOWN Fulton
JORDAN Onondaga
JORDANVILLE Herkimer
KANONA Steuben
KATONAH Westchester
KATTSKILL BAY (12844) Warren(91),
   Washington(8)
KAUNEONGA LAKE Sullivan
KEENE Essex
KEENE VALLEY Essex
KEESEVILLE (12944) Clinton(92),
   Essex(7)
KENDALL (14476) Orleans(95), Monroe(4)

KENNEDY (14747) Chautauqua(88),
   Cattaraugus(11)
KENOZA LAKE Sullivan
KENT Orleans
KERHONKSON Ulster
KEUKA PARK Yates
KIAMESHA LAKE Sullivan
KILL BUCK Cattaraugus
KILLAWOG Broome
KINDERHOOK Columbia
KING FERRY Cayuga
KINGS PARK Suffolk
KINGSTON Ulster
KIRKVILLE (13082) Madison(56),
   Onondaga(43)
KIRKWOOD Broome
KNAPP CREEK Cattaraugus
KNOWLESVILLE Orleans
KNOX Albany
KNOXBORO Oneida
LA FARGEVILLE Jefferson
LA FAYETTE Onondaga
LACONA Oswego
LAGRANGEVILLE Dutchess
LAKE CLEAR Franklin
LAKE GEORGE Warren
LAKE GROVE Suffolk
LAKE HILL Ulster
LAKE HUNTINGTON Sullivan
LAKE KATRINE Ulster
LAKE LUZERNE Warren
LAKE PEEKSKILL Putnam
LAKE PLACID Essex
LAKE PLEASANT Hamilton
LAKE VIEW Erie
LAKEMONT Yates
LAKEVILLE Livingston
LAKEWOOD Chautauqua
LANCASTER Erie
LANESVILLE Greene
LANSING (14882) Tompkins(98),
   Cayuga(1)
LARCHMONT Westchester
LATHAM Albany
LAUREL Suffolk
LAURENS Otsego
LAWRENCE Nassau
LAWRENCEVILLE St. Lawrence
LAWTONS Erie
LAWYERSVILLE Schoharie
LE ROY (14482) Genesee(95),
   Livingston(3)
LEBANON Madison
LEBANON SPRINGS Columbia
LEE CENTER Oneida
LEEDS Greene
LEICESTER (14481) Livingston(98),
   Wyoming(1)
LEON Cattaraugus
LEONARDSVILLE Madison
LEVITTOWN Nassau
LEW BEACH (12753) Ulster(58),
   Sullivan(38), Delaware(4)
LEWIS Essex
LEWISTON Niagara
LEXINGTON Greene
LIBERTY Sullivan
LILY DALE Chautauqua
LIMA (14485) Livingston(94), Ontario(5)
LIMERICK Jefferson
LIMESTONE Cattaraugus
LINCOLNDALE Westchester
LINDENHURST Suffolk
LINDLEY Steuben
LINWOOD Genesee
LISBON St. Lawrence
LISLE Broome
LITTLE FALLS Herkimer
LITTLE GENESEE Allegany
LITTLE VALLEY Cattaraugus
LITTLE YORK Cortland
LIVERPOOL Onondaga

LIVINGSTON Columbia
LIVINGSTON MANOR (12758) Sullivan(94), Ulster(5)
LIVONIA (14487) Livingston(93), Ontario(6)
LIVONIA CENTER Livingston
LOCH SHELDRAKE Sullivan
LOCKE (13092) Tompkins(96), Cayuga(3)
LOCKPORT Niagara
LOCKWOOD (14859) Tioga(59), Chemung(40)
LOCUST VALLEY Nassau
LODI Seneca
LONG BEACH Nassau
LONG EDDY (12760) Delaware(60), Sullivan(39)
LONG ISLAND CITY Queens
LONG LAKE Hamilton
LORRAINE Jefferson
LOWMAN Chemung
LOWVILLE Lewis
LYCOMING Oswego
LYNBROOK Nassau
LYNDONVILLE (14098) Orleans(97), Niagara(2)
LYON MOUNTAIN (12955) Clinton(97), Franklin(2)
LYONS (14489) Wayne(95), Ontario(2), Seneca(2)
LYONS FALLS Lewis
LYSANDER Onondaga
MACEDON (14502) Wayne(97), Monroe(2)
MACHIAS Cattaraugus
MADISON (13402) Madison(81), Oneida(18)
MADRID St. Lawrence
MAHOPAC (10541) Putnam(98), Westchester(1)
MAHOPAC FALLS Putnam
MAINE Broome
MALDEN BRIDGE Columbia
MALDEN ON HUDSON Ulster
MALLORY Oswego
MALONE Franklin
MALVERNE Nassau
MAMARONECK Westchester
MANCHESTER Ontario
MANHASSET Nassau
MANLIUS (13104) Onondaga(98), Madison(1)
MANNSVILLE Jefferson
MANORVILLE Suffolk
MAPLE SPRINGS Chautauqua
MAPLE VIEW Oswego
MAPLECREST Greene
MARATHON (13803) Cortland(94), Broome(5)
MARCELLUS Onondaga
MARCY Oneida
MARGARETVILLE Delaware
MARIETTA Onondaga
MARILLA Erie
MARION Wayne
MARLBORO (12542) Ulster(93), Orange(6)
MARTINSBURG Lewis
MARTVILLE (13111) Cayuga(88), Oswego(11)
MARYKNOLL Westchester
MARYLAND Otsego
MASONVILLE Delaware
MASSAPEQUA Nassau
MASSAPEQUA PARK Nassau
MASSENA St. Lawrence
MASTIC Suffolk
MASTIC BEACH Suffolk
MATTITUCK Suffolk
MATTYDALE Onondaga
MAYBROOK Orange
MAYFIELD Fulton
MAYVILLE Chautauqua
MC CONNELLSVILLE Oneida
MC DONOUGH Chenango
MC GRAW Cortland

MC LEAN Tompkins
MECHANICVILLE (12118) Saratoga(98), Rensselaer(1)
MECKLENBURG Schuyler
MEDFORD Suffolk
MEDINA Orleans
MEDUSA Albany
MELLENVILLE Columbia
MELROSE Rensselaer
MELVILLE Suffolk
MEMPHIS Onondaga
MENDON Monroe
MERIDALE Delaware
MERIDIAN Cayuga
MERRICK Nassau
MEXICO Oswego
MID HUDSON Orange
MID ISLAND Suffolk
MIDDLE FALLS Washington
MIDDLE GRANVILLE Washington
MIDDLE GROVE Saratoga
MIDDLE ISLAND Suffolk
MIDDLEBURGH (12122) Albany(55), Schoharie(44)
MIDDLEPORT (14105) Niagara(94), Orleans(4), Genesee(1)
MIDDLESEX Yates
MIDDLETOWN Orange
MIDDLEVILLE Herkimer
MILFORD Otsego
MILL NECK Nassau
MILLBROOK Dutchess
MILLER PLACE Suffolk
MILLERTON (12546) Dutchess(96), Columbia(3)
MILLPORT (14864) Chemung(85), Schuyler(14)
MILLWOOD Westchester
MILTON Ulster
MINEOLA Nassau
MINERVA Essex
MINETTO Oswego
MINEVILLE Essex
MINOA Onondaga
MODEL CITY Niagara
MODENA Ulster
MOHAWK Herkimer
MOHEGAN LAKE Westchester
MOIRA Franklin
MONGAUP VALLEY Sullivan
MONROE Orange
MONSEY Rockland
MONTAUK Suffolk
MONTEZUMA Cayuga
MONTGOMERY Orange
MONTICELLO Sullivan
MONTOUR FALLS Schuyler
MONTROSE Westchester
MOOERS Clinton
MOOERS FORKS Clinton
MORAVIA Cayuga
MORIAH Essex
MORIAH CENTER Essex
MORICHES Suffolk
MORRIS Otsego
MORRISONVILLE Clinton
MORRISTOWN St. Lawrence
MORRISVILLE Madison
MORTON Orleans
MOTTVILLE Onondaga
MOUNT KISCO Westchester
MOUNT MARION Ulster
MOUNT MORRIS Livingston
MOUNT SINAI Suffolk
MOUNT TREMPER Ulster
MOUNT UPTON (13809) Chenango(66), Otsego(33)
MOUNT VERNON Westchester
MOUNT VISION Otsego
MOUNTAIN DALE Sullivan
MOUNTAINVILLE Orange
MUMFORD Monroe

MUNNSVILLE Madison
NANUET Rockland
NAPANOCH Ulster
NAPLES (14512) Ontario(74), Yates(20), Steuben(3)
NARROWSBURG Sullivan
NASSAU Rensselaer
NATURAL BRIDGE (13665) Jefferson(72), Lewis(27)
NEDROW Onondaga
NELLISTON Montgomery
NESCONSET Suffolk
NEVERSINK Sullivan
NEW BALTIMORE Greene
NEW BERLIN Chenango
NEW CITY Rockland
NEW HAMPTON Orange
NEW HARTFORD Oneida
NEW HAVEN Oswego
NEW HYDE PARK Nassau
NEW KINGSTON Delaware
NEW LEBANON Columbia
NEW LISBON Otsego
NEW MILFORD Orange
NEW PALTZ Ulster
NEW ROCHELLE Westchester
NEW RUSSIA Essex
NEW SUFFOLK Suffolk
NEW WINDSOR Orange
NEW WOODSTOCK (13122) Onondaga(64), Madison(35)
NEW YORK New York
NEW YORK MILLS Oneida
NEWARK (14513) Wayne(97), Ontario(2)
NEWARK VALLEY (13811) Tioga(93), Broome(6)
NEWBURGH Orange
NEWCOMB Essex
NEWFANE Niagara
NEWFIELD Tompkins
NEWPORT Herkimer
NEWTON FALLS St. Lawrence
NEWTONVILLE Albany
NIAGARA FALLS Niagara
NIAGARA UNIVERSITY Niagara
NICHOLS Tioga
NICHOLVILLE St. Lawrence
NINEVEH (13813) Broome(90), Chenango(9)
NIOBE Chautauqua
NIVERVILLE Columbia
NORFOLK St. Lawrence
NORTH BABYLON Suffolk
NORTH BANGOR Franklin
NORTH BAY Oneida
NORTH BLENHEIM Schoharie
NORTH BOSTON Erie
NORTH BRANCH Sullivan
NORTH BROOKFIELD Madison
NORTH CHATHAM Columbia
NORTH CHILI Monroe
NORTH CLYMER Chautauqua
NORTH COHOCTON Steuben
NORTH COLLINS Erie
NORTH CREEK Warren
NORTH EVANS Erie
NORTH GRANVILLE Washington
NORTH GREECE Monroe
NORTH HOOSICK Rensselaer
NORTH HUDSON Essex
NORTH JAVA Wyoming
NORTH LAWRENCE (12967) St. Lawrence(98), Franklin(1)
NORTH NORWICH Chenango
NORTH PITCHER Chenango
NORTH RIVER Warren
NORTH ROSE Wayne
NORTH SALEM Westchester
NORTH TONAWANDA Niagara
NORTHPORT Suffolk
NORTHVILLE Fulton
NORTON HILL Greene

NORWICH Chenango
NORWOOD St. Lawrence
NUNDA Livingston
NYACK Rockland
OAK HILL Greene
OAKDALE Suffolk
OAKFIELD Genesee
OAKS CORNERS Ontario
OBERNBURG Sullivan
OCEAN BEACH Suffolk
OCEANSIDE Nassau
ODESSA Schuyler
OGDENSBURG St. Lawrence
OLCOTT Niagara
OLD BETHPAGE Nassau
OLD CHATHAM Columbia
OLD FORGE Herkimer
OLD WESTBURY Nassau
OLEAN Cattaraugus
OLIVEBRIDGE Ulster
OLIVEREA Ulster
OLMSTEDVILLE (12857) Essex(97), Warren(2)
ONCHIOTA Franklin
ONEIDA (13421) Madison(90), Oneida(9)
ONEONTA (13820) Otsego(96), Delaware(3)
ONTARIO (14519) Wayne(96), Monroe(3)
ONTARIO CENTER Wayne
ORAN Onondaga
ORANGEBURG Rockland
ORCHARD PARK Erie
ORIENT Suffolk
ORISKANY Oneida
ORISKANY FALLS Oneida
ORWELL Oswego
OSSINING Westchester
OSWEGATCHIE St. Lawrence
OSWEGO Oswego
OTEGO (13825) Otsego(97), Delaware(2)
OTISVILLE (10963) Orange(98), Sullivan(1)
OTTO Cattaraugus
OUAQUAGA Broome
OVID Seneca
OWASCO Cayuga
OWEGO Tioga
OWLS HEAD Franklin
OXBOW Jefferson
OXFORD Chenango
OYSTER BAY Nassau
PAINTED POST (14870) Steuben(97), Schuyler(2)
PALATINE BRIDGE Montgomery
PALENVILLE Greene
PALISADES Rockland
PALMYRA (14522) Wayne(89), Ontario(10)
PANAMA Chautauqua
PARADOX Essex
PARIS Oneida
PARISH Oswego
PARISHVILLE St. Lawrence
PARKSVILLE Sullivan
PATCHOGUE Suffolk
PATTERSON Putnam
PATTERSONVILLE Schenectady
PAUL SMITHS Franklin
PAVILION (14525) Genesee(61), Wyoming(33), Livingston(5)
PAWLING Dutchess
PEARL RIVER Rockland
PECONIC Suffolk
PEEKSKILL Westchester
PELHAM Westchester
PENFIELD Monroe
PENN YAN Yates
PENNELLVILLE Oswego
PERKINSVILLE Steuben
PERRY Wyoming
PERRYSBURG Cattaraugus
PERRYVILLE Madison
PERU Clinton

PETERBORO Madison
PETERSBURG Rensselaer
PHELPS (14532) Ontario(94), Seneca(5)
PHILADELPHIA Jefferson
PHILLIPSPORT Sullivan
PHILMONT Columbia
PHOENICIA Ulster
PHOENIX (13135) Oswego(90), Onondaga(9)
PIERCEFIELD St. Lawrence
PIERMONT Rockland
PIERREPONT MANOR Jefferson
PIFFARD Livingston
PIKE Wyoming
PINE BUSH (12566) Ulster(58), Orange(37), Sullivan(3)
PINE CITY (14871) Chemung(85), Steuben(14)
PINE HILL (12465) Ulster(92), Delaware(7)
PINE ISLAND Orange
PINE PLAINS (12567) Dutchess(91), Columbia(8)
PINE VALLEY Chemung
PISECO Hamilton
PITCHER (13136) Chenango(96), Cortland(3)
PITTSFORD Monroe
PLAINVIEW Nassau
PLAINVILLE Onondaga
PLATTEKILL Ulster
PLATTSBURGH Clinton
PLEASANT VALLEY Dutchess
PLEASANTVILLE Westchester
PLESSIS Jefferson
PLYMOUTH Chenango
POESTENKILL Rensselaer
POINT LOOKOUT Nassau
POLAND (13431) Oneida(90), Herkimer(9)
POMONA Rockland
POMPEY Onondaga
POND EDDY Sullivan
POOLVILLE Madison
POPLAR RIDGE Cayuga
PORT BYRON Cayuga
PORT CHESTER Westchester
PORT CRANE Broome
PORT EWEN Ulster
PORT GIBSON Ontario
PORT HENRY Essex
PORT JEFFERSON Suffolk
PORT JEFFERSON STATION Suffolk
PORT JERVIS Orange
PORT KENT Essex
PORT LEYDEN Lewis
PORT WASHINGTON Nassau
PORTAGEVILLE (14536) Wyoming(73), Allegany(26)
PORTER CORNERS Saratoga
PORTLAND Chautauqua
PORTLANDVILLE Otsego
PORTVILLE (14770) Cattaraugus(74), Allegany(25)
POTSDAM St. Lawrence
POTTERSVILLE Warren
POUGHKEEPSIE Dutchess
POUGHQUAG Dutchess
POUND RIDGE Westchester
PRATTS HOLLOW Madison
PRATTSBURGH (14873) Steuben(98), Yates(1)
PRATTSVILLE Greene
PREBLE (13141) Cortland(64), Onondaga(35)
PRESTON HOLLOW (12469) Albany(75), Greene(16), Schoharie(7)
PROSPECT Oneida
PULASKI Oswego
PULTENEY Steuben
PULTNEYVILLE Wayne
PURCHASE Westchester
PURDYS Westchester
PURLING Greene

PUTNAM STATION Washington
PUTNAM VALLEY Putnam
PYRITES St. Lawrence
QUAKER STREET Schenectady
QUEENS VILLAGE Queens
QUEENSBURY Warren
QUOGUE Suffolk
RAINBOW LAKE Franklin
RANDOLPH Cattaraugus
RANSOMVILLE Niagara
RAQUETTE LAKE Hamilton
RAVENA Albany
RAY BROOK Essex
RAYMONDVILLE St. Lawrence
READING CENTER Schuyler
RED CREEK (13143) Wayne(98), Cayuga(1)
RED HOOK (12571) Dutchess(98), Columbia(1)
REDFIELD (13437) Oswego(97), Lewis(2)
REDFORD Clinton
REDWOOD Jefferson
REMSEN (13438) Oneida(97), Herkimer(2)
REMSENBURG Suffolk
RENSSELAER Rensselaer
RENSSELAER FALLS St. Lawrence
RENSSELAERVILLE Albany
RETSOF Livingston
REXFORD (12148) Saratoga(96), Schenectady(3)
REXVILLE (14877) Steuben(98), Allegany(1)
RHINEBECK Dutchess
RHINECLIFF Dutchess
RICHBURG Allegany
RICHFIELD SPRINGS (13439) Otsego(91), Herkimer(8)
RICHFORD (13835) Tioga(56), Broome(30), Cortland(13)
RICHLAND Oswego
RICHMOND HILL Queens
RICHMONDVILLE (12149) Schoharie(88), Otsego(11)
RICHVILLE St. Lawrence
RIDGE Suffolk
RIFTON Ulster
RIPARIUS Warren
RIPLEY Chautauqua
RIVERHEAD Suffolk
ROCHESTER Monroe
ROCK CITY FALLS Saratoga
ROCK HILL Sullivan
ROCK STREAM (14878) Schuyler(70), Yates(29)
ROCK TAVERN Orange
ROCKLAND M P C Rockland
ROCKVILLE CENTRE Nassau
ROCKY POINT Suffolk
RODMAN (13682) Jefferson(95), Lewis(4)
ROME Oneida
ROMULUS Seneca
RONKONKOMA Suffolk
ROOSEVELT Nassau
ROOSEVELTOWN St. Lawrence
ROSCOE (12776) Sullivan(73), Delaware(26)
ROSE Wayne
ROSEBOOM Otsego
ROSENDALE Ulster
ROSLYN Nassau
ROSLYN HEIGHTS Nassau
ROSSBURG Allegany
ROTTERDAM JUNCTION Schenectady
ROUND LAKE Saratoga
ROUND TOP Greene
ROUSES POINT Clinton
ROXBURY Delaware
RUBY Ulster
RUSH Monroe
RUSHFORD Allegany
RUSHVILLE (14544) Yates(54), Ontario(45)

RUSSELL St. Lawrence
RYE Westchester
SABAEL Hamilton
SACKETS HARBOR Jefferson
SAG HARBOR Suffolk
SAGAPONACK Suffolk
SAINT BONAVENTURE Cattaraugus
SAINT JAMES Suffolk
SAINT JOHNSVILLE (13452) Montgomery(91), Fulton(8)
SAINT REGIS FALLS (12980) Franklin(98), St. Lawrence(1)
SALAMANCA Cattaraugus
SALEM (12865) Albany(86), Washington(13)
SALISBURY CENTER Herkimer
SALISBURY MILLS Orange
SALT POINT Dutchess
SANBORN Niagara
SAND LAKE Rensselaer
SANDUSKY Cattaraugus
SANDY CREEK Oswego
SANGERFIELD Oneida
SARANAC Clinton
SARANAC LAKE (12983) Franklin(82), Essex(17)
SARATOGA SPRINGS Saratoga
SARDINIA Erie
SAUGERTIES Ulster
SAUQUOIT (13456) Oneida(90), Herkimer(9)
SAVANNAH Wayne
SAVONA Steuben
SAYVILLE Suffolk
SCARSDALE Westchester
SCHAGHTICOKE Rensselaer
SCHENECTADY Schenectady
SCHENEVUS (12155) Otsego(97), Delaware(2)
SCHODACK LANDING (12156) Rensselaer(91), Columbia(9)
SCHOHARIE Schoharie
SCHROON LAKE (12870) Essex(89), Warren(10)
SCHUYLER FALLS Clinton
SCHUYLER LAKE Otsego
SCHUYLERVILLE Saratoga
SCIO Allegany
SCIPIO CENTER Cayuga
SCOTTSBURG Livingston
SCOTTSVILLE Monroe
SEA CLIFF Nassau
SEAFORD Nassau
SELDEN Suffolk
SELKIRK Albany
SENECA CASTLE Ontario
SENECA FALLS Seneca
SENNETT Cayuga
SEVERANCE Essex
SHANDAKEN (12480) Ulster(76), Greene(23)
SHARON SPRINGS (13459) Schoharie(94), Montgomery(5)
SHEDS Madison
SHELTER ISLAND Suffolk
SHELTER ISLAND HEIGHTS Suffolk
SHENOROCK Westchester
SHERBURNE Chenango
SHERIDAN Chautauqua
SHERMAN Chautauqua
SHERRILL Oneida
SHINHOPPLE Delaware
SHIRLEY Suffolk
SHOKAN Ulster
SHOREHAM Suffolk
SHORTSVILLE Ontario
SHRUB OAK Westchester
SHUSHAN Washington
SIDNEY (13838) Delaware(94), Otsego(5)
SIDNEY CENTER Delaware
SILVER BAY Warren
SILVER CREEK Chautauqua

SILVER LAKE Wyoming
SILVER SPRINGS Wyoming
SINCLAIRVILLE Chautauqua
SKANEATELES (13152) Onondaga(91), Cayuga(8)
SKANEATELES FALLS Onondaga
SLATE HILL Orange
SLATERVILLE SPRINGS Tompkins
SLINGERLANDS Albany
SLOANSVILLE Schoharie
SLOATSBURG Rockland
SMALLWOOD Sullivan
SMITHBORO Tioga
SMITHS LANDING Greene
SMITHTOWN Suffolk
SMITHVILLE FLATS (13841) Cortland(53), Chenango(43), Broome(3)
SMYRNA Chenango
SODUS Wayne
SODUS CENTER Wayne
SODUS POINT Wayne
SOLSVILLE Madison
SOMERS Westchester
SONYEA Livingston
SOUND BEACH Suffolk
SOUTH BETHLEHEM Albany
SOUTH BUTLER Wayne
SOUTH BYRON Genesee
SOUTH CAIRO Greene
SOUTH COLTON St. Lawrence
SOUTH DAYTON (14138) Cattaraugus(65), Chautauqua(34)
SOUTH EDMESTON Otsego
SOUTH FALLSBURG Sullivan
SOUTH GLENS FALLS Saratoga
SOUTH JAMESPORT Suffolk
SOUTH KORTRIGHT Delaware
SOUTH LIMA Livingston
SOUTH NEW BERLIN (13843) Chenango(98), Otsego(1)
SOUTH OTSELIC Chenango
SOUTH PLYMOUTH Chenango
SOUTH RUTLAND Jefferson
SOUTH SALEM Westchester
SOUTH SCHODACK Rensselaer
SOUTH WALES Erie
SOUTH WESTERLO Albany
SOUTHAMPTON Suffolk
SOUTHFIELDS Orange
SOUTHOLD Suffolk
SPARKILL Rockland
SPARROW BUSH (12780) Orange(81), Sullivan(18)
SPECULATOR Hamilton
SPENCER (14883) Tioga(79), Tompkins(19)
SPENCERPORT Monroe
SPENCERTOWN Columbia
SPEONK Suffolk
SPRAKERS Montgomery
SPRING BROOK Erie
SPRING GLEN Ulster
SPRING VALLEY Rockland
SPRINGFIELD CENTER Otsego
SPRINGVILLE (14141) Erie(94), Cattaraugus(5)
SPRINGWATER (14560) Livingston(51), Ontario(48)
STAATSBURG Dutchess
STAFFORD Genesee
STAMFORD (12167) Delaware(85), Schoharie(14)
STANFORDVILLE Dutchess
STANLEY (14561) Ontario(94), Yates(5)
STAR LAKE St. Lawrence
STATEN ISLAND Richmond
STEAMBURG Cattaraugus
STELLA NIAGARA Niagara
STEPHENTOWN Rensselaer
STERLING Cayuga
STERLING FOREST Orange
STILLWATER Saratoga

STITTVILLE Oneida
STOCKTON Chautauqua
STONE RIDGE Ulster
STONY BROOK Suffolk
STONY CREEK Warren
STONY POINT Rockland
STORMVILLE (12582) Dutchess(98),
    Putnam(1)
STOTTVILLE Columbia
STOW Chautauqua
STRATFORD (13470) Fulton(97),
    Herkimer(2)
STRYKERSVILLE (14145) Wyoming(92),
    Erie(7)
STUYVESANT Columbia
STUYVESANT FALLS Columbia
SUFFERN Rockland
SUGAR LOAF Orange
SUGARBUSH Franklin
SUMMIT Schoharie
SUMMITVILLE Sullivan
SUNDOWN Ulster
SURPRISE Greene
SWAIN Allegany
SWAN LAKE Sullivan
SYLVAN BEACH Oneida
SYOSSET Nassau
SYRACUSE Onondaga
TABERG Oneida
TALLMAN Rockland
TANNERSVILLE Greene
TAPPAN Rockland
TARRYTOWN Westchester
THENDARA Herkimer
THERESA Jefferson
THIELLS Rockland
THOMPSON RIDGE Orange
THOMPSONVILLE Sullivan
THORNWOOD Westchester
THOUSAND ISLAND PARK Jefferson
THREE MILE BAY Jefferson
TICONDEROGA Essex
TILLSON Ulster
TIOGA CENTER Tioga
TIVOLI (12583) Dutchess(62),
    Columbia(37)
TOMKINS COVE Rockland
TONAWANDA Erie
TREADWELL Delaware
TRIBES HILL Montgomery
TROUPSBURG Steuben
TROUT CREEK Delaware
TROY Albany
TRUMANSBURG (14886) Tompkins(61),
    Schuyler(25), Seneca(13)
TRUXTON Cortland
TUCKAHOE Westchester
TULLY (13159) Onondaga(87),
    Cortland(12)
TUNNEL Broome
TUPPER LAKE (12986) Franklin(93), St.
    Lawrence(6)
TURIN Lewis
TUXEDO PARK Orange

TYRONE Schuyler
ULSTER PARK Ulster
UNADILLA (13849) Otsego(77),
    Delaware(22)
UNION HILL Wayne
UNION SPRINGS Cayuga
UNIONDALE Nassau
UNIONVILLE Orange
UPPER JAY Essex
UPTON Suffolk
UTICA Oneida
VAILS GATE Orange
VALATIE Columbia
VALHALLA Westchester
VALLEY COTTAGE Rockland
VALLEY FALLS Rensselaer
VALLEY STREAM Nassau
VALOIS (14888) Schuyler(82), Seneca(17)
VAN BUREN POINT Chautauqua
VAN ETTEN (14889) Chemung(87),
    Schuyler(7), Tioga(5)
VAN HORNESVILLE (13475)
    Herkimer(83), Otsego(16)
VARYSBURG Wyoming
VERBANK Dutchess
VERMONTVILLE Franklin
VERNON Oneida
VERNON CENTER Oneida
VERONA Oneida
VERONA BEACH Oneida
VERPLANCK Westchester
VERSAILLES Cattaraugus
VESTAL Broome
VICTOR (14564) Ontario(97), Monroe(2)
VICTORY MILLS Saratoga
VOORHEESVILLE Albany
WACCABUC Westchester
WADDINGTON St. Lawrence
WADHAMS Essex
WADING RIVER Suffolk
WAINSCOTT Suffolk
WALDEN Orange
WALES CENTER Erie
WALKER VALLEY Ulster
WALLKILL (12589) Ulster(78), Orange(21)
WALTON Delaware
WALWORTH Wayne
WAMPSVILLE Madison
WANAKENA St. Lawrence
WANTAGH Nassau
WAPPINGERS FALLS Dutchess
WARNERS Onondaga
WARNERVILLE Schoharie
WARRENSBURG Warren
WARSAW Wyoming
WARWICK Orange
WASHINGTON MILLS Oneida
WASHINGTONVILLE Orange
WASSAIC Dutchess
WATER MILL Suffolk
WATERFORD Saratoga
WATERLOO Seneca
WATERPORT Orleans
WATERTOWN Jefferson

WATERVILLE (13480) Oneida(98),
    Madison(1)
WATERVLIET Albany
WATKINS GLEN Schuyler
WAVERLY (14892) Tioga(91), Chemung(8)
WAWARSING Ulster
WAYLAND (14572) Steuben(79),
    Livingston(20)
WAYNE Schuyler
WEBSTER Monroe
WEBSTER CROSSING Livingston
WEEDSPORT (13166) Cayuga(98),
    Onondaga(1)
WELLESLEY ISLAND Jefferson
WELLS Hamilton
WELLS BRIDGE (13859) Otsego(95),
    Delaware(4)
WELLSBURG Chemung
WELLSVILLE Allegany
WEST BABYLON Suffolk
WEST BLOOMFIELD Ontario
WEST BURLINGTON Otsego
WEST CAMP Ulster
WEST CHAZY Clinton
WEST CLARKSVILLE Allegany
WEST COPAKE Columbia
WEST COXSACKIE Greene
WEST DANBY Tompkins
WEST DAVENPORT Delaware
WEST EATON Madison
WEST EDMESTON (13485) Otsego(79),
    Madison(20)
WEST EXETER Otsego
WEST FALLS Erie
WEST FULTON Schoharie
WEST HARRISON Westchester
WEST HAVERSTRAW Rockland
WEST HEMPSTEAD Nassau
WEST HENRIETTA Monroe
WEST HURLEY Ulster
WEST ISLIP Suffolk
WEST KILL Greene
WEST LEBANON Columbia
WEST LEYDEN (13489) Lewis(98),
    Oneida(2)
WEST MONROE Oswego
WEST NYACK Rockland
WEST ONEONTA Otsego
WEST PARK Ulster
WEST POINT Orange
WEST SAND LAKE Rensselaer
WEST SAYVILLE Suffolk
WEST SHOKAN Ulster
WEST STOCKHOLM St. Lawrence
WEST VALLEY Cattaraugus
WEST WINFIELD (13491) Herkimer(89),
    Otsego(6), Oneida(2)
WESTBROOKVILLE Sullivan
WESTBURY Nassau
WESTDALE (13483) Oneida(97),
    Oswego(2)
WESTERLO Albany
WESTERN Oneida
WESTERNVILLE Oneida

WESTFIELD Chautauqua
WESTFORD Otsego
WESTHAMPTON Suffolk
WESTHAMPTON BEACH Suffolk
WESTMORELAND Oneida
WESTONS MILLS Cattaraugus
WESTPORT Essex
WESTTOWN Orange
WEVERTOWN Warren
WHALLONSBURG Essex
WHIPPLEVILLE Franklin
WHITE LAKE Sullivan
WHITE PLAINS Westchester
WHITE SULPHUR SPRINGS Sullivan
WHITEHALL Washington
WHITESBORO Oneida
WHITESVILLE (14897) Allegany(95),
    Steuben(4)
WHITNEY POINT Broome
WILLARD Seneca
WILLET (13863) Cortland(98), Broome(1)
WILLIAMSON Wayne
WILLIAMSTOWN Oswego
WILLISTON PARK Nassau
WILLOW Ulster
WILLSBORO Essex
WILLSEYVILLE (13864) Tioga(68),
    Tompkins(31)
WILMINGTON (12997) Essex(80),
    Saratoga(20)
WILSON Niagara
WINDHAM Greene
WINDSOR Broome
WINGDALE Dutchess
WINTHROP St. Lawrence
WITHERBEE Essex
WOLCOTT Wayne
WOODBOURNE (12788) Sullivan(97),
    Ulster(2)
WOODBURY Nassau
WOODGATE Oneida
WOODHULL Steuben
WOODMERE Nassau
WOODRIDGE Sullivan
WOODSTOCK Ulster
WOODVILLE Jefferson
WORCESTER Otsego
WURTSBORO Sullivan
WYANDANCH Suffolk
WYNANTSKILL Rensselaer
WYOMING (14591) Wyoming(87),
    Genesee(12)
YAPHANK Suffolk
YONKERS Westchester
YORK Livingston
YORKSHIRE Cattaraugus
YORKTOWN HEIGHTS Westchester
YORKVILLE Oneida
YOUNGSTOWN Niagara
YOUNGSVILLE Sullivan
YULAN Sullivan

ZIP/City Cross Reference

00401-00401	PLEASANTVILLE	
00501-00544	HOLTSVILLE	
06390-06390	FISHERS ISLAND	
09002-09894	APO or FPO	
10000-10292	NEW YORK	
10300-10314	STATEN ISLAND	
10400-10499	BRONX	
10501-10501	AMAWALK	
10502-10502	ARDSLEY	
10503-10503	ARDSLEY ON HUDSON	
10504-10504	ARMONK	
10505-10505	BALDWIN PLACE	
10506-10506	BEDFORD	
10507-10507	BEDFORD HILLS	
10509-10509	BREWSTER	
10510-10510	BRIARCLIFF MANOR	
10511-10511	BUCHANAN	
10512-10512	CARMEL	
10514-10514	CHAPPAQUA	
10516-10516	COLD SPRING	
10517-10517	CROMPOND	
10518-10518	CROSS RIVER	
10519-10519	CROTON FALLS	
10520-10521	CROTON ON HUDSON	
10522-10522	DOBBS FERRY	
10523-10523	ELMSFORD	
10524-10524	GARRISON	
10526-10526	GOLDENS BRIDGE	
10527-10527	GRANITE SPRINGS	
10528-10528	HARRISON	
10530-10530	HARTSDALE	
10532-10532	HAWTHORNE	
10533-10533	IRVINGTON	
10535-10535	JEFFERSON VALLEY	
10536-10536	KATONAH	
10537-10537	LAKE PEEKSKILL	
10538-10538	LARCHMONT	
10540-10540	LINCOLNDALE	
10541-10541	MAHOPAC	
10542-10542	MAHOPAC FALLS	
10543-10543	MAMARONECK	
10545-10545	MARYKNOLL	
10546-10546	MILLWOOD	
10547-10547	MOHEGAN LAKE	
10548-10548	MONTROSE	
10549-10549	MOUNT KISCO	
10550-10559	MOUNT VERNON	
10560-10560	NORTH SALEM	
10562-10562	OSSINING	
10566-10566	PEEKSKILL	
10567-10567	CORTLANDT MANOR	
10570-10572	PLEASANTVILLE	
10573-10573	PORT CHESTER	
10576-10576	POUND RIDGE	
10577-10577	PURCHASE	
10578-10578	PURDYS	
10579-10579	PUTNAM VALLEY	
10580-10581	RYE	
10583-10583	SCARSDALE	
10587-10587	SHENOROCK	

ZIP Range	Place	ZIP Range	Place	ZIP Range	Place	ZIP Range	Place
10588-10588	SHRUB OAK	10996-10997	WEST POINT	11714-11714	BETHPAGE	11853-11853	JERICHO
10589-10589	SOMERS	10998-10998	WESTTOWN	11715-11715	BLUE POINT	11854-11855	HICKSVILLE
10590-10590	SOUTH SALEM	11001-11002	FLORAL PARK	11716-11716	BOHEMIA	11901-11901	RIVERHEAD
10591-10592	TARRYTOWN	11003-11003	ELMONT	11717-11717	BRENTWOOD	11930-11930	AMAGANSETT
10594-10594	THORNWOOD	11004-11004	GLEN OAKS	11718-11718	BRIGHTWATERS	11931-11931	AQUEBOGUE
10595-10595	VALHALLA	11005-11005	FLORAL PARK	11719-11719	BROOKHAVEN	11932-11932	BRIDGEHAMPTON
10596-10596	VERPLANCK	11010-11010	FRANKLIN SQUARE	11720-11720	CENTEREACH	11933-11933	CALVERTON
10597-10597	WACCABUC	11020-11027	GREAT NECK	11721-11721	CENTERPORT	11934-11934	CENTER MORICHES
10598-10598	YORKTOWN HEIGHTS	11030-11030	MANHASSET	11722-11722	CENTRAL ISLIP	11935-11935	CUTCHOGUE
10600-10603	WHITE PLAINS	11040-11044	NEW HYDE PARK	11724-11724	COLD SPRING HARBOR	11937-11937	EAST HAMPTON
10604-10604	WEST HARRISON	11050-11055	PORT WASHINGTON	11725-11725	COMMACK	11939-11939	EAST MARION
10605-10650	WHITE PLAINS	11096-11096	INWOOD	11726-11726	COPIAGUE	11940-11940	EAST MORICHES
10700-10705	YONKERS	11099-11099	NEW HYDE PARK	11727-11727	CORAM	11941-11941	EASTPORT
10706-10706	HASTINGS ON HUDSON	11100-11120	LONG ISLAND CITY	11729-11729	DEER PARK	11942-11942	EAST QUOGUE
10707-10707	TUCKAHOE	11200-11256	BROOKLYN	11730-11730	EAST ISLIP	11944-11944	GREENPORT
10708-10708	BRONXVILLE	11300-11359	FLUSHING	11731-11731	EAST NORTHPORT	11946-11946	HAMPTON BAYS
10709-10709	EASTCHESTER	11359-11359	BAYSIDE	11732-11732	EAST NORWICH	11947-11947	JAMESPORT
10710-10710	YONKERS	11360-11380	FLUSHING	11733-11733	EAST SETAUKET	11948-11948	LAUREL
10800-10802	NEW ROCHELLE	11380-11380	ELMHURST	11735-11737	FARMINGDALE	11949-11949	MANORVILLE
10803-10803	PELHAM	11381-11390	FLUSHING	11738-11738	FARMINGVILLE	11950-11950	MASTIC
10804-10805	NEW ROCHELLE	11400-11418	JAMAICA	11739-11739	GREAT RIVER	11951-11951	MASTIC BEACH
10901-10901	SUFFERN	11418-11418	RICHMOND HILL	11740-11740	GREENLAWN	11952-11952	MATTITUCK
10910-10910	ARDEN	11419-11427	JAMAICA	11741-11741	HOLBROOK	11953-11953	MIDDLE ISLAND
10911-10911	BEAR MOUNTAIN	11427-11427	QUEENS VILLAGE	11742-11742	HOLTSVILLE	11954-11954	MONTAUK
10912-10912	BELLVALE	11428-11499	JAMAICA	11743-11743	HUNTINGTON	11955-11955	MORICHES
10913-10913	BLAUVELT	11501-11501	MINEOLA	11745-11745	SMITHTOWN	11956-11956	NEW SUFFOLK
10914-10914	BLOOMING GROVE	11507-11507	ALBERTSON	11746-11746	HUNTINGTON STATION	11957-11957	ORIENT
10915-10915	BULLVILLE	11509-11509	ATLANTIC BEACH	11747-11747	MELVILLE	11958-11958	PECONIC
10916-10916	CAMPBELL HALL	11510-11510	BALDWIN	11749-11749	FARMINGVILLE	11959-11959	QUOGUE
10917-10917	CENTRAL VALLEY	11514-11514	CARLE PLACE	11749-11749	ISLANDIA	11960-11960	REMSENBURG
10918-10918	CHESTER	11516-11516	CEDARHURST	11750-11750	HUNTINGTON STATION	11961-11961	RIDGE
10919-10919	CIRCLEVILLE	11518-11518	EAST ROCKAWAY	11751-11751	ISLIP	11962-11962	SAGAPONACK
10920-10920	CONGERS	11520-11520	FREEPORT	11752-11752	ISLIP TERRACE	11963-11963	SAG HARBOR
10921-10921	FLORIDA	11530-11536	GARDEN CITY	11753-11753	JERICHO	11964-11964	SHELTER ISLAND
10922-10922	FORT MONTGOMERY	11542-11542	GLEN COVE	11754-11754	KINGS PARK	11965-11965	SHELTER ISLAND HEIGHTS
10923-10923	GARNERVILLE	11545-11545	GLEN HEAD	11755-11755	LAKE GROVE	11967-11967	SHIRLEY
10924-10924	GOSHEN	11547-11547	GLENWOOD LANDING	11756-11756	LEVITTOWN	11968-11969	SOUTHAMPTON
10925-10925	GREENWOOD LAKE	11548-11548	GREENVALE	11757-11757	LINDENHURST	11970-11970	SOUTH JAMESPORT
10926-10926	HARRIMAN	11549-11551	HEMPSTEAD	11758-11758	MASSAPEQUA	11971-11971	SOUTHOLD
10927-10927	HAVERSTRAW	11552-11552	WEST HEMPSTEAD	11760-11760	HAUPPAUGE	11972-11972	SPEONK
10928-10928	HIGHLAND FALLS	11553-11553	UNIONDALE	11760-11760	ISLANDIA	11973-11973	UPTON
10930-10930	HIGHLAND MILLS	11554-11554	EAST MEADOW	11762-11762	MASSAPEQUA PARK	11975-11975	WAINSCOTT
10931-10931	HILLBURN	11555-11556	UNIONDALE	11763-11763	MEDFORD	11976-11976	WATER MILL
10932-10932	HOWELLS	11557-11557	HEWLETT	11764-11764	MILLER PLACE	11977-11977	WESTHAMPTON
10933-10933	JOHNSON	11558-11558	ISLAND PARK	11765-11765	MILL NECK	11978-11978	WESTHAMPTON BEACH
10940-10943	MIDDLETOWN	11559-11559	LAWRENCE	11766-11766	MOUNT SINAI	11980-11980	YAPHANK
10950-10950	MONROE	11560-11560	LOCUST VALLEY	11767-11767	NESCONSET	12007-12007	ALCOVE
10951-10951	ROCKLAND M P C	11561-11561	LONG BEACH	11768-11768	NORTHPORT	12008-12008	ALPLAUS
10952-10952	MONSEY	11563-11564	LYNBROOK	11769-11769	OAKDALE	12009-12009	ALTAMONT
10953-10953	MOUNTAINVILLE	11565-11565	MALVERNE	11770-11770	OCEAN BEACH	12010-12010	AMSTERDAM
10954-10954	NANUET	11566-11566	MERRICK	11771-11771	OYSTER BAY	12015-12015	ATHENS
10956-10956	NEW CITY	11568-11568	OLD WESTBURY	11772-11772	PATCHOGUE	12016-12016	AURIESVILLE
10958-10958	NEW HAMPTON	11569-11569	POINT LOOKOUT	11773-11773	SYOSSET	12017-12017	AUSTERLITZ
10959-10959	NEW MILFORD	11570-11571	ROCKVILLE CENTRE	11774-11774	FARMINGDALE	12018-12018	AVERILL PARK
10960-10960	NYACK	11572-11572	OCEANSIDE	11775-11775	MELVILLE	12019-12019	BALLSTON LAKE
10962-10962	ORANGEBURG	11575-11575	ROOSEVELT	11776-11776	PORT JEFFERSON	12020-12020	BALLSTON SPA
10963-10963	OTISVILLE	11576-11576	ROSLYN		STATION	12022-12022	BERLIN
10964-10964	PALISADES	11577-11577	ROSLYN HEIGHTS	11777-11777	PORT JEFFERSON	12023-12023	BERNE
10965-10965	PEARL RIVER	11579-11579	SEA CLIFF	11778-11778	ROCKY POINT	12024-12024	BRAINARD
10968-10968	PIERMONT	11580-11583	VALLEY STREAM	11779-11779	RONKONKOMA	12025-12025	BROADALBIN
10969-10969	PINE ISLAND	11588-11588	UNIONDALE	11780-11780	SAINT JAMES	12026-12026	BROOKVIEW
10970-10970	POMONA	11590-11590	WESTBURY	11782-11782	SAYVILLE	12027-12027	BURNT HILLS
10973-10973	SLATE HILL	11592-11592	ROCKVILLE CENTRE	11783-11783	SEAFORD	12028-12028	BUSKIRK
10974-10974	SLOATSBURG	11593-11595	WESTBURY	11784-11784	SELDEN	12029-12029	CANAAN
10975-10975	SOUTHFIELDS	11596-11596	WILLISTON PARK	11786-11786	SHOREHAM	12031-12031	CARLISLE
10976-10976	SPARKILL	11597-11597	WESTBURY	11787-11787	SMITHTOWN	12032-12032	CAROGA LAKE
10977-10977	SPRING VALLEY	11598-11598	WOODMERE	11788-11788	HAUPPAUGE	12033-12033	CASTLETON ON HUDSON
10979-10979	STERLING FOREST	11599-11599	GARDEN CITY	11789-11789	SOUND BEACH	12035-12035	CENTRAL BRIDGE
10980-10980	STONY POINT	11600-11695	FAR ROCKAWAY	11790-11790	STONY BROOK	12036-12036	CHARLOTTEVILLE
10981-10981	SUGAR LOAF	11696-11696	INWOOD	11791-11791	SYOSSET	12037-12037	CHATHAM
10982-10982	TALLMAN	11697-11697	FAR ROCKAWAY	11792-11792	WADING RIVER	12040-12040	CHERRY PLAIN
10983-10983	TAPPAN	11701-11701	AMITYVILLE	11793-11793	WANTAGH	12041-12041	CLARKSVILLE
10984-10984	THIELLS	11702-11702	BABYLON	11794-11794	STONY BROOK	12042-12042	CLIMAX
10985-10985	THOMPSON RIDGE	11703-11703	NORTH BABYLON	11795-11795	WEST ISLIP	12043-12043	COBLESKILL
10986-10986	TOMKINS COVE	11704-11704	WEST BABYLON	11796-11796	WEST SAYVILLE	12045-12045	COEYMANS
10987-10987	TUXEDO PARK	11705-11705	BAYPORT	11797-11797	WOODBURY	12046-12046	COEYMANS HOLLOW
10988-10988	UNIONVILLE	11706-11706	BAY SHORE	11798-11798	WYANDANCH	12047-12047	COHOES
10989-10989	VALLEY COTTAGE	11707-11707	WEST BABYLON	11801-11802	HICKSVILLE	12050-12050	COLUMBIAVILLE
10990-10990	WARWICK	11708-11708	AMITYVILLE	11803-11803	PLAINVIEW	12051-12051	COXSACKIE
10992-10992	WASHINGTONVILLE	11709-11709	BAYVILLE	11804-11804	OLD BETHPAGE	12052-12052	CROPSEYVILLE
10993-10993	WEST HAVERSTRAW	11710-11710	BELLMORE	11805-11805	MID ISLAND	12053-12053	DELANSON
10994-10995	WEST NYACK	11713-11713	BELLPORT	11815-11819	HICKSVILLE	12054-12054	DELMAR

12055-12055 DORMANSVILLE	12163-12163 SOUTH WESTERLO	12460-12460 OAK HILL	12566-12566 PINE BUSH
12056-12056 DUANESBURG	12164-12164 SPECULATOR	12461-12461 OLIVEBRIDGE	12567-12567 PINE PLAINS
12057-12057 EAGLE BRIDGE	12165-12165 SPENCERTOWN	12462-12462 OLIVEREA	12568-12568 PLATTEKILL
12058-12058 EARLTON	12166-12166 SPRAKERS	12463-12463 PALENVILLE	12569-12569 PLEASANT VALLEY
12059-12059 EAST BERNE	12167-12167 STAMFORD	12464-12464 PHOENICIA	12570-12570 POUGHQUAG
12060-12060 EAST CHATHAM	12168-12169 STEPHENTOWN	12465-12465 PINE HILL	12571-12571 RED HOOK
12061-12061 EAST GREENBUSH	12170-12170 STILLWATER	12466-12466 PORT EWEN	12572-12572 RHINEBECK
12062-12062 EAST NASSAU	12172-12172 STOTTVILLE	12468-12468 PRATTSVILLE	12574-12574 RHINECLIFF
12063-12063 EAST SCHODACK	12173-12173 STUYVESANT	12469-12469 PRESTON HOLLOW	12575-12575 ROCK TAVERN
12064-12064 EAST WORCESTER	12174-12174 STUYVESANT FALLS	12470-12470 PURLING	12577-12577 SALISBURY MILLS
12065-12065 CLIFTON PARK	12175-12175 SUMMIT	12471-12471 RIFTON	12578-12578 SALT POINT
12066-12066 ESPERANCE	12176-12176 SURPRISE	12472-12472 ROSENDALE	12580-12580 STAATSBURG
12067-12067 FEURA BUSH	12177-12177 TRIBES HILL	12473-12473 ROUND TOP	12581-12581 STANFORDVILLE
12068-12068 FONDA	12179-12183 TROY	12474-12474 ROXBURY	12582-12582 STORMVILLE
12069-12069 FORT HUNTER	12184-12184 VALATIE	12475-12475 RUBY	12583-12583 TIVOLI
12070-12070 FORT JOHNSON	12185-12185 VALLEY FALLS	12477-12477 SAUGERTIES	12584-12584 VAILS GATE
12071-12071 FULTONHAM	12186-12186 VOORHEESVILLE	12480-12480 SHANDAKEN	12585-12585 VERBANK
12072-12072 FULTONVILLE	12187-12187 WARNERVILLE	12481-12481 SHOKAN	12586-12586 WALDEN
12073-12073 GALLUPVILLE	12188-12188 WATERFORD	12482-12482 SOUTH CAIRO	12588-12588 WALKER VALLEY
12074-12074 GALWAY	12189-12189 WATERVLIET	12483-12483 SPRING GLEN	12589-12589 WALLKILL
12075-12075 GHENT	12190-12190 WELLS	12484-12484 STONE RIDGE	12590-12590 WAPPINGERS FALLS
12076-12076 GILBOA	12192-12192 WEST COXSACKIE	12485-12485 TANNERSVILLE	12592-12592 WASSAIC
12077-12077 GLENMONT	12193-12193 WESTERLO	12486-12486 TILLSON	12593-12593 WEST COPAKE
12078-12078 GLOVERSVILLE	12194-12194 WEST FULTON	12487-12487 ULSTER PARK	12594-12594 WINGDALE
12082-12082 GRAFTON	12195-12195 WEST LEBANON	12489-12489 WAWARSING	12600-12604 POUGHKEEPSIE
12083-12083 GREENVILLE	12196-12196 WEST SAND LAKE	12490-12490 WEST CAMP	12701-12701 MONTICELLO
12084-12084 GUILDERLAND	12197-12197 WORCESTER	12491-12491 WEST HURLEY	12719-12719 BARRYVILLE
12085-12085 GUILDERLAND CENTER	12198-12198 WYNANTSKILL	12492-12492 WEST KILL	12720-12720 BETHEL
12086-12086 HAGAMAN	12200-12288 ALBANY	12493-12493 WEST PARK	12721-12721 BLOOMINGBURG
12087-12087 HANNACROIX	12300-12345 SCHENECTADY	12494-12494 WEST SHOKAN	12722-12722 BURLINGHAM
12089-12089 HOOSICK	12401-12402 KINGSTON	12495-12495 WILLOW	12723-12723 CALLICOON
12090-12090 HOOSICK FALLS	12404-12404 ACCORD	12496-12496 WINDHAM	12724-12724 CALLICOON CENTER
12092-12092 HOWES CAVE	12405-12405 ACRA	12498-12498 WOODSTOCK	12725-12725 CLARYVILLE
12093-12093 JEFFERSON	12406-12406 ARKVILLE	12501-12501 AMENIA	12726-12726 COCHECTON
12094-12094 JOHNSONVILLE	12407-12407 ASHLAND	12502-12502 ANCRAM	12727-12727 COCHECTON CENTER
12095-12095 JOHNSTOWN	12409-12409 BEARSVILLE	12503-12503 ANCRAMDALE	12729-12729 CUDDEBACKVILLE
12106-12106 KINDERHOOK	12410-12410 BIG INDIAN	12504-12504 ANNANDALE ON HUDSON	12732-12732 ELDRED
12107-12107 KNOX	12411-12411 BLOOMINGTON	12506-12506 BANGALL	12733-12733 FALLSBURG
12108-12108 LAKE PLEASANT	12412-12412 BOICEVILLE	12507-12507 BARRYTOWN	12734-12734 FERNDALE
12110-12111 LATHAM	12413-12413 CAIRO	12508-12508 BEACON	12736-12736 FREMONT CENTER
12113-12113 LAWYERSVILLE	12414-12414 CATSKILL	12510-12510 BILLINGS	12737-12737 GLEN SPEY
12114-12114 LEBANON SPRINGS	12415-12415 CEMENTON	12511-12511 CASTLE POINT	12738-12738 GLEN WILD
12115-12115 MALDEN BRIDGE	12415-12415 SMITHS LANDING	12512-12512 CHELSEA	12739-12739 GODEFFROY
12116-12116 MARYLAND	12416-12416 CHICHESTER	12513-12513 CLAVERACK	12740-12740 GRAHAMSVILLE
12117-12117 MAYFIELD	12417-12417 CONNELLY	12514-12514 CLINTON CORNERS	12741-12741 HANKINS
12118-12118 MECHANICVILLE	12418-12418 CORNWALLVILLE	12515-12515 CLINTONDALE	12742-12742 HARRIS
12120-12120 MEDUSA	12419-12419 COTTEKILL	12516-12516 COPAKE	12743-12743 HIGHLAND LAKE
12121-12121 MELROSE	12420-12420 CRAGSMOOR	12517-12517 COPAKE FALLS	12745-12745 HORTONVILLE
12122-12122 MIDDLEBURGH	12421-12421 DENVER	12518-12518 CORNWALL	12746-12746 HUGUENOT
12123-12123 NASSAU	12422-12422 DURHAM	12520-12520 CORNWALL ON HUDSON	12747-12747 HURLEYVILLE
12124-12124 NEW BALTIMORE	12423-12423 EAST DURHAM	12521-12521 CRARYVILLE	12748-12748 JEFFERSONVILLE
12125-12125 NEW LEBANON	12424-12424 EAST JEWETT	12522-12522 DOVER PLAINS	12749-12749 KAUNEONGA LAKE
12128-12128 NEWTONVILLE	12427-12427 ELKA PARK	12523-12523 ELIZAVILLE	12750-12750 KENOZA LAKE
12130-12130 NIVERVILLE	12428-12428 ELLENVILLE	12524-12524 FISHKILL	12751-12751 KIAMESHA LAKE
12131-12131 NORTH BLENHEIM	12429-12429 ESOPUS	12525-12525 GARDINER	12752-12752 LAKE HUNTINGTON
12132-12132 NORTH CHATHAM	12430-12430 FLEISCHMANNS	12526-12526 GERMANTOWN	12753-12753 LEW BEACH
12133-12133 NORTH HOOSICK	12431-12431 FREEHOLD	12527-12527 GLENHAM	12754-12754 LIBERTY
12134-12134 NORTHVILLE	12432-12432 GLASCO	12528-12528 HIGHLAND	12758-12758 LIVINGSTON MANOR
12135-12135 NORTON HILL	12433-12433 GLENFORD	12529-12529 HILLSDALE	12759-12759 LOCH SHELDRAKE
12136-12136 OLD CHATHAM	12434-12434 GRAND GORGE	12530-12530 HOLLOWVILLE	12760-12760 LONG EDDY
12137-12137 PATTERSONVILLE	12435-12435 GREENFIELD PARK	12531-12531 HOLMES	12762-12762 MONGAUP VALLEY
12138-12138 PETERSBURG	12436-12436 HAINES FALLS	12533-12533 HOPEWELL JUNCTION	12763-12763 MOUNTAIN DALE
12139-12139 PISECO	12438-12438 HALCOTTSVILLE	12534-12534 HUDSON	12764-12764 NARROWSBURG
12140-12140 POESTENKILL	12439-12439 HENSONVILLE	12537-12537 HUGHSONVILLE	12765-12765 NEVERSINK
12141-12141 QUAKER STREET	12440-12440 HIGH FALLS	12538-12538 HYDE PARK	12766-12766 NORTH BRANCH
12143-12143 RAVENA	12441-12441 HIGHMOUNT	12540-12540 LAGRANGEVILLE	12767-12767 OBERNBURG
12144-12144 RENSSELAER	12442-12442 HUNTER	12541-12541 LIVINGSTON	12768-12768 PARKSVILLE
12147-12147 RENSSELAERVILLE	12443-12443 HURLEY	12542-12542 MARLBORO	12769-12769 PHILLIPSPORT
12148-12148 REXFORD	12444-12444 JEWETT	12543-12543 MAYBROOK	12770-12770 POND EDDY
12149-12149 RICHMONDVILLE	12446-12446 KERHONKSON	12544-12544 MELLENVILLE	12771-12771 PORT JERVIS
12150-12150 ROTTERDAM JUNCTION	12448-12448 LAKE HILL	12545-12545 MILLBROOK	12775-12775 ROCK HILL
12151-12151 ROUND LAKE	12449-12449 LAKE KATRINE	12546-12546 MILLERTON	12776-12776 ROSCOE
12153-12153 SAND LAKE	12450-12450 LANESVILLE	12547-12547 MILTON	12777-12777 FORESTBURGH
12154-12154 SCHAGHTICOKE	12451-12451 LEEDS	12548-12548 MODENA	12778-12778 SMALLWOOD
12155-12155 SCHENEVUS	12452-12452 LEXINGTON	12549-12549 MONTGOMERY	12779-12779 SOUTH FALLSBURG
12156-12156 SCHODACK LANDING	12453-12453 MALDEN ON HUDSON	12550-12552 NEWBURGH	12780-12780 SPARROW BUSH
12157-12157 SCHOHARIE	12454-12454 MAPLECREST	12553-12553 NEW WINDSOR	12781-12781 SUMMITVILLE
12158-12158 SELKIRK	12455-12455 MARGARETVILLE	12555-12555 MID HUDSON	12782-12782 SUNDOWN
12159-12159 SLINGERLANDS	12456-12456 MOUNT MARION	12561-12561 NEW PALTZ	12783-12783 SWAN LAKE
12160-12160 SLOANSVILLE	12457-12457 MOUNT TREMPER	12563-12563 PATTERSON	12784-12784 THOMPSONVILLE
12161-12161 SOUTH BETHLEHEM	12458-12458 NAPANOCH	12564-12564 PAWLING	12785-12785 WESTBROOKVILLE
12162-12162 SOUTH SCHODACK	12459-12459 NEW KINGSTON	12565-12565 PHILMONT	12786-12786 WHITE LAKE

ZIP Range	Place
12787-12787	WHITE SULPHUR SPRINGS
12788-12788	WOODBOURNE
12789-12789	WOODRIDGE
12790-12790	WURTSBORO
12791-12791	YOUNGSVILLE
12792-12792	YULAN
12801-12801	GLENS FALLS
12803-12803	SOUTH GLENS FALLS
12804-12804	QUEENSBURY
12808-12808	ADIRONDACK
12809-12809	ARGYLE
12810-12810	ATHOL
12811-12811	BAKERS MILLS
12812-12812	BLUE MOUNTAIN LAKE
12814-12814	BOLTON LANDING
12815-12815	BRANT LAKE
12816-12816	CAMBRIDGE
12817-12817	CHESTERTOWN
12819-12819	CLEMONS
12820-12820	CLEVERDALE
12821-12821	COMSTOCK
12822-12822	CORINTH
12823-12823	COSSAYUNA
12824-12824	DIAMOND POINT
12826-12826	EAST GREENWICH
12827-12827	FORT ANN
12828-12828	FORT EDWARD
12831-12831	GANSEVOORT
12832-12832	GRANVILLE
12833-12833	GREENFIELD CENTER
12834-12834	GREENWICH
12835-12835	HADLEY
12836-12836	HAGUE
12837-12837	HAMPTON
12838-12838	HARTFORD
12839-12839	HUDSON FALLS
12841-12841	HULETTS LANDING
12842-12842	INDIAN LAKE
12843-12843	JOHNSBURG
12844-12844	KATTSKILL BAY
12845-12845	LAKE GEORGE
12846-12846	LAKE LUZERNE
12847-12847	LONG LAKE
12848-12848	MIDDLE FALLS
12849-12849	MIDDLE GRANVILLE
12850-12850	MIDDLE GROVE
12851-12851	MINERVA
12852-12852	NEWCOMB
12853-12853	NORTH CREEK
12854-12854	NORTH GRANVILLE
12855-12855	NORTH HUDSON
12856-12856	NORTH RIVER
12857-12857	OLMSTEDVILLE
12858-12858	PARADOX
12859-12859	PORTER CORNERS
12860-12860	POTTERSVILLE
12861-12861	PUTNAM STATION
12862-12862	RIPARIUS
12863-12863	ROCK CITY FALLS
12864-12864	SABAEL
12865-12865	SALEM
12866-12866	SARATOGA SPRINGS
12870-12870	SCHROON LAKE
12871-12871	SCHUYLERVILLE
12872-12872	SEVERANCE
12873-12873	SHUSHAN
12874-12874	SILVER BAY
12878-12878	STONY CREEK
12879-12879	NEWCOMB
12883-12883	TICONDEROGA
12884-12884	VICTORY MILLS
12885-12885	WARRENSBURG
12886-12886	WEVERTOWN
12887-12887	WHITEHALL
12901-12903	PLATTSBURGH
12910-12910	ALTONA
12911-12911	KEESEVILLE
12912-12912	AU SABLE FORKS
12913-12913	BLOOMINGDALE
12914-12914	BOMBAY
12915-12915	BRAINARDSVILLE
12916-12916	BRUSHTON
12917-12917	BURKE
12918-12918	CADYVILLE
12919-12919	CHAMPLAIN
12920-12920	CHATEAUGAY
12921-12921	CHAZY
12922-12922	CHILDWOLD
12923-12923	CHURUBUSCO
12924-12924	KEESEVILLE
12926-12926	CONSTABLE
12927-12927	CRANBERRY LAKE
12928-12928	CROWN POINT
12929-12929	DANNEMORA
12930-12930	DICKINSON CENTER
12932-12932	ELIZABETHTOWN
12933-12933	ELLENBURG
12934-12934	ELLENBURG CENTER
12935-12935	ELLENBURG DEPOT
12936-12936	ESSEX
12937-12937	FORT COVINGTON
12938-12938	FORT JACKSON
12938-12938	NORTH LAWRENCE
12939-12939	GABRIELS
12940-12940	HOPKINTON
12941-12941	JAY
12942-12942	KEENE
12943-12943	KEENE VALLEY
12944-12944	KEESEVILLE
12945-12945	LAKE CLEAR
12946-12946	LAKE PLACID
12949-12949	LAWRENCEVILLE
12950-12950	LEWIS
12952-12952	LYON MOUNTAIN
12953-12953	MALONE
12955-12955	LYON MOUNTAIN
12956-12956	MINEVILLE
12957-12957	MOIRA
12958-12958	MOOERS
12959-12959	MOOERS FORKS
12960-12960	MORIAH
12961-12961	MORIAH CENTER
12962-12962	MORRISONVILLE
12964-12964	NEW RUSSIA
12965-12965	NICHOLVILLE
12966-12966	NORTH BANGOR
12967-12967	NORTH LAWRENCE
12968-12968	ONCHIOTA
12968-12968	SUGARBUSH
12968-12968	ONCHIOTA
12969-12969	OWLS HEAD
12970-12970	PAUL SMITHS
12972-12972	PERU
12973-12973	PIERCEFIELD
12974-12974	PORT HENRY
12975-12975	PORT KENT
12976-12976	RAINBOW LAKE
12977-12977	RAY BROOK
12978-12978	REDFORD
12979-12979	ROUSES POINT
12980-12980	SAINT REGIS FALLS
12981-12981	SARANAC
12982-12983	SARANAC LAKE
12985-12985	SCHUYLER FALLS
12986-12986	TUPPER LAKE
12987-12987	UPPER JAY
12989-12989	VERMONTVILLE
12990-12990	WADHAMS
12991-12991	BANGOR
12992-12992	WEST CHAZY
12993-12993	WESTPORT
12994-12994	BOUQUET
12994-12994	WHALLONSBURG
12995-12995	WHIPPLEVILLE
12996-12996	WILLSBORO
12997-12997	WILMINGTON
12998-12998	WITHERBEE
13020-13020	APULIA STATION
13021-13024	AUBURN
13026-13026	AURORA
13027-13027	BALDWINSVILLE
13028-13028	BERNHARDS BAY
13029-13029	BREWERTON
13030-13030	BRIDGEPORT
13031-13031	CAMILLUS
13032-13032	CANASTOTA
13033-13033	CATO
13034-13034	CAYUGA
13035-13035	CAZENOVIA
13036-13036	CENTRAL SQUARE
13037-13037	CHITTENANGO
13039-13039	CICERO
13040-13040	CINCINNATUS
13041-13041	CLAY
13042-13042	CLEVELAND
13043-13043	CLOCKVILLE
13044-13044	CONSTANTIA
13045-13045	CORTLAND
13050-13050	CUYLER
13051-13051	DELPHI FALLS
13052-13052	DE RUYTER
13053-13053	DRYDEN
13054-13054	DURHAMVILLE
13055-13055	EAST FREETOWN
13056-13056	EAST HOMER
13057-13057	EAST SYRACUSE
13060-13060	ELBRIDGE
13061-13061	ERIEVILLE
13062-13062	ETNA
13063-13063	FABIUS
13064-13064	FAIR HAVEN
13065-13065	FAYETTE
13066-13066	FAYETTEVILLE
13068-13068	FREEVILLE
13069-13069	FULTON
13071-13071	GENOA
13072-13072	GEORGETOWN
13073-13073	GROTON
13074-13074	HANNIBAL
13076-13076	HASTINGS
13077-13077	HOMER
13078-13078	JAMESVILLE
13080-13080	JORDAN
13081-13081	KING FERRY
13082-13082	KIRKVILLE
13083-13083	LACONA
13084-13084	LA FAYETTE
13085-13085	LEBANON
13087-13087	LITTLE YORK
13088-13090	LIVERPOOL
13092-13092	LOCKE
13093-13093	LYCOMING
13094-13094	LYSANDER
13101-13101	MC GRAW
13102-13102	MC LEAN
13103-13103	MALLORY
13104-13104	MANLIUS
13107-13107	MAPLE VIEW
13108-13108	MARCELLUS
13110-13110	MARIETTA
13111-13111	MARTVILLE
13112-13112	MEMPHIS
13113-13113	MERIDIAN
13114-13114	MEXICO
13115-13115	MINETTO
13116-13116	MINOA
13117-13117	MONTEZUMA
13118-13118	MORAVIA
13119-13119	MOTTVILLE
13120-13120	NEDROW
13121-13121	NEW HAVEN
13122-13122	NEW WOODSTOCK
13123-13123	NORTH BAY
13124-13124	NORTH PITCHER
13125-13125	ORAN
13126-13126	OSWEGO
13129-13129	GEORGETOWN
13130-13130	OWASCO
13131-13131	PARISH
13132-13132	PENNELLVILLE
13133-13133	PERRYVILLE
13134-13134	PETERBORO
13135-13135	PHOENIX
13136-13136	PITCHER
13137-13137	PLAINVILLE
13138-13138	POMPEY
13139-13139	POPLAR RIDGE
13140-13140	PORT BYRON
13141-13141	PREBLE
13142-13142	PULASKI
13143-13143	RED CREEK
13144-13144	RICHLAND
13145-13145	SANDY CREEK
13146-13146	SAVANNAH
13147-13147	SCIPIO CENTER
13148-13148	SENECA FALLS
13150-13150	SENNETT
13151-13151	SHEDS
13152-13152	SKANEATELES
13153-13153	SKANEATELES FALLS
13154-13154	SOUTH BUTLER
13155-13155	SOUTH OTSELIC
13156-13156	STERLING
13157-13157	SYLVAN BEACH
13158-13158	TRUXTON
13159-13159	TULLY
13160-13160	UNION SPRINGS
13162-13162	VERONA BEACH
13163-13163	WAMPSVILLE
13164-13164	WARNERS
13165-13165	WATERLOO
13166-13166	WEEDSPORT
13167-13167	WEST MONROE
13200-13210	SYRACUSE
13211-13211	MATTYDALE
13212-13290	SYRACUSE
13301-13301	ALDER CREEK
13302-13302	ALTMAR
13303-13303	AVA
13304-13304	BARNEVELD
13305-13305	BEAVER FALLS
13308-13308	BLOSSVALE
13309-13309	BOONVILLE
13310-13310	BOUCKVILLE
13312-13312	BRANTINGHAM
13313-13313	BRIDGEWATER
13314-13314	BROOKFIELD
13315-13315	BURLINGTON FLATS
13316-13316	CAMDEN
13317-13317	CANAJOHARIE
13318-13318	CASSVILLE
13319-13319	CHADWICKS
13320-13320	CHERRY VALLEY
13321-13321	CLARK MILLS
13322-13322	CLAYVILLE
13323-13323	CLINTON
13324-13324	COLD BROOK
13325-13325	CONSTABLEVILLE
13326-13326	COOPERSTOWN
13327-13327	CROGHAN
13328-13328	DEANSBORO
13329-13329	DOLGEVILLE
13331-13331	EAGLE BAY
13332-13332	EARLVILLE
13333-13333	EAST SPRINGFIELD
13334-13334	EATON
13335-13335	EDMESTON
13336-13336	FAIRFIELD
13337-13337	FLY CREEK
13338-13338	FORESTPORT
13339-13339	FORT PLAIN
13340-13340	FRANKFORT
13341-13341	FRANKLIN SPRINGS
13342-13342	GARRATTSVILLE
13343-13343	GLENFIELD
13345-13345	GREIG
13346-13346	HAMILTON
13348-13348	HARTWICK
13349-13349	HARTWICK SEMINARY
13350-13350	HERKIMER
13352-13352	HINCKLEY
13353-13353	HOFFMEISTER
13354-13354	HOLLAND PATENT
13355-13355	HUBBARDSVILLE
13357-13357	ILION
13360-13360	INLET
13361-13361	JORDANVILLE
13362-13362	KNOXBORO

13363-13363 LEE CENTER	13607-13607 ALEXANDRIA BAY	13695-13695 WANAKENA	13845-13845 TIOGA CENTER
13364-13364 LEONARDSVILLE	13608-13608 ANTWERP	13696-13696 WEST STOCKHOLM	13846-13846 TREADWELL
13365-13365 LITTLE FALLS	13609-13609 BALMAT	13697-13697 WINTHROP	13847-13847 TROUT CREEK
13367-13367 LOWVILLE	13610-13610 RODMAN	13698-13698 WOODVILLE	13848-13848 TUNNEL
13368-13368 LYONS FALLS	13611-13611 BELLEVILLE	13699-13699 POTSDAM	13849-13849 UNADILLA
13401-13401 MC CONNELLSVILLE	13612-13612 BLACK RIVER	13730-13730 AFTON	13850-13851 VESTAL
13402-13402 MADISON	13613-13613 BRASHER FALLS	13731-13731 ANDES	13856-13856 WALTON
13403-13403 MARCY	13614-13614 BRIER HILL	13732-13732 APALACHIN	13859-13859 WELLS BRIDGE
13404-13404 MARTINSBURG	13615-13615 BROWNVILLE	13733-13733 BAINBRIDGE	13860-13860 WEST DAVENPORT
13406-13406 MIDDLEVILLE	13616-13616 CALCIUM	13734-13734 BARTON	13861-13861 WEST ONEONTA
13407-13407 MOHAWK	13617-13617 CANTON	13736-13736 BERKSHIRE	13862-13862 WHITNEY POINT
13408-13408 MORRISVILLE	13618-13618 CAPE VINCENT	13737-13737 BIBLE SCHOOL PARK	13863-13863 WILLET
13409-13409 MUNNSVILLE	13619-13619 CARTHAGE	13738-13738 BLODGETT MILLS	13864-13864 WILLSEYVILLE
13410-13410 NELLISTON	13620-13620 CASTORLAND	13739-13739 BLOOMVILLE	13865-13865 WINDSOR
13411-13411 NEW BERLIN	13621-13621 CHASE MILLS	13740-13740 BOVINA CENTER	13900-13905 BINGHAMTON
13413-13413 NEW HARTFORD	13622-13622 CHAUMONT	13743-13743 CANDOR	14001-14001 AKRON
13415-13415 NEW LISBON	13623-13623 CHIPPEWA BAY	13744-13744 CASTLE CREEK	14003-14003 ALABAMA
13416-13416 NEWPORT	13624-13624 CLAYTON	13745-13745 CHENANGO BRIDGE	14004-14004 ALDEN
13417-13417 NEW YORK MILLS	13625-13625 COLTON	13746-13746 CHENANGO FORKS	14005-14005 ALEXANDER
13418-13418 NORTH BROOKFIELD	13626-13626 COPENHAGEN	13747-13747 COLLIERSVILLE	14006-14006 ANGOLA
13419-13419 WESTERN	13627-13627 DEER RIVER	13748-13748 CONKLIN	14008-14008 APPLETON
13420-13420 OLD FORGE	13628-13628 DEFERIET	13749-13749 CORBETTSVILLE	14009-14009 ARCADE
13421-13421 ONEIDA	13630-13630 DE KALB JUNCTION	13750-13750 DAVENPORT	14010-14010 ATHOL SPRINGS
13424-13424 ORISKANY	13631-13631 DENMARK	13751-13751 DAVENPORT CENTER	14011-14011 ATTICA
13425-13425 ORISKANY FALLS	13632-13632 DEPAUVILLE	13752-13752 DE LANCEY	14012-14012 BARKER
13426-13426 ORWELL	13633-13633 DE PEYSTER	13753-13753 DELHI	14013-14013 BASOM
13428-13428 PALATINE BRIDGE	13634-13634 DEXTER	13754-13754 DEPOSIT	14020-14021 BATAVIA
13429-13429 PARIS	13635-13635 EDWARDS	13755-13755 DOWNSVILLE	14024-14024 BLISS
13431-13431 POLAND	13636-13636 ELLISBURG	13756-13756 EAST BRANCH	14025-14025 BOSTON
13432-13432 POOLVILLE	13637-13637 EVANS MILLS	13757-13757 EAST MEREDITH	14026-14026 BOWMANSVILLE
13433-13433 PORT LEYDEN	13638-13638 FELTS MILLS	13758-13758 EAST PHARSALIA	14027-14027 BRANT
13434-13434 PRATTS HOLLOW	13639-13639 FINE	13760-13761 ENDICOTT	14028-14028 BURT
13435-13435 PROSPECT	13640-13640 WELLESLEY ISLAND	13762-13762 ENDWELL	14029-14029 CENTERVILLE
13436-13436 RAQUETTE LAKE	13641-13641 FISHERS LANDING	13763-13763 ENDICOTT	14030-14030 CHAFFEE
13437-13437 REDFIELD	13642-13642 GOUVERNEUR	13774-13774 FISHS EDDY	14031-14031 CLARENCE
13438-13438 REMSEN	13643-13643 GREAT BEND	13775-13775 FRANKLIN	14032-14032 CLARENCE CENTER
13439-13439 RICHFIELD SPRINGS	13645-13645 HAILESBORO	13776-13776 GILBERTSVILLE	14033-14033 COLDEN
13440-13449 ROME	13646-13646 HAMMOND	13777-13777 GLEN AUBREY	14034-14034 COLLINS
13450-13450 ROSEBOOM	13647-13647 HANNAWA FALLS	13778-13778 GREENE	14035-14035 COLLINS CENTER
13452-13452 SAINT JOHNSVILLE	13648-13648 HARRISVILLE	13780-13780 GUILFORD	14036-14036 CORFU
13454-13454 SALISBURY CENTER	13649-13649 HELENA	13782-13782 HAMDEN	14037-14037 COWLESVILLE
13455-13455 SANGERFIELD	13650-13650 HENDERSON	13783-13783 HANCOCK	14038-14038 CRITTENDEN
13456-13456 SAUQUOIT	13651-13651 HENDERSON HARBOR	13784-13784 HARFORD	14039-14039 DALE
13457-13457 SCHUYLER LAKE	13652-13652 HERMON	13786-13786 HARPERSFIELD	14040-14040 DARIEN CENTER
13459-13459 SHARON SPRINGS	13654-13654 HEUVELTON	13787-13787 HARPURSVILLE	14041-14041 DAYTON
13460-13460 SHERBURNE	13655-13655 HOGANSBURG	13788-13788 HOBART	14042-14042 DELEVAN
13461-13461 SHERRILL	13656-13656 LA FARGEVILLE	13790-13790 JOHNSON CITY	14043-14043 DEPEW
13464-13464 SMYRNA	13657-13657 LIMERICK	13794-13794 KILLAWOG	14047-14047 DERBY
13465-13465 SOLSVILLE	13658-13658 LISBON	13795-13795 KIRKWOOD	14048-14048 DUNKIRK
13466-13466 SOUTH EDMESTON	13659-13659 LORRAINE	13796-13796 LAURENS	14051-14051 EAST AMHERST
13468-13468 SPRINGFIELD CENTER	13660-13660 MADRID	13797-13797 LISLE	14052-14052 EAST AURORA
13469-13469 STITTVILLE	13661-13661 MANNSVILLE	13801-13801 MC DONOUGH	14054-14054 EAST BETHANY
13470-13470 STRATFORD	13662-13662 MASSENA	13802-13802 MAINE	14055-14055 EAST CONCORD
13471-13471 TABERG	13664-13664 MORRISTOWN	13803-13803 MARATHON	14056-14056 EAST PEMBROKE
13472-13472 THENDARA	13665-13665 NATURAL BRIDGE	13804-13804 MASONVILLE	14057-14057 EDEN
13473-13473 TURIN	13666-13666 NEWTON FALLS	13806-13806 MERIDALE	14058-14058 ELBA
13475-13475 VAN HORNESVILLE	13667-13667 NORFOLK	13807-13807 MILFORD	14059-14059 ELMA
13476-13476 VERNON	13668-13668 NORWOOD	13808-13808 MORRIS	14060-14060 FARMERSVILLE STATION
13477-13477 VERNON CENTER	13669-13669 OGDENSBURG	13809-13809 MOUNT UPTON	14061-14061 FARNHAM
13478-13478 VERONA	13670-13670 OSWEGATCHIE	13810-13810 MOUNT VISION	14062-14062 FORESTVILLE
13479-13479 WASHINGTON MILLS	13671-13671 OXBOW	13811-13811 NEWARK VALLEY	14063-14063 FREDONIA
13480-13480 WATERVILLE	13672-13672 PARISHVILLE	13812-13812 NICHOLS	14065-14065 FREEDOM
13482-13482 WEST BURLINGTON	13673-13673 PHILADELPHIA	13813-13813 NINEVEH	14066-14066 GAINESVILLE
13483-13483 WESTDALE	13674-13674 PIERREPONT MANOR	13814-13814 NORTH NORWICH	14067-14067 GASPORT
13484-13484 WEST EATON	13675-13675 PLESSIS	13815-13815 NORWICH	14068-14068 GETZVILLE
13485-13485 WEST EDMESTON	13676-13676 POTSDAM	13820-13820 ONEONTA	14069-14069 GLENWOOD
13486-13486 WESTERNVILLE	13677-13677 PYRITES	13825-13825 OTEGO	14070-14070 GOWANDA
13487-13487 WEST EXETER	13678-13678 RAYMONDVILLE	13826-13826 OUAQUAGA	14072-14072 GRAND ISLAND
13488-13488 WESTFORD	13679-13679 REDWOOD	13827-13827 OWEGO	14075-14075 HAMBURG
13489-13489 WEST LEYDEN	13680-13680 RENSSELAER FALLS	13830-13830 OXFORD	14079-14079 HELMUTH
13490-13490 WESTMORELAND	13681-13681 RICHVILLE	13832-13832 PLYMOUTH	14080-14080 HOLLAND
13491-13491 WEST WINFIELD	13682-13682 RODMAN	13833-13833 PORT CRANE	14081-14081 IRVING
13492-13492 WHITESBORO	13683-13683 ROOSEVELTOWN	13834-13834 PORTLANDVILLE	14082-14082 JAVA CENTER
13493-13493 WILLIAMSTOWN	13684-13684 RUSSELL	13835-13835 RICHFORD	14083-14083 JAVA VILLAGE
13494-13494 WOODGATE	13685-13685 SACKETS HARBOR	13837-13837 SHINHOPPLE	14085-14085 LAKE VIEW
13495-13495 YORKVILLE	13687-13687 SOUTH COLTON	13838-13838 SIDNEY	14086-14086 LANCASTER
13500-13599 UTICA	13688-13688 SOUTH RUTLAND	13839-13839 SIDNEY CENTER	14091-14091 LAWTONS
13601-13601 WATERTOWN	13690-13690 STAR LAKE	13840-13840 SMITHBORO	14092-14092 LEWISTON
13602-13602 FORT DRUM	13691-13691 THERESA	13841-13841 SMITHVILLE FLATS	14094-14095 LOCKPORT
13603-13603 WATERTOWN	13692-13692 THOUSAND ISLAND PARK	13842-13842 SOUTH KORTRIGHT	14098-14098 LYNDONVILLE
13605-13605 ADAMS	13693-13693 THREE MILE BAY	13843-13843 SOUTH NEW BERLIN	14101-14101 MACHIAS
13606-13606 ADAMS CENTER	13694-13694 WADDINGTON	13844-13844 SOUTH PLYMOUTH	14102-14102 MARILLA

14103-14103 MEDINA	14470-14470 HOLLEY	14590-14590 WOLCOTT	14805-14805 ALPINE
14105-14105 MIDDLEPORT	14471-14471 HONEOYE	14591-14591 WYOMING	14806-14806 ANDOVER
14107-14107 MODEL CITY	14472-14472 HONEOYE FALLS	14592-14592 YORK	14807-14807 ARKPORT
14108-14108 NEWFANE	14474-14474 INDUSTRY	14600-14694 ROCHESTER	14808-14808 ATLANTA
14109-14109 NIAGARA UNIVERSITY	14475-14475 IONIA	14701-14704 JAMESTOWN	14809-14809 AVOCA
14110-14110 NORTH BOSTON	14476-14476 KENDALL	14706-14706 ALLEGANY	14810-14810 BATH
14111-14111 NORTH COLLINS	14477-14477 KENT	14707-14707 ALLENTOWN	14812-14812 BEAVER DAMS
14112-14112 NORTH EVANS	14478-14478 KEUKA PARK	14708-14708 ALMA	14813-14813 BELMONT
14113-14113 NORTH JAVA	14479-14479 KNOWLESVILLE	14709-14709 ANGELICA	14814-14814 BIG FLATS
14120-14120 NORTH TONAWANDA	14480-14480 LAKEVILLE	14710-14710 ASHVILLE	14815-14815 BRADFORD
14125-14125 OAKFIELD	14481-14481 LEICESTER	14711-14711 BELFAST	14816-14816 BREESPORT
14126-14126 OLCOTT	14482-14482 LE ROY	14712-14712 BEMUS POINT	14817-14817 BROOKTONDALE
14127-14127 ORCHARD PARK	14485-14485 LIMA	14714-14714 BLACK CREEK	14818-14818 BURDETT
14129-14129 PERRYSBURG	14486-14486 LINWOOD	14715-14715 BOLIVAR	14819-14819 CAMERON
14130-14130 PIKE	14487-14487 LIVONIA	14716-14716 BROCTON	14820-14820 CAMERON MILLS
14131-14131 RANSOMVILLE	14488-14488 LIVONIA CENTER	14717-14717 CANEADEA	14821-14821 CAMPBELL
14132-14132 SANBORN	14489-14489 LYONS	14718-14718 CASSADAGA	14822-14822 CANASERAGA
14133-14133 SANDUSKY	14502-14502 MACEDON	14719-14719 CATTARAUGUS	14823-14823 CANISTEO
14134-14134 SARDINIA	14504-14504 MANCHESTER	14720-14720 CELORON	14824-14824 CAYUTA
14135-14135 SHERIDAN	14505-14505 MARION	14721-14721 CERES	14825-14825 CHEMUNG
14136-14136 SILVER CREEK	14506-14506 MENDON	14722-14722 CHAUTAUQUA	14826-14826 COHOCTON
14138-14138 SOUTH DAYTON	14507-14507 MIDDLESEX	14723-14723 CHERRY CREEK	14827-14827 COOPERS PLAINS
14139-14139 SOUTH WALES	14508-14508 MORTON	14724-14724 CLYMER	14830-14831 CORNING
14140-14140 SPRING BROOK	14510-14510 MOUNT MORRIS	14726-14726 CONEWANGO VALLEY	14836-14836 DALTON
14141-14141 SPRINGVILLE	14511-14511 MUMFORD	14727-14727 CUBA	14837-14837 DUNDEE
14143-14143 STAFFORD	14512-14512 NAPLES	14728-14728 DEWITTVILLE	14838-14838 ERIN
14144-14144 STELLA NIAGARA	14513-14513 NEWARK	14729-14729 EAST OTTO	14839-14839 GREENWOOD
14145-14145 STRYKERSVILLE	14514-14514 NORTH CHILI	14730-14730 EAST RANDOLPH	14840-14840 HAMMONDSPORT
14150-14151 TONAWANDA	14515-14515 NORTH GREECE	14731-14731 ELLICOTTVILLE	14841-14841 HECTOR
14166-14166 VAN BUREN POINT	14516-14516 NORTH ROSE	14732-14732 ELLINGTON	14842-14842 HIMROD
14167-14167 VARYSBURG	14517-14517 NUNDA	14733-14733 FALCONER	14843-14843 HORNELL
14168-14168 VERSAILLES	14518-14518 OAKS CORNERS	14735-14735 FILLMORE	14844-14845 HORSEHEADS
14169-14169 WALES CENTER	14519-14519 ONTARIO	14736-14736 FINDLEY LAKE	14846-14846 HUNT
14170-14170 WEST FALLS	14520-14520 ONTARIO CENTER	14737-14737 FRANKLINVILLE	14847-14847 INTERLAKEN
14171-14171 WEST VALLEY	14521-14521 OVID	14738-14738 FREWSBURG	14850-14853 ITHACA
14172-14172 WILSON	14522-14522 PALMYRA	14739-14739 FRIENDSHIP	14854-14854 JACKSONVILLE
14173-14173 YORKSHIRE	14525-14525 PAVILION	14740-14740 GERRY	14855-14855 JASPER
14174-14174 YOUNGSTOWN	14526-14526 PENFIELD	14741-14741 GREAT VALLEY	14856-14856 KANONA
14200-14280 BUFFALO	14527-14527 PENN YAN	14742-14742 GREENHURST	14857-14857 LAKEMONT
14300-14305 NIAGARA FALLS	14529-14529 PERKINSVILLE	14743-14743 HINSDALE	14858-14858 LINDLEY
14410-14410 ADAMS BASIN	14530-14530 PERRY	14744-14744 HOUGHTON	14859-14859 LOCKWOOD
14411-14411 ALBION	14532-14532 PHELPS	14745-14745 HUME	14860-14860 LODI
14413-14413 ALTON	14533-14533 PIFFARD	14747-14747 KENNEDY	14861-14861 LOWMAN
14414-14414 AVON	14534-14534 PITTSFORD	14748-14748 KILL BUCK	14863-14863 MECKLENBURG
14415-14415 BELLONA	14536-14536 PORTAGEVILLE	14749-14749 KNAPP CREEK	14864-14864 MILLPORT
14416-14416 BERGEN	14537-14537 PORT GIBSON	14750-14750 LAKEWOOD	14865-14865 MONTOUR FALLS
14418-14418 BRANCHPORT	14538-14538 PULTNEYVILLE	14751-14751 LEON	14867-14867 NEWFIELD
14420-14420 BROCKPORT	14539-14539 RETSOF	14752-14752 LILY DALE	14868-14868 NORTH COHOCTON
14422-14422 BYRON	14541-14541 ROMULUS	14753-14753 LIMESTONE	14869-14869 ODESSA
14423-14423 CALEDONIA	14542-14542 ROSE	14754-14754 LITTLE GENESEE	14870-14870 PAINTED POST
14424-14424 CANANDAIGUA	14543-14543 RUSH	14755-14755 LITTLE VALLEY	14871-14871 PINE CITY
14425-14425 FARMINGTON	14544-14544 RUSHVILLE	14756-14756 MAPLE SPRINGS	14872-14872 PINE VALLEY
14427-14427 CASTILE	14545-14545 SCOTTSBURG	14757-14757 MAYVILLE	14873-14873 PRATTSBURGH
14428-14428 CHURCHVILLE	14546-14546 SCOTTSVILLE	14758-14758 NIOBE	14874-14874 PULTENEY
14429-14429 CLARENDON	14547-14547 SENECA CASTLE	14759-14759 NORTH CLYMER	14876-14876 READING CENTER
14430-14430 CLARKSON	14548-14548 SHORTSVILLE	14760-14760 OLEAN	14877-14877 REXVILLE
14432-14432 CLIFTON SPRINGS	14549-14549 SILVER LAKE	14766-14766 OTTO	14878-14878 ROCK STREAM
14433-14433 CLYDE	14550-14550 SILVER SPRINGS	14767-14767 PANAMA	14879-14879 SAVONA
14435-14435 CONESUS	14551-14551 SODUS	14769-14769 PORTLAND	14880-14880 SCIO
14437-14437 DANSVILLE	14554-14554 SODUS CENTER	14770-14770 PORTVILLE	14881-14881 SLATERVILLE SPRINGS
14441-14441 DRESDEN	14555-14555 SODUS POINT	14772-14772 RANDOLPH	14882-14882 LANSING
14442-14442 EAGLE HARBOR	14556-14556 SONYEA	14774-14774 RICHBURG	14883-14883 SPENCER
14443-14443 EAST BLOOMFIELD	14557-14557 SOUTH BYRON	14775-14775 RIPLEY	14884-14884 SWAIN
14444-14444 EAST PALMYRA	14558-14558 SOUTH LIMA	14776-14776 ROSSBURG	14885-14885 TROUPSBURG
14445-14445 EAST ROCHESTER	14559-14559 SPENCERPORT	14777-14777 RUSHFORD	14886-14886 TRUMANSBURG
14449-14449 EAST WILLIAMSON	14560-14560 SPRINGWATER	14778-14778 SAINT BONAVENTURE	14887-14887 TYRONE
14450-14450 FAIRPORT	14561-14561 STANLEY	14779-14779 SALAMANCA	14888-14888 VALOIS
14452-14452 FANCHER	14563-14563 UNION HILL	14781-14781 SHERMAN	14889-14889 VAN ETTEN
14453-14453 FISHERS	14564-14564 VICTOR	14782-14782 SINCLAIRVILLE	14891-14891 WATKINS GLEN
14454-14454 GENESEO	14568-14568 WALWORTH	14783-14783 STEAMBURG	14892-14892 WAVERLY
14456-14456 GENEVA	14569-14569 WARSAW	14784-14784 STOCKTON	14893-14893 WAYNE
14461-14461 GORHAM	14571-14571 WATERPORT	14785-14785 STOW	14894-14894 WELLSBURG
14462-14462 GROVELAND	14572-14572 WAYLAND	14786-14786 WEST CLARKSVILLE	14895-14895 WELLSVILLE
14463-14463 HALL	14580-14580 WEBSTER	14787-14787 WESTFIELD	14896-14896 WEST DANBY
14464-14464 HAMLIN	14584-14584 WEBSTER CROSSING	14788-14788 WESTONS MILLS	14897-14897 WHITESVILLE
14466-14466 HEMLOCK	14585-14585 WEST BLOOMFIELD	14801-14801 ADDISON	14898-14898 WOODHULL
14467-14467 HENRIETTA	14586-14586 WEST HENRIETTA	14802-14802 ALFRED	14900-14975 ELMIRA
14468-14468 HILTON	14588-14588 WILLARD	14803-14803 ALFRED STATION	
14469-14469 BLOOMFIELD	14589-14589 WILLIAMSON	14804-14804 ALMOND	

North Carolina

General Help Numbers:

Governor's Office
20301 Mail Service Center
Raleigh, NC 27699-0301
www.governor.state.nc.us

919-733-4240
Fax 919-715-3175
8AM-6PM

Attorney General's Office
Justice Department
PO Box 629
Raleigh, NC 27602-0629
www.jus.state.nc.us

919-716-6400
Fax 919-716-6750
8AM-5PM

State Court Administrator
PO Box 2448
Raleigh, NC 27602-2448
www.nccourts.org/Courts/

919-733-7107
Fax 919-715-5779
8AM-5PM

State Archives
Archives & History Division
109 E Jones St
Raleigh, NC 27601-2807
www.ah.dcr.state.nc.us

919-733-3952
Fax 919-733-1354
8AM-5:30PM TU-F, 9-5 SA

State Specifics:

Capital: Raleigh
                                         Wake County

Time Zone: EST

Number of Counties: 100

Population: 8,186,268

Web Site: www.ncgov.com

State Agencies

Criminal Records

Access to Records is Restricted

State Bureau of Investigation, Identification Section, PO Box 29500, Raleigh, NC 27626 (Courier: 3320 Garner Rd, Raleigh, NC 27626-0500); 919-662-4500 x300, 919-662-4380 (Fax), 7:30AM-5PM.

http://sbi.jus.state.nc.us

Note: Sex offender data is at http://sbi.jus.state.nc.us/dojhaht/sor/. Record access is limited to criminal justice and other government agencies authorized by law. Employers are denied access unless subject is in the health or child care business. Contact agency for proper paperwork.

Corporation Records
Limited Partnerships
Limited Liability Company Records
Trademarks/Servicemarks

Secretary of State, Corporations Section, PO Box 29622, Raleigh, NC 27626-0622 (Courier: 2 S Salisbury, Raleigh, NC 27603); 919-807-2251 (Corporations), 919-807-2164 (Trademarks), 919-807-2039 (Fax), 8AM-5PM.

www.secretary.state.nc.us

Note: DBAs, Fictitious Names and Assumed Name records are found at the county Register of Deeds offices.

Indexing & Storage: Records are available from 1800's on. Most information is available on the computer database and on the agency's website. New records are available for inquiry immediately.

Searching: Information is open to the public. Include the following in your request: full name of business. Information contained in filings includes officers' names and addresses; registered agent; principal office; date of incorporation; and nature of the business.

Access by: mail, phone, fax, in person, online.

Fee & Payment: There is no search fee. Copies are $1.00 per page. Certification is $5.00. Fee payee: Secretary of State. Prepayment required. They will invoice except for in person searching. Personal checks accepted. No credit cards accepted.

Mail search: Expect 6-10 day turnaround time for corporation documents, 2-3 day turnaround time for trademark documents.

Phone search: There is no fee to do simple searches over the phone.

Fax search: They will invoice.

In person search: Turnaround time is immediate. There is a public access terminal to view records.

Online search: The web site offers a free search of status and registered agent by corporation name. The trademark database is not available online.

Other access: The state makes database information available for purchase via an FTP site. Contact Bonnie Elek at 919-807-2196 for details.

Uniform Commercial Code Federal Tax Liens

UCC Division, Secretary of State, Raleigh, NC 27626-0622 (Courier: 2 South Salisbury St, Raleigh, NC 27603-5909); 919-807-2111, 919-807-2120 (Fax), 8AM-5PM.

www.secretary.state.nc.us/UCC

Indexing & Storage: Records are available from 1967. Records are computerized since 1985. Records are normally destroyed after six years form lapse date.

Searching: Use search request form UCC-11. The search includes federal tax liens on businesses since 1985 if you request (add $5.00). You may search federal tax liens separately. Federal tax liens on individuals and all state tax liens are filed at Superior Courts. Include the following in your request: debtor name. Name will be searched as submitted; name variation printouts will be given.

Access by: mail, in person, online.

Fee & Payment: The search fee is $30.00 per debtor name plus $2.00 per page for copies or $2.00 per specific page request. $6.25 for certification plus $.200 each additional page. $.50 per reader printer copy, from customer reader printers. Fee payee: Secretary of State. Prepayment required. Prepayment is required. Underpayment requests will be rejected. Personal checks accepted. No credit cards accepted.

Mail search: Turnaround time: 3 days. A self addressed stamped envelope is requested.

In person search: Searching is available in person.

Online search: Free access is available at www.secretary.state.nc.us/ucc/. Click on "UCC research" or "Tax Liens." Search by ID number or debtor name.

Other access: The UCC or tax lien database can be purchased on either a weekly or monthly basis vai an FTP site. For more information, call 919-807-2196.

State Tax Liens

Records not maintained by a state level agency.

Note: Tax lien data is found at the county level.

Sales Tax Registrations

Access to Records is Restricted

Revenue Department, Sales & Use Tax Division, PO Box 25000, Raleigh, NC 27640 (Courier: 501 N Wilmington Street, Raleigh, NC 27604); 919-733-3661, 919-715-6086 (Fax), 8AM-5PM.

www.dor.state.nc.us

Birth Certificates

Center for health Statistics, Vital Records Branch, 1903 Mail Service Center, Raleigh, NC 27699-1903 (Courier: 225 N McDowell St, Raleigh, NC 27603); 919-733-3526, 800-669-8310 (Credit Card Orders), 919-829-1359 (Fax), 8AM-4PM.

www.schs.state.nc.us/SCHS

Note: Anyone can order an non-certified copy of a record. Only family members can order a certified copy. The fee is the same.

Indexing & Storage: Records are available from 1913 to present. Prior to 1913, the state did not keep records of births. It takes 90 days after birth before new records are available for inquiry. Records are indexed on microfiche, inhouse computer.

Searching: Investigative searches are permitted, but only non-certified copies are provided. Otherwise, requester must state relationship to subject and why record is needed. Include the following in your request: full name, names of parents, mother's maiden name, date of birth, place of birth. The following data is not released: adoption records or medical records.

Access by: mail, phone, in person.

Fee & Payment: Search fee is $10.00 per 5 years searched. Add $9.95 for using a credit card. Add $5.00 per copy for additional copies. Fee payee: North Carolina Vital Records. Prepayment required. Credit cards accepted for expedited service only. Personal checks accepted. Credit cards accepted: MasterCard, Visa.

Mail search: Turnaround time: 2 weeks. No self addressed stamped envelope is required.

Phone search: See expedited service.

In person search: Turnaround time is 30 minutes.

Expedited service: Expedited service is available for credit card searches. Turnaround time: overnight delivery. Total fee is $43.95 and includes overnight delivery and credit card fee.

Death Records

Dept of Environment, Health & Natural Resources, Vital Records Section, 1903 Mail Service Center, Raleigh, NC 27699-1903 (Courier: 225 N McDowell St, Raleigh, NC 27603); 919-733-3526, 919-829-1359 (Fax), 8AM-4PM.

www.schs.state.nc.us/SCHS

Note: Non-certified records may be obtained by the public; certified copies can only be purchased by family members. The fee is the same for either.

Indexing & Storage: Records are available from 1930 to present. It takes 90 days after death before new records are available for inquiry. Records are indexed on microfiche, inhouse computer.

Searching: Investigative searches are permitted, but only non-certified copies are provided. Include the following in your request: full name, date of death, place of death. Social Security Number is helpful.

Access by: mail, phone, in person.

Fee & Payment: The search fee is $10.00 for each 5 years searched. Add $9.95 for using a credit card. Add $5.00 per copy for additional copies. Fee payee: North Carolina Vital Records. Prepayment required. Credit cards accepted for phone service only. Personal checks accepted. Credit cards accepted: MasterCard, Visa, AmEx, Discover.

Mail search: Turnaround time: 2 weeks. No self addressed stamped envelope is required.

Phone search: See expedited service.

In person search: Turnaround time 30 minutes.

Expedited service: Expedited service is available for phone searches at 800-669-8310. Total fee is $43.95 and includes overnight delivery and fee for use of credit card.

Marriage Certificates

Dept of Environment, Health & Natural Resources, Vital Records Section, 1903 Mail Service Center, Raleigh, NC 27699-1903 (Courier: 225 N McDowell St, Raleigh, NC 27603); 919-733-3526, 919-829-1359 (Fax), 8AM-4PM.

www.schs.state.nc.us/SCHS

Note: Non-certified copies may be purchased by the public. Certified copies can be obtained by family members. The fee is the same for either report.

Indexing & Storage: Records are available from 1962 to present. New records are available for inquiry immediately. Records are indexed on microfiche, inhouse computer.

Searching: Investigative searches are permitted, but only non-certified copies are provided. Include the following in your request: names of husband and wife, date of marriage, place or county of marriage.

Access by: mail, phone, in person.

Fee & Payment: The search fee is $10.00 for each 5 years searched. Add $9.95 for using a credit card (expedited service only). Add $5.00 per copy for additional copies. Fee payee: North Carolina Vital Records. Prepayment required. Personal checks accepted. Credit cards accepted: MasterCard, Visa, AmEx, Discover.

Mail search: Turnaround time: 2 weeks. No self addressed stamped envelope is required.

Phone search: See expedited service.

In person search: Turnaround time 30 minutes.

Expedited service: Expedited service is available for phone searches. Total fee is $43.95 and includes overnight delivery and fee for use of credit card. Call 800-669-8310.

Divorce Records

Dept of Environment, Health & Natural Resources, Vital Records Section, 1903 Mail Service Center, Raleigh, NC 27699-1903 (Courier: 225 N McDowell St, Raleigh, NC 27603); 919-733-3526, 919-829-1359 (Fax), 8AM-4PM.

www.schs.state.nc.us/SCHS

Note: Non-certified copies are available to the public, certified copies to family members. The fee is the same for either report.

Indexing & Storage: Records are available from 1958 to present. New records are available for inquiry immediately. Records are indexed on microfiche, inhouse computer.

Searching: Investigative searches are permitted, but only non-certified copies are provided. Include the following in your request: names of husband and wife, date of divorce, place of divorce, case number (if known).

Access by: mail, phone, in person.

Fee & Payment: The search fee is $10.00 for each 5 years searched. Add $9.95 for using a credit card (expedited only). Add $5.00 per copy for additional copies. Fee payee: North Carolina Vital Records. Prepayment required. Personal checks accepted. Credit cards accepted: MasterCard, Visa, AmEx, Discover.

Mail search: Turnaround time: 2 weeks. No self addressed stamped envelope is required.

Phone search: See expedited service.

In person search: Turnaround time is 30 minutes.

Expedited service: Expedited service is available for phone searches only, use of creidt card required. Total fee is $43.95 and includes overnight delivery. Call 800-669-8310.

Workers' Compensation Records

NC Industrial Commission, 4340 Mail Service Center, Raleigh, NC 27699-4340; 919-807-2500, 8AM-5PM.

www.comp.state.nc.us

Indexing & Storage: Records are available from 1980.

Searching: Searches require a signed release or statement of purpose of request on letterhead. Only parties to claim will be allowed access. Records may not be used for pre-employment screening.

Access by: mail, in person.

Fee & Payment: There is no search fee. There is no copy fee unless the file is over 20 pages, then the fee is $1.00 per page (over 20). Fee payee: NC Industrial Commission. Personal checks accepted. No credit cards accepted.

Mail search: Turnaround time: 2 to 3 days.

In person search: Generally turnaround time is immediate, unless the case is closed and records must be researched.

Driver Records

Division of Motor Vehicles, Driver's License Section, 1100 New Bern Ave, Raleigh, NC 27697; 919-715-7000, 8AM-5PM.

www.dmv.dot.state.nc.us

Note: Records available include a limited three year (insurance purposes) and a complete seven year (employment purposes) record. Copies of tickets may be purchased from this same address for a fee of $5.00 per ticket.

Indexing & Storage: Records are available for 5 years or more for moving violations, 10 years or more for DWIs and suspensions. Records of surrendered licenses are kept for one year after the expiration date. North Carolina utilizes two point systems-one for the DMV, one for insurance purposes. It takes 30 days or less before new records are available for inquiry.

Searching: Large volume users are pre-approved and must file a certificate with the state. Form DL-DPPA-1 is required. Casual requesters can obtain records, but no personal information is released. Include the following in your request: driver's license number, full name, date of birth. Some search modes will look at the driver's license number first, then the name and DOB as a secondary search. Online requesters must have the license number to search. The following data is not released: medical information.

Access by: mail, in person, online.

Fee & Payment: The current fee is $5.00 per record. Certified records are an additional $2.00. Fee payee: Division of Motor Vehicles. Prepayment required. Personal checks accepted. No credit cards accepted.

Mail search: Turnaround time: 7 business days. No self addressed stamped envelope is required.

In person search: Up to 2 requests will be processed across the counter; the rest are available the next day.

Online search: To qualify for online availability, a client must be an insurance agent or insurance company support organization. The mode is interactive and is open from 7 AM to 10 PM. The DL# and name are needed when ordering. Records are $5.00 each. A minimum $500 security deposit is required.

Other access: Magnetic tape for high volume batch users is available. Requests must be pre-paid.

Vehicle Ownership
Vehicle Identification

Division of Motor Vehicles, Registration/ Correspondence Unit, 1100 New Bern Ave, Rm 100, Raleigh, NC 27697-0001; 919-715-7000, 8AM-5PM.

www.dmv.dot.state.nc.us

Indexing & Storage: Records are available from their first records for title records (on microfilm). Computer records are purged periodically according to plate activity. Records are maintained for mobile homes and boat trailers, also.

Searching: The state is in compliance with DPPA. Casual requesters receive records without personal information. Effective 01/01/00, only vehicle owners who have opted in, are placed on marketing list requests. Include the following in your request: vehicle description, name, and

signed release of subject on Form MVR-605A if not ongoing requester.

Access by: mail, in person.

Fee & Payment: The fee is $1.00 per record (includes lien data) or $5.00 for a certified record. Fee payee: Department of Motor Vehicles. Prepayment required. Personal checks accepted. No credit cards accepted.

Mail search: Turnaround time: 3 days. The use of Form MVR-605A is helpful. The requests require the requester's signature. A self addressed stamped envelope is requested.

In person search: Turnaround time is while you wait if you have the correct authorization.

Other access: North Carolina offers a bulk retrieval of ownership and registration information on magnetic tape. A written request specifying the purpose and details of the request is required. For more information, call 913-250-4230.

Accident Reports

Division of Motor Vehicles, Traffic Records Section, 3105 Mail Service Center, Raleigh, NC 27699-3105; 919-861-3098, 919-733-9605 (Fax), 8AM-5PM.

www.dmv.dot.state.nc.us/trafficrecords/faq

Indexing & Storage: Records are available from 1986 to present on computer, from 1990 to present on microfiche. Hard copies are available from 1994.

Searching: Records are not released on minor drivers. Using Form TR-67A, the requester should submit at least one of the names of the participants, the county of occurrence, date of occurrence, and the exception under which he/she qualifies to receive personal information in accordance with DPPA.

Access by: mail, in person.

Fee & Payment: The fee is $4.00 for a certified copy or no cost for a non-certified copy. Fee payee: Division of Motor Vehicles. Prepayment required. Personal checks accepted. No credit cards accepted.

Mail search: Turnaround time: 5 days.

In person search: Turnaround time is immediate if the record is available.

Other access: Bulk file purchase is available.

Vessel Ownership
Vessel Registration

North Carolina Wildlife Resources Commission, Transaction Management, 1709 Mail Service Center, Raleigh, NC 27699-1709; 800-628-3773, 919-662-4379 (Fax), 8AM-5PM.

http://216.27.49.98/

Indexing & Storage: Records are available from 1970 and are computerized. This is an optional title state. Lien information will show if the vessel is titled. All motorized boats and sailboats over 14 ft must be registered. New records are available for inquiry immediately.

Searching: Include the following in your request: Name, signed release. Submit the name or registration number or hull number.

Access by: mail, fax.

Fee & Payment: There is no search fee.

Mail search: Turnaround time: 1 to 2 weeks. No self addressed stamped envelope is required.

Fax search: Turnaround time is several days.

Other access: The agency sells a CD-ROM disk with registration information for $10.00 per disk.

Legislation Records

North Carolina General Assembly, State Legislative Bldg, 16 W. Jones Street, 1st Fl, Raleigh, NC 27603; 919-733-7779 (Bill Numbers), 919-733-3270 (Archives), 919-733-5648 (Order Desk), 8:30AM-5:30PM.

www.ncleg.net

Note: To get a copy of a bill, you must have a bill number first.

Indexing & Storage: Records are available for current and prior sessions only. Records are computer indexed since 1985, and are indexed on microfiche from 1969 to 1984.

Searching: Can search by 10 fields including bill number and subject.

Access by: mail, phone, in person, online.

Fee & Payment: There is no search fee, but copies are $.20 each. Fee payee: North Carolina General Assembly. Prepayment required. Money is only needed for the copy machine. Personal checks accepted. No credit cards accepted.

Mail search: Turnaround time: variable. No self addressed stamped envelope is required.

Phone search: Searches by phone are limited to between 5 and 8 bills depending on workload.

In person search: Turnaround time is immediate.

Online search: The Internet site has copies of bills, status, and state statutes.

Other access: This agency will mail lists of bills on computer printouts.

Voter Registration

State Board of Elections, PO Box 27255, Raleigh, NC 27611-7255; 919-733-7173, 919-715-0135 (Fax), 8AM-5PM.

www.sboe.state.nc.us

Note: There is now a statewide online system. Records are open to the public. Prior to 2002, records had to be be accessed at the county level through the County Director of Elections.

Indexing & Storage: Records are available for current and prior sessions only. Records are computer indexed since 1985, and are indexed on microfiche from 1969 to 1984.

Searching: Can search by 10 fields including bill number and subject.

Access by: mail, phone, in person, online.

Fee & Payment: The records are sold in database format in elecronic, magnetic or digital media. The maximum fee is $25.00.

Mail search: Turnaround time: variable. No self addressed stamped envelope is required.

Phone search: Searches by phone are limited depending on workload.

In person search: Turnaround time is immediate.

Online search: Online access to voter registration records is available free at www.sboe.state.nc.us/voterweb/seimsvot.htm.

Other access: The records are sold in database format in electronic, magnetic or digital media. The maximum fee is $25.00.

GED Certificates

Department of Community Colleges, GED Office, 5024 Mail Service Center, Raleigh, NC 27699-5024; 919-733-7051 x744, 919-715-5351 (Fax), 8AM-4PM.

www.ncccs.cc.nc.us

Indexing & Storage: Records are available from the 1940s, from 09/78 on microfilm.

Searching: There are no fees for verification or copies of transcripts. Include the following in your request: signed release, Social Security Number, date of birth. The year of the test is helpful.

Access by: mail, fax, in person.

Mail search: Turnaround time: 1 week.

Fax search: Searching is available by fax.

In person search: No fee for request.

Hunting License Information
Fishing License Information

Wildlife Resource Commission, Archdale Bldg, 512 N Salisbury Street, Raleigh, NC 27604-0118; 919-662-4370, 919-661-4878 (Fax), 8AM-5PM.

http://216.27.49.98

Indexing & Storage: Records are available for the past four years.

Searching: Requests must be in writing.

Access by: mail, phone, in person, online.

Fee & Payment: The are no fees.

Mail search: Turnaround time: variable. You may call them after mailing your request.

Fax search: You may have to call back for results, once you have faxed the request.

In person search: Turnaround time is immediate.

North Carolina State Licensing Agencies

Licenses Searchable Online

Acupuncturist #40 .... http://ncaaom.org/directory.php?sort=city
Anesthetist Nurse #8 .... www.docboard.org/nc/df/ncsearch.htm
Architect #3 .... www.member-base.com/ncbarch/public/lic/searchdb.asp
Architectural Firms #3 .... www.member-base.com/ncbarch/public/firms/searchdb.asp
Banking Division #17 .... www.banking.state.nc.us/banks.htm
Charitable/Sponsor Organization #52 .... www.secretary.state.nc.us/csl/index.html
Check Casher #17 .... www.banking.state.nc.us/checkcas.htm
Chiropractor #41 .... www.ncchiroboard.org/public/licensed_chiros.html
Clinical Nurse Specialist #8 .... www.docboard.org/nc/df/ncsearch.htm
Consumer Financer #17 .... www.banking.state.nc.us/cf.htm
Contractor, General #32 .... www.nclbgc.org/lic_fr.html (site may be down)
Dental Hygienist #42 .... www.ncdentalboard.org/ncdbe_search.asp
Dentist #42 .... www.ncdentalboard.org/ncdbe_search.asp
Electrical Contractor/Inspector #6 .... www.ncbeec.org/LicSearch.asp
Engineer #48 .... www.member-base.com/ncbels/public/searchdb.asp
Fire Sprinkler Contractor/Inspector #31 .... www.nclicensing.org/OnlineReg.htm
Fund Raiser Consultant/Solicitor #52 .... www.secretary.state.nc.us/csl/index.html
Geologist #46 .... www.ncblg.org/licensees.html
Hearing Aid Dispenser/Fitter #43 .... www.nchalb.org/getmembers.cfm
Heating Contractor #31 .... www.nclicensing.org/OnlineReg.htm
Landscape Architect #46 .... www.ncbola.org/rosternew.html
Lobbyist #51 .... www.secretary.state.nc.us/lobbyists/Lsearch.asp
Medical Doctor/Physician #47 .... www.docboard.org/nc/df/ncsearch.htm
Midwife Nurse #8 .... www.docboard.org/nc/df/ncsearch.htm
Mortgage Division #17 .... www.banking.state.nc.us/mbb.htm
Nurse Practitioner #8 .... www.docboard.org/nc/df/ncsearch.htm
Nurse-LPN #8 .... www.docboard.org/nc/df/ncsearch.htm
Nursing Home Administrator #5 .... www.ncbenha.org/searchdb.asp
Occupational Therapist #9 .... www.ncbot.org/fpdb/otimport.html
Occupational Therapist Assistant #9 .... www.ncbot.org/fpdb/otimport.html
Optometrist #18 .... www.ncoptometry.org/verify/index.asp
Osteopathic Physician #47 .... www.docboard.org/nc/df/ncsearch.htm
Pesticide Applicator #16 .... www.ncagr.com/aspzine/Fooddrug/data/advsearch.asp
Pesticide Consultant #16 .... www.ncagr.com/aspzine/Fooddrug/data/advsearch.asp
Pesticide Dealer #16 .... www.ncagr.com/aspzine/Fooddrug/data/advsearch.asp
Pharmacist #11 .... www.ncbop.org/names1.asp
Physician Assistant #47 .... www.docboard.org/nc/df/ncsearch.htm
Plumber #31 .... www.nclicensing.org/OnlineReg.htm
Podiatrist #12 .... www.ncbpe.org/search.php
Psychological Associate #36 .... www.ncpsychologyboard.org/search.htm
Psychologist #36 .... www.ncpsychologyboard.org/search.htm
Public Accountant-CPA #37 .... www.cpaboard.state.nc.us
Real Estate Broker/Dealer #39 .... www.memberbase.com/ncrec-new/licdb/indv/searchdb.asp
Real Estate Firm #39 .... www.memberbase.com/ncrec-new/licdb/firms/searchdb.asp
Surveyor, Land #48 .... www.member-base.com/ncbels/public/searchdb.asp

Licensing Quick Finder

Acupuncturist #40 919-773-0530	EDM #21 919-733-2285	Midwife Nurse #8...............................919-782-3211
Alarm Installer #1 919-875-3611	Electrical Contractor/Inspector #6 919-733-9042	Mortgage Division #17 919-733-3016
Alarm System Business #1...................919-875-3611	Electrologist #35 336-574-1414	Notary Public #58...............................919-733-3406
Alcoholic Beverage Control #20 919-779-0700	Electrology Instructor #35...................336-574-1414	Nurse Practitioner #8 919-782-3211
Ambulance Attendant #21 919-733-2285	Elevator Inspector #24 919-807-2770	Nurse-LPN #8.....................................919-782-3211
Amusement Device #24 919-807-2770	Embalmer #7 919-733-9380	Nursing Home #21 919-733-7461
Anesthetist Nurse #8 919-782-3211	Emergency Medical Service #21..........919-733-2285	Nursing Home Administrator #5............919-571-4164
Architect #3 919-733-9544	Emergency Medical Technician #21 919-733-2285	Occupational Therapist #9 919-832-1380
Architectural Firms #3.........................919-733-9544	Engineer #48 919-781-9499	Occupational Therapist Assistant #9 .. 919-832-1380
Armed Security Guard #53 919-875-3611	Esthetician Instructor/Apprentice/Practitioner #55	Optician #10 919-733-9321
Athletic Agent #51..............................919-807-2156	919-733-4117	Optometrist #18..................................919-285-3160
Attorney #45 919-828-4886	Family Therapist #57 336-794-3891	Osteopathic Physician #47..................919-326-1100
Auction Company #2 919-981-5066	Fire Sprinkler Contractor/Inspector #31 919-875-3612	Paramedic #21 919-733-2285
Auctioneer/Auctioneer Apprentice #2....919-981-5066	Firearms Trainer #53..........................919-875-3611	Pesticide Applicator #16.....................919-733-3556
Bail Bond Runner #23 919-733-2200	Fund Raiser Consultant/Solicitor #52...919-807-2214	Pesticide Consultant #16 919-733-3556
Bank #27...919-508-5973	Funeral Director #7.............................919-733-9380	Pesticide Dealer #16 919-733-3556
Banking Division #17 919-733-3016	Funeral Home/Chapel #7 919-733-9380	Pharmacist #11 919-942-4454
Barber Inspector #4 919-715-1159	Funeral Preneed Seller #7 919-733-9380	Pharmacy/Physician Pharmacy #11 919-942-4454
Barber Instructor #4 919-715-1159	Funeral Service #7 919-733-9380	Physical Therapist #49.......................919-490-6393
Barber/Barber Apprentice #4 919-715-1159	Fur Dealer #25....................................919-733-4984	Physician Assistant #47 919-326-1100
Beauty Shop/Salon #55.......................919-733-4117	Game Bird Propagator #25 919-733-4984	Plumber #31 919-875-3612
Bingo Operation #21............................919-733-3029	Geologist #46 919-850-9669	Podiatrist #12 919-787-5181
Boiler/Pressure Vessel Inspector #24 ...919-807-2760	Guard Dog Service #53 919-875-3611	Polygraph Examiner #53 919-875-3611
Bondsman, Professional/Surety #23 919-733-2200	Hearing Aid Dispenser/Fitter #43 919-981-5105	Private Investigator #53 919-875-3611
Building Inspector #23 919-733-3901	Heating Contractor #31 919-875-3612	Psychological Associate #36................828-262-2258
Cemetery #19 919-981-2536	Hospital #21..919-733-7461	Psychologist #36.................................828-262-2258
Cemetery Salesperson #19 919-981-2536	Hunting Preserve Operator #25 919-733-4984	Public Accountant-CPA #37.................919-733-4222
Charitable/Sponsor Organization #52 ...919-807-2214	Insurance Agent #23 919-733-7487	Real Estate Broker/Dealer #39 919-733-9580
Check Casher #17 919-733-3016	Insurance Company #23 919-733-7487	Real Estate Firm #39 919-733-9580
Chiropractor #41.................................704-782-0111	Investment Advisor #27 919-733-3924	Shorthand Reporter #29......................919-733-2927
Clinical Nurse Specialist #8 919-782-3211	Investment Represent./Advisor #26 919-733-3924	Social Worker #15...............................336-625-1679
Consumer Financer #17 919-733-3016	Jailer #56 919-716-6460	Solicitor #21..919-733-4510
Contractor, General #32 919-571-4183	Landscape Architect #46.....................919-850-9088	Solid Waste Facility Operator #34 919-733-0379
Cosmetologist Instructor/Apprentice/Practitioner #55	Librarian, Public #28...........................919-733-2570	Speech Pathologist/Audiologist #30 336-272-1828
....919-733-4117	Lobbyist #51 919-807-2156	Surveyor, Land #48.............................919-781-9499
Counselor #13 919-515-2244	Manicurist #54 919-850-2793	Taxidermist #25...................................919-733-4984
Crematory #7 919-733-9380	Manicurist Instructor/Apprentice/Practitioner #55	Veterinarian #50 919-733-7689
Day Care Administrator #21 919-622-4499	919-733-4117	Veterinary Technician #50 919-733-7689
Day Care Center Teacher #21 919-622-4499	Marriage & Family Therapist #33 336-794-3891	Waste Water Treatment Plant Operator #34
Dental Hygienist #42 919-781-4901	Medical Doctor/Physician #47..............919-326-1100	919-733-0379
Dentist #42...919-781-4901	Medical Program Director #21..............919-715-1872	Wildlife Collector #25 919-733-4984
DME (Rx Device) #11..........................919-942-4454	Medical Responder #21 919-733-2285	

Licensing Agency Information

#1 Alarm Systems Licensing Board, 1631 Midtown Pl #104, Raleigh, NC 27609; 919-875-3611, Fax: 919-875-3609. www.jus.state.nc.us/justice/pps/aslmain.htm. Agency email: PPSASL@mail.jus.state.nc.us.

#2 Auctioneer Licensing Board, 1001 Navajo Dr #105, Raleigh, NC 27609-7318; 919-981-5066, Fax: 919-981-5069. www.ncalb.org. Agency email: info@ncalb.org.

#3 Board of Architecture, 127 Hargett St #304, Raleigh, NC 27601; 919-733-9544, Fax: 919-733-1272. www.ncbarch.org Agency email: ncba@earthlink.net. Search database at www.ncbarch.org/dbase.asp. Mailing lists are also available, see "Directory" section at main web site.

#4 Board of Barber Examiners, 2321 Crabtree Blvd #110, Raleigh, NC 27604-2260; 919-715-1159, Fax: 919-715-4669.

#5 Board of Examiners for Nursing Home Administrators, 3733 National Drive #228, Raleigh, NC 27612; 919-571-4164, Fax: 919-571-4166. www.ncbenha.org. Search database at www.ncbenha.org/searchdb.asp

#6 Division of Enviornmental Health, Public Water Supply Section, Board of Examiners of Electrical Contractors, PO Box 18727 (1299 Front St.), Raleigh, NC 27619; 919-733-9042, Fax: 919-733-6105. www.ncbeec.org Agency email: info@ncbeec.org. Search database at www.ncbeec.org/LicSearch.asp

#7 Board of Mortuary Science, 2123 Crabtree Blvd #100, Raleigh, NC 27604; 919-733-9380, Fax: 919-733-8271. www.ncbms.org.

#8 Board of Nursing, PO Box 2129 (3724 National Dr.), Raleigh, NC 27602; 919-782-3211, Fax: 919-781-9461. www.ncbon.com Search database at www.docboard.org/nc/df/ncsearch.htm

#9 Board of Occupational Therapy, PO Box 2280, Raleigh, NC 27602; 919-832-1380, Fax: 919-833-1059. www.ncbot.org Agency email: administrator@ncbot.org. Search database at www.ncbot.org/fpdb/otimport.html

#10 Board of Opticians, PO Box 25336, Raleigh, NC 27611-5336; 919-733-9321, Fax: 919-733-0040.

#11 Board of Pharmacy, PO Box 459 (104 C Carrboro Plaza), Carrboro, NC 27510-0459; 919-942-4454, Fax: 919-967-5757. www.ncbop.org Agency email: csmith@ncbog.org. Search database at www.ncbop.org/names1.asp

#12 Board of Podiatry Examiners, 1500 Sunday Dr #102, Raleigh, NC 27607; 919-787-5181, Fax: 919-787-4916. www.ncbpe.org. Agency email: info@ncbpe.org. Search database at www.ncbpe.org/search.php

#13 Board of Registered Practicing Counselors, 893 Hwy 70 W #202, Garner, NC 27529; 919-661-0820, Fax: 919-779-5642. www.ncblpc.org Search database at www.ncblpc.org/searchform.cfm

#15 Certification Board for Social Workers, PO Box 1043, Asheboro, NC 27204; 336-625-1679, Fax: 336-625-1680. www.nccbsw.org Agency email: swboard@asheboro.com.

#16 Department of Agriculture, Pesticide Section, PO Box 27647 (2109 Blue Ridge Rd), Raleigh, NC 27611; 919-733-3556, Fax: 919-733-9796. www.agr.state.nc.us/fooddrug/pesticid/index.htm Search database at www.ncagr.com/aspzine/Food drug/data/advsearch.asp

#17 Department of Commerce, 4309 Mail Service Center (702 Oberlin Rd #400), Raleigh, NC 27699; 919-733-3016, Fax: 919-733-6918. www.banking.state.nc.us Search database at www.banking.state.nc.us

#18 Board of Examiners in Optometry, 109 N. Graham Street, Wallace, NC 28466; 910-285-3160, Fax: 910-285-4546. www.ncoptometry.org Agency email: ncsbeo@duplin.net. Search database at www.ncoptometry.org/verify/index.asp

#19 Department of Commerce, 1000 Navaho Dr GL-2, Raleigh, NC 27609; 919-981-2536, Fax: 919-981-2538.

#20 Department of Commerce, Alcoholic Beverage Control Commission, 4307 Mail Service Center, Raleigh, NC 27699-4307; 919-779-0700, Fax: 919-662-3583. www.ncabc.com

#21 Department of Health & Human Services, 2702 Mail Service Center (701 Barbour Drive), Raleigh, NC 27699-2707; 919-733-2285, Fax: 919-733-7021. www.dhhs.state.nc.us Agency email: ed.browning@ncmail.net.

#23 Department of Insurance, PO Box 26387, 430 N Salisbury St, Raleigh, NC 27611; 919-733-7487. www.ncdoi.com

#24 Department of Labor, 4 W Edenton St, Labor Bldg, Raleigh, NC 27601-1092; 919-733-7166, Fax: 919-733-6197. www.dol.state.nc.us.

#25 Department of Natural Resources & Environment, Wildlife Resources Commission, 512 N Salisbury St, Raleigh, NC 27604-1188; 919-733-4984. www.ncwildlife.org/fs_index_01_license.htm

#26 Department of State, Securities Division, 300 N Salisbury #404, Raleigh, NC 27603; 919-733-3924, Fax: 919-821-0818. www.secstate.state.nc.us Agency email: secdiv@sosnc.com.

#27 Department of State Treasurer, Investment & Banking Division, PO Box 29622 (300 N Salisbury St), Raleigh, NC 27626; 919-733-3924, Fax: 919-733-6918. www.sosnc.com

#28 Division of State Library, Department of Cultural Resources, 109 E Jones St, Raleigh, NC 27601-2807; 919-733-2570, Fax: 919-733-8714. http://statelibrary.dcr.state.nc.us

#29 Examiners for Court Reporting Standards & Testing, PO Box 2448 (2 E Morgan St), Raleigh, NC 27602; 919-733-7107, Fax: 919-715-5779.

#30 Examiners for Speech Pathologists & Audiologists, PO Box 16885, Greensboro, NC 27416-0885; 336-272-1828, Fax: 336-272-4353.

#31 Board of Examiners of Plumbing, Heating & Fire Sprinkler Contractors, 3801 Wake Forest Rd #201, Raleigh, NC 27609; 919-875-3612, Fax: 919-875-3616. www.nclicensing.org Agency email: info@nclicensing.org. Search database at www.nclicensing.org/OnlineReg.htm

#32 Licensing Board for General Contractors, PO Box 17187 (3739 National Dr #225), Raleigh, NC 27619; 919-571-4183, Fax: 919-571-4703. www.nclbgc.net

#33 Marital & Family Therapy Certification Board, 3000 Bethesda Pl #503, Winston-Salem, NC 27103-3327; 336-794-3891. http://jobs.esc.state.nc.us/lmi/ar/occuplic/MarFam Ther.htm. Agency email: mftlb@bellsouth.net.

#34 Water Treatment Facility Operators, Certification Board, 1635 Mail Service Center, Raleigh, NC 27699-1635; 919-733-0379, Fax: 919-715-2726.

#35 Board of Electrolysis Examiners, PO Box 13626, Greensboro, NC 27415-3626; 336-574-1414, Fax: 336-574-1414. Agency email: ncbeexam@yahoo.com.

#36 Psychology Board, 895 State Farm Road #101, Boone, NC 28607; 828-262-2258, Fax: 828-265-8611. www.ncpsychologyboard.org Agency email: ncpsybd@helicon.net. Search database at www.ncpsychologyboard.org/search.htm

#37 Board of CPA Examiners, PO Box 12827 (1101 Oberlin Rd, #104), Raleigh, NC 27605-2827; 919-733-4222. www.cpaboard.state.nc.us. Search database at www.cpaboard.state.nc.us

#39 Real Estate Commission, 1313 Navaho Dr, Raleigh, NC 27609-7460; 919-875-3700, Fax: 919-877-4222. www.ncrec.state.nc.us Agency email: records@ncrec.state.nc.us. Search database at www.ncrec.state.nc.us/licensees/licensees.asp

#40 Acupuncture Licensing Board, 893 US Highway 70 West, Garner, NC 27529; 919-773-0530, Fax: 919-779-5642. http://ncaaom.org Search database at http://ncaaom/org/directory.php?sort=city

#41 Board of Chiropractic Examiners, 174 Church St N, Concord, NC 28025; 704-782-0111. www.ncchiroboard.org. Agency email: ncchirobrd@juno.com. Search database at www.ncchiroboard.org/public/licensed_chiros.html

#42 Board of Dental Examiners, PO Box 32270 (37 National Dr, Spe. 221), Raleigh, NC 27622-2270; 919-781-4901, Fax: 919-571-4197. www.ncdentalboard.org. Agency email: info@ncdentalboard.org. Search database at www.ncdentalboard.org/ncdbe_search.asp

#43 Board of Hearing Aid Dealers & Fitters, 3733 Benson Drive, Raleigh, NC 27609; 919-981-5105, Fax: 919-981-5045. www.nchalb.org. Agency email: info@nchalb.org. Search database at www.nchalb.org/getmembers.cfm

#45 Board of Law Examiners, PO Box 2946 (208 Fayetteville St Mall), Raleigh, NC 27602; 919-828-4886, Fax: 919-828-2251. www.ncble.org.

#46 Landscape Architecture & Geologists Board, PO Box 41225 (3733 Benson Dr), Raleigh, NC 27629; 919-850-9669, Fax: 919-872-1598. www.ncbola.org Agency email: ncbla@bellsouth.net. Search database at www.ncbola.org/rosternew.html

#47 Board of Medical Examiners, PO Box 20007 (1201 Front St, 27609), Raleigh, NC 27619; 919-326-1100, Fax: 919-326-1130. www.docboard.org Agency email: info@ncmedboard.org. Search database at www.docboard.org/nc/df/ncsearch.htm

#48 Board of Registration for Prof Engineers & Land Surveyors, 310 W Mill Brook Rd, Raleigh, NC 27609; 919-841-4000, Fax: 919-841-4012. www.ncbels.org Agency email: lbpeace@ncbels.org. Search database at www.member-base.com/ncbels/public/searchdb.asp

#49 Examining Committee of Physical Therapy, 18 W Colony Pl #120, Durham, NC 27705; 919-490-6393, Fax: 919-490-5106. www.ncptboard.org Search database at www.ncptboard.org/search.asp

#50 Veterinary Medical Board, PO Box 12587, Raleigh, NC 27605; 919-733-7689. http://jobs.esc.state.nc.us/lmi/ar/occuplic/Veterinar i.htm

#51 Secretary of State, Lobbyist Registration, 2 N Salisbury St (PO Box 29622), Raleigh, NC 27626-0622; 919-807-2156, Fax: 919-807-2160. www.secstate.state.nc.us. Agency email: mkelly@mail.secstate.state.nc.us. Search database at www.secretary.state.nc.us/lobbyists/Lsearch.asp

#52 Secretary of State, Solicitation Licensing Section, PO Box 29622, Raleigh, NC 27626-0525; 919-807-2214, Fax: 919-807-2220. www.secretary.state.nc.us/sls/default.asp Agency email: solicit@mail.secretary.state.nc.us. Search database at www.secretary.state.nc.us/csl/index.html

#53 Private Protective Svcs Board, 1631 Midtown Pl #104, Raleigh, NC 27609; 919-875-3611, Fax: 919-875-3609. Agency email: PPSASL@mail.jus.state.nc.us.

#55 Board of Cosmetic Arts Examiners, 1201 Front St, #110, Raleigh, NC 27609; 919-733-4117, Fax: 919-733-4127. www.cosmetology.state.nc.us

#56 Department of Justice, Attorney General's Office, Sheriff's Standard Division, PO Drawer 629, Raleigh, NC 27602; 919-716-6460.

#57 Marital & Family Therapy Licensure Board, 3000 Bethesda Pl #503, Winston-Salem, NC 27103; 336-794-3891, Fax: 336-794-3116. Agency email: mftlb@bellsouth.net.

#58 Secretary of State, Notary Public Section, PO Box 29622, Raleigh, NC 27626-0622; 919-807-2131. www.sosnc.com Agency email: noarty@sosnc.com.

North Carolina Federal Courts

The following list indicates the district and division name for each county in the state. If the bankruptcy court location is different from the district court, then the location of the bankruptcy court appears in parentheses.

County/Court Cross Reference

County	District	Division
Alamance	Middle	Greensboro
Alexander	Western	Statesville (Charlotte)
Alleghany	Western	Statesville (Charlotte)
Anson	Western	Charlotte
Ashe	Western	Statesville (Charlotte)
Avery	Western	Asheville (Charlotte)
Beaufort	Eastern	Greenville-Eastern (Wilson)
Bertie	Eastern	Elizabeth City (Wilson)
Bladen	Eastern	Wilmington (Wilson)
Brunswick	Eastern	Wilmington (Wilson)
Buncombe	Western	Asheville (Charlotte)
Burke	Western	Shelby (Charlotte)
Cabarrus	Middle	Greensboro
Caldwell	Western	Statesville (Charlotte)
Camden	Eastern	Elizabeth City (Wilson)
Carteret	Eastern	Greenville-Eastern (Wilson)
Caswell	Middle	Greensboro
Catawba	Western	Statesville (Charlotte)
Chatham	Middle	Greensboro
Cherokee	Western	Bryson City (Charlotte)
Chowan	Eastern	Elizabeth City (Wilson)
Clay	Western	Bryson City (Charlotte)
Cleveland	Western	Shelby (Charlotte)
Columbus	Eastern	Wilmington (Wilson)
Craven	Eastern	Greenville-Eastern (Wilson)
Cumberland	Eastern	Greenville-Eastern (Wilson)
Currituck	Eastern	Elizabeth City (Wilson)
Dare	Eastern	Elizabeth City (Wilson)
Davidson	Middle	Greensboro (Winston-Salem)
Davie	Middle	Greensboro
Duplin	Eastern	Wilmington (Wilson)
Durham	Middle	Greensboro
Edgecombe	Eastern	Raleigh (Wilson)
Forsyth	Middle	Greensboro (Winston-Salem)
Franklin	Eastern	Raleigh
Gaston	Western	Charlotte
Gates	Eastern	Elizabeth City (Wilson)
Graham	Western	Bryson City (Charlotte)
Granville	Eastern	Raleigh
Greene	Eastern	Greenville-Eastern (Wilson)
Guilford	Middle	Greensboro
Halifax	Eastern	Greenville-Eastern (Wilson)
Harnett	Eastern	Raleigh
Haywood	Western	Asheville (Charlotte)
Henderson	Western	Asheville (Charlotte)
Hertford	Eastern	Elizabeth City (Wilson)
Hoke	Middle	Greensboro
Hyde	Eastern	Greenville-Eastern (Wilson)
Iredell	Western	Statesville (Charlotte)
Jackson	Western	Bryson City (Charlotte)
Johnston	Eastern	Raleigh
Jones	Eastern	Greenville-Eastern (Wilson)
Lee	Middle	Greensboro
Lenoir	Eastern	Greenville-Eastern (Wilson)
Lincoln	Western	Statesville (Charlotte)
Macon	Western	Bryson City (Charlotte)
Madison	Western	Asheville (Charlotte)
Martin	Eastern	Greenville-Eastern (Wilson)
McDowell	Western	Shelby (Charlotte)
Mecklenburg	Western	Charlotte
Mitchell	Western	Asheville (Charlotte)
Montgomery	Middle	Greensboro
Moore	Middle	Greensboro
Nash	Eastern	Raleigh (Wilson)
New Hanover	Eastern	Wilmington (Wilson)
Northampton	Eastern	Elizabeth City (Wilson)
Onslow	Eastern	Wilmington (Wilson)
Orange	Middle	Greensboro
Pamlico	Eastern	Greenville-Eastern (Wilson)
Pasquotank	Eastern	Elizabeth City (Wilson)
Pender	Eastern	Wilmington (Wilson)
Perquimans	Eastern	Elizabeth City (Wilson)
Person	Middle	Greensboro
Pitt	Eastern	Greenville-Eastern (Wilson)
Polk	Western	Shelby (Charlotte)
Randolph	Middle	Greensboro
Richmond	Middle	Greensboro
Robeson	Eastern	Wilmington (Wilson)
Rockingham	Middle	Greensboro
Rowan	Middle	Greensboro
Rutherford	Western	Shelby (Charlotte)
Sampson	Eastern	Wilmington (Wilson)
Scotland	Middle	Greensboro
Stanly	Middle	Greensboro
Stokes	Middle	Greensboro (Winston-Salem)
Surry	Middle	Greensboro (Winston-Salem)
Swain	Western	Bryson City (Charlotte)
Transylvania	Western	Asheville (Charlotte)
Tyrrell	Eastern	Elizabeth City (Wilson)
Union	Western	Charlotte
Vance	Eastern	Raleigh
Wake	Eastern	Raleigh
Warren	Eastern	Raleigh
Washington	Eastern	Elizabeth City (Wilson)
Watauga	Western	Statesville (Charlotte)
Wayne	Eastern	Raleigh (Wilson)
Wilkes	Western	Statesville (Charlotte)
Wilson	Eastern	Raleigh (Wilson)
Yadkin	Middle	Greensboro (Winston-Salem)
Yancey	Western	Asheville (Charlotte)

Standards for Federal Courts: The search fee is $20.00 per item (one party name or case number). Certification fee is $7.00 per document. Copy fee is $.50 per page. All fees standard unless noted in profile. Mail Search: always enclose a stamped self addressed envelope unless otherwise noted. Before releasing records, all courts require prepayment unless noted in profile.

Open records are located at the court unless otherwise noted. District courts index by defendant and plaintiff as well as by case number. Bankruptcy courts usually index by debtor and case number. While most courts now have their indexes on computer, many still maintain index card files as well.

The universal PACER sign-up number is 800-676-6856. Find PACER and the Party/Case Index on the Web at http://pacer.psc.uscourts.gov. PACER dial-up access is $.60 per minute. Also, courts offering internet access via RACER, PACER, Web-PACER or the new CM-ECF charge $.07 per page fee unless noted as free.

US District Court

Eastern District of North Carolina

Elizabeth City Division c/o Raleigh Division, PO Box 25670, Raleigh, NC 27611 (Courier Address: Room 574, 310 New Bern Ave, Raleigh, NC 27601), 919-856-4370.

www.nced.uscourts.gov

Counties: Bertie, Camden, Chowan, Currituck, Dare, Gates, Hertford, Northampton, Pasquotank, Perquimans, Tyrrell, Washington.

Indexing & Storage: New cases are available in the index after filing date. Open records are located at the Raliegh Division.

Fee & Payment Notes: Payment may be made by money order, cashier check, personal check.

Phone Search: Searching not available by phone.

Mail Search: A stamped self addressed envelope is not required.

In Person Search: In person searching available.

PACER: Toll-free dial-up access: 800-995-0313. Local dial-up access: 919-856-4768. Case records are available back to 1989. Records are purged when deemed necessary. New records are available online after 3 days.

Greenville-Eastern Division Room 209, 201 S Evans St, Greenville, NC 27858-1137 (Courier Address: Use mail address for courier delivery), 252-830-6009, Fax: 919-830-2793.

www.nced.uscourts.gov

Counties: Beaufort, Carteret, Craven, Edgecombe, Greene, Halifax, Hyde, Jones, Lenoir, Martin, Pamlico, Pitt.

Indexing & Storage: Cases are indexed by defendant, plaintiff, and case number. New cases are available in the index same day if possible after filing date. Civil records are retained for 2 years. All criminal records after 1979 are forwarded to Raleigh.

Fee & Payment Notes: Payment may be made by money order, cashier check, business check. In state personal checks are also accepted. Payee: Clerk, US District Court. You are allowed to make your own copies. These copies cost $.50 per page.

Phone Search: Only limited docket information is available by phone.

In Person Search: In person searching available.

PACER: Toll-free dial-up access: 800-995-0313. Local dial-up access: 919-856-4768. Case records are available back to 1989. Records are purged when deemed necessary. New records are available online after 3 days.

Raleigh Division Clerk's Office, PO Box 25670, Raleigh, NC 27611 (Courier Address: Room 574, 310 New Bern Ave, Raleigh, NC 27601), 919-856-4370, Fax: 919-856-4160.

www.nced.uscourts.gov

Counties: Cumberland, Franklin, Granville, Harnett, Johnston, Nash, Vance, Wake, Warren, Wayne, Wilson.

Indexing & Storage: Cases are indexed by defendant, plaintiff, and case number. New cases are available in the index 1 day after filing date. Records from a former office in Fayetteville that handled Cumberland and Harnett counties are maintained here. District wide searches are available after 1979 for criminal records through this court.

Fee & Payment Notes: Payment may be made by money order, cashier check, business check. In state personal checks are also accepted. Payee: Clerk, US District Court.

Phone Search: Only docket information is available by phone.

Mail Search: A stamped self addressed envelope is not required.

In Person Search: In person searching available.

PACER: Toll-free dial-up access: 800-995-0313. Local dial-up access: 919-856-4768. Case records are available back to 1989. Records are purged when deemed necessary. New records are available online after 3 days.

Wilmington Division PO Box 338, Wilmington, NC 28402 (Courier Address: Room 239, 2 Princess St, Wilmington, NC 28401), 910-815-4663, Fax: 910-815-4518.

www.nced.uscourts.gov

Counties: Bladen, Brunswick, Columbus, Duplin, New Hanover, Onslow, Pender, Robeson, Sampson.

Indexing & Storage: Cases are indexed by defendant, plaintiff, and case number. New cases are available in the index 1 day after filing date. Closed civil records are retained for 2 years. All criminal records after 1979 are located in Raleigh.

Fee & Payment Notes: Payment may be made by money order, cashier check, personal check. Payee: Clerk, US District Court. You are allowed to make your own copies. These copies cost $.50 per page.

Phone Search: Phone searches are only available for information from 1992 to the present.

Mail Search: A stamped self addressed envelope is not required.

In Person Search: In person searching available.

PACER: Toll-free dial-up access: 800-995-0313. Local dial-up access: 919-856-4768. Case records are available back to 1989. Records are purged when deemed necessary. New records are available online after 3 days.

US Bankruptcy Court

Eastern District of North Carolina

Raleigh Division PO Box 1441, Raleigh, NC 27602 (Courier Address: Room 209, Century Station Bldg, 300 Fayetteville St Mall, Raleigh, NC 27602), 919-856-4752.

www.nceb.uscourts.gov

Counties: Franklin, Granville, Harnett, Johnston, Vance, Wake, Warren.

Indexing & Storage: Cases are indexed by debtor as well as by case number. New cases are available in the index 1 day after filing date. Open records are located at this court.

Fee & Payment Notes: Payment may be made by money order, cashier check, business check, Visa or Mastercard. Personal checks are not accepted. Credit cards are accepted from companies only. Payee: Clerk, US Bankruptcy Court. You are allowed to make your own copies. These copies cost $.25 per page.

Phone Search: An automated voice case information service (VCIS) is available. Call VCIS at 888-847-9138 or 252-234-7655.

In Person Search: In person searching available.

PACER: Sign-up number is. Access fee is.

Other Online Access: Search records on the Internet using RACER at http://pacer.nceb.uscourts.gov. There is no fee.

Wilson Division PO Drawer 2807, Wilson, NC 27894-2807 (Courier Address: The Thomas Milton Moore Bldg, 1760 Parkwood Blvd, Wilson, NC 27894), 252-237-0248.

www.nceb.uscourts.gov

Counties: Beaufort, Bertie, Bladen, Brunswick, Camden, Carteret, Chowan, Columbus, Craven, Cumberland, Currituck, Dare, Duplin, Edgecombe, Gates, Greene, Halifax, Hertford, Hyde, Jones, Lenoir, Martin, Nash, New Hanover, Northampton, Onslow, Pamlico, Pasquotank, Pender, Perquimans, Pitt, Robeson, Sampson, Tyrrell, Washington, Wayne, Wilson.

Indexing & Storage: Cases are indexed by debtor as well as by case number. New cases are available in the index 1 day after filing date. Open records are located at this court.

Fee & Payment Notes: Payment may be made by money order, cashier check, business check, Visa or Mastercard. Personal checks are not accepted. Payee: Clerk, US Bankruptcy Court. You are allowed to make your own copies. These copies cost $.25 per page.

Phone Search: Only major dates such as the 341 date, discharge date and entry date will be released. An automated voice case information service (VCIS) is available. Call VCIS at 888-513-9765 or 252-234-7655.

In Person Search: In person searching available.

PACER: Sign-up number is. Access fee is.

Other Online Access: Search records on the Internet using RACER at http://pacer.nceb.uscourts.gov. There is no fee.

US District Court

Middle District of North Carolina

Greensboro Division Clerk's Office, PO Box 2708, Greensboro, NC 27402 (Courier Address: Room 311, 324 W Market St, Greensboro, NC 27401), 336-332-6000.

www.ncmd.uscourts.gov

Counties: Alamance, Cabarrus, Caswell, Chatham, Davidson, Davie, Durham, Forsyth, Guilford, Hoke, Lee, Montgomery, Moore, Orange, Person, Randolph, Richmond, Rockingham, Rowan, Scotland, Stanly, Stokes, Surry, Yadkin.

Indexing & Storage: Cases are indexed by defendant, plaintiff, and case number. New cases are available in the index 1 day after filing date. All other divisions in this district have been abolished as of July 1997.

Fee & Payment Notes: Payment may be made by money order, cashier check, business check. In state personal checks are also accepted. Payee: Clerk, US District Court.

Phone Search: Searching not available by phone. Only docket information is available by case number over the phone.

Mail Search: A stamped self addressed envelope is not required.

In Person Search: In person searching available.

PACER: Toll-free dial-up access: 800-372-8820. Local dial-up access: 336-332-6010. Case records are available back to September 1991. Records are never purged. New records are available online after 2 days. PACER is available online at http://pacer.ncmd.uscourts.gov.

US Bankruptcy Court

Middle District of North Carolina

Greensboro Division PO Box 26100, Greensboro, NC 27420-6100 (Courier Address: 101 S Edgeworth St, Greensboro, NC 27401), 336-333-5647.

www.ncmb.uscourts.gov

Counties: Alamance, Cabarrus, Caswell, Chatham, Davidson, Davie, Durham, Guilford, Hoke, Lee, Montgomery, Moore, Orange, Person, Randolph, Richmond, Rockingham, Rowan, Scotland, Stanly.

Indexing & Storage: Cases are indexed by debtor as well as by case number. New cases are available in the index 1-2 days after filing date. Only pre-BANCAP cases (cases filed prior to 7/17/89) are indexed on a separate computer program. District wide searches are available for information on cases filed after July 17, 1989 from this division on their VCIS system.

Fee & Payment Notes: Payment may be made by money order, cashier check, personal check. Debtor's checks are not accepted. Payee: Clerk, US Bankruptcy Court.

Phone Search: Only the name of the debtor, case number, date filed, trustee and attorney for the debtor will be released over the phone. An automated voice case information service (VCIS) is available. Call VCIS at 888-319-0455 or 336-333-5532.

In Person Search: In person searching available.

PACER: Toll-free dial-up access: 800-417-3571. Local dial-up access: 336-333-5389. Document images available on Pacer. Case records are available back to 1992. Records are purged every two years. New civil records are available online after 1 day. PACER is available online at http://pacer.ncmb.uscourts.gov. Document images available.

Electronic Filing: (Currently in the process of implementing CM/ECF.)

Winston-Salem Division 226 S Liberty St, Winston-Salem, NC 27101 (Courier Address: Use mail address for courier delivery), 336-631-5340.

www.ncmb.uscourts.gov

Counties: Forsyth, Stokes, Surry, Yadkin.

Indexing & Storage: Cases are indexed by debtor as well as by case number. New cases are available in the index 2 days after filing date. Open records are located at this court.

Fee & Payment Notes: Payment may be made by money order, cashier check, personal check. Debtor's checks are not accepted. Payee: Clerk, US Bankruptcy Court.

Phone Search: Basic docket information only is available by phone. An automated voice case information service (VCIS) is available. Call VCIS at 888-319-0455 or 336-333-5532.

In Person Search: In person searching available.

PACER: Toll-free dial-up access: 800-417-3571. Local dial-up access: 336-333-5389. Document images available. Case records are available back to 1992. Records are purged every two years. New civil records are available online after 1 day. PACER is available online at http://pacer.ncmb.uscourts.gov. Document images available.

Electronic Filing: (Currently in the process of implementing CM/ECF.)

US District Court

Western District of North Carolina

Asheville Division Clerk of the Court, Room 309, US Courthouse Bldg, 100 Otis St, Asheville, NC 28801-2611 (Courier Address: Use mail address for courier delivery), 828-771-7200, Fax: 828-271-4343.

www.ncwd.uscourts.gov

Counties: Avery, Buncombe, Haywood, Henderson, Madison, Mitchell, Transylvania, Yancey.

Indexing & Storage: Cases are indexed by defendant, plaintiff, and case number. New cases are available in the index 1 day after filing date. Not all records are entered on the in house automated system. This office also handles records for the Bryson City and Shelby Divisions.

Fee & Payment Notes: Payment may be made by money order, cashier check, personal check. Payee: Clerk, US District Court. You are allowed to make your own copies. These copies cost $.50 per page.

Phone Search: Only docket information is available by phone.

In Person Search: In person searching available.

PACER: Access fee is. Document images available. Case records are available back to 1991. New records are available online after 2 days.

WebPACER is available online at www.ncwd.uscourts.gov/index.html. Document images available.

Bryson City Division c/o Asheville Division, Clerk of the Court, Room 309, US Courthouse, 100 Otis St, Asheville, NC 28801-2611 (Courier Address: Use mail address for courier delivery), 828-771-7200.

www.ncwd.uscourts.gov

Counties: Cherokee, Clay, Graham, Jackson, Macon, Swain.

Indexing & Storage: New cases are available in the index after filing date. Open records are located at the Asheville Division.

Fee & Payment Notes: Payment may be made by money order, cashier check. Business checks are not accepted. Personal checks are not accepted.

Phone Search: Searching not available by phone.

In Person Search: In person searching available.

PACER: Access fee is. Case records are available back to 1991. New records are available online after 2 days. WebPACER is available online at www.ncwd.uscourts.gov/index.html. Document images available.

Charlotte Division Clerk, Room 210, 401 W Trade St, Charlotte, NC 28202 (Courier Address: Use mail address for courier delivery), 704-350-7400.

www.ncwd.uscourts.gov

Counties: Anson, Gaston, Mecklenburg, Union.

Indexing & Storage: Cases are indexed by defendant, plaintiff, and case number. New cases are available in the index 1-2 days after filing date. District wide searches are available for records from 1950 forward from this court.

Fee & Payment Notes: Payment may be made by money order, cashier check, personal check. Payee: Clerk, US District Court.

Phone Search: Searching not available by phone. Only docket information is available by phone.

Mail Search: A stamped self addressed envelope is not required.

In Person Search: In person searching available.

PACER: Access fee is. Case records are available back to 1991. New records are available online after 2 days. WebPACER is available online at www.ncwd.uscourts.gov/index.html. Document images available.

Shelby Division c/o Asheville Division, Clerk of the Court, Room 309, US Courthouse, 100 Otis St, Asheville, NC 28801-2611 (Courier Address: Use mail address for courier delivery), 828-771-7200.

www.ncwd.uscourts.gov

Counties: Burke, Cleveland, McDowell, Polk, Rutherford.

Indexing & Storage: New cases are available in the index after filing date. Open records are located at the Asheville Division.

Fee & Payment Notes: Payment may be made by money order, cashier check. Business checks are not accepted. Personal checks are not accepted.

Phone Search: Searching not available by phone.

In Person Search: In person searching available.

PACER: Access fee is. Case records are available back to 1991. New records are available online after 2 days. WebPACER is available online at www.ncwd.uscourts.gov/index.html. Document images available.

Statesville Division PO Box 466, Statesville, NC 28687 (Courier Address: Room 205, 200 W Broad St, Statesville, NC 28687), 704-883-1000.

www.ncwd.uscourts.gov

Counties: Alexander, Alleghany, Ashe, Caldwell, Catawba, Iredell, Lincoln, Watauga, Wilkes.

Indexing & Storage: Cases are indexed by defendant, plaintiff, and case number. New cases are available in the index 2 days after filing date. Open records are located at this court.

Fee & Payment Notes: Payment may be made by money order, cashier check, personal check. Payee: Clerk, US District Court. You are allowed to make your own copies. These copies cost - current fee is not known - per page.

Phone Search: Only docket information is available by phone.

Mail Search: A stamped self addressed envelope is not required.

In Person Search: In person searching available.

PACER: Access fee is. Case records are available back to 1991. New records are available online after 2 days. WebPACER is available online at www.ncwd.uscourts.gov/index.html. Document images available.

US Bankruptcy Court
Western District of North Carolina

Charlotte Division P.O. Box 34189, Charlotte, NC 28234-4189 (Courier Address: 401 W Trade St, Charlotte, NC 28202), 704-350-7500.

www.ncwb.uscourts.gov

Counties: Alexander, Alleghany, Anson, Ashe, Avery, Buncombe, Burke, Caldwell, Catawba, Cherokee, Clay, Cleveland, Gaston, Graham, Haywood, Henderson, Iredell, Jackson, Lincoln, Macon, Madison, McDowell, Mecklenburg, Mitchell, Polk, Rutherford, Swain,Transylvania, Union, Watauga, Wilkes, Yancey.

Indexing & Storage: Cases are indexed by debtor as well as by case number. New cases are available in the index 1-2 days after filing date. Open records are located at this court.

Fee & Payment Notes: Payment may be made by money order, cashier check, business check. Personal checks are not accepted. Debtor's checks are not accepted. Payee: Clerk, US Bankruptcy Court.

Phone Search: Only docket information available by telephone. An automated voice case information service (VCIS) is available. Call VCIS at 800-884-9868 or 704-350-7505.

In Person Search: In person searching available.

PACER:. Case records are available back to 1992. Records are purged every 2 years. New civil records are available online after 1 day.

Electronic Filing: Information is available online at https://ecf.ncwb.uscourts.gov

North Carolina County Courts

Court	Jurisdiction	No. of Courts	How Organized
Superior Courts*	General	0	46 Districts
District Courts*	Limited	0	39 Districts
Combined Courts*		100	

* Profiled in this Sourcebook.

	CIVIL								
Court	Tort	Contract	Real Estate	Min. Claim	Max. Claim	Small Claims	Es-tate	Eviction	Domestic Relations
Superior Courts*	X	X	X	$10,000	No Max		X		
District Courts*	X	X	X	$0	$10,000	4100		X	X

	CRIMINAL				
Court	Felony	Misdemeanor	DWI/DUI	Preliminary Hearing	Juvenile
Superior Courts*	X				
District Courts*		X	X	X	X

ADMINISTRATION

Administrative Office of the Courts, Justice Bldg, 2 E Morgan St, Raleigh, NC, 27602; 919-733-7107, Fax: 919-715-5779. www.nccourts.org

COURT STRUCTURE

The Superior Court is the court of general jurisdiction, the District Court is limited. The counties combine the courts, thus searching is done through one court, not two, within the county.

ONLINE ACCESS

Access active District/Superior Court criminal calendars on a county or statewide basis at http://www1.aoc.state.nc.us/www/calendars.html. Historical information is not available. While there is no statewide online access, web access to civil and criminal dockets are available at some individual courts.

ADDITIONAL INFORMATION

Many courts recommend that civil searches be done in person or by a retriever and that only criminal searches be requested in writing (for a $5.00 search fee). Many courts have archived their records prior to 1968 in the Raleigh State Archives, 919-733-5722. A list of companies offering North Carolina criminal records online can be accessed at www.nccourts.org/Citizens/GoToCourt/Default.asp?topic=1

PROBATE COURTS

Probate is handled by County Clerks.

Alamance County

Superior - District Court - Criminal 212 West Elm St, #105, Graham, NC 27253; 336-570-6867. Hours: 8AM-5PM (EST). *Felony, Misdemeanor.*

www.aoc.state.nc.us/www/public/courts/alamance.html

Criminal Records: Access: Mail, online, in person. Both court and visitors may perform in person searches. Search fee: $5.00 per name. Required to search: name, years to search, DOB; also helpful: address, SSN. Criminal records on computer since 1985, on index cards back to 1975. Search the active Criminal Calendar by defendant name at the web site.

General Information: Public access terminal is available. No sealed case records released. Turnaround time 1 week. Copy fee: $1.00 for first page, $.25 each add'l. Certification fee: $2.00. Fee payee: Clerk of Superior Court. Only cashiers checks and money orders accepted. Prepayment is required.

Superior-District Court - Civil 1 Court Square, Graham, NC 27253; 336-438-1002. Hours: 8AM-5PM (EST). *Civil, Eviction, Small Claims, Probate.*

Civil Records: Access: In person only. Visitors must perform in person searches for themselves. No search fee. Required to search: name, years to search. Civil cases indexed by defendant, plaintiff. Civil records computerized since 1985, prior indexed on books.

General Information: Public access terminal is available. No adoptions, sealed cases, juvenile, or mental records released. Copy fee: $1.00 for first page, $.25 each add'l. Certification fee: $2.00.

Alexander County

Superior - District Court PO Box 100, Taylorsville, NC 28681; 828-632-2215; Fax: 828-632-3550. Hours: 8AM-5PM (EST). *Felony, Misdemeanor, Civil, Eviction, Small Claims, Probate.*

www.aoc.state.nc.us/www/public/courts/alexander.htm

Civil Records: Access: Mail, in person. Both court and visitors may perform in person searches. Search fee: $5.00 per name. Required to search: name, years to search, address. Civil cases indexed by defendant, plaintiff. Civil records on computer since 10/1989, prior on books.

Criminal Records: Access: Mail, online, in person. Both court and visitors may perform in person searches. Search fee: $5.00 per name. Required to search: name, years to search, address, DOB, SSN. Criminal records on computer since 10/1989, prior on books. Search the active criminal calendar by defendant at the web site.

General Information: Public access terminal is available. No adoptions, sealed cases, juvenile, sex offenders, mental, expunged records released. SASE required. Turnaround time 1-3 days. Copy fee: $.25 per page. Certification fee: $2.00. Fee payee: Clerk of Superior Court. Business checks accepted. Prepayment is required.

Alleghany County

Superior - District Court PO Box 61, Sparta, NC 28675; 336-372-8949; Fax: 336-372-4899. Hours: 8AM-5PM (EST). *Felony, Misdemeanor, Civil, Eviction, Small Claims, Probate.*

www.aoc.state.nc.us/www/public/courts/alleghany.html

Civil Records: Access: In person only. Visitors must perform in person searches for themselves. Search fee: No search fee. Required to search: name, years to search; also helpful: address. Civil cases indexed by defendant, plaintiff. Civil records on computer from 11/1988, index books prior.

Criminal Records: Access: Fax, mail, online, in person. Only the court performs in person searches; visitors may not. Search fee: $5.00 per name. Required to search: name, years to search, DOB; also helpful: address, SSN. Criminal records on computer from 11/1988, index books prior. Search the active Criminal Calendar by defendant name at the web site.

General Information: No adoptions, sealed cases, juvenile, sex offenders, mental or expunged records released. SASE required. Turnaround time 2 days. Copy fee: $1.00 for first page, $.25 each add'l. Certification fee: $2.00. Fee payee: Clerk of Superior Court. Business checks accepted. Prepayment required.

Anson County

Superior - District Court PO Box 1064 (114 N Greene St), Wadesboro, NC 28170; 704-694-2314; Fax: 704-695-1161. Hours: 8AM-5PM (EST). *Felony, Misdemeanor, Civil, Eviction, Small Claims, Probate.*
www.aoc.state.nc.us/www/public/courts/anson.htm

Civil Records: Access: Mail, in person. Visitors must perform in person searches for themselves. Search fee: $5.00 per name. Required to search: name, years to search. Civil cases indexed by defendant, plaintiff. Civil records on computer since Oct. 1989, in books prior.
Criminal Records: Access: Mail, online, in person. Only the court performs in person searches; visitors may not. Search fee: $5.00 per name. Required to search: name, years to search, DOB; also helpful: SSN. Criminal records on computer since 10/89, on microfilm 1982-89, in books prior. Search the active Criminal Calendar by defendant name at the web site.
General Information: Public access terminal is available. (Estates & Special Proceedings only.) No adoptions, sealed cases, juvenile, mental, or expunged records released. SASE required. Turnaround time 2-5 days. Copy fee: $1.00 for first page, $.25 each add'l. Certification fee: $2.00. Fee payee: Clerk of Superior Court. Business checks accepted. Prepayment required.

Ashe County

Superior - District Court 150 Government Circle #3100, Jefferson, NC 28640-9378; 336-246-5641; Fax: 336-246-4276. 8AM-5PM (EST). *Felony, Misdemeanor, Civil, Eviction, Small Claims, Probate.*
www.aoc.state.nc.us/www/public/courts/ashe.html

Civil Records: Access: Mail, in person. Both court and visitors may perform in person searches. Search fee: $5.00 per name. Required to search: name, years to search. Civil cases indexed by defendant, plaintiff. Civil records on computer from 12/89, on index books back to 1900s.
Criminal Records: Access: Mail, online, in person. Both court and visitors may perform in person searches. Search fee: $5.00 per name. Required to search: name, years to search. Criminal records on computer from 12/89, on index books back to 1900s. Online access to the Criminal Calendar by defendant name is available at the web site. Court will search records after 1988; visitors or researchers must search themselves for records prior to 1988.
General Information: Public access terminal is available. No adoptions, sealed cases, juvenile, sex offenders, mental or expunged records released. Turnaround time 1-3 days. Copy fee: $1.00 for first page, $.25 each add'l. Certification fee: $2.00. Fee payee: Clerk of Superior Court. Only cashiers checks and money orders accepted.

Avery County

Superior-District Court PO Box 115, Newland, NC 28657; 828-733-2900; Fax: 828-733-8410. Hours: 8AM-4:30PM (EST). *Felony, Misdemeanor, Civil, Eviction, Small Claims, Probate.*
www.aoc.state.nc.us/www/public/courts/avery.htm

Civil Records: Access: Mail, in person, fax. Only the court performs in person searches; visitors may not. Search fee: $5.00 per name. Required to search: name, years to search; also helpful: address. Civil cases

indexed by defendant, plaintiff. Civil records on computer since 1988, on index books to 1968.
Criminal Records: Access: Mail, online, in person. Only the court performs in person searches; visitors may not. Search fee: $5.00 per name. Required to search: name, years to search; also helpful: address. Criminal records on computer from 11/88; on cards and books back to 1968. Search the active Criminal Calendar by defendant name at the web site.
General Information: No adoptions, sealed cases, juvenile, sex offenders, mental or expunged records released. Turnaround time 2-3 days. Copy fee: $.25 per page. Certification fee: $2.00. Fee payee: Clerk of Superior Court. Only cashiers checks and money orders accepted. Will bill copy fees.

Beaufort County

Superior - District Court PO Box 1403, Washington, NC 27889; 252-946-5184. Hours: 8:30AM-5:30PM (EST). *Felony, Misdemeanor, Civil, Eviction, Small Claims, Probate.*
www.aoc.state.nc.us/www/public/courts/beaufort.html

Civil Records: Access: In person only. Visitors must perform in person searches for themselves. No search fee. Required to search: name, years to search, address. Civil cases indexed by defendant, plaintiff. Civil records on computer since 6/87, docket books to 1800s.
Criminal Records: Access: Mail, online, in person. Both court and visitors may perform in person searches. Search fee: $5.00 per name. Required to search: name, years to search, address, DOB, SSN. Criminal records on computer since 6/87, docket books to 1800s. Search the active Criminal Calendar by defendant name at the web site.
General Information: Public access terminal is available. No adoptions, sealed cases, juvenile, sex offenders, mental or expunged records released. Turnaround time 5 days. Copy fee: $1.00 for first page, $.25 each add'l. Certification fee: $2.00. Fee payee: Clerk of Superior Court. Business checks accepted.

Bertie County

Superior - District Court PO Box 370, Windsor, NC 27983; 252-794-3039; Fax: 252-794-2482. Hours: 8AM-5PM (EST). *Felony, Misdemeanor, Civil, Eviction, Small Claims, Probate.*
www.aoc.state.nc.us/www/public/courts/bertie.html

Civil Records: Access: In person only. Visitors must perform in person searches for themselves. No search fee. Required to search: name, years to search. Civil cases indexed by defendant, plaintiff. Civil records on computer from 11/96, prior on books to 1968.
Criminal Records: Access: Mail, fax, online, in person. Both court and visitors may perform in person searches. Search fee: $5.00 per name. Required to search: name, years to search, DOB; also helpful: address, SSN. Criminal records on computer from 3/89, prior on books to 1968. Search the active Criminal Calendar by defendant name at the web site.
General Information: Public access terminal is available. No adoptions, sealed cases, juvenile, mental, expunged records released. SASE requested. Turnaround time 1-2 days. Fax notes: Fee to fax results is $1.00 first page; $.25 each add'l. Copy fee: $1.00 for first page, $.25 each add'l. Certification fee: Court will not certify any in-person searches, otherwise $2.00. Fee payee: Clerk of Superior Court. Only cashiers checks and money orders accepted. Prepayment is required.

Bladen County

Superior - District Court PO Box 2619, Elizabethtown, NC 28337; 910-862-2143. Hours: 8:30AM-5PM (EST). *Felony, Misdemeanor, Civil, Eviction, Small Claims, Probate.*
www.aoc.state.nc.us/www/public/courts/bladen.html

Civil Records: Access: In person only. Visitors must perform in person searches for themselves. No search fee. Required to search: name, years to search. Civil cases indexed by defendant, plaintiff. Civil records on computer since 1989, prior on judgment books back to 1896 (fire).
Criminal Records: Access: Mail, online, in person. Both court and visitors may perform in person searches. Search fee: $5.00 per name. Required to search: name, years to search, DOB. Criminal records on computer from 5/89, on books to 1968. Search the active Criminal Calendar by defendant name at the web site.
General Information: Public access terminal is available. No adoptions, sealed cases, juvenile, sex offenders, mental or expunged records released. Turnaround time 5 days. Copy fee: $1.00 for first page, $.25 each add'l. Certification fee: $2.00. Fee payee: Clerk of Superior Court. Only cashiers checks and money orders accepted. Prepayment is required.

Brunswick County

Superior - District Court PO Box 127, Bolivia, NC 28422; 910-253-8502; Fax: 910-253-7652. Hours: 8:30AM-5:00PM (EST). *Felony, Misdemeanor, Civil, Eviction, Small Claims, Probate.*
www.aoc.state.nc.us/www/public/courts/brunswick.html

Civil Records: Access: In person only. Visitors must perform in person searches for themselves. No search fee. Required to search: name, years to search. Civil cases indexed by defendant, plaintiff. Civil records on computer since 1989, prior on books to 1968.
Criminal Records: Access: Mail, online, in person. Both court and visitors may perform in person searches. Search fee: $5.00 per name. Required to search: name, years to search. Criminal records on computer since 1989, prior on books to 1968. Search the active Criminal Calendar by defendant name at the web site.
General Information: No adoptions, sealed cases, juvenile, mental or expunged records. Turnaround time 1-2 days. Copy fee: $1.00 for first page, $.25 each add'l. Certification fee: $2.00. Fee payee: Clerk of Court. Business checks accepted. Prepayment is required.

Buncombe County

Superior - District Court 60 Court Plaza, Asheville, NC 28801-3519; 828-232-2605; Fax: 828-251-6257. Hours: 8:30AM-5PM (EST). *Felony, Misdemeanor, Civil, Eviction, Small Claims, Probate.*
www.aoc.state.nc.us/www/public/courts/buncombe.html

Civil Records: Access: Mail, fax, in person. Both court and visitors may perform in person searches. Search fee: $5.00 per name. Required to search: name, years to search. Civil cases indexed by defendant, plaintiff. Civil records on computer since 1/89; on books or dockets to 1832; judgment books in archives.
Criminal Records: Access: Mail, fax, online, in person. Both court and visitors may perform in person searches. Search fee: $5.00 per name. Required to search: name, years to search, DOB. Criminal records on computer since 1/89; on books or dockets to 1832; judgment books in archives. Search the active Criminal Calendar by defendant name at the web site.
General Information: Public access terminal is available. No adoptions, sealed cases, juvenile, sex offenders, mental or expunged records required. SASE required. Turnaround time 1 week. Fax notes: Fee to fax results is $1.00 1st page; $.25 each add'l. Copy fee: $1.00 for first page, $.25 each add'l. Certification fee: $2.00. Fee payee: Clerk of Court. Only cashiers checks and money orders accepted. Prepayment is required.

Burke County

Superior - District Court PO Box 796, Morganton, NC 28680; 828-432-2800; Fax: 828-438-5460. Hours: 8AM-5PM (EST). *Felony, Misdemeanor, Civil, Eviction, Small Claims, Probate.*

www.aoc.state.nc.us/www/public/courts/burke.html

Civil Records: Access: Fax, mail, in person. Both court and visitors may perform in person searches. Search fee: $5.00 per name. Required to search: name, years to search; also helpful: address. Civil cases indexed by defendant, plaintiff. Civil records on computer since 10/88, on index books to 1890s.

Criminal Records: Access: Fax, mail, online, in person. Both court and visitors may perform in person searches. Search fee: $5.00 per name. Required to search: name, years to search, DOB; also helpful: address, SSN. Criminal records on computer since 6/86, on cards or books back to 1900s. Search the active Criminal Calendar by defendant name at the web site.

General Information: Public access terminal is available. No adoptions, sealed cases, juvenile, sex offenders, mental or expunged records released. SASE required. Turnaround time 1-2 days. Fax notes: Fee to fax results is $3.00 per document. Copy fee: $1.00 for first page, $.25 each add'l. Certification fee: $5.00. Fee payee: Clerk of Court. Business checks accepted. Prepayment is required.

Cabarrus County

Superior - District Court PO Box 70, Concord, NC 28026-0070; 704-786-4137 (Estates & Special Proceed); Civil phone: 704-786-4201; Criminal phone: 704-786-4138 (Superior); 786-4211 (Dist.). Hours: 8:30AM-5PM (EST). *Felony, Misdemeanor, Civil, Eviction, Small Claims, Probate.*

www.aoc.state.nc.us/www/public/courts/cabarrus.htm

Civil Records: Access: In person only. Visitors must perform in person searches for themselves. No search fee. Required to search: name, years to search; also helpful: address. Civil cases indexed by defendant, plaintiff. Civil records go back to 1900s'; on computer since 2/13/89.

Criminal Records: Access: Mail, online, in person. Both court and visitors may perform in person searches. Search fee: $5.00 per name. Required to search: name, DOB; also helpful: address, SSN, maiden name. Criminal records go back to 12/70; on computer back to 01/1/85. Search the active Criminal Calendar by defendant name at the web site.

General Information: Public access terminal is available. No adoptions, sealed cases, juvenile, sex offenders, mental or expunged records released. Turnaround time 2-3 days. Copy fee: $1.00 for first page, $.25 each add'l. Certification fee: $2.00. Fee payee: Clerk of Superior Court. Only cashiers checks and money orders accepted. Prepayment is required.

Caldwell County

Superior - District Court PO Box 1376, Lenoir, NC 28645; 828-757-1373; Fax: 828-757-1479. Hours: 8AM-5PM (EST). *Felony, Misdemeanor, Civil, Eviction, Small Claims, Probate.*

www.aoc.state.nc.us/www/public/courts/caldwell.html

Civil Records: Access: Mail, in person. Both court and visitors may perform in person searches. Search fee: $5.00 per name. Required to search: name, years to search. Civil cases indexed by defendant, plaintiff. Civil records on computer since Nov. 1988, prior on books to 1849.

Criminal Records: Access: Mail, online, in person. Both court and visitors may perform in person searches. Search fee: $5.00 per name. Required to search: name. Criminal records on computer from 8/86, prior in books to 1966. Search the active Criminal Calendar by defendant name at the web site.

General Information: Public access terminal is available. No adoptions, sealed cases, juvenile, sex offenders, mental or expunged records released. Turnaround time 1-2 days. Fax notes: Fee to fax results is $1.00 1st page; $.25 each add'l. Copy fee: $1.00 for

first page, $.25 each add'l. Certification fee: $2.00; $.500 for criminal. Fee payee: Clerk of Superior Court. Only cashiers checks and money orders accepted. Prepayment is required.

Camden County

Superior - District Court PO Box 219, Camden, NC 27921; 252-331-4871; Fax: 252-331-4827. Hours: 8AM-5PM (EST). *Felony, Misdemeanor, Civil, Eviction, Small Claims, Probate.*

www.aoc.state.nc.us/www/public/courts/camden.html

Civil Records: Access: In person only. Visitors must perform in person searches for themselves. Required to search: name, years to search. Civil cases indexed by defendant, plaintiff. Civil records on computer since Nov. 27 1989, prior on index books to 1966.

Criminal Records: Access: Mail, online, in person. Both court and visitors may perform in person searches. Search fee: $5.00 per name. Required to search: name, years to search, DOB. Criminal records on computer since Nov. 27 1989, prior on index books to 1966. Search the active Criminal Calendar by defendant name at the web site.

General Information: Public access terminal is available. No adoptions, sealed cases, juvenile, sex offenders, mental or expunged records released. Turnaround time 1-2 days. Copy fee: $1.00 for first page, $.25 each add'l. Certification fee: $2.00 if you do search, otherwise is included in search fee. Fee payee: Clerk of Superior Court. Business checks accepted. Prepayment is required.

Carteret County

Superior-District Court - Carteret County Courthouse Square, Beaufort, NC 28516; 252-728-8500; Fax: 252-728-6502. 8AM-5PM (EST). *Felony, Misdemeanor, Civil, Eviction, Small Claims, Probate.*

www.aoc.state.nc.us/www/public/courts/carteret.html

Civil Records: Access: In person only. Visitors must perform in person searches for themselves. No search fee. Required to search: name, years to search. Civil cases indexed by defendant, plaintiff. Civil records on computer back to 1988, prior on books to 1800s.

Criminal Records: Access: Mail, fax, online, in person. Both court and visitors may perform in person searches. Search fee: $5.00 per name. Required to search: name, years to search; also helpful: address, DOB, SSN. Criminal records on computer back to 1/87, prior on cards and books to 1800s. Search the active Criminal Calendar by defendant name at the web site.

General Information: Public access terminal is available. No adoptions, sealed cases, juvenile, sex offenders, mental or expunged records released. Turnaround time 1-2 days. Copy fee: $1.00 for first page, $.25 each add'l. Certification fee: $2.00. Fee payee: Clerk of Superior Court. Business checks accepted. Prepayment is required.

Caswell County

Superior-District Court PO Drawer 790, Yanceyville, NC 27379; 336-694-4171; Fax: 336-694-7338. Hours: 8AM-5PM (EST). *Felony, Misdemeanor, Civil, Eviction, Small Claims, Probate.*

www.aoc.state.nc.us/www/public/courts/caswell.html

Civil Records: Access: In person only. Visitors must perform in person searches for themselves. No search fee. Required to search: name, years to search. Civil cases indexed by defendant, plaintiff. Civil records on computer from 3/89 to present, on index books back to 1970, prior records in civil summons book.

Criminal Records: Access: Mail, online, in person. Both court and visitors may perform in person searches. Search fee: $5.00 per name. Required to search: name, years to search, DOB; also helpful: address. Criminal records on computer since 5/88, prior on books and

cards. Search the active Criminal Calendar by defendant name at the web site.

General Information: Public access terminal is available. No adoptions, sealed cases, juvenile, mental or expunged records released. SASE helpful. Turnaround time 1-2 days. Copy fee: $1.00 for first page, $.25 each add'l. Certification fee: $2.00. Fee payee: Clerk of Superior Court. Business checks accepted. Prepayment is required.

Catawba County

Superior-District Court PO Box 790, Newton, NC 28658; 828-466-6100. 8AM-5PM (EST). *Felony, Misdemeanor, Civil, Eviction, Small Claims, Probate.*

www.co.catawba.nc.us/state/clerk/clerklst.htm

Civil Records: Access: In person only. Visitors must perform in person searches for themselves. No search fee. Required to search: name, years to search. Civil cases indexed by defendant, plaintiff. Civil records on computer since 3/1988, prior on books.

Criminal Records: Access: Mail, online, in person. Both court and visitors may perform in person searches. Search fee: $5.00 per name. Required to search: name, years to search, DOB. Criminal records on computer since 4/85, on books to 1966, archived prior. Search the active Criminal Calendar by defendant at the web site.

General Information: Public access terminal is available. No adoptions, sealed cases, juvenile, sex offenders, mental or expunged records released. SASE required. Turnaround time 5 days. Copy fee: $1.00 for first page, $.25 each add'l. Certification fee: $2.00. Fee payee: Clerk of Court. Only cashiers checks and money orders accepted. Prepayment is required.

Chatham County

Superior-District Court PO Box 369, Pittsboro, NC 27312; 919-542-3240; Fax: 919-542-1402. Hours: 8AM-5PM (EST). *Felony, Misdemeanor, Civil, Eviction, Small Claims, Probate.*

www.aoc.state.nc.us/www/public/courts/chatham.html

Civil Records: Access: In person. Both court and visitors may perform in person searches. Search fee: $5.00 per name. Required to search: name, years to search. Civil cases indexed by defendant, plaintiff. Civil records on computer since 4/89, prior on books, archived 1968 back in Raleigh.

Criminal Records: Access: Mail, online, in person. Both court and visitors may perform in person searches. Search fee: $5.00 per name. Required to search: name, years to search; also helpful: address, DOB, SSN. Criminal records on computer since 7/87, prior on books or cards to 1968. Search the active Criminal Calendar by defendant name at the web site.

General Information: Public access terminal is available. No adoptions, sealed cases, juvenile, sex offenders, mental or expunged records released. Turnaround time 1 day. Copy fee: Included in criminal search fee. Will not certify civil. Fee payee: Clerk of Superior Court. Personal checks accepted. Prepayment is required.

Cherokee County

Superior-District Court 75 Peachtree St, Rm 201, Murphy, NC 28906; 828-837-2522. Hours: 8AM-5PM (EST). *Felony, Misdemeanor, Civil, Eviction, Small Claims, Probate.*

www.aoc.state.nc.us/www/public/courts/cherokee.html

Civil Records: Access: Mail, in person. Both court and visitors may perform in person searches. Search fee: $5.00 per name. Required to search: name, years to search, address. Civil cases indexed by defendant, plaintiff. Civil records on computer since 5/89, on index books to 1867.

Criminal Records: Access: Mail, online, in person. Only the court performs in person searches; visitors may not. Search fee: $5.00 per name. Required to search: name, years to search, DOB. Criminal records on computer since 5/89, index cards to 1985, index books to 1966. Search the active Criminal Calendar by defendant name at the web site. There is no public access terminal for searching criminal records.

General Information: Public access terminal is available. No adoptions, sealed cases, juvenile or mental records released. SASE required. Turnaround time 1-2 days. Fax notes: Fee to fax results is $1.00 1st page, $.25 each add'l. Copy fee: $1.00 for first page, $.25 each add'l. Certification fee: $4.00. Fee payee: Clerk of Superior Court. No personal checks accepted.

Chowan County

Superior-District Court N.C. Courier Box 106319, PO Box 588, Edenton, NC 27932; 252-482-2323; Fax: 252-482-2190. 9AM-5PM (EST). *Felony, Misdemeanor, Civil, Eviction, Small Claims, Probate.*
www.aoc.state.nc.us/www/public/courts/chowan.html

Civil Records: Access: In person only. Visitors must perform in person searches for themselves. No search fee. Required to search: name, years to search; also helpful: address. Civil cases indexed by defendant, plaintiff. Civil records on computer since 1990, prior on books to 1800s.

Criminal Records: Access: Mail, online, in person. Both court and visitors may perform in person searches. Search fee: $5.00 per name. Required to search: name, years to search, DOB; also helpful: address, SSN. Criminal records on computer from 1/90, prior as civil. Search the active Criminal Calendar by defendant name at the web site.

General Information: Public access terminal is available. No adoptions, sealed cases, juvenile, sex offenders, mental or expunged records released. SASE required. Turnaround time 3-5 days. Copy fee: $1.00 for first page, $.25 each add'l. Certification fee: $2.00. Fee payee: Clerk of Superior Court. Only cashiers checks and money orders accepted. Prepayment is required.

Clay County

Superior-District Court PO Box 506, Hayesville, NC 28904; 828-389-8334; Fax: 828-389-3329. Hours: 8AM-5PM (EST). *Felony, Misdemeanor, Civil, Eviction, Small Claims, Probate.*
www.aoc.state.nc.us/www/public/courts/clay.html

Civil Records: Access: Fax, mail, in person. Visitors must perform in person searches for themselves. Search fee: $5.00 per name. Required to search: name, years to search; also helpful: address. Civil cases indexed by defendant, plaintiff. Civil records on computer since 1989, on books since 1888.

Criminal Records: Access: Fax, mail, online, in person. Visitors must perform in person searches for themselves. Search fee: $5.00 per name. Required to search: name, years to search, DOB; also helpful: address, SSN. Criminal records on computer back to 1989, on books since 1888. Search the active Criminal Calendar by defendant name at the web site.

General Information: Public access terminal is available. No adoptions, sealed cases, juvenile, sex offenders, mental or expunged records released. Turnaround time 1-2 days. Fax notes: Fee to fax results is $.25 per page. Copy fee: $1.00 for first page, $.25 each add'l. Certification fee: $1.00. Fee payee: Clerk of Court. Business checks accepted. Prepayment required.

Cleveland County

Superior-District Court 100 Justice Place, Shelby, NC 28150; 704-484-4862; Fax: 704-480-5487. Hours: 8AM-5PM (EST). *Felony, Misdemeanor, Civil, Eviction, Small Claims, Probate.*
www.aoc.state.nc.us/www/public/courts/cleveland.html

Civil Records: Access: Mail, in person. Visitors must perform in person searches for themselves. No search

fee. Required to search: name, years to search; also helpful: address. Civil cases indexed by defendant, plaintiff. Civil records on computer since 1988, books to 1984, archived prior.

Criminal Records: Access: Fax, mail, online, in person. Both court and visitors may perform in person searches. Search fee: $5.00 per name. Required to search: name, years to search, DOB; also helpful: address, SSN. Criminal records on computer since 6/86, on books to 1972, archived prior. Search the active Criminal Calendar by defendant name at http://www1.aoc.state.nc.us/www/calendars/CriminalQuery.html. Includes an impaired driving query.

General Information: Public access terminal is available. No adoptions, sealed cases, juvenile, sex offenders, mental or expunged records released. SASE requested. Turnaround time 1-2 days. Fax notes: $1.00 for first page, $.25 each add'l. Copy fee: $1.00 for first page, $.25 each add'l. Certification fee: $2.00. Fee payee: Clerk of Superior Court. No out-of-state checks accepted. Prepayment is required.

Columbus County

Superior-District Court PO Box 1587, Whiteville, NC 28472; 910-641-3000; Fax: 910-641-3027. Hours: 8AM-5PM (EST). *Felony, Misdemeanor, Civil, Eviction, Small Claims, Probate.*
www.aoc.state.nc.us/www/public/courts/columbus.html

Civil Records: Access: Mail, fax, in person. Visitors must perform in person searches for themselves. No search fee. Required to search: name, years to search; also helpful: address. Civil cases indexed by defendant, plaintiff. Civil records on computer from 1989, prior on books to 1968.

Criminal Records: Access: Mail, fax, in person. Both court and visitors may perform in person searches. Search fee: $5.00 per name. Required to search: name, years to search, DOB; also helpful: address, SSN. Criminal records on computer from 1987, prior on books or cards to 1968. Search the active Criminal Calendar by defendant name at the web site.

General Information: Public access terminal is available. No adoptions, sealed, juvenile, sex offender, mental, expunged or dismissed. SASE required. Turnaround time 2-5 days. Fax notes: Do not fax. Copy fee: $1.00 per page. Certification fee: $2.00 per copy. Fee payee: Clerk of Superior Court. Only cashiers checks and money orders accepted. Prepayment is required.

Craven County

Superior-District Court PO Box 1187, New Bern, NC 28563; 252-514-4774; Fax: 252-514-4891. Hours: 8AM-5PM (EST). *Felony, Misdemeanor, Civil, Eviction, Small Claims, Probate.*
www.aoc.state.nc.us/www/public/courts/craven.htm

Civil Records: Access: Mail, in person. Both court and visitors may perform in person searches. Search fee: $5.00 per name. Required to search: name, years to search; also helpful: address. Civil cases indexed by defendant, plaintiff. Civil records on computer from 10/88, prior to 1968 are archived.

Criminal Records: Access: Mail, in person. Both court and visitors may perform in person searches. Search fee: $5.00 per name. Required to search: name, years to search, DOB; also helpful: address, SSN. Criminal records on computer since 1/87, prior on books and cards to 1968. Search the active Criminal Calendar by defendant name at the web site.

General Information: Public access terminal is available. No adoptions, sealed cases, juvenile, sex offenders, mental, expunged, or dismissed. SASE required. Turnaround time 1-2 days. Copy fee: $1.00 for first page, $.25 each add'l. Certification fee: $2.00. Fee payee: Clerk of Superior Court. Only cashiers checks and money orders accepted. Prepayment is required.

Cumberland County

Superior-District Court PO Box 363, Fayetteville, NC 28302; Civil phone: 910-678-2909; Criminal phone: 910-678-2906. Hours: 8:30AM-5PM (EST). *Felony, Misdemeanor, Civil, Eviction, Small Claims, Probate.*
www.aoc.state.nc.us/data/district12

Civil Records: Access: Mail, in person, online. Both court and visitors may perform in person searches. Search fee: $5.00 per name. Required to search: name, years to search; also helpful: address. Civil cases indexed by defendant, plaintiff. Civil records on computer since 1988, books back to 1956. Search active civil calendars by court date on the web site. The web site presents a list of online vendors to instant record access. Also, online name search dockets at http://www1.aoc.state.nc.us/www/calendars/Civil.html.

Criminal Records: Access: Mail, online, in person. Both court and visitors may perform in person searches. Search fee: $5.00 per name. Required to search: name, years to search; also helpful: address, DOB, SSN. Criminal records on computer since 5/82, books and cards to 1920s. Search the active Criminal Calendar by defendant name at the web site.

General Information: Public access terminal is available. No adoptions, sealed cases, juvenile, sex offenders, mental or expunged records released. Turnaround time 2 weeks. Copy fee: $2.00 per page. Certification fee: Included in search fee, unless in-person then $2.00. Fee payee: Clerk of Superior Court. Business checks accepted. Prepayment is required.

Currituck County

Superior-District Court PO Box 175, Currituck, NC 27929; 252-232-2010; Fax: 252-232-3722. Hours: 8AM-5PM (EST). *Felony, Misdemeanor, Civil, Eviction, Small Claims, Probate.*
www.aoc.state.nc.us/www/public/courts/currituck.html

Civil Records: Access: Fax, mail, in person. Both court and visitors may perform in person searches. No search fee. Required to search: name, years to search. Civil cases indexed by defendant, plaintiff. Civil records on computer back to 11/27/89, books to 1968, prior archived.

Criminal Records: Access: Fax, mail, online, in person. Both court and visitors may perform in person searches. Search fee: $5.00 per name. Required to search: name, years to search, DOB; also helpful-SSN, signed release. Criminal records on computer back to 11/27/89, books to 1968, prior archived. Search the active Criminal Calendar by defendant name at the web site.

General Information: Public access terminal is available. No adoptions, sealed cases, juvenile, sex offenders, mental or expunged records released. Copy fee: $1.00 for first page, $.25 each add'l. Certification fee: $2.00. Fee payee: Clerk of Superior Court. Only cashiers checks and money orders accepted. Prepayment is required.

Dare County

Superior-District Court PO Box 1849, Manteo, NC 27954; 252-473-2950; Fax: 252-473-1620. Hours: 8:30AM-5PM (EST). *Felony, Misdemeanor, Civil, Eviction, Small Claims, Probate.*
www.aoc.state.nc.us/www/public/courts/dare.htm

Civil Records: Access: Phone, mail, in person. Both court and visitors may perform in person searches. Search fee: $5.00 per name. Required to search: name, years to search; also helpful: address. Civil cases indexed by defendant, plaintiff. Civil records on computer since 1985, on books to 1968.

Criminal Records: Access: Mail, online, in person. Both court and visitors may perform in person searches. Search fee: $5.00 per name. Required to search: name, years to search, DOB or SSN. Criminal records on computer since 1987, on books and cards to 1968. Search the active Criminal Calendar by defendant name at the web site.

General Information: Public access terminal is available. No adoptions, sealed cases, juvenile, sex offenders, mental or expunged records released. Turnaround time 2 days. Fax notes: Fee to fax results is $.25 per page. Copy fee: $1.00 for first page, $.25 each add'l. Certification fee: $2.00. Fee payee: Superior District Court. Business checks accepted. Out of state business checks not accepted. Prepayment is required.

Davidson County

Superior - District Court PO Box 1064, Lexington, NC 27293-1064; 336-249-0351; Fax: 336-249-6951. Hours: 8AM-5PM (EST). *Felony, Misdemeanor, Civil, Eviction, Small Claims, Probate.* www.aoc.state.nc.us/www/public/courts/davidson.html

Civil Records: Access: In person only. Visitors must perform in person searches for themselves. No search fee. Required to search: name, years to search; also helpful: address. Civil cases indexed by defendant, plaintiff. Civil records on computer since 5/16/88, prior on books.

Criminal Records: Access: Mail, online, in person. Both court and visitors may perform in person searches. Search fee: $5.00 per name. Required to search: name, years to search; also helpful: address, DOB, SSN. Criminal records on computer since 10/85, on books and cards to 1952. Search the active Criminal Calendar by defendant name at the web site.

General Information: Public access terminal is available. No adoptions, sealed cases, juvenile, sex offenders, mental or expunged records released. SASE requested. Turnaround time 2-3 days. Copy fee: $1.00 for first page, $.25 each add'l. Certification fee: $2.00. Fee payee: Clerk of Superior Court. Business checks accepted. Prepayment is required.

Davie County

Superior - District Court 140 S Main St, Mocksville, NC 27028; Civil phone: 336-751-3507; Criminal phone: 336-751-3508; Fax: 336-751-4720. Hours: 8:30AM-5PM (EST). *Felony, Misdemeanor, Civil, Eviction, Small Claims, Probate.* www.aoc.state.nc.us/www/public/courts/davie.html

Civil Records: Access: Mail, in person. Both court and visitors may perform in person searches. Search fee: $5.00 per name. Required to search: name, years to search. Civil cases indexed by defendant, plaintiff. Civil records on computer back to 10/89; on books to 1970.

Criminal Records: Access: Mail, online, in person. Both court and visitors may perform in person searches. Search fee: $5.00 per name. Required to search: name, years to search, DOB, signed release. Criminal records on computer back to 10/89; on books to 1970. Search the active Criminal Calendar by defendant name at the web site.

General Information: Public access terminal is available. No adoptions, sealed cases, juvenile, sex offenders, mental or expunged records released. SASE required. Turnaround time 5 days. Copy fee: $1.00 for first page, $.25 each add'l. Certification fee: $2.00. Fee payee: Clerk of Superior Court. Personal checks accepted. Prepayment is required.

Duplin County

Superior-District Court PO Box 189, Kenansville, NC 28349; Civil phone: 910-296-1686; Criminal phone: 910-296-0110; Fax: 910-296-2310. Hours: 8AM-5PM (EST). *Felony, Misdemeanor, Civil, Eviction, Small Claims, Probate.* www.aoc.state.nc.us/www/public/courts/duplin.htm

Civil Records: Access: Phone, fax, mail, in person. Both court and visitors may perform in person searches.

Search fee: $5.00 per name. Required to search: name, years to search. Civil cases indexed by defendant, plaintiff. Civil records on computer since 1989, prior on books to early 1900s.

Criminal Records: Access: Phone, fax, mail, online, in person. Only the court performs in person searches; visitors may not. Search fee: $5.00 per name. Required to search: name, years to search, DOB. Criminal records on computer since 5/88, on cards and books to 1927. Search the active Criminal Calendar by defendant name at the web site.

General Information: Public access terminal is available. No adoptions, sealed cases, juvenile, sex offenders, mental or expunged records released. Turnaround time 1-2 days. Copy fee: $1.00 for first page, $.25 each add'l. Certification fee: $2.00. Fee payee: Clerk of Superior Court. Personal checks accepted. Prepayment is required.

Durham County

Superior-District Court 201 E Main St, Durham, NC 27702; Civil phone: 919-560-6823; Criminal phone: 919-560-6821. 8:30AM-5PM (EST). *Felony, Misdemeanor, Civil, Eviction, Small Claims, Probate.* www.aoc.state.nc.us/www/public/courts/durham.htm

Civil Records: Access: In person, online. Visitors must perform in person searches for themselves. No search fee. Required to search: name, years to search; also helpful: address. Civil cases indexed by defendant, plaintiff. Civil records on computer since 1/88, on books to late 1800s. Search active civil calendars by court date on the web site. Also, online name search dockets at http://www1.aoc.state.nc.us/www/calendars/Civil.html.

Criminal Records: Access: Mail, online, in person. Both court and visitors may perform in person searches. Search fee: $5.00 per name. Required to search: name, years to search, DOB; also helpful: address. Criminal records on microfiche since 1982, prior on books to 1979. Search the active Criminal Calendar by defendant name at the web site.

General Information: Public access terminal is available. No adoptions, sealed cases, juvenile, sex offenders, mental or expunged records released. SASE required. Turnaround time 3-4 days. Copy fee: $1.00 for first page, $.25 each add'l. Certification fee: Certification is $2.00 for civil, but is included in search fee for criminal. Fee payee: Clerk of Superior Court. Only cashiers checks and money orders accepted. Prepayment is required.

Edgecombe County

Superior-District Court PO Drawer 9, Tarboro, NC 27886; Civil phone: 252-823-6161; Criminal phone: 252-823-2056; Fax: 252-823-1278. Hours: 8AM-5PM (EST). *Felony, Misdemeanor, Civil, Eviction, Small Claims, Probate.* www.aoc.state.nc.us/www/public/courts/edgecombe.htm

Civil Records: Access: In person only. Visitors must perform in person searches for themselves. No search fee. Required to search: name, years to search, address. Civil cases indexed by defendant, plaintiff. Civil records on computer since 1988, prior on books to 1945, files to 1968.

Criminal Records: Access: Mail, online, in person. Both court and visitors may perform in person searches. Search fee: $5.00 per name. Required to search: name, years to search, DOB, SSN; also helpful: address. Criminal records on computer since 4/87, on books and cards to 1900s. Search the active Criminal Calendar by defendant name at the web site.

General Information: Public access terminal is available. No adoptions, sealed cases, juvenile, sex offenders, mental or expunged records required. Turnaround time 1-2 days. Copy fee: $1.00 for first page, $.25 each add'l. Certification fee: $2.00. Fee

payee: Clerk of Superior Court. Business checks accepted.

Forsyth County

Superior-District Court PO Box 20099, Winston Salem, NC 27120-0099; 336-761-2250; Civil phone: 336-761-2340; Criminal phone: 336-761-2366; Fax: 336-761-2018. Hours: 8AM-5PM (EST). *Felony, Misdemeanor, Civil, Eviction, Small Claims, Probate.* www.aoc.state.nc.us/www/public/courts/forsyth.html

Civil Records: Access: Mail, in person. Both court and visitors may perform in person searches. Search fee: $5.00 per name. Required to search: name, years to search. Civil cases indexed by defendant, plaintiff. Civil records on computer since 4/1988, prior on books to 1968, on microfiche prior.

Criminal Records: Access: Mail, online, in person. Both court and visitors may perform in person searches. Search fee: $5.00 per name. Required to search: name, years to search, DOB. Criminal records on computer since 10/1983, prior on books to 1968, on microfiche prior. Search the active Criminal Calendar by defendant name at the web site.

General Information: Public access terminal is available. No adoptions, sealed cases, juvenile, sex offenders, mental or expunged records released. SASE required. Turnaround time 1-2 days. Copy fee: $1.00 for first page, $.25 each add'l. Certification fee: $2.00. Fee payee: Clerk of Superior Court. Business checks accepted. Prepayment is required.

Franklin County

Superior-District Court 102 S Main St, Louisburg, NC 27549; 919-496-5104; Fax: 919-496-0407. Hours: 8:30AM-5PM (EST). *Felony, Misdemeanor, Civil, Eviction, Small Claims, Probate.* www.aoc.state.nc.us/www/public/courts/franklin.html

Civil Records: Access: Fax, mail, in person. Both court and visitors may perform in person searches. Search fee: $5.00 per name. Required to search: name, years to search; also helpful: address. Civil cases indexed by defendant, plaintiff. Civil records on computer since June 1989, prior on books.

Criminal Records: Access: Fax, mail, in person. Both court and visitors may perform in person searches. Search fee: $5.00 per name. Required to search: name, years to search, DOB; also helpful: address. Criminal records on computer since 1980, on index books back to 1968. Search the active Criminal Calendar by defendant name at the web site.

General Information: Public access terminal is available. No adoptions, sealed cases, juvenile, mental or expunged records released. SASE requested. Turnaround time 1-2 days. Copy fee: $1.00 for first page, $.25 each add'l. Certification fee: $2.00. Fee payee: Clerk of Superior Court. Personal checks accepted. Prepayment is required.

Gaston County

Superior-District Court PO Box 340, Gastonia, NC 28053; 704-852-3100. Hours: 8AM-5PM (EST). *Felony, Misdemeanor, Civil, Eviction, Small Claims, Probate.* www.aoc.state.nc.us/www/public/courts/gaston.htm

Civil Records: Access: In person only. Visitors must perform in person searches for themselves. No search fee. Required to search: name, years to search; also helpful: address. Civil cases indexed by defendant, plaintiff. Civil records on computer since 1988, prior on books to 1891.

Criminal Records: Access: Mail, online, in person. Both court and visitors may perform in person searches. Search fee: $5.00 per name. Required to search: name, address, DOB; also helpful: years to search, SSN. Criminal records on criminal to 1/83, on books and cards to 1973. Search the active Criminal Calendar by defendant name at the web site.

General Information: Public access terminal is available. No adoptions, sealed cases, juvenile, mental or expunged records released. Turnaround time 1-2 days. Copy fee: $.25 per page. Certification fee: $2.00. Fee payee: Clerk of Superior Court. Only cashiers checks and money orders accepted. No out of state checks. Prepayment is required.

Gates County

Superior-District Court PO Box 31, Gatesville, NC 27938; 252-357-1365; Fax: 252-357-1047. Hours: 8AM-5PM (EST). *Felony, Misdemeanor, Civil, Eviction, Small Claims, Probate.*

www.aoc.state.nc.us/www/public/courts/gates.html

Civil Records: Access: In person only. Visitors must perform in person searches for themselves. No search fee. Required to search: name, years to search; also helpful: address. Civil cases indexed by defendant, plaintiff. Civil records on computer since 1990, prior on books to 1966.

Criminal Records: Access: Mail, online, in person. Only the court performs in person searches; visitors may not. Search fee: $5.00 per name. Required to search: name, years to search, DOB; also helpful: address, SSN. Criminal records on computer since 1990, prior on books to 1966. Search the active Criminal Calendar by defendant name at the web site.

General Information: No adoptions, sealed cases, juvenile, sex offenders, mental or expunged records released. Turnaround time 1-2 days. Copy fee: $1.00 for first page, $.25 each add'l. Certification fee: $2.00. Fee payee: Clerk of Superior Court. Business checks accepted. Prepayment is required.

Graham County

Superior-District Court PO Box 1179, Robbinsville, NC 28771; 828-479-7986; Civil phone: X7974; Criminal phone: X7975; Fax: 828-479-6417. Hours: 8AM-5PM M-Th; 8AM-4:30PM Fri (EST). *Felony, Misdemeanor, Civil, Eviction, Small Claims, Probate.*

www.aoc.state.nc.us/www/public/courts/graham.html

Civil Records: Access: In person only. Visitors must perform in person searches for themselves. No search fee. Required to search: name, years to search. Civil cases indexed by defendant, plaintiff. Civil records on computer since 1989, on books since 1920s.

Criminal Records: Access: Mail, online, in person. Both court and visitors may perform in person searches. Search fee: $5.00 per name. Required to search: name, years to search; also helpful: address, DOB, SSN. Criminal records on computer since 1984, on books to 1920s. Search the active Criminal Calendar by defendant name at the web site.

General Information: Public access terminal is available. No adoptions, sealed cases, juvenile, sex offenders, mental or expunged records released. SASE required. Turnaround time 3-5 days. Copy fee: $1.00 for first page, $.25 each add'l. Certification fee: $2.00. Fee payee: Clerk of Superior Court. Only cashiers checks and money orders accepted. Prepayment is required.

Granville County

Superior-District Court Courthouse, 101 Main Street, Oxford, NC 27565; 919-693-2649; Fax: 919-693-8944. *Felony, Misdemeanor, Civil, Eviction, Small Claims, Probate.*

www.aoc.state.nc.us/www/public/courts/granville.html

Civil Records: Access: Phone, mail, in person. No search fee. Required to search: name, years to search; also helpful: address. Civil cases indexed by defendant, plaintiff. Civil records on computer since June 12, 1989, on books to 1968, prior files destroyed.

Criminal Records: Access: Mail, in person. Both court and visitors may perform in person searches. Search fee: $5.00 per name. Required to search: name, years to search, DOB; also helpful: address. Criminal records on computer since Feb. 29, 1988, prior on books on cards to 1968. Search the active Criminal Calendar by defendant name at the web site.

General Information: Public access terminal is available. No adoptions, sealed cases, juvenile, mental or expunged records released. SASE would be helpful. Turnaround time 1 day. Copy fee: $1.00 for first page, $.25 each add'l. Certification fee: $2.00. Fee payee: Clerk of Superior Court. Personal checks accepted. Prepayment is required.

Greene County

Superior-District Court PO Box 675, Snow Hill, NC 28580; 252-747-3505. 8AM-5PM (EST). *Felony, Misdemeanor, Civil, Eviction, Small Claims, Probate.*

www.aoc.state.nc.us/www/public/courts/greene.htm

Civil Records: Access: In person only. Visitors must perform in person searches for themselves. No search fee. Required to search: name, years to search; also helpful: address. Civil cases indexed by defendant, plaintiff. Civil records on computer since Oct. 1989, prior on books to 1865.

Criminal Records: Access: Mail, online, in person. Both court and visitors may perform in person searches. Search fee: $5.00 per name. Required to search: name, years to search; also helpful: address, DOB, SSN. Criminal records on computer since Oct. 1989, prior on books to 1865. Search the active Criminal Calendar by defendant name at the web site.

General Information: Public access terminal is available. No adoptions, sealed cases, juvenile, sex offenders, mental or expunged records released. Turnaround time 1-2 days. Fax notes: Fax back fee $1.00 per page. Copy fee: $1.00 for first page, $.25 each add'l. Certification fee: Included in search fee, unless in-person then $2.00. Fee payee: Clerk of Superior Court. Business checks accepted. Prepayment is required.

Guilford County

Superior-District Court 201 S Eugene, PO Box 3008, Greensboro, NC 27402; Civil phone: 336-574-4305; Criminal phone: 336-574-4307. Hours: 8:30AM-5PM (EST). *Felony, Misdemeanor, Civil, Eviction, Small Claims, Probate.*

www.aoc.state.nc.us/www/public/courts/guilford.html

Civil Records: Access: In person only. Visitors must perform in person searches for themselves. No search fee. Required to search: name, years to search; also helpful: address. Civil cases indexed by defendant, plaintiff. Civil records on computer since 9/88, on books to late 1800s.

Criminal Records: Access: Mail, online, in person. Both court and visitors may perform in person searches. Search fee: $5.00 per name. Required to search: name, years to search, DOB; also helpful: address, full name. Criminal records on computer since 5/83, on cards and books to late 1800s. Search the active Criminal Calendar by defendant name at the web site.

General Information: Public access terminal is available. No adoptions, sealed cases, juvenile, sex offenders, mental or expunged records released. SASE required. Turnaround time 1 week. Copy fee: $1.00 for first page, $.25 each add'l. Certification fee: $2.00. Fee payee: Clerk of Superior Court. Business checks accepted. Prepayment is required.

Halifax County

Superior-District Court PO Box 66, Halifax, NC 27839; 252-583-5061; Fax: 252-583-1005. Hours: 8:30AM-5PM (EST). *Felony, Misdemeanor, Civil, Eviction, Small Claims, Probate.*

www.aoc.state.nc.us/data/HALIFAX/index.html

Civil Records: Access: In person only. Visitors must perform in person searches for themselves. No search fee. Required to search: name, years to search; also helpful: address. Civil cases indexed by defendant, plaintiff. Civil records on computer since 1988, on books to 1968, prior archived.

Criminal Records: Access: Mail, online, in person. Both court and visitors may perform in person searches. Search fee: $5.00 per name. Required to search: name, years to search; also helpful: address, DOB, SSN. Criminal records on computer since 1988, on books to 1968, prior archived. Search the active Criminal Calendar by defendant name at the web site.

General Information: Public access terminal is available. (Civil only.) No adoptions, sealed cases, juvenile, sex offenders, mental or expunged records released. Turnaround time 1-2 days. Copy fee: $1.00 for first page, $.25 each add'l. Certification fee: $2.00. Fee payee: Clerk of Superior Court. Business checks accepted. Prepayment is required.

Harnett County

Superior-District Court PO Box 849, Lillington, NC 27546; 910-893-5164; Civil phone: 910-893-4961; Criminal phone: 910-893-5692; Probate phone: 910-893-5046; Fax: 910-893-3683. Hours: 8:30AM-5PM (EST). *Felony, Misdemeanor, Civil, Eviction, Small Claims, Probate.*

www.aoc.state.nc.us/www/public/courts/harnett.html

Civil Records: Access: In person only. Visitors must perform in person searches for themselves. No search fee. Required to search: name, years to search; also helpful: address. Civil cases indexed by defendant, plaintiff. Civil records on computer since April 17, 1989, prior on books from 1938.

Criminal Records: Access: Mail, in person. Both court and visitors may perform in person searches. Search fee: $5.00 per name. Required to search: name, years to search; also helpful: address, DOB, SSN. Criminal records on computer since 5/87, on books from 1968. Search the active Criminal Calendar by defendant name at the web site.

General Information: Public access terminal is available. No adoptions, sealed cases, juvenile, mental or expunged records released. SASE required. Turnaround time 1 week-10 days. Copy fee: $1.00 for first page, $.25 each add'l. Certification fee: $2.00. Fee payee: Clerk of Superior Court. Only cashiers checks and money orders accepted. Prepayment is required.

Haywood County

Superior-District Court 215 N. Main, Waynesville, NC 28786; 828-456-3540; Fax: 828-456-4937. Hours: 8:30AM-5PM (EST). *Felony, Misdemeanor, Civil, Eviction, Small Claims, Probate.*

www.aoc.state.nc.us/www/public/courts/haywood.html

Civil Records: Access: In person only. Visitors must perform in person searches for themselves. No search fee. Required to search: name, years to search; also helpful: address. Civil cases indexed by defendant, plaintiff. Civil records on computer since Oct. 13, 1988, prior on books to 1955.

Criminal Records: Access: Mail, online, in person. Both court and visitors may perform in person searches. Search fee: $5.00 per name. Required to search: name, years to search, DOB; also helpful: address, SSN. Criminal records on computer since 5/87, on books or cards from 1800s. Search the active Criminal Calendar by defendant name at the web site.

General Information: Public access terminal is available. No adoptions, sealed cases, juvenile, sex offenders, mental or expunged records released. Turnaround time 1-2 days. Copy fee: $1.25 for first page, $.25 each add'l. Fee payee: Clerk of Superior Court. Only cashiers checks and money orders accepted. Prepayment is required.

Henderson County

Superior-District Court PO Box 965, Hendersonville, NC 28793; Civil phone: 828-697-4851; Criminal phone: 828-697-4859. Hours: 8:30AM-5PM (EST). *Felony, Misdemeanor, Civil, Eviction, Small Claims, Probate.*

www.aoc.state.nc.us/www/public/courts/henderson.html

Civil Records: Access: Mail, in person. Both court and visitors may perform in person searches. Search fee: $5.00 per name. Required to search: name, years to search; also helpful: address. Civil cases indexed by defendant, plaintiff. Civil records on computer back to 1988, prior on books to 1968.
Criminal Records: Access: Mail, online, in person. Both court and visitors may perform in person searches. Search fee: $5.00 per name. Required to search: name, years to search, DOB; also helpful: address, SSN. Criminal records on computer back to 09/89, prior on books to 1968. Search the active Criminal Calendar by defendant name at the web site.
General Information: Public access terminal is available. No adoptions, sealed cases, juvenile, sex offenders, mental or expunged records released. SASE not required. Turnaround time 1 week. Copy fee: $.25 per page. Certification fee: $2.00. Fee payee: Clerk of Superior Court. Personal checks accepted. Prepayment is required.

Hertford County

Superior-District Court PO Box 86, Winton, NC 27986; 252-358-7845; Fax: 252-358-0793. Hours: 8AM-5PM (EST). *Felony, Misdemeanor, Civil, Eviction, Small Claims, Probate.*

www.aoc.state.nc.us/www/public/courts/hertford.html

Civil Records: Access: In person only. Visitors must perform in person searches for themselves. No search fee. Required to search: name, years to search; also helpful: address. Civil cases indexed by defendant, plaintiff. Civil records on computer back to 4/1989, prior on index cards and judgment books to 1968.
Criminal Records: Access: Mail, online, in person. Both court and visitors may perform in person searches. Search fee: $5.00 per name. Required to search: name, years to search, DOB; also helpful: address, SSN. Criminal records on computer back to 4/1989, prior on index cards or judgment books to 1968. Search the active Criminal Calendar by defendant at the web site.
General Information: Public access terminal is available. No adoptions, sealed cases, juvenile, sex offenders, mental or expunged records released. Turnaround time 1-2 days. Copy fee: $1.00 for first page, $.25 each add'l. Certification fee: Included in search fee, unless do it yourself then $2.00. Fee payee: Clerk of Superior Court. Only cashiers checks and money orders accepted. Local personal checks accepted. Prepayment is required.

Hoke County

Superior-District Court PO Drawer 1569, Raeford, NC 28376; 910-875-3728; Fax: 910-904-1708. Hours: 8:30AM-5PM (EST). *Felony, Misdemeanor, Civil, Eviction, Small Claims, Probate.*

www.aoc.state.nc.us/www/public/courts/hoke.html

Civil Records: Access: In person only. Visitors must perform in person searches for themselves. No search fee. Required to search: name, years to search; also helpful: address. Civil cases indexed by defendant, plaintiff. Civil records on computer since 10/89, on books to 1967.
Criminal Records: Access: Mail, online, in person. Only the court performs in person searches; visitors may not. Search fee: $5.00 per name. Required to search: name, years to search, DOB; also helpful: address, SSN. Criminal records on computer since

10/89, on books to 1967. Search the active Criminal Calendar by defendant name at the web site.
General Information: Public access terminal is available. No adoptions, sealed cases, juvenile, mental or expunged records released. SASE required. Turnaround time 1-2 days. Copy fee: $1.00 for first page, $.25 each add'l. Certification fee: $2.00. Fee payee: Clerk of Superior Court. Business checks accepted. Prepayment is required.

Hyde County

Superior-District Court PO Box 337, Swanquarter, NC 27885; 252-926-4101; Fax: 252-926-1002. Hours: 8:30AM-5:30PM (EST). *Felony, Misdemeanor, Civil, Eviction, Small Claims, Probate.*

www.aoc.state.nc.us/www/public/courts/hyde.html

Note: Phone requesting only for general inquires.

Civil Records: Access: Mail, in person. Both court and visitors may perform in person searches. Search fee: $5.00 per name. Required to search: name, years to search. Civil cases indexed by defendant, plaintiff. Civil records on computer since 7/89, on books to 1968; estate and special proceedings back to 1996.
Criminal Records: Access: Phone, mail, online, in person. Only the court performs in person searches; visitors may not. Search fee: $5.00 per name. Required to search: name, years to search, DOB; also helpful-signed release. Criminal records on computer since 7/89, on books to 1968. Search the active Criminal Calendar by defendant name at the web site.
General Information: Public access terminal is available. (Civil only.) No adoptions, sealed cases, juvenile, sex offenders, mental or expunged records released. SASE required. Turnaround time 2 days, phone searches 15 minutes. Fax notes: Fee to fax results is $1.00 1st page, $.25 each add'l. Copy fee: $1.00 for first page, $.25 each add'l. Certification fee: $2.00. Fee payee: Clerk of Superior Court. Only cashiers checks and money orders accepted. Prepayment is required.

Iredell County

Superior-District Court PO Box 186, Statesville, NC 28687; Civil phone: 704-878-4306; Criminal phone: 704-878-4204; Fax: 704-878-3261. Hours: 8AM-5PM (EST). *Felony, Misdemeanor, Civil, Eviction, Small Claims, Probate.*

www.aoc.state.nc.us/www/public/courts/iredell.htm

Civil Records: Access: Mail, in person. Both court and visitors may perform in person searches. Search fee: $5.00 per name. Required to search: name, years to search. Civil cases indexed by defendant, plaintiff. Civil records on computer since 1985, in books since, 1786, on microfiche since 1939.
Criminal Records: Access: Mail, online, in person. Both court and visitors may perform in person searches. Search fee: $5.00 per name. Required to search: name, years to search, DOB. Criminal records on computer since 1985, prior on books and cards to 1970. Search the active Criminal Calendar by defendant name at the web site.
General Information: Public access terminal is available. No adoptions, sealed cases, juvenile, sex offenders, mental or expunged records released. SASE required. Turnaround time 2 days. Copy fee: $1.00 for first page, $.25 each add'l. Certification fee: $2.00. Fee payee: Clerk of Superior Court. Only cashiers checks and money orders accepted. Prepayment is required.

Jackson County

Superior-District Court 401 Grindstaff Cove Rd, Sylva, NC 28779; 828-586-7512; Fax: 828-586-9009. Hours: 8:30AM-5PM (EST). *Felony, Misdemeanor, Civil, Eviction, Small Claims, Probate.*
www.aoc.state.nc.us/www/public/courts/jackson.html

Civil Records: Access: In person only. Visitors must perform in person searches for themselves. No search fee. Required to search: name, years to search; also helpful: address. Civil records on computer since May 29, 1989, prior on books from 1966.
Criminal Records: Access: Mail, online, in person. Both court and visitors may perform in person searches. Search fee: $5.00 per name. Required to search: name, years to search, DOB; also helpful: address, SSN. Criminal records on computer since May 29, 1989, prior on books from 1966. Search the active Criminal Calendar by defendant name at the web site.
General Information: Public access terminal is available. (Civil only.) No adoptions, sealed cases, juvenile, mental or expunged records released. SASE required. Turnaround time 1-2 days. Copy fee: $1.00 for first page, $.25 each add'l. Certification fee: $2.00. Fee payee: Clerk of Superior Court. Only cashiers checks and M.O.s accepted. Prepayment is required.

Johnston County

Superior-District Court PO Box 297, Smithfield, NC 27577; 919-934-3192; Fax: 919-934-5857. Hours: 8AM-5PM (EST). *Felony, Misdemeanor, Civil, Eviction, Small Claims, Probate.*

www.aoc.state.nc.us/www/public/courts/johnston.html

Civil Records: Access: In person only. Visitors must perform in person searches for themselves. No search fee. Required to search: name, years to search; also helpful: address. Civil cases indexed by defendant, plaintiff. Civil records on computer since 1989, prior on books to 1930s.
Criminal Records: Access: Mail, online, in person. Both court and visitors may perform in person searches. Search fee: $5.00 per name. Required to search: name, DOB; also helpful: years to search, address, SSN. Criminal records on computer from 5/86, prior on books and cards to 1968. Search the active Criminal Calendar by defendant name at the web site.
General Information: Public access terminal is available. No adoptions, sealed cases, juvenile, sex offenders, mental or expunged records released. SASE requested. Turnaround time 1-2 days. Copy fee: $1.00 for first page, $.25 each add'l. Certification fee: $2.00. Fee payee: Clerk of Superior Court. Business checks accepted. Prepayment is required.

Jones County

Superior-District Court PO Box 280, Trenton, NC 28585; 252-448-7351; Fax: 252-448-1607. Hours: 8AM-5PM (EST). *Felony, Misdemeanor, Civil, Eviction, Small Claims, Probate.*

www.aoc.state.nc.us/www/public/courts/jones.html

Civil Records: Access: In person. Visitors must perform in person searches. No search fee. Required to search: name, years to search. Civil cases indexed by defendant, plaintiff. Civil records on computer since 1989, prior on microfilm.
Criminal Records: Access: Mail, online, in person. Both court and visitors may perform in person searches. Search fee: $5.00 per name. Required to search: name, years to search, DOB. Criminal records on computer since 1989, prior on microfilm. Search the active Criminal Calendar by defendant name at the web site.
General Information: Public access terminal is available. No adoptions, sealed cases, juvenile, sex offenders, mental or expunged records released. SASE required. Turnaround time 5 days. Copy fee: $1.00 for first page, $.25 each add'l. Certification fee: $2.00. Fee payee: Clerk of Court. Only cashiers checks and money orders accepted. Prepayment is required.

Lee County

Superior-District Court PO Box 4209, Sanford, NC 27331; 919-708-4400; Fax: 919-775-3483. Hours: 8AM-5PM (EST). *Felony, Misdemeanor, Civil, Eviction, Small Claims, Probate.*
www.aoc.state.nc.us/www/public/courts/lee.html

Civil Records: Access: In person only. Visitors must perform in person searches for themselves. No search fee. Required to search: name, years to search. Civil cases indexed by defendant, plaintiff. Civil records on computer since 1989, prior on books to 1967, index to 1907.
Criminal Records: Access: Mail, online, in person. Visitors must perform in person searches for themselves No search fee. Required to search: name, years to search, DOB. Criminal records on computer since 6/87, prior on books to 12/68, index to criminal actions books from 8/84 to 6/87. Search the active Criminal Calendar by defendant name at the web site.
General Information: Public access terminal is available. No adoptions, sealed cases, juvenile, sex offenders, mental or expunged records released. Turnaround time 1-3 days. Copy fee: $1.00 for first page, $.25 each add'l. Certification fee: $2.00. Fee payee: Clerk of Superior Court. Only cashiers checks and money orders accepted. Prepayment is required.

Lenoir County

Superior-District Court PO Box 68, Kinston, NC 28502-0068; 252-527-6231; Fax: 252-527-9154. Hours: 8AM-5PM (EST). *Felony, Misdemeanor, Civil, Eviction, Small Claims, Probate.*
www.aoc.state.nc.us/www/public/courts/lenoir.htm
Civil Records: Access: In person only. Both court and visitors may perform in person searches. No search fee. Required to search: name, years to search; also helpful: address. Civil cases indexed by defendant, plaintiff. Civil records on computer since Oct. 24, 1988, prior on books to 1900s, prior destroyed due to fire.
Criminal Records: Access: Mail, online, in person. Both court and visitors may perform in person searches. Search fee: $5.00 per name. Required to search: name, years to search, DOB; also helpful: address. Criminal records on computer since 8/86, prior records on books and cards to 1925. Search the active Criminal Calendar by defendant name at the web site.
General Information: Public access terminal is available. No adoptions, sealed cases, juvenile, sex offenders, mental or expunged records released. SASE required. Turnaround time 1-2 days. Copy fee: $1.00 for first page, $.25 each add'l. Certification fee: Included in search fee, unless do it yourself then $2.00. Fee payee: Clerk of Superior Court. Only cashiers checks and money orders accepted. Prepayment is required.

Lincoln County

Superior-District Court PO Box 8, Lincolnton, NC 28093; 704-736-8566; Fax: 704-736-8718. Hours: 8AM-5PM (EST). *Felony, Misdemeanor, Civil, Eviction, Small Claims, Probate.*
www.aoc.state.nc.us/www/public/courts/lincoln.htm
Civil Records: Access: In person only. Visitors must perform in person searches for themselves. No search fee. Required to search: name, years to search. Civil cases indexed by defendant, plaintiff. Civil records on computer since 1988, in books since 1920s, on microfiche since 1988.
Criminal Records: Access: Mail, online, in person. Both court and visitors may perform in person searches. Search fee: $5.00 per name. Required to search: name, years to search, DOB. Criminal records on computer since 1986, prior on books and cards to 1968. Search the active Criminal Calendar by defendant name at the web site.
General Information: Public access terminal is available. No adoptions, sealed cases, juvenile, sex

offenders, mental or expunged records released. SASE required. Turnaround time 2 days to 1 week. Copy fee: $1.00 for first page, $.25 each add'l. Certification fee: $2.00. Fee payee: Clerk of Court. Business checks accepted. Prepayment is required.

Macon County

Superior-District Court PO Box 288, Franklin, NC 28744; 828-349-2000; Fax: 828-369-2515. Hours: 8:30AM-5PM (EST). *Felony, Misdemeanor, Civil, Eviction, Small Claims, Probate.*
www.aoc.state.nc.us/www/public/courts/macon.html

Civil Records: Access: In person only. Visitors must perform in person searches for themselves. No search fee. Required to search: name, years to search; also helpful: address. Civil cases indexed by defendant, plaintiff. Civil records on computer since May 1989, prior on books to 1968.
Criminal Records: Access: Mail, online, in person. Only the court performs in person searches; visitors may not. Search fee: $5.00 per name. Required to search: name, DOB; also helpful: years to search, address. Criminal records on computer since May 1989, prior on books to 1968. Search the active Criminal Calendar by defendant name at the web site.
General Information: Public access terminal is available. (Civil only.) No adoptions, sealed cases, juvenile, sex offenders, mental or expunged records released. Turnaround time 1-2 days. Copy fee: $.25 per page. Certification fee: $2.00. Fee payee: Clerk of Superior Court. Local personal checks accepted. Prepayment is required.

Madison County

Superior-District Court PO Box 217, Marshall, NC 28753; 828-649-2531; Fax: 828-649-2829. Hours: 8AM-5PM (EST). *Felony, Misdemeanor, Civil, Eviction, Small Claims, Probate.*
www.aoc.state.nc.us/www/public/courts/madison.htm

Civil Records: Access: In person only. Visitors must perform in person searches for themselves. No search fee. Required to search: name, years to search; also helpful: address. Civil cases indexed by defendant, plaintiff. Civil records on computer back to 10/88, prior on books to 1968.
Criminal Records: Access: Mail, online, in person. Only the court performs in person searches; visitors may not. Search fee: $5.00 per name. Required to search: name, DOB; also helpful: years to search. Criminal records on computer since 10/88, prior on books to 1968. Search the active Criminal Calendar by defendant name at the web site.
General Information: Public access terminal is available. No adoptions, sealed cases, juvenile, sex offenders, mental, expunged, or dismissed records released. Turnaround time 1-2 days. Copy fee: $1.00 for first page, $.25 each add'l. Certification fee: $2.00. Fee payee: Clerk of Superior Court. Only cashiers checks and money orders accepted. Prepayment is required.

Martin County

Superior-District Court PO Box 807, Williamston, NC 27892; 252-792-2515; Fax: 252-792-6668. Hours: 8AM-5PM (EST). *Felony, Misdemeanor, Civil, Eviction, Small Claims, Probate.*
www.aoc.state.nc.us/www/public/courts/martin.html

Civil Records: Access: Mail, in person. Both court and visitors may perform in person searches. Search fee: $5.00 per name. Required to search: name, years to search, address. Civil cases indexed by defendant, plaintiff. Civil records go back to 1800's, civil records on computer since 1989, in books since 1968.
Criminal Records: Access: Mail, online, in person. Both court and visitors may perform in person searches. Search fee: $5.00 per name. Required to search: name, years to search, address, DOB; also helpful: SSN.

Criminal records go back to 1800's criminal records on computer since 1996 in books since 1968. Search the active Criminal Calendar by defendant at the web site.
General Information: Public access terminal is available. No adoptions, sealed cases, juvenile, mental or expunged records released. SASE required. Turnaround time 1 week. Copy fee: $1.00 for first page, $.25 each add'l. Certification fee: $2.00. Fee payee: Clerk of Court. Only cashiers checks and money orders accepted. Prepayment is required.

McDowell County

Superior-District Court 21 S Main St, Marion, NC 28752; 828-652-7717; Fax: 828-659-2641. Hours: 8:30AM-5PM (EST). *Felony, Misdemeanor, Civil, Eviction, Small Claims, Probate.*
www.aoc.state.nc.us/www/public/courts/mcdowell.html

Civil Records: Access: Mail, in person. Both court and visitors may perform in person searches. No search fee. Required to search: name, years to search; also helpful: address. Civil cases indexed by defendant, plaintiff. Civil records on computer since 11/88, prior on books to 1930.
Criminal Records: Access: Mail, online, in person. Both court and visitors may perform in person searches. Search fee: $5.00 per name. Required to search: name, DOB; also helpful: years to search, address, SSN. Criminal records on computer since Oct. 1987, prior on books to 1968. Search the active Criminal Calendar by defendant name at the web site.
General Information: Public access terminal is available. No adoptions, sealed cases, juvenile, sex offenders, mental or expunged records released. SASE required. Turnaround time 1-2 days. Copy fee: $1.00 for first page, $.25 each add'l. Certification fee: $3.00. Fee payee: Clerk of Superior Court. Business checks accepted. Prepayment is required.

Mecklenburg County

Superior-District Court 800 E 4th St, PO Box 37971, Charlotte, NC 28237; Civil phone: 704-347-7814; Criminal phone: 704-347-7809. Hours: 8AM-5PM (EST). *Felony, Misdemeanor, Civil, Eviction, Small Claims, Probate.*
www.aoc.state.nc.us/www/public/courts/mecklenburg.htm

Civil Records: Access: In person, online. Visitors must perform in person searches for themselves. No search fee. Required to search: name. Civil cases indexed by defendant, plaintiff. Civil records on computer since April 1988, prior on books to 1940s. Search active civil calendars by court date on the web site. Also, online name search dockets at http://www1.aoc.state.nc.us/www/calendars/Civil.html.
Criminal Records: Access: Mail, online, in person. Both court and visitors may perform in person searches. Search fee: $5.00 per name. Required to search: name, years to search, address, DOB; also helpful: SSN. Criminal records on computer from 1/83, prior on cards and books to 1930s. Search the active Criminal Calendar by defendant name at the web site.
General Information: Public access terminal is available. No adoptions, sealed cases, juvenile, sex offenders, mental or expunged records released. SASE requested. Turnaround time 1-2 days. Copy fee: $1.00 for first page, $.25 each add'l. Certification fee: $2.00. Fee payee: Clerk of Superior Court. Only cashiers checks and money orders accepted.

Mitchell County

Superior-District Court PO Box 402, Bakersville, NC 28705; 828-688-2161; Fax: 828-688-2168. Hours: 8:30AM-5PM (EST). *Felony, Misdemeanor, Civil, Eviction, Small Claims, Probate.*
www.clerkofcourt.org

Civil Records: Access: Mail, in person. Both court and visitors may perform in person searches. Search fee:

$5.00 per name. Required to search: name, years to search; also helpful: address. Civil cases indexed by defendant, plaintiff. Civil records on computer since 1988, prior on books since 1968.

Criminal Records: Access: Mail, online, in person. Only the court performs in person searches; visitors may not. Search fee: $5.00 per name. Required to search: name, years to search, DOB, SSN; also helpful: address. Criminal records on computer since 1988, prior on books since 1968. Search the active Criminal Calendar by defendant name at www.aoc.state.nc.us/www/public/courts/mitchell.htm.

General Information: Public access terminal is available. (Civil only.) No adoptions, sealed cases, juvenile, sex offenders, mental or expunged records released. SASE required. Turnaround time 1-2 days. Copy fee: $1.00 for first page, $.25 each add'l. Certification fee: $2.00. Fee payee: Superior-District Court. Business checks accepted. Prepayment required.

Montgomery County

Superior - District Court PO Box 527, Troy, NC 27371; 910-576-4211; Fax: 910-576-5020. Hours: 8AM-5PM (EST). *Felony, Misdemeanor, Civil, Eviction, Small Claims, Probate.*
www.aoc.state.nc.us/www/public/courts/montgomery.html
Civil Records: Access: In person only. Visitors must perform in person searches for themselves. No search fee. Required to search: name, years to search. Civil cases indexed by defendant, plaintiff. Civil records on computer since April 1989, on books to 170, archived in Raleigh to 1843, prior records destroyed in fire.
Criminal Records: Access: Phone, fax, mail, online, in person. Both court and visitors may perform in person searches. Search fee: $5.00 per name. Required to search: name, years to search, address, DOB, signed release. Criminal records on computer since April 1989, on books to 170, archived in Raleigh to 1843, prior records destroyed in fire. Search the active Criminal Calendar by defendant name at the web site.
General Information: Public access terminal is available. No adoptions, sealed cases, juvenile, sex offenders, mental or expunged records released. Turnaround time 1-2 days. Copy fee: $.25 per page. Certification fee: $2.00. Fee payee: Clerk of Superior Court. Only cashiers checks and money orders accepted. Prepayment is required.

Moore County

Superior-District Court PO Box 936, Carthage, NC 28327; 910-947-2396; Fax: 910-947-1444. Hours: 8AM-5PM (EST). *Felony, Misdemeanor, Civil, Eviction, Small Claims, Probate.*
www.aoc.state.nc.us/www/public/courts/moore.html
Civil Records: Access: Mail, in person. Both court and visitors may perform in person searches. Search fee: $5.00 per name. Required to search: name, years to search. Civil cases indexed by defendant, plaintiff. Civil records on computer since March 1989, prior on books to 1968, older records in basement.
Criminal Records: Access: Mail, online, in person. Only the court performs in person searches; visitors may not. Search fee: $5.00 per name. Required to search: name, years to search, DOB, signed release; also helpful: address, SSN. Criminal records on computer since March 1989, prior on books to 1968, older records in basement. Search the active Criminal Calendar by defendant name at the web site.
General Information: Public access terminal is available. No adoptions, sealed cases, juvenile, sex offenders, mental or expunged records released. Turnaround time 2-4 days. Copy fee: $1.00 for first page, $.25 each add'l. Certification fee: $2.00. Fee payee: Clerk of Superior Court. Only cashiers checks and money orders accepted. Prepayment is required.

Nash County

Superior-District Court PO Box 759, Nashville, NC 27856; Civil phone: 252-459-4081; Criminal phone: 252-459-4085; Fax: 252-459-6050. Hours: 8AM-5PM (EST). *Felony, Misdemeanor, Civil, Eviction, Small Claims, Probate.*
www.aoc.state.nc.us/www/public/courts/nash.html
Civil Records: Access: Mail, in person. Both court and visitors may perform in person searches. No search fee. Required to search: name, years to search; also helpful: address. Civil cases indexed by defendant, plaintiff. Civil records on computer since 6/88, prior in books to 1988. Online access to the civil calendars is available at the web site.
Criminal Records: Access: Mail, online, in person. Both court and visitors may perform in person searches. Search fee: $5.00 per name. Required to search: name, years to search, DOB; also helpful: address. Criminal records on computer since 5/80, prior on books and cards dating back to late 1800s. Search the active Criminal Calendar by defendant name at the web site.
General Information: Public access terminal is available. No adoptions, sealed cases, juvenile, mental or expunged records released. SASE required. Turnaround time 1 week. Copy fee: $1.00 for first page, $.25 each add'l. Certification fee: $2.00. Fee payee: Rachel M Joyner, CSC. Only cashiers checks and money orders accepted. Prepayment is required.

New Hanover County

Superior-District Court PO Box 2023, Wilmington, NC 28402; 910-341-4430; Criminal phone: 910-341-4440; Fax: 910-251-2676. Hours: 8AM-5PM (EST). *Felony, Misdemeanor, Civil, Eviction, Small Claims, Probate.*
www.aoc.state.nc.us/www/public/courts/new_hanover.html
Civil Records: Access: In person only. Visitors must perform in person searches for themselves. No search fee. Required to search: name, years to search; also helpful: address. Civil cases indexed by defendant, plaintiff. Civil records on computer since 1988, on books to late 1800s.
Criminal Records: Access: Mail, online, in person. Both court and visitors may perform in person searches. Search fee: $5.00 per name. Required to search: name, years to search, DOB; also helpful: address, SSN. Criminal records on computer since 11/83, prior on books and files to late 1800s. Search the active Criminal Calendar by defendant name at the web site.
General Information: Public access terminal is available. No adoptions, sealed cases, juvenile, sex offenders, mental or expunged records released. SASE required. Turnaround time 1-2 days. Copy fee: $1.00 for first page, $.25 each add'l. Certification fee: $2.50. Fee payee: Clerk of Superior Court. Only cashiers checks and money orders accepted. Prepayment is required.

Northampton County

Superior-District Court PO Box 217, Jackson, NC 27845; 252-534-1631; Fax: 252-534-1308. Hours: 8:30AM-5PM (EST). *Felony, Misdemeanor, Civil, Eviction, Small Claims, Probate.*
www.aoc.state.nc.us/www/public/courts/northampton.html
Civil Records: Access: Mail, in person. Search fee: $5.00 per name. Required to search: name, years to search; also helpful: address. Civil cases indexed by defendant, plaintiff. Civil records on computer back to 1993, prior on books to 1968.
Criminal Records: Access: Mail, online, in person. Both court and visitors may perform in person searches. Search fee: $5.00 per name. Required to search: name, years to search, DOB; also helpful: address, SSN. Criminal records on computer back to 1989, prior on books to 1968. Search the active Criminal Calendar by defendant name at the web site.

General Information: Public access terminal is available. No adoptions, sealed cases, juvenile, sex offenders, mental or expunged records released. Turnaround time is 3-10 days. Copy fee: $1.00 for first page, $.25 each add'l. Certification fee: $2.50. Fee payee: Clerk of Superior Court. Business checks accepted. Prepayment is required.

Onslow County

Superior-District Court 625 Court St, Jacksonville, NC 28540; 910-455-4458. Hours: 8AM-5PM (EST). *Felony, Misdemeanor, Civil, Eviction, Small Claims, Probate.*
www.aoc.state.nc.us/www/public/courts/onslow.htm
Civil Records: Access: In person only. Visitors must perform in person searches for themselves. No search fee. Required to search: name, years to search; also helpful: address. Civil cases indexed by defendant, plaintiff. Civil records on computer since 1988, prior on books to 1920s.
Criminal Records: Access: Mail, online, in person. Both court and visitors may perform in person searches. Search fee: $5.00 per name. Required to search: name, years to search, DOB; also helpful: address, SSN. Criminal records on computer since 2/83, prior on books to 1920s. Search the active Criminal Calendar by defendant name at the web site.
General Information: Public access terminal is available. No adoptions, sealed cases, juvenile, sex offenders, mental or expunged records released. Turnaround time 1-2 days. Copy fee: $1.00 for first page, $.25 each add'l. Certification fee: $2.00. Fee payee: Clerk of Superior Court. Business checks accepted. Prepayment is required.

Orange County

Superior-District Court 106 E Margaret Lane, Hillsborough, NC 27278; 919-245-2210; Criminal phone: 919-245-2200; Fax: 919-644-3043. Hours: 8AM-5PM (EST). *Felony, Misdemeanor, Civil, Eviction, Small Claims, Probate.*
www.aoc.state.nc.us/www/public/courts/orange.htm
Civil Records: Access: Mail, in person. Both court and visitors may perform in person searches. Search fee: $5.00 per name. Required to search: name, years to search; also helpful: address. Civil cases indexed by defendant, plaintiff. Civil records on computer since May 1989, prior on books to early 1800s.
Criminal Records: Access: Mail, online, in person. Both court and visitors may perform in person searches. Search fee: $5.00 per name. Required to search: name, years to search, DOB; also helpful: address, SSN, race, sex. computer records go to 3/87. Search the active Criminal Calendar by defendant name at the web site.
General Information: Public access terminal is available. No adoptions, sealed cases, juvenile, sex offenders, mental or expunged records released. SASE required. Turnaround time 1-3 days. Copy fee: $1.00 for first page, $.25 each add'l. Certification fee: $2.00. Fee payee: Clerk of Superior Court. Business checks accepted. Prepayment is required.

Pamlico County

Superior-District Court PO Box 38, Bayboro, NC 28515; 252-745-6000; Fax: 252-745-6018. Hours: 8AM-5PM (EST). *Felony, Misdemeanor, Civil, Eviction, Small Claims, Probate.*
www.aoc.state.nc.us/www/public/courts/pamlico.html
Civil Records: Access: Mail, in person. Both court and visitors may perform in person searches. Search fee: $5.00 per name. Required to search: name, years to search, address. Civil cases indexed by defendant, plaintiff. Civil records go back to 1988; criminal records on computer since 9/89, prior on books to 1968.

Criminal Records: Access: Mail, online, in person. Only the court performs in person searches; visitors may not. Search fee: $5.00 per name. Required to search: name, years to search, DOB. Criminal records go back to 1990; criminal records on computer since 9/84, prior on books to 1968. Search the active Criminal Calendar by defendant name at the web site.

General Information: Public access terminal is available. No adoptions, sealed cases, juvenile, sex offenders, mental or expunged records released. SASE required. Turnaround time 1-2 days. Copy fee: $1.00 for first page, $.25 each add'l. Certification fee: $2.00. Fee payee: Clerk of Court. Only cashiers checks and money orders accepted. Prepayment is required.

Pasquotank County

Superior-District Court PO Box 449, Elizabeth City, NC 27907-0449; 252-331-4751. Hours: 8AM-5PM (EST). *Felony, Misdemeanor, Civil, Eviction, Small Claims, Probate.*

www.aoc.state.nc.us/www/public/courts/pasquotank.html

Civil Records: Access: In person only. Visitors must perform in person searches for themselves. No search fee. Required to search: name, years to search; also helpful: address. Civil cases indexed by defendant, plaintiff. Civil records on computer since March 6, 1989, books prior to 1800s (some in Raleigh).

Criminal Records: Access: Mail, online, in person. Both court and visitors may perform in person searches. Search fee: $5.00 per name. Required to search: name, years to search, DOB; also helpful: address, SSN, race, sex. Criminal records on computer since 4/88, prior on books and microfiche. Search the active Criminal Calendar by defendant name at the web site.

General Information: Public access terminal is available. No adoptions, sealed cases, juvenile, sex offenders, mental or expunged records released. Turnaround time 2 days. Copy fee: $1.00 for first page, $.25 each add'l. Certification fee: Included in search fee, court must do search. Fee payee: Clerk of Superior Court. Business checks accepted. Prepayment required.

Pender County

Superior-District Court PO Box 308, Burgaw, NC 28425; 910-259-1229; Fax: 910-259-1292. Hours: 8AM-5PM (EST). *Felony, Misdemeanor, Civil, Eviction, Small Claims, Probate.*

www.aoc.state.nc.us/www/public/courts/pender.html

Civil Records: Access: In person only. Visitors must perform in person searches for themselves. No search fee. Required to search: name, years to search; also helpful: address. Civil cases indexed by defendant, plaintiff. Civil records on computer since 9/89, prior in books from 1875.

Criminal Records: Access: Fax, mail, online, in person. Only the court performs in person searches; visitors may not. Search fee: $5.00 per name. Required to search: name, years to search, DOB; also helpful: address, SSN. Criminal records on computer since 9/89, prior in books from 1968. Search the active Criminal Calendar by defendant name at the web site.

General Information: Public access terminal is available. No adoptions, sealed cases, juvenile, sex offenders, mental or expunged records released. Turnaround time 1 week. Fax notes: $1.00 for first page, $.25 each add'l. Copy fee: $1.00 for first page, $.25 each add'l. Certification fee: Included in search fee, unless do it yourself then $2.00. Fee payee: Clerk of Superior Court. Business checks accepted. Prepayment is required.

Perquimans County

Superior-District Court PO Box 33, Hertford, NC 27944; 252-426-1505. Hours: 8AM-5PM (EST). *Felony, Misdemeanor, Civil, Eviction, Small Claims, Probate.*

www.aoc.state.nc.us/www/public/courts/perquimans.html

Civil Records: Access: In person only. Visitors must perform in person searches for themselves. No search fee. Required to search: name, years to search. Civil cases indexed by defendant, plaintiff. Civil records on computer since 1989, prior in books to 1966, rest archived and must be searched in person only.

Criminal Records: Access: Mail, online, in person. Both court and visitors may perform in person searches. Search fee: $5.00 per name. Required to search: name, years to search, DOB. Criminal records on computer since 1989, prior in books to 1966, rest archived and must be searched in person only. Search the active Criminal Calendar by defendant name at the web site.

General Information: Public access terminal is available. No adoptions, sealed cases, juvenile, sex offenders, mental or expunged records released. Turnaround time 1-2 days. Copy fee: $1.00 for first page, $.25 each add'l. Certification fee: $2.00. Fee payee: Clerk of Superior Court. Only cashiers checks and money orders accepted. Prepayment is required.

Person County

Superior-District Court 105 S Main St, Roxboro, NC 27573; Civil phone: 336-597-0554; Criminal phone: 336-597-0556; Fax: 336-597-0568. Hours: 8:30AM-5PM (EST). *Felony, Misdemeanor, Civil, Eviction, Small Claims, Probate.*

www.aoc.state.nc.us/www/public/courts/person.html

Civil Records: Access: In person only. Both court and visitors may perform in person searches. No search fee. Required to search: name, years to search. Civil cases indexed by defendant, plaintiff. Civil records on microfiche since 4/89, prior in index books to 1968.

Criminal Records: Access: Mail, online, in person. Both court and visitors may perform in person searches. Search fee: $5.00 per name. Required to search: name, years to search, DOB. Criminal records on computer since 3/88, index cards and books prior to 1968. Search the active Criminal Calendar by defendant name at the web site.

General Information: Public access terminal is available. No adoptions, sealed cases, juvenile, sex offenders, mental or expunged records released. SASE required. Turnaround time 1-2 days. Copy fee: $1.00 for first page, $.25 each add'l. Certification fee: Included in search fee, unless do it yourself then $2.00. Fee payee: Clerk of Superior Court. Business checks accepted.

Pitt County

Superior - District Court PO Box 6067, Greenville, NC 27835; 252-695-7100; Civil phone: 252-695-7150; Criminal phone: 252-695-7117; Fax: 252-830-7376. Hours: 8AM-5PM (EST). *Felony, Misdemeanor, Civil, Eviction, Small Claims, Probate.*

www.aoc.state.nc.us/www/public/courts/pitt.htm

Civil Records: Access: In person only. Visitors must perform in person searches for themselves. No search fee. Required to search: name, years to search; also helpful: address. Civil cases indexed by defendant, plaintiff. Civil records on computer back to 1988, on books to 1968.

Criminal Records: Access: Mail, online, in person. Both court and visitors may perform in person searches. Search fee: $5.00 per name. Required to search: name, years to search, DOB; also helpful: address, SSN. Criminal records on computer back to 2/85, on books and cards to early 1900s. Search the active Criminal Calendar by defendant name at the web site.

General Information:

General Information: Public access terminal is available. No adoptions, sealed cases, juvenile, sex offenders, mental or expunged records released. Turnaround time 1-2 days. Copy fee: $1.00 for first page, $.25 each add'l. Certification fee: $5.00. Fee payee: Clerk of Court. Business checks accepted. Prepayment is required.

Polk County

Superior-District Court PO Box 38, Columbus, NC 28722; 828-894-8231; Fax: 828-894-5752. Hours: 8AM-5PM (EST). *Felony, Misdemeanor, Civil, Eviction, Small Claims, Probate.*

www.aoc.state.nc.us/www/public/courts/polk.html

Civil Records: Access: Mail, in person. Both court and visitors may perform in person searches. Search fee: $5.00 per name. Required to search: name, years to search. Civil cases indexed by defendant, plaintiff. Civil records on computer since 5/89, prior on books to 1968.

Criminal Records: Access: Mail, online, in person. Only the court performs in person searches; visitors may not. Search fee: $5.00 per name. Required to search: name, years to search, DOB. Criminal records on computer since 5/89, prior on books to 1968. Search the active Criminal Calendar by defendant name at the web site.

General Information: No adoptions, sealed cases, juvenile, sex offenders, mental, expunged or dismissed records released. SASE required. Turnaround time 1-2 days. Copy fee: $1.00 for first page, $.25 each add'l. Certification fee: $2.00. Fee payee: Clerk of Superior Court. Business checks accepted. Prepayment is required.

Randolph County

Superior-District Court PO Box 1925, 176 E Salisbury St, Asheboro, NC 27203; 336-328-3000; Civil phone: 336-318-6750; Criminal phone: 336-318-6710; Fax: 336-328-3131. Hours: 8AM-5PM (EST). *Felony, Misdemeanor, Civil, Eviction, Small Claims, Probate.*

www.aoc.state.nc.us/www/public/courts/randolph.htm

Civil Records: Access: In person only. Visitors must perform in person searches for themselves. No search fee. Required to search: name, years to search. Civil cases indexed by defendant, plaintiff. Civil records on computer since 02/89, prior on books to 1800s.

Criminal Records: Access: Mail, online, in person. Only the court performs in person searches; visitors may not. Search fee: $5.00 per name. Required to search: name, years to search, address, DOB. Criminal records on computer since 06/85, prior on books and cards from 1970 to 1981. Microfilm from 1981 to 06/85. Search the active Criminal Calendar by defendant name at the web site.

General Information: Public access terminal is available. (Civil only.) No adoptions, sealed cases, juvenile, sex offenders, mental or expunged records released. SASE required. Turnaround time 1-2 days. Copy fee: $1.00 for first page, $.25 each add'l. Certification fee: $2.00. Fee payee: Clerk of Superior Court. Only cashiers checks and money orders accepted. Prepayment is required.

Richmond County

Superior-District Court 114 E Franklin St #103, Rockingham, NC 28379; Civil phone: 910-997-9102; Criminal phone: 910-997-9101; Fax: 910-997-9126. Hours: 8AM-5PM (EST). *Felony, Misdemeanor, Civil, Eviction, Small Claims, Probate.*

www.aoc.state.nc.us/www/public/courts/richmond.htm

Civil Records: Access: In person only. Visitors must perform in person searches for themselves. No search fee. Required to search: name, years to search; also helpful: address. Civil cases indexed by defendant, plaintiff. Civil records on computer since 4/89, prior on books since 1968.

Criminal Records: Access: Mail, online, in person. Both court and visitors may perform in person searches. Search fee: $5.00 per name. Required to search: name, years to search, DOB; also helpful: address, SSN. Criminal records on computer since 1977, cards to 1977, books to 1940, prior archived. Search the active Criminal Calendar by defendant name at the web site.

General Information: Public access terminal is available. No adoptions, sealed cases, juvenile, sex offenders, mental or expunged records released. SASE required. Turnaround time 1-2 days. Copy fee: $1.00 for first page, $.25 each add'l. Certification fee: $2.00. Fee payee: Clerk of Superior Court. Business checks accepted. Prepayment is required.

Robeson County

Superior-District Court PO Box 1084, Lumberton, NC 28359; 910-737-5035; Civil phone: 910-671-3372; Criminal phone: 910-671-3395; Fax: 910-618-5598. Hours: 8:30AM-5PM (EST). *Felony, Misdemeanor, Civil, Eviction, Small Claims, Probate.*

www.aoc.state.nc.us/www/public/courts/robeson.html

Civil Records: Access: In person only. Visitors must perform in person searches for themselves. No search fee. Required to search: name, years to search; also helpful: address. Civil cases indexed by defendant, plaintiff. Civil records on computer since 1988, prior on books since 1966.

Criminal Records: Access: Mail, in person. Both court and visitors may perform in person searches. Search fee: $5.00 per name. Required to search: name, years to search; also helpful: address, DOB. Criminal records on computer since 1983, index books prior. Search the active Criminal Calendar by defendant name at the web site.

General Information: Public access terminal is available. No sealed cases, juvenile, sex offenders, mental or expunged records released. SASE required. Turnaround time 1-2 days. Copy fee: $1.00 for first page, $.25 each add'l. Certification fee: $2.00; Exemplification is $5.00. Fee payee: Clerk of Superior Court. Business checks accepted. Prepayment is required.

Rockingham County

Superior-District Court PO Box 127, Wentworth, NC 27375; 336-342-8700. Hours: 8AM-5PM (EST). *Felony, Misdemeanor, Civil, Eviction, Small Claims, Probate.*

www.aoc.state.nc.us/www/public/courts/rockingham.html

Civil Records: Access: In person only. Both court and visitors may perform in person searches. No search fee. Required to search: name, years to search. Civil cases indexed by defendant, plaintiff. Civil records on computer since 2/89, prior on books.

Criminal Records: Access: Mail, online, in person. Both court and visitors may perform in person searches. No search fee. Required to search: name, years to search, DOB. Criminal records on computer since 5/85, prior on cards and books. Search the active Criminal Calendar by defendant name at the web site.

General Information: Public access terminal is available. No adoptions, sealed cases, juvenile, sex offenders, mental or expunged records released. Turnaround time 1-2 days. Copy fee: $1.00 for first page, $.25 each add'l. Certification fee: $2.00. Fee payee: Clerk of Superior Court. Only cashiers checks and money orders accepted. Prepayment is required.

Rowan County

Superior-District Court PO Box 4599, 210 N Main St, Salisbury, NC 28144; 704-639-7505. Hours: 8AM-5PM (EST). *Felony, Misdemeanor, Civil, Eviction, Small Claims, Probate.*

www.aoc.state.nc.us/www/public/courts/rowan.html

Civil Records: Access: In person, online. Both court and visitors may perform in person searches. No search fee. Required to search: name, years to search; also helpful: address. Civil cases indexed by defendant, plaintiff. Civil records on computer since 1989, prior on books to 1800s. Search active civil calendars by court date on the web site. Also, online name search dockets at http://www1.aoc.state.nc.us/www/calendars/Civil.html.

Criminal Records: Access: Mail, online, in person. Both court and visitors may perform in person searches. Search fee: $5.00 per name. Required to search: name, DOB; also helpful: years to search, address, SSN. Criminal records on computer from 5/85, prior on books and cards to 1970. Search the active Criminal Calendar by defendant name at the web site.

General Information: No adoptions, sealed cases, juvenile, sex offenders, mental or expunged records released. Turnaround time 1-3 days. Copy fee: $1.00 for first page, $.25 each add'l. Certification fee: Included in search fee, unless do it yourself then $2.00. Fee payee: Clerk of Superior Court. Business checks accepted. Prepayment is required.

Rutherford County

Superior-District Court PO Box 630, Rutherfordton, NC 28139; Civil phone: 828-286-9136; Criminal phone: 828-286-3243; Fax: 828-286-4322. Hours: 8:30AM-5PM (EST). *Felony, Misdemeanor, Civil, Eviction, Small Claims, Probate.*

www.aoc.state.nc.us/www/public/courts/rutherford.htm

Civil Records: Access: In person only. Visitors must perform in person searches for themselves. No search fee. Required to search: name, years to search; also helpful: address. Civil cases indexed by defendant, plaintiff. Civil records on computer Oct. 1988, prior on books, some records to 1700s.

Criminal Records: Access: Mail, online, in person. Both court and visitors may perform in person searches. Search fee: $5.00 per name. Required to search: name, years to search, DOB; also helpful: address, SSN. Criminal records on computer since 6/87, prior on microfiche and books dating to 1800s. Search the active Criminal Calendar by defendant name at the web site.

General Information: Public access terminal is available. No adoptions, sealed cases, juvenile, sex offenders, mental or expunged records released. Turnaround time 1-2 days. Copy fee: $1.00 for first page, $.25 each add'l. Certification fee: $2.00. Fee payee: Clerk of Superior Court. Business checks accepted. Prepayment is required.

Sampson County

Superior - District Court Courthouse, Clinton, NC 28328; 910-592-5191; Civil phone: 910-592-5192; Criminal phone: 910-592-6981; Fax: 910-592-5502. Hours: 8AM-5PM (EST). *Felony, Misdemeanor, Civil, Eviction, Small Claims, Probate.*

www.aoc.state.nc.us/www/public/courts/sampson.html

Civil Records: Access: In person only. Visitors must perform in person searches for themselves. No search fee. Required to search: name, years to search; also helpful: address. Civil cases indexed by defendant, plaintiff. Civil records on computer since 1989, prior on books.

Criminal Records: Access: Phone, mail, in person. Only the court performs in person searches; visitors may not. Search fee: $5.00 per name. Required to

search: name, years to search, DOB; also helpful: address, SSN. Criminal records on computer since 7/87, prior on books. Search the active Criminal Calendar by defendant name at the web site.

General Information: Public access terminal is available. No adoptions, sealed cases, juvenile, sex offenders, mental or expunged records released. SASE requested. Turnaround time 1-2 days. Copy fee: $1.00 for first page, $.25 each add'l. Certification fee: $2.00. Fee payee: Clerk of Superior Court. Personal checks accepted. Prepayment is required.

Scotland County

Superior-District Court PO Box 769, Laurinburg, NC 28353; 910-277-3240. Hours: 8:30AM-5PM (EST). *Felony, Misdemeanor, Civil, Eviction, Small Claims, Probate.*

www.aoc.state.nc.us/www/public/courts/scotland.html

Civil Records: Access: Mail, in person. Both court and visitors may perform in person searches. Search fee: $5.00 per name. Required to search: name, years to search. Civil cases indexed by defendant, plaintiff. Civil records on computer since 1988, in books since 1966, on microfiche since 1984.

Criminal Records: Access: Mail, online, in person. Only the court performs in person searches; visitors may not. Search fee: $5.00 per name. Required to search: name, years to search, DOB; SSN helpful. Criminal records on computer since 1988, in books since 1966, on microfiche since 1984. Search the active Criminal Calendar by defendant name at the web site.

General Information: Public access terminal is available. No adoptions, sealed cases, juvenile, sex offenders, mental or expunged records released. SASE required. Turnaround time 1-2 days. Copy fee: $1.00 for first page, $.25 each add'l. Certification fee: $2.00. Fee payee: Clerk of Court. Only cashiers checks and money orders accepted. Prepayment is required.

Stanly County

Superior-District Court PO Box 668, Albemarle, NC 28002-0668; 704-982-2161; Fax: 704-982-8107. Hours: 8:30AM-5PM (EST). *Felony, Misdemeanor, Civil, Eviction, Small Claims, Probate.*

www.aoc.state.nc.us/www/public/courts/stanly.htm

Civil Records: Access: In person only. Visitors must perform in person searches for themselves. No search fee. Required to search: name, years to search; also helpful: address. Civil cases indexed by defendant, plaintiff. Civil records on computer since 1989, books to 1968.

Criminal Records: Access: Mail, online, in person. Both court and visitors may perform in person searches. Search fee: $5.00 per name. Required to search: name, years to search, DOB; also helpful: address, SSN. Criminal records on computer since 1989, books to 1968. Search the active Criminal Calendar by defendant name at the web site.

General Information: Public access terminal is available. No adoptions, sealed cases, juvenile, sex offenders, mental or expunged records released. SASE required. Turnaround time 1-2 days. Copy fee: $1.00 for first page, $.25 each add'l. Certification fee: $2.00. Fee payee: Clerk of Superior Court. Only cashiers checks and money orders accepted. Prepayment is required.

Stokes County

Superior-District Court PO Box 250, Danbury, NC 27016; 336-593-2416. Hours: 8AM-5PM (EST). *Felony, Misdemeanor, Civil, Eviction, Small Claims, Probate.*

www.aoc.state.nc.us/www/public/courts/stokes.html

Civil Records: Access: In person only. Visitors must perform in person searches for themselves. No search fee. Required to search: name, years to search; also helpful: address. Civil cases indexed by defendant, plaintiff. Civil records on computer since 9/1988, prior on books to early 1900s. Civil background checks not performed.

Criminal Records: Access: Mail, online, in person. Both court and visitors may perform in person searches. Search fee: $5.00 per name. Required to search: name, years to search; also helpful: address, DOB. Criminal records on computer since 9/1988, prior on books to early 1900s. Search the active Criminal Calendar by defendant name at the web site.

General Information: Public access terminal is available. No adoptions, sealed cases, juvenile, sex offenders, mental or expunged records released. SASE required. Turnaround time 1 week. Copy fee: $1.00 for first page, $.25 each add'l. Certification fee: Included in search fee, unless do it yourself then $2.00. Fee payee: Clerk of Superior Court. Only cashiers checks and money orders accepted. Prepayment is required.

Surry County

Superior-District Court PO Box 345, Dobson, NC 27017; 336-386-8131; Fax: 336-386-9879. Hours: 8AM-5PM (EST). *Felony, Misdemeanor, Civil, Eviction, Small Claims, Probate.*

www.aoc.state.nc.us/www/public/courts/surry.html

Civil Records: Access: In person, mail. Visitors must perform in person searches for themselves. No search fee. Required to search: name, years to search, DOB; also helpful: address. Civil cases indexed by defendant, plaintiff. Civil records on computer since 10/88, on books to 1970, must know township for prior.

Criminal Records: Access: Mail, online, in person. Both court and visitors may perform in person searches. Search fee: $5.00 per name. Required to search: name, years to search, DOB. Criminal records on computer since 10/88, on books to 1970, must know township for prior. Search the active Criminal Calendar by defendant name at the web site.

General Information: Public access terminal is available. No adoptions, sealed cases, juvenile, sex offenders, mental or expunged records released. SASE required. Turnaround time 1-2 days. Copy fee: $1.00 for first page, $.25 each add'l. Certification fee: $2.00. Fee payee: Clerk of Superior Court. Business checks accepted. Prepayment is required.

Swain County

Superior-District Court PO Box 1397, Bryson City, NC 28713; 828-488-2288; Fax: 828-488-9360. Hours: 8:30AM-5PM (EST). *Felony, Misdemeanor, Civil, Eviction, Small Claims, Probate.*

www.aoc.state.nc.us/www/public/courts/swain.html

Civil Records: Access: Mail, in person. Both court and visitors may perform in person searches. Search fee: $5.00 per name. Required to search: name, years to search. Civil cases indexed by defendant, plaintiff. Civil records on computer since 5/1989, prior on books to 1920.

Criminal Records: Access: Mail, online, in person. Only the court performs in person searches; visitors may not. Search fee: $5.00 per name. Required to search: name, years to search, DOB; also helpful-SSN, signed release. Criminal records on computer back to 1989, prior on books to 1969. Search the active Criminal Calendar by defendant name at the web site.

General Information: Public access terminal is available. (Civil only.) No adoptions, sealed cases, juvenile, sex offenders, mental or expunged records released. SASE requested. Turnaround time 1-2 days. Copy fee: $1.00 for first page, $.25 each add'l. Certification fee: $2.00. Fee payee: Clerk of Superior Court. Only cashiers checks and money orders accepted. Prepayment is required.

Transylvania County

Superior-District Court 12 E Main St, Brevard, NC 28712; 828-884-3120; Fax: 828-883-2161. Hours: 8AM-5PM (EST). *Felony, Misdemeanor, Civil, Eviction, Small Claims, Probate.*

www.aoc.state.nc.us/www/public/courts/transylvania.html

Civil Records: Access: In person only. Visitors must perform in person searches for themselves. No search fee. Required to search: name, years to search; also helpful: address. Civil cases indexed by defendant, plaintiff. Civil records on computer from 6/89, on books 1968-1989.

Criminal Records: Access: Mail, online, in person. Visitors may perform in person searches for themselves. Search fee: $5.00 per name. Fee is for certified record check. Required to search: name, years to search, DOB; also helpful: address, SSN. Criminal records on computer from 6/89, on books 1968-1989. Search the active Criminal Calendar by defendant name at the web site.

General Information: No adoptions, sealed cases, juvenile, mental or expunged records released. SASE required. Turnaround time 1-3 days. Copy fee: $1.00 for first page, $.25 each add'l. Certification fee: $2.00. Fee payee: Clerk of Superior Court. Personal checks accepted. Prepayment is required.

Tyrrell County

Superior - District Court PO Box 406, Columbia, NC 27925; 252-796-6281; Fax: 252-796-0008. Hours: 8:30AM-5PM (EST). *Felony, Misdemeanor, Civil, Eviction, Small Claims, Probate.*

www.aoc.state.nc.us/www/public/courts/tyrrell.html

Civil Records: Access: In person only. Visitors must perform in person searches for themselves. No search fee. Required to search: name, years to search; also helpful: address. Civil cases indexed by defendant, plaintiff. Civil records on computer since 10/89, prior on microfilm to 1968.

Criminal Records: Access: Mail, online, in person. Both court and visitors may perform in person searches. Search fee: $5.00 per name. Required to search: name, years to search, DOB; also helpful: address, SSN. Criminal records on computer since 10/89, prior on books to 1968. Search the active Criminal Calendar by defendant name at the web site.

General Information: Public access terminal is available. No adoptions, sealed cases, juvenile, sex offenders, mental records expunged. Turnaround time 1-2 days. Copy fee: $1.00 for first page, $.25 each add'l. Certification fee: $2.00. Fee payee: Clerk of Superior Court. Business checks accepted. Prepayment is required.

Union County

Superior-District Court PO Box 5038, Monroe, NC 28111; 704-283-4313. Hours: 8AM-5PM (EST). *Felony, Misdemeanor, Civil, Eviction, Small Claims, Probate.*

www.aoc.state.nc.us/www/public/courts/union.htm

Civil Records: Access: In person only. Visitors must perform in person searches for themselves. No search fee. Required to search: name, years to search; also helpful: address. Civil cases indexed by defendant, plaintiff. Civil records on computer since 1987, prior on books to 1968.

Criminal Records: Access: Mail, online, in person. Both court and visitors may perform in person searches. Search fee: $5.00 per name. Required to search: name, years to search; also helpful: address, DOB, SSN. Criminal record on computer since 1987; prior on books to 1968. Search the active Criminal Calendar by defendant name at the web site.

General Information: Public access terminal is available. No adoptions, sealed cases, juvenile, sex offenders, mental or expunged records released. Turnaround time 1-2 days. Copy fee: $1.00 for first page, $.25 each add'l. Certification fee: Included in copy fee or search fee. Fee payee: Clerk of Superior Court. Only cashiers checks and money orders accepted. Local business checks only. Prepayment is required.

Vance County

Superior-District Court 156 Church St. #101, Henderson, NC 27536; 252-738-9000. Hours: 8AM-5PM (EST). *Felony, Misdemeanor, Civil, Eviction, Small Claims, Probate.*

www.aoc.state.nc.us/www/public/courts/vance.html

Civil Records: Access: In person only. Visitors must perform in person searches for themselves. No search fee. Required to search: name, years to search; also helpful: address. Civil cases indexed by defendant, plaintiff. Civil records on computer since 1989, prior on books to 1881.

Criminal Records: Access: Mail, online, in person. Both court and visitors may perform in person searches. Search fee: $5.00 per name. Required to search: name, years to search, address, DOB; also helpful: SSN. Criminal records on computer to 12/80, prior on books and cards to 1881. Search the active Criminal Calendar by defendant name at the web site.

General Information: Public access terminal is available. No adoptions, sealed cases, juvenile, sex offenders, mental or expunged records released. Turnaround time 1-2 days. Copy fee: $1.00 for first page, $.25 each add'l. Certification fee: Included in search fee, unless do it yourself then $2.00. Fee payee: Clerk of Superior Court. Business checks accepted. Prepayment is required.

Wake County

Superior - District Court PO Box 351, Raleigh, NC 27602; 919-755-4105; Civil phone: 919-755-4108; Criminal phone: 919-755-4112. Hours: 8:30AM-5:00PM (EST). *Felony, Misdemeanor, Civil, Eviction, Small Claims, Probate.*

www.aoc.state.nc.us/www/public/courts/wake.htm

Civil Records: Access: In person only. Visitors must perform in person searches for themselves. No search fee. Required to search: name, years to search. Civil cases indexed by defendant, plaintiff. Civil records on computer since 1988, prior on books to 1920s.

Criminal Records: Access: Mail, online, in person. Both court and visitors may perform in person searches. Search fee: $5.00 per name. Required to search: name, years to search. Criminal records on computer from 5/82, prior on books and cards from 1968. Search the active Criminal Calendar by defendant name at the web site.

General Information: Public access terminal is available. No adoptions, sealed cases, juvenile, sex offenders, mental or expunged records released. Turnaround time 1-2 days. Copy fee: $1.00 for first page, $.25 each add'l. Certification fee: $2.00. Fee payee: Clerk of Superior Court. Business checks accepted.

Warren County

Superior-District Court PO Box 709, Warrenton, NC 27589; 252-257-3261; Fax: 252-257-5529. Hours: 8:30AM-5PM (EST). *Felony, Misdemeanor, Civil, Eviction, Small Claims, Probate.*

www.aoc.state.nc.us/www/public/courts/warren.htm

Civil Records: Access: In person only. Visitors must perform in person searches for themselves. No search fee. Required to search: name, years to search. Civil cases indexed by defendant, plaintiff. Civil records on computer since 1989, prior on books to 1968.

Criminal Records: Access: Mail, online, in person. Both court and visitors may perform in person searches. Search fee: $5.00 per name. Required to search: name, years to search, DOB. Criminal records on computer from 5/81, prior on books to 1968. Search the active Criminal Calendar by defendant name at the web site.

General Information: Public access terminal is available. No adoptions, sealed cases, juvenile, sex offenders, mental or expunged records released. Turnaround time 1-2 days. Copy fee: $1.00 for first page, $.25 each add'l. Certification fee: $2.00. Fee payee: Clerk of Superior Court. Business checks accepted. Prepayment is required.

Washington County

Superior-District Court PO Box 901, Plymouth, NC 27962; 252-793-3013; Fax: 252-793-1081. Hours: 8AM-5PM (EST). *Felony, Misdemeanor, Civil, Eviction, Small Claims, Probate.*

www.aoc.state.nc.us/www/public/courts/washington.html

Civil Records: Access: In person only. Visitors must perform in person searches for themselves. No search fee. Required to search: name, years to search. Civil cases indexed by defendant, plaintiff. Civil records on computer back to 12/89, prior on books.

Criminal Records: Access: Mail, online, in person. Both court and visitors may perform in person searches. Search fee: $5.00 per name. Required to search: name, years to search; also helpful: address, DOB, SSN. Criminal records on computer back to 12/89, prior on books. Search the active Criminal Calendar by defendant name at the web site.

General Information: Public access terminal is available. No adoptions, sealed, juvenile, mental health, expunged or dismissed records released. SASE required. Turnaround time 2-3 days. Copy fee: $1.00 for first page, $.25 each add'l. Certification fee: $2.00. Fee payee: Clerk of Court. Business checks accepted. Prepayment is required.

Watauga County

Superior-District Court Courthouse #13, 842 West King St, Boone, NC 28607-3525; 828-265-5364; Fax: 828-262-5753. Hours: 8AM-5PM (EST). *Felony, Misdemeanor, Civil, Eviction, Small Claims, Probate.*

www.aoc.state.nc.us/www/public/courts/watauga.htm

Civil Records: Access: Mail, in person. Both court and visitors may perform in person searches. Search fee: $5.00 per name. Required to search: name, years to search. Civil cases indexed by defendant, plaintiff. Civil records on computer since 12/5/88, on books to 1872, prior destroyed by fire.

Criminal Records: Access: Mail, online, in person. Both court and visitors may perform in person searches. Search fee: $5.00 per name. Required to search: name, years to search, DOB, SSN. Criminal records on computer from 11/88, prior on cards and books to 1968. Search the active Criminal Calendar by defendant name at the web site.

General Information: Public access terminal is available. No adoptions, sealed, juvenile, sex offenders, mental, expunged or dismissed records released. SASE requested. Turnaround time 1-2 days. Copy fee: $1.00 for first page, $.25 each add'l. Certification fee: $2.00. Fee payee: Clerk of Court. Only cashiers checks and money orders accepted.

Wayne County

Superior-District Court PO Box 267, Goldsboro, NC 27530; Civil phone: 919-731-7919; Criminal phone: 919-731-7910; Fax: 919-731-2037. Hours: 8AM-5PM (EST). *Felony, Misdemeanor, Civil, Eviction, Small Claims, Probate.*

www.aoc.state.nc.us/www/public/courts/wayne.htm

Civil Records: Access: In person only. Visitors must perform in person searches for themselves. No search fee. Required to search: name, years to search; also helpful: address. Civil cases indexed by defendant, plaintiff. Civil records on computer since 7-18-88, on books since 1968, open to public prior. The court will not do a search unless book and page number or a year of judgment given.

Criminal Records: Access: Mail, online, in person. Both court and visitors may perform in person searches. Search fee: $5.00 per name. Required to search: name, years to search, DOB; also helpful: address, SSN, aliases. Criminal records on computer since 7-18-88, on books since 1968, open to public prior. Search the active Criminal Calendar by defendant name at the web site.

General Information: Public access terminal is available. No adoptions, sealed, juvenile, sex offenders, mental, expunged or dismissed. SASE requested. Turnaround time 1-2 days. Copy fee: $1.00 for first page, $.25 each add'l. Certification fee: $2.00. Fee payee: Clerk of Superior Court. Business checks accepted. Prepayment is required.

Wilkes County

Superior-District Court 500 Courthouse Drive, #1115, Wilkesboro, NC 28697; Civil phone: 336-667-1201; Criminal phone: 336-667-5266; Fax: 336-667-1985. Hours: 8AM-5PM (EST). *Felony, Misdemeanor, Civil, Eviction, Small Claims, Probate.*

www.aoc.state.nc.us/www/public/courts/wilkes.htm

Civil Records: Access: In person only. Visitors must perform in person searches for themselves. No search fee. Required to search: name, years to search. Civil cases indexed by defendant, plaintiff. Civil records on computer since 12/88, prior on books to early 1900s.

Criminal Records: Access: Mail, online, in person. Only the court performs in person searches; visitors may not. Search fee: $5.00 per name. Required to search: name, years to search, DOB; also helpful: address. Criminal records on computer since 12/88, prior on books to early 1900s. Search the active Criminal Calendar by defendant name at the web site.

General Information: Public access terminal is available. No adoptions, sealed cases, juvenile, sex offenders, mental or expunged records released. SASE requested. Turnaround time 1-2 days. Copy fee: $1.00 for first page, $.25 each add'l. Certification fee: $2.00. Fee payee: Clerk of Superior Court. Only cashiers checks and money orders accepted. Prepayment is required.

Wilson County

Superior-District Court PO Box 1608, Wilson, NC 27894; 252-291-7500; Fax: 252-291-8049 (Criminal) 291-8635 (Civil). Hours: 9AM-5PM (EST). *Felony, Misdemeanor, Civil, Eviction, Small Claims, Probate.*

www.aoc.state.nc.us/www/public/courts/wilson.html

Civil Records: Access: In person only. Visitors must perform in person searches for themselves. No search fee. Required to search: name, years to search; also helpful: address. Civil cases indexed by defendant,

plaintiff. Civil records on computer since 8/88, prior on books to 1968, public viewing from 1915 to 1968.

Criminal Records: Access: Mail, fax, online, in person. Both court and visitors may perform in person searches. Search fee: $5.00 per name. Required to search: name, years to search, DOB; also helpful: address, SSN. Criminal records on computer since 5/86, Index cards to 9/76, books to 1918. Search the active Criminal Calendar by defendant name at the web site.

General Information: Public access terminal is available. No adoptions, sealed cases, juvenile, sex offenders, mental, or expunged records released. SASE requested. Turnaround time 2-4 days. Copy fee: $1.00 for first page, $.25 each add'l. Certification fee: $2.00. Fee payee: Clerk of Court. Only cashiers checks and money orders accepted. In-state personal checks accepted. Prepayment is required.

Yadkin County

Superior-District Court PO Box 95, Yadkinville, NC 27055; 336-679-8838; Fax: 336-679-4378. Hours: 8AM-5PM (EST). *Felony, Misdemeanor, Civil, Eviction, Small Claims, Probate.*

www.aoc.state.nc.us/www/public/courts/yadkin.htm

Civil Records: Access: In person only. Visitors must perform in person searches for themselves. No search fee. Required to search: name, years to search; also helpful: address. Civil cases indexed by defendant, plaintiff. Civil records on computer since 8/89, prior on books to 1970.

Criminal Records: Access: Mail, online, in person. Both court and visitors may perform in person searches. Search fee: $5.00 per name. Required to search: name, years to search, DOB; also helpful: address. Criminal records on computer since 8/89, prior on books to 1970. Search the active Criminal Calendar by defendant name at the web site.

General Information: Public access terminal is available. No adoptions, sealed cases, juvenile, sex offenders, mental or expunged records released. SASE required. Turnaround time 1-2 days. Copy fee: $1.00 for first page, $.25 each add'l. Certification fee: $2.00. Fee payee: Clerk of Superior Court. Business checks accepted. Prepayment is required.

Yancey County

Superior-District Court 110 Town Square, Burnsville, NC 28714; 828-682-2122. Hours: 8:30AM-5PM (EST). *Felony, Misdemeanor, Civil, Eviction, Small Claims, Probate.*

www.aoc.state.nc.us/www/public/courts/yancey.htm

Civil Records: Access: In person only. Visitors must perform in person searches for themselves. No search fee. Required to search: name, years to search; also helpful: address. Civil cases indexed by defendant, plaintiff. Civil records on computer since 1988, prior on books.

Criminal Records: Access: Mail, online, in person. Only the court performs in person searches; visitors may not. Search fee: $5.00 per name. Required to search: name, years to search, DOB; also helpful: address, SSN. Criminal records on computer since 1988, prior on books. Search the active Criminal Calendar by defendant name at the web site.

General Information: No adoptions, sealed cases, juvenile, sex offenders, mental, expunged or dismissed records released. Turnaround time depends on ease of access, can take up to 2 weeks. Copy fee: $1.00 for first page, $.25 each add'l. Certification fee: $2.00. Fee payee: Clerk of Superior Court. Business checks accepted. Prepayment is required.

North Carolina Recording Offices

ORGANIZATION: 100 counties, 100 recording offices. The recording officers are Register of Deeds and Clerk of Superior Court (tax liens). The entire state is in the Eastern Time Zone (EST).

REAL ESTATE RECORDS: Counties will not perform real estate searches. Copy fees are usually $1.00 per page. Certification usually costs $3.00 for the first page and $1.00 for each additional page of a document.

UCC RECORDS: This was a dual filing state. Financing statements are were both at the state level and with the Register of Deeds, except for consumer goods, farm related and real estate related collateral. As of 7/1/2001, only real estate related collateral is filed at the county level. All counties will perform UCC searches on the records recorded prior to 7/1/2001. Use search request form UCC-11. Search fees were raised in 2001 to $30.00 per debtor name. Copies usually cost $1.00 per page.

TAX LIEN RECORDS: Federal tax liens on personal property of businesses are filed with the Secretary of State. Other federal and all state tax liens are filed with the county Clerk of Superior Court, not with the Register of Deeds. (Oddly, even tax liens on real property are also filed with the Clerk of Superior Court, not with the Register of Deeds.)

OTHER LIENS: Judgment, mechanics (all at Clerk of Superior Court).

ONLINE ACCESS: A growing number of counties offer free access to assessor and real estate records via the web.

Alamance County

Register of Deeds, PO Box 837, Graham, NC 27253. 336-570-6565 R/E Recording: 336-228-1312.
Will search UCC records prior to 7/2001 and current fixture (land) files. No tax liens filed here. Will not search real estate records. **Other Phone Numbers:** Assessor 336-228-1318; Treasurer 336-570-1318.

Alexander County

Register of Deeds, 201 First St SW, Suite 1, Taylorsville, NC 28681-2504. 828-632-3152 R/E Recording: 704-632-3152; Fax 828-632-1119.
Will search UCC records prior to 7/2001 and current fixture (land) files. No tax liens filed here. Will not search real estate records.

Alleghany County

Register of Deeds, PO Box 186, Sparta, NC 28675. 336-372-4342; Fax 336-372-2061. www.allcorod.com
Will search UCC records prior to 7/2001 and current fixture (land) files. No tax liens filed here. Will not search real estate records. **Online Access:** Real Estate, Grantor/Grantee Records. Access to the Register of Deeds database are available free at www.allcorod.com/cgi-bin/viewer/date.sh. Records go back to 12/1988. Also, search for property information on a GIS mapping site at www.webgis.net/Alleghany. **Other Phone Numbers:** Assessor 336-372-8291; Treasurer 336-372-4179; Appraiser/Auditor 336-372-8291; Elections 336-372-4557; Vital Records 336-372-4342.

Anson County

Register of Deeds, PO Box 352, Wadesboro, NC 28170-0352. Register of Deeds, R/E and UCC Recording 704-694-3212 UCC Recording: 704-694-7594; Fax 704-694-6135. www.co.anson.nc.us/servicesf0.htm
Will search UCC records prior to 7/2001 and current fixture (land) files. No tax liens filed here. Will not search real estate records. **Online Access:** Assessor, Real Estate Records. Records on the county Online Tax Inquiry System are available free online at www.co.anson.nc.us/pubcgi/taxinq. **Other Phone Numbers:** Assessor 704-694-2918; Treasurer 704-694-6219; Appraiser/Auditor 704-694-3072; Elections 704-694-7593.

Ashe County

Register of Deeds, 150 Government Circle, #2300, Jefferson, NC 28640. Register of Deeds, R/E and UCC Recording 336-219-2540; Fax 336-219-2564.
Will search UCC records prior to 7/2001 and current fixture (land) files. No tax liens filed here. Will not search real estate records. **Online Access:** Assessor, Real Estate Records. Access to records on the county Tax Parcel Information System are available free at www.webgis.net/ashe. **Other Phone Numbers:** Assessor 336-219-2554; Treasurer 336-219-2560; Appraiser/Auditor 336-219-2554; Elections 336-219-2570; Vital Records 336-219-2540.

Avery County

Register of Deeds, PO Box 87, Newland, NC 28657. 828-733-8260; Fax 828-733-8261.
Will search UCC records prior to 7/2001 and current fixture (land) files. No tax liens filed here. Will not search real estate records. **Other Phone Numbers:** Assessor 828-733-8216; Treasurer 828-732-8200.

Beaufort County

Register of Deeds, PO Box 514, Washington, NC 27889. Register of Deeds, R/E and UCC Recording 252-946-2323.
Will search UCC records prior to 7/2001 and current fixture (land) files. No tax liens filed here. Will not search real estate records. **Other Phone Numbers:** Vital Records 252-946-2323.

Bertie County

Register of Deeds, PO Box 340, Windsor, NC 27983. 252-794-5309; Fax 252-794-5327.
Will search UCC records prior to 7/2001 and current fixture (land) files. No tax liens filed here. Will not search real estate records. **Other Phone Numbers:** Assessor 252-794-5310.

Bladen County

Register of Deeds, PO Box 247, Elizabethtown, NC 28337. Register of Deeds, R/E and UCC Recording 910-862-6710; Fax 910-862-6716.
Will search UCC records prior to 7/2001 and current fixture (land) files. No tax liens filed here. Will not search real estate records. **Other Phone Numbers:** Assessor 910-862-6748.

Brunswick County

Register of Deeds, PO Box 87, Bolivia, NC 28422-0087. 910-253-2690 R/E Recording: 910-253-4371; Fax 910-253-2703.
Will search UCC records prior to 7/2001 and current fixture (land) files. No tax liens filed here. Will not search real estate records. **Other Phone Numbers:** Assessor 910-253-4351; Treasurer 910-253-4331.

Buncombe County

Register of Deeds, 60 Court Plaza, Room 110, Asheville, NC 28801-3563. 828-250-4300 R/E Recording: 828-250-4305 UCC Recording: 828-250-4302; Fax 828-255-5829. www.buncombecounty.org
Will search UCC records prior to 7/2001 and current fixture (land) files. No tax liens filed here. Will not search real estate records. **Online Access:** Assessor, Real Estate Records. Access to property information is available free on the gis mapping site at www.buncombecounty.org/GIS/Default.htm. Click on "Search methods" and search by owner name. Also, records from the county assessor are available free online at www.buncombetax.org. Property records are also available from a private company at www.propex.com/txrecd_ncbun.htm. **Other Phone Numbers:** Assessor 828-250-4940; Appraiser/Auditor 828-250-4900; Elections 828-250-4200; Vital Records 828-250-4301.

Burke County

Register of Deeds, PO Box 936, Morganton, NC 28680. Register of Deeds, R/E and UCC Recording 828-438-5450 UCC Recording: 828-438-5456; Fax 828-438-5463. www.co.burke.nc.us
Will search UCC records prior to 7/2001 and current fixture (land) files. No tax liens filed here. Will not search real estate records. **Online Access:** Real Estate, Assessor Records. Access to the property information is available free on the gis mapping site at www.webgis.net/burke. **Other Phone Numbers:** Assessor 828-438-5444; Treasurer 828-438-5446; Appraiser/Auditor 828-438-5403; Elections 828-433-1703; Vital Records 828-438-5453; Liens/Judgments 828-432-2804.

Cabarrus County

Register of Deeds, PO Box 707, Concord, NC 28026. 704-920-2112;				Fax			704-920-2898. www.co.cabarrus.nc.us
Will search UCC records prior to 7/2001. No tax liens filed here. Will not search real estate records. **Online Access:** Assessor, Real Estate Records. Search the tax assessor database for free online at www.co.cabarrus.nc.us/Pages/Tax/T_Disclaim.html. also, parcel information is available at http://166.82.128.222/ParcelInfo.html. **Other Phone Numbers:** Assessor 704-920-2166.

Caldwell County

Register of Deeds, 905 West Ave N.W., County Office Building, Lenoir, NC 28645. 828-757-1399 R/E Recording: 828-757-1311 UCC Recording: 828-757-1311; Fax 828-757-1294. www.co.caldwell.nc.us
Will search UCC records prior to 7/2001 and current fixture (land) files. No tax liens filed here. Will not search real estate records. **Online Access:** Assessor, Real Estate Records. Records on the county GIS map server site are available free online at http://maps.co.caldwell.nc.us. Click on "Start Spatial-data Explorer" then find query field at bottom of next page. **Other Phones:** Vital Records 828-757-1310.

Camden County

Register of Deeds, PO Box 190, Camden, NC 27921. 252-338-0066 R/E Recording: 252-338-1919.
Will search UCC records prior to 7/2001 and current fixture (land) files. No tax liens filed here. Real estate record owner searches available. **Other Phone Numbers:** Assessor 252-338-0066.

Carteret County

Register of Deeds, Courthouse Square, Beaufort, NC 28516-1898. Register of Deeds, R/E and UCC Recording 252-728-8474; Fax 252-728-7693.
Will search UCC records prior to 7/2001 and current fixture (land) files. No tax liens filed here. Will not search real estate records. **Other Phone Numbers:** Vital Records 252-728-8474.

Caswell County

Register of Deeds, PO Box 98, Yanceyville, NC 27379. 336-694-4197 R/E Recording: 336-694-4193; Fax 336-694-1405.
Will search UCC records prior to 7/2001 and current fixture (land) files. No tax liens filed here. Will not search real estate records.

Catawba County

Register of Deeds, PO Box 65, Newton, NC 28658-0065. 828-465-1573; www.co.catawba.nc.us
Will search UCC records prior to 7/2001 and current fixture (land) files. No tax liens filed here. Will not search real estate records. **Online Access:** Assessor, Real Estate Records. Records on the Catawba County Geographic Information System database are available free online at www.gis.catawba.nc.us. Click on map area; zoom in to find the parcel on the map, or search using query fields. **Other Phone Numbers:** Assessor 828-465-8421.

Chatham County

Register of Deeds, PO Box 756, Pittsboro, NC 27312. Register of Deeds, R/E and UCC Recording 919-542-8235.
Will search UCC records prior to 7/2001 and current fixture (land) files. No tax liens filed here. Will not search real estate records. **Other Phone Numbers:** Assessor 919-542-8250; Treasurer 919-542-8210; Appraiser/Auditor 919-542-8287; Elections 919-542-8206; Vital Records 919-542-8235; County Manager 919-542-8200.

Cherokee County

Register of Deeds, 53 Peachtree St, Murphy, NC 28906. Register of Deeds, R/E and UCC Recording 828-837-2613; Fax 828-837-8414.
Will search UCC records prior to 7/2001 and current fixture (land) files. No tax liens filed here. Will not search real estate records. **Other Phone Numbers:** Assessor 828-837-6626; Elections 828-837-6670.

Chowan County

Register of Deeds, PO Box 487, Edenton, NC 27932-0487. 252-482-2619 R/E Recording: 919-482-2619.
Will search UCC records prior to 7/2001 and current fixture (land) files. No tax liens filed here. Will not search real estate records.

Clay County

Register of Deeds, PO Box 118, Hayesville, NC 28904. 828-389-0087; Fax 828-389-9749.
Will search UCC records prior to 7/2001 and current fixture (land) files. No tax liens filed here. Will not search real estate records. **Other Phone Numbers:** Assessor 828-389-1266.

Cleveland County

Register of Deeds, PO Box 1210, Shelby, NC 28151-1210. Register of Deeds, R/E and UCC Recording 704-484-4834;				Fax			704-484-4909. www.clevelandcounty.com
Will search UCC records prior to 7/2001 and current fixture (land) files. No tax liens filed here. Will not search real estate records. **Online Access:** Real Estate, Assessor Records. Access to property information on a gis mapping site is available free at www.webgis.nct/Cleveland. Choose to search by name,address, parcel number, or map. **Other Phone Numbers:** Assessor 704-484-4847; Treasurer 704-484-4807; Vital Records 704-484-4834.

Columbus County

Register of Deeds, PO Box 1086, Whiteville, NC 28472-1086. 910-640-6625; Fax 910-640-2547.
This agency will not peform searches; no tax liens filed here. **Other Phone Numbers:** Assessor 910-640-6635.

Craven County

Register of Deeds, 226 Pollack St, New Bern, NC 28560. Register of Deeds, R/E and UCC Recording 252-636-6617; Fax 252-636-1937.
Will search UCC records prior to 7/2001 and current fixture (land) files. No tax liens filed here. Will not search real estate records. **Online Access:** Assessor, Real Estate Records. Records on the County Assessor database are available free online at http://gismaps.cravencounty.com/taxinfo.htm. **Other Phone Numbers:** Assessor 252-636-6605; Treasurer 252-636-6603; Appraiser/Auditor 252-636-6640; Elections 252-636-6610; Vital Records 252-636-6617.

Cumberland County

Register of Deeds, PO 2039, Fayetteville, NC 28302-2039. 910-678-7718 R/E Recording: 910-678-7783; Fax 910-323-1456. www.ccrod.org
Will search UCC records prior to 7/2001 and current fixture (land) files. No tax liens filed here. Will not search real estate records. **Online Access:** Land, Deed, Recording, UCC Records. Search two systems free at www.logansystems-cumberlandnc.com/welcome.asp. The land records index and images go back to 1984; images go back to 1/21/1975; UCCs are from 1995 tp June 29, 2001. **Other Phone Numbers:** Assessor 910-678-7506; Appraiser/Auditor 910-678-7507; Elections 910-678-7733; Vital Records 910-678-7767.

Currituck County

Register of Deeds, PO Box 71, Currituck, NC 27929. 252-232-3297; Fax 252-232-3906.
Will search UCC records prior to 7/2001. No tax liens filed here. Will not search real estate records. **Online Access:** Property Tax Records. Access to tax department requires that you download the terminal emulator, then the tax files at www.co.currituck.nc.us/Tax/taxdept.htm. **Other Phone Numbers:** Assessor 252-232-3005.

Dare County

Register of Deeds, PO Box 70, Manteo, NC 27954. 252-473-3438 R/E Recording: 252-473-1101; www.co.dare.nc.us
Will search UCC records prior to 7/2001 and current fixture (land) files. No tax liens filed here. Will not search real estate records. **Online Access:** Assessor, Real Estate Records. Records on the county Property Inquiry database are available free online at www.co.dare.nc.us/interactive/setup.htm. **Other Phone Numbers:** Assessor 252-473-1101; Treasurer 252-473-1101; Appraiser/Auditor 252-473-1101; Elections 252-473-1101.

Davidson County

Register of Deeds, PO Box 464, Lexington, NC 27293-0464.		336-242-2150;			Fax		336-238-2318. www.co.davidson.nc.us
Will search UCC records prior to 7/2001 and current fixture (land) files. No tax liens filed here. Will not search real estate records. **Online Access:** Assessor, Real Estate Records. Records on the county Tax Department database are available free online at www.co.davidson.nc.us/asp/taxsearch.asp.

Davie County

Register of Deeds, 123 S. Main St, Mocksville, NC 27028. 336-634-2513; www.co.davie.nc.us
Will search UCC records prior to 7/2001. No tax liens filed here. Will not search real estate records. **Other Phone Numbers:** Assessor 336-634-3416.

Duplin County

Register of Deeds, PO Box 970, Kenansville, NC 28349. Register of Deeds, R/E and UCC Recording 910-296-2108;				Fax			910-296-2344. www.duplincounty.org
Will search UCC records prior to 7/2001 and current fixture (land) files. No tax liens filed here. Will not search real estate records. **Other Phone Numbers:** Assessor 910-296-2110; Appraiser/Auditor 910-296-2110; Elections 910-296-2170; Vital Records 910-296-2108.

Durham County

Register of Deeds, PO Box 1107, Durham, NC 27702. 919-560-0494 R/E Recording: 919-560-0480 UCC Recording: 919-560-0480; Fax 919-560-0497. www.co.durham.nc.us/rgds
Will search UCC records prior to 7/2001. No tax liens filed here. Will not search real estate records. **Online Access:** Real Estate, Deed, Judgment, Recording, Voter Registration Records. Access to the Register of Deeds database is available free at http://207.4.222.118. Access to the tax accessor data is available free at http://207.4.222.117/tax/index.cfm. Also, search property records from the GIS mapping site free at http://199.72.142.253. After the disclaimer, click on "Spatial Data Explorer" to search. Also, search voter registration free at www.co.durham.nc.us/departments/elec/votersearch/VoterRecSearch.cfm. **Other Phone Numbers:** Assessor 919-560-0300; Vital Records 919-560-7670 (births/deaths); Vital Records (Marriages) 919-560-0480.

Edgecombe County

Register of Deeds, PO Box 386, Tarboro, NC 27886. Register of Deeds, R/E and UCC Recording 252-641-7924; Fax 252-641-1771.

Will search UCC records prior to 7/2001 and current fixture (land) files. No tax liens filed here. Will not search real estate records. **Other Phone Numbers:** Assessor 252-641-7855; Treasurer 252-641-7834; Elections 252-641-7854; Vital Records 252-641-7924.

Forsyth County

Register of Deeds, PO Box 20639, Winston-Salem, NC 27120-0639. 336-727-2903; Fax 336-727-2341.

Will search UCC records prior to 7/2001 and current fixture (land) files. No tax liens filed here. Will not search real estate records. **Online Access:** Real Estate, Land Records. Access to the county Geo-Data Explorer database is available free online at http://maps.co.forsyth.nc.us. Address and Parcel ID searching only. Includes Board of Adjustment and building permit records. Also, Register of Deed records are available on CD-ROM. Also, search tax liens by name lists for free at www.co.forsyth.nc.us/ tax/header.htm. Also, Online access to property and deeds indexes and images is available via a private company at http://auth.titlesearcher.com/ts/ts.asp or support@TitleSearcher.com. Fee/registration required; Monthly and per day available. **Other Phones:** Assessor 336-727-2513; Treasurer 336-727-2655.

Franklin County

Register of Deeds, PO Box 545, Louisburg, NC 27549-0545. Register of Deeds, R/E and UCC Recording 919-496-3500; Fax 919-496-1457. www.co.franklin.nc.us Will search UCC records prior to 7/2001 and current fixture (land) files. No tax liens filed here. Will not search real estate records. **Online Access:** Real Property Records. Access to the county spatial data explorer database is available free at www.co.franklin.nc.us/ docs/frame_tax.htm. Search the gis map or click on "text search" for name searching. **Other Phones:** Assessor 919-496-1497; Elections 919-496-3710.

Gaston County

Register of Deeds, PO Box 1578, Gastonia, NC 28053. 704-862-7681 R/E Recording: 704-866-3181 UCC Recording: 704-862-7583; Fax 704-862-7519.

Will search UCC records prior to 7/2001 and current fixture (land) files. No tax liens filed here. Will not search real estate records. **Other Phone Numbers:** Assessor 704-810-5838; Treasurer 704-866-3034; Appraiser/Auditor 704-810-5809; Elections 704-864-5858; Vital Records 704-862-7687; Deed Room 704-862-7683.

Gates County

Register of Deeds, PO Box 471, Gatesville, NC 27938-0471. Register of Deeds, R/E and UCC Recording 252-357-0850; Fax 252-357-0850.

Will search UCC records prior to 7/2001 and current fixture (land) files. No tax liens filed here. Will not search real estate records. **Other Phone Numbers:** Assessor 252-357-1360; Treasurer 252-357-1240; Appraiser/Auditor 252-357-1360; Elections 252-357-1780; Vital Records 252-357-0850.

Graham County

Register of Deeds, PO Box 406, Robbinsville, NC 28771-0406. Register of Deeds, R/E and UCC Recording 828-479-7971; Fax 828-479-7988.

Will search UCC records prior to 7/2001 and current fixture (land) files. No tax liens filed here. **Other Phone Numbers:** Assessor 828-479-7965; Treasurer 828-479-7962; Appraiser/Auditor 828-479-7963; Elections 828-479-7969; Vital Records 828-479-7971.

Granville County

Register of Deeds, PO Box 427, Oxford, NC 27565. Register of Deeds, R/E and UCC Recording 919-693-6314; Fax 919-603-1345.

Will search UCC records prior to 7/2001 and current fixture (land) files. No tax liens filed here. Will not search real estate records. **Other Phone Numbers:** Assessor 919-693-4181; Vital Records 919-693-2515.

Greene County

Register of Deeds, PO Box 86, Snow Hill, NC 28580. 252-747-3620 R/E Recording: 919-747-3620.

Will search UCC records prior to 7/2001 and current fixture (land) files. No tax liens filed here. Will not search real estate records.

Guilford County

Register of Deeds, PO Box 1467, High Point, NC 27261-1467. Register of Deeds, R/E and UCC Recording 336-884-7931; www.co.guilford.nc.us Will search UCC records prior to 7/2001 and current fixture (land) files. No tax liens filed here. Will not search real estate records. **Online Access:** Recorder, Assessor, Property, UCC, Vital Statistic Records. Access to the county e-gov databases is available free at www.co.guilford.nc.us/egov/index.html. Site may be down. **Other Phone Numbers:** Assessor 336-884-7911; Treasurer 336-884-7911; Appraiser/Auditor 336-884-7895; Elections 336-884-7931; Vital Records 336-373-7556.

Halifax County

Register of Deeds, PO Box 67, Halifax, NC 27839-0067. Register of Deeds, R/E and UCC Recording 252-583-2101; Fax 252-583-1273. www.halifaxnc.com/halinav.html Will search UCC records prior to 7/2001 and current fixture (land) files. No tax liens filed here. Will not search real estate records. **Other Phone Numbers:** Assessor 252-583-2121; Treasurer 252-583-3771; Appraiser/Auditor 252-583-2121; Elections 252-583-4391; Vital Records 252-583-2101.

Harnett County

Register of Deeds, PO Box 279, Lillington, NC 27546. Register of Deeds, R/E and UCC Recording 910-893-7540; Fax 910-814-3841. www.harnett.org/harnett/departments/rod.html Will search UCC records prior to 7/2001 and current fixture (land) files. No tax liens filed here. Will not search real estate records. **Online Access:** Real Estate, Grantor/Grantee, Sheriff Sales, Missing Person, Most Wanted Records. County real estate and property tax information is available free online at http://152.34.178.4/nc32. The sheriff's lists of most wanted, sheriff sales, and missing persons is available at www.harnettsheriff.com. **Other Phone Numbers:** Vital Records 910-893-7542.

Haywood County

Register of Deeds, Courthouse, 215 N. Main St., Waynesville, NC 28786. Register of Deeds, R/E and UCC Recording 828-452-6635; Fax 828-452-6762.

Will search UCC records prior to 7/2001 and current fixture (land) files. No tax liens filed here. Will not search real estate records. **Online Access:** Real Estate Records. Records on the Land Records Search database are available free online at www.undersys.com/haywood/haywood.html. Search will result in a map showing the parcel and owner, parcel number, and deed book & page information. **Other Phone Numbers:** Assessor 828-452-6635; Treasurer 828-452-6635.

Henderson County

Register of Deeds, Suite 129, 200 N. Grove St., Hendersonville, NC 28792. 828-697-4901.

Will search UCC records prior to 7/2001 and current fixture (land) files. No tax liens filed here. Will not search real estate records. **Online Access:** Land Records. Search property records at the GIS site free at www.henderson.lib.nc.us/county/ca/landrecord.html. Click on "4. Online Interactive GIS Web Site" the go to "GIS Online.". **Other Phone Numbers:** Assessor 828-697-4870.

Hertford County

Register of Deeds, PO Box 36, Winton, NC 27986. 252-358-7850 R/E Recording: 252-358-7805; Fax 252-358-7806.

Will search UCC records prior to 7/2001 and current fixture (land) files. No tax liens filed here. Will not search real estate records. **Other Phone Numbers:** Assessor 252-358-7810; Treasurer 252-358-7815; Elections 252-358-7812; Vital Records 252-358-7850.

Hoke County

Register of Deeds, 304 N. Main St., Raeford, NC 28376. Register of Deeds, R/E and UCC Recording 910-875-2035 UCC Recording: 910-875-0235; Fax 910-875-9515.

Will search UCC records prior to 7/2001 and current fixture (land) files. No tax liens filed here. Will not search real estate records. **Other Phones:** Assessor 910-875-8751; Appraiser/Auditor 910-875-8751; Elections 910-875-8751; Vital Records 910-875-2035.

Hyde County

Register of Deeds, PO Box 294, Swanquarter, NC 27885. 252-926-3011; Fax 252-926-3082.

Will search UCC records. No tax liens filed here. Will not search real estate records. **Other Phone Numbers:** Assessor 252-926-5151; Treasurer 252-926-4101.

Iredell County

Register of Deeds, PO Box 904, Statesville, NC 28687. 704-872-7468; Fax 704-878-3055.

Will search UCC records prior to 7/2001 and current fixture (land) files. No tax liens filed here. Will not search real estate records. **Other Phone Numbers:** Assessor 704-872-3021.

Jackson County

Register of Deeds, 401 Grindstaff Cove Rd., Sylva, NC 28779. 828-586-7530; Fax 828-586-6879. http://main.nc.us/jackson/jc50deed.htm Will search UCC records prior to 7/2001 and current fixture (land) files. No tax liens filed here. Will not search real estate records. **Other Phone Numbers:** Assessor 828-586-4055; Vital Records 828-568-7530.

Johnston County

Register of Deeds, Box 118, Smithfield, NC 27577. 919-989-5164.

Will search UCC records prior to 7/2001 and current fixture (land) files. No tax liens filed here. Will not search real estate records. **Other Phone Numbers:** Vital Records 919-989-5160.

Jones County

Register of Deeds, PO Box 189, Trenton, NC 28585-0189. 252-448-2551; Fax 252-448-1357.

Will search UCC records prior to 7/2001 and current fixture (land) files. No tax liens filed here. Will not search real estate records. **Other Phone Numbers:** Assessor 252-448-2546.

Lee County

Register of Deeds, PO Box 2040, Sanford, NC 27331-2040. 919-774-4821; Fax 919-774-5063.
Will search UCC records prior to 7/2001 and current fixture (land) files. No tax liens filed here. Will not search real estate records.

Lenoir County

Register of Deeds, PO Box 3289, Kinston, NC 28502. 252-559-6420 R/E Recording: 252-523-2390; Fax 252-523-6139.
Will search UCC records prior to 7/2001 and current fixture (land) files. No tax liens filed here. Will not search real estate records. **Other Phone Numbers:** Assessor 252-527-7174; Treasurer 252-527-7174.

Lincoln County

Register of Deeds, PO Box 218, Lincolnton, NC 28093-0218. 704-736-8530 R/E Recording: 704-736-8535 UCC Recording: 704-736-8533; Fax 704-732-9049.
Will search UCC records prior to 7/2001 and current fixture (land) files. No tax liens filed here. Will not search real estate records. **Other Phone Numbers:** Assessor 704-736-8540; Elections 704-736-8480; Vital Records 704-736-8530.

Macon County

Register of Deeds, 5 W. Main St, Franklin, NC 28734. 828-349-2095 R/E Recording: 828-524-6421; Fax 828-369-6382.
Will search UCC records prior to 7/2001 and current fixture (land) files. No tax liens filed here. Will not search real estate records. **Other Phone Numbers:** Assessor 828-524-6421.

Madison County

Register of Deeds, PO Box 66, Marshall, NC 28753. Register of Deeds, R/E and UCC Recording 828-649-3131.
Will search UCC records. No tax liens filed here. Will not search real estate records. **Other Phone Numbers:** Assessor 828-649-3014; Treasurer 828-649-2521; Appraiser/Auditor 828-649-3014; Elections 828-649-3731; Vital Records 828-649-3131.

Martin County

Register of Deeds, PO Box 348, Williamston, NC 27892. 252-792-1683 R/E Recording: 252-792-1901; Fax 252-792-1684.
Will search UCC records. No tax liens filed here. Will not search real estate records. **Other Phone Numbers:** Assessor 252-792-1031; Elections 252-792-5845; Vital Records 252-792-1683.

McDowell County

Register of Deeds, 21 S. Main St, Courthouse, Marion, NC 28752-3992. 828-652-4727; Fax 828-652-4727.
Will search UCC records prior to 7/2001 and current fixture (land) files. No tax liens filed here. Will not search real estate records. **Other Phone Numbers:** Assessor 828-652-7121; Treasurer 828-652-7121; Elections 828-652-7121; Vital Records 828-652-4727.

Mecklenburg County

Register of Deeds, 720 E. 4th St, Ste. 103, Charlotte, NC 28202. 704-336-2443; Fax 704-336-7699. http://meckrod.hartic.com
Will search UCC records prior to 7/2001 and current fixture (land) files. No tax liens filed here. Will not search real estate records. **Online Access:** Assessor, Real Estate, Grantor/Grantee, Judgment, Lien, Vital Statistic, Personal Property Records. Access to biirth, death, marriage, recordings, judgments, liens, and grantor/grantee indices are available free at http://meckrod.hartic.com/default.asp. Also, online access to the assessor records for real estate, personal property, and tax bills are available free at http://mcmf.co.mecklenburg.nc.us:3007/cics/txar/txar00 i. The sheriff's inmate lookup is available free at http://mcmf.co.mecklenburg.nc.us:3007/cjjl01w/cjjl/we bnull. Search warrants free at http://mcmf.co. mecklenburg.nc.us:3007/cjcr01w/cjjl/webnull.

Mitchell County

Register of Deeds, PO Box 82, Bakersville, NC 28705-0082. 828-688-2139 R/E Recording: 828-688-2139 x118; Fax 828-688-3666.
Will search UCC records prior to 7/2001 and current fixture (land) files. No tax liens filed here. Will not search real estate records. **Other Phone Numbers:** Assessor 828-688-2139 x122.

Montgomery County

Register of Deeds, PO Box 695, Troy, NC 27371-0695. 910-576-4271 R/E Recording: 919-576-4271; Fax 910-576-2209.
Will search UCC records prior to 7/2001 and current fixture (land) files. No tax liens filed here. Will not search real estate records.

Moore County

Register of Deeds, PO Box 1210, Carthage, NC 28327. 910-947-6370 R/E Recording: 910-947-6372 UCC Recording: 910-947-6372; Fax 910-947-6396. www.co.moore.nc.us
Will search UCC records prior to 7/2001 and current fixture (land) files. No tax liens filed here. Will not search real estate records. **Online Access:** Real Estate, Lien, Grantor/Grantee, Vital Statistic, DD214, Property Tax Records. Access to the recorder's Online Public Records (OPR) database is available free at http://rod.co.moore.nc.us/nc32. Also, access to county Tax Information System (TIS) data is available free online to registrants and subject to approval at www.co.moore.nc.us/property/TIS/Taxpayer%20Infor mation%20Login.htm. For information, call 910-947-6306. **Other Phone Numbers:** Treasurer 910-947-6310; Appraiser/Auditor 910-947-6412; Elections 910-947-3868; Vital Records 910-947-6370.

Nash County

Register of Deeds, PO Box 974, Nashville, NC 27856. 252-459-9836 R/E Recording: 252-459-4141 UCC Recording: 252-459-9825; Fax 252-459-9889.
Will search UCC records prior to 7/2001 and current fixture (land) files. No tax liens filed here. Will not search real estate records. **Other Phone Numbers:** Assessor 252-459-9824; Vital Records 252-459-9839.

New Hanover County

Register of Deeds, 316 Princess St, Room 216, Wilmington, NC 28401. 910-341-4530 R/E Recording: 919-341-4530; Fax 910-341-4169.
Will search UCC records prior to 7/2001 and current fixture (land) files. No tax liens filed here. Will not search real estate records. **Online Access:** Real Estate, Assessor, Grantor/Grantee, Lien, UCC, Judgment Records. Access to the register of deeds database is available free at http://srvrodweb.nhcgov.com/nc32/ RODsearch.asp. Also, online access to the real estate tax database is available free at www.nhcgov.com/HostPublisher/Oasinq/Oasinput.jsp. Also, you may search for property information on the GIB-mappings site at www.nhcgov.com/GIS/ GISservices.asp. **Other Phone Numbers:** Vital Records 910-341-4547.

Northampton County

Register of Deeds, PO Box 128, Jackson, NC 27845. 252-534-2511.
Will search UCC records prior to 7/2001 and current fixture (land) files. No tax liens filed here. Will not search real estate records. **Other Phone Numbers:** Assessor 252-534-2511.

Onslow County

Register of Deeds, 109 Old Bridge St, Jacksonville, NC 28540. 910-347-3451 R/E Recording: 910-347-3451; http://co.onslow.nc.us/register_of_deeds
Will search UCC records prior to 7/2001 and current fixture (land) files. No tax liens filed here. Will not search real estate records. **Online Access:** Real Estate Records. Access is to property information is available free at www.roktech.net/onslow. Enter the site and name search using the advanced search in the Parcel Query box.

Orange County

Register of Deeds, PO Box 8181, Hillsborough, NC 27278-8181. 919-732-8181; Fax 919-644-3018. www.co.orange.nc.us/deeds/
Will search UCC records prior to 7/2001 and current fixture (land) files. No tax liens filed here. Will not search real estate records. **Online Access:** Property Records. Access to property records on the GIS mapping site is available free at http://gis.co.orange.nc.us/gisdisclaimer.htm.

Pamlico County

Register of Deeds, PO Box 433, Bayboro, NC 28515. 252-745-4421.
Will search UCC records prior to 7/2001 and current fixture (land) files. No tax liens filed here. Will not search real estate records. **Other Phone Numbers:** Assessor 252-745-4125 x33.

Pasquotank County

Register of Deeds, PO Box 154, Elizabeth City, NC 27907-0154. Register of Deeds, R/E and UCC Recording 252-335-4367; Fax 252-335-5106.
Will search UCC records. No tax liens filed here. Will not search real estate records. **Other Phone Numbers:** Assessor 252-338-5169; Treasurer 252-335-4580; Elections 252-335-1739; Vital Records 252-335-4367.

Pender County

Register of Deeds, PO Box 43, Burgaw, NC 28425. 910-259-1225; Fax 910-259-1299.
Will search UCC records prior to 7/2001 and current fixture (land) files. No tax liens filed here. Will not search real estate records. **Other Phone Numbers:** Assessor 910-259-1225; Elections 910-259-1225; Vital Records 910-259-1458.

Perquimans County

Register of Deeds, PO Box 74, Hertford, NC 27944. 252-426-5660 R/E Recording: 252-426-8484; Fax 252-426-7443.
Will search UCC records prior to 7/2001 and current fixture (land) files. No tax liens filed here. Will not search real estate records. **Other Phone Numbers:** Assessor 252-426-5564.

Person County

Register of Deeds, Courthouse Square, Roxboro, NC 27573. Register of Deeds, R/E and UCC Recording 336-597-1733; www.personcounty.net/sections.php
Will search UCC records prior to 7/2001 and current fixture (land) files. No tax liens filed here. Will not search real estate records. **Other Phone Numbers:** Assessor 336-597-1712; Elections 336-597-1727; Vital Records 336-597-1727; Deed Vault 336-597-1729.

Pitt County

Register of Deeds, PO Box 35, Greenville, NC 27835-0035. Register of Deeds, R/E and UCC Recording 252-830-4128; www.co.pitt.nc.us/depts/
Will search UCC records. No tax liens filed here. Will not search real estate records. **Online Access:** Property,

Tax Sales Records. Access to property information on the GIS-mapping site is available free at http://opis.co.pitt.nc.us/opis. Also, online access to the county tax sales list is available free at www.co.pitt.nc.us/foreclosure. **Other Phone Numbers:** Assessor 252-830-4128; Treasurer 252-830-4128; Appraiser/Auditor 252-830-4128; Elections 252-830-4128; Vital Records 252-830-4128.

Polk County

Register of Deeds, PO Box 308, Columbus, NC 28722. 828-894-8450 R/E Recording: 828-894-8450; Fax 828-894-5781.
Will search UCC records prior to 7/2001 and current fixture (land) files. No tax liens filed here. Will not search real estate records. **Other Phone Numbers:** Assessor 828-894-8500; Treasurer 828-894-8500.

Randolph County

Register of Deeds, PO Box 4066, Asheboro, NC 27204. Register of Deeds, R/E and UCC Recording 336-318-6960; www.co.randolph.nc.us
Will search UCC records prior to 7/2001 and current fixture (land) files. No tax liens filed here. Will not search real estate records. **Online Access:** Real Property Records. Access to the gouncty GIS database is available free at www.co.randolph.nc.us/gis.htm. In the "Search functions" on the map page, click on "parcel owner.". **Other Phone Numbers:** Vital Records 336-318-6960.

Richmond County

Register of Deeds, 114 E Franklin St., Suite 101, Rockingham, NC 28379-3601. 910-997-8250; Fax 910-997-8499.
Will search UCC records prior to 7/2001. No tax liens filed here. Will not search real estate records. **Online Access:** Property Records. Access to County property records is available via a subscription service; registration and fees are required. For information, call 334-344-3333. **Other Phone Numbers:** Assessor 910-997-8274; Vital Records 910 997-8251.

Robeson County

Register of Deeds, Box 22 Courthouse-Room 102, Lumberton, NC 28358. 910-671-3046 R/E Recording: 910-671-3043; Fax 910-671-3041.
Will search UCC records prior to 7/2001 and current fixture (land) files. No tax liens filed here. Will not search real estate records. **Other Phone Numbers:** Assessor 910-671-3060; Elections 910-671-3080; Vital Records 910-671-4045.

Rockingham County

Register of Deeds, PO Box 56, Wentworth, NC 27375-0056. 336-342-8820 R/E Recording: 336-342-8820 UCC Recording: 336-342-8820; www.rockinghamcorod.org
Will search UCC records prior to 7/2001 and current fixture (land) files. No tax liens filed here. Will not search real estate records. **Online Access:** Land, Grantor/Grantee, Judgment, Tax Sales Records. Access to Register of Deeds database is available free at www.rockinghamcorod.org. Land indexes 1996 to present; and record images 1984 to present; plats 1907 to present. Also, online access to real estate and tax appraiser data is available free at www.co.rockingham.nc.us/taxinfo2.html. Also, online access to the tax sales property is available at www.co.rockingham.nc.us/forecl.htm. **Other Phone Numbers:** Assessor 336-342-8280; Treasurer 336-342-8120; Appraiser/Auditor 336-342-8280; Elections 336-342-8107; Vital Records 336-342-8820.

Rowan County

Register of Deeds, PO Box 2568, Salisbury, NC 28145. 704-638-3102; www.co.rowan.nc.us/rod
Will search UCC records prior to 7/2001 and current fixture (land) files. No tax liens filed here. Will not search real estate records. **Online Access:** Real Estate, Recording Records. Access to the Register of Dees land records database is available free at http://rod.co.rowan.nc.us. Records go back to 1975; financing statements back to 1993; images back to 6/2000. **Other Phone Numbers:** Assessor 704-633-4601; Treasurer 704-633-3871.

Rutherford County

Register of Deeds, PO Box 551, Rutherfordton, NC 28139. Register of Deeds, R/E and UCC Recording 828-287-6155; Fax 828-287-1229.
Will search UCC records prior to 7/2001 and current fixture (land) files. No tax liens filed here. Will not search real estate records. **Other Phone Numbers:** Assessor 828-287-6215.

Sampson County

Register of Deeds, PO Box 256, Clinton, NC 28329. Register of Deeds, R/E and UCC Recording 910-592-8026; Fax 910-592-1803.
Will search UCC records prior to 7/2001 and current fixture (land) files. No tax liens filed here. Will not search real estate records. **Other Phone Numbers:** Vital Records 910-592-8026.

Scotland County

Register of Deeds, PO Box 769, Laurinburg, NC 28353. Register of Deeds, R/E and UCC Recording 910-277-2575 UCC Recording: 910 277-2575; Fax 910-277-3133.
Will search UCC records prior to 7/2001 and current fixture (land) files. No tax liens filed here. Will not search real estate records. **Other Phone Numbers:** Assessor 910-277-3270; Treasurer 910-277-2410; Appraiser/Auditor 910-277-2566; Elections 910-277-2595; Vital Records 910-277-2575.

Stanly County

Register of Deeds, PO Box 97, Albemarle, NC 28002-0097. Register of Deeds, R/E and UCC Recording 704-986-3640; www.co.stanly.nc.us
Will search UCC records prior to 7/2001 and current fixture (land) files. No tax liens filed here. Will not search real estate records. **Online Access:** Real Estate, Assessor Records. Access to the county Property database is available free on the gis mapping site at www.webgis.net/stanly. Provides parcel ID and tax numbers, owner, address, year, land and building values. **Other Phone Numbers:** Assessor 704-586-3626; Vital Records 704-986-3640.

Stokes County

Register of Deeds, PO Box 67, Danbury, NC 27016. Register of Deeds, R/E and UCC Recording 336-593-2811; Fax 336-593-9360.
Will search UCC records prior to 7/2001 and current fixture (land) files. No tax liens filed here. Will not search real estate records. **Other Phones:** Assessor 336-593-2811; Appraiser/Auditor 336-593-2811; Elections 336-593-2811; Vital Records 336-593-2811.

Surry County

Register of Deeds, PO Box 303, Dobson, NC 27017-0303. 336-401-8150 R/E Recording: 336-386-9201; Fax 336-401-8151. www.co.surry.nc.us
Will search UCC records prior to 7/2001 and current fixture (land) files. No tax liens filed here. Will not search real estate records. **Other Phone Numbers:** Assessor 336-401-8100; Treasurer 336-386-9230.

Swain County

Register of Deeds, PO Box 1183, Bryson City, NC 28713. 828-488-9273; Fax 828-488-6947. www.swaincounty.org/page5.html
Will search UCC records prior to 7/2001 and current fixture (land) files. No tax liens filed here. Will not search real estate records. **Other Phone Numbers:** Assessor 828-488-9273 x223; Elections 828-488-6177; Vital Records 828-488-9273 x205.

Transylvania County

Register of Deeds, 12 E Main St, Courthouse, Brevard, NC 28712. Register of Deeds, R/E and UCC Recording 828-884-3162; www.landofsky.org/transylvania/county_departments.htm
Will search UCC records. No tax liens filed here. Will not search real estate records. **Other Phone Numbers:** Assessor 828-884-3197; Treasurer 828-884-3104; Appraiser/Auditor 828-884-3200; Elections 828-884-3114; Vital Records 828-884-3162.

Tyrrell County

Register of Deeds, PO Box 449, Columbia, NC 27925. 252-796-2901; Fax 252-796-0148.
Will search UCC records prior to 7/2001 and current fixture (land) files. No tax liens filed here. Will not search real estate records. **Other Phone Numbers:** Assessor 252-796-1371.

Union County

Register of Deeds, PO Box 248, Monroe, NC 28111-0248. Register of Deeds, R/E and UCC Recording 704-283-3727 UCC Recording: 704-283-3610; Fax 704-283-3569.
Will search UCC records prior to 7/2001 and current fixture (land) files. No tax liens filed here. Will not search real estate records. **Other Phones:** Vital Records 704-283-3610; Land Records 704-283-3728.

Vance County

Register of Deeds, 122 Young St, Courthouse, Suite F, Henderson, NC 27536. 252-738-2110 R/E Recording: 252-738-2110.
Will search UCC records prior to 7/2001. No tax liens filed here. Will not search real estate records.

Wake County

Register of Deeds, PO Box 1897, Raleigh, NC 27602. Register of Deeds, R/E and UCC Recording 919-856-5460 UCC Recording: 919-856-5464; Fax 919-856-5467. http://web.co.wake.nc.us/rdeeds/
Will search UCC records prior to 7/2001 and current fixture (land) files. No tax liens filed here. Will not search real estate records. **Online Access:** Real Estate, Assessor, Deed, Judgment, Lien, Voter Registration Records. Records from the County Department of Revenue are downloadable by township for free at http://web.co.wake.nc.us/revenue/wcmap.html. Also, a free real estate property search is available at http://aws1.co.wake.nc.us/realestate/search.asp. Also, online access to the Register of Deeds database is available free at http://rodweb01.co.wake.nc.us/books/genext/genextsearch.asp. Records go back to 10/1991. Registered voters can be found at http://web.co.wake.nc.us/bordelec/Waves/WavesOptions.asp. Also, Online access to Town of Cary property information is available free at a gis mapping site at www.webgis.net/cary. **Other Phone Numbers:** Assessor 919-856-6600; Treasurer 919-856-6600; Vital Records 919-733-3526.

Warren County

Register of Deeds, PO Box 506, Warrenton, NC 27589. Register of Deeds, R/E and UCC Recording 252-257-3265; Fax 252-257-1524.

Will search UCC records prior to 7/2001 and current fixture (land) files. No tax liens filed here. Will not search real estate records. **Other Phone Numbers:** Assessor 252-257-4158; Treasurer 252-257-3337; 2nd Fax 252-257-7011.

Washington County

Register of Deeds, PO Box 1007, Plymouth, NC 27962. 252-793-2325 R/E Recording: 252-793-5823; Fax 252-793-6982. www.washingtoncountygov.com

Will search UCC records prior to 7/2001 and current fixture (land) files. No tax liens filed here. Will not search real estate records. **Other Phone Numbers:** Assessor 252-793-1176.

Watauga County

Register of Deeds, 842 W. King St., Suite 9, Boone, NC 28607-3585. 828-265-8052 R/E Recording: 828-265-1300; Fax 828-265-7632. www.wataugacounty.org/deeds/index.html

Will search UCC records prior to 7/2001 and current fixture (land) files. No tax liens filed here. Will not search real estate records. **Online Access:** Grantor/Grantee, Judgment, Deed, UCC, Assessor, Property Records. Access to register of deeds database is available free at www.wataugacounty.org/deeds/disclaimer.shtml. Also, online access to county tax search data is available free at www.wataugacounty.org/tax/search_tax.shtml. **Other Phone Numbers:** Assessor 828-265-8036; Elections 828-265-8061; Vital Records 828-265-8052.

Wayne County

Register of Deeds, PO Box 267, Goldsboro, NC 27533-0267. 919-731-1449.

Will search UCC records prior to 7/2001 and current fixture (land) files. No tax liens filed here. Will not search real estate records. **Other Phone Numbers:** Assessor 919-731-1461.

Wilkes County

Register of Deeds, 500 Courthouse Dr, Ste. 1000, 500 Courthouse Dr., Wilkesboro, NC 28697. Register of Deeds, R/E and UCC Recording 336-651-7351.

Will search UCC records prior to 7/2001 and current fixture (land) files. No tax liens filed here. Will not search real estate records. **Other Phone Numbers:** Vital Records 336-651-7351.

Wilson County

Register of Deeds, PO Box 1728, Wilson, NC 27893. 252-399-2935; Fax 252-399-2942. www.wilson-co.com

Will search UCC records prior to 7/2001 and current fixture (land) files. No tax liens filed here. Will not search real estate records. **Online Access:** Assessor, Real Estate, Voter Registration Records. Records on the county Tax Administrator database are available free online at www.wilson-co.com/wctax.html. Records on the county registered voter database are available at www.wilson-co.com/wcbe_search.cfm. **Other Phone Numbers:** Assessor 252-399-2901; Treasurer 252-399-2902; Elections 252-399-2836.

Yadkin County

Register of Deeds, PO Box 211, Yadkinville, NC 27055. 336-679-4225 R/E Recording: 919-679-4225; Fax 336-679-3239. www.yadkincounty.gov/RegDeed.htm

Will search UCC records prior to 7/2001 and current fixture (land) files. No tax liens filed here. Will not search real estate records.

Yancey County

Register of Deeds, Courthouse, Room #4, Burnsville, NC 28714. 828-682-2174 R/E Recording: 704-682-2174; Fax 828-682-4520.

Will search UCC records. No tax liens filed here. Will not search real estate records.

North Carolina County Locator

You will usually be able to find the city name in the City/County Cross Reference below. In that case, it is a simple matter to determine the county from the cross reference. However, only the official US Postal Service city names are included in this index. There are an additional 40,000 place names that people use in their addresses. Therefore, we have also included a ZIP/City Cross Reference immediately following the City/County Cross Reference.

If you know the ZIP Code but the city name does not appear in the City/County Cross Reference index, look up the ZIP Code in the ZIP/City Cross Reference, find the city name, then look up the city name in the City/County Cross Reference. For example, you want to know the county for an address of Menands, NY 12204. There is no "Menands" in the City/County Cross Reference. The ZIP/City Cross Reference shows that ZIP Codes 12201-12288 are for the city of Albany. Looking back in the City/County Cross Reference, Albany is in Albany County.

City/County Cross Reference

ABERDEEN (28315) Moore(75), Hoke(24)
ADVANCE Davie
AHOSKIE Hertford
ALAMANCE Alamance
ALBEMARLE Stanly
ALBERTSON Duplin
ALEXANDER Buncombe
ALEXIS Gaston
ALLIANCE Pamlico
ALMOND (28702) Swain(97), Graham(2)
ALTAMAHAW Alamance
ANDREWS Cherokee
ANGIER (27501) Harnett(76), Johnston(22)
ANSONVILLE Anson
APEX (27502) Wake(90), Chatham(9)
AQUONE Macon
ARAPAHOE Pamlico
ARARAT Surry
ARDEN (28704) Buncombe(97), Henderson(1), Swain(1)
ASH Brunswick
ASHEBORO Randolph
ASHEVILLE Buncombe
ATKINSON Pender
ATLANTIC Carteret
ATLANTIC BEACH Carteret
AULANDER (27805) Bertie(67), Hertford(32)
AURORA Beaufort
AUTRYVILLE (28318) Sampson(86), Cumberland(13)
AVON Dare
AYDEN (28513) Pitt(92), Greene(7)
AYDLETT Currituck
BADIN Stanly
BAHAMA Durham
BAILEY (27807) Nash(64), Wilson(35)
BAKERSVILLE Mitchell
BALSAM Jackson
BALSAM GROVE Transylvania
BANNER ELK (28604) Avery(50), Watauga(49)
BARBER Rowan
BARCO Currituck
BARIUM SPRINGS Iredell
BARNARDSVILLE Buncombe
BARNESVILLE Robeson
BAT CAVE Henderson
BATH Beaufort
BATTLEBORO (27809) Edgecombe(55), Nash(44)
BAYBORO Pamlico
BEAR CREEK Chatham
BEAUFORT Carteret
BELEWS CREEK (27009) Forsyth(98), Stokes(1)
BELHAVEN Beaufort
BELLARTHUR Pitt
BELMONT Gaston
BELVIDERE (27919) Perquimans(89), Chowan(6), Gates(3)
BENNETT (27208) Chatham(57), Randolph(37), Moore(4)

BENSON (27504) Johnston(96), Harnett(3)
BESSEMER CITY Gaston
BETHANIA Forsyth
BETHEL (27812) Pitt(95), Edgecombe(4)
BEULAVILLE (28518) Duplin(90), Onslow(9)
BISCOE (27209) Montgomery(81), Moore(18)
BLACK CREEK Wilson
BLACK MOUNTAIN Buncombe
BLADENBORO (28320) Bladen(91), Columbus(8)
BLANCH Caswell
BLOUNTS CREEK Beaufort
BLOWING ROCK Watauga
BOILING SPRINGS Cleveland
BOLIVIA Brunswick
BOLTON (28423) Columbus(95), Bladen(4)
BONLEE Chatham
BOOMER Wilkes
BOONE Watauga
BOONVILLE Yadkin
BOSTIC Rutherford
BRASSTOWN (28902) Clay(93), Cherokee(6)
BREVARD Transylvania
BRIDGETON Craven
BROADWAY (27505) Harnett(80), Lee(19)
BROWNS SUMMIT Guilford
BRUNSWICK Columbus
BRYSON CITY Swain
BUIES CREEK Harnett
BULLOCK Granville
BUNN Franklin
BUNNLEVEL Harnett
BURGAW Pender
BURLINGTON Alamance
BURNSVILLE Yancey
BUTNER Granville
BUTTERS Bladen
BUXTON Dare
BYNUM Chatham
CALABASH Brunswick
CALYPSO Duplin
CAMDEN Camden
CAMERON (28326) Harnett(44), Moore(34), Lee(21)
CAMP LEJEUNE Onslow
CANDLER Buncombe
CANDOR Montgomery
CANTON Haywood
CAROLEEN Rutherford
CAROLINA BEACH New Hanover
CARRBORO Orange
CARTHAGE Moore
CARY Wake
CASAR (28020) Cleveland(85), Rutherford(14)
CASHIERS Jackson
CASTALIA (27816) Nash(76), Franklin(23)
CASTLE HAYNE New Hanover
CATAWBA Catawba
CEDAR FALLS Randolph

CEDAR GROVE Orange
CEDAR ISLAND Carteret
CEDAR MOUNTAIN Transylvania
CERRO GORDO Columbus
CHADBOURN Columbus
CHAPEL HILL Orange
CHARLOTTE Mecklenburg
CHEROKEE Swain
CHERRY POINT Craven
CHERRYVILLE (28021) Gaston(84), Lincoln(11), Cleveland(3)
CHIMNEY ROCK Rutherford
CHINA GROVE Rowan
CHINQUAPIN (28521) Duplin(95), Onslow(4)
CHOCOWINITY Beaufort
CLAREMONT Catawba
CLARENDON Columbus
CLARKTON (28433) Bladen(67), Columbus(32)
CLAYTON (27520) Johnston(97), Wake(2)
CLEMMONS (27012) Forsyth(74), Davidson(25)
CLEVELAND Rowan
CLIFFSIDE Rutherford
CLIMAX (27233) Randolph(67), Guilford(32)
CLINTON Sampson
CLYDE Haywood
COATS Harnett
COFIELD Hertford
COINJOCK Currituck
COLERAIN Bertie
COLFAX Guilford
COLLETTSVILLE (28611) Caldwell(93), Avery(6)
COLUMBIA Tyrrell
COLUMBUS Polk
COMFORT Jones
COMO Hertford
CONCORD Cabarrus
CONETOE Edgecombe
CONNELLYS SPRINGS Burke
CONOVER Catawba
CONWAY Northampton
COOLEEMEE Davie
CORAPEAKE Gates
CORDOVA Richmond
CORNELIUS Mecklenburg
COROLLA Currituck
COUNCIL Bladen
COVE CITY Craven
CRAMERTON Gaston
CRANBERRY Avery
CREEDMOOR (27522) Granville(88), Wake(11)
CRESTON Ashe
CRESWELL (27928) Washington(96), Tyrrell(3)
CROSSNORE Avery
CROUSE (28033) Lincoln(93), Gaston(6)
CRUMPLER Ashe
CULBERSON Cherokee

CULLOWHEE Jackson
CUMBERLAND Cumberland
CUMNOCK Lee
CURRIE Pender
CURRITUCK Currituck
DALLAS Gaston
DANA Henderson
DANBURY Stokes
DAVIDSON (28036) Mecklenburg(70), Cabarrus(28), Iredell(1)
DAVIS Carteret
DEEP GAP (28618) Watauga(95), Wilkes(4)
DEEP RUN (28525) Lenoir(88), Duplin(11)
DELCO Columbus
DENTON (27239) Davidson(76), Randolph(23)
DENVER (28037) Lincoln(83), Catawba(16)
DILLSBORO Jackson
DOBSON Surry
DOVER (28526) Craven(88), Jones(7), Lenoir(3)
DREXEL Burke
DUBLIN Bladen
DUDLEY Wayne
DUNN Harnett
DURANTS NECK Perquimans
DURHAM Durham
EAGLE ROCK Wake
EAGLE SPRINGS Moore
EARL Cleveland
EAST BEND Yadkin
EAST FLAT ROCK Henderson
EAST SPENCER Rowan
EDEN Rockingham
EDENTON Chowan
EDNEYVILLE Henderson
EDWARD Beaufort
EFLAND Orange
ELIZABETH CITY Pasquotank
ELIZABETHTOWN Bladen
ELK PARK Avery
ELKIN (28621) Surry(92), Wilkes(7)
ELLENBORO (28040) Rutherford(69), Hoke(15), Cleveland(14)
ELLERBE Richmond
ELM CITY (27822) Wilson(89), Nash(7), Edgecombe(3)
ELON COLLEGE (27244) Alamance(95), Guilford(4)
EMERALD ISLE Carteret
ENFIELD Halifax
ENGELHARD Hyde
ENKA Buncombe
ENNICE Alleghany
ERNUL Craven
ERWIN Harnett
ETHER Montgomery
ETOWAH Henderson
EURE Gates
EVERETTS Martin
EVERGREEN Columbus
FAIR BLUFF Columbus

FAIRFIELD (27826) Hyde(87), Tyrrell(12)
FAIRMONT Robeson
FAIRVIEW Buncombe
FAISON (28341) Sampson(76), Duplin(23)
FAITH Rowan
FALCON Cumberland
FALKLAND Pitt
FALLSTON Cleveland
FARMVILLE Pitt
FAYETTEVILLE Cumberland
FERGUSON Wilkes
FLAT ROCK Henderson
FLEETWOOD Ashe
FLETCHER (28732) Henderson(74),
   Buncombe(25)
FONTANA DAM (28733) Macon(78),
   Graham(21)
FOREST CITY Rutherford
FORT BRAGG Cumberland
FOUNTAIN (27829) Wilson(72), Pitt(21),
   Edgecombe(5)
FOUR OAKS (27524) Johnston(97),
   Wayne(2)
FRANKLIN Macon
FRANKLINTON (27525) Franklin(75),
   Granville(24)
FRANKLINVILLE Randolph
FREMONT (27830) Wayne(95), Wilson(4)
FRISCO Dare
FUQUAY VARINA (27526) Wake(72),
   Harnett(27)
GARLAND (28441) Sampson(58),
   Bladen(40)
GARNER (27529) Wake(81), Johnston(18)
GARYSBURG Northampton
GASTON Northampton
GASTONIA Gaston
GATES Gates
GATESVILLE Gates
GERMANTON (27019) Stokes(75),
   Forsyth(24)
GERTON Henderson
GIBSON Scotland
GIBSONVILLE (27249) Guilford(62),
   Alamance(28), Caswell(5),
   Rockingham(2)
GLADE VALLEY Alleghany
GLEN ALPINE Burke
GLENDALE SPRINGS Ashe
GLENDON Moore
GLENVILLE (28736) Jackson(98),
   Buncombe(1)
GLENWOOD McDowell
GLOUCESTER Carteret
GODWIN (28344) Sampson(80),
   Cumberland(19)
GOLD HILL (28071) Rowan(48),
   Cabarrus(29), Stanly(22)
GOLDSBORO Wayne
GOLDSTON Chatham
GRAHAM Alamance
GRANDY Currituck
GRANITE FALLS Caldwell
GRANITE QUARRY Rowan
GRANTSBORO Pamlico
GRASSY CREEK Ashe
GRAYSON Ashe
GREEN MOUNTAIN Yancey
GREENMOUNTAIN Yancey
GREENSBORO Guilford
GREENVILLE Pitt
GRIFTON (28530) Pitt(38), Lenoir(28),
   Craven(27), Greene(5)
GRIMESLAND (27837) Pitt(94), Beaufort(5)
GROVER Cleveland
GULF Chatham
GUMBERRY Northampton
HALIFAX Halifax
HALLSBORO Columbus
HAMILTON Martin
HAMLET (28345) Richmond(98),
   Scotland(1)

HAMPSTEAD Pender
HAMPTONVILLE (27020) Yadkin(81),
   Wilkes(18)
HARBINGER Currituck
HARKERS ISLAND Carteret
HARMONY (28634) Iredell(93), Davie(6)
HARRELLS (28444) Sampson(52),
   Bladen(46), Duplin(1)
HARRELLSVILLE Hertford
HARRIS Rutherford
HARRISBURG Cabarrus
HASSELL Martin
HATTERAS Dare
HAVELOCK Craven
HAW RIVER Alamance
HAYESVILLE Clay
HAYS Wilkes
HAZELWOOD Haywood
HENDERSON (27537) Vance(95),
   Franklin(3)
HENDERSONVILLE Henderson
HENRICO (27842) Northampton(93),
   Warren(6)
HENRIETTA Rutherford
HERTFORD Perquimans
HICKORY Catawba
HIDDENITE (28636) Alexander(96),
   Iredell(3)
HIGH POINT (27265) Guilford(79),
   Davidson(18), Forsyth(1)
HIGH SHOALS Gaston
HIGHFALLS Moore
HIGHLANDS Macon
HILDEBRAN Burke
HILLSBOROUGH (27278) Orange(96),
   Durham(3)
HOBBSVILLE (27946) Gates(97),
   Chowan(1)
HOBGOOD (27843) Halifax(88),
   Edgecombe(10), Martin(1)
HOBUCKEN Pamlico
HOFFMAN (28347) Richmond(92),
   Moore(7)
HOLLISTER Halifax
HOLLY RIDGE (28445) Onslow(57),
   Pender(42)
HOLLY SPRINGS (27540) Wake(90),
   Harnett(9)
HOOKERTON (28538) Greene(84),
   Lenoir(15)
HOPE MILLS Cumberland
HORSE SHOE Henderson
HOT SPRINGS Madison
HUBERT Onslow
HUDSON Caldwell
HUNTERSVILLE (28078) Mecklenburg(98),
   Cabarrus(1)
HURDLE MILLS (27541) Orange(50),
   Person(50)
HUSK Ashe
ICARD Burke
INDIAN TRAIL Union
INGOLD Sampson
IRON STATION (28080) Lincoln(98),
   Gaston(1)
IVANHOE (28447) Sampson(35),
   Pender(32), Bladen(32)
JACKSON Northampton
JACKSON SPRINGS (27281) Moore(61),
   Montgomery(38)
JACKSONVILLE Onslow
JAMESTOWN Guilford
JAMESVILLE Martin
JARVISBURG Currituck
JEFFERSON Ashe
JONAS RIDGE Burke
JONESVILLE (28642) Yadkin(92),
   Wilkes(7)
JULIAN (27283) Guilford(85), Randolph(14)
KANNAPOLIS (28083) Cabarrus(72),
   Rowan(27)
KELFORD Bertie

KELLY Bladen
KENANSVILLE Duplin
KENLY (27542) Wilson(60), Johnston(39)
KERNERSVILLE Forsyth
KILL DEVIL HILLS Dare
KING (27021) Stokes(97), Forsyth(2)
KINGS MOUNTAIN Cleveland
KINSTON Lenoir
KIPLING Harnett
KITTRELL (27544) Vance(88),
   Granville(11)
KITTY HAWK Dare
KNIGHTDALE Wake
KNOTTS ISLAND Currituck
KURE BEACH New Hanover
LA GRANGE (28551) Lenoir(66),
   Wayne(24), Greene(8)
LAKE JUNALUSKA Haywood
LAKE LURE Rutherford
LAKE TOXAWAY Transylvania
LAKE WACCAMAW Columbus
LAKEVIEW Moore
LANDIS Rowan
LANSING Ashe
LASKER Northampton
LATTIMORE Cleveland
LAUREL HILL Scotland
LAUREL SPRINGS (28644) Alleghany(57),
   Ashe(40)
LAURINBURG Scotland
LAWNDALE (28090) Cleveland(91),
   Lincoln(7)
LAWSONVILLE Stokes
LEASBURG Caswell
LEICESTER Buncombe
LELAND Brunswick
LEMON SPRINGS Lee
LENOIR (28645) Caldwell(98), Wilkes(1)
LEWISTON WOODVILLE Bertie
LEWISVILLE Forsyth
LEXINGTON Davidson
LIBERTY (27298) Randolph(59),
   Alamance(31), Guilford(8)
LILESVILLE Anson
LILLINGTON Harnett
LINCOLNTON Lincoln
LINDEN (28356) Cumberland(69),
   Harnett(30)
LINVILLE Avery
LINVILLE FALLS Burke
LINWOOD Davidson
LITTLE SWITZERLAND McDowell
LITTLETON (27850) Halifax(84),
   Warren(15)
LOCUST Stanly
LONGISLAND Catawba
LONGWOOD Brunswick
LOUISBURG Franklin
LOWELL Gaston
LOWGAP Surry
LOWLAND Pamlico
LUCAMA Wilson
LUMBER BRIDGE (28357) Robeson(54),
   Hoke(45)
LUMBERTON Robeson
LYNN Polk
MACCLESFIELD (27852) Wilson(83),
   Edgecombe(16)
MACON Warren
MADISON (27025) Rockingham(71),
   Stokes(28)
MAGGIE VALLEY Haywood
MAGNOLIA (28453) Duplin(72),
   Sampson(27)
MAIDEN Catawba
MAMERS Harnett
MANNS HARBOR Dare
MANSON (27553) Vance(97), Warren(2)
MANTEO Dare
MAPLE Currituck
MAPLE HILL (28454) Pender(78),
   Onslow(21)

MARBLE Cherokee
MARGARETTSVILLE Northampton
MARIETTA Robeson
MARION McDowell
MARS HILL (28754) Madison(88),
   Yancey(11)
MARSHALL Madison
MARSHALLBERG Carteret
MARSHVILLE Union
MARSTON (28363) Scotland(57),
   Richmond(42)
MATTHEWS Mecklenburg
MAURY Greene
MAXTON (28364) Robeson(73),
   Scotland(26)
MAYODAN Rockingham
MAYSVILLE (28555) Onslow(82),
   Jones(17)
MC ADENVILLE Gaston
MC FARLAN Anson
MC GRADY Wilkes
MC LEANSVILLE Guilford
MCCAIN Hoke
MCCUTCHEON FIELD Onslow
MEBANE (27302) Alamance(59),
   Orange(27), Caswell(13)
MERRITT Pamlico
MERRY HILL Bertie
MICAVILLE Yancey
MICRO Johnston
MIDDLEBURG Vance
MIDDLESEX (27557) Johnston(52),
   Nash(45), Wilson(1)
MIDLAND (28107) Cabarrus(89),
   Mecklenburg(6), Stanly(2), Union(1)
MIDWAY PARK Onslow
MILL SPRING Polk
MILLERS CREEK Wilkes
MILTON (27305) Caswell(98), Person(1)
MILWAUKEE Northampton
MINERAL SPRINGS Union
MINNEAPOLIS Avery
MISENHEIMER Stanly
MOCKSVILLE Davie
MONCURE Chatham
MONROE Union
MONTEZUMA Avery
MONTREAT Buncombe
MOORESBORO (28114) Rutherford(55),
   Cleveland(44)
MOORESVILLE Iredell
MORAVIAN FALLS (28654) Wilkes(97),
   Alexander(2)
MOREHEAD CITY Carteret
MORGANTON Burke
MORRISVILLE (27560) Wake(97),
   Durham(2)
MORVEN Anson
MOUNT AIRY (27030) Surry(97), Stokes(2)
MOUNT GILEAD (27306) Richmond(60),
   Montgomery(39)
MOUNT HOLLY Gaston
MOUNT MOURNE Iredell
MOUNT OLIVE (28365) Wayne(65),
   Duplin(30), Sampson(4)
MOUNT PLEASANT (28124) Cabarrus(98),
   Stanly(1)
MOUNT ULLA (28125) Rowan(95),
   Iredell(4)
MOUNTAIN HOME Henderson
MOYOCK Currituck
MURFREESBORO (27855) Hertford(96),
   Northampton(3)
MURPHY Cherokee
NAGS HEAD Dare
NAKINA Columbus
NAPLES Henderson
NASHVILLE Nash
NEBO (28761) McDowell(83), Burke(15)
NEW BERN Craven
NEW HILL (27562) Wake(56),
   Chatham(39), Harnett(3)

NEW LONDON (28127) Stanly(61),
   Montgomery(31), Davidson(6)
NEWELL Mecklenburg
NEWLAND (28657) Avery(87), Burke(12)
NEWPORT Carteret
NEWTON Catawba
NEWTON GROVE (28366) Sampson(81),
   Johnston(18)
NORLINA Warren
NORMAN Richmond
NORTH WILKESBORO Wilkes
NORTHSIDE Granville
NORWOOD Stanly
OAK CITY Martin
OAK ISLAND Brunswick
OAK RIDGE Guilford
OAKBORO Stanly
OCEAN ISLE BEACH Brunswick
OCRACOKE Hyde
OLD FORT McDowell
OLIN Iredell
OLIVIA Harnett
ORIENTAL Pamlico
ORRUM Robeson
OTTO Macon
OXFORD (27565) Granville(92), Vance(5),
   Person(1)
PALMYRA Halifax
PANTEGO Beaufort
PARKTON (28371) Robeson(82),
   Cumberland(17)
PARMELE Martin
PATTERSON Caldwell
PAW CREEK Mecklenburg
PEACHLAND (28133) Anson(77),
   Union(22)
PELHAM (27311) Caswell(98),
   Rockingham(1)
PEMBROKE Robeson
PENDLETON Northampton
PENLAND Mitchell
PENROSE Transylvania
PFAFFTOWN Forsyth
PIKEVILLE (27863) Wayne(70),
   Greene(29)
PILOT MOUNTAIN (27041) Surry(67),
   Stokes(32)
PINE HALL Stokes
PINE LEVEL Johnston
PINEBLUFF Moore
PINEHURST Moore
PINEOLA Avery
PINETOPS Edgecombe
PINETOWN Beaufort
PINEVILLE Mecklenburg
PINEY CREEK Alleghany
PINK HILL (28572) Duplin(53), Lenoir(33),
   Jones(11)
PINNACLE (27043) Stokes(87), Surry(12)
PISGAH FOREST Transylvania
PITTSBORO Chatham
PLEASANT GARDEN (27313) Guilford(58),
   Randolph(41)
PLEASANT HILL Northampton
PLUMTREE Avery
PLYMOUTH Washington
POINT HARBOR Currituck
POLKTON Anson
POLKVILLE Cleveland
POLLOCKSVILLE (28573) Jones(97),
   Craven(2)
POPE A F B Cumberland
POPLAR BRANCH Currituck
POTECASI Northampton
POWELLS POINT Currituck
POWELLSVILLE Bertie
PRINCETON (27569) Johnston(95),
   Wayne(4)
PROCTORVILLE Robeson
PROSPECT HILL Caswell
PROVIDENCE Caswell
PURLEAR Wilkes

RAEFORD Hoke
RALEIGH Wake
RAMSEUR Randolph
RANDLEMAN (27317) Randolph(98),
   Guilford(1)
RED OAK Nash
RED SPRINGS (28377) Robeson(62),
   Hoke(37)
REIDSVILLE Rockingham
REX Robeson
RHODHISS Caldwell
RICH SQUARE Northampton
RICHFIELD (28137) Stanly(51), Rowan(48)
RICHLANDS (28574) Onslow(93),
   Duplin(3), Jones(3)
RIDGECREST Buncombe
RIDGEWAY Warren
RIEGELWOOD (28456) Columbus(51),
   Bladen(42), Brunswick(6)
ROANOKE RAPIDS Halifax
ROARING GAP Alleghany
ROARING RIVER Wilkes
ROBBINS Moore
ROBBINSVILLE Graham
ROBERSONVILLE (27871) Pitt(84),
   Martin(15)
ROCKINGHAM Richmond
ROCKWELL (28138) Rowan(77),
   Cabarrus(22)
ROCKY MOUNT Nash
ROCKY POINT Pender
RODANTHE Dare
RODUCO Gates
ROLESVILLE Wake
RONDA Wilkes
ROPER Washington
ROSE HILL (28458) Duplin(68),
   Sampson(31)
ROSEBORO (28382) Sampson(78),
   Cumberland(20)
ROSMAN Transylvania
ROUGEMONT (27572) Orange(40),
   Person(30), Durham(23), Granville(5)
ROWLAND Robeson
ROXBORO Person
ROXOBEL Bertie
RUFFIN (27326) Rockingham(60),
   Caswell(39)
RURAL HALL Forsyth
RUTHERFORD COLLEGE Burke
RUTHERFORDTON Rutherford
SAINT PAULS (28384) Robeson(88),
   Bladen(11)
SALEMBURG Sampson
SALISBURY Rowan
SALTER PATH Carteret
SALUDA (28773) Polk(90), Henderson(8)
SALVO Dare
SANDY RIDGE Stokes
SANFORD (27332) Lee(57), Harnett(42)
SAPPHIRE (28774) Jackson(75),
   Transylvania(25)
SARATOGA Wilson
SAXAPAHAW Alamance
SCALY MOUNTAIN Macon
SCOTLAND NECK Halifax
SCOTTS Iredell
SCOTTVILLE Ashe
SCRANTON Hyde
SEABOARD (27876) Northampton(89),
   Pitt(10)
SEAGROVE (27341) Randolph(69),
   Moore(20), Montgomery(10)
SEALEVEL Carteret
SEDALIA Guilford
SELMA Johnston
SEMORA (27343) Person(67), Caswell(32)
SEVEN SPRINGS (28578) Wayne(69),
   Lenoir(17), Duplin(13)
SEVERN Northampton
SHALLOTTE Brunswick

SHANNON (28386) Robeson(59),
   Hoke(40)
SHARPSBURG Nash
SHAWBORO (27973) Camden(73),
   Currituck(26)
SHELBY Cleveland
SHERRILLS FORD (28673) Catawba(96),
   Lincoln(3)
SHILOH Camden
SILER CITY (27344) Chatham(96),
   Randolph(3)
SILOAM Surry
SIMPSON Pitt
SIMS (27880) Wilson(91), Nash(8)
SKYLAND Buncombe
SMITHFIELD Johnston
SMYRNA Carteret
SNEADS FERRY Onslow
SNOW CAMP (27349) Alamance(75),
   Chatham(24)
SNOW HILL Greene
SOPHIA Randolph
SOUTH BRUNSWICK Brunswick
SOUTH MILLS Camden
SOUTHERN PINES Moore
SOUTHMONT Davidson
SOUTHPORT Brunswick
SPARTA Alleghany
SPEED Edgecombe
SPENCER Rowan
SPINDALE Rutherford
SPRING HOPE Nash
SPRING LAKE (28390) Harnett(53),
   Cumberland(46)
SPRUCE PINE Mitchell
STACY Carteret
STALEY (27355) Randolph(73),
   Chatham(26)
STANFIELD Stanly
STANLEY (28164) Gaston(80), Lincoln(19)
STANTONSBURG (27883) Wilson(70),
   Wayne(18), Greene(11)
STAR (27356) Montgomery(85), Moore(14)
STATE ROAD (28676) Wilkes(86),
   Surry(13)
STATESVILLE Iredell
STEDMAN Cumberland
STELLA (28582) Onslow(54), Carteret(45)
STEM Granville
STOKES Pitt
STOKESDALE (27357) Rockingham(61),
   Guilford(38)
STONEVILLE Rockingham
STONEWALL Pamlico
STONY POINT Alexander
STOVALL Granville
STUMPY POINT Dare
SUGAR GROVE Watauga
SUMMERFIELD (27358) Guilford(68),
   Rockingham(31)
SUNBURY Gates
SUNSET BEACH Brunswick
SUPPLY Brunswick
SWANNANOA Buncombe
SWANQUARTER Hyde
SWANSBORO (28584) Carteret(60),
   Onslow(39)
SWEPSONVILLE Alamance
SYLVA Jackson
TABOR CITY Columbus
TAPOCO Graham
TAR HEEL Bladen
TARAWA TERRACE Onslow
TARBORO Edgecombe
TAYLORSVILLE Alexander
TEACHEY Duplin
TERRELL Catawba
THOMASVILLE Davidson
THURMOND (28683) Wilkes(95), Surry(4)
TILLERY Halifax
TIMBERLAKE (27583) Person(98),
   Orange(1)

TOAST Surry
TOBACCOVILLE (27050) Forsyth(81),
   Stokes(18)
TODD (28684) Ashe(50), Watauga(50)
TOPTON (28781) Macon(55),
   Cherokee(44)
TOWNSVILLE Vance
TRAPHILL Wilkes
TRENTON Jones
TRINITY Randolph
TRIPLETT Watauga
TROUTMAN Iredell
TROY (27371) Montgomery(74),
   Randolph(25)
TRYON Polk
TUCKASEGEE Jackson
TURKEY Sampson
TURNERSBURG Iredell
TUXEDO Henderson
TYNER (27980) Chowan(98),
   Perquimans(1)
UNION GROVE Iredell
UNION MILLS (28167) Rutherford(98),
   McDowell(1)
VALDESE Burke
VALE (28168) Lincoln(55), Catawba(44)
VALLE CRUCIS Watauga
VANCEBORO (28586) Craven(87), Pitt(6),
   Beaufort(6)
VANDEMERE Pamlico
VASS Moore
VAUGHAN Warren
VILAS Watauga
WACO Cleveland
WADE Cumberland
WADESBORO Anson
WAGRAM Scotland
WAKE FOREST Wake
WAKULLA Robeson
WALKERTOWN Forsyth
WALLACE (28466) Duplin(78), Pender(20),
   Sampson(1)
WALLBURG Davidson
WALNUT COVE (27052) Stokes(92),
   Forsyth(7)
WALSTONBURG (27888) Wilson(50),
   Greene(46), Pitt(2)
WANCHESE Dare
WARNE Clay
WARRENSVILLE Ashe
WARRENTON (27589) Warren(90),
   Franklin(9)
WARSAW Duplin
WASHINGTON (27889) Beaufort(97),
   Pitt(2)
WATHA Pender
WAVES Dare
WAXHAW Union
WAYNESVILLE Haywood
WEAVERVILLE (28787) Buncombe(94),
   Madison(5)
WEBSTER Jackson
WELCOME Davidson
WELDON Halifax
WENDELL (27591) Wake(84),
   Johnston(15)
WENTWORTH Rockingham
WEST END Moore
WEST JEFFERSON Ashe
WESTFIELD Surry
WHITAKERS (27891) Nash(87),
   Edgecombe(11), Halifax(1)
WHITE OAK Bladen
WHITE PLAINS Surry
WHITEHEAD Alleghany
WHITEVILLE Columbus
WHITSETT Guilford
WHITTIER Jackson
WILBAR Wilkes
WILKESBORO Wilkes
WILLARD (28478) Pender(92),
   Sampson(6)

WILLIAMSTON Martin
WILLISTON Carteret
WILLOW SPRING (27592) Wake(52), Johnston(43), Harnett(4)
WILMINGTON New Hanover
WILSON (27896) Wilson(84), Nash(15)
WILSONS MILLS Johnston
WINDSOR Bertie

WINFALL Perquimans
WINGATE Union
WINNABOW Brunswick
WINSTON SALEM Forsyth
WINSTON-SALEM Forsyth
WINTERVILLE Pitt
WINTON Hertford
WISE Warren

WOODLAND (27897) Northampton(91), Hertford(8)
WOODLEAF Rowan
WRIGHTSVILLE BEACH New Hanover
YADKINVILLE Yadkin
YANCEYVILLE Caswell
YOUNGSVILLE (27596) Franklin(86), Wake(9), Granville(4)

ZEBULON (27597) Wake(79), Franklin(14), Nash(4)
ZIONVILLE (28698) Watauga(95), Ashe(4)
ZIRCONIA Henderson

ZIP/City Cross Reference

27006-27006 ADVANCE	27253-27253 GRAHAM	27522-27522 CREEDMOOR	27822-27822 ELM CITY
27007-27007 ARARAT	27256-27256 GULF	27523-27523 EAGLE ROCK	27823-27823 ENFIELD
27008-27008 BARBER	27258-27258 HAW RIVER	27524-27524 FOUR OAKS	27824-27824 ENGELHARD
27009-27009 BELEWS CREEK	27259-27259 HIGHFALLS	27525-27525 FRANKLINTON	27825-27825 EVERETTS
27010-27010 BETHANIA	27260-27265 HIGH POINT	27526-27526 FUQUAY VARINA	27826-27826 FAIRFIELD
27011-27011 BOONVILLE	27278-27278 HILLSBOROUGH	27529-27529 GARNER	27827-27827 FALKLAND
27012-27012 CLEMMONS	27281-27281 JACKSON SPRINGS	27530-27534 GOLDSBORO	27828-27828 FARMVILLE
27013-27013 CLEVELAND	27282-27282 JAMESTOWN	27536-27537 HENDERSON	27829-27829 FOUNTAIN
27014-27014 COOLEEMEE	27283-27283 JULIAN	27540-27540 HOLLY SPRINGS	27830-27830 FREMONT
27016-27016 DANBURY	27284-27285 KERNERSVILLE	27541-27541 HURDLE MILLS	27831-27831 GARYSBURG
27017-27017 DOBSON	27288-27289 EDEN	27542-27542 KENLY	27832-27832 GASTON
27018-27018 EAST BEND	27291-27291 LEASBURG	27543-27543 KIPLING	27833-27836 GREENVILLE
27019-27019 GERMANTON	27292-27295 LEXINGTON	27544-27544 KITTRELL	27837-27837 GRIMESLAND
27020-27020 HAMPTONVILLE	27298-27298 LIBERTY	27545-27545 KNIGHTDALE	27838-27838 GUMBERRY
27021-27021 KING	27299-27299 LINWOOD	27546-27546 LILLINGTON	27839-27839 HALIFAX
27022-27022 LAWSONVILLE	27301-27301 MC LEANSVILLE	27549-27549 LOUISBURG	27840-27840 HAMILTON
27023-27023 LEWISVILLE	27302-27302 MEBANE	27551-27551 MACON	27841-27841 HASSELL
27024-27024 LOWGAP	27305-27305 MILTON	27552-27552 MAMERS	27842-27842 HENRICO
27025-27025 MADISON	27306-27306 MOUNT GILEAD	27553-27553 MANSON	27843-27843 HOBGOOD
27027-27027 MAYODAN	27310-27310 OAK RIDGE	27555-27555 MICRO	27844-27844 HOLLISTER
27028-27028 MOCKSVILLE	27311-27311 PELHAM	27556-27556 MIDDLEBURG	27845-27845 JACKSON
27030-27030 MOUNT AIRY	27312-27312 PITTSBORO	27557-27557 MIDDLESEX	27846-27846 JAMESVILLE
27031-27031 WHITE PLAINS	27313-27313 PLEASANT GARDEN	27559-27559 MONCURE	27847-27847 KELFORD
27040-27040 PFAFFTOWN	27314-27314 PROSPECT HILL	27560-27560 MORRISVILLE	27848-27848 LASKER
27041-27041 PILOT MOUNTAIN	27315-27315 PROVIDENCE	27562-27562 NEW HILL	27849-27849 LEWISTON WOODVILLE
27042-27042 PINE HALL	27316-27316 RAMSEUR	27563-27563 NORLINA	27850-27850 LITTLETON
27043-27043 PINNACLE	27317-27317 RANDLEMAN	27564-27564 NORTHSIDE	27851-27851 LUCAMA
27045-27045 RURAL HALL	27320-27323 REIDSVILLE	27565-27565 OXFORD	27852-27852 MACCLESFIELD
27046-27046 SANDY RIDGE	27325-27325 ROBBINS	27568-27568 PINE LEVEL	27853-27853 MARGARETTSVILLE
27047-27047 SILOAM	27326-27326 RUFFIN	27569-27569 PRINCETON	27854-27854 MILWAUKEE
27048-27048 STONEVILLE	27330-27332 SANFORD	27570-27570 RIDGEWAY	27855-27855 MURFREESBORO
27049-27049 TOAST	27340-27340 SAXAPAHAW	27571-27571 ROLESVILLE	27856-27856 NASHVILLE
27050-27050 TOBACCOVILLE	27341-27341 SEAGROVE	27572-27572 ROUGEMONT	27857-27857 OAK CITY
27051-27051 WALKERTOWN	27342-27342 SEDALIA	27573-27573 ROXBORO	27858-27858 GREENVILLE
27052-27052 WALNUT COVE	27343-27343 SEMORA	27576-27576 SELMA	27859-27859 PALMYRA
27053-27053 WESTFIELD	27344-27344 SILER CITY	27577-27577 SMITHFIELD	27860-27860 PANTEGO
27054-27054 WOODLEAF	27349-27349 SNOW CAMP	27581-27581 STEM	27861-27861 PARMELE
27055-27055 YADKINVILLE	27350-27350 SOPHIA	27582-27582 STOVALL	27862-27862 PENDLETON
27094-27099 RURAL HALL	27351-27351 SOUTHMONT	27583-27583 TIMBERLAKE	27863-27863 PIKEVILLE
27100-27100 WINSTON-SALEM	27355-27355 STALEY	27584-27584 TOWNSVILLE	27864-27864 PINETOPS
27100-27100 WINSTON SALEM	27356-27356 STAR	27586-27586 VAUGHAN	27865-27865 PINETOWN
27100-27100 WINSTON SALEM	27357-27357 STOKESDALE	27587-27588 WAKE FOREST	27866-27866 PLEASANT HILL
27101-27199 WINSTON SALEM	27358-27358 SUMMERFIELD	27589-27589 WARRENTON	27867-27867 POTECASI
27201-27201 ALAMANCE	27359-27359 SWEPSONVILLE	27591-27591 WENDELL	27868-27868 RED OAK
27202-27202 ALTAMAHAW	27360-27361 THOMASVILLE	27592-27592 WILLOW SPRING	27869-27869 RICH SQUARE
27203-27205 ASHEBORO	27370-27370 TRINITY	27593-27593 WILSONS MILLS	27870-27870 ROANOKE RAPIDS
27207-27207 BEAR CREEK	27371-27371 TROY	27594-27594 WISE	27871-27871 ROBERSONVILLE
27208-27208 BENNETT	27373-27373 WALLBURG	27596-27596 YOUNGSVILLE	27872-27872 ROXOBEL
27209-27209 BISCOE	27374-27374 WELCOME	27597-27597 ZEBULON	27873-27873 SARATOGA
27212-27212 BLANCH	27375-27375 WENTWORTH	27599-27599 CHAPEL HILL	27874-27874 SCOTLAND NECK
27213-27213 BONLEE	27376-27376 WEST END	27600-27699 RALEIGH	27875-27875 SCRANTON
27214-27214 BROWNS SUMMIT	27377-27377 WHITSETT	27700-27722 DURHAM	27876-27876 SEABOARD
27215-27220 BURLINGTON	27379-27379 YANCEYVILLE	27801-27804 ROCKY MOUNT	27877-27877 SEVERN
27228-27228 BYNUM	27400-27499 GREENSBORO	27805-27805 AULANDER	27878-27878 SHARPSBURG
27229-27229 CANDOR	27501-27501 ANGIER	27806-27806 AURORA	27879-27879 SIMPSON
27230-27230 CEDAR FALLS	27502-27502 APEX	27807-27807 BAILEY	27880-27880 SIMS
27231-27231 CEDAR GROVE	27503-27503 BAHAMA	27808-27808 BATH	27881-27881 SPEED
27233-27233 CLIMAX	27504-27504 BENSON	27809-27809 BATTLEBORO	27882-27882 SPRING HOPE
27235-27235 COLFAX	27505-27505 BROADWAY	27810-27810 BELHAVEN	27883-27883 STANTONSBURG
27237-27237 CUMNOCK	27506-27506 BUIES CREEK	27811-27811 BELLARTHUR	27884-27884 STOKES
27239-27239 DENTON	27507-27507 BULLOCK	27812-27812 BETHEL	27885-27885 SWANQUARTER
27242-27242 EAGLE SPRINGS	27508-27508 BUNN	27813-27813 BLACK CREEK	27886-27886 TARBORO
27243-27243 EFLAND	27509-27509 BUTNER	27814-27814 BLOUNTS CREEK	27887-27887 TILLERY
27244-27244 ELON COLLEGE	27510-27510 CARRBORO	27816-27816 CASTALIA	27888-27888 WALSTONBURG
27247-27247 ETHER	27511-27513 CARY	27817-27817 CHOCOWINITY	27889-27889 WASHINGTON
27248-27248 FRANKLINVILLE	27514-27517 CHAPEL HILL	27818-27818 COMO	27890-27890 WELDON
27249-27249 GIBSONVILLE	27518-27519 CARY	27819-27819 CONETOE	27891-27891 WHITAKERS
27251-27251 GLENDON	27520-27520 CLAYTON	27820-27820 CONWAY	27892-27892 WILLIAMSTON
27252-27252 GOLDSTON	27521-27521 COATS	27821-27821 EDWARD	27893-27896 WILSON

Zip	City	Zip	City	Zip	City	Zip	City
27897-27897	WOODLAND	28039-28039	EAST SPENCER	28328-28329	CLINTON	28445-28445	HOLLY RIDGE
27906-27909	ELIZABETH CITY	28040-28040	ELLENBORO	28330-28330	CORDOVA	28446-28446	INGOLD
27910-27910	AHOSKIE	28041-28041	FAITH	28331-28331	CUMBERLAND	28447-28447	IVANHOE
27915-27915	AVON	28042-28042	FALLSTON	28332-28332	DUBLIN	28448-28448	KELLY
27916-27916	AYDLETT	28043-28043	FOREST CITY	28333-28333	DUDLEY	28449-28449	KURE BEACH
27917-27917	BARCO	28051-28056	GASTONIA	28334-28335	DUNN	28450-28450	LAKE WACCAMAW
27919-27919	BELVIDERE	28070-28070	HUNTERSVILLE	28337-28337	ELIZABETHTOWN	28451-28451	LELAND
27920-27920	BUXTON	28071-28071	GOLD HILL	28338-28338	ELLERBE	28452-28452	LONGWOOD
27921-27921	CAMDEN	28072-28072	GRANITE QUARRY	28339-28339	ERWIN	28453-28453	MAGNOLIA
27922-27922	COFIELD	28073-28073	GROVER	28340-28340	FAIRMONT	28454-28454	MAPLE HILL
27923-27923	COINJOCK	28074-28074	HARRIS	28341-28341	FAISON	28455-28455	NAKINA
27924-27924	COLERAIN	28075-28075	HARRISBURG	28342-28342	FALCON	28456-28456	RIEGELWOOD
27925-27925	COLUMBIA	28076-28076	HENRIETTA	28343-28343	GIBSON	28457-28457	ROCKY POINT
27926-27926	CORAPEAKE	28077-28077	HIGH SHOALS	28344-28344	GODWIN	28458-28458	ROSE HILL
27927-27927	COROLLA	28078-28078	HUNTERSVILLE	28345-28345	HAMLET	28459-28459	SHALLOTTE
27928-27928	CRESWELL	28079-28079	INDIAN TRAIL	28347-28347	HOFFMAN	28460-28460	SNEADS FERRY
27929-27929	CURRITUCK	28080-28080	IRON STATION	28348-28348	HOPE MILLS	28461-28461	SOUTHPORT
27930-27930	DURANTS NECK	28081-28083	KANNAPOLIS	28349-28349	KENANSVILLE	28462-28462	SUPPLY
27932-27932	EDENTON	28086-28086	KINGS MOUNTAIN	28350-28350	LAKEVIEW	28463-28463	TABOR CITY
27935-27935	EURE	28088-28088	LANDIS	28351-28351	LAUREL HILL	28464-28464	TEACHEY
27936-27936	FRISCO	28089-28089	LATTIMORE	28352-28353	LAURINBURG	28465-28465	OAK ISLAND
27937-27937	GATES	28090-28090	LAWNDALE	28355-28355	LEMON SPRINGS	28466-28466	WALLACE
27938-27938	GATESVILLE	28091-28091	LILESVILLE	28356-28356	LINDEN	28467-28467	CALABASH
27939-27939	GRANDY	28092-28093	LINCOLNTON	28357-28357	LUMBER BRIDGE	28468-28468	SUNSET BEACH
27941-27941	HARBINGER	28097-28097	LOCUST	28358-28360	LUMBERTON	28469-28469	OCEAN ISLE BEACH
27942-27942	HARRELLSVILLE	28098-28098	LOWELL	28361-28361	MCCAIN	28470-28470	SOUTH BRUNSWICK
27943-27943	HATTERAS	28101-28101	MC ADENVILLE	28362-28362	MARIETTA	28471-28471	WATHA
27944-27944	HERTFORD	28102-28102	MC FARLAN	28363-28363	MARSTON	28472-28472	WHITEVILLE
27946-27946	HOBBSVILLE	28103-28103	MARSHVILLE	28364-28364	MAXTON	28478-28478	WILLARD
27947-27947	JARVISBURG	28104-28106	MATTHEWS	28365-28365	MOUNT OLIVE	28479-28479	WINNABOW
27948-27948	KILL DEVIL HILLS	28107-28107	MIDLAND	28366-28366	NEWTON GROVE	28480-28480	WRIGHTSVILLE BEACH
27949-27949	KITTY HAWK	28108-28108	MINERAL SPRINGS	28367-28367	NORMAN	28501-28504	KINSTON
27950-27950	KNOTTS ISLAND	28109-28109	MISENHEIMER	28368-28368	OLIVIA	28508-28508	ALBERTSON
27953-27953	MANNS HARBOR	28110-28112	MONROE	28369-28369	ORRUM	28509-28509	ALLIANCE
27954-27954	MANTEO	28114-28114	MOORESBORO	28370-28370	PINEHURST	28510-28510	ARAPAHOE
27956-27956	MAPLE	28115-28117	MOORESVILLE	28371-28371	PARKTON	28511-28511	ATLANTIC
27957-27957	MERRY HILL	28119-28119	MORVEN	28372-28372	PEMBROKE	28512-28512	ATLANTIC BEACH
27958-27958	MOYOCK	28120-28120	MOUNT HOLLY	28373-28373	PINEBLUFF	28513-28513	AYDEN
27959-27959	NAGS HEAD	28123-28123	MOUNT MOURNE	28374-28374	PINEHURST	28515-28515	BAYBORO
27960-27960	OCRACOKE	28124-28124	MOUNT PLEASANT	28375-28375	PROCTORVILLE	28516-28516	BEAUFORT
27962-27962	PLYMOUTH	28125-28125	MOUNT ULLA	28376-28376	RAEFORD	28518-28518	BEULAVILLE
27964-27964	POINT HARBOR	28126-28126	NEWELL	28377-28377	RED SPRINGS	28519-28519	BRIDGETON
27965-27965	POPLAR BRANCH	28127-28127	NEW LONDON	28378-28378	REX	28520-28520	CEDAR ISLAND
27966-27966	POWELLS POINT	28128-28128	NORWOOD	28379-28380	ROCKINGHAM	28521-28521	CHINQUAPIN
27967-27967	POWELLSVILLE	28129-28129	OAKBORO	28382-28382	ROSEBORO	28522-28522	COMFORT
27968-27968	RODANTHE	28130-28130	PAW CREEK	28383-28383	ROWLAND	28523-28523	COVE CITY
27969-27969	RODUCO	28133-28133	PEACHLAND	28384-28384	SAINT PAULS	28524-28524	DAVIS
27970-27970	ROPER	28134-28134	PINEVILLE	28385-28385	SALEMBURG	28525-28525	DEEP RUN
27972-27972	SALVO	28135-28135	POLKTON	28386-28386	SHANNON	28526-28526	DOVER
27973-27973	SHAWBORO	28136-28136	POLKVILLE	28387-28388	SOUTHERN PINES	28527-28527	ERNUL
27974-27974	SHILOH	28137-28137	RICHFIELD	28390-28390	SPRING LAKE	28528-28528	GLOUCESTER
27976-27976	SOUTH MILLS	28138-28138	ROCKWELL	28391-28391	STEDMAN	28529-28529	GRANTSBORO
27978-27978	STUMPY POINT	28139-28139	RUTHERFORDTON	28392-28392	TAR HEEL	28530-28530	GRIFTON
27979-27979	SUNBURY	28144-28147	SALISBURY	28393-28393	TURKEY	28531-28531	HARKERS ISLAND
27980-27980	TYNER	28150-28152	SHELBY	28394-28394	VASS	28532-28532	HAVELOCK
27981-27981	WANCHESE	28159-28159	SPENCER	28395-28395	WADE	28533-28533	CHERRY POINT
27982-27982	WAVES	28160-28160	SPINDALE	28396-28396	WAGRAM	28537-28537	HOBUCKEN
27983-27983	WINDSOR	28163-28163	STANFIELD	28397-28397	WAKULLA	28538-28538	HOOKERTON
27985-27985	WINFALL	28164-28164	STANLEY	28398-28398	WARSAW	28539-28539	HUBERT
27986-27986	WINTON	28166-28166	TROUTMAN	28399-28399	WHITE OAK	28540-28541	JACKSONVILLE
28001-28002	ALBEMARLE	28167-28167	UNION MILLS	28401-28412	WILMINGTON	28542-28542	CAMP LEJEUNE
28006-28006	ALEXIS	28168-28168	VALE	28420-28420	ASH	28543-28543	TARAWA TERRACE
28007-28007	ANSONVILLE	28169-28169	WACO	28421-28421	ATKINSON	28544-28544	MIDWAY PARK
28009-28009	BADIN	28170-28170	WADESBORO	28422-28422	BOLIVIA	28545-28545	MCCUTCHEON FIELD
28010-28010	BARIUM SPRINGS	28173-28173	WAXHAW	28423-28423	BOLTON	28546-28546	JACKSONVILLE
28012-28012	BELMONT	28174-28174	WINGATE	28424-28424	BRUNSWICK	28547-28547	CAMP LEJEUNE
28016-28016	BESSEMER CITY	28200-28299	CHARLOTTE	28425-28425	BURGAW	28551-28551	LA GRANGE
28017-28017	BOILING SPRINGS	28301-28306	FAYETTEVILLE	28428-28428	CAROLINA BEACH	28552-28552	LOWLAND
28018-28018	BOSTIC	28307-28307	FORT BRAGG	28429-28429	CASTLE HAYNE	28553-28553	MARSHALLBERG
28019-28019	CAROLEEN	28308-28308	POPE A F B	28430-28430	CERRO GORDO	28554-28554	MAURY
28020-28020	CASAR	28309-28309	FAYETTEVILLE	28431-28431	CHADBOURN	28555-28555	MAYSVILLE
28021-28021	CHERRYVILLE	28310-28310	FORT BRAGG	28432-28432	CLARENDON	28556-28556	MERRITT
28023-28023	CHINA GROVE	28311-28314	FAYETTEVILLE	28433-28433	CLARKTON	28557-28557	MOREHEAD CITY
28024-28024	CLIFFSIDE	28315-28315	ABERDEEN	28434-28434	COUNCIL	28560-28564	NEW BERN
28025-28027	CONCORD	28318-28318	AUTRYVILLE	28435-28435	CURRIE	28570-28570	NEWPORT
28031-28031	CORNELIUS	28319-28319	BARNESVILLE	28436-28436	DELCO	28571-28571	ORIENTAL
28032-28032	CRAMERTON	28320-28320	BLADENBORO	28438-28438	EVERGREEN	28572-28572	PINK HILL
28033-28033	CROUSE	28323-28323	BUNNLEVEL	28439-28439	FAIR BLUFF	28573-28573	POLLOCKSVILLE
28034-28034	DALLAS	28324-28324	BUTTERS	28441-28441	GARLAND	28574-28574	RICHLANDS
28035-28036	DAVIDSON	28325-28325	CALYPSO	28442-28442	HALLSBORO	28575-28575	SALTER PATH
28037-28037	DENVER	28326-28326	CAMERON	28443-28443	HAMPSTEAD	28577-28577	SEALEVEL
28038-28038	EARL	28327-28327	CARTHAGE	28444-28444	HARRELLS	28578-28578	SEVEN SPRINGS

28579-28579 SMYRNA	28644-28644 LAUREL SPRINGS	28695-28695 WHITEHEAD	28747-28747 LAKE TOXAWAY
28580-28580 SNOW HILL	28645-28645 LENOIR	28696-28696 WILBAR	28748-28748 LEICESTER
28581-28581 STACY	28646-28646 LINVILLE	28697-28697 WILKESBORO	28749-28749 LITTLE SWITZERLAND
28582-28582 STELLA	28647-28647 LINVILLE FALLS	28698-28698 ZIONVILLE	28750-28750 LYNN
28583-28583 STONEWALL	28648-28648 LONGISLAND	28699-28699 SCOTTS	28751-28751 MAGGIE VALLEY
28584-28584 SWANSBORO	28649-28649 MC GRADY	28701-28701 ALEXANDER	28752-28752 MARION
28585-28585 TRENTON	28650-28650 MAIDEN	28702-28702 ALMOND	28753-28753 MARSHALL
28586-28586 VANCEBORO	28651-28651 MILLERS CREEK	28703-28703 AQUONE	28754-28754 MARS HILL
28587-28587 VANDEMERE	28652-28652 MINNEAPOLIS	28704-28704 ARDEN	28755-28755 MICAVILLE
28589-28589 WILLISTON	28653-28653 MONTEZUMA	28705-28705 BAKERSVILLE	28756-28756 MILL SPRING
28590-28590 WINTERVILLE	28654-28654 MORAVIAN FALLS	28707-28707 BALSAM	28757-28757 MONTREAT
28594-28594 EMERALD ISLE	28655-28655 MORGANTON	28708-28708 BALSAM GROVE	28758-28758 MOUNTAIN HOME
28601-28603 HICKORY	28656-28656 NORTH WILKESBORO	28709-28709 BARNARDSVILLE	28760-28760 NAPLES
28604-28604 BANNER ELK	28657-28657 NEWLAND	28710-28710 BAT CAVE	28761-28761 NEBO
28605-28605 BLOWING ROCK	28658-28658 NEWTON	28711-28711 BLACK MOUNTAIN	28762-28762 OLD FORT
28606-28606 BOOMER	28659-28659 NORTH WILKESBORO	28712-28712 BREVARD	28763-28763 OTTO
28607-28608 BOONE	28660-28660 OLIN	28713-28713 BRYSON CITY	28765-28765 PENLAND
28609-28609 CATAWBA	28661-28661 PATTERSON	28714-28714 BURNSVILLE	28766-28766 PENROSE
28610-28610 CLAREMONT	28662-28662 PINEOLA	28715-28715 CANDLER	28768-28768 PISGAH FOREST
28611-28611 COLLETTSVILLE	28663-28663 PINEY CREEK	28716-28716 CANTON	28770-28770 RIDGECREST
28612-28612 CONNELLYS SPRINGS	28664-28664 PLUMTREE	28717-28717 CASHIERS	28771-28771 ROBBINSVILLE
28613-28613 CONOVER	28665-28665 PURLEAR	28718-28718 CEDAR MOUNTAIN	28772-28772 ROSMAN
28614-28614 CRANBERRY	28666-28666 ICARD	28719-28719 CHEROKEE	28773-28773 SALUDA
28615-28615 CRESTON	28667-28667 RHODHISS	28720-28720 CHIMNEY ROCK	28774-28774 SAPPHIRE
28616-28616 CROSSNORE	28668-28668 ROARING GAP	28721-28721 CLYDE	28775-28775 SCALY MOUNTAIN
28617-28617 CRUMPLER	28669-28669 ROARING RIVER	28722-28722 COLUMBUS	28776-28776 SKYLAND
28618-28618 DEEP GAP	28670-28670 RONDA	28723-28723 CULLOWHEE	28777-28777 SPRUCE PINE
28619-28619 DREXEL	28671-28671 RUTHERFORD COLLEGE	28724-28724 DANA	28778-28778 SWANNANOA
28621-28621 ELKIN	28672-28672 SCOTTVILLE	28725-28725 DILLSBORO	28779-28779 SYLVA
28622-28622 ELK PARK	28673-28673 SHERRILLS FORD	28726-28726 EAST FLAT ROCK	28780-28780 TAPOCO
28623-28623 ENNICE	28674-28674 NORTH WILKESBORO	28727-28727 EDNEYVILLE	28781-28781 TOPTON
28624-28624 FERGUSON	28675-28675 SPARTA	28728-28728 ENKA	28782-28782 TRYON
28625-28625 STATESVILLE	28676-28676 STATE ROAD	28729-28729 ETOWAH	28783-28783 TUCKASEGEE
28626-28626 FLEETWOOD	28677-28677 STATESVILLE	28730-28730 FAIRVIEW	28784-28784 TUXEDO
28627-28627 GLADE VALLEY	28678-28678 STONY POINT	28731-28731 FLAT ROCK	28785-28786 WAYNESVILLE
28628-28628 GLEN ALPINE	28679-28679 SUGAR GROVE	28732-28732 FLETCHER	28787-28787 WEAVERVILLE
28629-28629 GLENDALE SPRINGS	28680-28680 MORGANTON	28733-28733 FONTANA DAM	28788-28788 WEBSTER
28630-28630 GRANITE FALLS	28681-28681 TAYLORSVILLE	28734-28734 FRANKLIN	28789-28789 WHITTIER
28631-28631 GRASSY CREEK	28682-28682 TERRELL	28735-28735 GERTON	28790-28790 ZIRCONIA
28632-28632 GRAYSON	28683-28683 THURMOND	28736-28736 GLENVILLE	28791-28793 HENDERSONVILLE
28633-28633 LENOIR	28684-28684 TODD	28737-28737 GLENWOOD	28800-28816 ASHEVILLE
28634-28634 HARMONY	28685-28685 TRAPHILL	28738-28738 HAZELWOOD	28901-28901 ANDREWS
28635-28635 HAYS	28686-28686 TRIPLETT	28739-28739 HENDERSONVILLE	28902-28902 BRASSTOWN
28636-28636 HIDDENITE	28687-28687 STATESVILLE	28740-28740 GREENMOUNTAIN	28903-28903 CULBERSON
28337-28637 HILDEBRAN	28688-28688 TURNERSBURG	28740-28740 GREEN MOUNTAIN	28904-28904 HAYESVILLE
28638-28638 HUDSON	28689-28689 UNION GROVE	28741-28741 HIGHLANDS	28905-28905 MARBLE
28639-28639 HUSK	28690-28690 VALDESE	28742-28742 HORSE SHOE	28906-28906 MURPHY
28640-28640 JEFFERSON	28691-28691 VALLE CRUCIS	28743-28743 HOT SPRINGS	28909-28909 WARNE
28641-28641 JONAS RIDGE	28692-28692 VILAS	28744-28744 FRANKLIN	
28642-28642 JONESVILLE	28693-28693 WARRENSVILLE	28745-28745 LAKE JUNALUSKA	
28643-28643 LANSING	28694-28694 WEST JEFFERSON	28746-28746 LAKE LURE	

North Dakota

General Help Numbers:

Governor's Office
State Capitol
600 E Boulevard Ave, 1st Floor
Bismarck, ND 58505-0001
www.governor.state.nd.us

701-328-2200
Fax 701-328-2205
8AM-5PM

Attorney General's Office
State Capitol - Dept 125
600 E Boulevard Ave
Bismarck, ND 58505-0040
www.ag.state.nd.us

701-328-2210
Fax 701-328-2226
8AM-5PM

State Court Administrator
North Dakota Supreme Court
600 E Blvd Ave, Dept 180
Bismarck, ND 58505-0530
www.court.state.nd.us

701-328-4216
Fax 701-328-2092
8AM-5PM

State Archives
State Archives &
 Historical Research Library
N Dakota Heritage Center, 612 E Blvd Ave
Bismarck, ND 58505-0830
www.state.nd.us/hist/sal.htm

701-328-2666
Fax 701-328-3710
8AM-5PM

State Specifics:

Capital:	Bismark Burleigh County
Time Zone:	CST
Number of Counties:	53
Population:	634,448
Web Site:	http://discovernd.com

State Agencies

Criminal Records

Bureau of Criminal Investigation, PO Box 1054, Bismarck, ND 58502-1054 (Courier: 4205 N State St, Bismarck, ND 58501); 701-328-5500, 701-328-5510 (Fax), 8AM-5PM.

www.ag.state.nd.us

Note: A sexual offender registry is available online from the attorney general's office at www.ndsexoffender.com

Indexing & Storage: Records are available from 1930 to present. It takes 6 to 10 days before new records are available for inquiry. Records are indexed on computer if DOB is 1940 to present; prior in paper files. Records are normally destroyed after (records maintained indefinitely). 86% of all arrests in database have final dispositions recorded, 78% for those arrests within last 5 years.

Searching: Subject will be notified of the request. Include the following in your request: signed

release from subject, name, date of birth, current address, Social Security Number. Fingerprints optional, with additional fee. 100% of the records are fingerprint-supported. After one year, only records with convictions are released. Charges that are dismissed or sealed are not released.

Access by: mail, in person.

Fee & Payment: The search fee is $20.00 per name. Fingerprint searches are $22.00. Fee payee: ND Attorney General. Prepayment required.

Personal checks accepted. No credit cards accepted.

Mail search: Turnaround time: 3 to 5 days. No self addressed stamped envelope is required.

In person search: Turnaround time while you wait.

Corporation Records
Limited Liability Company Records
Limited Partnership Records
Limited Liability Partnership
Trademarks/Servicemarks
Fictitious Name & Assumed Name

Secretary of State, Business Information/ Registration, 600 E Boulevard Ave, Dept 108, Bismarck, ND 58505-0500; 701-328-4284, 800-352-0867, 701-328-2992 (Fax), 8AM-5PM.

www.state.nd.us/sec

Indexing & Storage: Records are available from 1890's on. Records are computerized since 1989. Records inactive prior to 1989 are maintained by state archives, and may take as long as two weeks to search. New records are available for inquiry immediately. Records are indexed on index cards, inhouse computer.

Searching: Include the following in your request: full name of business. In addition to the articles of incorporation, corporation records include the following information: Annual Reports, Officers, Directors, DBAs, Prior (merged) names, Inactive names, and Reserved names. The following data is not released: financial information.

Access by: mail, phone, fax, in person, online.

Fee & Payment: There is a search fee of $5.00 if a written confirmation is required or if data must be retrieved from the archives. Copies cost $1.00 for each 4 pages or fraction thereof. Certification is an additional $15.00. Fee payee: Secretary of State. Prepayment required. Personal checks accepted. Credit cards accepted: MasterCard, Visa, Discover.

Mail search: Turnaround time: 3 to 5 days. No self addressed stamped envelope is required.

Phone search: There is no fee for verbal confirmation on an active record, otherwise there is a $5.00 fee.

Fax search: Same fees as phone searching. Turnaround time is 1-3 days if written confirmation required. Add $1.00 per page for fax results.

In person search: No fee on active records, $5.00 fee on inactive records or if in archives. Turnaround time is while you wait.

Online search: The Secretary of State's registered business database may be viewed at the Internet for no charge. Records include corporations, limited liability companies, limited partnerships, limited liability partnerships, limited liability limited partnerships, partnership fictitious names, trade names, trademarks, and real estate investment trusts. The database includes all active records and those records inactivated within the past twelve months. Access by the first few words of a business name, by any significant word in a

business name, or by the System ID number assigned to the record.

Other access: The state provides a database purchase program. Costs are $35.00 per database and processing fees vary for type of media.

Uniform Commercial Code
Federal Tax Liens
State Tax Liens

UCC Division, Secretary of State, 600 E Boulevard Ave Dept 108, Bismarck, ND 58505-0500; 701-328-3662, 701-328-4214 (Fax), 8AM-5PM.

www.state.nd.us/sec

Note: The state has a Central Indexing System which allows UCC and tax lien searches at this office or at any of the county Register of Deeds (53).

Indexing & Storage: Records are available from 1966. Records are computerized on index statewide since 1992. Records are indexed on inhouse computer.

Searching: Use search request form UCC-11. Include the following in your request: debtor name.

Access by: mail, phone, fax, in person, online.

Fee & Payment: The search fee is $7.00 for the first 5 entries and $2.00 for each additional 5 entries or fraction thereof. A copy request with certificate is $7.00 for first 3 copies and $2.00 for each additional. All tax liens will show on the record request. Fee payee: Secretary of State. Will invoice, if requested. Monthly billing is offered to ongoing requesters. Personal checks accepted. Credit cards accepted: MasterCard, Visa.

Mail search: Turnaround time: 1 day. A self addressed stamped envelope is requested.

Phone search: General information is available without charge.

Fax search: There is an additional fee of $3.00 (maximum 20 pages). Please allow 20 minutes to 1 hour.

In person search: You may request information in person.

Online search: There is a limited free public search and a commercial system for professionals. Sign-up for access to the Central Indexing System includes an annual subscription $120 fee and a one-time $50.00 registration fee. The $7.00 fee applies, but documents will not be certified. Searches include UCC-11 information listing and farm product searches.

Sales Tax Registrations

State Tax Commission, Sales & Special Tax Division, State Capitol, 600 E Boulevard Ave, Bismarck, ND 58505-0599; 701-328-3470, 701-328-3700 (Fax), 8AM-5PM.

www.state.nd.us/taxdpt

Indexing & Storage: Records are available from 1996 to present, including inactive records. Records are indexed on computer.

Searching: This agency will only confirm if a business is registered and active. They will provide no other information as it is confidential. Include the following in your request: business name. They will also search by tax permit number or owner name.

Access by: mail, phone, fax.

Mail search: Turnaround time: 7 to 10 days. A self addressed stamped envelope is requested. No fee for mail request.

Phone search: No fee for telephone request.

Fax search: There is no fee.

Birth Certificates

ND Department of Health, Vital Records, State Capitol, 600 E Blvd, Dept 301, Bismarck, ND 58505-0200; 701-328-2360, 701-328-1850 (Fax), 7:30AM-5PM.

www.vitalnd.com

Indexing & Storage: Records are available from 1870 on. New records are available for inquiry immediately. Records are indexed on inhouse computer.

Searching: Must have a signed release from person of record if it is an out-of-wedlock birth. If under 18, parent or legal guardian signature needed. Include the following in your request: full name, names of parents, mother's maiden name, date of birth, place of birth, relationship to person of record, reason for information request.

Access by: mail, fax, in person, online.

Fee & Payment: The fee is $7.00 per name. Add $4.00 per name for second copies. Fee payee: North Dakota Department of Health. Prepayment required. Personal checks accepted. Credit cards accepted: MasterCard, Visa, AmEx, Discover.

Mail search: Turnaround time: 4 to 5 days. No self addressed stamped envelope is required.

Fax search: Use of credit card required. Turnaround time is same day if received by 10AM and request is marked for FedEx or UPS.

In person search: Turnaround time is less than 15 minutes.

Online search: Records may be ordered online from the Internet site, or via e-mail at vitalrec@state.nd.us for $7.00 per name. Records are not returned online.

Expedited service: Expedited service is available for fax or online searches. Turnaround time: overnight delivery. Expedited service options are available using a credit card and additional $15.00 fee for shipping.

Death Records

ND Department of Health, Vital Records, State Capitol, 600 E Blvd, Dept 301, Bismarck, ND 58505-0200; 701-328-2360, 701-328-1850 (Fax), 7:30AM-5PM.

www.vitalnd.com

Indexing & Storage: Records are available from 1881 on. Early records are few. New records are available for inquiry immediately. Records are indexed on inhouse computer.

Searching: Cause of death not shown on copy of Death Certificate if not a family member. Include the following in your request: full name, date of death, place of death, relationship to person of record, reason for information request.

Access by: mail, fax, in person, online.

Fee & Payment: The fee is $5.00 per name. Add $2.00 per name for second copies. Fee payee: North Dakota Department of Health. Prepayment required. Personal checks accepted. Credit cards accepted: MasterCard, Visa, AmEx, Discover.

Mail search: Turnaround time: 2 to 3 days. A self addressed stamped envelope is requested.

Fax search: This is considered expedited service. Turnaround time is same day if received by 10AM noon and request is marked for FedEx or UPS.

In person search: Turnaround time is 10 to 15 minutes.

Online search: Records may be ordered online from the Internet site, or via e-mail at vitalrec@state.nd.us for $5.00 per name. Records are not returned online.

Expedited service: Expedited service is available for fax searches. Turnaround time: overnight delivery. Expedited service options are available using a credit card and for additional $15.00 fee indicated for shipping.

Marriage Certificates

ND Department of Health, Vital Records, State Capitol, 600 E Blvd, Dept 301, Bismarck, ND 58505-0200; 701-328-2360, 701-328-1850 (Fax), 7:30AM-5PM.

www.vitalnd.com

Indexing & Storage: Records are available from July 1, 1925 to present. New records are available for inquiry immediately. Records are indexed on inhouse computer.

Searching: Include the following in your request: names of husband and wife, date of marriage, place or county of marriage, relationship to person of record, reason for information request, wife's maiden name.

Access by: mail, fax, in person, online.

Fee & Payment: The fee is $5.00 per name. Add $2.00 per name for second copies. Add $5.00 if credit card used. Fee payee: North Dakota Department of Health. Prepayment required. Personal checks accepted. Credit cards accepted: MasterCard, Visa, AmEx, Discover.

Mail search: Turnaround time: 4 to 5 days. No self addressed stamped envelope is required.

Fax search: Turnaround time is same day if received by 10 AM and request is being returned by FedEx or UPS.

In person search: Turnaround time is 10 to 15 minutes.

Online search: Records may be ordered online from the Internet site, or via e-mail at vitalrec@state.nd.us for $5.00 per name. Records are not returned online.

Expedited service: Expedited service is available for fax or online searches. Turnaround time: overnight delivery. Expedited service options are available using a credit card ($5.00 additional fee) and an additional $15.00 fee.

Divorce Records

Access to Records is Restricted

ND Department of Health, Vital Records, State Capitol, 600 E Blvd, Dept 301, Bismarck, ND 58505-0200; 701-328-2360.

www.vitalnd.com

Note: The State has an index to direct people to which county has the records. The index contains records from July 1, 1949 to present. Call or e-mail to vitalrec@state.nd.us.

Workers' Compensation Records

ND Workers Compensation, 500 E Front Ave, Bismarck, ND 58504-5685; 701-328-3800, 800-777-5033, 701-328-3820 (Fax), 8AM-5PM.

www.ndworkerscomp.com

Indexing & Storage: Records are available from 1919 but more reliable information is from 1975 on. It takes 24 hours before new records are available for inquiry. Records are indexed on inhouse computer.

Searching: Must have a signed release from person of record stating exactly what information is requested. Include the following in your request: claimant name, Social Security Number, date of birth. Also, a signed release by the subject is required, unless the requester is involved within the case.

Access by: mail.

Fee & Payment: Copies are $.35 per page. There is no search fee, unless file needs to be retrieved from off-site, then $5.00 is charged. Fee payee: Worker's Compensation Bureau. Prepayment required. Personal checks accepted.

Mail search: Turnaround time: 5 days. A self addressed stamped envelope is requested.

Driver Records

Department of Transportation, Driver License & Traffic Safety Division, 608 E Boulevard Ave, Bismarck, ND 58505-0700; 701-328-2603, 701-328-2435 (Fax), 8AM-5PM.

www.state.nd.us/dot

Note: Copies of tickets must be obtained from the local courts.

Indexing & Storage: Records are available for 3 years for moving violations, DWI and suspensions. Records available to the public will show neither violations less than 2 points nor accidents. The record will not show the driver's address to casual requesters without consent. It takes 1 day before new records are available for inquiry.

Searching: The Division sends an additional copy of the abstract to the driver whose record was requested, accompanied by a statement identifying the requester. The driver's license number, name, and DOB are required when ordering, but "two out of three" may produce a "hit."

Access by: mail, in person, online.

Fee & Payment: The fee is $3.00 per record. Fee payee: Driver License & Traffic Safety. Prepayment required. Personal checks accepted. Credit cards accepted: MasterCard, Visa, Discover.

Mail search: Turnaround time: 3 days. A self addressed stamped envelope is requested.

In person search: Up to eight requests will be processed while you wait.

Online search: The system is interactive and is open 24 hours daily. Fee is $3.00 per record, requesters must be approved. There is a minimum of 100 requests per month. For more information, call 701-328-4790.

Other access: Magnetic tape ordering is available for high volume users.

Vehicle Ownership
Vehicle Identification

Department of Transportation, Records Section/Motor Vehicle Div., 608 E Boulevard Ave, Bismarck, ND 58505-0780; 701-328-2725, 701-328-4156 (TTY:), 701-328-3500 (Fax), 8AM-4:50PM.

www.state.nd.us/dot

Note: Records on mobile homes are also maintained by this agency.

Indexing & Storage: Records are available from 1911 for license plate numbers. It takes 10 to 14 days before new records are available for inquiry.

Searching: Records are available with the prior authorization. Personal information is not released to casual requesters without consent. A written request or use of Form SFN-2963 is required. The following data is not released: Social Security Numbers or medical records.

Access by: mail, fax, in person.

Fee & Payment: The fee is $3.00 per record (includes lien data). There is a fee for a no record found. Fee payee: Motor Vehicle Division. Prepayment required. Personal checks accepted. Credit cards accepted: MasterCard, Visa.

Mail search: Turnaround time: 3 days. A self addressed stamped envelope is requested.

Fax search: fax requesting is available for pre-approved commercial accounts.

In person search: The state may limit the number of requests processed immediately, if busy.

Other access: North Dakota offers bulk or batch retrieval of VIN or ownership information of vehicles. The requester must explain purpose and intent; however, there are no restrictions placed upon requests of a legal nature. Customized or special runs are available.

Accident Reports

Driver License & Traffic Safety Division, CRASH Records Section, 608 E Boulevard Ave, Bismarck, ND 58505-0780; 701-328-4397, 701-328-2601, 701-328-2435 (Fax), 8AM-5PM.

www.state.nd.us/dot

Indexing & Storage: Records are available from 1994. Records are computer indexed since 1993. It takes 1-2 months before new records are available for inquiry.

Searching: The front page which includes drivers, witnesses, and insurance information, can be ordered by anyone with a written request. The investigating officer's report is also only to parties involved or their legal representative or insurer. Include the following in your request: date of accident, location of accident, full name of at least one driver, reason for information request.

Access by: mail, in person.

Fee & Payment: Fee is $3.00 for front page record (drivers, witnesses, etc.). Add $5.00 to receive the investigating officer's report. Fee payee: Driver License & Traffic Safety Division. Prepayment required. Personal checks accepted. Credit cards accepted: MasterCard, Visa.

Mail search: Turnaround time: 5 days. A self addressed stamped envelope is requested.

In person search: Turnaround time while you wait.

Vessel Ownership
Vessel Registration

North Dakota Game & Fish Department, 100 N Bismarck Expressway, Bismarck, ND 58501; 701-328-6335, 701-328-6352 (Fax), 8AM-5PM.

www.state.nd.us/gnf

Note: Liens are filed at same locations as UCCs.

Indexing & Storage: Records are available from 1975 to present. Records are computer indexed for the last five years. All motorized boat must be registered. No titles are issued.

Searching: To search, one of the following is required: hull ID #, registration #, decal #, or name.

Access by: mail, phone, fax, in person, online.

Fee & Payment: There is no fee for 1-2 names.

Mail search: Turnaround time: 1 day. No self addressed stamped envelope is required.

Phone search: Records are available by phone.

Fax search: Results can be faxed, mailed, or phoned.

In person search: Turnaround time is usually immediate.

Online search: There is a free public inquiry system on the home page. One can also search lottery hunting permit applications.

Other access: A printed list is available of all registered vessels.

Legislation Records

North Dakota Legislative Council, State Capitol, 600 E Boulevard Ave, Bismarck, ND 58505; 701-328-2916, 701-328-2900 (Secretary of State), 701-328-2992 (Sec of State fax), 8AM-5PM.

www.state.nd.us/lr

Note: Copies of "enrolled bills" are found at the Secretary of State's office (as well as online); search fee is $1.00 for each 4 pages. The legislature meets every odd year.

Indexing & Storage: Records are available from 1889 on. Records are on microfiche from 1969 to 2001, and computerized from 1997 forward. Records are indexed on inhouse computer, hard copy.

Searching: Include the following in your request: bill number.

Access by: mail, phone, fax, in person, online.

Fee & Payment: Fees is $1.00 for each 4 pages (through Sec of State). Fee payee: Secretary of State. Prepayment required. Personal checks accepted. Credit cards accepted: MasterCard, Visa, Discover.

Mail search: Turnaround time: 1 to 2 days. No self addressed stamped envelope is required.

Phone search: You may call for information.

Fax search: Fax to Secretary of State.

In person search: You may request information in person.

Online search: Their Internet site offers an extensive array of legislative information at no charge, including proposed and enacted legislation since 1997. Also, one may e-mail requests for information.

Voter Registration

Records not maintained by a state level agency.

Note: Records are maintained at the county level by the County Auditors in poll books. Records are open to the public.

GED Certificates

Department of Public Instruction, GED Testing, 600 E Blvd Ave, Bismarck, ND 58505-0440; 701-328-2393, 701-328-4770 (Fax), 8AM-4:30PM.

www.dpi.state.nd.us

Searching: A verification will only verify that a test was taken, but not if the subject passed the test. Include the following in your request: signed release, Social Security Number, date of birth.

Access by: mail, fax, in person, online.

Fee & Payment: There is no fee for a verification and a $2.00 fee for a copy of a transcript. Fee payee: Dept of Public Instruction. Prepayment required. Personal checks accepted. No credit cards accepted.

Mail search: Turnaround time: 1 week. No self addressed stamped envelope is required.

Fax search: Used only for verification.

In person search: Picture ID required.

Online search: One may request records via e-mail at JMarcell@mail.dpi.state.nd.us. There is no fee, unless a transcript is ordered.

Hunting License Information
Fishing License Information

ND Game & Fish Department, 100 N Bismarck Expressway, Bismarck, ND 58501-5095; 701-328-6300, 701-328-6335 (Licensing), 701-328-6352 (Fax), 8AM-5PM.

www.state.nd.us/gnf

Indexing & Storage: Records are available from 1992 on computer. Big Game Lottery Permits are only available for the current season. Records are indexed on inhouse computer.

Searching: Include the following in your request: full name, date of birth, Social Security Number. This agency also registers boats.

Access by: mail, fax, in person, online.

Fee & Payment: There is no search fee.

Mail search: Turnaround time: 1 to 3 days. A self addressed stamped envelope is requested.

Fax search: Same criteria as mail searches.

In person search: You can go in and access their records. They also make the boat registrations available.

Online search: One can search to see if a person has been chosen (lottery) for a specific hunt or passed hunter safety.

Other access: They sell mailing lists. Call Paul Schadewald at 701-328-6328 for more information.

North Dakota State Licensing Agencies

Licenses Searchable Online

Asbestos Abatement Contr./Worker #27 .... www.health.state.nd.us/ndhd/environ/ee/rad/asb/
Asbestos Abatement Insp./Monitor/Spvr. #27 .... www.health.state.nd.us/ndhd/environ/ee/rad/asb/
Asbestos Abatement Planner/Designer #27 .... www.health.state.nd.us/ndhd/environ/ee/rad/asb/
Attorney #41 .... www.court.state.nd.us/court/lawyers/index/frameset.htm
Bank #20 .... www.state.nd.us/dfi/Bank List.htm
Charitable Solicitation #39 .... www.state.nd.us/sec/charitableorganizationsearch.htm
Collection Agency #20 .... www.state.nd.us/dfi/Collection Agencies.htm
Consumer Finance Company #20 .... www.state.nd.us/dfi/Finance Companies.htm
Contractor/General Contractor #39 .... www.state.nd.us/sec/contractorsearch.htm
Credit Union #20 .... www.state.nd.us/dfi/Credit Union List.htm
Livestock Agent #19 .... www.agdepartment.com/Programs/Livestock/Agents.html
Livestock Auction Market #19 .... www.agdepartment.com/Programs/Livestock/markets.html
Livestock Dealer #19 .... www.agdepartment.com/Programs/Livestock/Dealers.html
Lobbyist #39 .... www.state.nd.us/sec/RegLobbyists/lobbyistregmnu.htm
Medical Doctor #47 .... www.docboard.org/nd/
Money Broker Firm #20 .... www.state.nd.us/dfi/Money Brokers.htm
Optometrist #49 .... www.ndsbopt.org/directory.asp
Pesticide Applicator/Dealer #19 .... www.ag.ndsu.nodak.edu/aginfo/pesticid/cert_info.htm
Physician Assistant #47 .... www.docboard.org/nd/
Public Accountant-CPA #42 .... www.state.nd.us/ndsba/database/sbasearch.asp
Public Accounting Firm #42 .... www.state.nd.us/ndsba/database/sbasearch.asp
Social Worker #18 .... www.ndbswe.com/list/main_pg.htm
Trust Company #20 .... www.state.nd.us/dfi/Trust Companies.htm

Licensing Quick Finder

Abstractor/Abstractor Company #1 701-947-2446	Day Care Service #22 701-328-4809	Livestock Dealer #19 701-328-4756
Adoption Service #22 701-328-4805	Debt Collector #20 701-328-9933	Lobbyist #39 701-328-3665
Aerial Applicator #30 701-328-9650	Dental Assistant #10 701-224-1815	Manicurist #8 701-224-9800
Aircraft Dealer #30 701-328-9650	Dental Hygienist #10 701-224-1815	Massage Therapist #46 701-255-1525
Aircraft Registration #30 701-328-9650	Dentist #10 701-224-1815	Medical Doctor #47 701-328-6500
Alcoholic Beverage Control #3 701-328-2329	Dietitian/Nutritionist #11 701-746-9171	Money Broker Firm #20 701-328-9933
Amusement Device, Coin-Operated #3.701-328-2329	Drug Manufacturer/Wholesaler #14 701-328-9535	Mortician #44 701-662-2511
Asbestos Abatement Contr./Worker #27	Electrician #25 701-328-9522	Notary Public #39 701-328-2901
....701-328-5188	Electrician Apprentice #25 701-328-9522	Nurse Assistant #31 701-328-9780
Asbestos Abatement Insp./Monitor/Supvr. #27	Embalmer #44 701-662-2511	Nurse-LPN #31 701-328-9777
....701-328-5188	Employment Agency (Permanent Placing) #23	Nurse-RN #31 701-328-9777
Asbestos Abatement Planner/Designer #27	701-328-2660	Nursing Home Administrator #13 701-222-4867
....701-328-5188	Engineer #36 701-258-0786	Nutritionist #11 701-746-9171
Athletic Trainer #5 701-857-5286	Esthetician #8 701-224-9800	Occupational Therapist #48 701-250-0847
Attorney #41 701-328-4201	Fireworks, Wholesale #3 701-328-2329	Oil & Gas Broker #40 701-328-2910
Auction Clerk #34 701-328-4097	Fishing Guide #26 701-328-6300	Oil & Gas Wellhead Welder #40 701-328-2910
Auctioneer #34 701-328-4097	Foster Care Program #22 701-328-3587	Optometrist #49 701-225-9333
Bank #20 701-328-9933	Fund Raiser, Professional #39 701-328-3665	Osteopathic Physician #47 701-328-6500
Barber #6 701-523-3327	Funeral Director #44 701-662-2511	Pesticide Applicator/Dealer #19 701-231-7180
Barber Shop #6 701-523-3327	Funeral Home #44 701-662-2511	Pharmacist #14 701-328-9535
Boxer/Boxing Professional #38 701-328-3665	Gaming #3 701-328-2329	Pharmacy #14 701-328-9535
Broker, Corporate #28 701-328-3548	Gaming Distributor/Mfg. #3 701-328-2329	Pharmacy Technician/Intern #14 701-328-9535
Charitable Solicitation #39 701-328-3665	Grain Buyer #34 701-328-4097	Physical Therapist/Assistant #51 701-352-0125
Check Seller #20 701-328-9933	Grain Warehouse #34 701-328-4097	Physician Assistant #47 701-328-6500
Chiropractor #7 701-352-1690	Hearing Aid Dealer/Fitter #45 701-237-9977	Plumber Journeyman/Apprentice/Master #32
Coal Mine, Surface #34 701-328-4096	Hunting Guide #26 701-328-6300	701-328-9977
Collection Agency #20 701-328-9933	Hunting/Fishing Guide Combo #26 701-328-6300	Podiatrist #15 701-232-5479
Consumer Finance Company #20 701-328-9933	Insurance Agency/Agent #28 701-328-3548	Polygraph Examiner #3 701-328-2329
Contractor/General Contractor #39 701-328-3665	Insurance Broker #28 701-328-3548	Private Investigation Agency #33 701-222-3063
Cosmetologist/Cosmetologist Instructor #8	Investment Advisor #40 701-328-2910	Private Investigator #33 701-222-3063
....701-224-9800	Kickboxer #38 701-328-3665	Psychologist #16 701-777-3792
Counselor, Addiction #4 701-255-1439	Laboratory Clinician #53 701-224-1815	Public Accountant-CPA #42 701-775-7100
Counselor, Professional #9 701-667-5969	Land Surveyor #36 701-258-0786	Public Accounting Firm #42 701-775-7100
Credit Union #20 701-328-9933	Livestock Agent #19 701-328-4756	Racing #3 701-328-4633
Crematorium #44 701-662-2511	Livestock Auction Market #19 701-328-4756	Real Estate Agent/Broker #35 701-328-9749

Respiratory Care Practitioner #37 701-222-1564	Social Worker #18 701-222-0255	Trust Company #20 701-328-9933
School Counselor/Designate #24 701-328-2260	Soil Classifier #17 701-225-3381	Veterinarian #29 701-328-9540
School Media Specialist #24 701-328-2260	Speech-Language Pathologist/Audiologist #12	Veterinary Technician #29 701-328-9540
School Principal/Assistant #24 701-328-2260	 701-777-4421	Water Conditioning Contractor/Installer #32
School Superintendent/Assistant #24 .. 701-328-2260	Taxidermist #26 701-328-6300	 701-328-9977
Securities Agent/Dealer #40 701-328-2910	Teacher #24 701-328-2260	Water Well Driller #50 701-328-2754
Security Employee #33 701-222-2063	Telecommunications Personnel #34 701-328-4076	Water Well Pump & Pitless Unit #50 701-328-2754
Security Provider/Company #33 701-222-3063	Tobacco, Retail/Wholesale #3 701-328-2329	Weather Modifier #2 701-328-2788
Sewer & Water Contractor/Installer #32 701-328-9977	Transient Merchant #3 701-328-2329	Well Contractor, Monitoring #50 701-328-2754

Licensing Agency Information

#1 Abstractors Board of Examiners, PO Box 551, New Rockford, ND 58356; 701-947-2446, Fax: 701-947-2443.

#2 Atmospheric Resource Board, Water Commission, 900 E Boulevard Ave, Bismarck, ND 58505; 701-328-4940, Fax: 701-328-4749. http://water.swc.state.nd.us

#3 Attorney General's Office, Licensing Division, 600 E Boulevard Ave, Dept 125, Bismarck, ND 58505-0040; 701-328-2392, Fax: 701-328-3535. www.ag.state.nd.us/buslic/bli.html

#4 Board of Addiction Counseling Examiners, PO Box 975, Bismarck, ND 58502-0975; 701-255-1439, Fax: 701-224-9824.
www.ndbace.org
Agency email: ndbace@aptnd.com.

#5 Board of Athletic Trainers, PO Box 5020, Minot, ND 58702; 701-857-5286, Fax: 701-857-5694.

#6 Board of Barber Examiners, PO Box 885, Bowman, ND 58623; 701-523-3327, Fax: 701-574-3126.

#7 c/o Jerry Blanchard, Board of Chiropractic Examiners, PO Box 185, Grafton, ND 58237; 701-352-1690, Fax: 701-352-2258.

#8 Board of Cosmetology, PO Box 2177 (1102 S Washington #200), Bismarck, ND 58502; 701-224-9800, Fax: 701-222-8756. Agency email: cosmo@gcentral.com.

#9 Board of Counselor Examiners, 2112 10th Av SE, Mandan, ND 58554-5066; 701-667-5969.
www.sendit.nodak.edu/ndbce
Agency email: ndbce@btigate.com.

#10 Board of Dental Examiners, PO Box 7246, Bismarck, ND 58507-7246; 701-224-1815, Fax: 701-224-9824.
www.nddentalboard.org
Agency email: ndsbde@aptnd.com.

#11 Board of Dietetic Practice, PO Box 6142, Grand Forks, ND 58206-6142; 701-777-2539, Fax: 701-777-3268.

#12 Board of Examiners in Audiology/Speech Pathology, 720 4th St N, Fargo, ND 58122; 701-777-4421, Fax: 701-777-4365.

#13 Board of Examiners in Nursing Home Adminstrators, 1900 N 11th St, Bismarck, ND 58501-1914; 701-222-4867, Fax: 701-223-0977. Agency email: hermanh@btigate.com.

#14 Board of Pharmacy, PO Box 1354, Bismarck, ND 58502-1354; 701-328-9535, Fax: 701-258-9312.
www.nodakpharmacy.com
Agency email: ndboph@btinet.net.

#15 Dr. Hofsommer, Board of Podiatric Medicine, 2631 12th Ave S, Fargo, ND 58103-2354; 701-232-5479.

#16 Board of Psychologist Examiners, PO Box 8380 or 9830, Grand Forks, ND 58202; 701-777-3792, Fax: 701-777-3454.
www.governor.state.nd.us/boards/boards-query.asp?Board_ID=88

#17 Board of Registry for Professional Soil Classifier, 2493 4th Ave W, Dickinson, ND 58601; 701-225-3381.

#18 Board of Social Worker Examiners, PO Box 914, Bismarck, ND 58502-0914; 701-222-0255, Fax: 701-224-9824.
www.ndbswe.com
Agency email: ndbswe@aptnd.com.
Search database at
www.ndbswe.com/list/main_pg.htm

#19 Department of Agriculture, Livestock & Pesticide Programs, 600 E Boulevard Ave,Dept 602, Bismarck, ND 58505-0020; 701-328-2231, Fax: 701-328-4567.
www.agdepartment.com
Agency email: gthompso@state.nd.us.
Search database at www.agdepartment.com/Programs/Livestock/Livestock.html

#20 Department of Banking & Financial Institutions, 2000 Schaefer St #G, Bismarck, ND 58501-1204; 701-328-9933, Fax: 701-328-9955.
www.state.nd.us/dfi
Agency email: banking@state.nd.us.

#22 Department of Human Services, Children & Family Services, 600 E Boulevard Ave, Bismarck, ND 58505-0250; 701-328-2310, Fax: 701-328-2359.

#23 Department of Labor, 600 E Blvd Ave, Dept 406, Bismarck, ND 58505-0340; 701-328-2660, Fax: 701-328-2031.
www.state.nd.us/labor/services/ea-licensing.
Agency email: labor@state.nd.us.

#24 Department of Public Instruction, 600 E Boulevard Ave, 1st Fl-Judicial Wing, Bismarck, ND 58505-0440; 701-328-2260, Fax: 701-328-2461.
www.dpi.state.nd.us

#25 Electrical Board, PO Box 857 (721 Memorial Highway), Bismarck, ND 58502; 701-328-9522, Fax: 701-328-9524.
www.state.nd.us/electric
Agency email: electric@state.nd.us.

#26 Game & Fish Department, 100 N Bismarck Exprwy, Bismarck, ND 58501-5095; 701-328-6300, Fax: 701-328-6352.
www.state.nd.us/gnf
Agency email: ndgf@state.nd.us.

#27 Department of Health, Asbestos Control Program, PO Box 5520 (1200 Missouri Ave), Bismarck, ND 58506-5520; 701-328-5188, Fax: 701-328-5200.
www.health.state.nd.us/ndhd/environ/ee/rad/asb/
Search database at
www.health.state.nd.us/ndhd/environ/ee/rad/asb

#28 Insurance Department, Producer/Agent Information, 600 E Boulevard Ave, Capitol Bldg, 1st Fl, Bismarck, ND 58505-0320; 701-328-2440, Fax: 701-328-4880.
www.state.nd.us/ndins/prodinfo/license.html.
Agency email: insuranc@state.nd.us.

#29 Board of Veterinarian ExaminERS, PO Box 5001, Bismarck, ND 58502-5001; 701-328-9540, Fax: 701-224-0435
Agency email: ndbvme@state.nd.us.

#30 Aeronautics Commission, PO Box 5020, Bismarck, ND 58502-5020; 701-328-9650, Fax: 701-328-9656.
www.state.nd.us/ndaero
Agency email: ndaero@state.nd.us.

#31 Board of Nursing, 919 S 7th St #504, Bismarck, ND 58504-5881; 701-328-9777, Fax: 701-328-9785.
www.ndbon.org

#32 State Board of Plumbing, 204 W Thayer Av, Bismarck, ND 58501; 701-328-9977, Fax: 701-328-9979.
http://governor.state.nd.us/boards/boards-query.asp?Board_ID=83
Agency email: ndplumb@state.nd.us.

#33 Private Investigation & Security Board, Private Investigators Licensing, 513 E Bismarck Expy, #5, Bismarck, ND 58504-6577; 701-222-3063, Fax: 701-222-3063.
http:www.state.nd.us./pisb
Agency email: ndpisb@midco.net.

#34 Public Service Commission, 600 E Boulevard Ave, Dept 408, Bismarck, ND 58505-0480; 701-328-4097, Fax: 701-328-2410.
www.psc.state.nd.us
Agency email: skr@oracle.psc.state.nd.us.

#35 Real Estate Commission, PO Box 727, Bismarck, ND 58502-0727; 701-328-9749, Fax: 701-328-9750. Agency email: ddschulz@pioneer.state.nd.us.

#36 Registration for Prof. Engineers & Land Surveyors, PO Box 1357, Bismarck, ND 58502-1357; 701-258-0786, Fax: 701-258-7471.

#37 Respiratory Care Examining Board, PO Box 2223, Bismarck, ND 58502; 701-222-1564, Fax: 701-255-9149.
www.governor.state.nd.us/boards/boards-query.asp?Board_ID=96
Agency email: ndsbrc@btigate.com.

#38 Secretary of State, Athletic Commissioner, Licensing Division, 600 East Blvd Ave, Dept 108, Bismarck, ND 58505-0040; 701-328-2900, Fax: 701-328-1690.
www.state.nd.us/sec
Agency email: sosadlic@state.nd.us.

#39 Secretary of State, Licensing Division, 600 East Blvd Ave, Dept 108, Bismarck, ND 58505-0500; 701-328-3665, Fax: 701-328-1690.
www.state.nd.us/sec
Agency email: sosadlic@state.nd.us.
Search database at www.state.nd.us/sec/administrativelicencing.htm

#40 Securities Commissioner, 600 E Blvd Ave, Dept 414, State Capitol, 5th Fl, Bismarck, ND 58505-0510; 701-328-2910, Fax: 701-255-3113.
www.state.nd.us/securities
Agency email: seccom@state.nd.us.

#41 Bar Board, 600 E Boulevard Ave, Dept. 180, Bismarck, ND 58505-0530; 701-328-4201, Fax: 701-328-4480.
www.court.state.nd.us
Search database at www.court.state.nd.us/court/lawyers/index/frameset.htm

#42 Board of Accountancy, 2701 S Columbia Rd, Grand Forks, ND 58201-6029; 800-532-5904, Fax: 701-775-7430.
www.state.nd.us/ndsba
Agency email: ndsba@pioneer.state.nd.us.
Search database at www.state.nd.us/ndsba/database/sbasearch.asp

#44 Board of Funeral Service, PO Box 633, Devil's Lake, ND 58301; 701-662-2511, Fax: 701-662-2501.

#45 Board of Examiners for Hearing Instrument Dispensers, 825 25th St SW, Fargo, ND 58103; 701-237-9977.

#46 Richard Radspinner, Board of Massage, 104 Georgia, Bismarck, ND 58504; 701-255-1525.

#47 Board of Medical Examiners, 418 E. Broadway #12, Bismarck, ND 58501; 701-328-6500, Fax: 701-328-6505.
www.ndbomex.com
Agency email: bomex@tic.bisman.com.
Search database at www.sdofnd.com/cart/ndbomex/Search%20Page.asp

#48 Board of Occupational Therapy Practice, PO Box 4005, Bismarck, ND 58502-4005; 701-250-0847, Fax: 701-224-9824.
www.ndotboard.com
Agency email: ndotboard@aptnd.com.

#49 Board of Optometry, 341 1st St E, Dickinson, ND 58601; 701-483-9141, Fax: 701-483-9501.
www.ndsbopt.org
Agency email: ndsbopt@dickinson.ctctel.com.
Search database at www.ndsbopt.org/directory.asp

#50 Board of Water Well Contractors, 900 E Boulevard Ave, Bismarck, ND 58505; 701-328-2754, Fax: 701-328-3696.

#51 Examining Committee of Physical Therapists, PO Box 69, Grafton, ND 58237; 701-352-0125, Fax: 701-352-3093. Agency email: ndsecpt@uslink.net.

#53 Board of Clinical Laboratory Practice, PO Box 4103, Bismarck, ND 58502-4103; 701-530-0199, Fax: 701-224-9824.
www.ndclinlab.com
Agency email: ndbclp@aptned.com.

North Dakota Federal Courts

The following list indicates the district and division name for each county in the state. If the bankruptcy court location is different from the district court, then the location of the bankruptcy court appears in parentheses.

County/Court Cross Reference

Adams	Bismarck-Southwestern (Fargo)	McLean	Bismarck-Southwestern (Fargo)
Barnes	Fargo-Southeastern (Fargo)	Mercer	Bismarck-Southwestern (Fargo)
Benson	Grand Forks-Northeastern (Fargo)	Morton	Bismarck-Southwestern (Fargo)
Billings	Bismarck-Southwestern (Fargo)	Mountrail	Minot-Northwestern (Fargo)
Bottineau	Minot-Northwestern (Fargo)	Nelson	Grand Forks-Northeastern (Fargo)
Bowman	Bismarck-Southwestern (Fargo)	Oliver	Bismarck-Southwestern (Fargo)
Burke	Minot-Northwestern (Fargo)	Pembina	Grand Forks-Northeastern (Fargo)
Burleigh	Bismarck-Southwestern (Fargo)	Pierce	Minot-Northwestern (Fargo)
Cass	Fargo-Southeastern (Fargo)	Ramsey	Grand Forks-Northeastern (Fargo)
Cavalier	Grand Forks-Northeastern (Fargo)	Ransom	Fargo-Southeastern (Fargo)
Dickey	Fargo-Southeastern (Fargo)	Renville	Minot-Northwestern (Fargo)
Divide	Minot-Northwestern (Fargo)	Richland	Fargo-Southeastern (Fargo)
Dunn	Bismarck-Southwestern (Fargo)	Rolette	Minot-Northwestern (Fargo)
Eddy	Fargo-Southeastern (Fargo)	Sargent	Fargo-Southeastern (Fargo)
Emmons	Bismarck-Southwestern (Fargo)	Sheridan	Minot-Northwestern (Fargo)
Foster	Fargo-Southeastern (Fargo)	Sioux	Bismarck-Southwestern (Fargo)
Golden Valley	Bismarck-Southwestern (Fargo)	Slope	Bismarck-Southwestern (Fargo)
Grand Forks	Grand Forks-Northeastern (Fargo)	Stark	Bismarck-Southwestern (Fargo)
Grant	Bismarck-Southwestern (Fargo)	Steele	Fargo-Southeastern (Fargo)
Griggs	Fargo-Southeastern (Fargo)	Stutsman	Fargo-Southeastern (Fargo)
Hettinger	Bismarck-Southwestern (Fargo)	Towner	Grand Forks-Northeastern (Fargo)
Kidder	Bismarck-Southwestern (Fargo)	Traill	Grand Forks-Northeastern (Fargo)
La Moure	Fargo-Southeastern (Fargo)	Walsh	Grand Forks-Northeastern (Fargo)
Logan	Bismarck-Southwestern (Fargo)	Ward	Minot-Northwestern (Fargo)
McHenry	Minot-Northwestern (Fargo)	Wells	Minot-Northwestern (Fargo)
McIntosh	Bismarck-Southwestern (Fargo)	Williams	Minot-Northwestern (Fargo)
McKenzie	Minot-Northwestern (Fargo)		

Standards for Federal Courts: The search fee is $20.00 per item (one party name or case number). Certification fee is $7.00 per document. Copy fee is $.50 per page. All fees standard unless noted in profile. Mail Search: always enclose a stamped self addressed envelope unless otherwise noted. Before releasing records, all courts require prepayment unless noted in profile. Open records are located at the court unless otherwise noted. District courts index by defendant and plaintiff as well as by case number. Bankruptcy courts usually index by debtor and case number. While most courts now have their indexes on computer, many still maintain index card files as well. The universal PACER sign-up number is 800-676-6856. Find PACER and the Party/Case Index on the Web at http://pacer.psc.uscourts.gov. PACER dial-up access is $.60 per minute. Also, courts offering internet access via RACER, PACER, Web-PACER or the new CM-ECF charge $.07 per page fee unless noted as free.

US District Court

District of North Dakota

Bismarck-Southwestern Division PO Box 1193, Bismarck, ND 58502 (Courier Address: 220 E Rosser Ave, Room 476, Bismarck, ND 58501), 701-530-2300, Fax: 701-530-2312.

www.ndd.uscourts.gov

Counties: Adams, Billings, Bowman, Burleigh, Dunn, Emmons, Golden Valley, Grant, Hettinger, Kidder, Logan, McIntosh, McLean, Mercer, Morton, Oliver, Sioux, Slope, Stark.

Indexing & Storage: Cases are indexed by defendant, plaintiff, and case number. New cases are available in the index 24 hours after filing date. Records are on computer and stored as hard copy records. Open records are located at this court.

Fee & Payment Notes: Payment may be made by money order, cashier check, in-state business check. In state personal checks are also accepted. Court will bill for copies. Payee: Clerk, US District Court.

Phone Search: Only docket information is available by phone.

Mail Search: A stamped self addressed envelope is not required.

In Person Search: In person searching available.

PACER: Toll-free dial-up access: 800-407-4453. Local dial-up access: 701-530-2367. Case records are available back to October 1990. Records are never purged. New records are available online after 1 day.

Fargo-Southeastern Division PO Box 870, Fargo, ND 58107 (Courier Address: 655 1st Ave N, Fargo, ND 58102), 701-297-7000, Fax: 701-297-7005.

www.ndd.uscourts.gov

Counties: Barnes, Cass, Dickey, Eddy, Foster, Griggs, La Moure, Ransom, Richland, Sargent, Steele, Stutsman. Rolette County cases prior to 1995 may be located here.

Indexing & Storage: Cases are indexed by defendant, plaintiff, and case number. New cases are available in the index 1 day after filing date. Civil cases prior to 10/90 are on index cards as well as all criminal records. Current records are on computer and stored as hard copy records. Open records are located at this court.

Fee & Payment Notes: Payment may be made by money order, cashier check, in-state business check. In state personal checks are also accepted. Payee: Clerk, US District Court.

Phone Search: Only docket information is available by phone.

Fax Search: Will accept fax search request, but results are held until payment received. Will fax results at $.50 per page paid in advance.

Mail Search: A stamped self addressed envelope is not required.

In Person Search: In person searching available.

PACER: Toll-free dial-up access: 800-407-4453. Local dial-up access: 701-530-2367. Case records are available back to October 1990. Records are never purged. New records are available online after 1 day.

Grand Forks-Northeastern Division c/o Fargo-Southeastern Division, 102 N 4th St, Grand Forks, ND 58201 (Courier Address: 655 1st Ave N, Fargo, ND 58102), 701-772-0511, Fax: 701-746-7544.

www.ndd.uscourts.gov

Counties: Benson, Cavalier, Grand Forks, Nelson, Pembina, Ramsey, Towner, Traill, Walsh.

Indexing & Storage: New cases are available in the index after filing date. Open records are located at the Fargo-SE Division.

Fee & Payment Notes: Payment may be made by money order, cashier check. Business checks are not accepted. Personal checks are not accepted.

Phone Search: Searching not available by phone.

Mail Search: A stamped self addressed envelope is not required.

In Person Search: In person searching available.

PACER: Toll-free dial-up access: 800-407-4453. Local dial-up access: 701-530-2367. Case records are available back to October 1990. Records are never purged. New records are available online after 1 day.

Minot-Northwestern Division c/o Bismarck Division, PO Box 1193, Bismarck, ND 58502 (Courier Address: 100 1st St SW, Minot, ND 58701), 701-839-6251, Fax: 701-838-3276.

www.ndd.uscourts.gov

Counties: Bottineau, Burke, Divide, McHenry, McKenzie, Mountrail, Pierce, Renville, Rolette, Sheridan, Ward, Wells, Williams. Case records from Rolette County prior to 1995 may be located in Fargo-Southeastern Division.

Indexing & Storage: New cases are available in the index after filing date. Open records are located at the Bismarck Division.

Fee & Payment Notes: Payment may be made by money order, cashier check. Business checks are not accepted. Personal checks are not accepted.

Phone Search: Searching not available by phone.

Mail Search: A stamped self addressed envelope is not required.

In Person Search: In person searching available.

PACER: Toll-free dial-up access: 800-407-4453. Local dial-up access: 701-530-2367. Case records are available back to October 1990. Records are never purged. New records are available online after 1 day.

US Bankruptcy Court

District of North Dakota

Fargo Division 655 1st Ave N #210, Fargo, ND 58102-4932 (Courier Address: Room 236, Federal Bldg & US Courthouse, Fargo, ND 58102), 701-297-7104.

www.ndb.uscourts.gov

Counties: All counties in North Dakota.

Indexing & Storage: Cases are indexed by debtor as well as by case number. New cases are available in the index 1 day after filing date. Open records are located at this court.

Fee & Payment Notes: Payment may be made by money order, cashier check, business check. Personal checks are not accepted. Exemplification costs $10.00 per document. The court will FAX in an emergency for $.50 per page sending or receiving. Payee: Clerk, US Bankruptcy Court.

Phone Search: Only docket information available by telephone. An automated voice case information service (VCIS) is available. Call VCIS at 701-297-7166.

Mail Search: A stamped self addressed envelope is not required.

In Person Search: In person searching available.

PACER: Toll-free dial-up access: 800-810-4092. Local dial-up access: 701-297-7164. Document images available on Pacer. Case records are available back to 1990. New civil records are available online after 1 day. PACER is available online at http://pacer.okwd.uscourts.gov.

Other Online Access: Search records on the Internet using RACER at https://racer.ndb.uscourts.gov/perl/bkplog.html.

North Dakota County Courts

Court	Jurisdiction	No. of Courts	How Organized
District Courts*	General	53	7 Judicial Districts
Municipal Courts	Municipal	76	76 Cities

* Profiled in this Sourcebook.

	CIVIL								
Court	Tort	Contract	Real Estate	Min. Claim	Max. Claim	Small Claims	Estate	Eviction	Domestic Relations
District Courts*	X	X	X	$0	No Max	$5000	X	X	X
Municipal Courts									

	CRIMINAL				
Court	Felony	Misdemeanor	DWI/DUI	Preliminary Hearing	Juvenile
District Courts*	X	X	X	X	X
Municipal Courts			X		

ADMINISTRATION
State Court Administrator, North Dakota Judiciary, 600 E Blvd, 1st Floor Judicial Wing, Dept. 180, Bismarck, ND, 58505-0530; 701-328-4216, Fax: 701-328-2092. www.ndcourts.com or www.court.state.nd.us

COURT STRUCTURE
In 1995, the County Courts merged with the District Courts statewide. County court records are maintained by the 53 District Court Clerks in the seven judicial districts. We recommend stating "include all County Court cases" in search requests. There are 76 Municipal Courts that handle traffic cases.

ONLINE ACCESS
A statewide computer system for internal purposes is in operation in most counties. You may now search North Dakota Supreme Court dockets and opinions at www.ndcourts.com. Search by docket number, party name, or anything else that may appear in the text. Records are from 1991 forward. Email notification of new opinions is also available.

ADDITIONAL INFORMATION
In the summer of 1997, the standard search fee in District Courts increased to $10.00 per name, and the certification fee increased to $10.00 per document. Copy fees remain at $.50 per page, but many courts charge only $.25.

📖📖📖📖📖📖📖

Adams County

Southwest Judicial District Court 602 Adams Ave, PO Box 469, Hettinger, ND 58639; 701-567-2460; Fax: 701-567-2910. Hours: 8:30AM-5PM (MST). *Felony, Misdemeanor, Civil, Eviction, Small Claims, Probate.*

Civil Records: Access: Fax, mail, in person. Both court and visitors may perform in person searches. Search fee: $10.00 per name. Required to search: name, years to search; also helpful: address. Civil cases indexed by defendant, plaintiff. Civil records on index cards from 1990, on docket books in vault from 1900s.

Criminal Records: Access: Fax, mail, in person. Both court and visitors may perform in person searches. Search fee: $10.00 per name. Required to search: name, years to search, DOB; also helpful: address. Criminal records on index cards from 1990, on docket books in vault from 1900s.

General Information: No adoptions, sealed, juvenile, mental health, expunged, DV or dismissed records released. SASE required. Turnaround time 1-2 days. Fax notes: Fee to fax results is $3.00 1st 2 pages, $.50 each add'l. Copy fee: $.25 per page. Certification fee:

$10.00. Fee payee: Clerk of District Court. Personal checks accepted. Prepayment is required.

Barnes County

Southeast Judicial District Court PO Box 774, Valley City, ND 58072; 701-845-8512; Fax: 701-845-1341. Hours: 8AM-5PM (CST). *Felony, Misdemeanor, Civil, Eviction, Small Claims, Probate.*

Civil Records: Access: Fax, mail, in person. Only the court performs in person searches; visitors may not. Search fee: $10.00 per name. Required to search: name, years to search; also helpful: address. Civil cases indexed by defendant, plaintiff. Civil records on index books from early 1900s; on computer back to 1996.

Criminal Records: Access: Fax, mail, in person. Only the court performs in person searches; visitors may not. Search fee: $10.00 per name. Required to search: name, years to search; also helpful: address, DOB, SSN. Criminal records maintained here for 10 years, archived on index books from early 1900s; on computer back to 1996.

General Information: No adoptions, paternity, sealed, juvenile, mental health, expunged or dismissed records released. SASE required. Turnaround time 1-2 days.

Fax notes: $10.00 per document. Copy fee: $.25 per page. Certification fee: $10.00. $5.00 for second copy. Fee payee: Clerk of District Court. Personal checks accepted. Prepayment is required.

Benson County

Northeast Judicial District Court PO Box 213, Minnewaukan, ND 58351; 701-473-5345; Fax: 701-473-5571. Hours: 8:30AM-4:30PM (CST). *Felony, Misdemeanor, Civil, Eviction, Small Claims, Probate.*

Civil Records: Access: Fax, mail, in person. Only the court performs in person searches; visitors may not. Search fee: $10.00 per name. Fee is for written confirmation. Required to search: name, years to search; also helpful: address. Civil cases indexed by defendant, plaintiff. Civil records on docket books and index books from early 1900s, on index cards from 6/10/91.

Criminal Records: Access: Fax, mail, in person. Only the court performs in person searches; visitors may not. Search fee: $10.00 per name. Fee is for written confirmation. Required to search: name, years to search, DOB, signed release; also helpful: address. Criminal records on docket books and index books from early

1900s, on index cards from 6/10/91. Signed release required for juvenile cases.

General Information: No adoptions, sealed, juvenile, mental health, expunged or dismissed records released. SASE not required. Turnaround time 5 days. Fax notes: $1.00 per page. Copy fee: $1.00 per page. Certification fee: $10.00. Fee payee: Benson County Court. Personal checks accepted. Prepayment is required.

Billings County

Southwest Judicial District Court PO Box 138, Medora, ND 58645; 701-623-4492; Fax: 701-623-4896. Hours: 9AM-Noon, 1-5PM (MST). *Felony, Misdemeanor, Civil, Eviction, Small Claims, Probate.*

Civil Records: Access: Fax, mail, in person. Both court and visitors may perform in person searches. Search fee: $10.00 per name. Required to search: name, years to search; also helpful: address. Civil cases indexed by defendant, plaintiff. Civil records on index cards from 1986, on index books from 1800s.

Criminal Records: Access: Fax, mail, in person. Both court and visitors may perform in person searches. Search fee: $10.00 per name. Required to search: name, years to search; also helpful: address, DOB, SSN. Criminal records in books.

General Information: No adoptions, sealed, juvenile, mental health, expunged or dismissed records released. SASE required. Turnaround time 2-3 days. Fax notes: Fax fee $2.00 1st 4 pages, $.50 each additional page. Copy fee: $.25 per page. Certification fee: $10.00 plus $5.00 each add'l page. Fee payee: Clerk of District Court. Personal checks accepted. Prepayment is required.

Bottineau County

Northeast Judicial District Court 314 W 5th St, Bottineau, ND 58318; 701-228-3983; Fax: 701-228-2336. *Felony, Misdemeanor, Civil, Eviction, Small Claims, Probate.*

Civil Records: Access: Fax, mail, in person. Only the court performs in person searches; visitors may not. Search fee: $10.00 per name. Required to search: name, years to search; also helpful: address. Civil cases indexed by defendant, plaintiff. Civil records on index cards from 1987, on docket books from 1972.

Criminal Records: Access: Fax, mail, in person. Only the court performs in person searches; visitors may not. Search fee: $10.00 per name. Required to search: name, years to search; also helpful: address, DOB, SSN. Criminal records on docket books from 1885.

General Information: No adoptions, paternity, sealed, juvenile, mental health, expunged or dismissed records released. SASE required. Turnaround time 1 day. Fax notes: $4.00 for first page, $2.00 each add'l. Copy fee: $.20 per page. Certification fee: $10.00. Fee payee: Clerk of the Court. Personal checks accepted. Prepayment is required.

Bowman County

Southwest Judicial District Court PO Box 379, Bowman, ND 58623; 701-523-3450; Fax: 701-523-5443. Hours: 8:00AM-Noon, 1-4:30PM (MST). *Felony, Misdemeanor, Civil, Eviction, Small Claims, Probate.*

Civil Records: Access: Mail, in person, phone, fax. Both court and visitors may perform in person searches. Search fee: $10.00 per name. Required to search: name, years to search; also helpful: address. Civil cases indexed by defendant, plaintiff. Civil records on microfiche from 1978, on dockets from 1907; computerized records back to 1995.

Criminal Records: Access: Mail, in person. Both court and visitors may perform in person searches. Search fee: $10.00 per name. Required to search: name, years to search, DOB; also helpful: address. Criminal records

on microfiche from 1978, on dockets from 1907; computerized records back to 1995.

General Information: No adoptions, sealed, juvenile, mental health, expunged or dismissed records released. SASE required. Turnaround time 1-2 days. Copy fee: $1.00 per page. Certification fee: $10.00. Fee payee: Clerk of Court. Personal checks accepted. Prepayment is required.

Burke County

Northwest Judicial District Court PO Box 219, Bowbells, ND 58721; 701-377-2718; Fax: 701-377-2020. Hours: 8:30AM-Noon, 1-5 PM (CST). *Felony, Misdemeanor, Civil, Eviction, Small Claims, Probate.*

Civil Records: Access: Mail, in person. Both court and visitors may perform in person searches. Search fee: $10.00 if a written reply is required. Required to search: name, years to search; also helpful: address. Civil cases indexed by defendant, plaintiff. Civil records for county civil, probate, and district from 1910, county criminal and small claims from 1980.

Criminal Records: Access: Mail, in person. Both court and visitors may perform in person searches. Search fee: $10.00 if a written reply is required. Required to search: name, years to search; also helpful: address, DOB, SSN. Criminal records for county civil, probate, and district from 1910, county criminal and small claims from 1980.

General Information: No adoptions, sealed, juvenile, mental health, expunged or dismissed records released. SASE not required. Turnaround time 1-3 days. Fax notes: Fee to fax results is $2.00 per page. Copy fee: $.50 per page. Certification fee: $10.00. Fee payee: Clerk of Court. Personal checks accepted. Prepayment is required.

Burleigh County

South Central Judicial District Court PO Box 1055, Bismarck, ND 58502; 701-222-6690; Criminal phone: Fax: 701-222-6758; Fax: 701-221-3756. Hours: 8AM-5PM (CST). *Felony, Misdemeanor, Civil, Eviction, Small Claims, Probate.*

Civil Records: Access: Mail, in person. Both court and visitors may perform in person searches. Search fee: $10.00 per name. Required to search: name; also helpful: years to search. Civil cases indexed by defendant, plaintiff. Civil records on computer back to 1/91; in books from 1800s.

Criminal Records: Access: Mail, in person. Both court and visitors may perform in person searches. Search fee: $10.00 per name. Required to search: name; also helpful: years to search, address, DOB, SSN. Criminal records on computer back to 1/91; in books from early 1900s.

General Information: Public access terminal is available. No adoptions, sealed, juvenile, mental health, expunged or dismissed records released. SASE required. Turnaround time 1-2 days. Copy fee: $.25 per page; $1 minimum. Certification fee: $10.00 plus $5.00 each add'l copy of same document, if needed. Fee payee: Clerk of Court. Personal checks accepted. Prepayment is required.

Cass County

East Central Judicial District Court 211 South 9th St, PO Box 2802, Fargo, ND 58108; 701-241-5645; Fax: 701-241-5636. Hours: 8AM-5PM (CST). *Felony, Misdemeanor, Civil, Eviction, Small Claims, Probate.*

Civil Records: Access: Mail, fax, in person. Only the court performs in person searches; visitors may not. Search fee: $10.00 per name. Required to search: name, years to search; also helpful: address. Civil cases indexed by defendant, plaintiff. Civil records on computer from 1988, on index books from late 1800s.

Criminal Records: Access: Mail,fax, in person. Only the court performs in person searches; visitors may not. Search fee: $10.00 per name. Required to search: name, years to search; also helpful: address, DOB, SSN. Criminal records on computer from 1988, on index cards from 1980.

General Information: No adoptions, sealed, juvenile, mental health, expunged or dismissed records released. SASE required. Turnaround time 3-5 days. Copy fee: $.25 per page. $1.00 minimum. Certification fee: $10.00. Fee payee: Clerk of District Court. Personal checks accepted. Prepayment is required.

Cavalier County

Northeast Judicial District Court 901 Third St, Langdon, ND 58249; 701-256-2124; Fax: 701-256-2124. Hours: 8:30AM-4:30PM (CST). *Felony, Misdemeanor, Civil, Eviction, Small Claims, Probate.*

Civil Records: Access: Fax, mail, in person. Only the court performs in person searches; visitors may not. Search fee: $10.00 per name. Required to search: name, years to search; also helpful: address. Civil cases indexed by defendant, plaintiff. Civil records going on computer, prior stored.

Criminal Records: Access: Fax, mail, in person. Only the court performs in person searches; visitors may not. Search fee: $10.00 per name. Required to search: name, years to search; also helpful: address, DOB, SSN. Criminal records for District Court on index books from 1937, for County Court on index books from 1983, prior stored.

General Information: No adoptions, sealed, juvenile, mental health, expunged or dismissed records released. SASE required. Turnaround time 1 week. Fax notes: No fee to fax results. Copy fee: $.25 per page. Certification fee: $10.00. Fee payee: Clerk of Court. Personal checks accepted. Prepayment is required.

Dickey County

Southeast Judicial District Court PO Box 336, Ellendale, ND 58436; 701-349-3249 X4; Fax: 701-349-3560. Hours: 9AM-Noon, 1-5PM (CST). *Felony, Misdemeanor, Civil, Eviction, Small Claims, Probate.*

Civil Records: Access: Mail, in person. Only the court performs in person searches; visitors may not. Search fee: $10.00 per name. Required to search: name, years to search; also helpful: address. Civil cases indexed by defendant, plaintiff. Civil records on index books from 1983; on computer back to 1997. Probate from 1800s. Old district court records have no index and are very hard to find.

Criminal Records: Access: Mail, in person. Both the court and visitors may performs in person searches. Search fee: $10.00 per name. Required to search: name, years to search, DOB; also helpful: address, SSN. Criminal records on index books from 1983, on computer back to 1997. Old district court records have no index and are very hard to find.

General Information: No adoptions, sealed, juvenile, mental health, expunged or dismissed records released. SASE not required. Turnaround time 1-2 days. Copy fee: $.25 per page. Certification fee: $10.00. Fee payee: Clerk of Court. Personal checks accepted. Prepayment is required.

Divide County

Northwest Judicial District Court PO Box 68, Crosby, ND 58730; 701-965-6831; Fax: 701-965-6943. Hours: 8:30AM-Noon, 1-5PM (CST). *Felony, Misdemeanor, Civil, Eviction, Small Claims, Probate.*

Civil Records: Access: Fax, mail, in person. Only the court performs in person searches; visitors may not. Search fee: $10.00 per name. Required to search: name, years to search; also helpful: address. Civil cases indexed by defendant, plaintiff. Civil records on index books from 1910. Visitor can check for judgments. Records for eviction, smalll claims and probate are an additonal $10.00 if full certification needed.

Criminal Records: Access: Fax, mail, in person. Only the court performs in person searches; visitors may not. Search fee: $10.00 per name. Required to search: name, years to search; also helpful: address, DOB, SSN. Criminal records on index books from 1910.

General Information: No adoptions, sealed, juvenile, mental health, expunged or dismissed records released. SASE required. Turnaround time 1-2 days. Fax notes: $3.00 for first page, $1.00 each add'l. There is also a charge of $1.00 per incoming fax page. Copy fee: $.25 per page. $1.00 minimum. Certification fee: Included in search fee. Fee payee: Clerk of District Court. Personal checks accepted. Prepayment is required.

Dunn County

District Court PO Box 136, Manning, ND 58642-0136; 701-573-4447; Fax: 701-573-4444. Hours: 8AM-Noon,12:30-4:30PM (MST). *Felony, Misdemeanor, Civil, Small Claims, Probate.*

Civil Records: Access: Fax, mail, in person. Both court and visitors may perform in person searches. Search fee: $10.00 per name. Required to search: name, years to search; also helpful: address. Civil cases indexed by defendant, plaintiff. Civil records on plaintiff/defendant index cards from 1988, on docket books from 1900s, on computer since 01/97. Fax requests must fax copy of the check to be mailed.

Criminal Records: Access: Fax, mail, in person. Both court and visitors may perform in person searches. Search fee: $10.00 per name. Required to search: name, years to search, DOB; also helpful: address, SSN. Criminal records on plaintiff/defendant index cards from 1988, on docket books from 1900s, on computer since 01/97. Fax requesters must fax copy of the check, which can be mailed.

General Information: Public access terminal is available. Adoptions, paternity, juvenile, mental health, deferred impositions, and termination of parental rights are restricted access files. SASE not required. Turnaround time 2 days. Fax notes: $2.00 plus $1.00 each page. Copy fee: $2.00 plus $.50 each page (mailed copies). Certification fee: $10.00. Fee payee: Dunn County Clerk of Court. Personal checks accepted. In state personal checks accepted. Prepayment is required.

Eddy County

Southeast Judicial District Court 524 Central Ave, New Rockford, ND 58356; 701-947-2813; Fax: 701-947-2067. Hours: 8AM-4PM (CST). *Felony, Misdemeanor, Civil, Eviction, Small Claims, Probate.*

Civil Records: Access: Fax, mail, in person. Only the court performs in person searches; visitors may not. Search fee: $10.00 per name. Required to search: name, years to search; also helpful: address. Civil cases indexed by defendant, plaintiff. Civil records on index cards from 4/92, on index books from early 1900s. All requests must be in writing.

Criminal Records: Access: Fax, mail, in person. Only the court performs in person searches; visitors may not. Search fee: $10.00 per name. Required to search: name, years to search; also helpful: address, DOB, SSN. Criminal records on index cards from 4/92, on index books from early 1900s. All requests must be in writing.

General Information: No adoptions, sealed, juvenile, mental health, expunged or dismissed records released. SASE required. Turnaround time 1-2 days. Fax notes: Fax fee $4.00 1st 3 pages, $1.00 each additional page. Copy fee: $1.00 per document. Certification fee: $10.00. Fee payee: Eddy County District Court. Personal checks accepted.

Emmons County

South Central Judicial District Court PO Box 905, Linton, ND 58552; 701-254-4812; Fax: 701-254-4012. Hours: 8:30AM-Noon, 1-5PM (CST). *Felony, Misdemeanor, Civil, Eviction, Small Claims, Probate.*

Civil Records: Access: Fax, mail, in person. Only the court performs in person searches; visitors may not. Search fee: $10.00 per name. Required to search: name, years to search; also helpful: address. Civil cases indexed by defendant, plaintiff. Civil records on index cards from 1988, on index books from 1914, on computer back to 1995.

Criminal Records: Access: Fax, mail, in person. Only the court performs in person searches; visitors may not. Search fee: $10.00 per name. Required to search: name, years to search, DOB; also helpful: address, SSN. Criminal records on index books back to 1983; on computer back to 1995.

General Information: No adoptions, sealed, juvenile, mental health, expunged or dismissed records released. SASE required. Turnaround time 1-2 days. Fax notes: Fee to fax results is $3.00 1st page, $1.00 each add'l. Copy fee: $.20 per page. Certification fee: $10.00. Fee payee: Clerk of Courts. Personal checks accepted. Prepayment is required.

Foster County

Southeast Judicial District Court PO Box 257, Carrington, ND 58421; 701-652-1001; Fax: 701-652-2173. Hours: 8:30AM-4:30PM (CST). *Felony, Misdemeanor, Civil, Eviction, Small Claims, Probate.*

Civil Records: Access: Mail, in person. Both court and visitors may perform in person searches. Search fee: $10.00 per name if court performs search. Required to search: name, years to search; also helpful: address. Civil cases indexed by defendant, plaintiff. Civil records on index books from early 1900s.

Criminal Records: Access: Mail, in person. Both court and visitors may perform in person searches. Search fee: $10.00 per name if court performs search. Required to search: name, years to search, DOB; also helpful: address. Criminal records on index books from early 1900s.

General Information: No adoptions, sealed, juvenile, mental health, expunged or dismissed records released. SASE required. Turnaround time 1-2 days. Fax notes: Fee to fax results is $3.00 per document. Copy fee: $1.00 per page. Certification fee: $10.00. Fee payee: Clerk of Courts. Personal checks accepted. Prepayment is required.

Golden Valley County

Southwest Judicial District Court PO Box 9, Beach, ND 58621-0009; 701-872-4352; Fax: 701-872-4383. Hours: 8-Noon, 1-4PM (MST). *Felony, Misdemeanor, Civil, Eviction, Small Claims, Probate.*

Civil Records: Access: Fax, mail, in person. Only the court performs in person searches; visitors may not. Search fee: $10.00 per name. Required to search: name, years to search; also helpful: address. Civil cases indexed by defendant, plaintiff. Civil records on index cards from 1987, on index books from 1913 to 1960. From 1960 to 1987, records are hard to find; there is no indexing and files are filed by number. Fax request must include copy of check.

Criminal Records: Access: Fax, mail, in person. Only the court performs in person searches; visitors may not. Search fee: $10.00 per name. Required to search: name, years to search, DOB; also helpful: address, SSN. Criminal records on index cards from 1987, on index books from 1913 to 1960. From 1960 to 1987, records are hard to find; there is no indexing and files are filed by number. Fax request must include copy of check.

General Information: No adoptions, sealed, juvenile, mental health, expunged or dismissed records released. SASE required. Turnaround time 3-4 days. Fax notes: $1.00 per page. Copy fee: $.50 per page. Certification fee: $10.00. Fee payee: Clerk of Court. Personal checks accepted. Prepayment is required.

Grand Forks County

Northeast Central Judicial District Court PO Box 5939, Grand Forks, ND 58206-5939; 701-780-8214; Fax: 701-780-8217. Hours: 8AM-5PM (CST). *Felony, Misdemeanor, Civil, Eviction, Small Claims, Probate.*

Civil Records: Access: Mail, in person. Both court and visitors may perform in person searches. Search fee: $10.00 per name. Required to search: name, years to search; also helpful: address. Civil cases indexed by defendant, plaintiff. Civil records on computer from 10/91, on index books from early 1900s.

Criminal Records: Access: Mail, in person. Both court and visitors may perform in person searches. Search fee: $10.00 per name. Required to search: name, years to search, DOB, signed release; also helpful: address, SSN. Criminal records on computer from 10/91, on index books from early 1900s.

General Information: Public access terminal is available. No adoptions, sealed, juvenile, mental health, expunged or dismissed records released. SASE required. Turnaround time 1-2 days. Fax notes: Fee to receive fax is $5.00. Fee to fax results is $1.00 per page, $3.00 minimum. Copy fee: $.25 per page; $1.00 minimum. Certification fee: $10.00. Fee payee: Clerk of District Court. Personal checks accepted. Prepayment is required.

Grant County

South Central Judicial District Court PO Box 258, Carson, ND 58529; 701-622-3615; Fax: 701-622-3717. Hours: 8AM-Noon, 12:30-4PM (MST). *Felony, Misdemeanor, Civil, Eviction, Small Claims, Probate.*

Civil Records: Access: Fax, mail, in person. Both court and visitors may perform in person searches. Search fee: $10.00 per name. Required to search: name, years to search; also helpful: address. Civil cases indexed by defendant, plaintiff. Civil records on index cards from 1990, on docket books in vault from 1900s.

Criminal Records: Access: Fax, mail, in person. Both court and visitors may perform in person searches. Search fee: $10.00 per name. Required to search: name, years to search; also helpful: address, DOB, SSN. Criminal records on index cards from 1990, on docket books in vault from 1900s.

General Information: No adoptions, sealed, juvenile, mental health, expunged or dismissed records released. SASE not required. Turnaround time 1 day. Fax notes: $3.00 per document. Copy fee: $.25 per page. Certification fee: $10.00. Fee payee: Clerk of Grant County Court. Personal checks accepted. Prepayment is required.

Griggs County

Southeast Judicial District Court PO Box 326, Cooperstown, ND 58425; 701-797-2772; Fax: 701-797-3587. Hours: 8AM-Noon, 1-4:30PM (CST). *Felony, Misdemeanor, Civil, Eviction, Small Claims, Probate.*

Civil Records: Access: Fax, mail, in person. Both court and visitors may perform in person searches. Search fee: $10.00 per name. Required to search: name, years to search; also helpful: address. Civil cases indexed by defendant, plaintiff. Civil records on docket books from 1890 for District and 1983 for County. Phone access discouraged.

Criminal Records: Access: Fax, mail, in person. Both court and visitors may perform in person searches.

Search fee: $10.00 per name. Required to search: name, years to search; also helpful: address, DOB, SSN. Criminal records on docket books from 1890 for District and 1983 for County. Phone access discouraged.

General Information: No adoptions, sealed, juvenile, mental health, expunged or dismissed records released. SASE required. Turnaround time 1-2 days. Fax notes: $1.00 per page. Incoming fax, $1.00 1st page, $.50 each additional page. Free for attorneys. Copy fee: $.25 per page. Certification fee: $10.00. Fee payee: Clerk of Courts. Personal checks accepted. Prepayment required.

Hettinger County

Southwest Judicial District Court PO Box 668, Mott, ND 58646; 701-824-2645; Fax: 701-824-2717. Hours: 8AM-Noon, 1-4:30PM (MST). *Felony, Misdemeanor, Civil, Eviction, Small Claims, Probate.*

Civil Records: Access: Fax, mail, in person. Only the court performs in person searches; visitors may not. Search fee: $10.00 per name. Required to search: name, years to search; also helpful: address. Civil cases indexed by defendant, plaintiff. Civil records on index cards from 1987, on index books from 1908.

Criminal Records: Access: Fax, mail, in person. Only the court performs in person searches; visitors may not. Search fee: $10.00 per name. Required to search: name, years to search, DOB; also helpful: address. Criminal records on index cards from 1987, on index books from 1908.

General Information: No adoptions, sealed, juvenile, mental health, expunged or dismissed records released. SASE required. Turnaround time 1 day. Fax notes: $3.00 per document. Fee is for up to 20 pages. Copy fee: $.25 per page. Certification fee: $10.00. Fee payee: Hettinger Court Clerk. Personal checks accepted. Prepayment is required.

Kidder County

District Court PO Box 66, Steele, ND 58482; 701-475-2632; Fax: 701-475-2202. Hours: 9AM-5PM (CST). *Felony, Misdemeanor, Civil, Eviction, Small Claims, Probate.*

Civil Records: Access: Fax, mail, in person. Both court and visitors may perform in person searches; visitors may not. Search fee: $10.00 per name. Required to search: name, years to search; also helpful: address. Civil cases indexed by defendant, plaintiff. Civil records on index book from 1800s, on computer since 1990.

Criminal Records: Access: Mail, in person. Both court and visitors may perform in person searches. Search fee: $10.00 per name. Required to search: name, years to search, DOB; also helpful: address. Records on index book from 1900s, on computer since 1990.

General Information: Public access terminal is available. No adoptions, sealed, juvenile, mental health, expunged or dismissed records released. SASE required. Turnaround time 1-2 days. Fax notes: Fee to fax is $3.00 per document. Copy fee: $1.00 per page. Certification fee: $10.00. Fee payee: Clerk of Court. Personal checks accepted. Prepayment is required.

La Moure County

Southeast Judicial District Court PO Box 128, LaMoure, ND 58458; 701-883-5193; Fax: 701-883-5304. Hours: 9AM-Noon, 1-5PM (CST). *Felony, Misdemeanor, Civil, Eviction, Small Claims, Probate.*

Civil Records: Access: Fax, mail, in person. Both court and visitors may perform in person searches. Search fee: $10.00 per name. Required to search: name, years to search; also helpful: address. Civil cases indexed by defendant, plaintiff. Civil records on docket books from 1800s; on computer back to 2002.

Criminal Records: Access: Fax, mail, in person. Both court and visitors may perform in person searches. Search fee: $10.00 per name. Required to search: name,

years to search; also helpful: address, DOB. Criminal records go back to 1987.

General Information: No adoptions, sealed, juvenile, mental health, expunged or dismissed records released. SASE required. Turnaround time 1 day. Fax notes: Will not fax results without pre-payment. Copy fee: $.25 for first page, $.10 each add'l. Certification fee: $10.00. Fee payee: Clerk of Court. Personal checks accepted. Prepayment is required.

Logan County

South Central Judicial District Court PO Box 6, Napoleon, ND 58561; 701-754-2751; Fax: 701-754-2270. Hours: 8:30AM-4:30PM (CST). *Felony, Misdemeanor, Civil, Eviction, Small Claims, Probate.*

Civil Records: Access: Fax, mail, in person. Both court and visitors may perform in person searches. Search fee: $10.00 per name. Required to search: name, years to search; also helpful: address, signed release. Civil cases indexed by defendant, plaintiff. Civil records on index books from 1884.

Criminal Records: Access: Fax, mail, in person. The court may perform in person searches. Search fee: $10.00 per name. Required to search: name, years to search, DOB; also helpful: address, signed release. Criminal records on index books from 1890.

General Information: No adoptions, sealed, juvenile, mental health, expunged or dismissed records released. SASE required. Turnaround time 1-2 days. Fax notes: Fee to fax is $3.00 for first page, $1.00 each add'l. Copy fee: $1.00 per page. Certification fee: $10.00. Fee payee: Clerk of Court. Business checks accepted. Prepayment is required.

McHenry County

Northeast Judicial District Court PO Box 117, Towner, ND 58788; 701-537-5729; Fax: 701-537-5969. Hours: 8AM-4:30PM (CST). *Felony, Misdemeanor, Civil, Eviction, Small Claims, Probate.*

Civil Records: Access: Fax, mail, in person. Both court and visitors may perform in person searches. Search fee: $10.00 per name. Required to search: name, years to search; also helpful: address. Civil cases indexed by defendant, plaintiff. Civil records on index cards from 1991, on index books from 1905.

Criminal Records: Access: Fax, mail, in person. Both court and visitors may perform in person searches. Search fee: $10.00 per name. Required to search: name, years to search; also helpful: address, DOB, SSN. Criminal records on index cards from 1991, on index books from 1905.

General Information: No adoptions, sealed, juvenile, mental health, expunged or dismissed records released. SASE required. Turnaround time 1-2 days. Fax notes: $1.00 for first page, $.25 each add'l. Copy fee: $.25 per page. Certification fee: $10.00. Fee payee: Clerk of Courts. Personal checks accepted. Prepayment is required.

McIntosh County

South Central Judicial District Court PO Box 179, Ashley, ND 58413; 701-288-3450; Fax: 701-288-3671. Hours: 8AM-4:30PM (CST). *Felony, Misdemeanor, Civil, Eviction, Small Claims, Probate.*

Civil Records: Access: Phone, fax, mail, in person. Visitors must perform in person searches for themselves. Search fee: $10.00 per name. Required to search: name, years to search; also helpful: address. Civil cases indexed by defendant, plaintiff. Civil records on index cards from 1987, on index books from 1930s.

Criminal Records: Access: Fax, mail, in person. Both court and visitors may perform in person searches. Search fee: $10.00 per name. Required to search: name, years to search, DOB; also helpful: address. Criminal records on index cards from 1987, on index books from 1930s.

General Information: No adoptions, sealed, juvenile, mental health, expunged or dismissed records released. SASE not required. Turnaround time 1-2 days. Copy fee: $.25 per page. Certification fee: $10.00. Fee payee: Clerk of Court. Only cashiers checks and money orders accepted. Prepayment is required.

McKenzie County

Northwest Judicial District Court PO Box 524, Watford City, ND 58854; 701-444-3452; Fax: 701-444-3916. Hours: 8:30AM-Noon, 1-5PM (CST). *Felony, Misdemeanor, Civil, Eviction, Small Claims, Probate.*

Civil Records: Access: Mail, in person. Both court and visitors may perform in person searches. Search fee: $10.00 per name. Required to search: name, years to search; also helpful: address, SSN. Civil cases indexed by defendant, plaintiff. Civil records on computer back to 01/96.

Criminal Records: Access: Mail, in person. Only the court performs in person searches; visitors may not. Search fee: $10.00 per name. Required to search: name, years to search, DOB, SSN. Criminal records on computer back to 12/87; on books back to 1908.

General Information: No adoptions, juvenile, mental health, expunged or dismissed records released. SASE required. Turnaround time 1-2 days. Fax notes: Fee to fax results is $2.00 per page. Copy fee: $.25 per page. Certification fee: $10.00. Fee payee: Clerk of Court, McKenzie County. Personal checks accepted. Prepayment is required.

McLean County

South Central Judicial District Court PO Box 1108, Washburn, ND 58577; 701-462-8541; Fax: 701-462-8212. Hours: 8AM-Noon, 12:30-4:30PM (CST). *Felony, Misdemeanor, Civil, Eviction, Small Claims, Probate.*

Civil Records: Access: Mail, in person. Both court and visitors may perform in person searches. Search fee: $10.00 per name. Required to search: name, years to search; also helpful: address. Civil cases indexed by defendant, plaintiff. Civil records on index books from early 1900s; on computer back to 1996.

Criminal Records: Access: Mail, in person. Both court and visitors may perform in person searches. Search fee: $10.00 per name. Required to search: name, years to search, DOB; also helpful: address, SSN. Criminal records on index cards from 1983, on index books from early 1900s; on computer back to 1996.

General Information: No adoptions, sealed, juvenile, mental health, expunged or deferred imposition dismissed records released. SASE required. Turnaround time 1-2 days. Copy fee: $.25 per page. Certification fee: $10.00. Fee payee: Clerk of Courts. Personal checks accepted. Prepayment is required.

Mercer County

District Court PO Box 39, Stanton, ND 58571; 701-745-3262; Fax: 701-745-3710. Hours: 8AM-4PM (MST). *Felony, Misdemeanor, Civil, Eviction, Small Claims, Probate.*

Civil Records: Access: Fax, mail, in person. Both court and visitors may perform in person searches. Search fee: $10.00 per name. Required to search: name, years to search; also helpful: address. Civil cases indexed by defendant, plaintiff. Civil records on index cards from 1979, on index books from 1889.

Criminal Records: Access: Fax, mail, in person. Both court and visitors may perform in person searches. Search fee: $10.00 per name. Required to search: name, years to search, signed release; also helpful: address, DOB, SSN. Criminal records on index cards from 1979, on index books from 1889.

General Information: Public access terminal is available. No adoptions, sealed, juvenile, mental health, expunged or dismissed records released. SASE required. Turnaround time 1-2 days. Fax notes: $5.00 per document. Copy fee: $.25 per page. Certification fee: $10.00. Fee payee: Mercer County Clerk of Court. Personal checks accepted. Prepayment is required.

Morton County

South Central Judicial District Court 210 2nd Ave NW, Mandan, ND 58554; 701-667-3358. Hours: 8AM-5PM (MST). *Felony, Misdemeanor, Civil, Eviction, Small Claims, Probate.*

Civil Records: Access: Mail, in person. Only the court performs in person searches; visitors may not. Search fee: $10.00 per name. Fee is for written search request. Required to search: name, years to search; also helpful: address. Civil cases indexed by defendant, plaintiff. Civil records on computer from 1990; on index books from 1985.

Criminal Records: Access: Mail, in person. Only the court performs in person searches; visitors may not. Search fee: $10.00 per name. Fee is for written search request. Required to search: name, years to search, DOB; also helpful: address. Criminal records on computer from 1990, on index books from 1985.

General Information: No adoptions, sealed, juvenile, mental health, expunged or dismissed records released. SASE required. Turnaround time 1-2 days. Copy fee: $5.00 per document. Certification fee: $10.00. Fee payee: Clerk of District Court. Personal checks accepted. Prepayment is required.

Mountrail County

Northwest Judicial District Court PO Box 69, Stanley, ND 58784; 701-628-2915; Fax: 701-628-3975. Hours: 8:30AM-4:30PM (CST). *Felony, Misdemeanor, Civil, Eviction, Small Claims, Probate.*

Civil Records: Access: Mail, in person, fax, phone. Both court and visitors may perform in person searches. Search fee: $10.00 per name. Fee is for written search. Required to search: name, years to search; also helpful: address. Civil cases indexed by defendant, plaintiff. Civil records on index books from 1909; on computer back to 1998.

Criminal Records: Access: Mail, in person. Both court and visitors may perform in person searches. Search fee: $10.00 per name. Fee is for written search. Required to search: name, years to search, DOB. Criminal records on index books from 1909; on computer back to 1998.

General Information: Public access terminal is available. No adoptions, sealed, juvenile, mental health, expunged or dismissed records released. SASE not required. Turnaround time 1-2 days. Fax notes: No fee to fax results. Copy fee: $.25 per page. Certification fee: $10.00. Fee payee: Clerk of District Court. Personal checks accepted. Prepayment is required.

Nelson County

Northeast Central Judicial District Court PO Box 565, Lakota, ND 58344; 701-247-2462; Fax: 701-247-2412. Hours: 8:30AM-5PM (CST). *Felony, Misdemeanor, Civil, Eviction, Small Claims, Probate.*

Note: Will accept e-mail record requests at rstevens@pioneer.state.nd.us.

Civil Records: Access: Fax, mail, in person. Both court and visitors may perform in person searches. Search fee: $10.00 per name. Required to search: name, years to search; also helpful: address. Civil cases indexed by defendant, plaintiff. Civil records on index books from 1883.

Criminal Records: Access: Fax, mail, in person. Only the court performs in person searches; visitors may not. Search fee: $10.00 per name. Required to search: name, years to search, DOB; also helpful: address, SSN. Criminal records on index books from 1883.

General Information: No adoptions, sealed, juvenile, mental health, expunged or dismissed records released. SASE required. Turnaround time 1-2 days. Fax notes: $3.00 per document. Copy fee: $1.00 per page. Certification fee: $10.00. Fee payee: Clerk of Courts. Personal checks accepted. Prepayment is required.

Oliver County

South Central Judicial District Court Box 125, Center, ND 58530; 701-794-8777; Fax: 701-794-3476. Hours: 8AM-4PM (CST). *Felony, Misdemeanor, Civil, Eviction, Small Claims, Probate.*

Civil Records: Access: Fax, mail, in person. Only the court performs in person searches; visitors may not. Search fee: $10.00 per name. Required to search: name, years to search; also helpful: address. Civil cases indexed by defendant. Civil records on docket books from 1980s.

Criminal Records: Access: Fax, mail, in person. Only the court performs in person searches; visitors may not. Search fee: $10.00 per name. Required to search: name, years to search, DOB; also helpful: address. Criminal records on docket books from 1980s.

General Information: No adoptions, sealed, juvenile, mental health, expunged or dismissed records released. SASE required. Turnaround time 1-2 days. Fax notes: $1.00 for first page, $.50 each add'l. Copy fee: $.25 per page. Certification fee: $10.00. Fee payee: Clerk of Court. Personal checks accepted. Prepayment required.

Pembina County

Pembina County District Court 301 Dakota St West #6, Cavalier, ND 58220-4100; 701-265-4275; Fax: 701-265-4876. Hours: 8:30AM-5PM (CST). *Felony, Misdemeanor, Civil, Eviction, Small Claims, Probate.*

Civil Records: Access: Fax, mail, in person. Both court and visitors may perform in person searches. Search fee: $10.00 per name. Required to search: name, years to search; also helpful: address, DOB, SSN. Civil cases indexed by defendant, plaintiff. Civil records on index books from 1880s; computerized records go back to 1992.

Criminal Records: Access: Fax, mail, in person. Both court and visitors may perform in person searches. Search fee: $10.00 per name. Required to search: name, years to search, DOB; also helpful: address, SSN. Felony records kept for 21 years, misdemeanor for 15 years; computerized records go back to 1997.

General Information: Public access terminal is available. No adoptions, sealed, juvenile, mental health, expunged or dismissed records released. SASE not required. Turnaround time 1-2 days. Copy fee: $.25 per page. Certification fee: $10.00. Fee payee: Pembina County Clerk of Court. Personal checks accepted. Prepayment is required.

Pierce County

Northeast Judicial District Court 240 SE 2nd St, Rugby, ND 58368; 701-776-6161; Fax: 701-776-5707. Hours: 9AM-5PM (CST). *Felony, Misdemeanor, Civil, Eviction, Small Claims, Probate.*

Civil Records: Access: Fax, mail, in person. Only the court performs in person searches; visitors may not. Search fee: $10.00 per name. Required to search: name, years to search; also helpful: address. Civil cases indexed by defendant, plaintiff. Civil records on computer from 1986, on index books and docket books from early 1900s.

Criminal Records: Access: Fax, mail, in person. Only the court performs in person searches; visitors may not. Search fee: $10.00 per name. Required to search: name, years to search, DOB; also helpful: address, SSN. Criminal records on computer from 1986, on index books and docket books from early 1900s.

Ramsey County

District Court 524 4th Ave #4, Devils Lake, ND 58301; 701-661-1309; Fax: 701-662-1303. Hours: 8AM-Noon; 1:00PM-5:00PM (CST). *Felony, Misdemeanor, Civil, Eviction, Small Claims, Probate.*

Civil Records: Access: Fax, mail, in person. Only the court performs in person searches; visitors may not. Search fee: $10.00 per name. Required to search: name; also helpful: years to search. Civil cases indexed by defendant, plaintiff. Civil records on index cards from 1985, on index books from early 1900s.

Criminal Records: Access: Fax, mail, in person. Only the court performs in person searches; visitors may not. Search fee: $10.00 per name. Required to search: name; also helpful: years to search, address, DOB, SSN. Criminal records on index cards from 1985, on index books from early 1900s.

General Information: No adoptions, sealed, juvenile, mental health, expunged or dismissed records released. SASE required. Turnaround time 1-2 days. Fax notes: No fee to fax results. Fax only available to businesses. Copy fee: $.50 per page. Certification fee: $10.00. Fee payee: Clerk of Courts. Personal checks accepted. Prepayment is required.

Ransom County

Southeast Judicial District Court PO Box 626, Lisbon, ND 58054; 701-683-5823 X120; Fax: 701-683-5826. Hours: 8:30AM-5PM (CST). *Felony, Misdemeanor, Civil, Eviction, Small Claims, Probate.*

Civil Records: Access: Fax, mail, in person. Both court and visitors may perform in person searches. Search fee: $10.00 per name. Required to search: name, years to search; also helpful: address. Civil cases indexed by defendant, plaintiff. Civil records on docket books.

Criminal Records: Access: Fax, mail, in person. Both court and visitors may perform in person searches. Search fee: $10.00 per name. Required to search: name, years to search, DOB; also helpful: address. Criminal records on index books.

General Information: No adoptions, sealed, juvenile, mental health, expunged or dismissed records released. SASE required. Turnaround time 3-4 days. Fax notes: No fee to fax results. Copy fee: $.20 per page. Certification fee: $10.00. Fee payee: Clerk of Court. Personal checks accepted. Prepayment is required.

Renville County

Northeast Judicial District Court PO Box 68, Mohall, ND 58761; 701-756-6398; Fax: 701-756-6398. Hours: 9AM-4:30PM (CST). *Felony, Misdemeanor, Civil, Eviction, Small Claims, Probate.*

Civil Records: Access: Fax, mail, in person. Both court and visitors may perform in person searches. Search fee: $10.00 per name. Required to search: name, years to search; also helpful: address. Civil cases indexed by defendant, plaintiff. Civil records on index books from 1910.

Criminal Records: Access: Fax, mail, in person. Both court and visitors may perform in person searches. Search fee: $10.00 per name. Required to search: name, years to search, DOB; also helpful: address. Criminal records on computer from 1/88, on index books from 1910 but not reliable before 1940.

General Information: No adoptions, sealed, juvenile, mental health, expunged or dismissed records released. SASE required. Turnaround time 1-2 days. Fax notes: $3.00 for first page, $1.00 each add'l. Copy fee: $1.00 per page. Certification fee: $10.00. Fee payee: Clerk of

Courts. Personal checks accepted. Prepayment is required.

Richland County

Southeast Judicial District Court 418 2nd Ave North, Wahpeton, ND 58074; 701-642-7818; Fax: 701-671-1512. Hours: 8AM-5PM (CST). *Felony, Misdemeanor, Civil, Eviction, Small Claims, Probate.*

Civil Records: Access: Mail, in person. Only the court performs in person searches; visitors may not. Search fee: $10.00 per name. Required to search: name, years to search; also helpful: address. Civil cases indexed by defendant. Civil records on index cards from 1985, on docket books from late 1800s, but not very accurate. Plaintiff and defendant names required to search.

Criminal Records: Access: Mail, in person. Only the court performs in person searches; visitors may not. Search fee: $10.00 per name. Required to search: name, years to search, DOB, SSN; also helpful: address. Criminal records on docket books from late 1800s but not very accurate.

General Information: No adoptions, sealed, juvenile, mental health, expunged or dismissed records released. SASE required. Turnaround time 1-2 days. Copy fee: $.25 per page. Certification fee: $10.00. Fee payee: Clerk of District Court. Personal checks accepted. Prepayment is required.

Rolette County

Northeast Judicial District Court PO Box 460, Rolla, ND 58367; 701-477-3816; Fax: 701-477-5770. Hours: 8:30AM-4:30PM (CST). *Felony, Misdemeanor, Civil, Eviction, Small Claims, Probate.*

Civil Records: Access: Fax, mail, in person. Both court and visitors may perform in person searches. Search fee: $10.00 per name. Required to search: name, years to search; also helpful: address. Civil cases indexed by defendant, plaintiff, stored since 1889; computerized since 2000.

Criminal Records: Access: Fax, mail, in person. Both court and visitors may perform in person searches. Search fee: $10.00 per name. Required to search: name, years to search; also helpful: address, DOB, SSN. Criminal records on dockets from 1970, computerized since 2000. Prior to 1970, records hard to find and not very accurate.

General Information: No adoptions, sealed, juvenile, mental health, expunged or dismissed records released. SASE required. Turnaround time 1-2 days. Fax notes: $5.00 per document. Copy fee: $.50 per page. Certification fee: $10.00. Fee payee: Clerk of Court. Business checks accepted. Prepayment is required.

Sargent County

Southeast Judicial District Court PO Box 176 (355 Main St), Forman, ND 58032; 701-724-6241 X115; Fax: 701-724-6244. Hours: 9AM-Noon, 12:30-4:30PM (CST). *Felony, Misdemeanor, Civil, Eviction, Small Claims, Probate.*

Civil Records: Access: Fax, mail, in person. Both court and visitors may perform in person searches. Search fee: $10.00 per name. Required to search: name, years to search; also helpful: address. Civil cases indexed by defendant. Civil records on books from early 1800s.

Criminal Records: Access: Fax, mail, in person. Both court and visitors may perform in person searches. Search fee: $10.00 per name. Required to search: name, years to search; also helpful-DOB. Criminal records on books from early 1800s.

General Information: No adoptions, sealed, juvenile, mental health, expunged or dismissed records released. SASE not required. Turnaround time 1-2 days. Fax notes: $3.00 for first page, $1.00 each add'l. Copy fee: $.10 per page. Certification fee: $10.00. Fee payee: Clerk of Court. Personal checks accepted. Prepayment is required.

Sheridan County

South Central Judicial District Court PO Box 409, McClusky, ND 58463; 701-363-2207; Fax: 701-363-2953. Hours: 9AM-Noon, 1-5PM (CST). *Felony, Misdemeanor, Civil, Eviction, Small Claims, Probate.*

Civil Records: Access: Mail, in person. Both court and visitors may perform in person searches. Search fee: $10.00 per name. Required to search: name, years to search; also helpful: address. Civil cases indexed by defendant, plaintiff. Civil records on index books from 1909.

Criminal Records: Access: Mail, in person. Both court and visitors may perform in person searches. Search fee: $10.00 per name. Required to search: name, years to search, signed release; also helpful: address, DOB, SSN. Criminal records on index books from 1909.

General Information: No adoptions, sealed, juvenile, mental health, expunged or dismissed records released. SASE not required. Turnaround time 1-2 days. Copy fee: $.25 per page. Certification fee: $10.00. Fee payee: Clerk of District Court. Business checks accepted. Prepayment is required.

Sioux County

South Central Judicial District Court Box L, Fort Yates, ND 58538; 701-854-3853; Fax: 701-854-3854. Hours: 9AM-5PM (CST). *Felony, Misdemeanor, Civil, Eviction, Small Claims, Probate.*

Civil Records: Access: Fax, mail, in person. Both court and visitors may perform in person searches. Search fee: $10.00 per name per year. Required to search: name, years to search; also helpful: address. Civil cases indexed by defendant, plaintiff. Civil records on index books from 1914.

Criminal Records: Access: Mail, in person. Both court and visitors may perform in person searches. Search fee: $10.00 per name per year. Required to search: name, years to search; also helpful: address, DOB, SSN. Criminal records on index books from 1914.

General Information: No adoptions, sealed, juvenile, mental health, expunged or dismissed records released. SASE required. Turnaround time 1-2 days. Fax notes: Fee to fax results is $3.00 per document. Copy fee: $.50 per page. Certification fee: $10.00. Fee payee: Clerk of Court. Personal checks accepted. All fees may be billed.

Slope County

Southwest Judicial District Court PO Box JJ, Amidon, ND 58620; 701-879-6275; Fax: 701-879-6278. Hours: 8:00AM-Noon; 1:00PM-5:00PM (MST). *Felony, Misdemeanor, Civil, Eviction, Small Claims, Probate.*

Civil Records: Access: Fax, mail, in person. Both court and visitors may perform in person searches. Search fee: $10.00 per name. Required to search: name, years to search; also helpful: address. Civil cases indexed by defendant, plaintiff. Civil records on index cards from 1989.

Criminal Records: Access: Fax, mail, in person. Both court and visitors may perform in person searches. Search fee: $10.00 per name. Required to search: name, years to search, DOB; also helpful: address. Criminal records on index books from 1915.

General Information: No adoptions, sealed, juvenile, mental health, expunged or dismissed records released. SASE required. Turnaround time 1-2 days. Fax notes: $3.00 per document. Copy fee: $.50 per page. Certification fee: $10.00. Fee payee: Clerk of Court. Personal checks accepted. Prepayment is required.

Stark County

District Court 51 Third St #106, Dickinson, ND 58602; 701-264-7637; Fax: 701-264-7640. Hours: 7AM-5PM (MST). *Felony, Misdemeanor, Civil, Eviction, Small Claims, Probate.*

Civil Records: Access: Mail, in person. Both court and visitors may perform in person searches. Search fee: $10.00 per name. Required to search: name, years to search. Civil cases indexed by defendant, plaintiff. Civil records on computer since 1/92, index cards since 1800s.

Criminal Records: Access: Mail, in person. Both court and visitors may perform in person searches. Search fee: $10.00 per name. Required to search: name, years to search, DOB; also helpful: SSN. Criminal records on computer since 1/92, index cards since 1800s.

General Information: Public access terminal is available. No adoptions, sealed, juvenile, mental health, expunged or dismissed records. SASE required. Turnaround time 1-2 days. Copy fee: $.25 per page; $1.00 minimum. Certification fee: $10.00. Fee payee: Clerk of Court. Personal checks accepted. Prepayment is required.

Steele County

East Central Judicial District Court PO Box 296, Finley, ND 58230; 701-524-2152; Fax: 701-524-1325. Hours: 8AM-Noon; 1-4:30PM (CST). *Felony, Misdemeanor, Civil, Eviction, Small Claims, Probate.*

Civil Records: Access: Mail, in person. Only the court performs in person searches; visitors may not. Search fee: $10.00 per name. Required to search: name, years to search; also helpful: address. Civil cases indexed by defendant, plaintiff. Civil records on docket books from approx 1894.

Criminal Records: Access: Mail, in person. Only the court performs in person searches; visitors may not. Search fee: $10.00 per name. Required to search: name, years to search, DOB, signed release; also helpful: address. Criminal records on docket books from approx 1894.

General Information: No adoptions, sealed, juvenile, mental health, expunged or dismissed records released. SASE required. Turnaround time 1-2 days. Copy fee: $1.00 per page. Certification fee: $10.00. Fee payee: Clerk of Court. Business checks accepted. Prepayment is required.

Stutsman County

Southeast Judicial District Court 511 2nd Ave SE, Jamestown, ND 58401; 701-252-9042; Fax: 701-251-1006. Hours: 8AM-5PM (CST). *Felony, Misdemeanor, Civil, Eviction, Small Claims, Probate.*

Civil Records: Access: Mail, fax, in person. Only the court performs in person searches; visitors may not. Search fee: $10.00 per name. Required to search: name, years to search; also helpful: address. Civil records on computer back to 1/87, on index books from 1800s.

Criminal Records: Access: Mail, fax, in person. Only the court performs in person searches; visitors may not. Search fee: $10.00 per name. Required to search: name, years to search, DOB; also helpful: address. Criminal records on computer back to 1/96, on index books from 1800s.

General Information: No adoptions, sealed, juvenile, mental health, expunged or dismissed records released. SASE required. Turnaround time 1-2 days. Fax notes: Fee to fax results is $3.00 per document. Copy fee: $.25 per page. Certification fee: $10.00. Fee payee: Clerk of Court. Personal checks accepted. Prepayment is required.

Towner County

Northeast Judicial District Court Box 517, Cando, ND 58324; 701-968-4340 Ext 3; Fax: 701-968-4344. Hours: 8:30AM-Noon; 1:00PM-5:00PM (CST). *Felony, Misdemeanor, Civil, Eviction, Small Claims, Probate.*

Civil Records: Access: Fax, mail, in person. Only the court performs in person searches; visitors may not. Search fee: $10.00 per name. Required to search: name, years to search; also helpful: address. Civil cases indexed by defendant, plaintiff. Civil records on index books from 1800s.

Criminal Records: Access: Fax, mail, in person. Only the court performs in person searches; visitors may not. Search fee: $10.00 per name. Required to search: name, years to search; also helpful: address, DOB, SSN. Criminal records on index books from 1800s.

General Information: No adoptions, sealed, juvenile, mental health, expunged or dismissed records released. SASE required. Turnaround time 1-2 days. Fax notes: $3.00 per document. Copy fee: $1,00 per page. Certification fee: $10.00. Fee payee: Clerk of District Court. Personal checks accepted. Prepayment is required.

Traill County

East Central Judicial District Court PO Box 805, Hillsboro, ND 58045; 701-636-4454; Fax: 701-636-5124. Hours: 8AM-4:30PM (CST). *Felony, Misdemeanor, Civil, Eviction, Small Claims, Probate.*

Civil Records: Access: Phone, fax, mail, in person. Only the court performs in person searches; visitors may not. Search fee: $10.00 per name. Required to search: name, years to search; also helpful: address. Civil cases indexed by defendant, plaintiff. Civil records on index books from 1800s.

Criminal Records: Access: Phone, fax, mail, in person. Only the court performs in person searches; visitors may not. Search fee: $10.00 per name. Required to search: name, years to search; also helpful: address, DOB, SSN. Criminal records on index books from 1800s.

General Information: No adoptions, sealed, juvenile, mental health, expunged or dismissed records released. SASE required. Turnaround time 1-2 days. Fax notes: $1.00 per page. Copy fee: $.25 per page. Certification fee: $10.00. Fee payee: Clerk of Court. Personal checks accepted. Prepayment is required.

Walsh County

Northeast Judicial District Court 600 Cooper Ave, Grafton, ND 58237; 701-352-0350; Fax: 701-352-4466. Hours: 8:30AM-5PM (CST). *Felony, Misdemeanor, Civil, Eviction, Small Claims, Probate.*

Civil Records: Access: Mail, in person. Both court and visitors may perform in person searches. Search fee: $10.00 per name. Required to search: name, years to search; also helpful: address. Civil cases indexed by defendant, plaintiff. Civil records on index books from early 1900s; on computer from 11/97.

Criminal Records: Access: Mail, in person. Only the court performs in person searches; visitors may not. Search fee: $10.00 per name. Required to search: name, years to search, DOB; also helpful: address, SSN. Criminal records on index books from early 1900s; on computer from 11/97.

General Information: No adoptions, sealed, juvenile, mental health, expunged or dismissed records released. SASE required. Turnaround time 5-10 days. Fax notes: Fee to fax results is $5.00 per document. Copy fee: $.25 per page; $1.00 minimum. Certification fee: $10.00, then $5.00 each add'l. Fee payee: Clerk of Court. Personal checks accepted. Prepayment is required.

Ward County

Northwest Judicial District Court PO Box 5005, Minot, ND 58702-5005; 701-857-6460; Fax: 701-857-6468. Hours: 8AM-4:30PM (CST). *Felony, Misdemeanor, Civil, Eviction, Small Claims, Probate.*

Civil Records: Access: Mail, in person. Both court and visitors may perform in person searches. Search fee: $10.00 per name. Required to search: name, years to search; also helpful: address. Civil cases indexed by defendant, plaintiff. Civil records on index cards from 1990, on index books from 1800s; computerized records go back to 1994.

Criminal Records: Access: Mail, in person. Both court and visitors may perform in person searches. Search fee: $10.00 per name. Required to search: name, years to search; also helpful: address, DOB, SSN. Criminal records on index cards from 1990, on index books from 1800s; computerized records go back to 1994.

General Information: Public access terminal is available. No adoptions, sealed, juvenile, mental health, expunged or dismissed records released. SASE not required. Turnaround time 5 days. Copy fee: $.25 per page (minimum $1.00). Certification fee: $10.00. Fee payee: Clerk of District Court. Business checks accepted. Prepayment is required.

Wells County

Southeast Judicial District Court PO Box 155, Fessenden, ND 58438; 701-547-3122; Fax: 701-547-3840. Hours: 8AM-4:30PM (CST). *Felony, Misdemeanor, Civil, Eviction, Small Claims, Probate.*

Civil Records: Access: Mail, in person. Only the court performs in person searches; visitors may not. Search fee: $10.00 per name. Required to search: name, years to search; also helpful: address. Civil cases indexed by defendant, plaintiff. Civil records on index books.

Criminal Records: Access: Mail, in person. Only the court performs in person searches; visitors may not. Search fee: $10.00 per name. Required to search: name, years to search; also helpful: address, DOB, SSN. Criminal records on index books from 1980.

General Information: No adoptions, sealed, juvenile, mental health, expunged or dismissed records released. SASE required. Turnaround time 1-2 days. Copy fee: $1.00 per document. Certification fee: $10.00. Fee payee: District Court. Personal checks accepted. Prepayment is required.

Williams County

Northwest Judicial District Court PO Box 2047, Williston, ND 58802; 701-572-1720; Fax: 701-572-1760. Hours: 8AM-5PM (CST). *Felony, Misdemeanor, Civil, Eviction, Small Claims, Probate.*

Civil Records: Access: Mail, in person. Both court and visitors may perform in person searches. Search fee: $10.00 per name. Required to search: name, years to search; also helpful: address. Civil cases indexed by defendant, plaintiff. Civil records computerized since 1/98, on index cards from 1/92, on index books from 1899.

Criminal Records: Access: Mail, in person. Both court and visitors may perform in person searches. Search fee: $10.00 per name. Required to search: name, years to search; also helpful: address, DOB, SSN. Criminal records computerized since 1/98, on index cards from 1/92, on index books from 1899.

General Information: No adoptions, sealed, juvenile, mental health, expunged or dismissed records released. SASE required. Turnaround time 1-2 days. Copy fee: $2.00 fee for $.25 per page with $1 minimum. Certification fee: $10.00. Fee payee: Clerk of Court. Personal checks accepted. Prepayment is required.

North Dakota Recording Offices

ORGANIZATION: 53 counties, 53 recording offices. The recording officer is the Register of Deeds. The entire state is in the Central Time Zone (CST).

REAL ESTATE RECORDS: Some counties will perform real estate searches by name or by legal description. Copy fees are usually $1.00 per page. Certified copies usually cost $5.00 for the first page and $2.00 for each additional page. Copies may be faxed.

UCC RECORDS: Since 07/1/2001, all financing statements must be filed at the state level, except for real estate related collateral, which are filed only with the Register of Deeds. Previously, the state was a dual filing state and reocrd could be filed at either place. The good news is that all counties access a statewide computer database of filings and will perform UCC searches. Use search request form UCC-11. Various search options are available, including by federal tax identification number or Social Security number The search with copies costs $7.00 per debtor name, including three pages of copies and $1.00 per additional page. Copies may be faxed for an additional fee of $3.00.

TAX LIEN RECORDS: Federal tax liens on personal property of businesses are filed with the Secretary of State. Other federal and all state tax liens are filed with the county Register of Deeds. All counties will perform tax lien searches. Some counties automatically include business federal tax liens as part of a UCC search because they appear on the statewide database. (Be careful - federal tax liens on individuals may only be in the county lien books, not on the statewide system.) Separate searches are usually available at $5.00-7.00 per name. Copy fees vary. Copies may be faxed.

OTHER LIENS: Mechanics, judgment, hospital, repair, egg cutter.

ONLINE ACCESS: The North Dakota Recorders Information Network (NDRIN) is a electronic central repository for about one-third of ND counties. Burleigh, Cass, Dunn, McKenzie, McLean, Stark, Ward and Walsh currently offer internet access. There are 12 other counties participating in the system. There is a $200 set-up fee and $50 monthly with $1.00 charge per image printed. Register or request information via the web site at www.ndrin.com

Adams County
Register of Deeds, PO Box 469, Hettinger, ND 58639-0469. 701-567-2460; Fax 701-567-2910.
Will search UCC records. **Other Phone Numbers:** Assessor 701-567-2900; Treasurer 701-567-2537; Elections 701-567-4363.

Barnes County
Register of Deeds, PO Box 684, Valley City, ND 58072. 701-845-8506; Fax 701-845-8538.
Participates in the ND Recorders Information Network, www.ndrin.com. Will search UCC records. Will not search real estate records. **Other Phone Numbers:** Assessor 701-845-8515; Treasurer 701-845-8505; Elections 701-845-8500.

Benson County
County Recorder, PO Box 193, Minnewaukan, ND 58351. 701-473-5332; Fax 701-473-5571.
Will search UCC records. Will search real estate records. **Other Phone Numbers:** Assessor 701-473-5524; Treasurer 701-473-5458; Elections 701-473-5340; Vital Records 701-473-5345.

Billings County
Recorder, PO Box 138, Medora, ND 58645-0138. 701-623-4491; Fax 701-623-4896.
Will search UCC records. Will not search real estate records. **Other Phone Numbers:** Assessor 701-623-4810; Treasurer 701-623-4484; Elections 701-623-4377.

Bottineau County
County Recorder, 314 W. 5th St, Bottineau, ND 58318-1265. 701-228-2786; Fax 701-228-3658.
Will search UCC records. Will not search real estate records. **Other Phone Numbers:** Treasurer 701-228-2035; Elections 701-228-2225.

Bowman County
Register of Deeds, PO Box 379, Bowman, ND 58623. Register of Deeds, R/E and UCC Recording 701-523-3450; Fax 701-523-5443.
Will search UCC records. **Other Phones:** Assessor 701-523-3129; Treasurer 701-523-3665; Appraiser/Auditor 701-523-3129; Elections 701-523-3130; Vital Records 701-328-2360; Auditor 701-523-3130.

Burke County
Register of Deeds, PO Box 219, Bowbells, ND 58721-0219. Register of Deeds, R/E and UCC Recording 701-377-2818; Fax 701-377-2020.
Will search UCC records. **Other Phone Numbers:** Assessor 701-377-2661; Treasurer 701-377-2917; Appraiser/Auditor 701-377-2661; Elections 701-377-2861; Vital Records 701-377-2718.

Burleigh County
Register of Deeds, PO Box 5518, Bismarck, ND 58506-5518. Register of Deeds, R/E and UCC Recording 701-222-6749; Fax 701-222-6717. www.ndrin.com
Will search UCC records. Will not search real estate records. **Online Access:** Real Estate Records. Access the recorder's land records are available by subscription to NDRIN's central repository at www.ndrin.com. See section introduction. **Other Phones:** Assessor 701-222-6691; Treasurer 222-6696; Appraiser/Auditor 222-6691; Elections 222-6718; Vital Records 222-2360.

Cass County
Register of Deeds, PO Box 2806, Fargo, ND 58108-2806. 701-241-5620; Fax 701-241-5621.
Will search UCC records. Will not search real estate records. **Online Access:** Real Estate Records. Access the recorder's land records are available by subscription to NDRIN's central repository at www.ndrin.com. See

section introduction. **Other Phones:** Assessor 701-241-5611; Treasurer 241-5611; Elections 241-5601.

Cavalier County
Register of Deeds, 901 3rd St, Langdon, ND 58249. Register of Deeds, R/E and UCC Recording 701-256-2136; Fax 701-256-2566.
Participates in the ND Recorders Information Network, www.ndrin.com. Will search UCC records. Will not search real estate records. **Other Phone Numbers:** Assessor 701-256-3826; Treasurer 701-256-2549; Elections 701-256-2229; Vital Records 701-256-2124.

Dickey County
Register of Deeds, PO Box 148, Ellendale, ND 58436. Register of Deeds, R/E and UCC Recording 701-349-3249; Fax 701-349-4639.
Will search UCC records. Will search real estate records. **Other Phone Numbers:** Assessor 701-349-3218; Elections 701-349-3249.

Divide County
Register of Deeds, PO Box 68, Crosby, ND 58730. 701-965-6661; Fax 701-965-6943.
Will search UCC records. Will not search real estate records. **Other Phones:** Assessor 701-965-6351; Treasurer 701-965-6312; Elections 701-965-6351.

Dunn County
Register of Deeds, PO Box 106, Manning, ND 58642-0106. Register of Deeds, R/E and UCC Recording 701-573-4443; Fax 701-573-4444. www.ndrin.com
Will search UCC records. Will not search real estate records. **Online Access:** Real Estate Records. Access the recorder's land records are available by subscription to NDRIN's central repository at www.ndrin.com. See section introduction. **Other Phone Numbers:** Assessor 701-573-4445; Treasurer 701-573-4446; Elections 701-573-4448 (Auditor); Vital Records 701-328-2360.

Eddy County

Register of Deeds, 524 Central Ave, New Rockford, ND 58356-1698. 701-947-2813; Fax 701-947-2067. Will search UCC records. **Other Phone Numbers:** Assessor 701-947-5220; Treasurer 701-947-5315; Elections 701-947-2434.

Emmons County

County Recorder, PO Box 905, Linton, ND 58552. 701-254-4812; Fax 701-254-4012. Will search UCC records. **Other Phone Numbers:** Assessor 701-254-4417; Treasurer 701-254-4802; Elections 701-254-4807.

Foster County

Register of Deeds, PO Box 257, Carrington, ND 58421. 701-652-2491; Fax 701-652-2173. Will search UCC records. **Other Phone Numbers:** Assessor 701-652-2441; Treasurer 701-652-2323; Elections 701-652-2441.

Golden Valley County

County Recorder, PO Box 130, Beach, ND 58621-0130. County Recorder, R/E and UCC Recording 701-872-3713; Fax 701-872-4383. Will search UCC records. **Other Phone Numbers:** Assessor 701-872-4673; Treasurer 701-872-4411; Elections 701-872-4331.

Grand Forks County

Register of Deeds, PO Box 5066, Grand Forks, ND 58206. 701-780-8261/8262 R/E Recording: 701-780-8200; Fax 701-780-8212. Will search UCC records. Will not search real estate records. **Other Phones:** Assessor 701-780-8261; Treasurer 701-780-8295; Elections 701-780-8200.

Grant County

Register of Deeds, PO Box 258, Carson, ND 58529. 701-622-3544; Fax 701-622-3717. Will search UCC records. **Other Phone Numbers:** Assessor 701-622-3275; Treasurer 701-622-3422; Elections 701-622-3275.

Griggs County

Register of Deeds, PO Box 237, Cooperstown, ND 58425. 701-797-2771; Fax 701-797-3587. Participates in the ND Recorders Information Network, www.ndrin.com. Will search UCC records. Will not search real estate records. **Other Phone Numbers:** Assessor 701-797-3211; Treasurer 701-797-2411; Elections 701-797-3117.

Hettinger County

Register of Deeds, PO Box 668, Mott, ND 58646. 701-824-2545/2645 R/E Recording: 701-824-2545 UCC Recording: 701-824-2545; Fax 701-824-2717. Will search UCC records. **Other Phone Numbers:** Assessor 701-824-2515; Treasurer 701-824-2655; Appraiser/Auditor 701-824-2515; Elections 701-824-2515; Vital Records 701-824-2545.

Kidder County

Register of Deeds, PO Box 66, Steele, ND 58482. Register of Deeds, R/E and UCC Recording 701-475-2632; Fax 701-475-2202. Will search UCC records. **Other Phone Numbers:** Assessor 701-475-2632; Treasurer 701-475-2632; Elections 701-475-2632.

La Moure County

Recorder, PO Box 128, La Moure, ND 58458-0128. 701-883-5301 R/E Recording: 701-883-5304; Fax 701-883-5304. Will search UCC records. Will search real estate records. **Other Phones:** Assessor 701-883-5301; Treasurer 701-883-5103; Elections 701-883-5301.

Logan County

Register of Deeds, PO Box 6, Napoleon, ND 58561-0006. 701-754-2751; Fax 701-754-2270. Will search UCC records. UCC search includes federal tax liens if requested. Real estate record owner and mortgage searches available. **Other Phone Numbers:** Assessor 701-754-2239; Treasurer 701-754-2286; Elections 701-754-2425.

McHenry County

Register of Deeds, PO Box 149, Towner, ND 58788. Register of Deeds, R/E and UCC Recording 701-537-5634; Fax 701-537-5969. www.state.nd.us Participates in the ND Recorders Information Network, www.ndrin.com. Will search UCC records. Will not search real estate records. **Other Phone Numbers:** Assessor 701-537-5359; Treasurer 701-537-5731; Elections 701-537-5724; Vital Records 701-537-5729.

McIntosh County

Register of Deeds, PO Box 179, Ashley, ND 58413. 701-288-3589/3450 R/E Recording: 701-288-3589; Fax 701-288-3671. Will search UCC records. **Other Phone Numbers:** Assessor 701-288-3347; Treasurer 701-288-3342; Elections 701-288-3347.

McKenzie County

Register of Deeds, PO Box 523, Watford City, ND 58854. 701-444-3453 R/E Recording: 701-842-3616 UCC Recording: 701-842-3453; Fax 701-844-3902. www.4eyes.net/county.htm Will search UCC records. Will not search real estate records. **Online Access:** Real Estate Records. Access the recorder's land records are available by subscription to NDRIN's central repository at www.ndrin.com. See section introduction. **Other Phones:** Assessor 701-842-6852; Treasurer 701-842-3457; Appraiser/Auditor 701-842-6852; Elections 701-842-3616; Vital Records 701-842-3452.

McLean County

Register of Deeds, PO Box 1108, Washburn, ND 58577-1108. 701-462-8541 x225/6 R/E Recording: 701-462-8541 X226, x225 UCC Recording: 701-462-8541; Fax 701-462-3633. Will search UCC records. **Online Access:** Real Estate Records. Access the recorder's land records are available by subscription to NDRIN's central repository at www.ndrin.com. See section introduction. **Other Phone Numbers:** Assessor 701-462-8541; Treasurer 701-462-8541 x223; Elections 701-462-8541 x216; Vital Records 701-462-8541 x228.

Mercer County

Register of Deeds, PO Box 39, Stanton, ND 58571. Register of Deeds, R/E and UCC Recording 701-745-3272; Fax 701-745-3364. Will search UCC records. Will not search real estate records. **Other Phone Numbers:** Assessor 701-745-3294; Elections 701-745-3292.

Morton County

Register of Deeds, 210 2nd Ave, Mandan, ND 58554. 701-667-3305; Fax 701-667-3453. Participates in the ND Recorders Information Network, www.ndrin.com. Will search UCC records. Will not search real estate records. **Other Phone Numbers:** Assessor 701-667-3300; Treasurer 701-667-3310; Elections 701-667-3300; Auditor 701-667-3300.

Mountrail County

Register of Deeds, PO Box 69, Stanley, ND 58784. Register of Deeds, R/E and UCC Recording 701-628-2945; Fax 701-628-3975.

Nelson County

Will search UCC records. Will not search real estate records. **Other Phones:** Assessor 701-826-2425; Treasurer 701-628-2935; Elections 701-628-2145.

Coounty Recorder, PO Box 565, Lakota, ND 58344. Coounty Recorder, R/E and UCC Recording 701-247-2433 UCC Recording: 701-247-2453; Fax 701-247-2412. Participates in the ND Recorders Information Network, www.ndrin.com. Will search UCC records. **Other Phone Numbers:** Assessor 701-247-2840; Treasurer 701-247-2453; Elections 701-247-2463; Vital Records 701-247-2462.

Oliver County

Register of Deeds, PO Box 125, Center, ND 58530-0125. 701-794-8777; Fax 701-794-3476. Will search UCC records. **Other Phone Numbers:** Assessor 701-794-8721; Treasurer 701-794-8737; Elections 701-794-8721.

Pembina County

Register of Deeds, 301 Dakota St W. #10, Cavalier, ND 58220. Register of Deeds, R/E and UCC Recording 701-265-4373; Fax 701-265-4876. Will search UCC records. Will not search real estate records. **Other Phone Numbers:** Assessor 701-265-4697; Treasurer 701-265-4465; Elections 701-265-4231.

Pierce County

Register of Deeds, 240 S.E. 2nd St, Rugby, ND 58368. 701-776-5206; Fax 701-776-5707. Will search UCC records. Will not search real estate records. **Other Phone Numbers:** Assessor 701-776-5225; Treasurer 701-776-6841; Elections 701-776-5225.

Ramsey County

Register of Deeds, 524 4th Ave #30, Devils Lake, ND 58301. 701-662-7018 R/E Recording: 701-62-7018; Fax 701-662-7093. Will search UCC records. Will not search real estate records. **Other Phone Numbers:** Assessor 701-662-7018; Treasurer 701-662-7021; Elections 701-62-7007.

Ransom County

Register of Deeds, PO Box 666, Lisbon, ND 58054-0666. 701-683-5823 R/E Recording: 701-683-5823 x115; Fax 701-683-5827. Participates in the ND Recorders Information Network, www.ndrin.com. Will search UCC records. **Other Phone Numbers:** Assessor 701-683-5823 x144; Treasurer 701-683-5823 x118; Elections 701-683-5823 x113; Vital Records 701-683-5823 x 120.

Renville County

Register of Deeds, PO Box 68, Mohall, ND 58761-0068. Register of Deeds, R/E and UCC Recording 701-756-6398; Fax 701-756-7158. www.renvillecounty.org Will search UCC records. UCC search includes federal tax liens. Will not search real estate records. **Other Phone Numbers:** Assessor 701-756-6368; Treasurer 701-756-6304; Appraiser/Auditor 701-756-6368; Elections 701-756-6301; Vital Records 701-756-6398.

Richland County

Register of Deeds, 418 2nd Ave North, Courthouse, Wahpeton, ND 58075-4400. Register of Deeds, R/E and UCC Recording 701-642-7800; Fax 701-642-7820. Participates in the ND Recorders Information Network, www.ndrin.com. Will search UCC records. **Other Phone Numbers:** Assessor 701-642-7805; Treasurer 701-642-7705; Elections 701-642-7700; Vital Records 701-642-7800.

Rolette County

Recorder, PO Box 276, Rolla, ND 58367. Recorder, R/E and UCC Recording 701-477-3166; Fax 701-477-5770.

Will search UCC records. Will search real estate records. **Other Phone Numbers:** Assessor 701-477-5665; Treasurer 701-477-3207; Elections 701-477-5665; Vital Records 701-477-3816.

Sargent County

Register of Deeds, PO Box 176, Forman, ND 58032-0176. 701-724-6241; Fax 701-724-6244.

Will search UCC records. Will not search real estate records. **Other Phone Numbers:** Assessor 701-724-6241 x15; Treasurer 701-724-6241 x13,14; Elections 701-724-6241.

Sheridan County

Register of Deeds, PO Box 668, McClusky, ND 58463-0668. 701-363-2207 UCC Recording: 603-895-2226; Fax 701-363-2953.

Will search UCC records. **Other Phone Numbers:** Assessor 701-363-2201; Treasurer 701-363-2206; Elections 701-363-2205; Vital Records 603-895-2207.

Sioux County

Register of Deeds, PO Box L, Fort Yates, ND 58538. 701-854-3853; Fax 701-854-3854.

Will search UCC records. **Other Phone Numbers:** Assessor 701-854-3424; Elections 701-854-3481.

Slope County

Register of Deeds, PO Box JJ, Amidon, ND 58620-0445. 701-879-6275 R/E Recording: 701-879-6276; Fax 701-879-6278.

Will search UCC records. Will not search real estate records. **Other Phones:** Assessor 701-879-6276; Treasurer 701-879-6271; Elections 701-879-6276.

Stark County

Register of Deeds, PO Box 130, Dickinson, ND 58601. 701-264-7645; Fax 701-264-7628.

Will search UCC records. Will not search real estate records. **Online Access:** Real Estate Records. Access the recorder's land records are available by subscription to NDRIN's central repository at www.ndrin.com. See section introduction. **Other Phone Numbers:** Assessor 701-264-7671; Elections 701-264-7630.

Steele County

Register of Deeds, PO Box 296, Finley, ND 58230. 701-524-2152 R/E Recording: 701-524-2790; Fax 701-524-1325.

Will search UCC records. Will not search real estate records. **Other Phones:** Assessor 701-524-2110; Treasurer 701-524-2890; Elections 701-524-2110.

Stutsman County

Register of Deeds, 511 2nd Ave S.E., Courthouse, Jamestown, ND 58401. 701-252-9034 R/E Recording: 701-252-9035; Fax 701-251-1603.

Participates in the ND Recorders Information Network, www.ndrin.com. Will search UCC records. Will not search real estate records. **Other Phone Numbers:** Assessor 701-252-9032; Treasurer 701-252-9036; Elections 701-252-9035.

Towner County

Register of Deeds, PO Box 517, Cando, ND 58324. 701-968-4343 R/E Recording: 701-968-4340 x5 UCC Recording: 701-968-4340 x5; Fax 701-968-4344.

Will search UCC records. Will not search real estate records. **Other Phones:** Assessor 701-968-4352; Treasurer 701-968-4347; Elections 701-968-4340.

Traill County

Register of Deeds, PO Box 399, Hillsboro, ND 58045. 701-636-4457 R/E Recording: 701-436-4457 UCC Recording: 701-436-4457; Fax 701-636-4457.

Will search UCC records. **Other Phone Numbers:** Assessor 701-436-5950; Treasurer 701-436-4459; Elections 701-436-4458; Vital Records 701-436-4454.

Walsh County

Register of Deeds, 600 Cooper Ave, Courthouse, Grafton, ND 58237. 701-352-2380; Fax 701-352-3340.

Will search UCC records. **Online Access:** Real Estate Records. Access the recorder's land records are available by subscription to NDRIN's central repository at www.ndrin.com. See section introduction. **Other Phone Numbers:** Assessor 701-352-2851; Treasurer 701-352-2541; Elections 701-352-2851.

Ward County

Register of Deeds, PO Box 5005, Courthouse, Minot, ND 58705-5005. 701-857-6410 R/E Recording: 701-857-6420; Fax 701-857-6414.

Will search UCC records. Will not search real estate records. **Online Access:** Real Estate Records. Access the recorder's land records are available by subscription to NDRIN's central repository at www.ndrin.com. See section introduction. **Other Phone Numbers:** Assessor 701-857-6430; Elections 701-857-6420.

Wells County

Register of Deeds, PO Box 125, Fessenden, ND 58438-0125. Register of Deeds, R/E and UCC Recording 701-547-3141; Fax 701-547-3719.

Participates in the ND Recorders Information Network, www.ndrin.com. Will search UCC records. Will search real estate records. **Other Phone Numbers:** Assessor 701-547-3220; Treasurer 701-547-3161; Elections 701-547-3521; Vital Records 701-547-3122.

Williams County

Recorder, PO Box 2047, Williston, ND 58802-2047. Recorder, R/E and UCC Recording 701-577-4540; Fax 701-577-4535. www.ndrin.com.

Participates in the ND Recorders Information Network, www.ndrin.com. Will search UCC records. Will not search real estate records. **Other Phone Numbers:** Assessor 701-577-4555; Treasurer 701-577-4530; Elections 701-577-4500; Vital Records 701-577-4580.

North Dakota County Locator

You will usually be able to find the city name in the City/County Cross Reference below. In that case, it is a simple matter to determine the county from the cross reference. However, only the official US Postal Service city names are included in this index. There are an additional 40,000 place names that people use in their addresses. Therefore, we have also included a ZIP/City Cross Reference immediately following the City/County Cross Reference.

If you know the ZIP Code but the city name does not appear in the City/County Cross Reference index, look up the ZIP Code in the ZIP/City Cross Reference, find the city name, then look up the city name in the City/County Cross Reference. For example, you want to know the county for an address of Menands, NY 12204. There is no "Menands" in the City/County Cross Reference. The ZIP/City Cross Reference shows that ZIP Codes 12201-12288 are for the city of Albany. Looking back in the City/County Cross Reference, Albany is in Albany County.

City/County Cross Reference

ABERCROMBIE Richland
ABSARAKA Cass
ADAMS Walsh
AGATE Rolette
ALAMO (58830) Williams(60), Divide(40)
ALEXANDER McKenzie
ALFRED La Moure
ALICE Cass
ALMONT (58520) Morton(72), Grant(27)
ALSEN Cavalier
AMBROSE Divide
AMENIA Cass
AMIDON (58620) Slope(98), Billings(1)
ANAMOOSE (58710) McHenry(61), Sheridan(22), Pierce(16)
ANETA (58212) Nelson(63), Griggs(25), Grand Forks(9), Steele(1)
ANTLER Bottineau
ARDOCH Walsh
ARENA (58412) Burleigh(98), Kidder(1)
ARGUSVILLE Cass
ARNEGARD McKenzie
ARTHUR Cass
ARVILLA Grand Forks
ASHLEY (58413) McIntosh(92), Dickey(7)
AYR Cass
BALDWIN Burleigh
BALFOUR McHenry
BALTA Pierce
BANTRY McHenry
BARNEY Richland
BARTON Pierce
BATHGATE Pembina
BEACH (58621) Golden Valley(95), McKenzie(3)
BELCOURT Rolette
BELFIELD (58622) Stark(72), Billings(27)
BENEDICT (58716) McLean(79), Ward(20)
BERLIN (58415) La Moure(98), Dickey(1)
BERTHOLD (58718) Ward(73), Mountrail(23), Renville(2)
BEULAH (58523) Mercer(94), Oliver(5)
BINFORD (58416) Griggs(97), Nelson(2)
BISBEE (58317) Towner(95), Rolette(3)
BISMARCK Burleigh
BLAISDELL Mountrail
BLANCHARD Traill
BOTTINEAU Bottineau
BOWBELLS Burke
BOWDON (58418) Wells(92), Kidder(7)
BOWMAN (58623) Bowman(85), Slope(14)
BRADDOCK (58524) Emmons(64), Kidder(23), Burleigh(11)
BREMEN Wells
BRINSMADE Benson
BROCKET (58321) Ramsey(51), Nelson(26), Walsh(22)
BUCHANAN Stutsman
BUFFALO Cass
BURLINGTON Ward
BUTTE (58723) McLean(74), McHenry(18), Sheridan(6)
BUXTON Traill
CALEDONIA Traill

CALVIN (58323) Cavalier(76), Towner(23)
CANDO Towner
CANNON BALL Sioux
CARPIO (58725) Renville(53), Ward(46)
CARRINGTON (58421) Foster(95), Stutsman(2), Wells(1)
CARSON Grant
CARTWRIGHT McKenzie
CASSELTON Cass
CATHAY Wells
CAVALIER Pembina
CAYUGA Sargent
CENTER Oliver
CHAFFEE Cass
CHASELEY (58423) Wells(83), Kidder(16)
CHRISTINE (58015) Richland(97), Cass(2)
CHURCHS FERRY (58325) Ramsey(61), Benson(38)
CLEVELAND Stutsman
CLIFFORD (58016) Traill(66), Steele(33)
COGSWELL Sargent
COLEHARBOR McLean
COLFAX Richland
COLUMBUS Burke
COOPERSTOWN Griggs
COURTENAY (58426) Stutsman(98), Foster(1)
CRARY Ramsey
CROSBY Divide
CRYSTAL Pembina
CRYSTAL SPRINGS Kidder
CUMMINGS Traill
DAHLEN (58224) Nelson(95), Walsh(4)
DAVENPORT Cass
DAWSON Kidder
DAZEY (58429) Barnes(97), Griggs(2)
DEERING (58731) McHenry(96), Ward(3)
DENHOFF Sheridan
DES LACS Ward
DEVILS LAKE Ramsey
DICKEY La Moure
DICKINSON Stark
DODGE (58625) Dunn(70), Mercer(29)
DONNYBROOK (58734) Ward(42), Mountrail(37), Renville(19)
DOUGLAS (58735) Ward(58), McLean(41)
DOYON Ramsey
DRAKE (58736) McHenry(88), Sheridan(11)
DRAYTON (58225) Pembina(82), Walsh(17)
DRISCOLL (58532) Burleigh(75), Kidder(24)
DUNN CENTER Dunn
DUNSEITH (58329) Rolette(82), Bottineau(17)
ECKELSON Barnes
EDGELEY (58433) La Moure(89), Dickey(10)
EDINBURG (58227) Walsh(56), Pembina(34), Cavalier(9)
EDMORE (58330) Ramsey(92), Walsh(4), Cavalier(3)
EGELAND Towner
ELGIN Grant
ELLENDALE Dickey
EMERADO Grand Forks

ENDERLIN (58027) Ransom(75), Cass(18), Barnes(5)
EPPING Williams
ERIE Cass
ESMOND (58332) Benson(87), Pierce(12)
FAIRDALE (58229) Walsh(68), Cavalier(27), Ramsey(3)
FAIRFIELD Billings
FAIRMOUNT Richland
FARGO Cass
FESSENDEN Wells
FINGAL (58031) Barnes(60), Cass(39)
FINLEY Steele
FLASHER (58535) Morton(78), Grant(21)
FLAXTON Burke
FORBES Dickey
FORDVILLE (58231) Walsh(72), Grand Forks(27)
FOREST RIVER (58233) Walsh(90), Grand Forks(9)
FORMAN Sargent
FORT RANSOM (58033) Ransom(98), La Moure(1)
FORT RICE Morton
FORT TOTTEN Benson
FORT YATES Sioux
FORTUNA Divide
FOXHOLM Ward
FREDONIA (58440) Logan(70), McIntosh(29)
FULLERTON Dickey
GACKLE (58442) Logan(85), Stutsman(14)
GALESBURG (58035) Traill(60), Cass(25), Steele(14)
GARDENA Bottineau
GARDNER Cass
GARRISON McLean
GILBY Grand Forks
GLADSTONE (58630) Stark(75), Dunn(24)
GLASSTON Pembina
GLEN ULLIN (58631) Morton(80), Grant(11), Mercer(7), Oliver(1)
GLENBURN (58740) Renville(70), Ward(26), Bottineau(1), McHenry(1)
GLENFIELD (58443) Foster(98), Griggs(1)
GOLDEN VALLEY Mercer
GOLVA Golden Valley
GOODRICH (58444) Sheridan(94), Burleigh(5)
GRACE CITY (58445) Foster(87), Eddy(12)
GRAFTON Walsh
GRAND FORKS Grand Forks
GRAND FORKS AFB Grand Forks
GRANDIN (58038) Cass(74), Traill(25)
GRANVILLE McHenry
GRASSY BUTTE (58634) McKenzie(93), Billings(6)
GREAT BEND Richland
GRENORA (58845) Williams(57), Divide(42)
GUELPH Dickey
GWINNER Sargent
HAGUE Emmons
HALLIDAY (58636) Dunn(97), Mercer(2)
HAMBERG Wells
HAMILTON Pembina

HAMPDEN (58338) Cavalier(50), Ramsey(49)
HANKINSON Richland
HANNAFORD (58448) Griggs(98), Barnes(1)
HANNAH Cavalier
HANSBORO Towner
HARVEY (58341) Wells(88), Pierce(9), Benson(1)
HARWOOD Cass
HATTON (58240) Traill(72), Steele(16), Grand Forks(10)
HAVANA Sargent
HAZELTON Emmons
HAZEN (58545) Mercer(94), Oliver(5)
HEATON (58450) Wells(86), Kidder(13)
HEBRON (58638) Morton(77), Mercer(9), Stark(8), Dunn(3)
HEIMDAL Wells
HENSEL Pembina
HENSLER Oliver
HETTINGER Adams
HILLSBORO Traill
HOOPLE (58243) Walsh(88), Pembina(12)
HOPE (58046) Steele(79), Barnes(17), Cass(3)
HORACE Cass
HUNTER (58048) Cass(95), Traill(4)
HURDSFIELD (58451) Wells(97), Sheridan(2)
INKSTER (58244) Grand Forks(96), Walsh(3)
JAMESTOWN Stutsman
JESSIE Griggs
JOLIETTE Pembina
JUD (58454) La Moure(79), Stutsman(19)
KARLSRUHE McHenry
KATHRYN (58049) Barnes(77), Ransom(16), La Moure(5)
KEENE McKenzie
KENMARE (58746) Ward(76), Renville(12), Burke(10)
KENSAL (58455) Stutsman(81), Foster(18)
KIEF (58747) Sheridan(70), McHenry(29)
KILLDEER (58640) Dunn(97), McKenzie(2)
KINDRED (58051) Cass(79), Richland(20)
KINTYRE (58549) Emmons(59), Logan(37), Kidder(3)
KNOX Benson
KRAMER (58748) Bottineau(96), McHenry(3)
KULM (58456) La Moure(76), Dickey(16), McIntosh(6)
LAKOTA (58344) Nelson(96), Ramsey(3)
LAMOURE (58458) La Moure(98), Dickey(1)
LANGDON Cavalier
LANKIN Walsh
LANSFORD (58750) Bottineau(63), Renville(36)
LARIMORE Grand Forks
LAWTON (58345) Ramsey(61), Walsh(38)
LEEDS (58346) Benson(91), Towner(7)
LEFOR Stark
LEHR (58460) McIntosh(55), Logan(44)
LEITH Grant
LEONARD (58052) Cass(80), Richland(15), Ransom(3)
LIDGERWOOD (58053) Richland(85), Sargent(14)

LIGNITE Burke
LINTON Emmons
LISBON Ransom
LITCHVILLE (58461) Barnes(74), La Moure(25)
LUVERNE (58056) Barnes(57), Steele(29), Griggs(12)
MADDOCK (58348) Benson(92), Wells(7)
MAIDA Cavalier
MAKOTI (58756) Ward(78), Mountrail(15), McLean(5)
MANDAN Morton
MANDAREE (58757) McKenzie(60), Dunn(39)
MANFRED Wells
MANNING (58642) Dunn(93), Billings(6)
MANTADOR Richland
MANVEL Grand Forks
MAPLETON Cass
MARION (58466) La Moure(77), Barnes(21), Stutsman(1)
MARMARTH (58643) Slope(56), Bowman(43)
MARSHALL Dunn
MARTIN (58758) Sheridan(68), Pierce(17), Wells(14)
MAX (58759) Ward(55), McLean(44)
MAXBASS Bottineau
MAYVILLE Traill
MCCANNA Grand Forks
MCCLUSKY Sheridan
MCGREGOR (58755) Williams(63), Divide(27), Burke(8)
MCHENRY (58464) Foster(50), Eddy(41), Griggs(7)
MCKENZIE Burleigh
MCLEOD (58057) Richland(72), Ransom(28)
MCVILLE Nelson
MEDINA (58467) Stutsman(94), Kidder(5)
MEDORA (58645) Billings(93), Golden Valley(6)
MEKINOCK Grand Forks
MENOKEN Burleigh
MERCER (58559) McLean(88), Sheridan(11)
MERRICOURT Dickey
MICHIGAN Nelson
MILNOR (58060) Sargent(80), Ransom(18)
MILTON (58260) Cavalier(94), Walsh(5)
MINNEWAUKAN (58351) Benson(95), Ramsey(4)
MINOT Ward
MINOT AFB Ward
MINTO (58261) Walsh(87), Grand Forks(12)
MOFFIT (58560) Burleigh(82), Emmons(17)
MOHALL (58761) Renville(72), Bottineau(27)
MONANGO Dickey
MONTPELIER (58472) Stutsman(68), La Moure(31)

MOORETON Richland
MOTT (58646) Hettinger(95), Adams(3)
MOUNTAIN (58262) Pembina(90), Cavalier(9)
MUNICH (58352) Cavalier(94), Towner(5)
MYLO Rolette
NAPOLEON Logan
NECHE Pembina
NEKOMA Cavalier
NEW ENGLAND (58647) Hettinger(58), Slope(34), Stark(6)
NEW LEIPZIG (58562) Grant(88), Hettinger(7), Adams(3)
NEW ROCKFORD (58356) Eddy(94), Wells(3), Foster(1)
NEW SALEM (58563) Morton(81), Oliver(17)
NEW TOWN (58763) Mountrail(71), McKenzie(28)
NEWBURG (58762) Bottineau(85), McHenry(14)
NIAGARA (58266) Grand Forks(82), Nelson(17)
NOME (58062) Barnes(80), Ransom(19)
NOONAN Divide
NORTHWOOD (58267) Grand Forks(98), Steele(1)
NORWICH (58768) McHenry(54), Ward(45)
OAKES (58474) Dickey(96), Sargent(3)
OBERON Benson
ORISKA Barnes
ORRIN Pierce
OSNABROCK Cavalier
OVERLY Bottineau
PAGE (58064) Cass(89), Barnes(9), Steele(1)
PALERMO Mountrail
PARK RIVER Walsh
PARSHALL (58770) Mountrail(82), McLean(17)
PEKIN Nelson
PEMBINA Pembina
PENN Ramsey
PERTH (58363) Towner(85), Rolette(14)
PETERSBURG Nelson
PETTIBONE (58475) Kidder(94), Stutsman(5)
PILLSBURY Barnes
PINGREE Stutsman
PISEK Walsh
PLAZA (58771) Mountrail(78), Ward(18), McLean(2)
PORTAL Burke
PORTLAND (58274) Traill(85), Steele(14)
POWERS LAKE (58773) Burke(73), Mountrail(26)
RALEIGH Grant
RAY Williams
REEDER (58649) Adams(86), Hettinger(7), Bowman(5)

REGAN Burleigh
REGENT (58650) Hettinger(94), Adams(5)
REYNOLDS (58275) Grand Forks(57), Traill(42)
RHAME (58651) Bowman(85), Slope(14)
RICHARDTON (58652) Stark(89), Dunn(10)
RIVERDALE McLean
ROBINSON Kidder
ROCKLAKE Towner
ROGERS Barnes
ROLETTE (58366) Rolette(97), Pierce(2)
ROLLA (58367) Rolette(91), Towner(8)
ROSEGLEN McLean
ROSS Mountrail
RUGBY (58368) Pierce(95), McHenry(2), Benson(2)
RUSO (58778) McLean(95), McHenry(4)
RUTLAND Sargent
RYDER (58779) McLean(54), Ward(45)
SAINT ANTHONY Morton
SAINT JOHN Rolette
SAINT MICHAEL Benson
SAINT THOMAS Pembina
SANBORN Barnes
SARLES (58372) Cavalier(59), Towner(40)
SAWYER Ward
SCRANTON (58653) Bowman(72), Slope(27)
SELFRIDGE Sioux
SELZ Pierce
SENTINEL BUTTE Golden Valley
SHARON Steele
SHELDON (58068) Ransom(98), Cass(1)
SHERWOOD (58782) Renville(95), Bottineau(4)
SHEYENNE (58374) Eddy(60), Benson(30), Wells(8)
SHIELDS Grant
SOLEN (58570) Morton(57), Sioux(42)
SOURIS Bottineau
SOUTH HEART Stark
SPIRITWOOD (58481) Stutsman(51), Barnes(48)
STANLEY (58784) Mountrail(95), Burke(4)
STANTON (58571) Mercer(76), Oliver(23)
STARKWEATHER (58377) Ramsey(77), Cavalier(11), Towner(10)
STEELE Kidder
STERLING Burleigh
STIRUM (58069) Sargent(95), Ransom(4)
STRASBURG Emmons
STREETER (58483) Stutsman(66), Logan(21), Kidder(11)
SURREY Ward
SUTTON (58484) Griggs(81), Foster(18)
SYKESTON (58486) Wells(91), Stutsman(8)
TAPPEN Kidder

TAYLOR (58656) Stark(83), Dunn(16)
THOMPSON Grand Forks
TIOGA (58852) Williams(91), Mountrail(8)
TOKIO Benson
TOLLEY (58787) Renville(96), Ward(3)
TOLNA (58380) Nelson(47), Eddy(43), Benson(8)
TOWER CITY (58071) Cass(80), Barnes(19)
TOWNER (58788) McHenry(95), Pierce(4)
TRENTON Williams
TROTTERS Golden Valley
TURTLE LAKE McLean
TUTTLE Kidder
UNDERWOOD McLean
UNION Cavalier
UPHAM (58789) McHenry(90), Bottineau(9)
VALLEY CITY Barnes
VELVA (58790) McHenry(93), Ward(6)
VENTURIA McIntosh
VERONA (58490) La Moure(86), Ransom(13)
VOLTAIRE McHenry
WAHPETON Richland
WALCOTT Richland
WALES Cavalier
WALHALLA (58282) Pembina(79), Cavalier(20)
WARWICK (58381) Benson(52), Eddy(47)
WASHBURN McLean
WATFORD CITY McKenzie
WEBSTER Ramsey
WEST FARGO Cass
WESTHOPE Bottineau
WHEATLAND Cass
WHITE EARTH (58794) Mountrail(98), Williams(2)
WILDROSE (58795) Divide(52), Williams(47)
WILLISTON Williams
WILLOW CITY (58384) Bottineau(65), Pierce(16), McHenry(11), Rolette(6)
WILTON (58579) McLean(51), Burleigh(48)
WIMBLEDON (58492) Barnes(78), Stutsman(12), Griggs(8)
WING Burleigh
WISHEK (58495) McIntosh(84), Logan(15)
WOLFORD (58385) Pierce(91), Rolette(8)
WOODWORTH Stutsman
WYNDMERE Richland
YORK (58386) Benson(74), Pierce(25)
YPSILANTI (58497) Stutsman(93), Barnes(6)
ZAHL (58856) Williams(66), Divide(33)
ZAP Mercer
ZEELAND McIntosh

ZIP/City Cross Reference

58001-58001	ABERCROMBIE
58002-58002	ABSARAKA
58003-58003	ALICE
58004-58004	AMENIA
58005-58005	ARGUSVILLE
58006-58006	ARTHUR
58007-58007	AYR
58008-58008	BARNEY
58009-58009	BLANCHARD
58011-58011	BUFFALO
58012-58012	CASSELTON
58013-58013	CAYUGA
58014-58014	CHAFFEE
58015-58015	CHRISTINE
58016-58016	CLIFFORD
58017-58017	COGSWELL
58018-58018	COLFAX
58021-58021	DAVENPORT
58027-58027	ENDERLIN
58029-58029	ERIE
58030-58030	FAIRMOUNT
58031-58031	FINGAL

58032-58032	FORMAN
58033-58033	FORT RANSOM
58035-58035	GALESBURG
58036-58036	GARDNER
58038-58038	GRANDIN
58039-58039	GREAT BEND
58040-58040	GWINNER
58041-58041	HANKINSON
58042-58042	HARWOOD
58043-58043	HAVANA
58045-58045	HILLSBORO
58046-58046	HOPE
58047-58047	HORACE
58048-58048	HUNTER
58049-58049	KATHRYN
58051-58051	KINDRED
58052-58052	LEONARD
58053-58053	LIDGERWOOD
58054-58054	LISBON
58056-58056	LUVERNE
58057-58057	MCLEOD
58058-58058	MANTADOR

58059-58059	MAPLETON
58060-58060	MILNOR
58061-58061	MOORETON
58062-58062	NOME
58063-58063	ORISKA
58064-58064	PAGE
58065-58065	PILLSBURY
58067-58067	RUTLAND
58068-58068	SHELDON
58069-58069	STIRUM
58071-58071	TOWER CITY
58072-58072	VALLEY CITY
58074-58076	WAHPETON
58077-58077	WALCOTT
58078-58078	WEST FARGO
58079-58079	WHEATLAND
58081-58081	WYNDMERE
58102-58126	FARGO
58201-58203	GRAND FORKS
58204-58205	GRAND FORKS AFB
58206-58208	GRAND FORKS
58210-58210	ADAMS

58212-58212	ANETA
58213-58213	ARDOCH
58214-58214	ARVILLA
58216-58216	BATHGATE
58218-58218	BUXTON
58219-58219	CALEDONIA
58220-58220	CAVALIER
58222-58222	CRYSTAL
58223-58223	CUMMINGS
58224-58224	DAHLEN
58225-58225	DRAYTON
58227-58227	EDINBURG
58228-58228	EMERADO
58229-58229	FAIRDALE
58230-58230	FINLEY
58231-58231	FORDVILLE
58233-58233	FOREST RIVER
58235-58235	GILBY
58236-58236	GLASSTON
58237-58237	GRAFTON
58238-58238	HAMILTON
58239-58239	HANNAH

ZIP Range	City
58240-58240	HATTON
58241-58241	HENSEL
58243-58243	HOOPLE
58244-58244	INKSTER
58246-58246	JOLIETTE
58249-58249	LANGDON
58250-58250	LANKIN
58251-58251	LARIMORE
58253-58253	MCCANNA
58254-58254	MCVILLE
58255-58255	MAIDA
58256-58256	MANVEL
58257-58257	MAYVILLE
58258-58258	MEKINOCK
58259-58259	MICHIGAN
58260-58260	MILTON
58261-58261	MINTO
58262-58262	MOUNTAIN
58265-58265	NECHE
58266-58266	NIAGARA
58267-58267	NORTHWOOD
58269-58269	OSNABROCK
58270-58270	PARK RIVER
58271-58271	PEMBINA
58272-58272	PETERSBURG
58273-58273	PISEK
58274-58274	PORTLAND
58275-58275	REYNOLDS
58276-58276	SAINT THOMAS
58277-58277	SHARON
58278-58278	THOMPSON
58279-58279	UNION
58281-58281	WALES
58282-58282	WALHALLA
58301-58301	DEVILS LAKE
58310-58310	AGATE
58311-58311	ALSEN
58313-58313	BALTA
58315-58315	BARTON
58316-58316	BELCOURT
58317-58317	BISBEE
58318-58318	BOTTINEAU
58319-58319	BREMEN
58320-58320	BRINSMADE
58321-58321	BROCKET
58323-58323	CALVIN
58324-58324	CANDO
58325-58325	CHURCHS FERRY
58327-58327	CRARY
58328-58328	DOYON
58329-58329	DUNSEITH
58330-58330	EDMORE
58331-58331	EGELAND
58332-58332	ESMOND
58335-58335	FORT TOTTEN
58337-58337	HAMBERG
58338-58338	HAMPDEN
58339-58339	HANSBORO
58341-58341	HARVEY
58342-58342	HEIMDAL
58343-58343	KNOX
58344-58344	LAKOTA
58345-58345	LAWTON
58346-58346	LEEDS
58348-58348	MADDOCK
58351-58351	MINNEWAUKAN
58352-58352	MUNICH
58353-58353	MYLO
58355-58355	NEKOMA
58356-58356	NEW ROCKFORD
58357-58357	OBERON
58359-58359	ORRIN
58360-58360	OVERLY
58361-58361	PEKIN
58362-58362	PENN
58363-58363	PERTH
58365-58365	ROCKLAKE
58366-58366	ROLETTE
58367-58367	ROLLA
58368-58368	RUGBY
58369-58369	SAINT JOHN
58370-58370	SAINT MICHAEL
58372-58372	SARLES
58373-58373	SELZ
58374-58374	SHEYENNE
58377-58377	STARKWEATHER
58379-58379	TOKIO
58380-58380	TOLNA
58381-58381	WARWICK
58382-58382	WEBSTER
58384-58384	WILLOW CITY
58385-58385	WOLFORD
58386-58386	YORK
58401-58405	JAMESTOWN
58411-58411	ALFRED
58412-58412	ARENA
58413-58413	ASHLEY
58415-58415	BERLIN
58416-58416	BINFORD
58418-58418	BOWDON
58420-58420	BUCHANAN
58421-58421	CARRINGTON
58422-58422	CATHAY
58423-58423	CHASELEY
58424-58424	CLEVELAND
58425-58425	COOPERSTOWN
58426-58426	COURTENAY
58427-58427	CRYSTAL SPRINGS
58428-58428	DAWSON
58429-58429	DAZEY
58430-58430	DENHOFF
58431-58431	DICKEY
58432-58432	ECKELSON
58433-58433	EDGELEY
58436-58436	ELLENDALE
58438-58438	FESSENDEN
58439-58439	FORBES
58440-58440	FREDONIA
58441-58441	FULLERTON
58442-58442	GACKLE
58443-58443	GLENFIELD
58444-58444	GOODRICH
58445-58445	GRACE CITY
58447-58447	GUELPH
58448-58448	HANNAFORD
58450-58450	HEATON
58451-58451	HURDSFIELD
58452-58452	JESSIE
58454-58454	JUD
58455-58455	KENSAL
58456-58456	KULM
58458-58458	LAMOURE
58460-58460	LEHR
58461-58461	LITCHVILLE
58463-58463	MCCLUSKY
58464-58464	MCHENRY
58465-58465	MANFRED
58466-58466	MARION
58467-58467	MEDINA
58469-58469	MERRICOURT
58471-58471	MONANGO
58472-58472	MONTPELIER
58474-58474	OAKES
58475-58475	PETTIBONE
58476-58476	PINGREE
58477-58477	REGAN
58478-58478	ROBINSON
58479-58479	ROGERS
58480-58480	SANBORN
58481-58481	SPIRITWOOD
58482-58482	STEELE
58483-58483	STREETER
58484-58484	SUTTON
58486-58486	SYKESTON
58487-58487	TAPPEN
58488-58488	TUTTLE
58489-58489	VENTURIA
58490-58490	VERONA
58492-58492	WIMBLEDON
58494-58494	WING
58495-58495	WISHEK
58496-58496	WOODWORTH
58497-58497	YPSILANTI
58501-58507	BISMARCK
58520-58520	ALMONT
58521-58521	BALDWIN
58523-58523	BEULAH
58524-58524	BRADDOCK
58528-58528	CANNON BALL
58529-58529	CARSON
58530-58530	CENTER
58531-58531	COLEHARBOR
58532-58532	DRISCOLL
58533-58533	ELGIN
58535-58535	FLASHER
58537-58537	FORT RICE
58538-58538	FORT YATES
58540-58540	GARRISON
58541-58541	GOLDEN VALLEY
58542-58542	HAGUE
58544-58544	HAZELTON
58545-58545	HAZEN
58547-58547	HENSLER
58549-58549	KINTYRE
58551-58551	LEITH
58552-58552	LINTON
58553-58553	MCKENZIE
58554-58554	MANDAN
58558-58558	MENOKEN
58559-58559	MERCER
58560-58560	MOFFIT
58561-58561	NAPOLEON
58562-58562	NEW LEIPZIG
58563-58563	NEW SALEM
58564-58564	RALEIGH
58565-58565	RIVERDALE
58566-58566	SAINT ANTHONY
58568-58568	SELFRIDGE
58569-58569	SHIELDS
58570-58570	SOLEN
58571-58571	STANTON
58572-58572	STERLING
58573-58573	STRASBURG
58575-58575	TURTLE LAKE
58576-58576	UNDERWOOD
58577-58577	WASHBURN
58579-58579	WILTON
58580-58580	ZAP
58581-58581	ZEELAND
58601-58602	DICKINSON
58620-58620	AMIDON
58621-58621	BEACH
58622-58622	BELFIELD
58623-58623	BOWMAN
58625-58625	DODGE
58626-58626	DUNN CENTER
58627-58627	FAIRFIELD
58630-58630	GLADSTONE
58631-58631	GLEN ULLIN
58632-58632	GOLVA
58634-58634	GRASSY BUTTE
58636-58636	HALLIDAY
58638-58638	HEBRON
58639-58639	HETTINGER
58640-58640	KILLDEER
58641-58641	LEFOR
58642-58642	MANNING
58643-58643	MARMARTH
58644-58644	MARSHALL
58645-58645	MEDORA
58646-58646	MOTT
58647-58647	NEW ENGLAND
58649-58649	REEDER
58650-58650	REGENT
58651-58651	RHAME
58652-58652	RICHARDTON
58653-58653	SCRANTON
58654-58654	SENTINEL BUTTE
58655-58655	SOUTH HEART
58656-58656	TAYLOR
58657-58657	TROTTERS
58701-58703	MINOT
58704-58705	MINOT AFB
58707-58707	MINOT
58710-58710	ANAMOOSE
58711-58711	ANTLER
58712-58712	BALFOUR
58713-58713	BANTRY
58716-58716	BENEDICT
58718-58718	BERTHOLD
58720-58720	BLAISDELL
58721-58721	BOWBELLS
58722-58722	BURLINGTON
58723-58723	BUTTE
58725-58725	CARPIO
58727-58727	COLUMBUS
58728-58728	BOWBELLS
58730-58730	CROSBY
58731-58731	DEERING
58733-58733	DES LACS
58734-58734	DONNYBROOK
58735-58735	DOUGLAS
58736-58736	DRAKE
58737-58737	FLAXTON
58738-58738	FOXHOLM
58739-58739	GARDENA
58740-58740	GLENBURN
58741-58741	GRANVILLE
58744-58744	KARLSRUHE
58746-58746	KENMARE
58747-58747	KIEF
58748-58748	KRAMER
58750-58750	LANSFORD
58752-58752	LIGNITE
58755-58755	MCGREGOR
58756-58756	MAKOTI
58757-58757	MANDAREE
58758-58758	MARTIN
58759-58759	MAX
58760-58760	MAXBASS
58761-58761	MOHALL
58762-58762	NEWBURG
58763-58763	NEW TOWN
58765-58765	NOONAN
58768-58768	NORWICH
58769-58769	PALERMO
58770-58770	PARSHALL
58771-58771	PLAZA
58772-58772	PORTAL
58773-58773	POWERS LAKE
58775-58775	ROSEGLEN
58776-58776	ROSS
58778-58778	RUSO
58779-58779	RYDER
58781-58781	SAWYER
58782-58782	SHERWOOD
58783-58783	SOURIS
58784-58784	STANLEY
58785-58785	SURREY
58787-58787	TOLLEY
58788-58788	TOWNER
58789-58789	UPHAM
58790-58790	VELVA
58792-58792	VOLTAIRE
58793-58793	WESTHOPE
58794-58794	WHITE EARTH
58795-58795	WILDROSE
58801-58802	WILLISTON
58830-58830	ALAMO
58831-58831	ALEXANDER
58833-58833	AMBROSE
58835-58835	ARNEGARD
58838-58838	CARTWRIGHT
58843-58843	EPPING
58844-58844	FORTUNA
58845-58845	GRENORA
58847-58847	KEENE
58849-58849	RAY
58852-58852	TIOGA
58853-58853	TRENTON
58854-58854	WATFORD CITY
58856-58856	ZAHL

General Help Numbers:

Governor's Office
77 S High St, 30th Floor   614-466-3555
Columbus, OH 43215   Fax 614-466-9354
www.state.oh.us/gov   8AM-5PM

Attorney General's Office
State Office Tower   614-466-4320
30 E Broad St, 17th Floor   Fax 614-644-6135
Columbus, OH 43215-3428   8AM-5PM
www.ag.state.oh.us

State Court Administrator
Supreme Court of Ohio   614-466-2653
30 E Broad St, 3rd Floor   Fax 614-752-8736
Columbus, OH 43266-0419   8AM-5PM
www.sconet.state.oh.us

State Archives
Archives/Library   614-297-2300
1982 Velma Ave   Fax 614-297-2546
Columbus, OH 43211-2497   9AM-5PM TH-SA: 10-5 SU
www.ohiohistory.org/ar_tools.html

State Specifics:

Capital: Columbus
    Franklin County

Time Zone: EST

Number of Counties: 88

Population: 11,373,541

Web Site: www.state.oh.us

State Agencies

Criminal Records

Ohio Bureau of Investigation, Civilian Background Section, PO Box 365, London, OH 43140 (Courier: 1560 State Rte 56, London, OH 43140); 740-845-2000 (General Info), 740-845-2375 (Civilian Background Cks), 740-845-2633 (Fax), 8AM-4:45PM.

www.ag.state.oh.us/bci/bcii.htm

Note: The state has an innovative system over the web for electronic transfer of fingerprints. Ohio's Sex Offender Registration and Notification Law (SORN) is administered within BCI's Identification Division.

Indexing & Storage: Records are available from 1921 on. Records from 1972 on are computerized. It takes 5 days, 15 with fingerprints before new records are available for inquiry. Records are indexed on inhouse computer. Records are normally destroyed after (records maintained indefinitely). 56% of all arrests in database have final dispositions recorded.

Searching: Include the following in your request: witnessed signed release from subject, fingerprints, name DOB, SSN. 100% of the records are fingerprint supported. Records without dispositions are not released.

Access by: mail.

Fee & Payment: The search fee is $15.00 per record. Stautorily-required checks may include an FBI fingerprint check for an additional $24.00. Fee payee: Treasurer - State of Ohio. Prepayment required. No credit cards accepted.

Mail search: Turnaround time: 30 days. No self addressed stamped envelope is required.

Corporation Records
Fictitious Name
Limited Partnership Records
Assumed Name
Trademarks/Servicemarks
Limited Liability Company Records

Secretary of State, Corporate Records - Customer Service, PO Box 130, Columbus, OH 43215 (Courier: 180 E Broad Street, 16th Fl, Columbus, OH 43215); 877-767-3453, 614-466-3910, 614-466-3899 (Fax), 8AM-5PM.

www.state.oh.us/sos

Note: Information regarding officers is available from the Department of Taxation at 614-438-5339. The Dept of Commerce offers a statewide search for unclaimed funds at http://www2.state.oh.us/com/unfd/thqry1.htm

Indexing & Storage: Records are available from the 1800's. New records are available for inquiry immediately. Records are indexed on microfilm, index cards, inhouse computer.

Searching: Include the following in your request: full name of business. In addition to the articles of incorporation, corporation records include the following information: Annual Reports, Prior (merged) names, Inactive and Reserved names.

Access by: mail, phone, fax, in person, online.

Fee & Payment: There is no search fee nor a fee for certification of a document. Copy fees are no charge up to 34 pages, then $1.05 for the 35th, and $.03 per copy thereafter. Good Standings are $5.00 each. There is no fee for a corporate printout of limited information. Fee payee: Secretary of State. Prepayment required. Personal checks accepted. No credit cards accepted.

Mail search: Turnaround time: 3 to 5 days. No self addressed stamped envelope is required.

Phone search: They will release limited information over the phone.

Fax search: No fee, turnaround time is 3-5 days.

In person search: There is no fee to look at records.

Online search: The agency provides free Internet searching for business and corporation records, the site also includes UCC and campaign finance.

Other access: The state makes the database available for purchase, call for details.

Uniform Commercial Code

UCC Records, Secretary of State, PO Box 2795, Columbus, OH 43216 (Courier: 180 E Broad Street, 16th Fl, Columbus, OH 43215); 877-767-3453, 614-466-3126, 614-466-2892 (Fax), 8AM-5PM.

www.state.oh.us/sos

Indexing & Storage: Records are available for only current or active filings. Records are indexed on inhouse computer.

Searching: Use search form UCC-11. All tax liens are filed at the county level. Include the following in your request: debtor name. Be sure to include the words "any and all addresses" in your search request.

Access by: mail, phone, in person, online.

Fee & Payment: The search fee is $20.00 per debtor name, copies included. Fee payee: Secretary of State. Prepayment required. Personal checks accepted. No credit cards accepted.

Mail search: Turnaround time: 5-8 days.

Phone search: Calls are limited to 10 filings, 3 debtor names per call. There is no charge for verbal information.

In person search: Searching is available in person.

Online search: The Internet site offers free online access to records.

Other access: The complete database is available on electronic media with weekly updates. Call for current pricing.

Federal Tax Liens
State Tax Liens
Records not maintained by a state level agency.

Note: Records are not housed by a state agency. You must secure from the local county recorder offices.

Sales Tax Registrations
Access to Records is Restricted

Taxation Department, Sale & Use Tax Division, 30 E Broad St, 20th Floor, Columbus, OH 43215; 614-466-7351, 888-405-4039, 614-466-4977 (Fax), 8AM-5PM M-F.

www.state.oh.us/tax

Note: This agency refuses to release any information about registrants.

Birth Certificates

Ohio Department of Health, Bureau of Vital Statistics, PO Box 15098, Columbus, OH 43216-0118 (Courier: 246 N High St, 1st Fl, Revenue Room, Columbus, OH 43215); 614-466-2531, 614-466-6604 (Fax), 7:45AM-4:30PM.

www.odh.state.oh.us/Birth/birthmain.htm

Indexing & Storage: Records are available from 01/45 1908 to present. Records from 12/20/08 to 12/31/44 are at the Ohio Historical Society at 614-297-2510. It takes 6 months before new records are available for inquiry.

Searching: Include the following in your request: full name, names of parents including mother's maiden name, date of birth, city and county of birth.

Access by: mail, in person.

Fee & Payment: The fee is $3.00 per name covering a ten year search. If a certified copy is needed, the fee is $10.00. Uncertified copies are $.05 per page plus postage. Fee payee: Treasurer, State of Ohio Prepayment required. Credit card use only for expedited service. Personal checks accepted. Credit cards accepted: MasterCard, Visa, AmEx, Discover.

Mail search: Turnaround time: 4 to 6 weeks. No self addressed stamped envelope is required.

In person search: Turnaround time 7 to 10 days.

Expedited service: Expedited service is available for fax searches through VitalChek at 877-553-2439 (fax), call 800-255-2414 for more information. Turnaround time: 5 days.

Death Records

Ohio Department of Health, Bureau of Vital Statistics, PO Box 15098, Columbus, OH 43215-0098 (Courier: 246 N High Street, 1st Fl, Revenue Room, Columbus, OH 43215); 614-466-2531, 7:45AM-4:30PM.

www.odh.state.oh.us/Birth/birthmain.htm

Indexing & Storage: Records are available from 1945 to present. Death records from 1908 to 1944 are found at Ohio Historical Society, 1982 Velma Ave, Columbus, OH 43211. Records prior to 1908 are located at the county level.

Searching: Requests must be in writing. Include the following in your request: full name, date of death, city and county of death.

Access by: mail, fax, in person, online.

Fee & Payment: The fee is $10.00 for a certified copy. The search includes a ten year period. There is an additional $3.00 for each 10 years searched. Uncertified copies are $.03 per page plus postage. Fee payee: Treasurer, State of Ohio. Prepayment required. Credit cards only accepted for expedited service. Personal checks accepted. Credit cards accepted: MasterCard, Visa, AmEx, Discover.

Mail search: Turnaround time: 4 to 6 weeks. No self addressed stamped envelope is required.

Fax search: See expedited service below.

In person: Turnaround time is 7 to 10 days.

Online search: The Ohio Historical Society Death Certificate Index Searchable Database at www.ohiohistory.org/dindex/search.cfm permits searching by name, county, index. Data is available from 1913 to 1937 only.

Expedited service: Expedited service is available from 800-255-2414 Turnaround time: 5 days. This is available from VitalChek. The fee is $26.75 which includes use of credit card and express delivery.

Marriage Certificates
Divorce Records
Access to Records is Restricted

Bureau of Vital Statistics., PO Box 15098, Columbus, OH 43215-0098.

www.odh.state.oh.us/Birth/birthmain.htm

Note: Marriage and Divorce records are found at county of issue.

Workers' Compensation Records

Bureau of Workers Compensation, Customer Assistance, 30 W Spring St, Fl 10, Columbus, OH 43215-2241; 800-644-6292, 877-520-6446 (Fax), 7:30AM-5:30PM.

www.ohiobwc.com

Indexing & Storage: Records are available for the past 10 years. Records are indexed on inhouse computer. Records are normally destroyed after 10 years if records are inactive.

Searching: All information is public except injured worker medical report and information pertaining to the employer's financial condition. Include the following in your request: claimant name, Social Security Number. Claim number is helpful. All requests must be in writing.

Access by: mail, phone, fax, in person, online.

Fee & Payment: There is no search fee, copy fee is $.25 per page. Fee payee: Ohio Bureau of Workers Compensation. Prepayment required. Personal checks accepted. No credit cards accepted.

Mail search: Turnaround time: 1 week. A self addressed stamped envelope is requested.

Phone search: They will provide the information immediately unless file is lengthy or excessive.

Fax search: Service is available with a 24 hour turnaround time.

In person search: Call for location of records before going in because there are 22 different office locations.

Online search: Injured workers, injured worker designees, representatives and managed care organizations (MCOs) can view a list of all claims associated with a given SSN, but are limited to viewing only the claims with which they are associated. Employers, their representatives or designees, and managed care organizations can view a list of all claims associated to their BWC policy number. Medical providers can view all claims associated with any given SSN. Access is through the web site listed above.

Other access: Bulk data is released to approved accounts; however, the legal department must approve requesters. The agency has general information available on a web site.

Driver Records

Department of Public Safety, Bureau of Motor Vehicles, 1970 W Broad St, Columbus, OH 43223-1102; 614-752-7600, 8AM-5:30PM M-T-W; 8AM-4:30PM TH-F.

www.ohiobmv.com

Note: Copies of tickets are available from the Bureau of Motor Vehicles, Transcript Records, PO Box 16520, Columbus 43266-0020. The fee is $1.00 per page.

Indexing & Storage: Records are available for 5 years for moving violations, DWI's and suspensions. Records are purged from public view after 7 years; insurance laws require 36 months of availability. It takes 2 to 5 weeks before new records are available for inquiry.

Searching: Use Record Request Form 1173 (downloadable from Internet). If requester does not have permissible use per DPPA, Form BMV 5008 is also required, which requires notarized consent of subject. Records w/o personal information are not released to the public. Include the following in your request: driver's license number, full name, date of birth, Social Security Number. Driver's address is included as part of the search report for permissible requesters, except for requests received from California. The following data is not released: mental health records, SSNs unless provided by requester (except government agency requesters).

Access by: mail, phone, fax, in person, online.

Fee & Payment: The fee is $2.00 per record. A license status check is available for $2.00. Fee payee: Treasurer, State of Ohio. Prepayment required. Personal checks accepted. No credit cards accepted.

Mail search: Turnaround time: 1 to 3 days. A self addressed stamped envelope is requested.

Phone search: Qualified, pre-approved accounts may order by phone. There is a $100.00 deposit.

Fax search: Same criteria as phone searches.

In person search: Up to eight records will be processed while you wait.

Online search: The system is called "Defender System" and is suggested for requesters who order 100 or more motor vehicle reports per day in batch mode. Turnaround is in 4-8 hours. The DL# or SSN and name are needed when ordering. Fee is $2.00 per record. For more information, call 614-752-7692.

Other access: Overnight magnetic tape service is available for larger accounts.

Vehicle Ownership
Vehicle Identification

Bureau of Motor Vehicles, Motor Vehicle Title Records, 1970 W Broad St, Columbus, OH 43223-1102; 614-752-7671, 614-752-8929 (Fax), 7:30AM-4:45PM.

www.ohiobmv.com/1

Indexing & Storage: Records are available for the current year plus six. It takes 1 to 2 days normally before new records are available for inquiry.

Searching: Use Record Request Form 1173 (downloadable from Internet). If requester does not have permissible use per DPPA, Form BMV 5008 is also required, which requires notarized consent of subject. Records w/o personal information are not released to the public. Lien information is not recorded on vehicle registration records in Ohio. The following data is not released: Social Security Numbers, unless included in request.

Access by: mail, in person, online.

Fee & Payment: The fee is $2.00 or each record searched. Fee payee: Treasurer, State of Ohio. Prepayment required. Personal checks accepted. No credit cards accepted.

Mail search: Turnaround time: 1 to 3 days. A self addressed stamped envelope is requested.

In person search: There may be a limit on the number of requests processed immediately, most are not available until the next day.

Online search: Ohio offers online access through AAMVAnet. All requesters must comply with a contractual agreement prior to release of data, which complies with DPPA regulations. Fee is $2.00 per record. Call 614-752-7692 for more information.

Accident Reports

Department of Public Safety, Central Records Unit, PO Box 182074, Columbus, OH 43218-2074; 614-752-1593, 614-644-9749 (Fax), 8AM-4:45PM.

Indexing & Storage: Records are available for 5 years to present. Records are indexed on computer. It takes 2 to 5 weeks before new records are available for inquiry.

Searching: Include the following in your request: full name, date of accident. Submitting the driver's license number or SSN is very helpful. The following data is not released: Social Security Numbers.

Access by: mail, in person.

Fee & Payment: The fee is $3.00 per record. There is a charge for a no record found. Fee payee: Department of Public Safety. Prepayment required. Personal checks accepted. No credit cards accepted.

Mail search: Turnaround time: 2 to 3 days.

In person search: Turnaround time is immediate if the record is on file.

Vessel Ownership
Vessel Registration

Natural Resources Department, Division of Watercraft, 4435 Fountain Square Dr Bldg A, Columbus, OH 43224-1300; 614-265-6480, 614-267-8883 (Fax), 8AM-5PM.

www.dnr.state.oh.us/watercraft/

Indexing & Storage: Records are available from 1960 to the present. Records are indexed on computer for the last 3 years. Any boat operated on public waters must be registered. All boats 14 ft or longer or having a 10+ hp motor must be titled.

Searching: To search, one of the following is required: name, hull ID #, registration #, or serial #. The following data is not released: Social Security Numbers.

Access by: mail, phone, fax, in person.

Fee & Payment: There is no search fee for registration records. There is a $2.00 fee for a title search. Fee payee: Division of Watercraft. Prepayment required. Personal checks accepted. No credit cards accepted.

Mail search: Turnaround time: 2 to 4 days. No self addressed stamped envelope is required.

Phone search: There is a limit of five names per call for registration information.

Fax search: Same criteria as mail searching.

In person search: Searching is available in person.

Legislation Records

Ohio House of Representatives, 77 S High Street, Columbus, OH 43266 (Courier: Ohio Senate, State House, Columbus, OH 43215); 614-466-8842 (In-State Only), 614-466-9745 (Out-of-State), 614-466-3357 (Clerk's Office), 614-644-8744 (Fax), 8:30AM-5PM.

www.legislature.state.oh.us

Note: Note the two addresses for the different bodies.

Indexing & Storage: Records are available from 1888 to present on microfiche and are computerized since 1990. Bills for the years 1888-1990 are available on microfilm at many libraries in Ohio.

Searching: Include the following in your request: bill number.

Access by: mail, phone, fax, in person, online.

Fee & Payment: There is no search fee.

Mail search: Turnaround time: 1 to 2 days.

Phone search: Records are available by phone.

Fax search: Records are available by fax.

In person search: Searching is available in person.

Online search: The Internet site offers access to bill text, status, and enactment back to 1997/98.

Other access: E-mail requests are accepted.

Voter Registration

Secretary of State, Elections Division, 180 E Broad St, 15th Fl, Columbus, OH 43215; 614-466-2585, 614-752-4360 (Fax), 8AM-5PM.

www.state.oh.us/sos

Indexing & Storage: Records are available for 6 years.

Searching: The state suggests that all individual requests be done at the county Board of Elections.

Access by: mail, in person.

Fee & Payment: There is no fee. Fee payee: Secretary of State. Prepayment required. No credit cards accepted.

Mail search: Turnaround time: 1 week to 10 days. No self addressed stamped envelope is required.

In person search: The state is not prepared to handle look-ups, but will assist as necessary.

Other access: Records may be purchased in a variety of formats. Lists are arranged in alpha order within precinct, unless otherwise indicated. For further information, contact Audrey Hatchett at 614-466-8895.

GED Certificates

Department of Education, State GED Office, 25 S Front St, 1st Fl, Columbus, OH 43215-4104; 614-466-1577, 614-752-9445 (Fax), 8AM-4:45PM.

Indexing & Storage: Records are available from 1984 to present. Prior records are on microfilm.

Searching: Include the following in your request: date of birth, Social Security Number, signed release, approx date of test. DOB is helpful.

Access by: fax, in person.

Fee & Payment: There is no fee for a verification, a $5.00 fee for a copy of a transcript. Fee payee: OH Dept of Education. Prepayment required. No credit cards accepted. No self addressed stamped envelope is required.

Fax search: Same criteria as mail searching.

In person search: Searching is available in person.

Hunting License Information
Fishing License Information

Ohio Department of Natural Resources, Division of Wildlife, 1840 Belcher Drive, Columbus, OH 43224 614-265-7040, 8AM-5PM.

Indexing & Storage: Records are available from from 1999 forward.

Searching: Request must be in writing, suggest placing "Attn: Cheryl" on envelope. Include the following in your request: date of birth, Social Security Number.

Access by: fax, in person.

Fee & Payment: There is no fee.

Mail search: Turnaround time is 1-3 days.

Ohio State Licensing Agencies

Licenses Searchable Online

Accounting Firm #1	www.state.oh.us/acc/search.html
Acupuncturist #28	www.state.oh.us/med/license/query.stm
Anesthesiologist Assistant #28	www.state.oh.us/med/license/query.stm
Architect #2	www.state.oh.us/arc/license/query.asp
Athletic Trainer #29	www.state.oh.us/scripts/pyt/query.asp
Audiologist/Audiologist Aide #8	www.state.oh.us/slp/licenses.htm
Barber School #26	www.state.oh.us/brb/barbsch.htm
Chiropractor #9	http://156.63.245.111/index.html
Clinical Nurse Specialist #6	www.state.oh.us/nur/Verification.stm
Coil Cleaner (Liquor/Beverage) #27	www.state.oh.us/com/liquor/liquor13.htm
Contractor #14	www.com.state.oh.us/odoc/dic/scripts/ociebqy.htm
Cosmetic Therapist #28	www.state.oh.us/med/license/query.stm
Counselor #11	www.state.oh.us/scripts/csw/query.asp
Dental Assistant Radiologist #33	www.state.oh.us/scripts/den/query.stm
Dental Hygienist #33	www.state.oh.us/scripts/den/query.stm
Dentist #33	www.state.oh.us/scripts/den/query.stm
Dialysis Technician #6	www.state.oh.us/nur/Dialysis.stm
Drug Wholesaler/Distributor #7	www.ohio.gov/pharmacy/license.htm
Electrician #14	www.com.state.oh.us/odoc/dic/scripts/ociebqy.htm
Lobbyist/Lobbyist Employer, Exec. Agency #30	www.jlec-olig.state.oh.us/agent_search_form.cfm
Heating/Refrigeration (HVAC) #14	www.com.state.oh.us/odoc/dic/scripts/ociebqy.htm
Hydronic #14	www.com.state.oh.us/odoc/dic/scripts/ociebqy.htm
Insurance Agent #20	www.ohioinsurance.gov/ConsumServ/ocs/agentloc.asp
Landscape Architect #2	www.state.oh.us/arc/license/query.asp
Legislative Agent/Agent Employer #30	www.jlec-olig.state.oh.us/agent_search_form.cfm
Liquor Distributor #27	www.state.oh.us/com/liquor/liquor15.htm
Liquor License #27	www.state.oh.us/com/liquor/phone.txt
Lottery Retailer #35	www.ohiolottery.com/frameset/games/retailer.html
Massage Therapist #28	www.state.oh.us/med/license/query.stm
Mechanotherapist #28	www.state.oh.us/med/license/query.stm
Medical Doctor #28	www.state.oh.us/med/license/query.stm
Midwife Nurse #6	www.state.oh.us/nur/Verification.stm
Naprapath #28	www.state.oh.us/med/license/query.stm
Nurse Anesthetist #6	www.state.oh.us/nur/Verification.stm
Nurse Practitioner #6	www.state.oh.us/nur/Verification.stm
Nurse-RN/LPN #6	www.state.oh.us/nur/Verification.stm
Occupational Therapist/Assistant #29	www.state.oh.us/scripts/pyt/query.asp
Optometrist #37	www.state.oh.us/scripts/opt/query.asp
Optometrist, Diagnostic/Therapeutic #37	www.state.oh.us/scripts/opt/query.asp
Osteopathic Physician #28	www.state.oh.us/med/license/query.stm
Pharmacist #7	www.ohio.gov/pharmacy/license.htm
Pharmacy/Pharmacy Dispensary #7	www.ohio.gov/pharmacy/license.htm
Physical Therapist/Assistant #29	www.state.oh.us/scripts/pyt/query.asp
Physician Assistant #28	www.state.oh.us/med/license/query.stm
Plumber #14	www.com.state.oh.us/odoc/dic/scripts/ociebqy.htm
Podiatrist #28	www.state.oh.us/med/license/query.stm
Polygraph Examiner #46	http://polygraph.org/states/oape/directory.htm
Prescriptive Authority #6	www.state.oh.us/nur/RxAuth.stm
Psychologist #36	http://www2.state.oh.us/psy/query.asp
Public Accountant-CPA #1	www.state.oh.us/acc/search.html
Real Estate Appraiser #15	www.asc.gov/content/category1/appr_by_state.asp
Real Estate Sales Agent #15	www.ohiorealtors.org/search/locate.html
Respiratory Therapist/Student #42	www.state.oh.us/scripts/rsp/license/query.asp
School Psychologist #36	http://www2.state.oh.us/psy/query.asp
Social Worker #11	www.state.oh.us/scripts/csw/query.asp
Speech Pathologist/Audiologist #8	www.state.oh.us/slp/licenses.htm
Teacher/Teacher's Aide #43	https://www.ode.state.oh.us/Teaching-Profession/Teacher/Certification_Licensure/certifact.asp
Veterinarian #45	www.state.oh.us/ovmlb/consumers.htm
Veterinary Technician #45	www.state.oh.us/ovmlb/consumers.htm

Licensing Quick Finder

Accounting Firm #1	614-466-4135	
Acupuncturist #28	614-644-3934	
Adoption Agency #19	614-466-9274	
Adult Care Home #18	614-466-7713	
Airline Liquor Permit #27	614-644-2360	
Anesthesiologist Assistant #28	614-644-3934	
Architect #2	614-466-2316	
Athlete Agent #32	330-742-5120	
Athletic Trainer #29	614-466-3774	
Attorney #44	614-466-1553	
Auctioneer #15	614-466-4130	
Audiologist/Audiologist Aide #8	614-466-3145	
Backflow Prevent Assembly Insp. #34	614-644-2223	
Bank #17	614-728-8400	
Barber #26	614-466-5003	
Barber Instructor #26	614-466-5003	
Barber School #26	614-466-5003	
Barber Shop #26	614-466-5003	
Bedding/Furniture Dealer/Dist. #38	614-644-2233	
Bedding/Furniture Mfg/Renovator #38	614-644-2233	
Boiler Inspector #34	614-644-2223	
Boiler Operator #34	614-644-2223	
Boxer/Boxing Professional #32	330-742-5120	
Boxing Event #32	330-742-5120	
Boxing Physician/Inspector #32	330-742-5120	
Boxing Promoter/Matchmaker #32	330-742-5120	
Building Inspector #3	614-644-2613	
Building Official #3	614-644-2613	
Cemetery #15	216-787-3100	
Check Cashing Service #17	614-728-8400	
Check Lending Service #17	614-728-8400	
Child Day Care Facility #19	614-466-9274	
Children's Residential Center #19	614-466-9274	
Children's Services Agency #19	614-466-9274	
Chiropractor #9	614-644-7032	
Clinical Nurse Specialist #6	614-466-3947	
Coil Cleaner (Liquor/Beverage) #27	614-644-2360	
Consumer Finance Company #17	614-728-8400	
Contractor #14	614-644-3493	
Cosmetic Therapist #28	614-466-3934	
Cosmetologist/Mgr.Cosmetologist #4	614-644-3834	
Cosmetology Instructor #4	614-644-3834	
Counselor #11	614-466-0912	
Credit Service Organization #13	614-466-2221	
Credit Union #13	614-466-2221or728-8400	
Crematory #5	614-466-4252	
Dairy Farm #12	614-466-5550	
Dental Assistant Radiologist #33	614-466-2580	
Dental Hygienist #33	614-466-2580	
Dentist #33	614-466-2580	
Dialysis Technician #6	614-466-3947	
Dietitian #31	614-466-3291	
Drug Wholesaler/Distributor #7	614-466-4143	
Electrical Safety Inspector #3	614-644-2613	
Electrical Safety Trainee #3	614-644-2613	
Electrician #14	614-644-3493	
Elevator Inspector #38	614-644-3524	
Embalmer/Embalming Facility #5	614-466-4252	
Emergency Medical Technician #22	614-466-9447	
EMT Instructor #22	614-466-9447	

Engineer #23	614-466-3650
Engineering/Surveying Company #23	614-466-3650
Esthetician/Managing Esthetician #4	614-644-3834
Explosives #34	614-752-7126
Family Foster Home #19	614-466-9274
Fire Alarm & Detection Inspector #34	614-644-7126
Fire Extinguisher (Portable) Insp. #34	614-644-7126
Fire Extinguisher Equip Inspector #34	614-644-7126
Firefighter/Firefighter Instructor #22	614-466-9447
Fireworks Exhibitor/Assistant #34	614-752-7126
Fishing Guide #21	419-625-8062
Foreign Real Estate Property #15	614-466-4100
Funeral Director #5	614-466-4252
Funeral Home #5	614-466-4252
Group Home Operator #19	614-466-9274
Health Care Facility #18	614-466-7713
Hearing Aid Dealer/Fitter #25	614-466-5215
Heating/Refrigeration (HVAC) #14	614-644-3493
Horse Racing Facility/Owner #41	614-466-2757
Hotel/Motel #34	614-752-7126
Hydronic #14	614-644-3493
Independent Living Arranger #19	614-466-9274
Insurance Agent #20	614-644-2665
Insurance Broker, Non-Resident #20	614-644-2665
Insurance Solicitor #20	614-644-2665
Investment Advisor/Advisor Rep. #16	614-644-3466
Landscape Architect #2	614-466-2316
Legislative Agent/Agent Employer #30	614-728-5100
Liquor Distributor #27	614-644-2360
Liquor License #27	614-644-2360
Lobbyist/Lobbyist Employer (Exec. Agency) #30	614-728-5100
Lottery Retailer #35	216-787-3200
Manicuring/Esthetician Instructor #4	614-644-3834
Manicurist/Managing Manicurist #4	614-644-3834
Massage Therapist #28	614-466-3934
Mechanical Inspector #3	614-644-2613
Mechanotherapist #28	614-644-3934
Medical Doctor #28	614-466-3934
Midwife Nurse #6	614-466-3947
Milk Hauler #12	614-466-5550
Milk Processor/Producer/Plant #12	614-466-5550
Milk Tester/Sampler #12	614-466-5550
Mortgage Broker #17	614-728-8400
Mortgage Broker, Real Estate #13	614-466-2221
Mortgage Loan Act #13	614-466-2221
Naprapath #28	614-644-3934
Notary Public #10	614-466-2566
Nurse Anesthetist #6	614-466-3947
Nurse Practitioner #6	614-466-3947
Nurse-RN/LPN #6	614-466-3947
Nursing Home #18	614-466-7713
Nursing Home Administrator #18	614-466-5114
Occupational Therapist/Assistant #29	614-466-3774
Ocularist/Ocularist Apprentice #39	614-466-9707
Optical Dispenser #39	614-466-9707
Optician/Optician Apprentice #39	614-466-9707
Optometrist #37	614-466-5115
Optometrist, Diagnostic/Therapeutic #37	614-466-5115

Osteopathic Physician #28	614-466-3934
Pawnbroker #17	614-728-8400
Pesticide Applicator #40	614-728-6987
Pesticide Dealer #40	614-728-6987
Pesticide Operator #40	614-728-6987
Pharmacist #7	614-466-4143
Pharmacy/Pharmacy Dispensary #7	614-466-4143
Physical Therapist/Assistant #29	614-466-3774
Physician Assistant #28	614-466-3934
Plan Examiner #3	614-644-2613
Plumber #14	614-644-3493
Podiatrist #28	614-644-3934
Polygraph Examiner #46	614-645-4174
Precious Metals Dealer #17	614-728-8400
Premium Finance Company #17	614-466-2221
Prescriptive Authority #6	614-466-3947
Pressure Piping Inspector #34	614-644-2223
Private Investigator #15	614-466-4130
Psychologist #36	614-466-8808
Public Accountant-CPA #1	614-752-8248
Public Adjuster #20	614-644-2665
Racetrack Personnel #41	614-466-2757
Racing Permit #41	614-466-2757
Real Estate Appraiser #15	216-787-3100
Real Estate Broker #15	614-466-4100
Real Estate Sales Agent #15	614-466-4100
Residential Care Facility #18	614-466-7713
Residential Parenting Organization #19	614-466-9274
Respiratory Therapist/Student #42	614-752-9218
Savings & Loan Association #17	614-728-8400
Savings Bank #17	614-728-8400
School Counselor #43	614-466-3593
School Principal/Administrator #43	614-466-3593
School Psychologist #36	614-466-8808
School Treasurer/Business Mgr. #43	614-466-3593
Scientific Collection Permit #21	614-265-6666
Securities Dealer/Salesperson #16	614-644-3466
Security Guard #15	614-466-4130
Social Worker #11	614-466-0912
Solid Waste Facility Operator #24	614-644-2621
Speech Pathologist Aide #8	614-466-3145
Speech Pathologist/Audiologist #8	614-466-3145
Sprinkler Equipment Inspector #34	614-644-7126
Sprinkler Inspector #3	614-644-2613
Sprinkler, Fire Alarm, Hazardous Designer #3	614-644-2613
Steam Engineer #34	614-644-2223
Steam, Stationary #34	614-644-2223
Surveyor, Land #23	614-466-3650
Teacher/Teacher's Aide #43	614-466-3593
Tough-Person Promoter #32	330-742-5120
Tour Promoter #34	614-644-2223
Travel Agent #34	614-644-2223
Underground Storage Tank #34	614-752-7938
Underground Tank Inspector #34	614-752-7921
Underground Tank Installer #34	614-752-7921
Veterinarian #45	614-644-5281
Veterinary Technician #45	614-644-5281
Water Supply Equip. Inspector 34	614-644-2223

Licensing Agency Information

#1 Accountancy Board of Ohio, 77 S High St, 18th Fl, Columbus, OH 43266-0301; 614-466-4135, Fax: 614-466-2628. www.state.oh.us/acc Search database at www.state.oh.us/acc/search.html

#2 Architects Board of Ohio, 77 S High St, 16th Fl, Columbus, OH 43266-0303; 614-466-2316, Fax: 614-644-9048. www.state.oh.us/arc Agency email: cmharch@aol.com. Search database at www.state.oh.us/arc/license/query.asp

#3 Department of Commerce, Board of Building Standards, 6606 Tussing Rd (PO Box 4009), Reynoldsburg, OH 43068; 614-644-2613, Fax: 614-644-3147.
www.com.state.oh.us/odoc/dic/dicbbs.htm.
Agency email: jwbrant@com.state.oh.us.

#4 Board of Cosmetology, 1010 Sland Mall, Columbus, OH 43207-4041; 614-466-3834, Fax: 614-644-6880. www.state.oh.us/cos. Agency email: ohiocosbd@das.state.oh.us. An online

search system is planned. Once available, the web address will be www.state.oh.us/cos/licensedb.htm

#5 Board of Embalmers & Funeral Directors of Ohio, 77 S High St, 16th Fl, Columbus, OH 43266; 614-466-4252, Fax: 614-728-6825.
www.state.oh.us/fun
Agency email: oh.emb.bd@exchange.state.oh.us.

#6 Board of Nursing, 17 S High St #400, Columbus, OH 43215; 614-466-3947, Fax: 614-466-0388. www.state.oh.us/nur *continued*

Search database at www.state.oh.us/nur/Verification.stm. Must search by license number or SSN. Prescriptive authority needs name or COA#.

#7 Board of Pharmacy, 77 S High St, 17th Fl, Columbus, OH 43266-0320; 614-466-4143, Fax: 614-752-4836. www.ohio.gov/pharmacy
Agency email: bob_butler@ohio.gov.
Search database at
www.ohio.gov/pharmacy/license.htm

#8 Board of Speech Pathology & Audiology, 77 S High St, 16th Fl, Columbus, OH 43215; 614-466-3145, Fax: 614-995-2286. www.state.oh.us/slp
Agency email: sallie.debolt@splaud.state.oh.us.
Search database at
www.state.oh.us/slp/licenses.htm

#9 Chiropractic Board, 77 S High St, 16th Fl, Columbus, OH 43266-0542; 614-644-7032, Fax: 614-752-2539.
www.state.oh.us/chr
Agency email: chirobd@mail.peps.state.oh.us.
Search database at
http://156.63.245.111/index.html

#10 Commission Clerk, 77 S High St, 19th Fl, Columbus, OH 43215; 614-466-2566.

#11 Counselor & Social Worker Board, 77 S High St, 16th Fl, Columbus, OH 43266-0340; 614-466-0912, Fax: 614-728-7790.
www.state.oh.us/csw
Agency email: csw_hackett@ohio.gov.
Search database at
www.state.oh.us/scripts/csw/query.asp

#12 Department of Agriculture, 8995 E Main St, Reynoldsburg, OH 43068-3399; 614-466-5550, Fax: 614-728-2652.
www.state.oh.us/agr/

#14 Ohio Department of Commerce, Construction Industry Examination Board, 6606 Tussing Rd, Reynoldsburg, OH 43068-9009; 614-644-3493, Fax: 614-728-1200.
www.com.state.oh.us/odoc/dic/default.htm
Search database at
www.com.state.oh.us/odoc/dic/scripts/ociebqy.htm

#15 Department of Commerce, Division of Real Estate & Professional Licensing, 77 S High St, 20th Fl, Columbus, OH 43266-0547; 614-466-4130, Fax: 614-466-0584.
www.com.state.oh.us/real
Agency email: WebMaster@com.state.oh.us.

#16 Department of Commerce, Division of Securities, 77 S High St, 22nd Fl, Columbus, OH 43215-0548; 614-644-7381, Fax: 614-466-3316.
www.securities.state.oh.us

#17 Department of Commerce, Division of Financial Institutions, 77 S High St, 21st Fl, Columbus, OH 43266-0121; 614-728-8400, Fax: 614-466-1631.
www.com.state.oh.us/dfi/default.htm
Agency email: WebMaster@com.state.oh.us.

#18 Department of Health, 246 N High St, Columbus, OH 43266-0118; 614-466-5114, Fax: 614-466-0271. www.odh.state.oh.us

#19 Office For Children & Families, 255 E Main, 3rd Fl, Columbus, OH 43215; 614-466-9274, Fax: 614-728-9682; 614-752-2580.
www.oh.state.us/odhs/oapl

#20 Department of Insurance, 2100 Stella Ct, Columbus, OH 43215-1067; 614-644-2665, Fax: 614-644-3475. www.ohioinsurance.gov

Search database at www.ohioinsurance.gov/ConsumServ/ocs/agentloc.asp

#21 Department of Natural Resources, 1840 Belcher Dr, Columbus, OH 43224; 614-265-7040, Fax: 614-262-1143. www.dnr.state.oh.us

#22 Department of Public Safety, PO Box 182073, Columbus, OH 43218-2073; 614-466-9447, Fax: 614-466-9461. www.state.oh.us/odps

#23 Engineers & Surveyors Board, 77 S High St, 16th Fl, Rm 1698, Columbus, OH 43266-0314; 614-466-3650, Fax: 614-728-3059.
www.ohiopeps.org
Agency email: board@mail.peps.state.oh.us.

#24 Hazardous Waste Facility Board, 122 S Front St, Columbus, OH 43215; 614-644-3020, Fax: 614-728-5315.
www.epa.state.oh.us/dsiwm

#25 Hearing Aid Dealers & Fitters Board, 246 N High St (PO Box 118), Columbus, OH 43266-0118; 614-466-5215, Fax: 614-466-8692.
www.odh.state.oh.us/odhprograms/hdlr/hdamain1.htm. Agency email: hearing@gw.odh.state.oh.us.

#26 Licensing Boards, Barber Board, 77 S High St, 16th Fl, Columbus, OH 43215; 614-466-5003, Fax: 614-387-1694. www.state.oh.us/brb

#27 Division of Liquor Control, 6606 Tussing Rd, Reynoldsburg, OH 43068-9005; 614-644-2360, Fax: 614-644-2480.
www.state.oh.us/com/liquor/liquor.htm
Agency email: agencyops@liquor.state.oh.us.

#28 Medical Board of Ohio, 77 S High St, 17th Fl, Columbus, OH 43266-0315; 614-466-3934, Fax: 614-728-5946. www.state.oh.us/med/
Search database at
www.state.oh.us/med/license/query.stm

#29 OTPTAT - Occupational Therapy - Physical Therapy Board, 77 S High St, 16th Fl, Columbus, OH 43266-0317; 614-466-3774, Fax: 614-644-8112. www.state.oh.us/pyt
Search database at
www.state.oh.us/scripts/pyt/query.asp

#30 Office of Legislative Inspector General, 50 W Broad St, #1308, Columbus, OH 43215-3365; 614-728-5100, Fax: 614-728-5074.
www.jlec-olig.state.oh.us
Agency email: info@jlec-olig.state.oh.us.
Search database at www.jlec-olig.state.oh.us/agent_search_form.cfm

#31 Board of Dietetics, 77 S High St, 18th Fl, Columbus, OH 43266-0337; 614-466-3291, Fax: 614-728-0723. www.state.oh.us/obd
Agency email: obd_mavko@ohio.gov.
#32 Boxing Commission, 2545 Belmont Ave, Union Square Plaza, Youngstown, OH 44505; 330-742-5120, Fax: 330-742-2571. Agency email: oacpaul@riffe.ciec.ohio.gov.

#33 Dental Board, 77 S High St, 18th Fl, Columbus, OH 43266-0306; 614-466-2580, Fax: 614-752-8995. www.state.oh.us/den
Search database at
www.state.oh.us/scripts/den/query.stm

#34 Ohio Department of Commerce, Testing and Registration, 6606 Tussing Rd, Reynoldsburg, OH 43068-9009; 614-644-2223, Fax: 614-644-2428.
www.com.state.oh.us/odoc/dic/default.htm

#35 Lottery Commission, 615 W Superior Ave, NW Frank J. Lausche Bldg, Cleveland, OH 44113; 216-787-3200, Fax: 216-787-3718.
www.ohiolottery.com
Agency email: olcwebmail@olc.state.oh.us.
Search database at www.ohiolottery.com/frameset/games/retailer.html

#36 Board of Psychology, 77 S High St, 18th Fl, Columbus, OH 43266-0321; 614-466-8808, Fax: 614-728-7081.
www.state.oh.us/psy
Agency email: psy.ce@exchange.state.oh.us.
Search database at http://www2.state.oh.us/psy/query.asp. If "SP" is part of a license number, that indicates a "school psychologist."

#37 Board of Optometry, 77 S High St, 16th Fl, Columbus, OH 43266-0318; 614-466-5115, Fax: 614-644-3937.
www.state.oh.us/opt
Agency email: optom_ott@ohio.gov.
Search database at
www.state.oh.us/scripts/opt/query.asp

#38 Bedding, Stuffed Toys & Upholstered Furniture Div., Industrial Complaince Division; Operations & Maintenance, 6606 Tussing Rd (PO Box 4009), Reynoldsburg, OH 43068-9009; 614-644-2223, Fax: 614-644-3580.
www.com.state.oh.us/odoc/dic/dicbedding.htm

#39 Optical Dispensers Board, 77 S High St, 16th Fl, Columbus, OH 43266-0328; 614-466-9707, Fax: 614-995-5392. www.state.oh.us/odb
Agency email: ohioopticalboard@hotmail.com.

#40 Pesticide Regulations, 8995 E Main St, Reynoldsburg, OH 43068-3399; 614-728-6200, Fax: 614-728-4235. www.state.oh.us/agr

#41 Racing Commission, 77 S High St, 18th Fl, Columbus, OH 43266-0416; 614-466-2757, Fax: 614-466-1900.

#42 Respiratory Care Board, 77 S High St, 16th Fl, Columbus, OH 43266-0777; 614-752-9218, Fax: 614-728-8691. www.state.oh.us/rsp
Agency email: rcb.logsdon@rcb.state.oh.us.
Search database at
www.state.oh.us/scripts/rsp/license/query.asp

#43 Department of Education, Office of Certification/Licensure, 25 S Front St, Columbus, OH 43215; 614-466-3593, Fax: 614-466-1999.
https://www.ode.state.oh.us
Search at https://www.ode.state.oh.us/Teaching-Profession/Teacher/Certification_Licensure/certifact.asp

#44 Supreme Court, 30 E Broad St, Columbus, OH 43266-0419; 614-644-1553, Fax: 614-728-0930.

#45 Veterinary Medical Board, 77 S High St, 16th Fl, Columbus, OH 43266-0116; 614-644-5281, Fax: 614-644-9038. www.state.oh.us/ovmlb
Agency email: info@ovmlb.state.oh.us.
Search database at www.state.oh.us/ovmlb/consumers.htm. Searching will be available at search site.

#46 Association of Polygraph Examiners, c/o Phillip Osborne, Columbus PD, 120 Marconi Blvd. 7th Fl, Columbus, OH 43215; 614-645-4174.
http://polygraph.org/states/oape/index.htm.
Agency email: posborne@insight.rr.com.
Search database at
http://polygraph.org/states/oape/directory.htm

Ohio Federal Courts

The following list indicates the district and division name for each county in the state. If the bankruptcy court location is different from the district court, then the location of the bankruptcy court appears in parentheses.

County/Court Cross Reference

County	District	Division
Adams	Southern	Cincinnati
Allen	Northern	Toledo
Ashland	Northern	Cleveland (Canton)
Ashtabula	Northern	Cleveland (Youngstown)
Athens	Southern	Columbus
Auglaize	Northern	Toledo
Belmont	Southern	Columbus
Brown	Southern	Cincinnati
Butler	Southern	Cincinnati (Dayton)
Carroll	Northern	Akron (Canton)
Champaign	Southern	Dayton
Clark	Southern	Dayton
Clermont	Southern	Cincinnati
Clinton	Southern	Cincinnati (Dayton)
Columbiana	Northern	Youngstown
Coshocton	Southern	Columbus
Crawford	Northern	Cleveland (Canton)
Cuyahoga	Northern	Cleveland
Darke	Southern	Dayton
Defiance	Northern	Toledo
Delaware	Southern	Columbus
Erie	Northern	Toledo
Fairfield	Southern	Columbus
Fayette	Southern	Columbus
Franklin	Southern	Columbus
Fulton	Northern	Toledo
Gallia	Southern	Columbus
Geauga	Northern	Cleveland
Greene	Southern	Dayton
Guernsey	Southern	Columbus
Hamilton	Southern	Cincinnati
Hancock	Northern	Toledo
Hardin	Northern	Toledo
Harrison	Southern	Columbus
Henry	Northern	Toledo
Highland	Southern	Cincinnati
Hocking	Southern	Columbus
Holmes	Northern	Akron (Canton)
Huron	Northern	Toledo
Jackson	Southern	Columbus
Jefferson	Southern	Columbus
Knox	Southern	Columbus
Lake	Northern	Cleveland
Lawrence	Southern	Cincinnati
Licking	Southern	Columbus
Logan	Southern	Columbus
Lorain	Northern	Cleveland
Lucas	Northern	Toledo
Madison	Southern	Columbus
Mahoning	Northern	Youngstown
Marion	Northern	Toledo
Medina	Northern	Cleveland (Akron)
Meigs	Southern	Columbus
Mercer	Northern	Toledo
Miami	Southern	Dayton
Monroe	Southern	Columbus
Montgomery	Southern	Dayton
Morgan	Southern	Columbus
Morrow	Southern	Columbus
Muskingum	Southern	Columbus
Noble	Southern	Columbus
Ottawa	Northern	Toledo
Paulding	Northern	Toledo
Perry	Southern	Columbus
Pickaway	Southern	Columbus
Pike	Southern	Columbus
Portage	Northern	Akron
Preble	Southern	Dayton
Putnam	Northern	Toledo
Richland	Northern	Cleveland (Canton)
Ross	Southern	Columbus
Sandusky	Northern	Toledo
Scioto	Southern	Cincinnati
Seneca	Northern	Toledo
Shelby	Southern	Dayton
Stark	Northern	Akron (Canton)
Summit	Northern	Akron
Trumbull	Northern	Youngstown
Tuscarawas	Northern	Akron (Canton)
Union	Southern	Columbus
Van Wert	Northern	Toledo
Vinton	Southern	Columbus
Warren	Southern	Cincinnati (Dayton)
Washington	Southern	Columbus
Wayne	Northern	Akron (Canton)
Williams	Northern	Toledo
Wood	Northern	Toledo
Wyandot	Northern	Toledo

Standards for Federal Courts: The search fee is $20.00 per item (one party name or case number). Certification fee is $7.00 per document. Copy fee is $.50 per page. All fees standard unless noted in profile. Mail Search: always enclose a stamped self addressed envelope unless otherwise noted. Before releasing records, all courts require prepayment unless noted in profile.

Open records are located at the court unless otherwise noted. District courts index by defendant and plaintiff as well as by case number. Bankruptcy courts usually index by debtor and case number. While most courts now have their indexes on computer, many still maintain index card files as well.

The universal PACER sign-up number is 800-676-6856. Find PACER and the Party/Case Index on the Web at http://pacer.psc.uscourts.gov. PACER dial-up access is $.60 per minute. Also, courts offering internet access via RACER, PACER, Web-PACER or the new CM-ECF charge $.07 per page fee unless noted as free.

US District Court

Northern District of Ohio

Akron Division 568 Federal Bldg, 2 S Main St, Akron, OH 44308 (Courier Address: Use mail address for courier delivery), 330-375-5705.

www.ohnd.uscourts.gov

Counties: Carroll, Holmes, Portage, Stark, Summit, Tuscarawas, Wayne. Cases filed prior to 1995 for counties in the Youngstown Division may be located here.

Indexing & Storage: Cases are indexed by defendant, plaintiff, and case number. New cases are available in the index immediately after filing date. Open cases may be located in another division in this district, depending on the judge assigned.

Fee & Payment Notes: Payment may be made by money order, cashier check, personal check. Payee: Clerk, US District Court.

Phone Search: Only docket information is available by phone.

In Person Search: In person searching available.

PACER: Toll-free dial-up access: 800-673-4409. Local dial-up access: 216-522-3669. Many cases prior to the indicated dates are also online. Case records are available back to January 1, 1990. Records are never purged. New records are available online after 1 day. PACER is available online at http://pacer.ohnd.uscourts.gov. Use the CM/ECF system (below) when PACER is phased out.

Electronic Filing: Information is available online at http://ecf.ohnd.uscourts.gov

Cleveland Division 201 Superior Ave, NE, Cleveland, OH 44114 (Courier Address: Use mail address for courier delivery), 216-522-4355, Fax: 216-522-2140.

www.ohnd.uscourts.gov

Counties: Ashland, Ashtabula, Crawford, Cuyahoga, Geauga, Lake, Lorain, Medina, Richland. Cases prior to July 1995 for the counties of Ashland, Crawford, Medina and Richland are located in the Akron Division. Cases filed prior to 1995 from the counties in the Youngstown Division may be located here.

Indexing & Storage: Cases are indexed by defendant, plaintiff, and case number. New cases are available in the index immediately after filing date. Open cases may be located in other divisions in this district, depending on the judge assigned.

Fee & Payment Notes: Payment may be made by money order, cashier check, personal check. Payee: Clerk, US District Court. You are allowed to make your own copies. These copies cost $.25 per page.

Phone Search: Only docket information is available by phone.

Mail Search: A stamped self addressed envelope is not required.

In Person Search: In person searching available.

PACER: Toll-free dial-up access: 800-673-4409. Local dial-up access: 216-522-3669. Many cases prior to the indicated dates are also online. Case records are available back to January 1, 1990. Records are never purged. New records are available online after 1 day. PACER is available online at http://pacer.ohnd.uscourts.gov. Use the CM/ECF system (below) when PACER is phased out.

Electronic Filing: Information is available online at http://ecf.ohnd.uscourts.gov

Toledo Division 114 US Courthouse, 1716 Spielbusch, Toledo, OH 43624 (Courier Address: Use mail address for courier delivery), 419-259-6412.

www.ohnd.uscourts.gov

Counties: Allen, Auglaize, Defiance, Erie, Fulton, Hancock, Hardin, Henry, Huron, Lucas, Marion, Mercer, Ottawa, Paulding, Putnam, Sandusky, Seneca, Van Wert, Williams, Wood, Wyandot.

Indexing & Storage: Cases are indexed by defendant, plaintiff, and case number. New cases are available in the index 1 day after filing date. Open records are located at this court.

Fee & Payment Notes: Payment may be made by money order, cashier check, personal check. Payee: Clerk, US District Court.

Phone Search: Only docket information is available by phone.

In Person Search: In person searching available.

PACER: Toll-free dial-up access: 800-673-4409. Local dial-up access: 216-522-3669. Many cases prior to the indicated dates are also online. Case records are available back to January 1, 1990. Records are never purged. New records are available online after 1 day. PACER is available online at http://pacer.ohnd.uscourts.gov. Use the CM/ECF system (below) when PACER is phased out.

Electronic Filing: Information is available online at http://ecf.ohnd.uscourts.gov

Youngstown Division 337 Federal Bldg, 125 Market St, Youngstown, OH 44503-1787 (Courier Address: Use mail address for courier delivery), 330-746-1906, Fax: 330-746-2027.

www.ohnd.uscourts.gov

Counties: Columbiana, Mahoning, Trumbull. This division was reactivated in the middle of 1995. Older cases will be found in Akron or Cleveland.

Indexing & Storage: Cases are indexed by defendant, plaintiff, and case number. New cases are available in the index immediately after filing date. Open cases may also be located in other

divisions in this district, depending upon the judge assigned.

Fee & Payment Notes: Payment may be made by money order, cashier check, personal check. Payee: Clerk, US District Court.

Phone Search: Only docket information is available by phone.

Fax Search: Prepayment is required for all fax requests.

In Person Search: In person searching available.

PACER: Toll-free dial-up access: 800-673-4409. Local dial-up access: 216-522-3669. Many cases prior to the indicated dates are also online. Case records are available back to January 1, 1990. Records are never purged. New records are available online after 1 day. PACER is available online at http://pacer.ohnd.uscourts.gov. Use the CM/ECF system (below) when PACER is phased out.

Electronic Filing: Information is available online at http://ecf.ohnd.uscourts.gov

US Bankruptcy Court

Northern District of Ohio

Akron Division 455 Federal Bldg, 2 S Main, Akron, OH 44308 (Courier Address: Use mail address for courier delivery), 330-375-5840.

www.ohnb.uscourts.gov

Counties: Medina, Portage, Summit.

Indexing & Storage: Cases are indexed by debtor as well as by case number. New cases are available in the index 1-2 days after filing date. Both computer and card indexes are maintained. Case records closed before 1993 were sent to the Chicago Federal Records Center. In Spring 1995, the 1994 closed cases were sent to Dayton.

Fee & Payment Notes: Payment may be made by money order, cashier check, personal check, Visa or Mastercard. Payee: Clerk, US Bankruptcy Court. You are allowed to make your own copies. These copies cost $.25 per page.

Phone Search: An automated voice case information service (VCIS) is available. Call VCIS at 800-898-6899 or 330-489-4731.

In Person Search: In person searching available.

PACER:. Case records are available back to January 1985. Records are purged only up to September 1990. New civil records are available online after 2 days. PACER is available online at http://pacer.ohnb.uscourts.gov.

Electronic Filing: Information is available online at https://ecf.ohnb.uscourts.gov

Canton Division Frank T Bow Federal Bldg, 201 Cleveland Ave SW, Canton, OH 44702 (Courier Address: Use mail address for courier delivery), 330-489-4426, Fax: 330-489-4434.

www.ohnb.uscourts.gov

Counties: Ashland, Carroll, Crawford, Holmes, Richland, Stark, Tuscarawas, Wayne.

Indexing & Storage: Cases are indexed by debtor as well as by case number. New cases are available in the index 48 hours after filing date. Records are indexed on computer from 1985 to the present. Records are indexed on index cards from 1982 to 1984, and also journalized in books from 1984 to 1990. Prior to 1995, closed. Case records were sent to the Chicago Federal Records Center.

Fee & Payment Notes: Payment may be made by money order, cashier check, personal check, Visa or Mastercard. Debtor's checks are not accepted. Payee: Clerk, US Bankruptcy Court. You are allowed to make your own copies. These copies cost $.25 per page.

Phone Search: An automated voice case information service (VCIS) is available. Call VCIS at 800-898-6899 or 330-489-4731.

Fax Search: Will accept fax search request, but will not process until fee is received.

In Person Search: In person searching available.

PACER:. Case records are available back to January 1985. Records are purged only up to September 1990. New civil records are available online after 2 days. PACER is available online at http://pacer.ohnb.uscourts.gov.

Electronic Filing: Information is available online at https://ecf.ohnb.uscourts.gov

Cleveland Division Key Tower, Room 3001, 127 Public Square, Cleveland, OH 44114 (Courier Address: Use mail address for courier delivery), 216-522-4373.

www.ohnb.uscourts.gov

Counties: Cuyahoga, Geauga, Lake, Lorain.

Indexing & Storage: Cases are indexed by debtor as well as by case number. New cases are available in the index 2 days after filing date. Records are also indexed on microfiche. Prior to 1995, closed. Case records were sent to the Chicago Federal Records Center.

Fee & Payment Notes: Payment may be made by money order, personal check. Debtor's checks are not accepted. Payee: Clerk, US Bankruptcy Court.

Phone Search: An automated voice case information service (VCIS) is available. Call VCIS at 800-898-6899 or 330-489-4731.

In Person Search: In person searching available.

PACER:. Case records are available back to January 1985. Records are purged only up to September 1990. New civil records are available online after 2 days. PACER is available online at http://pacer.ohnb.uscourts.gov.

Electronic Filing: Information is available online at https://ecf.ohnb.uscourts.gov

Toledo Division Room 411, 1716 Spielbusch Ave, Toledo, OH 43624 (Courier Address: Use mail address for courier delivery), 419-259-6440.

www.ohnb.uscourts.gov

Counties: Allen, Auglaize, Defiance, Erie, Fulton, Hancock, Hardin, Henry, Huron, Lucas, Marion, Mercer, Ottawa, Paulding, Putnam, Sandusky, Seneca, Van Wert, Williams, Wood, Wyandot.

Indexing & Storage: Cases are indexed by debtor as well as by case number. New cases are available in the index 24 hours after filing date. Prior to 1995, closed. Case records were sent to the Chicago Federal Records Center.

Fee & Payment Notes: Payment may be made by money order, cashier check, business check, Visa or Mastercard. Personal checks are not accepted. Payee: Clerk, US Bankruptcy Court.

Phone Search: An automated voice case information service (VCIS) is available. Call VCIS at 800-898-6899 or 330-489-4731.

In Person Search: In person searching available.

PACER:. Case records are available back to January 1985. Records are purged only up to

September 1990. New civil records are available online after 2 days. PACER is available online at http://pacer.ohnb.uscourts.gov.

Electronic Filing: Information is available online at https://ecf.ohnb.uscourts.gov

Youngstown Division PO Box 147, Youngstown, OH 44501 (Courier Address: 125 Market St, #210, Youngstown, OH 44503), 330-746-7027.

www.ohnb.uscourts.gov

Counties: Ashtabula, Columbiana, Mahoning, Trumbull.

Indexing & Storage: Cases are indexed by debtor and creditors as well as by case number. New cases are available in the index 24 hours after filing date. Prior to 1995, closed cases were sent to the Chicago Federal Records Center. Now. Case records are sent to the Dayton Federal Records Center every few years.

Fee & Payment Notes: Payment may be made by money order, cashier check, business check, Visa or Mastercard. Personal checks are not accepted. Payee: Clerk, US Bankruptcy Court.

Phone Search: An automated voice case information service (VCIS) is available. Call VCIS at 800-898-6899 or 330-489-4731.

Mail Search: A stamped self addressed envelope is not required.

In Person Search: In person searching available.

PACER:. Case records are available back to January 1985. Records are purged only up to September 1990. New civil records are available online after 2 days. PACER is available online at http://pacer.ohnb.uscourts.gov.

Electronic Filing: Information is available online at https://ecf.ohnb.uscourts.gov

US District Court
Southern District of Ohio

Cincinnati Division Clerk, US District Court, 324 Potter Stewart Courthouse, 100 E 5th St, Cincinnati, OH 45202 (Courier Address: Use mail address for courier delivery), 513-564-7500, Fax: 513-564-7505.

www.ohsd.uscourts.gov

Counties: Adams, Brown, Butler, Clermont, Clinton, Hamilton, Highland, Lawrence, Scioto, Warren.

Indexing & Storage: Cases are indexed by defendant, plaintiff, and case number. New cases are available in the index immediately after filing date. Open records are located at this court.

Fee & Payment Notes: Payment may be made by money order, cashier check, personal check. Give FedEx account number for expedited copy delivery. Payee: Clerk, US District Court.

Phone Search: Only docket information is available by phone.

Mail Search: A stamped self addressed envelope is not required.

In Person Search: In person searching available.

PACER: Access fee is $1.00 per minute. Toll-free dial-up access: 800-710-4939. Local dial-up access: 614-469-6990. Case records are available back to 1994. Records are never purged. New

records are available online after 1 day. PACER is available online at http://pacer.ohsd.uscourts.gov.

Columbus Division Office of the clerk, Room 260, 85 Marconi Blvd, Columbus, OH 43215 (Courier Address: Use mail address for courier delivery), 614-719-3000, Fax: 614-469-5953.

www.ohsd.uscourts.gov

Counties: Athens, Belmont, Coshocton, Delaware, Fairfield, Fayette, Franklin, Gallia, Guernsey, Harrison, Hocking, Jackson, Jefferson, Knox, Licking, Logan, Madison, Meigs, Monroe, Morgan, Morrow, Muskingum, Noble, Perry, Pickaway, Pike, Ross, Union, Vinton,Washington.

Indexing & Storage: Cases are indexed by defendant, plaintiff, and case number. New cases are available in the index 1-2 days after filing date. Records are also indexed on microfiche back to 1982. District wide searches are available from this division.

Fee & Payment Notes: Payment may be made by money order, cashier check, business check. Personal checks are not accepted. Payee: Clerk, US District Court.

Phone Search: Only docket information is available by phone.

In Person Search: In person searching available.

PACER: Access fee is $1.00 per minute. Toll-free dial-up access: 800-710-4939. Local dial-up access: 614-469-6990. Case records are available back to 1994. Records are never purged. New records are available online after 1 day. PACER is available online at http://pacer.ohsd.uscourts.gov.

Dayton Division Federal Bldg, 200 W 2nd, Room 712, Dayton, OH 45402 (Courier Address: Use mail address for courier delivery), 937-512-1400.

www.ohsd.uscourts.gov

Counties: Champaign, Clark, Darke, Greene, Miami, Montgomery, Preble, Shelby.

Indexing & Storage: Cases are indexed by defendant, plaintiff, and case number. New cases are available in the index 1 day after filing date. Records are also indexed on microfiche. The computer is only valid for cases that were open and pending from 1/90 to present. A view box is available to the public for cases filed for the present day that have not been entered into the computer. Open records are located at this court.

Fee & Payment Notes: Payment may be made by money order, cashier check, business check. Personal checks are not accepted. The Clerk's office will not respond to telephone requests that involve copywork. The searcher must provide a wide envelope for return of documents or, if documents are bulky, the searcher must provide access for bulk mailing. Payee: Clerk, US District Court.

Phone Search: Over the phone, this court will only reveal whether a case has been filed.

In Person Search: In person searching available.

PACER: Access fee is $1.00 per minute. Toll-free dial-up access: 800-710-4939. Local dial-up access: 614-469-6990. Case records are available back to 1994. Records are never purged. New records are available online after 1 day. PACER is available online at http://pacer.ohsd.uscourts.gov.

US Bankruptcy Court

Southern District of Ohio

Cincinnati Division Atrium Two, Suite 800, 221 E Fourth St, Cincinnati, OH 45202 (Courier Address: Use mail address for courier delivery), 513-684-2572.

www.ohsb.uscourts.gov

Counties: Adams, Brown, Clermont, Hamilton, Highland, Lawrence, Scioto and a part of Butler.

Indexing & Storage: Cases are indexed by debtor as well as by case number. New cases are available in the index 2 days after filing date. Prior to 1993, closed. Case records were sent to the Chicago Federal Records Center.

Fee & Payment Notes: Payment may be made by money order, cashier check. Business checks are not accepted, Visa or Mastercard. Personal checks are not accepted. Credit cards are accepted only from law firms. Debtor checks are not accepted. Payee: Clerk, US Bankruptcy Court.

Phone Search: Only docket information is available by phone. An automated voice case information service (VCIS) is available. Call VCIS at 800-726-1004 or 937-225-2544.

In Person Search: In person searching available.

PACER: Toll-free dial-up access: 800-793-7003. Local dial-up access: 937-225-7561. Case records are available back to 1990. Records are purged every six months. New civil records are available online after 1 day. PACER is available online at http://pacer.ohsb.uscourts.gov.

Electronic Filing: (Currently in the process of implementing CM/ECF.)

Columbus Division 170 N High St, Columbus, OH 43215 (Courier Address: Use mail address for courier delivery), 614-469-6638.

www.ohsb.uscourts.gov

Counties: Athens, Belmont, Coshocton, Delaware, Fairfield, Fayette, Franklin, Gallia, Guernsey, Harrison, Hocking, Jackson, Jefferson, Knox, Licking, Logan, Madison, Meigs, Monroe, Morgan, Morrow, Muskingum, Noble, Perry, Pickaway, Pike, Ross, Union, Vinton,Washington.

Indexing & Storage: New cases are available in the index 1 day after filing date. Prior to 1993, closed cases were sent to the Chicago Federal Records Facility.

Fee & Payment Notes: Payment may be made by money order, cashier check, business check. Personal checks are not accepted. Debtor's checks are not accepted. Payee: Clerk, US Bankruptcy Court.

Phone Search: An automated voice case information service (VCIS) is available. Call VCIS at 800-726-1006 or 513-225-2562.

Mail Search: A stamped self addressed envelope is not required.

In Person Search: In person searching available.

PACER: Toll-free dial-up access: 800-793-7003. Local dial-up access: 937-225-7561. Case records are available back to 1990. Records are purged every six months. New civil records are available online after 1 day. PACER is available online at http://pacer.ohsb.uscourts.gov.

Electronic Filing: (Currently in the process of implementing CM/ECF.)

Dayton Division 120 W 3rd St, Dayton, OH 45402 (Courier Address: Use mail address for courier delivery), 937-225-2516.

www.ohsb.uscourts.gov

Counties: Butler, Champaign, Clark, Clinton, Darke, Greene, Miami, Montgomery, Preble, Shelby, Warren; parts of Butler County are handled by Cincinnati Division.

Indexing & Storage: Cases are indexed by debtor as well as by case number. New cases are available in the index 1 day after filing date. Cases closed before June 1991 were sent to the Chicago Federal Records Facility.

Fee & Payment Notes: Payment may be made by money order, cashier check, in-state business check. Personal checks are not accepted. Debtor's checks are not accepted. Payee: Clerk, US Bankruptcy Court.

Phone Search: Only docket information is available by phone. An automated voice case information service (VCIS) is available. Call VCIS at 800-726-1004 or 937-225-2544.

In Person Search: In person searching available.

PACER: Toll-free dial-up access: 800-793-7003. Local dial-up access: 937-225-7561. Case records are available back to 1990. Records are purged every six months. New civil records are available online after 1 day. PACER is available online at http://pacer.ohsb.uscourts.gov.

Electronic Filing: (Currently in the process of implementing CM/ECF.)

Ohio County Courts

Court	Jurisdiction	No. of Courts	How Organized
Court of Common Pleas*	General	88	county
County Courts*	Limited	47	
Municipal Courts*	Municipal	118	
Mayors Courts	Municipal	400	
Court of Claims	Special	1	

* Profiled in this Sourcebook.

Court	CIVIL								
	Tort	Contract	Real Estate	Min. Claim	Max. Claim	Small Claims	Estate	Eviction	Domestic Relations
Court of Common Pleas*	X	X	X	$3000/ $10,000	No Max		X		X
County Courts*	X	X	X	$0	$15,000	$3000		X	
Municipal Courts*	X	X	X	$0	$15,000	$3000		X	
Mayors Courts									
Court of Claims					No Max				

Court	CRIMINAL				
	Felony	Misdemeanor	DWI/DUI	Preliminary Hearing	Juvenile
Court of Common Pleas*	X		Juvenile		X
County Courts*		X	X	X	
Municipal Courts*		X	X	X	
Mayors Courts		X	X		
Court of Claims					

ADMINISTRATION

Administrative Director, Supreme Court of Ohio, 30 E Broad St, 3rd Fl, Columbus, OH, 43266-0419; 614-466-2653, Fax: 614-752-8736. www.sconet.state.oh.us

COURT STRUCTURE

The Court of Common Pleas is the general jurisdiction court and County Courts have limited jurisdiction. Effective July 1, 1997, the dollar limits for civil cases in County and Municipal Courts were raised as follows: County Court - from $3,000 to $15,000; Municipal Court - from $10,000 to $15,000. In addition the small claims limit was raised from $2,000 to $3,000.

Effective in 2001, Ohio Common Pleas Courts may name their own civil action limits, though most of these courts have yet to make changes. In effect, these Common Pleas courts may take any civil cases. However, civil maximum limits for Ohio's County Courts and Municipal Courts remains the same: $15,000.

ONLINE ACCESS

There is no statewide computer system, but a number of counties offer online access.

PROBATE COURTS

Probate courts are separate from the Court of Common Pleas, but Probate Court phone numbers are given with that court in each county.

Adams County

Common Pleas Court 110 W Main, Rm 207, West Union, OH 45693; 937-544-2344; Probate phone: 937-544-2368; Fax: 937-544-8271. Hours: 8:30AM-4PM (EST). *Felony, Civil Actions Over $3,000, Probate.*

Civil Records: Access: In person only. Visitors must perform in person searches for themselves. Required to search: name, years to search. Civil cases indexed by defendant, plaintiff. Civil records on computer from April, 93, prior in books, archived from 1910.

Criminal Records: Access: Mail, in person. Visitors must perform in person searches for themselves. Search fee: $10.00. Required to search: name, years to search, signed release; also helpful: DOB, SSN. Criminal records on computer from April, 93, prior in books, archived from 1910.

General Information: Public access terminal is available. Copy fee: $.25 per page. Certification fee: $1.00. Fee payee: Clerk of Court. Personal checks accepted. Prepayment is required.

County Court 110 W Main, Rm 25, West Union, OH 45693; 937-544-2011; Fax: 937-544-8911. Hours: 8AM-4PM (EST). *Misdemeanor, Civil Actions Under $15,000, Small Claims.*

Civil Records: Access: Mail, in person. Both court and visitors may perform in person searches. Search fee: $10.00 per name. Required to search: name, years to search. Civil cases indexed by defendant, plaintiff. Civil records on computer from March, 93, index from 1958, prior on dockets and microfilm.

Criminal Records: Access: Mail, in person. Both court and visitors may perform in person searches. Search fee: $10.00 per name. Required to search: name, years to search; also helpful: SSN. Criminal records on computer from March, 93, index from 1958, prior on dockets and microfilm.

General Information: Public access terminal is available. SASE required. Turnaround time 1-2 days. Copy fee: $.50 per page. Certification fee: $1.00. Fee payee: Adams County Court. Business checks accepted. Prepayment is required.

Allen County

Common Pleas Court PO Box 1243, Lima, OH 45802; 419-228-3700; Fax: 419-222-8427. Hours: 8AM-4:30PM (EST). *Felony, Civil Actions Over $15,000, Probate.*

Note: Probate is a separate court.

Civil Records: Access: In person. Visitors may perform in person searches. No search fee. Required to search: name; also helpful: years to search, address. Civil cases indexed by defendant, plaintiff. Civil records on computer back to 1986; in books and archived prior.

Criminal Records: Access: Fax, mail, in person. Visitors may perform in person searches. No search fee. Required to search: name, years to search; also helpful: address, DOB, SSN. Criminal records on computer back to 1986; in books and archived prior.

General Information: Public access terminal is available. No secret indictment records released. SASE required. Turnaround time 1-2 days. Fax notes: $3.00 for first page, $1.00 each add'l. Copy fee: $1.00 for first page, $.25 each add'l. Certification fee: $3.00. Fee payee: Clerk of Court. Personal checks accepted. Prepayment is required.

Lima Municipal Court 109 N Union St (PO Box 1529), Lima, OH 45802; 419-221-5275; Civil phone: 419-221-5250; Fax: 419-998-5526. Hours: 8AM-5PM (EST). *Misdemeanor, Civil Actions Under $15,000, Eviction, Small Claims.*

www.limamunicipalcourt.org

Civil Records: Access: Phone, fax, mail, in person, email. Both court and visitors may perform in person searches. No search fee. Required to search: name, years to search; also helpful: address. Civil cases indexed by defendant, plaintiff. Civil records on computer from April, 90, microfilm from 1975, books and archived prior.

Criminal Records: Access: Phone, fax, mail, in person, email. Both court and visitors may perform in person searches. No search fee. Required to search: name, years to search; also helpful: address, DOB, SSN. Criminal records on computer from April, 90, microfilm from 1975, books and archived prior.

General Information: Public access terminal is available. SASE required. Turnaround time same day. Fax notes: Fee to fax results is $.25 per page. Copy fee: $.25 per page. Certification fee: $2.00. Fee payee: Clerk of Court. Business checks accepted. Credit cards accepted: Visa, MasterCard. Prepayment is required.

Ashland County

Common Pleas Court 142 W 2nd St, Ashland, OH 44805; 419-289-0000; Probate phone: 419-282-4284. Hours: 8AM-4PM (EST). *Felony, Civil Actions Over $10,000, Probate.*

Note: Probate court is a separate court at the same address.

Civil Records: Access: In person only. Visitors must perform in person searches for themselves. No search fee. Required to search: name, years to search. Civil cases indexed by defendant, plaintiff. Civil records in books and index from 1800s.

Criminal Records: Access: In person only. Visitors must perform in person searches for themselves. Required to search: name, years to search, DOB. Criminal records in books and index from 1800s.

General Information: Public access terminal is available. Copy fee: $.10 per page. Certification fee: $1.00. Fee payee: Clerk of Court. Personal checks accepted. Prepayment is required.

Ashland Municipal Court 1209 E Main St, Ashland, OH 44805; 419-289-8137; Fax: 419-289-8545. Hours: 8AM-5PM (EST). *Misdemeanor, Civil Actions Under $15,000, Eviction, Small Claims.*

www.ashland-ohio.com

Civil Records: Access: Phone, mail, fax, in person, email. Both court and visitors may perform in person searches. No search fee. Required to search: name, years to search. Civil cases indexed by defendant, plaintiff. Civil records on docket books from 1952, computerized since 1995.

Criminal Records: Access: Phone, mail, fax, in person, email. Both court and visitors may perform in person searches. No search fee. Required to search: name, years to search, SSN. Criminal records on docket books from 1952, computerized since 1995.

General Information: Public access terminal is available. SASE required. Turnaround time 1-3 days. Fax notes: Fee to fax results is $1.00 per page. Copy fee: $1.00 per page. Certification fee: $1.00. Fee payee: Municipal Court. Personal checks accepted. Prepayment is required.

Ashtabula County

Common Pleas Court 25 W Jefferson St, Jefferson, OH 44047; 440-576-3637; Probate phone: 440-576-3451; Fax: 440-576-2819. Hours: 8AM-4:30PM (EST). *Felony, Civil Actions Over $10,000, Probate.*

Civil Records: Access: In person only. Visitors must perform in person searches for themselves. No search fee. Required to search: name, years to search; also helpful: address. Civil cases indexed by defendant, plaintiff. Civil records on computer back to 5/93, in books back to the 1800s.

Criminal Records: Access: In person only. Visitors must perform in person searches for themselves. No search fee. Required to search: name, years to search; also helpful: address, DOB, SSN. Criminal records on computer back to 5/93, in books back to the 1800s.

General Information: Public access terminal is available. No expungments released. Copy fee: $.50 per page. Certification fee: $1.00. Fee payee: Clerk of Court. Personal checks accepted. Prepayment required.

County Court Eastern Division 25 W Jefferson St, Jefferson, OH 44047; 440-576-3617. Hours: 8AM-4:30PM (EST). *Misdemeanor, Civil Actions Under $15,000, Eviction, Small Claims.*

www.co.ashtabula.oh.us

Civil Records: Access: Mail, fax, in person. Both court and visitors may perform in person searches. No search fee. Required to search: name, years to search. Civil cases indexed by defendant, plaintiff. Civil records on computer since 01/09/95; in books back to 1960s.

Criminal Records: Access: Mail, fax, in person. Both court and visitors may perform in person searches. No search fee. Required to search: name, years to search, DOB or SSN. Criminal records on computer since 01/09/95; in books back to 1960s.

General Information: Public access terminal is available. SASE required. Turnaround time 1-2 days. Fax notes: Fee to fax results is $.50 per page. Copy fee: $.50 per page. Certification fee: $1.50. Fee payee: Eastern County Court. Only cashiers checks and money orders accepted. Prepayment is required.

County Court Western Division 117 W Main St, Geneva, OH 44041; 440-466-1184; Fax: 440-466-7171. Hours: 8AM-4:30PM (EST). *Misdemeanor, Civil Actions Under $15,000, Small Claims.*

Civil Records: Access: In person only. Visitors must perform in person searches for themselves. No search fee. Required to search: name, years to search. Civil cases indexed by defendant, plaintiff. Civil records on computer since 1994; prior records on docket books.

Criminal Records: Access: In person only. Visitors must perform in person searches for themselves. No search fee. Required to search: name, years to search, DOB, SSN, signed release. Criminal records on computer since 1994; prior records on docket books.

General Information: Public access terminal is available. No confidential records released. Copy fee: $1.00 per page. Certification fee: $1.00 per page. Fee payee: Western County Court. Only cashiers checks and money orders accepted. Prepayment is required.

Ashtabula Municipal Court 110 W 44th St, Ashtabula, OH 44004; 440-992-7110; Fax: 440-998-5786. Hours: 8AM-4:30PM (EST). *Misdemeanor, Civil Actions Under $15,000, Eviction, Small Claims.*

Note: 440-992-7109 gives a directory.

Civil Records: Access: In person only. Visitors must perform in person searches for themselves. No search fee. Required to search: name, years to search. Civil cases indexed by defendant, plaintiff. Civil records on computer from 1992, books back to 1971.

Criminal Records: Access: In person only. Visitors must perform in person searches for themselves. No search fee. Required to search: name, years to search, DOB, SSN, signed release. Criminal records on computer from 1992, books back to 1971.

General Information: Public access terminal is available. No expunged records released. Copy fee: $.10 per page. Certification fee: $5.00. Fee payee: Municipal Court. Personal checks accepted. Prepayment is required.

Athens County

Common Pleas Court PO Box 290, Athens, OH 45701-0290; 740-592-3242; Probate phone: 740-592-3251. Hours: 8AM-4PM (EST). *Felony, Civil Actions Over $10,000, Probate.*

www.athenscountycpcourt.org

Civil Records: Access: In person, online. Visitors must perform in person searches for themselves. No search fee. Required to search: name, years to search; also helpful: address. Civil cases indexed by defendant, plaintiff. Civil records on computer back to 1/92; prior in books. Online access to the CP court records is available free at the web site.

Criminal Records: Access: In person, online. Visitors must perform in person searches for themselves. No search fee. Required to search: name, years to search; also helpful: address, DOB, SSN. Criminal records on computer back to 1/92; prior in books. Online access to criminal records is the same as civil.

General Information: Public access terminal is available. Copy fee: $1.00 per page. Certification fee: $1.00. Fee payee: Clerk of Court. Business checks accepted. Prepayment is required.

Athens Municipal Court City Hall, 8 East Washington St, Athens, OH 45701; 740-592-3328; Fax: 740-592-3331. Hours: 8AM-4PM (EST). *Misdemeanor, Civil Actions Under $15,000, Eviction, Small Claims.*

Civil Records: Access: Mail, in person. Visitors must perform in person searches for themselves. No search fee. Required to search: name, years to search; also helpful: address. Civil cases indexed by defendant, plaintiff. Civil records on computer back to 1994, prior in books.

Criminal Records: Access: In person only. Visitors must perform in person searches for themselves. No search fee. Required to search: name, years to search; also helpful: address, DOB, SSN. Criminal records on computer back to 7/1993, prior in books back to 1974.

General Information: Public access terminal is available. No expunged or sealed records released. Copy fee: self serve copies: $.05. Certification fee: $1.00. Fee payee: ACMC. Personal checks accepted. Credit cards accepted: Visa, MasterCard. Prepayment is required.

Auglaize County

Common Pleas Court PO Box 409, Wapakoneta, OH 45895; 419-738-4219; Probate phone: 419-738-7710; Fax: 419-738-7953. Hours: 8AM-4:30PM (EST). *Felony, Civil Actions Over $10,000, Probate.*

Civil Records: Access: Fax, in person. Visitors must perform in person searches for themselves. No search fee. Required to search: name, years to search; also helpful: address. Civil cases indexed by defendant, plaintiff. Civil records on dockets from 1850, computerized since 02/00. Fax requests must be on company letterhead.

Criminal Records: Access: Fax, in person. Visitors must perform in person searches for themselves. No search fee. Required to search: name, years to search; also helpful: address, DOB, SSN. Criminal records on dockets from 1850, computerized since 02/00. Fax requests must be on company letterhead.

General Information: Public access terminal is available. Fax notes: Fee to fax results is $2.00 per page, plus $.25 each copy fee. Copy fee: $.50 per page. Certification fee: $1.00. Fee payee: Clerk of Court. Personal checks accepted. Prepayment is required.

Auglaize County Municipal Court PO Box 409, Wapakoneta, OH 45895; 419-738-2923. Hours: 8AM-4:30PM (EST). *Misdemeanor, Civil Actions Under $15,000, Eviction, Small Claims.*

Civil Records: Access: In person only. Visitors must perform in person searches for themselves. No search fee. Required to search: name, years to search; also helpful: address. Civil cases indexed by defendant, plaintiff. Civil records on computer from April, 1994, docket back to 1976.

Criminal Records: Access: In person only. Visitors must perform in person searches for themselves. No search fee. Required to search: name, years to search, signed release; also helpful: address, DOB, SSN. Criminal records on computer from October, 1993, docket back to 1976.

General Information: Public access terminal is available. No records released. Copy fee: $.50 per page. Certification fee: $1.00. Fee payee: Clerk of Court. Personal checks accepted. Prepayment is required.

Belmont County

Common Pleas Court Main St, Courthouse, St Clairsville, OH 43950; 740-695-2121; Probate phone: 740-695-2121 X202. Hours: 8:30AM-4:30PM (EST). *Felony, Civil Actions Over $3,000, Probate.*

Civil Records: Access: Mail, in person. Both court and visitors may perform in person searches. Search fee: $3.00 per name. Required to search: name, years to search. Civil cases indexed by defendant, plaintiff. Civil records in books, archived from 1896; computerized from 1995.

Criminal Records: Access: Mail, in person. Both court and visitors may perform in person searches. Search fee: $3.00 per name. Required to search: name, years to search. Criminal records in books, archived from 1896; computerized from 1995.

General Information: Public access terminal is available. No secret criminal records released. SASE required. Turnaround time 1 day. Copy fee: $1.00 per page. Certification fee: $5.00. Fee payee: Clerk of Court. Personal checks accepted. Prepayment is required.

County Court Eastern Division 400 W 26th St, Bellaire, OH 43906; 740-676-4490. Hours: 8AM-4PM (EST). *Misdemeanor, Civil Actions Under $15,000, Small Claims.*

Civil Records: Access: Mail, in person. Both court and visitors may perform in person searches. No search fee. Required to search: name, years to search. Civil cases indexed by defendant, plaintiff. Civil records on computer from September, 94, books back to 1950s. Mail access available to attorneys only.

Criminal Records: Access: Mail, in person. Both court and visitors may perform in person searches. No search fee. Required to search: name, years to search; also helpful: DOB, SSN. Criminal records on computer from September, 94, books back to 1950s.

General Information: Public access terminal is available. No sealed or confidential records released. SASE required. Copy fee: $1.00 per page. Fee payee: Eastern Division. Only cashiers checks and money orders accepted. Prepayment is required.

County Court Northern Division PO Box 40, Martins Ferry, OH 43935; 740-633-3147; Fax: 740-633-6631. Hours: 8AM-4PM (EST). *Misdemeanor, Civil Actions Under $15,000, Small Claims.*

Civil Records: Access: Mail, fax, in person. Both court and visitors may perform in person searches. No search fee. Required to search: name, years to search. Civil cases indexed by defendant, plaintiff. Civil records on computer from June, 1994, books back to 1950s.

Criminal Records: Access: Mail, fax, in person. Both court and visitors may perform in person searches. No search fee. Required to search: name, years to search,

DOB; also helpful: SSN, sex, signed release. Criminal records on computer from June, 1994, books back to 1950s.

General Information: Public access terminal is available. SASE not required. Turnaround time 5-7 days. No copy fee. Fee payee: Clerk of Court, Northern Division. Only cashiers checks and money orders accepted. Prepayment is required.

County Court Western Division 147 W Main St, St Clairsville, OH 43950; 740-695-2875; Fax: 740-695-7285. Hours: 8AM-4PM (EST). *Misdemeanor, Civil Actions Under $15,000, Small Claims.*

Civil Records: Access: Fax, mail, in person. Both court and visitors may perform in person searches. No search fee. Required to search: name, years to search, address. Civil cases indexed by defendant, plaintiff. Civil records on computer from 1994, books back to 1950s.

Criminal Records: Access: Fax, mail, in person. Both court and visitors may perform in person searches. No search fee. Required to search: name, years to search, address, DOB, SSN. Criminal records on computer from 1994, books back to 1950s.

General Information: Public access terminal is available. Pending case information not released. SASE required. Turnaround time 1 week. Fax notes: No fee to fax results. Copy fee: $1.00 per page. Certification fee: $1.00. Fee payee: Western Division Court. Only cashiers checks and money orders accepted. Prepayment is required.

Brown County

Common Pleas Court 101 S Main, Georgetown, OH 45121; 937-378-3100; Probate phone: 937-378-6549. Hours: 7:30AM-4:30PM (EST). *Felony, Civil Actions Over $3,000, Probate.*

Civil Records: Access: Mail, in person. Both court and visitors may perform in person searches. No search fee. Required to search: name, years to search; also helpful: address. Civil cases indexed by defendant, plaintiff. Civil records on computer since 1995, in books back to 1860s.

Criminal Records: Access: Mail, in person. Both court and visitors may perform in person searches. No search fee. Required to search: name, years to search; also helpful: address, DOB, SSN. Criminal records on computer since 1995, in books back to 1860s.

General Information: Public access terminal is available. No criminal expungment records released. SASE required. Turnaround time same day. Copy fee: $.25 per page. Certification fee: $1.00. Fee payee: Clerk of Court. Personal checks accepted. Prepayment is required.

County Court 770 Mount Orab Pike, Georgetown, OH 45121; 937-378-6358; Fax: 937-378-2462. Hours: 7:30AM-4:30PM M-F; 9AM-Noon S (EST). *Misdemeanor, Civil Actions Under $15,000, Eviction, Small Claims.*

www.browncountycourt.org

Civil Records: Access: Mail, in person. Both court and visitors may perform in person searches. No search fee. Required to search: name, years to search. Civil cases indexed by defendant, plaintiff. Civil records in books back to 1958, computerized since 1995.

Criminal Records: Access: Mail, in person. Both court and visitors may perform in person searches. No search fee. Required to search: name, years to search, DOB; also helpful: SSN. Criminal records in books back to 1958, computerized since 1995.

General Information: Public access terminal is available. SASE required. Copy fee: $.25. Fee payee: Brown County Court. Only cashiers checks and money orders accepted. Prepayment is required.

Butler County

Common Pleas Court 315 High St, General Division, Government Services Ctr, 3rd Fl, Hamilton, OH 45011; 513-887-3996; Probate phone: 513-887-3296; Fax: 513-887-3089. Hours: 8:30AM-4:30PM (EST). *Felony, Civil Actions Over $3,000, Probate.*

www.butlercountyclerk.org/

Note: Government Service Center phone number is 513-887-3288.

Civil Records: Access: Online, in person. Visitors must perform in person searches for themselves. No search fee. Required to search: name, years to search. Civil cases indexed by defendant, plaintiff. Civil records on computer from 1988, records go back to 1987. Online access to County Clerk of Courts records available free at http://24.123.15.5/pa/pa.urd/pamw6500-display. Search by name, dates, or case number and type. Online access to Probate Court records is available free at www.butlercountyohio.org/probate/estate.cfm. Search the Estate or Guardianship databases.

Criminal Records: Access: Online, in person. Visitors must perform in person searches for themselves. No search fee. Required to search: name, years to search, DOB; also helpful: SSN. Criminal records on computer from 1988, prior in books. Online access to criminal records is the same as civil.

General Information: Public access terminal is available. Copy fee: $.25 per page. Certification fee: $2.00. Fee payee: Clerk of Court. Personal checks accepted.

County Court Area #1 118 West High, Oxford, OH 45056; 513-523-4748; Fax: 513-523-4737. Hours: 8:30AM-4:30PM (EST). *Misdemeanor, Civil Actions Under $15,000, Small Claims.*

Civil Records: Access: Phone, mail, in person. Both court and visitors may perform in person searches. No search fee. Required to search: name, years to search. Civil cases indexed by defendant, plaintiff. Civil records on index back to 1983.

Criminal Records: Access: Phone, mail, in person. Both court and visitors may perform in person searches. No search fee. Required to search: name, years to search, DOB. Criminal records on index back to 1983.

General Information: No sealed records released. SASE required. Turnaround time 1-5 days. No copy fee.

County Court Area #2 Butler County Courthouse, 101 High St, 1st Fl, Hamilton, OH 45011; 513-887-3459. Hours: 8AM-5PM (EST). *Misdemeanor, Civil Actions Under $15,000, Small Claims.*

Civil Records: Access: Phone, in person. Visitors must perform in person searches for themselves. No search fee. Required to search: name, years to search. Civil cases indexed by defendant, plaintiff. Civil records on computer from 1993, books back to 1983.

Criminal Records: Access: Phone, in person. Visitors must perform in person searches for themselves. No search fee. Required to search: name, years to search. Criminal records on computer from 1993, books back to 1983.

General Information: Public access terminal is available. No sealed records released. No copy fee. Only cashiers checks and money orders accepted. Prepayment is required.

County Court Area #3 9113 Cincinnati, Dayton Rd, West Chester, OH 45069; 513-867-5070; Fax: 513-777-0558. Hours: 8:AM-5PM (EST). *Misdemeanor, Civil Actions Under $15,000, Small Claims.*

Civil Records: Access: Mail, in person. Both court and visitors may perform in person searches. No search fee. Required to search: name, years to search. Civil cases indexed by defendant, plaintiff. Civil records on computer from 1993, books back to 1983.

Criminal Records: Access: Mail, in person. Both court and visitors may perform in person searches. No search fee. Required to search: name, years to search. Criminal records on computer from 1993, books back to 1983.

General Information: Public access terminal is available. SASE required. Turnaround time 2-3 days. No copy fee. Certification fee: $1.00. Fee payee: Area #3 Court. Personal checks accepted. Prepayment is required.

Carroll County

Common Pleas Court PO Box 367, Carrollton, OH 44615; 330-627-4886; Probate phone: 330-627-2323; Fax: 330-627-6734. Hours: 8AM-4PM (EST). *Felony, Civil Actions Over $15,000, Probate.*

Note: Probate Court address is 199 Public Sq, Courthouse, Carrollton, OH.

Civil Records: Access: In person only. Visitors must perform in person searches for themselves. No search fee. Required to search: name, years to search. Civil cases indexed by defendant, plaintiff. Civil records in books back to 1900s.

Criminal Records: Access: In person only. Visitors must perform in person searches for themselves. No search fee. Required to search: name, years to search; also helpful: DOB, SSN. Criminal records in books back to 1900s.

General Information: Copy fee: $.05 per page. Certification fee: $1.00. Fee payee: Clerk of Court. Personal checks accepted. Prepayment is required.

County Court 119 S Lisbon St #301, Carrollton, OH 44615; 330-627-5049; Fax: 330-627-3662. Hours: 8AM-4PM (EST). *Misdemeanor, Civil Actions Under $15,000, Small Claims, Evictions.*

Civil Records: Access: In person only. Visitors must perform in person searches for themselves. No search fee. Required to search: name, years to search. Civil cases indexed by defendant, plaintiff. Civil records in books from 1958; on computer since 11/95.

Criminal Records: Access: In person only. Visitors must perform in person searches for themselves. No search fee. Required to search: name, years to search, DOB. Criminal records in books from 1958; on computer since 11/95.

General Information: No confidential records released. Copy fee: $.25 per page. Certification fee: $2.00. Fee payee: Carroll County Court. Personal checks accepted. Prepayment is required.

Champaign County

Common Pleas Court 200 N Main St, Urbana, OH 43078; 937-653-2746; Probate phone: 937-652-2108. Hours: 8AM-4PM (EST). *Felony, Civil Actions Over $10,000, Probate.*

Note: Probate is separate court at phone number given.

Civil Records: Access: Phone, mail, in person. Visitors must perform in person searches for themselves. No search fee. Required to search: name, years to search. Civil cases indexed by defendant, plaintiff. Civil records on computer from 06/92, books back to late 1800'. Will only do phone or mail searches with a case number.

Criminal Records: Access: Phone, mail, in person. Visitors must perform in person searches for themselves. No search fee. Required to search: name, years to search, DOB, SSN, signed release. Criminal records on computer from 06/92, books back to late 1800'. Will only do mail or phone searches with a case number.

General Information: Public access terminal is available. All records are public. SASE required. Copy fee: $.25 per page. Certification fee: $1.00. Fee payee: Clerk of Court. Personal checks accepted. Personal

checks over $10.00 not accepted. Prepayment is required.

Champaign County Municipal Court PO Box 85, Urbana, OH 43078; 937-653-7376. Hours: 8AM-4PM (EST). *Misdemeanor, Civil Actions Under $15,000, Eviction, Small Claims.*

Civil Records: Access: Mail, in person. Both court and visitors may perform in person searches. No search fee. Required to search: name, years to search. Civil cases indexed by defendant, plaintiff. Civil records on computer from June, 93, books back to late 1800s.

Criminal Records: Access: Mail, in person. Both court and visitors may perform in person searches. No search fee. Required to search: name, years to search; also helpful: DOB, SSN. Criminal records on computer from June, 93, books back to late 1800s.

General Information: No sealed records released. SASE required. Turnaround time 2-3 days. Copy fee: $.25 per page. Certification fee: $2.50. Fee payee: Municipal Court. Only cashiers checks and money orders accepted. Prepayment is required.

Clark County

Common Pleas Court 101 N Limestone St, Springfield, OH 45502; 937-328-2458; 937-328-4648 (Domestic); Probate phone: 937-328-2434; Fax: 937-328-2436. Hours: 8AM-4:30PM (EST). *Felony, Civil Actions Over $10,000, Probate.*

www.co.clark.oh.us

Note: Probate Court and records are at the same address, separate office and phone.

Civil Records: Access: In person, online. Visitors must perform in person searches for themselves. No search fee. Required to search: name, years to search. Civil cases indexed by defendant. Civil records on computer back to 1990, prior in index books. Online access to clerk's records are avaialble free at http://64.56.97.140/.

Criminal Records: Access: In person, online. Visitors must perform in person searches for themselves. No search fee. Required to search: name, years to search. Criminal records on computer back to 1990, prior in index books. Online access to clerk's records are avaialble free at http://64.56.97.140/.

General Information: Public access terminal is available. Fax notes: Fee to fax results is $1.00 per page. Copy fee: $.25 per page. Certification fee: $1.00. Fee payee: Clerk of Court. Business checks accepted. Prepayment is required.

Clark County Municipal Court 50 E Columbia St, Springfield, OH 45502; 937-328-3700. Hours: 8AM-5PM (EST). *Misdemeanor, Civil Actions Under $15,000, Eviction, Small Claims.*

www.clerkofcourts.municipal.co.clark.oh.us

Civil Records: Access: Phone, mail, in person, online. Both court and visitors may perform in person searches. No search fee. Required to search: name, years to search. Civil cases indexed by defendant, plaintiff. Civil records on computer since 3/90; prior records go back to 6/87. Online access to case information available free at www.clerkofcourts.municipal.co.clark.oh.us/cases/court cases.nsf. Name searching on "New Cases" other types require a case number.

Criminal Records: Access: Mail, in person, online. Both court and visitors may perform in person searches. No search fee. Required to search: name, years to search; also helpful: DOB, SSN. Criminal records on computer since 3/90; prior records go back to 6/87. Online access is the same as civil, see above.

General Information: Public access terminal is available. SASE required. Turnaround time 2-3 days. Copy fee: $.50 per page. Certification fee: $2.00. Fee payee: Clerk of Court. Personal checks not accepted. Prepayment is required.

Clermont County

Common Pleas Court 270 Main St, Batavia, OH 45103; 513-732-7130; Probate phone: 513-732-7243; Fax: 513-732-7050. Hours: 8:30AM-4:30PM (EST). *Felony, Civil Actions Over $10,000, Probate.*

Note: Probate court is located at 76 S Riverside Dr, Batavia 45103

Civil Records: Access: In person, online. Visitors must perform in person searches for themselves. No search fee. Required to search: name, years to search; also helpful: address. Civil cases indexed by defendant, plaintiff. Civil records on computer from 1987, some on microfiche from 1920s, index books from 1959. Online access to civil records is the same as criminal, see below.
Criminal Records: Access: In person, online. Visitors must perform in person searches for themselves. No search fee. Required to search: name, years to search, DOB; also helpful: address, SSN. Criminal records on computer from 1987, some on microfiche from 1920s, index books from 1959. Online access to court records is available free at www.clermontclerk.org/Case_Access.htm. Online records go back to 1/1998. Includes later Municipal Court records. The clerk refers criminal record requests to the Sheriff (513-732-7500) who will do searches for $5.00 per name.
General Information: Public access terminal is available. Copy fee: $.10 per page. Certification fee: $1.00 per page. Fee payee: Clerk of Court. Business checks accepted. Prepayment is required.

Clermont County Municipal Court 289 Main St, Civil court: 66 S Riverside Rd, Batavia, OH 45103; Civil phone: 513-732-7292; Criminal phone: 513-732-7290.   Hours: 8AM-4PM   (EST). *Misdemeanor, Civil Actions Under $15,000, Eviction, Small Claims.*

www.clermontclerk.org

Civil Records: Access: Mail, in person, online. Visitors must perform in person searches for themselves. Search fee: No search fee. Required to search: name, years to search. Civil cases indexed by defendant, plaintiff. Computerized records from 5/96, civil records in books and microfiche from 1959, docket books back to 1800s. Online access to court records is the same as criminal, see below.
Criminal Records: Access: Mail, in person, online. Visitors must perform in person searches for themselves. Search fee: No search fee. Required to search: name, years to search, DOB; also helpful: SSN. Computerized records back to 5/96, criminal records in books and microfiche from 1957, docket books back to 1800s. Online access to court records is available free at www.clermontclerk.org/Case_Access.htm.   Online records go back to 5/1/1996. Includes Common Pleas court records.
General Information: SASE required. Copy fee: $.25 per page. Certification fee: $4.25. Fee payee: Clerk of Court. Only cashiers checks and money orders accepted. Prepayment is required.

Clinton County

Clinton County Municipal Court 69 N South St, PO Box 71, Wilmington, OH 45177; 937-382-8985; Fax: 937-383-0130. Hours: 8AM-4PM (EST). *Misdemeanor, Civil Actions Under $15,000, Eviction, Small Claims.*

Civil Records: Access: Fax, mail, in person. Both court and visitors may perform in person searches. No search fee. Required to search: name, years to search. Civil cases indexed by defendant, plaintiff. Civil records in books from 1960; computerized records go back to 1995.
Criminal Records: Access: Fax, mail, in person. Both court and visitors may perform in person searches. No

search fee. Required to search: name, years to search, DOB; also helpful: SSN. Criminal records in books from 1960; computerized records go back to 1995.
General Information: SASE required. Turnaround time 1 day. Copy fee: $.25 per page after 10 pages. Fee payee: Clerk of Court. Only cashiers checks and money orders accepted.

Common Pleas Court 46 S South St, Wilmington, OH 45177; 937-382-2316; Probate phone: 937-382-2280; Fax: 937-383-3455. Hours: 7:30AM-4:30PM (EST). *Felony, Civil Actions Over $15,000, Probate.*

Note: Probate fax is 937-383-1158; hours are 8AM-4:30PM.

Civil Records: Access: Fax, mail, in person. Both court and visitors may perform in person searches. No search fee. Required to search: name, years to search; also helpful: address. Civil cases indexed by defendant, plaintiff. Civil records on computer since 1995; prior in books back to 1810.
Criminal Records: Access: Mail, in person. Both court and visitors may perform in person searches. Search fee: $5.00 per name. Required to search: name, years to search, DOD, SSN; also helpful: address. Criminal records on computer since 1995; prior in books back to 1810.
General Information: Public access terminal is available. No confidential records released. SASE required. Turnaround time 1 week. Copy fee: $.25 per page. Certification fee: $1.00. Fee payee: Clerk of Court. Personal checks accepted. Prepayment required.

Columbiana County

Common Pleas Court 105 S Market St, Lisbon, OH 44432; 330-424-7777; Fax: 330-424-3960. Hours: 8AM-4PM (EST). *Felony, Civil Actions Over $15,000, Probate.*

www.ccclerk.org

Civil Records: Access: In person, online. Visitors must perform in person searches for themselves. No search fee. Required to search: name, years to search; also helpful: address. Civil cases indexed by defendant, plaintiff. Civil records on computer since 1993; prior in books from 1968, archived back to 1800s. Free online access to all county court records is at www.ccclerk.org/case_access.htm.
Criminal Records: Access: In person, online. Visitors must perform in person searches for themselves. No search fee. Required to search: name, years to search, DOB; also helpful: address, SSN. Criminal records on computer since 1993; prior in books from 1968, archived back to 1800s. Free online access to all county court records is at www.ccclerk.org/case_access.htm.
General Information: Public access terminal is available. No secret indictment records released. Copy fee: $.50 per page. Certification fee: $1.00. Fee payee: Clerk of Court. Personal checks accepted. Prepayment is required.

Municipal Court Eastern Area 31 North Market St, East Palestine, OH 44413; 330-426-3774; Fax: 330-426-6328. Hours: 8AM-4PM (EST). *Misdemeanor, Civil Actions Under $15,000, Small Claims.*

www.ccclerk.org/the_courts.htm

Civil Records: Access: Mail, in person, online. Both court and visitors may perform in person searches. No search fee. Required to search: name, years to search. Civil cases indexed by defendant, plaintiff. Civil records in books from 1950s, archived from 1800s, recent records computerized. Free online access to all county court records at www.ccclerk.org/the_courts.htm.
Criminal Records: Access: Mail, in person, online. Both court and visitors may perform in person searches. No search fee. Required to search: name, years to

search. Criminal records in books from 1950s, archived from 1800s, recent records computerized. Free online access to all county court records at www.ccclerk.org/the_courts.htm.
General Information: Public access terminal is available. SASE required. Turnaround time 1 day. Copy fee: $.25 per page. Certification fee: $1.00. Fee payee: Clerk of Court. Only cashiers checks and money orders accepted. Prepayment is required.

Municipal Court Northwest Area 130 Penn Ave, Salem, OH 44460; 330-332-0297. Hours: 8AM-4PM (EST). *Misdemeanor, Civil Actions Under $15,000, Small Claims.*

Civil Records: Access: In person, online. Both court and visitors may perform in person searches. No search fee. Required to search: name, years to search. Civil cases indexed by defendant, plaintiff. Civil records in books from 1950s, archived from 1800s, computerized since 11/94. Free online access to all county court records at www.ccclerk.org/the_courts.htm.
Criminal Records: Access: Mail, in person, online. Both court and visitors may perform in person searches. No search fee. Required to search: name, years to search; also helpful: DOB. Criminal records in books from 1950s, archived from 1800s, computerized back to 11/94. Free online access to all county court records at www.ccclerk.org/the_courts.htm.
General Information: Public access terminal is available. SASE required. Turnaround time 2-3 days. Copy fee: $.25 per page. Certification fee: $1.00. Fee payee: Northwest Area Court. Only cashiers checks and money orders accepted. Prepayment is required.

Municipal Court Southwest Area 41 N Park Ave, Lisbon, OH 44432; 330-424-5326; Fax: 330-424-6658. Hours: 8AM-4PM (EST). *Misdemeanor, Civil Actions Under $15,000, Small Claims.*

www.ccclerk.org/the_courts.htm

Civil Records: Access: In person, online. Visitors must perform in person searches for themselves. No search fee. Required to search: name, years to search. Civil cases indexed by defendant, plaintiff. Civil records in books from 1950s, archived back to 1800s; on comptuer back to 1994. Free online access to all county court records at www.ccclerk.org/the_courts.htm.
Criminal Records: Access: In person, online. Visitors must perform in person searches for themselves. No search fee. Required to search: name, years to search; also helpful: DOB, SSN. Criminal records in books from 1950s, archived back to 1800s; on computer back to 1994. Free online access to all county court records at www.ccclerk.org/the_courts.htm.
General Information: Public access terminal is available. No expungment records released. Copy fee: $.50 per page. Certification fee: $1.00. Fee payee: Southwest Court. Only cashiers checks and money orders accepted. Prepayment is required.

East Liverpool Municipal Court 126 W 6th St, East Liverpool, OH 43920; 330-385-5151; Fax: 330-385-1566.   Hours: 8AM-4PM   (EST). *Misdemeanor, Civil Actions Under $15,000, Eviction, Small Claims.*

www.eastliverpool.com/court.html

Civil Records: Access: Phone, fax, mail, in person, online. Both court and visitors may perform in person searches. No search fee. Required to search: name, years to search. Civil cases indexed by defendant, plaintiff. Civil records in books from 1968, archived back to 1800s, computerized since 11/92. Free online access to all county court records at www.ccclerk.org/the_courts.htm.
Criminal Records: Access: Phone, fax, mail, in person, online. Both court and visitors may perform in person searches. No search fee. Required to search: name, years to search, signed release; also helpful:

DOB, SSN. Criminal records in books from 1968, archived back to 1800s, computerized since 11/92. Free online access to all county court records at www.ccclerk.org/the_courts.htm.
General Information: Public access terminal is available. No expungment records released. SASE required. Turnaround time 1-2 days. Fax notes: No fee to fax results. Copy fee: $.25 per page. Certification fee: $3.00. Fee payee: East Liverpool Municipal Court. No business or personal checks. Prepayment is required.

Coshocton County

Common Pleas Court 318 Main St, Coshocton, OH 43812; 740-622-1456; Probate phone: 740-622-1837. Hours: 8AM-4PM (EST). *Felony, Civil Actions Over $10,000, Probate.*

Civil Records: Access: Mail, in person. Both court and visitors may perform in person searches. No search fee. Required to search: name, years to search. Civil cases indexed by defendant, plaintiff. Civil records in books, microfilm back to 1985, archived back to 1800s; on computer back to 1998.
Criminal Records: Access: Mail, in person. Both court and visitors may perform in person searches. No search fee. Required to search: name, years to search, DOB; also helpful: SSN. Criminal records in books, microfilm back to 1985, archived back to 1800s; on computer back to 1998.
General Information: Public access terminal is available. No expunged records released. SASE not required. Turnaround time 2 days. Fax notes: Will not fax back results. Copy fee: $.25 per page. Certification fee: $1.00. Fee payee: Clerk of Court. Personal checks accepted. Prepayment is required.

Coshocton Municipal Court 760 Chesnut St, Coshocton, OH 43812; 740-622-2871; Fax: 740-623-5928. Hours: 8AM-4:30PM M-W,F; 8AM-Noon Th (EST). *Misdemeanor, Civil Actions Under $15,000, Eviction, Small Claims.*
www.coshoctonmunicipalcourt.com
Civil Records: Access: Phone, fax, mail, in person, online. Both court and visitors may perform in person searches. No search fee. Required to search: name, years to search. Civil cases indexed by defendant, plaintiff. Civil records on computer from 1989, books back to 1952. Online access to civil records is available at the web site. Search by name, case number, attorney, date.
Criminal Records: Access: Phone, fax, mail, in person, online. Both court and visitors may perform in person searches. No search fee. Required to search: name, years to search; also helpful: DOB, SSN. Criminal records on computer from 1989, books back to 1952. Online access to criminal records is the same as civil. Search by name, attorney, citation or case number.
General Information: Public access terminal is available. No expunged records released. SASE required. Turnaround time same day. Fax notes: No fee to fax results. Copy fee: $.50 per page. Certification fee: $5.00. Fee payee: Clerk of Court. Personal checks accepted. Prepayment is required.

Crawford County

Common Pleas Court 112 E Mansfield St #204, Bucyrus, OH 44820; 419-562-2766; Probate phone: 419-562-8891; Fax: 419-562-8011. Hours: 8:30AM-4:30PM *Felony, Civil Actions Over $3,000, Probate.*
www.crawford-co.org/Clerk/default.html
Civil Records: Access: Phone, mail, in person, online. Both court and visitors may perform in person searches. Search fee: $5.00 per name. Required to search: name, years to search; also helpful: address. Civil cases indexed by defendant, plaintiff. Civil records on computer back to 1990, some on microfiche and index books from 1800s. Online access to Common Please

court records is available free at www.crawford-co.org/Clerk/default.html and click on "Internet Inquiry.".
Criminal Records: Access: Mail, in person, online. Both court and visitors may perform in person searches. Search fee: $5.00 per name. Required to search: name, years to search; also helpful: address, DOB, SSN. Criminal records on computer back to 1990, some on microfiche and index books from 1800s. Online access to criminal cases is the same as civil.
General Information: Public access terminal is available. No divorce investigations. SASE required. Turnaround time 1-2 days. No copy fee. Certification fee: $1.00. Fee payee: Clerk of Court. Personal checks accepted. Prepayment is required.

Crawford County Municipal Court PO Box 550, Bucyrus, OH 44820; 419-562-2731; Fax: 419-562-7064. Hours: 8:30AM-4:30PM (EST). *Misdemeanor, Civil Actions Under $15,000, Eviction, Small Claims.*
Civil Records: Access: Phone, fax, mail, in person. Both court and visitors may perform in person searches. No search fee. Required to search: name, years to search. Civil cases indexed by defendant, plaintiff. Civil records in books back to 1978.
Criminal Records: Access: Mail, in person. Both court and visitors may perform in person searches. No search fee. Required to search: name, years to search, DOB. Criminal records in books back to 1978; on computer back to 1996.
General Information: No counseling report records released. SASE not required. Turnaround time within 1 week. Copy fee: $.10 per page. Certification fee: $2.00. Business checks accepted. Crawford county business checks accepted. Prepayment is required.

Crawford County Municipal Court Eastern Division 301 Harding Way East, Galion, OH 44833; 419-468-6819; Fax: 419-468-6828. Hours: 8AM-5PM (EST). *Misdemeanor, Civil Actions Under $15,000, Eviction, Small Claims.*
Civil Records: Access: Mail, in person. Both court and visitors may perform in person searches. No search fee. Required to search: name, years to search. Civil cases indexed by defendant, plaintiff. Civil records in books back to 1800s.
Criminal Records: Access: Mail, in person. Both court and visitors may perform in person searches. No search fee. Required to search: name, years to search, DOB, SSN, signed release. Criminal records in books back to 1800s.
General Information: SASE required. Turnaround time 2-3 days. Copy fee: $.10 per page. Certification fee: $5.00. Fee payee: Municipal Court. Only cashiers checks and money orders accepted. Prepayment is required.

Cuyahoga County

Common Pleas Court - General Division 1200 Ontario St, Cleveland, OH 44113; 216-443-8560; Civil phone: 216-443-7966; Criminal phone: 216-443-7985; Probate phone: 216-443-8764; Fax: 216-443-5424. Hours: 8:30AM-4:30PM (EST). *Felony, Civil Actions Over $10,000, Probate.*
www.cuyahoga.oh.us
Note: Probate is a separate division with separate records and personnel. 22 categories of Probate court records including marriages are available free online at http://198.30.212.11/pa.urd/pamw6500.display.
Civil Records: Access: Phone, mail, in person, online. Both court and visitors may perform in person searches. No search fee. Required to search: name, years to search; also helpful: address. Civil cases indexed by defendant, plaintiff. Civil records on index and dockets from 1968, archived from 1800s; computerized since

1975. Online access to Common Please civil courts is available by clicking on Civil Case Dockets at www.cuyahoga.oh.us/home/default.asp. Phone requests to 216-443-7966. Address mail requests to Gerald Fuerst, 1st Floor, Index Dept.
Criminal Records: Access: Phone, in person, online. Visitors must perform in person searches for themselves. No search fee. Required to search: name, years to search; also helpful: address, DOB, SSN. Criminal records on index and dockets from 1968, archived from 1800s; computerized since 1975. Online access to criminal records is available free at http://198.30.212.17/cpdock/. Address mail requests to Criminal Dept, 2nd Floor. Phone requests must have case number.
General Information: Public access terminal is available. No expungments or sealed records released. SASE required. Copy fee: $.25 per page. Certification fee: $1.00 per page. Fee payee: Clerk of Court. Business checks accepted. Prepayment is required.

Cleveland Municipal Court - Civil Division 1200 Ontario St, Cleveland, OH 44113; 216-664-4870; Fax: 216-664-4065. Hours: 8AM-3:50PM (EST). *Civil Actions Under $15,000, Eviction, Small Claims.*
Civil Records: Access: Fax, mail, in person. Both court and visitors may perform in person searches. No search fee. Required to search: name, years to search; also helpful: address. Civil cases indexed by defendant, plaintiff. Civil records on computer from 1988, docket books and index from 1950s, prior archived.
General Information: Public access terminal is available. SASE required. Turnaround time 2 days. Copy fee: $.25 per page. Certification fee: $1.00. Fee payee: Municipal Court. Personal checks accepted. Prepayment is required.

Cleveland Municipal Court - Criminal Division 1200 Ontario St, Cleveland, OH 44113; 216-664-4790. Hours: 8AM-3:50PM (EST). *Misdemeanor.*
Criminal Records: Access: I person. Both court and visitors may perform in person searches. No search fee. Required to search: name, years to search, DOB, SSN, signed release. Criminal records on computer since 1988, on books to 1950s, archived prior.
General Information: No adoption or juvenile records released. SASE required. Turnaround time 3-4 days. Copy fee: $.25 per page. Certification fee: $3.00. Fee payee: Municipal Court. Personal checks accepted. Prepayment is required.

Bedford Municipal Court 65 Columbus Rd, Bedford, OH 44146; 440-232-3420; Fax: 440-232-2510. Hours: 8:30AM-4:30PM (EST). *Misdemeanor, Civil Actions Under $15,000, Eviction, Small Claims.*
Civil Records: Access: Fax, mail, in person. Both court and visitors may perform in person searches. No search fee. Required to search: name, years to search. Civil cases indexed by defendant, plaintiff. Civil records on computer from 1990 docket books and index from 1970s, prior archived.
Criminal Records: Access: Fax, mail, in person. Both court and visitors may perform in person searches. No search fee. Required to search: name, years to search, signed release. Criminal records on computer from 1990, docket books and index from 1970s, prior archived.
General Information: SASE required. Turnaround time 3 days. Fax notes: No fee to fax results. Copy fee: $.50 per page. Certification fee: $2.00. Fee payee: Municipal Court. Only cashiers checks and money orders accepted. Prepayment is required.

Berea Municipal Court 11 Berea Commons, Berea, OH 44017; 440-826-5860; Fax: 440-891-3387.

Hours: 8AM-4:30PM (EST). *Misdemeanor, Civil Actions Under $15,000, Eviction, Small Claims.*

Civil Records: Access: Mail, fax, in person. Both court and visitors may perform in person searches. No search fee. Required to search: name, years to search. Civil cases indexed by defendant, plaintiff. Civil records on computer back to 1991, prior in books and archived.

Criminal Records: Access: Fax, mail, in person. Both court and visitors may perform in person searches. Search fee: $5.00 per name. Required to search: name, years to search; also helpful: address, DOB, SSN. Criminal records on computer back to 1991, prior in books and archived.

General Information: No probation records released. SASE required. Turnaround time 1 week-10 days. Fax notes: No fee to fax results. Copy fee: $1.00 per page. Certification fee: $5.00. Fee payee: Berea Municipal Court. Personal checks accepted. Credit cards accepted: Visa, MasterCard. Prepayment is required.

Cleveland Heights Municipal Court 40 Severance Circle, Cleveland Heights, OH 44118; 216-291-4901; Fax: 216-291-2459. Hours: 8AM-5PM (EST). *Misdemeanor, Civil Actions Under $15,000, Eviction, Small Claims.*

www.clevelandheightscourt.com

Civil Records: Access: Online, in person. Visitors must perform in person searches for themselves. No search fee. Required to search: name, years to search; also helpful: address. Civil cases indexed by defendant, plaintiff. Civil records on computer from 1990, prior in books to 1970s. Civil (to $15,000) or misdemeanor docket records for Municipal Court are available on the web site. Search by name or case number.

Criminal Records: Access: Online, in person. Visitors must perform in person searches for themselves. No search fee. Required to search: name, years to search; also helpful: address, DOB, SSN. Criminal records on computer from 1990, prior in books to 1970s. Online access to criminal records is the same as civil.

General Information: Public access terminal is available. No expungments or search warrant records released. Copy fee: $.10 per page. Certification fee: $3.00. Fee payee: Municipal Court. Personal checks accepted. Credit cards accepted: Visa, MasterCard. Visa, MC in person only. Prepayment is required.

East Cleveland Municipal Court 14340 Euclid Ave, East Cleveland, OH 44112; 216-681-2021/2022. 8:30AM-4:30PM (EST). *Misdemeanor, Civil Actions Under $15,000, Eviction, Small Claims.*

Civil Records: Access: In person only. Visitors must perform in person searches for themselves. No search fee. Required to search: name, years to search. Civil cases indexed by defendant, plaintiff. Civil records go back to 1979; on computer from 1989, docket books and index from 1950s, prior archived.

Criminal Records: Access: Mail, in person. Visitors must perform in person searches for themselves. No search fee. Required to search: name, years to search, DOB, SSN, signed release; also helpful: address. Criminal records on computer from 1997, docket books and index from 1950s, prior archived. Address mail requests to Police Record Room.

General Information: SASE required. Turnaround time 1-2 weeks. Copy fee: $1.00 per page. Certification fee: $3.00. Fee payee: Municipal Court. Personal checks not accepted on criminal cases. Prepayment is required.

Euclid Municipal Court 555 E 222 St, Euclid, OH 44123-2099; 216-289-2888; Fax: 216-289-8254. Hours: 8:30AM-4:30PM (EST). *Misdemeanor, Civil Actions Under $15,000, Eviction, Small Claims.*

Civil Records: Access: Mail, in person. Both court and visitors may perform in person searches. Search fee: $5.00 per name. Required to search: name, years to

search. Civil cases indexed by defendant, plaintiff. Civil records on computer from 1995, docket books and index from 1950s, prior archived.

Criminal Records: Access: Mail, in person. Both court and visitors may perform in person searches. Search fee: $5.00 per name. Required to search: name, years to search, DOB; also helpful: address, SSN. Criminal records on computer from 1995, docket books and index from 1950s, prior archived.

General Information: No expunged records released. SASE required. Turnaround time 1 week. Copy fee: $1.00 per page. Certification fee: $5.00 (included in search fee). Fee payee: Municipal Court. Personal checks accepted. Prepayment is required.

Garfield Heights Municipal Court 5555 Turney Rd, Garfield Heights, OH 44125; 216-475-1900. Hours: 8:30AM-4:30PM (EST). *Misdemeanor, Civil Actions Under $15,000, Eviction, Small Claims.*

www.ghmc.org

Civil Records: Access: Phone, mail, in person, online. Both court and visitors may perform in person searches. No search fee. Required to search: name, years to search; also helpful: address. Civil cases indexed by defendant, plaintiff. Civil records on computer from 11/91, docket books and index from 1996, prior archived. Phone access depends on age of case. Online access is limited to current dockets; search by name, date or case number at www.ghmc.org/docket.html.

Criminal Records: Access: Phone, mail, in person, online. Both court and visitors may perform in person searches. No search fee. Required to search: name, years to search, DOB; also helpful: address, SSN, signed release. Criminal records on computer from 1996, docket books and index from 1995, prior archived. Online access to criminal records is the same as civil.

General Information: Public access terminal is available. No expunged records released. SASE required. Turnaround time 2 weeks. Copy fee: $.05 per page. Certification fee: $1.00. Fee payee: Municipal Court. Personal checks accepted. Prepayment required.

Lakewood Municipal Court 12650 Detroit Ave, Lakewood, OH 44107; 216-529-6700; Fax: 216-529-7687. Hours: 8AM-5PM (EST). *Misdemeanor, Civil Actions Under $15,000, Eviction, Small Claims.*

www.lakewoodcourtoh.com

Civil Records: Access: Phone, fax, mail, in person. Both court and visitors may perform in person searches. No search fee. Required to search: name, years to search; also helpful: address. Civil cases indexed by defendant, plaintiff. Civil records on computer from 1987, prior in books. Weekly dockets are available at www.lakewoodcourtoh.com/CourtDockets.htm.

Criminal Records: Access: Fax, mail, in person. Both court and visitors may perform in person searches. No search fee. Required to search: name, years to search, DOB; also helpful: address, SSN. Criminal records on computer since 1983, prior in books. Weekly dockets are available at www.lakewoodcourtoh.com/CourtDockets.htm.

General Information: No confidential records released. SASE required. Turnaround time 1 week. Fax notes: No fee to fax results. Local faxing only. Copy fee: $.25 per page. Certification fee: $3.00. Fee payee: Municipal Court. Personal checks accepted. Prepayment is required.

Lyndhurst Municipal Court 5301 Mayfield Rd, Lyndhurst, OH 44124; 440-461-6500; Fax: 440-442-1910. Hours: 8:30AM-5PM M-TH; 8AM-4PM F (EST). *Misdemeanor, Civil Actions Under $15,000, Eviction, Small Claims.*

Civil Records: Access: Mail, in person. Both court and visitors may perform in person searches. No search fee. Required to search: name, years to search; also helpful:

address. Civil cases indexed by defendant, plaintiff. Civil records on computer from 1991, prior in books.

Criminal Records: Access: Mail, in person. Both court and visitors may perform in person searches. No search fee. Required to search: name, years to search, signed release; also helpful: address, DOB, SSN. Criminal records on computer from 1991, prior in books.

General Information: SASE required. Turnaround time 1 week. Copy fee: $1.00 per page. Certification fee: $5.00 per page. Fee payee: Municipal Court. Personal checks accepted. Prepayment is required.

Parma Municipal Court 5555 Powers Blvd, Parma, OH 44125; 440-887-7400; Fax: 440-887-7485. Hours: 8:30AM-4:30PM (EST). *Misdemeanor, Civil Actions Under $15,000, Eviction, Small Claims.*

Note: The court is making changes to block the SSN from appearing on record requests.

Civil Records: Access: Phone, fax, mail, in person. Both court and visitors may perform in person searches. Search fee: $1.00 for copy. Required to search: name, years to search; also helpful: address. Civil cases indexed by defendant, plaintiff. Civil records on computer from 1993, prior in books to 1977.

Criminal Records: Access: Phone, fax, mail, in person. Both court and visitors may perform in person searches. Search fee: $1.00 for copy. Required to search: name, years to search, DOB; also helpful: address, SSN. Criminal records on computer from 1993, prior in books to 1992.

General Information: Public access terminal is available. (The terminal is only for civil records.) SASE required. Turnaround time up to 1 week. Copy fee: $.10 per page. Certification fee: $1.00. Fee payee: Municipal Court. Personal checks accepted. Prepayment required.

Rocky River Municipal Court 21012 Hilliard Blvd, Rocky River, OH 44116; 440-333-0066; Fax: 440-356-5613. Hours: 8:30AM-4:30PM (EST). *Misdemeanor, Civil Actions Under $15,000, Eviction, Small Claims.*

Civil Records: Access: Phone, fax, mail, in person. Both court and visitors may perform in person searches. No search fee. Required to search: name, years to search. Civil cases indexed by defendant, plaintiff. Civil records on computer from 1987, prior in books to 1958.

Criminal Records: Access: Phone, fax, mail, in person. Both court and visitors may perform in person searches. No search fee. Required to search: name, years to search, DOB. Criminal records on computer back to 1987, prior in books to 1958.

General Information: Public access terminal is available. SASE required. Turnaround time 2 days. Copy fee: $.10 per page. Certification fee: $5.00. Fee payee: Municipal Court. Personal checks accepted. Prepayment is required.

Shaker Heights Municipal Court 3355 Lee Rd, Shaker Heights, OH 44120; 216-491-1300; Fax: 216-491-1314. Hours: 8:30AM-4:30PM (EST). *Misdemeanor, Civil Actions Under $15,000, Eviction, Small Claims.*

Note: Criminal Clerk open until 6:30PM on Mondays.

Civil Records: Access: Mail, fax, in person. Both court and visitors may perform in person searches. No search fee. Required to search: name, years to search; also helpful: address. Civil cases indexed by defendant, plaintiff. Civil records on computer from 06/86, prior in books for at least 25 years.

Criminal Records: Access: Phone, fax, mail, in person. Both court and visitors may perform in person searches. Search fee: None, however complete dockets are $10.00. Required to search: name, years to search, DOB or SSN. Criminal records on computer from 06/86, prior in books. For records prior to 1986 provide month & year to search. Phone access limited to gov't agencies.

General Information: Public access terminal is available. No medical or LEADS print-out records released. SASE required. Turnaround time 2 days. Fax notes: Fee to fax results is $.50 per page. Copy fee: $.05 per page. Certification fee: $5.00. Fee payee: Shaker Heights Municipal Court. Personal checks accepted. Credit cards accepted: Visa, MasterCard. Visa, MC accepted in person only. Prepayment is required.

South Euclid Municipal Court 1349 S Green Rd, South Euclid, OH 44121; 216-381-2880; Fax: 216-381-1195. Hours: 8:30AM-5PM (EST). *Misdemeanor, Civil Actions Under $15,000, Eviction, Small Claims.*

Civil Records: Access: Phone, fax, mail, in person. Both court and visitors may perform in person searches. No search fee. Required to search: name, years to search; also helpful: address. Civil cases indexed by defendant, plaintiff. Civil records on computer back to 10/97; prior in docket books to 1960s.

Criminal Records: Access: Mail, in person. Both court and visitors may perform in person searches. No search fee. Required to search: name, years to search, DOB, SSN, signed release; also helpful: address. Criminal records on computer back to 10/97; prior in docket books to 1960s.

General Information: Public access terminal is available. SASE required. Turnaround time 1 week. Copy fee: No charge until at least 10 pages, then $.10 per copy. Certification fee: $1.00 per page. Fee payee: Clerk of Court, South Euclid Municipal Court. Personal checks accepted. Visa/MC accepted. Prepayment is required.

Darke County

Common Pleas Court Courthouse, Greenville, OH 45331; 937-547-7325; Probate phone: 937-547-7345; Fax: 937-547-7305. Hours: 8:30AM-4:30PM (EST). *Felony, Civil Actions Over $3,000, Probate.*

Note: Probate is a separate court located at 300 Garst Ave at the number given.

Civil Records: Access: Mail, in person. Both court and visitors may perform in person searches. Search fee: $5.00 per name. Required to search: name, years to search. Civil cases indexed by defendant, plaintiff. Civil records in books to 1832, on microfiche from 1940s, computerized since 19993.

Criminal Records: Access: Mail, in person. Both court and visitors may perform in person searches. Search fee: $5.00 per name. Required to search: name, years to search. Criminal records in books to 1832, on microfiche from 1940s, computerized since 1987.

General Information: Public access terminal is available. No secret indictment records released. SASE required. Turnaround time 1-2 days. Copy fee: $.25 per page. Certification fee: $1.00. Fee payee: Clerk of Court. Business checks accepted. Prepayment required.

County Court Courthouse, Greenville, OH 45331-1990; 937-547-7340; Fax: 937-547-7378. Hours: 8:30AM-4:30PM (EST). *Misdemeanor, Civil Actions Under $15,000, Small Claims.*

Civil Records: Access: Mail, in person. Both court and visitors may perform in person searches. Search fee: $5.00 per name. Required to search: name, years to search. Civil cases indexed by defendant, plaintiff. Civil records in books since 1959.

Criminal Records: Access: Mail, in person. Both court and visitors may perform in person searches. Search fee: $5.00 per name. Required to search: name, years to search, DOB; also helpful: SSN. Criminal records in books since 1959.

General Information: Public access terminal is available. No sealed or confidential records released. SASE required. Turnaround time 1 week. Copy fee: $.25 per page. Certification fee: $1.00. Fee payee: Clerk of Court, Darke County. Only cashiers checks and money orders accepted. Credit cards accepted: Visa, MasterCard. Prepayment is required.

Defiance County

Common Pleas Court PO Box 716, Defiance, OH 43512; 419-782-1936; Probate phone: 419-782-4181. Hours: 8:30AM-4:30PM (EST). *Felony, Civil Actions Over $10,000, Probate.*

Civil Records: Access: Phone, in person. Visitors must perform in person searches for themselves. No search fee. Required to search: name, years to search; also helpful: address. Civil cases indexed by defendant, plaintiff. Civil Records on computer since 1995. Most recent records are kept here, usually up to 10 years.

Criminal Records: Access: Phone, in person. Visitors must perform in person searches for themselves. No search fee. Required to search: name, years to search; also helpful: address, DOB, SSN. Criminal records on computer since 1995; prior records on docket books.

General Information: Public access terminal is available. Fax notes: $3.00 for first page, $1.00 each add'l. Copy fee: $.25 per page. Certification fee: $1.00. Fee payee: Clerk of Court. Personal checks accepted. Prepayment is required.

Defiance Municipal Court 324 Perry St, Defiance, OH 43512; 419-782-5756; Civil phone: 419-782-4092; Fax: 419-782-2018. Hours: 8AM-5PM (EST). *Misdemeanor, Civil Actions Under $15,000, Eviction, Small Claims.*

Civil Records: Access: Mail, in person. Both court and visitors may perform in person searches. Search fee: $8.00 per name. Fee only for records prior to 1989. Required to search: name, years to search; also helpful: DOB, SSN, address. Civil cases indexed by defendant, plaintiff. Civil records on computer from 12/89, prior in books to 1958.

Criminal Records: Access: Mail, in person. Both court and visitors may perform in person searches. Search fee: $8.00 per name. Fee only for records prior to 1989. Required to search: name, years to search; also helpful: address, DOB, SSN. Criminal records on computer from 10/89, prior in books to 1958.

General Information: Public access terminal is available. No confidential records released. SASE required. Turnaround time 14 days. Copy fee: $.50 per page. Certification fee: $1.00. Fee payee: Municipal Court. Personal checks accepted. Credit cards accepted. Prepayment is required.

Delaware County

Common Pleas Court 91 N Sandusky, Delaware, OH 43015; 740-833-2500; Probate phone: 740-833-2680; Fax: 740-833-2499. Hours: 8:30AM-4:30PM *Felony, Civil Actions Over $10,000, Probate.*

www.co.delaware.oh.us/clerk/index.htm

Civil Records: Access: Mail, in person. Both court and visitors may perform in person searches. No search fee. Required to search: name, years to search; also helpful: address. Civil cases indexed by defendant, plaintiff. Civil records on computer from 1992, prior books go back to 1800s.

Criminal Records: Access: Mail, in person. Both court and visitors may perform in person searches. No search fee. Required to search: name, years to search, DOB; also helpful: address, SSN. Criminal records on computer from 1992, prior books go back to 1800s. Search the sheriff's county database of sex offenders, deadbeat parents, and most wanted list for free at www.delawarecountysheriff.com.

General Information: Public access terminal is available. No grand jury proceedings or expungment records released. SASE required. Turnaround time 1-2 days. Copy fee: $.25 per page. Certification fee: $1.00. Fee payee: Clerk of Court. Personal checks accepted. Prepayment is required.

Delaware Municipal Court 70 N Union St, Delaware, OH 43015; 740-363-1555/548-6707; Fax: 740-368-1583. Hours: 8AM-4:30PM (EST). *Misdemeanor, Civil Actions Under $15,000, Eviction, Small Claims.*

www.municipalcourt.org

Civil Records: Access: Phone, mail, in person. Both court and visitors may perform in person searches. Search fee: $5.00 per name. Fee is per 5 years searched. Required to search: name, years to search. Civil cases indexed by defendant, plaintiff. Civil records on computer from 1990, prior in books.

Criminal Records: Access: Phone, mail, in person. Both court and visitors may perform in person searches. No search fee. Required to search: name, years to search, DOB; also helpful: SSN. Criminal records on computer from 1992, prior in books.

General Information: Public access terminal is available. No assessment results or probation records released. SASE required. Turnaround time 1-2 weeks. Copy fee: $.05 per page. Certification fee: $1.00. Fee payee: Delaware Municipal Court. Personal checks accepted. Delaware County checks accepted. Prepayment is required.

Erie County

Common Pleas Court 323 Columbus Ave, Sandusky, OH 44870; 419-627-7705; Probate phone: 419-627-7759; Fax: 419-627-6873. Hours: 8AM-4PM M-Th/8AM-5PM F (EST). *Felony, Civil Actions Over $10,000, Probate.*

Civil Records: Access: In person only. Visitors must perform in person searches for themselves. No search fee. Required to search: name, years to search. Civil cases indexed by defendant, plaintiff. Civil records on books.

Criminal Records: Access: In person only. Visitors must perform in person searches for themselves. No search fee. Required to search: name, years to search, DOB, SSN, signed release. Criminal records on books; computerized records since 2001.

General Information: Public access terminal is available. Passports and expungments not released. Copy fee: $.25 per page. Certification fee: $1.00 1st page, $.25 for each add'l page. Fee payee: Clerk of Court. Personal checks accepted. Prepayment required.

Erie County Court 150 W Mason Rd, Milan, OH 44846; 419-499-4689; Fax: 419-499-3300. Hours: 8AM-4PM (EST). *Misdemeanor, Civil Actions Under $15,000, Small Claims.*

Civil Records: Access: Phone, mail, in person. Both court and visitors may perform in person searches. No search fee. Required to search: name, years to search; also helpful: address. Civil cases indexed by defendant, plaintiff. Civil records on computer back to 1990, microfiche back to 1982, index books from 1950s.

Criminal Records: Access: Phone, mail, in person. Both court and visitors may perform in person searches. No search fee. Required to search: name, years to search; also helpful: address, DOB. Criminal records on computer back to 1990, microfiche back to 1982, index books from 1950s.

General Information: Public access terminal is available. No sealed records released. SASE required. Turnaround time 3-4 days. Copy fee: $.05 per page. Fee payee: County Court. Business checks accepted. Prepayment required.

Sandusky Municipal Court 222 Meigs St, Sandusky, OH 44870; 419-627-5926; Civil phone: 419-627-5917; Criminal phone: 419-627-5975; Fax: 419-627-5950. Hours: 7AM-4PM (EST). *Misdemeanor, Civil Actions Under $15,000, Eviction, Small Claims.*

Civil Records: Access: Phone, fax, mail, in person. Both court and visitors may perform in person searches.

No search fee. Required to search: name, years to search; also helpful: case number. Civil cases indexed by defendant, plaintiff. Civil records on computer from 1987, prior in books.

Criminal Records: Access: Phone, fax, mail, in person. Both court and visitors may perform in person searches. No search fee. Required to search: name, years to search, DOB; also helpful: SSN, case number. Criminal records on computer from 1987, prior in books.

General Information: Public access terminal is available. No pending, (some) crimes of violence records, or expunged records released. SASE requested. Turnaround time 3-4 days. Copy fee: $.25 per page. Certification fee: $4.00. Fee payee: Sandusky Municipal Court.

Vermilion Municipal Court 687 Decatur Street, Vermilion, OH 44089; 440-967-6543; Fax: 440-967-1467. Hours: 8AM-4PM (EST). *Misdemeanor, Civil Actions Under $15,000, Eviction, Small Claims.*

www.vermilionmunicipalcourt.org

Civil Records: Access: Fax, mail, in person, online. Both court and visitors may perform in person searches. No search fee. Required to search: name, years to search. Civil cases indexed by defendant, plaintiff. Civil records on computer from 1992, prior in books. Online access to municipal court records is available at the web site or directly at http://209.142.158.114/search.html.

Criminal Records: Access: Fax, mail, in person, online. Both court and visitors may perform in person searches. No search fee. Required to search: name, years to search, DOB; also helpful: SSN. Criminal records on computer from 1992, prior in books. Online access to criminal records is the same as civil.

General Information: Public access terminal is available. SASE required. Turnaround time 1-5 days. Copy fee: $1.00 per page. The fee is for a computer printout. Certification fee: $2.00. Fee payee: Vermilion Municipal Court. Only cashiers checks and money orders accepted. Credit cards accepted: Visa, MasterCard. Prepayment is required.

Fairfield County

Common Pleas Court 224 E Main, Clerk's Office, Lancaster, OH 43130-0370; 740-687-7030; Probate phone: 740-687-7093. Hours: 8AM-4PM (EST). *Felony, Civil Actions Over $10,000, Probate.*

Note: Probate Court is separate from this court, at the same address and at the Probate phone number above.

Civil Records: Access: fax, mail, in person, online. Visitors must perform in person searches for themselves. No search fee. Required to search: name, years to search; also helpful: address. Civil cases indexed by defendant, plaintiff. Civil records on computer from 10/93, in books to 1970, prior archived to 1800s. Online access to County Clerk's court records database is available free at www.fairfieldcountyclerk.com/Search.

Criminal Records: Access: Phone, mail, in person, online. Visitors must perform in person searches for themselves. No search fee. Required to search: name, years to search; also helpful: address, DOB, SSN. Criminal records on computer from 10/93, in books to 1970, prior archived to 1800s. Online access to criminal records is the same as civil.

General Information: Public access terminal is available. No adoption or juvenile records released. SASE required. Turnaround time 1 week. Copy fee: $.05 per page. Certification fee: $5.00. Fee payee: Clerk of Court. Personal checks accepted. Credit cards accepted: Visa. Credit cards not accepted over the phone. Prepayment is required.

Fairfield County Municipal Court PO Box 2390, Lancaster, OH 43130; 740-687-6621. Hours:

8AM-4PM (EST). *Misdemeanor, Civil Actions Under $15,000, Eviction, Small Claims.*

Civil Records: Access: Mail, in person. Both court and visitors may perform in person searches. No search fee. Required to search: name, years to search. Civil cases indexed by defendant, plaintiff. Civil records on computer from 1990, prior in books.

Criminal Records: Access: Mail, in person. Both court and visitors may perform in person searches. No search fee. Required to search: name, years to search. Criminal records on computer from 1989, prior in books.

General Information: Public access terminal is available. SASE required. Turnaround time 2 days. No copy fee. Certification fee: $1.00. Fee payee: Fairfiled County Court. Personal checks accepted. Prepayment is required.

Fayette County

Common Pleas Court 110 E Court St, Washington Court House, OH 43160; 740-335-6371; Probate phone: 740-335-0640. Hours: 9AM-4PM (EST). *Felony, Civil Actions Over $10,000, Probate.*

Note: Probate is a separate court at number given.

Civil Records: Access: Mail, in person. Both court and visitors may perform in person searches. Search fee: $3.00 per name. Required to search: name, years to search. Civil cases indexed by defendant, plaintiff. Civil records on computer from 1992, prior in books to 1800s.

Criminal Records: Access: Mail, in person. Both court and visitors may perform in person searches. Search fee: $3.00 per name. Required to search: name, years to search, DOB, SSN. Criminal records on computer from 1992, prior in books to 1800s.

General Information: Public access terminal is available. No records released. SASE required. Turnaround time varies. Fax notes: Fee to fax results is $1.00 per page. Copy fee: $1.00 per page. Certification fee: $1.00. Fee payee: Clerk of Court. Personal checks accepted. Prepayment is required.

Municipal Court Washington Courthouse, 119 N Main St, Washington Court House, OH 43160; 740-636-2350; Fax: 740-636-2359. Hours: 8AM-4PM (EST). *Misdemeanor, Civil Actions Under $15,000, Eviction, Small Claims.*

Civil Records: Access: Mail, in person. Both court and visitors may perform in person searches. No search fee. Required to search: name, years to search. Civil cases indexed by defendant, plaintiff. Civil records on computer from 1990, prior in books to 1950s.

Criminal Records: Access: Mail, in person. Both court and visitors may perform in person searches. No search fee. Required to search: name, years to search, DOB; also helpful: SSN. Criminal records on computer from 1990, prior in books to 1950s.

General Information: Public access terminal is available. No records protected by the privacy act released. SASE required. Turnaround time 1 week. No copy fee. Certification fee: $5.00. Fee payee: Clerk of Court. Only cashiers checks and money orders accepted. Prepayment is required.

Franklin County

Common Pleas Court 369 S High St, Columbus, OH 43215-6311; Civil phone: 614-462-3621; Criminal phone: 614-462-3650; Probate phone: 614-462-3894; Fax: 614-462-4325 Civil; 614-462-6661 Crim. Hours: 8AM-5PM (EST). *Felony, Civil Actions Over $15,000, Probate.*

www.franklincountyclerk.com

Civil Records: Access: Online, in person. Visitors must perform in person searches for themselves. No search fee. Required to search: name, years to search. Civil cases indexed by defendant, plaintiff. Access records via the web site. Java-enable web browser required.

Online access to probate court records available free at www.co.franklin.oh.us/probate/ProbateSearch.html; search marriage records at www.co.franklin.oh.us/probate/PBMLSearch.html.

Criminal Records: Access: Mail, in person. Both court and visitors may perform in person searches. Search fee: $4.00 per name. Required to search: name, years to search.

General Information: No psych, adoption or estate tax records released. SASE required. Turnaround time to 7 days. Certification fee: $1.00 per page. Fee payee: Franklin County Probate Court (Civil); Clerk of Court (Criminal). Only cashiers checks and money orders accepted. Prepayment is required.

Franklin County Municipal Court - Civil Division 375 S High St, 3rd Flr, Columbus, OH 43215; 614-645-7220; Civil phone: 614-645-8161; Fax: 614-645-6919. Hours: 8AM-5PM (EST). *Civil Actions Under $15,000, Eviction, Small Claims.*

www.fcmcclerk.com

Civil Records: Access: Phone, fax, mail, online, in person. Both court and visitors may perform in person searches. No search fee. Required to search: name, years to search, SSN. Civil cases indexed by defendant, plaintiff. Civil records on computer from 1992, prior in books to 1970s. Records from the Clerk of Court Courtview database available free online at www.fcmcclerk.com/pa/pa.htm. Search by name, SSN, dates, ticket, DL or case numbers.

General Information: Public access terminal is available. No sealed or expunged records released. SASE required. Turnaround time 2-3 days. Copy fee: First 20 copies are free, then $.05 each. Certification fee: $1.00. Fee payee: Franklin County Municipal Court. Personal checks accepted. Credit cards accepted: Visa, MasterCard, Discover. Prepayment is required.

Franklin County Municipal Court - Criminal Division 375 S High St, 2nd Fl, Columbus, OH 43215; 614-645-8186. Hours: Open 24 hours a day (EST). *Misdemeanor.*

www.fcmcclerk.com

Criminal Records: Access: Phone, mail, online, in person. Both court and visitors may perform in person searches. No search fee. Required to search: name, years to search; also helpful: DOB, SSN. Criminal records go back to 1987; on computer back to 1992. Criminal and traffic records from the Clerk of Court Courtview 2000 database available free online at www.fcmcclerk.com/pa/pa.htm. Search by name, SSN, dates, ticket, DL or case numbers.

General Information: Public access terminal is available. No sealed or expunged records released. SASE required. Turnaround time 2 days. Copy fee: $.25 per page. Certification fee: $1.00. Fee payee: Franklin County Municipal Court. Personal checks accepted. Credit cards accepted: Visa, MasterCard. Prepayment is required.

Fulton County

Common Pleas Court 210 S Fulton, Wauseon, OH 43567; 419-337-9230; Probate phone: 419-337-9242. Hours: 8:30AM-4:30PM (EST). *Felony, Civil Actions Over $3,000, Probate.*

Civil Records: Access: In person only. Visitors must perform in person searches for themselves. No search fee. Required to search: name, years to search. Civil cases indexed by defendant, plaintiff. Civil records on computer from 9/88, prior in books to 1968, archived to 1800s.

Criminal Records: Access: In person only. Visitors must perform in person searches for themselves. No search fee. Required to search: name, years to search, DOB; also helpful: SSN. Criminal records on computer from 9/88, prior in books to 1968, archived to 1800s.

General Information: Public access terminal is available. Copy fee: $.25 per page. Certification fee: $1.00 per page. Fee payee: Mary Gype Clerk of Court. Personal checks accepted. Prepayment is required.

County Court Eastern District

128 N Main St, Swanton, OH 43558; 419-826-5636; Fax: 419-825-3324. Hours: 8:30AM-4:30PM (EST). *Misdemeanor, Civil Actions Under $15,000, Small Claims.*

www.fultoncountyoh.com/courts.htm

Civil Records: Access: Mail, in person. Both court and visitors may perform in person searches. No search fee. Required to search: name, years to search. Civil cases indexed by defendant, plaintiff. Civil records on computer from 1988, prior in books.

Criminal Records: Access: Mail, in person. Both court and visitors may perform in person searches. No search fee. Required to search: name, years to search, DOB. Criminal records on computer from 1988, prior in books.

General Information: No pending case records released. SASE required. Turnaround time 2 weeks. Copy fee: None, but must supply own paper for copies. Only cashiers checks and money orders accepted.

County Court Western District

224 S Fulton St, Wauseon, OH 43567; 419-337-9212; Fax: 419-337-9286. Hours: 8:30AM-4:30PM (EST). *Misdemeanor, Civil Actions Under $15,000, Small Claims.*

Civil Records: Access: Mail, in person. Both court and visitors may perform in person searches. No search fee. Required to search: name, years to search. Civil cases indexed by defendant, plaintiff. Civil records on computer from 1989, prior in books. In-person searchers should call first; Tuesdays are court day and computers in use.

Criminal Records: Access: Mail, in person. Both court and visitors may perform in person searches. No search fee. Required to search: name, years to search, DOB; also helpful: SSN. Criminal records on computer after 1988, indexed by name and DOB. In-person searchers should call first; be aware Tuesdays are busy and hard to get on computer to search.

General Information: Public access terminal is available. No pending case records released. SASE required. Turnaround time 2-3 days. Copy fee: $.10 per page. Certification fee: $1.00. Fee payee: County Court Western District. No personal checks.

Gallia County

Common Pleas Court - Gallia County Courthouse

18 Locust St, Rm 1290, Gallipolis, OH 45631-1290; 740-446-4612 x223; Probate phone: 740-446-4612 x240; Fax: 740-441-2094. Hours: 8AM-4PM (EST). *Felony, Civil Actions Over $10,000, Probate.*

Civil Records: Access: In person only. Visitors must perform in person searches for themselves. No search fee. Required to search: name, years to search. Civil cases indexed by defendant, plaintiff. Civil records on computer from 7/91, in books to 1968, archived to 1800s. Will fax copies for $1.00 per page if pre-paid.

Criminal Records: Access: In person only. Visitors must perform in person searches for themselves. No search fee. Required to search: name, years to search. Criminal records on computer from 7/91, in books to 1968, archived to 1800s. Will fax copies for $1.00 per page if pre-paid.

General Information: Public access terminal is available. No records released. Copy fee: $.25 per page. Certification fee: $1.00. Fee payee: Clerk of Court. Personal checks accepted. Prepayment is required.

Gallipolis Municipal Court

518 2nd Ave, Gallipolis, OH 45631; 740-446-9400; Fax: 740-446-2070. Hours: 9AM-4:30PM (EST). *Misdemeanor, Civil Actions Under $15,000, Eviction, Small Claims.*

Civil Records: Access: Phone, mail, in person. Both court and visitors may perform in person searches. No search fee. Required to search: name, years to search; also helpful: address. Civil cases indexed by defendant, plaintiff. Civil records on computer from 8/93, prior in books.

Criminal Records: Access: Phone, mail, in person. Both court and visitors may perform in person searches. No search fee. Required to search: name, years to search; also helpful: address, DOB, SSN. Criminal records on computer from 8/93, prior in books.

General Information: Public access terminal is available. No expunged records released. SASE required. Turnaround time 1 week. Copy fee: $.25 per page. Certification fee: $1.00. Fee payee: Municipal Court. Personal checks accepted. Prepayment required.

Geauga County

Common Pleas Court

100 Short Court, Chardon, OH 44024; 440-285-2222 X2380; Probate phone: 440-285-2222 X2000; Fax: 440-286-2127. Hours: 8AM-4:30PM (EST). *Felony, Civil Actions Over $10,000, Probate.*

www.co.geauga.oh.us

Civil Records: Access: In person, online. Visitors must perform in person searches for themselves. No search fee. Required to search: name, years to search. Civil cases indexed by defendant, plaintiff. Civil records on computer from 1990, in books from 1968, prior archived. Online access is available free from the Clerk of Courts at www.co.geauga.oh.us/departments/clerk_of_courts/docket/Courtintro.asp. Online records go back to 1990.

Criminal Records: Access: In person, online. Visitors must perform in person searches for themselves. No search fee. Required to search: name, years to search. Criminal records on computer from 1990, in books from 1968, prior archived. Online access is available free from the Clerk of Courts at www.co.geauga.oh.us/departments/clerk_of_courts/docket/Courtintro.asp. Online records go back to 1990.

General Information: Public access terminal is available. no sealed records released. Copy fee: $.25 per page. Certification fee: $1.00. Fee payee: Clerk of Court. Personal checks accepted. Credit cards accepted. Prepayment is required.

Chardon Municipal Court

111 Water St, Chardon, OH 44024; 440-286-2670/2684; Fax: 440-286-2679. Hours: 8AM-4:30PM (EST). *Misdemeanor, Civil Actions Under $15,000, Eviction, Small Claims.*

www.co.geauga.oh.us/departments/muni_court.htm

Civil Records: Access: Mail, in person. Both court and visitors may perform in person searches. No search fee. Required to search: name, years to search; also helpful: address. Civil cases indexed by defendant, plaintiff. Civil records on computer from 1990, prior in books.

Criminal Records: Access: Mail, in person. Both court and visitors may perform in person searches. No search fee. Required to search: name, years to search; also helpful: address, DOB, SSN. Criminal records on computer from 1988, prior in books to 1965.

General Information: Public access terminal is available. (Available 8AM-11:30AM, 1:30-4:30PM. Two hour maximum.) No expunged records released. SASE required. Turnaround time 2-4 days. Copy fee: $.25 per page. Certification fee: $1.50. Fee payee: Chardon Municipal Court. Personal checks accepted. Credit cards accepted: Visa, MasterCard. Accepted for criminal only. Prepayment is required.

Greene County

Common Pleas Court

45 N Detroit St (PO Box 156), Xenia, OH 45385; 937-562-5292; Probate phone: 937-376-5280; Fax: 937-562-5309. Hours: 8AM-4PM (EST). *Felony, Civil Actions Over $10,000, Probate.*

www.co.greene.oh.us/clerk.htm

Civil Records: Access: In person, online. Visitors must perform in person searches for themselves. No search fee. Required to search: name, years to search. Civil cases indexed by defendant, plaintiff. Civil records on computer from 1982, prior in books and on microfiche. Online access to clerk of court records is available free at http://198.30.12.229/pa/pa.htm. Search by name or case number.

Criminal Records: Access: In person, online. Visitors must perform in person searches for themselves. No search fee. Required to search: name, years to search; also helpful: DOB, SSN, case number. Criminal records on computer from 1982, prior in books and on microfiche. Online access to clerk of court records is available free at http://198.30.12.229/pa/pa.htm. Search by name or case number.

General Information: Public access terminal is available. No sealed records released. Fax notes: Fee to fax results is $1.00 per page. Copy fee: $.25 per page. Certification fee: $1.00 per page. Fee payee: Clerk of Court. Personal checks accepted. Credit cards accepted: Visa, MasterCard. Prepayment is required.

Fairborn Municipal Court

44 W Hebble Ave, Fairborn, OH 45324; Civil phone: 937-754-3044; Criminal phone: 937-754-3042; Fax: 937-879-4422. Hours: 7:30AM-4:30PM (EST). *Misdemeanor, Civil Actions Under $20,000, Eviction, Small Claims.*

Civil Records: Access: Mail, in person. Both court and visitors may perform in person searches. No search fee. Required to search: name, years to search; also helpful: address. Civil cases indexed by defendant, plaintiff. Civil records on computer from 1991, records go back to 1976.

Criminal Records: Access: Mail, in person. Both court and visitors may perform in person searches. No search fee. Required to search: name, years to search, SSN; also helpful: address, DOB. Criminal records on computer from mid 1991, records go back to 1976.

General Information: Public access terminal is available. SASE required. Turnaround time 1 week. Copy fee: $.25 per page. Certification fee: $2.00. Fee payee: Municipal Court. Personal checks accepted. Prepayment is required.

Xenia Municipal Court

101 N Detroit, Xenia, OH 45385; 937-376-7294; 376-7297 (Civil Clerk); Fax: 937-376-7288. Hours: 8AM-4:30PM (EST). *Misdemeanor, Civil Actions Under $15,000, Eviction, Small Claims.*

http://xmcwa.ci.xenia.oh.us

Civil Records: Access: Fax, mail, in person, online. Both court and visitors may perform in person searches. No search fee. Required to search: name, years to search; also helpful: address. Civil cases indexed by defendant, plaintiff. Civil records on computer from 1994, prior in books to 1966. Online access to Municipal Court records is available free through CourtView at http://xmcwa.ci.xenia.oh.us.

Criminal Records: Access: Fax, mail, in person, online. Both court and visitors may perform in person searches. No search fee. Required to search: name, years to search; also helpful: address, DOB, SSN. Criminal records on computer from 1994, prior in books to 1966. Online access is the same as civil, see above.

General Information: Public access terminal is available. No search warrant records released. SASE required. Fax notes: No fee to fax results. Copy fee: $.10 per page. Certification fee: $2.00. Fee payee:

Municipal Court. Business checks accepted. Credit cards accepted: Visa, MasterCard. Visa, MC. Prepayment is required.

Guernsey County

Common Pleas Court 801 E Wheeling Ave D-300, Cambridge, OH 43725; 740-432-9230; Probate phone: 740-432-9262; Fax: 740-432-7807. Hours: 8:30AM-4PM (EST). *Felony, Civil Actions Over $10,000, Probate.*

Note: Probate is a separate division with separate records and personnel.

Civil Records: Access: In person only. Visitors must perform in person searches for themselves. No search fee. Required to search: name, years to search. Civil cases indexed by defendant, plaintiff. Civil records on computer from 1990, prior in books, archived to 1800s.
Criminal Records: Access: In person only. Visitors must perform in person searches for themselves. No search fee. Required to search: name, years to search, DOB, SSN, signed release. Criminal records on computer from 1990, prior in books, archived to 1800s.
General Information: Public access terminal is available. No expunged records released. Copy fee: $.25 per page. Certification fee: $5.00. Fee payee: Clerk of Court. Personal checks accepted. Prepayment is required.

Cambridge Municipal Court 134 Southgate Parkway, Cambridge, OH 43725; 740-439-5585 x40; Fax: 740-439-5666. Hours: 8:30AM-4:30PM (EST). *Misdemeanor, Civil Actions Under $15,000, Eviction, Small Claims.*

Civil Records: Access: Phone, mail, in person. Both court and visitors may perform in person searches. No search fee. Required to search: name, years to search; also helpful: address. Civil cases indexed by defendant, plaintiff. Civil records on computer from 1988, prior in books.
Criminal Records: Access: Mail, in person. Visitors must perform in person searches for themselves. No search fee. Required to search: name, years to search, DOB, SSN; also helpful: address. Criminal records on computer from 1988, prior in books.
General Information: No confidential records released. SASE required. Turnaround time 3-5 days. Copy fee: No search fee. Certification fee: $2.00. Fee payee: Cambridge Municipal Court. Personal checks accepted. Credit cards accepted: Visa, MasterCard. Prepayment is required.

Hamilton County

Common Pleas Court 1000 Main St, Room 315, Cincinnati, OH 45202; Civil phone: 513-946-5635; Criminal phone: 513-946-5671; Probate phone: 513-946-3580; Fax: 513-632-7216. Hours: 8AM-4PM (EST). *Felony, Civil Actions Over $10,000, Probate.*

www.courtclerk.org

Note: Probate is separate court at telephone number given. Search probate records free online back to 1/2000 at www.probatect.org/case_search/cs-scripts/pimain.html.

Civil Records: Access: Phone, fax, mail, online, in person. Both court and visitors may perform in person searches. No search fee. Required to search: name, years to search. Civil cases indexed by defendant, plaintiff. Civil records indexed on computer since 1960s, prior in books and files. Records from the court clerk are available free online at the web site. Online civil index goes back to 1991.
Criminal Records: Access: Fax, mail, online, in person. Both court and visitors may perform in person searches. No search fee. Required to search: name, years to search, signed release; also helpful: DOB, SSN. Criminal records indexed on computer since 1960s,

prior in books and files. Online access to criminal records is the same as civil. Online criminal index goes back to 1986.
General Information: Public access terminal is available. Criminal histories not released. SASE required. Turnaround time 2-3 days. Copy fee: Fees vary by storage media of original. Certification fee: $1.00. Fee payee: Clerk of Court. Personal checks accepted. Credit cards accepted. Prepayment is required.

Hamilton County Municipal Court - Civil 1000 Main St, Rm 115, Cincinnati, OH 45202; 513-946-5700; Fax: 513-946-5710. Hours: 8AM-4PM *Civil Actions Under $15,000, Eviction, Small Claims.*

www.courtclerk.org

Civil Records: Access: Fax, mail, online, in person. Both court and visitors may perform in person searches. No search fee. Required to search: name; also helpful: years to search. Civil cases indexed by defendant, plaintiff. Civil records on computer from 1989, prior on microfilm. Records from the court clerk are available free online at the web site.
General Information: Public access terminal is available. No expungement records released. Turnaround time 5 days. Fax notes: No fee to fax results. Copy fee: $.25 per page. $4.00 for docket sheet (civil). Certification fee: $5.00. Fee payee: Clerk of Courts. Personal checks accepted. Credit cards accepted: Visa, MasterCard. Prepayment is required.

Hamilton County Municipal Court - Criminal 1000 Sycamore St #111, Cincinnati, OH 45202; 513-946-6040. Hours: 8AM-4PM (EST). *Misdemeanor.*

www.courtclerk.org

Criminal Records: Access: Fax, mail, in person. Visitors must perform in person searches for themselves. No search fee. Required to search: name, years to search, DOB; also helpful: SSN. Criminal records on computer back to 2000, prior on microfiche back to 1973.
General Information: Public access terminal is available. Turnaround time 2-3 days. Copy fee: $.10 per page. Fee payee: Clerk of Courts. Personal checks accepted. Credit cards accepted: Visa, MasterCard. Prepayment is required.

Hancock County

Common Pleas Court 300 S Main St, Findlay, OH 45840; 419-424-7037; Probate phone: 419-424-7079. Hours: 8:30AM-4:30PM (EST). *Felony, Civil Actions Over $10,000, Probate.*

Civil Records: Access: Mail, in person. Both court and visitors may perform in person searches. Search fee: $10.00 per name. Required to search: name, years to search. Civil cases indexed by defendant, plaintiff. Civil records on computer from 1985, microfiche from 1974, dockets archived to 1800s.
Criminal Records: Access: Mail, in person. Both court and visitors may perform in person searches. Search fee: $10.00 per name. Required to search: name, years to search. Criminal records on computer from 1985, microfiche from 1974, dockets archived to 1800s.
General Information: Public access terminal is available. No home investigations, medical records released. SASE required. Turnaround time 1-2 days. Certification fee: $1.00. Fee payee: Clerk of Court. Personal checks accepted. Prepayment is required.

Findlay Municipal Court PO Box 826, Findlay, OH 45839; 419-424-7141; Fax: 419-424-7803. Hours: 8AM-5PM; 8AM-7PM Tuesday only (EST). *Misdemeanor, Civil Actions Under $15,000, Eviction, Small Claims.*

Civil Records: Access: Mail, in person. Both court and visitors may perform in person searches. Search fee:

$2.00 per name. Required to search: name, years to search. Civil cases indexed by defendant, plaintiff. Civil records on computer from 1984.
Criminal Records: Access: Mail, in person. Both court and visitors may perform in person searches. Search fee: $2.00 per name. Required to search: name, years to search, DOB, SSN. Criminal records on computer from 1984.
General Information: Public access terminal is available. SASE required. Copy fee: $.25 per page. Certification fee: $1.00. Fee payee: Findlay Municipal Court. Only cashiers checks and money orders accepted. Local (Hancock County) personal checks accepted. Credit cards accepted: Visa, MasterCard. Prepayment is required.

Hardin County

Common Pleas Court Courthouse, Ste 310, Kenton, OH 43326; 419-674-2278; Probate phone: 419-674-2230; Fax: 419-674-2273. Hours: 8:30AM-4PM M-Th; 8:30AM-5PM F (EST). *Felony, Civil Actions Over $10,000.*

Civil Records: Access: Mail, in person. Both court and visitors may perform in person searches. No search fee. Required to search: name, years to search. Civil cases indexed by defendant, plaintiff. Current records on computer as of 1/95. Overall records go back to 1885.
Criminal Records: Access: Mail, in person. Both court and visitors may perform in person searches. No search fee. Required to search: name, years to search, DOB, signed release; also helpful: SSN. Current records on computer as of 1/95. Overall records go back to 1885.
General Information: Public access terminal is available. SASE required. Turnaround time 2-4 days. Fax notes: $2.00 1st page, $1.00 per page thereafter. Copy fee: $.25 per page. Certified copies $1.00 per page. Certification fee: $1.00 per page. Fee payee: Clerk of Court. No personal checks accepted. Prepayment is required.

Hardin County Municipal Court PO Box 250, Kenton, OH 43326; 419-674-4362; Fax: 419-674-4096. Hours: 8:30AM-4PM (EST). *Misdemeanor, Civil Actions Under $15,000, Eviction, Small Claims.*

Civil Records: Access: Mail, in person. Both court and visitors may perform in person searches. Search fee: $5.00. Required to search: name, years to search. Civil cases indexed by defendant, plaintiff. Civil records on computer since 1989, prior on books.
Criminal Records: Access: Mail, in person. Both court and visitors may perform in person searches. Search fee: $5.00. Required to search: name, years to search; also helpful: SSN. Criminal records on computer since 1989, prior on books.
General Information: Public access terminal is available. SASE required. Turnaround time 1-2 days. Copy fee: $.25 per page. Certification fee: $2.00. Fee payee: Hardin County Municipal Court. Business checks accepted. Prepayment is required.

Harrison County

Common Pleas Court 100 W Market, Cadiz, OH 43907; 740-942-8863; Fax: 740-942-4693. Hours: 8:30AM-4:30PM (EST). *Felony, Civil Actions Over $3,000, Probate.*

Civil Records: Access: Phone, fax, mail, in person. Both court and visitors may perform in person searches. No search fee. Required to search: name, years to search; also helpful: address. Civil cases indexed by defendant, plaintiff. Civil records on computer since 1994, in books back to 1800s.
Criminal Records: Access: In person only. Visitors must perform in person searches for themselves. No search fee. Required to search: name, years to search; also helpful: address, DOB, SSN. Criminal records on computer since 1994, in books back to 1800s.

General Information: Public access terminal is available. No secret records released. SASE required. Turnaround time 1-2 days. Fax notes: $.25 per page. Copy fee: $.25 per page. Certification fee: $1.00. Fee payee: Clerk of Court. Personal checks accepted. Prepayment is required.

Harrison County Court Courthouse, 100 W Market St, Cadiz, OH 43907; 740-942-8865; Fax: 740-942-3541. Hours: 8:00AM-4:30PM *Misdemeanor, Civil Actions Under $15,000, Small Claims.*

Civil Records: Access: In person only. Visitors must perform in person searches for themselves. No search fee. Required to search: name, years to search. Civil cases indexed by defendant, plaintiff. Civil records in books; on computer back to 1/2000 (older records being added).

Criminal Records: Access: In person only. Visitors must perform in person searches for themselves. No search fee. Required to search: name, years to search, DOB; also helpful: SSN. Criminal records in books; on computer back to 1/2000 (older records being added).

General Information: Public access terminal is available. Copy fee: $.25 per page. Certification fee: $1.00. Fee payee: Harrison County Court. Only cashiers checks and money orders accepted. Prepayment is required.

Henry County

Common Pleas Court PO Box 71, Napoleon, OH 43545; 419-592-5886; Probate phone: 419-592-7771; Fax: 419-592-4575. Hours: 8:30AM-4:30PM (EST). *Felony, Civil Actions Over $10,000, Probate.*

Note: Probate Court's address is PO Box 70, fax is 419-592-7000.

Civil Records: Access: Fax, mail, in person. Only visitors may perform in person searches. No search fee. Required to search: name, years to search. Civil cases indexed by defendant, plaintiff. Civil records on computer from 10/94, prior in books.

Criminal Records: Access: Fax, mail, in person. Only visitors may perform in person searches. No search fee. Required to search: name, years to search. Criminal records on computer from 10/94, prior in books.

General Information: Public access terminal is available. No adoption or mental records released. SASE required. Fax notes: $3.00 for first page, $1.00 each add'l. Copy fee: $1.00 per page. Certification fee: $1.00. Fee payee: Clerk of Court. Personal checks accepted. Prepayment is required.

Napoleon Municipal Court PO Box 502, Napoleon, OH 43545; 419-592-2851; Fax: 419-592-1805. Hours: 8AM-5PM (EST). *Misdemeanor, Civil Actions Under $15,000, Eviction, Small Claims.*

Civil Records: Access: Phone, fax, mail, in person. Both court and visitors may perform in person searches. No search fee. Required to search: name, years to search. Civil cases indexed by defendant, plaintiff. Civil records on computer from 1990, prior in books.

Criminal Records: Access: Phone, fax, mail, in person. Both court and visitors may perform in person searches. No search fee. Required to search: name, years to search, DOB; also helpful: SSN. Criminal records on computer from 1990, prior in books.

General Information: No alcohol treatment records released. SASE required. Turnaround time 1-2 days. Copy fee: $.05 per page. Certification fee: $1.00. Fee payee: Clerk of Court. Personal checks accepted. Credit cards accepted: Visa, MasterCard.

Highland County

Common Pleas Court PO Box 821, Hillsboro, OH 45133; 937-393-9957; Probate phone: 937-393-9981; Fax: 937-393-6878. Hours: 8AM-4:30PM (EST). *Felony, Civil Actions Over $10,000, Probate.*

Note: Probate is a separate court.

Civil Records: Access: Mail, fax, in person. Both court and visitors may perform in person searches. No search fee. Required to search: name, years to search; also helpful: address. Civil cases indexed by defendant, plaintiff. Civil records in books since 1800s; on computer since 1995.

Criminal Records: Access: Mail, fax, in person. Both court and visitors may perform in person searches. No search fee. Required to search: name, years to search, DOB, signed release; also helpful: SSN. Criminal records in books since 1800s; on computer since 1990.

General Information: Public access terminal is available. no sealed records released. SASE required. Turnaround time same day. Copy fee: $.10 per page. Certification fee: $1.00 per page. Fee payee: Clerk of Court. Personal checks accepted.

Hillsboro County Municipal Court 108 Governor Trimble Pl, Hillsboro, OH 45133; 937-393-3022; Fax: 937-393-3273. Hours: 7AM-3:30PM M,T,Th,F; 7AM-Noon W (EST). *Misdemeanor, Civil Actions Under $15,000, Eviction, Small Claims.*

Civil Records: Access: Phone, fax, mail, in person. Only the court performs in person searches; visitors may not. No search fee. Required to search: name, years to search. Civil cases indexed by defendant, plaintiff. Civil records on computer from 1991, prior in books.

Criminal Records: Access: Phone, fax, mail, in person. Only the court performs in person searches; visitors may not. No search fee. Required to search: name, years to search, DOB, SSN. Criminal records on computer from 1991, prior in books.

General Information: No expunged records released. Turnaround time 1-2 days. Fax notes: No fee to fax results. Local or toll free calls only. Copy fee: $.15 per page. Fee payee: Hillsboro Municipal Court. Personal checks accepted. Prepayment is required.

Hocking County

Common Pleas Court PO Box 108, Logan, OH 43138; 740-385-2616; Probate phone: 740-385-3022; Fax: 740-385-1822. Hours: 8:30AM-4PM (EST). *Felony, Civil Actions Over $10,000.*

Note: Probate is a separate court at the number given.

Civil Records: Access: Phone, fax, mail, in person. Both court and visitors may perform in person searches. No search fee. Required to search: name, years to search; also helpful: address. Civil cases indexed by defendant. Civil records on computer since 1996, in books to late 1800s.

Criminal Records: Access: Phone, fax, mail, in person. Both court and visitors may perform in person searches. No search fee. Required to search: name, years to search; also helpful: address, DOB, SSN. Criminal records date back to 1980 on docket books.

General Information: Public access terminal is available. No secret records released. SASE required. Turnaround time 1-2 days. Fax notes: $1.00 per page. Copy fee: $1.00 per page. Certification fee: $1.00. Fee payee: Clerk of Court. Business checks accepted. Prepayment is required.

Hocking County Municipal Court 1 E Main St (PO Box 950), Logan, OH 43138-1278; 740-385-2250; Fax: 740-385-3826. Hours: 8:30AM-4PM (EST). *Misdemeanor, Civil Actions Under $15,000, Eviction, Small Claims.*

Civil Records: Access: Mail, in person, fax. Both court and visitors may perform in person searches. No search

fee. Required to search: name, years to search. Civil cases indexed by defendant, plaintiff. Civil records on computer from 1990, prior in books.

Criminal Records: Access: Mail, in perso, fax. Both court and visitors may perform in person searches. No search fee. Required to search: name, years to search, DOB, SSN, signed release. Criminal records on computer from 1990 prior in books.

General Information: SASE required. Turnaround time 1-2 days. Copy fee: $.10 per page. Certification fee: $1.00 per page. Fee payee: Municipal Court. Personal checks accepted.

Holmes County

Common Pleas Court 1 E Jackson St #306, Millersburg, OH 44654; 330-674-1876; Probate phone: 330-674-5841; Fax: 330-674-0289. Hours: 8:30AM-4:30PM (EST). *Felony, Civil Actions Over $10,000, Probate.*

Note: Juvenile and probate court at Suite 201.

Civil Records: Access: Fax, mail, in person. Both court and visitors may perform in person searches. Search fee: $5.00 per name. Required to search: name, years to search; also helpful: address. Civil cases indexed by defendant, plaintiff. Civil records on computer from 6/30/94, prior in books to 1850.

Criminal Records: Access: Fax, mail, in person. Both court and visitors may perform in person searches. Search fee: $5.00 per name. Required to search: name, years to search; also helpful: address, DOB, SSN. Criminal records on computer from 6/30/94, prior in books to 1850.

General Information: Public access terminal is available. No court order, expunged records released. SASE required. Turnaround time 1-2 days. Fax notes: Fee to fax results is $1.00 per page. Copy fee: $1.00 per page. Certification fee: $1.00. Fee payee: Clerk of Court. Personal checks accepted. Prepayment required.

County Court 1 E Jackson St, Ste 101, Millersburg, OH 44654; 330-674-4901; Fax: 330-674-5514. Hours: 8:30AM-4:30PM (EST). *Misdemeanor, Civil Actions Under $15,000, Small Claims.*

Civil Records: Access: Phone, fax, mail, in person. Both court and visitors may perform in person searches. Search fee: $1.00 per name. Required to search: name, years to search. Civil cases indexed by defendant, plaintiff. Civil records in books going back to 1813; computerized records since 1994. Phone & fax access limited to 1 name.

Criminal Records: Access: Phone, fax, mail, in person. Both court and visitors may perform in person searches. Search fee: $1.00 per name. Required to search: name, years to search. Criminal records in books going back to 1813; computerized records since 1994. Same as civil.

General Information: Public access terminal is available. No search warrant records released. SASE required. Turnaround time 2-5 days. Copy fee: $.15 1-10 pages; $.10 10 plus pages. Certification fee: $1.00 per page. Fee payee: Holmes County Court. Personal checks accepted. Prepayment is required.

Huron County

Common Pleas Court 2 E Main St, Norwalk, OH 44857; 419-668-5113; Probate phone: 419-668-4383. Hours: 8AM-4:30PM (EST). *Felony, Civil Actions Over $10,000, Probate.*

www.huroncountyclerk.com

Note: Probate is separate court at phone number given.

Civil Records: Access: Mail, in person. Both court and visitors may perform in person searches. Search fee: $1.00 per name. Required to search: name, years to search; also helpful: address. Civil cases indexed by defendant, plaintiff. Civil records on computer from 1989, prior in books and on microfiche.

Criminal Records: Access: Mail, in person. Both court and visitors may perform in person searches. Search fee: $1.00 per name. Required to search: name, years to search, offense, date of offense; also helpful: address, DOB, SSN. Criminal records on computer since 1989, records from 1985 to present in actual files, 1930 to 1985 on microfiche.

General Information: Public access terminal is available. No secret records released. SASE required. Turnaround time 2 days. Fax notes: No fee to fax results. Copy fee: $.25 per page. Certification fee: $1.00. Fee payee: Clerk of Court. Personal checks accepted. Prepayment is required.

Bellevue Municipal Court 3000 Seneca Bend Pky, Bellevue, OH 44811; 419-483-5880; Fax: 419-484-8060. 8:30AM-4:30PM (EST). *Misdemeanor, Civil Actions Under $15,000, Eviction, Small Claims.*

Civil Records: Access: Phone, mail, in person. Both court and visitors may perform in person searches. No search fee. Required to search: name, years to search. Civil cases indexed by defendant, plaintiff. Civil records on index from 1988, prior in books. Will only do phone searching if not busy.

Criminal Records: Access: Phone, mail, in person. Both court and visitors may perform in person searches. No search fee. Required to search: name, years to search, DOB; also helpful: SSN. Criminal records on computer from 8/93. Court searches back to 8/93 only. Use an abstractor to go back further.

General Information: SASE required. Turnaround time 3-7 days. Certification fee: $1.00. Fee payee: Bellevue Municipal Court. Only cashiers checks and money orders accepted.

Norwalk Municipal Court 45 N Linwood, Norwalk, OH 44857; 419-663-6750; Fax: 419-663-6749. Hours: 8:30AM-4:30PM (EST). *Misdemeanor, Civil Actions Under $15,000, Eviction, Small Claims.*

Civil Records: Access: Fax, mail, in person. Both court and visitors may perform in person searches. Search fee: $1.00 per name. Required to search: name, years to search; also helpful: address. Civil cases indexed by defendant, plaintiff. Civil records on computer from 7/88; prior on docket book to 1976.

Criminal Records: Access: Fax, mail, in person. Both court and visitors may perform in person searches. Search fee: $1.00 per name. Required to search: name, years to search, DOB, SSN; also helpful: address. Criminal records on computer from 7/88, prior on docket books to 1976.

General Information: Public access terminal is available. SASE is required. Turnaround time 2-7 days. Fax notes: Fee to fax results is $1.00 per page. Copy fee: $.05 per page. Certification fee: $1.00 per page. Fee payee: Municipal Court. Personal checks accepted. Prepayment is required.

Jackson County

Common Pleas Court 226 Main St, Jackson, OH 45640; 740-286-2006; Probate phone: 740-286-1401; Fax: 740-286-4061. Hours: 8AM-4PM (EST). *Felony, Civil Actions Over $10,000, Probate.*

Civil Records: Access: Mail, in person. Both court and visitors may perform in person searches. No search fee. Required to search: name, years to search; also helpful: address. Civil cases indexed by defendant, plaintiff. Civil records go back to 1800s, computerized since 06/20/97.

Criminal Records: Access: Mail, in person. Both court and visitors may perform in person searches. Search fee: Searches only performed in emergency situations. Required to search: name, years to search; also helpful: address, DOB, SSN. Criminal records go back to 1/83; computerized since 06/20/97.

General Information: Public access terminal is available. No juvenile or search warrant record released. SASE required. Turnaround time varies. Copy fee: $.50 per page. Certification fee: $1.00. Fee payee: Clerk of Court. Personal checks accepted. Prepayment required.

Jackson County Municipal Court 350 Portsmouth St #101, Jackson, OH 45640-1764; 740-286-2718; Fax: 740-286-0679. Hours: 8AM-4PM (EST). *Misdemeanor, Civil Actions Under $15,000, Eviction, Small Claims.*

Civil Records: Access: In person only. Visitors must perform in person searches for themselves. No search fee. Required to search: name, years to search. Civil cases indexed by defendant, plaintiff. Civil records in books readily available for 8-10 years, prior archived.

Criminal Records: Access: In person only. Visitors must perform in person searches for themselves. No search fee. Required to search: name, years to search, DOB, SSN. Criminal records in books readily available for 8-10 years, prior archived.

General Information: Public access terminal is available. No victim records released. Copy fee: $.10 per page. Fee payee: Clerk of Municipal Court. Only cashiers checks and money orders accepted. Prepayment is required.

Jefferson County

County Court #1 1007 Franklin Ave, Toronto, OH 43964; 740-537-2020. Hours: 8:30AM-4:30PM (EST). *Misdemeanor, Civil Actions Under $15,000, Small Claims.*

www.uov.net/jeffcodp/court1.htm

Civil Records: Access: Mail, in person. Both court and visitors may perform in person searches. Search fee: $5.00 per name. Required to search: name, years to search. Civil cases indexed by defendant, plaintiff. Civil records in books, dating from 1813, computerized records from 6/98.

Criminal Records: Access: Mail, in person. Both court and visitors may perform in person searches. Search fee: $5.00 per name. Required to search: name, years to search, DOB, also helpful: SSN, sex, signed release. Criminal records in books, dating from 1813, computerized records from 6/98.

General Information: Public access terminal is available. All records are public. SASE required. Turnaround time 1-2 days. No copy fee. Fee payee: Jefferson County Court #1. Only cashiers checks and money orders accepted.

County Court #2 PO Box 2207, Wintersville, OH 43953; 740-264-7644. Hours: 8:30AM-4PM (EST). *Misdemeanor, Civil Actions Under $15,000, Small Claims.*

www.uov.net/jeffcodp/court1.htm

Civil Records: Access: Mail, in person. Both court and visitors may perform in person searches. Search fee: $5.00 per name. Required to search: name, years to search. Civil cases indexed by defendant, plaintiff. Civil records on computer back to 1998; in books from 1950s, prior archived.

Criminal Records: Access: Mail, in person. Both court and visitors may perform in person searches. Search fee: $5.00 per name. Required to search: name, years to search, DOB or SSN. Criminal records on computer back to 1998; in books from 1950s, prior archived.

General Information: SASE required. Turnaround time 1-2 days. Copy fee: $.25 per page. Certification fee: $1.00 per page. Fee payee: County Court #2. Only cashiers checks and money orders accepted. Prepayment is required.

County Court #3 PO Box 495, Dillonvale, OH 43917; 740-769-2903. 8AM-4PM *Misdemeanor, Civil Actions Under $15,000, Small Claims.*

www.uov.net/jeffcodp/court1.htm

Civil Records: Access: Mail, fax, in person. Both court and visitors may perform in person searches. Search fee: $5.00. Required to search: name, years to search. Civil cases indexed by defendant, plaintiff. Civil records on computer from 1998, prior manual dockets.

Criminal Records: Access: Mail, in person. Both court and visitors may perform in person searches. Search fee: $5.00. Required to search: name, years to search, DOB; also helpful: SSN. Criminal records on computer from 1998, prior manual dockets.

General Information: SASE required. Turnaround time 1-2 days. Copy fee: $1.00 per page. Certification fee: $1.00. Fee payee: County Court #3. Only cashiers checks and money orders accepted. Prepayment is required.

Steubenville Municipal Court 123 S 3rd St, Steubenville, OH 43952; 740-283-6020; Fax: 740-283-6167. Hours: 8:30AM-4PM (EST). *Misdemeanor, Civil Actions Under $15,000, Eviction, Small Claims.*

www.uov.net/jeffcodp/court1.htm

Civil Records: Access: Mail, in person. Both court and visitors may perform in person searches. No search fee. Required to search: name, years to search; also helpful: address. Civil cases indexed by defendant, plaintiff. Civil records on computer from 1991, prior in books.

Criminal Records: Access: Mail, in person. Both court and visitors may perform in person searches. No search fee. Required to search: name, years to search; also helpful: address, DOB, SSN. Criminal records on computer from 1991, prior in books.

General Information: Public access terminal is available. No expunged records released. SASE required. Turnaround time 1-5 days. Copy fee: $1.00 per page. Certification fee: $2.00. Fee payee: Steubenville Municipal Court. Only cashiers checks and money orders accepted. Prepayment is required.

Common Pleas Court 301 Market St (PO Box 1326), Steubenville, OH 43952; 740-283-8583. Hours: 8:30AM-4:30PM (EST). *Felony, Civil Actions Over $500, Probate.*

www.uov.net/jeffcodp/court1.htm

Note: Probate is at PO Box 649 and can be reached at 740-283-8653.

Civil Records: Access: In person only. Visitors must perform in person searches for themselves. No search fee. Required to search: name, years to search. Civil cases indexed by defendant, plaintiff. Civil records on books for 10 years or so, prior archived.

Criminal Records: Access: Mail, in person. Both court and visitors may perform in person searches. Search fee: $5.00 per name. Required to search: name, years to search, DOB, offense, date of offense. Criminal records on books for 10 years or so, prior archived.

General Information: Public access terminal is available. No sealed records released. SASE required. Turnaround time 1-2 days. Copy fee: $.25 per page. Certification fee: $1.00 per page. Fee payee: Jefferson County Clerk of Courts. Business checks accepted. Prepayment is required.

Knox County

Common Pleas Court 117 E High St #201, Mt Vernon, OH 43050; 740-393-6788; Probate phone: 740-393-6797. Hours: 8AM-4PM (EST). *Felony, Civil Actions Over $10,000.*

www.knoxcountyclerk.org

Note: Attention Clerk of Courts.

Civil Records: Access: Online, in person. Visitors must perform in person searches for themselves. No search fee. Required to search: name, years to search. Civil cases indexed by defendant, plaintiff. Civil records on computer since 9/86, on microfilm from 1960, prior archived. Search court index, dockets, calendars free

1145

The Sourcebook to Public Record Information

County Courts - Ohio

online at www.knoxcountycpcourt.org. Search by name or case number.

Criminal Records: Access: Online, in person. Visitors must perform in person searches for themselves. No search fee. Required to search: name, years to search. Criminal records on computer since 9/86, on microfilm from 1960, prior archived. Online access to criminal records is the same as civil.

General Information: Public access terminal is available. Copy fee: $.25 per page. Certification fee: $1.00. Fee payee: Common Pleas Court. Personal checks accepted.

Mount Vernon Municipal Court 5 North Gay St, Mount Vernon, OH 43050; 740-393-9510; Fax: 740-393-5349. Hours: 8AM-4PM (EST). *Misdemeanor, Civil Actions Under $15,000, Eviction, Small Claims.*

Civil Records: Access: Phone, fax, mail, in person. Both court and visitors may perform in person searches. No search fee. Required to search: name, years to search. Civil cases indexed by defendant, plaintiff. Civil records on computer from 06/89, prior in books.

Criminal Records: Access: Phone, fax, mail, in person. Both court and visitors may perform in person searches. No search fee. Required to search: name, years to search. Criminal records on computer from 06/89, prior in books.

General Information: SASE required. Turnaround time 1 week. No copy fee. Personal checks accepted. Credit cards accepted in some cases.

Probate Court 111 E High St, Mt Vernon, OH 43050; 740-393-6796; Fax: 740-393-6832. Hours: 8AM-4PM, 8AM-6PM Tues. (EST). *Probate.*

Lake County

Common Pleas Court PO Box 490, Painesville, OH 44077; 440-350-2658; Probate phone: 440-350-2624. Hours: 8AM-4:30PM (EST). *Felony, Civil Actions Over $10,000, Probate.*

www.lakecountyohio.org/clerk

Civil Records: Access: In person, online. Visitors must perform in person searches for themselves. No search fee. Required to search: name, years to search; also helpful: address. Civil cases indexed by defendant, plaintiff. Civil records on computer from 1990, microfilm from 1960, prior archived. Online access to court records, dockets, and quick index are available free at http://web2.lakecountyohio.org/clerk/search.htm. Includes domestic and appeals cases.

Criminal Records: Access: In person, online. Visitors must perform in person searches for themselves. No search fee. Required to search: name, years to search; also helpful: address, DOB, SSN. Criminal records on computer from 1990, microfilm from 1960, prior archived. Online access to criminal records is the same as civil.

General Information: Public access terminal is available. No adoption or juvenile records released. Copy fee: $.25 per page. Certification fee: $1.00. Fee payee: Clerk of Court. Business checks accepted. Prepayment is required.

Mentor Municipal Court 8500 Civic Center Blvd, Mentor, OH 44060-2418; Civil phone: 440-974-5744; Criminal phone: 440-974-5745; Fax: 440-974-5742. Hours: 8:30AM-4:30 PM (EST). *Misdemeanor, Civil Actions Under $15,000, Eviction, Small Claims.*

Civil Records: Access: In person only. Visitors must perform in person searches for themselves. No search fee. Required to search: name. Civil cases indexed by defendant, plaintiff. Civil records go back to 1972; on computer back to 11/1995.

Criminal Records: Access: In person only. Visitors must perform in person searches for themselves. No search fee. Required to search: name, years to search;

also helpful: DOB. Criminal records go back to 1972; on computer back to 11/1995.

General Information: Public access terminal is available. Copy fee: $1.00 per page. Certification fee: $1.00. Fee payee: Mentor Municipal Court. Only cashiers checks and money orders accepted. Prepayment is required.

Painesville Municipal Court 7 Richmond St (PO Box 601), Painesville, OH 44077; 440-639-4990; Fax: 440-352-0028. Hours: 8AM-4:30PM (EST). *Misdemeanor, Civil Actions Under $15,000, Eviction, Small Claims.*

www.painesvillemunicipalcourt.org/

Note: Civil & Probation Fax# 440-639-4932.

Civil Records: Access: Fax, mail, in person, online. Both court and visitors may perform in person searches. No search fee. Required to search: name, years to search; also helpful: address. Civil cases indexed by defendant, plaintiff. Civil records on computer from 7/90 (all divisions), prior on books or archived. Free online access to records at www.painesvillemunicipalcourt.org/search.html.

Criminal Records: Access: Fax, mail, in person, online. Both court and visitors may perform in person searches. No search fee. Required to search: name, years to search, address; also helpful: DOB, SSN. Criminal records on computer from 7/90 (all divisions), prior on books or archived. Free online access to records at www.painesvillemunicipalcourt.org/search.html.

General Information: Public access terminal is available. SASE not required. Turnaround time 1 week. Fax notes: Fax fee: local $1.00 per page; long distance $2.00 per page. Copy fee: $1.00 first page. $.20 each addl. Certification fee: $2.00 plus $1.00 per page after first. Fee payee: Municipal Court. Personal checks accepted. Credit cards accepted: Visa, MasterCard. Prepayment is required.

Willoughby Municipal Court One Public Square, Willoughby, OH 44094-7888; Civil phone: 440-953-4170; Criminal phone: 440-953-4150; Fax: 440-953-4149. Hours: 7:30AM-4:30 PM (till 7:30 on Mon) (EST). *Misdemeanor, Civil Actions Under $15,000, Eviction, Small Claims.*

www.willoughbycourt.com

Civil Records: Access: Mail, in person. Both court and visitors may perform in person searches. No search fee. Required to search: name, years to search. Civil cases indexed by defendant. Civil records on docket books since 1960, computerized back to 1986.

Criminal Records: Access: Mail, in person. Both court and visitors may perform in person searches. No search fee. Required to search: name; also helpful: DOB, SSN. Criminal records in docket books since 1960, computerized bacl to 1988.

General Information: Public access terminal is available. Turnaround time 2-3 days. Certification fee: $1.00 per page. Fee payee: Willoughby Municipal Court. Personal checks accepted. Prepayment is required.

Lawrence County

Common Pleas Court Clerk of the Courts, PO Box 208, Ironton, OH 45638; 740-533-4355/4329; Probate phone: 740-533-4340. Hours: 8:30AM-4PM (EST). *Felony, Civil Actions.*

www.lawrencecountyclkofcrt.org

Note: Probate is a separate court at Veterans Square in Ironton.

Civil Records: Access: Mail, in person, online. Visitors must perform in person searches for themselves. Search fee: No search fee. Required to search: name, years to search; also helpful: address. Civil cases indexed by

defendant, plaintiff. Civil records on computer back to 6/88, prior in books going back to 1800s. Online access to civil records is available free at the web site.

Criminal Records: Access: In person, online. Visitors must perform in person searches for themselves. Search fee: No search fee. Required to search: name, years to search; also helpful: address, DOB, SSN. Criminal records on computer back to 1/88, prior in books going back to 1800s. Online access to criminal records is available free at www.lawrencecountyclkofcrt.org.

General Information: Public access terminal is available. SASE required. Turnaround time 1 week. Copy fee: $.25 per page. Certification fee: $1.00. Fee payee: Clerk of Court. Personal checks accepted.

Lawrence County Municipal Court PO Box 126, Chesapeake, OH 45619; 740-867-3128/3127; Fax: 740-867-3547. Hours: 8:30AM-4PM (EST). *Misdemeanor, Civil Actions Under $15,000, Eviction, Small Claims.*

Civil Records: Access: Phone, fax, mail, in person. Both court and visitors may perform in person searches. Search fee: $5.00 per name. Required to search: name, years to search. Civil cases indexed by defendant, plaintiff. Civil records on computer from 1991.

Criminal Records: Access: Phone, fax, mail, in person. Both court and visitors may perform in person searches. Search fee: $5.00 per name. Required to search: name, years to search, DOB; also helpful: SSN. Criminal records on computer from 1991.

General Information: All records public. SASE required. Turnaround time 7-10 days. Copy fee: $.10 per page. Certification fee: $2.00. Fee payee: Lawrence County Municipal Court. Personal checks accepted. Prepayment is required.

Ironton Municipal Court PO Box 237, Ironton, OH 45638; 740-532-3062; Fax: 740-533-6088. Hours: 8:30AM-4PM (EST). *Misdemeanor, Civil Actions Under $15,000, Eviction, Small Claims.*

Civil Records: Access: Mail, in person. Both court and visitors may perform in person searches. No search fee. Required to search: name, years to search; also helpful: address. Civil cases indexed by defendant, plaintiff. Civil records on computer from 7/89, prior in books.

Criminal Records: Access: Mail, in person. Both court and visitors may perform in person searches. No search fee. Required to search: name, years to search; also helpful: address, DOB, SSN, singed release. Criminal records on computer from 7/89, prior in books.

General Information: Public access terminal is available. SASE required. Turnaround time 1-2 weeks. Certification fee: $1.00 per page. Fee payee: Municipal Court. Prepayment is required.

Licking County

Common Pleas Court PO Box 4370, Newark, OH 43058-4370; 740-349-6171; Probate phone: 740-349-6141; Fax: 740-349-6945. Hours: 8AM-4:30PM (EST). *Felony, Civil Actions Over $10,000, Probate.*

Note: Probate court has a separate clerk at the same address.

Civil Records: Access: In person only. Visitors must perform in person searches for themselves. No search fee. Required to search: name, years to search; also helpful: address. Civil cases indexed by defendant, plaintiff. Civil records on computer from 1992, prior in books.

Criminal Records: Access: In person only. Visitors must perform in person searches for themselves. No search fee. Required to search: name, years to search, DOB; also helpful: address, SSN. Criminal records on computer from 1992, prior in books.

General Information: Public access terminal is available. No sealed records released. Copy fee: $.05 per page. Certification fee: $1.00. Fee payee: Clerk of

Court. Business checks accepted. Prepayment is required.

Licking County Municipal Court 40 W Main St, Newark, OH 43055; 740-349-6627. Hours: 8AM-4:30PM (EST). *Misdemeanor, Civil Actions Under $15,000, Eviction, Small Claims.*

Civil Records: Access: Phone, fax, mail, in person, online. Both court and visitors may perform in person searches. No search fee. Required to search: name, years to search. Civil cases indexed by defendant, plaintiff. Civil records on computer from 1990, prior in books. Online access to Municipal Court records is available free at http://206.31.219.164.

Criminal Records: Access: Phone, fax, mail, in person, online. Both court and visitors may perform in person searches. No search fee. Required to search: name, years to search. Criminal records on computer from 1990, prior in books. Online access to criminal records is the same as civil.

General Information: Public access terminal is available. No sealed records released. SASE required. Turnaround time 2-3 days. Copy fee: $.25 per page. Certification fee: $2.00. Fee payee: Licking County Municipal Court. Personal checks accepted. Prepayment is required.

Logan County

Common Pleas Court 101 S Main St Rm 18, Bellefontaine, OH 43311-2097; 937-599-7260. Hours: 8:30AM-4:30PM (EST). *Felony, Civil Actions Over $10,000.*

Civil Records: Access: In person only. Visitors must perform in person searches for themselves. Search fee: No search fee. Required to search: name, years to search; also helpful: address. Civil cases indexed by defendant, plaintiff. Civil records on computer from 6/88, prior in books to 1943.

Criminal Records: Access: In person only. Visitors must perform in person searches for themselves. Search fee: No search fee. Required to search: name, years to search, DOB; also helpful: address, SSN. Criminal records on computer from 6/88, prior in books to 1943.

General Information: Public access terminal is available. All records public. Fax notes: Fee to fax results is $2.00 per page. Copy fee: $.25 per page after first 25 pages. Certification fee: $1.00 per page. Fee payee: Clerk of Court. Only cashiers checks and money orders accepted. Prepayment is required.

Bellefontaine Municipal Court 226 W Columbus Ave, Bellefontaine, OH 43311; 937-599-6127. Hours: 8AM-4:30PM (EST). *Misdemeanor, Civil Actions Under $15,000, Eviction, Small Claims.*

Civil Records: Access: In person only. Visitors must perform in person searches for themselves. No search fee. Required to search: name, years to search. Civil cases indexed by defendant, plaintiff. Civil records on computer from 1986, prior in books.

Criminal Records: Access: In person only. Visitors must perform in person searches for themselves. No search fee. Required to search: name, years to search, DOB, SSN, signed release; also helpful: address. Criminal records on computer from 1986, prior in books.

General Information: Public access terminal is available. All records are public. Copy fee: $.25 per page. Certification fee: $1.00. Fee payee: Bellefontaine Municipal Court. Personal checks accepted. Local checks accepted. Credit cards accepted: Visa, MasterCard. Accepted for traffic & criminal only. Prepayment is required.

Lorain County

Common Pleas Court 226 Middle Ave, Elyria, OH 44035; 440-329-5536; Probate phone: 440-329-5175; Fax: 440-329-5404. Hours: 8AM-4:30PM (EST). *Felony, Civil Actions Over $10,000, Probate.*

www.loraincounty.com/clerk

Civil Records: Access: Mail, online, in person. Both court and visitors may perform in person searches. No search fee. Required to search: name, years to search. Civil cases indexed by defendant, plaintiff. Civil records on computer from 1988, prior in books archived to 1800s. some records on microfiche to 1960. The web site offers free access to indices and dockets for civil and domestic relationship cases. Court will not do index searching, but they will pull specified records.

Criminal Records: Access: Mail, online, in person. Both court and visitors may perform in person searches. No search fee. Required to search: name, years to search. Criminal records on computer from 1988, prior in books archived to 1800s. some records on microfiche to 1960. Online access to criminal records is the same as civil. Court will not do index searching, but they will pull specified records.

General Information: Public access terminal is available. No juvenile records released. SASE required. Turnaround time 1-2 days. Copy fee: $.10 per page. Certification fee: $1.00. Fee payee: Clerk of Court. Personal checks accepted. Prepayment is required.

Avon Lake Municipal Court 32855 Walker Rd, Avon Lake, OH 44012; 440-930-4103. Hours: 8:30AM-4:30PM (EST). *Misdemeanor, Civil Actions Under $15,000, Eviction, Small Claims.*

Note: The court upgraded their computer system for 2000 and refrains from disclosing the SSN publicly.

Civil Records: Access: Phone, mail, in person. Only the court performs in person searches; visitors may not. No search fee. Required to search: name, years to search. Civil cases indexed by defendant, plaintiff. Civil records on computer from 5/92, records go back to 1976.

Criminal Records: Access: Phone, mail, in person. Only the court performs in person searches; visitors may not. No search fee. Required to search: name, years to search, DOB; also helpful: SSN. Criminal records on computer from 7/92, records go back to 1976.

General Information: No non-public records released. SASE required. Turnaround time 1-2 days. Fax notes: Fee to fax results is $3.00 per document. Copy fee: $.50 per page. Certification fee: $1.00. Fee payee: Avon Lake Municipal Court. Personal checks accepted. Prepayment is required.

Elyria Municipal Court 328 Broad St (PO Box 1498), Elyria, OH 44036; 440-323-5743; Criminal phone: 440-323-1328; Fax: 440-323-0785-Civil, 440-323-8095-Criminal. Hours: 8AM-4:30PM (EST). *Misdemeanor, Civil Actions Under $15,000, Eviction, Small Claims.*

www.elyriamunicourt.org

Civil Records: Access: Fax, mail, online, in person. Both court and visitors may perform in person searches. No search fee. Required to search: name, years to search; also helpful: address. Civil cases indexed by defendant, plaintiff. Civil records in books to 1956, computer from 1996. Search by e-mail to civil@elyriamunicourt.org.

Criminal Records: Access: Fax, mail, in person. Both court and visitors may perform in person searches. No search fee. Required to search: name, years to search; also helpful: address, DOB, SSN. Criminal records in books to 1956, computer from 1996. Search by e-mail to crtr@elyriamunicourt.org.

General Information: Public access terminal is available. All records are public. SASE required. Turnaround time 5 days. Fax notes: Will not fax results.

No copy fee. Certification fee: $2.00. Personal checks accepted.

Lorain Municipal Court 200 W Erie Ave, Lorain, OH 44052; 440-204-2140. Hours: 8:30AM-4:30PM (EST). *Misdemeanor, Civil Actions Under $15,000, Eviction, Small Claims.*

www.lorainmunicourt.org

Civil Records: Access: Online, in person. Visitors must perform in person searches for themselves. No search fee. Required to search: name, years to search; also helpful: address. Civil cases indexed by defendant, plaintiff. Civil records in books. Online access to municipal court records available free at www.lorainmunicourt.org/search.shtml. Search by name, date, case number, driver license number or attorney.

Criminal Records: Access: Online, in person. Visitors must perform in person searches for themselves. No search fee. Required to search: name, years to search; also helpful: address, DOB, SSN. Criminal records in books. Online access to criminal records is the same as civil.

General Information: Public access terminal is available. Copy fee: $1.00 per page. Certification fee: $2.00. Fee payee: Municipal Court. Prepayment is required.

Oberlin Municipal Court 85 S Main St, Oberlin, OH 44074; 440-775-1751; Fax: 440-775-0619. Hours: 8AM-4PM (EST). *Misdemeanor, Civil Actions Under $15,000, Eviction, Small Claims.*

Civil Records: Access: In person only. Visitors must perform in person searches for themselves. No search fee. Required to search: name, years to search; also helpful: address. Civil cases indexed by defendant, plaintiff. Civil records on computer from 1991, prior in books.

Criminal Records: Access: In person only. Visitors must perform in person searches for themselves. No search fee. Required to search: name, years to search; also helpful: address, DOB, SSN. Criminal records on computer from 1991, prior in books.

General Information: Public access terminal is available. Copy fee: $.10 per page. Certification fee: $1.00. Fee payee: Oberlin Municipal Court. Business checks accepted. Credit cards accepted: Visa, MasterCard. Prepayment is required.

Vermilion Municipal Court 687 Decatour St, Vermilion, OH 44089-1152; 440-967-6543; Fax: 440-967-1467. Hours: 8AM-4PM (EST). *Misdemeanor, Civil Actions Under $15,000, Eviction, Small Claims.*

www.vermilionmunicipalcourt.org

Civil Records: Access: Fax, mail, in person, online. Both court and visitors may perform in person searches. No search fee. Required to search: name, years to search; also helpful: address. Civil cases indexed by defendant, plaintiff. Civil records on computer since late 1991, indexed in books since 1966. Online access to municipal court records is available at the web site or directly at http://209.142.158.114/search.html.

Criminal Records: Access: Fax, mail, in person, online. Both court and visitors may perform in person searches. No search fee. Required to search: name, years to search; also helpful: SSN. Criminal records on computer since late 1991, indexed in books since 1966. Online access to criminal records is the same as civil.

General Information: Public access terminal is available. no addresses, victim info or confidential report records released. Fax notes: No fee to fax results. Copy fee: $.10 per page. Certification fee: $2.00. Fee payee: Municipal Court. Personal checks accepted. Credit cards accepted: Visa, MasterCard. Prepayment is required.

Lucas County

Common Pleas Court 700 Adams, Courthouse, Toledo, OH 43624; 419-213-4483 & 4484; Probate phone: 419-213-4775; Fax: 419-213-4487. Hours: 8AM-4:45PM (EST). *Felony, Civil Actions Over $10,000, Probate.*

www.co.lucas.oh.us/clerk

Note: Probate records must be searched separately; probate hours are 8:30-4:30 at the courthouse.

Civil Records: Access: Fax, mail, in person, online. Both court and visitors may perform in person searches. Search fee: $2.00 per name. Required to search: name, years to search. Civil cases indexed by defendant, plaintiff. Civil records computer from 1987, records go back to 1948, prior in books and on film. Online access to clerk of courts dockets is available free at www.co.lucas.oh.us/Clerk/dockets.asp. Online records go back to 9/1997.

Criminal Records: Access: Fax, mail, in person, online. Both court and visitors may perform in person searches. Search fee: $5.00 per name. Required to search: name, years to search, DOB, SSN; also helpful: sex, signed release. Criminal records computer from 1987, records go back to 1948, prior in books and on film. Online access to clerk of courts dockets is available free at www.co.lucas.oh.us/Clerk/dockets.asp. Online record go back to 9/1997.

General Information: Public access terminal is available. No expunged records released. SASE not required. Turnaround time 3 days. Fax notes: $1.00 per page plus $3.00 transmittal fee. Copy fee: $.25 per page. Certification fee: $3.00. Fee payee: Clerk of Court. Only cashiers checks and money orders accepted. Prepayment is required.

Maumee Municipal Court 400 Conant St, Maumee, OH 43537-3397; Civil phone: 419-897-7145; Criminal phone: 419-897-7136; Fax: 419-897-7129. Hours: 8AM-4:30PM (EST). *Misdemeanor, Civil Actions Under $15,000, Eviction, Small Claims.*

www.maumee.org/court/court.htm

Civil Records: Access: Phone, fax, mail, in person, online. Only the court performs in person searches; visitors may not. No search fee. Required to search: name; also helpful: years to search. Civil cases indexed by defendant, plaintiff. Civil records in docket books since 1964, on computer since 1989. Online access to the interactive web court system database is available free at www.maumee.org/court/courtsystem/index.html.

Criminal Records: Access: Phone, fax, mail, in person, online. Only the court performs in person searches; visitors may not. No search fee. Required to search: name, years to search, DOB; also helpful: SSN. Criminal records in docket books since 1964, on computer since 1987. Online access to criminal records is the same as civil.

General Information: Turnaround time 1 week. Fax notes: $3.00 per page. Copy fee: $.25 per page. Certification fee: $1.50. Fee payee: Maumee Municipal Court. Personal checks accepted. Credit cards accepted: Visa, MasterCard. Credit cards not accepted for phone orders. Prepayment is required.

Oregon Municipal Court 5330 Seaman Rd, Oregon, OH 43616; Civil phone: 419-698-7008; Criminal phone: 419-698-7173; Fax: 419-698-7013. 8:30AM-4:30PM (EST). *Misdemeanor, Civil Actions Under $15,000, Eviction, Small Claims, Traffic.*

www.ci.oregon.oh.us/ctydpt/court/court.htm

Civil Records: Access: Phone, fax, mail, in person, email. Both court and visitors may perform in person searches. No search fee. Required to search: name, years to search. Civil cases indexed by defendant, plaintiff. Civil records on books since 1960, computerized since 1989.

Criminal Records: Access: Phone, fax, mail, in person, email. Both court and visitors may perform in person searches. No search fee. Required to search: name, years to search; also helpful: DOB, SSN. Criminal records on books since 1960, computerized since 1989.

General Information: Turnaround time 1-2 days. Fax notes: No fee to fax results. Must be local call. Copy fee: $.50 for first page, $.10 each add'l. Certification fee: $2.50 per page. Fee payee: Oregon Municipal Court. Personal checks accepted. Credit cards accepted for criminal records only: Visa, MasterCard. For in person searching only. Prepayment is required.

Sylvania Municipal Court 6700 Monroe St, Sylvania, OH 43560-1995; 419-885-8975; Fax: 419-885-8987. Hours: 7:30AM-4PM (EST). *Misdemeanor, Civil Actions Under $15,000, Eviction, Small Claims.*

www.sylvaniacourt.com

Civil Records: Access: Fax, mail, in person. Visitors must perform in person searches for themselves. No search fee. Required to search: name, years to search. Civil cases indexed by defendant, plaintiff. Civil records on books since 1964, computerized since 1987.

Criminal Records: Access: Fax, mail, in person. Visitors must perform in person searches for themselves. No search fee. Required to search: name, years to search, DOB, SSN. Criminal records on books since 1964, computerized since 1987.

General Information: Public access terminal is available. Turnaround time 1 week. Fax notes: No fee to fax results. Local calls only. Copy fee: $.10 per page. Certification fee: $2.00 per page. Fee payee: Clerk of Court. Business checks accepted. Prepayment required.

Toledo Municipal Court 555 N Erie St, Toledo, OH 43624-1391; 419-245-1926 (Small Claims); Civil phone: 419-245-1927; Criminal phone: 419-936-3650; Fax: 419-245-1801. Hours: 8AM-4:30PM civil; 6AM-6PM M-F, 6-11:30AM Sat crim & traffic (EST). *Misdemeanor, Civil Actions Under $15,000, Eviction, Small Claims.*

www.tmc-clerk.com

Note: The daily docket is available online at the web site. Direct email requests to clerk@tmc-clerk.com.

Civil Records: Access: Mail, fax, in person, email. Both court and visitors may perform in person searches. No search fee. Required to search: name, years to search; also helpful: address. Civil cases indexed by defendant. Civil records on computer back to 1985, prior in books since 1960s.

Criminal Records: Access: Mail, fax, in person, email. Both court and visitors may perform in person searches. No search fee. Required to search: name, years to search, DOB, SSN; also helpful: address. Criminal records on computer back to 1985, prior in books since 1960s. Have either date of birth or SSN to request a search.

General Information: Public access terminal is available. (Civil only available.) No expunged records released. SASE required. Turnaround time 1 day with a case number; 5 days without a case number. Copy fee: $.25 per page. Certification fee: $6.00. Fee payee: Toledo Municipal Court. Personal checks accepted. Credit cards accepted: Visa, MasterCard. Prepayment is required.

Madison County

Common Pleas Court PO Box 557, London, OH 43140; 740-852-9776; Probate phone: 740-852-0756. Hours: 8AM-4PM (EST). *Felony, Civil Actions Over $10,000, Probate.*

Civil Records: Access: In person only. Visitors must perform in person searches for themselves. No search fee. Required to search: name, years to search. Civil

cases indexed by defendant, plaintiff. Civil records in books since 1981.

Criminal Records: Access: In person only. Visitors must perform in person searches for themselves. No search fee. Required to search: name, years to search; also helpful: address, DOB, SSN. Criminal records in books since 1981.

General Information: No secret indictment records released. Copy fee: $.25 per page. Fee payee: Clerk of Court. Personal checks accepted. Prepayment is required.

Madison County Municipal Court Main & High St, PO Box 646, London, OH 43140; 740-852-1669; Fax: 740-852-0812. Hours: 8AM-4PM (EST). *Misdemeanor, Civil Actions Under $15,000, Eviction, Small Claims.*

Civil Records: Access: Phone, fax, mail, in person. Both court and visitors may perform in person searches. No search fee. Required to search: name, years to search. Civil cases indexed by defendant, plaintiff. Civil records on computer from 1989, prior in books indexed from 1958.

Criminal Records: Access: Phone, fax, mail, in person. Both court and visitors may perform in person searches. No search fee. Required to search: name, years to search, DOB; also helpful: SSN. Criminal records on computer from 1989, prior in books indexed from 1958.

General Information: Public access terminal is available. No probation records released. SASE required. Turnaround time up to 2 weeks. Fax notes: No fee to fax results. Copy fee: $.25 per page. Certification fee: $1.00. Fee payee: Madison County Municipal Court. Only cashiers checks and money orders accepted. Prepayment is required.

Mahoning County

Common Pleas Court 120 Market St, Youngstown, OH 44503; 330-740-2310; Probate phone: 330-740-2312; Fax: 330-740-2105. Hours: 8AM-4PM (EST). *Felony, Civil Actions Over $15,000, Probate.*

Civil Records: Access: In person only. Visitors must perform in person searches for themselves. No search fee. Required to search: name, years to search; also helpful: address. Civil cases indexed by defendant, plaintiff. Civil records on computer from 1989, prior in books indexed from 1946.

Criminal Records: Access: Phone, fax, mail, in person. Both court and visitors may perform in person searches. No search fee. Required to search: name, years to search; also helpful: address, DOB, SSN. Criminal records on computer from 1989, prior in books indexed from 1946.

General Information: Public access terminal is available. No secret indictment records released. SASE required. Turnaround time 1 week. Fax notes: $2.00 for first page, $1.00 each add'l. Copy fee: $.10 per page. Certification fee: $1.00. Fee payee: Clerk of Court. Personal checks accepted. Prepayment is required.

County Court #2 127 Boardman Canfield Rd, Boardman, OH 44512; 330-726-5546; Fax: 330-740-2035. Hours: 8:30AM-4PM (EST). *Misdemeanor, Civil Actions Under $15,000, Small Claims.*

Civil Records: Access: Mail, fax, in person. Both court and visitors may perform in person searches. No search fee. Required to search: name, years to search. Civil cases indexed by defendant, plaintiff. Civil records in books and dockets from 1960; on computer back to 1995.

Criminal Records: Access: Mail, fax, in person. Both court and visitors may perform in person searches. No search fee. Required to search: name, years to search, DOB, SSN, signed release. Criminal records in books and dockets from 1960; on computer back to 1995.

Court will not perform party names searches for in-person requesters.

General Information: Public access terminal is available. Expunged records are not released. SASE required. Turnaround time 5-10 days. Copy fee: $.25 per page. Certification fee: $1.00. Fee payee: County Court #2. Personal checks accepted. Prepayment is required.

County Court #3 605 E Ohio Ave, Sebring, OH 44672; 330-938-9873; Fax: 330-938-6518. Hours: 8:30AM-4PM (EST). *Misdemeanor, Civil Actions Under $15,000, Small Claims.*

Civil Records: Access: Mail, in person. Both court and visitors may perform in person searches. No search fee. Required to search: name, years to search. Civil cases indexed by defendant, plaintiff. Civil records in books from 1958; on computer back to 8/95.

Criminal Records: Access: Mail, in person. Both court and visitors may perform in person searches. No search fee. Required to search: name, years to search, DOB; also helpful: SSN. Criminal records in books from 1989; on computer back to 8/95.

General Information: Public access terminal is available. No expunged records released. SASE required. Turnaround time 1 week. Copy fee: $.10 per page. Certification fee: $1.00 per page. Fee payee: Mahoning County Court #3. Personal checks accepted. Prepayment is required.

County Court #4 6000 Mahoning Ave, Youngstown, OH 44515-2288; 330-740-2001; Fax: 330-740-2036. Hours: 8:30AM-4PM (EST). *Misdemeanor, Civil Actions Under $15,000, Small Claims.*

Civil Records: Access: Fax, mail, in person. Both court and visitors may perform in person searches. No search fee. Required to search: name, years to search. Civil cases indexed by defendant, plaintiff. Civil records in books from the 1940s, on microfiche recent; computerized records since 1996. Phone, fax and mail access limited to out of town requests.

Criminal Records: Access: Fax, mail, in person. Both court and visitors may perform in person searches. No search fee. Required to search: name, years to search, DOB, SSN, signed release. Criminal records in books from the 1940s, on microfiche rec; computerized records since 1996.

General Information: Public access terminal is available. No expunged records released. SASE required. Turnaround time same day. Fax notes: $2.00 for first page, $.50 each add'l. Copy fee: $.10 per page. Certification fee: $1.00. Fee payee: County Court #4. Personal checks accepted. Prepayment is required.

County Court #5 72 N Broad St, Canfield, OH 44406; 330-533-3643; Fax: 330-740-2034. Hours: 8:30AM-4PM (EST). *Misdemeanor, Civil Actions Under $15,000, Small Claims.*

Civil Records: Access: Fax, mail, in person. Visitors must peform in person searches. No search fee. Required to search: name, years to search; also helpful: address. Civil cases indexed by defendant, plaintiff. Civil records on computer since 1995; overall records go back to 1991.

Criminal Records: Access: Fax, mail, in person. Both court and visitors may perform in person searches. Search fee: $5.00 per name. Fee includes certification. Required to search: name, years to search; also helpful: DOB, SSN. Criminal records on computer since 1995; overall records go back to 1991.

General Information: Public access terminal is available. No LEADS printout records released. SASE required. Turnaround time 1-2 days. Fax notes: $2.00 for first page, $1.00 each add'l. Copy fee: $.10 per page. Certification fee: $1.00. Fee payee: County Court #5. Only cashiers checks and money orders accepted. Prepayment is required.

Youngstown Municipal Court - Civil Records PO Box 6047, Youngstown, OH 44501-6047; 330-742-8863; Fax: 330-742-8786. Hours: 8AM-4PM (EST). *Civil Actions Under $15,000, Eviction, Small Claims.*

Civil Records: Access: Phone, fax, mail, in person. Both court and visitors may perform in person searches. No search fee. Required to search: name, years to search; also helpful: address. Civil cases indexed by defendant, plaintiff. Civil records in books since 1970; on computer since 1998.

General Information: Public access terminal is available. All records are public. SASE required. Turnaround time 1-2 days. Copy fee: $.10 per page. Certification fee: $1.00. Fee payee: Municipal Court. Personal checks accepted. Prepayment is required.

Youngstown Municipal Court - Criminal Records 26 S Phelps St, Youngstown, OH 44503; 330-742-8860; Fax: 330-742-8786. Hours: 8AM-4PM (EST). *Misdemeanor.*

Criminal Records: Access: Fax, mail, in person. Both court and visitors may perform in person searches. No search fee. Required to search: name, years to search, DOB; also helpful: SSN. Criminal records go back to 1966; kept available since 1981 on docket books, microfiche; also on computer since 1998.

General Information: No records released. SASE required. Turnaround time 1 day. Copy fee: $.10 per page. Certification fee: $1.00. Fee payee: Municipal Court. Only cashiers checks and money orders accepted. Prepayment is required.

Campbell Municipal Court 351 Tenney Ave, Campbell, OH 44405; 330-755-2165; Fax: 330-750-3058. Hours: 8AM-4PM (EST). *Misdemeanor, Civil Actions Under $15,000, Eviction, Small Claims.*

Civil Records: Access: Fax, mail, in person. Only the court performs in person searches; visitors may not. No search fee. Required to search: name, years to search. Civil cases indexed by defendant, plaintiff. Civil records in books from 1950s; on computer back to 1999. Mail and fax access limited to short searches.

Criminal Records: Access: Fax, mail, in person. Only the court performs in person searches; visitors may not. No search fee. Required to search: name, years to search; also helpful: DOB, SSN, signed release. Criminal records in books from 1950s; on computer back to 7/1999.

General Information: No sealed records released. SASE required. Turnaround time depends on workload. Fax notes: Will fax results to police agencies only. Copy fee: $.50 per page. Certification fee: $10.00. Fee payee: Campbell Municipal Court. Only cashiers checks and money orders accepted. Prepayment is required.

Struthers Municipal Court 6 Elm St, Struthers, OH 44471; 330-755-1800; Fax: 330-755-2790. Hours: 8AM-4PM; Public access only on Tuesday and Thursday (EST). *Misdemeanor, Civil Actions Under $15,000, Eviction, Small Claims.*

Civil Records: Access: Mail, in person. Both court and visitors may perform in person searches. No search fee. Required to search: name, years to search. Civil cases indexed by defendant, plaintiff. Civil records in books since 1965; on computer since 1996.

Criminal Records: Access: Mail, in person. Both court and visitors may perform in person searches. No search fee. Required to search: name, years to search; also helpful: SSN, DOB, signed release. Criminal records in books since 1965; on computer since 1996.

General Information: Public access terminal is available. (Terminal only available Tuesdays and Thursdays.) No pending case records released. SASE required. Turnaround time 2-3 days. No copy fee. Certification fee: $10.00. Fee payee: Municipal Court.

Only cashiers checks and money orders accepted. Prepayment is required.

Marion County

Common Pleas Court 100 N Main St, Marion, OH 43301-1823; 740-223-4270; Probate phone: 740-387-7614; Fax: 740-223-4260. Hours: 8:30AM-4:30PM (EST). *Felony, Civil Actions Over $10,000.*

Civil Records: Access: Mail, in person. Visitors must perform in person searches for themselves No search fee. Required to search: name, years to search. Civil cases indexed by defendant, plaintiff. Civil records on computer from 1991, prior in books since 1886. Mail is only used if you have the case number and request a specific document.

Criminal Records: Access: Mail, in person. Visitors must perform in person searches for themselves. No search fee. Required to search: name, years to search; also helpful: DOB, SSN. Criminal records on computer from 1991, prior in books since 1886. Mail is only used if you have the case number and request a specific document.

General Information: Public access terminal is available. No sealed, expunged records released. SASE required. Turnaround time 1-3 days. Fax notes: Fee to fax is $2.00 per transmission and $1.00 per page. Copy fee: $.25 per page. Certification fee: $1.00. Fee payee: Marion County Clerk of Courts. Personal checks accepted. Prepayment is required.

Marion Municipal Court 233 W Center St, Marion, OH 43302-0326; 740-387-2020; Fax: 740-382-5274. Hours: 8:30AM-4:30PM (EST). *Misdemeanor, Civil Actions Under $15,000, Eviction, Small Claims.*

Civil Records: Access: In person only. Visitors must perform in person searches for themselves. No search fee. Required to search: name, years to search. Civil cases indexed by defendant, plaintiff. Civil records on computer since 1995.

Criminal Records: Access: Mail, in person. Both court and visitors may perform in person searches. No search fee. Required to search: name, years to search; also helpful: DOB, SSN. Criminal records on computer from 1986, prior in books.

General Information: SASE required. Turnaround time 7 days. Copy fee: $.25 per page. Certification fee: $5.00. Fee payee: Municipal Court. Only cashiers checks and money orders accepted. Prepayment is required.

Medina County

Common Pleas Court 93 Public Square, Medina, OH 44256; 330-725-9720; Probate phone: 330-725-9703. Hours: 8AM-4:30PM (EST). *Felony, Civil Actions Over $10,000, Probate.*

Civil Records: Access: Mail, in person. No search fee. Required to search: name, years to search. Civil cases indexed by defendant, plaintiff. Civil records on computer from 10/92, in books to early 1960s, prior archived.

Criminal Records: Access: Mail, in person. Both court and visitors may perform in person searches. No search fee. Required to search: name, years to search. Criminal records on computer from 10/92, in books to early 1960s, prior archived.

General Information: Public access terminal is available. SASE required. Turnaround time 1-2 days. Copy fee: $.25 per page. Certification fee: $1.00. Fee payee: Clerk of Court. Personal checks accepted. Prepayment is required.

Medina Municipal Court 135 N Elmwood, Medina, OH 44256; 330-723-3287; Fax: 330-225-1108. Hours: 8AM-4:30PM (EST). *Misdemeanor, Civil Actions Under $15,000, Eviction, Small Claims.*

www.medinamunicipalcourt.org

Civil Records: Access: Mail, online, in person. Both court and visitors may perform in person searches. No search fee. Required to search: name, years to search. Civil cases indexed by defendant, plaintiff. Civil cases on computer from 1986, prior in books. Access to the online system requires Procomm Plus. There are no fees. Search by name or case number. The computer access number is 330-723-4337. For more information, call Rich Armstrong at ext. 230.

Criminal Records: Access: Mail, online, in person. Visitors must perform in person searches for themselves. No search fee. Required to search: name, years to search; also helpful: address, DOB, SSN. Criminal records on computer from 1986, prior in books. Online access to criminal records is the same as civil.

General Information: Public access terminal is available. No expunged records released. SASE required. Copy fee: $.50 per page. Certification fee: $1.50. Fee payee: Municipal Court. Personal checks accepted. Credit cards accepted: Visa, MasterCard for criminal and traffic records only.

Wadsworth Municipal Court 120 Maple St, Wadsworth, OH 44281-1825; 330-335-1596; Fax: 330-335-2723. Hours: 8AM-4PM (EST). *Misdemeanor, Civil Actions Under $15,000, Eviction, Small Claims.*

Civil Records: Access: Fax, mail, in person. Both court and visitors may perform in person searches. No search fee. Required to search: name, years to search. Civil cases indexed by defendant, plaintiff. Civil records on computer from 3/90, prior in books.

Criminal Records: Access: Fax, mail, in person. Both court and visitors may perform in person searches. No search fee. Required to search: name, years to search; also helpful: address, DOB, SSN. Criminal records on computer from 3/90, prior in books.

General Information: Public access terminal is available. No search warrant records released. SASE required. Turnaround time to 1 week. Fax notes: No fee to fax results. Local faxing only. Copy fee: $.25 per page. Certification fee: $1.00. Fee payee: Wadsworth Municipal Court. Personal checks accepted. Prepayment is required.

Meigs County

Common Pleas Court PO Box 151, Pomeroy, OH 45769; 740-992-5290; Probate phone: 740-992-3096; Fax: 740-992-4429. Hours: 8:30AM-4:30PM (EST). *Felony, Civil Actions Over $3,000, Probate.*

Note: Probate fax is 740-992-6727.

Civil Records: Access: In person only. Visitors must perform in person searches for themselves. No search fee. Required to search: name, years to search; also helpful: address. Civil cases indexed by defendant, plaintiff. Civil records on computer since 1996, in books to 1800s.

Criminal Records: Access: In person only. Visitors must perform in person searches for themselves. No search fee. Required to search: name, years to search, DOB; also helpful: address, SSN. Criminal records on computer since 1996, in books to 1800s.

General Information: Public access terminal is available. No secret records released. Copy fee: $.25 per page. Certification fee: $1.00. Fee payee: Clerk of Court. Personal checks accepted. Prepayment required.

Meigs County Court 2ns Street Courthouse, Pomeroy, OH 45769; 740-992-2279; Fax: 740-992-4570. Hours: 8:30AM-4:30PM (EST). *Misdemeanor, Civil Actions Under $15,000, Small Claims.*

Civil Records: Access: In person only. Visitors must perform in person searches for themselves. No search fee. Required to search: name, years to search. Civil cases indexed by defendant, plaintiff. Civil records on computer from 8/90, prior in docket books. Phone access limited to records from 1990 to present.

Criminal Records: Access: In person only. Visitors must perform in person searches for themselves. No search fee. Required to search: name, years to search, DOB, SSN, signed release. Criminal records on computer from 8/90, prior in docket books. Phone access limited to records from 1990 to present.

General Information: No sealed records released. Copy fee: $.10 per page. Certification fee: $2.00. Fee payee: Meigs County Court. Personal checks accepted. Out of state checks not accepted.

Mercer County

Common Pleas Court 101 N Main St, Rm 205, PO Box 28, Celina, OH 45822; 419-586-6461; Probate phone: 419-586-2418; Fax: 419-586-5826. Hours: 8:30AM-4PM (EST). *Felony, Civil Actions Over $10,000, Probate.*

Civil Records: Access: In person only. Visitors must perform in person searches for themselves. No search fee. Required to search: name, years to search; also helpful: address. Civil cases indexed by defendant, plaintiff. Civil records on computer back to 1997, microfiche up to and including 1985, prior in books.

Criminal Records: Access: In person only. Visitors must perform in person searches for themselves. No search fee. Required to search: name, years to search; also helpful: address, DOB, SSN. Criminal records on computer back to 1997, microfiche up to and including 1985, prior in books.

General Information: Public access terminal is available. No juvenile or sealed records released. Copy fee: $.25 per page. Certification fee: $1.00. Fee payee: Clerk of Court. Personal checks accepted. Prepayment is required.

Celina Municipal Court PO Box 362, Celina, OH 45822; 419-586-6491; Fax: 419-586-4735. Hours: 8AM-5PM (EST). *Misdemeanor, Civil Actions Under $15,000, Eviction, Small Claims.*

Civil Records: Access: Phone, fax, mail, in person. Both court and visitors may perform in person searches. No search fee. Required to search: name, years to search; also helpful: address. Civil cases indexed by defendant, plaintiff. Civil records on computer from 1990, prior in books.

Criminal Records: Access: Phone, fax, mail, in person. Both court and visitors may perform in person searches. No search fee. Required to search: name, years to search; also helpful: address, DOB, SSN. Criminal records are on computer since 1989, prior found in books and files.

General Information: Public access terminal is available. No confidential information released. SASE required. Turnaround time 2-3 days. Copy fee: $.05 per page. Certification fee: $1.00. Fee payee: Municipal Court. Personal checks accepted. Prepayment required.

Miami County

Common Pleas Court & Court of Appeals Safety Bldg, 201 West Main St, 3rd Flr, Troy, OH 45373; 937-332-6855; Probate phone: 937-332-6832; Fax: 937-332-7069. Hours: 8AM-4PM (EST). *Felony, Civil Actions Over $10,000, Probate.*

Note: Probate is a separate division at the phone number given above.

Civil Records: Access: Fax, mail, in person. Both court and visitors may perform in person searches. Search fee: $5.00 per name. Required to search: name, years to search; also helpful: address. Civil cases indexed by defendant, plaintiff. Civil records in books for past 30 years, prior are archived; on computer since 1984.

Criminal Records: Access: Fax, mail, in person. Both court sond visitors may perform in person searches. Search fee: $5.00 per name. Required to search: name, years to search, DOB, SSN; also helpful: address.

Criminal records in books for past 30 years, prior are archived; on computer since 1984.

General Information: Public access terminal is available. No expunged or sealed records released. Turnaround time 1-2 days. Fax notes: $1.00 per document. Copy fee: $.25 per page. Certification fee: $1.00. Fee payee: Miami County Clerk of Courts. Personal checks accepted. Prepayment is required.

Miami County Municipal Court 201 West Main St, Troy, OH 45373; 937-332-6920; Fax: 937-332-6932. Hours: 8AM-4PM (EST). *Misdemeanor, Civil Actions Under $15,000, Eviction, Small Claims.*

www.onthesquare.com/mc_muni

Note: If the SSN is not provided by the party doing the search, the court personnel will mask the SSN before providing copies.

Civil Records: Access: Mail, in person, online. Both court and visitors may perform in person searches. Search fee: $5.00 per name. Required to search: name, years to search. Civil cases indexed by defendant, plaintiff. Civil records in books go back 25 years; on computer back to 11/89. Online access to municipal court records is available free at www.co.miami.oh.us/pa.

Criminal Records: Access: Mail, in person, online. Both court and visitors may perform in person searches. Search fee: $5.00 per name. Required to search: name, years to search, SSN. Criminal records on computer back to 1985, prior in books. Online access to criminalr ecords is the same as civil.

General Information: Public access terminal is available. No search warrant records released. SASE required. Turnaround time 2-3 days. Fax notes: Fee to fax result is $1.00 per document. Copy fee: $1.00 per page. Certification fee: $2.00. Fee payee: Municipal Court. Credit cards accepted: Visa, MasterCard. Prepayment is required.

Monroe County

Common Pleas Court 101 N Main St Rm 26, Woodsfield, OH 43793; 740-472-0761; Probate phone: 740-472-1654; Fax: 740-472-2518/2549. Hours: 8:30AM-4:30PM (EST). *Felony, Civil Actions Over $3,000, Probate.*

Civil Records: Access: In person only. Visitors must perform in person searches for themselves. No search fee. Required to search: name, years to search; also helpful: address. Civil cases indexed by defendant, plaintiff. Civil records in books since 1800; no computerized records.

Criminal Records: Access: Mail, fax, in person. Both court and visitors may perform in person searches. Search fee: $2.00 per name. Will only search one name at a time. Required to search: name, years to search; also helpful: address, DOB, SSN. Criminal records in books since 1800; no computerized records. The court will not do party names searches for in-person requesters.

General Information: No secret indictment records released. SASE required. Turnaround time 3 days. Fax notes: Fee to fax results is $2.00 per page. Copy fee: $.25 per page. Certification fee: $1.00. Fee payee: Clerk of Court. Personal checks accepted. Prepayment is required.

County Court 101 N Main St, Rm 35, Woodsfield, OH 43793; 740-472-5181. Hours: 9AM-4:30PM (EST). *Misdemeanor, Civil Actions Under $15,000, Small Claims.*

Civil Records: Access: Phone, mail, in person. Both court and visitors may perform in person searches. No search fee. Required to search: name, years to search. Civil cases indexed by defendant, plaintiff. Civil records in books, indexed back to 1950; on computer back to 8/1999.

Criminal Records: Access: Phone, mail, in person. Both court and visitors may perform in person searches. No search fee. Required to search: name, years to search. Criminal records in books, indexed back to 1950; on computer back to 1999.

General Information: SASE required. Turnaround time 1-2 days. No copy fee. Personal checks accepted.

Montgomery County

Common Pleas Court 41 N Perry St, Dayton, OH 45422; 937-225-4512; Criminal phone: 937-225-4536; Probate phone: 937-225-4640; Fax: 937-496-7389/7220. Hours: 8:30AM-4:30PM (EST). *Felony, Civil Actions Over $10,000, Probate.*

www.clerk.co.montgomery.oh.us

Civil Records: Access: Fax, mail, in person, online. Both court and visitors may perform in person searches. No search fee. Required to search: name, years to search; also helpful: address. Civil cases indexed by defendant, plaintiff. Civil records on computer from 1970s, prior in books. Online access to the Courts county-wide PRO system is available free at www.clerk.co.montgomery.oh.us/pro/index.cfm. Address mail requests to Montgomery County Clerk of Court "Civil Records.".

Criminal Records: Access: In person, online. Visitors must perform in person searches for themselves. No search fee. Required to search: name, years to search; also helpful: address, DOB, SSN. Criminal records on computer from 1970s, prior in books. Online access to criminal and traffic records is the same as civil.

General Information: Public access terminal is available. No sealed records released. SASE required. Turnaround time 1 week. Copy fee: $.10 per page. Certification fee: $1.00 per page. Fee payee: Clerk of Court. Personal checks accepted. Credit cards accepted: Visa, MasterCard. Prepayment is required.

County Court - Area 1 195 S Clayton Rd, New Lebanon, OH 45345-9601; 937-687-9099; Fax: 937-687-7119. Hours: Noon-7PM M,W; 8AM-4PM T,Th,F (EST). *Misdemeanor, Civil Actions Under $15,000, Small Claims.*

http://areacourts.dnaco.net

Civil Records: Access: Mail, in person, online. Both court and visitors may perform in person searches. No search fee. Required to search: name, years to search. Civil cases indexed by defendant, plaintiff. Civil records on computer from 2/92, prior in books, Archives 937-225-6366. Search county-wide records online at www.clerk.co.montgomery.oh.us/clerk/pro/index.cfm. Also, online access to area civil/traffic records is available free at http://areacourts.dnaco.net/areaone. Click on "Public records online.".

Criminal Records: Access: Mail, in person, online. Both court and visitors may perform in person searches. No search fee. Required to search: name, years to search; also helpful: SSN. Criminal records on computer from 2/92, prior in books, Archives 937-225-6366. Online access to criminal records is the same as civil.

General Information: Public access terminal is available. No medical, PSI report or LEADS print-out records released. SASE required. Turnaround time 2-3 days. Copy fee: $.75 per page. Certification fee: $1.00. Fee payee: First District Court, Montgomery County. Only cashiers checks and money orders accepted. Prepayment is required.

County Court - Area 2 6111 Taylorsville Rd, Huber Heights, OH 45424; 937-496-7231; Fax: 937-496-7236. Hours: 8AM-4PM M,T,W,F; Noon-7PMTh (EST). *Misdemeanor, Civil Actions Under $15,000, Small Claims.*

http://areacourts.dnaco.net

Civil Records: Access: Phone, fax, mail, in person, online, e-mail. Both court and visitors may perform in person searches. No search fee. Required to search: name, years to search; also helpful: address. Civil cases indexed by defendant, plaintiff. Civil records on computer from 1992, prior in books back to 1974. Search county-wide records online at www.clerk.co.montgomery.oh.us/clerk/pro/index.cfm. Also, online access to area civil/traffic records is available free at http://areacourts.dnaco.net/areatwo. Click on "Public records online.".

Criminal Records: Access: Phone, fax, mail, in person, online, e-mail. Both court and visitors may perform in person searches. No search fee. Required to search: name, years to search; also helpful: address, DOB, SSN. Criminal records on computer from 1992, prior in books back to 1974. Online access to criminal records is the same as civil.

General Information: Public access terminal is available. No confidential, forensic evaluation or medical records released. SASE required. Turnaround time 2-7 days. Fax notes: No fee to fax results. Copy fee: $.25 per page. Certification fee: $1.00. Fee is for civil only. No fee for criminal. Fee payee: County Court Area Two. Business checks accepted. Prepayment is required.

Dayton Municipal Court - Civil Division 301 W 3rd St, PO Box 968, Dayton, OH 45402-0968; 937-333-4471; Fax: 937-333-4468. Hours: 8AM-4:30PM (EST). *Civil Actions Under $15,000, Eviction, Small Claims.*

www.daytonmunicipalcourt.org

Civil Records: Access: Phone, mail, in person, online. Both court and visitors may perform in person searches. No search fee. Required to search: name, years to search; also helpful: address. Civil cases indexed by defendant, plaintiff. Civil records on computer back to 1990, prior in books to 1971. Online access to municipal court records is available free at www.daytonmunicipalcourt.org/scripts/rgw.dll/Docket; includes traffic and criminal.

General Information: Public access terminal is available. No expunged case records released. SASE required. Turnaround time 2-3 days. Copy fee: $.25 per page. Fee payee: Clerk of Court. Personal checks accepted. Prepayment is required.

Dayton Municipal Court - Criminal Division 301 W 3rd St, Rm 331, Dayton, OH 45402; 937-333-4315; Fax: 937-333-4490. Hours: 8AM-4:30PM (EST). *Misdemeanor.*

www.daytonmunicipalcourt.org

Criminal Records: Access: In person, online. Visitors must perform in person searches for themselves. No search fee. Required to search: name, years to search, DOB; also helpful: address, SSN, signed release. Criminal records on computer back to 1992, prior in books. Online access to municipal court records is available free at www.daytonmunicipalcourt.org/scripts/rgw.dll/Docket; includes traffic and civil. Phone access is limited.

General Information: Public access terminal is available. All records are public. SASE required. Copy fee: $.25 per page. Fee payee: Dayton Municipal Court. Personal checks accepted. Credit cards accepted: Visa, MasterCard. Prepayment is required.

Dayton Municipal Court - Traffic Division 301 W 3rd St (PO Box 968), Dayton, OH 45402; 937-333-4313; Fax: 937-333-7558. Hours: 8AM-4:30PM (EST). *Misdemeanor.*

www.daytonmunicipalcourt.org

Note: It is difficult for the court to provide case information prior to 1995.

Kettering Municipal Court 3600 Shroyer Rd, Kettering, OH 45429; 937-296-2461; Fax: 937-534-7017. Hours: 8:30AM-4:30PM (EST). *Misdemeanor, Civil Actions Under $15,000, Eviction, Small Claims.*

www.ketteringcourt.org

Civil Records: Access: Phone, mail, fax, in person. Both court and visitors may perform in person searches. No search fee. Required to search: name, years to search. Civil cases indexed by defendant, plaintiff. Civil records on computer from 1989, prior in books.

Criminal Records: Access: Phone, mail, in person. Both court and visitors may perform in person searches. No search fee. Required to search: name, years to search, DOB; also helpful: SSN. Criminal records on computer from 1988.

General Information: No expungment records released. SASE required. Turnaround time 1-5 days. Copy fee: $.05 per page. Certification fee: $2.50 per page. Fee payee: Kettering Municipal Court. Business checks accepted. Attorney's check accepted. Credit cards accepted: Visa, MasterCard. Prepayment is required.

Miamisburg Municipal Court 10 N First St, Miamisburg, OH 45342; 937-866-2203; Fax: 937-866-0135. Hours: 8AM-4PM (EST). *Misdemeanor, Civil Actions Under $15,000, Eviction, Small Claims.*

Civil Records: Access: Mail, in person. Both court and visitors may perform in person searches. No search fee. Required to search: name, years to search; also helpful: address. Civil cases indexed by defendant, plaintiff. Civil records on computer from 1988, prior in books. Call in advance to schedule in person searching.

Criminal Records: Access: Mail, in person. Both court and visitors may perform in person searches. No search fee. Required to search: name, years to search; also helpful: address, DOB, SSN. Criminal records on computer from 1988, prior in books. Call in advance to schedule in person searching.

General Information: No police reports, search warrants with no returns records released. SASE required. Turnaround time 1-2 weeks. Copy fee: $.25 per page. Fee payee: Clerk of Court. Personal checks accepted. Prepayment is required.

Oakwood Municipal Court 30 Park Ave, Dayton, OH 45419; 937-293-3058. Hours: 8:30AM-4PM (EST). *Misdemeanor, Civil Actions Under $15,000, Eviction, Small Claims.*

Civil Records: Access: Mail, in person. Only the court performs in person searches; visitors may not. No search fee. Required to search: name, years to search; also helpful: address. Civil cases indexed by defendant, plaintiff. Civil records in books since 1976.

Criminal Records: Access: Mail, in person. Only the court performs in person searches; visitors may not. No search fee. Required to search: name, years to search; also helpful: address, DOB, SSN. Criminal records in books since 1976. Address mail search requests to the Police Records Section.

General Information: No sealed, expunged or confidential records released. SASE required. Turnaround time 1-2 weeks. Fee payee: City of Oakwood. Personal checks accepted. Local checks accepted. Prepayment is required.

Vandalia Municipal Court PO Box 429, Justice Center, 2nd Floor, Vandalia, OH 45377; 937-898-3996; Fax: 937-898-6648. Hours: 8AM-4PM (EST). *Misdemeanor, Civil Actions Under $15,000, Eviction, Small Claims.*

Civil Records: Access: Phone, fax, mail, in person. Both court and visitors may perform in person searches. Search fee: $1.00 per page for complete print out. Required to search: name, years to search. Civil cases indexed by defendant, plaintiff. Civil records on computer from 1986, prior in books.

Criminal Records: Access: Phone, fax, mail, in person. Both court and visitors may perform in person searches. No search fee. Required to search: name, years to search, DOB, SSN. Criminal records on computer from 1986, prior in books.

General Information: Public access terminal is available. No medical, psychological reports or domestic violence report records released. SASE required. Copy fee: $1.00 per page. Fee payee: Clerk of Court. Business checks accepted. Credit cards accepted. Prepayment is required.

Morgan County

Common Pleas Court 19 E Main St, McConnelsville, OH 43756; 740-962-4752, 740-962-3371 (clerk); Probate phone: 740-962-2861; Fax: 740-962-4589. Hours: 8AM-4PM M-Th; 8AM-5PM F (EST). *Felony, Civil Actions Over $3,000, Probate.*

Civil Records: Access: Mail, in person. Visitors must perform in person searches for themselves. Search fee: $2.00 per name. Required to search: name, years to search; also helpful: address. Civil cases indexed by defendant, plaintiff. Civil records in books, some back to 1850.

Criminal Records: Access: Mail, in person. Both court and visitors may perform in person searches. Search fee: $2.00 per name. Required to search: name, years to search; also helpful: address, DOB, SSN. Criminal records in books, some back to 1850.

General Information: No secret indictment records released. SASE required. Turnaround time 1-3 days. No copy fee. Certification fee: $1.00 per page. Fee payee: Clerk of Court. Personal checks accepted. Prepayment is required.

Morgan County Court 37 E Main St, McConnelsville, OH 43756; 740-962-4031; Fax: 740-962-2895. Hours: 8AM-4PM (EST). *Misdemeanor, Civil Actions Under $15,000, Small Claims.*

Civil Records: Access: Phone, fax, mail, in person. Both court and visitors may perform in person searches. No search fee. Required to search: name, years to search. Civil cases indexed by defendant, plaintiff. Civil records in books from 1958.

Criminal Records: Access: Phone, fax, mail, in person. Both court and visitors may perform in person searches. No search fee. Required to search: name, years to search, DOB; also helpful: SSN. Criminal records in books from 1958.

General Information: SASE required. Turnaround time 1-2 days. Fax notes: No fee to fax results. Copy fee: $.10 per page. Certification fee: $1.00. Fee payee: Morgan County Court. Personal checks accepted. Prepayment is required.

Morrow County

Common Pleas Court 48 E High St, Mount Gilead, OH 43338; 419-947-2085; Probate phone: 419-947-5575; Fax: 419-947-5421. Hours: 8AM-4:30PM (EST). *Felony, Civil Actions Over $3,000, Probate.*

Civil Records: Access: Phone, fax, mail, in person. Both court and visitors may perform in person searches. No search fee. Required to search: name, years to search; also helpful: address. Civil cases indexed by defendant, plaintiff. Civil records in books from 1960, computerized since 01/02.

Criminal Records: Access: Phone, fax, mail, in person. Both court and visitors may perform in person searches. No search fee. Required to search: name, years to search; also helpful: address, DOB, SSN. Criminal records in books from 1960, computerized since 01/02.

General Information: Public access terminal is available. SASE required. Turnaround time 1 day. Copy fee: $1.00 per page. Certification fee: $1.00. Fee payee:

Clerk of Court. Personal checks accepted. Prepayment is required.

County Court 48 E High St, Mount Gilead, OH 43338; 419-947-5045; Fax: 419-947-1860. Hours: 7:30AM-5PM (EST). *Misdemeanor, Civil Actions Under $15,000, Small Claims.*

Civil Records: Access: Mail, in person. Both court and visitors may perform in person searches. No search fee. Required to search: name, years to search; also helpful-DOB or SSN. Civil cases indexed by defendant, plaintiff. Civil records on computer back to 1997, indexed on books from 1970s, archived from 1800s.

Criminal Records: Access: Mail, in person. Both court and visitors may perform in person searches. No search fee. Required to search: name, years to search, DOB, SSN. Criminal records on computer since 1990, indexed on books from 1970s, archived from 1800s.

General Information: No confidential records released. Turnaround time 1-2 days. No copy fee.

Muskingum County

Common Pleas Court 401 Main St, Zanesville, OH 43701; 740-455-7104; Probate phone: 740-455-7113. Hours: 8:30AM-4:30PM (EST). *Felony, Civil Actions, Probate.*

Note: As of 1/1/2001, there is no dollar limit on civil actions; prior, the civil action minimum was $15,000.

Civil Records: Access: Mail, in person. Both court and visitors may perform in person searches. No search fee. Required to search: name, years to search; also helpful: address. Civil cases indexed by defendant, plaintiff. Civil records in original files back to 1800s.

Criminal Records: Access: Mail, in person. Both court and visitors may perform in person searches. No search fee. Required to search: name, years to search, DOB; also helpful: address, SSN. Criminal records on docket books to 1960, original files back to 1800s.

General Information: Public access terminal is available. No grand jury records released. SASE required. Turnaround time 2 weeks. Copy fee: $.25 per page. Certification fee: $1.00 per page. Fee payee: Clerk of Court. Personal checks accepted. Prepayment is required.

County Court 27 N 5th St, Zanesville, OH 43701; 740-455-7138; Fax: 740-455-7157. Hours: 8AM-4PM (EST). *Misdemeanor, Civil Actions Under $15,000, Small Claims.*

Civil Records: Access: Fax, mail, in person. Both court and visitors may perform in person searches. No search fee. Required to search: name, years to search; also helpful: address. Civil cases indexed by defendant, plaintiff. Civil records in books from 1958; on computer back to 1995.

Criminal Records: Access: Fax, mail, in person. Both court and visitors may perform in person searches. No search fee. Required to search: name, years to search, DOB; also helpful: address, SSN. Criminal records in books from 1958; on computer back to 1995.

General Information: Public access terminal is available. No expunged records released. SASE required. Turnaround time up to 1 week. Fax notes: No fee to fax results. Fax available in emergency only. Copy fee: There is a $1.00 fee for certified copies, but no fee for uncertified. Certification fee: $1.00. Fee payee: Muskingum County Clerk. Personal checks accepted.

Zanesville Municipal Court PO Box 566, Zanesville, OH 43702; 740-454-3269; Fax: 740-455-0739. Hours: 9AM-4:30PM (EST). *Misdemeanor, Civil Actions Under $15,000, Eviction, Small Claims.*

Civil Records: Access: Mail, in person. Both court and visitors may perform in person searches. No search fee. Required to search: name, years to search; also helpful:

address. Civil cases indexed by defendant, plaintiff. Civil records on computer since 1987.

Criminal Records: Access: Mail, in person. Both court and visitors may perform in person searches. No search fee. Required to search: name, years to search; also helpful: address, DOB, SSN. Criminal records on computer since 1993.

General Information: Public access terminal is available. SASE required. Turnaround time 1 week. Copy fee: No search fee. Certification fee: $1.00. Fee payee: Municipal Court. Personal checks accepted. Prepayment is required.

Noble County

Common Pleas Court 350 Courthouse, Caldwell, OH 43724; 740-732-4408; Probate phone: 740-732-5047; Fax: 740-732-5702. Hours: 8-11:30AM,12:30-4PM M-W; 8-Noon Th; 8-11:30AM, 12:30-6PM F (EST). *Felony, Civil Actions Over $3,000.*

Note: Probate office is separate from this court at noble County Probate Court, 270 Courthouse, Caldwell, OH 43724.

Civil Records: Access: Phone, fax, mail, in person. Both court and visitors may perform in person searches. No search fee. Required to search: name, years to search; also helpful: address. Civil cases indexed by defendant, plaintiff. Civil records in books, archived back to 1800s. Recent civil records are computerized.

Criminal Records: Access: Phone, fax, mail, in person. Both court and visitors may perform in person searches. No search fee. Required to search: name, years to search; also helpful: address, DOB, SSN. Criminal records in books, archived back to 1800s. Recent civil records are computerized.

General Information: No sealed records released. SASE required. Turnaround time 1-2 days. Fax notes: No fee to fax results. Copy fee: $.50 per page. Certification fee: $1.00. Fee payee: Clerk of Court. Personal checks accepted. Will bill all court rule copies.

Noble County Court 100 Courthouse, Caldwell, OH 43724; 740-732-5795; Fax: 740-732-1435. Hours: 8:30AM-4PM M-W,F; 8:30-11:30AM Th (EST). *Misdemeanor, Civil Actions Under $15,000, Small Claims.*

Civil Records: Access: Phone, fax, mail, in person. No search fee. Required to search: name, years to search. Civil cases indexed by defendant, plaintiff. Civil records in books since 1960, on computer back to 2002.

Criminal Records: Access: Fax, mail, in person. Both court and visitors may perform in person searches. No search fee. Required to search: name, years to search, DOB; also helpful- SSN, signed release. Criminal records in books since 1960; on computer back to 2002.

General Information: SASE required. Turnaround time up to 1 week. Copy fee: $.50 per page. Certification fee: $5.00. Fee payee: County Court. Only cashiers checks and money orders accepted. Prepayment is required.

Ottawa County

Common Pleas Court 315 Madison St, 3rd Fl, Port Clinton, OH 43452; 419-734-6755 (General Division); Probate phone: 419-734-6830. Hours: 8:30AM-4:30PM (EST). *Felony, Civil Actions Over $10,000, Probate.*

www.ottawacocpcourt.com

Note: Probate is a separate court at 315 Madison St.

Civil Records: Access: In person only. Visitors must perform in person searches for themselves. No search fee. Required to search: name, years to search; also helpful: address. Civil cases indexed by defendant, plaintiff. Civil records on computer from 8/89, prior in books to 1842.

Criminal Records: Access: In person only. Visitors must perform in person searches for themselves. No search fee. Required to search: name, years to search; also helpful: address, DOB, SSN. Criminal records on computer from 8/89, prior in books to 1842.

General Information: Public access terminal is available. No sealed records released. Copy fee: $1.00 per page. Certification fee: $1.00. Fee payee: Clerk of Courts. Personal checks accepted. Prepayment is required.

Ottawa County Municipal Court 1860 East Perry St, Port Clinton, OH 43452; 419-734-4143; Fax: 419-732-2862. Hours: 8:30AM-4:30PM (EST). *Misdemeanor, Civil Actions Under $15,000, Eviction, Small Claims.*

Civil Records: Access: In person only. Visitors must perform in person searches for themselves. No search fee. Required to search: name, years to search; also helpful: address. Civil cases indexed by defendant, plaintiff. Civil records on computer from 1989, prior in books.

Criminal Records: Access: In person only. Visitors must perform in person searches for themselves. No search fee. Required to search: name, years to search, DOB; also helpful: address, SSN. Criminal records on computer from 1989, prior in books.

General Information: Public access terminal is available. No sealed records released. Copy fee: $.25 per page. Certification fee: $3.00. Fee payee: Municipal Court. Only cashiers checks and money orders accepted. Prepayment is required.

Paulding County

Common Pleas Court 115 N Williams St Rm 104, Paulding, OH 45879; 419-399-8210; Probate phone: 419-339-8256; Fax: 419-399-8248. Hours: 8AM-4PM (EST). *Felony, Civil Actions Over $3,000, Probate.*

Civil Records: Access: Fax, mail, in person. Both court and visitors may perform in person searches. Search fee: $5.00 per name. Required to search: name, years to search. Civil cases indexed by defendant, plaintiff. Civil records in books, archived from 1800s.

Criminal Records: Access: Fax, mail, in person. Both court and visitors may perform in person searches. Search fee: $5.00 per name. Required to search: name, years to search; also helpful: address, DOB, SSN. Criminal records in books, archived from 1800s.

General Information: No mental, adoption records released. SASE required. Turnaround time same day. Fax notes: No fee to fax results. Copy fee: $.25 per page. Certification fee: $1.00. Fee payee: Clerk of Court. Personal checks accepted. Prepayment is required.

County Court 201 E Carolina St, #2, Paulding, OH 45879; 419-399-5370; Fax: 419-399-3421. Hours: 8AM-4PM (EST). *Misdemeanor, Civil Actions Under $15,000, Small Claims.*

Civil Records: Access: Fax, mail, in person. Both court and visitors may perform in person searches. Search fee: $5.00 per name. Required to search: name, years to search; also helpful: address. Civil cases indexed by defendant, plaintiff. Civil records in books since 1985; computerized records since 1997.

Criminal Records: Access: Fax, mail, in person. Both court and visitors may perform in person searches. Search fee: $5.00 per name. Required to search: name, years to search; also helpful: address, DOB, SSN. Criminal records in books since 1985; computerized records since 1997.

General Information: Public access terminal is available. SASE required. Turnaround time 2-4 days. Fax notes: No fee to fax results. Copy fee: $.50 per page. Certification fee: $2.00. Fee payee: County Court. Personal checks accepted. Prepayment is required.

Perry County

Common Pleas Court PO Box 67, New Lexington, OH 43764; 740-342-1022; Probate phone: 740-342-1493. Hours: 8AM-4PM (EST). *Felony, Civil Actions Over $3,000, Probate.*

Civil Records: Access: In person only. Visitors must perform in person searches for themselves. No search fee. Required to search: name, years to search; also helpful: address. Civil cases indexed by defendant, plaintiff. Civil records on computer since 3/96, in case files prior, indexed from 1940.

Criminal Records: Access: In person only. Visitors must perform in person searches for themselves. No search fee. Required to search: name, years to search; also helpful: address, DOB, SSN. Criminal records on computer since 3/96, in case files prior, indexed from 1940.

General Information: Public access terminal is available. Copy fee: $.05 per page. Certification fee: $1.00 per certification. Fee payee: Clerk of Court. Personal checks accepted. Prepayment is required.

Perry County Court PO Box 207, New Lexington, OH 43764-0207; 740-342-3156; Fax: 740-342-2189. Hours: 8:30AM-4:30PM M,W,F (EST). *Misdemeanor, Civil Actions Under $15,000, Small Claims.*

Civil Records: Access: In person only. Visitors must perform in person searches for themselves. No search fee. Required to search: name, years to search. Civil cases indexed by defendant, plaintiff. Civil records in books 10 to 12 years, computerized since 04/97.

Criminal Records: Access: In person only. Visitors must perform in person searches for themselves. No search fee. Required to search: name, years to search, DOB, SSN, signed release. Criminal records in books 10 to 12 years, computerized since 04/97.

General Information: Public access terminal is available. All records are public. Copy fee: $.10 per page. Certification fee: $1.00. Fee payee: Perry County Court. Personal checks accepted. Prepayment required.

Pickaway County

Common Pleas Court County Courthouse, 207 Court Street PO Box 270, Circleville, OH 43113; 740-474-5231; Probate phone: 740-474-3950. Hours: 8AM-4PM (EST). *Felony, Civil Actions Over $10,000, Probate.*

Civil Records: Access: Mail, in person. Both court and visitors may perform in person searches. No search fee. Required to search: name, years to search; also helpful: address. Civil cases indexed by defendant. Civil records on computer back to 1988, indexed to 1940s, archived from 1800s.

Criminal Records: Access: Mail, in person. Both court and visitors may perform in person searches. No search fee. Required to search: name, years to search; also helpful: address, DOB, SSN. Criminal records on computer back to 1988, indexed to 1940s, archived from 1800s.

General Information: Public access terminal is available. SASE required. Turnaround time 2-3 days. Copy fee: $.25 per page. Certification fee: $1.00 per page. Fee payee: Clerk of Court. Prepayment is required.

Circleville Municipal Court PO Box 128, Circleville, OH 43113; 740-474-3171; Fax: 740-477-8291. Hours: 8AM-4PM (EST). *Misdemeanor, Civil Actions Under $15,000, Eviction, Small Claims.*

Civil Records: Access: Phone, fax, mail, in person. Both court and visitors may perform in person searches. No search fee. Required to search: name, years to search. Civil cases indexed by defendant, plaintiff. Civil records on computer from 1989, prior in books.

Criminal Records: Access: Phone, fax, mail, in person. Both court and visitors may perform in person searches. No search fee. Required to search: name, years to search; also helpful: SSN. Criminal records on computer from 1987, prior in books back to 1983.

General Information: Public access terminal is available. No warrant records released. SASE required. Turnaround time 1-2 days. Copy fee: $.50 per page. Fee payee: Circleville Municipal Court. Personal checks accepted. Credit cards accepted: Visa, MasterCard. Prepayment is required.

Pike County

Common Pleas Court 100 East 2nd St, Waverly, OH 45690; 740-947-2715; Probate phone: 740-947-2560; Fax: 740-947-1729. Hours: 8:30AM-4PM (EST). *Felony, Civil Actions Over $15,000, Probate.*

Note: Probate is a separate court at the number given.

Civil Records: Access: In person only. Visitors must perform in person searches for themselves. No search fee. Required to search: name, years to search; also helpful: address. Civil cases indexed by defendant, plaintiff. Civil records in books back to 1815; on comptuer back to 1999.

Criminal Records: Access: In person only. Visitors must perform in person searches for themselves. No search fee. Required to search: name, years to search; also helpful: address, DOB, SSN. Criminal records in books back to 1815; on computer back to 1999.

General Information: No grand jury secret indictment records released. Copy fee: $.25 per page. Certification fee: $1.00. Fee payee: Clerk of Court. Personal checks accepted. Prepayment is required.

Pike County Court 230 Waverly Plaza, #900, Waverly, OH 45690; Criminal phone: 740-947-4003. Hours: 8:30AM-4PM (EST). *Misdemeanor, Civil Actions Under $15,000, Small Claims.*

Civil Records: Access: Phone, fax, mail, in person. Both court and visitors may perform in person searches. No search fee. Required to search: name, years to search. Civil cases indexed by defendant, plaintiff. Civil records in books indexed to 1958 1960.

Criminal Records: Access: Phone, fax, mail, in person. Both court and visitors may perform in person searches. No search fee. Required to search: name, years to search. Criminal records in books indexed to 1958, computerized since 1996.

General Information: Public access terminal is available. No sealed or expunged records released. SASE required. Turnaround time 1 week. Copy fee: $1.00 per page. Fee payee: Pike County Court. Personal checks accepted. Prepayment is required.

Portage County

Common Pleas Court PO Box 1035, Ravenna, OH 44266; 330-297-3644; Probate phone: 330-297-3870; Fax: 330-297-4554. Hours: 8AM-4PM (EST). *Felony, Civil Actions Over $10,000, Probate.*

Note: Probate Court address is PO Box 936, Ravenna, OH 44266-0936.

Civil Records: Access: In person only. Visitors must perform in person searches for themselves. No search fee. Required to search: name, years to search; also helpful: address. Civil cases indexed by defendant. Civil records on computer back to 1991, prior in books.

Criminal Records: Access: In person only. Visitors must perform in person searches for themselves. No search fee. Required to search: name, years to search; also helpful: address, DOB, SSN. Criminal records on computer back to 1991, prior in books.

General Information: Public access terminal is available. Copy fee: $.10 per page. Certification fee: $1.00. Fee payee: Clerk of Court. Personal checks accepted. Monthly accounts available.

Portage County Municipal Court PO Box 958, Ravenna, OH 44266; Civil phone: 330-297-3635; Criminal phone: 330-297-3639; Fax: 330-297-3526 (civ); 297-5867 (crim). Hours: 8AM-4PM (EST). *Misdemeanor, Civil Actions Under $15,000, Eviction, Small Claims.*

Civil Records: Access: In person only. Visitors must perform in person searches for themselves. No search fee. Required to search: name, years to search; also helpful: address. Civil cases indexed by defendant, plaintiff. Civil records on computer from 1992.
Criminal Records: Access: In person only. Visitors must perform in person searches for themselves. No search fee. Required to search: name, years to search; also helpful: address, DOB, SSN. Criminal records on computer from 1992.
General Information: Public access terminal is available. No records released. Copy fee: $.25 per page. Certification fee: $1.00. Fee payee: Municipal Court. Personal checks accepted.

Portage Municipal Court - Kent Branch 214 S Water, Kent, OH 44240; 330-678-9170/9101; Fax: 330-677-9944. Hours: 8AM-4PM (EST). *Misdemeanor, Civil Actions Under $15,000, Eviction, Small Claims.*

Civil Records: Access: In person only. Search fee: $1.00 per name. Required to search: name, years to search; also helpful: address. Civil cases indexed by defendant, plaintiff. Civil records on computer from 1992, prior in books.
Criminal Records: Access: In person only. Both court and visitors may perform in person searches. Search fee: $1.00 per name per year. Required to search: name, years to search; also helpful: address, DOB, SSN. Criminal records on computer from 1992, prior in books.
General Information: Public access terminal is available. No expunged records released. Copy fee: $.25 per page. Certification fee: $1.00. Fee payee: Portage County Municipal Court. Personal checks accepted. Credit cards accepted: Visa, MasterCard. Accepted for criminal only, and only if "in person". Prepayment is required.

Preble County

Common Pleas Court 101 E Main, 3rd Fl, Eaton, OH 45320; 937-456-8160; 456-8165 (common pleas); Probate phone: 937-456-8138; Fax: 937-456-9548. Hours: 8AM-4:30PM (EST). *Felony, Civil, Probate.*

Note: Probate office is separate from this court.

Civil Records: Access: In person only. Visitors must perform in person searches for themselves. No search fee. Required to search: name, years to search; also helpful: address. Civil cases indexed by defendant, plaintiff. Civil records on computer from 11/89, prior in books indexed to 1940s.
Criminal Records: Access: Mail, in person. Both court and visitors may perform in person searches. Search fee: $3.00 per name. Required to search: name, years to search; also helpful: address, DOB, SSN. Criminal records on computer from 11/89, prior in books indexed to 1940s.
General Information: Public access terminal is available. No secret records released. SASE required. Turnaround time 1 day. Copy fee: $.50 per page. Certification fee: $1.00. Fee payee: Clerk of Court. Personal checks accepted. Prepayment is required.

Eaton Municipal Court PO Box 65 (101 E Main St), Eaton, OH 45320; 937-456-4941/6204; Fax: 937-456-4685. Hours: 8AM-Noon, 1-4:30PM (EST). *Misdemeanor, Civil Actions Under $15,000, Eviction, Small Claims.*

www.eatonmunicipalcourt.com

Civil Records: Access: Mail, in person. Both court and visitors may perform in person searches. No search fee. Required to search: name, years to search. Civil cases indexed by defendant, plaintiff. Civil records on computer from 1989, prior in books indexed to 1959.
Criminal Records: Access: Mail, in person. Both court and visitors may perform in person searches. No search fee. Required to search: name, years to search; also helpful: SSN. Criminal records on computer from 1989, prior in books indexed to 1959.
General Information: Public access terminal is available. (For criminal only) No driving records released. SASE required. Turnaround time 1 week. Copy fee: $1.00 per page. Certification fee: $1.00. Fee payee: Eaton Municipal Court. Personal checks accepted. Credit cards accepted: Visa, MasterCard.

Putnam County

Common Pleas Court 245 E Main, Rm 301, Ottawa, OH 45875; 419-523-3110; Probate phone: 419-523-3012; Fax: 419-523-5284. Hours: 8:30AM-4:30PM (EST). *Felony, Civil Actions Over $3,000, Probate.*

Note: Probate is a separate court at number given.

Civil Records: Access: Fax, mail, in person. Both court and visitors may perform in person searches. Search fee: $10.00 per name. Required to search: name, years to search. Civil cases indexed by defendant, plaintiff. Civil records on computer from 1992 indexed on docket books back to 1800s.
Criminal Records: Access: Fax, mail, in person. Both court and visitors may perform in person searches. Search fee: $10.00 per name. Required to search: name, years to search; also helpful: address, DOB, SSN. Criminal records on computer from 1992 indexed on docket books back to 1800s.
General Information: Public access terminal is available. No sealed records released. SASE required. Turnaround time 1-4 days. Fax notes: No fee to fax results. Copy fee: $.50 per page. Certification fee: $1.00. Fee payee: Clerk of Court. Personal checks accepted. Putnam County personal checks accepted. Prepayment is required. Prepayment not required under $5.00.

Putnam County Court 245 E Main, Rm 303, Ottawa, OH 45875; 419-523-3110; Fax: 419-523-5284. Hours: 8:30AM-4:30PM (EST). *Misdemeanor, Civil Actions Under $15,000, Small Claims.*

Civil Records: Access: Mail, in person, fax. Both court and visitors may perform in person searches. Search fee: $10.00 per name. Required to search: name, years to search. Civil cases indexed by defendant, plaintiff. Civil records go back to 1800's; computerized records go back to 1992.
Criminal Records: Access: Mail, in person. Both court and visitors may perform in person searches. Search fee: $10.00 per name. Required to search: name, years to search. Criminal records go back to 1826; computerized records go back to 1992.
General Information: Public access terminal is available. SASE required. Turnaround time to 4 days. Copy fee: $.50 per page. Certification fee: $4.00. Fee payee: Clerk of Court. Only cashiers checks and money orders accepted. Prepayment is required.

Richland County

Common Pleas Court 50 Park Ave E, 2nd Floor, PO Box 127, Mansfield, OH 44901; 419-774-5549; Probate phone: 419-755-5583. Hours: 8AM-4PM (EST). *Felony, Civil Actions Over $10,000, Probate.*

Civil Records: Access: In person, mail, fax. Both court and visitors may perform in person searches. No search fee. Required to search: name, years to search; also helpful: address. Civil cases indexed by defendant,

plaintiff. Civil records on computer from 1989, prior in books and on microfiche to 1960.
Criminal Records: Access: In person, mail. Both court and visitors may perform in person searches. No search fee. Required to search: name, years to search, DOB, SSN, signed release; also helpful: address. Criminal records on computer from 1991, prior in books and on microfiche to 1960.
General Information: Public access terminal is available. No sealed records released. Copy fee: $.25 per page. Certification fee: $5.00. Fee payee: Clerk of Court. Personal checks accepted. Prepayment is required.

Mansfield Municipal Court PO Box 1228, Mansfield, OH 44901; 419-755-9617; Fax: 419-755-9647. Hours: 8AM-4PM (EST). *Misdemeanor, Civil Actions Under $15,000, Eviction, Small Claims.*

Civil Records: Access: Phone, fax, mail, in person. Both court and visitors may perform in person searches. No search fee. Required to search: name, years to search; also helpful: address. Civil cases indexed by defendant, plaintiff. Criminal records on computer from 1989. Overall records go back to 1940. Phone & fax access limited to short searches.
Criminal Records: Access: Phone, fax, mail, in person. Both court and visitors may perform in person searches. No search fee. Required to search: name, years to search; also helpful: address, DOB, SSN. Criminal records on computer from 1989. Overall records go back to 1940. Same as civil.
General Information: Public access terminal is available. No lead print out records released. SASE required. Turnaround time several 2-3 days. Fax notes: No fee to fax results. Copy fee: $.25 per page. Certification fee: $1.00. Fee payee: Clerk of Court or Mansfield Municipal Court. Personal checks accepted. Prepayment is required.

Ross County

Common Pleas Court County Courthouse, 2 N Paint St, Ste A, Chillicothe, OH 45601; 740-702-3010; Probate phone: 740-774-1179; Fax: 740-702-3018. Hours: 8AM-4PM (EST). *Felony, Civil Actions Over $10,000, Probate.*

Civil Records: Access: In person only. Both court and visitors may perform in person searches. No search fee. Required to search: name, years to search; also helpful: address. Civil cases indexed by defendant, plaintiff. Civil records on computer from 1989, prior in books to 1800s.
Criminal Records: Access: In person only. Both court and visitors may perform in person searches. No search fee. Required to search: name, years to search; also helpful: address, DOB, SSN. Criminal records on computer from 1989, prior in books to 1800s.
General Information: Public access terminal is available. No secret indictment records released. Copy fee: $1.00 per page. Certification fee: $1.00. Fee payee: Clerk of Court. Personal checks accepted. Prepayment is required.

Chillicothe Municipal Court 26 S Paint St, Chillicothe, OH 45601; 740-773-3515; Fax: 740-774-1101. Hours: 7:30AM-4:30PM (EST). *Misdemeanor, Civil Actions Under $15,000, Eviction, Small Claims.*

Civil Records: Access: Mail, in person. Both court and visitors may perform in person searches. No search fee. Required to search: name, years to search; also helpful: address. Civil cases indexed by defendant, plaintiff. Civil records on computer from 6/93, prior in books.
Criminal Records: Access: Mail, in person. Both court and visitors may perform in person searches. No search fee. Required to search: name, years to search, DOB, SSN; also helpful: address. Criminal records on computer from 6/93, prior in books.

General Information: Public access terminal is available. No confidential records released. SASE required. Turnaround time 10 days. Copy fee: $.05 per page. Certification fee: $1.00 per page. Fee payee: Municipal Court. Business checks accepted. Prepayment is required.

Sandusky County

Common Pleas Court 100 N Park Ave, Fremont, OH 43420; 419-334-6161/6163; Probate phone: 419-334-6217; Fax: 419-334-6164. Hours: 8AM-4:30PM (EST). *Felony, Civil Actions Over $3,000, Probate.*

Civil Records: Access: In person only. Visitors must perform in person searches for themselves. No search fee. Required to search: name, years to search; also helpful: address. Civil cases indexed by defendant, plaintiff. Civil records on computer from 1988, prior in books to 1800s.

Criminal Records: Access: In person only. Visitors must perform in person searches for themselves. No search fee. Required to search: name, years to search; also helpful: address, DOB, SSN. Criminal records on computer from 1988, prior in books to 1800s.

General Information: Public access terminal is available. No search warrant records released. Copy fee: $.10 per page. Certification fee: $1.00. Fee payee: Clerk of Court. Personal checks accepted. Prepayment is required.

County Court #1 847 E McPherson Hwy (PO Box 267), Clyde, OH 43410; 419-547-0915; Fax: 419-547-9198. Hours: 8AM-4:30PM (EST). *Misdemeanor, Civil Actions Under $15,000, Small Claims.*

www.sandusky-county.org/NEW/countycourts.asp

Civil Records: Access: Phone, fax, mail, in person. Both court and visitors may perform in person searches. No search fee. Required to search: name, years to search; also helpful: address. Civil cases indexed by defendant, plaintiff. Civil records on computer from 1988, prior in books.

Criminal Records: Access: Phone, fax, mail, in person. Both court and visitors may perform in person searches. No search fee. Required to search: name, years to search, DOB, SSN; also helpful: address. Criminal records on computer from 1988, prior in books.

General Information: SASE required. Turnaround time 2-3 days. Fax notes: No fee to fax results to toll-free number. Copy fee: $.25 per page. Certification fee: $1.00. Fee payee: County Court. Personal checks accepted. Credit cards accepted: Visa, MasterCard. Prepayment is required.

County Court #2 215 W Main St, Woodville, OH 43469; 419-849-3961; Fax: 419-849-3932. Hours: 8AM-4:30PM (EST). *Misdemeanor, Civil Actions Under $15,000, Small Claims.*

www.sandusky-county.org/NEW/countycourts.asp

Civil Records: Access: Phone, fax, mail, in person. Both court and visitors may perform in person searches. No search fee. Required to search: name, years to search; also helpful: address. Civil cases indexed by defendant, plaintiff. Civil records go back to 1983; on computer back to 1998.

Criminal Records: Access: Phone, fax, mail, in person. Only the court performs in person searches. No search fee. Required to search: name, years to search, SSN. Criminal records go back to 1995; on computer back to 1998.

General Information: No confidential records released. SASE required. Turnaround time 10 days, by phone 3 hours. Fax notes: $5.00 per document. Copy fee: $.10 per page. Certification fee: $1.00. Fee payee: County Court. Personal checks accepted. Credit cards accepted: Visa, MasterCard. Prepayment is required.

Fremont Municipal Court PO Box 886, Fremont, OH 43420-0071; 419-332-1579; Fax: 419-332-1570. Hours: 8AM-4:30PM (EST). *Misdemeanor, Civil Actions Under $15,000, Eviction, Small Claims.*

www.sandusky-county.org/NEW/countycourts.asp

Civil Records: Access: Fax, mail, in person. Both court and visitors may perform in person searches. No search fee. Required to search: name, years to search. Civil cases indexed by defendant, plaintiff. Civil records in books from 1960, computerized since 1992.

Criminal Records: Access: Fax, mail, in person. Both court and visitors may perform in person searches. No search fee. Required to search: name, years to search; also helpful: DOB, SSN. Criminal records in books from 1960, computerized since 1992.

General Information: Public access terminal is available. Turnaround time 2 days. Fax notes: No fee to fax results. Local calls only. Copy fee: $.25 per page. Fee payee: Fremont Municipal Court. Only cashiers checks and money orders accepted. Prepayment is required.

Scioto County

Common Pleas Court 602 7th St, Portsmouth, OH 45662; 740-355-8226; Probate phone: 740-355-8243. Hours: 8AM-4:30PM (EST). *Felony, Civil Actions Over $10,000, Probate.*

www.sciotocountycpcourt.org

Note: Probate is a separate office at the same address.

Civil Records: Access: In person, online. Visitors must perform in person searches for themselves. No search fee. Required to search: name, years to search; also helpful: address. Civil cases indexed by defendant, plaintiff. Civil records on computer from 1986, dockets to 1800s. Online access to civil records available free at www.sciotocountycpcourt.org/search.htm. Search by court calendar, quick index, general index or docket sheet.

Criminal Records: Access: In person, online. Visitors must perform in person searches for themselves. No search fee. Required to search: name, years to search; also helpful: address, DOB, SSN. Criminal records on computer from 1986, dockets to 1800s. Online access to criminal records is the same as civil.

General Information: Public access terminal is available. No sealed or secret records released. Fax notes: Fee to fax results is $1.00 per page. Copy fee: $1.00 per page. Certification fee: $1.00 per page. Fee payee: Clerk of Court. Personal checks accepted. Prepayment is required.

Portsmouth Municipal Court 728 2nd St, Portsmouth, OH 45662; 740-354-3283; Fax: 740-353-6645. Hours: 8AM-4PM (EST). *Misdemeanor, Civil Actions Under $15,000, Eviction, Small Claims.*

www.portsmouth-municipal-court.com

Civil Records: Access: Mail, in person, online. Both court and visitors may perform in person searches. Search fee: No fee for computer records search 1989 forward. Required to search: name, years to search. Civil cases indexed by defendant, plaintiff. Criminal records go back to 1985; on computer back to 1995. Online access is available free at www.portsmouth-municipal-court.com/disc.html.

Criminal Records: Access: Mail, in person, online. Both court and visitors may perform in person searches. Search fee: $20.00 per name if search includes years prior to 1989. No fee for computer records search 1989 forward. Required to search: name, years to search, SSN. Criminal records go back to 1985; on computer back to 1995. Online access to criminal records is available free at www.portsmouth-municipal-court.com/disc.html.

General Information: Public access terminal is available. No competency hearing, protection order

records released. SASE required. Turnaround time 2-3 days; older records up to 2 weeks. Fax notes: No fee to fax results. Copy fee: No search fee. Certification fee: $1.00 per page. Fee payee: Portsmouth Municipal Court. Prepayment is required.

Seneca County

Common Pleas Court 103 S Washington St, Tiffin, OH 44883; 419-447-0671; Probate phone: 419-447-3121; Fax: 419-443-7919. Hours: 8:30AM-4:30PM (EST). *Felony, Civil Actions Over $10,000, Probate.*

Civil Records: Access: Phone, fax, mail, in person. Both court and visitors may perform in person searches. No search fee. Required to search: name, years to search; also helpful: address. Civil cases indexed by defendant, plaintiff. Civil records on computer from 1/93, prior in books to 1900s, archived to 1800s.

Criminal Records: Access: Phone, fax, mail, in person. Both court and visitors may perform in person searches. No search fee. Required to search: name, years to search, SSN, date of offense. Criminal records on computer from 1/93, prior in books to 1900s, archived to 1800s.

General Information: Public access terminal is available. No sealed records released. SASE required. Turnaround time 1 week. Fax notes: Fee to fax results is $2.00 per transmission. Copy fee: $.25 per page. Certification fee: $1.00. Fee payee: Clerk of Court. Personal checks accepted. Prepayment is required.

Fostoria Municipal Court PO Box 985, Fostoria, OH 44830; 419-435-8139; Fax: 419-435-1150. Hours: 8:30AM-5PM (EST). *Misdemeanor, Civil Actions Under $15,000, Eviction, Small Claims.*

Civil Records: Access: Phone, fax, mail, in person. Both court and visitors may perform in person searches. No search fee. Required to search: name, years to search. Civil cases indexed by defendant, plaintiff. Civil records computerized since 1987.

Criminal Records: Access: Phone, fax, mail, in person. Both court and visitors may perform in person searches. No search fee. Required to search: name, years to search; also helpful: SSN. Criminal records computerized since 1987.

General Information: Public access terminal is available. Turnaround time 1-2 days. Fax notes: No fee if faxed to local or toll free number. Copy fee: $.10 per page. Certification fee: $1.00 per page. Fee payee: Fostoria Municipal Court. Personal checks accepted. Prepayment is required.

Tiffin Municipal Court PO Box 694, Tiffin, OH 44883; 419-448-5412; Civil phone: 419-448-5418; Criminal phone: 419-448-5411; Fax: 419-448-5419. Hours: 8:30AM-4:30PM (EST). *Misdemeanor, Civil Actions Under $15,000, Eviction, Small Claims.*

Civil Records: Access: Fax, mail, in person. Both court and visitors may perform in person searches. No search fee. Required to search: name, years to search; also helpful: address. Civil cases indexed by defendant, plaintiff. Civil records on computer from 8/90, prior in books.

Criminal Records: Access: Fax, mail, in person. Both court and visitors may perform in person searches. No search fee. Required to search: name, years to search, DOB, SSN, signed release; also helpful: address. Criminal records on computer from 8/90, prior in books.

General Information: Public access terminal is available. (Fee to fax results is $.05 per page.) No expunged records released. SASE required. Turnaround time 3 days. Fax notes: $.25 per page. Copy fee: $.05 per page. Certification fee: $1.00 per page. Fee payee: Municipal Court. Personal checks accepted. Prepayment is required.

Shelby County

Common Pleas Court PO Box 809, Sidney, OH 45365; 937-498-7221; Fax: 937-498-7824. Hours: 8:30AM-4:30PM M-Th; 8:30AM-6PM F (EST). *Felony, Civil Actions Over $10,000, Probate.*

www.co.shelby.oh.us/ClerkCourts/LegalDept.asp

Civil Records: Access: Fax, mail, in person. Both court and visitors may perform in person searches. Search fee: $1.00 per name. Required to search: name, years to search; also helpful: address. Civil cases indexed by defendant, plaintiff. Civil records on computer from 1987, on indexes from 1819.

Criminal Records: Access: Mail, in person. Visitors must perform in person searches for themselves. Search fee: $1.00 per name. Required to search: name, years to search DOB, SSN; also helpful: address. Criminal records on computer from 1987, on indexes from 1819.

General Information: Public access terminal is available. No grand jury tapes released. SASE required. Turnaround time 5 days. Fax notes: Fee to fax results is $3.00 per document. Copy fee: $.25 per page. Certification fee: $4.00. Fee payee: Shelby County Clerk of Courts. Personal checks accepted. Prepayment is required.

Sidney Municipal Court 201 W Poplar, Sidney, OH 45365; 937-498-0011; Fax: 937-498-8179. Hours: 8AM-4:30PM (EST). *Misdemeanor, Civil Actions Under $15,000, Eviction, Small Claims.*

www.sidneyoh.com

Note: Send mail requests to the address above; phone and in person searches are made at the court at 110 W Court St.

Civil Records: Access: Phone, fax, mail, in person. Both court and visitors may perform in person searches. No search fee. Required to search: name, years to search. Civil cases indexed by defendant, plaintiff. Civil records on computer from 1988; prior on books to 1958.

Criminal Records: Access: Phone, fax, mail, in person. Both court and visitors may perform in person searches. No search fee. Required to search: name, years to search; also helpful: address, DOB, SSN. Criminal records on computer from 1988; prior on books to 1958.

General Information: Public access terminal is available. Confidential and probation records are not released. SASE not required. Turnaround time 2 days. Copy fee: $.10 per page. Certification fee: $1.00 per page. Fee payee: Municipal Court. Personal checks accepted. Prepayment is required.

Stark County

Common Pleas Court - Civil Division PO Box 21160, Canton, OH 44701; 330-451-7795; Fax: 330-451-7853. Hours: 8:30AM-4:30PM (EST). *Civil Actions Over $15,000.*

www.starkclerk.org

Civil Records: Access: Phone, fax, mail, in person, online. Both court and visitors may perform in person searches. No search fee. Required to search: name, years to search. Civil cases indexed by defendant, plaintiff. Civil records on computer from 1985, prior in books form 1940s. Online access to the county online case docket database is available free at www.starkclerk.org/docket/index.html. Search by name, case number or SSN.

General Information: Public access terminal is available. No sealed records released. SASE required. Turnaround time up to 1 week. Fax notes: Fee to fax is $2.00 for 1st page, $1.00 each add'l. Copy fee: $.10 per page. Certification fee: $1.00. Fee payee: Clerk of Court. Personal checks accepted. Prepayment is required.

Common Pleas Court - Criminal Division PO Box 21160, Canton, OH 44701-1160; 330-451-7929; Fax: 330-451-7853. Hours: 8:30AM-4:30PM (EST). *Felony.*

www.starkclerk.org

Criminal Records: Access: Mail, in person, online. Both court and visitors may perform in person searches. No search fee. Required to search: name, years to search, DOB, SSN. Criminal records on computer back to 1985, prior in books to 1940s. Online access to the county online case docket database is available free at www.starkclerk.org/docket/index.html. Search by name, case number or SSN.

General Information: Public access terminal is available. No secret, expungment records released. SASE required. Turnaround time up to 2 weeks. Copy fee: $.10 per page. Certification fee: $1.00. Fee payee: Clerk of Courts. Personal checks accepted.

Canton Municipal Court 218 Cleveland Ave SW, PO Box 24218, Canton, OH 44702-4218; 330-489-3203; Fax: 330-489-3075 (civil) 489-3372 (criminal). Hours: 8AM-4:30PM (EST). *Misdemeanor, Civil Actions Under $15,000, Eviction, Small Claims.*

www.cantoncourt.org

Civil Records: Access: Phone, fax, mail, in person. Both court and visitors may perform in person searches. No search fee. Required to search: name, years to search. Civil cases indexed by defendant, plaintiff. Civil records on computer from 1991, prior in books to 1928.

Criminal Records: Access: Phone, fax, mail, in person. Both court and visitors may perform in person searches. No search fee. Required to search: name, years to search; also helpful: DOB, SSN. Criminal records on computer from 1986, books to 1928.

General Information: Public access terminal is available. No sealed records released. SASE required. Turnaround time 1-2 days. Fax notes: No fee to fax results. Copy fee: $.25 per page. Fee payee: Municipal Court. Personal checks accepted. Prepayment is required.

Massillon Municipal Court Two James Duncan Plaza, Massillion, OH 44646-6690; Civil phone: 330-830-1731; Criminal phone: 330-830-1732; Fax: 330-830-3648. Hours: 8:30AM-4:30PM (EST). *Misdemeanor, Civil Actions Under $15,000, Eviction, Small Claims.*

Civil Records: Access: Fax, mail, in person. Both court and visitors may perform in person searches. No search fee. Required to search: name. Civil cases indexed by defendant, plaintiff. Civil records on docket books from 1986, some records computerized.

Criminal Records: Access: Fax, mail, in person. Both court and visitors may perform in person searches. No search fee. Required to search: name, years to search; also helpful: DOB, SSN. computerized since 1991.

General Information: Public access terminal is available. (Criminal only.) Turnaround time 1 week. Fax notes: No fee to fax results. Copy fee: $.05 per page. Certification fee: $2.00 per page. Fee payee: Massillion Clerk of Court. Personal checks accepted. Prepayment is required.

Summit County

Common Pleas Court 209 S High St, Akron, OH 44308; 330-643-2201 (Divorce); Civil phone: 330-643-2217; Criminal phone: 330-643-2282; Probate phone: 330-643-2350; Fax: 330-643-7772. Hours: 9:30AM-4:15PM (EST). *Felony, Civil Actions Over $10,000, Probate.*

Note: Probate is a separate court at the phone number above.

Civil Records: Access: Mail, in person, online. Both court and visitors may perform in person searches. No search fee. Required to search: name, years to search. Civil cases indexed by defendant, plaintiff. Civil records on computer from 1982, prior in books, some microfiche. Access to County clerk of courts records is available free at www.cpclerk.co.summit.oh.us. Click on "Case Search.".

Criminal Records: Access: Mail, in person, online. Both court and visitors may perform in person searches. Search fee: $2.00 per name. Required to search: name, years to search, DOB; also helpful: SSN. Criminal records on computer from 1982, prior in books, some microfiche. Access to County clerk of courts records is available free at www.cpclerk.co.summit.oh.us. Click on "Case Search."

General Information: No secret indictment records released. SASE required. Turnaround time 1 week. Copy fee: $.05 per page. Certification fee: $1.00 per page. Fee payee: Clerk of Court. Only cashiers checks and money orders accepted. Prepayment is required.

Akron Municipal Court 217 S High St, Rm 837, Akron, OH 44308; Civil phone: 330-375-2920; Criminal phone: 330-375-2570; Fax: 330-375-2427. Hours: 8AM-4:30PM (EST). *Misdemeanor, Civil Actions Under $15,000, Eviction, Small Claims.*

http://courts.ci.akron.oh.us

Civil Records: Access: Mail, in person, online. Both court and visitors may perform in person searches. No search fee. Required to search: name, years to search. Civil cases indexed by defendant, plaintiff. Civil records on computer from 1988, prior in books to 1975. Online access to civil records is the same as criminal, see below.

Criminal Records: Access: Mail, in person, online. Both court and visitors may perform in person searches. No search fee. Required to search: name, years to search, DOB, SSN. Criminal records on computer from 1988, prior in books to 1960. Online access to court records is available free at http://courts.ci.akron.oh.us/disclaimer.htm.

General Information: Public access terminal is available. No sealed records released. SASE required. Turnaround time to 1 week. Copy fee: $.25 per page. Certification fee: $1.00. Fee payee: Municipal Court. Personal checks accepted. Prepayment is required.

Barberton Municipal Court Municipal Bldg, 576 W Park Ave, Barberton, OH 44203-2584; 330-753-2261; Fax: 330-848-6779. Hours: 8AM-5PM (civ); Crim/traffic to 8PM (EST). *Misdemeanor, Civil Actions Under $15,000, Eviction, Small Claims.*

www.cityofbarberton.com/clerkofcourts

Civil Records: Access: Phone, fax, mail, in person, online. Both court and visitors may perform in person searches. No search fee. Required to search: name, years to search. Civil cases indexed by defendant, plaintiff. Civil records computerized since 1994. Online access to civil records is the same as criminal, below.

Criminal Records: Access: Phone, fax, mail, in person, online. Both court and visitors may perform in person searches. No search fee. Required to search: name, years to search; also helpful: DOB, SSN. Criminal records computerized since 1994. Online records for Barberton, Green, Norton, Franklin, Clinton, Copley and Coventry are available free at http://24.93.200.18/.

General Information: Public access terminal is available. Turnaround time 1 week. Fax notes: No fee to fax results. Copy fee: $.10 per page. Certification fee: $1.00 per page. Fee payee: Barberton Municipal Court. Personal checks accepted. Prepayment is required.

Cuyahoga Falls Municipal Court 2310 Second St, Cuyahoga Falls, OH 44221; 330-971-8280; Civil phone: 330-971-8108; Criminal phone: 330-971-8109; Fax: 330-928-7722. Hours: 8AM-8PM (Criminal), 8AM-4:30PM (Civil) (EST).

Misdemeanor, Civil Actions Under $15,000, Eviction, Small Claims.

www.cfmunicourt.com

Civil Records: Access: Phone, mail, in person. Both court and visitors may perform in person searches. No search fee. Required to search: name, years to search. Civil cases indexed by defendant, plaintiff. Civil records indexed back to 1954. Current court docket information is available free online on the web site.

Criminal Records: Access: Phone, mail, in person. Both court and visitors may perform in person searches. No search fee. Required to search: name; also helpful: SSN. Criminal records indexed back to 1954. Current court docket information is available free online on the web site.

General Information: Public access terminal is available. Turnaround time 1 week. Copy fee: $.05 per page. Certification fee: $1.00 per page. Fee payee: Cuyahoga Falls Municipal Court. Business checks accepted. Prepayment is required.

Trumbull County

Common Pleas Court 160 High St, Warren, OH 44481; 330-675-2557; Probate phone: 330-675-2521. Hours: 8:30AM-4:30PM (EST). *Felony, Civil Actions Over $10,000, Probate.*

www.clerk.co.trumbull.oh.us

Civil Records: Access: Phone, mail, in person, online. Both court and visitors may perform in person searches. Search fee: $5.00 per name. Required to search: name, years to search. Civil cases indexed by defendant, plaintiff. Civil records indexed in books from 1977, archived from 1800s; on computer back to 5/96. Online access to court records is available free at www.clerk.co.trumbull.oh.us/search/search.htm. Records go back to May, 1996. Online access to probate court records is available free at www.trumbullprobate.org/paccessfront.htm.

Criminal Records: Access: Mail, in person, online. Both court and visitors may perform in person searches. Search fee: $5.00 per name. Required to search: name, years to search, DOB, SSN, signed release. Criminal records indexed in books from 1977, archived from 1800s; on computer back to 5/96. Online access to criminal records is the same as civil.

General Information: Public access terminal is available. No secret or sealed records released. SASE required. Turnaround time 1 week. Copy fee: $.10 per page. Certification fee: $1.00 per page. Fee payee: Clerk of Court. Business checks accepted. Prepayment is required.

Trumbull County Court Central 180 N Mecca St, Cortland, OH 44410; 330-637-5023; Fax: 330-637-5021. Hours: 8AM-4PM (EST). *Misdemeanor, Civil Actions Under $15,000, Eviction, Small Claims.*

Civil Records: Access: Phone, fax, mail, in person. Both court and visitors may perform in person searches. No search fee. Required to search: name, years to search.

Criminal Records: Access: Phone, fax, mail, in person. Both court and visitors may perform in person searches. No search fee. Required to search: name, years to search; also helpful: DOB, SSN. Same record keeping as civil.

General Information: Public access terminal is available. Turnaround time is 1-2 days. Fax notes: No fee to fax results. Local calls only. Copy fee: $.25 per page. Certification fee: $2.00 per page. Fee payee: Trumbull County Court Central. Personal checks accepted. Credit cards accepted: Visa, MasterCard. In person only. Prepayment is required.

Trumbull County Court East 7130 Brookwood Dr, Brookfield, OH 44403; 330-448-1726;

Fax: 330-448-6310. Hours: 8:30AM-4:30PM (EST). *Misdemeanor, Civil Under $15,000, Eviction, Small Claims.*

Civil Records: Access: Phone, fax, mail, in person. Both court and visitors may perform in person searches. No search fee. Required to search: name, years to search.

Criminal Records: Access: Phone, fax, mail, in person. Both court and visitors may perform in person searches. No search fee. Required to search: name, years to search; also helpful: DOB, SSN. Criminal Records in docket books since 1990, computerized since 1994.

General Information: Public access terminal is available. Turnaround time 1-2 days. Fax notes: No fee to fax results. Local calls only. Copy fee: $.25 per page. Fee payee: Trumbull County Court East. Personal checks accepted. Credit cards accepted: Visa, MasterCard. Prepayment is required.

Girard Municipal Court City Hall, 100 N Market St, #A, Girard, OH 44420-2559; Civil phone: 330-545-3177; Criminal phone: 330-545-0069; Fax: 330-545-7045. Hours: 8AM-4PM (EST). *Misdemeanor, Civil Actions Under $15,000, Eviction, Small Claims.*

Note: Traffic Records at 330-545-3049.

Civil Records: Access: Fax, mail, in person. Both court and visitors may perform in person searches. No search fee. Required to search: name, years to search. Civil cases indexed by defendant, plaintiff. Civil records on books since 1964, computerized since 09/96.

Criminal Records: Access: Fax, mail, in person. Both court and visitors may perform in person searches. No search fee. Required to search: name, years to search; also helpful: DOB, SSN. Criminal records on books since 1964, computerized since 09/96.

General Information: Public access terminal is available. Turnaround time 1 week. Fax notes: No fee to fax results. Copy fee: $1.00 per page 1st 10; $.10 per page each add'l. Certification fee: $10.00 per page. Fee payee: Girard Municipal Court. Business checks accepted. Prepayment is required.

Newton Falls Municipal Court 19 N Canal St, Newton Falls, OH 44444-1302; 330-872-0302; Fax: 330-872-3899. Hours: 8AM-4:30PM (EST). *Misdemeanor, Civil Actions Under $15,000, Eviction, Small Claims.*

Civil Records: Access: Fax, mail, in person. Both court and visitors may perform in person searches. No search fee. Required to search: name, years to search. Civil cases indexed by defendant, plaintiff. Civil records in books since 1970, computerized since 1992.

Criminal Records: Access: Fax, mail, in person. Both court and visitors may perform in person searches. No search fee. Required to search: name, years to search; also helpful: DOB, SSN. Criminal records in books since 1970, computerized since 1992.

General Information: Fax notes: No fee to fax results. Local calls only. Copy fee: $.10 per page. Certification fee: $1.00. Fee payee: Newton Falls Municipal Court. Only cashiers checks and money orders accepted. Prepayment is required.

Niles Municipal Court 15 East State St, Niles, OH 44446-5051; 330-652-5863; Fax: 330-544-9025. Hours: 8AM-4PM (EST). *Misdemeanor, Civil Actions Under $15,000, Eviction, Small Claims.*

Civil Records: Access: Fax, mail, in person. Both court and visitors may perform in person searches. Search fee: $10.00 per name. Required to search: name, years to search. Civil cases indexed by defendant, plaintiff. Civil records on computer since 10/96, in books since 1990, in storage from 1930.

Criminal Records: Access: Fax, mail, in person. Both court and visitors may perform in person searches. Search fee: $10.00 per name. Required to search: name,

years to search; also helpful: DOB, SSN. Criminal records on computer since 10/96, in books since 1990, in storage from 1930.

General Information: Public access terminal is available. Turnaround time will vary. Fax notes: No fee to fax results. Local calls only. Fee payee: Niles Municipal Court. Only cashiers checks and money orders accepted. Prepayment is required.

Warren Municipal Court 141 South St SE (PO Box 1550), Warren, OH 44482; Civil phone: 330-841-2527; Criminal phone: 330-841-2666; Fax: 330-841-2760. Hours: 8AM-4:30PM (EST). *Misdemeanor, Civil Actions Under $15,000, Eviction, Small Claims.*

Civil Records: Access: Fax, mail, in person. Both court and visitors may perform in person searches. No search fee. Required to search: name, years to search; also helpful: address. Civil cases indexed by defendant, plaintiff. Civil records on computer since 1995; prior in books to 1978.

Criminal Records: Access: Fax, mail, in person. Both court and visitors may perform in person searches. No search fee. Required to search: name, years to search, DOB, SSN, signed release; also helpful: address. Criminal records on computer since 1995; prior in books to 1978.

General Information: Public access terminal is available. No open case records released. SASE required. Turnaround time to 1-5 days. Fax notes: No fee to fax results. Copy fee: $.25 per page. Certification fee: $1.00 per document. Fee payee: Warren Municipal Court. Personal checks accepted. Credit cards accepted: Visa, MasterCard. Prepayment is required.

Tuscarawas County

Common Pleas Court 125 E High (PO Box 628), New Philadelphia, OH 44663; 330-364-8811 X243; Fax: 330-343-4682. Hours: 8AM-4:30PM (EST). *Felony, Civil Actions Over $15,000, Probate.*

www.co.tuscarawas.oh.us

Note: Probate is a separate court at 101 E High Ave.

Civil Records: Access: In person only. Visitors must perform in person searches for themselves. No search fee. Required to search: name, years to search; also helpful: address. Civil cases indexed by defendant, plaintiff. Civil records on computer from 1987, prior in books to 1808, archived prior.

Criminal Records: Access: In person only. Visitors must perform in person searches for themselves. No search fee. Required to search: name, years to search; also helpful: address, DOB, SSN. Criminal recods go back to 1868, criminal records on computer from 1987, prior in books to 1808, archived prior.

General Information: Public access terminal is available. Fax notes: Fee to fax results is $2.00 per document plus $1.00 per page. Copy fee: $.10 per page. Certification fee: $1.00 per page. Fee payee: Clerk of Court. Personal checks accepted. Credit cards accepted: Visa, MasterCard. Visa, MC. Prepayment is required.

County Court 220 E 3rd, Uhrichsville, OH 44683; 740-922-4795; Fax: 740-922-7020. Hours: 8AM-4:30PM (EST). *Misdemeanor, Civil Actions Under $15,000, Small Claims.*

Note: Probation Office phone: 740-922-3653 & 922-4360. Probation Office hours: 8AM-4:30PM.

Civil Records: Access: Fax, mail, in perso, fax. Both court and visitors may perform in person searches. No search fee. Required to search: name, years to search. Civil cases indexed by defendant, plaintiff. Civil records go back toi 19700's, civil records on computer from 2/94, prior in books.

Criminal Records: Access: Fax, mail, in person. Both court and visitors may perform in person searches. No search fee. Required to search: name, years to search,

DOB; also helpful: SSN. Criminal records on computer from 2/94, prior in books.

General Information: Public access terminal is available. SASE required. Turnaround time 1-2 days. Fax notes: No fee to fax results. Local faxing only. Copy fee: $1.00 per page. Fee payee: Tuscarawas County Court. Personal checks accepted. Tuscarawas County personal checks accepted. Prepayment is required.

New Philadelphia Municipal Court 166 E High Ave, New Philadelphia, OH 44663; 330-364-4491; Fax: 330-364-6885. Hours: 8AM-4:30PM (EST). *Misdemeanor, Civil Actions Under $15,000, Eviction, Small Claims.*

www.newphilaoh.com

Civil Records: Access: Mail, in person. Visitors must perform in person searches for themselves. No search fee. Required to search: name, years to search. Civil cases indexed by defendant, plaintiff. Civil records on computer back to 4/91, prior in books to 1976.

Criminal Records: Access: In person only. Visitors must perform in person searches for themselves. No search fee. Required to search: name, years to search, SSN. Criminal records on computer back to 4/91, prior in books to 1976.

General Information: Public access terminal is available. SASE required. Turnaround time 1-2 days. Copy fee: $.25 per page after first 10 free. Certification fee: $1.00 per page. Fee payee: Municipal Court. Personal checks accepted. Credit cards accepted: Visa, MasterCard. Prepayment is required.

Union County

Common Pleas Court County Courthouse, Clerk of Courts, 215 W 5th, PO Box 605, Marysville, OH 43040; 937-645-3006; Fax: 937-645-3162. Hours: 8:30AM-4PM (EST). *Felony, Civil Actions Over $10,000, Probate.*

www.co.union.oh.us/Clerk_of_Courts/clerk_of_courts.html

Civil Records: Access: In person, online. Visitors must perform in person searches for themselves. Required to search: name, years to search; also helpful: address. Civil cases indexed by defendant, plaintiff. Civil records on computer from 1990, records go back to 1850. Online access to the court clerk's public record and index is available free at http://www2.co.union.oh.us/clerkofcourts. Records go back to 1/1990, older added as accessed. Images go back to 1/2002.

Criminal Records: Access: Mail, in person, online. Visitors must perform in person searches for themselves. Search fee: $5.00 per name. Required to search: name, years to search, DOB, SSN; also helpful: address. Criminal records on computer from 1990, records go back to 1850. Online access to the court clerk's public record and index is available free at http://www2.co.union.oh.us/clerkofcourts. Records go back to 1/1990, older added as accessed. Images go back to 1/2002.

General Information: Public access terminal is available. Turnaround time 2 days. Fax notes: Fee to fax is $2.00 1st pg; $1.00 each add'l pg. Copy fee: $.50 per page. Certification fee: $1.00. Fee payee: Clerk of Court. Only cashiers checks and money orders accepted. Prepayment is required.

Marysville Municipal Court 125 East 6th Street, Marysville, OH 43040; 937-644-9102; Fax: 937-644-1228. Hours: 8AM-4PM (EST). *Misdemeanor, Civil Actions Under $15,000, Eviction, Small Claims.*

Civil Records: Access: Phone, fax, mail, in person. Both court and visitors may perform in person searches. No search fee. Required to search: name, years to search. Civil cases indexed by defendant, plaintiff. Civil records on computer from 1989, prior on microfilm.

Criminal Records: Access: Phone, fax, mail, in person. Both court and visitors may perform in person searches. No search fee. Required to search: name, years to search; also helpful: SSN. Criminal records on computer from 1989, prior on microfilm.

General Information: Public access terminal is available. No probation records released. SASE required. Turnaround time 1-2 days. Fax notes: No fee to fax results. No copy fee. No out-of-town checks accepted. Union County personal checks accepted. Credit cards accepted: Visa, MasterCard.

Van Wert County

Common Pleas Court 305 Courthouse, 121 E Main St, Van Wert, OH 45891; 419-238-6935; Probate phone: 419-238-0027; Fax: 419-238-2874; Clerk- 238-4760. Hours: 8AM-4PM (EST). *Felony, Civil Actions, Probate.*

www.vwcommonpleas.org

Note: Probate records are at the same address; call 419-238-0027.

Civil Records: Access: In person only. Visitors must perform in person searches for themselves. No search fee. Required to search: name, years to search. Civil cases indexed by defendant, plaintiff. Some early records on microfiche, have docket books and files, indexed on computer since 05/98. Court calendar available online.

Criminal Records: Access: In person only. Visitors must perform in person searches for themselves. No search fee. Required to search: name, years to search; also helpful: address, DOB, SSN. Some early years on microfiche, have docket books and files, indexed on computer since 05/98. Court calendar available online.

General Information: Public access terminal is available. (Records available from 05/98.) All records public. Copy fee: $.15 per page. Certification fee: $1.00. Fee payee: Clerk of Court. Personal checks accepted. Prepayment is required.

Van Wert Municipal Court 124 S Market, Van Wert, OH 45891; 419-238-5767. Hours: 8AM-4PM (EST). *Misdemeanor, Civil Actions Under $15,000, Eviction, Small Claims.*

Civil Records: Access: Mail, in person. Both court and visitors may perform in person searches. No search fee. Required to search: name, years to search. Civil cases indexed by defendant, plaintiff. Civil records on computer from 1989.

Criminal Records: Access: Mail, in person. Both court and visitors may perform in person searches. No search fee. Required to search: name, years to search; also helpful: SSN. Criminal records on computer from 1989.

General Information: Public access terminal is available. SASE required. Turnaround time 1-2 days. Fax notes: Fee to fax results is $1.00 per page. Copy fee: $1.00 per page. Certification fee: $1.00. Fee payee: Municipal Court. Personal checks accepted. Prepayment is required.

Vinton County

Common Pleas Court County Courthouse, 100 E Main St, McArthur, OH 45651; 740-596-3001; Probate phone: 740-596-3438; Fax: 740-596-9611. Hours: 8:30AM-4PM M-F (EST). *Felony, Civil Actions Over $3,000, Probate.*

Civil Records: Access: Mail, in person. Both court and visitors may perform in person searches. No search fee. Required to search: name, years to search. Civil cases indexed by defendant, plaintiff. Civil records in books since 1850.

Criminal Records: Access: Mail, in person. Both court and visitors may perform in person searches. No search fee. Required to search: name, years to search; also helpful: DOB, SSN. Criminal records in books since 1850.

General Information: No sealed records released. SASE required. Turnaround time 2-3 days. Copy fee: $.25 per page. Certification fee: $2.00. Fee payee: Clerk of Court. Personal checks accepted. Prepayment is required.

Vinton County Court County Courthouse, McArthur, OH 45651; 740-596-5000; Fax: 740-596-9721. Hours: 8:30AM-4PM (EST). *Misdemeanor, Civil Actions Under $15,000, Small Claims.*

Civil Records: Access: Phone, mail, in person. Both court and visitors may perform in person searches. No search fee. Required to search: name, years to search. Civil cases indexed by defendant, plaintiff. Civil records in books from 1980s, archived from 1800s.

Criminal Records: Access: Phone, mail, in person. Both court and visitors may perform in person searches. No search fee. Required to search: name, years to search, DOB; also helpful: SSN. Criminal records in books from 1980s, archived from 1800s.

General Information: SASE required. Turnaround time 1-2 days. No copy fee. Only cashiers checks and money orders accepted.

Warren County

Common Pleas Court PO Box 238, Lebanon, OH 45036; 513-695-1120; Probate phone: 513-695-1180; Fax: 513-695-2965. Hours: 8:30AM-4:30PM (EST). *Felony, Civil Actions Over $3,000, Probate.*

Civil Records: Access: Phone, mail, in person. Both court and visitors may perform in person searches. Search fee: $4.00 per name. Required to search: name, years to search. Civil cases indexed by defendant, plaintiff. Civil records on computer from 1974, archived from 1850.

Criminal Records: Access: Mail, in person. Both court and visitors may perform in person searches. Search fee: $4.00 per name. Required to search: name, years to search, DOB, signed release; also helpful: SSN. Criminal records on computer from 1974, archived from 1850.

General Information: Public access terminal is available. SASE required. Turnaround time 1-4 days. Copy fee: $.20 per page. Certification fee: $1.00. Fee payee: Clerk of Court. Personal checks accepted. Prepayment is required.

County Court 550 Justice Dr, Lebanon, OH 45036; 513-695-1370. Hours: 8AM-4:30PM (EST). *Misdemeanor, Civil Actions Under $15,000, Small Claims under $3000.*

www.co.warren.oh.us/countycourt

Civil Records: Access: Phone, mail, in person. Both court and visitors may perform in person searches. No search fee. Required to search: name, years to search; also helpful: address. Civil cases indexed by defendant, plaintiff. Civil records on computer from 1990, prior in books. No in person searches on Tuesdays or Thursdays.

Criminal Records: Access: Phone, mail, in person. Both court and visitors may perform in person searches. No search fee. Required to search: name, years to search, DOB; also helpful: SSN, address. Criminal records on computer from 1990, prior in books. No in person searches on Tuesdays or Thursdays.

General Information: Public access terminal is available. SASE required. Turnaround time 1-2 weeks. Copy fee: $.05 per page. Warren County checks accepted. Credit cards accepted: Visa, MasterCard. Prepayment is required.

Franklin Municipal Court 35 E 4th Street, Franklin, OH 45006-2484; 937-746-2858; Fax: 937-743-7751. Hours: 8:30AM-5PM (EST). *Misdemeanor, Civil Actions Under $15,000, Eviction, Small Claims.*

Civil Records: Access: Phone, fax, mail, in person. Both court and visitors may perform in person searches.

No search fee. Required to search: name, years to search. Civil cases indexed by defendant, plaintiff. Civil records in books since 1955, on computer back to 1990. **Criminal Records:** Access: Phone, fax, mail, in person. Both court and visitors may perform in person searches. No search fee. Required to search: name, years to search, signed release; also helpful: DOB, SSN. Criminal records in books since 1955, on computer back to 1990.

General Information: Turnaround time 1-2 days. Fax notes: Fee to fax results is $10.00 per document. Copy fee: $.50 per page. Certification fee: $1.00. Fee payee: Franklin Municipal Court. Personal checks accepted. Credit cards accepted: Visa, MasterCard. In person only. Prepayment is required.

Lebanon Muncipal Court City Building, 50 S Broadway, Lebanon, OH 45036-1777; 513-932-7210; Fax: 513-933-7212. Hours: 8AM-4PM (EST). *Misdemeanor, Civil Actions, Eviction, Small Claims.*

www.ci.lebanon.oh.us/departments/municourt/index.html

Civil Records: Access: Fax, mail, in person. Both court and visitors may perform in person searches. No search fee. Required to search: name, years to search. Civil cases indexed by defendant, plaintiff. Civil records on books since 1956, computerized since 1990. **Criminal Records:** Access: Fax, mail, in person. Both court and visitors may perform in person searches. No search fee. Required to search: name, years to search; also helpful: DOB, SSN. Criminal records on books since 1956, computerized since 1990.

General Information: Public access terminal is available. Turnaround time 2 days. Fax notes: No fee to fax results. Local calls only. Personal checks accepted. Only for criminal record searching, not civil.

Mason Municipal Court 202 W Main St, Mason, OH 45040-1620; 513-398-7901; Fax: 513-459-8085. Hours: 7:30AM-4PM (EST). *Misdemeanor, Civil Actions Under $15,000, Eviction, Small Claims.*

Civil Records: Access: Phone, fax, mail, in person. Both court and visitors may perform in person searches. Search fee: No search fee. Required to search: name, years to search. Civil cases indexed by defendant, plaintiff. Civil records in docket books since 1985, computerized since 1988. **Criminal Records:** Access: Phone, fax, mail, in person. Both court and visitors may perform in person searches. Search fee: No search fee. Required to search: name, years to search; also helpful: SSN. Criminal records in docket books since 1985, computerized since 1988.

General Information: Turnaround time 1-2 weeks. Fax notes: No fee to fax results. Local calls only. Certification fee: $3.00 per page. Fee payee: Mason Municipal Court. Only cashiers checks and money orders accepted. Credit cards accepted: Visa, MasterCard. In person criminal searching only. Prepayment is required.

Washington County

Common Pleas Court 205 Putnam St, Marietta, OH 45750; 740-373-6623; Probate phone: 740-373-6623. Hours: 8AM-4:15PM (EST). *Felony, Civil Actions Over $10,000, Probate.*

Civil Records: Access: In person only. Visitors must perform in person searches for themselves. No search fee. Required to search: name, years to search. Civil cases indexed by defendant, plaintiff. Civil records on computer since 1985, microfilm to 1977, index in books prior to 1795. **Criminal Records:** Access: In person only. Visitors must perform in person searches for themselves. No search fee. Required to search: name, years to search. Criminal records on computer since 1985, microfilm to 1977, index in books prior to 1795.

General Information: Public access terminal is available. No sealed, expunged records released. Copy fee: $.25 per page. Certification fee: $1.00. Fee payee: Clerk of Court. Personal checks accepted.

Marietta Municipal Court 301 S Putnam (PO Box 615), Marietta, OH 45750; 740-373-4474; Fax: 740-373-2547. Hours: 8AM-5PM (EST). *Misdemeanor, Civil Actions Under $15,000, Eviction, Small Claims.*

www.mariettacourt.com

Civil Records: Access: Mail, in person, online. Both court and visitors may perform in person searches. No search fee. Required to search: name, years to search. Civil cases indexed by defendant, plaintiff. Civil records on computer from 11/91, prior in books. Online access to courts records is to be available free at the web site. **Criminal Records:** Access: Mail, in person, online. Both court and visitors may perform in person searches. No search fee. Required to search: name, years to search. Criminal records on computer from 11/91, prior in books back to 1975. Online access to criminal records is the same as civil.

General Information: Public access terminal is available. SASE required. Turnaround time 1 week. Fax notes: Fee to fax results is $.50 per page. Copy fee: $.05 per page. Certification fee: $1.50. Fee payee: Municipal Court. Personal checks accepted. Prepayment is required.

Wayne County

Common Pleas Court PO Box 507, Wooster, OH 44691; 330-287-5590; Probate phone: 330-287-5575; Fax: 330-287-5416. Hours: 8AM-4:30PM (EST). *Felony, Civil Actions Over $15,000, Probate.*

http://waynecountyclerkofcourts.org/

Note: Probate is a separate court at number given.

Civil Records: Access: Mail, in person. Visitors must perform in person searches for themselves. No search fee. Required to search: name, years to search. Civil cases indexed by defendant, plaintiff. Civil records on computer since 1995, in books to 1800s. No name searches are performed by mail. **Criminal Records:** Access: Mail, in person. Visitors must perform in person searches for themselves. No search fee. Required to search: name, years to search. Criminal records on computer since 1995, in books to 1800s.

General Information: Public access terminal is available. No grand jury indictment records released. Copy fee: $.05 per page. Certification fee: $2.00. Fee payee: Clerk of Court. Personal checks accepted.

Wayne County Municipal Court 538 N Market St, Wooster, OH 44691; 330-287-5650; Fax: 330-263-4043. Hours: 8AM-4:30PM (EST). *Misdemeanor, Civil Actions Under $15,000, Eviction, Small Claims.*

Note: Court is scheduled to move to 215 Grant St in October, 2002.

Civil Records: Access: In person only. Visitors must perform in person searches for themselves. Search fee: No search fee. Required to search: name, years to search. Civil cases indexed by defendant, plaintiff. Civil records on computer back to 9/94; in books from 1975. **Criminal Records:** Access: In person only. Visitors must perform in person searches for themselves. No search fee. Required to search: name, years to search, offense, date of offense. Criminal records on computer back to 9/94; in books from 1975.

General Information: Public access terminal is available. Copy fee: $.10 per page. Certification fee: $2.00. Fee payee: Wayne County Municipal Court. In state personal checks accepted. Prepayment is required.

Williams County

Common Pleas Court 1 Courthouse Square, Clerk of Court of Common Pleas, Bryan, OH 43506; 419-636-1551; Probate phone: 419-636-1548; Fax: 419-636-7877. Hours: 8:30AM-4:30PM (EST). *Felony, Civil Actions Over $10,000, Probate.*

Note: Probate Court is at the same address, different phone number.

Civil Records: Access: Phone, fax, mail, in person. Both court and visitors may perform in person searches. No search fee. Required to search: name, years to search. Civil cases indexed by defendant, plaintiff. Civil records on computer from 1988, all records go back to 1840. **Criminal Records:** Access: Mail, in person. Both court and visitors may perform in person searches. No search fee. Required to search: name, years to search. Criminal records on computer from 1988, records go back to 1840.

General Information: Public access terminal is available. No expunged records released. SASE required. Turnaround time 1-2 days. Copy fee: $.25 per page. Certification fee: $1.00 per page. Fee payee: Clerk of Court. Personal checks accepted. Prepayment is required.

Bryan Municipal Court 1399 E High, PO Box 546, Bryan, OH 43506; 419-636-6939; Fax: 419-636-3417. Hours: 8:30AM-4:30PM (EST). *Misdemeanor, Civil Actions Under $15,000, Eviction, Small Claims.*

Civil Records: Access: Fax, mail, in person. Both court and visitors may perform in person searches. Search fee: $1.00 per name. Required to search: name, years to search. Civil cases indexed by defendant, plaintiff. Civil records on computer from 1988, prior in books to 1966, indexed prior. **Criminal Records:** Access: Fax, mail, in person. Both court and visitors may perform in person searches. Search fee: $1.00 per name. Required to search: name, years to search, DOB; also helpful: SSN. Criminal records on computer from 1988, prior in books to 1966, indexed prior.

General Information: Public access terminal is available. SASE required. Turnaround time 5 days. Fax notes: $2.00. Certification fee: $2.00. Fee payee: Municipal Court. Personal checks accepted. Credit cards accepted: Visa, MasterCard. Prepayment is required.

Wood County

Common Pleas Court Courthouse Square, Bowling Green, OH 43402; 419-354-9280; Probate phone: 419-354-9235; Fax: 419-354-9241. Hours: 8:30AM-4:30PM (EST). *Felony, Civil Actions Over $10,000, Probate.*

Note: Probate record searching and copy fees are different than those listed for civil and criminal records.

Civil Records: Access: Phone, fax, mail, in person. Both court and visitors may perform in person searches. Search fee: $3.00 per name. Required to search: name, years to search. Civil cases indexed by defendant, plaintiff. Civil records on computer from 7/90, in books and on microfilm from 1980, docket books, journals & microfilm back to 1800s. **Criminal Records:** Access: Fax, mail, in person. Both court and visitors may perform in person searches. Search fee: $3.00 per name. Required to search: name, years to search; also helpful: SSN. Criminal records on computer from 7/90, in books and on microfilm from 1980, docket books, journals and microfilm back to 1800s.

General Information: Public access terminal is available. No adoption commitment, parental rights, juvenile, mental illness records released. SASE required. Turnaround time same day. Fax notes: No fee to fax results. Copy fee: $.25 per page first 25 pages, $.10 thereafter. Certification fee: $1.00. Fee payee: Common Pleas Court. Business checks accepted. Prepayment is required.

Bowling Green Municipal Court
PO Box 326, Bowling Green, OH 43402; 419-352-5263; Fax: 419-352-9407. Hours: 8:30AM-4:30PM (EST). *Misdemeanor, Civil Actions Under $15,000, Eviction, Small Claims.*

www.bgcourt.org

Civil Records: Access: Phone, fax, mail, in person, online. Both court and visitors may perform in person searches. No search fee. Required to search: name, years to search. Civil cases indexed by defendant, plaintiff. Civil records on computer from 1988. Online access to be available in Fall, 2002 at the web site.
Criminal Records: Access: Phone, fax, mail, in person, online. Both court and visitors may perform in person searches. No search fee. Required to search: name, years to search, DOB; also helpful: SSN. Criminal records on computer from 1988. Online access to criminal records is the same as civil.
General Information: Public access terminal is available. SASE required. Turnaround time 3 days. Fax notes: No fee to fax results. Local faxing only. Copy fee: $.50 per page. Fee payee: Municipal Court. Personal checks accepted. Credit cards accepted: Visa, MasterCard.

Perrysburg Municipal Court
300 Walnut St, Perrysburg, OH 43551; 419-872-7900; Fax: 419-872-7905. Hours: 8AM-4:30PM (8AM-7PM Tues.) (EST). *Misdemeanor, Civil Actions Under $15,000, Eviction, Small Claims.*

www.perrysburgcourt.com

Civil Records: Access: Phone, fax, mail, online, in person. Both court and visitors may perform in person searches. Search fee: $3.00 per name. Fee is $15.00 to look in closed, stored files. Required to search: name, years to search; also helpful: address. Civil cases indexed by defendant, plaintiff. Civil records on computer from 1989, prior in books to 1982, archived from 1972. Online access to court records is available free at www.perrysburgcourt.com/disc.html.
Criminal Records: Access: Phone, fax, mail, online, in person. Both court and visitors may perform in person searches. Search fee: $3.00 per name. Fee is $15.00 to look in closed, stored files. Required to search: name, years to search; also helpful: DOB, SSN. Criminal records on computer from 1989, prior in books to 1982, archived from 1972. Online access to court records is available free at www.perrysburgcourt.com/disc.html.
General Information: Public access terminal is available. No expunged records released. SASE required. Turnaround time 2 days. Fax notes: Fee to fax results is $5.00 per document. Copy fee: $.10 per page. Certification fee: $3.00. Fee payee: Municipal Court. Personal checks accepted. Credit cards accepted: Visa, MasterCard. Not accepted over the phone. Prepayment is required.

Wyandot County

Common Pleas Court
109 S Sandusky Ave, Upper Sandusky, OH 43351; 419-294-1432; Probate phone: 419-294-2302; Fax: 419-294-6414. Hours: 8:30AM-4:30PM (EST). *Felony, Civil Actions Over $10,000, Probate.*

Civil Records: Access: In person. Visitors must perform in person searches No search fee. Required to search: name, years to search. Civil cases indexed by

defendant, plaintiff. Civil records on computer from 1990, prior in books from late 1800s.
Criminal Records: Access: Fax, mail, in perso, phone. Both court and visitors may perform in person searches. No search fee. Required to search: name, years to search; also helpful: SSN. Criminal records on computer from 1990, prior in books from late 1800s.
General Information: Public access terminal is available. SASE required. Turnaround time 1-2 days. Fax notes: Fo fee to fax results. Copy fee: $.25 per page. Certification fee: $1.00 per page. Fee payee: Clerk of Court. Personal checks accepted. Prepayment required.

Upper Sandusky Municipal Court
119 N 7th St, Upper Sandusky, OH 43351; 419-294-3809; Fax: 419-09-0474. Hours: 8AM-4:30PM (EST). *Misdemeanor, Civil Actions Under $15,000, Eviction, Small Claims.*

Civil Records: Access: Mail, in person. Both court and visitors may perform in person searches. Search fee: $10.00 per name. Required to search: name, years to search. Civil cases indexed by defendant, plaintiff. Civil records on computer from 5/90, prior in books.
Criminal Records: Access: Mail, in person. Both court and visitors may perform in person searches. Search fee: $10.00 per name. Required to search: name, years to search; also helpful: SSN. Criminal records on computer from 5/90, prior in books.
General Information: Public access terminal is available. No sealed records released. SASE required. Turnaround time 1-2 days. Copy fee: $.50 per page. Certification fee: $1.00. Fee payee: Upper Sandusky. Personal checks accepted. Credit cards accepted: Visa, MasterCard. Not accepted over the phone. Prepayment is required.

Ohio Recording Offices

ORGANIZATION: 88 counties, 88 recording offices. The recording officer is County Recorder and Clerk of Common Pleas Court (state tax liens). The entire state is in the Eastern Time Zone (EST).

REAL ESTATE RECORDS: Counties will not perform real estate searches. Copy fees are usually $1.00 per page. Certification usually costs $.50 per document. Tax records are located at the Auditor's Office.

UCC RECORDS: This was a dual filing state. Financing statements were filed both at the state level and with the County Recorder, except for consumer goods, farm related and real estate related collateral, which were filed only with the County Recorder. As of 7/1/2001, only real estate related collateral is filed at the county level. All counties will perform UCC searches. Use search request form UCC-11. Search fees are usually $20.00 per debtor name. Copies usually cost $1.00 per page.

TAX LIEN RECORDS: All federal tax liens are filed with the County Recorder. All state tax liens are filed with the Clerk of Common Pleas Court. Refer to County Court section for information about Ohio courts. Federal tax liens are filed in the "Official Records" of each county. Most counties will not perform a federal tax lien search.

OTHER LIENS: Mechanics, workers compensation, judgment.

ONLINE ACCESS: A growing number of Ohio counties offer online access via the Internet to assessor/real estate data.

Adams County

County Recorder, 110 W. Main, Courthouse, West Union, OH 45693. 937-544-2513 R/E Recording: 937-258-3315 or 544-5051 UCC Recording: 231-258-3315; Fax 937-544-4616.
Will search UCC records. Will not search real estate records. **Other Phone Numbers:** Assessor 937-544-2364; Treasurer 937-544-2317; Appraiser/Auditor 937-544-2364; Elections 937-544-2633; Vital Records 937-544-5547.

Allen County

County Recorder, PO Box 1243, Lima, OH 45802. 419-223-8517; Fax 419-222-8427.
Will search UCC records. This agency will not do a federal tax lien search. Will not search real estate records. **Other Phones:** Treasurer 419-223-8515.

Ashland County

County Recorder, Courthouse, 142 W. 2nd St., Ashland, OH 44805-2193. 419-282-4238; Fax 419-281-5715.
Will search UCC records. This agency will not do a federal tax lien search. Will not search real estate records. **Online Access:** Real Estate, Auditor Records. Property records on the county Auditor's database are available free online at www.ashlandcoauditor.org/ashland208/landrover.asp. **Other Phones:** Treasurer 419-282-4229; Appraiser/Auditor 419-282-4330; Elections 419-181-3172; Vital Records 419-282-4226.

Ashtabula County

County Recorder, 25 W. Jefferson St, Jefferson, OH 44047. County Recorder, R/E -UCC Recording 440-576-3762; Fax 440-576-3231. www.co.ashtabula.oh.us
Will search UCC records. Will not search real estate records. Can give specific information - filed date, deed volume/page, etc. over phone. **Online Access:** Real Estate, Auditor Records. Property records on the county Auditor's database are available free online at http://216.28.192.48/ashtabula208/LandRover.asp.
Other Phones: Treasurer 440-576-3727; Appraiser/Auditor 440-576-3789; Elections 440-576-6915; Vital Records 76-3627; Auditor 576-3783.

Athens County

County Recorder, 15 S Court St, Rm 236, Athens, OH 45701. 740-592-3228; Fax 740-592-3229.
Will search UCC records. Will not search real estate records. **Online Access:** Property, Deed, UCC Records. Access to county land and UCC records is available free at www.landaccess.com. Records go back to 1/1981. **Other Phone Numbers:** Treasurer 740-592-3231; Auditor 740-592-3223.

Auglaize County

County Recorder, Courthouse, Suite 101, 201 S. Willipie St., Wapakoneta, OH 45895-1972. 419-738-4318; Fax 419-738-4115.
Will search UCC records. Will not search real estate records. **Other Phone Numbers:** Treasurer 419-738-2110; Auditor 419-738-2511.

Belmont County

County Recorder, Courthouse, Room 105, 101 Main St., St. Clairsville, OH 43950. 740-699-2140.
Will search UCC records. This agency will not do a tax lien search. Mortgage searches available. **Other Phone Numbers:** Assessor 740-699-2130; Treasurer 740-695-2120 x211; Auditor 740-695-2120 x257.

Brown County

County Recorder, PO Box 149, Georgetown, OH 45121. 937-378-6478 UCC Recording: 937--378-6478; Fax 937-378-2848.
Will search UCC records. Will not search real estate records. **Online Access:** Property, Deed, UCC Records. Access to recordorings is available free at www.landaccess.com/sites/oh/brown/index.php.
Other Phone Numbers: Treasurer 937-378-6705; Appraiser/Auditor 937-378-6398.

Butler County

County Recorder, 130 High St, Hamilton, OH 45011. 513-887-3191 R/E Recording: 513-887-3192; Fax 513-887-3198. www.butlercountyohio.org/recorder
Will search UCC records. This agency will not do a federal tax lien search. Will not search real estate records. **Online Access:** Property, Deed, UCC, Probate, Voter Registration Records. County voter records are available at www.butlercountyohio.org/elections. County probate records are available at www.butlercountyohio.org/probate/estate.cfm. Search auditor records at http://propertysearch.butlercountyohio.org/butler. Also, online access to county land and UCC records is available free at www.landaccess.com. Records go back to 1/1987. Access to dog license tags is at www.butlercountyohio.org/auditor/dl_search.cfm; search county available property records at www.butlercountyohio.org/edabc/availand_index.html.
Other Phones: Treasurer 513-887-3181; Appraiser/Auditor 513-887-3147; Elections 513-887-3700; Vital Records 513-863-1770; Auditor 513-887-3295.

Carroll County

County Recorder, PO Box 550, Carrollton, OH 44615-0550. 330-627-4545; Fax 330-627-4295. www.ohiorecorders.com
Will search UCC records. This agency will not do a tax lien search. Will not search real estate records. **Other Phone Numbers:** Assessor 330-327-2250; Treasurer 330-627-4221; Appraiser/Auditor 330-627-2250; Elections 330-627-2610.

Champaign County

County Recorder, 512 S US Hwy 68 #B200, Urbana, OH 43078. 937-652-2263; Fax 937-652-1515.
Will search UCC records. **Other Phone Numbers:** Auditor 937-652-2264.

Clark County

County Recorder, PO Box 1406, Springfield, OH 45501. County Recorder, R/E and UCC Recording 937-328-2445; Fax 937-328-4620.
Will search UCC records. **Online Access:** Property, Deed, UCC Records. Access to county land and UCC records is available free at www.landaccess.com. Records go back to 1/1988. **Other Phone Numbers:** Treasurer 937-328-2432; Auditor 937-328-2423.

Clermont County

County Recorder, 101 E. Main St, Batavia, OH 45103-2958. County Recorder, R/E and UCC Recording 513-732-7236; Fax 513-732-7891. www.landaccess.com
Will search UCC records. **Online Access:** Property, Deed, UCC Records. Records from the assessor's county property database are available free online at http://clermont.akanda.com. Also, free access to the recorder's property, deed, and UCC records is available at www.landaccess.com/sites/oh/clermont/index.php.
Other Phone Numbers: Assessor 513-732-7150; Treasurer 513-732-7254; Elections 513-732-7275; Auditor 513-732-7150; Commissioners 513-732-7300;

Clinton County

County Recorder, 46 S. South St, Wilmington, OH 45177. 937-382-2067; Fax 937-383-6653.
Will search UCC records. This agency will not do a federal tax lien search. Will not search real estate records. **Other Phone Numbers:** Treasurer 937-382-2224; Elections 937-382-3537; Vital Records 937-382-3829; Auditor 937-382-2250.

Columbiana County

County Recorder, County Courthouse, Room 104, 105 S. Market St., Lisbon, OH 44432. 330-424-9517 x641; Fax 330-424-5067. www.columbianacntyauditor.org Will search UCC records. Will not do lien searches. Will not search real estate records. **Online Access:** Real Estate, Auditor Records. Property records on the county Auditor's database are available free online at www.columbianacntyauditor.org/columbv208/LandRover.asp.

Coshocton County

County Recorder, PO Box 817, Coshocton, OH 43812. County Recorder, R/E and UCC Recording 740-622-2817; Fax 740-622-0190.
Will search UCC records. Will not search real estate records. **Online Access:** Property, Deed, UCC Records. Access to county land and UCC records is available free at www.landaccess.com. Records go back to 1/1980. **Other Phone Numbers:** Treasurer 740-622-2713; Elections 740-622-1117; Auditor 740-622-1243.

Crawford County

County Recorder, PO Box 788, Bucyrus, OH 44820-0788. County Recorder, R/E and UCC Recording 419-562-6961; Fax 419-562-6061.
Will search UCC records. Will not search real estate records. **Other Phones:** Treasurer 419-562-7861; Appraiser/Auditor 562-7941; Elections 419-562-8721.

Cuyahoga County

County Recorder, 1219 Ontario St, Room 220, Cleveland, OH 44113. 216-443-7314 R/E Recording: 216-443-7300, 216-443-8194 UCCs: 216-443-7300; Fax 216-443-8193. www.cuyahoga.oh.us/recorder
Will search UCC records. This agency will not do a federal tax lien search. Will search real estate records. **Online Access:** Auditor/Assessor, Probate, Marriage, Real Estate, Tax Lien, Recording, Dog Tag, Most Wanted, Sexual Predator, Records. Access to the County Auditor Property Information database is available free at http://198.30.214.5/auditor/propinfo/Default.asp. Also, the Recorder's db has all land document records from 1965-2002. Online access to the Recorders database is available free at http://198.30.212.18/presearch.cfm. And, search 22 catagories of Probate records including marriages free at http://198.30.212.11/pa.urd/pamw6500.display. Also, the sexual predator data and most wanted lists are at www.cuyahoga.oh.us/sheriff/law/sou/sou_disclaimer.htm. Foreclosure sales: www.cuyahoga.oh.us/sheriff/foreclosures/sales.htm. Lost dogs: http://198.30.214.5/auditor/genservices/finddog.asp. **Other Phone Numbers:** Appraiser/Auditor 216-443-7092; Vital Records 216-664-2317.

Darke County

County Recorder, 504 S Broadway, Courthouse, Greenville, OH 45331. County Recorder, R/E and UCC Recording 937-547-7390.
Will search UCC records. This agency will not do a federal tax lien search. Will not search real estate records. **Online Access:** Real Estate, Deed, UCC Records. Property records on the Darke County database are available free online at www.darkecountyrealestate.org. Also, online access to county land and UCC records is available free at www.landaccess.com. Records go back to 1/1996. **Other Phone Numbers:** Treasurer 937-547-7365; Auditor 937-547-7310.

Defiance County

County Recorder, 221 Clinton St, Defiance, OH 43512. 419-782-4741; Fax 419-782-3421.
Will search real estate or UCC records. This agency will not do a federal tax lien search.

Delaware County

County Recorder, 91 N. Sandusky St, Courthouse, Delaware, OH 43015. 740-368-1835; Fax 740-833-2459. www.co.delaware.oh.us
Will search UCC records. This agency will not do a federal tax lien search. Will not search real estate records. **Online Access:** Real Estate, Auditor, Sheriff Sales Records. The Delaware Appraisal Land Information System Project (DALIS) maps with County Auditor records are available free online. At main site, click on "GIS mapping" in the lefthand menu bar, then select a search method. Once parcel is identified on the map, click on "identify" then on parcel map to get parcel information, values, sales, and building information. Also, access to the county auditor's property information is available free at www.delawarecountyauditor.org/delaware208/LandRover.asp. Sheriff sales information is available free at www.delawarecountysheriff.com. **Other Phones:** Treasurer 740-833-2460; Auditor 740-833-2460.

Erie County

County Recorder, Erie County Office Bldg, Room 225, 247 Columbus Ave., Sandusky, OH 44870-2635. 419-627-7686; Fax 419-627-6639.
Will search UCC records. UCC search does not include federal tax liens. Will not search real estate records. **Other Phones:** Treasurer 419-627-7201; Appraiser/Auditor 419-627-7746; Auditor 419-627-7741.

Fairfield County

County Recorder, PO Box 2420, Lancaster, OH 43130-5420. 740-687-7100; Fax 740-687-7104. www.co.fairfield.oh.us
Will search UCC records. This agency will not do a federal tax lien search. Will not search real estate records. **Online Access:** Property, Deed, UCC, Auditor Records. Access to county land and UCC records is available free at www.landaccess.com. Records go back to 8/1996. Also, online access to the Auditor's property database is free at http://realestate.co.fairfield.oh.us. Also, access to the sheriff's real estate sale list and sex offenders list is available free at www.sheriff.fairfield.oh.us. **Other Phone Numbers:** Treasurer 740-687-7094; Auditor 740-687-7090.

Fayette County

County Recorder, 133 S Main St, Courthouse Building, Washington Court House, OH 43160-1393. County Recorder, R/E and UCC Recording 740-335-1770; Fax 740-333-3521.
Will search UCC records. Will not search real estate records. **Other Phone Numbers:** Assessor 740-335-6461; Treasurer 740-335-4961; Elections 740-335-1190; Vital Records 740-335-5910.

Franklin County

County Recorder, 373 S. High St, 18th Floor, Columbus, OH 43215-6307. 614-462-3930, 614-462-3378 R/E Recording: 614-462-3930 UCC Recording: 614-462-3937; Fax 614-462-4312, 614-462-4299. www.co.franklin.oh.us/recorder/
Will search UCC records. Will not search real estate records. **Online Access:** Property, Auditor, Unclaimed Funds, Marriage Records. Access to the recordors data is available free at www.co.franklin.oh.us/recorder/documents.html. Free registration required. Search veterans graves at http://mvsp.co.franklin.oh.us:5080/cics/cwba/dfhwbtta/rg11. Search marriage licenses back to 1995 free at www.co.franklin.oh.us/probate/PBMLSearch.html. Also, search unclimed funds at www.co.franklin.oh.us/auditor/fiscal_services/unclaimed%20funds.html. Auditor's property database is at http://64.56.97.159/realestate/; and other county/municipal court databases are at www.co.franklin.oh.us. **Other Phones:** Auditor 614-462-3894.

Fulton County

County Recorder, 152 S Fulton St #175, 210 S. Fulton St., Wauseon, OH 43567. County Recorder, R/E and UCC Recording 419-337-9232; Fax 419-337-9282. www.fultoncountyoh.com
Will search UCC records. This agency will not do a federal tax lien search. Will not search real estate records. **Online Access:** Property, Deed, UCC Records. Access to property, deed, and UCC records is to be available free at www.landaccess.com. **Other Phones:** Treasurer 419-337-9200; Auditor 419-337-9200.

Gallia County

County Recorder, 18 Locust St, Room 1265, Gallipolis, OH 45631-1265. 740-446-4612 x248 R/E Recording: 740-446-4612 UCC Recording: 740-446-4612; Fax 740-446-4804. http://galliaauditor.ddti.net
Will search UCC records. Will not search real estate records. **Online Access:** Property, Real Estate Records. Property records on the county auditor real estate database are available free online at http://galliaauditor.ddti.net. Click on "attributes" for property information; click on "sales" to search by real estate attributes. **Other Phone Numbers:** Treasurer 740-446-6004; Auditor 740-446-4612.

Geauga County

County Recorder, 231 Main St, Ste. 1C, Courthouse Annex, Chardon, OH 44024-1235. County Recorder, R/E and UCC Recording 440-285-2222 x3680.
Will search UCC records. This agency will not do a federal tax lien search. Will not search real estate records. **Online Access:** Delinquent Property Tax Records. Search the treasurer's delinquent tax list free at www.co.geauga.oh.us/departments/treasurer/rp_tax_delq_lst.htm. **Other Phone Numbers:** Assessor 440-285-2222 x3450; Treasurer 440-285-2222 x3850; Appraiser/Auditor 440-285-2222 x4490; Elections 440-285-2222 x4020; Vital Records 440-285-2222 x6407.

Greene County

County Recorder, PO Box 100, Xenia, OH 45385-0100. 937-376-5270 R/E Recording: 937-562-5270 UCC Recording: 937-562-5275; Fax 937-376-5386. www.co.greene.oh.us/recorder.htm
Will search UCC records. This agency will not do a federal tax lien search. Will not search real estate records. **Online Access:** Real Estate, Auditor, Recording, Deed, Mortgage, Grantor/Grantee Records. Access to the recorders data is available free at http://198.30.12.229/recdoc.asp. Also, records on the county Internet Map Server are available free online at www.co.greene.oh.us/gismapserver.htm. Click on "Click here to enter. Server Site #1". Data includes owner, address, valuation, taxes, sales data, and parcel ID number. **Other Phones:** Treasurer 937-376-5065; Appraiser/Auditor 937-562-5278; Elections 937-562-5261; Vital Records 562-5686; Auditor 937-376-5065.

Guernsey County

County Recorder, Courthouse D-202, Wheeling Ave, Cambridge, OH 43725. County Recorder, R/E and UCC Recording 740-432-9275.
Will search UCC records. This agency will not do a federal tax lien search. Will not search real estate records. **Other Phones:** Assessor 740-432-9243; Treasurer 740-432-9278; Appraiser/Auditor 740-432-9243; Elections 432-2680; Vital Records 432-3577.

Hamilton County

County Recorder, 138 E Court St, Room 101-A, Cincinnati, OH 45202. 513-946-4588 R/E Recording: 513-946-4570; Fax 513-946-4577. www.recordersoffice.hamilton-co.org
Will search UCC records. UCC search does not include federal tax liens. Will not searh real estate records.

Online Access: Real Estate, Lien, Recording, Lien, Deed, Mortgage, UCC, Auditor Records. Access to county recorder records is available free at www.recordersoffice.hamilton-co.org. Also, online access to the auditor's tax records database is available free at www.hamiltoncountyauditor.org./realestate. Also, search probate records back to 1/2000 at www.probatect.org/case_search/cs-scripts/pimain.html. **Other Phone Numbers:** Treasurer 513-946-4800; Appraiser/Auditor 513-946-4000.

Hancock County

County Recorder, 300 S. Main St, Courthouse, Findlay, OH 45840. County Recorder, R/E and UCC Recording 419-424-7091; Fax 419-424-7828.
Will search UCC records. **Online Access:** Property Auditor Records. Search the auditor's property database free at http://hancock.iviewauditor.com. No name searching. **Other Phones:** Treasurer 419-424-7213; Appraiser/Auditor 419-424-7015; Elections 419-422-3245; Vital Records 424-7869; Auditor 419-424-7083.

Hardin County

County Recorder, One Courthouse Square, Suite 220, Kenton, OH 43326. County Recorder, R/E and UCC Recording 419-674-2250; Fax 419-675-2802. www.co.hardin.oh.us
Will search UCC records. This agency will not do a federal tax lien search. Will not search real estate records. **Online Access:** Property Records. Property records from the county database are available at the web site. Click on "Real Estate Internet Inquiry.". **Other Phones:** Treasurer 419-674-2246; Appraiser/Aud. 419-674-2211; Auditor 419-674-2239.

Harrison County

County Recorder, 100 W. Market St, Courthouse, Cadiz, OH 43907. County Recorder, R/E and UCC Recording 740-942-8869; Fax 740-942-4693.
Will search UCC records. This agency will not do a federal tax lien search. Will not search real estate records. **Other Phone Numbers:** Treasurer 740-942-8864; Elections 740-942-8866; Vital Records 740-942-8868; Auditor 740-942-8861; Engineer 740-942-8867;

Henry County

County Recorder, Courthouse, Room 202, 660 N. Perry St., Napoleon, OH 43545-1747. 419-592-1766; Fax 419-592-1652. www.ohiorecorders.com
Will search UCC records. This agency will not do a federal tax lien search. Will not search real estate records. **Other Phone Numbers:** Assessor 419-492-1956; Treasurer 419-592-1851; Elections 419-592-7956; Vital Records 419-599-5545.

Highland County

County Recorder, PO Box 804, Hillsboro, OH 45133. County Recorder, R/E and UCC Recording 937-393-9954; Fax 937-393-5855. www.ohiorecorders.com
Will search UCC records. This agency will not do a federal tax lien search. Will not search real estate records. **Online Access:** Property, Deed, UCC Records. Access to recordings is available free at www.landaccess.com/sites/oh/highland/index.php. **Other Phones:** Assessor 937-393-1915; Treasurer 937-393-9951; Appraiser/Auditor 937-393-1915; Elections 937-393-9961; Vital Records 937-393-1941.

Hocking County

County Recorder, PO Box 949, Logan, OH 43138-0949. County Recorder, R/E and UCC Recording 740-385-2031; Fax 740-385-0377.
Will search UCC records. Will not search real estate records. **Other Phone Numbers:** Assessor 740-385-2127; Treasurer 740-385-3517; Appraiser/Auditor 740-385-2127; Elections 740-385-0203; Vital Records 740-385-3030.

Holmes County

County Recorder, PO Box 213, Millersburg, OH 44654. 330-674-5916; Fax none.
Will search UCC records. This agency will not do a federal tax lien search. Will not search real estate records. **Other Phone Numbers:** Treasurer 330-674-1896; Auditor 330-674-1896.

Huron County

County Recorder, PO Box 354, Norwalk, OH 44857. 419-668-1916; Fax 419-663-4052.
Will search UCC records. Will not search real estate records.

Jackson County

County Recorder, 226 E. Main St., Courthouse, Suite 1, Jackson, OH 45640. County Recorder, R/E and UCC Recording 740-286-1919.
Will search UCC records. This agency will not do a federal tax lien search. Will not search real estate records. **Other Phone Numbers:** Treasurer 740-286-2402; Elections 740-286-2905; Auditor 740-286-4231.

Jefferson County

County Recorder, Jefferson County Recorder 301 Market St., Steubenville, OH 43952. 740-283-8566; Fax none.
Will search UCC records. UCC search includes federal tax liens if requested. Will not search real estate records. **Other Phone Numbers:** Assessor 614-283-8518; Treasurer 614-283-8511; Auditor 614-283-8511.

Knox County

County Recorder, 117 E. High St, Mount Vernon, OH 43050. 740-393-6755 R/E Recording: 740-393-6757 UCC Recording: 740-393-6757.
Will search UCC records. This agency will not do a federal tax lien search. Will not search real estate records. **Online Access:** Property Records. Records on the county auditor database are available free online at www.knoxcountyauditor.org/knox208/LandRover.asp. **Other Phone Numbers:** Assessor 740-397-6291; Treasurer 740-393-6740; Appraiser/Auditor 740-393-6750; Elections 740-393-6716; Vital Records 740-393-2200; Records Center 740-393-6781

Lake County

County Recorder, PO Box 490, Painesville, OH 44077-0490. County Recorder, R/E and UCC Recording 440-350-2510 UCC Recording: 440-350-2511; Fax 440-350-5940. www.lakecountyrecorder.org
Will search UCC records. Will not search tax liens. Will not search real estate records. **Online Access:** Real Estate, Auditor, Recording, Lien, Deed Records. Access to the Recorder's Document Index database is available free at http://web2.lakecountyohio.org/recorders/search/index.asp. Records go back to 1986. Also, access to the treasurer and auditor's real estate databases is available free at www.lake.iviewauditor.com. Click on "by attitude." Also, online access to Land Bank sales is available at www.lakecountyohio.org/auditor/index.htm and click on "Land Bank Sales". Access warrants and sex offenders lists at www.lakecountyohio.org/sheriff/index.htm. **Other Phone Numbers:** Treasurer 440-350-2517; Elections 440-350-2700; Vital Records 440-350-2549; Auditor 440-350-2528.

Lawrence County

County Recorder, PO Box 77, Ironton, OH 45638. Recorder, R/E /UCC Recording 740-533-4314; Fax 740-533-4411. www.lawrencecountyohiorecorder.org
Will search UCC records. Will not search real estate records. **Online Access:** Real Estate, Deed, Mortgage, Lien Records. Search the recorders data free at www.lawrencecountyohiorecorder.org/record_search.htm. Deeds go back to 1983; mortgages to 1988; liens

back to 1981; financing statements to 1989. Documents filed since 1/1997 can be printed.

Licking County

County Recorder, PO Box 520, Newark, OH 43058. County Recorder, R/E and UCC Recording 740-349-6061; Fax 740-349-1415. www.lcounty.com/rec/
Will search UCC records. This agency will not do a federal tax lien search. Will not search real estate records. **Online Access:** Real Estate, Tax Lien, Recording, Property Tax Records. Access to the county recorders database is available free at www.lcounty.com/recordings. Records with images go back to 1997. Also, online access to the Auditor's county property database is available free at www.lcounty.com/licking208.

Logan County

County Recorder, 100 S Madriver, Suite A, Suite A, Bellefontaine, OH 43311-2075. 937-599-7201 R/E Recording: 937-599-7202; Fax 937-599-7287. www.co.logan.oh.us/recorder/
Will search UCC records. Will not search real estate records. **Online Access:** Real Estate, Auditor Records. Records on the County Auditor's database are available free online at www2.co.logan.oh.us/logan208/LandRover.asp. Also, online access to the recorders database is free at http://www3.co.logan.oh.us/record30.asp. Click on "Document Search.". **Other Phone Numbers:** Treasurer 937-599-7223; Elections 937-599-7255; Auditor 937-599-7213.

Lorain County

County Recorder, 226 Middle Ave, Elyria, OH 44035-5643. County Recorder, R/E and UCC Recording 440-329-5148 UCC Recording: 440-329-5138; Fax 440-329-5477. www.loraincounty.com/government/
Will search UCC records. Will not search real estate records. **Online Access:** Real Estate, Lien, Auditor Records. Access to the county assessor database is available free at www.loraincounty.com/recorder/register. Free registration is required. Also, records on the County Auditor's database are available free at www.loraincountyauditor.org/lorain208/LandRover.asp

Lucas County

County Recorder, 1 Government Center #700, Jackson St, Toledo, OH 43604. 419-213-4400; Fax 419-213-4284. www.co.lucas.oh.us
Will search UCC records. UCC search includes federal tax liens if requested. Will not search real estate records. **Online Access:** Real Estate, Auditor, Unclaimed Funds, Sheriff Sale Records. Property records on the County Auditor's Real Estate Information System (AREIS) database are available free online at www.co.lucas.oh.us/Areis/areismain.asp. This replaces the old system. Also, online access to the treasurer's unclaimed funds and sheriff sale lists are available free at www.raytkest.com. **Other Phone Numbers:** Treasurer 419-213-4303; Vital Records 419-213-4100; Auditor 419-213-4424.

Madison County

County Recorder, Courthouse, Room 40, 1 N. Main St., London, OH 43140. County Recorder, R/E and UCC Recording 740-852-1854; Fax 740-845-1776. www.co.madison.oh.us/elected.htm
Will search UCC records. This agency will not do a federal tax lien search. Will not search real estate records. **Online Access:** Real Estate, Auditor, Deed, UCC Records. Records on the County Auditor's database are available free online at www.co.madison.oh.us/auditor/iView/iView.asp. Also, online access to county land and UCC records is available free at www.landaccess.com. Records go back to 5/1994. **Other Phone Numbers:** Treasurer 740-852-1936; Auditor 740-852-9717.

Mahoning County

County Recorder, PO Box 928, Youngstown, OH 44501. 330-740-2345; Fax 330-740-2006. www.mahoningcountyauditor.org
Will search UCC records. **Online Access:** Real Estate, Auditor, Deed, UCC Records. Property records on the County Auditor's database are available free online at www.mahoningcountyauditor.org/maho208/LandRover.asp. Also, property, deed, and UCC records are to be available free at www.landaccess.com. **Other Phones:** Treasurer 330-740-2460; Auditor 330-740-2010.

Marion County

County Recorder, 171 E. Center St., Marion, OH 43302-3089. County Recorder, R/E and UCC Recording 740-387-4521; www.co.marion.oh.us
Will search UCC records. This agency will not do a tax lien search. Will not search real estate records. **Online Access:** Real Estate, Auditor Records. Access to the county auditor real estate database is available free at www.co.marion.oh.us. Click on "Real Estate Inquiry.". **Other Phone Numbers:** Assessor 740-387-4811; Treasurer 740-387-7345; Appraiser/Auditor 740-387-4811; Elections 740-387-4058; Auditor 740-387-7345.

Medina County

County Recorder, County Administration Bldg, 144 N. Broadway, Medina, OH 44256-2295. County Recorder, R/E and UCC Recording 330-725-9782 UCC Records 330-725-9783; www.recorder.co.medina.oh.us
Will search UCC records. This agency will not do a federal tax lien search. Will not search real estate records. **Online Access:** Real Estate, Auditor Records. Access to indexes 1983 to present on the County Recorder database is available free at www.recorder.co.medina.oh.us/indexes2.htm. Click on "Indexes" and use "View" as user name and password. Also, online access to property records on the Medina County Auditor database are available free online at www.medinacountyauditor.org - "Public Records." Also, find a lost dog's owner at www.medinacountyauditor.org/finddog.htm. Sheriff's sex offender list is at www.medinasheriff.com. **Other Phone Numbers:** Assessor 330-725-9754.

Meigs County

County Recorder, 100 E. Second St, Courthouse, Pomeroy, OH 45769. 740-992-3806; Fax 740-992-2867.
Will search UCC records. This agency will not do a federal tax lien search. Will not search real estate records. **Other Phone Numbers:** Treasurer 740-992-2004; Auditor 740-992-5290.

Mercer County

County Recorder, 101 N. Main St, Courthouse Square-Room 203, Celina, OH 45822. 419-586-4232; Fax 419-586-3541. www.mercercountyohio.org
Will search UCC records. This agency will not do a federal tax lien search. Will not search real estate records. **Online Access:** Real Estate, Auditor Records. Property records on the County Auditor - Real Estate Department database are available free online at www.mercercountyohio.org/auditor/RealEstate/PcardInq/category.htm. **Other Phone Numbers:** Treasurer 419-586-2259; Appraiser/Auditor 419-586-6402; Elections 419-586-2215; Auditor 419-586-2259.

Miami County

County Recorder, PO Box 653, Troy, OH 45373. 937-332-6893 R/E Recording: 937-332-6912; Fax 937-332-6806.
Will search UCC records. This agency will not do a federal tax lien search. Will not search real estate records. **Other Phone Numbers:** Treasurer 937-332-6929; Elections 937-332-6926; Auditor 937-332-6964.

Monroe County

County Recorder, PO Box 152, Woodsfield, OH 43793-0152. 740-472-5264; Fax 740-472-2523.
Will search UCC records. This agency will not do a federal tax lien search. Will not search real estate records. **Other Phone Numbers:** Assessor 740-472-0763; Treasurer 740-472-1521; Auditor 740-472-0873.

Montgomery County

County Recorder, PO Box 972, Dayton, OH 45422. 937-225-4282 R/E Recording: 937-225-4275; Fax 937-225-5980. www.mcrecorder.org
dodgej@mcohio.org. Will search UCC records. Will not search real estate records. **Online Access:** Property, Real Estate, Lien, Recording Records. Access to the recorders data is available free at www.mcrecorder.org/search_selection.cfm. Property records on the county treasurer real estate tax information database are available free online at www.mctreas.org. **Other Phone Numbers:** Appraiser/Auditor 937-225-4002.

Morgan County

County Recorder, 19 E. Main St, McConnelsville, OH 43756. 740-962-4051; Fax 740-962-3364.
Will search UCC records. Will not search real estate records. **Other Phone Numbers:** Treasurer 740-962-4475; Elections 740-962-3116; Vital Records 740-962-4572; Auditor 740-962-4475.

Morrow County

County Recorder, 48 E. High St, Mount Gilead, OH 43338. 419-947-3060; Fax 419-947-3709. www.morrowcounty.info/morrowoff.htm
Will search UCC records. This agency will not do a tax lien search. Will not search real estate records. **Other Phone Numbers:** Treasurer 419-947-6070; Appraiser/Auditor 419-947-4060.

Muskingum County

County Recorder, PO Box 2333, Zanesville, OH 43702-2333. County Recorder, R/E and UCC Recording 740-455-7107; Fax 740-455-7943. www.muskingumcountyauditor.org
Will search UCC records. Will not search real estate records. **Online Access:** Real Estate, Assessor Records. Records on the county assesor database are available free at www.muskingumcountyauditor.org/realestate/LandRover.asp. **Other Phone Numbers:** Treasurer 740-455-7118; Auditor 740-455-7109.

Noble County

County Recorder, 260 Courthouse, Room 2E, Caldwell, OH 43724. County Recorder, R/E and UCC Recording 740-732-4319.
Will search UCC records. This agency will not do a tax lien search. Will not search real estate records. **Other Phone Numbers:** Treasurer 740-732-2457; Elections 740-732-2057; Vital Records 740-732-5047.

Ottawa County

County Recorder, 315 Madison St, Room 204, Port Clinton, OH 43452. 419-734-6730 R/E Recording: 419-734-6735 UCC Recording: 419-734-6735; Fax 419-734-6919.
Will search UCC records. Will not search tax liens. Will not search real estate records. **Other Phone Numbers:** Treasurer 419-734-6750; Appraiser/Auditor 419-734-6740; Vital Records 419-734-6800.

Paulding County

County Recorder, 115 N Williams St, 115 N. Williams St., Paulding, OH 45879. County Recorder, R/E and UCC Recording 419-399-8275; Fax 419-399-2862.
Will search UCC records. Will not search real estate records. **Other Phones:** Assessor 419-399-8205;

Treasurer 419-399-8280; Auditor 419-399-8205; Elections 419-399-8230; Vital Records 419-399-3921.

Perry County

County Recorder, PO Box 147, New Lexington, OH 43764. 740-342-2494 R/E Recording: 740-342-2444; Fax 740-342-5539.
Will search UCC records. This agency will not do a federal tax lien search. Will not search real estate records. **Other Phone Numbers:** Treasurer 740-342-2074; Auditor 740-342-2074.

Pickaway County

County Recorder, 207 S. Court St, Circleville, OH 43113. 740-474-5826; Fax 740-477-6361.
Will search UCC records. Will not search real estate records. **Other Phone Numbers:** Assessor 740-474-4765; Treasurer 740-474-2370; Elections 740-474-1100; Auditor 740-474-4765.

Pike County

County Recorder, Courthouse, 100 E. 2nd St., Waverly, OH 45690. 740-947-2622; Fax 740-947-7997.
Will search UCC records. Will not search real estate records. **Other Phone Numbers:** Assessor 740-947-4125; Treasurer 740-947-2713; Auditor 614-947-2713.

Portage County

County Recorder, 449 S. Meridian St, Ravenna, OH 44266. 330-297-3554 R/E Recording: 330-297-3553; Fax 330-297-7349.
Will search UCC records. This agency will not do a tax lien search. Will not search real estate records. **Other Phone Numbers:** Treasurer 330-297-3586; Appraiser/Auditor 330-297-3569.

Preble County

County Recorder, PO Box 371, Eaton, OH 45320-0371. 937-456-8173.
Will search UCC records. This agency will not do a federal tax lien search. Will not search real estate records. **Online Access:** Real Estate, Auditor Records. Property records on the County Auditor's database are available free at www.preblecountyauditor.org/preble208/LandRover.asp. **Other Phone Numbers:** Assessor 937-456-8148.

Putnam County

County Recorder, 245 E. Main St, Suite 202, Ottawa, OH 45875-1959. 419-523-6490; Fax 419-523-4403.
Will search UCC records. Will not search real estate records. **Other Phone Numbers:** Appraiser/Auditor 419-523-6686; Elections 419-523-3343.

Richland County

County Recorder, 50 Park Ave East, Mansfield, OH 44902. 419-774-5602/5600 R/E Recording: 419-774-5599; UCCs: 419-774-5601; Fax 419-774-5603.
Will search UCC records. UCC search includes federal tax liens if requested. Will not search real estate records. **Online Access:** Real Estate, Auditor, Deed, UCC Records. Property records from the County Auditor database are available free online at www.richlandcountyauditor.org. Also, online access to county land and UCC records is available free at www.landaccess.com. Records go back to 4/1989. **Other Phones:** Assessor 419-774-5502; Treasurer 419-774-5522; Appraiser/Auditor 419-774-5503; Elections 419-774-5530; Vital Records 419-774-5586.

Ross County

County Recorder, PO Box 6162, Chillicothe, OH 45601. 740-702-3000; Fax 740-702-3006.
Will search UCC records. This agency will not do a federal tax lien search. Will not search real estate records. **Online Access:** Property, Deed, UCC Records. Access to county land and UCC records is available free

at www.landaccess.com. Records go back to 1/1974. **Other Phone Numbers:** Assessor 740-702-3080; Appraiser/Auditor 740-702-3080.

Sandusky County

County Recorder, 100 N. Park Ave., Courthouse, Fremont, OH 43420-2477. 419-334-6226. Will search UCC records. This agency will not do a federal tax lien search. Mortgage searches available. **Other Phone Numbers:** Treasurer 419-334-6233; Auditor 419-334-6123.

Scioto County

County Recorder, 602 7th St, Rm 110, Room 110, Portsmouth, OH 45662-3950. County Recorder, R/E and UCC Recording 740-355-8304; Fax 740-353-7358. Will search UCC records. Will not search real estate records. **Other Phone Numbers:** Assessor 740-355-8264; Treasurer 740-355-8296; Appraiser/Auditor 740-355-8264; Elections 740-355-8217.

Seneca County

County Recorder, 109 S. Washington St, Box 667, Room 7, Tiffin, OH 44883. 419-447-4434. Will search UCC records. This agency will not do a federal tax lien search. Will not search real estate records.

Shelby County

County Recorder, 129 E. Court St, Shelby County Annex, Sidney, OH 45365. County Recorder, R/E and UCC Recording 937-498-7270; Fax 937-498-7272. Will search UCC records. Will not search real estate records. **Other Phone Numbers:** Treasurer 937-498-7281; Appraiser/Auditor 937-498-7202; Elections 937-498-7208 or 7209; Vital Records 937-498-7249 (Birth & Death Certificates); Probate (Wills) 937-498-7263; Clerk of Courts-Divorce & judgments 937-498-7221;

Stark County

County Recorder, 110 Central Plaza South, Suite 170, Canton, OH 44702-1409. 330-451-7440 R/E Recording: 330-451-7443 x4464 UCC Recording: 330-451-7443 x7933; Fax 330-451-7394. www.recorder.co.stark.oh.us Will search UCC records. This agency will not do a federal tax lien search. Will not search real estate records. **Online Access:** Real Estate, Deed, Recording Records. Access to the recorder's database is available free at www.recorder.co.stark.oh.us/DTS. Chose from simple, advanced or instrument search. Also, the elected officials list is available at www.stark.lib.oh.us/officials.html. Also, online access to the sheriff sales lists are at www.sheriff.co.stark.oh.us/RealEstate.htm. The sheriff's ex offenders list is at www.sheriff.co.stark.oh.us/OffenderLinks.htm. **Other Phone Numbers:** Treasurer 330-451-7814; Appraiser/Auditor 330-451-7814.

Summit County

Auditor, 175 S Main St, Akron, OH 44308-1355. 330-643-2720 R/E Recording: 330-643-2719 UCC Recording: 330-643-2719; Fax 330-643-2622. www.co.summit.oh.us Will search UCC records. This agency will not do a federal tax lien search. Will not search real estate records. **Online Access:** Real Estate, Auditor, Property Tax, Recording Records. Tax map information from the county auditor is available free online at http://scids.summitoh.net/taxmapsinternet, also property appraisal and tax information at www.summitoh.net. Access to the full document images database requires registration, password and one-time $150.00 fee. Call Summit County Data Center, Help Desk at 330-643-2687 for information and sign-up. Images are available from the recorder division at www.summitoh.net/rec/html/rcd4.html. The Sheriff's sex offenders list is at www.co.summit.oh.us/sheriff/sexoffenders01.htm.

Other Phones: Treasurer 330-643-2587; Auditor 330-643-2638; Auditor 330-643-2630.

Trumbull County

County Recorder, 160 High St NW, Warren, OH 44481. 330-675-2401, 330-393-2707 R/E Recording: 330-675-2401 UCC Recording: 330-675-2798; Fax 330-675-2404. Will search UCC records. This agency will not do a federal tax lien search. Will not search real estate records. **Online Access:** Auditor, Property Tax, Recording, Deed, Mortgage, Lien Records. Access to the recorder's database requires free registration and password at http://tcrecorder.co.trumbull.oh.us/index.cfm. Dog registration look-up is at www.dogtagsplus.com/Start.asp?CountyID=2. Also, real estate rcords from the County Auditor are available free at www.co.auditor.trumbull.oh.us/propertymax/LandRover.asp. Also, unclaimed funds list is available at www.trumbullprobate.org/UnclaimedFunds.htm. The Sheriff's warrants list is searchable at www.sheriff.co.trumbull.oh.us/warrants.htm. **Other Phone Numbers:** Treasurer 330-675-2736; Appraiser/Auditor 330-675-2420; Elections 330-675-4050; Auditor 330-675-2401 x216.

Tuscarawas County

County Recorder, 125 E. High Ave, New Philadelphia, OH 44663. 330-365-3284; www.co.tuscarawas.oh.us Will search UCC records. This agency will not do a federal tax lien search. Will not search real estate records. **Online Access:** Real Estate, Unclaimed Funds Records. County real estate records are available free at www.co.tuscarawas.oh.us/Auditor/realsearch.htm. The auditor's deliquent tax list is available in September. Also, the countyauditor's list of Unclaimed Funds is at www.co.tuscarawas.oh.us/Auditor/Unclaimed%20Funds.htm. Also, the clerk of court's page (see county main web site) can be searched free for unclaimed funds and outstanding checks. **Other Phone Numbers:** Treasurer 330-365-3254; Appraiser/Auditor 330-365-3220; Auditor 330-364-8811 x220.

Union County

County Recorder, 233 W. Sixth St., Marysville, OH 43040. County Recorder, R/E and UCC Recording 937-645-3032; Fax 937-642-3397. Will search UCC records. This agency will not do a federal tax lien search. Will not search real estate records. **Online Access:** Auditor, Property Tax, Real Estate, Recording, Delinquent Taxpayers Records. Access to the Auditors tax assessment/property records database and the appriaser property information is available free at http://www2.co.union.oh.us/PropInfoGuide.htm. You may also search for property information via the online GIS map. Search the treasurers list of delinquent taxpayers at www.co.union.oh.us/Treasurer/List_of_Delinquent_Taxpayers/list_of_delinquent_taxpayers.html. **Other Phones:** Treasurer 645-3029; Auditor 937-645-3003.

Van Wert County

County Recorder, 121 E Main St, Courthouse - Rm 206, Van Wert, OH 45891-1729. County Recorder, R/E and UCC Recording 419-238-2558; Fax 419-238-5410. Will search UCC records. This agency will not do a federal tax lien search. Will not search real estate records. **Online Access:** Property, Deed, UCC Records. Access to county land and UCC records is available free at www.landaccess.com. Records go back to 1/1994. **Other Phone Numbers:** Treasurer 419-238-5177; Elections 419-238-4192; Vital Records 419-238-0808; Auditor 419-238-0843.

Vinton County

County Recorder, PO Box 11, McArthur, OH 45651. 740-596-4314; Fax 740-596-2265.

Will search UCC records. This agency will not do a federal tax lien search. Will not search real estate records. **Other Phone Numbers:** Treasurer 740-596-5690; Elections 740-596-5855; Vital Records 740-596-5480; Auditor 740-596-5445.

Warren County

County Recorder, 406 Justice Dr., Lebanon, OH 45036. County Recorder, R/E and UCC Recording 513-695-1382 UCC Recording: 513-695-2638; Fax 513-695-2949. www.co.warren.oh.us Will search UCC records. Will not perform a tax lien search. Will not search real estate records. **Online Access:** Real Estate, Auditor Records. Access to the county auditor database is available free at www.co.warren.oh.us/auditor/index.htm. Click on Warren County Property Information Search at the bottom of web page. **Other Phone Numbers:** Assessor 513-695-1235; Treasurer 513-695-1300; Appraiser/Auditor 513-695-1218; Elections 513-695-1358; Auditor 513-695-1235.

Washington County

County Recorder, 205 Putnam St, Courthouse, Marietta, OH 45750. 740-373-6623 R/E Recording: 740-373-6623 x235; Fax 740-373-9643. www.ohiorecorders.com Will search UCC records. Will not search real estate records. **Online Access:** Property, Auditor, Deed, UCC Records. Access to the county auditor's Property search database free at www.washingtoncountyauditor.org/washington208/LandRover.asp. Also, access to property, deed, and UCC records is available free at www.landaccess.com/sites/oh/washington/index.php. **Other Phone Numbers:** Treasurer 740-373-6623 x256; Auditor 740-373-6623 x263.

Wayne County

County Recorder, 428 West Liberty St, Wooster, OH 44691-5097. County Recorder, R/E and UCC Recording 330-287-5460; Fax 330-287-5685. www.ohiorecorders.com Will search UCC records. This agency will not do a federal tax lien search. Will not search real estate records. **Other Phone Numbers:** Treasurer 330-287-5450; Elections 330-287-5480; Auditor 330-287-5430.

Williams County

County Recorder, 1 Courthouse Square, Bryan, OH 43506. 419-636-3259. Will search UCC records. This agency will not do a federal tax lien search. Will not search real estate records. **Other Phones:** Auditor 419-636-5639.

Wood County

County Recorder, 1 Courthouse Square, Bowling Green, OH 43402-2427. County Recorder, R/E and UCC Recording 419-354-9140. Will search UCC records. This agency will not do a tax lien search. Will not search real estate records. **Other Phone Numbers:** Assessor 419-354-9150; Treasurer 419-354-9130; Appraiser/Auditor 419-354-9150; Elections 419-354-9120; Vital Records 419-354-9130.

Wyandot County

County Recorder, Courthouse, 109 S. Sandusky Ave., Upper Sandusky, OH 43351. 419-294-1442 R/E Recording: 419-294-1531; Fax 419-294-6405. Will search UCC records. Will not search real estate records. **Online Access:** Real Estate, Auditor Records. Access to the Auditor's real estate database is available free at www.co.wyandot.oh.us/auditor/default.html. Click on "Real estate Internet Inquiry." Site may be down. **Other Phone Numbers:** Assessor 419-294-1531; Treasurer 419-294-2131; Elections 419-294-1226; Vital Records 419-294-2302.

Ohio County Locator

You will usually be able to find the city name in the City/County Cross Reference below. In that case, it is a simple matter to determine the county from the cross reference. However, only the official US Postal Service city names are included in this index. There are an additional 40,000 place names that people use in their addresses. Therefore, we have also included a ZIP/City Cross Reference immediately following the City/County Cross Reference.

If you know the ZIP Code but the city name does not appear in the City/County Cross Reference index, look up the ZIP Code in the ZIP/City Cross Reference, find the city name, then look up the city name in the City/County Cross Reference. For example, you want to know the county for an address of Menands, NY 12204. There is no "Menands" in the City/County Cross Reference. The ZIP/City Cross Reference shows that ZIP Codes 12201-12288 are for the city of Albany. Looking back in the City/County Cross Reference, Albany is in Albany County.

City/County Cross Reference

ABERDEEN Brown
ADA (45810) Hardin(94), Hancock(2), Allen(2)
ADAMSVILLE Muskingum
ADDYSTON Hamilton
ADELPHI Ross
ADENA (43901) Jefferson(74), Harrison(14), Belmont(10)
ADRIAN Seneca
AKRON Summit
ALBANY (45710) Athens(62), Meigs(20), Vinton(17)
ALEXANDRIA Licking
ALGER (45812) Hardin(91), Allen(8)
ALLEDONIA Belmont
ALLIANCE (44601) Stark(90), Mahoning(6), Columbiana(2)
ALPHA Greene
ALVADA (44802) Seneca(61), Hancock(37)
ALVORDTON Williams
AMANDA (43102) Fairfield(89), Hocking(9), Pickaway(1)
AMELIA Clermont
AMESVILLE (45711) Athens(92), Washington(6), Morgan(1)
AMHERST Lorain
AMLIN Franklin
AMSDEN Seneca
AMSTERDAM (43903) Carroll(56), Jefferson(43)
ANDOVER Ashtabula
ANNA Shelby
ANSONIA Darke
ANTWERP (45813) Paulding(98), Defiance(1)
APPLE CREEK Wayne
ARCADIA Hancock
ARCANUM (45304) Darke(94), Miami(5)
ARCHBOLD (43502) Fulton(89), Henry(10)
ARLINGTON Hancock
ASHLAND (44805) Ashland(98), Richland(1)
ASHLEY (43003) Delaware(56), Morrow(43)
ASHTABULA Ashtabula
ASHVILLE Pickaway
ATHENS Athens
ATTICA (44807) Seneca(86), Huron(13)
ATWATER (44201) Portage(97), Stark(2)
AUGUSTA Carroll
AURORA (44202) Portage(85), Summit(12), Geauga(1)
AUSTINBURG Ashtabula
AVA Noble
AVON Lorain
AVON LAKE Lorain
B F GOODRICH CO Summit
BAINBRIDGE (45612) Ross(65), Pike(22), Highland(12)
BAKERSVILLE Coshocton
BALTIC (43804) Holmes(56), Tuscarawas(24), Coshocton(18)
BALTIMORE Fairfield
BANNOCK Belmont
BARBERTON Summit

BARLOW Washington
BARNESVILLE Belmont
BARTLETT Washington
BARTON Belmont
BASCOM Seneca
BATAVIA Clermont
BATH Summit
BAY VILLAGE Cuyahoga
BEACH CITY (44608) Stark(76), Tuscarawas(23)
BEACHWOOD Cuyahoga
BEALLSVILLE (43716) Monroe(72), Belmont(27)
BEAVER (45613) Pike(82), Jackson(17)
BEAVERDAM Allen
BEDFORD Cuyahoga
BELLAIRE Belmont
BELLBROOK Greene
BELLE CENTER (43310) Logan(74), Hardin(25)
BELLE VALLEY Noble
BELLEFONTAINE Logan
BELLEVUE (44811) Huron(45), Sandusky(38), Seneca(10), Erie(5)
BELLVILLE (44813) Richland(85), Knox(7), Morrow(6)
BELMONT Belmont
BELMORE Putnam
BELOIT (44609) Mahoning(59), Columbiana(40)
BELPRE Washington
BENTON RIDGE Hancock
BENTONVILLE Adams
BEREA Cuyahoga
BERGHOLZ (43908) Jefferson(95), Carroll(4)
BERKEY (43504) Lucas(93), Fulton(6)
BERLIN Holmes
BERLIN CENTER Mahoning
BERLIN HEIGHTS Erie
BETHEL Clermont
BETHESDA Belmont
BETTSVILLE Seneca
BEVERLY (45715) Washington(95), Morgan(4)
BIDWELL Gallia
BIG PRAIRIE (44611) Holmes(94), Wayne(5)
BIRMINGHAM Erie
BLACKLICK Franklin
BLADENSBURG Knox
BLAINE Belmont
BLAKESLEE Williams
BLANCHESTER (45107) Clinton(84), Warren(8), Brown(3), Clermont(3)
BLISSFIELD Coshocton
BLOOMDALE (44817) Wood(92), Hancock(7)
BLOOMINGBURG Fayette
BLOOMINGDALE (43910) Jefferson(96), Harrison(3)
BLOOMVILLE (44818) Seneca(61), Crawford(38)
BLUE CREEK (45616) Adams(83), Scioto(16)

BLUE ROCK (43720) Muskingum(91), Morgan(8)
BLUFFTON (45817) Allen(83), Hancock(14), Putnam(1)
BOLIVAR (44612) Tuscarawas(94), Stark(5)
BOTKINS (45306) Shelby(94), Auglaize(5)
BOURNEVILLE Ross
BOWERSTON (44695) Harrison(55), Carroll(44)
BOWERSVILLE Greene
BOWLING GREEN Wood
BRADFORD (45308) Darke(54), Miami(45)
BRADNER (43406) Wood(91), Sandusky(8)
BRADY LAKE Portage
BRECKSVILLE (44141) Cuyahoga(93), Summit(6)
BREMEN (43107) Fairfield(91), Hocking(5), Perry(2)
BREWSTER Stark
BRICE Franklin
BRIDGEPORT Belmont
BRILLIANT Jefferson
BRINKHAVEN (43006) Holmes(41), Coshocton(39), Knox(19)
BRISTOLVILLE Trumbull
BROADVIEW HEIGHTS Cuyahoga
BROADWAY Union
BROOKFIELD Trumbull
BROOKPARK Cuyahoga
BROOKVILLE (45309) Montgomery(98), Darke(1)
BROWNSVILLE Licking
BRUNSWICK Medina
BRYAN (43506) Williams(94), Defiance(5)
BUCHTEL Athens
BUCKEYE LAKE Licking
BUCKLAND Auglaize
BUCYRUS Crawford
BUFFALO Guernsey
BUFORD Highland
BURBANK (44214) Wayne(71), Medina(28)
BURGHILL Trumbull
BURGOON (43407) Sandusky(97), Seneca(2)
BURKETTSVILLE Mercer
BURTON Geauga
BUTLER (44822) Richland(60), Knox(39)
BYESVILLE Guernsey
CABLE Champaign
CADIZ (43907) Harrison(98), Jefferson(1)
CAIRO Allen
CALDWELL (43724) Noble(97), Morgan(1)
CALEDONIA (43314) Marion(83), Morrow(10), Crawford(5)
CAMBRIDGE Guernsey
CAMDEN Preble
CAMERON Monroe
CAMP DENNISON Hamilton
CAMPBELL Mahoning
CANAL FULTON (44614) Stark(96), Summit(2), Wayne(1)
CANAL WINCHESTER (43110) Fairfield(54), Franklin(45)

CANFIELD Mahoning
CANTON Stark
CARBON HILL Hocking
CARBONDALE Athens
CARDINGTON (43315) Morrow(92), Marion(7)
CAREY (43316) Wyandot(82), Seneca(14), Hancock(2)
CARROLL Fairfield
CARROLLTON Carroll
CASSTOWN (45312) Miami(98), Champaign(1)
CASTALIA (44824) Erie(96), Sandusky(3)
CATAWBA Clark
CECIL (45821) Paulding(88), Defiance(11)
CEDARVILLE (45314) Greene(96), Clark(3)
CELINA Mercer
CENTERBURG (43011) Knox(63), Morrow(14), Delaware(11), Licking(10)
CHAGRIN FALLS Geauga
CHANDLERSVILLE Muskingum
CHARDON (44024) Geauga(97), Lake(2)
CHARM Holmes
CHATFIELD Crawford
CHAUNCEY Athens
CHERRY FORK Adams
CHESAPEAKE Lawrence
CHESHIRE (45620) Gallia(96), Meigs(3)
CHESTER Meigs
CHESTERHILL (43728) Morgan(91), Athens(8)
CHESTERLAND Geauga
CHESTERVILLE Morrow
CHICKASAW Mercer
CHILLICOTHE Ross
CHILO Clermont
CHIPPEWA LAKE Medina
CHRISTIANSBURG Champaign
CINCINNATI Hamilton
CIRCLEVILLE Pickaway
CLARINGTON Monroe
CLARKSBURG (43115) Ross(77), Pickaway(22)
CLARKSVILLE Clinton
CLAY CENTER Ottawa
CLAYTON Montgomery
CLEVELAND Cuyahoga
CLEVES Hamilton
CLIFTON Greene
CLINTON (44216) Summit(88), Stark(10)
CLOVERDALE (45827) Putnam(86), Paulding(13)
CLYDE (43410) Sandusky(96), Seneca(3)
COAL RUN Washington
COALTON Jackson
COLDWATER Mercer
COLERAIN Belmont
COLLEGE CORNER Butler
COLLINS (44826) Huron(83), Erie(16)
COLLINSVILLE Butler
COLTON Henry
COLUMBIA STATION Lorain
COLUMBIANA (44408) Columbiana(86), Mahoning(13)

COLUMBUS Franklin
COLUMBUS GROVE (45830) Putnam(79), Allen(20)
COMMERCIAL POINT Pickaway
CONESVILLE (43811) Coshocton(98), Muskingum(1)
CONNEAUT Ashtabula
CONOVER (45317) Miami(49), Champaign(40), Shelby(9)
CONTINENTAL (45831) Putnam(96), Defiance(1), Paulding(1)
CONVOY (45832) Van Wert(98), Paulding(1)
COOLVILLE (45723) Athens(86), Meigs(11), Washington(1)
CORNING (43730) Perry(97), Morgan(2)
CORTLAND Trumbull
COSHOCTON Coshocton
COVINGTON Miami
CREOLA (45622) Vinton(96), Hocking(3)
CRESTLINE (44827) Crawford(98), Richland(1)
CRESTON (44217) Wayne(89), Medina(10)
CROOKSVILLE (43731) Perry(86), Morgan(13)
CROTON Licking
CROWN CITY (45623) Gallia(83), Lawrence(16)
CUBA Clinton
CUMBERLAND (43732) Guernsey(73), Noble(17), Muskingum(7), Morgan(1)
CURTICE (43412) Lucas(56), Ottawa(43)
CUSTAR (43511) Wood(78), Henry(21)
CUTLER (45724) Washington(98), Athens(1)
CUYAHOGA FALLS Summit
CYGNET Wood
CYNTHIANA Pike
DALTON (44618) Wayne(91), Stark(8)
DAMASCUS Mahoning
DANVILLE (43014) Knox(98), Coshocton(1)
DAYTON Montgomery
DE GRAFF (43318) Logan(79), Champaign(20)
DECATUR Brown
DEERFIELD Portage
DEERSVILLE Harrison
DEFIANCE (43512) Defiance(95), Paulding(3)
DELAWARE Delaware
DELLROY Carroll
DELPHOS (45833) Allen(56), Van Wert(40), Putnam(3)
DELTA Fulton
DENNISON (44621) Tuscarawas(90), Harrison(7), Carroll(1)
DERBY Pickaway
DERWENT Guernsey
DESHLER (43516) Henry(81), Wood(12), Putnam(4), Hancock(1)
DEXTER CITY Noble
DIAMOND (44412) Portage(78), Mahoning(21)
DILLONVALE (43917) Jefferson(66), Belmont(33)
DOLA Hardin
DONNELSVILLE Clark
DORSET Ashtabula
DOVER Tuscarawas
DOYLESTOWN (44230) Wayne(98), Medina(1)
DRESDEN (43821) Muskingum(87), Coshocton(12)
DUBLIN (43017) Franklin(87), Delaware(12)
DUNBRIDGE Wood
DUNCAN FALLS Muskingum
DUNDEE (44624) Tuscarawas(59), Holmes(27), Wayne(11), Stark(1)
DUNKIRK Hardin
DUPONT Putnam

EAST CLARIDON Geauga
EAST FULTONHAM Muskingum
EAST LIBERTY (43319) Logan(97), Union(2)
EAST LIVERPOOL Columbiana
EAST PALESTINE Columbiana
EAST ROCHESTER (44625) Columbiana(81), Carroll(18)
EAST SPARTA (44626) Stark(95), Tuscarawas(4)
EAST SPRINGFIELD Jefferson
EASTLAKE Lake
EATON Preble
EDGERTON (43517) Williams(78), Defiance(21)
EDISON Morrow
EDON Williams
ELDORADO Preble
ELGIN Van Wert
ELKTON Columbiana
ELLSWORTH Mahoning
ELMORE (43416) Ottawa(92), Sandusky(7)
ELYRIA Lorain
EMPIRE Jefferson
ENGLEWOOD (45322) Montgomery(97), Miami(2)
ENON Clark
ETNA Licking
EUCLID Cuyahoga
EVANSPORT Defiance
FAIRBORN Greene
FAIRFIELD Butler
FAIRLAWN Summit
FAIRPOINT Belmont
FAIRVIEW Guernsey
FARMDALE Trumbull
FARMER Defiance
FARMERSVILLE (45325) Montgomery(98), Preble(1)
FAYETTE (43521) Fulton(97), Williams(2)
FAYETTEVILLE (45118) Brown(98), Clermont(1)
FEESBURG Brown
FELICITY Clermont
FINDLAY Hancock
FLAT ROCK Seneca
FLEMING Washington
FLETCHER Miami
FLUSHING (43977) Belmont(79), Harrison(20)
FOREST (45843) Hardin(61), Wyandot(19), Hancock(18)
FORT JENNINGS (45844) Putnam(90), Allen(5), Van Wert(4)
FORT LORAMIE (45845) Shelby(94), Auglaize(4)
FORT RECOVERY (45846) Mercer(85), Darke(14)
FORT SENECA Seneca
FOSTORIA (44830) Seneca(65), Hancock(17), Wood(16)
FOWLER Trumbull
FRANKFORT Ross
FRANKLIN (45005) Warren(98), Montgomery(1)
FRANKLIN FURNACE (45629) Scioto(93), Lawrence(6)
FRAZEYSBURG (43822) Muskingum(59), Licking(20), Coshocton(12), Knox(7)
FREDERICKSBURG (44627) Wayne(68), Holmes(31)
FREDERICKTOWN (43019) Knox(82), Morrow(16), Richland(1)
FREEPORT (43973) Guernsey(52), Harrison(46)
FREMONT Sandusky
FRESNO (43824) Coshocton(92), Tuscarawas(7)
FRIENDSHIP Scioto
FULTON Morrow
FULTONHAM Muskingum
GALENA Delaware

GALION (44833) Crawford(86), Morrow(9), Richland(3)
GALLIPOLIS Gallia
GALLOWAY (43119) Franklin(94), Madison(5)
GAMBIER Knox
GARRETTSVILLE (44231) Portage(88), Geauga(10), Trumbull(1)
GATES MILLS Cuyahoga
GENEVA (44041) Ashtabula(98), Lake(1)
GENOA (43430) Ottawa(95), Wood(3)
GEORGETOWN Brown
GERMANTOWN (45327) Montgomery(94), Preble(4), Butler(1)
GETTYSBURG Darke
GIBSONBURG (43431) Sandusky(98), Wood(1)
GIRARD Trumbull
GLANDORF Putnam
GLENCOE Belmont
GLENFORD (43739) Perry(64), Licking(35)
GLENMONT (44628) Holmes(62), Knox(37)
GLOUSTER (45732) Athens(92), Perry(5), Hocking(1)
GNADENHUTTEN Tuscarawas
GOMER Allen
GORDON Darke
GOSHEN Clermont
GRAFTON Lorain
GRAND RAPIDS (43522) Wood(52), Lucas(39), Henry(8)
GRAND RIVER Lake
GRANVILLE Licking
GRATIOT Licking
GRATIS Preble
GRAYSVILLE (45734) Monroe(79), Washington(20)
GRAYTOWN Ottawa
GREEN Summit
GREEN CAMP Marion
GREEN SPRINGS (44836) Seneca(57), Sandusky(42)
GREENFIELD Highland
GREENFORD Mahoning
GREENTOWN Stark
GREENVILLE Darke
GREENWICH (44837) Huron(77), Richland(12), Ashland(10)
GRELTON Henry
GROVE CITY Franklin
GROVEPORT Franklin
GROVER HILL (45849) Paulding(62), Van Wert(35), Putnam(1)
GUYSVILLE (45735) Athens(94), Meigs(5)
GYPSUM Ottawa
HALLSVILLE Ross
HAMDEN Vinton
HAMERSVILLE Brown
HAMILTON Butler
HAMLER Henry
HAMMONDSVILLE (43930) Jefferson(82), Columbiana(17)
HANNIBAL Monroe
HANOVERTON Columbiana
HARBOR VIEW Lucas
HARLEM SPRINGS Carroll
HARPSTER (43323) Wyandot(93), Marion(6)
HARRISBURG Franklin
HARRISON Hamilton
HARRISVILLE Harrison
HARROD (45850) Allen(78), Hardin(15), Auglaize(6)
HARTFORD Trumbull
HARTVILLE (44632) Stark(95), Portage(4)
HARVEYSBURG Warren
HASKINS Wood
HAVERHILL Scioto
HAVILAND Paulding
HAYDENVILLE Hocking
HAYESVILLE Ashland

HEBRON Licking
HELENA Sandusky
HICKSVILLE (43526) Defiance(96), Paulding(3)
HIGGINSPORT Brown
HIGHLAND Highland
HILLIARD Franklin
HILLSBORO (45133) Highland(97), Pike(2)
HINCKLEY Medina
HIRAM (44234) Portage(55), Geauga(44)
HOCKINGPORT Athens
HOLGATE (43527) Henry(89), Defiance(10)
HOLLAND Lucas
HOLLANSBURG Darke
HOLLOWAY Belmont
HOLMESVILLE Holmes
HOMER Licking
HOMERVILLE (44235) Medina(98), Ashland(1)
HOMEWORTH (44634) Columbiana(80), Stark(19)
HOOVEN Hamilton
HOPEDALE (43976) Harrison(98), Jefferson(1)
HOPEWELL (43746) Muskingum(88), Licking(12)
HOUSTON Shelby
HOWARD Knox
HOYTVILLE Wood
HUBBARD Trumbull
HUDSON Summit
HUNTSBURG (44046) Geauga(98), Ashtabula(1)
HUNTSVILLE Logan
HURON Erie
IBERIA Morrow
INDEPENDENCE Cuyahoga
IRONDALE (43932) Jefferson(92), Columbiana(7)
IRONTON (45638) Lawrence(94), Scioto(5)
IRWIN (43029) Union(75), Madison(24)
ISLE SAINT GEORGE Ottawa
JACKSON Monroe
JACKSON CENTER (45334) Shelby(90), Logan(5), Auglaize(4)
JACKSONTOWN Licking
JACKSONVILLE Athens
JACOBSBURG Belmont
JAMESTOWN (45335) Greene(95), Clinton(2), Fayette(1)
JASPER Pike
JEFFERSON Ashtabula
JEFFERSONVILLE Fayette
JENERA (45841) Hancock(94), Hardin(5)
JEROMESVILLE (44840) Ashland(98), Wayne(1)
JERRY CITY Wood
JERUSALEM (43747) Monroe(64), Belmont(35)
JEWELL Defiance
JEWETT (43986) Harrison(91), Carroll(8)
JOHNSTOWN (43031) Licking(97), Delaware(2)
JUNCTION CITY Perry
KALIDA Putnam
KANSAS (44841) Seneca(71), Sandusky(28)
KEENE Coshocton
KELLEYS ISLAND Erie
KENSINGTON (44427) Columbiana(58), Carroll(41)
KENT Portage
KENTON Hardin
KERR Gallia
KETTLERSVILLE Shelby
KIDRON Wayne
KILBOURNE Delaware
KILLBUCK (44637) Holmes(84), Coshocton(15)
KIMBOLTON (43749) Guernsey(93), Coshocton(4), Tuscarawas(2)

KINGS MILLS Warren
KINGSTON (45644) Ross(63),
   Pickaway(36)
KINGSVILLE Ashtabula
KINSMAN (44428) Trumbull(96),
   Ashtabula(3)
KIPLING Guernsey
KIPTON Lorain
KIRBY Wyandot
KIRKERSVILLE Licking
KITTS HILL Lawrence
KUNKLE Williams
LA RUE (43332) Marion(93), Hardin(4),
   Wyandot(2)
LACARNE Ottawa
LAFAYETTE Allen
LAFFERTY Belmont
LAGRANGE Lorain
LAINGS Monroe
LAKE MILTON (44429) Mahoning(98),
   Portage(1)
LAKEMORE Summit
LAKESIDE MARBLEHEAD Ottawa
LAKEVIEW (43331) Logan(94),
   Auglaize(4), Hardin(1)
LAKEVILLE (44638) Holmes(78),
   Ashland(14), Wayne(7)
LAKEWOOD Cuyahoga
LANCASTER Fairfield
LANGSVILLE Meigs
LANSING Belmont
LATHAM Pike
LATTY Paulding
LAURA (45337) Miami(84), Darke(15)
LAURELVILLE (43135) Hocking(70),
   Ross(12), Pickaway(12), Vinton(4)
LEAVITTSBURG Trumbull
LEBANON Warren
LEES CREEK Clinton
LEESBURG (45135) Highland(98),
   Fayette(1)
LEESVILLE Carroll
LEETONIA Columbiana
LEIPSIC (45856) Putnam(97), Henry(2)
LEMOYNE Wood
LEWIS CENTER Delaware
LEWISBURG Preble
LEWISTOWN Logan
LEWISVILLE Monroe
LIBERTY CENTER (43532) Henry(89),
   Fulton(6), Lucas(3)
LIMA Allen
LIMAVILLE Stark
LINDSEY (43442) Sandusky(96), Ottawa(3)
LISBON Columbiana
LITCHFIELD (44253) Medina(81),
   Lorain(18)
LITHOPOLIS Fairfield
LITTLE HOCKING (45742)
   Washington(92), Athens(7)
LOCKBOURNE (43137) Pickaway(58),
   Franklin(41)
LODI Medina
LOGAN (43138) Hocking(98), Perry(1)
LONDON (43140) Madison(98), Franklin(1)
LONDONDERRY Ross
LONG BOTTOM Meigs
LORAIN Lorain
LORE CITY Guernsey
LOUDONVILLE (44842) Ashland(90),
   Holmes(9)
LOUISVILLE Stark
LOVELAND (45140) Clermont(42),
   Hamilton(29), Warren(27)
LOWELL (45744) Washington(82),
   Noble(15), Morgan(2)
LOWELLVILLE Mahoning
LOWER SALEM (45745) Noble(54),
   Monroe(24), Washington(20)
LUCAS (44843) Richland(97), Ashland(?)
LUCASVILLE Scioto
LUCKEY (43443) Wood(97), Sandusky(2)

LUDLOW FALLS Miami
LYNCHBURG (45142) Highland(90),
   Clinton(8)
LYNX Adams
LYONS Fulton
MACEDONIA Summit
MACKSBURG (45746) Noble(57),
   Washington(42)
MADISON Lake
MAGNETIC SPRINGS Union
MAGNOLIA (44643) Stark(42),
   Tuscarawas(37), Carroll(20)
MAINEVILLE (45039) Warren(98),
   Hamilton(1)
MALAGA Monroe
MALINTA Henry
MALTA Morgan
MALVERN Carroll
MANCHESTER Adams
MANSFIELD Richland
MANTUA (44255) Portage(85), Geauga(14)
MAPLE HEIGHTS Cuyahoga
MAPLEWOOD Shelby
MARATHON Clermont
MARENGO (43334) Morrow(96),
   Delaware(3)
MARIA STEIN (45860) Mercer(98),
   Darke(1)
MARIETTA Washington
MARION Marion
MARK CENTER Defiance
MARSHALLVILLE (44645) Wayne(96),
   Stark(2), Summit(1)
MARTEL Marion
MARTIN (43445) Ottawa(63), Lucas(36)
MARTINS FERRY Belmont
MARTINSBURG Knox
MARTINSVILLE Clinton
MARYSVILLE Union
MASON Warren
MASSILLON Stark
MASURY Trumbull
MAUMEE Lucas
MAXIMO Stark
MAYNARD Belmont
MC ARTHUR Vinton
MC CLURE (43534) Henry(97), Wood(2)
MC COMB (45858) Hancock(97),
   Putnam(2)
MC CONNELSVILLE Morgan
MC CUTCHENVILLE (44844)
   Wyandot(60), Seneca(39)
MC DERMOTT Scioto
MC DONALD (44437) Trumbull(97),
   Mahoning(2)
MC GUFFEY Hardin
MECHANICSBURG (43044)
   Champaign(81), Clark(12), Madison(5)
MECHANICSTOWN Carroll
MEDINA Medina
MEDWAY Clark
MELMORE Seneca
MELROSE Paulding
MENDON (45862) Mercer(92), Auglaize(7)
MENTOR Lake
MESOPOTAMIA Trumbull
METAMORA Fulton
MIAMISBURG Montgomery
MIAMITOWN Hamilton
MIAMIVILLE Clermont
MIDDLE BASS Ottawa
MIDDLE POINT Van Wert
MIDDLEBRANCH Stark
MIDDLEBURG Logan
MIDDLEFIELD (44062) Geauga(80),
   Trumbull(16), Ashtabula(3)
MIDDLEPORT Meigs
MIDDLETOWN Butler
MIDLAND Clinton
MIDVALE Tuscarawas
MILAN (44846) Erie(93), Huron(6)
MILFORD Clermont

MILFORD CENTER (43045) Union(96),
   Champaign(3)
MILLBURY (43447) Wood(85), Ottawa(14)
MILLEDGEVILLE Fayette
MILLER CITY Putnam
MILLERSBURG (44654) Holmes(96),
   Coshocton(3)
MILLERSPORT (43046) Fairfield(91),
   Licking(8)
MILLFIELD Athens
MILTON CENTER Wood
MINERAL CITY (44656) Tuscarawas(96),
   Carroll(3)
MINERAL RIDGE (44440) Trumbull(83),
   Mahoning(16)
MINERVA (44657) Stark(50), Carroll(34),
   Columbiana(14)
MINFORD Scioto
MINGO Champaign
MINGO JUNCTION Jefferson
MINSTER (45865) Auglaize(77),
   Shelby(21)
MOGADORE (44260) Portage(69),
   Summit(24), Stark(5)
MONCLOVA Lucas
MONROE Butler
MONROEVILLE (44847) Huron(68),
   Erie(31)
MONTEZUMA Mercer
MONTPELIER Williams
MONTVILLE (44064) Geauga(97),
   Ashtabula(2)
MORRAL (43337) Marion(84), Wyandot(16)
MORRISTOWN Belmont
MORROW Warren
MOSCOW Clermont
MOUNT BLANCHARD (45867)
   Hancock(94), Wyandot(5)
MOUNT CORY (45868) Hancock(96),
   Putnam(3)
MOUNT EATON Wayne
MOUNT GILEAD Morrow
MOUNT HOPE Holmes
MOUNT LIBERTY Knox
MOUNT ORAB Brown
MOUNT PERRY (43760) Perry(70),
   Muskingum(22), Licking(6)
MOUNT PLEASANT Jefferson
MOUNT SAINT JOSEPH Hamilton
MOUNT STERLING (43143) Madison(74),
   Pickaway(16), Fayette(8)
MOUNT VERNON Knox
MOUNT VICTORY (43340) Hardin(89),
   Union(10)
MOWRYSTOWN Highland
MOXAHALA Perry
MUNROE FALLS Summit
MURRAY CITY Hocking
NANKIN Ashland
NAPOLEON (43545) Henry(98),
   Defiance(1)
NASHPORT (43830) Muskingum(87),
   Licking(11)
NASHVILLE Holmes
NAVARRE (44662) Stark(97), Wayne(2)
NEAPOLIS Lucas
NEFFS Belmont
NEGLEY Columbiana
NELSONVILLE (45764) Athens(88),
   Hocking(11)
NEVADA (44849) Wyandot(80),
   Crawford(19)
NEVILLE Clermont
NEW ALBANY (43054) Franklin(88),
   Delaware(11)
NEW ATHENS Harrison
NEW BAVARIA (43548) Henry(94),
   Defiance(2), Putnam(2)
NEW BLOOMINGTON Marion
NEW BREMEN (45869) Auglaize(91),
   Shelby(4), Mercer(4)

NEW CARLISLE (45344) Clark(82),
   Miami(13), Montgomery(2)
NEW CONCORD (43762) Muskingum(82),
   Guernsey(17)
NEW HAMPSHIRE Auglaize
NEW HAVEN Huron
NEW HOLLAND (43145) Pickaway(66),
   Fayette(33)
NEW KNOXVILLE (45871) Auglaize(83),
   Shelby(16)
NEW LEBANON Montgomery
NEW LEXINGTON Perry
NEW LONDON (44851) Huron(84),
   Lorain(11), Ashland(4)
NEW MADISON Darke
NEW MARSHFIELD (45766) Athens(88),
   Vinton(11)
NEW MATAMORAS (45767) Monroe(50),
   Washington(49)
NEW MIDDLETOWN Mahoning
NEW PARIS (45347) Preble(92), Darke(7)
NEW PHILADELPHIA Tuscarawas
NEW PLYMOUTH (45654) Vinton(72),
   Hocking(27)
NEW RICHMOND Clermont
NEW RIEGEL Seneca
NEW RUMLEY Harrison
NEW SPRINGFIELD (44443)
   Mahoning(95), Columbiana(5)
NEW STRAITSVILLE (43766) Perry(83),
   Hocking(16)
NEW VIENNA (45159) Clinton(96),
   Highland(3)
NEW WASHINGTON (44854)
   Crawford(92), Seneca(5), Huron(2)
NEW WATERFORD Columbiana
NEW WESTON Darke
NEWARK Licking
NEWBURY Geauga
NEWCOMERSTOWN (43832)
   Tuscarawas(84), Coshocton(13),
   Guernsey(1)
NEWPORT Washington
NEWTON FALLS (44444) Trumbull(93),
   Portage(4), Mahoning(1)
NEWTONSVILLE Clermont
NEY Defiance
NILES Trumbull
NORTH BALTIMORE (45872) Wood(98),
   Hancock(1)
NORTH BEND Hamilton
NORTH BENTON (44449) Portage(50),
   Mahoning(49)
NORTH BLOOMFIELD Trumbull
NORTH FAIRFIELD Huron
NORTH GEORGETOWN Columbiana
NORTH HAMPTON Clark
NORTH JACKSON Mahoning
NORTH KINGSVILLE Ashtabula
NORTH LAWRENCE (44666) Stark(79),
   Wayne(20)
NORTH LEWISBURG (43060) Union(53),
   Champaign(32), Logan(14)
NORTH LIMA Mahoning
NORTH OLMSTED Cuyahoga
NORTH RIDGEVILLE Lorain
NORTH ROBINSON Crawford
NORTH ROYALTON Cuyahoga
NORTH STAR Darke
NORTHFIELD Summit
NORTHWOOD Wood
NORWALK (44857) Huron(98), Erie(1)
NORWICH Muskingum
NOVA (44859) Ashland(94), Lorain(5)
NOVELTY Geauga
OAK HARBOR (43449) Ottawa(98),
   Sandusky(1)
OAK HILL (45656) Jackson(88), Gallia(7),
   Lawrence(3)
OAKWOOD Paulding
OBERLIN Lorain
OCEOLA Crawford

OHIO CITY Van Wert
OKEANA Butler
OKOLONA Henry
OLD FORT Seneca
OLD WASHINGTON Guernsey
OLMSTED FALLS Cuyahoga
ONTARIO Richland
ORANGEVILLE Trumbull
OREGON Lucas
OREGONIA Warren
ORIENT (43146) Pickaway(73),
    Franklin(24), Madison(1)
ORRVILLE Wayne
ORWELL (44076) Ashtabula(91),
    Trumbull(8)
OSGOOD Darke
OSTRANDER (43061) Delaware(81),
    Union(18)
OTTAWA Putnam
OTTOVILLE Putnam
OTWAY (45657) Scioto(79), Adams(17),
    Pike(2)
OVERPECK Butler
OWENSVILLE Clermont
OXFORD Butler
PAINESVILLE Lake
PALESTINE Darke
PANDORA (45877) Putnam(96), Allen(2)
PARIS Stark
PARKMAN Geauga
PATASKALA Licking
PATRIOT Gallia
PAULDING Paulding
PAYNE Paulding
PEDRO Lawrence
PEEBLES (45660) Adams(87), Pike(10),
    Highland(1)
PEMBERTON Shelby
PEMBERVILLE Wood
PENINSULA Summit
PERRY Lake
PERRYSBURG Wood
PERRYSVILLE (44864) Ashland(61),
    Richland(38)
PETERSBURG (44454) Mahoning(85),
    Columbiana(14)
PETTISVILLE Fulton
PHILLIPSBURG Montgomery
PHILO Muskingum
PICKERINGTON (43147) Fairfield(93),
    Franklin(5)
PIEDMONT (43983) Belmont(58),
    Guernsey(24), Harrison(14), Adams(2)
PIERPONT Ashtabula
PIKETON Pike
PINEY FORK Jefferson
PIONEER Williams
PIQUA (45356) Miami(96), Shelby(3)
PITSBURG Darke
PLAIN CITY (43064) Madison(53),
    Union(45), Franklin(1)
PLAINFIELD Coshocton
PLEASANT CITY (43772) Guernsey(58),
    Noble(41)
PLEASANT HILL Miami
PLEASANT PLAIN Warren
PLEASANTVILLE (43148) Fairfield(89),
    Perry(10)
PLYMOUTH (44865) Huron(50),
    Richland(45), Crawford(3)
POLK Ashland
POMEROY Meigs
PORT CLINTON Ottawa
PORT JEFFERSON Shelby
PORT WASHINGTON (43837)
    Tuscarawas(96), Guernsey(3)
PORT WILLIAM Clinton
PORTAGE Wood
PORTLAND Meigs
PORTSMOUTH Scioto
POTSDAM Miami

POWELL (43065) Delaware(71),
    Franklin(28)
POWHATAN POINT (43942) Belmont(92),
    Monroe(6)
PROCTORVILLE Lawrence
PROSPECT (43342) Marion(90),
    Delaware(7), Union(2)
PUT IN BAY Ottawa
QUAKER CITY (43773) Guernsey(53),
    Noble(40), Belmont(2), Monroe(2)
QUINCY (43343) Logan(77),
    Champaign(13), Shelby(8)
RACINE Meigs
RADCLIFF Vinton
RADNOR Delaware
RANDOLPH Portage
RARDEN (45671) Scioto(66), Pike(20),
    Adams(8), Fairfield(4)
RAVENNA Portage
RAWSON Hancock
RAY (45672) Vinton(69), Jackson(25),
    Ross(4)
RAYLAND (43943) Jefferson(96),
    Belmont(3)
RAYMOND Union
REEDSVILLE Meigs
REESVILLE Clinton
RENO Washington
REPUBLIC Seneca
REYNOLDSBURG Franklin
RICHFIELD Summit
RICHMOND Jefferson
RICHMOND DALE Ross
RICHWOOD (43344) Union(80),
    Marion(17), Delaware(2)
RIDGEVILLE CORNERS Henry
RIDGEWAY (43345) Hardin(61), Logan(38)
RIO GRANDE Gallia
RIPLEY Brown
RISINGSUN (43457) Wood(71),
    Sandusky(23), Seneca(4)
RITTMAN (44270) Wayne(94), Medina(5)
ROBERTSVILLE Stark
ROCK CAMP Lawrence
ROCK CREEK Ashtabula
ROCKBRIDGE Hocking
ROCKFORD (45882) Mercer(94), Van
    Wert(5)
ROCKY RIDGE Ottawa
ROCKY RIVER Cuyahoga
ROGERS Columbiana
ROME Ashtabula
ROOTSTOWN Portage
ROSEVILLE (43777) Muskingum(55),
    Perry(44)
ROSEWOOD Champaign
ROSS Butler
ROSSBURG Darke
ROSSFORD Wood
ROUNDHEAD Hardin
RUDOLPH Wood
RUSHSYLVANIA (43347) Logan(89),
    Hardin(10)
RUSHVILLE (43150) Fairfield(67),
    Perry(32)
RUSSELLS POINT Logan
RUSSELLVILLE Brown
RUSSIA Shelby
RUTLAND Meigs
SABINA (45169) Clinton(98), Fayette(1)
SAINT CLAIRSVILLE Belmont
SAINT HENRY (45883) Mercer(98),
    Darke(1)
SAINT JOHNS Auglaize
SAINT LOUISVILLE Licking
SAINT MARYS Auglaize
SAINT PARIS Champaign
SALEM (44460) Columbiana(89),
    Mahoning(10)
SALESVILLE (43778) Guernsey(97),
    Noble(2)

SALINEVILLE (43945) Columbiana(70),
    Carroll(20), Jefferson(9)
SANDUSKY Erie
SANDYVILLE Tuscarawas
SARAHSVILLE Noble
SARDINIA Brown
SARDIS Monroe
SAVANNAH Ashland
SCIO (43988) Harrison(71), Carroll(28)
SCIOTO FURNACE Scioto
SCOTT (45886) Van Wert(55),
    Paulding(44)
SCOTTOWN (45678) Lawrence(79),
    Gallia(20)
SEAMAN (45679) Adams(92), Highland(7)
SEBRING Mahoning
SEDALIA Madison
SENECAVILLE (43780) Guernsey(69),
    Noble(30)
SEVEN MILE Butler
SEVILLE Medina
SHADE (45776) Meigs(51), Athens(48)
SHADYSIDE Belmont
SHANDON Butler
SHARON CENTER Medina
SHARPSBURG Athens
SHAUCK Morrow
SHAWNEE Perry
SHEFFIELD LAKE Lorain
SHELBY (44875) Richland(96),
    Crawford(3)
SHERRODSVILLE (44675) Carroll(69),
    Tuscarawas(30)
SHERWOOD Defiance
SHILOH (44878) Richland(91), Huron(4),
    Ashland(3)
SHORT CREEK Harrison
SHREVE (44676) Wayne(82), Holmes(17)
SIDNEY Shelby
SINKING SPRING Highland
SMITHFIELD Jefferson
SMITHVILLE Wayne
SOLON Cuyahoga
SOMERDALE Tuscarawas
SOMERSET Perry
SOMERVILLE Butler
SOUTH BLOOMINGVILLE (43152)
    Hocking(83), Vinton(16)
SOUTH CHARLESTON (45368) Clark(95),
    Greene(4)
SOUTH LEBANON Warren
SOUTH POINT Lawrence
SOUTH SALEM Ross
SOUTH SOLON (43153) Madison(77),
    Fayette(10), Clark(6), Greene(5)
SOUTH VIENNA (45369) Clark(98),
    Madison(1)
SOUTH WEBSTER Scioto
SOUTHINGTON (44470) Trumbull(98),
    Portage(1)
SPARTA Morrow
SPENCER (44275) Medina(94), Lorain(5)
SPENCERVILLE (45887) Allen(75),
    Auglaize(14), Van Wert(7), Mercer(2)
SPRING HILL NURSERIES Miami
SPRING VALLEY Greene
SPRINGBORO Warren
SPRINGFIELD Clark
STAFFORD Monroe
STERLING Wayne
STEUBENVILLE Jefferson
STEWART Athens
STEWARTSVILLE Belmont
STILLWATER Tuscarawas
STOCKDALE Pike
STOCKPORT (43787) Morgan(95),
    Washington(4)
STONE CREEK (43840) Coshocton(67),
    Tuscarawas(32)
STONY RIDGE Wood
STOUT (45684) Scioto(66), Adams(33)

STOUTSVILLE (43154) Fairfield(79),
    Pickaway(20)
STOW Summit
STRASBURG Tuscarawas
STRATTON Jefferson
STREETSBORO Portage
STRONGSVILLE (44149) Cuyahoga(98),
    Medina(1)
STRUTHERS Mahoning
STRYKER (43557) Williams(81),
    Henry(12), Fulton(5)
SUGAR GROVE (43155) Fairfield(74),
    Hocking(25)
SUGARCREEK (44681) Tuscarawas(77),
    Holmes(22)
SULLIVAN (44880) Ashland(83),
    Lorain(13), Medina(3)
SULPHUR SPRINGS Crawford
SUMMERFIELD (43788) Noble(77),
    Monroe(22)
SUMMIT STATION Licking
SUMMITVILLE Columbiana
SUNBURY (43074) Delaware(97),
    Licking(1)
SWANTON (43558) Fulton(59), Lucas(40)
SYCAMORE (44882) Wyandot(62),
    Crawford(32), Seneca(5)
SYCAMORE VALLEY Monroe
SYLVANIA Lucas
SYRACUSE Meigs
TALLMADGE (44278) Summit(97),
    Portage(2)
TARLTON Pickaway
TERRACE PARK Hamilton
THE PLAINS Athens
THOMPSON (44086) Geauga(79),
    Lake(15), Ashtabula(5)
THORNVILLE (43076) Perry(44),
    Licking(31), Fairfield(24)
THURMAN (45685) Gallia(74), Jackson(25)
THURSTON Fairfield
TIFFIN Seneca
TILTONSVILLE Jefferson
TIPP CITY (45371) Miami(98),
    Montgomery(1)
TIPPECANOE (44699) Harrison(71),
    Tuscarawas(25), Guernsey(3)
TIRO Crawford
TOLEDO Lucas
TONTOGANY Wood
TORCH Athens
TORONTO Jefferson
TREMONT CITY Clark
TRENTON Butler
TRIMBLE Athens
TRINWAY Muskingum
TROY Miami
TUPPERS PLAINS Meigs
TUSCARAWAS Tuscarawas
TWINSBURG Summit
UHRICHSVILLE (44683) Tuscarawas(91),
    Harrison(8)
UNION CITY Darke
UNION FURNACE Hocking
UNIONPORT Jefferson
UNIONTOWN (44685) Stark(51),
    Summit(48)
UNIONVILLE Ashtabula
UNIONVILLE CENTER Union
UNIOPOLIS Auglaize
UPPER SANDUSKY Wyandot
URBANA Champaign
UTICA (43080) Licking(72), Knox(27)
VALLEY CITY (44280) Medina(95),
    Lorain(4)
VAN BUREN (45889) Hancock(98),
    Wood(1)
VAN WERT Van Wert
VANDALIA Montgomery
VANLUE Hancock
VAUGHNSVILLE Putnam

VENEDOCIA (45894) Van Wert(95),
   Mercer(3)
VERMILION (44089) Erie(56), Lorain(43)
VERONA Preble
VERSAILLES Darke
VICKERY (43464) Sandusky(74), Erie(25)
VIENNA Trumbull
VINCENT Washington
VINTON Gallia
WADSWORTH Medina
WAKEFIELD Pike
WAKEMAN (44889) Huron(67), Erie(20),
   Lorain(12)
WALBRIDGE Wood
WALDO (43356) Marion(77), Delaware(15),
   Morrow(7)
WALHONDING (43843) Coshocton(65),
   Knox(34)
WALNUT CREEK Holmes
WAPAKONETA Auglaize
WARNOCK Belmont
WARREN Trumbull
WARSAW (43844) Coshocton(94), Knox(5)
WASHINGTON COURT HOUSE (43160)
   Fayette(98), Ross(1)
WASHINGTONVILLE Columbiana
WATERFORD (45786) Washington(76),
   Morgan(23)
WATERLOO (45688) Lawrence(94),
   Gallia(5)
WATERTOWN Washington
WATERVILLE Lucas

WAUSEON Fulton
WAVERLY (45690) Pike(92), Ross(7)
WAYLAND Portage
WAYNE Wood
WAYNESBURG (44688) Stark(88),
   Carroll(11)
WAYNESFIELD (45896) Auglaize(81),
   Hardin(13), Allen(5)
WAYNESVILLE Warren
WELLINGTON Lorain
WELLSTON Jackson
WELLSVILLE Columbiana
WEST ALEXANDRIA (45381) Preble(95),
   Montgomery(4)
WEST CHESTER Butler
WEST ELKTON Preble
WEST FARMINGTON (44491)
   Trumbull(83), Geauga(14), Portage(1)
WEST JEFFERSON Madison
WEST LAFAYETTE Coshocton
WEST LIBERTY (43357) Logan(75),
   Champaign(24)
WEST MANCHESTER (45382) Preble(78),
   Darke(21)
WEST MANSFIELD (43358) Logan(58),
   Union(41)
WEST MILLGROVE Wood
WEST MILTON Miami
WEST POINT Columbiana
WEST PORTSMOUTH Scioto
WEST RUSHVILLE Fairfield

WEST SALEM (44287) Wayne(63),
   Ashland(29), Medina(6)
WEST UNION Adams
WEST UNITY (43570) Williams(95),
   Fulton(4)
WESTERVILLE Franklin
WESTFIELD CENTER Medina
WESTLAKE Cuyahoga
WESTON Wood
WESTVILLE Champaign
WHARTON Wyandot
WHEELERSBURG Scioto
WHIPPLE Washington
WHITE COTTAGE Muskingum
WHITEHOUSE Lucas
WICKLIFFE Lake
WILBERFORCE Greene
WILKESVILLE Vinton
WILLARD Huron
WILLIAMSBURG Clermont
WILLIAMSFIELD Ashtabula
WILLIAMSPORT (43164) Pickaway(95),
   Ross(4)
WILLIAMSTOWN Hancock
WILLISTON Ottawa
WILLOUGHBY Lake
WILLOW WOOD Lawrence
WILLSHIRE (45898) Van Wert(65),
   Mercer(34)
WILMINGTON Clinton
WILMOT (44689) Holmes(69), Stark(30)

WINCHESTER (45697) Adams(60),
   Brown(25), Highland(13)
WINDHAM (44288) Portage(98),
   Trumbull(1)
WINDSOR (44099) Ashtabula(85),
   Geauga(14)
WINESBURG Holmes
WINGETT RUN (45789) Washington(87),
   Monroe(12)
WINONA Columbiana
WINTERSVILLE Jefferson
WOLF RUN Jefferson
WOODSFIELD Monroe
WOODSTOCK (43084) Champaign(91),
   Union(8)
WOODVILLE (43469) Sandusky(93),
   Ottawa(5), Wood(1)
WOOSTER Wayne
WREN Van Wert
XENIA Greene
YELLOW SPRINGS (45387) Greene(93),
   Clark(6)
YORKSHIRE (45388) Darke(96),
   Shelby(2), Mercer(1)
YORKVILLE (43971) Jefferson(64),
   Belmont(35)
YOUNGSTOWN Mahoning
ZALESKI Vinton
ZANESFIELD Logan
ZANESVILLE Muskingum
ZOAR Tuscarawas

ZIP/City Cross Reference

43001-43001 ALEXANDRIA	43067-43067 RAYMOND	43144-43144 MURRAY CITY	43340-43340 MOUNT VICTORY
43002-43002 AMLIN	43068-43069 REYNOLDSBURG	43145-43145 NEW HOLLAND	43341-43341 NEW BLOOMINGTON
43003-43003 ASHLEY	43070-43070 ROSEWOOD	43146-43146 ORIENT	43342-43342 PROSPECT
43004-43004 BLACKLICK	43071-43071 SAINT LOUISVILLE	43147-43147 PICKERINGTON	43343-43343 QUINCY
43005-43005 BLADENSBURG	43072-43072 SAINT PARIS	43148-43148 PLEASANTVILLE	43344-43344 RICHWOOD
43006-43006 BRINKHAVEN	43073-43073 SUMMIT STATION	43149-43149 ROCKBRIDGE	43345-43345 RIDGEWAY
43007-43007 BROADWAY	43074-43074 SUNBURY	43150-43150 RUSHVILLE	43346-43346 ROUNDHEAD
43008-43008 BUCKEYE LAKE	43076-43076 THORNVILLE	43151-43151 SEDALIA	43347-43347 RUSHSYLVANIA
43009-43009 CABLE	43077-43077 UNIONVILLE CENTER	43152-43152 SOUTH BLOOMINGVILLE	43348-43348 RUSSELLS POINT
43010-43010 CATAWBA	43078-43078 URBANA	43153-43153 SOUTH SOLON	43349-43349 SHAUCK
43011-43011 CENTERBURG	43080-43080 UTICA	43154-43154 STOUTSVILLE	43350-43350 SPARTA
43013-43013 CROTON	43081-43082 WESTERVILLE	43155-43155 SUGAR GROVE	43351-43351 UPPER SANDUSKY
43014-43014 DANVILLE	43083-43083 WESTVILLE	43156-43156 TARLTON	43356-43356 WALDO
43015-43015 DELAWARE	43084-43084 WOODSTOCK	43157-43157 THURSTON	43357-43357 WEST LIBERTY
43016-43017 DUBLIN	43085-43085 COLUMBUS	43158-43158 UNION FURNACE	43358-43358 WEST MANSFIELD
43018-43018 ETNA	43086-43086 WESTERVILLE	43160-43160 WASHINGTON COURT	43359-43359 WHARTON
43019-43019 FREDERICKTOWN	43093-43093 NEWARK	HOUSE	43360-43360 ZANESFIELD
43021-43021 GALENA	43098-43098 HEBRON	43162-43162 WEST JEFFERSON	43402-43403 BOWLING GREEN
43022-43022 GAMBIER	43099-43099 BLACKLICK	43163-43163 WEST RUSHVILLE	43406-43406 BRADNER
43023-43023 GRANVILLE	43101-43101 ADELPHI	43164-43164 WILLIAMSPORT	43407-43407 BURGOON
43025-43025 HEBRON	43102-43102 AMANDA	43196-43199 GROVEPORT	43408-43408 CLAY CENTER
43026-43026 HILLIARD	43103-43103 ASHVILLE	43200-43299 COLUMBUS	43410-43410 CLYDE
43027-43027 HOMER	43105-43105 BALTIMORE	43301-43307 MARION	43412-43412 CURTICE
43028-43028 HOWARD	43106-43106 BLOOMINGBURG	43310-43310 BELLE CENTER	43413-43413 CYGNET
43029-43029 IRWIN	43107-43107 BREMEN	43311-43311 BELLEFONTAINE	43414-43414 DUNBRIDGE
43030-43030 JACKSONTOWN	43109-43109 BRICE	43314-43314 CALEDONIA	43416-43416 ELMORE
43031-43031 JOHNSTOWN	43110-43110 CANAL WINCHESTER	43315-43315 CARDINGTON	43420-43420 FREMONT
43032-43032 KILBOURNE	43111-43111 CARBON HILL	43316-43316 CAREY	43430-43430 GENOA
43033-43033 KIRKERSVILLE	43112-43112 CARROLL	43317-43317 CHESTERVILLE	43431-43431 GIBSONBURG
43035-43035 LEWIS CENTER	43113-43113 CIRCLEVILLE	43318-43318 DE GRAFF	43432-43432 GRAYTOWN
43036-43036 MAGNETIC SPRINGS	43115-43115 CLARKSBURG	43319-43319 EAST LIBERTY	43433-43433 GYPSUM
43037-43037 MARTINSBURG	43116-43116 COMMERCIAL POINT	43320-43320 EDISON	43434-43434 HARBOR VIEW
43040-43041 MARYSVILLE	43117-43117 DERBY	43321-43321 FULTON	43435-43435 HELENA
43044-43044 MECHANICSBURG	43119-43119 GALLOWAY	43322-43322 GREEN CAMP	43436-43436 ISLE SAINT GEORGE
43045-43045 MILFORD CENTER	43123-43123 GROVE CITY	43323-43323 HARPSTER	43437-43437 JERRY CITY
43046-43046 MILLERSPORT	43125-43125 GROVEPORT	43324-43324 HUNTSVILLE	43438-43438 KELLEYS ISLAND
43047-43047 MINGO	43126-43126 HARRISBURG	43325-43325 IBERIA	43439-43439 LACARNE
43048-43048 MOUNT LIBERTY	43127-43127 HAYDENVILLE	43326-43326 KENTON	43440-43440 LAKESIDE MARBLEHEAD
43050-43050 MOUNT VERNON	43128-43128 JEFFERSONVILLE	43330-43330 KIRBY	43441-43441 LEMOYNE
43054-43054 NEW ALBANY	43130-43132 LANCASTER	43331-43331 LAKEVIEW	43442-43442 LINDSEY
43055-43058 NEWARK	43135-43135 LAURELVILLE	43332-43332 LA RUE	43443-43443 LUCKEY
43060-43060 NORTH LEWISBURG	43136-43136 LITHOPOLIS	43333-43333 LEWISTOWN	43445-43445 MARTIN
43061-43061 OSTRANDER	43137-43137 LOCKBOURNE	43334-43334 MARENGO	43446-43446 MIDDLE BASS
43062-43062 PATASKALA	43138-43138 LOGAN	43335-43335 MARTEL	43447-43447 MILLBURY
43064-43064 PLAIN CITY	43140-43140 LONDON	43336-43336 MIDDLEBURG	43449-43449 OAK HARBOR
43065-43065 POWELL	43142-43142 MILLEDGEVILLE	43337-43337 MORRAL	43450-43450 PEMBERVILLE
43066-43066 RADNOR	43143-43143 MOUNT STERLING	43338-43338 MOUNT GILEAD	43451-43451 PORTAGE

43452-43452 PORT CLINTON	43722-43722 BUFFALO	43915-43915 CLARINGTON	44057-44057 MADISON
43456-43456 PUT IN BAY	43723-43723 BYESVILLE	43916-43916 COLERAIN	44060-44061 MENTOR
43457-43457 RISINGSUN	43724-43724 CALDWELL	43917-43917 DILLONVALE	44062-44062 MIDDLEFIELD
43458-43458 ROCKY RIDGE	43725-43725 CAMBRIDGE	43920-43920 EAST LIVERPOOL	44064-44064 MONTVILLE
43460-43460 ROSSFORD	43727-43727 CHANDLERSVILLE	43925-43925 EAST SPRINGFIELD	44065-44065 NEWBURY
43462-43462 RUDOLPH	43728-43728 CHESTERHILL	43926-43926 EMPIRE	44067-44067 NORTHFIELD
43463-43463 STONY RIDGE	43730-43730 CORNING	43927-43927 FAIRPOINT	44068-44068 NORTH KINGSVILLE
43464-43464 VICKERY	43731-43731 CROOKSVILLE	43928-43928 GLENCOE	44070-44070 NORTH OLMSTED
43465-43465 WALBRIDGE	43732-43732 CUMBERLAND	43930-43930 HAMMONDSVILLE	44072-44073 NOVELTY
43466-43466 WAYNE	43733-43733 DERWENT	43931-43931 HANNIBAL	44074-44074 OBERLIN
43467-43467 WEST MILLGROVE	43734-43734 DUNCAN FALLS	43932-43932 IRONDALE	44076-44076 ORWELL
43468-43468 WILLISTON	43735-43735 EAST FULTONHAM	43933-43933 JACOBSBURG	44077-44077 PAINESVILLE
43469-43469 WOODVILLE	43736-43736 FAIRVIEW	43934-43934 LANSING	44080-44080 PARKMAN
43501-43501 ALVORDTON	43738-43738 FULTONHAM	43935-43935 MARTINS FERRY	44081-44081 PERRY
43502-43502 ARCHBOLD	43739-43739 GLENFORD	43937-43937 MAYNARD	44082-44082 PIERPONT
43504-43504 BERKEY	43740-43740 GRATIOT	43938-43938 MINGO JUNCTION	44084-44084 ROCK CREEK
43505-43505 BLAKESLEE	43746-43746 HOPEWELL	43939-43939 MOUNT PLEASANT	44085-44085 ROME
43506-43506 BRYAN	43747-43747 JERUSALEM	43940-43940 NEFFS	44086-44086 THOMPSON
43510-43510 COLTON	43748-43748 JUNCTION CITY	43941-43941 PINEY FORK	44087-44087 TWINSBURG
43511-43511 CUSTAR	43749-43749 KIMBOLTON	43942-43942 POWHATAN POINT	44088-44088 UNIONVILLE
43512-43512 DEFIANCE	43750-43750 KIPLING	43943-43943 RAYLAND	44089-44089 VERMILION
43515-43515 DELTA	43752-43752 LAINGS	43944-43944 RICHMOND	44090-44090 WELLINGTON
43516-43516 DESHLER	43754-43754 LEWISVILLE	43945-43945 SALINEVILLE	44092-44092 WICKLIFFE
43517-43517 EDGERTON	43755-43755 LORE CITY	43946-43946 SARDIS	44093-44093 WILLIAMSFIELD
43518-43518 EDON	43756-43756 MC CONNELSVILLE	43947-43947 SHADYSIDE	44094-44094 WILLOUGHBY
43519-43519 EVANSPORT	43757-43757 MALAGA	43948-43948 SMITHFIELD	44095-44095 EASTLAKE
43520-43520 FARMER	43758-43758 MALTA	43950-43950 SAINT CLAIRSVILLE	44096-44096 WILLOUGHBY
43521-43521 FAYETTE	43759-43759 MORRISTOWN	43951-43951 LAFFERTY	44097-44097 EASTLAKE
43522-43522 GRAND RAPIDS	43760-43760 MOUNT PERRY	43952-43952 STEUBENVILLE	44099-44099 WINDSOR
43523-43523 GRELTON	43761-43761 MOXAHALA	43953-43953 WINTERSVILLE	44100-44106 CLEVELAND
43524-43524 HAMLER	43762-43762 NEW CONCORD	43960-43960 STEWARTSVILLE	44107-44107 LAKEWOOD
43525-43525 HASKINS	43764-43764 NEW LEXINGTON	43961-43961 STRATTON	44108-44115 CLEVELAND
43526-43526 HICKSVILLE	43766-43766 NEW STRAITSVILLE	43962-43962 SUMMITVILLE	44116-44116 ROCKY RIVER
43527-43527 HOLGATE	43767-43767 NORWICH	43963-43963 TILTONSVILLE	44117-44117 EUCLID
43528-43528 HOLLAND	43768-43768 OLD WASHINGTON	43964-43964 TORONTO	44118-44121 CLEVELAND
43529-43529 HOYTVILLE	43770-43770 STOCKPORT	43966-43966 UNIONPORT	44122-44122 BEACHWOOD
43530-43530 JEWELL	43771-43771 PHILO	43967-43967 WARNOCK	44123-44123 EUCLID
43531-43531 KUNKLE	43772-43772 PLEASANT CITY	43968-43968 WELLSVILLE	44124-44130 CLEVELAND
43532-43532 LIBERTY CENTER	43773-43773 QUAKER CITY	43970-43970 WOLF RUN	44131-44131 INDEPENDENCE
43533-43533 LYONS	43777-43777 ROSEVILLE	43971-43971 YORKVILLE	44132-44132 EUCLID
43534-43534 MC CLURE	43778-43778 SALESVILLE	43972-43972 BANNOCK	44133-44133 NORTH ROYALTON
43535-43535 MALINTA	43779-43779 SARAHSVILLE	43973-43973 FREEPORT	44134-44135 CLEVELAND
43536-43536 MARK CENTER	43780-43780 SENECAVILLE	43974-43974 HARRISVILLE	44136-44136 STRONGSVILLE
43537-43537 MAUMEE	43782-43782 SHAWNEE	43976-43976 HOPEDALE	44137-44137 MAPLE HEIGHTS
43540-43540 METAMORA	43783-43783 SOMERSET	43977-43977 FLUSHING	44138-44138 OLMSTED FALLS
43541-43541 MILTON CENTER	43786-43786 STAFFORD	43981-43981 NEW ATHENS	44139-44139 SOLON
43542-43542 MONCLOVA	43787-43787 STOCKPORT	43983-43983 PIEDMONT	44140-44140 BAY VILLAGE
43543-43543 MONTPELIER	43788-43788 SUMMERFIELD	43984-43984 NEW RUMLEY	44141-44141 BRECKSVILLE
43545-43545 NAPOLEON	43789-43789 SYCAMORE VALLEY	43985-43985 HOLLOWAY	44142-44142 BROOKPARK
43547-43547 NEAPOLIS	43791-43791 WHITE COTTAGE	43986-43986 JEWETT	44143-44144 CLEVELAND
43548-43548 NEW BAVARIA	43793-43793 WOODSFIELD	43988-43988 SCIO	44145-44145 WESTLAKE
43549-43549 NEY	43802-43802 ADAMSVILLE	43989-43989 SHORT CREEK	44146-44146 BEDFORD
43550-43550 OKOLONA	43803-43803 BAKERSVILLE	44001-44001 AMHERST	44147-44147 BROADVIEW HEIGHTS
43551-43552 PERRYSBURG	43804-43804 BALTIC	44003-44003 ANDOVER	44149-44149 STRONGSVILLE
43553-43553 PETTISVILLE	43805-43805 BLISSFIELD	44004-44005 ASHTABULA	44177-44199 CLEVELAND
43554-43554 PIONEER	43811-43811 CONESVILLE	44010-44010 AUSTINBURG	44201-44201 ATWATER
43555-43555 RIDGEVILLE CORNERS	43812-43812 COSHOCTON	44011-44011 AVON	44202-44202 AURORA
43556-43556 SHERWOOD	43821-43821 DRESDEN	44012-44012 AVON LAKE	44203-44203 BARBERTON
43557-43557 STRYKER	43822-43822 FRAZEYSBURG	44017-44017 BEREA	44210-44210 BATH
43558-43558 SWANTON	43824-43824 FRESNO	44021-44021 BURTON	44211-44211 BRADY LAKE
43560-43560 SYLVANIA	43828-43828 KEENE	44022-44023 CHAGRIN FALLS	44212-44212 BRUNSWICK
43565-43565 TONTOGANY	43830-43830 NASHPORT	44024-44024 CHARDON	44214-44214 BURBANK
43566-43566 WATERVILLE	43832-43832 NEWCOMERSTOWN	44026-44026 CHESTERLAND	44215-44215 CHIPPEWA LAKE
43567-43567 WAUSEON	43836-43836 PLAINFIELD	44028-44028 COLUMBIA STATION	44216-44216 CLINTON
43569-43569 WESTON	43837-43837 PORT WASHINGTON	44030-44030 CONNEAUT	44217-44217 CRESTON
43570-43570 WEST UNITY	43840-43840 STONE CREEK	44032-44032 DORSET	44221-44223 CUYAHOGA FALLS
43571-43571 WHITEHOUSE	43842-43842 TRINWAY	44033-44033 EAST CLARIDON	44224-44224 STOW
43600-43615 TOLEDO	43843-43843 WALHONDING	44035-44036 ELYRIA	44230-44230 DOYLESTOWN
43616-43616 OREGON	43844-43844 WARSAW	44039-44039 NORTH RIDGEVILLE	44231-44231 GARRETTSVILLE
43617-43617 TOLEDO	43845-43845 WEST LAFAYETTE	44040-44040 GATES MILLS	44232-44232 GREEN
43618-43618 OREGON	43901-43901 ADENA	44041-44041 GENEVA	44233-44233 HINCKLEY
43619-43619 NORTHWOOD	43902-43902 ALLEDONIA	44044-44044 GRAFTON	44234-44234 HIRAM
43620-43699 TOLEDO	43903-43903 AMSTERDAM	44045-44045 GRAND RIVER	44235-44235 HOMERVILLE
43701-43702 ZANESVILLE	43905-43905 BARTON	44046-44046 HUNTSBURG	44236-44238 HUDSON
43711-43711 AVA	43906-43906 BELLAIRE	44047-44047 JEFFERSON	44240-44240 KENT
43713-43713 BARNESVILLE	43907-43907 CADIZ	44048-44048 KINGSVILLE	44241-44241 STREETSBORO
43716-43716 BEALLSVILLE	43908-43908 BERGHOLZ	44049-44049 KIPTON	44242-44243 KENT
43717-43717 BELLE VALLEY	43909-43909 BLAINE	44050-44050 LAGRANGE	44250-44250 LAKEMORE
43718-43718 BELMONT	43910-43910 BLOOMINGDALE	44052-44053 LORAIN	44251-44251 WESTFIELD CENTER
43719-43719 BETHESDA	43912-43912 BRIDGEPORT	44054-44054 SHEFFIELD LAKE	44253-44253 LITCHFIELD
43720-43720 BLUE ROCK	43913-43913 BRILLIANT	44055-44055 LORAIN	44254-44254 LODI
43721-43721 BROWNSVILLE	43914-43914 CAMERON	44056-44056 MACEDONIA	44255-44255 MANTUA

44256-44259 MEDINA	44609-44609 BELOIT	44814-44814 BERLIN HEIGHTS	45056-45056 OXFORD
44260-44260 MOGADORE	44610-44610 BERLIN	44815-44815 BETTSVILLE	45061-45061 ROSS
44262-44262 MUNROE FALLS	44611-44611 BIG PRAIRIE	44816-44816 BIRMINGHAM	45062-45062 SEVEN MILE
44264-44264 PENINSULA	44612-44612 BOLIVAR	44817-44817 BLOOMDALE	45063-45063 SHANDON
44265-44265 RANDOLPH	44613-44613 BREWSTER	44818-44818 BLOOMVILLE	45064-45064 SOMERVILLE
44266-44266 RAVENNA	44614-44614 CANAL FULTON	44820-44820 BUCYRUS	45065-45065 SOUTH LEBANON
44270-44270 RITTMAN	44615-44615 CARROLLTON	44822-44822 BUTLER	45066-45066 SPRINGBORO
44272-44272 ROOTSTOWN	44617-44617 CHARM	44824-44824 CASTALIA	45067-45067 TRENTON
44273-44273 SEVILLE	44618-44618 DALTON	44825-44825 CHATFIELD	45068-45068 WAYNESVILLE
44274-44274 SHARON CENTER	44619-44619 DAMASCUS	44826-44826 COLLINS	45069-45069 WEST CHESTER
44275-44275 SPENCER	44620-44620 DELLROY	44827-44827 CRESTLINE	45070-45070 WEST ELKTON
44276-44276 STERLING	44621-44621 DENNISON	44828-44828 FLAT ROCK	45071-45071 WEST CHESTER
44278-44278 TALLMADGE	44622-44622 DOVER	44829-44829 FORT SENECA	45073-45099 MONROE
44280-44280 VALLEY CITY	44624-44624 DUNDEE	44830-44830 FOSTORIA	45101-45101 ABERDEEN
44281-44282 WADSWORTH	44625-44625 EAST ROCHESTER	44833-44833 GALION	45102-45102 AMELIA
44285-44285 WAYLAND	44626-44626 EAST SPARTA	44836-44836 GREEN SPRINGS	45103-45103 BATAVIA
44286-44286 RICHFIELD	44627-44627 FREDERICKSBURG	44837-44837 GREENWICH	45105-45105 BENTONVILLE
44287-44287 WEST SALEM	44628-44628 GLENMONT	44838-44838 HAYESVILLE	45106-45106 BETHEL
44288-44288 WINDHAM	44629-44629 GNADENHUTTEN	44839-44839 HURON	45107-45107 BLANCHESTER
44300-44317 AKRON	44630-44630 GREENTOWN	44840-44840 JEROMESVILLE	45110-45110 BUFORD
44318-44318 B F GOODRICH CO	44631-44631 HARLEM SPRINGS	44841-44841 KANSAS	45111-45111 CAMP DENNISON
44319-44334 AKRON	44632-44632 HARTVILLE	44842-44842 LOUDONVILLE	45112-45112 CHILO
44334-44334 FAIRLAWN	44633-44633 HOLMESVILLE	44843-44843 LUCAS	45113-45113 CLARKSVILLE
44372-44399 AKRON	44634-44634 HOMEWORTH	44844-44844 MC CUTCHENVILLE	45114-45114 CUBA
44401-44401 BERLIN CENTER	44636-44636 KIDRON	44845-44845 MELMORE	45115-45115 DECATUR
44402-44402 BRISTOLVILLE	44637-44637 KILLBUCK	44846-44846 MILAN	45118-45118 FAYETTEVILLE
44403-44403 BROOKFIELD	44638-44638 LAKEVILLE	44847-44847 MONROEVILLE	45119-45119 FEESBURG
44404-44404 BURGHILL	44639-44639 LEESVILLE	44848-44848 NANKIN	45120-45120 FELICITY
44405-44405 CAMPBELL	44640-44640 LIMAVILLE	44849-44849 NEVADA	45121-45121 GEORGETOWN
44406-44406 CANFIELD	44641-44641 LOUISVILLE	44850-44850 NEW HAVEN	45122-45122 GOSHEN
44408-44408 COLUMBIANA	44643-44643 MAGNOLIA	44851-44851 NEW LONDON	45123-45123 GREENFIELD
44410-44410 CORTLAND	44644-44644 MALVERN	44853-44853 NEW RIEGEL	45130-45130 HAMERSVILLE
44411-44411 DEERFIELD	44645-44645 MARSHALLVILLE	44854-44854 NEW WASHINGTON	45131-45131 HIGGINSPORT
44412-44412 DIAMOND	44646-44648 MASSILLON	44855-44855 NORTH FAIRFIELD	45132-45132 HIGHLAND
44413-44413 EAST PALESTINE	44650-44650 MAXIMO	44856-44856 NORTH ROBINSON	45133-45133 HILLSBORO
44415-44415 ELKTON	44651-44651 MECHANICSTOWN	44857-44857 NORWALK	45135-45135 LEESBURG
44416-44416 ELLSWORTH	44652-44652 MIDDLEBRANCH	44859-44859 NOVA	45138-45138 LEES CREEK
44417-44417 FARMDALE	44653-44653 MIDVALE	44860-44860 OCEOLA	45140-45140 LOVELAND
44418-44418 FOWLER	44654-44654 MILLERSBURG	44861-44861 OLD FORT	45142-45142 LYNCHBURG
44420-44420 GIRARD	44656-44656 MINERAL CITY	44862-44862 ONTARIO	45144-45144 MANCHESTER
44422-44422 GREENFORD	44657-44657 MINERVA	44864-44864 PERRYSVILLE	45145-45145 MARATHON
44423-44423 HANOVERTON	44659-44659 MOUNT EATON	44865-44865 PLYMOUTH	45146-45146 MARTINSVILLE
44424-44424 HARTFORD	44660-44660 MOUNT HOPE	44866-44866 POLK	45147-45147 MIAMIVILLE
44425-44425 HUBBARD	44661-44661 NASHVILLE	44867-44867 REPUBLIC	45148-45148 MIDLAND
44427-44427 KENSINGTON	44662-44662 NAVARRE	44870-44871 SANDUSKY	45150-45150 MILFORD
44428-44428 KINSMAN	44663-44663 NEW PHILADELPHIA	44874-44874 SAVANNAH	45152-45152 MORROW
44429-44429 LAKE MILTON	44665-44665 NORTH GEORGETOWN	44875-44875 SHELBY	45153-45153 MOSCOW
44430-44430 LEAVITTSBURG	44666-44666 NORTH LAWRENCE	44878-44878 SHILOH	45154-45154 MOUNT ORAB
44431-44431 LEETONIA	44667-44667 ORRVILLE	44880-44880 SULLIVAN	45155-45155 MOWRYSTOWN
44432-44432 LISBON	44669-44669 PARIS	44881-44881 SULPHUR SPRINGS	45156-45156 NEVILLE
44436-44436 LOWELLVILLE	44670-44670 ROBERTSVILLE	44882-44882 SYCAMORE	45157-45157 NEW RICHMOND
44437-44437 MC DONALD	44671-44671 SANDYVILLE	44883-44883 TIFFIN	45158-45158 NEWTONSVILLE
44438-44438 MASURY	44672-44672 SEBRING	44887-44887 TIRO	45159-45159 NEW VIENNA
44439-44439 MESOPOTAMIA	44675-44675 SHERRODSVILLE	44888-44888 WILLARD	45160-45160 OWENSVILLE
44440-44440 MINERAL RIDGE	44676-44676 SHREVE	44889-44889 WAKEMAN	45162-45162 PLEASANT PLAIN
44441-44441 NEGLEY	44677-44677 SMITHVILLE	44890-44890 WILLARD	45164-45164 PORT WILLIAM
44442-44442 NEW MIDDLETOWN	44678-44678 SOMERDALE	44900-44999 MANSFIELD	45165-45165 GREENFIELD
44443-44443 NEW SPRINGFIELD	44679-44679 STILLWATER	45001-45001 ADDYSTON	45166-45166 REESVILLE
44444-44444 NEWTON FALLS	44680-44680 STRASBURG	45002-45002 CLEVES	45167-45167 RIPLEY
44445-44445 NEW WATERFORD	44681-44681 SUGARCREEK	45003-45003 COLLEGE CORNER	45168-45168 RUSSELLVILLE
44446-44446 NILES	44682-44682 TUSCARAWAS	45004-45004 COLLINSVILLE	45169-45169 SABINA
44449-44449 NORTH BENTON	44683-44683 UHRICHSVILLE	45005-45005 FRANKLIN	45171-45171 SARDINIA
44450-44450 NORTH BLOOMFIELD	44685-44685 UNIONTOWN	45011-45013 HAMILTON	45172-45172 SINKING SPRING
44451-44451 NORTH JACKSON	44687-44687 WALNUT CREEK	45014-45014 FAIRFIELD	45174-45174 TERRACE PARK
44452-44452 NORTH LIMA	44688-44688 WAYNESBURG	45015-45015 HAMILTON	45176-45176 WILLIAMSBURG
44453-44453 ORANGEVILLE	44689-44689 WILMOT	45018-45018 FAIRFIELD	45177-45177 WILMINGTON
44454-44454 PETERSBURG	44690-44690 WINESBURG	45020-45026 HAMILTON	45200-45299 CINCINNATI
44455-44455 ROGERS	44691-44691 WOOSTER	45030-45030 HARRISON	45301-45301 ALPHA
44460-44460 SALEM	44693-44693 DEERSVILLE	45032-45032 HARVEYSBURG	45302-45302 ANNA
44470-44470 SOUTHINGTON	44695-44695 BOWERSTON	45033-45033 HOOVEN	45303-45303 ANSONIA
44471-44471 STRUTHERS	44697-44697 ZOAR	45034-45034 KINGS MILLS	45304-45304 ARCANUM
44473-44473 VIENNA	44699-44699 TIPPECANOE	45036-45036 LEBANON	45305-45305 BELLBROOK
44481-44488 WARREN	44700-44799 CANTON	45039-45039 MAINEVILLE	45306-45306 BOTKINS
44490-44490 WASHINGTONVILLE	44801-44801 ADRIAN	45040-45040 MASON	45307-45307 BOWERSVILLE
44491-44491 WEST FARMINGTON	44802-44802 ALVADA	45041-45041 MIAMITOWN	45308-45308 BRADFORD
44492-44492 WEST POINT	44803-44803 AMSDEN	45042-45044 MIDDLETOWN	45309-45309 BROOKVILLE
44493-44493 WINONA	44804-44804 ARCADIA	45050-45050 MONROE	45310-45310 BURKETTSVILLE
44500-44599 YOUNGSTOWN	44805-44805 ASHLAND	45051-45051 MOUNT SAINT JOSEPH	45311-45311 CAMDEN
44601-44601 ALLIANCE	44807-44807 ATTICA	45052-45052 NORTH BEND	45312-45312 CASSTOWN
44606-44606 APPLE CREEK	44809-44809 BASCOM	45053-45053 OKEANA	45314-45314 CEDARVILLE
44607-44607 AUGUSTA	44811-44811 BELLEVUE	45054-45054 OREGONIA	45315-45315 CLAYTON
44608-44608 BEACH CITY	44813-44813 BELLVILLE	45055-45055 OVERPECK	45316-45316 CLIFTON

45317-45317 CONOVER	45612-45612 BAINBRIDGE	45699-45699 LUCASVILLE	45822-45822 CELINA
45318-45318 COVINGTON	45613-45613 BEAVER	45701-45701 ATHENS	45826-45826 CHICKASAW
45319-45319 DONNELSVILLE	45614-45614 BIDWELL	45710-45710 ALBANY	45827-45827 CLOVERDALE
45320-45320 EATON	45616-45616 BLUE CREEK	45711-45711 AMESVILLE	45828-45828 COLDWATER
45321-45321 ELDORADO	45617-45617 BOURNEVILLE	45712-45712 BARLOW	45830-45830 COLUMBUS GROVE
45322-45322 ENGLEWOOD	45618-45618 CHERRY FORK	45713-45713 BARTLETT	45831-45831 CONTINENTAL
45323-45323 ENON	45619-45619 CHESAPEAKE	45714-45714 BELPRE	45832-45832 CONVOY
45324-45324 FAIRBORN	45620-45620 CHESHIRE	45715-45715 BEVERLY	45833-45833 DELPHOS
45325-45325 FARMERSVILLE	45621-45621 COALTON	45716-45716 BUCHTEL	45835-45835 DOLA
45326-45326 FLETCHER	45622-45622 CREOLA	45717-45717 CARBONDALE	45836-45836 DUNKIRK
45327-45327 GERMANTOWN	45623-45623 CROWN CITY	45719-45719 CHAUNCEY	45837-45837 DUPONT
45328-45328 GETTYSBURG	45624-45624 CYNTHIANA	45720-45720 CHESTER	45838-45838 ELGIN
45329-45329 GORDON	45628-45628 FRANKFORT	45721-45721 COAL RUN	45839-45840 FINDLAY
45330-45330 GRATIS	45629-45629 FRANKLIN FURNACE	45723-45723 COOLVILLE	45841-45841 JENERA
45331-45331 GREENVILLE	45630-45630 FRIENDSHIP	45724-45724 CUTLER	45843-45843 FOREST
45332-45332 HOLLANSBURG	45631-45631 GALLIPOLIS	45727-45727 DEXTER CITY	45844-45844 FORT JENNINGS
45333-45333 HOUSTON	45633-45633 HALLSVILLE	45729-45729 FLEMING	45845-45845 FORT LORAMIE
45334-45334 JACKSON CENTER	45634-45634 HAMDEN	45730-45730 JACKSON	45846-45846 FORT RECOVERY
45335-45335 JAMESTOWN	45636-45636 HAVERHILL	45732-45732 GLOUSTER	45848-45848 GLANDORF
45336-45336 KETTLERSVILLE	45638-45638 IRONTON	45734-45734 GRAYSVILLE	45849-45849 GROVER HILL
45337-45337 LAURA	45640-45640 JACKSON	45735-45735 GUYSVILLE	45850-45850 HARROD
45338-45338 LEWISBURG	45642-45642 JASPER	45739-45739 HOCKINGPORT	45851-45851 HAVILAND
45339-45339 LUDLOW FALLS	45643-45643 KERR	45740-45740 JACKSONVILLE	45853-45853 KALIDA
45340-45340 MAPLEWOOD	45644-45644 KINGSTON	45741-45741 LANGSVILLE	45854-45854 LAFAYETTE
45341-45341 MEDWAY	45645-45645 KITTS HILL	45742-45742 LITTLE HOCKING	45855-45855 LATTY
45342-45343 MIAMISBURG	45646-45646 LATHAM	45743-45743 LONG BOTTOM	45856-45856 LEIPSIC
45344-45344 NEW CARLISLE	45647-45647 LONDONDERRY	45744-45744 LOWELL	45858-45858 MC COMB
45345-45345 NEW LEBANON	45648-45648 LUCASVILLE	45745-45745 LOWER SALEM	45859-45859 MC GUFFEY
45346-45346 NEW MADISON	45650-45650 LYNX	45746-45746 MACKSBURG	45860-45860 MARIA STEIN
45347-45347 NEW PARIS	45651-45651 MC ARTHUR	45750-45750 MARIETTA	45861-45861 MELROSE
45348-45348 NEW WESTON	45652-45652 MC DERMOTT	45760-45760 MIDDLEPORT	45862-45862 MENDON
45349-45349 NORTH HAMPTON	45653-45653 MINFORD	45761-45761 MILLFIELD	45863-45863 MIDDLE POINT
45350-45350 NORTH STAR	45654-45654 NEW PLYMOUTH	45764-45764 NELSONVILLE	45864-45864 MILLER CITY
45351-45351 OSGOOD	45656-45656 OAK HILL	45766-45766 NEW MARSHFIELD	45865-45865 MINSTER
45352-45352 PALESTINE	45657-45657 OTWAY	45767-45767 NEW MATAMORAS	45866-45866 MONTEZUMA
45353-45353 PEMBERTON	45658-45658 PATRIOT	45768-45768 NEWPORT	45867-45867 MOUNT BLANCHARD
45354-45354 PHILLIPSBURG	45659-45659 PEDRO	45769-45769 POMEROY	45868-45868 MOUNT CORY
45356-45356 PIQUA	45660-45660 PEEBLES	45770-45770 PORTLAND	45869-45869 NEW BREMEN
45358-45358 PITSBURG	45661-45661 PIKETON	45771-45771 RACINE	45870-45870 NEW HAMPSHIRE
45359-45359 PLEASANT HILL	45662-45662 PORTSMOUTH	45772-45772 REEDSVILLE	45871-45871 NEW KNOXVILLE
45360-45360 PORT JEFFERSON	45663-45663 WEST PORTSMOUTH	45773-45773 RENO	45872-45872 NORTH BALTIMORE
45361-45361 POTSDAM	45669-45669 PROCTORVILLE	45775-45775 RUTLAND	45873-45873 OAKWOOD
45362-45362 ROSSBURG	45670-45670 RADCLIFF	45776-45776 SHADE	45874-45874 OHIO CITY
45363-45363 RUSSIA	45671-45671 RARDEN	45777-45777 SHARPSBURG	45875-45875 OTTAWA
45365-45365 SIDNEY	45672-45672 RAY	45778-45778 STEWART	45876-45876 OTTOVILLE
45366-45366 SPRING HILL NURSERIES	45673-45673 RICHMOND DALE	45779-45779 SYRACUSE	45877-45877 PANDORA
45367-45367 SIDNEY	45674-45674 RIO GRANDE	45780-45780 THE PLAINS	45879-45879 PAULDING
45368-45368 SOUTH CHARLESTON	45675-45675 ROCK CAMP	45781-45781 TORCH	45880-45880 PAYNE
45369-45369 SOUTH VIENNA	45677-45677 SCIOTO FURNACE	45782-45782 TRIMBLE	45881-45881 RAWSON
45370-45370 SPRING VALLEY	45678-45678 SCOTTOWN	45783-45783 TUPPERS PLAINS	45882-45882 ROCKFORD
45371-45371 TIPP CITY	45679-45679 SEAMAN	45784-45784 VINCENT	45883-45883 SAINT HENRY
45372-45372 TREMONT CITY	45680-45680 SOUTH POINT	45786-45786 WATERFORD	45884-45884 SAINT JOHNS
45373-45373 TROY	45681-45681 SOUTH SALEM	45787-45787 WATERTOWN	45885-45885 SAINT MARYS
45377-45377 VANDALIA	45682-45682 SOUTH WEBSTER	45788-45788 WHIPPLE	45886-45886 SCOTT
45378-45378 VERONA	45683-45683 STOCKDALE	45789-45789 WINGETT RUN	45887-45887 SPENCERVILLE
45380-45380 VERSAILLES	45684-45684 STOUT	45801-45807 LIMA	45888-45888 UNIOPOLIS
45381-45381 WEST ALEXANDRIA	45685-45685 THURMAN	45808-45808 BEAVERDAM	45889-45889 VAN BUREN
45382-45382 WEST MANCHESTER	45686-45686 VINTON	45809-45809 GOMER	45890-45890 VANLUE
45383-45383 WEST MILTON	45687-45687 WAKEFIELD	45810-45810 ADA	45891-45891 VAN WERT
45384-45384 WILBERFORCE	45688-45688 WATERLOO	45812-45812 ALGER	45893-45893 VAUGHNSVILLE
45385-45385 XENIA	45690-45690 WAVERLY	45813-45813 ANTWERP	45894-45894 VENEDOCIA
45387-45387 YELLOW SPRINGS	45692-45692 WELLSTON	45814-45814 ARLINGTON	45895-45895 WAPAKONETA
45388-45388 YORKSHIRE	45693-45693 WEST UNION	45815-45815 BELMORE	45896-45896 WAYNESFIELD
45389-45389 CHRISTIANSBURG	45694-45694 WHEELERSBURG	45816-45816 BENTON RIDGE	45897-45897 WILLIAMSTOWN
45390-45390 UNION CITY	45695-45695 WILKESVILLE	45817-45817 BLUFFTON	45898-45898 WILLSHIRE
45401-45490 DAYTON	45696-45696 WILLOW WOOD	45819-45819 BUCKLAND	45899-45899 WREN
45500-45506 SPRINGFIELD	45697-45697 WINCHESTER	45820-45820 CAIRO	45944-45999 CINCINNATI
45601-45601 CHILLICOTHE	45698-45698 ZALESKI	45821-45821 CECIL	

General Help Numbers:

Governor's Office
State Capitol, Suite 212   405-521-2342
Oklahoma City, OK 73105   Fax 405-521-3353
www.state.ok.us/~governor   8AM-5PM

Attorney General's Office
2300 N Lincoln, #112   405-521-3921
Oklahoma City, OK 73105   Fax 405-521-6246
www.oag.state.ok.us/   8:30AM-5PM
explorer.index.html

State Court Administrator
1915 N Stiles, #305   405-521-2450
Oklahoma City, OK 73105   Fax 405-521-6815
www.oscn.net   8AM-5PM

State Archives
Archives & Records Mgt Divisions   405-522-3577
200 NE 18th   Fax 405-525-7804
Oklahoma City, OK 73105-3298   8AM-5PM
www.odl.state.ok.us

State Specifics:

Capital:	Oklahoma City
	Oklahoma County
Time Zone:	CST
Number of Counties:	77
Population:	3,460,097
Web Site:	www.state.ok.us

State Agencies

Criminal Records

OK State Bureau of Investigation, Criminal History Reporting, 6600 N Harvey, Oklahoma City, OK 73116; 405-848-6724, 405-879-2503 (Fax), 8AM-5PM.

www.osbi.state.ok.us

Note: A record request form is available at the web site. A sex offender registry, maintained by the Dept. of Corrections, is not available online.

Indexing & Storage: Records are available from 1925 on. It takes 5 to 7 days before new records are available for inquiry. Records are normally destroyed after (records maintained indefinitely).

35% of all arrests in database have final dispositions recorded, 47% for those arrests within last 5 years.

Searching: Include the following in your request: DOB or approximate age. The SSN, sex or race are helpful and provide a better search, but not required. Fingerprints are optional. 100% of the records are fingerprint-supported. Arrest records without dispositions are released if the party was fingerprinted. Computer searches include arrests without dispositions.

Access by: mail, fax, in person.

Fee & Payment: The fee for a computer name search is $15.00. The fee for the fingerprint search

is $19.00. Fingerprint search does not include FBI fingerprint search; agency will not conduct an FBI search. Copies are $.25 per page. Fee payee: O.S.B.I. Prepayment required. Credit cards accepted: MasterCard, Visa.

Mail search: Turnaround time: 2 weeks. A self addressed stamped envelope is requested.

Fax search: Use of credit card and their "Credit Card Fax Form" is required. Call to have them fax you the form.

In person search: Name requests take 20 minutes, fingerprint searches take up to ten days to process.

Corporation Records
Limited Liability Company
     Records
Limited Partnerships
Trademarks/Servicemarks
Limited Liability
     Partnerships

Secretary of State, 2300 N Lincoln Blvd, Rm 101, Oklahoma City, OK 73105-4897; 405-521-3911, 900-825-2424 (Corporate Records), 405-521-3771 (Fax), 8AM-5PM.

www.sos.state.ok.us

Note: Officers are available from the Franchise Tax Dept. of the Oklahoma Tax Commission, 405-521-3161.

Indexing & Storage: Records are available from late 1800's on. Older records are kept at the State Archives. More recent records are maintained on a mainframe. New records are available for inquiry immediately.

Searching: The search includes correct name, status, date of registration, service agent and address, state of domicile, authorized shares and par value, amendments, name changes, mergers, and trade names. The records do not include owner. Include the following in your request: full name of business. Records include:corporations, limited partnerships, limited liability companies, limited liability partnerships, certificate of partnership fictitious name for general partnerships and trade names.

Access by: mail, phone, fax, in person.

Fee & Payment: The search fee is $5.00. Copies are provided by the Certification Dept at $1.00 per page. Fee payee: Secretary of State. Prepayment required. Personal checks accepted. The Discover Card is accepted.

Mail search: Turnaround time: 1 to 2 days. A self addressed stamped envelope is requested.

Phone search: They will give an immediate verbal verification only. Dial 1-900-555-2424. The fee is $5.00 per call and you are allowed up to 3 record searches per call.

Fax search: Turnaround time 1 to 2 days.

In person search: There is no fee to search records on a public access terminal.

Other access: A copy of the corporation database is available on cartridges or on magnetic tape for $500.

Uniform Commercial Code

UCC Recorder, Oklahoma County Clerk, 320 R.S. Kerr Ave, County Office Bldg, Rm 105, Oklahoma City, OK 73102; 405-713-1521, 405-713-1810 (Fax), 8AM-5PM.

www.oklahomacounty.org/countyclerk

Note: This county agency is the central filing agency for the state.

Indexing & Storage: Records are available for since 2/91 on UCC, 10 years on tax liens on computer. Records are on microfiche from 1977 to present. It takes 2 to 3 days before new records are available for inquiry.

Searching: Use search request form UCC-4. Include the following in your request: debtor name.

Access by: mail, in person, online.

Fee & Payment: The search fee is $5.00 per debtor name, the copy fee is $1.00 per page. Fee payee: Oklahoma County Clerk. Prepayment required. Personal checks accepted. No credit cards accepted, but may 07/01.

Mail search: Turnaround time: 2 days.

In person search: Searching is available in person.

Online search: Records of all UCC financing statements may be viewed free on the Internet at www.oklahomacounty.org/coclerk/default.htm. Neither certified searches nor record requests are accepted at the web.

Other access: The entire database is available on microfilm or computer tapes, prices start at $500.

Federal Tax Liens
State Tax Liens

Records not maintained by a state level agency.

Note: All state tax liens and federal tax liens are filed at the local level. Federal tax liens on businesses are filed with the Clerk of Oklahoma County.

Sales Tax Registrations

Taxpayer Assistance, 2501 N Lincoln Blvd, Oklahoma City, OK 73194; 405-521-3160, 405-521-3826 (Fax), 7:30AM-4:30PM.

www.oktax.state.ok.us

Indexing & Storage: Records are available for the most recent 10 years on computer, microfilmed back to the 1970's.

Searching: This agency will provide any information found on the face of the permit-business name, address, tax permit number, and SIC code. Payment history is not released. Include the following in your request: business name. They will also search by owner name, federal tax ID, or by tax permit number.

Access by: mail, phone, in person.

Fee & Payment: No search fees, but there is a copy fee of $.25 per page. Fee payee: Oklahoma Tax Commission. Prepayment required. If the card is used, there is an additional fee equal to 1.35% of the purchase. Personal checks accepted. No credit cards accepted.

Mail search: Turnaround time: within 2 weeks. A self addressed stamped envelope is requested.

Phone search: Records are available by phone.

In person search: Copies cost $.25 per page.

Other access: Current sales tax permit holders are permitted to purchase the sales tax database on microfiche or on 3.5 inch floppies. The annual subscription is $150.00 and is updated monthly.

Birth Certificates

State Department of Health, Vital Records Service, PO Box 53551, Oklahoma City, OK 73152-3551 (Courier: 1000 NE 10th St, Oklahoma City, OK 73117); 405-271-4040, 405-271-1646 (Order Line), 405-232-3311 (Fax), 8:30AM-4PM.

www.health.state.ok.us/program/vital/brec.html

Indexing & Storage: Records are available from 1908 on. Records are computerized since 1930. New records are available for inquiry immediately. Records are indexed on inhouse computer.

Searching: Must have a signed release from person of record or immediate family member. Include the following in your request: full name, names of parents, mother's maiden name, date of birth, place of birth, reason for information request, and copy of ID of requester. Also, daytime phone number.

Access by: mail, phone, fax, in person.

Fee & Payment: Fee is $5.00, add extra $5.50 for use of credit card. Fee payee: Oklahoma State Health Department. Prepayment required. Personal checks accepted. Credit cards accepted: MasterCard, Visa.

Mail search: Turnaround time: 1 to 2 weeks. A self addressed stamped envelope is requested.

Phone search: Use of credit card required.

Fax search: Use of credit card required.

In person search: Turnaround time is while you wait.

Expedited service: Expedited service is available for fax searches. Add 15.50 for express delivery. Use of credit card required.

Death Records

State Department of Health, Vital Records Service, PO Box 53551, Oklahoma City, OK 73152-3551 (Courier: 1000 NE 10th St, Oklahoma City, OK 73117); 405-271-4040, 405-271-1646 (Order Line), 405-232-3311 (Fax), 8:30AM-4PM.

www.health.state.ok.us/program/vital/brec.html

Indexing & Storage: Records are available from October 1908 on. Records are computerized since 1930. New records are available for inquiry immediately. Records are indexed on microfiche, inhouse computer.

Searching: Records are open to the public, Include the following in your request: full name, date of death, place of death, copy of ID of requester. Also, daytime phone number.

Access by: mail, phone, fax, in person.

Fee & Payment: Fee is $10.00 per record. Add $5.50 if credit card used. Fee payee: Oklahoma State Health Department. Prepayment required. Personal checks accepted. No credit cards accepted.

Mail search: Turnaround time: 1 to 2 weeks. A self addressed stamped envelope is requested.

Phone search: Credit card required.

Fax search: Credit card required.

In person search: Turnaround time is while you wait.

Expedited service: Expedited service is available for fax searches. Add $15.50 for express delivery. Use of credit card required.

Marriage Certificates Divorce Records

Records not maintained by a state level agency.

Note: Marriage and Divorce records are found at county level. The record should be requested from the county courthouse in the county where the marriage or divorce was filed or granted.

Workers' Compensation Records

Workers Compensation Court, 1915 N Stiles, Oklahoma City, OK 73105-4918; 405-522-8600, 405-522-8640 (Records Dept), 800-269-5353 (Enforcement), 405-552-8647 (Fax), 8AM-5PM.

www.owcc.state.ok.us

Indexing & Storage: Records are available since 1989 on computer. Index to case files are on print-outs and cards since the 1930's.

Searching: Claims information is considered public record. Anyone having a correct case number can access and review files. There are 2 searches involved-1st to get case number, then to do search. Any requests must be on their forms. Pending cases are available. Include the following in your request: claimant name, Social Security Number, claim number, date of birth, date of accident. To get the claim number, send a written request (Attn: Prior Claims) on their "Request for Information Form," and they will notify you of the case number. With a case number, you can request copies, but you must use their form.

Access by: mail, phone, in person.

Fee & Payment: Using their "Request for Information Form" (index card), you must include a $1 fee to get the case number, unless you are statutorily exempt. The copy fee is $1.00 for the first page and $.50 each add'l page if done by staff; $.25 if by searcher. Fee payee: Workers' Compensation Court. Prepayment required. In-state businesses can set up charge accounts; payment due within 30 days. Personal checks accepted. No credit cards accepted.

Mail search: Turnaround time: 5 days. Frequent requesters should set up an account. If payment not included, party will be billed and funds must be received before documents are mailed. A self addressed stamped envelope is requested.

Phone search: Only requests for forms will be answered over the phone.

In person search: One may search on the in-house computer in the basement level and also request and review a file, no fee. Files are pulled for the public from 8:15AM to 4:45PM.

Other access: PDF versions of most forms are available at the web site.

Driver Records

MVR Desk, Records Management Division, PO Box 11415, Oklahoma City, OK 73136 (Courier: 3600 Martin Luther King Blvd, Rm 206, Oklahoma City, OK 73111); 405-425-2262, 8AM-4:45PM.

www.dps.state.ok.us/dls

Note: Copies of tickets may be obtained for $.25 per page from the address listed above. Most tickets are two pages. For certification of copies, add $3.00.

Indexing & Storage: Records are available for 3 years for moving violations, DWIs and suspensions. All violations, except speeding less than ten mph over the limit, appear on the driving record. Accidents are reported if there is a conviction of citation. It takes 10 days to 6 months before new records are available for inquiry.

Searching: Information is available for law enforcement purposes. Anyone else requesting an MVR for another person is required to submit a consent to release records form signed by both parties. Ask for a State of Oklahoma Records Request Form. Include the following in your request: full name and date of birth, or driver's license number. The following data is not released: medical records, Social Security Numbers, addresses or personal information (height, weight, sex, eye color, etc.).

Access by: mail, in person.

Fee & Payment: The fee is $10.00 per driving record. There is a full fee for a no record found. Fee payee: Department of Public Safety. Prepayment required. Personal checks accepted. No credit cards accepted.

Mail search: Turnaround time: 1 week to 10 days. Oklahoma offers a monthly billing system for high volume requesters. A self addressed stamped envelope is requested.

In person search: Records may be requested at any Oklahoma Tag Agency statewide. Up to ten requests may be processed in one day or less. Many MV offices across the state will sell records.

Other access: Magnetic tape ordering is available for high volume users. Call 405-425-2222.

Vehicle Ownership & Identification
Vessel Ownership & Registration

Oklahoma Tax Commission, Motor Vehicle Division, Attn: Research, 2501 N Lincoln Blvd, Oklahoma City, OK 73194; 405-521-3221, 7:30AM-4:30PM.

www.oktax.state.ok.us/mvhome.html

Indexing & Storage: Records are available for 3 years (registration records); the state keeps title records internally for 20 years. All watercraft must be titled and registered. All motors in excess of 10 HP must be titled. Lien information appears on title records. It takes 2 up to 5 weeks before new records are available for inquiry.

Searching: Records are not released to casual requesters. Approved requesters must use the Vehicle Information Request Form. Name searches are not performed. The title number, VIN or current plate number is needed for a search.

Access by: mail, in person.

Fee & Payment: Current ownerhip/lienholder data is $1.00. A computer generated title history is $5.00, a microfilm title history is $7.50, and a certified microfilm title history is $10.00. Fee payee: Oklahoma Tax Commission, MVD. Prepayment required. Personal checks accepted. No credit cards accepted.

Mail search: Turnaround time: 7 to 10 days.

In person search: Turnaround time is while you wait, depending on the workload.

Other access: Oklahoma does not offer bulk delivery of vehicle and ownership information except for purposes such as vehicle recall.

Accident Reports

Department of Public Safety, Records Management Division, PO Box 11415, Oklahoma City, OK 73136 (Courier: 3600 Martin Luther King Blvd, Room 206, Oklahoma City, OK 73111); 405-425-2192, 405-425-2046 (Fax), 8AM-4:45PM.

www.dps.state.ok.us

Note: This agency refers to these reports as Collision Reports.

Indexing & Storage: Records are available for 3 years to present. It takes 10 to 14 days before new records are available for inquiry. Records are indexed on inhouse computer.

Searching: Include the following in your request: date of accident, location of accident, full name, county.

Access by: mail, phone, in person.

Fee & Payment: The fee is $7.00 for an uncertified copy and $10.00 for a certified copy. There is no charge for a no record found. Fee payee: Department of Public Safety. Prepayment required. Personal checks accepted. No credit cards accepted.

Mail search: Turnaround time: 24 hours. A self addressed stamped envelope is requested.

Phone search: No fee for telephone request. This agency will reveal whether there is an accident over the phone. No other information will be revealed over the phone.

In person search: Normal turnaround time is while you wait.

Legislation Records

Oklahoma Legislature, State Capitol, Bill Status Info-Rm B-30, Copies-Rm 310, Oklahoma City, OK 73105; 405-521-5642 (Bill Status Only), 405-521-5515 (Bill Distribution), 405-528-2546 (Bills in Progress), 405-521-5507 (Fax), 8:30AM-4:30PM.

www.lsb.state.ok.us

Note: For prior session bills, you may call the State Law Library at 405-521-2502, ext. 280.

Indexing & Storage: Records are available for current session only. Records are indexed on inhouse computer.

Searching: Include the following in your request: bill number.

Access by: mail, phone, in person, online.

Fee & Payment: There is no search fee.

Mail search: Turnaround time: same day. No self addressed stamped envelope is required.

Phone search: Turnaround time is same day.

In person search: Turnaround time is same day.

Online search: The web page provides a variety of legislative information including searching by topic or bill number.

Voter Registration

State Election Board, State Capitol-Rm B6, Box 53156, Oklahoma City, OK 73152; 405-521-2391, 405-521-6457 (Fax), 8AM-5PM.

www.state.ok.us/~elections

Indexing & Storage: Records are available for 4 years. It takes 7 to 10 days before new records are available for inquiry.

Searching: Records are open to the public and can be accessed at both the state and county levels. The following data is not released: phone numbers.

Access by: mail, phone, in person.

Fee & Payment: There is no fee for look-ups. Fee payee: OK State Board of Elections. Only certified funds or cashier's checks are accepted for database sales. No credit cards accepted.

Mail search: Turnaround time: 2 to 5 days. No self addressed stamped envelope is required.

Phone search: Limited information is given, depending on staff availability.

In person search: Searching is available in person.

Other access: A statewide database can be purchased on tape for a fee of $150. Large counties are available on tape for $50-75, and smaller counties or precincts are available on disk for $10-35.

GED Certificates

State Dept of Education, Lifelong Learning, 2500 N Lincoln Blvd, Oklahoma City, OK 73105; 405-521-3321, 405-521-6205 (Fax).

http://sde.state.ok.us

Searching: To search, all of the following is required: name, approximate year of test, date of birth, and Social Security Number.

Access by: mail, phone, fax, in person.

Fee & Payment: There is no fee for a verification. There is a $5.00 fee to obtain a transcript. If a duplicate certification is needed, that is $5.00 plus you must also purchase the transcript for $5.00. Fee payee: State Dept of Education. Prepayment required. Money orders and business checks are accepted. No credit cards accepted.

Mail search: Turnaround time: 1 to 2 days. No self addressed stamped envelope is required.

Phone search: This is for verification only.

Fax search: Same criteria as mail searching.

In person search: Turnaround time is typically 30 minutes for verification.

Hunting License Information
Fishing License Information
Access to Records is Restricted.

Note: They have a central database but do not release information to the public.

Oklahoma State Licensing Agencies

Licenses Searchable Online

Accounting Firm #15 .... www.state.ok.us/~oab/firms.html
Architect #23 .... www.state.ok.us/~architects/architects.html
Audiologist #6 .... www.obespa.state.ok.us/License%20Data.htm
Bank #35 .... www.state.ok.us/~osbd/
Consumer Finance Company #20 .... www.okdocc.state.ok.us/introSL.htm
Credit Services Organization #20 .... www.okdocc.state.ok.us/introCSO.htm
Credit Union #35 .... www.state.ok.us/~osbd/
Dental Hygienist #29 .... www.dentist.state.ok.us/lists/index.htm
Dental Laboratories #29 .... www.dentist.state.ok.us/lists/index.htm
Dentist/Dental Assistant #29 .... www.dentist.state.ok.us/lists/index.htm
Dietitian/Provisional Licensed Dietitian #8 .... www.okmedicalboard.org/medboard/index.php
Electrologist #8 .... www.okmedicalboard.org/medboard/index.php
Engineer #13 .... www.okpels.org/rosters.htm
Funeral Home #5 .... www.okfuneral.com/funeralhomedirectory/index.htm
Health Spa #20 .... www.okdocc.state.ok.us/introSpa.htm
Investment Company #34 .... www.securities.state.ok.us/_private/DB_Query/Corp_Fin_Search.htm
Landscape Architect #23 .... www.state.ok.us/~architects/landscape.html
Lobbyist #42 .... www.state.ok.us/~ethics/lobbyist.html
Medical Doctor #8 .... www.okmedicalboard.org/medboard/index.php
Midwife Nurse #30 .... www.youroklahoma.com/nursing/verify/
Money Order Agent #35 .... www.state.ok.us/~osbd/
Mortgage Banker #20 .... www.okdocc.state.ok.us/introMB.htm
Nurse #30 .... www.youroklahoma.com/nursing/verify/
Nurse Anesthetist #30 .... www.youroklahoma.com/nursing/verify/
Nurse Specialist, Clinical #30 .... www.youroklahoma.com/nursing/verify/
Nurse-RN/LPN #30 .... www.youroklahoma.com/nursing/verify/
Occupational Therapist/Assistant #8 .... www.okmedicalboard.org/medboard/index.php
Optometrist #7 .... www.odfinder.org/LicSearch.asp
Orthotist/Prosthetist #8 .... www.okmedicalboard.org/medboard/index.php
Osteopathic Physician #10 .... www.docboard.org/ok/df/oksearch.htm
Pawnbroker #20 .... www.okdocc.state.ok.us/introPB.htm
Perdorthist #8 .... www.okmedicalboard.org/medboard/index.php
Perfusionist #8 .... www.okmedicalboard.org/medboard/index.php
Physical Therapist/Assistant #8 .... www.okmedicalboard.org/medboard/index.php
Physician Assistant #8 .... www.okmedicalboard.org/medboard/index.php
Precious Metals & Gem Dealer #20 .... www.okdocc.state.ok.us/introPMD.htm
Private Investigator #19 .... www.opia.com/searches/search.html
Private Investigator Agency #19 .... www.opia.com/searches/search.html
Public Accountant-CPA #15 .... www.state.ok.us/~oab/twotier.html
Real Estate Appraiser #33 .... www.asc.gov/content/category1/appr_by_state.asp
Real Estate Broker #38 .... www.orec.state.ok.us/agents2.html
Real Estate Corp./Partnership #38 .... www.orec.state.ok.us/agents2.html
Real Estate Salesperson #38 .... www.orec.state.ok.us/agents2.html
Rent to Own Dealer #20 .... www.okdocc.state.ok.us/introRTO.htm
Respiratory Care Practitioner #8 .... www.okmedicalboard.org/medboard/index.php
Savings & Loan Association #35 .... www.state.ok.us/~osbd/
Speech Pathologist #6 .... www.obespa.state.ok.us/License%20Data.htm
Surveyor, Land #13 .... www.okpels.org/rosters.htm
Trust Company #35 .... www.state.ok.us/~osbd/

Licensing Quick Finder

Accounting Firm #15	405-521-2397
Airport Development Project #27	405-521-2377
Alarm Company/Employee #37	405-271-5217
Alcohol & Drug Influence Tester #17	405-425-2460
Animal Technician #18	405-524-9006
Architect #23	405-949-2383
Asbestos Abatement Worker #44	405-528-1500 x326
Athletic Trainer/Apprentice #8	405-848-6841
Attorney #28	405-524-2365
Audiologist #6	405-840-2774
Bail Bondsman #32	405-521-6610
Bank #35	405-521-2783
Barber Instructor #37	405-271-5217
Barber Shop #37	405-271-5217
Barber/Barber Apprentice #37	405-271-5217
Beauty School #4	405-521-2441
Beauty Shop/Salon #4	405-521-2441
Blacksmith #31	405-943-6472
Building Inspector #37	405-271-5217
Burglar Alarm Salesman #37	405-271-5217
Burglar Alarm Service/Installer #37	405-271-5217
Cemetery #35	405-521-2783
Children & Youth Agency, Private/Public #21	405-521-3561
Chiropractor #3	405-528-5505
Consumer Finance Company #20	405-521-3653
Cosmetology Instructor #4	405-521-2441
Cosmetology Student & Apprentice #4	405-521-2441
Counselor LPC/LM&T #43	405-271-6030
Credit Services Organization #20	405-521-3653
Credit Union #35	405-521-2783
Dental Hygienist #29	405-524-9037
Dental Laboratories #29	405-524-9037
Dentist/Dental Assistant #29	405-524-9037
Dietitian/Provisional Licensed Dietitian #8	405-848-6841
Electrical Contractor #37	405-271-5217
Electrical Inspector #37	405-271-5217
Electrician, Journeyman #37	405-271-5217
Electrologist #8	405-848-6841
Embalmer #5	405-522-1790
Emergency Medical Technician #37	405-271-4240
Engineer #13	405-521-2874
Facial Operator #4	405-521-2441

Firearm Permit for Retired Police Officer #19	405-425-2760
Forester #16	405-522-6147
Funeral Director #5	405-522-1790
Funeral Home #5	405-522-1790
Ground Water & Observation Water Well Driller #39	405-530-8800
Health Spa #20	405-521-3653
Hearing Aid Dealer/Fitter #37	405-271-5217
Horse Groom #31	405-943-6472
Horse Racing #31	405-943-6472
Horse Trainer #31	405-943-6472
Insurance Adjuster #32	405-521-2828
Insurance Agent/Representative #32	405-521-2828
Insurance Consultant #32	405-521-2828
Investment Adviser #34	405-280-7700
Investment Adviser Representative #34	405-280-7700
Investment Company #34	405-280-7700
Jockey #31	405-943-6472
Jockey Agent #31	405-943-6472
Journeyman #36	405-271-5217
Landscape Architect #23	405-949-2383
Liquor Industry #1	405-521-3484
Lobbyist #42	405-521-3451
LPG-Liquefied Petroleum Dealer/Mfg./Mgr #25	405-521-2458
LPG-Liquefied Petroleum System Installer #25	405-521-2458
Manicurist #4	405-521-2441
Mechanical Contractor #36	405-271-5217
Mechanical Inspector #36	405-271-5217
Medical Doctor #8	405-848-6841
Midwife Nurse #30	405-962-1800
Mining Operation #22	405-521-3859
Money Order Agent #35	405-521-2783
Mortgage Banker #20	405-521-3653
Notary Public #26	405-521-2516
Nurse #30	405-962-1800
Nurse Anesthetist #30	405-962-1800
Nurse Specialist, Clinical #30	405-962-1800
Nurse-RN/LPN #30	405-962-1800
Nursing Home Administrator #2	405-521-0991
Occupational Therapist/Assistant #8	405-848-6841
Optometrist #7	405-733-7836

Orthotist/Prosthetist #8	405-848-6841
Osteopathic Physician #10	405-528-8625
Pawnbroker #20	405-521-3653
Perdorthist #8	405-848-6841
Perfusionist #8	405-848-6841
Pharmacist #11	405-521-3815
Pharmacy #11	405-521-3815
Physical Therapist/Assistant #8	405-848-6841
Physician Assistant #8	405-848-6841
Placement Agency #21	405-521-3561
Plumbing Contractor/Inspector #36	405-271-5217
Podiatrist #12	405-848-6841
Police Officer #19	405-425-2755
Polygraph Examiner/Intern #40	405-425-2778
Polygraph Operator #19	405-425-2778
Precious Metals & Gem Dealer #20	405-521-3653
Private Investigator #19	405-425-2775
Private Investigator Agency #19	405-425-2775
Psychologist #14	405-271-6118
Public Accountant-CPA #15	405-521-2397
Pump Installer #39	405-530-8800
Real Estate Appraiser #33	405-521-6636
Real Estate Broker #38	405-521-3387
Real Estate Corp./Partnership #38	405-521-3387
Real Estate Salesperson #38	405-521-3387
Rent to Own Dealer #20	405-521-3653
Respiratory Care Practitioner #8	405-848-6841
Sanitarian/Environmental Specialist #37	405-271-5217
Savings & Loan Association #35	405-521-2783
School Accreditation #41	405-521-3301
School Transportation #41	405-521-3301
Securities Agent #34	405-280-7700
Securities Broker/Dealer #34	405-280-7700
Security Guard/Agency #19	405-425-2775
Shorthand Reporter #9	405-521-2450
Social Worker #24	405-946-7230
Speech Pathologist #6	405-840-2774
Surveyor, Land #13	405-521-2874
Teacher #41	405-521-3301
Trust Company #35	405-521-2783
Veterinarian #18	405-524-9006
Veterinary Technician #18	405-524-9006
Waste Water Operator #45	405-702-1000
Well Driller/Monitor #39	405-530-8800

Licensing Agency Information

#1 Alcoholic Beverage Laws Enforcement Commission, 4545 N Lincoln Blvd, #270, Oklahoma City, OK 73105; 405-521-3484, Fax: 405-521-6578. www.able.state.ok.us. Agency email: ablecomm@mhs.oklaosf.state.ok.us.

#2 Board for Nursing Home Administrators, 3033 N Walnut, #100E, Oklahoma City, OK 73105; 405-521-0991, Fax: 405-528-3483. Agency email: jclark@oklaosf.state.ok.us.

#3 Board of Chiropractic Examiners, 310 NE 28th St, #205, Oklahoma City, OK 73105; 405-524-6223, Fax: 405-522-6830. www.state.ok.us/~chiro/obce.htm Agency email: nramirez@oklaosf.state.ok.us.

#4 Board of Cosmetology, 2200 Classen Blvd, #1530, Oklahoma City, OK 73106; 405-521-2441, Fax: 405-528-8310. www.state.ok.us/~cosmo Agency email: bmoore@oklaosf.state.ok.us.

#5 Board of Embalmers & Funeral Directors, 4545 N Lincoln Blvd, #175, Oklahoma City, OK 73105; 405-522-1790, Fax: 405-522-1797. www.okfuneral.com Agency email: info@okfuneral.com.

#6 Board of Examiners for Speech Pathology/Audiology, 1140 NW 63rd, #305 (PO Box 53592), Oklahoma City, OK 73152-3592; 405-840-2774, Fax: 405-843-3489. www.obespa.state.ok.us Agency email: obespa@oklaosf.state.ok.us. Search database at www.obespa.state.ok.us/License%20Data.htm

#7 Board of Examiners in Optometry, 6912 E Reno Ave #302, Midwest City, OK 73110-2162; 405-733-7836, Fax: 405-741-3060. www.state.ok.us/~optometry Agency email: optboard@oklaosf.state.ok.us. Search database at www.odfinder.org/LicSearch.asp

#8 Board of Medical Licensure & Supervision, 5104 N Francis, #C (POB 18256 OK, OK 73154), Oklahoma City, OK 73118-0256; 405-848-6841, Fax: 405-848-8240. www.okmedicalboard.org/medboard/index.php. Agency email: executive@osbmls.state.ok.us. Search database at www.okmedicalboard.org/medboard/index.php

#9 Board of Official Shorthand Reporters, 1915 N Stiles, Rm 305, Oklahoma City, OK 73105; 405-521-2450, Fax: 405-521-3815. www.oscn.net.

#10 Board of Osteopathic Examiners, 4848 N Lincoln, #100, Oklahoma City, OK 73105; 405-528-8625, Fax: 405-557-0653. www.docboard.org/ok/ok.htm Search database at www.docboard.org/ok/df/oksearch.htm

#11 Board of Pharmacy, 4545 N Lincoln Blvd, North Terrace, #112, Oklahoma City, OK 73105-3488; 405-521-3815, Fax: 405-521-3758. www.state.ok.us/~pharmacy Agency email: pharmacy@oklaosf.state.ok.us

#12 Board of Podiatry, 5104 N Francis, #C, Oklahoma City, OK 73154-0256; 405-848-6841, Fax: 405-848-8240
Agency email: executive@osbmis.state.ok.us.

#13 Board of Professional Engineers & Land Surveyors, 201 NE 27th St, Rm 120, Oklahoma City, OK 73105; 405-521-2874, Fax: 405-523-3135.
www.okpels.org
Agency email: okpels@okpels.org.
Search database at www.okpels.org/rosters.htm

#14 Board of Psychologists Examiners, 201 NE 38th Terr #C, Oklahoma City, OK 73105; 405-271-6118, Fax: 405-271-6137.

#15 Board of Public Accountancy, 4545 N Lincoln Blvd, #165, Oklahoma City, OK 73105; 405-521-2397, Fax: 405-521-3118.
www.state.ok.us/~oab
Agency email: okaccybd@oklaosf.state.ok.us.

#16 Board of Registration for Foresters, 2800 N Lincoln Blvd, Agriculture Bldg, Oklahoma City, OK 73105-4298; 405-522-6147, Fax: 405-522-4583. Agency email: kurt@oda.state.ok.us.

#17 Board of Tests for Alcohol & Drug Influence, PO Box 11415, Oklahoma City, OK 73136-0415; 405-425-2460, Fax: 405-425-2490.
www.dps.state.ok.us/btadi
Agency email: msample@dos.state.ok.us.

#18 Board of Veterinary Medical Examiners, 201 NE 38th Terr. #1, Oklahoma City, OK 73105; 405-524-9006, Fax: 405-524-9012.
www.okvetboard.com
Agency email: information@okvetboard.com.

#19 Council on Law Enforcement Education & Training, 3530 N Martin Luther King Ave, Oklahoma City, OK 73136-0476; 405-425-2750, Fax: 405-425-2773.
www.cleet.state.ok.us
Agency email: nfloyd@cleet.state.ok.us.

#20 Department of Consumer Credit, 4545 N Lincoln Blvd, #104, Oklahoma City, OK 73105; 405-521-3653, Fax: 405-521-6740.
www.state.ok.us/~okdcc. Agency email: gwinston@oklaosf.state.ok.us.
Search database at www.okdocc.state.us/RosterPage.htm

#21 Department of Human Services, PO Box 25352, Oklahoma City, OK 73126; 405-521-3561, Fax: 405-522-2564.
www.okdhs.org/childcare/.

#22 Department of Mines, Mining Commission, 4040 N Lincoln, #107, Oklahoma City, OK 73105; 405-521-3859, Fax: 405-427-9646.

#23 Board of Governors/Licensed Architects & Landscape Architects, PO Box 53430 (3555 NW 58th St #640), Oklahoma City, OK 73152; 405-949-2383, Fax: 405-949-1690.
www.state.ok.us/~architects/
Search database at www.state.ok.us/~architects

#24 Licensed Social Workers Registration Board, 3535 NW 58th St, #765, Oklahoma City, OK 73112; 405-946-7230, Fax: 405-942-1070.
www.state.ok.us/~osblsw

#25 Liquefied Petroleum Gas Board, 2101 N Lincoln Blvd, Jim Thorpe Bldg, Rm B-45, Oklahoma City, OK 73105-4990; 405-521-2458, Fax: 405-521-6037.

#26 Office of Secretary of State, PO Box 53390, Oklahoma City, OK 73152-3390; 405-521-2516, Fax: 405-522-3555.
www.sos.state.ok.us. Agency email: mary.a.watts@oklaosf.state.ok.us.

#27 Aeronautics Commission, 200 NE 21st, B-7 1st Fl, Oklahoma City, OK 73105; 405-521-2377, Fax: 405-521-2379.
www.okladot.state.ok.us/hqdiv/aerot.htm. Agency email: bmiller@odot.org.

#28 Bar Association, (Attorney Certification), 1901 Lincoln Blvd, Oklahoma City, OK 73105; 405-524-2365, Fax: 405-524-7001.
www.okbar.org.

#29 Board of Dentistry, 201 N.E. 38th Terr, #2, Oklahoma City, OK 73105; 405-524-9037, Fax: 405-524-2223.
www.state.ok.us/~dentist
Agency email: dentist@oklaosf.state.ok.us.
Search database at www.dentist.state.ok.us/lists/index.htm

#30 Board of Nursing, 2915 N Classen Blvd, #524, Oklahoma City, OK 73106; 405-962-1800, Fax: 405-962-1821.
www.youroklahoma.com/nursing
Agency email: oklahoma@ncsbn.org.
Search database at www.youroklahoma.com/nursing/verify

#31 Horse Racing Commission, Shepherd Mall 2614 Villa Prom, Oklahoma City, OK 73107; 405-943-6472, Fax: 405-943-6474.
www.state.ok.us/~ohrc
Agency email: ohrc@socket.net.

#32 Insurance Department, PO Box 53408 (2401 N.W. 23 St #28), Oklahoma City, OK 73152-3408; 405-521-2828, Fax: 405-521-6652.
www.oid.state.ok.us   Tulsa office is 3105 E. Skelly Dr #305, Tulsa OK 74105, 918/747-7700.

#33 Real Estate Appraiser Board, PO Box 53408, Oklahoma City, OK 73152-3408; 405-521-6636, Fax: 405-521-6635.

www.oid.state.ok.us/agentbrokers/index.html

#34 Securities Commission, Department of Securities, 120 N Robinson, 1st National Center #860, Oklahoma City, OK 73102; 405-280-7700, Fax: 405-280-7742.
www.securities.state.ok.us
Agency email: jku@securities.state.ok.us.

#35 Banking Department, 4545 N Lincoln Blvd, #164, Oklahoma City, OK 73105-3427; 405-521-2782, Fax: 405-525-9701.
www.state.ok.us/~osbd
Search database at www.state.ok.us/~osbd

#37 Department of Health, 1000 NE 10th St, Oklahoma City, OK 73117-1299; 405-271-5217, Fax: 405-271-5254.
www.health.state.ok.us
Agency email: rockym@health.state.ok.us.

#38 Real Estate Commission, 2401 NW 23rd St #18, Oklahoma City, OK 73107; 405-521-3387, Fax: 405-521-2189.
www.orec.state.ok.us
Agency email: orec.help@orec.state.ok.us.
Search database at www.orec.state.ok.us/agents2.html

#39 Water Resources Board, 3800 N Classen Blvd, Oklahoma City, OK 73118; 405-530-8800, Fax: 405-530-8900.
www.state.ok.us/~owrb

#40 Polygraph Examiners Board, PO Box 11476, Oklahoma City, OK 73136-0476; 405-425-2778, Fax: 405-425-7314.

#41 Department of Education, 2500 N Lincoln Blvd, Oklahoma City, OK 73105-4599; 405-521-3301, Fax: 405-521-6205.
www.sde.state.ok.us

#42 Ethics Commission, Lobbyist Registration, Sec. of State, 2300 N Lincoln Blvd, RM B5, Oklahoma City, OK 73105-4812; 405-521-3451, Fax: 405-521-4905.
www.state.ok.us/~ethics

#43 Department of Health, 1000 NE 10th, Oklahoma City, OK 73117-1299; 405-271-6030, Fax: 405-271-1918.
www.health.state.ok.us

#44 Department of Labor, Asbestos Division, 4001 N Lincoln Blvd, Oklahoma City, OK 73105-5212; 405-528-1500, Fax: 405-528-3412.

#45 Department of Environmental Quality, 707 N robinson, Oklahoma City, OK 73102; 405-702-1000.

Oklahoma Federal Courts

The following list indicates the district and division name for each county in the state. If the bankruptcy court location is different from the district court, then the location of the bankruptcy court appears in parentheses.

County/Court Cross Reference

County	District	Location
Adair	Eastern	Muskogee (Okmulgee)
Alfalfa	Western	Oklahoma City
Atoka	Eastern	Muskogee (Okmulgee)
Beaver	Western	Oklahoma City
Beckham	Western	Oklahoma City
Blaine	Western	Oklahoma City
Bryan	Eastern	Muskogee (Okmulgee)
Caddo	Western	Oklahoma City
Canadian	Western	Oklahoma City
Carter	Eastern	Muskogee (Okmulgee)
Cherokee	Eastern	Muskogee (Okmulgee)
Choctaw	Eastern	Muskogee (Okmulgee)
Cimarron	Western	Oklahoma City
Cleveland	Western	Oklahoma City
Coal	Eastern	Muskogee (Okmulgee)
Comanche	Western	Oklahoma City
Cotton	Western	Oklahoma City
Craig	Northern	Tulsa
Creek	Northern	Tulsa
Custer	Western	Oklahoma City
Delaware	Northern	Tulsa
Dewey	Western	Oklahoma City
Ellis	Western	Oklahoma City
Garfield	Western	Oklahoma City
Garvin	Western	Oklahoma City
Grady	Western	Oklahoma City
Grant	Western	Oklahoma City
Greer	Western	Oklahoma City
Harmon	Western	Oklahoma City
Harper	Western	Oklahoma City
Haskell	Eastern	Muskogee (Okmulgee)
Hughes	Eastern	Muskogee (Okmulgee)
Jackson	Western	Oklahoma City
Jefferson	Western	Oklahoma City
Johnston	Eastern	Muskogee (Okmulgee)
Kay	Western	Oklahoma City
Kingfisher	Western	Oklahoma City
Kiowa	Western	Oklahoma City
Latimer	Eastern	Muskogee (Okmulgee)
Le Flore	Eastern	Muskogee (Okmulgee)
Lincoln	Western	Oklahoma City
Logan	Western	Oklahoma City
Love	Eastern	Muskogee (Okmulgee)
Major	Western	Oklahoma City
Marshall	Eastern	Muskogee (Okmulgee)
Mayes	Northern	Tulsa
McClain	Western	Oklahoma City
McCurtain	Eastern	Muskogee (Okmulgee)
McIntosh	Eastern	Muskogee (Okmulgee)
Murray	Eastern	Muskogee (Okmulgee)
Muskogee	Eastern	Muskogee (Okmulgee)
Noble	Western	Oklahoma City
Nowata	Northern	Tulsa
Okfuskee	Eastern	Muskogee (Okmulgee)
Oklahoma	Western	Oklahoma City
Okmulgee	Northern (Eastern)	Tulsa (Okmulgee)
Osage	Northern	Tulsa
Ottawa	Northern	Tulsa
Pawnee	Northern	Tulsa
Payne	Western	Oklahoma City
Pittsburg	Eastern	Muskogee (Okmulgee)
Pontotoc	Eastern	Muskogee (Okmulgee)
Pottawatomie	Western	Oklahoma City
Pushmataha	Eastern	Muskogee (Okmulgee)
Roger Mills	Western	Oklahoma City
Rogers	Northern	Tulsa
Seminole	Eastern	Muskogee (Okmulgee)
Sequoyah	Eastern	Muskogee (Okmulgee)
Stephens	Western	Oklahoma City
Texas	Western	Oklahoma City
Tillman	Western	Oklahoma City
Tulsa	Northern	Tulsa
Wagoner	Eastern	Muskogee (Okmulgee)
Washington	Northern	Tulsa
Washita	Western	Oklahoma City
Woods	Western	Oklahoma City
Woodward	Western	Oklahoma City

Standards for Federal Courts: The search fee is $20.00 per item (one party name or case number). Certification fee is $7.00 per document. Copy fee is $.50 per page. All fees standard unless noted in profile. Mail Search: always enclose a stamped self addressed envelope unless otherwise noted. Before releasing records, all courts require prepayment unless noted in profile. Open records are located at the court unless otherwise noted. District courts index by defendant and plaintiff as well as by case number. Bankruptcy courts usually index by debtor and case number. While most courts now have their indexes on computer, many still maintain index card files as well.

The universal PACER sign-up number is 800-676-6856. Find PACER and the Party/Case Index on the Web at http://pacer.psc.uscourts.gov. PACER dial-up access is $.60 per minute. Also, courts offering internet access via RACER, PACER, Web-PACER or the new CM-ECF charge $.07 per page fee unless noted as free.

US District Court

Eastern District of Oklahoma

Muskogee Division Clerk, PO Box 607, Muskogee, OK 74401 (Courier Address: 101 N 5th, Muskogee, OK 74401), 918-687-2471, Fax: 918-687-2400.

www.oked.uscourts.gov

Counties: Adair, Atoka, Bryan, Carter, Cherokee, Choctaw, Coal, Haskell, Hughes, Johnston, Latimer, Le Flore, Love, McCurtain, McIntosh, Marshall, Murray, Muskogee, Okfuskee, Pittsburg, Pontotoc, Pushmataha, Seminole, Sequoyah, Wagoner.

Indexing & Storage: Cases are indexed by defendant, plaintiff, and case number. New cases are available in the index 1 day after filing date. Open records are located at this court.

Fee & Payment Notes: Payment may be made by money order, cashier check. Business checks are not accepted. Personal checks are not accepted. Will bill law firms. Payee: Clerk, US District Court. You are allowed to make your own copies. These copies cost $.50 per page.

Phone Search: Only docket information is available by phone.

Mail Search: A stamped self addressed envelope is not required.

In Person Search: In person searching available.

PACER: Toll-free dial-up access: 866-863-3767. Local dial-up access: 918-687-2625. Case records are available back to 1996. Records are never purged. New records available online after 1 day.

US Bankruptcy Court

Eastern District of Oklahoma

Okmulgee Division PO Box 1347, Okmulgee, OK 74447 (Courier Address: PO & Federal Bldg, 111 4th St, Room 229, Okmulgee, OK 74447), 918-758-0126, Fax: 918-756-9248.

www.okeb.uscourts.gov

Counties: Adair, Atoka, Bryan, Carter, Cherokee, Choctaw, Coal, Haskell, Hughes, Johnston, Latimer, Le Flore, Love, Marshall, McCurtain, McIntosh, Murray, Muskogee, Okfuskee, Okmulgee, Pittsburg, Pontotoc, Pushmataha, Seminole, Sequoyah, Wagoner.

Indexing & Storage: Cases are indexed by debtor as well as by case number. New cases are available in the index immediately after filing date. Open records are located at this court.

Fee & Payment Notes: Payment may be made by money order, cashier check, personal check. Debtor's checks are not accepted. Payee: Clerk, US Bankruptcy Court.

Phone Search: Only docket information available by phone. An automated voice case information service (VCIS) is available. Call VCIS at 877-377-1221 or 918-756-8617.

Fax Search: The fee is $15.00 per name or item searched. The fee is $2.00 per page.

In Person Search: In person searching available.

PACER: Toll-free dial-up access: 866-863-3767. Local dial-up access: 918-756-4812. Case records are available back to 1986. Records are purged every six months. New civil records are available online after 1 day. PACER is available online at http://pacer.okeb.uscourts.gov. Document images available.

Electronic Filing: (Currently in the process of implementing CM/ECF.)

US District Court

Northern District of Oklahoma

Tulsa Division 411 US Courthouse, 333 W 4th St, Tulsa, OK 74103 (Courier Address: Use mail address for courier delivery), 918-699-4700, Fax: 918-699-4756.

www.oknd.uscourts.gov

Counties: Craig, Creek, Delaware, Mayes, Nowata, Okmulgee, Osage, Ottawa, Pawnee, Rogers, Tulsa, Washington.

Indexing & Storage: Cases are indexed by defendant, plaintiff, and case number. New cases are available in the index immediately after filing date. Open records are located at this court.

Fee & Payment Notes: Payment may be made by money order, cashier check, personal check, Visa, Mastercard. Credit cards are only accepted from in-person searchers. Payee: Clerk, US District Court. You are allowed to make your own copies. These copies cost $.50 per page.

Phone Search: Only docket information is available by phone.

In Person Search: In person searching available.

PACER: Toll-free dial-up access: 888-881-0574. Local dial-up access: 918-699-4742. Document images available. Case records are available back to 1992. New records are available online after 1 day. PACER is available online at http://pacer.oknd.uscourts.gov. Document images available.

Other Online Access: Search records on RACER at www.oknd.uscourts.gov/perl/bkplog.html.

US Bankruptcy Court

Northern District of Oklahoma

Tulsa Division 224 S. Boulder, Tulsa, OK 74103 (Courier: Use mail address for courier delivery), 918-699-4000, Fax: 918-699-4051.

www.oknb.uscourts.gov

Counties: Craig, Creek, Delaware, Mayes, Nowata, Osage, Ottawa, Pawnee, Rogers, Tulsa, Washington.

Indexing & Storage: Cases are indexed by debtor as well as by case number. New cases are available in the index same day if possible after filing date. District wide searches are available from this court.

Fee & Payment Notes: Payment may be made by money order, cashier check, personal check. Debtor's checks are not accepted. Payee: Clerk, US Bankruptcy Court. You are allowed to make your own copies. These copies cost $.15 per page.

Phone Search: Only docket information is available by phone, and only if it takes a minimum amount of time. An automated voice case information service (VCIS) is available. Call VCIS at 888-501-6977 or 918-699-4001.

Fax Search: The fees are the same as for mail searches. There is no fee for the fax, but copy fees must be prepaid.

Mail Search: A stamped self addressed envelope is not required.

In Person Search: In person searching available.

PACER: Toll-free dial-up access: 800-790-0860. Local dial-up access: 918-699-4033. Case records are available back to 1990. Records are never purged. New civil records are available online after 1 day.

Other Online Access: Search records on RACER at www.oknb.uscourts.gov/perl/bkplog.html.

US District Court

Western District of Oklahoma

Oklahoma City Division Clerk, Room 1210, 200 NW 4th St, Oklahoma City, OK 73102 (Courier Address: Use mail address for courier delivery), 405-609-5000, Fax: 405-609-5099.

www.okwd.uscourts.gov

Counties: Alfalfa, Beaver, Beckham, Blaine, Caddo, Canadian, Cimarron, Cleveland, Comanche, Cotton, Custer, Dewey, Ellis, Garfield, Garvin, Grady, Grant, Greer, Harmon, Harper, Jackson, Jefferson, Kay, Kingfisher, Kiowa, Lincoln, Logan, McClain, Major, Noble,Oklahoma, Payne, Pottawatomie, Roger Mills, Stephens, Texas, Tillman, Washita, Woods, Woodward.

Indexing & Storage: Cases are indexed by defendant, plaintiff, and case number. New cases are available in the index immediately after filing date. Records are also indexed on microfiche. District wide searches are available for records from 1907 from this court.

Fee & Payment Notes: Payment may be made by money order, cashier check, personal check. Will bill in some circumstances. Payee: Clerk, US District Court.

Phone Search: Information relating to docket entries will be given over the phone.

Mail Search: A stamped self addressed envelope is not required.

In Person Search: In person searching available.

PACER: Toll-free dial-up access: 888-699-7068. Local dial-up access: 405-231-4531. Case records are available back to 1991. Records are never purged. New records are available online after 2 days. PACER is available online at http://pacer.okwd.uscourts.gov.

US Bankruptcy Court

Western District of Oklahoma

Oklahoma City Division 1st Floor, Old Post Office Bldg, 215 Dean A McGee Ave, Oklahoma City, OK 73102 (Courier Address: Use mail address for courier delivery), 405-609-5700, Fax: 405-609-5752.

Counties: Alfalfa, Beaver, Beckham, Blaine, Caddo, Canadian, Cimarron, Cleveland, Comanche, Cotton, Custer, Dewey, Ellis, Garfield, Garvin, Grady, Grant, Greer, Harmon, Harper, Jackson, Jefferson, Kay, Kingfisher, Kiowa, Lincoln, Logan, Major, McClain, Noble,Oklahoma, Payne, Pottawatomie, Roger Mills, Stephens, Texas, Tillman, Washita, Woods, Woodward.

Indexing & Storage: Cases are indexed by debtor as well as by case number. New cases are available in the index 24 hours after filing date. Cases are also indexed by social security number. Open records are located at this court.

Fee & Payment Notes: Payment may be made by money order, cashier check, personal check. Debtor's checks are not accepted. Payee: Clerk, US Bankruptcy Court.

Phone Search: Docket information is available by phone. An automated voice case information service (VCIS) is available. Call VCIS at 800-872-1348 or 405-231-4768.

In Person Search: In person searching available.

PACER: Local dial-up access: 405-231-5064, 405-231-5065. Case records are available back to May 1, 1992. Records are purged every six months. New civil records are available online after 1 day.

Oklahoma County Courts

Court	Jurisdiction	No. of Courts	How Organized
District Courts*	General	80	26 Districts
Municipal Courts of Record	Municipal	2	
Municipal Courts Not of Record	Municipal	340	
Workers' Compensation Court	Special	1	

* Profiled in this Sourcebook.

Court	CIVIL								
	Tort	Contract	Real Estate	Min. Claim	Max. Claim	Small Claims	Estate	Eviction	Domestic Relations
District Courts*	X	X	X	$0	No Max	$4500	X	X	X
Municipal Courts of Record									
Municipal Courts Not of Record									
Workers' Compensation Court									

Court	CRIMINAL				
	Felony	Misdemeanor	DWI/DUI	Preliminary Hearing	Juvenile
District Courts*	X	X	X	X	X
Municipal Courts of Record			X		
Municipal Courts Not of Record			X		
Workers' Compensation Court					

ADMINISTRATION   Administrative Director of Courts, 1915 N Stiles #305, Oklahoma City, OK, 73105; 405-521-2450, Fax: 405-521-6815. www.oscn.net

COURT STRUCTURE   There are 80 District Courts in 26 judicial districts. Cities with populations in excess of 200,000 (Oklahoma City and Tulsa) have municipal criminal courts of record. Cities with less than 200,000 do not have such courts.

The small claims limit was raised from $3000 to $4500 in 1998.

ONLINE ACCESS   Free Internet access is available for eight District Courts and all Appellate courts at www.oscn.net. Both civil and criminal docket information is available. The counties are Canadian, Cleveland, Comanche, Garfield, Oklahoma, Payne, Rogers, and Tulsa.

One can search the Oklahoma Supreme Court Network by single cite or multiple cite (no name searches) from the Internet site.

Case information is available in bulk form for downloading to computer. For information, call the Administrative Director of Courts, 405-521-2450.

Adair County

15th Judicial District Court PO Box 426 (220 W Division), Stilwell, OK 74960; 918-696-7633. Hours: 8AM-4:30PM (CST). *Felony, Misdemeanor, Civil, Eviction, Small Claims, Probate.*

Civil Records: Access: Phone, fax, mail, in person. Both court and visitors may perform in person searches. Search fee: $5.00 per name. Fee is for 7 year search. Required to search: name, years to search. Civil cases indexed by defendant, plaintiff. Civil records archived since 1907.

Criminal Records: Access: Phone, fax, mail, in person. Both court and visitors may perform in person searches. Search fee: $5.00 per name. Fee is for 7 year search. Required to search: name, years to search, DOB; also helpful: SSN. Criminal records archived since 1907.

General Information: No juvenile, mental health or guardianship records released. SASE required. Turnaround time 1 day. Copy fee: $1.00 for first page, $.50 each add'l. Certification fee: $.50 per page. Fee payee: Adair County Court Clerk. Personal checks accepted. Prepayment is required.

Alfalfa County

4th Judicial District Court County Courthouse, 300 S Grand, Cherokee, OK 73728; 580-596-3523. Hours: 8:30AM-4:30PM (CST). *Felony, Misdemeanor, Civil, Eviction, Small Claims, Probate.*

Civil Records: Access: Mail, in person. Both court and visitors may perform in person searches. Search fee: $5.00 per name. Required to search: name, years to search. Civil cases indexed by defendant, plaintiff. Civil records archived to 1907; on computer back to 1998.

Criminal Records: Access: Mail, in person. Both court and visitors may perform in person searches. Search fee: $5.00 per name. Required to search: name, years to search. Criminal records archived to 1907; on computer back to 1998.

General Information: No confidential or guardianship records not released. SASE required. Turnaround time 1 day. Fax notes: Fee to fax results is $4.00 per page; $2.00 each add'l. Copy fee: $1.00 for first page, $.50 each add'l. Certification fee: $.50 per page. Fee payee: Court Clerk. Only cashiers checks and money orders accepted. Prepayment is required.

Atoka County

25th Judicial District Court 200 E. Court St, Atoka, OK 74525; 580-889-3565. Hours: 8:30AM-4:30PM (CST). *Felony, Misdemeanor, Civil, Eviction, Small Claims, Probate.*

Civil Records: Access: Mail, in person. Both court and visitors may perform in person searches. Search fee: $5.00 per name. Required to search: name, years to search. Civil cases indexed by defendant, plaintiff. Civil records on computer back to 1998; prior on books.

Criminal Records: Access: Mail, in person. Both court and visitors may perform in person searches. Search fee: $5.00 per name. Required to search: name, years to search, DOB or SSN. Criminal records on books from 1920; on computer back to 1998.

General Information: Public access terminal is available. No adoption, mental health or juvenile records released. SASE required. Turnaround time 1-2 days. Copy fee: $1.00 for first page, $.50 each add'l. Certification fee: $.50. Fee payee: Court Clerk. Personal checks accepted. Prepayment is required.

Beaver County

1st Judicial District Court PO Box 237, Beaver, OK 73932; 580-625-3191. Hours: 9AM-Noon, 1-5PM (CST). *Felony, Misdemeanor, Civil, Eviction, Small Claims, Probate.*

Civil Records: Access: Phone, mail, in person. Both court and visitors may perform in person searches. Search fee: $5.00 per name. Required to search: name, years to search. Civil cases indexed by defendant, plaintiff. Civil records on microfiche and archives from late 1800s, computerized back to 1997.

Criminal Records: Access: Mail, in person. Both court and visitors may perform in person searches. Search fee: $5.00 per name. Required to search: name, years to search. Criminal records on microfiche and archives from late 1800s, computerized back to 1997.

General Information: No adoption, mental health or juvenile records released. SASE required. Turnaround time 1-3 days. Copy fee: $1.00 for first page, $.50 each add'l. Certification fee: $.50. Fee payee: Court Clerk. Personal checks accepted. Prepayment is required.

Beckham County

2nd Judicial District Court PO Box 520, Sayre, OK 73662; 580-928-3330; Fax: 580-928-9278. Hours: 9AM-5PM (CST). *Felony, Misdemeanor, Civil, Eviction, Small Claims, Probate.*

Civil Records: Access: Fax, mail, in person. Both court and visitors may perform in person searches. Search fee: $5.00 per name. Required to search: name, years to search. Civil cases indexed by defendant, plaintiff. Civil records on microfiche back to 1907; on computer back to 1997.

Criminal Records: Access: Fax, mail, in person. Both court and visitors may perform in person searches. Search fee: $5.00 per name. Required to search: name, years to search. Criminal records on microfiche; on computer back to 1997.

General Information: Public access terminal is available. No juvenile, adoption or expunged records released. SASE required. Turnaround time 2 weeks. Fax notes: Fee to fax results is $1.00 per page. Copy fee: $1.00 for first page, $.50 each add'l. Certification fee: $.50. Fee payee: Court clerk. Personal checks accepted. Prepayment is required.

Blaine County

4th Judicial District Court 212 N. Weigle, Watonga, OK 73772; 580-623-5970. Hours: 8AM-4PM (CST). *Felony, Misdemeanor, Civil, Eviction, Small Claims, Probate.*

Civil Records: Access: Mail, in person. Both court and visitors may perform in person searches. Search fee: $5.00 per name. Required to search: name, years to search. Civil cases indexed by defendant, plaintiff. Civil records archived from 1900; on computer back to 1998.

Criminal Records: Access: Mail, in person. Both court and visitors may perform in person searches. Search fee: $5.00 per name. Required to search: name, years to search. Criminal records archived from 1900; on computer back to 1998.

General Information: Public access terminal is available. No juvenile or expunged records released. SASE required. Turnaround time 7-10 days. Copy fee: $1.00 for first page, $.50 each add'l. Certification fee: $.50. Fee payee: Court Clerk. Personal checks accepted. Prepayment is required.

Bryan County

19th Judicial District Court Courthouse 3rd Fl, Durant, OK 74701; 580-924-1446. Hours: 8:00AM-12:00PM,1:00PM-5:00PM (CST). *Felony, Misdemeanor, Civil, Eviction, Small Claims, Probate.*

Civil Records: Access: Mail, in person. Both court and visitors may perform in person searches. Search fee: $5.00 per name. Required to search: name, years to search, DOB. Civil cases indexed by defendant, plaintiff. Civil records archived from 1907; on comptuer back to 1994.

Criminal Records: Access: Mail, in person. Both court and visitors may perform in person searches. Search fee: $5.00 per name. Required to search: name, DOB, SSN, signed release. Criminal records archived from 1907; on comptuer back to 1994.

General Information: Public access terminal is available. No juvenile, mental health or adoption records released. SASE required. Turnaround time 2 days. Copy fee: $1.00 for first page, $.50 each add'l. Certification fee: $.50. Fee payee: Bryan County Court Clerk. Only cashiers checks and money orders accepted. Prepayment is required.

Caddo County

6th Judicial District Court PO Box 10, Anadarko, OK 73005; 405-247-3393. Hours: 8:30AM-4:30PM (CST). *Felony, Misdemeanor, Civil, Eviction, Small Claims, Probate.*

Civil Records: Access: Mail, in person. Both court and visitors may perform in person searches. Search fee: $10.00 per hour. Required to search: name, years to search. Civil cases indexed by defendant, plaintiff. Civil records on computer since 1997; prior on docket books to 1901.

Criminal Records: Access: Mail, in person. Both court and visitors may perform in person searches. Search fee: $10.00 per hour. Required to search: name, years to search. Criminal records on computer since 1997, prior on docket books to 1901.

General Information: Public access terminal is available. No adoption, mental health, juvenile, and some guardianship records released. SASE would be helpful. Turnaround time 1 week. Copy fee: $1.00 for first page, $.50 each add'l. Certification fee: $.50. Fee payee: Court Clerk. No foreign checks accepted. Prepayment is required.

Canadian County

26th Judicial District Court PO Box 730, El Reno, OK 73036; 405-262-1070 X172. Hours: 8AM-4:30PM (CST). *Felony, Misdemeanor, Civil, Eviction, Small Claims, Probate.*

Civil Records: Access: Mail, online, in person. Both court and visitors may perform in person searches. Search fee: $5.00 per name. Required to search: name, years to search. Civil cases indexed by defendant, plaintiff. Civil records on computer back to 1993, archived from 1907. Online access to court dockets available free online at www.oscn.net/applications/oscn/casesearch.asp. Dockets go back to 3/1983.

Criminal Records: Access: Mail, online, in person. Both court and visitors may perform in person searches. Search fee: $5.00 per name. Required to search: name, years to search, DOB or SSN. Criminal records on computer back to 1993, archived from 1907. Online access to criminal dockets is same as civil.

General Information: Public access terminal is available. No expunged criminal cases, juvenile, adoption, confidential portion of guardianship records released. Copy fee: $1.00 for first page, $.50 each add'l. Certification fee: $.50 per page. Fee payee: Court Clerk. Personal checks accepted. Prepayment is required.

Carter County

20th Judicial District Court PO Box 37, Court Clerk, Ardmore, OK 73402; 580-223-5253. Hours: 8AM-Noon, 1-5PM (CST). *Felony, Misdemeanor, Civil, Eviction, Small Claims, Probate.*

www.brightok.net/chickasaw/ardmore/county/crtclerk.html

Note: Bench warrants and current week dockets available at web site.

Civil Records: Access: Mail, in person. Both court and visitors may perform in person searches. Search fee: $5.00 per name. Required to search: name, years to search. Civil cases indexed by defendant, plaintiff. Civil records archived from 1907; on computer back to 1997.

Criminal Records: Access: Mail, in person. Both court and visitors may perform in person searches. Search fee: $5.00 per name. Required to search: name, years to search. Criminal records archived from 1907; on computer back to 1997.

General Information: Public access terminal is available. No juvenile, mental health, or adoption records released. SASE required. Turnaround time 2 weeks. Fax notes: Will not fax results. Copy fee: $1.00 for first page, $.50 each add'l. Certification fee: $.50. Fee payee: Carter County Court Clerk. Personal checks accepted. Prepayment is required.

Cherokee County

15th Judicial District Court 213 W. Delaware, Rm 302, Tahlequah, OK 74464; 918-456-0691; Fax: 918-458-6587. Hours: 8AM-4:30PM (CST). *Felony, Misdemeanor, Civil, Eviction, Small Claims, Probate.*

Civil Records: Access: Phone, mail, in person. Both court and visitors may perform in person searches. Search fee: $5.00 per name. Required to search: name, years to search. Civil cases indexed by defendant, plaintiff. Civil records on microfiche from 1907 (civil, probate, vital), computerized since 1999.

Criminal Records: Access: Phone, mail, in person. Both court and visitors may perform in person searches. Search fee: $5.00 per name. Required to search: name, years to search, DOB. Criminal records kept form 1969.

General Information: Public access terminal is available. No juvenile, adoption or mental health released. SASE required. Turnaround time 1-2 days. Copy fee: $1.00 for first page, $.50 each add'l. Certification fee: $.50 per page. Fee payee: Court Clerk. Personal checks accepted. Prepayment is required.

Choctaw County

17th Judicial District Court 300 E. Duke, Hugo, OK 74743; 580-326-7554 & 7555. Hours: 8AM-4PM (CST). *Felony, Misdemeanor, Civil, Eviction, Small Claims, Probate.*

Civil Records: Access: Phone, fax, mail, in person. Both court and visitors may perform in person searches. Search fee: $10.00 per name. Required to search: name, years to search. Civil cases indexed by defendant, plaintiff. Civil records archived from 1907.

Criminal Records: Access: Phone, fax, mail, in person. Both court and visitors may perform in person searches. Search fee: $10.00 per name. Required to search: name, years to search, DOB. Criminal records archived from 1907.

General Information: No juvenile, adoption, guardianship, wills or expunged records released. SASE required. Turnaround time 1 day. Fax notes: $7.50 per page. Copy fee: $1.00 for first page, $.50 each add'l. Certification fee: $.50. Fee payee: Court Clerk. Personal checks accepted. Prepayment is required.

Cimarron County

1st Judicial District Court PO Box 788, Boise City, OK 73933; 580-544-2221. Hours: 9AM-Noon,1-5PM (CST). *Felony, Misdemeanor, Civil, Eviction, Small Claims, Probate.*

Civil Records: Access: Phone, mail, in person. Only the court performs in person searches; visitors may not. Search fee: No search fee. Required to search: name, years to search. Civil cases indexed by defendant, plaintiff. Civil records archived from 1907; on computer back to 8/2001.

Criminal Records: Access: Phone, mail, in person. Only the court performs in person searches; visitors may not. Search fee: No search fee. Required to search: name, years to search. Criminal records archived from 1907.

General Information: No juvenile, adoption or mental health records released. SASE requested. Turnaround time 1 day. Copy fee: $1.00 for first page, $.50 each add'l. Certification fee: $.50. Fee payee: Court Clerk. Personal checks accepted. Prepayment is required.

Cleveland County

21st Judicial District Court - Civil Branch 200 S. Peters, Norman, OK 73069; 405-321-6402. Hours: 8AM-5PM (CST). *Civil, Eviction, Small Claims, Probate.*

Civil Records: Access: Mail, online, in person. Both court and visitors may perform in person searches. No search fee. Required to search: name, years to search. Civil cases indexed by defendant, plaintiff. Civil records on computer from 1989, on microfiche from 1800s, archived since 1970. Online access to court dockets available free online at www.oscn.net/applications/oscn/casesearch.asp. Dockets go back to 1/1989.

General Information: Public access terminal is available. No expunged, sealed records released. SASE required. Turnaround time 7-10 days. Copy fee: $1.00 for first page, $.50 each add'l. Certification fee: $.50. Fee payee: Court Clerk. Personal checks accepted. Prepayment is required.

21st Judicial District Court - Criminal 200 S. Peters, Norman, OK 73069; 405-321-6402. Hours: 8AM-5PM (CST). *Felony, Misdemeanor.*

Criminal Records: Access: Mail, online, in person. Both court and visitors may perform in person searches. No search fee. Required to search: name, years to search. Criminal records on computer from 1989, on microfiche from 1800s. Online access to criminal dockets is same as civil.

General Information: Public access terminal is available. No juvenile, adoption, or guardianship records released. Turnaround time 7-10 days. Copy fee: $1.00 for first page, $.50 each add'l. Certification fee: $.50. Fee payee: Cleveland County Court Clerk. Personal checks accepted. Local personal checks accepted. Prepayment is required.

Coal County

25th Judicial District Court 4 N Main #9, Coalgate, OK 74538; 580-927-2281. Hours: 8AM-5PM (CST). *Felony, Misdemeanor, Civil, Eviction, Small Claims, Probate.*

Civil Records: Access: In person only. Visitors must perform in person searches for themselves. No search fee. Required to search: name, years to search. Civil cases indexed by defendant, plaintiff. Civil records archived since 1907; computerized back to 1999.

Criminal Records: Access: In person only. Visitors must perform in person searches for themselves. No search fee. Required to search: name, years to search. Criminal records archived since 1907; computerized back to 1999.

General Information: Public access terminal is available. No juvenile, adoption, mental health, guardianship, wills or expunged records released. Fax notes: No fee to fax results. Copy fee: $1.00 for first page, $.50 each add'l. Certification fee: $1.00. Fee payee: Court Clerk. Personal checks accepted. Prepayment is required.

Comanche County

5th Judicial District Court 315 SW 5th Street, Rm 504, Lawton, OK 73501-4390; 580-355-4017. Hours: 8AM-5PM (CST). *Felony, Misdemeanor, Civil, Eviction, Small Claims, Probate.*

Civil Records: Access: Phone, mail, online, in person. Only the court performs in person searches; visitors may not. Search fee: $10.00 per name. Required to search: name, years to search; also helpful: address. Civil cases indexed by defendant, plaintiff. Civil records on computer from 8/88, prior in books to 1901. Online access to court dockets available free online at www.oscn.net/applications/oscn/casesearch.asp. Dockets go back to 8/1988.

Criminal Records: Access: Mail, online, in person. Only the court performs in person searches on computer; visitors may not. Search fee: $10.00 per name. Required to search: name, years to search; also helpful: address, DOB, SSN. Criminal records on computer from 8/88, prior in books to 1901. Online access to court dockets available free online at www.oscn.net/applications/oscn/casesearch.asp. Dockets go back to 8/1988.

General Information: No juvenile, mental health, adoption or some probate records released. SASE required. Turnaround time 1 day. Fax notes: Fee to fax results is $1.00 per page. Copy fee: $1.00 for first page, $.50 each add'l. Fee payee: District Court Clerk. Business checks accepted. Prepayment is required.

Cotton County

5th Judicial District Court 301 N. Broadway, Walters, OK 73572; 580-875-3029. Hours: 8AM-4:30PM (CST). *Felony, Misdemeanor, Civil, Eviction, Small Claims, Probate.*

Civil Records: Access: Mail, in person. Both court and visitors may perform in person searches. Search fee: $5.00 per name. Required to search: name, years to search. Civil cases indexed by defendant, plaintiff. Civil records archived from 1912; computerized back to 1997.

Criminal Records: Access: Mail, in person. Both court and visitors may perform in person searches. Search fee: $5.00 per name. Required to search: name, years to search, DOB. Criminal records archived from 1912; computerized back to 1997.

General Information: Public access terminal is available. No adoption, juvenile, and some guardianship records released. SASE not required. Turnaround time 2 day. Fax notes: No fax. Copy fee: $1.00 for first page, $.50 each add'l. Certification fee: $.50. Fee payee: Court Clerk. Personal checks accepted. Prepayment required.

Craig County

12th Judicial District Court 301 W. Canadian, Vinita, OK 74301; 918-256-6451. Hours: 8:30AM-4:30PM (CST). *Felony, Misdemeanor, Civil, Eviction, Small Claims, Probate.*

Note: SSNs are released to the public on criminal case matters, but not for civil cases.

Civil Records: Access: Mail, in person. Both court and visitors may perform in person searches. Search fee: $5.00 per name. Required to search: name, years to search. Civil cases indexed by defendant, plaintiff. Civil records on microfilm from 1902; on computer since 4/97.

Criminal Records: Access: Mail, in person. Both court and visitors may perform in person searches. Search

fee: $5.00 per name. Required to search: name, years to search; also helpful: SSN, DOB, sex. Criminal records on microfilm from 1902; on computer since 4/97.
General Information: Public access terminal is available. No mental or juvenile records released. SASE required. Turnaround time 1-3 days. Copy fee: $1.00 for first page, $.50 each add'l. Certification fee: $.50. Fee payee: Court Clerk. Personal checks accepted. Prepayment is required.

Creek County

24th Judicial District Court 222 E Dewey, #201, Sapulpa, OK 74067; 918-227-2525; Fax: 918-227-5030. Hours: 8AM-5PM (CST). *Felony, Misdemeanor, Civil, Eviction, Small Claims, Probate.*

Civil Records: Access: In person only. Visitors must perform in person searches for themselves. No search fee. Required to search: name, years to search; also helpful: address. Civil cases indexed by defendant, plaintiff. Computerized records back to Computerized records back to 1998, civil records on docket books and files back to 1907.
Criminal Records: Access: In person only. Visitors must perform in person searches for themselves. No search fee. Required to search: name, years to search; also helpful: address, DOB, SSN. Criminal records on docket books and files. They go back "many years, no exact date known".
General Information: Public access terminal is available. No juvenile, mental health, or adoption records released. Copy fee: $1.00 for first page, $.50 each add'l. Certification fee: $.50. Fee payee: Creek County Court Clerk. Personal checks accepted. Prepayment is required.

Custer County

2nd Judicial District Court Box D, Arapaho, OK 73620; 580-323-3233; Fax: 580-331-1121. Hours: 8AM-4PM (CST). *Felony, Misdemeanor, Civil, Eviction, Small Claims, Probate.*

Civil Records: Access: In person only. Visitors must perform in person searches for themselves Search fee: Court will not perform civil searches, but may assist. Required to search: name, years to search; also helpful: address. Civil cases indexed by defendant, plaintiff. Civil records go back to 1900's; records on computer go back to 1/95.
Criminal Records: Access: Mail, in person. Both court and visitors may perform in person searches. Search fee: $5.00 per name. Required to search: name, years to search; also helpful: DOB, SSN. Criminal records go back to 1900's; records on computer go back to 1/95.
General Information: Public access terminal is available. No adoptions, juvenile, or mental records released. SASE requested. Turnaround time 2-3 days. Copy fee: $1.00 for first page, $.50 each add'l. Certification fee: $.50. Fee payee: Court Clerk. Personal checks accepted. Prepayment is required.

Delaware County

13th Judicial District Court Box 407, Jay, OK 74346; 918-253-4420. Hours: 8:30AM-4:30PM (CST). *Felony, Misdemeanor, Civil, Eviction, Small Claims, Probate.*

Civil Records: Access: Mail, in person. Both court and visitors may perform in person searches. Search fee: $5.00 per name. Required to search: name, years to search. Civil cases indexed by defendant, plaintiff. Civil records on computer since 1996 and on microfilm from 1913.
Criminal Records: Access: Mail, in person. Both court and visitors may perform in person searches. Search fee: $5.00 per name. Required to search: name, years to search; also helpful: DOB, SSN. Criminal records on computer since 1991.

General Information: Public access terminal is available. No juvenile, adoption, guardianship or search warrant records released. SASE requested. Turnaround time 1-2 weeks. Copy fee: $1.00 for first page, $.50 each add'l. Certification fee: $.50. Fee payee: Delaware County Court Clerk. Business checks accepted. Prepayment is required.

Dewey County

4th Judicial District Court Box 278, Taloga, OK 73667; 580-328-5521. Hours: 8AM-4PM (CST). *Felony, Misdemeanor, Civil, Small Claims, Probate.*

Civil Records: Access: Mail, in person. Both court and visitors may perform in person searches. No search fee. Required to search: name, years to search. Civil cases indexed by defendant, plaintiff. Civil records archived from late 1800s, computerized records go back to 1995. All requests must be in writing.
Criminal Records: Access: Mail, in person. Both court and visitors may perform in person searches. No search fee. Required to search: name, years to search; also helpful: SSN. Criminal records archived from late 1800s, computerized records go back to 1995. All requests must be in writing.
General Information: No expunged, adoption, mental, guardianship, juvenile records released. SASE requested. Turnaround time 2 days. Copy fee: $1.00 for first page, $.50 each add'l. Certification fee: $.50. Fee payee: Dewey County Court Clerk. Personal checks accepted. Prepayment is required.

Ellis County

2nd Judicial District Court Box 217, Arnett, OK 73832; 580-885-7255. Hours: 8:30AM-4:30PM (CST). *Felony, Misdemeanor, Civil, Eviction, Small Claims, Probate.*

Civil Records: Access: Phone, mail, in person. Both court and visitors may perform in person searches. No search fee. Required to search: name, years to search. Civil cases indexed by defendant, plaintiff. Civil records on docket books from 1900.
Criminal Records: Access: Phone, mail, in person. Both court and visitors may perform in person searches. Search fee: $5.00 per name. Required to search: name, years to search; also helpful: SSN. Criminal records on docket books from 1900.
General Information: No expunged records released. SASE required. Turnaround time 1 day. Copy fee: $1.00 for first page, $.50 each add'l. Certification fee: $.50. Fee payee: Ellis County Court Clerk. Personal checks accepted. Prepayment is required.

Garfield County

4th Judicial District Court 114 W Broadway, Enid, OK 73701-4024; 580-237-0232. Hours: 8AM-4:30PM (CST). *Felony, Misdemeanor, Civil, Eviction, Small Claims, Probate.*

Civil Records: Access: Online, in person. Both court and visitors may perform in person searches. No search fee. Required to search: name, years to search. Civil cases indexed by defendant, plaintiff. Civil records on computer from 3-89, on microfiche from 1893. Online access to court dockets available free online at www.oscn.net/applications/oscn/casesearch.asp. Dockets go back to 3/1989.
Criminal Records: Access: Online, in person. Both court and visitors may perform in person searches. No search fee. Required to search: name, years to search, SSN. Criminal records on computer from 1989, on microfiche from 1893. Online access to criminal dockets is same as civil.
General Information: Public access terminal is available. No juvenile, mental health, or adoption records released. Copy fee: $1.00 for first page, $.50 each add'l. Certification fee: $.50. Fee payee: Court

Clerk. Personal checks accepted. Prepayment is required.

Garvin County

21st Judicial District Court PO Box 239, Pauls Valley, OK 73075; 405-238-5596. Hours: 8:30AM-4:30PM (CST). *Felony, Misdemeanor, Civil, Eviction, Small Claims, Probate.*

Civil Records: Access: Mail, in person. Both court and visitors may perform in person searches. Search fee: $10.00 per name. $7.00 mailing fee if SASE not enclosed. Required to search: name, years to search. Civil cases indexed by defendant, plaintiff. Civil records on computer since 1994, docket books from 1907.
Criminal Records: Access: Mail, in person. Both court and visitors may perform in person searches. Search fee: $10.00 per name. $7.00 mailing fee if SASE not enclosed. Required to search: name, years to search; also helpful: SSN, DOB. Criminal records on computer since 1994, docket books from 1907.
General Information: Public access terminal is available. No juvenile, adoption or guardianship released. SASE required. Turnaround time 1 day. Copy fee: $1.00 for first page, $.50 each add'l. Certification fee: $.50 per page. Fee payee: Garvin County Court Clerk. Only cashiers checks and money orders accepted. Prepayment is required.

Grady County

6th Judicial District Court PO Box 605, 328 Choctaw St, Chickasha, OK 73023; 405-224-7446. Hours: 8AM-4:30PM (CST). *Felony, Misdemeanor, Civil, Eviction, Small Claims, Probate.*

Civil Records: Access: In person only. Visitors must perform in person searches for themselves. No search fee. Required to search: name, years to search. Civil cases indexed by defendant, plaintiff. Civil records on microfiche from 1982, archived from 1907.
Criminal Records: Access: In person only. Visitors must perform in person searches for themselves. No search fee. Required to search: name, years to search; also helpful: address, DOB, SSN. Criminal records on microfiche from 1982, archived from 1907.
General Information: Public access terminal is available. No juvenile, adoption, guardianship or mental health records released. Copy fee: $1.00 for first page, $.50 each add'l. Certification fee: $.50 per document. Fee payee: Court Clerk. Personal checks accepted. Prepayment is required.

Grant County

4th Judicial District Court 112 E Guthrie, Medford, OK 73759; 580-395-2828. Hours: 8AM-4:30PM (CST). *Felony, Misdemeanor, Civil, Eviction, Small Claims, Probate.*

Civil Records: Access: Mail, in person. Both court and visitors may perform in person searches. Search fee: $5.00 per name. Required to search: name, years to search. Civil cases indexed by defendant, plaintiff. Civil records archived from 1893, in books since 1898.
Criminal Records: Access: Mail, in person. Both court and visitors may perform in person searches. Search fee: $5.00 per name. Required to search: name, years to search; also helpful: SSN. Criminal records archived from 1893, in books since 1898.
General Information: No juvenile, adoption, mental health, some guardianship or wills released. SASE helpful. Turnaround time 1-3 days. Copy fee: $1.00 for first page, $.50 each add'l. Certification fee: $.50 per page. Fee payee: Court Clerk. Personal checks accepted. No out of state personal checks accepted. Prepayment is required.

Greer County

2nd Judicial District Court PO Box 216, Courthouse Square, Mangum, OK 73554; 580-782-3665. Hours: 8:30AM-4:30PM (CST). *Felony, Misdemeanor, Civil, Eviction, Small Claims, Probate.*

Civil Records: Access: Mail, in person. Both court and visitors may perform in person searches. Search fee: $5.00 per name. Fee is per 15 minutes. Required to search: name, years to search. Civil cases indexed by defendant, plaintiff. Civil records on docket books from 1901; on computer back to 1997.

Criminal Records: Access: Mail, in person. Both court and visitors may perform in person searches. Search fee: $5.00 per name. Fee is per 15 minutes. Required to search: name, years to search, DOB; also helpful: SSN. Criminal records on docket books from 1901; on computer back to 1997.

General Information: Public access terminal is available. No juvenile, mental health, adoption or guardianship records released. SASE required. Turnaround time 1-2 days. Fax notes: Fee to fax results is $1.00 per document. Copy fee: $1.00 for first page, $.50 each add'l. Certification fee: $.50. Fee payee: Court Clerk. Personal checks accepted. Prepayment is required.

Harmon County

2nd Judicial District Court 114 W. Hollis, Hollis, OK 73550; 580-688-3617; Fax: 580-688-2900. Hours: 8AM-5PM (CST). *Felony, Misdemeanor, Civil, Eviction, Small Claims, Probate.*

Civil Records: Access: Mail, fax, in person. Both court and visitors may perform in person searches. Search fee: $5.00 per name. Required to search: name, years to search. Civil cases indexed by defendant, plaintiff. Civil records on docket books from 1909; on computer since 1996.

Criminal Records: Access: Mail, fax, in person. Both court and visitors may perform in person searches. Search fee: $5.00 per name. Required to search: name, years to search; also helpful: DOB, SSN, sex. Criminal records on docket books from 1909; on computer since 1996.

General Information: No juvenile, adoption, mental health, or guardianship records released. SASE requested. Turnaround time 1-2 days. Fax notes: Will fax results if provided pre-payment or proof of payment such as facsimile of check, etc. Copy fee: $1.00 for first page, $.50 each add'l. Certification fee: $.50 per page. Fee payee: Harmon County Court Clerk. Personal checks accepted. Prepayment is required.

Harper County

1st Judicial District Court Box 347, Buffalo, OK 73834; 580-735-2010. Hours: 8AM-4PM (CST). *Felony, Misdemeanor, Civil, Eviction, Small Claims, Probate.*

Civil Records: Access: Mail, in person. Both court and visitors may perform in person searches. Search fee: $5.00 per name. Required to search: name, years to search. Civil cases indexed by defendant, plaintiff. Civil records on docket books from 1907.

Criminal Records: Access: Mail, in person. Both court and visitors may perform in person searches. Search fee: $5.00 per name. Required to search: name, years to search. Criminal records on docket books from 1907.

General Information: No adoption, juvenile, conservatorship, mental health, guardianship, or expunged records released. SASE requested. Turnaround time 3 or 4 days. Copy fee: $1.00 for first page, $.50 each add'l. Certification fee: $.50 per page. Fee payee: Harper County Court Clerk. Personal checks not accepted. Cashier's check or money order. Prepayment is required.

Haskell County

16th Judicial District Court 202 E. Main, Stigler, OK 74462; 918-967-3323; Fax: 918-967-2819. Hours: 8AM-4:30PM (CST). *Felony, Misdemeanor, Civil, Eviction, Small Claims, Probate.*

Civil Records: Access: Phone, fax, mail, in person. Both court and visitors may perform in person searches. Search fee: $5.00. Required to search: name, years to search. Civil cases indexed by defendant, plaintiff. Civil records archived from 1907, they are in the process of placing files on microfiche starting with 1994; computerized since 1997.

Criminal Records: Access: Phone, fax, mail, in person. Both court and visitors may perform in person searches. Search fee: $5.00. Required to search: name, years to search; also helpful: SSN. Criminal records archived from 1907, they are in the process of placing files on microfiche starting with 1994; computerized since 1997.

General Information: Public access terminal is available. No juvenile, adoption or mental health records released. SASE required. Turnaround time 1 week. Copy fee: $1.00 for first page, $.50 each add'l. Certification fee: $2.00. Fee payee: Haskell County Court Clerk. Personal checks accepted.

Hughes County

22nd Judicial District Court 200 N Broadway, Box 32, Holdenville, OK 74848; 405-379-3384. Hours: 8AM-4:30PM (CST). *Felony, Misdemeanor, Civil, Eviction, Small Claims, Probate.*

Civil Records: Access: Mail, in person. Both court and visitors may perform in person searches. Search fee: $5.00 per name. Required to search: name, years to search. Civil cases indexed by defendant, plaintiff. Civil records archived from 1907, computerized records go back to 1998.

Criminal Records: Access: Mail, in person. Both court and visitors may perform in person searches. Search fee: $5.00 per name. Required to search: name, years to search; also helpful: SSN. Criminal records archived from 1907.

General Information: Public access terminal is available. No juvenile or adoption records released. SASE required. Turnaround time 2 days. Copy fee: $1.00 for first page, $.50 each add'l. Certification fee: $.50. Fee payee: Hughes County Court Clerk. Personal checks accepted. Prepayment is required.

Jackson County

3rd Judicial District Court PO Box 616, 101 N. Main, Rm. 303, Jackson County Courthouse, Altus, OK 73522; 580-482-0448. Hours: 8AM-4PM (CST). *Felony, Misdemeanor, Civil, Eviction, Small Claims, Probate.*

Civil Records: Access: Mail, in person. Both court and visitors may perform in person searches. Search fee: $5.00 per name. Required to search: name, years to search. Civil cases indexed by defendant, plaintiff. Civil records archived from early 1900; computerized records since 7/97.

Criminal Records: Access: Mail, in person. Both court and visitors may perform in person searches. Search fee: $5.00 per name. Required to search: name, years to search; also helpful: SSN. Criminal records archived from early 1900; computerized records since 7/97.

General Information: Public access terminal is available. No adoption, juvenile, mental health, or guardianship records released. SASE required. Turnaround time 3-4 days. Copy fee: $1.00 for first page, $.50 each add'l. Certification fee: $.50. Fee payee: Jackson County Court Clerk. Business checks accepted. Prepayment is required.

Jefferson County

5th Judicial District Court 220 N. Main, Room 302, Waurika, OK 73573; 580-228-2961. Hours: 8AM-4PM (CST). *Felony, Misdemeanor, Civil, Eviction, Small Claims, Probate.*

Civil Records: Access: Mail, in person. Both court and visitors may perform in person searches. Search fee: $5.00 per name. Required to search: name, years to search, DOB or SSN. Civil cases indexed by defendant, plaintiff. Civil records on docket books from 1907; on computer since October, 1997.

Criminal Records: Access: Mail, in person. Both court and visitors may perform in person searches. Search fee: $5.00 per name. Required to search: name, years to search, DOB; also helpful: SSN. Criminal records on docket books from 1907; on computer since October, 1997.

General Information: Public access terminal is available. No juvenile, adoption or guardianship records released. SASE required. Turnaround time 1 week. Copy fee: $1.00 for first page, $.50 each add'l. Certification fee: $.50. Fee payee: Court Clerk. Personal checks accepted. Prepayment is required.

Johnston County

20th Judicial District Court 403 W Main, #201, Tishomingo, OK 73460; 580-371-3281. Hours: 8:30AM-4:30PM (CST). *Felony, Misdemeanor, Civil, Eviction, Small Claims, Probate.*

Civil Records: Access: Phone, mail, in person. Both court and visitors may perform in person searches. Search fee: $5.00 per name. Required to search: name, years to search. Civil cases indexed by defendant, plaintiff. Civil records on docket books from 1907; on computer back to 1997. All requests must be in writing.

Criminal Records: Access: Mail, in person. Both court and visitors may perform in person searches. Search fee: $5.00 per name. Required to search: name, years to search; also helpful: DOB, SSN. Criminal records on docket books from 1907; on computer back to 1997. All requests must be in writing.

General Information: Public access terminal is available. No juvenile or mental health records released. SASE required. Turnaround time 2 days. Copy fee: $1.00 for first page, $.50 each add'l. Certification fee: $.50. Fee payee: Court. Personal checks accepted. Prepayment is required.

Kay County

8th Judicial District Court Box 428, Newkirk, OK 74647; 580-362-3350. Hours: 8:00AM-4:30PM (CST). *Felony, Misdemeanor, Civil, Eviction, Small Claims, Probate.*

Civil Records: Access: Phone, mail, in person. Both court and visitors may perform in person searches. Search fee: $5.00 per name. Required to search: name, years to search. Civil cases indexed by defendant, plaintiff. Civil records on microfiche and original records; computerized records since 1995.

Criminal Records: Access: Phone, mail, in person. Both court and visitors may perform in person searches. Search fee: $5.00 per name. Required to search: name, years to search; also helpful: DOB, SSN. Criminal records on microfiche and original records; computerized records since 1995.

General Information: Public access terminal is available. No juvenile, adoption, mental health, or sealed records released. Turnaround time 1 day. Copy fee: $1.00 for first page, $.50 each add'l. Certification fee: $.50. Fee payee: Kay County Court Clerk. Personal checks accepted. Prepayment is required.

Kingfisher County

4th Judicial District Court Box 328, Kingfisher, OK 73750; 405-375-3813. Hours: 8:00AM-4:30PM (CST). *Felony, Misdemeanor, Civil, Eviction, Small Claims, Probate.*

Civil Records: Access: Phone, mail, in person. Both court and visitors may perform in person searches. Search fee: $5.00. Required to search: name, years to search. Civil cases indexed by defendant, plaintiff. Civil records archived from 1900, computerized since 1998.

Criminal Records: Access: Mail, in person. Both court and visitors may perform in person searches. Search fee: $5.00. Required to search: name, years to search; also helpful: SSN. Criminal records archived from 1900, comuterized since 1998.

General Information: Public access terminal is available. No juvenile, mental or guardianship records released. Turnaround time 1-2 days. Copy fee: $1.00 for first page, $.50 each add'l. Certification fee: $.50. Fee payee: Court Clerk. Personal checks accepted. Prepayment is required.

Kiowa County

3rd Judicial District Court Box 854, Hobart, OK 73651; 580-726-5125. Hours: 9AM-5PM (CST). *Felony, Misdemeanor, Civil, Eviction, Small Claims, Probate.*

Civil Records: Access: Phone, mail, in person. Both court and visitors may perform in person searches. Search fee: $5.00 per name. Required to search: name, years to search. Civil cases indexed by defendant, plaintiff. Civil records archived from 1900, computerized reocrds from1996.

Criminal Records: Access: Phone, mail, in person. Both court and visitors may perform in person searches. Search fee: $5.00 per name. Required to search: name, years to search; also helpful: SSN. Criminal records archived from 1900, computerized records from 1996.

General Information: No juvenile or adoptions records released. SASE required. Turnaround time 1-2 days. Copy fee: $1.00 for first page, $.50 each add'l. Certification fee: $.50. Fee payee: Court Clerk. Only cashiers checks and money orders accepted. Prepayment is required.

Latimer County

16th Judicial District Court 109 N. Central, Rm 200, Wilburton, OK 74578; 918-465-2011. Hours: 8AM-4:30PM (CST). *Felony, Misdemeanor, Civil, Eviction, Small Claims, Probate.*

Civil Records: Access: Phone, mail, in person. Both court and visitors may perform in person searches. Search fee: $5.00 per name. Required to search: name, years to search. Civil cases indexed by defendant, plaintiff. Civil records in original files from 1907, computerized from 1999.

Criminal Records: Access: Phone, mail, in person. Both court and visitors may perform in person searches. Search fee: $5.00 per name. Required to search: name, years to search; also helpful: DOB, SSN. Criminal records in original files from 1907, computerized from 1999.

General Information: Public access terminal is available. No guardianship or juvenile records released. SASE not required. Turnaround time 2 days. Copy fee: $1.00 for first page, $.50 each add'l. Certification fee: $.50. Fee payee: Latimer County Court Clerk. Personal checks accepted. Will bill search fee to law firms.

Le Flore County

16th Judicial District Court PO Box 688, Poteau, OK 74953; 918-647-3181. Hours: 8AM-4:30PM (CST). *Felony, Misdemeanor, Civil, Eviction, Small Claims, Probate.*

Civil Records: Access: Mail, in person. Both court and visitors may perform in person searches. Search fee: $5.00 per name. Required to search: name, years to search. Civil cases indexed by defendant, plaintiff. Civil records on computer since July 1, 1997; prior records archived since 1904 in files and books.

Criminal Records: Access: Mail, in person. Both court and visitors may perform in person searches. Search fee: $5.00 per name. Required to search: name, years to search; also helpful: SSN. Criminal records on computer since July 1, 1997; prior records archived since 1904 in files and books.

General Information: No juvenile, adoptions, mental health or guardian records released. SASE required. Turnaround time 1 week. Copy fee: $1.00 for first page, $.50 each add'l. Certification fee: $.50. Fee payee: Court Clerk. Personal checks accepted.

Lincoln County

23rd Judicial District Court PO Box 307, Chandler, OK 74834; 405-258-1309. Hours: 8AM-4:30PM (CST). *Felony, Misdemeanor, Civil, Eviction, Small Claims, Probate.*

Civil Records: Access: Mail, in person. Both court and visitors may perform in person searches. Search fee: $5.00 per name. Required to search: name, years to search. Civil cases indexed by defendant, plaintiff. Civil records archived since 1891.

Criminal Records: Access: Mail, in person. Both court and visitors may perform in person searches. Search fee: $5.00 per name. Required to search: name, years to search, DOB, signed release; also helpful: SSN. Criminal records archived since 1891.

General Information: Public access terminal is available. No juvenile, adoption or guardianship records released. SASE required. Turnaround time can take 30 days or more. Record searching is a low priority. Copy fee: $1.00 for first page, $.50 each add'l. Fee payee: Court Clerk. Personal checks accepted. Prepayment is required.

Logan County

9th Judicial District Court 301 E. Harrison, Rm 201, Guthrie, OK 73044; 405-282-0123. Hours: 8:30AM-4:30PM (CST). *Felony, Misdemeanor, Civil, Eviction, Small Claims, Probate.*

Civil Records: Access: Mail, in person. Both court and visitors may perform in person searches. Search fee: $5.00 per name. Required to search: name, years to search. Civil cases indexed by defendant, plaintiff. Civil records on microfiche from 1907.

Criminal Records: Access: Mail, in person. Both court and visitors may perform in person searches. Search fee: $5.00 per name. Required to search: name, years to search; also helpful: SSN, DOB. Criminal records on microfiche from 1907.

General Information: No juvenile, mental health or adoption records released. SASE required. Turnaround time 2 days. Copy fee: $1.00 for first page, $.50 each add'l. Certification fee: $.50. Fee payee: Court Clerk. Personal checks accepted. Prepayment is required.

Love County

20th Judicial District Court 405 W. Main, Marietta, OK 73448; 580-276-2235. Hours: 8AM-4:30PM (CST). *Felony, Misdemeanor, Civil, Eviction, Small Claims, Probate.*

Civil Records: Access: Mail, in person. Both court and visitors may perform in person searches. Search fee: $5.00 per name. Required to search: name, years to

search. Civil cases indexed by defendant, plaintiff. Civil records on docket books from 1907, computer records back to 1997.

Criminal Records: Access: Mail, in person. Both court and visitors may perform in person searches. Search fee: $5.00 per name. Required to search: name, years to search; also helpful: DOB, SSN. Criminal records on docket books from 1907, computer records back to 1997.

General Information: No juvenile or adoptions records released. SASE required. Turnaround time 1-2 days. Copy fee: $1.00 for first page, $.50 each add'l. Certification fee: $.50. Fee payee: Court Clerk. Only cashiers checks and money orders accepted. Prepayment is required.

Major County

4th Judicial District Court 500 E Broadway, Fairview, OK 73737; 580-227-4690 X204. Hours: 8:30AM-4:30PM (CST). *Felony, Misdemeanor, Civil, Small Claims, Probate.*

Civil Records: Access: Phone, fax, mail, in person. Both court and visitors may perform in person searches. Search fee: $5.00 per name. Fee is per book. Required to search: name, years to search. Civil cases indexed by defendant, plaintiff. Civil records on docket books from 1907, on microfiche from 1970, on computer back to 1997.

Criminal Records: Access: Phone, fax, mail, in person. Both court and visitors may perform in person searches. Search fee: $5.00 per name. Fee is per book. Required to search: name, years to search, DOB; also helpful: SSN. Criminal records on docket books from 1907, on microfiche from 1970; on computer back to 1997.

General Information: No juvenile, adoptions or mental records released. SASE required. Turnaround time 3 days. Copy fee: $1.00 for first page, $.50 each add'l. Certification fee: $.50. Fee payee: Court Clerk. Personal checks accepted. Attorney's or firms with previous credit paid.

Marshall County

20th Judicial District Court Box 58, Madill, OK 73446; 580-795-3278 X240. Hours: 8:30AM-5PM (CST). *Felony, Misdemeanor, Civil, Eviction, Small Claims, Probate.*

Civil Records: Access: Phone, mail, in person. Both court and visitors may perform in person searches. Search fee: $5.00. Required to search: name, years to search. Civil cases indexed by defendant, plaintiff. Civil records on docket books from 1907; computerized since 1997.

Criminal Records: Access: Phone, mail, in person. Both court and visitors may perform in person searches. Search fee: $5.00. Required to search: name, years to search, DOB, SSN, signed release. Criminal records on docket books from 1907; computerized since 1997.

General Information: Public access terminal is available. No juvenile, adoptions, mental health or guardianship records released. SASE required. Turnaround time 3 days. Copy fee: $1.00 for first page, $.50 each add'l. Certification fee: $3.00. Fee payee: Court Clerk. Personal checks accepted.

Mayes County

12th Judicial District Court Box 867, Pryor, OK 74362; 918-825-0133. Hours: 9AM-5PM (CST). *Felony, Misdemeanor, Civil, Eviction, Small Claims, Probate.*

Civil Records: Access: Phone, mail, in person. Both court and visitors may perform in person searches. Search fee: $1.00 per name per year. Search fee is payable to employee doing research after hours. Required to search: name, years to search. Civil cases indexed by defendant, plaintiff. Civil records archived from 1907 on microfilm, computerized since 1998.

Criminal Records: Access: Phone, mail, in person. Both court and visitors may perform in person searches. Search fee: $1.00 per name per year. Search fee is payable to employee doing research after hours. Required to search: name, years to search; also helpful: DOB, SSN. Criminal records archived from 1907 on microfilm, computerized since 1998.

General Information: Public access terminal is available. No mental, adoption, most juvenile, and some reports in guardianship records not released. SASE required. Turnaround time 1 week. Copy fee: $1.00 for first page, $.50 each add'l. Certification fee: $.50. Fee payee: Clerk of Court. Personal checks accepted. Prepayment is required.

McClain County

21st Judicial District Court 121 N. 2nd Rm 231, Purcell, OK 73080; 405-527-3221. Hours: 8AM-4:30PM (CST). *Felony, Misdemeanor, Civil, Eviction, Small Claims, Probate.*

Civil Records: Access: Mail, in person. Both court and visitors may perform in person searches. Search fee: $10.00 per name. Required to search: name, years to search. Civil cases indexed by defendant, plaintiff. Civil records on docket books and cards from 1907, computerized since 01/97.

Criminal Records: Access: Mail, in person. Both court and visitors may perform in person searches. Search fee: $10.00 per name. Required to search: name, years to search; also helpful: DOB, SSN. Criminal records kept in individual docket files.

General Information: No adoptions, mental health or juvenile records released. SASE required. Turnaround time 2 days. Copy fee: $1.00 for first page, $.50 each add'l. Certification fee: $.50. Fee payee: Court Clerk. Personal checks accepted. Prepayment is required.

McCurtain County

17th Judicial District Court Box 1378, Idabel, OK 74745; 580-286-3693; Fax: 580-286-7095. Hours: 8AM-4PM (CST). *Felony, Misdemeanor, Civil, Eviction, Small Claims, Probate.*

Civil Records: Access: Mail, in person, online. Both court and visitors may perform in person searches. Search fee: $5.00 per name. Required to search: name, years to search. Civil cases indexed by defendant, plaintiff. Civil records on docket books from 1907; on computer back to 1998. Online access to court records via the statewide OSCN system is pending.

Criminal Records: Access: Mail, in person, online. Both court and visitors may perform in person searches. Search fee: $5.00. Required to search: name, years to search; also helpful: SSN. Criminal records on docket books from 1907; on computer back to 1998. Online access to court records via the statewide OSCN system is pending.

General Information: Public access terminal is available. No adoptions, guardianship or juvenile records released. SASE required. Turnaround time 1 day. Copy fee: $2.00 per page. Certification fee: $.50 per instrument. Fee payee: Court Clerk. Personal checks accepted. Prepayment is required.

McIntosh County

18th Judicial District Court Box 426, Eufaula, OK 74432; 918-689-2282. Hours: 8AM-4PM (CST). *Felony, Misdemeanor, Civil, Eviction, Small Claims, Probate.*

Civil Records: Access: Mail, in person. Both court and visitors may perform in person searches. Search fee: $5.00 per name. Required to search: name, years to search. Civil cases indexed by defendant, plaintiff. Civil records on microfilm since 1907; computerized back to 1996.

Criminal Records: Access: Mail, in person. Both court and visitors may perform in person searches. Search fee: $5.00 per name. Required to search: name, years to search; also helpful: SSN, DOB. Criminal records on microfilm since 1947; computerized back to 1996.

General Information: Public access terminal is available. No adoptions, mental health, guardianship or juvenile records released. SASE required. Turnaround time 3 days. Fax notes: Do not fax. Copy fee: $1.00 for first page, $.50 each add'l. Certification fee: $.50 per instrument. Fee payee: Court. No personal checks accepted; must be cashier's check or money order. Prepayment is required.

Murray County

20th Judicial District Court Box 578, Sulphur, OK 73086; 580-622-3223. Hours: 8AM-4:30PM, closed for lunch (CST). *Felony, Misdemeanor, Civil, Eviction, Small Claims, Probate.*

Civil Records: Access: Mail, in person. Both court and visitors may perform in person searches. Search fee: $5.00 per name. Required to search: name, years to search; also helpful: DOB. Civil cases indexed by defendant, plaintiff. Civil records on docket books from 1907, from 1973 back records are on microfilm; computerized back to 1997.

Criminal Records: Access: Mail, in person. Both court and visitors may perform in person searches. Search fee: $5.00 per name. Required to search: name, years to search; also helpful: SSN, DOB. Criminal records on docket books from 1907, from 1973 back records are on microfilm; computerized back to 1997.

General Information: Public access terminal is available. (For records since 1997.) No mental health, guardianship, juvenile or adoption records released. SASE required. Turnaround time 2 days, immediate if easily accessible. Fax notes: Do not fax. Copy fee: $1.00 for first page, $.50 each add'l. Certification fee: $5.00. Fee payee: Murray County Court Clerk. Personal checks accepted. Prepayment is required.

Muskogee County

15th Judicial District Court Box 1350, Muskogee, OK 74402; 918-682-7873. Hours: 8AM-4:30PM (CST). *Felony, Misdemeanor, Civil, Eviction, Small Claims, Probate.*

Civil Records: Access: Mail, in person. Both court and visitors may perform in person searches. Search fee: $10.00 per name. Required to search: name, years to search. Civil cases indexed by defendant, plaintiff. Civil records on docket books from 1907.

Criminal Records: Access: Mail, in person. Both court and visitors may perform in person searches. Search fee: $10.00 per name. Required to search: name, years to search, DOB; also helpful: SSN. Criminal records on docket books from 1907.

General Information: No adoptions, mental health, guardianship or juvenile records released. SASE required. Turnaround time 2-3 days. Copy fee: $1.00 for first page, $.50 each add'l. Certification fee: $.50. Fee payee: Court Clerk. Personal checks accepted. Prepayment is required.

Noble County

8th Judicial District Court 300 Courthouse Dr, Box 14, Perry, OK 73077; 580-336-5187. Hours: 8AM-4:30PM (CST). *Felony, Misdemeanor, Civil, Eviction, Small Claims, Probate.*

Civil Records: Access: Mail, in person. Both court and visitors may perform in person searches. Search fee: $5.00 per name. Required to search: name, years to search. Civil cases indexed by defendant, plaintiff. Civil records on microfiche from 1893; computerized back to 1997.

Criminal Records: Access: Mail, in person. Both court and visitors may perform in person searches. Search

fee: $5.00 per name. Required to search: name, years to search, DOB; also helpful: address, SSN. Criminal records on microfiche from 1893; computerized back to 1997.

General Information: Public access terminal is available. No adoptions, mental health, guardianship or juvenile records released. SASE appreciated. Turnaround time 1 day. Copy fee: $1.00 for first page, $.50 each add'l. Certification fee: $.50. Fee payee: Noble County Court Clerk. Personal checks accepted. Prepayment is required.

Nowata County

11th Judicial District Court 229 N. Maple, Nowata, OK 74048; 918-273-0127. Hours: 8AM-4:30PM (CST). *Felony, Misdemeanor, Civil, Eviction, Small Claims, Probate.*

Civil Records: Access: Mail, in person. Both court and visitors may perform in person searches. Search fee: $5.00 per name. Required to search: name, years to search. Civil cases indexed by defendant, plaintiff. Civil records on docket books from 1907; on computer since 1998.

Criminal Records: Access: Mail, in person. Both court and visitors may perform in person searches. Search fee: $5.00 per name. Required to search: name, years to search; also helpful: SSN. Criminal records on docket books from 1907; on computer since 1998.

General Information: No adoptions, mental health, guardianship or juvenile records released. SASE requested. Turnaround time 1 day. Copy fee: $1.00 for first page, $.50 each add'l. Certification fee: $.50 per page. Fee payee: Court Clerk. Personal checks accepted. Prepayment is required.

Okfuskee County

24th Judicial District Court Box 30, Okemah, OK 74859; 918-623-0525. Hours: 8:30AM-4:30PM (CST). *Felony, Misdemeanor, Civil, Eviction, Small Claims, Probate.*

Civil Records: Access: Mail, in person. Both court and visitors may perform in person searches. Search fee: $5.00 per name. Required to search: name, years to search. Civil cases indexed by defendant, plaintiff. Civil records in files and docket books from 1907, computerized since 1996.

Criminal Records: Access: Mail, in person. Both court and visitors may perform in person searches. Search fee: $5.00 per name. Required to search: name, years to search; also helpful: SSN. Criminal records in files and docket books from 1907, computerized since 1996.

General Information: No adoptions, mental health, guardianship or juvenile released. SASE required. Turnaround time 3 day. Copy fee: $1.00 for first page, $.50 each add'l. Certification fee: $.50 per page. Fee payee: Court Clerk. Personal checks accepted. Prepayment is required.

Oklahoma County

District Court 320 Robert S. Kerr St, Rm 409, Oklahoma City, OK 73102; 405-713-1705. Hours: 8AM-5PM (CST). *Felony, Misdemeanor, Civil, Eviction, Small Claims, Probate.*

Civil Records: Access: Mail, online, in person. Both court and visitors may perform in person searches. Search fee: Lengthy searches are $5.00 per half hour, otherwise no search fee. Required to search: name, years to search. Civil cases indexed by defendant, plaintiff. Civil records on microfiche from 1980, prior archived. Online access to court dockets available free online at www.oscn.net/applications/oscn/ casesearch.asp. Civil dockets go back to 12/1984.

Criminal Records: Access: Mail, online, in person. Both court and visitors may perform in person searches. Search fee: Lengthy searches $5.00 per half hour; commercial purpose searches: $25.00. Required to search: name, years to search, DOB; also helpful: SSN. Criminal records on microfiche from 1980, prior archived. Online access to criminal dockets is same as civil. Criminal dockets go back to 9/1988. The sheriff's current inmates and warrants list is available free at www.oklahomacounty.org/cosheriff.

General Information: Public access terminal is available. No juvenile, sealed, or expunged records released. SASE required. Turnaround time 5-10 days. Copy fee: $1.00 for first page, $.50 each add'l. Certification fee: $.50. Fee payee: District Court Clerk. Personal checks accepted. Prepayment is required.

Okmulgee County

24th Judicial District Court - Henryetta Branch
114 S 4th, Henryetta, OK 74437; 918-652-7142; Fax: 918-650-0287. Hours: 8:30AM-4:30PM (CST). *Felony, Misdemeanor, Civil, Eviction, Small Claims, Probate.*

Note: You must search both courts in this county, records are not co-mingled.

Civil Records: Access: Phone, mail, in person. Both court and visitors may perform in person searches. Search fee: $5.00 per name. Required to search: name, years to search. Civil cases indexed by defendant, plaintiff. Civil records on microfiche from 1970, computerized since 1977.

Criminal Records: Access: Phone, mail, in person. Both court and visitors may perform in person searches. Search fee: $5.00 per name. Required to search: name, years to search; also helpful: SSN. Criminal records on microfiche from 1970, books to 6-5-79, computerized since 1997.

General Information: No expunged or guardianship records released. SASE required. Turnaround time 1-2 days, limited phone searching immediate. Copy fee: $1.00 for first page, $.50 each add'l. Certification fee: $.50. Fee payee: Court Clerk. Business checks accepted. Prepayment is required.

24th Judicial District Court - Okmulgee Branch
314 W 7th, Okmulgee, OK 74447; 918-756-3042. Hours: 8AM-4:30PM (CST). *Felony, Misdemeanor, Civil, Eviction, Small Claims, Probate.*

Civil Records: Access: Phone, mail, in person. Both court and visitors may perform in person searches. Search fee: $5.00 per name. Required to search: name, years to search. Civil cases indexed by defendant, plaintiff. Civil records on microfiche from 1986, archived from 1907, computerized since 1997.

Criminal Records: Access: Phone, mail, in person. Both court and visitors may perform in person searches. Search fee: $5.00 per name. Required to search: name, years to search; also helpful: SSN. Criminal records on microfiche from 1986, archived from 1907, computerized since 1997.

General Information: Public access terminal is available. No juvenile, mental health, adoption or guardianship records released. SASE requested. Turnaround time 1-2 days. Copy fee: $1.00 for first page, $.50 each add'l. Certification fee: $.50. Fee payee: Court Clerk. Business checks accepted. Prepayment is required.

Osage County

10th Judicial District Court
County Courthouse, 600 Grandview, Pawhuska, OK 74056; 918-287-4104. Hours: 9AM-5PM (CST). *Felony, Misdemeanor, Civil, Eviction, Small Claims, Probate, Divorce.*

Civil Records: Access: Mail, in person. Both court and visitors may perform in person searches. Search fee: $5.00 per name. Required to search: name, years to search; also helpful: address. Civil cases indexed by defendant, plaintiff. Civil records archived from 1969.

Criminal Records: Access: Mail, in person. Both court and visitors may perform in person searches. Search fee: $5.00 per name. Required to search: name, years to search; also helpful: address. Criminal records archived from 1969.

General Information: Public access terminal is available. No juvenile or adoption records released. SASE required. Turnaround time 2 days. Copy fee: $1.00 for first page, $.50 each add'l. Certification fee: $.50. Fee payee: Court Clerk. Only cashiers checks and money orders accepted. Prepayment is required.

Ottawa County

13th Judicial District Court
102 E Central Ave, #300, Miami, OK 74354; 918-542-2801. Hours: 9:00AM-5:00PM (CST). *Felony, Misdemeanor, Civil, Eviction, Small Claims, Probate.*

Civil Records: Access: Phone, mail, in person. Both court and visitors may perform in person searches. Search fee: $5.00 per name. Required to search: name, years to search. Civil cases indexed by defendant, plaintiff. Civil records on docket books or cards from 1907, recent records computerized.

Criminal Records: Access: Mail, in person. Both court and visitors may perform in person searches. Search fee: $5.00. Required to search: name, years to search; also helpful: SSN. Criminal records on docket books or cards from 1907, recent records computerized.

General Information: Public access terminal is available. No juvenile, mental health, adoption or guardianship records released. SASE required. Turnaround time 1-2 days. Copy fee: $1.00 for first page, $.50 each add'l. Certification fee: $.50. Fee payee: Clerk of Court. Business checks accepted.

Pawnee County

14th Judicial District Court
Courthouse, 500 Harrison St, Pawnee, OK 74058; 918-762-2547. Hours: 8AM-4:30PM (CST). *Felony, Misdemeanor, Civil, Eviction, Small Claims, Probate.*

Civil Records: Access: Mail, in person. Both court and visitors may perform in person searches. Search fee: $5.00. Required to search: name, years to search. Civil cases indexed by defendant, plaintiff. Civil records on docket sheets to 1975, computerized from 1997.

Criminal Records: Access: Mail, in person. Both court and visitors may perform in person searches. Search fee: $5.00. Required to search: name, years to search; also helpful: SSN. Criminal records on docket sheets to 1975, computerized from 1997.

General Information: Public access terminal is available. No sealed records released. SASE required. Turnaround time 1-3 days. Copy fee: $1.00 for first page, $.50 each add'l. Certification fee: $.50. Fee payee: Court Clerk. Personal checks accepted. Prepayment is required.

Payne County

9th Judicial District Court
606 S. Husband Rm 308, Stillwater, OK 74074; 405-372-4774. Hours: 8AM-5PM (CST). *Felony, Misdemeanor, Civil, Eviction, Small Claims, Probate.*

Civil Records: Access: Mail, online, in person. Both court and visitors may perform in person searches. Search fee: $1.00 per name per year. Required to search: name, years to search. Civil cases indexed by defendant, plaintiff. Civil records on docket books from late 1800s, as of 1994 on computer. Online access to court dockets available free online at www.oscn.net/applications/oscn/casesearch.asp. Dockets go back to 1/1994.

Criminal Records: Access: Mail, online, in person. Both court and visitors may perform in person searches. Search fee: $1.00 per name per year. Required to search: name, years to search, DOB, SSN, signed release. Criminal records on docket books from late

1800s, as of 1994 on computer. Online access to criminal dockets is same as civil.

General Information: Public access terminal is available. No sealed records, juveniles or adoption records released. SASE required. Turnaround time 2 days. Copy fee: $1.00 for first page, $.50 each add'l. Certification fee: $.50 per page. Fee payee: Clerk of Court. Personal checks accepted. Prepayment is required.

Pittsburg County

18th Judicial District Court
Box 460, McAlester, OK 74502; 918-423-4859. Hours: 8AM-5PM (CST). *Felony, Misdemeanor, Civil, Eviction, Small Claims, Probate.*

Civil Records: Access: Mail, in person. Both court and visitors may perform in person searches. Search fee: $5.00 per name. Required to search: name, years to search. Civil cases indexed by defendant, plaintiff. Civil records on microfiche since 1907; on computer since 1997.

Criminal Records: Access: Mail, in person. Both court and visitors may perform in person searches. Search fee: $5.00 per name. Required to search: name, years to search, DOB. Criminal records on microfiche since 1907; on computer since 1997.

General Information: No juvenile, adoptions, mental health or guardianship records released. SASE required. Turnaround time 1-2 days. Copy fee: $1.00 for first page, $.50 each add'l. Certification fee: $.50. Fee payee: Court Clerk. Prepayment is required.

Pontotoc County

22nd Judicial District Court
Box 427, Ada, OK 74820; 580-332-5763; Fax: 580-436-5613. Hours: 8AM-5PM (CST). *Felony, Misdemeanor, Civil, Eviction, Small Claims, Probate.*

Civil Records: Access: Mail, in person. Both court and visitors may perform in person searches. Search fee: $5.00 per name. Required to search: name, years to search. Civil cases indexed by defendant, plaintiff. Civil records on card index from 1907; on computer back to 1997.

Criminal Records: Access: Mail, in person. Both court and visitors may perform in person searches. Search fee: $5.00 per name. Required to search: name, years to search; also helpful: DOB, SSN. Criminal records on card index from 1907; on computer back to 1990.

General Information: Public access terminal is available. No juvenile, adoptions, mental health or guardianship records released. SASE required. Turnaround time 2 days. Copy fee: $1.00 for first page, $.50 each add'l. Certification fee: $.50. Fee payee: Clerk of Court. Personal checks accepted. Must prepay if out of state. Will bill marriage license fees.

Pottawatomie County

23rd Judicial District Court
325 N. Broadway, Shawnee, OK 74801; 405-273-3624. Hours: 8:30AM-Noon, 1-5 PM (CST). *Felony, Misdemeanor, Civil, Eviction, Small Claims, Probate.*

Civil Records: Access: Mail, in person. Both court and visitors may perform in person searches. Search fee: $5.00 per name. Required to search: name, years to search. Civil cases indexed by defendant, plaintiff. Civil records on computer from 07/97; prior records on book of names from 1906.

Criminal Records: Access: Mail, in person. Both court and visitors may perform in person searches. Search fee: $5.00 per name. Required to search: name, years to search; also helpful: SSN. Criminal records on computer from 07/97; prior records on book of names from 1960.

General Information: Public access terminal is available. No juvenile, adoptions, mental health or guardianship records released. SASE requested.

Turnaround time 2 weeks or less. Copy fee: $1.00 for first page, $.50 each add'l. Certification fee: $.50. Fee payee: Court Clerk. Personal checks accepted. Prepayment is required.

Pushmataha County

17th Judicial District Court Push County Courthouse, 302 SW B, Antlers, OK 74523; 580-298-2274. Hours: 8AM-4:30PM (CST). *Felony, Misdemeanor, Civil, Eviction, Small Claims, Probate.*

Civil Records: Access: Mail, in person. Both court and visitors may perform in person searches. Search fee: $5.00 per name. Required to search: name, years to search. Civil cases indexed by defendant, plaintiff. Civil records on docket book from 1907.

Criminal Records: Access: Mail, in person. Both court and visitors may perform in person searches. Search fee: $5.00 per name. Required to search: name, years to search; also helpful: SSN. Criminal records on docket book from 1907.

General Information: No juvenile or adoption records released. SASE required. Turnaround time 1 day. Copy fee: $1.00 for first page, $.50 each add'l. Certification fee: $.50. Fee payee: Court Clerk. Personal checks accepted. Prepayment is required.

Roger Mills County

2nd Judicial District Court Box 409, Cheyenne, OK 73628; 580-497-3361. Hours: 8AM-Noon, 1-4:30PM (CST). *Felony, Misdemeanor, Civil, Eviction, Small Claims, Probate.*

Civil Records: Access: Phone, mail, in person. Both court and visitors may perform in person searches. No search fee. Required to search: name, years to search. Civil cases indexed by defendant, plaintiff. Civil records on computer since 1992, in books since 1893.

Criminal Records: Access: Phone, mail, fax, in person. Both court and visitors may perform in person searches. No search fee. Required to search: name, years to search, DOB; also helpful: SSN. Criminal records on computer since 1992, in books since 1893.

General Information: Public access terminal is available. No adoption, juvenile, mental health or guardianship records released. SASE required. Turnaround time 1 day. Copy fee: $1.00 for first page, $.50 each add'l. Certification fee: $.50. Fee payee: Court Clerk. Personal checks accepted. Prepayment is required.

Rogers County

12th Judicial District Court Box 839, 219 S Missouri, Claremore, OK 74018; 918-341-5711. Hours: 8AM-4:30PM (CST). *Felony, Misdemeanor, Civil, Eviction, Small Claims, Probate.*

Civil Records: Access: Phone, mail, online, in person. Both court and visitors may perform in person searches. Search fee: None, but phone and mail requests require case number. Required to search: name, years to search. Civil cases indexed by defendant, plaintiff. Civil records in card index since 1907, some computerized. Online access to court dockets available free online at www.oscn.net/applications/oscn/casesearch.asp. Dockets go back to 7/1997.

Criminal Records: Access: Phone, mail, online, in person. Both court and visitors may perform in person searches. Search fee: None, but phone and mail requests require case number. Required to search: name, years to search, DOB; also helpful: SSN. Criminal records on card index since 1907, some computerized. Online access to criminal dockets is the same as civil.

General Information: Public access terminal is available. No juvenile or adoption records released. SASE required. Turnaround time 1 day. Copy fee: $1.00 for first page, $.50 each add'l. Certification fee: $.50. Fee payee: Court Clerk. Personal checks accepted. Prepayment is required.

Seminole County

22nd Judicial District Court - Seminole Branch Box 1320, 401 Main St, Seminole, OK 74868; 405-382-3424. Hours: 8AM-Noon, 1-4PM (CST). *Civil, Small Claims, Probate.*

Note: Criminal records are now maintained at 22nd Judicial District Court, PO Box 130, Wewoka, OK, 405-257-6236.

Civil Records: Access: Phone, mail, in person. Only the court performs in person searches; visitors may not. Search fee: $5.00 per name. Required to search: name, years to search. Civil cases indexed by defendant, plaintiff. Civil records on index cards from 1931, probate from 1969; on computer back to 1996.

General Information: SASE required. Turnaround time 1 to 2 days. Fax notes: Will not fax results. Copy fee: $1.00 for first page, $.50 each add'l. Certification fee: $.50. Fee payee: Court Clerk. Only cashiers checks and money orders accepted. Prepayment is required.

22nd Judicial District Court - Wewoka Branch Box 130, Wewoka, OK 74884; 405-257-6236. Hours: 8AM-4PM (CST). *Felony, Misdemeanor, Civil, Eviction, Small Claims, Probate.*

Civil Records: Access: Mail, in person. Both court and visitors may perform in person searches. Search fee: $5.00 per name. Required to search: name, years to search. Civil cases indexed by defendant, plaintiff. Civil records indexed on computer since 1995; prior records on books to 1907.

Criminal Records: Access: Mail, in person. Both court and visitors may perform in person searches. Search fee: $5.00 per name. Required to search: name, years to search; also helpful: SSN. Criminal records indexed on computer since 1995; prior records on books to 1909. They maintain the criminal records for the Seminole Branch in Seminole, OK.

General Information: Public access terminal is available. No juvenile or adoption records released. SASE required. Turnaround time 1 day. Copy fee: $1.00 for first page, $.50 each add'l. Certification fee: $.50. Fee payee: Court Clerk. Personal checks accepted. Prepayment is required.

Sequoyah County

15th Judicial District Court 120 E Chickasaw, Sallisaw, OK 74955; 918-775-4411. Hours: 8AM-4PM (CST). *Felony, Misdemeanor, Civil, Eviction, Small Claims, Probate.*

Civil Records: Access: Mail, in person. Both court and visitors may perform in person searches. Search fee: $5.00 per name. Required to search: name, years to search. Civil cases indexed by defendant, plaintiff. Civil records in files and dockets from 1907; on computer back to 1997.

Criminal Records: Access: Phone, mail, in person. Both court and visitors may perform in person searches. Search fee: $5.00 per name. Required to search: name, years to search; also helpful: SSN. Some criminal records on computer back to 1997, prior in files and dockets.

General Information: Public access terminal is available. No juvenile, adoptions, mental health or guardianship records released. SASE required. Turnaround time 1 week. Copy fee: $1.00 for first page, $.50 each add'l. Certification fee: $2.00. Fee payee: Court Clerk. Personal checks accepted. Will bill mail requests.

Stephens County

5th Judicial District Court 101 S 11th Rm 301, Duncan, OK 73533; 580-470-2000. Hours: 8:30AM-4:30PM (CST). *Felony, Misdemeanor, Civil, Eviction, Small Claims, Probate.*

Civil Records: Access: Mail, in person. Both court and visitors may perform in person searches. Search fee: $5.00 per name. Required to search: name, years to search. Civil cases indexed by defendant, plaintiff. Civil records on computer from 10/95; prior records on docket books from 1907.

Criminal Records: Access: Mail, in person. Both court and visitors may perform in person searches. Search fee: $5.00 per name. Required to search: name, years to search; also helpful: address, DOB, SSN. Criminal records on computer from 10/95; prior records on docket books from 1907.

General Information: Public access terminal is available. No juvenile, adoptions, mental health or guardianship records released. SASE required. Turnaround time 1 day. Copy fee: $1.00 for first page, $.50 each add'l. Certification fee: $.50. Fee payee: Stephens County 5th Judicial Court. Personal checks npt accepted. Prepayment is required.

Texas County

1st Judicial District Court Box 1081, Guymon, OK 73942; 580-338-3003. Hours: 9AM-5PM (CST). *Felony, Misdemeanor, Civil, Eviction, Small Claims, Probate.*

Civil Records: Access: Mail, in person. Both court and visitors may perform in person searches. Search fee: $5.00 per name. Required to search: name, years to search. Civil cases indexed by defendant, plaintiff. Civil records on microfiche from 1976, archived prior, computerized since 03/95.

Criminal Records: Access: Mail, in person. Both court and visitors may perform in person searches. Search fee: $5.00 per name. Required to search: name, years to search; also helpful: SSN. Criminal records on microfiche from 1976, archived prior, computerized since 03/95.

General Information: Public access terminal is available. No juvenile, adoptions, mental health or guardianship records released. SASE required. Turnaround time 5 days, 1 day for phone. Copy fee: $1.00 for first page, $.50 each add'l. Certification fee: $.50. Fee payee: Court Clerk. Personal checks accepted. Prepayment is required.

Tillman County

3rd Judicial District Court Box 116, Frederick, OK 73542; 580-335-3023. Hours: 8AM-4PM (CST). *Felony, Misdemeanor, Civil, Eviction, Small Claims, Probate.*

Civil Records: Access: Mail, in person. Both court and visitors may perform in person searches. Search fee: $5.00 per name. Required to search: name, years to search. Civil cases indexed by defendant, plaintiff. Civil records on docket books from 1907; on computer back to 1998.

Criminal Records: Access: Mail, in person. Both court and visitors may perform in person searches. Search fee: $5.00 per name. Required to search: name, years to search, DOB; also helpful: SSN. Criminal records on docket books from 1907; on computer back to 1998.

General Information: No expunged records released. SASE required. Turnaround time 1 day. Copy fee: $1.00 for first page, $.50 each add'l. Copy charge is only if the person does their own search in person. Certification fee: $1.00. Fee payee: District Court. Business checks accepted. Will bill law firms.

Tulsa County

14th Judicial District Court 500 S. Denver, Tulsa, OK 74103-3832; 918-596-5000. Hours: 8:30AM-5PM (CST). *Felony, Misdemeanor, Civil, Eviction, Small Claims, Probate.*

Civil Records: Access: Mail, online, in person. Both court and visitors may perform in person searches. Search fee: $5.00 per name. Required to search: name, years to search. Civil cases indexed by defendant, plaintiff. Civil records on computer from 1984, on microfiche from 1907, archived from 1907. Online access to court dockets available free online at www.oscn.net/applications/oscn/casesearch.asp. Civil dockets go back to 10/1984.

Criminal Records: Access: Mail, online, in person. Both court and visitors may perform in person searches. Search fee: $5.00 per name. Required to search: name, years to search; also helpful: SSN. Criminal records on computer from 1984, on microfiche from 1907, archived from 1907. Online access to criminal dockets is same as civil. Criminal dockets go back to 1/1988.

General Information: Public access terminal is available. No juvenile, adoption or guardianship records released. SASE required. Turnaround time 1 week. Copy fee: $1.00 for first page, $.50 each add'l. Certification fee: $.50. Fee payee: Court Clerk. Will accept attorney personal checks. Prepayment required.

Wagoner County

15th Judicial District Court Box 249, Wagoner, OK 74477; 918-485-4508. Hours: 8:00AM-4:30PM (CST). *Felony, Misdemeanor, Civil, Eviction, Small Claims, Probate.*

Civil Records: Access: Mail, in person. Both court and visitors may perform in person searches. Search fee: $5.00 per name. Required to search: name, years to search. Civil cases indexed by defendant, plaintiff. Civil records on docket books from 1980; on computer back to 1997.

Criminal Records: Access: Mail, in person. Both court and visitors may perform in person searches. Search fee: $5.00 per name if assisted. Required to search: name, years to search; also helpful: SSN. Criminal records are in files and dockets back to 1907; on computer back to 1997.

General Information: Public access terminal is available. No juvenile, mental health, adoption or guardianship records released. SASE required. Turnaround time 1-2 days for civil, longer for criminal. Copy fee: $1.00 for first page, $.50 each add'l. Certification fee: $.50. Fee payee: Court Clerk. Personal checks accepted. Prepayment is required.

Washington County

11th Judicial District Court 420 S Johnstone, Rm 212, Bartlesville, OK 74003; 918-337-2870; Fax: 918-337-2897. Hours: 8AM-5PM (CST). *Felony, Misdemeanor, Civil, Eviction, Small Claims, Probate.*

Civil Records: Access: Phone, mail, in person. Both court and visitors may perform in person searches. Search fee: $5.00 per name. Required to search: name, years to search. Civil cases indexed by defendant, plaintiff. Civil records on microfiche from 1988, on docket books from 1907; computerized records since 1997.

Criminal Records: Access: Phone, mail, in person. Both court and visitors may perform in person searches. Search fee: $5.00 per name. Required to search: name, years to search, signed release; also helpful: DOB, SSN. Criminal records on microfiche from 1988, on docket books from 1907; computerized records since 1997.

General Information: Public access terminal is available. No juvenile, mental health, adoption or guardianship records released. Turnaround time 1-3 days. Copy fee: $1.00 for first page, $.50 each add'l. Certification fee: $.50. Fee payee: Court Clerk. Personal checks accepted. Prepayment is required.

Washita County

3rd Judicial District Court Box 397, Cordell, OK 73632,; 580-832-3836. Hours: 8AM-4PM (CST). *Felony, Misdemeanor, Civil, Small Claims, Probate.*

Note: Note: This court will change to 2nd Judicial District effective 01/06/03.

Civil Records: Access: Mail, in person. Both court and visitors may perform in person searches. Search fee: $5.00 per name. Required to search: name, years to search. Civil cases indexed by defendant, plaintiff. Civil records on computer since 1998; prior records on microfiche from 1980s & on docket books from 1892.

Criminal Records: Access: Mail, in person. Both court and visitors may perform in person searches. Search fee: $5.00 per name. Required to search: name, years to search; also helpful: DOB, SSN, aliases. Criminal records on computer since 1998; prior records on microfiche from 1980s & on docket books from 1892.

General Information: Public access terminal is available. No juvenile, mental health, adoption or guardianship records released. SASE required. Turnaround time same day. Copy fee: $1.00 for first page, $.50 each add'l. Certification fee: $.50. Fee payee: Court Clerk. Personal checks accepted. Prepayment is required.

Woods County

4th Judicial District Court Box 924, Alva, OK 73717; 580-327-3119. Hours: 9AM-5PM (CST). *Felony, Misdemeanor, Civil, Eviction, Small Claims, Probate.*

Civil Records: Access: Mail, in person. Both court and visitors may perform in person searches. Search fee: $5.00 per name. Required to search: name, years to search. Civil cases indexed by defendant, plaintiff. Civil records on docket books from 1890.

Criminal Records: Access: Mail, in person. Both court and visitors may perform in person searches. Search fee: $5.00 per name. Required to search: name, years to search. Criminal records on computer since 1987, on dockets and cards from 1890s.

General Information: No juvenile, mental health, adoption or guardianship records released. SASE required. Turnaround time 2 days. Copy fee: $1.00 for first page, $.50 each add'l. Certification fee: $.50. Fee payee: Clerk of Court. Personal checks accepted. Prepayment is required.

Woodward County

4th Judicial District Court 1600 Main, Woodward, OK 73801; 580-256-3413. Hours: 9AM-5PM (CST). *Felony, Misdemeanor, Civil, Eviction, Small Claims, Probate.*

Civil Records: Access: Mail, in person. Both court and visitors may perform in person searches. Search fee: $5.00 per name. Required to search: name, years to search. Civil cases indexed by defendant, plaintiff. Civil records on docket books from 1890, on microfiche from 1989; on computer from 1997.

Criminal Records: Access: Mail, in person. Both court and visitors may perform in person searches. Search fee: $5.00 per name. Required to search: name, years to search; also helpful: DOB, SSN. Criminal records on docket books from 1890, on microfiche from 1989; on computer from 1997.

General Information: Public access terminal is available. No mental, juvenile, adoption, guardianship records released. SASE required. Turnaround time 1-2 days unless older cases found. Fax notes: Fee to fax results is 1.00 per document. Copy fee: $1.00 for first page, $.50 each add'l. Certification fee: $.50 per page. $5.00 for whole file. Fee payee: Court Clerk. Personal checks accepted. Prepayment is required.

Oklahoma Recording Offices

ORGANIZATION: 77 counties, 77 recording offices. The recording officer is County Clerk. The entire state is in the Central Time Zone (CST).

REAL ESTATE RECORDS: Many counties will perform real estate searches by legal description. Copy fees are usually $1.00 per page. Certification usually costs $1.00 per document.

UCC RECORDS: Financing statements are filed centrally with the County Clerk of Oklahoma County. Prior to 7/2001, consumer goods, farm related, and real estate related collateral were dual filed with the local County Clerk as well as the County Clerk of Oklahoma County. Now only real estate related collateral is filed at the local level. All counties will perform UCC searches. Use search request form UCC-4. Search fees are usually $5.00 per debtor name for a written request and $3.00 per name by telephone. Copies usually cost $1.00 per page.

TAX LIEN RECORDS: Federal tax liens on personal property of businesses are filed with the County Clerk of Oklahoma County, which is the central filing office for the state. Other federal and all state tax liens are filed with the County Clerk. Usually state and federal tax liens on personal property are filed in separate indexes. Some counties will perform tax lien searches. Search fees vary.

OTHER LIENS: Judgment, mechanics, physicians, hospital.

ONLINE ACCESS: Very little is available online as of early months of year 2003..

Adair County

County Clerk, PO Box 169, Stilwell, OK 74960. 918-696-7198; Fax 918-696-2603.
Will search UCC records. Will not search real estate records. **Other Phone Numbers:** Assessor 918-696-2012; Treasurer 918-696-7551; Elections 918-696-7221.

Alfalfa County

County Clerk, 300 S. Grand, Cherokee, OK 73728. 580-596-3158.
Will search UCC records. This agency will not do a tax lien search. Will not search real estate records. **Other Phone Numbers:** Assessor 580-596-2145; Treasurer 580-596-3148; Elections 580-596-2718.

Atoka County

County Clerk, 200 E. Court St, Atoka, OK 74525. 580-889-5157; Fax 580-889-5063.
Will search UCC records. UCC search includes tax liens if requested. Will not search real estate records. **Other Phone Numbers:** Assessor 580-889-6036; Treasurer 580-889-5283.

Beaver County

County Clerk, PO Box 338, Beaver, OK 73932-0338. 580-625-3141 R/E Recording: 580-625-3418; Fax 580-625-3430.
Will search UCC records. Will not search real estate records. **Other Phone Numbers:** Assessor 580-625-3116; Treasurer 580-625-3161.

Beckham County

County Clerk, PO Box 428, Sayre, OK 73662-0428. 580-928-3383; Fax 580-928-5220.
Will search UCC records. This agency will not do a tax lien search. Will not search real estate records. **Other Phone Numbers:** Assessor 580-928-3329; Treasurer 580-928-2589.

Blaine County

County Clerk, PO Box 138, Watonga, OK 73772. County Clerk, R/E and UCC Recording 580-623-5890; Fax 580-623-5009.
This agency will not search real estate or UCC records. **Other Phone Numbers:** Assessor 580-623-5123; Treasurer 580-623-5007; Elections 580-623-5518.

Bryan County

County Clerk, PO Box 1789, Durant, OK 74702. County Clerk, R/E and UCC Recording 580-924-2202; Fax 580-924-2289.
Will search UCC records. **Other Phone Numbers:** Assessor 580-924-2166; Treasurer 580-924-0748; Appraiser/Auditor 580-924-2166; Elections 580-924-3228.

Caddo County

County Clerk, PO Box 68, Anadarko, OK 73005. County Clerk, R/E and UCC Recording 405-247-6609; Fax 405-247-6510.
Will search UCC records. Will not search real estate records. **Other Phone Numbers:** Assessor 405-247-2477; Treasurer 405-247-5151; Vital Records 405-271-4040; Real Estate 405-247-6510.

Canadian County

County Clerk, PO Box 458, El Reno, OK 73036. 405-262-1070; Fax 405-422-2411.
Will search UCC records. Will not search real estate records. **Other Phone Numbers:** Assessor 405-262-1070 x269; Treasurer 405-262-1070 x250.

Carter County

County Clerk, PO Box 1236, Ardmore, OK 73402. County Clerk, R/E and UCC Recording 580-223-8162; www.brightok.net/chickasaw/ardmore/county/coclerk.html
Will search UCC records. Will not search real estate records. **Online Access:** Assessor, Unsolved Case Records. The sheriff's unsolved mysteries page is available free at www.brightok.net/chickasaw/ardmore/county/unsolved.html. Search the county assessor data at www.cartercountyassessor.org/disclaim.htm. **Other Phone Numbers:** Assessor 580-223-9594, 800-231-8668 x594 (in county); Treasurer 580-223-9467.

Cherokee County

County Clerk, 213 W. Delaware, Room 200, Tahlequah, OK 74464. County Clerk, R/E and UCC Recording 918-456-3171 UCC Recording: 918-458-6512; Fax 918-458-6508.
Will search UCC records. UCC search includes tax liens if requested. Will not search real estate records. **Other Phone Numbers:** Assessor 918-456-3201; Treasurer 918-456-3321; Elections 918-456-2261.

Choctaw County

County Clerk, Courthouse, 300 E. Duke, Hugo, OK 74743. County Clerk, R/E and UCC Recording 580-326-3778; Fax 580-326-6787.
Will search UCC records. **Other Phone Numbers:** Assessor 580-326-2356; Treasurer 580-326-6142; Elections 580-326-5164; Vital Records 580-271-4040.

Cimarron County

County Clerk, PO Box 145, Boise City, OK 73933. County Clerk, R/E and UCC Recording 580-544-2251; Fax 580-544-2251.
Will search UCC records. Will not search real estate records. **Other Phones:** Assessor 580-544-2701; Treasurer 580-544-2261; Elections 580-544-3377.

Cleveland County

County Clerk, 201 S. Jones, Room 204, Norman, OK 73069-6099. County Clerk, R/E and UCC Recording 405-366-0240 UCC Recording: 405-366-0234; Fax 405-366-0229. www.okclev.cogov.net
Will search UCC records. Will not search real estate records. **Other Phone Numbers:** Assessor 405-366-0230; Treasurer 405-366-0217; Elections 405-26-0120; Vital Records 405-271-4040.

Coal County

County Clerk, 4 N. Main, Ste. 1, Suite 1, Coalgate, OK 74538. County Clerk, R/E and UCC Recording 580-927-2103; Fax 580-927-4003.
Will search UCC records. This agency will not do a tax lien search. Will not search real estate records. **Other Phone Numbers:** Assessor 580-927-3123; Treasurer 580-927-3121; Elections 580-927-3456; Vital Records 580-927-2281.

Comanche County

County Clerk, 315 SW 5th, Room 304, Lawton, OK 73501-4347. County Clerk, R/E and UCC Recording 580-355-5214.
Will search UCC records. UCC search does not include tax liens. Will not search real estate records. **Other Phone Numbers:** Assessor 580-355-1052; Treasurer 580-355-5763; Elections 580-353-1880; Vital Records 405-271-4040.

Cotton County

County Clerk, 301 N. Broadway, Walters, OK 73572. County Clerk, R/E and UCC Recording 580-875-3026; Fax 580-875-3756.
Will search UCC records. Will not search real estate records. **Other Phone Numbers:** Assessor 580-875-3289; Treasurer 580-875-3264; Elections 580-875-3403.

Craig County

County Clerk, PO Box 397, Vinita, OK 74301. 918-256-2507; Fax 918-256-3617.
Will search UCC records. Will not search real estate records. **Other Phone Numbers:** Assessor 918-256-3640; Treasurer 918-256-2286; Elections 918-256-7559.

Creek County

County Clerk, 317 E. Lee, First Floor, Sapulpa, OK 74066. 918-227-6306 R/E Recording: 918-227-4084.
Will search UCC records. This agency will not do a tax lien search. Will not search real estate records. **Other Phone Numbers:** Assessor 918-224-4508; Treasurer 918-227-4501.

Custer County

County Clerk, PO Box 300, Arapaho, OK 73620. County Clerk, R/E and UCC Recording 580-323-1221; Fax 580-323-4421.
Will search UCC records. Will not search real estate records. **Other Phone Numbers:** Assessor 580-323-3271; Treasurer 580-323-2292; Elections 580-323-2291; Vital Records 580-323-4040.

Delaware County

County Clerk, PO Box 309, Jay, OK 74346. 918-253-4520; Fax 918-253-8352.
Will search UCC records. Will not search real estate records. **Other Phone Numbers:** Assessor 918-328-5561.

Dewey County

County Clerk, PO Box 368, Taloga, OK 73667. 580-328-5361.
Will search UCC records. UCC search includes tax liens if requested. Real estate owner, mortgage, and property transfer searches available. **Other Phone Numbers:** Assessor 580-885-7975; Treasurer 580-328-5501.

Ellis County

County Clerk, PO Box 197, Arnett, OK 73832. County Clerk, R/E and UCC Recording 580-885-7301; Fax 580-885-7258.
Will search UCC records. Will search real estate records. **Other Phone Numbers:** Assessor 580-885-7975; Treasurer 580-885-7670; Elections 580-885-7721; Vital Records 580-885-7301.

Garfield County

County Clerk, PO Box 1664, Enid, OK 73702-1664. County Clerk, R/E and UCC Recording 580-237-0226; Fax 580-249-5951.
Will search UCC records. Will not search real estate records. **Other Phone Numbers:** Assessor 580-237-0220; Treasurer 580-237-0246; Elections 580-237-6016; Court Clerk 580-237-0232.

Garvin County

County Clerk, PO Box 926, Pauls Valley, OK 73075. 405-238-2772; Fax 405-238-6283.
Will search UCC records. Will not search real estate records. **Other Phone Numbers:** Assessor 405-238-2409; Treasurer 405-238-7301.

Grady County

County Clerk, PO Box 1009, Chickasha, OK 73023. 405-224-7388; Fax 405-222-4506.
www.gradycounty.net
Will search UCC records. Will not search real estate records. **Other Phone Numbers:** Assessor 405-224-4361; Treasurer 405-224-5337; Elections 405-224-1430; Vital Records 405-271-4040.

Grant County

County Clerk, PO Box 167, Medford, OK 73759-0167. County Clerk, R/E and UCC Recording 580-395-2274.
Will search UCC records. UCC search includes tax liens if requested. Lien searches performed by phone only, and if requested with UCC. Will not search real estate records. **Other Phone Numbers:** Assessor 580-395-2844; Treasurer 580-395-2284; Elections 580-395-2862.

Greer County

County Clerk, PO Box 207, Mangum, OK 73554. County Clerk, R/E and UCC Recording 580-782-3664; Fax 580-782-3803.
Will search UCC records. **Other Phone Numbers:** Assessor 580-782-2740; Treasurer 580-782-5515; Appraiser/Auditor 580-782-2454; Elections 580-782-2307; Vital Records 405-271-4040.

Harmon County

County Clerk, Courthouse, 14 W. Hollis, Hollis, OK 73550. 580-688-3658.
Will search UCC records. Property transfer searches available. **Other Phone Numbers:** Assessor 580-882-2529; Treasurer 580-882-3566.

Harper County

County Clerk, PO Box 369, Buffalo, OK 73834. 580-735-2012; Fax 580-735-2612.
Will search UCC records. UCC search includes tax liens if requested. Will search real estate records. **Other Phone Numbers:** Assessor 580-735-2343; Treasurer 580-735-2442.

Haskell County

County Clerk, 202 E. Main, Courthouse, Stigler, OK 74462. County Clerk, R/E and UCC Recording 918-967-2884; Fax 918-967-2885.
Will search UCC records. Will not search real estate records. **Other Phone Numbers:** Assessor 918-967-2611; Treasurer 918-967-2441; Appraiser/Auditor 918-967-8792.

Hughes County

County Clerk, 200 N. Broadway ST. #5, Holdenville, OK 74848-3400. 405-379-5487; Fax 405-379-6890.
Will search UCC records. UCC search includes tax liens if requested. Will not search real estate records. **Other Phone Numbers:** Assessor 405-379-3862; Treasurer 405-379-5371; Elections 405-379-2174.

Jackson County

County Clerk, PO Box 515, Altus, OK 73522. County Clerk, R/E and UCC Recording 580-482-4070.
Will search UCC records. UCC search includes tax liens if requested. Real estate owner, mortgage, and property transfer searches available. Legal description of property required **Other Phone Numbers:** Assessor 580-482-0787; Treasurer 580-482-4371; Elections 580-482-2370; Vital Records 580-482-4070.

Jefferson County

County Clerk, 220 N. Main, Courthouse - Room 103, Waurika, OK 73573. County Clerk, R/E and UCC Recording 580-228-2029; Fax 580-228-3418.

Will search UCC records. Will not search real estate records. **Other Phone Numbers:** Assessor 580-228-2377; Treasurer 580-228-2967.

Johnston County

County Clerk, 414 W. Main, Room 101, Tishomingo, OK 73460. County Clerk, R/E and UCC Recording 580-371-3184.
Will search UCC records. UCC search includes tax liens if requested. $3.00 per name for uncertified verbal search. Real estate owner, mortgage, and property transfer searches available. **Other Phone Numbers:** Assessor 580-371-3645; Treasurer 580-371-3082; Elections 580-371-3670.

Kay County

County Clerk, PO Box 450, Newkirk, OK 74647-0450. County Clerk, R/E and UCC Recording 580-362-2537; Fax 580-362-3300.
Will search UCC records. Search real estate land records by mail or phone for free. **Other Phone Numbers:** Assessor 580-362-2566; Treasurer 580-362-2523; Elections 580-362-2130.

Kingfisher County

County Clerk, 101 S. Main, Room #3, Kingfisher, OK 73750. 405-375-3887; Fax 405-375-6033.
Will search UCC records. **Other Phone Numbers:** Assessor 405-375-3884.

Kiowa County

County Clerk, PO Box 73, Hobart, OK 73651-0073. 580-726-5286; Fax 580-726-6033.
Will search UCC records. **Other Phone Numbers:** Assessor 580-726-2150; Treasurer 580-726-2362.

Latimer County

County Clerk, 109 North Central, Room 103, Wilburton, OK 74578. 918-465-3543; Fax 918-465-4001.
Will search UCC records. **Other Phone Numbers:** Assessor 918-465-3031; Treasurer 918-465-3450.

Le Flore County

County Clerk, PO Box 218, Poteau, OK 74953-0218. 918-647-5738; Fax 918-647-8930.
Will search UCC records. **Other Phone Numbers:** Assessor 918-647-3652; Treasurer 918-647-3525; Elections 918-647-3701.

Lincoln County

County Clerk, PO Box 126, Chandler, OK 74834-0126. County Clerk, R/E and UCC Recording 405-258-1264.
Will search UCC records. Tax liens not included in UCC search. Property transfer searches available. **Other Phone Numbers:** Assessor 405-258-1209; Treasurer 405-258-1491; Elections 405-258-1349.

Logan County

County Clerk, 301 E. Harrison, Suite 102, Guthrie, OK 73044-4999. County Clerk, R/E and UCC Recording 405-282-0266; Fax 405-282-0267.
Will search UCC records prior to 7/2001. UCC search includes tax liens if requested. **Other Phone Numbers:** Assessor 405-282-3509; Treasurer 405-282-3150; Elections 405-282-1900; Vital Records 405-271-4040.

Love County

County Clerk, 405 W. Main, Room 203, Marietta, OK 73448. 580-276-3059.
Will search UCC records. UCC search includes tax liens if requested. Will not search real estate records. **Other Phone Numbers:** Assessor 580-276-3059; Treasurer 580-276-2360.

Major County

County Clerk, PO Box 379, Fairview, OK 73737-0379. 580-227-4732 R/E Recording: 580-227-3918 UCC Recording: 580-227-3918; Fax 580-227-2736.
Will search UCC records. This agency will not do a tax lien search. Will not search real estate records. **Other Phone Numbers:** Assessor 580-227-4821; Treasurer 580-227-4782.

Marshall County

County Clerk, Marshall County Courthouse, Room 101, Madill, OK 73446. County Clerk, R/E and UCC Recording 580-795-3220; Fax 580-795-7596.
Will search UCC records. UCC search includes tax liens if requested. Real estate record owner searches available. Legal description and name required. **Other Phone Numbers:** Assessor 580-795-2398; Treasurer 580-792-2463; Appraiser/Auditor 580-795-2398; Elections 580-795-5460.

Mayes County

County Clerk, PO Box 97, Pryor, OK 74362. County Clerk, R/E and UCC Recording 918-825-2426; Fax 918-825-3803.
Will search UCC records. Will not search real estate records. **Other Phone Numbers:** Assessor 918-825-0625; Treasurer 918-825-0160; Appraiser/Auditor 918-825-0625; Elections 918-825-1826.

McClain County

County Clerk, PO Box 629, Purcell, OK 73080-0629. County Clerk, R/E and UCC Recording 405-527-3360.
Will search UCC records. This agency will not do a tax lien search. Real estate owner, mortgage, and property transfer searches available. **Other Phone Numbers:** Assessor 405-527-3520; Treasurer 405-527-3261.

McCurtain County

County Clerk, PO Box 1078, Idabel, OK 74745. County Clerk, R/E and UCC Recording 580-286-2370. Will search UCC records. UCC search includes tax liens. Will not search real estate records. **Other Phone Numbers:** Assessor 580-286-5272; Treasurer 580-286-5128; Elections 580-286-7405.

McIntosh County

County Clerk, PO Box 110, Eufaula, OK 74432-0110. 918-689-5419; Fax 918-689-3385.
Will search UCC records. Will not search real estate records. **Other Phone Numbers:** Assessor 918-689-5419; Treasurer 918-689-2491.

Murray County

County Clerk, PO Box 442, Sulphur, OK 73086. County Clerk, R/E and UCC Recording 580-622-3920; Fax 580-622-6209.
Will search UCC records. Will not search real estate records. **Other Phones:** Assessor 580-622-3433; Treasurer 580-622-5622; Elections 580-622-3920.

Muskogee County

County Clerk, PO Box 1008, Muskogee, OK 74401. 918-682-7781.
Will search UCC records. Tax liens not included in UCC search. Will not search real estate records. **Other Phones:** Assessor 682-8781; Treasurer 918-682-0811.

Noble County

County Clerk, 300 Courthouse Dr, Box 11, Courthouse, Box 11, Room 201, Perry, OK 73077. County Clerk, R/E and UCC Recording 580-336-2141; Fax 580-336-2481.
Will search UCC records. Will not search real estate records. **Other Phone Numbers:** Assessor 580-336-2185; Treasurer 580-336-2026; Elections 580-336-3527.

Nowata County

County Clerk, 229 N. Maple, Nowata, OK 74048. County Clerk, R/E and UCC Recording 918-273-2480; Fax 918-273-2481.
Will search UCC records. This agency will not do a tax lien search. Will not search real estate records. **Other Phone Numbers:** Assessor 918-273-0581; Treasurer 918-273-3562; Elections 918-273-0710; Vital Records 918-273-0127.

Okfuskee County

County Clerk, PO Box 108, Okemah, OK 74859-0108. County Clerk, R/E and UCC Recording 918-623-1724; Fax 918-623-0739.
Will search UCC records. Will not search real estate records. **Other Phone Numbers:** Assessor 918-623-1535; Treasurer 918-623-1494.

Oklahoma County

County Clerk, 320 Robert S. Kerr Ave, Courthouse - Room 107, Oklahoma City, OK 73102. 405-278-1538 R/E Recording: 405-713-1540 UCC Recording: 405-713-1522; Fax 405-278-2241. www.oklahomacounty.org
Will search UCC records. Will not search real estate records. **Online Access:** Real Estate, Assessor, Grantor/Grantee, UCC Records. Assessor and property information on the county assessor database are available free online at www.oklahomacounty.org/assessor/disclaim.htm. Real estate, UCC, grantor/grantee records on the county clerk database are available free online at www.oklahomacounty.org/coclerk. **Other Phone Numbers:** Assessor 405-278-3838; Treasurer 405-713-1300; Appraiser/Auditor 405-713-1200; Elections 405-713-1515.

Okmulgee County

County Clerk, PO Box 904, Okmulgee, OK 74447-0904. County Clerk, R/E and UCC Recording 918-756-0788; Fax 918-758-1261.
Will search UCC records. Will search real estate records. **Other Phone Numbers:** Assessor 918-758-1205; Treasurer 918-756-3848; Elections 918-756-2365.

Osage County

County Clerk, PO Box 87, Pawhuska, OK 74056. County Clerk, R/E and UCC Recording 918-287-3136; Fax 918-287-4979.
Will search UCC records. This agency will not do a tax lien search. Will not search real estate records. **Other Phone Numbers:** Assessor 918-287-3448; Treasurer 918-287-3101; Appraiser/Auditor 918-287-3448; Elections 918-287-3036.

Ottawa County

County Clerk, 102 E. Central, Suite 203, Miami, OK 74354-7043. County Clerk, R/E and UCC Recording 918-542-3332; Fax 918-542-8260.
Will search UCC records. This agency will not do a tax lien search. Will not search real estate records. **Other Phone Numbers:** Assessor 918-542-9418; Treasurer 918-542-8232; Elections 918-542-2893; Vital Records 918-571-2600.

Pawnee County

County Clerk, Courthouse, Room 202, 500 Harrison St., Pawnee, OK 74058. County Clerk, R/E and UCC Recording 918-762-2732.
Will search UCC records. Tax liens included in UCC search. Will not search real estate records. **Other Phone Numbers:** Assessor 918-762-2402; Treasurer 918-762-2418; Elections 918-762-2125.

Payne County

County Clerk, PO Box 7, Stillwater, OK 74076-0007. 405-747-8310 R/E Recording: 405-747-8345.
Will search UCC records. This agency will not do a tax lien search. Will not search real estate records. **Other Phone Numbers:** Assessor 405-747-8300; Treasurer 405-747-9411; Appraiser/Auditor 405-747-8300; Vital Records 405-271-4040; 405-747-8344.

Pittsburg County

County Clerk, PO Box 3304, McAlester, OK 74502. 918-423-6865; Fax 918-423-7304.
Will search UCC records. **Other Phone Numbers:** Assessor 918-423-4726; Treasurer 918-423-6895.

Pontotoc County

County Clerk, PO Box 1425, Ada, OK 74820. County Clerk, R/E and UCC Recording 580-332-1425; Fax 580-332-9509.
Will search UCC records. Will not search real estate records. **Other Phones:** Assessor 580-332-0317; Treasurer 580-332-0183; Vital Records 405-271-5600.

Pottawatomie County

County Clerk, PO Box 576, Shawnee, OK 74802. 405-273-8222; Fax 405-275-6898.
Will not search UCC records. **Other Phone Numbers:** Assessor 405-275-4740; Treasurer 405-273-0213; Elections 405-273-8367.

Pushmataha County

County Clerk, 302 SW 'B', Antlers, OK 74523. County Clerk, R/E and UCC Recording 580-298-3626; Fax 580-298-3626.
Will search UCC records. This agency will not do a tax lien search. Will not search real estate records. **Other Phone Numbers:** Assessor 580-298-3503; Treasurer 580-298-2580; Appraiser/Auditor 580-298-3504; Elections 580-298-3292.

Roger Mills County

County Clerk, PO Box 708, Cheyenne, OK 73628. 580-497-3395 R/E Recording: 580-497-3366 or 3395; Fax 580-497-3488.
This agency will not perform searches. **Other Phone Numbers:** Assessor 580-497-3350; Treasurer 580-497-3349; Elections 580-497-3330.

Rogers County

County Clerk, PO Box 1210, Claremore, OK 74018. 918-341-1860 R/E Recording: 918-341-2518 UCC Recording: 918-341-2518; Fax 918-341-4529.
Will search UCC records. This agency will not do a tax lien search. Will not search real estate records. **Other Phones:** Assessor 341-3290; Treasurer 918-341-3159.

Seminole County

County Clerk, PO Box 1180, Wewoka, OK 74884. 405-257-2501; Fax 405-257-6422.
Will search UCC records. Will not search real estate records. **Other Phone Numbers:** Assessor 405-257-3371; Treasurer 405-257-6262.

Sequoyah County

County Clerk, 120 E. Chickasaw, Sallisaw, OK 74955. 918-775-4516; Fax 918-775-1218.
Will search UCC records. Will not search real estate records. **Other Phones:** Assessor 918-775-2062; Treasurer 918-775-9321; Elections 918-775-2614.

Stephens County

County Clerk, 101 S. 11th St., Room 203, Duncan, OK 73533-4758. 580-255-0977; Fax 580-255-0991.
Will search UCC records. Will not search real estate records. **Other Phone Numbers:** Assessor 580-255-1542; Treasurer 580-255-0728.

Texas County

County Clerk, PO Box 197, Guymon, OK 73942-0197. County Clerk, R/E and UCC Recording 580-338-3141. Will search UCC records. This agency will not do a tax lien search. Will not search real estate records. **Other Phone Numbers:** Assessor 580-338-3060; Treasurer 580-338-7050; Elections 580-338-7644; Vital Records 405-271-4040.

Tillman County

County Clerk, PO Box 992, Frederick, OK 73542. County Clerk, R/E and UCC Recording 580-335-3421; Fax 580-335-3795. www.oklahomacounty.org/countyclerk
Will search UCC records. Will not search real estate records. **Other Phone Numbers:** Assessor 580-335-3424; Treasurer 580-335-3425; Elections 580-335-2287; Vital Records 405-271-4040.

Tulsa County

County Clerk, 500 S. Denver Ave, County Admin. Bldg.-Room 112, Tulsa, OK 74103-3832. County Clerk, R/E and UCC Recording 918-596-5801 UCC Recording: 918-596-5864; Fax 918-596-5867. www.tulsacounty.org
Will search UCC records. Will not search real estate records. **Other Phone Numbers:** Assessor 918-596-5828; Treasurer 918-596-5030.

Wagoner County

County Clerk, PO Box 156, Wagoner, OK 74477. County Clerk, R/E and UCC Recording 918-485-2216; Fax 918-485-8677.
Will search UCC records. Will not search real estate records. **Other Phones:** Assessor 918-485-2367; Treasurer 918-485-2149; Elections 918-485-2142.

Washington County

County Clerk, 420 S Johnstone, Suite 100, Bartlesville, OK 74003. 918-337-2840 R/E Recording: 918-337-2834 UCC Recording: 918-337-2834; Fax 918-337-2894. www.countycourthouse.org
Will search UCC records. Will not search real estate records. **Online Access:** Land, Deed, Mortgage, Lien, Sex Offender Records. Access to the recorders database is available for free at www.countycourthouse.org/countyclerk/disclaimer.htm Also, access to the sex offenders registry is available free at www.countycourthouse.org/registry/index.htm. **Other Phone Numbers:** Assessor 918-337-2830; Treasurer 918-337-2810; Elections 918-337-2850.

Washita County

County Clerk, PO Box 380, Cordell, OK 73632. 580-832-3548.
Will search UCC records. This agency will not do a tax lien search. Will not search real estate records. **Other Phone Numbers:** Assessor 580-832-2468; Treasurer 580-832-2667.

Woods County

County Clerk, PO Box 386, Alva, OK 73717-0386. 580-327-0998 R/E Recording: 580-327-6228; Fax 580-327-6230.
Will search UCC records. UCC search includes tax liens if requested. Real estate owner, mortgage, and property transfer searches available. **Other Phone Numbers:** Assessor 580-327-3118; Treasurer 580-327-0308; Elections 580-327-1452.

Woodward County

County Clerk, 1600 Main St, Ste. 8, Woodward, OK 73801-3051. 580-254-6800.
Will search UCC records. This agency will not do a tax lien search. Will not search real estate records. **Other Phone Numbers:** Assessor 580-254-5061; Treasurer 580-254-7404.

Oklahoma County Locator

You will usually be able to find the city name in the City/County Cross Reference below. In that case, it is a simple matter to determine the county from the cross reference. However, only the official US Postal Service city names are included in this index. There are an additional 40,000 place names that people use in their addresses. Therefore, we have also included a ZIP/City Cross Reference immediately following the City/County Cross Reference.

If you know the ZIP Code but the city name does not appear in the City/County Cross Reference index, look up the ZIP Code in the ZIP/City Cross Reference, find the city name, then look up the city name in the City/County Cross Reference. For example, you want to know the county for an address of Menands, NY 12204. There is no "Menands" in the City/County Cross Reference. The ZIP/City Cross Reference shows that ZIP Codes 12201-12288 are for the city of Albany. Looking back in the City/County Cross Reference, Albany is in Albany County.

City/County Cross Reference

ACHILLE Bryan
ADA Pontotoc
ADAIR Mayes
ADAMS Texas
ADDINGTON Jefferson
AFTON (74331) Delaware(63), Ottawa(34), Craig(1)
AGRA (74824) Lincoln(87), Payne(12)
ALBANY Bryan
ALBERT Caddo
ALBION Pushmataha
ALDERSON Pittsburg
ALEX (73002) Grady(91), McClain(8)
ALINE (73716) Alfalfa(58), Woods(32), Major(8)
ALLEN (74825) Pontotoc(89), Hughes(8), Coal(2)
ALTUS Jackson
ALTUS AFB Jackson
ALVA (73717) Woods(98), Alfalfa(1)
AMBER Grady
AMES (73718) Major(86), Garfield(11), Kingfisher(1)
AMORITA Alfalfa
ANADARKO Caddo
ANTLERS Pushmataha
APACHE (73006) Caddo(89), Comanche(10)
ARAPAHO Custer
ARCADIA (73007) Oklahoma(61), Logan(38)
ARDMORE Carter
ARKOMA Le Flore
ARNETT (73832) Ellis(89), Woodward(10)
ASHER Pottawatomie
ATOKA Atoka
ATWOOD Hughes
AVANT Osage
BACHE Pittsburg
BALKO (73931) Beaver(98), Texas(1)
BARNSDALL Osage
BARTLESVILLE Washington
BATTIEST McCurtain
BEAVER Beaver
BEGGS Okmulgee
BENNINGTON Bryan
BESSIE Washita
BETHANY Oklahoma
BETHEL McCurtain
BIG CABIN (74332) Craig(70), Mayes(15), Rogers(13)
BILLINGS (74630) Noble(87), Garfield(12)
BINGER Caddo
BISON Garfield
BIXBY Tulsa
BLACKWELL Kay
BLAIR Jackson
BLANCHARD (73010) McClain(58), Grady(41)
BLANCO Pittsburg
BLOCKER Pittsburg
BLUEJACKET (74333) Ottawa(75), Craig(24)

BOISE CITY Cimarron
BOKCHITO Bryan
BOKOSHE Le Flore
BOLEY Okfuskee
BOSWELL (74727) Choctaw(89), Bryan(9)
BOWLEGS Seminole
BOWRING Osage
BOYNTON (74422) Okmulgee(53), Muskogee(46)
BRADLEY Grady
BRAGGS Muskogee
BRAMAN Kay
BRAY Stephens
BRISTOW Creek
BROKEN ARROW (74014) Wagoner(98), Tulsa(1)
BROKEN BOW McCurtain
BROMIDE Johnston
BUFFALO Harper
BUNCH (74931) Cherokee(60), Adair(35), Sequoyah(4)
BURBANK Osage
BURLINGTON Alfalfa
BURNEYVILLE Love
BURNS FLAT Washita
BUTLER Custer
BYARS (74831) McClain(90), Pontotoc(8), Garvin(1)
BYRON Alfalfa
CACHE Comanche
CADDO (74729) Atoka(73), Bryan(26)
CALERA Bryan
CALUMET Canadian
CALVIN Hughes
CAMARGO Dewey
CAMERON Le Flore
CANADIAN Pittsburg
CANEY Atoka
CANTON (73724) Blaine(62), Dewey(37)
CANUTE Washita
CAPRON (73725) Woods(79), Alfalfa(20)
CARDIN Ottawa
CARMEN (73726) Alfalfa(80), Woods(20)
CARNEGIE (73015) Caddo(91), Washita(8)
CARNEY Lincoln
CARRIER Garfield
CARTER Beckham
CARTWRIGHT Bryan
CASHION (73016) Kingfisher(57), Logan(39), Canadian(3)
CASTLE Okfuskee
CATOOSA (74015) Rogers(75), Wagoner(24)
CEMENT (73017) Grady(49), Caddo(46), Comanche(4)
CENTRAHOMA Coal
CHANDLER Lincoln
CHATTANOOGA Comanche
CHECOTAH McIntosh
CHELSEA (74016) Rogers(93), Mayes(3), Nowata(1), Craig(1)
CHEROKEE Alfalfa

CHESTER (73838) Major(89), Woodward(10)
CHEYENNE Roger Mills
CHICKASHA Grady
CHOCTAW Oklahoma
CHOUTEAU (74337) Mayes(90), Wagoner(9)
CLAREMORE Rogers
CLARITA Coal
CLAYTON (74536) Pushmataha(95), Pittsburg(2), Latimer(1)
CLEARVIEW Okfuskee
CLEO SPRINGS (73729) Major(87), Woods(10), Alfalfa(2)
CLEVELAND Pawnee
CLINTON (73601) Custer(97), Washita(2)
COALGATE Coal
COLBERT Bryan
COLCORD Delaware
COLEMAN Johnston
COLLINSVILLE (74021) Tulsa(76), Rogers(19), Washington(4)
COLONY (73021) Washita(65), Caddo(34)
COMANCHE Stephens
COMMERCE Ottawa
CONCHO Canadian
CONNERVILLE Johnston
COOKSON Cherokee
COPAN (74022) Washington(97), Osage(2)
CORDELL Washita
CORN Washita
COUNCIL HILL (74428) McIntosh(60), Muskogee(39)
COUNTYLINE Stephens
COVINGTON Garfield
COWETA Wagoner
COYLE (73027) Logan(66), Payne(33)
CRAWFORD Roger Mills
CRESCENT (73028) Logan(92), Kingfisher(7)
CROMWELL Seminole
CROWDER Pittsburg
CUSHING (74023) Payne(95), Lincoln(3)
CUSTER CITY Custer
CYRIL Caddo
DACOMA (73731) Woods(94), Alfalfa(6)
DAISY (74540) Atoka(72), Pushmataha(27)
DAVENPORT Lincoln
DAVIDSON Tillman
DAVIS (73030) Murray(97), Garvin(2)
DEER CREEK Grant
DELAWARE Nowata
DEPEW (74028) Creek(98), Lincoln(1)
DEVOL Cotton
DEWAR Okmulgee
DEWEY Washington
DIBBLE McClain
DILL CITY Washita
DISNEY Mayes
DOUGHERTY Murray
DOUGLAS Garfield
DOVER Kingfisher

DRUMMOND (73735) Garfield(94), Major(5)
DRUMRIGHT (74030) Creek(98), Payne(1)
DUKE Jackson
DUNCAN Stephens
DURANT Bryan
DURHAM Roger Mills
DUSTIN (74839) Hughes(80), Okfuskee(14), McIntosh(4)
EAGLETOWN McCurtain
EAKLY Caddo
EARLSBORO (74840) Pottawatomie(68), Seminole(31)
EDMOND Oklahoma
EL RENO Canadian
ELDORADO (73537) Jackson(95), Harmon(4)
ELGIN Comanche
ELK CITY Beckham
ELMER Jackson
ELMORE CITY Garvin
ENID Garfield
ERICK Beckham
EUCHA Delaware
EUFAULA (74432) McIntosh(91), Pittsburg(8)
FAIRFAX Osage
FAIRLAND Ottawa
FAIRMONT Garfield
FAIRVIEW Major
FANSHAWE Le Flore
FARGO (73840) Ellis(66), Woodward(33)
FAXON Comanche
FAY (73646) Blaine(44), Dewey(41), Custer(14)
FELT Cimarron
FINLEY Pushmataha
FITTSTOWN Johnston
FITZHUGH Pontotoc
FLETCHER Comanche
FORGAN Beaver
FORT COBB Caddo
FORT GIBSON (74434) Muskogee(97), Wagoner(2)
FORT SILL Comanche
FORT SUPPLY Woodward
FORT TOWSON (74735) Choctaw(72), Pushmataha(27)
FOSS (73647) Washita(87), Custer(12)
FOSTER (73434) Stephens(66), Garvin(33)
FOX Carter
FOYIL Rogers
FRANCIS Pontotoc
FREDERICK Tillman
FREEDOM (73842) Woods(65), Woodward(25), Harper(9)
GAGE (73843) Ellis(95), Beaver(4)
GANS Sequoyah
GARBER Garfield
GARVIN McCurtain
GATE (73844) Beaver(67), Harper(32)
GEARY (73040) Blaine(76), Canadian(23)
GENE AUTRY Carter

GERONIMO Comanche
GLENCOE (74032) Payne(93), Pawnee(4),
    Noble(1)
GLENPOOL (74033) Tulsa(96), Creek(3)
GOLDEN McCurtain
GOLTRY (73739) Alfalfa(82), Garfield(17)
GOODWELL Texas
GORE (74435) Sequoyah(88),
    Muskogee(11)
GOTEBO (73041) Kiowa(76), Washita(23)
GOULD Harmon
GOWEN Latimer
GRACEMONT Caddo
GRAHAM Carter
GRANDFIELD Tillman
GRANITE Greer
GRANT Choctaw
GREENFIELD Blaine
GROVE Delaware
GUTHRIE Logan
GUYMON Texas
HAILEYVILLE Pittsburg
HALLETT Pawnee
HAMMON (73650) Roger Mills(77),
    Custer(22)
HANNA McIntosh
HARDESTY Texas
HARRAH (73045) Oklahoma(79),
    Lincoln(13), Pottawatomie(6)
HARTSHORNE (74547) Pittsburg(97),
    Latimer(2)
HASKELL (74436) Muskogee(62),
    Wagoner(21), Okmulgee(16)
HASTINGS (73548) Stephens(40),
    Jefferson(33), Cotton(26)
HAWORTH McCurtain
HAYWOOD Pittsburg
HEADRICK Jackson
HEALDTON Carter
HEAVENER Le Flore
HELENA Alfalfa
HENDRIX Bryan
HENNEPIN (73444) Carter(47), Garvin(41),
    Murray(11)
HENNESSEY (73742) Kingfisher(96),
    Garfield(3)
HENRYETTA Okmulgee
HILLSDALE Garfield
HINTON (73047) Caddo(73), Canadian(25)
HITCHCOCK (73744) Blaine(92),
    Kingfisher(7)
HITCHITA McIntosh
HOBART Kiowa
HODGEN Le Flore
HOLDENVILLE (74848) Hughes(98),
    Seminole(1)
HOLLIS Harmon
HOLLISTER Tillman
HOMINY Osage
HONOBIA (74549) Le Flore(92),
    Pushmataha(8)
HOOKER Texas
HOPETON Woods
HOWE Le Flore
HOYT Haskell
HUGO Choctaw
HULBERT Cherokee
HUNTER (74640) Garfield(81), Grant(18)
HYDRO (73048) Caddo(48), Custer(34),
    Blaine(17)
IDABEL McCurtain
INDIAHOMA Comanche
INDIANOLA Pittsburg
INOLA (74036) Rogers(96), Mayes(3)
ISABELLA Major
JAY Delaware
JENKS Tulsa
JENNINGS (74038) Pawnee(82),
    Creek(17)
JET Alfalfa
JONES Oklahoma
KANSAS (74347) Delaware(57), Adair(42)

KAW CITY Kay
KELLYVILLE Creek
KEMP Bryan
KENEFIC (74748) Bryan(46), Johnston(37),
    Atoka(16)
KENTON Cimarron
KEOTA (74941) Haskell(71), Le Flore(28)
KETCHUM Mayes
KEYES Cimarron
KIEFER Creek
KINGFISHER Kingfisher
KINGSTON Marshall
KINTA Haskell
KIOWA (74553) Pittsburg(70), Atoka(29)
KNOWLES Beaver
KONAWA (74849) Seminole(85),
    Pottawatomie(13)
KREBS Pittsburg
KREMLIN Garfield
LAHOMA (73754) Garfield(77), Major(21),
    Alfalfa(1)
LAMAR Hughes
LAMONT (74643) Grant(92), Kay(7)
LANE Atoka
LANGLEY Mayes
LANGSTON Logan
LAVERNE Harper
LAWTON Comanche
LEBANON Marshall
LEEDEY (73654) Dewey(60), Roger
    Mills(29), Custer(9)
LEFLORE Le Flore
LEHIGH (74556) Atoka(60), Coal(40)
LENAPAH Nowata
LEON Love
LEONARD Tulsa
LEQUIRE Haskell
LEXINGTON Cleveland
LINDSAY (73052) Garvin(91), McClain(5),
    Stephens(1)
LOCO Stephens
LOCUST GROVE (74352) Mayes(63),
    Sequoyah(30), Wagoner(3), Cherokee(2)
LOGAN Beaver
LONE GROVE Carter
LONE WOLF Kiowa
LONGDALE (73755) Blaine(61), Major(31),
    Dewey(6)
LOOKEBA Caddo
LOVELAND Tillman
LOYAL Kingfisher
LUCIEN Noble
LUTHER (73054) Oklahoma(79),
    Lincoln(12), Logan(8)
MACOMB Pottawatomie
MADILL Marshall
MANCHESTER (73758) Grant(81),
    Alfalfa(18)
MANGUM Greer
MANITOU Tillman
MANNFORD (74044) Creek(64),
    Pawnee(35)
MANNSVILLE Johnston
MARAMEC (74045) Pawnee(98), Payne(1)
MARBLE CITY Sequoyah
MARIETTA Love
MARLAND Noble
MARLOW (73055) Stephens(92), Grady(5),
    Comanche(2)
MARSHALL (73056) Logan(52),
    Garfield(38), Kingfisher(9)
MARTHA Jackson
MAUD (74854) Pottawatomie(58),
    Seminole(41)
MAY Harper
MAYFIELD Beckham
MAYSVILLE (73057) Garvin(70),
    McClain(29)
MAZIE Mayes
MC LOUD (74851) Pottawatomie(74),
    Lincoln(12), Cleveland(12)
MCALESTER Pittsburg

MCCURTAIN (74944) Haskell(76), Le
    Flore(23)
MCLOUD (74851) Pottawatomie(74),
    Lincoln(12), Cleveland(12)
MEAD Bryan
MEDFORD Grant
MEDICINE PARK Comanche
MEEKER (74855) Lincoln(89),
    Pottawatomie(10)
MEERS Comanche
MENO (73760) Major(99), Alfalfa(1)
MERIDIAN Logan
MIAMI Ottawa
MILBURN Johnston
MILFAY Creek
MILL CREEK (74856) Johnston(77),
    Murray(22)
MILLERTON McCurtain
MINCO (73059) Grady(67), Caddo(28),
    Canadian(4)
MOFFETT Sequoyah
MONROE Le Flore
MOODYS Cherokee
MOORELAND Woodward
MORRIS Okmulgee
MORRISON (73061) Noble(91), Pawnee(8)
MOUNDS (74047) Creek(66), Tulsa(26),
    Okmulgee(7)
MOUNTAIN PARK Kiowa
MOUNTAIN VIEW (73062) Kiowa(98),
    Comanche(1)
MOYERS Pushmataha
MULDROW Sequoyah
MULHALL (73063) Logan(82), Payne(17)
MUSE Le Flore
MUSKOGEE Muskogee
MUSTANG Canadian
MUTUAL Woodward
NARDIN (74646) Kay(90), Grant(9)
NASH (73761) Grant(92), Garfield(7)
NASHOBA Pushmataha
NEWALLA (74857) Cleveland(67),
    Oklahoma(30), Pottawatomie(1)
NEWCASTLE McClain
NEWKIRK Kay
NICOMA PARK Oklahoma
NINNEKAH Grady
NOBLE Cleveland
NORMAN (73072) Cleveland(96),
    McClain(3)
NORTH MIAMI Ottawa
NOWATA Nowata
OAKHURST Tulsa
OAKS (74359) Delaware(87),
    Cherokee(12)
OAKWOOD (73658) Dewey(90), Blaine(9)
OCHELATA (74051) Washington(98),
    Osage(1)
OILTON Creek
OKARCHE (73762) Canadian(51),
    Kingfisher(48)
OKAY Wagoner
OKEENE (73763) Blaine(89), Major(7),
    Kingfisher(2)
OKEMAH (74859) Okfuskee(93),
    Seminole(6)
OKLAHOMA CITY Oklahoma
OKMULGEE Okmulgee
OKTAHA Muskogee
OLUSTEE Jackson
OMEGA (73764) Kingfisher(60), Blaine(39)
OOLOGAH Rogers
ORLANDO (73073) Logan(73), Payne(17),
    Garfield(6), Noble(2)
OSAGE Osage
OSCAR Jefferson
OVERBROOK Love
OWASSO (74055) Tulsa(73), Rogers(26)
PADEN Okfuskee
PANAMA Le Flore
PANOLA Latimer
PAOLI (73074) Garvin(80), McClain(20)

PARK HILL Cherokee
PAULS VALLEY Garvin
PAWHUSKA Osage
PAWNEE Pawnee
PEGGS (74452) Cherokee(92), Mayes(7)
PERKINS (74059) Payne(96), Lincoln(3)
PERNELL Garvin
PERRY Noble
PHAROAH Okfuskee
PICHER Ottawa
PICKENS McCurtain
PIEDMONT Canadian
PITTSBURG (74560) Pittsburg(91),
    Atoka(8)
PLATTER Bryan
POCASSET (73079) Grady(87), Caddo(12)
POCOLA Le Flore
PONCA CITY (74604) Kay(70), Osage(29)
POND CREEK Grant
PORTER Wagoner
PORUM (74455) Muskogee(82),
    McIntosh(17)
POTEAU Le Flore
PRAGUE (74864) Lincoln(73),
    Pottawatomie(26)
PRESTON Okmulgee
PROCTOR Adair
PRUE Osage
PRYOR Mayes
PURCELL McClain
PUTNAM (73659) Dewey(98), Custer(1)
QUAPAW Ottawa
QUINTON (74561) Pittsburg(62),
    Haskell(37)
RALSTON (74650) Pawnee(66), Osage(33)
RAMONA Washington
RANDLETT Cotton
RATLIFF CITY (73481) Carter(73),
    Stephens(20), Garvin(6)
RATTAN Pushmataha
RAVIA Johnston
RED OAK Latimer
RED ROCK (74651) Noble(93), Pawnee(6)
REDBIRD Wagoner
RENTIESVILLE McIntosh
REYDON Roger Mills
RINGLING Jefferson
RINGOLD (74754) McCurtain(67),
    Pushmataha(30), Choctaw(2)
RINGWOOD Major
RIPLEY Payne
ROCKY (73661) Washita(97), Kiowa(2)
ROFF (74865) Pontotoc(67), Murray(25),
    Garvin(7)
ROLAND Sequoyah
ROOSEVELT (73564) Kiowa(97),
    Comanche(2)
ROSE (74364) Delaware(70), Mayes(18),
    Cherokee(10)
ROSSTON Harper
RUFE McCurtain
RUSH SPRINGS Grady
RYAN Jefferson
S COFFEYVILLE (74072) Nowata(98),
    Craig(1)
SAINT LOUIS Pottawatomie
SALINA (74365) Mayes(89), Delaware(10)
SALLISAW Sequoyah
SAND SPRINGS (74063) Tulsa(81),
    Osage(16), Creek(2)
SAPULPA Creek
SASAKWA (74867) Seminole(94),
    Hughes(5)
SAVANNA Pittsburg
SAWYER Choctaw
SAYRE (73662) Beckham(97), Roger
    Mills(2)
SCHULTER Okmulgee
SEILING Dewey
SEMINOLE Seminole
SENTINEL Washita
SHADY POINT Le Flore

SHAMROCK Creek
SHARON Woodward
SHATTUCK Ellis
SHAWNEE Pottawatomie
SHIDLER (74652) Osage(96), Kay(3)
SKIATOOK (74070) Osage(56), Tulsa(34), Washington(9)
SLICK Creek
SMITHVILLE (74957) McCurtain(56), Le Flore(43)
SNOW Pushmataha
SNYDER (73566) Kiowa(98), Tillman(1)
SOPER Choctaw
SOUTHARD Blaine
SPARKS Lincoln
SPAVINAW (74366) Mayes(86), Delaware(13)
SPENCER Oklahoma
SPENCERVILLE (74760) Choctaw(64), Pushmataha(35)
SPERRY (74073) Tulsa(76), Osage(23)
SPIRO Le Flore
SPRINGER Carter
STERLING Comanche
STIDHAM McIntosh
STIGLER (74462) Haskell(97), Pittsburg(2)
STILLWATER Payne
STILWELL Adair
STONEWALL (74871) Pontotoc(82), Coal(10), Johnston(7)
STRANG Mayes
STRATFORD (74872) Garvin(78), Pontotoc(18), McClain(2)
STRINGTOWN Atoka

STROUD (74079) Lincoln(94), Okfuskee(3), Creek(2)
STUART (74570) Hughes(56), Pittsburg(42), Coal(1)
SULPHUR Murray
SWEETWATER Roger Mills
SWINK Choctaw
TAFT Muskogee
TAHLEQUAH Cherokee
TALALA (74080) Rogers(67), Washington(32)
TALIHINA (74571) Latimer(50), Le Flore(46), Pushmataha(3)
TALOGA Dewey
TATUMS Carter
TECUMSEH Pottawatomie
TEMPLE Cotton
TERLTON (74081) Pawnee(92), Creek(7)
TERRAL Jefferson
TEXHOMA (73949) Cimarron(54), Texas(45)
TEXOLA Beckham
THACKERVILLE Love
THOMAS (73669) Custer(97), Blaine(1), Dewey(1)
TIPTON Tillman
TISHOMINGO Johnston
TONKAWA Kay
TRYON Lincoln
TULLAHASSEE Wagoner
TULSA Tulsa
TUPELO Coal
TURPIN (73950) Beaver(83), Texas(16)

TUSKAHOMA (74574) Pushmataha(51), Latimer(48)
TUSSY Carter
TUTTLE Grady
TWIN OAKS Delaware
TYRONE Texas
UNION CITY Canadian
VALLIANT (74764) McCurtain(90), Choctaw(9)
VELMA Stephens
VERA Washington
VERDEN (73092) Grady(71), Caddo(28)
VERNON McIntosh
VIAN Sequoyah
VICI (73859) Dewey(79), Woodward(18), Ellis(2)
VINITA Craig
VINSON Harmon
WAGONER Wagoner
WAINWRIGHT Muskogee
WAKITA Grant
WALTERS Cotton
WANETTE (74878) Pottawatomie(88), Cleveland(11)
WANN (74083) Nowata(98), Washington(1)
WAPANUCKA Johnston
WARDVILLE (74576) Atoka(53), Pittsburg(46)
WARNER (74469) Muskogee(95), McIntosh(4)
WASHINGTON McClain
WASHITA Caddo
WATONGA Blaine
WATSON McCurtain

WATTS (74964) Adair(83), Delaware(16)
WAUKOMIS Garfield
WAURIKA Jefferson
WAYNE McClain
WAYNOKA (73860) Woods(91), Major(9)
WEATHERFORD (73096) Custer(97), Washita(2)
WEBBERS FALLS Muskogee
WELCH Craig
WELEETKA (74880) Okfuskee(97), Okmulgee(2)
WELLING Cherokee
WELLSTON (74881) Lincoln(93), Logan(6)
WELTY Okfuskee
WESTVILLE Adair
WETUMKA (74883) Hughes(97), Okfuskee(2)
WEWOKA Seminole
WHEATLAND Oklahoma
WHITEFIELD Haskell
WHITESBORO Le Flore
WILBURTON Latimer
WILLOW (73673) Greer(78), Beckham(21)
WILSON (73463) Carter(95), Love(4)
WISTER (74966) Le Flore(92), Latimer(7)
WOODWARD Woodward
WRIGHT CITY McCurtain
WYANDOTTE (74370) Ottawa(91), Delaware(8)
WYNNEWOOD Garvin
WYNONA Osage
YALE Payne
YUKON Canadian

ZIP/City Cross Reference

73001-73001 ALBERT	73045-73045 HARRAH	73093-73093 WASHINGTON	73505-73507 LAWTON
73002-73002 ALEX	73046-73046 HENNEPIN	73094-73094 WASHITA	73520-73520 ADDINGTON
73003-73003 EDMOND	73047-73047 HINTON	73095-73095 WAYNE	73521-73522 ALTUS
73004-73004 AMBER	73048-73048 HYDRO	73096-73096 WEATHERFORD	73523-73523 ALTUS AFB
73005-73005 ANADARKO	73049-73049 JONES	73097-73097 WHEATLAND	73526-73526 BLAIR
73006-73006 APACHE	73050-73050 LANGSTON	73098-73098 WYNNEWOOD	73527-73527 CACHE
73007-73007 ARCADIA	73051-73051 LEXINGTON	73099-73099 YUKON	73528-73528 CHATTANOOGA
73008-73008 BETHANY	73052-73052 LINDSAY	73100-73199 OKLAHOMA CITY	73529-73529 COMANCHE
73009-73009 BINGER	73053-73053 LOOKEBA	73401-73403 ARDMORE	73530-73530 DAVIDSON
73010-73010 BLANCHARD	73054-73054 LUTHER	73425-73425 COUNTYLINE	73531-73531 DEVOL
73011-73011 BRADLEY	73055-73055 MARLOW	73430-73430 BURNEYVILLE	73532-73532 DUKE
73012-73012 BRAY	73056-73056 MARSHALL	73432-73432 COLEMAN	73533-73536 DUNCAN
73013-73013 EDMOND	73057-73057 MAYSVILLE	73433-73433 ELMORE CITY	73537-73537 ELDORADO
73014-73014 CALUMET	73058-73058 MERIDIAN	73434-73434 FOSTER	73538-73538 ELGIN
73015-73015 CARNEGIE	73059-73059 MINCO	73435-73435 FOX	73539-73539 ELMER
73016-73016 CASHION	73061-73061 MORRISON	73436-73436 GENE AUTRY	73540-73540 FAXON
73017-73017 CEMENT	73062-73062 MOUNTAIN VIEW	73437-73437 GRAHAM	73541-73541 FLETCHER
73018-73018 CHICKASHA	73063-73063 MULHALL	73438-73438 HEALDTON	73542-73542 FREDERICK
73019-73019 NORMAN	73064-73064 MUSTANG	73439-73439 KINGSTON	73543-73543 GERONIMO
73020-73020 CHOCTAW	73065-73065 NEWCASTLE	73440-73440 LEBANON	73544-73544 GOULD
73021-73021 COLONY	73066-73066 NICOMA PARK	73441-73441 LEON	73546-73546 GRANDFIELD
73022-73022 CONCHO	73067-73067 NINNEKAH	73442-73442 LOCO	73547-73547 GRANITE
73023-73023 CHICKASHA	73068-73068 NOBLE	73443-73443 LONE GROVE	73548-73548 HASTINGS
73024-73024 CORN	73069-73072 NORMAN	73444-73444 HENNEPIN	73549-73549 HEADRICK
73025-73025 COUNTYLINE	73073-73073 ORLANDO	73446-73446 MADILL	73550-73550 HOLLIS
73026-73026 NORMAN	73074-73074 PAOLI	73447-73447 MANNSVILLE	73551-73551 HOLLISTER
73027-73027 COYLE	73075-73075 PAULS VALLEY	73448-73448 MARIETTA	73552-73552 INDIAHOMA
73028-73028 CRESCENT	73076-73076 PERNELL	73449-73449 MEAD	73553-73553 LOVELAND
73029-73029 CYRIL	73077-73077 PERRY	73450-73450 MILBURN	73554-73554 MANGUM
73030-73030 DAVIS	73078-73078 PIEDMONT	73453-73453 OVERBROOK	73555-73555 MANITOU
73031-73031 DIBBLE	73079-73079 POCASSET	73455-73455 RAVIA	73556-73556 MARTHA
73032-73032 DOUGHERTY	73080-73080 PURCELL	73456-73456 RINGLING	73557-73557 MEDICINE PARK
73033-73033 EAKLY	73081-73081 RATLIFF CITY	73458-73458 SPRINGER	73558-73558 MEERS
73034-73034 EDMOND	73082-73082 RUSH SPRINGS	73459-73459 THACKERVILLE	73559-73559 MOUNTAIN PARK
73035-73035 ELMORE CITY	73083-73083 EDMOND	73460-73460 TISHOMINGO	73560-73560 OLUSTEE
73036-73036 EL RENO	73084-73084 SPENCER	73461-73461 WAPANUCKA	73561-73561 OSCAR
73037-73037 NORMAN	73085-73085 YUKON	73463-73463 WILSON	73562-73562 RANDLETT
73038-73038 FORT COBB	73086-73086 SULPHUR	73476-73476 PERNELL	73564-73564 ROOSEVELT
73039-73039 FOSTER	73087-73087 TATUMS	73481-73481 RATLIFF CITY	73565-73565 RYAN
73040-73040 GEARY	73088-73088 TUSSY	73487-73487 TATUMS	73566-73566 SNYDER
73041-73041 GOTEBO	73089-73089 TUTTLE	73488-73488 TUSSY	73567-73567 STERLING
73042-73042 GRACEMONT	73090-73090 UNION CITY	73491-73491 VELMA	73568-73568 TEMPLE
73043-73043 GREENFIELD	73091-73091 VELMA	73501-73502 LAWTON	73569-73569 TERRAL
73044-73044 GUTHRIE	73092-73092 VERDEN	73503-73503 FORT SILL	73570-73570 TIPTON

Zip Range	City	Zip Range	City	Zip Range	City	Zip Range	City
73571-73571	VINSON	73766-73766	POND CREEK	74054-74054	OSAGE	74452-74452	PEGGS
73572-73572	WALTERS	73768-73768	RINGWOOD	74055-74055	OWASSO	74454-74454	PORTER
73573-73573	WAURIKA	73770-73770	SOUTHARD	74056-74056	PAWHUSKA	74455-74455	PORUM
73575-73575	DUNCAN	73771-73771	WAKITA	74058-74058	PAWNEE	74456-74456	PRESTON
73601-73601	CLINTON	73772-73772	WATONGA	74059-74059	PERKINS	74457-74457	PROCTOR
73620-73620	ARAPAHO	73773-73773	WAUKOMIS	74060-74060	PRUE	74458-74458	REDBIRD
73622-73622	BESSIE	73801-73802	WOODWARD	74061-74061	RAMONA	74459-74459	RENTIESVILLE
73624-73624	BURNS FLAT	73832-73832	ARNETT	74062-74062	RIPLEY	74460-74460	SCHULTER
73625-73625	BUTLER	73834-73834	BUFFALO	74063-74063	SAND SPRINGS	74461-74461	STIDHAM
73626-73626	CANUTE	73835-73835	CAMARGO	74066-74067	SAPULPA	74462-74462	STIGLER
73627-73627	CARTER	73838-73838	CHESTER	74068-74068	SHAMROCK	74463-74463	TAFT
73628-73628	CHEYENNE	73840-73840	FARGO	74070-74070	SKIATOOK	74464-74465	TAHLEQUAH
73632-73632	CORDELL	73841-73841	FORT SUPPLY	74071-74071	SLICK	74466-74466	TULLAHASSEE
73638-73638	CRAWFORD	73842-73842	FREEDOM	74072-74072	S COFFEYVILLE	74467-74467	WAGONER
73639-73639	CUSTER CITY	73843-73843	GAGE	74073-74073	SPERRY	74468-74468	WAINWRIGHT
73641-73641	DILL CITY	73844-73844	GATE	74074-74078	STILLWATER	74469-74469	WARNER
73642-73642	DURHAM	73847-73847	KNOWLES	74079-74079	STROUD	74470-74470	WEBBERS FALLS
73644-73644	ELK CITY	73848-73848	LAVERNE	74080-74080	TALALA	74471-74471	WELLING
73645-73645	ERICK	73849-73849	LOGAN	74081-74081	TERLTON	74472-74472	WHITEFIELD
73646-73646	FAY	73851-73851	MAY	74082-74082	VERA	74477-74477	WAGONER
73647-73647	FOSS	73852-73852	MOORELAND	74083-74083	WANN	74501-74502	MCALESTER
73648-73648	ELK CITY	73853-73853	MUTUAL	74084-74084	WYNONA	74521-74521	ALBION
73650-73650	HAMMON	73855-73855	ROSSTON	74085-74085	YALE	74522-74522	ALDERSON
73651-73651	HOBART	73857-73857	SHARON	74100-74194	TULSA	74523-74523	ANTLERS
73654-73654	LEEDEY	73858-73858	SHATTUCK	74301-74301	VINITA	74525-74525	ATOKA
73655-73655	LONE WOLF	73859-73859	VICI	74330-74330	ADAIR	74526-74526	BACHE
73656-73656	MAYFIELD	73860-73860	WAYNOKA	74331-74331	AFTON	74528-74528	BLANCO
73658-73658	OAKWOOD	73901-73901	ADAMS	74332-74332	BIG CABIN	74529-74529	BLOCKER
73659-73659	PUTNAM	73931-73931	BALKO	74333-74333	BLUEJACKET	74530-74530	BROMIDE
73660-73660	REYDON	73932-73932	BEAVER	74335-74335	CARDIN	74531-74531	CALVIN
73661-73661	ROCKY	73933-73933	BOISE CITY	74337-74337	CHOUTEAU	74533-74533	CANEY
73662-73662	SAYRE	73937-73937	FELT	74338-74338	COLCORD	74534-74534	CENTRAHOMA
73663-73663	SEILING	73938-73938	FORGAN	74339-74339	COMMERCE	74535-74535	CLARITA
73664-73664	SENTINEL	73939-73939	GOODWELL	74340-74340	DISNEY	74536-74536	CLAYTON
73666-73666	SWEETWATER	73942-73942	GUYMON	74342-74342	EUCHA	74538-74538	COALGATE
73667-73667	TALOGA	73944-73944	HARDESTY	74343-74343	FAIRLAND	74540-74540	DAISY
73668-73668	TEXOLA	73945-73945	HOOKER	74344-74345	GROVE	74542-74542	ATOKA
73669-73669	THOMAS	73946-73946	KENTON	74346-74346	JAY	74543-74543	FINLEY
73673-73673	WILLOW	73947-73947	KEYES	74347-74347	KANSAS	74545-74545	GOWEN
73701-73706	ENID	73949-73949	TEXHOMA	74349-74349	KETCHUM	74546-74546	HAILEYVILLE
73716-73716	ALINE	73950-73950	TURPIN	74350-74350	LANGLEY	74547-74547	HARTSHORNE
73717-73717	ALVA	73951-73951	TYRONE	74352-74352	LOCUST GROVE	74548-74548	HAYWOOD
73718-73718	AMES	74001-74001	AVANT	74353-74353	MAZIE	74549-74549	HONOBIA
73719-73719	AMORITA	74002-74002	BARNSDALL	74354-74355	MIAMI	74552-74552	KINTA
73720-73720	BISON	74003-74006	BARTLESVILLE	74358-74358	NORTH MIAMI	74553-74553	KIOWA
73722-73722	BURLINGTON	74008-74008	BIXBY	74359-74359	OAKS	74554-74554	KREBS
73723-73723	BYRON	74009-74009	BOWRING	74360-74360	PICHER	74555-74555	LANE
73724-73724	CANTON	74010-74010	BRISTOW	74361-74362	PRYOR	74556-74556	LEHIGH
73725-73725	CAPRON	74011-74014	BROKEN ARROW	74363-74363	QUAPAW	74557-74557	MOYERS
73726-73726	CARMEN	74015-74015	CATOOSA	74364-74364	ROSE	74558-74558	NASHOBA
73727-73727	CARRIER	74016-74016	CHELSEA	74365-74365	SALINA	74559-74559	PANOLA
73728-73728	CHEROKEE	74017-74018	CLAREMORE	74366-74366	SPAVINAW	74560-74560	PITTSBURG
73729-73729	CLEO SPRINGS	74020-74020	CLEVELAND	74367-74367	STRANG	74561-74561	QUINTON
73730-73730	COVINGTON	74021-74021	COLLINSVILLE	74368-74368	TWIN OAKS	74562-74562	RATTAN
73731-73731	DACOMA	74022-74022	COPAN	74369-74369	WELCH	74563-74563	RED OAK
73733-73733	DOUGLAS	74023-74023	CUSHING	74370-74370	WYANDOTTE	74565-74565	SAVANNA
73734-73734	DOVER	74026-74026	DAVENPORT	74401-74403	MUSKOGEE	74567-74567	SNOW
73735-73735	DRUMMOND	74027-74027	DELAWARE	74421-74421	BEGGS	74569-74569	STRINGTOWN
73736-73736	FAIRMONT	74028-74028	DEPEW	74422-74422	BOYNTON	74570-74570	STUART
73737-73737	FAIRVIEW	74029-74029	DEWEY	74423-74423	BRAGGS	74571-74571	TALIHINA
73738-73738	GARBER	74030-74030	DRUMRIGHT	74425-74425	CANADIAN	74572-74572	TUPELO
73739-73739	GOLTRY	74031-74031	FOYIL	74426-74426	CHECOTAH	74574-74574	TUSKAHOMA
73741-73741	HELENA	74032-74032	GLENCOE	74427-74427	COOKSON	74576-74576	WARDVILLE
73742-73742	HENNESSEY	74033-74033	GLENPOOL	74428-74428	COUNCIL HILL	74577-74577	WHITESBORO
73743-73743	HILLSDALE	74034-74034	HALLETT	74429-74429	COWETA	74578-74578	WILBURTON
73744-73744	HITCHCOCK	74035-74035	HOMINY	74430-74430	CROWDER	74601-74604	PONCA CITY
73746-73746	HOPETON	74036-74036	INOLA	74431-74431	DEWAR	74630-74630	BILLINGS
73747-73747	ISABELLA	74037-74037	JENKS	74432-74432	EUFAULA	74631-74631	BLACKWELL
73749-73749	JET	74038-74038	JENNINGS	74434-74434	FORT GIBSON	74632-74632	BRAMAN
73750-73750	KINGFISHER	74039-74039	KELLYVILLE	74435-74435	GORE	74633-74633	BURBANK
73753-73753	KREMLIN	74041-74041	KIEFER	74436-74436	HASKELL	74636-74636	DEER CREEK
73754-73754	LAHOMA	74042-74042	LENAPAH	74437-74437	HENRYETTA	74637-74637	FAIRFAX
73755-73755	LONGDALE	74043-74043	LEONARD	74438-74438	HITCHITA	74640-74640	HUNTER
73756-73756	LOYAL	74044-74044	MANNFORD	74440-74440	HOYT	74641-74641	KAW CITY
73757-73757	LUCIEN	74045-74045	MARAMEC	74441-74441	HULBERT	74643-74643	LAMONT
73758-73758	MANCHESTER	74046-74046	MILFAY	74442-74442	INDIANOLA	74644-74644	MARLAND
73759-73759	MEDFORD	74047-74047	MOUNDS	74444-74444	MOODYS	74646-74646	NARDIN
73760-73760	MENO	74048-74048	NOWATA	74445-74445	MORRIS	74647-74647	NEWKIRK
73761-73761	NASH	74050-74050	OAKHURST	74446-74446	OKAY	74650-74650	RALSTON
73762-73762	OKARCHE	74051-74051	OCHELATA	74447-74447	OKMULGEE	74651-74651	RED ROCK
73763-73763	OKEENE	74052-74052	OILTON	74450-74450	OKTAHA	74652-74652	SHIDLER
73764-73764	OMEGA	74053-74053	OOLOGAH	74451-74451	PARK HILL	74653-74653	TONKAWA

74701-74702 DURANT	74760-74760 SPENCERVILLE	74851-74851 MCLOUD	74932-74932 CAMERON
74720-74720 ACHILLE	74761-74761 SWINK	74852-74852 MACOMB	74935-74935 FANSHAWE
74721-74721 ALBANY	74764-74764 VALLIANT	74854-74854 MAUD	74936-74936 GANS
74722-74722 BATTIEST	74766-74766 WRIGHT CITY	74855-74855 MEEKER	74937-74937 HEAVENER
74723-74723 BENNINGTON	74801-74804 SHAWNEE	74856-74856 MILL CREEK	74939-74939 HODGEN
74724-74724 BETHEL	74818-74818 SEMINOLE	74857-74857 NEWALLA	74940-74940 HOWE
74726-74726 BOKCHITO	74820-74821 ADA	74859-74859 OKEMAH	74941-74941 KEOTA
74727-74727 BOSWELL	74824-74824 AGRA	74860-74860 PADEN	74942-74942 LEFLORE
74728-74728 BROKEN BOW	74825-74825 ALLEN	74862-74862 PHAROAH	74943-74943 LEQUIRE
74729-74729 CADDO	74826-74826 ASHER	74863-74863 FITTSTOWN	74944-74944 MCCURTAIN
74730-74730 CALERA	74827-74827 ATWOOD	74864-74864 PRAGUE	74945-74945 MARBLE CITY
74731-74731 CARTWRIGHT	74829-74829 BOLEY	74865-74865 ROFF	74946-74946 MOFFETT
74733-74733 COLBERT	74830-74830 BOWLEGS	74866-74866 SAINT LOUIS	74947-74947 MONROE
74734-74734 EAGLETOWN	74831-74831 BYARS	74867-74867 SASAKWA	74948-74948 MULDROW
74735-74735 FORT TOWSON	74832-74832 CARNEY	74868-74868 SEMINOLE	74949-74949 MUSE
74736-74736 GARVIN	74833-74833 CASTLE	74869-74869 SPARKS	74951-74951 PANAMA
74737-74737 GOLDEN	74834-74834 CHANDLER	74871-74871 STONEWALL	74953-74953 POTEAU
74738-74738 GRANT	74835-74835 CLEARVIEW	74872-74872 STRATFORD	74954-74954 ROLAND
74740-74740 HAWORTH	74836-74836 CONNERVILLE	74873-74873 TECUMSEH	74955-74955 SALLISAW
74741-74741 HENDRIX	74837-74837 CROMWELL	74875-74875 TRYON	74956-74956 SHADY POINT
74743-74743 HUGO	74838-74838 SHAWNEE	74877-74877 VERNON	74957-74957 SMITHVILLE
74745-74745 IDABEL	74839-74839 DUSTIN	74878-74878 WANETTE	74959-74959 SPIRO
74747-74747 KEMP	74840-74840 EARLSBORO	74880-74880 WELEETKA	74960-74960 STILWELL
74748-74748 KENEFIC	74842-74842 FITTSTOWN	74881-74881 WELLSTON	74962-74962 VIAN
74750-74750 MILLERTON	74843-74843 FITZHUGH	74882-74882 WELTY	74963-74963 WATSON
74752-74752 PICKENS	74844-74844 FRANCIS	74883-74883 WETUMKA	74964-74964 WATTS
74753-74753 PLATTER	74845-74845 HANNA	74884-74884 WEWOKA	74965-74965 WESTVILLE
74754-74754 RINGOLD	74848-74848 HOLDENVILLE	74901-74901 ARKOMA	74966-74966 WISTER
74755-74755 RUFE	74849-74849 KONAWA	74902-74902 POCOLA	
74756-74756 SAWYER	74850-74850 LAMAR	74930-74930 BOKOSHE	
74759-74759 SOPER	74851-74851 MC LOUD	74931-74931 BUNCH	

General Help Numbers:

Governor's Office
State Capitol Bldg.   503-378-4582
900 Court St NE   Fax 503-378-4863
Salem, OR 97301-4047   8AM-5PM
www.governor.state.or.us

Attorney General's Office
Department of Justice   503-378-4400
1162 Court St NE   Fax 503-378-4017
Salem, OR 97310   8AM-5PM
www.doj.state.or.us

State Court Administrator
Supreme Court Bldg, 1163 State St   503-986-5500
Salem, OR 97310   Fax 503-986-5503
www.ojd.state.or.us/osca   8AM-5PM

State Archives
Archives Division   503-373-0701
800 Summer St NE   Fax 503-373-0953
Salem, OR 97301   8AM-4:45PM
http://arcweb.sos.state.or.us

State Specifics:

Capital: Salem
                                  Marion County

Time Zone: PST

Number of Counties: 36

Population: 3,472,867

Web Site: www.oregon.gov

State Agencies

Criminal Records

Oregon State Police, Unit 11, Identification Services Section, PO Box 4395, Portland, OR 97208-4395 (Courier: 3772 Portland Rd NE, Bldg C, Salem, OR 97303); 503-378-3070, 503-378-2121 (Fax), 8AM-5PM.

www.osp.state.or.us

Note: A sex offender registry is not available online. Direct inquiries to the Sex Offender Registration Unit, 503-378-3720.

Indexing & Storage: Records are available from 1941 on and are computerized. It takes up to 8

days before new records are available for inquiry. Records are indexed on inhouse computer. Records are normally destroyed after (records maintained indefinitely). Approximately 50% of all arrests in database have final dispositions recorded.

Searching: Three types of searches exist: open records search, own record search, and statutorily-required search. The latter can include an FBI fingerprint check for an additional $24.00 fee. Include the following in your request: name, date of birth. Submitting the SSN is helpful, but not required. Fingerprints are required only when subject submits the request. If record exists, person

of record will be notified of the request and the record will not be released for 14 additional days. Open record information includes all records with convictions and also all arrests within the past year without disposition. Statutorily-required record searches and own record searches include all records.

Access by: mail, fax, online.

Fee & Payment: Open record search fee is $15.00 per individual name. If someone is submitting a search on oneself, the fee is $12.00 and fingerprints are required. Statutorily-required searches are $12.00 plus FBI fingerprint fee, if required. $5.00 fee to notarize. Fee payee: Oregon State Police. Prepayment required. Personal checks accepted. No credit cards accepted.

Mail search: Clean records are returned in 7-10 days, records with activity take 3 weeks to return. A self addressed stamped envelope is requested.

Fax search: Requesters must be pre-approved.

Online search: A web based site is available for requesting and receiving criminal records. Web site is ONLY for high-volume requesters who must be pre-approved. Results are posted as "No Record" or "In Process" ("In Process" means a record will be mailed in 14 days). Use the "open records" link to get into the proper site. Fee is $12.00 per record. Call 503-373-1808, ext 230 to receive the application, or visit the web site.

Corporation Records
Limited Partnership Records
Trademarks/Servicemarks
Fictitious Name
Assumed Name
Limited Liability Company Records

Corporation Division, Public Service Building, 255 Capital St NE, #151, Salem, OR 97310-1327; 503-986-2200, 503-378-4381 (Fax), 8AM-5PM.

www.filinginoregon.com

Indexing & Storage: Records are available on the computer screen for 10 years after inactive. Assumed names are only available for 5 years after inactive. The records prior to 20 years ago are stored in the State Archives back to the 1800's for corporations only. New records are available for inquiry immediately. Records are indexed on microfilm, inhouse computer.

Searching: All information is public record. Include the following in your request: full name of business. In addition to the articles of incorporation, corporation records include the following information: Annual Reports, Prior (merged) names, Articles of Amendment.

Access by: mail, phone, fax, in person, online.

Fee & Payment: There is no search fee. Copies cost $5.00 per business name or $15.00 if certified, otherwise there is a $1.00 fee per business name for a computer printout. A Good Standing certificate is $10.00. Fee payee: Corporation Division. Prepayment required. Personal checks accepted. Credit cards accepted: MasterCard, Visa.

Mail search: Turnaround time: 7 to 10 days. A self addressed stamped envelope is requested.

Phone search: There is a limit of 3 searches per phone call.

Fax search: Requesters must use a credit card, turnaround time is 5 days or less.

In person search: Turnaround time while you wait.

Online search: There is free, limited access at the web site for business registry information. A commercial dial-up system is also available. Call 503-229-5133 for details. In addition, the complete database can be purchased with monthly updates via e-mail, call 503-986-2343.

Other access: A subscription service for new business lists and tapes of the database are available for $15.00 per month or $150.00 for an annual subscription. Call 503-986-2343 for more information.

Expedited service: Expedited service is available for phone and in person searches. Turnaround time: 1 day. They will ship overnight if you supply your shipper's account number. Fax requests are expedited only if phoned in first.

Uniform Commercial Code
Federal Tax Liens
State Tax Liens

UCC Division, Secretary of State, 255 Capitol St NE, Suite 151, Salem, OR 97310-1327; 503-986-2200, 503-373-1166 (Fax), 8AM-5PM.

www.sos.state.or.us/corporation

Note: State tax liens on personal property are filed here; state tax liens on real property are filed at the county level.

Indexing & Storage: Records are available on microfiche to 1963. It takes 2 to 4 days before new records are available for inquiry.

Searching: Use search request form UCC-11. The search includes tax liens filed here. Include the following in your request: debtor name.

Access by: mail, phone, fax, in person, online.

Fee & Payment: The search fee is $10.00 per name, with copies is $15.00 per name. A document number request is $5.00. A state seal certificate is $15.00. CD service is $20.00 per CDl. Special research projects are $20.00 per hour. Fee payee: Secretary of State. Prepayment required. Personal checks accepted. Credit cards accepted: MasterCard, Visa.

Mail search: Turnaround time: 1 to 4 days.

Phone search: Limited information is available.

Fax search: A credit card is required. Results are mailed.

In person search: Searching is available in person.

Online search: UCC index information can be obtained for free from the web site. You can search by debtor name or by lien number. You can also download forms from here.

Other access: Monthly UCC information is released via e-mail or diskette. Prices start at $15.00 per month or $150.00 annually for new filings, or $200 per month for all active filings. For more information, call Program Services at 503-986-2212.

Sales Tax Registrations
State does not impose sales tax.

Birth Certificates

Department of Human Services, Vital Records, PO Box 14050, Portland, OR 97293-0050 (Courier: 800 NE Oregon St, #205, Portland, OR 97232); 503-731-4095 (Recorded Message), 503-731-4108, 503-234-8417 (Fax), 8AM-4:30PM.

www.ohd.hr.state.or.us/chs/welcome.htm

Note: While records cannot be ordered online from this agency, you may order directly on Vital Chek's web page at www.VitalChek.com

Indexing & Storage: Records are available from July 1903 to present. There are some delayed filed, unindexed records with DOBs from 1885 to 1902.

Birth indexes prior to 1902 available at the State Archives. It takes 2 to 4 weeks before new records are available for inquiry.

Searching: Investigative searches must have a signed, notarized release form from person of record or immediate family member, unless record over 100 years old. Records only available to legal guardians & legal representatives with proof of such Include the following in your request: full name, names of parents, mother's maiden name, date of birth, place of birth, relationship to person of record. Must request "long form" if time of birth, hospital or physician's names is needed. The following data is not released: original records of adoption, except to adoptee over age of 21.

Access by: mail, phone, fax, in person.

Fee & Payment: The search fee is $15.00. Add $12.00 for each additional copy. Fee payee: Oregon Health Division. Prepayment required. Personal checks accepted. Credit cards accepted: MasterCard, Visa, AmEx, Discover.

Mail search: Turnaround time: 2 to 3 weeks. Express mail requests are handled immediately. No self addressed stamped envelope is required.

Phone search: Fax and phone orders are billed to credit cards and processed the next day. There is an additional $10.50 service fee.

Fax search: Same criteria as phone searching.

In person search: Turnaround time is under 20 minutes.

Expedited service: Expedited service is available for fax and phone searches. Turnaround time: overnight delivery. Orders are charged to credit cards. Fee depends on delivery service.

Death Records

Department of Human Services, Vital Records, PO Box 14050, Portland, OR 97293-0050 (Courier: 800 NE Oregon St, #205, Portland, OR 97232); 503-731-4095 (Recorded Message), 503-731-4108, 503-234-8417 (Fax), 8AM-4:30PM.

www.ohd.hr.state.or.us/chs/welcome.htm

Note: While records cannot be ordered online from this agency, you may order directly on Vital Chek's web page at www.VitalChek.com

Indexing & Storage: Records are available from July 1903 to present. It takes 2 to 4 weeks before new records are available for inquiry.

Searching: Investigative searches must have a signed, notarized release from immediate family member or legal representative or person with a personal property right. After 50 years, a record becomes public record and there are no restrictions. Include the following in your request: full name, date of death, place of death, relationship to person of record, reason for information request. The name of the spouse is helpful. The date of birth is helpful for common names.

Access by: mail, phone, fax, in person.

Fee & Payment: The search fee is $15.00 and additional copies are $12.00 each. Fee payee: DHS Vital Records. Prepayment required. Personal checks accepted. Credit cards accepted: MasterCard, Visa, AmEx, Discover.

Mail search: Turnaround time: 2 to 3 weeks. Express mail requests are processed immediately. No self addressed stamped envelope is required.

Phone search: Phone and fax orders require use of a credit card and an additional $10.50 service fee. Turnaround time is generally in 24 hours.

Fax search: Same criteria as phone searching.

In person search: Turnaround time is within 20 minutes.

Other access: Indexes are available at many state libraries.

Expedited service: Expedited service is available for fax and phone searches. Turnaround time: overnight delivery. Carrier chosen to return documents determines fees. Use of credit card is required.

Marriage Certificates

Department of Human Services, Vital Records, PO Box 14050, Portland, OR 97293-0050 (Courier: 800 NE Oregon St, #205, Portland, OR 97232); 503-731-4095 (Recorded Message), 503-731-4108, 503-234-8417 (Fax), 8AM-4:30PM.

www.ohd.hr.state.or.us/chs/welcome.htm

Note: While records cannot be ordered online from this agency, you may order directly on Vital Chek's web page at www.VitalChek.com

Indexing & Storage: Records are available from 1906 to present. Early records are in an abbreviated form called "Return of Marriage." It takes 4 to 8 weeks before new records are available for inquiry.

Searching: Records less than 50 years old are only available to family members, legal representatives or those with a personal or property right. Include the following in your request: names of husband and wife, date of marriage, place or county of marriage. Include daytime phone number and as many identifiers as possible.

Access by: mail, phone, fax, in person.

Fee & Payment: The search fee is $15.00, additional copies $12.00 per record. Fee payee: DHS Vital Records Prepayment required. Personal checks accepted. Credit cards accepted: MasterCard, Visa, AmEx, Discover.

Mail search: Turnaround time: 2 to 3 weeks. If request is expressed, it will be answered ASAP. No self addressed stamped envelope is required.

Phone search: There is an additional $10.50 quick service search fee per telephone or fax order. Use of a credit card is required.

Fax search: Results are sent by mail. Turnaround time is next working day.

In person search: Turnaround time is usually within 20 minutes.

Other access: Many state libraries offer record indexes.

Expedited service: Expedited service is available for mail, phone and fax searches. Turnaround time: overnight delivery. Additional fees will be added, depending on carrier. For mail requests, enclose a prepaid, self-addressed envelope for overnight carrier.

Divorce Records

Department of Human Services, Vital Records, Suite 205, PO Box 14050, Portland, OR 97293-0050 (Courier: 800 NE Oregon St, #205, Portland, OR 97232); 503-731-4095 (Recorded Message), 502-731-4108, 503-234-8417 (Fax), 8AM-4:30PM.

www.ohd.hr.state.or.us/chs/welcome.htm

Note: While records cannot be ordered online from this agency, you may order directly on Vital Chek's web page at www.VitalChek.com

Indexing & Storage: Records are available from 1925 to present. It takes 4 to 8 weeks before new records are available for inquiry.

Searching: Records less than 50 years old are only available to family members, legal representatives and those with a personal or property right. Include the following in your request: date of divorce. Also include names of husband and wife, and reason for request.

Access by: mail, phone, fax, in person.

Fee & Payment: The search fee is $15.00, additional copies are $12.00 each. Fee payee: DHS Vital Records. Prepayment required. Using personal checks (with guarantee card) may delay processing by 2 weeks. For a mail request, enclose a prepaid, self-addressed envelope for overnight carrier. Personal checks accepted. Credit cards accepted: MasterCard, Visa, AmEx, Discover.

Mail search: Turnaround time: 2 to 3 weeks. Send request by overnight delivery and it will be processed ASAP. No self addressed stamped envelope is required.

Phone search: There is an additional $15.00 service fee for ordering by fax or phone and you must use a credit card.

Fax search: Results are sent by mail. Turnaround time next working day.

In person search: Turnaround time is usually within 20 minutes.

Other access: Indexes are available in many state libraries.

Expedited service: Expedited service is available for fax and phone searches. Turnaround time: overnight delivery.

Workers' Compensation Records

Department of Consumer & Business Srvs, Workers Compensation Division, 350 Winter Street NE Rm 27, Salem, OR 97301-3879; 503-947-7818, 503-947-7993 (TTY), 503-945-7630 (Fax), 8AM-5PM M-F.

www.oregonwcd.org

Indexing & Storage: Records are available from June 1980 on. Records from 1966 to June 1980 are in the State Archives. It takes 4 days or less before new records are available for inquiry. Records are indexed on inhouse computer.

Searching: Per ORS 192.502(18), claims records are exempt from public disclosure. Access to records is at the discretion of the Director. In general, those with a legitimate business purpose are granted access. Include the following in your request: claimant name, Social Security Number, claim number, name and address of requester. A signed release by subject is honored. The web site features rules, bulletins, forms, and publications.

Access by: mail, fax, in person.

Fee & Payment: The Department has the authority to charge for staff time and resources for any record request. Records releases only after disclosure requirements are met. Fee payee: DCBS. Prepayment required. Personal checks accepted. No credit cards accepted.

Mail search: Turnaround time: 1 to 5 days. No self addressed stamped envelope is required.

Fax search: Fax requests are accepted if disclosure requirements are met. Completed report may be mailed back.

In person search: Completed report may need to be mailed back. Turnaround time: 1 to 5 days.

Driver Records

Driver and Motor Vehicle Services, Record Services, 1905 Lana Ave, NE, Salem, OR 97314; 503-945-5000, 8AM-5PM.

www.oregondmv.com

Note: Oregon differentiates between "employment" and "non-employment" records. Ongoing requesters with a permissible use and quailfy to receive personal information per state law may establish a Record Inquiry Account.

Indexing & Storage: Records are available for 3 or 5 years for minor convictions; 10 years for DUIs and major convictions; and 3 or 5 years after reinstatement for suspensions. It takes 2-3 weeks normally before new records are available for inquiry.

Searching: Permissible use requesters must open a Record Inquiry Account and are then approved to access via one of the automated systems. Casual requesters who do not present written consent may receive a "sanitized record." Include the following in your request: full name, date of birth, driver's license number. A driver's license report is available which lists the driver's name, address, date of birth, license number, issue and expiration dates, original business date, restrictions, status, and, if applicable, the ID card expiration date. The following data is not released: medical information, SSNs, photos.

Access by: mail, phone, fax.

Fee & Payment: Fee for a 3 year non-employment driving record is $1.50; $2.00 for a 3 year employment driving record; $3.00 for a "court print" record; $1.50 per record for a driver license information report. There is a charge of $1.50 for no record found. Fee payee: DMV Services. Prepayment required. Personal checks accepted. No credit cards accepted.

Mail search: Turnaround time: 1 day from receipt. A record request form and record fee list is available online. No self addressed stamped envelope is required.

Phone search: Oregon offers "DAVE" (DMV's Interactive Voice Response System) which reads information from computer files in a human sounding voice. A variety of records are available on DAVE 24 hours a day. Call 503-945-7950 for more information.

Fax search: Records are available by fax.

Other access: The agency offers an automated "flag program" that inform customers of activity on a name list. Call the Automated Reporting System at 503-945-5312 for more information.

Vehicle Ownership
Vehicle Identification

Driver and Motor Vehicle Services, Record Services Unit, 1905 Lana Ave, NE, Salem, OR 97314; 503-945-5000, 503-945-5425 (Fax), 8AM-5PM.

www.oregondmv.com

Note: Ongoing requesters with a permissibile use and quality for personal information per state law may establish a Record Inquiry Account.

Indexing & Storage: Records are available from 1963 to present. Vehicle title and registration records are archived on microfilm and microfiche. It takes 2-3 weeks from issue before new records are available for inquiry.

Searching: Title and registration ownership records are open to the public, for a fee. By law, only certain entities may receive records with personal info. Casual requesters cannot obtain records with personal information without written consent of subject. DOB is helpful. The following data is not released: medical information, SSNs.

Access by: mail, phone.

Fee & Payment: Vehicle record prints are $4.00, information given orally is $2.50 (to account holders). A complete vehicle title history is $22.50. An insurance information search is $10.00. Generally, $2.50 is charged if no record is found. Fee payee: Driver & Motor Services (DMV). Prepayment required. Personal checks accepted. No credit cards accepted.

Mail search: Turnaround time: 1 day. A self addressed stamped envelope is requested.

Phone search: The automated system called "DAVE" is open 24 hours a day. An account is necessary. Call 503-945-7950 for more information.

Accident Reports

Motor Vehicle Division, Accident Reports & Information, 1905 Lana Ave, NE, Salem, OR 97314; 503-945-5098, 503-945-5267 (Fax), 8AM-5PM.

www.oregondmv.com

Indexing & Storage: Records are available for 5 years to present. It takes 2-4 weeks before new records are available for inquiry.

Searching: Qualified requesters include legal representatives, involved insurance companies and those involved with property damage or injury. Include the following in your request: full name, date of accident, location of accident. The police report is provided without personal information unless the requester qualifies for personal information under OR law.

Access by: mail, fax, in person.

Fee & Payment: The fee is $8.50 for the police accident report. There is a $1.50 charge for a "no record found." Fee payee: MVD Services. Prepayment required. Personal checks accepted. No credit cards accepted.

Mail search: Turnaround time: 3 to 5 days. No self addressed stamped envelope is required.

Fax search: This is only available for account holders. Same fees and turnaround time (3-5 days).

In person search: Turnaround time will vary, record may not be available same day.

Other access: Bulk release of police accident reports is available for sale. Records are unsorted and include all counties.

Vessel Ownership
Vessel Registration

Oregon State Marine Board, PO Box 14145, Salem, OR 97309 (Courier: 435 Commercial St NE, #400, Salem, OR 97301); 503-378-8587, 503-378-4597 (Fax), 8AM-5PM M-F.

www.boatoregon.com

Indexing & Storage: Records are available from 1997 to present for titles. Records are indexed on computer for the last 3 years. Records are on microfiche from the 1978 to the present. Titles and registrations are issued on all motorized boats and sailboats over 12 ft. It takes about one day before new records are available for inquiry.

Searching: Extremely large boats which move along the OR-WA-CA border for 60 days or more are registered with the US Coast Guard. Call (800) 799-8362 for more information. To search, one of the following is required: name, Oregon #, or hull ID #. Requests can be made via e-mail, from the web site,

Access by: mail, phone, fax, in person.

Fee & Payment: There is no fee for 1 search. Fees for lists are dependent on the time involved. Fee payee: State Marine Board. Prepayment required. Personal checks accepted. No credit cards accepted.

Mail search: Turnaround time: 7 to 10 days. No self addressed stamped envelope is required.

Phone search: Limited registration information is released over the phone.

Fax search: Records are available by fax.

In person search: If the search is lengthy, the results will be sent by mail.

Other access: Records are available CD starting at $165 and on labels starting at $250.

Legislation Records

Oregon Legislative Assembly, Legislative Publications, 900 Court St, #49, Salem, OR 97310; 503-986-1180 (Current Bill Information), 503-373-0701 (Archives), 503-373-1527 (Fax), 8AM-5PM.

www.leg.state.or.us

Note: Older passed bills are located at the State Archives, 503-373-0701.

Indexing & Storage: Records are available for current session only. Records are indexed on inhouse computer.

Searching: Enrolled bills are available back to 1997. Include the following in your request: bill number, year.

Access by: mail, phone, fax, in person, online.

Fee & Payment: There are no fees for copies of current bills. Copies of enrolled bills and bills from Archives are $.25 per page copy fee and other charges depending on the search requirement.

Mail search: Turnaround time: same day. No self addressed stamped envelope is required.

Phone search: Records are available by phone.

Fax search: Fax searching available.

In person: Searching is available in person.

Online search: Text and histories of measures can be found at the Internet site for no charge.

Voter Registration

Records not maintained by a state level agency.

Note: Records are maintained at the county level and cannot be purchased for commercial reasons.

GED Certificates

Dept of Community Colleges/ Workforce Development, GED Program, 255 Capitol St NE, Salem, OR 97310; 503-378-8648 x369, 503-378-8434 (Fax), 8AM-5PM M-F.

www.odccwd.state.or.us

Searching: To verify, the following is a required: name, date/year of test, DOB, and Social Security Number. If a copy of a transcript is requested, include the above plus a signed release.

Access by: mail, phone, fax, in person.

Fee & Payment: There is no fee for verification. Copies of transcripts are $5.00 each. Fee payee: State of Oregon Prepayment required. Money orders are accepted. Personal checks accepted. No credit cards accepted.

Mail search: Turnaround time is 10-12 days. No self addressed stamped envelope is required. No fee for mail request.

Phone search: No fee for telephone request.

Fax search: You may request a verification of transcript by fax.

In person search: Turnaround time is typically 5 minutes.

Hunting License Information
Fishing License Information

Fish & Wildlife Department, Licensing Division, PO Box 59, Portland, OR 97207 (Courier: 2501 SW 1st Ave, Portland, OR 97201); 503-872-5275, 503-872-5261 (Fax), 8AM-5PM.

www.dfw.state.or.us

Indexing & Storage: Records are available from 1996 on computer.

Searching: Include the following in your request: full name, DOB. Fishing licenses and hunting licenses are in the same building in different divisions. The following data is not released: phone numbers or Social Security Numbers.

Access by: mail, fax, in person.

Fee & Payment: The fee for a search is $5.00. The record is certified. Fee payee: O.D.F.W. Prepayment required. Personal checks accepted. Credit cards accepted: MasterCard, Visa, Discover.

Mail search: Turnaround time: 1 to 3 days. No self addressed stamped envelope is required.

Fax search: Same fees and turnaround time as mail requests.

In person search: Records are usually returned by mail.

Other access: The state will release bulk lists for a fee. Call 503-872-5267 x5617.

Oregon State Licensing Agencies

Licenses Searchable Online

Acupuncturist #29 .... www.bme.state.or.us/search.html
Animal Feed (Livestock) #22 .... www.oda.state.or.us/dbs/licenses/search.lasso?&division=commercial_feed
Animal Food Processor #22 .... www.oda.state.or.us/dbs/licenses/search.lasso?&division=ahid
Architect #6 .... www.architect-board.state.or.us/A-B.htm
Architectural Firm #6 .... www.architect-board.state.or.us/ARFirms.htm
Attorney #43 .... www.osbcle.org/members/start.asp
Audiologist #58 .... http://bspa.ohd.hr.state.or.us
Bakery #23 .... www.oda.state.or.us/dbs/licenses/search.lasso?&division=fsd
Bank #26 .... www.cbs.state.or.us/external/dfcs/banking/regagent.htm
Brand (Livestock - Available) #22 .... www.oda.state.or.us/dbs/search.lasso
Brand Inspector #22 .... www.oda.state.or.us/dbs/brandinspector/search.lasso
Building Official #19 .... www.cbs.state.or.us/external/imd/database/bcd/licensing/index.html
Check & Money Order Seller #26 .... www.oregondfcs.org/e_commerce/m_tran/m_tran.htm
Chiropractor/Chiropractic Assistant #8 .... www.obce.state.or.us
Christmas Tree Grower #25 .... www.oda.state.or.us/dbs/licenses/search.lasso?&division=nursery
Collection Agency #26 .... www.oregondfcs.org/ca/ca.htm
Construction Contractor/Subcontractor #21 .... www.ccb.state.or.us/newq_start.htm
Consumer Finance Company #26 .... www.cbs.state.or.us/external/dfcs/cf/cfdatabase/search_main.htm
Credit Service Organization #26 .... www.oregondfcs.org/cso/cso.htm
Credit Union #26 .... www.cbs.state.or.us/external/dfcs/cu/cuagents.htm
Dairy Industries #23 .... www.oda.state.or.us/dbs/licenses/search.lasso?&division=fsd
Debt Consolidation Agency #26 .... www.cbs.state.or.us/external/dfcs/dca/lic_dca.htm
Dentist #55 .... www.oregondentistry.org/
Egg Handler/Breaker #23 .... www.oda.state.or.us/dbs/licenses/search.lasso?&division=fsd
Electrical Installation #19 .... www.cbs.state.or.us/external/imd/database/bcd/licensing/index.html
Fertilizer/Mineral/Lime Registrants #24 .... www.oda.state.or.us/dbs/search.lasso
Florist #25 .... www.oda.state.or.us/dbs/licenses/search.lasso?&division=nursery
Food Establishment, Retail #23 .... www.oda.state.or.us/dbs/licenses/search.lasso?&division=fsd
Food Exporter #23 .... www.oda.state.or.us/dbs/licenses/search.lasso?&division=fsd
Food Processing Facility #23 .... www.oda.state.or.us/dbs/licenses/search.lasso?&division=fsd
Food Producer/Distributor #23 .... www.oda.state.or.us/dbs/licenses/search.lasso?&division=fsd
Food Storage Facility #23 .... www.oda.state.or.us/dbs/licenses/search.lasso?&division=fsd
Frozen Desert Industry #23 .... www.oda.state.or.us/dbs/licenses/search.lasso?&division=fsd
Geologist #12 .... www.open.org/~osbge/registrants.htm
Geologist, Engineering #12 .... www.open.org/~osbge/registrants.htm
Greenhouse Grower of Herbaceous Plants #25 ..... www.oda.state.or.us/dbs/licenses/search.lasso?&division=nursery
Inspector #19 .... www.cbs.state.or.us/external/imd/database/bcd/licensing/index.html
Inspector, Structural/Mechanical #19 .... www.cbs.state.or.us/external/imd/database/bcd/licensing/index.html
Insurance Adjuster #26 .... www.cbs.state.or.us/external/imd/database/inslic/main.htm
Insurance Agency #26 .... www.cbs.state.or.us/external/imd/database/inslic/agency_main.htm
Insurance Agent #26 .... www.cbs.state.or.us/external/imd/database/inslic/main.htm
Insurance Company #26 .... www.cbs.state.or.us/external/imd/database/inslic/comp_main.htm
Insurance Consultant #26 .... www.cbs.state.or.us/external/imd/database/inslic/main.htm
Investment Advisor #26 .... www.cbs.state.or.us/external/imd/database/lear/adviser_search_main.htm
Landscape Business #21 .... www.ccb.state.or.us/lcbmenu.htm
Landscaper #25 .... www.oda.state.or.us/dbs/licenses/search.lasso?&division=nursery
Livestock Industry (Feedlot, Transport, etc.) #22 ... www.oda.state.or.us/dbs/licenses/search.lasso?&division=ahid
LPG Meter #20 .... www.oda.state.or.us/dbs/licenses/search.lasso?&division=msd
Manufactured Housing Construction #19 .... www.cbs.state.or.us/external/imd/database/bcd/licensing/index.html
Medical Doctor/Surgeon #29 .... www.bme.state.or.us/search.html
Milk Hauler/Milk Stabilization/Handler #23 .... www.oda.state.or.us/dbs/licenses/search.lasso?&division=fsd
Money Transmitter #26 .... www.oregondfcs.org/e_commerce/m_tran/m_tran.htm
Mortgage Banker/Broker/Lender #26 .... www.cbs.state.or.us/external/imd/database/lear/search_main.htm
Non-Alcoholic Beverage Plant #23 .... www.oda.state.or.us/dbs/licenses/search.lasso?&division=fsd
Nursery Dealer #25 .... www.oda.state.or.us/dbs/licenses/search.lasso?&division=nursery
Nursery Stock/Native Plants Collector #25 .... www.oda.state.or.us/dbs/licenses/search.lasso?&division=nursery
Occupational Therapist #36 .... www.otlb.state.or.us/licensees.htm
Occupational Therapist Assistant #36 .... www.otlb.state.or.us/licensees.htm
Optometrist #14 .... www.obo.state.or.us/doctorinfo.htm
Oregon Product #22 .... www.oda.state.or.us/dbs/oregon_products/search.lasso
Osteopathic Physician/Surgeon #29 .... www.bme.state.or.us/search.html
Pawnbroker #26 .... www.cbs.state.or.us/external/dfcs/pawn/pawnshop.htm
Pesticide Applicator/Trainee #24 .... www.oda.state.or.us/dbs/licenses/search.lasso?&division=pest

Pesticide Dealer/Company./Consultant #24 ....www.oda.state.or.us/dbs/licenses/search.lasso?&division=pest
Pesticide Product #24 ....www.oda.state.or.us/dbs/licenses/search.lasso?&division=pest
Physician Assistant #29 ....www.bme.state.or.us/search.html
Plans Examiner #19...www.cbs.state.or.us/external/imd/database/bcd/licensing/index.html
Police Chief #18...www.oregonvos.net/dpsst/downloads/misc/Address.txt
Plumber #19 ....www.cbs.state.or.us/external/imd/database/bcd/licensing/index.html
Podiatrist #29...www.bme.state.or.us/search.html
Psychologist #16..www.obpe.state.or.us/licensee_applicant.htm
Psychologist Associate #16 ....www.obpe.state.or.us/licensee_applicant.htm
Public Accountant-CPA #5..www.boa.state.or.us/search.htm
Pump Installation Contractor (Limited) #21 ....www.cbs.state.or.us/external/imd/database/bcd/licensing/index.html
Real Estate Appraiser #4 ....http://oregonaclb.org/app_search.lasso
Refrigerated Plant #23 ....www.oda.state.or.us/dbs/licenses/search.lasso?&division=fsd
Scales/Weigher #20..www.oda.state.or.us/dbs/licenses/search.lasso?&division=msd
Shellfish Industries #23 ....www.oda.state.or.us/dbs/licenses/search.lasso?&division=fsd
Sign Contractor (Limited) #21 ....www.cbs.state.or.us/external/imd/database/bcd/licensing/index.html
Slaughterhouse #23..www.oda.state.or.us/dbs/licenses/search.lasso?&division=fsd
Speech Language Pathologist #58 ....http://bspa.ohd.hr.state.or.us
Teacher #53 ....www.tspc.state.or.us/lookup_query.asp
Trust Company #26..www.cbs.state.or.us/external/dfcs/banking/regagent.htm
Veterinary Clinic, Livestock #22.............................www.oda.state.or.us/dbs/clinics/search.lasso
Veterinary Product, Livestock #22 ....www.oda.state.or.us/dbs/licenses/search.lasso?&division=vet_products

Licensing Quick Finder

Acupuncturist #29 503-229-5770
Aircraft Registration #3 503-378-4880
Airport/Aircraft Landing Area #3 503-378-4880
Amusement Ride Inspector #19..............503-378-4133
Animal Euthanasia Technician #54 503-731-4051
Animal Feed (Livestock) #22.................503-986-4691
Animal Food Processor #22 503-986-4680
Animal Health Technician #54...............503-731-4051
Architect #6...503-378-4270
Architectural Firm #6 503-378-4270
Athletic Trainer #57.............................503-378-8667
Attorney #43..503-620-0222
Audiologist #58 503-731-4050
Auditor, Municipal #5...........................503-378-4181
Bakery #23..503-986-4720
Bank #26...503-378-4387
Barber #7 503-378-8667
Body Piercer #57 503-378-8667
Boilermaker #19..................................503-373-1268
Boxer #44 503-378-8739
Brand (Livestock - Available) #22.....503-986-4681
Brand Inspector #22 503-986-4681
Brewery #41...503-872-5124
Building Official #19.............................503-373-1248
Cemetery #52 ....503-731-4040 x26
Check & Money Order Seller #26........503-378-4387
Chiropractor/Chiropractic Assistant #8..503-378-5816
Christmas Tree Grower #25 503-986-4644
Collection Agency #26.........................503-378-4387
Construction Contractor/Subcontractor #21
....503-378-4621 x4900
Consumer Finance Company #26........503-378-4387
Corrections Officer #18........................503-378-2100
Cosmetologist #57...............................503-378-8667
Counselor (Marriage & Family) #28 ...503-378-5499
Court Reporter #59..............................503-986-5500
Credit Service Organization #26 503-378-4387
Credit Union #26.................................503-378-4387
Crematorium #52.....................503-731-4040 x26
Dairy Industries #23............................503-986-4720
Debt Consolidation Agency #26 503-378-4387
Dental Hygienist #55...........................503-229-5520
Dental Specialist #55...........................503-229-5520
Dentist #55...503-229-5520
Denture Technologist #57....................503-378-8667
Denturist #9 503-378-8667

Diagnostic Radiologic Technologist #39
....503-731-4088
Diagnostic/Therapeutic Technologist #39
....503-731-4088
Dietitian #11..503-731-4085
Dog Racing #42...................................503-731-4052
Drug Manufacturer/Wholesaler #15 503-731-4032
Drug Outlet, Over-the-Counter #15......503-731-4032
Egg Handler/Breaker #23.....................503-986-4720
Electrical Installation #19.....................503-373-1268
Electrician #19.....................................503-373-1268
Electrologist #7...................................503-378-8667
Electrologist #57.................................503-378-8667
Electrology Facility #1 503-378-8667
Electrology Instructor/School #1 503-378-8667
Embalmer/Embalmer Apprentice #52
....503-731-4040 x26
EMD #18...503-378-2100
Engineer #10.......................................503-362-2666
Escrow Agent/Agency #46 503-378-4170
Facial Technician/Technologist #57.....503-378-8667
Farm Labor Contractor #21 503-731-4200
Firefighter #18 503-378-2100
Florist #25...503-986-4644
Food Establishment, Retail #23 503-986-4720
Food Exporter #23...............................503-986-4720
Food Processing Facility #23 503-986-4720
Food Producer/Distributor #23 503-986-4720
Food Storage Facility #23 503-986-4720
Forest Labor Contractor #21 503-731-4200
Frozen Desert Industry #23.................503-986-4720
Funeral Establishment #52............503-731-4040 x26
Funeral Preneed Salesperson #52 503-731-4040 x26
Funeral Service Practitioner/Apprentice #52
....503-731-4040 x26
Geologist #12 503-566-2837
Geologist, Engineering #12 503-566-2837
Greenhouse Grower of Herbaceous Plants #25
....503-986-4644
Hair Salon #7 503-378-8667
Hair Stylist (Designer) #57 503-378-8667
Hairdresser #7....................................503-378-8667
Hearing Aid Dealer/Dispenser #2........503-378-8667
Heliport #3 503-378-4880
Home Inspector #21 ....503-378-4621 x4900
Horse Racing #42................................503-731-4052

Immediate Disposition Company #52 .. 503-731-4040
x26
Inspector #19.......................................503-373-1248
Inspector, Structural/Mechanical #19... 503-373-1248
Insurance Adjuster #26 503-378-4387
Insurance Agency #26 503-378-4387
Insurance Agent #26 503-378-4387
Insurance Company #26 503-378-4387
Insurance Consultant #26 503-378-4387
Interpreter, Legal #59 503-986-5695
Investment Advisor #26.......................503-378-4140
Landscape Architect #50.....................503-589-0093
Landscape Business #21 503-378-4621
Landscaper #25...................................503-986-4644
Liquor Control #41...............................503-872-5000
Liquor Salesman/Agent #41.................503-872-5123
Liquor, Wide Shipper #41.....................503-872-5124
Livestock Industry (Feedlot, Transport, etc.) #22
....503-986-4680
Lobbyist #40..503-378-5105
LPG Meter #20....................................503-986-4670
Manicurist/Nail Technician #7 503-378-8667
Manufactured Housing Construction #19
....503-373-1248
Marriage & Family Therapist #28.........503-378-5499
Massage Therapist #38........................503-365-8657
Medical Doctor/Surgeon #29...............503-229-5770
Medical Examiner #51..........................503-280-6061
Midwife #57 503-378-8667
Milk Hauler/Milk Stabilization/Handler #23
....503-986-4720
Money Transmitter #26 503-378-4387
Mortgage Banker/Broker/Lender #26... 503-378-4387
Nail Technician #57 503-378-8667
Naturopathic Physician #34 503-731-4045
Non-Alcoholic Beverage Plant #23 503-986-4720
Notary Public #37................................503-986-2593
Nurse #13..503-731-3459
Nurse-LPN #13....................................503-731-3459
Nursery Dealer #25 503-986-4644
Nursery Stock/Native Plants Collector #25
....503-986-4644
Nursing Assistant #13 503-731-3459
Nursing Home Administrator #35.........503-731-4046
Occupational Therapist #36.................503-731-4048
Occupational Therapist Assistant #36 . 503-731-4048
Optometrist #14...................................503-373-7721

Oral Pathology Endorsement #9	503-378-8667
Oregon Product #22	503-986-4680
Osteopathic Physician/Surgeon #29	503-229-5770
Parole/Probation Officer #18	503-378-2100
Pawnbroker #26	503-378-4387
Permanent Color Technician #57	503-378-8667
Pharmacist #15	503-731-4032
Pharmacy #15	503-731-4032
Physical Therapist/Assistant #45	503-731-4047
Physician Assistant #30	503-229-5770
Physician Assistant #29	503-229-5770
Pilot #3	503-378-4880
Plans Examiner #19	503-373-1248
Plumber #19	503-373-7479
Podiatrist #31	502-229-5770
Podiatrist #29	503-229-5770
Police Chief #18	503-378-2100
Police Officer #18	503-378-2100
Polygraph Examiner #18	503-378-2100
Private Security Officer #18	503-378-2100
Property Manager #46	503-378-4170
Psychologist #16	503-378-4154
Psychologist Associate #16	503-378-4154
Public Accountant-CPA #5	503-378-4181
Pump Installation Contractor (Limited) #21	503-731-4072
Radiologic Technologist Limited Permit #39	503-731-4088
Radiologic Therapy Technologist #39	503-731-4088
Real Estate Appraiser #4	503-373-1505
Real Estate Branch Office #46	503-378-4170
Real Estate Broker #46	503-378-4170
Real Estate Salesperson #46	503-378-4170
Refrigerated Plant #23	503-986-4720
Respiratory Care Practitioner #32	503-378-8667x4330
Respiratory Care Therapist #57	503-378-8667
Sanitarian #47	503-378-8667
Sanitarian/Sanitarian Trainee #57	503-378-8667
Savings & Loan Association #26	503-378-4387
Scales/Weigher #20	503-986-4670
School Counselor/Supervisor #53	503-378-6813
School Superintendent/Admin. #53	503-378-6813
Securities Broker/Dealer #26	503-378-4140
Securities Salesperson #26	503-378-4387
Shellfish Industries #23	503-986-4720
Sign Contractor (Limited) #21	503-731-4072
Slaughterhouse #23	503-986-4720
Social Worker, Clinical #48	503-378-5735
Special Qualifications Corporation #26	503-378-4387
Speech Language Pathologist #58	503-731-4050
Surveyor, Land #10	503-362-2666
Tattoo Artist #57	503-378-8667
Tax Consultant/Preparer #17	503-378-4034
Teacher #53	503-378-6813
Telecommunicator #18	503-378-2100
Travel Agent #26	503-378-4387
Trust Company #26	503-378-4387
Veterinarian #54	503-731-4051
Veterinary Clinic, Livestock #22	503-986-4680
Veterinary Product, Livestock #22	503-986-4680
Veterinary Technician #54	503-731-4051
Waste Water Treatment System Operator #61	503-229-5622
Water Rights Examiner #10	503-362-2666
Water Well Constructor #60	503-378-8455
Winery #41	503-872-5124
Wrestler #44	503-378-8739

Licensing Agency Information

#2 Advisory Council on Hearing Aids, 700 Summer St, #320, Salem, OR 97301-1287; 503-378-8667, Fax: 503-585-9114.
www.hdlp.hr.state.or.us/hdhome.htm
Agency email: hdlp.mail@state.or.us.

#3 Department of Aviation, Aeronautics Section, 3040 25th S SE, Salem, OR 97310; 503-378-4880, Fax: 503-373-1688.
www.aviation.state.or.us

#4 Appraiser Certification & Licensure Board, 1860 Hawthorne Avenue NE #200, Salem, OR 97303; 503-485-2555, Fax: 503-485-2559.
http://oregonaclb.org
Agency email: jan@oregonaclb.org.
Search database at
http://oregonaclb.org/app_search.lasso

#5 Board of Accountancy, 3218 Pringle Rd SE, #110, Salem, OR 97302-6307; 503-378-4181, Fax: 503-378-3575.
www.boa.state.or.us/boa.html
Agency email: carol.halford@state.or.us.

#6 Board of Architect Examiners, 750 Front St NE #260, Salem, OR 97301; 503-378-4270, Fax: 503-378-6091.
www.architect-board.state.or.us
Agency email: architect.board@state.or.us.
Search database at www.architect-board.state.or.us

#7 Board of Barbers & Hairdressers, 700 Summer St NE #320, Salem, OR 97301-1287; 503-378-8667, Fax: 503-585-9004.
www.hdlp.hr.state.or.us/bhhome.htm
Agency email: hdlp.mail@state.or.us.

#8 Board of Chiropractic Examiners, 3218 Pringle Rd SE, #150, Salem, OR 97302-6311; 503-378-5816, Fax: 503-362-1260.
www.obce.state.or.us
Agency email: jill.bauer@state.or.us.

#9 Board of Denture Technology, 700 Summer St, #320, Salem, OR 97301-1287; 503-378-8667, Fax: 503-585-9114.
www.hdlp.hr.state.or.us/dthome.htm. Agency email: hdlp.mail@state.or.us.

#10 Board of Examiners for Engineer & Land Surveyors, 728 Hawthorne Ave NE, Salem, OR 97301; 503-362-2666, Fax: 503-362-5454.
www.osbeels.org. Agency email: osbeels@osbeels.org.
Search database at www.osbeels.org

#11 Board of Examiners of Licensed Dieticians, 800 NE Oregon, #407, Portland, OR 97232; 503-731-4085, Fax: 503-731-4207.
www.bld.state.or.us
Agency email: ann.aaluna@state.or.us.

#12 Board of Geologist Examiners, 707 13th St SE #275, Salem, OR 97301; 503-566-2837, Fax: 503-362-6393.
www.osbge.org. Agency email: osbge@open.org.
Search database at
www.open.org/~osbge/registrants.htm

#13 Board of Nursing, 800 NE Oregon St, #465, Portland, OR 97232-2162; 503-731-4745, Fax: 503-731-4755.
www.osbn.state.or.us
Agency email: oregon.bn.info@state.or.us.

#14 Board of Optometry, 3218 Pringle Rd SE, #270, Salem, OR 97310-6306; 503-373-7721, Fax: 503-378-3616.
www.obo.state.or.us
Agency email: david.plunkett@state.or.us.
Search database at
www.obo.state.or.us/doctorinfo.htm

#15 Board of Pharmacy, 800 NE Oregon St, State Office Bldg, #9, Rm 425, Portland, OR 97232; 503-731-4032, Fax: 503-731-4067.
www.pharmacy.state.or.us
Agency email: pharmacy.board@state.or.us.

#16 Board of Psychologist Examiners, 3218 Pringle Road, #130, Salem, OR 97301-6309; 503-378-4154, Fax: 503-378-3575.
www.obpe.state.or.us
Search database at
www.obpe.state.or.us/licensee_applicant.htm

#17 Board of Tax Service Examiners, 3218 Pringle Road, #120, Salem, OR 97302; 503-378-4034, Fax: 503-378-3575.
www.open.org/~ortaxbrd
Agency email: tax.bd@state.or.us.

#18 Department of Public Safety Standards & Training, 550 N Monmouth Ave, Monmouth, OR 97361; 503-378-2100, Fax: 503-838-8907.
www.OregonVOS.net/dpsst
Agency email: Rance.Downer@state.or.us.

#19 Department of Consumer & Business Svcs, Building Codes Division, PO Box 14470, Salem, OR 97309-0404; 503-378-4133, Fax: 503-378-2322.
www.oregonbcd.org
Agency email: bcd.webmaster@state.or.us.
Search database at
www.cbs.state.or.us/external/imd/database/bcd/licensing/index.html

#20 Department of Agriculture, Measurements Standards Division, 635 Capitol St NE, Salem, OR 97310-0110; 503-986-4670, Fax: 503-986-4784.
www.oda.state.or.us/Measurement_Standards/MSDINFO.html
Agency email: pestx@oda.state.or.us.
Search database at www.oda.state.or.us/dbs/licenses/search.lasso?&division=msd

#21 Construction & Landscape Contractors Boards, 700 Summer St NE #300, Salem, OR 97309-5052; 503-378-4621 x4900, Fax: 503-373-2007. www.ccb.state.or.us. Agency email: ccbinfo@ccb.state.or.us. 24-hour Contractor Inquiry Line - 503-378-4610 or 888-366-5635.

#22 Department of Agriculture, Animal Health & Identification Division (State Vet.), 635 Capitol St NE, Salem, OR 97310-0110; 503-986-4680, Fax: 503-986-4734.
www.oda.state.or.us/Livestock_Health_ID/ahid_home.html. Agency email: csorrels@oda.state.or.us.
Search database at www.oda.state.or.us/cgi/fm/animal_health/Search.html

#23 Department of Agriculture, Food Safety Division, 635 Capitol St NE, Salem, OR 97301; 503-986-4720, Fax: 503-986-4729.
www.oda.state.or.us/Food_Safety/FSDINFO.html.
Agency email: rmckay@oda.state.or.us.
Search database at
www.oda.state.or.us/dbs/licenses/search.lasso?&division=fsd. Updated weekly. Mailing labels available (database formatted ASCII files)

#24 Department of Agriculture, Pesticides Division, 635 Capitol St NE, Salem, OR 97310-0110; 503-986-4635, Fax: 503-986-4735. www.oda.state.or.us/pesticide. Agency email: pestx@oda.state.or.us.
Search database at www.oda.state.or.us/pest/license/search.lasso

#25 Department of Agriculture, Plant Division, 635 Capitol St NE, Salem, OR 97310-0110; 503-986-4644, Fax: 503-986-4786.
www.oda.state.or.us
Search database at www.oda.state.or.us/dbs/licenses/search.lasso?&division=nursery

#26 Department of Consumer & Business Svcs, Division of Finance and Corporate Securities, 350 Winter St, Labor & Industries Bldg, Rm 410, Salem, OR 97301-3881; 503-378-4140, Fax: 503-947-7862.
www.oregondfcs.org
Search database at www.oregondfcs.org

#28 Licensed Professional Counselors & Therapists, 3218 Pringle Rd SE, #160, Salem, OR 97302-6312; 503-378-5499.
www.oblpct.state.or.us
Agency email: lpc.lmft@state.or.us.

#29 Board of Medical Examiners, 1500 SW 1st Ave #620, Portland, OR 97201; 503-229-5770, Fax: 503-229-6543.
www.bme.state.or.us/welcome.html
Agency email: bme.info@state.or.us.
Search database at www.bme.state.or.us/search.html

#32 Respiratory Therapist Licensing Board, 700 Summer St NE #320, Salem, OR 97310; 503-378-8667 x4330, Fax: 503-229-6543.
www.hdlp.hr.state.or.us/rthome.htm
Agency email: hdlp.mail@state.or.us.

#34 Naturopathic Board of Examiners, 800 NE Oregon, #407, Portland, OR 97232; 503-731-4045, Fax: 503-731-4207.
www.state.or.us/agencies.ns/83300/00060/index.html. Agency email: obne.info@state.or.us.

#35 Nursing Home Board, 800 NE Oregon, #407, Portland, OR 97232; 503-731-4046, Fax: 503-731-4207.
www.state.or.us/agencies.ns
Agency email: Barbara.Orazio@state.or.us.

#36 Occupational Therapy Licensing, 800 NE Oregon, #407, Portland, OR 97232; 503-731-4048, Fax: 503-731-4207.
www.otlb.state.or.us
Agency email: otlb.info@state.or.us.
Search database at www.otlb.state.or.us/licensees.htm

#37 Office of Secretary of State, 255 Capitol St NE, #151, Salem, OR 97310; 503-986-2593, Fax: 503-986-2300.
www.filinginoregon.com/notary/index.htm.
Agency email: oregon.notary@state.or.us.

#38 Board of Massage Technicians, 3218 Pringle Rd SE, #250, Salem, OR 97302; 503-365-8657, Fax: 503-385-4465.
www.oregonmassage.org
Agency email: jacqueline.mccal@state.or.us.

#39 Board of Radiologic Technology, 800 NE Oregon, #407, Portland, OR 97232; 503-731-4088, Fax: 503-731-4207.
www.obrt.state.or.us
Agency email: chris.w.stewart@state.or.us.

#40 Government Standards & Pracrices Commission, 100 High St SE, #220, Salem, OR 97310; 503-378-5105, Fax: 503-373-1456.
www.gspc.state.or.us

#41 Liquor Control Commission, 9079 SE McLoughlin Blvd, Portland, OR 97222-7355; 503-872-5000, Fax: 503-872-5018.
www.olcc.state.or.us
Agency email: Shannon.KILEY@state.or.us.

#42 Racing Commission, 800 NE Oregon, #11, Portland, OR 97232; 503-731-4052, Fax: 503-731-4053.
www.oregonvos.net/~orc
Agency email: sbarham@OregonVOS.net.

#43 State Bar Association, 5200 SW Meadows Rd, Lake Oswego, OR 97035; 503-620-0222, Fax: 503-684-1366.
www.osbar.org. Agency email: info@osbar.org.
Search database at www.osbcle.org/members/start.asp

#44 Boxing & Wrestling Commission, 3400 State St #G750, Salem, OR 97301; 503-378-8739, Fax: 503-304-9157. Agency email: jim.cassidy@state.or.us.

#45 Physical Therapist Licensing Board, 800 NE Oregon St, #407, Portland, OR 97232-2162; 503-731-4047, Fax: 503-731-4207.
www.ptboard.state.or.us
Agency email: patti.gustafson@state.or.us.

#46 Real Estate Agency, 1177 Center St NE, Salem, OR 97310-2503; 503-378-4170, Fax: 503-378-2491.
www.rea.state.or.us

#47 Sanitarians Registration Board, 700 Summer St NE, #320, Salem, OR 97301-1287; 503-378-8667, Fax: 503-585-9114.
www.hdlp.hr.state.or.us/snhome.htm
Agency email: hdlp.mail@state.or.us.

#48 Board of Clinical Social Workers, 3218 Pringle Rd SE, #240, Salem, OR 97302-6310; 503-378-5735, Fax: 503-378-3575.
http://bcsw.state.or.us. Agency email: bcsw@state.or.us.

#50 Landscape Architect Board, 1193 Royvonne Ave SE #19, Salem, OR 97302; 503-589-0093, Fax: 503-589-0545. Agency email: oslab@uswest.net.

#52 Mortuary & Cemetery Board, 800 NE Oregon, #430, Portland, OR 97232-2162; 503-731-4040 X26, Fax: 503-731-4494. Agency email: mortuary.board@state.or.us.

#53 Teacher Standards & Practices Commission, 465 Commercial St. NE, Salem, OR 97301; 503-378-6813, Fax: 503-378-4448.
www.tspc.state.or.us. Agency email: Matt.Garrett@state.or.us.
Search database at www.tspc.state.or.us/lookup_query.asp

#54 Veterinary Medical Board, 800 NE Oregon, #407, Portland, OR 97232; 503-731-4051, Fax: 503-731-4207. Agency email: ovmeb@info@state.or.us.

#55 Board of Dentistry, 1515 SW 5th #602, Portland, OR 97201; 503-229-5520, Fax: 503-229-6606.
www.oregondentistry.org
Search database at www.oregondentistry.org

#57 Health Licensing Offc, Admin Svcs Div Mgr, 700 Summer St NE #320, Salem, OR 97310-1287; 503-378-8667, Fax: 503-585-9114.
www.hlo.state.or.us
Agency email: hlo.mail@state.or.us.

#58 Board of Examiners for Speech-Language Pathology & Audiology, 800 NE Oregon St #21, State Office Bldg, Portland, OR 97232; 503-731-4050, Fax: 503-731-4207.
http://bspa.ohd.hr.state.or.us
Agency email: brenda.felber@state.or.us.

#59 Judicial Department, Office of the State Court Administrator, 1163 State St, Salem, OR 97310-0260; 503-986-5500.

#60 Department of Water Resources, 158 12th St NE, Commerce Bldg, Salem, OR 97310; 503-378-8455.

#61 Department of Environmental Quality, Operator Certification Program, Water Quality Division, 811 SW 6th Ave, Portland, OR 97204; 503-229-5696, Fax: 503-229-6037.

Oregon Federal Courts

The following list indicates the district and division name for each county in the state. If the bankruptcy court location is different from the district court, then the location of the bankruptcy court appears in parentheses.

County/Court Cross Reference

Baker	Portland	Lake	Medford (Eugene)
Benton	Eugene	Lane	Eugene
Clackamas	Portland	Lincoln	Eugene
Clatsop	Portland	Linn	Eugene
Columbia	Portland	Malheur	Portland
Coos	Eugene	Marion	Eugene
Crook	Portland	Morrow	Portland
Curry	Medford (Eugene)	Multnomah	Portland
Deschutes	Eugene (Portland)	Polk	Portland (Eugene)
Douglas	Eugene	Sherman	Portland
Gilliam	Portland	Tillamook	Portland
Grant	Portland	Umatilla	Portland
Harney	Portland	Union	Portland
Hood River	Portland	Wallowa	Portland
Jackson	Medford (Eugene)	Wasco	Portland
Jefferson	Portland	Washington	Portland
Josephine	Medford (Eugene)	Wheeler	Portland
Klamath	Medford (Eugene)	Yamhill	Portland

Standards for Federal Courts: The search fee is $20.00 per item (one party name or case number). Certification fee is $7.00 per document. Copy fee is $.50 per page. All fees standard unless noted in profile. Mail Search: always enclose a stamped self addressed envelope unless otherwise noted. Before releasing records, all courts require prepayment unless noted in profile.

Open records are located at the court unless otherwise noted. District courts index by defendant and plaintiff as well as by case number. Bankruptcy courts usually index by debtor and case number. While most courts now have their indexes on computer, many still maintain index card files as well.

The universal PACER sign-up number is 800-676-6856. Find PACER and the Party/Case Index on the Web at http://pacer.psc.uscourts.gov. PACER dial-up access is $.60 per minute. Also, courts offering internet access via RACER, PACER, Web-PACER or the new CM-ECF charge $.07 per page fee unless noted as free.

US District Court

District of Oregon

Eugene Division 100 Federal Bldg, 211 E 7th Ave, Eugene, OR 97401 (Courier Address: Use mail address for courier delivery), 541-465-6423, Fax: 541-465-6344.

www.ord.uscourts.gov

Counties: Benton, Coos, Deschutes, Douglas, Lane, Lincoln, Linn, Marion.

Indexing & Storage: Cases are indexed by defendant, plaintiff, and case number. New cases are available in the index immediately after filing date. Records are also indexed on microfiche for criminal records older than 1986. District wide searches are available from this division.

Fee & Payment Notes: Payment may be made by money order, cashier check, personal check, Visa, Mastercard. Payee: Clerk, US District Court.

Phone Search: Only docket information is available by phone.

Mail Search: A stamped self addressed envelope is not required.

In Person Search: In person searching available.

PACER: Local dial-up access: 503-326-8903. Case records are available back to September 1988. Records are never purged. New records are available online after 1 day. PACER is available online at http://pacer.ord.uscourts.gov.

Electronic Filing: Information is available online at https://ecf.ord.uscourts.gov.

Other Online Access: Logon to ECF/PACER at https://ecf.ord.uscourts.gov/cgi-bin/login.pl.

Medford Division 201 James A Redden US Courthouse, 310 W 6th St, Medford, OR 97501 (Courier Address: Use mail address for courier delivery), 541-776-3926, Fax: 541-776-3925.

www.ord.uscourts.gov

Counties: Curry, Jackson, Josephine, Klamath, Lake. Court set up in April 1994; Cases prior to that time were tried in Eugene.

Indexing & Storage: Cases are indexed by defendant, plaintiff, and case number. New cases are available in the index 1 day after filing date. Open records are located at this court.

Fee & Payment Notes: Payment may be made by money order, cashier check, personal check, Visa, Mastercard. Payee: Clerk, USDC.

Phone Search: Only docket information is available by phone.

Fax Search: Will accept fax search request with $15.00 fee. Will fax docket listings at no extra charge.

Mail Search: A stamped self addressed envelope is not required.

In Person Search: In person searching available.

PACER: Local dial-up access: 503-326-8903. Case records are available back to September 1988. Records are never purged. New records are available online after 1 day. PACER is available online at http://pacer.ord.uscourts.gov.

Electronic Filing: Information is available online at https://ecf.ord.uscourts.gov

Other Online Access: Logon to ECF/PACER at https://ecf.ord.uscourts.gov/cgi-bin/login.pl.

Portland Division Clerk, 740 US Courthouse, 1000 SW 3rd Ave, Portland, OR 97204-2902 (Courier Address: Use mail address for courier delivery), 503-326-8000, Fax: 503-326-8010.

www.ord.uscourts.gov

Counties: Baker, Clackamas, Clatsop, Columbia, Crook, Gilliam, Grant, Harney, Hood River, Jefferson, Malheur, Morrow, Multnomah, Polk, Sherman, Tillamook, Umatilla, Union, Wallowa, Wasco, Washinton, Wheeler, Yamhill.

Indexing & Storage: Cases are indexed by defendant, plaintiff, and case number. New cases are available in the index 24 hours after filing date. Records are also indexed on microfiche. District wide searches are available from this court. All civil cases after 8/88 and all criminal cases after 3/91 are maintained in this division for the other divisions.

Fee & Payment Notes: Payment may be made by money order, cashier check, personal check. Payee: Clerk, USDC. You are allowed to make your own copies. These copies cost $.15 per page.

Phone Search: If the case number is known, docket information will be released over the phone.

Fax Search: Will accept fax to determine fee for a search.

Mail Search: A stamped self addressed envelope is not required.

In Person Search: In person searching available.

PACER: Local dial-up access: 503-326-8903. Case records are available back to September 1988. Records are never purged. New records are available online after 1 day. PACER is available online at http://pacer.ord.uscourts.gov.

Electronic Filing: Information is available online at https://ecf.ord.uscourts.gov

Other Online Access: Logon to ECF/PACER at https://ecf.ord.uscourts.gov/cgi-bin/login.pl.

US Bankruptcy Court

District of Oregon

Eugene Division PO Box 1335, Eugene, OR 97440 (Courier Address: 151 W 7th St, #300, Eugene, OR 97401), 541-465-6448.

www.orb.uscourts.gov

Counties: Benton, Coos, Curry, Deschutes, Douglas, Jackson, Josephine, Klamath, Lake, Lane, Lincoln, Linn, Marion.

Indexing & Storage: Cases are indexed by debtor as well as by case number. New cases are available in the index 1 day after filing date. Open records are located at this court.

Fee & Payment Notes: Payment may be made by money order, cashier check, personal check. Payee: Clerk, US Bankruptcy Court. You are allowed to make your own copies. These copies cost $.15 per page.

Phone Search: Only docket information available by telephone. An automated voice case information service (VCIS) is available. Call VCIS at 800-726-2227 or 503-326-2249.

Mail Search: A stamped self addressed envelope is not required.

In Person Search: In person searching available.

PACER: Toll-free dial-up access: 800-610-9315. Local dial-up access: 503-326-5650. Case records are available back to 1989. Records are purged every six months. New civil records are available online after 1 day. PACER is available online at http://pacer.orb.uscourts.gov.

Electronic Filing: (Currently in the process of implementing CM/ECF.)

Portland Division %%OR601%%, 1001 SW 5th Ave, #700, Portland, OR 97204 (Courier Address: Use mail address for courier delivery), 503-326-2231.

www.orb.uscourts.gov

Counties: Baker, Clackamas, Clatsop, Columbia, Crook, Gilliam, Grant, Harney, Hood River, Jefferson, Malheur, Morrow, Multnomah, Polk, Sherman, Tillamook, Umatilla, Union, Wallowa, Wasco, Washington, Wheeler, Yamhill.

Indexing & Storage: Cases are indexed by debtor as well as by case number. New cases are available in the index 1 day after filing date. Open records are located at this court.

Fee & Payment Notes: Payment may be made by money order, cashier check, personal check. Payee: Clerk, US Bankruptcy Court. You are allowed to make your own copies. These copies cost $.15 per page.

Phone Search: Only docket information is available by phone. An automated voice case information service (VCIS) is available. Call VCIS at 800-726-2227 or 503-326-2249.

In Person Search: In person searching available.

PACER: Toll-free dial-up access: 800-610-9315. Local dial-up access: 503-326-5650. Case records are available back to 1989. Records are purged every six months. New civil records are available online after 1 day. PACER is available online at http://pacer.orb.uscourts.gov.

Electronic Filing: (Currently in the process of implementing CM/ECF.)

Oregon County Courts

Court	Jurisdiction	No. of Courts	How Organized
Circuit Courts*	General	38	27 Districts
County Courts*	Probate	6	6 Counties
Justice Courts	Municipal	35	
Municipal Courts	Municipal	112	
Tax Court	Special	1	

* Profiled in this Sourcebook.

Court	CIVIL								
	Tort	Contract	Real Estate	Min. Claim	Max. Claim	Small Claims	Estate	Eviction	Domestic Relations
Circuit Courts*	X	X	X	$0	No Max	$2500	X	X	X
County Courts*							X		X
Justice Courts	X	X	X	$200	$2500	$2500			
Municipal Courts									
Tax Court									

Court	CRIMINAL				
	Felony	Misdemeanor	DWI/DUI	Preliminary Hearing	Juvenile
Circuit Courts*	X	X	X	X	X
County Courts*					X
Justice Courts		X	X	X	
Municipal Courts		X	X		
Tax Court					

ADMINISTRATION
Court Administrator, Supreme Court Building, 1163 State St, Salem, OR, 97310; 503-986-5500, Fax: 503-986-5503. www.ojd.state.or.us

COURT STRUCTURE
Effective January 15, 1998, the District and Circuit Courts were combined into "Circuit Courts." At the same time, 3 new judicial districts were created by splitting existing ones.

ONLINE ACCESS
Online computer access is available through the Oregon Judicial Information Network (OJIN). OJIN Online includes almost all cases filed in the Oregon state courts. Generally, the OJIN database contains criminal, civil, small claims, probate, and some but not all juvenile records. However, it does not contain any records from municipal nor county courts. There is a one-time setup fee of $295.00, plus a monthly usage charge (minimum $10.00) based on transaction type, type of job, shift, and number of units/pages (which averages $10-13 per hour). For further information and/or a registration packet, write to: Oregon Judicial System, Information Systems Division, ATTN: Technical Support, 1163 State Street, Salem OR 97310, or call 800-858-9658, or visit www.ojd.state.or.us/ojin

ADDITIONAL INFORMATION
Many Oregon courts indicated that in person searches would markedly improve request turnaround time as court offices are understaffed or spread very thin. Most Circuit Courts that have records on computer do have a public access terminal that will speed up in-person or retriever searches. Most records offices close from Noon to 1PM Oregon time for lunch. No staff is available during that period.

PROBATE COURTS
Probate is handled by the Circuit Court except in 6 counties (Gilliam, Grant, Harney, Malheur, Sherman, and Wheeler) where Probate in handled by County Courts.

Baker County

Circuit Court 1995 3rd St, #220, Baker City, OR 97814; 541-523-6305; Fax: 541-523-9738. Hours: 8AM-Noon, 1-4PM (PST). *Felony, Misdemeanor, Civil, Probate.*

www.ojd.state.or.us/baker

Civil Records: Access: Phone, fax, mail, in person. Both court and visitors may perform in person searches. No search fee. Required to search: name, years to search. Civil cases indexed by defendant, plaintiff. Civil records on computer from 1987, archives back to 1865. Index available remotely online on the statewide OJIN system, call 800-858-9658 for information.

Criminal Records: Access: Phone, fax, mail, in person. Both court and visitors may perform in person searches. No search fee. Required to search: name, years to search. Criminal records on computer from 1987, archives back to 1865. Online access to criminal records is the same as civil.

General Information: Public access terminal is available. No adoption, mental, juvenile or sealed records released. SASE required. Turnaround time 10 days. Fax notes: Fee to fax results is $5.00 minimum per document. Copy fee: $.25 per page. Certification fee: $5.00. Fee payee: State of Oregon. Personal checks accepted. Prepayment is required.

Benton County

Circuit Court Box 1870 (120 NW Fourth Street), Corvallis, OR 97339; 541-766-6828; Fax: 541-766-6028. Hours: 8AM-5PM (PST). *Felony, Misdemeanor, Civil, Eviction, Small Claims, Probate.*

www.ojd.state.or.us/benton

Civil Records: Access: Phone, mail, online, in person. Both court and visitors may perform in person searches. No search fee. Required to search: name, years to search; also helpful: address. Civil cases indexed by defendant, plaintiff. Civil records on computer from 1987, archives back to the 1900s. Index available remotely online on the statewide OJIN system, call 800-858-9658 for information.

Criminal Records: Access: Phone, mail, online, in person. Both court and visitors may perform in person searches. No search fee. Required to search: name, years to search, DOB, offense; also helpful: address, SSN. Criminal records on computer from 1987, archives back to the 1900s. Online access to criminal records is the same as civil.

General Information: Public access terminal is available. No adoption, juvenile, sealed by judge, expunged, mental health records released. SASE not required. Turnaround time up to 1 week. Copy fee: $.25 per page. Certification fee: $5.00. Fee payee: State of Oregon. Personal checks accepted. Prepayment is required.

Clackamas County

Circuit Court 807 Main St, Oregon City, OR 97045; 503-655-8447. Hours: 10AM-5PM M-TH (PST). *Felony, Misdemeanor, Civil, Eviction, Small Claims, Probate.*

Civil Records: Access: Mail, online, in person. Both court and visitors may perform in person searches. No search fee. Required to search: name, years to search. Civil cases indexed by defendant, plaintiff. Civil records on computer from 1986, index back to 1980. Index available remotely online on the statewide OJIN system, call 800-858-9658 for information.

Criminal Records: Access: Mail, online, in person. Both court and visitors may perform in person searches. No search fee. Required to search: name, years to search, DOB. Criminal records on computer from 1986, index back to 1980. Online access to criminal records is the same as civil.

General Information: Public access terminal is available. No adoption, juvenile, sealed by judge, expunged, mental health records released. SASE required. Turnaround time 4-6 weeks. Copy fee: $.25 per page. Certification fee: $5.00. Fee payee: State of Oregon. Personal checks accepted. Credit cards accepted: Visa, MasterCard. Prepayment is required.

Clatsop County

Circuit Court Box 835, Astoria, OR 97103; 503-325-8583; Fax: 503-325-9300. 8AM-Noon, 1-5PM (PST). *Felony, Civil Actions Over $10,000, Probate.*

Civil Records: Access: Phone, mail, online, in person. Both court and visitors may perform in person searches. No search fee. Required to search: name, years to search. Civil cases indexed by defendant, plaintiff. Civil records on computer from 1986, archives back to 1900. Index available remotely online on the statewide OJIN system, call 800-858-9658 for information.

Criminal Records: Access: Phone, mail, online, in person. Both court and visitors may perform in person searches. No search fee. Required to search: name, years to search, DOB. Criminal records on computer from 1987, archives back to 1900. Online access to criminal records is the same as civil.

General Information: Public access terminal is available. No adoption, juvenile, sealed by judge, expunged, paternity or mental health records released. SASE required. Turnaround time 1 week. Copy fee: $.25 per page. Certification fee: $5.00. Fee payee: Clatsop County Circuit Court. Personal checks accepted. Prepayment is required.

Circuit Court Box 659, Astoria, OR 97103; 503-325-8536; Fax: 503-325-9300. Hours: 8AM-5PM (PST). *Misdemeanor.*

Criminal Records: Access: Phone, mail, online, in person. Both court and visitors may perform in person searches. No search fee. Required to search: name, years to search, DOB. Criminal records on computer back to 1987, archives back to 1900. Online access to criminal records is the same as civil.

General Information: Public access terminal is available. No adoptions, juvenile, sealed by Judge, expunged, paternity or mental health records released. SASE required. Turnaround time 3-5 days. Copy fee: $.25 per page. Certification fee: $5.00. Fee payee: Circuit Court. Personal checks accepted. Prepayment is required.

Columbia County

Circuit Court Columbia County Courthouse, 244 Strand St, St. Helens, OR 97051; 503-397-2327; Fax: 503-397-3226. Hours: 8:30AM-5PM (PST). *Felony, Misdemeanor, Civil, Eviction, Small Claims, Probate.*

Civil Records: Access: Mail, fax, online, in person. Both court and visitors may perform in person searches. No search fee. Required to search: name, years to search; also helpful: address. Civil cases indexed by defendant, plaintiff. Civil records on computer from September, 1987, archives back to 1900. Index available remotely online on the statewide OJIN system, call 800-858-9658 for information.

Criminal Records: Access: Mail, fax, online, in person. Both court and visitors may perform in person searches. No search fee. Required to search: name, years to search, DOB; also helpful: address, SSN, signed release. Criminal records on computer from September, 1987, archives back to 1900. Online access to criminal records is the same as civil.

General Information: Public access terminal is available. No adoptions, juvenile, sealed by Judge, expunged, mental health records released. SASE required. Turnaround time 4-5 days. Copy fee: $.25 per page. Certification fee: $5.00. Fee payee: State of

Oregon. Personal checks accepted. Prepayment is required.

Coos County

Circuit Court Courthouse, Coquille, OR 97423; 541-396-3121; Civil phone: X343; Criminal phone: X251; Fax: 541-396-3456. Hours: 8AM-Noon,1-5PM (PST). *Felony, Misdemeanor, Civil, Eviction, Small Claims, Probate.*

http://cooscurrycourts.org

Note: Eviction, Small Claims and Probate records are available at 541-756-2020 ext556. Circuit Court Annex at 1975 McPherson, Noth Bend oR 97459.

Civil Records: Access: Phone, mail, online, in person. Both court and visitors may perform in person searches. No search fee. Required to search: name, years to search; also helpful: address. Civil cases indexed by defendant, plaintiff. Civil records on computer from 1987, archives back to 1800. Index available remotely online on the statewide OJIN system, call 800-858-9658 for information.

Criminal Records: Access: Phone, mail, online, in person. Both court and visitors may perform in person searches. No search fee. Required to search: name, years to search, DOB; also helpful: address, SSN. Criminal records on computer from 1987, archives back to 1800. Online access to criminal records is the same as civil.

General Information: Public access terminal is available. No adoptions, sealed by Judge, expunged, paternity or mental health records released. SASE required. Turnaround time 1-2 days. Copy fee: $.25 per page. Certification fee: $5.00. Fee payee: State Courts. Personal checks accepted. Credit cards accepted: Visa, MasterCard. Visa, MC. Not accepted for filing fees. Prepayment is required.

Crook County

Circuit Court Crook County Courthouse, 300 NE Third St, Prineville, OR 97754; 541-447-6541. Hours: 8AM-5PM (PST). *Felony, Misdemeanor, Civil, Eviction, Small Claims, Probate.*

Civil Records: Access: Phone, mail, in person, online. Both court and visitors may perform in person searches. No search fee. Required to search: name, years to search; also helpful: address. Civil cases indexed by defendant, plaintiff. Civil records on computer from 1986, microfiche from 1907, archives from 1907. Index available remotely online on the statewide OJIN system, call 800-858-9658 for information.

Criminal Records: Access: Phone, mail, in person, online. Both court and visitors may perform in person searches. No search fee. Required to search: name, years to search, DOB; also helpful: address, SSN. Criminal records on computer from 1986, microfiche from 1907, archives from 1907. Online access to criminal records is the same as civil.

General Information: No adoptions, juvenile, sealed by Judge, expunged, paternity or mental health records released. SASE required. Turnaround time 2-4 days. Copy fee: $.25 per page. Certification fee: $5.00. Fee payee: State of Oregon. Personal checks accepted. Prepayment is required.

Curry County

Circuit Court Box 810, Gold Beach, OR 97444; 541-247-4511. Hours: 8AM-5PM M; 8AM-3:30PM T-F (PST). *Felony, Misdemeanor, Civil, Eviction, Small Claims, Probate.*

www.cooscurrycourts.org

Civil Records: Access: Phone, mail, online, in person. Both court and visitors may perform in person searches. No search fee. Required to search: name, years to search; also helpful: address. Civil cases indexed by defendant, plaintiff. Civil records on computer from

1987, archives back to 1891. Index available remotely online on the statewide OJIN system, call 800-858-9658 for information.

Criminal Records: Access: Phone, mail, online, in person. Both court and visitors may perform in person searches. No search fee. Required to search: name, years to search, DOB; also helpful: address, SSN. Criminal records on computer from 1987, archives back to 1891. Online access to criminal records is the same as civil.

General Information: Public access terminal is available. No adoptions, sealed by Judge, expunged, paternity or mental health records released. SASE required. Turnaround time 1-2 days from receipt of payment. Copy fee: $.25 per page. Add postage if SASE not enclosed. Certification fee: $5.00 for 1st page and $.25 for each add'l page. Fee payee: State Courts. Personal checks accepted. Credit card accepted: Visa, MC. Prepayment is required.

Deschutes County

Deschutes County Courts 1100 NW Bond, Bend, OR 97701; 541-388-5300. Hours: 8AM-5PM (PST). *Felony, Misdemeanor, Civil, Eviction, Small Claims, Probate.*

www.deschutescircuitcourt.org

Civil Records: Access: Phone, mail, online, in person. Both court and visitors may perform in person searches. No search fee. Required to search: name, years to search. Civil cases indexed by defendant, plaintiff. Civil records on computer from 9/87, books from 1976, archived from 1916 on microfiche. Index available remotely online on the statewide OJIN system, call 800-858-9658 for information. Also, current calendars are available free at www.ojd.state.or.us/des/calendar.nsf/

Criminal Records: Access: Phone, mail, online, in person. Both court and visitors may perform in person searches. No search fee. Required to search: name, years to search, SSN. Criminal records on computer from 9/87, books from 1976, archived from 1916 on microfiche. Criminal Index available remotely online on the statewide OJIN system, call 800-858-9658. Records from 07/86 forward. Also, current calendars are available free at www.ojd.state.or.us/des/calendar.nsf/

General Information: Public access terminal is available. No adoptions, juvenile, sealed by Judge, expunged, mental health records released. SASE required. Turnaround time 3-5 days. Copy fee: $.25 per page. Certification fee: $5.00. Fee payee: State of Oregon. Personal checks accepted. Prepayment is required.

Douglas County

Circuit Court 1036 S E Douglas, Roseburg, OR 97470; 541-957-2470; Fax: 541-957-2462. Hours: 8AM-noon, 3-5PM (PST). *Felony, Misdemeanor, Civil, Eviction, Small Claims, Probate.*

www.ojd.state.or.us/douglas

Civil Records: Access: Phone, mail, online, in person. Both court and visitors may perform in person searches. No search fee. Required to search: name, years to search. Civil cases indexed by defendant, plaintiff. Civil records on computer back to 10/1987, microfiche from 1974 (district) 1962 (circuit), archived from 1910. Index available remotely online on the statewide OJIN system, call 800-858-9658 for information.

Criminal Records: Access: Phone, mail, online, in person. Both court and visitors may perform in person searches. No search fee. Required to search: name, years to search, DOB. Criminal records on computer back to 10/1987, microfiche from 1974 (district) 1962 (circuit), archived from 1910. Online access to criminal records is the same as civil.

General Information: Public access terminal is available. No adoptions, juvenile, sealed by Judge, expunged or mental health records released. SASE

required. Turnaround time 5-10 days. Copy fee: $.25 per page. Certification fee: $5.00. Fee payee: Oregon Judicial Department. Personal checks accepted. Prepayment is required.

Gilliam County

Circuit Court Box 622, Condon, OR 97823; 541-384-3572; Fax: 541-384-2166. Hours: 1-5PM (PST). *Felony, Misdemeanor, Civil.*

http://seventhdistrict.ojd.state.or.us/

Civil Records: Access: Phone, mail, online, in person. Both court and visitors may perform in person searches. No search fee. Required to search: name, years to search. Civil cases indexed by defendant, plaintiff. Civil records on computer from 1989, index cards back to 1800s. Index available remotely online on the statewide OJIN system, call 800-858-9658 for information.

Criminal Records: Access: Phone, mail, online, in person. Both court and visitors may perform in person searches. No search fee. Required to search: name, years to search; also helpful: DOB. Criminal records on computer from 1989, index cards back to 1800s. Online access to criminal records is the same as civil.

General Information: No adoptions, juvenile, sealed by Judge, expunged, mental health records released. SASE required. Turnaround time 1-2 days. Copy fee: $.25 per page. Certification fee: $5.00. Fee payee: Gilliam Circuit Court. Personal checks accepted. Prepayment is required.

County Court 221 S Oregon, PO Box 427, Condon, OR 97823; 541-384-2311; Fax: 541-384-2166. Hours: 8:30AM-Noon, 1-5PM (PST). *Probate.*

Grant County

Circuit Court Box 159 (205 S. Humbolt Street), Canyon City, OR 97820; 541-575-1438; Fax: 541-575-2165. Hours: 8AM-Noon, 1-5PM (PST). *Felony, Misdemeanor, Civil.*

www.ojd.state.or.us/grant

Civil Records: Access: Mail, online, in person. Only the court performs in person searches; visitors may not. No search fee. Required to search: name, years to search. Civil cases indexed by defendant, plaintiff. Civil records on computer from 1987, microfiche from 1950-1965, archives back to 1880. Index available remotely online on the statewide OJIN system, call 800-858-9658 for information.

Criminal Records: Access: Mail, online, in person. Only the court performs in person searches; visitors may not. No search fee. Required to search: name, years to search. Criminal records on computer from 1987, microfiche from 1950-1965, archives back to 1880. Online access to criminal records is the same as civil.

General Information: No adoptions, juvenile, sealed by Judge, expunged, mental health records released. SASE required. Turnaround time 3-5 days. Copy fee: $.25 per page. Certification fee: $5.00. Fee payee: Grant County Circuit Court. Personal checks accepted. Prepayment is required.

County Court 201 Humbolt St #290, Canyon City, OR 97820-6186; 541-575-1675; Fax: 541-575-2248. Hours: 8AM-5PM (PST). *Probate.*

Harney County

Circuit Court 450 N. Buena Vista, Burns, OR 97720; 541-573-5207; Fax: 541-573-5715. 8AM-12PM; 1PM-5PM (PST). *Felony, Misdemeanor, Civil.*

www.ojd.state.or.us/harney

Civil Records: Access: Phone, fax, mail, online, in person. Both court and visitors may perform in person searches. No search fee. Required to search: name, years to search. Civil cases indexed by defendant, plaintiff. Civil records on computer from 1988, microfiche from 1970-1979, archives back to 1880.

Index available remotely online on the statewide OJIN system, call 800-858-9658 for information.

Criminal Records: Access: Phone, fax, mail, online, in person. Both court and visitors may perform in person searches. No search fee. Required to search: name, years to search. Criminal records on computer from 1988, microfiche from 1970-1979, archives back to 1880. Online access to criminal records is the same as civil.

General Information: Public access terminal is available. No adoptions, juvenile, sealed by Judge, expunged, paternity or mental health records released. SASE required. Turnaround time 1-2 days. Fax notes: $2.00 for first page, $1.00 each add'l. Copy fee: $.25 per page. Certification fee: $5.00. Fee payee: Harney Circuit Court. Personal checks accepted. Prepayment is required.

County Court 450 N Buena Vista Ave, Burns, OR 97720-1518; 541-573-6641; Fax: 541-573-8370. Hours: 8:30AM-Noon, 1-5PM (PST). *Probate.*

www.co.harney.or.us

Hood River County

Circuit Court 309 State St., Hood River, OR 97031; 541-386-1862; Fax: 541-386-3465. Hours: 8AM-Noon, 1-5PM (PST). *Felony, Misdemeanor, Civil, Eviction, Small Claims, Probate.*

http://seventhdistrict.ojd.state.or.us/

Civil Records: Access: Phone, fax, mail, online, in person. Both court and visitors may perform in person searches. No search fee. Required to search: name, years to search. Civil cases indexed by defendant, plaintiff. Civil records on computer from 1989, docket books from 1950. Index available remotely online on the statewide OJIN system, call 800-858-9658 for information.

Criminal Records: Access: Phone, fax, mail, online, in person. Both court and visitors may perform in person searches. No search fee. Required to search: name, years to search, DOB. Criminal records on computer from 1989, docket books from 1950. Online access to criminal records is the same as civil.

General Information: Public access terminal is available. No adoptions, juvenile, sealed by Judge, expunged, paternity or mental health records released. Turnaround time 1-2 days. Copy fee: $.25 per page. Certification fee: $5.00. Fee payee: Hood River Trial Courts. Personal checks accepted. Credit cards accepted. Prepayment is required.

Jackson County

Circuit Court 100 S. Oakdale, Medford, OR 97501; 541-776-7171; Fax: 541-776-7057. Hours: 8AM-5PM (PST). *Felony, Misdemeanor, Civil Actions, Eviction, Small Claims, Probate.*

http://jackson-court.ojd.state.or.us/

Civil Records: Access: Mail, online, in person. Visitors must perform in person searches for themselves. No search fee. Required to search: name, years to search. Civil cases indexed by defendant, plaintiff. Civil records on computer from 1988, prior records on docket books and microfilm. Index available remotely online on the statewide OJIN system, call 800-858-9658 for information.

Criminal Records: Access: Mail, online, in person. Visitors must perform in person searches for themselves. No search fee. Required to search: name, years to search, DOB. Criminal records on computer from 1988, prior records on docket books and microfilm. Online access to criminal records is the same as civil.

General Information: Public access terminal is available. No adoptions, juvenile, sealed by Judge, expunged, mental health records released. SASE required. Turnaround time 1 week. Copy fee: $.25 per page. Certification fee: $5.00. Fee payee: Jackson County Courts. Personal checks accepted. Credit cards accepted. Prepayment is required.

Jefferson County

Circuit Court 75 SE C St., Madras, OR 97741-1750; 541-475-3317; Fax: 541-475-3421. Hours: 8AM-5PM (PST). *Felony, Misdemeanor, Civil, Eviction, Small Claims, Probate.*

Civil Records: Access: Mail, online, in person. Both court and visitors may perform in person searches. No search fee. Required to search: name, years to search. Civil cases indexed by defendant, plaintiff. Civil records on computer from Oct 1986, archives from 1916-1986. Index available remotely online on the statewide OJIN system, call 800-858-9658 for information.
Criminal Records: Access: Mail, online, in person. Both court and visitors may perform in person searches. No search fee. Required to search: name, years to search, DOB. Criminal records on computer from Oct 1986, archives from 1916-1986. Online access to criminal records is the same as civil.
General Information: Public access terminal is available. No adoptions, juvenile, sealed by Judge, expunged, mental health records released. SASE required. Turnaround time 1-2 weeks. Copy fee: $.25 per page. Certification fee: $5.00. Fee payee: State of Oregon. Personal checks accepted.

Josephine County

Circuit Court Josephine County Courthouse, Rm 254, 500 NW 6th St, Grants Pass, OR 97526; 541-476-2309; Fax: 541-471-2079. Hours: 8AM-4PM (PST). *Felony, Misdemeanor, Civil, Eviction, Small Claims, Probate.*

Civil Records: Access: Fax, mail, online, in person. Both court and visitors may perform in person searches. No search fee. Required to search: name, years to search. Civil cases indexed by defendant, plaintiff. Civil records on computer from 1987, microfilm prior to 1980, archives from 1920, index books. Index available remotely online on the statewide OJIN system, call 800-858-9658 for information.
Criminal Records: Access: Fax, mail, online, in person. Both court and visitors may perform in person searches. No search fee. Required to search: name, years to search, DOB. Criminal records on computer from 1987, microfilm prior to 1980, archives from 1920, index books. Online access to criminal records is the same as civil.
General Information: Public access terminal is available. No adoptions, juvenile, sealed by Judge, expunged, mental health records released. SASE required. Turnaround time 10-15 working days. Fax notes: No fee to fax results. Copy fee: $.25 per page. Certification fee: $5.00. Fee payee: Josephine County Court. Personal checks accepted. Credit cards accepted: Visa, MasterCard. Prepayment is required.

Klamath County

Circuit Court 316 Main Street, Klamath Falls, OR 97601; 541-883-5503; Fax: 541-882-6109. Hours: 8AM-5PM (PST). *Felony, Misdemeanor, Civil, Eviction, Small Claims, Probate.*

http://klamath-court.ojd.state.or.us

Civil Records: Access: Mail, fax, online, in person. Both court and visitors may perform in person searches. Search fee: $7.50 if requested by mail. Required to search: name, years to search. Civil cases indexed by defendant, plaintiff. Civil records on computer from 1988, microfiche from 1940-1980. Index available remotely online on the statewide OJIN system, call 800-858-9658 for information.
Criminal Records: Access: Mail, fax, online, in person. Both court and visitors may perform in person searches. Search fee: $7.50 if requested by mail.

Required to search: name, years to search. Criminal records on computer from 1988, microfiche from 1940-1980. Online access to criminal records is the same as civil.
General Information: Public access terminal is available. No adoptions, juvenile, sealed by Judge, expunged, paternity or mental health records released. SASE required. Turnaround time 2 weeks. Fax notes: Fee to fax results is $2.00 per page and $1.00 each add'l. Copy fee: $.25 per page. Certification fee: $5.00. Fee payee: Klamath County Circuit Court. No personal checks accepted. Credit cards accepted: Visa, MasterCard. Prepayment is required.

Lake County

Circuit Court 513 Center St., Lakeview, OR 97630; 541-947-6051; Fax: 541-947-3724. Hours: 8AM-5PM (PST). *Felony, Misdemeanor, Civil, Eviction, Small Claims, Probate.*

Civil Records: Access: Mail, online, in person. Both court and visitors may perform in person searches. No search fee. Required to search: name, years to search. Civil cases indexed by defendant, plaintiff. Civil records on computer from 1988, index cards prior. Index available remotely online on the statewide OJIN system, call 800-858-9658 for information.
Criminal Records: Access: Mail, online, in person. Both court and visitors may perform in person searches. No search fee. Required to search: name, years to search. Criminal records on computer from 1988, index cards prior. Online access to criminal records is the same as civil.
General Information: Public access terminal is available. No adoptions, juvenile, sealed by Judge, expunged or mental health records released. SASE required. Turnaround time 1 week. Fax notes: Will fax back only if local and prepaid. Copy fee: $.25 per page. Certification fee: $5.00. Fee payee: Lake County Circuit Court. Personal checks accepted. Prepayment required.

Lane County

Circuit Court 125 E. 8th Ave., Eugene, OR 97401; 541-682-4020. Hours: 8AM-5PM (PST). *Felony, Misdemeanor, Civil, Eviction, Small Claims, Probate.*

Civil Records: Access: Online, in person. Visitors must perform in person searches for themselves. No search fee. Required to search: name, years to search. Civil cases indexed by defendant, plaintiff. Civil records on computer from 1983, index books prior. Index available remotely online on the statewide OJIN system, call 800-858-9658 for information.
Criminal Records: Access: Online, in person. Visitors must perform in person searches for themselves. No search fee. Required to search: name, years to search. Criminal records on computer from 1983, index books prior. Online access to criminal records is the same as civil.
General Information: Public access terminal is available. No adoptions, juvenile, sealed by Judge, expunged, mental health records released. Copy fee: $.25 per page. Certification fee: $3.75 plus $.25 per page. Fee payee: Lane County Circuit Court or Lane County Courts. Personal checks accepted. Credit cards accepted. Accepted in person only. Prepayment is required.

Lincoln County

Lincoln County Courts PO Box 100, Newport, OR 97365; 541-265-4236; Fax: 541-265-7561. Hours: 8AM-5PM (PST). *Felony, Misdemeanor, Civil, Eviction, Small Claims, Probate.*

www.ojd.state.or.us/lincoln

Civil Records: Access: Mail, online, in person. Visitors must perform in person searches for themselves. No search fee. Required to search: name. Civil cases indexed by defendant, plaintiff. Civil records on

computer from 2/88, archives back to 1893, prior to 1988, years to search must be specified. Index available remotely online on the statewide OJIN system, call 800-858-9658 for information.
Criminal Records: Access: Mail, online, in person. Visitors must perform in person searches for themselves. No search fee. Required to search: name, years to search. Criminal records on computer from 2/88, archives back to 1893, prior to 1988, years to search must be specified. Online access to criminal records is the same as civil.
General Information: Public access terminal is available. No adoptions, sealed by Judge, expunged, or mental health records released. SASE required. Turnaround time 1 week. Copy fee: $.25 per page. Certification fee: $5.00. Fee payee: State of Oregon. Personal checks accepted. Credit cards accepted: Visa, MasterCard. $1.00 minimum charge. Prepayment is required.

Linn County

Circuit Court PO Box 1749, Albany, OR 97321; 541-967-3845. Hours: 8AM-5PM (PST). *Felony, Misdemeanor, Civil, Eviction, Small Claims, Probate.*

www.ojd.state.or.us/linn-circuit

Civil Records: Access: Mail, online, in person. Both court and visitors may perform in person searches. No search fee. Required to search: name, years to search. Civil cases indexed by defendant, plaintiff. Civil records on computer from June 1987, archives back to 1863. Index available remotely online on the statewide OJIN system, call 800-858-9658 for information.
Criminal Records: Access: Mail, online, in person. Both court and visitors may perform in person searches. No search fee. Required to search: name, years to search, DOB. Criminal records on computer from June 1987, archives back to 1863. Online access to criminal records is the same as civil.
General Information: Public access terminal is available. No adoptions, juvenile, sealed by judge, expunged, paternity or mental health records released. SASE required. Turnaround time 5-10 days. Copy fee: $.25 per page. Certification fee: $5.00. Fee payee: Linn County Courts. Personal checks accepted. Prepayment is required.

Malheur County

Circuit Court 251 B St West, Vale, OR 97918; 541-473-5171; Fax: 541-473-2213. Hours: 8AM-5PM; 9AM-Noon, 1-4PM (Record Inquiry) (MST). *Felony, Misdemeanor, Civil, Eviction, Small Claims.*

www.ojd.state.or.us/malheur

Civil Records: Access: Mail, online, in person. Both court and visitors may perform in person searches. Search fee: No fee, unless access needed to archived records. Required to search: name, years to search. Civil cases indexed by defendant, plaintiff. Civil records on computer from July 1988, archived from 1887. Index available remotely online on the statewide OJIN system, call 800-858-9658 for information.
Criminal Records: Access: Mail, online, in person. Both court and visitors may perform in person searches. Search fee: None fee unless archived records needed. Required to search: name, years to search, DOB. Criminal records on computer from July 1988, archived from 1887. Online access to criminal records is the same as civil.
General Information: Public access terminal is available. No adoptions, juvenile, sealed by Judge, expunged, mental health records released. SASE requested. Turnaround time 2 weeks minimum. Fax notes: Fee to fax results is $1.00 per page. Copy fee: $.25 per page. Certification fee: $5.00. Fee payee: Trial Court Clerk. Personal checks accepted. Credit cards accepted: Visa, MasterCard. Accepted for filing fees only. Prepayment is required.

County Court 251 B St W #5, Vale, OR 97918; 541-473-5123; Fax: 541-473-5523. Hours: 8:30AM-Noon, 1-5:00PM (MST). *Probate.*

www.malheurco.org

Marion County

Circuit Court PO Box 12869 (100 High St NE), Salem, OR 97309; 503-588-5101; Fax: 503-373-4360. Hours: 8AM-5PM (PST). *Felony, Misdemeanor, Civil, Eviction, Small Claims, Probate.*

http://marion-court.ojd.state.or.us

Civil Records: Access: Mail, online, in person. Both court and visitors may perform in person searches. No search fee. Required to search: name, years to search. Civil cases indexed by defendant, plaintiff. Civil records on computer from 1986, prior to 1986 on microfiche. Index available remotely online on the statewide OJIN system, call 800-858-9658 for information.

Criminal Records: Access: Mail, online, in person. Both court and visitors may perform in person searches. No search fee. Required to search: name, years to search, signed release; also helpful: DOB, SSN. Criminal records on computer from 1986, prior to 1986 on microfiche. Online access to criminal records is the same as civil. Online access to the County sexual offenders registry is available free at www.open.org/~msheriff/sexnotif.htm.

General Information: Public access terminal is available. No adoptions, juvenile, sealed by Judge, expunged, paternity or mental health records released. SASE required. Turnaround time 1-2 days. Copy fee: $.25 per page. Certification fee: $3.00. Fee payee: State of Oregon. Personal checks accepted. Prepayment is required.

Morrow County

Circuit Court PO Box 609, Heppner, OR 97836; 541-676-5264; Fax: 541-676-9902. Hours: 8AM-Noon, 1-4:45PM (PST). *Felony, Misdemeanor, Civil, Eviction, Small Claims, Probate.*

www.ojd.state.or.us/morrow

Civil Records: Access: Phone, fax, mail, in person. Both court and visitors may perform in person searches. No search fee. Required to search: name, years to search. Civil cases indexed by defendant, plaintiff. Civil records on computer from 1987, archives back to 1940, index cards, docket books by case #. Index available remotely online on the statewide OJIN system, call 800-858-9658 for information.

Criminal Records: Access: Phone, fax, mail, online, in person. Both court and visitors may perform in person searches. No search fee. Required to search: name, years to search, DOB. Criminal records on computer from 1987, archives back to 1940, index cards, docket books by case #. Online access to criminal records is the same as civil.

General Information: Public access terminal is available. No adoptions, juvenile, sealed by Judge, expunged, paternity or mental health records released. SASE required. Turnaround time 1-3 days. Fax notes: No fee to fax results. Copy fee: $.25 per page. Certification fee: $5.00. Fee payee: Circuit Court. Personal checks accepted. Prepayment is required.

Multnomah County

Circuit Court 1021 SW 4th Ave, Rm 131, Portland, OR 97204; 503-988-3003. Hours: 8AM-4:30PM (PST). *Felony, Misdemeanor, Civil Actions Over $10,000, Probate.*

Civil Records: Access: Mail, online, in person. Both court and visitors may perform in person searches. No search fee. Required to search: name, years to search. Civil cases indexed by defendant, plaintiff. Civil records on computer from 1988, microfiche, index books, docket books back to 1857. Index available remotely online on the statewide OJIN system, call 800-858-9658 for information.

Criminal Records: Access: Mail, online, in person. Both court and visitors may perform in person searches. No search fee. Required to search: name, years to search; also helpful: DOB. Criminal records on computer from 1988, microfiche, index books, docket books back to 1857. Online access to criminal records is the same as civil.

General Information: Public access terminal is available. No adoptions, juvenile, sealed by Judge, expunged or mental health records released. SASE required. Turnaround time 4-5 days. Copy fee: $.25 per page. Certification fee: $5.00. Fee payee: State of Oregon. Personal checks accepted. Prepayment is required.

Circuit Court - Civil Division 1021 SW 4th Ave, Rm 210, Portland, OR 97204; 503-988-3022. Hours: 8AM-4PM (Tele: 8-11AM; 1-3:30PM) (PST). *Civil Actions Under $10,000, Eviction, Small Claims.*

www.ojd.state.or.us/multnomah

Civil Records: Access: Phone, mail, online, in person. Both court and visitors may perform in person searches. Some limitations may apply. No search fee. Required to search: name, years to search. Civil cases indexed by defendant, plaintiff. Civil records on computer from 1988, microfiche 1984-1988, docket cards by case # and yr. Index available remotely online on the statewide OJIN system, call 800-858-9658 for information.

General Information: Public access terminal is available. No adoptions, juvenile, sealed by Judge, expunged, paternity or mental health records released. SASE required. Turnaround time 5 days. Copy fee: $.25 per page. Certification fee: $5.00 per document; exemplified-$10.00. Fee payee: State of Oregon. Personal checks accepted. Prepayment is required.

Polk County

Circuit Court Polk County Courthouse, Rm 301, 850 Main St, Dallas, OR 97338; Civil phone: 503-623-6614; Criminal phone: 503-831-1778; Fax: 503-831-1779. Hours: 8AM-Noon, 1-5PM (PST). *Felony, Misdemeanor, Civil, Eviction, Small Claims, Probate.*

Note: Fax for criminal is 503-831-1779.

Civil Records: Access: Phone, fax, mail, online, in person. Both court and visitors may perform in person searches. No search fee. Required to search: name, years to search. Civil cases indexed by defendant, plaintiff. Civil records on computer from 1985, microfilm, archives from 1969 (District) back to 1800s (Circuit). Index available remotely online on the statewide OJIN system, call 800-858-9658 for information.

Criminal Records: Access: Phone, fax, mail, online, in person. Both court and visitors may perform in person searches. No search fee. Required to search: name, years to search, DOB; also helpful: SSN. Criminal records on computer from 1985, microfilm, archives from 1969 (District) back to 1800s (Circuit). Online access to criminal records is the same as civil.

General Information: Public access terminal is available. No adoptions, juvenile, sealed by Judge, expunged, mental health records released. SASE required. Turnaround time 2 weeks. Fax notes: No fee to fax results. Copy fee: $.25 per page. Certification fee: $5.00. Fee payee: Trial Court Administrator. Personal checks accepted. Credit cards accepted: Visa, MasterCard. Credit cards accepted in person only. Prepayment is required.

Sherman County

Circuit Court PO Box 402, Moro, OR 97039; 541-565-3650. Hours: 1-5PM (PST). *Felony, Misdemeanor, Civil.*

Civil Records: Access: Phone, mail, online, in person. Both court and visitors may perform in person searches. No search fee. Required to search: name, years to search. Civil cases indexed by defendant, plaintiff. Civil records on computer from 1992, microfiche up to 1987, index books, judgment docket books. Index available remotely online on the statewide OJIN system, call 800-858-9658 for information.

Criminal Records: Access: Phone, mail, online, in person. Both court and visitors may perform in person searches. No search fee. Required to search: name, years to search, DOB. Criminal records on computer from 1992, microfiche up to 1987, index books, judgment docket books. Online access to criminal records is the same as civil.

General Information: Public access terminal is available. No adoptions, juvenile, sealed by Judge, expunged, paternity or mental health records released. SASE required. Turnaround time 2-5 days. Fax notes: Will not fax results. Copy fee: $.25 per page. Certification fee: $5.00. Fee payee: Sherman County Circuit Court. Personal checks accepted. Prepayment is required.

County Court PO Box 365, Moro, OR 97039; 541-565-3606; Fax: 541-565-3312. Hours: 8AM-5PM (PST). *Probate.*

Tillamook County

Circuit Court 201 Laurel Ave, Tillamook, OR 97141; 503-842-8014; Fax: 503-842-2597. Hours: 8AM-Noon; 1PM-5PM (PST). *Felony, Misdemeanor, Civil, Eviction, Small Claims, Probate.*

Civil Records: Access: Mail, fax, online, in person. Both court and visitors may perform in person searches. No search fee. Required to search: name, years to search. Civil cases indexed by defendant, plaintiff. Civil records on computer from 1987, prior on case files. Index available remotely online on the statewide OJIN system, call 800-858-9658 for information.

Criminal Records: Access: Mail, fax, online, in person. Both court and visitors may perform in person searches. No search fee. Required to search: name, years to search. Criminal records on computer from 1987, prior on case files. Online access to criminal records is the same as civil.

General Information: Public access terminal is available. No adoptions, juvenile, sealed by Judge, expunged, paternity or mental health records released. SASE required. Turnaround time 2-3 days. Copy fee: $.25 per page. Certification fee: $5.00. Fee payee: Trial Court Administrator. Personal checks accepted. Credit cards accepted. Prepayment is required.

Umatilla County

Circuit Court PO Box 1307, Pendleton, OR 97801; 541-278-0341; Fax: 541-278-2071. Hours: 8AM-5PM (PST). *Felony, Misdemeanor, Civil, Eviction, Small Claims, Probate.*

www.ojd.state.or.us/morrow

Civil Records: Access: Mail, online, in person. Both court and visitors may perform in person searches. No search fee. Required to search: name, years to search. Civil cases indexed by defendant, plaintiff. Civil records on computer from 11/86, microfiche, index card, docket books. Index available remotely online on the statewide OJIN system, call 800-858-9658 for information.

Criminal Records: Access: Mail, online, in person. Both court and visitors may perform in person searches. No search fee. Required to search: name, years to search. Criminal records on computer from 11/86, microfiche, index card, docket books. Online access to criminal records is the same as civil.

General Information: Public access terminal is available. No adoptions, juvenile, sealed by Judge, expunged, paternity or mental health records released. SASE required. Turnaround time 1-3 weeks. Copy fee: $.25 per page. Certification fee: $5.00. Fee payee: Trial Court Administrator. Personal checks accepted. Credit cards accepted. Prepayment is required.

Union County

Circuit Court 1008 K Ave, La Grande, OR 97850; 541-962-9500; Fax: 541-963-0444. Hours: 8AM-Noon, 1-5PM (PST). *Felony, Misdemeanor, Civil, Eviction, Small Claims, Probate.*

www.ojd.state.or.us/union

Civil Records: Access: Mail, online, in person. Both court and visitors may perform in person searches. No search fee. Required to search: name, years to search. Civil cases indexed by defendant, plaintiff. Civil records on computer from 1986, archives back to 1800s, on ledger books/docket books. Index available remotely online on the statewide OJIN system, call 800-858-9658 for information.

Criminal Records: Access: Mail, online, in person. Both court and visitors may perform in person searches. No search fee. Required to search: name, years to search, DOB. Criminal records on computer from 1986, archives back to 1800s, on ledger books/docket books. Online access to criminal records is the same as civil.

General Information: Public access terminal is available. No adoptions, juvenile, sealed by Judge, expunged, paternity or mental health records released. SASE required. Turnaround time 1-2 weeks. Copy fee: $.25 per page. Certification fee: $5.00. Fee payee: Circuit Court. Personal checks accepted. Credit cards accepted: Visa, MasterCard. Prepayment is required.

Wallowa County

Circuit Court 101 S River St, Rm 204, Enterprise, OR 97828; 541-426-4991; Fax: 541-426-4992. Hours: 8AM-5PM (PST). *Felony, Misdemeanor, Civil, Eviction, Small Claims, Probate.*

Civil Records: Access: Phone, mail, online, in person. Both court and visitors may perform in person searches. No search fee. Required to search: name, years to search. Civil cases indexed by defendant, plaintiff. Civil records on computer from 1987, prior on docket books. Index available remotely online on the statewide OJIN system, call 800-858-9658 for information.

Criminal Records: Access: Phone, mail, online, in person. Both court and visitors may perform in person searches. No search fee. Required to search: name, years to search. Criminal records on computer from 1987, prior on docket books. Online access to criminal records is the same as civil.

General Information: Public access terminal is available. No adoptions, juvenile, sealed by Judge, expunged, paternity or mental health records released. SASE required. Turnaround time 1-3 days. Copy fee: $.25 per page. Certification fee: $5.00. Fee payee:

Circuit Court. Personal checks accepted. Copy fees will be billed.

Wasco County

Circuit Court PO Box 1400, The Dalles, OR 97058-1400; 541-296-3154; Fax: 541-298-5611. Hours: 8AM-Noon,1-5PM (PST). *Felony, Misdemeanor, Civil, Eviction, Small Claims, Probate.*

http://seventhdistrict.ojd.state.or.us/html/wasco.html

Civil Records: Access: Phone, fax, mail, online, in person. Both court and visitors may perform in person searches. No search fee. Required to search: name, years to search. Civil cases indexed by defendant, plaintiff. Civil records on computer from 1989, prior records in docket books by case # and year back to 1900s. Index available remotely online on the statewide OJIN system, call 800-858-9658 for information.

Criminal Records: Access: Phone, fax, mail, online, in person. Both court and visitors may perform in person searches. No search fee. Required to search: name, years to search, DOB. Criminal records on computer from 1989, prior records in docket books by case # and year back to 1900s. Online access to criminal records is the same as civil.

General Information: Public access terminal is available. No adoptions, juvenile, sealed by Judge, expunged, paternity or mental health records released. SASE required. Turnaround time 2-3 days. Fax notes: Fee to fax results is $.25 per page. Copy fee: $.25 per page. Certification fee: $5.00. Fee payee: Trial Court Administrator. Personal checks accepted. Credit cards accepted: Visa, MasterCard. Prepayment is required.

Washington County

Circuit Court 150 N 1st, Hillsboro, OR 97124; 503-846-8888 x2302 (civ) x6060 (crim); Fax: 503-846-6087. Hours: 8-11:30AM, 12:30-3PM (PST). *Felony, Misdemeanor, Civil, Eviction, Small Claims, Probate.*

Civil Records: Access: Phone, mail, online, in person. Both court and visitors may perform in person searches. No search fee. Required to search: name, years to search. Civil cases indexed by defendant, plaintiff. Civil records on computer from 1982, prior on docket books. Index available remotely online on the statewide OJIN system, call 800-858-9658 for information.

Criminal Records: Access: Phone, mail, online, in person. Both court and visitors may perform in person searches. No search fee. Required to search: name, years to search, DOB. Criminal records on computer from 1982, prior on docket books. Online access to criminal records is the same as civil.

General Information: Public access terminal is available. No adoptions, juvenile, sealed by Judge, expunged, paternity or mental health records released. Turnaround time 2-5 days. Copy fee: $.25 per page. Certification fee: $5.00. Fee payee: State of Oregon. Personal checks accepted. Prepayment is required.

Wheeler County

Circuit Court PO Box 308, Fossil, OR 97830; 541-763-2541; Fax: 541-763-2026. Hours: 8:30AM-11:30AM (PST). *Felony, Misdemeanor, Civil.*

http://seventhdistrict.ojd.state.or.us/

Civil Records: Access: Phone, mail, online, in person. Both court and visitors may perform in person searches. No search fee. Required to search: name, years to search. Civil cases indexed by defendant. Civil records on computer from 1989, docket books by case # and yr. Index available remotely online on the statewide OJIN system, call 800-858-9658 for information.

Criminal Records: Access: Phone, mail, online, in person. Both court and visitors may perform in person searches. No search fee. Required to search: name, years to search, DOB. Criminal records on computer from 1989, docket books by case # and yr. Online access to criminal records is the same as civil.

General Information: Public access terminal is available. No adoptions, juvenile, sealed by Judge, expunged, paternity or mental health records released. SASE required. Turnaround time 1 week. Copy fee: $.25 per page. Certification fee: $5.00. Fee payee: Wheeler Circuit Court. Personal checks accepted. Prepayment is required.

County Court PO Box 327 (701 Adams, Rm 204), Fossil, OR 97830; 541-763-2400; Fax: 541-763-2026. Hours: 9-5PM (PST). *Probate.*

Yamhill County

Circuit Court 535 NE Fifth, McMinnville, OR 97128; 503-434-7530; Fax: 503-472-5805. Hours: 8AM-Noon, 1-5PM (PST). *Felony, Misdemeanor, Civil, Eviction, Small Claims, Probate.*

http://yamhill-court.ojd.state.or.us/

Civil Records: Access: Mail, online, in person. Both court and visitors may perform in person searches. No search fee. Required to search: name, years to search. Civil cases indexed by defendant, plaintiff. Civil records on computer from 1987, microfiche (10 yrs Dist, unlimited Circuit), archives back to 1900s, docket books by case # and yr. Index available remotely online on the statewide OJIN system, call 800-858-9658 for information.

Criminal Records: Access: Mail, online, in person. Both court and visitors may perform in person searches. No search fee. Required to search: name, years to search, DOB. Criminal records on computer from 1987, microfiche (10 yrs Dist, unlimited Circuit), archives back to 1900s, docket books by case # and yr. Online access to criminal records is the same as civil.

General Information: Public access terminal is available. No adoptions, juvenile, sealed by Judge, expunged or mental health records released. SASE requested. Turnaround time 1-7 days. Copy fee: $.25 per page. Certification fee: $5.00. Fee payee: Trial Court. Personal checks accepted. Two party, payroll checks not accepted. Credit cards accepted: Visa, MasterCard. Prepayment is required.

Oregon Recording Offices

ORGANIZATION: 36 counties, 36 recording offices. The recording officer is County Clerk. 35 counties are in the Pacific Time Zone (PST) and one is in the Mountain Time Zone (MST).

REAL ESTATE RECORDS: Some counties will not perform real estate searches. Search fees vary. Many counties will search all liens together for $12.50 per name. Copy fees are usually $.25 per page. Certification usually costs $3.75 per document. The Assessor keeps tax and ownership records.

UCC RECORDS: Financing statements are filed at the state level, except for real estate related collateral. Many county clerks will perform UCC searches, fees vary from $3.50 to $13.50, we suggest to call first.

TAX LIEN RECORDS: All federal and state tax liens on personal property are filed with the Secretary of State. Other federal and state tax liens are filed with the County Clerk. Most counties will perform tax lien searches and include both with a UCC search for an extra $7.50 per name. Search fees vary widely.

OTHER LIENS: County tax, public utility, construction, judgment, hospital.

ONLINE ACCESS: A few counties offer Internet access to assessor records. There is no statewide system available.

Baker County

County Clerk, 1995 Third St, Suite 150, Baker, OR 97814-3398. County Clerk, R/E and UCC Recording 541-523-8207; Fax 541-523-8240. www.bakercounty.org
Will search UCC records. **Other Phone Numbers:** Assessor 541-523-8203; Treasurer 541-523-8233; Appraiser/Auditor 541-523-8203; Elections 541-523-8207; Vital Records 541-731-4095.

Benton County

County Clerk, 120 NW 4th St, Room 4, Corvallis, OR 97330. County Clerk, R/E and UCC Recording 541-766-6831; Fax 541-766-6675. www.co.benton.or.us
Will search UCC records. **Online Access:** Real Estate Records. The County is developing a Geographic Information System Internet site for viewing property information at www.co.benton.or.us/irm/gis/GISpage.htm. Search fee is $3.75 per record found. A law enforcement case system may soon offer open case data. **Other Phone Numbers:** Assessor 541-766-6855; Treasurer 766-6808; Appraiser/Auditor 541-766-6855; Elections 541-766-6756; Vital Records 503-731-4108.

Clackamas County

County Clerk, 104 11th St, Room 104, Oregon City, OR 97045. County Clerk, R/E and UCC Recording 503-655-8551; www.co.clackamas.or.us/clerk
This agency will not search real estate or UCC records. **Other Phone Numbers:** Assessor 503-655-8671; Treasurer 503-655-8915; Elections 503-655-8510; Vital Records 503-731-4095.

Clatsop County

County Clerk, PO Box 178, Astoria, OR 97103-0178. County Clerk, R/E and UCC Recording 503-325-8511; Fax 503-325-9307. www.co.clatsop.or.us/contact.htm
Will search UCC records. **Other Phone Numbers:** Assessor 503-325-8522; Treasurer 503-325-8565; Appraiser/Auditor 503-325-8522; Elections 503-325-8511; Vital Records 503-325-8511.

Columbia County

County Clerk, Courthouse, St. Helens, OR 97051-2041. County Clerk, R/E and UCC Recording 503-397-3796; Fax 503-397-7266.
Will search UCC records. Will not search real estate records. **Other Phone Numbers:** Assessor 503-397-7210; Treasurer 503-397-0344; Appraiser/Auditor 503-397-2240; Elections 503-397-7214 & 3796; Vital Records 503-397-3796.

Coos County

County Clerk, Courthouse, 250 N. Baxter, Coquille, OR 97423-1899. 541-396-3121 R/E Recording: 541-396-3121 x223 UCC Recording: 541-396-3121 x223; Fax 541-396-6551.
Will search UCC records. This agency will not do a tax lien search. Will not search real estate records. **Other Phone Numbers:** Assessor 541-396-3121 x274; Treasurer 541-396-3121 x333; Appraiser/Auditor 541-396-3121 x274; Elections 541-396-3121 x301.

Crook County

County Clerk, 300 E. Third, Prineville, OR 97754. 541-447-6553; Fax 541-447-1051.
Will search UCC records. Will search real estate records. **Other Phone Numbers:** Assessor 541-447-4133; Treasurer 541-447-6554; Elections 541-447-6553.

Curry County

County Clerk, PO Box 746, Gold Beach, OR 97444. County Clerk, R/E and UCC Recording 541-247-7011 x209; Fax 541-247-6440. www.co.curry.or.us
Will search UCC records. **Other Phone Numbers:** Assessor 541-247-7011; Treasurer 541-247-7011; Appraiser/Auditor 541-247-7011 x230; Elections 541-247-7011 x223.

Deschutes County

County Clerk, 1340 NW Wall St., Bend, OR 97701. County Clerk, R/E and UCC Recording 541-388-6549; Fax 541-389-6830. http://recordings.co.deschutes.or.us
Will search UCC records. Will not search real estate records. **Online Access:** Real Estate, Tax Assessor Records. To access records on the Deschutes County "Assessor Inquiry System" web site, click on DIAL on the menu bar. Tax information, assessment, appraisal details, ownership, sales information, transaction histories, account histories, land use records, and lot numbers are available for no fee. **Other Phone Numbers:** Assessor 541-388-6508; Treasurer 541-388-6535; Elections 541-388-6546.

Douglas County

County Clerk, PO Box 10, Roseburg, OR 97470. 541-440-4322 R/E Recording: 541-440-4320; Fax 541-440-4408.
Will search UCC records by written request only. **Other Phone Numbers:** Assessor 541-440-4222; Treasurer 541-440-3311; Elections 541-440-4252.

Gilliam County

County Clerk, PO Box 427, Condon, OR 97823. County Clerk, R/E and UCC Recording 541-384-2311; Fax 541-384-2166.
Will search UCC records. This agency will not do a tax lien search. Will not search real estate records. **Other Phone Numbers:** Assessor 541-384-3781; Treasurer 541-384-6321; Appraiser/Auditor 541-384-3781; Elections 541-384-2311; Vital Records 541-384-2311.

Grant County

County Clerk, 201 S. Humbolt, Suite 290, Canyon City, OR 97820. County Clerk, R/E and UCC Recording 541-575-1675; Fax 541-575-2248.
Will search UCC records. **Other Phone Numbers:** Assessor 541-575-0107; Treasurer 541-575-1798; Appraiser/Auditor 541-575-0107; Elections 541-575-1675.

Harney County

County Clerk, 450 N. Buena Vista, Burns, OR 97720. 541-573-6641 R/E Recording: 541-573-6411 UCC Recording: 541-573-6411; Fax 541-573-8370.
Will not search UCC records. **Other Phone Numbers:** Assessor 541-573-8367; Treasurer 541-573-6541; Appraiser/Auditor 541-573-8368; Elections 541-573-6411.

Hood River County

County Clerk, 309 State St, Hood River, OR 97031-2093. County Clerk, R/E and UCC Recording 541-386-1442; Fax 541-386-9392.
This agency will not search real estate or UCC records. **Other Phone Numbers:** Assessor 541-386-3970; Elections 541-386-1442.

Jackson County

County Clerk, 10 S. Oakdale, Room 216A, Medford, OR 97501. 541-774-6151.
Will search UCC records. Tax liens included with UCC search for total fee of $12.50. Will not search real estate records. **Other Phones:** Assessor 541-776-7077.

Jefferson County

County Clerk, 75 S.E. C St, Madras, OR 97741. County Clerk, R/E and UCC Recording 541-475-4451; Fax 541-475-4454.
Will search UCC records. **Other Phone Numbers:** Assessor 541-475-2443; Treasurer 541-475-4458; Appraiser/Auditor 541-475-2443; Elections 541-475-4451.

Josephine County

County Clerk, PO Box 69, Grants Pass, OR 97528. 541-474-5240; Fax 541-476-5246.
This agency will not search real estate or UCC records. **Other Phone Numbers:** Assessor 541-474-5260; Treasurer 541-474-5235; Appraiser/Auditor 541-474-5260; Elections 541-474-5243.

Klamath County

County Clerk, 305 Main St., Klamath Falls, OR 97601. 541-883-5134; Fax 541-885-6757.
Will not search UCC records. This agency will do a federal tax lien search only. Mortgage searches available. **Other Phones:** Assessor 541-883-5111.

Lake County

County Clerk, 513 Center St, Lakeview, OR 97630-1539. 541-947-6006; Fax 541-947-6015.
Will search UCC records. Tax liens included in UCC search if requested for $12.50 total fee. Real estate owner, mortgage, and property transfer searches available. **Other Phones:** Assessor 541-947-6000.

Lane County

County Clerk, 125 E. 8th Ave, Eugene, OR 97401. 541-682-3654; Fax 541-682-3330.
Will search UCC records. Tax liens not included in UCC search. Will do real estate record searches by mail only. **Online Access:** Assessor, Real Estate Records. Property records on the County Tax Map site are at www.co.lane.or.us/taxmap/TaxMapSelect.asp. **Other Phone Numbers:** Assessor 541-687-4321.

Lincoln County

County Clerk, 225 W. Olive St, Room 201, Newport, OR 97365-3869. 541-265-4121; Fax 541-265-4950.
Will search UCC records. UCC search includes tax liens if requested. Will not search real estate records. **Other Phone Numbers:** Assessor 541-265-4102.

Linn County

County Clerk, PO Box 100, Albany, OR 97321. 541-967-3829; Fax 541-926-5109. www.co.linn.or.us
Will search UCC records. **Online Access:** Assessor, Real Estate Records. Records on the County Property Records database are available free online at the web site. **Other Phone Numbers:** Assessor 541-967-3808.

Malheur County

County Clerk, 251 B St West, #4, Vale, OR 97918. County Clerk, R/E and UCC Recording 541-473-5151; Fax 541-473-5523. www.malheurco.org
Will search UCC records. Will search real estate records. **Other Phones:** Assessor 541-473-5117; Treasurer 541-473-5165; Vital Records 541-889-7279.

Marion County

County Clerk, 100 High St NE, Room 1331, Salem, OR 97301. 503-588-5225; Fax 503-588-5237.
This agency will not search real estate or UCC records. **Other Phone Numbers:** Assessor 503-588-5236.

Morrow County

Chief Deputy Clerk, PO Box 338, Heppner, OR 97836. 541-676-9061 R/E Recording: 541-676-5604 UCC Recording: 541-676-5604; Fax 541-676-9876. www.rootsweb.com/~ormorrow/MorrowCountyCourthouse.htm
Will search UCC records. Will not search real estate records. **Other Phone Numbers:** Assessor 541-676-5607; Treasurer 541-676-5630; Appraiser/Auditor 541-676-9061; Elections 541-676-9061; Vital Records 541-676-5603.

Multnomah County

County Clerk, PO Box 5007, Portland, OR 97208-5007. County Clerk, R/E and UCC Recording 503-988-3034; Fax 503-988-3330. www.co.multnomah.or.us/dss/at/index.html
This agency will not perform searches. Records prior to 1850 are at Clackamas County. **Online Access:** Real Property Records. Records on the County Metromap database are available free online at http://metromap.metro-region.org/public. No name searching. **Other Phone Numbers:** Assessor 503-988-3326; Appraiser/Auditor 503-988-3367; Elections 503-988-3720; Vital Records 503-731-4095 (State); Tax information line 503-988-3326.

Polk County

County Clerk, Courthouse, 850 Main St., Dallas, OR 97338-3179. County Clerk, R/E and UCC Recording 503-623-9217; Fax 503-623-0717.
This agency will not search real estate or UCC records. **Other Phone Numbers:** Assessor 503-623-8391; Treasurer 503-623-9264; Appraiser/Auditor 503-623-8391; Elections 503-623-9217; Vital Records 503-731-0495 (Portland).

Sherman County

Deputy Clerk, PO Box 365, Moro, OR 97039. Deputy Clerk, R/E and UCC Recording 541-565-3606; Fax 541-565-3312.
Will search UCC records. Will search real estate records. **Other Phone Numbers:** Assessor 541-565-3505; Treasurer 541-565-3553; Appraiser/Auditor 541-565-3605; Elections 541-565-3606.

Tillamook County

County Clerk, 201 Laurel Ave, Tillamook, OR 97141. County Clerk, R/E and UCC Recording 503-842-3402; Fax 503-842-1599. www.co.tillamook.or.us/gov/clerk/default.htm
Will search UCC records. **Online Access:** Assessor, Real Estate Records. Assessment and taxation records on the County Property database are available free online at www.co.tillamook.or.us/Documents/Search/query.asp. Search by property ID number or by name in the general query. Also, search for property information on the GIS-mapping service site at http://gisweb.co.tillamook.or.us. **Other Phone Numbers:** Assessor 503-842-3400/3424; Treasurer 503-842-3425; Appraiser/Auditor 503-842-3400/3424; Elections 503-842-3402; Vital Records 503-731-4095.

Umatilla County

County Clerk, PO Box 1227, Pendleton, OR 97801-1227. 541-278-6236; Fax 541-278-5463.
Will search UCC records. Will not search real estate records. **Other Phone Numbers:** Assessor 541-276-7111 x214.

Union County

County Clerk, 1001 4th St., Suite "D", La Grande, OR 97850. County Clerk, R/E and UCC Recording 541-963-1006; Fax 541-963-1013.
This agency will not search real estate or UCC records. **Other Phones:** Assessor 541-963-1002; Treasurer 541-963-1018; Appraiser/Auditor 541-963-1002; Elections 541-963-1006; Vital Records 541-963-1006.

Wallowa County

County Clerk, 101 S. River, ROom 100 Door 16, Enterprise, OR 97828. County Clerk, R/E and UCC Recording 541-426-4543 x15; Fax 541-426-5901.
Will search UCC records. Will not search real estate records. **Other Phone Numbers:** Assessor 541-426-4543; Treasurer 541-426-4543 x14; Appraiser/Auditor 541-426-4543 x36; Elections 541-426-4543 x15; State 503-731-4095.

Wasco County

County Clerk, 511 Washington St., Courthouse, The Dalles, OR 97058-2237. County Clerk, R/E and UCC Recording 541-296-6159; Fax 541-298-3607.
This agency will not search real estate or UCC records. **Other Phones:** Assessor 541-296-5477; Treasurer 541-296-3327; Appraiser/Auditor 541-296-5477; Elections 541-296-6159; Vital Records 541-296-6159.

Washington County

County Clerk, 155 N. First Ave., Mail Stop 9, Hillsboro, OR 97124. County Clerk, R/E and UCC Recording 503-846-8752; www.co.washington.or.us
Will search UCC records. UCC search includes tax liens if requested. Will not search real estate records. **Online Access:** Real Estate Records. Records on County GIS Intermap database are available free online at www.co.washington.or.us/gisaps/cfdocs/gisweb/par_2.htm. General Recording Office information is available at www.co.washington.or.us/deptmts/at/recordng/record.htm. **Other Phone Numbers:** Assessor 503-846-8741; Appraiser/Auditor 503-846-8826; Elections 503-846-8670; Vital Records 503-846-3538.

Wheeler County

County Clerk, PO Box 327, Fossil, OR 97830-0327. 541-763-2400; Fax 541-763-2026.
Will search UCC records. Will not search real estate records. **Other Phone Numbers:** Assessor 541-763-4266; Treasurer 541-763-2078; Appraiser/Auditor 541-763-4266; Elections 541-763-2400; Vital Records 541-763-2400.

Yamhill County

County Clerk, 535 NE 5th St, Rm 119, McMinnville, OR 97128-4593. 503-434-7518; Fax 503-434-7520. www.co.yamhill.or.us/clerk
This agency will not search real estate or UCC records. **Other Phone Numbers:** Assessor 503-434-7521; Treasurer 503-434-7533; Appraiser/Auditor 503-434-7521; Vital Records 503-434-7523.

Oregon County Locator

You will usually be able to find the city name in the City/County Cross Reference below. In that case, it is a simple matter to determine the county from the cross reference. However, only the official US Postal Service city names are included in this index. There are an additional 40,000 place names that people use in their addresses. Therefore, we have also included a ZIP/City Cross Reference immediately following the City/County Cross Reference.

If you know the ZIP Code but the city name does not appear in the City/County Cross Reference index, look up the ZIP Code in the ZIP/City Cross Reference, find the city name, then look up the city name in the City/County Cross Reference. For example, you want to know the county for an address of Menands, NY 12204. There is no "Menands" in the City/County Cross Reference. The ZIP/City Cross Reference shows that ZIP Codes 12201-12288 are for the city of Albany. Looking back in the City/County Cross Reference, Albany is in Albany County.

City/County Cross Reference

ADAMS Umatilla
ADEL Lake
ADRIAN Malheur
AGNESS Curry
ALBANY (97321) Linn(88), Benton(11)
ALLEGANY Coos
ALSEA (97324) Benton(92), Lincoln(7)
ALVADORE Lane
AMITY (97101) Yamhill(83), Polk(16)
ANTELOPE Wasco
ARCH CAPE Clatsop
ARLINGTON Gilliam
AROCK Malheur
ASHLAND Jackson
ASHWOOD Jefferson
ASTORIA Clatsop
ATHENA Umatilla
AUMSVILLE Marion
AURORA (97002) Marion(76),
   Clackamas(23)
AZALEA Douglas
BAKER CITY (97814) Baker(95), Union(4)
BANDON Coos
BANKS Washington
BATES Grant
BAY CITY Tillamook
BEATTY Klamath
BEAVER Tillamook
BEAVERCREEK Clackamas
BEAVERTON Washington
BEND Deschutes
BLACHLY Lane
BLODGETT (97326) Lincoln(61),
   Benton(38)
BLUE RIVER Lane
BLY Klamath
BOARDMAN Morrow
BONANZA Klamath
BORING Clackamas
BRIDAL VEIL Multnomah
BRIDGEPORT Baker
BRIGHTWOOD Clackamas
BROADBENT Coos
BROGAN Malheur
BROOKINGS Curry
BROTHERS Deschutes
BROWNSVILLE Linn
BURNS Harney
BUTTE FALLS Jackson
BUXTON Washington
CAMAS VALLEY Douglas
CAMP SHERMAN Jefferson
CANBY Clackamas
CANNON BEACH Clatsop
CANYON CITY Grant
CANYONVILLE Douglas
CARLTON Yamhill
CASCADE LOCKS (97014)
   Multnomah(57), Hood River(42)
CASCADIA Linn
CAVE JUNCTION Josephine
CAYUSE Umatilla
CENTRAL POINT Jackson

CHEMULT (97731) Douglas(64),
   Klamath(35)
CHESHIRE Lane
CHILOQUIN Klamath
CHRISTMAS VALLEY Lake
CLACKAMAS Clackamas
CLATSKANIE (97016) Columbia(81),
   Clatsop(18)
CLOVERDALE Tillamook
COLTON Clackamas
COLUMBIA CITY Columbia
CONDON Gilliam
COOS BAY Coos
COQUILLE Coos
CORBETT Multnomah
CORNELIUS Washington
CORVALLIS Benton
COTTAGE GROVE Lane
COVE Union
CRABTREE Linn
CRANE Harney
CRATER LAKE Klamath
CRAWFORDSVILLE Linn
CRESCENT Klamath
CRESCENT LAKE Klamath
CRESWELL Lane
CULP CREEK Lane
CULVER Jefferson
CURTIN Douglas
DAIRY Klamath
DALLAS Polk
DAYS CREEK Douglas
DAYTON Yamhill
DAYVILLE (97825) Grant(97), Wheeler(2)
DEADWOOD Lane
DEER ISLAND Columbia
DEPOE BAY Lincoln
DETROIT Marion
DEXTER Lane
DIAMOND Harney
DILLARD Douglas
DONALD Marion
DORENA Lane
DRAIN Douglas
DREWSEY Harney
DUFUR Wasco
DUNDEE Yamhill
DURKEE Baker
EAGLE CREEK Clackamas
EAGLE POINT Jackson
ECHO Umatilla
EDDYVILLE Lincoln
ELGIN Union
ELKTON Douglas
ELMIRA Lane
ENTERPRISE Wallowa
ESTACADA Clackamas
EUGENE Lane
FAIRVIEW Multnomah
FALL CREEK Lane
FALLS CITY Polk
FIELDS Harney
FLORENCE Lane

FOREST GROVE Washington
FORT KLAMATH Klamath
FORT ROCK Lake
FOSSIL Wheeler
FOSTER Linn
FOX Grant
FRENCHGLEN Harney
GALES CREEK Washington
GARDINER Douglas
GARIBALDI Tillamook
GASTON (97119) Washington(76),
   Yamhill(23)
GATES (97346) Marion(75), Linn(25)
GERVAIS Marion
GILCHRIST Klamath
GLADSTONE Clackamas
GLENDALE Douglas
GLENEDEN BEACH Lincoln
GLIDE Douglas
GOLD BEACH Curry
GOLD HILL Jackson
GOVERNMENT CAMP Clackamas
GRAND RONDE (97347) Polk(64),
   Yamhill(33), Tillamook(1)
GRANTS PASS Josephine
GRASS VALLEY (97029) Wasco(95),
   Sherman(4)
GREENLEAF Lane
GRESHAM (97080) Multnomah(95),
   Clackamas(4)
HAINES Baker
HALFWAY Baker
HALSEY Linn
HAMMOND Clatsop
HARPER Malheur
HARRISBURG (97446) Linn(98), Lane(1)
HEBO Tillamook
HELIX Umatilla
HEPPNER Morrow
HEREFORD Baker
HERMISTON Umatilla
HILLSBORO Washington
HINES Harney
HOOD RIVER Hood River
HUBBARD (97032) Marion(91),
   Clackamas(8)
HUNTINGTON (97907) Malheur(67),
   Baker(32)
IDANHA (97350) Marion(72), Linn(27)
IDLEYLD PARK Douglas
IMBLER Union
IMNAHA Wallowa
INDEPENDENCE Polk
IONE Morrow
IRONSIDE Malheur
IRRIGON Morrow
JACKSONVILLE Jackson
JAMIESON Malheur
JEFFERSON Marion
JOHN DAY Grant
JORDAN VALLEY Malheur
JOSEPH Wallowa

JUNCTION CITY (97448) Lane(98),
   Benton(1)
JUNTURA Malheur
KEIZER Marion
KENO Klamath
KENT Sherman
KERBY Josephine
KIMBERLY Grant
KLAMATH FALLS Klamath
LA GRANDE Union
LA PINE (97739) Deschutes(75),
   Klamath(24)
LAFAYETTE Yamhill
LAKE OSWEGO (97035) Clackamas(92),
   Multnomah(5), Washington(1)
LAKESIDE Coos
LAKEVIEW Lake
LANGLOIS Curry
LAWEN Harney
LEBANON Linn
LEXINGTON Morrow
LINCOLN CITY Lincoln
LOGSDEN Lincoln
LONG CREEK Grant
LORANE Lane
LOSTINE Wallowa
LOWELL Lane
LYONS (97358) Linn(68), Marion(31)
MADRAS Jefferson
MALIN Klamath
MANNING Washington
MANZANITA Tillamook
MAPLETON Lane
MARCOLA Lane
MARION Marion
MARYLHURST Clackamas
MAUPIN Wasco
MCMINNVILLE Yamhill
MEACHAM Umatilla
MEDFORD Jackson
MEHAMA Marion
MERLIN Josephine
MERRILL Klamath
MIDLAND Klamath
MIKKALO Gilliam
MILL CITY (97360) Linn(65), Marion(34)
MILTON FREEWATER Umatilla
MITCHELL Wheeler
MOLALLA Clackamas
MONMOUTH (97361) Polk(97), Benton(2)
MONROE Benton
MONUMENT Grant
MORO (97039) Wasco(58), Sherman(41)
MOSIER Wasco
MOUNT ANGEL (97362) Marion(95),
   Clackamas(4)
MOUNT HOOD PARKDALE Hood River
MOUNT VERNON Grant
MULINO Clackamas
MURPHY Josephine
MYRTLE CREEK Douglas
MYRTLE POINT Coos

NEHALEM (97131) Tillamook(98), Clatsop(2)
NEOTSU Lincoln
NESKOWIN Tillamook
NETARTS Tillamook
NEW PINE CREEK (97635) Lake(71), Morrow(28)
NEWBERG (97132) Yamhill(98), Washington(1)
NEWPORT Lincoln
NORTH BEND Coos
NORTH PLAINS (97133) Washington(96), Multnomah(3)
NORTH POWDER (97867) Union(92), Baker(7)
NORWAY Coos
NOTI Lane
NYSSA Malheur
O BRIEN Josephine
OAKLAND Douglas
OAKRIDGE Lane
OCEANSIDE Tillamook
ODELL Hood River
ONTARIO Malheur
OPHIR Curry
OREGON CITY Clackamas
OTIS (97368) Lincoln(72), Tillamook(27)
OTTER ROCK Lincoln
OXBOW Baker
PACIFIC CITY Tillamook
PAISLEY Lake
PAULINA Crook
PENDLETON Umatilla
PHILOMATH Benton
PHOENIX Jackson
PILOT ROCK Umatilla
PLEASANT HILL Lane
PLUSH Lake
PORT ORFORD Curry
PORTLAND Multnomah
POST Crook

POWELL BUTTE Crook
POWERS Coos
PRAIRIE CITY Grant
PRINCETON Harney
PRINEVILLE Crook
PROSPECT Jackson
RAINIER Columbia
REDMOND Deschutes
REEDSPORT Douglas
REMOTE Coos
RHODODENDRON Clackamas
RICHLAND Baker
RICKREALL Polk
RIDDLE Douglas
RILEY Harney
RITTER Grant
RIVERSIDE Malheur
ROCKAWAY BEACH Tillamook
ROGUE RIVER Jackson
ROSE LODGE Lincoln
ROSEBURG Douglas
RUFUS Sherman
SAGINAW Lane
SAINT BENEDICT Marion
SAINT HELENS Columbia
SAINT PAUL Marion
SALEM Marion
SANDY Clackamas
SCAPPOOSE (97056) Columbia(98), Multnomah(1)
SCIO Linn
SCOTTS MILLS (97375) Marion(81), Clackamas(18)
SCOTTSBURG Douglas
SEAL ROCK Lincoln
SEASIDE Clatsop
SELMA Josephine
SENECA Grant
SHADY COVE Jackson
SHANIKO Wasco
SHEDD Linn

SHERIDAN (97378) Yamhill(85), Polk(14)
SHERWOOD (97140) Washington(75), Clackamas(20), Yamhill(3)
SILETZ Lincoln
SILVER LAKE Lake
SILVERTON Marion
SISTERS (97759) Deschutes(81), Jefferson(17), Linn(1)
SIXES Curry
SOUTH BEACH Lincoln
SPRAGUE RIVER Klamath
SPRAY Wheeler
SPRINGFIELD Lane
STANFIELD Umatilla
STAYTON (97383) Marion(96), Linn(3)
SUBLIMITY Marion
SUMMER LAKE Lake
SUMMERVILLE Union
SUMPTER Baker
SUTHERLIN Douglas
SWEET HOME Linn
SWISSHOME Lane
TALENT Jackson
TANGENT Linn
TENMILE Douglas
TERREBONNE (97760) Jefferson(55), Deschutes(40), Crook(3)
THE DALLES Wasco
THURSTON Lane
TIDEWATER (97390) Lincoln(89), Lane(10)
TILLAMOOK Tillamook
TILLER Douglas
TIMBER Washington
TOLEDO Lincoln
TOLOVANA PARK Clatsop
TRAIL Jackson
TROUTDALE Multnomah
TUALATIN (97062) Washington(83), Clackamas(16)
TURNER Marion
TYGH VALLEY Wasco

UKIAH Umatilla
UMATILLA Umatilla
UMPQUA Douglas
UNION Union
UNITY Baker
VALE Malheur
VENETA Lane
VERNONIA Columbia
VIDA Lane
WALDPORT Lincoln
WALLOWA Wallowa
WALTERVILLE Lane
WALTON Lane
WARM SPRINGS Jefferson
WARREN Columbia
WARRENTON Clatsop
WASCO Sherman
WEDDERBURN Curry
WELCHES Clackamas
WEST LINN Clackamas
WESTFALL Malheur
WESTFIR Lane
WESTLAKE Lane
WESTON Umatilla
WHEELER Tillamook
WHITE CITY Jackson
WILBUR Douglas
WILDERVILLE Josephine
WILLAMINA (97396) Yamhill(55), Polk(44)
WILLIAMS Josephine
WILSONVILLE (97070) Clackamas(88), Washington(11)
WINCHESTER Douglas
WINSTON Douglas
WOLF CREEK Josephine
WOODBURN (97071) Marion(97), Clackamas(2)
YACHATS Lincoln
YAMHILL Yamhill
YONCALLA Douglas

ZIP/City Cross Reference

97001-97001 ANTELOPE	97048-97048 RAINIER	97119-97119 GASTON	97336-97336 CRAWFORDSVILLE
97002-97002 AURORA	97049-97049 RHODODENDRON	97121-97121 HAMMOND	97338-97338 DALLAS
97004-97004 BEAVERCREEK	97050-97050 RUFUS	97122-97122 HEBO	97339-97339 CORVALLIS
97005-97008 BEAVERTON	97051-97051 SAINT HELENS	97123-97124 HILLSBORO	97341-97341 DEPOE BAY
97009-97009 BORING	97053-97053 WARREN	97125-97125 MANNING	97342-97342 DETROIT
97010-97010 BRIDAL VEIL	97054-97054 DEER ISLAND	97127-97127 LAFAYETTE	97343-97343 EDDYVILLE
97011-97011 BRIGHTWOOD	97055-97055 SANDY	97128-97128 MCMINNVILLE	97344-97344 FALLS CITY
97013-97013 CANBY	97056-97056 SCAPPOOSE	97130-97130 MANZANITA	97345-97345 FOSTER
97014-97014 CASCADE LOCKS	97057-97057 SHANIKO	97131-97131 NEHALEM	97346-97346 GATES
97015-97015 CLACKAMAS	97058-97058 THE DALLES	97132-97132 NEWBERG	97347-97347 GRAND RONDE
97016-97016 CLATSKANIE	97060-97060 TROUTDALE	97133-97133 NORTH PLAINS	97348-97348 HALSEY
97017-97017 COLTON	97062-97062 TUALATIN	97134-97134 OCEANSIDE	97350-97350 IDANHA
97018-97018 COLUMBIA CITY	97063-97063 TYGH VALLEY	97135-97135 PACIFIC CITY	97351-97351 INDEPENDENCE
97019-97019 CORBETT	97064-97064 VERNONIA	97136-97136 ROCKAWAY BEACH	97352-97352 JEFFERSON
97020-97020 DONALD	97065-97065 WASCO	97137-97137 SAINT PAUL	97355-97355 LEBANON
97021-97021 DUFUR	97067-97067 WELCHES	97138-97138 SEASIDE	97357-97357 LOGSDEN
97022-97022 EAGLE CREEK	97068-97068 WEST LINN	97140-97140 SHERWOOD	97358-97358 LYONS
97023-97023 ESTACADA	97070-97070 WILSONVILLE	97141-97141 TILLAMOOK	97359-97359 MARION
97024-97024 FAIRVIEW	97071-97071 WOODBURN	97143-97143 NETARTS	97360-97360 MILL CITY
97026-97026 GERVAIS	97075-97078 BEAVERTON	97144-97144 TIMBER	97361-97361 MONMOUTH
97027-97027 GLADSTONE	97080-97080 GRESHAM	97145-97145 TOLOVANA PARK	97362-97362 MOUNT ANGEL
97028-97028 GOVERNMENT CAMP	97101-97101 AMITY	97146-97146 WARRENTON	97364-97364 NEOTSU
97029-97029 GRASS VALLEY	97102-97102 ARCH CAPE	97147-97147 WHEELER	97365-97365 NEWPORT
97030-97030 GRESHAM	97103-97103 ASTORIA	97148-97148 YAMHILL	97366-97366 SOUTH BEACH
97031-97031 HOOD RIVER	97106-97106 BANKS	97149-97149 NESKOWIN	97367-97367 LINCOLN CITY
97032-97032 HUBBARD	97107-97107 BAY CITY	97200-97299 PORTLAND	97368-97368 OTIS
97033-97033 KENT	97108-97108 BEAVER	97301-97306 SALEM	97369-97369 OTTER ROCK
97034-97035 LAKE OSWEGO	97109-97109 BUXTON	97307-97307 KEIZER	97370-97370 PHILOMATH
97036-97036 MARYLHURST	97110-97110 CANNON BEACH	97308-97314 SALEM	97371-97371 RICKREALL
97037-97037 MAUPIN	97111-97111 CARLTON	97321-97321 ALBANY	97372-97372 ROSE LODGE
97038-97038 MOLALLA	97112-97112 CLOVERDALE	97324-97324 ALSEA	97373-97373 SAINT BENEDICT
97039-97039 MORO	97113-97113 CORNELIUS	97325-97325 AUMSVILLE	97374-97374 SCIO
97040-97040 MOSIER	97114-97114 DAYTON	97326-97326 BLODGETT	97375-97375 SCOTTS MILLS
97041-97041 MOUNT HOOD PARKDALE	97115-97115 DUNDEE	97327-97327 BROWNSVILLE	97376-97376 SEAL ROCK
97042-97042 MULINO	97116-97116 FOREST GROVE	97329-97329 CASCADIA	97377-97377 SHEDD
97044-97044 ODELL	97117-97117 GALES CREEK	97330-97333 CORVALLIS	97378-97378 SHERIDAN
97045-97045 OREGON CITY	97118-97118 GARIBALDI	97335-97335 CRABTREE	97380-97380 SILETZ

97381-97381 SILVERTON	97459-97459 NORTH BEND	97621-97621 BEATTY	97828-97828 ENTERPRISE
97383-97383 STAYTON	97460-97460 NORWAY	97622-97622 BLY	97830-97830 FOSSIL
97384-97384 MEHAMA	97461-97461 NOTI	97623-97623 BONANZA	97831-97831 FOX
97385-97385 SUBLIMITY	97462-97462 OAKLAND	97624-97624 CHILOQUIN	97833-97833 HAINES
97386-97386 SWEET HOME	97463-97463 OAKRIDGE	97625-97625 DAIRY	97834-97834 HALFWAY
97388-97388 GLENEDEN BEACH	97464-97464 OPHIR	97626-97626 FORT KLAMATH	97835-97835 HELIX
97389-97389 TANGENT	97465-97465 PORT ORFORD	97627-97627 KENO	97836-97836 HEPPNER
97390-97390 TIDEWATER	97466-97466 POWERS	97630-97630 LAKEVIEW	97837-97837 HEREFORD
97391-97391 TOLEDO	97467-97467 REEDSPORT	97632-97632 MALIN	97838-97838 HERMISTON
97392-97392 TURNER	97468-97468 REMOTE	97633-97633 MERRILL	97839-97839 LEXINGTON
97394-97394 WALDPORT	97469-97469 RIDDLE	97634-97634 MIDLAND	97840-97840 OXBOW
97396-97396 WILLAMINA	97470-97470 ROSEBURG	97635-97635 NEW PINE CREEK	97841-97841 IMBLER
97401-97405 EUGENE	97472-97472 SAGINAW	97636-97636 PAISLEY	97842-97842 IMNAHA
97406-97406 AGNESS	97473-97473 SCOTTSBURG	97637-97637 PLUSH	97843-97843 IONE
97407-97407 ALLEGANY	97476-97476 SIXES	97638-97638 SILVER LAKE	97844-97844 IRRIGON
97408-97408 EUGENE	97477-97478 SPRINGFIELD	97639-97639 SPRAGUE RIVER	97845-97845 JOHN DAY
97409-97409 ALVADORE	97479-97479 SUTHERLIN	97640-97640 SUMMER LAKE	97846-97846 JOSEPH
97410-97410 AZALEA	97480-97480 SWISSHOME	97641-97641 CHRISTMAS VALLEY	97848-97848 KIMBERLY
97411-97411 BANDON	97481-97481 TENMILE	97701-97709 BEND	97850-97850 LA GRANDE
97412-97412 BLACHLY	97482-97482 THURSTON	97710-97710 FIELDS	97856-97856 LONG CREEK
97413-97413 BLUE RIVER	97484-97484 TILLER	97711-97711 ASHWOOD	97857-97857 LOSTINE
97414-97414 BROADBENT	97486-97486 UMPQUA	97712-97712 BROTHERS	97859-97859 MEACHAM
97415-97415 BROOKINGS	97487-97487 VENETA	97720-97720 BURNS	97861-97861 MIKKALO
97416-97416 CAMAS VALLEY	97488-97488 VIDA	97721-97721 PRINCETON	97862-97862 MILTON FREEWATER
97417-97417 CANYONVILLE	97489-97489 WALTERVILLE	97722-97722 DIAMOND	97864-97864 MONUMENT
97419-97419 CHESHIRE	97490-97490 WALTON	97730-97730 CAMP SHERMAN	97865-97865 MOUNT VERNON
97420-97420 COOS BAY	97491-97491 WEDDERBURN	97731-97731 CHEMULT	97867-97867 NORTH POWDER
97423-97423 COQUILLE	97492-97492 WESTFIR	97732-97732 CRANE	97868-97868 PILOT ROCK
97424-97424 COTTAGE GROVE	97493-97493 WESTLAKE	97733-97733 CRESCENT	97869-97869 PRAIRIE CITY
97425-97425 CRESCENT LAKE	97494-97494 WILBUR	97734-97734 CULVER	97870-97870 RICHLAND
97426-97426 CRESWELL	97495-97495 WINCHESTER	97735-97735 FORT ROCK	97872-97872 RITTER
97427-97427 CULP CREEK	97496-97496 WINSTON	97736-97736 FRENCHGLEN	97873-97873 SENECA
97428-97428 CURTIN	97497-97497 WOLF CREEK	97737-97737 GILCHRIST	97874-97874 SPRAY
97429-97429 DAYS CREEK	97498-97498 YACHATS	97738-97738 HINES	97875-97875 STANFIELD
97430-97430 DEADWOOD	97499-97499 YONCALLA	97739-97739 LA PINE	97876-97876 SUMMERVILLE
97431-97431 DEXTER	97501-97501 MEDFORD	97740-97740 LAWEN	97877-97877 SUMPTER
97432-97432 DILLARD	97502-97502 CENTRAL POINT	97741-97741 MADRAS	97880-97880 UKIAH
97434-97434 DORENA	97503-97503 WHITE CITY	97750-97750 MITCHELL	97882-97882 UMATILLA
97435-97435 DRAIN	97504-97504 MEDFORD	97751-97751 PAULINA	97883-97883 UNION
97436-97436 ELKTON	97520-97520 ASHLAND	97752-97752 POST	97884-97884 UNITY
97437-97437 ELMIRA	97522-97522 BUTTE FALLS	97753-97753 POWELL BUTTE	97885-97885 WALLOWA
97438-97438 FALL CREEK	97523-97523 CAVE JUNCTION	97754-97754 PRINEVILLE	97886-97886 WESTON
97439-97439 FLORENCE	97524-97524 EAGLE POINT	97756-97756 REDMOND	97901-97901 ADRIAN
97440-97440 EUGENE	97525-97525 GOLD HILL	97758-97758 RILEY	97902-97902 AROCK
97441-97441 GARDINER	97526-97528 GRANTS PASS	97759-97759 SISTERS	97903-97903 BROGAN
97442-97442 GLENDALE	97530-97530 JACKSONVILLE	97760-97760 TERREBONNE	97904-97904 DREWSEY
97443-97443 GLIDE	97531-97531 KERBY	97761-97761 WARM SPRINGS	97905-97905 DURKEE
97444-97444 GOLD BEACH	97532-97532 MERLIN	97801-97801 PENDLETON	97906-97906 HARPER
97445-97445 GREENLEAF	97533-97533 MURPHY	97810-97810 ADAMS	97907-97907 HUNTINGTON
97446-97446 HARRISBURG	97534-97534 O BRIEN	97812-97812 ARLINGTON	97908-97908 IRONSIDE
97447-97447 IDLEYLD PARK	97535-97535 PHOENIX	97813-97813 ATHENA	97909-97909 JAMIESON
97448-97448 JUNCTION CITY	97536-97536 PROSPECT	97814-97814 BAKER CITY	97910-97910 JORDAN VALLEY
97449-97449 LAKESIDE	97537-97537 ROGUE RIVER	97817-97817 BATES	97911-97911 JUNTURA
97450-97450 LANGLOIS	97538-97538 SELMA	97818-97818 BOARDMAN	97913-97913 NYSSA
97451-97451 LORANE	97539-97539 SHADY COVE	97819-97819 BRIDGEPORT	97914-97914 ONTARIO
97452-97452 LOWELL	97540-97540 TALENT	97820-97820 CANYON CITY	97917-97917 RIVERSIDE
97453-97453 MAPLETON	97541-97541 TRAIL	97821-97821 CAYUSE	97918-97918 VALE
97454-97454 MARCOLA	97543-97543 WILDERVILLE	97823-97823 CONDON	97920-97920 WESTFALL
97455-97455 PLEASANT HILL	97544-97544 WILLIAMS	97824-97824 COVE	
97456-97456 MONROE	97601-97603 KLAMATH FALLS	97825-97825 DAYVILLE	
97457-97457 MYRTLE CREEK	97604-97604 CRATER LAKE	97826-97826 ECHO	
97458-97458 MYRTLE POINT	97620-97620 ADEL	97827-97827 ELGIN	

Pennsylvania

General Help Numbers:

Governor's Office

225 Main Capitol Bldg   717-787-2500
Harrisburg, PA 17120   Fax 717-772-8284
www.state.pa.us/PA_Exec/   9AM-4:30PM
Governor/organization.html

Attorney General's Office

Strawberry Square, 16th Floor   717-787-3391
Harrisburg, PA 17120   Fax 717-787-1190
www.attorneygeneral.gov   8AM-5PM

State Court Administrator

PO Box 229   717-795-2000
Mechanicsburg, PA 17055   Fax 717-795-2050
www.courts.state.pa.us   9AM-5PM

State Archives

Bureau of Archives & History   717-783-3281
350 North St   Fax 717-787-4822
Harrisburg, PA 17120   9AM-4PM TU-F
www.phmc.state.pa.us

State Specifics:

Capital: Harrisburg
    Dauphin County

Time Zone: EST

Number of Counties: 67

Population: 12,287,150

Web Site: www.state.pa.us

State Agencies

Criminal Records

State Police Central Repository, 1800 Elmerton Ave, Harrisburg, PA 17110-9758; 717-783-5494, 717-783-9973, 717-705-8840 (Fax), 8:15AM-4:15PM.

www.psp.state.pa.us/psp/site/default.asp

Note: A sex offender registry is not available online.

Indexing & Storage: Records are available from the 1920s. Records are available for all convictions. It takes 1 day before new records are available for inquiry. Records are indexed on fingerprint cards and inhouse computer. Records are normally destroyed after 3 years after individual is confirmed deceased by fingerprints. 60% of all arrests in database have final dispositions recorded, 31% for those arrests within last 5 years.

Searching: Must make request on Request Form SP4-164 or the request will be returned. Include the following in your request: full name, date of birth, Social Security Number, sex, race, any aliases. A release is not required. The record database is 100% fingerprint-supported. Statutorily-required fingerprint searches include an FBI fingerprint search. Records include felony and misdemeanor convictions, also cases without dispositions less than 3 years old.

Access by: mail.

Fee & Payment: Fee is $10.00 per name search. Add $24.00 if for a statutorily-required FBI fingerprint check. Fee payee: Commonwealth of Pennsylvania. Prepayment required. No personal checks accepted. No credit cards accepted.

Mail search: Turnaround time: 2-3 weeks. Turnaround can be 6 weeks if a record has a hit. No self addressed stamped envelope is required.

Corporation Records
Limited Partnership Records
Trademarks/Servicemarks
Fictitious Name
Assumed Name
Limited Liability Company Records
Limited Liability Partnerships

Corporation Bureau, Department of State, PO Box 8722, Harrisburg, PA 17105-8722 (Courier: 206 North Office Bldg, Harrisburg, PA 17120); 717-787-1057, 717-783-2244 (Fax), 8AM-5PM.

http://corps.state.pa.us/corps.htm

Indexing & Storage: Records are available from 1700's on. Records are indexed on computer since the 1800's.

Searching: Include the following in your request: full name of business. Corporation records include: Articles of Incorporation, Officers, Directors, DBAs, Prior (merged) names, Withdrawn and Reserved (120 days) names. Annual Reports on for-profit corporations are not required by the Department of State.

Access by: mail, phone, fax, in person, online.

Fee & Payment: The search fee is $12.00, copies are $2.00 per page. Fee payee: Department of State. Prepayment required. Ongoing requesters should open a customer deposit account. Personal checks accepted. No credit cards accepted.

Mail search: Turnaround time: 3 to 5 days. No self addressed stamped envelope is required.

Phone search: No fee for telephone request. They will provide basic information only.

Fax search: You must have an account to have materials returned by fax, same fees as above.

In person search: There are 2 computer terminals available for public use.

Online search: There is free general searching by entity name or number from the web site. Searching by name provides a list of entities whose name starts with the search name entered.Users can click on any one entity in the list displayed to get more detailed information regarding that entity.

Other access: Business lists, UCC on microfilm, and financing statements are available in bulk for $.25 per name.

Expedited service: Expedited service is available for mail and phone searches. Add $52.00 per transaction. If ordered before 1 PM, the record will be available by 5 PM.

Uniform Commercial Code

UCC Division, Department of State, PO Box 8721, Harrisburg, PA 17105-8721 (Courier: North Office Bldg, Rm 206, Harrisburg, PA 17120); 717-787-1057 x2, 717-783-2244 (Fax), 8AM-5PM.

www.dos.state.pa.us/corps/site/default.asp

Indexing & Storage: Records are available from 1964 to present on microfiche and computer. It takes 2 to 3 days before new records are available for inquiry.

Searching: Use search request form UCC-11. All federal and state tax liens are filed at the Prothonotary of each county. Include the following in your request: debtor name.

Access by: mail, fax, in person, online.

Fee & Payment: The search fee is $12.00 per debtor name, copies cost $2.00 per page. Fee payee: Pennsylvania Department of State. Prepayment required. Deposit accounts are accepted. Personal checks accepted. No credit cards accepted.

Mail search: Turnaround time: 3 to 5 days. A self addressed stamped envelope is requested.

Fax search: There is an additional $2.00 per page fee if returned by fax. A customer deposit account is required.

In person search: If the search is conducted by the customer, there is no $12.00 search fee.

Online search: The web site allows a search of UCC-1 financing statements filed with the Corporation Bureau by debtor name, which displays a list of financing statements. Users can refine the search further by entering a city and/or state for the search. The site also allows a search of financing statement records filed with the Corporation Bureau by financing statement number.

Other access: Daily computer tapes and copies of microfilm are available. Call the number above for details.

Federal Tax Liens
State Tax Liens

Records not maintained by a state level agency.

Note: All federal and state tax liens are filed at the Prothonotary of each county.

Sales Tax Registrations

Revenue Department, Sales Tax Division, Dept 280901, Harrisburg, PA 17128-0901; 717-783-9360, 717-783-5274 (Fax), 7:30AM-5PM.

www.revenue.state.pa.us

Indexing & Storage: Records are available from 1971 to present, seachable form 1995 forward.

Searching: This agency will only confirm that a business is registered, unless a signed release is proviced. They will only search with a tax permit number.

Access by: mail, phone, fax.

Fee & Payment: There is no search fee.

Mail search: Turnaround time: 2 to 7 days. A self addressed stamped envelope is requested.

Phone search: Records are available by phone.

Fax search: Same criteria as mail searches.

Birth Certificates

PA Department of Health, Division of Vital Records, PO Box 1528, New Castle, PA 16103-1528 (Courier: 101 S Mercer St, Room 401, New Castle, PA 16101); 724-656-3100 (Message Phone), 724-652-8951 (Fax), 8AM-4PM.

www.health.state.pa.us/vitalrecords

Indexing & Storage: Records are available from 1906 to present.

Searching: Must have a signed release form from person of record or immediate family member. Include the following in your request: full name, names of parents, mother's maiden name, date of birth, place of birth, relationship to person of record, reason for information request. Must include daytime phone number.

Access by: mail, phone, fax, in person.

Fee & Payment: The fee is $4.00 per record. Fee payee: Vital Records. Prepayment required. Personal checks accepted. Credit cards accepted: MasterCard, Visa, AmEx, Discover.

Mail search: Turnaround time: 3 weeks. Credit cards not accepted for mail requests. A self addressed stamped envelope is requested.

Phone search: Phone requests accepted with a credit card for an additional $7.00 fee. Turnaround time is 2-4 days.

Fax search: See expedited services

In person search: Turnaround time is 1 hour.

Expedited service: Expedited service is available for fax requests. Use of the state form (downloadable from web site) is recommended. Turnaround time: 2 to 3 days. Add $7.00 for credit card use; add fees for express delivery, if desired.

Death Records

Department of Health, Division of Vital Records, PO Box 1528, New Castle, PA 16103-1528 (Courier: 101 S Mercer St, Room 401, New Castle, PA 16101); 724-656-3100 (Message Phone), 724-652-8951 (Fax), 8AM-4:30PM.

www.health.state.pa.us/vitalrecords

Note: Statewide records are avilable from this office. Records from 1994 forward are available from these cities (only for that particular city): Erie, Harrisburg, Philadelphia, Pittsburgh, and Scranton. Visit web site for address information.

Indexing & Storage: Records are available from 1906 to present.

Searching: Must have a signed release form from immediate family member, or give tangible evidence of need. Requester must be at least 18 years of age. Include the following in your request: full name, date of death, place of death, relationship to person of record, reason for information request. SSN helpful, if known. Include daytime phone number.

Access by: mail, fax, in person.

Fee & Payment: The fee is $3.00 per record. Fee payee: Vital Records. Prepayment required. Personal checks accepted. Credit cards accepted: MasterCard, Visa, AmEx, Discover.

Mail search: Turnaround time: 3 to 4 weeks. A self addressed stamped envelope is requested.

Fax search: See Expedited Service.

In person search: Turnaround time 1 hour.

Expedited service: Expedited service is available for fax requests. Use of the state form (downloadable from web site) is recommended. Turnaround time: 2 to 3 days. Add $7.00 for use of credit card and cost of express delivery if desired.

Marriage Certificates
Divorce Records

Records not maintained by a state level agency.

Note: Marriage and divorce records are found at county level at Prothonotary of issue.

Workers' Compensation Records

Bureau of Workers' Compensation, Physical Records Section, 1171 S Cameron St, Rm 103, Harrisburg, PA 17104-2501; 717-772-4447, 7:30AM-4PM.

www.dli.state.pa.us/landi/site/default.asp

Indexing & Storage: Records are available for past 4 years. It takes 1 to 3 days before new records are available for inquiry. Records are indexed on inhouse computer.

Searching: Only the party to the record is allowed full access without a subpoena or a signed release. They will indicate whether they have a record for a person, but will not give any other information to the public. Include the following in your request: claimant name, year, date of accident, Social Security Number. If not a party to claim, then include a signed release.

Access by: mail.

Fee & Payment: No fees involved for simple requests.

Mail search: Turnaround time: 14 days. No self addressed stamped envelope is required.

Driver Records

Department of Transportation, Driver Record Services, PO Box 68695, Harrisburg, PA 17106-8695 (Courier: 1101 S Front Street, Harrisburg, PA 17104); 717-391-6190, 800-932-4600 (In-state only), 7:30AM-4:30PM.

www.dmv.state.pa.us

Note: Copies of tickets may be purchased from this location for a fee of $5.00 each.

Indexing & Storage: Records are available for minimum of 3 calendar years for moving violations and departmental actions, minimum of 7 years for DWIs, and indefinite for suspensions. Accidents are reported on record as involvement only. The driver's address appears on the record. It takes 60 days from receipt before new records are available for inquiry.

Searching: The state must pre-authorize all customers of MVR vendor companies. Include the following in your request: driver's license number, full name, date of birth. Casual requesters submit Form DL-503, which requires the signature of the subject, and notarized signature of the requester. Large volume requesters must sign an agreement stating the individual authorizations are on file.

Access by: mail, in person, online.

Fee & Payment: The fee is $5.00 for each record, add $10.00 for certification. A 10 year employment record for commercial drivers is available. Fee payee: Department of Transportation. Prepayment required. Personal checks accepted. No credit cards accepted.

Mail search: Turnaround time: 5 to 7 days. No self addressed stamped envelope is required.

In person search: The state will process one record request while you wait, additional requests are mailed back to the requester.

Online search: The online system is available to high volume requesters only. Fee is $5.00 per record. Call 717-787-7154 for more information. The sale of records over the Internet is strictly forbidden.

Vehicle Ownership
Vehicle Identification

Department of Transportation, Vehicle Record Services, PO Box 68691, Harrisburg, PA 17106-8691 (Courier: 1101 South Front St, Harrisburg, PA 17104); 717-391-6190, 800-932-6000 (In-state), 7:30AM-4:30PM.

www.dmv.state.pa.us

Note: This agency also holds records for unattached mobile homes.

Searching: The requester must submit Form DL-135. The state does not authorize the bulk delivery or commercial use of ownership and vehicle information.

Access by: mail.

Fee & Payment: The fee is $5.00 per transaction. Title history may have more than one transaction per vehicle. You can call first to determine the number. There is an additional $5.00 for certification. Fee payee: Department of Transportation. Prepayment required. Personal checks accepted. No credit cards accepted.

Mail search: Turnaround time: 7 to 10 days. You can order a record in person, but results will be mailed. No SASE is required.

Other access: Bulk information is not sold for commercial purposes. Certain statistical type user requests will be honored.

Accident Reports

State Police Headquarters, Crash Reports Unit, 1800 Elmerton Ave, Harrisburg, PA 17110; 717-783-5516, 8AM-5PM.

www.psp.state.pa.us

Note: Order form is available at the Web site.

Indexing & Storage: Records are available for 5 years to present. It takes 60 days before new records are available for inquiry. Records are indexed on inhouse computer.

Searching: Only those involved, their attorney or insurer may request a copy of the accident report. Include the following in your request: full name, date of accident, State Police incident number. The following data is not released: medical information or expunged records.

Access by: mail.

Fee & Payment: Reports are $8.00 per record. Fee payee: Commonwealth of Pennsylvania. Prepayment required. Personal checks accepted. No credit cards accepted.

Mail search: Turnaround time: 6 weeks or more.

Vessel Ownership
Vessel Registration

Access to Records is Restricted

Fish and Boat Commission, Licensing & Registration Section, PO Box 68900, Harrisburg, PA 17106-8900; 717-705-7940.

www.fish.state.pa.us

Note: Boat registration and ownership information is not open to the public. Liens are filed at UCC filing locations.

Legislation Records

Pennsylvania General Assembly, Legislative Reference Bureau, Main Capitol Bldg, Room 641, Harrisburg, PA 17120; 717-787-2342 (History Room), 717-787-5320 (House Bills), 717-787-6732 (Senate Bills), House-8:30AM-4:30PM/Senate-8:30AM-5PM.

www.legis.state.pa.us

Note: Call the History Room first to get the bill number, print number, and status.

Indexing & Storage: Records are available from 1981 to present. Records are indexed on inhouse computer.

Searching: Include the following in your request: the topic of bill (bill number is not required).

Access by: mail, phone, in person, online.

Fee & Payment: There is no search fee.

Mail search: Turnaround time: 2 days. No self addressed stamped envelope is required.

Phone search: Limited information is released.

In person search: Searching available in person.

Online search: Free access to bill text is available at the Electronic Bill Room found at the web page by selecting "Session Information."

Voter Registration

Records not maintained by a state level agency.

Note: Records are kept at the county level and cannot be sold for commercial purposes.

GED Certificates

Commonwealth Diploma Program, GED Testing, 333 Market St 12th Fl, Harrisburg, PA 17126-0333; 717-787-6747, 8:30AM-4:30PM.

www.paadulted.org/able/site/default.asp

Searching: For all requests the following is required: a signed release, name, approximate year of test, date of birth, Social Security Number, city of test, and a phone where you can be reached.

Access by: mail.

Fee & Payment: Verifications and copies of transcripts are $3.00 each. The fee is non-refundable. Fee payee: Commonwealth of PA. Prepayment required. Cashier's checks and money orders are accepted. No credit cards or personal checks accepted.

Mail search: Turnaround time: 3 to 4 weeks. No self addressed stamped envelope is required.

Hunting License Information

Records not maintained by a state level agency.

Note: Hunting license information is not released to the public.

Fishing License Information

Access to Records is Restricted

Fish & Boat Commission, Fishing License Division, PO Box 67000, Harrisburg, PA 17106 (Courier: 3532 Walnut St, Harrisburg, PA 17106); 717-705-7930 (Fishing License Division), 717-787-4250 (Hunting License Division), 717-705-7931 (Fax), 8AM-4PM.

Pennsylvania State Licensing Agencies

Licenses Searchable Online

Acupuncturist #20	http://licensepa.state.pa.us/default.asp
Amphetamine Program #20	http://licensepa.state.pa.us/default.asp
Animal Health Technician #20	http://licensepa.state.pa.us/default.asp
Appraiser, Residential #20	http://licensepa.state.pa.us/default.asp
Architect #20	http://licensepa.state.pa.us/default.asp
Athletic Agent #22	http://web.dos.state.pa.us/sac/cgi-bin/aalist.cgi
Auctioneer #20	http://licensepa.state.pa.us/default.asp
Auctioneer, Real Estate #20	http://licensepa.state.pa.us/default.asp
Audiologist #20	http://licensepa.state.pa.us/default.asp
Bank #4	www.banking.state.pa.us/PA_Exec/Banking/organiz.htm#exambureau
Barber #20	http://licensepa.state.pa.us/default.asp
Boxer #22	www.dos.state.pa.us/sac/cwp/view.asp?a=1090&q=436810&sacNav=|
Chiropractor #20	http://licensepa.state.pa.us/default.asp
Cosmetologist/Cosmetician #20	http://licensepa.state.pa.us/default.asp
Counselor, Professional #20	http://licensepa.state.pa.us/default.asp
Credit Union #4	www.banking.state.pa.us/PA_Exec/Banking/resource/cufrm.pdf
Dental Assistant, Expanded Function #18	www.licensepa.state.pa.us/default.asp
Dentist/Dental Hygienist #18	www.licensepa.state.pa.us/default.asp
Engineer #20	http://licensepa.state.pa.us/default.asp
Funeral Director #20	http://licensepa.state.pa.us/default.asp
Geologist #20	http://licensepa.state.pa.us/default.asp
Hearing Examiners #20	http://licensepa.state.pa.us/default.asp
Insurance Company #11	www.insurance.state.pa.us/html/licensed.html
Landscape Architect #20	http://licensepa.state.pa.us/default.asp
Manicurist #20	http://licensepa.state.pa.us/default.asp
Marriage & Family Therapist #20	http://licensepa.state.pa.us/default.asp
Medical Doctor #20	http://licensepa.state.pa.us/default.asp
Midwife #20	http://licensepa.state.pa.us/default.asp
Nuclear Medicine Technologist #20	http://licensepa.state.pa.us/default.asp
Nurse #20	http://licensepa.state.pa.us/default.asp
Nursing Home Administrator #20	http://licensepa.state.pa.us/default.asp
Occupational Therapist/Assistant #20	http://licensepa.state.pa.us/default.asp
Optometrist #20	http://licensepa.state.pa.us/default.asp
Osteopathic Physician/Phys. Assistant #20	http://licensepa.state.pa.us/default.asp
Pharmacist #20	http://licensepa.state.pa.us/default.asp
Physical Therapist/Assistant #20	http://licensepa.state.pa.us/default.asp
Physician Assistant #20	http://licensepa.state.pa.us/default.asp
Podiatrist #20	http://licensepa.state.pa.us/default.asp
Psychologist #20	http://licensepa.state.pa.us/default.asp
Public Accountant-CPA #20	http://licensepa.state.pa.us/default.asp
Public Accounting Partnership/Corp. #20	http://licensepa.state.pa.us/default.asp
Radiation Therapy Technician #20	http://licensepa.state.pa.us/default.asp
Radiologic Technologist #20	http://licensepa.state.pa.us/default.asp
Real Estate Appraiser/Broker #20	http://licensepa.state.pa.us/default.asp
Real Estate Salesperson #20	http://licensepa.state.pa.us/default.asp
Respiratory Care Practitioner #20	http://licensepa.state.pa.us/default.asp
Savings Association #4	www.banking.state.pa.us/PA_Exec/Banking/organiz.htm#exambureau
Social Worker #20	http://licensepa.state.pa.us/default.asp
Speech-Language Pathologist #20	http://licensepa.state.pa.us/default.asp
Surveyor, Land #20	http://licensepa.state.pa.us/default.asp
Teacher #6	https://www.tcs.ed.state.pa.us/validchk.asp
Trust Company #4	www.banking.state.pa.us/PA_Exec/Banking/organiz.htm#exambureau
Veterinarian #20	http://licensepa.state.pa.us/default.asp
Veterinary Technician #20	http://licensepa.state.pa.us/default.asp

Licensing Quick Finder

Acupuncturist #20	717-783-1400	Athletic Event Occupation #22	717-787-5720	Barber #20	717-783-3402
Ambulance Service #8	717-787-8740	Athletic Physician/Trainer #22	717-787-5720	Boat Registration #13	717-705-7940
Amphetamine Program #20	717-787-2568	Attorney #1	717-731-7073	Boxer #22	717-787-5720
Animal Health Technician #20	717-783-7134	Auctioneer #20	717-783-3397	Boxing Judge/Promoter/Second #22	717-787-5720
Appraiser, Residential #20	717-783-4866	Auctioneer, Real Estate #20	717-783-3658	Check Casher #4	717-787-3717
Architect #20	717-783-3397	Audiologist #20	717-783-1389	Child Day Care Facility #12	717-787-8691
Athletic Agent #22	717-787-5720	Bank #4	717-787-3717	Chiropractor #20	717-783-7155

License	Phone
Consumer Discount Company #4	717-787-3717
Cosmetologist/Cosmetician #20	717-783-7130
Counselor, Professional #20	717-783-1389
Credit Services Loan Broker #4	717-787-3717
Credit Union #4	717-787-3717
Debt Collector, Repossessor #4	717-787-3717
Dental Assistant, Expanded Function #18	717-783-7162
Dental Hygienist #18	717-783-7162
Dentist #18	717-783-7162
Education Specialist #6	717-787-2967
Emergency Medical Technician #8	717-787-8740
Engineer #20	717-783-7049
First Responder EMT #8	717-787-8740
Funeral Director #20	717-783-3397
Geologist #20	717-783-7049
Harness Racing #3	717-787-5789
Health Professional #8	717-787-8740
Hearing Aid Dealer #7	717-783-1389
Hearing Aid Fitter/Fitter Apprentice #7	717-783-1389
Hearing Examiners #20	717-783-1389
Horse Racing #3	717-783-8726
Installment Loan Seller #4	717-787-3717
Installment Seller #4	717-787-3717
Insurance Agent #11	717-787-3840
Insurance Broker/Supervisor #11	717-787-3840
Insurance Company #11	717-787-2735
Investment Adviser #16	717-783-4211
Kickboxer #22	717-787-5720
Laboratory, Medical #10	610-363-8500
Landscape Architect #20	717-772-8528
Liquor Distributor/Retailer/Wholesaler #14	717-783-8250
Lobbyist #17	717-787-5920
Manicurist #20	717-783-7130
Marriage & Family Therapist #20	717-783-1389
Medical Doctor #20	717-787-2381
Midwife #20	717-783-1400
Money Transmitter #4	717-787-3717
Mortgage (1st) Banker #4	717-787-3717
Mortgage (1st) Broker/Banker #4	717-787-3717
Mortgage (1st) Limited Broker #4	717-787-3717
Mortgage (1st) Loan Correspondent #4	717-787-3717
Mortgage (2nd) Lender #4	717-787-3717
Mortgage (2nd) Loan Broker/Agent #4	717-787-3717
Mortgage (Accelerated) Payment Provider #4	717-787-3717
Notary Public #21	717-787-5280
Nuclear Medicine Technologist #20	717-787-4858
Nurse #20	717-783-7142
Nursing Home #9	610-594-8041
Nursing Home Administrator #20	717-783-7155
Occupational Therapist/Assistant #20	717-783-1389
Optometrist #20	717-783-7155
Osteopathic Physician #20	717-783-4858
Osteopathic Physician Assistant #20	717-783-4858
Paramedic #8	717-787-8740
Pawnbroker #4	717-787-3717
Pest Management Consultant #2	717-787-5231x2
Pesticide Applicator/Technician #2	717-787-5231 x2
Pesticide Dealer #2	717-787-5231 x2
Pharmacist #20	717-783-7156
Physical Therapist/Assistant #20	717-783-7134
Physician Assistant #20	717-787-2381
Podiatrist #20	717-783-4858
Pre-Hospital RN #8	717-787-8740
Private Investigator #15	717-255-2692
Private School Staff #6	717-783-8228
Psychologist #20	717-783-7134
Public Accountant Corporation #20	717-783-1404
Public Accountant-CPA #20	717-783-1404
Public Accounting Partnership #20	717-783-1404
Radiation Therapy Technician #20	717-783-4858
Radiologic Technologist #20	717-783-4858
Real Estate Appraiser #20	717-783-4866
Real Estate Broker #20	717-783-3658
Real Estate Salesperson #20	717-783-3658
Referee #22	717-787-5720
Respiratory Care Practitioner #20	717-783-4858
Sales Finance Company #4	717-787-3717
Savings Association #4	717-787-3717
School Admin./Superintendent #6	717-787-2967
School Intermediate Unit Director #6	717-787-2967
School Supervisor #6	717-787-2967
Securities Agent #16	717-783-4212
Securities Broker/Dealer #16	717-783-4213
Social Worker #20	717-783-1389
Speech-Language Pathologist #20	717-783-1389
Surveyor, Land #20	717-783-7049
Tablefunder, Wholesale #4	717-787-3717
Teacher #6	717-787-2967
Teacher #5	717-787-2967
Trust Company #4	717-787-3717
Vehicle Dealer/Manufacturer #19	717-783-1697
Vehicle Salesperson #19	717-783-1697
Veterinarian #20	717-783-7134
Veterinary Technician #20	717-783-7134
Wrestling Promoter #22	717-787-5720

Licensing Agency Information

#1 Disciplinary Board of the Supreme Court of Pennsylvania, 2 Lemoyne Dr, First Fl, Lemoyne, PA 17055; 717-731-7073, Fax: 717-731-7080.

#2 Department of Agriculture, Bureau of Plant Industry, 2301 N Cameron St, Harrisburg, PA 17110-9408; 717-772-5231, Fax: 717-783-3275. http://sites.state.pa.us/PA_Exec/Agriculture/bureaus/plant_industry/index.html Agency email: dascott@state.pa.us.

#3 Department of Agriculture, (Racing License Division), 2301 N Cameron St, Agriculture Office Bldg, Harrisburg, PA 17110-9408; 717-787-5196, Fax: 717-787-2271. www.pda.state.pa.us

#4 Department of Banking, 333 Market St, 16th Fl, Harrisburg, PA 17111-2290; 717-787-2665, Fax: 717-787-8773. www.banking.state.pa.us Agency email: pabanking@banking.state.pa.us.

#6 Department of Education, 333 Market St, 3rd Fl, Harrisburg, PA 17126-0333; 717-787-2967, Fax: 717-783-6736. www.pde.state.pa.us Agency email: sstewart@state.pa.us. Search database at https://www.tcs.ed.state.pa.us/validchk.asp Use a teacher's SSN to verify certifications.

#7 Board of Examiners in Speech-Language and Hearing, Bureau of Profession and Occ. Affairs, PO Box 2649, Harrisburg, PA 17105; 717-783-1389, Fax: 717-787-7769. www.dos.state.pa.us/bpoa/cwp/view.asp?a=1104&q=433191 Agency email: speech@pados.dos.state.pa.us.

#8 Department of Health, Emergency Medical Services, PO Box 90 (7th & Forster), Harrisburg, PA 17108; 717-787-8740, Fax: 717-772-0910. www.webserver.health.state.pa.us/health/site

#9 Department of Health, Long Term Care Division, 110 Pickering Way, Lionville, PA 19353; 610-594-8041, Fax: 610-436-3346. www.health.state.pa.us/qa/ltc

#10 Department of Health, Bureau of Labs, PO Box 500, Exton, PA 19341-0500; 610-363-8500, Fax: 610-436-3346. www.health.state.pa.us/HPA/labinvst.htm

#11 Department of Insurance, 1300 Strawberry Sq, Harrisburg, PA 17120; 717-787-2735, Fax: 717-787-8557. www.insurance.state.pa.us Search database at www.insurance.state.pa.us/html/licensed.html

#12 Department of Public Welfare, 1401 N Market St, Harrisburg, PA 17105; 717-787-8691, Fax: 717-787-1529. www.dpw.state.pa.us/ocyf/dpwocyf.asp

#13 Fish & Boat Commission, 1601 Elmerton Ave, Harrisburg, PA 17110-9299; 717-705-7940, Fax: 717-705-7931. www.fish.state.pa.us

#14 Liquor Control Board, PO Box 8940 (Capitol & Forester St), Harrisburg, PA 17105-8940; 717-783-8250, Fax: 717-772-2165. wwww.lcb.state.pa.us

#16 Securities Commission, 1010 N 7th St, Eastgate-2nd Fl, Harrisburg, PA 17102-1410; 717-787-8061, Fax: 717-783-5122.www.psc.state.pa.us

#17 State Ethics Commission, 309 Finance Bldg, PO Box 11470, Harrisburg, PA 17108-1470; 717-783-1610. www.ethics.state.pa.us

#18 Department of State, Board of Dentistry, PO Box 2649 (124 Pine St), Harrisburg, PA 17105-2649; 717-783-7162, Fax: 717-787-7769. www.dos.state.pa.us/bpoa/denbd/mainpage.htm. Agency email: dentistr@pados.dos.state.pa.us. Search database at www.licensepa.state.pa.us/default.asp

#19 Dept. of State, Professional & Occupational Affairs, Board of Vehicle Manufacturers, Dealers & Salespersons, Box 2649PO Box 2649 (124 Pine St, Trans & Safety Bldg, 6th Fl), Harrisburg, PA 17105; 717-783-1697, Fax: 717-787-0250. www.dos.state.pa.us/bpoa/cwp/view.asp?a=1104&q=433233. Agency email: vehicle@pados.dos.state.pa.us. For verifications you may contact the Board via e-mail.

#20 Department of State, Professional & Occupational Affairs, P.O. Box 2649 (124 Pine St), Harrisburg, PA 17105; 717-787-8503, Fax: 717-787-7769. www.dos.state.pa.us/bpoa/site/default.asp Search database at http://licensepa.state.pa.us/default.asp

#21 Department of State, Elections & Legislation, North Office Bldg, Rm 304, Harrisburg, PA 17120; 717-787-5280, Fax: 717-787-2854. www.dos.state.pa.us Agency email: rcole@state.pa.us.

#22 Department of State, Athletic Commission, 116 Pine St, 3rd Fl, Harrisburg, PA 17101; 717-787-5720, Fax: 717-783-0824. www.dos.state.pa.us/sac/sac.html. Agency email: sac@pados.dos.state.pa.us.

Pennsylvania Federal Courts

The following list indicates the district and division name for each county in the state. If the bankruptcy court location is different from the district court, then the location of the bankruptcy court appears in parentheses.

County/Court Cross Reference

County	District	Location	County	District	Location
Adams	Middle	Harrisburg	Lackawanna	Middle	Scranton (Wilkes-Barre)
Allegheny	Western	Pittsburgh	Lancaster	Eastern	Allentown/Reading (Reading)
Armstrong	Western	Pittsburgh	Lawrence	Western	Pittsburgh
Beaver	Western	Pittsburgh	Lebanon	Middle	Harrisburg
Bedford	Western	Johnstown (Pittsburgh)	Lehigh	Eastern	Allentown/Reading (Reading)
Berks	Eastern	Allentown/Reading (Reading)	Luzerne	Middle	Scranton (Wilkes-Barre)
Blair	Western	Johnstown (Pittsburgh)	Lycoming	Middle	Williamsport (Wilkes-Barre)
Bradford	Middle	Scranton (Wilkes-Barre)	McKean	Western	Erie
Bucks	Eastern	Philadelphia	Mercer	Western	Pittsburgh (Erie)
Butler	Western	Pittsburgh	Mifflin	Middle	Harrisburg
Cambria	Western	Johnstown (Pittsburgh)	Monroe	Middle	Scranton (Wilkes-Barre)
Cameron	Middle	Williamsport (Wilkes-Barre)	Montgomery	Eastern	Philadelphia
Carbon	Middle	Scranton (Wilkes-Barre)	Montour	Middle	Williamsport (Harrisburg)
Centre	Middle	Williamsport (Harrisburg)	Northampton	Eastern	Allentown/Reading (Reading)
Chester	Eastern	Philadelphia	Northumberland	Middle	Williamsport (Harrisburg)
Clarion	Western	Pittsburgh (Erie)	Perry	Middle	Williamsport (Harrisburg)
Clearfield	Western	Johnstown (Pittsburgh)	Philadelphia	Eastern	Philadelphia
Clinton	Middle	Williamsport (Wilkes-Barre)	Pike	Middle	Scranton (Wilkes-Barre)
Columbia	Middle	Williamsport (Wilkes-Barre)	Potter	Middle	Williamsport (Wilkes-Barre)
Crawford	Western	Erie	Schuylkill	Eastern	Allentown/Reading (Reading)
Cumberland	Middle	Harrisburg	Snyder	Middle	Williamsport (Harrisburg)
Dauphin	Middle	Harrisburg	Somerset	Western	Johnstown (Pittsburgh)
Delaware	Eastern	Philadelphia	Sullivan	Middle	Williamsport (Wilkes-Barre)
Elk	Western	Erie	Susquehanna	Middle	Scranton (Wilkes-Barre)
Erie	Western	Erie	Tioga	Middle	Williamsport (Wilkes-Barre)
Fayette	Western	Pittsburgh	Union	Middle	Williamsport (Harrisburg)
Forest	Western	Erie	Venango	Western	Erie
Franklin	Middle	Harrisburg	Warren	Western	Erie
Fulton	Middle	Harrisburg	Washington	Western	Pittsburgh
Greene	Western	Pittsburgh	Wayne	Middle	Scranton (Wilkes-Barre)
Huntingdon	Middle	Harrisburg	Westmoreland	Western	Pittsburgh
Indiana	Western	Pittsburgh	Wyoming	Middle	Scranton (Wilkes-Barre)
Jefferson	Western	Pittsburgh (Erie)	York	Middle	Harrisburg
Juniata	Middle	Harrisburg			

US District Court

Eastern District of Pennsylvania

Allentown/Reading Division c/o Philadelphia Division, Room 2609, US Courthouse, 601 Market St, Philadelphia, PA 19106-1797 (Use mail address for courier delivery), 215-597-7704, Fax: 215-597-6390.

www.paed.uscourts.gov

Counties: Berks, Lancaster, Lehigh, Northampton, Schuylkill.

Indexing & Storage: New cases are available in the index after filing date. Open records are located at the Philadelphia Division.

Fee & Payment Notes: Payment may be made by money order, cashier check. Business checks are not accepted. Personal checks are not accepted.

Phone Search: Searching not available by phone.

In Person Search: In person searching available.

PACER: Sign-up number is 215-597-5710. Toll-free dial-up access: 800-458-2993. Local dial-up access: 215-597-0258. Case records are available back to July 1, 1990. Records are never purged.

New records are available online after 1 day. PACER is available online at http://pacer.paed.uscourts.gov.

Electronic Filing: Information is available online at https://ecf.paed.uscourts.gov

Opinions Online: Court opinions are available online at www.paed.uscourts.gov/contents.shtml

Other Online Access: Online access is available free at www.paed.uscourts.gov/us04000.shtml. No fee to search; select document type and enter name as search string.

Philadelphia Division Room 2609, US Courthouse, 601 Market St, Philadelphia, PA 19106-1797 (Use mail address for courier delivery), 215-597-7704, Fax: 215-597-6390.

www.paed.uscourts.gov

Counties: Bucks, Chester, Delaware, Montgomery, Philadelphia.

Indexing & Storage: Cases are indexed by defendant, plaintiff, and case number. New cases are available in the index immediately after filing date. The computer index is from 1990 on. Records are also indexed on microfiche. Indexes by judgment and by nature of suit are also

available. District wide searches are available from this division.

Fee & Payment Notes: Payment may be made by money order, cashier check, personal check, Visa, Mastercard. Payee: Clerk, US District Court.

Phone Search: Docket information available by phone if case number is known.

Fax Search: Will accept fax searches at $15.00 per name. Will fax docket listing at $.50 per page.

In Person Search: In person searching available.

PACER: Sign-up number is 215-597-5710. Toll-free dial-up access: 800-458-2993. Local dial-up access: 215-597-0258. Case records are available back to July 1, 1990. Records are never purged. New records are available online after 1 day. PACER is available online at http://pacer.paed.uscourts.gov.

Electronic Filing: Information is available online at https://ecf.paed.uscourts.gov

Opinions Online: Court opinions are available online at www.paed.uscourts.gov/contents.shtml

Other Online Access: Online access is available free at www.paed.uscourts.gov/us04000.shtml. No fee to search; select document type and enter name as search string.

Standards for Federal Courts: The search fee is $20.00 per item (one party name or case number). Certification fee is $7.00 per document. Copy fee is $.50 per page. All fees standard unless noted in profile. Mail Search: always enclose a stamped self addressed envelope unless otherwise noted. Before releasing records, all courts require prepayment unless noted in profile. Open records are located at the court unless otherwise noted. District courts index by defendant and plaintiff as well as by case number. Bankruptcy courts usually index by debtor and case number. While most courts now have their indexes on computer, many still maintain index card files as well. The universal PACER sign-up number is 800-676-6856. Find PACER and the Party/Case Index on the Web at http://pacer.psc.uscourts.gov. PACER dial-up access is $.60 per minute. Also, courts offering internet access via RACER, PACER, Web-PACER or the new CM-ECF charge $.07 per page fee unless noted as free.

US Bankruptcy Court

Eastern District of Pennsylvania

Philadelphia Division 4th Floor, 900 Market St, Philadelphia, PA 19107 (Courier Address: Use mail address for courier delivery), 215-408-2800.

www.paeb.uscourts.gov

Counties: Bucks, Chester, Delaware, Montgomery, Philadelphia.

Indexing & Storage: Cases are indexed by debtor and creditors as well as by case number. New cases are available in the index 1 day after filing date. A microfiche index is also maintained. Open records are located at this court.

Fee & Payment Notes: Payment may be made by money order, cashier check, business check, Visa or Mastercard. Personal checks are not accepted. Payee: Clerk, US Bankruptcy Court. You are allowed to make your own copies. These copies cost $.25 per page. In person searchers may not search the card index.

Phone Search: An automated voice case information service (VCIS) is available. Call VCIS at 215-597-2244.

In Person Search: In person searching available.

PACER: Toll-free dial-up access: 888-381-2921. Local dial-up access: 215-597-3501. Case records are available back to 1988. Records are purged every 6 months. New civil records are available online after 1 day. PACER is available online at http://pacer.paeb.uscourts.gov.

Electronic Filing: (Currently in the process of implementing CM/ECF.)

Reading Division Suite 300, The Madison, 400 Washington St, Reading, PA 19601 (Courier Address: Use mail address for courier delivery), 610-320-5255.

www.paeb.uscourts.gov

Counties: Berks, Lancaster, Lehigh, Northampton, Schuylkill.

Indexing & Storage: Cases are indexed by debtor as well as by case number. New cases are available in the index 1 day after filing date. Open records are located at this court.

Fee & Payment Notes: Payment may be made by money order, cashier check, business check, Visa

or Mastercard. Personal checks are not accepted. Payee: Clerk, US Bankruptcy Court.

Phone Search: Only docket information is available by phone. An automated voice case information service (VCIS) is available. Call VCIS at 215-597-2244.

In Person Search: In person searching available.

PACER: Toll-free dial-up access: 888-381-2921. Local dial-up access: 215-597-3501. Case records are available back to 1988. Records are purged every 6 months. New civil records are available online after 1 day. PACER is available online at http://pacer.paeb.uscourts.gov.

Electronic Filing: (Currently in the process of implementing CM/ECF.)

US District Court

Middle District of Pennsylvania

Harrisburg Division PO Box 983, Harrisburg, PA 17108-0983 (Courier Address: US Courthouse & Federal Bldg, 228 Walnut St, Harrisburg, PA 17108), 717-221-3920, Fax: 717-221-3959.

www.pamd.uscourts.gov

Counties: Adams, Cumberland, Dauphin, Franklin, Fulton, Huntingdon, Juniata, Lebanon, Mifflin, York.

Indexing & Storage: Cases are indexed by defendant, plaintiff, and case number. New cases are available in the index immediately after filing date. Open records are located at this court.

Fee & Payment Notes: Payment may be made by money order, cashier check, personal check, American Express, Visa, Mastercard. Payee: Clerk, US District Court.

Phone Search: Searching not available by phone. Only accession numbers for a specific case are available by phone.

Fax Search: Will accept fax search requests for $25.00. The fee is $1.00 per page.

Mail Search: A stamped self addressed envelope is not required.

In Person Search: In person searching available.

PACER: Toll-free dial-up access: 800-658-8381. Local dial-up access: 570-347-8286. Document images available. Case records are available back to May 1989. Records are never purged. New records are available online after 1 day. PACER is available online at http://pacer.pamd.uscourts.gov. Document images available.

Electronic Filing: (CM/ECF available late 2002)

Other Online Access: Search records on the Internet using RACER at https://racer.pamd.uscourts.gov/perl/bkplog.html.

Scranton Division Clerk's Office, William J Nealon Fedearl Bldg & US Courthouse, PO Box 1148, Scranton, PA 18501 (Courier Address: 235 N Washington Ave, Room 101, Scranton, PA 18503), 570-207-5680, Fax: 717-207-5689.

www.pamd.uscourts.gov

Counties: Bradford, Carbon, Lackawanna, Luzerne, Monroe, Pike, Susquehanna, Wayne, Wyoming.

Indexing & Storage: Cases are indexed by defendant, plaintiff, and case number. New cases are available in the index 1 day after filing date. Records are also indexed on microfiche. Records

are stored on an in-house computer from 1989. District wide searches are available for information from 1901 from this court.

Fee & Payment Notes: Payment may be made by money order, cashier check, personal check, Visa, Mastercard. Payee: Clerk, US District Court.

Phone Search: Only minimal docket information will be released over the phone.

Fax Search: Will accept fax search with credit card number.

Mail Search: A stamped self addressed envelope is not required.

In Person Search: In person searching available.

PACER: Toll-free dial-up access: 800-658-8381. Local dial-up access: 570-347-8286. Case records are available back to May 1989. Records are never purged. New records are available online after 1 day. PACER is available online at http://pacer.pamd.uscourts.gov. Document images available.

Electronic Filing: (CM/ECF available late 2002)

Other Online Access: Search records on the Internet using RACER at https://racer.pamd.uscourts.gov/perl/bkplog.html.

Williamsport Division PO Box 608, Williamsport, PA 17703 (Courier Address: Federal Bldg, ROom 402, 240 W 3rd St, Williamsport, PA 17701), 570-323-6380, Fax: 717-323-0636.

www.pamd.uscourts.gov

Counties: Cameron, Centre, Clinton, Columbia, Lycoming, Montour, Northumberland, Perry, Potter, Snyder, Sullivan, Tioga, Union.

Indexing & Storage: Cases are indexed by defendant, plaintiff, and case number. New cases are available in the index immediately after filing date. Open records are located at this court.

Fee & Payment Notes: Payment may be made by money order, cashier check, personal check, Visa, Mastercard. Payee: Clerk, US District Court.

Phone Search: Only docket information is available by phone.

Fax Search: Fax requests require the original signature and prepayment.

In Person Search: In person searching available.

PACER: Toll-free dial-up access: 800-658-8381. Local dial-up access: 570-347-8286. Case records are available back to May 1989. Records are never purged. New records are available online after 1 day. PACER is available online at http://pacer.pamd.uscourts.gov. Document images available.

Electronic Filing: (CM/ECF available late 2002)

Other Online Access: Search records on the Internet using RACER at https://racer.pamd.uscourts.gov/perl/bkplog.html.

US Bankruptcy Court

Middle District of Pennsylvania

Harrisburg Division PO Box 908, Harrisburg, PA 17108 (Courier: 228 Walnut St, 3rd Floor, Harrisburg, PA 17101), 717-901-2800.

www.pamd.uscourts.gov

Counties: Adams, Centre, Cumberland, Dauphin, Franklin, Fulton, Huntingdon, Juniata, Lebanon, Mifflin, Montour, Northumberland, Perry, Schuylkill, Snyder, Union, York.

Indexing & Storage: Cases are indexed by debtor as well as by case number. New cases are available in the index 1 day after filing date. Open records are located at this court.

Fee & Payment Notes: Payment may be made by money order, cashier check, personal check. Debtor's checks are not accepted. Payee: Clerk, US Bankruptcy Court.

Phone Search: Only docket information is available by phone. An automated voice case information service (VCIS) is available. Call VCIS at 877-440-2699.

In Person Search: In person searching available.

PACER: Toll-free dial-up access: 800-882-6899. Local dial-up access: 570-901-2835. Case records are available back to August 1986. Records are never purged. New civil records are available online after 1 day. PACER is available online at http://pacer.pamb.uscourts.gov. Document images available.

Electronic Filing: (Currently in the process of implementing CM/ECF.)

Wilkes-Barre Division
Clerk's Office, Max Rosen US Courthouse, 197 S Main St, Wilkes-Barre, PA 18701 (Courier Address: Use mail address for courier delivery), 570-826-6450.

www.paeb.uscourts.gov

Counties: Bradford, Cameron, Carbon, Clinton, Columbia, Lackawanna, Luzerne, Lycoming, Monroe, Pike, Potter, Schuylkill, Sullivan, Susquehanna, Tioga, Wayne, Wyoming.

Indexing & Storage: Cases are indexed by debtor as well as by case number. New cases are available in the index 1-3 days after filing date. Open records are located at this court.

Fee & Payment Notes: Payment may be made by money order, cashier check, personal check. Debtor's checks are not accepted. Make checks payable to the Clerk for services other than copy services; for copies, make checks payable to Louise Cannon Copy Service. Payee: Clerk, US Bankruptcy Court. You are allowed to make your own copies.

Phone Search: Phone searches can be done if the name, social security number, or case number is provided. Only docket information will be released. An automated voice case information service (VCIS) is available. Call VCIS at 877-440-2699.

In Person Search: In person searching available.

PACER: Toll-free dial-up access: 800-640-3037. Local dial-up access: 570-821-4033. Use of PC Anywhere v4.0 suggested. Case records are available back to 1987. New civil records are available online after 1 day. PACER is available online at http://pacer.pamb.uscourts.gov. Document images available.

Electronic Filing: (Currently in the process of implementing CM/ECF.)

US District Court
Western District of Pennsylvania

Erie Division PO Box 1820, Erie, PA 16507 (Courier Address: 102 US Courthouse, 617 State St, Erie, PA 16501), 814-453-4829.

www.pawd.uscourts.gov

Counties: Crawford, Elk, Erie, Forest, McKean, Venango, Warren.

Indexing & Storage: Cases are indexed by defendant, plaintiff, and case number. New cases are available in the index 1 day after filing date. The court prefers that you perform searches through the Pittsburgh Division. Open records are located at this court.

Fee & Payment Notes: Payment may be made by money order, cashier check, personal check, Visa, Mastercard. Payee: Clerk, US District Court.

Phone Search: Only the number, caption and attorneys' names will be released over the phone.

In Person Search: In person searching available.

PACER: Toll-free dial-up access: 800-770-4745. Local dial-up access: 412-208-7588. Case records are available back to 1989. Records are never purged. New records are available online after 1 day. PACER is available online at http://pacer.pawd.uscourts.gov.

Johnstown Division
Penn Traffic Bldg, Room 208, 319 Washington St, Johnstown, PA 15901 (Courier: Use mail address for courier delivery), 814-533-4504, Fax: 814-533-4519.

www.pawd.uscourts.gov

Counties: Bedford, Blair, Cambria, Clearfield, Somerset.

Indexing & Storage: Cases are indexed by defendant, plaintiff, and case number. New cases are available in the index 1 day after filing date. On computer since June 1992. Card index from 1989 to 1992. Open records are located at this court.

Fee & Payment Notes: Payment may be made by money order, cashier check, personal check, Visa. Payee: Clerk, US District Court.

Phone Search: Only the number, caption and attorneys' names will be released over the phone.

Mail Search: A stamped self addressed envelope is not required.

In Person Search: In person searching available.

PACER: Toll-free dial-up access: 800-770-4745. Local dial-up access: 412-208-7588. Case records are available back to 1989. Records are never purged. New records are available online after 1 day. PACER is available online at http://pacer.pawd.uscourts.gov.

Pittsburgh Division
US Post Office & Courthouse, Room 829, 7th Ave & Grant St, Pittsburgh, PA 15219 (Courier Address: Use mail address for courier delivery), 412-644-3527.

www.pawd.uscourts.gov

Counties: Allegheny, Armstrong, Beaver, Butler, Clarion, Fayette, Greene, Indiana, Jefferson, Lawrence, Mercer, Washington, Westmoreland.

Indexing & Storage: Cases are indexed by defendant, plaintiff, and case number. New cases are available in the index 2 days after filing date. The Erie and Johnstown Divisions send complete paper copies of. Case records to Pittsburgh, so that all. Case records for the District are available here.

Fee & Payment Notes: Payment may be made by money order, cashier check, personal check, Visa, Mastercard. Payee: Clerk, US District Court.

Phone Search: Only docket information is available by phone.

In Person Search: In person searching available.

PACER: Toll-free dial-up access: 800-770-4745. Local dial-up access: 412-208-7588. Case records are available back to 1989. Records are never purged. New records are available online after 1 day. PACER is available online at http://pacer.pawd.uscourts.gov.

US Bankruptcy Court
Western District of Pennsylvania

Erie Division 717 State St, #501, Erie, PA 16501 (Courier Address: Use mail address for courier delivery), 814-453-7580.

www.pawb.uscourts.gov

Counties: Clarion, Crawford, Elk, Erie, Forest, Jefferson, McKean, Mercer, Venango, Warren.

Indexing & Storage: Cases are indexed by debtor as well as by case number. New cases are available in the index 1 day after filing date. Open records are located at this court.

Fee & Payment Notes: Payment may be made by money order, cashier check, personal check. Payee: Clerk, US Bankruptcy Court.

Phone Search: Docket information is available by phone. An automated voice case information service (VCIS) is available. Call VCIS at 412-355-3210.

In Person Search: In person searching available.

PACER: Toll-free dial-up access: 800-795-2829. Local dial-up access: 412-355-2588. Case records are available back to 1991. Records are purged every six months. New civil records are available online after 1 day. PACER is available online at http://pacer.pawb.uscourts.gov.

Electronic Filing: (Currently in the process of implementing CM/ECF.)

Pittsburgh Division
600 Grant St #5414, Pittsburgh, PA 15219-2801 (Courier Address: Use mail address for courier delivery), 412-644-2700.

www.pawb.uscourts.gov

Counties: Allegheny, Armstrong, Beaver, Bedford, Blair, Butler, Cambria, Clearfield, Fayette, Greene, Indiana, Lawrence, Somerset, Washington, Westmoreland.

Indexing & Storage: Cases are indexed by debtor as well as by case number. New cases are available in the index 1 day after filing date. Records are also indexed on microfiche. District wide searches are available for information from 1986 from this division.

Fee & Payment Notes: Payment may be made by money order, personal check. Debtor's checks are not accepted. Payee: Clerk, US Bankruptcy Court.

Phone Search: Docket information is available by phone. An automated voice case information service (VCIS) is available. Call VCIS at 412-355-3210.

In Person Search: In person searching available.

PACER: Toll-free dial-up access: 800-795-2829. Local dial-up access: 412-355-2588. Case records are available back to 1991. Records are purged every six months. New civil records are available online after 1 day. PACER is available online at http://pacer.pawb.uscourts.gov.

Electronic Filing: (Currently in the process of implementing CM/ECF.)

Pennsylvania County Courts

Court	Jurisdiction	No. of Courts	How Organized
Court of Common Pleas*	General	103	60 Districts
Philadelphia Municipal Court*	Municipal	1	1st District
Philadelphia Traffic Court	Municipal	1	1st District
Pittsburgh Magistrates Court	Municipal	1	Pittsburgh
Register of Wills*	Probate	67	
Magisterial District Courts	Limited	550	

* Profiled in this Sourcebook.

CIVIL								
Court	Tort	Contract	Real Estate	Min. Claim	Max. Claim	Small Claims	Estate	Eviction	Domestic Relations
Court of Common Pleas*	X	X	X	$0	No Max			X	X
Philadelphia Municipal Court*	X	X	X	$0	$10,000	$5000		X	X
Philadelphia Traffic Court									
Pittsburgh City Magistrates Court			X	$0	No Max				
Register of Wills*							X		
Magisterial District Courts	X	X	X	$0	$8000	$8000			

CRIMINAL					
Court	Felony	Misdemeanor	DWI/DUI	Preliminary Hearing	Juvenile
Court of Common Pleas*	X	X	X	X	X
Philadelphia Municipal Court*	X	X	X	X	
Philadelphia Traffic Court					
Pittsburgh City Magistrates Court		X	X		
Register of Wills*					
Magisterial District Courts		X	X	X	

ADMINISTRATION
Administrative Office of Pennsylvania Courts, PO Box 719, Mechanicsburg, PA, 17055; 717-795-2000, Fax: 717-795-2050. www.courts.state.pa.us

COURT STRUCTURE
The Courts of Common Pleas are the general trial courts, with jurisdiction over both civil and criminal matters and appellate jurisdiction over matters disposed of by the special courts. The civil records clerk of the Court of Common Pleas is called the Prothonotary.

Small claims cases are, usually, handled by the Magistrates and Magisterial District Courts (formerly known as District Justice Courts). These Magisterial Courts, which are designated as "special courts," also handle civil cases up to $8,000. However, all small claims and civil actions are recorded through the Prothonotary Section (civil) of the Court of Common Pleas, which then holds the records. It is not necessary to check with each Magisterial District Court, but rather to check with the Prothonotary for the county.

ONLINE ACCESS

The state's Magisterial District Courts are served by a statewide, automated case management system; online access to the case management system is not available. However, public access to statutorily authorized information is available from the Special Courts, filing offices of Appellate Courts, and from the AOPC. The courts are considering ways to implement a unified, statewide system in the criminal division of the Courts of Common Pleas.

The Infocon County Access System provides direct dial-up access to court record information for 15 counties - Armstrong, Bedford, Blair, Butler, Clarion, Clinton, Erie, Franklin, Huntingdon, Juaniata, Lawrence, Mercer, Mifflin, Pike, and Potter. Set up entails a $25.00 base set-up fee plus $25.00 per county. The monthly usage fee minimum is $25.00, plus time charges. For Information, call Infocon at 814-472-6066.

ADDITIONAL INFORMATION

Fees vary widely among jurisdictions. Many courts will not conduct searches due to a lack of personnel or, if they do search, turnaround time may be excessively lengthy. Many courts have public access terminals for in-person searches.

PROBATE COURTS

Probate is handled by the Register of Wills.

Adams County

Court of Common Pleas - Civil 111-117 Baltimore St Rm 104, Gettysburg, PA 17325; 717-334-6781 X285. Hours: 8AM-4:30PM (EST). *Civil, Eviction.*

Civil Records: Access: In person. Visitors must perform in person searches. No search fee. Required to search: name, years to search. Civil cases indexed by defendant, plaintiff. Civil records on computer from 1988, some microfiche (dates unsure), on index from 1800s.

General Information: Public access terminal is available. No mental health, sealed records released. SASE required. Turnaround time 1-2 days. Copy fee: $.25 per page. Certification fee: $4.50 per document. Fee payee: Prothonotary. Personal checks accepted. Prepayment is required.

Court of Common Pleas - Criminal 111-117 Baltimore St, Gettysburg, PA 17325; 717-337-9806. Hours: 8AM-4:30PM (EST). *Felony, Misdemeanor.*

Criminal Records: Access: Mail, in person. Both court and visitors may perform in person searches. Search fee: $8.00 per name. Required to search: name, years to search, DOB. Criminal records on computer since 1986 on microfiche since 1974, previous records on microfilm to 1800's.

General Information: Public access terminal is available. No juvenile records released. SASE required. Turnaround time 1 day. Copy fee: $.25 per page. Certification fee: $8.00. Fee payee: Clerk of Courts. Personal checks accepted. No third party checks. Prepayment is required.

Register of Wills 111-117 Baltimore St Rm 102, Gettysburg, PA 17325; 717-337-9826; Fax: 717-334-1758. Hours: 8AM-4:30PM (EST). *Probate.*

Allegheny County

Court of Common Pleas - Civil City County Bldg, 414 Grant St, First Floor, Pittsburgh, PA 15219; 412-350-4200; Fax: 412-350-5260. Hours: 8:30AM-4:30PM (EST). *Civil.*

www.county.allegheny.pa.us

Civil Records: Access: Mail, in person, online. Both court and visitors may perform in person searches. Search fee: $25.00 per name. Required to search: name, years to search. Civil cases indexed by defendant, plaintiff. Civil records archived from 1700s; on computer since. Online access to prothonotary civil records available free at http://prothonotary. county.allegheny.pa.us/allegheny/welcome.htm. Registration required; search by case number. Also, the Techi provides court records services for those with PA Bar ID at www.techi.org/login.CFM.

General Information: Public access terminal is available. No juvenile records released. SASE required. Turnaround time 10 days. Copy fee: $.50 per page. Certification fee: $8.00. Fee payee: Prothonotary of Allegheny County. Business checks accepted. Prepayment is required. Business accounts may set up a draw down account.

Court of Common Pleas - Criminal 220 Courthouse, 436 Grant Street, Pittsburgh, PA 15219; 412-350-5322. Hours: 8:30AM-4:30PM (EST). *Felony, Misdemeanor.*

Criminal Records: Access: Mail, in person, online. Both court and visitors may perform in person searches. Search fee: $15.00 per name. Required to search: name, years to search, DOB; also helpful: SSN. Criminal records on files, microfilm back to 1800s; on computer since. Online access to Common Pleas court records is available at http://prothonotary.county.allegheny.pa.us/allegheny/welcome.htm. Registration required; search by case number. Also, the Techi provides court records services for those with PA Bar ID at www.techi.org/login.CFM.

General Information: All records public. SASE required. Turnaround time 2 days. Copy fee: $.50 per page. Certification fee: $10.00. Fee payee: Clerk of Courts. Personal checks accepted. Prepayment required.

Register of Wills 414 Grant St, City County Bldg, PIttsburgh, PA 15219; 412-350-4183. Hours: 8:30AM-4:30PM (EST). *Probate.*

www.county.allegheny.pa.us/regwills/index.asp

Armstrong County

Court of Common Pleas - Civil 500 E Market St, Kittanning, PA 16201; 724-548-3251; Fax: 724-548-3236. Hours: 8AM-4:30PM (EST). *Civil, Eviction.*

www.geocities.com/acprothonotary

Civil Records: Access: Online, in person. Visitors must perform in person searches for themselves. No search fee. Required to search: name, years to search. Civil cases indexed by defendant, plaintiff. Civil records on files, microfiche since 1930; on computer since. Online access is available through a private company. For information, call Infocon at 814-472-6066.

General Information: Public access terminal is available. No juvenile, civil commitment records released. Copy fee: $1.00 per page. Certification fee: $3.00. Fee payee: Prothonotary. Personal checks accepted. Prepayment is required.

Court of Common Pleas - Criminal 500 Market St, Kittanning, PA 16201; 724-548-3252. Hours: 8AM-4:30PM (EST). *Felony, Misdemeanor.*

www.geocities.com/acprothonotary

Criminal Records: Access: Mail, online, in person. Both court and visitors may perform in person searches. Search fee: $10.00 per name. Required to search: name, years to search; also helpful: DOB, SSN. Criminal records in card file from early 1930; on computer since 1994. Online access is available through a private company. For information, call Infocon at 814-472-6066.

General Information: Public access terminal is available. No juvenile or mental health records released. SASE required. Turnaround time same day. Copy fee: $1.00 per page. Certification fee: $5.00 first page; $1.00 each add'l. Fee payee: Clerk of Courts. Personal checks accepted. Prepayment is required.

Register of Wills 500 Market St, Armstrong County Courthouse, Kittanning, PA 16201; 724-548-3256 X220; Fax: 724-548-3236. Hours: 8AM-4:30PM (EST). *Probate.*

Beaver County

Court of Common Pleas - Civil Beaver County Courthouse, 810 3rd St, Beaver, PA 15009; 724-728-5700. Hours: 8:30AM-4:30PM (EST). *Civil, Eviction.*

www.co.beaver.pa.us/prothonotary

Civil Records: Access: In person, mail. Both court and visitors may perform in person searches. No search fee. Required to search: name, years to search. Civil cases indexed by defendant, plaintiff. Civil records go back to 1800; on computer back to 1995.

General Information: Public access terminal is available. No sealed records released. SASE required. Turnaround time 1 week. Copy fee: $.25 per page. Certification fee: $5.00. Fee payee: Prothonotary. Personal checks accepted. Prepayment is required.

Court of Common Pleas - Criminal Beaver County Courthouse, 810 3rd St, Beaver, PA 15009; 724-728-5700; Fax: 724-728-8853. Hours: 8:30AM-4:30PM (EST). *Felony, Misdemeanor.*

www.co.beaver.pa.us

Criminal Records: Access: Fax, mail, in person. Both court and visitors may perform in person searches. Search fee: $16.00 per name. Required to search: name, years to search; also helpful: DOB, SSN. Criminal records on computer back to 1973, on microfiche since 1802.

General Information: Public access terminal is available. Records sealed by court order not released. SASE required. Turnaround time 1 week. Fax notes: Fee to fax results is $1.00 per page. Copy fee: $.50 per page. Certification fee: $8.00. Fee payee: Clerk of Courts Office. Personal checks accepted. Prepayment is required.

Register of Wills Beaver County Courthouse, 3rd St, Beaver, PA 15009; 724-728-5700 X11265, X11274; Fax: 724-728-9810. 8:30AM-4:30PM (EST). *Probate.*

Bedford County

Court of Common Pleas - Criminal/Civil
Bedford County Courthouse, Bedford, PA 15522; 814-623-4833; Fax: 814-623-4831. Hours: 8:30AM-4:30PM (EST). *Felony, Misdemeanor, Civil, Eviction.*

Civil Records: Access: Mail, in person. Both court and visitors may perform in person searches. Search fee: $18.00 per name. Required to search: name, years to search. Civil cases indexed by defendant, plaintiff. Civil records on file from late 1700s. Online access is available through a private company. For information, call Infocon at 814-472-6066.

Criminal Records: Access: Mail, online, in person. Both court and visitors may perform in person searches. Search fee: $18.00 per name. Required to search: name, years to search, DOB. Criminal records on file from late 1700s. Online access to criminal is the same as civil.

General Information: No sex related or juvenile records released. SASE required. Turnaround time 2 weeks. Copy fee: $.50 per page. Certification fee: $3.00. Fee payee: Prothonotary of Beford County. Personal checks accepted. Prepayment is required.

Register of Wills 200 S Juliana St, Bedford, PA 15522; 814-623-4836; Fax: 814-624-0488. Hours: 8:30AM-4:30PM (EST). *Probate.*

Berks County

Court of Common Pleas - Civil 2nd Floor, 633 Court St, Reading, PA 19601; 610-478-6970; Fax: 610-478-6969. 8AM-4PM (EST). *Civil, Eviction.*

Civil Records: Access: Fax, mail, in person. Both court and visitors may perform in person searches. No search fee. Required to search: name, years to search. Civil cases indexed by defendant, plaintiff. Civil records partially on microfiche, on manual index files from 1750. Mail access limited to docket information only. The Registry of Wills has a free searchable website at www.berksregofwills.com including marriage, estate, birth and death records for the county. The estate and marriage records are current.

General Information: Public access terminal is available. No mental, sealed records released. SASE required. Turnaround time 1-2 days. Fax notes: $5.00 for first page, $1.00 each add'l. For emergency use only. Copy fee: $.50 per page. Certification fee: $3.75. Fee payee: Prothonotary. Personal checks accepted. Prepayment is required.

Court of Common Pleas - Criminal 4th Floor, 633 Court St, Reading, PA 19601; 610-478-6550; Fax: 610-478-6570. Hours: 8AM-5PM (EST). *Felony, Misdemeanor.*

Criminal Records: Access: In person only. Visitors must perform in person searches for themselves. No search fee. Required to search: name, years to search; also helpful: DOB, SSN. Criminal records on computer from 1985 in files from 1991, prior archived.

General Information: Public access terminal is available. No juvenile records released. Copy fee: $.25 per page. Add $1.00 for each page after first 10. Certification fee: $5.00. Fee payee: Berks County Clerk of Courts. Only cashiers checks and money orders accepted. Credit cards accepted for payments on criminal cases only.

Register of Wills 633 Court St 2nd Floor, Reading, PA 19601; 610-478-6600; Fax: 610-478-6251. Hours: 8AM-5PM (EST). *Probate.*

www.berksregofwills.com

Blair County

Court of Common Pleas - Criminal/Civil
423 Allegheny Street #144, Hollidaysburg, PA 16648; 814-693-3080. Hours: 8AM-4:30PM (EST). *Felony, Misdemeanor, Civil, Eviction.*

Civil Records: Access: Online, in person. Visitors must perform in person searches for themselves. No search fee. Required to search: name, years to search. Civil cases indexed by defendant, plaintiff. Civil records on computer from 1989, on index books from 1846 to 1989. Online access is available through a private company. For information, call Infocon at 814-472-6066.

Criminal Records: Access: Mail, online, in person. Both court and visitors may perform in person searches. Search fee: $10.00 per name. Required to search: name, years to search, DOB; also helpful: SSN. Criminal records on computer from 1989, on index books from 1846 to 1989. Online access is available through a private company. For information, call Infocon at 814-472-6066.

General Information: Public access terminal is available. No adoption records released. SASE required. Turnaround time 2 days. Copy fee: $.50 per page. Certification fee: $5.00. Fee payee: Blair County Prothonotary. Personal checks accepted. Prepayment is required.

Register of Wills 423 Allegheny #145, Hollidaysburg, PA 16648-2022; 814-693-3095. Hours: 8AM-4PM (EST). *Probate.*

Bradford County

Court of Common Pleas - Criminal/Civil
Courthouse, 301 Main St, Towanda, PA 18848; 570-265-1705. Hours: 9AM-5PM (EST). *Felony, Misdemeanor, Civil, Eviction.*

Civil Records: Access: Mail, in person. Both court and visitors may perform in person searches. Search fee: $5.00 per name. Required to search: name, years to search. Civil cases indexed by defendant, plaintiff. Civil records on computer from 1986, on microfiche from mid 1800s, archived from mid-1940s.

Criminal Records: Access: Mail, in person. Both court and visitors may perform in person searches. Search fee: $8.00 per name. Required to search: name, years to search, DOB. Criminal records on computer from 1986, on microfiche from mid 1800s, archived from mid-1940s.

General Information: Public access terminal is available. SASE required. Turnaround time 1-2 days. Copy fee: $.25 per page. Certification fee: $3.00. $5.00 for criminal records. Fee payee: Prothonotary. Personal checks accepted. Prepayment is required.

Register of Wills 301 Main St., Towanda, PA 18848; 570-265-1702. 9AM-5PM (EST). *Probate.*

Bucks County

Court of Common Pleas - Civil 55 E Court St, Doylestown, PA 18901; 215-348-6191. Hours: 8:15AM-4:15PM (EST). *Civil, Eviction.*

www.buckscounty.org

Civil Records: Access: Online, in person. Visitors must perform in person searches for themselves. No search fee. Required to search: name, years to search. Civil cases indexed by defendant, plaintiff. Civil records on computer back to 1980, prior on dockets. Access to the remote online system requires Sprint ID ($24). The per minute fee is $.60 with 2 minute minimum. Contact John Morris at 215-348-6579 for more information.

General Information: Public access terminal is available. No mental, sealed records released. Copy fee: $.25 per page. Certification fee: $4.50. Fee payee:

Prothonotary. Personal checks accepted. Prepayment is required.

Court of Common Pleas - Criminal Bucks County Courthouse, 55 E Court St, Doylestown, PA 18901; 215-348-6389; Fax: 215-348-6740. Hours: 8AM-4:30PM (EST). *Felony, Misdemeanor.*

www.buckscounty.org/departments/public_access

Criminal Records: Access: Mail, online, in person. Both court and visitors may perform in person searches. Search fee: $10.00 per name. Required to search: name, years to search, DOB. Criminal records on computer from 1980, some records on microfiche, on card index from 1932 to 1979. Access to the criminal online system requires Sprint ID ($25). The per minute fee is $.60 with a 2 minute minimum. Search by name or case number. Contact John Morris at 215-348-6579 for more information or visit www.buckscounty.org/departments/public_access/.

General Information: Public access terminal is available. No sealed, juvenile or mental records released. SASE required. Turnaround time same day. Fax notes: Fee to fax results is $1.50 per page. No copy fee. Certification fee: $7.50. Fee payee: Clerk of Courts Criminal Division. Personal checks accepted.

Register of Wills Bucks County Courthouse, Doylestown, PA 18901; 215-348-6265; Fax: 215-348-6156. Hours: 8AM-4:30PM (EST). *Probate.*

www.buckscounty.org

Butler County

Court of Common Pleas - Civil Butler County Courthouse, PO Box 1208, Butler, PA 16001-1208; 724-284-5214. Hours: 8:30AM-4:30PM (EST). *Civil, Eviction.*

Civil Records: Access: Phone, mail, online, in person. Visitors must perform in person searches for themselves. No search fee. Required to search: name, years to search. Civil cases indexed by defendant, plaintiff. Civil records on computer from 1993, prior on docket books back to 1800. Online access is available through a private company. For information, call Infocon at 814-472-6066.

General Information: Public access terminal is available. No mental records released. Copy fee: $.25 per page. Certification fee: $4.00. Fee payee: Prothonotary. Personal checks accepted. Prepayment is required.

Court of Common Pleas - Criminal PO Box 1208, Butler County Courthouse, 124 W Diamond St, Butler, PA 16003-1208; 724-284-5233; Fax: 724-284-5244. Hours: 8:30AM-4:30PM (EST). *Felony, Misdemeanor.*

www.co.butler.pa.us/CoC.htm

Criminal Records: Access: Mail, online, in person. Both court and visitors may perform in person searches. Search fee: $16.00 per name. Required to search: name, DOB; also helpful: years to search, SSN. Original records in office for 10 years. Computerized from 1988 to present, prior in Russell Index. Online access is available through a private company. For information, call Infocon at 814-472-6066.

General Information: Public access terminal is available. No mental, sealed, juvenile (16 & under) victim records released. SASE required. Turnaround time 1-2 days. Copy fee: $.50 per page. Certification fee: $8.00 per page. Fee payee: Clerk of Courts. Personal checks accepted. Prepayment is required.

Register of Wills Butler County Courthouse, PO Box 1208, Butler, PA 16003-1208; 724-284-5348; Fax: 724-284-5278. 8:30AM-4:30PM (EST). *Probate.*

Cambria County

Court of Common Pleas - Civil 200 S Center St, Ebensburg, PA 15931; 814-472-1636; Fax: 814-472-5632. Hours: 9AM-4PM (EST). *Civil, Eviction.*

Civil Records: Access: Phone, mail, fax, in person. Both court and visitors may perform in person searches. No search fee. Required to search: name, years to search. Civil cases indexed by defendant, plaintiff. Civil records on computer from 1/1/94, prior on dockets from 1800s.

General Information: Public access terminal is available. No divorce or mental records released. SASE requested. Fax notes: Fee to fax results is $1.00 per page. Copy fee: $.25 per page. Certification fee: $3.00. Fee payee: Prothonotary. Personal checks accepted. Prepayment is required.

Court of Common Pleas - Criminal Cambria County Courthouse S Center St, Ebensburg, PA 15931; 814-472-1540. Hours: 9AM-4PM (EST). *Felony, Misdemeanor.*

Criminal Records: Access: Mail, in person. Only the court performs in person searches; visitors may not. Search fee: $4.00 per name. Required to search: name, years to search, DOB; also helpful: SSN. Criminal conviction records are computerized, indexed from 1800s.

General Information: No sealed or child victim records released. Turnaround time 3 days. Copy fee: $.50 per page. Certification fee: $8.00. Fee payee: Clerk of Court. Personal checks accepted. Third party checks not accepted. Prepayment is required.

Register of Wills 200 S Center St, Ebensburg, PA 15931; 814-472-5440 X1440; Probate phone: 814-472-1438; Fax: 814-472-0762. 9AM-4PM (EST). *Probate.*

www.co.cambria.pa.us

Cameron County

Court of Common Pleas - Civil Cameron County Courthouse, 20 East 5th St, Emporium, PA 15834; 814-486-3355; Fax: 814-468-0464. Hours: 8:30AM-4:30PM (EST). *Civil, Eviction.*

Civil Records: Access: Phone, fax, mail, in person. Both court and visitors may perform in person searches. No search fee. Required to search: name, years to search. Civil cases indexed by defendant, plaintiff. Civil records on computer from 1988, archived from 1860 to present.

General Information: Public access terminal is available. No adoption, military discharge records released. SASE required. Turnaround time same day. Copy fee: $.50 per page. Certification fee: $5.00. Fee payee: Prothonotary. Personal checks accepted. Credit cards accepted: Visa, MasterCard. Will bill fees with prior permission form Clerk.

Court of Common Pleas - Criminal 20 East 5th St, Emporium, PA 15834; 814-486-3349; Fax: 814-486-0464. Hours: 8:30AM-4PM (EST). *Felony, Misdemeanor.*

Criminal Records: Access: Phone, fax, mail, in person. Both court and visitors may perform in person searches. No search fee. Required to search: name, years to search; also helpful: address, DOB, SSN. Criminal records archived from 1860.

General Information: No juvenile, mental health records released. SASE required. Turnaround time same day. Copy fee: $.50 per page. Certification fee: $5.00. Fee payee: Clerk of Court. Personal checks accepted. Credit cards accepted: Visa, MasterCard. Prepayment is required.

Register of Wills Cameron County Courthouse, East 5th St., Emporium, PA 15834; 814-486-3355; Fax: 814-486-0464. Hours: 8:30AM-4PM (EST). *Probate.*

Carbon County

Court of Common Pleas - Civil PO Box 130, Courthouse, Jim Thorpe, PA 18229; 570-325-2481; Fax: 570-325-8047. Hours: 8:30AM-4:30PM (EST). *Civil, Eviction.*

Civil Records: Access: In person, online. Visitors must perform in person searches for themselves. No search fee. Required to search: name. Civil cases indexed by defendant, plaintiff. Civil records on computer from 1/84, financing statements from 1/87, on microfiche from 1/84, prior archived. Online access to the clerk of courts docket records is available free at www.carboncourts.com/pubacc.htm. Registration is required.

General Information: Public access terminal is available. No abuse, mental health records released. Copy fee: $.25 per page. Certification fee: $8.15. Fee payee: Prothonotary of Carbon County. Personal checks accepted. Prepayment is required.

Register of Wills PO Box 286, Jim Thorpe, PA 18229; 570-325-2261; Fax: 570-325-5098. Hours: 8:30AM-4:30PM (EST). *Probate.*

Note: Docket information is available free online at www.carboncourts.com/pubacc.htm. Registration is required.

Court of Common Pleas - Criminal County Courthouse, Jim Thorpe, PA 18229; 570-325-3637; Fax: 570-325-5705. Hours: 8:30AM-4PM (EST). *Felony, Misdemeanor.*

Criminal Records: Access: Phone, mail, in person, online. Only the court performs in person searches; visitors may not. No search fee. Required to search: name, years to search, DOB; also helpful: SSN. Criminal records on computer from 1973, on microfiche from 1800. Online access to the clerk of courts docket records is available free at www.carboncourts.com/pubacc.htm. Registration is required.

General Information: No juvenile, mental health records released. SASE required. Turnaround time 1 day. Certification fee: $5.00. Fee payee: Clerk of Courts Carbon County. Personal checks accepted.

Centre County

Court of Common Pleas - Criminal/Civil Centre County Courthouse, Bellefonte, PA 16823; 814-355-6796. Hours: 8:30AM-5PM (EST). *Felony, Misdemeanor, Civil, Eviction.*

www.co.centre.pa.us/271.htm

Civil Records: Access: Mail, in person. Both court and visitors may perform in person searches. Search fee: $7.00 per name. Required to search: name, years to search, DOB. Civil cases indexed by defendant, plaintiff. Civil records on computer from 7-1-94, on card files and docket books from 1986, on microfiche and archived from 1800 to 1986.

Criminal Records: Access: Mail, in person. Both court and visitors may perform in person searches. Search fee: $7.00 per name. Required to search: name, years to search, DOB. Criminal records on computer from 7-1-94, on card files and docket books from 1986, on microfiche and archived from 1800 to 1986.

General Information: Public access terminal is available. No sex related, juvenile, mental records released. SASE helpful. Turnaround time 3-5 days. Fax notes: Do not fax. Copy fee: $.50 per page. Certification fee: $4.00. Fee payee: Clerk of Court. Personal checks accepted. Prepayment is required.

Register of Wills Willowbank Office Bldg, 414 Holmes Ave #2, Bellefonte, PA 16823; 814-355-6724, 355-6760. Hours: 8:30AM-5PM (EST). *Probate.*

www.co.centre.pa.us/224.htm

Chester County

Court of Common Pleas - Civil 2 North High St, Ste 130, West Chester, PA 19380; 610-344-6300. Hours: 8:30AM-4:30PM (EST). *Civil, Eviction.*

www.chesco.org

Civil Records: Access: Online, in person. Visitors must perform in person searches for themselves. No search fee. Required to search: name, years to search. Civil cases indexed by defendant, plaintiff. Civil records on dockets from 1985 to present, on microfiche from 1981 to 1984, archived from 1700s. Internet access to county records including court records requires a sign-up and credit card payment. Application fee: $50. There is a $10.00 per month minimum (no charge for no activity); and $.10 each transaction beyond 100. Sign-up and/or logon at http://epin.chesco.org.

General Information: Public access terminal is available. No sealed records released. Copy fee: $.25 per page. Certification fee: $3.00. Fee payee: Prothonotary. Business checks accepted. Prepayment is required.

Court of Common Pleas - Criminal 2 North High St #160, West Chester, PA 19380; 610-344-6135. 8:30AM-4:30PM (EST). *Felony, Misdemeanor.*

www.chesco.org

Criminal Records: Access: Mail, online, in person. Both court and visitors may perform in person searches. Search fee: $10.00 per name. Required to search: name, years to search; also helpful: DOB. Criminal records on computer and microfiche from mid-70s, archived from the 1700s. Internet access to county records including criminal records requires a sign-up and credit card payment. Application fee: $50. There is a $10.00 per month minimum (no charge for no activity); and $.10 each transaction beyond 100. Sign-up and/or logon at http://epin.chesco.org.

General Information: Public access terminal is available. No juvenile records released. Turnaround time 1 day. Copy fee: $1.00 per page. Certification fee: $5.00. Fee payee: Clerk of Courts. Business checks accepted. Prepayment is required.

Register of Wills 2 North High St, #109, West Chester, PA 19380-3073; 610-344-6335; Fax: 610-344-6218. Hours: 8:30AM-4:30PM (EST). *Probate.*

Note: Internet access to probate records requires a sign-up/payment. Sign-up/logon at http://epin.chesco.org.

Clarion County

Court of Common Pleas - Civil Clarion County Courthouse, Main St, Clarion, PA 16214; 814-226-1119; Fax: 814-226-8069. Hours: 8:30AM-4:30PM (EST). *Civil, Eviction.*

Civil Records: Access: Phone, fax, mail, online, in person. Both court and visitors may perform in person searches. Search fee: $10.00 per name. Required to search: name, years to search. Civil cases indexed by defendant, plaintiff. Civil records on computer from mid-1990s, on dockets from 1800s. Online access is available through a private company. For information, call Infocon at 814-472-6066.

General Information: Public access terminal is available. No juvenile, mental health records released. Fax notes: No fee to fax results. No copy fee. Certification fee: $5.00. Fee payee: Prothonotary. Personal checks accepted. Prepayment is required.

Court of Common Pleas - Criminal Clarion County Courthouse, Main St, Clarion, PA 16214; 814-226-4000; Fax: 814-226-8069. Hours: 8AM-4:30PM (EST). *Felony, Misdemeanor.*

Criminal Records: Access: Phone, fax, mail, online, in person. Both court and visitors may perform in person searches. Search fee: $10.00 per name. Required to search: name, years to search, DOB. Criminal records on computer and microfiche from 1990, on docket books from 1800s. Online access is available through a private company. For information, call Infocon at 814-472-6066.

General Information: Public access terminal is available. No juvenile, mental health records released. Turnaround time same day. Fax notes: No fee to fax results. Copy fee: $.50 per page. Certification fee: $5.00. Fee payee: Clerk of Court. Personal checks accepted.

Register of Wills Clarion County Courthouse, Corner of 5th & Main, Clarion, PA 16214; 814-226-4000 X2500; Fax: 814-226-1117. Hours: 8:30AM-4:30PM (EST). *Probate.*

Clearfield County

Court of Common Pleas - Criminal/Civil

PO Box 549 (1 N 2nd St), Clearfield, PA 16830; 814-765-2641 X1330; Fax: 814-765-7659. Hours: 8:30AM-4PM (EST). *Felony, Misdemeanor, Civil, Eviction.*

Civil Records: Access: Mail, in person. Both court and visitors may perform in person searches. Search fee: $7.00 per name, 5-years search. Required to search: name, years to search; also helpful: address. Civil cases indexed by defendant, plaintiff. Civil records indexed (Russell System) on dockets from 1820s; on computer back to 11/01.

Criminal Records: Access: Mail, in person. Both court and visitors may perform in person searches. Search fee: $7.00 per name, 5-year search. Required to search: name, years to search, address, DOB, SSN, signed release. Criminal records indexed (Russell System) on dockets from 1820s; on computer back to 11/01.

General Information: Public access terminal is available. No juvenile, sealed or mental health records released. SASE required. Turnaround time 2 days. Copy fee: $.25 per page. Certification fee: $1.50. Fee payee: Prothonotary. Personal checks accepted. Prepayment is required.

Register of Wills & Clerk of Orphans Court PO Box 361, Clearfield, PA 16830; 814-765-2641 X1350/1; Fax: 814-765-6089. Hours: 8:30AM-4PM (EST). *Probate.*

Clinton County

Court of Common Pleas - Criminal/Civil

230 E Water St, Lock Haven, PA 17745; 570-893-4007. Hours: 8AM-5PM M, T, Th, F; 8AM-12:30PM Wed (EST). *Felony, Misdemeanor, Civil, Eviction.*

Civil Records: Access: Online, in person. Visitors must perform in person searches for themselves. No search fee. Required to search: name, years to search. Civil cases indexed by defendant, plaintiff. Civil records on computer from 1992, on files from 1839. Online access is available through a private company. For information, call Infocon at 814-472-6066.

Criminal Records: Access: Online, in person. Visitors must perform in person searches for themselves. No search fee. Required to search: name, years to search, DOB, SSN, signed release. Criminal records on computer from 1992, on files from 1839. Online access is available through a private company. For information, call Infocon at 814-472-6066.

General Information: Public access terminal is available. No sealed, mental health or minor victim abuse cases records released. Copy fee: $.50 per page. Certification fee: $4.50. Fee payee: Clerk of Court or Prothonotary. Personal checks accepted. Will bill Federal Liens fees.

Register of Wills PO Box 943, Lock Haven, PA 17745; 570-893-4010; Fax: 570-893-4273. 8:30AM-5PM M,T,Th,F; 8AM-12:30PM Wed (EST). *Probate.* www.clintoncountypa.com

Columbia County

Court of Common Pleas - Criminal/Civil

PO Box 380, Bloomsburg, PA 17815; 570-389-5600. Hours: 8AM-4:30PM (EST). *Felony, Misdemeanor, Civil, Eviction.*

Civil Records: Access: In person only. Both court and visitors may perform in person searches. Search fee: $20.00 per name. Required to search: name, years to search. Civil cases indexed by defendant, plaintiff. Civil records on computer to 1992, on microfiche from 1814 to present, on dockets from 1814.

Criminal Records: Access: Mail, in person. Both court and visitors may perform in person searches. Search fee: $20.00 per name. Required to search: name, years to search; also helpful: DOB. Criminal records on computer to 1992, on microfiche from 1814 to present, on dockets from 1814.

General Information: Public access terminal is available. No juvenile, adoption, mental health petition or OAPSA records released. SASE required. Turnaround time same day. Copy fee: $.50 per page. Certification fee: $4.00. Fee payee: Prothonotary or Clerk of Court. Personal checks accepted. Prepayment is required.

Register of Wills 35 W Main St, PO Box 380, Bloomsburg, PA 17815; 570-389-5635/32; Fax: 570-389-5636. Hours: 8AM-4:30PM (EST). *Probate.*

Crawford County

Court of Common Pleas - Civil

Crawford County Courthouse, Meadville, PA 16335; 814-333-7324. Hours: 8:30AM-4:30PM (EST). *Civil, Eviction.*

Civil Records: Access: Mail, in person. Both court and visitors may perform in person searches. Search fee: $7.50 per name. Required to search: name, years to search. Civil cases indexed by defendant, plaintiff. Civil records on dockets from 1800s.

General Information: No mental health, sealed records released. SASE required. Turnaround time 3 days. Copy fee: $.75 per page. Docket copy $1.50 per page. Certification fee: $1.50. Fee payee: Prothonotary Crawford County. Personal checks accepted. Checks accepted with ID. Prepayment is required.

Court of Common Pleas - Criminal

Crawford County Courthouse, Meadville, PA 16335; 814-333-7442; Fax: 814-337-7349. Hours: 8:30AM-4:30PM (EST). *Felony, Misdemeanor.*

Criminal Records: Access: Mail, in person. Both court and visitors may perform in person searches. Search fee: $10.00 per name. Required to search: name, years to search, signed release; also helpful: DOB. Criminal records on microfiche from 1974, on dockets from 1914, archived from 1880s.

General Information: No juvenile records released. SASE required. Turnaround time 10-14 days. Copy fee: $1.00 per page. Certification fee: $5.00 per page. Fee payee: Clerk of Courts. Personal checks accepted. Prepayment is required.

Register of Wills 903 Diamond Park, Meadville, PA 16335; 814-373-2537, 814-333-7338; Fax: 814-337-5296. Hours: 8:30AM-4:30PM (EST). *Probate.*

Cumberland County

Court of Common Pleas - Civil

Cumberland County Courthouse, Rm 100, One Courthouse Square, Carlisle, PA 17013-3387; 717-240-6195; Fax: 717-240-6573. Hours: 8AM-4:30PM (EST). *Civil, Eviction.* www.ccpa.net

Civil Records: Access: In person only. Visitors must perform in person searches for themselves. No search fee. Required to search: name, years to search; also helpful: address. Civil cases indexed by defendant,

plaintiff. Civil records on computer from 1994, on microfiche from 1966-1986, on dockets from 1800s.

General Information: Public access terminal is available. No mental health records released. Copy fee: $.50 per page. Fee payee: Office of Prothonotary. No checks accepted for copies. Prepayment is required.

Court of Common Pleas - Criminal

Cumberland County Courthouse, East Wing, 1 Courthouse Sq, Carlisle, PA 17013-3387; 717-240-6250; Fax: 717-240-6571. Hours: 8AM-4:30PM (EST). *Felony, Misdemeanor.*

www.ccpa.net

Criminal Records: Access: Mail, in person. Both court and visitors may perform in person searches. Search fee: $15.00 per name. Required to search: name, years to search, DOB or SSN. Criminal records on computer from 1994, on files from 1976, archived from 1800s.

General Information: Public access terminal is available. No juvenile records released (Including any case with a juvenile as the victim). SASE required. Turnaround time same day. Copy fee: $1.00 per page. Certification fee: $1.00 per page. Fee payee: Clerk of Courts. Personal checks accepted. Prepayment required.

Register of Wills Cumberland County Courthouse, Rm 102, 1 Courthouse Sq, Carlisle, PA 17013; 717-240-6345; Fax: 717-240-6490. Hours: 8AM-4:30PM (EST). *Probate.*

Dauphin County

Court of Common Pleas - Civil

PO Box 945, Harrisburg, PA 17108; 717-780-6520. Hours: 8AM-4:30PM (EST). *Civil, Eviction.*

Civil Records: Access: Phone, mail, in person. Both court and visitors may perform in person searches. Search fee: $7.75 per name. Fee is per 5 years searched. Required to search: name, years to search. Civil cases indexed by defendant, plaintiff. Civil records on microfilm and dockets from 1970s, archived from 1700s; on computer back to 11/2001.

General Information: Public access terminal is available. No mental health released. SASE required. Turnaround time 1 day. Copy fee: $.75 per page. Certification fee: $4.75 1st pg; $1.50 each add'l. Fee payee: Dauphin County Prothonotary. Business checks accepted. Prepayment is required.

Court of Common Pleas - Criminal

Front & Market St, Harrisburg, PA 17101; 717-255-2692; Fax: 717-255-2694. Hours: 8:30AM-5PM (EST). *Felony, Misdemeanor.*

Criminal Records: Access: Mail, in person. Both court and visitors may perform in person searches. Search fee: $20.00 per name. Required to search: name, years to search; also helpful: DOB, SSN. Criminal records on dockets and computer from 1950, archived from 1700s.

General Information: Public access terminal is available. No juvenile, mental records released. SASE not required. Turnaround time 1 week. Copy fee: $.50 per page. Certification fee: $5.00. Fee payee: Clerk of Court. Business checks accepted. Prepayment required.

Register of Wills PO Box 1295, Harrisburg, PA 17101; 717-780-6505; Fax: 717-780-6474. Hours: 8AM-4:30PM (EST). *Probate.* www.dauphinc.org

Delaware County

Court of Common Pleas - Criminal/Civil

201 W Front St, Media, PA 19063; 610-891-4370. Hours: 8:30AM-4:30PM *Felony, Misdemeanor, Civil, Eviction.*

www.co.delaware.pa.us

Civil Records: Access: Online, in person. Visitors must perform in person searches for themselves. No search fee. Required to search: name, years to search. Civil cases indexed by defendant, plaintiff. Civil records on computer from early 1990, on card file from 1920s, archived from 1800s. Online access to court civil records available free at www2.co.delaware.pa.us/pa/default.htm. For more information, call 610-891-4675. Search online by name or document type.

Criminal Records: Access: Mail, in person. Both court and visitors may perform in person searches. No search fee. Required to search: name, years to search; also helpful: DOB, SSN. Criminal records on computer from late 1970s, prior on files. No online access to criminal records.

General Information: Public access terminal is available. No juvenile, mental health records released. SASE required. Turnaround time 1-3 days. Copy fee: $1.00 per page. Certification fee: $4.50 first page and $1.00 thereafter. Fee payee: Office of Judical Support. Business checks accepted. Prepayment is required.

Register of Wills Delaware County Courthouse, 201 W Front St, Media, PA 19063; 610-891-4400; Fax: 610-891-4812. 8:30AM-4:30PM (EST). *Probate.*

www.co.delaware.pa.us

Elk County

Court of Common Pleas - Criminal/Civil PO Box 237, Ridgway, PA 15853; 814-776-5344; Fax: 814-776-5303. Hours: 8:30AM-4PM (EST). *Felony, Misdemeanor, Civil, Eviction.*

Civil Records: Access: Phone, fax, mail, in person. Both court and visitors may perform in person searches. Search fee: $7.50 per name. Required to search: name, years to search. Civil cases indexed by defendant, plaintiff. Civil records on dockets from 1843, on comptuer back to 1998.

Criminal Records: Access: Phone, fax, mail, in person. Both court and visitors may perform in person searches. Search fee: $10.00 per name. Required to search: name, years to search, DOB. Criminal records on dockets from 1843, on computer back to 1998.

General Information: Public access terminal is available. No mental health or juvenile records released. SASE not required. Turnaround time 1 day. Copy fee: $.50 per page. Certification fee: $4.50. Fee payee: Elk County Prothonotary. Personal checks accepted. Prepayment is required.

Register of Wills PO Box 314, Ridgway, PA 15853; 814-776-5349; Fax: 814-776-5379. Hours: 8:30AM-4PM (EST). *Probate.*

Erie County

Court of Common Pleas - Civil Erie County Courthouse, 140 West 6th St., Erie, PA 16501; 814-451-6076. 8:30AM-4:30PM (EST). *Civil, Eviction.*

www.eriecountygov.org

Civil Records: Access: Mail, online, in person. Both court and visitors may perform in person searches. No search fee. Required to search: name, years to search. Civil cases indexed by defendant, plaintiff. Civil records on computer from 1992, on dockets from 1971, on microfilm/microfiche from 1800s. Online access is available through a private company. For information, call Infocon at 814-472-6066.

General Information: Public access terminal is available. No sealed records released. SASE required. Turnaround time less than one week. Copy fee: $.50 per page. Computer page $1.00 per page. Certification fee: $3.00. Fee payee: Prothonotary. Personal checks accepted. Prepayment is required.

Court of Common Pleas - Criminal Erie County Courthouse, 140 West 6th St, Erie, PA 16501; 814-451-6229; Fax: 814-451-6420. Hours: 8:30AM-4:30PM (EST). *Felony, Misdemeanor.*

Criminal Records: Access: Mail, online, in person. Both court and visitors may perform in person searches.

Search fee: $10.00 per name. Required to search: name, years to search, DOB. Criminal records go back to 1960; records computerized back to 1992. Online access is available through a private company. For information, call Infocon at 814-472-6066.

General Information: Public access terminal is available. No juvenile or ARD records released. SASE not required. Turnaround time 1 week. Copy fee: $.10 per page. Fee payee: Clerk of Courts. Personal checks accepted. Prepayment is required.

Register of Wills Erie County Courthouse 140 W 6th St, Erie, PA 16501; 814-451-6260. Hours: 8:30AM-4:30PM (EST). *Probate.*

Fayette County

Court of Common Pleas - Civil 61 East Main St, Uniontown, PA 15401; 724-430-1272; Fax: 724-430-4555. Hours: 8AM-4:30PM (EST). *Civil, Eviction.*

Civil Records: Access: Mail, in person. Both court and visitors may perform in person searches. Search fee: $5.00 per name. Required to search: name, years to search. Civil cases indexed by defendant, plaintiff. Civil records on computer from 1999, archived from 1700s.

General Information: No mental records released. SASE not required. Turnaround time 2 weeks. Copy fee: $.50 per page. Certification fee: $10.00. Fee payee: Prothonotary. Personal checks accepted. Prepayment is required.

Court of Common Pleas - Criminal 61 East Main St, Uniontown, PA 15401; 724-430-1253; Fax: 724-438-8410. Hours: 8AM-4:30PM (EST). *Felony, Misdemeanor.*

Criminal Records: Access: Fax, mail, in person. Both court and visitors may perform in person searches. Search fee: $15.00 for 5-year search; $30.00 for 5-yr. plus. Required to search: name, years to search, DOB; also helpful: SSN. Criminal records on computer from 1993, on files from 1800s.

General Information: Public access terminal is available. No sex related or juvenile records released. SASE not required. Turnaround time 5-10 days. Fax notes: $3.00 per document. Copy fee: $.50 per page. Certification fee: $16.50. Fee payee: Clerk of Courts. Personal checks accepted. Prepayment is required.

Register of Wills 61 East Main St, Uniontown, PA 15401; 724-430-1206; Fax: 724-430-1275. Hours: 8AM-4:30PM (EST). *Probate.*

Forest County

Court of Common Pleas 526 Elm St #2, Forest County Courthouse, Tionesta, PA 16353; 814-755-3526; Fax: 814-755-8837. Hours: 9AM-4PM (EST). *Felony, Misdemeanor, Civil, Eviction, Probate.*

Note: Computerized records includes the Register of Wills.

Civil Records: Access: Mail, fax, in person. Both court and visitors may perform in person searches. No search fee. Required to search: name, years to search. Civil cases indexed by defendant, plaintiff. Computerized records from 2002, civil records on dockets since 1995, archived from 1857.

Criminal Records: Access: Mail, fax, in person. Both court and visitors may perform in person searches. Search fee: $10.00 per name. Required to search: name, years to search; also helpful: DOB, SSN. Computerized records from 2002, criminal records on dockets since 1995, archived from 1857.

General Information: Public access terminal is available. No adoption records released. SASE required. Turnaround time same day. Fax notes: Fee to fax results is $4.00 per document. Copy fee: $2.00 per page. Certification fee: $2.00. Fee payee: Clerk of Courts. Personal checks accepted. Prepayment is required.

Franklin County

Court of Common Pleas - Civil 157 Lincoln Way East, Chambersburg, PA 17201; 717-261-3858; Fax: 717-264-6772. Hours: 8:30AM-4:30PM (EST). *Civil, Eviction.*

Civil Records: Access: In person only. Visitors must perform in person searches for themselves. Search fee: No search fee. Required to search: name, years to search. Civil cases indexed by defendant, plaintiff. Civil records on file from 1985; on computer back to 4/1/1999.

General Information: No mental records released. Fax notes: Fee to fax results is $1.00 per page. Copy fee: $1.00 per page. Certification fee: $5.00 for 1st pg; $1.00 each add'l. Fee payee: Prothonotary. Personal checks accepted. Prepayment is required.

Court of Common Pleas - Criminal 157 Lincoln Way East, Chambersburg, PA 17201; 717-261-3805; Fax: 717-261-3896. Hours: 8:30AM-4:30PM (EST). *Felony, Misdemeanor.*

Criminal Records: Access: Mail, in person. Both court and visitors may perform in person searches. Search fee: $10.00 per name. Required to search: name, years to search, DOB. Computerized back to 1995; criminal records on files for 50 years, archived from 1800s.

General Information: Public access terminal is available. No juvenile records released. SASE requested. Turnaround time same day. Copy fee: $.25 per page. Certification fee: $5.00. Fee payee: Clerk of Courts. Personal checks accepted. Prepayment is required.

Register of Wills 157 Lincoln Way East, Chambersburg, PA 17201; 717-261-3872; Fax: 717-267-3438. Hours: 8:30AM-4:30PM (EST). *Probate.*

Fulton County

Court of Common Pleas - Criminal/Civil Fulton County Courthouse, 201 N 2nd St, McConnellsburg, PA 17233; 717-485-4212; Fax: 717-485-5568 Attn: Court of Common Pleas. Hours: 8:30AM-4:30PM (EST). *Felony, Misdemeanor, Civil, Eviction.*

Civil Records: Access: In person only. Visitors must perform in person searches for themselves. No search fee. Required to search: name, years to search. Civil cases indexed by defendant, plaintiff. Civil records on docket index from 1850s; on computer back to 1999.

Criminal Records: Access: Mail, in person. Both court and visitors may perform in person searches. Search fee: $5.00 per name. Required to search: name, years to search. Criminal records on docket index from 1850s; on computer back to 1994.

General Information: Public access terminal is available. No juvenile, adoption records released. SASE required. Turnaround time 3-5 days. Fax notes: $5.00 per document. Copy fee: $.25 per page. Certification fee: $5.00. Fee payee: Prothonotary. Personal checks accepted. Prepayment is required.

Register of Wills 201 N 2nd St, McConnellsburg, PA 17233; 717-485-4212; Fax: 717-485-5568. Hours: 8:30AM-4:30PM (EST). *Probate.*

Greene County

Court of Common Pleas Greene County Courthouse, Room 105, Waynesburg, PA 15370; 724-852-5289. Hours: 8:30AM-4:30PM (EST). *Civil, Eviction.*

Civil Records: Access: Mail, in person. Visitors must perform in person searches for themselves. No search fee. Required to search: name, years to search. Civil cases indexed by defendant, plaintiff. Civil records go back to 1797; on computer back to 1996.

General Information: Public access terminal is available. No mental health records released. SASE required. Turnaround time 1 week. Copy fee: $.50 per page. Certification fee: $6.00. Fee payee: Prothonotary. Personal checks accepted. Prepayment is required.

Court of Common Pleas - Criminal Greene County Courthouse, Waynesburg, PA 15370; 724-852-5281; Fax: 724-852-5316. Hours: 8:30AM-4:30PM (EST). *Felony, Misdemeanor.*

Criminal Records: Access: Mail, in person. Both court and visitors may perform in person searches. Search fee: $10.00 per name. Required to search: name, years to search, DOB, signed release; also helpful: SSN. Criminal records on index books from 1940s, on computer since 1996.

General Information: Public access terminal is available. (Limited number of cases only.) No juvenile, adoption records released. SASE required. Turnaround time same day. Fax notes: Fee to fax results is $2.00 1st page; $1.00 each add'l page. Copy fee: $.50 per page. Certification fee: $8.00. Fee payee: Clerk of Courts. Personal checks accepted. Prepayment is required.

Register of Wills Greene County Courthouse, 10 E High St, Waynesburg, PA 15370; 724-852-5283. Hours: 8:30AM-4PM (EST). *Probate.*

Huntingdon County

Court of Common Pleas - Criminal/Civil PO Box 39, Courthouse, Huntingdon, PA 16652; 814-643-1610; Fax: 814-643-4172. Hours: 8:30AM-4:30PM (EST). *Felony, Misdemeanor, Civil, Eviction.*

Civil Records: Access: Phone, mail, fax, in person. Both court and visitors may perform in person searches. No search fee. Required to search: name, years to search; also helpful: address. Civil cases indexed by defendant, plaintiff. Civil records on computer from 08/03/92, on dockets from 1700s. Online access is available through a private company. For information, call Infocon at 814-472-6066.

Criminal Records: Access: Phone, mail, fax, in person. Both court and visitors may perform in person searches. No search fee. Required to search: name, years to search; also helpful: DOB, SSN. Criminal records on computer from 08/03/92, on dockets from 1700s. Online access is available through a private company. For information, call Infocon at 814-472-6066.

General Information: Public access terminal is available. No juvenile records released. SASE required. Turnaround time 1-2 days. Copy fee: $.25 per page. Certification fee: $4.50. Fee payee: Kay Coons, Prothonotary. Personal checks accepted. Prepayment is required.

Register of Wills Courthouse, 223 Penn St, Huntingdon, PA 16652; 814-643-2740. Hours: 8:30AM-4:30PM (EST). *Probate.*

Indiana County

Court of Common Pleas - Criminal/Civil County Courthouse, 825 Philadelphia St, Indiana, PA 15701; 724-465-3855/3858; Fax: 724-465-3968. Hours: 8AM-4PM *Felony, Misdemeanor, Civil, Eviction.*

Civil Records: Access: Fax, mail, in person. Both court and visitors may perform in person searches. Search fee: $10.00 per name. Will not conduct judgment searches. Required to search: name, years to search. Civil cases indexed by defendant, plaintiff. Civil records on computer from 1994, prior on index files to 1806.

Criminal Records: Access: Fax, mail, in person. Both court and visitors may perform in person searches. Search fee: $10.00 per name. Required to search: name, years to search, DOB, signed release. Criminal records on computer from 1994, prior on index files to 1806.

General Information: Public access terminal is available. No juvenile, commitment records released. Turnaround time same day. Fax notes: $.25 per page. Copy fee: $.25 per page. Certification fee: $3.00. Fee payee: Clerk of Court or Prothonotary. Personal checks accepted. Prepayment is required.

Register of Wills County Courthouse, 825 Philadelphia St, Indiana, PA 15701; 724-465-3860; Fax: 724-465-3863. 8AM-4:30PM (EST). *Probate.*

Jefferson County

Court of Common Pleas - Criminal/Civil Courthouse, 200 Main St, Brookville, PA 15825; 814-849-1606 X225; Fax: 814-849-1607. Hours: 8:30AM-4:30PM (EST). *Felony, Misdemeanor, Civil, Eviction.*

Civil Records: Access: Mail, in person. Both court and visitors may perform in person searches. Search fee: $5.00 per name. Required to search: name, years to search. Civil cases indexed by defendant, plaintiff. Civil records on computer back to 1987; all incoming records microfilmed, records since 1823 on microfilm.

Criminal Records: Access: Mail, in person. Both court and visitors may perform in person searches. Search fee: $5.00 per name. Required to search: name, years to search, DOB; also helpful: SSN. Criminal records on computer back to 1987; all incoming records microfilmed, records since 1947 on microfilm.

General Information: Public access terminal is available. No juvenile, mental health, records released, including criminal cases with a minor as a victim. SASE required. Turnaround time 2 days. Copy fee: $.50 per page. Certification fee: $1.50. Fee payee: Clerk of Courts. Personal checks okay. Prepayment required.

Register of Wills Jefferson County Courthouse, 200 Main St, Brookville, PA 15825; 814-849-1610; Fax: 814-849-1677. 8:30AM-4:30PM (EST). *Probate.*

Note: $5.00 serach fee, $1.00 per copy.

Juniata County

Court of Common Pleas - Criminal/Civil Juniata County Courthouse, Mifflintown, PA 17059; 717-436-7715; Fax: 717-436-7734. Hours: 8AM-4:30PM (EST). *Felony, Misdemeanor, Civil, Eviction.*

Civil Records: Access: Mail, in person. Both court and visitors may perform in person searches. Search fee: $5.00 per name. Required to search: name, years to search. Civil cases indexed by defendant, plaintiff. Civil records on computer go back to 1993, on dockets from 1836.

Criminal Records: Access: Phone, mail, in person. Both court and visitors may perform in person searches. Search fee: $5.00 per name. Required to search: name, years to search, DOB, SSN, signed release. Criminal records on computer go back to 1993, on dockets from 1894.

General Information: Public access terminal is available. No juvenile records released. SASE required. Turnaround time 1 week. Copy fee: $.50 per page. Certification fee: $1.00 per page. Fee payee: Prothonotary or Clerk of Courts. Personal checks accepted. Prepayment is required.

Register of Wills Juniata County Courthouse, PO Box 68, Mifflintown, PA 17059; 717-436-7709; Fax: 717-436-7756. Hours: 8AM-4:30PM M-F, 8AM-12PM Wed (June-Sept) (EST). *Probate.*

Lackawanna County

Court of Common Pleas - Civil Clerk of Judicial Records, PO Box 133, Scranton, PA 18503; 570-963-6724; Civil phone: 717-963-6723. Hours: 9AM-4PM (EST). *Civil, Eviction.*

Civil Records: Access: In person only. Visitors must perform in person searches for themselves. No searches

performed by this court but exceptions are made. Required to search: name, years to search. Civil cases indexed by defendant, plaintiff. Civil records computerized since 09/95, dockets from 1920s, archived from 1800s. Case number is required.

General Information: Public access terminal is available. No juvenile records released. Fax notes: Copy fee: $.25 if self service; $.50 if done by Clerk; $1.00 for mail requesters first copy, $.50 each add'l. Certification fee: $4.50. Fee payee: Clerk of Judicial Records. Business checks accepted. Prepayment is required.

Court of Common Pleas - Criminal Lackawanna County Courthouse, Scranton, PA 18503; 570-963-6759; Fax: 570-963-6459. Hours: 9AM-4PM (EST). *Felony, Misdemeanor.*

Criminal Records: Access: Mail, fax, in person. Both court and visitors may perform in person searches. Search fee: $10.00 per name. Required to search: name, years to search, DOB, SSN. Criminal records computerized since 10/95, on dockets from 1983, archived from 1941, indexed by defendant only.

General Information: Public access terminal is available. No juvenile records released. SASE required. Turnaround time 1-2 days. Fax notes: Will not fax results. Copy fee: $.50 per page. Certification fee: $8.00. Fee payee: Clerk of Judicial Records. Business checks accepted. Prepayment is required.

Register of Wills Register of Wills, County Courthouse, 200 N Washington Ave, Scranton, PA 18503; 570-963-6702; Fax: 570-963-6377. Hours: 9AM-4PM (EST). *Probate.*

Lancaster County

Court of Common Pleas - Civil 50 N Duke St, PO Box 83480, Lancaster, PA 17608-3480; 717-299-8282; Fax: 717-293-7210. Hours: 8:30AM-5PM (EST). *Civil, Eviction.*

www.co.lancaster.pa.us/courts/site/default.asp

Civil Records: Access: Online, in person. Visitor must perform in person searches for themselves. No search fee. Required to search: name, years to search; also helpful: address. Civil cases indexed by defendant, plaintiff. Civil records on computer from 7/87, in files from 1987, judgments on dockets from 1800s, others archived from 1800s. Access to remote online records requires a $25.00 monthly fee plus $.18 per minute. Search by name or case number. Call Kathy Harris at 717-299-8252 for more information.

General Information: Public access terminal is available. No naturalization records released. SASE required. Turnaround time 2-3 days. Fax notes: $2.00 for first page, $1.00 each add'l. Fee higher for out of state faxing. Copy fee: $1.00 per page. Certification fee: $3.00. Fee payee: Prothonotary. Business checks accepted. Prepayment is required.

Court of Common Pleas - Criminal Clerk of Courts, 50 North Duke St, Lancaster, PA 17602; 717-299-8275. Hours: 8:30AM-5PM (EST). *Felony, Misdemeanor.*

Criminal Records: Access: Mail, in person. Both court and visitors may perform in person searches. Search fee: $15.00 per name. Required to search: name, years to search. Criminal records on computer from 1988, archived from 1901.

General Information: Public access terminal is available. No juvenile records released. SASE required. Turnaround time 2 days. Copy fee: $.50 per copy or $1.00 for docket page including disposition; however, there is no copy fee if court does the search. Certification fee: $8.00. Fee payee: Clerk of Courts. Only cashiers checks and money orders accepted. Prepayment is required.

Register of Wills 50 N. Duke St., Lancaster, PA 17602; 717-299-8243; Fax: 717-295-5914. Hours: 8:30AM-5PM (EST). *Probate.*
www.co.lancaster.pa.us

Lawrence County

Court of Common Pleas - Criminal/Civil
430 Court St, New Castle, PA 16101-3593; 724-656-2143; Fax: 724-656-1988. Hours: 8AM-4PM (EST). *Felony, Misdemeanor, Civil, Eviction.*
www.co.lawrence.pa.us

Civil Records: Access: Fax, mail, online, in person. Both court and visitors may perform in person searches. Search fee: $10.00 per name. Required to search: name, years to search. Civil cases indexed by defendant, plaintiff. Civil records on computer from 1987, on Russell Index from 1885. Online access is available through a private company. For information, call Infocon at 814-472-6066.

Criminal Records: Access: Fax, mail, online, in person. Both court and visitors may perform in person searches. Search fee: $10.00 per name. Required to search: name, years to search, signed release; also helpful: DOB, SSN. Criminal records on computer from 1987, on Russell Index from 1885. Online access is available through a private company. For information, call Infocon at 814-472-6066.

General Information: Public access terminal is available. No adoption, juvenile, impounded, or juvenile sex crime victim records released. SASE requested. Turnaround time ASAP. Fax notes: No fee to fax results. Fax Fee: Local $1.00 plus $.50 per pg; Long distance $3.00 plus $.50 per pg. Copy fee: $.50 per page. Certification fee: $1.50. Fee payee: Prothonotary. Business checks accepted. Prepayment is required.

Register of Wills 430 Court St, New Castle, PA 16101-3593; 724-656-2128/2159; Fax: 724-656-1966. Hours: 8AM-4PM (EST). *Probate.*

General Information: Public access terminal is available. . Fee payee: Register of Wills, Lawrence County. Prepayment is required.

Lebanon County

Court of Common Pleas - Civil Municipal Bldg, Rm 104, 400 S 8th St, Lebanon, PA 17042; 717-274-2801 X2120. Hours: 8:30AM-4:30PM (EST). *Civil, Eviction.*

Civil Records: Access: Main, in person. Visitors must perform in person searches for themselves. No search fee. Required to search: name, years to search; also helpful: address. Civil cases indexed by defendant, plaintiff. Civil records on computer from 1985, on files from 1883. Docket number required for phone access.

General Information: Public access terminal is available. No mental health records released. Copy fee: $.50 per page. Certification fee: $8.00. Fee payee: Prothonotary. Personal checks accepted. Prepayment is required.

Court of Common Pleas - Criminal Municipal Bldg Rm 102, 400 S 8th St, Lebanon, PA 17042; 717-274-2801 X2118. Hours: 8:30AM-4:30PM (EST). *Felony, Misdemeanor.*

Criminal Records: Access: Phone, mail, in person. Both court and visitors may perform in person searches. Search fee: $16.00 per name. Required to search: name, years to search. Criminal records on computer from 1986, indexed from 1800s. Action number required for phone access.

General Information: Public access terminal is available. No juvenile records released. SASE required. Turnaround time varies. Copy fee: $.50 per page. Certification fee: $8.00. Fee payee: Clerk of Court. Personal checks accepted. Prepayment is required.

Register of Wills Municipal Bldg, Rm 105, 400 S 8th St, Lebanon, PA 17042; 717-274-2801 X2215; Fax: 717-274-8094. 8:30AM-4:30PM (EST). *Probate.*

Lehigh County

Court of Common Pleas - Civil 455 W Hamilton St, Allentown, PA 18101-1614; 610-782-3148; Fax: 610-770-3840. Hours: 8:30AM-4:30PM (EST). *Civil, Eviction.*
www.lccpa.org

Civil Records: Access: Mail, online, in person. Both the court and visitors may perform in person searches. No search fee. Required to search: name, years to search, DOB or SSN. Civil cases indexed by defendant, plaintiff. Civil records on computer since 1990, on microfilm from 1812, some in books. Access to the county online system requires monthly usage fee. Search by name or case number. Call Lehigh Cty Computer Svcs Dept at 610-782-3286 for more information.

General Information: Public access terminal is available. No sealed, confidential, or impounded records released. Copy fee: $.50 per page; docket printout $3.00. Certification fee: $4.50. Fee payee: Clerk of Courts-Civil. Personal checks accepted.

Court of Common Pleas - Criminal 455 W Hamilton St, Allentown, PA 18101-1614; 610-782-3077; Fax: 610-770-6797. Hours: 8:30AM-4:30PM (EST). *Felony, Misdemeanor.*
www.lccpa.org

Criminal Records: Access: mail, online, in person. Both court and visitors may perform in person searches. Search fee: $20.00 per name. Fee includes copy of certified docket. Required to search: name, years to search, DOB; SSN helpful. Criminal records on computer from 1990, on alpha index from 1962 to 1990, on microfilm from 1812. Access to the countywide online system requires monthly usage fee. Search by name or case number. Call Lehigh Cty Computer Svcs Dept at 610-782-3286 for more information. Also, free online access is under development; currently calendars and bench warrants are available online at www.lehighcountycourt.org under "Calendars & Schedules.".

General Information: Public access terminal is available. No juvenile or impounded records released. SASE required. Turnaround time 1 week. Fax notes: No fee to fax results. Copy fee: $.50. Docket printout mailed $2.00. Certification fee: $8.00. Fee payee: Clerk of Courts-Criminal. Personal checks accepted. Prepayment is required.

Register of Wills 455 W Hamilton, Allentown, PA 18101-1614; 610-820-3170; Fax: 610-820-3439. Hours: 8AM-4PM (EST). *Probate.*

Luzerne County

Court of Common Pleas - Civil 200 N River St, Wilkes Barre, PA 18711-1001; 570-825-1745; Fax: 570-825-1757. 9AM-4:30PM (EST). *Civil, Eviction.*

Civil Records: Access: Phone, mail, in person. Both court and visitors may perform in person searches. Search fee: $15.75 per name for 5 years, $1.50 each add'l year, and $1.50 each reference cited. Required to search: name, years to search, address. Civil cases indexed by defendant, plaintiff. Civil records partially on microfiche and archives, on dockets from 1935.

General Information: No mental, sealed records released. SASE required. Turnaround time 3 days. Fax notes: Fee to fax results is $1.50 per page. Copy fee: $1.00 per page. Certification fee: $4.75. Fee payee: Prothonotary. Personal checks accepted. Credit cards accepted: Visa, MasterCard, AmEx. Prepayment is required.

Court of Common Pleas - Criminal 200 N River St, Wilkes Barre, PA 18711; 570-825-1585; Fax: 570-825-1843. Hours: 8AM-4:30PM (EST). *Felony, Misdemeanor.*

Criminal Records: Access: Phone, fax, mail, in person. Only the court performs in person searches. Search fee: $15.00 per name. Required to search: name, years to search, DOB or SSN. Criminal records on computer, microfiche and archived from 1989, on files from 1972. Records from 1933 to 1959 destroyed in flood. Index starts in 1918.

General Information: No "M" number (confidential custody case) records released. SASE not required. Turnaround time 1-2 days. Fax notes: No fee to fax results. Copy fee: $.35 per page. Certification fee: $7.00. Fee payee: Clerk of Courts. Personal checks accepted. Credit cards accepted: Visa, MasterCard, Discover. Prepayment is required.

Register of Wills 200 N River St, Wilkes Barre, PA 18711; 570-825-1672, 570-825-1500 X670. Hours: 9AM-4:30PM (EST). *Probate.*

Lycoming County

Court of Common Pleas - Criminal/Civil 48 W 3rd St, Williamsport, PA 17701; 570-327-2251. Hours: 8:30AM-5PM (EST). *Felony, Misdemeanor, Civil, Eviction.*

Civil Records: Access: In person only. Visitors must perform in person searches for themselves. No search fee. Required to search: name, years to search; also helpful: address. Civil cases indexed by defendant, plaintiff. Civil records on computer from 1983, on dockets from 1795.

Criminal Records: Access: Mail, in person. Both court and visitors may perform in person searches. Search fee: $10.00 per name. Required to search: name, years to search, DOB; also helpful: address. Criminal records on computer from 1910.

General Information: Public access terminal is available. No juvenile, cases involving minors, mental records released. SASE required. Turnaround time same day. Copy fee: $.50 per page. Certification fee: $5.00. Fee payee: Prothonotary. Personal checks accepted. Prepayment is required.

Register of Wills Lycoming Co Courthouse, 48 W 3rd St, Williamsport, PA 17701; 570-327-2263, 327-2258; Fax: 570-327-2455. 8:30AM-5PM *Probate.*

McKean County

Court of Common Pleas - Criminal & Civil PO Box 273, Smethport, PA 16749; 814-887-3270; Fax: 814-887-3219. Hours: 8:30AM-4:30PM (EST). *Felony, Misdemeanor, Civil, Eviction.*

Civil Records: Access: Phone, fax, mail, in person. Both court and visitors may perform in person searches. Search fee: $12.00 per name. Required to search: name, years to search. Civil cases indexed by defendant, plaintiff. Civil records on computer since 1994, on microfiche from 1952 to 1962, on dockets from 1872.

Criminal Records: Access: Mail, in person. Both court and visitors may perform in person searches. Search fee: $10.00 per name. Required to search: name, years to search, DOB. Criminal records on computer since 1994, on dockets from 1872.

General Information: Public access terminal is available. No sex related, juvenile, mental health records released. SASE required. Turnaround time same day. Fax notes: $2.00 per page. Copy fee: $.50 per page. Computer search copy fee: $1.00 per page. Certification fee: $3.50. Fee payee: Prothonotary or Clerk of Courts. Personal checks accepted. Prepayment is required.

Register of Wills PO Box 202, Smethport, PA 16749-0202; 814-887-3263; Fax: 814-887-3255. Hours: 8:30AM-4:30PM (EST). *Probate.*

Mercer County

Court of Common Pleas - Civil 105 Mercer County Courthouse, Mercer, PA 16137; 724-662-3800. Hours: 8:30AM-4:30PM (EST). *Civil, Eviction.*

Civil Records: Access: In person. Visitors must perform in person searches. No search fee. Required to search: name, years to search. Civil cases indexed by defendant, plaintiff. Civil records on computer since 1994; prior records on dockets from 1930s, archived from 1700s. Include SSN and DOB in your search. Online access is available through a private company. For information, call Infocon at 814-472-6066.

General Information: Public access terminal is available. No mental, sealed records released. SASE required. Turnaround time 1-2 days. Copy fee: $2.00 per page. Certification fee: $4.50. Fee payee: Prothonotary or Clerk of Courts. Business checks accepted. Prepayment is required.

Court of Common Pleas - Criminal 112 Mercer County Courthouse, Mercer, PA 16137; 724-662-3800 X2248. Hours: 8:30AM-4:30PM (EST). *Felony, Misdemeanor.*

www.mcc.co.mercer.pa.us/LOCRULES.htm

Criminal Records: Access: Mail, in person, online. Both court and visitors may perform in person searches. Search fee: $10.00 per name. Required to search: name, years to search; also helpful: DOB, SSN. Criminal records on computer since 1993, indexed since 1920, on files from 1980. Online access is available through a private company. For information, call Infocon at 814-472-6066.

General Information: Public access terminal is available. No juvenile records released. SASE required. Turnaround time 1 day. Fax notes: Fee to fax results is $1.00 per page. Copy fee: $1.00 for first page, $.50 each add'l. Certification fee: $5.00. Fee payee: Clerk of Courts. Personal checks accepted. Prepayment required.

Register of Wills 112 Mercer County Courthouse, Mercer, PA 16137; 724-662-3800 X2248; Fax: 724-662-1604. Hours: 8:30AM-4:30PM (EST). *Probate.*

Mifflin County

Court of Common Pleas - Criminal & Civil 20 N Wayne St, Lewistown, PA 17044; 717-248-8146; Fax: 717-248-5275. Hours: 8AM-4:30PM (EST). *Felony, Misdemeanor, Civil, Eviction.*

http://mifflincounty.lcworkshop.com/

Note: The web site contains court opinions. Click on "Row Offices" then "Court of Common Pleas."

Civil Records: Access: In person only. Visitors must perform in person searches for themselves. No search fee. Required to search: name, years to search. Civil cases indexed by defendant, plaintiff. Civil records on computer from 1993, on microfiche from 1971-1990 prior on books. Online access is available through a private company. For information, call Infocon at 814-472-6066.

Criminal Records: Access: In person only. Visitors must perform in person searches for themselves. No search fee. Required to search: name, years to search. Criminal records on computer from 1993, on microfiche from 1971-1990prior on books. Online access is available through a private company. For information, call Infocon at 814-472-6066.

General Information: Public access terminal is available. No juvenile, mental health records released. Fax notes: Will fax back if fees are prepaid. Copy fee: $.50 per page. Certification fee: $4.50. Fee payee: Clerk

of Courts. Personal checks accepted. Prepayment is required.

Register of Wills 20 N. Wayne St., Lewistown, PA 17044; 717-242-1449. Hours: 8AM-4:30PM (EST). *Probate.*

Monroe County

Court of Common Pleas - Civil Monroe County Courthouse - Prothonotary, 7th & Monroe St, Stroudsburg, PA 18360; 570-517-3370; 570-420-3570; Fax: 570-420-3582. Hours: 8:30AM-4:30PM (EST). *Civil, Eviction.*

Civil Records: Access: Mail, in person. Both court and visitors may perform in person searches. Search fee: $5.00. Required to search: name, years to search; also helpful:DOB, SSN, signed release. Civil cases indexed by defendant, plaintiff. Civil records indexed on computer 1995 to present, prior in dockets.

General Information: Public access terminal is available. No juvenile records released. SASE not required. Turnaround time 1 day. Copy fee: $.50 per page. Certification fee: $3.00. Fee payee: Monroe County Prothonotary. Only cashiers checks and money orders accepted. Prepayment is required.

Court of Common Pleas - Criminal Monroe County Courthouse Rm 312, Stroudsburg, PA 18360-2190; 570-517-3385. Hours: 8:30AM-4:30PM (EST). *Felony, Misdemeanor.*

Criminal Records: Access: Mail, in person. Both court and visitors may perform in person searches. Search fee: $5.00 per name. Required to search: name, years to search; also helpful: address, DOB, SSN. Criminal records on computer since 1995; prior on dockets.

General Information: Public access terminal is available. No sex related, juvenile, adoption records released. SASE not required. Turnaround time 1 day. Copy fee: $1.00 per page. Certification fee: $5.00. Fee payee: Clerk of Court. Only cashiers checks and money orders accepted. Prepayment is required.

Register of Wills Monroe County Courthouse, Stroudsburg, PA 18360; 570-517-3359; Fax: 570-420-3537. Hours: 8:30AM-4:30PM (EST). *Probate.*

Note: Online access to wills is available through a private company at www.landex.com/remote/. Fee is $.20 per minute and $.50 per fax page. Wills go back to 11/1836.

Montgomery County

Court of Common Pleas - Civil PO Box 311, Airy & Swede St, Norristown, PA 19404-0311; 610-278-3360. 8:30AM-4:15PM (EST). *Civil, Eviction.*

www.montcopa.org

Civil Records: Access: Online, in person. Visitors must perform in person searches for themselves. No search fee. Required to search: name, years to search. Civil cases indexed by defendant, plaintiff. Civil records on computer from 4/82, on microfilm from 1800s. Court and other records are available free online at www1.montcopa.org. System is experimental and may or may not be adapted full time. A pay service, offering remote dial-up, is also available.

General Information: Public access terminal is available. No mental health, divorce, sealed records released. SASE required. Copy fee: $.25 per page. Certification fee: $4.50. Fee payee: Prothonotary. Personal checks accepted. Prepayment is required.

Court of Common Pleas - Criminal PO Box 311, Airy & Swede St, Norristown, PA 19404-0311; 610-278-3346. Hours: 8:30AM-4:15PM (EST). *Felony, Misdemeanor.*

www.montcopa.org

Criminal Records: Access: Mail, online, in person. Both court and visitors may perform in person searches. Search fee: $15.00 per name. Required to search: name, years to search, DOB, signed release. Criminal records on computer from 10/84, prior archived and on microfiche. Criminal court and other records are available free online at www.montcopa.org/mway/index.html. Includes purged cases. This replaces the pay remote dial-up service at at 610-292-4931.

General Information: Public access terminal is available. No impounded, sealed records released. SASE required. Turnaround time 5 days. Copy fee: $1.00 per page. Certification fee: $7.00. Fee payee: Clerk of Courts. Business checks accepted. Credit cards accepted: Visa, MasterCard, Discover. Accepted in person only. Prepayment is required.

Register of Wills Airy & Swede St, PO Box 311, Norristown, PA 19404; 610-278-3400; Fax: 610-278-3240. Hours: 8:30AM-4:15PM (EST). *Probate.*

www.montcopa.org

Montour County

Court of Common Pleas - Criminal & Civil Montour County Courthouse, 29 Mill St, Danville, PA 17821; 570-271-3010; Fax: 570-271-3089. Hours: 9AM-4PM (EST). *Felony, Misdemeanor, Civil, Eviction.*

Civil Records: Access: Phone, fax, mail, in person. Both court and visitors may perform in person searches. Search fee: $10.00 per name. Required to search: name, years to search. Civil cases indexed by defendant, plaintiff. Civil records on books since 1991, on microfiche since 1939, on computer back to 1995. Actual files kept for 20 years.

Criminal Records: Access: Phone, fax, mail, in person. Both court and visitors may perform in person searches. Search fee: $10.00 per name. Required to search: name, years to search, DOB. Criminal records on books since 1991, on microfiche since 1939, on computer back to 1995. Actual files kept for 20 years.

General Information: Public access terminal is available. No sex related, juvenile or adoption records released. SASE required. Turnaround time 1-2 days. Copy fee: $.50 per page. Certification fee: $3.00. Fee payee: Prothonotary. Personal checks accepted. Prepayment is required.

Register of Wills 29 Mill St, Danville, PA 17821; 570-271-3012; Fax: 570-271-3071. Hours: 9AM-4PM (EST). *Probate.*

Northampton County

Court of Common Pleas - Civil Gov't Center, 669 Washington St Rm 207, Easton, PA 18042-7498; 610-559-3060. Hours: 8:30AM-4:30PM (EST). *Civil, Eviction.*

Civil Records: Access: In person only. Visitors must perform in person searches for themselves. No search fee. Required to search: name, years to search; also helpful: address. Civil cases indexed by defendant, plaintiff. Civil records on computer since 1/85 (Civil) and 2/90 (Judgments).

General Information: Public access terminal is available. No impounded or PFA abuse records released. Copy fee: $1.00 per page. Certification fee: $4.75. Fee payee: Clerk of Court-Civil or Prothonotary's Office. Business checks, certified check accepted; no personal checks accepted. Prepayment is required.

Court of Common Pleas - Criminal 669 Washington St, Easton, PA 18042-7494; 610-559-3000 X2114; Fax: 610-262-4391. Hours: 8:30AM-4:30PM (EST). *Felony, Misdemeanor.*

Criminal Records: Access: Mail, in person. Both court and visitors may perform in person searches. Search fee: $10.00 per name. Required to search: name, years

to search, DOB; also helpful: SSN. Criminal records on computer from 1984, on files from 1800s.

General Information: Public access terminal is available. No juvenile, expunged records released. SASE not required. Turnaround time same day. Copy fee: $.50 per page. Certification fee: $8.00. Fee payee: Criminal Division. Business checks accepted. Credit cards accepted: Visa, MasterCard. Prepayment is required.

Register of Wills Governmnent Center, 669 Washington St, Easton, PA 18042; 610-559-3094; Fax: 610-559-3735. 8:30AM-4:30PM (EST). *Probate.*

Northumberland County

Court of Common Pleas - Civil County Courthouse, 201 Market St, Rm #7, Sunbury, PA 17801-3468; 570-988-4151. Hours: 9AM-5PM M; 9AM-4:30PM T-F (EST). *Civil, Eviction.*

Civil Records: Access: Phone, mail, in person. Both court and visitors may perform in person searches. Search fee: $7.00 per name. Required to search: name, years to search. Civil cases indexed by defendant, plaintiff. Civil records on file from 1772; on computer back to 1998.

General Information: Public access terminal is available. No adult abuse, involuntary treatment records released. SASE required. Turnaround time 1-2 days. Copy fee: $1.00 2st page; $.25. Each add'l. Certification fee: $4.00 plus $1.00 each add'l page. Fee payee: Northumberland Prothonotary. Business checks accepted. Prepayment is required.

Court of Common Pleas - Criminal County Courthouse, 201 Market St, Rm 7, Sunbury, PA 17801-3468; 570-988-4148. Hours: 9AM-5PM M; 9AM-4:30PM T-F (EST). *Felony, Misdemeanor.*

Criminal Records: Access: Mail, in person. Both court and visitors may perform in person searches. Search fee: $10.00 per name. Required to search: name, years to search, DOB; also helpful: SSN. Criminal records indexed in office from 1945, on dockets from 1772, archived from 1700s to 1945, on computer to 1998.

General Information: Public access terminal is available. No juvenile records released. SASE required. Turnaround time 1-2 days. Copy fee: $1.00 for first page, $.25 each add'l. First copy for in person requests is $.25. Certification fee: $4.00 plus $1.00 each additional page. Fee payee: Clerk of Courts Office. Personal checks accepted. Prepayment is required.

Register of Wills County Courthouse, 201 Market St, Sunbury, PA 17801; 570-988-4143 and 5760-988-4140. Hours: 9AM-4:30PM (EST). *Probate.*

Perry County

Court of Common Pleas - Criminal & Civil PO Box 325, New Bloomfield, PA 17068; 717-582-2131 X240. Hours: 8AM-4PM (EST). *Felony, Misdemeanor, Civil, Eviction.*

Civil Records: Access: In person only. Visitors must perform in person searches for themselves. No search fee. Required to search: name, years to search. Civil cases indexed by defendant, plaintiff. Civil records on dockets from 1800s.

Criminal Records: Access: Phone, fax, mail, in person. Both court and visitors may perform in person searches. Search fee: $10.00 per name. Required to search: name, years to search; also helpful: DOB, SSN. Criminal records on dockets from 1950.

General Information: No juvenile records released. SASE required. Turnaround time 1 week, phone turnaround immediate. Fax notes: No fee to fax results. Copy fee: $.40 per page. Certification fee: $5.00. Fee payee: Prothonotary or Clerk of Courts. Personal checks accepted. Will bill to attorneys & abstract companies upon approval.

Register of Wills PO Box 223, New Bloomfield, PA 17068; 717-582-2131; Fax: 717-582-8570. Hours: 8AM-4PM (EST). *Probate.*

Philadelphia County

Court of Common Pleas - Civil First Judicial District of PA, Room 284, City Hall, Philadelphia, PA 19107; 215-686-6656; Fax: 215-567-7380. Hours: 9AM-5PM (EST). *Civil.*

Civil Records: Access: Mail, online, in person. Both court and visitors may perform in person searches. Search fee: $35.00 per name. Required to search: name, years to search. Civil cases indexed by defendant, plaintiff. Civil records on computer from 1/82 to present, archived on files from 1700s to 1982. Access to 1st Judicial District Civil Trial records available free online at http://dns2.phila.gov:8080. Search by name, judgment and docket information.

General Information: Public access terminal is available. No mental health, divorce, abuse, adoption records released. SASE required. Turnaround time 1-5 days. Copy fee: $.50 per page. Certification fee: $30.00. Fee payee: Prothonotary. Business checks accepted. Prepayment is required.

Clerk of Quarter Session 1301 Filbert St #310, Philadelphia, PA 19107; 215-683-7700 X01 & X02. Hours: 8AM-5PM (EST). *Felony, Misdemeanor.*

Criminal Records: Access: Mail, in person. Both court and visitors may perform in person searches. Search fee: $10.00 per name. Required to search: name, years to search, DOB, signed release; also helpful: address, SSN, race, sex. Criminal records on computer and microfiche from 1969, archived from 1800s.

General Information: No sealed, grand jury, mental records released. SASE required. Turnaround time 1-2. Copy fee: $.25 per page. Certification fee: $12.50. Fee payee: Clerk of Quarter Sessions. Business checks accepted. Prepayment is required.

Municipal Court 34 S 11th St, 5th floor, Philadelphia, PA 19107; 215-686-7997; Fax: 215-569-9254. Hours: 9AM-5PM (EST). *Felony, Misdemeanor, Civil Actions Under $10,000, Eviction.*

Note: Court has jurisdiction over certain criminal offenses with jail terms up to five years.

Civil Records: Access: Mail, in person. Only the court performs in person searches; visitors may not. No search fee. Required to search: name, years to search, address. Civil cases indexed by defendant, plaintiff. Civil records on computer from 1969. Include SSN and DOB if possible.

Criminal Records: Access: Mail, in person. Only the court performs in person searches; visitors may not. No search fee. Required to search: name, years to search, address, DOB, signed release. Criminal records on computer from 1969.

General Information: SASE required. Turnaround time 1-5 days. Copy fee: $.50 per page. Certification fee: $3.00. Fee payee: Prothonotary. Only cashiers checks and money orders accepted. Prepayment is required.

Register of Wills City Hall Rm 180, Philadelphia, PA 19107; 215-686-6250/6282; Fax: 215-686-6293. Hours: 8:30AM-4:30PM (EST). *Probate.*

Pike County

Court of Common Pleas - Criminal & Civil 412 Broad St, Milford, PA 18337; 570-296-7231. Hours: 8:30AM-4:30PM (EST). *Felony, Misdemeanor, Civil, Eviction.*

Civil Records: Access: Phone, mail, online, in person. Both court and visitors may perform in person searches. No search fee. Required to search: name, years to search. Civil cases indexed by defendant, plaintiff. Civil

records on files for 100 yrs, computerized since 1995. Online access is available through a private company. See note at beginning of section. The court will only do searches from 01/95 forward.

Criminal Records: Access: Phone, mail, online, in person. Both court and visitors may perform in person searches. Search fee: $10.00 per name. Required to search: name, years to search. Criminal records on files for 100 yrs, computerized since 1995. Online access to criminal records is available through a private company. For information, call Infocon at 814-472-6066. The court will only do searches from 01/95 forward.

General Information: Public access terminal is available. No juvenile, adoption, sealed records released. SASE required. Turnaround time varies. Copy fee: $.25 per page. Certification fee: $2.50 per page. Fee payee: Prothonotary. Personal checks accepted. Personal checks not exceeding $25.00 accepted. Prepayment is required.

Register of Wills 506 Broad St, Milford, PA 18337; 570-296-3508. 8:30AM-4:30PM *Probate.*

Potter County

Court of Common Pleas - Criminal & Civil 1 E 2nd St Rm 23, Coudersport, PA 16915; 814-274-9740; Fax: 814-274-3361. Hours: 8:30AM-4:30PM (EST). *Felony, Misdemeanor, Civil, Eviction.*

Civil Records: Access: Phone, fax, mail, in person. Both court and visitors may perform in person searches. No search fee. Required to search: name, years to search. Civil cases indexed by defendant, plaintiff. Civil records on dockets from early 1833 to 11/97; on computer since 11/97.

Criminal Records: Access: Phone, fax, mail, in person. Both court and visitors may perform in person searches. No search fee. Required to search: name, years to search, DOB. Criminal records on card index from 1983 to 6/27/97; on computer since 6/27/97; archived since 1839.

General Information: Public access terminal is available. No juvenile records released. SASE required. Turnaround time 2 weeks, phone turnaround immediate (unless lengthy search). Fax notes: No fee to fax results if limited. Copy fee: $.25 per page. Certification fee: $5.00. Fee payee: Prothonotary or Clerk of Courts. Personal checks accepted. Prepayment is required.

Register of Wills 1 E 2nd St, Coudersport, PA 16915; 814-274-8370. 8:30AM-4:30PM *Probate.*

Schuylkill County

Court of Common Pleas - Civil 401 N 2nd St, Pottsville, PA 17901-2528; 570-628-1270; Fax: 570-628-1261. 8:30AM-4:30PM (EST). *Civil, Eviction.*

www.co.schuylkill.pa.us/Offices/Courts/CourtAdministration.htm

Civil Records: Access: Mail, in person. Both court and visitors may perform in person searches. Search fee: $5.00 per name. Required to search: name, years to search. Civil cases indexed by defendant, plaintiff. Civil records (suits) on computer from 1989, judgments on computer from 199 and on dockets from 1800s.

General Information: Public access terminal is available. No master reports or sealed records released. SASE requested. Turnaround time 1 day. Copy fee: $.25 per page. Certification fee: $4.00 per page. Fee payee: Prothonotary. Personal checks accepted. Will bill copy fees.

Court of Common Pleas - Criminal 410 N 2nd St, Pottsville, PA 17901; 570-622-5570 X1133; Fax: 570-628-1143. Hours: 9AM-4PM (EST). *Felony, Misdemeanor.*

Criminal Records: Access: Fax, mail, in person. Both court and visitors may perform in person searches.

Search fee: $10.00 plus $5.00 automation fee per name. Required to search: name, years to search, DOB; also helpful: SSN. Criminal records on computer from 4/88, on dockets from 1800s.

General Information: No juvenile records released. SASE not required. Turnaround time same day. Fax notes: No fee to fax results. Copy fee: $.25 per page. Certification fee: $8.00. Fee payee: Clerk of Courts. Business checks accepted. Prepayment is required.

Register of Wills Courthouse 401 N 2nd St, Pottsville, PA 17901-2520; 570-628-1377; Fax: 570-628-1384. Hours: 8:30AM-4:30PM (EST). *Probate.*

Snyder County

Court of Common Pleas - Criminal & Civil Snyder County Courthouse, PO Box 217, Middleburg, PA 17842; 570-837-4202. Hours: 8:30AM-4PM *Felony, Misdemeanor, Civil, Eviction.*

Civil Records: Access: Mail, in person. Both court and visitors may perform in person searches. Search fee: $10.00 per name. Required to search: name, years to search. Civil cases indexed by defendant, plaintiff. Civil records on dockets from 1800s, some on microfilm.

Criminal Records: Access: Mail, in person. Both court and visitors may perform in person searches. Search fee: $15.00 per name. Required to search: name, years to search. Criminal records on dockets from 1800s, some on microfilm.

General Information: No juvenile records released. SASE required. Turnaround time 2 days. Copy fee: $.35 per page. Certification fee: $4.00. Fee payee: Prothonotary or Clerk of Courts. No personal checks. Prepayment is required.

Register of Wills County Courthouse-W. Market St, PO Box 217, Middleburg, PA 17842; 570-837-4224/6. Hours: 8:30AM-4PM (EST). *Probate.*

Somerset County

Court of Common Pleas - Civil 111 E Union St #190, Somerset, PA 15501; 814-445-1428; Fax: 814-444-9270. Hours: 8:30AM-4PM (EST). *Civil, Eviction.*

Civil Records: Access: Phone, fax, mail, in person. Both court and visitors may perform in person searches. Search fee: $12.00 per name. Required to search: name, years to search. Civil cases indexed by defendant, plaintiff. Civil records on computer from 1/92, on microfiche from 1920 to 1972, on dockets (Russell System for all other years prior to 1992). Hard copy must follow fax request.

General Information: Public access terminal is available. No commitment records released. SASE required. Turnaround time 2-3 days. Fax notes: $.50 per page. Copy fee: $.50 per page. Certification fee: $2.00. Fee payee: Prothonotary of Somerset Co. Business checks accepted. Prepayment is required.

Court of Common Pleas - Criminal 111 E Union St #180, Somerset, PA 15501; 814-445-1435. Hours: 8:30AM-4PM (EST). *Felony, Misdemeanor.*

Criminal Records: Access: Phone, mail, in person. Both court and visitors may perform in person searches. Search fee: $5.00 per name. Required to search: name, years to search, DOB; also helpful: SSN. Criminal records on microfilm from 1920, archive dates uncertain, computerized since 1996.

General Information: No impounded records released. SASE not required. Turnaround time same day, phone turnaround immediate. Copy fee: $.50 per copy. Certification fee: $1.00. Fee payee: Clerk of Courts. Personal checks accepted. Will bill copy fees.

Register of Wills 111 E Union St #170, Somerset, PA 15501-0586; 814-445-1548; Fax: 814-445-7991. Hours: 8:30AM-4PM (EST). *Probate.*

Sullivan County

Court of Common Pleas - Criminal & Civil Main Street, Laporte, PA 18626; 570-946-7351; Probate phone: 570-946-7351. Hours: 8:30AM-4PM (EST). *Felony, Misdemeanor, Civil, Eviction, Probate.*

Note: Includes the Register of Wills.

Civil Records: Access: Mail, in person. Visitors must perform in person searches for themselves. No search fee. Required to search: name, years to search. Civil cases indexed by defendant, plaintiff. Civil records on dockets from 1847 to present and on computer from August 2000.

Criminal Records: Access: Mail, in person. Visitors must perform in person searches for themselves. No search fee. Required to search: name, years to search; also helpful: SSN. Criminal records on dockets from 1847 to present and on computer from August 2000.

General Information: No juvenile records released. SASE required. Turnaround time same day. Copy fee: $2.00 per page. Certification fee: $3.00 per page. Fee payee: Prothonotary or Clerk of Courts. Personal checks accepted. Prepayment is required.

Susquehanna County

Court of Common Pleas - Civil Susquehanna Courthouse, PO Box 218, Montrose, PA 18801; 570-278-4600 X120. Hours: 8:30AM-4:30PM (EST). *Civil, Eviction.*

Civil Records: Access: Mail, fax, in person. Both court and visitors may perform in person searches. No search fee. Required to search: name, years to search. Civil cases indexed by defendant, plaintiff. Civil records on dockets from 1800s.

General Information: Public access terminal is available. No juvenile records released. SASE required. Turnaround time same day. Copy fee: $1.00 per page. Certification fee: $3.00. Fee payee: Prothonotary. Personal checks accepted. Prepayment is required.

Court of Common Pleas - Criminal Susquehanna Courthouse, PO Box 218, Montrose, PA 18801; 570-278-4600 X321, X320. Hours: 8:30AM-4:30PM (EST). *Felony, Misdemeanor.*

Criminal Records: Access: Mail, in person. Both court and visitors may perform in person searches. Search fee: $5.00 per name. Required to search: name, years to search; also helpful: DOB, SSN. Criminal records on dockets from 1800s, archived from 1971, computerized since 08/96.

General Information: Public access terminal is available. No juvenile records released. SASE required. Turnaround time same day. Certification fee: $3.00. Fee payee: Clerk of Courts. Personal checks accepted. Prepayment is required.

Register of Wills Susquehanna County Courthouse, PO Box 218, Montrose, PA 18801; 570-278-4600 X112; Fax: 570-278-9268. Hours: 8:30AM-4:30PM (EST). *Probate.*

Tioga County

Court of Common Pleas - Criminal & Civil 116 Main St, Wellsboro, PA 16901; 570-724-9281. Hours: 9AM-4:30PM (EST). *Felony, Misdemeanor, Civil, Eviction.*

Civil Records: Access: In person only. Visitors must perform in person searches for themselves. No search fee. Required to search: name. Civil cases indexed by defendant. Civil records on dockets from 1827; computerized records since 1997.

Criminal Records: Access: Mail, in person. Both court and visitors may perform in person searches. Search fee: $5.00 per name per year. Required to search: name, years to search, signed release. Criminal records on dockets from 1827; computerized records since 1965.

General Information: No mental health, juvenile, abuse (14 or younger) records released. SASE required. Turnaround time same day when possible. Copy fee: $.25 per page. Certification fee: $4.50. Fee payee: Tioga County Prothonotary. Personal checks accepted. Prepayment is required.

Register of Wills 116 Main St, Wellsboro, PA 16901; 570-724-9260. 9AM-4:30PM (EST). *Probate.*

Note: Online access to wills is available through a private company at www.landex.com/remote. Fee is $.20 per minute and $.50 per fax page. Images and wills go back to 2/1999.

Union County

Court of Common Pleas - Criminal & Civil 103 S 2nd St, Lewisburg, PA 17837; 570-524-8751. Hours: 8:30AM-4:30PM (EST). *Felony, Misdemeanor, Civil, Eviction.*

Civil Records: Access: Phone, mail, in person. Both court and visitors may perform in person searches. No search fee. Required to search: name, years to search. Civil cases indexed by defendant, plaintiff. Civil records on computer from 1988, on microfiche (orphans court 1813 to 1988, marriage 1885 to 1998), on dockets from 1800s to 1988.

Criminal Records: Access: Phone, mail, in person. Both court and visitors may perform in person searches. No search fee. Required to search: name, years to search. Criminal records on computer from 1988, on microfiche (orphans court 1813 to 1988, marriage 1885 to 1998), on dockets from 1800s to 1988.

General Information: Public access terminal is available. No juvenile records released. SASE required. Turnaround time same day. Copy fee: $.25 per page. Certification fee: $4.00. Fee payee: Prothonotary or Clerk of Courts. Personal checks accepted. Prepayment is required.

Register of Wills 103 S 2nd St, Lewisburg, PA 17837-1996; 570-524-8761. Hours: 8:30AM-4:30PM (EST). *Probate.*

Venango County

Court of Common Pleas - Criminal & Civil Venango County Courthouse, 1168 Liberty St, Franklin, PA 16323; 814-432-9577; Fax: 814-432-9573. Hours: 8:30AM-4:30PM (EST). *Felony, Misdemeanor, Civil, Eviction.*

www.co.venango.pa.us

Civil Records: Access: Mail, in person. Both court and visitors may perform in person searches. Search fee: $5.00 per name. Required to search: name, years to search. Civil cases indexed by defendant, plaintiff. Civil records on computer from 1993, on dockets from 1800s.

Criminal Records: Access: Mail, in person. Both court and visitors may perform in person searches. Search fee: $5.00 per name. Required to search: name, years to search, DOB; also helpful: SSN. Criminal records on computer from 1993, on dockets from 1800s.

General Information: Public access terminal is available. No juvenile records released. SASE required. Turnaround time same day. Fax notes: Fee to fax results is $1.00 per page. Copy fee: $.50 per page. Certification fee: $7.00. Fee payee: Clerk of Courts. Personal checks accepted. Prepayment is required.

Register of Wills/Recorder of Deeds 1168 Liberty St, Franklin, PA 16323; 814-432-9534; Fax: 814-432-9569. 8:30AM-4:30PM (EST). *Probate.*

Warren County

Court of Common Pleas - Criminal & Civil 4th & Market St, Warren, PA 16365; 814-728-3440; Fax: 814-728-3459. Hours: 8:30AM-4:30PM (EST). *Felony, Misdemeanor, Civil, Eviction.*

http://users.penn.com/~wrncourt

Civil Records: Access: Fax, mail, in person. Both court and visitors may perform in person searches. Search fee: $20.00 per name. Required to search: name, years to search. Civil cases indexed by defendant, plaintiff. Civil records on computer from 1987, on dockets from 1800s.

Criminal Records: Access: Fax, mail, in person. Both court and visitors may perform in person searches. Search fee: $20.00 per name. Required to search: name, years to search; also helpful: DOB. Criminal records on computer from 1987, on dockets from 1800s.

General Information: No juvenile records released. SASE required. Turnaround time 2 days. Fax notes: No fee to fax results. Copy fee: $1.00 per page. Certification fee: $4.00. Fee payee: Prothonotary or Clerk of Courts. Business checks accepted. Prepayment is required.

Register of Wills Courthouse, 204 4th Ave, Warren, PA 16365; 814-728-3430. Hours: 8:30AM-4:30PM (EST). *Probate.*

Washington County

Court of Common Pleas - Civil 1 S Main St #1001, Washington, PA 15301; 724-228-6770. Hours: 9AM-4:30PM (EST). *Civil, Eviction.*

www.co.washington.pa.us

Civil Records: Access: Online, in person. Visitors must perform in person searches for themselves. No search fee. Required to search: name, years to search. Civil cases indexed by defendant, plaintiff. Civil records on computer from 1987, prior on dockets to 1800s. Civil records online access to be available in 2002. See the web site.

General Information: Public access terminal is available. Fax notes: Fee to fax results is $1.50 per page. Copy fee: $1.50 per page. Certification fee: $4.50. Fee payee: Prothonotary. Only cashiers checks and money orders accepted. Checks from attorneys accepted. Prepayment is required.

Court of Common Pleas - Criminal Courthouse Ste 1005, 1 S Main St, Washington, PA 15301; 724-228-6787; Fax: 724-228-6890. Hours: 9AM-4:30PM (EST). *Felony, Misdemeanor.*

www.co.washington.pa.us

Criminal Records: Access: Mail, in person. Both court and visitors may perform in person searches. Search fee: $10.00 per name. Required to search: name, years to search, DOB; also helpful: address, SSN. Criminal records on computer since 10/87, prior on dockets, archived from 1800s.

General Information: Public access terminal is available. No juvenile records released. SASE required. Turnaround time over 1 week. Copy fee: $.50 per page. Certification fee: $8.00. Fee payee: Clerk of Courts. Personal checks accepted. Prepayment is required.

Register of Wills Courthouse, 1 S Main St #1002, Washington, PA 15301; 724-228-6775. Hours: 9AM-4:30PM (EST). *Probate.*

Wayne County

Court of Common Pleas - Criminal & Civil 925 Court St, Honesdale, PA 18431; 570-253-5970 X200; Fax: 570-253-0687. Hours: 8:30AM-4:30PM (EST). *Felony, Misdemeanor, Civil, Eviction.*

Civil Records: Access: In person only. Visitors must perform in person searches for themselves. No search

fee. Required to search: name, years to search. Civil cases indexed by defendant, plaintiff. Civil records on daily docket entries, computerized since 1996.

Criminal Records: Access: In person only. Visitors must perform in person searches for themselves. No search fee. Required to search: name, years to search. Criminal records on daily docket entries, computerized since 1996.

General Information: Public access terminal is available. Juvenile records not released. Copy fee: $.50 per page. Personal checks accepted. Prepayment is required.

Register of Wills 925 Court St, Honesdale, PA 18431; 570-253-5970 X212; Probate phone: ext. 213. Hours: 8:30AM-4:30PM (EST). *Probate.*

www.co-wayne-pa-us.org

Westmoreland County

Court of Common Pleas - Civil Courthouse Sq, Rm 501, PO Box 1630, Greensburg, PA 15601-1168; 724-830-3502; Fax: 724-830-3517. Hours: 8:30AM-4PM (EST). *Civil, Eviction.*

Civil Records: Access: Online, in person. Visitors must perform in person searches for themselves. No search fee. Required to search: name, years to search. Civil cases indexed by defendant, plaintiff. Civil records on computer from 9/85, on dockets from 1700s. Access to the remote online system requires $100 setup (no set-up if accessed via Internet) plus $20 monthly minimum fee. System includes civil, criminal, prothonotary indexes, and recorder information. For information, call 724-830-3874.

General Information: Public access terminal is available. No final divorce, mental health records released. Copy fee: $.50 per page. Computer print out: $1.00 per page. Certification fee: $4.75. Fee payee: Prothonotary. Business checks accepted. Prepayment is required.

Court of Common Pleas - Criminal Criminal Division, 203 Courthouse Square, Greensburg, PA 15601-1168; 724-830-3734; Fax: 724-830-3472/850-3979. Hours: 8:30AM-4PM (EST). *Felony, Misdemeanor.*

Criminal Records: Access: Fax, mail, online, in person. Both court and visitors may perform in person searches. Search fee: $10.00 per name. Required to search: name, years to search, signed release; also helpful: DOB, SSN. Criminal records on computer from 1941, on microfiche from 1793 to 1950, archived from 1773. Access to the criminal online system requires $100 setup plus $20 monthly minimum fee. System includes civil, criminal, prothonotary indexes. For information, call 724-830-3734.

General Information: Public access terminal is available. No juvenile records released. SASE not required. Turnaround time 1 day. Fax notes: $10.00 per document. Copy fee: $.50 per page. Computer copy $.50 per page. Certification fee: $5.00. Fee payee: Clerk of Courts. Personal checks accepted. Attorney's check accepted. Prepayment is required.

Register of Wills 2 N Main St, #301, Greensburg, PA 15601; 724-830-3177; Fax: 724-850-3976. Hours: 8:30AM-4PM (EST). *Probate.*

Wyoming County

Court of Common Pleas - Criminal & Civil Wyoming County Courthouse, Tunkhannock, PA 18657; 570-836-3200 X232-234. Hours: 8:30AM-4PM (EST). *Felony, Misdemeanor, Civil, Eviction.*

Civil Records: Access: In person only. Visitors must perform in person searches for themselves. No search fee. Required to search: name, years to search. Civil

cases indexed by defendant, plaintiff. Civil records on dockets from 1800s.

Criminal Records: Access: In person only. Visitors must perform in person searches for themselves. No search fee. Required to search: name, years to search; also helpful: DOB. Criminal records on dockets from 1800s.

General Information: Public access terminal is available. No juvenile records released. Copy fee: $.25 per page. Certification fee: $7.00. Fee payee: Prothonotary or Clerk of Courts. Personal checks accepted. Prepayment is required.

Register of Wills County Courthouse, 1 Courthouse Sq, Tunkhannock, PA 18657; 570-836-3200 X2235. Hours: 8:30AM-4PM (EST). *Probate.*

York County

Court of Common Pleas - Civil York County Courthouse, 28 E Market St, York, PA 17401; 717-771-9611. Hours: 8:30AM-4:30PM (EST). *Civil.*

www.york-county.org/departments/courts/crtf1.htm

Civil Records: Access: Online, in person, mail. Visitors must perform in person searches for themselves. No search fee. Required to search: name, years to search. Civil cases indexed by defendant, plaintiff. Civil records on computer from mid-1988, on dockets from 1800s, archived from mid-1700s. Access to the remote online system is set-up through Information Services and requires $.75 per minute plus a $200.00 setup fee. For more information, call 717-771-9235.

General Information: Public access terminal is available. No mental health records released. SASE required. Turnaround time 1 day. Copy fee: $1.00 per page. Certification fee: $4.50. Fee payee: Prothonotary. Only cashiers checks and money orders accepted. Prepayment is required.

Court of Common Pleas - Criminal York County Courthouse, 28 E Market St, York, PA 17401; 717-771-9612; Fax: 717-771-9096. Hours: 8:30AM-4:30PM (EST). *Felony, Misdemeanor.*

www.york-county.org/departments/courts/crtf1.htm

Criminal Records: Access: Fax, mail, online, in person. Both court and visitors may perform in person searches. Search fee: $5.00 per name. Required to search: name, years to search. Criminal records on computer from 1987, on dockets from 1942, archived from 1700s. Access is available to Information Service's remote online system for criminal records from mid-1988 forward. Usage fee is $.75 per minute plus a $200.00 setup fee. For more information, call 717-771-9321.

General Information: Public access terminal is available. No sex crime, juvenile records released. SASE required. Turnaround time 1-2 weeks. Fax notes: No fee to fax results. Copy fee: $.50 per page. Certification fee: $10.00. Fee payee: Clerk of Courts. Personal checks accepted. Prepayment is required.

Register of Wills York County Courthouse 28 E Market St, York, PA 17401; 570-771-9263; Fax: 570-771-4678. Hours: 8:30AM-4:15PM (EST). *Probate.*

Note: Online access to wills is available through a private company at www.landex.com/remote. Fee is $.20 per minute and $.50 per fax page. Images and wills go back to 2/1999.

Pennsylvania Recording Offices

ORGANIZATION: 67 counties, 67 recording offices and 134 UCC filing offices. Each county has two different recording offices: the Prothonotary - their term for "Clerk" - accepted UCC and tax lien filings until 07/01/2001, and the Recorder of Deeds maintains real estate records. The entire state is in the Eastern Time Zone (EST).

REAL ESTATE RECORDS: County Recorders of Deeds will not perform real estate searches. Copy fees and certification fees vary.

UCC RECORDS: This was a dual filing state. Until 07/1/2001, Financing statements were filed both at the state level and with the Prothonotary, except for real estate related collateral, which were filed with the Recorder of Deeds. Now, only real estate related collateral is filed locally. Some county offices will not perform UCC searches. Use search request form UCC-11. Search fees are usually $59.00 per debtor name. Copies usually cost $.50-$2.00 per page. Counties also charge $5.00 per financing statement found on a search.

TAX LIEN RECORDS: All federal and state tax liens on personal property and on real property are filed with the Prothonotary. Usually, tax liens on personal property are filed in the judgment index of the Prothonotary. Some Prothonotaries will perform tax lien searches. Search fees are usually $5.00 per name.

OTHER LIENS: Judgment, municipal, mechanics.

ONLINE ACCESS: A number of counties provide web access to assessor data. The Infocon County Access System provides Internet and direct dial-up access to recorded record information for 15 Pennsylvania counties - Armstrong, Bedford, Blair, Butler, Clarion, Clinton, Erie, Franklin, Huntingdon, Juaniata, Lawrence, Mercer, Mifflin, Pike, and Potter. Fees are involved. Document images are available. For information, call Infocon at 814-472-6066 or visit www.ic-access.com

Adams County Prothonotary

County Prothonotary, 111-117 Baltimore St, Gettysburg, PA 17325. 717-334-6781; Fax 717-334-0532.
Will search UCC records. See Recorder for real estate records. **Other Phone Numbers:** Assessor 717-337-9837.

Adams County Recorder

County Recorder of Deeds, 111-117 Baltimore St, County Courthouse Room 102, Gettysburg, PA 17325. 717-337-9826; Fax 717-334-1758.
This agency will not peform searches. **Other Phone Numbers:** Assessor 717-334-6781 x216; Treasurer 717-334-6781 x221.

Allegheny County Prothonotary

County Prothonotary, 414 Grant St, City County Building, Pittsburgh, PA 15219. 412-350-4203 R/E Recording: 412-355-4226; http://www2.county.allegheny.pa.us/realestate/
Will search UCC records. UCC search includes tax liens if requested. See Recorder for real estate records. **Online Access:** Civil Court, UCC, Tax Lien, Real Estate, Assessor Records. Access to Comon Pleas Civil records is available free at http://prothonotary.county.allegheny.pa.us/allegheny/welcome.htm. Registration is required. UCC records are pre-7-1-2001. Online access to the certified values database is available free at the web site. Also, online access to Allegheny County real estate database is available free at http://www2.county.allegheny.pa.us/realestate/Search.asp. **Other Phone Numbers:** Assessor 412-350-4625.

Allegheny County Recorder

County Recorder of Deeds, 101 County Office Building, 542 Forbes Ave, Pittsburgh, PA 15219-2947. 412-350-4226; Fax 412-350-6877.
Will search UCC records, but only real estate related UCC filed here. No tax liens filed here. Will not search real estate records. **Other Phone Numbers:** Assessor 412-355-4625; Treasurer 412-355-4100.

Armstrong County Prothonotary

County Prothonotary, County Courthouse, 500 E. Market St, Kittanning, PA 16201. 724-543-2500 R/E Recording: 724-548-3280 UCC Recording: 724-548-3251; Fax 724-548-3351.
Will search UCC records. This agency will not do a tax lien search. See Recorder for real estate records. **Online Access:** Tax Lien Records. Online search: see Register of Deeds. **Other Phone Numbers:** Assessor 724-548-3487; Treasurer 724-548-3271; Elections 724-548-3222.

Armstrong County Recorder

County Recorder of Deeds, County Courthouse, 500 Market St., Kittanning, PA 16201-1495. 724-548-3256; Fax 724-548-3236.
Will search UCC records. No tax liens filed here. Will not search real estate records. **Online Access:** Real Estate, Marriage, Probate Records. Access is available through a private company. For information, call Infocon at 814-472-6066. **Other Phone Numbers:** Assessor 724-548-3489.

Beaver County Prothonotary

County Prothonotary, Third St, County Courthouse, Beaver, PA 15009. 724-728-5700; Fax 724-728-3360. http://co.beaver.pa.us/prothonotary
Will not search UCC records. This agency will not do a tax lien search. See Recorder for real estate records.

Beaver County Recorder

County Recorder of Deeds, 3rd St, County Courthouse, Beaver, PA 15009. County Recorder of Deeds, R/E and UCC Recording 724-728-5700; Fax 724-728-3630. www.co.beaver.pa.us
This agency will not peform searches. **Online Access:** Real Estate, Deed, Mortgage Records. Access to the Recorder's database is to be available free at http://co.beaver.pa.us/RecorderofDeeds/Disclaimer.htm. Registration is required. Deed records go back to 1957; Mortgages to 7/1974; images to 6/1998. **Other Phone Numbers:** Assessor 724-728-5700; Treasurer 724-728-5700; Elections 724-728-5700.

Bedford County Prothonotary

County Prothonotary, County Courthouse, Corner of Penn & Julliana, Bedford, PA 15522. 814-623-4833; Fax 814-623-4831.
Will search UCC records. UCC search includes tax liens if requested. See Recorder for real estate records. **Online Access:** Tax Lien Records. Online search: see Register of Deeds.

Bedford County Recorder

County Recorder, 200 S. Juliana St, County Courthouse, Bedford, PA 15522. County Recorder, R/E and UCC Recording 814-623-4836; Fax 814-624-0488. www.bedford.net/regrec/home.html
Will search UCC records. No tax liens filed here. Will not search real estate records. **Online Access:** Real Estate, Assessor, Probate, Marriage Records. Access is available through a private company. For information, call Infocon at 814-472-6066. **Other Phone Numbers:** Assessor 814-623-4842; Treasurer 814-623-4846; Elections 814-623-4807; Vital Records 814-623-4833.

Berks County Prothonotary

County Prothonotary, 633 Court St., Reading, PA 19601. 610-478-6980 R/E Recording: 610-478-3380; Fax 610-478-6969.
Will search UCC records. See Recorder for real estate records. **Other Phones:** Assessor 610-478-6262; Treasurer 610-478-6640; Elections 610-478-6490.

Berks County Recorder

Recorder of Deeds, 633 Court St., 3rd Floor, Reading, PA 19601. Recorder of Deeds, R/E and UCC Recording 610-478-3380; Fax 610-478-3359. www.berksrecofdeeds.com
This agency will not peform searches; no tax liens filed here. **Online Access:** Vital Statistic, Probate Records. Access to the Registry of Wills' databases are available free at www.berksregofwills.com including county marriage, estate, birth and death records. Estate and marriage records are current. **Other Phone Numbers:** Assessor 610-478-6262; Treasurer 610-478-6640; Elections 610-478-6490.

Blair County Prothonotary

County Prothonotary, 423 Allegheny St Suite 144, Hollidaysburg, PA 16648. 814-693-3080.
Will search UCC records. This agency will not do a tax lien search. See Recorder for real estate records. **Online Access:** Tax Lien Records. Online search: see Register of Deeds.

Blair County Recorder

County Recorder of Deeds, 423 Allegheny St., Suite 145, Hollidaysburg, PA 16648. County Recorder of Deeds, R/E and UCC Recording 814-693-3095.
Will search UCC records, but only real estate related UCC filed here. No tax liens filed here. Will not search real estate records. **Online Access:** Real Estate, Marriage, Probate Records. Access is available through a private company. For information, call Infocon at 814-472-6066. **Other Phones:** Assessor 695-5541 x223.

Bradford County Prothonotary

County Prothonotary, Courthouse, 301 Main St., Towanda, PA 18848. 570-265-1705.
Will search UCC records prior to 7/2002. This agency will not do a tax lien search. See Recorder for real estate records. **Other Phones:** Assessor 570-265-1714.

Bradford County Recorder

County Recorder of Deeds, 301 Main St, Courthouse, Towanda, PA 18848. County Recorder of Deeds, R/E and UCC Recording 570-265-1702; Fax 570-265-1721.
Will search UCC records. No tax liens filed here. Will not search real estate records. **Other Phone Numbers:** Assessor 570-265-1714; Treasurer 570-265-1700.

Bucks County Prothonotary

County Prothonotary, 55 E. Court St., Courthouse, Doylestown, PA 18901. 215-348-6198 UCC Recording: 215-348-6183; Fax 215-348-6184. www.buckscounty.org/courts/
Will search UCC records. This agency will not do a tax lien search. See Recorder for real estate records. **Online Access:** Recording, Judgment, Courts, Sheriff Sales, Assessor, Voter Registration Records. Access to County records requires a Sprint ID number and payment of $25 annual Sprint fee, plus $.60 per minute of use. Records go back to 1980. Lending agency, Register of Wills, liens, sheriff sales, voter registration, criminal also available. For information, contact Jack Morris at 215-348-6579 or visit www.buckscounty.org/departments/public_access.

Bucks County Recorder

County Recorder of Deeds, Courthouse, 55 E. Court St., Doylestown, PA 18901-4367. 215-348-6209; www.buckscounty.org/departments/registerofwills/index.html
Will search UCC records, but only real estate related UCC filed here. No tax liens filed here. Will not do a real estate search. **Online Access:** Assessor, Real Estate, Tax Lien, Probate Records. Access to County records requires a Sprint ID number and payment of $25 annual Sprint fee, plus $.60 per minute of use. Records go back to 1980. Lending agency, Register of Wills, liens, sheriff sales, voter registration, courts, prothonotary available. For information, contact Jack Morris at 215-348-6579 or visit www.buckscounty.org/departments/public_access. **Other Phone Numbers:** Assessor 215-348-6219; Treasurer 215-348-6244.

Butler County Prothonotary

County Prothonotary, PO Box 1208, Butler, PA 16003-1208. 724-284-5214.
Will search UCC records. This agency will not do a tax lien search. See Recorder for real estate records. **Online Access:** Tax Lien Records. Online search: see Register of Deeds.

Butler County Recorder

County Recorder of Deeds, PO Box 1208, Butler, PA 16003-1208. 724-284-5340 R/E Recording: 724-285-4731; Fax 724-285-9099. www.butlercounty.com/court/index.htm
Will search UCC records. No tax liens filed here. **Online Access:** Marriage, Probate Records. Marriage and probate records also available through a private company. For information, call Infocon at 814-472-6066. **Other Phone Numbers:** Assessor 724-284-5316; Treasurer 724-284-5149.

Cambria County Prothonotary

County Prothonotary, 200 S. Center St., Ebensburg, PA 15931. 814-472-1637 R/E Recording: 814-472-1473; Fax 814-472-5632.
Will search UCC records. This agency will not do a tax lien search. See Recorder for real estate records. **Other Phone Numbers:** Assessor 814-472-1451; Treasurer 814-472-1643; Elections 814-472-1460.

Cambria County Recorder

Recorder of Deeds, Cambria County Courthouse, 200 S. Center St., Ebensburg, PA 15931. 814-472-1470 R/E Recording: 814-472-1473 UCC Recording: 814-472-1473; Fax 814-472-1412.
Will search UCC records. No tax liens filed here. **Other Phone Numbers:** Assessor 814-472-5440 x450; Treasurer 814-472-5440 x345; Elections 814-472-1464; Register of Wills 814-472-1440.

Cameron County Prothonotary

County Prothonotary, 20 E. 5th St, Emporium, PA 15834. 814-486-3349; Fax 814-486-0464.
Will search UCC records. See Recorder for real estate records.

Cameron County Recorder

County Recorder of Deeds, 20 E. 5th St, Emporium, PA 15834. 814-486-3349; Fax 814-486-0464.
Will search UCC records. No tax liens filed here. **Other Phone Numbers:** Assessor 814-486-0723; Treasurer 814-486-3348.

Carbon County Prothonotary

County Prothonotary, PO Box 130, Jim Thorpe, PA 18229-0127. 570-325-2481 R/E Recording: 570-325-2651 (Recorder of Deeds) UCC Recording: 570-325-2481 (Prothonotary); Fax 570-325-8047.
Will not search UCC records. This agency will not do a tax lien search. See Recorder for real estate records. **Online Access:** Tax Lien, UCC Records. Access to the county's remote public access dial-up database is available free; 570-325-3288; instructions and registration are at www.carboncourts.com/pubacc. **Other Phone Numbers:** Assessor 570-325-5254; Treasurer 570-325-2251; Elections 570-325-4801.

Carbon County Recorder

County Recorder of Deeds, PO Box 87, Jim Thorpe, PA 18229. 570-325-2651; Fax 570-325-2726.
This agency will not peform searches. **Online Access:** Real Estate, Probate, Grantor/Grantee Records. Access to docket information on the county's remote public access dial-up database is available free; 570-325-3288; instructions and registration are found at www.carboncourts.com/pubacc.htm. **Other Phone Numbers:** Assessor 570-325-5254; Treasurer 570-325-2251; Elections 570-325-4801.

Centre County Prothonotary

County Prothonotary, Allegheny & High, County Courthouse, Bellefonte, PA 16823. 814-355-6796 R/E Recording: 814-355-6801.
Will search UCC records. This agency will not do a tax lien search. See Recorder for real estate records. **Other Phone Numbers:** Assessor 814-355-6721; Treasurer 814-355-6810; Elections 814-355-6703.

Centre County Recorder

County Recorder of Deeds, 414 Holmes Ave. #1, Bellefonte, PA 16823. 814-355-6801 R/E Recording: 814-355-6701; Fax 814-355-8680.
Will search UCC records. No tax liens filed here. Will not search real estate records. **Other Phone Numbers:** Assessor 814-355-6721; Treasurer 814-355-6810.

Chester County Prothonotary

County Prothonotary, PO Box 2748, West Chester, PA 19380-0991. 610-344-6111 R/E Recording: 610-344-6330; Fax 610-344-5903. www.chesco.org/prothy.html
Will not search UCC records. See Recorder for real estate records. **Online Access:** Court Dockets, Property Tax, Warrant, Lien, Assessor Records. Access to the prothonotary database is available at www.chesco.org/prothy.html. Click on "SEARCH:~." There is a $50 set up fee and $10 each month of use (if over 100 transcation per/mo, $.10 per document). Registration/password at 610-344-6884. Prothonotary records go back to 1990. **Other Phone Numbers:** Assessor 610-344-6105; Treasurer 610-344-6370; Appraiser/Auditor 610-344-6105; Elections 610-344-6410; Vital Records 717-783-2548.

Chester County Recorder

County Recorder of Deeds, 235 W Market St. #100, West Chester, PA 19382-2616. 610-344-6330; Fax 610-344-6408. www.chesco.org/recorder
Will search UCC records. No tax liens filed here. Will not search real estate records. **Online Access:** Recording, Deed, Court, Vital Statistic Records. Searching countywide records including court records requires a sign-up and credit card payment. Application fee is $50. with $10.00 per month minimum (no charge for no activity); and $.10 each transaction beyond 100. Sign-up and/or logon at http://epin.chesco.org. County data is also available as reports, labels, magnetic tape, and diskette. Also, genealogical and older vital statistics are available free at www.chesco.org/archives. All Recorder of Deeds records will shortly be on Internet; no fee planned. **Other Phone Numbers:** Assessor 610-344-6105; Treasurer 610-344-6370; BLR (Bureau of Land Records-for help with UPI #) 610-344-5968.

Clarion County Prothonotary

County Prothonotary, Main St, Courthouse, Clarion, PA 16214-1092. 814-226-4000; Fax 814-226-8069.
Will search UCC records for one name only. See Recorder for real estate records. **Online Access:** Tax Lien Records. Online search: see Register of Deeds.

Clarion County Recorder

County Recorder of Deeds, Courthouse, Corner of 5th Ave. & Main St., Clarion, PA 16214. 814-226-4000 x2500 R/E Recording: 814-226-4000 x2501 UCC Recording: 814-226-4000 x2501; Fax 814-226-1117.
Will search UCC records. No tax liens filed here. Will not search real estate records. **Online Access:** Assessor, Real Estate, Voter Registration Records. Access is available through a private company. For information, call Infocon at 814-472-6066. **Other Phone Numbers:** Assessor 814-226-4000 x2301; Treasurer 814-226-4000 x2861.

Clearfield County Prothonotary

County Prothonotary, PO Box 549, Clearfield, PA 16830. 814-765-2641 UCC Recording: 814-765-2641 x1330; Fax 814-765-6089.
Will search UCC records. See Recorder for real estate records. **Other Phone Numbers:** Assessor 814-765-2641 x1128; Treasurer 814-765-2641 x1381; Appraiser/Auditor 814-765-2641 x1129; Elections 814-765-2641 x1140.

Clearfield County Recorder

County Recorder of Deeds, PO Box 361, Clearfield, PA 16830. County Recorder of Deeds, R/E and UCC Recording 814-765-2641 x1350; Fax 814-765-6089. Will search UCC records. No tax liens filed here. Will not search real estate records. **Other Phone Numbers:** Assessor 814-765-2641 x5997; Treasurer 814-765-2641 x5985; Elections 814-765-2641 x5996.

Clinton County Prothonotary

County Prothonotary, 230 E. Water St., Courthouse, Lock Haven, PA 17745. 570-893-4007. Will search UCC records. This agency will not do a tax lien search. See Recorder for real estate records. **Online Access:** Tax Lien Records. Online search: see Register of Deeds. **Other Phones:** Assessor 570-893-4033.

Clinton County Recorder

County Recorder of Deeds, PO Box 943, Lock Haven, PA 17745. 570-893-4010 R/E Recording: 570-893-4020 UCC Recording: 570-893-4020; Fax 570-893-4273. Will search UCC records, but only real estate related UCC filed here. No tax liens filed here. Will not search real estate records. **Online Access:** Real Estate, Probate Records. Access is available through a private company. For information, call Infocon at 814-472-6066. **Other Phone Numbers:** Assessor 570-893-4034; Treasurer 570-893-4004.

Columbia County Prothonotary

County Prothonotary, PO Box 380, Bloomsburg, PA 17815. 570-389-5614 R/E Recording: 570-389-5635 UCC Recording: 570-389-5617. Will search UCC records. This agency will not do a tax lien search. See Recorder for real estate records. **Other Phone Numbers:** Assessor 570-389-5646; Treasurer 570-389-5626; Elections 570-389-5640.

Columbia County Recorder

County Recorder of Deeds, PO Box 380, Bloomsburg, PA 17815. County Recorder of Deeds, R/E and UCC Recording 570-389-5632; Fax 570-389-5636. www.columbiapa.org/county/offices.html This agency will not peform searches; no tax liens filed here. **Other Phone Numbers:** Assessor 570-389-5645; Treasurer 570-389-5626; Appraiser/Auditor 570-389-5645; Elections 570-389-5640.

Crawford County Prothonotary

County Prothonotary, 903 Diamond Park, County Courthouse, Meadville, PA 16335. 814-333-7324 R/E Recording: 814-373-2537; Fax 814-337-5416. Will search UCC records. See Recorder for real estate records. **Other Phones:** Assessor 814-333-7302; Treasurer 814-333-7332; Elections 814-333-7307.

Crawford County Recorder

County Recorder of Deeds, Courthouse, 903 Diamond Park, Meadville, PA 16335. 814-373-2537; Fax 814-337-5296. Will search UCC records, but only real estate related UCC filed here. No tax liens filed here. Will not search real estate records. **Other Phone Numbers:** Assessor 814-333-7302; Treasurer 814-333-7332.

Cumberland County Prothonotary

County Prothonotary, 1 Courthouse Square, County Courthouse, Carlisle, PA 17013-3387. 717-240-7832. Will search UCC records. This agency will not do a tax lien search. See Recorder for real estate records.

Cumberland County Recorder

County Recorder of Deeds, County Courthouse, 1 Courthouse Square, Carlisle, PA 17013. County Recorder of Deeds, R/E and UCC Recording 717-240-

6370 UCC Recording: 717-240-5370; Fax 717-240-6490. This agency will not peform searches; no tax liens filed here. **Other Phone Numbers:** Assessor 717-240-6350; Treasurer 717-240-6380; Elections 717-240-6385.

Dauphin County Prothonotary

County Prothonotary, PO Box 945, Harrisburg, PA 17108. 717-255-2697. Will search UCC records. Tax liens not included in UCC search. See Recorder for real estate records.

Dauphin County Recorder

County Recorder of Deeds, PO Box 12000, Harrisburg, PA 17108. 717-255-2802; Fax 717-257-1521. This agency will not peform searches; no tax liens filed here. **Other Phone Numbers:** Assessor 717-255-2735; Treasurer 717-255-2676.

Delaware County Prothonotary

County Prothonotary, Delaware County Government Center Bldg., 201 W. Front St., Room 127, Media, PA 19063. 610-891-5009. Will search UCC records. This agency will not do a tax lien search. See Recorder for real estate records. **Other Phone Numbers:** Assessor 610-891-4891/4897.

Delaware County Recorder

County Recorder of Deeds, 201 W. Front St, Room 107, Government Center Building, Media, PA 19063. 610-891-4148 R/E Recording: 610-891-4144; http://www2.co.delaware.pa.us/pa/default.htm This agency will not peform searches. **Online Access:** Assessor, Deed, Real Estate Records. Access to the public access system is available free - temporarily - at the web site. Records go back to 1982. Also, property tax records are available free on the Internet at http://taxrecords.com. **Other Phone Numbers:** Assessor 610-891-4880; Treasurer 610-891-4272; Elections 610-891-4938.

Elk County Prothonotary

County Prothonotary, PO Box 237, Ridgway, PA 15853-0237. 814-776-5344; Fax 814-776-5303. Will search UCC records. See Recorder for real estate records. **Other Phone Numbers:** Assessor 814-776-5340; Treasurer 814-776-5322; Elections 814-776-5337.

Elk County Recorder

County Recorder of Deeds, PO Box 314, Ridgway, PA 15853-0314. County Recorder of Deeds, R/E and UCC Recording 814-776-5349; Fax 814-776-5382. Will search UCC records, but only real estate related UCC filed here. No tax liens filed here. Will not search real estate records. **Other Phone Numbers:** Assessor 814-776-5340; Treasurer 814-776-5322; Elections 814-776-5337.

Erie County Prothonotary

County Prothonotary, 140 W. 6th St, Room 120, Erie, PA 16501-1080. 814-451-6078. Will search UCC records. This agency will not do a tax lien search. Cannot search UCCs filed after June 30, 2001. See Recorder for real estate records. **Online Access:** Tax Lien Records. Online search: see Register of Deeds.

Erie County Recorder

County Recorder of Deeds, PO Box 1849, Erie, PA 16507-0849. 814-451-6246; Fax 814-451-6213. This agency will not peform searches; no tax liens filed here. **Online Access:** Real Estate, Marriage, Probate Records. Access is available through a private company. For information, call Infocon at 814-472-6066. Also, online access to property records data is available free at www.mypropertyrecords.com/

eriecountypa. **Other Phone Numbers:** Assessor 814-451-6225; Treasurer 814-451-6080.

Fayette County Prothonotary

County Prothonotary, 61 E. Main St, Courthouse, Uniontown, PA 15401. 724-430-1272 R/E Recording: 724-430-1238. Will search UCC records. This agency will not do a tax lien search. See Recorder for real estate records. **Other Phone Numbers:** Assessor 724-430-7350; Treasurer 724-430-1256; Appraiser/Auditor 724-430-1350; Elections 724-432-1289; Vital Records 724-432-1206.

Fayette County Recorder

County Recorder of Deeds, 61 E. Main St, Courthouse, Uniontown, PA 15401-3389. County Recorder of Deeds, R/E and UCC Recording 724-430-1238 UCC Recording: 724-430-1272; Fax 724-430-1238. Will search UCC records. No tax liens filed here. Will not search real estate records. **Online Access:** Property, Assessor Records. Access to property assessments is available free at www.fayetteproperty.org/assessor. **Other Phone Numbers:** Assessor 724-430-1350; Treasurer 724-430-1256; Elections 724-430-1289; Vital Records 724-430-1206.

Forest County Prothonotary

County Prothonotary, PO Box 423, Tionesta, PA 16353. 814-755-3526; Fax 814-755-8837. Will search UCC records. See Recorder for real estate records.

Forest County Recorder

County Recorder of Deeds, PO Box 423, Tionesta, PA 16353. 814-755-3526 R/E Recording: 814-755-3537; Fax 814-755-8837. Will search UCC records. No tax liens filed here. Will not search real estate records. **Other Phone Numbers:** Assessor 814-755-3532; Treasurer 814-755-3536.

Franklin County Prothonotary

County Prothonotary, 157 Lincoln Way East, County Court House, Chambersburg, PA 17201. 717-261-3860 R/E Recording: 717-261-3872; Fax 717-264-6772. Will search UCC records. See Recorder for real estate records. **Online Access:** Tax Lien Records. Online search: see Register of Deeds. **Other Phone Numbers:** Assessor 717-261-3801; Treasurer 717-261-3119; Elections 717-261-3886; UCC/Personal Property 717-261-3858.

Franklin County Recorder

County Recorder of Deeds, 157 Lincoln Way East, Chambersburg, PA 17201. 717-264-4125; Fax 717-267-3438. Will search UCC records. No tax liens filed here. Will not search real estate records. **Online Access:** Real Estate, Probate Records. Access is available through a private company. For information, call Infocon at 814-472-6066. **Other Phone Numbers:** Assessor 717-261-3801; Treasurer 717-261-3120.

Fulton County Prothonotary

County Prothonotary, 201 N. Second St, Fulton County Courthouse, McConnellsburg, PA 17233-1198. 717-485-4212. Will not search UCC records. UCC search includes tax liens if requested. See Recorder for real estate records.

Fulton County Recorder

County Recorder of Deeds, 201 N. Second St, Fulton County Courthouse, McConnellsburg, PA 17233-1198. County Recorder of Deeds, R/E and UCC Recording 717-485-4212. This agency will not peform searches; no tax liens filed here. **Other Phone Numbers:** Assessor 717-485-3208; Treasurer 717-485-4454.

Greene County Prothonotary

County Prothonotary, 10 E. High St., Room 105, Waynesburg, PA 15370. 724-852-5289.
Will not search UCC records. UCC search includes tax liens if requested. See Recorder for real estate records.

Greene County Recorder

County Recorder of Deeds, 10 E High St, Courthouse, Waynesburg, PA 15370. County Recorder of Deeds, R/E and UCC Recording 724-852-5283 UCC Recording: 724-852-5289; http://county.greenepa.net
Will search UCC records, but only real estate related UCC filed here. No tax liens filed here. Will not search real estate records. **Other Phone Numbers:** Assessor 724-852-5211; Treasurer 724-852-5225; Elections 724-852-5230.

Huntingdon County Prothonotary

County Prothonotary, PO Box 39, Huntingdon, PA 16652-1486. 814-643-1610 R/E Recording: 814-643-2740; Fax 814-643-4271.
Will search UCC records. See Recorder for real estate records. **Online Access:** Tax Lien Records. Online search: see Register of Deeds. **Other Phone Numbers:** Assessor 814-643-1000; Treasurer 814-643-3523; Elections 814-643-3091.

Huntingdon County Recorder

County Recorder of Deeds, 223 Penn St, Courthouse, Huntingdon, PA 16652. County Recorder of Deeds, R/E and UCC Recording 814-643-2740; Fax 814-643-8152.
This agency will not peform searches; no tax liens filed here. **Online Access:** Real Estate, Marriage, Probate Records. Access is available through a private company. For information, call Infocon at 814-472-6066. **Other Phone Numbers:** Assessor 814-643-1000; Treasurer 814-643-3523; Elections 814-643-3091.

Indiana County Prothonotary

Prothonotary & Clerk of Courts, 825 Philadelphia St, Courthouse, 1st Floor, Indiana, PA 15701-3934. 724-465-3855 R/E Recording: 724-465-3860; Fax 724-465-3868.
Will search UCC records. See Recorder for real estate records. **Other Phone Numbers:** Assessor 724-465-3812; Treasurer 724-465-3845; Elections 724-465-3852; Vital Records 724-656-3100.

Indiana County Recorder

County Recorder of Deeds, 825 Philadelphia St, Courthouse, Indiana, PA 15701. County Recorder of Deeds, R/E and UCC Recording 724-465-3860; Fax 724-465-3863.
Will search UCC records. No tax liens filed here. Will not search real estate records. **Other Phone Numbers:** Assessor 724-465-3812; Treasurer 724-465-3845.

Jefferson County Prothonotary

County Prothonotary, 200 Main St, Court House, Room 102, Brookville, PA 15825. 814-849-1606 R/E Recording: 814-849-1610 UCC Recording: 814-849-1625; Fax 814-849-1607.
Will search UCC records. This agency will not do a tax lien search. See Recorder for real estate records.

Jefferson County Recorder

County Recorder of Deeds, 200 Main St, Courthouse, Brookville, PA 15825. County Recorder of Deeds, R/E and UCC Recording 814-849-1610; Fax 814-849-1677.
Will search UCC records. No tax liens filed here. Will not search real estate records. **Other Phone Numbers:** Assessor 814-849-1637; Treasurer 814-849-1609; Elections 814-849-1603.

Juniata County Prothonotary

County Prothonotary, Courthouse, Mifflintown, PA 17059. 717-436-7715 R/E Recording: 717-436-7709; Fax 717-436-7734.
Will search UCC records. This agency will not do a tax lien search. See Recorder for real estate records. **Other Phone Numbers:** Assessor 717-436-7740; Treasurer 717-436-7742; Elections 717-436-7706.

Juniata County Recorder

County Recorder of Deeds, PO Box 68, Mifflintown, PA 17059. County Recorder of Deeds, R/E and UCC Recording 717-436-7709; Fax 717-436-7756.
This agency will not peform searches; no tax liens filed here. **Online Access:** Real Estate, Marriage, Probate Records. Access is available through a private company. For information, call Infocon at 814-472-6066. **Other Phones:** Assessor 717-436-7740; Treasurer 717-436-7742; Prothonotary 717-436-7715.

Lackawanna County Prothonotary

County Clerk of Judicial Records, PO Box 133, Scranton, PA 18503. 570-963-6723; Fax none.
Will not search UCC records. This agency will not do a tax lien search. See Recorder for real estate records. **Other Phone Numbers:** Assessor 570-963-6728.

Lackawanna County Recorder

County Recorder of Deeds, 200 N. Washington, Courthouse, Scranton, PA 18503. County Recorder of Deeds, R/E and UCC Recording 570-963-6775.
Will search UCC records, but only real estate related UCC filed here. No tax liens filed here. Will not search real estate records. **Other Phone Numbers:** Assessor 570-963-6728; Treasurer 570-963-6731.

Lancaster County Prothonotary

County Prothonotary, PO Box 83480, Lancaster, PA 17608-3480. 717-299-8282 R/E Recording: 717-299-8238; Fax 717-293-7210. www.co.lancaster.pa.us
Will search UCC records. See Recorder for real estate records. **Online Access:** Real Estate, Recording, UCC, Tax Lien, PFA, Termination List Records. See Register of Deeds. The PFA (protection from abuse) records data kept by the Prothonotary is searchable for free at www.co.lancaster.pa.us/scripts/PFAWebQuery.exe. Also, search the court case termination list (argument report) for the prior year from the Prothonotary's web page. **Other Phones:** Assessor 717-299-8381; Treasurer 717-299-8222; Elections 717-299-8293.

Lancaster County Recorder

County Recorder of Deeds, 50 N. Duke St, Lancaster, PA 17602. County Recorder of Deeds, R/E and UCC Recording 717-299-8238; Fax 717-299-8393. www.co.lancaster.pa.us
Will search UCC records, but only real estate related UCC filed here. No tax liens filed here. Will not search real estate records. **Online Access:** Assessor, Real Estate, Recording, Tax Lien Records. Access to county property information is available free from the GIS Dept. at www.co.lancaster.pa.us/GIS/disclaimer.html. Access to deeds, UCCs and other recordings is available free at http://198.51.78.24/splash.jsp. **Other Phones:** Assessor 717-299-8381; Treasurer 717-299-8222.

Lawrence County Prothonotary

County Prothonotary, 430 Court St, Government Center, New Castle, PA 16101-3593. 724-656-1943 R/E Recording: 724-656-2128 UCC Recording: 724-656-2143; Fax 724-656-1988.
Will not search UCC records. This agency will not do a tax lien search. See Reorder for real estate records. **Online Access:** Tax Lien Records. Online search: see Register of Deeds. **Other Phone Numbers:** Assessor

724-656-2191; Treasurer 724-656-1978; Elections 724-656-2161; Vital Records 724-656-3100.

Lawrence County Recorder

County Recorder of Deeds, 430 Court St, Government Center, New Castle, PA 16101. 724-656-2127; Fax 724-656-1966.
Will search UCC records. No tax liens filed here. Will not search real estate records. **Online Access:** Real Estate, Assessor, Marriage, Probate Records. Access is available through a private company. For information, call Infocon at 814-472-6066. **Other Phone Numbers:** Assessor 724-656-2191; Treasurer 724-656-2183.

Lebanon County Prothonotary

County Prothonotary, 400 S. 8th St, Lebanon, PA 17042. County Prothonotary, R/E and UCC Recording 717-274-2801.
Will search UCC records. This agency will not do a tax lien search. See Recorder for real estate records. **Other Phone Numbers:** Assessor 717-274-2801; Treasurer 717-274-2801; Appraiser/Auditor 717-274-2801; Elections 717-274-2801; Vital Records 717-274-2801.

Lebanon County Recorder

County Recorder of Deeds, 400 S. 8th St, Room 107, Lebanon, PA 17042. 717-274-2801 R/E Recording: 717-274-2801 x2224 UCC Recording: 717-274-2801 x2225.
This agency will not peform searches; no tax liens filed here. **Other Phone Numbers:** Assessor 717-274-2801 x2250; Treasurer 717-274-2801 x2229.

Lehigh County Prothonotary

County Prothonotary, 455 W. Hamilton St., Allentown, PA 18101-1614. 610-782-3148; Fax 610-770-3840. www.lccpa.org/depts/clerkofcourtsgeninfo.html
The City of Bethlehem is in both Northampton and Lehigh counties. Will search UCC records. This agency will not do a tax lien search. See Recorder for real estate records.

Lehigh County Recorder

County Recorder of Deeds, 17 South St, Room 350, Allentown, PA 18101. 610-782-3162 R/E Recording: 610-820-3162; Fax 610-782-3116.
This agency will not peform searches; no tax liens filed here. **Online Access:** Assessor, Real Estate, Tax Lien, Marriage Records. The system is open 24 hours daily; there are set-up and usage fees. Records go back to 1984. Lending agency information is available. Court records are also available. Call Lehigh City Computer Svcs Dept at 610-782-3286 for more information. **Other Phone Numbers:** Assessor 610-820-3038; Treasurer 610-820-3113; Elections 610-820-3194.

Luzerne County Prothonotary

County Prothonotary, 200 N. River St, County Court House, Wilkes-Barre, PA 18711-1001. 570-825-6189 UCC Recording: 570-825-1749; Fax 570-825-1757.
Will search UCC records. See Recorder for real estate records.

Luzerne County Recorder

County Recorder of Deeds, 200 N. River St, Courthouse, Wilkes-Barre, PA 18711. County Recorder of Deeds, R/E and UCC Recording 570-825-1641; Fax 570-970-4580.
Will search UCC records, but only real estate related UCC filed here. No tax liens filed here. Will not search real estate records. **Other Phone Numbers:** Assessor 570-825-1539; Treasurer 570-825-1786.

Lycoming County Prothonotary

County Prothonotary, 48 W. Third St, Williamsport, PA 17701. 570-327-2251.
Will search UCC records. This agency will not do a tax lien search. See Recorder for real estate records.

Lycoming County Recorder

County Recorder of Deeds, 48 W. Third St, Williamsport, PA 17701. Recorder, R/E and UCC Recording 570-327-2263; Fax 570-327-2511.
Will search UCC records, but only real estate related UCC filed here. No tax liens filed here. Will not search real estate records. **Other Phone Numbers:** Assessor 570-327-2302; Treasurer 570-327-2249.

McKean County Prothonotary

County Prothonotary, PO Box 273, Smethport, PA 16749. 814-887-3271 R/E Recording: 814-887-3253; Fax 814-887-3219.
Will search UCC records. See Recorder for real estate records. **Other Phones:** Assessor 814-887-3214; Treasurer 814-887-3220; Elections 814-887-3203.

McKean County Recorder

Recorder of Deeds, PO Box 3426, Smethport, PA 16749. 814-887-3253 R/E Recording: 814-887-3250 UCC Recording: 814-887-3250; Fax 814-887-3255.
This agency will not peform searches; no tax liens filed here. **Other Phone Numbers:** Assessor 814-887-3215; Treasurer 814-887-3220; Elections 814-887-3203; Vital Records 814-887-3260.

Mercer County Prothonotary

County Prothonotary, 105 Mercer County Courthouse, Mercer, PA 16137-0066. 724-662-3800; Fax none.
Will not search UCC records. This agency will not do a tax lien search. See Recorder for real estate records. **Online Access:** Tax Lien Records. Online search: see Register of Deeds. **Other Phone Numbers:** Assessor 724-662-3800.

Mercer County Recorder

County Recorder of Deeds, 109 Courthouse, Mercer, PA 16137-1293. 724-662-3800; Fax 724-662-2096.
Will search UCC records. No tax liens filed here. Will not search real estate records. **Online Access:** Real Estate, Assessor Records. Access is available through a private company. For information, call Infocon at 814-472-6066. **Other Phone Numbers:** Assessor 724-662-3800 x505; Treasurer 724-662-3800 x257.

Mifflin County Prothonotary

County Prothonotary, 20 N. Wayne St, Lewistown, PA 17044. 717-248-8146; Fax 717-248-5275.
Will not search UCC records. See Recorder for real estate records. **Online Access:** Tax Lien Records. Online search: see Register of Deeds.

Mifflin County Recorder

County Recorder of Deeds, 20 N. Wayne St, Lewistown, PA 17044. 717-242-1449 R/E Recording: 717-248-6733;   Fax   717-248-3695. http://mifflincounty.lcworkshop.com/rowoffices/register_and_recorder/default.asp
Will search UCC records, but only real estate related UCC filed here. No tax liens filed here. Will not search real estate records. **Online Access:** Real Estate, Assessor, Probate Records. Access is available through a private company. For information, call Infocon at 814-472-6066. Also, proiperty assessment and occupational tax records are available free on the Internet at http://mifflincounty.lcworkshop.com/departments/assesment. Also available is a advanced fee-based system with greater land and property records; fee is $99 per year. Sign up is available online. **Other Phones:** Assessor 717-248-5783; Treasurer 717-248-8439.

Monroe County Prothonotary

County Prothonotary, N. 7th & Monroe St, Courthouse, Room 303, Stroudsburg, PA 18360-2190. 570-420-3570.
Will not search UCC records. See Recorder for real estate records.

Monroe County Recorder

County Recorder of Deeds, 7th & Monroe St, Courthouse, Stroudsburg, PA 18360-2185. 570-420-3530 R/E Recording: 570-420-3400; Fax 570-420-3537.
Will search UCC records. No tax liens filed here. Will not search real estate records. **Online Access:** Real Estate, Wills Records. Access is available through a private company at www.landex.com/remote. Fee is $.20 per minute and $.50 per fax page. Land Index goes back to 1/1979; wills go back to 11/1836; images go back to 8/1997. **Other Phone Numbers:** Assessor 570-420-3412; Treasurer 570-420-3510.

Montgomery County Prothonotary

County Prothonotary, PO Box 311, Norristown, PA 19404. 610-278-3360; Fax 610-278-5994.
Will search UCC records. This agency will not do a tax lien search. See Recorder for real estate records. **Other Phone Numbers:** Assessor 610-278-3761.

Montgomery County Recorder

County Recorder of Deeds, PO Box 311, Norristown, PA 19404-0311. 610-278-3289 R/E Recording: 610-278-3868; Fax 610-278-3869. www.montcopa.org
Will search UCC records, but only real estate related UCC filed here. No tax liens filed here. Will not search real estate records. **Online Access:** Assessor, Real Estate, Tax Lien Records. Two sources are available. Access to County online records requires a $10 sign up fee plus $.15 per minute of use. Records date back to 1990. Lending agency and prothonotary information are available on the system. For information or to sign up, contact Berkheimer Assoc. at 800-360-8989. Also, records on the County PIR database are available free on the Internet at www.montcopa.org/reassessment/boahome0.htm. Click on "Instructions" to learn how to use the search features, then search by parcel number, name, address, or municipality. **Other Phone Numbers:** Assessor 610-278-3761; Treasurer 610-278-3066; Elections 610-278-3075.

Montour County Prothonotary

County Prothonotary, 29 Mill St, Courthouse, Danville, PA 17821. 570-271-3010 R/E Recording: 570-271-3012; Fax 570-271-3089.
Will search UCC records. Tax liens not included in UCC search. See Recorder for real estate records. **Other Phone Numbers:** Assessor 570-271-3006; Treasurer 570-271-3016; Elections 570-271-3000; Vital Records 570-271-3010.

Montour County Recorder

Register & Recorder, 29 Mill St, Courthouse, Danville, PA 17821. 570-271-3012; Fax 570-271-3071.
Will search UCC records. No tax liens filed here. **Other Phone Numbers:** Assessor 570-271-3006; Treasurer 570-271-3016; Appraiser/Auditor 570-271-3006; Elections 570-271-3000.

Northampton County Prothonotary

County Prothonotary, 669 Washington St., 2nd Floor, Room 207, Easton, PA 18042-7498. 610-559-3060.
The City of Bethlehem is in both Northampton and Lehigh counties. Will search UCC records. This agency will not do a tax lien search. See Recorder for real estate records.

Northampton County Recorder

County Recorder of Deeds, 669 Washington St, Government Center, Easton, PA 18042. 610-559-3077; Fax 610-559-3103.
The City of Bethlehem is in both Northampton and Lehigh counties. Will search UCC records, but only real estate related UCC filed here. No tax liens filed here. Will not search real estate records. **Online Access:** Deed, Mortgage, Misc. Recording, Property, Assessor Records. Two sources are available. One is a private company at www.landex.com/remote. Fee is $.20 per minute and $.50 per fax page. Deeds data goes back to 11/85; mortgages to 2/88; faxable images go back to 5/94. Also, online access to assessor's property records data is available free at www.ncpub.org. **Other Phone Numbers:** Assessor 610-559-3160.

Northumberland County Prothonotary

County Prothonotary, 201 Market St, Courthouse, Room 7, Sunbury, PA 17801-3468. 570-988-4151 R/E Recording: 570-988-4143.
Will search UCC records. This agency will not do a tax lien search. See Recorder for real estate records. **Other Phone Numbers:** Assessor 570-988-4112; Treasurer 570-988-4161; Elections 570-988-4211.

Northumberland County Recorder

County Recorder of Deeds, 2nd & Market Streets, Court House, Sunbury, PA 17801. 570-988-4140.
Will search UCC records, but only real estate related UCC filed here. No tax liens filed here. Will not search real estate records. **Other Phone Numbers:** Assessor 570-988-4312; Treasurer 570-988-4160.

Perry County Prothonotary

County Prothonotary, PO Box 325, New Bloomfield, PA 17068-0325. 717-582-2131.
Will search UCC records. This agency will not do a tax lien search. See Recorder for real estate records.

Perry County Recorder

County Recorder of Deeds, PO Box 223, New Bloomfield, PA 17068. 717-582-2131.
Will search UCC records, but only real estate related UCC filed here. No tax liens filed here. Will not search real estate records. **Other Phone Numbers:** Assessor 717-582-8984 x3; Treasurer 717-582-8984 x4.

Philadelphia County Prothonotary

County Prothonotary, Broad & Market Streets, City Hall Room 262, Philadelphia, PA 19107. 215-686-6664.
Will search UCC records. Tax liens not included in UCC search. See Recorder for real estate records. **Other Phone Numbers:** Assessor 215-686-4334.

Philadelphia County Recorder

County Recorder of Deeds, Broad & Market Streets, City Hall Room 153, Philadelphia, PA 19107. 215-686-2260 R/E Recording: 215-686-2291.
Will search UCC records, but only real estate related UCC filed here. No tax liens filed here. Will not search real estate records. **Online Access:** Death Records. Search the Philadelphia area obituaries for free at www.legacy.com/philly/LegacyHome.asp. **Other Phone Numbers:** Assessor 215-686-4334; Treasurer 215-686-2312.

Pike County Prothonotary

County Prothonotary, 412 Broad St, Milford, PA 18337. 570-296-7231; Fax none.
Will not search UCC records. This agency will not do a tax lien search. See Recorder for real estate records. **Online Access:** Tax Lien Records. Online search: see

Register of Deeds. **Other Phone Numbers:** Assessor 570-296-3417; Elections 570-296-3426.

Pike County Recorder

County Recorder of Deeds, 506 Broad St, Milford, PA 18337. 570-296-3508; Fax 570-296-3514.
Will search UCC records, but only real estate related UCC filed here. No tax liens filed here. Will not search real estate records. **Online Access:** Probate Records. Access is available through a private company. For information, call Infocon at 814-472-6066. **Other Phone Numbers:** Assessor 570-296-3417; Treasurer 570-296-3441.

Potter County Prothonotary

County Prothonotary, Courthouse, Room 23, 1 E. 2nd St., Coudersport, PA 16915. 814-274-9740 R/E Recording: 814-274-8370; Fax 814-274-8284.
Will search UCC records. See Recorder for real estate records. **Online Access:** Tax Lien Records. Online search: see Register of Deeds. **Other Phone Numbers:** Assessor 814-274-0488; Treasurer 814-274-9775; Elections 814-274-8467; Vital Records 814-274-9740.

Potter County Recorder

County Recorder of Deeds, Courthouse, Room 20, Coudersport, PA 16915. 814-274-8370.
Will search UCC records, but only real estate related UCC filed here. No tax liens filed here. Will not search real estate records. **Online Access:** Real Estate, Assessor, Probate Records. Access is available through a private company. For information, call Infocon at 814-472-6066. **Other Phone Numbers:** Assessor 814-247-0488; Treasurer 814-274-9775.

Schuylkill County Prothonotary

County Prothonotary, 401 N. Second St., Pottsville, PA 17901-2520. 570-628-1270 R/E Recording: 570-628-1480; Fax 570-628-1261.
Will search UCC records. UCC search includes tax liens if requested. $5.00 per 5 year judgment search. See Recorder for real estate records. **Other Phone Numbers:** Assessor 570-628-1025; Treasurer 570-628-1433; Elections 570-628-3040.

Schuylkill County Recorder

County Recorder of Deeds, 401 N. Second St., Pottsville, PA 17901. County Recorder of Deeds, R/E and UCC Recording 570-628-1480.
Will search UCC records, but only real estate related UCC filed here. No tax liens filed here. Will not search real estate records. **Other Phone Numbers:** Assessor 570-628-1024; Treasurer 570-628-1433.

Snyder County Prothonotary

County Prothonotary, PO Box 217, Middleburg, PA 17842-0217. 570-837-4202; Fax 570-837-4275.
Will not search UCC records. See Recorder for real estate records. **Other Phone Numbers:** Assessor 570-837-4216.

Snyder County Recorder

County Recorder of Deeds, PO Box 217, Middleburg, PA 17842-0217. County Recorder of Deeds, R/E and UCC Recording 570-837-4225; Fax 570-837-4299.
Will not search real estate records. **Other Phones:** Assessor 570-837-4218; Treasurer 570-837-4221.

Somerset County Prothonotary

County Prothonotary, 111 E. Union St., Suite 190, Somerset, PA 15501. 814-445-1428 R/E Recording: 814-445-1547; Fax 814-444-9270.
Will search UCC records. Will not search tax liens. See Recorder for real estate records. **Other Phone Numbers:** Assessor 814-445-1536; Treasurer 814-445-1482; Elections 814-445-1549.

Somerset County Recorder

County Recorder of Deeds, 300 N Center Ave, #400, Suite 140, Somerset, PA 15501. 814-445-1547.
Will search UCC records, but only real estate related UCC filed here. No tax liens filed here. Will not search real estate records. **Other Phone Numbers:** Assessor 814-445-8931; Treasurer 814-445-2071.

Sullivan County Prothonotary

County Prothonotary, Main St, Courthouse, Laporte, PA 18626. County Prothonotary, R/E and UCC Recording 570-946-7351.
Will not search UCC records. This agency will not do a tax lien search. See Recorder for real estate records. **Other Phone Numbers:** Assessor 570-946-5061; Treasurer 570-946-7331; Elections 570-946-5201.

Sullivan County Recorder

County Recorder of Deeds, Main St, Courthouse, Laporte, PA 18626. County Recorder of Deeds, R/E and UCC Recording 570-946-7351.
This agency will not peform searches. **Other Phone Numbers:** Assessor 570-946-5061; Treasurer 570-946-7331; Elections 570-946-5201.

Susquehanna County Prothonotary

County Prothonotary, PO Box 218, Montrose, PA 18801-0218. 570-278-4600 x121; Fax 570-278-9268.
Will not search UCC records. See Recorder for real estate records. **Other Phone Numbers:** Assessor 570-278-4600 x151.

Susquehanna County Recorder

Recorder of Deeds, PO Box 218, Montrose, PA 18801. 570-278-4600 x112/3 R/E Recording: 570-278-4600 x112 UCC Recording: 570-278-4600 x112; Fax 570-278-9268.
Will search UCC records. No tax liens filed here. Will not search real estate records. **Other Phone Numbers:** Assessor 570-278-4600 x150; Treasurer 570-278-4600 x130; Vital Records 570-278-4600 x112.

Tioga County Prothonotary

County Prothonotary, 116 Main St, Courthouse, Wellsboro, PA 16901. 570-724-9281.
Will not search UCC records. This agency will not do a tax lien search. See Recorder for real estate records.

Tioga County Recorder

County Recorder of Deeds, 116 Main St, Courthouse, Wellsboro, PA 16901. 570-724-9260 R/E Recording: 570-724-1906.
Will search UCC records, but only real estate related UCC filed here. No tax liens filed here. Will not search real estate records. **Online Access:** Real Estate, Recording, Wills Records. Access is available through a private company at www.landex.com/remote. Fee is $.20 per minute and $.50 per fax page. Recorders data goes back to 1977; images and wills go back to 2/1999. **Other Phone Numbers:** Assessor 570-724-9117; Treasurer 570-723-9213.

Union County Prothonotary

County Prothonotary, 103 S. 2nd St, Courthouse, Lewisburg, PA 17837. 570-524-8751 R/E Recording: 570-524-8761 UCC Recording: 570-524-8761.
Will not search UCC records. UCC search does not include tax liens. See Recorder for real estate records. **Other Phone Numbers:** Assessor 570-524-8611; Treasurer 570-524-8781.

Union County Recorder

County Recorder of Deeds, 103 S. 2nd St, Courthouse, Lewisburg, PA 17837-1996. 570-524-8761; www.unionco.org
This agency will not peform searches. **Other Phones:** Assessor 570-524-8611; Treasurer 570-524-8781.

Venango County Prothonotary

County Prothonotary, Courthouse, Franklin, PA 16323. 814-432-9577 R/E Recording: 814-432-9534 UCC Recording: 814-432-9534; Fax 814-432-9573.
Will search UCC records. UCC search includes tax liens if requested. See Recorder for real estate records. **Other Phone Numbers:** Assessor 814-432-9515; Treasurer 814-432-9525; Elections 814-432-9514.

Venango County Recorder

County Recorder of Deeds, PO Box 831, Franklin, PA 16323. 814-432-9539 R/E Recording: 814-437-6871; Fax 814-432-9569. www.co.venango.pa.us/Directory/index.htm
This agency will not peform searches; no tax liens filed here. **Other Phone Numbers:** Assessor 814-432-9516; Treasurer 814-432-9525; Elections 814-432-9514; Vital Records 814-432-9535.

Warren County Prothonotary

County Prothonotary, 4th & Market Streets, Courthouse, Warren, PA 16365. 814-723-7550 UCC Recording: 814-723-7550 x4; Fax 814-723-8115.
Will not search UCC records. See Recorder for real estate records. **Other Phone Numbers:** Treasurer 814-723-7550 x3.

Warren County Recorder

County Recorder of Deeds, 4th & Market Streets, Courthouse, Warren, PA 16365. 814-723-7550.
Will search UCC records, but only real estate related UCC filed here. No tax liens filed here. Will not search real estate records. **Other Phone Numbers:** Assessor 814-723-7550; Treasurer 814-723-7550.

Washington County Prothonotary

County Prothonotary, 1 S. Main St., Suite 1001, Courthouse, Washington, PA 15301. 724-228-6770.
Will search UCC records. This agency will not do a tax lien search. See Recorder for real estate records.

Washington County Recorder

County Prothonotary, Washington County Courthouse, 1 S. Main St., Room 1006, Washington, PA 15301. County Prothonotary, R/E and UCC Recording 724-228-6806 UCC Recording: 724-228-6770; Fax 724-228-6737. www.co.washington.pa.us
Will search UCC records. No tax liens filed here. **Online Access:** Assessor, Real Estate Records. Records are available on the county online system. Records date back to 1952. Register of Wills information and lending agency information is also available. For information, call 724-228-6766. **Other Phone Numbers:** Assessor 724-228-6850; Treasurer 724-228-6780; Elections 724-228-6750.

Wayne County Prothonotary

County Prothonotary, 925 Court St, Courthouse, Honesdale, PA 18431-1996. 570-253-5970 x200/5 R/E Recording: 570-253-5970 x212 UCC Recording: 570-253-5970 x205; Fax 570-253-0687.
Will search UCC records. This agency will not do a tax lien search. See Recorder for real estate records. **Other Phone Numbers:** Assessor 570-253-5970 x216; Treasurer 570-253-5970 x125; Elections 570-253-5970 x165; Vital Records 570-253-5970 x200.

Wayne County Recorder

County Recorder of Deeds, 925 Court St, Honesdale, PA 18431-1996. County Recorder of Deeds, R/E and UCC Recording 570-253-5970 x212; www.co-wayne-pa-us.org

Will search UCC records, but only real estate related UCC filed here. No tax liens filed here. Will not search real estate records. **Other Phone Numbers:** Assessor 570-253-5970 x216; Treasurer 570-253-5970 x125; Elections 570-253-5970 x165.

Westmoreland County Prothonotary

County Prothonotary, PO Box 1630, Courthouse Square Room 501, Greensburg, PA 15601. 724-830-3516.

Will search UCC records. UCC search includes tax liens if requested. See Recorder for real estate records.

Westmoreland County Recorder

, 2 N Main St #503, Greensburg, PA 15601. 724-830-3526 R/E Recording: 724-830-3518 UCC Recording: 724-830-3518;   Fax   724-853-4657. www.co.westmoreland.pa.us

Will search UCC records. No tax liens filed here. Will not search real estate records. **Online Access:** Real Estate, Tax Lien Records. The online system costs $100 setup plus $20 per month minimum fee, and a per minute charge of $.50 after 40 minutes. The system also includes civil, criminal, prothonotary indexes. Recorder information dates back to 1957. No tax lien information is available, only UCC liens. For information, call 724-830-3874. **Other Phones:** Assessor 724-830-3490; Treasurer 724-830-3173; Elections 724-830-3150.

Wyoming County Prothonotary

County Prothonotary, 1 Courthouse Square, Wyoming County Courthouse, Tunkhannock, PA 18657-1219. 717-836-3200 R/E Recording: 717-836-3200 x235.

Will search UCC records. This agency will not do a tax lien search. See Recorder for real estate records. **Other Phone Numbers:** Assessor 717-836-3200; Treasurer 717-836-3200; Elections 717-836-3200; Vital Records 717-836-3200.

Wyoming County Recorder

County Recorder of Deeds, 1 Courthouse Square, Tunkhannock, PA 18657. 717-836-3200 x235/6 R/E Recording: 717-836-3200.

Will search UCC records, but only real estate related UCC filed here. No tax liens filed here. Will not search real estate records. **Other Phone Numbers:** Assessor 717-836-3200 x261; Treasurer 717-836-3200 x287.

York County Prothonotary

County Prothonotary, 28 E. Market St, York, PA 17401. 717-771-9611; Fax 717-771-4629.

Will search UCC records. See Recorder for real estate records.

York County Recorder

Recorder of Deeds, 28 E. Market St, York, PA 17401. 717-771-9608;   Fax   717-771-9582. www.york-county.org/departments/deeds/deeds.htm

This agency will not peform searches; no tax liens filed here. **Online Access:** Assessor, Real Estate Records. Two sources are available. Online access to the assessors database is available free at www.york-county.org/test/manager.htm. Also, online access is available through Landex at www.landex.com/remote. Some records are free, others on a pay per time usage. Records go back to 1990; images to 1994. Also, parcel numbers are available to the public at www.york-county.org/departments/assessment/tx_asmnt.htm.

Other Phone Numbers: Assessor 717-771-9220; Treasurer 717-771-9603.

Pennsylvania County Locator

You will usually be able to find the city name in the City/County Cross Reference below. In that case, it is a simple matter to determine the county from the cross reference. However, only the official US Postal Service city names are included in this index. There are an additional 40,000 place names that people use in their addresses. Therefore, we have also included a ZIP/City Cross Reference immediately following the City/County Cross Reference.

If you know the ZIP Code but the city name does not appear in the City/County Cross Reference index, look up the ZIP Code in the ZIP/City Cross Reference, find the city name, then look up the city name in the City/County Cross Reference. For example, you want to know the county for an address of Menands, NY 12204. There is no "Menands" in the City/County Cross Reference. The ZIP/City Cross Reference shows that ZIP Codes 12201-12288 are for the city of Albany. Looking back in the City/County Cross Reference, Albany is in Albany County.

City/County Cross Reference

AARONSBURG Centre
ABBOTTSTOWN (17301) Adams(81), York(18)
ABINGTON Montgomery
ACKERMANVILLE Northampton
ACME (15610) Westmoreland(96), Fayette(3)
ACOSTA Somerset
ADAH Fayette
ADAMSBURG Westmoreland
ADAMSTOWN Lancaster
ADAMSVILLE (16110) Crawford(90), Mercer(9)
ADDISON Somerset
ADRIAN Armstrong
AIRVILLE York
AKRON Lancaster
ALBA Bradford
ALBION Erie
ALBRIGHTSVILLE (18210) Carbon(86), Monroe(13)
ALBURTIS (18011) Berks(61), Lehigh(38)
ALDENVILLE Wayne
ALEPPO Greene
ALEXANDRIA Huntingdon
ALIQUIPPA Beaver
ALLENPORT Washington
ALLENSVILLE (17002) Mifflin(89), Huntingdon(10)
ALLENTOWN Lehigh
ALLENWOOD (17810) Lycoming(86), Union(13)
ALLISON Fayette
ALLISON PARK Allegheny
ALLPORT Clearfield
ALTOONA Blair
ALUM BANK Bedford
ALVERDA Indiana
ALVERTON Westmoreland
AMBERSON Franklin
AMBLER Montgomery
AMBRIDGE (15003) Beaver(94), Allegheny(5)
AMITY Washington
ANALOMINK Monroe
ANDREAS (18211) Schuylkill(86), Carbon(13)
ANITA Jefferson
ANNVILLE Lebanon
ANTES FORT Lycoming
APOLLO (15613) Armstrong(51), Westmoreland(48)
AQUASHICOLA Carbon
ARCADIA Indiana
ARCHBALD Lackawanna
ARCOLA Montgomery
ARDARA Westmoreland
ARDMORE (19003) Montgomery(62), Delaware(37)
ARENDTSVILLE Adams
ARISTES Columbia
ARMAGH Indiana
ARMBRUST Westmoreland
ARNOT Tioga

ARONA Westmoreland
ARTEMAS (17211) Bedford(93), Fulton(6)
ASHFIELD Carbon
ASHLAND Schuylkill
ASHVILLE (16613) Cambria(98), Blair(1)
ASPERS Adams
ASTON Delaware
ATGLEN (19310) Chester(98), Lancaster(1)
ATHENS Bradford
ATLANTIC Crawford
ATLASBURG Washington
AUBURN Schuylkill
AUDUBON Montgomery
AULTMAN Indiana
AUSTIN (16720) Potter(48), Cameron(44), McKean(7)
AVELLA Washington
AVIS Clinton
AVONDALE Chester
AVONMORE Westmoreland
BADEN (15005) Beaver(87), Allegheny(12)
BAINBRIDGE Lancaster
BAIRDFORD Allegheny
BAKERS SUMMIT Bedford
BAKERSTOWN Allegheny
BALA CYNWYD Montgomery
BALLY Berks
BANGOR Northampton
BARNESBORO (15714) Cambria(79), Indiana(20)
BARNESVILLE Schuylkill
BART Lancaster
BARTO (19504) Berks(67), Montgomery(32)
BARTONSVILLE Monroe
BATH Northampton
BAUSMAN Lancaster
BEACH HAVEN Luzerne
BEACH LAKE (18405) Wayne(92), Pike(7)
BEALLSVILLE Washington
BEAR CREEK Luzerne
BEAR LAKE Warren
BEAVER Beaver
BEAVER FALLS Beaver
BEAVER MEADOWS (18216) Carbon(50), Luzerne(50)
BEAVER SPRINGS Snyder
BEAVERDALE Cambria
BEAVERTOWN Snyder
BECCARIA Clearfield
BECHTELSVILLE (19505) Montgomery(96), Berks(3)
BEDFORD Bedford
BEDMINSTER Bucks
BEECH CREEK (16822) Centre(71), Clinton(28)
BELLE VERNON (15012) Fayette(57), Westmoreland(41), Washington(1)
BELLEFONTE Centre
BELLEVILLE Mifflin
BELLWOOD Blair
BELSANO Cambria
BENDERSVILLE Adams

BENEZETT Elk
BENSALEM Bucks
BENTLEYVILLE Washington
BENTON (17814) Columbia(63), Luzerne(27), Lycoming(7), Sullivan(2)
BERLIN Somerset
BERNVILLE Berks
BERRYSBURG Dauphin
BERWICK (18603) Columbia(79), Luzerne(20)
BERWYN (19312) Chester(98), Delaware(1)
BESSEMER Lawrence
BETHEL Berks
BETHEL PARK Allegheny
BETHLEHEM Lehigh
BEYER Indiana
BIG COVE TANNERY Fulton
BIG RUN Jefferson
BIGLER Clearfield
BIGLERVILLE (17307) Adams(98), Cumberland(1)
BIRCHRUNVILLE Chester
BIRD IN HAND Lancaster
BIRDSBORO Berks
BLACK LICK Indiana
BLAIN Perry
BLAIRS MILLS Huntingdon
BLAIRSVILLE (15717) Indiana(94), Westmoreland(5)
BLAKESLEE (18610) Monroe(97), Luzerne(2)
BLANCHARD Centre
BLANDBURG Cambria
BLANDON Berks
BLOOMING GLEN Bucks
BLOOMSBURG Columbia
BLOSSBURG Tioga
BLUE BALL Lancaster
BLUE BELL Montgomery
BLUE RIDGE SUMMIT Franklin
BOALSBURG Centre
BOBTOWN Greene
BODINES Lycoming
BOILING SPRINGS Cumberland
BOLIVAR Westmoreland
BOSWELL Somerset
BOVARD Westmoreland
BOWERS Berks
BOWMANSDALE Cumberland
BOWMANSTOWN Carbon
BOWMANSVILLE Lancaster
BOYERS Butler
BOYERTOWN (19512) Berks(95), Montgomery(4)
BOYNTON Somerset
BRACKENRIDGE Allegheny
BRACKNEY Susquehanna
BRADDOCK Allegheny
BRADENVILLE Westmoreland
BRADFORD McKean
BRADFORDWOODS Allegheny
BRANCHDALE Schuylkill
BRANCHTON Butler

BRANDAMORE Chester
BRANDY CAMP Elk
BRAVE Greene
BREEZEWOOD Bedford
BREINIGSVILLE Lehigh
BRIDGEPORT Montgomery
BRIDGEVILLE (15017) Allegheny(92), Washington(7)
BRIER HILL Fayette
BRISBIN Clearfield
BRISTOL Bucks
BROAD TOP Huntingdon
BROCKPORT (15823) Elk(95), Jefferson(4)
BROCKTON Schuylkill
BROCKWAY (15824) Jefferson(97), Clearfield(1)
BRODHEADSVILLE Monroe
BROGUE York
BROOKHAVEN Delaware
BROOKLYN Susquehanna
BROOKVILLE Jefferson
BROOMALL Delaware
BROWNFIELD Fayette
BROWNSTOWN Lancaster
BROWNSVILLE (15417) Fayette(62), Washington(37)
BRUIN Butler
BRUSH VALLEY Indiana
BRYN ATHYN Montgomery
BRYN MAWR (19010) Delaware(53), Montgomery(46)
BUCK HILL FALLS Monroe
BUCKINGHAM Bucks
BUENA VISTA Allegheny
BUFFALO MILLS (15534) Bedford(98), Somerset(1)
BULGER Washington
BUNOLA Allegheny
BURGETTSTOWN Washington
BURLINGTON Bradford
BURNHAM Mifflin
BURNSIDE Clearfield
BURNT CABINS (17215) Fulton(85), Huntingdon(15)
BUSHKILL Pike
BUTLER Butler
BYRNEDALE Elk
CABOT (16023) Butler(98), Armstrong(1)
CADOGAN Armstrong
CAIRNBROOK Somerset
CALIFORNIA Washington
CALLENSBURG Clarion
CALLERY Butler
CALUMET Westmoreland
CALVIN Huntingdon
CAMBRA Luzerne
CAMBRIDGE SPRINGS (16403) Crawford(93), Erie(6)
CAMP HILL Cumberland
CAMPBELLTOWN Lebanon
CAMPTOWN Bradford
CANADENSIS (18325) Monroe(70), Pike(29)
CANONSBURG Washington

CANTON (17724) Bradford(84), Lycoming(7), Tioga(7)
CARBONDALE (18407) Lackawanna(98), Susquehanna(1)
CARDALE Fayette
CARLISLE Cumberland
CARLTON (16311) Mercer(87), Venango(12)
CARMICHAELS Greene
CARNEGIE Allegheny
CARROLLTOWN Cambria
CARVERSVILLE Bucks
CASHTOWN Adams
CASSANDRA Cambria
CASSVILLE Huntingdon
CASTANEA Clinton
CATASAUQUA (18032) Lehigh(69), Northampton(30)
CATAWISSA (17820) Columbia(98), Montour(1)
CECIL Washington
CEDAR RUN Lycoming
CEDARS Montgomery
CENTER VALLEY Lehigh
CENTERPORT Berks
CENTERVILLE Crawford
CENTRAL CITY Somerset
CENTRALIA Columbia
CENTRE HALL Centre
CHADDS FORD (19317) Delaware(63), Chester(36)
CHALFONT Bucks
CHALK HILL Fayette
CHALKHILL Fayette
CHAMBERSBURG Franklin
CHAMBERSVILLE Indiana
CHAMPION (15622) Westmoreland(81), Fayette(10), Somerset(8)
CHANDLERS VALLEY Warren
CHARLEROI Washington
CHATHAM Chester
CHELTENHAM Montgomery
CHERRY TREE (15724) Indiana(65), Clearfield(26), Cambria(7)
CHERRYVILLE Northampton
CHEST SPRINGS Cambria
CHESTER Delaware
CHESTER HEIGHTS Delaware
CHESTER SPRINGS Chester
CHESTNUT RIDGE Fayette
CHESWICK Allegheny
CHEYNEY (19319) Delaware(97), Chester(2)
CHICORA (16025) Butler(96), Armstrong(3)
CHINCHILLA Lackawanna
CHRISTIANA Lancaster
CLAIRTON Allegheny
CLARENCE Centre
CLARENDON Warren
CLARIDGE Westmoreland
CLARINGTON (15828) Jefferson(92), Forest(5), Elk(2)
CLARION Clarion
CLARK Mercer
CLARKS MILLS Mercer
CLARKS SUMMIT Lackawanna
CLARKSBURG Indiana
CLARKSVILLE (15322) Greene(58), Washington(41)
CLAYSBURG (16625) Bedford(77), Blair(22)
CLAYSVILLE Washington
CLEARFIELD Clearfield
CLEARVILLE Bedford
CLIFFORD Susquehanna
CLIFTON HEIGHTS Delaware
CLIMAX Armstrong
CLINTON (15026) Beaver(77), Allegheny(15), Washington(6)
CLINTONVILLE Venango
CLUNE Indiana
CLYMER Indiana

COAL CENTER Washington
COAL TOWNSHIP Northumberland
COALDALE Schuylkill
COALPORT (16627) Clearfield(93), Cambria(6)
COATESVILLE Chester
COBURN Centre
COCHRANTON (16314) Crawford(94), Mercer(5)
COCHRANVILLE Chester
COCOLAMUS Juniata
CODORUS York
COGAN STATION Lycoming
COKEBURG Washington
COLEBROOK Lebanon
COLLEGEVILLE Montgomery
COLMAR Montgomery
COLUMBIA Lancaster
COLUMBIA CROSS ROADS (16914) Bradford(92), Tioga(7)
COLUMBUS Warren
COLVER Cambria
COMMODORE Indiana
CONCORD Franklin
CONCORDVILLE Delaware
CONESTOGA Lancaster
CONFLUENCE (15424) Somerset(78), Fayette(21)
CONNEAUT LAKE Crawford
CONNEAUTVILLE Crawford
CONNELLSVILLE Fayette
CONNOQUENESSING Butler
CONSHOHOCKEN Montgomery
CONWAY Beaver
CONYNGHAM Luzerne
COOKSBURG (16217) Clarion(91), Forest(8)
COOLSPRING Jefferson
COOPERSBURG (18036) Lehigh(87), Bucks(12)
COOPERSTOWN (16317) Venango(93), Crawford(6)
COPLAY Lehigh
CORAL Indiana
CORAOPOLIS Allegheny
CORNWALL Lebanon
CORRY (16407) Erie(87), Warren(7), Crawford(5)
CORSICA (15829) Jefferson(74), Clarion(25)
COUDERSPORT Potter
COULTERS Allegheny
COUPON Cambria
COURTNEY Washington
COVINGTON Tioga
COWANESQUE Tioga
COWANSVILLE Armstrong
CRABTREE Westmoreland
CRALEY York
CRANBERRY (16319) Venango(58), Clarion(41)
CRANBERRY TWP Butler
CRANESVILLE Erie
CREAMERY Montgomery
CREEKSIDE (15732) Indiana(98), Armstrong(1)
CREIGHTON Allegheny
CRESCENT Allegheny
CRESCO Monroe
CRESSON Cambria
CRESSONA Schuylkill
CROSBY McKean
CROSS FORK (17729) Potter(84), Clinton(15)
CROWN Clarion
CROYDON Bucks
CRUCIBLE Greene
CRUM LYNNE Delaware
CRYSTAL SPRING Fulton
CUDDY Allegheny
CUMBOLA Schuylkill
CURLLSVILLE Clarion

CURRYVILLE Blair
CURTISVILLE Allegheny
CURWENSVILLE Clearfield
CUSTER CITY McKean
CYCLONE McKean
DAGUS MINES Elk
DAISYTOWN Washington
DALLAS Luzerne
DALLASTOWN York
DALMATIA (17017) Northumberland(62), Dauphin(37)
DALTON (18414) Lackawanna(78), Wyoming(21)
DAMASCUS Wayne
DANBORO Bucks
DANIELSVILLE Northampton
DANVILLE Montour
DARBY Delaware
DARLINGTON Beaver
DARRAGH Westmoreland
DAUBERVILLE Berks
DAUPHIN Dauphin
DAVIDSVILLE Somerset
DAWSON Fayette
DAYTON (16222) Indiana(37), Jefferson(36), Armstrong(25)
DE LANCEY Jefferson
DE YOUNG Elk
DEFIANCE Bedford
DELANO Schuylkill
DELAWARE WATER GAP Monroe
DELMONT Westmoreland
DELTA York
DENBO Washington
DENVER Lancaster
DERRICK CITY McKean
DERRY Westmoreland
DEVAULT Chester
DEVON Chester
DEWART Northumberland
DICKERSON RUN Fayette
DICKINSON Cumberland
DICKSON CITY Lackawanna
DILLINER Greene
DILLSBURG York
DILLTOWN Indiana
DIMOCK Susquehanna
DINGMANS FERRY Pike
DISTANT Armstrong
DIXONVILLE Indiana
DONEGAL Westmoreland
DONORA Washington
DORNSIFE Northumberland
DOUGLASSVILLE Berks
DOVER York
DOWNINGTOWN Chester
DOYLESBURG Franklin
DOYLESTOWN Bucks
DRAVOSBURG Allegheny
DRESHER Montgomery
DREXEL HILL Delaware
DRIFTING Clearfield
DRIFTON Luzerne
DRIFTWOOD (15832) Cameron(95), Elk(4)
DRUMORE Lancaster
DRUMS Luzerne
DRY RUN Franklin
DU BOIS Clearfield
DUBLIN Bucks
DUDLEY Huntingdon
DUKE CENTER McKean
DUNBAR Fayette
DUNCANNON Perry
DUNCANSVILLE Blair
DUNLEVY Washington
DUNLO Cambria
DUQUESNE Allegheny
DURHAM Bucks
DURYEA Luzerne
DUSHORE (18614) Sullivan(97), Wyoming(2)
DYSART (16636) Cambria(97), Blair(2)

EAGLES MERE Sullivan
EAGLEVILLE Montgomery
EARLINGTON Montgomery
EARLVILLE Berks
EAST BERLIN (17316) Adams(76), York(23)
EAST BRADY (16028) Clarion(74), Armstrong(25)
EAST BUTLER Butler
EAST EARL Lancaster
EAST FREEDOM Blair
EAST GREENVILLE (18041) Montgomery(72), Lehigh(22), Bucks(3), Berks(1)
EAST HICKORY Forest
EAST MC KEESPORT Allegheny
EAST MILLSBORO Fayette
EAST PETERSBURG Lancaster
EAST PITTSBURGH Allegheny
EAST PROSPECT York
EAST SMETHPORT McKean
EAST SMITHFIELD Bradford
EAST SPRINGFIELD Erie
EAST STROUDSBURG Monroe
EAST TEXAS Lehigh
EAST VANDERGRIFT Westmoreland
EAST WATERFORD (17021) Juniata(88), Huntingdon(4), Franklin(3), Perry(2)
EASTON Northampton
EAU CLAIRE Butler
EBENSBURG Cambria
EBERVALE Luzerne
EDGEMONT Delaware
EDINBORO Erie
EDINBURG Lawrence
EDMON Armstrong
EFFORT Monroe
EIGHTY FOUR Washington
ELCO Washington
ELDERSVILLE Washington
ELDERTON Armstrong
ELDRED McKean
ELGIN Erie
ELIZABETH Allegheny
ELIZABETHTOWN (17022) Lancaster(88), Dauphin(11)
ELIZABETHVILLE Dauphin
ELKINS PARK Montgomery
ELKLAND Tioga
ELLIOTTSBURG Perry
ELLSWORTH Washington
ELLWOOD CITY (16117) Lawrence(53), Beaver(46)
ELM Lancaster
ELMHURST Lackawanna
ELMORA Cambria
ELRAMA Washington
ELTON Cambria
ELVERSON (19520) Chester(68), Berks(31)
ELYSBURG (17824) Northumberland(88), Columbia(11)
EMEIGH Cambria
EMIGSVILLE York
EMLENTON (16373) Venango(48), Clarion(48), Butler(3)
EMMAUS Lehigh
EMPORIUM (15834) Cameron(92), Elk(7)
ENDEAVOR Forest
ENOLA Cumberland
ENON VALLEY (16120) Lawrence(80), Beaver(19)
ENTRIKEN Huntingdon
EPHRATA Lancaster
EQUINUNK Wayne
ERIE Erie
ERNEST Indiana
ERWINNA Bucks
ESSINGTON Delaware
ETTERS York
EVANS CITY Butler
EVERETT Bedford

EVERSON Fayette
EXCELSIOR Northumberland
EXPORT Westmoreland
EXTON Chester
FACTORYVILLE (18419) Wyoming(81),
    Lackawanna(17)
FAIRBANK Fayette
FAIRCHANCE Fayette
FAIRFIELD Adams
FAIRHOPE Somerset
FAIRLESS HILLS Bucks
FAIRMOUNT CITY Clarion
FAIRVIEW Erie
FAIRVIEW VILLAGE Montgomery
FALLENTIMBER (16639) Cambria(83),
    Clearfield(16)
FALLS (18615) Wyoming(89), Luzerne(8),
    Lackawanna(2)
FALLS CREEK (15840) Jefferson(98),
    Clearfield(1)
FANNETTSBURG Franklin
FARMINGTON Fayette
FARRANDSVILLE Clinton
FARRELL Mercer
FAWN GROVE York
FAYETTE CITY Fayette
FAYETTEVILLE (17222) Franklin(94),
    Adams(5)
FEASTERVILLE TREVOSE Bucks
FELTON York
FENELTON Butler
FERNDALE Bucks
FINLEYVILLE (15332) Washington(93),
    Allegheny(6)
FIRST NAT BANK Erie
FISHER Clarion
FISHERTOWN Bedford
FLEETVILLE Lackawanna
FLEETWOOD Berks
FLEMING Centre
FLICKSVILLE Northampton
FLINTON Cambria
FLOURTOWN Montgomery
FOGELSVILLE Lehigh
FOLCROFT Delaware
FOLSOM Delaware
FOMBELL (16123) Beaver(97),
    Lawrence(2)
FORBES ROAD Westmoreland
FORCE Elk
FORD CITY Armstrong
FORD CLIFF Armstrong
FOREST CITY (18421) Susquehanna(58),
    Wayne(24), Lackawanna(16)
FOREST GROVE Bucks
FORESTVILLE Butler
FORKSVILLE Sullivan
FORT HILL Somerset
FORT LITTLETON Fulton
FORT LOUDON Franklin
FORT WASHINGTON Bucks
FOUNTAINVILLE Bucks
FOXBURG Clarion
FRACKVILLE Schuylkill
FRANCONIA Montgomery
FRANKLIN Venango
FRANKLINTOWN York
FREDERICK Montgomery
FREDERICKSBURG (17026) Lebanon(88),
    Berks(11)
FREDERICKTOWN Washington
FREDONIA Mercer
FREEBURG Snyder
FREEDOM Beaver
FREELAND Luzerne
FREEPORT (16229) Armstrong(66),
    Butler(25), Westmoreland(6),
    Allegheny(1)
FRENCHVILLE Clearfield
FRIEDENS Somerset
FRIEDENSBURG Schuylkill
FRIENDSVILLE Susquehanna

FROSTBURG Jefferson
FRYBURG Clarion
FURLONG Bucks
GAINES (16921) Tioga(92), Potter(7)
GALETON Potter
GALLITZIN (16641) Cambria(96), Blair(3)
GANS Fayette
GAP (17527) Lancaster(91), Chester(8)
GARARDS FORT Greene
GARDENVILLE Bucks
GARDNERS (17324) Adams(63),
    Cumberland(36)
GARLAND Warren
GARRETT Somerset
GASTONVILLE Washington
GEIGERTOWN Berks
GENESEE Potter
GEORGETOWN Beaver
GERMANSVILLE Lehigh
GETTYSBURG Adams
GIBBON GLADE Fayette
GIBSON Susquehanna
GIBSONIA (15044) Allegheny(95), Butler(4)
GIFFORD McKean
GILBERT Monroe
GILBERTON Schuylkill
GILBERTSVILLE Montgomery
GILLETT Bradford
GIPSY Indiana
GIRARD Erie
GIRARDVILLE Schuylkill
GLADWYNE Montgomery
GLASGOW Cambria
GLASSPORT Allegheny
GLEN CAMPBELL (15742) Indiana(90),
    Clearfield(9)
GLEN HOPE Clearfield
GLEN LYON Luzerne
GLEN MILLS (19342) Delaware(97),
    Chester(2)
GLEN RICHEY Clearfield
GLEN RIDDLE LIMA Delaware
GLEN ROCK York
GLENMOORE Chester
GLENOLDEN Delaware
GLENSHAW Allegheny
GLENSIDE Montgomery
GLENVILLE York
GLENWILLARD Allegheny
GOODVILLE Lancaster
GORDON Schuylkill
GORDONVILLE Lancaster
GOULDSBORO (18424) Wayne(48),
    Lackawanna(32), Luzerne(16),
    Monroe(2)
GOWEN CITY Northumberland
GRADYVILLE Delaware
GRAMPIAN Clearfield
GRAND VALLEY Warren
GRANTHAM Cumberland
GRANTVILLE (17028) Dauphin(90),
    Lebanon(9)
GRANVILLE Mifflin
GRANVILLE SUMMIT Bradford
GRAPEVILLE Westmoreland
GRASSFLAT Clearfield
GRATZ Dauphin
GRAY Somerset
GRAYSVILLE Greene
GREAT BEND Susquehanna
GREELEY Pike
GREEN LANE (18054) Montgomery(83),
    Bucks(16)
GREEN PARK Perry
GREENCASTLE Franklin
GREENOCK Allegheny
GREENSBORO Greene
GREENSBURG Westmoreland
GREENTOWN Pike
GREENVILLE (16125) Mercer(95),
    Crawford(4)
GRINDSTONE Fayette

GROVE CITY (16127) Mercer(89),
    Venango(5), Butler(4)
GROVER Bradford
GUYS MILLS Crawford
GWYNEDD Montgomery
GWYNEDD VALLEY Montgomery
HADLEY Mercer
HALIFAX Dauphin
HALLSTEAD Susquehanna
HAMBURG Berks
HAMILTON Jefferson
HAMLIN Wayne
HANNASTOWN Westmoreland
HANOVER York
HARBORCREEK Erie
HARFORD Susquehanna
HARLEIGH Luzerne
HARLEYSVILLE Montgomery
HARMONSBURG Crawford
HARMONY (16037) Butler(91),
    Lawrence(4), Beaver(3)
HARRISBURG Dauphin
HARRISON CITY Westmoreland
HARRISON VALLEY Potter
HARRISONVILLE Fulton
HARRISVILLE (16038) Venango(55),
    Butler(44)
HARTLETON Union
HARTSTOWN Crawford
HARVEYS LAKE (18618) Luzerne(87),
    Wyoming(12)
HARWICK Allegheny
HASTINGS (16646) Cambria(94),
    Clearfield(5)
HATBORO (19040) Montgomery(95),
    Bucks(4)
HATFIELD (19440) Montgomery(91),
    Bucks(8)
HAVERFORD (19041) Montgomery(74),
    Delaware(25)
HAVERTOWN Delaware
HAWK RUN Clearfield
HAWLEY (18428) Wayne(68), Pike(31)
HAWTHORN Clarion
HAZEL HURST McKean
HAZLETON Luzerne
HEGINS Schuylkill
HEILWOOD Indiana
HELFENSTEIN Schuylkill
HELLERTOWN (18055) Northampton(97),
    Bucks(2)
HENDERSONVILLE Washington
HENRYVILLE Monroe
HEREFORD Berks
HERMAN Butler
HERMINIE Westmoreland
HERMITAGE Mercer
HERNDON (17830) Northumberland(98),
    Dauphin(1)
HERRICK CENTER Susquehanna
HERSHEY (17033) Dauphin(96),
    Lebanon(3)
HESSTON Huntingdon
HIBBS Fayette
HICKORY Washington
HIDDEN VALLEY Somerset
HIGHSPIRE Dauphin
HILLER Fayette
HILLIARDS Butler
HILLSDALE Indiana
HILLSGROVE (18619) Sullivan(82),
    Lycoming(18)
HILLSVILLE Lawrence
HILLTOWN Bucks
HOLBROOK Greene
HOLICONG Bucks
HOLLIDAYSBURG Blair
HOLLSOPPLE Somerset
HOLMES Delaware
HOLTWOOD Lancaster
HOME Indiana
HOMER CITY Indiana

HOMESTEAD Allegheny
HONESDALE Wayne
HONEY BROOK (19344) Chester(89),
    Lancaster(10)
HONEY GROVE (17035) Juniata(98),
    Perry(1)
HOOKSTOWN Beaver
HOOVERSVILLE Somerset
HOP BOTTOM Susquehanna
HOPELAND Lancaster
HOPEWELL Bedford
HOPWOOD Fayette
HORSHAM Montgomery
HOSTETTER Westmoreland
HOUSTON Washington
HOUTZDALE Clearfield
HOWARD Centre
HUGHESVILLE Lycoming
HUMMELS WHARF Snyder
HUMMELSTOWN Dauphin
HUNKER Westmoreland
HUNLOCK CREEK Luzerne
HUNTINGDON Huntingdon
HUNTINGDON VALLEY (19006)
    Montgomery(93), Bucks(6)
HUNTINGTON MILLS Luzerne
HUSTONTOWN (17229) Fulton(96),
    Huntingdon(3)
HUTCHINSON Westmoreland
HYDE Clearfield
HYDE PARK Westmoreland
HYDETOWN Crawford
HYNDMAN (15545) Bedford(77),
    Somerset(22)
HYNER Clinton
ICKESBURG Perry
IDAVILLE Adams
IMLER (16655) Bedford(98), Blair(1)
IMMACULATA Chester
IMPERIAL Allegheny
INDIAN HEAD Fayette
INDIANA Indiana
INDIANOLA Allegheny
INDUSTRY Beaver
INGOMAR Allegheny
INTERCOURSE Lancaster
IRVINE Warren
IRVONA Clearfield
IRWIN Westmoreland
ISABELLA Fayette
JACKSON Susquehanna
JACKSON CENTER Mercer
JACOBS CREEK Westmoreland
JAMES CITY Elk
JAMES CREEK (16657) Huntingdon(98),
    Bedford(1)
JAMESTOWN (16134) Crawford(90),
    Mercer(9)
JAMISON Bucks
JEANNETTE Westmoreland
JEFFERSON Greene
JENKINTOWN Montgomery
JENNERS Somerset
JENNERSTOWN Somerset
JERMYN Lackawanna
JEROME Somerset
JERSEY MILLS Lycoming
JERSEY SHORE (17740) Lycoming(85),
    Clinton(14)
JESSUP Lackawanna
JIM THORPE Carbon
JOFFRE Washington
JOHNSONBURG Elk
JOHNSTOWN Cambria
JONES MILLS Westmoreland
JONESTOWN Lebanon
JOSEPHINE Indiana
JULIAN Centre
JUNEAU Indiana
JUNEDALE Carbon
KANE McKean
KANTNER Somerset

KARNS CITY (16041) Butler(88), Armstrong(11)
KARTHAUS (16845) Clearfield(68), Centre(31)
KEISTERVILLE Fayette
KELAYRES Schuylkill
KELTON Chester
KEMBLESVILLE Chester
KEMPTON (19529) Berks(51), Lehigh(48)
KENNERDELL Venango
KENNETT SQUARE Chester
KENT Indiana
KERSEY Elk
KIMBERTON Chester
KING OF PRUSSIA Chester
KINGSLEY Susquehanna
KINGSTON Luzerne
KINTNERSVILLE Bucks
KINZERS Lancaster
KIRKWOOD Lancaster
KITTANNING Armstrong
KLEINFELTERSVILLE Lebanon
KLINGERSTOWN (17941) Schuylkill(77), Northumberland(22)
KNOX Clarion
KNOX DALE Jefferson
KNOXVILLE Tioga
KOPPEL Beaver
KOSSUTH Clarion
KREAMER Snyder
KRESGEVILLE Monroe
KULPMONT Northumberland
KULPSVILLE Montgomery
KUNKLETOWN (18058) Monroe(69), Carbon(30)
KUTZTOWN (19530) Berks(90), Lehigh(9)
KYLERTOWN Clearfield
LA BELLE Fayette
LA JOSE Clearfield
LA PLUME Lackawanna
LACEYVILLE (18623) Wyoming(47), Bradford(36), Susquehanna(16)
LACKAWAXEN Pike
LAFAYETTE HILL Montgomery
LAHASKA Bucks
LAIRDSVILLE Lycoming
LAKE ARIEL (18436) Wayne(69), Lackawanna(30)
LAKE CITY Erie
LAKE COMO Wayne
LAKE HARMONY Carbon
LAKE LYNN Fayette
LAKE WINOLA Wyoming
LAKEVILLE Wayne
LAKEWOOD Wayne
LAMAR Clinton
LAMARTINE Clarion
LAMPETER Lancaster
LANCASTER Lancaster
LANDENBERG Chester
LANDINGVILLE Schuylkill
LANDISBURG Perry
LANDISVILLE Lancaster
LANESBORO Susquehanna
LANGELOTH Washington
LANGHORNE Bucks
LANSDALE Montgomery
LANSDOWNE Delaware
LANSE Clearfield
LANSFORD Carbon
LAPORTE Sullivan
LARIMER Westmoreland
LATROBE Westmoreland
LATTIMER MINES Luzerne
LAUGHLINTOWN Westmoreland
LAURELTON Union
LAURYS STATION Lehigh
LAVELLE Schuylkill
LAWN Lebanon
LAWRENCE Washington
LAWRENCEVILLE Tioga
LAWTON Susquehanna

LE RAYSVILLE (18829) Bradford(93), Susquehanna(6)
LEBANON Lebanon
LECK KILL (17836) Northumberland(89), Schuylkill(10)
LECKRONE Fayette
LECONTES MILLS Clearfield
LEDERACH Montgomery
LEECHBURG (15656) Armstrong(57), Westmoreland(42)
LEEPER Clarion
LEESPORT Berks
LEETSDALE Allegheny
LEHIGH VALLEY Northampton
LEHIGHTON Carbon
LEHMAN Luzerne
LEISENRING Fayette
LEMASTERS Franklin
LEMONT Centre
LEMONT FURNACE Fayette
LEMOYNE Cumberland
LENHARTSVILLE Berks
LENNI Delaware
LENOXVILLE Susquehanna
LEOLA Lancaster
LEROY Bradford
LEVITTOWN Bucks
LEWIS RUN McKean
LEWISBERRY York
LEWISBURG Union
LEWISTOWN Mifflin
LEWISVILLE Chester
LIBERTY (16930) Tioga(82), Lycoming(17)
LIBRARY Allegheny
LICKINGVILLE Clarion
LIGHT STREET Columbia
LIGONIER Westmoreland
LILLY Cambria
LIMEKILN Berks
LIMEPORT Lehigh
LIMESTONE Clarion
LINCOLN UNIVERSITY Chester
LINDEN Lycoming
LINE LEXINGTON (18932) Bucks(93), Montgomery(6)
LINESVILLE Crawford
LIONVILLE Chester
LISTIE Somerset
LITITZ Lancaster
LITTLE MEADOWS (18830) Susquehanna(94), Bradford(5)
LITTLESTOWN Adams
LIVERPOOL (17045) Perry(78), Juniata(17), Snyder(3)
LLEWELLYN Schuylkill
LOCK HAVEN (17745) Clinton(98), Lycoming(1)
LOCUST GAP Northumberland
LOCUSTDALE Schuylkill
LOGANTON Clinton
LOGANVILLE York
LONG POND Monroe
LOPEZ Sullivan
LORETTO Cambria
LOST CREEK Schuylkill
LOWBER Westmoreland
LOYALHANNA Westmoreland
LOYSBURG Bedford
LOYSVILLE Perry
LUCERNEMINES Indiana
LUCINDA Clarion
LUDLOW McKean
LUMBERVILLE Bucks
LURGAN Franklin
LUTHERSBURG Clearfield
LUXOR Westmoreland
LUZERNE Luzerne
LYKENS Dauphin
LYNDELL Chester
LYNDORA Butler
LYON STATION Berks
MACKEYVILLE Clinton

MACUNGIE (18062) Lehigh(89), Berks(10)
MADERA Clearfield
MADISON Westmoreland
MADISONBURG Centre
MAHAFFEY (15757) Clearfield(98), Indiana(1)
MAHANOY CITY Schuylkill
MAHANOY PLANE Schuylkill
MAINESBURG Tioga
MAINLAND Montgomery
MALVERN Chester
MAMMOTH Westmoreland
MANCHESTER York
MANHEIM (17545) Lancaster(98), Lebanon(1)
MANNS CHOICE Bedford
MANOR Westmoreland
MANORVILLE Armstrong
MANSFIELD Tioga
MAPLETON DEPOT Huntingdon
MAR LIN Schuylkill
MARBLE Clarion
MARCHAND Indiana
MARCUS HOOK Delaware
MARIANNA Washington
MARIENVILLE (16239) Forest(60), Clarion(39)
MARIETTA Lancaster
MARION Franklin
MARION CENTER Indiana
MARION HEIGHTS Northumberland
MARKLETON Somerset
MARKLEYSBURG Fayette
MARS (16046) Butler(86), Allegheny(13)
MARSHALLS CREEK Monroe
MARSTELLER Cambria
MARTIN Fayette
MARTINDALE Lancaster
MARTINS CREEK Northampton
MARTINSBURG (16662) Blair(69), Bedford(30)
MARY D Schuylkill
MARYSVILLE (17053) Perry(97), Cumberland(2)
MASONTOWN Fayette
MATAMORAS Pike
MATHER Greene
MATTAWANA Mifflin
MAXATAWNY Berks
MAYPORT (16240) Clarion(70), Jefferson(22), Armstrong(6)
MAYTOWN Lancaster
MC ALISTERVILLE Juniata
MC CLELLANDTOWN Fayette
MC CLURE (17841) Mifflin(86), Snyder(13)
MC CONNELLSBURG Fulton
MC CONNELLSTOWN Huntingdon
MC DONALD (15057) Washington(86), Allegheny(13)
MC ELHATTAN Clinton
MC EWENSVILLE Northumberland
MC GRANN Armstrong
MC INTYRE Indiana
MC KEAN Erie
MC KEES ROCKS Allegheny
MC KEESPORT Allegheny
MC KNIGHTSTOWN Adams
MC SHERRYSTOWN Adams
MC VEYTOWN Mifflin
MCADOO (18237) Schuylkill(98), Carbon(1)
MEADOW LANDS Washington
MEADVILLE Crawford
MECHANICSBURG (17055) Cumberland(97), York(2)
MECHANICSVILLE Bucks
MEDIA Delaware
MEHOOPANY Wyoming
MELCROFT Fayette
MENDENHALL Chester
MENGES MILLS York
MENTCLE Indiana

MERCER Mercer
MERCERSBURG (17236) Franklin(91), Fulton(8)
MERION STATION Montgomery
MERRITTSTOWN Fayette
MERTZTOWN (19539) Berks(87), Lehigh(12)
MESHOPPEN (18630) Wyoming(54), Susquehanna(45)
MEXICO Juniata
MEYERSDALE Somerset
MIDDLEBURG Snyder
MIDDLEBURY CENTER Tioga
MIDDLEPORT Schuylkill
MIDDLETOWN Dauphin
MIDLAND Beaver
MIDWAY Washington
MIFFLIN Juniata
MIFFLINBURG Union
MIFFLINTOWN Juniata
MIFFLINVILLE Columbia
MILAN Bradford
MILANVILLE Wayne
MILDRED Sullivan
MILESBURG Centre
MILFORD Pike
MILFORD SQUARE Bucks
MILL CREEK (17060) Huntingdon(87), Mifflin(12)
MILL HALL Clinton
MILL RUN Fayette
MILL VILLAGE Erie
MILLERSBURG Dauphin
MILLERSTOWN (17062) Perry(92), Juniata(7)
MILLERSVILLE Lancaster
MILLERTON (16936) Tioga(87), Bradford(12)
MILLHEIM Centre
MILLMONT Union
MILLRIFT Pike
MILLS Potter
MILLSBORO Washington
MILLVILLE (17846) Columbia(98), Lycoming(1)
MILNESVILLE Luzerne
MILROY Mifflin
MILTON (17847) Northumberland(96), Montour(3)
MINERAL POINT Cambria
MINERAL SPRINGS Clearfield
MINERSVILLE Schuylkill
MINGOVILLE Centre
MINISINK HILLS Monroe
MIQUON Montgomery
MODENA Chester
MOHNTON (19540) Berks(93), Lancaster(6)
MOHRSVILLE Berks
MONACA Beaver
MONESSEN Westmoreland
MONOCACY STATION Berks
MONONGAHELA (15063) Washington(96), Allegheny(3)
MONROETON Bradford
MONROEVILLE Allegheny
MONT ALTO Franklin
MONT CLARE Montgomery
MONTANDON Northumberland
MONTGOMERY Lycoming
MONTGOMERYVILLE Montgomery
MONTOURSVILLE Lycoming
MONTROSE Susquehanna
MOOSIC (18507) Lackawanna(98), Luzerne(1)
MORANN Clearfield
MORGAN Allegheny
MORGANTOWN (19543) Berks(76), Lancaster(20), Chester(3)
MORRIS (16938) Tioga(69), Lycoming(30)
MORRIS RUN Tioga
MORRISDALE Clearfield

MORRISVILLE Bucks
MORTON Delaware
MOSCOW (18444) Lackawanna(91), Wayne(8)
MOSHANNON Centre
MOUNT AETNA Berks
MOUNT BETHEL Northampton
MOUNT BRADDOCK Fayette
MOUNT CARMEL Northumberland
MOUNT GRETNA Lebanon
MOUNT HOLLY SPRINGS Cumberland
MOUNT JEWETT McKean
MOUNT JOY Lancaster
MOUNT MORRIS Greene
MOUNT PLEASANT (15666) Westmoreland(83), Fayette(16)
MOUNT PLEASANT MILLS (17853) Snyder(87), Juniata(12)
MOUNT POCONO Monroe
MOUNT UNION (17066) Huntingdon(67), Mifflin(32)
MOUNT WOLF York
MOUNTAIN TOP Luzerne
MOUNTAINHOME Monroe
MOUNTVILLE Lancaster
MUIR Schuylkill
MUNCY (17756) Lycoming(94), Northumberland(3), Montour(1)
MUNCY VALLEY (17758) Sullivan(67), Lycoming(32)
MUNSON (16860) Clearfield(76), Centre(23)
MURRYSVILLE Westmoreland
MUSE Washington
MYERSTOWN (17067) Lebanon(89), Berks(10)
NANTICOKE Luzerne
NANTY GLO Cambria
NARBERTH Montgomery
NARVON (17555) Lancaster(98), Berks(1)
NATRONA HEIGHTS Allegheny
NAZARETH Northampton
NEEDMORE Fulton
NEELYTON Huntingdon
NEFFS Lehigh
NELSON Tioga
NEMACOLIN Greene
NESCOPECK (18635) Luzerne(69), Columbia(30)
NESQUEHONING (18240) Carbon(85), Schuylkill(14)
NEW ALBANY (18833) Bradford(89), Sullivan(10)
NEW ALEXANDRIA Westmoreland
NEW BALTIMORE Somerset
NEW BEDFORD Lawrence
NEW BERLIN Union
NEW BERLINVILLE Berks
NEW BETHLEHEM (16242) Clarion(92), Armstrong(7)
NEW BLOOMFIELD Perry
NEW BRIGHTON Beaver
NEW BUFFALO Perry
NEW CASTLE Lawrence
NEW COLUMBIA Union
NEW CUMBERLAND (17070) Cumberland(58), York(41)
NEW DERRY Westmoreland
NEW EAGLE Washington
NEW ENTERPRISE Bedford
NEW FLORENCE (15944) Indiana(81), Westmoreland(18)
NEW FREEDOM York
NEW FREEPORT Greene
NEW GALILEE (16141) Beaver(66), Lawrence(33)
NEW GENEVA Fayette
NEW GERMANTOWN Perry
NEW HOLLAND Lancaster
NEW HOPE Bucks
NEW KENSINGTON Westmoreland
NEW KINGSTOWN Cumberland

NEW LONDON Chester
NEW MILFORD Susquehanna
NEW MILLPORT Clearfield
NEW OXFORD Adams
NEW PARIS Bedford
NEW PARK York
NEW PHILADELPHIA Schuylkill
NEW PROVIDENCE Lancaster
NEW RINGGOLD Schuylkill
NEW SALEM Fayette
NEW STANTON Westmoreland
NEW TRIPOLI Lehigh
NEW WILMINGTON Lawrence
NEWBURG (17240) Cumberland(72), Franklin(27)
NEWELL Fayette
NEWFOUNDLAND (18445) Wayne(82), Pike(16)
NEWMANSTOWN Lebanon
NEWPORT Perry
NEWRY Blair
NEWTON HAMILTON Mifflin
NEWTOWN Bucks
NEWTOWN SQUARE (19073) Delaware(97), Chester(2)
NEWVILLE Cumberland
NICHOLSON (18446) Wyoming(55), Susquehanna(41), Lackawanna(2)
NICKTOWN Cambria
NINEVEH Greene
NISBET Lycoming
NORMALVILLE Fayette
NORRISTOWN Chester
NORTH APOLLO Armstrong
NORTH BEND Clinton
NORTH EAST Erie
NORTH SPRINGFIELD Erie
NORTH VERSAILLES Allegheny
NORTH WALES Montgomery
NORTH WASHINGTON Butler
NORTHAMPTON Northampton
NORTHPOINT Indiana
NORTHUMBERLAND Northumberland
NORVELT Westmoreland
NORWOOD Delaware
NOTTINGHAM (19362) Chester(98), Lancaster(1)
NOXEN (18636) Wyoming(75), Luzerne(24)
NU MINE Armstrong
NUANGOLA Luzerne
NUMIDIA Columbia
NUREMBERG (18241) Luzerne(56), Schuylkill(43)
OAK RIDGE Armstrong
OAKDALE Allegheny
OAKLAND MILLS Juniata
OAKMONT Allegheny
OAKS Montgomery
OHIOPYLE Fayette
OIL CITY Venango
OLANTA Clearfield
OLD FORGE Lackawanna
OLD ZIONSVILLE Lehigh
OLEY Berks
OLIVEBURG Jefferson
OLIVER Fayette
OLYPHANT Lackawanna
ONEIDA Schuylkill
ONO Lebanon
ORANGEVILLE Columbia
ORBISONIA (17243) Huntingdon(95), Fulton(3), Juniata(1)
OREFIELD Lehigh
ORELAND Montgomery
ORRSTOWN Franklin
ORRTANNA Adams
ORSON Wayne
ORVISTON Centre
ORWIGSBURG Schuylkill
OSCEOLA Tioga

OSCEOLA MILLS (16666) Clearfield(91), Centre(7), Blair(1)
OSTERBURG Bedford
OTTSVILLE Bucks
OXFORD (19363) Chester(93), Lancaster(6)
PALM (18070) Montgomery(54), Berks(45)
PALMERTON Carbon
PALMYRA (17078) Lebanon(93), Dauphin(6)
PAOLI Chester
PARADISE Lancaster
PARDEESVILLE Luzerne
PARKER (16049) Clarion(81), Butler(14), Armstrong(3)
PARKER FORD Chester
PARKESBURG Chester
PARKHILL Cambria
PARRYVILLE Carbon
PATTON Cambria
PAUPACK Pike
PAXINOS Northumberland
PAXTONVILLE Snyder
PEACH BOTTOM Lancaster
PEACH GLEN Adams
PECKVILLE Lackawanna
PEN ARGYL Northampton
PENFIELD Clearfield
PENN Westmoreland
PENN RUN Indiana
PENNS CREEK Snyder
PENNS PARK Bucks
PENNSBURG (18073) Montgomery(91), Bucks(8)
PENNSYLVANIA FURNACE (16865) Centre(88), Huntingdon(11)
PENRYN Lancaster
PEQUEA Lancaster
PERKASIE Bucks
PERKIOMENVILLE Montgomery
PERRYOPOLIS Fayette
PETERSBURG Huntingdon
PETROLIA Butler
PHILADELPHIA Philadelphia
PHILIPSBURG (16866) Centre(59), Clearfield(40)
PHOENIXVILLE (19460) Chester(98), Montgomery(1)
PICTURE ROCKS Lycoming
PILLOW Dauphin
PINE BANK Greene
PINE FORGE Berks
PINE GROVE Schuylkill
PINE GROVE MILLS Centre
PINEVILLE Bucks
PIPERSVILLE Bucks
PITCAIRN Allegheny
PITMAN (17964) Schuylkill(92), Northumberland(7)
PITTSBURGH Allegheny
PITTSFIELD Warren
PITTSTON Luzerne
PLAINFIELD Cumberland
PLEASANT HALL Franklin
PLEASANT MOUNT Wayne
PLEASANT UNITY Westmoreland
PLEASANTVILLE (16341) Venango(92), Forest(7)
PLUMSTEADVILLE Bucks
PLUMVILLE Indiana
PLYMOUTH Luzerne
PLYMOUTH MEETING Montgomery
POCONO LAKE Monroe
POCONO LAKE PRESERVE Monroe
POCONO MANOR Monroe
POCONO PINES Monroe
POCONO SUMMIT Monroe
POCOPSON Chester
POINT MARION Fayette
POINT PLEASANT Bucks
POLK (16342) Venango(97), Mercer(2)
POMEROY Chester

PORT ALLEGANY (16743) McKean(86), Potter(13)
PORT CARBON Schuylkill
PORT CLINTON Schuylkill
PORT MATILDA Centre
PORT ROYAL Juniata
PORT TREVORTON Snyder
PORTAGE (15946) Cambria(94), Blair(2), Bedford(2)
PORTERS SIDELING York
PORTERSVILLE (16051) Butler(80), Lawrence(20)
PORTLAND Northampton
POTTERSDALE (16871) Clearfield(84), Clinton(15)
POTTS GROVE Northumberland
POTTSTOWN Chester
POTTSVILLE Schuylkill
POYNTELLE Wayne
PRESTO Allegheny
PRESTON PARK Wayne
PRICEDALE Westmoreland
PROMPTON Wayne
PROSPECT Butler
PROSPECT PARK Delaware
PROSPERITY (15329) Washington(84), Greene(15)
PULASKI (16143) Lawrence(59), Mercer(40)
PUNXSUTAWNEY (15767) Jefferson(91), Indiana(8)
QUAKAKE Schuylkill
QUAKERTOWN Bucks
QUARRYVILLE Lancaster
QUECREEK Somerset
QUEEN Bedford
QUENTIN Lebanon
QUINCY Franklin
RAILROAD York
RALSTON Lycoming
RAMEY Clearfield
RANSOM Lackawanna
RAVINE Schuylkill
REA Washington
READING Berks
REAMSTOWN Lancaster
REBERSBURG Centre
REBUCK Northumberland
RECTOR Westmoreland
RED HILL Montgomery
RED LION York
REEDERS Monroe
REEDSVILLE Mifflin
REFTON Lancaster
REHRERSBURG Berks
REINHOLDS (17569) Lancaster(80), Berks(19)
RENFREW Butler
RENO Venango
RENOVO Clinton
REPUBLIC Fayette
REVERE Bucks
REVLOC Cambria
REW McKean
REXMONT Lebanon
REYNOLDSVILLE Jefferson
RHEEMS Lancaster
RICES LANDING Greene
RICEVILLE Crawford
RICHBORO Bucks
RICHEYVILLE Washington
RICHFIELD (17086) Juniata(54), Snyder(45)
RICHLAND (17087) Berks(51), Lebanon(48)
RICHLANDTOWN Bucks
RIDDLESBURG Bedford
RIDGWAY Elk
RIDLEY PARK Delaware
RIEGELSVILLE (18077) Bucks(89), Northampton(10)
RILLTON Westmoreland

RIMERSBURG Clarion
RINGGOLD Jefferson
RINGTOWN Schuylkill
RIVERSIDE Northumberland
RIXFORD McKean
ROARING BRANCH (17765) Tioga(87), Lycoming(11)
ROARING SPRING (16673) Blair(69), Bedford(30)
ROBERTSDALE (16674) Huntingdon(98), Fulton(1)
ROBESONIA (19551) Berks(93), Lebanon(4), Lancaster(1)
ROBINSON Indiana
ROCHESTER Beaver
ROCHESTER MILLS Indiana
ROCK GLEN Luzerne
ROCKHILL FURNACE Huntingdon
ROCKTON Clearfield
ROCKWOOD Somerset
ROGERSVILLE Greene
ROME Bradford
RONCO Fayette
RONKS Lancaster
ROSCOE Washington
ROSSITER (15772) Indiana(98), Jefferson(1)
ROSSVILLE York
ROULETTE Potter
ROUSEVILLE Venango
ROUZERVILLE Franklin
ROWLAND Pike
ROXBURY Franklin
ROYERSFORD Montgomery
RUFFS DALE Westmoreland
RURAL RIDGE Allegheny
RURAL VALLEY Armstrong
RUSHLAND Bucks
RUSHVILLE Susquehanna
RUSSELL Warren
RUSSELLTON Allegheny
SABINSVILLE (16943) Tioga(80), Potter(19)
SACRAMENTO Schuylkill
SADSBURYVILLE Chester
SAEGERTOWN Crawford
SAGAMORE Armstrong
SAINT BENEDICT Cambria
SAINT BONIFACE Cambria
SAINT CLAIR Schuylkill
SAINT JOHNS Luzerne
SAINT MARYS Elk
SAINT MICHAEL Cambria
SAINT PETERS Chester
SAINT PETERSBURG Clarion
SAINT THOMAS Franklin
SALFORD Montgomery
SALFORDVILLE Montgomery
SALINA Westmoreland
SALISBURY Somerset
SALIX Cambria
SALONA Clinton
SALTILLO Huntingdon
SALTSBURG (15681) Indiana(97), Westmoreland(2)
SANDY LAKE Mercer
SANDY RIDGE Centre
SARVER (16055) Butler(94), Armstrong(4)
SASSAMANSVILLE Montgomery
SAXONBURG Butler
SAXTON (16678) Bedford(94), Huntingdon(5)
SAYLORSBURG Monroe
SAYRE Bradford
SCENERY HILL Washington
SCHAEFFERSTOWN Lebanon
SCHELLSBURG Bedford
SCHENLEY Armstrong
SCHNECKSVILLE Lehigh
SCHUYLKILL HAVEN Schuylkill
SCHWENKSVILLE Montgomery
SCIOTA Monroe

SCOTLAND Franklin
SCOTRUN Monroe
SCOTTDALE (15683) Westmoreland(85), Fayette(14)
SCRANTON Lackawanna
SEANOR Somerset
SELINSGROVE Snyder
SELLERSVILLE Bucks
SELTZER Schuylkill
SEMINOLE Armstrong
SENECA Venango
SEVEN VALLEYS York
SEWARD (15954) Indiana(90), Westmoreland(9)
SEWICKLEY Allegheny
SHADE GAP Huntingdon
SHADY GROVE Franklin
SHAMOKIN Northumberland
SHAMOKIN DAM Snyder
SHANKSVILLE Somerset
SHARON Mercer
SHARON HILL Delaware
SHARPSVILLE Mercer
SHARTLESVILLE Berks
SHAVERTOWN Luzerne
SHAWANESE Luzerne
SHAWNEE ON DELAWARE Monroe
SHAWVILLE Clearfield
SHEAKLEYVILLE Mercer
SHEFFIELD Warren
SHELOCTA (15774) Indiana(77), Armstrong(22)
SHENANDOAH Schuylkill
SHEPPTON Schuylkill
SHERMANS DALE (17090) Perry(93), Cumberland(6)
SHICKSHINNY (18655) Luzerne(92), Columbia(7)
SHINGLEHOUSE (16748) Potter(89), McKean(10)
SHIPPENSBURG (17257) Cumberland(63), Franklin(36)
SHIPPENVILLE Clarion
SHIPPINGPORT Beaver
SHIRLEYSBURG Huntingdon
SHOEMAKERSVILLE Berks
SHOHOLA Pike
SHREWSBURY York
SHUNK Sullivan
SIDMAN Cambria
SIGEL (15860) Jefferson(93), Clarion(5), Elk(1)
SILVER SPRING Lancaster
SILVERDALE Bucks
SINNAMAHONING Cameron
SIPESVILLE Somerset
SIX MILE RUN Bedford
SKIPPACK Montgomery
SKYTOP Monroe
SLATE RUN Lycoming
SLATEDALE Lehigh
SLATINGTON Lehigh
SLICKVILLE Westmoreland
SLIGO Clarion
SLIPPERY ROCK (16057) Butler(92), Lawrence(4), Mercer(2)
SLOVAN Washington
SMETHPORT McKean
SMICKSBURG (16256) Indiana(98), Jefferson(1)
SMITHFIELD Fayette
SMITHMILL Clearfield
SMITHTON Westmoreland
SMOCK Fayette
SMOKERUN Clearfield
SMOKETOWN Lancaster
SNOW SHOE Centre
SNYDERSBURG Clarion
SNYDERTOWN Northumberland
SOLEBURY Bucks
SOMERSET Somerset
SONESTOWN Sullivan

SOUDERSBURG Lancaster
SOUDERTON (18964) Montgomery(95), Bucks(4)
SOUTH CANAAN Wayne
SOUTH FORK Cambria
SOUTH GIBSON Susquehanna
SOUTH HEIGHTS Beaver
SOUTH MONTROSE Susquehanna
SOUTH MOUNTAIN Franklin
SOUTH PARK Allegheny
SOUTH STERLING Wayne
SOUTHAMPTON Bucks
SOUTHEASTERN Chester
SOUTHVIEW Washington
SOUTHWEST Westmoreland
SPANGLER Cambria
SPARTANSBURG (16434) Crawford(96), Warren(3)
SPINNERSTOWN Bucks
SPRAGGS Greene
SPRANKLE MILLS Jefferson
SPRING CHURCH Armstrong
SPRING CITY Chester
SPRING CREEK Warren
SPRING GLEN (17978) Schuylkill(98), Dauphin(1)
SPRING GROVE York
SPRING HOUSE Montgomery
SPRING MILLS Centre
SPRING MOUNT Montgomery
SPRING RUN Franklin
SPRINGBORO Crawford
SPRINGDALE Allegheny
SPRINGFIELD Delaware
SPRINGS Somerset
SPRINGTOWN Bucks
SPRINGVILLE (18844) Susquehanna(98), Wyoming(1)
SPROUL Blair
SPRUCE CREEK Huntingdon
STAHLSTOWN Westmoreland
STAR JUNCTION Fayette
STARFORD Indiana
STARLIGHT Wayne
STARRUCCA (18462) Wayne(97), Susquehanna(2)
STATE COLLEGE Centre
STATE LINE Franklin
STEELVILLE Chester
STERLING (18463) Wayne(70), Pike(29)
STEVENS Lancaster
STEVENSVILLE Bradford
STEWARTSTOWN York
STILLWATER (17878) Columbia(83), Luzerne(16)
STOCKDALE Washington
STOCKERTOWN Northampton
STONEBORO (16153) Mercer(97), Venango(2)
STONY RUN Berks
STOYSTOWN Somerset
STRABANE Washington
STRASBURG Lancaster
STRATTANVILLE Clarion
STRAUSSTOWN Berks
STRONGSTOWN (15957) Indiana(60), Cambria(39)
STROUDSBURG Monroe
STUMP CREEK Jefferson
STURGEON Allegheny
SUGAR GROVE Warren
SUGAR RUN Bradford
SUGARLOAF Luzerne
SUMMERDALE Cumberland
SUMMERHILL Cambria
SUMMERVILLE (15864) Clarion(84), Jefferson(15)
SUMMIT HILL Carbon
SUMMIT STATION Schuylkill
SUMNEYTOWN Montgomery
SUNBURY Northumberland
SUPLEE Chester

SUSQUEHANNA (18847) Susquehanna(97), Wayne(2)
SUTERSVILLE Westmoreland
SWARTHMORE Delaware
SWEET VALLEY Luzerne
SWENGEL Union
SWIFTWATER Monroe
SYBERTSVILLE Luzerne
SYCAMORE Greene
SYKESVILLE (15865) Jefferson(93), Clearfield(6)
SYLVANIA Bradford
TAFTON Pike
TALMAGE Lancaster
TAMAQUA Schuylkill
TAMIMENT Pike
TANNERSVILLE Monroe
TARENTUM Allegheny
TARRS Westmoreland
TATAMY Northampton
TAYLOR Lackawanna
TAYLORSTOWN Washington
TELFORD (18969) Montgomery(59), Bucks(40)
TEMPLE Berks
TEMPLETON Armstrong
TERRE HILL Lancaster
THOMASVILLE York
THOMPSON (18465) Susquehanna(87), Wayne(12)
THOMPSONTOWN Juniata
THORNDALE Chester
THORNTON Delaware
THREE SPRINGS (17264) Huntingdon(96), Fulton(3)
TIDIOUTE (16351) Warren(96), Forest(3)
TIMBLIN Jefferson
TIOGA Tioga
TIONA Warren
TIONESTA (16353) Clarion(72), Forest(15), Venango(11)
TIPTON Blair
TIRE HILL Somerset
TITUSVILLE (16354) Crawford(64), Venango(34)
TOBYHANNA Monroe
TODD Huntingdon
TOPTON Berks
TORRANCE Westmoreland
TOUGHKENAMON Chester
TOWANDA Bradford
TOWER CITY (17980) Schuylkill(95), Dauphin(4)
TOWNVILLE Crawford
TRAFFORD (15085) Westmoreland(98), Allegheny(1)
TRANSFER Mercer
TREICHLERS Northampton
TREMONT Schuylkill
TRESCKOW Carbon
TREVORTON Northumberland
TREXLERTOWN Lehigh
TROUT RUN Lycoming
TROUTVILLE Clearfield
TROXELVILLE Snyder
TROY (16947) Bradford(94), Tioga(5)
TRUMBAUERSVILLE Bucks
TUNKHANNOCK Wyoming
TURBOTVILLE (17772) Montour(68), Northumberland(29)
TURKEY CITY Clarion
TURTLE CREEK Allegheny
TURTLEPOINT McKean
TUSCARORA Schuylkill
TWIN ROCKS Cambria
TYLER HILL Wayne
TYLERSBURG Clarion
TYLERSPORT Montgomery
TYLERSVILLE Clinton
TYRONE (16686) Blair(73), Huntingdon(20), Centre(6)
ULEDI Fayette

ULSTER Bradford
ULYSSES Potter
UNION CITY (16438) Crawford(60), Erie(39)
UNION DALE (18470) Susquehanna(92), Wayne(7)
UNIONTOWN Fayette
UNIONVILLE Chester
UNITED Westmoreland
UNITY HOUSE Pike
UNITYVILLE (17774) Lycoming(98), Columbia(1)
UNIVERSITY PARK Centre
UPPER BLACK EDDY Bucks
UPPER DARBY Delaware
UPPERSTRASBURG Franklin
URSINA Somerset
UTICA (16362) Venango(86), Mercer(11), Crawford(1)
UWCHLAND Chester
VALENCIA (16059) Butler(92), Allegheny(7)
VALIER Jefferson
VALLEY FORGE Chester
VALLEY VIEW Schuylkill
VAN VOORHIS Washington
VANDERBILT Fayette
VANDERGRIFT (15690) Westmoreland(63), Armstrong(36)
VENANGO Crawford
VENETIA Washington
VENUS (16364) Venango(69), Clarion(30)
VERONA Allegheny
VESTABURG Washington
VICKSBURG Union
VILLA MARIA Lawrence
VILLANOVA (19085) Delaware(53), Montgomery(46)
VINTONDALE (15961) Indiana(92), Cambria(7)
VIRGINVILLE Berks
VOLANT (16156) Lawrence(51), Mercer(48)
VOWINCKEL (16260) Clarion(95), Forest(4)
WAGONTOWN Chester
WALLACETON Clearfield
WALLINGFORD Delaware
WALNUT BOTTOM Cumberland

WALNUTPORT Northampton
WALSTON Jefferson
WALTERSBURG Fayette
WAMPUM (16157) Lawrence(65), Beaver(34)
WAPWALLOPEN Luzerne
WARFORDSBURG Fulton
WARMINSTER Bucks
WARREN Warren
WARREN CENTER Bradford
WARRENDALE Allegheny
WARRINGTON Bucks
WARRIORS MARK (16877) Centre(50), Huntingdon(49)
WASHINGTON Washington
WASHINGTON BORO Lancaster
WASHINGTON CROSSING Bucks
WASHINGTONVILLE Montour
WATERFALL Fulton
WATERFORD (16441) Erie(94), Crawford(5)
WATERVILLE Lycoming
WATSONTOWN (17777) Northumberland(96), Montour(3)
WATTSBURG Erie
WAVERLY Lackawanna
WAYMART Wayne
WAYNE Delaware
WAYNESBORO Franklin
WAYNESBURG Greene
WEATHERLY (18255) Carbon(98), Luzerne(1)
WEBSTER Westmoreland
WEEDVILLE Elk
WEIKERT Union
WELLERSBURG Somerset
WELLS TANNERY Fulton
WELLSBORO Tioga
WELLSVILLE York
WENDEL Westmoreland
WERNERSVILLE Berks
WEST ALEXANDER Washington
WEST CHESTER Chester
WEST DECATUR Clearfield
WEST ELIZABETH Allegheny
WEST FINLEY (15377) Washington(90), Greene(9)
WEST GROVE Chester
WEST HICKORY Forest

WEST LEBANON Indiana
WEST LEISENRING Fayette
WEST MIDDLESEX (16159) Mercer(96), Lawrence(3)
WEST MIDDLETOWN Washington
WEST MIFFLIN Allegheny
WEST MILTON Union
WEST NEWTON (15089) Westmoreland(97), Allegheny(2)
WEST PITTSBURG Lawrence
WEST POINT Montgomery
WEST SALISBURY Somerset
WEST SPRINGFIELD Erie
WEST SUNBURY Butler
WEST WILLOW Lancaster
WESTFIELD Tioga
WESTLAND Washington
WESTLINE McKean
WESTMORELAND CITY Westmoreland
WESTON Luzerne
WESTOVER Clearfield
WESTPORT Clinton
WESTTOWN Chester
WEXFORD Allegheny
WHEATLAND Mercer
WHITE Fayette
WHITE DEER Union
WHITE HAVEN (18661) Luzerne(92), Carbon(7)
WHITE MILLS Wayne
WHITEHALL Lehigh
WHITNEY Westmoreland
WICKHAVEN Fayette
WICONISCO Dauphin
WIDNOON Armstrong
WILBURTON Columbia
WILCOX (15870) McKean(52), Elk(47)
WILDWOOD Allegheny
WILKES BARRE Luzerne
WILLIAMSBURG (16693) Blair(98), Huntingdon(1)
WILLIAMSON Franklin
WILLIAMSPORT Lycoming
WILLIAMSTOWN Dauphin
WILLOW GROVE Montgomery
WILLOW HILL Franklin
WILLOW STREET Lancaster
WILMERDING Allegheny
WILMORE Cambria

WINBURNE Clearfield
WIND GAP Northampton
WIND RIDGE Greene
WINDBER (15963) Somerset(85), Cambria(14)
WINDSOR York
WINFIELD (17889) Union(59), Snyder(40)
WITMER Lancaster
WOMELSDORF Berks
WOOD Bedford
WOODBURY Bedford
WOODLAND Clearfield
WOODLYN Delaware
WOODWARD Centre
WOOLRICH Clinton
WORCESTER Montgomery
WORTHINGTON (16262) Armstrong(97), Butler(2)
WORTHVILLE Jefferson
WOXALL Montgomery
WRIGHTSVILLE York
WYALUSING Bradford
WYANO Westmoreland
WYCOMBE Bucks
WYNCOTE Montgomery
WYNNEWOOD (19096) Montgomery(95), Delaware(4)
WYOMING Luzerne
WYSOX Bradford
YATESBORO Armstrong
YEAGERTOWN Mifflin
YORK York
YORK HAVEN York
YORK NEW SALEM York
YORK SPRINGS (17372) Adams(96), York(3)
YOUNGSTOWN Westmoreland
YOUNGSVILLE Warren
YOUNGWOOD Westmoreland
YUKON Westmoreland
ZELIENOPLE (16063) Butler(84), Beaver(15)
ZIEGLERVILLE Montgomery
ZION GROVE (17985) Schuylkill(94), Columbia(5)
ZIONHILL Bucks
ZIONSVILLE (18092) Lehigh(95), Berks(4)
ZULLINGER Franklin

ZIP/City Cross Reference

ZIP Range	City
15001-15001	ALIQUIPPA
15003-15003	AMBRIDGE
15004-15004	ATLASBURG
15005-15005	BADEN
15006-15006	BAIRDFORD
15007-15007	BAKERSTOWN
15009-15009	BEAVER
15010-15010	BEAVER FALLS
15012-15012	BELLE VERNON
15014-15014	BRACKENRIDGE
15015-15015	BRADFORDWOODS
15017-15017	BRIDGEVILLE
15018-15018	BUENA VISTA
15019-15019	BULGER
15020-15020	BUNOLA
15021-15021	BURGETTSTOWN
15022-15022	CHARLEROI
15024-15024	CHESWICK
15025-15025	CLAIRTON
15026-15026	CLINTON
15027-15027	CONWAY
15028-15028	COULTERS
15029-15029	COURTNEY
15030-15030	CREIGHTON
15031-15031	CUDDY
15032-15032	CURTISVILLE
15033-15033	DONORA
15034-15034	DRAVOSBURG
15035-15035	EAST MC KEESPORT
15036-15036	ELDERSVILLE
15037-15037	ELIZABETH
15038-15038	ELRAMA
15042-15042	FREEDOM
15043-15043	GEORGETOWN
15044-15044	GIBSONIA
15045-15045	GLASSPORT
15046-15046	GLENWILLARD
15046-15046	CRESCENT
15047-15047	GREENOCK
15049-15049	HARWICK
15050-15050	HOOKSTOWN
15051-15051	INDIANOLA
15052-15052	INDUSTRY
15053-15053	JOFFRE
15054-15054	LANGELOTH
15055-15055	LAWRENCE
15056-15056	LEETSDALE
15057-15057	MC DONALD
15059-15059	MIDLAND
15060-15060	MIDWAY
15061-15061	MONACA
15062-15062	MONESSEN
15063-15063	MONONGAHELA
15064-15064	MORGAN
15065-15065	NATRONA HEIGHTS
15066-15066	NEW BRIGHTON
15067-15067	NEW EAGLE
15068-15069	NEW KENSINGTON
15071-15071	OAKDALE
15072-15072	PRICEDALE
15074-15074	ROCHESTER
15075-15075	RURAL RIDGE
15076-15076	RUSSELLTON
15077-15077	SHIPPINGPORT
15078-15078	SLOVAN
15081-15081	SOUTH HEIGHTS
15082-15082	STURGEON
15083-15083	SUTERSVILLE
15084-15084	TARENTUM
15085-15085	TRAFFORD
15086-15086	WARRENDALE
15087-15087	WEBSTER
15088-15088	WEST ELIZABETH
15089-15089	WEST NEWTON
15090-15090	WEXFORD
15091-15091	WILDWOOD
15095-15096	WARRENDALE
15101-15101	ALLISON PARK
15102-15102	BETHEL PARK
15104-15104	BRADDOCK
15106-15106	CARNEGIE
15108-15108	CORAOPOLIS
15110-15110	DUQUESNE
15112-15112	EAST PITTSBURGH
15116-15116	GLENSHAW
15120-15120	HOMESTEAD
15122-15123	WEST MIFFLIN
15126-15126	IMPERIAL
15127-15127	INGOMAR
15129-15129	LIBRARY
15129-15129	SOUTH PARK
15130-15135	MC KEESPORT
15136-15136	MC KEES ROCKS
15137-15137	NORTH VERSAILLES
15139-15139	OAKMONT
15140-15140	PITCAIRN
15142-15142	PRESTO
15143-15143	SEWICKLEY
15144-15144	SPRINGDALE
15145-15145	TURTLE CREEK
15146-15146	MONROEVILLE
15147-15147	VERONA
15148-15148	WILMERDING
15189-15189	SEWICKLEY
15200-15295	PITTSBURGH
15301-15301	WASHINGTON
15310-15310	ALEPPO
15311-15311	AMITY
15312-15312	AVELLA
15313-15313	BEALLSVILLE
15314-15314	BENTLEYVILLE
15315-15315	BOBTOWN

15316-15316 BRAVE	15442-15442 GRINDSTONE	15564-15564 WELLERSBURG	15713-15713 AULTMAN
15317-15317 CANONSBURG	15443-15443 HIBBS	15565-15565 WEST SALISBURY	15714-15714 BARNESBORO
15320-15320 CARMICHAELS	15444-15444 HILLER	15601-15606 GREENSBURG	15715-15715 BIG RUN
15321-15321 CECIL	15445-15445 HOPWOOD	15610-15610 ACME	15716-15716 BLACK LICK
15322-15322 CLARKSVILLE	15446-15446 INDIAN HEAD	15611-15611 ADAMSBURG	15717-15717 BLAIRSVILLE
15323-15323 CLAYSVILLE	15447-15447 ISABELLA	15612-15612 ALVERTON	15720-15720 BRUSH VALLEY
15324-15324 COKEBURG	15448-15448 JACOBS CREEK	15613-15613 APOLLO	15721-15721 BURNSIDE
15325-15325 CRUCIBLE	15449-15449 KEISTERVILLE	15615-15615 ARDARA	15722-15722 CARROLLTOWN
15327-15327 DILLINER	15450-15450 LA BELLE	15616-15616 ARMBRUST	15723-15723 CHAMBERSVILLE
15329-15329 PROSPERITY	15451-15451 LAKE LYNN	15617-15617 ARONA	15724-15724 CHERRY TREE
15330-15330 EIGHTY FOUR	15454-15454 LECKRONE	15618-15618 AVONMORE	15725-15725 CLARKSBURG
15331-15331 ELLSWORTH	15455-15455 LEISENRING	15619-15619 BOVARD	15727-15727 CLUNE
15332-15332 FINLEYVILLE	15456-15456 LEMONT FURNACE	15620-15620 BRADENVILLE	15728-15728 CLYMER
15333-15333 FREDERICKTOWN	15458-15458 MC CLELLANDTOWN	15621-15621 CALUMET	15729-15729 COMMODORE
15334-15334 GARARDS FORT	15459-15459 MARKLEYSBURG	15622-15622 CHAMPION	15730-15730 COOLSPRING
15336-15336 GASTONVILLE	15460-15460 MARTIN	15623-15623 CLARIDGE	15731-15731 CORAL
15337-15337 GRAYSVILLE	15461-15461 MASONTOWN	15624-15624 CRABTREE	15732-15732 CREEKSIDE
15338-15338 GREENSBORO	15462-15462 MELCROFT	15625-15625 DARRAGH	15733-15733 DE LANCEY
15339-15339 HENDERSONVILLE	15463-15463 MERRITTSTOWN	15626-15626 DELMONT	15734-15734 DIXONVILLE
15340-15340 HICKORY	15464-15464 MILL RUN	15627-15627 DERRY	15736-15736 ELDERTON
15341-15341 HOLBROOK	15465-15465 MOUNT BRADDOCK	15628-15628 DONEGAL	15737-15737 ELMORA
15342-15342 HOUSTON	15466-15466 NEWELL	15629-15629 EAST VANDERGRIFT	15738-15738 EMEIGH
15344-15344 JEFFERSON	15467-15467 NEW GENEVA	15630-15630 EDMON	15739-15739 ERNEST
15345-15345 MARIANNA	15468-15468 NEW SALEM	15631-15631 EVERSON	15740-15740 FROSTBURG
15346-15346 MATHER	15469-15469 NORMALVILLE	15632-15632 EXPORT	15741-15741 GIPSY
15347-15347 MEADOW LANDS	15470-15470 OHIOPYLE	15633-15633 FORBES ROAD	15742-15742 GLEN CAMPBELL
15348-15348 MILLSBORO	15472-15472 OLIVER	15634-15634 GRAPEVILLE	15744-15744 HAMILTON
15349-15349 MOUNT MORRIS	15473-15473 PERRYOPOLIS	15635-15635 HANNASTOWN	15745-15745 HEILWOOD
15350-15350 MUSE	15474-15474 POINT MARION	15636-15636 HARRISON CITY	15746-15746 HILLSDALE
15351-15351 NEMACOLIN	15475-15475 REPUBLIC	15637-15637 HERMINIE	15747-15747 HOME
15352-15352 NEW FREEPORT	15476-15476 RONCO	15638-15638 HOSTETTER	15748-15748 HOMER CITY
15353-15353 NINEVEH	15477-15477 ROSCOE	15639-15639 HUNKER	15750-15750 JOSEPHINE
15354-15354 PINE BANK	15478-15478 SMITHFIELD	15640-15640 HUTCHINSON	15751-15751 JUNEAU
15356-15356 REA	15479-15479 SMITHTON	15641-15641 HYDE PARK	15752-15752 KENT
15357-15357 RICES LANDING	15480-15480 SMOCK	15642-15642 IRWIN	15753-15753 LA JOSE
15358-15358 RICHEYVILLE	15482-15482 STAR JUNCTION	15644-15644 JEANNETTE	15754-15754 LUCERNEMINES
15359-15359 ROGERSVILLE	15483-15483 STOCKDALE	15646-15646 JONES MILLS	15756-15756 MC INTYRE
15360-15360 SCENERY HILL	15484-15484 ULEDI	15647-15647 LARIMER	15757-15757 MAHAFFEY
15361-15361 SOUTHVIEW	15485-15485 URSINA	15650-15650 LATROBE	15758-15758 MARCHAND
15362-15362 SPRAGGS	15486-15486 VANDERBILT	15655-15655 LAUGHLINTOWN	15759-15759 MARION CENTER
15363-15363 STRABANE	15488-15488 WALTERSBURG	15656-15656 LEECHBURG	15760-15760 MARSTELLER
15364-15364 SYCAMORE	15489-15489 WEST LEISENRING	15658-15658 LIGONIER	15761-15761 MENTCLE
15365-15365 TAYLORSTOWN	15490-15490 WHITE	15660-15660 LOWBER	15762-15762 NICKTOWN
15366-15366 VAN VOORHIS	15492-15492 WICKHAVEN	15661-15661 LOYALHANNA	15763-15763 NORTHPOINT
15367-15367 VENETIA	15501-15501 SOMERSET	15662-15662 LUXOR	15764-15764 OLIVEBURG
15368-15368 VESTABURG	15502-15502 HIDDEN VALLEY	15663-15663 MADISON	15765-15765 PENN RUN
15370-15370 WAYNESBURG	15510-15510 SOMERSET	15664-15664 MAMMOTH	15767-15767 PUNXSUTAWNEY
15376-15376 WEST ALEXANDER	15520-15520 ACOSTA	15665-15665 MANOR	15770-15770 RINGGOLD
15377-15377 WEST FINLEY	15521-15521 ALUM BANK	15666-15666 MOUNT PLEASANT	15771-15771 ROCHESTER MILLS
15378-15378 WESTLAND	15522-15522 BEDFORD	15668-15668 MURRYSVILLE	15772-15772 ROSSITER
15379-15379 WEST MIDDLETOWN	15530-15530 BERLIN	15670-15670 NEW ALEXANDRIA	15773-15773 SAINT BENEDICT
15380-15380 WIND RIDGE	15531-15531 BOSWELL	15671-15671 NEW DERRY	15774-15774 SHELOCTA
15401-15401 UNIONTOWN	15532-15532 BOYNTON	15672-15672 NEW STANTON	15775-15775 SPANGLER
15410-15410 ADAH	15533-15533 BREEZEWOOD	15673-15673 NORTH APOLLO	15776-15776 SPRANKLE MILLS
15411-15411 ADDISON	15534-15534 BUFFALO MILLS	15674-15674 NORVELT	15777-15777 STARFORD
15412-15412 ALLENPORT	15535-15535 CLEARVILLE	15675-15675 PENN	15778-15778 TIMBLIN
15413-15413 ALLISON	15536-15536 CRYSTAL SPRING	15676-15676 PLEASANT UNITY	15779-15779 TORRANCE
15415-15415 BRIER HILL	15537-15537 EVERETT	15677-15677 RECTOR	15780-15780 VALIER
15416-15416 BROWNFIELD	15538-15538 FAIRHOPE	15678-15678 RILLTON	15781-15781 WALSTON
15417-15417 BROWNSVILLE	15539-15539 FISHERTOWN	15679-15679 RUFFS DALE	15783-15783 WEST LEBANON
15419-15419 CALIFORNIA	15540-15540 FORT HILL	15680-15680 SALINA	15784-15784 WORTHVILLE
15420-15420 CARDALE	15541-15541 FRIEDENS	15681-15681 SALTSBURG	15801-15801 DU BOIS
15421-15421 CHALKHILL	15542-15542 GARRETT	15682-15682 SCHENLEY	15821-15821 BENEZETT
15421-15421 CHALK HILL	15544-15544 GRAY	15683-15683 SCOTTDALE	15822-15822 BRANDY CAMP
15422-15422 CHESTNUT RIDGE	15545-15545 HYNDMAN	15684-15684 SLICKVILLE	15823-15823 BROCKPORT
15423-15423 COAL CENTER	15546-15546 JENNERS	15685-15685 SOUTHWEST	15824-15824 BROCKWAY
15424-15424 CONFLUENCE	15547-15547 JENNERSTOWN	15686-15686 SPRING CHURCH	15825-15825 BROOKVILLE
15425-15425 CONNELLSVILLE	15548-15548 KANTNER	15687-15687 STAHLSTOWN	15827-15827 BYRNEDALE
15427-15427 DAISYTOWN	15549-15549 LISTIE	15688-15688 TARRS	15828-15828 CLARINGTON
15428-15428 DAWSON	15550-15550 MANNS CHOICE	15689-15689 UNITED	15829-15829 CORSICA
15429-15429 DENBO	15551-15551 MARKLETON	15690-15690 VANDERGRIFT	15831-15831 DAGUS MINES
15430-15430 DICKERSON RUN	15552-15552 MEYERSDALE	15691-15691 WENDEL	15832-15832 DRIFTWOOD
15431-15431 DUNBAR	15553-15553 NEW BALTIMORE	15692-15692 WESTMORELAND CITY	15834-15834 EMPORIUM
15432-15432 DUNLEVY	15554-15554 NEW PARIS	15693-15693 WHITNEY	15840-15840 FALLS CREEK
15433-15433 EAST MILLSBORO	15555-15555 QUECREEK	15695-15695 WYANO	15841-15841 FORCE
15434-15434 ELCO	15557-15557 ROCKWOOD	15696-15696 YOUNGSTOWN	15845-15845 JOHNSONBURG
15435-15435 FAIRBANK	15558-15558 SALISBURY	15697-15697 YOUNGWOOD	15846-15846 KERSEY
15436-15436 FAIRCHANCE	15559-15559 SCHELLSBURG	15698-15698 YUKON	15847-15847 KNOX DALE
15437-15437 FARMINGTON	15560-15560 SHANKSVILLE	15701-15705 INDIANA	15848-15848 LUTHERSBURG
15438-15438 FAYETTE CITY	15561-15561 SIPESVILLE	15710-15710 ALVERDA	15849-15849 PENFIELD
15439-15439 GANS	15562-15562 SPRINGS	15711-15711 ANITA	15851-15851 REYNOLDSVILLE
15440-15440 GIBBON GLADE	15563-15563 STOYSTOWN	15712-15712 ARCADIA	15853-15853 RIDGWAY

15856-15856 ROCKTON
15857-15857 SAINT MARYS
15860-15860 SIGEL
15861-15861 SINNAMAHONING
15863-15863 STUMP CREEK
15864-15864 SUMMERVILLE
15865-15865 SYKESVILLE
15866-15866 TROUTVILLE
15868-15868 WEEDVILLE
15870-15870 WILCOX
15901-15915 JOHNSTOWN
15920-15920 ARMAGH
15921-15921 BEAVERDALE
15922-15922 BELSANO
15923-15923 BOLIVAR
15924-15924 CAIRNBROOK
15925-15925 CASSANDRA
15926-15926 CENTRAL CITY
15927-15927 COLVER
15928-15928 DAVIDSVILLE
15929-15929 DILLTOWN
15930-15930 DUNLO
15931-15931 EBENSBURG
15934-15934 ELTON
15935-15935 HOLLSOPPLE
15936-15936 HOOVERSVILLE
15937-15937 JEROME
15938-15938 LILLY
15940-15940 LORETTO
15942-15942 MINERAL POINT
15943-15943 NANTY GLO
15944-15944 NEW FLORENCE
15945-15945 PARKHILL
15946-15946 PORTAGE
15948-15948 REVLOC
15949-15949 ROBINSON
15951-15951 SAINT MICHAEL
15952-15952 SALIX
15953-15953 SEANOR
15954-15954 SEWARD
15955-15955 SIDMAN
15956-15956 SOUTH FORK
15957-15957 STRONGSTOWN
15958-15958 SUMMERHILL
15959-15959 TIRE HILL
15960-15960 TWIN ROCKS
15961-15961 VINTONDALE
15962-15962 WILMORE
15963-15963 WINDBER
16001-16003 BUTLER
16016-16020 BOYERS
16021-16021 BRANCHTON
16022-16022 BRUIN
16023-16023 CABOT
16024-16024 CALLERY
16025-16025 CHICORA
16027-16027 CONNOQUENESSING
16028-16028 EAST BRADY
16029-16029 EAST BUTLER
16030-16030 EAU CLAIRE
16033-16033 EVANS CITY
16034-16034 FENELTON
16035-16035 FORESTVILLE
16036-16036 FOXBURG
16037-16037 HARMONY
16038-16038 HARRISVILLE
16039-16039 HERMAN
16040-16040 HILLIARDS
16041-16041 KARNS CITY
16045-16045 LYNDORA
16046-16046 MARS
16048-16048 NORTH WASHINGTON
16049-16049 PARKER
16050-16050 PETROLIA
16051-16051 PORTERSVILLE
16052-16052 PROSPECT
16053-16053 RENFREW
16054-16054 SAINT PETERSBURG
16055-16055 SARVER
16056-16056 SAXONBURG
16057-16057 SLIPPERY ROCK
16058-16058 TURKEY CITY

16059-16059 VALENCIA
16061-16061 WEST SUNBURY
16063-16063 ZELIENOPLE
16066-16066 CRANBERRY TWP
16101-16108 NEW CASTLE
16110-16110 ADAMSVILLE
16111-16111 ATLANTIC
16112-16112 BESSEMER
16113-16113 CLARK
16114-16114 CLARKS MILLS
16115-16115 DARLINGTON
16116-16116 EDINBURG
16117-16117 ELLWOOD CITY
16120-16120 ENON VALLEY
16121-16121 FARRELL
16123-16123 FOMBELL
16124-16124 FREDONIA
16125-16125 GREENVILLE
16127-16127 GROVE CITY
16130-16130 HADLEY
16131-16131 HARTSTOWN
16132-16132 HILLSVILLE
16133-16133 JACKSON CENTER
16134-16134 JAMESTOWN
16136-16136 KOPPEL
16137-16137 MERCER
16140-16140 NEW BEDFORD
16141-16141 NEW GALILEE
16142-16142 NEW WILMINGTON
16143-16143 PULASKI
16145-16145 SANDY LAKE
16146-16146 SHARON
16148-16148 HERMITAGE
16150-16150 SHARPSVILLE
16151-16151 SHEAKLEYVILLE
16153-16153 STONEBORO
16154-16154 TRANSFER
16155-16155 VILLA MARIA
16156-16156 VOLANT
16157-16157 WAMPUM
16159-16159 WEST MIDDLESEX
16160-16160 WEST PITTSBURG
16161-16161 WHEATLAND
16172-16172 NEW WILMINGTON
16201-16201 KITTANNING
16210-16210 ADRIAN
16211-16211 BEYER
16212-16212 CADOGAN
16213-16213 CALLENSBURG
16214-16214 CLARION
16215-16215 KITTANNING
16216-16216 CLIMAX
16217-16217 COOKSBURG
16218-16218 COWANSVILLE
16220-16220 CROWN
16221-16221 CURLLSVILLE
16222-16222 DAYTON
16223-16223 DISTANT
16224-16224 FAIRMOUNT CITY
16225-16225 FISHER
16226-16226 FORD CITY
16228-16228 FORD CLIFF
16229-16229 FREEPORT
16230-16230 HAWTHORN
16232-16232 KNOX
16233-16233 LEEPER
16234-16234 LIMESTONE
16235-16235 LUCINDA
16236-16236 MC GRANN
16238-16238 MANORVILLE
16239-16239 MARIENVILLE
16240-16240 MAYPORT
16242-16242 NEW BETHLEHEM
16244-16244 NU MINE
16245-16245 OAK RIDGE
16246-16246 PLUMVILLE
16248-16248 RIMERSBURG
16249-16249 RURAL VALLEY
16250-16250 SAGAMORE
16253-16253 SEMINOLE
16254-16254 SHIPPENVILLE
16255-16255 SLIGO

16256-16256 SMICKSBURG
16257-16257 SNYDERSBURG
16258-16258 STRATTANVILLE
16259-16259 TEMPLETON
16260-16260 VOWINCKEL
16261-16261 WIDNOON
16262-16262 WORTHINGTON
16263-16263 YATESBORO
16301-16301 OIL CITY
16311-16311 CARLTON
16312-16312 CHANDLERS VALLEY
16313-16313 CLARENDON
16314-16314 COCHRANTON
16316-16316 CONNEAUT LAKE
16317-16317 COOPERSTOWN
16319-16319 CRANBERRY
16321-16321 EAST HICKORY
16322-16322 ENDEAVOR
16323-16323 FRANKLIN
16326-16326 FRYBURG
16327-16327 GUYS MILLS
16328-16328 HYDETOWN
16329-16329 IRVINE
16331-16331 KOSSUTH
16332-16332 LICKINGVILLE
16333-16333 LUDLOW
16334-16334 MARBLE
16335-16335 MEADVILLE
16340-16340 PITTSFIELD
16341-16341 PLEASANTVILLE
16342-16342 POLK
16343-16343 RENO
16344-16344 ROUSEVILLE
16345-16345 RUSSELL
16346-16346 SENECA
16347-16347 SHEFFIELD
16350-16350 SUGAR GROVE
16351-16351 TIDIOUTE
16352-16352 TIONA
16353-16353 TIONESTA
16354-16354 TITUSVILLE
16360-16360 TOWNVILLE
16361-16361 TYLERSBURG
16362-16362 UTICA
16364-16364 VENUS
16365-16367 WARREN
16368-16368 IRVINE
16368-16368 WARREN
16369-16369 IRVINE
16369-16369 WARREN
16370-16370 WEST HICKORY
16371-16371 YOUNGSVILLE
16372-16372 CLINTONVILLE
16373-16373 EMLENTON
16374-16374 KENNERDELL
16375-16375 LAMARTINE
16388-16388 MEADVILLE
16401-16401 ALBION
16402-16402 BEAR LAKE
16403-16403 CAMBRIDGE SPRINGS
16404-16404 CENTERVILLE
16405-16405 COLUMBUS
16406-16406 CONNEAUTVILLE
16407-16407 CORRY
16410-16410 CRANESVILLE
16411-16411 EAST SPRINGFIELD
16412-16412 EDINBORO
16413-16413 ELGIN
16415-16415 FAIRVIEW
16416-16416 GARLAND
16417-16417 GIRARD
16420-16420 GRAND VALLEY
16421-16421 HARBORCREEK
16422-16422 HARMONSBURG
16423-16423 LAKE CITY
16424-16424 LINESVILLE
16426-16426 MC KEAN
16427-16427 MILL VILLAGE
16428-16428 NORTH EAST
16430-16430 NORTH SPRINGFIELD
16432-16432 RICEVILLE
16433-16433 SAEGERTOWN

16434-16434 SPARTANSBURG
16435-16435 SPRINGBORO
16436-16436 SPRING CREEK
16438-16438 UNION CITY
16440-16440 VENANGO
16441-16441 WATERFORD
16442-16442 WATTSBURG
16443-16443 WEST SPRINGFIELD
16444-16444 EDINBORO
16475-16475 ALBION
16500-16565 ERIE
16566-16566 FIRST NAT BANK
16601-16603 ALTOONA
16611-16611 ALEXANDRIA
16613-16613 ASHVILLE
16614-16614 BAKERS SUMMIT
16616-16616 BECCARIA
16617-16617 BELLWOOD
16619-16619 BLANDBURG
16620-16620 BRISBIN
16621-16621 BROAD TOP
16622-16622 CALVIN
16623-16623 CASSVILLE
16624-16624 CHEST SPRINGS
16625-16625 CLAYSBURG
16627-16627 COALPORT
16629-16629 COUPON
16630-16630 CRESSON
16631-16631 CURRYVILLE
16633-16633 DEFIANCE
16634-16634 DUDLEY
16635-16635 DUNCANSVILLE
16636-16636 DYSART
16637-16637 EAST FREEDOM
16638-16638 ENTRIKEN
16639-16639 FALLENTIMBER
16640-16640 FLINTON
16641-16641 GALLITZIN
16644-16644 GLASGOW
16645-16645 GLEN HOPE
16646-16646 HASTINGS
16647-16647 HESSTON
16648-16648 HOLLIDAYSBURG
16650-16650 HOPEWELL
16651-16651 HOUTZDALE
16652-16652 HUNTINGDON
16655-16655 IMLER
16656-16656 IRVONA
16657-16657 JAMES CREEK
16659-16659 LOYSBURG
16660-16660 MC CONNELLSTOWN
16661-16661 MADERA
16662-16662 MARTINSBURG
16663-16663 MORANN
16664-16664 NEW ENTERPRISE
16665-16665 NEWRY
16666-16666 OSCEOLA MILLS
16667-16667 OSTERBURG
16668-16668 PATTON
16669-16669 PETERSBURG
16670-16670 QUEEN
16671-16671 RAMEY
16672-16672 RIDDLESBURG
16673-16673 ROARING SPRING
16674-16674 ROBERTSDALE
16675-16675 SAINT BONIFACE
16677-16677 SANDY RIDGE
16678-16678 SAXTON
16679-16679 SIX MILE RUN
16680-16680 SMITHMILL
16681-16681 SMOKERUN
16682-16682 SPROUL
16683-16683 SPRUCE CREEK
16684-16684 TIPTON
16685-16685 TODD
16686-16686 TYRONE
16689-16689 WATERFALL
16691-16691 WELLS TANNERY
16692-16692 WESTOVER
16693-16693 WILLIAMSBURG
16694-16694 WOOD
16695-16695 WOODBURY

ZIP Range	Town
16698-16698	HOUTZDALE
16699-16699	CRESSON
16701-16701	BRADFORD
16720-16720	AUSTIN
16724-16724	CROSBY
16725-16725	CUSTER CITY
16726-16726	CYCLONE
16727-16727	DERRICK CITY
16728-16728	DE YOUNG
16729-16729	DUKE CENTER
16730-16730	EAST SMETHPORT
16731-16731	ELDRED
16732-16732	GIFFORD
16733-16733	HAZEL HURST
16734-16734	JAMES CITY
16735-16735	KANE
16738-16738	LEWIS RUN
16740-16740	MOUNT JEWETT
16743-16743	PORT ALLEGANY
16744-16744	REW
16745-16745	RIXFORD
16746-16746	ROULETTE
16748-16748	SHINGLEHOUSE
16749-16749	SMETHPORT
16750-16750	TURTLEPOINT
16751-16751	WESTLINE
16801-16801	STATE COLLEGE
16802-16802	UNIVERSITY PARK
16803-16805	STATE COLLEGE
16820-16820	AARONSBURG
16821-16821	ALLPORT
16822-16822	BEECH CREEK
16823-16823	BELLEFONTE
16825-16825	BIGLER
16826-16826	BLANCHARD
16827-16827	BOALSBURG
16828-16828	CENTRE HALL
16829-16829	CLARENCE
16830-16830	CLEARFIELD
16832-16832	COBURN
16833-16833	CURWENSVILLE
16834-16834	DRIFTING
16835-16835	FLEMING
16836-16836	FRENCHVILLE
16837-16837	GLEN RICHEY
16838-16838	GRAMPIAN
16839-16839	GRASSFLAT
16840-16840	HAWK RUN
16841-16841	HOWARD
16843-16843	HYDE
16844-16844	JULIAN
16845-16845	KARTHAUS
16847-16847	KYLERTOWN
16848-16848	LAMAR
16849-16849	LANSE
16850-16850	LECONTES MILLS
16851-16851	LEMONT
16852-16852	MADISONBURG
16853-16853	MILESBURG
16854-16854	MILLHEIM
16855-16855	MINERAL SPRINGS
16856-16856	MINGOVILLE
16858-16858	MORRISDALE
16859-16859	MOSHANNON
16860-16860	MUNSON
16861-16861	NEW MILLPORT
16863-16863	OLANTA
16864-16864	ORVISTON
16865-16865	PENNSYLVANIA FURNACE
16866-16866	PHILIPSBURG
16868-16868	PINE GROVE MILLS
16870-16870	PORT MATILDA
16871-16871	POTTERSDALE
16872-16872	REBERSBURG
16873-16873	SHAWVILLE
16874-16874	SNOW SHOE
16875-16875	SPRING MILLS
16876-16876	WALLACETON
16877-16877	WARRIORS MARK
16878-16878	WEST DECATUR
16879-16879	WINBURNE
16880-16880	BELLEFONTE
16881-16881	WOODLAND
16882-16882	WOODWARD
16901-16901	WELLSBORO
16910-16910	ALBA
16911-16911	ARNOT
16912-16912	BLOSSBURG
16914-16914	COLUMBIA CROSS ROADS
16915-16915	COUDERSPORT
16917-16917	COVINGTON
16918-16918	COWANESQUE
16920-16920	ELKLAND
16921-16921	GAINES
16922-16922	GALETON
16923-16923	GENESEE
16925-16925	GILLETT
16926-16926	GRANVILLE SUMMIT
16927-16927	HARRISON VALLEY
16928-16928	KNOXVILLE
16929-16929	LAWRENCEVILLE
16930-16930	LIBERTY
16932-16932	MAINESBURG
16933-16933	MANSFIELD
16935-16935	MIDDLEBURY CENTER
16936-16936	MILLERTON
16937-16937	MILLS
16938-16938	MORRIS
16939-16939	MORRIS RUN
16940-16940	NELSON
16941-16941	GENESEE
16942-16942	OSCEOLA
16943-16943	SABINSVILLE
16945-16945	SYLVANIA
16946-16946	TIOGA
16947-16947	TROY
16948-16948	ULYSSES
16950-16950	WESTFIELD
17001-17001	CAMP HILL
17002-17002	ALLENSVILLE
17003-17003	ANNVILLE
17004-17004	BELLEVILLE
17005-17005	BERRYSBURG
17006-17006	BLAIN
17007-17007	BOILING SPRINGS
17008-17008	BOWMANSDALE
17009-17009	BURNHAM
17010-17010	CAMPBELLTOWN
17011-17012	CAMP HILL
17013-17013	CARLISLE
17014-17014	COCOLAMUS
17015-17015	COLEBROOK
17016-17016	CORNWALL
17017-17017	DALMATIA
17018-17018	DAUPHIN
17019-17019	DILLSBURG
17020-17020	DUNCANNON
17021-17021	EAST WATERFORD
17022-17022	ELIZABETHTOWN
17023-17023	ELIZABETHVILLE
17024-17024	ELLIOTTSBURG
17025-17025	ENOLA
17026-17026	FREDERICKSBURG
17027-17027	GRANTHAM
17028-17028	GRANTVILLE
17029-17029	GRANVILLE
17030-17030	GRATZ
17031-17031	GREEN PARK
17032-17032	HALIFAX
17033-17033	HERSHEY
17034-17034	HIGHSPIRE
17035-17035	HONEY GROVE
17036-17036	HUMMELSTOWN
17037-17037	ICKESBURG
17038-17038	JONESTOWN
17039-17039	KLEINFELTERSVILLE
17040-17040	LANDISBURG
17041-17041	LAWN
17042-17042	LEBANON
17043-17043	LEMOYNE
17044-17044	LEWISTOWN
17045-17045	LIVERPOOL
17046-17046	LEBANON
17047-17047	LOYSVILLE
17048-17048	LYKENS
17049-17049	MC ALISTERVILLE
17050-17050	MECHANICSBURG
17051-17051	MC VEYTOWN
17052-17052	MAPLETON DEPOT
17053-17053	MARYSVILLE
17054-17054	MATTAWANA
17055-17055	MECHANICSBURG
17056-17056	MEXICO
17057-17057	MIDDLETOWN
17058-17058	MIFFLIN
17059-17059	MIFFLINTOWN
17060-17060	MILL CREEK
17061-17061	MILLERSBURG
17062-17062	MILLERSTOWN
17063-17063	MILROY
17064-17064	MOUNT GRETNA
17065-17065	MOUNT HOLLY SPRINGS
17066-17066	MOUNT UNION
17067-17067	MYERSTOWN
17068-17068	NEW BLOOMFIELD
17069-17069	NEW BUFFALO
17070-17070	NEW CUMBERLAND
17071-17071	NEW GERMANTOWN
17072-17072	NEW KINGSTOWN
17073-17073	NEWMANSTOWN
17074-17074	NEWPORT
17075-17075	NEWTON HAMILTON
17076-17076	OAKLAND MILLS
17077-17077	ONO
17078-17078	PALMYRA
17080-17080	PILLOW
17081-17081	PLAINFIELD
17082-17082	PORT ROYAL
17083-17083	QUENTIN
17084-17084	REEDSVILLE
17085-17085	REXMONT
17086-17086	RICHFIELD
17087-17087	RICHLAND
17088-17088	SCHAEFFERSTOWN
17089-17089	CAMP HILL
17090-17090	SHERMANS DALE
17091-17091	CAMP HILL
17093-17093	SUMMERDALE
17094-17094	THOMPSONTOWN
17097-17097	WICONISCO
17098-17098	WILLIAMSTOWN
17099-17099	YEAGERTOWN
17100-17177	HARRISBURG
17201-17201	CHAMBERSBURG
17210-17210	AMBERSON
17211-17211	ARTEMAS
17212-17212	BIG COVE TANNERY
17213-17213	BLAIRS MILLS
17214-17214	BLUE RIDGE SUMMIT
17215-17215	BURNT CABINS
17217-17217	CONCORD
17218-17218	DICKINSON
17219-17219	DOYLESBURG
17220-17220	DRY RUN
17221-17221	FANNETTSBURG
17222-17222	FAYETTEVILLE
17223-17223	FORT LITTLETON
17224-17224	FORT LOUDON
17225-17225	GREENCASTLE
17228-17228	HARRISONVILLE
17229-17229	HUSTONTOWN
17231-17231	LEMASTERS
17232-17232	LURGAN
17233-17233	MC CONNELLSBURG
17235-17235	MARION
17236-17236	MERCERSBURG
17237-17237	MONT ALTO
17238-17238	NEEDMORE
17239-17239	NEELYTON
17240-17240	NEWBURG
17241-17241	NEWVILLE
17243-17243	ORBISONIA
17244-17244	ORRSTOWN
17246-17246	PLEASANT HALL
17247-17247	QUINCY
17249-17249	ROCKHILL FURNACE
17250-17250	ROUZERVILLE
17251-17251	ROXBURY
17252-17252	SAINT THOMAS
17253-17253	SALTILLO
17254-17254	SCOTLAND
17255-17255	SHADE GAP
17256-17256	SHADY GROVE
17257-17257	SHIPPENSBURG
17260-17260	SHIRLEYSBURG
17261-17261	SOUTH MOUNTAIN
17262-17262	SPRING RUN
17263-17263	STATE LINE
17264-17264	THREE SPRINGS
17265-17265	UPPERSTRASBURG
17266-17266	WALNUT BOTTOM
17267-17267	WARFORDSBURG
17268-17268	WAYNESBORO
17270-17270	WILLIAMSON
17271-17271	WILLOW HILL
17272-17272	ZULLINGER
17294-17294	BLUE RIDGE SUMMIT
17301-17301	ABBOTTSTOWN
17302-17302	AIRVILLE
17303-17303	ARENDTSVILLE
17304-17304	ASPERS
17306-17306	BENDERSVILLE
17307-17307	BIGLERVILLE
17309-17309	BROGUE
17310-17310	CASHTOWN
17311-17311	CODORUS
17312-17312	CRALEY
17313-17313	DALLASTOWN
17314-17314	DELTA
17315-17315	DOVER
17316-17316	EAST BERLIN
17317-17317	EAST PROSPECT
17318-17318	EMIGSVILLE
17319-17319	ETTERS
17320-17320	FAIRFIELD
17321-17321	FAWN GROVE
17322-17322	FELTON
17323-17323	FRANKLINTOWN
17324-17324	GARDNERS
17325-17326	GETTYSBURG
17327-17327	GLEN ROCK
17329-17329	GLENVILLE
17331-17334	HANOVER
17337-17337	IDAVILLE
17339-17339	LEWISBERRY
17340-17340	LITTLESTOWN
17342-17342	LOGANVILLE
17343-17343	MC KNIGHTSTOWN
17344-17344	MC SHERRYSTOWN
17345-17345	MANCHESTER
17346-17346	MENGES MILLS
17347-17347	MOUNT WOLF
17349-17349	NEW FREEDOM
17350-17350	NEW OXFORD
17352-17352	NEW PARK
17353-17353	ORRTANNA
17354-17354	PORTERS SIDELING
17355-17355	RAILROAD
17356-17356	RED LION
17358-17358	ROSSVILLE
17360-17360	SEVEN VALLEYS
17361-17361	SHREWSBURY
17362-17362	SPRING GROVE
17363-17363	STEWARTSTOWN
17364-17364	THOMASVILLE
17365-17365	WELLSVILLE
17366-17366	WINDSOR
17368-17368	WRIGHTSVILLE
17370-17370	YORK HAVEN
17371-17371	YORK NEW SALEM
17372-17372	YORK SPRINGS
17375-17375	PEACH GLEN
17400-17415	YORK
17501-17501	AKRON
17502-17502	BAINBRIDGE
17503-17503	BART
17504-17504	BAUSMAN
17505-17505	BIRD IN HAND

17506-17506 BLUE BALL	17751-17751 MILL HALL	17887-17887 WHITE DEER	18060-18060 LIMEPORT
17507-17507 BOWMANSVILLE	17752-17752 MONTGOMERY	17888-17888 WILBURTON	18062-18062 MACUNGIE
17508-17508 BROWNSTOWN	17754-17754 MONTOURSVILLE	17889-17889 WINFIELD	18063-18063 MARTINS CREEK
17509-17509 CHRISTIANA	17756-17756 MUNCY	17901-17901 POTTSVILLE	18064-18064 NAZARETH
17512-17512 COLUMBIA	17758-17758 MUNCY VALLEY	17920-17920 ARISTES	18065-18065 NEFFS
17516-17516 CONESTOGA	17759-17759 NISBET	17921-17921 ASHLAND	18066-18066 NEW TRIPOLI
17517-17517 DENVER	17760-17760 NORTH BEND	17922-17922 AUBURN	18067-18067 NORTHAMPTON
17518-17518 DRUMORE	17762-17762 PICTURE ROCKS	17923-17923 BRANCHDALE	18068-18068 OLD ZIONSVILLE
17519-17519 EAST EARL	17763-17763 RALSTON	17925-17925 BROCKTON	18069-18069 OREFIELD
17520-17520 EAST PETERSBURG	17764-17764 RENOVO	17927-17927 CENTRALIA	18070-18070 PALM
17521-17521 ELM	17765-17765 ROARING BRANCH	17929-17929 CRESSONA	18071-18071 PALMERTON
17522-17522 EPHRATA	17767-17767 SALONA	17930-17930 CUMBOLA	18072-18072 PEN ARGYL
17527-17527 GAP	17768-17768 SHUNK	17931-17932 FRACKVILLE	18073-18073 PENNSBURG
17528-17528 GOODVILLE	17769-17769 SLATE RUN	17933-17933 FRIEDENSBURG	18074-18074 PERKIOMENVILLE
17529-17529 GORDONVILLE	17770-17770 SONESTOWN	17934-17934 GILBERTON	18076-18076 RED HILL
17532-17532 HOLTWOOD	17771-17771 TROUT RUN	17935-17935 GIRARDVILLE	18077-18077 RIEGELSVILLE
17533-17533 HOPELAND	17772-17772 TURBOTVILLE	17936-17936 GORDON	18078-18078 SCHNECKSVILLE
17534-17534 INTERCOURSE	17773-17773 TYLERSVILLE	17938-17938 HEGINS	18079-18079 SLATEDALE
17535-17535 KINZERS	17774-17774 UNITYVILLE	17939-17939 HELFENSTEIN	18080-18080 SLATINGTON
17536-17536 KIRKWOOD	17776-17776 WATERVILLE	17941-17941 KLINGERSTOWN	18081-18081 SPRINGTOWN
17537-17537 LAMPETER	17777-17777 WATSONTOWN	17942-17942 LANDINGVILLE	18083-18083 STOCKERTOWN
17538-17538 LANDISVILLE	17778-17778 WESTPORT	17943-17943 LAVELLE	18084-18084 SUMNEYTOWN
17540-17540 LEOLA	17779-17779 WOOLRICH	17944-17944 LLEWELLYN	18085-18085 TATAMY
17543-17543 LITITZ	17801-17801 SUNBURY	17945-17945 LOCUSTDALE	18086-18086 TREICHLERS
17545-17545 MANHEIM	17810-17810 ALLENWOOD	17946-17946 LOST CREEK	18087-18087 TREXLERTOWN
17547-17547 MARIETTA	17812-17812 BEAVER SPRINGS	17948-17948 MAHANOY CITY	18088-18088 WALNUTPORT
17549-17549 MARTINDALE	17813-17813 BEAVERTOWN	17949-17949 MAHANOY PLANE	18091-18091 WIND GAP
17550-17550 MAYTOWN	17814-17814 BENTON	17951-17951 MAR LIN	18092-18092 ZIONSVILLE
17551-17551 MILLERSVILLE	17815-17815 BLOOMSBURG	17952-17952 MARY D	18098-18099 EMMAUS
17552-17552 MOUNT JOY	17820-17820 CATAWISSA	17953-17953 MIDDLEPORT	18100-18195 ALLENTOWN
17554-17554 MOUNTVILLE	17821-17822 DANVILLE	17954-17954 MINERSVILLE	18201-18202 HAZLETON
17555-17555 NARVON	17823-17823 DORNSIFE	17957-17957 MUIR	18210-18210 ALBRIGHTSVILLE
17557-17557 NEW HOLLAND	17824-17824 ELYSBURG	17959-17959 NEW PHILADELPHIA	18211-18211 ANDREAS
17560-17560 NEW PROVIDENCE	17825-17825 EXCELSIOR	17960-17960 NEW RINGGOLD	18212-18212 ASHFIELD
17562-17562 PARADISE	17827-17827 FREEBURG	17961-17961 ORWIGSBURG	18214-18214 BARNESVILLE
17563-17563 PEACH BOTTOM	17828-17828 GOWEN CITY	17963-17963 PINE GROVE	18216-18216 BEAVER MEADOWS
17564-17564 PENRYN	17829-17829 HARTLETON	17964-17964 PITMAN	18218-18218 COALDALE
17565-17565 PEQUEA	17830-17830 HERNDON	17965-17965 PORT CARBON	18219-18219 CONYNGHAM
17566-17566 QUARRYVILLE	17831-17831 HUMMELS WHARF	17966-17966 RAVINE	18220-18220 DELANO
17567-17567 REAMSTOWN	17832-17832 MARION HEIGHTS	17967-17967 RINGTOWN	18221-18221 DRIFTON
17568-17568 REFTON	17833-17833 KREAMER	17968-17968 SACRAMENTO	18222-18222 DRUMS
17569-17569 REINHOLDS	17834-17834 KULPMONT	17970-17970 SAINT CLAIR	18223-18223 EBERVALE
17570-17570 RHEEMS	17835-17835 LAURELTON	17972-17972 SCHUYLKILL HAVEN	18224-18224 FREELAND
17572-17573 RONKS	17836-17836 LECK KILL	17974-17974 SELTZER	18225-18225 HARLEIGH
17575-17575 SILVER SPRING	17837-17837 LEWISBURG	17976-17976 SHENANDOAH	18229-18229 JIM THORPE
17576-17576 SMOKETOWN	17839-17839 LIGHT STREET	17978-17978 SPRING GLEN	18230-18230 JUNEDALE
17577-17577 SOUDERSBURG	17840-17840 LOCUST GAP	17979-17979 SUMMIT STATION	18231-18231 KELAYRES
17578-17578 STEVENS	17841-17841 MC CLURE	17980-17980 TOWER CITY	18232-18232 LANSFORD
17579-17579 STRASBURG	17842-17842 MIDDLEBURG	17981-17981 TREMONT	18234-18234 LATTIMER MINES
17580-17580 TALMAGE	17843-17843 BEAVER SPRINGS	17982-17982 TUSCARORA	18235-18235 LEHIGHTON
17581-17581 TERRE HILL	17844-17844 MIFFLINBURG	17983-17983 VALLEY VIEW	18237-18237 MCADOO
17582-17582 WASHINGTON BORO	17845-17845 MILLMONT	17985-17985 ZION GROVE	18239-18239 MILNESVILLE
17583-17583 WEST WILLOW	17846-17846 MILLVILLE	18001-18003 LEHIGH VALLEY	18240-18240 NESQUEHONING
17584-17584 WILLOW STREET	17847-17847 MILTON	18010-18010 ACKERMANVILLE	18241-18241 NUREMBERG
17585-17585 WITMER	17850-17850 MONTANDON	18011-18011 ALBURTIS	18242-18242 ONEIDA
17600-17699 LANCASTER	17851-17851 MOUNT CARMEL	18012-18012 AQUASHICOLA	18243-18243 PARDEESVILLE
17701-17705 WILLIAMSPORT	17853-17853 MOUNT PLEASANT MILLS	18013-18013 BANGOR	18244-18244 PARRYVILLE
17720-17720 ANTES FORT	17855-17855 NEW BERLIN	18014-18014 BATH	18245-18245 QUAKAKE
17721-17721 AVIS	17856-17856 NEW COLUMBIA	18015-18025 BETHLEHEM	18246-18246 ROCK GLEN
17722-17722 BODINES	17857-17857 NORTHUMBERLAND	18030-18030 BOWMANSTOWN	18247-18247 SAINT JOHNS
17723-17723 JERSEY SHORE	17858-17858 NUMIDIA	18031-18031 BREINIGSVILLE	18248-18248 SHEPPTON
17724-17724 CANTON	17859-17859 ORANGEVILLE	18032-18032 CATASAUQUA	18249-18249 SUGARLOAF
17726-17726 CASTANEA	17860-17860 PAXINOS	18034-18034 CENTER VALLEY	18250-18250 SUMMIT HILL
17727-17727 CEDAR RUN	17861-17861 PAXTONVILLE	18035-18035 CHERRYVILLE	18251-18251 SYBERTSVILLE
17728-17728 COGAN STATION	17862-17862 PENNS CREEK	18036-18036 COOPERSBURG	18252-18252 TAMAQUA
17729-17729 CROSS FORK	17864-17864 PORT TREVORTON	18037-18037 COPLAY	18254-18254 TRESCKOW
17730-17730 DEWART	17865-17865 POTTS GROVE	18038-18038 DANIELSVILLE	18255-18255 WEATHERLY
17731-17731 EAGLES MERE	17866-17866 COAL TOWNSHIP	18039-18039 DURHAM	18256-18256 WESTON
17734-17734 FARRANDSVILLE	17867-17867 REBUCK	18040-18040 EASTON	18301-18301 EAST STROUDSBURG
17735-17735 GROVER	17868-17868 RIVERSIDE	18041-18041 EAST GREENVILLE	18320-18320 ANALOMINK
17737-17737 HUGHESVILLE	17870-17870 SELINSGROVE	18042-18045 EASTON	18321-18321 BARTONSVILLE
17738-17738 HYNER	17872-17872 SHAMOKIN	18046-18046 EAST TEXAS	18322-18322 BRODHEADSVILLE
17739-17739 JERSEY MILLS	17876-17876 SHAMOKIN DAM	18049-18049 EMMAUS	18323-18323 BUCK HILL FALLS
17740-17740 JERSEY SHORE	17877-17877 SNYDERTOWN	18050-18050 FLICKSVILLE	18324-18324 BUSHKILL
17742-17742 LAIRDSVILLE	17878-17878 STILLWATER	18051-18051 FOGELSVILLE	18325-18325 CANADENSIS
17743-17743 LEROY	17880-17880 SWENGEL	18052-18052 WHITEHALL	18326-18326 CRESCO
17744-17744 LINDEN	17881-17881 TREVORTON	18053-18053 GERMANSVILLE	18327-18327 DELAWARE WATER GAP
17745-17745 LOCK HAVEN	17882-17882 TROXELVILLE	18054-18054 GREEN LANE	18328-18328 DINGMANS FERRY
17747-17747 LOGANTON	17883-17883 VICKSBURG	18055-18055 HELLERTOWN	18330-18330 EFFORT
17748-17748 MC ELHATTAN	17884-17884 WASHINGTONVILLE	18056-18056 HEREFORD	18331-18331 GILBERT
17749-17749 MC EWENSVILLE	17885-17885 WEIKERT	18058-18058 KUNKLETOWN	18332-18332 HENRYVILLE
17750-17750 MACKEYVILLE	17886-17886 WEST MILTON	18059-18059 LAURYS STATION	18333-18333 KRESGEVILLE

18334-18334 LONG POND	18473-18473 WHITE MILLS	18840-18840 SAYRE	19013-19013 CHESTER
18335-18335 MARSHALLS CREEK	18500-18505 SCRANTON	18842-18842 SOUTH GIBSON	19014-19014 ASTON
18336-18336 MATAMORAS	18507-18507 MOOSIC	18843-18843 SOUTH MONTROSE	19015-19015 BROOKHAVEN
18337-18337 MILFORD	18508-18515 SCRANTON	18844-18844 SPRINGVILLE	19016-19016 CHESTER
18340-18340 MILLRIFT	18517-18517 TAYLOR	18845-18845 STEVENSVILLE	19017-19017 CHESTER HEIGHTS
18341-18341 MINISINK HILLS	18518-18518 OLD FORGE	18846-18846 SUGAR RUN	19018-19018 CLIFTON HEIGHTS
18342-18342 MOUNTAINHOME	18519-18519 DICKSON CITY	18847-18847 SUSQUEHANNA	19019-19019 PHILADELPHIA
18343-18343 MOUNT BETHEL	18522-18577 SCRANTON	18848-18848 TOWANDA	19020-19020 BENSALEM
18344-18344 MOUNT POCONO	18601-18601 BEACH HAVEN	18850-18850 ULSTER	19021-19021 CROYDON
18346-18346 POCONO SUMMIT	18602-18602 BEAR CREEK	18851-18851 WARREN CENTER	19022-19022 CRUM LYNNE
18347-18347 POCONO LAKE	18603-18603 BERWICK	18853-18853 WYALUSING	19023-19023 DARBY
18348-18348 POCONO LAKE PRESERVE	18610-18610 BLAKESLEE	18854-18854 WYSOX	19025-19025 DRESHER
18349-18349 POCONO MANOR	18611-18611 CAMBRA	18901-18901 DOYLESTOWN	19026-19026 DREXEL HILL
18350-18350 POCONO PINES	18612-18612 DALLAS	18910-18910 BEDMINSTER	19027-19027 ELKINS PARK
18351-18351 PORTLAND	18614-18614 DUSHORE	18911-18911 BLOOMING GLEN	19028-19028 EDGEMONT
18352-18352 REEDERS	18615-18615 FALLS	18912-18912 BUCKINGHAM	19029-19029 ESSINGTON
18353-18353 SAYLORSBURG	18616-18616 FORKSVILLE	18913-18913 CARVERSVILLE	19030-19030 FAIRLESS HILLS
18354-18354 SCIOTA	18617-18617 GLEN LYON	18914-18914 CHALFONT	19031-19031 FLOURTOWN
18355-18355 SCOTRUN	18618-18618 HARVEYS LAKE	18915-18915 COLMAR	19032-19032 FOLCROFT
18356-18356 SHAWNEE ON DELAWARE	18619-18619 HILLSGROVE	18916-18916 DANBORO	19033-19033 FOLSOM
18357-18357 SKYTOP	18621-18621 HUNLOCK CREEK	18917-18917 DUBLIN	19034-19034 FORT WASHINGTON
18360-18360 STROUDSBURG	18622-18622 HUNTINGTON MILLS	18918-18918 EARLINGTON	19035-19035 GLADWYNE
18370-18370 SWIFTWATER	18623-18623 LACEYVILLE	18920-18920 ERWINNA	19036-19036 GLENOLDEN
18371-18371 TAMIMENT	18624-18624 LAKE HARMONY	18921-18921 FERNDALE	19037-19037 GLEN RIDDLE LIMA
18372-18372 TANNERSVILLE	18625-18625 LAKE WINOLA	18922-18922 FOREST GROVE	19038-19038 GLENSIDE
18373-18373 UNITY HOUSE	18626-18626 LAPORTE	18923-18923 FOUNTAINVILLE	19039-19039 GRADYVILLE
18401-18401 ALDENVILLE	18627-18627 LEHMAN	18924-18924 FRANCONIA	19040-19040 HATBORO
18403-18403 ARCHBALD	18628-18628 LOPEZ	18925-18925 FURLONG	19041-19041 HAVERFORD
18405-18405 BEACH LAKE	18629-18629 MEHOOPANY	18926-18926 GARDENVILLE	19043-19043 HOLMES
18407-18407 CARBONDALE	18630-18630 MESHOPPEN	18927-18927 HILLTOWN	19044-19044 HORSHAM
18410-18410 CHINCHILLA	18631-18631 MIFFLINVILLE	18928-18928 HOLICONG	19046-19046 JENKINTOWN
18411-18411 CLARKS SUMMIT	18632-18632 MILDRED	18929-18929 JAMISON	19047-19048 LANGHORNE
18413-18413 CLIFFORD	18634-18634 NANTICOKE	18930-18930 KINTNERSVILLE	19048-19048 FORT WASHINGTON
18414-18414 DALTON	18635-18635 NESCOPECK	18931-18931 LAHASKA	19049-19049 LANGHORNE
18415-18415 DAMASCUS	18636-18636 NOXEN	18932-18932 LINE LEXINGTON	19049-19049 FORT WASHINGTON
18416-18416 ELMHURST	18637-18637 NUANGOLA	18933-18933 LUMBERVILLE	19050-19050 LANSDOWNE
18417-18417 EQUINUNK	18640-18641 PITTSTON	18934-18934 MECHANICSVILLE	19052-19052 LENNI
18419-18419 FACTORYVILLE	18642-18642 DURYEA	18935-18935 MILFORD SQUARE	19053-19053 FEASTERVILLE TREVOSE
18420-18420 FLEETVILLE	18643-18643 PITTSTON	18936-18936 MONTGOMERYVILLE	19054-19059 LEVITTOWN
18421-18421 FOREST CITY	18644-18644 WYOMING	18938-18938 NEW HOPE	19061-19061 MARCUS HOOK
18424-18424 GOULDSBORO	18651-18651 PLYMOUTH	18940-18940 NEWTOWN	19063-19063 MEDIA
18425-18425 GREELEY	18653-18653 RANSOM	18942-18942 OTTSVILLE	19064-19064 SPRINGFIELD
18426-18426 GREENTOWN	18654-18654 SHAWANESE	18943-18943 PENNS PARK	19065-19065 MEDIA
18427-18427 HAMLIN	18655-18655 SHICKSHINNY	18944-18944 PERKASIE	19066-19066 MERION STATION
18428-18428 HAWLEY	18656-18656 SWEET VALLEY	18946-18946 PINEVILLE	19067-19067 MORRISVILLE
18430-18430 HERRICK CENTER	18657-18657 TUNKHANNOCK	18947-18947 PIPERSVILLE	19070-19070 MORTON
18431-18431 HONESDALE	18660-18660 WAPWALLOPEN	18949-18949 PLUMSTEADVILLE	19072-19072 NARBERTH
18433-18433 JERMYN	18661-18661 WHITE HAVEN	18950-18950 POINT PLEASANT	19073-19073 NEWTOWN SQUARE
18434-18434 JESSUP	18690-18690 DALLAS	18951-18951 QUAKERTOWN	19074-19074 NORWOOD
18435-18435 LACKAWAXEN	18700-18703 WILKES BARRE	18953-18953 REVERE	19075-19075 ORELAND
18436-18436 LAKE ARIEL	18704-18704 KINGSTON	18954-18954 RICHBORO	19076-19076 PROSPECT PARK
18437-18437 LAKE COMO	18705-18706 WILKES BARRE	18955-18955 RICHLANDTOWN	19078-19078 RIDLEY PARK
18438-18438 LAKEVILLE	18707-18707 MOUNTAIN TOP	18956-18956 RUSHLAND	19079-19079 SHARON HILL
18439-18439 LAKEWOOD	18708-18708 SHAVERTOWN	18957-18957 SALFORD	19080-19080 WAYNE
18440-18440 LA PLUME	18709-18709 LUZERNE	18958-18958 SALFORDVILLE	19081-19081 SWARTHMORE
18441-18441 LENOXVILLE	18710-18774 WILKES BARRE	18960-18960 SELLERSVILLE	19082-19082 UPPER DARBY
18443-18443 MILANVILLE	18801-18801 MONTROSE	18962-18962 SILVERDALE	19083-19083 HAVERTOWN
18444-18444 MOSCOW	18810-18810 ATHENS	18963-18963 SOLEBURY	19085-19085 VILLANOVA
18445-18445 NEWFOUNDLAND	18812-18812 BRACKNEY	18964-18964 SOUDERTON	19086-19086 WALLINGFORD
18446-18446 NICHOLSON	18813-18813 BROOKLYN	18966-18966 SOUTHAMPTON	19087-19089 WAYNE
18447-18448 OLYPHANT	18814-18814 BURLINGTON	18968-18968 SPINNERSTOWN	19090-19090 WILLOW GROVE
18449-18449 ORSON	18815-18815 CAMPTOWN	18969-18969 TELFORD	19091-19091 MEDIA
18451-18451 PAUPACK	18816-18816 DIMOCK	18970-18970 TRUMBAUERSVILLE	19092-19093 PHILADELPHIA
18452-18452 PECKVILLE	18817-18817 EAST SMITHFIELD	18971-18971 TYLERSPORT	19094-19094 WOODLYN
18453-18453 PLEASANT MOUNT	18818-18818 FRIENDSVILLE	18972-18972 UPPER BLACK EDDY	19095-19095 WYNCOTE
18454-18454 POYNTELLE	18820-18820 GIBSON	18974-18974 WARMINSTER	19096-19096 WYNNEWOOD
18455-18455 PRESTON PARK	18821-18821 GREAT BEND	18976-18976 WARRINGTON	19098-19098 HOLMES
18456-18456 PROMPTON	18822-18822 HALLSTEAD	18977-18977 WASHINGTON CROSSING	19099-19255 PHILADELPHIA
18457-18457 ROWLAND	18823-18823 HARFORD	18979-18979 WOXALL	19301-19301 PAOLI
18458-18458 SHOHOLA	18824-18824 HOP BOTTOM	18980-18980 WYCOMBE	19310-19310 ATGLEN
18459-18459 SOUTH CANAAN	18825-18825 JACKSON	18981-18981 ZIONHILL	19311-19311 AVONDALE
18460-18460 SOUTH STERLING	18826-18826 KINGSLEY	18991-18991 WARMINSTER	19312-19312 BERWYN
18461-18461 STARLIGHT	18827-18827 LANESBORO	19001-19001 ABINGTON	19316-19316 BRANDAMORE
18462-18462 STARRUCCA	18828-18828 LAWTON	19002-19002 AMBLER	19317-19317 CHADDS FORD
18463-18463 STERLING	18829-18829 LE RAYSVILLE	19003-19003 ARDMORE	19318-19318 CHATHAM
18464-18464 TAFTON	18830-18830 LITTLE MEADOWS	19004-19004 BALA CYNWYD	19319-19319 CHEYNEY
18465-18465 THOMPSON	18831-18831 MILAN	19006-19006 HUNTINGDON VALLEY	19320-19320 COATESVILLE
18466-18466 TOBYHANNA	18832-18832 MONROETON	19007-19007 BRISTOL	19330-19330 COCHRANVILLE
18469-18469 TYLER HILL	18833-18833 NEW ALBANY	19008-19008 BROOMALL	19331-19331 CONCORDVILLE
18470-18470 UNION DALE	18834-18834 NEW MILFORD	19009-19009 BRYN ATHYN	19333-19333 DEVON
18471-18471 WAVERLY	18837-18837 ROME	19010-19010 BRYN MAWR	19335-19335 DOWNINGTOWN
18472-18472 WAYMART	18839-18839 RUSHVILLE	19012-19012 CHELTENHAM	19339-19340 CONCORDVILLE

19341-19341 EXTON	19401-19404 NORRISTOWN	19460-19460 PHOENIXVILLE	19522-19522 FLEETWOOD
19342-19342 GLEN MILLS	19405-19405 BRIDGEPORT	19462-19462 PLYMOUTH MEETING	19523-19523 GEIGERTOWN
19343-19343 GLENMOORE	19406-19406 KING OF PRUSSIA	19464-19465 POTTSTOWN	19525-19525 GILBERTSVILLE
19344-19344 HONEY BROOK	19407-19407 AUDUBON	19468-19468 ROYERSFORD	19526-19526 HAMBURG
19345-19345 IMMACULATA	19408-19408 EAGLEVILLE	19470-19470 SAINT PETERS	19529-19529 KEMPTON
19346-19346 KELTON	19409-19409 FAIRVIEW VILLAGE	19472-19472 SASSAMANSVILLE	19530-19530 KUTZTOWN
19347-19347 KEMBLESVILLE	19415-19415 EAGLEVILLE	19473-19473 SCHWENKSVILLE	19533-19533 LEESPORT
19348-19348 KENNETT SQUARE	19420-19420 ARCOLA	19474-19474 SKIPPACK	19534-19534 LENHARTSVILLE
19350-19350 LANDENBERG	19421-19421 BIRCHRUNVILLE	19475-19475 SPRING CITY	19535-19535 LIMEKILN
19351-19351 LEWISVILLE	19422-19422 BLUE BELL	19477-19477 SPRING HOUSE	19536-19536 LYON STATION
19352-19352 LINCOLN UNIVERSITY	19423-19423 CEDARS	19478-19478 SPRING MOUNT	19538-19538 MAXATAWNY
19353-19353 LIONVILLE	19424-19424 BLUE BELL	19480-19480 UWCHLAND	19539-19539 MERTZTOWN
19354-19354 LYNDELL	19425-19425 CHESTER SPRINGS	19481-19485 VALLEY FORGE	19540-19540 MOHNTON
19355-19355 MALVERN	19426-19426 COLLEGEVILLE	19486-19486 WEST POINT	19541-19541 MOHRSVILLE
19357-19357 MENDENHALL	19428-19429 CONSHOHOCKEN	19487-19487 KING OF PRUSSIA	19542-19542 MONOCACY STATION
19358-19358 MODENA	19430-19430 CREAMERY	19488-19489 NORRISTOWN	19543-19543 MORGANTOWN
19360-19360 NEW LONDON	19432-19432 DEVAULT	19490-19490 WORCESTER	19544-19544 MOUNT AETNA
19362-19362 NOTTINGHAM	19435-19435 FREDERICK	19492-19492 ZIEGLERVILLE	19545-19545 NEW BERLINVILLE
19363-19363 OXFORD	19436-19436 GWYNEDD	19493-19496 VALLEY FORGE	19547-19547 OLEY
19365-19365 PARKESBURG	19437-19437 GWYNEDD VALLEY	19501-19501 ADAMSTOWN	19548-19548 PINE FORGE
19366-19366 POCOPSON	19438-19438 HARLEYSVILLE	19503-19503 BALLY	19549-19549 PORT CLINTON
19367-19367 POMEROY	19440-19440 HATFIELD	19504-19504 BARTO	19550-19550 REHRERSBURG
19369-19369 SADSBURYVILLE	19441-19441 HARLEYSVILLE	19505-19505 BECHTELSVILLE	19551-19551 ROBESONIA
19370-19370 STEELVILLE	19442-19442 KIMBERTON	19506-19506 BERNVILLE	19554-19554 SHARTLESVILLE
19371-19371 SUPLEE	19443-19443 KULPSVILLE	19507-19507 BETHEL	19555-19555 SHOEMAKERSVILLE
19372-19372 THORNDALE	19444-19444 LAFAYETTE HILL	19508-19508 BIRDSBORO	19557-19557 STONY RUN
19373-19373 THORNTON	19446-19446 LANSDALE	19510-19510 BLANDON	19559-19559 STRAUSSTOWN
19374-19374 TOUGHKENAMON	19450-19450 LEDERACH	19511-19511 BOWERS	19560-19560 TEMPLE
19375-19375 UNIONVILLE	19451-19451 MAINLAND	19512-19512 BOYERTOWN	19562-19562 TOPTON
19376-19376 WAGONTOWN	19452-19452 MIQUON	19516-19516 CENTERPORT	19564-19564 VIRGINVILLE
19380-19383 WEST CHESTER	19453-19453 MONT CLARE	19517-19517 DAUBERVILLE	19565-19565 WERNERSVILLE
19390-19390 WEST GROVE	19454-19455 NORTH WALES	19518-19518 DOUGLASSVILLE	19567-19567 WOMELSDORF
19395-19395 WESTTOWN	19456-19456 OAKS	19519-19519 EARLVILLE	19600-19640 READING
19397-19399 SOUTHEASTERN	19457-19457 PARKER FORD	19520-19520 ELVERSON	

Puerto Rico County Locator

ZIP/City Cross Reference

00601-00601 ADJUNTAS	00664-00664 JAYUYA	00721-00721 PALMER	00778-00778 GURABO
00602-00602 AGUADA	00667-00667 LAJAS	00723-00723 PATILLAS	00780-00780 COTO LAUREL
00603-00605 AGUADILLA	00669-00669 LARES	00725-00727 CAGUAS	00782-00782 COMERIO
00606-00606 MARICAO	00670-00670 LAS MARIAS	00728-00728 PONCE	00783-00783 COROZAL
00610-00610 ANASCO	00674-00674 MANATI	00729-00729 CANOVANAS	00784-00785 GUAYAMA
00611-00611 ANGELES	00676-00676 MOCA	00730-00734 PONCE	00786-00786 LA PLATA
00612-00614 ARECIBO	00677-00677 RINCON	00735-00735 CEIBA	00791-00792 HUMACAO
00616-00616 BAJADERO	00678-00678 QUEBRADILLAS	00736-00737 CAYEY	00794-00794 BARRANQUITAS
00617-00617 BARCELONETA	00680-00682 MAYAGUEZ	00738-00738 FAJARDO	00795-00795 JUANA DIAZ
00622-00622 BOQUERON	00683-00683 SAN GERMAN	00739-00739 CIDRA	00901-00933 SAN JUAN
00623-00623 CABO ROJO	00685-00685 SAN SEBASTIAN	00740-00740 PUERTO REAL	00934-00934 FORT BUCHANAN
00624-00624 PENUELAS	00687-00687 MOROVIS	00741-00741 PUNTA SANTIAGO	00935-00940 SAN JUAN
00627-00627 CAMUY	00688-00688 SABANA HOYOS	00742-00742 ROOSEVELT ROADS	00949-00951 TOA BAJA
00631-00631 CASTANER	00690-00690 SAN ANTONIO	00744-00744 RIO BLANCO	00952-00952 SABANA SECA
00636-00636 ROSARIO	00692-00692 VEGA ALTA	00745-00745 RIO GRANDE	00953-00954 TOA ALTA
00637-00637 SABANA GRANDE	00693-00694 VEGA BAJA	00751-00751 SALINAS	00955-00955 SAN JUAN
00638-00638 CIALES	00698-00698 YAUCO	00754-00754 SAN LORENZO	00956-00961 BAYAMON
00641-00641 UTUADO	00703-00703 AGUAS BUENAS	00757-00757 SANTA ISABEL	00962-00963 CATANO
00646-00646 DORADO	00704-00704 AGUIRRE	00765-00765 VIEQUES	00964-00964 SAN JUAN
00647-00647 ENSENADA	00705-00705 AIBONITO	00766-00766 VILLALBA	00965-00971 GUAYNABO
00650-00650 FLORIDA	00707-00707 MAUNABO	00767-00767 YABUCOA	00975-00975 SAN JUAN
00652-00652 GARROCHALES	00714-00714 ARROYO	00769-00769 COAMO	00976-00977 TRUJILLO ALTO
00653-00653 GUANICA	00715-00715 MERCEDITA	00771-00771 LAS PIEDRAS	00978-00978 SAINT JUST
00656-00656 GUAYANILLA	00716-00717 PONCE	00772-00772 LOIZA	00978-00978 ST JUST
00659-00659 HATILLO	00718-00718 NAGUABO	00773-00773 LUQUILLO	00978-00978 SAINT JUST CONTRACT
00660-00660 HORMIGUEROS	00719-00719 NARANJITO	00775-00775 CULEBRA	00979-00999 CAROLINA
00662-00662 ISABELA	00720-00720 OROCOVIS	00777-00777 JUNCOS	

Rhode Island

General Help Numbers:

Governor's Office
222 State House
Providence, RI 02903-1196
www.governor.state.ri.us

401-222-2080
Fax 401-861-5894
8:30AM-4:30PM

Attorney General's Office
150 S Main St
Providence, RI 02903
www.riag.state.ri.us

401-274-4400
Fax 401-222-1331
8:30AM-4:30PM

State Court Administrator
Supreme Court
250 Benefit St
Providence, RI 02903
www.courts.state.ri.us/

401-222-3272
Fax 401-222-3599
8:30AM-4:30PM

State Archives
State Archives & Public Records Admin.   401-222-2353
337 Westminster St   Fax 401-222-3199
Providence, RI 02903   8:30AM-4:30PM M-SA
www.state.ri.us/archives

State Specifics:

Capital: Providence
                     Providence County

Time Zone: EST

Number of Counties: 5

Population: 1,058,920

Web Site: www.state.ri.us

State Agencies

Criminal Records

Department of Attorney General, Bureau of Criminal Identification, 150 S Main Street, Providence, RI 02903; 401-274-4400 x2353, 8:30AM-4;30PM.

www.riag.state.ri.us

Note: The state Sexual Offender Registry is not available to the public.

Indexing & Storage: It takes 1-7 days before new records are available for inquiry. 60% of all arrests in database have final dispositions recorded.

Searching: Criminal records are only released to law enforcement agencies, the subject, or, rarely,

to those with a signed notarized authorization from the subject. Records may be obtained at the county level. Include the following in your request: signed notarized release from subject, SSN, picture ID of the requester. Fingerprints are optional. They will call the Notary on the authorization for verification. 100% of the records are fingerprint-supported. All arrests and convictions are reported.

Access by: mail, in person, online.

Fee & Payment: The fee is $5.00 per name. If required, the FBI fingerprint search is $24.00. Fee payee: Department of Attorney General. Prepayment required. Personal checks accepted. No credit cards accepted.

Mail search: Turnaround time: up to 2 weeks. A self addressed stamped envelope is requested.

In person search: Turnaround time is while you wait.

Online search: Online access to the Adult Criminal Information Database is available at http://courtconnect.courts.state.ri.us/pls/ri_adult/ck_public_qry_main.cp_main_idx. Search by name or case number.

Corporation Records
Fictitious Name
Limited Partnerships
Limited Liability Companys
Limited Liability
Partnerships
Not For Profit Entities

Secretary of State, Corporations Division, 100 N Main St, Providence, RI 02903-1335; 401-222-3040, 401-222-1309 (Fax), 8:30AM-4:30PM.

http://155.212.254.78/corporations.htm

Indexing & Storage: Records are available from the beginning of the Division. Records are computerized since 1984. It takes less 5 days before new records are available for inquiry. Records are indexed on an inhouse computer.

Searching: Include the following in your request: full name of business.

Access by: mail, phone, in person, online.

Fee & Payment: The copy fee is $.15 per page. Certification costs $5.00 per document plus copy fees. There is no search fee. Fee payee: Secretary of State. Prepayment required. Personal checks accepted. No credit cards accepted.

Mail search: Turnaround time: variable. A self addressed stamped envelope is heplful.

Phone search: They will give date of incorporation, registered agent, one officer, status, and whether domestic or foreign. Certified copies and documents can be ordered, but must be picked up in person, takes 48 hours.

In person search: Certified copies and certifications may not be available same day.

Online search: At the web, search filings for active and inactive Rhode Island and foreign business corporations, non-profit corporations, limited partnerships, limited liability companies, and limited liability partnerships. Weekly lisiting of new corporations are also available. There is no fee.

Other access: The corporation database may be purchased on CD.

Trademarks/Servicemarks

Secretary of State, Trademark Section, 100 N Main St, Providence, RI 02903-1335; 401-222-1487, 401-222-3879 (Fax), 8:30AM-4:30PM.

www.corps.state.ri.us/trademarks.htm

Indexing & Storage: Records are available from the beginning of the Division. It takes less than one day before new records are available for inquiry.

Searching: All records are open to the public. Include the following in your request: trademark/servicemark name, registration number and applicant name, if known.

Access by: mail, phone, fax.

Fee & Payment: There is no search fee. The copy fee is $.15 per page.

Mail search: Turnaround time: 3 to 5 days. No self addressed stamped envelope is required.

Phone search: No fee for telephone request. Limited verification information available.

Fax search: Fax searching available.

Uniform Commercial Code

UCC Division, Secretary of State, 100 North Main St, Providence, RI 02903; 401-222-2249, 401-222-3040, 8:30AM-4:30PM.

http://155.212.254.78/corporations.htm

Indexing & Storage: Records are indexed on hard copy.

Searching: Use search request form UCC-11. All tax liens are filed at the city/town level. Include the following in your request: debtor name.

Access by: mail, in person.

Fee & Payment: The search fee is $5.00 per name, copies are $.15 each. Add $5.00 for certification. Fee payee: Secretary of State. Prepayment required. Personal checks accepted. No credit cards accepted.

Mail search: Turnaround time: 5 to 10 working days.

In person search: If you do the search yourself, there is no search fee.

Federal Tax Liens
State Tax Liens
Records not maintained by a state level agency.

Note: All records are located at the county level.

Sales Tax Registrations

Taxation Division, Sales & Use Tax Office, One Capitol Hill, Providence, RI 02908-5800; 401-222-2937, 401-222-6006 (Fax), 8:30AM-4PM.

www.tax.state.ri.us

Indexing & Storage: Records are available from the 1960's. All current permits are on the computer, all inactive records are kept on microfiche. New records are available for inquiry immediately.

Searching: This agency will only confirm that a business is registered. They will provide no other information. Include the following in your request: business name. They will also search by tax permit number.

Access by: mail, phone, fax, in person.

Fee & Payment: There is no search fee nor a copy fee, unless extensive documents are requested.

Mail search: Turnaround time: 7 to 10 days. A self addressed stamped envelope is requested.

Phone search: It will take 24 hours for a response.

Fax search: Same criteria as mail searching.

In person search: It will take 24 hours for a response.

Birth Certificates

State Department of Health, Division of Vital Records, 3 Capitol Hill, Room 101, Providence, RI 02908-5097; 401-222-2812, 401-222-2811, 8:30AM-4:30PM.

www.healthri.org/

Note: If the record is less than 100 years old, it can also be obtained from the city or town where birth occurred.

Indexing & Storage: Records are available from 1902 to present. New records are available for

inquiry immediately. Records are indexed on microfiche, inhouse computer.

Searching: Investigative searches must have a signed release form from person of record or immediate family member. Include the following in your request: full name, names of parents, mother's maiden name, date of birth, place of birth.

Access by: mail, phone, in person.

Fee & Payment: The fee is $15.00 for 2 years searched and $.50 for each additional year. Fee payee: General Treasurer, State of Rhode Island. Prepayment required. Credit cards for emergencies only. Personal checks accepted. Credit cards accepted: MasterCard, Visa, AmEx, Discover.

Mail search: Turnaround time: 4 to 6 weeks. A self addressed stamped envelope is requested. Include photo copy of requester's ID (DL, passport, etc).

Phone search: This is for emergency, expedited needs only.

In person search: Turnaround time while you wait.

Expedited service: Expedited service is available for mail and phone searches. For a 1 week service, mark "rush" on envelope and send in an extra $5.00. For emergencies, add an additional $5.00 for using a credit card and $15.50 for shipping.

Death Records

State Department of Health, Division of Vital Records, 3 Capitol Hill, Room 101, Providence, RI 02908-5097; 401-222-2812, 401-222-2811, 8:30AM-4:30PM.

www.healthri.org/

Note: Records less than 50 years old can be obtained at the town or city where death took place.

Indexing & Storage: Records are available from 1952 to present. For records from 1853 to 1951, contact RI Archives at 401-222-2353. New records are available for inquiry immediately. Records are indexed on microfiche, inhouse computer.

Searching: Investigative searches must have a signed release from immediate family member. Include the following in your request: full name, date of death, place of death, names of parents, mother's maiden name. Any other identifying information is helpful.

Access by: mail, phone, in person.

Fee & Payment: The fee is $15.00 for 2 years searched and $.50 for each additional year. Fee payee: General Treasurer, State of Rhode Island. Prepayment required. Credit cards are for emergency use only. Personal checks accepted. Credit cards accepted: MasterCard, Visa, AmEx, Discover.

Mail search: Turnaround time: 4 to 6 weeks. A self addressed stamped envelope is requested. Include photo copy of requester's ID (DL, passport, etc).

Phone search: See expedited services.

In person search: Searching is available in person.

Expedited service: Expedited service is available for mail and phone searches. You must mark "RUSH" on the outside of the envelope and enclose an extra $5.00, if you want 1 week turnaround time. For true emergencies, you can phone in. Add $5.00 fee for use of credit card and provide return express pre-paid package.

Marriage Certificates

State Department of Health, Division of Vital Records, 3 Capitol Hill, Room 101, Providence, RI 02908-5097; 401-222-2812, 401-222-2811, 8:30AM-4:30PM M-F.

www.healthri.org/

Note: The record may be obtained from the town or city where the marriage took place, if the record is less than 100 years old.

Indexing & Storage: Records are available from 1902 to present. New records are available for inquiry immediately. Records are indexed on microfiche, inhouse computer.

Searching: Investigative searches must have a signed release form from persons of record or immediate family member. Include the following in your request: names of husband and wife, date of marriage, place or county of marriage, wife's maiden name.

Access by: mail, phone, in person.

Fee & Payment: The search fee is $15.00 for 2 years searched and $.50 for each additional year. Fee payee: General Treasurer, State of Rhode Island. Prepayment required. Credit card use is for emergencies only. Personal checks accepted. Credit cards accepted: MasterCard, Visa, AmEx, Discover.

Mail search: Turnaround time: 4 to 6 weeks. A self addressed stamped envelope is requested. Include photo copy of requester's ID (DL, passport, etc).

Phone search: See expedited services.

In person search: Searching is available in person.

Expedited service: Expedited service is available for mail and phone searches. For 1 week turnaround, send an extra $5.00 and mark "RUSH" on the outside of the envelope. For true emergencies, you can order by phone. Add $5.00 fee for use of credit card and provide return express pre-paid package.

Divorce Records

Records not maintained by a state level agency.

Note: Divorce records are found at one of the 4 county Family Courts.

Workers' Compensation Records

Department of Labor & Training, Division of Workers' Compensation, PO Box 20190, Cranston, RI 02920 (Courier: 1511 Pontiac Ave, Cranston, RI 02920); 401-462-8100, 8:30AM-4PM.

www.dlt.state.ri.us

Indexing & Storage: Records are available from 1950s. New records are available for inquiry immediately. Records are indexed on inhouse computer.

Searching: Records are not available for employment screening. A first report of injury is not public, by law. Records are released to claimant, attorneys, employer and insurer only if connected to case. Include the following in your

request: claimant name, Social Security Number, file number (if known), reason for information request, specific records that you need copies of. Records of insurance carrier coverage only are available for no charge by phone or mail. The following data is not released: medical records.

Access by: mail, in person.

Fee & Payment: The search fee is $15.00 per hour. Copies are $.15 per page. There is a $.40 per page fee for return by fax. Fee payee: Department of Labor & Training. Prepayment is required for first time requesters. Personal checks accepted. No credit cards accepted.

Mail search: Turnaround time: 1 to 2 weeks. A self addressed stamped envelope is requested.

In person search: Proof of identity is required.

Driver Records

Division of Motor Vehicles, Driving Record Clerk, Operator Control, 286 Main Street, Pawtucket, RI 02860; 401-588-3010, 8:30AM-4:30PM.

www.dmv.state.ri.us

Note: Copies of tickets may be obtained without fee by writing to the Traffic Tribunal at the address listed above.

Indexing & Storage: Records are available for 3 years for accidents and moving violations, 5 years for alcohol-related violations or suspensions, 3 years after reinstatement for suspensions. Surrendered licenses are purged 3 years after expiration. It takes 20 days after received from courts before new records are available for inquiry.

Searching: Information is not made available for the purpose of commercial solicitation or trade. A description of proposed use must be submitted in advance for departmental approval of high volume requesters. Include the following in your request: driver's license number, full name, date of birth. The following data is not released: Social Security Numbers.

Access by: mail, in person, online.

Fee & Payment: The fee is $16.00 per record request, $18.00 if online. This is the highest fee in the nation for a driving record. Fee payee: Division of Motor Vehicles. Prepayment required. Personal checks accepted. No credit cards accepted.

Mail search: Turnaround time: 1 week. A self addressed stamped envelope is requested.

In person search: Although you may request a record in person, results must be picked up the next day or mailed back.

Online search: Driving records are available online for permissible users from the state's web portal. The fee is $18.00 per record. All users must be approved by the DMV's Administrator's Office. For details, please call Ms. Elaine Phillips.

Vehicle Ownership
Vehicle Identification

Registry of Motor Vehicles, c/o Registration Files, 286 Main Street, Pawtucket, RI 02860; 401-588-3020 x2552, 8:30AM-3:30PM.

www.dmv.state.ri.us

Indexing & Storage: Records are available for 3 years for title information, for 10 years for registration information. It takes 1 week before new records are available for inquiry.

Searching: Request must be in writing and the purpose stated. Records will not be released for commercial or solicitation purposes. Casual requesters cannot obtain records.

Access by: mail, in person.

Fee & Payment: The fee is $10.00 per record request for registration and license data, and $25.00 for title information. The state will release lien information. There is a full charge for a no record found request. Fee payee: Registry of Motor Vehicles. Prepayment required. Personal checks accepted. No credit cards accepted.

Mail search: Turnaround time: 1 week. A self addressed stamped envelope is requested.

In person search: Records are not released in person, but are mailed.

Other access: Bulk retrieval of vehicle and ownership information is limited to statistical purposes.

Accident Reports

Rhode Island State Police, Accident Record Division, 311 Danielson Pike, North Scituate, RI 02857; 401-444-1143, 401-444-1133 (Fax), 10AM-4PM M,T,F; till 6:30PM on Wed.

www.risp.state.ri.us

Indexing & Storage: Records are available for the past 2 years plus the current year. Accidents before that are stored in archives. Hard copy files are indexed. It takes 7-14 days before new records are available for inquiry.

Searching: Include the following in your request: reason for information request, full name, date of accident, location of accident.

Access by: mail, phone, in person.

Fee & Payment: The fee is $10.00 per record. Fee payee: Treasurer - State of Rhode Island. Prepayment required. Personal checks accepted. No credit cards accepted.

Mail search: Turnaround time: 1 week. A self addressed stamped envelope is requested.

Phone search: No fee for telephone request. The office will let a requester know if a report is available, but information will not be given over the phone.

In person search: Same day processing is available, provided report has been received.

Vessel Ownership
Vessel Registration

Dept of Environmental Management, Office of Boat Registration, 235 Promenade, Rm 360, Providence, RI 02908; 401-222-6647, 401-222-1181 (Fax), 8:30AM-3:30PM M-F.

www.state.ri.us/dem

Indexing & Storage: Records are available from the late 1970s to the present. Records are computer indexed for the last 3 years. This is a title state, lien information shows on the title record. All boats over 14 ft must be titled and registered.

Searching: All requests must be in writing on the agency's request form. Call or write for the form. Records cannot be purchased for solicitation or commercial purposes. The name or registration number or RI number is needed for a request. They will not release the name and address of the lien holder, but will indicate if a lien exists.

Access by: mail, in person.

Fee & Payment: There is no fee, unless extensive searching is involved which is a $15.00 per hour charge.

Mail search: Turnaround time: 1 to 2 weeks. No self addressed stamped envelope is required.

In person search: Turnaround time varies.

Legislation Records

Secretary of State, State House, Room 38, Public Information Center, Providence, RI 02903; 401-222-3983 (Bill Status Only), 401-222-2473 (State Library), 401-222-1404 (Fax), 8:30AM-4:30PM.

www.rilin.state.ri.us

Note: All bills are available at the State Law Library. Current session bills are available from the Office of Public Information.

Indexing & Storage: Records are available for current session only.

Searching: One may search by bill number, subject, word, sponsor, etc.

Access by: mail, phone, fax, in person, online.

Fee & Payment: Copies are made by the Office of Public Information, $.15 per page. There is no search fee.

Mail search: No self addressed stamped envelope is required.

Phone search: Records are available by phone.

Fax search: Fax searching available.

In person search: There are public access terminals available.

Online search: The web site provides excellent means to search enactments and measures by keywords or bill numbers.

Voter Registration
Records not maintained by a state level agency.

Note: The Local Board of Canvassers keeps records at the town and city level. Although records are open they may not be purchased for commercial purposes. This agency offers the statewide database available on CD ($.25 per name) for permitted requesters.

GED Certificates

Department of Education, GED Testing, 255 Westminster, Providence, RI 02908; 401-222-4600 x2181, 7:30AM-4PM.

Searching: Include the following in your request: Social Security Number, date of birth, year of testing name at time of test. A signed release is also required for a verification or transcript copy.

Access by: mail, phone, in person.

Fee & Payment: The fee for a transcript is $3.00 or duplicate diploma. There is no fee for a verification. Fee payee: General Treasurer, State of Rhode Island. Prepayment required. Personal checks accepted. No credit cards accepted.

Mail search: Turnaround time: 1 week. No self addressed stamped envelope is required.

Phone search: Limited data is available.

In person search: Searching is available in person.

Hunting License Information
Fishing License Information

RI DEM, Boat Registration & Licensing, 235 Promenade, Providence, RI 02908; 401-222-3576 (License Issue Only), 401-222-1181 (Fax), 8:30AM-3:30PM.

www.state.ri.us/dem

Indexing & Storage: Records are available for the current year only. Agents have hard copies.

Searching: Although all records are considered open, commercial use of the records is not permitted. Include the following in your request: date of application, date of birth, address. Also, include where purchased. Requests must be in writing.

Access by: mail, phone, fax, in person.

Fee & Payment: There is no fee for a short search or confirmation. Otherwise, for extensive searches the rate $15.00 per hour. Fee payee: RI DEM. Prepayment required. Personal checks accepted. No credit cards accepted.

Mail search: Turnaround time: 1 week to 10 days.

Phone search: They will confirm only.

Fax search: Same criteria as mail searches.

In person search: They will return by mail.

Rhode Island State Licensing Agencies

Licenses Searchable Online

Acupuncturist #13	http://63.72.31.182/
Ambulatory Care Facility #13	http://63.72.31.182/
Asbestos Abatement Worker #13	http://63.72.31.182/
Athletic Trainer #13	http://63.72.31.182/
Audiologist #13	http://63.72.31.182/
Barber Shop #13	http://63.72.31.182/
Barber/Barber Instructor #13	http://63.72.31.182/
Birth Center #13	http://63.72.31.182/
Blood Test Screener #13	http://63.72.31.182/
Cable Installer #4	www.crb.state.ri.us/search.asp
Charter School #16	www.ridoe.net/charterschools/list.htm
Chimney Sweep #4	www.crb.state.ri.us/search.asp
Chiropractor #13	http://63.72.31.182/
Clinical Lab Scientist, Cytogenetic #7	http://63.72.31.182
Clinical Lab Scientist/Technician #7	http://63.72.31.182
Contractor, Residential Building #4	www.crb.state.ri.us/search.asp
Cytotechnologist #7	http://63.72.31.182
Day Care, Children #22	www.dcyf.state.ri.us/cgi-bin/dcyf.cgi
Dental Hygienist #13	http://63.72.31.182/
Dentist #13	http://63.72.31.182/
Dietitian/Nutritionist #13	http://63.72.31.182/
Electrologist #13	http://63.72.31.182/
Electron Microscopy, Clinical Lab Scientist #7	http://63.72.31.182
Embalmer #13	http://63.72.31.182/
Emergency Care Facility #13	http://63.72.31.182/
Emergency Medical Technician/Svcs #13	http://63.72.31.182/
Esthetician #13	http://63.72.31.182/
Funeral Director #13	http://63.72.31.182/
Group Home #13	http://63.72.31.182/
Hairdresser/Hairdresser Instructor #13	http://63.72.31.182/
Hazardous Waste Transporter #9	www.state.ri.us/dem/programs/benviron/waste/transpor/index.htm
Hearing Aid Dispenser #13	http://63.72.31.182/
Histologic Technician, Clinical #7	http://63.72.31.182
Home Care Providers #13	http://63.72.31.182/
Home Nursing Care #13	http://63.72.31.182/
Hospice Provider #13	http://63.72.31.182/
Hospital #13	http://63.72.31.182/
Interpretor for Deaf #13	http://63.72.31.182/
Laboratory, Medical #13	http://63.72.31.182/
Lobbyist #25	www.corps.state.ri.us/lobby/default.asp
Manicurist #13	http://63.72.31.182/
Manicurist Shop #13	http://63.72.31.182/
Marriage & Family Therapist #13	http://63.72.31.182/
Massage Therapist #13	http://63.72.31.182/
Medical Doctor #13	www.docboard.org/ri/df/search.htm
Medical Waste Transporter #9	www.state.ri.us/dem/programs/benviron/waste/transpor/index.htm
Mental Health Counselor #13	http://63.72.31.182/
Midwife #13	http://63.72.31.182/
Notary Public #15	www.corps.state.ri.us/notaries/notaries.htm
Nuclear Medicine Technologist #13	http://63.72.31.182/
Nurse #13	http://63.72.31.182/
Nurse-LPN #13	http://63.72.31.182/
Nursing Assistant #13	http://63.72.31.182/
Nursing Home Administrator #13	http://63.72.31.182/
Nursing Service #13	http://63.72.31.182/
Occupational Therapist #13	http://63.72.31.182/
Office Operatories (Medical) #13	http://63.72.31.182/
Optician #13	http://63.72.31.182/
Optometrist #13	http://63.72.31.182/
Osteopathic Physician #13	www.docboard.org/ri/df/search.htm
Outpatient Rehabilitation #13	http://63.72.31.182/
Pharmacist/Pharmacy Technician #3	http://63.72.31.182/
Pharmacy, Residential/Non-Resi. #3	http://63.72.31.182/
Phlebotomy Station #13	http://63.72.31.182/

Physical Therapist #13 ....http://63.72.31.182/
Physical Therapist Assistant #13 ....http://63.72.31.182/
Physician #13 ....http://63.72.31.182/
Physician Assistant #13 ....http://63.72.31.182/
Podiatrist #13...http://63.72.31.182/
Portable X-ray #13 ....http://63.72.31.182/
Prevention Specialist/Spvr./Advanced #6 ....http://63.72.31.182
Prosthetist #13 ....http://63.72.31.182/
Psychologist #13 ....http://63.72.31.182/
Radiation Therapist #13 ....http://63.72.31.182/
Radiographer #13 ....http://63.72.31.182/
Real Estate Appraiser #5 ....www.asc.gov/content/category1/appr_by_state.asp
Res. Care/Assisted Living Facility #13.............http://63.72.31.182/
Respiratory Care Practitioner #13....................http://63.72.31.182/
Sanitarian #13...http://63.72.31.182/
Security Alarm Installer #4 ....www.crb.state.ri.us/search.asp
Septic Transporter #9 ....www.state.ri.us/dem/programs/benviron/waste/transpor/index.htm
Social Worker #13 ....http://63.72.31.182/
Speech/Language Pathologist #13 ....http://63.72.31.182/
Surgery Center, Freestanding #13....................http://63.72.31.182/
Tanning Facility #13..http://63.72.31.182/
Tattoo Artist #13 ....http://63.72.31.182/
Underground Sprinkler Installer #4 ....www.crb.state.ri.us/search.asp
Veterinarian #13 ....http://63.72.31.182/
X-ray Facility #13 ....http://63.72.31.182/

Licensing Quick Finder

Acupuncturist #13 401-222-2827
Alarm Agent/Company #11 401-222-3857
Ambulatory Care Facility #13 401-222-2827
Arborist #10 401-647-3367
Architect #5...401-222-2565
Asbestos Abatement Worker #13.........401-222-3601
Athletic Trainer #13.............................401-222-5888
Attorney #21 401-222-4233
Auctioneer #11....................................401-222-3857
Audiologist #13 401-222-2827
Automobile Body Shop #11 401-222-3857
Automobile Glass Installer #11............401-222-3857
Automobile Wrecker #11......................401-222-3857
Bank #5...401-222-2405
Barber Shop #13.................................401-222-2827
Barber/Barber Instructor #13...............401-222-2827
Beekeeper #9 ....401-222-2781 x4510
Birth Center #13..................................401-222-2827
Blaster #19..401-294-0861
Blood Test Screener #13.....................401-222-2827
Bondsman #18.....................................401-222-3212
Boxer #5..401-222-6541
Cable Installer #4................................401-222-1268
Cattle Dealer #9.................401-222-2781 x4510
Charter School #16..............................401-222-4600
Chemical Dependency Clinical Supervisor #6
....401-233-2215
Chemical Dependency Prof./Advanced #6
....401-233-2215
Chimney Sweep #4..............................401-222-1268
Chiropractor #13 401-222-2827
Clinical Lab Scientist, Cytogenetic #7 .401-222-2827
Clinical Lab Scientist/Technician #7.....401-222-2877
Clinical Supervisor, Recognized #6......401-233-2215
Contractor, Residential Building #4 401-222-1268
Controlled Substance Wholesaler #3....401-222-2837
Court Reporter #26..............................401-222-3215
Cytotechnologist #7.............................401-222-2827
Day Care, Children #22.......................401-528-3624
Dental Hygienist #13 401-222-2151
Dentist #13..401-222-2151
Dietitian/Nutritionist #13......................401-222-2827
Electrician #8 401-462-8527
Electrologist #13 401-222-2827

Electron Microscopy, Clinical Lab Scientist #7
....401-222-2827
Elevator Inspector #8 401-462-8527
Elevator Mechanic #8..........................401-462-8527
Embalmer #13......................................401-222-2827
Emergency Care Facility #13 401-222-2827
Emergency Medical Technician/Services #13
....401-222-2401
Engineer #2 401-222-2038
Esthetician #13....................................401-222-2827
Facility Designer #9.............................401-222-6820
Family/Group Day Care Home Provider #22
....401-528-3608
Fire Alarm Installer #19 401-294-0861
Fire Extinguisher Installer/Service #19..401-294-0861
Fireworks Shooter #19.........................401-294-0861
Fisher, Commercial #9 401-222-6647
Foster Care/Homes #22 401-528-3620
Funeral Director #13............................401-222-2827
Fur Buyer #9 401-222-6647
Group Home #13 401-222-2827
Hairdresser/Hairdresser Instructor #13 .401-222-2827
Hazardous Waste Transporter #9401-222-4700x7517
Hearing Aid Dispenser #13 401-222-2827
Histologic Technician, Clinical #7.........401-222-2827
Hoisting Engineer #8 401-462-8527
Home Care Providers #13....................401-222-2827
Home Nursing Care #13.......................401-222-2827
Hospice Provider #13...........................401-222-2827
Hospital #13...401-222-2827
Hypodermic Dispenser #3 401-222-2837
Insurance Adjuster #5 401-222-2223
Insurance Appraiser #5 401-222-2223
Insurance Broker/Producer #5 401-222-2223
Insurance Solicitor #5..........................401-222-2223
Interpreter for the Deaf #13 401-222-2827
Investment Advisor #5..........................401-222-3048
Laboratory, Medical #13 401-222-2827
Land Surveyor Firm #2.........................401-222-2038
Landscape Architect #2........................401-222-2038
Landscaper #5.....................................401-222-2565
Lifeguard #12.......................................401-222-2632
Liquor Control #5.................................401-222-2562
Lobbyist #25..401-222-6616

Manicurist #13 401-222-2827
Manicurist Shop #13 401-222-2827
Marriage & Family Therapist #13..........401-222-2827
Massage Therapist #13........................401-222-2827
Medical Doctor #13..............................401-222-2827
Medical Waste Transporter #9.. 401-222-4700 x7517
Mental Health Counselor #13 401-222-2827
Midwife #13 401-222-5700
Mobile Home Park #11.........................401-222-3857
Mobile/Manufactured Home Mfg./Dealer #11
....401-222-3857
Money Broker #5.................................401-222-2405
Mortgage Broker #5.............................401-222-2405
Notary Public #15................................401-222-1487
Nuclear Medicine Technologist #13.....401-222-5700
Nurse #13..401-222-5700
Nurse-LPN #13....................................401-222-5700
Nurseryman #9 ....401-222-2781 x4510
Nursing Assistant #13 401-222-5888
Nursing Home Administrator #13..........401-222-5888
Nursing Service #13.............................401-222-2827
Occupational Therapist #13 401-222-2827
Office Operatories (Medical) #13.........401-222-2827
Optician #13 401-222-2827
Optometrist #13...................................401-222-2827
Osteopathic Physician #13..................401-222-3855
Outpatient Rehabilitation #13...............401-222-2827
Park Ranger #12 401-222-2632
Pesticide Applicator #9.............. 401-222-2781 x4510
Pharmacist/Pharmacy Technician #3 .. 401-222-2837
Pharmacy, Residential/Non-Resi. #3... 401-222-2837
Phlebotomy Station #13 401-222-2827
Physical Therapist #13 401-222-2827
Physical Therapist Assistant #13 401-222-2827
Physician #13......................................401-222-2827
Physician Assistant #13 401-222-2827
Physicians Controlled Substance #3 ... 401-222-2837
Pipefitter #8 401-462-8527
Plumber/Master Plumber/Journeyman #8
....401-462-8527
Podiatrist #13 401-222-2827
Portable X-ray #13 401-222-2827
Prevention Specialist/Spvr./Advd. #6... 401-233-2215
Prosthetist #13....................................401-222-2827

Psychologist #13.....................................401-222-2827
Public Accountant-CPA #1 401-222-3185
Pyrotechnic Operator #19.....................401-294-0861
Radiation Therapist #13 401-222-2827
Radiographer #13..................................401-222-2827
Reading Specialist #16..........................401-222-2675
Real Estate Appraiser #5.......................401-222-2255
Real Estate Broker/Salesperson #5 401-222-2255
Refrigeration Technician #8...................401-462-8527
Res. Care/Assisted Living Facility #13 ..401-222-2827
Respiratory Care Practitioner #13........401-222-2827
Salvage Yard #11 401-222-3857
Sanitarian #13.......................................401-222-2827
School Coach #16 401-222-2675
School Guidance Counselor #16..........401-222-2675

School Principal/Superintendent/Supervisor #16
....401-222-2675
School Psychologist/Social Worker #16 401-222-2675
Securities Broker/Dealer #5 401-222-3048
Securities Broker/Dealer Sales Rep. #5 401-222-3048
Securities Sales Representative #5 401-222-3048
Security Alarm Installer #4 401-222-1268
Septic Transporter #9...............401-222-4700 x7517
Sewage Disposal System Installer #9...401-222-6820
Sheet Metal Technician/Worker #8 401-462-8527
Ship Pilot #20 401-783-5551
Social Worker #13 401-222-2827
Speech/Language Pathologist #13 401-222-2827
Surgery Center, Freestanding #13.......401-222-2827
Surveyor, Land #5 401-222-2565
Tanning Facility #13 401-222-2827

Tattoo Artist #13 401-222-2827
Teacher #16 401-222-2675
Telecommunications Technician #8.....401-462-8527
Trapper #9..401-222-6647
Travel Agent #5 401-222-3857
Underground Sprinkler Installer #4 401-222-1268
Vendor Employee #5............................401-222-2405
Veterinarian #13 401-222-2827
Waste Water Treatment Plant Operator #9
....401-222-6820
Wildlife Propagator #9 401-222-6647
Wildlife Rehabilitator #23 401-789-0281
Woods Operator #10.............................401-647-3367
Wrestler #5 401-222-6541
X-ray Facility #13.................................401-222-2827

Licensing Agency Information

#1 Department of Business Regulation, Board of Accountancy, 233 Richmond St, Providence, RI 02903-4236; 401-222-3185, Fax: 401-222-6654. www.dbr.state.ri.us/account.html

#3 Board of Pharmacy, 3 Capitol Hill, Rm 205, Providence, RI 02908; 401-222-2837, Fax: 401-222-2158.
www.health.state.ri.us
Search database at http://63.72.31.182

#4 Contractors' Registration Board, 1 Capitol Hill, 2nd Fl, Providence, RI 02908; 401-222-1268, Fax: 401-222-2599.
www.crb.state.ri.us
Search database at www.crb.state.ri.us/search.asp

#5 Business Regulation Department, Division of Commercial Licensing & Regulation, 233 Richmond St, Providence, RI 02903-4232; 401-222-2246.
www.dbr.state.ri.us

#6 Certification of Chemical Dependency Professionals, 345 Waterman Ave, Smithfield, RI 02917; 401-233-2215, Fax: 401-233-0690. Agency email: ricert@msn.com.
Search database at http://63.72.31.182

#7 Clinical Laboratory Advisory Board, 3 Capitol Hill, Rm 104, Providence, RI 02908; 401-222-2827, Fax: 401-222-1272.
www.health.state.ri.us
Search database at http://63.72.31.182

#8 Department of Labor & Training, Division of Prof. Regulation - Bldg #70, PO Box 20247 (1511 Pontiac Av), Providence, RI 02920-0943; 401-462-8527, Fax: 401-462-8528.

#9 Department of Environmental Management, 235 Promenade St, #260, Providence, RI 02908-5767; 401-222-4700, Fax: 401-222-6802.
www.state.ri.us/dem/programs/index.htm

#10 Division of Forest Environment, Department of Environmental Management, 1037 Hartford Pike, North Scituate, RI 02857; 401-647-3367, Fax: 401-647-3590.
www.state.ri.us/dem/programs/bnatres/forest/index.htm. Agency email: riforestry@edgenet.net.

#11 Division of Licensing & Consumer Protection, Business Registrations, 233 Richmond St, Providence, RI 02903; 401-222-3857, Fax: 401-222-6654.
www.dbr.state.ri.us

#12 Division of Parks & Recreation, 2321 Hartford Ave, Johnston, RI 02919; 401-222-2632, Fax: 401-934-0610.
www.riparks.com/employment.htm
Agency email: riparks@earthlink.net.

#13 Health Department, Professional Regulation Division, 3 Capitol Hill, Rm 205, Providence, RI 02908-5097; 401-222-2827, Fax: 401-222-1272.
www.health.state.ri.us. Agency email: library@health.state.ri.us.
Search database at http://63.72.31.182

#15 Office of Secretary of State, Notary Public Section, 100 N Main St, Providence, RI 02903; 401-222-2249, Fax: 401-222-3879.
www.state.ri.us
Search database at www.state.ri.us. To Search, there are separate buttons for the Notary Public Section or Lobbyist.

#16 Office of Teacher Certification, Department of Education, 255 Westminster St, Providence, RI 02903; 401-222-4600, Fax: 401-222-2048.
www.ridoe.net

#18 Superior Court, Bondsman Registration, 250 Benefit St, Rm 533, Providence, RI 02903; 401-222-3212, Fax: 401-272-4645. Direct written requests to Judge Jos. F. Rodgers, Jr.

#19 State Fire Marshall's Office, 24 Conway Ave, Quansit-Davisville Industrial Park, Davisville/North Kingston, RI 02852; 401-294-0861, Fax: 401-295-9092.

#20 Pilotage Commission, 301 Great Island Rd, Galilee, RI 02882; 401-783-5551, Fax: 401-783-7285.

#21 Supreme Court, Board of Bar Examiners, 250 Benefit St, Providence, RI 02903; 401-222-4233, Fax: 401-222-3599.
www.courts.state.ri.us/supreme/bar/barexaminers.htm. Agency email: kcacchiotti@courts.state.ri.us.

#22 Department of Children, Youth & Famillies, 101 Friendship St #101, Providence, RI 02903; 401-528-3624.
www.dcyf.state.ri.us
Search database at www.dcyf.state.ri.us/cgi-bin/dcyf.cgi

#23 Department of Environmental Management, Division of Fish & Wildlife, Box 218, West Kingston, RI 02892; 401-789-0281, Fax: 401-783-7490.
www.state.ri.us/dem

#25 Office of Secretary of State, Lobbyist Registration, 100 N Main St, Providence, RI 02903; 401-222-2249, Fax: 401-222-3879.
www.state.ri.us/
Search database at www.state.ri.us. To Search, there are separate buttons for the Notary Public Section or Lobbyist.

#26 Court Administrator Office, 250 Benefit St, #506, Providence, RI 02903; 401-222-3215.

Rhode Island Federal Courts

The following list indicates the district and division name for each county in the state.

County/Court Cross Reference

Bristol...Providence

Kent...Providence

Newport...Providence

Providence...Providence

Washington..Providence

US District Court

District of Rhode Island

Providence Division Clerk's Office, Two Exchange Terrace, Federal Bldg, Providence, RI 02903 (Courier Address: Use mail address for courier delivery), 401-752-7200, Fax: 401-752-7247.

www.rid.uscourts.gov

Counties: All counties in Rhode Island.

Indexing & Storage: Cases are indexed by defendant, plaintiff, and case number. New cases are available in the index 1-2 days after filing date. Computer indexing is since 1991. Anything prior to that is maintained on card index. District wide searches are available from this court.

Fee & Payment Notes: Payment may be made by money order, cashier check, personal check. Payee: Clerk, US District Court. You are allowed to make your own copies. These copies cost $.25 per page. Naturalization records are at the Federal Records Center in Waltham, MA.

Phone Search: Only the case number or name will be released over the phone.

In Person Search: In person searching available.

PACER: Toll-free dial-up access: 888-421-6861. Local dial-up access: 401-752-7262. Case records are available back to December 1988. Records are never purged. New records are available online after 2 days. PACER is available online at http://pacer.rid.uscourts.gov.

US Bankruptcy Court

District of Rhode Island

Providence Division 6th Floor, 380 Westminster St, Providence, RI 02903 (Courier Address: Use mail address for courier delivery), 401-528-4477, Fax: 401-528-4470.

www.rib.uscourts.gov

Counties: All counties in Rhode Island.

Indexing & Storage: Cases are indexed by debtor and creditors as well as by case number. New cases are available in the index 1 day after filing date. Open records are located at this court.

Fee & Payment Notes: Payment may be made by money order, cashier check, personal check, Visa or Mastercard. Debtors checks are not accepted. Payee: Clerk, US Bankruptcy Court. You are allowed to make your own copies. These copies cost $.20 per page.

Phone Search: Only docket information is available by phone. An automated voice case information service (VCIS) is available. Call VCIS at 800-843-2841 or 401-528-4476.

Fax Search: The fees for a fax request are the same as for a mail request. The fee is $15.00 per item.

In Person Search: In person searching available.

PACER: Toll-free dial-up access: 800-610-9310. Local dial-up access: 401-528-4062. Case records are available back to 1990. Records are purged every three years. New civil records are available online after 1 day. PACER is available online at http://pacer.rib.uscourts.gov. Document images available.

Electronic Filing: (Currently in the process of implementing CM/ECF.)

Standards for Federal Courts: The search fee is $20.00 per item (one party name or case number). Certification fee is $7.00 per document. Copy fee is $.50 per page. All fees standard unless noted in profile. Mail Search: always enclose a stamped self addressed envelope unless otherwise noted. Before releasing records, all courts require prepayment unless noted in profile.

Open records are located at the court unless otherwise noted. District courts index by defendant and plaintiff as well as by case number. Bankruptcy courts usually index by debtor and case number. While most courts now have their indexes on computer, many still maintain index card files as well.

The universal PACER sign-up number is 800-676-6856. Find PACER and the Party/Case Index on the Web at http://pacer.psc.uscourts.gov. PACER dial-up access is $.60 per minute. Also, courts offering internet access via RACER, PACER, Web-PACER or the new CM-ECF charge $.07 per page fee unless noted as free.

Rhode Island County Courts

Court	Jurisdiction	No. of Courts	How Organized
Superior Courts*	General	4	4 Divisions
District Courts*	Limited	4	6 Divisions
Municipal Courts	Municipal	16	
Probate Courts*	Probate	39	39 Cities/ Towns
Family Courts	Special	4	4 Divisions
Workers' Compensation Court	Special	1	

* Profiled in this Sourcebook.

CIVIL									
Court	Tort	Contract	Real Estate	Min. Claim	Max. Claim	Small Claims	Estate	Eviction	Domestic Relations
Superior Courts*	X	X	X	$5000	No Max				
District Courts*	X	X	X	$1500	$10,000	$1500		X	
Municipal Courts									
Probate Courts*							X		
Family Courts									X
Workers' Compensation Court									

CRIMINAL					
Court	Felony	Misdemeanor	DWI/DUI	Preliminary Hearing	Juvenile
Superior Courts*	X				
District Courts*		X	X	X	
Municipal Courts					
Probate Courts*					
Family Courts					X
Workers' Compensation Court					

ADMINISTRATION Court Administrator, Supreme Court, 250 Benefit St, Providence, RI, 02903; 401-222-3272, Fax: 401-222-3599. www.courts.state.ri.us

COURT STRUCTURE Rhode Island has five counties, but only four Superior/District Court Locations (2nd-Newport, 3rd-Kent, 4th-Washignton, and 6th-Providence/Bristol Districts). Bristol and Providence counties are completely merged at the Providence location. Civil claims between $5000 and $10,000 may be filed in either Superior or District Court at the discretion of the filer.

ONLINE ACCESS The Rhode Island Judiciary offers free Internet access to court criminal records statewide at http://courtconnect.courts.state.ri.us. A word of caution, this website is provided as an informational service only and should not be relied upon as an official record of the court.

Superior (civil, family) and Appellate courts are online internally for court personnel only.

PROBATE COURTS Probate is handled by the Town Clerk at the 39 cities and towns across Rhode Island.

Bristol County

Superior & District Courts c/o Bristol Town Hall, 10 Court St, Bristol, RI 02809; Probate phone: 401-253-7000.

Note: Do not send criminal or civil (except probate) record requests here. All civil and criminal cases are handled by the Providence County courts.

Barrington Town Hall 283 County Road, Barrington, RI 02806; 401-247-1900 x4; Fax: 401-245-5003. Hours: 8:30AM-4:30PM (EST). *Probate.*

Bristol Town Hall 10 Court Street, Bristol, RI 02809; 401-253-7000 x21; Fax: 401-253-3080. Hours: 8:30AM-4PM (EST). *Probate.*

Warren Town Hall 514 Main Street, Warren, RI 02885; 401-245-7340; Fax: 401-245-7421. Hours: 9AM-4PM (EST). *Probate.*

Kent County

Superior Court 222 Quaker Lane, Warwick, RI 02886; 401-822-1311. Hours: 8:30AM-4:30PM (EST). *Felony, Civil Actions Over $10,000.*

www.courts.state.ri.us

Civil Records: Access: In person only. Visitors must perform in person searches for themselves. No search fee. Required to search: name, years to search. Civil cases indexed by defendant, plaintiff. Civil records on computer from 1987.

Criminal Records: Access: In person, online. Visitors must perform in person searches for themselves. No search fee. Required to search: name, years to search, signed release; also helpful: DOB. Criminal records on computer from 1987. Free Internet access is available at http://courtconnect.courts.state.ri.us. This website is provided as an informational service only and should not be relied upon as an official record of the court.

General Information: Public access terminal is available. (Records available from 1997.) No adoption, confidential or sealed records released. Copy fee: $.15 per page. Certification fee: $3.00. Exemplified copies $9.00 and $3.00 per page. Fee payee: Clerk of Superior Court. Personal checks accepted. Prepayment is required.

3rd Division District Court 222 Quaker Lane, Warwick, RI 02886-0107; 401-822-1771. Hours: 8:30AM-4:30PM (EST). *Misdemeanor, Civil Actions Under $10,000, Eviction, Small Claims.*

Civil Records: Access: In person only. Visitors must perform in person searches for themselves. No search fee. Required to search: name, years to search. Civil cases indexed by defendant, plaintiff. Civil records for 1995-1997 on index cards. Archives stored at Rhode Island Judicial Records Center, 1 Hill St, Pawtucket, RI 02860, 401-277-3249. Records destroyed after 10 years, but remain in docket books.

Criminal Records: Access: In person, online. Visitors must perform in person searches for themselves. No search fee. Required to search: name, years to search, DOB, signed release. Criminal records for 1995-1997 on index cards. Archives stored at Rhode Island Judicial Records Center. Records destroyed after 10 years, but remain in docket books. Free Internet access is available at http://courtconnect.courts.state.ri.us. This website is provided as an informational service only and should not be relied upon as an official record of the court.

General Information: No mental or sealed records released. Copy fee: $1.00 per page. Certification fee: $1.00 per page. Fee payee: 3rd District Court. Personal checks accepted. Credit cards accepted: Visa, AmEx. Prepayment is required.

Coventry Town Hall 1670 Flat River Road, Coventry, RI 02816; 401-822-9174; Fax: 401-822-9132. Hours: 8:30AM-4:30PM (EST). *Probate.*

East Greenwich Town Hall 125 Main St (PO Box 111), East Greenwich, RI 02818; 401-886-8607; 8604; Fax: 401-886-8625. Hours: 8:30AM-4:30PM (EST). *Probate.*

Warwick City Hall 3275 Post Road, Warwick, RI 02886; 401-738-2000 (x6213); Fax: 401-738-6639. Hours: 8:30AM-4:30PM (EST). *Probate.*

West Greenwich Town Hall 280 Victory Highway, West Greenwich, RI 02817; 401-392-3800; Fax: 401-392-3805. Hours: 9AM-4PM M,T,Th,F; 9AM-4PM, 7-9PM W (EST). *Probate.*

West Warwick Town Hall 1170 Main Street, West Warwick, RI 02893-4829; 401-822-9201; Fax: 401-822-9266. Hours: 8:30AM-4:30PM; 8:30AM-4PM June 1st-Labor Day (EST). *Probate.*

Newport County

Superior Court Florence K Murray Judicial Complex, 45 Washington Sq, Newport, RI 02840; 401-841-8330. Hours: 8:30AM-4:30PM (July and August till 4PM) (EST). *Felony, Civil Actions Over $10,000.*

Civil Records: Access: Mail, in person. Both court and visitors may perform in person searches. No search fee. Required to search: name, years to search. Civil cases indexed by defendant, plaintiff. Civil records on computer from 1989. Prior records archived at Rhode Island Records Center.

Criminal Records: Access: Mail, in person, online. Both court and visitors may perform in person searches. No search fee. Required to search: name, years to search, DOB. Criminal records on computer from 1983, index from 1968. Prior records archived at Records Center. Free Internet access is available at http://courtconnect.courts.state.ri.us. This website is provided as an informational service only and should not be relied upon as an official record of the court.

General Information: Public access terminal is available. No child molestation or sexual assault records released. SASE required. Turnaround time 1 day. Copy fee: $.50 per page. Certification fee: $1.00. Fee payee: Clerk Superior Court. Personal checks accepted. Prepayment is required.

2nd District Court 45 Washington Square, Newport, RI 02840; 401-841-8350. Hours: 8:30AM-4:30PM (4PM-summer months) (EST). *Misdemeanor, Civil Actions Under $10,000, Eviction, Small Claims.*

Civil Records: Access: In person only. Visitors must perform in person searches for themselves. No search fee. Required to search: name, years to search. Civil cases indexed by defendant, plaintiff. Civil records on index cards for past 3 years, prior archived at Pawtucket Judicial Records Center.

Criminal Records: Access: In person, online. Visitors must perform in person searches for themselves. No search fee. Required to search: name. Overall records from 1998-2002. Computerized records from 1999-2002. Free Internet access is available at http://courtconnect.courts.state.ri.us. This website is provided as an informational service only and should not be relied upon as an official record of the court.

General Information: No juvenile, family court, sealed, expunged or ordered by judge or adoption records released. Copy fee: $.15 per page. Certification fee: $1.00. Fee payee: 2nd District Court. Personal checks accepted. Prepayment is required.

Jamestown Town Hall 93 Narragansett Avenue, Jamestown, RI 02835; 401-423-7200; Fax: 401-423-7230. Hours: 8AM-4:30PM (EST). *Probate.*

Little Compton Town Hall 40 Commons, PO Box 226, Little Compton, RI 02837; 401-635-4400; Fax: 401-635-2470. Hours: 8AM-4PM (EST). *Probate.*

Middletown Town Hall 350 East Main Road, Middletown, RI 02842; 401-847-0009; Fax: 401-845-0406. Hours: 8AM-5PM (EST). *Probate.*

Newport City Hall 43 Broadway, Newport, RI 02840; 401-846-9600; Fax: 401-849-8757. Hours: 8:30AM-5PM (EST). *Probate.*

Portsmouth Town Hall 2200 East Main Road, PO Box 115, Portsmouth, RI 02871; 401-683-2101. Hours: 9AM-4PM (EST). *Probate.*

Tiverton Town Hall 343 Highland Road, Tiverton, RI 02878; 401-625-6700; Fax: 401-625-6705. Hours: 8:30AM-4PM (EST). *Probate.*

Providence County

Providence/Bristol Superior Court 250 Benefit St, Providence, RI 02903; 401-222-3250. Hours: 8:30AM-4:30PM (EST). *Felony, Civil Actions Over $10,000.*

www.courts.state.ri.us

Note: All civil and criminal cases are handled by the Providence County courts.

Civil Records: Access: Phone, mail, in person. Visitors must perform in person searches for themselves. No search fee. Required to search: name, years to search. Civil cases indexed by defendant, plaintiff. Civil records on computer since 1983.

Criminal Records: Access: In person, online. Visitors must perform in person searches for themselves. No search fee. Required to search: name, years to search, DOB. Criminal records on computer since 1983. Free Internet access at http://courtconnect.courts.state.ri.us. This website is provided as an informational service only and should not be relied upon as an official record of the court.

General Information: Public access terminal is available. No adoption, confidential or sealed records released. Copy fee: $.15 per page. Certification fee: $3.00. Fee payee: Providence Superior Court. Personal checks accepted. Prepayment is required.

6th Division District Court 1 Dorrance Plaza 2nd Floor, Providence, RI 02903; 401-458-5400. Hours: 8:30AM-4:30PM (EST). *Misdemeanor, Civil Actions Under $10,000, Eviction, Small Claims.*

Note: All civil and criminal cases are handled by the Providence County courts.

Civil Records: Access: Mail, phone, in person. Both court and visitors may perform in person searches. No search fee. Required to search: name, years to search. Civil cases indexed by defendant, plaintiff. Civil records on card files to present. Phone access limited to one name.

Criminal Records: Access: Mail, phone, in person, online. Both court and visitors may perform in person searches. No search fee. Required to search: name, years to search. Criminal records for misdemeanor on computer from 1989. Phone requests limited to one name. Free Internet access is available at http://courtconnect.courts.state.ri.us. This website is provided as an informational service only and should not be relied upon as an official record of the court.

General Information: No adoption, confidential or sealed records released. SASE required. Turnaround time varies. Copy fee: $.50 per page. Certification fee: $1.00. Fee payee: 6th Division District Court. Personal checks accepted. Prepayment is required.

Burrillville Town Hall 105 Harrisville Main Street, Harrisville, RI 02830; 401-568-4300; Fax: 401-568-0490. Hours: 8:30AM-4:30PM (EST). *Probate.*

Central Falls City Hall 580 Broad Street, Central Falls, RI 02863; 401-727-7400; Fax: 401-727-7406. Hours: 8:30AM-4:30PM (EST). *Probate.*

Cranston City Hall 869 Park Avenue, Cranston, RI 02910; 401-461-1000; Fax: 401-461-9650. Hours: 8:30AM-4:30PM (EST). *Probate.*

Cumberland Town Hall 45 Broad Street, PO Box 7, Cumberland, RI 02864; 401-728-2400 x37; Fax: 401-724-1103. Hours: 8:30AM-4:30PM (EST). *Probate.*

East Providence City Hall 145 Taunton Avenue, East Providence, RI 02914; 401-435-7500; Fax: 401-438-7501. Hours: 8AM-4PM (EST). *Probate.*

Foster Town Hall 181 Howard Hill Road, Foster, RI 02825; 401-392-9200; Fax: 401-392-9201. Hours: 9AM-4PM (EST). *Probate.*

Glocester Town Hall 1145 Putnam Pike, Glocester/ Chepachet, RI 02814; 401-568-6206; Fax: 401-568-5850. Hours: 8AM-4:30PM (EST). *Probate.*

Johnston Town Hall 1385 Hartford Avenue, Johnston, RI 02919; 401-351-6618/401-553-8830 (Direct Phone); Fax: 401-553-8835. Hours: 8:30AM-4:30PM (EST). *Probate.*

Note: Online access to probate court records is available at http://johnston-ri.com/probate.asp. Search by last name.

Lincoln Town Hall 100 Old River Road, Lincoln, RI 02865; 401-333-1100; 333-8451; Fax: 401-333-3648. Hours: 9AM-4:30PM (EST). *Probate.*

www.lincolnri.org/clerksoffice.shtml

Note: Court meets fourth Monday at 9 AM.

North Providence Town Hall 2000 Smith Street, North Providence, RI 02911; 401-232-0900; Fax: 401-233-1409. Hours: 8:30AM-4:30PM (EST). *Probate.*

North Smithfield Town Hall Municipal Annex, 575 Smithfield Rd, North Smithfield, RI 02896; 401-767-2200 x216; Fax: 401-767-2840. Hours: 8AM-4PM M, Tu, W; 8AM-7PM Th; 8AM-noon F (EST). *Probate.*

Pawtucket City Hall 137 Roosevelt Avenue, Pawtucket, RI 02860; 401-728-0500; Fax: 401-728-8932. Hours: 8:30AM-4:30PM (EST). *Probate.*

Providence City Hall 25 Dorrance Street, Providence, RI 02903; 401-421-7740; Fax: 401-861-6208. Hours: 8:45AM-4:15PM (EST). *Probate.*

Note: All civil and criminal cases are handled by the Providence County courts.

Scituate Town Hall 195 Danielson Pike, PO Box 328, North Scituate, RI 02857; 401-647-2822; Fax: 401-647-7220. Hours: 8:30AM-4PM (EST). *Probate.*

Smithfield Town Hall 64 Farnum Pike, Smithfield, RI 02917; 401-233-1000 X111; Fax: 401-232-7244. Hours: 9AM-4PM (EST). *Probate.*

Woonsocket City Hall 169 Main Street, Woonsocket, RI 02895; 401-762-6400; Fax: 401-765-0022. Hours: 8:30AM-4PM (EST). *Probate.*

Washington County

Superior Court 4800 Towerhill Rd, Wakefield, RI 02879; 401-782-4121. Hours: 8:30AM-4:30PM (Sept-June) 8:30AM-4PM (July & Aug) (EST). *Felony, Civil Actions Over $10,000.*

Civil Records: Access: Phone, mail, in person. Both court and visitors may perform in person searches. No search fee. Required to search: name, years to search. Civil cases indexed by defendant, plaintiff. Civil records on computer from 1984, on index prior to 1984. Archived at Record Center, 401-277-3249. Phone requests taken only after 3PM.

Criminal Records: Access: Mail, in person, online. Both court and visitors may perform in person searches. No search fee. Required to search: name, years to search; also helpful: DOB. Criminal records on computer from 1984, on index prior to 1984. Archived at Record Center, 401-277-3249. Free Internet access is available at http://courtconnect.courts.state.ri.us. This website is provided as an informational service only and should not be relied upon as an official record of the court.

General Information: No confidential or sealed records released. SASE required. Turnaround time 1 week. Copy fee: $.15 per page. Certification fee: $3.00. Fee payee: Washington Superior Court. Personal checks accepted.

4th District Court 4800 Towerhill Rd, Wakefield, RI 02879; 401-782-4131. Hours: 8:30AM-4:30PM (EST). *Misdemeanor, Civil Actions Under $10,000, Eviction, Small Claims.*

Civil Records: Access: In person only. Visitors must perform in person searches for themselves. No search fee. Required to search: name, years to search. Civil cases indexed by defendant, plaintiff. Civil records on index cards.

Criminal Records: Access: In person, online. Visitors must perform in person searches for themselves. No

search fee. Required to search: name, years to search, DOB. Criminal records available on computer beginning in 1996. Free Internet access is available at http://courtconnect.courts.state.ri.us. This website is provided as an informational service only and should not be relied upon as an official record of the court.

General Information: Public access terminal is available. (Terminal is for criminal records only.) No family court records released. Copy fee: $.50 per page. Certification fee: $1.00. Fee payee: Court Clerk. Personal checks accepted. Prepayment is required.

Charlestown Town Hall 4540 South County Trail, Charlestown, RI 02813; 401-364-1200; Fax: 401-364-1238. Hours: 8:30AM-4:30PM (EST). *Probate.*

Exeter Town Hall 675 Ten Rod Road, Exeter, RI 02822; 401-294-3891 (295-7500); Fax: 401-295-1248. Hours: 9AM-4PM (EST). *Probate.*

Note: Probate Court held fourth Monday monthly at 2:00 PM.

Hopkinton Town Hall 1 Town House Road, Hopkinton, RI 02833; 401-377-7777; Fax: 401-377-7788. Hours: 8:30AM-4:30PM or by appointment (EST). *Probate.*

Narragansett Town Hall 25 Fifth Avenue, Narragansett, RI 02882; 401-789-1044 X621; Fax: 401-783-9637. Hours: 8:30AM-4:30PM (EST). *Probate.*

New Shoreham Town Hall Old Town Road, PO Drawer 220, Block Island, RI 02807; 401-466-3200; Fax: 401-466-3219. Hours: 9AM-3PM (EST). *Probate.*

North Kingstown Town Hall 80 Boston Neck Road, North Kingstown, RI 02852-5762; 401-294-3331; Fax: 401-885-7373. Hours: 8:30AM-4:30PM (EST). *Probate.*

www.northkingstown.org

Richmond Town Hall 5 Richmond Townhouse Rd., Wyoming, RI 02898; 401-539-2497; Fax: 401-539-1089. Hours: 9AM-4PM; 8:30 AM on second Tuesday (EST). *Probate.*

South Kingstown Town Hall 180 High Street, Wakefield, RI 02879; 401-789-9331; Fax: 401-789-5280. Hours: 8:30AM-4:30PM (EST). *Probate.*

Westerly Town Hall 45 Broad Street, Westerly, RI 02891; 401-348-2500; Fax: 401-348-2571. Hours: 8:30AM-4:30PM (EST). *Probate.*

Rhode Island Recording Offices

ORGANIZATION: 5 counties and 39 towns, 39 recording offices. The recording officer is Town/City Clerk (Recorder of Deeds). The Town/City Clerk usually also serves as the Recorder of Deeds. There is no county administration in Rhode Island that handles recording. The entire state is in the Eastern Time Zone (EST). Be aware that the recordings in the counties of Bristol, Newport, and Providence can relate to property located in other cities/ towns even though each of these three cities bears the same name as the county.

Towns will not perform real estate searches. Copy fees are usually $1.50 per page. Certification usually costs $3.00 per document.

REAL ESTATE RECORDS: Towns will not perform real estate searches. Copy fees are usually $1.50 per page. Certification usually costs $3.00 per document.

UCC RECORDS: Financing statements are filed at the state level, except for farm related and real estate related collateral, which are filed with the Town/City Clerk. Most recording offices will not perform UCC searches. Use search request form UCC-11. Copy fees are usually $1.50 per page. Certification usually costs $3.00 per document.

TAX LIEN RECORDS: All federal and state tax liens on personal property and on real property are filed with the Recorder of Deeds. Towns will not perform tax lien searches.

OTHER LIENS: Mechanics, municipal, lis pendens.

ONLINE ACCESS: A private vendor has placed on the Internet the assessor records from a number of towns. Visit http://data.visionappraisal.com

Barrington Town

Town Clerk, 283 County Road, Town Hall, Barrington, RI 02806. Town Clerk, R/E and UCC Recording 401-247-1900; Fax 401-245-5003.
Will search UCC records. This agency will not do a tax lien search. Will not search real estate records. **Other Phone Numbers:** Assessor 401-247-1900; Treasurer 401-247-1900; Appraiser/Auditor 401-247-1900; Elections 401-247-1900; Vital Records 401-247-1900.

Bristol Town

Town Clerk, 10 Court St, Town Hall, Bristol, RI 02809. 401-253-7000 R/E Recording: 401-253-7000 x36; Fax 401-253-3080. www.onlinebristol.com
Will search UCC records. This agency will not do a tax lien search. Will not search real estate records. **Other Phone Numbers:** Assessor 401-253-7000 x38; Treasurer 401-253-7000 x16; Elections 401-253-7000 x35; Vital Records 401-253-7000 x21.

Burrillville Town

Town Clerk, 105 Harrisville Main St, Town Hall, Harrisville, RI 02830-1499. 401-568-4300 R/E Recording: 401-568-4300 x13 UCC Recording: 401-568-4300 x13; Fax 401-568-0490.
This agency will not search real estate or UCC records. **Other Phone Numbers:** Assessor 401-568-9452; Treasurer 401-568-9451; Appraiser/Auditor 401-568-9452; Elections 401-568-9454; Vital Records 401-568-4300 x11.

Central Falls City

City Clerk, 580 Broad St, City Hall, Central Falls, RI 02863. City Clerk, R/E and UCC Recording 401-727-7400; Fax 401-727-7406.
This agency will not perform searches. **Other Phone Numbers:** Assessor 401-727-7430; Treasurer 401-727-7470; Elections 401-727-7450; Vital Records 401-727-7400.

Charlestown Town

Town Clerk, 4540 South County Trail, Charlestown, RI 02813. 401-364-1200; Fax 401-364-1238. www.charlestownri.org
This agency will not search real estate or UCC records. **Other Phone Numbers:** Assessor 401-364-1233.

Coventry Town

Town Clerk, 1670 Flat River Road, Town Hall, Coventry, RI 02816-8911. 401-822-9174; Fax 401-822-9132.
Will search UCC records. Will not search real estate records. **Online Access:** Assessor, Property Records. Access is to be available in 2002 at www.town.coventry.ri.us/assess.htm. **Other Phone Numbers:** Assessor 401-822-9163.

Cranston City

City Clerk, 869 Park Ave, City Hall, Cranston, RI 02910. 401-461-1000 x3130.
Will search UCC records. This agency will not do a tax lien search. Will not search real estate records. **Other Phone Numbers:** Assessor 401-461-1000 x3181.

Cumberland Town

Town Clerk, PO Box 7, Cumberland, RI 02864-0808. 401-728-2400 R/E Recording: 401-728-2400 x35 UCC Recording: 401-728-2400 x35; Fax 401-724-1103.
Will search UCC records. This agency will not do a tax lien search. Will not search real estate records. **Other Phone Numbers:** Assessor 401-728-2400 x13; Treasurer 401-728-2400 x28; Appraiser/Auditor 401-728-2400 x15; Elections 401-728-2400 x40; Vital Records 401-728-2400 x33.

East Greenwich Town

Town Clerk, PO Box 111, East Greenwich, RI 02818. 401-886-8603 R/E Recording: 401-886-8602 UCC Recording: 401-886-8602; Fax 401-886-8625. www.eastgreenwichri.com
Will search UCC records. Will not search real estate records. **Online Access:** Property Records. Limited Finance Dept. property sales information is listed at www.eastgreenwichri.com/finance.htm. See bottom of web page. **Other Phone Numbers:** Assessor 401-886-8614; Treasurer 401-886-8608; Elections 401-886-8603; Vital Records 401-886-8602.

East Providence City

Town Clerk, 145 Taunton Ave, City Hall, East Providence, RI 02914. 401-435-7500 R/E Recording: 401-435-7594 UCC Recording: 401-435-7594; Fax 401-435-7501. www.eastprovidence.com

Will search UCC records. Will not search real estate records. **Other Phone Numbers:** Assessor 401-435-7574; Treasurer 401-435-7560; Elections 401-435-7503; Vital Records 401-435-7596.

Exeter Town

Town Clerk, 675 Ten Rod Road, Town Hall, Exeter, RI 02822. Town Clerk, R/E and UCC Recording 401-294-3891; Fax 401-295-1248. www.town.exeter.ri.us
Will search UCC records. Will not search real estate records. **Online Access:** Assessor, Property Records. Access is may be available from a private company at http://data.visionappraisal.com/ExeterRI. Free registration is required to view full data. **Other Phone Numbers:** Assessor 401-294-5734; Treasurer 401-267-1024; Appraiser/Auditor 401-294-2287; Elections 401-294-3891; Vital Records 401-884-4740.

Foster Town

Town Clerk, 181 Howard Hill Road, Town Hall, Foster, RI 02825-1227. Town Clerk, R/E and UCC Recording 401-392-9200; Fax 401-392-9201.
Will search UCC records. This agency will not do a tax lien search. Will not search real estate records. **Other Phone Numbers:** Assessor 401-392-9202; Treasurer 401-392-9207; Elections 401-392-9200; Vital Records 401-392-9200.

Glocester Town

Town Clerk, PO Drawer B, Glocester/ Chepachet, RI 02814-0702. Town Clerk, R/E and UCC Recording 401-568-6206; Fax 401-568-5850. www.glocesterri.org/townclerk.htm
This agency will not search real estate or UCC records. **Other Phone Numbers:** Assessor 401-568-3329; Treasurer 401-568-3342; Elections 401-568-6206; Vital Records 401-568-6206; Tax Collector 401-568-5110.

Hopkinton Town

Town Clerk, 1 Town House Road, Town Hall, Hopkinton, RI 02833. Town Clerk, R/E and UCC Recording 401-377-7777; Fax 401-377-7788.
This agency will not search real estate or UCC records. **Other Phone Numbers:** Assessor 401-377-7780; Treasurer 401-377-7766; Elections 401-377-7777; Vital Records 401-377-7777.

Jamestown Town

Town Clerk, 93 Narragansett Ave, Town Hall, Jamestown, RI 02835. Town Clerk, R/E and UCC Recording 401-423-7200; Fax 401-423-7230.
Will search UCC records. Will not search real estate records. **Other Phones:** Assessor 401-423-7200; Treasurer 401-423-7200; Appraiser 401-423-7200; Elections 401-423-7200; Vital Records 401-423-7200.

Johnston Town

Town Clerk, 1385 Hartford Ave, Town Hall, Johnston, RI 02919. 401-351-6618; Fax 401-331-4271. www.johnston-ri.com Will search UCC records. Will not search real estate records.

Lincoln Town

Town Clerk, PO Box 100, Lincoln, RI 02865. Town Clerk, R/E and UCC Recording 401-333-1100; Fax 401-333-3648. www.lincolnri.com
Will not search real estate records. **Other Phone Numbers:** Assessor 401-333-1100; Treasurer 401-333-1100; Appraiser/Auditor 401-333-1100; Elections 401-333-1100; Vital Records 401-333-1100.

Little Compton Town

Town Clerk, PO Box 226, Little Compton, RI 02837-0226. 401-635-4400; Fax 401-635-2470. Will search UCC records. Will not search real estate records.

Middletown Town

Town Clerk, 350 E. Main Road, Town Hall, Middletown, RI 02842. 401-847-0009; Fax 401-848-0500.
Will search UCC records. Will not search real estate records. **Online Access:** Assessor, Property Records. Records on the Town of Middletown assessor database are available online at http://data.visionappraisal.com/ MiddletownRI. Free registration is required for full data. **Other Phone Numbers:** Assessor 401-847-7300.

Narragansett Town

Town Clerk, 25 Fifth Ave, Town Hall, Narragansett, RI 02882. 401-789-1044 R/E Recording: 401-789-1044 x623; Fax 401-783-9637.
This agency will not perform searches. **Online Access:** Assessor Records. Access may soon be available via a private company, see www.narragansettri.com/ townhall/assessor.htm. **Other Phone Numbers:** Assessor 401-789-1044 x236.

New Shoreham Town

Town Clerk, PO Drawer 220, Block Island, RI 02807. 401-466-3200; Fax 401-466-3219.
This agency will not search real estate or UCC records. **Other Phone Numbers:** Assessor 401-466-3217.

Newport City

City Clerk, 43 Broadway, Town Hall, Newport, RI 02840-2798. 401-846-9600 R/E Recording: 401-846-9600 x209 UCC Recording: 401-846-9600 x209; www.cityofnewport.com
This agency will not perform searches. **Online Access:** Assessor, Property Records. Access is available via a private company at http://data.visionappraisal.com/ NewportRI. Free registration is required for full data. **Other Phones:** Assessor 401-846-9600 x229 or 228 or 313; Elections 401-846-9600 x319 or 320 or 318; Vital Records 401-846-9600 x327 or 328 or 329 or 326.

North Kingstown Town

Town Clerk, 80 Boston Neck Road, Town Hall, North Kingstown, RI 02852. 401-294-3331 R/E Recording: 401-294-3331 x125 UCC Recording: 401-294-3331 x125; Fax 401-885-7373. www.northkingstown.org
Will search UCC records. Will not search real estate records. **Online Access:** Assessor, Property Records.

Access is available via a private company at http://data.visionappraisal.com/NorthkingstownRI. Free registration is required for full data. **Other Phone Numbers:** Assessor 401-294-3331 x110; Treasurer 401-294-3331 x148; Elections 401-294-3331 x129; Vital Records 401-294-3331 x122.

North Providence Town

Town Clerk, 2000 Smith St, Town Hall, North Providence, RI 02911. 401-232-0900; Fax 401-233-1409.
Will search UCC records. This agency will not do a tax lien search. Will not search real estate records. **Other Phone Numbers:** Assessor 401-232-0900 x245; Treasurer 401-232-0900 x218.

North Smithfield Town

Town Clerk, 1 Main St, Town Hall, Slatersville, RI 02876. Town Clerk, R/E and UCC Recording 401-767-2200; Fax 401-766-0016.
This agency will not search real estate or UCC records. **Online Access:** Assessor, Property Records. Access is available via a private company at http://data.visionappraisal.com/NorthsmithfieldRI. Free registration is required to view full data. **Other Phones:** Assessor 401-767-2202; Elections 401-767-2200 x316.

Pawtucket City

Town Clerk, 137 Roosevelt Ave, City Hall, Pawtucket, RI 02860. 401-728-0500 R/E Recording: 401-728-0500 x262 UCC Recording: 401-728-0500 x262; Fax 401-728-8932.
Will search UCC records. Will not search real estate records. **Other Phone Numbers:** Assessor 401-728-0500 x338; Treasurer 401-728-0500 x244; Elections 401-728-0500 x207; Vital Records 401-728-0500 x224.

Portsmouth Town

Town Clerk, PO Box 155, Portsmouth, RI 02871. 401-683-2101.
This agency will not perform searches. **Online Access:** Assessor, Property Records. Records on the Town of Portsmouth assessor database are available online at http://data.visionappraisal.com/PortsmouthRI. Free registration is required to view full data. **Other Phone Numbers:** Assessor 401-683-1536.

Providence City

City Clerk, 25 Dorrance St, City Hall, Providence, RI 02903. 401-421-7740 x312.
This agency will not perform searches. **Other Phone Numbers:** Assessor 401-421-5900.

Richmond Town

Town Clerk, 5 Richmond Townhouse Rd., Town Hall, Wyoming, RI 02898. Town Clerk, R/E and UCC Recording 401-539-2497; Fax 401-539-1089.
Will search UCC records. Will not search real estate records. **Other Phone Numbers:** Assessor 401-539-2130; Treasurer 401-539-2498; Elections 401-539-2497; Vital Records 401-539-2497.

Scituate Town

Town Clerk, PO Box 328, North Scituate, RI 02857-0328. Town Clerk, R/E and UCC Recording 401-647-2822; Fax 401-647-7220. www.scituateri.org/ townhall.htm
This agency will not perform searches. **Other Phones:** Assessor 401-647-2919; Treasurer 401-647-2547.

Smithfield Town

Town Clerk, 64 Farnum Pike, Town Hall, Esmond, RI 02917. Town Clerk, R/E and UCC Recording 401-233-1000; Fax 401-232-7244.
Will search UCC records. Will not search real estate records. **Other Phone Numbers:** Assessor 401-233-

1014; Treasurer 401-233-1005; Elections 401-233-1000; Vital Records 401-233-1000.

South Kingstown Town

Town Clerk, PO Box 31, Wakefield, RI 02880. 401-789-9331 R/E Recording: 401-789-9331 x234; Fax 401-788-9792. www.southkingstownri.com
Will search UCC records. This agency will not do a tax lien search. Will not search real estate records. **Online Access:** Real Estate, Assessor Records. Access to the property values database is available free at www.southkingstownri.com/code/propvalues_search.cf m. **Other Phone Numbers:** Assessor 401-789-9331 x220; Treasurer 401-789-9331 x209; Elections 401-789-9331 x231; Vital Records 401-789-9331 x230.

Tiverton Town

Town Clerk, 343 Highland Road, Town Hall, Tiverton, RI 02878. 401-625-6700; Fax 401-624-8640.
Will search UCC records. This agency will not do a tax lien search. Will not search real estate records. **Other Phone Numbers:** Assessor 401-625-5609.

Warren Town

Town Clerk, 514 Main St, Town Hall, Warren, RI 02885. Town Clerk, R/E and UCC Recording 401-245-7340; Fax 401-245-7421.
Will search UCC records. Will not search real estate records. **Other Phone Numbers:** Assessor 401-245-7342; Treasurer 401-245-7341; Appraiser/Auditor 401-245-7342; Elections 401-245-7340; Vital Records 401-245-7340; Town Manager 401-245-7554.

Warwick City

City Clerk, 3275 Post Road, Warwick, RI 02886. 401-738-2000 R/E Recording: 401-738-2000 x6218 UCC Recording: 401-738-2000 x6218; Fax 401-738-6639. www.warwickri.com
Will search UCC records. Will not search real estate records. **Other Phones:** Assessor 401-738-2000 x6016; Treasurer 401-738-2000 x6228; Elections 401-738-2000 x6223; Vital Records 401-738-2000 x6215.

West Greenwich Town

Town Clerk, 280 Victory Highway, Town Hall, West Greenwich, RI 02817. 401-397-5016; Fax 401-392-3805.
This agency will not perform searches. **Other Phone Numbers:** Assessor 401-397-5016 x3.

West Warwick Town

Town Clerk, 1170 Main St, Town Hall, West Warwick, RI 02893-4829. Town Clerk, R/E and UCC Recording 401-822-9201; Fax 401-822-9266.
Will search UCC records. Will not search real estate records. **Other Phone Numbers:** Assessor 401-822-9208; Treasurer 401-822-9216; Elections 401-822-9201; Vital Records 401-822-9201.

Westerly Town

Town Clerk, 45 Broad St, Town Hall, Westerly, RI 02891. Town Clerk, R/E and UCC Recording 401-348-2500; Fax 401-348-2571.
Will search UCC records. Will not search real estate records. **Other Phones:** Assessor 401-348-2500.

Woonsocket City

Town Clerk, 169 Main St, City Hall, Woonsocket, RI 02895. 401-762-6400 R/E Recording: 401-767-9248 UCC Recording: 401-767-9248; Fax 401-765-4569.
Will search UCC records. Will not search real estate records. **Other Phone Numbers:** Assessor 401-762-6400 x109; Treasurer 401-767-9280; Elections 401-767-9224; Vital Records 401-767-8875.

Rhode Island County Locator

You will usually be able to find the city name in the City/County Cross Reference below. In that case, it is a simple matter to determine the county from the cross reference. However, only the official US Postal Service city names are included in this index. There are an additional 40,000 place names that people use in their addresses. Therefore, we have also included a ZIP/City Cross Reference immediately following the City/County Cross Reference.

If you know the ZIP Code but the city name does not appear in the City/County Cross Reference index, look up the ZIP Code in the ZIP/City Cross Reference, find the city name, then look up the city name in the City/County Cross Reference. For example, you want to know the county for an address of Menands, NY 12204. There is no "Menands" in the City/County Cross Reference. The ZIP/City Cross Reference shows that ZIP Codes 12201-12288 are for the city of Albany. Looking back in the City/County Cross Reference, Albany is in Albany County.

City/County Cross Reference

ADAMSVILLE Newport	EXETER Washington	MANVILLE Providence	RUMFORD Providence
ALBION Providence	FISKEVILLE Providence	MAPLEVILLE Providence	SAUNDERSTOWN Washington
ASHAWAY Washington	FORESTDALE Providence	MIDDLETOWN Newport	SHANNOCK Washington
BARRINGTON Bristol	FOSTER Providence	NARRAGANSETT Washington	SLATERSVILLE Providence
BLOCK ISLAND Washington	GLENDALE Providence	NEWPORT Newport	SLOCUM Washington
BRADFORD Washington	GREENE Kent	NORTH KINGSTOWN Washington	SMITHFIELD Providence
BRISTOL Bristol	GREENVILLE Providence	NORTH PROVIDENCE Providence	TIVERTON Newport
CAROLINA Washington	HARMONY Providence	NORTH SCITUATE Providence	WAKEFIELD Washington
CENTRAL FALLS Providence	HARRISVILLE Providence	NORTH SMITHFIELD Providence	WARREN Bristol
CHARLESTOWN Washington	HOPE Providence	OAKLAND Providence	WARWICK Kent
CHEPACHET Providence	HOPE VALLEY Washington	PASCOAG Providence	WEST GREENWICH Kent
CLAYVILLE Providence	HOPKINTON Washington	PAWTUCKET Providence	WEST KINGSTON Washington
COVENTRY Kent	JAMESTOWN Newport	PEACE DALE Washington	WEST WARWICK Kent
CRANSTON Providence	JOHNSTON Providence	PORTSMOUTH Newport	WESTERLY Washington
CUMBERLAND Providence	KENYON Washington	PROVIDENCE Providence	WOOD RIVER JUNCTION Washington
EAST GREENWICH Kent	KINGSTON Washington	PRUDENCE ISLAND Bristol	WOONSOCKET Providence
EAST PROVIDENCE Providence	LINCOLN Providence	RIVERSIDE Providence	WYOMING Washington
ESCOHEAG Washington	LITTLE COMPTON Newport	ROCKVILLE Washington	

ZIP/City Cross Reference

02801-02801 ADAMSVILLE	02826-02826 GLENDALE	02860-02862 PAWTUCKET	02892-02892 WEST KINGSTON
02802-02802 ALBION	02827-02827 GREENE	02863-02863 CENTRAL FALLS	02893-02893 WEST WARWICK
02804-02804 ASHAWAY	02828-02828 GREENVILLE	02864-02864 CUMBERLAND	02894-02894 WOOD RIVER JUNCTION
02806-02806 BARRINGTON	02829-02829 HARMONY	02865-02865 LINCOLN	02895-02895 WOONSOCKET
02807-02807 BLOCK ISLAND	02830-02830 HARRISVILLE	02871-02871 PORTSMOUTH	02896-02896 NORTH SMITHFIELD
02808-02808 BRADFORD	02831-02831 HOPE	02872-02872 PRUDENCE ISLAND	02898-02898 WYOMING
02809-02809 BRISTOL	02832-02832 HOPE VALLEY	02873-02873 ROCKVILLE	02900-02909 PROVIDENCE
02812-02812 CAROLINA	02833-02833 HOPKINTON	02874-02874 SAUNDERSTOWN	02910-02910 CRANSTON
02813-02813 CHARLESTOWN	02835-02835 JAMESTOWN	02875-02875 SHANNOCK	02911-02911 NORTH PROVIDENCE
02814-02814 CHEPACHET	02836-02836 KENYON	02876-02876 SLATERSVILLE	02912-02912 PROVIDENCE
02815-02815 CLAYVILLE	02837-02837 LITTLE COMPTON	02877-02877 SLOCUM	02914-02914 EAST PROVIDENCE
02816-02816 COVENTRY	02838-02838 MANVILLE	02878-02878 TIVERTON	02915-02915 RIVERSIDE
02817-02817 WEST GREENWICH	02839-02839 MAPLEVILLE	02879-02880 WAKEFIELD	02916-02916 RUMFORD
02818-02818 EAST GREENWICH	02840-02841 NEWPORT	02881-02881 KINGSTON	02917-02917 SMITHFIELD
02821-02821 ESCOHEAG	02842-02842 MIDDLETOWN	02882-02882 NARRAGANSETT	02918-02918 PROVIDENCE
02822-02822 EXETER	02852-02854 NORTH KINGSTOWN	02883-02883 PEACE DALE	02919-02919 JOHNSTON
02823-02823 FISKEVILLE	02857-02857 NORTH SCITUATE	02885-02885 WARREN	02920-02921 CRANSTON
02824-02824 FORESTDALE	02858-02858 OAKLAND	02886-02889 WARWICK	02940-02940 PROVIDENCE
02825-02825 FOSTER	02859-02859 PASCOAG	02891-02891 WESTERLY	

South Carolina

General Help Numbers:

Governor's Office
PO Box 11829
Columbia, SC 29211
www.state.sc.us/governor

803-734-9400
Fax 803-734-9413
8AM-6PM

Attorney General's Office
PO Box 11549
Columbia, SC 29211
www.scattorneygeneral.org

803-734-3970
Fax 803-734-4323
8:30AM-5:30PM

State Court Administrator
1015 Sumter St, 2nd Floor
Columbia, SC 29201
www.judicial.state.sc.us/

803-734-1800
Fax 803-734-1821
8:30AM-5PM M-F

State Archives
8301 Parklane Rd
Columbia, SC 29223
www.state.sc.us/scdah

803-896-6100
Fax 803-896-6198
8:30AM-5PM M-F

State Specifics:

Capital: Columbia
Richland County

Time Zone: EST

Number of Counties: 46

Population: 4,063,011

Web Site: www.myscgov.com

State Agencies

Criminal Records

South Carolina Law Enforcement Division (SLED), Criminal Records Section, PO Box 21398, Columbia, SC 29221 (Courier: 4400 Broad River Rd, Columbia, SC 29210); 803-896-7043, 803-896-7022 (Fax), 8:30AM-5PM.

www.sled.state.sc.us

Note: Sex offender data is available online at www.scattorneygeneral.com; click on "Sex Offender Registry."

Indexing & Storage: Records are available from the 1960s. It takes 3 to 12 days before new records are available for inquiry. Records are indexed on inhouse computer. Records are normally destroyed after (records maintained indefinitely unless expunged). 72% of all arrests in database have final dispositions recorded, 85% for those arrests within last 5 years.

Searching: Criminal records are open without restrictions. Include the following in your request: full name, any aliases, date of birth, sex, race. The SSN is optional. 100% of the records are fingerprint supported. They will not do fingerprint searches. All records are released, including those without dispositions.

Access by: mail, in person, online.

Fee & Payment: The search fee is $25.00 per individual. The fee is $8.00 for non-profit organizations, pre-approval is required. Fee payee: SLED. Prepayment required. Business and company checks are accepted. No credit cards accepted.

Mail search: Turnaround time: 5 to 7 days. They will return by overnight delivery service if prepaid and materials provided. A self addressed stamped envelope is requested.

In person search: Turnaround time is within minutes.

Online search: SLED offers commercial access to criminal record history from 1960 forward on the web site. Fees are $25.00 per screening or $8.00 if for a charitable organization. Credit card ordering accepted. Visit the web site or call 803-896-7219 for details.

Fictitious Name
Assumed Name
Trade Names

Records not maintained by a state level agency.

Note: Records are found at the county level.

Corporation Records
Trademarks/Servicemarks
Limited Partnerships
Limited Liability Companys
Limited Liability Partnerships

Corporation Division, Capitol Complex, PO Box 11350, Columbia, SC 29211 (Courier: Edgar A. Brown Bldg, Room 525, Columbia, SC 29201); 803-734-2158, 803-734-2164 (Fax), 8:30PM-5PM.

www.scsos.com

Note: This office also handles not-for-profit entity records. Trademarks and service marks are not on the computer but are in this department.

Indexing & Storage: Records are available from 1800's on. In house computer records are from 1985 on. Older records are stored at the State Archives. New records are available for inquiry immediately. Records are indexed on microfilm, inhouse computer.

Searching: This office will not release company's officer's names and addresses. For that information, call the Dept of Revenue at 803-898-5751. Include the following in your request: full name of business. In addition to the articles of incorporation, corporation records include the following information: Prior (merged) names, Inactive and Reserved names. Annual Reports, Officer and Directors are kept in the State Department of Revenue.

Access by: mail, phone, in person, online.

Fee & Payment: $1.00 per page for the first document and $.50 per page for each additional document. If record is to be certified, then fee is $3.00 for first page. Fee payee: Secretary of State. Prepayment required. Personal checks accepted. No credit cards accepted.

Mail search: Turnaround time: 1 to 2 days. A self addressed stamped envelope is requested.

Phone search: No fee for telephone request. They will provide basic information only.

In person search: Information requests are available.

Online search: This free web-based program is called the Online Business Filings search page at www.scsos.com/corp_search.htm. The database provides access to basic filing information about any entity filed with the office. Registered agents' names and addresses, dates of business filings and types of filings are all available. The database is updated every 48 hours.

Annual Reports
Directors and Officers

Department of Revenue, Office Services/Records, 301 Gervias St, Columbia, SC 29201; 803-898-5751, 803-898-5888 (Fax), 8:30AM-5PM.

www.sctax.org/DOR/default.htm

Indexing & Storage: Records are available from 1990 on. Records are indexed on inhouse computer, hard copy.

Searching: Information on partnerships and on taxes is not public. Include the following in your request: full name of business. They will give officers and registered agent information only if it appears on the annual report. Request forms can be downloaded from the web site.

Access by: mail, fax, in person.

Fee & Payment: The fee is $2.63 which is on a per year basis for the annual reports. Fee payee: South Carolina Department of Revenue. Prepayment required. Personal checks accepted. No credit cards accepted.

Mail search: Turnaround time: 1 week. A self addressed stamped envelope is requested.

Fax search: Turnaround is usually in 1 day.

In person search: You may request information in person, but will not receive copies the same day.

Uniform Commercial Code

UCC Division, Secretary of State, PO Box 11350, Columbia, SC 29211 (Courier: Edgar Brown Bldg, 1205 Pendelton St #525, Columbia, SC 29201); 803-734-1961, 803-734-2164 (Fax), 8:30AM-5PM.

www.scsos.com/Uniform_Commercial_Code.htm

Indexing & Storage: Records are available from 1968. Records are computerized since 1985.

Searching: The agency prefers UCC-11 forms, but will still accept UCC-4 for in-state requests. All tax liens are filed at the county level. Include the following in your request: debtor name.

Access by: mail, phone, fax, in person, online.

Fee & Payment: The search fee is $5.00, there is no search fee if file number given. Copies are $2.00 for the first page, plus $1.00 for each page of attachments. Certification is $2.00 per copy. Fee payee: Secretary of State. Prepayment required. Personal checks accepted. No credit cards accepted.

Mail search: Turnaround time: 5 to 10 days. A self addressed stamped envelope is requested.

Phone search: No fee for telephone request. The staff will look-up file numbers at no charge.

Fax search: There is an additional $5.00 fee for faxing in and $10.00 fee for faxing back.

In person search: You may request information in person.

Online search: "Direct Access" is open 24 hours daily, there are no fees. Inquiry is by debtor name. The system provides for copies to be faxed automatically. Call 803-734-2345 for registration information.

Federal Tax Liens
State Tax Liens

Records not maintained by a state level agency.

Note: Tax lien data is found at the county level.

Sales Tax Registrations

Revenue Department, Sales Tax Registration Section, PO Box 125, Columbia, SC 29214 (Courier: 301 Gervais St, Columbia, SC 29214); 803-898-5872, 803-898-5888 (Fax), 8:30AM-4:45PM.

www.dor.state.sc.us

Indexing & Storage: Records are available for 4 to 5 years, then are archived on hard copy. Records are indexed on inhouse computer.

Searching: This agency will only confirm that a business is registered. They will provide no other information. Include the following in your request: business name. They can also search by tax permit number, owner name, or federal ID.

Access by: mail, phone, fax, in person.

Mail search: Turnaround time: 7 days. A self addressed stamped envelope is requested. No fee for mail request.

Phone search: No fee for telephone request.

Fax search: Fax searching available.

In person search: No fee for request.

Birth Certificates

South Carolina DHEC, Vital Records, 2600 Bull St, Columbia, SC 29201-1797; 803-898-3630, 803-898-3631 (Order Line), 877-284-1008 (Expedite), 803-799-0301 (Fax), 8:30AM-4:30PM.

www.scdhec.net/vr/index.htm

Note: A "short form" wallet size birth certificate can be obtained from any SC county. This form will not show parent names.

Indexing & Storage: Records are available from January 1, 1915 to present. It takes 2 months before new records are available for inquiry. Records are indexed on microfiche, inhouse computer.

Searching: Records will only be released to the registrant (if 18 or older), parents, guardian or legal representative. Include the following in your request: full name, names of parents, mother's maiden name, date of birth, place of birth. Two types of certificates are issued: wallet-size; photocopy certification (actual birth certificate).

Access by: mail, phone, fax, in person.

Fee & Payment: The fee is $12.00 per name. Add $3.00 per copy for additional copies of same certificate. Add $5.00 for use of credit card. Fee payee: DHEC. Prepayment required. Credit cards accepted for phone and fax requests only. Personal checks accepted. Credit cards accepted: MasterCard, Visa, Discover.

Mail search: Turnaround time: 3 to 4 weeks. No self addressed stamped envelope is required.

Phone search: Phone requests are accepted, using a credit card. See expedited service.

Fax search: Same criteria as phone searches. Is considered expedited.

In person search: Turnaround time is within 1 hour.

Expedited service: Expedited service is available for mail, phone and fax searches. To have search "expedited" to a 3-4 day turnaround, fee is an extra $5.00 and must use a credit card for add'l $5.00. Overnight shipping is available for an extra fee.

Death Records

South Carolina DHEC, Vital Records, 2600 Bull St, Columbia, SC 29201-1797; 803-898-3630, 803-898-3631 (Order Line), 803-799-0301 (Fax), 8:30AM-4:30PM.

www.scdhec.net/vr/index.htm

Indexing & Storage: Records are available from January 1, 1915 to date. New records are available for inquiry immediately. Records are indexed on microfiche, inhouse computer.

Searching: Copies are available to those who show a direct, tangible interest in a determination of a personal or property right. If less than 5 years, records are at county also. Include the following in your request: full name, date of death, place of death.

Access by: mail, phone, fax, in person.

Fee & Payment: The search fee is $12.00 per name. Add $3.00 per copy for additional copies. Add $5.00 for use of credit card. Fee payee: DHEC. Prepayment required. Credit cards accepted for phone and fax requests only. Personal checks accepted. Credit cards accepted: MasterCard, Visa, AmEx, Discover.

Mail search: Turnaround time: 3 to 4 weeks. No self addressed stamped envelope is required.

Phone search: Phone requests are accepted, using a credit card. See expedited service.

Fax search: See expedited service.

In person search: Turnaround time within 1 hour.

Expedited service: Expedited service is available for mail, phone and fax searches. To have the request expedited (3-4 days turnaround), fee is $5.00. To use a credit card there is an additional $5.00 fee. Add pre-paid overnight shipping if desired.

Marriage Certificates

South Carolina DHEC, Vital Records, 2600 Bull St, Columbia, SC 29201-1797; 803-898-3630, 803-898-3631 (Order Line), 803-799-0301 (Fax), 8:30AM-4:30PM.

www.scdhec.net/vr/index.htm

Note: Copies may also be obtained from the Probate Judge in the county where license was issued.

Indexing & Storage: Records are available from July 1, 1950 to present. New records are available for inquiry immediately. Records are indexed on microfiche, inhouse computer.

Searching: Records are released only to the subjects, their adult children, former or present spouses and legal representatives. Others may obtain a statement of marriage date and place. Include the following in your request: names of husband and wife, date of marriage, place or county of marriage.

Access by: mail, phone, fax, in person.

Fee & Payment: The search fee is $12.00 per name, add $3.00 for each additional copy. Use of credit card is additional $5.00. Fee payee: DHEC. Prepayment required. Credit cards accepted for phone and fax searches only. Personal checks

accepted. Credit cards accepted: MasterCard, Visa, AmEx, Discover.

Mail search: Turnaround time: 3 weeks. No self addressed stamped envelope is required.

Phone search: Phone requests are accepted, using a credit card. See expedited service.

Fax search: See expedited service.

In person search: Turnaround time within 1 hour.

Expedited service: Expedited service is available for mail, phone and fax searches. To have request expedited is an additional $5.00 plus $5.00 credit card fee. Add pre-paid overnight shipping if desired.

Divorce Records

South Carolina DHEC, Vital Records, 2600 Bull St, Columbia, SC 29201-1797; 803-898-3630, 803-898-3631 (Order Line), 803-799-0301 (Fax), 8:30AM-4:30PM.

www.scdhec.net/vr/index.htm

Indexing & Storage: Records are available from July 1, 1962 to present. New records are available for inquiry immediately. Records are indexed on microfiche, inhouse computer.

Searching: Records are available only to the parties, their adult children, a present or former spouse, and their legal representatives. Others may obtain a statement of the date and county of the event. Include the following in your request: names of husband and wife, date of divorce, place of divorce.

Access by: mail, phone, fax, in person.

Fee & Payment: The fee is $12.00 per name. Add $3.00 per copy for additional copies. Use of credit card is $5.00. Fee payee: DHEC. Prepayment required. Credit cards accepted for phone and fax requests only. Personal checks accepted. Credit cards accepted: MasterCard, Visa, AmEx, Discover.

Mail search: Turnaround time: 3 weeks. No self addressed stamped envelope is required.

Phone search: Phone requests are accepted, using a credit card. See expedited service.

Fax search: See expedited service.

In person search: Turnaround time within 1 hour.

Expedited service: Expedited service is available for mail, phone and fax searches. The fee for expedited service of 3-4 days turnaround time is $5.00. Use of a credit card is an additional $5.00. Add pre-paid overnight shipping if desired.

Workers' Compensation Records

Workers Compensation Commission, PO Box 1715, Columbia, SC 29202 (Courier: 1612 Marion St, Columbia, SC 29201); 803-737-5700, 803-737-5768 (Fax), 8:30AM-5PM.

www.wcc.state.sc.us

Indexing & Storage: Records are available from 1983 on the computer. Some of the older records are at this office and the rest are at the State Archives. Call office first for location of records. New records are available for inquiry immediately. Records are indexed on inhouse computer, books (volumes). Records are normally destroyed after 5 years after closing.

Searching: Must have a signed release form from claimant and you must specify what records you

want. Include the following in your request: claimant name, Social Security Number, date of accident.

Access by: mail, fax, in person.

Fee & Payment: The search fee is $6.00 per record and includes a computer printout. File copies cost $20.00 for the first up to 20 pages and $.50 for each additional page. Fee payee: SC Workers Compensation Commission. Prepayment required. Personal checks accepted. No credit cards accepted.

Mail search: Turnaround time: 1 week. A self addressed stamped envelope is requested.

Fax search: You can request by fax, but reply is sent by mail, same turnaround time.

In person search: Records are still returned by mail.

Driver License Information
Driver Records

Division of Motor Vehicles, Driver Records Section, PO Box 1498, Columbia, SC 29216-0035 (Courier: 955 Park St, Columbia, SC 29201); 803-737-4000, 803-737-1077 (Fax), 8:30AM-5PM.

www.scdps.org/

Note: Copies of tickets are available from this department for a fee of $6.00 per record.

Indexing & Storage: Records are available for up to 10 years for moving violations, DWIs and suspensions. Records provided to the public are limited to 3 or 10 years. The state will show moving violations regardless of whether the fine was not paid and license suspended. It takes 1 to 4 weeks before new records are available for inquiry.

Searching: Driving records and Identification card information is confidential by statute. Requests must fall within the guidelines of DPPA. Casual requesters must submit consent of subject if personal information is to be released. The driver's license number or full name and DOB are required to order a record. The following data is not released: Social Security Numbers or personal information (height, weight, sex, eye color, etc.).

Access by: mail, in person, online.

Fee & Payment: The fee is $6.00 per record request. Fee payee: Department of Public Safety. Prepayment required. Personal checks accepted. No credit cards accepted.

Mail search: Turnaround time: 5 days. Fee and return address must be submitted with each request. No self addressed stamped envelope is required.

In person search: Most DMV Branch offices in the state will process up to 10 records while you wait.

Online search: The online system offers basic driver data, for a 3 year or a 10 year record. This is a single inquiry process. Network charges will be incurred as well as initial set-up and a security deposit. The system is up between 8 AM and 7 PM. Fee is $6.00 per record. Access is through the AAMVAnet (IBMIN), which requesters much "join." Call Wanda DeLeon at 803-737-1546 for further information.

Other access: Magnetic tape and cassette batch processing is available.

Vehicle Ownership
Vehicle Identification

Division of Motor Vehicles, Title and Registration Records Section, PO Box 1498, Columbia, SC 29216 (Courier: 955 Park St, Columbia, SC 29201); 803-737-4000, 8:30AM-5PM.

www.state.sc.us/dps/dmv

Note: For Registration, use PO Box address with ZIP 29216-0022; use ZIP 29216-0024 for Titles.

Indexing & Storage: Records are available for 10 years for titles, 3 years for registration. The index to the records is computerized since 1984. It takes one day before new records are available for inquiry.

Searching: Information regarding the name, address and telephone number will not be released to the public, unless the requester completes form provided by department. Information is not provided to casual requesters. Requesters must be in compliance with DPPA.

Access by: mail, phone, fax, in person.

Fee & Payment: The fee is $6.00 per record request for all records, including lien information. Fee payee: Department of Public Safety. Prepayment required. A deposit account is available for ongoing requesters by mail or phone. Personal checks accepted. No credit cards accepted.

Mail search: Turnaround time: 3 days. No self addressed stamped envelope is required.

Phone search: Telephone searching is available for pre-approved, ongoing requesters. A deposit is required.

Fax search: This is only available to pre-approved, ongoing requesters. A deposit is required.

In person search: You may search in person.

Other access: South Carolina offers a variety of bulk retrieval programs where permitted by law. There is a minimum charge of $1,000.00. For more information, call customer service department for automated searches.

Expedited service: Expedited service is available for fax searches. Turnaround time: 1 to 2 days. Must have a deposit account. The fax number is 803-737-2299.

Accident Reports

Accident Reports, PO Box 1498, Columbia, SC 29216-0040 (Courier: 955 Park St, Columbia, SC 29201); 803-737-4000, 803-737-4483 (Fax), 8:30AM-5PM.

Indexing & Storage: Records are available for 10 years to present. The records are indexed on computer. It takes one week after receipt from enforcement agency before new records are available for inquiry. Records are indexed on inhouse computer.

Searching: Must have full name of all the drivers involved in the accident. Include the following in your request: full name, date of accident, driver's license number, county.

Access by: mail, phone, in person.

Fee & Payment: The fee is $6.00 for an accident research or insurance research. You may call to find out if record is on file. Fee payee: Department of Public Safety. Ongoing requesters may open an account with a $100.00 deposit and then will be billed monthly. Personal checks accepted. No credit cards accepted now, but may the near future.

Mail search: Turnaround time: 7 to 10 days. Information requests are available. A self addressed stamped envelope is requested.

Phone search: Five records per day may be requested with a pre-approved account.

In person search: Records will be processed while you wait.

Vessel Ownership
Vessel Registration

Dept of Natural Resources, Registration & Titles, PO Box 167, Columbia, SC 29202 (Courier: 1000 Assembly St, Room 104, Columbia, SC 29201); 803-734-3857, 803-734-4138 (Fax), 8:30AM-5PM.

www.dnr.state.sc.us

Indexing & Storage: Records are available from 1958 to present. Active records remain on computer as long as they are active. Inactive records are put on microfiche seven years after becoming inactive. It takes 30 days before new records are available for inquiry.

Searching: State law prohibits the release of records for commercial solicitation. All motorized boats must be titled and registered. Sailboats lest than 14' must be titled, and if used with propulsion then registered. To search, one of the following is required: name and address, hull ID #, title #, or SC (serial) #. The following data is not released: Social Security Numbers.

Access by: mail, fax, in person.

Fee & Payment: The search fee for all types of searches is $3.00 per record if no motor, and $6.00 per record if motor. Fee payee: SC Dept of Natural Resources. Prepayment required. Personal checks accepted. No credit cards accepted.

Mail search: Turnaround time: 7 to 20 days. No self addressed stamped envelope is required.

Fax search: Fax requests must be prepaid.

In person search: Turnaround time is usually same day.

Other access: Bulk data is available. The fee is $200 for up to 20,000 records, then $10 for each 1,000 additional records.

Legislation Records

South Carolina Legislature, 937 Assembly Street, Rm 220, Columbia, SC 29201; 803-734-2060, 803-734-2145 (Older Bills), 9AM-5PM.

www.scstatehouse.net

Note: Older passed bills are found at the Legislative Council on the 2nd floor, 803-734-2145.

Indexing & Storage: Records are available for current session only. The session is a 2 year session.

Access by: mail, phone, in person, online.

Mail search: Turnaround time: variable. Information requests are available. No self addressed stamped envelope is required.

Phone search: You may call for copies of bills.

In person search: Searching is available in person.

Online search: At the web site, search by bill number, subject, or sponsor. The site has a myriad of data including state codes, laws and regulations.

Voter Registration

State Election Commission, Records, PO Box 5987, Columbia, SC 29205; 803-734-9060, 803-734-9366 (Fax), 8:30AM-5PM.

www.state.sc.us/scsec

Indexing & Storage: Records are available for all active records.

Searching: Records are open to the public. To search, provide the name with the county or DOB. The following data is not released: Social Security Numbers.

Access by: mail, phone, fax, in person.

Fee & Payment: There is no search fee unless extensive time involved. Copies are $.20 each. Fee payee: State Election Commission. Prepayment required. No credit cards accepted.

Mail search: Turnaround time: 1 to 2 days.

Phone search: Records are available by phone.

Fax search: Same criteria as mail searching. There is a $.20 fee per page to return by fax.

In person search: Searching is available in person.

Other access: Lists, labels, diskettes, and magnetic tapes are available with a variety of sort features. The minimum charge varies from $75 to $160 depending on the media.

GED Certificates

GED Testing Office, 402 Rutledge Bldg, 1429 Senate St, Columbia, SC 29201; 803-734-8347, 803-734-8336 (Fax), 8:30AM-5PM M-F.

www.state.sc.us/sde

Indexing & Storage: It takes 6 weeks before new records are available for inquiry.

Searching: To search, all of the following is required: a signed release, name, Social Security Number, and approximate date of. Specify if for civilian or military use.

Access by: mail, fax.

Fee & Payment: There is no fee for a verification. There is a $5.00 fee for a copy of a transcript by mail, $3.00 if by fax. Fee payee: SC Dept of Education. Prepayment required. Cash and money orders are accepted. No credit cards accepted.

Mail search: Turnaround time is 3-5 days. No self addressed stamped envelope is required.

Fax search: Must call for verification within a day of faxed release.

Hunting License Information
Fishing License Information

Records not maintained by a state level agency.

Note: They do not have a central database. Licenses are kept on file within the License Division by the county and agent where the license was sold; however the records are not open to the public.

South Carolina State Licensing Agencies

Licenses Searchable Online

Accounting Practitioner-AP #2	http://lookup.llronline.com/index.asp
Acupuncturist #39	http://lookup.llronline.com/Lookup/Medical.asp
Airport Contact #35	www.scaeronautics.com/directorysearch.asp
Alcoholic Beverage Sunday Sales #34	www.sctax.org/DOR/Tax+Information/tax/sundaysales.html
Animal Health Technician #43	http://lookup.llronline.com/Lookup/Mh.asp
Architect #3	http://lookup.llronline.com/Lookup/Architects.asp
Architectural Partnership/Corp #3	http://lookup.llronline.com/Lookup/Architects.asp
Attorney #48	http://gandalf.scbar.org/lawyer_directory/default.asp
Auction Company #50	http://lookup.llronline.com/Lookup/Auctioneers.asp
Auctioneer/Auctioneer Apprentice #50	http://lookup.llronline.com/Lookup/Auctioneers.asp
Aviation Facility #35	www.scaeronautics.com/AirportSearch.asp
Barber Instructor/School #47	http://lookup.llronline.com/lookup/barbers.asp
Barber/Barber Apprentice #47	http://lookup.llronline.com/lookup/barbers.asp
Bodywork Therapist #47	http://lookup.llronline.com/Lookup/Massage.asp
Building Inspector/Official #21	http://lookup.llronline.com/Lookup/BuildingCodes.asp
Burglar Alarm Contractor #24	http://lookup.llronline.com/index.asp
Chiropractor #4	http://lookup.llronline.com/lookup/Chiropractic.asp
Contractor, General & Mechanical #24	http://lookup.llronline.com/Lookup/Contractors.asp
Cosmetologist #5	http://lookup.llronline.com/lookup/cosmetology.asp
Counselor, Professional #8	http://lookup.llronline.com/lookup/Counselors.asp
Dentist #6	http://lookup.llronline.com/Lookup/Dentistry.asp
Embalmer #11	http://lookup.llronline.com/Lookup/Funeral.asp
Emergency Medical Svc (Ambulance Co) #27	www.scems.com/emsassn/members.html
Engineer #7	http://lookup.llronline.com/lookup/Engineers.asp
Forester #38	http://lookup.llronline.com/Lookup/Foresters.asp
Funeral Director #11	http://lookup.llronline.com/Lookup/Funeral.asp
Funeral Home #11	http://lookup.llronline.com/Lookup/Funeral.asp
Geologist #20	http://lookup.llronline.com/Lookup/Geologists.asp
Hair Care Master Specialist #47	http://lookup.llronline.com/lookup/barbers.asp
Hearing Aid Dispenser/Fitter #29	http://lookup.llronline.com/Lookup/Speech.asp
Home Builder, Residential #45	http://lookup.llronline.com/Lookup/ResidentialBuilders.asp
Housing Inspector #21	http://lookup.llronline.com/Lookup/BuildingCodes.asp
Inspector, Mech./Elec./Plumb./Prov. #21	http://lookup.llronline.com/Lookup/BuildingCodes.asp
Insurance Agency/Company/Filing #31	www.doi.state.sc.us/Eng/Public/Static/DBSearch.asp
Insurance Agent #31	www.doi.state.sc.us/Eng/Public/Static/DBSearch.asp
Landscape Architect #40	www.dnr.state.sc.us/water/envaff/prolicense/prolicense.html
Lobbyist #37	www.lpitr.state.sc.us/reports/ethrpt.htm
Manicure Assistant #47	http://lookup.llronline.com/lookup/barbers.asp
Manufactured House Mfg/Dealer/Rep #41	http://lookup.llronline.com/Lookup/Mh.asp
Manufactured House Sales/Install/Repair #41	http://lookup.llronline.com/Lookup/Mh.asp
Marriage & Family Therapist #8	http://lookup.llronline.com/lookup/Counselors.asp
Massage Therapist #47	http://lookup.llronline.com/Lookup/Massage.asp
Medical Doctor #39	http://lookup.llronline.com/lookup/Medical.asp
Nurse #12	http://lookup.llronline.com/lookup/nurses.asp
Nurse-LPN #12	http://lookup.llronline.com/lookup/nurses.asp
Nursing Home Administrator #32	http://lookup.llronline.com/Lookup/LTC.asp
Occupational Therapist/Assistant #13	http://lookup.llronline.com/Lookup/OT.asp
Optician #14	http://lookup.llronline.com/Lookup/Opticians.asp
Optometrist #9	http://lookup.llronline.com/Lookup/Optometry.asp
Osteopathic Physician #39	http://lookup.llronline.com/Lookup/Medical.asp
Percolation Test Technician #36	http://lookup.llronline.com/Lookup/Environmental.asp
Pharmacist/Pharmacy Technician #15	http://lookup.llronline.com/lookup/pharmacy.asp
Pharmacy/Drug Outlet #15	http://lookup.llronline.com/lookup/pharmacy.asp
Physical Therapist/Therapist Asst #16	http://lookup.llronline.com/Lookup/PT.asp
Physician Assistant #39	http://lookup.llronline.com/Lookup/Medical.asp
Plans Examiner #21	http://lookup.llronline.com/Lookup/BuildingCodes.asp
Podiatrist #17	http://lookup.llronline.com/Lookup/Podiatry.asp
Psycho-Educational Specialist #8	http://lookup.llronline.com/lookup/Counselors.asp
Psychologist #18	http://lookup.llronline.com/Lookup/Psychology.asp
Public Accountant-CPA #2	http://lookup.llronline.com/index.asp
Real Estate Appraiser #44	www.asc.gov/content/category1/appr_by_state.asp
Residential Care, Community #32	http://lookup.llronline.com/Lookup/LTC.asp
Respiratory Care Practitioner #39	http://lookup.llronline.com/Lookup/Medical.asp

Roadside Market #25..www.scda.state.sc.us/Consinfo/rsmktdir00.html
Shampoo Assistant #47..http://lookup.llronline.com/lookup/barbers.asp
Social Worker #18 ....http://lookup.llronline.com/Lookup/SW.asp
Soil Classifier #40..www.dnr.state.sc.us/water/envaff/prolicense/prolicense.html
Solid Waste Landfill #30 ....www.scdhec.net/lwm/html/min.html
Specialty Food Producer #25....................................www.scda.state.sc.us/Consinfo/scsfp00mem.html
Specialty Contractor, Residential #45.......................http://lookup.llronline.com/Lookup/RhbSpecialty.asp
Speech-Language Pathologist #22...........................http://lookup.llronline.com/Lookup/Speech.asp
Sprinkler Systems Contractor #24 ....http://lookup.llronline.com/index.asp
Surveyor, Land #7 ....http://lookup.llronline.com/lookup/Engineers.asp
Swimming Pool/Spa Operator #36.............................http://lookup.llronline.com/Lookup/Environmental.asp
Veterinarian #43 ....http://lookup.llronline.com/Lookup/Mh.asp
Waste Water Treatment Plant Operator #36 ....http://lookup.llronline.com/Lookup/Environmental.asp
Water Treatment (registration) #36...........................http://lookup.llronline.com/Lookup/Environmental.asp
Well Driller #36 ....http://lookup.llronline.com/Lookup/Environmental.asp
Wholesalers/Shippers (Food) #25 ....www.scda.state.sc.us/Ship/wholeandship.htm

Licensing Quick Finder

Accounting Practitioner-AP #2 803-896-4492
Acupuncturist #39....................................803-896-4500
Agricultural Dealer/Handler #25 803-737-9696
Airport Contact #35.................................803-896-6270
Alcoholic Beverage Sunday Sales #34 . 803-898-5880
Alcoholic Beverage Vendor/Mfg./Whlse. #34
....803-898-5864
Amusement Ride #46 803-734-9711
Animal Health Technician #43................803-896-4598
Architect #3...803-896-4408
Architectural Partnership/Corp #3 803-896-4408
Athletic Contest #49 803-896-4498
Athletic Trainer #49................................803-896-4498
Attorney #48 803-799-6653
Auction Company #50.............................803-896-4853
Auctioneer/Auctioneer Apprentice #50..803-896-4853
Audiologist #22.......................................803-896-4650
Aviation Facility #35...............................803-896-6270
Bank #10..803-734-2001
Barber Instructor/School #47.................803-896-4588
Barber Shop #47.....................................803-896-4588
Barber/Barber Apprentice #47...............803-896-4588
Bodywork Therapist #47.........................896-896-4498
Boxer/Boxing Professional #49 803-896-4498
Building Inspector/Official #21...............803-896-4688
Burglar Alarm Contractor #24................803-896-4686
Butterfat Tester #25................................803-737-9700
Chiropractor #4 803-896-4587
Constable #51...803-896-7014
Contact Lens License #14......................803-896-4681
Contractor, General & Mechanical #24 . 803-896-4686
Cosmetologist #5....................................803-896-4494
Cosmetology Instructor/School #5 803-896-4494
Counselor, Professional #8 803-896-4658
Dental Hygienist #6.................................803-896-4599
Dental Specialist #6................................803-896-4599
Dental Technician #6 803-896-4599
Dentist #6..803-896-4599
Electrician #42..803-933-1209
Elevator Service #46 803-734-9711
Embalmer #11 803-896-4497
Emergency Medical Svc. (Ambulance Co) #27
....803-737-7204
Emergency Medical Technician #27 803-737-7204
Engineer #7 803-896-4422
Esthetician #5 803-896-4494
Feed Manufacturer/Product #25............803-737-9700
Financial Institution #10........................803-734-2001

Forester #38 803-896-4498
Funeral Director #11..............................803-896-4497
Funeral Home #11..................................803-896-4497
Geologist #20 803-896-4498
Hair Care Master Specialist #47 803-896-4588
Hearing Aid Dispenser/Fitter #29.........803-896-4650
Heating & Air/Gas Fitting #42...............803-933-1209
Home Builder, Residential #45..............803-896-4696
Housing Inspector #21 803-896-4688
Inspector, Mech./Elec./Plumb./etc. #21. 803-896-4688
Insurance Agency/Company/Filing #31 803-737-6221
Insurance Agent #31 803-737-6095
Investment Advisor #1...........................803-734-9916
Landscape Architect #40.......................803-734-9100
Liquor Permit, Special Event #34.........803-898-5864
Lobbyist #37...803-253-4192
Manicure Assistant #47 803-896-4588
Manicurist #5 803-896-4494
Manufactured House Mfg/Dealer/Rep #41
....803-896-4682
Manufactured House Sales/Install/Repair #41
....803-896-4682
Marriage & Family Therapist #8 803-896-4658
Massage Therapist #47.........................803-896-4498
Medical Doctor #39................................803-896-4500
Mine Site #30...803-896-4000
Nail Technician #5.................................803-896-4494
Nurse #12 803-896-4550
Nurse-LPN #12.......................................803-896-4550
Nursing Home Administrator #32 803-896-4544
Occupational Therapist/Assistant #13... 803-896-4683
Optician #14...803-896-4681
Optician Apprentice #14........................803-896-4681
Optometrist #9 803-869-4679
Osteopathic Physician #39....................803-896-4500
Percolation Test Technician #36..........803-896-4430
Pesticide Applicator #33.......................803-646-2155
Pesticide Dealer #33 803-646-2155
Pharmacist/Pharmacy Technician #15.. 803-896-4700
Pharmacy/Drug Outlet #15....................803-896-4700
Physical Therapist/Therapist Asst #16.. 803-896-4655
Physician Assistant #39 803-896-4500
Pilot #35..803-896-6280
Pipefitter #42 803-933-1209
Plans Examiner #21 803-896-4688
Plumbing #42..803-933-1209
Podiatrist #17...803-896-4685
Polygraph Examiner #51 803-896-7292

Private Detective #51 803-896-7014
Property Manager #44 803-896-4400
Psycho-Educational Specialist #8........803-896-4658
Psychologist #18....................................803-896-4661
Public Accountant-CPA #2.....................803-896-4492
Pyrotechnic Technician #19..................803-896-4420
Pyrotechnic Wholesaler/Facility/Jobber #19
....803-896-4420
Real Estate Appraiser #44.....................803-896-4400
Real Estate Broker #44 803-896-4400
Residential Care, Community #32 803-896-4544
Respiratory Care Practitioner #39........803-896-4500
Roadside Market #25.............................803-734-2225
Sanitarian #28 803-896-0646
School Guidance Counselor #26 803-896-3224
School Media Communications Specialist #26
....803-896-3224
School Principal/Supervisor/Superintendent #26
....803-896-3224
Securities Agent #1 803-734-9916
Securities Broker/Dealer #1 803-734-9916
Security Guard/Security Company #51. 803-896-7014
Seed Salesperson #25...........................803-737-9690
Shampoo Assistant #47 803-896-4588
Sheet Metal #42 803-933-1209
Social Worker #18..................................803-896-4665
Soil Classifier #40..................................803-734-9100
Solid Waste Landfill #30........................803-896-4149
Solid Waste Landfill Operator #30 803-896-4149
Specialty Contractor, Residential #45... 803-896-4696
Specialty Food Producer #25................803-734-2182
Speech-Language Pathologist #22......803-896-4650
Sprinkler Systems Contractor #24 803-896-4686
Surveyor, Land #7..................................803-896-4422
Swimming Pool/Spa Operator #36.......803-896-4430
Teacher #26 803-896-3224
Timeshare/Land Salesperson #44 803-896-4400
Veterinarian #43 803-896-4598
Waste Water Treatment Plant Operator #36
....803-896-4430
Water Treatment #36 803-896-4430
Weighman #25 803-737-9700
Weighmaster #25 803-737-9696
Well Driller #36.......................................803-896-4430
Wholesalers/Shippers (Food) #25 803-737-9700
Wrestler/Wrestling Professional #49..... 803-896-4498

Licensing Agency Information

#1 Attorney Generals Office, Securities Division, PO Box 11549 (1000 Assembly St, Rembert C. Dennis Building), Columbia, SC 29211-1549; 803-734-9916, Fax: 803-734-0032. www.scsecurities.org/index.html

#2 Department of Labor, Licensing & Regulation, Board of Accountancy, PO Box 11329 (110 Centerview Dr.), Columbia, SC 29211; 803-896-4770, Fax: 803-896-4554. www.llr.state.sc.us/pol.asp Agency email: mcwhortm@mail.llr.state.sc. Search database at http://lookup.llronline.com/index.asp

#3 Department of Labor, Licensing & Regulation, Board of Architectural Examiners, PO Box 11419 (110 Centerview Dr, #201), Columbia, SC 29211; 803-896-4408, Fax: 803-734-4410. www.llr.state.sc.us/pol.asp Search database at http://lookup.llronline.com/index.asp

#4 Department of Labor, Licensing & Regulation, Division of Chiropractic Examiners, PO Box 11329 (110 Centerview Dr, #306), Columbia, SC 29211-1329; 803-896-4587, Fax: 803-896-4719. www.llr.state.sc.us/pol.asp Agency email: holmesa@mail.llr.state.sc.us. Search database at http://lookup.llronline.com/index.asp

#5 Department of Labor, Licensing & Regulation, Board of Cosmetology, PO Box 11329 (110 Centerview Dr), Columbia, SC 29211-1329; 803-896-4494, Fax: 803-896-4484. www.llr.state.sc.us/pol.asp Search database at http://lookup.llronline.com/index.asp. See also Board of Barber examiners for Shampoo Assistant and Master Hair Care Specialist.

#6 Department of Labor, Licensing & Regulation, Board of Dentistry, PO Box 11329 (110 Centerview Dr), Columbia, SC 29211-1329; 803-896-4599, Fax: 803-896-4596. www.llr.state.sc.us/pol.asp Agency email: joness@mail.llr.state.sc.us. Search database at http://lookup.llronline.com/index.asp

#7 Department of Labor, Licensing & Regulation, Board of Prof. Engineers & Land Surveyors, PO Box 11597 (110 Centerview Dr, #201), Columbia, SC 29211-1597; 803- 896-4422, Fax: 803-896-4427. www.llr.state.sc.us/pol.asp Search database at http://lookup.llronline.com/index.asp

#8 Department of Labor, Licensing & Regulation, Board of Examiners of Prof. Counselors / Family Therapists, PO Box 11329 (110 Centerview, #306), Columbia, SC 29211; 803-896-4658, Fax: 803-896-4719. www.llr.state.sc.us/pol.asp Agency email: harringtons@mail.llr.state.sc.us. Search database at http://lookup.llronline.com/index.asp

#9 Department of Labor, Licensing & Regulation, Board of Examiners in Optometry, PO Box 11329 (110 Centerview Dr.), Columbia, SC 29211-1329; 803-896-4679, Fax: 803-896-4719. www.llr.state.sc.us/pol.asp Agency email: combsa@mail.llr.state.sc.us.

Search database at http://lookup.llronline.com/index.asp. Online disciplinary records only go back to 1994.

#10 Board of Financial Institutions, PO Box 12549 (1015 Sumter St, Rm 309), Columbia, SC 29201; 803-734-2001, Fax: 803-734-2013.

#11 Department of Labor, Licensing & Regulation, Board of Funeral Service, PO Box 11329 (110 Centerview Dr, #104), Columbia, SC 29211-1329; 803-896-4497, Fax: 803-896-4554. www.llr.state.sc.us/pol.asp Search database at http://lookup.llronline.com/index.asp

#12 Department of Labor, Licensing & Regulation, Board of Nursing, PO Box 12367 (110 Centerview Dr, #202), Columbia, SC 29211-2367; 803-896-4550, Fax: 803-896-4525. www.llr.state.sc.us/pol.asp Agency email: bolandr@mail.llr.state.sc.us. Search database at http://lookup.llronline.com/index.asp

#13 Department of Labor, Licensing & Regulation, Board of Occupational Therapy, PO Box 11329 (110 Centerview Dr, #306), Columbia, SC 29211; 803-896-4683, Fax: 803-896-4719. www.llr.state.sc.us/pol.asp Agency email: owensb@mail.llr.state.sc.us. Search database at http://lookup.llronline.com/index.asp. Online records only go back to 1994.

#14 Department of Labor, Licensing & Regulation, Board of Opticinary Examiners, PO Box 11329 (110 Centerview Dr.), Columbia, SC 29211-1329; 803-896-4681, Fax: 803-896-4719. www.llr.state.sc.us/pol.asp. Agency email: combsa@mail.llr.state.sc.us. Search database at http://lookup.llronline.com/index.asp. Online records only go back to 1994.

#15 Department of Labor, Licensing & Regulation, Board of Pharmacy, 110 Centerview Dr, Kingstree Bldg, #306, Columbia, SC 29211-1927; 803-896-4700, Fax: 803-896-4596. www.llr.state.sc.us/pol.asp Agency email: funderbm@mail.llr.state.sc.us. Search database at http://lookup.llronline.com/index.asp

#16 Department of Labor, Licensing & Regulation, Board of Physical Therapy Examiners, PO Box 11329 (110 Centerview Dr,), Columbia, SC 29211; 803-896-4655, Fax: 803-896-4719. www.llr.state.sc.us/pol.asp Agency email: owensb@mail.llr.state.sc.us. Search database at http://lookup.llronline.com/index.asp

#17 Department of Labor, Licensing & Regulation, Board of Podiatry Examiners, PO Box 11289 (110 Centerview Dr, #202), Columbia, SC 29211-1289; 803-896-4685, Fax: 803-896-4515. www.llr.state.sc.us/pol.asp Agency email: podiatry@mail.llr.state.sc.us. Search database at http://lookup.llronline.com/index.asp

#18 Department of Labor, Licensing & Regulation, Board of Examiners in Psychology/Social Work Examiners, PO Box 11329 (100 Centerview Dr), Columbia, SC 29211-1329; 803-896-4664, Fax: 803-896-4687. www.llr.state.sc.us/pol.asp Agency email: glennp@mail.llr.state.sc.us.

Search database at http://lookup.llronline.com/index.asp. Online psychologist records only go bck to 1994.

#19 Department of Labor, Licensing & Regulation, Board of Pyrotechnic Safety, PO Box 11847 (110 Centerview Dr, #201), Columbia, SC 29211-1329; 803-896-4400, Fax: 803-896-4404. www.llr.state.sc.us/POL/Pyrotechnic

#20 Department of Labor, Licensing & Regulation, Board of Registration for Geologists, PO Box 11329 (110 Centerview Dr, #104), Columbia, SC 29211-1329; 803-896-4498, Fax: 803-896-4484. www.llr.state.sc.us/pol.asp Agency email: pyattl@mail.llr.state.sc.us. Search database at http://lookup.llronline.com/index.asp

#21 Department of Labor, Licensing & Regulation, Building Codes Council, PO Box 11329 (110 Centerview Dr, #102), Columbia, SC 29211-1329; 803-896-4688, Fax: 803-896-4814. www.llr.state.sc.us/pol.asp Agency email: reynoldsv@mail.llr.state.sc.us. Search database at http://lookup.llronline.com/index.asp

#22 Department of Labor, Licensing & Regulation, Board of Examiners for Speech-Language Pathology & Audiology, PO Box 11329 (110 Centerview Dr, #306), Columbia, SC 29211-1329; 803-896-4650, Fax: 803-896-4719. www.llr.state.sc.us/pol.asp Agency email: reynoldsv@mail.llr.state.sc.us. Search database at http://lookup.llronline.com/index.asp

#24 Department of Labor, Licensing & Regulation, Contractor's Licensing Board, PO Box 11329 (110 Centerview Dr, #201), Columbia, SC 29211-1329; 803-896-4686, Fax: 803-896-4364. www.llr.state.sc.us/pol.asp Search database at http://lookup.llronline.com/index.asp

#25 Department of Agriculture, PO Box 11280, Columbia, SC 29211; 803-734-2182, Fax: 803-734-2192. www.scda.state.sc.us

#26 Department of Education, Office of Teacher Certification, 1429 Senate St, Columbia, SC 29201; 803-734-8466, Fax: 803-734-2873. www.scteachers.org

#27 Department of Health & Environmental Control, EMS Department, 2600 Bull St, Columbia, SC 29201; 803-737-7204, Fax: 803-545-4212. www.scems.com

#28 Department of Health & Environmental Control, Department of Licensing - Sanitarians, 2600 Bull St, Columbia, SC 29201; 803-896-0646, Fax: 803-896-0645. www.scdhec.net

#29 Board of Examiners in Speech-Language Pathology & Audiology, PO Box 11329 (100 Centerview Dr #306), Columbia, SC 29211; 803-896-4650, Fax: 803-896-4719. www.llr.state.sc.us/POL/speech/INDEX.ASP. Agency email: reynoldsv@mail.llr.state.sc.us.

#30 Department of Health & Environmental Control, Bureau of Land and Waste Management,

2600 Bull St, Columbia, SC 29201; 803-896-4000, Fax: 803-896-4001.
www.scdhec.net
Search database at www.scdhec.net/lwm/html/min.html. For landfill operators, search by county.

#31 Department of Insurance, PO Box 100105 (300 Arbor Lake Dr., #1200), Columbia, SC 29202-3105; 803-737-6095, Fax: 803-737-6231. www.doi.state.sc.us. Agency email: AgntMail@doi.state.sc.us.
Search database at www.doi.state.sc.us/Eng/Public/Static/DBSearch.asp

#32 Department of Labor, Licensing & Regulation, Board of Long Term Care Administrators, PO Box 11329, Columbia, SC 29211; 803-896-4544, Fax: 803-896-4555. www.llr.state.sc.us/pol.asp
Agency email: welbornd@mail.llr.state.sc.us.
Search database at http://lookup.llronline.com/index.asp

#33 Department of Pesticide Regulation, 511 Winghouse Rd, Pendelton, SC 29670; 864-646-2155, Fax: 864-646-2179.

#34 Department of Revenue & Taxation, Alcoholic Beverage Section, PO Box 125, Columbia, SC 29214; 803-898-5864, Fax: 803-898-5899.
www.sctax.org/tax/abl.html

#35 Division of Aeronautics, PO Box 280068 (2553 Airport Blvd, West Columbia), Columbia, SC 29228-0068; 803-896-6270, Fax: 803-896-6277. Agency email: bcoward@aeronautics.state.sc.us.

#36 Department of Labor, Licensing & Regulation, Environmental Certification Board, PO Box 11329, Columbia, SC 29211; 803-896-4430, Fax: 803-896-4424.
www.llr.state.sc.us/pol.asp
Search database at http://lookup.llronline.com/Lookup/Environmental.asp

#37 Ethics Commission, 5000 Thurmond Mall #250, Columbia, SC 29201; 803-253-4192, Fax: 803-253-7539.
www.state.sc.us/ethics/
Search database at www.lpitr.state.sc.us/reports/ethrpt.htm

#38 Department of Labor, Licensing & Regulation, Board of Registration for Foresters,

PO Box 11329, Columbia, SC 29211-1329; 803-896-4498, Fax: 803-896-4595.
www.llr.state.sc.us/pol.asp
Agency email: pyattl@mail.llr.state.sc.us.
Search database at http://lookup.llronline.com/Lookup/Foresters.asp

#39 Department of Labor, Licensing & Regulation, Board of Medical Examiners, PO Box 11289 (110 Centerview Dr, #202), Columbia, SC 29211-1289; 803-896-4500, Fax: 803-896-4515.
www.llr.state.sc.us/POL/Medical. Agency email: medboard@mail.llr.state.sc.us.
Search database at http://lookup.llronline.com/Lookup/Medical.asp

#40 Department of Natural Resources, Land, Water & Conservation Div., Licensing Program, 2221 Devine St, #222, Columbia, SC 29205-2474; 803-734-9100, Fax: 803-734-9200.
www.dnr.state.sc.us
Agency email: moorer@water.dnr.state.sc.us.
Search database at www.dnr.state.sc.us/water/envaff/prolicense/prolicense.html

#41 Department of Labor, Licensing & Regulation, Manufactured Housing Board, PO Box 11329 (110 Centerview Dr, #102), Columbia, SC 29211-1329; 803-896-4682, Fax: 803-896-4814.
www.llr.state.sc.us/pol.asp
Agency email: wigginsg@mail.llr.state.sc.us.
Search database at http://lookup.llronline.com/index.asp

#42 Municipal Association of South Carolina, Trades Certification Program, PO Box 12109 (1411 Gervais St), Columbia, SC 29211; 803-779-9574, Fax: 803-933-1299.
www.masc.sc/trades/trades.htm

#43 Department of Labor, Licensing & Regulation, Board of Veterinary Medical Examiners, PO Box 11329, Columbia, SC 29211-1329; 803-896-4598, Fax: 803-896-4719.
www.llr.state.sc.us/pol.asp
Agency email: holmesa@mail.llr.state.sc.us.
Search database at http://lookup.llronline.com/index.asp

#44 Real Estate Commission, PO Box 11847 (110 Centerview Dr #201), Columbia, SC 29211-1847; 803-896-4400, Fax: 803-896-4404.
www.llr.state.sc.us/pol.asp
Agency email: selmanr@mail.llr.state.sc.us.

#45 Department of Labor, Licensing & Regulation, Residential Home Builders Commission, PO Box 11329 (110 Centerview Dr, #201), Columbia, SC 29211-1329; 803-896-4696, Fax: 803-896-4656.
www.llr.state.sc.us/pol.asp. Agency email: driverc@mail.llr.state.sc.us.
Search database at http://lookup.llronline.com/index.asp

#46 Department of Labor, Licensing & Regulation, Office of Elevators and Amusement Rides, PO Box 11329, Columbia, SC 29211-1329; 803-734-9711, Fax: 803-737-9119.
www.llr.state.sc.us

#47 Department of Labor, Licensing & Regulation, Board of Barber Examiners, Massage/Bodywork Therapy, PO Box 11329 (110 Centerview Dr, #104), Columbia, SC 29211-1329; 803-896-4491, Fax: 803-896-4484.
www.llr.state.sc.us/POL/Barber
Agency email: jonese@mail.llr.state.sc.us.
Search database at http://lookup.llronline.com/index.asp

#48 Supreme Court, PO Box 608 (950 Taylor St), Columbia, SC 29202; 803-799-6653, Fax: 803-799-4118.
www.scbar.org
Search database at http://gandalf.scbar.org/lawyer_directory/default.asp

#49 Department of Labor, Licensing & Regulation, Athletic Commission, PO Box 11329 (110 Centerview Dr), Columbia, SC 29211; 803-896-4498, Fax: 803-896-4595.
www.llr.state.sc.us/pol.asp
Agency email: halll@mail.llr.state.sc.us.

#50 Department of Labor, Licensing & Regulation, Auctioneer's Commission, PO Box 11329 (110 Centerview Dr, #104), Columbia, SC 29211-1329; 803-896-4853, Fax: 803-896-4484.
www.llr.state.sc.us/pol.asp
Agency email: pyatt@mail.llr.state.sc.us.
Search database at http://lookup.llronline.com/index.asp

#51 Law Enforcement Division, Regulatory Department, 4400 Broad River Rd, Columbia, SC 29210; 803-737-9000, Fax: 803-896-7037.

South Carolina Federal Courts

The following list indicates the district and division name for each county in the state. If the bankruptcy court location is different from the district court, then the location of the bankruptcy court appears in parentheses.

County/Court Cross Reference

County	Court	County	Court
Abbeville	Greenwood (Columbia)	Greenwood	Greenwood (Columbia)
Aiken	Greenwood (Columbia)	Hampton	Beaufort (Columbia)
Allendale	Greenwood (Columbia)	Horry	Florence (Columbia)
Anderson	Anderson (Columbia)	Jasper	Beaufort (Columbia)
Bamberg	Greenwood (Columbia)	Kershaw	Columbia
Barnwell	Greenwood (Columbia)	Lancaster	Greenwood (Columbia)
Beaufort	Beaufort (Columbia)	Laurens	Greenville (Columbia)
Berkeley	Charleston (Columbia)	Lee	Columbia
Calhoun	Greenwood (Columbia)	Lexington	Columbia
Charleston	Charleston (Columbia)	Marion	Florence (Columbia)
Cherokee	Spartanburg (Columbia)	Marlboro	Florence (Columbia)
Chester	Spartanburg (Columbia)	McCormick	Greenwood (Columbia)
Chesterfield	Florence (Columbia)	Newberry	Greenwood (Columbia)
Clarendon	Charleston (Columbia)	Oconee	Anderson (Columbia)
Colleton	Charleston (Columbia)	Orangeburg	Greenwood (Columbia)
Darlington	Florence (Columbia)	Pickens	Anderson (Columbia)
Dillon	Florence (Columbia)	Richland	Columbia
Dorchester	Charleston (Columbia)	Saluda	Greenwood (Columbia)
Edgefield	Greenwood (Columbia)	Spartanburg	Spartanburg (Columbia)
Fairfield	Greenwood (Columbia)	Sumter	Columbia
Florence	Florence (Columbia)	Union	Spartanburg (Columbia)
Georgetown	Charleston (Columbia)	Williamsburg	Florence (Columbia)
Greenville	Greenville (Columbia)	York	Spartanburg (Columbia)

Standards for Federal Courts: The search fee is $20.00 per item (one party name or case number). Certification fee is $7.00 per document. Copy fee is $.50 per page. All fees standard unless noted in profile. Mail Search: always enclose a stamped self addressed envelope unless otherwise noted. Before releasing records, all courts require prepayment unless noted in profile.

Open records are located at the court unless otherwise noted. District courts index by defendant and plaintiff as well as by case number. Bankruptcy courts usually index by debtor and case number. While most courts now have their indexes on computer, many still maintain index card files as well.

The universal PACER sign-up number is 800-676-6856. Find PACER and the Party/Case Index on the Web at http://pacer.psc.uscourts.gov. PACER dial-up access is $.60 per minute. Also, courts offering internet access via RACER, PACER, Web-PACER or the new CM-ECF charge $.07 per page fee unless noted as free.

US District Court

District of South Carolina

Anderson Division c/o Greenville Division, PO Box 10768, Greenville, SC 29603 (Courier Address: 300 E Washington St, Greenville, SC 29601), 864-241-2700.

www.scd.uscourts.gov

Counties: Anderson, Oconee, Pickens.

Indexing & Storage: New cases are available in the index after filing date. Open records are located at the Greenville Division.

Fee & Payment Notes: Payment may be made by money order, cashier check. Business checks are not accepted. Personal checks are not accepted.

Phone Search: Searching not available by phone.

Mail Search: A stamped self addressed envelope is not required.

In Person Search: In person searching available.

PACER: Toll-free dial-up access: 800-831-6162. Local dial-up access: 803-765-5871. Case records are available back to January 1990. Records are never purged. New records are available online after 1 day. PACER is available online at http://pacer.scd.uscourts.gov.

Opinions Online: Court opinions are available online at www.law.sc.edu/dsc/dsc.htm

Beaufort Division c/o Charleston Division, PO Box 835, Charleston, SC 29402 (Courier Address: 85 Broad St, Hollings Judicial Center, Charleston, SC 29401), 843-579-1401, Fax: 803-579-1402.

www.scd.uscourts.gov

Counties: Beaufort, Hampton, Jasper.

Indexing & Storage: New cases are available in the index after filing date. Open records are located at the Charleston Division. Civil records are sent to Federal Records Center 1 year after case close. Criminal records are sent 5 years after case close.

Fee & Payment Notes: Payment may be made by money order, cashier check. Business checks are not accepted. Personal checks are not accepted.

Phone Search: Searching not available by phone.

In Person Search: In person searching available.

PACER: Toll-free dial-up access: 800-831-6162. Local dial-up access: 803-765-5871. Case records are available back to January 1990. Records are never purged. New records are available online after 1 day. PACER is available online at http://pacer.scd.uscourts.gov.

Opinions Online: Court opinions are available online at www.law.sc.edu/dsc/dsc.htm

Charleston Division PO Box 835, Charleston, SC 29402 (Courier Address: 85 Broad St, Hollings Judicial Center, Charleston, SC 29401), 843-579-1401, Fax: 803-579-1402.

www.scd.uscourts.gov

Counties: Berkeley, Charleston, Clarendon, Colleton, Dorchester, Georgetown.

Indexing & Storage: Cases are indexed by defendant, plaintiff, and case number. New cases are available in the index 1-2 days after filing date. Older records are indexed on cards and microfiche. District wide searches are available for information from 1980 from this court.

Fee & Payment Notes: Payment may be made by money order, cashier check, personal check. Payee: US District Court.

Phone Search: Only docket information is available by phone.

In Person Search: In person searching available.

PACER: Toll-free dial-up access: 800-831-6162. Local dial-up access: 803-765-5871. Case records are available back to January 1990. Records are never purged. New records are available online after 1 day. PACER is available online at http://pacer.scd.uscourts.gov.

Opinions Online: Court opinions are available online at www.law.sc.edu/dsc/dsc.htm

Columbia Division 1845 Assembly St, Columbia, SC 29201 (Courier Address: Use mail address for courier delivery), 803-765-5816.

www.scd.uscourts.gov

Counties: Kershaw, Lee, Lexington, Richland, Sumter.

Indexing & Storage: Cases are indexed by defendant, plaintiff, and case number. New cases are available in the index 1 month after filing date. Older records are also indexed on microfiche. District wide searches are available from this court.

Fee & Payment Notes: Payment may be made by money order, cashier check, personal check. Payee: Clerk, US District Court.

Phone Search: Searching not available by phone. If a case number, caption and judge are provided, docket information is given. The court will not search case numbers or captions on the phone.

Fax Search: Will accept fax search request. Response will be sent through the mail when payment is received.

Mail Search: A stamped self addressed envelope is not required.

In Person Search: In person searching available.

PACER: Toll-free dial-up access: 800-831-6162. Local dial-up access: 803-765-5871. Case records are available back to January 1990. Records are never purged. New records are available online after 1 day. PACER is available online at http://pacer.scd.uscourts.gov.

Opinions Online: Court opinions are available online at www.law.sc.edu/dsc/dsc.htm

Florence Division PO Box 2317, Florence, SC 29503 (Courier Address: 401 W Evans St, McMillan Federal Bldg., Room 361, Florence, SC 29501), 843-676-3820, Fax: 843-676-3831.

www.scd.uscourts.gov

Counties: Chesterfield, Darlington, Dillon, Florence, Horry, Marion, Marlboro, Williamsburg.

Indexing & Storage: Cases are indexed by defendant, plaintiff, and case number. New cases are available in the index 24-48 hours after filing date. District wide searches are available from this court.

Fee & Payment Notes: Payment may be made by money order, cashier check, personal check. Payee: Clerk, US District Court.

Phone Search: Searching not available by phone.

Fax Search: Will accept fax for price quote.

In Person Search: In person searching available.

PACER: Toll-free dial-up access: 800-831-6162. Local dial-up access: 803-765-5871. Case records are available back to January 1990. Records are never purged. New records are available online after 1 day. PACER is available online at http://pacer.scd.uscourts.gov.

Opinions Online: Court opinions are available online at www.law.sc.edu/dsc/dsc.htm

Greenville Division PO Box 10768, Greenville, SC 29603 (Courier Address: 300 E Washington St, Greenville, SC 29601), 864-241-2700, Fax: 864-241-2711.

www.scd.uscourts.gov

Counties: Greenville, Laurens.

Indexing & Storage: Cases are indexed by defendant, plaintiff, and case number. New cases are available in the index 24 hours after filing date. The computer index is from 1991 on. Older records are indexed on microfiche. Open records are located at this court.

Fee & Payment Notes: Payment may be made by money order, cashier check, personal check. Payee: Clerk, US District Court.

Phone Search: Only the case number, parties and attorneys' names will be released over the phone.

Mail Search: A stamped self addressed envelope is not required.

In Person Search: In person searching available.

PACER: Toll-free dial-up access: 800-831-6162. Local dial-up access: 803-765-5871. Case records are available back to January 1990. Records are never purged. New records are available online after 1 day. PACER is available online at http://pacer.scd.uscourts.gov.

Opinions Online: Court opinions are available online at www.law.sc.edu/dsc/dsc.htm

Greenwood Division c/o Greenville Division, PO Box 10768, Greenville, SC 29603 (Courier: 300 E Washington St, Greenville, SC 29601), 864-241-2700, Fax: 864-241-2711.

www.scd.uscourts.gov

Counties: Abbeville, Aiken, Allendale, Bamberg, Barnwell, Calhoun, Edgefield, Fairfield, Greenwood, Lancaster, McCormick, Newberry, Orangeburg, Saluda.

Indexing & Storage: New cases are available in the index after filing date. Open records are located at the Greenville Division.

Fee & Payment Notes: Payment may be made by money order, cashier check. Business checks are not accepted. Personal checks are not accepted.

Phone Search: Searching not available by phone.

Mail Search: A stamped self addressed envelope is not required.

In Person Search: In person searching available.

PACER: Toll-free dial-up access: 800-831-6162. Local dial-up access: 803-765-5871. Case records are available back to January 1990. Records are never purged. New records are available online after 1 day. PACER is available online at http://pacer.scd.uscourts.gov.

Opinions Online: Court opinions are available online at www.law.sc.edu/dsc/dsc.htm

Spartanburg Division c/o Greenville Division, PO Box 10768, Greenville, SC 29603 (Courier: 300 E Washington St, Greenville, SC 29601), 864-241-2700, Fax: 864-241-2711.

www.scd.uscourts.gov

Counties: Cherokee, Chester, Spartanburg, Union, York.

Indexing & Storage: New cases are available in the index after filing date. Open records are located at the Greenville Division.

Fee & Payment Notes: Payment may be made by money order, cashier check. Business checks are not accepted. Personal checks are not accepted.

Phone Search: Searching not available by phone.

Mail Search: A stamped self addressed envelope is not required.

In Person Search: In person searching available.

PACER: Toll-free dial-up access: 800-831-6162. Local dial-up access: 803-765-5871. Case records are available back to January 1990. Records are never purged. New records are available online after 1 day. PACER is available online at http://pacer.scd.uscourts.gov.

Opinions Online: Court opinions are available online at www.law.sc.edu/dsc/dsc.htm

US Bankruptcy Court

District of South Carolina

Columbia Division PO Box 1448, Columbia, SC 29202 (Courier Address: 1100 Laurel St, Columbia, SC 29201), 803-765-3004.

www.scb.uscourts.gov

Counties: All counties in South Carolina.

Indexing & Storage: Cases are indexed by debtor as well as by case number. New cases are available in the index 1-2 days after filing date. Creditor lists are available through PACER. The bankruptcy information maintained at the US Bankruptcy Court, Columbia Division encompasses all bankruptcy information available for the District of South Carolina.

Fee & Payment Notes: Payment may be made by money order, cashier check, personal check. Debtor's checks are not accepted. Payee: Clerk, US Bankruptcy Court.

Phone Search: An automated voice case information service (VCIS) is available. Call VCIS at 800-669-8767 or 803-765-5211.

In Person Search: In person searching available.

PACER: Toll-free dial-up access: 800-410-2988. Local dial-up access: 803-765-5965. Case records are available back to November 1988. Records are never purged. New civil records are available online after 1 day. PACER is available online at http://pacer.scb.uscourts.gov. Document images available.

Electronic Filing: (Currently in the process of implementing CM/ECF.)

South Carolina County Courts

Court	Jurisdiction	No. of Courts	How Organized
Circuit Courts*	General	46	16 Circuits
Magistrate Courts*	Limited	182	
Municipal Courts	Municipal	160	
Probate Courts*	Probate	46	
Family Courts	Special	46	16 Circuits

* Profiled in this Sourcebook.

CIVIL									
Court	Tort	Contract	Real Estate	Min. Claim	Max. Claim	Small Claims	Estate	Eviction	Domestic Relations
Circuit Courts*	X	X	X	$5000	No Max	$7500			
Magistrate Courts	X		X	$0	$7500	$7500		X	
Municipal Courts									
Probate Courts*							X		
Family Courts									X

CRIMINAL					
Court	Felony	Misdemeanor	DWI/DUI	Preliminary Hearing	Juvenile
Circuit Courts*	X	X	X		
Magistrate Courts*		X	X	X	
Municipal Courts		X	X	X	
Probate Courts*					
Family Courts					X

ADMINISTRATION

Court Administration, 1015 Sumter St, 2nd Floor, Columbia, SC, 29201; 803-734-1800, Fax: 803-734-1355. www.judicial.state.sc.us

COURT STRUCTURE

The 46 SC counties are divided among sixteen judicial circuits. The circuit courts are in operation at the county level and consist of a court of general sessions (criminal) and a court of common pleas (civil). A family court is also in operation at the county level. The over 300 Magistrate and Municipal Courts (often referred to as "Summary Courts") only handle misdemeanor cases involving a $500.00 fine and/or 30 days or less jail time.

The maximum civil claim monetary amount for the Magistrate Courts increased from $2500 to $5000 as of January 1, 1996. In 2001, this civil limit was raised to $7,500.

ONLINE ACCESS

The judicial Department is developing a statewide court case management system. At present only Charleston County offers Internet access to Circuit Court records and Sumter County to Family Court records.

ADDITIONAL INFORMATION

If requesting a record in writing, it is recommended that the words "request that General Session, Common Pleas, and Family Court records be searched" be included in the request.

Most South Carolina courts will not conduct searches. However, if a name and case number are provided, many will pull and copy the record. Search fees vary widely as they are set by each county individually.

Abbeville County

Circuit Court PO Box 99, Abbeville, SC 29620; 864-459-5074; Fax: 864-459-9188. Hours: 9AM-5PM (EST). *Felony, Misdemeanor, Civil Actions Over $7,500.*
Civil Records: Access: In person only. Visitors must perform in person searches for themselves. No search fee. Required to search: name, years to search. Civil cases indexed by defendant, plaintiff. Civil records on card index from 1870.
Criminal Records: Access: In person only. Visitors must perform in person searches for themselves. No search fee. Required to search: name, years to search; also helpful: SSN. Criminal records on card index from 1870.
General Information: No adoption, juvenile, sealed or expunged records released. Copy fee: $.25 per page. Fee payee: Clerk of Court. Personal checks accepted. Prepayment is required.

Abbeville Magistrate Court 101 Church St, PO Drawer 1156, Abbeville, SC 29620; 864-459-2080/2053; Fax: 864-459-8245. Hours: 9AM-5PM (EST). *Misdemeanor, Civil Actions Under $7,500, Eviction, Small Claims.*

Probate Court PO Box 70, Abbeville, SC 29620; 864-459-4626; Fax: 864-459-4023. Hours: 9AM-5PM (EST). *Probate.*

Aiken County

Circuit Court PO Box 583, Aiken, SC 29802; 803-642-1715. Hours: 8:30AM-5PM (EST). *Felony, Misdemeanor, Civil Actions Over $7,500.*
Civil Records: Access: In person only. Both court and visitors may perform in person searches. No search fee. Required to search: name, years to search. Civil cases indexed by defendant, plaintiff. Civil records on computer from 1988; on microfiche, archives and card index from 1800s.
Criminal Records: Access: In person only. Both court and visitors may perform in person searches. Search fee: $10.00 per hour. Required to search: name, years to search, DOB; also helpful: SSN. Criminal records on computer from 1990; on microfiche, archives and card index from 1800s.
General Information: Public access terminal is available. No adoption, juvenile, sealed or expunged records released. Copy fee: $.25 per page. Certification fee: $1.00. Fee payee: Clerk of Court. Only cashiers checks and money orders accepted. Prepayment is required.

Aiken Magistrate Court 1680 Richland Ave W, Ste 70, Aiken, SC 29801; 803-642-1744/1747. Hours: 9AM-5PM (EST). *Civil Actions Under $7,500, Eviction, Small Claims.*

Graniteville Magistrate Court 50 Canal St #14, Graniteville, SC 29829; 803-663-6634/6635; Fax: 803-663-6635. Hours: 9AM-5PM (EST). *Civil Actions Under $7,500, Misdemeanor, Eviction, Small Claims.*
Note: Misdemeanor records accessed same as civil

Langley Magistrate Court PO Box 769, Langley, SC 29834; 803-593-5171/5172; Fax: 803-593-8402. *Civil Actions Under $7,500, Eviction, Small Claims.*

Monetta Magistrate Court 5697 Columbia Hwy N, PO Box 190, Monetta, SC 29105; 803-685-7125; Fax: 803-685-7988. *Civil Actions Under $7,500, Eviction, Small Claims.*

New Ellenton Magistrate Court PO Box 40, New Ellenton, SC 29809; 803-652-3609; Fax: 803-652-

2653. Hours: 9AM-2:30PM; 1:30PM-5:00PM (EST). *Civil Actions Under $7,500, Eviction, Small Claims.*

North Augusta Magistrate Court PO Box 6493, North Augusta, SC 29861; 803-202-3580/3581; Fax: 803-202-3583. Hours: 9AM-5PM (EST). *Civil Actions Under $7,500, Eviction, Small Claims.*

Probate Court PO Box 1576 (109 Park Ave), Aiken, SC 29802; 803-642-2000; Fax: 803-642-2007. Hours: 8:30AM-5PM (EST). *Probate.*

Allendale County

Circuit Court PO Box 126, Allendale, SC 29810; 803-584-2737; Fax: 803-584-7058. Hours: 9AM-5PM (EST). *Felony, Misdemeanor, Civil Actions Over $7,500.*
Civil Records: Access: Phone, mail, in person. Both court and visitors may perform in person searches. Search fee: $5.00 per name. Required to search: name, years to search. Civil cases indexed by defendant, plaintiff. Civil records on computer 1988, card index from 1919.
Criminal Records: Access: Phone, mail, in person. Both court and visitors may perform in person searches. Search fee: $5.00 per name. Required to search: name, years to search, DOB, signed release; also helpful: SSN. Criminal records kept on computer for 3 years.
General Information: Public access terminal is available. No adoption, juvenile, sealed or expunged records released. SASE required. Turnaround time 2 days. Copy fee: $.50 per page. Certification fee: $2.00. Fee payee: Clerk of Court. Personal checks accepted. Prepayment is required.

Allendale Magistrate Court 939 N Main St, Allendale, SC 29810; 803-584-3755; Fax: 803-584-7980. Hours: 9AM-5PM (EST). *Civil Actions Under $7,500, Eviction, Small Claims.*

Fairfax Magistrate Court 115 N Hampton Ave, PO Box 421, Fairfax, SC 29827; 803-632-3871/3468; Fax: 803-632-2113. *Civil Actions Under $7,500, Eviction, Small Claims.*

Probate Court PO Box 603, Courthouse Complex, Allendale, SC 29810; 803-584-3157; Fax: 803-584-7042. Hours: 9AM-5PM (EST). *Probate.*

Anderson County

Circuit Court PO Box 8002, Anderson, SC 29622; 864-260-4053; Fax: 864-260-4715. Hours: 8:30AM-5PM (EST). *Felony, Misdemeanor, Civil Actions Over $7,500.*
Civil Records: Access: In person only. Visitors must perform in person searches for themselves. No search fee. Required to search: name, years to search. Civil cases indexed by defendant, plaintiff. Civil records on computer back to 1994, prior on cards. Mail searches available to state agencies only.
Criminal Records: Access: In person only. Visitors must perform in person searches for themselves. No search fee. Required to search: name, years to search, DOB, SSN, signed release. Criminal records on computer back to 1994, prior on cards. Same as civil.
General Information: Public access terminal is available. No adoption, juvenile, sealed or expunged records released. Copy fee: $.50 per page. Fee payee: Clerk of Court. Personal checks accepted. Prepayment is required.

Anderson Magistrate Court PO Box 8002, Anderson, SC 29622; 864-260-4156/4055; Fax: 864-260-4144. Hours: 8:30AM-5PM (EST). *Civil Actions Under $7,500, Eviction, Small Claims.*

Honea Path Magistrate Court PO Box 505, Honea Path, SC 29654; 864-369-0015; Fax: 864-369-0015. Hours: 8:30AM-2PM M, T, TH; 8:30AM-Noon W (EST). *Civil Actions Under $7,500, Eviction, Small Claims.*

Iva Magistrate Court 719 E Front St, PO Box 1163, Iva, SC 29655; 864-348-3456; Fax: 864-348-3456. *Civil Actions Under $7,500, Eviction, Small Claims.*

www.scscja.com/judges/andersoncounty/andersoncountymaglist.htm
Note: The court holds warrants and criminal actions with sentences of 30 days and/or $500 fine.

Pelzer Magistrate Court PO Box 824, Pelzer, SC 29669; 864-947-5225; Fax: 864-947-5225. *Civil Actions Under $7,500, Eviction, Small Claims, Misdemeanor.*

Pendleton Magistrate Court 2301 Six and Twenty Rd, Pendleton, SC 29670; 864-646-6701. *Civil Actions Under $7,500, Eviction, Small Claims.*

Piedmont Magistrate Court PO Box 51312, Piedmont, SC 296; 864-295-2651; Fax: 864-295-5962. Hours: 9AM-5PM (EST). *Civil Actions Under $7,500, Eviction, Small Claims.*
Note: Physical address is 104 Annex Way, Easley SC 29642.

Starr Magistrate Court 7626 Hwy 81 South, PO Box 247, Starr, SC 29684; 864-352-3157; Fax: 864-352-3157. *Civil Actions Under $7,500, Eviction, Small Claims.*

Williamston Magistrate Court 12 W Main St, PO Box 125, Williamston, SC 29697; 864-847-8580; Fax: 864-847-8580. Hours: 9AM-Noon; 1PM-5PM T, W, TH (EST). *Civil Actions Under $7,500, Eviction, Small Claims.*

Probate Court PO Box 8002, Anderson, SC 29622; 864-260-4049; Fax: 864-260-4811. Hours: 8AM-5PM (EST). *Probate.*

Bamberg County

Circuit Court PO Box 150, Bamberg, SC 29003; 803-245-3025; Fax: 803-245-3088. Hours: 9AM-5PM (EST). *Felony, Misdemeanor, Civil Actions Over $7,500.*
Civil Records: Access: Mail, in person. Both court and visitors may perform in person searches. Search fee: $5.00 per name. Required to search: name, years to search. Civil cases indexed by defendant, plaintiff. Civil records on index books, files back to 1890.
Criminal Records: Access: Mail, in person. Both court and visitors may perform in person searches. Search fee: $5.00 per name. Required to search: name, years to search, DOB; also helpful: SSN. Criminal records on index books, files back to 1890.
General Information: No adoption, juvenile, sealed or expunged records released. SASE required. Turnaround time 1-2 days. Copy fee: $.25 per page. Fee payee: Clerk of Court. Personal checks accepted. Prepayment is required.

Bamberg Magistrate Court PO Box 187, Bamberg, SC 29003; 803-245-3016; Fax: 803-245-3085. Hours: 9AM-5PM M-F (EST). *Civil Actions Under $7,500, Eviction, Small Claims.*

Probate Court PO Box 180, Bamberg, SC 29003; 803-245-3008; Fax: 803-245-3008. Hours: 9AM-5PM (EST). *Probate.*

Barnwell County

Circuit Court PO Box 723, Barnwell, SC 29812; 803-541-1020; Fax: 803-541-1025. Hours: 9AM-5PM (EST). *Felony, Misdemeanor, Civil Actions Over $7,500.*

Civil Records: Access: In person only. Visitors must perform in person searches for themselves. No search fee. Required to search: name, years to search. Civil cases indexed by defendant. Civil records on computer from 1988.

Criminal Records: Access: In person only. Visitors must perform in person searches for themselves. No search fee. Required to search: name, years to search, DOB, SSN. Criminal records on computer from 1988.

General Information: Public access terminal is available. No adoption, juvenile, sealed or expunged records released. Copy fee: $.50 per page. Certification fee: $1.00. Fee payee: Clerk of Court. Personal checks accepted. Prepayment is required.

Barnwell Magistrate Court PO Box 1205, Barnwell, SC 29812; 803-541-1035; Fax: 83-541-1055. Hours: 9AM-Noon, 1-5PM (EST). *Civil Actions Under $7,500, Eviction, Small Claims.*

Blackville Magistrate Court 5997 Lartique St, Blackville, SC 29817; 803-284-2765; Fax: 803-284-9107. Hours: 8AM-5PM M, T, TH, F; 8AM-Noon W (EST). *Civil Actions Under $7,500, Eviction, Small Claims.*

Williston Magistrate Court PO Box 485, Williston, SC 29853; 803-266-3700; Fax: 803-266-5496. Hours: 9AM-5PM (EST). *Civil Actions Under $7,500, Eviction, Small Claims.*

Probate Court Room 108, County Courthouse, Barnwell, SC 29812; 803-541-1032; Fax: 803-541-1012. Hours: 9AM-5PM (EST). *Probate.*

Beaufort County

Circuit Court PO Drawer 1128 (128 Ribaut Rd, Rm 208), Beaufort, SC 29901; 843-470-5218; Fax: 843-470-5248. Hours: 8AM-5PM (EST). *Felony, Misdemeanor, Civil Actions Over $7,500.*

www.bcgov.org/Clerk_Court/clerk_court.htm

Civil Records: Access: Mail, in person. Both court and visitors may perform in person searches. Search fee: $10.00 per name. Required to search: name, years to search. Civil cases indexed by defendant, plaintiff. Civil records on computer back to 1985; prior in index books.

Criminal Records: Access: In person only. Both court and visitors may perform in person searches. Search fee: $10.00 per name. Required to search: name, years to search, DOB; also helpful: SSN. Criminal records on computer back to 1985; prior in index books.

General Information: Public access terminal is available. No adoption, juvenile, sealed or expunged records released. Copy fee: $.25 per page. Certification fee: $1.00. Fee payee: Clerk of Court. Personal checks accepted. Prepayment is required.

Beaufort Magistrate Court PO Box 2207, Beaufort, SC 29901-2207; 843-470-5202 (470-5204); Fax: 843-470-5206. Hours: 8AM-4PM (EST). *Misdemeanors, Civil Actions Under $7,500, Eviction, Small Claims, Traffic.*

Bluffton Magistrate Court PO Box 840, Bluffton, SC 29910; 843-757-1500; Fax: 843-757-1527. *Misdemeanors, Civil Actions Under $7,500, Eviction, Small Claims.*

Hilton Head Magistrate Court PO Box 22895, Hilton Head, SC 29925; 843-842-4260; Fax: 843-842-4261. *Civil Actions Under $7,500, Eviction, Small Claims.*

Lobeco Magistrate Court PO Box 845, Lobeco, SC 29931-0845; 843-846-3902; Fax: 843-846-0823. Hours: 5:30PM-7:30PM M, W (EST). *Civil Actions Under $7,500, Eviction, Small Claims.*

St Helena Island Magistrate Court PO Box 1271, St Helena Island, SC 29920; 843-838-3212; Fax: 843-838-3212. *Civil Actions Under $7,500, Eviction, Small Claims.*

Probate Court PO Box 1083, Beaufort, SC 29901-1083; 843-470-5319; Fax: 843-470-5324. Hours: 8AM-5PM (EST). *Probate.*

Berkeley County

Circuit Court PO Box 219, Moncks Corner, SC 29461; 843-719-4400. Hours: 9AM-5PM (EST). *Felony, Misdemeanor, Civil Actions Over $7,500.*

Civil Records: Access: In person only. Visitors must perform in person searches for themselves. No search fee. Required to search: name, years to search. Civil cases indexed by defendant, plaintiff. Civil records on computer from early 1980s, prior on books.

Criminal Records: Access: In person only. Visitors must perform in person searches for themselves. No search fee. Required to search: name, years to search, DOB, SSN. Criminal records on computer from early 1980s, prior on books.

General Information: Public access terminal is available. No adoption, juvenile, sealed or expunged records released. Personal checks accepted.

Goose Creek Magistrate Court 538 Redbank Rd, Goose Creek, SC 29445; 843-553-7080; Fax: 843-553-7074. Hours: 9AM-5PM (EST). *Civil Actions Under $7,500, Eviction, Small Claims.*

Moncks Corner Magistrate Court 103 Gulledge St, Moncks Corner, SC 29461; 843-719-4220 or 723-3800 X4220; Fax: 843-719-4534. Hours: 9AM-5PM (EST). *Civil Actions Under $7,500, Eviction, Small Claims.*

St Stephen Magistrate Court PO Box 1433, St Stephen, SC 29479; 843-567-7400; Fax: 843-567-6028. *Civil Actions Under $7,500, Eviction, Small Claims.*

Summerville Magistrate Court 1306 Alexander Circle, Summerville, SC 29483; 843-719-4385; Fax: 843-719-4834. *Civil Actions Under $7,500, Eviction, Small Claims.*

Probate Court 300 B California Ave, Moncks Corner, SC 29461; 843-719-4519; Fax: 843-719-4527. Hours: 9AM-5PM (EST). *Probate.*

Calhoun County

Circuit Court 302 S Huff Dr, St Matthews, SC 29135; 803-874-3524; Fax: 803-874-1942. Hours: 9AM-5PM (EST). *Felony, Misdemeanor, Civil Actions Over $7,500.*

Civil Records: Access: Mail, in person. Both court and visitors may perform in person searches. Search fee: $5.00 per name. Required to search: name, years to search. Civil cases indexed by defendant, plaintiff. Civil records on computer from 1982, prior on index books from 1912.

Criminal Records: Access: Mail, in person. Both court and visitors may perform in person searches. Search fee: $5.00 per name. Required to search: name, years to search, DOB. Criminal records on computer from 1982, prior on index books from 1912.

General Information: Public access terminal is available. No adoption, juvenile, sealed or expunged records released. SASE required. Turnaround time 1 day. Copy fee: $.25 per page. Fee payee: Clerk of

Court. Personal checks accepted. Prepayment is required.

Cameron Magistrate Court Cameron Town Hall, PO Box 663, Cameron, SC 29030; 803-823-2266; Fax: 803-823-2328. Hours: 1PM-5PM T, TH (EST). *Civil Actions Under $7,500, Eviction, Small Claims.*

Cameron/Lone Starr Magistrate Court PO Box 663, Cameron, SC 29030; 803-823-2266. Hours: 1-5PM Tues & Thur (EST). *Civil Actions Under $7,500, Eviction, Small Claims.*

St Matthews Magistrate Court 112 W Bridge St, PO Box 191, St Matthews, SC 29135; 803-874-1112; Fax: 803-874-1111. Hours: 9AM-5PM (EST). *Civil Actions Under $7,500, Eviction, Small Claims.*

Probate Court 302 South F.R. Huff Dr, St Matthews, SC 29135; 803-874-3514; Fax: 803-874-1942. *Probate.*

Charleston County

Circuit Court PO Box 70219, Charleston, SC 29415; 843-740-5700; Fax: 843-740-5887. Hours: 8:30AM-5PM (EST). *Felony, Misdemeanor, Civil Actions Over $7,500.*

http://www3.charlestoncounty.org

Civil Records: Access: Mail, online, in person. Both court and visitors may perform in person searches. Search fee: $10.00 per name. Required to search: name, years to search. Civil cases indexed by defendant, plaintiff. Civil records on computer from 1988, microfiche and archives from mid 1800s. Access to civil records (1988 forward), judgments and lis pendens are available free online at www3.charlestoncounty.org/connect. Online document images go back to 1/1/1999.

Criminal Records: Access: Mail, online, in person. Both court and visitors may perform in person searches. Search fee: $10.00 per name. Required to search: name, years to search, DOB; also helpful: SSN. Criminal records on computer from 4/90, prior on books and microfilm from 1900s. The Internet offers access to records from 04/92 forward. Search by name or case number. There is no fee.

General Information: Public access terminal is available. No adoption, juvenile, sealed or expunged records released. SASE required. Turnaround time 3 days. Fax notes: No fee to fax results. Copy fee: $.25 per page. Certification fee: $1.00. Fee payee: Clerk of Court. Business checks accepted. Prepayment is required.

Charleston Magistrate Court 1720 Sam Rittenberg Blvd Unit 11, PO Box 31861, Charleston, SC 29417; 843-766-6531; Fax: 843-571-4751. *Civil Actions Under $7,500, Eviction, Small Claims, Misdemeanors.*

www.charlestoncounty.org

Note: County magistrate courts records from 1998 forward can be searched free at www3.charlestoncounty.org/connect?ref=Magistrates.

Charleston Magistrate Court 4045 Bridgeview Dr, PO Box 60037, Charleston, SC 29419; 843-202-6610; Fax: 843-202-6620. Hours: 8:30AM-4:30PM (EST). *Civil Actions Under $7,500, Misdemeanor, Eviction, Small Claims.*

Note: County magistrate courts records from 1998 forward can be searched free at www3.charlestoncounty.org/connect?ref=Magistrates.

Charleston Magistrate Court 995 Morrison Dr, PO Box 941, Charleston, SC 29402; 843-724-6719; Fax: 843-745-6785. Hours: 8:30-5PM (EST). *Civil Actions Under $7,500, Eviction.*

Note: County magistrate courts records from 1998 forward can be searched free at www3.charlestoncounty.org/connect?ref=Magistrates.

East Cooper Magistrate Court
1189 Iron Bridge Rd, Ste 300, PO Box 584, Mt Pleasant, SC 29465; 843-856-1205; Fax: 843-856-1188. Hours: 8AM-12, 1-4:30PM (EST). *Misdemeanor, Civil Actions Under $7,500, Eviction.*
http://www3.charlestoncounty.org/docs/CoC/index.html
Note: County magistrate courts records from 1998 forward can be searched free at www3.charlestoncounty.org/connect?ref=Magistrates.

Edisto Island Magistrate Court
8070 Indigo Hill Rd, PO Box 216, Edisto Island, SC 29438; 843-869-2909; Fax: 843-869-4460. Hours: 4:30PM-6PM M, W (EST). *Civil Actions Under $7,500, Eviction, Traffic.*
Note: County magistrate courts records from 1998 forward can be searched free at www3.charlestoncounty.org/connect?ref=Magistrates.

James Island Magistrate Court
PO Box 12226, James Island, SC 29422; 843-795-1140; Fax: 843-406-2753. Hours: 8:30AM-5PM (EST). *Misdemeanor, Civil Actions Under $7,500, Eviction, Small Claims.*
Note: County magistrate courts records from 1998 forward can be searched free at www3.charlestoncounty.org/connect?ref=Magistrates.

Johns Island Magistrate Court
1521 Main Rd, Johns Island, SC 29455; 843-559-1218; Fax: 843-559-2378. Hours: 8:30AM-5PM T, Th; 9AM-7PM M, W, F (EST). *Civil Actions Under $7,500, Eviction, Small Claims.*
Note: County magistrate courts records from 1998 forward can be searched free at www3.charlestoncounty.org/connect?ref=Magistrates.

McClellanville Magistrate Court
9888 Randall Rd, PO Box 7, McClellanville, SC 29458; 843-887-3334; Fax: 843-887-3901. Hours: 9AM-Noon, 1-4PM M,Th (EST). *Civil Actions Under $7,500, Eviction, Small Claims.*
Note: County magistrate courts records from 1998 forward can be searched free at www3.charlestoncounty.org/connect?ref=Magistrates.

North Charleston Magistrate Court
2036 Cherokee St, PO Box 71316, North Charleston, SC 29416; 843-745-2215; Fax: 843-745-2334. Hours: 8:30AM-1PM; 2PM-5PM M-F (EST). *Civil Actions Under $7,500, Eviction, Small Claims.*
Note: County magistrate courts records from 1998 forward can be searched free at www3.charlestoncounty.org/connect?ref=Magistrates.

North Charleston Magistrate Court
7272 Cross County Rd, North Charleston, SC 29419; 843-767-2743; Fax: 843-760-6887. Hours: 8:30AM-4:30PM (EST). *Civil Actions Under $7,500, Eviction, Small Claims.*
Note: County magistrate courts records from 1998 forward can be searched free at www3.charlestoncounty.org/connect?ref=Magistrates.

North Charleston Magistrate Court
4045 Bridge View Dr, North Charleston, SC 29405; 843-740-5860. Hours: 8:30AM-4:30PM (EST). *Civil Actions Under $7,500, Small Claims.*
Note: County magistrate courts records from 1998 forward can be searched free at www3.charlestoncounty.org/connect?ref=Magistrates.

Ravenel Magistrate Court
5962 Hwy 165, #200, Ravenel, SC 29470; 843-889-8332; Fax: 843-889-9202. Hours: 8:30AM-4:30PM (EST). *Civil Actions Under $7,500, Eviction, Small Claims.*
Note: County magistrate courts records from 1998 forward can be searched free at www3.charlestoncounty.org/connect?ref=Magistrates.

Probate Court
2144 Melbourne Ave, North Charleston, SC 29405; 843-740-5890; Fax: 843-740-5897. Hours: 8:30AM-5PM (EST). *Probate.*

Cherokee County

Circuit Court
PO Drawer 2289, Gaffney, SC 29342; 864-487-2571; Fax: 864-487-2754. Hours: 8:30AM-5PM (EST). *Felony, Misdemeanor, Civil Actions Over $7,500.*
Civil Records: Access: In person only. Visitors must perform in person searches for themselves. No search fee. Required to search: name, years to search. Civil cases indexed by defendant, plaintiff. Civil records go back to 1897; computerized records go back to 1994.
Criminal Records: Access: In person only. Visitors must perform in person searches for themselves. No search fee. Required to search: name, years to search. Criminal records on computer from 1994, prior on books.
General Information: Public access terminal is available. No adoption, juvenile, sealed or expunged records released. Copy fee: $1.00 per page. Certification fee: $1.00. Fee payee: Clerk of Court. Business checks accepted. Prepayment is required.

Blacksburg Magistrate Court
101 S Shelby St, PO Box 427, Blacksburg, SC 29702; 864-839-2492; Fax: 864-839-3415. Hours: 8:30AM-5PM (EST). *Civil Actions Under $7,500, Eviction, Small Claims.*

Cherokee County Magistrate Court
312 E Frederick St, PO Box 336, Gaffney, SC 29342-0336; 864-487-2533/2501; Fax: 864-902-8425. Hours: 8:30AM-5PM (EST). *Misdemeanors, Civil Actions Under $7,500, Eviction, Small Claims.*

www.cherokeemagistrate.com
Note: Civil Action minimum raises to $7,500 on January 1, 2001.

Probate Court
1434 N Limestone St, Peachtree Ctr, Gaffney, SC 29340; 864-487-2583; Fax: 864-902-8426. Hours: 9AM-5PM (EST). *Probate.*

Chester County

Circuit Court
PO Drawer 580, Chester, SC 29706; 803-385-2605; Fax: 803-581-7975. Hours: 8:30AM-5PM (EST). *Felony, Misdemeanor, Civil Actions Over $7,500.*
Civil Records: Access: In person. Visitors must perform in person searches. No search fee. Required to search: name, years to search, address. Civil cases indexed by defendant, plaintiff. Civil records on computer from 1989, microfiche from 1927.
Criminal Records: Access: In person. Visitors must perform in person searches. No search fee. Required to search: name, years to search, DOB, signed release; also helpful: SSN. Criminal records on computer from 1994, docket books prior.
General Information: Public access terminal is available. (Public Access for Civil only) No adoption, juvenile, sealed or expunged records released. Copy fee: $.50 per page. Certification fee: $1.00. Fee payee: Clerk of Court. Personal checks accepted. Prepayment is required.

Chester Magistrate Court
2740 Dawson Dr, PO Box 727, Chester, SC 29706; 803-581-5136; 581-

3040; Fax: 803-581-5552. *Civil Actions Under $7,500, Eviction, Small Claims.*

Probate Court
PO Drawer 580, Chester, SC 29706; 803-385-2604; Fax: 803-581-5180. Hours: 8:30AM-5PM (EST). *Probate.*

Chesterfield County

Circuit Court
PO Box 529, Chesterfield, SC 29709; 843-623-2574; Fax: 843-623-6944. Hours: 8:30AM-5PM (EST). *Felony, Misdemeanor, Civil Actions Over $7,500.*
Civil Records: Access: Mail, in person. Both court and visitors may perform in person searches. Search fee: $5.00 per name. Required to search: name, years to search. Civil cases indexed by defendant, plaintiff. Civil records on computer back to 1986, prior on docket books.
Criminal Records: Access: Mail, in person. Both court and visitors may perform in person searches. Search fee: $5.00 per name. Required to search: name, years to search, DOB, SSN. Criminal records on computer back to 1986, prior on docket books.
General Information: No adoption, juvenile, sealed or expunged records released. SASE required. Turnaround time 3 days. Copy fee: $2.00 per document and $.25 per page after 1st 4 pages. Fee payee: Clerk of Court. Personal checks accepted. Prepayment is required.

Cheraw Magistrate Court
105 State Rd, PO Box 364, Cheraw, SC 29520; 843-537-3323; Fax: 843-537-1670. *Civil Actions Under $7,500, Eviction, Small Claims.*

Cheraw Magistrate Court
Hinson Hill Rd, Rt 1 Box 366-A, Cheraw, SC 29520; 843-623-2955. *Civil Actions Under $7,500, Eviction, Small Claims.*

Cheraw Magistrate Court
Route 2, Box 727, Cheraw, SC 29520; 843-537-7139; Fax: 843-537-8404. Hours: 8:30AM-5PM (EST). *Civil Actions Under $7,500, Eviction, Small Claims.*

Chesterfield Magistrate Court
Rte 1 Box 40, Chesterfield, SC 29709; 843-623-7929; Fax: 843-623-7929. *Civil Actions Under $7,500, Eviction, Small Claims.*

McBee Magistrate Court
Rt 2 Box 650, McBee, SC 29101; 843-623-7929. *Civil Actions Under $7,500, Eviction, Small Claims.*

Pageland Magistrate Court
310 W McGregor St, PO Box 133, Pageland, SC 29728; 843-672-5685. Hours: 10AM-3PM (EST). *Civil Actions Under $7,500, Eviction, Small Claims.*

Patrick Magistrate Court
Rt 1 Box 385, Patrick, SC 29584; 843-498-6398. Hours: 4PM-8PM M-TH *Civil Actions Under $7,500, Eviction, Small Claims.*

Ruby Magistrate Court
300 Deaton St, PO Box 131, Ruby, SC 29741; 843-634-6597. *Civil Actions Under $7,500, Eviction, Small Claims, Misdemeanors.*

Probate Court
County Courthouse, 200 W Main St, Chesterfield, SC 29709; 843-623-2376; Fax: 843-623-9886. Hours: 8:30AM-5PM (EST). *Probate.*

Clarendon County

Circuit Court
PO Drawer E, Manning, SC 29102; 803-435-4444. Hours: 8:30AM-5PM (EST). *Felony, Misdemeanor, Civil Actions Over $7,500.*
Civil Records: Access: Mail, in person. Both court and visitors may perform in person searches. Search fee: $27.00. Includes all copy fees. Required to search: name, years to search. Civil cases indexed by defendant,

plaintiff. Civil records on computer from 1988, index books from 1865.

Criminal Records: Access: Mail, in person. Both court and visitors may perform in person searches. Search fee: $27.00. Includes copy fees. Required to search: name, years to search. Criminal records on computer from 1983, index books from 1865.

General Information: Public access terminal is available. No adoption, juvenile, sealed or expunged records released. SASE required. Turnaround time 5 days. Copy fee: $.25 per page. Certification fee: $1.00. Fee payee: Clerk of Court. Personal checks accepted. Prepayment is required.

Manning Magistrate Court 10 Keitt St, PO Box 371, Manning, SC 29102; 803-435-2670/8925; Fax: 803-435-8905. Hours: 8:30AM-5PM (EST). *Civil Actions Under $7,500, Eviction, Small Claims.*

Summerton Magistrate Court 216 Main St, PO Box 386, Summerton, SC 29148; 803-485-8228. Hours: 9AM-Noon T, W, TH (EST). *Civil Actions Under $7,500, Eviction, Small Claims.*

Probate Court PO Box 307, Manning, SC 29102; 803-435-8774; Fax: 803-435-8698. Hours: 8:30AM-5PM (EST). *Probate.*

Colleton County

Circuit Court PO Box 620, Walterboro, SC 29488; 843-549-5791; Fax: 843-549-2875. Hours: 8:00AM-5PM (EST). *Felony, Misdemeanor, Civil Actions Over $7,500.*

Civil Records: Access: Phone, fax, mail, in person. Both court and visitors may perform in person searches. Search fee: $5.00 per name. Required to search: name, years to search. Civil cases indexed by defendant, plaintiff. Civil records on computer from 1986, on index books from 1865.

Criminal Records: Access: Phone, fax, mail, in person. Both court and visitors may perform in person searches. Search fee: $5.00 per name. Required to search: name, years to search; also helpful: SSN, DOB. Criminal records on computer from 1986, on index books from 1865.

General Information: No adoption, juvenile, PTI, sealed or expunged records released. SASE required. Turnaround time 2 days. Fax notes: Extra fee to fax back results. Copy fee: $.25 per page. Certification fee: $1.00. Fee payee: Clerk of Court. Business checks accepted. Prepayment is required.

Green Pond Magistrate Court 8464 Ace Basin Prky, Green Pond, SC 29446; 843-844-8486; Fax: 843-844-8835. Hours: 9AM-4:30PM (EST). *Civil Actions Under $7,500, Eviction, Small Claims.*

Walterboro Magistrate Court 217 Brown St, Walterboro, SC 29488; 843-549-2417; Fax: 843-549-2211. *Civil Actions Under $7,500, Eviction, Small Claims.*

Walterboro Magistrate Court 492 Benton Farm Rd, Walterboro, SC 29488; 843-538-3637/3903; Fax: 843-538-5173. Hours: 8:30AM-5PM (EST). *Civil Actions Under $7,500, Eviction, Small Claims.*

Walterboro Magistrate Court 40-B Klein St, PO Box 1732, Walterboro, SC 29488; 843-549-1122; Fax: 843-549-9010. Hours: 8AM-5PM (EST). *Civil Actions Under $7,500, Eviction, Small Claims.*

Probate Court PO Box 1036, Walterboro, SC 29488-0031; 843-549-7216; Fax: 843-549-5571. Hours: 8:00AM-5PM (EST). *Probate.*

Darlington County

Circuit Court PO Box 1177, Darlington, SC 29540; 843-398-4339. Hours: 8:30AM-5PM (EST). *Felony, Misdemeanor, Civil Actions Over $7,500.*

Civil Records: Access: In person only. Visitors must perform in person searches for themselves. No search fee. Required to search: name, years to search. Civil cases indexed by defendant, plaintiff. Civil records on computer from 1989, on index books from 1805.

Criminal Records: Access: In person only. Visitors must perform in person searches for themselves. No search fee. Required to search: name, years to search; also helpful: DOB, SSN. Criminal records on computer from 1989, on index books from 1805. Will give disposition & sentence over phone if case number given.

General Information: No adoption, juvenile, sealed or expunged records released. Copy fee: $.10 per page. Fee payee: Clerk of Court. Business checks accepted. Prepayment is required.

Darlington Magistrate Court PO Box 782 (200 Camp Rd), Darlington, SC 29540; 843-398-4220; Fax: 843-332-7212. Hours: 8:30AM-5PM (EST). *Civil Actions Under $7,500, Eviction, Small Claims.*

Hartsville Magistrate Court 404 S 4th St, PO Box 1765, Hartsville, SC 29550; 843-332-9661; Fax: 843-332-1603. Hours: 8:30AM-5PM (EST). *Civil Actions Under $7,500, Eviction, Small Claims.*

Lamar Magistrate Court 103 Warren Ave, PO Box 38, Lamar, SC 29069; 843-326-5441; Fax: 843-326-5280. Hours: 8AM-6PM T, W, TH (EST). *Civil Actions Under $7,500, Eviction, Small Claims.*

Society Hill Magistrate Court PO Box 447, Society Hill, SC 29593; 843-378-4601. *Civil Actions Under $7,500, Eviction, Small Claims.*

Probate Court #1 Public Sq - Courthouse Rm 208, Darlington, SC 29532; 843-398-4310; Fax: 843-398-4172. Hours: 8:30AM-5PM (EST). *Probate.*

Dillon County

Circuit Court PO Drawer 1220, Dillon, SC 29536; 843-774-1425. Hours: 8:30AM-5PM (EST). *Felony, Misdemeanor, Civil Actions Over $7,500.*

Civil Records: Access: Mail, in person. Both court and visitors may perform in person searches. Search fee: $10.00 per name. Required to search: name, years to search. Civil cases indexed by defendant, plaintiff. Civil records on computer from 1990, on docket books prior.

Criminal Records: Access: Mail, in person. Both court and visitors may perform in person searches. Search fee: $10.00 per name. Required to search: name, years to search; also helpful: DOB, SSN. Criminal records on computer from 1990, on docket books prior.

General Information: No adoption, juvenile, sealed or expunged records released. SASE required. Turnaround time 1 day. Copy fee: $.50 per page. Certification fee: $1.00. Fee payee: Clerk of Court. Personal checks accepted. Prepayment is required.

Dillon Magistrate Court 200 S 5th Ave, PO Box 1016, Dillon, SC 29536; 843-774-1407; Fax: 843-774-1453. Hours: 8:30AM-5PM (EST). *Civil Actions Under $7,500, Eviction, Small Claims.*

Dillon Magistrate Court 200 S 5th Ave, PO Box 1061, Dillon, SC 29536; 843-774-1406. Hours: 8:30AM-5PM (EST). *Civil Actions Under $7,500, Eviction, Small Claims.*

Hamer Magistrate Court

Hamer Magistrate Court 143 Elkins Road, PO Box 1, Hamer, SC 29547; 843-774-2041; Fax: 843-774-1453. Hours: None (EST). *Civil Actions Under $7,500, Eviction, Small Claims.*

Note: Court only has records prior to 1996; later records are at Dillon Magistrate Court, where court now resides.

Lake View Magistrate Court PO Box 272, Lake View, SC 29563; 843-759-2181. *Civil Actions Under $7,500, Eviction, Small Claims.*

Probate Court PO Box 189, Dillon, SC 29536; 843-774-1423; Fax: 843-841-3732. Hours: 8:30AM-5PM (EST). *Probate.*

Dorchester County

Circuit Court 101 Ridge St, St George, SC 29477; 843-563-0160. Hours: 8:30AM-5PM (EST). *Felony, Misdemeanor, Civil Actions Over $7,500.*

Civil Records: Access: In person only. Visitors must perform in person searches for themselves. No search fee. Required to search: name, years to search. Civil cases indexed by defendant, plaintiff. Civil records on index books back to 1950s, on computer since 1994.

Criminal Records: Access: In person only. Visitors must perform in person searches for themselves. No search fee. Required to search: name, years to search, DOB, signed release; also helpful: SSN. Criminal records on index books back to 1950s, on computer since 1944.

General Information: No adoption, juvenile, sealed or expunged records released. Copy fee: $.50 per page. Fee payee: Clerk of Court. Personal checks accepted. Prepayment is required.

Dorchester County Court 101 Ridge St, St George, SC 29477; 843-563-0130; Fax: 843-563-0123. Hours: 8AM-5PM (EST). *Civil Actions Under $7,500, Eviction, Small Claims.*

Civil Records: Access: Mail. No search fee.

General Information: Turnaround time 5-7 days. Fee payee: County Treasurer. Prepayment is required.

St George Magistrate Court 101 Ridge St, St. George, SC 29477; 843-832-0130; Fax: 843-563-0123. Hours: 8:30AM-5PM (EST). *Civil Actions Under $7,500, Eviction, Small Claims.*

Summerville Magistrate Court 212 Deming Way, Box 10, Summerville, SC 29483; 843-832-0370; Fax: 843-832-0123. *Civil Actions Under $7,500, Eviction, Small Claims.*

Probate Court 101 Ridge St, County Courthouse, St George, SC 29477; 843-563-0105; Fax: 843-563-0245. Hours: 8:30AM-5PM (EST). *Probate.*

Edgefield County

Circuit Court PO Box 34, Edgefield, SC 29824; 803-637-4082; Fax: 803-637-4117. Hours: 8:30AM-5PM (EST). *Felony, Misdemeanor, Civil Actions Over $7,500.*

Civil Records: Access: Mail, in person. Both court and visitors may perform in person searches. Search fee: $5.00 per name. Required to search: name, years to search. Civil cases indexed by defendant, plaintiff. Civil records archived from 1839; on computer back to 1987.

Criminal Records: Access: Mail, in person. Both court and visitors may perform in person searches. Search fee: $5.00 per name. Required to search: name, years to search, DOB; also helpful: SSN. Criminal records archived from 1839; on computer back to 1987.

General Information: No adoption, juvenile, sealed or expunged records released. SASE required. Turnaround time 1 day. Fax notes: Will not fax results. Copy fee: $.50 per page. Certification fee: $1.00. Fee payee: Clerk of Court. Business checks accepted. Prepayment is required.

Edgefield Magistrate Court 129 Courthouse Sq, #212, PO Box 664, Edgefield, SC 29824; 803-637-4090; Fax: 803-637-4101. Hours: 8:30AM-4:30PM (EST). *Civil Actions Under $7,500, Eviction, Small Claims.*

Probate Court 124 Courthouse Square, Edgefield, SC 29824; 803-637-4076; Fax: 803-637-7157. Hours: 8:30AM-5PM (EST). *Probate.*

Fairfield County

Circuit Court PO Drawer 299, Winnsboro, SC 29180; 803-712-6526. Hours: 9AM-5PM (EST). *Felony, Misdemeanor, Civil Actions Over $7,500.*

Civil Records: Access: In person only. Visitors must perform in person searches for themselves. No search fee. Required to search: name, years to search. Civil cases indexed by defendant, plaintiff. Civil records on docket books. The court provides an index, but will not do record searching.

Criminal Records: Access: In person only. Visitors must perform in person searches for themselves. No search fee. Required to search: name, years to search, DOB; also helpful: SSN. Criminal records on docket books.

General Information: No adoption, juvenile, sealed or expunged records released. Fax notes: Will not fax results. Copy fee: $.25 per page. Certification fee: $1.00. Fee payee: Clerk of Court. Personal checks accepted. Prepayment is required.

Winnsboro Magistrate Court 115-B South Congress St, Winnsboro, SC 29180; 803-635-4525; Fax: 803-635-5717. Hours: 9AM-5PM (EST). *Civil Actions Under $7,500, Eviction, Small Claims.*

Probate Court PO Box 385, Winnsboro, SC 29180; 803-712-6519; Fax: 803-712-6939. Hours: 9AM-5PM (EST). *Probate.*

Florence County

Circuit Court Drawer E, City County Complex (180 N Irby St), Florence, SC 29501; 843-665-3031. Hours: 8:30AM-5PM (EST). *Felony, Misdemeanor, Civil Actions Over $7,500.*

www.florenceco.org/clerk.html

Civil Records: Access: Mail, in person. Both court and visitors may perform in person searches. Search fee: $5.00 per name. Required to search: name, years to search. Civil cases indexed by defendant, plaintiff. Civil records on computer from 1984, on microfiche and docket books from 1900s.

Criminal Records: Access: Mail, in person. Both court and visitors may perform in person searches. Search fee: $5.00 per name. Required to search: name, years to search, DOB; also helpful: SSN. Criminal records on computer from 1984, on microfiche and docket books from 1900s.

General Information: No adoption, juvenile, sealed or expunged records released. SASE required. Turnaround time 10-14 days. Copy fee: $.50. Certification fee: $1.00. Fee payee: Clerk of Court. Personal checks accepted. Prepayment is required.

Florence Magistrate Court 180 N Irby St (MSC-W), Florence, SC 29501; 843-665-0031; Fax: 843-661-7800. Hours: 8:30AM-4:45PM M-TH; 8:30AM-4:30PM F (EST). *Civil Actions Under $7,500, Eviction, Small Claims.*

Johnsonville Magistrate Court 461 S Railroad Ave, Johnsonville, SC 29555; 843-665-0031; Fax: 843-386-3623. Hours: 8:30AM-5PM M,T,W (EST). *Civil Actions Under $7,500, Eviction, Small Claims.*

Lake City Magistrate Court PO Box 39, Lake City, SC 29560; 843-394-5461; Fax: 843-394-3865. Hours: 8:30AM-5PM (EST). *Civil Actions Under $7,500, Eviction, Small Claims.*

Olanta Magistrate Court PO Box 362, Olanta, SC 29114; 843-396-9056. Hours: 8:30AM-5PM (EST). *Civil Actions Under $7,500, Eviction, Small Claims.*

Pamplico Magistrate Court 124 Third Ave East, PO Box 367, Pamplico, SC 29583; 843-493-0072; Fax: 843-493-5391. Hours: 8:30AM-4:30PM T, W, TH; 8:30AM-2PM M (EST). *Civil Actions Under $7,500, Misdemeanor, Eviction, Small Claims, Traffic.*

Timmonsville Magistrate Court 307 Smith St, PO Box 190, Timmonsville, SC 29161; 843-346-7472; Fax: 843-346-0660. Hours: 8:30-5PM (EST). *Civil Actions Under $7,500, Eviction, Small Claims.*

Probate Court 180 N Irby, MSC-L, Florence, SC 29501; 843-665-3085; Fax: 843-665-3068. Hours: 8:30AM-5PM (EST). *Probate.*

Georgetown County

Circuit Court PO Box 421270, Georgetown, SC 29442; 843-546-5011; Civil phone: 843-545-3041; Criminal phone: 843-545-3053; Fax: 843-546-3281. Hours: 8:30AM-5PM (EST). *Felony, Misdemeanor, Civil Actions Over $7,500.*

Civil Records: Access: In person only. Visitors must perform in person searches for themselves. No search fee. Required to search: name, years to search. Civil cases indexed by defendant, plaintiff. Civil records on index from 1926.

Criminal Records: Access: In person only. Visitors must perform in person searches for themselves. No search fee. Required to search: name, years to search, DOB; also helpful: SSN. Criminal records on index from 1926, computerized since 2001.

General Information: Public access terminal is available. No adoption, juvenile, sealed or expunged records released. Copy fee: $.50 per page. Certification fee: $1.00 per page. Fee payee: Clerk of Court. Business checks accepted. Prepayment is required.

Andrews Magistrate Court 110 N Morgan Ave, Andrews, SC 29510; 843-264-8811; Fax: 843-264-5177. Hours: 8:30AM-5PM (EST). *Civil Actions Under $7,500, Eviction, Small Claims.*

Georgetown Magistrate Court 333 Cleland St, PO Box 807, Georgetown, SC 29442; 843-546-4650; Fax: 843-527-1703. Hours: 8:30AM-5PM (EST). *Civil Actions Under $7,500, Eviction, Small Claims.*

Georgetown Magistrate Court 1277 N Frasier St, PO Box 1838, Georgetown, SC 29442; 843-545-8140; Fax: 843-545-8142. *Civil Actions Under $7,500, Eviction, Small Claims.*

Note: This court now handles only traffic offenses.

Murrells Inlet Magistrate Court 4450 Murrells Inlet Rd, PO Box 859, Murrells Inlet, SC 29576; 843-651-6292; Fax: 843-651-6685. Hours: 8AM-5PM (EST). *Civil Actions Under $7,500, Eviction, Small Claims.*

Pawleys Island Magistrate Court 291 Parkersville Rd, PO Box 1830, Pawleys Island, SC 29585; 843-237-8995; Fax: 843-237-3244. Hours: 8AM-5PM (EST). *Civil Actions Under $7,500, Eviction, Small Claims.*

Plesant Hill Magistrate Court 9174 Pleasant Hill Dr, Hemingway, SC 29554; 843-558-9711; Fax: 843-558-5827. *Misdemeanors, Civil Actions Under $7,500, Eviction, Small Claims.*

Probate Court PO Box 421270, Georgetown, SC 29442; 843-545-3274; Fax: 843-545-3292. Hours: 8:30AM-5PM (EST). *Probate.*

Greenville County

Circuit Court 305 E. North St, RM 227, Greenville, SC 29601; 864-467-8551; Fax: 864-467-8540. Hours: 8:30AM-5PM (EST). *Felony, Misdemeanor, Civil Actions Over $7,500.*

www.greenvillecounty.org

Civil Records: Access: In person only. Visitors must perform in person searches for themselves. No search fee. Required to search: name, years to search. Civil cases indexed by defendant, plaintiff. Civil records on computer from 1985, on docket books from 1900s.

Criminal Records: Access: In person only. Visitors must perform in person searches for themselves. No search fee. Required to search: name, years to search, DOB, SSN, signed release. Criminal records on computer from 1985, on docket books from 1900s.

General Information: Public access terminal is available. No adoption, juvenile, sealed or expunged records released. Copy fee: $.25 per page. Certification fee: $1.00. Fee payee: Clerk of Court. Prepayment is required.

Gantt Magistrate Court 1103 White Horse Rd, Greenville, SC 29605; Civil phone: 864-277-0856; Criminal phone: 864-277-4429; Fax: 864-277-4376. Hours: 8:30AM-5PM (EST). *Misdemeanors, Civil Actions Under $7,500, Eviction, Small Claims.*

http://greenvillecounty.org/Magistrates/Gantt.htm

Greenville Magistrate Courts #1 & #2 4 McGhee St, LEC Room 116A, Greenville, SC 29601; 864-467-5312 (City #1), 864-467-5302 (City #2); Fax: 864-467-5105. Hours: 8:30AM-5PM (EST). *Civil Actions Under $7,500, Eviction, Small Claims.*

http://greenvillecounty.org/Magistrates/City1.htm

Piedmont Magistrate Court 8150 August Rd, Piedmont, SC 29673; 864-277-9555; Fax: 864-277-8345. Hours: 8:30AM-5PM (EST). *Civil Actions Under $7,500, Eviction, Small Claims.*

http://greenvillecounty.org/Magistrates/SouthGC.htm

Simpsonville Magistrate Court 3600 Grandview Dr, Simpsonville, SC 296180; 864-963-3457; Fax: 864-963-0029. Hours: 8:30AM-5:00PM (EST). *Civil Actions Under $7,500, Eviction, Small Claims.*

http://greenvillecounty.org/Magistrates/FairAustin.htm

Taylors Magistrate Court 2801 Wade Hampton Blvd, Taylors, SC 29687; 864-244-2922; Fax: 864-268-1333. Hours: 8:30AM-5PM (EST). *Civil Actions Under $7,500, Eviction, Small Claims.*

http://greenvillecounty.org/Magistrates/ChickSprings.htm

Travelers Rest Magistrate Court 114 N Poinsett Hwy, Travelers Rest, SC 29690; 864-834-6910; Fax: 864-834-6911. Hours: 9AM-4PM (EST). *Civil Actions Under $7,500, Eviction, Small Claims.*

http://greenvillecounty.org/Magistrates/Bates.htm

West Greenville Magistrate Court 6247 White Horse Rd, Greenville, SC 29611; 864-294-4810; Fax: 864-294-4801. Hours: 8:30AM-5PM (EST). *Misdemeanors, Civil Actions Under $7,500, Eviction, Small Claims.*

http://greenvillecounty.org/Magistrates/WestGC.htm

Probate Court 301 University Ridge, Ste 1200, Greenville, SC 29601; 864-467-7170; Fax: 864-467-7198. Hours: 8:30AM-5PM (EST). *Probate.*

www.greenvillecounty.org/probate/index.htm

Greenwood County

Circuit Court Courthouse, Rm 114, 528 Monument St, Greenwood, SC 29646; 864-942-8547; Fax: 864-943-8693. Hours: 8:30AM-5PM (EST). *Felony, Misdemeanor, Civil Actions Over $7,500.*

Civil Records: Access: Mail, in person. Visitors must perform in person searches for themselves. Search fee: $2.00 per name. Required to search: name, years to search. Civil cases indexed by defendant, plaintiff. Civil records on docket books from 1897; on computer back to 2000.

Criminal Records: Access: Mail, in person. Visitors must perform in person searches for themselves. Search fee: $2.00 per name. Required to search: name, years to search, DOB; also helpful: SSN. Criminal records on alpha index from 1897; on computer back to 2000. The court will not perform party name searches for in-person requesters.

General Information: Public access terminal is available. (Only civil searching is available.) No adoption, juvenile, sealed or expunged records released. SASE required. Turnaround time 1-2 days. Copy fee: $.25 per page. Certification fee: $2.00. Fee payee: Clerk of Court. Business checks accepted. Prepayment is required.

Greenwood Magistrate Court Greenood County Courthouse, Rm 100, Greenwood, SC 29646; 864-942-8655; Fax: 864-942-8663. Hours: 7:30AM-5PM (EST). *Civil Actions Under $7,500, Eviction, Small Claims.*

Probate Court PO Box 1210, Greenwood, SC 29648; 864-942-8625; Fax: 864-942-8620. Hours: 8:30AM-5PM (EST). *Probate.*

Hampton County

Circuit Court PO Box 7, Hampton, SC 29924; 803-943-7510. Hours: 8AM-5PM (EST). *Felony, Civil Actions Over $7,500.*

Civil Records: Access: In person only. Visitors must perform in person searches for themselves. No search fee. Required to search: name, years to search. Civil cases indexed by defendant, plaintiff. Civil records on docket books, archived from 1878.

Criminal Records: Access: In person only. Visitors must perform in person searches for themselves. No search fee. Required to search: name, years to search, DOB; also helpful: SSN. Criminal records on docket books, archived from 1878.

General Information: No adoption, juvenile, sealed or expunged records released. Copy fee: $.50 per page. Certification fee: $1.00. Fee payee: Clerk of Court. Personal checks accepted. Prepayment is required.

Estill Magistrate Court 140 E Railroad Ave, PO Box 969, Estill, SC 29918; 803-625-3232; Fax: 803-625-2148. Hours: 9AM-5PM (EST). *Civil Actions Under $7,500, Eviction, Small Claims.*

Varnville Magistrate Court Law Enforcement Ctr, 411 Cemetery Rd, PO Box 1299, Varnville, SC 29944; 803-943-7511; Fax: 843-943-7557. Hours: 8:30AM-4:30PM (EST). *Misdemeanor, Civil Actions Under $7,500, Eviction, Small Claims.*

Probate Court PO Box 601, Hampton, SC 29924; 803-943-7512; Fax: 803-943-7596, 803-943-7540. Hours: 8AM-5PM (EST). *Probate.*

Horry County

Circuit Court PO Box 677, Conway, SC 29526; 843-248-1270; Fax: 843-248-1341. Hours: 8AM-5PM (EST). *Felony, Misdemeanor, Civil Actions Over $7,500.*

Civil Records: Access: Phone, mail, in person. Both court and visitors may perform in person searches.

Search fee: $3.00 per name. Required to search: name, years to search. Civil cases indexed by defendant, plaintiff. Civil records on computer from 1987, on alpha index from 1920s.

Criminal Records: Access: Phone, mail, in person. Both court and visitors may perform in person searches. Search fee: $3.00 per name. Required to search: name, years to search, DOB, SSN, signed release. Criminal records on computer from 1987, on alpha index from 1920s.

General Information: Public access terminal is available. No adoptions, juvenile, sealed or expunged records released. SASE required. Turnaround time 2 days. Copy fee: $.50 per page. Certification fee: $1.00. Fee payee: Clerk of Court. Business checks accepted.

Aynor Magistrate Court PO Box 115, Aynor, SC 29511; 843-358-5508; Fax: 843-358-0704. Hours: 8AM-5PM (EST). *Civil Actions Under $7,500, Eviction, Small Claims.*

Conway Magistrate Court 1316 First Ave, PO Box 1236, Conway, SC 29528; 843-248-1373; Fax: 843-248-1536. Hours: 8AM-5PM (EST). *Civil Actions Under $7,500, Eviction, Small Claims.*

Conway Magistrate Court 1316 1st Ave, Conway, SC 29526; 843-248-1373; Fax: 843-248-1536. *Civil Actions Under $7,500, Eviction, Small Claims.*

Green Sea Magistrate Court 5527 Hwy #9, PO Box 153, Green Sea, SC 29545; 843-392-1219; Fax: 843-392-1834. *Civil Actions Under $7,500, Eviction, Small Claims.*

Little River Summary Court 107 Highway 57 N, Little River, SC 29566; 843-399-5443; Fax: 843-399-6792. Hours: 8AM-5PM (EST). *Civil Actions Under $7,500, Eviction, Small Claims.*

Civil Records: Access: Phone, fax, mail, in person. No search fee. Records computerized since 1988.

General Information: Turnaround time 5-7 days. Fee payee: Magistrate District 7.

Loris Magistrate Court 3817 Walnut St, Loris, SC 29569; 843-756-7918/6674; Fax: 843-756-1355. *Civil Actions Under $7,500, Eviction, Small Claims.*

Myrtle Beach Magistrate Court 1201 21st North Ave, Myrtle Beach, SC 29577; 843-444-6127; Fax: 843-444-6131. Hours: 8AM-5PM (EST). *Civil Actions Under $7,500, Eviction, Small Claims.*

Surfside Beach Magistrate Court 1106 Glenns Bay Rd, Surfside Beach, SC 29575; 843-238-3277/3677; Fax: 843-238-3591. Hours: 8AM-5PM (EST). *Misdemeanor, Civil Actions Under $7,500, Eviction, Small Claims.*

Probate Court PO Box 288, Conway, SC 29528; 843-248-1294; Fax: 843-248-1298. Hours: 8AM-5PM (EST). *Probate.*

Jasper County

Circuit Court PO Box 248, Ridgeland, SC 29936; 843-726-7710. Hours: 8:30AM-5PM (EST). *Felony, Misdemeanor, Civil Actions Over $7,500.*

Civil Records: Access: Mail, in person. Both court and visitors may perform in person searches. No search fee. Required to search: name, years to search. Civil cases indexed by defendant, plaintiff. Civil records on computer back to 1999; prior on books.

Criminal Records: Access: Mail, in person. Both court and visitors may perform in person searches. Search fee: $5.00 per name. Required to search: name, years to search, DOB; also helpful: SSN, signed release. Criminal records on computer back to 1999; prior on books.

General Information: Public access terminal is available. No adoption, juvenile, sealed or expunged records released. SASE required. Turnaround time 2 days. Fax notes: Fee to fax results is $2.00 per document. Copy fee: $1.00 per page. Certification fee: $1.00. Fee payee: Clerk of Court. Personal checks accepted. Prepayment is required.

Hardeeville Magistrate Court 21 Martin St, PO Box 248, Hardeeville, SC 29927; 843-726-7710. Hours: 9AM-5Pm (EST). *Civil Actions Under $7,500, Eviction, Small Claims.*

Ridgeland Magistrate Court 111 W Adams St, PO Box 665, Ridgeland, SC 29936; 843-726-7737; Fax: 843-726-7745. Hours: 9AM-Noon; 1PM-5PM (EST). *Civil Actions Under $7,500, Eviction, Small Claims.*

Ridgeland Magistrate Court Route 2, Box 73, Pineland, SC 29936; 843-726-8590; Fax: 843-726-7745. *Civil Actions Under $7,500, Eviction, Small Claims.*

Probate Court PO Box 1028, Ridgeland, SC 29936; 843-726-7719; Fax: 843-726-7782. Hours: 9AM-5PM (EST). *Probate.*

Kershaw County

Circuit Court County Courthouse, Rm 313, PO Box 1557, Camden, SC 29020; 803-425-1500 x623; Fax: 803-425-1505. Hours: 8:30AM-5PM (EST). *Felony, Misdemeanor, Civil Actions Over $7,500.*

Civil Records: Access: Mail, in person. Visitors must perform in person searches for themselves. No search fee. Required to search: name, years to search. Civil cases indexed by defendant, plaintiff. Civil records archived from 1797, computerized records from 1994.

Criminal Records: Access: In person only. Visitors must perform in person searches for themselves. No search fee. Required to search: name, years to search, DOB; also helpful: SSN. Criminal records archived from 1890, computerized records from 1994.

General Information: Public access terminal is available. No adoption, juvenile, sealed or expunged records released. Copy fee: $.50 per page. Certification fee: $1.00. Fee payee: Clerk of Court. Personal checks accepted. Prepayment is required.

Bethune Magistrate Court 202 N Main St, PO Box 215, Bethune, SC 29009; 843-334-8460; Fax: 843-334-8450. *Civil Actions Under $7,500, Eviction, Small Claims.*

Camden Magistrate Court County Courthouse #118, 1121 Broad St, PO Box 1528, Camden, SC 29020; 803-425-1500 X386; Fax: 803-425-6044. Hours: 9AM-5PM (EST). *Civil Actions Under $7,500, Eviction, Small Claims.*

Probate Court 1121 Broad St, Rm 302, Camden, SC 29020; 803-425-1500; Fax: 803-425-1526. Hours: 9AM-5PM (EST). *Probate.*

Lancaster County

Circuit Court PO Box 1809, Lancaster, SC 29721; 803-285-1581; Fax: 803-416-9388. Hours: 8:30AM-5PM (EST). *Felony, Misdemeanor, Civil Actions Over $7,500.*

Civil Records: Access: Mail, in person. Both court and visitors may perform in person searches. Search fee: $5.00 per name. Required to search: name, years to search. Civil cases indexed by defendant, plaintiff. Civil records on computer from 1987, microfiche from 1937, alpha index from 1764.

Criminal Records: Access: Mail, in person. Both court and visitors may perform in person searches. Search fee: $5.00 per name. Required to search: name, years to

search, DOB; also helpful: SSN. Criminal records on computer from 1987, microfiche from 1937, alpha index from 1764.

General Information: No adoption, juvenile, sealed or expunged records released. SASE required. Turnaround time 5 days. Copy fee: $.25 per page. Certification fee: $2.50. Fee payee: Clerk of Court. Personal checks accepted. Prepayment is required.

Lancaster Magistrate Court 101 South Wylie St, Lancaster, SC 29720; 803-283-3983; Fax: 803-285-3361. Hours: 8:30AM-5PM (EST). *Civil Actions Under $7,500, Eviction, Small Claims.*

Probate Court PO Box 1809, Lancaster, SC 29721; 803-283-3379; Fax: 803-283-3370. Hours: 8:30AM-5PM (EST). *Probate.*

Laurens County

Circuit Court PO Box 287, Laurens, SC 29360; 864-984-3538. Hours: 9AM-5PM (EST). *Felony, Misdemeanor, Civil Actions Over $7,500.*

Civil Records: Access: Mail, in person. Both court and visitors may perform in person searches. Search fee: $5.00 per name. Required to search: name, years to search. Civil cases indexed by defendant, plaintiff. Civil records on index books back to 1800s; on computer back to 1980.

Criminal Records: Access: Mail, in person. Both court and visitors may perform in person searches. Search fee: $5.00 per name. Required to search: name, years to search, DOB; also helpful: SSN. Criminal records on index books back to 1950s; on computer back to 1980.

General Information: No adoption, juvenile, sealed or expunged records released. SASE required. Turnaround time 2-3 days. Copy fee: $.50 per page. Certification fee: $1.00 per page. Fee payee: Clerk of Court. Personal checks accepted. Prepayment is required.

Clinton Magistrate Court 203 W Pitts St, Clinton, SC 29325; 864-833-5879; Fax: 864-833-7502. Hours: 8AM-5PM M, T; 8AM-Noon W; 8AM-10AM F (EST). *Civil Actions Under $7,500, Eviction, Small Claims.*

Gray Court Magistrate Court 329 Main St, Town Hall, PO Box 438, Gray Court, SC 29645; 864-876-4390. *Civil Actions Under $7,500, Eviction, Small Claims.*

Laurens Magistrate Court PO Box 925, Laurens, SC 29360; 864-683-4485. *Civil Actions Under $7,500, Eviction, Small Claims.*

Probate Court PO Box 194 (100 Hillcrest Sq #A), Laurens, SC 29360; 864-984-7315; Probate phone: 864-984-7731; Fax: 864-984-3779. Hours: 9AM-5PM (EST). *Probate.*

Lee County

Circuit Court PO Box 387, Bishopville, SC 29010; 803-484-5341; Fax: 803-484-1632. Hours: 9AM-5PM (EST). *Felony, Misdemeanor, Civil Actions Over $7,500.*

Civil Records: Access: Mail, in person. Both court and visitors may perform in person searches. Search fee: $5.00 per name. Required to search: name, years to search. Civil cases indexed by defendant, plaintiff. Civil records on computer from 1991, on archives from 1900s.

Criminal Records: Access: Mail, in person. Both court and visitors may perform in person searches. Search fee: $2.00 per name. Required to search: name, years to search, DOB; also helpful: SSN. Criminal records on computer from 1991, on archives from 1900s.

General Information: No adoption, juvenile, sealed or expunged records released. SASE required. Turnaround time 2 days. Copy fee: $.25 per page. $1.00 minimum.

Certification fee: $1.00. Fee payee: Clerk of Court. Business checks accepted. Prepayment is required.

Bishopville Magistrate Court 115 Gregg St, PO Box 2, Bishopville, SC 29010; 803-484-6463, 484-9184; Fax: 803-484-5163. *Civil Actions Under $7,500, Eviction, Small Claims.*

Dalzell Magistrate Court PO Box 2, Bishopville, SC 29010; 803-484-6463; Fax: 803-484-5043. Hours: 9AM-5PM (EST). *Civil Actions Under $7,500, Eviction, Small Claims.*

Mayesville Magistrate Court 475 Lower Lee School Rd, Mayesville, SC 29104; 803-428-6762; Fax: 803-484-6463. *Civil Actions Under $7,500, Eviction, Small Claims.*

Probate Court PO Box 24, Bishopville, SC 29010; 803-484-5341 X338, X339, X361; Fax: 803-484-6881. Hours: 9AM-5PM (EST). *Probate.*

Lexington County

Circuit Court Lexington County Courthouse, Rm 107, 139 East Main St, Lexington, SC 29072; 803-359-8212; Fax: 803-359-8314. Hours: 8AM-5PM (EST). *Felony, Misdemeanor, Civil Actions Over $7,500.*

Civil Records: Access: Mail, in person. Both court and visitors may perform in person searches. Search fee: $3.00 per name. Required to search: name, years to search. Civil cases indexed by defendant, plaintiff. Civil records on index from 1936.

Criminal Records: Access: Fax, mail, in person. Both court and visitors may perform in person searches. Search fee: $3.00 per name. Required to search: name, years to search, DOB, SSN. Criminal records on computer since 1983.

General Information: No adoption, juvenile, sealed or expunged records released. SASE required. Turnaround time 3 days. Copy fee: $.25 per page. Certification fee: $1.00. Fee payee: County of Lexington. Personal checks accepted. Prepayment is required.

Batesburg Leesville Magistrate Court 231 W Church St, Batesburg, SC 29006; 803-359-8330/532-9204/9205; Fax: 803-532-0357. Hours: 8:AM-4:30PM (EST). *Civil Actions Under $7,500, Eviction, Small Claims.*

Cayce Magistrate Court 650 Knox Abbott Dr, Cayce, SC 29033; 803-796-7100; Fax: 803-796-7635. Hours: 8AM-4:30PM (EST). *Civil Actions Under $7,500, Eviction, Small Claims.*

Columbia Magistrate Court 108 Harbison Blvd, Columbia, SC 29212; 803-781-7584/7585; Fax: 803-749-4050. *Misdemeanor, Civil Actions Under $7,500, Eviction, Small Claims.*

Lexington Magistrate Court 605 W Main St #100, Magistrate's Office, Lexington, SC 29072; 803-359-8221; Fax: 803-359-8155. Hours: 8:30AM-4:30PM (EST). *Civil Actions Under $7,500, Eviction, Small Claims.*

Swansea Magistrate Court 500 Charlie Rast Rd, PO Box 457, Swansea, SC 29160; 803-568-3616; Fax: 803-568-4078. Hours: 8:30AM-4:30PM (EST). *Civil Actions Under $7,500, Eviction, Small Claims.*

Probate Court County Courthouse, Rm 110, 139 E Main St, Lexington, SC 29072-3488; 803-359-8324; Fax: 803-359-8199. Hours: 8AM-5PM (EST). *Probate.*

Marion County

Circuit Court PO Box 295, Marion, SC 29571; 843-423-8240. Hours: 8:30AM-5PM (EST). *Felony, Misdemeanor, Civil Actions Over $7,500.*

Civil Records: Access: In person only. Visitors must perform in person searches for themselves. No search fee. Required to search: name, years to search. Civil cases indexed by defendant, plaintiff. Civil records on computer since 1988; prior records on index cards from 1800s.

Criminal Records: Access: In person only. Visitors must perform in person searches for themselves. No search fee. Required to search: name, years to search, DOB; also helpful: SSN. Criminal records on computer since 1988; prior records on index cards from 1800s.

General Information: No adoption, juvenile, sealed or expunged records released. Copy fee: $.25 per page. Certification fee: $1.00.

Gresham Magistrate Court PO Box 35, Gresham, SC 29546; 843-362-0180. Hours: 8:30AM-5PM (EST). *Civil Actions Under $7,500, Eviction, Small Claims.*

Marion Magistrate Court 2715 W Highway 76, #B, Mullins, SC 29574-6015; 843-423-8208; Fax: 843-423-8394. Hours: 8:30AM-5PM (EST). *Civil Actions Under $7,500, Eviction, Small Claims.*

Mullins Magistrate Court 2715 US Highway 76, #B, Mullins, SC 29574; 843-423-8208 X231; Fax: 843-423-8394. Hours: 8:30AM-5PM (EST). *Civil Actions Under $7,500, Eviction, Small Claims.*

Probate Court PO Box 583, Marion, SC 29571; 843-423-8244; Fax: 843-431-5026. Hours: 8:30AM-5PM (EST). *Probate.*

Marlboro County

Circuit Court PO Drawer 996, Bennettsville, SC 29512; 843-479-5613; Fax: 843-479-5640. Hours: 8:30AM-5PM (EST). *Felony, Misdemeanor, Civil Actions Over $7,500.*

Civil Records: Access: Mail, in person. Only visitors may perform in person searches. Search fee: $5.00 per name. Required to search: name, years to search. Civil cases indexed by defendant, plaintiff. Civil records on computer from 1985, on index from 1786.

Criminal Records: Access: Mail, in person. Only visitors may perform in person searches. Search fee: $5.00 per name. Required to search: name, years to search, DOB; also helpful: SSN. Criminal records on computer from 1985, on index from 1786.

General Information: Public access terminal is available. No adoption, juvenile, sealed or expunged records released. SASE required. Turnaround time 1 day. Copy fee: $.25 per page. Certification fee: $2.00. Fee payee: Clerk of Court. Personal checks accepted. Prepayment is required.

Bennettsville Magistrate Court 211 N Marlboro St, PO Box 418, Bennettsville, SC 29512; 843-479-5620; Fax: 843-479-5646. Hours: 10AM-5PM M-Th; Civil 4-5PM (EST). *Civil Actions Under $7,500, Eviction, Small Claims.*

Note: Court is again active.

Marlboro County Summary Court PO Box 418, Bennettsville, SC 29512; 843-479-5620/5621; Fax: 843-479-5646. Hours: 8:30AM-4:30PM (EST). *Civil Actions Under $7,500, Eviction, Small Claims.*

Civil Records: Access: Mail. No search fee.

General Information: Turnaround time 5-7 days. Fee payee: County Treasurer. Prepayment is required.

Probate Court PO Box 455, Bennettsville, SC 29512; 843-479-5610; Fax: 843-479-5668. Hours: 8:30AM-5PM (EST). *Probate.*

McCormick County

Circuit Court 133 S Mine St, McCormick, SC 29835; 864-465-2195; Fax: 864-465-0071. Hours: 9AM-5PM (EST). *Felony, Misdemeanor, Civil Actions Over $7,500.*

Civil Records: Access: In person. Visitors must perform in person searches for themselves. No search fee. Required to search: name, years to search. Civil cases indexed by defendant, plaintiff. Civil records on index books from 1916.

Criminal Records: Access: In person. Both court and visitors may perform in person searches. No search fee. Required to search: name, years to search, DOB; also helpful: SSN. Criminal records on index books from 1916.

General Information: No adoption, juvenile, sealed or expunged records released. Copy fee: $.35 per page. Certification fee: $1.00. Fee payee: Clerk of Court. Prepayment is required.

McCormick Magistrate Court 201 Augusta St, PO Box 1116, McCormick, SC 29835; 864-465-2316; Fax: 864-465-2582. Hours: 9AM-5PM (EST). *Civil Actions Under $7,000, Eviction, Small Claims.*

Probate Court 133 S Mine St #101, McCormick, SC 29835; 864-465-2630; Fax: 864-465-0071. Hours: 9AM-5PM (EST). *Probate.*

Newberry County

Circuit Court PO Box 278, Newberry, SC 29108; 803-321-2110; Fax: 803-321-2102. Hours: 8:30AM-5PM (EST). *Felony, Misdemeanor, Civil Actions Over $7,500.*

Civil Records: Access: Mail, in person. Both court and visitors may perform in person searches. No search fee. Required to search: name, years to search. Civil cases indexed by defendant, plaintiff. Civil records on computer from 1983, docket books from 1776.

Criminal Records: Access: In person only. Visitors must perform in person searches for themselves. No search fee. Required to search: name, years to search, DOB; also helpful: SSN. Criminal records on computer from 1983, docket books from 1776.

General Information: Public access terminal is available. No adoption, juvenile, sealed, PTI or expunged records released. Turnaround time 1 week. Copy fee: $.20 per page. Certification fee: $1.00. Fee payee: Clerk of Court. Only cashiers checks and money orders accepted. Prepayment is required.

Little Mountain Magistrate Court 824 Main St, PO Box 95, Little Mountain, SC 29075; 803-345-1040; Fax: 803-945-7222. Hours: 2PM-5PM T, W (EST). *Civil Actions Under $7,500, Eviction, Small Claims.*

Newberry Magistrate Court 3239 Louis Rich Rd, Newberry, SC 29108; 803-321-2144/2145; Fax: 803-321-2172. Hours: 8:30-5PM (EST). *Civil Actions Under $7,500, Eviction, Small Claims, Misdemeanor, Traffic.*

Whitmire Magistrate Court 116 Duncan St, Whitmire, SC 29178; 803-321-2144. Hours: 8:30AM-5PM (EST). *Civil Actions Under $7,500, Eviction, Small Claims.*

Probate Court PO Box 442, Newberry, SC 29108; 803-321-2118; Fax: 803-321-2119. Hours: 8:30AM-5PM (EST). *Probate.*

www.newberrycounty.net

Oconee County

Circuit Court PO Box 678, Walhalla, SC 29691; 864-638-4280. Hours: 8:30AM-5PM (EST). *Felony, Misdemeanor, Civil Actions Over $7,500.*

Civil Records: Access: In person only. Visitors must perform in person searches for themselves. No search fee. Required to search: name, years to search. Civil cases indexed by defendant, plaintiff. Civil records on index cards from 1868; on computer back to 1994.

Criminal Records: Access: In person only. Visitors must perform in person searches for themselves. No search fee. Required to search: name, years to search; also helpful: DOB, SSN, signed release. Criminal records on index cards from 1868; on computer back to 1994.

General Information: Public access terminal is available. No adoption, juvenile, sealed or expunged records released. Copy fee: $1.00 for first page, $.50 each add'l. Fee payee: Clerk of Court. Personal checks accepted. Prepayment is required.

County Summary Court 208 Booker Dr, Walhalla, SC 29691; 864-638-4125; Fax: 864-638-4127. *Civil Actions Under $7,500, Eviction, Small Claims.*

Civil Records: Access: Mail. No search fee.

General Information: Turnaround time 5-7 days. Fee payee: County Treasurer. Prepayment is required.

Walhalla Magistrate Court 208 Booker Dr, Walhalla, SC 29691; 864-638-4127; Fax: 864-638-4229. Hours: 8:30AM-5PM (EST). *Civil Actions Under $7,500, Eviction, Small Claims.*

Probate Court PO Box 471, Walhalla, SC 29691; 864-638-4275; Fax: 864-638-4278. Hours: 8:30AM-5PM (EST). *Probate.*

Orangeburg County

Circuit Court PO Box 9000, Orangeburg, SC 29116; 803-533-6260; Fax: 803-534-3848. Hours: 8:30AM-5PM (EST). *Felony, Misdemeanor, Civil Actions Over $7,500.*

Civil Records: Access: In person only. Visitors must perform in person searches for themselves. No search fee. Required to search: name, years to search. Civil cases indexed by defendant, plaintiff. Civil records on index cards from 1924.

Criminal Records: Access: In person only. Visitors must perform in person searches for themselves. No search fee. Required to search: name, years to search, DOB; also helpful: SSN. Criminal records on index cards from 1924.

General Information: No adoption, juvenile, sealed or expunged records released. Copy fee: $.50 per page. Certification fee: $1.00. Fee payee: Clerk of Court. Personal checks accepted.

Bowman Magistrate Court 6803 Charleston Highway, PO Box 365, Bowman, SC 29018; 803-829-2831. *Civil Actions Under $7,500, Eviction, Small Claims.*

Branchville Magistrate Court 7644 Freedom Rd, PO Box 85, Branchville, SC 29432; 803-274-8820; Fax: 803-274-8820. Hours: 4PM-7PM M & W (EST). *Civil Actions Under $7,500, Eviction, Small Claims.*

Elloree Magistrate Court 2614 Cleveland St, PO Box 436, Elloree, SC 29047; 803-897-4626; Fax: 803-897-2165. *Civil Actions Under $7,500, Eviction, Small Claims.*

Eutawville Magistrate Court 300 Porcher Ave, PO Box 188, Eutawville, SC 29048; 803-492-3697/533-5879; Fax: 803-496-5850. *Civil Actions Under $7,500, Eviction, Small Claims.*

Holly Hill Magistrate Court 1006 Peake St, PO Box 154, Holly Hill, SC 29059; 803-496-9533; Fax: 803-496-9533. Hours: 11AM-4PM T & TH (EST). *Civil Actions Under $7,500, Eviction, Small Claims.*

North Magistrate Court 9305 North Rd, PO Box 399, North, SC 29112; 803-247-2101. Hours: 8:30AM-4:30PM M-TH; 8:30AM-3PM F (EST). *Civil Actions Under $7,500, Eviction, Small Claims.*

Norway Magistrate Court 8413 Savannah Hwy, PO Box 67, Norway, SC 29113; 803-263-4100; Fax: 803-263-4292. *Civil Actions Under $7,500, Eviction, Small Claims.*

Orangeburg County Magistrate Court 1520 Ellis Ave NE, PO Box 9000, Orangeburg, SC 29116; 803-533-5880/5879; Fax: 803-533-5806. Hours: 8:30AM-5PM (EST). *Civil Actions Under $7,500, Eviction, Small Claims.*

Orangeburg Magistrate Court 2308 Norway Rd, Orangeburg, SC 29115; 803-533-5843. Hours: 11AM-4Pm M & TH (EST). *Civil Actions Under $7,500, Eviction, Small Claims.*

Springfield Magistrate Court 7304 Festival Trail Rd, PO Box 125, Springfield, SC 29146; 803-258-1002; Fax: 803-258-1006. Hours: 9AM-5PM (EST). *Civil Actions Under $7,500, Eviction, Small Claims.*

Probate Court PO Drawer 9000, Orangeburg, SC 29116-9000; 803-533-6280; Fax: 803-533-6279. Hours: 8:30AM-5PM (EST). *Probate.*

Pickens County

Circuit Court PO Box 215, Pickens, SC 29671; 864-898-5866; Fax: 864-898-5863. Hours: 8:30AM-5PM (EST). *Felony, Misdemeanor, Civil Actions Over $7,500.*

Civil Records: Access: In person. Both court and visitors may perform in person searches. No search fee. Required to search: name, years to search. Civil cases indexed by defendant, plaintiff. Civil records on computer from 1990, on index from 1970.

Criminal Records: Access: In person. Both court and visitors may perform in person searches. No search fee. Required to search: name, years to search, DOB; also helpful: SSN. Criminal records on computer from 1990, on index from 1970.

General Information: No adoption, juvenile, sealed or expunged records released. Copy fee: $.50 per page. Certification fee: $1.00. Fee payee: Clerk of Court. Personal checks accepted. Prepayment is required.

Clemson Magistrate Court 115-B Commons Way, Central, SC 29630; 864-639-8084; Fax: 864-639-8084. Hours: 8:30AM-4PM (EST). *Civil Actions Under $7,500, Eviction, Small Claims.*

Easley Magistrate Court 135 Folger Ave, West End Hall, Easley, SC 29640; 864-850-7076; Fax: 864-850-7075. Hours: 8:30AM-Noon; 1PM-4:30PM (EST). *Civil Actions Under $7,500, Eviction, Small Claims.*

Liberty Magistrate Court 431 E Main St, Liberty, SC 29657; 864-850-3500; Fax: 864-850-3501. Hours: 8:30AM-5PM (EST). *Misdemeanor, Civil Actions Under $7,500, Eviction, Small Claims.*

Pickens Magistrate Court 216-A, Law Enforcement Ctr Rd, Pickens, SC 29671; 864-898-5551/5552; Fax: 864-898-5546. Hours: 8:30AM-5PM (EST). *Civil Actions Under $7,500, Eviction, Small Claims.*

Probate Court 222 McDaniel Ave B-16, Pickens, SC 29671; 864-898-5903; Fax: 864-898-5924. Hours: 8:30AM-5PM (EST). *Probate.*

Richland County

Circuit Court PO Box 2766, Columbia, SC 29202; 803-576-1999; Fax: 803-748-5039. 8:30AM-5PM *Felony, Misdemeanor, Civil Actions Over $7,500.*

Civil Records: Access: Mail, in person. Both court and visitors may perform in person searches. Search fee: $2.00 per name. Required to search: name, years to search. Civil cases indexed by defendant, plaintiff. Civil records on computer from 1987. Many prior records indexed to 1920's.

Criminal Records: Access: In person only. Visitors may perform in person searches for themselves. No search fee. Required to search: name, years to search; also helpful: DOB, SSN. Criminal records on index to 1920's, computerized since 1987.

General Information: Public access terminal is available. No adoption, juvenile, sealed or expunged records released. SASE required. Turnaround time 1 day. Copy fee: $.50 for first page, $.15 each add'l. Fee payee: Richland County Clerk. Personal checks accepted. Prepayment is required.

Columbia Magistrate Court Richland Central Court, 1400 Huger St, PO Box 192, Columbia, SC 29202; 803-576-2300; Fax: 803-7576-2325. Hours: 8:30AM-5PM M-F (EST). *Civil Actions Under $7,500, Eviction, Small Claims.*

Columbia Magistrate Court 6941 A North Trenholm Rd, Columbia, SC 29206; 803-782-2807; Fax: 803-782-2923. *Civil Actions Under $7,500, Eviction, Small Claims.*

Columbia Magistrate Court 1731 L, PO Box 192, Columbia, SC 29202; 803-576-2510; Fax: 803-576-2519. *Civil Actions Under $7,500, Eviction, Small Claims.*

Columbia Magistrate Court 4919 Rhett St, Columbia, SC 29203; 803-754-2250; Fax: 803-754-8783. Hours: 8:30-Noon; 1:15PM-5PM (EST). *Civil Actions Under $7,500, Eviction, Small Claims.*

Columbia Magistrate Court 1601 B Shop Rd, PO Box 9305, Columbia, SC 29201; 803-799-1779; Fax: 803-748-5009. Hours: 8:30AM-5PM (EST). *Civil Actions Under $7,500, Eviction, Small Claims.*

Dutch Fork Magistrate Court 1223 St Andrews Rd, Columbia, SC 29210; 803-772-6464/6465; Fax: 803-798-6144. Hours: 9AM-5PM (EST). *Misdemeanor, Civil Actions Under $7,500, Eviction, Small Claims.*

Elgin Magistrate Court 10509 Two Notch Rd, Elgin, SC 29045; 803-788-8232; Fax: 803-865-0889. Hours: 8:30AM-4:30PM (EST). *Civil Actions Under $7,500, Eviction, Small Claims.*

Hopkins Magistrate Court 6108 Cabin Creek Rd, PO Box 70, Hopkins, SC 29061; 803-576-2530; Fax: 803-576-2535. Hours: 8:30AM-5PM (EST). *Misdemeanors, Civil Actions Under $7,500, Eviction, Small Claims.*

Lykesland Magistrate Court 1403 Caroline Rd, PO Box 9523, Columbia, SC 29290; 803-776-0454; Fax: 803-783-2667. Hours: 9AM-5PM (EST). *Civil Actions Under $7,500, Eviction, Small Claims.*

Waverly Magistrate Court 2712 Middleburg Dr #106, Columbia, SC 29204; 803-738-9017/9019; Fax: 803-738-7020. *Civil Actions Under $7,500, Eviction, Small Claims.*

Probate Court PO Box 192 (1701 Main St #207), Columbia, SC 29202; 803-576-1961; Fax: 803-576-1987. Hours: 8:30AM-5PM (EST). *Probate.* www.richlandonline.com/probate.htm

Saluda County

Circuit Court County Courthouse, 100 E Church St #6, Saluda, SC 29138; 864-445-3303/2168; Fax: 864-445-3772. Hours: 8:30AM-5PM (EST). *Felony, Misdemeanor, Civil Actions Over $7,500.*

Civil Records: Access: In person. Both court and visitors may perform in person searches. No search fee. Required to search: name, years to search, address. Civil cases indexed by defendant, plaintiff. Civil records on computer from 1995, on index from 1897.

Criminal Records: Access: In person. Both court and visitors may perform in person searches. No search fee. Required to search: name, years to search, address, DOB, signed release; also helpful: SSN. Criminal records on computer from 1995, on index from 1897. Request must be in writing.

General Information: Public access terminal is available. No adoption, juvenile, sealed or expunged records released. Copy fee: $.25 per page. Certification fee: $1.00. Fee payee: Clerk of Court. Personal checks accepted. Prepayment is required.

Saluda Magistrate Court 120 S Main St, Courthouse Annex, Saluda, SC 29138; 864-445-2846; Fax: 864-445-3684. Hours: 8AM-4:30PM (EST). *Civil Actions Under $7,500, Eviction, Small Claims.*

Probate Court 100 E Church St, Saluda, SC 29138; 864-445-7110; Fax: 864-445-9726. Hours: 8:30AM-5PM (EST). *Probate.*

Spartanburg County

Circuit Court County Courthouse, 180 Magnolia St, Spartanburg, SC 29306; 864-596-2591; Fax: 864-596-2239. Hours: 8:30AM-5PM (EST). *Felony, Misdemeanor, Civil Actions Over $7,500.*

Civil Records: Access: In person only. Visitors must perform in person searches for themselves. No search fee. Required to search: name, years to search. Civil cases indexed by defendant, plaintiff. Civil records on computer from 1975, on microfiche from 1960, on alpha index from 1800s.

Criminal Records: Access: In person only. Visitors must perform in person searches for themselves. No search fee. Required to search: name, years to search, DOB, SSN, signed release. Criminal records on computer from 1975, on microfiche from 1960, on alpha index from 1800s. An index is available for the public to search.

General Information: Public access terminal is available. (Civil only.) No adoption, juvenile, sealed or expunged records released. Copy fee: $.25 per page. Certification fee: $1.00. Fee payee: Clerk of Court. Personal checks accepted. Prepayment is required.

Chesnee Magistrate Court 201 Cherokee St, Chesnee, SC 29323; 864-461-3402; Fax: 864-596-3622. *Civil Actions Under $7,500, Eviction, Small Claims.*

Inman Magistrate Court 7 Mill St, Inman, SC 29349; 864-472-4447/6247; Fax: 864-596-3622. Hours: 9AM-8PM M; 8AM-Noon T (EST). *Civil Actions Under $7,500, Eviction, Small Claims.*

Landrum Magistrate Court 137-B N Howard Ave, Landrum, SC 29356; 864-457-7245; Fax: 864-596-3622. Hours: (variable) (EST). *Civil Actions Under $7,500, Eviction, Small Claims.*

Pacolet Magistrate Court 980 Sunny Acres Rd, PO Box 416, Pacolet Mills, SC 29373; 864-474-0344/3391; Fax: 864-503-2417. Hours: 6PM-10PM M & W, 6PM-9PM Th (EST). *Civil Actions Under $7,500, Eviction, Small Claims.*

Reidville Magistrate Court 7450 Reidville Rd, PO Box 124, Reidville, SC 29375; 864-433-9223. Hours: 10:30AM-6:30PM Tues.; 8:30AM-2:30PM Th (EST). *Civil Actions Under $7,500, Eviction, Small Claims.*

Spartanburg Magistrate Court County Courthouse, Rm 105, 180 Magnolia St, Spartanburg, SC 29306; 864-596-2564; Fax: 864-596-3622. *Civil Actions Under $7,500, Eviction, Small Claims.*

Probate Court 180 Magnolia St, Room 300, Spartanburg, SC 29306-2392; 864-596-2556; Fax: 864-596-2011. Hours: 8:30AM-5PM (EST). *Probate.*

Sumter County

Circuit Court 141 N Main, Sumter, SC 29150; 803-436-2227; Fax: 803-436-2223. Hours: 8:30AM-5PM (EST). *Felony, Misdemeanor, Civil Actions Over $7,500.*

www.sumtercountysc.org

Civil Records: Access: Mail, in person, online. Only Family Court records are online at this time. Both court and visitors may perform in person searches. Search fee: $5.00 per name. Required to search: name, years to search; also helpful: address. Civil cases indexed by defendant, plaintiff. Civil records on computer from 1987, microfiche and books from 1900s.

Criminal Records: Access: Mail, in person. Both court and visitors may perform in person searches. Search fee: $5.00 per name. Required to search: name, years to search, DOB, SSN, signed release; also helpful: address. Criminal records in books.

General Information: No adoption, juvenile, sealed or expunged records released. SASE required. Turnaround time 2 days. Copy fee: $.25 per page. Certification fee: $5.00. Fee payee: Sumter County Treasurer. Business checks accepted. Prepayment is required.

Mayesville Magistrate Court PO Box 236, Town Hall, Mayesville, SC 29104; 803-436-9372. *Civil Actions Under $7,500, Eviction, Small Claims.*

Pinewood Magistrate Court PO Box 41, Pinewood, SC 29125; Fax: 803-452-6467. *Civil Actions Under $7,500, Eviction, Small Claims.*

Sumter Magistrate Court 115 N Harvin St, PO Box 1428, Sumter, SC 29151; 803-436-2280; Fax: 803-436-2300. *Civil Actions Under $7,500, Eviction, Small Claims.*

Probate Court 141 N Main, Rm 111, Sumter, SC 29150; 803-436-2166; Fax: 803-436-2407. Hours: 8:30AM-5PM (EST). *Probate.*

Union County

Circuit Court PO Box 703 (210 W Main St), Union, SC 29379; 864-429-1630; Fax: 864-429-1715. Hours: 9AM-5PM (EST). *Felony, Misdemeanor, Civil Actions Over $7,500.*

Civil Records: Access: In person only. Visitors must perform in person searches for themselves. No search fee. Required to search: name, years to search. Civil cases indexed by defendant, plaintiff. All records on computer.

Criminal Records: Access: In person only. Visitors must perform in person searches for themselves. No search fee. Required to search: name, years to search; also helpful: SSN, DOB. Criminal records on computer.

General Information: Public access terminal is available. No adoption, juvenile, sealed or expunged records released. Copy fee: $.50 per page. Certification fee: $2.00. Fee payee: Clerk of Court. Personal checks accepted. Prepayment is required.

Jonesville Magistrate Court 440 Pacolet St, PO Box 33, Jonesville, SC 29353; 864-674-5426; Fax: 864-674-6634. *Civil Actions Under $7,500, Eviction, Small Claims.*

Lockhart Magistrate Court 210 Main St, Union, SC 29379; 864-545-2338. *Civil Actions Under $7,500, Eviction, Small Claims.*

Union Magistrate Court 210 Main St, Courthouse, Union, SC 29379; 864-429-1648; Fax: 864-429-1685. *Civil Actions Under $7,500, Eviction, Small Claims.*

Carlisle Magistrate Court 210 W Main St, c/o Union Magistrate Court, Union, SC 29379; 864-429-1648. *Civil Actions Under $7,500, Eviction, Small Claims.*

Note: This court is closed. Records are at the address and phone number given above.

Probate Court PO Box 447, Union, SC 29379; 864-429-1625; Fax: 864-429-1627. Hours: 9AM-5PM (EST). *Probate.*

Williamsburg County

Circuit Court 125 W Main St, Kingstree, SC 29556; 843-355-9321 X552; Fax: 843-354-7821. Hours: 8:30AM-5PM (EST). *Felony, Misdemeanor, Civil Actions Over $7,500.*

Civil Records: Access: In person. Both court and visitors may perform in person searches. Search fee: $5.00 per name. Required to search: name, years to search. Civil cases indexed by defendant, plaintiff. Civil records on books, archived from 1980-1989, indexed from 1806; computerized records since 1993.

Criminal Records: Access: In person. Both court and visitors may perform in person searches. No search fee. Required to search: name, years to search, DOB; also helpful: SSN. Criminal records on books, archived from 1980-1989, indexed from 1806; computerized records since 1993.

General Information: No adoption, juvenile, sealed or expunged records released. Copy fee: $.25 per page. Fee payee: Clerk of Court. Personal checks accepted. Prepayment is required.

Hemingway Magistrate Court 206 E Broad St, PO Box 416, Hemingway, SC 29554; 843-558-2116; Fax: 843-5578-5314. *Civil Actions Under $7,500, Eviction, Small Claims.*

Kingstree Magistrate Court #10 Courthouse Sq, Kingstree, SC 29556; 843-355-9321. Hours: 8:30AM-5Pm (EST). *Civil Actions Under $7,500, Eviction, Small Claims.*

Kingstree Magistrate Court 10 Courthouse Sq, PO Box 673, Kingstree, SC 29556; 843-354-9602/9603, 843-355-9321 X179; Fax: 843-355-6444. *Civil Actions Under $7,500, Eviction, Small Claims.*

Lane Magistrate Court PO Box 39, Lane, SC 29564; 843-387-5151. *Civil Actions Under $7,500, Eviction, Small Claims.*

Nesmith Magistrate Court 10 Courthouse Square, Kingstree, SC 29556; 843-355-9321 ext 179; Fax: 843-355-6444. *Civil Actions Under $7,500, Eviction, Small Claims.*

Probate Court PO Box 1005, Kingstree, SC 29556; 843-355-9321 x558; Fax: 843-355-9350. Hours: 8:30AM-5PM (EST). *Probate.*

York County

Circuit Court PO Box 649, York, SC 29745; 803-688-8506. Hours: 8AM-5PM (EST). *Felony, Misdemeanor, Civil Actions Over $7,500.*

Civil Records: Access: Mail, in person. Both court and visitors may perform in person searches. Search fee: $5.00 per name. Required to search: name, years to search. Civil cases indexed by defendant, plaintiff. Civil records on computer from 1982, in books from 1932.

Criminal Records: Access: Fax, mail, in person. Both court and visitors may perform in person searches. Search fee: $5.00 per name. Required to search: name, years to search, DOB; also helpful: SSN. Criminal records on computer from 1982, in books from 1932.

General Information: No adoption, juvenile, sealed or expunged records released. SASE required. Turnaround time 1 day. Fax notes: $5.00 per document. Copy fee: $.40 per page. Certification fee: $1.00. Fee payee: Clerk of Court. Personal checks accepted. Prepayment is required.

Clover Magistrate Court 201 S Main St, PO Box 165, Clover, SC 29710; 803-222-9404. Hours: 8AM-5PM (EST). *Civil Actions Under $7,500, Eviction, Small Claims.*

Fort Mill Magistrate Court 114 Springs St, Fort Mill, SC 29715; 803-547-5572/5573; Fax: 803-547-6344. Hours: 8AM-5PM (EST). *Civil Actions Under $7,500, Eviction, Small Claims.*

Hickory Grove Magistrate Court PO Box 37, Hickory Grove, SC 29717; 803-925-2815. *Civil Actions Under $7,500, Eviction, Small Claims.*

York Magistrate Court 1675 York Highway, York, SC 29745; 803-628-3095; Fax: 803-328-8353. Hours: 8AM-5PM (EST). *Civil Actions Under $7,500, Eviction, Small Claims.*

York Magistrate Court 1675 York Hwy, York, SC 29745; 803-628-3095. *Civil Actions Under $7,500, Eviction, Small Claims.*

Probate Court PO Box 219, York, SC 29745; 803-684-8513 X8630; Fax: 803-684-8536. Hours: 8AM-5PM (EST). *Probate.*

South Carolina Recording Offices

ORGANIZATION: 46 counties, 46 recording offices. The recording officer is. Register of Mesne Conveyances or Clerk of Court (This varies by county). The entire state is in the Eastern Time Zone (EST).

REAL ESTATE RECORDS: Most counties will not perform real estate searches. Copy and certification fees vary. The Assessor keeps tax records.

UCC RECORDS: Financing statements are filed at the state level, except for real estate related collateral, which are filed with the Register. However, prior to 07/2001, consumer goods and farm collateral were also filed at the Register and these older records can be searched there. As a general rule, all recording offices will perform UCC searches. Search fees are usually $5.00 per debtor name. Copy fees are usually $1.00 per page.

TAX LIEN RECORDS: All federal and state tax liens on personal property and on real property are filed with the Register of Mesne Conveyances (Clerk of Court). Some counties will perform tax lien searches. Search fees and copy fees vary.

ONLINE ACCESS: There is no statewide system, buy several counties have placed free record data on their web sites.

Abbeville County

Clerk of Court, PO Box 99, Abbeville, SC 29620. 864-459-5074 R/E Recording: 864-459-4944 UCC Recording: 864-459-4944; Fax 864-459-9188.
Will search UCC records. This agency will not do a tax lien search. Will not search real estate records. **Other Phones:** Assessor 864-459-4921; Treasurer 459-2539; Appraiser/Auditor 459-4921; Elections 864-459-5083.

Aiken County

County Register of Mesne Conveyances, PO Box 537, Aiken, SC 29802-0537. County Register of Mesne Conveyances, R/E and UCC Recording 803-642-2072 UCC Recording: 803-642-2075.
Will search UCC records. Tax liens not included in UCC search. Real estate record owner and mortgage searches available. **Other Phones:** Assessor 803-642-1576; Treasurer 803-642-2055; Appraiser/Auditor 803-642-1576; Elections 803-642-2028.

Allendale County

Clerk of Court, PO Box 126, Allendale, SC 29810. 803-584-2737; Fax 803-584-7058.
Will search UCC records. This agency will not do a tax lien search. Will not search real estate records. **Other Phones:** Assessor 803-584-2572; Treasurer 584-3876.

Anderson County

Register of Deeds, PO Box 8002, Anderson, SC 29622. Register of Deeds, R/E and UCC Recording 864-260-4054; Fax 864-260-4443. www.andersoncountysc.org
This agency will not search real estate or UCC records. **Other Phones:** Assessor 864-260-4028; Treasurer 864-260-4033; Anderson County Operator 864-260-4444.

Bamberg County

Clerk of Court, PO Box 150, Bamberg, SC 29003. Clerk of Court, R/E and UCC Recording 803-245-3025; Fax 803-245-3088.
This agency will not search real estate or UCC records. **Other Phones:** Assessor 803-245-3010; Treasurer 803-245-3003; Appraiser 245-3010; Elections 245-3028; Probate Court 803-245-3008; Auditor 803-245-3006;

Barnwell County

Clerk of Court, PO Box 723, Barnwell, SC 29812-0723. 803-541-1020; Fax 803-541-1025. Will search UCC records. Will not search real estate records. **Other Phones:** Assessor 541-1011; Treasurer 541-1050.

Beaufort County

Clerk of Court, PO Drawer 1197, Beaufort, SC 29901-1197. Clerk of Court, R/E and UCC Recording 843-470-2700 UCC Recording: 843-470-2715; Fax 843-470-2709. www.co.beaufort.sc.us
Will search UCC records. **Online Access:** Property, Assessor Records. Access to the public records search database is at http://rodweb.co.beaufort.sc.us. Also, search county property information at the GIS mapping database at http://maps.co.beaufort.sc.us/Search.htm. A fuller records subscription service requiring registration, fees, and logon is under development. **Other Phone Numbers:** Assessor 843-470-2513; Treasurer 843-470-2766; Elections 843-470-3753.

Berkeley County

Clerk of Court, 223 N. Live Oak Drive, Moncks Corner, SC 29461. 843-719-4084; Fax 843-719-4139.
Will search UCC records. Will not search real estate records. **Other Phone Numbers:** Assessor 843-761-6900 x4061; Treasurer 843-761-3800.

Calhoun County

Clerk of Court, 302 S. F.R. Huff Drive, St. Matthews, SC 29135. 803-874-3524; Fax 803-874-1942.
Will search UCC records. Will not search real estate records. **Other Phone Numbers:** Assessor 803-874-3613; Treasurer 803-874-3519.

Charleston County

Clerk of Court, PO Box 726, Charleston, SC 29402. Clerk of Court, R/E and UCC Recording 843-958-4800; Fax 843-958-4803. www.charlestoncounty.org
Will search UCC records. Will not search real estate records. **Online Access:** Real Estate, Property Tax Records. Access to the county's GIS mapping database of property records is available free at http://gisweb.charlestoncounty.org. Also, online access the the auditor & tresurer's tax system database is available free at http://taxweb.charlestoncounty.org. **Other Phones:** Assessor 843-958-4100; Treasurer 843-958-4360; elections 745-2226; vital records 740-0801.

Cherokee County

Clerk of Court, PO Drawer 2289, Gaffney, SC 29342. Clerk of Court, R/E and UCC Recording 864-487-2571; Fax 864-487-2754.
Will search UCC records. This agency will not do a tax lien search. Will not search real estate records. **Other Phones:** Assessor 864-487-2552; Treasurer 864-487-2551; Elections 487-2563; Vital Records 487-2571.

Chester County

Clerk of Court, PO Drawer 580, Chester, SC 29706. 803-385-2605; Fax 803-581-7975.
Will search UCC records. Will not search real estate records. **Other Phone Numbers:** Assessor 803-377-4177; Treasurer 803-385-2608.

Chesterfield County

Clerk of Court, PO Box 529, Chesterfield, SC 29709. Clerk of Court, R/E and UCC Recording 843-623-2574 UCC Recording: 843-623-7853; Fax 843-623-3945.
Will search UCC records. Will not search real estate records. **Other Phones:** Assessor 843-623-7362; Treasurer 843-623-2563; Appraiser 843-623-7362; Elections 843-623-2265; Vital Records 843-623-2117.

Clarendon County

Clerk of Court, PO Drawer E, Manning, SC 29102. 803-435-4443 R/E Recording: 803-435-4444 UCC Recording: 803-435-4444; Fax 803-435-8258.
This agency will not search real estate or UCC records. **Other Phone Numbers:** Assessor 803-435-4423.

Colleton County

Clerk of Court, PO Box 620, Walterboro, SC 29488-0028. Clerk of Court, R/E and UCC Recording 843-549-5791; Fax 843-549-2875. Will search UCC records. Will not search real estate records. **Other Phones:** Assessor 843-549-1213; Treasurer 843-549-2233; Elections 549-2842; Vital Records 549-1516.

Darlington County

Clerk of Court, PO Box 1177, Darlington, SC 29540. Clerk of Court, R/E and UCC Recording 843-398-4330; Fax 843-398-4172. This agency will not search real estate or UCC records. **Other Phone Numbers:** Assessor 843-398-4180; Treasurer 843-398-4160.

Dillon County

Clerk of Court, PO Drawer 1220, Dillon, SC 29536. Clerk of Court, R/E and UCC Recording 843-774-1425; Fax 843-774-1443.
Will search UCC records. UCC search includes tax liens if requested. Will not search real estate records. **Other Phone Numbers:** Assessor 843-774-1412; Treasurer 843-774-1416; Appraiser/Auditor 843-774-1412; Elections 843-774-1403; Vital Records 843-774-5611; Auditor 843-774-1418; Probate 8437741423;

Dorchester County

Clerk of Court, PO Box 38, St. George, SC 29477. 843-563-0106 R/E Recording: 843-832-0153 UCC Recording: 843-832-0153; Fax 843-563-0277.
Will search UCC records. Will not search real estate records. **Other Phones:** Assessor 843-563-0156; Treasurer 843-563-0165; Appraiser/Auditor 843-563-0156; Elections 563-0132; Vital Records 563-0107.

Edgefield County

Clerk of Court, PO Box 34, Edgefield, SC 29824. 803-637-4080 R/E Recording: 803-637-4049 UCC Recording: 803-637-4049; Fax 803-637-4117.

Will search UCC records. Will not search real estate records. **Other Phone Numbers:** Assessor 803-637-4066; Treasurer 803-637-4069; Appraiser/Auditor 803-637-4057; Elections 803-637-4072.

Fairfield County

Clerk of Court, PO Drawer 299, Winnsboro, SC 29180. 803-635-1411.
Will search UCC records. This agency will not do a tax lien search. Will not search real estate records. **Other Phones:** Assessor 803-635-1411; Treasurer 635-1411.

Florence County

Clerk of Court, MSC-E City/County Complex, Florence, SC 29501. Clerk of Court, R/E and UCC Recording 843-665-3031; Fax 843-665-3097.
Will search UCC records. Will not search real estate records. **Other Phone Numbers:** Assessor 843-665-3056; Treasurer 843-665-3041.

Georgetown County

Register of Deeds, PO Drawer 1270, Georgetown, SC 29442. 843-545-3088.
This agency will not perform searches. **Other Phones:** Assessor 843-545-3014; Treasurer 843-545-3098.

Greenville County

Register of Deeds, 301 University Ridge, #1300, County Square Suite 1300, Greenville, SC 29601-3655. Register of Deeds, R/E and UCC Recording 864-467-7240 UCC Recording: 864-467-7180; Fax 864-467-7107. www.greenvillecounty.org
Will not search UCC records. Effective July 2, 2001- Will not search tax liens. Will not search real estate records. **Online Access:** Real Property Records. Search the Register of Deeds database free online at www.greenvillecounty.org. **Other Phone Numbers:** Assessor 864-467-7300; Treasurer 864-467-7210.

Greenwood County

Clerk of Court, Courthouse, 528 Monument St., Greenwood, SC 29646. Clerk of Court, R/E and UCC Recording 864-942-8551 UCC Recording: 864-942-8613; Fax 864-942-8693. www.co.greenwood.sc.us
This agency will not perform searches. **Online Access:** Property Records. Records on the County Parcel Search database are available at http://165.166.39.5/website/gis/viewer.htm. Click on search and choose to search by owner name. An interactive map is included. **Other Phone Numbers:** Assessor 864-942-8532; Treasurer 864-942-8528; Appraiser/Auditor 864-942-8532; Elections 864-942-8521.

Hampton County

Clerk of Court, PO Box 7, Hampton, SC 29924. Clerk of Court, R/E and UCC Recording 803-943-7510; Fax 803-943-7596. Will not do search UCC records. Will not do tax lien searches. Will not search real estate records. **Other Phone Numbers:** Assessor 803-943-7507; Treasurer 803-943-7509; Appraiser/Auditor 803-943-7507; Vital Records 803-943-3878.

Horry County

Clerk of Court, PO Box 470, Conway, SC 29528. 843-248-1252; Fax 843-248-1566. Will search UCC records. Will not search real estate records. **Other Phones:** Assessor 843-248-1361.

Jasper County

Clerk of Court, PO Box 248, Ridgeland, SC 29936. 843-726-7710; Fax 843-726-7782.
Will search UCC records. Will not search real estate records. **Other Phones:** Assessor 843-726-7725.

Kershaw County

Clerk of Court, PO Box 1557, Camden, SC 29020-1557. 803-425-1500 R/E Recording: 803-425-1500 x623 UCC Recording: 803-425-1500 x623; Fax 803-425-1505.
This agency will not search real estate or UCC records. **Other Phones:** Assessor 803-425-1504; Treasurer 803-425-1500 x605; Appraiser/Auditor 803-425-1500 x611.

Lancaster County

Clerk of Court, PO Box 1809, Lancaster, SC 29721. Clerk of Court, R/E and UCC Recording 803-285-1581; Fax 803-416-9388. Will search UCC records. **Other Phone Numbers:** Assessor 803-285-6964; Treasurer 803-285-7939; Appraiser/Auditor 803-285-6964; Elections 285-2969; Vital Records 286-9948.

Laurens County

Clerk of Court, PO Box 287, Laurens, SC 29360. 864-984-3538. This agency will not perform searches. **Other Phone Numbers:** Assessor 864-984-6546.

Lee County

Register of Deeds, PO Box 387, Bishopville, SC 29010. 803-484-5341 R/E Recording: 803-484-5341 x333 UCC Recording: 803-484-5341 x378; Fax 803-484-1632. Will search UCC records. Will not search real estate records. **Other Phone Numbers:** Assessor 803-484-5341 x362; Treasurer 803-484-5341 x327.

Lexington County

Register of Deeds, 212 South Lake Drive, Lexington, SC 29072. 803-359-8404 R/E Recording: 803-359-8168 UCC Recording: 803-359-8168; Fax 803-359-8189. www.lex-co.com/my_lex.html
Will search UCC records. Will not search real estate records. **Online Access:** Tax Assessor Records. Access to county Reassessment Information is available free at www.lex-co.com/my_lex.html. Click on "Assessment Information.". **Other Phone Numbers:** Assessor 803-359-8190; Treasurer 803-359-8217.

Marion County

Clerk of Court, PO Box 295, Marion, SC 29571. 843-423-8240; Fax 843-423-8306.
Will search UCC records. This agency will not do a tax lien search. Will not search real estate records. **Other Phone Numbers:** Assessor 843-423-8225.

Marlboro County

Clerk of Court, PO Drawer 996, Bennettsville, SC 29512. 843-479-5613; Fax 843-479-5640.
Will search UCC records. UCC search includes tax liens if requested. Will not search real estate records.

McCormick County

Clerk of Court, 133 S. Mine St Room 102, Courthouse, Room 102, McCormick, SC 29835. Clerk of Court, R/E and UCC Recording 864-465-2195; Fax 864-465-0071. This agency will not search real estate or UCC records. **Other Phone Numbers:** Assessor 864-465-2931; Treasurer 864-465-2332.

Newberry County

Court Clerk, PO Box 278, Newberry, SC 29108. Court Clerk, R/E and UCC Recording 803-321-2110; Fax 803-321-2111. Will search UCC records. Will not search real estate records. **Other Phone Numbers:** Assessor 803-321-2125; Treasurer 803-321-2130.

Oconee County

Register of Deeds, 415 S Pine St, Walhalla, SC 29691. Reg. Deeds, R/E and UCC Recording 864-638-4285. This agency will not perform searches. **Other Phones:** Assessor 864-638-4150; Treasurer 864-638-4162.

Orangeburg County

Register of Deeds, Box 9000, Orangeburg, SC 29116-9000. Register of Deeds, R/E and UCC Recording 803-533-6236; Fax 803-534-2354.

This agency will not search real estate or UCC records. **Other Phone Numbers:** Assessor 803-533-6220; Treasurer 803-533-6130.

Pickens County

Register of Deeds, 222 McDaniel Ave. B-5, Pickens, SC 29671. Register of Deeds, R/E and UCC Recording 864-898-5868; Fax 864-898-5924.
Will search UCC records prior to 7/2001. Will not search real estate records. **Other Phone Numbers:** Assessor 864-898-5871; Treasurer 864-898-5883; Appraiser/Auditor 864-898-5878; Elections 864-898-5848; Vital Records 864-898-5965.

Richland County

Clerk of Court, PO Box 192, Columbia, SC 29202. 803-748-4800; Fax 803-748-4807.
Will search UCC records. Will not search real estate records. **Other Phones:** Assessor 803-748-5038.

Saluda County

Clerk of Court, Courthouse, Saluda, SC 29138. Clerk of Court, R/E and UCC Recording 864-445-3303; Fax 864-445-3772.
Will search UCC records. Will not search real estate records. **Other Phone Numbers:** Assessor 864-445-8121; Treasurer 864-445-2875.

Spartanburg County

County Register of Mesne Conveyances, 366 N. Church St, County Administrative Offices, Spartanburg, SC 29303. 864-596-2514.
Will search UCC records. This agency will not do a tax lien search. Will not search real estate records. **Other Phone Numbers:** Assessor 864-596-2544; Treasurer 864-596-2603.

Sumter County

Register of Deeds, Courthouse, Room 202, 141 N. Main St., Sumter, SC 29150. Register of Deeds, R/E and UCC Recording 803-436-2177 UCC Recording: 803-436-2179.
Will search UCC records. This agency will not do a tax lien search. Will not search real estate records. **Online Access:** Real Estate, Recording, Deed, Property Tax Records. Search county e-gov data free at www.sumtercountysc.org/disclaim.htm. **Other Phone Numbers:** Assessor 803-436-2112; Treasurer 803-436-2213; Appraiser/Auditor 803-436-2112; Elections 803-436-2310.

Union County

Clerk of Court, PO Box 200, Union, SC 29379. Clerk of Court, R/E and UCC Recording 864-429-1630; Fax 864-429-1715. www.judicial.state.sc.us/clerks/union
Will search UCC records. This agency will not do a tax lien search. Will not search real estate records. **Other Phone Numbers:** Assessor 864-429-1650; Treasurer 864-429-1606; Elections 864-429-1616; Vital Records 864-429-1690.

Williamsburg County

Clerk of Court, 125 W. Main St, Kingstree, SC 29556. 843-354-6855; Fax 843-354-5813.
Will search UCC records. Will not search real estate records. **Other Phone Numbers:** Assessor 843-354-7059.

York County

Clerk of Court, PO Box 649, York, SC 29745. 803-684-8510.
Will search UCC records. This agency will not do a tax lien search. Will not search real estate records. **Other Phone Numbers:** Assessor 803-684-8526; Treasurer 803-684-8528.

South Carolina County Locator

You will usually be able to find the city name in the City/County Cross Reference below. In that case, it is a simple matter to determine the county from the cross reference. However, only the official US Postal Service city names are included in this index. There are an additional 40,000 place names that people use in their addresses. Therefore, we have also included a ZIP/City Cross Reference immediately following the City/County Cross Reference.

If you know the ZIP Code but the city name does not appear in the City/County Cross Reference index, look up the ZIP Code in the ZIP/City Cross Reference, find the city name, then look up the city name in the City/County Cross Reference. For example, you want to know the county for an address of Menands, NY 12204. There is no "Menands" in the City/County Cross Reference. The ZIP/City Cross Reference shows that ZIP Codes 12201-12288 are for the city of Albany. Looking back in the City/County Cross Reference, Albany is in Albany County.

City/County Cross Reference

ABBEVILLE Abbeville
ADAMS RUN (29426) Charleston(78), Dorchester(21)
AIKEN Aiken
ALCOLU (29001) Clarendon(92), Sumter(7)
ALLENDALE Allendale
ANDERSON Anderson
ANDREWS (29510) Georgetown(51), Williamsburg(48)
ARCADIA Spartanburg
AWENDAW Charleston
AYNOR Horry
BALLENTINE Richland
BAMBERG Bamberg
BARNWELL Barnwell
BATESBURG (29006) Lexington(51), Saluda(30), Aiken(18)
BATH Aiken
BEAUFORT Beaufort
BEECH ISLAND Aiken
BELTON (29627) Anderson(93), Greenville(5)
BENNETTSVILLE Marlboro
BETHERA Berkeley
BETHUNE (29009) Kershaw(87), Lee(8), Chesterfield(3)
BISHOPVILLE Lee
BLACKSBURG Cherokee
BLACKSTOCK (29014) Fairfield(50), Chester(49)
BLACKVILLE (29817) Barnwell(79), Bamberg(20)
BLAIR Fairfield
BLENHEIM Marlboro
BLUFFTON Beaufort
BLYTHEWOOD (29016) Richland(94), Fairfield(5)
BONNEAU Berkeley
BORDEN Sumter
BOWLING GREEN York
BOWMAN (29018) Orangeburg(93), Dorchester(6)
BRADLEY (29819) Greenwood(98), McCormick(1)
BRANCHVILLE (29432) Orangeburg(71), Bamberg(21), Dorchester(5)
BRUNSON Hampton
BUFFALO Union
CADES Williamsburg
CALHOUN FALLS (29628) Abbeville(97), McCormick(2)
CAMDEN (29020) Kershaw(94), Lee(5)
CAMERON (29030) Calhoun(71), Orangeburg(28)
CAMPOBELLO (29322) Spartanburg(98), Greenville(1)
CANADYS Colleton
CARLISLE (29031) Union(45), Chester(33), Fairfield(20)
CASSATT (29032) Kershaw(69), Lee(30)
CATAWBA York
CAYCE Lexington
CENTENARY Marion
CENTRAL (29630) Pickens(93), Anderson(6)

CHAPIN (29036) Lexington(72), Richland(21), Newberry(5)
CHAPPELLS (29037) Newberry(68), Saluda(28), Laurens(3)
CHARLESTON Berkeley
CHARLESTON AFB Charleston
CHERAW Chesterfield
CHEROKEE FALLS Cherokee
CHESNEE (29323) Spartanburg(88), Cherokee(11)
CHESTER Chester
CHESTERFIELD Chesterfield
CLARKS HILL (29821) McCormick(90), Edgefield(9)
CLEARWATER Aiken
CLEMSON Pickens
CLEVELAND (29635) Greenville(72), Pickens(27)
CLIFTON Spartanburg
CLINTON Laurens
CLIO (29525) Marlboro(97), Dillon(2)
CLOVER York
COLUMBIA Richland
CONESTEE Greenville
CONVERSE Spartanburg
CONWAY Horry
COOSAWATCHIE Jasper
COPE Orangeburg
CORDESVILLE Berkeley
CORDOVA Orangeburg
COTTAGEVILLE Colleton
COWARD Florence
COWPENS (29330) Spartanburg(64), Cherokee(35)
CROCKETVILLE Hampton
CROSS (29436) Berkeley(96), Orangeburg(3)
CROSS ANCHOR Spartanburg
CROSS HILL (29332) Laurens(91), Newberry(8)
DALE Beaufort
DALZELL (29040) Sumter(80), Lee(19)
DARLINGTON Darlington
DAUFUSKIE ISLAND Beaufort
DAVIS STATION Clarendon
DENMARK Bamberg
DILLON Dillon
DONALDS (29638) Abbeville(86), Greenwood(13)
DORCHESTER Dorchester
DRAYTON Spartanburg
DUE WEST Abbeville
DUNCAN Spartanburg
EARLY BRANCH (29916) Hampton(90), Jasper(9)
EASLEY (29642) Pickens(68), Anderson(31)
EASTOVER Richland
EDGEFIELD Edgefield
EDGEMOOR Chester
EDISTO ISLAND (29438) Colleton(59), Charleston(40)
EFFINGHAM Florence
EHRHARDT (29081) Bamberg(92), Colleton(7)

ELGIN (29045) Kershaw(56), Richland(39), Fairfield(3)
ELKO Barnwell
ELLIOTT Lee
ELLOREE (29047) Orangeburg(51), Calhoun(48)
ENOREE (29335) Spartanburg(72), Laurens(24), Union(3)
ESTILL Hampton
EUTAWVILLE Orangeburg
FAIR PLAY (29643) Oconee(80), Anderson(19)
FAIRFAX (29827) Allendale(97), Hampton(2)
FAIRFOREST Spartanburg
FINGERVILLE Spartanburg
FLORENCE Florence
FLOYD DALE Dillon
FOLLY BEACH Charleston
FORK Dillon
FORT LAWN Chester
FORT MILL York
FOUNTAIN INN (29644) Laurens(59), Greenville(40)
FURMAN Hampton
GABLE (29051) Clarendon(52), Sumter(47)
GADSDEN Richland
GAFFNEY Cherokee
GALIVANTS FERRY Horry
GARNETT (29922) Hampton(96), Jasper(3)
GASTON (29053) Lexington(90), Calhoun(9)
GEORGETOWN Georgetown
GIFFORD Hampton
GILBERT Lexington
GLENDALE Spartanburg
GLOVERVILLE Aiken
GOOSE CREEK Berkeley
GRAMLING Spartanburg
GRANITEVILLE Aiken
GRAY COURT Laurens
GREAT FALLS (29055) Chester(70), Fairfield(29)
GREELEYVILLE (29056) Williamsburg(90), Clarendon(9)
GREEN POND Colleton
GREEN SEA Horry
GREENVILLE Greenville
GREENWOOD (29649) Greenwood(98), Abbeville(1)
GREER Greenville
GRESHAM Marion
GROVER Dorchester
HAMER Dillon
HAMPTON Hampton
HARDEEVILLE (29927) Jasper(98), Beaufort(1)
HARLEYVILLE Dorchester
HARTSVILLE Darlington
HEATH SPRINGS (29058) Lancaster(94), Kershaw(5)
HEMINGWAY (29554) Williamsburg(49), Georgetown(48), Florence(1)
HICKORY GROVE York
HILDA Barnwell

HILTON HEAD ISLAND Beaufort
HODGES Greenwood
HOLLY HILL (29059) Orangeburg(96), Berkeley(3)
HOLLYWOOD Charleston
HONEA PATH (29654) Anderson(60), Abbeville(21), Laurens(10), Greenville(7)
HOPKINS Richland
HORATIO Sumter
HUGER Berkeley
INMAN Spartanburg
IRMO (29063) Richland(92), Lexington(7)
ISLANDTON Colleton
ISLE OF PALMS Charleston
IVA (29655) Anderson(58), Abbeville(41)
JACKSON Aiken
JACKSONBORO Colleton
JAMESTOWN Berkeley
JEFFERSON Chesterfield
JENKINSVILLE Fairfield
JOANNA Laurens
JOHNS ISLAND Charleston
JOHNSONVILLE (29555) Florence(93), Williamsburg(6)
JOHNSTON (29832) Edgefield(98), Saluda(1)
JONESVILLE Union
KERSHAW (29067) Lancaster(73), Kershaw(26)
KINARDS (29355) Newberry(54), Laurens(45)
KINGS CREEK Cherokee
KINGSTREE Williamsburg
KLINE Barnwell
LA FRANCE Anderson
LADSON (29456) Berkeley(44), Dorchester(35), Charleston(19)
LAKE CITY (29560) Florence(68), Williamsburg(17), Clarendon(13)
LAKE VIEW Dillon
LAMAR (29069) Darlington(84), Lee(15)
LANCASTER Lancaster
LANDO Chester
LANDRUM (29356) Spartanburg(58), Greenville(41)
LANE Williamsburg
LANGLEY Aiken
LATTA (29565) Dillon(86), Marion(10), Marlboro(2)
LAURENS Laurens
LEESVILLE (29070) Lexington(75), Saluda(24)
LEXINGTON Lexington
LIBERTY (29657) Pickens(86), Anderson(13)
LIBERTY HILL Kershaw
LITTLE MOUNTAIN (29075) Newberry(80), Richland(13), Lexington(6)
LITTLE RIVER Horry
LITTLE ROCK Dillon
LIVINGSTON Orangeburg
LOBECO Beaufort
LOCKHART Union
LODGE (29082) Colleton(92), Bamberg(7)
LONE STAR Calhoun

LONG CREEK Oconee
LONGS Horry
LORIS Horry
LOWNDESVILLE Abbeville
LUGOFF (29078) Kershaw(96), Richland(3)
LURAY (29932) Allendale(55), Hampton(44)
LYDIA Darlington
LYMAN Spartanburg
LYNCHBURG (29080) Lee(50), Sumter(50)
MANNING (29102) Clarendon(98), Sumter(1)
MARIETTA (29661) Greenville(76), Pickens(23)
MARION Marion
MARTIN (29836) Allendale(98), Barnwell(1)
MAULDIN Greenville
MAYESVILLE (29104) Sumter(51), Lee(48)
MAYO Spartanburg
MC BEE (29101) Chesterfield(50), Darlington(49)
MC CLELLANVILLE Charleston
MC COLL Marlboro
MC CONNELLS York
MC CORMICK McCormick
MILEY Hampton
MINTURN Dillon
MODOC (29838) McCormick(84), Edgefield(15)
MONCKS CORNER Berkeley
MONETTA (29105) Aiken(83), Saluda(16)
MONTICELLO Fairfield
MONTMORENCI Aiken
MOORE Spartanburg
MOUNT CARMEL McCormick
MOUNT CROGHAN Chesterfield
MOUNT PLEASANT Charleston
MOUNTAIN REST Oconee
MOUNTVILLE Laurens
MULLINS Marion
MURRELLS INLET (29576) Horry(55), Georgetown(44)
MYRTLE BEACH Horry
NEESES Orangeburg
NESMITH Williamsburg
NEW ELLENTON Aiken
NEW ZION (29111) Clarendon(92), Williamsburg(7)
NEWBERRY Newberry
NEWRY Oconee
NICHOLS (29581) Horry(81), Marion(10), Dillon(8)
NINETY SIX (29666) Greenwood(95), Saluda(4)
NORRIS Pickens
NORTH (29112) Orangeburg(90), Calhoun(6), Lexington(2)

NORTH AUGUSTA Aiken
NORTH CHARLESTON Charleston
NORTH MYRTLE BEACH Horry
NORWAY Orangeburg
OLANTA (29114) Florence(57), Sumter(41)
OLAR (29843) Bamberg(93), Barnwell(6)
ORANGEBURG (29118) Orangeburg(95), Calhoun(4)
PACOLET (29372) Spartanburg(69), Union(16), Cherokee(14)
PACOLET MILLS Spartanburg
PAGELAND Chesterfield
PAMPLICO Florence
PARKSVILLE McCormick
PATRICK Chesterfield
PAULINE (29374) Spartanburg(93), Union(6)
PAWLEYS ISLAND Georgetown
PEAK Newberry
PELION Lexington
PELZER (29669) Anderson(65), Greenville(34)
PENDLETON (29670) Anderson(98), Pickens(1)
PERRY Aiken
PICKENS Pickens
PIEDMONT (29673) Greenville(51), Anderson(48)
PINELAND (29934) Hampton(80), Jasper(19)
PINEVILLE Berkeley
PINEWOOD (29125) Clarendon(55), Sumter(44)
PINOPOLIS Berkeley
PLUM BRANCH (29845) McCormick(97), Edgefield(2)
POMARIA Newberry
PORT ROYAL Beaufort
POSTON Horry
PROSPERITY (29127) Newberry(95), Saluda(4)
RAINS Marion
RAVENEL (29470) Charleston(88), Dorchester(11)
REEVESVILLE Dorchester
REIDVILLE Spartanburg
REMBERT (29128) Sumter(77), Lee(15), Kershaw(7)
RICHBURG Chester
RICHLAND Oconee
RIDGE SPRING (29129) Aiken(50), Saluda(40), Edgefield(8)
RIDGELAND (29936) Jasper(79), Beaufort(20)
RIDGEVILLE (29472) Dorchester(63), Colleton(20), Berkeley(15)

RIDGEWAY (29130) Fairfield(85), Kershaw(12), Richland(1)
RIMINI (29131) Sumter(65), Clarendon(34)
RION Fairfield
ROCK HILL York
ROEBUCK Spartanburg
ROUND O Colleton
ROWESVILLE Orangeburg
RUBY Chesterfield
RUFFIN Colleton
RUSSELLVILLE Berkeley
SAINT GEORGE Dorchester
SAINT HELENA ISLAND Beaufort
SAINT MATTHEWS (29135) Calhoun(97), Orangeburg(2)
SAINT STEPHEN Berkeley
SALEM Oconee
SALLEY (29137) Aiken(85), Orangeburg(14)
SALTERS Williamsburg
SALUDA (29138) Saluda(97), Greenwood(1)
SANDY SPRINGS Anderson
SANTEE Orangeburg
SARDINIA Clarendon
SCOTIA Hampton
SCRANTON Florence
SEABROOK Beaufort
SELLERS (29592) Dillon(66), Marion(33)
SENECA Oconee
SHARON York
SHAW A F B Sumter
SHELDON Beaufort
SILVERSTREET Newberry
SIMPSONVILLE Greenville
SIX MILE Pickens
SLATER Greenville
SMOAKS (29481) Colleton(95), Bamberg(4)
SMYRNA York
SOCIETY HILL (29593) Darlington(54), Chesterfield(45)
SPARTANBURG Spartanburg
SPRINGFIELD (29146) Orangeburg(69), Aiken(30)
STARR Anderson
STARTEX Spartanburg
STATE PARK Richland
SULLIVANS ISLAND Charleston
SUMMERTON Clarendon
SUMMERVILLE (29485) Dorchester(89), Charleston(10)
SUMTER Sumter
SUNSET Pickens
SWANSEA (29160) Lexington(66), Calhoun(32)
SYCAMORE Allendale

TAMASSEE Oconee
TATUM Marlboro
TAYLORS Greenville
TIGERVILLE Greenville
TILLMAN Jasper
TIMMONSVILLE (29161) Florence(81), Darlington(18)
TOWNVILLE (29689) Anderson(89), Oconee(10)
TRAVELERS REST Greenville
TRENTON (29847) Edgefield(57), Aiken(42)
TRIO Williamsburg
TROY (29848) Greenwood(87), McCormick(8), Saluda(3)
TURBEVILLE Clarendon
ULMER Allendale
UNA Spartanburg
UNION Union
VAN WYCK Lancaster
VANCE Orangeburg
VARNVILLE Hampton
VAUCLUSE Aiken
WADMALAW ISLAND Charleston
WAGENER Aiken
WALHALLA Oconee
WALLACE Marlboro
WALTERBORO Colleton
WARD Saluda
WARE SHOALS (29692) Laurens(66), Greenwood(24), Abbeville(9)
WARRENVILLE Aiken
WATERLOO Laurens
WEDGEFIELD Sumter
WELLFORD Spartanburg
WEST COLUMBIA Lexington
WEST UNION Oconee
WESTMINSTER Oconee
WESTVILLE Kershaw
WHITE OAK Fairfield
WHITE ROCK Richland
WHITE STONE Spartanburg
WHITMIRE (29178) Newberry(78), Union(16), Laurens(5)
WILLIAMS Colleton
WILLIAMSTON Anderson
WILLISTON (29853) Barnwell(59), Aiken(40)
WINDSOR Aiken
WINNSBORO (29180) Fairfield(97), Richland(2)
WISACKY Lee
WOODRUFF (29388) Spartanburg(93), Laurens(6)
YEMASSEE (29945) Hampton(44), Colleton(39), Beaufort(15)
YORK York

ZIP/City Cross Reference

ZIP	City
29001-29001	ALCOLU
29002-29002	BALLENTINE
29003-29003	BAMBERG
29006-29006	BATESBURG
29009-29009	BETHUNE
29010-29010	BISHOPVILLE
29014-29014	BLACKSTOCK
29015-29015	BLAIR
29016-29016	BLYTHEWOOD
29017-29017	BORDEN
29018-29018	BOWMAN
29020-29020	CAMDEN
29030-29030	CAMERON
29031-29031	CARLISLE
29032-29032	CASSATT
29033-29033	CAYCE
29036-29036	CHAPIN
29037-29037	CHAPPELLS
29038-29038	COPE
29039-29039	CORDOVA
29040-29040	DALZELL
29041-29041	DAVIS STATION
29042-29042	DENMARK
29044-29044	EASTOVER
29045-29045	ELGIN
29046-29046	ELLIOTT
29047-29047	ELLOREE
29048-29048	EUTAWVILLE
29051-29051	GABLE
29052-29052	GADSDEN
29053-29053	GASTON
29054-29054	GILBERT
29055-29055	GREAT FALLS
29056-29056	GREELEYVILLE
29058-29058	HEATH SPRINGS
29059-29059	HOLLY HILL
29061-29061	HOPKINS
29062-29062	HORATIO
29063-29063	IRMO
29065-29065	JENKINSVILLE
29067-29067	KERSHAW
29069-29069	LAMAR
29070-29070	LEESVILLE
29071-29073	LEXINGTON
29074-29074	LIBERTY HILL
29075-29075	LITTLE MOUNTAIN
29076-29076	LIVINGSTON
29077-29077	LONE STAR
29078-29078	LUGOFF
29079-29079	LYDIA
29080-29080	LYNCHBURG
29081-29081	EHRHARDT
29082-29082	LODGE
29101-29101	MC BEE
29102-29102	MANNING
29104-29104	MAYESVILLE
29105-29105	MONETTA
29106-29106	MONTICELLO
29107-29107	NEESES
29108-29108	NEWBERRY
29111-29111	NEW ZION
29112-29112	NORTH
29113-29113	NORWAY
29114-29114	OLANTA
29115-29118	ORANGEBURG
29122-29122	PEAK
29123-29123	PELION
29124-29124	PERRY
29125-29125	PINEWOOD
29126-29126	POMARIA
29127-29127	PROSPERITY
29128-29128	REMBERT
29129-29129	RIDGE SPRING
29130-29130	RIDGEWAY
29131-29131	RIMINI
29132-29132	RION
29133-29133	ROWESVILLE
29135-29135	SAINT MATTHEWS
29137-29137	SALLEY
29138-29138	SALUDA
29142-29142	SANTEE
29143-29143	SARDINIA
29145-29145	SILVERSTREET
29146-29146	SPRINGFIELD

Zip Range	City	Zip Range	City	Zip Range	City	Zip Range	City
29147-29147	STATE PARK	29439-29439	FOLLY BEACH	29588-29588	POSTON	29724-29724	LANDO
29148-29148	SUMMERTON	29440-29442	GEORGETOWN	29588-29588	MYRTLE BEACH	29726-29726	MC CONNELLS
29150-29151	SUMTER	29445-29445	GOOSE CREEK	29589-29589	RAINS	29727-29727	MOUNT CROGHAN
29152-29152	SHAW A F B	29446-29446	GREEN POND	29590-29590	SALTERS	29728-29728	PAGELAND
29153-29154	SUMTER	29447-29447	GROVER	29591-29591	SCRANTON	29729-29729	RICHBURG
29160-29160	SWANSEA	29448-29448	HARLEYVILLE	29592-29592	SELLERS	29730-29734	ROCK HILL
29161-29161	TIMMONSVILLE	29449-29449	HOLLYWOOD	29593-29593	SOCIETY HILL	29741-29741	RUBY
29162-29162	TURBEVILLE	29450-29450	HUGER	29594-29594	TATUM	29742-29742	SHARON
29163-29163	VANCE	29451-29451	ISLE OF PALMS	29595-29595	TRIO	29743-29743	SMYRNA
29164-29164	WAGENER	29452-29452	JACKSONBORO	29596-29596	WALLACE	29744-29744	VAN WYCK
29166-29166	WARD	29453-29453	JAMESTOWN	29597-29598	NORTH MYRTLE BEACH	29745-29745	YORK
29168-29168	WEDGEFIELD	29455-29455	JOHNS ISLAND	29601-29617	GREENVILLE	29801-29808	AIKEN
29169-29172	WEST COLUMBIA	29456-29456	LADSON	29620-29620	ABBEVILLE	29809-29809	NEW ELLENTON
29175-29175	WESTVILLE	29457-29457	JOHNS ISLAND	29621-29626	ANDERSON	29810-29810	ALLENDALE
29176-29176	WHITE OAK	29458-29458	MC CLELLANVILLE	29627-29627	BELTON	29812-29812	BARNWELL
29177-29177	WHITE ROCK	29461-29461	MONCKS CORNER	29628-29628	CALHOUN FALLS	29813-29813	HILDA
29178-29178	WHITMIRE	29464-29466	MOUNT PLEASANT	29630-29630	CENTRAL	29814-29814	KLINE
29180-29180	WINNSBORO	29468-29468	PINEVILLE	29631-29634	CLEMSON	29816-29816	BATH
29183-29183	WISACKY	29469-29469	PINOPOLIS	29635-29635	CLEVELAND	29817-29817	BLACKVILLE
29200-29292	COLUMBIA	29470-29470	RAVENEL	29636-29636	CONESTEE	29819-29819	BRADLEY
29301-29319	SPARTANBURG	29471-29471	REEVESVILLE	29638-29638	DONALDS	29821-29821	CLARKS HILL
29320-29320	ARCADIA	29472-29472	RIDGEVILLE	29639-29639	DUE WEST	29822-29822	CLEARWATER
29321-29321	BUFFALO	29474-29474	ROUND O	29640-29642	EASLEY	29824-29824	EDGEFIELD
29322-29322	CAMPOBELLO	29475-29475	RUFFIN	29643-29643	FAIR PLAY	29826-29826	ELKO
29323-29323	CHESNEE	29476-29476	RUSSELLVILLE	29644-29644	FOUNTAIN INN	29827-29827	FAIRFAX
29324-29324	CLIFTON	29477-29477	SAINT GEORGE	29645-29645	GRAY COURT	29828-29828	GLOVERVILLE
29325-29325	CLINTON	29479-29479	SAINT STEPHEN	29646-29649	GREENWOOD	29829-29829	GRANITEVILLE
29329-29329	CONVERSE	29481-29481	SMOAKS	29650-29652	GREER	29831-29831	JACKSON
29330-29330	COWPENS	29482-29482	SULLIVANS ISLAND	29653-29653	HODGES	29832-29832	JOHNSTON
29331-29331	CROSS ANCHOR	29483-29485	SUMMERVILLE	29654-29654	HONEA PATH	29834-29834	LANGLEY
29332-29332	CROSS HILL	29487-29487	WADMALAW ISLAND	29655-29655	IVA	29835-29835	MC CORMICK
29333-29333	DRAYTON	29488-29488	WALTERBORO	29656-29656	LA FRANCE	29836-29836	MARTIN
29334-29334	DUNCAN	29492-29492	CHARLESTON	29657-29657	LIBERTY	29838-29838	MODOC
29335-29335	ENOREE	29493-29493	WILLIAMS	29658-29658	LONG CREEK	29839-29839	MONTMORENCI
29336-29336	FAIRFOREST	29501-29506	FLORENCE	29659-29659	LOWNDESVILLE	29840-29840	MOUNT CARMEL
29338-29338	FINGERVILLE	29510-29510	ANDREWS	29661-29661	MARIETTA	29841-29841	NORTH AUGUSTA
29340-29342	GAFFNEY	29511-29511	AYNOR	29662-29662	MAULDIN	29842-29842	BEECH ISLAND
29346-29346	GLENDALE	29512-29512	BENNETTSVILLE	29664-29664	MOUNTAIN REST	29843-29843	OLAR
29348-29348	GRAMLING	29516-29516	BLENHEIM	29665-29665	NEWRY	29844-29844	PARKSVILLE
29349-29349	INMAN	29518-29518	CADES	29666-29666	NINETY SIX	29845-29845	PLUM BRANCH
29351-29351	JOANNA	29519-29519	CENTENARY	29667-29667	NORRIS	29846-29846	SYCAMORE
29353-29353	JONESVILLE	29520-29520	CHERAW	29669-29669	PELZER	29847-29847	TRENTON
29355-29355	KINARDS	29525-29525	CLIO	29670-29670	PENDLETON	29848-29848	TROY
29356-29356	LANDRUM	29526-29528	CONWAY	29671-29671	PICKENS	29849-29849	ULMER
29360-29360	LAURENS	29530-29530	COWARD	29672-29672	SENECA	29850-29850	VAUCLUSE
29364-29364	LOCKHART	29532-29532	DARLINGTON	29673-29673	PIEDMONT	29851-29851	WARRENVILLE
29365-29365	LYMAN	29536-29536	DILLON	29675-29675	RICHLAND	29853-29853	WILLISTON
29368-29368	MAYO	29540-29540	DARLINGTON	29676-29676	SALEM	29856-29856	WINDSOR
29369-29369	MOORE	29541-29541	EFFINGHAM	29677-29677	SANDY SPRINGS	29860-29861	NORTH AUGUSTA
29370-29370	MOUNTVILLE	29542-29542	FLOYD DALE	29678-29679	SENECA	29899-29899	MC CORMICK
29372-29372	PACOLET	29543-29543	FORK	29680-29681	SIMPSONVILLE	29901-29906	BEAUFORT
29373-29373	PACOLET MILLS	29544-29544	GALIVANTS FERRY	29682-29682	SIX MILE	29910-29910	BLUFFTON
29374-29374	PAULINE	29545-29545	GREEN SEA	29683-29683	SLATER	29911-29911	BRUNSON
29375-29375	REIDVILLE	29546-29546	GRESHAM	29684-29684	STARR	29912-29912	COOSAWATCHIE
29376-29376	ROEBUCK	29547-29547	HAMER	29685-29685	SUNSET	29913-29913	CROCKETVILLE
29377-29377	STARTEX	29550-29551	HARTSVILLE	29686-29686	TAMASSEE	29914-29914	DALE
29378-29378	UNA	29554-29554	HEMINGWAY	29687-29687	TAYLORS	29915-29915	DAUFUSKIE ISLAND
29379-29379	UNION	29555-29555	JOHNSONVILLE	29688-29688	TIGERVILLE	29916-29916	EARLY BRANCH
29384-29384	WATERLOO	29556-29556	KINGSTREE	29689-29689	TOWNVILLE	29918-29918	ESTILL
29385-29385	WELLFORD	29560-29560	LAKE CITY	29690-29690	TRAVELERS REST	29920-29920	SAINT HELENA ISLAND
29386-29386	WHITE STONE	29563-29563	LAKE VIEW	29691-29691	WALHALLA	29921-29921	FURMAN
29388-29388	WOODRUFF	29564-29564	LANE	29692-29692	WARE SHOALS	29922-29922	GARNETT
29390-29391	DUNCAN	29565-29565	LATTA	29693-29693	WESTMINSTER	29923-29923	GIFFORD
29395-29395	JONESVILLE	29566-29566	LITTLE RIVER	29695-29695	HODGES	29924-29924	HAMPTON
29401-29403	CHARLESTON	29567-29567	LITTLE ROCK	29696-29696	WEST UNION	29925-29926	HILTON HEAD ISLAND
29404-29404	CHARLESTON AFB	29568-29568	LONGS	29697-29697	WILLIAMSTON	29927-29927	HARDEEVILLE
29405-29410	CHARLESTON	29569-29569	LORIS	29698-29698	GREENVILLE	29928-29928	HILTON HEAD ISLAND
29410-29410	NORTH CHARLESTON	29570-29570	MC COLL	29702-29702	BLACKSBURG	29929-29929	ISLANDTON
29411-29415	CHARLESTON	29571-29571	MARION	29703-29703	BOWLING GREEN	29931-29931	LOBECO
29415-29415	NORTH CHARLESTON	29572-29572	MYRTLE BEACH	29704-29704	CATAWBA	29932-29932	LURAY
29416-29425	CHARLESTON	29573-29573	MINTURN	29705-29705	CHEROKEE FALLS	29933-29933	MILEY
29426-29426	ADAMS RUN	29574-29574	MULLINS	29706-29706	CHESTER	29934-29934	PINELAND
29429-29429	AWENDAW	29575-29575	MYRTLE BEACH	29708-29708	FORT MILL	29935-29935	PORT ROYAL
29430-29430	BETHERA	29576-29576	MURRELLS INLET	29709-29709	CHESTERFIELD	29936-29936	RIDGELAND
29431-29431	BONNEAU	29577-29579	MYRTLE BEACH	29710-29710	CLOVER	29938-29938	HILTON HEAD ISLAND
29432-29432	BRANCHVILLE	29580-29580	NESMITH	29712-29712	EDGEMOOR	29939-29939	SCOTIA
29433-29433	CANADYS	29581-29581	NICHOLS	29714-29714	FORT LAWN	29940-29940	SEABROOK
29434-29434	CORDESVILLE	29582-29582	NORTH MYRTLE BEACH	29715-29716	FORT MILL	29941-29941	SHELDON
29435-29435	COTTAGEVILLE	29583-29583	PAMPLICO	29717-29717	HICKORY GROVE	29943-29943	TILLMAN
29436-29436	CROSS	29584-29584	PATRICK	29718-29718	JEFFERSON	29944-29944	VARNVILLE
29437-29437	DORCHESTER	29585-29585	PAWLEYS ISLAND	29719-29719	KINGS CREEK	29945-29945	YEMASSEE
29438-29438	EDISTO ISLAND	29587-29587	MYRTLE BEACH	29720-29722	LANCASTER	29948-29948	HILTON HEAD ISLAND

General Help Numbers:

Governor's Office

State Capitol, 500 E Capitol Ave	605-773-3212
Pierre, SD 57501-5070	Fax 605-773-4711
www.state.sd.us/governor/	8AM-5PM

Attorney General's Office

State Capitol, 500 E Capitol Ave	605-773-3215
Pierre, SD 57501-5070	Fax 605-773-4106
www.state.sd.us/attorney/index.htm	8AM-5PM

State Court Administrator

State Capitol Bldg	605-773-3474
500 E Capitol Ave	Fax 605-773-5627
Pierre, SD 57501-5059	8AM-5PM
www.sdjudicial.com	

State Archives

Cultural Heritage Center/State Archives	605-773-3804
900 Governors Dr	Fax 605-773-6041
Pierre, SD 57501-2217	9AM-4:30PM
www.state.sd.us/deca/cultural/archives.htm	

State Specifics:

Capital: Pierre
Hughes County

Time Zone: CST*

* South Dakota's eighteen western-most counties are MST: They are: Bennett, Butte, Corson, Custer, Dewey, Fall River, Haakon, Harding, Jackson, Lawrence, Meade, Mellette, Pennington, Perkins, Shannon, Stanley, Todd, Ziebach,

Number of Counties: 66

Population: 756,600

Web Site: www.state.sd.us

State Agencies

Criminal Records

Division of Criminal Investigation, Identification Section, 500 E Capitol, Pierre, SD 57501-5070; 605-773-3331, 605-773-4629 (Fax), 8AM-5PM.

www.state.sd.us/attorney/attorney.html

Note: The State Court Administrator's Office has a statewide database of criminal record information from the state's circuit courts. For more information about setting up a commercial account, contact Jill Gusso at 605-773-3474.

Indexing & Storage: Records are available for 10 years for misdemeanors and lifetime for felonies. It takes 1 day before new records are available for inquiry. Records are indexed on inhouse computer (90+%); only older records not computerized. Records are normally destroyed after 10 years, if a misdemeanor. 98% of all arrests in database have final dispositions recorded.

Searching: Sexual Offender Registry at www.sddci.com/administration/id/sexoffender/index.htm. Include the following in your request: date of birth, full name, set of fingerprints, signed release form. The form requires identifying information: color of hair and eyes, height, weight, date of birth, Social Security Number. The following data is not released: juvenile records, minor traffic violations or out-of-state or federal charges. Records without dispositions are not released, unless the case is still open.

Access by: mail.

Fee & Payment: The fee is $15.00 per name. Statutorily-required fingerprint checks will include an FBI fingerprint check for an additional $24.00. Fee payee: Division of Criminal Investigation. Prepayment required. Personal checks accepted. No credit cards accepted.

Mail search: Turnaround time: 5 to 10 working days. Upon receipt of those requirements, they will conduct a search of their files and supply a copy of any criminal history that is found or a statement that there is no criminal history. A self addressed stamped envelope is requested.

Fictitious Name
Assumed Name

Records not maintained by a state level agency.

Note: Records are located at the county level.

Corporation Records
Limited Partnerships
Limited Liability Company Records
Trademarks/Servicemarks

Corporation Division, Secretary of State, 500 E Capitol Ave, Suite B-05, Pierre, SD 57501-5070; 605-773-4845, 605-773-5666 (Trademarks), 605-773-4550 (Fax), 8AM-5PM.

www.state.sd.us/sos/sos.htm

Indexing & Storage: Records are available from the founding of the state. New records are available for inquiry immediately. Records are indexed on microfiche, inhouse computer.

Searching: Trademarks may be search via e-mail at kea.warne@state.sd.us. Include the following in your request: full name of business. In addition to the articles of incorporation, corporation records include the following information: Annual Reports, Officers, Directors, Prior (merged) names, Inactive and Reserved names.

Access by: mail, phone, fax, in person, online.

Fee & Payment: There is no fee for a general search. A Certificate of Good Standing is available for a fee of $10.00. Copies are $1.00 per page, add $5.00 for certification. Fee payee: Secretary of State. Prepayment required. Personal checks accepted. Credit cards accepted: MasterCard, Visa.

Mail search: Turnaround time: 1 to 3 days. A self addressed stamped envelope is requested.

Phone search: They will provide basic information only.

Fax search: Records can be retruned by fax for $1.00 per page.

In person search: Turnaround time is immediate.

Online search: Search the Secretary of State Corporations Div. Database free at www.state.sd.us/applications/st02corplook/corpfile.asp

Expedited service: Expedited service is available for an additional $10.00 per request. Add $10.00 per request.

Uniform Commercial Code
Federal Tax Liens

UCC Division, Secretary of State, 500 East Capitol, Pierre, SD 57501-5077; 605-773-4422, 605-773-4550 (Fax), 8AM-5PM.

www.state.sd.us/sos/sos.htm

Note: Federal tax liens on business filed here, if on individuals then filed at county level.

Indexing & Storage: Records are available for all active records. It takes 1-2 days before new records are available for inquiry. Records are indexed on computer.

Searching: Use search request form UCC-11. The search includes federal tax liens on businesses. Federal tax liens on businesses and all state tax liens on individuals are filed at the county level. Include the following in your request: debtor name.

Access by: mail, phone, fax, in person, online.

Fee & Payment: The fee is $12.00 per debtor name ($10.00 if online), copies are $1.00 per page. There is an additional $5.00 if certification of document desired. Fee payee: Secretary of State. Prepayment required. Credit cards accepted: MasterCard, Visa.

Mail search: Turnaround time: 1 to 2 days. A self addressed stamped envelope is requested.

Phone search: Limited information is given over the phone. Reports can be ordered.

Fax search: Use of a credit card is required. Fee is additional $1.00 per page to fax back.

In person search: Searching is available in person.

Online search: Dakota Fast File is the filing and searching service available from the web site. This is a commercial service that requires registration and a $120-360 fee per year. A certified search is also available.

Expedited service: Expedited service is available for mail, phone and fax searches. Turnaround time: 1 day. Add $10.00 per debtor name.

State Tax Liens
Federal Tax Liens

Records not maintained by a state level agency.

Note: All state tax liens and federal yax liens on individuals are filed at the county level.

Sales Tax Registrations

Revenue Department, Business Tax Division, 445 E Capitol, Pierre, SD 57501-3100; 605-773-3311, 605-773-5129 (Fax), 8AM-5PM.

www.state.sd.us/revenue

Indexing & Storage: Records are available from 1992 on computer. Records have been placed on microfilm from 1970 to 1996.

Searching: This agency will only confirm if a business is registered and licensed. They will provide no other information. Include the following in your request: business name. Also search by tax permit number or owner name.

Access by: mail, phone, fax, in person.

Mail search: Turnaround time: 2 to 3 weeks. A self addressed stamped envelope is requested. No fee for mail request.

Phone search: No fee for telephone request.

Fax search: There is no fee, turnaround time is 2-3 weeks.

In person search: No fee for request. Usually requests can be processed while you wait.

Birth Certificates

South Dakota Department of Health, Vital Records, 600 E Capitol, Pierre, SD 57501-2536; 605-773-4961, 605-773-5683 (Fax), 8AM-5PM.

www.state.sd.us/doh/VitalRec/index.htm

Indexing & Storage: Records are available from 1906 to present. New records are available for inquiry immediately.

Searching: Include the following in your request: full name, names of parents, mother's maiden name, date of birth, place of birth. Any county Register of Deeds can provide a computer generated birth certificate for the same fee. The following data is not released: sealed records.

Access by: mail, phone, in person, online.

Fee & Payment: The fee is $10.00. Use of a credit card is an additional $10.00 expedited fee. Fee payee: South Dakota Department of Health. Prepayment required. Personal checks accepted. Credit cards accepted: MasterCard, Visa, AmEx, Discover.

Mail search: Turnaround time: 2 to 3 days. No self addressed stamped envelope is required.

Phone search: You must use a credit card, considered expedited service.

In person search: Turnaround time 30 minutes.

Online search: You can search free at the web site for birth records over 100 years old. You can order recent (less than 100 years) birth records at the web site, for a fee.

Expedited service: Expedited service is available for web and phone searches. Turnaround time: overnight delivery. Add delivery fee and use of credit card fee.

Death Records

South Dakota Department of Health, Vital Records, 600 E Capitol, Pierre, SD 57501-2536; 605-773-4961, 605-773-5683 (Fax), 8AM-5PM.

www.state.sd.us/doh/VitalRec/index.htm

Indexing & Storage: Records are available from 1905 to present. New records are available for inquiry immediately.

Searching: Include the following in your request: full name, date of death, place of death. The following data is not released: sealed records.

Access by: mail, phone, in person, online.

Fee & Payment: The fee is $10.00 per record. There is an additional $10.00 fee if a credit card is used. Fee payee: South Dakota Department of Health. Prepayment required. Personal checks accepted. Credit cards accepted: MasterCard, Visa, AmEx, Discover.

Mail search: Turnaround time: 2 to 3 days. No self addressed stamped envelope is required.

Phone search: You must use a credit card.

In person search: Turnaround time is 30 minutes.

Online search: Records may be ordered online at the web site.

Expedited service: Expedited service is available for Internet and phone searches. Turnaround time: overnight delivery. Add delivery fee and use of credit card fee.

Marriage Certificates

South Dakota Department of Health, Vital Records, 600 E Capitol, Pierre, SD 57501-2536; 605-773-4961, 605-773-5683 (Fax), 8AM-5PM.

www.state.sd.us/doh/VitalRec/index.htm

Indexing & Storage: Records are available from 1905 to present. New records are available for inquiry immediately.

Searching: Include the following in your request: names of husband and wife, date of marriage, place or county of marriage. Also include wife's maiden name.

Access by: mail, phone, in person, online.

Fee & Payment: The fee is $7.00 per record. There is an additional $10.00 expedited fee if a credit card is used. Fee payee: South Dakota Department of Health. Prepayment required. Personal checks accepted. Credit cards accepted: MasterCard, Visa, AmEx, Discover.

Mail search: Turnaround time: 2 to 3 days. No self addressed stamped envelope is required.

Phone search: You must use a credit card.

In person search: Turnaround time is 30 minutes.

Online search: Records may be ordered online at the web site.

Expedited service: Expedited service is available for Internet and phone searches. Turnaround time: overnight delivery. Add delivery fee and use of credit card fee.

Divorce Records

South Dakota Department of Health, Vital Records, 600 E Capitol, Pierre, SD 57501-2536; 605-773-4961, 605-773-5683 (Fax), 8AM-5PM.

www.state.sd.us/doh/VitalRec/index.htm

Indexing & Storage: Records are available from 1905 to present. New records are available for inquiry immediately.

Searching: Include the following in your request: names of husband and wife, date of divorce, place of divorce. The following data is not released: sealed records.

Access by: mail, phone, in person, online.

Fee & Payment: The fee is $7.00 per record. There is an additional $10.00 expedited fee if a credit card is used. Fee payee: South Dakota Department of Health. Prepayment required. Personal checks accepted. Credit cards accepted: MasterCard, Visa, AmEx, Discover.

Mail search: Turnaround time: 2 to 3 days. No self addressed stamped envelope is required.

Phone search: You must use a credit card.

In person search: Turnaround time 30 minutes.

Online search: Records may be ordered at the web site.

Expedited service: Expedited service is available for Internet and phone searches. Turnaround time: overnight delivery. Add delivery fee and use of credit card fee.

Workers' Compensation Records

Labor Department, Workers Compensation Division, 700 Governors Dr, Pierre, SD 57501; 605-773-3681, 605-773-4211 (Fax), 8AM-5PM.

www.state.sd.us/dol/dlm/dlm-home.htm

Indexing & Storage: Records are available from 1973. New records are available for inquiry immediately. Records are indexed on inhouse computer.

Searching: Must have a signed release form from the claimant. Must also specify which records you are requesting. A computer search will only go back to July 1989. Fraud reports and sealed files are not released. Include the following in your request: claimant name, Social Security Number, date of accident, body part injured.

Access by: mail.

Fee & Payment: Search fee is $20.00 per file or date of injury, copies are included. Fee payee: Division of Labor Management. Prepayment required. Personal checks accepted. No credit cards accepted.

Mail search: Turnaround time: 1 week.

Driver Records

Dept of Commerce & Regulation, Office of Driver Licensing, 118 W Capitol, Pierre, SD 57501; 605-773-6883, 605-773-3018 (Fax), 8AM-5PM.

www.state.sd.us/dcr/dl/sddriver.htm

Note: Ticket information is maintained at the local courts, not at the state.

Indexing & Storage: Records are available for 3 years for moving violations and DWIs. Speeding violations less than 10 mph over and out-of-state speeding violations (except for commercial drivers), suspensions and revocations are not listed on the record. It takes 1 to 3 weeks before new records are available for inquiry.

Searching: Casual requesters can only obtain records with the written permission of the subject. All other requesters must certify for what reason they are obtaining the information and comply with DPPA policies. Request forms can be downloaded from web site. Include the following in your request: full name, date of birth. If for a non-permissible (DPPA) use, then notarized signature of driver needed. A secondary search will be done with the license number if no record is found on the name search. The following data is not released: Social Security Numbers.

Access by: mail, phone, in person, online.

Fee & Payment: The fee is $4.00 per record. The agency charges sales tax, if record request comes from a South Dakota address. Fee payee: Dept of Commerce and Regulation. Prepayment required. Personal checks accepted. No credit cards accepted.

Mail search: Turnaround time: 48 hours. The DL#, name, and DOB are all needed when requesting records via mail. A self addressed stamped envelope is requested.

Phone search: Pre-approved accounts may order via the telephone. This is a very limited access.

In person search: Turnaround time while you wait.

Online search: The system is open for batch requests 24 hours a day. There is a minimum of 250 requests daily. It generally takes 10 minutes to process a batch. The current fee is $4.00 per record and there are some start-up costs. For more information, call 605-773-6883.

Other access: Lists are available to the insurance industry.

Vehicle Ownership & Identification
Vessel Ownership & Registration

Division of Motor Vehicles, Information Section, 445 E Capitol Ave, Pierre, SD 57501-3100; 605-773-3541, 605-773-5129 (Fax), 8AM-5PM.

www.state.sd.us/revenue/motorvcl.htm

Note: The DMV took over the registration and title process for boats in 1992. All boats (except canoes, inflatables, kayaks, sailboards) over 12 ft in length must be titled and registered. Motorized boats 12 foot and under need to be registered.

Indexing & Storage: Records are available for 20 years to present. It takes 2 weeks before new records are available for inquiry.

Searching: The state requires all requests for vehicle related records be on the Division DPPA Form. Casual requesters (individuals) can only obtain information with written permission of the subject. All requests must be in writing.

Access by: mail, in person.

Fee & Payment: The fee for VIN, plate, owner, title, or lien searches is $2.00 per record. A complete title history from microfiche is $5.00. Fee payee: Division of Motor Vehicles. Prepayment required. Personal checks accepted. No credit cards accepted.

Mail search: Turnaround time: 1 day to 1 week. Must provide DPPA request form (details regarding the reasons for requesting the information). A self addressed stamped envelope is requested.

In person search: You may request records in person, but the request must be in writing on the Division DPPA Form.

Accident Reports

Department of Transportation, Accident Records, 700 E. Broadway, Pierre, SD 57501-2586; 605-773-3868, 605-773-4870 (Fax), 8AM-5PM.

Indexing & Storage: Records are available for 10 years to present. It takes 2 weeks from receipt from law enforcement agency before new records are available for inquiry.

Searching: Include the following in your request: full name, date of accident, location of accident.

Access by: mail, in person.

Fee & Payment: The fee is $4.00 per record. Fee payee: Accident Records. Prepayment required. Personal checks accepted. No credit cards accepted.

Mail search: Turnaround time: 5 days. A self addressed stamped envelope is requested.

In person search: Normal turnaround time is immediate if the record is on file.

Legislation Records

South Dakota Legislature, Capitol Bldg - Legislative Research Council, 500 E Capitol Ave, Pierre, SD 57501; 605-773-3251, 605-773-4576 (Fax), 8AM-5PM.

http://legis.state.sd.us

Note: Signed bills are found at the Secretary of State's office, 605-773-3537. Pending legislation may be obtained here during the session.

Indexing & Storage: Records are available from 1951 on. New records are available for inquiry immediately.

Searching: Search by bill number, subject, sponsor or by keyword.

Access by: mail, phone, in person, online.

Fee & Payment: Fees are not charged for documents, unless one purchases a subscription to all the bills or journals.

Mail search: Turnaround time: same day. Single copies of legislation can be requested by mail. No self addressed stamped envelope is required.

Phone search: You may order bills by phone.

In person search: Searching is available in person.

Online search: Information is available at their web site at no charge. The site is very thorough and has enrolled version of bills.

Voter Registration

Records not maintained by a state level agency.

Note: The county auditors hold records. There are no restrictions on usage.

GED Certificates

Department of Labor, AEL/GED/Literacy, 700 Governors Drive, Pierre, SD 57501-2291; 605-773-3101, 605-773-6184 (Fax), 8AM-5PM.

www.state.sd.us/dol/GED/index.html

Note: You may e-mail requests to marcia.hess@state.sd.us.

Indexing & Storage: Records are available from 1942 to present. It takes 6 weeks before new records are available for inquiry.

Searching: The SSN, approximate date of test and DOB are needed to verify a record. In addition, a signed release is required for a copy of a transcript.

Access by: mail, fax, in person.

Fee & Payment: There is no fee for verifications, but a $5.00 fee per transcript. Prepayment required. Personal checks not accepted.

Mail search: Turnaround time: 1 day. No self addressed stamped envelope is required. No fee for mail request.

Fax search: Results will available in 1 hour, but will only send transcript after $5.00 fee received.

In person search: No fee for request. You can wait for results.

Hunting License Information
Fishing License Information

Game, Fish & Parks Department, License Division, 412 W Missouri, Pierre, SD 57501; 605-773-3926, 605-773-5842 (Fax), 8AM-5PM.

www.state.sd.us/gfp

Indexing & Storage: Records are available for current and previous years only.

Searching: Requests must be in writing. They will release address data. The DOB and address are helpful.

Access by: in person.

Fee & Payment: The fee depends on the extent of the names and the search. The state refuses to quote a price at this time.

In person search: There is no fee, if the search request is simple.

Other access: Mailing lists are available, list is $100.00 per 1000 names. They have records for big game licensees.

South Dakota State Licensing Agencies

Licenses Searchable Online

Abstractor Business #1 .... www.state.sd.us/dcr/abstractors/roster.htm
Ambulance Service #20 .... www.state.sd.us/doh/ems/direct.pdf
Animal Remedy (medicine/drug for animals) #19 ... www.state.sd.us/doa/das/hp-af-ar.htm
Architect #23 .... www.state.sd.us/dcr/engineer/Roster/index.cfm
Assessor #23 .... www.state.sd.us/dcr/engineer/Roster/index.cfm
Auctioneer #28 .... www.state.sd.us/dcr/realestate/roster/index.cfm
Bank #2 .... www.state.sd.us/dcr/bank
Barber Shop #4 .... www.state.sd.us/dcr/barber/roster.htm
Counselor #6 .... www.state.sd.us/dcr/counselor/roster.htm
Engineer #23 .... www.state.sd.us/dcr/engineer/Roster/index.cfm
Engineer, Petroleum Environmental #23 .... www.state.sd.us/dcr/engineer/Roster/index.cfm
Fertilizer #19 .... www.state.sd.us/doa/das/hp-fert.htm
Home Inspector #28 .... www.state.sd.us/dcr/realestate/roster/index.cfm
Landscape Architect #23 .... www.state.sd.us/dcr/engineer/Roster/index.cfm
Lobbyist #27 .... www.state.sd.us/sos/lobbyist/lobbyist.htm
Marriage & Family Therapist #6 .... www.state.sd.us/dcr/counselor/roster.htm
Mortgage Broker #2 .... www.state.sd.us/dcr/bank
Mortgage Lender #2 .... www.state.sd.us/dcr/bank
Nurse #11 .... https://www.state.sd.us/applications/bn99/secure/Entry.asp
Nurse-RN #11 .... https://www.state.sd.us/applications/bn99/secure/Entry.asp
Optometrist #9 .... www.odfinder.org/LicSearch.asp
Pesticide Applicator/Dealer #19 .... www.state.sd.us/doa/das/
Petroleum Release Remediator #23 .... www.state.sd.us/dcr/engineer/Roster/index.cfm
Podiatrist #14 .... www.state.sd.us/dcr/podiatry/pod-home.htm
Property Manager #28 .... www.state.sd.us/dcr/realestate/roster/index.cfm
Public Accountant-CPA #3 .... www.state.sd.us/dcr/accountancy/annreg.pdf
Real Estate Broker #28 .... www.state.sd.us/dcr/realestate/roster/index.cfm
Real Estate Salesperson #28 .... www.state.sd.us/dcr/realestate/roster/index.cfm
Remediator #23 .... www.state.sd.us/dcr/engineer/Roster/index.cfm
Surveyor, Land #23 .... www.state.sd.us/dcr/engineer/Roster/index.cfm
Timeshare Real Estate #28 .... www.state.sd.us/dcr/realestate/roster/index.cfm
Waste Water Collection System Operator #12 .... www.state.sd.us/denr/databases/operator/index.cfm
Waste Water Treatment Plant Operator #12 .... www.state.sd.us/denr/databases/operator/index.cfm
Water Distributor #12 .... www.state.sd.us/denr/databases/operator/index.cfm
Water Treatment Operator #39 .... www.state.sd.us/denr/enviro/wastewtr.htm
Water Treatment Plant Operator #12 .... www.state.sd.us/denr/databases/operator/index.cfm
Well Driller #36 .... www.state.sd.us/denr/des/waterrights/drillers.htm

Licensing Quick Finder

Abstractor #1 605-869-2269
Abstractor Business #1 605-869-2269
Acupuncturist #5 605-343-7440
Alcoholic Beverage Distributor #21 605-773-3311
Ambulance Service #20 605-773-4031
Animal Feed Seller/Producer #19 605-773-4432
Animal Remedy (medicine/drug for animals) #19
.... 605-773-4432
Appliance Contractor/Journeyman/Apprentice #34
.... 605-773-3429
Architect #23 605-394-2510
Asbestos Abatement Worker #36 605-773-3153
Assessor #23 605-394-2510
Athletic Trainer #10 605-334-8343
Attorney #32 605-224-7554
Auctioneer #28 605-773-3600
Audiologist #30 605-642-1600
Bail Bond Agent #37 605-773-3513
Bank #2 605-773-3421
Barber #4 605-642-1600
Barber Shop #4 605-642-1600

Beauty Shop/Salon #18 605-773-6193
Brokerage Firm #31 605-733-4013
Bus Driver #17 605-773-6883
Business Opportunities Broker #31 605-733-4823
Chiropractor #5 605-343-7440
Cigarette Wholesaler #21 605-773-3311
Clinical Nurse Specialist #11 605-362-2760
Cosmetologist #18 605-773-6193
Cosmetology Instructor #18 605-773-6193
Cosmetology Salon #18 605-773-6193
Counselor #6 605-331-2927
Court/Shorthand Reporter #38 605-773-3474
Dental Assistant #7 605-224-1282
Dental Hygienist #7 605-224-1282
Dentist #7 605-224-1282
Dietitian/Nutritionist #10 605-334-8343
Drug Wholesaler #13 605-362-2737
Electrical Inspector #33 605-773-3573
Electrician #33 605-773-3573
Emergency Medical Technician #20 605-773-4031
Engineer #23 605-394-2510

Engineer, Petroleum Environment #23 . 605-394-2510
Esthetician #18 605-773-6193
Fertilizer #19 605-773-4432
Franchise Sales #31 605-733-4823
Funeral Director/Embalmer #29 605-642-1600
Funeral Establishment #29 605-642-1600
Funeral Service #15 605-642-1600
Gaming #24 605-773-6050
Hearing Aid Dispenser #30 605-642-1600
Home Inspector #28 605-773-3600
Insurance Agent #17 605-773-3513
Investment Advisor #31 605-733-4013
Land Surveyor #17 605-394-2510
Landscape Architect #23 605-394-2510
Law Enforcement Officer #25 605-773-3584
Livestock Dealer #16 605-773-3321
Loan Production #2 605-773-3421
Lobbyist #27 605-773-5666
Manicurist/Nail Technician #18 605-773-6193
Marriage & Family Therapist #6 605-331-2927
Medical Assistant #10 605-334-8343

Medical Doctor #10	605-334-8343
Midwife Nurse #11	605-362-2760
Milk Grader/Hauler #19	605-773-4294
Milk Tester/Sampler #19	605-773-4294
Mobile Home Contractor #34	605-773-3429
Money Lending License #2	605-773-3421
Money Order Business #2	605-773-3421
Mortgage Broker #2	605-773-3421
Mortgage Lender #2	605-773-3421
Nail Salon #18	605-773-6193
Notary Public #27	605-773-5666
Nurse #11	605-362-2760
Nurse Anesthetist #11	605-362-2760
Nurse-RN #11	605-362-2760
Nurses' Aide #35	605-362-2762
Nurses' Aide Applicant #35	605-339-2071
Nursing Home Administrator #8	605-331-5040
Occupational Therapist/Assistant #10	605-334-8343
Optometrist #9	605-347-2136
Osteopathic Physician #10	605-334-8343
Paramedic #20	605-773-4031
Pesticide Applicator/Dealer #19	605-773-4432

Petroleum Release Remediator #23	605-394-2510
Pharmacist/Pharmacy #13	605-362-2737
Physical Therapist/Assistant #10	605-334-8343
Physician/Medical Assistant #10	605-334-8343
Plumber #34	605-773-3429
Podiatrist #14	605-642-1600
Polygraph Examiner #25	605-773-3584
Property Manager #28	605-773-3600
Psychologist #26	605-642-1600
Public Accountant-CPA #3	605-367-5770
Racing #24	605-773-6050
Radiologist (Chiro.) #5	605-343-7440
Radiology (Dental) #7	605-224-1282
Real Estate Broker #28	605-773-3600
Real Estate Salesperson #28	605-773-3600
Remediator #23	605-394-2510
Respiratory Care Practitioner #10	605-334-8343
School Bus Driver #17	605-773-6883
School Counselor #22	605-773-3553
School Principal/Superintendent #22	605-773-3553
Securities Agent/Broker/Dealer #31	605-733-4013

Sewage & Water Installation Contractor/Installer #34	605-773-3429
Social Worker #15	605-642-1600
Surveyor, Land #23	605-394-2510
Teacher #22	605-773-3553
Timeshare Real Estate #28	605-773-3600
Truck Driver #17	605-773-6883
Veterinarian/Veterinary Technician #16	605-773-3321
Veterinary Corporation #16	605-773-3321
Waste Water Collection System Operator #12	605-773-4208
Waste Water Treatment Plant Operator #12	605-773-4208
Water Conditioning Plumbing Installer #34	605-773-3429
Water Distributor #12	605-773-4208
Water Treatment Operator #39	605-773-4208
Water Treatment Plant Operator #12	605-773-4205
Weapon, Concealed #27	605-773-3537
Well Driller #36	605-773-3153

Licensing Agency Information

#1 Abstractors Board of Examiners, PO Box 187, Kennebec, SD 57544-0187; 605-869-2269, Fax: 605-869-2269.
www.state.sd.us/dcr/abstractors/abst-hom.htm.
Agency email: lctc@wcenet.com.
Search database at
www.state.sd.us/dcr/abstractors/abst-hom.htm

#2 Department of Commerce & Regulation, Division of Banking, 217 1/2 W Missouri, Pierre, SD 57501-4590; 605-773-3421, Fax: 605-773-5367.
www.state.sd.us/dcr/bank
Agency email: judy.keating@state.sd.us.
Search database at www.state.sd.us/dcr/bank

#3 Board of Accountancy, 301 E 14th St, #200, Sioux Falls, SD 57104-5022; 605-367-5770, Fax: 605-367-5773.
www.state.sd.us/dcr/accountancy
Agency email: sdbdact@dtgnet.com.
Search database at www.state.sd.us/dcr/account ancy/annreg.pdf. To search, scroll down through the alphabetical listings.

#4 Board of Barber Examiners, c/o Carol Tellinghuisen, Executive Secretary, 135 E Illinois, Spearfish, SD 57783; 605-642-1600, Fax: 605-642-1756.
www.state.sd.us/dcr/barber/barber-h.htm
Agency email: proflic@rushmore.com.
Search database at
www.state.sd.us/dcr/barber/roster.htm

#5 Board of Chiropractic Examiners, 2603 Ella Lane, Yankton, SD 57078; 605-668-9017, Fax: 605-668-9017.
www.state.sd.us/dcr/chiropractic
Agency email: sdbce@dtgnet.com.

#6 Board of Counselor Examiners, PO Box 1822, Sioux Falls, SD 57101-1822; 605-331-2927, Fax: 605-331-2043.
www.state.sd.us/dcr/counselor/couns-ho.htm
Search database at
www.state.sd.us/dcr/counselor/roster.htm

#7 Board of Dentistry, 106 W Capitol, #7, Pierre, SD 57501; 605-224-1282, Fax: 605-224-7426.
www.state.sd.us/dcr/dentistry/dent-hom.htm

#8 Board of Examiners for Nursing Home Administrators, PO Box 632, Sioux Falls, SD 57101-0632; 605-331-5040, Fax: 605-331-2043.
www.state.sd.us/dcr/nursinghome/

#9 Board of Examiners in Optometry, PO Box 370, Sturgis, SD 57785-0370; 605-347-2136, Fax: 605-347-5823.
www.state.sd.us/dcr/optometry/optom-ho.htm.
Agency email: sdoptbd_99@yahoo.com.
Search database at
www.odfinder.org/LicSearch.asp

#10 Board of Medical & Osteopathic Examiners, 1323 S Minnesota Ave, Sioux Falls, SD 57105-0685; 605-334-8343, Fax: 605-336-0270.
www.state.sd.us/dcr/medical/med-hom.htm.
Agency email: jphalen@sdsma.org.

#11 Board of Nursing, 4300 S Louise Ave, Sioux Falls, SD 57106-3124; 605-362-2760, Fax: 605-362-2768.
www.state.sd.us/dcr/nursing/nurs-hom.htm.
Agency email: carey.duffy@state.sd.us.
Search database at https://www.state.sd.us/applic ations/bn99/secure/Entry.asp. SSN or license number required to search online.

#12 Board of Operator Certification, 523 E Capitol Ave, Foss Bldg, Pierre, SD 57501; 605-773-3754, Fax: 605-773-5286.
www.state.sd.us/denr/enviro/wastewtr.htm.
Agency email: rob.kittay@state.sd.us.
Search database at www.state.sd.us/denr/datab ases/operator/index.cfm

#13 Board of Pharmacy, 4305 S Louise Ave, #104, Sioux Falls, SD 57106-3115; 605-362-2737, Fax: 605-362-2738.
www.state.sd.us/dcr/pharmacy/pharm-ho.htm.
Agency email: dennis.jones@state.sd.us.

#14 Board of Podiatry Examiners, 135 E Illinois, #214, Spearfish, SD 57783; 605-642-1600, Fax: 605-642-1756.
www.state.sd.us/dcr/podiatry/pod-home.htm.
Agency email: proflic@mato.com.
Search database at
www.state.sd.us/dcr/podiatry/pod-home.htm

#15 Board of Social Work Examiners, 135 E Illinois, #214, Spearfish, SD 57783; 605-642-1600, Fax: 605-642-1756.
www.state.sd.us/dcr/socialwork/soc-hom.htm.
Agency email: proflic@mato.com.

#16 Board of Veterinary Medical Examiners, 411 S Fort St, Pierre, SD 57501-4503; 605-773-3321, Fax: 605-773-5459. Agency email: dr.holland@state.sd.us.

#17 Department of Commerce & Regulation, 118 W Capitol Ave, Pierre, SD 57501-2000; 605-773-3178, Fax: 605-773-3018.
www.state.sd.us/dcr.html
Agency email: nancy.carroll@state.sd.us.

#18 Cosmetology Commission, 500 E Capitol, Pierre, SD 57501-5070; 605-773-6193, Fax: 605-773-7175.
www.state.sd.us/dcr/cosmo
Agency email: sdcosmo@sd.cybernex.net.

#19 Department of Agriculture, Division of Ag Services, 523 E Capitol, Foss Bldg, Pierre, SD 57501-3182; 605-773-3724, Fax: 605-773-3481.
www.state.sd.us/doa/das/

#20 Department of Health, Emergency Medical Services, 600 E Capitol Ave, Pierre, SD 57501-3185; 605-773-4031, Fax: 605-773-5904.
www.state.sd.us/doh/ems

#21 Department of Revenue, 445 E Capitol Ave, Pierre, SD 57501-3185; 605-773-3311, Fax: 605-773-5129. www.state.sd.us/revenue

#22 Education & Cultural Affairs Department, Office of Policy & Accountability, 700 Governors Dr, Pierre, SD 57501-2291; 605-773-3553, Fax: 605-773-6139.
www.state.sd.us/deca
Agency email: janelle.toman@state.sd.us.

#23 Engineering, Board of Technical Professions, 2040 W Main St, #304, Rapid City, SD 57702-2447; 605-394-2510, Fax: 605-395-2509.
www.state.sd.us/dcr/engineer. Agency email: ann.whipple@state.sad.us.
Search database at
www.state.sd.us/dcr/engineer/Roster/index.cfm

#24 Gaming Commission, 118 W Capitol, Pierre, SD 57501-5070; 605-773-6050, Fax: 605-773-6053.
www.state.sd.us/dcr/gaming/gam-hom.htm

#25 Law Enforcement Standards & Training Commission, Division of Criminal Justice Training Center, Pierre, SD 57501; 605-773-3584, Fax: 605-773-4629.

#27 Office of Secretary of State, 500 E Capitol Ave, State Capitol Bldg, #204, Pierre, SD 57501-5070; 605-773-3537, Fax: 605-773-6580.
www.state.sd.us/state/executive/sos/SOS.HTM
Notary web site is www.state.sd.us/state/execut ive/sos/Notaries/notarycover.htm

#28 Real Estate Commission, 118 W Capitol, Pierre, SD 57501; 605-773-3600, Fax: 605-773-4356.
www.state.sd.us/dcr/realestate/Real-hom.htm.
Agency email: deejones@state.sd.us.
Search database at
www.state.sd.us/dcr/realestate/roster/index.cfm

#29 Board of Funeral Services, 135 E Illinois, #214, Spearfish, SD 57783; 605-642-1600, Fax: 605-642-1756.
www.state.sd.us/dcr/funeral/fun-hom.htm. Agency email: proflic@mato.com.

#30 Board of Licensing, 135 E Illinois Way, Spearfish, SD 57783-0654; 605-642-1600, Fax: 605-642-1756.
www.state.sd.us/dcr/hearing/hear-hom.htm.
Agency email: proflic@mato.com.

#31 Division of Securities, 118 W Capitol Ave, Pierre, SD 57501-2017; 605-773-4823, Fax: 605-773-5953.
www.state.sd.us/dcr/securities/security.htm.
Agency email: jennifer.deyo@state.sd.us.

#32 State Bar, 222 E Capitol Ave, Pierre, SD 57501-2596; 605-224-7554, Fax: 605-224-0282.
www.sdbar.org. Agency email:
tbarnett@sdbar.org.

#33 Electrical Commission, 118 W Capitol, Pierre, SD 57501-5070; 605-773-3573, Fax: 605-773-6213.
www.state.sd.us/dcr/electrical/ELEC_HOM.htm

#34 Plumbing Commission, 118 W Capitol Ave, Pierre, SD 57501; 605-773-3429, Fax: 605-773-5405.
www.state.sd.us/dcr/plumbing
Agency email: mike.richards@state.sd.us.

#35 Healthcare Administration, Nurses Aide Testing, 804 N Western Av, Souix Falls, SD 57104-2098; 605-339-2071, Fax: 605-339-1354.
www.sdhca.org
Agency email: sdhca@worldnet.att.net.

#36 Department of Environment & Natural Resources, Division of Environmental Svcs, 523 E Capitol Ave, Pierre, SD 57501-3182; 605-773-3153.
www.state.sd.us

#37 Department of Commerce & Regulation, Division of Insurance, 118 W Capitol, Pierre, SD 57501; 605-773-3563, Fax: 605-773-5369.
www.state.sd.us/dcr/insurance

#38 Supreme Court, Unified Judicial Court Administrators Office, Capitol Bldg, 500 E Capitol, Pierre, SD 57501; 605-773-3474, Fax: 605-773-5627.
www.ujs.state.sd.us

#39 Department of Environment & Natural Resources, Division of Environmental Svcs, Drinking Water Program, 523 E Capitol Ave, Pierre, SD 57501; 605-773-4208.
www.state sd.us/denr/enviro

South Dakota Federal Courts

The following list indicates the district and division name for each county in the state. If the bankruptcy court location is different from the district court, then the location of the bankruptcy court appears in parentheses.

County/Court Cross Reference

County	Court	County	Court
Aurora	Sioux Falls	Hyde	Pierre
Beadle	Sioux Falls	Jackson	Pierre
Bennett	Rapid City (Pierre)	Jerauld	Pierre
Bon Homme	Sioux Falls	Jones	Pierre
Brookings	Sioux Falls	Kingsbury	Sioux Falls
Brown	Aberdeen (Pierre)	Lake	Sioux Falls
Brule	Sioux Falls	Lawrence	Rapid City (Pierre)
Buffalo	Pierre	Lincoln	Sioux Falls
Butte	Aberdeen (Pierre)	Lyman	Pierre
Campbell	Aberdeen (Pierre)	Marshall	Aberdeen (Pierre)
Charles Mix	Sioux Falls	McCook	Sioux Falls
Clark	Aberdeen (Pierre)	McPherson	Aberdeen (Pierre)
Clay	Sioux Falls	Meade	Rapid City (Pierre)
Codington	Aberdeen (Pierre)	Mellette	Pierre
Corson	Aberdeen (Pierre)	Miner	Sioux Falls
Custer	Rapid City (Pierre)	Minnehaha	Sioux Falls
Davison	Sioux Falls	Moody	Sioux Falls
Day	Aberdeen (Pierre)	Pennington	Rapid City (Pierre)
Deuel	Aberdeen (Pierre)	Perkins	Rapid City (Pierre)
Dewey	Pierre	Potter	Pierre
Douglas	Sioux Falls	Roberts	Aberdeen (Pierre)
Edmunds	Aberdeen (Pierre)	Sanborn	Sioux Falls
Fall River	Rapid City (Pierre)	Shannon	Rapid City (Pierre)
Faulk	Pierre	Spink	Aberdeen (Pierre)
Grant	Aberdeen (Pierre)	Stanley	Pierre
Gregory	Pierre	Sully	Pierre
Haakon	Pierre	Todd	Pierre
Hamlin	Aberdeen (Pierre)	Tripp	Pierre
Hand	Pierre	Turner	Sioux Falls
Hanson	Sioux Falls	Union	Sioux Falls
Harding	Rapid City (Pierre)	Walworth	Aberdeen (Pierre)
Hughes	Pierre	Yankton	Sioux Falls
Hutchinson	Sioux Falls	Ziebach	Pierre

Standards for Federal Courts: The search fee is $20.00 per item (one party name or case number). Certification fee is $7.00 per document. Copy fee is $.50 per page. All fees standard unless noted in profile. Mail Search: always enclose a stamped self addressed envelope unless otherwise noted. Before releasing records, all courts require prepayment unless noted in profile.

Open records are located at the court unless otherwise noted. District courts index by defendant and plaintiff as well as by case number. Bankruptcy courts usually index by debtor and case number. While most courts now have their indexes on computer, many still maintain index card files as well.

The universal PACER sign-up number is 800-676-6856. Find PACER and the Party/Case Index on the Web at http://pacer.psc.uscourts.gov. PACER dial-up access is $.60 per minute. Also, courts offering internet access via RACER, PACER, Web-PACER or the new CM-ECF charge $.07 per page fee unless noted as free.

US District Court

District of South Dakota

Aberdeen Division c/o Pierre Division, Federal Bldg & Courthouse, 225 S Pierre St, Room 405, Pierre, SD 57501 (Courier Address: Use mail address for courier delivery), 605-224-5849, Fax: 605-224-0806.

www.sdd.uscourts.gov

Counties: Brown, Butte, Campbell, Clark, Codington, Corson, Day, Deuel, Edmunds, Grant, Hamlin, McPherson, Marshall, Roberts, Spink, Walworth. Judge Battey's closed. Case records are located at the Rapid City Division.

Indexing & Storage: New cases are available in the index after filing date. Open records are located at the Pierre Division.

Fee & Payment Notes: Payment may be made by money order, cashier check. Business checks are not accepted. Personal checks are not accepted.

Phone Search: Searching not available by phone.

In Person Search: In person searching available.

PACER:. Case records are available back to 1991. Records are purged every six months. New records are available online after 1 day. PACER is available online at http://pacer.sdd.uscourts.gov. Court does not allow electronic access to criminal cases. Civil document images available.

Other Online Access: Access available on Racer at http://racer.sdd.uscourts.gov/perl/bkplog.html. Includes document images.

Pierre Division Federal Bldg & Courthouse, Room 405, 225 S Pierre St, Pierre, SD 57501 (Courier Address: Use mail address for courier delivery), 605-224-5849, Fax: 605-224-0806.

www.sdd.uscourts.gov

Counties: Buffalo, Dewey, Faulk, Gregory, Haakon, Hand, Hughes, Hyde, Jackson, Jerauld, Jones, Lyman, Mellette, Potter, Stanley, Sully, Todd, Tripp, Ziebach.

Indexing & Storage: Cases are indexed by defendant, plaintiff, and case number. New cases are available in the index 1 day after filing date. Open records are located at this court.

Fee & Payment Notes: Payment may be made by money order, cashier check, personal check. Payee: Clerk, US District Court.

Phone Search: Only docket information is available by phone.

Fax Search: Will accept fax for a price quote only.

In Person Search: In person searching available.

PACER:. Case records are available back to 1991. Records are purged every six months. New records are available online after 1 day. PACER is available online at http://pacer.sdd.uscourts.gov. Court does not allow electronic access to criminal cases. Civil document images available.

Other Online Access: Access available on Racer at http://racer.sdd.uscourts.gov/perl/bkplog.html. $.07 per page fees charged; includes document images.

Rapid City Division Clerk's Office, Room 302, 515 9th St, Rapid City, SD 57701 (Courier Address: Use mail address for courier delivery), 605-342-3066, Fax: 605-343-4367.

www.sdd.uscourts.gov

Counties: Bennett, Custer, Fall River, Harding, Lawrence, Meade, Pennington, Perkins, Shannon. Judge Battey's closed cases are located here.

Indexing & Storage: Cases are indexed by defendant, plaintiff, and case number. New cases are available in the index 24 hours after filing date. Open records are located at this court.

Fee & Payment Notes: Payment may be made by money order, cashier check, business check. Personal checks are not accepted. Payee: Clerk, US District Court.

Phone Search: Only docket information available by telephone.

Mail Search: A stamped self addressed envelope is not required.

In Person Search: In person searching available.

PACER:. Case records are available back to 1991. Records are purged every six months. New records are available online after 1 day. PACER is available online at http://pacer.sdd.uscourts.gov. Court does not allow electronic access to criminal cases. Civil document images available.

Other Online Access: Access available on Racer at http://racer.sdd.uscourts.gov/perl/bkplog.html. $.07 per page fees charged; includes document images.

Sioux Falls Division P.O. Box 5060, Sioux Falls, SD 57117-5060 (Courier Address: Room 128, US Courthouse, 400 S Phillips Ave, Sioux Falls, SD 57104-6851), 605-330-4447, Fax: 605-330-4312.

www.sdd.uscourts.gov

Counties: Aurora, Beadle, Bon Homme, Brookings, Brule, Charles Mix, Clay, Davison, Douglas, Hanson, Hutchinson, Kingsbury, Lake, Lincoln, McCook, Miner, Minnehaha, Moody, Sanborn, Turner, Union, Yankton.

Indexing & Storage: Cases are indexed by defendant, plaintiff, and case number. New cases are available in the index 1 day after filing date. Open records are located at this court.

Fee & Payment Notes: Payment may be made by money order, cashier check, personal check. Payee: Clerk, US District Court.

Phone Search: Only docket information for civil cases will be released over the phone.

Fax Search: To send a fax request, you must set up an account with the court. The fee for a fax request is $15.00 per name and $1.50 per page sent. The fee is $1.50 per page sent.

In Person Search: In person searching available.

PACER:. Case records are available back to 1991. Records are purged every six months. New records are available online after 1 day. PACER is available online at http://pacer.sdd.uscourts.gov. Court does not allow electronic access to criminal cases. Civil document images available.

Other Online Access: Access is also available through Racer at http://racer.sdd.uscourts.gov/perl/bkplog.html; $.07 per page fees charged; includes document images.

US Bankruptcy Court

District of South Dakota

Pierre Division Clerk, Room 203, Federal Bldg, 225 S Pierre St, Pierre, SD 57501 (Courier Address: Use mail address for courier delivery), 605-224-6013, Fax: 605-224-9808.

www.sdb.uscourts.gov

Counties: Bennett, Brown, Buffalo, Butte, Campbell, Clark, Codington, Corson, Custer, Day, Deuel, Dewey, Edmunds, Fall River, Faulk, Grant, Gregory, Haakon, Hamlin, Hand, Harding, Hughes, Hyde, Jackson, Jerauld, Jones, Lawrence, Lyman, Marshall, McPherson, Meade,Mellette, Pennington, Perkins, Potter, Roberts,Shannon, Spink, Stanley, Sully, Todd, Tripp, Walworth, Ziebach.

Indexing & Storage: Cases are indexed by debtor and creditors as well as by case number. New cases are available in the index immediately after

filing date. District wide searches are available for information from 10/1/91 from this court.

Fee & Payment Notes: Payment may be made by money order, cashier check, in-state business check. Personal checks are not accepted. Payee: Clerk, US Bankruptcy Court.

Phone Search: Only docket information is available by phone. An automated voice case information service (VCIS) is available. Call VCIS at 800-768-6218 or 605-330-4559.

Fax Search: Will accept fax searches. Will fax docket listings at no extra charge.

In Person Search: In person searching available.

PACER: Toll-free dial-up access: 800-410-2988. Local dial-up access: 803-765-5965. Case records are available back to October 1, 1991. Records are never purged. New civil records are available online after 1 day. PACER is available online at http://pacer.sdb.uscourts.gov. Document images available.

Electronic Filing: Information is available online at https://ecf.sdb.uscourts.gov

Sioux Falls Division PO Box 5060, Sioux Falls, SD 57117-5060 (Courier Address: Room 104, 400 S Phillips Ave, Sioux Falls, SD 57102), 605-330-4541, Fax: 605-330-4548.

www.sdb.uscourts.gov

Counties: Aurora, Beadle, Bon Homme, Brookings, Brule, Charles Mix, Clay, Davison, Douglas, Hanson, Hutchinson, Kingsbury, Lake, Lincoln, McCook, Miner, Minnehaha, Moody, Sanborn, Turner, Union, Yankton.

Indexing & Storage: Cases are indexed by debtor and creditors as well as by case number. New cases are available in the index 1 day after filing date. District wide searches are available for information from 10/1/91 from this court.

Fee & Payment Notes: Payment may be made by money order, cashier check, in-state business check. Personal checks are not accepted. Payee: Clerk, US Bankruptcy Court.

Phone Search: Only docket information is available by phone. An automated voice case information service (VCIS) is available. Call VCIS at 800-768-6218 or 605-330-4559.

Fax Search: Will accept fax search at $15.00 fee. Will fax docket listing at no extra charge.

In Person Search: In person searching available.

PACER: Toll-free dial-up access: 800-410-2988. Local dial-up access: 803-765-5965. Case records are available back to October 1, 1991. Records are never purged. New civil records are available online after 1 day. PACER is available online at http://pacer.sdb.uscourts.gov. Document images available.

Electronic Filing: Information is available online at https://ecf.sdb.uscourts.gov

South Dakota County Courts

Court	Jurisdiction	No. of Courts	How Organized
Circuit Courts*	General	66	7 Circuits
Magistrate Courts		66	

* Profiled in this Sourcebook.

Court					CIVIL				
	Tort	Contract	Real Estate	Min. Claim	Max. Claim	Small Claims	Estate	Eviction	Domestic Relations
Circuit Courts*	X	X	X	$0	No Max	$8000	X	X	X
Magistrate Courts				$0	$10,000	$8000	X	X	X

Court		CRIMINAL			
	Felony	Misdemeanor	DWI/DUI	Preliminary Hearing	Juvenile
Circuit Courts*	X	X	X	X	X
Magistrate Courts		X	X	X	

ADMINISTRATION

State Court Administrator, State Capitol Building, 500 E Capitol Av, Pierre, SD, 57501; 605-773-3474, Fax: 605-773-5627. www.sdjudicial.com

COURT STRUCTURE

The state re-aligned their circuits from 8 to 7 effective June, 2000.

South Dakota has a statewide criminal record search database, administrated by the State Court Administrator's Office in Pierre. All criminal record information from July 1, 1989 forward, statewide, is contained in the database. To facilitate quicker access for the public, the state has designated 10 county record centers to process all mail or ongoing commercial accounts' criminal record requests. All mail requests are forwarded to, and commercial account requests are assigned to one of 10 specific county court clerks for processing a statewide search. For faster service on mail requests, use Hanson or Miner Counties. Note that walk-in requesters seeking a single or minimum of requests may still obtain a record from their local county court. Five counties (Buffalo, Campbell, Dewey, McPherson, and Ziebach) do not have computer terminals in-house. The criminal records from these counties are entered into the database by court personnel from another location.

The search fee is $15.00 per record. State authorized commercial accounts may order and receive records by fax, there is an additional $5.00 fee unless a non-toll free line is used.

Requesters who wish to set up a commercial account are directed to contact Jill Gusso at the Court Administrator's Office in Pierre at the address mentioned above, or at jill.gusso@ujs.state.sd.us

ONLINE ACCESS

There is no statewide online access computer system currently available. Larger courts are being placed on computer systems at a rate of 4 to 5 courts per year. Access is intended for internal use only. Smaller courts place their information on computer cards that are later sent to Pierre for input by the state office.

ADDITIONAL INFORMATION

Most South Dakota courts do not allow the public to perform searches, but rather require the court clerk to do them for a fee of $15.00 per name (increased from $5.00 as of July 1, 1997). A special Record Search Request Form must be used. Searches will be returned with a disclaimer stating that the clerk is not responsible for the completeness of the search. Clerks are not required to respond to telephone or Fax requests. Many courts are not open all day so they prefer written requests.

Aurora County

Circuit Court PO Box 366, Plankinton, SD 57368; 605-942-7165; Fax: 605-942-7170. Hours: 8AM-Noon, 1-5PM (CST). *Felony, Misdemeanor, Civil, Eviction, Small Claims, Probate.*

Civil Records: Access: Fax, mail, in person. Both court and visitors may perform in person searches. Search fee: $15.00 per name. Required to search: name, years to search; also helpful: address. Civil cases indexed by defendant, plaintiff. Civil records on manual index since 1879, some computerized since 1988.

Criminal Records: Access: Fax, mail, in person. Only the court performs in person searches; visitors may not. Search fee: $15.00 per name. Required to search: name, years to search, signed release; also helpful: address, DOB, SSN. Criminal records are computerized since 07/89 on a statewide system. Mail requests are forwarded to Douglas County for processing.

General Information: No juvenile, sealed, dismissed, adoption or mental health records released. SASE required. Turnaround time 1 day. Fax notes: $1.00 per page to fax back, $5.00 minimum. Copy fee: $.20 per page. Certification fee: $2.00. Fee payee: Aurora County Clerk of Court. Business checks accepted. Prepayment is required.

Beadle County

Circuit Court PO Box 1358, Huron, SD 57350; 605-353-7165. Hours: 8AM-5PM (CST). *Felony, Misdemeanor, Civil, Eviction, Small Claims, Probate.*

Civil Records: Access: Mail, in person. Only the court performs in person searches; visitors may not. Search fee: $15.00 per name. Required to search: name, years to search. Civil cases indexed by defendant, plaintiff. Civil records on computer from 1990 (limited), cards from 1900. Not for public use.

Criminal Records: Access: Mail, in person. Only the court performs in person searches; visitors may not. Search fee: $15.00 per name. Required to search: name, years to search, DOB; also helpful: SSN. Criminal records are computerized since 07/89 on a statewide system. Mail requests are forwarded to Hand County for processing.

General Information: No juvenile, sealed, dismissed, adoption, or mental health records released. Turnaround time up to 2 weeks. Copy fee: $.20 per page. Certification fee: $2.00. Fee payee: Beadle County Clerk of Court. Personal checks accepted. Out of state checks not accepted. Prepayment is required.

Bennett County

Circuit Court PO Box 281, Martin, SD 57551; 605-685-6969. Hours: 8AM-4:30PM (MST). *Felony, Misdemeanor, Civil, Eviction, Small Claims, Probate.*

Civil Records: Access: Mail, in person. Only the court performs in person searches; visitors may not. Search fee: $15.00 per name. Required to search: name, years to search; also helpful: address. Civil cases indexed by defendant, plaintiff. Civil records on index from 1912.

Criminal Records: Access: Mail, in person. Only the court performs in person searches; visitors may not. Search fee: $15.00 per name. Required to search: name, years to search, DOB; also helpful: address. Criminal records are computerized since 07/89 on a statewide system. All mail requests are forwarded to Potter County for processing.

General Information: No juvenile, sealed, dismissed, or mental health records released. SASE required. Turnaround time 48 hours. Application form available. Copy fee: $.20 per page. Certification fee: $3.00. Fee payee: Bennett County Clerk of Courts. Business checks accepted. Prepayment is required.

Bon Homme County

Circuit Court PO Box 6, Tyndall, SD 57066; 605-589-4215; Fax: 605-589-4245. Hours: 8AM-4:30PM (CST). *Felony, Misdemeanor, Civil, Eviction, Small Claims, Probate.*

Civil Records: Access: Fax, mail, in person. Both court and visitors may perform in person searches. Search fee: $15.00 per name. Required to search: name, years to search; also helpful: address. Civil cases indexed by defendant, plaintiff. Civil records on alpha index books from 1877. Requests should be in writing.

Criminal Records: Access: Mail, in person. Only the court performs in person searches; visitors may not. Search fee: $15.00 per name. Required to search: name, years to search, DOB, signed release; also helpful: address, SSN. Criminal records are computerized since 07/89 on a statewide system. All mail requests are forwarded to Douglas County for processing.

General Information: No juvenile, sealed, dismissed, or mental health records released. SASE required. Turnaround time 3 days to 1 week. Fax notes: $1.00 per page. $5.00 minimum, unless call is local or toll free. Copy fee: $.25 per page. Certification fee: $2.00. Fee payee: Bon Homme County Clerk of Court. Personal checks accepted. Prepayment is required.

Brookings County

Circuit Court 314 6th Ave, Brookings, SD 57006; 605-688-4200; Fax: 605-688-4952. Hours: 8AM-5PM (CST). *Felony, Misdemeanor, Civil, Eviction, Small Claims, Probate.*

Civil Records: Access: Mail, in person. Only the court performs in person searches; visitors may not. Search fee: $15.00 per name. Required to search: name, years to search; also helpful: address. Civil cases indexed by defendant, plaintiff. Civil records on alpha index books from 1900s.

Criminal Records: Access: Mail, in person. Only the court performs in person searches; visitors may not. Search fee: $15.00 per name. Required to search: name, years to search, DOB; also helpful: address, SSN. Criminal records on computer since July 1989 on a statewide system. All mail requests are forwarded to Hand County for processing.

General Information: No juvenile, sealed, dismissed, or mental health records released. SASE required. Turnaround time 3 days. Fax notes: Fee to fax results is $1.00 per page; $5.00 minimum. Copy fee: $.20 per page. Certification fee: $2.00. Fee payee: Brookings County Clerk of Court. Only cashiers checks and money orders accepted. Prepayment is required.

Brown County

Circuit Court 101 1st Ave SE, Aberdeen, SD 57401; 605-626-2451; Fax: 605-626-2491. Hours: 8AM-5PM (CST). *Felony, Misdemeanor, Civil, Eviction, Small Claims, Probate.*

Civil Records: Access: Mail, in person. Both court and visitors may perform in person searches. Search fee: $15.00 per name. Required to search: name, years to search; also helpful: address. Civil cases indexed by defendant, plaintiff. Civil records on registers from 1975 (misdemeanor), registers from 1900s (civil).

Criminal Records: Access: Mail, in person. Only the court performs in person searches; visitors may not. Search fee: $15.00 per name. Required to search: name, years to search, DOB; also helpful: address, signed release, SSN. Criminal records on computer since 07/89 on a statewide system. All mail requests are forwarded to Edmunds County for processing.

General Information: No juvenile, sealed, dismissed, or mental health records released. SASE required. Turnaround time 1-3 days. Copy fee: $.20 per page. Certification fee: $2.00. Fee payee: Brown County

Clerk of Court. Personal checks accepted. Prepayment is required.

Brule County

Circuit Court 300 S Courtland #111, Chamberlain, SD 57325-1599; 605-734-4580; Fax: 605-734-5443. Hours: 8AM-Noon, 1-5PM (CST). *Felony, Misdemeanor, Civil, Eviction, Small Claims, Probate.*

Civil Records: Access: Fax, mail, in person. Both court and visitors may perform in person searches. Search fee: $15.00 per name. Required to search: name, years to search; also helpful: address. Civil cases indexed by defendant, plaintiff. Civil records on index books or docket books from 1875.

Criminal Records: Access: Fax, mail, in person. Only the court performs in person searches; visitors may not. Search fee: $15.00 per name. Required to search: name, years to search, DOB; also helpful: address, SSN. Criminal records on computer since July 1989 on a statewide system. All mail requests are forwarded to Miner County for processing. Fax requests accepted for commercial accounts only and are forwarded as well.

General Information: No juvenile, sealed, dismissed, or mental health records released. SASE required. Turnaround time 3-5 days. Fax notes: $1.00 per page. $5.00 minimum. Copy fee: $.20 per page. Certification fee: $2.00. Fee payee: Brule County Clerk of Court. Personal checks accepted. Prepayment is required.

Buffalo County

Circuit Court PO Box 148, Gann Valley, SD 57341; 605-293-3234; Fax: 605-293-3240. Hours: 9AM-Noon (CST). *Felony, Misdemeanor, Civil, Eviction, Small Claims, Probate.*

Note: Only records prior to 2000 are at Gann Valley. Records after 2000 are at the Brule Circuit Court Clerk, 300 S. Courtland #111, Chamberlin SD 57325, 605-734-4586.

Civil Records: Access: Mail, in person. Only the court performs in person searches; visitors may not. Search fee: $15.00 per name. Required to search: name, years to search; also helpful: address. Civil cases indexed by defendant, plaintiff. All data on alpha index from 1915 to 2000 only.

Criminal Records: Access: Mail, in person. Only the court performs in person searches; visitors may not. Search fee: $15.00 per name. Required to search: name, years to search, DOB; also helpful: address, SSN. Criminal records are on books to 2000, but computerized on the statewide computer system since 07/89. All mail requests are forwarded to Miner County for processing.

General Information: No juvenile, sealed, dismissed, or mental health records released. SASE required. Turnaround time 1 week. Copy fee: $.20 per page. Certification fee: $2.00. Fee payee: Buffalo County Clerk of Court. Personal checks accepted. Prepayment is required.

Butte County

Circuit Court PO Box 237, Belle Fourche, SD 57717; 605-892-2516; Fax: 605-892-2836. Hours: 8AM-Noon, 1-5PM (MST). *Felony, Misdemeanor, Civil, Eviction, Small Claims, Probate.*

Civil Records: Access: Mail, in person. Only the court performs in person searches; visitors may not. Search fee: $15.00 per name. Required to search: name, years to search; also helpful: address. Civil cases indexed by defendant, plaintiff. All data on alpha index from 1900s.

Criminal Records: Access: Mail, in person. Only the court performs in person searches; visitors may not. Search fee: $15.00 per name. Required to search: name, years to search; also helpful: address. Criminal records on computer since 07/89 on a statewide system. All mail requests are forwarded to Lawrence County for processing.

General Information: No juvenile, sealed, dismissed, or mental health records released. SASE required. Turnaround time varies. Copy fee: $.20 per page. Certification fee: $2.00. Fee payee: Butte County Clerk of Court. Personal checks accepted. Prepayment is required.

Campbell County

Circuit Court PO Box 146, Mound City, SD 57646; 605-955-3536; Fax: 605-955-3308. Hours: 8AM-Noon T-W-F (CST). *Felony, Misdemeanor, Civil, Small Claims, Probate.*

Civil Records: Access: Mail, in person. Both court and visitors may perform in person searches. Search fee: $15.00 per name. Required to search: name, years to search; also helpful: address. Civil cases indexed by defendant, plaintiff. All data on alpha index from 1800s.
Criminal Records: Access: Mail, in person. Only the court performs in person searches; visitors may not. Search fee: $15.00 per name. Required to search: name, years to search, DOB; also helpful: address, SSN. Although records are computerized at the state level, this office has records and indices on paper. All mail requests are forwarded to Edmunds County for processing.
General Information: No juvenile, sealed, dismissed, or mental health records released. SASE required. Turnaround time varies. Copy fee: $.20 per page. Certification fee: $2.00. Fee payee: Campbell County Clerk of Court. Only cashiers checks and money orders accepted. Prepayment is required.

Charles Mix County

Circuit Court PO Box 640, Lake Andes, SD 57356; 605-487-7511; Fax: 605-487-7547. Hours: 8AM-4:30PM (CST). *Felony, Misdemeanor, Civil, Eviction, Small Claims, Probate.*

Civil Records: Access: Fax, mail, in person. Both court and visitors may perform in person searches. Search fee: $15.00 per name. Required to search: name, years to search; also helpful: address. Civil cases indexed by defendant, plaintiff. Civil records on alpha index books from 1917.
Criminal Records: Access: Fax, mail, in person. Only the court performs in person searches; visitors may not. Search fee: $15.00 per name. Required to search: name, years to search, DOB; also helpful: address, SSN. Criminal records on computer since 07/89 on a statewide system located in Douglas County. All mail and fax requests are forwarded to Douglas County for processing.
General Information: No juvenile, sealed, dismissed, or mental health records released. SASE required. Turnaround time 2-5 days. Fax notes: $1.00 per page. $5.00 minimum. Copy fee: $.20 per page. Certification fee: $2.00. Fee payee: Charles Mix County Clerk of Court. Personal check accepted with SSN or DL#. Prepayment is required.

Clark County

Circuit Court PO Box 294, Clark, SD 57225; 605-532-5851. Hours: 8AM-Noon, 1-5PM (CST). *Felony, Misdemeanor, Civil, Eviction, Small Claims, Probate.*

Civil Records: Access: Mail, in person. Only the court performs in person searches; visitors may not. Search fee: $15.00 per name. Required to search: name, years to search; also helpful: address. Civil cases indexed by defendant, plaintiff. Civil records on alpha index cards from 1969.
Criminal Records: Access: Mail, in person. Only the court performs in person searches; visitors may not. Search fee: $15.00 per name. Required to search: name, years to search, DOB; also helpful: address, SSN. Criminal records on computer since 1986 on a statewide system. All mail requests are forwarded to

Hand County for processing, PO Box 122, Miller, SD 57362-0122.
General Information: No juvenile, sealed, dismissed, or mental health records released. SASE required. Turnaround time 1-4 days. Copy fee: $.20 per page. Certification fee: $2.00. Fee payee: Clark County Clerk of Court. Personal checks accepted. Prepayment is required.

Clay County

Circuit Court PO Box 377, Vermillion, SD 57069; 605-677-6755; Fax: 605-677-8885. Hours: 8AM-5PM (CST). *Felony, Misdemeanor, Civil, Eviction, Small Claims, Probate.*

Civil Records: Access: Mail, in person. Both court and visitors may perform in person searches. Search fee: $15.00 per name. Required to search: name, years to search; also helpful: address. Civil cases indexed by defendant, plaintiff. Civil records on computer from 1993, in books to 1920, and archived from 1800s.
Criminal Records: Access: Mail, in person. Only the court performs in person searches; visitors may not. Search fee: $15.00 per name. Required to search: name, years to search, DOB; also helpful: address, SSN. Criminal records on computer from 1989, in books to 1920, and archived from 1800s. All mail requests are forwarded to Douglas County for processing.
General Information: No juvenile, sealed, dismissed, or mental health records released. SASE required. Turnaround time 2-4 days. Copy fee: $.20 per page. Certification fee: $2.00. Fee payee: Clay County Clerk of Court. Personal checks accepted. Prepayment is required.

Codington County

Circuit Court PO Box 1054, Watertown, SD 57201; 605-882-5095; Fax: 605-882-5106. Hours: 8AM-5PM (CST). *Felony, Misdemeanor, Civil, Eviction, Small Claims, Probate.*

Civil Records: Access: Mail, in person. Only the court performs in person searches; visitors may not. Search fee: $15.00 per name. Required to search: name, years to search. Civil cases indexed by defendant, plaintiff. Civil records on computer from 1991 and alpha index cards back to 1890.
Criminal Records: Access: Mail, in person. Only the court performs in person searches; visitors may not. Search fee: $15.00 per name. Required to search: name, years to search, DOB. Criminal records on computer since 07/89 on a statewide system. Mail requests for dates 1989 to present are forwarded to Hand County for processing. Prior to 1989 processed in Codington County.
General Information: No juvenile, sealed, dismissed, or mental health records released. SASE required. Turnaround time 2 days. Copy fee: $.20 per page. Certification fee: $2.00. Fee payee: Codington County Clerk of Court. Business checks accepted. Prepayment is required.

Corson County

Circuit Court PO Box 175, McIntosh, SD 57641; 605-273-4201; Fax: 605-273-4597. Hours: 9:30AM-2:30PM (MST). *Felony, Misdemeanor, Civil, Eviction, Small Claims, Probate.*

Civil Records: Access: Mail, fax, in person. Both court and visitors may perform in person searches. Search fee: $15.00 per name. Required to search: name, years to search; also helpful: address. Civil cases indexed by defendant, plaintiff. All data on alpha index from 1940s.
Criminal Records: Access: Mail, fax, in person. Only the court performs in person searches; visitors may not. Search fee: $15.00 per name. Required to search: name, years to search, DOB; also helpful: address, SSN. Criminal records on computer back to 1989. All phone

requests are forwarded to Lawrence County for processing.
General Information: No juvenile, sealed, dismissed, adoption or mental health records released. SASE not required. Turnaround time 1 day. Copy fee: $.20 per page. Certification fee: $2.00. Fee payee: Corson County Clerk of Court. Personal checks accepted. Prepayment is required.

Custer County

Circuit Court 420 Mt Rushmore Rd, Custer, SD 57730; 605-673-4816; Fax: 605-673-3416. Hours: 8AM-5PM (MST). *Felony, Misdemeanor, Civil, Eviction, Small Claims, Probate.*

Civil Records: Access: Mail, in person. Only the court performs in person searches; visitors may not. Search fee: $15.00 per name. Required to search: name, years to search, SSN; also helpful: address. Civil cases indexed by defendant, plaintiff. Probate on microfiche from 1915, all other data on docket books and index cards from 1960s.
Criminal Records: Access: Mail, in person. Only the court performs in person searches; visitors may not. Search fee: $15.00 per name. Required to search: name, years to search, DOB, SSN, signed release; also helpful: address. Criminal records on computer since 07/89 on a statewide system. Criminal searches are performed through the Search Center at Harding County Clerk, POB 534, Buffalo, SD 57720.
General Information: No juvenile, sealed, dismissed, or mental health records released. SASE required. Turnaround time 2 days. Copy fee: $.25 per page. Certification fee: $2.00. Fee payee: Custer County Clerk of Court. Personal checks accepted. Prepayment is required.

Davison County

Circuit Court PO Box 927, Mitchell, SD 57301; 605-995-4705; Fax: 605-995-8105. Hours: 8AM-5PM (CST). *Felony, Misdemeanor, Civil, Eviction, Small Claims, Probate.*

Civil Records: Access: Mail, in person. Both court and visitors may perform in person searches. Search fee: $15.00 per name. Required to search: name, years to search; also helpful: address. Civil cases indexed by defendant. All data on alpha index from 1900s.
Criminal Records: Access: Mail, in person. Only the court performs in person searches; visitors may not. Search fee: $15.00 per name. Required to search: name, years to search, DOB; also helpful: address, SSN. Criminal records are computerized since 07/89 on a statewide system. All mail request are forwarded to Miner County for processing.
General Information: No juvenile, sealed, dismissed, or mental health records released. SASE required. Turnaround time 1 week. Copy fee: $.20 per page. Certification fee: $2.00. Fee payee: Davison County Clerk of Court. Personal checks accepted. Out of state checks not accepted. Prepayment is required.

Day County

Circuit Court 710 W 1st St, Webster, SD 57274; 605-345-3771; Fax: 605-345-3818. Hours: 8AM-5PM (CST). *Felony, Misdemeanor, Civil, Small Claims, Probate.*

Civil Records: Access: Mail, in person. Only the court performs in person searches; visitors may not. Search fee: $15.00 per name. Required to search: name, years to search; also helpful: address. Civil cases indexed by defendant. Civil records on docket books from 1800s.
Criminal Records: Access: Mail, in person. Only the court performs in person searches; visitors may not. Search fee: $15.00 per name. Required to search: name, years to search, DOB; also helpful: address, SSN. Criminal records on computer since 1982 on a

statewide system. All mail requests are forwarded to Edmunds County for processing.

General Information: No juvenile, sealed, dismissed, or mental health records released. SASE required. Turnaround time 1 week. Copy fee: $.20 per page. Certification fee: $2.00. Fee payee: Day County Clerk of Court. Prepayment is required.

Deuel County

Circuit Court PO Box 308, Clear Lake, SD 57226; 605-874-2120. Hours: 8AM-5PM (CST). *Felony, Misdemeanor, Civil, Eviction, Small Claims, Probate.*

Civil Records: Access: Mail, in person. Only the court performs in person searches; visitors may not. Search fee: $15.00 per name. Required to search: name, years to search; also helpful: address. Civil cases indexed by defendant, plaintiff. Civil records on docket books from late 1800s.

Criminal Records: Access: Mail, in person. Only the court performs in person searches; visitors may not. Search fee: $15.00 per name. Required to search: name, years to search, DOB, signed release; also helpful: address, SSN. Criminal records on computer since 07/89 on a statewide system. All mail requests are forwarded to Hand County for processing.

General Information: No juvenile, sealed, dismissed, or mental health records released. SASE required. Turnaround time 1-2 days. Copy fee: $.20 per page. Certification fee: $2.00. Fee payee: Deuel County Clerk of Court. Personal checks accepted. Prepayment is required.

Dewey County

Circuit Court PO Box 96, Timber Lake, SD 57656; 605-865-3566. Hours: 9:30AM-Noon, 1-2:30PM (MST). *Felony, Misdemeanor, Civil, Eviction, Small Claims, Probate.*

Civil Records: Access: Mail, in person. Both court and visitors may perform in person searches. Search fee: $15.00 per name. Required to search: name, years to search; also helpful: address. Civil cases indexed by defendant, plaintiff. All data on alpha index and docket books from 1900s; computerized back to 1999.

Criminal Records: Access: Mail, in person. Only the court performs in person searches; visitors may not. Search fee: $15.00 per name. Required to search: name, years to search, DOB; also helpful: address, SSN, signed release. Criminal records data on alpha index and docket books from 1900s; computerized back to 1999. All mail requests are forwarded to Lawrence County for processing.

General Information: No juvenile, adoption, sealed, dismissed, or mental health records released. SASE required. Turnaround time 2 days to 1 week. Fax notes: Fee to fax results is $1.00 per page; $5.00 per document. Copy fee: $.25 per page. Certification fee: $2.00. Fee payee: Dewey County Clerk of Court. Personal checks accepted. Prepayment is required.

Douglas County

Circuit Court PO Box 36, Armour, SD 57313; 605-724-2585. Hours: 8:30AM-1:30PM M-Th (CST). *Felony, Misdemeanor, Civil, Eviction, Small Claims, Probate.*

Civil Records: Access: Mail, in person. Both court and visitors may perform in person searches. Search fee: $15.00 per name. Required to search: name, years to search; also helpful: address. Civil cases indexed by defendant. Civil records on docket books from late 1800s.

Criminal Records: Access: Fax, mail, in person. Only the court performs in person searches; visitors may not. Search fee: $15.00 per name. Required to search: name, years to search, DOB, signed release; also helpful: address, SSN. Criminal records are computerized since

---

07/89 on a statewide system. Fax requests are for commercial accounts only.

General Information: No juvenile, sealed, dismissed, or mental health records released. SASE required. Turnaround time 1-2 weeks. Will release limited civil data over phone. Copy fee: $.25 per page. Certification fee: $2.00. Fee payee: Douglas County Clerk of Court. Personal checks accepted. Prepayment is required.

Edmunds County

Circuit Court PO Box 384, Ipswich, SD 57451; 605-426-6671; Fax: 605-426-6323. Hours: 8AM-Noon, 1-5PM (CST). *Felony, Misdemeanor, Civil, Eviction, Small Claims, Probate.*

Civil Records: Access: Fax, mail, in person. Both court and visitors may perform in person searches. Search fee: $15.00 per name. Required to search: name, years to search; also helpful: address. Civil cases indexed by defendant, plaintiff. Civil records on docket books from late 1800s.

Criminal Records: Access: Fax, mail, in person. Only the court performs in person searches; visitors may not. Search fee: $15.00 per name. Required to search: name, years to search, DOB; also helpful: SSN, signed release. Criminal records on computer since 07/89; prior records on docket books. Fax requests are for commercial accounts only. Results are statewide.

General Information: No juvenile, sealed or mental health records released. SASE required. Turnaround time 1 day to 1 week. Copy fee: $.25 per page. Certification fee: $2.00. Fee payee: Edmunds County Clerk of Court. Personal checks accepted. Prepayment is required.

Fall River County

Circuit Court 906 N River St, Hot Springs, SD 57747; 605-745-5131. Hours: 8AM-5PM (MST). *Felony, Misdemeanor, Civil, Eviction, Small Claims, Probate.*

Note: Also handles cases for Shannon County. Specify which county in any search request.

Civil Records: Access: Mail, in person. Only the court performs in person searches; visitors may not. Search fee: $15.00 per name. Required to search: name, years to search; also helpful: DOB. Civil cases indexed by defendant, plaintiff. Civil records on computer from 1992, files from 1800s archived off site.

Criminal Records: Access: Mail, in person. Only the court performs in person searches; visitors may not. Search fee: $15.00 per name. Required to search: name, years to search, DOB; also helpful: address, SSN. Criminal records on computer since 07/89 on a statewide system.

General Information: No juvenile, sealed, adoption, or mental health records released. SASE required. Turnaround time 1 week. Copy fee: $.25 per page. Certification fee: $2.00. Fee payee: Clerk of Court. Personal checks accepted. Prepayment is required.

Faulk County

Circuit Court PO Box 357, Faulkton, SD 57438; 605-598-6223; Fax: 605-598-6680. Hours: 1:00PM-5:00PM (CST). *Felony, Misdemeanor, Civil, Eviction, Small Claims, Probate.*

Civil Records: Access: Mail, in person. Both court and visitors may perform in person searches. Search fee: $15.00 per name. Required to search: name, years to search; also helpful: address. Civil cases indexed by defendant. Civil records on docket books from 1900s.

Criminal Records: Access: Mail, in person. Only the court performs in person searches; visitors may not. Search fee: $15.00 per name. Required to search: name, years to search, DOB; also helpful: address, SSN. Criminal records are computerized since 07/89 on a statewide system. All mail requests are forwarded to Edmunds County for processing.

General Information: No juvenile, sealed, dismissed, adoption, or mental health records released. SASE required. Turnaround time 2-3 days. Copy fee: $.20 per page. Certification fee: $2.00. Fee payee: Faulk County Clerk of Court. Personal checks accepted. Prepayment is required.

Grant County

Circuit Court PO Box 509, Milbank, SD 57252; 605-432-5482. Hours: 8AM-Noon, 1-5PM (CST). *Felony, Misdemeanor, Civil, Eviction, Small Claims, Probate.*

Civil Records: Access: Mail, in person. Only the court performs in person searches; visitors may not. Search fee: $15.00 per name. Required to search: name, years to search; also helpful: address. Civil cases indexed by defendant, plaintiff. Civil records on computer from 1995, docket books from 1800s.

Criminal Records: Access: Mail, in person. Only the court performs in person searches; visitors may not. Search fee: $15.00 per name. Required to search: name, years to search, DOB; also helpful: address, SSN. Criminal records on computer since 07/89 on a statewide system. All mail requests are forwarded to and processed by Hand County.

General Information: No juvenile, sealed, dismissed, adoption or mental health records released. SASE required. Turnaround time 1 week by mail, immediate by phone if on computer. Copy fee: $.25 per page. Certification fee: $2.00. Fee payee: Grant County Clerk of Court. Prepayment is required.

Gregory County

Circuit Court PO Box 430, Burke, SD 57523; 605-775-2665. Hours: 8AM-Noon, 1-5PM (CST). *Felony, Misdemeanor, Civil, Eviction, Small Claims, Probate.*

Civil Records: Access: Mail, in person. Only the court performs in person searches; visitors may not. Search fee: $15.00 per name. Required to search: name, years to search; also helpful: address. Civil cases indexed by defendant, plaintiff. Civil records on docket books from late 1800s, computerized since 1999.

Criminal Records: Access: Mail, in person. Only the court performs in person searches; visitors may not. Search fee: $15.00 per name. Required to search: name, years to search, DOB, signed release; also helpful: address, SSN. Criminal records on computer back to 07/89 on a statewide system. All mail requests are forwarded to Potter County for processing.

General Information: No juvenile, sealed, dismissed, or mental health records released. SASE required. Turnaround time 1 week. Fax notes: Will fax results for a fee. Copy fee: $.20 per page. Certification fee: $2.00. Fee payee: Gregory County Clerk of Court. Only cashiers checks and money orders accepted. Prepayment is required.

Haakon County

Circuit Court PO Box 70, Philip, SD 57567; 605-859-2627. Hours: 8AM-Noon (MST). *Felony, Misdemeanor, Civil, Eviction, Small Claims, Probate.*

Civil Records: Access: Mail, in person. Only the court performs in person searches; visitors may not. Search fee: $15.00 per name. Required to search: name, years to search; also helpful: address. Civil cases indexed by defendant, plaintiff. Civil records on register from 1915.

Criminal Records: Access: Mail, in person. Only the court performs in person searches; visitors may not. Search fee: $15.00 per name. Required to search: name, years to search, DOB; also helpful: address, SSN. Criminal records are computerized since 07/89 on a statewide system. All mail requests are forwarded to Potter County for processing.

General Information: No juvenile, sealed, dismissed, or mental health records released. SASE required. Turnaround time 1 day. Fax notes: Fee to fax results is

$1.00 per page; $5.00 minimum. Copy fee: $.20 per page. Certification fee: $2.00. Fee payee: Haakon County Clerk of Court. Personal checks accepted. Local checks accepted. Prepayment is required.

Hamlin County

Circuit Court PO Box 256, Hayti, SD 57241; 605-783-3751; Fax: 605-783-3201. Hours: 9AM-Noon, 1-4PM (CST). *Felony, Misdemeanor, Civil, Eviction, Small Claims, Probate.*

Civil Records: Access: Mail, in person. Only the court performs in person searches; visitors may not. Search fee: $15.00 per name. Required to search: name, years to search; also helpful: address. Civil cases indexed by defendant, plaintiff. Civil records on docket books from 1800s.

Criminal Records: Access: Mail, in person. Only the court performs in person searches; visitors may not. Search fee: $15.00 per name. Required to search: name, years to search, DOB; also helpful: address, SSN. Criminal records on computer since 07/89 on a statewide system.

General Information: No juvenile, sealed, dismissed, or mental health records released. SASE required. Turnaround time 1 day. Copy fee: $.20 per page. Certification fee: $2.00. Fee payee: Hamlin County Clerk of Court. Personal checks accepted. Prepayment is required.

Hand County

Circuit Court PO Box 122, Miller, SD 57362; 605-853-3337; Fax: 605-853-3779. Hours: 8AM-5PM (CST). *Felony, Misdemeanor, Civil, Small Claims, Probate.*

Civil Records: Access: Mail, in person. Only the court performs in person searches; visitors may not. Search fee: $15.00 per name. Required to search: name, years to search; also helpful: address. Civil cases indexed by defendant. All data on alpha index and docket books from late 1800s.

Criminal Records: Access: Fax, mail, in person. Only the court performs in person searches; visitors may not. Search fee: $15.00 per name. Required to search: name, years to search, DOB; also helpful: address, SSN. Criminal records on computer since 07/89 on a statewide system. Fax requesting for commercial accounts only.

General Information: No juvenile, sealed, dismissed, or mental health records released. SASE required. Turnaround time 1 day. Copy fee: $.20 per page. Certification fee: $2.00. Fee payee: Hand County Clerk of Court. Business checks accepted. Prepayment is required.

Hanson County

Circuit Court PO Box 127, Alexandria, SD 57311; 605-239-4446; Fax: 605-239-9446. Hours: 8AM-5PM (CST). *Felony, Misdemeanor, Civil, Small Claims, Probate.*

Civil Records: Access: Fax, mail, in person. Only the court performs in person searches; visitors may not. Search fee: $15.00 per name. Required to search: name, years to search; also helpful: address. Civil cases indexed by defendant, plaintiff. Civil records on docket books from 1902; on computer back to 2000.

Criminal Records: Access: Mail, in person. Only the court performs in person searches; visitors may not. Search fee: $15.00 per name. Required to search: name, years to search, DOB; also helpful: address, SSN. Criminal records computerized since 07/89 on a statewide system.

General Information: No juvenile, sealed, dismissed, adoption or mental health records released. SASE required. Turnaround time varies. Fax notes: $5.00 per document. $1.00 per page after 5 pages. Copy fee: $.15 per page. Certification fee: $2.00. Fee payee: Hanson

County Clerk of Court. Personal checks accepted. Prepayment is required.

Harding County

Circuit Court PO Box 534, Buffalo, SD 57720; 605-375-3351. Hours: 9:30AM-Noon, 1-2:30PM (MST). *Felony, Misdemeanor, Civil, Eviction, Small Claims, Probate.*

Note: This court is the designated search center of Harding and Pennington County criminal records. For eviction information the court says to contact Harding County Sheriff, PO Box 207, Buffalo SD 57720.

Civil Records: Access: Mail, in person. Both court and visitors may perform in person searches. Search fee: $15.00 per name. Required to search: name, years to search; also helpful: address. Civil cases indexed by defendant. Civil records in archives from 1909 to 1920, index books from 1920.

Criminal Records: Access: Fax, mail, in person. Only the court performs in person searches; visitors may not. Search fee: $15.00 per name. Required to search: name, years to search, DOB; also helpful: address, SSN. Criminal records are computerized since 07/89 on a statewide system. Fax requests for commercial accounts only.

General Information: No juvenile, sealed, dismissed, or mental health records released. SASE required. Turnaround time 1 week. Fax notes: $1.00 per page. $5.00 minimum, unless call is local or toll free. Copy fee: $.20 per page. Certification fee: $2.00. Fee payee: Harding County Clerk of Court. Personal checks accepted. Prepayment is required.

Hughes County

Circuit Court 104 E Capital, Pierre, SD 57501; 605-773-3713. Hours: 8AM-5PM (CST). *Felony, Misdemeanor, Civil, Eviction, Small Claims, Probate.*

Civil Records: Access: Mail, in person. Only the court performs in person searches; visitors may not. Search fee: $15.00 per name. Required to search: name, years to search; also helpful: address. Civil cases indexed by defendant, plaintiff. Civil records on microfiche from 1948 to 1973. From 1974 forward have hard copy file, starting 1991 index and docketing on computer.

Criminal Records: Access: Mail, in person. Only the court performs in person searches; visitors may not. Search fee: $15.00 per name. Required to search: name, years to search, DOB; also helpful: address. Criminal records on computer since 1988 on a statewide system. All mail requests are forwarded to Potter County for processing.

General Information: No juvenile, adoption, any record sealed by the Court or mental health records released. SASE required. Turnaround time approx 2 days. Copy fee: $.20 per page. Certification fee: $2.00. Fee payee: Hughes County Clerk of Court. Personal checks accepted. Prepayment is required.

Hutchinson County

Circuit Court 140 Euclid Rm 36, Olivet, SD 57052-2103; 605-387-4215; Fax: 605-387-4209. Hours: 8AM-Noon, 1-5PM (CST). *Felony, Misdemeanor, Civil, Eviction, Small Claims, Probate.*

Civil Records: Access: Fax, mail, in person. Only the court performs in person searches; visitors may not. Search fee: $15.00 per name. Required to search: name, years to search; also helpful: address. Civil cases indexed by defendant, plaintiff. Civil records on docket books and index cards from 1800s, on computer since 1994.

Criminal Records: Access: Fax, mail, in person. Only the court performs in person searches; visitors may not. Search fee: $15.00 per name. Required to search: name, years to search, DOB; also helpful: address, SSN. Older records on docket books and index cards, records since 07/89 are computerized on a statewide system. All fax

and mail requests are forwarded to Douglas County for processing.

General Information: No juvenile, sealed, dismissed, adoption or mental health records released. SASE required. Turnaround time 1 day. Fax notes: $5.00 per document. No fee if call is toll free, for commercial accounts only. Copy fee: $.10 per page. Certification fee: $2.00. Fee payee: Hutchinson County Clerk of Court. Business checks accepted. Prepayment is required.

Hyde County

Circuit Court PO Box 306, Highmore, SD 57345; 605-852-2512; Fax: 605-852-2767. Hours: 8AM-12PM (CST). *Felony, Misdemeanor, Civil, Eviction, Small Claims, Probate.*

Civil Records: Access: Fax, mail, in person. Only the court performs in person searches; visitors may not. Search fee: $15.00 per name. Required to search: name, years to search; also helpful: address. Civil cases indexed by defendant, plaintiff. Civil records on docket books from 1920s, computerized from 2000.

Criminal Records: Access: Fax, mail, in person. Only the court performs in person searches; visitors may not. Search fee: $15.00 per name. Required to search: name, years to search, DOB, signed release; also helpful: address, SSN. Criminal records are computerized since 07/89 on a statewide system. All fax and mail requests are forwarded to Potter County for processing.

General Information: No juvenile, sealed, dismissed, or mental health records released. SASE required. Turnaround time 1-3 days. Fax notes: $5.00 per document. There is no fee if call is local or toll free. Copy fee: $.25 per page. Certification fee: $2.00. Fee payee: Hyde County Clerk of Courts. Personal checks accepted. Prepayment is required.

Jackson County

Circuit Court PO Box 128, Kadoka, SD 57543; 605-837-2122. Hours: 8AM-Noon, 1-5PM (MST). *Felony, Misdemeanor, Civil, Eviction, Small Claims, Probate.*

Civil Records: Access: Mail, in person. Only the court performs in person searches; visitors may not. Search fee: $15.00 per name. Required to search: name, years to search; also helpful: address. Civil cases indexed by defendant. Civil records on "Register of Action" from 1915; on comptuer back to 1993.

Criminal Records: Access: Mail, in person. Only the court performs in person searches; visitors may not. Search fee: $15.00 per name. Required to search: name, years to search, DOB; also helpful: address, SSN. Criminal records on computer back to 07/89 on a statewide system; other records go back to 1920. All mail requests are forwarded to Potter County for processing.

General Information: No juvenile, sealed, dismissed, or mental health records released. SASE required. Turnaround time 1-2 days. Copy fee: $.20 per page. Certification fee: $2.00. Fee payee: Jackson County Clerk of Court. Personal checks accepted. Prepayment is required.

Jerauld County

Circuit Court PO Box 435, Wessington Springs, SD 57382; 605-539-1202; Fax: 605-539-1203. Hours: 8AM-5PM (CST). *Felony, Misdemeanor, Civil, Eviction, Small Claims, Probate.*

Civil Records: Access: Mail, in person. Only the court performs in person searches; visitors may not. Search fee: $15.00 per name. Required to search: name, years to search; also helpful: address. Civil cases indexed by defendant. Civil records on docket books from 1900s.

Criminal Records: Access: Fax, mail, in person. Only the court performs in person searches; visitors may not. Search fee: $15.00 per name. Required to search: name, years to search, DOB; also helpful: address, SSN. Criminal records are computerized since 1989 on a statewide system. Fax requesting for commercial accounts only.

General Information: No juvenile, sealed, dismissed, or mental health records released. SASE required. Turnaround time 2 days. Fax notes: $5.00 per page. No fee is call is local or toll free. Copy fee: $.25 per page. Certification fee: $2.00. Fee payee: Jerauld County Clerk of Court. Personal checks accepted. Prepayment is required.

Jones County

Circuit Court PO Box 448, Murdo, SD 57559; 605-669-2361. Hours: 8AM-Noon, 1-5PM (CST). *Felony, Misdemeanor, Civil, Eviction, Small Claims, Probate.*

Note: Criminal cases and records at Potter County.

Civil Records: Access: Mail, in person. Only the court performs in person searches; visitors may not. Search fee: $15.00 per name. Required to search: name, years to search; also helpful: address. Civil cases indexed by defendant, plaintiff. Civil records on docket books from 1900s.

Criminal Records: Access: Mail, in person. Only the court performs in person searches; visitors may not. Search fee: $15.00 per name. Required to search: name, years to search, DOB, SSN; also helpful: address. Criminal records are computerized since 07/89 on a statewide system. Records on books go back to 1917. All requests are forwarded to Potter County for processing.

General Information: No juvenile, sealed, dismissed, or mental health records released. SASE required. Turnaround time 3 days to 1 week. Fax notes: Fee to fax results is $1.00 per page; minimum $5.00. Copy fee: $.20 per page. Certification fee: $2.00. Fee payee: Jones County Clerk of Court (civil cases); Potter County Clerk of Court (criminal cases). Business checks accepted. Prepayment is required.

Kingsbury County

Circuit Court PO Box 176, De Smet, SD 57231-0176; 605-854-3811; Fax: 605-854-3811. Hours: 8AM-Noon, 1-5PM (CST). *Felony, Misdemeanor, Civil, Eviction, Small Claims, Probate.*

Civil Records: Access: Mail, in person. Both court and visitors may perform in person searches. Search fee: $15.00 per name. Required to search: name, years to search; also helpful: address. Civil cases indexed by defendant, plaintiff. Civil records on computer printed index from 1978 and bound books from 1890.

Criminal Records: Access: Mail, in person. Only the court performs in person searches; visitors may not. Search fee: $15.00 per name. Required to search: name, years to search, DOB; also helpful: address, SSN. Criminal records on computer since 07/89 on a statewide system. All mail requests are forwarded to Hand County for processing.

General Information: No juvenile, sealed, dismissed, adoption or mental health records released. SASE required. Turnaround time same day. Copy fee: $.20 per page. Certification fee: $2.00. Fee payee: Kingsbury County Clerk of Court. Personal checks accepted. Prepayment is required.

Lake County

Circuit Court 200 E Center St, Madison, SD 57042; 605-256-5644. Hours: 8AM-Noon, 1-5PM (CST). *Felony, Misdemeanor, Civil, Eviction, Small Claims, Probate.*

Civil Records: Access: Mail, in person. Only the court performs in person searches; visitors may not. Search fee: $15.00 per name. Required to search: name, years to search; also helpful: address. Civil cases indexed by defendant. Civil records on computer from 1985, docket books from 1800s.

Criminal Records: Access: Mail, in person. Only the court performs in person searches; visitors may not. Search fee: $15.00 per name. Required to search: name, years to search, DOB, signed release; also helpful: address, SSN. Criminal records on computer since 1989 on a statewide system; prior records on docket books since 1800s. All mail requests are forwarded to Miner County for processing.

General Information: No juvenile, sealed, dismissed, or mental health records released. SASE required. Turnaround time 1 day. Copy fee: $.20 per page. Certification fee: $2.00. Fee payee: Lake County Clerk of Court. Personal checks accepted. Prepayment is required.

Lawrence County

Circuit Court PO Box 626, Deadwood, SD 57732; 605-578-2040. Hours: 8AM-5PM (MST). *Felony, Misdemeanor, Civil, Eviction, Small Claims, Probate.*

Civil Records: Access: Mail, in person. Only the court performs in person searches; visitors may not. Search fee: $15.00 per name. Required to search: name, years to search; also helpful: address. Civil cases indexed by defendant, plaintiff. Civil records on computer from 1989 and index books from 1800s.

Criminal Records: Access: Fax, mail, in person. Only the court performs in person searches; visitors may not. Search fee: $15.00 per name. Required to search: name, years to search, DOB; also helpful: address, SSN. Criminal records on computer since 07/89 on a statewide system. Fax requesting only available for commercial accounts.

General Information: No juvenile, sealed, dismissed, or mental health records released. SASE required. Turnaround time 2 weeks. Fax notes: $5.00 per document. No fee for local or toll free calls. Copy fee: $.20 per page. Certification fee: $2.00. Fee payee: Lawrence County Clerk of Court. Personal checks accepted. Prepayment is required.

Lincoln County

Circuit Court Clerk of Courts, 100 E 5th St, Canton, SD 57013; 605-987-5891. 8AM-5PM *Felony, Misdemeanor, Civil, Eviction, Small Claims, Probate.*

Civil Records: Access: Mail, in person. Only the court performs in person searches; visitors may not. Search fee: $15.00 per name. Required to search: name, years to search; also helpful: address. Civil cases indexed by defendant, plaintiff. Civil records on docket books from 1900s. Visitor may search written index pre-1993; only the court searches computer records 1994 forward.

Criminal Records: Access: Mail, in person. Only the court performs in person searches; visitors may not. Search fee: $15.00 per name. Required to search: name, years to search, DOB; also helpful: address, SSN. Criminal records on computer since 07/89 on a statewide system. All mail requests are forwarded to Douglas County.

General Information: No juvenile, sealed, dismissed, adoption or mental health records released. SASE required. Turnaround time 2 days, longer for probate. Copy fee: $.20 per page. Certification fee: $2.00. Fee payee: Lincoln County Clerk of Court. Personal checks accepted. Prepayment is required.

Lyman County

Circuit Court PO Box 235, Kennebec, SD 57544; 605-869-2277. Hours: 8AM-5PM (CST). *Felony, Misdemeanor, Civil, Eviction, Small Claims, Probate.*

Civil Records: Access: Mail, in person. Both court and visitors may perform in person searches. Search fee: $15.00 per name. Required to search: name, years to search; also helpful: address. Civil cases indexed by defendant, plaintiff. Civil records on docket books from 1900s; on computer back one year.

Criminal Records: Access: Mail, in person. Only the court performs in person searches; visitors may not. Search fee: $15.00 per name. Required to search: name, years to search, DOB; also helpful: address, SSN. Criminal records on computer since 07/89 on a statewide system. All mail requests forwarded to Potter county for processing.

General Information: No juvenile, sealed, dismissed, or mental health records released. SASE required. Turnaround time 1 week. Fax notes: Fee to fax results is $1.00 per page. Copy fee: $.20 per page. Certification fee: $2.00. Fee payee: Lyman County Clerk of Court. Personal checks accepted. Prepayment is required.

Marshall County

Circuit Court PO Box 130, Britton, SD 57430; 605-448-5213. Hours: 8AM-Noon, 1-5PM (CST). *Felony, Misdemeanor, Civil, Eviction, Small Claims, Probate.*

Civil Records: Access: Mail, in person. Only the court performs in person searches; visitors may not. Search fee: $15.00 per name. Required to search: name, years to search; also helpful: address. Civil cases indexed by defendant, plaintiff. Civil records on docket books from 1800s.

Criminal Records: Access: Phone, mail, in person. Only the court performs in person searches; visitors may not. Search fee: $15.00 per name. Required to search: name, years to search, DOB; also helpful: address, SSN. Criminal records are computerized since 07/89 on a statewide system. All mail requests forwarded to Edmunds County for processing.

General Information: No juvenile, sealed, dismissed, or mental health records released. SASE required. Turnaround time 1 week. Copy fee: $.20 per page. Certification fee: $2.00. Fee payee: Marshall County Clerk of Court. Personal checks accepted. Prepayment is required.

McCook County

Circuit Court PO Box 504, Salem, SD 57058; 605-425-2781; Fax: 605-425-3144. Hours: 8AM-5PM (CST). *Felony, Misdemeanor, Civil, Eviction, Small Claims, Probate.*

Civil Records: Access: Mail, in person. Both court and visitors may perform in person searches. Search fee: $15.00 per name. Required to search: name, years to search; also helpful: address. Civil cases indexed by defendant, plaintiff. Civil records in index and docket books from late 1800s.

Criminal Records: Access: Mail, in person. Only the court performs in person searches; visitors may not. Search fee: $15.00 per name. Required to search: name, years to search, DOB, signed release; also helpful: address, SSN. Criminal records are computerized since 07/89 on a statewide system. All mail requests are forwarded to Miner County for processing. In person requests must be written.

General Information: No juvenile, sealed, dismissed, or mental health records released. SASE required. Turnaround time 1 day. Copy fee: $.20 per page. Certification fee: $2.00. Fee payee: McCook County Clerk of Court. Personal checks accepted. Prepayment is required.

McPherson County

Circuit Court PO Box 248, Leola, SD 57456; 605-439-3361; Fax: 605-439-3394. Hours: 8AM-Noon (CST). *Felony, Misdemeanor, Civil, Eviction, Small Claims, Probate.*

Civil Records: Access: Mail, in person. Both court and visitors may perform in person searches. Search fee: $15.00 per name. Required to search: name, years to search; also helpful: address. Civil cases indexed by defendant, plaintiff. Civil records on register of action from 1910, records are not computerized. There is no fee if case number is known for in person searchers.

Criminal Records: Access: Mail, in person. Only the court performs in person searches; visitors may not. Search fee: $15.00 per name. Required to search: name, years to search, DOB, signed release; also helpful: address, SSN. Criminal records on register of action from 1910, records are not computerized. All mail requests are forwarded to Edmunds County for processing.

General Information: No juvenile, sealed, dismissed, adoption or mental health records released. SASE required. Turnaround time 1 day to 1 week. Copy fee: $.25 per page. Certification fee: $2.00. Fee payee: McPherson County Clerk of Court. Personal checks accepted. Prepayment is required.

Meade County

Circuit Court PO Box 939, Sturgis, SD 57785; 605-347-4411; Fax: 605-347-3526. Hours: 8AM-Noon, 1-5PM (MST). *Felony, Misdemeanor, Civil, Eviction, Small Claims, Probate.*

Civil Records: Access: Mail, in person. Both court and visitors may perform in person searches. Search fee: $15.00 per name. Required to search: name, years to search; also helpful: address. Civil cases indexed by defendant, plaintiff. Civil records on index cards and docket books from 1800s.

Criminal Records: Access: Mail, in person. Only the court performs in person searches; visitors may not. Search fee: $15.00 per name. Required to search: name, years to search, DOB, signed release; also helpful: address, SSN. Criminal records on computer since 07/89 on a statewide system. All mail requests are forwarded to Lawrence County for processing.

General Information: No juvenile, sealed, dismissed, or mental health records released. SASE required. Turnaround time 1 day to 2 weeks. Copy fee: $.20 per page. Certification fee: $2.00. Fee payee: Meade County Clerk of Courts. Personal checks accepted. Prepayment is required.

Mellette County

Circuit Court PO Box 257, White River, SD 57579; 605-259-3230; Fax: 605-259-3194. Hours: 8AM-Noon (CST). *Felony, Misdemeanor, Civil, Eviction, Small Claims, Probate.*

Civil Records: Access: Phone, mail, in person. Both court and visitors may perform in person searches. Search fee: $15.00 per name. Required to search: name, years to search; also helpful: address. Civil cases indexed by defendant. Civil records on index cards and docket books from 1900s.

Criminal Records: Access: Phone, mail, in person. Only the court performs in person searches; visitors may not. Search fee: $15.00 per name. Required to search: name, years to search, DOB, signed release; also helpful: address, SSN. Criminal records are computerized since 07/89 on a statewide system. All mail requests are forwarded to Potter County for processing.

General Information: No juvenile, sealed, dismissed, or mental health records released. SASE not required. Turnaround time 3 days, Probate up to 1 month. Copy fee: $.20 per page. Certification fee: $2.00. Fee payee: Mellette County Clerk of Court. Personal checks accepted. Prepayment is required.

Miner County

Circuit Court PO Box 265, Howard, SD 57349; 605-772-4612; Fax: 605-772-4412. Hours: 8AM-noon; 1-5PM (CST). *Felony, Misdemeanor, Civil, Eviction, Small Claims, Probate.*

Civil Records: Access: Mail, in person. Both court and visitors may perform in person searches. Search fee: $15.00 per name. Required to search: name, years to search. Civil cases indexed by defendant, plaintiff. Civil records on docket books from 1900's.

Criminal Records: Access: Fax, mail, in person. Only the court performs in person searches; visitors may not. Search fee: $15.00 per name. Required to search: name, years to search, DOB; also helpful: SSN. Criminal records are computerized since 1989. This is a statewide search.

General Information: No juvenile, sealed, dismissed or mental health records released. SASE required. Turnaround time 2 days. Fax notes: $5.00 per document. There is no fee is call is local or toll free. Copy fee: $.25 per page. Certification fee: $2.00 per page. Fee payee: Miner County Clerk of Court. Personal checks accepted. Prepayment is required.

Minnehaha County

Circuit Court 425 N Dakota Ave, Sioux Falls, SD 57104; 605-367-5900; Fax: 605-367-5916. Hours: 8AM-5PM (CST). *Felony, Misdemeanor, Civil, Eviction, Small Claims, Probate.*

Civil Records: Access: Mail, in person. Only the court performs in person searches; visitors may not. Search fee: $15.00 per name. Required to search: name, years to search; also helpful: address. Civil cases indexed by defendant, plaintiff. Civil records on computer from 1989, docket books from 1800s.

Criminal Records: Access: Mail, in person. Only the court performs in person searches; visitors may not. Search fee: $15.00 per name. Required to search: name, years to search, DOB, signed release; also helpful: address, SSN. Criminal records on computer since 07/89. All mail requests are forwarded to either Jerauld or Sanborn counties for processing. This is a statewide system.

General Information: No juvenile, sealed, dismissed or mental health records released. SASE required. Turnaround time 2 weeks. Copy fee: $.20 per page. Certification fee: $2.00. Fee payee: Minnehaha County Clerk of Court. Personal checks accepted. Prepayment is required.

Moody County

Circuit Court 101 E Pipestone, Flandreau, SD 57028; 605-997-3181; Fax: 605-997-3861. Hours: 8AM-5PM (CST). *Felony, Misdemeanor, Civil, Eviction, Small Claims, Probate.*

Civil Records: Access: Mail, in person. Only the court performs in person searches; visitors may not. Search fee: $15.00 per name. Required to search: name, years to search; also helpful: address. Civil cases indexed by defendant, plaintiff. Civil records on computer from 1992 and docket books from 1800s.

Criminal Records: Access: Mail, in person. Only the court performs in person searches; visitors may not. Search fee: $15.00 per name. Required to search: name, years to search, DOB; also helpful: address, SSN. Criminal records on computer since 07/89 on a statewide index. All mail requests are forwarded to Miner County of processing.

General Information: No juvenile, sealed, dismissed, adoption or mental health records released. SASE required. Turnaround time 2-3 days. Copy fee: $.20 per page. Certification fee: $2.00. Fee payee: Moody County Clerk of Court. Personal checks accepted. Prepayment is required.

Pennington County

Circuit Court PO Box 230, Rapid City, SD 57709; 605-394-2575. Hours: 8AM-5PM (MST). *Felony, Misdemeanor, Civil, Eviction, Small Claims, Probate.*

Civil Records: Access: Mail, in person. Only the court performs in person searches; visitors may not. Search fee: $15.00 per name. Required to search: name, years to search; also helpful: address. Civil records on computer from 1991, cards and docket books from 1800s.

Criminal Records: Access: Mail, in person. Only the court performs in person searches; visitors may not. Search fee: $15.00 per name. Required to search: name, years to search, DOB; also helpful: address, SSN. Criminal records are computerized since 1989 on a statewide system. If prior to 1989, mail requests should be sent to Pennington County Clerk - arrest date and charge is required to conduct search. If 1989 to present, mail to Harding County Clerk, POB 534, Buffalo, SD 57720, 605-375-3351.

General Information: No juvenile, sealed, dismissed, or mental health records released. SASE required. Turnaround time 2 weeks. Copy fee: $.25 per page. Certification fee: $2.00. Fee payee: Clerk of Courts. Personal checks accepted. Prepayment is required.

Perkins County

Circuit Court PO Box 426, Bison, SD 57620-0426; 605-244-5626; Fax: 605-244-7110. Hours: 8AM-Noon, 1-5PM (MST). *Felony, Misdemeanor, Civil, Eviction, Small Claims, Probate.*

Civil Records: Access: Fax, mail, in person. Both court and visitors may perform in person searches. Search fee: $15.00 per name. Required to search: name, years to search. Civil cases indexed by defendant, plaintiff. Civil records on docket books from 1908; on computer back to 1999.

Criminal Records: Access: Fax, mail, in person. Only the court performs in person searches; visitors may not. Search fee: $15.00 per name. Required to search: name, years to search, DOB, signed release. Criminal records are computerized back to 07/89 on a statewide system. All fax and mail requests are forwarded to Lawrence County for processing.

General Information: No juvenile, sealed or mental health records released. SASE requested. Turnaround time varies. Fax notes: $1.00 per page. $5.00 minimum, no fee for toll free calls. Copy fee: $.25 per page. Certification fee: $2.00. Fee payee: Perkins County Clerk of Courts. Only cashiers checks and money orders accepted. Prepayment is required.

Potter County

Circuit Court 201 S Exene, Gettysburg, SD 57442; 605-765-9472. Hours: 8AM-Noon, 1-5PM (CST). *Felony, Misdemeanor, Civil, Eviction, Small Claims, Probate.*

Civil Records: Access: Mail, in person. Only the court performs in person searches; visitors may not. Search fee: $15.00 per name. Required to search: name, years to search; also helpful: address. Civil cases indexed by defendant, plaintiff. Civil records on index cards and docket books from 1889.

Criminal Records: Access: Fax, mail, in person. Only the court performs in person searches; visitors may not. Search fee: $15.00 per name. Required to search: name, years to search, DOB, signed release; also helpful: address, SSN. Criminal records are indexed on computer since 07/89 on a statewide system.

General Information: No juvenile, sealed, dismissed, adoption or mental health records released. SASE required. Turnaround time 1-2 days. Fax notes: $5.00 per document. Faxing is for commercial accounts only, no fee if call is toll free. Copy fee: $.20 per page. Certification fee: $2.00. Fee payee: Potter County Clerk of Court. Personal checks accepted. Prepayment is required.

Roberts County

Circuit Court 411 2nd Ave E, Sisseton, SD 57262; 605-698-3395; Fax: 605-698-7894. Hours: 8AM-5PM (CST). *Felony, Misdemeanor, Civil, Eviction, Small Claims, Probate.*

Civil Records: Access: Mail, in person. Only the court performs in person searches; visitors may not. Search fee: $15.00 per name. Required to search: name, years to search; also helpful: address. Civil cases indexed by defendant, plaintiff. Civil records on computer from 1992, microfilm from 1920 to 1975 and original files from 1986.

Criminal Records: Access: Mail, in person. Only the court performs in person searches; visitors may not. Search fee: $15.00 per name. Required to search: name, years to search, DOB; also helpful: address, SSN. Criminal records on computer since 1988 on a statewide system. Criminal search requests should be sent to Edmunds County (PO Box 384, Ipswich SD 57451; 605-426-6323 fax) for processing.

General Information: No juvenile, sealed, dismissed, adoption or mental health records released. SASE required. Turnaround time 2-3 days. Copy fee: $.20 per page. Certification fee: $2.00. Fee payee: Roberts County Clerk of Court (or, Edmunds City Clerk, if a criminal search. Personal checks accepted. Prepayment is required.

Sanborn County

Circuit Court PO Box 56, Woonsocket, SD 57385; 605-796-4515; Fax: 605-796-4509. Hours: 8AM-5PM (CST). *Felony, Misdemeanor, Civil, Eviction, Small Claims, Probate.*

Civil Records: Access: Mail, in person. Only the court performs in person searches; visitors may not. Search fee: $15.00 per name. Required to search: name, years to search; also helpful: address. Civil cases indexed by defendant, plaintiff. Civil records on docket books from 1890s.

Criminal Records: Access: Fax, mail, in person. Only the court performs in person searches; visitors may not. Search fee: $15.00 per name. Required to search: name, years to search, DOB; also helpful: address, SSN. Criminal records are computerized since 1989 on a statewide system.

General Information: No juvenile, sealed, dismissed, or mental health records released. SASE required. Turnaround time 1 week. Fax notes: $1.00 per page. $5.00 minimum, no fee if toll free. Copy fee: $.25 per page. Certification fee: $2.00. Fee payee: Sanborn County Clerk of Courts. Personal checks accepted. No two party checks. Prepayment is required.

Shannon County

Circuit Court 906 N River St, Hot Springs, SD 57747; 605-745-5131. Hours: 8AM-5PM (MST). *Felony, Misdemeanor, Civil, Eviction, Small Claims, Probate.*

Note: Also handles cases for Fall River County. Specify which county in your search request.

Civil Records: Access: Mail, in person. Only the court performs in person searches; visitors may not. Search fee: $15.00 per name. Required to search: name, years to search; also helpful: address. Civil cases indexed by defendant, plaintiff. Civil records on computer from 1991, index books from 1889.

Criminal Records: Access: Mail, in person. Only the court performs in person searches; visitors may not. Search fee: $15.00 per name. Required to search: name, years to search, DOB; also helpful: address, SSN. Criminal records on computer since 07/89 on a statewide system. All mail requests are forwarded to Fall River County for processing.

General Information: No juvenile, sealed, adoption, or mental health records released. SASE required. Turnaround time 1 week. Copy fee: $.25 per page. Certification fee: $2.00. Fee payee: Shannon County Clerk of Court. Personal checks accepted. Prepayment is required.

Spink County

Circuit Court 210 E 7th Ave, Redfield, SD 57469; 605-472-4535; Fax: 605-472-4352. Hours: 8AM-5PM (CST). *Felony, Misdemeanor, Civil, Eviction, Small Claims, Probate.*

Civil Records: Access: Phone, fax, mail, in person. Only the court performs in person searches; visitors may not. Search fee: $15.00 per name. Required to search: name, years to search; also helpful: address. Civil cases indexed by defendant, plaintiff. Civil records on docket books from 1882.

Criminal Records: Access: Phone, fax, mail, in person. Only the court performs in person searches; visitors may not. Search fee: $15.00 per name. Required to search: name, years to search, DOB; also helpful: address, SSN. Criminal records on computer since 1988 on a statewide system. All fax and mail requests are forwarded to Edmunds County for processing.

General Information: No juvenile, sealed, dismissed, or mental health records released. SASE required. Turnaround time 1 day. Fax notes: $5.00 per document. No fee if call is toll free, must be a commercial account. Copy fee: $.20 per page. Certification fee: $2.00. Fee payee: Spink County Clerk of Court. Personal checks accepted. Prepayment is required.

Stanley County

Circuit Court PO Box 758, Fort Pierre, SD 57532; 605-223-7735; Fax: 605-223-7738. Hours: 8AM-5PM (CST). *Felony, Misdemeanor, Civil, Eviction, Small Claims, Probate.*

Civil Records: Access: Mail, in person. Both court and visitors may perform in person searches. Search fee: $15.00 per name. Required to search: name, years to search; also helpful: address. Civil cases indexed by defendant, plaintiff. Civil records on docket books from 1973.

Criminal Records: Access: Mail, in person. Only the court performs in person searches; visitors may not. Search fee: $15.00 per name. Required to search: name, years to search, DOB; also helpful: address, SSN. Criminal records on computer since 1989 on a statewide system. All mail requests are forwarded to Potter County for processing.

General Information: No juvenile, sealed, dismissed, or mental health records released. SASE required. Turnaround time 1-2 days. Copy fee: $.20 per page. Certification fee: $2.00. Fee payee: Stanley County Clerk of Court. Personal checks accepted. Prepayment is required.

Sully County

Circuit Court PO Box 188, Onida, SD 57564; 605-258-2535; Fax: 605-258-2270. Hours: 8AM-Noon (CST). *Felony, Misdemeanor, Civil, Eviction, Small Claims, Probate.*

Civil Records: Access: Mail, in person. Only the court performs in person searches; visitors may not. Search fee: $15.00 per name. Required to search: name, years to search; also helpful: address. Civil cases indexed by defendant, plaintiff. Civil records on docket books from 1900s.

Criminal Records: Access: Mail, in person. Only the court performs in person searches; visitors may not. Search fee: $15.00 per name. Required to search: name, years to search; also helpful: address. Criminal records on computer since 07/89 on statewide system; local computer back to 2000. All mail requests are forwarded to Potter County for processing.

General Information: No juvenile, sealed, dismissed, or mental health records released. SASE required. Turnaround time 1-2 days. Copy fee: $.25 per page. Certification fee: $2.00. Fee payee: Sully County Clerk of Court. No personal checks accepted. Prepayment is required.

Todd County

Circuit Court 200 E 3rd St, PO Box 311, Winner, SD 57580; 605-842-2266; Fax: 605-842-2267. Hours: 8AM-5PM (MST). *Felony, Misdemeanor, Civil, Eviction, Small Claims, Probate.*

Civil Records: Access: Mail, in person. Only the court performs in person searches; visitors may not. Search fee: $15.00 per name. Required to search: name, years to search; also helpful: address. Civil cases indexed by defendant, plaintiff. Civil records on docket books from 1920s.

Criminal Records: Access: Mail, in person. Only the court performs in person searches; visitors may not. Search fee: $15.00 per name. Required to search: name, years to search, DOB, signed release; also helpful: address, SSN. Criminal records on computer since 07/89 on statewide system. All mail requests are forwarded to Potter County for processing.

General Information: No juvenile, sealed, dismissed, or mental health records released. SASE required. Turnaround time 2 days. Copy fee: $.20 per page. Certification fee: $2.00. Fee payee: Todd County Clerk of Court. Personal checks accepted. Prepayment is required.

Tripp County

Circuit Court 200 E 3rd St, PO Box 311, Winner, SD 57580; 605-842-2266; Fax: 605-842-2267. Hours: 8AM-5PM (CST). *Felony, Misdemeanor, Civil, Eviction, Small Claims, Probate.*

Civil Records: Access: Mail, in person. Only the court performs in person searches; visitors may not. Search fee: $15.00 per name. Required to search: name, years to search; also helpful: address. Civil cases indexed by defendant, plaintiff. Civil records on docket books from 1920s.

Criminal Records: Access: Mail, in person. Only the court performs in person searches; visitors may not. Search fee: $15.00 per name. Required to search: name, years to search, DOB, signed release; also helpful: address, SSN. Criminal records on computer since 1989 on statewide system. All mail requests are forwarded to Potter County for processing.

General Information: No juvenile, sealed, dismissed, or mental health records released. SASE required. Turnaround time 2 days. Copy fee: $.20 per page. Certification fee: $2.00. Fee payee: Tripp County Clerk of Court. Personal checks accepted. Prepayment is required.

Turner County

Circuit Court PO Box 446, Parker, SD 57053; 605-297-3115; Fax: 605-297-2115. Hours: 8AM-5PM (CST). *Felony, Misdemeanor, Civil, Eviction, Small Claims, Probate.*

Civil Records: Access: Mail, in person. Only the court performs in person searches; visitors may not. Search fee: $15.00 per name. Required to search: name, years to search; also helpful: address. Civil cases indexed by defendant, plaintiff. Civil records on index cards and docket books from 1900s.

Criminal Records: Access: Mail, in person. Only the court performs in person searches; visitors may not. Search fee: $15.00 per name. Required to search: name, years to search, DOB, signed release; also helpful: address, SSN. Criminal records on computer since 07/89 on a statewide system. All mail requests are forwarded to Douglas County for processing.

General Information: No juvenile, sealed, dismissed, or mental health records released. SASE required. Turnaround time 2 days. Fax notes: Fee to fax results is $1.00 per page; $5.00 minimum. Copy fee: $.25 per page. Certification fee: $2.00. Fee payee: Turner County Clerk of Courts. Prepayment is required.

Union County

Circuit Court PO Box 757, Elk Point, SD 57025; 605-356-2132; Fax: 605-356-3687. Hours: 8:30AM-5PM (CST). *Felony, Misdemeanor, Civil, Eviction, Small Claims, Probate.*

Civil Records: Access: Fax, mail, in person. Only the court performs in person searches; visitors may not. Search fee: $15.00 per name. Required to search: name, years to search; also helpful: address. Civil cases indexed by defendant, plaintiff. Civil records on computer from 1990, docket books from 1900s.

Criminal Records: Access: Fax, mail, in person. Only the court performs in person searches; visitors may not. Search fee: $15.00 per name. Required to search: name, years to search, DOB; also helpful: address, SSN. Criminal records on computer since 1988 on a statewide system, on docket books from 1900s. All mail requests for years 1988 to present are forwarded to Douglas County for processing.

General Information: No juvenile, sealed, dismissed, or mental health records released. SASE required. Turnaround time 1-2 days. Fax notes: Fee to fax results is $5.00 or $1.00 per page, whichever is greater. Copy fee: $.20 per page. Certification fee: $2.00. Fee payee: Union County Clerk of Court. Personal checks accepted. Prepayment is required.

Walworth County

Circuit Court PO Box 328, Selby, SD 57472; 605-649-7311; Fax: 605-649-7624. Hours: 8AM-5PM (CST). *Felony, Misdemeanor, Civil, Eviction, Small Claims, Probate.*

Civil Records: Access: Mail, in person. Only the court performs in person searches; visitors may not. Search fee: $15.00 per name. Required to search: name, years to search; also helpful: address. Civil cases indexed by defendant, plaintiff. Civil records on index cards and docket books from 1900s.

Criminal Records: Access: Mail, in person. Only the court performs in person searches; visitors may not. Search fee: $15.00 per name. Required to search: name, years to search, DOB, signed release; also helpful: address, SSN. Criminal records on computer since 07/89 in a statewide system. All mail requests are forwarded to Edmunds County for processing.

General Information: No juvenile, sealed, dismissed, or mental health records released. SASE required. Turnaround time 1-2 days. Copy fee: $.20 per page. Certification fee: $2.00. Fee payee: Walworth County Clerk of Court. Personal checks accepted. Prepayment is required.

Yankton County

Circuit Court PO Box 155, Yankton, SD 57078; 605-668-3080; Fax: 605-668-5411. Hours: 8AM-5PM (CST). *Felony, Misdemeanor, Civil, Small Claims (and Eviction), Probate.*

Civil Records: Access: Mail, in person. Both court and visitors may perform in person searches. Search fee: $15.00 per name. Required to search: name, years to search; also helpful: address. Civil cases indexed by defendant, plaintiff. Civil records on computer from 1991, docket books from 1900s. Visitors only have access to the book index.

Criminal Records: Access: Mail, in person. Both court and visitors may perform in person searches. Search fee: $15.00 per name. Must be a state authorized account. Required to search: name, years to search, DOB; also helpful: address, SSN. Criminal records on computer since 07/89 on a statewide system, Class II offenses not accessible on computer to public. Visitors only have access to the book index. All mail requests are forwarded to Douglas County for processing.

General Information: No juvenile, sealed, dismissed, or mental health records released. SASE required. Turnaround time 1 week. Fax notes: Will fax results for $1 per page, $5 minimum. Copy fee: $.20 per page. Certification fee: $2.00. Fee payee: Yankton County Clerk of Court. Personal checks accepted. Prepayment is required.

Ziebach County

Circuit Court PO Box 306, Dupree, SD 57623; 605-365-5159. Hours: 9:30AM-Noon, 1-2:30PM (MST). *Felony, Misdemeanor, Civil, Eviction, Small Claims, Probate.*

Civil Records: Access: Mail, in person. Only the court performs in person searches; visitors may not. Search fee: $15.00 per name. Required to search: name, years to search; also helpful: address. Civil cases indexed by defendant. Civil records on index books from 1900s.

Criminal Records: Access: Mail, in person. Only the court performs in person searches; visitors may not. Search fee: $15.00 per name. Required to search: name, years to search, DOB; also helpful: address, SSN. Criminal records on index books from 1900s. All mail requests are forwarded to Lawrence County for processing.

General Information: No juvenile, sealed, dismissed, adoption or mental health records released. SASE required. Turnaround time 2-3 days. Copy fee: $.10 per page. Certification fee: $2.00. Fee payee: Ziebach County Clerk of Court. Personal checks accepted. Prepayment is required.

South Dakota Recording Offices

ORGANIZATION: 66 counties, 66 recording offices. The recording officer is. Register of Deeds. 48 counties are in the Central Time Zone (CST) and 18 are in the Mountain Time Zone (MST).

REAL ESTATE RECORDS: Many counties will perform real estate searches. Search fees and copy fees vary. Certification usually costs $1.00 per document.

UCC RECORDS: Financing statements are filed at the state level, except for real estate related collateral, which are filed with the Register of Deeds. All recording offices will perform UCC searches. All counties have access to a statewide database of UCC filings. Use search request form UCC-11. Searches fees are usually $12.00 per debtor name, $10.00 if online. Copy fees are usually $1.00 per page. Certification is $5.00.

TAX LIEN RECORDS: Federal and state tax liens on personal property of businesses are filed with the Secretary of State. Other federal and state tax liens are filed with the county Register of Deeds. Most counties will perform tax lien searches. Search fees and copy fees vary.

OTHER LIENS: Mechanics, motor vehicle, materials.

ONLINE ACCESS: Access to UCC records are available online through the SOS's Fast File Internet Access System at www.state.sd.us/sos/ucc.htm. Registration and annual fee is required. A certified search is also available. A new system named "Expa" is soon to be available for the occasional user.

Aurora County

Register of Deeds, PO Box 397, Plankinton, SD 57368. Register of Deeds, R/E and UCC Recording 605-942-7161; Fax 605-942-7751.
Will search UCC records. Will not search real estate records. **Other Phone Numbers:** Assessor 605-942-7164; Treasurer 605-942-7162; Vital Records 605-942-7161.

Beadle County

Register of Deeds, PO Box 55, Huron, SD 57350-0055. 605-353-8412 R/E Recording: 605-352-3168; Fax 605-353-8402.
Will search UCC records. Will not search real estate records. **Other Phone Numbers:** Assessor 605-353-8408; Treasurer 605-353-8405; Elections 605-353-8400; Vital Records 605-353-8412.

Bennett County

Register of Deeds, PO Box 433, Martin, SD 57551-0433. 605-685-6054; Fax 605-685-6311.
Will search UCC records. Will not search real estate records. **Other Phone Numbers:** Assessor 605-685-6991; Treasurer 605-685-6092.

Bon Homme County

Register of Deeds, PO Box 3, Tyndall, SD 57066. 605-589-4217 R/E Recording: 605-589-3302.
Will search UCC records. UCC search includes tax liens if requested. Will not search real estate records. **Other Phone Numbers:** Assessor 605-589-3462.

Brookings County

Register of Deeds, 314 6th Ave, Courthouse, Brookings, SD 57006-2084. 605-696-8240 R/E Recording: 605-692-2724; Fax 605-696-8245.
Will search UCC records. UCC search includes tax liens if requested. Real estate record owner and mortgage searches available. **Other Phone Numbers:** Assessor 605-696-8220; Treasurer 605-696-8250; Appraiser/Auditor 605-696-8301; Elections 605-696-8220; Vital Records 605-696-8240.

Brown County

Register of Deeds, PO Box 1307, Aberdeen, SD 57402-1307. 605-626-7140 R/E Recording: 605-622-7140; Fax 605-626-4010.
Will search UCC records. Will not search real estate records. **Other sNumbers:** Assessor 605-622-7133.

Brule County

Register of Deeds, 300 S. Courtland, Suite 110, Chamberlain, SD 57325. 605-734-4434; Fax 605-734-4434.
Will search UCC records. Will not search real estate records. **Other Phone Numbers:** Assessor 605-734-4432; Treasurer 605-734-4436; Elections 605-734-4430; Vital Records 605-734-4434.

Buffalo County

Register of Deeds, PO Box 174, Gannvalley, SD 57341. 605-293-3239; Fax 605-293-3240.
Will search UCC records. Will not search real estate records. **Other Phone Numbers:** Assessor 605-293-3236; Treasurer 605-293-3236.

Butte County

Register of Deeds, 839 Fifth Ave, Belle Fourche, SD 57717. 605-892-2912.
Will search UCC records. Will not search real estate records. **Other Phone Numbers:** Assessor 605-892-3950; Treasurer 605-892-4456.

Campbell County

Register of Deeds, PO Box 148, Mound City, SD 57646-0148. Register of Deeds, R/E and UCC Recording 605-955-3505; Fax 605-955-3308.
Will search UCC records. Will not search real estate records. **Other Phone Numbers:** Assessor 605-955-3577; Treasurer 605-955-3388; Appraiser/Auditor 605-955-3577; Elections 605-955-3366; Vital Records 605-955-3505.

Charles Mix County

Register of Deeds, PO Box 206, Lake Andes, SD 57356-0206. Register of Deeds, R/E and UCC Recording 605-487-7141; Fax 605-487-7221.
Will search UCC records. **Other Phone Numbers:** Assessor 605-487-7382; Treasurer 605-487-7142; Elections 605-487-7131; Vital Records 605-487-7141.

Clark County

Register of Deeds, PO Box 294, Clark, SD 57225-0294. 605-532-5363 R/E Recording: 605-632-5363 UCC Recording: 605-632-5363; Fax 605-532-5931.
Will search UCC records. Will not search real estate records. **Other Phone Numbers:** Assessor 605-532-3751; Treasurer 605-532-5911; Elections 605-532-5921; Vital Records 605-632-5363.

Clay County

Register of Deeds, 211 W. Main St, Suite 202, Vermillion, SD 57069. 605-677-7130 R/E Recording: 605-624-2871.
Will search UCC records. UCC search includes tax liens if requested. Will not search real estate records. **Other Phone Numbers:** Assessor 605-677-7140; Treasurer 605-677-7123; Elections 605-677-7120; Vital Records 605-677-7130.

Codington County

Register of Deeds, 14 1st Ave S.E., Watertown, SD 57201-3695. 605-882-6278 R/E Recording: 605-886-4719; Fax 602-882-5230.
Will search UCC records. Will not search real estate records. **Other Phone Numbers:** Assessor 605-886-6274; Treasurer 605-886-6285; Elections 605-882-6297; Vital Records 605-882-6278.

Corson County

Register of Deeds, PO Box 256, McIntosh, SD 57641-0256. 605-273-4395; Fax 605-273-4304.
Will search UCC records. Will not search real estate records. **Other Phone Numbers:** Assessor 605-273-4354; Treasurer 605-273-4552.

Custer County

Register of Deeds, 420 Mount Rushmore Road, Custer, SD 57730-1934. 605-673-2784 R/E Recording: 605-673-8171; Fax 605-673-3439.
Will search UCC records. Will not search real estate records. **Other Phone Numbers:** Assessor 605-673-8172; Treasurer 605-673-8170.

Davison County

Register of Deeds, 200 E. 4th, Courthouse, Mitchell, SD 57301-2692. 605-995-8616 R/E Recording: 605-996-2209; Fax 605-995-8648. www.davisoncounty.org/registerofdeeds.html
Will search UCC records. Tax Lien search available. Will not search real estate records. **Other Phone Numbers:** Assessor 605-995-8613; Treasurer 605-995-8617; Appraiser/Auditor 605-995-8613; Elections 605-995-8608; Vital Records 605-995-8616; Court Clerk 605-995-8105.

Day County

Register of Deeds, 711 W. First St, Webster, SD 57274-1396. Register of Deeds, R/E and UCC Recording 605-345-4162; Fax 605-345-4162.
Will search UCC records. UCC search includes tax liens if requested. Will not search real estate records. **Other Phone Numbers:** Assessor 605-345-3151; Treasurer 605-345-3081; Elections 605-345-3103; Vital Records 605-345-4162.

Deuel County

Register of Deeds, PO Box 307, Clear Lake, SD 57226. Register of Deeds, R/E and UCC Recording 605-874-2268; Fax 605-874-1306.
Will search UCC records. **Other Phone Numbers:** Assessor 605-874-2229; Treasurer 605-874-2483; Elections 605-874-2312; Vital Records 605-874-2268.

Dewey County

Register of Deeds, PO Box 117, Timber Lake, SD 57656-0117. Register of Deeds, R/E and UCC Recording 605-865-3661; Fax 605-865-3691.
Will search UCC records. Will search real estate records. **Other Phone Numbers:** Assessor 605-865-3573; Treasurer 605-865-3501; Appraiser/Auditor 605-865-3730; Elections 605-865-3672; Vital Records 605-865-3661.

Douglas County

Register of Deeds, PO Box 267, Armour, SD 57313-0267. 605-724-2204; Fax 605-724-2204.
Will search UCC records. **Other Phone Numbers:** Assessor 605-724-2688.

Edmunds County

Register of Deeds, PO Box 386, Ipswich, SD 57451-0386. Register of Deeds, R/E and UCC Recording 605-426-6431; Fax 605-426-6257.
Will search UCC records. This agency will not do a tax lien search. Will not search real estate records. **Other Phone Numbers:** Assessor 605-426-6841; Treasurer 605-426-6801; Appraiser/Auditor 605-426-6841; Elections 605-426-6762; Vital Records 605-426-6431.

Fall River County

Register of Deeds, 906 N. River St, Hot Springs, SD 57747. 605-745-5139; Fax 605-745-6835.
Will search UCC records. **Other Phone Numbers:** Assessor 605-745-5136; Treasurer 605-745-5145.

Faulk County

Register of Deeds, PO Box 309, Faulkton, SD 57438. 605-598-6228; Fax 605-598-6680.
Will search UCC records. This agency will not do a tax lien search. Real estate owner, mortgage, and property transfer searches available. **Other Phone Numbers:** Assessor 605-598-6225; Treasurer 605-598-6232; Vital Records 605-598-6228.

Grant County

Register of Deeds, PO Box 587, Milbank, SD 57252. Register of Deeds, R/E and UCC Recording 605-432-4752.
Will search UCC records. UCC search includes tax liens if requested. Will not search real estate records. **Other Phone Numbers:** Assessor 605-432-6532; Treasurer 605-432-5651; Appraiser/Auditor 605-432-6532; Elections 605-432-6711; Vital Records 605-432-4752.

Gregory County

Register of Deeds, PO Box 437, Burke, SD 57523. 605-775-2624; Fax 605-775-2596.
Will search UCC records. Will not search real estate records. **Other Phone Numbers:** Assessor 605-775-2673; Treasurer 605-775-2605.

Haakon County

Register of Deeds, PO Box 100, Philip, SD 57567-0100. 605-859-2785.
Will search UCC records. UCC search includes tax liens if requested. Will not search real estate records. **Other Phone Numbers:** Assessor 605-859-2824; Treasurer 605-859-2612.

Hamlin County

Register of Deeds, PO Box 56, Hayti, SD 57241. 605-783-3206.
This agency will not perform searches. **Other Phone Numbers:** Assessor 605-783-3331; Treasurer 605-783-3441.

Hand County

Register of Deeds, 415 W. 1st Ave, Miller, SD 57362-1346. Register of Deeds, R/E and UCC Recording 605-853-3512; Fax 605-853-2769.
Will search UCC records. Will not search real estate records. **Other Phone Numbers:** Assessor 605-853-2115; Treasurer 605-853-2136; Appraiser/Auditor 605-853-2182; Vital Records 605-853-3512.

Hanson County

Register of Deeds, PO Box 500, Alexandria, SD 57311-0500. Register of Deeds, R/E and UCC Recording 605-239-4512; Fax 605-239-4296.
Will search UCC records. **Other Phone Numbers:** Assessor 605-239-4445; Treasurer 605-239-4723; Appraiser/Auditor 605-239-4445; Elections 605-239-4714; Vital Records 605-239-4512.

Harding County

Register of Deeds, PO Box 101, Buffalo, SD 57720. 605-375-3321; Fax 605-375-3318.
Will search UCC records. Tax liens not included in UCC search. Real estate record owner and mortgage searches available. **Other Phone Numbers:** Assessor 605-375-3234; Treasurer 605-375-3542.

Hughes County

Register of Deeds, 104 E. Capital, Pierre, SD 57501. 605-773-7495 R/E Recording: 605-224-7891; Fax 605-773-7479.
Will search UCC records. Will search real estate records. **Other Phone Numbers:** Assessor 605-224-5883; Treasurer 605-224-9231; Elections 605-773-7451; Vital Records 605-773-7495.

Hutchinson County

Register of Deeds, 140 Euclid St, Room 37, Olivet, SD 57052-2103. 605-387-4217 R/E Recording: 605-387-2838; Fax 605-387-4209.
Will search UCC records. Will not search real estate records. **Other Phone Numbers:** Assessor 605-387-4210; Treasurer 605-387-4213; Appraiser/Auditor 605-387-4210; Elections 605-387-4217.

Hyde County

Register of Deeds, PO Box 342, Highmore, SD 57345. 605-852-2517.
Will search UCC records. UCC search includes tax liens if requested. Will not search real estate records. **Other Phone Numbers:** Assessor 605-852-2570; Treasurer 605-852-2510.

Jackson County

Register of Deeds, PO Box 248, Kadoka, SD 57453. 605-837-2420.
Will search UCC records. UCC search includes tax liens if requested. Will not search real estate records. **Other Phone Numbers:** Assessor 605-837-2424; Treasurer 605-837-2423.

Jerauld County

Register of Deeds, PO Box 452, Wessington Springs, SD 57382-0452. 605-539-1221.
Will search UCC records. UCC search includes tax liens if requested. Real estate owner, mortgage, and property transfer searches available. **Other Phones:** Assessor 605-539-9701; Treasurer 605-539-1241.

Jones County

Register of Deeds, PO Box 446, Murdo, SD 57559. 605-669-2132.
Will search UCC records. UCC search includes tax liens if requested. Will not search real estate records. **Other Phone Numbers:** Assessor 605-669-2122; Treasurer 605-669-2122.

Kingsbury County

Register of Deeds, PO Box 146, De Smet, SD 57231-0146. 605-854-3591; Fax 605-854-3833.
Will search UCC records. Will not search real estate records. **Other Phones:** Assessor 605-854-3593; Treasurer 605-854-3411; Elections 605-854-3832.

Lake County

Register of Deeds, PO Box 266, Madison, SD 57042. 605-256-7614 R/E Recording: 605-256-2068; Fax 605-256-7622.
Will search UCC records. **Other Phone Numbers:** Assessor 605-256-7605; Treasurer 605-256-7618.

Lawrence County

Register of Deeds, PO Box 565, Deadwood, SD 57732. 605-578-3930.
Will search UCC records. Tax liens not included in UCC search. Real estate record owner searches available. **Other Phone Numbers:** Assessor 605-578-3680.

Lincoln County

Register of Deeds, 100 E. 5th, Canton, SD 57013-1789. Register of Deeds, R/E and UCC Recording 605-764-5661; Fax 605-764-5932.
Will search UCC records. UCC search includes tax liens if requested. Real estate owner, mortgage, and property transfer searches available. **Other Phone Numbers:** Assessor 605-764-2571; Treasurer 605-764-5701; Elections 605-764-2581; Vital Records 605-764-5661.

Lyman County

Register of Deeds, PO Box 98, Kennebec, SD 57544-0098. Register of Deeds, R/E and UCC Recording 605-869-2297; Fax 605-869-2203.
Will search UCC records. **Other Phone Numbers:** Assessor 605-869-2206; Treasurer 605-869-2295; Appraiser/Auditor 605-869-2206; Elections 605-869-2247; Vital Records 605-869-2297.

Marshall County

Register of Deeds, PO Box 130, Britton, SD 57430. Register of Deeds, R/E and UCC Recording 605-448-2352; Fax 605-448-2116.
Will search UCC records. Will not search real estate records unless provided with legal description. **Other Phone Numbers:** Assessor 605-448-5291; Treasurer 605-448-2451; Elections 605-448-2401; Vital Records 605-448-2352.

McCook County

Register of Deeds, PO Box 338, Salem, SD 57058-0338. 605-425-2701; Fax 605-425-2534.
Will search UCC records. Tax liens not included in UCC search. Real estate record owner searches available. **Other Phone Numbers:** Assessor 605-425-2681; Treasurer 605-425-2721.

McPherson County

Register of Deeds, PO Box 129, Leola, SD 57456. 605-439-3151; Fax 605-439-3394.
Will search UCC records. Will not search real estate records. **Other Phone Numbers:** Assessor 605-439-3663; Treasurer 605-439-3544.

Meade County

Register of Deeds, 1425 Sherman St, Sturgis, SD 57785. 605-347-2356; Fax 605-347-5925.
Will search UCC records. Will not search real estate records. **Other Phone Numbers:** Assessor 605-347-3818; Treasurer 605-347-5871.

Mellette County

Register of Deeds, PO Box 183, White River, SD 57579-0183. 605-259-3371.
Will search UCC records. UCC search includes tax liens if requested. Real estate record owner and mortgage searches available. **Other Phone Numbers:** Assessor 605-259-3150; Treasurer 605-259-3151.

Miner County

Register of Deeds, PO Box 546, Howard, SD 57349. 605-772-5621;   Fax   605-772-4148. www.howardsd.com
Will search UCC records. **Other Phone Numbers:** Assessor 605-772-4241; Treasurer 605-772-4652.

Minnehaha County

Register of Deeds, 415 North Dakota Ave, Sioux Falls, SD 57104-2465. Register of Deeds, R/E and UCC Recording 605-367-4223; Fax 605-367-8314.
Will search UCC records. UCC search includes federal tax liens only. Will not search real estate records. **Other Phone Numbers:** Assessor 605-367-4228; Treasurer 605-367-4212; Appraiser/Auditor 605-367-4228; Elections 605-367-4220; Vital Records 605-367-4223.

Moody County

Register of Deeds, PO Box 247, Flandreau, SD 57028-0247. Register of Deeds, R/E and UCC Recording 605-997-3151.
Will search UCC records. This agency will not do a tax lien search. Will not search real estate records. **Other Phone Numbers:** Assessor 605-997-3101; Treasurer 605-997-3171.

Pennington County

Register of Deeds, 315 St. Joe St, Rapid City, SD 57701. Register of Deeds, R/E and UCC Recording 605-394-2177.
Will search UCC records. Tax liens not included in UCC search. Real estate record owner searches available. **Other Phone Numbers:** Assessor 605-394-2175; Treasurer 605-394-2161; Elections 605-394-2153; Vital Records 605-394-2177.

Perkins County

Register of Deeds, PO Box 127, Bison, SD 57620. Register of Deeds, R/E and UCC Recording 605-244-5620; Fax 605-244-7289.
Will search UCC records. **Other Phone Numbers:** Assessor 605-244-5623; Treasurer 605-244-5613.

Potter County

Register of Deeds, 201 S. Exene, Gettysburg, SD 57442. 605-765-9467; Fax 605-765-2836.
Will search UCC records. Will not search real estate records. **Other Phone Numbers:** Assessor 605-765-2481; Treasurer 605-765-9403; Elections 605-765-9408; Vital Records 605-765-9467.

Roberts County

Register of Deeds, 411 E. 2nd Ave, Sisseton, SD 57262. 605-698-7152.
Will search UCC records. UCC search includes tax liens if requested. Mortgage searches available. **Other Phone Numbers:** Assessor 605-698-3205; Treasurer 605-698-7245.

Sanborn County

Register of Deeds, PO Box 295, Woonsocket, SD 57385. 605-796-4516; Fax 605-796-4509.
Will search UCC records. Will not search real estate records. **Other Phone Numbers:** Assessor 605-796-4514; Treasurer 605-796-4512.

Shannon County

Register of Deeds, 906 N. River St, Hot Springs, SD 57747. 605-745-5139.
Will search UCC records. UCC search includes tax liens if requested. No separate searches. Real estate owner, mortgage, and property transfer searches available. **Other Phone Numbers:** Assessor 605-745-5141; Treasurer 605-745-5145.

Spink County

Register of Deeds, PO Box 266, Redfield, SD 57469-0266. Register of Deeds, R/E and UCC Recording 605-472-0150; Fax 605-472-2410.
Will search UCC records. **Other Phone Numbers:** Assessor 605-472-2891; Treasurer 605-472-0880; Elections 605-472-1825; Vital Records 605-472-0150.

Stanley County

Register of Deeds, PO Box 596, Fort Pierre, SD 57532. Register of Deeds, R/E and UCC Recording 605-223-2610; Fax 605-223-9948.
Will search UCC records. UCC search includes tax liens if requested. Real estate owner, mortgage, and property transfer searches available. **Other Phones:** Assessor 605-223-2746; Treasurer 605-223-2648; Elections 605-223-2673; Vital Records 605-223-2610.

Sully County

Register of Deeds, PO Box 265, Onida, SD 57564. Register of Deeds, R/E and UCC Recording 605-258-2331; Fax 605-258-2884.

Will search UCC records. Will not search real estate records. **Other Phone Numbers:** Assessor 605-258-2522; Treasurer 605-258-2444; Appraiser/Auditor 605-258-2522; Elections 605-258-2541; Vital Records 605-258-2331.

Todd County

Register of Deeds, 200 E 3rd St, 200 E. 3rd St., Winner, SD 57580-1806. 605-842-2208; Fax 605-842-3621.
Will search UCC records. **Other Phone Numbers:** Assessor 605-856-4633; Treasurer 605-842-1700.

Tripp County

Register of Deeds, 200 E 3rd St, Courthouse, 200 E. 3rd St., Winner, SD 57580-1806. 605-842-2208; Fax 605-842-3621.
Will search UCC records. Property transfer searches available. **Other Phone Numbers:** Assessor 605-842-2300; Treasurer 605-842-1700.

Turner County

Register of Deeds, PO Box 485, Parker, SD 57053-0485. 605-297-3443; Fax 605-297-5556.
Will search UCC records. Will not search real estate records. **Other Phone Numbers:** Assessor 605-297-4420; Treasurer 605-297-4425.

Union County

Register of Deeds, PO Box 490, Elk Point, SD 57025-0490. 605-356-2191 R/E Recording: 605-356-2041; Fax 605-356-3047.
Will search UCC records. Will not search real estate records. **Other Phone Numbers:** Assessor 605-356-2252; Treasurer 605-356-2391; Elections 605-356-2101; Vital Records 605-356-2191.

Walworth County

Register of Deeds, PO Box 159, Selby, SD 57472-0159. 605-649-7057 R/E Recording: 605-649-7311; Fax 605-649-7867.
Will search UCC records. This agency will not do a tax lien search. Real estate record owner and mortgage searches available. **Other Phone Numbers:** Assessor 605-649-7737; Treasurer 605-649-7737.

Yankton County

Register of Deeds, PO Box 694, Yankton, SD 57078. 605-665-2422 R/E Recording: 605-65-2422; Fax 605-668-9682.
Will search UCC records. Tax liens not included in UCC search. Will not search real estate records for last deed of record only. **Other Phone Numbers:** Assessor 605-665-5962; Treasurer 605-665-2143.

Ziebach County

Register of Deeds, PO Box 68, Dupree, SD 57623. 605-365-5165.
Will search UCC records. This agency will not do a tax lien search. Will not search real estate records. **Other Phone Numbers:** Assessor 605-365-5129; Treasurer 605-365-5173.

South Dakota County Locator

You will usually be able to find the city name in the City/County Cross Reference below. In that case, it is a simple matter to determine the county from the cross reference. However, only the official US Postal Service city names are included in this index. There are an additional 40,000 place names that people use in their addresses. Therefore, we have also included a ZIP/City Cross Reference immediately following the City/County Cross Reference.

If you know the ZIP Code but the city name does not appear in the City/County Cross Reference index, look up the ZIP Code in the ZIP/City Cross Reference, find the city name, then look up the city name in the City/County Cross Reference. For example, you want to know the county for an address of Menands, NY 12204. There is no "Menands" in the City/County Cross Reference. The ZIP/City Cross Reference shows that ZIP Codes 12201-12288 are for the city of Albany. Looking back in the City/County Cross Reference, Albany is in Albany County.

City/County Cross Reference

ABERDEEN Brown
AGAR Sully
AKASKA Walworth
ALCESTER (57001) Union(94), Lincoln(5)
ALEXANDRIA (57311) Hanson(97), Hutchinson(1)
ALLEN Bennett
ALPENA (57312) Jerauld(58), Beadle(40), Sanborn(2)
AMHERST (57421) Marshall(91), Brown(8)
ANDOVER (57422) Day(95), Brown(4)
ARDMORE Fall River
ARLINGTON (57212) Kingsbury(69), Brookings(26), Hamlin(3)
ARMOUR (57313) Douglas(79), Charles Mix(20)
ARTESIAN Sanborn
ASHTON (57424) Spink(93), Faulk(6)
ASTORIA (57213) Deuel(77), Brookings(22)
AURORA (57002) Brookings(95), Moody(4)
AVON (57315) Bon Homme(98), Charles Mix(1)
BADGER Kingsbury
BALTIC Minnehaha
BANCROFT Kingsbury
BARNARD Brown
BATESLAND (57716) Shannon(90), Bennett(10)
BATH Brown
BEAVER CREEK Tripp
BELLE FOURCHE Butte
BELVIDERE (57521) Jackson(68), Mellette(32)
BERESFORD (57004) Union(62), Lincoln(29), Clay(8)
BETHLEHEM Meade
BIG STONE CITY (57216) Grant(86), Roberts(13)
BISON Perkins
BLACK HAWK (57718) Meade(98), Pennington(1)
BLUNT (57522) Hughes(90), Sully(9)
BONESTEEL Gregory
BOWDLE (57428) Edmunds(79), Walworth(20)
BOX ELDER (57719) Pennington(84), Meade(15)
BRADLEY Clark
BRANDON Minnehaha
BRANDT Deuel
BRENTFORD Spink
BRIDGEWATER (57319) McCook(71), Turner(14), Hutchinson(13)
BRISTOL Day
BRITTON Marshall
BROOKINGS Brookings
BRUCE Brookings
BRYANT (57221) Hamlin(85), Clark(11), Kingsbury(3)
BUFFALO Harding
BUFFALO GAP (57722) Custer(70), Fall River(21), Shannon(7)
BUFFALO RIDGE Minnehaha

BULLHEAD Corson
BURBANK (57010) Clay(72), Union(27)
BURKE Gregory
CAMP CROOK Harding
CANISTOTA McCook
CANOVA (57321) Hanson(46), Miner(43), McCook(10)
CANTON Lincoln
CAPUTA Pennington
CARPENTER (57322) Beadle(42), Clark(37), Spink(20)
CARTER (57526) Tripp(75), Todd(18), Mellette(5)
CARTHAGE (57323) Miner(90), Kingsbury(8)
CASTLEWOOD (57223) Hamlin(97), Deuel(2)
CAVOUR Beadle
CEDARBUTTE Mellette
CENTERVILLE (57014) Turner(72), Clay(14), Lincoln(13)
CHAMBERLAIN Brule
CHANCELLOR (57015) Turner(96), Minnehaha(3)
CHERRY CREEK Ziebach
CHESTER (57016) Lake(93), Minnehaha(6)
CLAIRE CITY Roberts
CLAREMONT (57432) Brown(81), Marshall(18)
CLARK (57225) Clark(90), Deuel(9)
CLEAR LAKE (57226) Deuel(96), Hamlin(3)
COLMAN (57017) Moody(95), Lake(4)
COLOME Tripp
COLTON (57018) Minnehaha(94), Lake(5)
COLUMBIA Brown
CONDE (57434) Spink(67), Brown(16), Day(8), Clark(7)
CORONA (57227) Roberts(94), Grant(5)
CORSICA Douglas
CORSON Minnehaha
CREIGHTON Pennington
CRESBARD (57435) Faulk(90), Edmunds(9)
CROCKER Clark
CROOKS Minnehaha
CUSTER (57730) Custer(96), Pennington(3)
DALLAS (57529) Tripp(54), Gregory(45)
DANTE Charles Mix
DAVIS (57021) Turner(98), Lincoln(1)
DE SMET Kingsbury
DEADWOOD Lawrence
DELL RAPIDS (57022) Minnehaha(80), Moody(19)
DELMONT (57330) Douglas(72), Charles Mix(18), Hutchinson(8)
DIMOCK (57331) Hutchinson(66), Douglas(18), Davison(15)
DOLAND Spink
DRAPER (57531) Jones(98), Lyman(1)
DUPREE (57623) Ziebach(90), Dewey(9)
EAGLE BUTTE Dewey

EDEN (57232) Marshall(97), Day(2)
EDGEMONT (57735) Custer(61), Fall River(38)
EGAN Moody
ELK POINT Union
ELKTON (57026) Brookings(76), Moody(23)
ELLSWORTH AFB Meade
ELM SPRINGS Meade
EMERY (57332) Hutchinson(46), Hanson(40), McCook(13)
ENNING Meade
ERWIN (57233) Kingsbury(96), Hamlin(3)
ESTELLINE (57234) Hamlin(65), Deuel(31), Brookings(2)
ETHAN (57334) Davison(64), Hanson(25), Hutchinson(9)
EUREKA (57437) McPherson(75), Campbell(24)
FAIRBURN Custer
FAIRFAX Gregory
FAIRVIEW Lincoln
FAITH (57626) Meade(51), Perkins(42), Ziebach(5)
FAULKTON Faulk
FEDORA (57337) Miner(94), Sanborn(5)
FERNEY Brown
FIRESTEEL (57628) Corson(50), Dewey(50)
FLANDREAU Moody
FLORENCE (57235) Codington(93), Day(6)
FORT MEADE Meade
FORT PIERRE (57532) Stanley(98), Lyman(1)
FORT THOMPSON Buffalo
FRANKFORT Spink
FREDERICK Brown
FREEMAN (57029) Hutchinson(75), Turner(24)
FRUITDALE Butte
FULTON (57340) Hanson(90), Miner(9)
GANN VALLEY (57341) Buffalo(96), Brule(3)
GARDEN CITY Clark
GARRETSON Minnehaha
GARY Deuel
GAYVILLE (57031) Yankton(80), Clay(19)
GEDDES (57342) Charles Mix(98), Douglas(1)
GETTYSBURG (57442) Potter(96), Dewey(2), Sully(1)
GLAD VALLEY Ziebach
GLENCROSS (57630) Dewey(91), Corson(8)
GLENHAM (57631) Walworth(92), Campbell(7)
GOODWIN (57238) Deuel(69), Codington(25), Hamlin(3)
GREGORY Gregory
GRENVILLE Day
GROTON Brown
HAMILL (57534) Tripp(88), Lyman(11)
HARRISBURG Lincoln
HARRISON Douglas

HARROLD (57536) Hughes(85), Sully(12), Hyde(2)
HARTFORD Minnehaha
HAYES (57537) Stanley(92), Haakon(7)
HAYTI Hamlin
HAZEL (57242) Hamlin(78), Codington(21)
HECLA Brown
HENRY (57243) Codington(95), Clark(4)
HERMOSA (57744) Custer(50), Pennington(47), Shannon(1)
HERREID Campbell
HERRICK Gregory
HETLAND Kingsbury
HIGHMORE (57345) Hyde(95), Faulk(4)
HILL CITY Pennington
HITCHCOCK (57348) Beadle(65), Spink(34)
HOLABIRD Hyde
HOSMER (57448) Edmunds(76), McPherson(23)
HOT SPRINGS (57747) Fall River(97), Custer(2)
HOUGHTON Brown
HOVEN (57450) Potter(59), Walworth(40)
HOWARD Miner
HOWES Meade
HUDSON (57034) Lincoln(94), Union(5)
HUMBOLDT (57035) Minnehaha(97), McCook(2)
HURLEY Turner
HURON Beadle
IDEAL Tripp
INTERIOR (57750) Jackson(93), Pennington(6)
IONA (57542) Lyman(98), Gregory(1)
IPSWICH Edmunds
IRENE (57037) Yankton(68), Turner(18), Clay(13)
IROQUOIS (57353) Kingsbury(65), Beadle(32), Clark(1)
ISABEL (57633) Dewey(64), Corson(30), Ziebach(5)
JAVA (57452) Walworth(74), Campbell(26)
JEFFERSON Union
KADOKA Jackson
KAYLOR Hutchinson
KELDRON Corson
KENNEBEC (57544) Lyman(98), Tripp(1)
KEYSTONE Pennington
KIMBALL (57355) Jerauld(56), Brule(40), Buffalo(2)
KRANZBURG Codington
KYLE (57752) Shannon(88), Jackson(11)
LABOLT Grant
LAKE ANDES Charles Mix
LAKE CITY Marshall
LAKE NORDEN (57248) Hamlin(86), Kingsbury(13)
LAKE PRESTON Kingsbury
LANE Jerauld
LANGFORD (57454) Marshall(79), Day(20)
LANTRY Dewey
LEAD Lawrence
LEBANON Potter

LEMMON (57638) Perkins(97), Corson(2)
LENNOX (57039) Lincoln(94), Turner(5)
LEOLA (57456) McPherson(98), Edmunds(1)
LESTERVILLE (57040) Yankton(95), Bon Homme(4)
LETCHER (57359) Sanborn(76), Aurora(11), Davison(10), Jerauld(1)
LINN (57483) Hand(48), Faulk(35), Spink(16)
LITTLE EAGLE Corson
LODGEPOLE Perkins
LONG VALLEY Jackson
LONGLAKE McPherson
LOWER BRULE Lyman
LUDLOW Harding
LYONS Minnehaha
MADISON Lake
MAHTO Corson
MANDERSON Shannon
MANSFIELD (57460) Brown(60), Spink(19), Faulk(10), Edmunds(9)
MARCUS Meade
MARION (57043) Turner(94), McCook(3), Hutchinson(1)
MARTIN Bennett
MARTY Charles Mix
MARVIN (57251) Grant(96), Roberts(3)
MC INTOSH Corson
MC LAUGHLIN Corson
MEADOW (57644) Perkins(79), Corson(14), Ziebach(5)
MECKLING Clay
MELLETTE (57461) Spink(98), Brown(2)
MENNO (57045) Hutchinson(85), Yankton(12), Turner(1)
MIDLAND (57552) Haakon(49), Stanley(33), Jackson(10), Mellette(5)
MILBANK Grant
MILESVILLE Haakon
MILLER (57362) Hand(98), Buffalo(1)
MINA (57462) Edmunds(86), Brown(13)
MISSION Todd
MISSION HILL Yankton
MISSION RIDGE Stanley
MITCHELL (57301) Davison(98), Hanson(1)
MOBRIDGE Walworth
MONROE (57047) McCook(61), Turner(38)
MONTROSE (57048) McCook(89), Minnehaha(9)
MORRISTOWN (57645) Corson(84), Grant(15)
MOUND CITY Campbell
MOUNT VERNON (57363) Davison(91), Aurora(4), Sanborn(3)
MUD BUTTE (57758) Meade(80), Perkins(16), Butte(3)
MURDO (57559) Jones(94), Mellette(5)
NEMO Lawrence
NEW EFFINGTON Roberts
NEW HOLLAND Douglas
NEW UNDERWOOD (57761) Pennington(59), Meade(40)

NEWELL (57760) Butte(95), Harding(3), Meade(1)
NISLAND Butte
NORRIS (57560) Mellette(59), Bennett(33), Jackson(7)
NORTH SIOUX CITY Union
NORTHVILLE (57465) Spink(60), Faulk(39)
NUNDA Lake
OACOMA Lyman
OELRICHS Fall River
OGLALA Shannon
OKATON Jones
OKREEK Todd
OLDHAM (57051) Kingsbury(91), Miner(5), Lake(3)
OLIVET Hutchinson
ONAKA (57466) Faulk(79), Edmunds(17), Potter(2)
ONIDA (57564) Sully(97), Hyde(2)
OPAL Meade
ORAL Fall River
ORIENT (57467) Hand(68), Faulk(31)
ORTLEY (57256) Grant(66), Roberts(20), Day(7), Codington(6)
OWANKA (57767) Pennington(63), Meade(36)
PARADE Dewey
PARKER (57053) Turner(95), McCook(3), Minnehaha(1)
PARKSTON (57366) Hutchinson(94), Douglas(5)
PARMELEE (57566) Todd(75), Mellette(25)
PEEVER Roberts
PHILIP (57567) Haakon(77), Jackson(22)
PICKSTOWN Charles Mix
PIEDMONT Meade
PIERPONT Day
PIERRE (57501) Hughes(96), Sully(3)
PINE RIDGE Shannon
PLANKINTON Aurora
PLATTE (57369) Charles Mix(95), Aurora(2), Douglas(2)
POLLOCK Campbell
PORCUPINE Shannon
PRAIRIE CITY (57649) Perkins(89), Harding(10)
PRESHO Lyman
PRINGLE Custer
PROVO Fall River
PUKWANA (57370) Brule(83), Buffalo(16)
QUINN (57775) Pennington(71), Haakon(18), Jackson(10)
RALPH Harding
RAMONA (57054) Lake(96), Kingsbury(2)
RAPID CITY Pennington
RAVINIA Charles Mix
RAYMOND (57258) Clark(87), Spink(12)
RED OWL Meade
REDFIELD (57469) Spink(96), Hand(3)
REDIG Harding
REE HEIGHTS (57371) Hand(95), Hyde(2), Buffalo(1)
RELIANCE Lyman
RENNER Minnehaha

REVA (57651) Harding(66), Perkins(33)
REVILLO (57259) Grant(68), Deuel(31)
RIDGEVIEW Dewey
ROCHFORD Pennington
ROCKHAM (57470) Faulk(54), Hand(45)
ROSCOE Edmunds
ROSEBUD Todd
ROSHOLT Roberts
ROSLYN (57261) Day(98), Marshall(1)
ROWENA Minnehaha
RUTLAND (57057) Lake(98), Moody(1)
SAINT CHARLES Gregory
SAINT FRANCIS Todd
SAINT LAWRENCE Hand
SAINT ONGE (57779) Lawrence(92), Butte(7)
SALEM (57058) McCook(93), Miner(5)
SCENIC (57780) Pennington(94), Shannon(6)
SCOTLAND (57059) Bon Homme(88), Hutchinson(11)
SELBY Walworth
SENECA (57473) Faulk(75), Potter(24)
SHADEHILL Perkins
SHERMAN Minnehaha
SINAI Brookings
SIOUX FALLS Minnehaha
SISSETON (57262) Roberts(95), Marshall(4)
SMITHWICK Fall River
SOUTH SHORE (57263) Codington(79), Grant(20)
SPEARFISH Lawrence
SPENCER (57374) Hanson(52), McCook(47)
SPRINGFIELD Bon Homme
STEPHAN Hyde
STICKNEY (57375) Aurora(96), Davison(2)
STOCKHOLM (57264) Grant(98), Codington(1)
STRANDBURG (57265) Grant(70), Deuel(26), Codington(4)
STRATFORD (57474) Brown(93), Spink(6)
STURGIS (57785) Meade(98), Lawrence(1)
SUMMIT (57266) Grant(55), Roberts(44)
TABOR (57063) Bon Homme(84), Yankton(15)
TEA (57064) Lincoln(96), Turner(3)
TIMBER LAKE Dewey
TOLSTOY (57475) Potter(59), Edmunds(39)
TORONTO (57268) Deuel(75), Brookings(24)
TRAIL CITY (57657) Corson(90), Dewey(9)
TRENT Moody
TRIPP (57376) Hutchinson(86), Bon Homme(12), Charles Mix(1)
TULARE (57476) Spink(86), Hand(13)
TURTON Spink
TUTHILL Bennett
TWIN BROOKS Grant
TYNDALL Bon Homme
UNION CENTER Meade
UTICA Yankton

VALE (57788) Meade(64), Butte(35)
VALLEY SPRINGS Minnehaha
VEBLEN (57270) Marshall(91), Roberts(8)
VERMILLION Clay
VIBORG (57070) Turner(92), Yankton(7)
VIENNA (57271) Clark(77), Hamlin(22)
VIRGIL (57379) Beadle(80), Jerauld(20)
VIVIAN (57576) Lyman(91), Jones(8)
VOLGA (57071) Brookings(92), Lake(5), Moody(1)
VOLIN (57072) Yankton(78), Clay(21)
WAGNER Charles Mix
WAKONDA (57073) Clay(94), Turner(5)
WAKPALA Corson
WALKER Corson
WALL Pennington
WALLACE (57272) Codington(87), Clark(10), Day(2)
WANBLEE (57577) Jackson(96), Bennett(3)
WARD Moody
WARNER Brown
WASTA (57791) Pennington(74), Meade(25)
WATAUGA Corson
WATERTOWN Codington
WAUBAY (57273) Day(93), Roberts(6)
WAVERLY Codington
WEBSTER (57274) Day(98), Clark(1)
WENTWORTH (57075) Lake(98), Moody(1)
WESSINGTON (57381) Beadle(60), Hand(39)
WESSINGTON SPRINGS (57382) Jerauld(93), Aurora(4), Beadle(2)
WESTPORT (57481) Brown(59), McPherson(29), Edmunds(10)
WEWELA Tripp
WHITE Brookings
WHITE LAKE (57383) Aurora(98), Brule(1)
WHITE OWL Meade
WHITE RIVER Mellette
WHITEHORSE Dewey
WHITEWOOD (57793) Lawrence(83), Meade(16)
WILLOW LAKE Clark
WILMOT Roberts
WINFRED (57076) Miner(51), Lake(48)
WINNER Tripp
WITTEN Tripp
WOLSEY Beadle
WOOD Mellette
WOONSOCKET (57385) Sanborn(83), Jerauld(14), Aurora(1)
WORTHING Lincoln
WOUNDED KNEE Shannon
YALE Beadle
YANKTON Yankton
ZEONA (57795) Perkins(66), Butte(33)

ZIP/City Cross Reference

57001-57001 ALCESTER	57201-57201 WATERTOWN	57331-57331 DIMOCK	57456-57456 LEOLA
57002-57002 AURORA	57202-57202 WAVERLY	57332-57332 EMERY	57457-57457 LONGLAKE
57003-57003 BALTIC	57212-57212 ARLINGTON	57334-57334 ETHAN	57460-57460 MANSFIELD
57004-57004 BERESFORD	57213-57213 ASTORIA	57335-57335 FAIRFAX	57461-57461 MELLETTE
57005-57005 BRANDON	57214-57214 BADGER	57337-57337 FEDORA	57462-57462 MINA
57006-57007 BROOKINGS	57216-57216 BIG STONE CITY	57339-57339 FORT THOMPSON	57465-57465 NORTHVILLE
57010-57010 BURBANK	57217-57217 BRADLEY	57340-57340 FULTON	57466-57466 ONAKA
57012-57012 CANISTOTA	57218-57218 BRANDT	57341-57341 GANN VALLEY	57467-57467 ORIENT
57013-57013 CANTON	57219-57219 BRISTOL	57342-57342 GEDDES	57468-57468 PIERPONT
57014-57014 CENTERVILLE	57220-57220 BRUCE	57344-57344 HARRISON	57469-57469 REDFIELD
57015-57015 CHANCELLOR	57221-57221 BRYANT	57345-57345 HIGHMORE	57470-57470 ROCKHAM
57016-57016 CHESTER	57223-57223 CASTLEWOOD	57346-57346 STEPHAN	57471-57471 ROSCOE
57017-57017 COLMAN	57224-57224 CLAIRE CITY	57348-57348 HITCHCOCK	57472-57472 SELBY
57018-57018 COLTON	57225-57225 CLARK	57349-57349 HOWARD	57473-57473 SENECA
57019-57019 CORSON	57226-57226 CLEAR LAKE	57350-57350 HURON	57474-57474 STRATFORD
57020-57020 CROOKS	57227-57227 CORONA	57353-57353 IROQUOIS	57475-57475 TOLSTOY
57021-57021 DAVIS	57229-57229 CROCKER	57354-57354 KAYLOR	57476-57476 TULARE
57022-57022 DELL RAPIDS	57231-57231 DE SMET	57355-57355 KIMBALL	57477-57477 TURTON
57024-57024 EGAN	57232-57232 EDEN	57356-57356 LAKE ANDES	57479-57479 WARNER
57025-57025 ELK POINT	57233-57233 ERWIN	57357-57357 RAVINIA	57481-57481 WESTPORT
57026-57026 ELKTON	57234-57234 ESTELLINE	57358-57358 LANE	57483-57483 LINN
57027-57027 FAIRVIEW	57235-57235 FLORENCE	57359-57359 LETCHER	57501-57501 PIERRE
57028-57028 FLANDREAU	57236-57236 GARDEN CITY	57361-57361 MARTY	57520-57520 AGAR
57029-57029 FREEMAN	57237-57237 GARY	57362-57362 MILLER	57521-57521 BELVIDERE
57030-57030 GARRETSON	57238-57238 GOODWIN	57363-57363 MOUNT VERNON	57522-57522 BLUNT
57031-57031 GAYVILLE	57239-57239 GRENVILLE	57364-57364 NEW HOLLAND	57523-57523 BURKE
57032-57032 HARRISBURG	57241-57241 HAYTI	57365-57365 OACOMA	57526-57526 CARTER
57033-57033 HARTFORD	57242-57242 HAZEL	57366-57366 PARKSTON	57527-57527 CEDARBUTTE
57034-57034 HUDSON	57243-57243 HENRY	57367-57367 PICKSTOWN	57528-57528 COLOME
57035-57035 HUMBOLDT	57244-57244 HETLAND	57368-57368 PLANKINTON	57529-57529 DALLAS
57036-57036 HURLEY	57245-57245 KRANZBURG	57369-57369 PLATTE	57531-57531 DRAPER
57037-57037 IRENE	57246-57246 LABOLT	57370-57370 PUKWANA	57532-57532 FORT PIERRE
57038-57038 JEFFERSON	57247-57247 LAKE CITY	57371-57371 REE HEIGHTS	57533-57533 GREGORY
57039-57039 LENNOX	57248-57248 LAKE NORDEN	57373-57373 SAINT LAWRENCE	57534-57534 HAMILL
57040-57040 LESTERVILLE	57249-57249 LAKE PRESTON	57374-57374 SPENCER	57536-57536 HARROLD
57041-57041 LYONS	57251-57251 MARVIN	57375-57375 STICKNEY	57537-57537 HAYES
57042-57042 MADISON	57252-57253 MILBANK	57376-57376 TRIPP	57538-57538 HERRICK
57043-57043 MARION	57255-57255 NEW EFFINGTON	57379-57379 VIRGIL	57540-57540 HOLABIRD
57044-57044 MECKLING	57256-57256 ORTLEY	57380-57380 WAGNER	57541-57541 IDEAL
57045-57045 MENNO	57257-57257 PEEVER	57381-57381 WESSINGTON	57542-57542 IONA
57046-57046 MISSION HILL	57258-57258 RAYMOND	57382-57382 WESSINGTON SPRINGS	57543-57543 KADOKA
57047-57047 MONROE	57259-57259 REVILLO	57383-57383 WHITE LAKE	57544-57544 KENNEBEC
57048-57048 MONTROSE	57260-57260 ROSHOLT	57384-57384 WOLSEY	57545-57545 BEAVER CREEK
57049-57049 NORTH SIOUX CITY	57261-57261 ROSLYN	57385-57385 WOONSOCKET	57547-57547 LONG VALLEY
57050-57050 NUNDA	57262-57262 SISSETON	57386-57386 YALE	57548-57548 LOWER BRULE
57051-57051 OLDHAM	57263-57263 SOUTH SHORE	57399-57399 HURON	57551-57551 MARTIN
57052-57052 OLIVET	57264-57264 STOCKHOLM	57401-57402 ABERDEEN	57552-57552 MIDLAND
57053-57053 PARKER	57265-57265 STRANDBURG	57420-57420 AKASKA	57553-57553 MILESVILLE
57054-57054 RAMONA	57266-57266 SUMMIT	57421-57421 AMHERST	57555-57555 MISSION
57055-57055 RENNER	57268-57268 TORONTO	57422-57422 ANDOVER	57557-57557 MISSION RIDGE
57056-57056 ROWENA	57269-57269 TWIN BROOKS	57424-57424 ASHTON	57559-57559 MURDO
57057-57057 RUTLAND	57270-57270 VEBLEN	57426-57426 BARNARD	57560-57560 NORRIS
57058-57058 SALEM	57271-57271 VIENNA	57427-57427 BATH	57562-57562 OKATON
57059-57059 SCOTLAND	57272-57272 WALLACE	57428-57428 BOWDLE	57563-57563 OKREEK
57060-57060 SHERMAN	57273-57273 WAUBAY	57429-57429 BRENTFORD	57564-57564 ONIDA
57061-57061 SINAI	57274-57274 WEBSTER	57430-57430 BRITTON	57566-57566 PARMELEE
57062-57062 SPRINGFIELD	57276-57276 WHITE	57432-57432 CLAREMONT	57567-57567 PHILIP
57063-57063 TABOR	57278-57278 WILLOW LAKE	57433-57433 COLUMBIA	57568-57568 PRESHO
57064-57064 TEA	57279-57279 WILMOT	57434-57434 CONDE	57569-57569 RELIANCE
57065-57065 TRENT	57301-57301 MITCHELL	57435-57435 CRESBARD	57570-57570 ROSEBUD
57066-57066 TYNDALL	57311-57311 ALEXANDRIA	57436-57436 DOLAND	57571-57571 SAINT CHARLES
57067-57067 UTICA	57312-57312 ALPENA	57437-57437 EUREKA	57572-57572 SAINT FRANCIS
57068-57068 VALLEY SPRINGS	57313-57313 ARMOUR	57438-57438 FAULKTON	57574-57574 TUTHILL
57069-57069 VERMILLION	57314-57314 ARTESIAN	57439-57439 FERNEY	57576-57576 VIVIAN
57070-57070 VIBORG	57315-57315 AVON	57440-57440 FRANKFORT	57577-57577 WANBLEE
57071-57071 VOLGA	57316-57316 BANCROFT	57441-57441 FREDERICK	57578-57578 WEWELA
57072-57072 VOLIN	57317-57317 BONESTEEL	57442-57442 GETTYSBURG	57579-57579 WHITE RIVER
57073-57073 WAKONDA	57319-57319 BRIDGEWATER	57445-57445 GROTON	57580-57580 WINNER
57074-57074 WARD	57321-57321 CANOVA	57446-57446 HECLA	57584-57584 WITTEN
57075-57075 WENTWORTH	57322-57322 CARPENTER	57448-57448 HOSMER	57585-57585 WOOD
57076-57076 WINFRED	57323-57323 CARTHAGE	57449-57449 HOUGHTON	57601-57601 MOBRIDGE
57077-57077 WORTHING	57324-57324 CAVOUR	57450-57450 HOVEN	57620-57620 BISON
57078-57079 YANKTON	57325-57326 CHAMBERLAIN	57451-57451 IPSWICH	57621-57621 BULLHEAD
57100-57110 SIOUX FALLS	57328-57328 CORSICA	57452-57452 JAVA	57622-57622 CHERRY CREEK
57115-57115 BUFFALO RIDGE	57329-57329 DANTE	57454-57454 LANGFORD	57623-57623 DUPREE
57116-57198 SIOUX FALLS	57330-57330 DELMONT	57455-57455 LEBANON	57625-57625 EAGLE BUTTE

57626-57626 FAITH	57656-57656 TIMBER LAKE	57737-57737 ENNING	57769-57769 PIEDMONT
57628-57628 FIRESTEEL	57657-57657 TRAIL CITY	57738-57738 FAIRBURN	57770-57770 PINE RIDGE
57629-57629 GLAD VALLEY	57658-57658 WAKPALA	57741-57741 FORT MEADE	57772-57772 PORCUPINE
57630-57630 GLENCROSS	57659-57659 WALKER	57742-57742 FRUITDALE	57773-57773 PRINGLE
57631-57631 GLENHAM	57660-57660 WATAUGA	57744-57744 HERMOSA	57774-57774 PROVO
57632-57632 HERREID	57661-57661 WHITEHORSE	57745-57745 HILL CITY	57775-57775 QUINN
57633-57633 ISABEL	57701-57703 RAPID CITY	57747-57747 HOT SPRINGS	57776-57776 REDIG
57634-57634 KELDRON	57706-57706 ELLSWORTH AFB	57748-57748 HOWES	57777-57777 RED OWL
57636-57636 LANTRY	57708-57708 BETHLEHEM	57750-57750 INTERIOR	57778-57778 ROCHFORD
57638-57638 LEMMON	57709-57709 RAPID CITY	57751-57751 KEYSTONE	57779-57779 SAINT ONGE
57639-57639 LITTLE EAGLE	57714-57714 ALLEN	57752-57752 KYLE	57780-57780 SCENIC
57640-57640 LODGEPOLE	57715-57715 ARDMORE	57754-57754 LEAD	57782-57782 SMITHWICK
57641-57641 MC INTOSH	57716-57716 BATESLAND	57755-57755 LUDLOW	57783-57783 SPEARFISH
57642-57642 MC LAUGHLIN	57717-57717 BELLE FOURCHE	57756-57756 MANDERSON	57785-57785 STURGIS
57643-57643 MAHTO	57718-57718 BLACK HAWK	57757-57757 MARCUS	57787-57787 UNION CENTER
57644-57644 MEADOW	57719-57719 BOX ELDER	57758-57758 MUD BUTTE	57788-57788 VALE
57645-57645 MORRISTOWN	57720-57720 BUFFALO	57759-57759 NEMO	57790-57790 WALL
57646-57646 MOUND CITY	57722-57722 BUFFALO GAP	57760-57760 NEWELL	57791-57791 WASTA
57647-57647 PARADE	57724-57724 CAMP CROOK	57761-57761 NEW UNDERWOOD	57792-57792 WHITE OWL
57648-57648 POLLOCK	57725-57725 CAPUTA	57762-57762 NISLAND	57793-57793 WHITEWOOD
57649-57649 PRAIRIE CITY	57729-57729 CREIGHTON	57763-57763 OELRICHS	57794-57794 WOUNDED KNEE
57650-57650 RALPH	57730-57730 CUSTER	57764-57764 OGLALA	57795-57795 ZEONA
57651-57651 REVA	57732-57732 DEADWOOD	57765-57765 OPAL	57799-57799 SPEARFISH
57652-57652 RIDGEVIEW	57735-57735 EDGEMONT	57766-57766 ORAL	
57653-57653 SHADEHILL	57736-57736 ELM SPRINGS	57767-57767 OWANKA	

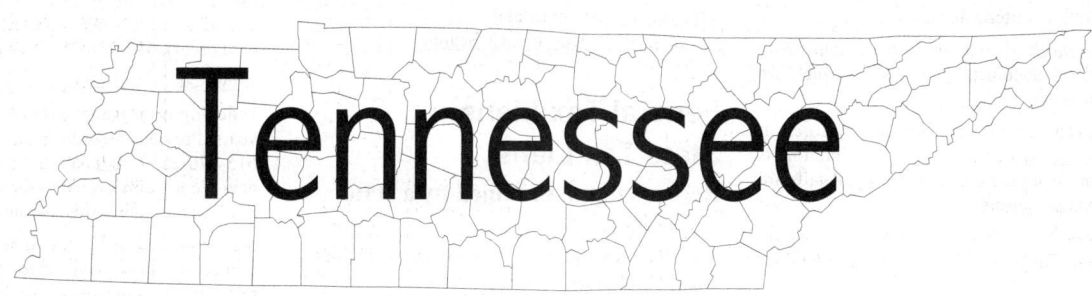

General Help Numbers:

Governor's Office

State Capitol, 1st Floor
Nashville, TN 37243-0001
www.state.tn.us/governor

615-741-2001
Fax 615-532-1353
8AM-5PM

Attorney General's Office

PO Box 20207
Nashville, TN 37202-0207
www.attorneygeneral.state.tn.us

615-741-3491
Fax 615-741-2009
8AM-4:30PM

State Court Administrator

Nashville City Center
511 Union St, Suite 600
Nashville, TN 37219
www.tsc.state.tn.us

615-741-2687
Fax 615-741-6285
8AM-4:30PM

State Archives

State Library & Archives Division
403 7th Ave N
Nashville, TN 37243-0312
www.state.tn.us/sos/statelib/tslahome.htm

615-741-7996
Fax 615-532-9293
8AM-6PM M-SA

State Specifics:

Capital:

Nashville
Davidson County

Time Zone:

CST*

* Tennessee's twenty-nine eastern-most counties are EST: They are: Anderson, Blount, Bradley, Campbell, Carter, Claiborne, Cocke, Grainger, Greene, Hamilton, Hancock, Hawkins, Jefferson, Johnson, Knox, Loudon, McMinn, Meigs, Monroe, Morgan, Polk, Rhea, Roane, Scott, Sevier, Sullivan, Unicoi, Union, Washington.

Number of Counties:

95

Population:

5,740,021

Web Site:

www.state.tn.us

State Agencies

Criminal Records

Access to Records is Restricted

Tennessee Bureau of Investigation, Records and Identification Unit, 901 R S Gass Blvd., Nashville, TN 37216; 615-744-4000, 615-744-4653 (Fax), 24 hours daily.

www.tbi.state.tn.us

Note: The record database is not open to the general public or employers. It can only be accessed by those - state agencies and law enforcement, mostly - who have specific authorization per state law. The state maintains a web site at www.ticic.state.tn.us for searching of sexual offenders, missing children, and people placed on parole who reside in TN. Search sexual offenders after 7/1/1997 at www.ticic.state.tn.us/SEX_ofndr/search_short.asp

Corporation Records
Limited Partnership Records
Fictitious Name
Assumed Name
Limited Liability Company Records

Division of Business Svcs; Corporations, Department of State, 312 Eighth Ave. N, 6th Fl, Nashville, TN 37243; 615-741-2286, 615-741-7310 (Fax), 8AM-4:30PM.

www.state.tn.us/sos/service.htm

Indexing & Storage: Records are available from 1875 to present. Records are computerized and are on microfilm from 1979. Records are indexed on inhouse computer.

Searching: All information is considered public record. Include the following in your request: full name of business. In addition to the articles of incorporation, corporation records include the following information: Annual Reports, Officers, Directors, DBAs (assumed names only), Prior (merged) names, Inactive and Reserved names.

Access by: mail, phone, fax, in person, online.

Fee & Payment: Certification costs $20.00. Corp., LLC, LP, and LLP records cost $20.00 per entity, which includes certification. Fee payee: Secretary of State. Prepayment required. Personal checks accepted. No credit cards accepted.

Mail search: Turnaround time: 1 to 3 days. Certificates are usually processed in 1 day. No self addressed stamped envelope is required.

Phone search: Limited information is given over the phone. Requests for certificates must be in writing.

Fax search: Sam criteria as mail searching.

In person search: Turnaround time is immediate unless certified documents are ordered which are ready the next day.

Online search: There is a free online search at www.tennesseeanytime.org/sosname. While this is intended for business name availability, details are given on existing entities.

Other access: Some data can be purchased in bulk or list format. Call 615-532-9007 for more details.

Trademarks/Servicemarks Trade Names

Secretary of State, Trademarks/Tradenames Division, 312 8th Ave North, 6th Fl, Nashville, TN 37243-0306; 615-741-0531, 615-741-7310 (Fax), 8AM-4:30PM.

www.state.tn.us/sos/service.htm

Indexing & Storage: Records are available from the 1950s to present. It takes 2 to 3 days before new records are available for inquiry. Records are indexed on microfilm.

Searching: Include the following in your request: trademark/servicemark name, name of owner, date of application.

Access by: mail, phone, in person, online.

Fee & Payment: There is $20.00 search fee, add $2.00 for certification. Fee payee: Secretary of State. Personal checks accepted. No credit cards accepted.

Mail search: Turnaround time: 1 to 3 days. A self addressed stamped envelope is requested.

Phone search: No fee for telephone request.

In person search: Turnaround time is while you wait.

Online search: The Internet provides a record search of TN Trademarks, newest records are 3 days old.

Other access: The agency will provide a file update every three months for $1.00 per page. Requests must be in writing.

Uniform Commercial Code

Division 0f Business Services, Secretary of State, 312 Eighth Ave N, 6th Fl, Nashville, TN 37243; 615-741-3276, 615-741-7310 (Fax), 8AM-4:30PM.

www.state.tn.us/sos

Note: State and federal tax liens are filed at the county level with the Register of Deeds where the lienee or its property is located.

Indexing & Storage: Records are available from 1964. Records are computerized from 03/01/96.

Searching: Use search request form UCC-11. Include the following in your request: debtor name.

Access by: mail, in person, online.

Fee & Payment: The fee is $15.00 per debtor or debtor address, copies are $1.00 per page. Fee payee: Secretary of State. Prepayment required. Personal checks accepted. No credit cards accepted.

Mail search: Turnaround time: 1 to 2 days. A self addressed stamped envelope is requested.

In person search: The results are mailed in 2-3 days.

Online search: Free access at http://ndweb.state.tn.us/cgi-bin/nd_CGI_50/ietm/PgUCCSearch

Federal Tax Liens
State Tax Liens

Records not maintained by a state level agency.

Note: Records are filed at the county level with the Register of Deeds.

Sales Tax Registrations

Access to Records is Restricted

Revenue Department, Tax Enforcement Division, Andrew Jackson Bldg, 500 Deaderick St, Nashville, TN 37242-0100; 615-741-7071, 615-532-6339 (Fax), 8AM-4:30PM.

Note: This agency refuses to make any information about registrants available.

Birth Certificates

Tennessee Department of Health, Office of Vital Records, 421 5th Ave North, 1st floor, Nashville, TN 37247; 615-741-1763, 615-741-0778 (Credit card order), 615-726-2559 (Fax), 8AM-4PM.

www.state.tn.us/health/vr

Indexing & Storage: Records are available from 1914 to present. For birth records prior to 1914, contact the State Library and Archives at 615-741-2764. Short forms are only available since 1949. New records are available for inquiry immediately. Records are indexed on index cards, inhouse computer.

Searching: Must have a signed release form from person of record or immediate family member for certified copy. Medical and health information is not released. Include the following in your request: full name, names of parents, mother's maiden name, date of birth, place of birth, relationship to person of record. Daytime phone helpful.

Access by: mail, phone, fax, in person, online.

Fee & Payment: $10.00 for the long (copy of actual certificate) form; $5.00 for the short computerized form. Add $2.00 per name per copy for additional copies. Fee payee: Tennessee Vital Records. Prepayment required. Personal checks accepted. Credit cards accepted: MasterCard, Visa, AmEx, Discover.

Mail search: Turnaround time: 2 to 3 weeks. No self addressed stamped envelope is required.

Phone search: You must use credit cards with fax or phone requests. There is an additional $10.00 fee. Phone service is available from 8AM to 4PM.

Fax search: Fax requests are handled like phone requests.

In person search: Wait time is 15 minutes.

Online search: Records may be ordered from the web site, but are returned by mail.

Expedited service: Expedited service is available for phone, fax or online searches. Turnaround time: 1 day. Phone and fax records ordered by credit card, for $10.00 extra, can be returned overnight for an additional fee.

Death Records

Tennessee Department of Health, Office of Vital Records, 421 5th Ave North, 1st floor, Nashville, TN 37247; 615-741-1763, 615-741-0778 (Credit card order), 615-726-2559 (Fax), 8AM-4PM.

www.state.tn.us/health/vr

Indexing & Storage: Records are available for 50 years. Previous records are at the State Archives at 615-726-2559. It takes 3 months or less before new records are available for inquiry. Records are indexed on index cards, inhouse computer.

Searching: Must have a signed release form from immediate family member. Cause of death is restricted to immediate family members or their representatives and must be specifically requested. Include the following in your request: full name, names of parents, mother's maiden name, date of death, place of death, reason for information request, relationship to person of record. Daytime phone helpful.

Access by: mail, phone, fax, in person, online.

Fee & Payment: The fee is $5.00 per name. Fee payee: Tennessee Vital Records. Prepayment required. Personal checks accepted. Credit cards accepted: MasterCard, Visa, AmEx, Discover.

Mail search: Turnaround time: 2 to 3 weeks. No self addressed stamped envelope is required.

Phone search: You must use a credit card for an additional fee of $10.00. Turnaround time is one day.

Fax search: Same criteria as phone requests.

In person search: Wait is 15 minutes.

Online search: Records may be ordered online at the web site, but are returned by mail. The Cleveland (Tennessee) Public Library staff and volunteers have published the 1914-1925 death records of thirty-three counties at www.state.tn.us/sos/statelib/pubsvs/death.htm#index. It should be noted that the records of children under two years of age have been omitted from this project.

Expedited service: Expedited service is available for phone, fax or online searches. Turnaround time: 24 hours. Add $10.00 per request. For credit card orders only. Add fees for overnight shipping.

Marriage Certificates

Tennessee Department of Health, Office of Vital Records, 421 5th Ave North, 1st floor, Nashville, TN 37247; 615-741-1763, 615-741-0778 (Credit card order), 615-726-2559 (Fax), 8AM-4PM.

www.state.tn.us/health/vr

Indexing & Storage: Records are available for 50 years. It takes 1 month before new records are available for inquiry. Records are indexed on index cards, inhouse computer.

Searching: Must have a signed release form from persons of record or immediate family member for certified copy. Information on race or previous marriages is only released for statistical purposes. Include the following in your request: names of husband and wife, date of marriage, place or county of marriage.

Access by: mail, phone, fax, in person, online.

Fee & Payment: The search fee is $10.00. Add $2.00 for each additional copy. Fee payee: Tennessee Vital Records. Prepayment required. Personal checks accepted. Credit cards accepted: MasterCard, Visa, AmEx, Discover.

Mail search: Turnaround time: 2 to 3 weeks. No self addressed stamped envelope is required.

Phone search: You must use a credit card for an additional $10.00 fee. Records are processed in 24 hours.

Fax search: Same criteria as phone searching.

In person search: Wait time is about 15 minutes.

Online search: Records may be ordered from the web site, but are returned by mail.

Expedited service: Expedited service is available for phone, fax or online searches. Turnaround time: 24 hours if received. Add $10.00 per name. You must use a credit card. Add fees if overnight shipping desired ($11.75).

Divorce Records

Tennessee Department of Health, Office of Vital Records, 421 5th Ave North, 1st floor, Nashville, TN 37247; 615-741-1763, 615-741-0778 (Credit card order), 615-726-2559 (Fax), 8AM-4PM.

www.state.tn.us/health/vr

Indexing & Storage: Records are available for 50 years. It takes 2 weeks to 2 months before new records are available for inquiry. Records are indexed on index cards, inhouse computer.

Searching: Must have a signed release form from person of record or immediate family member. Information on previous marriages and education is released for statistical use only. Include the following in your request: names of husband and wife, date of divorce, place of divorce.

Access by: mail, phone, fax, in person, online.

Fee & Payment: The search fee is $10.00. There is an additional $2 charge for an extra copy. Fee payee: Tennessee Vital Records. Prepayment required. Personal checks accepted. Credit cards accepted: MasterCard, Visa, AmEx, Discover.

Mail search: Turnaround time: 2 to 3 weeks. No self addressed stamped envelope is required.

Phone search: You must use a credit card and there is an additional fee of $10.00. Records are processed in one day.

Fax search: Same criteria as phone searching.

In person search: Wait time is about 15 minutes.

Online search: Records may be ordered online, but are returned by mail.

Expedited service: Expedited service is available for phone, fax or online searches. Turnaround time: 24 hours. Add $10.00 per request. This requires use of credit card. Add fees if overnight delivery is desired ($11.75).

Workers' Compensation Records

Tennessee Department of Labor, Workers Compensation Division, 710 James Robertson Pwy, 2nd Floor, Nashville, TN 37243-0661; 615-741-2395, 615-532-1468 (Fax), 8AM-4:30PM.

www.state.tn.us/labor-wfd

Indexing & Storage: Records are available from 09/91 on computer, from 1987 to present on microfiche. Prior records are maintained on index cards.

Searching: Unless you have a signed authorization from the injured party or are an attorney representing the injured party, a court order is required to obtain records. This information is not considered public record;

however, they'll tell if a claim is on file. The SSN, company name, date of injury, and claim # is required for searching records after 1987, prior record searching requires the name of the company involved.

Access by: mail, fax, in person.

Fee & Payment: The search fee is $5.00, copy fee is $.25 per page. Fee payee: State of Tennessee Treasurer. Personal checks accepted. No credit cards accepted.

Mail search: Turnaround time: within 2 weeks. They will invoice you for copies and postage. No self addressed stamped envelope is required.

Fax search: This will not effect turnaround time.

In person search: Records are still returned in 2 weeks, but you can pick them up.

Driver Records

Dept. of Safety, Financial Responsibility Section, Attn: Driving Records, 1150 Foster Ave, Nashville, TN 37210; 615-741-3954, 8AM-4:30PM.

www.state.tn.us/safety

Note: Tickets are available from this office for a $5.00 fee per record.

Indexing & Storage: Records are available for past 3 years for convictions, if valid; 7 years if the license is suspended, restricted, or revoked. It takes 30 days or more before new records are available for inquiry.

Searching: Tennessee passed legislation similar to DPPA. Casual requesters must have written notarized authorization to receive record information with address data. The driver's license number and last name or DOB are needed when ordering.

Access by: mail, in person, online.

Fee & Payment: The fee is $5.00 per record. Fee payee: Tennessee Department of Safety. Prepayment required. Certified checks or money orders are preferred. MasterCard & Visa accepted in person only.

Mail search: Turnaround time: 2 weeks. No self addressed stamped envelope is required.

In person search: Up to 10 requests will be processed while you wait at this location or at offices in Nashville, Memphis, Knoxville, Chattanooga, and various Driver License Testing Centers.

Online search: Driving records are available to subscribers, signup at www.tennesseeanytime.org. There is a $75 registration fee. Records are available 24 hours daily on an interactive basis. Records are $5.00 each. Suggested only for ongoing users. Call 1-866-886-3468 for more information.

Other access: Magnetic tape retrieval is available for high volume users. Purchase of the DL file is available for approved requesters.

Vehicle Ownership
Vehicle Identification

Titling and Registration Division, Information Unit, 44 Vantage Way #160, Nashville, TN 37243-8050; 615-741-3101 (Titles), 888-871-3171, 8AM-4:30PM.

www.state.tn.us/safety

Indexing & Storage: Records are available for 5 years to present. It takes 12 weeks before new records are available for inquiry.

Searching: The state follows the DPPA guidelines for permissible requesters. Records are not released to casual requesters without consent. The state recommends use of their form-SF1255. Include the following in your request: purpose of request, copy of requester's photo ID, and requester's signature.

Access by: mail, in person.

Fee & Payment: The fee is $1.00 for general inquiry, $5.00 for current title data, and $15.00 for a complete title history. Fee payee: Titling and Registration. Prepayment required. Personal checks accepted. No credit cards accepted.

Mail search: Turnaround time: 2 to 4 weeks. A self addressed stamped envelope is requested.

In person search: Turnaround time is while you wait, unless photocopy of actual document is required. The office closes at 4PM for walk-in customers. Photo ID required.

Accident Reports

Financial Responsibility Section, Records Unit, 1150 Foster Avenue, Nashville, TN 37210; 615-741-3954, 8AM-4:30PM.

www.state.tn.us/safety

Note: Also, you can obtain accident reports from the investigating agency.

Indexing & Storage: Records are available from 1991 to present. It takes 30 days before new records are available for inquiry.

Searching: Include the following in your request: full name, date of accident, location of accident. Also, include the county of the accident and DL of driver(s).

Access by: mail, in person.

Fee & Payment: The fee is $4.00 per record copy. Fee payee: Tennessee Department of Safety. Prepayment required. Agency prefers money orders and certified checks. Personal checks not accepted. MasterCard & Visa accepted for in person only.

Mail search: Turnaround time: 2 weeks. No self addressed stamped envelope is required.

In person search: Turnaround time is generally while you wait.

Vessel Ownership
Vessel Registration

Wildlife Resources Agency, Boating Division, PO Box 40747, Nashville, TN 37204; 615-781-6585, 615-741-4606 (Fax), 8AM-4:30PM.

www.state.tn.us/twra

Note: All liens are filed with the Secretary of State.

Indexing & Storage: Records are available for the past 3 years. Records are indexed on computer. The state does not issue titles. All motorized boats and all sailboats must be registered. It takes 30 days before new records are available for inquiry.

Searching: To search, one of the following is required: Tennessee ID #, hull id #, name, or SSN.

Access by: mail, phone, fax, in person.

Fee & Payment: There is no fee to do 1 or 2 searches; however, large lists may incur a charge.

Mail search: Turnaround time: 2 days. No self addressed stamped envelope is required.

Phone search: Whether a phone search will be performed depends on how busy the personnel is at the time of the call. Phone searches are only verbal verifications and require a Tennessee ID # to search.

Fax search: Turnaround time is 2 days. Results will be sent by mail.

In person search: Turnaround time is usually immediate, when staff available.

Other access: Records can be purchased in bulk. There is a minimum $272.50 fee if on labels and $240.00 minimum fee if on tape. Call Charlie Freeman at 615-781-6500 for more details.

Legislation Records

Tennessee General Assembly, Office of Legislative Information Services, Rachel Jackson Bldg, 1st Floor, Nashville, TN 37243; 615-741-3511 (Status), 615-741-0927 (Bill Room), 8AM-4:30PM.

www.legislature.state.tn.us

Indexing & Storage: Records are available for the current and past session only. Earlier records are maintained in the State Library & Archives.

Searching: Include the following in your request: bill number, topic of bill.

Access by: mail, phone, in person, online.

Fee & Payment: No fee to search, copy fee is $.25 per page. Fee payee: State of Tennessee. Personal checks accepted. No credit cards accepted.

Mail search: Turnaround time: same day. No self addressed stamped envelope is required.

Phone search: You may call for information.

In person search: You may request information in person.

Online search: Bill information can be viewed at the Internet site. The Tennessee Code is also available from the web page.

Voter Registration
Access to Records is Resticted.

Note: The statewide database cannot be accessed. However records are held by the Administrator of Elections at the county level. Records can only be purchased for politically-related purposes.

GED Certificates

Department of Labor & Workforce Development, GED Records - Davy Crockett Tower, 500 James Robertson Parkway, 2nd Fl, Nashville, TN 37245; 615-741-7054, 615-532-4899 (Fax), 8AM-4:30PM.

www.state.tn.us/labor-wfd/AE/aeged.htm

Searching: Include the following in your request: date of birth, Social Security Number, signed release. Include your daytime telephone number. Year diploma issued also helpful.

Access by: mail, fax, in person.

Fee & Payment: There is no fee for a verification.

Mail search: Turnaround time: 7 to 10 working days. No self addressed stamped envelope is required.

Fax search: Turnaround time is generally in 3 days.

In person search: Searching is available in person.

Hunting License Information
Fishing License Information
Access to Records is Restricted

Wildlife Resources Agency, Sportsman License Division, PO Box 40747, Nashville, TN 37204; 615-781-6585, 615-741-4606 (Fax), 8AM-4:30PM.

www.state.tn.us/twra

Note: There is not a central database of hunting or fishing licenses except the Sportman License Division holds information on 45,000 sportsman licenses (boating, etc).

Otherwise, you must contact the vendor where the license was sold.

Tennessee State Licensing Agencies

Licenses Searchable Online

Accounting Firm #3	www.state.tn.us/cgi-bin/commerce/roster2.pl
Alarm Contractor #3	www.state.tn.us/cgi-bin/commerce/roster2.pl
Alcohol & Drug Abuse Counselor #7	http://www2.state.tn.us/health/licensure/index.htm
Animal Euthanasia Technician #7	http://www2.state.tn.us/health/licensure/index.htm
Architect #3	www.state.tn.us/cgi-bin/commerce/roster2.pl
Athletic Trainer #7	http://www2.state.tn.us/health/licensure/index.htm
Auction Company #3	www.state.tn.us/cgi-bin/commerce/roster2.pl
Auctioneer #3	www.state.tn.us/cgi-bin/commerce/roster2.pl
Audiologist #7	http://www2.state.tn.us/health/licensure/index.htm
Barber School/Barber Shop #3	www.state.tn.us/cgi-bin/commerce/roster2.pl
Barber/Barber Technician #3	www.state.tn.us/cgi-bin/commerce/roster2.pl
Boxing/Racing Personnel #3	www.state.tn.us/cgi-bin/commerce/roster2.pl
Chiropractor/Chiropractic Therapy Assist. #7	http://www2.state.tn.us/health/licensure/index.htm
Clinical Lab Technician/Personnel #6	http://www2.state.tn.us/health/licensure/index.htm
Collection Agent/Manager #3	www.state.tn.us/cgi-bin/commerce/roster2.pl
Contractor #3	www.state.tn.us/cgi-bin/commerce/roster2.pl
Cosmetologist/Cosmetology Shop #3	www.state.tn.us/cgi-bin/commerce/roster2.pl
Cosmetology School #3	www.state.tn.us/cgi-bin/commerce/roster2.pl
Counselor, Associate/Professional #7	http://www2.state.tn.us/health/licensure/index.htm
Dental Hygienist #7	http://www2.state.tn.us/health/licensure/index.htm
Dentist/Dental Assistant #7	http://www2.state.tn.us/health/licensure/index.htm
Dietitian/Nutritionist #7	http://www2.state.tn.us/health/licensure/index.htm
Electrologist #7	http://www2.state.tn.us/health/licensure/index.htm
Electrology Instructor/School #7	http://www2.state.tn.us/health/licensure/index.htm
Embalmer #3	www.state.tn.us/cgi-bin/commerce/roster2.pl
Emergency Medical Personnel/Dispatcher #7	http://www2.state.tn.us/health/licensure/index.htm
Emergency Medical Service #7	http://www2.state.tn.us/health/licensure/index.htm
Engineer #3	www.state.tn.us/cgi-bin/commerce/roster2.pl
First Responder EMS #7	http://www2.state.tn.us/health/licensure/index.htm
Funeral & Burial Director/Apprentice #3	www.state.tn.us/cgi-bin/commerce/roster2.pl
Funeral & Burial Est./Cemetery #3	www.state.tn.us/cgi-bin/commerce/roster2.pl
Geologist #3	www.state.tn.us/cgi-bin/commerce/roster2.pl
Hearing Aid Dispenser #7	http://www2.state.tn.us/health/licensure/index.htm
Home Improvement #3	www.state.tn.us/cgi-bin/commerce/roster2.pl
Insurance Agent #3	www.state.tn.us/cgi-bin/commerce/roster2.pl
Insurance Firm #3	www.state.tn.us/cgi-bin/commerce/roster2.pl
Interior Designer #3	www.state.tn.us/cgi-bin/commerce/roster2.pl
Landscape Architect #3	www.state.tn.us/cgi-bin/commerce/roster2.pl
Landscape Architect Firm #3	www.state.tn.us/cgi-bin/commerce/roster2.pl
Lobbyist #10	www.state.tn.us/tref/lobbyists/lobbyists.htm
Marriage & Family Therapist #7	http://www2.state.tn.us/health/licensure/index.htm
Massage Therapist/Establishment #7	http://www2.state.tn.us/health/licensure/index.htm
Medical Doctor #6	http://www2.state.tn.us/health/licensure/index.htm
Medical Laboratory Personnel #6	http://www2.state.tn.us/health/licensure/index.htm
Med. Disciplinary Tracking (Abuse Registry) #6	http://www2.state.tn.us/health/abuseregistry/index.html
Midwife #7	http://www2.state.tn.us/health/licensure/index.htm
Motor Vehicle Auction #3	www.state.tn.us/cgi-bin/commerce/roster2.pl
Motor Vehicle Dealer/Salesperson #3	www.state.tn.us/cgi-bin/commerce/roster2.pl
Nurse-RN/LPN #6	http://www2.state.tn.us/health/licensure/index.htm
Nurses' Aide #6	http://www2.state.tn.us/health/licensure/index.htm
Nursing Home Administrator #7	http://www2.state.tn.us/health/licensure/index.htm
Occupational Therapist/Assistant #7	http://www2.state.tn.us/health/licensure/index.htm
Optician, Dispensing #7	http://www2.state.tn.us/health/licensure/index.htm
Optometrist #7	http://www2.state.tn.us/health/licensure/index.htm
Orthopedic Physician Assistant #6	http://www2.state.tn.us/health/licensure/index.htm
Osteopathic Physician #6	http://www2.state.tn.us/health/licensure/index.htm
Pastoral Therapist, Clinical #7	http://www2.state.tn.us/health/licensure/index.htm
Personnel Leasing #3	www.state.tn.us/cgi-bin/commerce/roster2.pl
Pharmacist #3	www.state.tn.us/cgi-bin/commerce/roster2.pl
Pharmacy #3	www.state.tn.us/cgi-bin/commerce/roster2.pl
Pharmacy Researcher #3	www.state.tn.us/cgi-bin/commerce/roster2.pl
Physical Therapist/Assistant #6	http://www2.state.tn.us/health/licensure/index.htm
Physician Assistant #6	http://www2.state.tn.us/health/licensure/index.htm

Podiatrist #7 .... http://www2.state.tn.us/health/licensure/index.htm
Polygraph Examiner #3 .... www.state.tn.us/cgi-bin/commerce/roster2.pl
Private Investigative Company #3 .... www.state.tn.us/cgi-bin/commerce/roster2.pl
Private Investigator #3 .... www.state.tn.us/cgi-bin/commerce/roster2.pl
Psychological Examiner #7 .... http://www2.state.tn.us/health/licensure/index.htm
Psychologist #7 .... http://www2.state.tn.us/health/licensure/index.htm
Public Accountant-CPA #3 .... www.state.tn.us/cgi-bin/commerce/roster2.pl
Racetrack #3 .... www.state.tn.us/cgi-bin/commerce/roster2.pl
Real Estate Appraiser #3 .... www.state.tn.us/cgi-bin/commerce/roster2.pl
Real Estate Broker #3 .... www.state.tn.us/cgi-bin/commerce/roster2.pl
Real Estate Firm #3 .... www.state.tn.us/cgi-bin/commerce/roster2.pl
Real Estate Sales Agent #3 .... www.state.tn.us/cgi-bin/commerce/roster2.pl
Respiratory Care Therapist/Tech./Assist. #6 .... http://www2.state.tn.us/health/licensure/index.htm
Security Company #3 .... www.state.tn.us/cgi-bin/commerce/roster2.pl
Security Guard #3 .... www.state.tn.us/cgi-bin/commerce/roster2.pl
Security Trainer #3 .... www.state.tn.us/cgi-bin/commerce/roster2.pl
Social Worker, Master/Clinical #7 .... http://www2.state.tn.us/health/licensure/index.htm
Speech Pathologist #7 .... http://www2.state.tn.us/health/licensure/index.htm
Teacher #5 .... https://www.k-12.state.tn.us/tcertinf/Search.asp
Timeshare Agent #3 .... www.state.tn.us/cgi-bin/commerce/roster2.pl
Veterinarian #7 .... http://www2.state.tn.us/health/licensure/index.htm
X-ray Operator #6 .... http://www2.state.tn.us/health/licensure/index.htm
X-ray Technologist, Podiatry #6 .... http://www2.state.tn.us/health/licensure/index.htm

Licensing Quick Finder

Accounting Firm #3 615-741-9771
Aesthetician #3 615-741-2515
Alarm Contractor #3 615-741-9771
Alcohol & Drug Abuse Counselor #7 ... 615-532-5097
Alcohol Package Store #1 615-741-1602
Alcohol Server #1 615-741-1602
Animal Euthanasia Technician #7 615-532-3202
Animal/Livestock Dealer #11 615-837-5241
Architect #3 615-741-3221
Athletic Trainer #7 615-532-3202
Attorney #12 615-741-3234
Auction Company #3 615-741-9771
Auctioneer #3 615-741-3226
Audiologist #7 615-532-3202
Barber School/Barber Shop #3 615-741-9771
Barber/Barber Technician #3 615-741-9771
Bed & Breakfast #14 615-741-7206
Boiler Operator #8 901-385-5077
Boxing/Racing Personnel #3 615-741-9771
Camp #14 615-741-7206
Chiropractor/Chiropractic Therapy Assist. #7
.... 615-532-3202
Clinical Lab Technician/Personnel #6 ... 615-532-3202
Collection Agent/Manager #3 615-741-1741
Contractor #3 615-741-8307
Cosmetologist/Cosmetology Shop #3 ... 615-741-2515
Cosmetology School #3 615-741-9771
Counselor, Associate/Professional #7 ... 615-532-3202
Court Reporter/Stenographer #2 423-756-0221
Dental Hygienist #7 615-532-3202
Dentist/Dental Assistant #7 615-532-3202
Dietitian/Nutritionist #7 615-532-3202
Electrologist #7 615-532-3202
Electrology Instructor/School #7 615-532-3202
Elevator Inspector #15 615-741-2123
Embalmer #3 615-741-9771
Emergency Medical Personnel/Dispatcher #7
.... 615-532-3202
Emergency Medical Service #7 615-532-3202
Engineer #3 615-741-3221
Environmentalist #7 615-532-3202
Fire Protection Sprinkler System Contractor #3
.... 615-741-7190
First Responder EMS #7 615-532-3202
Food Service Establishment #14 615-741-7206
Funeral & Burial Director/Apprentice #3 615-741-9771

Funeral & Burial Est./Cemetery #3 615-741-9771
Geologist #3 615-741-9771
Health Care Facility #6 615-532-3202
Hearing Aid Dispenser #7 615-532-3202
Home Improvement #3 615-741-9771
Hotel #14 615-741-7206
Insurance Agent #3 615-741-2693
Insurance Firm #3 615-741-2693
Interior Designer #3 615-741-9771
Investment Advisor #3 615-741-2947
Landscape Architect #3 615-741-3221
Landscape Architect Firm #3 615-741-9771
Liquor Sale/Permit #1 615-741-1602
Livestock Brand #11 615-837-5241
Lobbyist #10 615-741-7959
Manicurist #3 615-741-2515
Marriage & Family Therapist #7 615-532-3202
Massage Therapist/Establishment #7 ... 615-532-5083
Med. Disciplinary Tracking (Abuse Registry) #6
.... 615-532-3202
Medical Doctor #6 615-532-3202
Medical Laboratory Personnel #6 615-532-3202
Midwife #7 615-532-3202
Milk Tester/Sampler #11 615-837-5151
Motor Vehicle Auction #3 615-741-9771
Motor Vehicle Dealer/Salesperson #3 ... 615-741-9771
Notary Public #9 615-741-3699
Nurse-RN/LPN #6 615-532-3202
Nursery #11 615-837-5512
Nursery Plant Dealer #11 615-837-5512
Nurses' Aide #6 615-532-3202
Nursing Home Administrator #7 615-532-3202
Occupational Therapist/Assistant #7 ... 615-532-3202
Optician, Dispensing #7 615-532-3202
Optometrist #7 615-532-3202
Orthopedic Physician Assistant #6 615-532-3202
Osteopathic Physician #6 615-532-3202
Pastoral Therapist, Clinical #7 615-532-3202
Personnel Leasing #3 615-741-9771
Pest Control Operator #11 615-837-5138
Pharmacist #3 615-741-9771
Pharmacy #3 615-741-9771
Pharmacy Researcher #3 615-741-9771
Physical Therapist/Assistant #6 615-532-3202
Physician Assistant #6 615-532-3202
Plumber/Plumbing Company #8 901-385-5077

Podiatrist #7 615-532-3202
Polygraph Examiner #3 615-741-9771
Private Investigative Company #3 615-741-9771
Private Investigator #3 615-741-9771
Private Security Guard #3 615-741-4827
Psychological Examiner #7 615-532-3202
Psychologist #7 615-532-3202
Public Accountant-CPA #3 615-741-2550
Racetrack #3 615-741-9771
Radiation Therapy Technician #6 615-532-3202
Radiologic Technologist #6 615-532-3202
Real Estate Appraiser #3 615-741-9771
Real Estate Broker #3 615-741-9771
Real Estate Firm #3 615-741-9771
Real Estate Sales Agent #3 615-741-1831
Refrigeration Installer/Contractor #8 ... 901-385-5077
Respiratory Care Therapist/Tech./Assist.ant #6
.... 615-532-3202
School Administrative Supervisor #5 ... 615-532-4885
School Counselor #5 615-532-4885
School Librarian #5 615-532-4885
Securities Agent #3 615-741-2947
Securities Broker/Dealer #3 615-741-2947
Security Company #3 615-741-9771
Security Guard #3 615-741-9771
Security Trainer #3 615-741-9771
Service Technician (weigh scales) #11. 615-837-5109
Shampoo Technician #3 615-741-2515
Shorthand Reporter #2 423-756-0221
Social Worker, Master/Clinical #7 615-532-3202
Speech Pathologist #7 615-532-3202
Surveyor, Land #3 615-741-3611
Swimming Pool #14 615-741-7206
Tattoo Artist/Apprentice #14 615-741-7206
Teacher #5 615-532-4885
Timeshare Agent #3 615-741-2273
Veterinarian #7 615-532-3202
Water Treatment Plant Operator #13 ... 615-898-8090
Weigher, Public (Bulk Products, Aggregates) #11
.... 615-837-5109
Weighmaster #11 615-837-5109
Wine Production/Sale/Transport #1 615-741-1602
X-ray Operator #6 615-532-3202
X-ray Technologist, Podiatry #6 615-532-6280

Licensing Agency Information

#1 Alcoholic Beverage Commission, 226 Capitol Blvd Bldg, #300, Nashville, TN 37243-0755; 615-741-1602, Fax: 615-741-0847.
www.state.tn.us/abc
Agency email: stallman@mail.state.tn.us.

#3 Department of Commerce & Insurance, 500 James Robertson Pky, 2nd Fl, Nashville, TN 37243; 615-741-9771, Fax: 615-532-2965.
www.state.tn.us/commerce. Agency email: dci@mail.state.tn.us.
Search database at www.state.tn.us/cgi-bin/commerce/roster2.pl.

#5 Department of Education, 710 James Robertson Pky, Andrew Johnson Tower, 5th Fl, Nashville, TN 37243-0377; 615-532-4885, Fax: 615-532-1448.
www.state.tn.us/education/lic_home.htm
Search database at https://www.k-12.state.tn.us/tcertinf

#6 Department of Health, Medical Professions, 425 5th Ave N, Cordell Hull Bldg, 1st Fl, Nashville, TN 37247-1010; 615-532-3202.
http://www2.state.tn.us/health

Search database at
http://www2.state.tn.us/health/licensure/index.htm

#7 Department of Health, (Allied Health Professions), 425 5th Ave N, Cordell Hull Bldg, 1st Fl, Nashville, TN 37247-1010; 615-532-3202.
http://www2.state.tn.us/health
Search database at
http://www2.state.tn.us/health/licensure/index.htm

#8 Mechanical Licensing Board, (Shelby County/Western Tennesee), 6465 Mullins Station Rd, Memphis, TN 38134; 901-385-5054, Fax: 901-385-5198.

#9 Office of Secretary of State, 312 8th Av N, 6th Fl, W R Snodgrass Tower, Nashville, TN 37243-0306; 615-741-3699, Fax: 615-741-7310.
www.state.tn.us/sos/sos.htm

#10 Registry of Election Finance, 404 James Robertson Pky, #1614, Nashville, TN 37243; 615-741-7959, Fax: 615-532-8902.
www.state.tn.us/tref
Agency email: drawlins@mail.state.tn.us.
Search database at
www.state.tn.us/tref/lobbyists/lobbyists.htm

#11 Department of Agriculture, Melrose Station, Nashville, TN 37204; 615-837-5120, Fax: 615-837-5335.
www.state.tn.us/agriculture

#12 Board of Law Examiners, 706 Church St, #100, Nashville, TN 37243-0740; 615-741-3234, Fax: 615-741-5867.
www.state.tn.us/lawexaminers
Agency email: ib27ble02@smtpaoc.tsc.state.tn.us.

#13 Water & Wastewater Certification Program, 2022 Blanton Dr, Fleming Training Ctr, Murfreesboro, TN 37129; 615-898-8090, Fax: 615-818-8064.

#14 Department of Health, Division of General Environmental Health, 415 5th Ave N, Cordell Hull Bldg 6th Fl, Nashville, TN 37247-3901; 615-741-7206, Fax: 615-741-8510.
www.state.tn.us/health

#15 Department of Labor, Boiler & Elevator Division, Board of Boiler Rules, 710 James Robertson Pky, Andrew Johnson Tower 4th Fl, Nashville, TN 37243; 615-741-2123.
www.state.tn.us/labor-wfd/bediv.html

Tennessee Federal Courts

The following list indicates the district and division name for each county in the state. If the bankruptcy court location is different from the district court, then the location of the bankruptcy court appears in parentheses.

County/Court Cross Reference

County	District	Division
Anderson	Eastern	Knoxville
Bedford	Eastern	Winchester (Chattanooga)
Benton	Western	Jackson
Bledsoe	Eastern	Chattanooga
Blount	Eastern	Knoxville
Bradley	Eastern	Chattanooga
Campbell	Eastern	Knoxville
Cannon	Middle	Nashville
Carroll	Western	Jackson
Carter	Eastern	Greeneville (Knoxville)
Cheatham	Middle	Nashville
Chester	Western	Jackson
Claiborne	Eastern	Knoxville
Clay	Middle	Cookeville (Nashville)
Cocke	Eastern	Greeneville (Knoxville)
Coffee	Eastern	Winchester (Chattanooga)
Crockett	Western	Jackson
Cumberland	Middle	Cookeville (Nashville)
Davidson	Middle	Nashville
De Kalb	Middle	Cookeville (Nashville)
Decatur	Western	Jackson
Dickson	Middle	Nashville
Dyer	Western	Memphis
Fayette	Western	Memphis
Fentress	Middle	Cookeville (Nashville)
Franklin	Eastern	Winchester (Chattanooga)
Gibson	Western	Jackson
Giles	Middle	Columbia (Nashville)
Grainger	Eastern	Knoxville
Greene	Eastern	Greeneville (Knoxville)
Grundy	Eastern	Winchester (Chattanooga)
Hamblen	Eastern	Greeneville (Knoxville)
Hamilton	Eastern	Chattanooga
Hancock	Eastern	Greeneville (Knoxville)
Hardeman	Western	Jackson
Hardin	Western	Jackson
Hawkins	Eastern	Greeneville (Knoxville)
Haywood	Western	Jackson
Henderson	Western	Jackson
Henry	Western	Jackson
Hickman	Middle	Columbia (Nashville)
Houston	Middle	Nashville
Humphreys	Middle	Nashville
Jackson	Middle	Cookeville (Nashville)
Jefferson	Eastern	Knoxville
Johnson	Eastern	Greeneville (Knoxville)
Knox	Eastern	Knoxville
Lake	Western	Jackson
Lauderdale	Western	Memphis
Lawrence	Middle	Columbia (Nashville)
Lewis	Middle	Columbia (Nashville)
Lincoln	Eastern	Winchester (Chattanooga)
Loudon	Eastern	Knoxville
Macon	Middle	Cookeville (Nashville)
Madison	Western	Jackson
Marion	Eastern	Chattanooga
Marshall	Middle	Columbia (Nashville)
Maury	Middle	Columbia (Nashville)
McMinn	Eastern	Chattanooga
McNairy	Western	Jackson
Meigs	Eastern	Chattanooga
Monroe	Eastern	Knoxville
Montgomery	Middle	Nashville
Moore	Eastern	Winchester (Chattanooga)
Morgan	Eastern	Knoxville
Obion	Western	Jackson
Overton	Middle	Cookeville (Nashville)
Perry	Western	Jackson
Pickett	Middle	Cookeville (Nashville)
Polk	Eastern	Chattanooga
Putnam	Middle	Cookeville (Nashville)
Rhea	Eastern	Chattanooga
Roane	Eastern	Knoxville
Robertson	Middle	Nashville
Rutherford	Middle	Nashville
Scott	Eastern	Knoxville
Sequatchie	Eastern	Chattanooga
Sevier	Eastern	Knoxville
Shelby	Western	Memphis
Smith	Middle	Cookeville (Nashville)
Stewart	Middle	Nashville
Sullivan	Eastern	Greeneville (Knoxville)
Sumner	Middle	Nashville
Tipton	Western	Memphis
Trousdale	Middle	Nashville
Unicoi	Eastern	Greeneville (Knoxville)
Union	Eastern	Knoxville
Van Buren	Eastern	Winchester (Chattanooga)
Warren	Eastern	Winchester (Chattanooga)
Washington	Eastern	Greeneville (Knoxville)
Wayne	Middle	Columbia (Nashville)
Weakley	Western	Jackson
White	Middle	Cookeville (Nashville)
Williamson	Middle	Nashville
Wilson	Middle	Nashville

Standards for Federal Courts: The search fee is $20.00 per item (one party name or case number). Certification fee is $7.00 per document. Copy fee is $.50 per page. All fees standard unless noted in profile. Mail Search: always enclose a stamped self addressed envelope unless otherwise noted. Before releasing records, all courts require prepayment unless noted in profile.

Open records are located at the court unless otherwise noted. District courts index by defendant and plaintiff as well as by case number. Bankruptcy courts usually index by debtor and case number. While most courts now have their indexes on computer, many still maintain index card files as well.

The universal PACER sign-up number is 800-676-6856. Find PACER and the Party/Case Index on the Web at http://pacer.psc.uscourts.gov. PACER dial-up access is $.60 per minute. Also, courts offering internet access via RACER, PACER, Web-PACER or the new CM-ECF charge $.07 per page fee unless noted as free.

US District Court

Eastern District of Tennessee

Chattanooga Division Clerk's Office, PO Box 591, Chattanooga, TN 37401 (Courier Address: Room 309, 900 Georgia Ave, Chattanooga, TN 37402), 423-752-5200.

www.tned.uscourts.gov

Counties: Bledsoe, Bradley, Hamilton, McMinn, Marion, Meigs, Polk, Rhea, Sequatchie.

Indexing & Storage: Cases are indexed by defendant, plaintiff, and case number. New cases are available in the index 1-2 days after filing date. Open records are located at this court.

Fee & Payment Notes: Payment may be made by money order, cashier check, personal check. Payee: Clerk, US District Court.

Phone Search: Only docket information available by telephone.

In Person Search: In person searching available.

PACER: Access fee is. Toll-free dial-up access: 800-869-1265. Local dial-up access: 865-545-4647. Case records are available back to 1994. Records are never purged. New records are available online after 1 day. PACER is available online at http://pacer.tned.uscourts.gov.

Greeneville Division 101 Summer St W, Greeneville, TN 37743 (Courier Address: Use mail address for courier delivery), 423-639-3105.

www.tned.uscourts.gov

Counties: Carter, Cocke, Greene, Hamblen, Hancock, Hawkins, Johnson, Sullivan, Unicoi, Washington.

Indexing & Storage: Cases are indexed by defendant, plaintiff, and case number. New cases are available in the index immediately after filing date. Open records are located at this court.

Fee & Payment Notes: Payment may be made by money order, cashier check, personal check. Payee: Clerk, US District Court.

Phone Search: Only docket information is available by phone.

Mail Search: A stamped self addressed envelope is not required.

In Person Search: In person searching available.

PACER: Access fee is. Toll-free dial-up access: 800-869-1265. Local dial-up access: 865-545-4647. Case records are available back to 1994. Records are never purged. New records are available online after 1 day. PACER is available online at http://pacer.tned.uscourts.gov.

Knoxville Division Clerk's Office, 800 Market St, Knoxville, TN 37902 (Courier: Use mail address for courier delivery), 865-545-4279.

www.tned.uscourts.gov

Counties: Anderson, Blount, Campbell, Claiborne, Grainger, Jefferson, Knox, Loudon, Monroe, Morgan, Roane, Scott, Sevier, Union.

Indexing & Storage: Cases are indexed by defendant, plaintiff, and case number. New cases are available in the index 1-2 days after filing date. Computerized index as of June 1, 1992. Index cards prior to June 1, 1992. Open records are located at this court.

Fee & Payment Notes: Payment may be made by money order, cashier check, personal check. Payee: Clerk, US District Court.

Phone Search: Only docket information is available by phone.

Mail Search: A stamped self addressed envelope is not required.

In Person Search: In person searching available.

PACER: Access fee is. Toll-free dial-up access: 800-869-1265. Local dial-up access: 423-545-4647. Case records are available back to 1994. Records are never purged. New records are available online after 1 day. PACER is available online at http://pacer.ohsd.uscourts.gov.

Winchester Division PO Box 459, Winchester, TN 37398 (Courier Address: 200 S Jefferson St, Room 201, Winchester, TN 37397), 931-967-1444.

www.tned.uscourts.gov

Counties: Bedford, Coffee, Franklin, Grundy, Lincoln, Moore, Van Buren, Warren.

Indexing & Storage: Cases are indexed by defendant, plaintiff, and case number. New cases are available in the index 1-2 days after filing date. Office has just begun maintaining records in 1997.

Fee & Payment Notes: Payment may be made by money order, cashier check, personal check. Payee: Clerk, US District Court.

Phone Search: Only docket information available by telephone.

In Person Search: In person searching available.

PACER: Access fee is. Toll-free dial-up access: 800-869-1265. Local dial-up access: 423-545-4647. Case records are available back to 1994. Records are never purged. New records are available online after 1 day. PACER is available online at http://pacer.tned.uscourts.gov.

US Bankruptcy Court

Eastern District of Tennessee

Chattanooga Division Historic US Courthouse, 31 E 11th St, Chattanooga, TN 37402 (Courier Address: same), 423-752-5163.

www.tneb.uscourts.gov

Counties: Bedford, Bledsoe, Bradley, Coffee, Franklin, Grundy, Hamilton, Lincoln, Marion, McMinn, Meigs, Moore, Polk, Rhea, Sequatchie, Van Buren, Warren.

Indexing & Storage: Cases are indexed by debtor and creditors as well as by case number. New cases are available in the index 2 days after filing date. The court needs the name of the debtor and to obtain positive identification, a social security number or address is needed. Open records are located at this court.

Fee & Payment Notes: Payment may be made by money order, cashier check, business check. Personal checks are not accepted. Will invoice for copy fees only. Payee: US Bankruptcy Court.

Phone Search: The court will only confirm bankruptcy filings over the phone and will only honor up to three requests per phone call per day. An automated voice case information service (VCIS) is available. Call VCIS at 800-767-1512 or 423-752-5272.

Mail Search: A stamped self addressed envelope is not required.

In Person Search: In person searching available.

PACER: Toll-free dial-up access: 888-833-9512. Local dial-up access: 423-752-5136. Case records are available back to January 1986. Records are purged as deemed necessary. New civil records are available online after 1 day. PACER is available online at http://pacer.tneb.uscourts.gov.

Knoxville Division 800 Market St #330, Howard H Baker Jr US Courthouse, Knoxville, TN 37902 (Courier Address: Use mail address for courier delivery), 865-545-4279.

www.tneb.uscourts.gov

Counties: Anderson, Blount, Campbell, Carter, Claiborne, Cocke, Grainger, Greene, Hamblen,

Hancock, Hawkins, Jefferson, Johnson, Knox, Loudon, Monroe, Morgan, Roane, Scott, Sevier, Sullivan, Unicoi, Union, Washington.

Indexing & Storage: Cases are indexed by debtor as well as by case number. New cases are available in the index 2-3 days after filing date. District wide searches are possible for limited information from 1/86 from this court.

Fee & Payment Notes: Payment may be made by money order, cashier check, personal check. Payee: Clerk, US Bankruptcy Court.

Phone Search: The court will only confirm debtor names, SSN, address, attorney, trustee, chapter filed, date of filing, date of discharge/dismissal, date case closed, in addition to limited information regarding motions, hearings, etc. An automated voice case information service (VCIS) is available. Call VCIS at 800-767-1512 or 423-752-5272.

In Person Search: In person searching available.

PACER: Toll-free dial-up access: 888-833-9512. Local dial-up access: 423-752-5136. Case records are available back to January 1986. Records are purged as deemed necessary. New civil records are available online after 1 day. PACER is available online at http://pacer.tneb.uscourts.gov.

US District Court

Middle District of Tennessee

Columbia Division c/o Nashville Division, 800 US Courthouse, 801 Broadway, Nashville, TN 37203 (Courier Address: Use mail address for courier delivery), 615-736-5498.

www.tnmd.uscourts.gov

Counties: Giles, Hickman, Lawrence, Lewis, Marshall, Maury, Wayne.

Indexing & Storage: New cases are available in the index after filing date. Open records are located at the Nashville Division.

Fee & Payment Notes: Payment may be made by money order, cashier check. Business checks are not accepted. Personal checks are not accepted.

Phone Search: Searching not available by phone.

Mail Search: A stamped self addressed envelope is not required.

In Person Search: In person searching available.

PACER: Toll-free dial-up access: 800-458-2994. Local dial-up access: 615-736-7164. Case records are available back three years. Records are purged every year. New records are available online after 1 day. PACER is available online at http://pacer.tnmd.uscourts.gov.

Cookeville Division c/o Nashville Division, 800 US Courthouse, 801 Broadway, Nashville, TN 37203 (Courier Address: Use mail address for courier delivery), 615-736-5498, Fax: 615-736-7488.

www.tnmd.uscourts.gov

Counties: Clay, Cumberland, De Kalb, Fentress, Jackson, Macon, Overton, Pickett, Putnam, Smith, White.

Indexing & Storage: Cases are indexed by defendant, plaintiff, and case number. New cases are available in the index 1 month after filing date. Records are also indexed on microfiche. Open records are located at the Nashville Division.

Fee & Payment Notes: Payment may be made by money order, cashier check, business check.

Personal checks are not accepted. Payee: Clerk, US District Court.

Phone Search: Only docket information is available by phone.

In Person Search: In person searching available.

PACER: Toll-free dial-up access: 800-458-2994. Local dial-up access: 615-736-7164. Case records are available back three years. Records are purged every year. New records are available online after 1 day. PACER is available online at http://pacer.tnmd.uscourts.gov.

Nashville Division 800 US Courthouse, 801 Broadway, Nashville, TN 37203 (Courier Address: Use mail address for courier delivery), 615-736-5498, Fax: 615-736-7488.

www.tnmd.uscourts.gov

Counties: Cannon, Cheatham, Davidson, Dickson, Houston, Humphreys, Montgomery, Robertson, Rutherford, Stewart, Sumner, Trousdale, Williamson, Wilson.

Indexing & Storage: Cases are indexed by defendant, plaintiff, and case number. New cases are available in the index immediately after filing date. Records are also indexed on microfiche. Open records are located at this court.

Fee & Payment Notes: Payment may be made by money order, cashier check, personal check. Payee: Clerk, US District Court.

Phone Search: Only docket information is available by phone.

Fax Search: Will accept fax search at $15.00 per name.

Mail Search: A stamped self addressed envelope is not required.

In Person Search: In person searching available.

PACER: Toll-free dial-up access: 800-458-2994. Local dial-up access: 615-736-7164. Case records are available back three years. Records are purged every year. New records are available online after 1 day. PACER is available online at http://pacer.tnmd.uscourts.gov.

US Bankruptcy Court

Middle District of Tennessee

Nashville Division PO Box 24890, Nashville, TN 37202-4890 (Courier Address: Customs House, Room 200, 701 Broadway, Nashville, TN 37203), 615-736-5584.

www.tnmb.uscourts.gov

Counties: Cannon, Cheatham, Clay, Cumberland, Davidson, De Kalb, Dickson, Fentress, Giles, Hickman, Houston, Humphreys, Jackson, Lawrence, Lewis, Macon, Marshall, Maury, Montgomery, Overton, Pickett, Putnam, Robertson, Rutherford, Smith, Stewart, Sumner, Trousdale, Wayne, White, Williamson, Wilson.

Indexing & Storage: Cases are indexed by debtor as well as by case number. New cases are available in the index 24 hours after filing date. Open records are located at this court.

Fee & Payment Notes: Payment may be made by money order, cashier check, business check. Personal checks are not accepted. Payee: Clerk, US Bankruptcy Court.

Phone Search: Only docket information is available by phone.

In Person Search: In person searching available.

PACER: Sign-up number is 615-736-5577. Access fee is. Case records are available back to September 1989. Records are never purged. New civil records are available online after 1 day. PACER is available online at http://pacer.tnmb.uscourts.gov. To search for free you may request an exemption by downloading a registration form from: http://pacer.psc.uscourts.gov/faxform.html. Fax the form to (210) 301-6441.

Electronic Filing: (Currently in the process of implementing CM/ECF.)

Other Online Access: Search "mega cases" at the web site main page; in the database selection box choose "Mega Cases" and follow prompts. Court calendars are also available. Court does not participate in the U.S. party case index.

US District Court

Western District of Tennessee

Jackson Division Rm 26, US Courthouse 262, 111 S Highland, Jackson, TN 38301 (Courier: same), 731-421-9200, Fax: 731-421-9210.

www.tnwd.uscourts.gov

Counties: Benton, Carroll, Chester, Crockett, Decatur, Gibson, Hardeman, Hardin, Haywood, Henderson, Henry, Lake, McNairy, Madison, Obion, Perry, Weakley.

Indexing & Storage: Cases are indexed by defendant, plaintiff, and case number. New cases are available in the index 1-2 days after filing date. Open records are located at this court.

Fee & Payment Notes: Payment may be made by money order, cashier check, personal check, Visa, Mastercard. Payee: Clerk, US District Court.

Phone Search: Only docket information is available by phone.

In Person Search: In person searching available.

PACER: Toll-free dial-up access: 800-407-4456. Local dial-up access: 901-495-1259. Case records are available back to 1993. Records are purged as deemed necessary. New records are available online after 2 days.

Memphis Division Federal Bldg, Room 242, 167 N Main, Memphis, TN 38103 (Courier Address: Use mail address for courier delivery), 901-495-1200, Fax: 901-495-1250.

www.tnwd.uscourts.gov

Counties: Dyer, Fayette, Lauderdale, Shelby, Tipton.

Indexing & Storage: Cases are indexed by defendant, plaintiff, and case number. New cases are available in the index 1-2 days after filing date. Open records are located at this court.

Fee & Payment Notes: Payment may be made by money order, cashier check, personal check, Visa, Mastercard. Payee: Clerk, US District Court.

Phone Search: Only docket information is available by phone.

Fax Search: Will accept fax searches with credit card. Will fax docket listings at $.50 per page.

In Person Search: In person searching available.

PACER: Toll-free dial-up access: 800-407-4456. Local dial-up access: 901-495-1259. Case records are available back to 1993. Records are purged as deemed necessary. New records are available online after 2 days.

US Bankruptcy Court

Western District of Tennessee

Jackson Division Room 107, 111 S Highland Ave, Jackson, TN 38301 (Courier Address: Use mail address for courier delivery), 731-421-9300.

www.tnwb.uscourts.gov

Counties: Benton, Carroll, Chester, Crockett, Decatur, Gibson, Hardeman, Hardin, Haywood, Henderson, Henry, Lake, Madison, McNairy, Obion, Perry, Weakley.

Indexing & Storage: Cases are indexed by debtor as well as by case number. New cases are available in the index 1-2 days after filing date. Open records are located at this court.

Fee & Payment Notes: Payment may be made by money order, cashier check, business check. Personal checks are not accepted. A search fee is charged only when certification of the search is issued. Payee: US Bankruptcy Court.

Phone Search: Only docket information is available by phone. An automated voice case information service (VCIS) is available. Call VCIS at 800-767-1512 or 423-752-5272.

Mail Search: A stamped self addressed envelope is not required.

In Person Search: In person searching available.

PACER: Toll-free dial-up access: 800-406-0190. Local dial-up access: 901-328-3617. Case records are available back to 1989. Records are never purged. New civil records are available online after 2 days.

Memphis Division Suite 413, 200 Jefferson Ave, Memphis, TN 38103 (Courier Address: Use mail address for courier delivery), 901-328-3500, Fax: 901-328-3500.

www.tnwb.uscourts.gov

Counties: Dyer, Fayette, Lauderdale, Shelby, Tipton.

Indexing & Storage: Cases are indexed by debtor as well as by case number. New cases are available in the index 2 days after filing date. Open records are located at this court.

Fee & Payment Notes: Payment may be made by money order, cashier check, business check. Personal checks are not accepted. In general, if the cost of copies exceeds the amount of the check, the court will bill for the excess by mail. Payee: Clerk, US Bankruptcy Court.

Phone Search: Only docket information is available by phone. An automated voice case information service (VCIS) is available. Call VCIS at 888-381-4961.

Mail Search: A stamped self addressed envelope is not required.

In Person Search: In person searching available.

PACER: Toll-free dial-up access: 800-406-0190. Local dial-up access: 901-328-3617. Case records are available back to 1989. Records are never purged. New civil records are available online after 2 days. PACER is available online at http://pacer.tnwb.uscourts.gov.

Electronic Filing: (Currently in the process of implementing CM/ECF.)

Tennessee County Courts

Court	Jurisdiction	No. of Courts	How Organized
Circuit Courts*	General	15	31 Districts
Chancery Courts*	General	87	31 Districts
General Sessions Courts*	Limited	16	By County
Combined Circuit/ General Sessions*		87	By County
Municipal Courts	Municipal	300	
Probate Courts*	Probate	5	By County
Juvenile Courts	Special	17	By County

* Profiled in this Sourcebook.

CIVIL									
Court	Tort	Contract	Real Estate	Min. Claim	Max. Claim	Small Claims	Estate	Eviction	Domestic Relations
Circuit Courts*	X	X	X	$0	No Max				X
Chancery Court*	X	X	X	$0	No Max		X		X
General Sessions Courts*	X	X	X	$0	$15,000	X	X		X
Municipal Courts									
Probate Courts*							X		
Juvenile Courts									X

CRIMINAL					
Court	Felony	Misdemeanor	DWI/DUI	Preliminary Hearing	Juvenile
Circuit Courts*	X	X	X		
Criminal Courts*	X	X	X		
Chancery Court*					
General Sessions Courts*		X	X	X	X
Municipal Courts		X	X		
Probate Courts*					
Juvenile Courts					X

ADMINISTRATION   Administrative Office of the Courts, 511 Union St (Nashville City Center) #600, Nashville, TN, 37219; 615-741-2687, Fax: 615-741-6285. www.tsc.state.tn.us

COURT STRUCTURE   Criminal cases are handled by the Circuit Courts and General Sessions Courts. Generally, misdemeanor cases are heard by General Sessions, but in Circuit Court if connected to a felony. All General Sessions Courts have raised the maximum civil case limit to $15,000 from $10,000. The Chancery Courts, in addition to handling probate, also hear certain types of equitable civil cases. Combined courts vary by county, and the counties of Davidson, Hamilton, Knox, and Shelby have separate Criminal Courts.

ONLINE ACCESS   The Administrative Office of Courts provides access to Appellate Court opinions at the web site www.tsc.state.tn.us. Several counties offer online access to court records.

PROBATE COURTS   Probate is handled in the Chancery or County Courts, except in Shelby and Davidson Counties where it is handled by the Probate Court.

Anderson County

7th District Circuit & General Sessions

Court 100 Main St, Clinton, TN 37716; 865-457-5400. Hours: 8AM-4:30PM (EST). *Felony, Misdemeanor, Civil, Eviction, Small Claims.*

Civil Records: Access: In person only. Visitors must perform in person searches for themselves. No search fee. Required to search: name, years to search. Civil cases indexed by defendant, plaintiff. Civil records on computer from 1988, archived from 1947.

Criminal Records: Access: In person only. Visitors must perform in person searches for themselves. No search fee. Required to search: name, years to search, DOB, SSN. Criminal records on computer from 1988, archived from 1947.

General Information: Public access terminal is available. No juvenile records released. Copy fee: $1.00 per page. Certification fee: $4.00. Fee payee: Circuit Court Clerk or General Sessions Clerk. Personal checks accepted. Prepayment is required.

Chancery Court Anderson County Courthouse, PO Box 501, Clinton, TN 37717; 865-457-5400; Fax: 865-457-6267. 8:30AM-4:30PM (EST). *Civil, Probate.*

Civil Records: Access: Phone, mail, in person. Both court and visitors may perform in person searches. No search fee. Required to search: name, years to search. Civil cases indexed by defendant, plaintiff. Civil records on computer 1992 to present, prior records on another system.

General Information: No adoption or mental health records released. Copy fee: $2.00 for first page, $1.00 each add'l. Certification fee: $4.00. Fee payee: Clerk and Master. Personal checks accepted. Prepayment is required.

Bedford County

17th District Circuit & General Sessions

Court 1 Public Sq, #200, Shelbyville, TN 37160; 931-684-3223. Hours: 8AM-4PM M-Th, 8AM-5PM Fri (CST). *Felony, Misdemeanor, Civil, Eviction, Small Claims.*

Civil Records: Access: In person only. Visitors must perform in person searches for themselves. No search fee. Required to search: name, years to search. Civil cases indexed by defendant, plaintiff. Civil records on archives and books from 1934; computerized records since 1994.

Criminal Records: Access: In person only. Visitors must perform in person searches for themselves. No search fee. Required to search: name, years to search, DOB; also helpful: SSN. Criminal records on archives and books from 1934; computerized records since 1994.

General Information: Public access terminal is available. No juvenile, adoptions, mental health, expunged or sealed records released. Copy fee: $.50 per page. Fee payee: Thomas Smith, Clerk. Personal checks accepted. Prepayment is required.

Chancery Court Chancery Court, 1 Public Sq, #302, Shelbyville, TN 37160; 931-684-1672. Hours: 8AM-4PM M-Th, 8AM-5PM Fri (CST). *Civil, Probate.*

Civil Records: Access: In person only. Visitors must perform in person searches for themselves. No search fee. Required to search: name, years to search. Civil cases indexed by defendant, plaintiff. Civil records on books from 9/82 (probate), prior records back to 1800s filed in county clerk's office.

General Information: No adoption records released. Turnaround time same day. Copy fee: $.50 per page. Certification fee: $5.00. Fee payee: Clerk and Master. Personal checks accepted. Prepayment is required.

Benton County

24th District Circuit & General Sessions

Court 1 East Court Sq Rm 207, Camden, TN 38320; 731-584-6711; Fax: 731-584-0475. Hours: 8AM-4PM M-Th; 8AM-5PM F (CST). *Felony, Misdemeanor, Civil, Eviction, Small Claims.*

Civil Records: Access: In person only. Both court and visitors may perform in person searches. No search fee. Required to search: name, years to search. Civil cases indexed by defendant, plaintiff. Civil records computerized since 1995. Public can only use docket books to search, older records archived to 1800s.

Criminal Records: Access: In person only. Both court and visitors may perform in person searches. No search fee. Required to search: name, years to search. Criminal records computerized since 1995. Public can only use docket books to search, older records archived to 1800s.

General Information: No juvenile records released without judge approval. Copy fee: $1.00 per page. Certification fee: $5.00. Fee payee: Circuit Court Clerk or General Session. Business checks accepted. Prepayment is required.

Chancery Court 1 E Court Sq, Courthouse Rm 206, Camden, TN 38320; 731-584-4435; Fax: 731-584-1407. Hours: 8AM-4PM M-Th; 8AM-5PM F (CST). *Civil, Probate.*

Civil Records: Access: In person only. Visitors must perform in person searches for themselves. No search fee. Required to search: name, years to search. Civil cases indexed by defendant, plaintiff. Civil records in books since 1880.

General Information: Public access terminal is available. No adoption or sealed records released. Certification fee: $6.00. Fee payee: Clerk & Master. No personal checks accepted. Prepayment is required.

Bledsoe County

12th District Circuit & General Sessions

Court PO Box 455, Pikeville, TN 37367; 423-447-6488; Fax: 423-447-6856. Hours: 8AM-4PM (CST). *Felony, Misdemeanor, Civil, Eviction, Small Claims.*

Civil Records: Access: In person only. Visitors must perform in person searches for themselves. No search fee. Required to search: name, years to search. Civil cases indexed by plaintiff. Civil records archived from 1920 in books.

Criminal Records: Access: In person only. Visitors must perform in person searches for themselves. Search fee: No search fee. Required to search: name, years to search, DOB. Criminal records archived from 1920 in books.

General Information: Public access terminal is available. (Only criminal records are available.) No juvenile records released. Copy fee: $.25 per page. Prepayment is required.

Chancery Court PO Box 389, Pikeville, TN 37367; 423-447-2484; Fax: 423-447-6856. Hours: 8AM-4PM M,T,W,F; 8AM-Noon Sat (CST). *Civil, Probate.*

Civil Records: Access: Fax, mail, in person. Both court and visitors may perform in person searches. No search fee. Required to search: name, years to search. Civil cases indexed by defendant, plaintiff. Civil records on books since 1856.

General Information: No juvenile or adoption records released. Turnaround time 3 days. Copy fee: $1.00 per page. Certification fee: $2.00 per page. Fee payee: Bledsoe County Clerk and Master. Personal checks accepted.

Blount County

5th District Circuit & General Sessions

Court 926 E Lamar Alexander Pkwy, Maryville, TN 37804-6201; 865-273-5450; Fax: 865-273-5411. Hours: 8AM-4:30PM (EST). *Felony, Misdemeanor, Civil, Eviction, Small Claims.*

Civil Records: Access: Mail, in person. Both court and visitors may perform in person searches. Search fee: $15.00 per name. Required to search: name, years to search. Civil cases indexed by defendant, plaintiff. Civil records archived in books back to 1991; on computer back to 1996.

Criminal Records: Access: Mail, in person. Only visitors may perform in person searches. Required to search: name, years to search. Criminal records archived in books back to 1991; on computer back to 1996.

General Information: No juvenile records released. Turnaround time 3-6 days. Copy fee: $1.00 per page. Certification fee: $5.00. Fee payee: Circuit Court Clerk or General Session. Business checks accepted. Prepayment is required.

Circuit Court 926 E Lamar Alexander Parkway, Maryville, TN 37804; 865-273-5400; Fax: 865-273-5411. 8AM-4:30PM (EST). *Misdemeanor, Civil.*

Civil Records: Access: Mail, in person. Both court and visitors may perform in person searches. Search fee: $15.00 per name. Required to search: name, years to search. Civil cases indexed by defendant. Civil records on books.

Criminal Records: Access: In person only. Visitors must perform in person searches for themselves. Search fee: $15.00 per name. Required to search: name, years to search. Criminal records on books.

General Information: Public access terminal is available. No juvenile records released. Copy fee: $1.00 per page. Certification fee: $2.00. Fee payee: Circuit Court Clerk. Only cashiers checks and money orders accepted. Prepayment is required.

Bradley County

10th District Circuit & General Sessions

Court Courthouse, Rm 205, 155 N Ocoee St, Cleveland, TN 37311-5068; 423-476-0692; Fax: 423-476-0488. Hours: 8:30AM-4:30PM M-Th, 8:30AM-5PM Fri (EST). *Felony, Misdemeanor, Civil, Eviction, Small Claims.*

Civil Records: Access: Mail, in person. Both court and visitors may perform in person searches. Search fee: $25.00 per name. Required to search: name, years to search. Civil cases indexed by defendant, plaintiff. Civil records archived from 1990, on computer from 1990.

Criminal Records: Access: Mail, in person. Both court and visitors may perform in person searches. Search fee: $25.00 per name plus $2.00 data charge. Required to search: name, years to search, signed release. Criminal records archived from 1990, on computer from 1990.

General Information: No juvenile records released. Turnaround time 10 days. Fax notes: Fee to fax results is $1.00 per page. Copy fee: $.30 per page. Certification fee: $10.00. Fee payee: Circuit Court Clerk or General Session. Personal checks accepted. Prepayment is required.

Chancery Court Chancery Court, 155 N. Ocoee St, Cleveland, TN 37311; 423-476-0526. Hours: 8:30AM-4:30PM M-Th, 8:30AM-5PM Fri (EST). *Civil, Probate.*

Civil Records: Access: Phone, in person. Both court and visitors may perform in person searches. No search fee. Required to search: name, years to search. Civil cases indexed by defendant, plaintiff. Civil records filed in books back to 1861.

General Information: No adoption records released. Turnaround time same day. Copy fee: $.25 per page. Certification fee: $10.00. Fee payee: Clerk and Master. Personal checks accepted.

Campbell County

8th District Circuit & General Sessions Court PO Box 26, Jacksboro, TN 37757; 423-562-2624. Hours: 8AM-4:30PM (EST). *Felony, Misdemeanor, Civil, Eviction, Small Claims.*

Civil Records: Access: Mail, in person. Both court and visitors may perform in person searches. No search fee. Required to search: name, years to search. Civil cases indexed by defendant, plaintiff. Civil records on computer since 1991. On microfiche from 1987 and archived since court started located at La Follette Library, La Follette, TN 37766.

Criminal Records: Access: Mail, in person. Both court and visitors may perform in person searches. No search fee. Required to search: name, years to search, DOB, SSN. Criminal records on computer since 1991. On microfiche from 1987 and archived since court started located at La Follette Library, La Follette, TN 37766.

General Information: Public access terminal is available. No juvenile, adoption and judicial hospitalization records released. Turnaround time depends on type of search. Copy fee: $1.00 per page. Certification fee: $3.00. Fee payee: Circuit Court Clerk or General Session. Business checks accepted. Prepayment is required.

Chancery Court PO Box 182 (570 Main St, #110), Jacksboro, TN 37757; 423-562-3496. Hours: 8AM-4:30PM (EST). *Civil, Probate.*

Civil Records: Access: In person, mail. Visitors must perform in person searches for themselves. No search fee. Required to search: name, years to search. Civil cases indexed by defendant, plaintiff. Civil records filed in books, microfiche available at LaFollette Library since 1842.

General Information: No adoption records released. SASE preferred. Turnaround time 1-2 days. Fax notes: Fee to fax results is $1.00 per page and $.50 per document. Copy fee: $1.00 per page. Certification fee: $4.00. Fee payee: Clerk and Master. Business checks accepted.

Cannon County

16th District Circuit & General Sessions Court County Courthouse Public Sq, Woodbury, TN 37190; 615-563-4461; Fax: 615-563-6391. Hours: 8AM-4PM M,T,Th,F; 8AM-Noon Wed (CST). *Felony, Misdemeanor, Civil, Eviction, Small Claims.*

Civil Records: Access: In person only. Visitors must perform in person searches for themselves. No search fee. Required to search: name, years to search. Civil cases indexed by defendant, plaintiff. Civil records archived on books from 1980s.

Criminal Records: Access: In person only. Visitors must perform in person searches for themselves. No search fee. Required to search: name, years to search, DOB. Criminal records archived on books from 1980s.

General Information: No juvenile records released. Copy fee: $1.00 per page. Certification fee: $3.00. Fee payee: Circuit Court Clerk or General Session. Personal checks accepted. Prepayment is required.

County Court County Courthouse Public Square, Woodbury, TN 37190; 615-563-4278/5936; Fax: 615-563-5696. Hours: 8AM-4PM M,T,Th,F; 8AM-Noon Sat (CST). *Probate.*

Carroll County

24th District Circuit & General Sessions Court 99 Court Sq #103, Huntingdon, TN 38344; 731-986-1929. Hours: 8AM-4PM (CST). *Felony, Misdemeanor, Civil, Eviction, Small Claims.*

Civil Records: Access: In person only. Only the court may perform the searches Search fee: $5.00 per name. Required to search: name, years to search. Civil cases indexed by defendant, plaintiff. Civil records archived from 1924; on computer from 1989.

Criminal Records: Access: In person only. Only the court may perform the searches Search fee: $5.00 per name. Required to search: name, years to search, DOB. Criminal records archived from 1925; on computer from 1989.

General Information: Copy fee: $.50 per page. No copies by mail. Certification fee: $6.00. Fee payee: Circuit Court Clerk or General Session. Only cashiers checks and money orders accepted. Prepayment is required.

Chancery Court 99 Court Sq, #105, Huntingdon, TN 38344; 731-986-1920. Hours: 8AM-4PM M-F (CST). *Civil, Probate.*

Civil Records: Access: Mail, in person. Both court and visitors may perform in person searches. Search fee: $15.00. Required to search: name, years to search. Civil cases indexed by defendant, plaintiff. Civil records on computer since 6/88, records go back to 1822.

General Information: No adoption or sealed documents released. SASE required ($.52 postage). Turnaround time 5-10 days. Copy fee: $1.00 per page and $3.00 per document. Certification fee: $6.00. Fee payee: Clerk and Master. No out-of-state checks, money orders and cashiers checks accepted. Prepayment is required.

Carter County

1st District Circuit & General Sessions Court Carter County Justice Center, 900 E Elk Ave, Elizabethton, TN 37643; 423-542-1835; Fax: 423-542-3742. Hours: 8AM-5PM (EST). *Felony, Misdemeanor, Civil, Eviction, Small Claims.*

Civil Records: Access: In person only. Visitors must perform in person searches for themselves. No search fee. Required to search: name, years to search. Civil cases indexed by defendant, plaintiff. Civil records archived from 1800s (partial lost in fire), on computer from 4-92.

Criminal Records: Access: In person only. Visitors must perform in person searches for themselves. No search fee. Required to search: name, years to search. Criminal records archived from 1800s (partial lost in fire), on computer from 4-92.

General Information: Public access terminal is available. No juvenile, psychiatric or expunged records released. Certification fee: $4.00 plus $1.00 each add'l page. Fee payee: Circuit Court Clerk or General Session. Personal checks okay. Prepayment is required.

County Court 801 E Elk, Elizabethton, TN 37643; 423-542-1814; Fax: 423-547-1502. Hours: 8AM-5PM (EST). *Probate.*

Cheatham County

23rd District Circuit Court 100 Public Sq, RM 225, Ashland City, TN 37015; 615-792-3272; Fax: 615-792-3203. Hours: 8AM-4PM (CST). *Felony, Civil Actions over $15,000, Misdemeanors.*

Note: Circuit Court is Rm 225, General Sessions is Rm 223 (615-792-4866); they must be searched separately. Circuit court handles felony, civil actions over $15,000, some misdemeanors; General Sessions handles misdemeanors, small claims, civil under $15,000.

Civil Records: Access: Mail, in person. Both court and visitors may perform in person searches. Search fee: $5.00 per name. Required to search: name, years to search. Civil cases indexed by defendant, plaintiff. Civil records archived on books from 1946 in office, since court started in storage and on computer from 1990.

Criminal Records: Access: Mail, in person. Both court and visitors may perform in person searches. Search fee: $5.00 per name. Required to search: name, years to search. Criminal records archived on books from 1946 in office, since court started in storage and on computer from 1990.

General Information: No juvenile records released. SASE required. Turnaround time 2-3 days. Copy fee: $2.50 per document (or $1.00 per page). Certification fee: $5.00. Fee payee: Circuit Court Clerk. Prepayment is required.

General Sessions 100 Public Sq, RM 223, Ashland City, TN 37015; 615-792-4866; Fax: 615-792-3203. Hours: 8AM-4PM (CST). *Misdemeanor, Civil under $15,000, Eviction, Small Claims.*

Civil Records: Access: Mail, in person. Both court and visitors may perform in person searches. Search fee: $5.00 per name. Required to search: name, years to search. Civil cases indexed by defendant, plaintiff. Civil records archived on books from 1946 in office, since court started in storage and on computer from 1990.

Criminal Records: Access: Mail, in person. Both court and visitors may perform in person searches. Search fee: $5.00 per name. Required to search: name, years to search. Criminal records archived on books from 1946 in office, since court started in storage and on computer from 1990.

General Information: No juvenile records released. SASE required. Turnaround time 2-3 days. Copy fee: $2.50 per document (or $1.00 per page). Certification fee: $5.00. Fee payee: General Sessions Clerk. Prepayment is required.

Chancery Court Clerk & Master, #106, Ashland City, TN 37015; 615-792-4620. Hours: 8AM-4PM (CST). *Civil, Probate.*

Civil Records: Access: In person only. Visitors must perform in person searches for themselves. No search fee. Required to search: name, years to search. Civil cases indexed by defendant, plaintiff. Civil records on computer.

General Information: No adoption records released. SASE required. Turnaround time same day. Copy fee: $1.00 per page. Certification fee: $2.00. Fee payee: Chancery Court. Personal checks accepted. Prepayment is required.

Chester County

26th District Circuit & General Sessions Court PO Box 133, Henderson, TN 38340; 731-989-2454. Hours: 8AM-4PM (CST). *Felony, Misdemeanor, Civil, Eviction, Small Claims.*

Civil Records: Access: Mail, in person. Both court and visitors may perform in person searches. Search fee: $20.00. Required to search: name, years to search. Civil cases indexed by defendant, plaintiff. Civil records in books and archived from 1892.

Criminal Records: Access: Mail, in person. Both court and visitors may perform in person searches. Search fee: $20.00 per name. Required to search: name, years to search, DOB. Criminal records in books and archived from 1892.

General Information: No juvenile records released. Turnaround time 2 days. Copy fee: $1.00 per page. Certification fee: $5.00. Fee payee: Circuit Court, or General Sessions Clerk. Prepayment is required.

Chancery Court Clerk & Master, PO Box 262, Henderson, TN 38340; 731-989-7171; Fax: 731-989-7176. Hours: 8AM-4PM (CST). *Civil, Probate.*

Civil Records: Access: In person only. Visitors must perform in person searches for themselves. No search fee. Required to search: name, years to search. Civil cases indexed by defendant, plaintiff. Civil records on books.

General Information: No adoption or sealed records released. Copy fee: $1.00 per page. Certification fee: $3.00. Fee payee: Clerk and Master. Personal checks accepted.

Claiborne County

8th District Criminal, Circuit & General Sessions Court 1740 Main Street, #201, Tazewell, TN 37879; 423-626-8181; Fax: 423-626-5631. Hours: 8:30AM-4PM M-F, 9AM-Noon Sat (EST). *Felony, Misdemeanor, Civil, Eviction, Small Claims.*

Civil Records: Access: Mail, fax, in person. Both court and visitors may perform in person searches. Search fee: $10.00 per name. Required to search: name, years to search. Civil cases indexed by defendant, plaintiff. Civil records archived since 1932; on computer back to 1986.

Criminal Records: Access: Mail, fax, in person. Both court and visitors may perform in person searches. Search fee: $10.00 per name. Required to search: name, years to search. Criminal records archived since 1932; on computer back to 1986.

General Information: Public access terminal is available. No adoption records released. SASE required. Turnaround time 2-3 days. Fax notes: Fee to fax results is $.25 per page. Copy fee: $.25 per page. Certification fee: $5.00. Fee payee: Circuit Court Clerk or General Sessions. Business checks accepted. In-state personal checks accepted. Prepayment is required.

Chancery Court PO Box 180, Tazewell, TN 37879; 423-626-3284; Fax: 423-626-3604. Hours: 8:30AM-Noon, 1-4PM (EST). *Civil, Probate.*

Civil Records: Access: Mail, in person. Both court and visitors may perform in person searches. No search fee. Required to search: name, years to search. Civil cases indexed by defendant, plaintiff. Civil records kept on books back to 1932; recent on computer.

General Information: No adoption records released. Turnaround time 1-2 days. Copy fee: $.25 per page. Certification fee: $5.00. Fee payee: Clerk and Master. Personal checks accepted. Prepayment is required.

Clay County

13th District Circuit & General Sessions Court PO Box 749, Celina, TN 38551; 931-243-2557. Hours: 8AM-4PM (CST). *Felony, Misdemeanor, Civil, Eviction, Small Claims.*

Civil Records: Access: In person only. Visitors must perform in person searches for themselves. No search fee. Required to search: name, years to search. Civil cases indexed by defendant, plaintiff. Civil records archived from early 1900s, on microfiche from 1986.

Criminal Records: Access: In person only. Visitors must perform in person searches for themselves. No search fee. Required to search: name, years to search; also helpful: SSN. Criminal records archived from early 1900s, on microfiche from 1986.

General Information: No juvenile records released. Copy fee: $.25 per page. Fee payee: Circuit Court, or General Sessions Clerk. Personal checks accepted. Prepayment is required.

Chancery Court PO Box 332, Celina, TN 38551; 931-243-3145. Hours: 8AM-4PM M,T,Th,F; 8AM-Noon W (CST). *Civil, Probate.*

Civil Records: Access: Mail, in person. Both court and visitors may perform in person searches. No search fee.

Required to search: name, years to search. Civil cases indexed by defendant, plaintiff. Civil records on books.

General Information: No juvenile records released. Turnaround time 1 week. Copy fee: No search fee. Fee payee: Clerk & Master. Personal checks accepted. Prepayment is required.

Cocke County

4th District Circuit Court 111 Court Ave Rm 201, Newport, TN 37821; 423-623-6124; Fax: 423-625-3889. Hours: 8:30AM-5PM (EST). *Felony, Misdemeanor, Civil Actions Over $15,000.*

Civil Records: Access: Phone, fax, mail, in person. Both court and visitors may perform in person searches. Search fee: $3.00 per name. Required to search: name, years to search. Civil cases indexed by defendant, plaintiff. Civil records archived from late 1800s.

Criminal Records: Access: Phone, fax, mail, in person. Both court and visitors may perform in person searches. Search fee: $3.00 per name. Required to search: name, years to search, DOB. Criminal records archived from late 1800s.

General Information: No divorce or sealed records released. SASE not required. Turnaround time ASAP. Copy fee: $.25 per page. Certification fee: $5.00. Fee payee: Circuit Court. Personal checks accepted.

General Sessions Court 111 Court Ave, Newport, TN 37821; 423-623-8619; Fax: 423-623-9808. Hours: 8AM-4PM (EST). *Misdemeanor, Civil Actions Under $15,000, Eviction, Small Claims.*

Civil Records: Access: Phone, mail, in person. Both court and visitors may perform in person searches. Search fee: $3.00 per name. Required to search: name, years to search. Civil cases indexed by defendant, plaintiff. Civil records on books at least 10 years.

Criminal Records: Access: Phone, mail, in person. Both court and visitors may perform in person searches. Search fee: $3.00 per name. Required to search: name, years to search. DOB, SSN. Criminal records on books at least 10 years.

General Information: SASE required. Turnaround time varies. Copy fee: $3.00 per document. Certification fee: $3.00. Fee payee: General Sessions Court. Business checks accepted. Prepayment is required.

Chancery Court Courthouse Annex, 360 E Main St, Suite 103, Newport, TN 37821; 423-623-3321; Fax: 423-625-3642. Hours: 8AM-4:30PM (EST). *Civil, Probate.*

Civil Records: Access: Phone, mail, in person. Only the court performs in person searches; visitors may not. No search fee. Required to search: name, years to search. Civil cases indexed by defendant, plaintiff. Civil records on computer since 1984, on books from 1930.

General Information: No sealed records released. Turnaround time 1 week. Copy fee: $1.00 per document. Certification fee: $3.00. Fee payee: Chancery Court, Clerk and Master. Personal checks accepted. Prepayment is required.

Coffee County

14th District Circuit & General Sessions Court PO Box 629, Manchester, TN 37349; 931-723-5110. Hours: 8AM-4:30PM (CST). *Felony, Misdemeanor, Civil, Eviction, Small Claims.*

Civil Records: Access: Mail, in person. Both court and visitors may perform in person searches. Search fee: $5.00 if July 1, 1996 to present; 10 year check is $10.00; beyond 10 years add $5.00 per year. Required to search: name, years to search. Civil cases indexed by defendant, plaintiff. Civil records archived from late 1800s, indexed chronologically by court date.

Criminal Records: Access: Mail, in person. Both court and visitors may perform in person searches. Search fee: Same fees as civil. Required to search: name, years

to search, DOB; also helpful: SSN. Criminal records archived from late 1800s, indexed chronologically by court date.

General Information: Public access terminal is available. No juvenile record released. Turnaround time 1 week. Copy fee: $1.00 per page. Certification fee: $3.50. Fee payee: General Sessions Clerk. Personal checks accepted. Prepayment is required.

Chancery Court 300 Hillsboro Blvd, Rm 102, Manchester, TN 37355; 931-723-5132. Hours: 8AM-4:30PM (CST). *Civil, Probate.*

Civil Records: Access: Mail, in person. Both court and visitors may perform in person searches. No search fee. Required to search: name, years to search. Civil cases indexed by defendant, plaintiff. Civil records on books after 1980, before 1980 filed in County Clerk's Office.

General Information: No juvenile or adoption records released. Copy fee: $.50 per page. Certification fee: $2.00. Fee payee: Chancery Court. Personal checks accepted. Prepayment is required.

Crockett County

Circuit & General Sessions Court 1 South Bell St, Ste 6 Courthouse, Alamo, TN 38001; 731-696-5462; Fax: 731-696-2605. Hours: 8AM-4PM (CST). *Felony, Misdemeanor, Civil, Eviction, Small Claims.*

Civil Records: Access: Mail, fax, in person. Both court and visitors may perform in person searches. Search fee: $10.00 per name. Required to search: name, years to search. Civil cases indexed by defendant, plaintiff. Civil records archived since court started, records prior to 1986 on docket books. All requests must be in writing.

Criminal Records: Access: Mail, fax, in person. Both court and visitors may perform in person searches. Search fee: $10.00 per name. Required to search: name, years to search, DOB; also helpful: SSN, sex. Criminal records on docket books, on computer from 1993. All requests must be in writing.

General Information: Public access terminal is available. No adoption or mental records released. SASE requested. Turnaround time 1-2 days. Copy fee: $1.00 per page. Certification fee: $6.00. Fee payee: Circuit Court, or General Sessions Clerk. Business checks accepted. Prepayment is required.

Chancery Court 1 South Bells St, #5, Alamo, TN 38001; 731-696-5458; Fax: 731-696-3028. Hours: 8AM-4PM (CST). *Civil, Probate.*

Civil Records: Access: Mail, in person. Both court and visitors may perform in person searches. No search fee. Required to search: name, years to search. Civil cases indexed by defendant, plaintiff. Civil records on books bacl to 1872.

General Information: No adoption records released. SASE required. Turnaround time 1-3 days. Fax notes: Fax back $1.00. Copy fee: $1.00 per page. Certification fee: $4.00. Fee payee: Chancery Court Clerk. Personal checks accepted. Prepayment is required.

Cumberland County

13th District Circuit & General Sessions Court 2 N Main St, #302, Crossville, TN 38555; 931-484-6647; Fax: 931-456-5013. Hours: 8AM-4PM (CST). *Felony, Misdemeanor, Civil, Eviction, Small Claims.*

Civil Records: Access: In person only. Visitors must perform in person searches for themselves. No search fee. Required to search: name, years to search. Civil cases indexed by defendant, plaintiff. Civil records archived on books from 1940s approx.; on computer back to 1996.

Criminal Records: Access: In person only. Visitors must perform in person searches for themselves. No search fee. Required to search: name, years to search,

DOB; also helpful: SSN. Criminal records archived on books from 1940s approx.; on computer back to 1996.
General Information: Public access terminal is available. No sealed records released. Only cashiers checks and money orders accepted. Prepayment is required.

Chancery Court 2 N Main St, #101, Crossville, TN 38555-4583; 931-484-4731. Hours: 8AM-4PM (CST). *Civil, Probate.*

Civil Records: Access: Mail, in person. Only the court performs in person searches; visitors may not. No search fee. Required to search: name, years to search. Civil cases indexed by defendant, plaintiff. Civil records on computer since 1991, on books since 1900s.
General Information: No juvenile, adoption records released. SASE requested. Turnaround time 2 days. Copy fee: $.50 per page. Certification fee: $2.00 per document. Fee payee: Clerk and Master. Personal checks accepted. Prepayment is required.

Davidson County

20th District Criminal Court Metro Courthouse, Rm 305, Nashville, TN 37201; 615-862-5600; Fax: 615-862-5676. Hours: 8AM-4PM (CST). *Felony, Misdemeanor.*
www.nashville.org/ccrt

Criminal Records: Access: Mail, online, in person. Both court and visitors may perform in person searches. Search fee: $15.00 per name. Required to search: name, years to search, DOB, signed release; also helpful: SSN, race. Records from Metropolitan Nashville and Davidson County Criminal Court database are available free online at www.nashville.org/ccrt. Search the criminal court dockets by date. Also, the City of Nashville sponsors an Internet site at www.police.nashville.org/justice/default.asp.
General Information: No records unauthorized by statutes released. SASE required. Turnaround time 2-3 days. Copy fee: $.25 per page. Certification fee: $6.00. Fee payee: Circuit Court Clerk. Personal checks accepted. Credit cards accepted: Visa, MasterCard, Discover. Visa, MC, Discover. Prepayment is required.

Circuit Court 506 Metro Courthouse, Nashville, TN 37201; 615-862-5181. 8AM-4:30PM (CST). *Civil.*
www.nashville.org/cir

Civil Records: Access: Mail, in person. Both court and visitors may perform in person searches. No search fee. Required to search: name, years to search. Civil cases indexed by defendant, plaintiff. Civil records archived on books from 1800s, on computer from 1974.
General Information: Public access terminal is available. No juvenile or adoption records released. Turnaround time 2-3 days. Copy fee: $.50 per page. Certification fee: $2.00 per page. Fee payee: Circuit Court Clerk. Prepayment is required.

General Sessions Court 211 Union St, #202, Nashville, TN 37201; 615-862-5195; Fax: 615-862-5924. Hours: 8AM-4:30PM (CST). *Civil Actions Under $15,000, Eviction, Small Claims.*
www.nashville.org/cir

Civil Records: Access: In person only. Visitors must perform in person searches for themselves. No search fee. Required to search: name, years to search.
General Information: Public access terminal is available. No juvenile records released. Copy fee: $1.00 per page. Certification fee: $3.00 per page. Fee payee: General Sessions Court Clerk. Prepayment is required.

Probate Court 408 Metro Courthouse #105, Nashville, TN 37201; 615-862-5980; Fax: 615-862-5994. Hours: 8AM-4:30 (CST). *Probate.*

De Kalb County

13th District Circuit & General Sessions Court 1 Public Sq, Rm 303, Smithville, TN 37166; 615-597-5711. Hours: 8AM-4:30PM M,T,W,Th; 8AM-5PM Fri (CST). *Felony, Misdemeanor, Civil, Eviction, Small Claims.*

Civil Records: Access: In person only. Both court and visitors may perform in person searches. No search fee. Required to search: name, years to search. Civil cases indexed by defendant, plaintiff. Civil records archived in office last 10 years. Prior to 1982, records are not very accurate because of fire. Dist Court records on computer back to 2001; General Sessions to mid-2000.
Criminal Records: Access: In person only. Visitors must perform in person searches for themselves. No search fee. Required to search: name, years to search, DOB; also helpful: SSN. Criminal records archived in office last 10 years. Prior to 1982, records are not very accurate because of fire. Dist Court records on computer back to 2001; General Sessions to mid-2000.
General Information: Public access terminal is available. No juvenile records released. Copy fee: $1.00 per page. Certification fee: $6.00. Fee payee: Circuit Court, or General Sessions Clerk. Personal checks accepted. Prepayment is required.

Chancery Court 1 Public Square, Rm 302, Smithville, TN 37166; 615-597-4360. Hours: 8AM-4PM (CST). *Civil, Probate.*

Civil Records: Access: In person only. Visitors must perform in person searches for themselves. No search fee. Required to search: name, years to search. Civil cases indexed by defendant, plaintiff. Civil records on books, computerized as of 6/00.
General Information: Public access terminal is available. No adoption, juvenile records released. Fax notes: Do not fax. Copy fee: $1.00 per page. Certification fee: $6.00. Fee payee: Clerk and Master. Personal checks accepted. Prepayment is required.

Decatur County

24th District Circuit & General Sessions Court PO Box 488, Decaturville, TN 38329; 731-852-3125; Fax: 731-852-2130. Hours: 8AM-4PM M,T,Th,F; 8AM-Noon W & Sat (CST). *Felony, Misdemeanor, Civil, Eviction, Small Claims.*

Civil Records: Access: In person only. Visitors must perform in person searches for themselves. No search fee. Required to search: name, years to search. Civil cases indexed by defendant, plaintiff. Civil records archived on books from 192; computerized records since 1996.
Criminal Records: Access: In person only. Visitors must perform in person searches for themselves. No search fee. Required to search: name, years to search, DOB, SSN, signed release. Criminal records archived on books from 1927; computerized records since 1996.
General Information: No adoption records released. Copy fee: $.25 per page. Fee payee: Circuit Court. Business checks accepted. Prepayment is required.

Chancery Court Clerk & Master, Decaturville, TN 38329; 731-852-3422; Fax: 731-852-2130. Hours: 9M-4PM M,T,Th,F; 9AM-Noon Sat (CST). *Civil, Probate.*

Civil Records: Access: In person only. Visitors must perform in person searches for themselves. No search fee. Required to search: name, years to search. Civil cases indexed by plaintiff. Probate records in books since 1869 for probate, civil records in books since 1958.
General Information: No adoption records released. SASE required. Turnaround time 2 days. Copy fee: $.25 per page. Certification fee: $2.00. Fee payee: Elizabeth Carpenter, Clerk and Master. Personal checks accepted.

Dickson County

23rd District Circuit Court Court Square, PO Box 220, Charlotte, TN 37036; 615-789-7010; Probate phone: 615-789-4171; Fax: 615-789-7018. Hours: 8AM-4PM (CST). *Felony, Misdemeanor, Civil Actions Over $15,000.*

Civil Records: Access: Phone, fax, mail, in person. Both court and visitors may perform in person searches. Search fee: $6.00 per name. Required to search: name, years to search. Civil cases indexed by defendant, plaintiff. Civil records archived from 1800s, on computer from 1986, some records back to 1974.
Criminal Records: Access: Phone, fax, mail, in person. Both court and visitors may perform in person searches. Search fee: $6.00 per name. Required to search: name, years to search; also helpful: DOB. Criminal records archived from 1800s, on computer from 1986, some records back to 1974.
General Information: No adoption records released. SASE required. Turnaround time 1 day. Fax notes: $6.00 per document. Copy fee: $.25 per page. Certification fee: $2.00. Fee payee: Circuit Court Clerk. Personal checks accepted. Prepayment is required.

General Sessions PO Box 217, Charlotte, TN 37036; 615-789-5414; Fax: 615-789-3456. Hours: 8AM-4PM (CST). *Civil Actions Under $15,000, Eviction, Small Claims.*

Civil Records: Access: Phone, mail, in person. Both court and visitors may perform in person searches. Search fee: $6.00. Required to search: name, years to search. Civil cases indexed by defendant. Civil records archived since court began, on computer from Aug 1991.
General Information: No sealed or expunged records released. SASE required. Turnaround time 2-3 days. Copy fee: $.50 per page. Certification fee: $3.00. Fee payee: General Sessions. Personal checks accepted. Prepayment is required.

County Court Court Square, PO Box 220, Charlotte, TN 37036; 615-789-0250. Hours: 8AM-4PM (CST). *Probate.*

Dyer County

29th District Circuit & General Sessions Court PO Box 1360, Dyersburg, TN 38025; 731-286-7809; Fax: 731-288-7728. Hours: 8:30AM-4:30PM *Felony, Misdemeanor, Civil, Eviction, Small Claims.*

Civil Records: Access: Mail, in person. Both court and visitors may perform in person searches. Search fee: $25.00 per name. Required to search: name, years to search. Civil cases indexed by defendant, plaintiff. Civil records archived since 1990.
Criminal Records: Access: Mail, in person. Both court and visitors may perform in person searches. Search fee: $25.00 per name. Required to search: name, years to search, DOB, SSN. Criminal records archived since 1990.
General Information: Public access terminal is available. No juvenile records released. SASE not required. Turnaround time 1 week. No copy fee. Fee payee: Circuit Court, or General Sessions Clerk. Personal checks accepted. Prepayment is required.

Chancery Court PO Box 1360, Dyersburg, TN 38024; 731-286-7818; Fax: 731-288-7706. Hours: 8:30AM-4:30PM M-F (CST). *Civil, Probate.*

Civil Records: Access: Mail, in person. Both court and visitors may perform in person searches. No search fee. Required to search: name, years to search. Civil cases indexed by defendant, plaintiff. Civil records on books.
General Information: No adoption, juvenile records released. SASE requested. Turnaround time 1 week. Copy fee: $.50 per page. Certification fee: $1.00. Fee

payee: Chancery Court Clerk. Personal checks accepted. Prepayment is required.

Fayette County

25th District Circuit & General Sessions
Court PO Box 670, Somerville, TN 38068; 901-465-5205; Fax: 901-465-5215. Hours: 9AM-5PM (CST). *Felony, Misdemeanor, Civil, Eviction, Small Claims.*

Civil Records: Access: Mail, in person. Both court and visitors may perform in person searches. Search fee: $10.00. Required to search: name, years to search. Civil cases indexed by defendant, plaintiff. Civil records on computer since 1991, prior records archived since court began, some older records destroyed by fire.

Criminal Records: Access: Mail, in person. Both court and visitors may perform in person searches. Search fee: $10.00. Required to search: name, years to search, DOB, SSN. Criminal records on computer since 1991, prior records archived since court began, some older records destroyed by fire.

General Information: Public access terminal is available. No adoption or sealed records released. SASE required. Turnaround time 2-5 days to search books, immediate for computer records. Copy fee: $.25 per page. Certification fee: $6.00. Fee payee: Circuit Court, or General Sessions Clerk. Personal checks accepted. Prepayment is required.

Chancery Court PO Drawer 220, Somerville, TN 38068; 901-465-5220; Fax: 901-465-5215. Hours: 9AM-5PM (CST). *Civil, Probate.*

Civil Records: Access: In person only. Visitors must perform in person searches for themselves. No search fee. Required to search: name, years to search. Civil cases indexed by defendant, plaintiff. Civil records on computer since 10/92; on books.

General Information: No adoption records released. Copy fee: $1.00 per page. Certification fee: $4.00 first page, $2.00 every add'l page. Fee payee: Clerk and Master. Personal checks accepted.

Fentress County

8th District Circuit & General Sessions
Court PO Box 699, Jamestown, TN 38556; 931-879-7919. Hours: 8AM-4PM M-F; 8AM-Noon Sat (CST). *Felony, Misdemeanor, Civil, Eviction, Small Claims.*

Civil Records: Access: Mail, in person. Both court and visitors may perform in person searches. Search fee: $25.00 per name. Required to search: name, years to search. Civil cases indexed by defendant, plaintiff. Civil records archived from 1800s.

Criminal Records: Access: Mail, in person. Both court and visitors may perform in person searches. Search fee: $25.00 per name. Required to search: name, years to search, DOB, SSN. Criminal records archived from 1800s.

General Information: No juvenile records released. SASE required. Turnaround time 5 days. Copy fee: $.25 per page. Certification fee: $2.00. Fee payee: Circuit Court Clerk or General Session. Personal checks accepted.

Chancery Court PO Box 66, Jamestown, TN 38556; 931-879-8615; Fax: 931-879-4236. Hours: 9AM-5PM M,T,Th,F; 9AM-Noon Wed (CST). *Civil, Probate.*

Civil Records: Access: Mail, in person. Both court and visitors may perform in person searches. No search fee. Required to search: name, years to search. Civil cases indexed by defendant, plaintiff. Civil records in books.

General Information: No sealed or adoption records released. Turnaround time 1-5 days. Copy fee: $.25 per page. Certification fee: $4.00. Fee payee: Clerk and Master. Personal checks accepted. Prepayment is required.

Franklin County

12th District Circuit Court & General
Sessions 1 South Jefferson St, Winchester, TN 37398; 931-967-2923; Fax: 931-962-1479. Hours: 8AM-4:30PM (CST). *Felony, Misdemeanor, Civil, Eviction, Small Claims.*

Civil Records: Access: Mail, in person. Both court and visitors may perform in person searches. Search fee: $10.00 per name. Required to search: name, years to search. Civil cases indexed by defendant, plaintiff. Civil records archived on docket books from 1940s, on computer since mid 1991.

Criminal Records: Access: Mail, in person. Both court and visitors may perform in person searches. Search fee: $10.00 per name. Required to search: name, years to search, DOB; also helpful: SSN. Criminal records archived on docket books from 1940s, on computer since mid 1991.

General Information: Public access terminal is available. No juvenile records released. Turnaround time 1 week. Copy fee: $.25 per page. Certification fee: $4.00. Fee payee: Circuit Court Clerk or General Session. Business checks accepted.

County Court 1 South Jefferson St, Winchester, TN 37398; 931-962-1485; Fax: 931-962-3394. Hours: 8AM-4:30PM; *AM-Noon Sat (CST). *Probate.*

Gibson County

28th District Circuit & General Sessions
Court 295 N College, PO Box 147, Trenton, TN 38382; 731-855-7615; Fax: 731-855-7676. Hours: 8AM-4:30PM (CST). *Felony, Misdemeanor, Civil, Eviction, Small Claims.*

Civil Records: Access: Fax, mail, in person. Both court and visitors may perform in person searches. Search fee: $5.00 per name. Required to search: name, years to search; also helpful: address. Civil cases indexed by defendant, plaintiff. Civil records archived in vault mid 1800s, in office since 1982. On computer since 1990.

Criminal Records: Access: Fax, mail, in person. Both court and visitors may perform in person searches. Search fee: $5.00 per name. Required to search: name, years to search; also helpful: address, DOB, SSN. Criminal records archived in vault mid 1800s, in office since 1982. On computer since 1990.

General Information: Public access terminal is available. No adoption or expunged records released. SASE requested. Turnaround time 1-3 days. Fax notes: No fee to fax results. Copy fee: $.25 per page. $3.00 maximum fee. Certification fee: $5.00. Fee payee: Circuit Court Clerk. Business checks accepted. In-state checks accepted.

Chancery Court Clerk & Master, PO Box 290, Trenton, TN 38382; 731-855-7639; Fax: 731-855-7655. Hours: 8AM-4:30PM (CST). *Civil, Probate.*

Civil Records: Access: In person only. Visitors must perform in person searches for themselves. Required to search: name, years to search. Civil cases indexed by defendant, plaintiff. Probate records in this office since 9/82, prior records filed in County Clerk's office, computerized records go back to 1967.

General Information: No adoption, commitment records released. SASE requested. Turnaround time 1 week. Fax notes: $10.00 per document. Copy fee: $1.00 per page. Certification fee: $4.00. Fee payee: Clerk & Master. Money orders or certified checks accepted. No personal checks. Prepayment is required.

Giles County

22nd District Circuit & General Sessions
Court PO Box 678, Pulaski, TN 38478; 931-363-5311; Fax: 931-424-4790. Hours: 8AM-4PM (CST). *Felony, Misdemeanor, Civil, Eviction, Small Claims.*

Civil Records: Access: mail, fax, in-person. Both court and visitors may perform in person searches. Search fee: $20.00 per name if pre-1990; $5.00 if 1990 to present. Required to search: name, years to search. Civil cases indexed by defendant, plaintiff. Civil records on computer from 1/90, remaining records filed in docket books.

Criminal Records: Access: Phone, mail, fax, in person. Both court and visitors may perform in person searches. Search fee: $20.00 per name if pre-1990; $5.00 if 1990 to present. Required to search: name, years to search, DOB; also helpful: SSN. Criminal records on computer from 1/90, remaining records filed in docket books.

General Information: Public access terminal is available. No juvenile records released without signed release. SASE required. Turnaround time 1 week. Copy fee: $.25 per page. Certification fee: $6.00. Fee payee: Circuit Court Clerk. Prepayment is required.

County Court PO Box 678, Pulaski, TN 38478; 931-363-1509; Fax: 931-424-6101. Hours: 8AM-4PM M-F (CST). *Probate.*

Grainger County

4th District Circuit & General Sessions
Court PO Box 157, Rutledge, TN 37861; 865-828-3605; Hours: 8:30AM-4:30PM (EST). *Felony, Misdemeanor, Civil, Eviction, Small Claims.*

Civil Records: Access: In person only. Visitors must perform in person searches for themselves. No search fee. Required to search: name, years to search. Civil cases indexed by defendant, plaintiff. Civil records archived from 1977 in office.

Criminal Records: Access: In person only. Visitors must perform in person searches for themselves. No search fee. Required to search: name, years to search, DOB, SSN. Criminal records archived from 1977 in office.

General Information: No sealed records released. Copy fee: $.25 per page. Certification fee: $4.00. Fee payee: Circuit Court Clerk. Business checks accepted. Prepayment is required.

Chancery Court Clerk & Master, PO Box 160, Rutledge, TN 37861; 865-828-4436; Fax: 865-828-8714. Hours: 8:30AM-4:30PM M,T,Th,F, 8:30AM-Noon Wed (EST). *Civil, Probate.*

Civil Records: Access: Phone, fax, mail, in person. Both court and visitors may perform in person searches. No search fee. Required to search: name, years to search. Civil cases indexed by defendant, plaintiff. Civil records on books.

General Information: No adoption records released. SASE requested. Turnaround time varies. Copy fee: $1.00 per page. Certification fee: $4.00. Fee payee: Clerk & Master. Personal checks accepted. Prepayment is required.

Greene County

3rd District Circuit & General Sessions
Court 101 S Main, Geene County Courthouse, Greeneville, TN 37743; 423-798-1760; Fax: 423-798-1763. Hours: 8AM-4:30PM (EST). *Felony, Misdemeanor, Civil, Eviction, Small Claims.*

Civil Records: Access: In person only. Visitors must perform in person searches for themselves. No search fee. Required to search: name, years to search. Civil cases indexed by defendant, plaintiff. Civil records archived since court started, on computer from end of 1990.

Criminal Records: Access: In person only. Visitors must perform in person searches for temselves. No search fee. Required to search: name, years to search. Criminal records archived since court started, on computer from end of 1990.

General Information: Public access terminal is available. No adoption records released. Copy fee: $1.00 per page. Certification fee: $3.00. Fee payee: Circuit Court Clerk. Personal checks accepted. Prepayment is required.

County Court 204 N Cutler St, #200, County Courthouse Annex, Greeneville, TN 37745; 423-798-1708, 798-1709; Fax: 423-798-1822. Hours: 8AM-4:30PM (EST). *Probate.*

Grundy County

12th District Circuit & General Sessions Court PO Box 161, Altamont, TN 37301; 931-692-3368; Fax: 931-692-2414. Hours: 8AM-4PM M-Th; 8AM-5PM F (CST). *Felony, Misdemeanor, Civil, Eviction, Small Claims.*

Civil Records: Access: Mail, fax, in person. Both court and visitors may perform in person searches. Search fee: $10.00 per name. Fee is per court. Required to search: name, years to search. Civil cases indexed by defendant, plaintiff. Civil records on computer since 1993, prior records in books to 1990. Before 1990 on microfiche since 1868.

Criminal Records: Access: Mail, fax, in person. Both court and visitors may perform in person searches. Search fee: $10.00 per name. Fee is per court. Required to search: name, years to search, DOB; also helpful: SSN. Criminal records on computer since 1993, prior records in books to 1990. Before 1990 on microfiche since 1868.

General Information: No juvenile records released. Turnaround time 5 days. Fax notes: Fee to fax results is $4.00 per document. Copy fee: $1.00 per page. Certification fee: $5.00. Fee payee: Circuit Court Clerk. Prepayment is required.

Chancery Court PO Box 174, Altamont, TN 37301; 931-692-3455; Fax: 931-692-4125. Hours: 8AM-4PM M-Th; 8AM-5pm F (CST). *Civil, Probate.*

Civil Records: Access: Phone, mail, in person. Both court and visitors may perform in person searches. Search fee: $5.00 per name. Required to search: name, years to search. Civil cases indexed by defendant, plaintiff. Civil records on computer since 1993, on books back to 1990.

General Information: No adoption records released. SASE requested. Turnaround time 5 days. Copy fee: $.25 per page. Certification fee: $2.00. Fee payee: Clerk & Master. Personal checks accepted. Prepayment is required.

Hamblen County

3rd District Circuit & General Sessions Court 510 Allison St, Morristown, TN 37814; 423-586-5640; Fax: 423-585-2764. Hours: 8AM-4PM M-Th, 8AM-5PM Fri, 9-11:30AM Sat (CST). *Felony, Misdemeanor, Civil, Eviction, Small Claims.*

Civil Records: Access: Mail, in person. Both court and visitors may perform in person searches. Search fee: $5.00 per name. Required to search: name, years to search. Civil cases indexed by defendant, plaintiff. Civil records archived from early 1900s, on computer from 1989.

Criminal Records: Access: Mail, in person. Both court and visitors may perform in person searches. Search fee: $5.00 per name. Required to search: name, years to search, DOB; also helpful: SSN. Criminal records archived from early 1900s, on computer from 1989.

General Information: Public access terminal is available. No adoption records released. SASE required. Turnaround time 1 day. Copy fee: $.25 per page. Certification fee: $4.00. Fee payee: Circuit Court Clerk or General Sessions. Personal checks accepted. Prepayment is required.

Chancery Court 511 West 2nd North St, Morristown, TN 37814; 423-586-9112; Fax: 423-318-2510. Hours: 8AM-4PM M-Th; 8AM-4:30PM F (EST). *Civil.*

Civil Records: Access: Phone, fax, mail, in person. Both court and visitors may perform in person searches. No search fee. Required to search: name, years to search. Civil cases indexed by defendant, plaintiff. Civil records on computer from 1979; prior on books back to 1870's.

General Information: No adoption records released. Turnaround time 3-5 days. Fax notes: $1.00 per page. Copy fee: $.50 per page. Certification fee: $2.00. Fee payee: Clerk & Master. Only cashiers checks and money orders accepted. Prepayment is required.

Hamilton County

11th District Civil Court Room 500 Courthouse, 625 Georgia Ave, Chattanooga, TN 37402; 423-209-6700; Fax: 423-209-6701. Hours: 8AM-4PM (EST). *Civil Actions Over $15,000.*

www.hamiltontn.gov/courts

Civil Records: Access: Phone, fax, mail, in person, online. Both court and visitors may perform in person searches. No search fee. Required to search: name, years to search. Civil cases indexed by defendant, plaintiff. Civil records archived from 1921, on computer back to 7/89. Court minutes are on microfiche. Online access to current court dockets are available free at www.hamiltontn.gov/courts/CircuitClerk/dockets/default.htm.

General Information: Public access terminal is available. No adoptions or judicial hospitalization records released. Turnaround time 1 week. Fax notes: Will fax results to local numbers only. Copy fee: $2.00 per page. Certification fee: $4.00. Fee payee: Circuit Court Clerk. Personal checks accepted. Prepayment is required.

11th District General Sessions Court Civil Division, 600 Market St, Room 111, Chattanooga, TN 37402; 423-209-7630; Fax: 423-209-7631. Hours: 8AM-4PM (EST). *Civil Actions Under $15,000, Eviction, Small Claims.*

www.hamiltontn.gov/courts/sessions/default.htm

Civil Records: Access: Phone, mail, in person, online. Both court and visitors may perform in person searches. No search fee. Required to search: name, years to search. Civil cases indexed by defendant, plaintiff. Civil records archived on docket books, on computer from 6/1985. Online access to current court dockets is available free at www.hamiltontn.gov/courts/CircuitClerk/dockets/default.htm.

General Information: Public access terminal is available. No mental health records released. Turnaround time 3-4 days. Copy fee: $1.00 per page. Certification fee: $4.00. Fee payee: Sessions Court Clerk. Personal checks accepted. Prepayment is required.

11th District Criminal Court 600 Market St, Room 102, Chattanooga, TN 37402; 423-209-7500; Fax: 423-209-7501. Hours: 8AM-4PM (EST). *Felony, Misdemeanor.*

www.hamiltontn.gov/courts/

Criminal Records: Access: Mail, in person, online. Both court and visitors may perform in person searches. Search fee: $10.00 per name. Required to search: name, years to search, DOB, signed release; also helpful: SSN. Criminal records on computer since 1985, prior records in books. Online access to current court dockets are available free at www.hamiltontn.gov/courts/CircuitClerk/dockets/default.htm.

General Information: Public access terminal is available. No juvenile records released. Turnaround time 1 week. Copy fee: No search fee. Fee payee:

Circuit Court Clerk. Personal checks accepted. Prepayment is required.

Chancery Court Chancery Court, Clerk & Master, 201 E 7th St, Rm 300, Chattanooga, TN 37402; 423-209-6600; Fax: 423-209-6601. Hours: 8AM-4PM (EST). *Civil, Probate.*

www.hamiltontn.gov/Courts/ClerkMaster/default.htm

Civil Records: Access: Phone, mail, in person. Both court and visitors may perform in person searches. No search fee. Required to search: name, years to search. Civil cases indexed by defendant, plaintiff. Civil records on index cards from 1919, on dockets from 6/56, microfilm: wills since 1862, inventories since 1911, settlements since 1869, bonds and letters since 1878.

General Information: Public access terminal is available. No mental health, adoption records released. SASE required. Turnaround time 2-3 days. Fax notes: $1.00 per page. Copy fee: $1.00 per page 1-5 pages; $2.00 each 5-10 pages; $.25 over 10. Certification fee: $4.00 ($10 if Act of Congress) plus $2.00 per page. Fee payee: Hamilton County Clerk and Master. Personal checks accepted. Prepayment is required.

Hancock County

3rd District Circuit & General Sessions Court PO Box 347, Sneedville, TN 37869; 423-733-2954; Fax: 423-733-2119. Hours: 8AM-4PM (EST). *Felony, Misdemeanor, Civil, Eviction, Small Claims.*

Civil Records: Access: Mail, in person. Both court and visitors may perform in person searches. Search fee: $4.00 per name. Required to search: name, years to search. Civil cases indexed by plaintiff. Civil records archived on books from 1934.

Criminal Records: Access: Mail, in person. Both court and visitors may perform in person searches. Search fee: $4.00 per name. Required to search: name, years to search, DOB; also helpful: SSN. Criminal records archived on books from 1934.

General Information: Public access terminal is available. No juvenile records released. Turnaround time 3-4 days. Copy fee: $.50 per page. Fee payee: Circuit Court Clerk. Personal checks accepted. Prepayment is required.

Chancery Court PO Box 277, Sneedville, TN 37869; 423-733-4524; Fax: 423-733-2762. Hours: 9AM-4PM (EST). *Civil, Probate.*

Civil Records: Access: Mail, in person. Both court and visitors may perform in person searches. No search fee. Required to search: name, years to search. Civil cases indexed by defendant, plaintiff. Civil records on books.

General Information: No adoption records released. SASE requested. Turnaround time 2 days. Copy fee: $.50 per page. Certification fee: $1.00. Fee payee: Clerk & Master. Personal checks accepted. Prepayment is required.

Hardeman County

25th District Circuit & General Sessions Court Courthouse, 100 N Main, Bolivar, TN 38008; 731-658-6524; Fax: 731-658-4584. Hours: 8:30AM-4:30PM M-Th, 8AM-5PM Fri (CST). *Felony, Misdemeanor, Civil, Eviction, Small Claims.*

Civil Records: Access: In person only. Visitors must perform in person searches for themselves. No search fee. Required to search: name, years to search. Civil cases indexed by defendant, plaintiff. Civil records on computer since 12/92, archived General Sessions from 1960 and Circuit from 1800s.

Criminal Records: Access: In person only. Visitors must perform in person searches for themselves. No search fee. Required to search: name, years to search, DOB, SSN, signed release. Criminal records on computer since 12/92, archived General Sessions from 1960 and Circuit from 1800s.

General Information: No juvenile records released. Copy fee: $1.00 per page. Certification fee: $4.00 per document. Fee payee: Circuit Court Clerk. Only cashiers checks and money orders accepted. Hardeman county personal checks accepted. Prepayment is required.

Chancery Court PO Box 45, Bolivar, TN 38008; 731-658-3142; Fax: 731-658-4580. Hours: 8:30AM-4:30PM M-Th, 8:30AM-5PM Fri *Civil, Probate.*

Civil Records: Access: Phone, mail, fax, in person. Both court and visitors may perform in person searches. No search fee. Required to search: name, years to search. Civil cases indexed by defendant, plaintiff. Civil records on books back to 1825; computerized back to 1975.

General Information: No mental health, adoption records released. SASE requested. Turnaround time 1 day. Fax notes: Fee to fax results is $.25 per page. Copy fee: $.25 per page. Additional fee for postage. Certification fee: $4.00. Fee payee: Chancery Court Clerk. Business checks accepted. Prepayment required.

Hardin County

24th District Circuit & General Sessions Court 601 Main St, Savannah, TN 38372; 731-925-3583; Fax: 731-926-2955. Hours: 8AM-4:30PM M,T,Th,F, 8AM-Noon Wed (CST). *Felony, Misdemeanor, Civil, Eviction, Small Claims.*

Civil Records: Access: In person only. Visitors must perform in person searches for themselves. No search fee. Required to search: name, years to search. Civil cases indexed by defendant, plaintiff. Civil records archived on books and on microfiche from 1800s, on computer from 1996.

Criminal Records: Access: In person only. Visitors must perform in person searches for themselves. No search fee. Required to search: name, years to search. Criminal records archived on books and on microfiche from 1800s, on computer from 1996.

General Information: No juvenile records released. Certification fee: $5.00. Fee payee: Circuit Court Clerk. Hardin county personal checks accepted. Prepayment required.

County Court 601 Main St, Savannah, TN 38372; 731-925-3921; Fax: 731-926-4313. 8AM-4:30PM M,T,TH,F, 8AM-12PM Wed & Sat (CST). *Probate.*

Hawkins County

3rd District Circuit & General Sessions Court 100 E Main St, Rogersville, TN 37857; 423-272-3397; Fax: 423-272-9646. Hours: 8AM-4PM (EST). *Felony, Misdemeanor, Civil, Eviction, Small Claims.*

Civil Records: Access: In person only. Visitors must perform in person searches for themselves. No search fee. Required to search: name, years to search. Civil cases indexed by defendant, plaintiff. Civil records archived on books from 1800s.

Criminal Records: Access: In person only. Visitors must perform in person searches for themselves. No search fee. Required to search: name, years to search. Criminal records archived on books from 1800s.

General Information: No juvenile records released. Copy fee: $1.00 per page. Certification fee: $4.00 ($6 if Acts of Congress) plus $2.00 per page. Fee payee: Circuit Court Clerk. No personal checks accepted.

Chancery Court PO Box 908, Rogersville, TN 37857; 423-272-8150. Hours: 8AM-4PM (EST). *Civil, Probate.*

Civil Records: Access: In person only. Visitors must perform in person searches for themselves. No search fee. Required to search: name, years to search. Civil cases indexed by defendant, plaintiff. Civil records on index books from 1927 to present.

General Information: No adoption records released. Copy fee: $1.00 per page. Certification fee: $2.00. Fee payee: Hawkins County Clerk and Master. Personal checks accepted. Prepayment is required.

Haywood County

28th District Circuit & General Sessions Court 1 N Washington Ave, Brownsville, TN 38012; 731-772-1112; Fax: 731-772-8139. Hours: 8:30AM-5PM (CST). *Felony, Misdemeanor, Civil, Eviction, Small Claims.*

Civil Records: Access: Phone, mail, fax, in person. Both court and visitors may perform in person searches. No search fee. Required to search: name, years to search. Civil cases indexed by defendant, plaintiff. Civil records on computer since 8/1991, prior archived since the 1800s.

Criminal Records: Access: Phone, mail, fax, in person. Both court and visitors may perform in person searches. No search fee. Required to search: name, years to search, DOB; also helpful: SSN. Criminal records on computer since 8/1991, prior archived since the 1800s.

General Information: No juvenile records released. Turnaround time dependent upon search. Copy fee: $1.00 per page. Certification fee: $3.50. Fee payee: Circuit Court Clerk. No personal checks accepted. Prepayment is required.

Chancery Court 1 N Washington, PO Box 356, Brownsville, TN 38012; 731-772-0122; Fax: 731-772-3864. Hours: 8:30AM-5PM (CST). *Civil, Probate.*

Civil Records: Access: In person only. Visitors must perform in person searches for themselves. No search fee. Required to search: name, years to search. Civil cases indexed by defendant, plaintiff. Probate records on books since 9/82; other records go back to 1800s.

General Information: No adoption or sealed records released. Turnaround time 2 days. Copy fee: $1.00 per page. Certification fee: $5.00. Fee payee: Chancery Court. Personal checks accepted. Prepayment is required.

Henderson County

26th District Circuit & General Sessions Court 17 Monroe Ave #9, Henderson County Courthouse, Lexington, TN 38351; 731-968-2031; Fax: 731-967-9441 (criminal). Hours: 8AM-4:30PM M,T,Th,F (CST). *Felony, Misdemeanor, Civil, Eviction, Small Claims.*

Civil Records: Access: Mail, in person. Both court and visitors may perform in person searches. Search fee: $6.00 per name. Required to search: name, years to search. Civil cases indexed by defendant, plaintiff. Civil records on cards or books, archived from 1800s; on computer back 5 years.

Criminal Records: Access: Mail, in person. Both court and visitors may perform in person searches. Search fee: $6.00 per name. Required to search: name, years to search, DOB; also helpful: SSN. Criminal records on cards or books, archived from 1800s; on computer back 5 years.

General Information: Public access terminal is available. No sealed indictment records released. SASE required. Turnaround time 1-2 weeks. Fax notes: Fee to fax results is $10.00 per document. Copy fee: $2.00 per page. Certification fee: $6.00. Fee payee: Circuit Court Clerk. Personal checks accepted. Prepayment is required.

Chancery Court 17 Monroe Rm 2, 2nd Fl, Lexington, TN 38351; 731-968-2801; Fax: 731-967-5380. Hours: 8AM-4:30PM (till noon on Wed) (CST). *Civil, Probate.*

Civil Records: Access: Phone, mail, fax, in person. Both court and visitors may perform in person searches.

Court will only do recent searches that may be found on computer. Search fee: No search fee. Required to search: name, years to search. Civil cases indexed by defendant, plaintiff. Civil records on computer back to 6/2000; prior in books to 1895.

General Information: No confidential adoption records released. SASE required. Turnaround time dependent on search length. Fax notes: Fee to fax results is $2.00 per page. Copy fee: $2.00 per page. Certification fee: $2.00. Fee payee: Chancery Court. Only cashiers checks and money orders accepted. Prepayment is required.

Henry County

24th District Circuit & General Sessions Court PO Box 429, Paris, TN 38242; 731-642-0461. Hours: 8AM-4:30PM (CST). *Felony, Misdemeanor, Civil, Eviction, Small Claims.*

Civil Records: Access: Phone, fax, mail, in person. Both court and visitors may perform in person searches. No search fee. Required to search: name, years to search. Civil cases indexed by defendant, plaintiff. Civil records archived from 1820s (you search) or 1900s (they search); General Sessions on computer from 1991.

Criminal Records: Access: Phone, mail, in person. Both court and visitors may perform in person searches. No search fee. Required to search: name, years to search; also helpful: SSN, DOB. Criminal records archived from 1820s (you search) or 1900s (they search); General Sessions on computer from 1991.

General Information: Public access terminal is available. No juvenile records released. Turnaround time 1-2 weeks. Copy fee: $.25 per page. Certification fee: $2.00. Fee payee: Circuit Court Clerk or General Sessions. Personal checks accepted.

County Court PO Box 24, Paris, TN 38242; 731-642-2412; Fax: 731-644-0947. Hours: 8AM-4:30PM (CST). *Probate.*

Hickman County

21st District Circuit & General Sessions Court 104 College Ave #204, Centerville, TN 37033; 931-729-2211; Fax: 931-729-6141. Hours: 8AM-4PM (CST). *Felony, Misdemeanor, Civil, Eviction, Small Claims.*

Civil Records: Access: In person only. Visitors must perform in person searches for themselves. Required to search: name, years to search. Civil cases indexed by defendant, plaintiff. Civil records on computer since 1991, prior records on books to 1849.

Criminal Records: Access: In person only. Visitors must perform in person searches for themselves. Required to search: name, years to search. Criminal records on computer since 1991, prior records on books to 1849.

General Information: No juvenile records released. Copy fee: $1.00 per page. Certification fee: $5.00. Fee payee: Circuit Court Clerk. No personal checks accepted. Prepayment is required.

Chancery Court 104 College Ave #202, Centerville, TN 37033; 931-729-2522; Fax: 931-729-6141. Hours: 8AM-4PM (CST). *Civil, Probate.*

Civil Records: Access: Mail, in person. Both court and visitors may perform in person searches. No search fee. Required to search: name, years to search. Civil cases indexed by defendant, plaintiff. Civil records on books since 1965; computerized records since 1984.

General Information: No confidential or adoption records released. SASE requested. Turnaround time 1 week. Copy fee: $.25 per page. Certification fee: $3.00. Fee payee: Clerk & Master. Personal checks accepted.

Houston County

23rd District Circuit & General Sessions
Court PO Box 403, Erin, TN 37061; 931-289-4673; Fax: 931-289-5182. Hours: 8AM-4:30PM (CST). *Felony, Misdemeanor, Civil, Eviction, Small Claims.*

Civil Records: Access: Phone, fax, mail, in person. Only the court performs in person searches; visitors may not. Search fee: $5.00 per name. Required to search: name, years to search. Civil cases indexed by defendant, plaintiff. Civil records archived from 1930s in books.

Criminal Records: Access: Phone, fax, mail, in person. Only the court performs in person searches; visitors may not. Search fee: $5.00 per name. Required to search: name, years to search, DOB; also helpful: SSN. Criminal records archived from 1930s in books.

General Information: No juvenile records released. SASE required. Turnaround time 1-2 days. Copy fee: $.25 per page. Certification fee: $3.50. Fee payee: Circuit Court Clerk. Personal checks accepted. Prepayment is required.

Chancery Court PO Box 332, Erin, TN 37061; 931-289-3870; Fax: 931-289-5679. Hours: 8AM-4PM (CST). *Civil, Probate.*

Civil Records: Access: Mail, in person. Both court and visitors may perform in person searches. No search fee. Required to search: name, years to search. Civil cases indexed by defendant, plaintiff. Civil records on books.

General Information: No adoption records released. Turnaround time 2 days. Copy fee: $.25 per page. Certification fee: $3.50. Fee payee: Clerk & Master. Personal checks accepted. Prepayment is required.

Humphreys County

23rd District Circuit & General Sessions
Court Room 106, Waverly, TN 37185; 931-296-2461; Fax: 931-296-1651. Hours: 8AM-4:30PM (CST). *Felony, Misdemeanor, Civil, Eviction, Small Claims.*

Civil Records: Access: Phone, fax, mail, in person. Both court and visitors may perform in person searches. Search fee: $1.00 per name per year. If more than 15 years, the fee is a flat $25.00. Required to search: name, years to search. Civil cases indexed by defendant, plaintiff. Civil records archived from early 1900s, on computer back to 1989.

Criminal Records: Access: Phone, fax, mail, in person. Both court and visitors may perform in person searches. Search fee: $1.00 per name per year. If more than 15 years, the fee is a flat $25.00. Required to search: name, years to search, DOB, SSN, signed release. Criminal records archived from early 1900s, on computer back to 1989.

General Information: No expunged records released. SASE required. Turnaround time same day. Copy fee: $.25 per page. Certification fee: $2.00 for the document seal plus $2.00 per page. Fee payee: Rm 106 Courthouse, Waverly TN. Business checks accepted. Prepayment is required.

County Court Clerk, Room 2 Courthouse Annex, Waverly, TN 37185; 931-296-7671, 931-296-6503; Fax: 931-296-5011. 8AM-4:30PM (CST). *Probate.*

Jackson County

15th District Circuit & General Sessions
Court PO Box 205, Gainesboro, TN 38562; 931-268-9314; Fax: 931-268-4555. Hours: 8AM-4PM M,T,Th,F; 8AM-3PM W; 8AM-Noon Sat (CST). *Felony, Misdemeanor, Civil, Eviction, Small Claims.*

Civil Records: Access: Fax, mail, in person. Both court and visitors may perform in person searches. Search fee: $5.00 per name. Required to search: name, years to search. Civil cases indexed by defendant, plaintiff. Civil

records archived from 1900s in books, computerized since 2000.

Criminal Records: Access: Fax, mail, in person. Both court and visitors may perform in person searches. Search fee: $5.00 per name. Required to search: name, years to search, DOB; also helpful: SSN. Criminal records archived from 1900s in books, computerized since 2000.

General Information: No juvenile records released. SASE required. Turnaround time 1 week. Copy fee: $.50 per page (first 24 are free). Certification fee: $5.00. Fee payee: Circuit Court Clerk. Business checks accepted. Prepayment is required.

Chancery Court PO Box 733, Gainesboro, TN 38562-0733; 931-268-9516; Fax: 931-268-9512. 8AM-4PM M,T,Th,F; 8AM-3PM W (CST). *Probate.*

www.jacksonco.com

Jefferson County

4th District Circuit & General Sessions
Court PO Box 671, Dandridge, TN 37725; 865-397-2786; Fax: 865-397-4894. Hours: 8AM-4PM M-F; 8-11AM Sat (EST). *Felony, Misdemeanor, Civil, Eviction, Small Claims.*

Civil Records: Access: Mail, in person. Both court and visitors may perform in person searches. No search fee. Required to search: name, years to search. Civil cases indexed by defendant, plaintiff. Civil records archived from early 1900s on books.

Criminal Records: Access: Mail, in person. Both court and visitors may perform in person searches. No search fee. Required to search: name, years to search, DOB, SSN, signed release. Criminal records archived from early 1900s on books.

General Information: No adoption or juvenile records released. Turnaround time 1 week. Copy fee: $.25 per page. Certification fee: $3.00. Copy fee included in cert fee. Fee payee: Circuit Court Clerk. Personal checks accepted.

County Court PO Box 710, Dandridge, TN 37725; 865-397-2935; Fax: 865-397-3839. Hours: 8AM-4PM M-F, 8AM-11PM Sat (EST). *Probate.*

Johnson County

1st District Circuit & General Sessions
Court PO Box 73, Mountain City, TN 37683; 423-727-9012; Fax: 423-727-7047. Hours: 8:30AM-5PM (EST). *Felony, Misdemeanor, Civil, Eviction, Small Claims.*

Civil Records: Access: Phone, mail, in person. Both court and visitors may perform in person searches. Search fee: $5.00 per name. Required to search: name, years to search. Civil cases indexed by defendant, plaintiff. Civil records in docket books, sessions 1976, criminal & circuit 1800s.

Criminal Records: Access: Phone, mail, in person. Both court and visitors may perform in person searches. Search fee: $5.00 per name. Required to search: name, years to search, DOB. Criminal records in docket books, sessions 1976, criminal & circuit 1800s.

General Information: No adoption, expunged or juvenile records released. SASE required. Turnaround time 2-3 days. Copy fee: $2.00 per page. Certification fee: $2.00. Fee payee: Circuit Court Clerk. Only cashiers checks and money orders accepted. Prepayment is required.

Chancery Court PO Box 196, Mountain City, TN 37683; 423-727-7853; Fax: 423-727-7047. Hours: 8:30AM-5PM (EST). *Civil, Probate.*

Civil Records: Access: Mail, in person. Both court and visitors may perform in person searches. No search fee. Required to search: name, years to search. Civil cases

indexed by defendant, plaintiff. Civil records on books and files.

General Information: No adoption records released. SASE required. Turnaround time same day. Copy fee: $1.00 per page. Certification fee: $2.00 plus $2.00 per page. Fee payee: Clerk & Master. Only cashiers checks and money orders accepted. Prepayment is required.

Knox County

6th District Criminal Court
400 Main Ave, Room 149, Knoxville, TN 37902; 865-215-2492; Fax: 865-215-4291. Hours: 8AM-5PM M-Th; 8AM-4:30PM F (EST). *Felony, Misdemeanor.*

www.knoxcounty.org

Criminal Records: Access: Fax, mail, in person. Only the court performs in person searches; visitors may not. Search fee: $5.00 per name. Required to search: name, years to search, DOB; also helpful: address, SSN, signed release. Criminal records on computer back to 1980; on books from 1962.

General Information: No sealed records released. SASE not required. Turnaround time 48 hours. Fax notes: $2.00 for first page, $1.00 each add'l. Copy fee: $2.00 per page. Certification fee: $2.00. Fee payee: Criminal Court Clerk. Personal checks accepted. Prepayment is required.

Circuit Court 400 Main Ave, Room M-30, PO Box 379, Knoxville, TN 37901; 865-215-2400; Fax: 865-215-4251. Hours: 8AM-5PM; 4:30 PM Fri. (EST). *Civil Actions Over $15,000.*

Civil Records: Access: Phone, fax, mail, in person. Both court and visitors may perform in person searches. Search fee: $5.00. Required to search: name, years to search. Civil cases indexed by defendant, plaintiff. Civil records on computer from 1986, prior records archived and on microfilm.

General Information: Public access terminal is available. No adoption or sealed records released. Turnaround time 2-3 days. Copy fee: $1.00 per page. Certification fee: $2.00. Fee payee: Circuit Court Clerk. Personal checks accepted. Credit cards accepted: Visa, MC. Prepayment is required.

General Sessions Court 300 Main Ave, RM 318, PO Box 379, Knoxville, TN 37901; 865-215-2518. Hours: 8AM-4:30PM (EST). *Civil Actions Under $15,000, Eviction, Small Claims.*

www.knoxcounty.org

Civil Records: Access: Mail, in person. Both court and visitors may perform in person searches. Search fee: $5.00. Required to search: name, years to search. Civil cases indexed by defendant, plaintiff. Civil records on books and computer.

General Information: No juvenile or adoption records released. Turnaround time 1 week. Copy fee: $1.50 per page. Certification fee: $3.50. Fee payee: General Sessions Court. Personal checks accepted. Credit cards accepted: Visa, MasterCard. Prepayment is required.

Chancery Court 400 Main Ave, Knoxville, TN 37902; 865-215-2555 (Chancery); Probate phone: 865-215-2389; Fax: 865-215-2920. Hours: 8AM-4:30PM (EST). *Civil, Probate.*

www.knoxcounty.org

Civil Records: Access: Phone, fax, mail, in person. Visitors must perform in person searches for themselves. No search fee. Required to search: name, years to search. Civil cases indexed by defendant, plaintiff. Civil records on computer since 1978, prior records on books.

General Information: No commitment or adoption records released. Turnaround time 1-2 days. Fax notes: $1.00 per page. Copy fee: $1.00 per page. Certification fee: $2.00. Fee payee: Chancery or Probate Court. Personal checks accepted. Prepayment is required.

Lake County

29th District Circuit & General Sessions Court 227 Church St, PO Box 11, Tiptonville, TN 38079; 731-253-7137; Fax: 731-253-8930. Hours: 8AM-4PM M-W & F; 8AM-Noon Th (CST). *Felony, Misdemeanor, Civil, Eviction, Small Claims.*

Civil Records: Access: In person only. Visitors must perform in person searches for themselves. Search fee: No search fee. Required to search: name, years to search. Civil cases indexed by defendant, plaintiff. Civil records archived on books in office up to 30 yrs, vault records before 1960; General Sessions computerized records go back to 1997.

Criminal Records: Access: In person only. Visitors must perform in person searches for themselves. Search fee: No search fee. Required to search: name, years to search, DOB; also helpful: SSN. Criminal records archived on books in office up to 30 yrs, vault records before 1960.

General Information: No sealed records released. Copy fee: $1.00 per page. Certification fee: $3.00. Fee payee: Circuit Court Clerk. Personal checks accepted.

Chancery Court 229 Church Lake County Courthouse, Box 12, Tiptonville, TN 38079; 731-253-8926. Hours: 9AM-4PM M-W & F, 8AM-Noon Th (CST). *Probate.*

Civil Records: Access: Mail, in person. Both court and visitors may perform in person searches. No search fee. Required to search: name, years to search. Civil cases indexed by defendant. Civil records on books and files from 1984, prior records filed in county clerks office.

General Information: Turnaround time 3-5 days. Copy fee: $.50 per page. Certification fee: $6.00. Fee payee: Clerk and Master. Personal checks accepted. Prepayment is required.

Lauderdale County

25th District Circuit Court Lauderdale County Justice Center, 675 Hwy 51 S, PO Box 509, Ripley, TN 38063; 731-635-0101; Fax: 731-221-8663. Hours: 8AM-4:30PM (CST). *Felony, Misdemeanor, Civil Actions Over $15,000.*

Civil Records: Access: Phone, mail, in person. Both court and visitors may perform in person searches. Search fee: $10.00 per name. Required to search: name, years to search. Civil cases indexed by defendant, plaintiff. Civil records archived on books from 1800s; on computer back to 1992.

Criminal Records: Access: Mail, in person. Both court and visitors may perform in person searches. Search fee: $10.00 per name. Required to search: name, years to search; also helpful: DOB, SSN. Criminal records archived on books from 1800s; on computer back to 1992.

General Information: Public access terminal is available. No sealed or adoption records released. SASE required. Turnaround time 2-3 days. Copy fee: $1.00 per page. Certification fee: $10.00. Fee payee: Circuit Court Clerk. Business checks accepted. Prepayment is required.

General Sessions Court PO Box 509, Ripley, TN 38063; 731-635-2572; Fax: 731-221-8663. Hours: 8AM-4:30PM (till noon on Wed) (CST). *Civil Actions Under $15,000, Eviction, Small Claims.*

Civil Records: Access: Mail, in person. Both court and visitors may perform in person searches. Search fee: $10.00 per name. Required to search: name, years to search. Civil cases indexed by defendant, plaintiff. Civil records on computer since 1992, records prior to 1984 on docket books.

General Information: Public access terminal is available. No confidential records released. SASE required. Turnaround time 2-3 days. Copy fee: $1.00 per page. Certification fee: $5.00. Fee payee: General

Sessions. Business checks accepted. Prepayment is required.

County Court Courthouse, 100 Court Sq, Ripley, TN 38063; 731-635-2561. Hours: 8AM-4:30PM M,T,Th,F; 8AM-Noon W & Sat (CST). *Probate.*

Lawrence County

22nd District Circuit & General Sessions Court NBU #12 240 W Gaines, Lawrenceburg, TN 38464; 931-762-4398; Fax: 931-766-4471. Hours: 8AM-4:30PM (CST). *Felony, Misdemeanor, Civil, Eviction, Small Claims.*

Civil Records: Access: In person only. Visitors must perform in person searches for themselves. No search fee. Required to search: name, years to search. Civil cases indexed by defendant, plaintiff. Civil records archived on books since court started in 1940s.

Criminal Records: Access: In person only. Visitors must perform in person searches for themselves. No search fee. Required to search: name, years to search, DOB, SSN. Criminal records archived on books since court started in 1940s.

General Information: Public access terminal is available. No expunged records released. Certification fee: $5.00. Fee payee: Circuit Court Clerk. Business checks accepted. Prepayment is required.

County Clerk 240 W Gaines St, NBU #2, Lawrenceburg, TN 38464; 931-762-7700; ext 116. Hours: 8AM-4:30PM (CST). *Probate.*

Lewis County

21st District Circuit & General Sessions Court Courthouse 110 Park Avenue N, Rm 201, Hohenwald, TN 38462; 931-796-3724; Fax: 931-796-6021. Hours: 8AM-4:30PM (CST). *Felony, Misdemeanor, Civil, Eviction, Small Claims.*

Civil Records: Access: In person only. Visitors must perform in person searches for themselves. No search fee. Required to search: name, years to search. Civil cases indexed by defendant, plaintiff. Civil records archived 15 years in office, 1800s in vault.

Criminal Records: Access: In person only. Visitors must perform in person searches for themselves. No search fee. Required to search: name, years to search; also helpful: SSN. Criminal records archived 15 years in office, 1800s in vault.

General Information: No juvenile, adoption records released. Copy fee: $1.00 per page. Certification fee: $2.00 per document plus $2.00 per page. Fee payee: Circuit Court Clerk. Personal checks accepted.

Chancery Court Lewis County Courthouse, 110 Park Ave N, Rm 208, Hohenwald, TN 38462; 931-796-3734; Fax: 931-796-6010. Hours: 8AM-4:30PM (CST). *Civil, Probate.*

Civil Records: Access: In person only. Visitors must perform in person searches for themselves. No search fee. Required to search: name, years to search. Civil cases indexed by defendant, plaintiff. Civil records on computer since 10/94, prior records on books.

General Information: No juvenile or adoption records released. Copy fee: $1.00 per page. Certification fee: $2.00. Fee payee: Clerk & Master. Personal checks accepted. Prepayment is required.

Lincoln County

17th District Circuit & General Sessions Court 112 Main Ave S, Rm 203, Fayetteville, TN 37334; 931-433-2334; Fax: 931-438-1577. Hours: 8AM-4PM (CST). *Felony, Misdemeanor, Civil, Eviction, Small Claims.*

Civil Records: Access: Phone, fax, mail, in person. Both court and visitors may perform in person searches. Search fee: $10.00 per name. Fee is for 5 years. Add

$1.00 for each add'l year. Required to search: name, years to search. Civil cases indexed by defendant, plaintiff. Civil records archived on books since court started; files go back 10 years; on computer back to 1995.

Criminal Records: Access: Phone, fax, mail, in person. Both court and visitors may perform in person searches. Search fee: $10.00 per name. Fee is for 5 years. Add $1.00 for each add'l year. Required to search: name, years to search, DOB, SSN, signed release. Criminal records archived on books since court started; files go back 10 years; on computer back to 1995.

General Information: Public access terminal is available. No probation records released. SASE required. Turnaround time 1-2 days. Fax notes: $2.00 per page. Copy fee: $1.00 per page. Certification fee: $4.00. Fee payee: Circuit Court Clerk. Business checks accepted.

Chancery Court 112 Main Ave, Rm B109, Fayetteville, TN 37334; 931-433-1482; Fax: 931-433-9979. Hours: 8AM-4PM (CST). *Civil, Probate.*

Civil Records: Access: In person only. Visitors must perform in person searches for themselves. No search fee. Required to search: name, years to search. Civil cases indexed by defendant, plaintiff. Civil records archived on books.

General Information: No adoption, divorce records released. Fax notes: Fee to fax results is $1.00 per page. Certification fee: $4.00 plus $2.00 per page. Fee payee: Clerk & Master. Personal checks accepted.

Loudon County

9th District Criminal & Circuit Court PO Box 280, Loudon, TN 37774; 865-458-2042; Fax: 865-458-2043. Hours: 8AM-4:30PM (EST). *Felony, Misdemeanor, Civil, Eviction, Small Claims.*

www.loudoncounty.com/ccc.htm

Note: General Sessions (Eviction, small claims, and juvenile court) located at 12680 Hwy 11 W Suite 3, Lenoir City, TN 37771, 423-986-3505.

Civil Records: Access: Phone, fax, mail, in person. Both court and visitors may perform in person searches. Search fee: $5.00 per name. Required to search: name, years to search. Civil cases indexed by defendant, plaintiff. Civil records archived from 1870 on books, on computer from 8/1990.

Criminal Records: Access: Phone, fax, mail, in person. Both court and visitors may perform in person searches. Search fee: $5.00 per name. Required to search: name, years to search. Criminal records archived from 1800s on books, on computer from 8/1990.

General Information: No juvenile, adoption records released. SASE requested. Turnaround time 2-4 days. Copy fee: $1.00 per page. Certification fee: $2.00. Fee payee: Circuit Court or general Sessions Court. Prepayment is required.

County Court 101 Mulberry St #200, Loudon, TN 37774; 865-458-2726; Fax: 865-458-9891. 8AM-5:30PM Mon, 8AM-4:30PM T-F (EST). *Probate.*

Macon County

15th District Circuit & General Sessions Court Court Clerk, 904 Highway 52 Bypass, Lafayette, TN 37083; 615-666-2354; Fax: 615-666-3001. Hours: 8AM-4:30PM M-Th; 8AM-5PM F *Felony, Misdemeanor, Civil, Eviction, Small Claims.*

Civil Records: Access: In person only. Visitors must perform in person searches for themselves. Required to search: name, years to search. Civil cases indexed by defendant, plaintiff. Civil records archived in office from 1975, rest in records room from 1960; on computer since 1997.

Criminal Records: Access: In person only. Visitors must perform in person searches for themselves. Required to search: name, years to search, DOB; also helpful: SSN. Criminal records archived in office from 1975, rest in records room from 1960, on computer since1997.

General Information: Public access terminal is available. No juvenile or adoption records released. Copy fee: $1.00 per page. Certification fee: $5.00. Fee payee: Circuit Court Clerk. Personal checks accepted. Prepayment is required.

County Court County Court Clerk, Rm 104, Lafayette, TN 37083; 615-666-2333; Fax: 615-666-2202. Hours: 8AM-4:30PM M-W, Closed Thu, 8AM-5PM Fri, 8AM-1:30PM Sat (CST). *Probate, Juvenile.*

Madison County

26th District Circuit Court 515 S Liberty St, Jackson, TN 38301; 731-423-6035. Hours: 8AM-4PM *Felony, Misdemeanor, Civil Actions Over $15,000.*

Note: Misdemeanor cases here are usually accompanied by felonies.

Civil Records: Access: In person only. Visitors must perform in person searches for themselves. No search fee. Required to search: name, years to search. Civil cases indexed by defendant, plaintiff. Civil records archived on books in office from 1963; on computer back to 1995.

Criminal Records: Access: In person only. Visitors must perform in person searches for themselves. No search fee. Required to search: name, years to search; also helpful: DOB, SSN. Criminal records computerized since 1995, on books from 1965.

General Information: Public access terminal is available. No sealed records released. Copy fee: $.50 per page. Searcher can bring own paper then no charges for copies. Certification fee: $5.00. Fee payee: Circuit Court Clerk. Only cashiers checks and money orders accepted. Prepayment is required.

General Sessions Court 515 S Liberty St, Jackson, TN 38301; 731-423-6018. Hours: 8AM-4PM (CST). *Misdemeanor, Civil Actions Under $15,000, Eviction, Small Claims.*

Civil Records: Access: Mail, in person. Visitors must perform in person searches for themselves. Search fee: No search fee. Required to search: name, years to search. Civil cases indexed by defendant, plaintiff. Civil records computerized since 04/98, archived on books in office from 1982, rest stored elsewhere from 1950s.

Criminal Records: Access: In person only. Visitors must perform in person searches for themselves. Search fee: No search fee. Required to search: name.

General Information: Public access terminal is available. Turnaround time 1 week. Copy fee: $1.50 per page. Certification fee: $4.00. Fee payee: General Sessions Court. Only cashiers checks and money orders accepted.

Probate Division - General Sessions Division II 110 Irby St, PO Box 1504, Jackson, TN 38302-1504; 731-988-3025; Fax: 731-423-6044. Hours: 8:30-12, 1-4:30PM (CST). *Probate.*

Marion County

12th District Circuit & General Sessions Court PO Box 789, Courthouse Sq, Jasper, TN 37347; 423-942-2134; Fax: 423-942-4160. Hours: 8AM-4PM (CST). *Felony, Misdemeanor, Civil, Eviction, Small Claims.*

Civil Records: Access: Phone, mail, in person. Both court and visitors may perform in person searches. No search fee. Required to search: name, years to search. Civil cases indexed by defendant, plaintiff. Civil records

on computer from 1988, prior records archived on books and microfiche since 1922.

Criminal Records: Access: Phone, mail, in person. Both court and visitors may perform in person searches. No search fee. Required to search: name, years to search, DOB; also helpful: SSN. Criminal records on computer from 1988, prior records archived on books and microfiche since 1922.

General Information: Public access terminal is available. No adoption records released. Turnaround time 1 week. Copy fee: $.50 per page. Certification fee: $3.00. Fee payee: Circuit Court Clerk. Personal checks accepted.

Chancery Court PO Box 789, Jasper, TN 37347; 423-942-2601; Fax: 423-942-0291. Hours: 8AM-4PM (CST). *Civil, Probate.*

Civil Records: Access: Mail, in person. Both court and visitors may perform in person searches. No search fee. Required to search: name, years to search. Civil cases indexed by defendant, plaintiff. Civil records on computer since 03/94, prior records on books.

General Information: No adoption records released. SASE requested. Turnaround time 1 day. Copy fee: $.50 per page. Certification fee: $3.00. Fee payee: Clerk and Master. Personal checks accepted. Prepayment is required.

Marshall County

17th District Circuit & General Sessions Court Courthouse, Lewisburg, TN 37091; 931-359-0536; Fax: 931-359-0543. Hours: 8AM-4PM (CST). *Felony, Misdemeanor, Civil, Eviction, Small Claims.*

Civil Records: Access: In person only. Visitors must perform in person searches for themselves. No search fee. Required to search: name, years to search. Civil cases indexed by plaintiff. Civil records archived on books; also on computer back to 2000.

Criminal Records: Access: In person only. Visitors must perform in person searches for themselves. No search fee. Required to search: name, years to search; also helpful: DOB, SSN. Criminal records in docket books back to 1987; on comptuer back to 2000.

General Information: Public access terminal is available. No adoption records released. Copy fee: $1.00 per page. Certification fee: $5.00. Fee payee: Circuit Court Clerk. No personal checks accepted. Prepayment is required.

Chancery Court 1107 Courthouse Annex, Lewisburg, TN 37091; 931-359-2181; Fax: 931-359-0543. Hours: 8AM-4PM (CST). *Probate.*

Note: Probate is handled by the Clerk & Master.

Maury County

Circuit & General Sessions Court Maury County Courthouse, 41 Public Square, Columbia, TN 38401; 931-381-3690; Fax: 931-381-3985. Hours: 8AM-4PM (CST). *Felony, Misdemeanor, Civil, Eviction, Small Claims.*

Civil Records: Access: Phone, fax, mail, in person. Visitors must perform in person searches for themselves. No search fee. Required to search: name, years to search. Civil cases indexed by defendant, plaintiff. Civil records on books since 1984; on computer back to 1989.

Criminal Records: Access: In person only. Visitors must perform in person searches for themselves. No search fee. Required to search: name, years to search; also helpful: DOB, SSN. Criminal records on computer back to 1989; others go back to early 1900s.

General Information: Public access terminal is available. No juvenile records released. Turnaround time 1 week. Fax notes: $1.00 per page. Copy fee: $1.00 per page. Certification fee: $6.00. Fee payee: Circuit Court Clerk. Personal checks accepted.

Probate Court Maury County Courthouse, Clerk & Masters Office, 41 Public Square, Columbia, TN 38401; 931-381-3690 x515; Fax: 931-308-5614. Hours: 8AM-4PM. *Probate.*

Note: Records on computer go back to 1991.

McMinn County

10th District Circuit & General Sessions Court PO Box 506, Athens, TN 37303; 423-745-1923; Fax: 423-745-1642. Hours: 8:30AM-4PM (EST). *Felony, Misdemeanor, Civil, Eviction, Small Claims, Probate.*

Civil Records: Access: Phone, fax, mail, in person. Both court and visitors may perform in person searches. Search fee: $3.00 per name. Required to search: name, years to search; also helpful: address. Civil cases indexed by defendant, plaintiff. Civil records archived approximately 20 years; computerized back to 1996. Phone access is limited to three names.

Criminal Records: Access: Phone, fax, mail, in person. Both court and visitors may perform in person searches. Search fee: $3.00. Required to search: name, years to search, DOB, SSN; also helpful: address. Criminal records archived approximately 20 years; computerized back to 1996. Phone access is limited to three names.

General Information: No juvenile, adoption records released. Turnaround time 5-10 days. Fax notes: Fee to fax results is $2.00 per page. Copy fee: $2.00 per page. Certification fee: $4.00. Fee payee: Circuit Court Clerk. Business checks accepted.

McNairy County

25th District Circuit & General Sessions Court 300 Industrial Drive, Selmer, TN 38375; 731-645-1015; Fax: 731-645-1003. Hours: 8AM-4:30PM M-F; 8AM-Noon Sat (CST). *Felony, Misdemeanor, Civil, Eviction, Small Claims.*

Civil Records: Access: Mail, in person. Both court and visitors may perform in person searches. Search fee: $5.00 per name. Required to search: name, years to search. Civil cases indexed by defendant, plaintiff. Civil records archived on docket books since 1966; computerized records since 2/95.

Criminal Records: Access: Mail, in person. Both court and visitors may perform in person searches. Search fee: $5.00 per name. Required to search: name, years to search, DOB, SSN. Criminal records archived on docket books since 1966; on computer back to 2/95.

General Information: Public access terminal is available. No juvenile records released. Turnaround time 1-2 days. Copy fee: $.25 per page. Certification fee: $3.00. Fee payee: Circuit Court Clerk. Personal checks accepted. Prepayment is required.

Chancery Court Chancery Court, Clerk & Master, Courthouse, Rm 205, Selmer, TN 38375; 731-645-5446; Fax: 731-645-3656. Hours: 8AM-4PM M,T,Th,F; Closed W (CST). *Civil, Probate.*

Civil Records: Access: In person only. Visitors must perform in person searches for themselves. No search fee. Required to search: name, years to search. Civil cases indexed by defendant, plaintiff. Civil records on books.

General Information: No adoption records released. Copy fee: $.50. Certification fee: $5.00. Fee payee: Clerk & Master. Personal checks accepted.

Meigs County

9th District Circuit & General Sessions Court PO Box 205, Decatur, TN 37322; 423-334-5821; Fax: 423-334-4819. Hours: 8AM-5PM M,T,Th,F; 8AM-12PM Sat (EST). *Felony, Misdemeanor, Civil, Eviction, Small Claims.*

Civil Records: Access: Mail, in person. Both court and visitors may perform in person searches. No search fee. Required to search: name, years to search. Civil cases indexed by defendant, plaintiff. Civil records archived in office from 1930s, records in storage go further. They refer all name searches to an outside agency.

Criminal Records: Access: Mail, in person. Both court and visitors may perform in person searches. No search fee. Required to search: name, years to search. Criminal records archived in office from 1930s, records in storage go further. They refer all name searches to an outside agency.

General Information: No juvenile records released. SASE requested. Turnaround time 24 hours. Copy fee: $.25 per page. Certification fee: $5.00. Fee payee: Circuit Court Clerk. Personal checks accepted. Prepayment is required.

Chancery Court PO Box 5, Decatur, TN 37322; 423-334-5243. Hours: 8AM-5PM M,T,Th,F; 8:30AM-Noon Wed (EST). *Civil, Probate.*

Civil Records: Access: In person only. Visitors must perform in person searches for themselves. No search fee. Required to search: name, years to search. Civil cases indexed by defendant, plaintiff. Civil records on dockets since 1940.

General Information: No adoption records released. Copy fee: $.25 per page. Certification fee: $5.00. Fee payee: Meigs County Chancery Court. Personal checks accepted. Prepayment is required.

Monroe County

10th District Circuit & General Sessions Court 105 College St, Madisonville, TN 37354; 423-442-2396; Fax: 423-442-9538. Hours: 8AM-4:30PM *Felony, Misdemeanor, Civil, Eviction, Small Claims.*

Civil Records: Access: Mail, in person. Both court and visitors may perform in person searches. Search fee: $10.00 per name. Required to search: name, years to search. Civil cases indexed by defendant, plaintiff. Civil records on computer since 1991, records on books in office for 10 years, unspecified prior to then.

Criminal Records: Access: Mail, in person. Both court and visitors may perform in person searches. Search fee: $10.00 per name. Required to search: name, years to search. Criminal records on computer since 1991, records on books in office for 10 years, unspecified prior to then.

General Information: Public access terminal is available. No juvenile records released. Turnaround time 2 days. Copy fee: $1.00 per page. Certification fee: $4.00. Fee payee: Circuit Court Clerk. Personal checks accepted. Prepayment is required.

Chancery Court 105 College St #2, Madisonville, TN 37354; 423-442-2644; Probate phone: 423-442-4573; Fax: 423-420-0048. Hours: 8:30AM-4:30PM (EST). *Civil, Probate.*

Civil Records: Access: Mail, in person. Both court and visitors may perform in person searches. No search fee. Required to search: name, years to search. Civil cases indexed by plantiff and defendant. Civil records on computer since 1993, prior records on books.

General Information: No adoption, sealed records released. SASE requested. Turnaround time 2-3 days. Copy fee: $2.00 per page. Certification fee: $4.00. Fee payee: Chancery Court. Personal checks accepted. Prepayment is required.

Montgomery County

19th District Circuit Court PO Box 384, Clarksville, TN 37041-0384; 931-648-5700; Fax: 931-648-5731. Hours: 8:30AM-4:30PM (CST). *Felony, Civil Actions Over $10,000, Misdemeanor.*

Note: Genneral Sessions also has misdemeanor cases.

Civil Records: Access: Mail, in person. Visitors must perform in person searches for themselves. Search fee: $10.00 per name. Required to search: name, years to search. Civil cases indexed by defendant, plaintiff. Civil records on computer back to 11/1999, archived on books in office from 1970s, on microfiche from 1950s.

Criminal Records: Access: Mail, in person. Visitors must perform in person searches for themselves. Search fee: $10.00 per name. Required to search: name, years to search, DOB; also helpful-signed release, SSN. Criminal records on computer back to 1985; prior records archived on books from 1970s, on microfiche from 1950s.

General Information: Public access terminal is available. (Only criminal records are available.) No juvenile records released. SASE required. Copy fee: $.50 per page. Certification fee: $6.00. Fee payee: Circuit Court Clerk. Business checks accepted. Prepayment is required.

General Sessions Court 120 Commerce St, Clarksville, TN 37040; Civil phone: 931-648-5769; Criminal phone: 931-648-5771. Hours: 8:30AM-4:30PM (CST). *Misdemeanor, Civil Actions Under $15,000, Eviction, Small Claims.*

Civil Records: Access: Phone, mail, in person. Both court and visitors may perform in person searches. Search fee: $10 per name. Required to search: name, years to search. Civil cases indexed by defendant, plaintiff. Civil records on books, archived.

Criminal Records: Access: Fax, mail, in person. Both court and visitors may perform in person searches. Search fee: $10.00 per name. Required to search: name, years to search, DOB; also helpful: SSN. Criminal records on books, archives; on computer back to 1985.

General Information: Public access terminal is available. Turnaround time 1-2 weeks. Fax notes: Will fax results for $2.00 per page. Copy fee: $.50 per page. Certification fee: $6.00. Fee payee: General Sessions Court. Business checks accepted. Prepayment is required.

Chancery Court Chancery Court, Clerk & Master, Montgomery County Courthouse 329 Main St, Clarksville, TN 37040; 931-648-5703. Hours: 8AM-4:30PM (CST). *Civil, Probate.*

Civil Records: Access: In person only. Visitors must perform in person searches for themselves. No search fee. Required to search: name, years to search. Civil cases indexed by defendant, plaintiff. Civil records on books and microfilm.

General Information: Public access terminal is available. No adoption or sealed records released. Copy fee: $1.00 per page. Certification fee: $2.00 per page. Fee payee: Clerk & Master. Business checks accepted. Prepayment is required.

Moore County

17th District Circuit & General Sessions Court Courthouse, PO Box 206, Lynchburg, TN 37352; 931-759-7208; Fax: 931-759-5673. Hours: 8AM-4:30PM MTWF; 8AM-Noon Sat (CST). *Felony, Misdemeanor, Civil, Eviction, Small Claims.*

Civil Records: Access: Mail, in person. Both court and visitors may perform in person searches. Search fee: $5.00 per name. Required to search: name, years to search. Civil cases indexed by defendant, plaintiff. Civil records archived to 1862, on docket books and microfiche from 1862 to 1980s.

Criminal Records: Access: Mail, in person. Both court and visitors may perform in person searches. Search fee: $5.00 per name. Required to search: name, years to search. Criminal records archived to 1862, on docket books and microfiche from 1862 to 1980s.

General Information: No juvenile records released. SASE required. Turnaround time 7-10 days. Copy fee: $2.00 per page. Certification fee: $2.00. Fee payee:

Circuit Court Clerk. Only cashiers checks and money orders accepted. Prepayment is required.

Chancery Court PO Box 206, Lynchburg, TN 37352; 931-759-7028; Fax: 931-759-5610. Hours: 8AM-4:30PM M-W,F; 8AM-Noon Sat (CST). *Civil, Probate.*

Civil Records: Access: In person only. Visitors must perform in person searches for themselves. No search fee. Required to search: name, years to search. Civil cases indexed by plaintiff. Civil records on books.

General Information: No adoption or sealed records released. Copy fee: $.50 per page. Certification fee: $5.00. Fee payee: Clerk and Master. Only cashiers checks and money orders accepted. Prepayment is required.

Morgan County

9th District Circuit & General Sessions Court PO Box 163, Wartburg, TN 37887; 423-346-3503. Hours: 8AM-4PM (EST). *Felony, Misdemeanor, Civil, Eviction, Small Claims.*

Civil Records: Access: In person only. Visitors must perform in person searches for themselves. No search fee. Required to search: name, years to search. Civil cases indexed by defendant, plaintiff. Civil records archived on books from 1855.

Criminal Records: Access: In person only. Visitors must perform in person searches for themselves. No search fee. Required to search: name, years to search; also helpful: DOB, SSN. Criminal records archived on books from 1855; computerized since 2/01.

General Information: No sealed records released. Copy fee: $1.00 per page. Certification fee: $6.00. Fee payee: Circuit Court Clerk. Only cashiers checks and money orders accepted. Prepayment is required.

Chancery Court PO Box 789, Wartburg, TN 37887; 423-346-3881. Hours: 8AM-4PM (EST). *Civil, Probate.*

Civil Records: Access: Phone, mail, in person. Both court and visitors may perform in person searches. No search fee. Required to search: name, years to search. Civil cases indexed by defendant, plaintiff. Civil records in books since 1883, on microfiche since 1939 at state archives.

General Information: No adoption or conservatorship records released. SASE required. Turnaround time 1-8 days. Copy fee: $.50 per page. Certification fee: $10.00. Fee payee: Clerk & Master. Personal checks accepted. Prepayment is required.

Obion County

27th District Circuit Court 7 Bill Burnett Circle, Union City, TN 38261; 731-885-1372; Fax: 731-885-7515. Hours: 8:30AM-4:30PM (CST). *Felony, Misdemeanor, Civil Actions Over $10,000.*

Civil Records: Access: Mail, in person. Both court and visitors may perform in person searches. Search fee: $5.00 per name. Required to search: name, years to search. Civil cases indexed by defendant, plaintiff. Civil records for criminal archived on books from 1969, civil on books from 1974, rest are located elsewhere.

Criminal Records: Access: Mail, in person. Both court and visitors may perform in person searches. Search fee: $5.00. Misdemeanor records are $5.00 per year. Required to search: name, years to search, DOB, SSN. Criminal records for criminal archived on books from 1969, civil on books from 1974, rest are located elsewhere.

General Information: No adoption records released. SASE required. Turnaround time 2 days. Copy fee: $1.00 per page. Certification fee: $3.00. Fee payee: Circuit Court. Business checks accepted. Prepayment is required.

General Sessions Court 9 Bill Burnett Circle, Union City, TN 38281-0236; 731-885-1811; Fax: 731-885-7515. Hours: 8:30AM-4:30PM (CST). *Civil Actions Under $15,000, Eviction, Small Claims.*

Civil Records: Access: Mail, in person. Both court and visitors may perform in person searches. Search fee: $5.00 5 years & under; $10.00 over 5 years. Required to search: name. Civil cases indexed by defendant, plaintiff. Civil records kept in office for last 10 years. **General Information:** No juvenile or adoption records released. SASE required. Turnaround time 2 days. Copy fee: $1.00 per page. Certification fee: $3.00. Fee payee: Circuit Court Clerk. Personal checks accepted. Prepayment is required.

Chancery Court PO Box 187, Union City, TN 38281; 731-885-2562; Fax: 731-885-7515. Hours: 8:30AM-4:30PM (CST). *Civil, Probate.*

Civil Records: Access: Phone, mail, in person. Both court and visitors may perform in person searches. No search fee. Required to search: name, years to search. Civil cases indexed by defendant, plaintiff. Civil records (probate) from 9/82 on books in Chancery office, prior records on books in County Clerk's office. **General Information:** No adoption or sealed records released. Fax notes: Fee to fax results is $3.00 per document. Copy fee: $1.00 per page. Certification fee: $4.00. Fee payee: Clerk and Master. Personal checks accepted. Prepayment is required.

Overton County

13th District Circuit & General Sessions Court Overton County Courthouse, 100 Joan Tom Poindexter Dr, Livingston, TN 38570; 931-823-2312; Fax: 931-823-9728. Hours: 8AM-4:30PM M,T,Th,F, 8AM-Noon Wed & Sat (CST). *Felony, Misdemeanor, Civil, Eviction, Small Claims.*

Civil Records: Access: Mail, in person. Both court and visitors may perform in person searches. No search fee. Required to search: name, years to search. Civil cases indexed by defendant, plaintiff. Civil records archived on books from late 1800s; computerized records since 1996. **Criminal Records:** Access: Mail, in person. Both court and visitors may perform in person searches. No search fee. Required to search: name, years to search, DOB, SSN, signed release. Criminal records archived on books from late 1800s; computerized records since 1996. **General Information:** No juvenile records released. Turnaround time 3-5 days. Copy fee: $.50 per page. Certification fee: $5.00 per page. Fee payee: Circuit Court Clerk. Business checks accepted. Prepayment is required.

County Court Courthouse Annex, University St, Livingston, TN 38570; 931-823-2631; Fax: 931-823-7036. Hours: 8AM-4:30PM M,T,Th,F; 8AM-Noon W & Sat (CST). *Probate.*

Perry County

21st District Circuit & General Sessions Court PO Box 91, Linden, TN 37096; 931-589-2218. Hours: 8AM-4PM (CST). *Felony, Misdemeanor, Civil, Eviction, Small Claims.*

Civil Records: Access: Mail, in person, phone. Both court and visitors may perform in person searches. No search fee. Required to search: name, years to search. Civil cases indexed by defendant, plaintiff. Civil records archived on books from 1941, on microfiche (limited) at library. **Criminal Records:** Access: Mail, in person, phone. Both court and visitors may perform in person searches. No search fee. Required to search: name, years to search, DOB, SSN. Criminal records archived on books from 1941, on microfiche (limited) at library.

General Information: No adoption records released. SASE required. Turnaround time 2-3 days. Copy fee: No search fee. Fee payee: Circuit Court Clerk. Personal checks accepted.

Chancery Court PO Box 251, Linden, TN 37096; 931-589-2217; Fax: 931-589-2350. Hours: 8AM-4PM (CST). *Civil, Probate.*

Civil Records: Access: In person only. Visitors must perform in person searches for themselves. No search fee. Required to search: name, years to search. Civil cases indexed by defendant, plaintiff. Civil records (probate) on books from 1982, prior records in County Clerks office. **General Information:** No adoption records released. SASE required. Copy fee: $1.50 per page. Certification fee: $5.00. Fee payee: Clerk and Master. Local checks accepted. Prepayment is required.

Pickett County

13th District Circuit & General Sessions Court PO Box 5, Byrdstown, TN 38549; 931-864-3958; Fax: 931-864-6885. Hours: 8AM-4PM (CST). *Felony, Misdemeanor, Civil, Eviction, Small Claims.*

Civil Records: Access: Mail, in person. Both court and visitors may perform in person searches. Search fee: $10.00 per name. Required to search: name, years to search. Civil cases indexed by defendant. Civil records archived on books but not specific. **Criminal Records:** Access: Mail, in person. Both court and visitors may perform in person searches. Search fee: $10.00 per name. Required to search: name, years to search; also helpful: SSN. Criminal records not computerized, all on books. **General Information:** No adoption or juvenile records released. Turnaround time 3-4 days. Copy fee: No search fee. Fee payee: Circuit Court Clerk. Personal checks accepted.

County Court PO Box 5 Courthoue Square, Byrdstown, TN 38549; 931-864-3879. Hours: 8AM-4PM M,T,Th,F, 8AM-Noon W & Sat (CST). *Probate.*

Polk County

10th District Circuit & General Sessions Court PO Box 256, Benton, TN 37307; 423-338-4524; Fax: 423-338-8611. Hours: 8:30AM-4:30PM M-F (EST). *Felony, Misdemeanor, Civil, Eviction, Small Claims.*

Civil Records: Access: Mail, in person. Both court and visitors may perform in person searches. Search fee: $5.00 per name. Required to search: name, years to search. Civil cases indexed by defendant, plaintiff. Civil records archived from 1936. **Criminal Records:** Access: Mail, in person. Both court and visitors may perform in person searches. Search fee: $5.00 per name. Required to search: name, years to search, DOB, SSN. Criminal records archived from 1936. **General Information:** No juvenile records released. SASE requested. Turnaround time 3 days. Copy fee: $5.00 per document. Certification fee: Certification fee varies according to document size. Fee payee: Circuit Court Clerk. Personal checks accepted. Prepayment is required.

Chancery Court PO Drawer L, Benton, TN 37307; 423-338-4522; Fax: 423-338-4553. Hours: 8:30AM-4:30PM (EST). *Civil, Probate.*

Civil Records: Access: Mail, in person. Both court and visitors may perform in person searches. Search fee: $5.00 per name. Fee varies by document. Required to search: name, years to search. Civil cases indexed by defendant, plaintiff. Civil records on books tp;ate 1800's, computerized since 10/2000.

General Information: No adoption records released. Copy fee: $1.00 per page. Certification fee: $5.50. Fee payee: Chancery Court. Personal checks accepted.

Putnam County

13th District Circuit & General Sessions Court 421 E Spring St, 1C-49A, Cookeville, TN 38501; 931-528-1508. Hours: 8AM-4PM (CST). *Felony, Misdemeanor, Civil, Eviction, Small Claims.*

Civil Records: Access: In person. Visitors must perform in person searches. No search fee. Required to search: name, years to search. Civil cases indexed by defendant, plaintiff. Civil records archived in office from 1980s, unknown before then; computerized records since 1995. Books can only be searches Tuesday & Thursday. **Criminal Records:** Access: In person. Visitors must perform in person searches. No search fee. Required to search: name, years to search; also helpful: SSN. Criminal records computerized since 1995. Books can only be searched Tuesday & Thursday. **General Information:** Public access terminal is available. No juvenile or adoption records released. Copy fee: $.25 per page. Certification fee: $4.50. Fee payee: Circuit Court Clerk. Business checks accepted. Prepayment is required.

County Court PO Box 220, Cookeville, TN 38503-0220; 931-526-7106; Fax: 931-372-8201. Hours: 8AM-4:30PM (CST). *Probate.*

Rhea County

12th District Circuit & General Sessions Court 1475 Market St Rm 200, Dayton, TN 37321; 423-775-7805; Probate phone: 423-775-7806; Fax: 423-775-7895. Hours: 8AM-4:30PM (EST). *Felony, Misdemeanor, Civil, Eviction, Small Claims, Probate.*

Note: Probate located at the Rhea County Clerk and Master's Office.

Civil Records: Access: In person only. Visitors must perform in person searches for themselves. No search fee. Required to search: name, years to search. Civil cases indexed by defendant, plaintiff. Civil records in docket books. **Criminal Records:** Access: Mail, fax, in person. Both court and visitors may perform in person searches. However, court will only do name searches if current or within past year. No search fee. Required to search: name, years to search; also helpful: DOB, SSN. Criminal records in docket books. **General Information:** Public access terminal is available. (Very limited, recent; civil cases only.) No adoption records released. Copy fee: $.25 per page. Certification fee: $4.50. Fee payee: Circuit Court Clerk. Local personal checks accepted (no out of state). Prepayment is required.

Roane County

9th District Circuit & General Sessions Court PO Box 73, Kingston, TN 37763; 865-376-2390; Fax: 865-717-4141. Hours: 8:30AM-6PM Mon; 8:30AM-4:30PM T-F (EST). *Felony, Misdemeanor, Civil, Eviction, Small Claims.*

Note: General Sessions phone is 865-376-5584, their records are separate from Circuit Court records.

Civil Records: Access: Mail, fax, in person. Both court and visitors may perform in person searches. Search fee: $5.00 per name. Required to search: name, years to search. Civil cases indexed by defendant, plaintiff. Civil records archived since court started, General Sessions and Circuit are on computer since 1991. **Criminal Records:** Access: Mail, fax, in person. Both court and visitors may perform in person searches. Search fee: $5.00 per name. Required to search: name, years to search, DOB; also helpful, SSN, signed release.

Criminal records archived since court started, General Sessions and Circuit are on computer since 1991.

General Information: No adoption, expunged records released. SASE required. Turnaround time 2-3 days. Copy fee: $.50 per page. Certification fee: $5.00. Fee payee: Circuit Court Clerk. Business checks accepted. Prepayment is required.

Chancery Court PO Box 402, Kingston, TN 37763; 865-376-2487; Fax: 865-376-1228. Hours: 8:30AM-6PM Mon, 8:30AM-4:30PM T-F (EST). *Civil, Probate.*

Civil Records: Access: Phone, mail, in person. Both court and visitors may perform in person searches. No search fee. Required to search: name, years to search. Civil cases indexed by defendant, plaintiff. Civil records on books; on computer since 7/95. Tax records on computer since 1982.

General Information: No adoption records released. SASE not required. Turnaround time same day. Fax notes: Fee to fax results is $1.00 per page. Copy fee: $.50 per page. Certification fee: $2.00. Fee payee: Clerk and Master. Personal checks accepted.

Robertson County

19th District Circuit & General Sessions Court
Room 200, Springfield, TN 37172; 615-382-2324; Fax: 615-384-8246. Hours: 8AM-4:30PM (CST). *Felony, Misdemeanor, Civil, Eviction, Small Claims.*

Civil Records: Access: Phone, fax, mail, in person. Both court and visitors may perform in person searches. Search fee: $5.00 per name. Required to search: name, years to search. Civil cases indexed by defendant, plaintiff. Civil records archived in office from 1980s, archived from 1800s located elsewhere.

Criminal Records: Access: Phone, fax, mail, in person. Both court and visitors may perform in person searches. Search fee: $5.00 per name. Required to search: name, years to search; also helpful: DOB, SSN. Criminal records archived in office from 1980s, archived from 1800s located elsewhere. No long distance outgoing faxing.

General Information: Public access terminal is available. No sealed records released. SASE required. Turnaround time 15 days. Copy fee: $.25 per page. Certification fee: $5.00. Fee payee: Circuit Court Clerk. Personal checks accepted. Prepayment is required.

Chancery Court 501 Main Street - 101 Robertson, County Courthouse, Springfield, TN 37172; 615-384-5650. Hours: 8AM-4:30PM (CST). *Civil, Probate.*

Civil Records: Access: Mail, in person. Both court and visitors may perform in person searches. No search fee. Required to search: name, years to search. Civil cases indexed by defendant, plaintiff. Civil records in books since 1982, computerized from 09/94 to present, all chancery records on books.

General Information: No adoption records released. SASE required. Turnaround time 1-2 days. Copy fee: $1.00 per page. Certification fee: $2.00. Fee payee: Clerk & Master. Personal checks accepted. Prepayment is required.

Rutherford County

16th District Circuit Court
Room 201, Murfreesboro, TN 37130; Civil phone: 615-898-7820; Criminal phone: 615-898-7812; Fax: 615-849-9553. Hours: 8AM-4:15PM (CST). *Felony, Misdemeanor, Civil Actions Over $15,000.*

Civil Records: Access: In person only. Visitors must perform in person searches for themselves. No search fee. Required to search: name, years to search. Civil cases indexed by defendant, plaintiff. Civil records archived since court started, criminal on computer since 1986.

Criminal Records: Access: In person only. Visitors must perform in person searches for themselves. No search fee. Required to search: name, years to search, DOB, signed release; also helpful: SSN. Criminal records archived since court started, criminal on computer since 1990.

General Information: Public access terminal is available. No expunged, sealed criminal records released. Copy fee: $1.00 per page. Certification fee: $2.00 per page. Fee payee: Circuit Court Clerk. Personal checks accepted.

General Sessions Court Judicial Bldg, Room 101, Murfreesboro, TN 37130; 615-898-7831; Fax: 615-898-7835. Hours: 8AM-4:15PM (CST). *Civil Actions Under $10,000, Eviction, Small Claims.*

Civil Records: Access: In person only. Visitors must perform in person searches for themselves. No search fee. Required to search: name, years to search, DOB, SSN. Civil cases indexed by defendant, plaintiff. Civil records go back to 1948; on computer from 1986.

General Information: Public access terminal is available. No juvenile records released. Copy fee: $1.00 per page. Certification fee: $4.00 plus copy fee. Fee payee: General Sessions Court. No personal checks accepted. Prepayment is required.

County Court 319 N Maple St, Murfreesboro, TN 37130; 615-898-7798; Fax: 615-898-7830. Hours: 8AM-4PM M-Th; 8AM-5PM F (CST). *Probate.*

Scott County

8th District Circuit & General Sessions Court
PO Box 330, Huntsville, TN 37756; 423-663-2440. Hours: 8AM-4:30PM (EST). *Felony, Misdemeanor, Civil, Eviction, Small Claims, Probate.*

Civil Records: Access: Phone, mail, in person. Both court and visitors may perform in person searches. Search fee: $10.00 per name per year. Required to search: name, years to search. Civil cases indexed by defendant, plaintiff. Civil records archived in docket books but not specified, on computer from 1991.

Criminal Records: Access: Phone, mail, in person. Both court and visitors may perform in person searches. Search fee: $10.00 per name per year. Fee varies according to info requested. Required to search: name, years to search, DOB; also helpful: SSN. Criminal records archived in docket books but not specified, on computer from 1991.

General Information: No juvenile records released. SASE required. Turnaround time same week. Fax notes: No fee to fax results. Copy fee: $.25 per page. Certification fee: $2.00. Fee payee: Circuit Court Clerk. Personal checks accepted.

Sequatchie County

12th District Circuit & General Sessions Court
PO Box 551, Dunlap, TN 37327; 423-949-2618; Fax: 423-949-2902. Hours: 8AM-4PM (CST). *Felony, Misdemeanor, Civil, Eviction, Small Claims.*

Civil Records: Access: Phone, fax, mail, in person. Both court and visitors may perform in person searches. No search fee. Required to search: name, years to search. Civil cases indexed by defendant, plaintiff. Civil records archived on books but not specified.

Criminal Records: Access: Phone, fax, mail, in person. Both court and visitors may perform in person searches. No search fee. Required to search: name, years to search, DOB; also helpful: SSN. Criminal records not computerized.

General Information: No adoption records released. Turnaround time 1 week. Fax notes: No fee to fax results. Copy fee: $.25 per page. Fee payee: Circuit Court Clerk. Personal checks accepted.

Chancery Court PO Box 1651, Dunlap, TN 37327; 423-949-3670; Fax: 423-949-2579. Hours: 8AM-4PM (CST). *Civil, Probate.*

Civil Records: Access: Fax, mail, in person. Both court and visitors may perform in person searches. No search fee. Required to search: name, years to search. Civil cases indexed by defendant, plaintiff. Civil records on books.

General Information: No sealed or adoption records released. Turnaround time 1 week. Fax notes: $1.00 per page. Copy fee: $1.00 per page. Certification fee: $2.00. Fee payee: Clerk and Master. Personal checks accepted. Prepayment is required.

Sevier County

Circuit Court 125 Court Ave 204 E, 2nd Fl, Sevierville, TN 37862; 865-453-5536; Fax: 865-774-9792. Hours: 8AM-4:30PM M-Th, 8AM-6PM Fri (EST). *Felony, Misdemeanor, Civil actions over $15,000.*

Civil Records: Access: Fax, mail, in person. Both court and visitors may perform in person searches. Search fee: $1.00 per name. Required to search: name, years to search. Civil cases indexed by defendant, plaintiff. Civil records computerized since 1994. Records before 1980s difficult to locate.

Criminal Records: Access: Fax, mail, in person. Both court and visitors may perform in person searches. Search fee: $1.00 per name. Required to search: name, years to search; also helpful: SSN. Criminal records computerized since 1990.

General Information: No expunged records released. SASE not required. Turnaround time 1 week. Fax notes: $1.00 per page. Copy fee: $1.00 per page. Certification fee: $3.00. Fee payee: Circuit Court or General Sessions Clerk. Personal checks accepted.

General Sessions Court 125 Court Ave 107 E, 1st Fl, Sevierville, TN 37862; 865-453-6116; Fax: 865-774-3842. Hours: 8AM-4:30PM M-Th, 8AM-6PM Fri (EST). *Misdemeanor, Civil actions under $15,000, Eviction, Small Claims.*

Note: This court is now separate from the Circuit Court, which is on the 2nd floor.

Civil Records: Access: Phone, fax, mail, in person. Only the court performs in person searches. Search fee: $15.00 per name. Required to search: name, years to search. Civil cases indexed by defendant, plaintiff. Civil records computerized back to 1995; prior records go back to 1973.

Criminal Records: Access: Fax, mail, in person. Only the court performs in person searches. Search fee: $15.00 per name. Required to search: name, years to search, DOB; also helpful: SSN, date of arrest. Criminal records computerized since 1995; prior records go back to 1973.

General Information: No expunged records released. SASE not required. Turnaround time 1 week. Fax notes: $1.00 per page. Copy fee: $1.00 per page. Certification fee: $5.00. Fee payee: Circuit Court or General Sessions Clerk. No personal checks accepted.

County Court 125 Court Ave, #202, Sevierville, TN 37862; 865-453-5502; Fax: 865-453-6830. Hours: 8AM-4:30PM (EST). *Probate.*

Shelby County

Circuit Court 140 Adams Ave, Rm 224, Memphis, TN 38103; 901-545-4006; Fax: 901-545-3952. Hours: 8AM-4:30PM (CST). *Civil Actions Over $15,000.*

Civil Records: Access: Fax, mail, in person, online. Both court and visitors may perform in person searches. Search fee: $5.00 per name. Required to search: name; also helpful: years to search. Civil cases indexed by defendant, plaintiff. Civil records archived from early 1900s, on computer from 1991, on microfiche from 1980. Search the clerk's circuit court records for free at http://jssi.co.shelby.tn.us/.

General Information: No juvenile or adoption records released. Turnaround time 5-8 days. Fax notes: $1.00 per page. Copy fee: $.50 per page. Certification fee: $5.00 instate, $8.00 out of state. Fee payee: Circuit Court Clerk. Personal checks accepted. Prepayment is required.

30th District Criminal Court 201 Poplar, Room 401, 4th Flr, Memphis, TN 38103; 901-545-5001; Fax: 901-545-3679. Hours: 8AM-4:30PM (CST). *Felony.*

www.co.shelby.tn.us/county_gov/court_clerks/criminal_court/index.html

Criminal Records: Access: Fax, mail, in person, online. Both court and visitors may perform in person searches. Search fee: $5.00 per name. Required to search: name, years to search, DOB, SSN. Criminal records on computer for approximately 15 years, prior records archived since court started. Search the criminal court records for free at http://jssi.co.shelby.tn.us/.

General Information: Public access terminal is available. No expunged or sealed records released. Turnaround time 2 days. Fax notes: Fee to fax results is $5.00 per document. Copy fee: $2.00 per page. Certification fee: $5.00. Fee payee: Criminal Court Clerk. Business checks accepted. Credit cards accepted: Visa, MasterCard. Prepayment is required.

General Sessions - Civil 140 Adams, Room 106, Memphis, TN 38103; 901-576-4031. Hours: 8AM-4:30PM (CST). *Civil Actions Under $25,000, Eviction, Small Claims.*

http://generalsessionscourt.co.shelby.tn.us

Civil Records: Access: In person, online. Visitors must perform in person searches for themselves. No search fee. Required to search: name, years to search. Civil cases indexed by defendant, plaintiff. Civil records archived 10 years in office, (prior records unsure), some microfiche and on computer from 1982. Search the court records for free at http://jssi.co.shelby.tn.us.

General Information: Public access terminal is available. No mental commitment records released. SASE requested. Turnaround time 1 week. Copy fee: $1.50 per page. Certification fee: $6.00. Fee payee: General Sessions Court Clerk. Personal checks accepted. Prepayment is required.

General Sessions - Criminal 201 Poplar, Room 81, Memphis, TN 38103; 901-545-5100; Fax: 901-545-3655. 8AM-4:30PM (CST). *Misdemeanor.*

http://generalsessionscourt.co.shelby.tn.us

Criminal Records: Access: Mail, in person, online. Both court and visitors may perform in person searches. Search fee: $10.00 per name. Use of terminal is $10.00 each 20 minutes. Required to search: name, years to search, DOB; also helpful: SSN. Criminal records on computer since 1982, prior records archived since court started. Search the criminal court records for free at http://jssi.co.shelby.tn.us/.

General Information: Public access terminal is available. No mental records released. SASE not required. Turnaround time 2-5 days. Copy fee: $1.50 per page. Fee payee: General Sessions Court. Personal checks accepted. Prepayment is required.

Chancery Court 140 Adams Ave, Rm 308, Memphis, TN 38103; 901-545-4002; Fax 901-545-3309; Hours: 8AM-4:30PM (CST). *Civil Actions Under $25,000, Equity Cases (also, lower Circuit Court Civil issues).*

Civil Records: Access: Fax, mail, in person, online. Only the court may perform in person searches. Search fee: $5.00 per name. Required to search: name, years to search. Civil cases indexed by defendant, plaintiff. Search the chancery court records for free at http://jssi.co.shelby.tn.us/.

General Information: No juvenile or adoption records released. Turnaround time 1 week. Copy fee: $1.00 per page. Certification fee: $10.00. Fee payee: Chancery Court Clerk. Prepayment is required.

Probate Court 140 Adams, Room 124, Memphis, TN 38103; 901-576-4040; Fax: 901-576-4746. Hours: 8AM-4:30PM (CST). *Probate.*

www.probate.co.shelby.tn.us

Smith County

15th District Circuit & General Sessions Court 211 Main St, Carthage, TN 37030; 615-735-0500; Fax: 615-735-8261. Hours: 8AM-4PM M-F (CST). *Felony, Misdemeanor, Civil, Eviction, Small Claims.*

Civil Records: Access: Mail, in person. Both court and visitors may perform in person searches. No search fee. Required to search: name, years to search. Civil cases indexed by defendant, plaintiff. Civil records on computer from 3/92, prior records archived on books, questionable to dates.

Criminal Records: Access: Phone, mail, in person. Both court and visitors may perform in person searches. No search fee. Required to search: name, years to search. Criminal records on computer from 3/92, prior records archived on books, questionable to dates.

General Information: No juvenile records released. Turnaround time 1-2 days. Copy fee: $.25 per page. Certification fee: $6.00. Fee payee: Circuit Court Clerk. Only cashiers checks and money orders accepted. Prepayment is required.

Chancery Court 211 N Main St, Carthage, TN 37030; 615-735-2092; Fax: 615-735-8261. Hours: 8AM-4PM (CST). *Civil, Probate.*

Civil Records: Access: Fax, mail, in person. Only the court performs in person searches; visitors may not. No search fee. Required to search: name, years to search. Civil cases indexed by defendant, plaintiff. Civil records on books back to 1825.

General Information: No adoption records released. SASE requested. Turnaround time 1 day. Fax notes: Fee to fax results is $1.00 per page. Copy fee: $.50 per page. Certification fee: $4.00. Fee payee: Clerk and Master. Personal checks accepted. Prepayment is required.

Stewart County

23rd District Circuit & General Sessions Court PO Box 193, Dover, TN 37058; 931-232-7042; Fax: 931-232-3111. Hours: 8AM-4:30PM (CST). *Felony, Misdemeanor, Civil, Eviction, Small Claims.*

Civil Records: Access: Mail, in person. Visitors must perform in person searches. No search fee. Required to search: name, years to search. Civil cases indexed by plaintiff. Civil records archived on books from 1800s, on computer through 8/1993.

Criminal Records: Access: Mail, in person. Visitors must perform in person searches. No search fee. Required to search: name, years to search. Criminal records archived on books from 1800s, on computer through 8/1993.

General Information: No expunged records released. Turnaround time 1-10 days.

Chancery Court PO Box 102, Dover, TN 37058; 931-232-5665; Fax: 931-232-3111. Hours: 8AM-4:30PM (CST). *Civil, Probate.*

Civil Records: Access: Mail, in person. Only the court performs in person searches; visitors may not. No search fee. Required to search: name, years to search. Civil cases indexed by defendant, plaintiff. Civil records on books to 1865; computerized since 1994.

General Information: No adoption records released. SASE required. Turnaround time 1 week. Copy fee: $.25 per page. Certification fee: $4.00. Fee payee: Clerk and Master. Personal checks accepted. Prepayment is required.

Sullivan County

Bristol Circuit Court - Civil Division Courthouse, Rm 131, 801 Anderson St, Bristol, TN 37620; 423-989-4354. Hours: 8AM-5PM (EST). *Civil.*

Civil Records: Access: In person. Both court and visitors may perform in person searches. No search fee. Required to search: name, years to search. Civil cases indexed by defendant, plaintiff. Civil records archived from 1930s (minute books, unsure of docket books), on computer from 1986.

General Information: Public access terminal is available. No adoption or sealed records released. Turnaround time 1-2 weeks. Copy fee: $1.00 per page. Certification fee: $5.00 for the seal and $1.00 per page. Fee payee: Circuit Court Clerk. Personal checks accepted.

Kingsport Circuit Court - Civil Division 225 W Center St, Kingsport, TN 37660; 423-224-1724. Hours: 8AM-5PM (EST). *Civil Actions Over $15,000.*

Civil Records: Access: Phone, mail, in person. Both court and visitors may perform in person searches. No search fee. Required to search: name, years to search. Civil cases indexed by defendant, plaintiff. Civil records archived from 1920s, on computer from 1985.

General Information: No juvenile, adoption records released. SASE requested. Turnaround time 2-3 days. Copy fee: $1.00 per page. Certification fee: $5.00. Fee payee: Circuit Court Clerk. Personal checks accepted. Prepayment is required.

2nd District Circuit Court 140 Blockville ByPass, PO Box 585, Blountville, TN 37617; 423-323-5158. Hours: 8AM-5PM (EST). *Felony, Misdemeanor.*

Criminal Records: Access: Mail, in person. Both court and visitors may perform in person searches. No search fee. Required to search: name, years to search, DOB; also helpful: SSN. Criminal records on computer since 12/83; prior records archived since the 1800s.

General Information: Public access terminal is available. No juvenile records released. Turnaround time 1 week. Copy fee: $1.00 per page. Certification fee: $7.00 per page. Fee payee: Circuit Court Clerk. Personal checks accepted.

Bristol General Sessions Court Courthouse, 801 Anderson St, Rm 131, Bristol, TN 37620; 423-989-4352. Hours: 8AM-5PM (EST). *Misdemeanor, Civil Actions Under $15,000, Eviction, Small Claims.*

Civil Records: Access: Phone, mail, in person. Both court and visitors may perform in person searches. No search fee. Required to search: name, years to search. Civil cases indexed by defendant, plaintiff. Civil records archived since court started (stored in Blountville), on computer from 1986.

Criminal Records: Access: Phone, mail, in person. Both court and visitors may perform in person searches. No search fee. Required to search: name, years to search, DOB, SSN. Criminal records archived since court started (stored in Blountville), on computer from 1986.

General Information: Public access terminal is
available. No juvenile records released. SASE required.
Turnaround time depends on search. Copy fee: $1.00
per page. Certification fee: $5.00. Fee payee: Circuit
Court Clerk. Personal checks accepted.

Chancery Court PO Box 327, Blountville, TN
37617; 423-323-6483; Fax: 423-279-3280. Hours:
8AM-5PM (EST). *Civil, Probate.*

Civil Records: Access: Mail, in person. Both court and
visitors may perform in person searches. No search fee.
Required to search: name, years to search. Civil cases
indexed by defendant, plaintiff. Civil records on books
back to 1867; computerized records go back to 1996.
General Information: No adoption records released.
Copy fee: Varies by length of document. Certification
fee: $5.00. Fee payee: Chancery Court. Personal checks
accepted.

Kingsport General Sessions 200 Shelby St,
Kingsport, TN 37660; 423-224-1711. Hours: 8AM-
5PM (EST). *Misdemeanor, Civil Actions Under
$15,000, Eviction, Small Claims.*

Civil Records: Access: Phone, mail, in person. Visitors
must perform in person searches. No search fee.
Required to search: name, years to search. Civil cases
indexed by defendant, plaintiff. Civil records archived
in office from 1973, on computer from 1981.
Criminal Records: Access: In person. Visitors must
perform in person searches. No search fee. Required to
search: name, years to search; also helpful: SSN.
Criminal records archived in office from 1973, on
computer from 1981.
General Information: Public access terminal is
available. No juvenile records released. Turnaround
time 2-3 days. Copy fee: $1.00 per page. Certification
fee: $7.00 per page. Fee payee: General Sessions Clerk.
Personal checks accepted. Prepayment is required.

Sumner County

18th District Circuit & General Sessions
Court Public Sq, PO Box 549, Gallatin, TN 37066;
615-452-4367; Fax: 615-451-6027. Hours: 8AM-
4:30PM (CST). *Felony, Misdemeanor, Civil, Eviction,
Small Claims.*

Civil Records: Access: In person only. Visitors must
perform in person searches for themselves. No search
fee. Required to search: name, years to search. Civil
cases indexed by defendant, plaintiff. Civil records
archived on books in office from 1950.
Criminal Records: Access: In person only. Visitors
must perform in person searches for themselves. No
search fee. Required to search: name, years to search.
Criminal records archived on books in office from
1950; computerized back to 1997.
General Information: Public access terminal is
available. No juvenile, adoption records released. Copy
fee: $1.00 per page. Certification fee: $4.00. Fee payee:
Circuit Court Clerk. Only cashiers checks and money
orders accepted. Prepayment is required.

Chancery Court Room 300, Sumner County
Courthouse, Gallatin, TN 37066; 615-452-4282; Fax:
615-451-6031. Hours: 8AM-4:30PM (CST). *Civil,
Probate.*

Civil Records: Access: Phone, fax, mail, in person.
Both court and visitors may perform in person searches.
Search fee: $5.00. Required to search: name, years to
search. Civil cases indexed by defendant, plaintiff. Civil
records go back to 1981.
General Information: No juvenile or adoption records
released. Turnaround time 1-2 days. Copy fee: $1.00
per page. Certification fee: $4.00 plus $2.00 per page.
Fee payee: Clerk and Master. Only money orders, cash
or business checks. Prepayment is required.

Tipton County

25th District Circuit & General Sessions
Court 1801 S College, Rm 102, Covington, TN
38019; 901-475-3310. Hours: 8AM-5PM (CST).
Felony, Misdemeanor, Civil, Eviction, Small Claims.

Civil Records: Access: Mail, in person. Both court and
visitors may perform in person searches. Search fee:
$10.00 per name per court. $25.00 for computer info
before 07/91. Required to search: name, years to search.
Civil cases indexed by defendant, plaintiff. Civil records
on computer from July 1991, prior records on docket
books.
Criminal Records: Access: Mail, in person. Both court
and visitors may perform in person searches. Search
fee: $10.00 per name per court. Required to search:
name, years to search, DOB; also helpful: SSN.
Criminal records on computer from July 1992, prior
records on docket books.
General Information: Public access terminal is
available. No juvenile or adoption records released.
SASE requested. Turnaround time 1 week. Copy fee:
$.50 per page. Certification fee: $5.00. Fee payee:
Circuit Court Clerk or General Sessions. Personal
checks accepted. Prepayment is required.

Chancery Court Tipton County Justice Ctr., 1801
S College #110, Covington, TN 38019; 901-476-0209;
Fax: 901-476-0246. Hours: 8AM-5PM (CST). *Civil,
Probate.*

Civil Records: Access: Phone, fax, mail, in person.
Both court and visitors may perform in person searches.
No search fee. Required to search: name, years to
search. Civil cases indexed by defendant, plaintiff. Civil
records on books since 1800's, on computer since 1991.
General Information: No adoption records released.
SASE required. Turnaround time ASAP. Copy fee:
$.50 per page. Certification fee: $4.00 plus $2.00 per
page. Fee payee: Tipton County Chancery Court.
Personal checks accepted. Prepayment is required.

Trousdale County

15th District Circuit & General Sessions
Court 200 East Main St, Rm 5, Hartsville, TN 37074;
615-374-3411; Fax: 615-374-1100. Hours: 8AM-
4:30PM (CST). *Felony, Misdemeanor, Civil, Eviction,
Small Claims.*

Civil Records: Access: In person only. Visitors must
perform in person searches for themselves. No search
fee. Required to search: name, years to search. Civil
cases indexed by defendant, plaintiff. Civil records
archived on books since 1927.
Criminal Records: Access: In person only. Visitors
must perform in person searches for themselves. No
search fee. Required to search: name, years to search.
Criminal records archived on books since 1927.
General Information: No juvenile or adoption records
released. Copy fee: $1.00 per page. Certification fee:
$3.00. Fee payee: Circuit Court Clerk. Only cashiers
checks and money orders accepted. Prepayment is
required.

Chancery Court Courthouse Room 1, 200 E Main
St, Hartsville, TN 37074; 615-374-2996; Fax: 615-374-
1100. Hours: 8AM-4:30PM (CST). *Civil, Probate.*

Civil Records: Access: In person only. Visitors must
perform in person searches for themselves. No search
fee. Required to search: name, years to search. Civil
cases indexed by defendant, plaintiff. Civil records on
book since 9/80, prior records in County Clerks office.
General Information: No adoption or sealed records
released. Copy fee: $.50 per page. Certification fee:
$3.00. Plus $.50 per page. Fee payee: Clerk and Master.
Personal checks accepted. Prepayment is required.

Unicoi County

1st District Circuit & General Sessions
Court PO Box 2000, Erwin, TN 37650; 423-743-
3541. Hours: 8AM-5PM (EST). *Felony,
Misdemeanor, Civil, Eviction, Small Claims.*

Civil Records: Access: Mail, in person. Both court and
visitors may perform in person searches. Search fee:
$10.00 per name. Required to search: name, years to
search. Civil cases indexed by defendant, plaintiff. Civil
records archived on books from 1932 (felonies) and
1961 (misdemeanors); only general sessions is on
computer back to 3-4 years.
Criminal Records: Access: Mail, in person. Both court
and visitors may perform in person searches. Search
fee: $10.00 per name. Required to search: name, years
to search, DOB. Criminal records archived on books
from 1932 (felonies) and 1961 (misdemeanors); only
general sessions is on computer back to 3-4 years.
General Information: Public access terminal is
available. No adoption records released. Turnaround
time 2 days. Copy fee: $.25 per page. Certification fee:
$4.50 per document plus $.50 per page. Fee payee:
Circuit Court Clerk. Personal checks accepted.
Prepayment is required.

Probate Court PO Box 340, Erwin, TN 37650;
423-743-3381; Fax: 423-743-5430. Hours: 9AM-5PM
M-F, 9AM-Noon Sat (EST). *Probate.*

Union County

8th District Circuit & General Sessions
Court 901 E Main Street, #220, Maynardville, TN
37807; 865-992-5493. Hours: 8AM-4PM Mon-Thur;
8AM-6PM Fri (EST). *Felony, Misdemeanor, Civil,
Eviction, Small Claims.*

Civil Records: Access: Mail, in person. Both court and
visitors may perform in person searches. Search fee:
$10.00 per name. Required to search: name, years to
search. Civil cases indexed by defendant, plaintiff. Civil
records archived on books from 1969.
Criminal Records: Access: Mail, in person. Both court
and visitors may perform in person searches. Search
fee: $10.00 per name. Required to search: name, years
to search, DOB, SSN. Criminal records archived on
books from 1969.
General Information: No sealed records released.
Turnaround time 1 week. Copy fee: $.25 per page.
Certification fee: $4.00. Fee payee: Circuit Court Clerk.
Personal checks accepted.

Chancery Court 901 Main St #215, Maynardville,
TN 37807-3510; 865-992-5942. Hours: 8AM-4PM
(6PM F) (EST). *Civil, Probate.*

Civil Records: Access: Phone, mail, in person. Both
court and visitors may perform in person searches. No
search fee. Required to search: name, years to search.
Civil cases indexed by plaintiff. Civil records on books
back to 1969.
General Information: No adoption records released.
Turnaround time 1 week. Fax notes: Fee to fax results is
$.50 per page. Copy fee: $.50 per page. Certification
fee: $4.00. Fee payee: Union County Clerk and Master.
Personal checks accepted.

Van Buren County

31st District Circuit & General Sessions
Court PO Box 126, Spencer, TN 38585; 931-946-
2153; Fax: 931-946-7572. Hours: 8AM-5PM (CST).
Felony, Misdemeanor, Civil, Eviction, Small Claims.

Civil Records: Access: Mail, in person. Both court and
visitors may perform in person searches. Search fee:
$10.00 per name. Required to search: name, years to
search. Civil cases indexed by defendant. Civil records
archived on books, date unspecified.

Criminal Records: Access: Mail, in person. Both court and visitors may perform in person searches. Search fee: $10.00 per name. Required to search: name, years to search, DOB; also helpful: SSN. Criminal records archived on books, date unspecified.

General Information: No juvenile records released. Turnaround time 2 weeks. Copy fee: $.25 per page. Certification fee: $3.00. Fee payee: Circuit Court Clerk. Only cashiers checks and money orders accepted.

County Court PO Box 126, Spencer, TN 38585; 931-946-2121; Fax: 931-946-2388. Hours: 8AM-4PM M,T,Th,F, 8AM-Noon Wed & Sat (CST). *Probate.*

Warren County

31st District Circuit & General Sessions
Court 111 Court Sq, PO Box 639, McMinnville, TN 37111; 931-473-2373; Fax: 931-473-3726. Hours: 8AM-4:30PM M-Th; 8AM-5PM F (CST). *Felony, Misdemeanor, Civil, Eviction, Small Claims.*

Civil Records: Access: Mail, in person. Both court and visitors may perform in person searches. Search fee: $5.00 per name. Required to search: name, years to search. Civil cases indexed by defendant, plaintiff. Civil records on computer since 1988 (general sessions), archived in office from 1939 (Circuit).

Criminal Records: Access: Mail, in person. Both court and visitors may perform in person searches. Search fee: $5.00 per name. Required to search: name, years to search, DOB, SSN, offense, date of offense. Criminal records on computer since 1988 (general sessions), archived in office from 1939 (Circuit).

General Information: No adoption or juvenile records released. Turnaround time 1-2 days. Copy fee: $1.00 per page. Certification fee: $2.00. Fee payee: Circuit Court Clerk. Personal checks accepted. Prepayment is required.

Chancery Court PO Box 639, McMinnville, TN 37111; 931-473-2364; Fax: 931-473-3232. 8AM-4:30PM M-Th, 8AM-5PM F (CST). *Civil, Probate.*

Civil Records: Access: Mail, in person. Both court and visitors may perform in person searches. No search fee. Required to search: name, years to search. Civil cases indexed by defendant, plaintiff. Civil records on books.

General Information: No adoption records released. SASE required. Turnaround time 1 week. Copy fee: $2.00 per page. Certification fee: Certification is $4.00 for first page, $2.00 each add'l. Fee payee: Clerk and Master. Personal checks accepted.

Washington County

1st District Circuit & General Sessions
Court PO Box 356, Jonesborough, TN 37659; 423-753-1611; Fax: 423-753-1809. Hours: 8AM-5PM *Felony, Misdemeanor, Civil, Eviction, Small Claims.*

Civil Records: Access: Mail, in person. Both court and visitors may perform in person searches. Search fee: $5.00 per name. Required to search: name, years to search. Civil cases indexed by defendant, plaintiff. Civil records archived from 1800s, on computer from 1989.

Criminal Records: Access: Mail, in person. Both court and visitors may perform in person searches. Search fee: $5.00 per name. Required to search: name, years to search, DOB, SSN. Criminal records archived from 1800s, on computer from 1989.

General Information: Public access terminal is available. No sealed, juvenile, adoption records released. SASE requested. Turnaround time 1 week. Copy fee: $2.00 per page. Certification fee: $4.00. Fee payee: Circuit Court Clerk. Personal checks accepted. Prepayment is required.

General Sessions 101 E Market St, Johnson City, TN 37604; 423-461-1412; Fax: 423-926-4862. Hours: 8AM-5PM (EST). *Civil Actions Under $15,000, Eviction, Small Claims.*

Civil Records: Access: Mail, in person. Both court and visitors may perform in person searches. Search fee: $5.00 per name. Required to search: name, years to search. Civil cases indexed by defendant, plaintiff. Civil records archived since court started, computerized since 1990.

General Information: Public access terminal is available. No sealed records released. SASE requested. Turnaround time 1-2 weeks. Copy fee: $2.00 per page. Certification fee: $8.00. Fee payee: Circuit Court Clerk. In-state checks accepted. Prepayment is required.

Johnson City Law Court - Civil 101 E Market St, Johnson City, TN 37604; 423-461-1475; Fax: 423-926-4862. Hours: 8AM-5PM (EST). *Civil Actions Over $15,000.*

Civil Records: Access: Mail, in person. Both court and visitors may perform in person searches. Search fee: $5.00 per name. Required to search: name, years to search. Civil cases indexed by defendant, plaintiff. Civil records on computer from 1988.

General Information: No sealed records released. SASE requested. Turnaround time 1 week. Copy fee: $2.00 per page. Certification fee: $4.00. Fee payee: Circuit Court Clerk. Personal checks accepted. Out of state checks not accepted. Prepayment is required.

Probate Court PO Box 218, Jonesborough, TN 37659; 423-753-1623; Fax: 423-753-4716. Hours: 8AM-5PM (EST). *Probate.*

Wayne County

22nd District Circuit & General Sessions
Court PO Box 869, Waynesboro, TN 38485; 931-722-5519; Fax: 931-722-5994. Hours: 8AM-4PM M,T,Th,F, 8AM-Noon W & Sat (CST). *Felony, Misdemeanor, Civil, Eviction, Small Claims.*

Civil Records: Access: Phone, mail, in person. Both court and visitors may perform in person searches. Search fee: $5.00 per name. Required to search: name, years to search. Civil cases indexed by defendant, plaintiff. Civil records archived on books from 1800s.

Criminal Records: Access: Phone, mail, in person. Both court and visitors may perform in person searches. Search fee: $5.00 per name. Required to search: name, years to search, DOB, SSN. Criminal records archived on books from 1800s.

General Information: No juvenile or adoption records released. Turnaround time 7-10 days. Certification fee: Same as copy fee. Fee payee: Circuit Court Clerk. Personal checks accepted. Prepayment is required.

Chancery Court PO Box 101, Waynesboro, TN 38485; 931-722-5517; Fax: 931-722-5994. Hours: 8AM-4PM (CST). *Civil, Probate.*

Civil Records: Access: Mail, in person. Both court and visitors may perform in person searches. No search fee. Required to search: name, years to search. Civil cases indexed by defendant, plaintiff. Civil records on books; computerized since 12/92.

General Information: No adoption records released. SASE requested. Turnaround time 2 days. No copy fee. Certification fee: $3.00 minimum or $1.00 per page. Fee payee: Clerk and Master. Personal checks accepted. Prepayment is required.

Weakley County

27th District Circuit & General Sessions
Court PO Box 28, Dresden, TN 38225; 731-364-3455; Fax: 731-364-6765. Hours: 8AM-4:30PM (CST). *Felony, Misdemeanor, Civil, Eviction, Small Claims.*

Civil Records: Access: In person only. Visitors must perform in person searches for themselves. No search fee. Required to search: name, years to search. Civil cases indexed by defendant, plaintiff. Civil records archived on since court started, on books; computerized since 1997.

Criminal Records: Access: In person only. Visitors must perform in person searches for themselves. No search fee. Required to search: name, years to search, DOB; also helpful: SSN. Criminal records archived on since court started, on books; computerized since 1997.

General Information: Public access terminal is available. No adoption or sealed records released. Copy fee: $2.00 per page. Certification fee: $6.00. Fee payee: Circuit Court Clerk. No personal checks accepted. Prepayment is required.

Chancery Court PO Box 197, Dresden, TN 38225; 731-364-3454; Fax: 731-364-5247. Hours: 8AM-4:30PM (CST). *Civil, Probate.*

Note: Court will not do searches for geneaology.

Civil Records: Access: Mail, in person. Both court and visitors may perform in person searches. No search fee. Required to search: name, years to search. Civil cases indexed by defendant, plaintiff. Civil records on computer since 1982, prior records in books to 1930; Probate to 1800s.

General Information: No adoption or sealed records released. Turnaround time 1 week. Copy fee: $1.00 per page. Certification fee: $5.00. Fee payee: Clerk and Master. Personal checks accepted. Prepayment is required.

White County

13th District Circuit & General Sessions
Court 111 Dept St Ste 1, Sparta, TN 38583; 931-836-3205; Fax: 931-836-3526. Hours: 8AM-5PM (CST). *Felony, Misdemeanor, Civil, Eviction, Small Claims.*

Civil Records: Access: In person only. Visitors must perform in person searches for themselves. No search fee. Required to search: name, years to search. Civil cases indexed by defendant, plaintiff. Civil records archived since court started, computerized since 1996.

Criminal Records: Access: In person only. Visitors must perform in person searches for themselves. No search fee. Required to search: name, years to search, DOB; also helpful: SSN. Criminal records archived since court started; computerized records since 19996.

General Information: No juvenile, adoption records released. Certification fee: $3.50. Fee payee: Circuit Court Clerk. Personal checks accepted. Prepayment is required.

Chancery Court White County Courthouse, Room 303, Sparta, TN 38583; 931-836-3787. Hours: 8AM-4PMn (CST). *Civil, Probate.*

Civil Records: Access: Phone, in person. Visitors must perform in person searches for themselves. No search fee. Required to search: name, years to search. Civil cases indexed by defendant, plaintiff. Overall records go back to 1842.

General Information: No adoption records released. Certification fee: $2.00. Fee payee: Clerk and Master. Personal checks accepted. Prepayment is required.

Williamson County

21st District Circuit & General Sessions Court

Room 107, Franklin, TN 37064; 615-790-5454; Fax: 615-790-5432. Hours: 8AM-4:30PM (CST). *Felony, Misdemeanor, Civil, Eviction, Small Claims.*

Civil Records: Access: Mail, in person. Both court and visitors may perform in person searches. Search fee: $15.00 per name. Required to search: name, years to search. Civil cases indexed by defendant, plaintiff. Civil records archived on books from 1810, on computer from 1992.

Criminal Records: Access: Mail, in person. Both court and visitors may perform in person searches. Search fee: $12.00 per name. Misdemeanor search is $30.00. Required to search: name, years to search, DOB; also helpful: SSN. Criminal records archived on books from 1810, on computer from 1992.

General Information: SASE not required. Turnaround time 3 days. Certification fee: $4.00. Fee payee: Circuit Court Clerk. Personal checks accepted. Prepayment is required.

Chancery Court

Clerk & Master, PO Box 1666, Franklin, TN 37064; 615-790-5428; Fax: 615-790-5626. Hours: 8AM-4:30PM (CST). *Civil, Probate.*

Civil Records: Access: Phone, mail, in person. Both court and visitors may perform in person searches. No search fee. Required to search: name, years to search. Civil cases indexed by defendant, plaintiff. Civil records on computer since 1991, prior records on books since 1800s (no probate on computer).

General Information: No adoption, sealed records released. SASE requested. Copy fee: $1.00 per page. Certification fee: $2.00 per document. Fee payee: Clerk and Master. Local checks accepted.

Wilson County

15th District Circuit & General Sessions Court

PO Box 518, Lebanon, TN 37088-0518; 615-444-2042; Fax: 615-449-3420. Hours: 8AM-4PM M-Th, 8AM-5PM F (CST). *Felony, Misdemeanor, Civil, Eviction, Small Claims.*

Civil Records: Access: In person only. Visitors must perform in person searches for themselves. No search fee. Required to search: name, years to search. Civil cases indexed by defendant, plaintiff. Civil records archived in office from 1982, from 1800s located elsewhere, on computer from 1990, on microfiche from 1940s.

Criminal Records: Access: In person only. Visitors must perform in person searches for themselves. No search fee. Required to search: name, years to search, DOB, SSN. Criminal records archived in office from 1982, from 1800s located elsewhere, on computer from 1190, on microfiche from 1940s.

General Information: Public access terminal is available. No adoption, juvenile records released. Copy fee: $.25 per page. Certification fee: $6.00. Plus $2.00 each additional page. Fee payee: Circuit Court Clerk. Business checks accepted. Prepayment is required.

County Court

PO Box 950, Lebanon, TN 37088-0918; 615-443-2627; Fax: 615-443-2628. Hours: 8AM-4:30PM M-Th, 8AM-5PM Fri (CST). *Probate.*

Tennessee Recording Offices

ORGANIZATION: 95 counties, 96 recording offices. The recording officer is. Register of Deeds. Sullivan County has two offices. 66 counties are in the Central Time Zone (CST) and 29 are in the Eastern Time Zone (EST).

REAL ESTATE RECORDS: Counties will not perform real estate searches. Certified copies usually cost $1.00 per page. Tax records are kept at the Assessor's Office.

UCC RECORDS: Financing statements are filed at the state level, except for real estate related collateral, which are filed with the Register of Deeds. However, prior to 07/2001, consumer goods and farm collateral were also filed at the Register of Deeds and these older records can be searched there. Many recording offices will not perform UCC searches. Use search request form UCC-11. Search fee is usually $12-15, the copy fee is $1.00.

TAX LIEN RECORDS: All federal tax liens are filed with the county Register of Deeds. State tax liens are filed with the Secretary of State or the Register of Deeds. Counties will not perform tax lien searches.

OTHER LIENS: Judgment, materialman, mechanics, trustee.

ONLINE ACCESS: The State Comptroller of the Treasury Real Estate Assessment Database can be searched free at http://170.142.31.248/. Select a county then search by name for real property infromation. Counties not on the system are Davidson, Hamilton, Knox, Shelby, and Unicoi.

Online access to forty counties' property and deeds indexes and images is available via a private company at http://auth.titlesearcher.com/ts/ts.asp or email support@TitleSearcher.com. Registration, login, and monthly $35 fee per county required, plus $20. set up. A $5 per day plan is also available.

Also, online access to 22 counties' property, deeds, judgment, liens, and UCCs is available via a private company at www.ustitlesearch.com or call 615-223-5420. Registration, login, and monthly $25 fee required, plus $50 set up. Use DEMO username to try system.

Finally, www.tnrealestate.com offers free and fee services for real estate information from all counties.

Anderson County

Register of Deeds, 100 N Main St, Room 205, Clinton, TN 37716-3688. 865-457-5400; Fax 865-457-1638.
Will search UCC records prior to 7/2001 and current fixture (land) files. Will not search real estate records. **Online Access:** Land Records. Access to property and deeds indexes and images is available via a private company at http://auth.titlesearcher.com/ts/ts.asp. Fee/registration required; see state introduction. **Other Phone Numbers:** Assessor 865-457-5400 x225.

Bedford County

Register of Deeds, 108 Northside Square, Shelbyville, TN 37160. Reg. Deeds, R/E and UCC Recording 931-684-5719; Fax 931-685-2086. http://titlesearcher.com
Will search UCC records prior to 7/2001 and current fixture (land) files. Will not search real estate records. **Online Access:** Land Records. Access to property and deeds indexes and images is available via a private company at http://auth.titlesearcher.com/ts/ts.asp. Fee/registration required; see state introduction. **Other Phones:** Assessor 931-684-6390; Treasurer 931-684-4303; Appraiser 684-4303; Elections 684-0531.

Benton County

Register of Deeds, 1 E. Court Sq., Suite 105, Camden, TN 38320-2070. 731-584-6661.
Will search UCC records prior to 7/2001 and current fixture (land) files. This agency will not do a tax lien search. Will not search real estate records. **Online Access:** Real Estate, Deed, Judgment, Lien, UCC Records. Access to indexes and images is available via a private company at www.ustitlesearch.com. Registration and monthly fee required; see state introduction. **Other Phones:** Assessor 731-584-7615.

Bledsoe County

Register of Deeds, PO Box 385, Pikeville, TN 37367. Register of Deeds, R/E and UCC Recording 423-447-2020; Fax 423-447-6856.
Will search UCC records prior to 7/2001 and current fixture (land) files. Will not search real estate records. **Other Phones:** Assessor 423-447-6548; Treasurer 447-2369; Appraiser 447-6548; Elections 423-447-2776.

Blount County

Register of Deeds, 349 Court St, Maryville, TN 37804-5906. 865-273-5880; Fax 865-273-5890. www.blount.state.tn.us/register.htm
Will search UCC records prior to 7/2001 and current fixture (land) files. Will not search real estate records. **Other Phone Numbers:** Assessor 865-982-5130.

Bradley County

Register of Deeds, PO Box 579, Cleveland, TN 37364-0579. 423-476-0513; Fax 423-478-8888.
This agency will not search real estate or UCC records. **Online Access:** Land Records. Access to property and deeds indexes and images is available via a private company at http://auth.titlesearcher.com/ts/ts.asp. Fee/registration required; see state introduction. **Other Phone Numbers:** Assessor 423-476-0505.

Campbell County

Register of Deeds, PO Box 85, Jacksboro, TN 37757. 423-562-3864; Fax 423-562-9833.
Will search UCC records prior to 7/2001 and current fixture (land) files. Tax liens not included in UCC search. Will not search real estate records. **Other Phones:** Assessor 423-562-3201; Treasurer 562 5185.

Cannon County

Register of Deeds, Courthouse, Woodbury, TN 37190. 615-563-2041; Fax 615-563-5696.
Will search UCC records prior to 7/2001 and current fixture (land) files. **Online Access:** Real Estate, Deed, Judgment, Lien, UCC Records. Access to real estate records is available at www.ustitlesearch.com. Registration and fee required; information at web site; also see state introduction. **Other Phone Numbers:** Assessor 615-563-5437.

Carroll County

Register of Deeds, Carroll County Office Complex, 625 High St., Suite 104, Huntingdon, TN 38344. 731-986-1952; Fax 731-986-1955.
Will search UCC records prior to 7/2001 and current fixture (land) files. Will not search real estate records. **Online Access:** Real Estate, Deed, Judgment, Lien,

UCC Records. Access to indexes and images is available via a company at www.ustitlesearch.com. Registration and monthly fee required; see state introduction. **Other Phones:** Assessor 731-986-1975.

Carter County

Register of Deeds, 801 E. Elk Ave, Elizabethton, TN 37643. 423-542-1830.
This agency will not perform searches. **Online Access:** Land Records. Access to property and deeds indexes and images is available via a private company at http://auth.titlesearcher.com/ts/ts.asp. Fee and registration required; see state introduction. **Other Phone Numbers:** Assessor 423-542-1806.

Cheatham County

Register of Deeds, PO Box 453, Ashland City, TN 37015. 615-792-4317; Fax 615-792-2039.
Will search UCC records prior to 7/2001 and current fixture (land) files. Will not search real estate records. **Online Access:** Real Estate, Deed, Judgment, Lien, UCC Records. Access to indexes and images is available via a private company at www.ustitlesearch.com. Registration and monthly fee required; see state introduction. **Other Phones:** Assessor 615-792-5371; Treasurer 615-792-4298.

Chester County

Register of Deeds, PO Box 292, Henderson, TN 38340. Reg. Deeds, R/E and UCC Recording 731-989-4991.
This agency will not perform searches. **Online Access:** Real Estate, Deed, Judgment, Lien, UCC Records. Access to indexes and images is available via a private company at www.ustitlesearch.com. Registration and monthly fee required; see state introduction. **Other Phones:** Assessor 731-989-4882; Treasurer 989-3993.

Claiborne County

Register of Deeds, PO Box 117, Tazewell, TN 37879. 423-626-3325.
Will search UCC records prior to 7/2001 and current fixture (land) files. This agency will not do a tax lien search. Real estate record owner and property searches available. **Online Access:** Land Records. Access to property and deeds indexes and images is available via

a private company at http://auth.titlesearcher.com/ts/ts.asp. Fee/registration required; see state introduction. **Other Phone Numbers:** Assessor 423-626-3276; Treasurer 423-626-3275.

Clay County

Register of Deeds, PO Box 430, Celina, TN 38551. 931-243-3298.
Will search UCC records prior to 7/2001 and current fixture (land) files. UCC search includes tax liens. Will not search real estate records. **Online Access:** Land Records. Access to property and deeds indexes and images is available via a private company at http://auth.titlesearcher.com/ts/ts.asp. Fee/registration required; see state introduction. **Other Phones:** Assessor 931-243-2599; Treasurer 931-243-2310.

Cocke County

Register of Deeds, 111 Court Ave., Room 102, Courthouse, Newport, TN 37821-3102. 423-623-7540.
Will search UCC records prior to 7/2001 and current fixture (land) files. This agency will not do a tax lien search. Will not search real estate records. **Online Access:** Land Records. Access to property and deeds indexes and images is available via a private company at http://auth.titlesearcher.com/ts/ts.asp. Fee/registration required; see state introduction. **Other Phones:** Assessor 423-623-7024; Trustee 423-623-3037.

Coffee County

Register of Deeds, PO Box 178, Manchester, TN 37349. 931-723-5130; Fax 931-723-8232.
Will search UCC records prior to 7/2001 and current fixture (land) files. Will not search real estate records. **Online Access:** Land Records. Access to property and deeds indexes and images is available via a private company at http://auth.titlesearcher.com/ts/ts.asp. Fee/registration required; see state introduction. **Other Phone Numbers:** Assessor 931-723-5126.

Crockett County

Register of Deeds, County Courthouse, 1 S Bells St #2, 1 S. Bells St., Suite 2, Alamo, TN 38001. 731-696-5455; Fax 731-696-3028.
This agency will not search real estate or UCC records. **Other Phone Numbers:** Assessor 731-696-5456; Treasurer 731-696-5454.

Cumberland County

Register of Deeds, 2 N. Main St., Suite 204, Crossville, TN 38555-4583. 931-484-5559.
This agency will not perform searches. **Online Access:** Land Records. Access to property and deeds indexes and images is available via a private company at http://auth.titlesearcher.com/ts/ts.asp. Fee/registration required; see state introduction. **Other Phone Numbers:** Assessor 931-484-5745; Elections 931-484-4919; Trustee 931-484-5730.

Davidson County

Register of Deeds, 103 Metro Courthouse, Nashville, TN 37201-5028. 615-862-6790; Fax 615-880-2039. www.nashville.org
This agency will not search real estate or UCC records. **Online Access:** Property Records. Property records on the Metropolitan Planning Commission City of Nashville database are available free online at www.nashville.org/mpc/maps/index.html. Click on "Go straight to maps." There is also a commercial online service that allows subscribers to download information via an FTP site. **Other Phones:** Assessor 862-6080.

De Kalb County

Register of Deeds, 1 Public Square, #201, Smithville, TN 37166. 615-597-4153; Fax 615-597-7420.
Will search UCC records prior to 7/2001 and current fixture (land) files. This agency will not do a tax lien

search. Will not search real estate records. **Other Phones:** Assessor 615-597-5925; Trustee 597-5176.

Decatur County

Register of Deeds, PO Box 488, Decaturville, TN 38329. 731-852-3712.
Will search UCC records prior to 7/2001 and current fixture (land) files. This agency will not do a tax lien search. Will not search real estate records. **Online Access:** Land Records. Access to property and deeds indexes and images is available via a private company at http://auth.titlesearcher.com/ts/ts.asp. Fee/registration required; see state introduction. **Other Phones:** Assessor 731-852-3117; Treasurer 731-852-3723.

Dickson County

Register of Deeds, PO Box 220, Charlotte, TN 37036. 615-789-4171; Fax 615-789-3893.
Will search UCC records prior to 7/2001 and current fixture (land) files. Will not search real estate records. **Online Access:** Real Estate, Deed, Judgment, Lien, UCC Records. Access to indexes and images is available via a private company at www.ustitlesearch.com. Registration and monthly fee required; see state introduction. Also, a 2nd private company offers online access to property and deeds indexes and images at http://auth.titlesearcher.com/ts/ts.asp. Fee/registration required; see state introduction. **Other Phones:** Assessor 615-789-4171.

Dyer County

Register of Deeds, PO Box 1360, Dyersburg, TN 38025-1360. 731-286-7806; Fax 731-288-7724. www.co.dyer.tn.us
Will search UCC records prior to 7/2001 and current fixture (land) files. This agency will not do a tax lien search. Will not search real estate records. **Online Access:** Real Estate, Deed, Judgment, Lien, UCC, Property Tax Records. Access to indexes and images is available via a company at www.ustitlesearch.com. Registration and monthly fee required; see state introduction. Also, property tax information is available free online at https://dyer.tn.ezgov.com/property/review_search.jsp however, no name searching. **Other Phones:** Assessor 731-286-7805; Treasurer 731-286-7802; Elections 286-4268; Vital Records 286-7814.

Fayette County

Register of Deeds, PO Box 99, Somerville, TN 38068-0099. 901-465-5251.
Will search UCC records prior to 7/2001 and current fixture (land) files. This agency will not do a tax lien search. Will not search real estate records. **Online Access:** Land Records. Access to property and deeds indexes and images is available via a private company at http://auth.titlesearcher.com/ts/ts.asp. Fee/registration required; see state introduction. **Other Phone Numbers:** Assessor 901-465-5226; Treasurer 901-465-5224; Elections 901-465-5223.

Fentress County

Register of Deeds, PO Box 341, Jamestown, TN 38556. Register of Deeds, R/E and UCC Recording 931-879-7818; Fax 931-879-1579.
This agency will not search real estate or UCC records. **Online Access:** Land Records. Access to property and deeds indexes and images is available via a private company at http://auth.titlesearcher.com/ts/ts.asp. Fee/registration required; see state introduction. **Other Phone Numbers:** Assessor 931-879-9194; Treasurer 931-879-7717; Appraiser/Auditor 931-879-8294; Elections 931-879-7162; Vital Records 931-879-8014.

Franklin County

Register of Deeds, PO Box 101, Winchester, TN 37398-0101. 931-967-2840; www.titlesearcher.com

This agency will not perform searches. **Online Access:** Land Records. Access is through a private company at www.titlesearcher.com. Registration and password required; signup at web site. Per day usage available; see state introduction. Also, online access to property and deeds indexes and images is available via a private company at http://auth.titlesearcher.com/ts/ts.asp. Fee/registration required; see state introduction. **Other Phones:** Assessor 931-967-3869; Treasurer 967-2962.

Gibson County

Register of Deeds, Courthouse, 1 Court Square, Trenton, TN 38382. 731-855-7628; Fax 731-855-7650.
This agency will not search real estate or UCC records. **Online Access:** Real Estate, Deed, Judgment, Lien, UCC Records. Access to indexes and images is available via a private company at www.ustitlesearch.com. Registration and monthly fee required; see state introduction. **Other Phones:** Assessor 731-855-7634; Elections 731-855-7669.

Giles County

Register of Deeds, PO Box 678, Pulaski, TN 38478. Reg. Deeds, R/E and UCC Recording 931-363-5137; Fax 931-424-6101. www.usit.net/giles/Government/register.htm
Will search UCC records prior to 7/2001 and current fixture (land) files. This agency will not do a tax lien search. Will not search real estate records. **Online Access:** Land Records. Access to property and deeds indexes and images is available via a private company at http://auth.titlesearcher.com/ts/ts.asp. Fee/registration required; see state introduction. **Other Phone Numbers:** Assessor 931-363-2166; Treasurer 931-363-1676; Appraiser/Auditor 931-363-2166; Elections 931-363-2424; Trustee 931-363-1676.

Grainger County

Register of Deeds, PO Box 174, Rutledge, TN 37861. 865-828-3523; Fax 865-828-4284.
Will search UCC records prior to 7/2001 and current fixture (land) files. **Online Access:** Land Records. Access to property and deeds indexes and images is available via a private company at http://auth.titlesearcher.com/ts/ts.asp. Fee/registration required; see state introduction. **Other Phones:** Assessor 865-828-5858; Trustee 865-828-3514.

Greene County

Register of Deeds, Courthouse, 101 S. Main St. #201, Greeneville, TN 37743. 423-639-0196 R/E Recording: 423-639-1726 UCC Recording: 423-639-1726.
This agency will not perform searches. **Online Access:** Land Records. Access to property and deeds indexes and images is available via a private company at http://auth.titlesearcher.com/ts/ts.asp. Fee/registration required; see state introduction. **Other Phones:** Assessor 423-638-1738; Treasurer 423-639-1705.

Grundy County

Register of Deeds, PO Box 35, Altamont, TN 37301-0035. 931-692-3621; Fax 931-692-3627.
Will search UCC records prior to 7/2001 and current fixture (land) files. Will not search real estate records. **Online Access:** Land Records. Access to property and deeds indexes and images is available via a private company at http://auth.titlesearcher.com/ts/ts.asp. Fee/registration required; see state introduction. **Other Phone Numbers:** Assessor 931-692-3596.

Hamblen County

Register of Deeds, 511 W. 2nd North St, Morristown, TN 37814. 423-586-6551; Fax 423-587-9798.
Will search UCC records prior to 7/2001 and current fixture (land) files. Will not search real estate records. **Online Access:** Land Records. Access to property and deeds indexes and images is available via a private

company at http://auth.titlesearcher.com/ts/ts.asp. Fee/registration required; see state introduction.

Hamilton County

Register of Deeds, 625 Georgia Ave., Court House, Room 400, Chattanooga, TN 37402. 423-209-6560; Fax 423-209-6561. www.hamiltontn.gov/register Will search UCC records prior to 7/2001 and current fixture (land) files. This agency will not do a tax lien search. Will not search real estate records. **Online Access:** Real Estate, Recording, Deeds, Property Assessor, Delinquent Tax Records. The County Register of Deeds subscription service is available online for $50 per month and $1.00 per fax page. Search by name, address, or book & page. For further information, call 423-209-6560. Also, property assessor records are available free online at www.hamiltontn.gov/DataServices/default.htm. Click on "Assessor of Property Inquiry." Also, search the county trustees back taxes list at www.hamiltontn.gov/Trustee/backtax.htm. **Other Phones:** Assessor 423-209-7300; Treasurer 423-209-7270.

Hancock County

Register of Deeds, PO Box 72, Sneedville, TN 37869. 423-733-4545.
Will search UCC records prior to 7/2001 and current fixture (land) files. This agency will not do a tax lien search. Will not search real estate records. **Other Phone Numbers:** Assessor 423-733-2332.

Hardeman County

Register of Deeds, Courthouse, 100 N Main St., Bolivar, TN 38008. 731-658-3476; Fax 731-658-3075. This agency will not perform searches. **Online Access:** Real Estate, Deed, Judgment, Lien, UCC Records. Access to indexes and images is available via a private company at www.ustitlesearch.com. Registration and monthly fee required; see state introduction. **Other Phone Numbers:** Assessor 731-658-6522.

Hardin County

Register of Deeds, Courthouse, Savannah, TN 38372. 731-925-4936.
Will search UCC records prior to 7/2001 and current fixture (land) files. This agency will not do a tax lien search. Will not search real estate records. **Online Access:** Real Estate, Deed, Judgment, Lien, UCC Records. Access to indexes and images is available via a private company at www.ustitlesearch.com. Registration and monthly fee required; see state introduction. **Other Phone Numbers:** Assessor 731-925-9031; Treasurer 731-925-8180.

Hawkins County

Register of Deeds, PO Box 235, Rogersville, TN 37857. Register of Deeds, R/E and UCC Recording 423-272-8304; Fax 423-921-3170.
This agency will not search real estate or UCC records. **Other Phone Numbers:** Assessor 423-272-8505; Elections 423-272-8061.

Haywood County

Register of Deeds, 1 N. Washington, Courthouse, Brownsville, TN 38012. 731-772-0332.
Will search UCC records prior to 7/2001 and current fixture (land) files. This agency will not do a tax lien search. Will not search real estate records. **Other Phone Numbers:** Assessor 731-772-0432; Treasurer 731-772-1722.

Henderson County

Register of Deeds, Courthouse, Lexington, TN 38351. 731-968-2941.
Will search UCC records prior to 7/2001 and current fixture (land) files. This agency will not do a tax lien search. Will not search real estate records. **Online

Access: Real Estate, Deed, Judgment, Lien, UCC Records. Access to indexes and images is available via a private company at www.ustitlesearch.com. Registration and monthly fee required; see state introduction.

Henry County

Register of Deeds, PO Box 44, Paris, TN 38242. Register of Deeds, R/E & UCC Recording 731-642-4081; Fax 731-642-2123. www.ustitlesearch.com This agency will not search real estate or UCC records. **Online Access:** Real Estate, Deed, Judgment, Lien, UCC Records. Access to indexes and images is available via a private company at www.ustitlesearch.com. Registration and monthly fee required; see state introduction. **Other Phone Numbers:** Assessor 731-642-0162; Elections 731-642-0411; Trustee 731-642-6633.

Hickman County

Register of Deeds, #1 Courthouse, Centerville, TN 37033-1639. Register of Deeds, R/E and UCC Recording 931-729-4882.
Will search UCC records prior to 7/2001 and current fixture (land) files. This agency will not do a tax lien search. Will not search real estate records. **Online Access:** Land Records. Access to property and deeds indexes and images is available via a private company at http://auth.titlesearcher.com/ts/ts.asp. Fee/registration required; see state introduction. **Other Phone Numbers:** Assessor 931-729-2169.

Houston County

Register of Deeds, PO Box 412, Erin, TN 37061. 931-289-3510; Fax 931-289-4240.
Will search UCC records prior to 7/2001 and current fixture (land) files. Will not search real estate records. **Other Phone Numbers:** Assessor 931-289-3929.

Humphreys County

Register of Deeds, 102 Thompson St, Courthouse Annex, Room 3, Waverly, TN 37185. Register of Deeds, R/E and UCC Recording 931-296-7681.
This agency will not perform searches. **Online Access:** Land Records. Access to property and deeds indexes and images is available via a private company at http://auth.titlesearcher.com/ts/ts.asp. Fee/registration required; see state introduction. **Other Phones:** Assessor 931-615-2919; Treasurer 931-296-2414.

Jackson County

Register of Deeds, PO Box 301, Gainesboro, TN 38562. Register of Deeds, R/E and UCC Recording 931-268-9012.
This agency will not perform searches. **Online Access:** Land Records. Access to property and deeds indexes and images is available via a private company at http://auth.titlesearcher.com/ts/ts.asp. Fee/registration required; see state introduction. **Other Phone Numbers:** Assessor 931-268-0246; Treasurer 931-268-9417; Elections 931-268-9284.

Jefferson County

Register of Deeds, PO Box 58, Dandridge, TN 37725. 865-397-2918.
Will not search UCC records, but will do an index name search back 3 years only. This agency will not do a tax lien search. Will not search real estate records. **Online Access:** Land Records. Access to property and deeds indexes and images is available via a private company at http://auth.titlesearcher.com/ts/ts.asp. Fee/registration required; see state introduction. **Other Phones:** Assessor 865-397-3326; Treasurer 865-397-2101.

Johnson County

Register of Deeds, 222 Main St, Mountain City, TN 37683. 423-727-7841; Fax 423-727-7047.

This agency will not search real estate or UCC records. **Other Phone Numbers:** Assessor 423-727-7692; Treasurer 423-727-9062; Elections 423-727-8592.

Knox County

Register of Deeds, 400 W. Main Ave, Room 224, Knoxville, TN 37902. 865-215-2330; www.knoxcounty.org/rod/default.asp Will search UCC records prior to 7/2001 and current fixture (land) files. This agency will not do a tax lien search. Will not search real estate records. **Online Access:** Real Estate, Property Tax Records. Search the property tax rolls for free at www.knoxcounty.org/tax_search. **Other Phones:** Assessor 865-521-2360; Treasurer 865-521-2305.

Lake County

Register of Deeds, 229 Church St., Box 5, Courthouse, Tiptonville, TN 38079. Register of Deeds, R/E and UCC Recording 731-253-7462; Fax 731-253-6815. Will search UCC records. Will not search real estate records. **Online Access:** Real Estate, Deed, Judgment, Lien, UCC Records. Access to indexes and images is available via a private company at www.ustitlesearch.com. Registration and monthly fee required; see state introduction. **Other Phone Numbers:** Assessor 731-253-7200.

Lauderdale County

Register of Deeds, Courthouse, Ripley, TN 38063. 731-635-2171; Fax 731-635-9682.
Will search UCC records prior to 7/2001 and current fixture (land) files. Will not search real estate records. **Online Access:** Real Estate, Deed, Judgment, Lien, UCC Records. Access to indexes and images is available via a private company at www.ustitlesearch.com. Registration and monthly fee required; see state introduction. **Other Phones:** Assessor 731-635-9561; Treasurer 731-635-0712.

Lawrence County

Register of Deeds, 240 W. Gaines St, N.B.U. #18, Lawrenceburg, TN 38464. Register of Deeds, R/E and UCC Recording 931-766-4100; Fax 931-766-5602. www.titlesearcher.com Will search UCC records prior to 7/2001 and current fixture (land) files. Will not search real estate records. **Online Access:** Land Records. Access to property and deeds indexes and images is available via a private company at http://auth.titlesearcher.com/ts/ts.asp. Fee/registration required; see state introduction. **Other Phone Numbers:** Assessor 931-766-4104; Treasurer 931-766-4110; Appraiser/Auditor 931-766-4104; Elections 931-766-4130; Vital Records 615-741-1763.

Lewis County

Register of Deeds, Courthouse, Room 104, 110 N. Park Ave., Hohenwald, TN 38462. 931-796-2255.
Will search UCC records. This agency will not do a tax lien search. Will not search real estate records. **Online Access:** Real Estate, Deed, Judgment, Lien, UCC Records. Access to indexes and images is available via a private company at www.ustitlesearch.com. Registration and monthly fee required; see state introduction. **Other Phone Numbers:** Assessor 931-796-5848; Elections 931-796-362.

Lincoln County

Register of Deeds, 112 Main Ave S, Rm 104, 112 Main St., Fayetteville, TN 37334. Register of Deeds, R/E and UCC Recording 931-433-5366; Fax 931-433-9312.
This agency will not perform searches. **Online Access:** Land Records. Access to property and deeds indexes and images is available via a private company at http://auth.titlesearcher.com/ts/ts.asp. Fee/registration required; see state introduction. **Other Phone**

Numbers: Assessor 931-433-5409; Treasurer 931-433-1371; Elections 931-433-6220.

Loudon County

Register of Deeds, PO Box 395, Loudon, TN 37774. 865-458-2605; Fax 865-458-9028.
This agency will not search real estate or UCC records. **Other Phone Numbers:** Assessor 865-458-2050; Elections 865-458-2560.

Macon County

Register of Deeds, Courthouse, Room 102, Lafayette, TN 37083. 615-666-2353; Fax 615-666-5323.
Will search UCC records prior to 7/2001 and current fixture (land) files. Will not search real estate records. **Online Access:** Land Records. Access to property and deeds indexes and images is available via a private company at http://auth.titlesearcher.com/ts/ts.asp. Fee/registration required; see state introduction. **Other Phones:** Assessor 615-666-3688; Trustee 666-3624.

Madison County

Register of Deeds, Courthouse, Room 109, 100 Main St., Jackson, TN 38301. 731-423-6028; Fax 731-422-1171.
Will search UCC records prior to 7/2001 and current fixture (land) files only. Will not search real estate records. **Online Access:** Land Records. Access to property and deeds indexes and images is available via a private company at http://auth.titlesearcher.com/ts/ts.asp. Fee/registration required; see state introduction. **Other Phone Numbers:** Assessor 731-423-6100; Treasurer 731-423-6027.

Marion County

Register of Deeds, PO Box 789, Jasper, TN 37347. 423-942-2573.
This agency will not perform searches. **Online Access:** Land Records. Access to property and deeds indexes and images is available via a private company at http://auth.titlesearcher.com/ts/ts.asp. Fee/registration required; see state introduction. **Other Phone Numbers:** Assessor 423-942-3494.

Marshall County

Register of Deeds, 1103 Courthouse Annex, Lewisburg, TN 37091. 931-359-4933.
This agency will not perform searches. **Online Access:** Land Records. Access to property and deeds indexes and images is available via a private company at http://auth.titlesearcher.com/ts/ts.asp. Fee/registration required; see state introduction. **Other Phone Numbers:** Assessor 931-359-3238.

Maury County

Register of Deeds, PO Box 769, Columbia, TN 38402-0769. 931-381-3690 x358 R/E Recording: 931-381-3690 x355 UCC Recording: 931-381-3690 x355; www.titlesearcher.com
Will search UCC records. This agency will not do a tax lien search. Will not search real estate records. **Online Access:** Land Records. Access to property and deeds indexes and images is available via a private company at http://auth.titlesearcher.com/ts/ts.asp. Fee/registration required; see state introduction. **Other Phone Numbers:** Assessor 931-381-3690 x253.

McMinn County

Register of Deeds, PO Box 1074, Athens, TN 37371-1074. 423-745-1232; Fax 423-745-0095.
Will search UCC records prior to 7/2001 and current fixture (land) files. Will not search real estate records. **Online Access:** Real Estate, Deed, Judgment, Lien, UCC Records. Access to indexes and images is available via a private company at www.ustitlesearch.com. Registration and monthly fee required; see state introduction. Records go back to 9-1-

99. **Other Phones:** Assessor 423-745-2743; Treasurer 423-745-4103; Elections 423-745-0843; Trustee 423-745-1291; Circuit Court Clerk 423-745-1923;

McNairy County

Register of Deeds, PO Box 158, Selmer, TN 38375. 731-645-3656; Fax 731-645-3656.
Will search UCC records prior to 7/2001 and current fixture (land) files. Tax liens not included in UCC search. Real estate record owner and mortgage searches available. **Online Access:** Real Estate, Deed, Judgment, Lien, UCC Records. Access to indexes and images is available via a private company at www.ustitlesearch.com. Registration and monthly fee required; see state introduction. **Other Phone Numbers:** Assessor 731-645-5146.

Meigs County

Register of Deeds, PO Box 245, Decatur, TN 37322. 423-334-5228; Fax 423-334-5228.
Will search UCC records prior to 7/2001 and current fixture (land) files. This agency will not do a tax lien search. Will not search real estate records. **Other Phones:** Assessor 423-334-5231; Trustee 334-5119.

Monroe County

Register of Deeds, 103 College St - Suite 4, Madisonville, TN 37354. 423-442-2440.
Will search UCC records prior to 7/2001 and current fixture (land) files. This agency will not do a tax lien search. Will not search real estate records. **Online Access:** Land Records. Access to property and deeds indexes and images is available via a private company at http://auth.titlesearcher.com/ts/ts.asp. Fee/registration required; see state introduction. **Other Phones:** Assessor 423-442-2440; Treasurer 423-442-2920.

Montgomery County

Register of Deeds, 350 Pageant Ln, #404, Clarksville, TN 37040. 931-648-5713; Fax 931-553-5157.
Will search UCC records prior to 7/2001 and current fixture (land) files. Will not search real estate records. **Other Phone Numbers:** Assessor 931-648-5709; Trustee 931-648-5710.

Moore County

Register of Deeds, PO Box 206, Lynchburg, TN 37352. 931-759-7913; Fax 931-759-6394.
Will search UCC records prior to 7/2001 and current fixture (land) files. This agency will not do a tax lien search. Will not search real estate records. **Other Phone Numbers:** Assessor 931-759-7044.

Morgan County

Register of Deeds, PO Box 311, Wartburg, TN 37887. 423-346-3105.
Will search UCC records prior to 7/2001 and current fixture (land) files. This agency will not do a tax lien search. Will not search real estate records. **Other Phone Numbers:** Assessor 423-346-3130.

Obion County

Register of Deeds, PO Box 514, Union City, TN 38261. Register of Deeds, R/E and UCC Recording 731-885-9351; Fax 731-885-7515.
This agency will not search real estate or UCC records. **Other Phone Numbers:** Assessor 731-885-2931; Elections 731-885-1901.

Overton County

Register of Deeds, 317 E. University St., Room 150, Livingston, TN 38570. 931-823-4011.
This agency will not perform searches.

Perry County

Register of Deeds, PO Box 62, Linden, TN 37096-0062. Register of Deeds, R/E and UCC Recording 931-589-2210; Fax 931-589-2215.
Will search UCC records prior to 7/2001 and current fixture (land) files. UCC search includes tax liens if requested. Will not search real estate records. **Online Access:** Land Records. Access to property and deeds indexes and images is available via a private company at http://auth.titlesearcher.com/ts/ts.asp. Fee/registration required; see state introduction. **Other Phones:** Assessor 931-589-2277; Treasurer 931-589-2313.

Pickett County

Register of Deeds, PO Box 5, Byrdstown, TN 38549. 931-864-3316; Fax 931-864-6615.
Will search UCC records prior to 7/2001 and current fixture (land) files. Will not search real estate records. **Other Phone Numbers:** Assessor 931-864-3114.

Polk County

Register of Deeds, PO Box 293, Benton, TN 37307. 423-338-4537.
Will search UCC records prior to 7/2001 and current fixture (land) files. This agency will not do a tax lien search. Will not search real estate records. **Other Phones:** Assessor 423-338-4505; Trustee 338-4545.

Putnam County

Register of Deeds, PO Box 487, Cookeville, TN 38503-0487. 931-526-7101.
Will search UCC records prior to 7/2001 and current fixture (land) files. This agency will not do a tax lien search. Will not search real estate records. **Other Phones:** Assessor 931-528-8428; Treasurer 528-8845.

Rhea County

Register of Deeds, 1475 Market St, Dayton, TN 37321. Register of Deeds, R/E and UCC Recording 423-775-7841; Fax 423-775-7895.
Will search UCC records prior to 7/2001 and current fixture (land) files. This agency will not do a tax lien search. Will not search real estate records. **Other Phones:** Assessor 423-775-7840; Treasurer 775-7810.

Roane County

Register of Deeds, PO Box 181, Kingston, TN 37763. 865-376-4673.
This agency will not perform searches. **Other Phones:** Assessor 865-376-4362; Trustee 865-376-4938.

Robertson County

Register of Deeds, 525 S. Brown St., Springfield, TN 37172. Register of Deeds, R/E and UCC Recording 615-384-3772.
This agency will not perform searches. **Online Access:** Real Estate, Deed, Judgment, Lien, UCC Records. Access to indexes and images is available via a private company at www.ustitlesearch.com. Registration and monthly fee required; see state introduction. **Other Phones:** Assessor 615-384-4311; Elections 384-5592.

Rutherford County

Register of Deeds, PO Box 5050, Murfreesboro, TN 37133-5050. 615-898-7870; Fax 615-898-7987.
Will search UCC records prior to 7/2001 and current fixture (land) files. Will not search real estate records. **Other Phone Numbers:** Assessor 615-898-7750.

Scott County

Register of Deeds, PO Box 61, Huntsville, TN 37756. 423-663-2417.
Will search UCC records prior to 7/2001 and current fixture (land) files. This agency will not do a tax lien search. Will not search real estate records. **Other Phones:** Assessor 423-663-2420; Treasurer 663-2598.

Sequatchie County

Register of Deeds, PO Box 174, Dunlap, TN 37327. Register of Deeds, R/E and UCC Recording 423-949-2512; Fax 423-949-6554.

This agency will not search real estate or UCC records. **Online Access:** Land Records. Access to property and deeds indexes and images is available via a private company at http://auth.titlesearcher.com/ts/ts.asp. Fee/registration required; see state introduction. **Other Phone Numbers:** Assessor 423-949-3534.

Sevier County

Register of Deeds, 125 Court Ave, Courthouse Suite 209W, Sevierville, TN 37862. Register of Deeds, R/E and UCC s 865-453-2758.

This agency will not perform searches. **Online Access:** Land Records. Access to property and deeds indexes and images is available via a private company at http://auth.titlesearcher.com/ts/ts.asp. Fee/registration required; see state introduction. **Other Phones:** Assessor 865-453-3242; Appraiser/Auditor 865-453-3242; Elections 865-453-6985; Trustee 865-453-2767.

Shelby County

Register of Deeds, 160 N. Main St., Room 519, Memphis, TN 38173-0823. 901-545-4366; Fax 901-545-3837. http://register.shelby.tn.us

This agency will not search real estate or UCC records. **Online Access:** Real Estate, Lien, UCC, Recording, Property Tax Records. Access to the register database is available free online at http://auth.titlesearcher.com/shelby/menu.asp. Images go back to 12/3/01; indexes to 1986 Also, online access to the assessor property appraisal database is available free at www.assessor.shelby.tn.us. Also, a commercial site at http://64.132.246.16/default.asp allows for 20 public record database searches. Most records go back to 1990. Low monthly fee; apply at web site. **Other Phone Numbers:** Assessor 901-373-7444.

Smith County

Register of Deeds, 122 Turner High Circle, Suite 113, Carthage, 37030. 615-735-1760; Fax 615-735-8263.

Will search UCC records prior to 7/2001 and current fixture (land) files. Will not search real estate records. **Online Access:** Land Records. Access to property and deeds indexes and images is available via a private company at http://auth.titlesearcher.com/ts/ts.asp. Fee/registration required; see state introduction. **Other Phone Numbers:** Assessor 615-735-1750.

Stewart County

Register of Deeds, PO Box 57, Dover, TN 37058. 931-232-5990.

Will search UCC records prior to 7/2001 and current fixture (land) files. This agency will not do a tax lien search. Will not search real estate records. **Other Phones:** Assessor 931-232-5252; Trustee 232-7026.

Sullivan County (Blountville Office)

Register of Deeds, 3411 Hwy 126, #101, Blountville, TN 37617. Register of Deeds, R/E and UCC Recording 423-323-6420; Fax 423-279-2771.

This agency will not search real estate or UCC records. **Other Phones:** Assessor 423-323-6455; Appraiser 423-323-6455; Elections 423-323-6444; Vital Records 423-279-2777; Trustee 423-323-6464.

Sullivan County (Bristol Office)

Register of Deeds, 801 Anderson St., Bristol, TN 37620. Register of Deeds, R/E and UCC Recording 423-989-4370.

Will search UCC records prior to 7/2001 and current fixture (land) files. This agency will not do a tax lien search. Will not search real estate records. **Other Phones:** Assessor 423-323-6455; Treasurer 323-6464.

Sumner County

Register of Deeds, PO Box 299, Gallatin, TN 37066-0299. Register of Deeds, R/E and UCC Recording 615-452-3892; www.deeds.sumnertn.org

Will search UCC records prior to 7/2001 and current fixture (land) files. This agency will not do a tax lien search. Will not search real estate records. **Online Access:** Property, Recording Records. Access to the Register of Deeds website requires a $25.00 set-up fee and $50.00 monthly user fee. For information, call the Registrar at 615-452-3892 or download the User Agreement from the website. **Other Phone Numbers:** Assessor 615-452-2412; Trustee 615-452-1260.

Tipton County

Register of Deeds, PO Box 644, Covington, TN 38019-0644. Register of Deeds, R/E and UCC Recording 901-476-0204; Fax 901-476-0227.

This agency will not perform searches. **Online Access:** Real Estate, Deed, Judgment, Lien, UCC Records. Access to indexes and images is available via a private company at www.ustitlesearch.com. Registration and monthly fee required; see state introduction. **Other Phone Numbers:** Assessor 901-476-0213; Treasurer 901-476-0211; Elections 901-476-0223.

Trousdale County

Register of Deeds, 200 E. Main St. #8, Hartsville, TN 37074-1706. 615-374-2921; Fax 615-374-1100.

Will search UCC records prior to 7/2001 and current fixture (land) files. This agency will not do a tax lien search. Will not search real estate records. **Other Phone Numbers:** Assessor 615-374-2553.

Unicoi County

Register of Deeds, PO Box 305, Erwin, TN 37650-0305. 423-743-6104.

This agency will not perform searches. **Other Phone Numbers:** Assessor 423-743-3801.

Union County

Register of Deeds, 901 Main St #108, Maynardville, TN 37807. 865-992-8024.

Will search UCC records prior to 7/2001 and current fixture (land) files. This agency will not do a tax lien search. Will not search real estate records. **Other Phones:** Assessor 865-992-3211; Trustee 992-5943.

Van Buren County

Register of Deeds, PO Box 9, Spencer, TN 38585. 931-946-7363; Fax 931-946-7363.

This agency will not search real estate or UCC records. **Online Access:** Land Records. Access to property and deeds indexes and images is available via a private company at http://auth.titlesearcher.com/ts/ts.asp. Fee/registration required; see state introduction. **Other Phone Numbers:** Assessor 931-946-2451.

Warren County

Register of Deeds, PO Box 128, McMinnville, TN 37111. Register of Deeds, R/E and UCC Recording 931-473-2926 UCC Recording: 931-473-8663; Fax 931-474-2114.

Will search UCC records prior to 7/2001 and current fixture (land) files. This agency will not do a tax lien search. Will not search real estate records. **Online Access:** Real Estate, Deed, Judgment, Lien, UCC Records. Access to indexes and images is available via a private company at www.ustitlesearch.com. Registration and monthly fee required; see state introduction. **Other Phones:** Assessor 931-473-3450.

Washington County

Register of Deeds, PO Box 69, Jonesboro, TN 37659. 423-753-1644 R/E Recording: 423-753-1645 UCC Recording: 423-753-1648; Fax 423-753-1743.

This agency will not search real estate or UCC records. **Online Access:** Land Records. Access to property and deeds indexes and images is available via a private company at http://auth.titlesearcher.com/ts/ts.asp. Fee/registration required; see state introduction. **Other Phone Numbers:** Assessor 423-753-1670; Treasurer 423-753-1610; Appraiser/Auditor 423-753-1670; Elections 423-753-1688; Vital Records 423-753-1621.

Wayne County

Register of Deeds, PO Box 465, Waynesboro, TN 38485. 931-722-5518; Fax 931-722-5518.

Will search UCC records prior to 7/2001 and current fixture (land) files. Will not search real estate records. **Online Access:** Land Records. Access to property and deeds indexes and images is available via a private company at http://auth.titlesearcher.com/ts/ts.asp. Fee/registration required; see state introduction. **Other Phone Numbers:** Assessor 931-722-5282; Treasurer 931-722-3269; Appraiser/Auditor 931-722-5282; Elections 931-722-3517.

Weakley County

Register of Deeds, PO Box 45, Dresden, TN 38225-0045. 731-364-3646; Fax 731-364-5389.

Will search UCC records prior to 7/2001 and current fixture (land) files. Will not search real estate records. **Online Access:** Land Records. Access to property and deeds indexes and images is available via a private company at http://auth.titlesearcher.com/ts/ts.asp. Fee/registration required; see state introduction. **Other Phones:** Assessor 731-364-3677; Trustee 364-3643.

White County

Register of Deeds, PO Box 86, Sparta, TN 38583-0086. 931-836-2817; Fax 931-836-8418.

Will search UCC records prior to 7/2001 and current fixture (land) files. Will not search real estate records. **Online Access:** Land Records. Access to property and deeds indexes and images is available via a private company at http://auth.titlesearcher.com/ts/ts.asp. Fee/registration required; see state introduction. **Other Phone Numbers:** Assessor 931-836-3840.

Williamson County

Register of Deeds, PO Box 808, Franklin, TN 37065-0808. Register of Deeds, R/E and UCC Recording 615-790-5706; www.rod.williamson-tn.org

Will search UCC records. This agency will not do a tax lien search. Will not search real estate records. **Online Access:** Deed, Property, Tax Assessor Records. Access to the Professional Access database is available for a $50 per month fee. Information and sign-up at http://williamson-tn.org/co_gov/profacc.htm. **Other Phones:** Assessor 615-790-5708; Treasurer 615-790-5709; Appraiser 615-790-5708; Elections 790-5712.

Wilson County

Register of Deeds, PO Box 176, Lebanon, TN 37087-0176. Reg. Deeds, R/E and UCCs 615-443-2611; Fax 615-443-3288. www.register.co.wilson.tn.us

This agency will not search real estate or UCC records. **Online Access:** Real Estate, Lien, Recording Records. Access to the Register of Deeds database requires a $10 registration fee then $25.00 per month usage fee. Includes indexes and images back to 11/1999, expanding to include 1994. Also, Online access to property and deeds indexes and images is available via a private company at http://auth.titlesearcher.com/ts/ts.asp. A per day only fee/registration required; see state introduction. **Other Phone Numbers:** Assessor 615-444-8661; Treasurer 615-444-0894.

Tennessee County Locator

You will usually be able to find the city name in the City/County Cross Reference below. In that case, it is a simple matter to determine the county from the cross reference. However, only the official US Postal Service city names are included in this index. There are an additional 40,000 place names that people use in their addresses. Therefore, we have also included a ZIP/City Cross Reference immediately following the City/County Cross Reference.

If you know the ZIP Code but the city name does not appear in the City/County Cross Reference index, look up the ZIP Code in the ZIP/City Cross Reference, find the city name, then look up the city name in the City/County Cross Reference. For example, you want to know the county for an address of Menands, NY 12204. There is no "Menands" in the City/County Cross Reference. The ZIP/City Cross Reference shows that ZIP Codes 12201-12288 are for the city of Albany. Looking back in the City/County Cross Reference, Albany is in Albany County.

City/County Cross Reference

ADAMS (37010) Robertson(60), Montgomery(39)
ADAMSVILLE (38310) McNairy(56), Hardin(43)
AFTON Greene
ALAMO Crockett
ALCOA Blount
ALEXANDRIA (37012) De Kalb(77), Wilson(11), Smith(10)
ALLARDT Fentress
ALLONS (38541) Overton(65), Clay(34)
ALLRED Overton
ALPINE (38543) Overton(81), Pickett(18)
ALTAMONT Grundy
ANDERSONVILLE (37705) Anderson(68), Union(31)
ANTIOCH Davidson
APISON Hamilton
ARDMORE (38449) Giles(68), Lincoln(31)
ARLINGTON (38002) Shelby(89), Fayette(9)
ARNOLD AFB Coffee
ARRINGTON (37014) Williamson(59), Rutherford(40)
ARTHUR Claiborne
ASHLAND CITY (37015) Cheatham(94), Davidson(3), Montgomery(1)
ATHENS McMinn
ATOKA (38004) Tipton(94), Shelby(5)
ATWOOD (38220) Carroll(94), Gibson(5)
AUBURNTOWN (37016) Cannon(72), Wilson(27)
BAKEWELL Hamilton
BATH SPRINGS Decatur
BAXTER (38544) Putnam(91), De Kalb(8)
BEAN STATION Grainger
BEECH BLUFF (38313) Madison(52), Henderson(25), Chester(22)
BEECHGROVE (37018) Coffee(97), Bedford(2)
BEERSHEBA SPRINGS Grundy
BELFAST Marshall
BELL BUCKLE (37020) Bedford(80), Rutherford(19)
BELLS (38006) Crockett(78), Haywood(15), Madison(5)
BELVIDERE Franklin
BENTON Polk
BETHEL SPRINGS (38315) McNairy(84), Chester(15)
BETHPAGE (37022) Sumner(73), Trousdale(24), Macon(2)
BIG ROCK Stewart
BIG SANDY Benton
BIRCHWOOD (37308) Hamilton(61), Meigs(38)
BLAINE (37709) Union(57), Grainger(40), Knox(2)
BLOOMINGTON SPRINGS (38545) Jackson(62), Putnam(37)
BLOUNTVILLE Sullivan
BLUFF CITY Sullivan
BOGOTA Dyer

BOLIVAR Hardeman
BON AQUA (37025) Hickman(78), Dickson(16), Williamson(4)
BRADEN Fayette
BRADFORD Gibson
BRADYVILLE (37026) Cannon(90), Coffee(9)
BRENTWOOD (37027) Williamson(80), Davidson(19)
BRICEVILLE Anderson
BRIGHTON (38011) Tipton(96), Shelby(3)
BRISTOL Sullivan
BROWNSVILLE Haywood
BRUCETON (38317) Carroll(94), Benton(5)
BRUNSWICK Shelby
BRUSH CREEK Smith
BUCHANAN Henry
BUENA VISTA (38318) Carroll(97), Benton(2)
BUFFALO VALLEY (38548) Putnam(77), Smith(22)
BULLS GAP (37711) Greene(60), Hawkins(35), Hamblen(3)
BUMPUS MILLS Stewart
BURLISON Tipton
BURNS Dickson
BUTLER (37640) Johnson(66), Carter(33)
BYBEE Cocke
BYRDSTOWN (38549) Pickett(98), Fentress(1)
CALHOUN (37309) McMinn(83), Polk(16)
CAMDEN Benton
CAMPAIGN Warren
CARTHAGE Smith
CARYVILLE Campbell
CASTALIAN SPRINGS (37031) Sumner(57), Trousdale(42)
CEDAR GROVE Carroll
CEDAR HILL (37032) Robertson(94), Cheatham(4)
CELINA (38551) Clay(98), Jackson(1)
CENTERVILLE Hickman
CHAPEL HILL (37034) Marshall(84), Bedford(16)
CHAPMANSBORO (37035) Cheatham(98), Montgomery(1)
CHARLESTON (37310) Bradley(98), Polk(1)
CHARLOTTE (37036) Dickson(93), Cheatham(6)
CHATTANOOGA Hamilton
CHESTNUT MOUND Smith
CHEWALLA McNairy
CHRISTIANA Rutherford
CHUCKEY (37641) Greene(88), Washington(11)
CHURCH HILL Hawkins
CLAIRFIELD (37715) Claiborne(82), Campbell(17)
CLARKRANGE Fentress
CLARKSBURG Carroll
CLARKSVILLE Montgomery
CLEVELAND Bradley

CLIFTON (38425) Wayne(67), Hardin(26), Perry(5)
CLINTON Anderson
COALFIELD Morgan
COALMONT Grundy
COKERCREEK Monroe
COLLEGE GROVE (37046) Williamson(84), Rutherford(14), Marshall(1)
COLLEGEDALE Hamilton
COLLIERVILLE Shelby
COLLINWOOD Wayne
COLUMBIA Maury
COMO Henry
CONASAUGA Polk
COOKEVILLE (38506) Putnam(80), Overton(14), White(5)
COPPERHILL Polk
CORDOVA Shelby
CORNERSVILLE (37047) Marshall(78), Giles(20), Lincoln(1)
CORRYTON (37721) Knox(79), Union(20)
COSBY (37722) Cocke(82), Sevier(17)
COTTAGE GROVE (38224) Henry(95), Weakley(4)
COTTONTOWN (37048) Sumner(91), Robertson(8)
COUNCE Hardin
COVINGTON Tipton
COWAN Franklin
CRAB ORCHARD Cumberland
CRAWFORD Overton
CROCKETT MILLS Crockett
CROSS PLAINS Robertson
CROSSVILLE Cumberland
CRUMP Hardin
CULLEOKA (38451) Maury(87), Marshall(12)
CUMBERLAND CITY (37050) Stewart(78), Montgomery(15), Houston(6)
CUMBERLAND FURNACE (37051) Dickson(66), Montgomery(33)
CUMBERLAND GAP Claiborne
CUNNINGHAM (37052) Montgomery(97), Dickson(2)
CYPRESS INN Wayne
DANDRIDGE (37725) Jefferson(97), Sevier(1)
DARDEN (38328) Henderson(75), Decatur(24)
DAYTON Rhea
DECATUR (37322) McMinn(74), Meigs(25)
DECATURVILLE (38329) Decatur(94), Henderson(5)
DECHERD (37324) Franklin(97), Grundy(2)
DEER LODGE (37726) Morgan(85), Fentress(14)
DEL RIO Cocke
DELANO (37325) Polk(80), McMinn(15), Hamilton(4)
DELLROSE Lincoln
DENMARK Madison
DENVER Humphreys

DICKSON Dickson
DIXON SPRINGS (37057) Trousdale(48), Macon(28), Smith(22)
DOVER Stewart
DOWELLTOWN De Kalb
DOYLE (38559) White(90), Van Buren(9)
DRESDEN Weakley
DRUMMONDS Tipton
DUCK RIVER Hickman
DUCKTOWN Polk
DUFF Campbell
DUKEDOM Weakley
DUNLAP (37327) Sequatchie(93), Bledsoe(6)
DYER Gibson
DYERSBURG Dyer
EADS (38028) Fayette(56), Shelby(43)
EAGAN Claiborne
EAGLEVILLE (37060) Rutherford(86), Bedford(8), Williamson(4)
EATON Gibson
EIDSON (37731) Hawkins(89), Hancock(10)
ELBRIDGE Obion
ELGIN Scott
ELIZABETHTON Carter
ELKTON Giles
ELLENDALE Shelby
ELMWOOD Smith
ELORA (37328) Lincoln(82), Franklin(17)
ENGLEWOOD (37329) McMinn(93), Monroe(6)
ENVILLE (38332) Chester(89), McNairy(10)
ERIN (37061) Houston(95), Humphreys(3)
ERWIN (37650) Unicoi(95), Washington(4)
ESTILL SPRINGS (37330) Franklin(93), Coffee(6)
ETHRIDGE (38456) Lawrence(78), Giles(21)
ETOWAH McMinn
EVA Benton
EVENSVILLE Rhea
FAIRVIEW (37062) Williamson(96), Dickson(2)
FALL BRANCH (37656) Greene(48), Washington(43), Sullivan(7)
FARNER Polk
FAYETTEVILLE (37334) Lincoln(98), Bedford(1)
FINGER (38334) McNairy(80), Chester(19)
FINLEY Dyer
FIVE POINTS Lawrence
FLAG POND Unicoi
FLINTVILLE (37335) Lincoln(97), Franklin(1)
FOSTERVILLE Rutherford
FOWLKES Dyer
FRANKEWING (38459) Giles(56), Lincoln(43)
FRANKLIN Williamson
FRIENDSHIP (38034) Crockett(81), Dyer(18)

FRIENDSVILLE (37737) Blount(92), Loudon(7)
FRUITVALE Crockett
GADSDEN Crockett
GAINESBORO Jackson
GALLATIN Sumner
GALLAWAY Fayette
GATES (38037) Lauderdale(67), Haywood(32)
GATLINBURG Sevier
GEORGETOWN (37336) Bradley(42), Hamilton(37), Meigs(20)
GERMANTOWN Shelby
GIBSON Gibson
GLADEVILLE Wilson
GLEASON (38229) Weakley(98), Henry(1)
GOODLETTSVILLE (37072) Davidson(58), Sumner(29), Robertson(11)
GOODSPRING Giles
GORDONSVILLE Smith
GRAND JUNCTION (38039) Hardeman(72), Fayette(27)
GRANDVIEW (37337) Rhea(48), Cumberland(43), Pickett(8)
GRANVILLE (38564) Jackson(90), Putnam(9)
GRAYSVILLE (37338) Rhea(59), Sequatchie(20), Bledsoe(13), Hamilton(6)
GREENBACK (37742) Loudon(73), Blount(26)
GREENBRIER Robertson
GREENEVILLE Greene
GREENFIELD Weakley
GRIMSLEY Fentress
GRUETLI LAAGER Grundy
GUILD Marion
GUYS McNairy
HALLS (38040) Lauderdale(83), Crockett(11), Dyer(4)
HAMPSHIRE (38461) Maury(60), Lewis(38), Hickman(1)
HAMPTON Carter
HARRIMAN (37748) Roane(89), Morgan(10)
HARRISON Hamilton
HARROGATE Claiborne
HARTFORD Cocke
HARTSVILLE (37074) Trousdale(86), Macon(13)
HEISKELL (37754) Anderson(53), Knox(40), Union(5)
HELENWOOD Scott
HENDERSON (38340) Chester(91), Hardeman(8)
HENDERSONVILLE Sumner
HENNING Lauderdale
HENRY Henry
HERMITAGE (37076) Davidson(94), Wilson(5)
HICKMAN (38567) Smith(95), De Kalb(4)
HICKORY VALLEY (38042) Hardeman(97), Fayette(2)
HICKORY WITHE Fayette
HILHAM (38568) Overton(59), Clay(24), Jackson(15)
HILLSBORO Coffee
HIXSON Hamilton
HOHENWALD Lewis
HOLLADAY (38341) Benton(82), Decatur(13), Henderson(3)
HOLLOW ROCK Carroll
HORNBEAK Obion
HORNSBY (38044) Hardeman(91), McNairy(5), Chester(3)
HUMBOLDT (38343) Gibson(76), Crockett(15), Madison(7)
HUNTINGDON Carroll
HUNTLAND Franklin
HUNTSVILLE Scott
HURON Henderson
HURRICANE MILLS Humphreys

IDLEWILD Gibson
INDIAN MOUND (37079) Stewart(81), Montgomery(18)
IRON CITY (38463) Lawrence(64), Wayne(35)
ISABELLA Polk
JACKS CREEK Chester
JACKSBORO Campbell
JACKSON Madison
JAMESTOWN Fentress
JASPER Marion
JEFFERSON CITY Jefferson
JELLICO Campbell
JOELTON (37080) Davidson(59), Cheatham(40)
JOHNSON CITY Washington
JONESBOROUGH Washington
KELSO Lincoln
KENTON (38233) Gibson(68), Obion(31)
KINGSPORT Sullivan
KINGSTON Roane
KINGSTON SPRINGS Cheatham
KNOXVILLE Knox
KODAK (37764) Sevier(85), Knox(10), Jefferson(3)
KYLES FORD Hancock
LA FOLLETTE Campbell
LA GRANGE Fayette
LA VERGNE Rutherford
LACONIA Fayette
LAFAYETTE Macon
LAKE CITY (37769) Anderson(79), Campbell(20)
LANCASTER (38569) Smith(77), De Kalb(22)
LANCING Morgan
LASCASSAS (37085) Rutherford(77), Wilson(22)
LAUREL BLOOMERY Johnson
LAVINIA Carroll
LAWRENCEBURG (38464) Lawrence(93), Giles(3), Wayne(2)
LEBANON (37090) Wilson(97), Smith(2)
LENOIR CITY Loudon
LENOX Dyer
LEOMA (38468) Lawrence(90), Giles(10)
LEWISBURG (37091) Marshall(96), Bedford(3)
LEXINGTON Henderson
LIBERTY (37095) De Kalb(77), Cannon(19), Wilson(3)
LIMESTONE (37681) Greene(55), Washington(44)
LINDEN (37096) Perry(92), Wayne(6)
LIVINGSTON Overton
LOBELVILLE (37097) Perry(95), Humphreys(4)
LONE MOUNTAIN Claiborne
LOOKOUT MOUNTAIN Hamilton
LORETTO Lawrence
LOUDON (37774) Loudon(94), Roane(4)
LOUISVILLE Blount
LOWLAND Hamblen
LUPTON CITY Hamilton
LURAY Chester
LUTTRELL (37779) Union(92), Knox(6), Grainger(1)
LUTTS Wayne
LYLES Hickman
LYNCHBURG Moore
LYNNVILLE (38472) Giles(92), Marshall(7)
MACON Fayette
MADISON Davidson
MADISONVILLE (37354) Monroe(98), McMinn(1)
MANCHESTER Coffee
MANSFIELD Henry
MARTIN Weakley
MARYVILLE Blount
MASCOT (37806) Knox(96), Grainger(3)
MASON (38049) Fayette(79), Tipton(20)
MAURY CITY Crockett

MAYNARDVILLE (37807) Union(98), Knox(1)
MC DONALD (37353) Bradley(89), Hamilton(10)
MC EWEN (37101) Humphreys(94), Houston(2), Hickman(2)
MC KENZIE (38201) Carroll(75), Weakley(14), Henry(10)
MC LEMORESVILLE Carroll
MC MINNVILLE Warren
MEDINA (38355) Gibson(54), Madison(45)
MEDON (38356) Madison(56), Hardeman(32), Chester(10)
MEMPHIS Shelby
MERCER (38392) Madison(66), Hardeman(32)
MICHIE (38357) McNairy(80), Hardin(19)
MIDDLETON Hardeman
MIDWAY Greene
MILAN Gibson
MILLEDGEVILLE (38359) Chester(74), McNairy(22), Hardin(2)
MILLIGAN COLLEGE Carter
MILLINGTON Shelby
MILTON (37118) Rutherford(66), Wilson(24), Cannon(9)
MINOR HILL Giles
MISTON Dyer
MITCHELLVILLE Sumner
MOHAWK Greene
MONROE (38573) Overton(64), Pickett(35)
MONTEAGLE (37356) Marion(84), Grundy(15)
MONTEREY (38574) Putnam(66), Overton(15), Cumberland(14), Fentress(4)
MOORESBURG (37811) Hawkins(96), Grainger(3)
MORLEY Campbell
MORRIS CHAPEL (38361) Hardin(89), McNairy(10)
MORRISON (37357) Warren(58), Coffee(29), Cannon(9), Grundy(1)
MORRISTOWN Hamblen
MOSCOW Fayette
MOSHEIM Greene
MOSS Clay
MOUNT CARMEL Hawkins
MOUNT JULIET (37122) Wilson(96), Rutherford(3)
MOUNT PLEASANT (38474) Maury(94), Lewis(3), Giles(1)
MOUNT VERNON Monroe
MOUNTAIN CITY Johnson
MOUNTAIN HOME Washington
MULBERRY (37359) Moore(50), Lincoln(49)
MUNFORD Tipton
MURFREESBORO Rutherford
NASHVILLE Davidson
NEW JOHNSONVILLE Humphreys
NEW MARKET Jefferson
NEW TAZEWELL (37825) Claiborne(88), Union(11)
NEWBERN Dyer
NEWCOMB Campbell
NEWPORT Cocke
NIOTA (37826) McMinn(94), Meigs(5)
NOLENSVILLE (37135) Williamson(92), Rutherford(4), Davidson(3)
NORENE Wilson
NORMANDY (37360) Coffee(45), Bedford(39), Moore(14)
NORRIS Anderson
NUNNELLY Hickman
OAK RIDGE Anderson
OAKDALE Morgan
OAKFIELD Madison
OAKLAND Fayette
OBION (38240) Obion(93), Dyer(6)
OCOEE Polk

OLD HICKORY (37138) Davidson(68), Wilson(31)
OLDFORT (37362) Bradley(74), Polk(25)
OLIVEHILL (38475) Hardin(85), Wayne(14)
OLIVER SPRINGS (37840) Morgan(45), Roane(33), Anderson(21)
ONEIDA Scott
ONLY Hickman
OOLTEWAH Hamilton
ORLINDA Robertson
OZONE Cumberland
PALL MALL (38577) Fentress(50), Pickett(49)
PALMER (37365) Grundy(90), Sequatchie(5), Marion(1)
PALMERSVILLE Weakley
PALMYRA Montgomery
PARIS (38242) Henry(98), Weakley(1)
PARROTTSVILLE Cocke
PARSONS Decatur
PEGRAM (37143) Cheatham(86), Davidson(13)
PELHAM Grundy
PETERSBURG (37144) Lincoln(56), Marshall(33), Bedford(7), Moore(1)
PETROS Morgan
PHILADELPHIA (37846) Loudon(59), Roane(23), Monroe(15), McMinn(1)
PICKWICK DAM Hardin
PIGEON FORGE Sevier
PIKEVILLE (37367) Bledsoe(83), Cumberland(10), Van Buren(5)
PINEY FLATS Sullivan
PINSON (38366) Madison(54), Chester(45)
PIONEER (37847) Scott(63), Campbell(36)
PLEASANT HILL Cumberland
PLEASANT SHADE (37145) Smith(72), Macon(15), Jackson(11)
PLEASANT VIEW (37146) Cheatham(70), Robertson(29)
PLEASANTVILLE Hickman
POCAHONTAS (38061) Hardeman(63), McNairy(36)
PORTLAND (37148) Sumner(94), Robertson(5)
POWDER SPRINGS (37848) Grainger(61), Union(38)
POWELL (37849) Knox(82), Anderson(17)
PRIMM SPRINGS (38476) Williamson(37), Hickman(35), Maury(27)
PROSPECT Giles
PRUDEN Claiborne
PULASKI Giles
PURYEAR Henry
QUEBECK White
RAMER McNairy
READYVILLE (37149) Rutherford(64), Cannon(35)
REAGAN (38368) Henderson(77), Chester(22)
RED BOILING SPRINGS (37150) Macon(75), Clay(24)
RELIANCE (37369) Polk(80), Monroe(19)
RICEVILLE McMinn
RICKMAN Overton
RIDDLETON Smith
RIDGELY (38080) Lake(76), Dyer(18), Obion(5)
RIDGETOP Robertson
RIPLEY (38063) Lauderdale(93), Haywood(6)
RIVES Obion
ROAN MOUNTAIN Carter
ROBBINS (37852) Scott(90), Morgan(9)
ROCK ISLAND (38581) Warren(89), Van Buren(10)
ROCKFORD (37853) Blount(94), Knox(5)
ROCKVALE (37153) Rutherford(91), Bedford(8)
ROCKWOOD (37854) Roane(71), Cumberland(16), Morgan(11)
ROGERSVILLE Hawkins

ROSSVILLE Fayette
RUGBY Morgan
RUSSELLVILLE Hamblen
RUTHERFORD Gibson
RUTLEDGE Grainger
SAINT ANDREWS Franklin
SAINT BETHLEHEM Montgomery
SAINT JOSEPH Lawrence
SALE CREEK Hamilton
SALTILLO (38370) Hardin(95), Henderson(4)
SAMBURG Obion
SANTA FE Maury
SARDIS (38371) Hardin(65), Henderson(34)
SAULSBURY Hardeman
SAVANNAH Hardin
SCOTTS HILL (38374) Decatur(98), Henderson(1)
SELMER McNairy
SEQUATCHIE Marion
SEVIERVILLE (37876) Sevier(97), Jefferson(2)
SEWANEE Franklin
SEYMOUR (37865) Sevier(79), Blount(20)
SHADY VALLEY Johnson
SHARON Weakley
SHARPS CHAPEL Union
SHAWANEE Claiborne
SHELBYVILLE Bedford
SHERWOOD Franklin
SHILOH (38376) Hardin(79), McNairy(20)
SIGNAL MOUNTAIN (37377) Hamilton(94), Sequatchie(5)
SILERTON Hardeman
SILVER POINT (38582) Putnam(71), De Kalb(28)
SLAYDEN Dickson
SMARTT Warren
SMITHVILLE (37166) De Kalb(89), Warren(9), Cannon(1)
SMYRNA Rutherford

SNEEDVILLE (37869) Hancock(78), Hawkins(17), Claiborne(3)
SODDY DAISY Hamilton
SOMERVILLE Fayette
SOUTH FULTON (38257) Obion(94), Weakley(5)
SOUTH PITTSBURG Marion
SOUTHSIDE Montgomery
SPARTA (38583) White(85), De Kalb(6), Putnam(3), Cumberland(3)
SPEEDWELL (37870) Claiborne(75), Campbell(12), Union(11)
SPENCER Van Buren
SPRING CITY Rhea
SPRING CREEK Madison
SPRING HILL (37174) Maury(68), Williamson(30)
SPRINGFIELD (37172) Robertson(98), Sumner(1)
SPRINGVILLE Henry
STANTON (38069) Haywood(90), Fayette(9)
STANTONVILLE McNairy
STEWART (37175) Houston(72), Stewart(27)
STRAWBERRY PLAINS (37871) Knox(45), Jefferson(38), Sevier(15)
SUGAR TREE (38380) Decatur(67), Benton(32)
SUMMERTOWN (38483) Lawrence(75), Lewis(20), Giles(2), Maury(1)
SUMMITVILLE Coffee
SUNBRIGHT (37872) Morgan(95), Scott(4)
SURGOINSVILLE Hawkins
SWEETWATER (37874) Monroe(88), McMinn(6), Loudon(5)
TAFT Lincoln
TALBOTT (37877) Hamblen(61), Jefferson(38)
TALLASSEE Blount
TAZEWELL Claiborne
TELFORD Washington

TELLICO PLAINS Monroe
TEN MILE (37880) Roane(59), Meigs(39)
TENNESSEE RIDGE (37178) Houston(84), Stewart(15)
THOMPSONS STATION Williamson
THORN HILL (37881) Grainger(86), Hancock(10), Hawkins(2)
TIGRETT Dyer
TIPTON Tipton
TIPTONVILLE Lake
TOONE Hardeman
TOWNSEND Blount
TRACY CITY Grundy
TRADE Johnson
TREADWAY Hancock
TRENTON Gibson
TREZEVANT Carroll
TRIMBLE (38259) Dyer(86), Obion(8), Gibson(4)
TROY Obion
TULLAHOMA (37388) Coffee(72), Franklin(18), Moore(7)
TURTLETOWN Polk
UNICOI Unicoi
UNION CITY Obion
UNIONVILLE (37180) Bedford(94), Rutherford(5)
VANLEER (37181) Dickson(93), Houston(6)
VIOLA Warren
VONORE (37885) Monroe(97), Loudon(2)
WALLAND Blount
WALLING White
WARTBURG Morgan
WARTRACE (37183) Bedford(73), Coffee(18), Moore(8)
WASHBURN (37888) Grainger(77), Union(22)
WATAUGA (37694) Carter(76), Sullivan(18), Washington(4)
WATERTOWN (37184) Wilson(96), Smith(3)

WATTS BAR DAM Rhea
WAVERLY Humphreys
WAYNESBORO (38485) Wayne(98), Lewis(1)
WESTMORELAND (37186) Sumner(59), Macon(40)
WESTPOINT (38486) Lawrence(83), Wayne(16)
WESTPORT (38387) Carroll(90), Benton(9)
WHITE BLUFF (37187) Dickson(93), Cheatham(6)
WHITE HOUSE (37188) Robertson(58), Sumner(41)
WHITE PINE (37890) Jefferson(92), Hamblen(7)
WHITES CREEK Davidson
WHITESBURG (37891) Hamblen(69), Hawkins(30)
WHITESIDE Marion
WHITEVILLE (38075) Hardeman(70), Haywood(14), Fayette(14)
WHITLEYVILLE (38588) Jackson(76), Clay(16), Macon(7)
WHITWELL (37397) Marion(95), Sequatchie(4)
WILDER Fentress
WILDERSVILLE Henderson
WILLIAMSPORT (38487) Maury(69), Hickman(30)
WILLISTON Fayette
WINCHESTER (37398) Franklin(98), Moore(1)
WINFIELD Scott
WINONA Scott
WOODBURY (37190) Cannon(98), Warren(1)
WOODLAND MILLS Obion
WOODLAWN Montgomery
WYNNBURG Lake
YORKVILLE Gibson
YUMA (38390) Carroll(80), Henderson(19)

ZIP/City Cross Reference

37010-37010	ADAMS
37011-37011	ANTIOCH
37012-37012	ALEXANDRIA
37013-37013	ANTIOCH
37014-37014	ARRINGTON
37015-37015	ASHLAND CITY
37016-37016	AUBURNTOWN
37018-37018	BEECHGROVE
37019-37019	BELFAST
37020-37020	BELL BUCKLE
37022-37022	BETHPAGE
37023-37023	BIG ROCK
37024-37024	BRENTWOOD
37025-37025	BON AQUA
37026-37026	BRADYVILLE
37027-37027	BRENTWOOD
37028-37028	BUMPUS MILLS
37029-37029	BURNS
37030-37030	CARTHAGE
37031-37031	CASTALIAN SPRINGS
37032-37032	CEDAR HILL
37033-37033	CENTERVILLE
37034-37034	CHAPEL HILL
37035-37035	CHAPMANSBORO
37036-37036	CHARLOTTE
37037-37037	CHRISTIANA
37040-37044	CLARKSVILLE
37046-37046	COLLEGE GROVE
37047-37047	CORNERSVILLE
37048-37048	COTTONTOWN
37049-37049	CROSS PLAINS
37050-37050	CUMBERLAND CITY
37051-37051	CUMBERLAND FURNACE
37052-37052	CUNNINGHAM
37054-37054	DENVER

37055-37056	DICKSON
37057-37057	DIXON SPRINGS
37058-37058	DOVER
37059-37059	DOWELLTOWN
37060-37060	EAGLEVILLE
37061-37061	ERIN
37062-37062	FAIRVIEW
37063-37063	FOSTERVILLE
37064-37065	FRANKLIN
37066-37066	GALLATIN
37067-37069	FRANKLIN
37070-37070	GOODLETTSVILLE
37071-37071	GLADEVILLE
37072-37072	GOODLETTSVILLE
37073-37073	GREENBRIER
37074-37074	HARTSVILLE
37075-37075	HENDERSONVILLE
37076-37076	HERMITAGE
37077-37077	HENDERSONVILLE
37078-37078	HURRICANE MILLS
37079-37079	INDIAN MOUND
37080-37080	JOELTON
37082-37082	KINGSTON SPRINGS
37083-37083	LAFAYETTE
37085-37085	LASCASSAS
37086-37086	LA VERGNE
37087-37088	LEBANON
37089-37089	LA VERGNE
37090-37090	LEBANON
37091-37091	LEWISBURG
37095-37095	LIBERTY
37096-37096	LINDEN
37097-37097	LOBELVILLE
37098-37098	LYLES
37101-37101	MC EWEN

37110-37111	MC MINNVILLE
37115-37116	MADISON
37118-37118	MILTON
37119-37119	MITCHELLVILLE
37121-37122	MOUNT JULIET
37127-37133	MURFREESBORO
37134-37134	NEW JOHNSONVILLE
37135-37135	NOLENSVILLE
37136-37136	NORENE
37137-37137	NUNNELLY
37138-37138	OLD HICKORY
37140-37140	ONLY
37141-37141	ORLINDA
37142-37142	PALMYRA
37143-37143	PEGRAM
37144-37144	PETERSBURG
37145-37145	PLEASANT SHADE
37146-37146	PLEASANT VIEW
37147-37147	PLEASANTVILLE
37148-37148	PORTLAND
37149-37149	READYVILLE
37150-37150	RED BOILING SPRINGS
37151-37151	RIDDLETON
37152-37152	RIDGETOP
37153-37153	ROCKVALE
37155-37155	SAINT BETHLEHEM
37160-37162	SHELBYVILLE
37165-37165	SLAYDEN
37166-37166	SMITHVILLE
37167-37167	SMYRNA
37171-37171	SOUTHSIDE
37172-37172	SPRINGFIELD
37174-37174	SPRING HILL
37175-37175	STEWART
37178-37178	TENNESSEE RIDGE

37179-37179	THOMPSONS STATION
37180-37180	UNIONVILLE
37181-37181	VANLEER
37183-37183	WARTRACE
37184-37184	WATERTOWN
37185-37185	WAVERLY
37186-37186	WESTMORELAND
37187-37187	WHITE BLUFF
37188-37188	WHITE HOUSE
37189-37189	WHITES CREEK
37190-37190	WOODBURY
37191-37191	WOODLAWN
37200-37250	NASHVILLE
37301-37301	ALTAMONT
37302-37302	APISON
37303-37303	ATHENS
37304-37304	BAKEWELL
37305-37305	BEERSHEBA SPRINGS
37306-37306	BELVIDERE
37307-37307	BENTON
37308-37308	BIRCHWOOD
37309-37309	CALHOUN
37310-37310	CHARLESTON
37311-37312	CLEVELAND
37313-37313	COALMONT
37314-37314	COKERCREEK
37315-37315	COLLEGEDALE
37316-37316	CONASAUGA
37317-37317	COPPERHILL
37318-37318	COWAN
37320-37320	CLEVELAND
37321-37321	DAYTON
37322-37322	DECATUR
37323-37323	CLEVELAND
37324-37324	DECHERD

37325-37325 DELANO	37657-37657 FLAG POND	37830-37831 OAK RIDGE	38048-38048 MACON
37326-37326 DUCKTOWN	37658-37658 HAMPTON	37840-37840 OLIVER SPRINGS	38049-38049 MASON
37327-37327 DUNLAP	37659-37659 JONESBOROUGH	37841-37841 ONEIDA	38050-38050 MAURY CITY
37328-37328 ELORA	37660-37669 KINGSPORT	37842-37842 OZONE	38052-38052 MIDDLETON
37329-37329 ENGLEWOOD	37680-37680 LAUREL BLOOMERY	37843-37843 PARROTTSVILLE	38053-38055 MILLINGTON
37330-37330 ESTILL SPRINGS	37681-37681 LIMESTONE	37845-37845 PETROS	38056-38056 MISTON
37331-37331 ETOWAH	37682-37682 MILLIGAN COLLEGE	37846-37846 PHILADELPHIA	38057-38057 MOSCOW
37332-37332 EVENSVILLE	37683-37683 MOUNTAIN CITY	37847-37847 PIONEER	38058-38058 MUNFORD
37333-37333 FARNER	37684-37684 MOUNTAIN HOME	37848-37848 POWDER SPRINGS	38059-38059 NEWBERN
37334-37334 FAYETTEVILLE	37686-37686 PINEY FLATS	37849-37849 POWELL	38060-38060 OAKLAND
37335-37335 FLINTVILLE	37687-37687 ROAN MOUNTAIN	37851-37851 PRUDEN	38061-38061 POCAHONTAS
37336-37336 GEORGETOWN	37688-37688 SHADY VALLEY	37852-37852 ROBBINS	38063-38063 RIPLEY
37337-37337 GRANDVIEW	37690-37690 TELFORD	37853-37853 ROCKFORD	38066-38066 ROSSVILLE
37338-37338 GRAYSVILLE	37691-37691 TRADE	37854-37854 ROCKWOOD	38067-38067 SAULSBURY
37339-37339 GRUETLI LAAGER	37692-37692 UNICOI	37857-37857 ROGERSVILLE	38068-38068 SOMERVILLE
37340-37340 GUILD	37694-37694 WATAUGA	37860-37860 RUSSELLVILLE	38069-38069 STANTON
37341-37341 HARRISON	37699-37699 PINEY FLATS	37861-37861 RUTLEDGE	38070-38070 TIGRETT
37342-37342 HILLSBORO	37701-37701 ALCOA	37862-37862 SEVIERVILLE	38071-38071 TIPTON
37343-37343 HIXSON	37705-37705 ANDERSONVILLE	37863-37863 PIGEON FORGE	38074-38074 BOLIVAR
37345-37345 HUNTLAND	37707-37707 ARTHUR	37864-37864 SEVIERVILLE	38075-38075 WHITEVILLE
37346-37346 ISABELLA	37708-37708 BEAN STATION	37865-37865 SEYMOUR	38076-38076 WILLISTON
37347-37347 JASPER	37709-37709 BLAINE	37866-37866 SHARPS CHAPEL	38077-38077 WYNNBURG
37348-37348 KELSO	37710-37710 BRICEVILLE	37867-37867 SHAWANEE	38079-38079 TIPTONVILLE
37349-37349 MANCHESTER	37711-37711 BULLS GAP	37868-37868 PIGEON FORGE	38080-38080 RIDGELY
37350-37350 LOOKOUT MOUNTAIN	37713-37713 BYBEE	37869-37869 SNEEDVILLE	38083-38083 MILLINGTON
37351-37351 LUPTON CITY	37714-37714 CARYVILLE	37870-37870 SPEEDWELL	38088-38088 CORDOVA
37352-37352 LYNCHBURG	37715-37715 CLAIRFIELD	37871-37871 STRAWBERRY PLAINS	38100-38137 MEMPHIS
37353-37353 MC DONALD	37716-37717 CLINTON	37872-37872 SUNBRIGHT	38138-38139 GERMANTOWN
37354-37354 MADISONVILLE	37719-37719 COALFIELD	37873-37873 SURGOINSVILLE	38140-38182 MEMPHIS
37355-37355 MANCHESTER	37721-37721 CORRYTON	37874-37874 SWEETWATER	38183-38183 GERMANTOWN
37356-37356 MONTEAGLE	37722-37722 COSBY	37876-37876 SEVIERVILLE	38184-38197 MEMPHIS
37357-37357 MORRISON	37723-37723 CRAB ORCHARD	37877-37877 TALBOTT	38201-38201 MC KENZIE
37358-37358 MOUNT VERNON	37724-37724 CUMBERLAND GAP	37878-37878 TALLASSEE	38220-38220 ATWOOD
37359-37359 MULBERRY	37725-37725 DANDRIDGE	37879-37879 TAZEWELL	38221-38221 BIG SANDY
37360-37360 NORMANDY	37726-37726 DEER LODGE	37880-37880 TEN MILE	38222-38222 BUCHANAN
37361-37361 OCOEE	37727-37727 DEL RIO	37881-37881 THORN HILL	38223-38223 COMO
37362-37362 OLDFORT	37729-37729 DUFF	37882-37882 TOWNSEND	38224-38224 COTTAGE GROVE
37363-37363 OOLTEWAH	37730-37730 EAGAN	37883-37883 TREADWAY	38225-38225 DRESDEN
37364-37364 CLEVELAND	37731-37731 EIDSON	37885-37885 VONORE	38226-38226 DUKEDOM
37365-37365 PALMER	37732-37732 ELGIN	37886-37886 WALLAND	38227-38227 ELBRIDGE
37366-37366 PELHAM	37733-37733 RUGBY	37887-37887 WARTBURG	38229-38229 GLEASON
37367-37367 PIKEVILLE	37737-37737 FRIENDSVILLE	37888-37888 WASHBURN	38230-38230 GREENFIELD
37369-37369 RELIANCE	37738-37738 GATLINBURG	37890-37890 WHITE PINE	38231-38231 HENRY
37370-37370 RICEVILLE	37742-37742 GREENBACK	37891-37891 WHITESBURG	38232-38232 HORNBEAK
37371-37371 ATHENS	37743-37745 GREENEVILLE	37892-37892 WINFIELD	38233-38233 KENTON
37372-37372 SAINT ANDREWS	37748-37748 HARRIMAN	37893-37893 WINONA	38235-38235 MC LEMORESVILLE
37373-37373 SALE CREEK	37752-37752 HARROGATE	37900-37999 KNOXVILLE	38236-38236 MANSFIELD
37374-37374 SEQUATCHIE	37753-37753 HARTFORD	38001-38001 ALAMO	38237-38238 MARTIN
37375-37375 SEWANEE	37754-37754 HEISKELL	38002-38002 ARLINGTON	38240-38240 OBION
37376-37376 SHERWOOD	37755-37755 HELENWOOD	38004-38004 ATOKA	38241-38241 PALMERSVILLE
37377-37377 SIGNAL MOUNTAIN	37756-37756 HUNTSVILLE	38006-38006 BELLS	38242-38242 PARIS
37378-37378 SMARTT	37757-37757 JACKSBORO	38007-38007 BOGOTA	38251-38251 PURYEAR
37379-37379 SODDY DAISY	37760-37760 JEFFERSON CITY	38008-38008 BOLIVAR	38253-38253 RIVES
37380-37380 SOUTH PITTSBURG	37762-37762 JELLICO	38010-38010 BRADEN	38254-38254 SAMBURG
37381-37381 SPRING CITY	37763-37763 KINGSTON	38011-38011 BRIGHTON	38255-38255 SHARON
37382-37382 SUMMITVILLE	37764-37764 KODAK	38012-38012 BROWNSVILLE	38256-38256 SPRINGVILLE
37383-37383 SEWANEE	37765-37765 KYLES FORD	38014-38014 BRUNSWICK	38257-38257 SOUTH FULTON
37384-37384 SODDY DAISY	37766-37766 LA FOLLETTE	38015-38015 BURLISON	38258-38258 TREZEVANT
37385-37385 TELLICO PLAINS	37769-37769 LAKE CITY	38016-38016 CORDOVA	38259-38259 TRIMBLE
37387-37387 TRACY CITY	37770-37770 LANCING	38017-38017 COLLIERVILLE	38260-38260 TROY
37388-37388 TULLAHOMA	37771-37772 LENOIR CITY	38018-38018 CORDOVA	38261-38261 UNION CITY
37389-37389 ARNOLD AFB	37773-37773 LONE MOUNTAIN	38019-38019 COVINGTON	38271-38271 WOODLAND MILLS
37391-37391 TURTLETOWN	37774-37774 LOUDON	38021-38021 CROCKETT MILLS	38281-38281 UNION CITY
37394-37394 VIOLA	37777-37777 LOUISVILLE	38023-38023 DRUMMONDS	38301-38308 JACKSON
37395-37395 WATTS BAR DAM	37778-37778 LOWLAND	38024-38025 DYERSBURG	38310-38310 ADAMSVILLE
37396-37396 WHITESIDE	37779-37779 LUTTRELL	38027-38027 COLLIERVILLE	38311-38311 BATH SPRINGS
37397-37397 WHITWELL	37801-37804 MARYVILLE	38028-38028 EADS	38313-38313 BEECH BLUFF
37398-37398 WINCHESTER	37806-37806 MASCOT	38029-38029 ELLENDALE	38314-38314 JACKSON
37400-37499 CHATTANOOGA	37807-37807 MAYNARDVILLE	38030-38030 FINLEY	38315-38315 BETHEL SPRINGS
37501-37501 MEMPHIS	37809-37809 MIDWAY	38033-38033 FOWLKES	38316-38316 BRADFORD
37601-37615 JOHNSON CITY	37810-37810 MOHAWK	38034-38034 FRIENDSHIP	38317-38317 BRUCETON
37616-37616 AFTON	37811-37811 MOORESBURG	38036-38036 GALLAWAY	38318-38318 BUENA VISTA
37617-37617 BLOUNTVILLE	37812-37812 MORLEY	38037-38037 GATES	38320-38320 CAMDEN
37618-37618 BLUFF CITY	37813-37816 MORRISTOWN	38039-38039 GRAND JUNCTION	38321-38321 CEDAR GROVE
37620-37625 BRISTOL	37818-37818 MOSHEIM	38040-38040 HALLS	38324-38324 CLARKSBURG
37640-37640 BUTLER	37819-37819 NEWCOMB	38041-38041 HENNING	38326-38326 COUNCE
37641-37641 CHUCKEY	37820-37820 NEW MARKET	38042-38042 HICKORY VALLEY	38327-38327 CRUMP
37642-37642 CHURCH HILL	37821-37822 NEWPORT	38043-38043 HICKORY WITHE	38328-38328 DARDEN
37643-37644 ELIZABETHTON	37824-37825 NEW TAZEWELL	38044-38044 HORNSBY	38329-38329 DECATURVILLE
37645-37645 MOUNT CARMEL	37826-37826 NIOTA	38045-38045 LACONIA	38330-38330 DYER
37650-37650 ERWIN	37828-37828 NORRIS	38046-38046 LA GRANGE	38331-38331 EATON
37656-37656 FALL BRANCH	37829-37829 OAKDALE	38047-38047 LENOX	38332-38332 ENVILLE

38333-38333 EVA	38372-38372 SAVANNAH	38463-38463 IRON CITY	38552-38552 CHESTNUT MOUND
38334-38334 FINGER	38374-38374 SCOTTS HILL	38464-38464 LAWRENCEBURG	38553-38553 CLARKRANGE
38336-38336 FRUITVALE	38375-38375 SELMER	38468-38468 LEOMA	38554-38554 CRAWFORD
38337-38337 GADSDEN	38376-38376 SHILOH	38469-38469 LORETTO	38555-38555 CROSSVILLE
38338-38338 GIBSON	38377-38377 SILERTON	38471-38471 LUTTS	38556-38556 JAMESTOWN
38339-38339 GUYS	38378-38378 SPRING CREEK	38472-38472 LYNNVILLE	38557-38558 CROSSVILLE
38340-38340 HENDERSON	38379-38379 STANTONVILLE	38473-38473 MINOR HILL	38559-38559 DOYLE
38341-38341 HOLLADAY	38380-38380 SUGAR TREE	38474-38474 MOUNT PLEASANT	38560-38560 ELMWOOD
38342-38342 HOLLOW ROCK	38381-38381 TOONE	38475-38475 OLIVEHILL	38562-38562 GAINESBORO
38343-38343 HUMBOLDT	38382-38382 TRENTON	38476-38476 PRIMM SPRINGS	38563-38563 GORDONSVILLE
38344-38344 HUNTINGDON	38387-38387 WESTPORT	38477-38477 PROSPECT	38564-38564 GRANVILLE
38345-38345 HURON	38388-38388 WILDERSVILLE	38478-38478 PULASKI	38565-38565 GRIMSLEY
38346-38346 IDLEWILD	38389-38389 YORKVILLE	38481-38481 SAINT JOSEPH	38567-38567 HICKMAN
38347-38347 JACKS CREEK	38390-38390 YUMA	38482-38482 SANTA FE	38568-38568 HILHAM
38348-38348 LAVINIA	38391-38391 DENMARK	38483-38483 SUMMERTOWN	38569-38569 LANCASTER
38351-38351 LEXINGTON	38392-38392 MERCER	38485-38485 WAYNESBORO	38570-38570 LIVINGSTON
38352-38352 LURAY	38393-38393 CHEWALLA	38486-38486 WESTPOINT	38571-38572 CROSSVILLE
38355-38355 MEDINA	38401-38402 COLUMBIA	38487-38487 WILLIAMSPORT	38573-38573 MONROE
38356-38356 MEDON	38425-38425 CLIFTON	38488-38488 TAFT	38574-38574 MONTEREY
38357-38357 MICHIE	38449-38449 ARDMORE	38501-38503 COOKEVILLE	38575-38575 MOSS
38358-38358 MILAN	38450-38450 COLLINWOOD	38504-38504 ALLARDT	38577-38577 PALL MALL
38359-38359 MILLEDGEVILLE	38451-38451 CULLEOKA	38505-38506 COOKEVILLE	38578-38578 PLEASANT HILL
38361-38361 MORRIS CHAPEL	38452-38452 CYPRESS INN	38541-38541 ALLONS	38579-38579 QUEBECK
38362-38362 OAKFIELD	38453-38453 DELLROSE	38542-38542 ALLRED	38580-38580 RICKMAN
38363-38363 PARSONS	38454-38454 DUCK RIVER	38543-38543 ALPINE	38581-38581 ROCK ISLAND
38365-38365 PICKWICK DAM	38455-38455 ELKTON	38544-38544 BAXTER	38582-38582 SILVER POINT
38366-38366 PINSON	38456-38456 ETHRIDGE	38545-38545 BLOOMINGTON SPRINGS	38583-38583 SPARTA
38367-38367 RAMER	38457-38457 FIVE POINTS	38547-38547 BRUSH CREEK	38585-38585 SPENCER
38368-38368 REAGAN	38459-38459 FRANKEWING	38548-38548 BUFFALO VALLEY	38587-38587 WALLING
38369-38369 RUTHERFORD	38460-38460 GOODSPRING	38549-38549 BYRDSTOWN	38588-38588 WHITLEYVILLE
38370-38370 SALTILLO	38461-38461 HAMPSHIRE	38550-38550 CAMPAIGN	38589-38589 WILDER
38371-38371 SARDIS	38462-38462 HOHENWALD	38551-38551 CELINA	

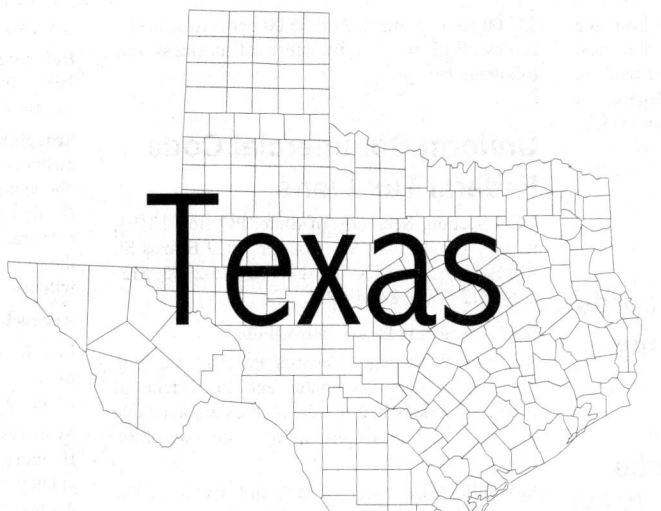

General Help Numbers:

Governor's Office
PO Box 12428   512-463-2000
Austin, TX 78711-2428   Fax 512-463-1849
www.governor.state.tx.us   7:30AM-5:30PM

Attorney General's Office
PO Box 12548   512-463-2100
Austin, TX 78711-2548   Fax 512-463-2063
www.oag.state.tx.us   7:30AM-5:30PM

State Court Administrator
PO Box 12066   512-463-1625
Austin, TX 78711-2066   Fax 512-463-1648
www.courts.state.tx.us/oca   8AM-5PM

State Archives
PO Box 12927   512-463-5455
Austin, TX 78711-2927   Fax 512-463-5436
www.tsl.state.tx.us   8AM-5PM
Genealogy 8-5 TU-SA

State Specifics:

Capital: Austin
Travis County

Time Zone: CST*

* Texas' two western-most counties are MST:
They are: El Paso and Hudspeth,

Number of Counties: 254

Population: 21,325,018

Web Site: www.state.tx.us

State Agencies

Criminal Records

Dept of Public Safety, Correspondence Section, Crime Records Service, PO Box 15999, Austin, TX 78761-5999 (Courier: 5805 N Lamar, Bldg G, Austin, TX 78752); 512-424-2474, 8AM-5PM.

http://records.txdps.state.tx.us

Note: Sex offender data is available online at http://records.txdps.state.tx.us/soSearch/soSearch.cfm. There is no charge for a sex offender search.

Indexing & Storage: Records are available from 1930 to present. It takes 1 day before new records are available for inquiry. Records are indexed on inhouse computer. 55% of all arrests in database have final dispositions recorded.

Searching: To obtain ALL arrest information (conviction and non-conviction), must have a signed release and full set of fingerprints from the person of record. To obtain conviction and deferred adjudication data only, submit full name, sex, race, and DOB. The SSN is helpful, but not required. No letter of authorization is needed for the conviction only report. The following data is not released: Juvenile records are not considered public information and are not released. Fingerprint searches show complete record; name search is conviction only. Since 1/1/93, records include complete information regarding charge, disposition, date of conviction, and county. Data prior to this date may not be complete.

Access by: mail, in person, online.

Fee & Payment: The fee is $15.00 for the full search using fingerprints, and $10.00 for a name-based search. If required, the FBI fingerprint check is an additional $24.00. Fee payee: Texas Department of Public Safety. Prepayment required. Credit cards are accepted for online searches only. Personal checks accepted. Credit cards accepted: MasterCard, Visa.

Mail search: The turnaround time for both fingerprint and name-based searches is approximately three weeks. No self addressed stamped envelope is required.

In person search: Records requested at the Dept. of Public Safety Crime Records Service in Austin usually takes 1-2 business days.

Online search: Records can be pulled from the web site. Requesters may use a credit card or must establish an account and have a pre-paid bank to work from. The fee established by the Department (Sec. 411.135(b)) is $3.15 per request plus a $.57 handling fee.

Corporation Records
Fictitious Name
Limited Partnership Records
Limited Liability Company Records
Assumed Name
Trademarks/Servicemarks

Secretary of State, Corporation Section, PO Box 13697, Austin, TX 78711-3697 (Courier: J Earl Rudder Bldg, 1019 Brazos, B-13, Austin, TX 78701); 512-463-5555 (Information), 512-463-5578 (Copies), 512-463-5709 (Fax), 8AM-5PM.

www.sos.state.tx.us

Indexing & Storage: Records are available from the 1800s. Records are indexed on inhouse computer, online.

Searching: New records are available immediately on the computer, but it takes 12 days before new records are available to be copied. Requests may be ordered via e-mail from the web site. Include the following in your request: full name of business, corporation file number. In addition to the articles of incorporation, corporation records include the following information: Public Information Reports (extracted information from the database only), Officers, Directors, DBAs, Prior (merged) names, Inactive and Reserved names.

Access by: mail, phone, fax, in person, online.

Fee & Payment: Certification is $10.00 plus $1.00 per document page. Copies are $.10 per page. Fee payee: Secretary of State. Credit card transaction charge is 2.1% of the total amount charged. Frequent requesters may set up a pre-paid billing account. Personal checks accepted. Credit cards accepted: MasterCard, Visa, Discover.

Mail search: Turnaround time: 3 to 5 days. No self addressed stamped envelope is required.

Phone search: No fee for telephone request.

Fax search: Fax requests cost an additional $2.00 per page plus expedited fees.

In person search: Public access terminals are available for walk-in requesters.

Online search: There are several online methods available. Web access is available 24 hours daily. There is a $1.00 fee for each record searched. Filing procedures and forms are available from the web site or from 900-263-0060 ($1.00 per minute). Also, Corporate and other TX Sec of State data is available via SOSDirect on the Web; visit www.sos.state.tx.us/corp/sosda/index.shtml. SOSDA accounts are converted to SOSDirect. Printing and certifying capabilities. Also, general corporation information is available at no fee at http://ecpa.cpa.state.tx.us/coa/coaStart.html from the State Comptroller office.

Other access: The agency makes portions of its database available for purchase. Call 512-475-2755 for more information.

Expedited service: Expedited service is available for mail, phone and in person searches. Add

$25.00 per document. Add $5.00 per certificate for copies. Will process by close of business day following receipt.

Uniform Commercial Code
Federal Tax Liens

UCC Section, Secretary of State, PO Box 13193, Austin, TX 78711-3193 (Courier: 1019 Brazos St, Rm B-13, Austin, TX 78701); 512-475-2705, 512-475-2812 (Fax), 8AM-5PM.

www.sos.state.tx.us/ucc/index.shtml

Indexing & Storage: Records are available from 1966, indexed on computer and microfiche. It takes 3 to 5 days before new records are available for inquiry. Records are indexed on microfilm, inhouse computer.

Searching: Use search request form UCC-11. The search includes all tax liens on businesses. Federal tax liens on individuals and all state tax liens are filed at the county level. Include the following in your request: debtor name.

Access by: mail, phone, fax, in person, online.

Fee & Payment: Using the approved form - $10.00 per debtor name; other forms - $25.00 per debtor name; copies - $1.50 per page with a minimum of $5.00. Effective 01/01/00, a version of the UCC-11 was designated as the standard form. Fee payee: Secretary of State. Personal checks accepted.

Mail search: Turnaround time: 1 to 2 weeks. No self addressed stamped envelope is required.

Phone search: Debtor names, up to 10 filings per debtor searched, will be released. No collateral is listed.

Fax search: There is an additional fee of $15.00.

In person search: You may request information in person.

Online search: There are two systems. Direct dial-up is open from 7 AM to 6 PM. The fee is $3.00 per search, $10.00 for a secured party search. Also, UCC and other TX Sec of State data is available via SOSDirect on the Web; visit www.sos.state.tx.us/corp/sosda/index.shtml. UCC records are $1.00 per search, with printing ($1.00 per page) and certifying ($10.00), also. General information and forms can be found at the web site.

Other access: The state offers the database for sale, contact the Information Services Dept at 512-463-5609 for further details.

Expedited service: Expedited service is available for mail, in-person and phone searches. Turnaround time: 24 hours. Add $15.00 per from. Expedited mail service is offered. Also, you can include your Fed Ex number for fastest return.

State Tax Liens

Records not maintained by a state level agency.

Note: Records are located at the county level.

Sales Tax Registrations

Comptroller of Public Accounts, PO Box 13528, Austin, TX 78711-3528 (Courier: LBJ Office Bldg, 111 E 17th St, Austin, TX 78774); 800-252-5555, 800-252-1386 (Searches), 512-475-1610 (Fax), 8AM-5PM.

www.window.state.tx.us

Indexing & Storage: Records are available from 1980 to present. It takes 6 weeks before new records are available for inquiry.

Searching: This agency will provide the following business information: business name, address, phone number, tax permit number, a list of officers & directors, and the registered agent for a corporation. Audit results are not released. Include the following in your request: business name. They will also search by tax permit number.

Access by: mail, phone, in person, online.

Fee & Payment: There is no search fee. Fee payee: Comptroller of Public Accounts. Personal checks accepted. No credit cards accepted.

Mail search: Turnaround time: 10 working days. If more than 3 businesses are requested, the agency prefers that you request by mail. No self addressed stamped envelope is required. No fee for mail request.

Phone search: No fee for telephone request. The agency will provide responses to 3 business names or less over the phone.

In person search: No fee for request. They will verify information or will mail a letter.

Online search: Go to http://aixtcp.cpa.state.tx.us/star/ to search 16,000+ documents by index or collection. This office makes general corporation information available at http://ecpa.cpa.state.tx.us/coa/coaStart.html. There is no fee.

Birth Certificates

Texas Department of Health, Bureau of Vital Statistics, PO Box 12040, Austin, TX 78711-2040 (Courier: 1100 W 49th St, Austin, TX 78756-3191); 512-458-7111, 512-458-7506 (Fax), 8AM-5PM.

www.tdh.state.tx.us/bvs

Indexing & Storage: Records are available from 1903 to present. It takes receipt from local registration officials before new records are available for inquiry. Records are indexed on microfiche, index cards, inhouse computer.

Searching: Must have a signed, notarized release form from person of record or immediate family member and name and address of requester for records less than 50 years old. Include the following in your request: full name, names of parents, mother's maiden name, date of birth, place of birth, relationship to person of record, reason for information request. Must send a copy of requester's photo ID or show a photo ID for in-person searches. The following data is not released: Social Security Numbers.

Access by: mail, fax, in person.

Fee & Payment: The search fee is $11.00 per name. Fee payee: Bureau of Vital Statistics. Prepayment required. Credit cards accepted for fax requests only. Personal checks accepted. Credit cards accepted: MasterCard, Visa.

Mail search: Turnaround time: 6 to 8 weeks. No self addressed stamped envelope is required.

Fax search: See expedited service.

In person search: Turnaround time 1-2 hours.

Other access: Birth Indexes from 1926-1995 are available on CD-Rom and microfiche.

Expedited service: Expedited service is available for fax searches. Turnaround time: 48 to 96 hours. The total fee for expedited service is $24.00; ($11.00 for search, $5.00 for expedited service, and $8.00 for overnight service fee), add $6.75 if delivery to PO box or rural route.

Death Records

Texas Department of Health, Bureau of Vital Statistics, PO Box 12040, Austin, TX 78711-2040 (Courier: 1100 W 49th St, Austin, TX 78756-3191); 512-458-7111, 512-458-7506 (Fax), 8AM-5PM.

www.tdh.state.tx.us/bvs

Indexing & Storage: Records are available from 1903 to present. It takes receipt from local registration officials before new records are available for inquiry. Records are indexed on microfiche, index cards, inhouse computer.

Searching: Must have a signed release form from immediate family member and requester's name and current address for records less than 25 years old. Include the following in your request: full name, date of death, place of death, Social Security Number, relationship to person of record, reason for information request. You must include a copy of requesters' photo ID or show a photo ID for in person requests. The following data is not released: Social Security Numbers.

Access by: mail, fax, in person.

Fee & Payment: The search fee is $9.00 per name. Add $3.00 per name per copy for each additional copy. Fee payee: Bureau of Vital Statistics. Prepayment required. Credit cards accepted for fax requests only. Personal checks accepted. Credit cards accepted: MasterCard, Visa.

Mail search: Turnaround time: 6 to 8 weeks. No self addressed stamped envelope is required.

Fax search: See expedited service.

In person search: Turnaround time 1-2 hours.

Other access: Death Indexes from 1964-1998 are available on CD-Rom and microfiche.

Expedited service: Expedited service is available for fax searches. Turnaround time: 48 to 96 hours. The total expedited service fee is $22.00; ($9.00 search fee, $5.00 expedited service fee, and $8.00 overnight service fee), add $6.75 if delivery to PO box or rural route.

Marriage Certificates

Texas Department of Health, Bureau of Vital Statistics, 1100 W 49th St, Austin, TX 78756 (Courier: 1100 W 49th St, Austin, TX 78756-3191); 512-458-7111, 512-458-7506 (Fax), 8AM-5PM.

www.tdh.state.tx.us/bvs

Indexing & Storage: Records are available from 1966 to present. It takes delivery from the county clerk before new records are available for inquiry. Records are indexed on microfiche, index cards, inhouse computer.

Searching: They only have a copy of the application form and an index to the county record. The actual certificate must be obtained from the county recorder of record. Include the following in your request: names of husband and wife, date of marriage, place or county of marriage. The following data is not released: Social Security Numbers.

Access by: mail, fax, in person.

Fee & Payment: The search fee is $9.00 per record. Fee payee: Bureau of Vital Statistics. Prepayment required. Credit cards accepted for fax

requests only. Personal checks accepted. Credit cards accepted: MasterCard, Visa.

Mail search: Turnaround time: 6 to 12 weeks. No self addressed stamped envelope is required.

Fax search: See expedited service.

In person: Turnaround time while you wait.

Expedited service: Expedited service is available for fax searches. Turnaround time: 48 to 96 hours. Total expedited service fee is $22.00; ($9.00 search fee, $5.00 expedited service fee, and $8.00 overnight service fee), add $6.75 if delivery to PO box or rural route.

Divorce Records

Texas Department of Health, Bureau of Vital Statistics, PO Box 12040, Austin, TX 78711-2040 (Courier: 1100 W 49th St, Austin, TX 78756-3191); 512-458-7111, 512-458-7506 (Fax), 8AM-5PM.

www.tdh.state.tx.us/bvs

Note: Note, there is a private entity site. The divorce records database 1968-1997 of the Department of Health is available at http://userdb.rootsweb.com/tx/divorce/search.cgi. May be temporarily unavailable. Search by husband or wife name, county, or year.

Indexing & Storage: Records are available from 1968 to present. It takes delivery from the county district clerk before new records are available for inquiry. Records are indexed on microfiche, index cards, inhouse computer.

Searching: They only have the report of divorce form and an index that directs you to the county district court of record. A copy of the actual record must be obtained at the county level. Include the following in your request: names of husband and wife, date of divorce, year divorce case began, case number (if known).

Access by: mail, fax, in person.

Fee & Payment: The search fee is $9.00 per name. Fee payee: Bureau of Vital Statistics. Prepayment required. Credit cards accepted for fax requests only. Personal checks accepted. Credit cards accepted: MasterCard, Visa.

Mail search: Turnaround time: 6 to 12 weeks. No self addressed stamped envelope is required.

Fax search: See expedited service.

In person search: Turnaround time 1-2 hours.

Expedited service: Expedited service is available for fax searches. Turnaround time: 48 to 96 hours. The total expedited service fee is $22.00; ($9.00 search fee, $5.00 expedited service fee, and $8.00 overnight service fee), add $6.75 if delivery to PO box or rural route.

Workers' Compensation Records

Texas Workers' Compensation Commission, Southfield Building, 4000 South, IH-35, MS-92B, Austin, TX 78704-7491; 512-804-4000, 512-804-4990 (Reprographics Department), 512-804-4993 (Fax), 8AM-5PM.

www.twcc.state.tx.us

Indexing & Storage: Records are available from 1962. Records are indexed on inhouse computer.

Searching: A signed, notarized release is required to obtain file copies. Use Form TWCC-153. Include the following in your request: claimant

name, Social Security Number, date of accident. The file number is required to receive copies. If you don't know the file number or date of accident, you must submit Form TWCC-155.

Access by: mail, fax.

Fee & Payment: The fees for TWCC-153 are $1.00 for certification, $1.00 for the first page and $.30 each additional page. The fees for TWCC-155 are $15.00 search fee and $1.00 for certification. Fee payee: Texas Workers' Compensation Commission. Prepayment required. An invoice will be sent, copies are held until payment received. Personal checks accepted. No credit cards accepted.

Mail search: Turnaround time: 4 to 6 weeks. No self addressed stamped envelope is required.

Fax search: Same as by mail, but only TWCC-153 available by fax

Expedited service: Expedited service is available for mail and phone searches. They will call and advise exact fees needed to pre-pay.

Driver Records

Department of Public Safety, Driver Records Section, PO Box 15999, Austin, TX 78761-5999 (Courier: 5805 N Lamar Blvd, Austin, TX 78752); 512-424-2032, 8AM-5PM.

www.txdps.state.tx.us

Note: Tickets are only available from the court system.

Indexing & Storage: Records are available for 5 years for moving violations and suspensions, indefinite for DWIs, 11 years for SR judgments. Non-moving violations do not appear on the record. It takes 30 days before new records are available for inquiry.

Searching: Requesters must use Form DR-1. This form contains space for written consent if personal information is requested by a casual user. The name and driver's license number or date of birth, are needed when ordering. Class type listings from the driver's record are not provided. The following data is not released: Social Security Numbers or medical records.

Access by: mail, in person.

Fee & Payment: Driving record fees are $6.00 for a 3 year driving record, $10.00 if certified or $5.00 if by tape. A license statue including latest address is $4.00 per report. There is a full charge for a "no record found." Fee payee: Texas Department of Public Safety. Prepayment required. Personal checks accepted. No credit cards accepted.

Mail search: Turnaround time: 7 to 10 days. No self addressed stamped envelope is required.

In person search: Normal turnaround time is same day.

Other access: Magnetic tape retrieval is available for high volume users.

Vehicle Ownership
Vehicle Identification

Department of Transportation, Vehicle Titles and Registration Division, 40th and Jackson Ave, Austin, TX 78779-0001; 512-465-7611, 512-465-7736 (Fax), 8AM-5PM.

www.dot.state.tx.us

Note: A "Request for Texas Motor Vehicle Information" Form VTR-275, which includes a signed statement certifying that the information will be used in compliance with state and federal laws and that the information, is needed for a "lawful and legitimate purpose

Indexing & Storage: Records are available as an active files until there is no activity for 2 years, upon which records become inactive. After 4 years of inactivity, records are archived. Title history information is available on microfiche for 16 years to present. It takes 48 hours after entry into the system before new records are available for inquiry.

Searching: For plate checks, include a signed statement showing the information is needed for "lawful and legitimate purposes." The state does not permit name searches. Personal information is not released to casual requesters without written consent of subject. Use Form VTR-275 for ordering a vehicle history. The following data is not released: Social Security Numbers.

Access by: mail, online.

Fee & Payment: The current fee for VIN and plate checks is $2.30 per record. The fee for a title search is $5.75 or $6.75 certified. Fee payee: Department of Transportation. Prepayment required. Personal checks accepted. No credit cards accepted.

Mail search: Turnaround time: 7 to 10 days. Use of the state form is required.

Online search: Online access is available for pre-approved accounts. A $200 deposit is required, there is a $23.00 charge per month and $.12 fee per inquiry. Searching by name is not permitted. For more information, contact Production Data Control.

Other access: The state offers tape cartridge retrieval for customized searches or based on the entire database, to eligible organizations. Weekly updates are available. There are approximately 26,000,000 records in the database.

Accident Reports

Texas Department of Public Safety, Accident Records Bureau, PO Box 15999, Austin, TX 78761-5999 (Courier: 5805 N Lamar Blvd, Austin, TX 78752); 512-424-2600, 8AM-5PM.

www.txdps.state.tx.us

Indexing & Storage: Records are available for 10 years to present. It takes 30 days before new records are available for inquiry.

Searching: Accident reports investigated by law enforcement agencies and driver reports are open to the public. Items required to search include two or more of following: full name of any person involved, specific city/county location, and date of incident.

Access by: mail, in person.

Fee & Payment: Fee is $6.00 per uncertified report and $8.00 per certified report. There is a $6.00 charge for a no record found search. Fee payee: Texas Department of Public Safety. Prepayment required. Personal checks accepted. No credit cards accepted.

Mail search: Turnaround time: 4 to 6 weeks. No self addressed stamped envelope is required.

In person search: Up to 5 requests will be processed immediately.

Vessel Ownership
Vessel Registration

Parks & Wildlife Dept, 4200 Smith School Rd, Austin, TX 78744; 512-389-4828, 800-262-8755, 8AM-5PM.

www.tpwd.state.tx.us/boat/boat.htm

Indexing & Storage: Records are available from 1976 to 1988 for titled boats, then from 1989 to present for all boats. Records are indexed on computer. All motorized boats must be registered and titled. All sailboats 14 ft and over must be registered and titled. Lien data shows on all reports.

Searching: The written request must include: name & address of requestor, TX #, motor # and/or serial numbers, and the statement "The use of the information obtained will be for lawful purposes." If the history needs to be certified for court, request must show that you need a "certified history."

Access by: mail, in person.

Fee & Payment: There is a $1.50 fee for a record check and a $6.00 fee for a complete history from microfilm. Fee payee: TX Parks & Wildlife Dept. Prepayment required. Personal checks accepted. No credit cards accepted.

Mail search: Turnaround time: 2 to 3 weeks. Turnaround time is often longer in the summer. No self addressed stamped envelope is required.

In person search: Histories are returned by mail.

Other access: Records are released in bulk format; however, requesters are screened for lawful purpose. The agency requires a copy of any item mailed or distributed as a result of purchase. media includes tape, labels, and printed lists.

Legislation Records

Legislative Reference Library, PO Box 12488, Austin, TX 78711-2488 (Courier: State Capitol Building, 2N.3, 1100 Congress, Austin, TX 78701); 512-463-1252 (Bill Status), 512-463-0252 (Senate Bill Copies), 512-463-1144 (House Bill Copies), 512-475-4626 (Fax), 8AM-5PM.

www.lrl.state.tx.us

Note: They ask that you call first to obtain location of bills. The sessions meet in odd number years from January through May.

Indexing & Storage: Records are available from the beginning of the Legislature in the Library. Records are computerized since 1989 and are on microfiche from 1973 to 1980.

Searching: Include the following in your request: bill number, year.

Access by: mail, fax, in person, online.

Fee & Payment: There is no search fee. Ther copy fee is $.20 per page plus any shipping costs. Will express ship with requester's proper account number of the shipping company. Fee payee: Legislative Reference Library. Prepayment required. Business checks or money orders are preferred. No credit cards accepted.

Mail search: Turnaround time: variable. No self addressed stamped envelope is required.

Fax search: Result will be returned by fax if under 25 pages at a cost of $1.00 per page.

In person search: Searching is available in person.

Online search: The web is a thorough searching site of bills and status.

Voter Registration
Access to Records is Restricted

Secretary of State, Elections Division, PO Box 12060, Austin, TX 78711-2060; 800-252-8683, 512-475-2811 (Fax), 8AM-5PM.

www.sos.state.tx.us

Note: To do individual look-ups, one must go to the Tax Assessor-Collector at the county level Records are open. The state will sell the entire database, for non-commercial purposes, in a variety of media and sort formats.

GED Certificates

Texas Education Agency, GED Records, 1701 N Congress Ave, Austin, TX 78701-1494; 512-463-9292, 512-305-9493 (Fax), 7AM-6PM.

www.tea.state.tx.us/ged

Indexing & Storage: Records are available from 1944 to present. It takes 2 weeks before new records are available for inquiry. Records are indexed on mainframe computer.

Searching: Include the following in your request: name, DOB, and SSN.

Access by: mail, phone, fax, in person.

Fee & Payment: There is no fee for verification, but $5.00 fee for a double record of transcripts. Also, if the subject did not pay the GED fees and the record is prior to 1994, a fee may be charged to the requester,

Mail search: Turnaround time: 1 to 2 days. No self addressed stamped envelope is required.

Phone search: Verifications are available by phone.

Fax search: Fax requests require a signed release. Turnaround time: Same day.

In person search: Searching is available in person.

Hunting License Information
Fishing License Information

TX Parks & Wildlife Department, License Section, 4200 Smith School Rd, Austin, TX 78744; 512-389-4820, 512-389-4330 (Fax), 8AM-5PM.

www.tpwd.state.tx.us

Indexing & Storage: Records are available from 09/01/96 forward and are computerized.

Searching: All requests must be in writing on their official Form, unless request is for self. They will release address, status, and date of issue. Include the driver's license number and/or SSN and or DOB. Requests must be in writing and signed by requester. Include requester's address and phone.

Access by: mail, fax.

Fee & Payment: There is no fee.

Mail search: Turnaround time: 1 to 3 days. Up to 5 names can be requested by mail.

Fax search: Up to 5 names can be requested by fax. Results are mailed unless you have a toll free fax number.

Other access: The license database is for sale. For fees and procedures call 512-389-8069.

Texas State Licensing Agencies

Licenses Searchable Online

Air Conditioning/Refrigeration Contractor #14 .... www.license.state.tx.us/LicenseSearch/
Architectural Barrier #14 .... www.license.state.tx.us/LicenseSearch/
Athletic Trainer #21 .... www.tdh.state.tx.us/hcqs/plc/at_rost.txt
Attorney #40 .... www.texasbar.com/members/onlinetools/qrymbr.asp
Auctioneer #14 .... www.license.state.tx.us/LicenseSearch/
Audiologist #22 .... www.tdh.state.tx.us/hcqs/plc/speech.htm
Bank Agency, Foreign #1 .... www.banking.state.tx.us/asp/fba/lookup.asp
Bank, State Chartered #1 .... www.banking.state.tx.us/asp/bank/lookup.asp
Barber School #2 .... www.tsbbe.state.tx.us/schoolr.htm
Boiler Inspector/Installer #14 .... www.license.state.tx.us/LicenseSearch/
Boxing/Combative Sports Event #14 .... www.license.state.tx.us/LicenseSearch/
Career Counselor #14 .... www.license.state.tx.us/LicenseSearch/
Check Seller #1 .... www.banking.state.tx.us/asp/soc/lookup.asp
Chiropractor #25 .... www.tbce.state.tx.us
Counselor, Professional #41 .... www.tdh.state.tx.us/hcqs/plc/lpcrost.txt
Currency Exchange #1 .... www.banking.state.tx.us/asp/cex/lookup.asp
Dental Hygienist #23 .... www.tsbde.state.tx.us/dbsearch/
Dental Laboratory #23 .... www.tsbde.state.tx.us/dbsearch/
Dentist #23 .... www.tsbde.state.tx.us/dbsearch/
Dietitian #22 .... www.tdh.state.tx.us/hcqs/plc/dtrost.txt
ECA #27 .... http://160.42.108.3/ems_web/blh_html_page1.htm
Elevator/Escalator #14 .... www.license.state.tx.us/LicenseSearch/
Emergency Medical Technician #27 .... http://160.42.108.3/ems_web/blh_html_page1.htm
Engineer #5 .... www.tbpe.state.tx.us/downloads.htm
Engineering Firm #5 .... www.tbpe.state.tx.us/downloads.htm
Funeral Establ./Preneed Funeral Home #15 .... www.banking.state.tx.us/asp/pfc/lookup.asp
Funeral Prepaid Permit Holder #1 .... www.banking.state.tx.us/asp/pfc/lookup.asp
Health Facility, Occupation'l/Physical Therapy #17 .www.ecptote.state.tx.us/license/ftverif.php
Hearing Instrument Dispenser/Fitter #22 .... www.tdh.state.tx.us/hcqs/plc/fdhi.htm
Industrialized Housing #14 .... www.license.state.tx.us/LicenseSearch/
Insurance Adjuster #48 .... www.tdi.state.tx.us/general/forms/colists.html
Insurance Agency #48 .... www.tdi.state.tx.us/general/forms/colists.html
Insurance Agent #48 .... www.tdi.state.tx.us/general/forms/agentlists.html
Insurance Company #48 .... www.tdi.state.tx.us/general/forms/colists.html
Lead Training Program Providers #55 .... www.tdh.state.tx.us/beh/lead/TRnlist.htm
Lobbyist #50 .... www.ethics.state.tx.us/php/index.html
Marriage & Family Therapist #31 .... www.tdh.state.tx.us/hcqs/plc/mft.htm#rosters
Massage Therapist #28 .... www.tdh.state.tx.us/hcqs/plc/mtrost.txt
Massage Therapist, Temporary #28 .... www.tdh.state.tx.us/hcqs/plc/mtrostt.txt
Massage Therapy Establishment #28 .... www.tdh.state.tx.us/hcqs/plc/mtroste.txt
Massage Therapy School #28 .... www.tdh.state.tx.us/hcqs/plc/mtrosts.txt
Massage Therapy School Instructor #28 .... www.tdh.state.tx.us/hcqs/plc/mtrosti.txt
Medical Doctor #30 .... http://204.65.101.19/OnLineVerif/Phys_SearchVerif.asp
Medical Specialty (Doctor) #30 .... http://204.65.101.19/OnLineVerif/Phys_SearchVerif.asp
Occupational Therapist/Assistant #17 .... www.ecptote.state.tx.us/license/otverif.php
Optometrist #51 .... www.odfinder.org/LicSearch.asp
Orthotics & Prosthetics Facility #26 .... www.tdh.state.tx.us/hcqs/plc/op_fac.htm
Orthotist/Prosthetist #26 .... www.tdh.state.tx.us/hcqs/plc/op.htm
PAC List #50 .... www.ethics.state.tx.us/dfs/paclists.htm
Paramedic #27 .... http://160.42.108.3/ems_web/blh_html_page1.htm
Perfusionist #26 .... www.tdh.state.tx.us/hcqs/plc/perfusn.htm
Perpetual Care Cemetery #1 .... www.banking.state.tx.us/asp/pcc/lookup.asp
Personal Employment Service #14 .... www.license.state.tx.us/LicenseSearch/
Pharmacist/Pharmacist Intern #24 .... www.tsbp.state.tx.us/dbsearch/Default.htm
Pharmacy #24 .... www.tsbp.state.tx.us/dbsearch/Default.htm
Physical Therapist/Assistant #17 .... www.ecptote.state.tx.us/license/ptverif.php
Physicist, Medical #26 .... www.tdh.state.tx.us/hcqs/plc/mprost.txt
Podiatrist #20 .... www.foot.state.tx.us/verifications.htm
Political Contributor #50 .... http://txprod.ethics.state.tx.us/tx00/
Polygraph Examiner #34 .... http://polygraph.org/states/tape/members_roster.htm
Polygraph Examiner of Sex Offenders #26 .... www.tdh.state.tx.us/hcqs/plc/csp.htm
Property Tax Consultant #14 .... www.license.state.tx.us/LicenseSearch/
Public Accountant-CPA #43 .... www.tsbpa.state.tx.us

Radiologic Technologist #25 .... www.tdh.state.tx.us/hcqs/plc/mrtrost.txt
Radiology Technician #26 .... www.tdh.state.tx.us/hcqs/plc/mrtrost.txt
Real Estate Appraiser #47 .... www.talcb.state.tx.us
Real Estate Broker/Salesperson #52 .... www.trec.state.tx.us/publicinfo/
Real Estate Inspector #52 .... www.trec.state.tx.us/publicinfo/
Representative Offices (Banking) #1 .... www.banking.state.tx.us/asp/rep/lookup.asp
Respiratory Care Practitioner #29 .... www.tdh.state.tx.us/hcqs/plc/rcrost.txt
Service Contract Provider #14 .... www.license.state.tx.us/LicenseSearch/
Sex Offender Treatment Provider #22 .... www.tdh.state.tx.us/hcqs/plc/csot.htm
Social Worker #26 .... www.tdh.state.tx.us/hcqs/plc/lsw/lsw_default.htm#roster
Speech-Language Pathologist #22 .... www.tdh.state.tx.us/hcqs/plc/speech.htm
Staff Leasing #14 .... www.license.state.tx.us/LicenseSearch/
STAP Vendor #6 .... www.puc.state.tx.us/relay/stap/vendors.cfm
Talent Agency #14 .... www.license.state.tx.us/LicenseSearch/
Temporary Common Worker #14 .... www.license.state.tx.us/LicenseSearch/
Transportation Service Provider #54 .... www.license.state.tx.us/LicenseSearch/
Trust Company #1 .... www.banking.state.tx.us/asp/trustco/lookup.asp
Underground Storage Tank Installer #60 .... www.tnrcc.state.tx.us/enforcement/csd/ics/ustlicense.html
Vehicle Protection Provider #14 .... www.license.state.tx.us/LicenseSearch/
Water Well & Pump Installer #14 .... www.license.state.tx.us/LicenseSearch/
Weather Modification Service #14 .... www.license.state.tx.us/LicenseSearch/

Licensing Quick Finder

Acupuncturist #30 512-305-7030
Agricultural Specialties, Perishable #11 512-463-7604
Air Conditioning/Refrigeration Contractor #14
....512-463-6599
Alcoholic Beverage Dist./Mfg./Retailer #46
....512-206-3360
Architect #61 512-305-9000
Architectural Barrier #14 512-463-6599
Asbestos Abatement Contractor #12 . 512-834-6600
Asbestos Air Monitoring Technician #12 512-834-6600
Asbestos Consultant/Inspector #12 512-834-6600
Asbestos Mgmt Planner #12 512-834-6600
Asbestos Worker #12 512-834-6600
Athletic Agent #38 512-475-1769
Athletic Trainer #21 512-834-6615
Attorney #40 512-463-1463
Auctioneer #14 512-463-6599
Audiologist #22 512-834-6627
Audiology Assistant #25 512-834-6627
Bank Agency, Foreign #1 512-475-1300
Bank, State Chartered #1 512-475-1300
Barber #2 512-305-8475
Barber School #2 512-305-8475
Barber Shop #2 512-305-8475
Beauty Shop/Salon #8 512-467-8206
Boiler Inspector/Installer #14 800-722-7843
Boxing/Combative Sports Event #14 ... 512-463-5101
Career Counselor #14 512-463-6599
Check Seller #1 512-475-1290
Child Care Facility/Administrator #49 . 512-438-3269
Chiropractor #25 512-305-6700
Contact Lens Dispenser #26 512-834-4515
Cosmetologist #8 512-467-8206
Counselor, Professional #41 512-834-6658
County Librarian #44 512-463-5466
Court Reporter #9 512-463-1630
Currency Exchange #1 512-475-1290
Day Care Center #49 512-438-3269
Day Care, Residential #49 512-438-3269
Dental Assistant #23 512-463-6400
Dental Hygienist #23 512-434-6400
Dental Laboratory #23 512-463-6400
Dentist #23 512-463-6400
Dietitian #22 512-834-6601
Dog Racing/Dog Racing Professional #36
....512-833-6697
ECA #27 512-834-6700
Elevator/Escalator #14 512-463-6599
Emergency Medical Technician #27 512-834-6700

Engineer #5 512-440-7723
Engineering Firm #5 512-440-7723
Family Home Day Care #49 512-438-3269
Farm/Agricultural Service Company #11 512-462-1441
Fire Alarm System Contractor #53 512-305-7931
Fire Extinguisher Contractor #53 512-305-7931
Fire Inspector #56 512-918-7100
Fire Investigator #56 512-918-7100
Fire Protection Sprinkler System Contractor #53.512-
305-7931
Fire Suppression Specialist #56 512-918-7100
Firefighter #56 512-918-7100
Fireworks Display #53 512-305-7931
Fish Farmer #11 512-463-7602
Fishing Guide #45 512-389-4818
Funeral Director #15 512-936-2474
Funeral Establ./Preneed Funeral Home #15
....512-936-2474
Funeral Prepaid Permit Holder #1 512-475-1290
Health Facility, Occupational/Physical Therapy #17
....512-305-6900
Health Related Registry #26 512-834-6602
Hearing Instrument Disp./Fitter #22 ... 512-834-6784
Home Equity & Secondary Mortgage Lenders #7
....512-936-7600
Home Health Agency #26 512-834-6646
Horse Racing/Horse Racing Professional #36
....512-833-6697
Industrialized Housing #14 512-463-7353
Insurance Adjuster #48 512-322-3503
Insurance Agency #48 512-322-3503
Insurance Agent #48 512-322-3503
Insurance Company #48 512-322-3507
Interior Designer #61 512-305-9000
Interpreter for the Deaf #6 512-407-3250
Investment Advisor #39 512-305-8332
Irrigator #57 512-239-6719
Laboratory Certification #25 512-463-6400
Landscape Architect #61 512-305-9000
Law Enforcement Officer #58 512-936-7700
Lead Abatement Project Designer #55 . 512-834-6612
Lead Abatement Worker #55 512-834-6612
Lead Firm #55 512-834-6612
Lead Risk Assessor/Inspector #55 512-834-6612
Lead Supervisor #55 512-834-6612
Lead Training Program Providers #55 .. 512-834-6612
Loan Company #7 512-936-7600
Lobbyist #50 512-463-5800

LPG-Liquefied Petroleum Gas Technician #11
....512-462-1441
Manicurist/Manicurist Shop #2 512-305-8475
Marriage & Family Therapist #31 512-834-6657
Massage Therapist #28 512-834-6616
Massage Therapist, Temporary #28 512-834-6616
Massage Therapy Establishment #28.. 512-834-6616
Massage Therapy School #28 512-834-6616
Massage Therapy Sch. Instructor #28 .. 512-834-6616
Medical Doctor #30 512-305-7030
Medical Laboratory Practitioner #22 512-834-6602
Medical Specialty (Doctor) #30 512-305-7030
Medication Aide #13 512-231-5827
Midwife, Direct Entry #25 512-458-7700
Notary Public #33 512-463-5705
Nurse, Advance Regist. Practice #25 .. 512-305-7400
Nurse-RN #25 512-231-5829
Nurses' Aide #13 512-231-5829
Nursing Home Admin./Facility #13 512-231-5825
Occupational Therapist/Assistant #17 . 512-305-6900
Optician #26 512-834-6661
Optometrist #51 512-305-8500
Orthotics & Prosthetics Facility #26 512-834-4520
Orthotist/Prosthetist #26 512-834-4520
PAC List #50 512-463-5800
Paramedic #27 512-834-6700
Pawn Shop #7 512-936-7600
Perfusionist #26 512-834-6751
Perpetual Care Cemetery #1 512-475-1290
Personal Employment Service #14 512-463-6599
Pesticide Applicator/Dealer #10 512-475-1639
Pharmacist/Pharmacist Intern #24 512-305-8000
Pharmacy #24 512-305-8000
Physical Therapist/Assistant #17 512-305-6900
Physician Assistant #30 512-305-7030
Physicist, Medical #26 512-834-6655
Plumber Master/Journeyman #3 .. 512-458-2145 x227
Plumbing Inspector #3 .... 512-458-2145 x227
Podiatrist #20 512-305-7000
Political Contributor #50 512-463-5800
Polygraph Examiner #34 512-424-2058
Polygraph Examiner of Sex Offenders #26
....512-834-6655
Private Investigator #35 512-463-5545
Property Tax Consultant #14 512-463-6599
Psychological Associate #19 512-305-7700
Psychologist #19 512-305-7700
Psychologist Associate #25 512-305-7700
Public Accountant-CPA #43 512-305-7853

Radiologic Technologist #25	512-834-6617
Radiology Technician #26	512-834-6617
Real Estate Appraiser #47	512-465-3950
Real Estate Broker/Salesperson #52	512-459-6544
Real Estate Inspector #52	512-459-6544
Representative Offices (Banking) #1	512-475-1300
Respiratory Care Practitioner #29	512-834-6632
Sanitarian #22	512-834-6635
Sanitation Code Enforcement Officer #22	512-834-6635
Savings & Loan Association #37	512-475-1350
Savings Bank #37	512-475-1350
School Psychology Specialist #19	512-305-7700
School Psychology Specialist #25	512-305-7700

Securities Agent/Salesperson #39	512-305-8332
Securities Broker #39	512-305-8332
Securities Dealer #39	512-305-8332
Security Agency, Private #35	512-463-5545
Seed Dealer #11	979-542-3691
Service Contract Provider #14	512-463-6599
Sex Offender Treatment Provider #22	512-834-4530
Shorthand Reporter #9	512-463-1630
Social Worker #26	512-719-3521
Speech-Language Pathologist #22	512-834-6627
Staff Leasing #14	512-475-2896
STAP Vendor #6	512-407-3250
Surveyor, Land #4	512-452-9427
Talent Agency #14	512-463-6599

Tax Appraisal Professional #59	512-305-7300
Teacher #42	512-469-3000
Temporary Common Worker #14	512-463-6599
Transportation Service Provider #54	512-465-3500
Trust Company #1	512-475-1300
Underground Storage Tank Intall. #60	512-239-2191
Vehicle Protection Provider #14	512-463-6599
Veterinarian #18	512-305-7555
Water Well & Pump Installer #14	512-463-7880
Weather Modification Service #14	512-463-6599
Weigher, Public #11	512-463-7607
Wig Specialist #2	512-305-8475

Licensing Agency Information

#1 Banking Department, 2601 N Lamar Blvd, Austin, TX 78705-4294; 512-475-1300, Fax: 512-475-1313.
www.banking.state.tx.us
Search database at
www.banking.state.tx.us/itds.htm

#2 Board of Barber Examiners, 333 Guadalupe, #2-110, Austin, TX 78701; 512-305-8475, Fax: 512-305-6800.
www.tsbbe.state.tx.us Cost of bulk record request is estimated based on amount of information requested.

#3 Board of Plumbing Examiners, PO Box 4200, Austin, TX 78765-4200; 512-458-2145, Fax: 512-450-0637.
www.tsbpe.state.tx.us
Agency email: info@tsbpe.state.tx.us.

#4 Board of Professional Land Surveying, 7701 N Lamar, #400, Austin, TX 78752; 512-452-9427, Fax: 512-452-7711.
www.txls.state.tx.us

#5 Board of Registration for Professional Engineers, 1917 IH35 S (78760), Austin, TX 78741; 512-440-7723, Fax: 512-442-1414.
www.tbpe.state.tx.us
Agency email: peboard@tbpe.state.tx.us.
Search database at www.tbpe.state.tx.us/downloads.htm. Licensing data available as pdf downloads; lists updated twice monthly.

#6 Commission for the Deaf & Hard of Hearing, PO Box 12904, Austin, TX 78711; 512-407-3250 Voice; 512-407-3251 TTY, Fax: 512-451-9316.
www.tcdhh.state.tx.us
Agency email: angelab@tcdhh.tx.us.

#7 Office of Consumer Credit Commissioner, 2601 N Lamar Blvd, Austin, TX 78705-4207; 512-936-2600, Fax: 512-936-7610.
www.occc.state.tx.us
Agency email: info@occc.state.tx.us.

#8 Cosmetology Commission, 5717 Balcones Dr, Austin, TX 78755; 512-467-8206, Fax: 512-419-9914.

#9 Court Reporter Certification Board, PO Box 131131, Austin, TX 78711-3131; 512-463-1630, Fax: 512-463-1117.
www.crcb.state.tx.us
Agency email: info@crcb.state.tx.us.

#10 Department of Agriculture, Pesticide Program, P.O. Box 12847 (1700 Congress Ave), Austin, TX 78711; 512-475-1639, Fax: 512-475-1618.
www.agr.state.tx.us/pesticide/index.htm
Agency email: contact@agr.state.tx.us.

#11 Department of Agriculture, PO Box 12847 (1700 N Congress, Stephen F Austin Bldg), Austin, TX 78711; 512-463-7476, Fax: 512-463-1104.
www.agr.state.tx.us

#12 Department of Health, Asbestos Programs Branch, 1100 W 49th St, Austin, TX 78756; 512-834-6600, Fax: 512-834-6644.
www.tdh.state.tx.us/beh/asbmain.htm
Agency email: todd.wingler@tdh.state.tx.us.

#13 Department of Human Services, Long Term Care Regulatory Credentialing Dept, PO Box 149030, Mail Code Y979 (701 W. 51st St), Austin, TX 78714-9030; 512-231-5800, Fax: 512-834-6764.
www.dhs.state.tx.us/programs/ltc/credentialing/index.html. Agency email: ltcr@dhs.state.tx.us.

#14 Department of Licensing & Regulation, PO Box 12157 (920 Colorado), Austin, TX 78711-2157; 512-463-6599, Fax: 512-475-2854.
www.license.state.tx.us
Search database at
www.license.state.tx.us/LicenseSearch

#15 Funeral Service Commission, 510 S Congress Ave, #206, Austin, TX 78704-1718; 512-936-2474, Fax: 512-479-5064.
www.tfsc.state.tx.us
Agency email: tfsc@tfsc.state.tx.us.

#17 Executive Council on Physical Therapy & Occupational Therapy Examiners, 333 Guadalupe St, Tower 2, #510, Austin, TX 78701; 512-305-6900, Fax: 512-305-6951.
www.ecptote.state.tx.us
Agency email: ecptote@mail.capnet.state.tx.us.
Search database at
www.ecptote.state.tx.us/serv/verification/default.html

#18 Health Department, State Veterinary Board, 333 Guadalupe, Tower 2, #330, Austin, TX 78701-3998; 512-305-7555, Fax: 512-305-7556.
www.texasonline.state.tx.us/tbvme. Agency email: Vet.Board@tbvme.state.tx.us.

#19 Board of Examiners of Psychologists, 333 Guadalupe, #2-450, Austin, TX 78701; 512-305-7700, Fax: 512-305-7701.
www.tsbep.state.tx.us. Agency email: Janice.Alvarez@tsbep.state.tx.us.

#20 Board of Podiactric Medical Examiners, 333 Guadalupe, #2-320, Austin, TX 78701; 512-305-7000, Fax: 512-305-7003.
www.foot.state.tx.us. Agency email: michele.wooldridge@foot.state.tx.us.
Search database at
www.foot.state.tx.us/verifications.htm

#21 Health Department, Advisory Board of Athletic Trainers, 1100 W 49th St, Austin, TX 78756; 512-834-6615, Fax: 512-834-6677.
www.tdh.state.tx.us/hcqs/plc/at.htm. Agency email: at@tdh.state.tx.us.
Search database at
www.tdh.state.tx.us/hcqs/plc/at_rost.txt

#22 Health Department, Professional Licensure & Certification, 1100 W 49th St, Austin, TX 78756-3183; 512-834-6635, Fax: 512-834-6707.
www.tdh.state.tx.us/license.htm
Agency email: registry@licc.tdh.state.tx.us.

#23 Health Department, 333 Guadalupe, Tower 3, #800, Austin, TX 78701; 512-463-6400, Fax: 512-463-7452.
www.tsbde.state.tx.us. Agency email: webmaster@tsbde.state.tx.us.
Search database at www.tsbde.state.tx.us/dbsearch

#24 Health Department, Board of Pharmacy, 333 Guadalupe, Box 21, Tower 3, #600, Austin, TX 78701-3942; 512-305-8000, Fax: 512-305-8082.
www.tsbp.state.tx.us
Agency email: openrec@tsbp.state.tx.us.
Search database at
www.tsbp.state.tx.us/dbsearch/Default.htm

#25 Health Department, 323 Guadalupe, Tower 3, #825, Austin, TX 78701; 512-458-7111, Fax: 512-305-6705.
www.tdh.state.tx.us

#26 Department of Health, Professional Licensing & Certification Div, 1100 W 49th St, Austin, TX 78756-3180; 512-834-6658, Fax: 512-834-6789.
www.tdh.state.tx.us/hcqs/plc/plcd.htm
Agency email: lpc@licc.tdh.state.tx.us.

#27 Health Department, Bureau of Emergency Management, 1100 W 49th St, Austin, TX 78756; 512-458-6700, Fax: 512-834-6736.
www.tdh.state.tx.us/hcqs/ems/emshome.htm.
Agency email: emscert@ems.tdh.state.tx.us.
Search database at
http://160.42.108.3/ems_web/blh_html_page1.htm

#28 Health Department, Professional Licensure & Certification, 1100 W 49th St, Austin, TX 78756; 512-834-6616, Fax: 512-834-6677.
www.tdh.state.tx.us/hcqs/plc/massage.htm.
Agency email: massage@licc.tdh.state.tx.us.

#29 Health Department, Professional Licensure & Certification, 1100 W 49th St, Austin, TX 78756; 512-834-6632, Fax: 512-834-4518.
www.tdh.state.tx.us/hcqs/plc/resp.htm. Agency email: resp@licc.tdh.state.tx.us.

#30 Board of Medical Examiners, MC 240, PO Box 2018, Austin, TX 78768-2018; 512-305-7030, Fax: 512-463-9416.
www.tsbme.state.tx.us
Agency email: verifcic@tsbme.state.tx.us.
Search database at http://204.65.101.19/OnLineVerif/Phys_SearchVerif.asp

#31 Health Department, Professional Licensure & Certification, 1100 W 49th St, Austin, TX 78756; 512-834-6628, Fax: 512-834-6677.
www.tdh.state.tx.us/hcqs/plc/mft.htm
Agency email: mft@licc.tdh.state.tx.us.
Search database at www.tdh.state.tx.us/hcqs/plc/mft.htm#rosters

#33 Office of Secretary of State, PO Box 13375 (1019 Brazos, Rm 214), Austin, TX 78711; 512-463-5705.
www.sos.state.tx.us/statdoc/index.shtml

#34 Polygraph Examiner Board, PO Box 4087, Austin, TX 78773-4087; 512-424-2058, Fax: 512-424-5739.
http://polygraph.org/states/tape. Agency email: polygraph.board@mail.capnet.state.tx.us.
Search database at http://polygraph.org/states/tape/members_roster.htm

#35 Private Investigators/Security Agencies Board, 4930 S Congress, Capitol Station, Austin, TX 78711; 512-463-5545, Fax: 512-707-2041.
www.tcps.state.tx.us

#36 Racing Commission, 8505 Cross Park Dr, #110, Austin, TX 78754; 512-833-6699, Fax: 512-833-6907.
www.txrc.state.tx.us

#37 Savings & Loan Department, 2601 N Lamar Blvd, #201, Austin, TX 78705-4241; 112-475-1350, Fax: 512-475-1360.
www.tsld.state.tx.us

#38 Secretary of State, Statutory Documents Section, PO Box 12887 (10119 Bravos), Austin, TX 78711-2887; 512-475-1769, Fax: 512-475-2815.
www.sos.state.tx.us

#39 Securities Board, 200 E 10th St, 5th Fl, Austin, TX 78701; 512-305-8300, Fax: 512-305-8310.
www.ssb.state.tx.us
Agency email: webmaster@ssb.state.tx.us.

#40 State Bar of Texas, 1414 Colorado, #300, Austin, TX 78701-1627; 512-463-1463 x1383, Fax: 512-462-1475.
www.texasbar.com
Search database at www.texasbar.com/members/onlinetools/qrymbr.asp

#41 Board of Examiners for Professional Counselors, 1100 W 49th St, Austin, TX 78756; 512-834-6658, Fax: 512-834-6789.
www.tdh.state.tx.us/hcqs/plc/lpc.htm
Agency email: lpc@tdh.state.tx.us.

#42 Board for Educator Certification, 1001 Trinity, Austin, TX 78701-2603; 512-469-3000, Fax: 512-469-3018.
www.sbec.state.tx.us.

#43 Board of Public Accountancy, 333 Guadalupe St, Tower III, #900, Austin, TX 78701; 512-305-7800, Fax: 512-505-7875.
www.tsbpa.state.tx.us
Search database at www.tsbpa.state.tx.us

#44 Library & Archives Commission, 1201 Brazos, Austin, TX 78711-2927; 512-463-5466, Fax: 512-463-8800.
www.tsl.state.tx.us
Agency email: ld@tsl.state.tx.su.

#45 State Parks & Wildlife Department, 4200 Smith School Rd, Austin, TX 78744; 512-389-4818, Fax: 512-389-4349.
www.tpwd.state.tx.us

#46 Alcoholic Beverage Commission, PO Box 13127 (5806 Mesa Dr), Austin, TX 78711; 512-206-3333, Fax: 512-451-0240.
www.tabc.state.tx

#47 Appraisers Licensing & Certification Board, 1101 Camino La Costa, Austin, TX 78752; 512-465-3950, Fax: 512-465-3953.
www.talcb.state.tx.us
Search database at www.talcb.state.tx.us

#48 Department of Insurance, 333 Guadalupe, Austin, TX 78701; 512-463-6169, Fax: 512-475-2025.
www.tdi.state.tx.us. Agency email: consumer_protection@tdi.state.tx.us.
Search database at www.tdi.state.tx.us/general/forms/colists.html

#49 Department of Protective & Regulatory Services, Child Care Licensing Division, 701 W 51st St, #E-550, Austin, TX 78714-9030; 512-438-4800, Fax: 512-438-3848.
www.tdprs.state.tx.us

#50 Ethics Commission, PO Box 12070, Austin, TX 78711-2070; 512-463-5800, Fax: 512-463-5777.
www.ethics.state.tx.us
Agency email: disclosure@ethics.state.tx.us.
Search database at http://txprod.ethics.state.tx.us/tx00

#51 Optometry Board, 333 Guadalupe St, #2-420, Austin, TX 78701-3942; 512-305-8500, Fax: 512-305-8501.

www.tded.state.tx.us/guide/regulatorybodies.html.
Agency email: lisa.ake@mail.capnet.st.tx.us.
Search database at www.odfinder.org/LicSearch.asp

#52 Real Estate Commission, PO Box 12188, Austin, TX 78711-2188; 512-459-6544, Fax: 512-465-3698.
www.trec.state.tx.us
Agency email: glen.bridge@trec.state.tx.us.
Search database at www.trec.state.tx.us/publicinfo

#53 State Fire Marshal, 333 Guadalupe, Austin, TX 78701; 512-305-7900, Fax: 512-305-7922.
www.tdi.state.tx.us/fire/fmli.html.

#54 Department of Transportation, (Transportation Service Licensing Dept.), 4203 Bull Creek, Austin, TX 78731; 512-465-3500, Fax: 512-465-3535.
www.dot.state.tx.us

#55 Department of Health, Toxic Substances Control Division, Environmental Lead Branch, 1100 W 49th St, Austin, TX 78756-3199; 512-834-6612, Fax: 512-834-6644.
www.tdh.state.tx.us/beh/TSCD
Agency email: peter.tadin@tdh.state.tx.us.

#56 Commission on Fire Protection, 12675 Research Blvd, PO Box 2286, Austin, TX 78768-2286; 512-918-7100, Fax: 512-239-4917.
www.tcfp.state.tx.us
Agency email: info@tcfp.state.tx.us.

#57 Natural Resource Conservation Comm MC178, PO Box 13087, Austin, TX 78711-3087; 512-239-6719, Fax: 512-239-0533.
www.tnrcc.state.tx.us
Agency email: irrclerk@tnrcc.state.tx.us.

#58 Commission on Law Enforcement Officer, 6330 U.S. 290 East #200, Austin, TX 78723; 512-936-7700, Fax: 512-936-7714.
www.tcleose.state.tx.us
Agency email: kris.faldyn@mail.capnet.state.tx.us.

#59 Board of Tax Professional Examiners, 333 Guadalupe St, Tower II #520, Austin, TX 78701; 512-305-7300, Fax: 512-305-7304.
http://www/txbtpe/state/tx/us
Agency email: btpe@mail.compact.state.tx.us.
Search database at www.txbtpe.state.tx.us

#60 Natural Resource Conservation Commission, PO Box 13087, Austin, TX 78711-3087; 512-239-2191, Fax: 512-239-0533.
www.tnrcc.state.tx.us
Agency email: wkurio@tnrcc.state.tx.us.
Search database at www.tnrcc.state.tx.us/enforcement/csd/ics/ustlicense.html

#61 Board of Architectural Examiners, PO Box 12337, Austin, TX 78711-2337; 512-305-9000, Fax: 512-305-8900.
www.tbae.state.tx.us

Texas Federal Courts

The following list indicates the district and division name for each county in the state. If the bankruptcy court location is different from the district court, then the location of the bankruptcy court appears in parentheses.

County/Court Cross Reference

County	District	Division
Anderson	Eastern	Tyler
Andrews	Western	Midland (Midland/Odessa)
Angelina	Eastern	Texarkana (Beaumont)
Aransas	Southern	Corpus Christi
Archer	Northern	Wichita Falls
Armstrong	Northern	Amarillo
Atascosa	Western	San Antonio
Austin	Southern	Houston
Bailey	Northern	Lubbock
Bandera	Western	San Antonio
Bastrop	Western	Austin
Baylor	Northern	Wichita Falls
Bee	Southern	Corpus Christi
Bell	Western	Waco
Bexar	Western	San Antonio
Blanco	Western	Austin
Borden	Northern	Lubbock
Bosque	Western	Waco
Bowie	Eastern	Texarkana
Brazoria	Southern	Galveston (Houston)
Brazos	Southern	Houston
Brewster	Western	Pecos (Midland/Odessa)
Briscoe	Northern	Amarillo
Brooks	Southern	Corpus Christi
Brown	Northern	San Angelo (Lubbock)
Burleson	Western	Austin
Burnet	Western	Austin
Caldwell	Western	Austin
Calhoun	Southern	Victoria (Corpus Christi)
Callahan	Northern	Abilene (Lubbock)
Cameron	Southern	Brownsville (Corpus Christi)
Camp	Eastern	Marshall
Carson	Northern	Amarillo
Cass	Eastern	Marshall
Castro	Northern	Amarillo
Chambers	Southern	Galveston (Houston)
Cherokee	Eastern	Tyler
Childress	Northern	Amarillo
Clay	Northern	Wichita Falls
Cochran	Northern	Lubbock
Coke	Northern	San Angelo (Lubbock)
Coleman	Northern	San Angelo (Lubbock)
Collin	Eastern	Sherman (Plano)
Collingsworth	Northern	Amarillo
Colorado	Southern	Houston
Comal	Western	San Antonio
Comanche	Northern	Fort Worth
Concho	Northern	San Angelo (Lubbock)
Cooke	Eastern	Sherman (Plano)
Coryell	Western	Waco
Cottle	Northern	Wichita Falls
Crane	Western	Midland (Midland/Odessa)
Crockett	Northern	San Angelo (Lubbock)
Crosby	Northern	Lubbock
Culberson	Western	Pecos (Midland/Odessa)
Dallam	Northern	Amarillo
Dallas	Northern	Dallas
Dawson	Northern	Lubbock
De Witt	Southern	Victoria (Houston)
Deaf Smith	Northern	Amarillo
Delta	Eastern	Sherman (Plano)
Denton	Eastern	Sherman (Plano)
Dickens	Northern	Lubbock
Dimmit	Western	San Antonio
Donley	Northern	Amarillo
Duval	Southern	Corpus Christi
Eastland	Northern	Abilene (Lubbock)
Ector	Western	Midland (Midland/Odessa)
Edwards	Western	Del Rio (San Antonio)
El Paso	Western	El Paso
Ellis	Northern	Dallas
Erath	Northern	Fort Worth
Falls	Western	Waco
Fannin	Eastern	Sherman (Plano)
Fayette	Southern	Houston
Fisher	Northern	Abilene (Lubbock)
Floyd	Northern	Lubbock
Foard	Northern	Wichita Falls
Fort Bend	Southern	Houston
Franklin	Eastern	Texarkana
Freestone	Western	Waco
Frio	Western	San Antonio
Gaines	Northern	Lubbock
Galveston	Southern	Galveston (Houston)
Garza	Northern	Lubbock
Gillespie	Western	Austin
Glasscock	Northern	San Angelo (Lubbock)
Goliad	Southern	Victoria (Corpus Christi)
Gonzales	Western	San Antonio
Gray	Northern	Amarillo
Grayson	Eastern	Sherman (Plano)
Gregg	Eastern	Tyler
Grimes	Southern	Houston
Guadalupe	Western	San Antonio
Hale	Northern	Lubbock
Hall	Northern	Amarillo
Hamilton	Western	Waco
Hansford	Northern	Amarillo
Hardeman	Northern	Wichita Falls
Hardin	Eastern	Beaumont
Harris	Southern	Houston
Harrison	Eastern	Marshall
Hartley	Northern	Amarillo
Haskell	Northern	Abilene (Lubbock)
Hays	Western	Austin
Hemphill	Northern	Amarillo
Henderson	Eastern	Tyler
Hidalgo	Southern	McAllen (Corpus Christi)
Hill	Western	Waco
Hockley	Northern	Lubbock
Hood	Northern	Fort Worth
Hopkins	Eastern	Sherman (Plano)
Houston	Eastern	Texarkana (Beaumont)
Howard	Northern	Abilene (Lubbock)
Hudspeth	Western	Pecos (Midland/Odessa)
Hunt	Northern	Dallas

County	District	Court
Hutchinson	Northern	Amarillo
Irion	Northern	San Angelo (Lubbock)
Jack	Northern	Fort Worth
Jackson	Southern	Victoria (Corpus Christi)
Jasper	Eastern	Beaumont
Jeff Davis	Western	Pecos (Midland/Odessa)
Jefferson	Eastern	Beaumont
Jim Hogg	Southern	Laredo (Houston)
Jim Wells	Southern	Corpus Christi
Johnson	Northern	Dallas
Jones	Northern	Abilene (Lubbock)
Karnes	Western	San Antonio
Kaufman	Northern	Dallas
Kendall	Western	San Antonio
Kenedy	Southern	Corpus Christi
Kent	Northern	Lubbock
Kerr	Western	San Antonio
Kimble	Western	Austin
King	Northern	Wichita Falls
Kinney	Western	Del Rio (San Antonio)
Kleberg	Southern	Corpus Christi
Knox	Northern	Wichita Falls
La Salle	Southern	Laredo (Corpus Christi)
Lamar	Eastern	Sherman (Plano)
Lamb	Northern	Lubbock
Lampasas	Western	Austin
Lavaca	Southern	Victoria (Houston)
Lee	Western	Austin
Leon	Western	Waco
Liberty	Eastern	Beaumont
Limestone	Western	Waco
Lipscomb	Northern	Amarillo
Live Oak	Southern	Corpus Christi
Llano	Western	Austin
Loving	Western	Pecos (Midland/Odessa)
Lubbock	Northern	Lubbock
Lynn	Northern	Lubbock
Madison	Southern	Houston
Marion	Eastern	Marshall
Martin	Western	Midland (Midland/Odessa)
Mason	Western	Austin
Matagorda	Southern	Galveston (Houston)
Maverick	Western	Del Rio (San Antonio)
McCulloch	Western	Austin
McLennan	Western	Waco
McMullen	Southern	Laredo (Houston)
Medina	Western	San Antonio
Menard	Northern	San Angelo (Lubbock)
Midland	Western	Midland (Midland/Odessa)
Milam	Western	Waco
Mills	Northern	San Angelo (Lubbock)
Mitchell	Northern	Abilene (Lubbock)
Montague	Northern	Wichita Falls
Montgomery	Southern	Houston
Moore	Northern	Amarillo
Morris	Eastern	Marshall
Motley	Northern	Lubbock
Nacogdoches	Eastern	Texarkana (Beaumont)
Navarro	Northern	Dallas
Newton	Eastern	Beaumont
Nolan	Northern	Abilene (Lubbock)
Nueces	Southern	Corpus Christi
Ochiltree	Northern	Amarillo
Oldham	Northern	Amarillo
Orange	Eastern	Beaumont
Palo Pinto	Northern	Fort Worth
Panola	Eastern	Tyler
Parker	Northern	Fort Worth
Parmer	Northern	Amarillo
Pecos	Western	Pecos (Midland/Odessa)
Polk	Eastern	Texarkana (Beaumont)
Potter	Northern	Amarillo
Presidio	Western	Pecos (Midland/Odessa)
Rains	Eastern	Tyler
Randall	Northern	Amarillo
Reagan	Northern	San Angelo (Lubbock)
Real	Western	San Antonio
Red River	Eastern	Sherman (Plano)
Reeves	Western	Pecos (Midland/Odessa)
Refugio	Southern	Victoria (Corpus Christi)
Roberts	Northern	Amarillo
Robertson	Western	Waco
Rockwall	Northern	Dallas
Runnels	Northern	San Angelo (Lubbock)
Rusk	Eastern	Tyler
Sabine	Eastern	Texarkana (Beaumont)
San Augustine	Eastern	Texarkana (Beaumont)
San Jacinto	Southern	Houston
San Patricio	Southern	Corpus Christi
San Saba	Western	Austin
Schleicher	Northern	San Angelo (Lubbock)
Scurry	Northern	Lubbock
Shackelford	Northern	Abilene (Lubbock)
Shelby	Eastern	Texarkana (Beaumont)
Sherman	Northern	Amarillo
Smith	Eastern	Tyler
Somervell	Western	Waco
Starr	Southern	McAllen (Corpus Christi)
Stephens	Northern	Abilene (Lubbock)
Sterling	Northern	San Angelo (Lubbock)
Stonewall	Northern	Abilene (Lubbock)
Sutton	Northern	San Angelo (Lubbock)
Swisher	Northern	Amarillo
Tarrant	Northern	Fort Worth
Taylor	Northern	Abilene (Lubbock)
Terrell	Western	Del Rio (San Antonio)
Terry	Northern	Lubbock
Throckmorton	Northern	Abilene (Lubbock)
Titus	Eastern	Texarkana
Tom Green	Northern	San Angelo (Lubbock)
Travis	Western	Austin
Trinity	Eastern	Texarkana (Beaumont)
Tyler	Eastern	Texarkana (Beaumont)
Upshur	Eastern	Marshall
Upton	Western	Midland (Midland/Odessa)
Uvalde	Western	Del Rio (San Antonio)
Val Verde	Western	Del Rio (San Antonio)
Van Zandt	Eastern	Tyler
Victoria	Southern	Victoria (Corpus Christi)
Walker	Southern	Houston
Waller	Southern	Houston
Ward	Western	Pecos (Midland/Odessa)
Washington	Western	Austin
Webb	Southern	Laredo (Houston)
Wharton	Southern	Houston
Wheeler	Northern	Amarillo
Wichita	Northern	Wichita Falls
Wilbarger	Northern	Wichita Falls
Willacy	Southern	Brownsville (Corpus Christi)
Williamson	Western	Austin
Wilson	Western	San Antonio
Winkler	Western	Pecos (Midland/Odessa)
Wise	Northern	Fort Worth
Wood	Eastern	Tyler
Yoakum	Northern	Lubbock
Young	Northern	Wichita Falls
Zapata	Southern	Laredo (Houston)
Zavala	Western	Del Rio (San Antonio)

Standards for Federal Courts: The search fee is $20.00 per item (one party name or case number). Certification fee is $7.00 per document. Copy fee is $.50 per page. All fees standard unless noted in profile. Mail Search: always enclose a stamped self addressed envelope unless otherwise noted. Before releasing records, all courts require prepayment unless noted in profile.

Open records are located at the court unless otherwise noted. District courts index by defendant and plaintiff as well as by case number. Bankruptcy courts usually index by debtor and case number. While most courts now have their indexes on computer, many still maintain index card files as well.

The universal PACER sign-up number is 800-676-6856. Find PACER and the Party/Case Index on the Web at http://pacer.psc.uscourts.gov. PACER dial-up access is $.60 per minute. Also, courts offering internet access via RACER, PACER, Web-PACER or the new CM-ECF charge $.07 per page fee unless noted as free.

US District Court

Eastern District of Texas

Beaumont Division PO Box 3507, Beaumont, TX 77704 (Courier Address: Room 104, 300 Willow, Beaumont, TX 77701), 409-654-7000.

www.txed.uscourts.gov

Counties: Delta*, Fannin*, Hardin, Hopkins*, Jasper, Jefferson, Lamar*, Liberty, Newton, Orange, Red River. Counties marked with an asterisk are called the Paris Division, whose. Case records are maintained here.

Indexing & Storage: Cases are indexed by defendant, plaintiff, and case number. New cases are available in the index immediately after filing date. Records are also indexed on microfiche. District wide searches are available for records from 3/86 from this division. This division maintains records for the Paris Division also.

Fee & Payment Notes: Payment may be made by money order, cashier check, personal check. Payee: Clerk, US District Court. You are allowed to make your own copies. These copies cost $.25 per page. Copies are made from a public copy machine. Certified search requests are $25.00.

Phone Search: Only docket information is available by phone.

Mail Search: A stamped self addressed envelope is not required.

In Person Search: In person searching available.

PACER:. Case records are available back to 1992. Records are purged once per year. New records are available online after 1 day. PACER is available online at http://pacer.txed.uscourts.gov.

Lufkin Division 104 N. Third St., Lufkin, TX 75901 (Courier Address: Use mail address for courier delivery), 936-632-2739.

www.txed.uscourts.gov

Counties: Angelina, Houston, Nacogdoches, Polk, Sabine, San Augustine, Shelby, Trinity, Tyler.

Indexing & Storage: Cases are indexed by defendant, plaintiff, and case number. New cases are available in the index 1 day after filing date. Records are also indexed on microfiche. Open records are located at this court.

Fee & Payment Notes: Payment may be made by money order, cashier check, personal check. Payee: US District Court. You are allowed to make your own copies. These copies cost $.50 per page.

Phone Search: Only docket information is available by phone.

In Person Search: In person searching available.

PACER: Access fee is. New records are available online after 1 day. PACER is available online at http://pacer.txed.uscourts.gov.

Marshall Division PO Box 1499, Marshall, TX 75671-1499 (Courier Address: 100 E Houston, Marshall, TX 75670), 903-935-2912, Fax: 903-938-2651.

www.txed.uscourts.gov

Counties: Camp, Cass, Harrison, Marion, Morris, Upshur.

Indexing & Storage: Cases are indexed by defendant, plaintiff, and case number. New cases are available in the index 1 day after filing date. Records are also indexed on microfiche. Open records are located at this court.

Fee & Payment Notes: Payment may be made by money order, cashier check, personal check. Payee: US District Court. You are allowed to make your own copies. These copies cost $.50 per page.

Phone Search: Only docket information is available by phone.

In Person Search: In person searching available.

PACER:. Case records are available back to 1992. Records are purged once per year. New records are available online after 1 day. PACER is available online at http://pacer.txed.uscourts.gov.

Sherman Division 101 E Pecan St, Sherman, TX 75090 (Courier Address: Use mail address for courier delivery), 903-892-2921.

www.txed.uscourts.gov

Counties: Collin, Cooke, Denton, Grayson.

Indexing & Storage: Cases are indexed by defendant, plaintiff, and case number. New cases are available in the index 1 day after filing date. Records are also indexed on microfiche. District wide searches are available from this division.

Fee & Payment Notes: Payment may be made by money order, cashier check, personal check. Payee: Clerk, US District Court.

Phone Search: Docket information available by phone.

In Person Search: In person searching available.

PACER:. Case records are available back to 1992. Records are purged once per year. New records are available online after 1 day. PACER is available online at http://pacer.txed.uscourts.gov.

Texarkana Division Clerk's Office, 500 State Line Ave, Room 301, Texarkana, TX 75501 (Courier Address: Use mail address for courier delivery), 903-794-8561, Fax: 903-794-0600.

www.txed.uscourts.gov

Counties: Bowie, Franklin, Titus.

Indexing & Storage: Cases are indexed by defendant, plaintiff, and case number. New cases are available in the index 1-2 days after filing date. Records are also indexed on microfiche. There is no set time when cases are sent to the Fort Worth Federal Records Center.

Fee & Payment Notes: Payment may be made by money order, cashier check, personal check. Payee: Clerk, US District Court.

In Person Search: In person searching available.

PACER:. Case records are available back to 1992. Records are purged once per year. New records are available online after 1 day. PACER is available online at http://pacer.txed.uscourts.gov.

Tyler Division Clerk, Room 106, 211 W Ferguson, Tyler, TX 75702 (Courier Address: Use mail address for courier delivery), 903-590-1000.

www.txed.uscourts.gov

Counties: Anderson, Cherokee, Gregg, Henderson, Panola, Rains, Rusk, Smith, Van Zandt, Wood.

Indexing & Storage: Cases are indexed by defendant, plaintiff, and case number. New cases are available in the index 1-2 days after filing date. Records are also indexed on microfiche. There is no set time when cases are sent to the Fort Worth Federal Records Center.

Fee & Payment Notes: Payment may be made by money order, cashier check, personal check. Payee: Clerk, US District Court. You are allowed to make your own copies. These copies cost $.25 per page.

Phone Search: Only docket information is available by phone.

Mail Search: A stamped self addressed envelope is not required.

In Person Search: In person searching available.

PACER:. Case records are available back to 1992. Records are purged once per year. New records are available online after 1 day. PACER is available online at http://pacer.txed.uscourts.gov.

US Bankruptcy Court

Eastern District of Texas

Beaumont Division Suite 100, 300 Willow, Beaumont, TX 77701 (Courier Address: Use mail address for courier delivery), 409-839-2617.

www.txeb.uscourts.gov

Counties: Angelina, Hardin, Houston, Jasper, Jefferson, Liberty, Nacogdoches, Newton, Orange, Polk, Sabine, San Augustine, Shelby, Trinity, Tyler.

Indexing & Storage: Cases are indexed by debtor as well as by case number. New cases are available in the index 1 day after filing date. Open records are located at this court.

Fee & Payment Notes: Payment may be made by money order, cashier check, personal check. Debtor's checks are not accepted. Payee: Clerk, US Bankruptcy Court. You are allowed to make your own copies. These copies cost $.25 per page. The searcher must fill out a card with their phone number, the date and the case number.

Phone Search: Only docket information is available by phone. An automated voice case information service (VCIS) is available. Call VCIS at 800-466-1694 or 903-590-1217.

In Person Search: In person searching available.

PACER: Toll-free dial-up access: 800-466-1681. Local dial-up access: 903-590-1220. Case records are available back to 1989. Records are purged every six months. New civil records are available online after 1 day. PACER is available online at http://pacer.txeb.uscourts.gov. Document images available.

Electronic Filing: Information is available online at https://ecf.txeb.uscourts.gov

Marshall Division c/o Tyler Division, 200 E Ferguson, Tyler, TX 75702 (Courier Address: Use mail address for courier delivery), 903-590-1212, Fax: 903-590-1226.

www.txeb.uscourts.gov

Counties: Camp, Cass, Harrison, Marion, Morris, Upshur.

Indexing & Storage: New cases are available in the index after filing date. Open records are located at the Tyler Division.

Fee & Payment Notes: Payment may be made by money order, cashier check. Business checks are not accepted. Personal checks are not accepted.

Phone Search: An automated voice case information service (VCIS) is available. Call VCIS at 800-466-1694 or 903-590-1217.

Mail Search: A stamped self addressed envelope is not required.

In Person Search: In person searching available.

PACER: Toll-free dial-up access: 800-466-1681. Local dial-up access: 903-590-1220. Case records are available back to 1989. Records are purged every six months. New civil records are available online after 1 day. PACER is available online at http://pacer.txeb.uscourts.gov. Document images available.

Electronic Filing: Information is available online at https://ecf.txeb.uscourts.gov

Plano Division Suite 300B, 660 N Central Expressway, Plano, TX 75074 (Courier Address: Use mail address for courier delivery), 972-509-1240, Fax: 972-509-1245.

www.txeb.uscourts.gov

Counties: Collin, Cooke, Delta, Denton, Fannin, Grayson, Hopkins, Lamar, Red River.

Indexing & Storage: Cases are indexed by debtor and creditors as well as by case number. New cases are available in the index 24 hours after filing date. Open records are located at this court.

Fee & Payment Notes: Payment may be made by money order, cashier check, personal check. Payee: Clerk, US Bankruptcy Court. You are allowed to make your own copies. These copies cost $.25 per page.

Phone Search: Only docket information is available by phone. An automated voice case information service (VCIS) is available. Call VCIS at 800-466-1694 or 903-590-1217.

In Person Search: In person searching available.

PACER: Toll-free dial-up access: 800-466-1681. Local dial-up access: 903-590-1220. Case records are available back to 1989. Records are purged every six months. New civil records are available online after 1 day. PACER is available online at http://pacer.txeb.uscourts.gov. Document images available.

Electronic Filing: Information is available online at https://ecf.txeb.uscourts.gov

Texarkana Division c/o Plano Division, Suite 300B, 660 N Central Expressway, Plano, TX 75074 (Courier Address: Use mail address for courier delivery), 972-509-1240, Fax: 972-509-1245.

www.txeb.uscourts.gov

Counties: Bowie, Franklin, Titus.

Indexing & Storage: New cases are available in the index after filing date. Open records are located at the Plano Division.

Fee & Payment Notes: Payment may be made by money order, cashier check. Business checks are not accepted. Personal checks are not accepted.

Phone Search: An automated voice case information service (VCIS) is available. Call VCIS at 800-466-1694 or 903-590-1217.

Mail Search: A stamped self addressed envelope is not required.

In Person Search: In person searching available.

PACER: Toll-free dial-up access: 800-466-1681. Local dial-up access: 903-590-1220. Case records are available back to 1989. Records are purged every six months. New civil records are available online after 1 day. PACER is available online at http://pacer.txeb.uscourts.gov/. Document images available.

Electronic Filing: Information is available online at https://ecf.txeb.uscourts.gov

Tyler Division 200 E Ferguson, 2nd Floor, Tyler, TX 75702 (Courier Address: Use mail address for courier delivery), 903-590-1212, Fax: 903-590-1226.

www.txeb.uscourts.gov

Counties: Anderson, Cherokee, Gregg, Henderson, Panola, Rains, Rusk, Smith, Van Zandt, Wood.

Indexing & Storage: Cases are indexed by debtor as well as by case number. New cases are available in the index 1 day after filing date. Records are also indexed on microfiche. Card index is only for cases prior to October 1987. District wide searches are available for information from 10/87 from this court. This court maintains automated. Case records and all finance records for the other divisions in this district.

Fee & Payment Notes: Payment may be made by money order, cashier check, personal check. Payee: Clerk, US Bankruptcy Court. You are allowed to make your own copies. These copies cost $.25 per page.

Phone Search: This court will answer questions pertaining to information not available from VCIS. An automated voice case information service (VCIS) is available. Call VCIS at 800-466-1694 or 903-590-1217.

Mail Search: A stamped self addressed envelope is not required.

In Person Search: In person searching available.

PACER: Toll-free dial-up access: 800-466-1681. Local dial-up access: 903-590-1220. Case records are available back to 1989. Records are purged every six months. New civil records are available online after 1 day. PACER is available online at http://pacer.txeb.uscourts.gov. Document images available.

Electronic Filing: Information is available online at https://ecf.txeb.uscourts.gov

US District Court

Northern District of Texas

Abilene Division PO Box 1218, Abilene, TX 79604 (Courier Address: Room 2008, 341 Pine St, Abilene, TX 79601), 915-677-6311.

www.txnd.uscourts.gov

Counties: Callahan, Eastland, Fisher, Haskell, Howard, Jones, Mitchell, Nolan, Shackelford, Stephens, Stonewall, Taylor, Throckmorton.

Indexing & Storage: Cases are indexed by defendant, plaintiff, and case number. New cases are available in the index 2 days after filing date. A computer index is planned for early 1996. District wide searches can be conducted from this court for information from 1983.

Fee & Payment Notes: Payment may be made by money order, cashier check, personal check. Payee: Clerk, US District Court.

Phone Search: Only a name or case number will be released over the phone.

Mail Search: A stamped self addressed envelope is not required.

In Person Search: In person searching available.

PACER: Toll-free dial-up access: 800-684-2393. Local dial-up access: 214-753-2449. Case records are available back to June 1991. Records are purged once per year. New records are available online after 1 day. PACER is available online at http://pacer.txnd.uscourts.gov. Document images available.

Electronic Filing: (Currently in the process of implementing CM/ECF.)

Amarillo Division 205 E 5th St, Amarillo, TX 79101 (Courier Address: Use mail address for courier delivery), 806-324-2352.

www.txnd.uscourts.gov

Counties: Armstrong, Briscoe, Carson, Castro, Childress, Collingsworth, Dallam, Deaf Smith, Donley, Gray, Hall, Hansford, Hartley, Hemphill, Hutchinson, Lipscomb, Moore, Ochiltree, Oldham, Parmer, Potter, Randall, Roberts, Sherman, Swisher, Wheeler.

Indexing & Storage: Cases are indexed by defendant, plaintiff, and case number. New cases are available in the index immediately after filing date. Records are also indexed on microfiche. Open records are located at this court.

Fee & Payment Notes: Payment may be made by money order, cashier check, personal check. Payee: Clerk, US District Court.

Phone Search: No party information is released over the phone. Only pleadings are released over the phone.

Mail Search: A stamped self addressed envelope is not required.

In Person Search: In person searching available.

PACER: Toll-free dial-up access: 800-684-2393. Local dial-up access: 214-753-2449. Case records are available back to June 1991. Records are purged once per year. New records are available online after 1 day. PACER is available online at http://pacer.txnd.uscourts.gov. Document images available.

Electronic Filing: (Currently in the process of implementing CM/ECF.)

Dallas Division Room 14A20, 1100 Commerce St, Dallas, TX 75242 (Courier Address: Use mail address for courier delivery), 214-753-2200.

www.txnd.uscourts.gov

Counties: Dallas, Ellis, Hunt, Johnson, Kaufman, Navarro, Rockwall.

Indexing & Storage: Cases are indexed by defendant, plaintiff, and case number. New cases are available in the index 2 days after filing date. Computer index goes back to 1990 for the entire district. Records are also indexed on microfiche since 1957. District wide searches are available for information from 1957 forward from this division.

Fee & Payment Notes: Payment may be made by money order, cashier check, personal check, Visa, Mastercard. Payee: Clerk, US District Court. You are allowed to make your own copies. These copies cost $.25 per page.

Phone Search: Only computerized docket information will be released over the phone.

In Person Search: In person searching available.

PACER: Toll-free dial-up access: 800-684-2393. Local dial-up access: 214-753-2449. Document images available. Case records are available back to June 1991. Records are purged once per year. New records are available online after 1 day. PACER is available online at http://pacer.txnd.uscourts.gov. Document images available.

Electronic Filing: (Currently in the process of implementing CM/ECF.)

Fort Worth Division Clerk's Office, 501 W Tenth St, Room 310, Fort Worth, TX 76102 (Courier Address: Use mail address for courier delivery), 817-978-3132.

www.txnd.uscourts.gov

Counties: Comanche, Erath, Hood, Jack, Palo Pinto, Parker, Tarrant, Wise.

Indexing & Storage: Cases are indexed by defendant, plaintiff, and case number. New cases are available in the index 1 day after filing date. Computer records go back to 1990 for civil cases and 1993 for criminal cases. Records are also indexed on microfiche. District wide searches for information from 1957 are available from this court.

Fee & Payment Notes: Payment may be made by money order, cashier check, personal check. Payee: Clerk, US District Court. You are allowed to make your own copies. These copies cost $.25 per page.

Phone Search: The court will only release minimal information about a case when the caller already has a case number. They will not search for case numbers over the phone.

Mail Search: A stamped self addressed envelope is not required.

In Person Search: In person searching available.

PACER: Toll-free dial-up access: 800-684-2393. Local dial-up access: 214-753-2449. Case records are available back to June 1991. Records are purged once per year. New records are available online after 1 day. PACER is available online at http://pacer.txnd.uscourts.gov. Document images available.

Electronic Filing: (Currently in the process of implementing CM/ECF.)

Lubbock Division Clerk, Room 209, 1205 Texas Ave, Lubbock, TX 79401 (Courier: Use mail address for courier delivery), 806-472-7624.

www.txnd.uscourts.gov

Counties: Bailey, Borden, Cochran, Crosby, Dawson, Dickens, Floyd, Gaines, Garza, Hale, Hockley, Kent, Lamb, Lubbock, Lynn, Motley, Scurry, Terry, Yoakum.

Indexing & Storage: Cases are indexed by defendant, plaintiff, and case number. New cases are available in the index 1 day after filing date. Records are also indexed on microfiche. No records have been sent to the Federal Records Center.

Fee & Payment Notes: Payment may be made by money order, cashier check, personal check. Payee: Clerk, US District Court.

In Person Search: In person searching available.

PACER: Toll-free dial-up access: 800-684-2393. Local dial-up access: 214-753-2449. Case records are available back to June 1991. Records are purged once per year. New records are available online after 1 day. PACER is available online at http://pacer.txnd.uscourts.gov. Document images available.

Electronic Filing: (Currently in the process of implementing CM/ECF.)

San Angelo Division Clerk's Office, Room 202, 33 E Twohig, San Angelo, TX 76903 (Courier Address: Use mail address for courier delivery), 915-655-4506, Fax: 915-658-6826.

www.txnd.uscourts.gov

Counties: Brown, Coke, Coleman, Concho, Crockett, Glasscock, Irion, Menard, Mills, Reagan, Runnels, Schleicher, Sterling, Sutton, Tom Green.

Indexing & Storage: Cases are indexed by defendant, plaintiff, and case number. New cases are available in the index immediately after filing date. Records are also indexed on microfiche. Civil records are retained for 3 years. Criminal records are retained for 7 to 8 years.

Fee & Payment Notes: Payment may be made by money order, cashier check, personal check. Payee: Clerk, US District Court.

Phone Search: Only docket information available by telephone.

Fax Search: Fax requests cost the same as mail requests and require prepayment.

In Person Search: In person searching available.

PACER: Toll-free dial-up access: 800-684-2393. Local dial-up access: 214-753-2449. Case records are available back to June 1991. Records are purged once per year. New records are available online after 1 day. PACER is available online at http://pacer.txnd.uscourts.gov. Document images available.

Electronic Filing: (Currently in the process of implementing CM/ECF.)

Wichita Falls Division PO Box 1234, Wichita Falls, TX 76307 (Courier Address: Room 203, 1000 Lamar, Wichita Falls, TX 76301), 940-767-1902, Fax: 940-767-2526.

www.txnd.uscourts.gov

Counties: Archer, Baylor, Clay, Cottle, Foard, Hardeman, King, Knox, Montague, Wichita, Wilbarger, Young.

Indexing & Storage: Cases are indexed by defendant, plaintiff, and case number. New cases

are available in the index immediately after filing date. Records are also indexed on microfiche. Open records are located at this court.

Fee & Payment Notes: Payment may be made by money order, cashier check, personal check. Payee: Clerk, US District Court.

Phone Search: Only docket information is available by phone.

Fax Search: Will accept fax for price quote only.

In Person Search: In person searching available.

PACER: Toll-free dial-up access: 800-684-2393. Local dial-up access: 214-753-2449. Case records are available back to June 1991. Records are purged once per year. New records are available online after 1 day. PACER is available online at http://pacer.txnd.uscourts.gov. Document images available.

Electronic Filing: (Currently in the process of implementing CM/ECF.)

US Bankruptcy Court

Northern District of Texas

Amarillo Division PO Box 15960, Amarillo, TX 79105 (Courier Address: 624 Polk St, Suite 100, Amarillo, TX 79101), 806-324-2302.

www.txnb.uscourts.gov

Counties: Armstrong, Briscoe, Carson, Castro, Childress, Collingsworth, Dallam, Deaf Smith, Donley, Gray, Hall, Hansford, Hartley, Hemphill, Hutchinson, Lipscomb, Moore, Ochiltree, Oldham, Parmer, Potter, Randall, Roberts, Sherman, Swisher, Wheeler.

Indexing & Storage: Cases are indexed by debtor as well as by case number. New cases are available in the index immediately after filing date. Card index available prio to June 1988. Open records are located at this court.

Fee & Payment Notes: Payment may be made by money order, cashier check, business check. Personal checks are not accepted. Law firm checks are accepted. Payee: Clerk, US Bankruptcy Court. You are allowed to make your own copies. These copies cost $.50 per page. The search fee is required should the court have to pull the file and count pages and the fee is $15.00 per case file. The court does not charge to do a name search.

Phone Search: Only docket information is available by phone. An automated voice case information service (VCIS) is available. Call VCIS at 800-886-9008 or 214-753-2128.

In Person Search: In person searching available.

PACER: Toll-free dial-up access: 888-225-1738. Local dial-up access: 214-753-2134. Case records are available back to 1994. Records are purged every six months. New civil records are available online after 1 day. PACER is available online at https://pacer.txnb.uscourts.gov. Document images available.

Electronic Filing: (Currently in the process of implementing CM/ECF.)

Dallas Division 1100 Commerce St, Suite 12A24, Dallas, TX 75242-1496 (Courier: Use mail address for courier delivery), 214-753-2000.

www.txnb.uscourts.gov

Counties: Dallas, Ellis, Hunt, Johnson, Kaufman, Navarro, Rockwall.

Indexing & Storage: Cases are indexed by debtor and creditors as well as by case number. New cases are available in the index 1-2 days after filing date. District wide searches are available for records from 8/92 to the present from this division. This court maintains records for the Wichita Falls Division.

Fee & Payment Notes: Payment may be made by money order. Business checks are not accepted. Personal checks are not accepted. There is no search fee for searching docket sheets or claim registers. Payee: Clerk, US Bankruptcy Court.

Phone Search: Only docket information is available by phone. An automated voice case information service (VCIS) is available. Call VCIS at 800-886-9008 or 214-753-2128.

In Person Search: In person searching available.

PACER: Toll-free dial-up access: 888-225-1738. Local dial-up access: 214-753-2134. Case records are available back to 1994. Records are purged every six months. New civil records are available online after 1 day. PACER is available online at https://pacer.txnb.uscourts.gov. Document images available.

Electronic Filing: (Currently in the process of implementing CM/ECF.)

Fort Worth Division 501 W 10th, Suite 147, Fort Worth, TX 76102 (Courier Address: Use mail address for courier delivery), 817-333-6000, Fax: 817-333-6001.

www.txnb.uscourts.gov

Counties: Comanche, Erath, Hood, Jack, Palo Pinto, Parker, Tarrant, Wise.

Indexing & Storage: Cases are indexed by debtor as well as by case number. New cases are available in the index 1-2 days after filing date. Records up to 1986 are on index cards. Complete August 1, 1992 through the present are indexed on computer. From 1987 to August 1, 1992, records are indexed manually. Closed cases are held in house as long as there is space to store them. They are sent opnce at year end to the Fort Worth Federal Records Center.

Fee & Payment Notes: Payment may be made by money order, cashier check, personal check. Debtor's checks are not accepted. Payee: Clerk, US Bankruptcy Court. You are allowed to make your own copies. These copies cost $.25 per page.

Phone Search: Only docket information is available by phone. A record can be searched over the phone by debtor's name for records from 1987 to the present. An automated voice case information service (VCIS) is available. Call VCIS at 800-886-9008 or 214-753-2128.

In Person Search: In person searching available.

PACER: Toll-free dial-up access: 888-225-1738. Local dial-up access: 214-753-2134. Case records are available back to 1994. Records are purged every six months. New civil records are available online after 1 day. PACER is available online at https://pacer.txnb.uscourts.gov. Document images available.

Electronic Filing: (Currently in the process of implementing CM/ECF.)

Lubbock Division 306 Federal Bldg, 1205 Texas Ave, Lubbock, TX 79401-4002 (Courier Address: Use mail address for courier delivery), 806-472-5000.

www.txnb.uscourts.gov

Counties: Bailey, Borden, Brown, Callahan, Cochran, Cooke, Coleman, Concho, Crockett, Crosby, Dawson, Dickens, Eastland, Fisher, Floyd, Gaines, Garza, Glasscock, Hale, Haskell, Hockley, Howard, Irion, Jones, Kent, Lamb, Lubbock, Lynn, Menard, Mills, Mitchell,Motley, Nolan, Reagan, Runnels, Schleicher, Scurry, Shackelford, Stephens, Sterling, Stonewall, Sutton, Taylor, Terry, Throckmorton, Tom Green, Yoakum.

Indexing & Storage: Cases are indexed by debtor as well as by case number. New cases are available in the index 1-2 days after filing date. Open records are located at this court.

Fee & Payment Notes: Payment may be made by money order, cashier check, business check. Personal checks are not accepted. Debtor's checks are not accepted. Payee: Clerk, US Bankruptcy Court.

Phone Search: Only docket information is available by phone. A record can be searched over the phone by debtor's name for records from 1987 to the present. An automated voice case information service (VCIS) is available. Call VCIS at 800-886-9008 or 214-753-2128.

In Person Search: In person searching available.

PACER: Toll-free dial-up access: 888-225-1738. Local dial-up access: 214-753-2134. Case records are available back to 1994. Records are purged every six months. New civil records are available online after 1 day. PACER is available online at https://pacer.txnb.uscourts.gov. Document images available.

Electronic Filing: (Currently in the process of implementing CM/ECF.)

Wichita Falls Division c/o Dallas Division, Suite 12A24, 1100 Commerce St, Dallas, TX 75242-1496 (Courier Address: Use mail address for courier delivery), 214-753-2000.

www.txnb.uscourts.gov

Counties: Archer, Baylor, Clay, Cottle, Foard, Hardeman, King, Knox, Montague, Wichita, Wilbarger, Young.

Indexing & Storage: New cases are available in the index after filing date. Open records are located at the Dallas Division.

Fee & Payment Notes: Payment may be made by money order, cashier check. Business checks are not accepted. Personal checks are not accepted.

Phone Search: An automated voice case information service (VCIS) is available. Call VCIS at 800-886-9008 or 214-753-2128.

In Person Search: In person searching available.

PACER: Toll-free dial-up access: 888-225-1738. Local dial-up access: 214-753-2134. Case records are available back to 1994. Records are purged every six months. New civil records are available online after 1 day. PACER is available online at https://pacer.txnb.uscourts.gov. Document images available.

Electronic Filing: (Currently in the process of implementing CM/ECF.)

US District Court

Southern District of Texas

Brownsville Division 600 E Harrison St Rm 101, Brownsville, TX 78520-7114 (Courier Address: Use mail address for courier delivery., 600 E Harrison St #101,), 956-548-2500, Fax: 956-548-2598.

www.txsd.uscourts.gov

Counties: Cameron, Willacy.

Indexing & Storage: Cases are indexed by defendant, plaintiff, and case number. New cases are available in the index 2 days after filing date. Records are also indexed on microfiche. Open records are located at this court.

Fee & Payment Notes: Payment may be made by money order, cashier check, personal check. Payee: Clerk, US District Court.

Phone Search: Only docket information is available by phone.

In Person Search: In person searching available.

PACER: Toll-free dial-up access: 800-998-9037. Local dial-up access: 713-250-5000. Case records are available back to June 1990. Records are purged every six months. New records are available online after 1 day. PACER is available online at http://pacer.txs.uscourts.gov. Document images available.

Corpus Christi Division Clerk's Office, 1133 N. Shoreline Blvd., #208, Corpus Christi, TX 78401 (Courier Address: Use mail address for courier delivery), 361-888-3142.

www.txsd.uscourts.gov

Counties: Aransas, Bee, Brooks, Duval, Jim Wells, Kenedy, Kleberg, Live Oak, Nueces, San Patricio.

Indexing & Storage: Cases are indexed by defendant, plaintiff, and case number. New cases are available in the index 3 to 5 days after filing date. Records are also indexed on microfiche. Open records are located at this court.

Fee & Payment Notes: Payment may be made by money order, cashier check, personal check. Payee: Clerk, US District Court.

Phone Search: Searching not available by phone.

In Person Search: In person searching available.

PACER: Toll-free dial-up access: 800-998-9037. Local dial-up access: 713-250-5000. Case records are available back to June 1990. Records are purged every six months. New records are available online after 1 day. PACER is available online at http://pacer.txs.uscourts.gov. Document images available.

Galveston Division Clerk's Office, PO Drawer 2300, Galveston, TX 77553 (Courier Address: 601 Rosenberg, Room 411, Galveston, TX 77550), 409-766-3530.

www.txsd.uscourts.gov

Counties: Brazoria, Chambers, Galveston, Matagorda.

Indexing & Storage: Cases are indexed by defendant, plaintiff, and case number. New cases are available in the index 1 day after filing date. Records are also indexed on microfiche. Open records are located at this court.

Fee & Payment Notes: Payment may be made by money order, cashier check, business check.

Personal checks are not accepted. Payee: Clerk, US District Court. You are allowed to make your own copies. These copies cost $.50 per page.

Phone Search: Only the status of the case and the trial settings will be released over the phone.

In Person Search: In person searching available.

PACER: Toll-free dial-up access: 800-998-9037. Local dial-up access: 713-250-5000. Case records are available back to June 1990. Records are purged every six months. New records are available online after 1 day. PACER is available online at http://pacer.txs.uscourts.gov. Document images available.

Houston Division PO Box 61010, Houston, TX 77208 (Courier Address: Room 1217, 515 Rusk, Houston, TX 77002), 713-250-5500.

www.txsd.uscourts.gov

Counties: Austin, Brazos, Colorado, Fayette, Fort Bend, Grimes, Harris, Madison, Montgomery, San Jacinto, Walker, Waller, Wharton.

Indexing & Storage: Cases are indexed by defendant, plaintiff, and case number. New cases are available in the index 2 days after filing date. Mail searches must be coordinated through the court's copy service (IKON). Call 713-236-0903. They charge $8.12 per search plus $.29 per page for copies. Records are also indexed on microfiche. District wide searches are available for information from 1979 forward from this court. Criminal docketing for the district is performed in Houston.

Fee & Payment Notes: Payment may be made by money order, cashier check, personal check. Payee: Clerk, US District Court.

Phone Search: Searching not available by phone.

Mail Search: A stamped self addressed envelope is not required.

In Person Search: In person searching available.

PACER: Toll-free dial-up access: 800-998-9037. Local dial-up access: 713-250-5000. Case records are available back to June 1990. Records are purged every six months. New records are available online after 1 day. PACER is available online at http://pacer.txs.uscourts.gov. Document images available.

Laredo Division PO Box 597, Laredo, TX 78042-0597 (Courier Address: Room 319, 1300 Matamoros, Laredo, TX 78040), 956-723-3542, Fax: 956-726-2289.

www.txsd.uscourts.gov

Counties: Jim Hogg, La Salle, McMullen, Webb, Zapata.

Indexing & Storage: Cases are indexed by defendant, plaintiff, and case number. New cases are available in the index immediately after filing date. The style of the case is needed to search. Open records are located at this court.

Fee & Payment Notes: Payment may be made by cashier check. Business checks are not accepted. Personal checks are not accepted. Payee: Clerk, US District Court.

Phone Search: Searching not available by phone.

Mail Search: A stamped self addressed envelope is not required.

In Person Search: In person searching available.

PACER: Toll-free dial-up access: 800-998-9037. Local dial-up access: 713-250-5000. Case records are available back to June 1990. Records are

purged every six months. New records are available online after 1 day. PACER is available online at http://pacer.txs.uscourts.gov. Document images available.

McAllen Division Suite 1011, 1701 W Business Hwy 83, McAllen, TX 78501 (Courier Address: Use mail address for courier delivery), 956-618-8065.

www.txsd.uscourts.gov

Counties: Hidalgo, Starr.

Indexing & Storage: Cases are indexed by defendant, plaintiff, and case number. New cases are available in the index 1 day after filing date. This court has only been in operation for about 4 years. They have sent no records to the Fort Worth Federal Records Center.

Fee & Payment Notes: Payment may be made by money order, cashier check, business check. Personal checks are not accepted. Payee: Clerk, US District Court.

Phone Search: Only docket information available by phone.

In Person Search: In person searching available.

PACER: Toll-free dial-up access: 800-998-9037. Local dial-up access: 713-250-5000. Case records are available back to June 1990. Records are purged every six months. New records are available online after 1 day. PACER is available online at http://pacer.txs.uscourts.gov. Document images available.

Victoria Division Clerk US District Court, PO Box 1638, Victoria, TX 77902 (Courier Address: Room 406, 312 S Main, Victoria, TX 77901), 361-788-5000.

www.txsd.uscourts.gov

Counties: Calhoun, De Witt, Goliad, Jackson, Lavaca, Refugio, Victoria.

Indexing & Storage: Cases are indexed by defendant, plaintiff, and case number. New cases are available in the index 2 days after filing date. Open records are located at this court.

Fee & Payment Notes: Payment may be made by money order, cashier check, personal check. Payee: Clerk, US District Court. You are allowed to make your own copies. These copies cost $.50 per page.

Phone Search: Only docket information is available by phone.

In Person Search: In person searching available.

PACER: Toll-free dial-up access: 800-998-9037. Local dial-up access: 713-250-5000. Case records are available back to June 1990. Records are purged every six months. New records are available online after 1 day. PACER is available online at http://pacer.txs.uscourts.gov. Document images available.

US Bankruptcy Court

Southern District of Texas

Corpus Christi Division 1133 N. Shoreline Blvd. - 3rd Fl., Corpus Christi, TX 78401 (Courier Address: Use mail address for courier delivery), 361-888-3484.

www.txsd.uscourts.gov

Counties: Aransas, Bee, Brooks, Calhoun, Cameron, Duval, Goliad, Hidalgo, Jackson, Jim

Wells, Kenedy, Kleberg, Lavaca, Live Oak, Nueces, Refugio, San Patricio, Starr, Victoria, Willacy.Files from Brownsville, Corpus Christi, and McAllen are maintained here.

Indexing & Storage: Cases are indexed by debtor as well as by case number. New cases are available in the index 1-2 days after filing date. Records are also indexed on microfiche. Until further notice as of 9/1/97, this office will continue to hold. Case records for the Victoria Division.

Fee & Payment Notes: Payment may be made by money order, cashier check, personal check. Payee: Clerk, US Bankruptcy Court. You are allowed to make your own copies. These copies cost $.25 per page. There are dollar and coin-operated copiers available for public use.

Phone Search: An automated voice case information service (VCIS) is available. Call VCIS at 800-745-4459 or 713-250-5049.

In Person Search: In person searching available.

PACER: Toll-free dial-up access: 800-998-9037. Local dial-up access: 713-250-5000. Case records are available back to June 1, 1991. Records are purged every six months. New civil records are available online after 1-3 days. PACER is available online at http://pacer.txs.uscourts.gov. Document images available.

Electronic Filing: Information is available online at https://ecf.txsb.uscourts.gov

Houston Division Room 1217, 515 Rusk Ave, Houston, TX 77002 (Courier Address: Use mail address for courier delivery), 713-250-5500.

www.txsd.uscourts.gov

Counties: Austin, Brazoria, Brazos, Chambers, Colorado, De Witt, Fayette, Fort Bend, Galveston, Grimes, Harris, Jim Hogg*, La Salle*, Madison, Matagorda, McMullen*, Montgomery, San Jacinto, Walker,Waller, Wharton, Webb* Zapata*. Open. Case records for the counties marked with an asterisk are being moved to the Laredo Division.

Indexing & Storage: Cases are indexed by debtor as well as by case number. New cases are available in the index 1-2 days after filing date. Records are also indexed on microfiche. Some case files are maintained here from as early as 1978. Case files for the new Laredo Division are being moved to 1300 Matamors, Laredo, TX 78040, 956-726-2236 as of 9/1/97.

Fee & Payment Notes: Payment may be made by money order, cashier check, personal check. Payee: Clerk, US Bankruptcy Court.

Phone Search: Only docket information is available by phone. An automated voice case information service (VCIS) is available. Call VCIS at 800-745-4459 or 713-250-5049.

In Person Search: In person searching available.

PACER: Toll-free dial-up access: 800-998-9037. Local dial-up access: 713-250-5000. Case records are available back to June 1, 1991. Records are purged every six months. New civil records are available online after 1-3 days. PACER is available online at http://pacer.txs.uscourts.gov. Document images available.

Electronic Filing: Information is available online at https://ecf.txsb.uscourts.gov

US District Court

Western District of Texas

Austin Division Room 130, 200 W 8th St, Austin, TX 78701 (Courier Address: Use mail address for courier delivery), 512-916-5896.

www.txwd.uscourts.gov

Counties: Bastrop, Blanco, Burleson, Burnet, Caldwell, Gillespie, Hays, Kimble, Lampasas, Lee, Llano, McCulloch, Mason, San Saba, Travis, Washington, Williamson.

Indexing & Storage: Cases are indexed by defendant, plaintiff, and case number. New cases are available in the index 1 day after filing date. Records are also indexed on microfiche. Open records are located at this court.

Fee & Payment Notes: Payment may be made by money order, cashier check, personal check. Payee: Clerk, US District Court. You are allowed to make your own copies. These copies cost $.35 per page.

Phone Search: Only docket information is available by phone. The caller must have the case number.

In Person Search: In person searching available.

PACER: Toll-free dial-up access: 888-869-6365. Local dial-up access: 210-472-5256. Case records are available back to 1994. Records are purged every six months. New records are available online after 1 day. PACER is available online at http://pacer.txwd.uscourts.gov.

Del Rio Division Room L100, 111 E Broadway, Del Rio, TX 78840 (Courier Address: Use mail address for courier delivery), 830-703-2054.

www.txwd.uscourts.gov

Counties: Edwards, Kinney, Maverick, Terrell, Uvalde, Val Verde, Zavala.

Indexing & Storage: Cases are indexed by defendant, plaintiff, and case number. New cases are available in the index 1 month after filing date. Open records are located at this court.

Fee & Payment Notes: Payment may be made by money order, cashier check, personal check. Payee: Clerk, US District Court.

Phone Search: Only docket information is available by phone.

In Person Search: In person searching available.

PACER: Toll-free dial-up access: 888-869-6365. Local dial-up access: 210-472-5256. Case records are available back to 1994. Records are purged every six months. New records are available online after 1 day. PACER is available online at http://pacer.txwd.uscourts.gov.

El Paso Division US District Clerk's Office, Room 350, 511 E San Antonio, El Paso, TX 79901 (Courier Address: Use mail address for courier delivery), 915-534-6725.

www.txwd.uscourts.gov

Counties: El Paso.

Indexing & Storage: Cases are indexed by defendant, plaintiff, and case number. New cases are available in the index 1-2 days after filing date. Microfiche also available. Open records are located at this court.

Fee & Payment Notes: Payment may be made by money order, cashier check, personal check.

Payee: Clerk, US District Court. You are allowed to make your own copies. These copies cost $.25 per page.

Phone Search: Only docket information is available by phone.

In Person Search: In person searching available.

PACER: Toll-free dial-up access: 888-869-6365. Local dial-up access: 210-472-5256. Case records are available back to 1994. Records are purged every six months. New records are available online after 1 day. PACER is available online at http://pacer.txwd.uscourts.gov.

Midland Division Clerk, US District Court, 200 E Wall St, Rm 107, Midland, TX 79701 (Courier Address: Use mail address for courier delivery), 915-686-4001.

www.txwd.uscourts.gov

Counties: Andrews, Crane, Ector, Martin, Midland, Upton.

Indexing & Storage: Cases are indexed by defendant, plaintiff, and case number. New cases are available in the index immediately after filing date. Records are also indexed on microfiche. Open records are located at this court.

Fee & Payment Notes: Payment may be made by money order, cashier check, personal check. Payee: Clerk, US District Court. You are allowed to make your own copies. These copies cost $.25 per page. To do your own copies, you must bring your own change. They will not provide change.

Phone Search: Most information will be released over the phone.

In Person Search: In person searching available.

PACER: Toll-free dial-up access: 888-869-6365. Local dial-up access: 210-472-5256. Case records are available back to 1994. Records are purged every six months. New records are available online after 1 day. PACER is available online at http://pacer.txwd.uscourts.gov.

Pecos Division US Courthouse, 410 S Cedar St, Pecos, TX 79772 (Courier Address: Use mail address for courier delivery), 915-445-4228.

www.txwd.uscourts.gov

Counties: Brewster, Culberson, Hudspeth, Jeff Davis, Loving, Pecos, Presidio, Reeves, Ward, Winkler.

Indexing & Storage: Cases are indexed by defendant, plaintiff, and case number. New cases are available in the index immediately after filing date. Open records are located at this court.

Fee & Payment Notes: Payment may be made by money order, cashier check, personal check. Debtor's checks are not accepted. Payee: Clerk, US District Court. You are allowed to make your own copies. These copies cost $.25 per page.

Phone Search: Searching not available by phone.

In Person Search: In person searching available.

PACER: Toll-free dial-up access: 888-869-6365. Local dial-up access: 210-472-5256. Case records are available back to 1994. Records are purged every six months. New records are available online after 1 day. PACER is available online at http://pacer.txwd.uscourts.gov.

San Antonio Division US Clerk's Office, 655 E Durango Blvd, Suite G-65, San Antonio, TX 78206 (Courier Address: Use mail address for courier delivery), 210-472-6550.

www.txwd.uscourts.gov

Counties: Atascosa, Bandera, Bexar, Comal, Dimmit, Frio, Gonzales, Guadalupe, Karnes, Kendall, Kerr, Medina, Real, Wilson.

Indexing & Storage: Cases are indexed by defendant, plaintiff, and case number. New cases are available in the index 1-2 days after filing date. Records are also indexed on microfiche. Open records are located at this court.

Fee & Payment Notes: Payment may be made by money order, cashier check, personal check. Payee: Clerk, US District Court. You are allowed to make your own copies. These copies cost $.35 per page.

Phone Search: Only docket information is available by phone.

In Person Search: In person searching available.

PACER: Toll-free dial-up access: 888-869-6365. Local dial-up access: 210-472-5256. Case records are available back to 1994. Records are purged every six months. New records are available online after 1 day. PACER is available online at http://pacer.txwd.uscourts.gov.

Waco Division Clerk, Room 303, 800 Franklin, Waco, TX 76701 (Courier Address: Use mail address for courier delivery), 254-750-1501.

www.txwd.uscourts.gov

Counties: Bell, Bosque, Coryell, Falls, Freestone, Hamilton, Hill, Leon, Limestone, McLennan, Milam, Robertson, Somervell.

Indexing & Storage: Cases are indexed by defendant, plaintiff, and case number. New cases are available in the index 1-2 days after filing date. Open records are located at this court.

Fee & Payment Notes: Payment may be made by money order, cashier check, personal check. Payee: Clerk, US District Court. You are allowed to make your own copies. These copies cost $.25 per page.

Phone Search: Only docket information is available by phone.

In Person Search: In person searching available.

PACER: Toll-free dial-up access: 888-869-6365. Local dial-up access: 210-472-5256. Case records are available back to 1994. Records are purged every six months. New records are available online after 1 day. PACER is available online at http://pacer.txwd.uscourts.gov.

US Bankruptcy Court

Western District of Texas

Austin Division Homer Thornberry Judicial Bldg, 903 San Antonio, Room 322, Austin, TX 78701 (Courier Address: Use mail address for courier delivery), 512-916-5237.

www.txwb.uscourts.gov

Counties: Bastrop, Blanco, Burleson, Burnet, Caldwell, Gillespie, Hays, Kimble, Lampasas, Lee, Llano, Mason, McCulloch, San Saba, Travis, Washington, Williamson.

Indexing & Storage: Cases are indexed by debtor and creditors as well as by case number. New cases are available in the index 24 hours after filing date. Records are also indexed on microfiche. Open records are located at this court.

Fee & Payment Notes: Payment may be made by money order, cashier check, personal check, Visa or Mastercard. Debtor's checks are not accepted.

Payee: US Bankruptcy Court. You are allowed to make your own copies. These copies cost $.25 per page. Xerox copy service available in lobby. Fee is $.25 per page plus tax.

Phone Search: Only docket information is available by phone. An automated voice case information service (VCIS) is available. Call VCIS at 888-436-7477 or 210-472-4023.

In Person Search: In person searching available.

PACER: Toll-free dial-up access: 888-372-5708. Local dial-up access: 210-472-6262. Case records are available back to May 1, 1987. Records are purged every 6-8 months. New civil records are available online after 1 day. PACER is available online at http://pacer.txwb.uscourts.gov.

Electronic Filing: Information is available online at http://ecf.txwb.uscourts.gov

El Paso Division PO Box 971040, El Paso, TX 79925 (Courier Address: 8515 Lockheed, El Paso, TX 79997-1040), 915-779-7362, Fax: 915-779-5693.

www.txwb.uscourts.gov

Counties: El Paso.

Indexing & Storage: Cases are indexed by debtor as well as by case number. New cases are available in the index 24 hours after filing date. The computer index goes back to 1987. Prior to that there is a card index to 1987 and microfiche up to 1980. Open records are located at this court.

Fee & Payment Notes: Payment may be made by money order, cashier check, personal check. Payee: Clerk, US Bankruptcy Court. You are allowed to make your own copies. These copies cost $.25 per page.

Phone Search: Only docket information is available by phone. An automated voice case information service (VCIS) is available. Call VCIS at 888-436-7477 or 210-472-4023.

In Person Search: In person searching available.

PACER: Toll-free dial-up access: 888-372-5708. Local dial-up access: 210-472-6262. Case records are available back to May 1, 1987. Records are purged every 6-8 months. New civil records are available online after 1 day. PACER is available online at http://pacer.txwb.uscourts.gov.

Electronic Filing: Information is available online at http://ecf.txwb.uscourts.gov

Midland/Odessa Division US Post Office Annex, Room P-163, 100 E Wall St, Midland, TX 79701 (Courier Address: Use mail address for courier delivery), 915-683-1650.

www.txwb.uscourts.gov

Counties: Andrews, Brewster, Crane, Culberson, Ector, Hudspeth, Jeff Davis, Loving, Martin, Midland, Pecos, Presidio, Reeves, Upton, Ward, Winkler.

Indexing & Storage: Cases are indexed by debtor as well as by case number. New cases are available in the index immediately after filing date. Records are also indexed on microfiche. Records from the Pecos Division, which has been closed, have been transferred here.

Fee & Payment Notes: Payment may be made by money order, cashier check, personal check. Payee: Clerk, US Bankruptcy Court. You are allowed to make your own copies. These copies cost $.25 per page. To do your own copies, you must bring your own change. They will not provide change.

Phone Search: Only docket information is available by phone. An automated voice case information service (VCIS) is available. Call VCIS at 888-436-7477 or 210-472-4023.

In Person Search: In person searching available.

PACER: Toll-free dial-up access: 888-372-5708. Local dial-up access: 210-472-6262. Case records are available back to May 1, 1987. Records are purged every 6-8 months. New civil records are available online after 1 day. PACER is available online at http://pacer.txwb.uscourts.gov.

Electronic Filing: Information is available online at http://ecf.txwb.uscourts.gov

San Antonio Division PO Box 1439, San Antonio, TX 78295 (Courier Address: 615 E Houston St, San Antonio, TX 78205), 210-472-6720, Fax: 210-472-5916.

www.txsd.uscourts.gov/

Counties: Atascosa, Bandera, Bexar, Comal, Dimmit, Edwards, Frio, Gonzales, Guadalupe, Karnes, Kendall, Kerr, Kinney, Maverick, Medina, Real, Terrell, Uvalde, Val Verde, Wilson, Zavala.

Indexing & Storage: Cases are indexed by debtor as well as by case number. New cases are available in the index 24 hours after filing date. District wide searches are available for records within a 10 year span from this division.

Fee & Payment Notes: Payment may be made by cashier check. Business checks are not accepted, American Express, Visa, or Mastercard. Personal checks are not accepted. You are allowed to make your own copies. These copies cost $.35 per page. There is a copy service on site.

Phone Search: An automated voice case information service (VCIS) is available. Call VCIS at 888-436-7477 or 210-472-4023.

In Person Search: In person searching available.

PACER: Toll-free dial-up access: 888-372-5708. Local dial-up access: 210-472-6262. Case records are available back to May 1, 1987. Records are purged every 6-8 months. New civil records are available online after 1 day.

Electronic Filing: Information is available online at http://ecf.txwb.uscourts.gov

Waco Division St. Charles Place, Ste. 20, 600 Austin Ave, Waco, TX 76701 (Courier Address: Use mail address for courier delivery), 254-754-1481, Fax: 254-754-8385.

www.txwb.uscourts.gov

Counties: Bell, Bosque, Coryell, Falls, Freestone, Hamilton, Hill, Leon, Limestone, McLennan, Milam, Robertson, Somervell.

Indexing & Storage: Cases are indexed by debtor as well as by case number. New cases are available in the index 1 day after filing date. Records are also indexed on microfiche. Open records are located at this court.

Fee & Payment Notes: Payment may be made by money order, cashier check, personal check. Payee: Clerk, US Bankruptcy Court. You are allowed to make your own copies. These copies cost $.25 per page.

Phone Search: Only docket information is available by phone. An automated voice case information service (VCIS) is available. Call VCIS at 888-436-7477 or 210-472-4023.

In Person Search: In person searching available.

PACER: Toll-free dial-up access: 888-372-5708. Local dial-up access: 210-472-6262. Case records are available back to May 1, 1987. Records are purged every 6-8 months. New civil records are available online after 1 day. PACER is available online at http://pacer.txwb.uscourts.gov.

Electronic Filing: Information is available online at http://ecf.txwb.uscourts.gov

Texas County Courts

Court	Jurisdiction	No. of Courts	How Organized
District Courts*	General	416	416 Districts
County Courts*	Limited	182	
Combined Courts*		72	
Justice of the Peace Courts	By Precinct	834	
Municipal Courts	Municipal	863	
Probate Courts*	Probate	15	

* Profiled in this Sourcebook.

CIVIL									
Court	Tort	Contract	Real Estate	Min. Claim	Max. Claim	Small Claims	Estate	Eviction	Domestic Relations
District Courts*	X	X	X	$200	No Max				X
County Courts*	X	X	X	$200	Varies		X		X
Justice of the Peace Courts	X	X		$0	$5000	$5000		X	
Municipal Courts									
Probate Courts*							X		

CRIMINAL					
Court	Felony	Misdemeanor	DWI/DUI	Preliminary Hearing	Juvenile
District Courts*	X				X
County Courts*		X	X		X
Justice of the Peace Courts		X		X	
Municipal Courts		X			
Probate Courts*					

ADMINISTRATION   Office of Court Administration, PO Box 12066, Austin, TX, 78711; 512-463-1625, Fax: 512-463-1648. www.courts.state.tx.us

COURT STRUCTURE   The legal court structure for Texas takes up 30 pages in the "Texas Judicial Annual Report." Generally, Texas District Courts have general civil jurisdiction and exclusive felony jurisdiction, along with typical variations such as contested probate and divorce.

The County Court structure includes two forms of courts - "Constitutional" and "at Law" - which come in various configurations depending upon the county. County Courts' upper claim limits vary from $5,000 to $100,000. For civil matters up to $5000, we recommend searchers start at the Constitutional County Court as they, generally, offer a shorter waiting time for cases in urban areas. In addition, keep in mind that the Municipal Courts have, per the Texas manual, "limited civil penalties in cases involving dangerous dogs." In some counties the District Court or County Court handles evictions.

District Courts handle felonies. County Courts handle misdemeanors and general civil cases.

ONLINE ACCESS   Statewide appellate court case information is searchable for free on the Internet at www.info.courts.state.tx.us/appindex/appindex.exe. A number of individual county courts also offer online access to their records.

PROBATE COURTS   Probate is handled in Probate Court in the 18 largest counties and in District Courts or County Courts at Law elsewhere. However, the County Clerk is responsible for the records in every county.

Anderson County

District Court PO Box 1159, Palestine, TX 75802-1159; 903-723-7412. Hours: 8AM-Noon, 1-5PM (CST). *Felony, Civil.*

Civil Records: Access: Phone, mail, in person. Both court and visitors may perform in person searches. Search fee: $5.00 per name. Required to search: name, years to search. Civil cases indexed by defendant, plaintiff. Civil records on computer from 1984; prior on card index back to 1946.

Criminal Records: Access: Mail, in person. Both court and visitors may perform in person searches. Search fee: $5.00 per name. Required to search: name, years to search, DOB, SSN. Criminal records on computer from 1984; prior on card index.

General Information: Public access terminal is available. No juvenile or adoption records released. SASE required. Turnaround time 2 days. Fax notes: Do not fax. Copy fee: $1.00 per page. Certification fee: $1.00 per page. Fee payee: Anderson County District Clerk. Personal checks accepted. Prepayment is required.

County Court 500 N Church, Palestine, TX 75801; 903-723-7432. Hours: 8AM-5PM (CST). *Misdemeanor, Civil, Probate.*

Civil Records: Access: Mail, in person. Both court and visitors may perform in person searches. Search fee: $5.00 per name. Required to search: name, years to search. Civil cases indexed by defendant, plaintiff. Civil records on computer from 1982, land cases from 1983.

Criminal Records: Access: Mail, in person. Both court and visitors may perform in person searches. Search fee: $5.00 per name. Required to search: name, years to search, DOB. Criminal records on computer from 1969.

General Information: Public access terminal is available. SASE required. Turnaround time 1 week. Copy fee: $1.00 per page. Certification fee: $5.00. Fee payee: County Clerk. Personal checks accepted. Prepayment is required.

Andrews County

District Court PO Box 328, Andrews, TX 79714; 915-524-1417. Hours: 8AM-5PM (CST). *Felony, Civil.*

Civil Records: Access: Mail, in person. Only the court performs in person searches; visitors may not. Search fee: $5.00 per name. Required to search: name, years to search. Civil cases indexed by defendant, plaintiff. Civil records computerized since 1975.

Criminal Records: Access: Mail, in person. Only the court performs in person searches; visitors may not. Search fee: $5.00 per name. Required to search: name, years to search, DOB; also helpful: SSN. Criminal records computerized since 1975; prior to 1910.

General Information: No juvenile, mental, sealed, terminations or adoption records released. SASE required. Turnaround time 1 day. Fax notes: Do not fax. Copy fee: $1.00 for first page, $.25 each add'l. Certification fee: $2.00. Fee payee: District Clerk. Personal checks accepted. Prepayment is required.

County Court PO Box 727, Andrews, TX 79714; 915-524-1426. Hours: 8AM-5PM (CST). *Misdemeanor, Civil, Probate.*

Civil Records: Access: Phone, mail, in person. Both court and visitors may perform in person searches. Search fee: $5.00 per name. Required to search: name, years to search. Civil cases indexed by defendant, plaintiff. Civil records on computer since 1980; prior records in manual index.

Criminal Records: Access: Phone, mail, in person. Both court and visitors may perform in person searches. Search fee: $5.00 per name. Required to search: name, years to search, DOB or SSN; also helpful: sex. Criminal records on computer since 1985; prior records in manual index.

General Information: No juvenile, mental, sealed, or adoption records released. SASE not required. Turnaround time 1 day. Copy fee: $1.00 per page. Certification fee: $5.00. Fee payee: F. Wm. Hoermann County Clerk. Personal checks accepted if instate. Prepayment is required.

Angelina County

District Court PO Box 908, Lufkin, TX 75902; 936-634-4312; Fax: 936-634-5915. Hours: 8AM-5PM (CST). *Felony, Civil.*

Civil Records: Access: Mail, in person. Both court and visitors may perform in person searches. Search fee: $5.00 per name. Required to search: name, years to search. Civil cases indexed by defendant, plaintiff. Civil records on computer for 10 years, on index books from 1800s. Must state whether search is on plaintiff or defendant.

Criminal Records: Access: Mail, in person. Both court and visitors may perform in person searches. Search fee: $5.00 per name. Required to search: name, years to search, DOB; also helpful: SSN. Criminal records on computer from 1984, on index books from 1800s.

General Information: Public access terminal is available. No juvenile, mental, sealed, or adoption records released. SASE required. Turnaround time 2-3 days. Copy fee: $1.00 per page. Certification fee: $2.00. Fee payee: District Clerk. Personal checks accepted. Prepayment is required.

County Court PO Box 908, Lufkin, TX 75902; 936-634-8339; Fax: 936-634-8460. Hours: 8AM-5PM (CST). *Misdemeanor, Civil, Probate.*

Civil Records: Access: Mail, in person. Both court and visitors may perform in person searches. Search fee: $10.00 per name. Will search back to 1984. Required to search: name, years to search. Civil cases indexed by defendant, plaintiff. Civil records ogo back to 1972; computerized records go back to 1990.

Criminal Records: Access: Mail, in person. Both court and visitors may perform in person searches. Search fee: $10.00 per name. Will search back to 1984. Required to search: name, years to search; also helpful: DOB. Criminal records go back to 1910; computerized records go back to 1983.

General Information: No juvenile, mental, sealed, or adoption records released. SASE required. Turnaround time 1-2 days. Copy fee: $1.00 per page. Certification fee: $5.00. Fee payee: County Clerk. Business checks accepted. Prepayment is required.

Aransas County

District Court 301 North Live Oak, Rockport, TX 78382; 361-790-0128; Fax: 361-790-5211. Hours: 8AM-5PM (CST). *Felony, Civil.*

Civil Records: Access: Mail, in person. Both court and visitors may perform in person searches. Search fee: $5.00 per name. Required to search: name, years to search. Civil cases indexed by defendant, plaintiff. Civil records in index books from 1800s, computerized since 1999.

Criminal Records: Access: Mail, in person. Both court and visitors may perform in person searches. Search fee: $5.00 per name. Required to search: name, years to search. Criminal records in index books from 1800s, computerized since 1999.

General Information: Public access terminal is available. No juvenile, mental, sealed, or adoption records released. SASE required. Turnaround time 1-2 days. Copy fee: $1.00 per page. Certification fee: $1.00. Fee payee: District Clerk. Personal checks accepted. Prepayment is required.

County Court 301 N Live Oak, Rockport, TX 78382; 361-790-0122. Hours: 8AM-4:30PM (CST). *Misdemeanor, Civil, Probate.*

Civil Records: Access: Mail, fax, in person. Both court and visitors may perform in person searches. Search fee: $5.00 per name. Required to search: name, years to search. Civil cases indexed by defendant, plaintiff. Civil records in index books from 1947, computerized records go back to 1998.

Criminal Records: Access: Mail, fax, in person. Both court and visitors may perform in person searches. Search fee: $5.00 per name. Required to search: name, years to search, DOB. Criminal records in index books from 1947; computerized records go back to 1995.

General Information: Public access terminal is available. No juvenile, mental, sealed, or adoption records released. SASE is required. Turnaround time 2 days. Copy fee: $1.00 per page. Certification fee: $5.00. Fee payee: County Clerk. Personal checks accepted. Prepayment is required.

Archer County

District & County Court PO Box 815, Archer City, TX 76351; 940-574-4615. Hours: 8:30AM-5PM (CST). *Felony, Misdemeanor, Civil, Probate.*

Civil Records: Access: Phone, mail, in person. Both court and visitors may perform in person searches. Search fee: $5.00 per name. Fee is per index searched. Required to search: name, years to search. Civil cases indexed by defendant, plaintiff. Civil records in index books from 1900s.

Criminal Records: Access: Phone, mail, in person. Both court and visitors may perform in person searches. Search fee: $5.00 per name. Fee is per index searched. Required to search: name, years to search. Criminal records in index books from 1900s.

General Information: No juvenile, mental, sealed, or adoption records released. SASE required. Turnaround time 1 day. Copy fee: $1.00 per page. Certification fee: $1.00. County Court certification fee is $5.00. Fee payee: County Clerk or District Clerk. Personal checks accepted. Prepayment is required.

Armstrong County

District & County Court PO Box 309, Claude, TX 79019; 806-226-2081; Fax: 806-226-5301. Hours: 8AM-Noon, 1-5PM (CST). *Felony, Misdemeanor, Civil, Probate.*

Civil Records: Access: Mail, in person. Both court and visitors may perform in person searches. Search fee: $5.00 per name. Required to search: name, years to search. Civil cases indexed by defendant, plaintiff. Civil records in index books from 1800s.

Criminal Records: Access: Mail, in person. Both court and visitors may perform in person searches. Search fee: $5.00 per name. Required to search: name, years to search. Criminal records in index books from 1800s; computerized back to 1992.

General Information: No juvenile, mental, sealed, or adoption records released. SASE required. Turnaround time 1-2 days. Copy fee: $1.00 per page. Certification fee: $5.00. Fee payee: County Clerk. Personal checks accepted. Prepayment is required.

Atascosa County

District Court #52 Courthouse Circle, Jourdanton, TX 78026; 830-769-3011. Hours: 8AM-Noon, 1-5PM (CST). *Felony, Civil.*

Civil Records: Access: Mail, in person. Both court and visitors may perform in person searches. Search fee: $5.00 per name. Required to search: name, years to search; also helpful: address. Civil cases indexed by defendant, plaintiff. Civil records in index books from 1857.

Criminal Records: Access: Mail, in person. Both court and visitors may perform in person searches. Search fee: $5.00 per name. Required to search: name, years to search; also helpful: DOB, SSN. Criminal records in index books from 1857.

General Information: No juvenile, mental, sealed, or adoption records released. SASE required. Turnaround time 6 days. Fax notes: Fee to fax results is $2.00 per page. Copy fee: $1.00 per page. Certification fee: $1.00. Fee payee: District Clerk. Personal checks accepted.

County Court Circle Dr Rm 6-1, Jourdanton, TX 78026; 830-767-2511. Hours: 8AM-5PM (CST). *Misdemeanor, Civil, Probate.*

Civil Records: Access: Mail, in person. Both court and visitors may perform in person searches. No search fee. Required to search: name, years to search. Civil cases indexed by defendant, plaintiff. Civil records in index books from 1900s; on computer back to 2000.

Criminal Records: Access: In person only. Visitors must perform in person searches for themselves. No search fee. Required to search: name, years to search. Criminal records in index books from 1900s; on computer back to 2000.

General Information: No juvenile, mental, sealed, or adoption records released. SASE required. Turnaround time same day. Copy fee: $1.00 per page. Certification fee: $5.00. Fee payee: County Clerk. Personal checks accepted. Prepayment is required.

Austin County

District Court 1 East Main, Bellville, TX 77418-1598; 979-865-5911 X121. Hours: 8AM-Noon, 1-5PM (CST). *Felony, Civil.*

www.austincountyonline.com/dclerk.html

Civil Records: Access: Mail, in person. Both court and visitors may perform in person searches. Search fee: $5.00 per name. Required to search: name, years to search. Civil cases indexed by defendant, plaintiff. Civil records in index books from 1843; on computer back to 1995.

Criminal Records: Access: Mail, in person. Both court and visitors may perform in person searches. Search fee: $5.00 per name. Required to search: name, years to search; also helpful: DOB, SSN. Criminal records in index books from 1843; on computer back to 1996.

General Information: Public access terminal is available. No juvenile, mental, sealed, or adoption records released. SASE required. Turnaround time same day. Fax notes: Fee to fax results is $2.00 per document. Copy fee: $1.00 per page. Certification fee: Included in copy fee, if document complete. Fee payee: District Clerk. Personal checks accepted. Prepayment is required.

County Court at Law 1 E Main, Bellville, TX 77418; 979-865-5911; Fax: 979-865-0336. Hours: 8AM-5PM (CST). *Misdemeanor, Civil, Probate.*

Civil Records: Access: Mail, in person. Both court and visitors may perform in person searches. Search fee: $5.00 per name. Required to search: name, years to search. Civil cases indexed by defendant, plaintiff. Civil records on computer from 06/95, index books from 1843.

Criminal Records: Access: Mail, in person. Both court and visitors may perform in person searches. Search fee: $5.00 per name. Required to search: name, years to search, DOB; also helpful: SSN. Criminal records on computer from 05/95, index books from 1876.

General Information: No juvenile, mental, sealed, or adoption records released. SASE required. Turnaround time 2 days. Copy fee: $1.00 per page. Certification fee: $5.00. Fee payee: Carrie Gregor, County Clerk. Personal checks accepted. Prepayment is required.

Bailey County

District Court 300 S 1st St, Muleshoe, TX 79347; 806-272-3165; Fax: 806-272-3124. Hours: 8AM-5PM (CST). *Felony, Civil.*

Civil Records: Access: Phone, mail, fax, in person, online. Both court and visitors may perform in person searches. Search fee: $5.00 per name. Required to search: name, years to search. Civil cases indexed by defendant, plaintiff. Civil records in index books, archived from 1925, computerized back to 1995. Online access is through www.idocket.com; registration and password required. Records go back to 12/31/1995.

Criminal Records: Access: Phone, mail, in person, online. Both court and visitors may perform in person searches. Search fee: $5.00 per name. Required to search: name, years to search. Criminal records in index books, archived from 1925, computerized back to 1995. Online access is through www.idocket.com; registration and password required. Records go back to 12/31/1995.

General Information: No juvenile, mental, sealed, or adoption records released. SASE required. Turnaround time 1 day. Copy fee: $1.00 per page. Certification fee: $1.00. Fee payee: District Clerk. Personal checks accepted. Prepayment is required.

County Court 300 S 1st St, Muleshoe, TX 79347; 806-272-3044; Fax: 806-272-3538. Hours: 8AM-5PM (CST). *Misdemeanor, Civil, Probate.*

Civil Records: Access: Mail, in person, online. Both court and visitors may perform in person searches. Search fee: $10.00 per name. Required to search: name, years to search. Civil cases indexed by defendant, plaintiff. Civil records in index books, archived from 1925. Online access is through www.idocket.com; registration and password required. Records go back to 12/31/1995.

Criminal Records: Access: Mail, in person, online. Both court and visitors may perform in person searches. Search fee: $10.00 per name. Required to search: name, years to search. Criminal records in index books, archived from 1925. Online access is through www.idocket.com; registration and password required. Records go back to 12/31/1995.

General Information: No juvenile, mental, sealed, or adoption records released. SASE required. Turnaround time 10 days. Copy fee: $1.00 per page. Certification fee: $5.00. Fee payee: County Clerk. Personal checks accepted. Prepayment is required.

Bandera County

District Court PO Box 2688 (500 Main St), Bandera, TX 78003; 830-796-4606; Fax: 830-796-8323. 7:30AM-4:30PM (CST). *Felony, Civil, Probate.*

Civil Records: Access: Phone, fax, mail, in person, online. Both court and visitors may perform in person searches. Search fee: $5.00 per name. Required to search: name, years to search; also helpful: address. Civil cases indexed by defendant, plaintiff. Civil records on computer back to 1988, index books from 1857. Civil case information is available free online at www.idocket.com. Free searching is limited. Records go back to 12/31/1990.

Criminal Records: Access: Fax, mail, in person, online. Both court and visitors may perform in person searches. Search fee: $5.00 per name. Required to search: name, years to search, signed release; also helpful: address, DOB, SSN. Criminal records on computer back to 1988, index books from 1857. Online access is through www.idocket.com; registration and password required. Records go back to 12/31/1990.

General Information: Public access terminal is available. No juvenile, mental or sealed records released. SASE required. Turnaround time 2 days. Fax notes: Fee to fax results is $2.00 for first page, $1.00 each add'l. Copy fee: $1.00 per page certified; non-certified is $1.00 1st pg, $.25 each add'l. Certification fee: $5.00. Fee payee: Bandera County District Clerk. Personal checks accepted. Prepayment is required.

County Court PO Box 823 (500 Main St), Bandera, TX 78003; 830-796-3332; Fax: 830-796-8323. Hours: 8AM-4:30PM (CST). *Misdemeanor, Civil, Eviction, Probate.*

Note: The District Clerk can be reached at PO Box 2688 and 830-796-4606. PO Box and phone above is for County Clerk.

Civil Records: Access: Fax, mail, in person. Both court and visitors may perform in person searches. Search fee: $5.00 per name. Required to search: name, years to search; also helpful: address. Civil cases indexed by defendant, plaintiff. Civil records on computer from 1988, index books from 1857.

Criminal Records: Access: Fax, mail, in person. Both court and visitors may perform in person searches. Search fee: $5.00 per name. Required to search: name, years to search, signed release; also helpful: address, DOB, SSN. Criminal records on computer from 1988, index books from 1857.

General Information: No juvenile, mental or sealed records released. SASE required. Turnaround time 2 days. Fax notes: Fee to fax results is $2.00 for first page, $1.00 each add'l. Copy fee: $1.00 per page certified; non-certified is $1.00 1st pg, $.25 each add'l. Certification fee: $5.00. Fee payee: Bandera County Court Clerk. Personal checks accepted. Prepayment is required.

Bastrop County

District Court PO Box 770, Bastrop, TX 78602; 512-332-7244. Hours: 8AM-5PM (CST). *Felony, Civil.*

Civil Records: Access: Mail, in person. Both court and visitors may perform in person searches. Search fee: $5.00 per name. Required to search: name, years to search. Civil cases indexed by defendant, plaintiff. Civil records on microfilm from 1986, archived from early 1800s.

Criminal Records: Access: Mail, in person. Both court and visitors may perform in person searches. Search fee: $5.00 per name. Required to search: name, years to search, signed release. Criminal records on computer since 1989; prior on microfilm from 1986, archived from early 1800s.

General Information: No juvenile, mental, sealed, or adoption records released. SASE required. Turnaround time 1 day. Copy fee: $.25 per page. Certification fee: $1.00. Fee payee: District Clerk. Personal checks accepted.

County Court PO Box 577, Bastrop, TX 78602; 512-332-7234. Hours: 8AM-5:PM (CST). *Misdemeanor, Probate.*

Criminal Records: Access: Phone, mail, in person. Both court and visitors may perform in person searches. Search fee: $5.00 per name. Required to search: name, years to search, DOB, SSN. Criminal records on computer since 1986, prior on index books.

General Information: No juvenile, mental, sealed, or adoption records released. SASE required. Turnaround time 1-2 days. Fax notes: Fee to fax results is $5.00. Copy fee: $1.00 per page. Certification fee: $5.00. Fee payee: Bastrop County Clerk. Personal checks accepted. Prepayment is required.

Baylor County

District & County Court PO Box 689, Seymour, TX 76380; 940-888-3322. Hours: 8:30AM-5PM (CST). *Felony, Misdemeanor, Civil, Probate.*

Civil Records: Access: Phone, mail, in person. Both court and visitors may perform in person searches. Search fee: $10.00 per name. Required to search: name, years to search. Civil cases indexed by defendant, plaintiff. Civil records in books from 1900s.

Criminal Records: Access: Phone, mail, in person. Both court and visitors may perform in person searches. Search fee: $10.00 per name. Required to search: name, years to search. Criminal records in books from 1900s.

General Information: No juvenile, mental, sealed, or adoption records released. SASE required. Turnaround time 1-2 days. Copy fee: $1.00 per page. Certification fee: $2.00 felony, $5.00 misdemeanor for County Court certification. Fee payee: Baylor County Clerk. Personal checks accepted. Prepayment is required.

Bee County

District Court PO Box 666, Beeville, TX 78104-0666; 361-362-3242; Fax: 361-362-3282. Hours: 8AM-5PM (CST). *Felony, Civil.*

Civil Records: Access: Mail, in person. Both court and visitors may perform in person searches. Search fee: $5.00 per name. Required to search: name, years to search. Civil cases indexed by defendant, plaintiff. Civil records on index books from 1911.
Criminal Records: Access: Mail, in person. Both court and visitors may perform in person searches. Search fee: $5.00 per name. Required to search: name, years to search, signed release. Criminal records on index books from 1911.
General Information: No juvenile, mental, sealed, or adoption records released. SASE required. Turnaround time 1-3 days. Copy fee: $1.00 per page. Certification fee: $2.00. Fee payee: District Clerk. Personal checks accepted.

County Court 105 W Corpus Christi St, Rm 103, Beeville, TX 78102; 361-362-3245; Fax: 361-362-3247. Hours: 8AM-Noon, 1-5PM (CST). *Misdemeanor, Civil, Probate.*

Civil Records: Access: Phone, fax, mail, in person. Both court and visitors may perform in person searches. Search fee: $5.00 per name. Required to search: name, years to search. Civil cases indexed by defendant, plaintiff. Civil records on index books from 1900; computerized since 1995.
Criminal Records: Access: Phone, fax, mail, in person. Both court and visitors may perform in person searches. Search fee: $5.00 per name. Add $1.00 for certificate. Required to search: name, years to search, DOB; also helpful: SSN. Criminal records on index books from 1900; computerized since 1995.
General Information: No juvenile, mental, sealed, or adoption records released. SASE required. Turnaround time 1 day. Fax notes: Fee to fax results is $2.00 per page. Copy fee: $1.00 per page. Certification fee: $5.00. Fee payee: County Clerk. Personal checks accepted. Prepayment is required.

Bell County

District Court 104 S Main St, PO Box 909, Belton, TX 76513; 254-933-5197; Fax: 254-933-5199. Hours: 8AM-5PM (CST). *Felony, Civil.*

Civil Records: Access: Mail, in person. Both court and visitors may perform in person searches. Search fee: $10.00 per name. Required to search: name, years to search. Civil cases indexed by defendant, plaintiff. Civil records on computer back to 1987, alpha index from 1982, chrono from 1800.
Criminal Records: Access: Mail, in person. Both court and visitors may perform in person searches. Search fee: $10.00 per name. Required to search: name, years to search, DOB; also helpful, SSN, signed release, cause number. Criminal records on computer back to 1987, alpha index from 1982, chrono from 1800.
General Information: Public access terminal is available. No juvenile, mental, sealed, or adoption records released. SASE required. Turnaround time 1-2 days. Copy fee: $.50 per page. Certification fee: $1.00 per page. Fee payee: District Clerk, Bell County. Only cashiers checks and money orders accepted. Prepayment is required.

County Court PO Box 480, Belton, TX 76513; 254-933-5165; Civil phone: 254-933-5174; Criminal phone: 254-933-5170; Fax: 254-933-5176. Hours: 8AM-5PM (CST). *Misdemeanor, Civil, Probate.*

Civil Records: Access: Mail, in person. Both court and visitors may perform in person searches. Search fee:

$5.00 per name. Required to search: name, years to search. Civil cases indexed by defendant, plaintiff. Civil records on computer since September, 1989.
Criminal Records: Access: Mail, in person. Both court and visitors may perform in person searches. Search fee: $5.00 per name. Required to search: name, years to search, DOB, SSN. Criminal records on computer since 1986.
General Information: Public access terminal is available. No juvenile, mental, sealed, or adoption records released. SASE not required. Turnaround time 3-5 days. Copy fee: $1.00 per page. Certification fee: $1.00. Fee payee: County Clerk. Local checks only. Prepayment is required.

Bexar County

District Court - Central Records 100 Dolorosa, County Courthouse, Chief Court Clerk/Records, San Antonio, TX 78205; 210-335-2001; Civil phone: 210-335-2662; Criminal phone: 210-335-2217. Hours: 8AM-5PM (CST). *Felony, Civil.*

www.co.bexar.tx.us/dclerk

Note: There is a separate court clerk for civil and criminal, and fee for searching in each, though records are centralized.

Civil Records: Access: Mail, fax, online, in person. Both court and visitors may perform in person searches. Search fee: $5.00 per name. Required to search: name, years to search. Civil cases indexed by defendant, plaintiff. Civil records on computer from 1982-present, chrono index from 1909. Access to the remote online system requires $100 setup fee, plus a $25 monthly fee, plus inquiry fees. Call Jennifer Mann at 210-335-0212 for more information. Also, free online access to records is being implemented. Check www.co.bexar.tx.us/dclerk/e-Services/e-services.htm for updates. For fax requests, call court to request form, then submit form with payment with Discover Card.
Criminal Records: Access: Mail, fax, online, in person. Both court and visitors may perform in person searches. Search fee: $5.00 per name. Required to search: name, years to search, signed release, DOB. Criminal records on computer back to 1974, chrono index from 1909. Online access to criminal records is the same as civil. For fax requests, call court to request form, then submit form with payment with Discover card.
General Information: Public access terminal is available. No juvenile, mental, sealed, or adoption records released. SASE required. Turnaround time up to 10 days. Fax notes: Fee to fax results is $.50 per page. Copy fee: $.50 per page. Certification fee: $1.00 per page. Fee payee: District Clerk. Only cashiers checks and money orders accepted. Prepayment is required.

County Court - Civil Central Filing Dept. 100 Dolorosa, San Antonio, TX 78205-3083; 210-335-2231. 8AM-5PM (CST). *Civil.*

Note: There are twelve hearing locations in this county where open cases are held. All closed cases are forwarded here.

Civil Records: Access: Phone, mail, in person. Both court and visitors may perform in person searches. Search fee: $5.00 per name. Fee is for 10 year search. Required to search: name, years to search. Civil cases indexed by defendant, plaintiff. Civil records on computer go back 10 years, index books prior. Open and closed records maintained.
General Information: Public access terminal is available. No mental, sealed records released. SASE required. Turnaround time 1-2 days. Copy fee: $1.00 per page. Certification fee: $5.00. Fee payee: County Clerk. Personal checks accepted. Prepayment required.

County Court - Criminal 300 Dolorosa, #4101, San Antonio, TX 78205; 210-335-2238. Hours: 8AM-5PM (CST). *Misdemeanor.*

www.co.bexar.tx.us/dclerk

Criminal Records: Access: Mail, online, in person. Both court and visitors may perform in person searches. Search fee: $5.00 per name. Fee is per ten year period. $1.00 for each addt'l year. Required to search: name, years to search, DOB, signed release; also helpful: SSN. Criminal records on computer since 1983, alpha index since 1983, on card index form 1909, records go back to 1899. Access to the criminal online system requires $100 setup fee, plus a $25 monthly fee, plus inquiry fees. Call Jennifer Mann at 210-335-0212 for more information.
General Information: Public access terminal is available. No sealed records released. SASE requested. Turnaround time 2-3 days. Copy fee: $1.00 per page. Certification fee: $5.00 plus $1.00 per page. Fee payee: County Clerk. Personal checks accepted. Checks must be in state. Prepayment is required.

Probate Court #2 100 Dolorosa St, Rm 117, San Antonio, TX 78205; 210-335-2546. Hours: 8AM-5PM (CST). *Probate.*

www.co.bexar.tx.us/pcourt/probatecourts.htm

Blanco County

District & County Court PO Box 65, Johnson City, TX 78636; 830-868-7357. Hours: 8AM-4:30PM (CST). *Felony, Misdemeanor, Civil, Probate.*

Civil Records: Access: Mail, in person. Both court and visitors may perform in person searches. Search fee: $5.00 per name. Required to search: name, years to search. Civil cases indexed by defendant, plaintiff. Civil records on computer from 1994, index books back to 1876.
Criminal Records: Access: Mail, in person. Both court and visitors may perform in person searches. Search fee: $5.00 per name. Required to search: name, years to search, DOB, SSN. Criminal records on computer from 1994, index books back to 1876.
General Information: Public access terminal is available. No juvenile, mental, sealed, or adoption records released. SASE required. Turnaround time 1 day. Copy fee: $1.00 per page. Certification fee: $5.00. Fee payee: County Clerk. Personal checks accepted. Prepayment is required.

Borden County

District & County Court PO Box 124, Gail, TX 79738; 806-756-4312. Hours: 8AM-5PM (CST). *Felony, Misdemeanor, Civil, Probate.*

Civil Records: Access: Mail, in person. Both court and visitors may perform in person searches. Search fee: $5.00 per name. Required to search: name, years to search. Civil cases indexed by defendant, plaintiff. Civil records in index books, archived from 1900.
Criminal Records: Access: Mail, in person. Only the court performs in person searches; visitors may not. Search fee: $5.00 per name. Required to search: name, years to search. Criminal records in index books, archived from 1900.
General Information: No juvenile, mental, sealed, or adoption records released. SASE required. Turnaround time 1 week. Fax notes: Fee to fax results is $1.00 per page. Copy fee: $1.00 per page. Certification fee: $1.00. Fee payee: District Clerk. Personal checks accepted. Prepayment is required.

Bosque County

District Court Main & Morgan St, PO Box 674, Meridian, TX 76665; 254-435-2334. Hours: 8AM-5PM (CST). *Felony, Civil.*

Civil Records: Access: Mail, in person. Both court and visitors may perform in person searches. Search fee: $5.00 per name. Required to search: name, years to search. Civil cases indexed by defendant, plaintiff. Civil records on computer from 1984, files/books from 1870s.

Criminal Records: Access: Mail, in person. Both court and visitors may perform in person searches. Search fee: $5.00 per name. Required to search: name, years to search, DOB or SSN. Computerized from 1984, criminal records on books/files from 1856.

General Information: No juvenile, mental, sealed, or adoption records released. SASE required. Turnaround time 1 day. Copy fee: $1.00 per page. Certification fee: $1.00. Fee payee: District Clerk. Personal checks accepted.

County Court PO Box 617, Meridian, TX 76665; 254-435-2201; Fax: 254-435-2152. Hours: 8AM-5PM (CST). *Misdemeanor, Civil, Probate.*

Civil Records: Access: Mail, in person. Both court and visitors may perform in person searches. Search fee: $5.00 per name. Required to search: name, years to search. Civil cases indexed by defendant, plaintiff. Civil records in index books from 1854; on computer back to 1997.

Criminal Records: Access: Mail, in person. Both court and visitors may perform in person searches. Search fee: $5.00 per name. Required to search: name, years to search, DOB, SSN. Criminal records in index books from 1854; on computer back to 1997.

General Information: Public access terminal is available. No juvenile, mental, sealed, or adoption records released. SASE required. Turnaround time 1-2 days. Copy fee: $1.00 per page. Certification fee: $5.00. Fee payee: County Clerk. Personal checks accepted. In state checks only. Prepayment is required.

Bowie County

District & County Court 710 James Bowie Dr, PO Box 248, New Boston, TX 75570; 903-628-6750; Probate phone: 903-628-6740. Hours: 8AM-5PM (CST). *Felony, Misdemeanor, Civil, Probate.*

Note: Probate records are at this address in the County Clerk's office.

Civil Records: Access: Mail, in person. Both court and visitors may perform in person searches. Search fee: $5.00 per name. Required to search: name, years to search. Civil cases indexed by defendant, plaintiff. Civil records on computer from 1978, on microfiche from 1900s, chrono index from 1800s.

Criminal Records: Access: Mail, in person. Both court and visitors may perform in person searches. Search fee: $5.00 per name. Required to search: name, years to search, DOB. Criminal records on computer from 1978, on microfiche from 1900s, chrono index from 1800s.

General Information: No juvenile, mental, sealed, or adoption records released. SASE required. Turnaround time 1 day. Copy fee: $1.00 per page. Certification fee: $2.00. Fee payee: District Clerk. Personal checks accepted.

Brazoria County

District Court 111 E Locus #500, Angleton, TX 77515-4678; 979-864-1316. Hours: 8AM-5PM (CST). *Felony, Civil.*

www.brazoria-county.com/dclerk

Civil Records: Access: Phone, mail, in person. Both court and visitors may perform in person searches. Search fee: $5.00 per name. Fee is per 10 year period. Required to search: name, years to search. Civil cases indexed by defendant, plaintiff. Civil records on computer from 1986, index chrono from 1900, prior alpha.

Criminal Records: Access: Phone, mail, in person. Both court and visitors may perform in person searches. Search fee: $5.00 per name. Fee is per 10 year period. Required to search: name, years to search, DOB, signed release; also helpful: SSN. Criminal records on

computer from 1986, index chrono from 1900, prior alpha.

General Information: Public access terminal is available. No juvenile, mental, sealed, or adoption records released. SASE required. Turnaround time up to 1 week. Copy fee: $1.00 per page. Certification fee: $1.00. Fee payee: District Clerk. Only cashiers checks and money orders accepted. Prepayment is required.

County Court 111 E Locust #200, Angleton, TX 77515; Civil phone: 979-864-1385; Criminal phone: 979-864-1380; Fax: 979-848-1031 (civil); -1020 (Crim.). 8AM-5PM (CST). *Misdemeanor, Civil.*

Civil Records: Access: Fax, mail, in person. Both court and visitors may perform in person searches. Search fee: $5.00 per name. Required to search: name, years to search. Civil cases indexed by defendant, plaintiff. Civil records on computer from 1984; prior on books or microfiche back to 1800s. Fee must be prepaid before faxing search request.

Criminal Records: Access: Fax, mail, in person. Both court and visitors may perform in person searches. Search fee: $5.00 per name. Required to search: name, years to search, DOB. Criminal records on computer from 1984; prior on books or microfiche back to 1800s.

General Information: Public access terminal is available. No juvenile, mental, sealed records released. SASE required. Turnaround time 2 days. Copy fee: $1.00 per page. Certification fee: $5.00 per document. Fee payee: Joyce Hudman, County Clerk. Personal checks accepted. Prepayment is required.

Probate Court 111 E Locust #200, Angleton, TX 77515; 979-864-1367; Fax: 979-864-1830. Hours: 8AM-5PM (CST). *Probate.*

Brazos County

District Court 300 E 26th St #216 (PO Box 2208), Bryan, TX 77806; 979-361-4233; Fax: 979-361-0197. Hours: 8AM-5PM (CST). *Felony, Civil.*

www.co.brazos.tx.us/disclerk

Civil Records: Access: Mail, in person. Both court and visitors may perform in person searches. Search fee: $5.00 per name. Required to search: name, years to search. Civil cases indexed by defendant, plaintiff. Civil records on computer, index chrono from 1800s.

Criminal Records: Access: Mail, in person. Both court and visitors may perform in person searches. Search fee: $5.00 per name. Required to search: name, years to search; also helpful: DOB, SSN. Criminal records on computer, index chrono from 1800s.

General Information: No juvenile, mental, sealed, or adoption records released. SASE required. Turnaround time 1-2 days. Copy fee: $.50 per page. Certification fee: $1.00 per page. Fee payee: District Clerk. Personal checks accepted. Prepayment is required.

County Court 300 E 26th St #120, Bryan, TX 77803; 979-361-4128. Hours: 8AM-5PM (CST). *Misdemeanor, Civil under $500, Probate.*

Note: County Clerk holds misdemeanor records prior to 1986 only. Newer cases are filed at the District Clerks Office.

Civil Records: Access: Mail, in person. Both court and visitors may perform in person searches. Search fee: $5.00 per name. Required to search: name, years to search. Civil cases indexed by defendant, plaintiff. Civil records on computer from 1986, index chrono from 1958.

Criminal Records: Access: Mail, in person. Both court and visitors may perform in person searches. Search fee: $5.00 per name. Required to search: name, years to search, DOB. Criminal records on computer from 1986, index chrono from 1958.

General Information: Public access terminal is available. No juvenile, mental, sealed, or adoption records released. SASE required. Turnaround time 2-3

days. Copy fee: $1.00 per page. Certification fee: $5.00. Fee payee: County Clerk or District Clerk. Only cashiers checks and money orders accepted. Prepayment is required.

Brewster County

District Court PO Box 1024, Alpine, TX 79831; 915-837-6216; Fax: 915-837-6217. Hours: 9AM-12, 1-5PM (CST). *Felony, Civil.*

Civil Records: Access: Phone, fax, mail, in person. Both court and visitors may perform in person searches. No search fee. Required to search: name; also helpful: years to search. Civil cases indexed by defendant, plaintiff. Civil records are computerized since 1994, indexed from 1899.

Criminal Records: Access: Phone, fax, mail, in person. Both court and visitors may perform in person searches. No search fee. Required to search: name, DOB; also helpful: years to search. Criminal records are computerized since 1994, indexed from 1899.

General Information: Turnaround time 1-2 days. Fax notes: No fee for local calls. Copy fee: $1.00 per page. Certification fee: $1.00. Fee payee: District Clerk. Personal checks accepted. Prepayment is required.

County Court PO Box 119 (201 W Avenue E), Alpine, TX 79831; 915-837-3366; Fax: 915-837-6217. 9AM-5PM (CST). *Misdemeanor, Civil Probate.*

Civil Records: Access: Mail, fax, in person. Both court and visitors may perform in person searches. Search fee: $10.00 per name. Required to search: name, years to search. Civil cases indexed by defendant, plaintiff. Civil records in index books from 1800s; computerized since 1994.

Criminal Records: Access: Mail, fax, in person. Both court and visitors may perform in person searches. Search fee: $10.00 per name. Required to search: name, years to search, DOB, signed release; also helpful: SSN. Criminal records in index books from 1800s, computerized since 1994.

General Information: No juvenile, mental, sealed, or adoption records released. SASE required. Turnaround time 1 week. Fax notes: Fee to fax results is $2.00 per page. Copy fee: $1.00 per page. Certification fee: $5.00. Fee payee: County Clerk. Personal checks accepted. Prepayment is required.

Briscoe County

District & County Court PO Box 555, Silverton, TX 79257; 806-823-2134; Fax: 806-823-2359. Hours: 8AM-5PM *Felony, Misdemeanor, Civil, Probate.*

Civil Records: Access: Fax, mail, in person. Both court and visitors may perform in person searches. Search fee: $5.00 per name. Required to search: name, years to search. Civil cases indexed by defendant, plaintiff. Civil records in index books from 1892.

Criminal Records: Access: Fax, mail, in person. Both court and visitors may perform in person searches. Search fee: $5.00 per name. Required to search: name, years to search, DOB. Criminal records in index books from 1892.

General Information: No juvenile, mental, sealed, or adoption records released. SASE required. Turnaround time 1 day. Copy fee: $1.00 per page. Certification fee: $5.00. Fee payee: District or County Clerk. Personal checks accepted. Prepayment is required.

Brooks County

District Court PO Box 534, Falfurrias, TX 78355; 361-325-5604; Fax: 361-325-5679. Hours: 8AM-5PM (CST). *Felony, Civil.*

Civil Records: Access: Phone, fax, mail, online, in person. Both court and visitors may perform in person searches. Search fee: $5.00 per name. Required to search: name, years to search; also helpful: address. Civil cases indexed by defendant, plaintiff. Civil records on computer back to 1992, index books since 1920. Civil case information is available online at www.idocket.com. Free searching is limited. Records go back to 12/31/1993.

Criminal Records: Access: Phone, fax, mail, online, in person. Both court and visitors may perform in person searches. Search fee: $5.00 per name. Required to search: name, years to search, DOB, SSN; also helpful: address. Criminal records on computer back to 1992, index books since 1920, microfiche since 1939. Online access is through www.idocket.com; registration and password required. Records go back to 12/31/1993.

General Information: No juvenile, mental, sealed, or adoption records released. SASE required. Turnaround time 1 week. Fax notes: Fee to fax results is $1.00 per page. Copy fee: $1.00 per page. Certification fee: $2.00. Fee payee: District Clerk. Business checks accepted. Prepayment is required.

County Court PO Box 427, Falfurrias, TX 78355; 361-325-5604 X245,246,248. Hours: 8AM-5PM (CST). *Misdemeanor, Civil, Probate.*

Civil Records: Access: Phone, fax, mail, in person. Both court and visitors may perform in person searches. Search fee: $10.00 per name. Required to search: name, years to search. Civil cases indexed by plaintiff. Civil records in index books since 1911.

Criminal Records: Access: Phone, fax, mail, in person. Both court and visitors may perform in person searches. Search fee: $10.00 per name. Required to search: name, years to search, DOB. Criminal records in index books since 1911.

General Information: No juvenile, mental, sealed, or adoption records released. SASE required. Turnaround time 1-2 days. Fax notes: $5.00 for first page, $2.00 each add'l. Copy fee: $1.00 per page. Certification fee: $5.00. Payee: County Clerk. Personal checks accepted.

Brown County

District Court 200 S Broadway, Brownwood, TX 76801; 915-646-5514. Hours: 8:30AM-5PM (CST). *Felony, Civil.*

Civil Records: Access: Mail, in person. Both court and visitors may perform in person searches. Search fee: $5.00 per name. Required to search: name, years to search. Civil cases indexed by defendant, plaintiff. Civil records on computer since 1995; prior records on books to 1930s.

Criminal Records: Access: Mail, in person, phone. Both court and visitors may perform in person searches. Search fee: $5.00 per name. Required to search: name, years to search. Criminal records on computer since 1995; prior records on books to 1930s.

General Information: Public access terminal is available. No juvenile, mental, sealed, or adoption records released. SASE required. Turnaround time 2-3 days. Fax notes: Do not fax. Copy fee: $1.00 per page. Certification fee: $1.00 per page. Fee payee: District Clerk. Business checks accepted. Prepayment is required.

County Court 200 S Broadway, Brownwood, TX 76801; 915-643-2594. Hours: 8:30AM-5PM (CST). *Misdemeanor, Civil, Probate.*

Civil Records: Access: Mail, in person. Both court and visitors may perform in person searches. Search fee: $5.00 per name. Required to search: name, years to search. Civil cases indexed by defendant, plaintiff. Civil records on computer from 1988 on microfiche from 1900s.

Criminal Records: Access: Mail, in person. Both court and visitors may perform in person searches. Search fee: $5.00 per name. Required to search: name, years to search; also helpful: DOB, SSN. Criminal records on computer from 1988, on microfiche from 1900s.

General Information: Public access terminal is available. No juvenile, mental, sealed records released.

SASE required. Turnaround time 1-2 days. Copy fee: $1.00 per page. Certification fee: $5.00. Fee payee: Brown County Clerk. Personal checks accepted. Prepayment is required.

Burleson County

District Court 100 West Buck #303, Caldwell, TX 77836; 979-567-2336. Hours: 8AM-12, 1-5PM (CST). *Felony, Civil.*

Civil Records: Access: Mail, in person. Both court and visitors may perform in person searches. Search fee: $5.00 per name. Required to search: name, years to search. Civil cases indexed by defendant, plaintiff. Civil records on microfilm from 1980, index books prior.

Criminal Records: Access: Mail, in person. Both court and visitors may perform in person searches. Search fee: $5.00 per name. Required to search: name, years to search. Criminal records on microfilm from 1980, index books prior.

General Information: No juvenile, mental, sealed, or adoption records released. SASE or toll-free phone number required. Turnaround time 1-2 days. Fax notes: Will fax to toll-free number. Copy fee: $1.00 per page. Certification fee: $1.00 per page. Fee payee: District Clerk. Personal checks accepted. Prepayment required.

County Court 100 West Buck, Ste 203, Caldwell, TX 77836; 979-567-2329; Fax: 979-567-2376. Hours: 8AM-5PM (CST). *Misdemeanor, Civil, Probate.*

Civil Records: Access: Phone, mail, fax, in person. Visitors must perform in person searches for themselves. No search fee. Required to search: name, years to search. Civil cases indexed by defendant, plaintiff. Civil records indexed to 1900, records archived to 1900s.

Criminal Records: Access: Mail, fax, in person. Visitors must perform in person searches for themselves. No search fee. Required to search: name, years to search, DOB, SSN. Criminal records indexed to 1900, records archived to 1900s.

General Information: No juvenile, mental, or sealed records released. SASE required. Turnaround time 2-4 days. Fax notes: Fee to fax results is $1.00 per page. Copy fee: $1.00 per page. Certification fee: $5.00. Fee payee: County Clerk. Personal checks accepted. Prepayment is required.

Burnet County

District Court 220 S Pierce, Burnet, TX 78611; 512-756-5450. Hours: 8AM-5PM (CST). *Felony, Civil.*

Civil Records: Access: Mail, in person. Both court and visitors may perform in person searches. Search fee: $5.00 per name. Required to search: name, years to search. Civil cases indexed by defendant, plaintiff. Civil records on computer from 1991, index books from 1856.

Criminal Records: Access: Mail, in person. Both court and visitors may perform in person searches. Search fee: $5.00 per name. Required to search: name, years to search; also helpful: DOB, SSN. Criminal records on computer from 1988, index book from 1856.

General Information: No juvenile, mental, sealed, or adoption records released. SASE required. Turnaround time 2 days. Copy fee: $1.00 per page. Certification fee: $2.00. Fee payee: District Clerk. Personal checks accepted. Prepayment is required.

County Court 220 S Pierce, Burnet, TX 78611; 512-756-5403; Fax: 512-756-5410. Hours: 8AM-5PM (CST). *Misdemeanor, Civil, Probate.*

Civil Records: Access: Fax, mail, in person. Both court and visitors may perform in person searches. Search fee: $10.00 per name. Required to search: name, years to search. Civil cases indexed by defendant, plaintiff. Civil records on computer from 1989, on microfiche from 1852.

Criminal Records: Access: Fax, mail, in person. Both court and visitors may perform in person searches. Search fee: $10.00 per name. Required to search: name, years to search, offense, date of offense. Criminal records on computer from 1989, on microfiche from 1852.

General Information: Public access terminal is available. No juvenile, mental, sealed, or adoption records released. SASE required. Turnaround time 2 days. Fax notes: $1.00 per page. Copy fee: $1.00 per page. Certification fee: $5.00. Fee payee: County Clerk. Personal checks accepted. Prepayment is required.

Caldwell County

District Court 201 E San Antonio St, Lockhart, TX 78644; 512-398-1806. Hours: 8:30AM-Noon, 1-5PM (CST). *Felony, Civil.*

Civil Records: Access: Phone, fax, mail, in person. Both court and visitors may perform in person searches. Search fee: $5.00 per name. Required to search: name, years to search. Civil cases indexed by defendant, plaintiff. Civil records on computer since 1988, index books from 1900s.

Criminal Records: Access: Phone, fax, mail, in person. Both court and visitors may perform in person searches. Search fee: $5.00 per name. Required to search: name, years to search; also helpful: DOB, SSN. Criminal records on computer since 1988, index books from 1900s.

General Information: No juvenile, mental, sealed, or adoption records released. SASE required. Turnaround time 1-3 days. Copy fee: $1.00 per page. Certification fee: $1.00. Fee payee: District Clerk. Personal checks accepted. Prepayment is required.

County Court PO Box 906, Lockhart, TX 78644; 512-398-1804. Hours: 8:30AM-Noon, 1-5PM (CST). *Misdemeanor, Civil, Probate.*

Civil Records: Access: Mail, in person. Both court and visitors may perform in person searches. Search fee: $5.00 per name. Required to search: name, years to search. Civil cases indexed by defendant, plaintiff. Civil records in index books since 1967.

Criminal Records: Access: Mail, in person. Both court and visitors may perform in person searches. Search fee: $5.00 per name. Required to search: name, years to search, DOB, offense, date of offense. Criminal records in index books since 1967.

General Information: Public access terminal is available. No juvenile, mental, sealed, or adoption records released. SASE not required. Turnaround time 2-4 days. Copy fee: $1.00 per page. Certification fee: $5.00. Fee payee: Caldwell County Clerk. Personal checks accepted. Prepayment is required.

Calhoun County

District Court PO Box 658 (c/o District Clerk), Port Lavaca, TX 77979; 361-553-8698. Hours: 8AM-5PM (CST). *Felony, Civil.*

Civil Records: Access: Mail, in person. Both court and visitors may perform in person searches. Search fee: $5.00 per name. Required to search: name, years to search. Civil cases indexed by defendant, plaintiff. Civil records in index books from 1852.

Criminal Records: Access: Mail, in person. Both court and visitors may perform in person searches. Search fee: $5.00 per name. Required to search: name, years to search, signed release; also helpful: DOB. Criminal records in index books from 1852.

General Information: No juvenile, mental, sealed, or adoption records released. SASE required. Turnaround time 1 day. Copy fee: $1.00 per page. Certification fee: $1.00. Fee payee: District Clerk. Personal checks accepted. Prepayment is required.

County Court 211 S Ann, Port Lavaca, TX 77979; 361-553-4411; Fax: 361-553-4420. Hours: 8AM-5PM (CST). *Misdemeanor, Civil, Probate.*

Note: Established 11/1986.

Civil Records: Access: Phone, mail, in person. Both court and visitors may perform in person searches. Search fee: $5.00 per name. Required to search: name, years to search. Civil cases indexed by defendant, plaintiff. Civil records in index books from 11/1986; indexed on computer back to 2000.

Criminal Records: Access: Phone, mail, in person. Both court and visitors may perform in person searches. Search fee: $5.00 per name. Required to search: name, years to search. Criminal records in index books from 11/1986; indexed on computer back to 1993.

General Information: No juvenile, mental, sealed, or adoption records released. SASE required. Turnaround time 1-2 days. Copy fee: $1.00 per page. Certification fee: $5.00. Fee payee: County Clerk. Personal checks accepted. Prepayment is required.

Callahan County

District Court 100 W 4th St #300, Baird, TX 79504-5396; 915-854-1800. Hours: 8AM-5PM (CST). *Felony, Civil.*

Civil Records: Access: Mail, in person. Both court and visitors may perform in person searches. Search fee: $5.00 per name. Required to search: name, years to search. Civil cases indexed by defendant, plaintiff. Civil records in index books since 1879.

Criminal Records: Access: Mail, in person. Both court and visitors may perform in person searches. Search fee: $5.00 per name. Required to search: name, years to search. Criminal records in index books since 1879.

General Information: No juvenile, mental, sealed, or adoption records released. SASE required. Turnaround time 1-2 days. Copy fee: $1.00 per page. Fee payee: District Clerk. Personal checks accepted. Prepayment is required.

County Court 100 W 4th St, #104, Baird, TX 79504-5300; 915-854-1217; Fax: 915-854-1227. Hours: 8AM-5PM (CST). *Misdemeanor, Civil, Probate.*

Civil Records: Access: Mail, in person. Both court and visitors may perform in person searches. Search fee: $6.00 per name. Required to search: name, years to search. Civil cases indexed by defendant, plaintiff. Civil records go back to 1877; computerized records go back to 1992.

Criminal Records: Access: Phone, fax, mail, in person. Both court and visitors may perform in person searches. Search fee: $6.00 per name. Required to search: name, years to search. Criminal records go back to 1877; computerized records go to 1992.

General Information: Public access terminal is available. (Public access for land records only.) No juvenile, mental, sealed, or adoption records released. SASE required. Turnaround time 1 day. Fax notes: Fee to fax results is $1.50 per page. Copy fee: $1.00 per page. Certification fee: $5.00. Fee payee: Jeanie Bohannon, County Clerk. Personal checks accepted. Prepayment is required.

Cameron County

District Court 974 E Harrison St, Brownsville, TX 78520; 956-544-0839. Hours: 8AM-Noon, 1-5PM (CST). *Felony, Civil.*

Civil Records: Access: Mail, online, in person. Both court and visitors may perform in person searches. Search fee: $5.00 per name. Required to search: name, years to search. Civil cases indexed by defendant, plaintiff. Civil records on computer from 1989. Online access is available 24 hours daily. $125 setup fee includes software, there is a $30 monthly access fee also. For more information, call Eric at 956-544-0838

X475. Online access is through www.idocket.com; registration and password required. Records go back to 12/31/1988.

Criminal Records: Access: Mail, in person, online. Only the court performs in person searches; visitors may not. Search fee: $5.00 per name. Required to search: name, years to search, DOB, SSN, signed release, offense. Criminal records on computer since 1987. Online access may be available at www.idocket.com; registration and password required. Records may go back to 12/31/1988.

General Information: Public access terminal is available. (Civil only.) No juvenile, mental, sealed, or adoption records released. SASE required. Turnaround time 1 week. On cases prior to 1990 turnaround time could be more than 1 week. Copy fee: $1.00 per page. Fee payee: Cameron County District Clerk. Personal checks accepted. Prepayment is required.

County Court No. 1, 2 & 3 PO Box 2178, Brownsville, TX 78522-2178; 956-544-0848; Fax: 956-544-0894. Hours: 8AM-5PM (CST). *Misdemeanor, Civil, Probate.*

Civil Records: Access: Fax, mail, in person. Both court and visitors may perform in person searches. Search fee: $5.00 per name. Required to search: name, years to search. Civil cases indexed by defendant, plaintiff. Civil records on optical imaging since 1994, on computer from 1987, index books from 1912.

Criminal Records: Access: Fax, mail, in person. Both court and visitors may perform in person searches. Search fee: $5.00 per name. Required to search: name, years to search, DOB. Criminal records on optical imaging since 1994, on computer from 1987, index books from 1912.

General Information: Public access terminal is available. No juvenile, mental, sealed, or adoption records released. SASE required. Turnaround time 1-2 days. Fax notes: $4.25 for first page, $2.25 each add'l. Must receive payment prior to faxing. Copy fee: $1.00 per page. Certification fee: $5.00. Fee payee: Joe G Rivera, County Clerk. Personal checks accepted. Prepayment is required.

Camp County

District Court 126 Church St Rm 203, Pittsburg, TX 75686; 903-856-3221; Fax: 903-856-0560. Hours: 8AM-5PM (CST). *Felony, Civil.*

Civil Records: Access: Mail, fax, in person. Both court and visitors may perform in person searches. Search fee: $5.00 per name. Required to search: name, years to search. Civil cases indexed by defendant, plaintiff. Civil records in index books from 1874; computerized since 1995.

Criminal Records: Access: Mail, in person. Both court and visitors may perform in person searches. Search fee: $5.00 per name. Required to search: name, years to search, signed release. Criminal records in index books from 1874; computerized since 1993.

General Information: No juvenile, mental, sealed, or adoption records released. SASE not required. Turnaround time 1 week. Fax notes: Fee to fax results is $.25 per page. Copy fee: $.25 per page. Certification fee: $2.00 for 1st page, $.25 each add'l. Fee payee: District Clerk. Personal checks accepted. Prepayment is required.

County Court 126 Church St Rm 102, Pittsburg, TX 75686; 903-856-2731; Fax: 903-856-2309. Hours: 8AM-Noon, 1-5PM *Misdemeanor, Civil, Probate.*

Civil Records: Access: Fax, mail, in person. Both court and visitors may perform in person searches. Search fee: $10.00 per name. Required to search: name, years to search. Civil cases indexed by defendant, plaintiff. Civil records in index books from 1960; computerized since 1999. Fax access is only allowed with prepayment of fees.

Criminal Records: Access: Fax, mail, in person. Both court and visitors may perform in person searches. Search fee: $10.00 per name. Required to search: name, years to search, signed release, offense. Criminal records in index books from 1960; computerized since 1999.

General Information: No juvenile, mental, sealed, or adoption records released. SASE required. Turnaround time 1 day. Copy fee: $1.00 per page. Certification fee: $5.00 plus $1.00 per page. Fee payee: Camp County Clerk. Personal checks accepted. Prepayment required.

Carson County

District & County Court PO Box 487, Panhandle, TX 79068; 806-537-3623; Fax: 806-537-3724. Hours: 8AM-Noon, 1-5PM (CST). *Felony, Misdemeanor, Civil, Probate.*

Civil Records: Access: Mail, fax, in person. Both court and visitors may perform in person searches. Search fee: $5.00 per name. Required to search: name, years to search. Civil cases indexed by defendant, plaintiff. Civil records on computer from 1981, index books from 1800s.

Criminal Records: Access: Mail, fax, in person. Both court and visitors may perform in person searches. Search fee: $5.00 per name. Required to search: name, years to search. Criminal records on computer from 1981, index books from 1800s.

General Information: No juvenile, mental, sealed, or adoption records released. SASE required. Turnaround time 1 day. Copy fee: $1.00 per page. Certification fee: $5.00 per page. Fee payee: Carson County Clerk. Personal checks accepted. Prepayment is required.

Cass County

District Court PO Box 510, Linden, TX 75563; 903-756-7514. Hours: 8AM-5PM (CST). *Felony, Civil.*

Civil Records: Access: Mail, in person. Both court and visitors may perform in person searches. Search fee: $5.00 per name. Required to search: name, years to search. Civil cases indexed by defendant, plaintiff. Civil records on computer from 1985, index books from 1900s.

Criminal Records: Access: Mail, in person. Both court and visitors may perform in person searches. Search fee: $5.00 per name. Required to search: name, years to search. Criminal records on computer from 1985, index books from 1900s.

General Information: Public access terminal is available. No juvenile, mental, sealed, or adoption records released. SASE required. Turnaround time 1 day. Fax notes: Fee to fax results is $.25 per minute; minimum $3.00. Copy fee: $1.00 per page. Certification fee: $1.00 per page. Fee payee: District Clerk. Personal checks accepted. Prepayment is required.

County Court PO Box 449, Linden, TX 75563; 903-756-5071. Hours: 8AM-5PM (CST). *Misdemeanor, Probate.*

Criminal Records: Access: Mail, in person. Both court and visitors may perform in person searches. Search fee: $10.00 per name. Required to search: name, years to search. Criminal records in index books from 1983.

General Information: No juvenile, mental, sealed, or adoption records released. SASE required. Turnaround time 1 day. Copy fee: $1.00 per page. Certification fee: $5.00 plus $1.00 per page. Fee payee: County Clerk. Monery order or cashier check. Prepayment is required.

Castro County

District & County Court 100 E Bedford, Rm 101, Dimmitt, TX 79027; 806-647-3338. Hours: 8AM-5PM (CST). *Felony, Misdemeanor, Civil, Probate.*

Civil Records: Access: Mail, in person. Both court and visitors may perform in person searches. No search fee. Required to search: name, years to search. Civil cases indexed by defendant, plaintiff. Civil records in index books.

Criminal Records: Access: Mail, in person. Both court and visitors may perform in person searches. Search fee: $5.00 per name. Required to search: name, years to search; also helpful: DOB, SSN. Criminal records in index books; computerized records since 2000.

General Information: No juvenile, mental, sealed, or adoption records released. SASE required. Turnaround time 1 day. Copy fee: $1.00 per page. Certification fee: $5.00 (county) per document, $1.00 (district) per page. Fee payee: County or District Court Clerk. Personal checks accepted. Prepayment is required.

Chambers County

District Clerk Drawer NN, Anahuac, TX 77514; 409-267-8276. Hours: 8AM-Noon, 1-5PM (CST). *Felony, Civil.*

Civil Records: Access: Mail, in person. Both court and visitors may perform in person searches. Search fee: $5.00 per name. Required to search: name, years to search. Civil cases indexed by defendant, plaintiff. Civil records on computer back to 1800s.

Criminal Records: Access: Mail, in person. Both court and visitors may perform in person searches. Search fee: $5.00 per name. Required to search: name, years to search, DOB, SNN. Criminal records on computer back to 1940s.

General Information: No juvenile, mental, sealed, or adoption records released. SASE required. Turnaround time 1 day. Copy fee: $1.00 per page. Certification fee: $5.00. Fee payee: R B Scherer Jr, District Clerk. Personal checks accepted. Prepayment is required.

County Court PO Box 728, Anahuac, TX 77514; 409-267-8309; Fax: 409-267-4453. Hours: 8AM-5PM (CST). *Misdemeanor, Civil, Probate.*

www.co.chambers.tx.us

Civil Records: Access: Mail, in person. Both court and visitors may perform in person searches. Search fee: $5.00 per name. Required to search: name, years to search; also helpful: address. Civil cases indexed by defendant, plaintiff. Civil records on computer from 1987, index books from 1875.

Criminal Records: Access: Mail, in person. Both court and visitors may perform in person searches. Search fee: $5.00 per name. Required to search: name, years to search, DOB, offense; also helpful: address. Criminal records on computer from 1987, index books from 1875.

General Information: No juvenile or mental records released. SASE required. Turnaround time 2-3 days. Copy fee: $1.00 per page. Certification fee: $5.00. Fee payee: Chambers County Clerk. Personal checks accepted. Prepayment is required.

Cherokee County

District Court Drawer C, Rusk, TX 75785; 903-683-4533. 8AM-Noon, 1-5PM (CST). *Felony, Civil.*

Civil Records: Access: Mail, fax, in person. Both court and visitors may perform in person searches. Search fee: $5.00 per name. Required to search: name, years to search. Civil cases indexed by defendant, plaintiff. Civil records on computer from 1991, index books from 1848.

Criminal Records: Access: Mail, fax, in person. Both court and visitors may perform in person searches. Search fee: $5.00 per name. Required to search: name, years to search. Criminal records on computer from 1991, index books from 1848.

General Information: No juvenile, mental, sealed, or adoption records released. SASE required. Turnaround time 1-2 days. Copy fee: $.50 per page. Certification fee: $1.00 per page. Fee payee: District Clerk. Personal checks accepted. Prepayment is required.

County Court Cherokee County Clerk, PO Box 420, Rusk, TX 75785; 903-683-2350; Fax: 903-683-5931. 8AM-5PM . *Misdemeanor, Civil, Probate.*

Civil Records: Access: Mail, in person. Both court and visitors may perform in person searches. Search fee: $5.00 per name. Required to search: name, years to search. Civil cases indexed by defendant, plaintiff. Civil records on computer back to 1987, index books from 1846.

Criminal Records: Access: Mail, in person. Both court and visitors may perform in person searches. Search fee: $10.00 per name. Required to search: name, years to search. Criminal records on computer back to 1987, index books from 1920s.

General Information: No juvenile, mental, sealed, or adoption records released. SASE required. Turnaround time 2-4 days. Copy fee: $1.00 per page. Certification fee: $5.00. Fee payee: County Clerk. Personal checks accepted. Prepayment is required.

Childress County

District & County Court Courthouse Box 4, Childress, TX 79201; 940-937-6143; Fax: 940-937-3479. Hours: 8:30AM-Noon, 1-5PM (CST). *Felony, Misdemeanor, Civil, Probate.*

Civil Records: Access: Mail, in person. Both court and visitors may perform in person searches. Search fee: $5.00 per name. Required to search: name, years to search. Civil cases indexed by defendant, plaintiff. Civil records on computer from 1995, index books from 1920.

Criminal Records: Access: Mail, in person. Both court and visitors may perform in person searches. Search fee: $5.00 per name. Required to search: name, years to search, DOB. Criminal records on computer from 1995, index books from 1920.

General Information: No juvenile, mental, sealed, or adoption records released. SASE not required. Turnaround time 1 day. Copy fee: $1.00 per page. Certification fee: $1.00. County Court certification fee is $5.00. Fee payee: District or County Clerk. Personal checks accepted. Prepayment is required.

Clay County

District Clerk PO Box 568, Henrietta, TX 76365; 940-538-4561; Fax: 940-538-4431. Hours: 8AM-Noon, 1-5PM (CST). *Felony, Civil.*

Civil Records: Access: Mail, in person. Both court and visitors may perform in person searches. Search fee: $5.00 per name. Required to search: name, years to search. Civil cases indexed by defendant, plaintiff. Civil records in index books from 1873.

Criminal Records: Access: Mail, in person. Both court and visitors may perform in person searches. Search fee: $5.00 per name. Required to search: name, years to search. Criminal records in index books from 1873.

General Information: No juvenile, mental, sealed, or adoption records released. SASE required. Turnaround time 1-2 days. Fax notes: Will not fax results. Copy fee: $.50 per page. Certification fee: $1.00 per page. Fee payee: District Clerk. Personal checks accepted. Prepayment is required.

County Court PO Box 548, Henrietta, TX 76365; 940-538-4631. Hours: 8AM-5PM (CST). *Misdemeanor, Civil, Probate.*

Civil Records: Access: Mail, in person, fax. Both court and visitors may perform in person searches. Search fee: $5.00 per name. Required to search: name, years to search. Civil cases indexed by defendant, plaintiff. Civil records in index books from 1873, reecords go back to 1910; no computerized records.

Criminal Records: Access: Mail, in person. Both court and visitors may perform in person searches. Search fee: $5.00 per name. Required to search: name, years to

search. Criminal records in index books from 1873, records go back to 1910; no computerized records.

General Information: No juvenile, mental, sealed, or adoption records released. SASE required. Turnaround time 2-4 days. Copy fee: $1.00 per page. Certification fee: $5.00. Fee payee: County Clerk. Personal checks accepted. Prepayment is required.

Cochran County

District & County Court County Courthouse Rm 102, Morton, TX 79346; 806-266-5450; Fax: 806-266-9027. Hours: 8AM-5PM (CST). *Felony, Misdemeanor, Civil, Probate.*

Note: E-mail address for search requests is cclerk@door.net.

Civil Records: Access: Phone, fax, mail, in person. Both court and visitors may perform in person searches. Search fee: $5.00 per name. Required to search: name, years to search. Civil cases indexed by defendant, plaintiff. Civil records in index books go back to 1925.

Criminal Records: Access: Fax, mail, in person. Both court and visitors may perform in person searches. Search fee: $5.00 per name. Required to search: name, years to search, DOB; also helpful: sex. Criminal records in index books go back to 1925.

General Information: No juvenile, mental, sealed, or adoption records released. SASE required. Turnaround time 1 day. Fax notes: Will fax back results to 800 # only. Copy fee: $1.00 per page. Certification fee: $1.00. Fee payee: District or County Clerk. Personal checks accepted. Prepayment is required.

Coke County

District & County Court PO Box 150, Robert Lee, TX 76945; 915-453-2631; Fax: 915-453-2650. Hours: 8AM-5PM (CST). *Felony, Misdemeanor, Civil, Probate.*

Civil Records: Access: Mail, in person. Both court and visitors may perform in person searches. Search fee: $5.00 per name. Required to search: name, years to search. Civil cases indexed by defendant, plaintiff. Civil records in index books since 1889, computerized since 1993.

Criminal Records: Access: Mail, in person. Both court and visitors may perform in person searches. Search fee: $5.00 per name. Required to search: name, years to search. Criminal records in index books since 1889.

General Information: No juvenile, mental, sealed, or adoption records released. SASE not required. Turnaround time 2 days. Fax notes: $2.00 per page. Copy fee: $1.00 per page. Certification fee: $5.00. Fee payee: Coke County Clerk. Personal checks accepted. Prepayment is required.

Coleman County

District Court PO Box 512, Coleman, TX 76834; 915-625-2568. 8AM-4:30PM (CST). *Felony, Civil.*

Civil Records: Access: Mail, in person. Both court and visitors may perform in person searches. Search fee: $5.00 per name. Required to search: name, years to search. Civil cases indexed by defendant, plaintiff. Civil records in index books since 1934; earlier records not indexed.

Criminal Records: Access: Mail, in person. Both court and visitors may perform in person searches. Search fee: $5.00 per name. Required to search: name, years to search, DOB, SSN. Criminal records in index books since 1931; earlier records not indexed.

General Information: No juvenile, mental, sealed, or adoption records released. SASE required. Turnaround time up to 5 days. Fax notes: Do not fax. Copy fee: $1.00 per page. Certification fee: $1.00. Fee payee: District Clerk. Personal checks accepted. Prepayment is required.

County Court PO Box 591, Coleman, TX 76834; 915-625-2889. Hours: 8AM-5PM (CST). *Misdemeanor, Civil, Probate.*

Civil Records: Access: Mail, in person. Both court and visitors may perform in person searches. Search fee: $5.00 per name. Required to search: name, years to search. Civil cases indexed by defendant, plaintiff. Civil records in index books from 1971.

Criminal Records: Access: Mail, in person. Both court and visitors may perform in person searches. Search fee: $5.00 per name. Required to search: name, years to search. Criminal records in index books from 1977, archived ffrom 1900s.

General Information: No juvenile, mental, sealed, or adoption records released. SASE required. Turnaround time 1-2 days. Copy fee: $1.00 per page. Certification fee: $5.00. Fee payee: County Clerk. Personal checks accepted. Prepayment is required.

Collin County

District Clerk PO Box 578, McKinney, TX 75070; Civil phone: 972-548-4320; Criminal phone: 972-548-4430. Hours: 8AM-4:30PM (CST). *Felony, Civil.*

Civil Records: Access: Mail, online, in person. Both court and visitors may perform in person searches. Search fee: $5.00 per name. Required to search: name, years to search. Civil cases indexed by defendant, plaintiff. Civil records on computer and microfiche from 1986 (some records are on computer through the 1970s), index books from 1846. Online is available 7am to 7pm M-Sat, 6 to 6 on Sun. Access fee is $.12 a minute, there is a monthly minimum of $31.13. Procomm Plus is suggested. Subscribers also receive fax call-back service. Call Patty Ostrom at 972-548-4503 for subscription information.

Criminal Records: Access: Mail, online, in person. Both court and visitors may perform in person searches. Search fee: $5.00 per name. Required to search: name, years to search, DOB. Criminal records on computer and microfiche from 1986 (some records are on computer through the 1970s), index books from 1846. Online access to criminal records is the same as civil.

General Information: Public access terminal is available. No juvenile, mental, sealed, or adoption records released. SASE required. Turnaround time 2-3 days. Copy fee: $1.00 per page. Fee payee: District Clerk. Personal checks accepted. Prepayment required.

County Court 1800 N Graves #110, McKinney, TX 75069; 972-548-6420; Fax: 972-548-6433. Hours: 8AM-5PM (CST). *Misdemeanor, Civil, Probate.*

Civil Records: Access: Mail, online, in person. Both court and visitors may perform in person searches. Search fee: $5.00 per name. Required to search: name, years to search. Civil cases indexed by defendant, plaintiff. Civil records on computer and microfiche from 1975, index books prior. Online is available 7am to 7pm M-Sat, 6 to 6 on Sun. Access fee is $.12 a minute, there is a monthly minimum of $31.13. Procomm Plus is suggested. Call Patty Ostrom at 972-548-4503 for subscription information.

Criminal Records: Access: Mail, online, in person. Both court and visitors may perform in person searches. Search fee: $5.00 per name. Required to search: name, DOB. Criminal records computerized since early 1970s. Online access to misdemeanor records is the same as civil.

General Information: Public access terminal is available. No juvenile, mental, sealed, or adoption records released. SASE required. Turnaround time 2-4 days. Copy fee: $1.00 per page. Certification fee: $5.00. Fee payee: County Clerk. Personal checks accepted. Prepayment is required.

Collingsworth County

District & County Court County Courthouse, Rm 3, 800 West Ave, Box 10, Wellington, TX 79095; 806-447-2408; Fax: 806-447-5418. Hours: 9AM-5PM (CST). *Felony, Misdemeanor, Civil, Probate.*

Civil Records: Access: Phone, fax, mail, in person. Both court and visitors may perform in person searches. Search fee: $10.00 per name. Required to search: name, years to search. Civil cases indexed by defendant, plaintiff. Civil records on index books from 1800s.

Criminal Records: Access: Mail, in person. Both court and visitors may perform in person searches. Search fee: $10.00 per name. Required to search: name, years to search, DOB. Criminal records on index books from 1800s.

General Information: No juvenile, mental health, sealed, or adoption records released. SASE required. Turnaround time 2 days. Copy fee: $1.00 per page. Certification fee: $5.00. Fee payee: Collingsworth County Clerk. Personal checks accepted. Prepayment is required.

Colorado County

District Court County Courthouse, RM 210E, 400 Spring St, Columbus, TX 78934; 979-732-2536. Hours: 8AM-Noon, 1-5PM (CST). *Felony, Civil.*

Civil Records: Access: Mail, in person. Both court and visitors may perform in person searches. Search fee: $5.00 per name. Required to search: name, years to search. Civil cases indexed by defendant, plaintiff. Civil records in index books from 1837.

Criminal Records: Access: Mail, in person. Both court and visitors may perform in person searches. Search fee: $5.00 per name. Required to search: name, years to search. Criminal records in index books from 1837.

General Information: No juvenile, mental, sealed, or adoption records released. SASE required. Turnaround time 1 day. Copy fee: $1.00 per page. Certification fee: $2.00. Fee payee: District Clerk. Personal checks accepted. Prepayment is required.

County Court PO Box 68, County Courthouse, Columbus, TX 78934; 979-732-2155; Fax: 979-732-8852. 8AM-5PM . *Misdemeanor, Civil, Probate.*

Civil Records: Access: Mail, in person. Both court and visitors may perform in person searches. Search fee: $10.00 per name. Required to search: name, years to search. Civil cases indexed by defendant, plaintiff. Civil records in index books from 1850.

Criminal Records: Access: Mail, in person. Both court and visitors may perform in person searches. Search fee: $10.00 per name. Required to search: name, years to search. Criminal records in index books from 1850.

General Information: No juvenile, mental, sealed, or adoption records released. SASE required. Turnaround time 1-2 days. Copy fee: $1.00 per page. Certification fee: $5.00. Fee payee: County Clerk. Personal checks accepted. Prepayment is required.

Comal County

District Court 150 N Seguin Ste 304, New Braunfels, TX 78130-5161; 830-620-5574; Fax: 830-608-2006. Hours: 8AM-4:30PM (CST). *Felony, Civil.*

www.co.comal.tx.us

Civil Records: Access: Fax, mail, in person, online. Both court and visitors may perform in person searches. Search fee: $5.00 per name. Required to search: name, years to search. Civil cases indexed by defendant, plaintiff. Civil records on computer from 1984, index books from 1846. Online access to county judicial records is available free at www.co.comal.tx.us/Search/judsrch.htm. Search by either party name.

Criminal Records: Access: Fax, mail, in person, online. Both court and visitors may perform in person

searches. Search fee: $5.00 per name. Required to search: name, years to search, DOB; also helpful: SSN, sex. Criminal records on computer from 1984, index books from 1846. Online access to county criminal judicial records is available free at www.co.comal.tx.us/Search/judsrch.htm. Search by defendant name.

General Information: Public access terminal is available. No juvenile, sealed, or adoption records released. SASE required. Turnaround time 3 days. Fax notes: $5.00 per page. Fee is for incoming & outgoing faxes. Copy fee: $1.00 for first page, $.25 each add'l. Certification fee: $1.00 per page. Fee payee: District Clerk. Personal checks accepted. Prepayment required.

County Court at Law 100 Main Plaza, Ste 303, New Braunfels, TX 78130; 830-620-5582; Fax: 830-608-2021. Hours: 8AM-4:30PM (CST). *Misdemeanor, Civil, Probate.*

www.comalcounty.net

Civil Records: Access: Phone, fax, mail, in person, online. Both court and visitors may perform in person searches. Search fee: $5.00 per name. Required to search: name, years to search. Civil cases indexed by defendant, plaintiff. Civil records on computer since 1977. Online access to county judicial records is available free at www.comalcounty.net/JudicialSearch/JudSrch.htm. Search by either party name.

Criminal Records: Access: Phone, fax, mail, in person. Both court and visitors may perform in person searches. Search fee: $5.00 per name. Required to search: name, years to search; also helpful: address, DOB. Criminal records on computer since 1977. Online access to county criminal judicial records is available at www.comalcounty.net/JudicialSearch/JudSrch.htm. Search by defendant name.

General Information: Public access terminal is available. No juvenile, mental, sealed or adoption records released. Turnaround time 1 week. Fax notes: $1.00 per page. Copy fee: $1.00 per page. Certification fee: $5.00. Fee payee: County Court at Law. Only cashiers checks and money orders accepted. Prepayment is required.

Comanche County

District Court County Courthouse, Box 206, Comanche, TX 76442; 915-356-2342; Fax: 915-356-2150. Hours: 8:30AM-Noon, 1-5PM (CST). *Felony, Civil.*

Civil Records: Access: Mail, in person. Only the court performs in person searches; visitors may not. Search fee: $5.00 per name. Required to search: name, years to search. Civil cases indexed by defendant, plaintiff. Civil records on computer back 1 year, index books from 1876.

Criminal Records: Access: Mail, in person. Only the court performs in person searches; visitors may not. Search fee: $5.00 per name. Required to search: name, years to search. Criminal records on computer from 1990, index books from 1876.

General Information: No juvenile, mental, sealed, or adoption records released. SASE required. Turnaround time 1 day. Copy fee: $1.00 per page. Certification fee: $2.00. Fee payee: District Clerk. Personal checks accepted. Prepayment is required.

County Court County Courthouse, Comanche, TX 76442; 915-356-2655. Hours: 8:30AM-5PM (CST). *Misdemeanor, Civil, Probate.*

Civil Records: Access: Mail, in person. Both court and visitors may perform in person searches. Search fee: $5.00 per name. Required to search: name, years to search. Civil cases indexed by defendant, plaintiff. Civil records in index books from 1856.

Criminal Records: Access: Mail, in person. Both court and visitors may perform in person searches. Search

fee: $5.00 per name. Required to search: name, years to search. Criminal records in index books from 1856.

General Information: No juvenile, mental, sealed, or adoption records released. SASE required. Turnaround time 1 day. Copy fee: $1.00 per page. Certification fee: $5.00. Fee payee: County Clerk. Personal checks accepted. Prepayment is required.

Concho County

District & County Court PO Box 98, Paint Rock, TX 76866; 915-732-4322; Fax: 915-732-2040. Hours: 8:30AM-5PM (CST). *Felony, Misdemeanor, Civil, Probate.*

Civil Records: Access: Phone, mail, in person. Both court and visitors may perform in person searches. Search fee: $5.00 per name. Required to search: name, years to search. Civil cases indexed by defendant, plaintiff. Civil records in index books from 1879; computerized back to 1994.

Criminal Records: Access: Phone, mail, in person. Only the court performs in person searches; visitors may not. Search fee: $5.00 per name. Required to search: name, years to search, DOB; also helpful: SSN. Criminal records in index books from 1879; computerized back to 1994.

General Information: No juvenile, mental, sealed, or adoption records released. SASE required. Turnaround time 1 week. Fax notes: Fee to fax results is $1.00 per page. Copy fee: $1.00 per page. Certification fee: $5.00. Fee payee: District or County Clerk. Personal checks accepted. Prepayment is required.

Cooke County

District Court County Courthouse, 100 S Dixon, Gainesville, TX 76240; 940-668-5450. Hours: 8AM-5PM (CST). *Felony, Civil.*

Civil Records: Access: Mail, in person. Both court and visitors may perform in person searches. Search fee: $5.00 per name. Required to search: name, years to search. Civil cases indexed by defendant, plaintiff. Civil records on microfiche from late 1900s, index books from 1800s. Must request specifically if you wish to go back more than 10 years.

Criminal Records: Access: Mail, in person. Both court and visitors may perform in person searches. Search fee: $5.00 per name. Required to search: name, years to search. Criminal records on microfiche from late 1900,s, index books from 1800s.

General Information: No juvenile, mental, sealed, or adoption records released. SASE required. Turnaround time 2 days. Copy fee: $.50 per page. Certification fee: $1.00. Fee payee: District Clerk. Personal checks accepted. Prepayment is required.

County Court County Courthouse, Gainesville, TX 76240; 940-668-5422. Hours: 8AM-5PM (CST). *Misdemeanor, Civil, Probate.*

Civil Records: Access: Mail, in person. Both court and visitors may perform in person searches. Search fee: $5.00 per name. Required to search: name, years to search. Civil cases indexed by defendant, plaintiff. Civil records in index books and original papers from late 1850s.

Criminal Records: Access: Mail, in person. Both court and visitors may perform in person searches. Search fee: $5.00 per name. Required to search: name, years to search, DOB. Criminal records go back to 1969.

General Information: No juvenile, mental, sealed, or adoption records released. SASE not required. Turnaround time 1 day. Copy fee: $1.00 per page. Certification fee: $5.00. Fee payee: Cooke County Clerk. Personal checks accepted. Prepayment required.

Coryell County

District Court PO Box 4, Gatesville, TX 76528; 254-865-5911; Fax: 254-865-5064. Hours: 8AM-5PM (CST). *Felony, Civil.*

Civil Records: Access: Fax, mail, in person. Both court and visitors may perform in person searches. Search fee: $5.00 per name. Required to search: name, years to search. Civil cases indexed by defendant, plaintiff. Civil records in index books from 1854; computerized back to 2000.

Criminal Records: Access: Fax, mail, in person. Both court and visitors may perform in person searches. Search fee: $5.00 per name. Required to search: name, years to search, DOB, SSN. Criminal records in index books from 1854; computerized back to 2000.

General Information: Public access terminal is available. No juvenile, sealed, or adoption records released. SASE required. Turnaround time 1 day. Fax notes: Fee to fax results is $1.00 per page. Copy fee: $1.00 per page. Fee payee: District Clerk. Personal checks accepted from Coryell County residents only. Money order or cashiers check for other residents. Prepayment is required.

County Court PO Box 237, Gatesville, TX 76528; 254-865-5016; Fax: 254-865-8631. Hours: 8AM-Noon, 1-5PM (CST). *Misdemeanor, Civil, Probate.*

Civil Records: Access: Mail, in person. Visitors must perform in person searches for themselves. Search fee: $10.00 per name per 10 years. Required to search: name, years to search. Civil cases indexed by defendant, plaintiff. Civil records on computer back to 1995, index books from 1846.

Criminal Records: Access: Mail, in person. Visitors must perform in person searches for themselves. Search fee: $10.00 per name per 10 years. Required to search: name, years to search, DOB, SSN. Criminal records on computer back to 1995; index books from 1846.

General Information: Public access terminal is available. No juvenile, mental, sealed, or adoption records released. SASE required. Turnaround time 1-5 days. Fax notes: $1.00 per page. Fax fee for out of county request is $5.00 plus $1.00 per page. Copy fee: $1.00 per page. Certification fee: $5.00 plus $1.00 per page. Fee payee: County Clerk. Business checks accepted. Personal checks must be in county. Prepayment is required.

Cottle County

District & County Court PO Box 717, Paducah, TX 79248; 806-492-3823. Hours: 9AM-Noon, 1-5PM (CST). *Felony, Misdemeanor, Civil, Probate.*

Civil Records: Access: Mail, in person. Both court and visitors may perform in person searches. Search fee: $5.00 per name. Required to search: name, years to search. Civil cases indexed by defendant, plaintiff. Civil records in index books from 1892.

Criminal Records: Access: Mail, in person. Both court and visitors may perform in person searches. Search fee: $5.00 per name. Required to search: name, years to search. Criminal records in index books from 1892.

General Information: No juvenile, mental, sealed, or adoption records released. SASE required. Turnaround time 2-3 days. Copy fee: $1.00 per page. Certification fee: $1.00. Fee payee: Cottle County Clerk. Personal checks accepted. Prepayment is required.

Crane County

District & County Court PO Box 578, Crane, TX 79731; 915-558-3581. Hours: 9AM-12 1-5PM (CST). *Felony, Misdemeanor, Civil, Probate.*

Civil Records: Access: In person only. Visitors must perform in person searches for themselves. Required to search: name, years to search. Civil cases indexed by

defendant, plaintiff. Limited civil records on computer from 1990; index books from 1927.

Criminal Records: Access: Mail, fax, in person. Both court and visitors may perform in person searches. Search fee: $5.00 per name. Ten year search only. Required to search: name, years to search, offense. Limited criminal records on computer from 1990; index books from 1927.

General Information: Public access terminal is available. No juvenile, mental, sealed or adoption records released. SASE required. Turnaround time 2-5 days. Copy fee: $1.00 per page. Certification fee: County = $5.00. District Court = $1.00. Fee payee: District or County Clerk. Only cashiers checks and money orders accepted. Prepayment is required.

Crockett County

District & County Court PO Drawer C, Ozona, TX 76943; 915-392-2022. Hours: 8AM-5PM (CST). *Felony, Misdemeanor, Civil, Probate.*

Civil Records: Access: Mail, in person. Both court and visitors may perform in person searches. Search fee: $10.00 per name. Required to search: name, years to search. Civil cases indexed by defendant, plaintiff. Civil records on computer from 1982, index books from 1800s.

Criminal Records: Access: Mail, in person. Both court and visitors may perform in person searches. Search fee: $10.00 per name. Required to search: name, years to search, DOB, SSN, signed release. Criminal records on computer from 1982, index books from 1800s.

General Information: No juvenile, mental, sealed, or adoption records released. SASE not required. Turnaround time 1 week. Fax notes: Fee to fax results is $1.00 per page. Copy fee: $1.00 per page. Certification fee: $5.00. Fee payee: District or County Clerk. Personal checks accepted. Prepayment is required.

Crosby County

District Court 201 W Aspen St #207, Crosbyton, TX 79322-2500; 806-675-2071; Fax: 806-675-2433. Hours: 8AM-Noon, 1-5PM (CST). *Felony, Civil.*

Civil Records: Access: Phone, fax, mail, in person. Both court and visitors may perform in person searches. Search fee: $5.00 per name. Required to search: name, years to search. Civil cases indexed by defendant, plaintiff. Civil records in index books from 1896.

Criminal Records: Access: Phone, fax, mail, in person. Both court and visitors may perform in person searches. Search fee: $5.00 per name. Required to search: name, years to search. Criminal records in index books from 1896.

General Information: No juvenile, mental, sealed, or adoption records released. SASE required. Turnaround time 1 day. Fax notes: No fee to fax results. Only for local or toll free calls. Copy fee: $1.00 per page. Certification fee: $1.00. Fee payee: District Clerk. Personal checks accepted. Prepayment is required.

County Court 201 W Aspen St #102, Crosbyton, TX 79322-2500; 806-675-2334. Hours: 8AM-noon, 1:00PM-5PM (CST). *Misdemeanor, Civil, Probate.*

Civil Records: Access: Mail, in person. Both court and visitors may perform in person searches. No search fee. Required to search: name, years to search. Civil cases indexed by defendant, plaintiff. Civil records on microfiche from 1990, index books from 1886.

Criminal Records: Access: Mail, in person. Both court and visitors may perform in person searches. Search fee: $5.00 per name. Required to search: name, years to search. Criminal records on microfiche from 1990, index books from 1886.

General Information: No juvenile, mental, sealed, or adoption records released. SASE not required. Turnaround time 1 day. Copy fee: $1.00 per page.

Certification fee: $5.00. Fee payee: County Clerk. Personal checks accepted. Prepayment is required.

Culberson County

District & County Court PO Box 158, Van Horn, TX 79855; 915-283-2058. Hours: 8AM-5PM (CST). *Felony, Misdemeanor, Civil, Probate.*

Civil Records: Access: Phone, mail, fax, in person. Both court and visitors may perform in person searches. Search fee: $5.00 per name. Required to search: name, years to search. Civil cases indexed by defendant, plaintiff. Civil records in index books since 1911.

Criminal Records: Access: Phone, mail, fax, in person. Both court and visitors may perform in person searches. Search fee: $5.00 per name. Required to search: name, years to search, signed release. Criminal records in index books since 1911.

General Information: No juvenile, mental, sealed, or adoption records released. SASE required. Turnaround time 2 days. Fax notes: Fee to fax results is $1.00 per page. Copy fee: $1.00 per page. Certification fee: $5.00. Fee payee: District or County Clerk. Personal checks accepted. Prepayment is required.

Dallam County

District & County Court PO Box 1352, Dalhart, TX 79022; 806-249-4751; Fax: 806-249-2252. Hours: 9AM-5PM (CST). *Felony, Misdemeanor, Civil, Probate.*

Civil Records: Access: Fax, mail, in person. Both court and visitors may perform in person searches. Search fee: $5.00 per name. Required to search: name, years to search. Civil cases indexed by defendant, plaintiff. Civil records in index books from 1800s; computerized since 1991.

Criminal Records: Access: Fax, mail, in person. Both court and visitors may perform in person searches. Search fee: $5.00 per name. Required to search: name, years to search. Criminal records in index books from 1800s; computerized since 1991.

General Information: No juvenile, mental, sealed, or adoption records released. SASE required. Turnaround time 1 day. Fax notes: $5.00 for first page, $1.00 each add'l. Copy fee: $1.00 per page. Certification fee: $5.00. Fee payee: Dallam County Clerk. Personal checks accepted. Prepayment is required.

Dallas County

District Court - Civil 600 Commerce St, Dallas, TX 75202-4606; 214-653-7421. Hours: 8AM-6:00PM (CST). *Civil.*

www.dallascounty.org

Civil Records: Access: Mail, online, in person. Both court and visitors may perform in person searches. Search fee: $5.00 per name. Required to search: name, years to search, DOB. Civil cases indexed by defendant, plaintiff. Civil records on computer since 1967; on dockets back to 1940; records prior to 1940 are maintained by Texas Historical Div. of the Dallas Public Library. Public Access System allows remote access at $1.00 per minute to these and other court/public records. Will invoice to your telephone bill. Access number is 900-263-INFO. ProComm Plus is recommended. Searching is by name or case number. Call the Public Access Administrator at 214-653-7717 for more information.

General Information: Public access terminal is available. No sealed records released. Fax notes: Fee to fax results is $1.00 per page. Copy fee: $1.00 per page. Fee payee: District Clerk. Only cashiers checks and money orders accepted. Prepayment is required.

District Court - Criminal 133 N Industrial Blvd, Dallas, TX 75207-4313; 214-653-5950; Fax: 214-653-5986. Hours: 8AM-4:30PM (CST). *Felony.*

www.dallascounty.org

Criminal Records: Access: Mail, online, in person. Both court and visitors may perform in person searches. Search fee: $5.00 per name. Required to search: name, years to search, DOB. Criminal records on computer from 1972, on microfiche from 1979. Public Access System allows remote access at $1.00 per minute to these and other court/public records. Will invoice to your telephone bill. Access number is 900-263-INFO. ProComm Plus is recommended. The system is open 8am to 4:30pm. Searching is by name or case number. Call the Public Access Administrator at 214-653-6807 for more information.

General Information: Public access terminal is available. No juvenile, mental, sealed, or adoption records released. SASE required. Turnaround time 1-2 days. Copy fee: $1.00 per page. Certification fee: $1.00 per page. Fee payee: District Clerk. Only cashiers checks and money orders accepted. Prepayment is required.

County Court - Misdemeanor 133 N Industrial Blvd LB43, Dallas, TX 75207-4313; 214-653-5740. Hours: 8AM-4:30PM (CST). *Misdemeanor.*

www.dallascounty.org

Criminal Records: Access: Mail, online, in person. Both court and visitors may perform in person searches. Search fee: $5.00 per name. Required to search: name, years to search, DOB. Criminal records on computer from 1972; prior on microfiche. For older searches call 214-653-5763. Public Access System allows remote access at $1.00 per minute to these and other court/public records. Will invoice to your telephone bill. Access number is 900-263-INFO. ProComm Plus is recommended. Searching is by name or case number. Call the Public Access Administrator at 214-653-6807 for more information.

General Information: Public access terminal is available. No juvenile, mental, sealed, or adoption records released. SASE required. Turnaround time 2-3 weeks. Copy fee: $1.00 per page. Certification fee: $5.00. Fee payee: County Clerk. Only cashiers checks and money orders accepted or cash if in person. Prepayment is required.

County Court - Civil 509 W Main 3rd Floor, Dallas, TX 75202; 214-653-7131. Hours: 8AM-4:30PM (CST). *Civil.*

www.dallascounty.org

Note: No civil claims limit as of 05/23/97 in Dallas County

Civil Records: Access: Phone, mail, online, in person. Both court and visitors may perform in person searches. Search fee: $5.00 per name per 10 years. Required to search: name, years to search. Civil cases indexed by defendant, plaintiff. Civil records on computer from 1964, index books from 1800s. Public Access System allows remote access at $1.00 per minute to these and other court/public records. Will invoice to your telephone bill. Access number is 900-263-INFO. ProComm Plus is recommended. Searching is by name or case number. Call the Public Access Administrator at 214-653-6807 for more information.

General Information: Public access terminal is available. No juvenile, mental, sealed, or adoption records released. SASE required. Turnaround time 1 day. Copy fee: $1.00 per page. Certification fee: $5.00. Fee payee: Earl Bullock, County Clerk. Personal checks accepted. Prepayment is required.

Probate Court #3 Records Bldg, 2nd Floor, Dallas, TX 75202; 214-653-6166. Hours: 8AM-4:30PM (CST). *Probate.*

Note: Remote access system for civil and criminal records in this county includes probate records.

Dawson County

District Court Drawer 1268, Lamesa, TX 79331; 806-872-7373; Fax: 806-872-9513. Hours: 8:30AM-5PM (CST). *Felony, Civil.*

Civil Records: Access: Mail, in person. Both court and visitors may perform in person searches. Search fee: $5.00 per name. Required to search: name, years to search. Civil cases indexed by defendant, plaintiff. Civil records in index books/files from 1900; computerized records since 1995.

Criminal Records: Access: Mail, in person. Both court and visitors may perform in person searches. Search fee: $5.00 per name. Required to search: name, years to search, signed release. Criminal records in index books/files from 1900s; computerized records since 1995.

General Information: No juvenile, mental, sealed, or adoption records released. SASE not required. Turnaround time 1 day. Fax notes: $1.00 per page. Copy fee: $1.00 per page. Certification fee: $1.00 per page. Fee payee: Dawson County District Clerk. Personal checks accepted. Prepayment is required.

County Court Drawer 1268, Lamesa, TX 79331; 806-872-3778; Fax: 806-872-2473. Hours: 8:30AM-5PM (CST). *Misdemeanor, Civil, Probate.*

Civil Records: Access: Fax, mail, in person. Both court and visitors may perform in person searches. Search fee: $5.00 per name. Required to search: name, years to search. Civil cases indexed by defendant, plaintiff. Civil records in index files since 1905; on computer back to 1992. Fees must be prepaid before fax access is allowed.

Criminal Records: Access: Mail, in person. Both court and visitors may perform in person searches. Search fee: $5.00 per name. Required to search: name, years to search, DOB; also helpful-signed release, offense, date of offense. Criminal records in index files since 1905; on computer back to 1992. Fees must be prepaid before fax access is allowed.

General Information: No juvenile, mental or sealed records released. SASE not required. Turnaround time 1 day. Fax notes: Fee to fax results is $5.00 per document and $1.00 per page. Copy fee: $1.00 per page. Certification fee: $5.00. Fee payee: County Clerk. Personal checks accepted. Prepayment is required.

De Witt County

County Court 307 N Gonzales, Cuero, TX 77954; 361-275-3724; Fax: 361-275-8994. Hours: 8AM-5PM (CST). *Misdemeanor, Probate.*

Civil Records: Access: Phone, fax, mail, in person. Search fee: $5.00 per name. Required to search: name, years to search. Civil cases indexed by defendant, plaintiff. Civil records go back to 1960s; on computer back to 1998.

Criminal Records: Access: Mail, in person. Both court and visitors may perform in person searches. Search fee: $5.00 per name. Required to search: name, years to search; also helpful: DOB, SSN. Criminal records go back to 1960s; on computer back to 1998.

General Information: No juvenile, mental, sealed, or adoption records released. SASE required. Fax notes: Fee to fax results is $1.00 per page. Copy fee: $1.00 per page. Certification fee: $1.00. Fee payee: DeWitt County Clerk. Personal checks accepted. Prepayment is required.

District Court PO Box 845, Cuero, TX 77954; 361-275-2221. Hours: 8AM-5PM (CST). *Felony, Civil.*

Civil Records: Access: Mail, in person. Both court and visitors may perform in person searches. Search fee: $5.00 per name. Required to search: name, years to search. Civil cases indexed by defendant, plaintiff.

Criminal Records: Access: Mail, in person. Both court and visitors may perform in person searches. Search

fee: $5.00 per name. Required to search: name, years to search, DOB, SSN, signed release. Criminal records maintained on books.

General Information: No juvenile, mental, sealed, or adoption records released. SASE required. Turnaround time 1 week. Copy fee: $1.00 per page. Certification fee: $1.00. Fee payee: District Clerk. Personal checks accepted. Prepayment is required.

Deaf Smith County

District Court 235 E Third St Rm 304, Hereford, TX 79045; 806-364-3901; Fax: 806-363-7007. Hours: 8AM-5PM (CST). *Felony, Civil.*

Civil Records: Access: Fax, mail, in person. Both court and visitors may perform in person searches. Search fee: $5.00 per name. Required to search: name, years to search. Civil cases indexed by defendant, plaintiff. Civil records on computer from 2/1993; prior on microfiche from 5/15/1981.

Criminal Records: Access: Fax, mail, in person. Both court and visitors may perform in person searches. Search fee: $5.00 per name. Required to search: name, years to search; also helpful: DOB, SSN, case number. Criminal records on computer from 2/1993; prior on microfiche from 5/15/1981.

General Information: Public access terminal is available. No juvenile, mental, sealed, or adoption records released. SASE required. Turnaround time 1 day. Fax notes: Fee to fax results is $2.00 per page. Copy fee: $1.00 per page. Certification fee: $1.00. Fee payee: District Clerk. Personal checks accepted. Prepayment is required.

County Court Deaf Smith Courthouse, 235 E Third, Room 203, Hereford, TX 79045; 806-363-7077. 8AM-5PM (CST). *Misdemeanor, Civil, Probate.*

Civil Records: Access: Mail, in person. Both court and visitors may perform in person searches. Search fee: $5.00 per name. Required to search: name, years to search. Civil cases indexed by defendant, plaintiff. Civil records on computer from 1989, microfiche from 1981, index books from early 1900s.

Criminal Records: Access: Mail, in person. Both court and visitors may perform in person searches. Search fee: $5.00 per name. Required to search: name, years to search. Criminal records on computer from 1989, microfiche from 1981, index books from early 1900s.

General Information: Public access terminal is available. No juvenile, mental, sealed, or adoption records released. SASE not required. Turnaround time 1 day. Copy fee: $1.00 per page. Certification fee: $5.00. Fee payee: County Clerk. Personal checks accepted. Prepayment is required.

Delta County

District & County Court PO Box 455, Cooper, TX 75432; 903-395-4400 x223; Fax: 903-395-2178. Hours: 8AM-5PM (CST). *Felony, Misdemeanor, Civil, Probate.*

Civil Records: Access: Phone, mail, in person. Both court and visitors may perform in person searches. Search fee: $5.00 per name. Required to search: name, years to search. Civil cases indexed by defendant, plaintiff. Civil records in index books from late 1800s. Phone searches must be pre-paid.

Criminal Records: Access: Phone, mail, in person. Both court and visitors may perform in person searches. Search fee: $5.00 per name. Required to search: name, years to search, DOB. Criminal records in index books from late 1800s. Phone searches must be prepaid.

General Information: No juvenile, mental, sealed, or adoption records released. SASE required. Turnaround time 1 day. Fax notes: Fee to fax is $2.50 per page plus $1.00 per document. Copy fee: $1.00 per page. Certification fee: $5.00. Fee payee: County or District Clerk. Personal checks accepted. Prepayment required.

Denton County

District Court PO Box 2146, Denton, TX 76202; 940-349-2200; Fax: 940-349-2201. Hours: 8AM-4:30PM (CST). *Felony, Civil.*

http://dentoncounty.com/dept/main.asp?Dept=26

Civil Records: Access: Phone, mail, fax, online, in person. Both court and visitors may perform in person searches. Search fee: $5.00 per name. Required to search: name, years to search. Civil cases indexed by defendant, plaintiff. Civil records on computer from 1990, archived from 1936. Civil searches available at http://justice.dentoncounty.com at no charge. Search by name or cause number.

Criminal Records: Access: Mail, fax, online, in person. Both court and visitors may perform in person searches. Search fee: $5.00 per name. Required to search: name, years to search, DOB. Criminal records on computer from 1990, archived from 1936. Criminal searches are available at http://justice.dentoncounty.com at no charge. Records available from 1994 forward. Access also includes sheriff bond and jail records.

General Information: Public access terminal is available. No juvenile, mental, sealed, expunctions or adoption records released. SASE required. Turnaround time 1-2 weeks. Fax notes: Fee to fax results is $1.00 per page. Copy fee: $1.00 per page. Certification fee: $1.00. Fee payee: District Clerk. Personal checks accepted. Credit cards accepted: Visa, MasterCard.

County Court Attn: County Clerk, PO Box 2187, Denton, TX 76202-2187; Civil phone: 940-565-8518; Criminal phone: 940-565-8520; Probate phone: 940-349-2036. Hours: 8AM-5PM (CST). *Misdemeanor, Civil, Probate.*

www.dentoncounty.com/dept/ccl.htm

Civil Records: Access: Mail, in person, online. Both court and visitors may perform in person searches. Search fee: $5.00 per name. Add $1.00 per year over first 5. Required to search: name, years to search. Civil cases indexed by defendant, plaintiff. Civil records on computer from 1989, microfiche from 1968. Online access to civil court records is available free online at http://justice.dentoncounty.com/CivilSearch/civfrmd.htm.

Criminal Records: Access: Mail, in person, online. Both court and visitors may perform in person searches. Search fee: $5.00 per name. Add $1.00 per year over first 5. Required to search: name, years to search, DOB. Criminal records on computer from 1989, microfiche from 1968. Online access to county criminal records available free at http://justice.dentoncounty.com/CrimSearch/crimfrmd.htm. Jail, bond, and parole records are also available at http://justice.dentoncounty.com. Search for registered sex offenders by zip code at http://sherrif.dentoncounty.com/sex_offenders/default.htm.

General Information: Public access terminal is available. No juvenile, mental, sealed, or adoption records released. SASE required. Turnaround time 1-2 weeks. Copy fee: $1.00 per page. Certification fee: $5.00. Fee payee: Denton County Clerk. Only cashiers checks and money orders accepted. Prepayment is required.

Dickens County

District & County Court PO Box 120, Dickens, TX 79229; 806-623-5531; Fax: 806-623-5319. Hours: 8AM-5PM (CST). *Felony, Misdemeanor, Civil, Probate.*

Civil Records: Access: Mail, fax, phone, in person. Both court and visitors may perform in person searches. Search fee: $5.00 per name. Required to search: name, years to search, DOB, SSN and signed release. Civil cases indexed by defendant, plaintiff. Civil records in index books since late 1891.

Criminal Records: Access: Mail, fax, phone, in person. Both court and visitors may perform in person searches. Search fee: $5.00 per name. Required to search: name, years to search; also helpful: DOB, SSN and signed release. Criminal records in index books since late 1891.

General Information: No juvenile, mental, sealed or adoption records released. SASE required. Turnaround time 1-2 days. Fax notes: Will not fax results. Copy fee: $1.00 per page. Certification fee: $5.00. Fee payee: District Court. Personal checks accepted. Prepayment is required.

Dimmit County

District Court 303 S 5th, Carrizo Springs, TX 78834; 830-876-2323 #244; Fax: 830-876-5036. Hours: 8AM-Noon; 1PM-5PM (CST). *Felony, Civil.*

Civil Records: Access: Mail, in person. Both court and visitors may perform in person searches. Search fee: $5.00 per name. Required to search: name, years to search; also helpful: address. Civil cases indexed by defendant, plaintiff. Civil records in index books, archived from 1936.

Criminal Records: Access: Mail, in person. Both court and visitors may perform in person searches. Search fee: $5.00 per name. Required to search: name, years to search; also helpful: DOB, SSN. Criminal records in index books, archived from 1936.

General Information: No juvenile, mental, sealed, or adoption records released. SASE required. Turnaround time 2-3 days. Copy fee: $1.00 per page. Certification fee: $1.00 per page. Fee payee: District Clerk. Personal checks accepted. Prepayment is required.

County Court 103 N 5th, Carrizo Springs, TX 78834; 830-876-2323 x232; Fax: 830-876-4205. Hours: 8AM-5PM (CST). *Misdemeanor, Civil, Probate.*

Civil Records: Access: Phone, fax, mail, in person. Both court and visitors may perform in person searches. Search fee: $5.00 per name. Required to search: name, years to search. Civil cases indexed by defendant, plaintiff. Civil records on microfiche from 1992, index books prior.

Criminal Records: Access: Phone, fax, mail, in person. Both court and visitors may perform in person searches. Search fee: $5.00 per name. Required to search: name, years to search, signed release, DOB; also helpful: sex, SSN. Criminal records on microfiche from 1992, index books prior.

General Information: No juvenile, mental, sealed, or adoption records released. SASE required. Turnaround time 1 day. Fax notes: Fee to fax results is $2.00 1st page; $1.00 each add'l. Copy fee: $1.00 per page. Certification fee: $5.00. Fee payee: County Clerk. Personal checks accepted. Prepayment is required.

Donley County

District & County Court PO Drawer U, Clarendon, TX 79226; 806-874-3436; Fax: 806-874-5146. Hours: 8AM-Noon, 1-5PM (CST). *Felony, Misdemeanor, Civil, Probate.*

Civil Records: Access: Mail, in person. Both court and visitors may perform in person searches. Search fee: $5.00 per name. Required to search: name, years to search. Civil cases indexed by defendant, plaintiff. Civil records on computer from 1991, index books from 1890s.

Criminal Records: Access: Mail, in person. Both court and visitors may perform in person searches. Search fee: $5.00 per name. Required to search: name, years to search, DOB, signed release, aliases; also helpful: SSN. Criminal records on computer from 1991, index books from 1890s.

General Information: Public access terminal is available. No juvenile, mental, sealed, or adoption records released. SASE required. Turnaround time 1 day. Copy fee: $1.00 per page. Certification fee: $1.00. Fee payee: County Clerk. Personal checks accepted. Prepayment is required.

Duval County

District Court PO Drawer 428, San Diego, TX 78384; 361-279-3322 X239. Hours: 8AM-5PM (CST). *Felony, Civil.*

Civil Records: Access: Mail, in person. Both court and visitors may perform in person searches. Search fee: $15.00 per name. Fee is for large cases. Required to search: name, years to search. Civil cases indexed by defendant, plaintiff. Civil records on index books from 1900s.
Criminal Records: Access: Phone, mail, in person. Both court and visitors may perform in person searches. Search fee: $15.00 per name. Fee is for large cases. Required to search: name, years to search. Criminal records not computerized, indexed in books since 1900's.
General Information: No sealed, or adoption records released. SASE required. Turnaround time 1-2 days. Copy fee: $1.00 per page. Certification fee: $3.00. Fee payee: District Clerk. Personal checks accepted. Prepayment is required.

County Court PO Box 248, San Diego, TX 78384; 361-279-3322. Hours: 8AM-Noon, 1-5PM (CST). *Misdemeanor, Civil, Probate.*

Civil Records: Access: Mail, in person. Both court and visitors may perform in person searches. Search fee: $10.00 per name. Required to search: name, years to search. Civil cases indexed by defendant, plaintiff. Civil records in index books from 1800s, records go back to the early 1900's.
Criminal Records: Access: Mail, in person. Both court and visitors may perform in person searches. Search fee: $10.00 per name. Required to search: name, years to search, offense, date of offense. Criminal records in index books from 1800s.
General Information: No juvenile, mental, sealed, or adoption records released. SASE required. Turnaround time 2 days. Copy fee: $1.00 per page. Certification fee: $5.00. Fee payee: County Clerk. Personal checks accepted. Prepayment is required.

Eastland County

District Court PO Box 670, Eastland, TX 76448; 254-629-2664; Fax: 254-629-1558. Hours: 8AM-5PM (CST). *Felony, Civil.*

Civil Records: Access: Phone, fax, mail, online, in person. Both court and visitors may perform in person searches. No search fee. Required to search: name, years to search. Civil cases indexed by defendant, plaintiff. Civil records on computer from 1930. Civil case information is available online at www.idocket.com. Free searching is limited. Records go back to 12/31/1940.
Criminal Records: Access: Phone, fax, mail, online, in person. Both court and visitors may perform in person searches. No search fee. Required to search: name, years to search. Criminal records on computer from 1976, archived from 1875. Online access is through www.idocket.com; registration and password required. Records go back to 12/31/1966.
General Information: No juvenile, mental, sealed, or adoption records released. SASE required. Turnaround time 1 day. Copy fee: $1.00 per page. Fee payee: District Clerk. Personal checks accepted. Prepayment is required.

County Court PO Box 110, Eastland, TX 76448; 254-629-1583. Hours: 8AM-5PM (CST). *Misdemeanor, Probate.*

Note: No civil records after 1977; criminal and probate records only thereafter.

Criminal Records: Access: Mail, in person. Both court and visitors may perform in person searches. Search fee: $5.00 per name. Required to search: name, years to search, DOB; also helpful: SSN. Signed release required if subject is a minor. Criminal records in index books from 1873. Name searches only.
General Information: No juvenile, mental, sealed, or adoption records released. SASE not required. Turnaround time 1-2 days. Copy fee: $1.00 per page. Certification fee: $5.00. Fee payee: Eastland County Clerk. Personal checks accepted. Checks accepted (must have phone number & DL # on check). Prepayment is required.

Ector County

District Court County Courthouse, 300 N Grant, Rm 301, Odessa, TX 79761; 915-498-4290; Fax: 915-498-4292. Hours: 8AM-5PM (CST). *Felony, Civil.*

Civil Records: Access: Phone, fax, mail, in person. Both court and visitors may perform in person searches. Search fee: $5.00 per name. Required to search: name, years to search. Civil cases indexed by defendant, plaintiff. Civil records on computer from 1989, index books from 1880.
Criminal Records: Access: Phone, mail, in person. Only the court performs in person searches; visitors may not. Search fee: $5.00 per name. Required to search: name, years to search. Criminal records on computer from 1989, index books from 1880.
General Information: Public access terminal is available. No juvenile, mental, sealed, or adoption records released. SASE required. Turnaround time 2 weeks. Fax notes: $2.00 per page. Copy fee: $.25 per page. Certification fee: $1.00 per page. Fee payee: Ector County District Clerk. Business checks accepted. Prepayment is required.

County Court PO Box 707, Odessa, TX 79760; 915-498-4130. Hours: 8AM-4:30PM (CST). *Misdemeanor, Civil, Probate.*

Civil Records: Access: Mail, in person. Both court and visitors may perform in person searches. Search fee: $5.00 per name. Required to search: name, years to search. Civil cases indexed by defendant, plaintiff. Civil records on computer from 1992, index books from 1900s.
Criminal Records: Access: Mail, in person. Both court and visitors may perform in person searches. Search fee: $5.00 per name. Required to search: name, years to search; also helpful: DOB, SSN. Criminal records on computer from 1989, index books from 1900s.
General Information: Public access terminal is available. No juvenile, mental, sealed, or adoption records released. SASE required. Turnaround time 2 days. Fax notes: Fee to fax back $2.00 per document. Copy fee: $1.00 per page. Certification fee: $5.00. Fee payee: County Clerk. Personal checks accepted. Prepayment is required.

Edwards County

District & County Court PO Box 184, Rocksprings, TX 78880; 830-683-2235; Fax: 830-683-5376. Hours: 8AM-Noon, 1-5PM (CST). *Felony, Misdemeanor, Civil, Probate.*

Civil Records: Access: Phone, fax, mail, in person. Both court and visitors may perform in person searches. Search fee: $5.00 per name. Required to search: name, years to search. Civil cases indexed by defendant, plaintiff. Civil records on computer from 1991, Real Property on computer from 1960, index books from 1885.
Criminal Records: Access: Phone, fax, mail, in person. Both court and visitors may perform in person searches. Search fee: $10.00 per name. Required to search: name, years to search. Criminal records on computer from 1991, index books from 1960.

General Information: No juvenile, mental, sealed, or adoption records released. SASE required. Turnaround time 1 day. Fax notes: Fee to fax results is $2.50 for first page, $.50 per page thereafter. Copy fee: $1.00 per page. Certification fee: $5.00. Payee: Edwards County Clerk. Personal checks okay. Prepayment required.

El Paso County

District Court 500 East San Antonio Rm 103, El Paso, TX 79901; 915-546-2021. Hours: 8AM-4:45PM (MST). *Felony, Civil.*

Civil Records: Access: Mail, in person, online. Both court and visitors may perform in person searches. Search fee: $5.00 per name. Fee is per 10 year period. Required to search: name, years to search. Civil cases indexed by defendant, plaintiff. Civil records on computer from 1976, microfiche from 1971, index books from 1800s. Online access to civil court records is available free at www.co.el-paso.tx.us/search.htm. (pending cases only).
Criminal Records: Access: Mail, in person, online. Both court and visitors may perform in person searches. Search fee: $5.00 per name. Fee is per 10 year period. Required to search: name, years to search, DOB, signed release; also helpful: sex. Criminal records on computer from 1986, microfiche from 1971, index books from 1800s. Online access to criminal records is available at free at www.co.el-paso.tx.us/search.htm. Also, online access is through www.idocket.com; registration and password required; records go back to 6/1/2002.
General Information: Public access terminal is available. No juvenile, mental, sealed, or adoption records released. SASE required. Turnaround time 1-3 days. Copy fee: $.25 per page. Certification fee: $1.00. Fee payee: District Clerk. Business checks accepted. Credit cards accepted: Visa, MasterCard. Prepayment is required.

County Court 500 E San Antonio St Rm 105, El Paso, TX 79901; 915-546-2072. Hours: 8AM-4:45PM (MST). *Misdemeanor, Civil.*

Civil Records: Access: Mail, fax, in person, online. Both court and visitors may perform in person searches. Search fee: $5.00 per name. Required to search: name, years to search. Civil cases indexed by defendant, plaintiff. Civil records on computer from 1989, on microfiche and archived from 1952. Online access to civil court records is available free at www.co.el-paso.tx.us/search.htm.
Criminal Records: Access: Phone, mail, fax, in person, online. Both court and visitors may perform in person searches. Search fee: $5.00 per name. Required to search: name, years to search, DOB, SSN. Criminal records computerized since 1989. Online access to criminal records is the same as civil.
General Information: Public access terminal is available. No juvenile, mental, sealed, or adoption records released. SASE required. Turnaround time up to 1 week. Copy fee: $1.00 per page. Certification fee: $5.00. Fee payee: County Clerk. Personal checks accepted. Prepayment is required.

Probate Court 500 E San Antonio, Rm 1201 A, El Paso, TX 79901; 915-546-2161; Fax: 915-533-4448. Hours: 8AM-5PM (MST). *Probate.*

Ellis County

District Court 1201 N Hiway 77 #B, Waxahachie, TX 75165; 972-923-5000. 8AM-5PM *Felony, Civil.*

Civil Records: Access: Mail, in person. Both court and visitors may perform in person searches. Search fee: $5.00 per name. Required to search: name, years to search. Civil cases indexed by defendant, plaintiff. Civil records on computer from 1992, index books from 1800s.
Criminal Records: Access: Mail, in person. Both court and visitors may perform in person searches. Search

fee: $5.00 per name. Required to search: name, years to search, DOB, offense. Criminal records on computer from 1992, index books from 1800s.

General Information: Public access terminal is available. No juvenile, mental, sealed, or adoption records released. SASE required. Turnaround time 1 week. Copy fee: $.50 per page. Certification fee: $1.00 per page. Fee payee: District Clerk's Office. Only cashiers checks and money orders accepted. Prepayment is required.

County Court PO Box 250, Waxahachie, TX 75168; 972-923-5070. Hours: 8AM-4:45PM (CST). *Misdemeanor, Civil, Probate.*

Civil Records: Access: Mail, in person. Both court and visitors may perform in person searches. Search fee: $10.00 per name. Fee is per 5 year period. Required to search: name, years to search, DOB, SSN, Signed release. Civil cases indexed by defendant, plaintiff. Civil records on computer go back to 1995. Prior to computer records go back to 1969.

Criminal Records: Access: Mail, in person. Both court and visitors may perform in person searches. Search fee: $10.00 per name. Fee is per 5 year period. Required to search: name, years to search. Criminal records on computer since 1992, index books from 1959.

General Information: Public access terminal is available. No juvenile, mental, sealed, or adoption records released. SASE required. Turnaround time 1-5 days. Copy fee: $1.00 per page. Certification fee: $5.00. Fee payee: Ellis County Clerk. Personal checks accepted. Prepayment is required.

Erath County

District Court 112 W College, Courthouse Annex, Stephenville, TX 76401; 254-965-1486; Fax: 254-965-7156. Hours: 8AM-Noon, 1-5PM (CST). *Felony, Civil.*

Civil Records: Access: Mail, fax, in person. Both court and visitors may perform in person searches. Search fee: $5.00 per name. Fee is per name per search. Required to search: name, years to search. Civil cases indexed by defendant, plaintiff. Limited civil records on computer last 10 years, in person must be done using docket books.

Criminal Records: Access: Mail, fax, in person. Both court and visitors may perform in person searches. Search fee: $5.00 per name. Required to search: name, years to search, DOB; also helpful: SSN. Limited criminal records on computer last 10 years, in person must be done using docket books.

General Information: No juvenile, mental, sealed, or adoption records released. SASE required. Turnaround time 1-2 days. Fax notes: Fee to fax results is $1.00 per page. Copy fee: $1.00 per page. Certification fee: $5.00. Fee payee: District Clerk. Personal checks accepted. Prepayment is required.

County Court Erath County Courthouse, Stephenville, TX 76401; 254-965-1482. Hours: 8AM-4PM (CST). *Misdemeanor, Civil, Probate.*

Civil Records: Access: Mail, in person. Both court and visitors may perform in person searches. Search fee: $10.00 per name. Required to search: name, years to search. Civil cases indexed by defendant, plaintiff. Civil records on computer back to 1993, index books to 1970.

Criminal Records: Access: Mail, in person. Both court and visitors may perform in person searches. Search fee: $10.00 per name. Required to search: name, years to search, DOB. Criminal records on computer back to 1993, index books from 1960.

General Information: Public access terminal is available. No juvenile, mental, sealed, or adoption records released. SASE required. Turnaround time 1 week. Copy fee: $1.00 per page. Certification fee: $5.00 plus $1.00 per page. Fee payee: County Clerk. Personal checks accepted. Prepayment is required.

Falls County

District Court 3rd Floor, NW Corner, 125 Bridge St. Room 301, Marlin, TX 76661; 254-883-1419. Hours: 8AM-Noon, 1-5PM (CST). *Felony, Civil.*

Civil Records: Access: Mail, in person. Both court and visitors may perform in person searches. Search fee: $5.00 per name. Required to search: name, years to search. Civil cases indexed by defendant, plaintiff. Overall records go back to 1850's. Computerized records go back to 1998.

Criminal Records: Access: Mail, in person. Both court and visitors may perform in person searches. Search fee: $5.00 per name. Required to search: name, years to search; also helpful: DOB. Criminal records in index books.

General Information: No juvenile, mental, sealed, child support or adoption records released. SASE required. Turnaround time 1-5 days. Copy fee: $1.00 per page. Fee payee: District Clerk. Personal checks accepted. Prepayment is required.

County Court PO Box 458, Marlin, TX 76661; 254-883-1408. Hours: 8AM-5PM (CST). *Misdemeanor, Civil, Probate.*

Civil Records: Access: Phone, mail, in person. Both court and visitors may perform in person searches. Search fee: $5.00 per name. Required to search: name, years to search. Civil cases indexed by defendant, plaintiff. Civil records in index books from 1985. Phone search only available if fee prepaid.

Criminal Records: Access: Phone, mail, in person. Both court and visitors may perform in person searches. Search fee: $5.00 per name. Required to search: name, years to search, DOB, SSN. Criminal records in index books from 1985. Phone search only available if fee prepaid.

General Information: No juvenile, mental, sealed, or adoption records released. SASE required. Turnaround time 1 day. Copy fee: $1.00 per page. Certification fee: $5.00. Fee payee: County Clerk. Business checks accepted. Local personal and business checks accepted. Prepayment is required.

Fannin County

District Court Fannin County Courthouse Ste 201, Bonham, TX 75418; 903-583-7459 X33; Fax: 903-640-1826. 8AM-Noon, 1-5PM (CST). *Felony, Civil.*

Civil Records: Access: Fax, mail, in person. Both court and visitors may perform in person searches. Search fee: $5.00 per name. Required to search: name, years to search. Civil cases indexed by defendant, plaintiff. Civil records in index books, archived from 1865.

Criminal Records: Access: Fax, mail, in person. Both court and visitors may perform in person searches. Search fee: $5.00 per name. Fee is for felonies only. Required to search: name, years to search, address, DOB, SSN. Criminal records on computer from 1985, books from 1975, archived from 1865.

General Information: No juvenile, mental, sealed, or adoption records released. SASE required. Turnaround time 2 days. Fax notes: No fee to fax results. Fax available to 800 numbers only. Copy fee: $1.00 per page. Fee payee: District Clerk, Fannin County. Personal checks accepted. Prepayment is required.

County Court County Courthouse, 101 E Sam Rayburn Ste 102, Bonham, TX 75418; 903-583-7486; Fax: 903-583-7811. Hours: 8AM-5PM (CST). *Misdemeanor, Civil, Probate.*

Civil Records: Access: Phone, mail, in person. Both court and visitors may perform in person searches. Search fee: $5.00 per name. Required to search: name, years to search. Civil cases indexed by defendant, plaintiff. Civil records in index books.

Criminal Records: Access: Phone, mail, in person. Both court and visitors may perform in person searches.

Search fee: $5.00 per name. Required to search: name, years to search, DOB; also helpful-SSN. Criminal records on computer back to 1979; prior on index books. Phone search limited to 1 year.

General Information: No juvenile, mental, sealed, or adoption records released. SASE required. Turnaround time 1 day. Copy fee: $1.00 per page. Certification fee: $5.00. Fee payee: County Clerk. Personal checks accepted. Prepayment is required.

Fayette County

District Court Fayette County Courthouse, 151 N Washington, La Grange, TX 78945; 979-968-3548; Fax: 979-968-2618. Hours: 8AM-5PM (CST). *Felony, Civil.*

Civil Records: Access: Mail, in person. Both court and visitors may perform in person searches. Search fee: $5.00 per name. Required to search: name, years to search. Civil cases indexed by defendant, plaintiff. Civil records in index books, on computer since 1992.

Criminal Records: Access: Mail, in person. Both court and visitors may perform in person searches. Search fee: $5.00 per name. Required to search: name, years to search. Criminal records in index books, on computer since 1992.

General Information: No juvenile, mental, sealed, or adoption records released. SASE required. Turnaround time 2-3 days. Copy fee: $1.00 per page. Certification fee: $2.00. Fee payee: Fayette County District Clerk. Personal checks accepted. Prepayment is required.

County Court PO Box 59, La Grange, TX 78945; 979-968-3251. Hours: 8AM-5PM (CST). *Misdemeanor, Civil, Probate.*

Civil Records: Access: Phone, mail, in person. Both court and visitors may perform in person searches. Search fee: $5.00 per name. Required to search: name, years to search. Civil cases indexed by defendant, plaintiff. Civil records in index books, archived to 1970.

Criminal Records: Access: Phone, mail, in person. Both court and visitors may perform in person searches. Search fee: $5.00 per name. Required to search: name, years to search. Criminal records on computer from 1980, index books prior.

General Information: No juvenile, mental, sealed, or adoption records released. SASE required. Turnaround time 1 day. Copy fee: $1.00 per page. Certification fee: $5.00 plus $1.00 per page. Fee payee: County Clerk. Personal checks accepted. Prepayment is required.

Fisher County

32nd District Court PO Box 88, Roby, TX 79543; 915-776-2279; Fax: 915-776-2815. Hours: 8AM-5PM (CST). *Felony, Civil.*

Civil Records: Access: Mail, fax, in person. Both court and visitors may perform in person searches. Search fee: $10.00 per name. Required to search: name, years to search; also helpful: address. Civil cases indexed by defendant, plaintiff. Civil records in index books to 1886.

Criminal Records: Access: Mail, fax, in person. Both court and visitors may perform in person searches. Search fee: $10.00 per name. Required to search: name, years to search, signed release; also helpful: address, DOB. Criminal records in index books from 1886.

General Information: No juvenile, mental, sealed, or adoption records released. SASE required. Turnaround time 1-2 days. Fax notes: Fee to fax results is $1.00 per page. Copy fee: $1.00 per page. Certification fee: $1.00. Fee payee: District Clerk. Business checks accepted. Prepayment is required.

County Court Box 368, Roby, TX 79543-0368; 915-776-2401. Hours: 8AM-Noon, 1-5PM (CST). *Misdemeanor, Civil, Probate.*

Civil Records: Access: Mail, in person, phone, fax. Both court and visitors may perform in person searches.

Search fee: $5.00 per name. Required to search: name, years to search. Civil cases indexed by defendant, plaintiff. Civil records on computer from 1990 index books from 1880.

Criminal Records: Access: Mail, in person. Both court and visitors may perform in person searches. Search fee: $5.00 per name. Required to search: name, years to search, signed release, offense. Criminal records on computer from 1989, index books from 1886.

General Information: No juvenile, mental, sealed, or adoption records released. SASE required. Turnaround time 1 day. Copy fee: $1.00 per page. Certification fee: $5.00. Fee payee: Fisher County Clerk. Personal checks accepted. Prepayment is required.

Floyd County

District Court PO Box 67, Floydada, TX 79235; 806-983-4923. Hours: 8:30AM-Noon, 1-4:45PM (CST). *Felony, Civil.*

Civil Records: Access: Phone, mail, in person. Both court and visitors may perform in person searches. Search fee: $5.00 per name. Required to search: name, years to search. Civil cases indexed by defendant, plaintiff. Civil records in index books from early 1891.

Criminal Records: Access: Mail, in person. Both court and visitors may perform in person searches. Search fee: $5.00 per name. Required to search: name, years to search. Criminal records in index books to early 1891.

General Information: No juvenile, mental, sealed, or adoption records released. SASE required. Turnaround time 1 day. Copy fee: $.25 per page. Certification fee: $1.00. Fee payee: District Clerk. Personal checks accepted. Prepayment is required.

County Court Courthouse, Rm 101, Main Street, Floydada, TX 79235; 806-983-4900. Hours: 8:30AM-Noon, 1-5PM (CST). *Misdemeanor, Civil, Probate.*

Civil Records: Access: Phone, mail, in person. Both court and visitors may perform in person searches. Search fee: $10.00 per name. Required to search: name, years to search. Civil cases indexed by defendant, plaintiff. Civil records in index books from 1897.

Criminal Records: Access: Phone, mail, in person. Both court and visitors may perform in person searches. Search fee: $10.00 per name. Required to search: name, years to search, DOB, SSN. Criminal records in index books from 1897.

General Information: No juvenile, mental, sealed, or adoption records released. SASE not required. Turnaround time 1-5 days. Fax notes: Fax back $1.00 per page. Copy fee: $1.00 per page. Certification fee: $5.00. Fee payee: County Clerk. Personal checks accepted. Prepayment is required.

Foard County

District & County Court PO Box 539, Crowell, TX 79227; 940-684-1365. Hours: 9AM-4:30PM (CST). *Felony, Misdemeanor, Civil, Probate.*

Civil Records: Access: Mail, in person. Both court and visitors may perform in person searches. Search fee: $10.00 per name. Required to search: name, years to search. Civil cases indexed by defendant, plaintiff. Civil records go back to 1908, civil records in index books from 1910; on computer from 1989.

Criminal Records: Access: Mail, in person. Both court and visitors may perform in person searches. Search fee: $10.00 per name. Required to search: name, years to search, DOB. Crominal records go back to 1908, criminal records in index books from 1910; on computer from 1989.

General Information: No juvenile, mental, sealed, or adoption records released. SASE required. Turnaround time varies. Fax notes: Fee to fax results is $.25 per page. Copy fee: $1.00 per page. Certification fee: $5.00. Fee payee: District or County Clerk. Personal checks accepted. Prepayment is required.

Fort Bend County

District Court 301 Jackson, Richmond, TX 77469; 281-341-4515; Civil phone: 281-341-4562; Criminal phone: 281-341-4542; Fax: 281-341-4519. Hours: 8AM-5PM (CST). *Felony, Civil.*

www.co.fort-bend.tx.us/Admin_of_just
ice/district_clerkdistrict_courts.htm

Note: Physical court location is 401 Jackson.

Civil Records: Access: Phone, mail, online, in person. Both court and visitors may perform in person searches. Search fee: $5.00 per name. Required to search: name, years to search. Civil cases indexed by defendant, plaintiff. Civil records on computer from 1991, index books from early 1900s. Online searching available through a 900 number service. Access fee is $.55 per minute plus a deposit. Call 281-341-4522 for information.

Criminal Records: Access: Phone, mail, online, in person. Both court and visitors may perform in person searches. Search fee: $5.00 per name. Required to search: name, years to search, DOB, SSN. Criminal records on computer from 1981, index books from early 1900s. Criminal records from 1987 are available on the same online system described in civil records.

General Information: Public access terminal is available. (Located at 401 Jackson, Rm 100, Richmond, TX 77469.) No juvenile, mental, sealed, termination or adoption records released. SASE required. Turnaround time 2-3 weeks. Copy fee: $.50 per page. Include $1.00 for postage. Fee for microfilm copies $.50 per page. Fee payee: District Clerk. Personal checks accepted. For legal ease account info call 281-341-4508. Prepayment is required.

County Court 301 Jackson St, #101, Richmond, TX 77469; 281-341-8685; Fax: 281-341-4520. Hours: 8AM-4PM (CST). *Misdemeanor, Civil, Probate.*

www.co.fort-bend.tx.us

Civil Records: Access: Mail, online, in person. Both court and visitors may perform in person searches. Search fee: $10.00 per name. Search fee is for each type record to be searched. Required to search: name, years to search. Civil cases indexed by defendant, plaintiff. Civil records on computer from 1984, microfiche from 1983-1994, 1984-present optical imaged. Online access to the civil records index available free at www.co.fort-bend.tx.us/Admin_of_Justice/County_Clerk/index_info_research.htm. Includes Probate records index online.

Criminal Records: Access: Mail, online, in person. Both court and visitors may perform in person searches. Search fee: $10.00 per name. A search fee for each type record to be searched required. Required to search: name, years to search, DOB. Criminal records on computer from 1983, microfiche from 1983-1994, 1994-present optical imaged. Online access to the criminal index is the same as civil.

General Information: Public access terminal is available. No juvenile, mental, sealed, or adoption records released. SASE not required. Turnaround time 1-2 days. Fax notes: Fee to fax results is $1.00 per page. Copy fee: $1.00 per page. Certification fee: $5.00. Fee payee: Ft Bend County Clerk. Personal checks accepted. Credit cards accepted: Visa, MC. Prepayment is required.

Franklin County

District Court PO Box 750, Mount Vernon, TX 75457; 903-537-4786. Hours: 8AM-5PM (CST). *Felony, Civil.*

Civil Records: Access: Mail, in person. Both court and visitors may perform in person searches. Search fee: $5.00 per name. Required to search: name, years to search. Civil cases indexed by defendant, plaintiff. Civil records on computer from 1987, on microfiche from 1986, index books from 1800s.

Criminal Records: Access: Mail, in person. Both court and visitors may perform in person searches. Search fee: $5.00 per name. Required to search: name, years to search; also helpful: DOB, SSN. Criminal records on computer from 1987, on microfiche from 1986, index books from 1800s.

General Information: No juvenile, mental, sealed, or adoption records released. SASE required. Turnaround time 1 day. Copy fee: $1.00 per page. Certification fee: $5.00. Fee payee: District Clerk. Personal checks accepted. Prepayment is required.

County Court PO Box 68, Mount Vernon, TX 75457; 903-537-4252; Fax: 903-537-2418. Hours: 8AM-5PM (CST). *Misdemeanor, Civil, Probate.*

Civil Records: Access: Mail, in person. Both court and visitors may perform in person searches. Search fee: $5.00 per name. Required to search: name, years to search. Civil cases indexed by defendant, plaintiff. Civil records on computer from 1993 index books from 1847.

Criminal Records: Access: Mail, in person. Both court and visitors may perform in person searches. Search fee: $5.00 per name. Required to search: name, years to search, DOB and SSN. Criminal records on computer from 1993, index books from 1847.

General Information: No juvenile, mental, sealed, or adoption records released. SASE required. Turnaround time 1 day. Fax notes: Fee to fax results is $1.00 per page. Copy fee: $1.00 per page. Certification fee: $5.00. Fee payee: County Clerk. Personal checks accepted. Prepayment is required.

Freestone County

District Court PO Box 722, Fairfield, TX 75840; 903-389-2534. Hours: 8AM-5PM (CST). *Felony, Civil.*

Civil Records: Access: Phone, mail, in person. Both court and visitors may perform in person searches. Search fee: $5.00 per name. Required to search: name, years to search. Civil cases indexed by defendant, plaintiff. Civil records in index books from 1830s.

Criminal Records: Access: Phone, mail, in person. Both court and visitors may perform in person searches. Search fee: $5.00 per name. Required to search: name, years to search. Criminal records in index books from 1830a.

General Information: No juvenile, mental, sealed, or adoption records released. SASE required. Turnaround time 1 day. Copy fee: $1.00 per page. Certification fee: $1.00. Fee payee: District Clerk. Personal checks accepted.

County Court PO Box 1011, Fairfield, TX 75840; 903-389-2635. Hours: 8AM-5PM (CST). *Misdemeanor, Civil, Probate.*

Civil Records: Access: Mail, in person. Both court and visitors may perform in person searches. Search fee: $5.00 per name. Required to search: name, years to search. Civil cases indexed by defendant, plaintiff. Civil records in index books from 1967.

Criminal Records: Access: Mail, in person. Both court and visitors may perform in person searches. Search fee: $5.00 per name. Required to search: name, years to search. Criminal records in index books from 1967.

General Information: No juvenile, mental, sealed, or adoption records released. SASE required. Turnaround time 2 days. Copy fee: $1.00 per page. Certification fee: $5.00. Fee payee: Freestone County Clerk. Personal checks accepted. Prepayment is required.

Frio County

District Court 500 E San Antonio Box 8, Pearsall, TX 78061; 830-334-8073; Fax: 830-334-0047. Hours: 8AM-5PM (CST). *Felony, Civil.*

Civil Records: Access: Mail, in person. Both court and visitors may perform in person searches. Search fee: $5.00 per name. Required to search: name, years to search; also helpful: address. Civil cases indexed by defendant, plaintiff. Civil records in index books from 1890s.

Criminal Records: Access: Mail, in person. Both court and visitors may perform in person searches. Search fee: $5.00 per name. Required to search: name, years to search, DOB; also helpful: address. Criminal records in index books from 1950.

General Information: No juvenile, mental, sealed, or adoption records released. SASE required. Turnaround time 2-3 days. Fax notes: Fee to fax results is $2.00 per page. Copy fee: $1.00 per page. Certification fee: $1.00. Fee payee: District Clerk. Business checks accepted. Prepayment is required.

County Court 500 E San Antonio St #6, Pearsall, TX 78061; 830-334-2214; Fax: 830-334-0021. Hours: 8AM-5PM (CST). *Misdemeanor, Civil, Probate.*

Civil Records: Access: Fax, mail, in person. Both court and visitors may perform in person searches. Search fee: $5.00 per name. Required to search: name, years to search. Civil cases indexed by defendant, plaintiff. Civil records go back to 1800's, civil records in index books from 1876, no computerized records.

Criminal Records: Access: Fax, mail, in person. Both court and visitors may perform in person searches. Search fee: $5.00 per name. Required to search: name, years to search. Criminal records go back to 1800's, criminal records in index books from 1876; no computerized records.

General Information: No juvenile, mental, sealed, or adoption records released. SASE required. Turnaround time 2-4 days. Fax notes: $2.00 per page. Copy fee: $1.00 per page. Certification fee: $5.00. Fee payee: County Clerk. Personal checks accepted. Prepayment is required.

Gaines County

District Court 101 S Main Rm 213, Seminole, TX 79360; 915-758-4013; Fax: 915-758-4036. Hours: 8AM-Noon, 1-5PM (CST). *Felony, Civil.*

Civil Records: Access: Phone, mail, in person. Only the court performs in person searches; visitors may not. Search fee: $5.00 per name. Required to search: name, years to search. Civil cases indexed by defendant, plaintiff. Civil records on computer from 1980, index books from 1900s.

Criminal Records: Access: Phone, mail, in person. Only the court performs in person searches; visitors may not. Search fee: $5.00 per name. Required to search: name, years to search. Criminal records on computer from 1980, index books from 1900s.

General Information: No juvenile, mental, sealed, or adoption records released. SASE required. Turnaround time 1 day. Copy fee: $1.00 per page. Fee payee: District Clerk. Personal checks accepted. Prepayment is required.

County Court 101 S Main Rm 107, Seminole, TX 79360; 915-758-4003. Hours: 8AM-5PM (CST). *Misdemeanor, Civil, Probate.*

Civil Records: Access: Mail, in person. Both court and visitors may perform in person searches. No search fee. Required to search: name, years to search. Civil cases indexed by defendant, plaintiff.

Criminal Records: Access: Mail, in person. Both court and visitors may perform in person searches. No search fee. Required to search: name, years to search.

General Information: No juvenile, mental, sealed, or adoption records released. SASE required. Turnaround time 1 day. Copy fee: $1.00 per page. Certification fee: $1.00. Fee payee: County Clerk. Personal checks accepted. Prepayment is required.

Galveston County

District Court 722 Moody St Rm 404, Galveston, TX 77550; 409-766-2424; Fax: 409-766-2292. Hours: 8AM-5PM (CST). *Felony, Civil.*

www.co.galveston.tx.us/District_Courts/default.htm

Civil Records: Access: Fax, mail, in person. Search fee: $5.00 per name. Required to search: name, years to search. Civil cases indexed by defendant, plaintiff. Civil records on computer from 1984, on microfiche from 1982, archived from 1849. Online access to Judge's daily calendars is available free at the web site. Fax access is only allowed with prepaid accounts.

Criminal Records: Access: Fax, mail, in person. Both court and visitors may perform in person searches. Search fee: $5.00 per name. Required to search: name, years to search, DOB. Criminal records on computer from 1984, on microfiche from 1982, archived from 1849. Online access to Judge's daily calendars is available free at the web site.

General Information: Public access terminal is available. No juvenile, mental, sealed, or adoption records released. SASE required. Turnaround time 2-5 days. Copy fee: $1.00 per page. Certification fee: $2.00 for an affidavit. Fee payee: District Clerk. Personal checks accepted. Prepayment is required.

County Court PO Box 2450, Galveston, TX 77553-2450; Civil phone: 409-766-2203; Criminal phone: 409-770-5112; Probate phone: 409-766-2022. 8AM-5PM (CST). *Misdemeanor, Civil, Probate.*

www.co.galveston.tx.us/County_Courts

Civil Records: Access: Mail, online, in person. Both court and visitors may perform in person searches. Search fee: $5.00 per name. Required to search: name, years to search. Civil cases indexed by defendant, plaintiff. Civil records on computer from 1984, index books from 1947. Access to the GCNET remote online service has been suspended. Requires $200 escrow account plus a $.25 per minute fee. For more information, call 409-770-5115.

Criminal Records: Access: Mail, online, in person. Both court and visitors may perform in person searches. Search fee: $5.00 per name. Required to search: name, years to search, DOB; also helpful: SSN. Criminal records on computer from 1984, index books from 1947. Online access is through the GCNET Service as described in civil records.

General Information: Public access terminal is available. No juvenile, mental, sealed, or adoption records released. SASE required. Turnaround time 1-2 days. Copy fee: $1.00 per page. Certification fee: $5.00 per document. Fee payee: County Clerk. Prepayment is required.

Garza County

District & County Court PO Box 366, Post, TX 79356; 806-495-4430; Fax: 806-495-4431. Hours: 8AM-Noon,1-5PM (CST). *Felony, Misdemeanor, Civil, Probate.*

Civil Records: Access: Mail, in person. Both court and visitors may perform in person searches. Search fee: $5.00 per name. Required to search: name, years to search. Civil cases indexed by defendant, plaintiff. Civil records on index books.

Criminal Records: Access: Mail, in person. Both court and visitors may perform in person searches. Search fee: $5.00 per name. Required to search: name, years to search, DOB or SSN. Criminal records on index books.

General Information: No criminal records released. Turnaround time 2-3 days. Fax notes: Fee to fax results is $4.00 per document. Copy fee: $1.00 per page. Certification fee: $5.00. Fee payee: District or County Clerk. Personal checks accepted. Prepayment is required.

Gillespie County

District Court 101 W Main Rm 204, Fredericksburg, TX 78624; 830-997-6517. Hours: Public hours 8AM-5PM (CST). *Felony, Civil.*

Civil Records: Access: Mail, in person. Both court and visitors may perform in person searches. Search fee: $5.00 per name. Required to search: name, years to search. Civil cases indexed by defendant, plaintiff. Civil records in index books from 1800s. Index #1 from 1800s-1927, Index #2 from 1927-1988, Index #3 from 1989-present.

Criminal Records: Access: Mail, in person. Both court and visitors may perform in person searches. Search fee: $5.00 per name. Required to search: name, years to search; also helpful: DOB, SSN. Criminal records in index books from 1800s. Index #1 from 1800s-1927, Index #2 from 1927-1988, Index #3 from 1989-present.

General Information: No juvenile, mental, sealed, or adoption records released. SASE required. Turnaround time 1-2 days. Copy fee: $1.00 for first page, $.25 each add'l. Certification fee: $1.00 per page. Fee payee: Gillespie County District Clerk. Personal checks accepted. Prepayment is required.

County Court 101 W Main Unit #13, Fredericksburg, TX 78624; 830-997-6515; Fax: 830-997-9958. Hours: 8AM-4PM (CST). *Misdemeanor, Civil, Probate.*

Civil Records: Access: Mail, in person. Both court and visitors may perform in person searches. Search fee: $5.00 per name. Required to search: name, years to search; also helpful: address. Civil cases indexed by defendant, plaintiff. Civil records on computer from 1988, on microfiche from 1990, index books from 1900s.

Criminal Records: Access: Mail, in person. Both court and visitors may perform in person searches. Search fee: $5.00 per name. Required to search: name, years to search, aliases; also helpful: DOB, SSN. Criminal records on computer from 1988, on microfiche from 1990, index books from 1900s.

General Information: No juvenile, mental, sealed, or adoption record released. SASE required. Turnaround time 1-2 days. Copy fee: $1.00 per page. Certification fee: $10.00. Fee payee: Debbie Wahl County Clerk. No out-of-town checks accepted. Prepayment is required.

Glasscock County

District & County Court PO Box 190, 117 E Currie, Garden City, TX 79739; 915-354-2371. Hours: 8AM-4PM (CST). *Felony, Misdemeanor, Civil, Probate.*

Civil Records: Access: Mail, in person. Both court and visitors may perform in person searches. Search fee: $10.00 per name. Required to search: name, years to search. Civil cases indexed by defendant, plaintiff. Civil records in index books from 1893.

Criminal Records: Access: Mail, in person. Both court and visitors may perform in person searches. Search fee: $10.00 per name. Required to search: name, years to search, DOB. Criminal records in index books from 1893.

General Information: No juvenile, mental, or adoption records released. SASE required. Turnaround time 2 days. Copy fee: $1.00 per page. Certification fee: $5.00. Fee payee: District or County Clerk. Personal checks accepted. Prepayment is required.

Goliad County

District & County Court PO Box 50 (127 N Courthouse Sq.), Goliad, TX 77963; 361-645-2443/3294; Fax: 361-645-3858. Hours: 8AM-5PM (CST). *Felony, Misdemeanor, Civil, Probate.*

Note: May be at 218 S Commercial St through 2003.

Civil Records: Access: Mail, in person. Both court and visitors may perform in person searches. Search fee: $5.00 per name. Fee is per court. Required to search: name, years to search; also helpful: address. Civil cases indexed by defendant, plaintiff. Civil records on computer since 1983 (real property only), on microfiche and index books from 1870.

Criminal Records: Access: Mail, in person. Both court and visitors may perform in person searches. Search fee: $5.00 per name. Fee is per court. Required to search: name, years to search; also helpful: address, DOB, SSN, offense. Criminal records on microfiche and index books from 1870.

General Information: Public access terminal is available. No juvenile, mental, sealed, or adoption records released. SASE not required. Turnaround time 1-2 days. Fax notes: Fee to fax results is $1.00 per page. Copy fee: $1.00 per page. Certification fee: Certification: Fee is $5.00 for County Court; $1.00 for District Court plus $1.00 per page. Fee payee: Goliad County/District Clerk. Personal checks accepted. Prepayment is required.

Gonzales County

District Court PO Box 34, Gonzales, TX 78629-0034; 830-672-2326; Fax: 830-672-9313. Hours: 8AM-Noon 1-5PM (CST). *Felony, Civil.*

Civil Records: Access: Phone, fax, mail, in person. Both court and visitors may perform in person searches. Search fee: $5.00 per name. Required to search: name, years to search; also helpful: address. Civil cases indexed by defendant, plaintiff. Civil records on computer from 1991, index books from 1800s.

Criminal Records: Access: Phone, fax, mail, in person. Both court and visitors may perform in person searches. Search fee: $5.00 per name. Required to search: name, years to search; also helpful: address, DOB, SSN. Criminal records on computer from 1991, index books from 1800s.

General Information: No juvenile, mental, sealed, or adoption records released. SASE required. Turnaround time 1-2 days. Fax notes: Fee to fax results is $1.00 per page. Copy fee: $1.00 per page. Fee payee: District Clerk. Personal checks accepted.

County Court PO Box 77, Gonzales, TX 78629; 830-672-2801; Fax: 830-672-2636. Hours: 8AM-5PM (CST). *Misdemeanor, Civil, Probate.*

Civil Records: Access: Fax, mail, in person. Both court and visitors may perform in person searches. Search fee: $5.00 per name. Required to search: name, years to search. Civil cases indexed by defendant, plaintiff. Civil records on computer since 1993, original jackets since 1975, index books from 1900s.

Criminal Records: Access: Mail, in person. Both court and visitors may perform in person searches. Search fee: $5.00 per name. Required to search: name, years to search, offense, date of offense. Criminal records on computer since 1993, original jackets, index books from 1900s.

General Information: No mental or drug dependant commitment records released. SASE required. Turnaround time 1-2 days. Fax notes: Fee to fax results is $5.00. Copy fee: $1.00 per page. Certification fee: $5.00. Fee payee: County Clerk. Personal checks accepted. Prepayment is required.

Gray County

District Court PO Box 1139, Pampa, TX 79066-1139; 806-669-8010; Fax: 806-669-8053. Hours: 8:30AM-5PM (CST). *Felony, Civil.*

Civil Records: Access: Fax, mail, in person. Both court and visitors may perform in person searches. Search fee: $5.00 per name. Required to search: name, years to search, DOB. Civil cases indexed by defendant,

plaintiff. Civil records on computer from 1940, index books from 1910. All requests must be in writing.

Criminal Records: Access: Fax, mail, in person. Both court and visitors may perform in person searches. Search fee: $5.00 per name. Required to search: name, years to search; also helpful: DOB. Criminal records go back to 1930; criminal records on computer from 1965. All requests must be in writing.

General Information: No juvenile, mental, sealed, or adoption records released. SASE required. Turnaround time 1-2 days. Fax notes: $1.00 per page. Copy fee: $.25 per page. Certification fee: $1.00 per page. Fee payee: District Clerk. Personal checks accepted. Prepayment is required.

County & Probate Court PO Box 1902, Pampa, TX 79066-1902; 806-669-8004; Fax: 806-669-8054. Hours: 8:30AM-5PM (CST). *Misdemeanor, Civil, Probate.*

Civil Records: Access: Phone, fax, mail, in person. Both court and visitors may perform in person searches. Search fee: $10.00 per name. Fee is per index. Required to search: name, years to search. Civil cases indexed by defendant, plaintiff. Civil records on type written indices from 1900s.

Criminal Records: Access: Phone, fax, mail, in person. Both court and visitors may perform in person searches. Search fee: $10.00 per name. Fee is per index. Required to search: name, years to search, DOB. Criminal records on type written indices from 1900s.

General Information: No juvenile, mental, sealed, or adoption records released. They will not release any records with the SSN on it. SASE required. Turnaround time 1-2 days. Fax notes: $2.50 for first page, $1.00 each add'l. Copy fee: $1.00 per page. Certification fee: $5.00. Fee payee: Susan Winborne, County Clerk. Personal checks accepted. Prepayment is required.

Grayson County

District Court 200 S Crockett Rm 120-A, Sherman, TX 75090; 903-813-4352. Hours: 8AM-5PM (CST). *Felony, Civil, Family.*

Civil Records: Access: Mail, in person. Both court and visitors may perform in person searches. Search fee: $5.00 per name. Required to search: name, years to search. Civil cases indexed by defendant, plaintiff. Civil records on computer from 1988, microfilm since 1939, index books since 1900s.

Criminal Records: Access: Mail, in person. Both court and visitors may perform in person searches. Search fee: $5.00 per name. Required to search: name, years to search, DOB; also helpful: SSN. Criminal records on computer since 1988, microfilm since 1939, index books since 1900s.

General Information: Public access terminal is available. No juvenile, mental, sealed, expunction or adoption records released. SASE required. Turnaround time 1-2 days. Copy fee: $1.00 per page. Certification fee: $2.00. Fee payee: District Clerk. Personal checks accepted. Prepayment is required.

County Court 200 S Crockett, Sherman, TX 75090; 903-813-4336; Fax: 903-892-8300. Hours: 8AM-5PM (CST). *Misdemeanor, Civil, Probate.*

www.co.grayson.tx.us

Civil Records: Access: Mail, in person, online. Both court and visitors may perform in person searches. Search fee: $5.00 per name. Required to search: name, years to search. Civil cases indexed by defendant, plaintiff. Civil records on computer since 1992, index books since 1952. Online access to civil records available free online at http://209.151.115.130:3004/judsrch.asp. Also includes sheriffs' bail, and sheriff's jail searching.

Criminal Records: Access: Mail, in person, online. Both court and visitors may perform in person searches. Search fee: $5.00 per name. Required to search: name,

years to search, also helpful: DOB, SSN. Criminal records on computer from 1982. Online access to criminal records is the same as civil.

General Information: Public access terminal is available. No juvenile, mental, sealed, or adoption records released. SASE required. Turnaround time 1-2 days. Fax notes: Will fax results if prepaid. Copy fee: $1.00 per page. Certification fee: $5.00. Fee payee: County Clerk. Personal checks accepted. Prepayment is required.

Gregg County

District Court PO Box 711, Longview, TX 75606; 903-237-2663. Hours: 8AM-5PM (CST). *Felony, Civil.*

www.co.gregg.tx.us/government/courts.asp

Civil Records: Access: Phone, fax, mail, in person, online. Both court and visitors may perform in person searches. Search fee: $5.00 per name. Required to search: name, years to search. Civil cases indexed by defendant, plaintiff. Civil records on computer back to 1981, index books from 1873. Online access to county judicial records is available free at www.co.gregg.tx.us/judsrch.htm. Search by name, cause number, status.

Criminal Records: Access: Phone, fax, mail, in person, online. Both court and visitors may perform in person searches. Search fee: $5.00 per name. Required to search: name, years to search. Criminal records on computer back to 1977, index books from 1873. Online access to criminal records is the same as civil. Also includes jail and bond search.

General Information: Public access terminal is available. No juvenile, mental, sealed, or adoption records released. SASE required. Turnaround time 1-2 days. Fax notes: $1.00 per page. Copy fee: $1.00 per page. Certification fee: $1.00 per page. Fee payee: District Clerk. Only cashiers checks and money orders accepted. Prepayment is required.

County Court PO Box 3049, Longview, TX 75606; 903-236-8430. Hours: 8AM-5PM (CST). *Misdemeanor, Civil, Probate.*

www.co.gregg.tx.us/government/commissionersCourt/county_judge.asp

Civil Records: Access: Mail, in person, online. Both court and visitors may perform in person searches. Search fee: $5.00 per name. Required to search: name, years to search. Civil cases indexed by defendant, plaintiff. Civil records on computer from 1983, index books after 1962. Online access to county judicial records is available free at www.co.gregg.tx.us/judsrch.htm. Search by name, cause number, or status.

Criminal Records: Access: Mail, in person, online. Both court and visitors may perform in person searches. Search fee: $5.00 per name. Required to search: name, years to search, DOB or SSN. Criminal records on computer from 1983, index books after 1932. Online access to criminal records is the same as civil. Jail and bond search also available.

General Information: Public access terminal is available. No juvenile, mental, sealed, or adoption records released. SASE required. Turnaround time 1 week. Fax notes: Fee to fax results is $1.00 per page. Copy fee: $1.00 per page. Certification fee: $5.00. Fee payee: Gregg County Clerk. Only in-state personal checks accepted. Prepayment is required.

Grimes County

District Court PO Box 234, Anderson, TX 77830; 936-873-2111; Fax: 936-873-2415. Hours: 8AM-4:45PM (CST). *Felony, Civil.*

Civil Records: Access: Phone, fax, mail, in person. Both court and visitors may perform in person searches. Search fee: $5.00 per name. Required to search: name, years to search. Civil cases indexed by defendant, plaintiff. Civil records on computer from 1990, index books from 1800s.

Criminal Records: Access: Phone, fax, mail, in person. Both court and visitors may perform in person searches. Search fee: $5.00 per name. Required to search: name, years to search, DOB, SSN. Criminal records on computer from 1990, index books from 1800s.

General Information: No juvenile, mental, sealed, or adoption records released. SASE not required. Turnaround time 1-2 days. Copy fee: $1.00 per page. Certification fee: $1.00. Fee payee: District Clerk. Personal checks accepted. Prepayment is required.

County Court PO Box 209, Anderson, TX 77830; 936-873-2606 X251. Hours: 8AM-4:45PM (CST). *Misdemeanor, Civil, Probate.*

Civil Records: Access: Mail, in person. Only the court performs in person searches; visitors may not. Search fee: $5.00 per name. Required to search: name, years to search. Civil cases indexed by defendant, plaintiff. Civil records in index books from 1850.

Criminal Records: Access: Mail, in person. Only the court performs in person searches; visitors may not. Search fee: $5.00 per name. Required to search: name, years to search, offense, date of offense. Criminal records in index books from 1850.

General Information: No juvenile, mental, sealed, or adoption records released. SASE required. Turnaround time 1-2 days. Copy fee: $1.00 per page. Certification fee: $5.00. Fee payee: County Clerk. Personal checks accepted.

Guadalupe County

District Court 101 E Court St, Seguin, TX 78155; 830-303-4188; Fax: 830-379-1943. Hours: 8AM-5PM (CST). *Felony, Civil.*

www.co.guadalupe.tx.us/districtclerk.htm

Civil Records: Access: In person, online. Visitors must perform in person searches for themselves. No search fee. Required to search: name, years to search. Civil cases indexed by defendant, plaintiff. Civil records on computer from 1990, index books from 1846. Online access is available at www.idocket.com; one free search per day; subscription required for more. Online records go back to 12/31/1991.

Criminal Records: Access: In person, online. Visitors must perform in person searches for themselves. No search fee. Required to search: name, years to search, DOB; also helpful: SSN. Criminal records on computer from 1990, index books from 1846. Online access is through www.idocket.com; registration and password required. Records go back to 12/31/1991.

General Information: Public access terminal is available. No juvenile, mental, sealed, or adoption records released. Copy fee: $.20 per page. Certification fee: $1.00 per page. Fee payee: District Clerk. Personal checks accepted. Credit cards accepted: Visa, MasterCard, AmEx. Prepayment is required.

County Court 101 E Court St, Seguin, TX 78155; 830-303-4188 X266,234,232; Fax: 830-372-1206. Hours: 8AM-4:30PM *Misdemeanor, Civil, Probate.*

Civil Records: Access: Mail, in person. Both court and visitors may perform in person searches. Search fee: $5.00 per name. Required to search: name, years to search. Civil cases indexed by defendant, plaintiff. Civil records on computer from 1990, index books from 1968.

Criminal Records: Access: Mail, in person. Both court and visitors may perform in person searches. Search fee: $5.00 per name. Required to search: name, years to search, DOB; also helpful: SSN. Criminal records on computer from 1990, index books from 1968.

General Information: No juvenile, mental, sealed, or adoption records released. SASE required. Turnaround time 5 days. Copy fee: $1.00 per page. Certification fee:

$5.00. Fee payee: County Clerk. Personal checks accepted. Checks accepted for civil fees. Prepayment is required.

Hale County

District Court 500 Broadway #200, Plainview, TX 79072-8050; 806-291-5226; Fax: 806-291-5206. Hours: 8AM-Noon; 1-5PM (CST). *Felony, Civil.*

Civil Records: Access: Phone, fax, mail, in person. Both court and visitors may perform in person searches. Search fee: $5.00 per name. Required to search: name, years to search. Civil cases indexed by defendant, plaintiff. Civil records on computer back to 1989; index cards from 1975; prior back to 1897.

Criminal Records: Access: Phone, fax, mail, in person. Both court and visitors may perform in person searches. Search fee: $5.00 per name. Required to search: name, years to search, SSN; also helpful: DOB. Criminal records on computer back to 1988, index cards from 1975; prior back to 1897.

General Information: Public access terminal is available. No juvenile, mental, sealed, or adoption records released. SASE required. Turnaround time 1-2 days. Fax notes: Fee to fax results is $2.00 per document. Copy fee: $1.00 1st 4 pages, $.25 each additional page. Certification fee: $1.00 each. Fee payee: District Clerk. Personal checks accepted. Prepayment is required.

County Court 500 Broadway #140, Plainview, TX 79072-8030; 806-291-5261; Fax: 806-291-9810. Hours: 8AM-Noon, 1-5PM (CST). *Misdemeanor, Civil, Probate.*

Civil Records: Access: Mail, fax, in person. Both court and visitors may perform in person searches. Search fee: $5.00 per name. Required to search: name, years to search, address. Civil cases indexed by defendant, plaintiff. Civil records in index books from 1928; on computer back to 1995.

Criminal Records: Access: Mail, fax, in person. Both court and visitors may perform in person searches. Search fee: $5.00 per name. Required to search: name, years to search, DOB. Criminal records in index books from 1928; on computer back to 1995, limited records back to 1990.

General Information: Public access terminal is available. No juvenile, mental, sealed, or adoption records released. SASE required. Turnaround time 1-2 days. Copy fee: $1.00 per page. Certification fee: $5.00. Fee payee: County Clerk. No personal checks accepted except for vital records. Prepayment is required.

Hall County

District & County Court County Courthouse, 512 Main St #8, Memphis, TX 79245; 806-259-2627; Fax: 806-259-5078. Hours: 8:30AM-Noon; 1-5PM (CST). *Felony, Misdemeanor, Civil, Probate.*

Civil Records: Access: Phone, mail, in person. Both court and visitors may perform in person searches. Search fee: $5.00 per name. Required to search: name, years to search. Civil cases indexed by defendant, plaintiff. Civil records on computer from 1992, index books from 1890.

Criminal Records: Access: Phone, mail, in person. Both court and visitors may perform in person searches. Search fee: $5.00 per name. Required to search: name, years to search, offense. Criminal records on computer from 1992, index books from 1890.

General Information: No juvenile, mental, sealed, or adoption records released. SASE required. Turnaround time 1-2 days. Copy fee: $1.00 per page. Certification fee: $5.00. Fee payee: Hall County Clerk. Personal checks accepted. Prepayment is required.

Hamilton County

District Court County Courthouse, Hamilton, TX 76531; 254-386-3417; Fax: 254-386-8610. Hours: 8AM-5PM M-Th; 8AM-4:30PM F. *Felony, Civil.*

Civil Records: Access: Fax, mail, in person. Both court and visitors may perform in person searches. Search fee: $5.00 per name. Required to search: name, years to search. Civil cases indexed by defendant, plaintiff. Civil records since 1985 in index books, computerized since 1999.

Criminal Records: Access: Fax, mail, in person. Both court and visitors may perform in person searches. Search fee: $5.00 per name. Required to search: name, years to search. Criminal records in index books since 1985, computerized since 1999.

General Information: No juvenile, mental, sealed, or adoption records released. SASE required. Turnaround time 2-4 days. Fax notes: No fee to fax results. Copy fee: $1.00 per page. Certification fee: $2.00. Fee payee: District Clerk. Personal checks accepted.

County Court County Courthouse, Hamilton, TX 76531; 254-386-3518; Fax: 254-386-8727. Hours: 8AM-5PM (CST). *Misdemeanor, Civil, Probate.*

Civil Records: Access: Mail, fax, in person. Both court and visitors may perform in person searches. Search fee: $5.00 per name. Required to search: name, years to search. Civil cases indexed by defendant, plaintiff. Civil records in index books; on computer since.

Criminal Records: Access: Mail, fax, in person. Both court and visitors may perform in person searches. Search fee: $5.00 per name. Required to search: name, years to search, DOB or SSN. Criminal records in index books; on computer since.

General Information: No juvenile, mental, sealed, or adoption records released. SASE required. Turnaround time 1-2 days. Fax notes: Will fax results for fee. Copy fee: $1.00 per page. Certification fee: $1.00. Fee payee: County Clerk. Personal checks accepted. Prepayment is required.

Hansford County

District & County Court PO Box 397, Spearman, TX 79081; 806-659-4110; Fax: 806-659-4168. Hours: 8:00AM-5PM (CST). *Felony, Misdemeanor, Civil, Probate.*

Civil Records: Access: Phone, fax, mail, in person. Both court and visitors may perform in person searches. Search fee: $5.00 per name. Required to search: name, years to search. Civil cases indexed by defendant, plaintiff. Civil records on computer from 01/92, index books from 1900s.

Criminal Records: Access: Phone, fax, mail, in person. Both court and visitors may perform in person searches. Search fee: $5.00 per name. Required to search: name, years to search; also helpful: DOB, SSN. Criminal records on computer since 06/92, archived form 1900s.

General Information: Public access terminal is available. No juvenile, mental, sealed, or adoption records released. SASE required. Turnaround time 1-2 days. Fax notes: $4.00 for 1st page, $1.00 each add'l. Copy fee: $1.00 per page. Certification fee: $2.00 for District Court records; $5.00 for County Court records. Payee: District/County Clerk. Personal checks accepted.

Hardeman County

District & County Court PO Box 30, Quanah, TX 79252; 940-663-2901. Hours: 8:30AM-5PM (CST). *Felony, Misdemeanor, Civil, Probate.*

Civil Records: Access: Mail, in person. Both court and visitors may perform in person searches. Search fee: $10.00 per name. Required to search: name, years to search. Civil cases indexed by defendant, plaintiff. Civil records in index books from 1900s.

Criminal Records: Access: Mail, in person. Both court and visitors may perform in person searches. Search fee: $10.00 per name. Required to search: name, years to search. Criminal records in index books from 1920.

General Information: No juvenile, mental, sealed, or adoption records released. SASE required. Turnaround time 1-2 days. Copy fee: $1.00 per page. Certification fee: $5.00. Fee payee: District Clerk. Personal checks accepted. Prepayment is required.

Hardin County

District Court PO Box 2997, Kountze, TX 77625; 409-246-5150. Hours: 8AM-4PM (CST). *Felony, Civil.*

Civil Records: Access: Phone, mail, in person. Both court and visitors may perform in person searches. Search fee: $5.00 per name. Required to search: name, years to search. Civil cases indexed by defendant, plaintiff. Civil records in index books since 1920, computerized since 1997.

Criminal Records: Access: Phone, mail, in person. Both court and visitors may perform in person searches. Search fee: $5.00 per name. Required to search: name, years to search, DOB; also helpful: SSN, sex. Criminal records in index books since 1920, computer to 1997.

General Information: No juvenile, mental, sealed, or adoption records released. SASE required. Turnaround time 1-2 days. Fax notes: Fee to fax results is $1.00 per page. Copy fee: $1.00 per page. Certification fee: $2.00. Fee payee: District Clerk. Business checks accepted. Prepayment is required.

County Court PO Box 38, Kountze, TX 77625; 409-246-5185. Hours: 8AM-5PM (CST). *Misdemeanor, Civil, Probate.*

Civil Records: Access: Mail, in person, phone. Both court and visitors may perform in person searches. Search fee: $5.00 per name. Required to search: name, years to search. Civil cases indexed by defendant, plaintiff. Civil records in index books since 1850.

Criminal Records: Access: Mail, in person, phone. Both court and visitors may perform in person searches. Search fee: $5.00 per name. Required to search: name, years to search. Criminal records on computer since 1992, index books from 1850.

General Information: No juvenile, mental, sealed, or adoption records released. SASE not required. Turnaround time 1-2 days. Copy fee: $1.00 per page. Certification fee: $5.00. Fee payee: Hardin County Clerk. Personal checks accepted. Prepayment required.

Harris County

District Court PO Box 4651, Houston, TX 77210; Civil phone: 713-755-5711; Criminal phone: 713-755-5734; Fax: 713-755-5480 (civil). Hours: 8AM-6PM (CST). *Felony, Civil Over $100,000.*

www.hcdistrictclerk.com

Civil Records: Access: Phone, mail, online, in person, email. Both court and visitors may perform in person searches. Search fee: $5.00 per name. Required to search: name, years to search. Civil cases indexed by defendant, plaintiff. Civil records on computer from 1969. The online subscriber fee site is now replaced by the free-to-view e-docs service at https://e-docs.hcdistrictclerk.com/FormsLogin.asp?/. There is a $1 per page charge (credit cards accepted) for documents and you may choose the delivery method. Online records go back to 10/1989. Also, civil court general information is available on the Internet at www.ccl.co.harris.tx.us/civil/default.htm.

Criminal Records: Access: Phone, mail, online, in person, email. Both court and visitors may perform in person searches. Search fee: $5.00 per name. Required to search: name, years to search, DOB; also helpful: SSN. Criminal records on computer since 1976. Online access to criminal records is the same as civil, see above. Also, Internet access to criminal records

available to qualified JIMs subscribers at www.co.harris.tx.us/subscriber/cb/submenu.htm. Records include felonies and A & B class misdemeanors.

General Information: Public access terminal is available. No juvenile, sealed, or adoption records released. SASE required. Fax notes: Fax service requires credit card pre-payment. Copy fee: $1.00 per page. Fax requesters must be pre-approved Certification fee: $1.00. Fee payee: District Clerk, Harris County. Business check accepted from attorney with TX Bar Card number, corporate or company check with Harris Co address. Prepayment is required.

County Court, PO Box 1525, Houston, TX 77251-1525; 713-755-6421. Hours: 8AM-4:30PM (CST). *Civil Under $100,000.*

www.cclerk.hctx.net

Civil Records: Access: Phone, mail, online, in person. Both court and visitors may perform in person searches. Search fee: $5.00 for mail requests; $3.00 if in person and court performs search. Required to search: name, years to search. Civil cases indexed by defendant, plaintiff. Civil records on computer and microfiche from 1963. Online access is free at the www.cclerk.hctx.net/coolice/default.asp?Category=RealProperty&Service=mastermenu. Includes civil data search and county civil settings inquiry and other county clerk functions. For further information, visit the web site, send email request to dcsa@dco.co.harris.tx.us, or call 713-755-6421.

General Information: Public access terminal is available. (Public access terminal for Civil and Probate records only.) SASE required. Turnaround time 24-48 hours. Copy fee: $1.00 per page. Certification fee: $5.00. Fee payee: Harris County Clerk. Business checks accepted. Credit cards accepted: Visa, MasterCard, Discover, AmEx. Prepayment is required.

Probate Court 1115 Congress, 6th Floor, Houston, TX 77002; 713-755-6084; Probate phone: 713-755-6425; Fax: 713-755-4349. 6AM-5PM (CST). *Probate.*

Note: Probate dockets are available through the Harris County online system. Call (713) 755-7815 for information. Also, probate dockets are available free at www.cclerk.hctx.net/coolice/default.asp?Category=ProbateCourt&Service=pc_inquiry. Records on their computer go back to 1837.

Harrison County

71st District Court PO Box 1119, Marshall, TX 75671-1119; 903-935-4845. Hours: 8AM-5PM (CST). *Felony, Civil.*

www.co.harrison.tx.us

Civil Records: Access: Mail, in person. Both court and visitors may perform in person searches. Search fee: $5.00 per name. Required to search: name, years to search; also helpful: address. Civil cases indexed by defendant, plaintiff. Civil records on computer from 1988, index books from 1845.

Criminal Records: Access: Mail, in person. Both court and visitors may perform in person searches. Search fee: $5.00 per name. Required to search: name, years to search, DOB; also helpful: address, SSN. Criminal records on computer back to 1988, index books from 1845.

General Information: Public access terminal is available. No juvenile, mental, sealed, or adoption records released. SASE required. Turnaround time 1-2 days. Copy fee: $1.00 per page. Fee payee: Harrison County District Clerk. Personal checks accepted. Prepayment is required.

County Court PO Box 1365, Marshall, TX 75671; 903-935-4858. 8AM-5PM (CST). *Misdemeanor, Civil, Probate.*

Civil Records: Access: Mail, in person. Both court and visitors may perform in person searches. Search fee: $5.00 per name. Required to search: name, years to search. Civil cases indexed by defendant, plaintiff. Civil records in docket books from 1800; on computer back to 2002.

Criminal Records: Access: Mail, in person. Both court and visitors may perform in person searches. Search fee: $5.00 per name. Required to search: name, years to search, DOB. Criminal records in docket books from 1800; on computer back to 1995.

General Information: No juvenile, mental, sealed, birth, death or adoption records released. SASE not required. Turnaround time 10 days. Fax notes: Fee to fax results is $1.00 per page. Copy fee: $1.00 per page. Certification fee: $5.00 plus $1.00 per page. Fee payee: County Clerk. Personal checks accepted. In state checks only. Prepayment is required.

Hartley County

District & County Court PO Box Q, Channing, TX 79018; 806-235-3582; Fax: 806-235-2316. Hours: 8:30AM-Noon, 1-5PM (CST). *Felony, Misdemeanor, Civil, Probate.*

Civil Records: Access: Mail, in person. Both court and visitors may perform in person searches. Search fee: $5.00 per name. Charge is for each book searched. Required to search: name, years to search. Civil cases indexed by defendant, plaintiff. Civil records on computer from 1994, index books from 1890. Results can be faxed if pre-paid and local call.

Criminal Records: Access: Mail, in person. Both court and visitors may perform in person searches. Search fee: $5.00 per name, per book searched (misdemeanor or felony). Required to search: name, years to search, DOB. Criminal records on computer from 1994, index books from 1890. Results can be faxed if pre-paid and local call.

General Information: No juvenile, mental, sealed, or adoption records released. SASE required. Turnaround time 1-2 days. Copy fee: $1.00 per page. Certification fee: $5.00. Fee payee: Hartley County Clerk. Personal checks accepted. Prepayment is required.

Haskell County

District Court PO Box 27, Haskell, TX 79521; 940-864-2030. Hours: 8AM-Noon, 1-5PM M-Th; 8AM-4:30PM F (CST). *Felony, Civil.*

Civil Records: Access: Mail, in person. Both court and visitors may perform in person searches. Search fee: $5.00 per name. Required to search: name, years to search. Civil cases indexed by defendant, plaintiff. Civil records on computer from 1992, index books from 1896.

Criminal Records: Access: Mail, in person. Both court and visitors may perform in person searches. Search fee: $5.00 per name. Required to search: name, years to search, signed release. Criminal records on computer from 1992, index books from 1896.

General Information: No juvenile, mental, sealed, or adoption records released. SASE required. Turnaround time 1-2 days. Copy fee: $1.00 per page. Certification fee: $1.00. Fee payee: District Clerk. Business checks accepted. In-state checks okay. Prepayment required.

County Court PO Box 725, Haskell, TX 79521; 940-864-2451. Hours: 8AM-Noon, 1-5PM (CST). *Misdemeanor, Civil, Probate.*

Civil Records: Access: Phone, fax, mail, in person. Both court and visitors may perform in person searches. Search fee: $5.00 per name. Required to search: name, years to search. Civil cases indexed by defendant, plaintiff. Civil records in index books from 1903; computerized records since 1994.

Criminal Records: Access: Fax, mail, in person. Both court and visitors may perform in person searches.

Search fee: $5.00 per name. Required to search: name, years to search. Criminal records in index books from 19; computerized records since 1994.

General Information: No juvenile, mental, sealed, or adoption records released. SASE required. Turnaround time 1-2 days. Fax notes: $2.00 per page. Copy fee: $1.00 per page. Certification fee: $5.00. Fee payee: County Clerk. Personal checks accepted. Prepayment is required.

Hays County

District Court 110 E Martin Luther King, #123, Attn: District Clerk, San Marcos, TX 78666; 512-393-7660; Fax: 512-393-7674. Hours: 8AM-5PM (CST). *Felony, Civil.*

www.co.hays.tx.us

Civil Records: Access: Phone, fax, mail, in person, online. Both court and visitors may perform in person searches. Search fee: $5.00 per name. Required to search: name, years to search. Civil cases indexed by defendant, plaintiff. Civil records on computer from 1987, index books from 1890s. Online access is through www.idocket.com; registration and password required. Records go back to 12/31/1986.

Criminal Records: Access: Phone, fax, mail, in person, online. Both court and visitors may perform in person searches. Search fee: $5.00 per name. Required to search: name, years to search; also helpful: DOB, SSN. Criminal records on computer from 1987, index books from 1890s. Online access is through www.idocket.com; registration and password required. Records go back to 12/31/1986.

General Information: Public access terminal is available. No sealed or adoption records released. SASE required. Turnaround time 1-5 days. Copy fee: $.50 per page. Certification fee: $1.00 plus $1.00 per page. Fee payee: District Clerk. Personal checks accepted. Prepayment is required.

County Court Justice Center, 110 E Martin L King Dr, San Marcos, TX 78666; 512-393-7738; Fax: 512-393-7735. Hours: 8AM-5PM (CST). *Misdemeanor, Civil, Probate.*

www.co.hays.tx.us

Civil Records: Access: Mail, in person, online. Both court and visitors may perform in person searches. Search fee: $5.00 per name. Required to search: name, years to search. Civil cases indexed by defendant, plaintiff. Civil records on computer from 1988, index books from 1848. Online access is through www.idocket.com; registration and password required. Records go back to 12/31/1987. Includes probate.

Criminal Records: Access: Mail, in person, online. Both court and visitors may perform in person searches. Search fee: $5.00 per name. Required to search: name, years to search, DOB. Criminal records on computer from 1988, index books from 1848. Online access is through www.idocket.com; registration and password required. Records go back to 12/31/1987.

General Information: Public access terminal is available. No juvenile, mental, sealed, or adoption records released. SASE not required. Turnaround time 1-2 weeks. Copy fee: $1.00 per page. Certification fee: $5.00. Fee payee: Hays County Clerk. Personal checks accepted. Prepayment is required.

Hemphill County

District & County Court PO Box 867, Canadian, TX 79014; 806-323-6212. Hours: 8AM-5PM (CST). *Felony, Misdemeanor, Civil, Probate.*

Civil Records: Access: Phone, mail, in person. Both court and visitors may perform in person searches. Search fee: $10.00 per name. Required to search: name, years to search. Civil cases indexed by defendant, plaintiff. Civil records in index books from 1890s.

Criminal Records: Access: Phone, mail, in person. Both court and visitors may perform in person searches. Search fee: $10.00 per name. Required to search: name, years to search, DOB. Criminal records in index books from 1890s.

General Information: Public access terminal is available. No juvenile, mental, sealed, or adoption records released. SASE required. Turnaround time 1-2 days. Fax notes: Fee to fax results is $1.00 per page. Copy fee: $1.00 per page. Certification fee: $5.00 per page. Fee payee: Hemphill County Clerk. Personal checks accepted. Prepayment is required.

Henderson County

District Court Henderson County Courthouse, Athens, TX 75751; 903-675-6115. Hours: 8AM-5PM (CST). *Felony, Civil.*

Civil Records: Access: Mail, in person, phone, fax. Both court and visitors may perform in person searches. Search fee: $5.00 per name. Required to search: name, years to search. Civil cases indexed by defendant, plaintiff. Civil records on computer from 1987, index books from 1849.

Criminal Records: Access: Mail, in person. Both court and visitors may perform in person searches. Search fee: $5.00 per name. Required to search: name, years to search, DOB; also helpful: SSN. Criminal records on computer from 1987, index books from 1849.

General Information: Public access terminal is available. No juvenile, mental, sealed, or adoption records released. SASE required. Turnaround time 1-2 days. Copy fee: $1.00 per page. Certification fee: $2.00. Fee payee: District Clerk. Personal checks accepted. Prepayment is required.

County Court PO Box 632, Athens, TX 75751; 903-675-6140. Hours: 8AM-5PM (CST). *Misdemeanor, Civil, Probate.*

Civil Records: Access: Phone, mail, in person. Both court and visitors may perform in person searches. Search fee: $5.00 per name. Required to search: name, years to search. Civil cases indexed by defendant, plaintiff. Civil records on computer back to 1984, index books from 1900s.

Criminal Records: Access: Mail, fax, in person. Both court and visitors may perform in person searches. Search fee: $5.00 per name. Required to search: name, years to search, DOB, SSN. Criminal records on computer back to 1984, index books from 1900s.

General Information: No juvenile, mental, sealed, or adoption records released. SASE required. Turnaround time 1-2 weeks. Fax notes: Fee to fax results is $2.00 per page. Copy fee: $1.00 per page. Fee payee: County Clerk. Personal checks accepted. Prepayment required.

Hidalgo County

District Court 100 N Closner, Box 87, Edinburg, TX 78540; 956-318-2200. Hours: 8AM-5PM (CST). *Felony, Civil.*

Civil Records: Access: Mail, in person, online. Only the court performs in person searches; visitors may not. Search fee: $5.00 per name. Required to search: name, years to search. Civil cases indexed by defendant, plaintiff. Civil records on computer from 1987. Online access is through www.idocket.com; registration and password required. Records go back to 12/31/1986.

Criminal Records: Access: Mail, in person, online. Only the court performs in person searches; visitors may not. Search fee: $5.00 per name. Required to search: name, years to search, DOB. Criminal records on computer from 1987. Online access is through www.idocket.com; registration and password required. Records go back to 12/31/1986.

General Information: No juvenile, mental, sealed, or adoption records released. SASE required. Turnaround time 1-2 days. Copy fee: $1.00 per page. Certification

fee: $1.00. Fee payee: District Clerk. Business checks accepted. Prepayment is required.

County Court PO Box 58, Edinburg, TX 78540; 956-318-2100. Hours: 7:30AM-5:30PM (CST). *Misdemeanor, Civil, Probate.*

Civil Records: Access: Mail, in person, online. Both court and visitors may perform in person searches. Search fee: $5.00 per name. Required to search: name, years to search. Civil cases indexed by defendant, plaintiff. Civil records on computer from 1985, index books before 1985. Online access is through www.idocket.com; registration and password required. Civil and probate records go back to 12/31/1986.

Criminal Records: Access: Mail, in person, online. Both court and visitors may perform in person searches. Search fee: $5.00 per name. Required to search: name, years to search. Criminal records on computer from 1985, index books after 1985. Online access is through www.idocket.com; registration and password required. Records go back to 12/31/1991.

General Information: Public access terminal is available. (Criminal only.) No juvenile, mental, sealed, or adoption records released. SASE required. Turnaround time 1-2 days. Copy fee: $1.00 per page. Certification fee: $5.00. Fee payee: County Clerk. Business checks accepted. Prepayment is required.

Hill County

District Court PO Box 634, Hillsboro, TX 76645; 254-582-4042. Hours: 8AM-5PM (CST). *Felony, Civil.*

Civil Records: Access: Mail, in person, online. Both court and visitors may perform in person searches. Search fee: $5.00 per name. Required to search: name, years to search. Civil cases indexed by defendant, plaintiff. Civil records on optical imaging from September, 1993, on computer from 1991, microfilm from 1930s to 1950s, index books from 1900s. Online access to court records is available through idocket.com. One search a day is free; subcription required for more. Records go back to 12/31/1990.

Criminal Records: Access: Mail, in person. Both court and visitors may perform in person searches. Search fee: $5.00 per name. Required to search: name, years to search; also helpful: DOB, SSN. Criminal records on optical imaging from September, 1993, on computer from 1989, microfilm from 1930s to 1950s, index books from 1900s. Online access is through www.idocket.com; registration and password required. Records go back to 12/31/1990.

General Information: Public access terminal is available. (Aloows for civil searches only.) No juvenile, mental, sealed, or adoption records released. SASE required. Turnaround time 1-2 days. Copy fee: $1.00 per page. Certification fee: $1.00. Fee payee: District Clerk. Personal checks accepted. Prepayment is required.

County Court PO Box 398, Hillsboro, TX 76645; 254-582-4030. Hours: 8AM-5PM (CST). *Misdemeanor, Probate.*

General Information: Turnaround time 1-2 days. Fee payee: County Clerk. Prepayment is required.

Hockley County

District Court 802 Houston St, Ste 316, Levelland, TX 79336; 806-894-8527; Fax: 806-894-3891. Hours: 9AM-5PM (CST). *Felony, Civil.*

Civil Records: Access: Phone, mail, in person. Both court and visitors may perform in person searches. Search fee: $5.00 per name. Required to search: name, years to search. Civil cases indexed by defendant, plaintiff. Civil records on computer from 1990, achived from 1929.

Criminal Records: Access: Phone, mail, in person. Both court and visitors may perform in person searches. Search fee: $5.00 per name. Required to search: name, years to search. Criminal records on computer from 1990, archived from 1929.

General Information: Public access terminal is available. No juvenile, mental, sealed, or adoption records released. SASE required. Turnaround time 1-2 days. Copy fee: $1.00 per page. Certification fee: $2.00. Fee payee: District Clerk. Personal checks accepted. Prepayment is required.

County Court County Courthouse, 802 Houston St Ste 213, Levelland, TX 79336; 806-894-3185. Hours: 9AM-5PM (CST). *Misdemeanor, Civil, Probate.*

Civil Records: Access: Mail, in person. Both court and visitors may perform in person searches. No search fee. Required to search: name, years to search. Civil cases indexed by defendant, plaintiff. Civil records on computer from 1990, index books from 1960.

Criminal Records: Access: Mail, in person. Both court and visitors may perform in person searches. Search fee: $5.00 per name. Required to search: name, years to search; also helpful: DOB. Criminal records on computer from 1990, index books from 1960.

General Information: Public access terminal is available. No juvenile, mental, sealed, or adoption records released. SASE required. Turnaround time 1-2 days. Copy fee: $1.00 per page. Certification fee: $5.00. Payee: Hockley County Clerk. Personal checks okay.

Hood County

District Court County Courthouse, 100 E Pearl #21, Granbury, TX 76048; 817-579-3236; Fax: 817-579-3239. Hours: 8AM-5PM (CST). *Felony, Civil.*

Civil Records: Access: Mail, in person. Both court and visitors may perform in person searches. Search fee: $5.00 per name. Required to search: name, years to search. Civil cases indexed by defendant, plaintiff. Civil records on computer and microfiche from 1983, index books before 1983.

Criminal Records: Access: Mail, in person. Both court and visitors may perform in person searches. Search fee: $5.00 per name. Required to search: name, years to search, DOB, SSN, signed release. Criminal records on computer and microfiche from 1983, index books before 1983.

General Information: No juvenile, mental, sealed, or adoption records released. SASE required. Turnaround time 1-2 days. Copy fee: $1.00 per page. Certification fee: $1.00. Fee payee: District Clerk. Personal checks accepted. Prepayment is required.

County Court PO Box 339, Granbury, TX 76048; 817-579-3222; Fax: 817-579-3227. Hours: 8AM-5PM (CST). *Misdemeanor, Civil, Probate.*

Civil Records: Access: Mail, in person. Both court and visitors may perform in person searches. Search fee: $5.00 per name. Required to search: name, years to search. Civil cases indexed by defendant, plaintiff. Civil records in index books.

Criminal Records: Access: Mail, in person. Both court and visitors may perform in person searches. Search fee: $5.00 per name. Required to search: name, years to search; also helpful: DOB. Criminal records on computer and microfiche from 1982, index books before 1982.

General Information: Public access terminal is available. No juvenile, mental, sealed, or adoption records released. SASE required. Turnaround time 1 day. Copy fee: $1.00 per page. Certification fee: $5.00. Fee payee: Hood County Clerk. Personal checks accepted. Prepayment is required.

Hopkins County

District Court PO Box 391 (411 College St), Sulphur Springs, TX 75482; 903-438-4081. Hours: 8AM-5PM (CST). *Felony, Civil.*

Civil Records: Access: Mail, in person. Both court and visitors may perform in person searches. Search fee:

$5.00 per name. Required to search: name, years to search. Civil cases indexed by defendant, plaintiff. Civil records on computer from 1987, index books from 1840, archived from 1890.

Criminal Records: Access: Mail, in person. Both court and visitors may perform in person searches. Search fee: $5.00 per name. Required to search: name, years to search. Criminal records on computer from 1987, index books from 1840, archived from 1890.

General Information: Public access terminal is available. No juvenile, mental, sealed, or adoption records released. SASE required. Turnaround time 2 days. Copy fee: $1.00 per page. Certification fee: $2.00. Fee payee: District Clerk. Personal checks accepted. Prepayment is required.

County Court PO Box 288, Sulphur Springs, TX 75483; 903-438-4074; Fax: 903-438-4007. Hours: 8AM-5PM (CST). *Misdemeanor, Civil, Probate.*

www.hopkinscountytx.org/departments.htm

Civil Records: Access: Mail, in person. Both court and visitors may perform in person searches. Search fee: $5.00 per name. Required to search: name, years to search. Civil cases indexed by defendant, plaintiff. Civil records on computer since 1992, index books from 1846.

Criminal Records: Access: Mail, in person. Both court and visitors may perform in person searches. Search fee: $5.00 per name. Required to search: name, years to search; also helpful-DOB, SSN, signed release. Criminal records on computer from 1985, index books from 1846.

General Information: Public access terminal is available. No juvenile, mental, sealed, or adoption records released. SASE required. Turnaround time 1-2 days. Fax notes: Will not fax results. Copy fee: $1.00 per page. Certification fee: $5.00. Fee payee: County Clerk. Personal checks accepted. Prepayment required.

Houston County

District Court County Courthouse, 401 E Houston, PO Box 1186, Crockett, TX 75835; 936-544-3255 x222; Fax: 936-544-9523. Hours: 8AM-4:30PM (CST). *Felony, Civil.*

Civil Records: Access: Fax, mail, in person. Both court and visitors may perform in person searches. Search fee: $5.00 per name. Required to search: name, years to search. Civil cases indexed by plaintiff. Civil records on computer from 10/99, index books since 1800s.

Criminal Records: Access: Fax, mail, in person. Both court and visitors may perform in person searches. Search fee: $5.00 per name. Required to search: name, years to search, signed release; also helpful: DOB, SSN. Criminal records on computer since 10/99, index books since 1800s.

General Information: No juvenile, mental, sealed, or adoption records released. SASE required. Turnaround time 1-2 days. Fax notes: $3.50 for first page, $.50 each add'l. Copy fee: $1.00 per page. Fee payee: District Clerk. Personal checks okay. Prepayment is required.

County Court PO Box 370, Crockett, TX 75835; 936-544-3255; Fax: 936-546-9605. Hours: 8AM-4:30 (CST). *Misdemeanor, Civil, Probate.*

Civil Records: Access: Mail, in person. Both court and visitors may perform in person searches. Search fee: $5.00 per name. Required to search: name, years to search. Civil cases indexed by defendant, plaintiff. Civil records on computer since 2000, microfiche since 1983, index books since 1881 (probate).

Criminal Records: Access: Mail, in person. Both court and visitors may perform in person searches. Search fee: $5.00 per name. Required to search: name, years to search. Criminal records on computer since 2000, index books since 1881.

General Information: Public access terminal is available. No juvenile, mental, sealed, or adoption

records released. SASE not required. Turnaround time 1-2 days. Fax notes: Will not fax results. Copy fee: $1.00 per page. Certification fee: $5.00. Fee payee: County Clerk. Personal checks accepted. Prepayment is required.

Howard County

District Court PO Box 2138, Big Spring, TX 79721; 915-264-2223; Fax: 915-264-2256. Hours: 8AM-5PM (CST). *Felony, Civil.*

Civil Records: Access: Mail, in person. Both court and visitors may perform in person searches. Search fee: $5.00 per name. Required to search: name, years to search. Civil cases indexed by defendant, plaintiff. Civil records on computer from 1990, index books to 1881.

Criminal Records: Access: Mail, in person. Both court and visitors may perform in person searches. Search fee: $5.00 per name. Required to search: name, years to search. Criminal records on computer from 1990, index books from 1881.

General Information: No juvenile, mental, sealed or adoption records released. SASE required. Turnaround time 1-2 days. Fax notes: Fee to fax results is $1.00 per page. Copy fee: $1.00 per page. Certification fee: $1.00 per page. Fee payee: District Clerk. Personal checks accepted. Prepayment is required.

County Court PO Box 1468, Big Spring, TX 79721; 915-264-2213; Fax: 915-264-2215. Hours: 8AM-5PM (CST). *Misdemeanor, Civil, Probate.*

Civil Records: Access: Phone, mail, in person. Both court and visitors may perform in person searches. Search fee: $5.00 per name. Required to search: name, years to search. Civil cases indexed by defendant, plaintiff. Civil records in index books since 1881.

Criminal Records: Access: Phone, mail, in person. Both court and visitors may perform in person searches. Search fee: $5.00 per name. Required to search: name, years to search. Criminal records index books to 1881.

General Information: No juvenile, mental, sealed, or adoption records released. SASE not required. Turnaround time 1-2 days. Fax notes: $5.00 per document. Copy fee: $1.00 per page. Certification fee: $5.00. Fee payee: County Clerk. Business checks accepted. Prepayment is required.

Hudspeth County

District & County Court PO Drawer 58, Sierra Blanca, TX 79851; 915-369-2301; Fax: 915-369-3005. Hours: 8AM-5PM (MST). *Felony, Misdemeanor, Civil, Probate.*

Civil Records: Access: Phone, fax, mail, in person. Both court and visitors may perform in person searches. Search fee: $5.00 per name. Required to search: name, years to search. Civil cases indexed by defendant, plaintiff. Civil records in index books from 1900s; on computer since 1988.

Criminal Records: Access: Phone, fax, mail, in person. Both court and visitors may perform in person searches. Search fee: $5.00 per name. Required to search: name, years to search, DOB. Criminal records in index books from 1900s; on computer since 1998.

General Information: Public access terminal is available. No juvenile, mental, sealed, or adoption records released. SASE required. Turnaround time 1-2 days. Fax notes: $1.00 per page. Copy fee: $1.00 per page. Certification fee: $5.00. Fee payee: District/County Clerk. Personal checks accepted. Prepayment is required.

Hunt County

District Court PO Box 1437, Greenville, TX 75403; 903-408-4172. 8AM-5PM. *Felony, Civil.*

Civil Records: Access: Mail, in person. Both court and visitors may perform in person searches. Search fee: $5.00 per name. Required to search: name, years to

search. Civil cases indexed by defendant, plaintiff. Civil records on computer from 1992, microfiche from 1973, index books from 1900s.

Criminal Records: Access: Mail, in person. Both court and visitors may perform in person searches. Search fee: $5.00 per name. Required to search: name, years to search, DOB. Criminal records on computer from 1992, microfilm from 1973, index books from 1900s.

General Information: Public access terminal is available. No juvenile, sealed, or adoption records released. SASE required. Turnaround time 1-2 days. Copy fee: $1.00 per page. Certification fee: $1.00. Fee payee: District Clerk. Personal checks accepted. Prepayment is required.

County Court PO Box 1316, Greenville, TX 75403-1316; 903-408-4130. Hours: 8AM-5PM (CST). *Misdemeanor, Civil, Probate.*

Civil Records: Access: Mail, in person. Both court and visitors may perform in person searches. Search fee: $5.00 per name. Required to search: name, years to search. Civil cases indexed by defendant, plaintiff. Civil records on computer since 1986, index books from 1940; on microfilm prior to 1986.

Criminal Records: Access: Mail, in person. Both court and visitors may perform in person searches. Search fee: $5.00 per name. Required to search: name, years to search, DOB. Criminal records on computer since 1986, index books from 1940; on microfilm prior to 1986.

General Information: Public access terminal is available. No juvenile, mental, sealed, or adoption records released. SASE required. Turnaround time 1-2 days. Fax notes: No fax results available. Copy fee: $1.00 per page. Certification fee: $5.00. Fee payee: County Clerk. Personal checks accepted. Prepayment is required.

Hutchinson County

District Court PO Box 580, Stinnett, TX 79083; 806-878-4017; Fax: 806-878-4042. Hours: 9AM-5PM (CST). *Felony, Civil.*

Civil Records: Access: Mail, in person. Both court and visitors may perform in person searches. Search fee: $5.00 per name. Required to search: name, years to search. Civil cases indexed by defendant, plaintiff. Civil records on computer from 1989, docket books from 1920.

Criminal Records: Access: Mail, in person. Both court and visitors may perform in person searches. Search fee: $5.00 per name. Required to search: name, years to search, signed release; also helpful: DOB, SSN. Criminal records on computer from 1989, docket books from 1920.

General Information: Public access terminal is available. No juvenile, mental, sealed, or adoption records released. SASE required. Turnaround time 2 days. Fax notes: Fee to fax results is $1.00 per page. Copy fee: $.25 per page. $1.00 minimum. Certification fee: $1.00 per page. Fee payee: District Clerk. Personal checks accepted. Prepayment is required.

County Court PO Box 1186, Stinnett, TX 79083; 806-878-4002. Hours: 9AM-5PM (CST). *Misdemeanor, Civil, Probate.*

Civil Records: Access: Mail, in person. Both court and visitors may perform in person searches. Search fee: $5.00 per name. Required to search: name, years to search. Civil cases indexed by defendant, plaintiff. Civil records in index books from 1900s.

Criminal Records: Access: Mail, in person. Both court and visitors may perform in person searches. Search fee: $5.00 per name. Required to search: name, years to search, signed release, DOB or SSN. Criminal records on computer since 1990, index books from 1900s.

General Information: Public access terminal is available. No juvenile, mental, sealed, or adoption records released. SASE not required. Turnaround time 2

days. Copy fee: $1.00 per page. Certification fee: $5.00. Fee payee: Carol Ann Herbst, Hutchinson County Clerk. Business checks accepted. Prepayment required.

Irion County

District & County Court PO Box 736, Mertzon, TX 76941-0736; 915-835-2421; Fax: 915-835-2008. Hours: 8AM-5PM (CST). *Felony, Misdemeanor, Civil, Probate.*

Civil Records: Access: Mail, fax, n person. Both court and visitors may perform in person searches. Search fee: $5.00 per name. Fee is per court. Required to search: name, years to search. Civil cases indexed by defendant, plaintiff. Civil records in index books from 1886.

Criminal Records: Access: Mail, fax, in person. Both court and visitors may perform in person searches. Search fee: $5.00 per name. Fee is per court. Required to search: name, years to search; also helpful: DOB, SSN. Criminal records on index books from 1886.

General Information: No juvenile, mental, or sealed records released. SASE required. Turnaround time 5-20 days. Fax notes: $1.00 per page. Copy fee: $1.00 per page. Certification fee: $1.00. County Court certification fee $5.00. Fee payee: District/County Clerk. Personal checks accepted. Prepayment required.

Jack County

District Court 100 Main, County Courthouse, Jacksboro, TX 76458; 940-567-2141; Fax: 940-567-2696. Hours: 8AM-5PM (CST). *Felony, Civil.*

Civil Records: Access: Mail, in person. Both court and visitors may perform in person searches. Search fee: $10.00 per name. Required to search: name, years to search. Civil cases indexed by defendant, plaintiff. Civil records in index books from 1857.

Criminal Records: Access: Mail, in person. Both court and visitors may perform in person searches. Search fee: $10.00 per name. Required to search: name, years to search. Criminal records in index books from 1857.

General Information: No juvenile, mental, sealed, or adoption records released. SASE required. Turnaround time 2 days. Copy fee: $.50 per page. Certification fee: $10.00. Fee payee: Jack County District Clerk. Personal checks accepted. Prepayment is required.

County Court 100 Main, Jacksboro, TX 76458; 940-567-2111. Hours: 8AM-5PM (CST). *Misdemeanor, Civil, Probate.*

Civil Records: Access: Phone, mail, in person. Both court and visitors may perform in person searches. Search fee: $5.00 per name. Required to search: name, years to search. Civil cases indexed by defendant, plaintiff. Civil records in index books from 1856.

Criminal Records: Access: Phone, mail, in person. Both court and visitors may perform in person searches. Search fee: $5.00 per name. Required to search: name, years to search. Criminal records in index books from 1856, computerized since 1999.

General Information: No juvenile, mental, sealed, or adoption records released. SASE required. Turnaround time 1-2 days. Copy fee: $1.00 per page. Certification fee: $5.00. Fee payee: Jack County Clerk. Personal checks accepted. Prepayment is required.

Jackson County

District Court 115 W Main Rm 203, Edna, TX 77957; 361-782-3812. 8AM-5PM *Felony, Civil.*

Civil Records: Access: Phone, mail, in person. Both court and visitors may perform in person searches. Search fee: $5.00 per name. Required to search: name, years to search. Civil cases indexed by defendant, plaintiff. Civil records in index books from 1850.

Criminal Records: Access: Phone, mail, in person. Both court and visitors may perform in person searches. Search fee: $5.00 per name. Required to search: name,

years to search. Criminal records on microfiche from 1981, index books from 1850.

General Information: No juvenile, mental, sealed, or adoption records released. SASE required. Turnaround time 1-2 days. Copy fee: $1.00 per page. Certification fee: $1.00. Fee payee: District Clerk. Personal checks accepted. Prepayment is required.

County Court 115 W Main Rm101, Edna, TX 77957; 361-782-3563. Hours: 8AM-5PM (CST). *Misdemeanor, Civil, Probate.*

Civil Records: Access: Mail, in person. Both court and visitors may perform in person searches. Search fee: $5.00 per name. Required to search: name, years to search. Civil cases indexed by defendant, plaintiff. Civil records in index books from 1900s; computerized back to 1993.

Criminal Records: Access: In person only. Both court and visitors may perform in person searches. Search fee: $5.00 per name. Required to search: name, years to search, DOB, offense, date of offense. Criminal records in index books from 1900s; deed records computerized back to 1993.

General Information: No juvenile, mental, sealed, or adoption records released. SASE not required. Turnaround time 1-2 days. Fax notes: Fee to fax results is $4.25 for the 1st page and $2.25 per page thereafter. Copy fee: $1.00 per page. Certification fee: $5.00. Fee payee: County Clerk. Personal checks accepted. Prepayment is required.

Jasper County

District Court County Courthouse #202, PO Box 2088, Jasper, TX 75951; 409-384-2721. Hours: 8AM-4:30PM (CST). *Felony, Civil.*

Civil Records: Access: Mail, in person. Only the court performs in person searches; visitors may not. Search fee: $5.00 per name. Required to search: name, years to search. Civil cases indexed by defendant, plaintiff. Civil records on computer since 1991, index books and microfilm since 1850s.

Criminal Records: Access: Mail, in person. Only the court performs in person searches; visitors may not. Search fee: $5.00 per name. Required to search: name, years to search. Criminal records on computer since 12/96; index books and microfilm since 1850s.

General Information: No juvenile, mental, sealed, or adoption records released. SASE required. Turnaround time 1-2 days. Copy fee: $1.00 per page. Fee payee: District Clerk/Court. Personal checks accepted. Prepayment is required.

County Court Rm 103, Courthouse, Main at Lamar, PO Box 2070, Jasper, TX 75951; 409-384-9481; Fax: 409-384-7198. Hours: 8AM-5PM (CST). *Misdemeanor, Civil, Probate.*

Civil Records: Access: Phone, mail, fax, in person. Both court and visitors may perform in person searches. Search fee: $10.00 per name. There is no fee if you do the search yourself. Required to search: name, years to search. Civil cases indexed by defendant, plaintiff. Civil records in index books; on computer back to 1987.

Criminal Records: Access: Phone, mail, fax, in person. Both court and visitors may perform in person searches. Search fee: $10.00 per name. There is no fee if you do the search yourself. Required to search: name, years to search, DOB; also helpful: SSN. Criminal records in index books; on computer back to 1987.

General Information: Public access terminal is available. No juvenile, mental, sealed, or adoption records released. SASE not required. Turnaround time 1 day. Fax notes: Fee to fax results is $3.00 1st page; $1.00 each add'l. Copy fee: $1.00 per page. Certification fee: $5.00. Fee payee: Debbie Newman County Clerk. Personal checks accepted. Personal checks require drivers license. Prepayment is required.

Jeff Davis County

District & County Court PO Box 398, Fort Davis, TX 79734; 915-426-3251; Fax: 915-426-3760. Hours: 9AM-Noon, 1-5PM (CST). *Felony, Misdemeanor, Civil, Probate.*

Civil Records: Access: Mail, in person. Both court and visitors may perform in person searches. Search fee: $5.00 per name. Required to search: name, years to search. Civil cases indexed by defendant, plaintiff. Civil records in index books.

Criminal Records: Access: Mail, in person. Both court and visitors may perform in person searches. Search fee: $5.00 per name. Required to search: name, years to search. Criminal records in index books.

General Information: No juvenile, mental, sealed, or adoption records released. SASE required. Turnaround time 2 days. Copy fee: $1.00 per page. Certification fee: $5.00. Fee payee: County Clerk. Personal checks accepted. Prepayment is required.

Jefferson County

District Court PO Box 3707 (Pearl St Courthouse), Beaumont, TX 77704; 409-835-8580; Fax: 409-835-8527. Hours: 8AM-5PM (CST). *Felony, Civil.*

www.co.jefferson.tx.us

Civil Records: Access: Mail, online, in person. Both court and visitors may perform in person searches. Search fee: $5.00 per name. Required to search: name, years to search. Civil cases indexed by defendant, plaintiff. Civil records on computer and index books since 1940s. Online access to civil index available at www.co.jefferson.tx.us/dclerk/civil_index/main.htm. Search by defendant or plaintiff by year 1985 to present. Search results are not certified unless done by the court itself.

Criminal Records: Access: Mail, online, in person. Both court and visitors may perform in person searches. Search fee: $5.00 per name. Required to search: name, years to search; also helpful: DOB, SSN. Criminal records on computer and index books since 1940s. Online access to the criminal records index is available at www.co.jefferson.tx.us/dclerk/criminal_index/main.htm. Search by name by year 1981 to present.

General Information: Public access terminal is available. (Civil, Family & E-file on selected cases.) No juvenile, mental, sealed, or adoption records released. SASE required. Turnaround time 2-4 days. Copy fee: $1.00 per page. Certification fee: $1.00. Fee payee: District Clerk. Personal checks accepted. Prepayment is required.

County Court PO Box 1151, Beaumont, TX 77704; 409-835-8479; Fax: 409-839-2394. Hours: 8AM-5PM (CST). *Misdemeanor, Civil, Probate.*

www.co.jefferson.tx.us

Civil Records: Access: Mail, in person. Both court and visitors may perform in person searches. Search fee: $5.00 per name. Required to search: name, years to search. Civil cases indexed by defendant, plaintiff. Civil records on computer since 11/1/95, index books to 1836.

Criminal Records: Access: Mail, in person. Both court and visitors may perform in person searches. Search fee: $5.00 per name. Required to search: name, years to search, DOB. Criminal records on computer since 2/25/91, index books to 1836.

General Information: Public access terminal is available. No juvenile, mental, sealed, or adoption records released. SASE not required. Turnaround time 1 day. Fax notes: $2.50 for first page, $.50 each add'l. Copy fee: $1.00 per page. Certification fee: $5.00. Fee payee: County Clerk. Personal checks accepted. Credit cards accepted. Prepayment is required.

Jim Hogg County

District & County Court PO Box 878, Hebbronville, TX 78361; 361-527-4031; Fax: 361-527-5843. Hours: 9AM-5PM (CST). *Felony, Misdemeanor, Civil, Probate.*

Civil Records: Access: Mail, fax, in person. Both court and visitors may perform in person searches. Search fee: $15.00 per name. Required to search: name, years to search. Civil cases indexed by defendant, plaintiff. Civil records in index books.

Criminal Records: Access: In person only. Visitors must perform in person searches for themselves. No search fee. Required to search: name, years to search. Criminal records in index books.

General Information: No juvenile, mental, sealed, or adoption records released. SASE required. Turnaround time 2-4 days. Fax notes: Fee to fax results is $3.00 per page. Copy fee: $1.00 per page. Certification fee: $5.00. Fee payee: District Clerk. Personal checks accepted. Prepayment is required.

Jim Wells County

79th District Court PO Drawer 2219, Alice, TX 78333; 361-668-5717. Hours: 8AM-Noon, 1-5PM (CST). *Felony, Civil.*

Civil Records: Access: Mail, in person. Both court and visitors may perform in person searches. Search fee: $5.00 per name. Required to search: name, years to search. Civil cases indexed by defendant, plaintiff. Civil records on computer since 1992, index books since 1912.

Criminal Records: Access: Mail, in person. Both court and visitors may perform in person searches. Search fee: $5.00 per name. Required to search: name, years to search; also helpful: SSN. Criminal records on computer since 1992, index books since 1912.

General Information: No juvenile, mental, sealed, or adoption records released. SASE required. Turnaround time 2 days. Copy fee: $1.00 per page. Certification fee: $2.00. Fee payee: District Clerk. Personal checks accepted. Prepayment is required.

County Court PO Box 1459, 200 N Almond, Alice, TX 78333; 361-668-5702. Hours: 8:00AM-Noon, 1-5PM (CST). *Misdemeanor, Civil, Probate.*

Civil Records: Access: Mail, in person. Both court and visitors may perform in person searches. Search fee: $10.00 per name. Required to search: name, years to search. Civil cases indexed by defendant, plaintiff. Civil records in index books from 1911.

Criminal Records: Access: Phone, mail, in person. Both court and visitors may perform in person searches. Search fee: $10.00 per name. Required to search: name, years to search, address, DOB. Criminal records on computer since 1992, index books from 1911.

General Information: No juvenile, mental, sealed, or adoption records released. SASE not required. Turnaround time 1 day. Copy fee: $1.00 per page. Certification fee: $5.00. Fee payee: County Clerk. Personal checks accepted. Prepayment is required.

Johnson County

District Court PO Box 495, Cleburne, TX 76033-0495; 817-556-6843; Fax: 817-556-6120. Hours: 8AM-5PM (CST). *Felony, Civil.*

Civil Records: Access: Fax, mail, in person. Both court and visitors may perform in person searches. Search fee: $5.00 per name. Required to search: name; also helpful: years to search. Civil cases indexed by defendant, plaintiff. Civil records on computer from 1989, index books back to 1800s.

Criminal Records: Access: Fax, mail, in person. Both court and visitors may perform in person searches. Search fee: $5.00 per name. Required to search: name;

also helpful: years to search, aliases. Criminal records on computer from 1989, index books back to 1800s.

General Information: Public access terminal is available. No juvenile, mental, sealed, or adoption records released. SASE required. Turnaround time 2-4 days. Fax notes: Fee to fax results is $1.00 per page. Copy fee: $.50 per page. Certification fee: $1.00. Fee payee: District Clerk. Business checks accepted. Prepayment is required.

County Court Room 104, PO Box 662, Cleburne, TX 76033-0662; 817-556-6300. Hours: 8AM-Noon, 1-4:30PM (CST). *Misdemeanor, Civil, Probate.*

Civil Records: Access: Mail, in person. Both court and visitors may perform in person searches. Search fee: $5.00 per name. Required to search: name, years to search. Civil cases indexed by defendant, plaintiff. Civil records on computer since 1988, index books from 1985.

Criminal Records: Access: Mail, in person. Both court and visitors may perform in person searches. Search fee: $5.00 per name. Required to search: name, years to search, and DOB or SSN. Criminal records on computer since 1988, index books from 1985.

General Information: Public access terminal is available. No juvenile, mental, sealed, or adoption records released. SASE required. Turnaround time 1-2 days. Copy fee: $1.00 per page. Certification fee: $5.00. Fee payee: County Clerk. Business checks accepted. Prepayment is required.

Jones County

District Court PO Box 308, Anson, TX 79501; 915-823-3731; Fax: 915-823-3513 (Attn: Nona Carter). 8AM-5PM (CST). *Felony, Misdemeanor, Civil.*

Civil Records: Access: Mail, in person. Both court and visitors may perform in person searches. Search fee: $5.00 per name. Required to search: name, years to search. Civil cases indexed by defendant, plaintiff. Civil records on computer since 1990, index books to 1881.

Criminal Records: Access: Mail, in person. Both court and visitors may perform in person searches. Search fee: $5.00 per name. Required to search: name, years to search, DOB. Criminal records on computer since 1986, index books since 1881.

General Information: No juvenile, mental, sealed, or adoption records released. SASE required. Turnaround time same day. Copy fee: $1.00 per page. Certification fee: $2.00. Fee payee: Nona Carter, District Clerk. Personal checks accepted. Can set up deposit account. Prepayment is required.

Karnes County

District Court County Courthouse, 101 N Panna Maria Ave, Karnes City, TX 78118-2930; 830-780-2562; Fax: 830-780-3227. Hours: 8AM-Noon, 1-5PM (CST). *Felony, Civil.*

Civil Records: Access: Mail, in person, fax. Both court and visitors may perform in person searches. Search fee: $5.00 per name. Required to search: name, years to search. Civil cases indexed by defendant, plaintiff. Civil records in index books form 1858.

Criminal Records: Access: Mail, in person. Both court and visitors may perform in person searches. Search fee: $5.00 per name. Required to search: name, years to search. Criminal records in index books form 1906.

General Information: No juvenile, mental, sealed, or adoption records released. SASE required. Turnaround time 1-2 days. Copy fee: $1.00 per page. Certification fee: $2.00. Fee payee: District Clerk. Personal checks accepted. Prepayment is required.

County Court 101 N Panna Maria Ave #9 Courthouse, Karnes City, TX 78118-2929; 830-780-3938; Fax: 830-780-4576. Hours: 8AM-5PM (CST). *Misdemeanor, Civil, Probate.*

Civil Records: Access: Mail, in person. Both court and visitors may perform in person searches. Search fee: $10.00 per name. Required to search: name, years to search. Civil cases indexed by defendant, plaintiff. Civil records in index books, no computerization.

Criminal Records: Access: Mail, in person. Both court and visitors may perform in person searches. Search fee: $10.00 per name. Required to search: name, years to search. Criminal records in index books, no computerization.

General Information: No juvenile, mental, sealed, or adoption records released. SASE required. Turnaround time 2 days. Fax notes: Fee to fax results is $2.00 per page. Copy fee: $1.00 per page. Certification fee: $5.00. Fee payee: Elizabeth Swize, County Clerk. Personal checks accepted. Prepayment is required.

Kaufman County

District Court County Courthouse, 100 W Mulberry St, Kaufman, TX 75142; 972-932-4331 x214. Hours: 8AM-5PM (CST). *Felony, Civil.*

Civil Records: Access: Mail, in person. Both court and visitors may perform in person searches. Search fee: $5.00 per name. Required to search: name, years to search. Civil cases indexed by defendant, plaintiff. Civil records on computer or books from 1849.

Criminal Records: Access: Mail, in person. Both court and visitors may perform in person searches. Search fee: $5.00 per name. Required to search: name, years to search. Criminal records on computer or books from 1849.

General Information: No sealed, or adoption records released. SASE required. Turnaround time up to 1 week. Copy fee: $1.00 per page. Certification fee: $1.00. Fee payee: Kaufman Distric Clerk. Personal checks accepted. Prepayment is required.

County Court County Courthouse, Kaufman, TX 75142; 972-932-4331 x220. Hours: 8AM-4:30PM (CST). *Misdemeanor, Civil, Probate.*

Civil Records: Access: Mail, in person. Both court and visitors may perform in person searches. Search fee: $5.00 per name. Required to search: name, years to search. Civil cases indexed by defendant, plaintiff. Civil records on computer from 1985, index books before 1985.

Criminal Records: Access: Mail, in person. Both court and visitors may perform in person searches. Search fee: $5.00 per name. Required to search: name, years to search. Criminal records on computer from 1985, index books before 1985.

General Information: Public access terminal is available. No juvenile, mental, sealed, or adoption records released. SASE required. Turnaround time 10 days. Copy fee: $1.00 per page. Certification fee: $5.00. Fee payee: County Clerk. Personal checks accepted. Prepayment is required.

Kendall County

District Court 201 E. San Antonia, #201, Boerne, TX 78006; 830-249-9343. Hours: 8AM-Noon, 1-5PM (CST). *Felony, Civil.*

Civil Records: Access: Mail, in person. Both court and visitors may perform in person searches. Search fee: $5.00 per name. Required to search: name, years to search. Civil cases indexed by defendant, plaintiff. Civil records in index books back to early 1900s.

Criminal Records: Access: Mail, in person. Both court and visitors may perform in person searches. Search fee: $5.00 per name. Required to search: name, DOB, years to search, signed release; also helpful: SSN. Criminal records in index books back to early 1900s.

General Information: No juvenile, mental, sealed, or adoption records released. SASE required. Turnaround time 2-4 days. Copy fee: $.50 per page. Certification

fee: $1.00 per page. Fee payee: District Clerk. Personal checks accepted. Prepayment is required.

County Court 201 E San Antonio #127, Boerne, TX 78006; 830-249-9343; Fax: 830-249-3472. Hours: 8AM-5PM (CST). *Misdemeanor, Probate.*

Civil Records: Access: Mail, in person. Both court and visitors may perform in person searches. Search fee: $10.00 per name. Required to search: name, years to search. Civil cases indexed by defendant, plaintiff. Civil records in index books from 1860s.

Criminal Records: Access: Mail, in person. Both court and visitors may perform in person searches. Search fee: $10.00 per name. Required to search: name, years to search. Criminal records in index books from 1860s.

General Information: No juvenile, mental, sealed, or adoption records released. SASE required. Turnaround time 2-4 days. Fax notes: No fee to fax results. Copy fee: $1.00 per page. Certification fee: $5.00. Fee payee: County Clerk. Personal checks accepted. Prepayment is required.

Kenedy County

District & County Court PO Box 227, Sarita, TX 78385; 361-294-5220; Fax: 361-294-5218. Hours: 8:30AM-Noon, 1PM-4:30PM (CST). *Felony, Misdemeanor, Civil, Probate.*

Civil Records: Access: Phone, mail, in person. Both court and visitors may perform in person searches. Search fee: $5.00 per name. Required to search: name, years to search. Civil cases indexed by defendant, plaintiff. Civil records on microfilm since 1991, minute books since 1921.

Criminal Records: Access: Phone, mail, in person. Both court and visitors may perform in person searches. Search fee: $5.00 per name. Required to search: name, years to search. Criminal records on microfilm since 1991, minute books since 1921.

General Information: No juvenile, mental, sealed, or adoption records released. SASE not required. Turnaround time 5 days. Copy fee: $1.00 per page. Certification fee: $5.00. Fee payee: District/County Clerk. Personal checks accepted. Prepayment required.

Kent County

District & County Court PO Box 9, Jayton, TX 79528; 806-237-3881; Fax: 806-237-2632. Hours: 8:30AM-Noon, 1-5PM (CST). *Felony, Misdemeanor, Civil, Probate.*

Civil Records: Access: Mail, in person. Both court and visitors may perform in person searches. Search fee: $5.00 per name. Required to search: name, years to search. Civil cases indexed by defendant, plaintiff. Civil records in index books.

Criminal Records: Access: Mail, in person. Both court and visitors may perform in person searches. Search fee: $5.00 per name. Required to search: name, years to search. Criminal records in index books.

General Information: No juvenile, mental, sealed, or adoption records released. SASE required. Turnaround time as soon as possible. Copy fee: $1.00 per page. Certification fee: $5.00 plus $1.00 per page. Fee payee: County Clerk. Only cashiers checks and money orders accepted. Prepayment is required.

Kerr County

District Court 700 Main, County Courthouse, Kerrville, TX 78028; 830-792-2281. Hours: 8AM-5PM (CST). *Felony, Civil.*

Civil Records: Access: Mail, in person. Both court and visitors may perform in person searches. Search fee: $5.00 per name. Required to search: name, years to search. Civil cases indexed by defendant, plaintiff. Civil records on computer from late 1991, index books after 1991.

Criminal Records: Access: Mail, in person. Both court and visitors may perform in person searches. Search fee: $5.00 per name. Required to search: name, years to search, DOB, SSN. Criminal records on computer from late 1990, index books prior.

General Information: No juvenile, mental, sealed, or adoption records released. SASE required. Turnaround time 2-4 days. Fax notes: Fee to fax results is $1.00 per page. Copy fee: $1.00 1st page; $.25 each add'l. Certification fee: $1.00 per page. Fee payee: District Clerk. Personal checks accepted. 1989. Prepayment is required.

County Court & County Court at Law 700 Main St, #122, Kerrville, TX 78028-5389; 830-792-2262; Probate phone: 830-792-2298; Fax: 830-792-2274. Hours: 8AM-5PM (CST). *Misdemeanor, Civil, Probate.*

Civil Records: Access: Phone, mail, fax, in person. Both court and visitors may perform in person searches. Search fee: $5.00 per name. Required to search: name, years to search. Civil cases indexed by defendant, plaintiff. Civil records on computer since 1988, microfiche since 1985, index books prior to 1985.

Criminal Records: Access: Phone, mail, fax, in person. Both court and visitors may perform in person searches. Search fee: $5.00 per name. Required to search: name, years to search, DOB; also helpful: SSN. Criminal records on computer since 1985, index books prior to 1918.

General Information: Public access terminal is available. No juvenile, mental, sealed, or adoption records released. SASE not required. Turnaround time 3 days. Fax notes: Fee to fax results is $1.00 per page. Copy fee: $1.00 per page. Certification fee: $5.00. Fee payee: Kerr County Clerk. Only cashiers checks and money orders accepted. Prepayment is required.

Kimble County

District & County Court 501 Main St, Junction, TX 76849; 915-446-3353; Fax: 915-446-2986. Hours: 8AM-Noon, 1-5PM (CST). *Felony, Misdemeanor, Civil, Probate.*

Civil Records: Access: Mail, in person. Both court and visitors may perform in person searches. Search fee: $5.00 per name. Required to search: name, years to search. Civil cases indexed by defendant, plaintiff. Civil records in index books (records are micro-filmed for security only).

Criminal Records: Access: Mail, in person. Both court and visitors may perform in person searches. Search fee: $5.00 per name. Required to search: name, years to search, DOB. Criminal records in index books (records are micro-filmed for security only).

General Information: No juvenile, mental, sealed, or adoption records released. SASE not required. Turnaround time 3-4 days. Copy fee: $1.00 per page. Certification fee: $5.00. Fee payee: Kimble County/District Clerk. Personal checks accepted. Prepayment is required.

King County

District & County Court PO Box 135, Guthrie, TX 79236; 806-596-4412; Fax: 806-596-4664. 9AM-Noon, 1-5PM *Felony, Misdemeanor, Civil, Probate.*

Civil Records: Access: Mail, in person. Both court and visitors may perform in person searches. Search fee: $5.00 per name. Required to search: name, years to search. Civil cases indexed by defendant, plaintiff. Civil records in index books.

Criminal Records: Access: Mail, in person. Both court and visitors may perform in person searches. Search fee: $5.00 per name. Required to search: name, years to search, DOB. Criminal records in index books.

General Information: No juvenile, mental, sealed, or adoption records released. SASE required. Turnaround time 2-4 days. Fax notes: Fee to fax results is $1.00 per document. Copy fee: $1.00 per page. Certification fee: $5.00. Fee payee: District Clerk. Personal checks accepted. Prepayment is required.

Kinney County

District & County Court PO Drawer 9, Brackettville, TX 78832; 830-563-2521; Fax: 830-563-2644. Hours: 8AM-5PM (CST). *Felony, Misdemeanor, Civil, Probate.*

Civil Records: Access: Phone, fax, mail, in person. Both court and visitors may perform in person searches. Search fee: $10.00 per name. Required to search: name, years to search. Civil cases indexed by defendant, plaintiff. Civil records in index books from late 1800s; computerized back to 1980s.

Criminal Records: Access: Phone, fax, mail, in person. Both court and visitors may perform in person searches. Search fee: $10.00 per name. Required to search: name, years to search, DOB. Criminal records in index books from late 1800s; computerized records back to 1980s.

General Information: No juvenile, mental, sealed, or adoption records released. SASE required. Turnaround time 1 week. Fax notes: $3.00 for 1st page; $2.00 each add'l. Copy fee: $1.00 per page. Certification fee: Certification fee: $5.00 County; $1.00 District. Fee payee: County & District Clerk. Personal checks accepted. Prepayment is required.

Kleberg County

District & County Court at Law PO Box 312, Kingsville, TX 78364-0312; 361-595-8561; Fax: 361-595-8525. 8AM-Noon, 1-5 PM (CST). *Felony, Civil.*

Civil Records: Access: Phone, fax, mail, in person. Both court and visitors may perform in person searches. Search fee: $5.00 per name. Required to search: name, years to search. Civil cases indexed by defendant, plaintiff. Civil records in index books since 1916. Computerized records go back to 1992.

Criminal Records: Access: Phone, fax, mail, in person. Both court and visitors may perform in person searches. Search fee: $5.00 per name. Required to search: name, years to search; also helpful: DOB, SSN. Criminal records in index books since 1916. Computerized records go to 1992.

General Information: No sealed or adoption records released. SASE required. Turnaround time 2-3 days. Fax notes: $5.00 per document. Incoming fax fee $1.00. Copy fee: $1.00 per page. Certification fee: $1.00. Fee payee: District Clerk. Personal checks accepted. (local personal checks only). Prepayment is required.

County Court - Criminal PO Box 1327, Kingsville, TX 78364; 361-595-8548. Hours: 8AM-noon; 1-5PM (CST). *Misdemeanor, Probate.*

Note: Court also handles civil cases dealing with occupational licenses and bond forfeitures.

Criminal Records: Access: Phone, mail, in person. Both court and visitors may perform in person searches. Search fee: $10.00 per name per 10 years. Required to search: name, years to search, DOB. Criminal records on computer since 1989, index books since 1913.

General Information: No juvenile or mental records released. SASE required. Turnaround time same day. Copy fee: $1.00 per page. Certification fee: $5.00. Fee payee: Kleberg County Clerk. Business checks accepted. Prepayment is required.

Knox County

District & County Court PO Box 196, Benjamin, TX 79505; 940-454-2441. Hours: 8AM-Noon, 1-5PM (CST). *Felony, Misdemeanor, Civil, Probate.*

Civil Records: Access: Mail, in person. Both court and visitors may perform in person searches. Search fee: $5.00 per name. Required to search: name, years to

search. Civil cases indexed by defendant, plaintiff. Civil records in index books.

Criminal Records: Access: Mail, in person. Both court and visitors may perform in person searches. Search fee: $5.00 for a misdemeanor search; $5.00 for a felony search. Required to search: name, years to search, DOB, SSN, signed release. Criminal records in index books back to 1885.

General Information: No juvenile, mental, sealed, or adoption records released. SASE required. Turnaround time 1 day. Fax notes: Fee to fax results is $1.00 per page. Copy fee: $1.00 per page. Certification fee: $5.00. Fee payee: District/County Clerk. Personal checks accepted. Prepayment is required.

La Salle County

District Court PO Box 340, Cotulla, TX 78014; 830-879-4434. Hours: 8AM-5PM (CST). *Felony, Civil.*

Civil Records: Access: Phone, mail, in person. Both court and visitors may perform in person searches. Search fee: $5.00 per name. Required to search: name, years to search. Civil cases indexed by defendant, plaintiff. Civil records on computer back to 1990, prior in index books.

Criminal Records: Access: Mail, in person. Both court and visitors may perform in person searches. Search fee: $5.00 per name. Required to search: name, years to search. Criminal records on computer back to 1990, prior in index books.

General Information: No juvenile, mental, sealed, or adoption records released. SASE required. Turnaround time 1-2 days. Copy fee: $1.00 per page. Certification fee: $5.00. Fee payee: District Clerk. Personal checks accepted. Prepayment is required.

District & County Courts PO Box 340, Cotulla, TX 78014; 830-879-4432; Fax: 830-879-2933. Hours: 8AM-5PM (CST). *Misdemeanor, Civil, Probate.*

Civil Records: Access: Mail, in person. Both court and visitors may perform in person searches. Search fee: $5.00 per name. Required to search: name, years to search. Civil cases indexed by defendant, plaintiff. Civil records on computer since 1994, prior on index books.

Criminal Records: Access: Mail, in person. Both court and visitors may perform in person searches. Search fee: $5.00 per name. Required to search: name, years to search. Criminal records on computer since 1994, prior on index books to 1988.

General Information: No juvenile, mental, sealed, or adoption records released. SASE required. Turnaround time 1-2 days. Copy fee: $1.00 per page. Certification fee: $5.00. Fee payee: County Clerk. Personal checks accepted. Prepayment is required.

Lamar County

District Court 119 N Main Rm 306, Paris, TX 75460; 903-737-2427. 8AM-5PM . *Felony, Civil.*

Civil Records: Access: Mail, in person. Both court and visitors may perform in person searches. Search fee: $5.00 per name. Required to search: name, years to search. Civil cases indexed by defendant, plaintiff. Civil records on computer since January, 1994, index books prior to 1994.

Criminal Records: Access: Mail, in person. Both court and visitors may perform in person searches. Search fee: $5.00 per name. Required to search: name, years to search. Criminal records on computer since January, 1994, index books prior to 1994.

General Information: Public access terminal is available. No juvenile, mental, sealed, or adoption records released. SASE required. Turnaround time 1-2 days. Copy fee: $1.00 per page. Fee payee: District Clerk. Personal checks accepted. Prepayment is required.

County Court 119 N Main, Paris, TX 75460; 903-737-2420. Hours: 8AM-5PM (CST). *Misdemeanor, Civil, Probate.*

Civil Records: Access: Phone, fax, mail, in person. Both court and visitors may perform in person searches. Search fee: $5.00 per name. Required to search: name, years to search. Civil cases indexed by defendant, plaintiff. Civil records in index books since 1913; on computer back to 1998.

Criminal Records: Access: Phone, fax, mail, in person. Both court and visitors may perform in person searches. Search fee: $5.00 per name. Required to search: name, years to search, DOB; also helpful- SSN, drivers license number. Criminal records on computer back to 1988, index books since 1913.

General Information: No juvenile, mental, sealed, or adoption records released. SASE not required. Turnaround time 2-3 days. Copy fee: $1.00 per page. Certification fee: $5.00. Fee payee: County Clerk. Business checks accepted. Personal checks must be local. Prepayment is required.

Lamb County

District Court 100 6th Rm 212, Courthouse, Littlefield, TX 79339; 806-385-4222. Hours: 8AM-Noon, 1-5PM (CST). *Felony, Civil.*

Civil Records: Access: Mail, in person. Both court and visitors may perform in person searches. Search fee: $5.00 per name. Required to search: name, years to search. Civil cases indexed by defendant, plaintiff. Civil records on computer since 1987; on index books back to 1940.

Criminal Records: Access: Mail, in person. Both court and visitors may perform in person searches. Search fee: $10.00 per name. Required to search: name, years to search; also helpful: DOB, SSN. Criminal records in index books to 1940s; on computer since 1987.

General Information: No juvenile, mental, sealed, or adoption records released. SASE required. Turnaround time 2-3 days. Copy fee: $1.00 per page. Certification fee: $1.00 per page. Fee payee: District Court. Personal checks accepted. Prepayment is required.

County Court County Courthouse, Rm 103, Box 3, Littlefield, TX 79339-3366; 806-385-4222 X214; Fax: 806-385-6485. Hours: 8AM-5PM (CST). *Misdemeanor, Civil, Probate.*

Civil Records: Access: Mail, in person. Both court and visitors may perform in person searches. Search fee: $5.00 per name. Required to search: name, years to search. Civil cases indexed by defendant, plaintiff. Civil records in index books.

Criminal Records: Access: Mail, in person. Both court and visitors may perform in person searches. Search fee: $5.00 per name. Required to search: name, years to search; also helpful: DOB, SSN. Criminal records in index books.

General Information: No juvenile, mental, sealed, or adoption records released. SASE required. Turnaround time 1-2 days. Copy fee: $1.00 per page. Certification fee: $5.00. Fee payee: Lamb County Clerk. Personal checks accepted. Prepayment is required.

Lampasas County

District Court PO Box 327, Lampasas, TX 76550; 512-556-8271 X22; Fax: 512-556-9463. Hours: 8AM-5PM (CST). *Felony, Civil.*

Civil Records: Access: Mail, in person. Both court and visitors may perform in person searches. Search fee: $5.00 per name. Required to search: name, years to search. Civil cases indexed by defendant, plaintiff. Civil records in index books, computerized since 1997.

Criminal Records: Access: Mail, in person. Both court and visitors may perform in person searches. Search fee: $5.00 per name. Required to search: name, years to

search. Criminal records in index books; on computer for 5 years.

General Information: No juvenile, mental, sealed, or adoption records released. SASE required. Turnaround time 2-4 days. Fax notes: Fee to fax results is $1.00 per page. Copy fee: $1.00 per page. Certification fee: $2.00. Fee payee: District Clerk. Business checks accepted. Prepayment is required.

County Court PO Box 347, Lampasas, TX 76550; 512-556-8271 X37. Hours: 8AM-5PM (CST). *Misdemeanor, Civil, Probate.*

Civil Records: Access: Mail, in person. Both court and visitors may perform in person searches. Search fee: $5.00 per name. Required to search: name, years to search. Civil cases indexed by defendant, plaintiff. Civil records in index books.

Criminal Records: Access: Mail, in person. Both court and visitors may perform in person searches. Search fee: $5.00 per name. Required to search: name, years to search; also helpful: DOB, SSN. Criminal records in index books.

General Information: Public access terminal is available. No juvenile, mental, sealed, or adoption records released. SASE required. Turnaround time 1-2 days. Copy fee: $1.00 per page. Certification fee: $5.00. Fee payee: County Clerk. Personal checks accepted. Checks must be in state. Prepayment is required.

Lavaca County

District Court PO Box 306, Hallettsville, TX 77964; 361-798-2351. Hours: 8AM-Noon, 1-5PM (CST). *Felony, Civil.*

Civil Records: Access: Phone, mail, in person. Both court and visitors may perform in person searches. Search fee: $5.00 per name. Required to search: name, years to search. Civil cases indexed by defendant, plaintiff. Civil records in index books from 1847. Information released to attorneys only.

Criminal Records: Access: Mail, in person. Both court and visitors may perform in person searches. Search fee: $5.00 per name. Required to search: name, years to search. Criminal records in index books from 1847. Information released to law enforcement only.

General Information: No juvenile, Department of Human Services, adoptions and expunction records released. SASE required. Turnaround time same day. Copy fee: $1.00 per page. Certification fee: $2.00. Fee payee: Lavaca County District Clerk. Personal checks accepted. Prepayment is required.

County Court PO Box 326, Hallettsville, TX 77964; 361-798-3612. Hours: 8AM-5PM (CST). *Misdemeanor, Civil, Probate.*

Civil Records: Access: Mail, in person. Both court and visitors may perform in person searches. Search fee: $5.00 per name per 5 years. Required to search: name, years to search, DOB; also helpful: address, SSN, DL#. Civil cases indexed by defendant, plaintiff. Civil records on computer go back to late 1993; earlier in index books.

Criminal Records: Access: Mail, in person. Both court and visitors may perform in person searches. Search fee: $5.00 per name per 5 years. Required to search: name, years to search; also helpful: address, DOB, DL#, SSN. Civil records on computer go back to late 1993; earlier in index books.

General Information: No mental health or sealed records released. SASE not required. Turnaround time same day as received. Copy fee: $1.00 per page. Certification fee: $5.00 plus 1.00 per page. Fee payee: County Clerk. Personal checks accepted. Prepayment is required.

Lee County

District Court PO Box 176, Giddings, TX 78942; 979-542-2947; Fax: 979-542-2444. Hours: 8AM-Noon, 1-5PM (CST). *Felony, Civil.*

Civil Records: Access: Mail, in person. Both court and visitors may perform in person searches. Search fee: $5.00 per name. Required to search: name, years to search. Civil cases indexed by defendant, plaintiff. Civil records on index books from 1800s.

Criminal Records: Access: Mail, in person. Both court and visitors may perform in person searches. Search fee: $5.00 per name. Required to search: name, years to search; also helpful: DOB, SSN. Criminal records on computer since 1989.

General Information: No juvenile or adoption records released. Turnaround time 1-2 days. Copy fee: $1.00 per page. Certification fee: $2.00. Fee payee: District Clerk, Lee County. Personal checks accepted. Prepayment is required.

County Court PO Box 419, Giddings, TX 78942; 979-542-3684; Fax: 979-542-2623. Hours: 8AM-5PM (CST). *Misdemeanor, Civil, Probate.*

Civil Records: Access: Mail, in person. Both court and visitors may perform in person searches. Search fee: $5.00 per name. Required to search: name, years to search. Civil cases indexed by defendant, plaintiff. Civil records in index books since 1874 (beginning 1995 on computer).

Criminal Records: Access: Mail, in person. Both court and visitors may perform in person searches. Search fee: $5.00 per name. Required to search: name, years to search. Criminal records on computer since 1992, index books since 1874.

General Information: No juvenile, mental, sealed or adoption records released. SASE required. Turnaround time 1-3 days. Copy fee: $1.00 per page. Certification fee: $5.00. Fee payee: County Clerk. Personal checks accepted. Prepayment is required.

Leon County

District Court PO Box 39, Centerville, TX 75833; 903-536-2227. Hours: 8AM-5PM (CST). *Felony, Civil.*

Civil Records: Access: Mail, in person. Both court and visitors may perform in person searches. Search fee: $5.00 per name. Required to search: name, years to search. Civil cases indexed by defendant, plaintiff. Civil records in index books.

Criminal Records: Access: Mail, in person. Only the court performs in person searches; visitors may not. Search fee: $5.00 per name. Required to search: name, years to search. Criminal records in index books.

General Information: No juvenile, mental, sealed, or adoption records released. SASE required. Turnaround time 2-4 days. Copy fee: $1.00 per page. Certification fee: $2.00. Fee payee: District Clerk. Personal checks accepted. Prepayment is required.

County Court PO Box 98, Centerville, TX 75833; 903-536-2352. Hours: 8AM-5PM (CST). *Misdemeanor, Civil, Probate.*

Civil Records: Access: Mail, in person. Both court and visitors may perform in person searches. Search fee: $5.00 per name. Required to search: name, years to search. Civil cases indexed by defendant, plaintiff. Civil records in index books.

Criminal Records: Access: Mail, in person. Both court and visitors may perform in person searches. Search fee: $5.00 per name. Required to search: name, years to search, signed release. Criminal records in index books.

General Information: No juvenile, mental, sealed, or adoption records released. SASE required. Turnaround time 1-3 days. Copy fee: $1.00 per page. Certification fee: $5.00. Fee payee: Leon County Clerk. Business checks accepted. Personal checks accepted in person only. Prepayment is required.

Liberty County

District Court 1923 Sam Houston Rm 303, Liberty, TX 77575; 936-336-4600. Hours: 8AM-Noon, 1-5PM (CST). *Felony, Civil.*

Civil Records: Access: Mail, in person. Both court and visitors may perform in person searches. Search fee: $5.00 per name. Required to search: name, years to search. Civil cases indexed by defendant, plaintiff. Civil records on computer since 1994, index books prior.

Criminal Records: Access: Mail, in person. Both court and visitors may perform in person searches. Search fee: $5.00 per name. Required to search: name, years to search. Criminal records on computer since 1994, index books prior.

General Information: No juvenile, mental, sealed, or adoption records released. SASE required. Turnaround time 2-4 days. Copy fee: $1.00 per page. Fee payee: District Clerk. Personal checks accepted. Prepayment is required.

County Court PO Box 369, Liberty, TX 77575; 936-336-4670. Hours: 8AM-5PM (CST). *Misdemeanor, Civil, Probate.*

Civil Records: Access: Mail, in person. Both court and visitors may perform in person searches. Search fee: $5.00 per name. Required to search: name, years to search. Civil cases indexed by defendant, plaintiff. Civil records in index books; later on computer.

Criminal Records: Access: Mail, in person. Both court and visitors may perform in person searches. Search fee: $5.00 per name. Required to search: name, years to search, DOB, SSN, signed release. Criminal records in index books; later on computer.

General Information: No juvenile, mental, sealed, or adoption records released. SASE required. Turnaround time 2-4 days. Copy fee: $1.00 per page. Certification fee: $5.00. Fee payee: County Clerk. Business checks accepted. Personal checks accepted in person only. Prepayment is required.

Limestone County

District Court PO Box 230, Groesbeck, TX 76642; 254-729-3206; Fax: 254-729-2960. Hours: 8AM-5PM (CST). *Felony, Civil.*

Civil Records: Access: Phone, fax, mail, in person. Both court and visitors may perform in person searches. Search fee: $5.00 per name. Required to search: name, years to search. Civil cases indexed by defendant, plaintiff. Civil records on computer since September 1990, index books since 1883.

Criminal Records: Access: Phone, fax, mail, in person. Both court and visitors may perform in person searches. Search fee: $5.00 per name. Required to search: name, years to search, DOB; also helpful: SSN. Criminal records on computer since September 1990, index books since 1911.

General Information: No juvenile, mental, sealed, or adoption records released. SASE not required. Turnaround time 1 week. Fax notes: $1.00 for first page, $.25 each add'l. Copy fee: $1.00 per document or $.50 per single page. Certification fee: $2.00. Fee payee: District Clerk. Personal checks accepted.

County Court PO Box 350, Groesbeck, TX 76642; 254-729-5504; Fax: 254-729-2951. Hours: 8AM-5PM (CST). *Misdemeanor, Civil, Probate.*

Civil Records: Access: Mail, in person. Both court and visitors may perform in person searches. Search fee: $5.00 per name. Required to search: name, years to search. Civil cases indexed by defendant, plaintiff. Civil records in index books.

Criminal Records: Access: Mail, in person. Both court and visitors may perform in person searches. Search fee: $5.00 per name. Required to search: name, years to search; also helpful: DOB, SSN, signed release. Criminal records in index books.

General Information: Public access terminal is available. No juvenile, mental, sealed, or adoption records released. SASE not required. Turnaround time 2 days. Fax notes: Fee to fax results is $2.00 per page. Copy fee: $1.00 per page. Certification fee: $5.00. Fee payee: Limestone County Clerk. Personal checks accepted. Prepayment is required.

Lipscomb County

District & County Court PO Box 70, Lipscomb, TX 79056; 806-862-3091; Fax: 806-862-3004. Hours: 8:30AM-Noon, 1-5PM (CST). *Felony, Misdemeanor, Civil, Probate.*

Civil Records: Access: Fax, mail, in person. Both court and visitors may perform in person searches. Search fee: $5.00 per name. Required to search: name. Civil cases indexed by defendant, plaintiff. Civil records in index books since 1887; on computer back to 1999.
Criminal Records: Access: Fax, mail, in person. Both court and visitors may perform in person searches. Search fee: $5.00 per name. Required to search: name; also helpful: DOB. Criminal records in index books since 1887; on computer back to 1999.
General Information: No juvenile, mental, sealed, or adoption records released. SASE not required. Turnaround time 2 days. Fax notes: $1.00 for first page, $.50 each add'l. Copy fee: $1.00 per page. Certification fee: $5.00 and $1.00 per district. Fee payee: County Clerk. Personal checks accepted. Prepayment required.

Live Oak County

District Court PO Drawer 440, George West, TX 78022; 361-449-2733 X105. Hours: 8AM-5PM (CST). *Felony, Civil.*

Civil Records: Access: Phone, fax, mail, in person. Both court and visitors may perform in person searches. Search fee: $10.00 per name. Required to search: name, years to search. Civil cases indexed by defendant, plaintiff. Civil records in index books and microfiche since 1850s.
Criminal Records: Access: Phone, fax, mail, in person. Both court and visitors may perform in person searches. Search fee: $10.00 per name. Required to search: name, years to search, DOB; also helpful: SSN. Criminal records in index books and microfiche since 1850s.
General Information: No juvenile, mental, sealed, or adoption records released. SASE required. Turnaround time 1-2 days. Copy fee: $1.00 per page. Certification fee: $1.00. Fee payee: District Clerk. Personal checks accepted. Prepayment is required.

County Court PO Box 280, George West, TX 78022; 361-449-2733 X3. Hours: 8AM-5PM (CST). *Misdemeanor, Civil, Probate.*

Civil Records: Access: Mail, in person. Both court and visitors may perform in person searches. Search fee: $10.00 per name. Required to search: name, years to search. Civil cases indexed by defendant, plaintiff. Civil records in index books.
Criminal Records: Access: Mail, in person. Both court and visitors may perform in person searches. Search fee: $10.00 per name. Required to search: name, years to search. Criminal records in index books.
General Information: No juvenile, mental, sealed, or adoption records released. SASE required. Turnaround time 1-2 days. Copy fee: $1.00 per page. Certification fee: $5.00. Fee payee: County Clerk. Personal checks accepted. Prepayment is required.

Llano County

District Clerk PO Box 877, Llano, TX 78643-0877; 915-247-5036; Fax: 915-248-0492. Hours: 8AM-4:30PM (CST). *Felony, Civil.*

Civil Records: Access: Mail, in person. Both court and visitors may perform in person searches. Search fee:

$5.00 per name. Fee is per 5 year period. Required to search: name, years to search. Civil cases indexed by defendant, plaintiff. Civil records in index books back to 1900, computerized back to 1995.
Criminal Records: Access: Mail, in person. Both court and visitors may perform in person searches. Search fee: $5.00 per name. Fee is per 5 year period. Required to search: name, years to search. Criminal records in index books back to 1900, computerized back to 1995.
General Information: No juvenile, mental, sealed, or adoption records released. SASE required. Turnaround time 1-3 days. Copy fee: $1.00 per page. Certification fee: $1.00 per page. Fee payee: Llano County District Clerk. Personal checks accepted. Credit cards accepted: Visa, MasterCard. 5% handling fee charged. Prepayment is required.

County Court PO Box 40, Llano, TX 78643-0040; 915-247-4455. Hours: 8AM-4:30PM (CST). *Misdemeanor, Civil, Probate.*

Civil Records: Access: Phone, mail, in person. Both court and visitors may perform in person searches. Search fee: $5.00 per name. Required to search: name, years to search. Civil cases indexed by defendant, plaintiff. Civil records on computer since 1985, index books prior.
Criminal Records: Access: Phone, mail, in person. Both court and visitors may perform in person searches. Search fee: $5.00 per name. Required to search: name, years to search; also helpful: DOB. Criminal records on computer since 1985, index books prior.
General Information: Public access terminal is available. No juvenile, mental, sealed, or adoption records released. SASE not required. Turnaround time 2-4 days. Copy fee: $1.00 per page. Certification fee: $5.00. Fee payee: County Clerk. Personal checks okay.

Loving County

District & County Court PO Box 194, Mentone, TX 79754; 915-377-2441; Fax: 915-377-2701. Hours: 9AM-Noon, 1-5PM (CST). *Felony, Misdemeanor, Civil, Probate.*

Civil Records: Access: Phone, fax, mail, in person. Both court and visitors may perform in person searches. Search fee: $5.00 per name. Required to search: name, years to search. Civil cases indexed by defendant, plaintiff. Civil records in index books from 1935; computerized back to 1987.
Criminal Records: Access: Phone, fax, mail, in person. Both court and visitors may perform in person searches. Search fee: $5.00 per name. Required to search: name, years to search. Criminal records in index books from 1935; computerized back to 1987.
General Information: No juvenile, mental, sealed, or adoption records released. SASE required. Turnaround time 2 days. Fax notes: Fee to fax results is $1.50 per page. Copy fee: $1.00 per page. Certification fee: $5.00. Fee payee: Loving County Clerk. Personal checks accepted. Prepayment is required.

Lubbock County

District Court PO Box 10536, Lubbock, TX 79408-3536; 806-775-1623; Fax: 806-775-1382. Hours: 8AM-5PM (CST). *Felony, Civil.*

www.districtclerk.com

Civil Records: Access: Fax, mail, in person. Both court and visitors may perform in person searches. Search fee: $5.00 per name. Required to search: name, years to search. Civil cases indexed by defendant, plaintiff. Civil records on computer back to 1983, in index books to 1908.
Criminal Records: Access: Fax, mail, in person. Both court and visitors may perform in person searches. Search fee: $5.00 per name. Required to search: name, years to search, DOB; also helpful: SSN, signed release.

Criminal records on computer back to 1983, in index books to 1908.
General Information: Public access terminal is available. No juvenile, mental, sealed, or adoption records released. SASE required. Fax notes: $5.00 per document. Copy fee: $1.00 per page. Certification fee: $1.00. Fee payee: District Clerk. Personal checks accepted. Prepayment is required.

County Courts Courthouse, Room 207, PO Box 10536, Lubbock, TX 79408; 806-775-1051. Hours: 8:30AM-5PM (CST). *Misdemeanor, Civil, Probate.*

www.co.lubbock.tx.us/CCourt/c_courts.htm

Civil Records: Access: Mail, in person. Both court and visitors may perform in person searches. Search fee: $10.00 per name. Fee is for each 5 year period. Required to search: name, years to search. Civil cases indexed by defendant, plaintiff. Civil records on computer back to 1986, index books prior.
Criminal Records: Access: Mail, in person. Both court and visitors may perform in person searches. Search fee: $5.00 per name. Fee is for each 5 year period; $7.00 for more than 5 years. Required to search: name, years to search. Criminal records on computer back to 1986, index books prior.
General Information: Public access terminal is available. No juvenile, mental, sealed, or adoption records released. SASE required. Turnaround time 3-5 days. Fax notes: Will not fax results. Copy fee: $1.00 per page. Certification fee: $5.00. Fee payee: County Clerk. Personal checks accepted. Prepayment required.

Lynn County

District Court PO Box 939, Tahoka, TX 79373; 806-561-4274; Fax: 806-561-4151. Hours: 8:30AM-5PM (CST). *Felony, Civil.*

Civil Records: Access: Fax, mail, in person. Both court and visitors may perform in person searches. Search fee: $5.00 per name. Required to search: name, years to search. Civil cases indexed by defendant, plaintiff. Civil records on computer from 1997, index books from 1916.
Criminal Records: Access: Fax, mail, in person. Both court and visitors may perform in person searches. Search fee: $5.00 per name. Required to search: name, years to search. Criminal records on computer from 1997, index books from 1916.
General Information: No juvenile, mental, sealed, or adoption records released. SASE is required. Turnaround time 2 days. Fax notes: $2.00 per page. Copy fee: $1.00 per page. Certification fee: $1.00 per page. Fee payee: District Clerk. Personal checks accepted. Prepayment is required.

County Court PO Box 937, Tahoka, TX 79373; 806-561-4750; Fax: 806-561-4988. Hours: 8:30AM-5PM (CST). *Misdemeanor, Civil, Probate.*

Civil Records: Access: Mail, in person. Both court and visitors may perform in person searches. Search fee: $5.00. Required to search: name, years to search. Civil cases indexed by defendant, plaintiff. Civil records in index books from 1903; on computer back to 1997.
Criminal Records: Access: Mail, in person. Both court and visitors may perform in person searches. Search fee: $5.00. Required to search: name, years to search. Criminal records in index books from 1903; on computer back to 1997.
General Information: No juvenile, mental, sealed, or adoption records released. SASE required. Turnaround time 2-4 days. Fax notes: Fee to fax results is $2.00 per page. Copy fee: $1.00 per page. Certification fee: $5.00. Fee payee: Lynn County Clerk. Personal checks accepted. Prepayment is required.

Madison County

District Court 101 W Main Rm 226, Madisonville, TX 77864; 936-348-9203. Hours: 8AM-Noon, 1-5PM (CST). *Felony, Civil.*

Civil Records: Access: Mail, in person. Both court and visitors may perform in person searches. Search fee: $5.00 per name. Required to search: name, years to search. Civil cases indexed by defendant, plaintiff. Civil records in index books to 1967.

Criminal Records: Access: Mail, in person. Both court and visitors may perform in person searches. Search fee: $5.00 per name. Required to search: name, years to search. Criminal records in index books to 1835.

General Information: No juvenile, mental, sealed, or adoption records released. SASE required. Turnaround time 1 day. Copy fee: $1.00 per page. Fee payee: District Clerk. Personal checks accepted. Prepayment is required.

County Court 101 W Main Rm 102, Madisonville, TX 77864; 936-348-2638; Fax: 936-348-5858. Hours: 8AM-4:30PM (CST). *Misdemeanor, Civil, Probate.*

Civil Records: Access: Mail, in person, fax. Both court and visitors may perform in person searches. Search fee: $10.00 per name. Required to search: name, years to search. Civil cases indexed by defendant. Civil records on computer from 1/00; index books back to 1970.

Criminal Records: Access: Mail, in person. Both court and visitors may perform in person searches. Search fee: $10.00 per name. Required to search: name, years to search, DOB. Criminal records on computer from 1982; records go back to early 1900's (not indexed).

General Information: No juvenile, mental, sealed, or adoption records released. SASE required. Turnaround time as soon as fees are paid. Fax notes: Fee to fax results is $1.00 per page. Copy fee: $1.00 per page. Certification fee: $5.00. Fee payee: Madison County Clerk. Personal checks accepted. Prepayment is required.

Marion County

District Court PO Box 628, Jefferson, TX 75657; 903-665-2441/2013. Hours: 8AM-5PM (CST). *Felony, Civil.*

Civil Records: Access: Mail, in person. Both court and visitors may perform in person searches. Search fee: $5.00 per name. Required to search: name, years to search. Civil cases indexed by defendant, plaintiff. Civil records on computer from 1997, index books up to 1986.

Criminal Records: Access: Mail, in person. Both court and visitors may perform in person searches. Search fee: $5.00 per name. Required to search: name, years to search. Criminal records on computer from 1997, index books up to 1986.

General Information: No juvenile, mental, sealed, or adoption records released. SASE required. Turnaround time 1 week. Copy fee: $1.00 per page. Certification fee: $1.00. Fee payee: District Clerk. Personal checks accepted. Prepayment is required.

County Court PO Box 763, Jefferson, TX 75657; 903-665-3971. Hours: 8AM-Noon, 1-5PM (CST). *Misdemeanor, Probate.*

Criminal Records: Access: Phone, mail, in person. Both court and visitors may perform in person searches. No search fee. Required to search: name, years to search. Criminal records in index books from 1966; computerized back to 1973.

General Information: No juvenile, mental, sealed, or adoption records released. SASE required. Turnaround time 2-4 days. Copy fee: $1.00 per page. Certification fee: $5.00. Fee payee: County Clerk. Personal checks accepted. Prepayment is required.

Martin County

District & County Court PO Box 906, Stanton, TX 79782; 915-756-3412. Hours: 8AM-Noon, 1-5PM (CST). *Felony, Misdemeanor, Civil, Probate.*

Civil Records: Access: Mail, in person. Both court and visitors may perform in person searches. Search fee: $5.00 per name. Required to search: name, years to search. Civil cases indexed by defendant, plaintiff. Civil records in index books to 1900.

Criminal Records: Access: Mail, in person. Both court and visitors may perform in person searches. Search fee: $5.00 per name. Required to search: name, years to search. Criminal records in index books to 1900, computerized since 1980.

General Information: No juvenile, mental, sealed, or adoption records released. SASE required. Turnaround time 2-4 days. Fax notes: Fee to fax results is $1.00 per page. Copy fee: $1.00 per page. Certification fee: $5.00. Fee payee: County/District Clerk. Personal checks accepted. Prepayment is required.

Mason County

District & County Court PO Box 702, Mason, TX 76856; 915-347-5253; Fax: 915-347-6868. Hours: 8AM-Noon, 1-4PM (CST). *Felony, Misdemeanor, Civil, Probate.*

Civil Records: Access: Mail, in person. Both court and visitors may perform in person searches. Search fee: $10.00 per name. Required to search: name, years to search. Civil cases indexed by defendant, plaintiff. Civil records in index books to 1858; on computer back to 1993.

Criminal Records: Access: Mail, in person. Both court and visitors may perform in person searches. Search fee: $10.00 per name. Required to search: name, years to search; also helpful: DOB, SSN. Criminal records igo back to 1877; on computer back to 1993.

General Information: No juvenile, mental, sealed, or adoption records released. SASE required. Turnaround time 2 days. Fax notes: Will not fax results. Copy fee: $1.00 per page. Certification fee: $5.00. Fee payee: County/District Clerk. Personal checks accepted. Prepayment is required.

Matagorda County

District Court 1700 7th St Rm 307, Bay City, TX 77414-5092; 979-244-7621. Hours: 8AM-Noon, 1-5PM (CST). *Felony, Civil.*

Civil Records: Access: Mail, in person. Both court and visitors may perform in person searches. Search fee: $5.00 per name. Required to search: name, years to search. Civil cases indexed by defendant, plaintiff. Civil records in index books and card files back to 1910; computerized back to 1994.

Criminal Records: Access: Mail, in person. Both court and visitors may perform in person searches. Search fee: $5.00 per name. Required to search: name, years to search, DOB. Criminal records in index books and card files back to 1910; computerized back to 1994.

General Information: No juvenile, sealed, or adoption records released. SASE required. Turnaround time 1-2 days. Fax notes: Do not fax. Copy fee: $1.00 per page. Certification fee: $2.00. Fee payee: District Clerk. Personal checks accepted. Prepayment is required.

County Court 1700 7th St Rm 202, Bay City, TX 77414-5094; 979-244-7680; Fax: 979-244-7688. Hours: 8AM-5PM (CST). *Misdemeanor, Civil, Probate.*

Civil Records: Access: Mail, in person. Both court and visitors may perform in person searches. Search fee: $5.00 per name. Required to search: name, years to search. Civil cases indexed by defendant, plaintiff. Civil records on computer from 1994, index books prior.

Criminal Records: Access: Mail, in person. Both court and visitors may perform in person searches. Search fee: $5.00 per name. Required to search: name, years to search, DOB, SSN. Criminal records on computer from 1994, index books prior.

General Information: Public access terminal is available. No juvenile, mental, sealed, or adoption records released. SASE required. Turnaround time 1-2 days. Fax notes: Fee to fax results is $2.00 per document. Copy fee: $1.00 per page. Certification fee: $5.00. Fee payee: County Clerk. Personal checks accepted. Credit cards accepted: Visa, MasterCard. Prepayment is required.

Maverick County

District Court PO Box 3659, Eagle Pass, TX 78853; 830-773-2629. Hours: 8AM-5PM (CST). *Felony, Civil.*

Civil Records: Access: Mail, in person. Both court and visitors may perform in person searches. Search fee: $5.00 per name. Required to search: name, years to search. Civil cases indexed by defendant, plaintiff. Civil records in index books; recent records computerized.

Criminal Records: Access: Mail, in person. Both court and visitors may perform in person searches. Search fee: $5.00 per name. Required to search: name, years to search. Criminal records in index books; recent records computerized.

General Information: No juvenile, mental, sealed, or adoption records released. SASE required. Turnaround time 2-4 days. Fax notes: Fee to fax results is $1.00 per page. Copy fee: $1.00 per page. Certification fee: $5.00. Fee payee: District Clerk. Personal checks accepted. Prepayment is required.

County Court PO Box 4050, Eagle Pass, TX 78853; 830-773-2829. Hours: 8AM-5PM (CST). *Misdemeanor, Civil, Probate.*

Civil Records: Access: Mail, in person. Both court and visitors may perform in person searches. Search fee: $10.00 per name. Required to search: name, years to search. Civil cases indexed by defendant, plaintiff. Civil records on index books.

Criminal Records: Access: Mail, in person. Both court and visitors may perform in person searches. Search fee: $10.00 per name. Required to search: name, years to search, DOB, SSN. Criminal records on index books.

General Information: No juvenile, mental, sealed, or adoption records released. SASE not required. Turnaround time 1-2 days. Fax notes: Fee to fax results is 1.00 per page. Copy fee: $1.00 per page. Certification fee: $5.00. Fee payee: County Clerk. Personal checks accepted. Prepayment is required.

McCulloch County

District Court County Courthouse Rm 205, Brady, TX 76825; 915-597-0733; Fax: 915-597-0606. Hours: 8:30AM-5PM (CST). *Felony, Civil.*

Civil Records: Access: Mail, fax, in person, online. Both court and visitors may perform in person searches. Search fee: $5.00 per name. Required to search: name, years to search. Civil cases indexed by defendant, plaintiff. Civil records in index books. Civil case information is available free online at www.idocket.com. Free searching is limited. Records go back to 12/31/1995.

Criminal Records: Access: Mail, fax, in person, online. Both court and visitors may perform in person searches. Search fee: $5.00 per name. Required to search: name, years to search; also helpful: DOB, SSN. Criminal records in index books back to 1990; on computer back to 1995. Online access is through www.idocket.com; registration and password required. Records go back to 12/31/1995.

General Information: Public access terminal is available. No juvenile, mental, sealed, or adoption records released. SASE required. Turnaround time 2-4 days. Fax notes: Will not fax results. Copy fee: $1.00 per page. Certification fee: $2.00. Fee payee: District Clerk. Personal checks accepted. Prepayment required.

County Court County Courthouse, Brady, TX 76825; 915-597-0733. Hours: 8AM-5PM (CST). *Misdemeanor, Civil, Probate.*

Civil Records: Access: Mail, in person, online. Both court and visitors may perform in person searches. Search fee: $5.00 per name. Required to search: name, years to search. Civil cases indexed by defendant, plaintiff. Civil records in index books. Online access is through www.idocket.com; registration and password required. Records go back to 12/31/1996; includes probate records.

Criminal Records: Access: Mail, in person, online. Both court and visitors may perform in person searches. Search fee: $5.00 per name. Required to search: name, years to search. Criminal records in index books. Online access is through www.idocket.com; registration and password required. Records go back to 12/31/1996.

General Information: No juvenile, mental, sealed, or adoption records released. SASE required. Turnaround time 1-2 days. Copy fee: $1.00 per page. Certification fee: $1.00. Fee payee: County Clerk. Personal checks accepted. Prepayment is required.

McLennan County

District Court PO Box 2451, Waco, TX 76703; Civil phone: 254-757-5057; Criminal phone: 254-757-5054; Fax: 254-757-5060. Hours: 8AM-Noon, 1-5PM (CST). *Felony, Civil.*

Civil Records: Access: Fax, mail, in person. Both court and visitors may perform in person searches. Search fee: $5.00 per name. Required to search: name, years to search. Civil cases indexed by defendant, plaintiff. Civil records on computer since 1986, index books to 1850.

Criminal Records: Access: Fax, mail, in person. Both court and visitors may perform in person searches. Search fee: $5.00 per name. Required to search: name, years to search. Criminal records on computer since 1959, index books from 1850.

General Information: No juvenile, mental, sealed, or adoption records released. SASE required. Turnaround time 2 days. Copy fee: $1.00 per page. Fee payee: Joe Johnson, District Clerk. Personal checks accepted. Credit cards accepted: Visa, MasterCard. Prepayment is required.

County Court PO Box 1727, Waco, TX 76703; 254-757-5185; Fax: 254-757-5146. Hours: 8AM-5PM (CST). *Misdemeanor, Civil, Probate.*

Civil Records: Access: Mail, in person. Both court and visitors may perform in person searches. Search fee: $5.00 per name. Required to search: name, years to search. Civil cases indexed by defendant, plaintiff. Civil records in index books back to 1876; Probate to 1850.

Criminal Records: Access: Mail, in person. Both court and visitors may perform in person searches. Search fee: $5.00 per name. Required to search: name, years to search; also helpful: DOB, SSN. Criminal records on computer since 1993; in index books to 1935.

General Information: No juvenile, mental, sealed, or adoption records released. SASE required. Turnaround time 2-4 days. Copy fee: $1.00 per page. Certification fee: $5.00. Fee payee: County Clerk. Business checks accepted. Prepayment is required. Will fax results to toll-free numbers only.

McMullen County

District & County Court PO Box 235, Tilden, TX 78072; 361-274-3215; Fax: 361-274-3858. Hours: 8AM-4PM (CST). *Felony, Misdemeanor, Civil, Probate.*

Civil Records: Access: Mail, in person. Both court and visitors may perform in person searches. Search fee:

$5.00 per name. Required to search: name, years to search. Civil cases indexed by defendant, plaintiff. Civil records in index books from 1918.

Criminal Records: Access: Mail, in person. Both court and visitors may perform in person searches. Search fee: $5.00 per name. Required to search: name, years to search. Criminal records in index books form 1918.

General Information: No juvenile, mental, sealed, or adoption records released. SASE required. Turnaround time 2-4 days. Fax notes: Will fax results for a fee. Copy fee: $1.00 per page. Certification fee: $5.00. Fee payee: County Clerk. Personal checks accepted. Prepayment is required.

Medina County

District Court County Courthouse Rm 209, Hondo, TX 78861; 830-741-6070. Hours: 8AM-Noon, 1-5PM (CST). *Felony, Civil.*

Civil Records: Access: Phone, mail, in person. Both court and visitors may perform in person searches. Search fee: $5.00 per name. Required to search: name, years to search. Civil cases indexed by defendant, plaintiff. Civil records on computer since 1990, index books since 1849.

Criminal Records: Access: Mail, in person. Both court and visitors may perform in person searches. Search fee: $5.00 per name. Required to search: name, years to search, DOB, SSN. Criminal records on computer since 1990, index books since 1849.

General Information: Public access terminal is available. No juvenile, mental, sealed, or adoption records released. SASE required. Turnaround time 1 week. Fax notes: Will not fax results. Copy fee: $1.00 1st page; $.50 each add'l. Certification fee: $1.00 per page. Fee payee: District Clerk. Only cashiers checks and money orders accepted. Out-of-state checks not accepted. Prepayment is required.

County Court at Law 1100 16th St, Rm 203, Hondo, TX 78861; 830-741-6061. Hours: 8AM-Noon, 1-5PM (CST). *Misdemeanor, Civil, Probate.*

Civil Records: Access: Phone, mail, in person. Both court and visitors may perform in person searches. Search fee: $5.00 per name. Required to search: name, years to search. Civil cases indexed by defendant, plaintiff. Civil records on computer since late 1993, index books prior.

Criminal Records: Access: Phone, mail, in person. Both court and visitors may perform in person searches. Search fee: $5.00 per name. Required to search: name, years to search; also helpful: address, DOB, SSN. Criminal records on computer since late 1993, index books prior.

General Information: No juvenile, mental, or sealed records released. SASE required. Turnaround time 1-2 days. Copy fee: $1.00 per page. Certification fee: $5.00. Fee payee: County Clerk. Personal checks accepted. Prepayment is required.

Menard County

District & County Court PO Box 1038, Menard, TX 76859; 915-396-4682; Fax: 915-396-2047. Hours: 8AM-Noon, 1-5PM (CST). *Felony, Misdemeanor, Civil, Probate.*

Civil Records: Access: Fax, mail, in person. Both court and visitors may perform in person searches. Search fee: $9.00 per name. Required to search: name, years to search. Civil cases indexed by defendant, plaintiff. Civil records in index books.

Criminal Records: Access: Mail, in person. Both court and visitors may perform in person searches. Search fee: $9.00 per name. Required to search: name, years to search. Criminal records in index books.

General Information: No juvenile, mental, sealed, or adoption records released. SASE required. Turnaround time 2-4 days. Fax notes: $1.00 per page. Copy fee:

$1.00 per page. Certification fee: $5.00. Fee payee: District/County Clerk. Personal checks accepted. Prepayment is required.

Midland County

District Court 200 W Wall #301, Midland, TX 79701; 915-688-1107. 8AM-5PM *Felony, Civil.*

www.co.midland.tx.us/DC/default.asp

Civil Records: Access: Mail, in person, online. Both court and visitors may perform in person searches. Search fee: $5.00 per name. Required to search: name, years to search. Civil cases indexed by defendant, plaintiff. Civil records on computer back to 1965, index books prior. Online access to the district Clerk database is available at www.co.midland.tx.us/CC/Database/default.asp. Registration and password is required; contact the clerk for access restrictions.

Criminal Records: Access: Mail, in person, online. Both court and visitors may perform in person searches. Search fee: $5.00 per name. Required to search: name, years to search. Criminal records on computer back to 1940, index books prior. Online access to criminal records is the same as civil.

General Information: Public access terminal is available. No juvenile, mental, sealed, or adoption records released. SASE required. Turnaround time 2 days. Fax notes: Fee to fax results is $1.00 per page. Copy fee: $1.00 per page. Fee payee: District Clerk. Business checks accepted. Prepayment is required.

County Court PO Box 211, Midland, TX 79702; 915-688-1070; Fax: 915-688-8973. Hours: 8AM-5PM (CST). *Misdemeanor, Civil, Probate.*

www.co.midland.tx.us/CC/default.asp

Civil Records: Access: Mail, in person, online. Both court and visitors may perform in person searches. Search fee: $5.00 per name. Required to search: name; also helpful: years to search, address. Civil cases indexed by defendant, plaintiff. Civil records on computer since 1987, index books since 1885. Probate records on computer since 1887. Online access to the County Clerk database is available free at www.co.midland.tx.us/CC/Database/default.asp.

Criminal Records: Access: Mail, in person, online. Both court and visitors may perform in person searches. Search fee: $5.00 per name. Required to search: name; also helpful: years to search, address, DOB, SSN. Criminal records on computer since 1978, index books since 1885. Online access to criminal records is the same as civil.

General Information: Public access terminal is available. No juvenile, mental, sealed, or adoption records released. SASE not required. Turnaround time 1-2 days. Copy fee: $1.00 per page. Certification fee: $5.00. Fee payee: County Clerk. Only cashiers checks and money orders accepted. Prepayment is required.

Milam County

District Court PO Box 999, Cameron, TX 76520; 254-697-7052. Hours: 8AM-5PM (CST). *Felony, Civil.*

Civil Records: Access: Mail, in person. Both court and visitors may perform in person searches. Search fee: $5.00 per name. Required to search: name, years to search. Civil cases indexed by defendant, plaintiff. Civil records on microfilm and index books.

Criminal Records: Access: Mail, in person. Both court and visitors may perform in person searches. Search fee: $5.00 per name. Required to search: name, years to search. Criminal records on microfilm and index books.

General Information: No juvenile, mental, sealed, or adoption records released. SASE required. Turnaround time same day. Copy fee: $1.00 per page. Certification fee: $1.00. Fee payee: District Clerk. Only cashiers checks and money orders accepted. Prepayment is required.

County Court PO Box 191, Cameron, TX 76520; 254-697-7049; Fax: 254-697-7055. Hours: 8AM-5PM (CST). *Misdemeanor, Civil, Probate.*

Civil Records: Access: Mail, in person. Both court and visitors may perform in person searches. Search fee: $5.00 per name. Required to search: name, years to search. Civil cases indexed by defendant, plaintiff. Civil records in books go back to 1874.

Criminal Records: Access: Mail, in person. Both court and visitors may perform in person searches. Search fee: $5.00 per name. Required to search: name, years to search, signed release, SSN. Criminal records in books go back to 1874.

General Information: No juvenile, mental, sealed, or adoption records released. SASE not required. Turnaround time 1-2 days. Fax notes: Fee to fax results is $2.00 plus $1.00 per page. Copy fee: $1.00 per page. Certification fee: $5.00. Fee payee: Milam County Clerk. Personal checks accepted. Prepayment required.

Mills County

District & County Court PO Box 646, Goldthwaite, TX 76844; 915-648-2711; Fax: 915-648-3251. Hours: 8AM-Noon, 1-5PM (CST). *Felony, Misdemeanor, Civil, Probate.*

Civil Records: Access: Fax, mail, in person. Both court and visitors may perform in person searches. Search fee: $5.00 per name. Required to search: name, years to search; also helpful: cause number. Civil cases indexed by defendant, plaintiff. Civil records in index books since 1887; no computerized records.

Criminal Records: Access: Mail, fax, in person. Both court and visitors may perform in person searches. Search fee: $5.00 per name. Required to search: name, years to search, DOB, signed release; also helpful: cause number. Criminal records in index books since 1887; no computerized records.

General Information: No juvenile, mental, sealed, or adoption records released. SASE required. Turnaround time 1-2 days. Copy fee: $1.00 per page. Certification fee: $5.00. Fee payee: County-District Clerk. Personal checks accepted. Prepayment is required.

Mitchell County

District Court County Courthouse, Colorado City, TX 79512; 915-728-5918. Hours: 8AM-5PM (CST). *Felony, Civil.*

Civil Records: Access: Mail, in person. Both court and visitors may perform in person searches. Search fee: $5.00 per name. Required to search: name, years to search. Civil cases indexed by defendant, plaintiff. Civil records in index books.

Criminal Records: Access: Mail, in person. Only the court performs in person searches; visitors may not. Search fee: $5.00 per name. Required to search: name, years to search. Criminal records in index books.

General Information: No juvenile, mental, sealed, or adoption records released. SASE required. Turnaround time 1 day. Copy fee: $.35 per page. Certification fee: $1.00 per page. Fee payee: District Clerk. Personal checks accepted. Prepayment is required.

County Court 349 Oak St Rm 103, Colorado City, TX 79512; 915-728-3481; Fax: 915-728-5322. Hours: 8AM-Noon, 1-5PM (CST). *Misdemeanor, Civil, Probate.*

Civil Records: Access: Fax, mail, in person. Both court and visitors may perform in person searches. Search fee: $5.00 per name. Required to search: name, years to search. Civil cases indexed by defendant, plaintiff. Civil records in index books, on computer from 9-1-1998 to present.

Criminal Records: Access: Mail, in person. Both court and visitors may perform in person searches. Search fee: $5.00 per name. Required to search: name, years to

search; also helpful: DOB. Criminal records in index books, on computer from 9-1-1998 to present.

General Information: Public access terminal is available. (Land records on computer back to 5/1985.) No juvenile, mental, sealed, or adoption, commitment records released. Turnaround time 2-4 days. Fax notes: Fee to fax results is $3.00 for the 1st page and $1.00 per page thereafter. Copy fee: $1.00 per page. Certification fee: $5.00. Fee payee: Mitchell County Clerk. Personal checks accepted. No out of state personal checks. Money order accepted. Prepayment is required.

Montague County

District Court PO Box 155, Montague, TX 76251; 940-894-2571. Hours: 8AM-5PM (CST). *Felony, Civil.*

Civil Records: Access: Mail, in person. Both court and visitors may perform in person searches. Search fee: $5.00 per name. Required to search: name, years to search. Civil cases indexed by defendant, plaintiff. Civil records on computer and index books.

Criminal Records: Access: Mail, in person. Both court and visitors may perform in person searches. Search fee: $5.00 per name. Required to search: name, years to search. Criminal records on computer and index books.

General Information: No juvenile, mental, sealed, or adoption records released. SASE required. Turnaround time 2-4 days. Copy fee: $1.00 per page. Certification fee: $5.00. Fee payee: District Clerk. Personal checks accepted. Prepayment is required.

County Court PO Box 77, Montague, TX 76251; 940-894-2461. Hours: 8AM-5PM (CST). *Misdemeanor, Civil, Probate.*

Civil Records: Access: Mail, in person. Both court and visitors may perform in person searches. Search fee: $5.00 per name. Required to search: name, years to search. Civil cases indexed by defendant, plaintiff. Civil records on computer since 1993, index books prior.

Criminal Records: Access: Mail, in person. Both court and visitors may perform in person searches. Search fee: $5.00 per name. Required to search: name, years to search, DOB. Criminal records on computer since 1993, index books prior.

General Information: No juvenile, mental, sealed, or adoption records released. SASE required. Turnaround time 1-2 days. Fax notes: Fee to fax results is $2.50 1st page, $.75 each add'l page. Copy fee: $1.00 per page. Certification fee: $5.00. Fee payee: County Clerk. Personal checks accepted. Prepayment is required.

Montgomery County

District Court PO Box 2985, Conroe, TX 77305; 936-539-7855. Hours: 8AM-5PM M-T,Th-F; 8AM-4:30PM W (CST). *Felony, Civil.*

Civil Records: Access: Mail, in person. Both court and visitors may perform in person searches. Search fee: $5.00 per name. Required to search: name, years to search. Civil cases indexed by defendant, plaintiff. Civil records in index books since 1900, on computer since 1990.

Criminal Records: Access: Mail, in person. Both court and visitors may perform in person searches. Search fee: $5.00 per name. Required to search: name, years to search. Criminal records in index books since 1900, on computer since 1990.

General Information: Public access terminal is available. No juvenile, mental, sealed, or adoption records released. SASE not required. Turnaround time 3-6 days. Copy fee: $1.00 per page. Fee payee: Barbara Adamick, District Clerk. Personal checks not accepted. Prepayment is required.

County Court PO Box 959, Conroe, TX 77305; 936-539-7885; Fax: 936-760-6990. Hours: 8AM-5PM (CST). *Misdemeanor, Civil, Probate.*

www.co.montgomery.tx.us

Civil Records: Access: Mail, in person. Both court and visitors may perform in person searches. Search fee: $5.00 per name. Required to search: name, years to search. Civil cases indexed by defendant, plaintiff. Civil records on computer since 1971, and in index books.

Criminal Records: Access: Mail, in person. Both court and visitors may perform in person searches. Search fee: $5.00 per name. Required to search: name, years to search, and identifers such as DOB or SSN. Criminal records on computer since 1985, and in index books.

General Information: Public access terminal is available. No mental or sealed records released. SASE required. Turnaround time 2 days. Fax notes: Fee to fax results is $2.00 per page. Copy fee: $1.00 per page. Certification fee: $5.00. Fee payee: County Clerk. Personal checks accepted. Prepayment is required.

Moore County

District Court 715 Dumas Ave #109, Dumas, TX 79029; 806-935-4218; Fax: 806-935-6325. Hours: 8:30AM-5PM (CST). *Felony, Civil.*

Civil Records: Access: Mail, in person. Both court and visitors may perform in person searches. Search fee: $5.00 per name. Required to search: name, years to search. Civil cases indexed by defendant, plaintiff. Civil records on computer back to 1990; docket books and original files prior.

Criminal Records: Access: Mail, in person. Both court and visitors may perform in person searches. Search fee: $5.00 per name. Required to search: name, years to search, DOB; also helpful: SSN. Criminal records on computer back to 1990; docket books and original files prior.

General Information: No juvenile, mental, sealed, or adoption records released. SASE required. Turnaround time 1 day. Copy fee: $1.00 per page. Certification fee: $1.00. Fee payee: District Clerk. Personal checks accepted. Prepayment is required.

County Court 715 Dumas Ave Rm 105, Dumas, TX 79029; 806-935-6164/2009; Fax: 806-935-9004. 8:30AM-5PM (CST). *Misdemeanor, Civil, Probate.*

Civil Records: Access: Mail, i n person. Both court and visitors may perform in person searches. Search fee: $5.00 per name. Required to search: name, years to search. Civil cases indexed by defendant, plaintiff. Civil records on computer back to 1996, in index books prior.

Criminal Records: Access: Mail, fax, in person. Both court and visitors may perform in person searches. Search fee: $5.00 per name. Required to search: name, years to search, signed release, DOB or SSN. Criminal records on computer back to 1987, in index books prior.

General Information: Public access terminal is available. No juvenile, mental, sealed, or adoption records released. SASE required. Turnaround time 24 hours. Fax notes: Fee to fax results is $5.00 plus $1.00 per page. Copy fee: $1.00 per page. Certification fee: $5.00. Fee payee: Moore County Clerk. Business checks accepted. Prepayment is required.

Morris County

District Court 500 Broadnax, Daingerfield, TX 75638; 903-645-2321. Hours: 8AM-5PM (CST). *Felony, Civil.*

Civil Records: Access: Mail, in person. Both court and visitors may perform in person searches. Search fee: $5.00 per name. Required to search: name, years to search. Civil cases indexed by defendant, plaintiff. Civil records in index books and file folders from 1930s. Plaintiff index only for active cases.

Criminal Records: Access: Mail, in person. Both court and visitors may perform in person searches. Search fee: $5.00 per name. Required to search: name, years to search, DOB. Criminal records in index books and file folders from 1930s. Plaintiff index only for active cases.

General Information: No juvenile, mental, sealed, or adoption records released. SASE required. Turnaround time 1 day. Copy fee: $1.00 per page. Fee payee: Morris County District Clerk. Personal checks accepted. Prepayment is required.

County Court 500 Broadnax, Daingerfield, TX 75638; 903-645-3911. Hours: 8AM-5PM (CST). *Misdemeanor, Probate.*

Criminal Records: Access: Mail, in person. Both court and visitors may perform in person searches. Search fee: $5.00 per name. Required to search: name, years to search. Criminal record on index books.

General Information: No juvenile, mental, sealed, or adoption records released. SASE not required. Turnaround time 1 day. Copy fee: $1.00 per page. Certification fee: $5.00. Fee payee: County Clerk. Personal checks accepted. Prepayment is required.

Motley County

District & County Court PO Box 660, Matador, TX 79244; 806-347-2621; Fax: 806-347-2220. Hours: 9AM-Noon, 1-5PM (CST). *Felony, Misdemeanor, Civil, Probate.*

Civil Records: Access: Mail, fax, in person. Both court and visitors may perform in person searches. Search fee: $10.00 per name. Required to search: name, years to search, address. Civil cases indexed by defendant, plaintiff. Civil records in docket books, archived from 1891.

Criminal Records: Access: Mail, fax, in person. Only the court performs in person searches; visitors may not. Search fee: $10.00 per name. Required to search: name, years to search, DOB. Criminal records in docket books, archived from 1891.

General Information: No juvenile, mental, sealed or adoption records released. SASE required. Turnaround time 1-2 days. Copy fee: $1.00 per page. Certification fee: $2.00. Fee payee: Motley County Clerk. Personal checks accepted. Prepayment is required.

Nacogdoches County

District Court 101 W Main #215, Nacogdoches, TX 75961; 936-560-7730; Fax: 936-560-7839. Hours: 8AM-5PM (CST). *Felony, Civil.*

Civil Records: Access: Mail, in person. Both court and visitors may perform in person searches. Search fee: $5.00 per name. Required to search: name, years to search. Civil cases indexed by defendant, plaintiff. Civil records on computer from 1987, index books prior.

Criminal Records: Access: Mail, in person. Both court and visitors may perform in person searches. Search fee: $5.00 per name. Required to search: name, years to search, signed release. Criminal records on computer from 1987, index books prior.

General Information: No juvenile, mental, sealed, or adoption records released. SASE required. Turnaround time 5-6 days. Copy fee: $1.00 per page. Fee payee: Nacogdoches County. Business checks accepted. Prepayment is required.

County Court 101 W Main, Rm 205, Nacogdoches, TX 75961; 936-560-7733. Hours: 8AM-5PM (CST). *Misdemeanor, Civil, Probate.*

Civil Records: Access: Mail, in person. Both court and visitors may perform in person searches. Search fee: $5.00 per name. Required to search: name, years to search. Civil cases indexed by defendant, plaintiff. Civil records on computer since 1986, index books prior.

Criminal Records: Access: Mail, in person. Both court and visitors may perform in person searches. Search fee: $5.00 per name. Required to search: name, years to search. Criminal records on computer since 1987, index books prior.

General Information: Public access terminal is available. No juvenile, mental, sealed, or adoption records released. SASE required. Turnaround time 2-4

days. Copy fee: $1.00 per page. Certification fee: $5.00. Fee payee: County Clerk. Personal checks accepted. Prepayment is required.

Navarro County

District Court PO Box 1439, Corsicana, TX 75151; 903-654-3040; Fax: 903-654-3088. Hours: 8AM-5PM (CST). *Felony, Civil.*

Civil Records: Access: Phone, fax, mail, online, in person. Both court and visitors may perform in person searches. Search fee: $5.00 per name. Required to search: name, years to search. Civil cases indexed by defendant, plaintiff. Civil records on computer since 1990, index books and microfiche since 1900s. Civil case information is available online at www.idocket.com. Free searching is limited. Records go back to 12/31/1990.

Criminal Records: Access: Phone, fax, mail, in person, online. Both court and visitors may perform in person searches. Search fee: $5.00 per name. Required to search: name, years to search. Criminal records on computer since 1990, index books and microfiche since 1900s. Online access is through www.idocket.com; registration and password required. Records go back to 12/31/1990.

General Information: No juvenile, sealed, or adoption records released. SASE required. Turnaround time 1-2 days. Fax notes: $5.00 for first page, $1.00 each add'l. Copy fee: $1.00 for first page, $.25 each add'l. Certification fee: $1.00 per page. Fee payee: District Clerk. Personal checks accepted. Prepayment is required.

County Court PO Box 423, Corsicana, TX 75151; 903-654-3035. Hours: 8AM-5PM (CST). *Misdemeanor, Civil, Probate.*

Civil Records: Access: Mail, in person. Both court and visitors may perform in person searches. Search fee: $5.00 per name. Fee is for 10 year period. Required to search: name, years to search. Civil cases indexed by defendant, plaintiff. Civil records in index books to 1960's; on computer back to 1999.

Criminal Records: Access: Mail, in person. Both court and visitors may perform in person searches. Search fee: $5.00 per name. Fee is for 10 year period. Required to search: name, years to search, DOB or SSN. Criminal records in index books to 1930's; on computer back to 1999.

General Information: Public access terminal is available. No juvenile, mental, sealed, or adoption records released. SASE required. Turnaround time 2-4 days. Copy fee: $1.00 per page. Certification fee: $5.00. Fee payee: County Clerk. Personal checks accepted. Prepayment is required.

Newton County

District Court PO Box 535, Newton, TX 75966; 409-379-3951. 8AM-4:30PM (CST). *Felony, Civil.*

Civil Records: Access: Mail, in person. Both court and visitors may perform in person searches. Search fee: $5.00 per name. Required to search: name, years to search. Civil cases indexed by defendant, plaintiff. Civil records in index books.

Criminal Records: Access: Mail, in person. Both court and visitors may perform in person searches. Search fee: $5.00 per name. Required to search: name, years to search. Criminal records in index books.

General Information: No juvenile, mental, sealed, or adoption records released. SASE required. Turnaround time same day. Fax notes: Fee to fax results is $2.00 per page. Copy fee: $1.00 per page. Certification fee: $2.00. Fee payee: District Clerk. Personal checks accepted. Prepayment is required.

County Court PO Box 484, Newton, TX 75966; 409-379-5341; Fax: 409-379-9049. Hours: 8AM-4:30PM (CST). *Misdemeanor, Civil, Probate.*

Civil Records: Access: Mail, in person. Both court and visitors may perform in person searches. Search fee: $5.00 per name. Required to search: name, years to search. Civil cases indexed by defendant, plaintiff. Civil records on index books from 1953.

Criminal Records: Access: Mail, in person. Both court and visitors may perform in person searches. Search fee: $5.00 per name. Required to search: name, years to search. Criminal records on index books from 1953.

General Information: No juvenile, mental, sealed, or adoption records released. SASE not required. Turnaround time 1-2 days. Fax notes: Fee to fax results is $.50 per page. Copy fee: $1.00 per page. Certification fee: $5.00. Fee payee: County Clerk. Personal checks accepted. Prepayment is required.

Nolan County

District Court 100 E 3rd 200A, Sweetwater, TX 79556; 915-235-2111. Hours: 8:30AM-Noon, 1-5PM (CST). *Felony, Civil.*

Civil Records: Access: Mail, in person. Both court and visitors may perform in person searches. Search fee: $5.00 per name. Required to search: name, years to search. Civil cases indexed by defendant, plaintiff. Civil records in index books, records are not computerized.

Criminal Records: Access: Mail, in person. Only the court performs in person searches; visitors may not. Search fee: $5.00 per name. Required to search: name, years to search. Criminal records in index books, records are not computerized. Include which years to search.

General Information: No juvenile, mental, sealed, or adoption records released. SASE required. Turnaround time same day. Copy fee: $1.00 for first page, $.50 each add'l. Certification fee: $1.00 per page. Fee payee: District Clerk. Personal checks accepted. Prepayment is required.

County Court 100 East 3rd St #108, Sweetwater, TX 79556-4546; 915-235-2462. Hours: 8:30AM-Noon, 1-5PM (CST). *Misdemeanor, Civil, Probate.*

Civil Records: Access: Mail, in person. Both court and visitors may perform in person searches. Search fee: $5.00 per name. Required to search: name, years to search. Civil cases indexed by defendant, plaintiff. Civil records in index books, computerized since 1982.

Criminal Records: Access: Mail, in person. Both court and visitors may perform in person searches. Search fee: $5.00 per name. Required to search: name, years to search. Criminal records in index books, computerized since 1982.

General Information: Public access terminal is available. No juvenile, mental, sealed, or adoption records released. SASE required. Turnaround time 2-4 days. Copy fee: $1.00 per page. Certification fee: $5.00. Fee payee: County Clerk. Personal checks accepted. Prepayment is required.

Nueces County

District Court PO Box 2987, Corpus Christi, TX 78403-2987; 361-888-0450; Fax: 361-888-0571. Hours: 8AM-5PM (CST). *Felony, Civil.*

www.co.nueces.tx.us/districtclerk

Civil Records: Access: Mail, in person, online. Both court and visitors may perform in person searches. Search fee: $5.00 per name. Required to search: name, years to search. Civil cases indexed by defendant, plaintiff. Civil records on computer since 1980, index books prior. Online access to civil District Court records are available free online at the web site. Search by name, company, or cause number.

Criminal Records: Access: Mail, in person, online. Both court and visitors may perform in person searches. Search fee: $5.00 per name. Required to search: name, years to search. Criminal records on computer since 1980, index books prior. Online access to criminal

District Court records are available free online at the web site. Search by name, SID #, or cause number.

General Information: Public access terminal is available. (Civil only.) No juvenile, mental, sealed, or adoption records released. SASE required. Turnaround time 2-4 days. Copy fee: $1.00 per page for civil, $.1.00 per page for criminal. Certification fee: $1.00. Fee payee: District Clerk. Personal checks accepted. Prepayment is required.

County Court PO Box 2987, Corpus Christi, TX 78403-2987; Civil phone: 361-888-0450; Criminal phone: 361-888-0681; Probate phone: 361-888-0365; Fax: 361-888-0571. Hours: 8AM-5PM (CST). *Misdemeanor, Civil, Probate.*

www.co.nueces.tx.us/districtclerk

Civil Records: Access: Mail, in person, online. Both court and visitors may perform in person searches. Search fee: $5.00 per name. Required to search: name, years to search. Civil cases indexed by defendant, plaintiff. Civil records on computer since 1993, index books prior. Online access to civil County Court records are available free online at the web site. Search by name, company, or cause number.

Criminal Records: Access: Mail, in person, online. Both court and visitors may perform in person searches. Search fee: $5.00 per name. Required to search: name, years to search, DOB. Criminal records on computer since 1987, index books prior. Online access to criminal County Court records are available free online at the web site. Search by name, SID #, or cause number.

General Information: Public access terminal is available. (Civil & Criminal only.) No juvenile, mental, sealed, or adoption records released. SASE required. Turnaround time 2-4 days. Copy fee: $1.00 per page. Certification fee: $1.00. Fee payee: County Clerk. Personal checks accepted. Prepayment is required.

Ochiltree County

District Court 511 S Main, Perryton, TX 79070; 806-435-8054; Fax: 806-435-8058. Hours: 8:30AM-5PM (CST). *Felony, Civil.*

Civil Records: Access: Fax, mail, in person. Both court and visitors may perform in person searches. Search fee: $5.00 per name. Required to search: name, years to search. Civil cases indexed by defendant, plaintiff. Civil records in index books; on computer back to 1995.

Criminal Records: Access: Fax, mail, in person. Only the court performs in person searches; visitors may not. Search fee: $5.00 per name. Required to search: name, years to search. Criminal records in index books; on computer back to 1995.

General Information: No juvenile, mental, sealed, or adoption records released. SASE required. Turnaround time 2-4 days. Fax notes: No fee to fax results. Copy fee: $1.00 per page. Certification fee: $1.00. Fee payee: District Clerk. Personal checks accepted. Prepayment is required.

County Court 511 S Main St, Perryton, TX 79070; 806-435-8031; Fax: 806-435-2081. Hours: 8:30AM-Noon, 1-5PM (CST). *Misdemeanor, Civil, Probate.*

Civil Records: Access: Fax, mail, in person. Both court and visitors may perform in person searches. Search fee: $5.00 per name. Required to search: name, years to search. Civil cases indexed by defendant, plaintiff. Civil records in index books.

Criminal Records: Access: Fax, mail, in person. Both court and visitors may perform in person searches. Search fee: $5.00 per name. Required to search: name, years to search. Criminal records in index books.

General Information: No juvenile, mental, sealed, or adoption records released. SASE not required. Turnaround time usually mailed out same day of receipt. Fax notes: $3.00 for first page, $2.00 each add'l. Copy fee: $1.00 per page. Certification fee: $5.00. Fee

payee: Ochiltree County Clerk. Personal checks accepted. Fax fees may be billed.

Oldham County

District & County Court PO Box 360, Vega, TX 79092; 806-267-2667. Hours: 8:30AM-Noon, 1-5PM (CST). *Felony, Misdemeanor, Civil, Probate.*

Civil Records: Access: Mail, in person. Both court and visitors may perform in person searches. Search fee: $5.00 per name. Required to search: name, years to search. Civil cases indexed by defendant, plaintiff. Civil records in index books.

Criminal Records: Access: Mail, in person. Both court and visitors may perform in person searches. Search fee: $5.00 per name. Required to search: name, years to search. Criminal records in index books.

General Information: No juvenile, mental, sealed, or adoption records released. SASE required. Turnaround time 2-4 days. Copy fee: $1.00 per page. Certification fee: $5.00 for county, $1.00 for district. Fee payee: Oldham County/District Clerk. Personal checks accepted. Prepayment is required.

Orange County

District Court PO Box 427, Orange, TX 77630; 409-883-7740. Hours: 8AM-5PM (CST). *Felony, Civil.*

Civil Records: Access: Mail, in person. Both court and visitors may perform in person searches. Search fee: $5.00 per name. Required to search: name, years to search. Civil cases indexed by defendant, plaintiff. Civil records on computer since 1985, index books prior.

Criminal Records: Access: Mail, in person. Both court and visitors may perform in person searches. Search fee: $5.00 per name. Required to search: name, years to search. Criminal records computerized since 1989.

General Information: Public access terminal is available. No juvenile, mental, sealed, or adoption records released. SASE required. Turnaround time 2-4 days. Copy fee: $1.00 per page. Certification fee: $1.00. Fee payee: District Clerk. Only cashiers checks and money orders accepted. Prepayment is required.

County Court PO Box 1536, Orange, TX 77631-1536; 409-882-7055; Fax: 409-882-0379. Hours: 8:30AM-5PM (CST). *Misdemeanor, Civil, Probate.*

www.co.orange.tx.us

Civil Records: Access: Phone, fax, mail, in person. Both court and visitors may perform in person searches. No search fee. Required to search: name, years to search. Civil cases indexed by defendant, plaintiff. Civil records back to 1852; on computer back to 1897.

Criminal Records: Access: Phone, fax, mail, in person. Both court and visitors may perform in person searches. No search fee. Required to search: name, years to search. Criminal records back to 1897, on computer back to 1897.

General Information: Public access terminal is available. No juvenile, mental, sealed. Turnaround time 7-10 days. Fax notes: Fee to fax results is $1.00 per page. Copy fee: $1.00 per page. Certification fee: $5.00. Fee payee: Karen Jo Vance, County Clerk. Personal checks accepted. Prepayment is required.

Palo Pinto County

District Court PO Box 189, Palo Pinto, TX 76484-0189; 940-659-1279. 8AM-4:30PM *Felony, Civil.*

Civil Records: Access: Mail, in person. Both court and visitors may perform in person searches. Search fee: $5.00 per name. Required to search: name, years to search. Civil cases indexed by defendant, plaintiff. Civil records on computer since 1993, index books prior.

Criminal Records: Access: Mail, in person. Both court and visitors may perform in person searches. Search fee: $5.00 per name. Required to search: name, years to search. Criminal records on computer since 1993, index books prior.

General Information: No juvenile, mental, sealed, or adoption records released. SASE required. Turnaround time 1-2 days. Copy fee: $1.00 per page. Certification fee: $1.00. Fee payee: District Clerk. Personal checks accepted. Prepayment is required.

County Court PO Box 219, Palo Pinto, TX 76484; 940-659-1277; Fax: 940-659-2590. Hours: 8:30AM-4:30PM (CST). *Misdemeanor, Civil, Probate.*

Civil Records: Access: Mail, in person, phone. Both court and visitors may perform in person searches. Search fee: $5.00 per name. Required to search: name, years to search. Civil cases indexed by defendant, plaintiff. Civil records on computer back to 1998 index books from 1857.

Criminal Records: Access: Mail, in person. Both court and visitors may perform in person searches. Search fee: $5.00 per name. Required to search: name, years to search, DOB; also helpful: SSN. Criminal records on computer back to 1986; index books from 1857.

General Information: No juvenile, mental, sealed, or adoption records released. SASE not required. Turnaround time next day. Copy fee: $1.00 per page. Certification fee: $5.00. Fee payee: County Clerk. Personal checks accepted in person, not by mail. Prepayment is required.

Panola County

District Court County Courthouse Rm 227, Carthage, TX 75633; 903-693-0306; Fax: 903-693-6914. Hours: 8AM-5PM (CST). *Felony, Civil.*

Civil Records: Access: Mail, in person. Both court and visitors may perform in person searches. Search fee: $5.00 per name. Required to search: name, years to search. Civil cases indexed by defendant, plaintiff. Civil records in index books from 1865; computerized back to 1994.

Criminal Records: Access: Mail, in person. Both court and visitors may perform in person searches. Search fee: $5.00 per name. Required to search: name, years to search, DOB. Criminal records in index books from 1900's; computerized back to 1994.

General Information: No juvenile, mental, sealed, or adoption records released. SASE required. Turnaround time 3 days. Fax notes: Fee to fax results is $1.00 per page. Copy fee: $1.00 per page. Certification fee: $1.00 fee per page. Fee payee: District Clerk. Personal checks accepted. Prepayment is required.

County Court County Courthouse Rm 201, Carthage, TX 75633; 903-693-0302. Hours: 8AM-5PM (CST). *Misdemeanor, Civil, Probate.*

Civil Records: Access: Mail, in person. Both court and visitors may perform in person searches. Search fee: $5.00 per name. Required to search: name, years to search. Civil cases indexed by defendant, plaintiff. Civil records in index books; computerized since 1996.

Criminal Records: Access: Mail, in person. Both court and visitors may perform in person searches. Search fee: $5.00 per name. Required to search: name, years to search, DOB. Criminal records in index books; computerized since 1996.

General Information: No juvenile, mental, sealed, or adoption records released. SASE not required. Turnaround time 2-4 days. Copy fee: $1.00 per page. Certification fee: $5.00. Fee payee: County Clerk. Personal checks accepted. Personal checks require ID. Prepayment is required.

Parker County

District Court 117 Ft. Worth Ave (PO Box 340), Weatherford, TX 76086; 817-598-6114 (clerk); 599-6591 (swtbd); Criminal phone: X6200/x6214. Hours: 8AM-5PM (CST). *Felony, Civil.*

Civil Records: Access: Mail, in person. Both court and visitors may perform in person searches. Search fee: $5.00 per name. Required to search: name, years to

search, and/or cause number. Civil cases indexed by defendant, plaintiff. Civil records in index books.
Criminal Records: Access: Mail, in person. Both court and visitors may perform in person searches. Search fee: $5.00 per name. Required to search: name, years to search, DOB, and/or cause number; also helpful: SSN. Criminal records in index books; on comptuer back to 7/1988.
General Information: No juvenile, mental, sealed, or adoption records released. SASE required. Turnaround time same day. Copy fee: $1.00 per page. Certification fee: $1.00 per page. Fee payee: District Clerk. Personal checks accepted. Prepayment is required.

County Court County Clerk - Court Division, PO Box 819, Weatherford, TX 76086-0819; 817-594-1632. Hours: 8AM-Noon, 1-5PM (CST). *Misdemeanor, Civil.*

Civil Records: Access: Phone, mail, fax, in person. Both court and visitors may perform in person searches. Search fee: $5.00 per name. Required to search: name, years to search. Civil cases indexed by defendant, plaintiff. Civil records in index books; on computer since 8/1985.
Criminal Records: Access: Phone, mail, fax, in person. Both court and visitors may perform in person searches. Search fee: $5.00 per name. Required to search: name, years to search, DOB; also helpful - SSN, signed release. Criminal records on computer since 8/1985, index books and archived since 1900s.
General Information: Public access terminal is available. No juvenile, mental, sealed, or adoption records released. SASE required. Turnaround time 1-2 days. Copy fee: $1.00 per page. Certification fee: $1.00. Fee payee: County Clerk. Personal checks accepted. Prepayment is required.

Probate Court 1112 Santa Fe Dr, PO Box 819, Weatherford, TX 76086; 817-594-7461. Hours: 8AM-5PM (CST). *Probate.*

Parmer County

District Court PO Box 195, Farwell, TX 79325-0195; 806-481-3419; Fax: 806-481-9416. Hours: 8:30AM-Noon, 1-5PM (CST). *Felony, Civil.*

Civil Records: Access: Fax, mail, in person, online. Both court and visitors may perform in person searches. Search fee: $5.00 per name. Required to search: name, years to search. Civil cases indexed by defendant, plaintiff. Civil records in index books since 1917. Online access is through www.idocket.com; registration and password required. Records go back to 12/31/1995.
Criminal Records: Access: Fax, mail, in person, online. Both court and visitors may perform in person searches. Search fee: $5.00 per name. Required to search: name, years to search. Criminal records in index books since 1917. Online access is through www.idocket.com; registration and password required. Records go back to 12/31/95.
General Information: No juvenile, mental, sealed, or adoption records released. SASE required. Turnaround time 1 day. Fax notes: $1.00 per page. Copy fee: $1.00 per page. Fee payee: District Clerk. Personal checks accepted. Prepayment is required.

County Court PO Box 356, Farwell, TX 79325; 806-481-3691. Hours: 8:30AM-5PM (CST). *Misdemeanor, Civil, Probate.*

Civil Records: Access: Mail, in person. Both court and visitors may perform in person searches. Search fee: $5.00 per name. Required to search: name, years to search. Civil cases indexed by defendant, plaintiff. Civil records in index books to 1901, computerized since 1996.
Criminal Records: Access: Mail, in person. Both court and visitors may perform in person searches. Search fee: $5.00 per name. Required to search: name, years to

search. Criminal records in index books to 1901, computerized since 1996.
General Information: No juvenile, mental, sealed, or adoption records released. SASE required. Turnaround time 2-4 days. Copy fee: $1.00 per page. Certification fee: $5.00. Fee payee: County Clerk. Personal checks accepted. Prepayment is required.

Pecos County

District Court 400 S Nelson, Fort Stockton, TX 79735; 915-336-3503; Fax: 915-336-6437. Hours: 8AM-5PM (CST). *Felony, Civil.*

Civil Records: Access: Fax, mail, in person. Both court and visitors may perform in person searches. Search fee: $5.00 per name. Required to search: name, years to search. Civil cases indexed by defendant, plaintiff. Civil records on computer since 1987, index books prior.
Criminal Records: Access: Fax, mail, in person. Both court and visitors may perform in person searches. Search fee: $5.00 per name. Required to search: name, years to search, DOB, signed release; also helpful-address, SSN. Criminal records on computer since 1987, index books prior.
General Information: No juvenile, mental, sealed, or adoption records released. SASE required. Turnaround time 2-4 days. Fax notes: Fee to fax results is $1.00 per page. Copy fee: $1.00 per page. Fee payee: District Clerk. Personal checks accepted. Prepayment is required.

County Court 103 W Callaghan, Fort Stockton, TX 79735; 915-336-7555; Fax: 915-336-7575. Hours: 8AM-5PM (CST). *Misdemeanor, Civil, Probate.*

Civil Records: Access: Mail, in person. Both court and visitors may perform in person searches. Search fee: $8.00 per name. Required to search: name, years to search. Civil cases indexed by defendant, plaintiff. Civil records on computer and index books to 1955.
Criminal Records: Access: Mail, in person. Both court and visitors may perform in person searches. Search fee: $8.00 per name. Required to search: name, years to search. Criminal records on computer and index books to 1955.
General Information: No juvenile, mental, sealed, or adoption records released. SASE required. Turnaround time same day. Fax notes: Fee to fax results is $1.00 per page. Copy fee: $1.00 per page. Certification fee: $5.00. Fee payee: County Clerk. Personal checks accepted. Prepayment is required.

Polk County

District Court 101 W Church, Livingston, TX 77351; 936-327-6814. 8AM-5PM *Felony, Civil.*

Civil Records: Access: Mail, in person. Both court and visitors may perform in person searches. Search fee: $5.00 per name. Fee is per 10 year period. Required to search: name, years to search. Civil cases indexed by defendant, plaintiff. Civil records in index books.
Criminal Records: Access: Mail, in person. Both court and visitors may perform in person searches. Search fee: $5.00 per name. Fee is per 10 year period. Required to search: name, years to search; also helpful: DOB. Criminal records in index books.
General Information: No juvenile, mental, sealed, or adoption records released. SASE required. Turnaround time 2-4 days. Copy fee: $1.00 per page. Certification fee: $2.00. Fee payee: District Clerk. Personal checks accepted. Prepayment is required.

County Court PO Drawer 2119, Livingston, TX 77351; 936-327-6804; Fax: 936-327-6874. Hours: 8AM-5PM (CST). *Misdemeanor, Civil, Probate.*

Civil Records: Access: Mail, in person. Both court and visitors may perform in person searches. Search fee: $5.00 per name. Required to search: name, years to search. Civil cases indexed by defendant, plaintiff. Civil records in index books, on computer since 1988.

Criminal Records: Access: Mail, in person. Both court and visitors may perform in person searches. Search fee: $5.00 per name. Required to search: name, years to search; also helpful: DOB, SSN. Criminal records in index books; on computer back to 1982.
General Information: No juvenile, mental, sealed, or adoption records released. SASE required. Turnaround time 2-4 days. Fax notes: Fee to fax results is $2.00 per document and $1.00 per page. Copy fee: $1.00 per page. Certification fee: $5.00. Fee payee: County Clerk. Personal checks accepted. Prepayment is required.

Potter County

District Court PO Box 9570, Amarillo, TX 79105-9570; 806-379-2300. 7:30AM-5:30PM *Felony, Civil.*

www.co.potter.tx.us/districtclerk

Civil Records: Access: Phone, fax, mail, online, in person. Both court and visitors may perform in person searches. Search fee: $5.00 per name. Required to search: name, years to search. Civil cases indexed by defendant, plaintiff. Civil records on computer since 9/87, index books prior. Civil case information from 1988 forward is available online at www.idocket.com. Free case searching is limited.
Criminal Records: Access: Phone, fax, mail, online, in person. Both court and visitors may perform in person searches. Search fee: $5.00 per name. Required to search: name, years to search. Criminal records on computer since 9/87, index books prior. Online access to criminal records is the same as civil.
General Information: Public access terminal is available. No juvenile, mental, sealed, or adoption records released. SASE required. Turnaround time 2-4 days. Fax notes: $1.00 per page plus 5% of transaction total for credit card fee. Copy fee: $.25 per page. Certification fee: $1.00 per page. Fee payee: District Clerk. Business checks accepted. Credit cards accepted: Visa, MasterCard. Prepayment is required.

County Court & County Courts at Law 1 & 2 PO Box 9638, Amarillo, TX 79105; 806-379-2285; Fax: 806-379-2296. Hours: 8AM-5PM (CST). *Misdemeanor, Civil, Probate.*

www.co.potter.tx.us/countyclerk/index.html

Note: Limited civil records filed here, most are with the District Clerk.

Civil Records: Access: Mail, in person. Both court and visitors may perform in person searches. Search fee: $10.00 per name. Required to search: exact name, years to search. Civil cases indexed by defendant, plaintiff. Civil records on computer since 1990, index books and microfiche since 1889. Probate records available since 1800's. Civil case information is available from idocket at http://idocket.com/counties.htm. Free searching is limited.
Criminal Records: Access: Mail, in person. Both court and visitors may perform in person searches. Search fee: $10.00 per name. Required to search: exact name, years to search, DOB. Criminal records on computer since 1990, index books and microfiche since 1889. Criminal case information is available from idocket at http://idocket.com/counties.htm.
General Information: Public access terminal is available. No juvenile, mental or sealed records released. SASE required. Turnaround time 1-2 days. Copy fee: $1.00 per page. Certification fee: $5.00. Fee payee: Potter County Clerk. Personal checks accepted. Credit cards accepted: Visa, MC. Prepayment required.

Presidio County

District & County Court PO Box 789, Marfa, TX 79843; 915-729-4812; Fax: 915-729-4313. Hours: 8AM-Noon, 1-4PM (CST). *Felony, Misdemeanor, Civil, Probate.*

Civil Records: Access: Mail, in person. Both court and visitors may perform in person searches. Search fee:

$5.00 per name. Required to search: name, years to search. Civil cases indexed by defendant, plaintiff. Civil records in index books.

Criminal Records: Access: Mail, in person. Both court and visitors may perform in person searches. Search fee: $5.00 per name. Required to search: name, years to search. Criminal records in index books.

General Information: No juvenile, mental, sealed, or adoption records released. SASE required. Turnaround time 2-4 days. Copy fee: $1.00 per page. Certification fee: $5.00. Fee payee: District Clerk. Personal checks accepted. Prepayment is required.

Rains County

District & County Court PO Box 187, Emory, TX 75440; 903-474-9999 x14, x15, x16. Fax 903-474-9390; Hours: 8AM-5PM (CST). *Felony, Misdemeanor, Civil, Probate.*

Civil Records: Access: Mail, fax, in person. Both court and visitors may perform in person searches. Search fee: $5.00 per name. Required to search: name. Civil cases indexed by defendant, plaintiff. Civil records on computer back to 1989, index books back to 1880.

Criminal Records: Access: Mail, fax, in person. Both court and visitors may perform in person searches. Search fee: $5.00 per name. Required to search: name; also helpful: DOB. Criminal records on computer back to 1989, index books back to 1903.

General Information: No juvenile, mental, sealed, or adoption records released. SASE required. Turnaround time same day. Copy fee: $1.00 per page. Certification fee: $5.00. Fee payee: Linda Wallace, District/County Clerk. Personal checks accepted. Prepayment required.

Randall County

District Courts PO Box 1096, Canyon, TX 79015; 806-468-5600; Fax: 806-468-5604. Hours: 8AM-5PM (CST). *Felony, Civil.*

www.randallcounty.org

Civil Records: Access: Fax, mail, online, in person. Both court and visitors may perform in person searches. Search fee: $5.00 per name. Required to search: name, years to search. Civil cases indexed by defendant, plaintiff. Civil records in index books. Records on computer since 1982. Civil case information is available free online at www.idocket.com. Free searching is limited.

Criminal Records: Access: Fax, mail, online, in person. Both court and visitors may perform in person searches. Search fee: $5.00 per name. Required to search: name, years to search. Criminal records on computer since 1985; prior in docket books. Online access to criminal records is the same as civil.

General Information: Public access terminal is available. (Criminal only.) No juvenile, mental, sealed, or adoption records released. SASE not required. Turnaround time 1-2 days. Fax notes: Fee to fax results is $5.00 1st pg; $1.00 each add'l. Copy fee: $.50 per page. Certification fee: $1.00 per page. Fee payee: District Clerk. Personal checks accepted. Credit cards accepted: Visa, MasterCard. Prepayment is required.

County Court PO Box 660, Canyon, TX 79015; 806-655-6330; Hours: 8AM-5PM (CST). *Misdemeanor, Civil, Probate.*

www.randallcounty.org/cclerk/default.htm

Civil Records: Access: Phone, mail, fax, in person, email. Both court and visitors may perform in person searches. Search fee: $10.00 per name. Required to search: name, years to search, SASE. Civil cases indexed by defendant, plaintiff. Civil records in index books 1900 to present. Civil case information is available online from idocket at http://idocket.com/counties.htm. Free searching is limited. Records go back to 12/31/1999; probate back to 12/31/1969.

Criminal Records: Access: Phone, mail, fax, in person, online, email. Both court and visitors may perform in person searches. Search fee: $10.00 per name. Required to search: name, years to search; also helpful: DOB. Criminal records on computer since 1984; prior records in index books. Criminal case information is available online from idocket at http://idocket.com/counties.htm. Online records go back to 12/31/1991.

General Information: Public access terminal is available. No juvenile, mental, sealed, or adoption records released. SASE required. Turnaround time 2-4 days. Fax notes: Fee to fax results is $1.00 per page. Copy fee: $1.00 per page. Certification fee: $5.00. Fee payee: Randall County Clerk. Personal checks accepted.

Reagan County

District & County Court PO Box 100, Big Lake, TX 76932; 915-884-2442; Fax: 915-884-1503. Hours: 8:30AM-5PM (CST). *Felony, Misdemeanor, Civil, Probate.*

Civil Records: Access: Mail, in person. Both court and visitors may perform in person searches. Search fee: $5.00 per name. Required to search: name, years to search. Civil cases indexed by defendant, plaintiff. Civil records in index books.

Criminal Records: Access: Mail, in person. Both court and visitors may perform in person searches. Search fee: $5.00 per name. Required to search: name, years to search. Criminal records in index books.

General Information: No juvenile, mental, sealed, or adoption records released. SASE required. Turnaround time same day. Fax notes: $5.00 per document; no fee to fax to toll-free number. Copy fee: $1.00 per page. Certification fee: $5.00. Fee payee: County/District Clerk. Personal checks accepted. Prepayment required.

Real County

District & County Court PO Box 750, Leakey, TX 78873; 830-232-5202; Fax: 830-232-6888. Hours: 8AM-5PM (CST). *Felony, Misdemeanor, Civil, Probate.*

Civil Records: Access: In person only. Visitors must perform in person searches for themselves. No search fee. Required to search: name, years to search. Civil cases indexed by defendant, plaintiff. Civil records in index books.

Criminal Records: Access: In person only. Visitors must perform in person searches for themselves. No search fee. Required to search: name, years to search, DOB. Criminal records in index books.

General Information: No juvenile, mental, sealed, or adoption records released. Fax notes: Fee to fax results is $1.00 per page. Copy fee: $1.00 per page. Certification fee: $5.00. Fee payee: District/County Court. Personal checks accepted. Prepayment required.

Red River County

District Court 400 N Walnut, Clarksville, TX 75426; 903-427-3761; Fax: 903-427-1201. Hours: 8:30AM-Noon, 1-5PM (CST). *Felony, Civil.*

Civil Records: Access: Mail, fax, in person. Both court and visitors may perform in person searches. Search fee: $5.00 per name. Required to search: name, years to search. Civil cases indexed by defendant, plaintiff. Civil records in index books and on microfilm to 1800s.

Criminal Records: Access: Mail, fax, in person. Both court and visitors may perform in person searches. Search fee: $5.00 per name. Required to search: name, years to search. Criminal records in index books and on microfilm to 1800s.

General Information: No juvenile, mental, sealed, or adoption records released. SASE required. Turnaround time same day. Copy fee: $1.00 per page. Certification fee: $2.00. Fee is for in person certification only. Fee

payee: District Clerk. Personal checks accepted. Prepayment is required.

County Court 200 N Walnut, Clarksville, TX 75426; 903-427-2401. Hours: 8:30AM-5PM (CST). *Misdemeanor, Probate.*

Criminal Records: Access: Mail, in person. Both court and visitors may perform in person searches. Search fee: $5.00 per name. Required to search: name, years to search, SSN. Criminal records on computer (name only) since 1980, in index books since 1960s.

General Information: Public access terminal is available. No mental, sealed, or adoption records released. SASE required. Turnaround time 1-2 days. Copy fee: $1.00 per page. Certification fee: $5.00. Fee payee: County Clerk. Personal checks accepted. Prepayment is required.

Reeves County

District Court PO Box 848, Pecos, TX 79772; 915-445-2714; Fax: 915-445-7455. Hours: 8AM-Noon, 1-5PM (CST). *Felony, Civil.*

Civil Records: Access: Phone, mail, in person. Both court and visitors may perform in person searches. Search fee: $5.00 per name. Required to search: name, years to search. Civil cases indexed by defendant, plaintiff. Civil records on computer since 01/91, index books prior.

Criminal Records: Access: Mail, in person. Both court and visitors may perform in person searches. Search fee: $5.00 per name. Required to search: name, years to search. Criminal records on computer back to 01/90, index books prior.

General Information: No juvenile, mental, sealed, or adoption records released. SASE required. Turnaround time 2-4 days. Copy fee: $.25 per page. Certification fee: $1.00 per page. Fee payee: District Clerk Reeves County. Personal checks okay. Prepayment required.

County Court PO Box 867, Pecos, TX 79772; 915-445-5467. Hours: 8AM-5PM (CST). *Misdemeanor, Civil, Probate.*

Civil Records: Access: Mail, in person. Both court and visitors may perform in person searches. Search fee: $10.00 per name. Required to search: name, years to search; also helpful: address. Civil cases indexed by defendant, plaintiff. Civil records on computer go back 10 years, index books prior.

Criminal Records: Access: Mail, in person. Both court and visitors may perform in person searches. Search fee: $10.00 per name. Required to search: name, years to search, DOB; also helpful: address. Criminal records on computer go back 10 years; index books prior.

General Information: No juvenile, mental, sealed, or adoption records released. SASE required. Turnaround time 5 days. Fax notes: $.50 per page. Copy fee: $1.00 per page. Certification fee: $5.00. Fee payee: Reeves County Clerk. Personal checks accepted.

Refugio County

District Court PO Box 736, Refugio, TX 78377; 361-526-2721. Hours: 8AM-Noon, 1-5PM (CST). *Felony, Civil.*

Civil Records: Access: Mail, in person. Both court and visitors may perform in person searches. Search fee: $5.00 per name. Required to search: name, years to search. Civil cases indexed by defendant, plaintiff. Civil records on computer since 1992, index books back to 1879.

Criminal Records: Access: Mail, in person. Both court and visitors may perform in person searches. Search fee: $5.00 per name. Required to search: name, years to search, date of birth. Criminal records on computer since 1992, index books back to 1879.

General Information: No juvenile, mental, sealed, or adoption records released. SASE required. Turnaround time 2-4 days. Copy fee: $1.00 per page. Certification fee: $1.00. Fee payee: District Clerk. Personal checks accepted. Prepayment is required.

County Court PO Box 704, Refugio, TX 78377; 361-526-2233. Hours: 8AM-5PM (CST). *Misdemeanor, Civil, Probate.*

Civil Records: Access: Mail, in person. Both court and visitors may perform in person searches. Search fee: $5.00 per name. Required to search: name, years to search. Civil cases indexed by defendant, plaintiff. Civil records in index books.

Criminal Records: Access: Mail, in person. Both court and visitors may perform in person searches. Search fee: $5.00 per name. Required to search: name, years to search. Criminal records on computer since 1992, index books prior.

General Information: No juvenile, mental, sealed, or adoption records released. SASE not required. Turnaround time 5-10 days. Copy fee: $1.00 per page. Certification fee: $5.00. Fee payee: Janelle Morgan, County Clerk. Personal checks accepted. Prepayment is required.

Roberts County

District & County Court PO Box 477, Miami, TX 79059; 806-868-2341. Hours: 8AM-Noon, 1-5PM (CST). *Felony, Misdemeanor, Civil, Probate.*

Civil Records: Access: Mail, in person. Both court and visitors may perform in person searches. Search fee: $5.00 per name. Required to search: name, years to search. Civil cases indexed by defendant, plaintiff. Civil records in index books.

Criminal Records: Access: Mail, in person. Both court and visitors may perform in person searches. Search fee: $5.00 per name. Required to search: name, years to search, DOB, SSN. Criminal records in index books.

General Information: No juvenile, mental, sealed, or adoption records released. SASE required. Turnaround time 2-4 days. Fax notes: $3.00 first pg; $1.00 each add'l. Copy fee: $1.00 per page. Include postage with copy fee. Certification fee: County Court certification fee is $5.00, District is $1.00. Fee payee: Roberts County. Personal checks accepted. Prepayment is required.

Robertson County

District Court PO Box 250, Franklin, TX 77856; 979-828-3636. Hours: 8AM-5PM (CST). *Felony, Civil.*

Civil Records: Access: Mail, in person. Both court and visitors may perform in person searches. Search fee: $5.00 per name. Required to search: name, years to search. Civil cases indexed by defendant, plaintiff. Civil records on computer since 1984 and index books.

Criminal Records: Access: Mail, in person. Both court and visitors may perform in person searches. Search fee: $5.00 per name. Required to search: name, years to search, DOB; also helpful: SSN. Criminal records on computer since 1984 and index books.

General Information: No juvenile, sealed, or adoption records released. SASE required. Turnaround time 1-2 days. Copy fee: $1.00 per page. Certification fee: $1.00 per page. Fee payee: Robertson County District Clerk. Personal checks accepted. Prepayment is required.

County Court PO Box 1029, Franklin, TX 77856; 979-828-4130. Hours: 8AM-5PM (CST). *Misdemeanor, Civil, Probate.*

Civil Records: Access: Mail, fax, in person. Both court and visitors may perform in person searches. Search fee: $5.00 per name. Required to search: name, years to search. Civil cases indexed by defendant, plaintiff. Civil records on computer back to 1982, index books from 1988.

Criminal Records: Access: Mail, fax, in person. Both court and visitors may perform in person searches. Search fee: $5.00 per name. Required to search: name,

years to search, DOB. Criminal records on computer back to 1982, index books from 1988.

General Information: Public access terminal is available. No juvenile, mental, sealed, or adoption records released. SASE not required. Turnaround time same day. Fax notes: Will not fax results. Copy fee: $1.00 per page. Certification fee: $5.00. Fee payee: Robertson County Clerk. Personal checks accepted. Prepayment is required.

Rockwall County

District Court 1101 Ridge Rd #209, Rockwall, TX 75087; 972-882-0260; Fax: 972-882-0268. Hours: 8AM-5PM (CST). *Felony, Civil.*

Civil Records: Access: Mail, in person. Both court and visitors may perform in person searches. Search fee: $5.00 per name. Fee is per 5 year period. Required to search: name, years to search. Civil cases indexed by defendant, plaintiff. Civil records on computer back to 1994, index books prior.

Criminal Records: Access: Mail, in person. Both court and visitors may perform in person searches. Search fee: $5.00 per name. Required to search: name, years to search, DOB. Criminal records on computer back to 1980, index books prior.

General Information: Public access terminal is available. No juvenile, mental, sealed, or adoption records released. SASE required. Turnaround time 2-4 days. Copy fee: $1.00 per page. Certification fee: $1.00. Fee payee: District Clerk. Personal checks accepted. Prepayment is required.

County Court 1101 Ridge Rd #101, Rockwall, TX 75087; 972-882-0220; Fax: 972-882-0229. Hours: 8AM-5PM (CST). *Misdemeanor, Civil, Probate.*

Civil Records: Access: Phone, mail, in person. Both court and visitors may perform in person searches. Search fee: $5.00 per name. Required to search: name, years to search. Civil cases indexed by defendant, plaintiff. Civil records on computer back to 1983 and in index books from 1800s.

Criminal Records: Access: Phone, mail, in person. Both court and visitors may perform in person searches. Search fee: $5.00 per name. Required to search: name, years to search. Criminal records on computer back to 1983 and in index books from 1800s.

General Information: Public access terminal is available. No juvenile, mental, sealed, or adoption records released. SASE required. Turnaround time 2-4 days. Fax notes: Fee to fax results is $5.00 per document. Copy fee: $1.00 per page. Certification fee: $5.00. Fee payee: County Clerk. Personal checks accepted. Prepayment is required.

Runnels County

District Court PO Box 166, Ballinger, TX 76821; 915-365-2638; Fax: 915-365-4933. Hours: 8:30AM-5PM (CST). *Felony, Civil.*

Civil Records: Access: Phone, fax, mail, in person. Both court and visitors may perform in person searches. Search fee: $5.00 per name. Required to search: name; also helpful: years to search. Civil cases indexed by defendant, plaintiff. Civil records in index books since 1882.

Criminal Records: Access: Phone, fax, mail, in person. Both court and visitors may perform in person searches. Search fee: $5.00 per name. Required to search: name; also helpful: years to search, DOB, SSN. Criminal records in index books since 1882.

General Information: No juvenile, mental, sealed or adoption records released. SASE required. Turnaround time 1-2 days. Fax notes: $1.00 per page. Copy fee: $1.00 per page. Certification fee: $1.00. Fee payee: District Clerk. Personal checks accepted. Prepayment is required.

County Court PO Box 189, Ballinger, TX 76821; 915-365-2720. Hours: 8:30AM-Noon, 1-5PM (CST). *Misdemeanor, Civil, Probate.*

Civil Records: Access: Phone, mail, in person. Both court and visitors may perform in person searches. Search fee: $5.00. Required to search: name, years to search. Civil cases indexed by defendant, plaintiff. Civil records in docket books with alphabetical index and file jacket by number; computerized since 1992.

Criminal Records: Access: Phone, mail, in person. Both court and visitors may perform in person searches. Search fee: $5.00. Required to search: name, years to search; also helpful: DOB. Criminal records in docket books with alphabetical index and file jacket by number; computerized since 1992.

General Information: No juvenile or mental records released. SASE not required. Turnaround time 1-2 days. Copy fee: $1.00 per page. Certification fee: $5.00. Fee payee: County Clerk, Runnels County. Personal checks accepted. Prepayment is required.

Rusk County

District Court PO Box 1687, Henderson, TX 75653; 903-657-0353. Hours: 8AM-5PM (CST). *Felony, Civil.*

Civil Records: Access: Mail, in person. Both court and visitors may perform in person searches. Search fee: $5.00 per name. Required to search: name, years to search. Civil cases indexed by defendant, plaintiff. Civil records in index books; on computer back to 1973.

Criminal Records: Access: Mail, in person. Both court and visitors may perform in person searches. Search fee: $5.00 per name. Required to search: name, years to search, DOB, SSN, signed release. Criminal records in index books; on computer back to 1973.

General Information: No juvenile, mental, sealed, or adoption records released. SASE required. Turnaround time 2-4 days. Copy fee: $1.00 per page. Certification fee: $1.00. Fee payee: District Clerk. Only cashiers checks and money orders accepted. Prepayment is required.

County Court at Law PO Box 1687, Henderson, TX 75653-1687; 903-657-0353 (X0348 Fam Court Records). Hours: 8AM-5PM (CST). *Misdemeanor, Civil, Probate.*

Note: Misdemeanor & Probate records are at County Clerk, PO Box 758, phone 903-657-0330.

Civil Records: Access: Mail, in person. Both court and visitors may perform in person searches. Search fee: $5.00 per name. Required to search: name, years to search. Civil cases indexed by defendant, plaintiff. Civil records in index books.

Criminal Records: Access: Mail, in person. Both court and visitors may perform in person searches. Search fee: $5.00 per name. Required to search: name, years to search, DOB, SSN. Criminal records are not computerized, are indexed in books.

General Information: No juvenile, mental, sealed, or adoption records released. SASE required. Turnaround time 2-4 days. Copy fee: $1.00 per page. Fee payee: District Clerk. Business checks accepted. Prepayment is required.

Sabine County

District Court PO Box 850, Hemphill, TX 75948; 409-787-2912. Hours: 8AM-4PM (CST). *Felony, Civil.*

Civil Records: Access: Mail, in person. Both court and visitors may perform in person searches. Search fee: $10.00 per name. Required to search: name, years to search. Civil cases indexed by defendant, plaintiff. Civil records on computer since 1992. Overall records go back to 1900.

Criminal Records: Access: Mail, in person. Both court and visitors may perform in person searches. Search fee: $10.00 per name. Required to search: name, years

to search. Criminal records on computer since 1992. Overall records go back to 1900.

General Information: No juvenile, mental, sealed, or adoption records released. SASE required. Turnaround time 1-2 days. Copy fee: $1.00 per page. Fee payee: District Clerk. Personal checks accepted. Prepayment is required.

County Court PO Drawer 580, Hemphill, TX 75948-0580; 409-787-3786. Hours: 8AM-4PM (CST). *Misdemeanor, Probate.*

Criminal Records: Access: Mail, in person. Both court and visitors may perform in person searches. Search fee: $10.00 per name. Required to search: name, years to search. Criminal records on computer since 1992, index books prior.

General Information: No juvenile, mental, sealed, or adoption records released. SASE not required. Turnaround time 2 days. Copy fee: $1.00 per page. Certification fee: $5.00. Fee payee: Sabine County Clerk. Business checks accepted. Prepayment required.

San Augustine County

District Court County Courthouse Rm 202, San Augustine, TX 75972; 936-275-2231; Fax: 936-275-9579. Hours: 8AM-4:15PM (CST). *Felony, Civil.*

Civil Records: Access: Phone, mail, in person. Both court and visitors may perform in person searches. Search fee: $5.00 per name. Required to search: name, years to search. Civil cases indexed by plaintiff. Civil records in index books.

Criminal Records: Access: Phone, mail, in person. Only the court performs in person searches; visitors may not. Search fee: $5.00 per name. Required to search: name, years to search. Criminal records in index books.

General Information: No juvenile, mental, sealed, or adoption records released. SASE required. Turnaround time 2-4 days. Copy fee: $1.00 per page. Certification fee: $1.00. Fee payee: District Clerk. Personal checks accepted.

County Court County Courthouse Rm 106, San Augustine, TX 75972; 936-275-2452; Fax: 936-275-9579. Hours: 8AM-4:30PM (CST). *Misdemeanor, Civil, Probate.*

Civil Records: Access: Mail, in person. Both court and visitors may perform in person searches. Search fee: $5.00 per name. Required to search: name, years to search; also helpful: address. Civil cases indexed by defendant, plaintiff. Civil records go back to 1988; no computerized records.

Criminal Records: Access: Phone, mail, in person. Both court and visitors may perform in person searches. Search fee: $5.00 per name. Required to search: name, years to search; also helpful: address, DOB, SSN. Criminal records go back to 1984; on computer since 1990. Criminal information may be obtained over the phone, but copies must be paid for in advance. Will fax back if $5.00 paid in advance.

General Information: No juvenile, mental, sealed, or adoption records released. SASE required. Turnaround time 2-3 days. Copy fee: $1.00 per page. Certification fee: $5.00. Fee payee: County Clerk. Personal checks accepted. Prepayment is required.

San Jacinto County

District Court PO Box 369, Coldspring, TX 77331; 936-653-2909. 8AM-Noon, 1-5PM *Felony, Civil.*

Civil Records: Access: Mail, in person. Both court and visitors may perform in person searches. Search fee: $5.00 per name. Required to search: name, years to search. Civil cases indexed by defendant, plaintiff. Civil records in index books.

Criminal Records: Access: Mail, in person. Both court and visitors may perform in person searches. Search

fee: $5.00 per name. Required to search: name, years to search. Criminal records on computer since 1986.

General Information: Public access terminal is available. No juvenile, mental, sealed, or adoption records released. SASE required. Turnaround time 2-4 days. Copy fee: $1.00 per page. Certification fee: $5.00. Fee payee: District Clerk. Personal checks accepted. Prepayment is required.

County Court PO Box 669, Coldspring, TX 77331; 936-653-2324. Hours: 8AM-4:30PM (CST). *Misdemeanor, Civil, Probate.*

www.co.san-jacinto.tx.us

Civil Records: Access: Mail, in person. Both court and visitors may perform in person searches. Search fee: $5.00 per name. Required to search: name, years to search. Civil cases indexed by defendant, plaintiff. Civil records in index books.

Criminal Records: Access: Mail, in person. Both court and visitors may perform in person searches. Search fee: $5.00 per name. Required to search: name, years to search; also helpful: address, DOB, SSN. Criminal records in index books.

General Information: No juvenile, mental, sealed, or adoption records released. SASE required. Turnaround time 2 weeks. Copy fee: $1.00 per page. Certification fee: $5.00. Fee payee: County Clerk. Personal checks accepted. Only cashiers checks and money orders accepted for criminal searches. Prepayment is required.

San Patricio County

District Court PO Box 1084, Sinton, TX 78387; 361-364-6225. Hours: 8AM-5PM (CST). *Felony, Civil.*

Civil Records: Access: Mail, in person. Both court and visitors may perform in person searches. Search fee: $5.00 per name. Fee is per division. Required to search: name, years to search. Civil cases indexed by defendant, plaintiff. Civil records in index books from 1800s; computerized back to 1993.

Criminal Records: Access: Mail, in person. Both court and visitors may perform in person searches. Search fee: $5.00 per name. Fee is per division. Required to search: name, years to search. Criminal records in index books from 1800s; computerized back to 1993.

General Information: Public access terminal is available. No juvenile, mental, sealed, or adoption records released. SASE required. Turnaround time 2-4 days. Copy fee: $1.00 per page. Certification fee: $1.00. Fee payee: District Clerk. Business checks accepted. Prepayment is required.

County Court PO Box 578, Sinton, TX 78387; 361-364-6290; Fax: 361-364-6112. Hours: 8AM-5PM (CST). *Misdemeanor, Civil, Probate.*

Civil Records: Access: Phone, mail, in person. Both court and visitors may perform in person searches. Search fee: $5.00 per name. Required to search: name, years to search; also helpful: address. Civil cases indexed by defendant, plaintiff. Civil records in index books and microfilm; computerizing in 2002.

Criminal Records: Access: Phone, mail, in person. Both court and visitors may perform in person searches. Search fee: $5.00 per name. Required to search: name, years to search; also helpful: address, DOB, SSN, anything. Criminal records in index books and microfilm; computerizing in 2002.

General Information: No juvenile, mental, or sealed records released. SASE required. Turnaround time 2-3 days. Copy fee: $1.00 per page. Certification fee: $5.00. Fee payee: County Clerk. Personal checks accepted. Prepayment is required.

San Saba County

District & County Court County Courthouse, 500 E Wallace #202, San Saba, TX 76877; 915-372-3375. Hours: 8AM-Noon, 1-4:30PM (CST). *Felony, Misdemeanor, Civil, Probate.*

Civil Records: Access: Phone, mail, in person. Both court and visitors may perform in person searches. Search fee: $10.00 per name. Required to search: name, years to search. Civil cases indexed by defendant, plaintiff. Civil records in index books.

Criminal Records: Access: Mail, in person. Both court and visitors may perform in person searches. Search fee: $10.00 per name. Required to search: name, years to search; also helpful: DOB. Criminal records in index books.

General Information: No juvenile, mental, sealed, or adoption records released. SASE required. Turnaround time 2-3 days. Copy fee: $1.00 per page. Certification fee: $5.00. Fee payee: District/County Clerk. Personal checks accepted. Prepayment is required.

Schleicher County

District & County Court PO Drawer 580, Eldorado, TX 76936; 915-853-2833; Fax: 915-853-2603. Hours: 9AM-Noon, 1-5PM (CST). *Felony, Misdemeanor, Civil, Probate.*

Civil Records: Access: Mail, in person. Both court and visitors may perform in person searches. Search fee: $10.00 per name. Required to search: name, years to search. Civil cases indexed by defendant, plaintiff. Civil records in index books.

Criminal Records: Access: Mail, in person. Both court and visitors may perform in person searches. Search fee: $10.00 per name. Required to search: name, years to search. Criminal records in index books.

General Information: No juvenile, mental, sealed, or adoption records released. SASE required. Turnaround time 2-3 days. Copy fee: $1.00 per page. Certification fee: $5.00. Fee payee: District/County Clerk. Personal checks accepted. Prepayment is required.

Scurry County

132nd District Court 1806 25th St #402, Snyder, TX 79549; 915-573-5641. 8AM-5PM *Felony, Civil.*

Civil Records: Access: Mail, in person. Both court and visitors may perform in person searches. Search fee: $5.00 per name. Required to search: name, years to search. Civil cases indexed by defendant, plaintiff. Civil records go back to 1890; computerized records since 1994. All requests must be in writing.

Criminal Records: Access: Mail, in person. Both court and visitors may perform in person searches. Search fee: $5.00 per name. Required to search: name, years to search, address, DOB, SSN, sex. Criminal records go back to 1890; computerized records since 1994. All requests must be in writing.

General Information: No juvenile, mental, sealed, or adoption records released. SASE required. Turnaround time 2-3 days. Fax notes: Fee to fax results is $1.00 per page. Copy fee: $1.00 for first page, $.25 each add'l. Certification fee: $1.00 per page. Fee payee: District Clerk. Personal checks accepted. Prepayment required.

County Court County Courthouse, 1806 25th St Ste 300, Snyder, TX 79549; 915-573-5332. Hours: 8:30AM-5PM (CST). *Misdemeanor, Civil, Probate.*

Civil Records: Access: Mail, in person. Both court and visitors may perform in person searches. Search fee: $10.00 per name. Required to search: name, years to search. Civil cases indexed by defendant, plaintiff. Civil records in index books since 1900s; on computer back to 1995.

Criminal Records: Access: Mail, in person. Both court and visitors may perform in person searches. Search fee: $5.00 per name. Fee includes copies. Required to search: name, years to search; also helpful: address, DOB, SSN. Criminal records in index books since 1900s; on computer back to 1995. Written request always required.

General Information: Public access terminal is available. No mental or sealed records released. SASE required. Turnaround time 1-2 days. Fax notes: Fee to fax results is $1.00 per page. Copy fee: $1.00 per page. Certification fee: $5.00. Fee payee: County Clerk Scurry County. Personal checks accepted. Personal checks must be in-state. Prepayment is required.

Shackelford County

District & County Court PO Box 247, Albany, TX 76430; 915-762-2232. Hours: 8:30AM-5PM (CST). *Felony, Misdemeanor, Civil, Probate.*

Civil Records: Access: Mail, in person. Both court and visitors may perform in person searches. Search fee: $5.00 per name. Fee is per court. Required to search: name, years to search. Civil cases indexed by defendant, plaintiff. Civil records on computer since 1987, index books since 1867.

Criminal Records: Access: Mail, in person. Both court and visitors may perform in person searches. Search fee: $5.00 per name. Fee is per court. Required to search: name, years to search. Criminal records on computer since 1987, index books since 1867.

General Information: No juvenile, mental, sealed, or adoption records released. SASE required. Turnaround time 3 days after receipt. Copy fee: $1.00 per page. Certification fee: $5.00. Fee payee: Clerk, Shackelford County. Personal checks okay. Prepayment required.

Shelby County

District Court PO Drawer 1953, Center, TX 75935; 936-598-4164. 8AM-4:30PM (CST). *Felony, Civil.*

Civil Records: Access: Mail, in person. Both court and visitors may perform in person searches. Search fee: $5.00 per name. Required to search: name, years to search. Civil cases indexed by defendant, plaintiff. Civil records in index books; on computer back to 2000.

Criminal Records: Access: Mail, in person. Both court and visitors may perform in person searches. Search fee: $5.00 per name. Required to search: name, years to search, signed release. Criminal records in index books; on computer back to 2000.

General Information: No juvenile, mental, sealed, or adoption records released. SASE required. Turnaround time 2-3 days. Copy fee: $1.00 per page. Certification fee: $1.00. Fee payee: District Clerk. Only cashiers checks and money orders accepted. Will accept attorney's check. Prepayment is required.

County Court PO Box 1987, Center, TX 75935; 936-598-6361; Fax: 936-598-3701. Hours: 8AM-4:30PM (CST). *Misdemeanor, Civil, Probate.*

Civil Records: Access: Mail, fax, in person. Both court and visitors may perform in person searches. Search fee: $10.00 per name. Required to search: name, years to search. Civil cases indexed by defendant, plaintiff. Civil records in index books back to 1882; on computer back to 1990.

Criminal Records: Access: Mail, in person. Both court and visitors may perform in person searches. Search fee: $10.00 per name. Required to search: name, years to search, SSN, DOB; also helpful: signed release. Criminal records in index books back to 1920; on comptuer back to 1990. All requests must be in writing.

General Information: Public access terminal is available. No juvenile, mental, sealed, or adoption records released. SASE required. Turnaround time 1-2 days. Copy fee: $1.00 per page. Certification fee: $5.00. Fee payee: Shelby County Clerk. Personal checks accepted. Prepayment is required.

Sherman County

District & County Court PO Box 270, Stratford, TX 79084; 806-366-2371; Fax: 806-366-5670. Hours: 8AM-Noon, 1-5PM (CST). *Felony, Misdemeanor, Civil, Probate.*

Civil Records: Access: Mail, in person. Both court and visitors may perform in person searches. Search fee:

$5.00 per name. Required to search: name, years to search. Civil cases indexed by defendant. Civil records on computer since 1994, index books prior.

Criminal Records: Access: Mail, in person. Both court and visitors may perform in person searches. Search fee: $5.00 per name. Required to search: name, years to search. Criminal records on computer since 1994, index books prior.

General Information: No juvenile, mental, sealed, or adoption records released. SASE required. Turnaround time 2-3 days. Copy fee: $1.00 per page. Certification fee: $5.00. Fee payee: Sherman County Clerk. Personal checks accepted. Prepayment is required.

Smith County

District Court PO Box 1077, Tyler, TX 75710; 903-535-0666; Fax: 903-535-0683. Hours: 8AM-5PM (CST). *Felony, Civil.*

Civil Records: Access: Mail, in person. Both court and visitors may perform in person searches. Search fee: $5.00 per name. Required to search: name, years to search. Civil cases indexed by defendant, plaintiff. Civil records in index books.

Criminal Records: Access: Mail, in person. Both court and visitors may perform in person searches. Search fee: $5.00 per name. Required to search: name, years to search. Criminal records in index books to 1846, computerized since 1/99.

General Information: No juvenile, mental, sealed, or adoption records released. SASE required. Turnaround time 2-3 days. Copy fee: $1.00 per page. Certification fee: $1.00. Fee payee: District Clerk. Cashiers checks and money orders accepted. Prepayment is required.

County Court PO Box 1018, Tyler, TX 75710; 903-535-0630; Fax: 903-535-0684. Hours: 8AM-5PM (CST). *Misdemeanor, Civil, Probate.*

Civil Records: Access: Mail, in person. Both court and visitors may perform in person searches. Search fee: $5.00 per name. Required to search: name, years to search. Civil cases indexed by defendant, plaintiff. Civil records in index books.

Criminal Records: Access: Mail, in person. Both court and visitors may perform in person searches. Search fee: $5.00 per name. Required to search: name, years to search; also helpful: DOB, SSN. Criminal records in index books.

General Information: No juvenile, mental, sealed, or adoption records released. SASE required. Turnaround time 2-4 days. Copy fee: $1.00 per page. $5.00 certified copies. Certification fee: $5.00. Fee payee: Smith County Clerk. Personal checks accepted. Prepayment is required.

Somervell County

District & County Court PO Box 1098, Glen Rose, TX 76043; 254-897-4427; Fax: 254-897-3233. Hours: 8AM-5PM (CST). *Felony, Misdemeanor, Civil, Probate.*

Note: Evictions are handled by Justice of the Peace, POB 237, Glen Rose, TX 76043, 254-897-2120.

Civil Records: Access: Mail, in person. Both court and visitors may perform in person searches. Search fee: $5.00 per name. Required to search: name, years to search; also helpful: address. Civil cases indexed by defendant, plaintiff. Civil records on computer since 1991, microfilm since 1980, index books since 1875.

Criminal Records: Access: Mail, in person. Both court and visitors may perform in person searches. Search fee: $5.00 per name. Required to search: name, years to search, DOB, SSN, signed release; also helpful: address. Criminal records on computer since 1991, microfilm since 1980, index books since 1875.

General Information: No juvenile, mental, sealed, or adoption records released. SASE preferred. Turnaround time same day. Fax notes: Fee to fax results is $1.00 per

page. Copy fee: $1.00 per page. Certification fee: $5.00. Fee payee: County/District Clerk. Personal checks accepted. Prepayment is required.

Starr County

District & County Court Starr County Courthouse, Room 304, Rio Grande City, TX 78582; 956-487-8482 (Dist) 487-8485 (County); Fax: 956-487-8493. Hours: 8AM-5PM (CST). *Felony, Misdemeanor, Civil, Probate.*

Note: Handles civil county court cases.

Civil Records: Access: Phone, fax, mail, in person. Both court and visitors may perform in person searches. Search fee: $7.00 per name. Required to search: name, years to search. Civil cases indexed by defendant, plaintiff. Civil records on index books from 1920s, computerized since 1992.

Criminal Records: Access: Phone, fax, mail, in person. Only the court performs in person searches; visitors may not. Search fee: $7.00 per name. Required to search: name, years to search, SSN; also helpful: DOB. Criminal records on computer since 1992; in docket books to 1800s.

General Information: No adoption records released. SASE required. Turnaround time 2 days. Fax notes: $5.00 for 1st copy; $1.00 each add'l. Copy fee: $1.00 per page. Certification fee: $5.00. Fee payee: District Clerk. Personal checks accepted. Prepayment required.

County Court Starr County Courthouse, Room 201, Rio Grande City, TX 78582; 956-487-8032; Fax: 956-487-8674. 8AM-5PM *Misdemeanor, Probate.*

Note: See District & County Court for civil county court cases.

Civil Records: Access: Phone, fax, mail, in person. Both court and visitors may perform in person searches. Search fee: $10.00 per name. Required to search: name, years to search. Civil cases indexed by defendant, plaintiff. Civil records in index books since 1920s.

Criminal Records: Access: Mail, in person. Both court and visitors may perform in person searches. Search fee: $10.00 per name. Required to search: name, years to search; also helpful: SSN, DOB. Criminal records on computer since 1972, in index books since 1920s.

General Information: No juvenile, mental, sealed, or adoption records released. SASE requested. Turnaround time 2-4 days. Fax notes: Fee to fax results is $1.00 per page. Copy fee: $1.00 per page. Certification fee: $5.00. Fee payee: County Clerk. Personal checks accepted. Prepayment is required.

Stephens County

District Court 200 W Walker, Breckenridge, TX 76424; 254-559-3151; Fax: 254-559-8127. Hours: 8:30AM-5PM (CST). *Felony, Civil, Misdemeanor.*

Civil Records: Access: Fax, mail, in person. Both court and visitors may perform in person searches. Search fee: $5.00 per name. Required to search: name, years to search. Civil cases indexed by defendant, plaintiff. Civil records in index books, archived from 1900; on comptuer back to 1995.

Criminal Records: Access: Fax, mail, in person. Both court and visitors may perform in person searches. Search fee: $5.00 per name. Required to search: name, years to search, DOB. Criminal records in index books, archived from 1900; on comptuer back to 1995.

General Information: No juvenile, mental, sealed, or adoption records released. SASE required. Turnaround time same day. Fax notes: $1.00 per page. Available to local and 800 numbers only. Copy fee: $1.00 per page. Certification fee: $1.00. Fee payee: District Clerk. Personal checks accepted. Prepayment is required.

County Court 200 W Walker, Breckenridge, TX 76424; 254-559-3700. Hours: 8:30AM-5PM (CST). *Probate, Misdemeanor.*

Sterling County

District & County Court PO Box 55, Sterling City, TX 76951; 915-378-5191. Hours: 8:30AM-Noon, 1-5PM (CST). *Felony, Misdemeanor, Civil, Probate.*

Civil Records: Access: Mail, in person. Both court and visitors may perform in person searches. No search fee. Required to search: name, years to search; also helpful: address. Civil cases indexed by defendant, plaintiff. Civil records in index books from 1900s.

Criminal Records: Access: Mail, in person. Both court and visitors may perform in person searches. No search fee. Required to search: name, years to search; also helpful: DOB, SSN. Criminal records in index books from 1900s.

General Information: No juvenile, mental, sealed, or adoption records released. SASE required. Turnaround time 1-2 days. Fax notes: Fee to fax results is $1.00 per page. Copy fee: $1.00 per page. Certification fee: $5.00. Fee payee: Sterling County/District Clerk. Personal checks accepted. Prepayment is required.

Stonewall County

District & County Court PO Drawer P, Aspermont, TX 79502; 940-989-2272. 8AM-Noon, 1-4:30PM (CST). *Felony, Misdemeanor, Civil, Probate.*

Civil Records: Access: Phone, mail, in person. Both court and visitors may perform in person searches. No search fee. Required to search: name, years to search. Civil cases indexed by defendant, plaintiff. Civil records in index books to 1900's.

Criminal Records: Access: Phone, mail, in person. Both court and visitors may perform in person searches. No search fee. Required to search: name, years to search. Criminal records in index books to 1900's.

General Information: No juvenile, mental, sealed, or adoption records released. SASE required. Fax notes: Fax fee is $2.00 per page. Copy fee: $1.00 per page. Certification fee: $5.00. Fee payee: County Clerk. Personal checks accepted.

Sutton County

District & County Court 300 E Oak, Ste 3, Sonora, TX 76950; 915-387-3815. Hours: 8:30AM-4:30PM (CST). *Felony, Misdemeanor, Civil, Probate.*

Civil Records: Access: Phone, mail, in person. Both court and visitors may perform in person searches. Search fee: $10.00 per name. Required to search: name, years to search. Civil cases indexed by defendant, plaintiff. Civil records on computer back to 1992, index books prior.

Criminal Records: Access: Mail, in person. Both court and visitors may perform in person searches. Search fee: $10.00 per name. Required to search: name, years to search. Criminal records on computer back to 1992, index books prior.

General Information: No juvenile, mental, sealed, or adoption records released. SASE required. Turnaround time 2-4 days. Copy fee: $1.00 per page. Certification fee: $5.00. Fee payee: County Clerk. Personal checks accepted. Prepayment is required.

Swisher County

District & County Court County Courthouse, 119 S Maxwell, Tulia, TX 79088; 806-995-4396; Fax: 806-995-4121. Hours: 8AM-5PM (CST). *Felony, Misdemeanor, Civil, Probate.*

Civil Records: Access: Mail, fax, in person, email. Both court and visitors may perform in person searches. Search fee: $5.00 per name. Required to search: name, years to search. Civil cases indexed by defendant, plaintiff. Civil records on computer since 1992, index books prior.

Criminal Records: Access: Mail, fax, in person, email. Both court and visitors may perform in person searches. Search fee: $5.00 per name. Required to search: name,

years to search, DOB and SSN. Criminal records on computer since 1992, index books prior to early 1900's.

General Information: No juvenile, mental, sealed, or adoption records released. SASE requested. Turnaround time 1-2 days. Fax notes: Fee to fax results is $1.00 per page. If the call is long distance, add $5.00. Copy fee: $1.00 per page. Certification fee: $1.00 per page plus $5.00 (only $.50 if Family Law case). Fee payee: County/District Clerk. Personal checks accepted. Prepayment is required.

Tarrant County

District Court 401 W Belknap, Tarrant County District Clerk's Office, Fort Worth, TX 76196-0402; 817-884-1574 (884-1265 Family Division); Civil phone: 817-884-1240; Criminal phone: 817-884-1342; Fax: 817-884-1484. 8AM-5PM (CST). *Felony, Civil.*

www.tarrantcounty.com

Civil Records: Access: Mail, online, in person. Both court and visitors may perform in person searches. Search fee: $5.00 per name if the office does the search. Required to search: full name, years to search or case number. Civil cases indexed by defendant, plaintiff. Civil records on computer since 1989, file jackets prior to 1989; records go back to 1800's. Access to the remote online system requires $50 setup, $25 monthly fee and $.05 per minute access. Call Peter Lee Hinojosa at 817-884-1419 for more information.

Criminal Records: Access: Mail, online, in person. Both court and visitors may perform in person searches. Search fee: $5.00 per name if the office does the search. Required to search: full name, years to search, DOB; also helpful: SSN. Criminal records on computer back to 1975, microfilm since 1970, index books and case files since 1800's. Access to the remote online system requires $50 setup, $25 monthly fee and $.05 per minute access. Call Peter Lee Hinojosa at 817-884-1419 for more information.

General Information: Public access terminal is available. No juvenile, mental, sealed, or adoption records released. SASE not required. Turnaround time 1-3 days. Copy fee: $.30 per page. Certification fee: $1.00 per page. Fee payee: Thomas A Wilder, District Clerk. Business checks accepted. Prepayment is required.

County Court - Criminal 401 W Belknap, Tarrant County District Clerk's Office, Fort Worth, TX 76196-0402; 817-884-1195. Hours: 7:30AM-4:30PM (CST). *Misdemeanor.*

www.tarrantcounty.com

Note: Small Claims, Evictions, and low-level civil cases are handled by JP/Municipal Courts.

Criminal Records: Access: Mail, online, in person. Both court and visitors may perform in person searches. Search fee: $5.00 per name. Required to search: name, years to search, DOB. Criminal records on computer back to 1980s. Access to the remote online system requires $50 setup, $25 monthly fee and $.05 per minute access. Call Peter Lee Hinojosa at 817-884-1419 for more information.

General Information: Public access terminal is available. No juvenile, mental, sealed, or adoption records released. SASE required. Turnaround time 1-3 days. Fax notes: Will not fax results. Copy fee: $.30 per page. Certification fee: $5.00. Business checks accepted. Prepayment is required.

Probate Court County Courthouse, 100 W Weatherford St, Probate Court #1 Rm 260A, Fort Worth, TX 76196; 817-884-1200; Fax: 817-884-3178. Hours: 8AM-4:30PM (CST). *Probate.*

Taylor County

District Court 300 Oak St, Abilene, TX 79602; 915-674-1316. Hours: 8AM-Noon, 1-5PM (CST). *Felony, Civil.*

Civil Records: Access: Mail, in person. Both court and visitors may perform in person searches. Search fee: $5.00 per name. Required to search: name, years to search. Civil cases indexed by defendant, plaintiff. Civil records on computer since 1996; prior records in index books to 1885.

Criminal Records: Access: Mail, in person. Both court and visitors may perform in person searches. Search fee: $5.00 per name. Required to search: name, years to search, DOB; also helpful: SSN. Criminal records on computer since 1996; prior records in index books to 1885.

General Information: Public access terminal is available. No juvenile, mental, sealed, or adoption records released. SASE required. Turnaround time 4 days. Copy fee: $1.00 per page. Fee payee: Taylor County District Clerk. Business checks accepted. Prepayment is required.

County Court PO Box 5497, Abilene, TX 79608; 915-674-1202; Fax: 915-674-1279. Hours: 8AM-5PM (CST). *Misdemeanor, Civil, Probate.*

www.taylorcountytexas.org

Civil Records: Access: Mail, in person. Both court and visitors may perform in person searches. Search fee: $5.00 per name. Fee is per 10 years. Required to search: name, years to search. Civil cases indexed by defendant, plaintiff. Civil records on computer less than ten years, index books prior.

Criminal Records: Access: Mail, in person. Both court and visitors may perform in person searches. Search fee: $5.00 per name. Fee is per 10 years. Required to search: name, years to search, DOB; also helpful: address, SSN. Criminal records on computer back to 1980; overall records go back to 1949.

General Information: Public access terminal is available. No juvenile, mental, sealed, or adoption records released. SASE required. Turnaround time 2-4 days. Fax notes: Fee to fax results is $1.00 per page, $2.00 per doc. Copy fee: $1.00 per page. Certification fee: $5.00. Fee payee: County Clerk. Personal checks accepted. Prepayment is required.

Terrell County

District & County Court PO Drawer 410, Sanderson, TX 79848; 915-345-2391; Fax: 915-345-2653. Hours: 9AM-Noon, 1-5PM (CST). *Felony, Misdemeanor, Civil, Probate.*

Civil Records: Access: Mail, in person. Both court and visitors may perform in person searches. No search fee. Required to search: name, years to search. Civil cases indexed by defendant, plaintiff. Civil records in index books.

Criminal Records: Access: Mail, in person. Both court and visitors may perform in person searches. Search fee: $5.00 per name. Required to search: name, years to search. Criminal records in index books.

General Information: No juvenile, mental, sealed, or adoption records released. Turnaround time 2-4 days. Fax notes: $8.00 for first page, $2.00 each add'l. Copy fee: $1.00 per page. Fee payee: County Clerk. Personal checks accepted. Prepayment is required.

Terry County

District Court 500 W Main Rm 209E, Brownfield, TX 79316; 806-637-4202. Hours: 8:30AM-5PM (CST). *Felony, Civil.*

Civil Records: Access: Mail, in person. Both court and visitors may perform in person searches. Search fee: $5.00 per name. Required to search: name, years to

search. Civil cases indexed by defendant, plaintiff. Civil records in index books.

Criminal Records: Access: Mail, in person. Only the court performs in person searches; visitors may not. Search fee: $5.00 per name. Required to search: name, years to search, DOB; also helpful: SSN. Criminal records in index books.

General Information: No juvenile, mental, sealed, or adoption records released. SASE required. Turnaround time same day. Copy fee: $1.00 per page. Certification fee: $1.00. Fee payee: District Clerk. Personal checks accepted. Prepayment is required.

County Court 500 W Main Rm 105, Brownfield, TX 79316-4398; 806-637-8551; Fax: 806-637-4874. Hours: 8:30AM-5PM (CST). *Misdemeanor, Civil, Probate.*

Civil Records: Access: Mail, in person. Both court and visitors may perform in person searches. Search fee: $10.00 per name. Required to search: name, years to search. Civil cases indexed by defendant, plaintiff. Civil records in index books to 1904, computerized since 1981.

Criminal Records: Access: Mail, in person. Both court and visitors may perform in person searches. Search fee: $10.00 per name. Required to search: name, years to search; also helpful: address, DOB, SSN. Criminal records in index books back to 1904, computerized since 1981.

General Information: No juvenile, mental, sealed, or adoption records released. SASE required. Turnaround time 1-2 days. Fax notes: Fee to fax results is $1.00 per page. Copy fee: $1.00 per page. Certification fee: $5.00. Fee payee: County Clerk. Personal checks accepted. Prepayment is required.

Throckmorton County

District & County Court PO Box 309, Throckmorton, TX 76483; 940-849-2501. Hours: 8AM-Noon, 1-5PM (CST). *Felony, Misdemeanor, Civil, Probate.*

Civil Records: Access: Phone, mail, in person. Both court and visitors may perform in person searches. Search fee: $10.00 per name. Required to search: name, years to search; also helpful: address. Civil cases indexed by defendant, plaintiff. Civil records in index books; computerized records go back to 1990.

Criminal Records: Access: Mail, in person. Both court and visitors may perform in person searches. Search fee: $10.00 per name. Required to search: name, years to search. Criminal records in index books; computerized records go back to 1990.

General Information: No juvenile, mental, sealed, or adoption records released. SASE required. Turnaround time 2-4 days. Copy fee: $1.00 per page. Fee payee: County/District Clerk. Personal checks accepted. Prepayment is required.

Titus County

District Court 105 W 1st St, PO Box 492, Mount Pleasant, TX 75455; 903-577-6721. Hours: 8AM-5PM (CST). *Felony, Civil.*

Civil Records: Access: Phone, mail, in person. Both court and visitors may perform in person searches. Search fee: $5.00 per name. Required to search: name, years to search. Civil cases indexed by defendant, plaintiff. Civil records in index books from 1895; computerized back to 1992.

Criminal Records: Access: Phone, mail, in person. Both court and visitors may perform in person searches. Search fee: $5.00 per name. Required to search: name, years to search. Criminal records in index books from 1895; computerized back to 1992.

General Information: Public access terminal is available. No juvenile, mental, sealed, or adoption records released. SASE required. Turnaround time 2-3

days. Copy fee: $1.00 per page. Certification fee: $5.00. Fee payee: District Clerk. Personal checks accepted. Prepayment is required.

County Court 100 W 1st St #204, Mount Pleasant, TX 75455; 903-577-6796; Fax: 903-577-6793. Hours: 8AM-5PM (CST). *Misdemeanor, Civil, Probate.*

Civil Records: Access: Mail, in person. Both court and visitors may perform in person searches. Search fee: $10.00 per name. Required to search: name, years to search; also helpful: address. Civil cases indexed by defendant, plaintiff. Civil records on computer since January 1994, index books since 1895.

Criminal Records: Access: Mail, in person. Both court and visitors may perform in person searches. Search fee: $10.00 per name. Required to search: name, years to search; also helpful: address, DOB, SSN. Criminal records on computer since January 1994, index books since 1895.

General Information: No juvenile, mental, sealed, or adoption records released. SASE required. Turnaround time 1 week to 10 days. Copy fee: $1.00 per page. Certification fee: $5.00. Fee payee: County Clerk. Business checks accepted. Prepayment is required.

Tom Green County

District Court County Courthouse, 112 W Beauregard, San Angelo, TX 76903; 915-659-6579; Fax: 915-659-3241. 8AM-5PM (CST). *Felony, Civil.*

http://justice.co.tom-green.tx.us

Civil Records: Access: Mail, in person, online. Both court and visitors may perform in person searches. Search fee: $5.00 per name. Required to search: name, years to search; also helpful. Civil cases indexed by defendant, plaintiff. Civil records in index books from 1900s; on computer back to 1993. Online access to civil case records back to 1994 is available online at the web site. Search by name, case number, DOB.

Criminal Records: Access: Mail, in person, online. Both court and visitors may perform in person searches. Search fee: $5.00 per name. Required to search: name, years to search, DOB. Criminal records in index books from 1900s; on computer back to 1993. Online access to criminal records is the same as civil.

General Information: Public access terminal is available. No juvenile, mental, sealed, or adoption records released. SASE required. Turnaround time 1 week. Fax notes: Fee to fax results is $1.00 per page. Copy fee: $1.00 per page. Fee payee: District Clerk. Personal checks accepted. Prepayment is required.

County Court 124 W Beauregard, San Angelo, TX 76903; 915-659-6555. Hours: 8AM-4:30PM (CST). *Misdemeanor, Civil, Probate.*

http://justice.co.tom-green.tx.us

Civil Records: Access: Mail, in person, online. Both court and visitors may perform in person searches. Search fee: $5.00 per name. Required to search: name, years to search; also helpful: address. Civil cases indexed by defendant, plaintiff. Civil records on computer since 1994, index books prior. Online access to civil records back to 1994 is available free at the web site.

Criminal Records: Access: Mail, in person, online. Both court and visitors may perform in person searches. Search fee: $5.00 per name. Required to search: name, years to search, DOB; also helpful: address, SSN. Criminal records on computer since 1994, index books prior. Online access to criminal records is the same as civil. Web site also includes Sheriff jail and bond records.

General Information: Public access terminal is available. No juvenile, mental, sealed, or adoption records released. SASE required. Turnaround time same day. Copy fee: $1.00 per page. Certification fee: $5.00. Fee payee: County Clerk. Prepayment is required.

Travis County

District Court PO Box 1748, Austin, TX 78767; Civil phone: 512-854-9457; Criminal phone: 512-854-9420; Fax: 512-854-9549 Civil; 512-854-4566 Crim. Hours: 8AM-5PM (CST). *Felony, Civil.*

Civil Records: Access: Phone, mail, in person. Both court and visitors may perform in person searches. Search fee: $5.00 per name. Add $2.00 per year prior to 1988. Required to search: name, years to search. Civil cases indexed by defendant, plaintiff. Civil records on computer since 1986, microfiche and index books.

Criminal Records: Access: Phone, mail, in person. Both court and visitors may perform in person searches. Search fee: $5.00 per name. Add $2.00 per year prior to 1988. Required to search: name, years to search, DOB. Criminal records on computer since 1988, index books prior to 1988.

General Information: Public access terminal is available. No juvenile, mental, sealed, or adoption records released (all felony cases are public record). SASE required. Turnaround 2-3 days, normally. Copy fee: $.50 per page. Fee payee: District Clerk. Personal checks accepted. Credit cards accepted: Visa, MasterCard, Discover. Prepayment is required.

County Court PO Box 1748, Austin, TX 78767-1748; Civil phone: 512-854-9090; Criminal phone: 512-854-9440; Probate phone: 512-854-9595; Fax: 512-854-4220. Hours: 8AM-5PM (CST). *Misdemeanor, Civil, Probate.*

www.co.travis.tx.us

Note: Records include appeals from the Travis County JP Courts.

Civil Records: Access: Phone, mail, in person. Both court and visitors may perform in person searches. Search fee: $5.00 per name. Fee applies to cases opened prior to June 1986. Required to search: name, years to search. Civil cases indexed by defendant, plaintiff. Civil records on computer since 06/86, microfilm prior to 1845, probate from 1992 forward.

Criminal Records: Access: Phone, mail, in person. Both court and visitors may perform in person searches. Search fee: $5.00 per name. $10.00 per name for microfilm. Required to search: name, years to search; also helpful: address, DOB, SSN. Criminal misdemeanor records on computer since 1981; prior records on microfilm to 1845.

General Information: Public access terminal is available. No juvenile, mental, sealed, or adoption records released. SASE not required. Turnaround time 2-5 days. Copy fee: $1.00 per page. Certification fee: $5.00 per document. Fee payee: Travis County Clerk. Personal checks accepted. Prepayment is required.

Trinity County

District Court PO Box 548, Groveton, TX 75845; 936-642-1118. Hours: 8AM-5PM (CST). *Felony, Civil.*

Civil Records: Access: In person, mail. Both court and visitors may perform in person searches. Search fee: $5.00 per name. Required to search: name, years to search. Civil cases indexed by defendant, plaintiff. Civil records on computer since 1980, index books prior.

Criminal Records: Access: In person, mail. Both court and visitors may perform in person searches. Search fee: $5.00 per name. Required to search: name, years to search. Criminal records on computer since 1980, index books prior.

General Information: No juvenile, mental, sealed, or adoption records released. Fax notes: Do not fax. Copy fee: $1.00 per page. Certification fee: $1.00 per page. Fee payee: District Clerk. Personal checks accepted. Prepayment is required.

County Court PO Box 456, Groveton, TX 75845; 936-642-1208; Fax: 936-642-3004. Hours: 8AM-5PM (CST). *Misdemeanor, Civil, Probate.*

Civil Records: Access: Mail, in person. Both court and visitors may perform in person searches. Search fee: $10.00 per name. Required to search: name, years to search; also helpful: address. Civil cases indexed by defendant, plaintiff. Civil records in index books back to 1982. Date of birth required for searching.

Criminal Records: Access: Mail, in person. Both court and visitors may perform in person searches. Search fee: $10.00 per name. Required to search: name, years to search, SSN; also helpful: address, DOB, sex. Computerized records back to 1980; criminal records in index books back to 1982. Date of birth required for searching.

General Information: No juvenile, mental, sealed, or adoption records released. SASE required. Turnaround time 1-2 days. Fax notes: Fee to fax results is $1.00 per page. Copy fee: $1.00 per page. Certification fee: $5.00. Fee payee: County Clerk. Personal checks accepted. Prepayment is required.

Tyler County

District Court 203 Courthouse, 100 W Bluff, Woodville, TX 75979; 409-283-2162. Hours: 8AM-Noon, 1-4:30PM (CST). *Felony, Civil.*

Civil Records: Access: Mail, in person. Both court and visitors may perform in person searches. Search fee: $5.00 per name. Required to search: name, years to search. Civil cases indexed by defendant, plaintiff. Civil records in index books.

Criminal Records: Access: Mail, in person. Both court and visitors may perform in person searches. Search fee: $5.00. Required to search: name, years to search. Criminal records in index books.

General Information: No juvenile, mental, sealed, or adoption records released. SASE required. Turnaround time same day. Copy fee: $1.00 per page. Fee payee: District Clerk. Business checks accepted. Prepayment is required.

County Court County Courthouse, Rm 110, 100 W Bluff, Woodville, TX 75979; 409-283-2281; Fax: 409-283-6305. Hours: 8AM-4:30PM (CST). *Misdemeanor, Civil, Probate.*

Civil Records: Access: Phone, mail, in person. Both court and visitors may perform in person searches. Search fee: $5.00 per name. Required to search: name, years to search. Civil cases indexed by defendant, plaintiff. Civil records on computer back to 1989, microfilm since 1973, index books from 1800s.

Criminal Records: Access: Mail, in person. Both court and visitors may perform in person searches. Search fee: $5.00 per name. Required to search: name, years to search; also helpful: address, DOB, SSN. Criminal records on computer back to 1989, microfilm since 1973, index books from 1800s.

General Information: Public access terminal is available. No juvenile, mental, sealed or adoption records released. SASE not required. Turnaround time 1-2 days. Copy fee: $1.00 per page. Certification fee: $5.00. Fee payee: County Clerk. Personal checks accepted. Prepayment is required.

Upshur County

District Court PO Box 950, Gilmer, TX 75644; 903-843-5031; Fax: 903-843-3540. Hours: 8AM-5PM (CST). *Felony, Misdemeanor, Civil, Probate.*

Civil Records: Access: Mail, in person. Both court and visitors may perform in person searches. Search fee: $5.00 per name. Required to search: name, years to search. Civil cases indexed by defendant, plaintiff. Civil records in index books to 1800s.

Criminal Records: Access: Mail, in person. Both court and visitors may perform in person searches, but in

county court, only the court may search. Search fee: $5.00 per name. Required to search: name, years to search. Criminal records in index books to 1800s.

General Information: No juvenile, mental, sealed or adoption records released. SASE required. Turnaround time same day. Copy fee: $1.00 per page. Certification fee: $1.00 per document. Fee payee: County Clerk. No checks accepted. Prepayment is required.

County Court PO Box 730, Gilmer, TX 75644; 903-843-4015. Hours: 8AM-5PM (CST). *Misdemeanor, Civil, Probate.*

Civil Records: Access: Mail, in person. Both court and visitors may perform in person searches. Search fee: $10.00 per name. Fee is per 5 year period. Required to search: name, years to search. Civil cases indexed by defendant, plaintiff. Civil records in index books to 1936; on computer back to 1997.

Criminal Records: Access: Mail, in person. Both court and visitors may perform in person searches, but in county court, only the court may search. Search fee: $10.00 per name. Fee is per 5 year period. Required to search: name, years to search, DOB, offense, signed release. Criminal records in index books to 1936; on computer back to 1997.

General Information: Public access terminal is available. No juvenile, mental, sealed or adoption records released. SASE required. Turnaround time same day. Copy fee: $1.00 per page. Certification fee: $5.00. Fee payee: County Clerk. Personal checks accepted. Prepayment is required.

Upton County

District & County Court PO Box 465, Rankin, TX 79778; 915-693-2861; Fax: 915-693-2129. Hours: 8AM-5PM *Felony, Misdemeanor, Civil, Probate.*

Civil Records: Access: Fax, mail, in person. Both court and visitors may perform in person searches. Search fee: $5.00 per name. Required to search: name, years to search. Civil cases indexed by defendant, plaintiff. Civil records on computer back to 1987; in index books to 1910.

Criminal Records: Access: Fax, mail, in person. Both court and visitors may perform in person searches. Search fee: $5.00 per name. Required to search: name, years to search, signed release; also helpful: address, DOB. Criminal records on computer back to 1987; in index books to 1910.

General Information: No juvenile, mental, sealed, or adoption records released. SASE required. Turnaround time 1-2 days. Fax notes: Fee to fax results is $2.00 per page. Copy fee: $1.00 per page. Certification fee: $5.00. Fee payee: District/County Clerk. Personal checks accepted. Prepayment is required.

Uvalde County

District Court County Courthouse ##15, Uvalde, TX 78801; 830-278-3918. Hours: 8AM-5PM (CST). *Felony, Civil.*

Civil Records: Access: Phone, mail, in person. Both court and visitors may perform in person searches. Search fee: $5.00 per name. Required to search: name, years to search. Civil cases indexed by defendant, plaintiff. Civil records in index books. Phone access available to those with an account.

Criminal Records: Access: Phone, mail, in person. Both court and visitors may perform in person searches. Search fee: $5.00 per name. Required to search: name, years to search, DOB, SSN. Criminal records in index books.

General Information: No juvenile, mental, sealed, or adoption records released. SASE required. Turnaround time 2-3 days. Copy fee: $.75 per page. Certification fee: $1.00 per page. Fee payee: District Clerk. Personal checks accepted. Prepayment is required.

County Clerk PO Box 284, Uvalde, TX 78802; 830-278-6614. Hours: 8AM-5PM (CST). *Misdemeanor, Civil, Probate.*

Civil Records: Access: Mail, in person. Both court and visitors may perform in person searches. Search fee: $10.00 per name. The fee covers a 10 year search. Required to search: name, years to search. Civil cases indexed by defendant, plaintiff. Civil records in index books from 1856, computerized records from 1997.

Criminal Records: Access: Mail, in person. Both court and visitors may perform in person searches. Search fee: $10.00 per name. The fee covers a 10 year search. Required to search: name, years to search, DOB, SSN. Criminal records in index books from 1856, computerized records from 1997.

General Information: Public access terminal is available. No juvenile, mental, sealed, or adoption records released. SASE not required. Turnaround time 1-2 days. Copy fee: $1.00 per page. Certification fee: $5.00. Fee payee: Lucille C Hutcherson, Uvalde County Clerk. Personal checks accepted. Prepayment required.

Val Verde County

District Court PO Box 1544, Del Rio, TX 78841; 830-774-7538. Hours: 8AM-4:30PM (CST). *Felony, Civil.*

Civil Records: Access: Mail, in person. Both court and visitors may perform in person searches. Search fee: $5.00 per name. Required to search: name, years to search. Civil cases indexed by defendant, plaintiff. Civil records on computer since 1990, index books prior.

Criminal Records: Access: Mail, in person. Both court and visitors may perform in person searches. Search fee: $5.00 per name. Required to search: name, years to search. Criminal records on computer since 1990, index books prior.

General Information: Public access terminal is available. No juvenile, mental, sealed, or adoption records released. SASE required. Turnaround time 2-5 days. Copy fee: $.50 per page. Certification fee: $1.00 per page. Fee payee: District Clerk. Business checks accepted. Local checks accepted. Prepayment is required.

County Court PO Box 1267, Del Rio, TX 78841-1267; 830-774-7564. Hours: 8AM-4:30PM (CST). *Misdemeanor, Civil, Probate.*

Civil Records: Access: Mail, in person. Both court and visitors may perform in person searches. Search fee: $5.00 per name. Civil cases indexed by defendant, plaintiff. Civil records in index books back to 1885.

Criminal Records: Access: Mail, in person. Both court and visitors may perform in person searches. Search fee: $5.00 per name. Required to search: name, years to search; also helpful: address, DOB, SSN. Criminal records in index books.

General Information: No juvenile, mental, sealed, or adoption records released. SASE required. Turnaround time 1-2 days. Copy fee: $1.00 per page. Certification fee: $5.00. Fee payee: County Clerk. Personal checks accepted. Prepayment is required.

Van Zandt County

District Court 121 E Dallas St Rm 302, Canton, TX 75103; 903-567-6576; Fax: 903-567-4700. Hours: 8AM-5PM (CST). *Felony, Civil.*

Civil Records: Access: Phone, fax, mail, in person. Both court and visitors may perform in person searches. Search fee: $5.00 per name. Required to search: name, years to search. Civil cases indexed by defendant, plaintiff. Civil records in index books back to 1800's; on computer back to 1980.

Criminal Records: Access: Mail, fax, in person. Both court and visitors may perform in person searches. Search fee: $5.00 per name. Required to search: name, years to search, DOB, SSN. Criminal records in index books back to 1800's; on computer back to 1980.

General Information: No juvenile, mental, sealed, or adoption records released. SASE required. Turnaround time 2-4 days. Copy fee: $1.00 per page. Fee payee: District Clerk. Personal checks accepted. Prepayment is required.

County Court 121 E Dallas St #202, Canton, TX 75103; 903-567-6503; Fax: 903-567-6722. Hours: 8AM-5PM (CST). *Misdemeanor, Civil, Probate.*

Civil Records: Access: Mail, in person. Both court and visitors may perform in person searches. Search fee: $5.00 per name. Required to search: name, years to search. Civil cases indexed by defendant, plaintiff. Civil records in index books to 1850s; on computer back to 1987.

Criminal Records: Access: Mail, in person. Both court and visitors may perform in person searches. Search fee: $5.00 per name. Required to search: name, years to search; also helpful: address, DOB, SSN. Criminal records in index books back to 1850s; on computer back to 1987.

General Information: Public access terminal is available. No juvenile, mental, sealed, or adoption records released. SASE required. Turnaround time 2-4 days. Fax notes: Fee to fax is $5.00 per doc, plus $1 per page. Copy fee: $1.00 per page. Certification fee: $5.00. Fee payee: County Clerk. Personal checks accepted. Prepayment is required.

Victoria County

District Court PO Box 2238, Victoria, TX 77902; 361-575-0581; Fax: 361-572-5682. Hours: 8AM-5PM (CST). *Felony, Civil.*

Civil Records: Access: Fax, mail, in person. Both court and visitors may perform in person searches. Search fee: $5.00 per name. Required to search: name, years to search. Civil cases indexed by defendant, plaintiff. Civil records on computer since 1989, index books since 1838.

Criminal Records: Access: Fax, mail, in person. Both court and visitors may perform in person searches. Search fee: $5.00 per name. Required to search: name, years to search, DOB. Criminal records on computer since 1989, index books since 1838s.

General Information: No juvenile, mental, sealed, or adoption records released. SASE required. Turnaround time 1-2 days. Fax notes: No fee for local fax; Long distance fax fee $5.00 plus $1.00 per pg. Copy fee: $1.00 per page. Certification fee: $1.00. Fee payee: District Clerk. Personal checks accepted. Prepayment is required.

County Court 115 N Bridge, Rm 103, Victoria, TX 77901; 361-575-1478; Fax: 361-575-6276. Hours: 8AM-5PM (CST). *Misdemeanor, Civil, Probate.*

Civil Records: Access: Phone, mail, in person. Both court and visitors may perform in person searches. Search fee: $10.00 per name. Required to search: name, years to search. Civil cases indexed by defendant, plaintiff. Civil records on Cox index back to 1836; on comptuer back to 1991.

Criminal Records: Access: Phone, fax, mail, in person. Both court and visitors may perform in person searches. Search fee: $5.00 per name. Required to search: name, years to search; also helpful: address, DOB, SSN. Criminal records on Cox index back to 1836; on computer back to 1989.

General Information: Public access terminal is available. No juvenile, mental, sealed, birth, death or adoption records released. SASE required. Turnaround time 1 day. Fax notes: $3.50 per doc (plus copy fee) or $3.50 plus $1.50 per page (plus copy fee) to non toll-free. Copy fee: $1.00 per page. Certification fee: $5.00. Fee payee: Victoria County Clerk. Personal checks accepted. Prepayment is required.

Walker County

District Court 1100 University Ave Rm 301, Huntsville, TX 77340; 936-436-4972. Hours: 8AM-Noon, 1-4:30PM (CST). *Felony, Civil.*

Civil Records: Access: Mail, in person. Both court and visitors may perform in person searches. Search fee: $5.00 per name. Required to search: name, years to search. Civil cases indexed by defendant, plaintiff. Civil records on index books.

Criminal Records: Access: Mail, in person. Both court and visitors may perform in person searches. Search fee: $5.00 per name. Required to search: name, years to search. Criminal records on index books.

General Information: No juvenile, mental, sealed, abortion or adoption records released. SASE required. Turnaround time 1-2 days. Copy fee: $1.00 per page. Fee payee: District Clerk. Business checks accepted. Prepayment is required.

County Court PO Box 210, Huntsville, TX 77342-0210; 936-436-4922; Fax: 936-436-4928. Hours: 8AM-4:45PM (CST). *Misdemeanor, Civil, Probate.*

Civil Records: Access: Mail, in person. Both court and visitors may perform in person searches. Search fee: $5.00 per name. Required to search: name, years to search. Civil cases indexed by defendant, plaintiff. Civil records in index books.

Criminal Records: Access: Mail, in person. Both court and visitors may perform in person searches. Search fee: $5.00 per name. Required to search: name, years to search; also helpful: address, DOB, SSN. Criminal records in index books.

General Information: No juvenile, mental, sealed, or adoption records released. SASE required. Turnaround time 2-3 days. Copy fee: $1.00 per page. Certification fee: $5.00. Fee payee: County Clerk. Personal checks accepted. Prepayment is required.

Waller County

District Court 836 Austin St Rm 318, Hempstead, TX 77445; 979-826-7735. Hours: 8AM-Noon, 1-5PM (CST). *Felony, Civil.*

Civil Records: Access: Mail, in person. Both court and visitors may perform in person searches. Search fee: $5.00 per name. Required to search: name, years to search, DOB, SSN. Civil cases indexed by defendant, plaintiff. Civil records on index books to 1866, computerized in 2002.

Criminal Records: Access: Mail, in person. Both court and visitors may perform in person searches. Search fee: $5.00 per name. Required to search: name, years to search, DOB, SSN. Criminal records on computer since 9/99, archived to early 1900s.

General Information: Public access terminal is available. (Terminal is for civil only.) No juvenile, mental, sealed, or adoption records released. SASE required. Turnaround time 2 days. Copy fee: $1.00 per page. Certification fee: $1.00. Fee payee: District Clerk. Personal checks accepted. Prepayment is required.

County Court 836 Austin St, Rm 217, Hempstead, TX 77445; 936-826-3357. Hours: 8AM-Noon, 1-5PM (CST). *Misdemeanor, Civil, Probate.*

Civil Records: Access: Mail, in person. Both court and visitors may perform in person searches. Search fee: $5.00 per name. Required to search: name, years to search. Civil cases indexed by defendant, plaintiff. Civil records in index books; on computer back to 1994.

Criminal Records: Access: Mail, in person. Both court and visitors may perform in person searches. Search fee: $5.00 per name. Required to search: name, years to search, signed release; also helpful: DOB, SSN. Criminal records in index books; on computer back to 1994.

General Information: No juvenile, mental, sealed, or adoption records released. SASE required. Turnaround

time 2-3 days. Copy fee: $1.00 per page. Certification fee: $5.00. Fee payee: Waller County Clerk. No personal checks accepted for copies. Prepayment is required.

Ward County

District Court PO Box 440, Monahans, TX 79756; 915-943-2751; Fax: 915-943-3810. Hours: 8AM-5PM (CST). *Felony, Civil.*

Civil Records: Access: Mail, fax, in person. Both court and visitors may perform in person searches. Search fee: $5.00 per name. Required to search: name, years to search. Civil cases indexed by defendant, plaintiff. Civil records on computer since 1980, index books prior.

Criminal Records: Access: Mail, fax, in person. Both court and visitors may perform in person searches. Search fee: $5.00 per name. Required to search: name, years to search, signed release, also DOB or SSN. Criminal records on books, computerized since 1980.

General Information: No juvenile, mental, sealed, or adoption records released. SASE required. Turnaround time 1-2 days. Copy fee: $.50 per page. Certification fee: $1.00 per page. Fee payee: District Clerk. Business checks accepted. Prepayment is required.

County Court County Courthouse, Monahans, TX 79756; 915-943-3294; Fax: 915-943-6054. Hours: 8AM-5PM (CST). *Misdemeanor, Civil, Probate.*

Civil Records: Access: Mail, in person. Both court and visitors may perform in person searches. Search fee: $5.00 per name. Required to search: name, years to search. Civil cases indexed by defendant, plaintiff. Civil records in index books; computerized records go back 10 years. In person requests must be accompanied by written request.

Criminal Records: Access: Mail, in person. Both court and visitors may perform in person searches. Search fee: $5.00 per name. Required to search: name, years to search, DOB, signed release; also helpful: address, SSN. Criminal records in index books; computerized records go back 10 years. In person requests must be accompanied by a written request.

General Information: No juvenile, mental, sealed, or adoption records released. SASE required. Turnaround time 1-2 days. Fax notes: Fee to fax results is $3.00 per page. Copy fee: $1.00 per page. Certification fee: $5.00 plus $1.00 per page. Fee payee: County Clerk. Personal checks accepted. Prepayment is required.

Washington County

District Court 100 E Main #304, Brenham, TX 77833-3753; 979-277-6200. Hours: 8AM-5PM (CST). *Felony, Civil.*

Civil Records: Access: Mail, in person. Both court and visitors may perform in person searches. Search fee: $5.00 per name. Required to search: name, years to search. Civil cases indexed by defendant, plaintiff. Civil records in index books since 1800s; on computer back to 1988.

Criminal Records: Access: Mail, in person. Both court and visitors may perform in person searches. Search fee: $5.00 per name. Required to search: name, years to search; also helpful: DOB. Criminal records in index books since 1800s; on computer back to 1988.

General Information: Public access terminal is available. No juvenile, mental, sealed, or adoption records released. SASE not required. Turnaround time 1-2 days. Copy fee: $.50 per page. Certification fee: $1.00 per page. Fee payee: District Clerk. Personal checks accepted. Prepayment is required.

County Court 100 E Main #102, Brenham, TX 77833; 979-277-6200; Fax: 979-277-6278. Hours: 8AM-5PM (CST). *Misdemeanor, Civil, Probate.*

Civil Records: Access: Mail, in person. Both court and visitors may perform in person searches. Search fee: $5.00 per name. Required to search: name, years to

search. Civil cases indexed by defendant, plaintiff. Civil records in index books from 1868; computerized back to 1985. In person request must be accompanied by a written request.

Criminal Records: Access: Mail, in person. Both court and visitors may perform in person searches. Search fee: $5.00 per name. Required to search: name, years to search; also helpful: address, DOB, SSN. Criminal records in index books from 1870; computerized back to 1992. In person requests must be accompanied by a written request.

General Information: Public access terminal is available. No juvenile, mental, sealed, or adoption records released. SASE required. Turnaround time 1-2 days. Fax notes: Fee to fax results is $1.00 per page and must be pre-paid. Copy fee: $1.00 per page. Certification fee: $5.00 per instrument. Fee payee: Washington County Clerk. Personal checks accepted. Prepayment is required.

Webb County

District Court PO Box 667, Laredo, TX 78042-0667; 956-523-4268; Fax: 956-523-5063. Hours: 8AM-5PM (CST). *Felony, Civil.*

www.webbcounty.com

Civil Records: Access: Phone, mail, fax, in person, online. Both court and visitors may perform in person searches. Search fee: $5.00 per name. Required to search: name, years to search, address; also helpful: DOB, SSN. Civil cases indexed by defendant, plaintiff. Civil records on computer back to 11/1988, index books prior. Online access is through www.idocket.com; registration and password required. Records go back to 12/31/1988.

Criminal Records: Access: Mail, fax, in person, online. Both court and visitors may perform in person searches. Search fee: $5.00 per name. Required to search: name, years to search, DOB or SSN, signed release. Criminal records on computer back to 11/1988, index books prior. Online access is through www.idocket.com; registration and password required. Records go back to 12/31/1988.

General Information: Public access terminal is available. No juvenile, mental, sealed, or adoption records released. SASE required. Turnaround time 1 week. Copy fee: $1.00 per page. Certification fee: $1.00. Fee is per page of document. Fee payee: District Clerk. Personal checks accepted. Prepayment required.

County Court 1110 Victoria #201, Laredo, TX 78040; 956-721-2640; Civil phone: 956-721-2653; Criminal phone: 956-721-2651; Probate phone: 956-721-2656; Fax: 956-721-2288. Hours: 8AM-5PM (CST). *Misdemeanor, Civil Under $5,000, Probate.*

Civil Records: Access: Mail, in person, online. Both court and visitors may perform in person searches. Search fee: $5.00 per name. Required to search: name, years to search. Civil cases indexed by defendant, plaintiff. Civil records on computer since 1988, index books prior. Online access is through www.idocket.com; registration and password required. Records go back to 12/31/1989. Includes probate.

Criminal Records: Access: Mail, in person, online. Both court and visitors may perform in person searches. Search fee: $5.00 per name. Required to search: name, years to search, DOB; also helpful: address, SSN. Criminal records on computer since 1988, index books prior. Online access is through www.idocket.com; registration and password required. Records go back to 12/31/1989.

General Information: Public access terminal is available. No juvenile, mental, sealed, or adoption records released. SASE required. Turnaround time 2-3 days. Copy fee: $1.00 per page. Certification fee: $5.00. Fee payee: County Clerk. Personal checks accepted. Prepayment is required.

Wharton County

District Court PO Drawer 391, Wharton, TX 77488; 979-532-5542; Fax: 979-532-1299. Hours: 8AM-5PM (CST). *Felony, Civil.*

Civil Records: Access: Mail, fax, in person. Both court and visitors may perform in person searches. Search fee: $5.00 per name. Required to search: name, years to search. Civil cases indexed by defendant, plaintiff. Civil records on computer since 1989, index books prior to 1848.

Criminal Records: Access: Mail, fax, in person. Both court and visitors may perform in person searches. Search fee: $5.00 per name. Required to search: name, years to search. Criminal records on computer since 1989, index books prior to 1932.

General Information: No juvenile, mental, sealed, or adoption records released. SASE required. Turnaround time same day. Copy fee: $1.00 per page. Certification fee: $2.00. Fee payee: District Clerk of Wharton. Personal checks accepted. Prepayment is required.

County Court PO Box 69, Wharton, TX 77488; 979-532-2381. Hours: 8AM-5PM (CST). *Misdemeanor, Civil, Probate.*

Civil Records: Access: Mail, in person. Both court and visitors may perform in person searches. Search fee: $5.00 per name per 10 years searched. Required to search: name, years to search. Civil cases indexed by defendant, plaintiff. Civil records on computer since 1991, index books since 1978, prior indexes in storage.

Criminal Records: Access: Mail, in person. Both court and visitors may perform in person searches. Search fee: $5.00 per name per 10 years searched. Required to search: name, years to search, DOB, signed release; also helpful: address, SSN, copy of ID. Criminal records on computer since 1991, index books since 1978, prior indexes in storage.

General Information: Public access terminal is available. No juvenile, mental, sealed, or adoption records released. SASE required. Turnaround time 1-2 days. Fax notes: Fee to fax results is $2.00 plus $1.00 per page. Copy fee: $1.00 per page. Certification fee: $5.00. Fee payee: County Clerk. Business checks accepted. Prepayment is required.

Wheeler County

District Court PO Box 528, Wheeler, TX 79096; 806-826-5931; Fax: 806-826-5503. Hours: 8AM-5PM (CST). *Felony, Civil.*

Civil Records: Access: Phone, mail, in person. Both court and visitors may perform in person searches. Search fee: $5.00 per name. Required to search: name, years to search. Civil cases indexed by defendant, plaintiff. Civil records in index books.

Criminal Records: Access: Phone, mail, in person. Both court and visitors may perform in person searches. Search fee: $5.00 per name. Required to search: name, years to search. Criminal records in index books.

General Information: No juvenile, mental, sealed, or adoption records released. SASE not required. Turnaround time 2-3 days. Copy fee: $1.00. Fee is for first 10 pages. Add $.25 per add'l page. Certification fee: $1.00. Fee payee: District Clerk. Personal checks accepted.

County Court PO Box 465, Wheeler, TX 79096; 806-826-5544; Fax: 806-826-3282. Hours: 8AM-5PM (CST). *Misdemeanor, Civil, Probate.*

Civil Records: Access: Mail, in person. Both court and visitors may perform in person searches. Search fee: $10.00 per name. Required to search: name, years to search. Civil cases indexed by defendant, plaintiff. Civil records on computer and index books back to 1800's.

Criminal Records: Access: Mail, in person. Both court and visitors may perform in person searches. Search fee: $10.00 per name. Required to search: name, years

to search; also helpful: DOB, SSN. Criminal records on computer and index books.

General Information: No juvenile, mental, sealed, or adoption records released. Turnaround time 1 day. Fax notes: Fax back $1.00 per page. Copy fee: $1.00 per page. Certification fee: $5.00. Fee payee: County Clerk. Business checks accepted. Prepayment is required.

Wichita County

District Court PO Box 718, Wichita Falls, TX 76307; 940-766-8190. Hours: 8AM-5PM (CST). *Felony, Civil.*

Civil Records: Access: Phone, mail, in person. Both court and visitors may perform in person searches. Search fee: $5.00 per name. Required to search: name, years to search. Civil cases indexed by defendant, plaintiff. Civil records on computer since 1984, index books prior. Phone searches must be prepaid.

Criminal Records: Access: Phone, mail, in person. Both court and visitors may perform in person searches. Search fee: $5.00 per name. Required to search: name, years to search. Criminal records on computer since 1984, index books before. Phone searches must be prepaid.

General Information: No juvenile, mental, sealed, or adoption records released. SASE required. Turnaround time 2-3 days. Copy fee: $1.00 per page. Certification fee: $1.00. Fee payee: District Clerk. Personal checks accepted. Prepayment is required.

County Court PO Box 1679, Wichita Falls, TX 76307; 940-766-8173; Probate phone: 940-766-8172. Hours: 8AM-5PM (CST). *Misdemeanor, Probate.*

Criminal Records: Access: Phone, mail, in person. Both court and visitors may perform in person searches. Search fee: $10.00 per name searched. Required to search: name, years to search; also helpful: DOB, SSN. Criminal records on computer or printed index from 1980 to present.

General Information: Public access terminal is available. No juvenile, mental, sealed, or adoption records released. Mental can be released with an order from the judge. SASE required. Turnaround time within 1 week or less. Copy fee: $1.00 per page. Certification fee: $5.00 per document. Fee payee: Wichita County Clerk. No checks accepted. Prepayment is required.

Wilbarger County

District Court 1700 Wilbarger Rm 33, Vernon, TX 76384; 940-553-3411; Fax: 940-553-2316. Hours: 8AM-5PM (CST). *Felony, Civil.*

Civil Records: Access: Mail, in person. Both court and visitors may perform in person searches. Search fee: $5.00 per name. Required to search: name, years to search. Civil cases indexed by defendant, plaintiff. Civil records go back to 1800's; computerized records go back 4 years.

Criminal Records: Access: Mail, in person. Both court and visitors may perform in person searches. Search fee: $5.00 per name. Required to search: name, years to search, DOB. Criminal records go back to 1800's; computerized records go back 4 years.

General Information: No juvenile, mental, sealed, or adoption records released. Will return results by fax or phone if an 800 number is provided. SASE required. Turnaround time 2-3 days. Fax notes: Will fax results to toll-free number. Copy fee: $1.00 per page. Certification fee: $5.00. Fee payee: District Clerk. Business checks accepted. Prepayment is required.

County Court 1700 Wilbarger Rm 15, Vernon, TX 76384; 940-552-5486. Hours: 8AM-5PM (CST). *Misdemeanor, Civil, Probate.*

Civil Records: Access: Mail, in person. Both court and visitors may perform in person searches. Search fee: $10.00 per name. Required to search: name, years to

search. Civil cases indexed by defendant. Civil records go back to 1990's; no computerized records.

Criminal Records: Access: Mail, in person. Both court and visitors may perform in person searches. Search fee: $10.00 per name. Required to search: name, years to search; also helpful: address, DOB, SSN. Criminal records go back to 1900's; computerized records go back to 1999.

General Information: No juvenile, mental, sealed, or adoption records released. SASE required. Turnaround time same day. Fax notes: Fee to fax results is $1.00 per page. Copy fee: $1.00 per page. Certification fee: $5.00 plus $1.00 per page. Fee payee: County Clerk. Personal checks accepted. Prepayment is required.

Willacy County

District Court County Courthouse, Raymondville, TX 78580; 956-689-2532; Fax: 956-689-5713. Hours: 8AM-5PM (CST). *Felony, Civil.*

Civil Records: Access: Mail, in person, phone, fax. Both court and visitors may perform in person searches. Search fee: $8.00 per name. Required to search: name, years to search. Civil cases indexed by defendant, plaintiff. Civil records in index books.

Criminal Records: Access: Mail, in person. Both court and visitors may perform in person searches. Search fee: $8.00 per name. Required to search: name, years to search. Criminal records in index books.

General Information: No juvenile, mental, sealed, or adoption records released. SASE required. Turnaround time 2-3 days. Copy fee: $1.00 per page. Certification fee: $2.00 per page. Fee payee: District Clerk. Personal checks accepted. Prepayment is required.

County Court 540 W Hidalgo, Raymondville, TX 78580; 956-689-2710. Hours: 8AM-Noon, 1-5PM (CST). *Misdemeanor, Civil, Probate.*

Civil Records: Access: Mail, in person. Both court and visitors may perform in person searches. Search fee: $5.00 per name. Required to search: name, years to search; also helpful: address. Civil cases indexed by defendant, plaintiff. Civil records go back to 1920's.

Criminal Records: Access: Mail, in person. Both court and visitors may perform in person searches. Search fee: $5.00 per name. Required to search: name, years to search; also helpful: address, DOB, SSN. Criminal records go back to 1920's.

General Information: No juvenile, mental, sealed, or adoption records released. SASE required. Turnaround time 2-3 days. Fax notes: Fee to fax results is $2.00 per page. Copy fee: $1.00 per page. Certification fee: $5.00. Fee payee: County Clerk. Personal checks accepted. Prepayment is required.

Williamson County

District Court PO Box 24, Georgetown, TX 78627; 512-943-1212; Fax: 512-943-1222. Hours: 8AM-5PM (CST). *Felony, Civil.*

www.williamson-county.org

Civil Records: Access: Mail, in person. Both court and visitors may perform in person searches. Search fee: $5.00 per name. Required to search: name, years to search. Civil cases indexed by defendant, plaintiff. Civil records on computer since 1989, index books prior.

Criminal Records: Access: Mail, in person. Both court and visitors may perform in person searches. Search fee: $5.00 per name. Required to search: name, years to search, DOB, signed release; also helpful: SSN. Criminal records on computer since 1989, index books prior.

General Information: No juvenile, mental, sealed, or adoption records released. SASE required. Turnaround time 2-3 days. Copy fee: $1.00 1st pg; $.25 each add'l. Certification fee: $1.00. Fee payee: District Clerk. Personal checks accepted. Prepayment is required.

County Court 405 MLK St, Box 14, Georgetown, TX 78626; Civil phone: 512-943-1150; Criminal phone: 512-943-1150; Probate phone: 512-943-1140; Fax: 512-943-1154. Hours: 8AM-5PM (CST). *Misdemeanor, Civil, Probate.*

Civil Records: Access: Mail, in person. Both court and visitors may perform in person searches. Search fee: $10.00 per name. Required to search: name, years to search. Civil cases indexed by defendant, plaintiff. Civil records on computer since 1985, index books since 1848.GA.

Criminal Records: Access: Mail, in person. Both court and visitors may perform in person searches. Search fee: $10.00 per name. Required to search: name, years to search; also helpful: DOB, SSN. Criminal records on computer since 1983. Overall records go back to 1800.

General Information: Public access terminal is available. No juvenile, mental, sealed, or adoption records released. SASE required. Turnaround time 2 days. Fax notes: Fee to fax results is $1.00 per page. Copy fee: $1.00 per page. Certification fee: $5.00. Fee payee: County Clerk. Personal checks accepted. Prepayment is required.

Wilson County

District Court PO Box 812, Floresville, TX 78114; 830-393-7322; Fax: 830-393-7319. Hours: 8AM-Noon, 1-5PM (CST). *Felony, Civil.*

Civil Records: Access: Fax, mail, in person. Both court and visitors may perform in person searches. Search fee: $5.00 per name. Required to search: name, years to search. Civil cases indexed by defendant, plaintiff. Civil records go back to 1960.

Criminal Records: Access: Fax, mail, in person. Both court and visitors may perform in person searches. Search fee: $5.00 per name. Required to search: name, years to search; also helpful: DOB. Criminal records go back to 1975.

General Information: No juvenile, mental, sealed, or adoption records released. SASE required. Turnaround time 2 days. Fax notes: Fee to fax results is $3.00 for first page, $1.00 per page thereafter. Copy fee: $1.00 per page. Certification fee: $1.00. Fee payee: District Clerk. Personal checks accepted. Prepayment is required.

County Court PO Box 27, Floresville, TX 78114; 830-393-7308. Hours: 8AM-5PM (CST). *Misdemeanor, Civil, Probate.*

Civil Records: Access: Phone, mail, fax, in person. Both court and visitors may perform in person searches. No search fee. Required to search: name, years to search. Civil cases indexed by defendant, plaintiff. Civil records available from 1862.

Criminal Records: Access: Phone, mail, fax, in person. Both court and visitors may perform in person searches. No search fee. Required to search: name, years to search, DOB. Criminal records stored since 1917, computerized since 1992.

General Information: No juvenile, mental, sealed, or adoption records released. SASE required. Turnaround time same day. Fax notes: Do not fax. Copy fee: $1.00 per page. Certification fee: $5.00. Fee payee: Eva S Martinez, County Clerk. Personal checks accepted. Prepayment is required.

Winkler County

District Court PO Box 1065, Kermit, TX 79745; 915-586-3359. Hours: 8AM-5PM (CST). *Felony, Civil.*

Civil Records: Access: Phone, mail, in person. Both court and visitors may perform in person searches. Search fee: $5.00 per name. Required to search: name, years to search. Civil cases indexed by defendant, plaintiff. Civil records on computer since 1991 (child-support only), index books prior.

Criminal Records: Access: Mail, in person. Both court and visitors may perform in person searches. Search

fee: $5.00 per name. Required to search: name, years to search, DOB, SSN. Criminal records on computer since 1991, index books prior.

General Information: No juvenile, mental, sealed, or adoption records released. SASE required. Turnaround time 1-2 days. Copy fee: $1.00 per page. Fee payee: District Clerk. Personal checks accepted. Prepayment is required.

County Court PO Box 1007, Kermit, TX 79745; 915-586-3401. Hours: 8AM-5PM (CST). *Misdemeanor, Civil, Probate.*

Civil Records: Access: Mail, in person. Only visitors may perform in person searches. Search fee: $5.00 per name. Required to search: name, years to search. Civil cases indexed by defendant, plaintiff. All civil records in index books.

Criminal Records: Access: Mail, in person. Only visitors may perform in person searches. Search fee: $5.00 per name. Required to search: name, years to search; also helpful: address, DOB, SSN. Criminal records on computer back to 1991; prior in index books.

General Information: No juvenile, mental, sealed, or adoption records released. SASE required. Turnaround time 2-3 days. Copy fee: $1.00 per page. Certification fee: $5.00. Fee payee: County Clerk. Business checks accepted. Prepayment is required.

Wise County

District Court PO Box 308, Decatur, TX 76234; 940-627-5535; Fax: 940-627-0705. Hours: 8AM-5PM (CST). *Felony, Civil.*

Civil Records: Access: Mail, in person. Both court and visitors may perform in person searches. Search fee: $5.00 per name. Required to search: name, years to search. Civil cases indexed by defendant, plaintiff. Civil records in index books since 1895, computerized since 1999.

Criminal Records: Access: Mail, in person. Both court and visitors may perform in person searches. Search fee: $5.00 per name. Required to search: name, years to search, DOB, SSN, signed release. Criminal records in docket books to 1896, computerized since 1999.

General Information: No juvenile, mental, sealed, or adoption records released. SASE required. Turnaround time same day. Copy fee: $1.00 per page. Certification fee: $2.00. Fee payee: Wise County District Clerk. Personal checks accepted. Prepayment is required.

County Court at Law PO Box 359, Decatur, TX 76234; 940-627-3351; Fax: 940-627-2138. Hours: 8AM-5PM (CST). *Misdemeanor, Civil, Probate.*

Civil Records: Access: Mail, in person. Both court and visitors may perform in person searches. Search fee: $10.00 per name. Required to search: name, years to search. Civil cases indexed by defendant, plaintiff. Civil records in index books since sovereignty; on computer back to 1998.

Criminal Records: Access: Mail, in person. Both court and visitors may perform in person searches. Search fee: $10.00 per name. Required to search: name, years to search; also helpful: DOB, SSN. Criminal records in index books since sovereignty; on computer back to 1997.

General Information: Public access terminal is available. No mental health or sealed records released. SASE required. Turnaround time 1 day. Copy fee: $1.00 per page. Certification fee: $5.00. Fee payee: Wise County Clerk. Personal checks accepted. Prepayment is required.

Wood County

District Court PO Box 1707, Quitman, TX 75783; 903-763-2361; Fax: 903-763-1511. Hours: 8AM-Noon, 1-5PM (CST). *Felony, Civil.*

Civil Records: Access: Mail, fax, in person. Both court and visitors may perform in person searches. Search fee: $5.00 per name. Required to search: name, years to search. Civil cases indexed by defendant, plaintiff. Civil records on computer since 1990, microfilm since 1981, index books since 1890.

Criminal Records: Access: Mail, fax, in person. Both court and visitors may perform in person searches. Search fee: $5.00 per name. Required to search: name, years to search; also helpful: DOB, SSN. Criminal records on computer since 1990, microfilm since 1981, index books since 1890.

General Information: Public access terminal is available. No juvenile, mental, sealed, or adoption records released. SASE required. Turnaround time 2-3 days. Copy fee: $1.00 per page. Certification fee: $1.00. Fee payee: District Clerk. Personal checks accepted. Prepayment is required.

County Court PO Box 1796, Quitman, TX 75783; 903-763-2711; Fax: 903-763-5641. Hours: 8AM-5PM (CST). *Misdemeanor, Civil, Probate.*

Civil Records: Access: Mail, in person. Both court and visitors may perform in person searches. Search fee: $5.00 per name. Required to search: name, years to search. Civil cases indexed by defendant, plaintiff. Civil records on computer since 1980; index books since early 1900s.

Criminal Records: Access: Mail, in person. Both court and visitors may perform in person searches. Search fee: $5.00 per name. Required to search: name, years to search; also helpful DOB, SSN, signed release, DL#. Criminal records on computer back to 1986; index books from 1965, archived to 1900.

General Information: No mental or sealed records released. SASE required. Turnaround time same day. Copy fee: $1.00 per page. Certification fee: $5.00. Fee payee: Wood County Clerk. Personal checks accepted. Prepayment is required.

Yoakum County

District Court PO Box 899, Plains, TX 79355; 806-456-7453; Fax: 806-456-8767. Hours: 8AM-5PM (CST). *Felony, Civil.*

Civil Records: Access: Fax, mail, in person. Both court and visitors may perform in person searches. Search fee: $5.00 per name. Required to search: name, years to search. Civil cases indexed by defendant, plaintiff. Civil records on computer since 1980, index books since 1907.

Criminal Records: Access: Fax, mail, in person. Both court and visitors may perform in person searches. Search fee: $5.00 per name. Required to search: name, years to search, DOB; also helpful: SSN. Criminal records on computer since 1980, index books since 1930.

General Information: Public access terminal is available. No juvenile, mental, sealed, or adoption records released. SASE required. Turnaround time same day. Fax notes: $2.00 for first page, $1.00 each add'l. Copy fee: $1.00 per page. Certification fee: $1.00. Fee payee: District Clerk. Personal checks accepted. Prepayment is required.

County Court PO Box 309, Plains, TX 79355; 806-456-2721; Fax: 806-456-6175 (County Judge Office). Hours: 8AM-5PM (CST). *Misdemeanor, Civil, Probate.*

Civil Records: Access: Phone, mail, in person. Both court and visitors may perform in person searches. Search fee: $5.00 per name. Required to search: name, years to search; also helpful: address. Civil cases indexed by defendant, plaintiff. Civil records in minutes books and microfilm since 9/1986; on computer back to 1/1986.

Criminal Records: Access: Mail, in person. Only the court may perform in person searches. Search fee: $5.00 per name. Required to search: name, years to search, DOB; also helpful: address, SSN. Criminal minutes books and microfilm since 9/1986; on computer back to 1/1986.

General Information: Public access terminal is available. No juvenile or mental records released. SASE not required. Turnaround time same day. Copy fee: $1.00 per page. Certification fee: $5.00. Fee payee: County Clerk, Yoakum County. Personal checks accepted. Prepayment is required.

Young County

District Court 516 4th St Rm 201, Courthouse, Graham, TX 76450; 940-549-0029; Fax: 940-549-4874. Hours: 8:30AM-Noon, 1-5PM (CST). *Felony, Civil.*

Civil Records: Access: Phone, fax, mail, in person. Both court and visitors may perform in person searches. Search fee: $5.00 per name. Required to search: name, years to search. Civil cases indexed by defendant, plaintiff. Civil records on computer since 1988, index books prior. Search fee must be prepaid before fax access is allowed.

Criminal Records: Access: Phone, fax, mail, in person. Both court and visitors may perform in person searches. Search fee: $5.00 per name. Required to search: name, years to search; also helpful: DOB, SSN. Criminal records on computer since 1988, index books prior.

General Information: No juvenile, mental, sealed, or adoption records released. SASE required. Turnaround time 1-2 days. Fax notes: No fee to fax results. Copy fee: $1.00 for first page, $.25 each add'l. Certification fee: $1.00 per page. Fee payee: District Clerk. Personal checks accepted. Prepayment is required.

County Court 516 4th St Rm 104, Graham, TX 76450; 940-549-8432; Fax: 940-521-0305. Hours: 8:30AM-Noon, 1-5PM (CST). *Misdemeanor, Civil, Probate.*

Civil Records: Access: Mail, in person. Both court and visitors may perform in person searches. Search fee: $10.00 per name. Required to search: name, years to search. Civil cases indexed by defendant, plaintiff. Civil records on computer since 1991, index books prior to 1800's.

Criminal Records: Access: Mail, in person. Both court and visitors may perform in person searches. Search fee: $5.00 per name. Required to search: name, years to search. Criminal records on computer since 1991, index books prior to 1800's.

General Information: Public access terminal is available. No juvenile, mental, sealed, or adoption records released. SASE not required. Turnaround time upon receipt. Fax notes: Fee to fax results is $1.00 per page. Copy fee: $1.00 per page. Certification fee: $5.00. Fee payee: Shirley Choate, County Clerk. Personal checks accepted. Prepayment is required.

Zapata County

District Court PO Box 788, Clerk's Office, Zapata, TX 78076; 956-765-9930; Fax: 956-765-9931. Hours: 8AM-Noon, 1-5PM (CST). *Felony, Civil.*

Civil Records: Access: Fax, mail, in person. Both court and visitors may perform in person searches. Search fee: $5.00 per name. Required to search: name, years to search. Civil cases indexed by plaintiff. Civil records in index books.

Criminal Records: Access: Fax, mail, in person. Both court and visitors may perform in person searches.

Search fee: $5.00 per name. Required to search: name, years to search. Criminal records in index books.

General Information: No juvenile, mental, sealed, or adoption records released. SASE required. Turnaround time 1-3 days. Fax notes: $1.00 for first page, $1.00 each add'l. Copy fee: $1.00 per page. Certification fee: $5.00. Fee payee: District Clerk/County Clerk. Personal checks accepted. Prepayment is required.

County Court PO Box 789, Zapata, TX 78076; 956-765-9915; Fax: 956-765-9933. Hours: 8AM-Noon, 1-5PM (CST). *Misdemeanor, Civil, Probate.*

Civil Records: Access: Mail, in person. Both court and visitors may perform in person searches. Search fee: $5.00 per name. Required to search: name, years to search. Civil cases indexed by defendant, plaintiff. Civil records in index books since 1800's, computerized records back to 1980.

Criminal Records: Access: Mail, in person. Both court and visitors may perform in person searches. Search fee: $5.00 per name. Required to search: name, years to search, DOB, SSN. Criminal records in index books since 1800's, computerized records back to 1930.

General Information: No juvenile, mental, sealed, or adoption records released. SASE not required. Turnaround time 1-2 days. Fax notes: Fee to fax results is $4.00 for 1st page, $1.00 each add'l. Copy fee: $1.00 per page. Certification fee: $5.00. Fee payee: Consuelo R Villarreal, County Clerk. Personal checks accepted. Prepayment is required.

Zavala County

District Court PO Box 704, Crystal City, TX 78839; 830-374-3456. Hours: 8AM-Noon, 1-5PM (CST). *Felony, Civil.*

Civil Records: Access: Phone, mail, in person. Both court and visitors may perform in person searches. Search fee: $5.00 per name. Required to search: name, years to search. Civil cases indexed by defendant, plaintiff. Civil records in index books from 1900s.

Criminal Records: Access: Phone, mail, in person. Both court and visitors may perform in person searches. Search fee: $5.00 per name. Required to search: name, years to search. Criminal records in index books from 1900s.

General Information: No juvenile, mental, sealed, or adoption records released. SASE required. Turnaround time 1-2 days. Copy fee: $1.00 per page. Fee payee: Zavala County District Clerk. Personal checks accepted.

County Court Zavala County Courthouse, 200 E Uvalde, Crystal City, TX 78839; 830-374-2331; Fax: 830-374-5955. Hours: 8AM-5PM (CST). *Misdemeanor, Civil, Probate.*

Civil Records: Access: Mail, in person. Both court and visitors may perform in person searches. Search fee: $10.00 per name. Required to search: name, years to search. Civil cases indexed by defendant, plaintiff. Civil records in index books from 1880s.

Criminal Records: Access: Mail, in person. Both court and visitors may perform in person searches. Search fee: $10.00 per name. Required to search: name, years to search, DOB. Criminal records in index books from 1880s.

General Information: No juvenile, mental, sealed, or adoption records released. SASE required. Turnaround time 1-2 days. Copy fee: $1.00 per page. Certification fee: $1.00. Fee payee: Zavala County Clerk. Personal checks accepted. Prepayment is required.

Texas Recording Offices

ORGANIZATION: 254 counties, 254 recording offices. The recording officer is County Clerk. 252 counties are in the Central Time Zone (CST) and 2 are in the Mountain Time Zone (MST).

REAL ESTATE RECORDS: Some counties will perform real estate searches. Copy fees are usually $1.00 per page. Certification usually costs $5.00 per document. Each county has an "Appraisal District" which is responsible for collecting taxes.

UCC RECORDS: Financing statements are filed at the state level, except for real estate related collateral, which are filed with the County Clerk. Most all recording offices will perform UCC searches. Searches fees are usually $10.00 per debtor name using the approved UCC-11 request form, plus $15.00 for using a non-Texas form. Copy fees are usually $1.00-2.00 per page with a minimum copy fee of $5.00.

TAX LIEN RECORDS: Federal tax liens on personal property of businesses are filed with the Secretary of State. Other federal and all state tax liens are filed with the County Clerk. All counties will perform tax lien searches. Search fees and copy fees can vary, but records are usually provided as part of the UCC search.

OTHER LIENS: Mechanics, judgment, hospital, labor, lis pendens.

ONLINE ACCESS: Numerous counties offer online access to assessor and recordered document data. There are two private companies that offer access via the web to multiple counties' tax assessor data. Visit www.txcountydata.com or www.taxnetusa.com. Some counties can be accessed from either site.

www.txcountydata.com - Assessor and property information records for over fifty Texas counties on the TXCOUNTYDATA site are available for no fee. At this site click on "County Search" then use the pull down menu in the county field to select the county to search. The County Info page for each county lists the Appraiser, mailing address, phone, fax, web site, e-mail. Generally, you can search any county account, owner name, address, or property ID number. Search allows you to access owner address, property address, legal description, taxing entities, exemptions, deed, account number, abstract/subdivision, neighborhood, valuation info, and more.

www.taxnetusa.com - TaxNetUSA offers free appraisal district and property information records for a growing number of Texas counties as well as a few counties in other states. The site also offers advanced and subscriptions services for many of the counties.

At the TaxNetUSA site, user chooses "advanced search subscribers login" (fee service) or "Appraisal Districts Online Basic Search" (no fee). For a basic search, use the pull down menu in the county field to select the county to search. Select county and click go. At the county Assessor/Tax site, follow the directions for that county. Generally, but in varying degrees from county to county, the basic search allows you to access general property information: name, address, valuation, etc., and you may search by parcel number, owner name, or address. Depending on the county, more "detailed" information may be available.

TaxNetUSA's Advanced Search Information (fee) allows most counties to be searched by any combination of criteria. Fees vary and can range from a simple $25 search to multiple county subscriptions as high as $1,500.

Anderson County

County Clerk, 500 N. Church St, Palestine, TX 75801. 903-723-7432 R/E Recording: 903-723-7484 UCC Recording: 903-723-7484; Fax 903-723-7801.
Will search UCC records prior to 7/2001 and current fixture (land) files. This agency will not do a tax lien search. Will not search real estate records. **Online Access:** Assessor, Property Tax Records. See note at beginning of section. **Other Phone Numbers:** Assessor 903-723-7433; Treasurer 903-723-7408; Appraiser/Auditor 903-723-2949; Elections 903-723-7438; Vital Records 903-723-7430.

Andrews County

County Clerk, PO Box 727, Andrews, TX 79714. County Clerk, R/E and UCC Recording 915-524-1426; Fax 915-524-1473.
Will search UCC records prior to 7/2001 and current fixture (land) files. Will not search real estate records. **Other Phone Numbers:** Assessor 915-524-1409; Appraiser/Auditor 915-523-9111; Elections 915-524-1426; Vital Records 915-524-1426.

Angelina County

County Clerk, PO Box 908, Lufkin, TX 75902-0908. 936-634-8339; Fax 936-634-8460.
Will search UCC records prior to 7/2001 and current fixture (land) files. Tax liens not included in UCC search. Will not search real estate records. **Online Access:** Assessor, Property Tax Records. See note at beginning of section. **Other Phones:** Assessor 936-634-8456; Appraiser/Auditor 936-634-8456.

Aransas County

County Clerk, 301 N. Live Oak, Rockport, TX 78382. County Clerk, R/E and UCC Recording 361-790-0122.
Will search UCC records prior to 7/2001 and current fixture (land) files. Tax liens not included in UCC search. Will not search real estate records. **Online Access:** Recording, Birth, Death, Assessor, Property Tax Records. Access to recordings, land records, births, deaths is available free at http://apolloplus.com then click on member counties to access Washington Co. Also, assessor and property tax information is available at www.aransascad.org, also see note at beginning of section. **Other Phone Numbers:** Assessor 361-790-9733; Treasurer 361-790-0132; Appraiser/Auditor 361-729-9733; Elections 361-729-7431; Vital Records 361-790-0122.

Archer County

County Clerk, PO Box 815, Archer City, TX 76351. 940-574-4615; Fax 940-574-4625.
Will search UCC records prior to 7/2001 and current fixture (land) files. Tax liens not included in UCC search. Will not search real estate records. **Online Access:** Property Tax Records. See note at beginning of section. **Other Phone Numbers:** Assessor 940-574-4224; Treasurer 940-574-4822; Appraiser/Auditor 940-574-2172.

Armstrong County

County Clerk, PO Box 309, Claude, TX 79019-0309. County Clerk, R/E and UCC Recording 806-226-2081; Fax 806-226-5301.
Will search UCC records prior to 7/2001 and current fixture (land) files. Tax liens not included in UCC search. Will not search real estate records. **Other Phone Numbers:** Assessor 806-226-4481; Treasurer 806-226-3651; Appraiser/Auditor 806-226-4481; Elections 806-226-2081; Vital Records 806-226-2081.

Atascosa County

County Clerk, Circle Drive, Room 6-1, Jourdanton, TX 78026. 830-769-2511 R/E Recording: 830-767-2511.
Will search UCC records prior to 7/2001 and current fixture (land) files. UCC search includes tax liens if requested. Will not search real estate records. **Online Access:** Assessor, Property Tax Records. See note at beginning of section. **Other Phone Numbers:** Assessor 830-769-3620; Treasurer 830-769-3024; Appraiser/Auditor 830-742-3591.

Austin County

County Clerk, 1 E. Main, Bellville, TX 77418-1551. County Clerk, R/E and UCC Recording 979-865-5911; Fax 979-865-0336.

Will search UCC records prior to 7/2001 and current fixture (land) files. This agency will not do a tax lien search. Will not search real estate records. **Online Access:** Assessor, Property Tax Records. See note at beginning of section. **Other Phone Numbers:** Assessor 979-865-9124; Treasurer 979-865-5911; Appraiser/Auditor 409-865-9124; Elections 979-865-5911; Vital Records 979-865-5911.

Bailey County

County Clerk, 300 S. First, Suite 200, Muleshoe, TX 79347. County Clerk, R/E and UCC Recording 806-272-3044; Fax 806-272-3538.

Will search UCC records prior to 7/2001 and current fixture (land) files. **Other Phone Numbers:** Assessor 806-272-3022; Treasurer 806-272-3239; Appraiser/Auditor 806-272-5501.

Bandera County

County Clerk, PO Box 823, Bandera, TX 78003. 830-796-3332; Fax 830-796-8323.

Will search UCC records prior to 7/2001 and current fixture (land) files. UCC search includes tax liens if requested. Real estate owner, mortgage, and property transfer searches available. **Online Access:** Property Tax Records. See note at beginning of section. **Other Phone Numbers:** Assessor 830-796-3039; Appraiser/Auditor 830-796-3030.

Bastrop County

County Clerk, PO Box 577, Bastrop, TX 78602. County Clerk, R/E and UCC Recording 512-332-7234; Fax 512-332-7241.

Will search UCC records prior to 7/2001 and current fixture (land) files. UCC search includes tax liens if requested. Real estate owner, mortgage, and property transfer searches available. **Online Access:** Assessor, Property Tax Records. See notes at beginning of section. **Other Phone Numbers:** Assessor 512-303-3536; Treasurer 512-332-7204; Appraiser/Auditor 512-303-3536; Elections 512-332-7234; Vital Records 512-332-7234; Voter Registrar 512-332-7261.

Baylor County

County Clerk, PO Box 689, Seymour, TX 76380-0689. County Clerk, R/E and UCC Recording 940-889-3322. Will search UCC records prior to 7/2001 and current fixture (land) files. UCC search includes tax liens if requested. Real estate owner, mortgage, and property transfer searches available. **Other Phone Numbers:** Assessor 940-889-3169; Treasurer 940-889-1846; Appraiser/Auditor 940-888-5636; Elections 940-889-3322; Vital Records 940-889-3322.

Bee County

County Clerk, 105 W. Corpus Christi St, Room 103, Beeville, TX 78102. 361-362-3245; Fax 361-362-3247. Will search UCC records prior to 7/2001 and current fixture (land) files. UCC search includes tax liens if requested. Will not search real estate records. **Online Access:** Property Tax Records. See note at beginning of section. **Other Phone Numbers:** Assessor 361-362-3250; Appraiser/Auditor 361-358-0193.

Bell County

County Clerk, PO Box 480, Belton, TX 76513-0480. 254-933-5171; Fax 254-933-5176.

Will search UCC records prior to 7/2001 and current fixture (land) files. Tax liens not included in UCC search. Will not search real estate records. **Online Access:** Assessor, Property Tax Records. TexasTax provides two methods of access to county records.

Access to "Advanced Search" records requires a login and subscription fee. Subs are allowed in monthly increments. Advanced Search includes full data, maps, and Excel spreadsheet. For information, see www.texasstax.com/bell/subscriptioninfo.asp. Records on "Quick Search - FREE" at www.texasstax.com/bell/index/asp allows access to these County records: tax ID number, owner, parcel address, land value data. Search FREE by tax ID number, address, name, city or value. View details. **Other Phones:** Assessor 817-771-1108; Treasurer 817-933-5255; Appraiser/Auditor 254-939-5841.

Bexar County

County Clerk, Bexar County Courthouse, 100 Dolorosa, Room 108, San Antonio, TX 78205-3083. County Clerk, R/E and UCC Recording 210-335-2581; Fax 210-335-2813. www.bexar.org

Will search UCC records prior to 7/2001 and current fixture (land) files. Tax liens not included in UCC search. Real estate owner, mortgage, and property transfer searches available. **Online Access:** Grantor/Grantee, Marriage, UCC, Assumed Name, Recording, Property Tax, Assessor Records. Access to the County Clerk database is available free at www.countyclerk.bexar.landata.com. Also, Online access to the county Central Appraisal District database is available free at www.bcad.org/property.htm. **Other Phone Numbers:** Assessor 210-335-2251; Appraiser/Auditor 210-224-8511; Elections 210-335-0362; Vital Records 210-335-2585.

Blanco County

County Clerk, PO Box 65, Johnson City, TX 78636. 830-868-7357.

Will search UCC records prior to 7/2001 and current fixture (land) files. Will search tax liens-$5.00 per record. Will not search real estate records. **Online Access:** Assessor, Property Tax Records. See note at beginning of section. **Other Phone Numbers:** Assessor 830-868-7178; Treasurer 830-868-4566; Appraiser/Auditor 830-868-4624.

Borden County

County Clerk, PO Box 124, Gail, TX 79738-0124. County Clerk, R/E and UCC Recording 806-756-4312; Fax 806-756-4405.

Will search UCC records prior to 7/2001 and current fixture (land) files. Tax liens not included in UCC search. Will not search real estate records. **Other Phone Numbers:** Assessor 806-756-4415; Treasurer 806-756-4386; Appraiser/Auditor 806-756-4484; Elections 806-756-4312; Vital Records 806-756-4312.

Bosque County

County Clerk, PO Box 617, Meridian, TX 76665. 254-435-2201.

Will search UCC records prior to 7/2001 and current fixture (land) files. UCC search includes tax liens if requested. Real estate owner, mortgage, and property transfer searches available. **Other Phone Numbers:** Assessor 254-435-2201 x15; Treasurer 254-435-2201 x20; Appraiser/Auditor 254-435-2301; Elections 254-435-2201; Vital Records 254-435-2201.

Bowie County

County Clerk, P.O.Box 248, New Boston, TX 75570. 903-628-6740; Fax 903-628-6729.

Will search UCC records prior to 7/2001 and current fixture (land) files. Will not search real estate records. **Other Phone Numbers:** Assessor 903-628-2571 x229; Treasurer 903-628-2571 x230; Appraiser/Auditor 903-628-5493; Elections 903-628-6809; Vital Records 903-628-6744.

Brazoria County

County Clerk, 111 E. Locust, Suite 200, Angleton, TX 77515-4654. 979-849-5711; Fax 979-864-1358. www.brazoria-county.com

Will search UCC records prior to 7/2001 and current fixture (land) files. **Online Access:** Assessor, Property Tax Records. Access to the county Central Appraisal District database is available free at www.brazoriacad.org. Click on "appraisal roll." Also, see notes at beginning of section. **Other Phone Numbers:** Assessor 979-849-7792; Treasurer 979-849-5711; Appraiser/Auditor 979-849-7792.

Brazos County

County Clerk, 300 E. 26th St, Suite 120, Bryan, TX 77803. 979-361-4132 R/E Recording: 979-361-4132; Fax 979-361-4125.

Will search UCC records prior to 7/2001 and current fixture (land) files. UCC search includes tax liens if requested. Mortgage and property transfer searches available. **Online Access:** Assessor, Property Tax Records. See notes at beginning of section. **Other Phone Numbers:** Assessor 979-361-4480; Treasurer 979-361-4340; Appraiser/Auditor 979-774-4100.

Brewster County

County Clerk, PO Box 119, Alpine, TX 79831. County Clerk, R/E and UCC Recording 915-837-3366; Fax 915-837-6217.

Will search UCC records prior to 7/2001 and current fixture (land) files. Will search real estate records. **Other Phone Numbers:** Assessor 915-837-2214; Treasurer 915-837-6200; Appraiser/Auditor 915-837-2558; Vital Records 915-837-3366.

Briscoe County

County Clerk, PO Box 555, Silverton, TX 79257. County Clerk, R/E and UCC Recording 806-823-2134; Fax 806-823-2359.

Will search UCC records prior to 7/2001 and current fixture (land) files. **Other Phone Numbers:** Assessor 806-823-2136; Treasurer 806-823-2131; Appraiser/Auditor 806-823-2161; Elections 806-823-2134; Vital Records 806-823-2134.

Brooks County

County Clerk, PO Box 427, Falfurrias, TX 78355. 361-325-5604 R/E Recording: 361-325-5604 x1; Fax 361-325-4944.

Will search UCC records. **Other Phone Numbers:** Assessor 361-325-5604 x226; Treasurer 361-325-5604 x229; Appraiser/Auditor 361-325-5681.

Brown County

County Clerk, 200 S. Broadway, Courthouse, Brownwood, TX 76801. County Clerk, R/E and UCC Recording 915-643-2594.

Will search UCC records. Tax liens not included in UCC search. Will not search real estate records. **Online Access:** Assessor, Property Tax Records. See note at beginning of section. **Other Phone Numbers:** Assessor 915-643-1646 (Tax); Treasurer 915-646-6033; Appraiser/Auditor 915-643-5676; Elections 915-643-2594; Vital Records 915-643-2594.

Burleson County

County Clerk, 100 W Buck St #203, Caldwell, TX 77836. 979-567-2329 R/E Recording: 979-567-2329; Fax 979-567-2376.

Will search UCC records prior to 7/2001 and current fixture (land) files. Tax liens not included in UCC search. Will not search real estate records. **Online Access:** Assessor, Property Tax Records. See note at beginning of section. **Other Phone Numbers:** Assessor 979-567-4671; Appraiser/Auditor 979-567-2318.

Burnet County

County Clerk, 220 S. Pierce St, Burnet, TX 78611. 512-756-5406; Fax 512-756-5410.

Will search UCC records prior to 7/2001 and current fixture (land) files. Tax liens not included in UCC search. Will not search real estate records. **Online Access:** Assessor, Property Tax Records. See note at beginning of section. **Other Phone Numbers:** Assessor 512-756-8291; Appraiser/Auditor 512-756-8291.

Caldwell County

County Clerk, PO Box 906, Lockhart, TX 78644-0906. 512-398-1804; www.caldwellcad.org

Will search UCC records prior to 7/2001 and current fixture (land) files. Tax liens not included in UCC search. Real estate owner, mortgage, and property transfer searches available. **Online Access:** Assessor, Property Tax, Personal Property Records. Access to the county Appraisal District database is available free at www.caldwellcad.org/search.htm. Also, see notes at beginning of section. **Other Phone Numbers:** Assessor 512-398-2391; Treasurer 512-398-1800; Appraiser/Auditor 512-398-0550.

Calhoun County

County Clerk, 211 S. Ann, Port Lavaca, TX 77979. County Clerk, R/E and UCC Recording 361-553-4411; Fax 361-553-4420.

Will search UCC records. Will not search real estate records. **Other Phone Numbers:** Assessor 361-552-8808; Treasurer 361-553-4620; Appraiser/Auditor 361-552-8808; Elections 361-553-4440; Vital Records 361-553-4411.

Callahan County

County Clerk, 100 W. 4th, Ste. 104, Courthouse, Baird, TX 79504. 915-854-1217; Fax 915-854-1227.

Will search UCC records. Tax liens not included in UCC search. Will not search real estate records. **Other Phone Numbers:** Treasurer 915-854-1399; Appraiser/Auditor 915-854-1165.

Cameron County

County Clerk, PO Box 2178, Brownsville, TX 78520. County Clerk, R/E and UCC Recording 956-544-0815 UCC Recording: 956-550-1329; Fax 956-554-0813.

Will search UCC records prior to 7/2001 and current fixture (land) files. **Online Access:** Assessor, Property Tax Records. See note at beginning of section. **Other Phone Numbers:** Assessor 956-544-0800; Treasurer 956-544-0819; Appraiser/Auditor 956-399-9322; Elections 956-544-0809; Vital Records 956-544-0817.

Camp County

County Clerk, 126 Church St, Room 102, Pittsburg, TX 75686. County Clerk, R/E and UCC Recording 903-856-2731; Fax 903-856-2309.

Will search UCC records prior to 7/2001 and current fixture (land) files. Will not search real estate records. **Other Phone Numbers:** Assessor 903-856-3391; Treasurer 903-856-7862; Appraiser/Auditor 903-856-6538; Elections 903-856-2731; Vital Records 903-856-2731.

Carson County

County Clerk, PO Box 487, Panhandle, TX 79068. County Clerk, R/E and UCC Recording 806-537-3873; Fax 806-537-3623.

Will search UCC records prior to 7/2001 and current fixture (land) files. UCC search includes tax liens if requested. Will not search real estate records. **Other Phone Numbers:** Assessor 806-537-3412; Treasurer 806-537-3753; Appraiser/Auditor 806-537-3569; Elections 806-537-3873; Vital Records 806-537-3873.

Cass County

County Clerk, PO Box 449, Linden, TX 75563. County Clerk, R/E and UCC Recording 903-756-5071; Fax 903-756-5732.

Will search UCC records prior to 7/2001 and current fixture (land) files. **Other Phone Numbers:** Assessor 903-756-5311; Treasurer 903-756-7626; Appraiser/Auditor 903-756-7545; Elections 903-756-5071; Vital Records 903-756-5071.

Castro County

County Clerk, 100 E. Bedford, Room 101, Dimmitt, TX 79027-2643. County Clerk, R/E and UCC Recording 806-647-3338.

Will search UCC records prior to 7/2001 and current fixture (land) files. UCC search includes tax liens if requested. Will not search real estate records. **Other Phone Numbers:** Assessor 806-647-5336; Treasurer 806-647-5534; Appraiser/Auditor 806-647-5131; Elections 806-647-3338; Vital Records 806-647-3338.

Chambers County

County Clerk, PO Box 728, Anahuac, TX 77514. 409-267-8309; Fax 409-267-4453.

Will search UCC records prior to 7/2001 and current fixture (land) files. UCC search includes tax liens if requested. Will not search real estate records. **Online Access:** Property Tax, Appraiser Records. Search the appraiser property tax database for free at www.chamberscad.org. Also, see note at beginning of section. **Other Phone Numbers:** Assessor 409-267-8304; Treasurer 409-267-8286; Appraiser/Auditor 409-267-3795.

Cherokee County

County Clerk, PO Box 420, Rusk, TX 75785. County Clerk, R/E and UCC Recording 903-683-2350; Fax 903-683-5931.

Will search UCC records prior to 7/2001 and current fixture (land) files. **Other Phone Numbers:** Assessor 903-683-5478; Treasurer 903-683-4935; Appraiser/Auditor 903-683-2296; Elections 903-683-2350; Vital Records 903-683-2350.

Childress County

County Clerk, Courthouse Box 4, Childress, TX 79201. County Clerk, R/E and UCC Recording 940-937-6143; Fax 940-937-3479.

Will search UCC records. **Other Phone Numbers:** Assessor 940-937-6062; Treasurer 940-937-6271; Appraiser/Auditor 940-937-6062; Elections 940-937-6143; Vital Records 940-937-6143.

Clay County

County Clerk, PO Box 548, Henrietta, TX 76365. 940-538-4631.

Will search UCC records prior to 7/2001 and current fixture (land) files. This agency will not do a tax lien search. Real estate owner, mortgage, and property transfer searches available. **Online Access:** Property Tax Records. See note at beginning of section. **Other Phone Numbers:** Assessor 940-538-4311; Appraiser/Auditor 940-538-4311.

Cochran County

County Clerk, 100 N. Main, Courthouse, Morton, TX 79346-2598. 806-266-5450; Fax 806-266-9027.

Will search UCC records prior to 7/2001 and current fixture (land) files. Tax liens not included in UCC search. Real estate owner, mortgage, and property transfer searches available. **Other Phone Numbers:** Assessor 806-266-5171; Treasurer 806-266-5161; Appraiser/Auditor 806-266-5584.

Coke County

County Clerk, PO Box 150, Robert Lee, TX 76945. 915-453-2631; Fax 915-453-2650.

Will search UCC records prior to 7/2001 and current fixture (land) files. UCC search includes tax liens if requested. Will not search real estate records. **Other Phone Numbers:** Assessor 915-453-2614; Treasurer 915-453-2713; Appraiser/Auditor 915-453-4528.

Coleman County

County Clerk, PO Box 591, Coleman, TX 76834. 915-625-2889.

Will search UCC records. This agency will not do a tax lien search. Will not search real estate records. **Other Phone Numbers:** Assessor 915-625-4155; Treasurer 915-625-4221; Appraiser/Auditor 915-625-4155.

Collin County

County Clerk, 200 S. McDonald, Annex "A", Suite 120, McKinney, TX 75069. County Clerk, R/E and UCC Recording 972-548-4134 UCC Recording: 972-548-4151; www.co.collin.tx.us

Will search UCC records prior to 7/2001 and current fixture (land) files. UCC search includes tax liens if requested. Will not search real estate records. **Online Access:** Property Tax, Assessor, Business Personal Property Records. Search the assessor's property tax and business property database for free at www.collincad.org/search.cfm. Also, see note at beginning of section. **Other Phone Numbers:** Assessor 972-547-5020; Treasurer 972-548-4202; Appraiser/Auditor 972-578-5200; Elections 972-548-3214; Vital Records 972-548-4134.

Collingsworth County

County Clerk, Courthouse, Room 3, 800 West Ave., Wellington, TX 79095. County Clerk, R/E and UCC Recording 806-447-2408; Fax 806-447-5418.

Will search UCC records prior to 7/2001 and current fixture (land) files. Tax liens not included in UCC search. Real estate record owner searches available. **Other Phone Numbers:** Assessor 806-447-5606; Treasurer 806-447-2616; Appraiser/Auditor 806-447-5172; Elections 806-447-2408; Vital Records 806-447-2408.

Colorado County

County Clerk, PO Box 68, Columbus, TX 78934. 979-732-2155 R/E Recording: 979-732-6561 or 2155; Fax 979-732-8852.

Will not search UCC records. Will search real estate records. **Other Phone Numbers:** Assessor 979-732-8222; Treasurer 979-732-2865; Appraiser/Auditor 979-732-8222.

Comal County

County Clerk, 150 N Seguin, Suite 101, Suite 104, New Braunfels, TX 78130. 830-620-5513; Fax 830-620-3410. www.co.comal.tx.us

Will search UCC records prior to 7/2001 and current fixture (land) files. **Other Phone Numbers:** Assessor 830-620-5521; Treasurer 830-620-5506; Appraiser/Auditor 830-625-8597; Elections 830-620-5538; Vital Records 830-620-5515.

Comanche County

County Clerk, Courthouse, Comanche, TX 76442. 915-356-2655; Fax 915-356-3710.

Will search UCC records prior to 7/2001 and current fixture (land) files. UCC search includes tax liens if requested. Will not search real estate records. **Online Access:** Assessor, Property Tax Records. See note at beginning of section. **Other Phone Numbers:** Assessor 915-356-3101; Treasurer 915-356-2838; Appraiser/Auditor 915-356-5253.

Concho County

County Clerk, PO Box 98, Paint Rock, TX 76866-0098. County Clerk, R/E and UCC Recording 915-732-4322; Fax 915-732-2040.

Will search UCC records prior to 7/2001 and current fixture (land) files. UCC search includes tax liens if requested. Real estate record owner and mortgage searches available. **Other Phone Numbers:** Assessor 915-732-4460; Treasurer 915-732-4279; Appraiser/Auditor 915-732-4389; Elections 915-732-4322; Vital Records 915-732-4322.

Cooke County

County Clerk, Courthouse, Gainesville, TX 76240. County Clerk, R/E and UCC Recording 940-668-5420 UCC Recording: 940-668-5474; Fax 940-668-5440.

Will search UCC records prior to 7/2001 and current fixture (land) files. Will not search real estate records. **Other Phones:** Assessor 940-665-7651; Treasurer 940-668-5423; Appraiser/Auditor 940-665-7651; Elections 940-668-5420; Vital Records 940-668-5421.

Coryell County

County Clerk, PO Box 237, Gatesville, TX 76528. 254-865-5016 R/E Recording: 254-865-5016 x3; Fax 254-865-8631.

Will search UCC records prior to 7/2001 and current fixture (land) files. Will not search real estate records. **Online Access:** Recording, Land Records. Access may be available at http://apolloplus.com in late 2002. **Other Phone Numbers:** Assessor 254-865-6593; Appraiser/Auditor 254-865-6593.

Cottle County

County Clerk, PO Box 717, Paducah, TX 79248. 806-492-3823.

Will search UCC records. UCC search includes tax liens if requested. Real estate owner, mortgage, and property transfer searches available. **Other Phone Numbers:** Assessor 806-492-3345; Treasurer 806-492-3738; Appraiser/Auditor 806-492-3345.

Crane County

County Clerk, PO Box 578, Crane, TX 79731. 915-558-3581.

Will search UCC records prior to 7/2001 and current fixture (land) files. This agency will not do a tax lien search. Will not search real estate records. **Other Phone Numbers:** Assessor 915-558-2622; Treasurer 915-558-3372; Appraiser/Auditor 915-558-1021.

Crockett County

County Clerk, PO Drawer C, Ozona, TX 76943. County Clerk, R/E and UCC Recording 915-392-2022; Fax 915-392-3742.

Will search UCC records prior to 7/2001 and current fixture (land) files. Will not search real estate records. **Other Phones:** Assessor 915-392-2674; Treasurer 915-392-3376; Appraiser/Auditor 915-392-2674; Elections 915-392-2022; Vital Records 915-392-2022.

Crosby County

County Clerk, 201 W Aspen St, Room 102, Crosbyton, TX 79322. 806-675-2334.

Will search UCC records prior to 7/2001 and current fixture (land) files. Tax liens not included in UCC search. Will not search real estate records. **Other Phone Numbers:** Assessor 806-675-2356; Appraiser/Auditor 806-675-2356.

Culberson County

County Clerk, PO Box 158, Van Horn, TX 79855. 915-283-2058 R/E Recording: 915-283-2059; Fax 915-283-9234.

Will search UCC records prior to 7/2001 and current fixture (land) files. Will search real estate records.

Other Phones: Assessor 915-283-2977; Treasurer 915-283-2115; Appraiser/Auditor 915-283-2977; Elections 915-283-2058; Vital Records 915-283-2058.

Dallam County

County Clerk, PO Box 1352, Dalhart, TX 79022. 806-249-4751 R/E Recording: 806-244-4751 UCC Recording: 806-244-4751; Fax 806-249-2252.

Will search UCC records. Will not search real estate records. **Other Phone Numbers:** Assessor 806-244-2801; Appraiser/Auditor 806-249-6767; Elections 806-244-4751; Vital Records 806-244-4751.

Dallas County

County Clerk, Records Bldg, 2nd Floor, 509 Main St., Dallas, TX 75202-3502. 214-653-7131; www.dallascounty.org/html/citizen-serv/county-clerk/

Will search UCC records prior to 7/2001 and current fixture (land) files. Tax liens not included in UCC search. Will not search real estate records. **Online Access:** Property Tax, Personal Property, Voter Registration, Marriage, UCC, Assumed Name Records. Access to the County Voter Registration Records is available free online at www.openrecords.org/records/voting/dallas_voting. Search by name or partial name. Also, online access to the Central Appraisal District data is free at www.dallascad.org/search.htm. Business personal property searches are available. Also, see note at beginning of section. Also, search marriages, assumed names, UCCs back to 1977 on the online records search system, either per item or $75 annual fee. Credit cards accepted; see www.dallascounty.org/applications/english/record-search/intro.html. Has probate and court records also. **Other Phones:** Assessor 214-653-0520; Appraiser/Auditor 214-631-0520.

Dawson County

County Clerk, PO Drawer 1268, Lamesa, TX 79331. 806-872-3778; Fax 806-872-2473.

Will search UCC records prior to 7/2001 and current fixture (land) files. UCC search includes tax liens if requested. Will not search real estate records. **Other Phone Numbers:** Assessor 806-872-7060; Treasurer 806-872-7474; Appraiser/Auditor 806-872-7060; Elections 806-872-2124.

De Witt County

County Clerk, 307 N. Gonzales, Courthouse, Cuero, TX 77954. 361-275-3724; Fax 361-275-8994.

Will search UCC records prior to 7/2001 and current fixture (land) files. Tax liens not included in UCC search, must search each location. Will not search real estate records. **Other Phone Numbers:** Appraiser/Auditor 361-275-5753.

Deaf Smith County

County Clerk, 235 E. 3rd, Room 203, Hereford, TX 79045-5542. 806-363-7077; Fax 806-363-7007.

Will search UCC records prior to 7/2001 and current fixture (land) files. Tax liens not included in UCC search. Will not search real estate records. **Other Phone Numbers:** Treasurer 806-364-0399; Appraiser/Auditor 806-364-0625.

Delta County

County Clerk, PO Box 455, Cooper, TX 75432. County Clerk, R/E and UCC Recording 903-395-4110; Fax 903-395-2178.

Will search UCC records. UCC search includes tax liens if requested. Real estate owner, mortgage, and property transfer searches available. **Other Phone Numbers:** Assessor 903-395-2718; Treasurer 903-395-4315; Appraiser/Auditor 903-395-4118; Elections 903-395-4110; Vital Records 903-395-4110.

Denton County

County Clerk, PO Box 2187, Denton, TX 76202-2187. County Clerk, R/E and UCC Recording 940-349-2010; www.dentoncounty.com/dept/ccl.htm

Will search UCC records prior to 7/2001 and current fixture (land) files. Tax liens not included in UCC search. Real estate record owner searches available. **Online Access:** Real Estate, Property, Recording, Voter Registration, Most Wanted, Parollee, Sex Offender, Bond, Jail, Conviction Records. Access to the county property database indices is available free for name/instrument searches. There is for fee for access, but to print is $1.00 per page. Visit www.texaslandrecords.com/Denton/index.jsp. And, with a full subscription, you can search full indices and download images. Also, search the voter registration rolls for free at http://elections.dentoncounty.com/VRSearch/default.asp. Search the "justice" database for free at http://justice.dentoncounty.com. Includes Parollees, sex offenders, most wanted lists, bond, jail, convictions and court records databases. **Other Phone Numbers:** Assessor 940-349-3500; Treasurer 940-349-3500; Elections 940-349-3200; Vital Records 940-349-2018.

Dickens County

County Clerk, PO Box 120, Dickens, TX 79229. 806-623-5531; Fax 806-623-5319.

Will search UCC records prior to 7/2001 and current fixture (land) files. UCC search includes tax liens if requested. Will search real estate records. **Other Phone Numbers:** Assessor 806-623-5216; Appraiser/Auditor 806-623-5216; Elections 806-623-5531.

Dimmit County

County Clerk, 103 N. 5th St, Carrizo Springs, TX 78834. 830-876-2323 x233 R/E Recording: 830-876-3569; Fax 830-876-4205.

Will search UCC records prior to 7/2001 and current fixture (land) files. Will not search real estate records. **Other Phone Numbers:** Assessor 830-876-2323 x228; Treasurer 830-876-2323 x226; Appraiser/Auditor 830-876-3420; Vital Records 830-876-2323 x233.

Donley County

County Clerk, PO Drawer U, Clarendon, TX 79226. County Clerk, R/E and UCC Recording 806-874-3436; Fax 806-874-5146.

Will search UCC records prior to 7/2001 and current fixture (land) files. **Other Phone Numbers:** Assessor 806-874-2193; Treasurer 806-874-2328; Appraiser/Auditor 806-874-2744; Elections 806-874-3436; Vital Records 806-874-3436.

Duval County

County Clerk, PO Box 248, San Diego, TX 78384. 361-279-3322 x271/2 R/E Recording: 361-279-3322 x272 UCC Recording: 361-279-3322 x272; Fax 361-279-3159.

Will search UCC records prior to 7/2001 and current fixture (land) files. UCC search includes tax liens if requested. Will not search real estate records. **Other Phone Numbers:** Assessor 361-279-3322; Treasurer 361-279-6128; Appraiser/Auditor 361-279-3305; Elections 361-279-3322 x272; Vital Records 361-279-3322 x272.

Eastland County

County Clerk, PO Box 110, Eastland, TX 76448-0110. 254-629-1583; Fax 254-629-8125.

Will search UCC records. Will not search real estate records. **Other Phone Numbers:** Assessor 254-629-1564; Treasurer 254-629-2672; Appraiser/Auditor 254-629-8597.

Ector County

County Clerk, PO Box 707, Odessa, TX 79760. 915-498-4130; Fax 915-498-4177.

Will search UCC records. Will not search real estate records. **Online Access:** Real Estate, Appraiser, Personal Property Records. Search the county appraisal district database for free at www.ectorcad.org/real_name.html. **Other Phone Numbers:** Assessor 915-498-4050; Treasurer 915-498-4060; Appraiser/Auditor 915-332-6834; Elections 915-498-4030.

Edwards County

County Clerk, PO Box 184, Rocksprings, TX 78880-0184. 830-683-2235; Fax 830-683-5376.

Will search UCC records. UCC search includes tax liens if requested. Will not search real estate records. **Other Phone Numbers:** Assessor 830-683-2337; Treasurer 830-683-5116; Appraiser/Auditor 830-683-4189.

El Paso County

County Clerk, 500 E. San Antonio, Room 105, El Paso, TX 79901-2496. 915-546-2074.

Will search UCC records prior to 7/2001 and current fixture (land) files. UCC search includes tax liens if requested. Real estate owner, mortgage, and property transfer searches available. **Online Access:** Assumed Name, Property Tax, Real Estate, Vital Statistic Records. Search vital statistics (birth, death, marriage), assumed names, and property (land) records free at www.co.el-paso.tx.us/search.htm. Also, search property tax data at www.elpasocad.org. Also, see note at beginning of section. **Other Phone Numbers:** Assessor 915-541-4054; Appraiser/Auditor 915-780-2000.

Ellis County

County Clerk, PO Box 250, Waxahachie, TX 75168. County Clerk, R/E and UCC Recording 972-923-5070; Fax 972-923-5075.

Will search UCC records prior to 7/2001 and current fixture (land) files. UCC search includes tax liens if requested. Real estate owner, mortgage, and property transfer searches available. **Online Access:** Appraiser, Property Tax Records. Search the property appraiser database for free at www.elliscad.org. Also, see note a beginning of section. **Other Phone Numbers:** Assessor 972-923-5150; Treasurer 972-923-5125; Appraiser/Auditor 972-937-3552; Elections 972-923-5195; Vital Records 972-923-5070.

Erath County

County Clerk, Courthouse, 100 W. Washington St., Stephenville, TX 76401. County Clerk, R/E and UCC Recording 254-965-1482; Fax 254-965-5732.

Will search UCC records prior to 7/2001 and current fixture (land) files. UCC search includes tax liens if requested. Will not search real estate records. **Online Access:** Property Tax Records. See note at beginning of section. **Other Phone Numbers:** Assessor 254-965-7301; Treasurer 254-965-1483; Appraiser/Auditor 254-965-7301
254-965-1482; Elections 254-965-1482; Vital Records 254-965-1410.

Falls County

County Clerk, PO Box 458, Marlin, TX 76661. County Clerk, R/E and UCC Recording 254-883-1408; Fax 254-883-1406.

Will search UCC records prior to 7/2001 and current fixture (land) files. Tax liens not included in UCC search. Will not search real estate records. **Other Phone Numbers:** Assessor 254-883-1436; Treasurer 254-883-1433; Appraiser/Auditor 254-883-2543; Elections 254-883-1408; Vital Records 254-883-1408.

Fannin County

County Clerk, Courthouse, Suite 102, 101 E. Sam Rayburn Dr., Bonham, TX 75418-4346. 903-583-7486; Fax 903-583-7811.

Will search UCC records prior to 7/2001 and current fixture (land) files. UCC search includes tax liens if requested. Will not search real estate records. **Online Access:** Assessor, Property Tax Records. See notes at beginning of section. **Other Phone Numbers:** Assessor 903-583-9546; Appraiser/Auditor 903-583-8701.

Fayette County

County Clerk, PO Box 59, La Grange, TX 78945. 979-968-3251 R/E Recording: 409-968-3251.

Will search UCC records. Tax liens not included in UCC search. Will not search real estate records. **Online Access:** Recording, Land Records. Access may be available at http://apolloplus.com in late 2002. **Other Phone Numbers:** Assessor 979-968-3164; Treasurer 979-968-3055; Appraiser/Auditor 979-968-8383; Elections 979-968-3251; Vital Records 979-968-3251.

Fisher County

County Clerk, PO Box 368, Roby, TX 79543-0368. 915-776-2401; Fax 915-776-2815.

Will search UCC records. **Other Phone Numbers:** Assessor 915-776-2181; Treasurer 915-776-2351; Appraiser/Auditor 915-776-2733; Elections 915-776-2401; Vital Records 915-776-2401.

Floyd County

County Clerk, Courthouse, Room 101, 105 Main St., Floydada, TX 79235. County Clerk, R/E and UCC Recording 806-983-4900; Fax 806-983-4909.

Will search UCC records prior to 7/2001 but no current fixture (land) files. UCC search includes tax liens if requested. Will not search real estate records. **Other Phone Numbers:** Assessor 806-983-5256; Treasurer 806-983-4910; Appraiser/Auditor 806-983-5256.

Foard County

County Clerk, PO Box 539, Crowell, TX 79227. County Clerk, R/E and UCC Recording 940-684-1365; Fax 940-684-1947.

Will search UCC records prior to 7/2001 and current fixture (land) files. Will search real estate records. **Other Phone Numbers:** Assessor 940-684-1225; Treasurer 940-684-1818; Appraiser/Auditor 940-684-1225; Elections 940-684-1365; Vital Records 940-684-1365.

Fort Bend County

County Clerk, 301 Jackson, Suite 101, Richmond, TX 77469. County Clerk, R/E and UCC Recording 281-341-8685; Fax 281-341-8669. www.co.fort-bend.tx.us

Will search UCC records prior to 7/2001 and current fixture (land) files. Tax liens not included in UCC search. Will not search real estate records. **Online Access:** Real Estate, Lien, Assessor, UCC, Marriage, Death, Birth Records. Access to the county clerk database is available free at www.co.fort-bend.tx.us/admin_of_justice/County_Clerk/index_info_research.htm. Search the property index by name, or the plat index. And, search county UCCs, probate and court records. Also, for full records, their fee remote system is available, including images. Access fee is $.25 per minute plus set-up. For information, contact Diane Shepard at 281-341-8664. Also, see note at beginning of section for add'l fee service for tax records. **Other Phone Numbers:** Assessor 281-341-3735; Treasurer 281-341-3750; Appraiser/Auditor 281-341-8623; Elections 281-341-8670; Vital Records 281-341-8685.

Franklin County

County Clerk, PO Box 68, Mount Vernon, TX 75457-0068. 903-537-4252 R/E Recording: 903-537-4252 x6 UCC Recording: 903-537-4252 ext 6; Fax 903-537-2982.

Will search UCC records prior to 7/2001 and current fixture (land) files. Tax liens not included in UCC search. Real estate owner, mortgage, and property transfer searches available. **Online Access:** Property Tax Records. See note at beginning of section. **Other Phones:** Assessor 903-537-4252 x3; Treasurer 903-537-2206 x8; Appraiser/Auditor 903-537-2286; Elections 903-537-4252 x3; Vital Records 903-537-4252 ext 6.

Freestone County

County Clerk, PO Box 1017, Fairfield, TX 75840. 903-389-2635.

Will search UCC records. Tax liens not included in UCC search. Will not search real estate records. **Online Access:** Assessor, Property Tax Records. Search the assessor's property tax database for free at www.freestonecad.org/search.html. **Other Phone Numbers:** Assessor 903-389-2336; Treasurer 903-389-2180; Appraiser/Auditor 903-389-5510; Elections 903-389-2635; Vital Records 903-389-2635.

Frio County

County Clerk, 500 E. San Antonio St, # 6, Pearsall, TX 78061. County Clerk, R/E and UCC Recording 830-334-2214; Fax 830-334-0021.

Will search UCC records prior to 7/2001 and current fixture (land) files. Will not search real estate records. **Other Phones:** Assessor 830-334-2152; Treasurer 830-334-0040; Appraiser/Auditor 830-334-4163; Elections 830-334-2214; Vital Records 830-334-2214.

Gaines County

County Clerk, 101 S. Main, Room 107, Seminole, TX 79360. County Clerk, R/E and UCC Recording 915-758-4003 UCC Recording: 915-758-4033.

Will search UCC records. UCC search includes tax liens if requested. Will not search real estate records. **Other Phone Numbers:** Assessor 915-758-4008; Treasurer 915-758-4009; Appraiser/Auditor 915-758-3263; Vital Records 915-758-4033.

Galveston County

County Clerk, PO Box 2450, Galveston, TX 77553-2450. 409-766-2208 R/E Recording: 409-76-2208; www.galvestoncad.org

Will search UCC records prior to 7/2001 and current fixture (land) files. UCC search includes tax liens if requested. Will not search real estate records. **Online Access:** Real Estate, Lien, Assessor Records. Several sources exist. Access to County online records requires $200 escrow deposit, $25 monthly fee, plus $.25 per minute. Index records date back to 1965; image documents to 1/95. Lending agency information and fax back services are available. For information, contact Robert Dickinson at 409-770-5115. Also, access to the Central Appraisal District database is available free at www.galvestoncad.org/search.htm. Also, see note at beginning of section. Also, online access to sheriff sales is free at www.co.galveston.tx.us/sheriff/sheriff.htm. **Other Phone Numbers:** Assessor 409-762-8621 x481; Treasurer 409-762-8621 x345; Appraiser/Auditor 409-935-1980.

Garza County

County Clerk, PO Box 366, Post, TX 79356-0366. County Clerk, R/E and UCC Recording 806-495-4430; Fax 806-495-4431.

Will search UCC records prior to 7/2001 and current fixture (land) files. Tax liens not included in UCC search. Will not search real estate records. **Other Phone**

Numbers: Assessor 806-495-4427; Treasurer 806-495-4423; Appraiser/Auditor 806-495-3518; Elections 806-495-4430; Vital Records 806-495-4430.

Gillespie County

County Clerk, 101 W. Main, Room 109, Unit #13, Fredericksburg, TX 78624. 830-997-6515; Fax 830-997-9958.

Will search UCC records prior to 7/2001 and current fixture (land) files. UCC search includes tax liens if requested. Will not search real estate records. **Online Access:** Assessor, Property Tax Records. See note at beginning of section. **Other Phone Numbers:** Assessor 830-997-6519; Treasurer 830-997-6521; Appraiser/Auditor 830-997-9807; Elections 830-997-6515; Vital Records 830-997-6515.

Glasscock County

County Clerk, PO Box 190, Garden City, TX 79739. County Clerk, R/E and UCC Recording 915-354-2371. Will search UCC records prior to 7/2001 and current fixture (land) files. UCC search includes tax liens if requested. Real estate owner, mortgage, and property transfer searches available. **Other Phone Numbers:** Assessor 915-354-2580; Treasurer 915-354-2415; Appraiser/Auditor 915-354-2580; Elections 915-354-2371; Vital Records 915-354-2371.

Goliad County

County Clerk, PO Box 50, Goliad, TX 77963. County Clerk, R/E and UCC Recording 361-645-3294; Fax 361-645-3858.

Will search UCC records prior to 7/2001 and current fixture (land) files. **Other Phone Numbers:** Assessor 361-645-2492; Treasurer 361-645-3551; Appraiser/Auditor 361-645-2492; Elections 361-645-3294; Vital Records 361-645-3294.

Gonzales County

County Clerk, PO Box 77, Gonzales, TX 78629. County Clerk, R/E and UCC Recording 830-672-2801; Fax 830-672-2636.

Will search UCC records. Will not search real estate records. **Other Phone Numbers:** Assessor 830-627-2841; Treasurer 830-627-2621; Appraiser/Auditor 830-672-2879; Vital Records 830-672-2801.

Gray County

County Clerk, PO Box 1902, Pampa, TX 79066-1902. County Clerk, R/E and UCC Recording 806-669-8004; Fax 806-669-8054.

Will search UCC records. UCC search includes tax liens if requested with extra fee. Will not search real estate records. **Other Phone Numbers:** Assessor 806-665-0791; Treasurer 806-669-8009; Appraiser/Auditor 806-665-0791; Elections 806-669-8004; Vital Records 806-669-8004.

Grayson County

County Clerk, 100 W. Houston #17, Sherman, TX 75090. County Clerk, R/E and UCC Recording 903-813-4239; Fax 903-870-0829. www.co.grayson.tx.us

Will search UCC records prior to 7/2001 and current fixture (land) files. UCC search includes tax liens. Will not search real estate records. **Online Access:** Property Tax Records. See note at beginning of section. **Other Phone Numbers:** Assessor 903-893-9673; Treasurer 903-813-4251; Appraiser/Auditor 903-893-9673; Vital Records 903-813-4239.

Gregg County

County Clerk, PO Box 3049, Longview, TX 75606. 903-236-8430 R/E Recording: 903-236-8430 x746 UCC Recording: 903-236-8430 X746; Fax 903-237-2574. www.co.gregg.tx.us

Will search UCC records prior to 7/2001 and current fixture (land) files. UCC search does not include tax liens. Will not search real estate records. **Online Access:** Property Tax Records. See note at beginning of section. **Other Phone Numbers:** Assessor 903-759-0015; Treasurer 903-236-8430 X853; Appraiser/Auditor 903-238-8823; Elections 903-237-2654; Vital Records 903-236-8430 X637.

Grimes County

County Clerk, PO Box 209, Anderson, TX 77830. County Clerk, R/E and UCC Recording 936-873-2111 UCC Recording: 936-873-2606 x252.

Will search UCC records prior to 7/2001 and current fixture (land) files. This agency will not do a tax lien search. Will not search real estate records. **Other Phones:** Assessor 936-873-2606 x231; Treasurer 936-873-2606 x233; Appraiser/Auditor 936-873-2163; Elections 873-2606x246; Vital Records 873-2606x250.

Guadalupe County

County Clerk, PO Box 990, Seguin, TX 78156-0990. County Clerk, R/E and UCC Recording 830-303-4188 x236; Fax 830-401-0300. www.guadalupecad.org

Will search UCC records prior to 7/2001 and current fixture (land) files. Tax liens not included in UCC search. Will not search real estate records. **Online Access:** Property Tax, Assessor Records. Access to the county Appraisal District database is available free at www.guadalupecad.org/gadname.html. Name search here, but other methods are allowed at the web site above. Also, see note at beginning of section. **Other Phones:** Assessor 830-303-3421 x354; Treasurer 830-303-4188 x374; Appraiser/Auditor 830-372-2871; Elections 303-4188x280; Vital Records 303-4188x233.

Hale County

County Clerk, 500 Broadway #140, Plainview, TX 79072-8030. County Clerk, R/E and UCC Recording 806-291-5261 UCC Recording: 806-291-5248; Fax 806-296-9810.

Will search UCC records prior to 7/2001 and current fixture (land) files. Tax liens not included in UCC search. Will search real estate records. Written requests only. **Other Phones:** Assessor 806-291-5278; Treasurer 806-291-5213; Appraiser/Auditor 806-293-4226; Elections 291-5261; Vital Records 291-5219.

Hall County

County Clerk, Courthouse, Box 8, Memphis, TX 79245. 806-259-2627; Fax 806-259-5078.

Will search UCC records prior to 7/2001 and current fixture (land) files. Tax liens not included in UCC search. Real estate owner, mortgage, and property transfer searches available. **Other Phone Numbers:** Assessor 806-259-2125; Treasurer 806-259-2421; Appraiser/Auditor 806-259-2393.

Hamilton County

County Clerk, Main St, Courthouse, Hamilton, TX 76531. County Clerk, R/E and UCC Recording 254-386-3518; Fax 254-386-8727.

Will search UCC records prior to 7/2001 and current fixture (land) files. Will not search real estate records. **Other Phone Numbers:** Assessor 254-386-5114; Treasurer 254-386-5315; Appraiser/Auditor 254-386-8945; Elections 254-386-3518; Vital Records 254-386-3518.

Hansford County

County Clerk, PO Box 397, Spearman, TX 79081. County Clerk, R/E and UCC Recording 806-659-4110; Fax 806-659-4168.

Will search UCC records prior to 7/2001 and current fixture (land) files. Will not search real estate records. **Other Phone Numbers:** Assessor 806-659-4120; Treasurer 806-659-4125; Appraiser/Auditor 806-659-5575; Elections 806-659-4110.

Hardeman County

County Clerk, PO Box 30, Quanah, TX 79252-0030. County Clerk, R/E and UCC Recording 940-663-2901; Fax 940-663-5161.

Will search UCC records prior to 7/2001 and current fixture (land) files. UCC search includes tax liens if requested. Will not search real estate records. **Other Phone Numbers:** Assessor 940-663-5221; Treasurer 940-663-5401; Appraiser/Auditor 940-663-2532.

Hardin County

County Clerk, PO Box 38, Kountze, TX 77625. County Clerk, R/E and UCC Recording 409-246-5185.

Will search UCC records. This agency will not do a tax lien search. Will not search real estate records. **Other Phone Numbers:** Assessor 409-246-5180; Treasurer 409-246-5121; Appraiser/Auditor 409-246-2507.

Harris County

County Clerk, PO Box 1525, Houston, TX 77251-1525. 713-755-6405 R/E Recording: 713-755-6411 UCC Recording: 713-755-6439; Fax 713-755-4977. www.co.harris.tx.us/cclerk

Personal checks are not accepted for mail requests. Will search UCC records prior to 7/2001 and current fixture (land) files. Tax liens not included in UCC search. Will not search real estate records. **Online Access:** Real Estate, Lien, Assessor, Voter, UCC, Assumed Name, Grantor/Grantee, Vital Statistic Records. Two sources for County Clerk information exist. Access to the County online subscription service requires a $300 deposit and $40 per hour of use. For info, call Ken Peabody at 713-755-7151. Also, free access to records is available free on the web. Assumed Name records, UCC filings, vital statistic, and Real Property are at www.cclerk.hctx.net/coolice/default.asp?Category=RealProperty&Service=mastermenu. Assessor records are at www.hcad.org/Records. County Court Civil, marriage and informal marriage records are also available there. Also, search the Assessor-Collector database free at www.tax.co.harris.tx.us/dbsearch.htm. **Other Phone Numbers:** Assessor 713-683-9200; Appraiser/Auditor 713-957-5291; Elections 713-755-5792; Vital Records 713-755-6438.

Harrison County

County Clerk, PO Box 1365, Marshall, TX 75671. County Clerk, R/E and UCC Recording 903-935-4858; Fax 903-935-4877.

Will search UCC records prior to 7/2001 and current fixture (land) files. UCC search includes tax liens if requested. Will not search real estate records. **Online Access:** Property Tax Records. Search the appraiser database for free at www.harrisoncad.org. Also, see note at beginning of section. **Other Phone Numbers:** Assessor 903-935-1991; Treasurer 903-935-4820; Appraiser/Auditor 903-935-1991; Elections 903-935-4822; Vital Records 903-935-4858.

Hartley County

County Clerk, PO Box Q, Channing, TX 79018. County Clerk, R/E and UCC Recording 806-235-2603 UCC Recording: 806-235-3582; Fax 806-235-2316.

Will search UCC records prior to 7/2001 and current fixture (land) files. Will not search real estate records. **Other Phone Numbers:** Assessor 806-235-4515; Treasurer 806-235-3572; Appraiser/Auditor 806-235-4515; Elections 806-235-3582; Vital Records 806-235-3582; Judge 806-235-3142.

Haskell County

County Clerk, PO Box 725, Haskell, TX 79521-0725. 940-864-2451; Fax 940-864-6164.

Will search UCC records prior to 7/2001 and current fixture (land) files. Will search real estate records. **Other Phones:** Assessor 940-864-2181; Treasurer 940-

864-3448; Appraiser/Auditor 940-864-3805; Elections 940-864-2451; Vital Records 940-864-2451.

Hays County

County Clerk, 137 N. Guadalupe, Hays County Records Building, San Marcos, TX 78666. 512-393-7330; Fax 512-393-7337. www.co.hays.tx.us/departments/departments.asp
Will search UCC records prior to 7/2001 and current fixture (land) files. **Online Access:** Assessor, Property Tax Records. See notes at beginning of section. **Other Phone Numbers:** Assessor 512-268-2522; Treasurer 512-392-3669; Appraiser/Auditor 512-268-2522; Elections 512-393-7310.

Hemphill County

County Clerk, PO Box 867, Canadian, TX 79014. County Clerk, R/E and UCC Recording 806-323-6212. Will search UCC records. UCC search includes tax liens if requested. Real estate owner, mortgage, and property transfer searches available. **Other Phone Numbers:** Assessor 806-323-5161; Treasurer 806-323-6671; Appraiser/Auditor 806-323-8022; Elections 806-323-6212; Vital Records 806-323-6212.

Henderson County

County Clerk, PO Box 632, Athens, TX 75751-0632. 903-675-6140; Fax 903-675-6105.
Will search UCC records prior to 7/2001 and current fixture (land) files. Tax liens not included in UCC search. Will not search real estate records. **Online Access:** Property Tax Records. See note at beginning of section. **Other Phone Numbers:** Assessor 903-675-9296; Treasurer 903-675-6119; Appraiser/Auditor 903-675-9296.

Hidalgo County

County Clerk, PO Box 58, Edinburg, TX 78540. 956-318-2100; Fax 956-318-2105. www.co.hidalgo.tx.us
Will search UCC records prior to 7/2001 and current fixture (land) files. This agency will not do a tax lien search. Will not search real estate records. **Online Access:** Assessor, Property Tax Records. See note at beginning of section. **Other Phones:** Assessor 956-318-2180; Appraiser/Auditor 956-782-2255.

Hill County

County Clerk, PO Box 398, Hillsboro, TX 76645. 254-582-2161.
Will search UCC records prior to 7/2001 and current fixture (land) files. Tax liens not included in UCC search. Real estate owner, mortgage, and property transfer searches available. **Online Access:** Property Tax Records. See note at beginning of section. **Other Phone Numbers:** Assessor 254-582-3862; Treasurer 254-582-2632; Appraiser/Auditor 254-582-2508.

Hockley County

County Clerk, 800 Houston St., Ste 213, Levelland, TX 79336. County Clerk, R/E and UCC Recording 806-894-3185.
Will search UCC records prior to 7/2001 and current fixture (land) files. UCC search includes tax liens if requested. Will not search real estate records. **Other Phone Numbers:** Assessor 806-894-4938; Treasurer 806-894-3718; Appraiser/Auditor 806-894-9654; Elections 806-894-3185; Vital Records 806-894-3185.

Hood County

County Clerk, PO Box 339, Granbury, TX 76048-0339. 817-579-3222; Fax 817-579-3227.
Will search UCC records prior to 7/2001 and current fixture (land) files. Tax liens not included in UCC search. Real estate owner, mortgage, and property transfer searches available. **Online Access:** Assessor, Property Tax Records. Search the county appraisal roll for free at www.hoodcad.org. Also, see note at

beginning of section. **Other Phone Numbers:** Assessor 817-579-3295; Treasurer 817-579-3208; Appraiser/Auditor 817-573-2471.

Hopkins County

County Clerk, PO Box 288, Sulphur Springs, TX 75483. 903-438-4074 R/E Recording: 903-885-3929; Fax 903-438-9007. www.hopkinscountytx.org
Will search UCC records prior to 7/2001 and current fixture (land) files. UCC search includes tax liens if requested. Will not search real estate records. **Other Phone Numbers:** Assessor 903-438-4063; Treasurer 903-438-4003; Appraiser/Auditor 903-885-2173; Elections 903-438-4074; Vital Records 903-438-4074; Voter Registrar 903-438-4063.

Houston County

County Clerk, PO Box 370, Crockett, TX 75835-0370. 936-544-3255 R/E Recording: 936-544-3255 x241 UCC Recording: 936-544-3255 x241; Fax 936-544-8053.
Will search UCC records prior to 7/2001 and current fixture (land) files. UCC search includes tax liens if requested. Real estate owner, mortgage, and property transfer searches available. **Other Phone Numbers:** Assessor 936-544-3255 x258; Treasurer 936-544-3255 x236; Appraiser/Auditor 936-544-9655; Elections 936-544-3255 x241; Vital Records 936-544-3255 x241.

Howard County

County Clerk, PO Box 1468, Big Spring, TX 79721-1468. County Clerk, R/E and UCC Recording 915-264-2213 UCC Recording: 915-264-2214; Fax 915-264-2215. www.howard-county.net
Will search UCC records prior to 7/2001. Tax liens not included in UCC search. Will not search real estate records. **Other Phone Numbers:** Assessor 915-264-2232; Treasurer 915-264-2218; Appraiser/Auditor 915-263-8301; Elections 915-264-2214; Vital Records 915-264-2214.

Hudspeth County

County Clerk, PO Drawer A, Sierra Blanca, TX 79851. County Clerk, R/E and UCC Recording 915-369-2301; Fax 915-369-2361.
Will search UCC records prior to 7/2001 and current fixture (land) files. **Other Phone Numbers:** Assessor 915-369-2331; Treasurer 915-369-3511; Appraiser/Auditor 915-369-4118; Elections 915-369-2301; Vital Records 915-369-2301.

Hunt County

County Clerk, PO Box 1316, Greenville, TX 75403-1316. County Clerk, R/E and UCC Recording 903-408-4130.
Will search UCC records prior to 7/2001 and current fixture (land) files. Tax liens not included in UCC search. Will not search real estate records. **Online Access:** Assessor, Property Tax Records. See notes at beginning of section. **Other Phone Numbers:** Assessor 903-408-4150; Treasurer 903-408-4171; Appraiser/Auditor 903-408-3510; Elections 903-408-4130; Vital Records 903-408-4130.

Hutchinson County

County Clerk, PO Box 1186, Stinnett, TX 79083. County Clerk, R/E and UCC Recording 806-878-4002. Will search UCC records. UCC search includes tax liens if requested. Will not search real estate records. **Other Phone Numbers:** Assessor 806-878-4005; Treasurer 806-878-4010; Appraiser/Auditor 806-274-2294; Elections 806-878-4002; Vital Records 806-878-4002.

Irion County

County Clerk, PO Box 736, Mertzon, TX 76941-0736. County Clerk, R/E and UCC Recording 915-835-2421; Fax 915-835-2008.
Will search UCC records prior to 7/2001 and current fixture (land) files. Will search state tax liens-$5.00 per name. Will search real estate records. **Other Phone Numbers:** Assessor 915-835-7771; Treasurer 915-835-4111; Appraiser/Auditor 915-835-3551; Elections 915-835-2421; Vital Records 915-835-2421.

Jack County

County Clerk, 100 Main St, Jacksboro, TX 76458. County Clerk, R/E and UCC Recording 940-567-2111. Will search UCC records. UCC search includes tax liens if requested. Will not search real estate records. **Other Phones:** Assessor 940-567-6301; Treasurer 940-567-2251; Appraiser/Auditor 940-567-6301; Elections 940-567-2111; Vital Records 940-567-2111.

Jackson County

County Clerk, 115 W. Main, Room 101, Edna, TX 77957. 361-782-3563; Fax 361-782-3645.
Will search UCC records prior to 7/2001 and current fixture (land) files. UCC search includes tax liens if requested. Will not search real estate records. **Other Phone Numbers:** Assessor 361-782-7115; Treasurer 361-782-3402; Appraiser/Auditor 361-782-7115.

Jasper County

Deputy Clerk, PO Box 2070, Jasper, TX 75951. Deputy Clerk, R/E and UCC Recording 409-384-2632; Fax 409-384-7198.
Will search UCC records prior to 7/2001 and current fixture (land) files. Will not search real estate records. **Other Phone Numbers:** Assessor 409-384-6896; Treasurer 409-384-2461; Appraiser/Auditor 409-384-2544; Elections 409-384-3399; Vital Records 409-384-2632.

Jeff Davis County

County Clerk, PO Box 398, Fort Davis, TX 79734. 915-426-3251; Fax 915-426-3760.
Will search UCC records prior to 7/2001 and current fixture (land) files. Will not search real estate records. **Other Phone Numbers:** Assessor 915-426-3213; Treasurer 915-426-3242; Appraiser/Auditor 915-857-3333.

Jefferson County

County Clerk, PO Box 1151, Beaumont, TX 77704-1151. County Clerk, R/E and UCC Recording 409-835-8475; Fax 409-839-2394. www.co.jefferson.tx.us
Will search UCC records prior to 7/2001 and current fixture (land) files. State tax liens not included in UCC search. Will search only federal tax liens. Will not search real estate records. **Online Access:** Property Tax Records. Search the appraiser database for free at www.jcad.org/search2.asp. Also, see note at beginning of section. **Other Phone Numbers:** Assessor 409-835-8516; Treasurer 409-835-8509; Appraiser/Auditor 409-835-4611; Elections 409-835-8760; Vital Records 409-835-8475.

Jim Hogg County

County Clerk, PO Box 878, Hebbronville, TX 78361. County Clerk, R/E and UCC Recording 361-527-4031; Fax 361-527-5843.
Will search UCC records prior to 7/2001 and current fixture (land) files. **Other Phone Numbers:** Assessor 361-527-3237; Treasurer 361-527-3164; Appraiser/Auditor 361-527-4033; Elections 361-527-4031; Vital Records 361-527-4031.

Jim Wells County

County Clerk, PO Box 1459, Alice, TX 78333. 361-668-5702.
Will search UCC records prior to 7/2001 and current fixture (land) files. UCC search includes tax liens if requested. Will not search real estate records. **Other Phone Numbers:** Assessor 361-668-9656; Treasurer 361-668-5713; Appraiser/Auditor 361-668-9656.

Johnson County

County Clerk, PO Box 662, Cleburne, TX 76033-0662. County Clerk, R/E & UCC Recording 817-556-6314 UCC Recording: 817-556-6310; Fax 817-556-6326. www.johnsoncad.com/search.htm
Will search UCC records prior to 7/2001 and current fixture (land) files. **Online Access:** Assessor, Property Tax Records. Records from the County Appraiser are available fee online at the web site. Also, see note at beginning of section. **Other Phone Numbers:** Assessor 817-556-6100; Treasurer 817-566-6341; Appraiser/Auditor 817-558-8100; Elections 817-556-6311; Vital Records 817-556-6314.

Jones County

County Clerk, PO Box 552, Anson, TX 79501-0552. County Clerk, R/E and UCC Recording 915-823-3762; Fax 915-823-4223.
Will search UCC records prior to 7/2001 and current fixture (land) files. Will not search real estate records. **Other Phones:** Assessor 915-823-2422; Treasurer 915-823-3742; Appraiser/Auditor 915-823-2422; Elections 915-823-3762; Vital Records 915-823-3762.

Karnes County

County Clerk, 101 N. Panna Maria Ave., Courthouse - Suite 9, Karnes City, TX 78118-2929. County Clerk, R/E and UCC Recording 830-780-3938; Fax 830-780-4576.
Will search UCC records prior to 7/2001 and current fixture (land) files. **Other Phone Numbers:** Assessor 830-780-2431; Treasurer 830-780-2312; Appraiser/Auditor 830-780-2433; Elections 830-780-3938; Vital Records 830-780-3938.

Kaufman County

County Clerk, Courthouse, Kaufman, TX 75142. County Clerk, R/E and UCC Recording 972-932-4331; Fax 972-932-7628.
Will search UCC records prior to 7/2001 and current fixture (land) files. UCC search includes tax liens if requested. Real estate owner, mortgage, and property transfer searches available. **Online Access:** Assessor, Property Tax Records. See note at beginning of section. **Other Phone Numbers:** Assessor 972-932-6081; Treasurer 972-932-4331; Appraiser/Auditor 972-932-6081; Elections 972-932-4331; Vital Records 972-932-4331.

Kendall County

County Clerk, 201 E. San Antonio, Suite 127, Boerne, TX 78006. County Clerk, R/E and UCC Recording 830-249-9343; Fax 830-249-3472.
Will search UCC records. Tax liens not included in UCC search. Real estate owner, mortgage, and property transfer searches available. **Online Access:** Appraiser, Property Tax Records. See note at beginning of section. **Other Phones:** Assessor 830-249-9343; Treasurer 830-249-9343; Appraiser/Auditor 830-249-8012; Elections 830-249-9343; Vital Records 830-249-9343.

Kenedy County

County Clerk, PO Box 227, Sarita, TX 78385-0227. County Clerk, R/E and UCC Recording 361-294-5220; Fax 361-294-5218.
Will search UCC records prior to 7/2001 and current fixture (land) files. UCC search includes tax liens if requested. Real estate owner, mortgage, and property transfer searches available. **Other Phone Numbers:** Assessor 361-294-5202; Treasurer 361-294-5304; Appraiser/Auditor 361-321-1695; Elections 361-294-5220; Vital Records 361-294-5220.

Kent County

County Clerk, PO Box 9, Jayton, TX 79528-0009. 806-237-3881; Fax 806-237-2632.
Will search UCC records prior to 7/2001 and current fixture (land) files. UCC search includes tax liens if requested. Mortgage searches available. **Other Phone Numbers:** Assessor 806-237-3066; Treasurer 806-237-3075; Appraiser/Auditor 806-237-3036.

Kerr County

County Clerk, Courthouse, Room 122, 700 Main, Kerrville, TX 78028-5389. County Clerk, R/E and UCC Recording 830-792-2255; Fax 830-792-2274. www.ktc.com
Will search UCC records prior to 7/2001 and current fixture (land) files. **Online Access:** Assessor, Property Tax Records. See note at beginning of section. **Other Phone Numbers:** Assessor 830-895-5223; Treasurer 830-257-7972; Appraiser/Auditor 830-895-5223; Elections 830-792-2255; Vital Records 830-792-2255.

Kimble County

County Clerk, 501 Main St, Junction, TX 76849. County Clerk, R/E and UCC Recording 915-446-3353; Fax 915-446-2986.
Will search UCC records. UCC search includes tax liens if requested. Will not search real estate records. **Other Phones:** Assessor 915-446-3717; Treasurer 915-446-2847; Appraiser/Auditor 915-446-3717; Elections 915-446-3353; Vital Records 915-446-3353.

King County

County Clerk, PO Box 135, Guthrie, TX 79236. County Clerk, R/E and UCC Recording 806-596-4412; Fax 806-596-4664.
Will search UCC records prior to 7/2001 and current fixture (land) files. Tax liens not included in UCC search. Will not search real estate records. **Other Phone Numbers:** Assessor 806-596-4318; Treasurer 806-596-4319; Appraiser/Auditor 806-596-4318; Elections 806-596-4412; Vital Records 806-596-4412.

Kinney County

County Clerk, PO Drawer 9, Brackettville, TX 78832. County Clerk, R/E and UCC Recording 830-563-2521; Fax 830-563-2644.
Will search UCC records. Will not search real estate records. **Other Phone Numbers:** Assessor 830-563-2323; Treasurer 830-563-2777; Appraiser/Auditor 830-563-2323; Elections 830-563-2521; Vital Records 830-563-2521.

Kleberg County

County Clerk, PO Box 1327, Kingsville, TX 78364-1327. County Clerk, R/E and UCC Recording 361-595-8548.
Will search UCC records prior to 7/2001 and current fixture (land) files. UCC search includes tax liens if requested. Will not search real estate records. **Online Access:** Property Tax Records. See note at beginning of section. **Other Phone Numbers:** Assessor 361-595-8541; Treasurer 361-595-8535; Appraiser/Auditor 361-595-5775; Elections 361-595-8548; Vital Records 361-595-8548.

Knox County

County Clerk, PO Box 196, Benjamin, TX 79505. County Clerk, R/E and UCC Recording 940-454-2441; Fax 940-454-2005.
Will search UCC records prior to 7/2001 and current fixture (land) files. UCC search includes tax liens if requested. Will not search real estate records. **Other Phone Numbers:** Treasurer 817-454-2251; Appraiser/Auditor 940-454-3891.

La Salle County

County Clerk, PO Box 340, Cotulla, TX 78014. 830-879-4432; Fax 830-879-2933.
Will search UCC records prior to 7/2001 and current fixture (land) files. Will not search real estate records. **Other Phone Numbers:** Assessor 830-879-4437; Treasurer 830-879-4440; Appraiser/Auditor 830-879-2547; Elections 830-879-4432; Vital Records 830-879-4432.

Lamar County

County Clerk, Courthouse, 119 N. Main #109, Paris, TX 75460. County Clerk, R/E and UCC Recording 903-737-2420; Fax 903-782-1100.
Will search UCC records prior to 7/2001 and current fixture (land) files. Tax liens not included in UCC search. Will not search real estate records. **Online Access:** Death Records. Cemetery records in Lamar County are available free online at http://userdb.rootsweb.com/cemeteries/TX/Lamar. **Other Phone Numbers:** Assessor 903-785-7822; Treasurer 903-737-2418; Appraiser/Auditor 903-785-7822; Elections 903-737-2420; Vital Records 903-737-2420.

Lamb County

County Clerk, 100 6th St, Room 103 Box 3, Littlefield, TX 79339-3366. 806-385-4222 x210 R/E Recording: 806-385-4222; Fax 806-385-6485.
Will search UCC records prior to 7/2001 and current fixture (land) files. Tax liens not included in UCC search. Will not search real estate records. **Online Access:** Assessor, Property Tax Records. See note at beginning of section. **Other Phone Numbers:** Assessor 806-385-6474; Treasurer 806-385-3770; Appraiser/Auditor 806-385-6474.

Lampasas County

County Clerk, PO Box 347, Lampasas, TX 76550. 512-556-8271.
Will search UCC records prior to 7/2001 and current fixture (land) files. Tax liens not included in UCC search. Property transfer searches available. **Other Phone Numbers:** Assessor 512-556-8058; Treasurer 512-556-8058; Appraiser/Auditor 512-556-8058.

Lavaca County

County Clerk, PO Box 326, Hallettsville, TX 77964-0326. County Clerk, R/E and UCC Recording 361-798-3612.
Will search UCC records. This agency will not do a tax lien search. Will not search real estate records. **Other Phone Numbers:** Assessor 361-798-3600; Treasurer 361-798-2181; Appraiser/Auditor 361-798-4396; Elections 361-798-3612; Vital Records 361-798-3612.

Lee County

County Clerk, PO Box 419, Giddings, TX 78942. County Clerk, R/E and UCC Recording 979-542-3684; Fax 979-542-2623.
Will search UCC records prior to 7/2001 and current fixture (land) files. This agency will not do a tax lien search. Real estate owner, mortgage, and property transfer searches available. **Other Phones:** Assessor 979-542-2640; Treasurer 979-542-2161; Appraiser/Auditor 979-542-9618; Elections 979-542-3684.

Leon County

County Clerk, PO Box 98, Centerville, TX 75833. County Clerk, R/E and UCC Recording 903-536-2352; Fax 903-536-2431.
Will search UCC records prior to 7/2001 and current fixture (land) files. Will not search real estate records.

Other Phones: Assessor 903-536-2543; Treasurer 903-536-2915; Appraiser/Auditor 903-536-2252; Elections 903-536-2352; Vital Records 903-536-2352.

Liberty County

County Clerk, PO Box 369, Liberty, TX 77575. 936-336-4673 R/E Recording: 409-336-4673.
Will search UCC records prior to 7/2001 and current fixture (land) files. UCC search includes tax liens if requested. Will not search real estate records. **Online Access:** Assessor, Property Tax Records. See note at beginning of section. **Other Phones:** Assessor 936-336-4673; Appraiser/Auditor 409-336-5722.

Limestone County

County Clerk, PO Box 350, Groesbeck, TX 76642. 254-729-5504 R/E Recording: 254-729-3009; Fax 254-729-2951.
Will search UCC records prior to 7/2001 and current fixture (land) files. Tax liens not included in UCC search. Real estate record owner searches available. **Online Access:** Assessor, Property Tax Records. See notes at beginning of section. **Other Phone Numbers:** Assessor 254-729-3009; Treasurer 254-729-3314; Appraiser/Auditor 254-729-5504.

Lipscomb County

County Clerk, PO Box 70, Lipscomb, TX 79056. 806-862-3091; Fax 806-862-3004.
Will search UCC records. **Other Phone Numbers:** Assessor 806-624-2881; Treasurer 806-862-3821; Appraiser/Auditor 806-624-2881.

Live Oak County

County Clerk, PO Box 280, George West, TX 78022. 361-449-2733 x3 R/E Recording: 361-449-2733 UCC Recording: 361-449-2733 x103 or 129.
Will not search UCC records. Tax liens not included in UCC search. Will not search real estate records. **Other Phone Numbers:** Assessor 361-449-2641; Treasurer 361-449-2641 x109; Appraiser/Auditor 361-449-2641; Elections 361-449-2733 x129 or 103; Vital Records 361-449-2733 x129 or 103.

Llano County

County Clerk, 107 W. Sandstone, Llano, TX 78643-2318. 915-247-4455; Fax 915-247-2406.
Will search UCC records prior to 7/2001 and current fixture (land) files. UCC search includes tax liens if requested. Will not search real estate records. **Online Access:** Assessor, Property Tax Records. See note at beginning of section. **Other Phone Numbers:** Assessor 915-247-3065; Treasurer 915-247-5056; Appraiser/Auditor 915-247-3065.

Loving County

County Clerk, PO Box 194, Mentone, TX 79754. County Clerk, R/E and UCC Recording 915-377-2441; Fax 915-377-2701.
Will search UCC records. Will not search real estate records. **Other Phones:** Assessor 915-377-2411; Treasurer 915-377-2311; Appraiser/Auditor 915-377-2201; Elections 377-2441; Vital Records 377-2441.

Lubbock County

County Clerk, PO Box 10536, Lubbock, TX 79408-0536. 806-775-1060; Fax 806-775-1660. www.co.lubbock.tx.us
Will search UCC records prior to 7/2001. Will not search real estate records. **Online Access:** Elections, Appraiser, Property Tax Records. Access to the county clerks records is limited to election results at www.co.lubbock.tx.us/CClerk/county_clerk.htm. Also, search the property appraiser database for free at www.lubbockcad.org/search.cfm. **Other Phone Numbers:** Assessor 806-762-5000; Treasurer 806-775-1018; Appraiser/Auditor 806-762-5000; Elections 806-

775-1057 (election), 806-775-1339 (voter); Vital Records 806-775-2926 (birth/death), 806-775-1054 (marriage).

Lynn County

County Clerk, PO Box 937, Tahoka, TX 79373. County Clerk, R/E and UCC Recording 806-998-4750; Fax 806-998-4988.
Will search UCC records prior to 7/2001 and current fixture (land) files. UCC search includes tax liens if requested. Will not search real estate records. **Other Phone Numbers:** Assessor 806-998-4112; Treasurer 806-998-4055; Appraiser/Auditor 806-998-5477; Elections 806-998-4750; Vital Records 806-998-4750.

Madison County

County Clerk, 101 W. Main, Room 102, Madisonville, TX 77864. County Clerk, R/E and UCC Recording 936-348-2638; Fax 936-348-5858.
Will search UCC records. UCC search includes tax liens if requested. Will not search real estate records. **Other Phones:** Assessor 936-348-2783; Treasurer 936-348-5141; Appraiser/Auditor 936-348-2783; Elections 936-348-2638; Vital Records 936-348-2638.

Marion County

County Clerk, PO Box 763, Jefferson, TX 75657. County Clerk, R/E and UCC Recording 903-665-3971; Fax 903-665-8732.
Will search UCC records prior to 7/2001 and current fixture (land) files. Tax liens not included in UCC search. Real estate owner, mortgage, and property transfer searches available. **Other Phone Numbers:** Assessor 903-665-3281; Treasurer 903-665-2472; Appraiser/Auditor 903-665-2519; Elections 903-665-3971; Vital Records 903-665-3971.

Martin County

County Clerk, PO Box 906, Stanton, TX 79782. County Clerk, R/E and UCC Recording 915-756-3412; Fax 915-756-2992.
Will search UCC records prior to 7/2001 and current fixture (land) files. UCC search includes tax liens if requested. Will not search real estate records. **Other Phone Numbers:** Assessor 915-756-3396; Treasurer 915-756-3631; Appraiser/Auditor 915-756-2823; Elections 915-756-3412; Vital Records 915-756-3412.

Mason County

County Clerk, PO Box 702, Mason, TX 76856-0702. County Clerk, R/E and UCC Recording 915-347-5253; Fax 915-347-6868.
Will search UCC records prior to 7/2001 and current fixture (land) files. UCC search includes tax liens if requested. Will not search real estate records. **Other Phone Numbers:** Assessor 915-347-5989; Treasurer 915-347-5251; Appraiser/Auditor 915-347-5989; Elections 915-347-5253; Vital Records 915-347-5253.

Matagorda County

County Clerk, 1700 7th St, Room 202, Bay City, TX 77414. County Clerk, R/E and UCC Recording 979-244-7680; Fax 979-244-7688.
Will search UCC records prior to 7/2001 and current fixture (land) files. Will not search real estate records. **Other Phones:** Assessor 979-244-7670; Treasurer 979-244-7609; Appraiser/Auditor 979-244-2031; Elections 979-244-7680; Vital Records 979-244-7680.

Maverick County

County Clerk, PO Box 4050, Eagle Pass, TX 78853-4050. County Clerk, R/E and UCC Recording 830-773-2829; Fax 830-773-0129.
Will Search UCC records prior to 7/2001 and current fixture (land) files. UCC search includes tax liens if requested. Will not search real estate records. **Online Access:** Assessor, Property Tax Records. See note at

beginning of section. **Other Phone Numbers:** Assessor 830-773-9273; Treasurer 830-773-2413; Appraiser/Auditor 830-773-0255; Elections 830-773-2829; Vital Records 830-773-2829.

McCulloch County

County Clerk, Courthouse, Brady, TX 76825. County Clerk, R/E and UCC Recording 915-597-0733; Fax 915-597-1731.
Will search UCC records prior to 7/2001 and current fixture (land) files. Will search real estate records. **Other Phones:** Assessor 915-597-7607; Treasurer 915-597-0773 x116; Appraiser/Auditor 915-597-1627; Elections 915-597-7607; Vital Records 915-597-0733.

McLennan County

County Clerk, PO Box 1727, Waco, TX 76703-1727. 254-757-5078; Fax 254-757-5146.
Will search UCC records prior to 7/2001 and current fixture (land) files. Tax liens not included in UCC search. Will not search real estate records. **Online Access:** Property Tax Records. See note at beginning of section. **Other Phone Numbers:** Appraiser/Auditor 254-752-9864.

McMullen County

County Clerk, PO Box 235, Tilden, TX 78072-0235. 361-274-3215; Fax 361-274-3618.
Will search UCC records prior to 7/2001 and current fixture (land) files. Tax liens not included in UCC search. Property transfer searches available. **Other Phone Numbers:** Assessor 361-274-3214; Treasurer 361-274-3685; Appraiser/Auditor 361-274-3233.

Medina County

County Clerk, Courthouse, Room 109, 16th St., Hondo, TX 78861. County Clerk, R/E and UCC Recording 830-741-6041; Fax 830-741-6015.
Will search UCC records prior to 7/2001 and current fixture (land) files. **Other Phone Numbers:** Assessor 830-741-6100; Treasurer 830-741-6110; Appraiser/Auditor 830-741-3035; Elections 830-741-6040; Vital Records 830-741-6041.

Menard County

County Clerk, PO Box 1028, Menard, TX 76859. 915-396-4682 R/E Recording: 915-396-4784; Fax 915-396-2047.
Will search UCC records prior to 7/2001 and current fixture (land) files. Will search real estate records. **Other Phone Numbers:** Assessor 915-396-4523; Appraiser/Auditor 915-396-4682.

Midland County

County Clerk, PO Box 211, Midland, TX 79702. County Clerk, R/E and UCC Recording 915-688-1059; Fax 915-688-8914.
Will search UCC records prior to 7/2001 and current fixture (land) files. Tax liens not included in UCC search. Will not search real estate records. **Online Access:** Property Assessor, Voter Registration Records. Access to the property tax database is available free at www.co.midland.tx.us/Tax/Property/Database/search.asp. Also, search property data on the mapping page at www.midcad.org/Search/index.htm. Online access to the voter registration database is available free at www.co.midland.tx.us/Elections/VoterDatabase/input.asp. **Other Phones:** Assessor 915-699-4991; Treasurer 915-688-1235; Appraiser/Auditor 915-699-4991; Elections 915-688-1222; Vital Records 915-688-1059.

Milam County

County Clerk, PO Box 191, Cameron, TX 76520. 254-697-7049 R/E Recording: 254-697-6596; Fax 254-697-7055.
Will search UCC records prior to 7/2001 and current fixture (land) files. UCC search includes tax liens if

requested. Will not search real estate records. **Online Access:** Assessor, Property Tax Records. See note at beginning of section. **Other Phone Numbers:** Assessor 254-697-7017; Treasurer 254-697-7032; Appraiser/Auditor 254-697-6638; Elections 254-697-7049; Vital Records 254-697-7049.

Mills County

County Clerk, PO Box 646, Goldthwaite, TX 76844-0646. County Clerk, R/E and UCC Recording 915-648-2711; Fax 915-648-3251.
Will not search UCC records. Tax liens not included in UCC search. Will not search real estate records. **Other Phone Numbers:** Assessor 915-648-2253; Treasurer 915-648-2636; Appraiser/Auditor 915-648-2253; Elections 915-648-2711; Vital Records 915-648-2711.

Mitchell County

County Clerk, 349 Oak St. #103, Colorado City, TX 79512-6213. County Clerk, R/E and UCC Recording 915-728-3481; Fax 915-728-5322.
Will search UCC records prior to 7/2001 and current fixture (land) files. Tax liens not included in UCC search. Real estate owner, mortgage, and property transfer searches available. **Other Phone Numbers:** Assessor 915-728-2606; Treasurer 915-728-8356; Appraiser/Auditor 915-728-5028; Elections 915-728-2606; Vital Records 915-728-3481.

Montague County

County Clerk, PO Box 77, Montague, TX 76251-0077. 940-894-2461; Fax 940-894-3110.
Will search UCC records prior to 7/2001 and current fixture (land) files. Will not search real estate records. **Other Phone Numbers:** Assessor 940-894-6011; Appraiser/Auditor 940-894-2081.

Montgomery County

County Clerk, PO Box 959, Conroe, TX 77305. 936-539-7893 R/E Recording: 936-539-7885 UCC Recording: 936-539-7885; Fax 936-760-6990. www.co.montgomery.tx.us
Will search UCC records prior to 7/2001 and current fixture (land) files. Tax liens not included in UCC search. Will not search real estate records. **Online Access:** Assessor, Property Tax Records. See notes at beginning of section. **Other Phone Numbers:** Assessor 936-756-3354; Treasurer 936-759-7844; Appraiser/Auditor 936-756-3354; Elections 936-539-7843; Vital Records 936-538-8114.

Moore County

County Clerk, 715 Dumas Ave., Rm. 105, Dumas, TX 79029. 806-935-2009; Fax 806-935-9004.
Will search UCC records prior to 7/2001 and current fixture (land) files. UCC search includes tax liens if requested. Will not search real estate records. **Other Phone Numbers:** Assessor 806-935-4193; Treasurer 806-935-2019; Appraiser/Auditor 806-935-4193.

Morris County

County Clerk, 500 Broadnax St, Daingerfield, TX 75638. County Clerk, R/E and UCC Recording 903-645-3911.
Will search UCC records prior to 7/2001 and current fixture (land) files. UCC search includes tax liens if requested. Will not search real estate records. **Other Phone Numbers:** Assessor 903-645-2440; Treasurer 903-645-2916; Appraiser/Auditor 903-645-5061; Elections 903-645-3911; Vital Records 903-645-3911.

Motley County

County Clerk, PO Box 66, Matador, TX 79244. County Clerk, R/E and UCC Recording 806-347-2621; Fax 806-347-2220.
Will search UCC records. **Other Phone Numbers:** Assessor 806-347-2252; Treasurer 806-347-2800;

Appraiser/Auditor 806-347-2273; Elections 806-347-2621; Vital Records 806-347-2621.

Nacogdoches County

County Clerk, 101 W. Main, Room 205, Nacogdoches, TX 75961. County Clerk, R/E and UCC Recording 936-560-7733; Fax 936-559-5926.
Will search UCC records prior to 7/2001 and current fixture (land) files. Tax liens not included in UCC search. Will not search real estate records. **Online Access:** Property Tax Records. Access to the county Central Appraisal District Appriasal Roll from TaxNetUSA is available free at www.taxnetusa.com/nacogdoches. **Other Phone Numbers:** Assessor 936-560-3447; Treasurer 936-560-7703; Appraiser/Auditor 409-560-3447; Elections 936-560-7825; Vital Records 936-560-7733.

Navarro County

County Clerk, PO Box 423, Corsicana, TX 75151. 903-654-3035.
Will search UCC records prior to 7/2001 and current fixture (land) files. UCC search includes tax liens if requested. Will not search real estate records. **Online Access:** Assessor, Property Tax Records. See note at beginning of section for "Advanced" fee service. **Other Phone Numbers:** Assessor 903-872-6161; Treasurer 903-654-3090; Appraiser/Auditor 903-872-2476.

Newton County

County Clerk, PO Box 484, Newton, TX 75966-0484. County Clerk, R/E and UCC Recording 409-379-5341; Fax 409-379-9049.
Will search UCC records prior to 7/2001 and current fixture (land) files. UCC search includes tax liens if requested. Will not search real estate records. **Online Access:** Assessor, Property Tax, Death Records. For assessor/property tax: see note at beginning of section. Death records in this county may be accessed over the Internet at www.jas.net/jas.htm (site may be temporarily down). **Other Phone Numbers:** Assessor 409-379-3710; Treasurer 409-379-8127; Appraiser/Auditor 409-379-3710; Vital Records 409-379-5341.

Nolan County

County Clerk, 100 E 3rd St #108, Sweetwater, TX 79556-0098. 915-235-2462.
Will search UCC records prior to 7/2001 and current fixture (land) files. Tax liens not included in UCC search. Will not search real estate records. **Other Phone Numbers:** Assessor 915-235-8421; Treasurer 915-236-6932; Appraiser/Auditor 915-235-8421.

Nueces County

County Clerk, PO Box 2627, Corpus Christi, TX 78403. County Clerk, R/E and UCC Recording 361-888-0611 UCC Recording: 361-888-0580; Fax 361-888-0329. www.co.nueces.tx.us
Will search UCC records prior to 7/2001 and current fixture (land) files. Tax liens not included in UCC search. Will not search real estate records. **Online Access:** Assessor, Property Tax Records. Records from the County Appraiser are available fee online at www.nuecescad.org/nueces3.html. Also, see notes at beginning of section. **Other Phone Numbers:** Assessor 361-888-0230; Treasurer 361-888-0515; Appraiser/Auditor 361-881-8022; Elections 361-888-0483; Vital Records 361-888-0580.

Ochiltree County

County Clerk, 511 S. Main, Perryton, TX 79070. County Clerk, R/E and UCC Recording 806-435-8039; Fax 806-435-2081.
Will search UCC records prior to 7/2001 and current fixture (land) files. UCC search includes tax liens if requested. Will not search real estate records. **Other Phone Numbers:** Assessor 806-435-8025; Treasurer

806-435-8046; Appraiser/Auditor 806-435-9623; Elections 806-435-8039; Vital Records 806-435-8039.

Oldham County

County Clerk, PO Box 360, Vega, TX 79092. 806-267-2667.
Will search UCC records prior to 7/2001 and current fixture (land) files. UCC search includes tax liens if requested. Will not search real estate records. **Other Phone Numbers:** Appraiser/Auditor 806-267-2442.

Orange County

County Clerk, PO Box 1536, Orange, TX 77631-1536. County Clerk, R/E and UCC Recording 409-882-7055; Fax 409-882-0379.
Will search UCC records. Will not search real estate records. **Other Phones:** Assessor 409-882-7971; Treasurer 409-882-7991; Appraiser/Auditor 409-745-4777; Elections 882-7055; Vital Records 882-7055.

Palo Pinto County

County Clerk, PO Box 219, Palo Pinto, TX 76484. County Clerk, R/E and UCC Recording 940-659-1277.
Will search UCC records. Tax liens not included in UCC search. Will not search real estate records. **Other Phone Numbers:** Assessor 940-659-1281; Treasurer 940-659-1260; Appraiser/Auditor 940-659-1281; Elections 940-659-1277; Vital Records 940-659-1277.

Panola County

County Clerk, Sabine & Sycamore, Courthouse Bldg., Room 201, Carthage, TX 75633. County Clerk, R/E and UCC Recording 903-693-0302; Fax 903-693-2726.
Will search UCC records prior to 7/2001 and current fixture (land) files. UCC search includes tax liens if requested. Will not search real estate records. **Other Phone Numbers:** Assessor 903-693-0340; Treasurer 903-693-0325; Appraiser/Auditor 903-693-2891; Elections 903-693-0370; Vital Records 903-693-0302.

Parker County

County Clerk, PO Box 819, Weatherford, TX 76086. 817-599-6591.
Will search UCC records prior to 7/2001 and current fixture (land) files. UCC search includes tax liens if requested. Will not search real estate records. **Online Access:** Assessor, Property Tax Records. See note at beginning of section for "Advanced" fee service. **Other Phone Numbers:** Assessor 817-599-7671; Treasurer 817-596-0078; Appraiser/Auditor 817-596-0077.

Parmer County

County Clerk, PO Box 356, Farwell, TX 79325. County Clerk, R/E and UCC Recording 806-481-3691; Fax 806-481-9154.
Will search UCC records prior to 7/2001 and current fixture (land) files. UCC search includes tax liens if requested. Will not search real estate records. **Other Phone Numbers:** Assessor 806-481-3845; Treasurer 806-481-9152; Appraiser/Auditor 806-481-1405; Elections 806-481-3691; Vital Records 806-481-3691.

Pecos County

County Clerk, 103 W. Callaghan St, Fort Stockton, TX 79735. 915-336-7555; Fax 915-336-7557.
Will search UCC records prior to 7/2001 and current fixture (land) files. Will not search real estate records. **Other Phones:** Assessor 915-336-7587; Treasurer 915-336-3461; Appraiser/Auditor 915-336-7587; Elections 915-336-7555; Vital Records 915-336-7555.

Polk County

County Clerk, PO Drawer 2119, Livingston, TX 77351. County Clerk, R/E and UCC Recording 936-327-6804; Fax 936-327-6874.
Will search UCC records prior to 7/2001 and current fixture (land) files. Tax liens not included in UCC

search. Will not search real estate records. **Other Phone Numbers:** Assessor 936-327-6801; Treasurer 936-327-6816; Appraiser/Auditor 936-327-2174; Elections 936-327-6852; Vital Records 936-327-6804; Court Clerk 936-327-6805.

Potter County

County Clerk, PO Box 9638, Amarillo, TX 79105. 806-379-2275; Fax 806-379-2296. www.prad.org
Will search UCC records prior to 7/2001 and current fixture (land) files. Tax liens not included in UCC search. Will not search real estate records. **Online Access:** Assessor, Property Tax Records. Two sources exist. Records on the Potter-Randall Appraisal District database are available free online at www.prad.org/search.html. Records periodically updated; for current tax information call Potter (806-342-2600) or Randall (806-665-6287). See note at beginning of section for "Advanced" fee service. **Other Phone Numbers:** Assessor 806-358-1601; Treasurer 806-379-2236; Appraiser/Auditor 806-358-1601.

Presidio County

County Clerk, PO Box 789, Marfa, TX 79843. County Clerk, R/E and UCC Recording 915-729-4812; Fax 915-729-4313.
Will search UCC records prior to 7/2001 and current fixture (land) files. **Other Phone Numbers:** Assessor 915-729-4081; Treasurer 915-729-4076; Appraiser/Auditor 915-729-3431; Elections 915-729-4812; Vital Records 915-729-4812.

Rains County

County Clerk, PO Box 187, Emory, TX 75440. County Clerk, R/E and UCC Recording 903-473-2461.
Will search UCC records prior to 7/2001 and current fixture (land) files. UCC search does not include tax liens. Will not search real estate records. **Other Phone Numbers:** Assessor 903-473-2391; Treasurer 903-473-2310; Appraiser/Auditor 903-473-2391; Elections 903-473-2461; Vital Records 903-473-2461.

Randall County

County Clerk, PO Box 660, Canyon, TX 79015. County Clerk, R/E and UCC Recording 806-655-6330; Fax 806-656-6430. www.prad.org
Will search UCC records prior to 7/2001 and current fixture (land) files. Tax liens not included in UCC search. Will not search real estate records. **Online Access:** Assessor, Property Tax Records. Two sources exist. Randall County records are combined online with Potter County; see Potter County for access information. Also, see notes at beginning of section. **Other Phone Numbers:** Assessor 806-358-1414; Treasurer 806-655-6256; Appraiser/Auditor 806-358-1601; Elections 806-655-6363; Vital Records 806-655-6332.

Reagan County

County Clerk, PO Box 100, Big Lake, TX 76932. County Clerk, R/E and UCC Recording 915-884-2442; Fax 915-884-1503.
Will search UCC records prior to 7/2001 and current fixture (land) files. UCC search includes tax liens if requested. Will not search real estate records. **Other Phone Numbers:** Assessor 915-884-2131; Treasurer 915-884-2090; Appraiser/Auditor 915-884-3275; Elections 915-884-2442; Vital Records 915-884-2442.

Real County

County Clerk, PO Box 750, Leakey, TX 78873-0750. 830-232-5202; Fax 830-232-6888. www.realcountytexas.com
Will search UCC records prior to 7/2001 and current fixture (land) files. **Other Phone Numbers:** Assessor 830-232-6210; Treasurer 830-232-6627; Appraiser/Auditor 830-232-6248.

Red River County

County Clerk, 200 N. Walnut, Courthouse Annex, Clarksville, TX 75426-3075. County Clerk, R/E and UCC Recording 903-427-2401; Fax 903-427-5510.
Will search UCC records prior to 7/2001 and current fixture (land) files. Tax liens not included in UCC search. Real estate record owner searches available. **Other Phone Numbers:** Assessor 903-427-3009; Treasurer 903-427-3748; Appraiser/Auditor 903-427-4181; Elections 903-427-2401; Vital Records 903-427-2401.

Reeves County

County Clerk, PO Box 867, Pecos, TX 79772. County Clerk, R/E and UCC Recording 915-445-5467; Fax 915-445-5096.
Will search UCC records prior to 7/2001 and current fixture (land) files. Will not search real estate records. **Other Phone Numbers:** Assessor 915-445-5122; Treasurer 915-445-2631; Appraiser/Auditor 915-445-5122; Elections 915-445-5467; Vital Records 915-445-5467.

Refugio County

County Clerk, PO Box 704, Refugio, TX 78377. 361-526-1325 R/E Recording: 361-526-2233.
Will search UCC records prior to 7/2001 and current fixture (land) files. UCC search includes tax liens if requested. Real estate record owner and property searches available. **Other Phone Numbers:** Assessor 361-526-5994; Treasurer 361-526-4223; Appraiser/Auditor 361-526-5994.

Roberts County

County Clerk, PO Box 477, Miami, TX 79059-0477. 806-868-2341; Fax 806-868-3381.
This agency will not search real estate or UCC records. **Other Phone Numbers:** Assessor 806-868-3611; Treasurer 806-868-3201; Appraiser/Auditor 806-868-5281; Vital Records 806-868-2341.

Robertson County

County Clerk, PO Box 1029, Franklin, TX 77856. County Clerk, R/E and UCC Recording 979-828-4130; Fax 979-828-1260.
Will search UCC records prior to 7/2001 and current fixture (land) files. UCC search includes tax liens if requested. Will not search real estate records. **Other Phone Numbers:** Assessor 979-828-3337; Treasurer 979-828-3201; Appraiser/Auditor 979-828-5800; Elections 979-828-4130; Vital Records 979-828-4130.

Rockwall County

County Clerk, 1101 Ridge Rd., S-101, Rockwall, TX 75087. County Clerk, R/E and UCC Recording 972-882-0220 UCC Recording: 972-882-0225; Fax 972-882-0229.
Will search UCC records prior to 7/2001 and current fixture (land) files. UCC search includes tax liens if requested. Will not search real estate records. **Online Access:** Assessor, Property Tax Records. See notes at beginning of section. **Other Phone Numbers:** Assessor 972-882-0250; Treasurer 972-882-0290; Appraiser/Auditor 972-771-2034; Elections 972-882-0220; Vital Records 972-882-0220.

Runnels County

County Clerk, PO Box 189, Ballinger, TX 76821-0189. County Clerk, R/E and UCC Recording 915-365-2720; Fax 915-365-3408.
Will search UCC records prior to 7/2001 and current fixture (land) files. Tax liens not included in UCC search. Will not search real estate records. **Other Phone Numbers:** Assessor 915-365-3583; Treasurer 915-365-2428; Appraiser/Auditor 915-365-3583; Elections 915-365-2720; Vital Records 915-365-2720.

Rusk County

County Clerk, PO Box 758, Henderson, TX 75653-0758. County Clerk, R/E and UCC Recording 903-657-0330.
Will search UCC records prior to 7/2001 and current fixture (land) files. UCC search includes tax liens if requested. Will not search real estate records. **Online Access:** Property Tax Records. See note at beginning of section. **Other Phone Numbers:** Assessor 903-657-0338; Treasurer 903-657-0352; Appraiser/Auditor 903-657-3578; Elections 903-657-0301; Vital Records 903-657-0301; 903-657-0327.

Sabine County

County Clerk, PO Drawer 580, Hemphill, TX 75948-0580. County Clerk, R/E and UCC Recording 409-787-3786; Fax 409-787-2044.
Will search UCC records. **Other Phone Numbers:** Assessor 409-787-2777; Treasurer 409-787-2210; Appraiser/Auditor 409-787-2777; Elections 409-787-3786; Vital Records 409-787-3786.

San Augustine County

County Clerk, 106 Courthouse, 100 W. Columbia, San Augustine, TX 75972-1335. 936-275-2452 R/E Recording: 409-275-2452; Fax 936-275-9579.
Will search UCC records prior to 7/2001 and current fixture (land) files. Will not search real estate records. **Other Phone Numbers:** Assessor 936-275-2300; Treasurer 936-275-9472; Appraiser/Auditor 936-275-3496.

San Jacinto County

County Clerk, PO Box 669, Coldspring, TX 77331. County Clerk, R/E and UCC Recording 936-653-2324.
Will search UCC records prior to 7/2001 and current fixture (land) files. This agency will not do a tax lien search. Real estate owner, mortgage, and property transfer searches available. **Online Access:** Assessor, Property Tax Records. See note at beginning of section. **Other Phone Numbers:** Assessor 936-653-3292; Treasurer 936-653-2353; Appraiser/Auditor 936-653-4481; Elections 936-653-2324; Vital Records 936-653-2324.

San Patricio County

County Clerk, PO Box 578, Sinton, TX 78387. 361-364-6290 R/E Recording: 361-364-6290 x241 UCC Recording: 361-364-6290 x241; Fax 361-364-3825.
Will search UCC records prior to 7/2001 and current fixture (land) files. Tax liens not included in UCC search. Will not search real estate records. **Online Access:** Assessor, Property Tax, Personal Property Records. Searh the assessor data for free at www.sanpatriciocad.org/sanpatsearch.htm. Also see note at beginning of section. **Other Phone Numbers:** Assessor 361-364-6150; Treasurer 361-364-6228; Appraiser/Auditor 361-364-5402; Elections 361-364-6290 x238; Vital Records 361-364-6290 x238.

San Saba County

County Clerk, 500 E. Wallace, San Saba, TX 76877. 915-372-3614; Fax 915-372-5746.
Will search UCC records prior to 7/2001 and current fixture (land) files. Will not search real estate records. **Other Phone Numbers:** Assessor 915-372-5325; Treasurer 915-372-3337; Appraiser/Auditor 915-372-5031; Vital Records 915-372-3614.

Schleicher County

County Clerk, PO Drawer 580, Eldorado, TX 76936. 915-853-2833; Fax 915-853-2603.
Will search UCC records prior to 7/2001 and current fixture (land) files. Will not search real estate records. **Other Phone Numbers:** Assessor 915-853-3066; Appraiser/Auditor 915-853-2671.

Scurry County

County Clerk, 1806 25th St, Suite 300, Snyder, TX 79549-2530. 915-573-5332; Fax 915-573-7396.
Will search UCC records prior to 7/2001 and current fixture (land) files. Will not search real estate records. **Other Phone Numbers:** Assessor 915-573-9316; Treasurer 915-573-5382; Appraiser/Auditor 915-573-8549.

Shackelford County

County Clerk, PO Box 247, Albany, TX 76430. County Clerk, R/E and UCC Recording 915-762-2232.
Will search UCC records. Tax liens not included in UCC search. **Other Phone Numbers:** Assessor 915-762-2207; Treasurer 915-762-2232; Appraiser/Auditor 915-762-2207; Elections 915-762-2232; Vital Records 915-762-2232.

Shelby County

County Clerk, PO Box 1987, Center, TX 75935. 936-598-6361 R/E Recording: 409-598-6361; Fax 936-598-3701.
Will search UCC records prior to 7/2001 and current fixture (land) files. UCC search includes tax liens if requested. Will not search real estate records. **Other Phone Numbers:** Assessor 936-598-4441; Treasurer 936-598-3581; Appraiser/Auditor 409-598-6171.

Sherman County

County Clerk, PO Box 270, Stratford, TX 79084. 806-366-2371; Fax 806-366-5670.
Will search UCC records prior to 7/2001 and current fixture (land) files. **Other Phones:** Assessor 806-396-2150; Treasurer 396-5842; Appraiser 396-5566.

Smith County

County Clerk, PO Box 1018, Tyler, TX 75710. 903-535-0650; Fax 903-535-0684.
Will search UCC records prior to 7/2001. **Online Access:** Property Tax Records. See note at beginning of section. **Other Phones:** Assessor 903-535-0835; Treasurer 903-535-0555; Appraiser/Auditor 903-510-8600; Elections 535-0657; Vital Records 535-0650.

Somervell County

County/District Clerk, PO Box 1098, Glen Rose, TX 76043. County/District Clerk, R/E and UCC Recording 254-897-4427; Fax 254-897-3233.
Will search UCC records prior to 7/2001 and current fixture (land) files. This agency will not do a tax lien search. Will not search real estate records. **Online Access:** Assessor, Property Tax Records. See note at beginning of section. **Other Phone Numbers:** Assessor 254-897-2419; Treasurer 254-897-4814; Appraiser/Auditor 254-897-4094; Elections 254-897-4427; Vital Records 254-897-4427.

Starr County

County Clerk, Courthouse, Rio Grande City, TX 78582. 956-487-2954; Fax 956-487-6227.
Will search UCC records. UCC search includes tax liens if requested. Real estate owner, mortgage, and property transfer searches available. **Other Phone Numbers:** Appraiser/Auditor 956-487-5613; Vital Records 956-487-2101.

Stephens County

County Clerk, Courthouse, Breckenridge, TX 76424. County Clerk, R/E and UCC Recording 254-559-3700.
Will search UCC records prior to 7/2001 and current fixture (land) files. UCC search includes tax liens if requested. Will not search real estate records. **Other Phone Numbers:** Assessor 254-559-2732; Treasurer 254-559-3181; Appraiser/Auditor 254-559-8233; Elections 254-559-3700; Vital Records 254-559-3700.

Sterling County

County Clerk, PO Box 55, Sterling City, TX 76951-0055. 915-378-5191.
Will search UCC records prior to 7/2001 and current fixture (land) files. UCC search includes tax liens if requested. Will not search real estate records. **Other Phone Numbers:** Assessor 915-378-7711; Treasurer 915-378-8511; Appraiser/Auditor 915-378-7711.

Stonewall County

County Clerk, PO Drawer P, Aspermont, TX 79502. 940-989-2272.
Will search UCC records prior to 7/2001 and current fixture (land) files. UCC search includes tax liens if requested. Real estate owner, mortgage, and property transfer searches available. **Other Phone Numbers:** Assessor 940-989-2633; Treasurer 940-989-3520; Appraiser/Auditor 940-989-3363.

Sutton County

County Clerk, Sutton County Annex, 300 E. Oak, Suite 3, Sonora, TX 76950. 915-387-3815.
Will search UCC records prior to 7/2001 and current fixture (land) files. UCC search includes tax liens if requested. Real estate owner, mortgage, and property transfer searches available. **Other Phone Numbers:** Assessor 915-387-2809; Treasurer 915-387-2886; Appraiser/Auditor 915-387-2809.

Swisher County

County Clerk, Courthouse, 119 S. Maxwell, Tulia, TX 79088. 806-995-3294; Fax 806-995-4121.
Will search UCC records. UCC search includes tax liens if requested. Will not search real estate records. **Online Access:** Assessor, Property Tax Records. Search the appraisal tax rolls for free at www.txcountydata.com/county.asp?County=219. Also see notes at beginning of section. **Other Phone Numbers:** Appraiser/Auditor 806-995-4118.

Tarrant County

County Clerk, 100 W. Weatherford, Courthouse, Room 180, Ft. Worth, TX 76196. 817-884-1550; www.tarrantcounty.com/tc_countyclerk/site/default.asp
Will search UCC records prior to 7/2001 and current fixture (land) files. This agency will not do a tax lien search. Will not search real estate records. **Online Access:** Property Tax, Assessor, Real Estate, Grantor/Grantee Records. Access to the county Appraisal District Property data is available free at www.tad.org/Datasearch/datasearch.htm. Also, online access to the county clerk's real estate and grantor/grantee index is available free at www.tarrantcounty.com/tc_countyclerk/lib/tc_countyclerk/search.asp. Also, online access to property tax data is available free at www.tad.org/Datasearch/datasearch.htm. Also, see note at beginning of section. **Other Phone Numbers:** Assessor 817-284-0024; Appraiser/Auditor 817-284-0024.

Taylor County

County Clerk, PO Box 5497, Abilene, TX 79608. 915-674-1202; Fax 915-674-1279. www.taylorcad.org
Will search UCC records prior to 7/2001 and current fixture (land) files. Tax liens not included in UCC search. Will not search real estate records. **Online Access:** Assessor, Property Tax, Personal Property, Unclaimed Property Records. Access to the county Central Appraisal District database is available free at www.taylorcad.org/tayname.html. Search is by name, but other methods are available via the web site listed above. Search business personal property at www.taylorcad.org/taypname.html. Also, search the treasurer's database of unclaimed property free at www.taylorcountytexas.org/unclaime.html. Also, see note at beginning of section. **Other Phone Numbers:**

Assessor 915-672-4870; Treasurer 915-674-1231; Appraiser/Auditor 915-676-9381; Elections 915-674-1216; Vital Records 915-674-1202.

Terrell County

County Clerk, PO Drawer 410, Sanderson, TX 79848. County Clerk, R/E and UCC Recording 915-345-2391; Fax 915-345-2653.
Will search UCC records prior to 7/2001 and current fixture (land) files. **Other Phone Numbers:** Assessor 915-345-2251; Appraiser/Auditor 915-345-2251.

Terry County

County Clerk, 500 W. Main, Room 105, Brownfield, TX 79316-4398. County Clerk, R/E and UCC Recording 806-637-8551; Fax 806-637-4874.
Will search UCC records prior to 7/2001 and current fixture (land) files. Will not search real estate records. **Other Phones:** Assessor 806-637-6966; Treasurer 806-637-3616; Appraiser/Auditor 806-637-6966; Elections 806-637-8551; Vital Records 806-637-8551.

Throckmorton County

County Clerk, PO Box 309, Throckmorton, TX 76483. County Clerk, R/E and UCC Recording 940-849-2501; Fax 940-849-3220.
Will search UCC records prior to 7/2001 and current fixture (land) files. **Other Phones:** Assessor 940-849-9421; Treasurer 940-849-2921; Appraiser/Auditor 940-849-5691; Elections 940-849-2501; Vital Records 940-849-2501.

Titus County

County Clerk, 100 W. 1 St., 2nd Floor, Suite 204, Mount Pleasant, TX 75455. 903-577-6796; Fax 903-572-5078.
Will search UCC records prior to 7/2001 and current fixture (land) files. UCC search includes tax liens if requested. Will not search real estate records. **Other Phone Numbers:** Assessor 903-572-6712; Treasurer 903-572-8723; Appraiser/Auditor 903-577-7939.

Tom Green County

County Clerk, 124 W. Beauregard, San Angelo, TX 76903-5835. 915-659-6552 R/E Recording: 915-659-3262.
This agency will not search real estate or UCC records. **Other Phone Numbers:** Appraiser/Auditor 915-658-5575; Vital Records 915-659-6556.

Travis County

County Clerk, PO Box 1748, Austin, TX 78701. 512-854-9188; R/E and UCC Recording: 512-854-9188; Fax 512-854-9075. www.traviscad.org
Will search UCC records prior to 7/2001 and current fixture (land) files. Tax liens not included in UCC search. Real estate owner, mortgage, and property transfer searches available. **Online Access:** Assessor, Property Tax, Business Property, Voter Registration Records. Access to the Central Appraisal District database is available free at www.traviscad.org/search.htm. Also search business personal property. Also, See note at beginning of section. Also, search the voter registration rolls free at www.texasonline.com/travisco/voter/home.htm. **Other Phone Numbers:** Assessor 512-854-9473; Treasurer 512-854-9000; Appraiser/Auditor 512-854-9317; Elections 512-854-4996; Vital Records 512-458-7111.

Trinity County

County Clerk, PO Box 456, Groveton, TX 75845. County Clerk, R/E and UCC Recording 936-642-1208; Fax 936-642-3004.
Will search UCC records. Tax liens not included in UCC search. Will not search real estate records. **Other Phone Numbers:** Assessor 936-642-1637; Treasurer

936-642-1443; Appraiser/Auditor 936-642-1502; Elections 936-642-1208; Vital Records 936-642-1208.

Tyler County

County Clerk, 110 W. Bluff, Room 110, Woodville, TX 75979. 409-283-2281 R/E Recording: 409-283-2281 x10 UCC Recording: 409-283-2281 x13.

Will search UCC records prior to 7/2001 and current fixture (land) files. Tax liens not included in UCC search. Real estate owner, mortgage, and property transfer searches available. **Other Phone Numbers:** Assessor 409-283-2734; Treasurer 409-283-3054; Appraiser/Auditor 409-283-3736; Elections 409-283-2281 x10; Vital Records 409-283-2281 x15.

Upshur County

County Clerk, PO Box 730, Gilmer, TX 75644. 903-843-4014 R/E and UCC Recording: 903-843-4015; Fax 903-843-5492.

Will search UCC records prior to 7/2001 and current fixture (land) files. Tax liens not included in UCC search. Real estate owner, mortgage, and property transfer searches available. **Online Access:** Assessor, Property Tax Records. See note at beginning of section. **Other Phone Numbers:** Assessor 903-843-3083; Treasurer 903-843-4027; Appraiser/Auditor 903-843-3041; Elections 903-843-1614; Vital Records 903-843-4015.

Upton County

County Clerk, PO Box 465, Rankin, TX 79778. County Clerk, R/E and UCC Recording 915-693-2861; Fax 915-693-2129.

Will search UCC records. **Other Phone Numbers:** Assessor 915-652-3222; Treasurer 915-693-2401; Appraiser/Auditor 915-652-3221; Elections 915-693-2861; Vital Records 915-693-2861.

Uvalde County

County Clerk, PO Box 284, Uvalde, TX 78802-0284. County Clerk, R/E and UCC Recording 830-278-6614. Will search UCC records prior to 7/2001 and current fixture (land) files. UCC search includes tax liens if requested. Real estate owner, mortgage, and property transfer searches available. **Other Phone Numbers:** Assessor 830-278-3225; Treasurer 830-278-5821; Appraiser/Auditor 830-278-1106; Elections 830-278-6614; Vital Records 830-278-6614.

Val Verde County

County Clerk, PO Box 1267, Del Rio, TX 78841-1267. 830-774-7564.

Will search UCC records prior to 7/2001 and current fixture (land) files. Tax liens not included in UCC search. Will search real estate records. **Other Phone Numbers:** Treasurer 210-774-4602; Appraiser/Auditor 830-774-4602.

Van Zandt County

County Clerk, 121 E. Dallas St, Courthouse - Room 202, Canton, TX 75103. County Clerk, R/E and UCC Recording 903-567-6503; Fax 903-567-6722.

Will search UCC records prior to 7/2001 and current fixture (land) files. UCC search includes tax liens if requested. Will not search real estate records. **Online Access:** Property Appraisal Records. Search the county appraisal rolls for free at www.vanzandtcad.org. Also includes plat maps online. Also see note at beginning of section. **Other Phone Numbers:** Assessor 903-567-6171; Treasurer 903-567-2551; Appraiser/Auditor 903-567-6171; Elections 903-567-6503; Vital Records 903-567-6503.

Victoria County

County Clerk, PO Box 2410, Victoria, TX 77902. County Clerk, R/E and UCC Recording 361-575-1478; Fax 361-575-6276.

Will search UCC records prior to 7/2001 and current fixture (land) files. Tax liens not included in UCC search. Will not search real estate records. **Online Access:** Assessor, Property Tax Records. See notes at beginning of section. **Other Phone Numbers:** Assessor 361-576-3671; Treasurer 361-576-8588; Appraiser/Auditor 361-576-3621; Elections 361-576-0124; Vital Records 361-575-1478.

Walker County

County Clerk, PO Box 210, Huntsville, TX 77342-0210. 936-436-4922; Fax 936-436-4928.

Will search UCC records prior to 7/2001 and current fixture (land) files. UCC search includes tax liens if requested. Real estate owner, mortgage, and property transfer searches available. **Other Phone Numbers:** Appraiser/Auditor 936-295-0402.

Waller County

County Clerk, 836 Austin St, Room 217, Hempstead, TX 77445. County Clerk, R/E and UCC Recording 979-826-7711.

Will search UCC records prior to 7/2001 and current fixture (land) files. This agency will not do a tax lien search. Will not search real estate records. **Online Access:** Assessor, Property Tax Records. See note at beginning of section. **Other Phone Numbers:** Assessor 979-826-7620; Treasurer 979-826-7707; Appraiser/Auditor 409-396-6100; Elections 979-826-7643; Vital Records 979-826-7711.

Ward County

County Clerk, Corner of 4 & Allen, Monahans, TX 79756. County Clerk, R/E and UCC Recording 915-943-3294; Fax 915-942-6054.

Will search UCC records. Will not search real estate records. **Other Phone Numbers:** Assessor 915-943-3224; Treasurer 915-943-2841; Appraiser/Auditor 915-943-3224; Elections 915-943-3294; Vital Records 915-943-3294.

Washington County

County Clerk, 100 E. Main, Suite 102, Brenham, TX 77833. 979-277-6200; Fax 979-277-6278.

Will search UCC records prior to 7/2001 and current fixture (land) files. Will not search real estate records. **Online Access:** Recording, Land, Marriage, Death, Birth, Military Discharge Records. Access is available free at http://apolloplus.com then click on member counties to access Washington Co. **Other Phone Numbers:** Assessor 979-836-5674; Treasurer 979-277-6200; Appraiser/Auditor 979-277-6528.

Webb County

County Clerk, PO Box 29, Laredo, TX 78042. 956-721-2640; Fax 956-721-2288. www.webbcad.org

Will search UCC records prior to 7/2001 and current fixture (land) files. UCC search includes tax liens if requested. Real estate owner, mortgage, and property transfer searches available. **Online Access:** Appraiser, Property Tax Records. Search the county Central Appraisal District database available at www.webbcad.org/search1.htm. Also, See note at beginning of section. **Other Phone Numbers:** Assessor 956-721-2323; Treasurer 956-721-2215; Appraiser/Auditor 956-718-4091.

Wharton County

County Clerk, PO Box 69, Wharton, TX 77488. County Clerk, R/E and UCC Recording 979-532-2381; Fax 979-532-8426.

Will search UCC records prior to 7/2001 and current fixture (land) files. UCC search includes tax liens if requested. Will not search real estate records. **Online Access:** Assessor, Property Tax Records. See note at beginning of section. **Other Phone Numbers:**

Appraiser/Auditor 979-532-8931; Vital Records 979-532-2381.

Wheeler County

County Clerk, PO Box 465, Wheeler, TX 79096. 806-826-5544; Fax 806-826-3282.

Will search UCC records prior to 7/2001 and current fixture (land) files. **Other Phone Numbers:** Assessor 806-826-3131; Treasurer 806-826-3122; Appraiser/Auditor 806-826-5900.

Wichita County

County Clerk, PO Box 1679, Wichita Falls, TX 76307-1679. County Clerk, R/E and UCC Recording 940-766-8160; Fax 940-716-8554.

Will search UCC records prior to 7/2001 and current fixture (land) files. Tax liens not included in UCC search. Will not search real estate records. **Online Access:** Property Tax Records. See note at beginning of section. **Other Phone Numbers:** Assessor 940-322-2435; Treasurer 940-766-8245; Appraiser/Auditor 940-322-2435; Elections 940-766-8174; Vital Records 940-766-81644.

Wilbarger County

County Clerk, Courthouse, 1700 Main St. #15, Vernon, TX 76384. County Clerk, R/E and UCC Recording 940-552-5486.

Will search UCC records prior to 7/2001 and current fixture (land) files. UCC search includes tax liens if requested. Real estate owner, mortgage, and property transfer searches available. **Online Access:** Property Tax, Personal Property Records. Search the appraisal rolls for free at www.taxnetusa.com/wilbarger. Also see note at beginning of section. **Other Phone Numbers:** Assessor 940-552-9341; Treasurer 940-553-2302; Appraiser/Auditor 940-553-1857; Elections 940-552-5486; Vital Records 940-552-5486.

Willacy County

County Clerk, 540 W. Hidalgo Ave, Courthouse Building, First Floor, Raymondville, TX 78580. County Clerk, R/E and UCC Recording 956-689-2710; Fax 956-689-0937.

Will search UCC records prior to 7/2001 and current fixture (land) files. Tax liens not included in UCC search. Will not search real estate records. **Other Phone Numbers:** Assessor 956-689-3621; Treasurer 956-689-2772; Appraiser/Auditor 956-689-5979; Elections 956-689-2710; Vital Records 956-689-2710.

Williamson County

County Clerk, PO Box 18, Georgetown, TX 78627-0018. County Clerk, R/E and UCC Recording 512-943-1515 UCC Recording: 512-943-1514; Fax 512-943-1616. www.wilco.org

Will search UCC records prior to 7/2001. Tax liens not included in UCC search. Will not search real estate records. **Online Access:** Assessor, Property Tax, Tax Sales Records. TexasTax provides free access to county tax assessor information online at www.texastax.com/search/default.asp?County=william son. Also, see note at beginning of section. Also, online access to the appraiser database is available free at www.wcad.org/Search/Quicksearch.asp. Also, online access to the monthly delinquent tax sale list is available free at www.williamson-county.org/Assessor/Tax.html. **Other Phones:** Assessor 512-943-1603; Treasurer 512-943-1587; Appraiser/Auditor 512-930-3787; Elections 512-943-1630; Vital Records 512-943-1512.

Wilson County

County Clerk, PO Box 27, Floresville, TX 78114. County Clerk, R/E and UCC Recording 830-393-7308; Fax 830-393-7334.

Will search UCC records prior to 7/2001 and current fixture (land) files. UCC search includes tax liens if requested. Real estate record owner searches available. **Online Access:** Assessor, Property Tax Records. See note at beginning of section. **Other Phone Numbers:** Assessor 830-393-7313; Treasurer 830-393-7310; Appraiser/Auditor 830-393-3065; Elections 830-393-7368; Vital Records 830-393-7308.

Winkler County

County Clerk, PO Box 1007, Kermit, TX 79745. 915-586-3401.

Will search UCC records prior to 7/2001 and current fixture (land) files. Tax liens not included in UCC search. Will not search real estate records. **Other Phone Numbers:** Assessor 915-586-3465; Treasurer 915-586-6604; Appraiser/Auditor 915-586-2832.

Wise County

County Clerk, PO Box 359, Decatur, TX 76234. 940-627-3351; Fax 940-627-2138.

Will search UCC records prior to 7/2001 and current fixture (land) files. Will not search real estate records. **Online Access:** Property Tax Records. See note at beginning of section. **Other Phone Numbers:** Assessor 940-627-3523; Treasurer 940-627-3540; Appraiser/Auditor 940-627-3081.

Wood County

County Clerk, PO Box 1756, Quitman, TX 75783. 903-763-2711; Fax 903-763-5641.

Will search UCC records prior to 7/2001 and current fixture (land) files. UCC search includes tax liens if requested. Will not search real estate records. **Online Access:** Assessor, PropertyTax Records. See note at beginning of section. **Other Phone Numbers:** Assessor 903-763-4946; Treasurer 903-763-4186; Appraiser/Auditor 903-763-4891.

Yoakum County

County Clerk, PO Box 309, Plains, TX 79335. 806-456-2721; Fax 806-456-2258.

Will search UCC records prior to 7/2001 and current fixture (land) files. UCC search includes tax liens if requested. Real estate record owner and property transfer searches available. **Other Phone Numbers:** Assessor 806-456-7102; Treasurer 806-456-8794; Appraiser/Auditor 806-456-7101.

Young County

County Clerk, 516 Fourth St #104, 516 Fourth St., Room 104, Graham, TX 76450-3063. 940-549-8432 R/E Recording: 940-539-8432 UCC Recording: 940-539-8432; Fax 940-521-0305.

Will search UCC records prior to 7/2001 and current fixture (land) files. Tax liens not included in UCC

search. Will not search real estate records. **Other Phone Numbers:** Assessor 940-549-1393; Treasurer 940-549-2633; Appraiser/Auditor 940-549-2392; Elections 940-549-5132; Vital Records 940-539-8432; 940-539-8433.

Zapata County

County Clerk, PO Box 789, Zapata, TX 78076. 956-765-9915; Fax 956-765-9933.

Will search UCC records prior to 7/2001 and current fixture (land) files. UCC search includes tax liens if requested. Real estate owner, mortgage, and property transfer searches available. **Online Access:** Property Tax Records. See note at beginning of section. **Other Phone Numbers:** Assessor 956-765-9971; Treasurer 956-765-9925; Appraiser/Auditor 956-765-9971.

Zavala County

County Clerk, Zavala Courthouse, Crystal City, TX 78839. County Clerk, R/E and UCC Recording 830-374-2331; Fax 830-374-5955.

Will search UCC records prior to 7/2001 and current fixture (land) files. UCC search includes tax liens if requested. Real estate owner, mortgage, and property transfer searches available. **Other Phone Numbers:** Assessor 830-347-2351; Treasurer 830-374-2442; Appraiser/Auditor 830-374-3476.

Texas County Locator

You will usually be able to find the city name in the City/County Cross Reference below. In that case, it is a simple matter to determine the county from the cross reference. However, only the official US Postal Service city names are included in this index. There are an additional 40,000 place names that people use in their addresses. Therefore, we have also included a ZIP/City Cross Reference immediately following the City/County Cross Reference.

If you know the ZIP Code but the city name does not appear in the City/County Cross Reference index, look up the ZIP Code in the ZIP/City Cross Reference, find the city name, then look up the city name in the City/County Cross Reference. For example, you want to know the county for an address of Menands, NY 12204. There is no "Menands" in the City/County Cross Reference. The ZIP/City Cross Reference shows that ZIP Codes 12201-12288 are for the city of Albany. Looking back in the City/County Cross Reference, Albany is in Albany County.

City/County Cross Reference

ABBOTT (76621) Hill(97), McLennan(2)
ABERNATHY (79311) Hale(73), Lubbock(26)
ABILENE Taylor
ACE Polk
ACKERLY (79713) Dawson(54), Martin(22), Howard(18), Borden(4)
ADDISON Dallas
ADKINS (78101) Bexar(77), Wilson(22)
ADRIAN (79001) Oldham(73), Deaf Smith(26)
AFTON Dickens
AGUA DULCE Nueces
AIKEN Floyd
ALAMO Hidalgo
ALANREED Gray
ALBA (75410) Wood(70), Rains(29)
ALBANY Shackelford
ALEDO (76008) Parker(84), Tarrant(15)
ALICE Jim Wells
ALIEF Harris
ALLEN Collin
ALLEYTON Colorado
ALLISON Wheeler
ALPINE Brewster
ALTAIR Colorado
ALTO Cherokee
ALVARADO Johnson
ALVIN Brazoria
ALVORD Wise
AMARILLO Potter
AMHERST Lamb
ANAHUAC Chambers
ANDERSON Grimes
ANDREWS Andrews
ANGLETON Brazoria
ANNA Collin
ANNONA Red River
ANSON Jones
ANTHONY El Paso
ANTON (79313) Hockley(76), Lamb(18), Lubbock(3), Hale(1)
APPLE SPRINGS Trinity
AQUILLA Hill
ARANSAS PASS (78336) San Patricio(74), Aransas(24)
ARCHER CITY Archer
ARGYLE Denton
ARLINGTON Tarrant
ARMSTRONG Kenedy
ARP Smith
ART Mason
ARTESIA WELLS La Salle
ARTHUR CITY Lamar
ASHERTON Dimmit
ASPERMONT Stonewall
ATASCOSA Bexar
ATHENS (75752) Henderson(94), Van Zandt(5)
ATLANTA Cass
AUBREY Denton
AUSTIN Travis
AUSTWELL Refugio

AVALON Ellis
AVERY (75554) Red River(90), Bowie(9)
AVINGER (75630) Marion(56), Cass(43)
AXTELL (76624) McLennan(97), Limestone(2)
AZLE Parker
BACLIFF Galveston
BAGWELL Red River
BAILEY Fannin
BAIRD Callahan
BALLINGER Runnels
BALMORHEA Reeves
BANDERA Bandera
BANGS (76823) Brown(86), Coleman(13)
BANQUETE Nueces
BARDWELL Ellis
BARKER Harris
BARKSDALE (78828) Edwards(71), Real(28)
BARNHART (76930) Irion(54), Crockett(45)
BARRY Navarro
BARSTOW Ward
BARTLETT (76511) Bell(68), Williamson(28), Milam(3)
BASTROP Bastrop
BATESVILLE Zavala
BATSON Hardin
BAY CITY Matagorda
BAYSIDE Refugio
BAYTOWN Harris
BEASLEY Fort Bend
BEAUMONT Jefferson
BEBE Gonzales
BECKVILLE Panola
BEDFORD Tarrant
BEDIAS Grimes
BEEVILLE Bee
BELLAIRE Harris
BELLEVUE (76228) Clay(94), Montague(5)
BELLS Grayson
BELLVILLE Austin
BELMONT Gonzales
BELTON Bell
BEN ARNOLD Milam
BEN BOLT Jim Wells
BEN FRANKLIN Delta
BEN WHEELER Van Zandt
BENAVIDES Duval
BEND San Saba
BENJAMIN Knox
BERCLAIR Goliad
BERGHEIM Kendall
BERTRAM Burnet
BIG BEND NATIONAL PARK Brewster
BIG LAKE Reagan
BIG SANDY Upshur
BIG SPRING Howard
BIG WELLS Dimmit
BIGFOOT Frio
BIROME Hill
BISHOP Nueces
BIVINS Cass
BLACKWELL (79506) Nolan(63), Coke(36)

BLANCO (78606) Blanco(84), Comal(13), Kendall(2)
BLANKET (76432) Brown(94), Comanche(5)
BLEDSOE Cochran
BLEIBLERVILLE Austin
BLESSING Matagorda
BLOOMBURG Cass
BLOOMING GROVE (76626) Navarro(98), Ellis(1)
BLOOMINGTON Victoria
BLOSSOM Lamar
BLUE RIDGE (75424) Collin(97), Fannin(2)
BLUEGROVE Clay
BLUFF DALE (76433) Erath(67), Hood(20), Somervell(11)
BLUFFTON Llano
BLUM Hill
BOERNE (78015) Bexar(61), Kendall(33), Comal(4)
BOGATA Red River
BOLING (77420) Wharton(93), Matagorda(5)
BON WIER Newton
BONHAM Fannin
BOOKER (79005) Lipscomb(63), Ochiltree(36)
BORGER Hutchinson
BOVINA Parmer
BOWIE (76230) Montague(97), Jack(1)
BOYD (76023) Wise(95), Parker(4)
BOYS RANCH (79010) Oldham(83), Potter(16)
BRACKETTVILLE Kinney
BRADY McCulloch
BRANDON Hill
BRASHEAR (75420) Hopkins(96), Rains(3)
BRAZORIA Brazoria
BRECKENRIDGE Stephens
BREMOND (76629) Robertson(95), Falls(4)
BRENHAM Washington
BRIDGE CITY Orange
BRIDGEPORT (76426) Wise(95), Jack(4)
BRIGGS Burnet
BRISCOE (79011) Hemphill(64), Wheeler(36)
BROADDUS San Augustine
BRONSON (75930) Sabine(72), San Augustine(27)
BRONTE (76933) Coke(59), Runnels(40)
BROOKELAND (75931) Sabine(63), Jasper(36)
BROOKESMITH (76827) Brown(98), Coleman(1)
BROOKSHIRE (77423) Waller(85), Fort Bend(14)
BROOKSTON Lamar
BROWNFIELD Terry
BROWNSBORO (75756) Henderson(94), Van Zandt(5)
BROWNSVILLE Cameron
BROWNWOOD Brown

BRUCEVILLE (76630) McLennan(97), Falls(2)
BRUNI (78344) Webb(91), Duval(8)
BRYAN (77808) Brazos(91), Robertson(8)
BRYSON Jack
BUCHANAN DAM Llano
BUCKHOLTS Milam
BUDA (78610) Hays(84), Travis(15)
BUFFALO (75831) Leon(96), Freestone(3)
BUFFALO GAP Taylor
BULA (79320) Bailey(81), Lamb(18)
BULLARD (75757) Smith(71), Cherokee(28)
BULVERDE Comal
BUNA Jasper
BURKBURNETT Wichita
BURKETT Coleman
BURKEVILLE Newton
BURLESON Johnson
BURLINGTON (76519) Milam(90), Bell(5), Falls(3)
BURNET (78611) Burnet(96), Llano(3)
BURTON Washington
BUSHLAND Potter
BYERS Clay
BYNUM Hill
CACTUS Moore
CADDO Stephens
CADDO MILLS Hunt
CALDWELL Burleson
CALL (75933) Newton(70), Jasper(29)
CALLIHAM McMullen
CALVERT Robertson
CAMDEN Polk
CAMERON Milam
CAMP WOOD Real
CAMPBELL Hunt
CAMPBELLTON (78008) Atascosa(97), Live Oak(2)
CANADIAN (79014) Hemphill(94), Lipscomb(5)
CANTON Van Zandt
CANUTILLO El Paso
CANYON Randall
CANYON LAKE Comal
CARBON Eastland
CAREY Childress
CARLSBAD Tom Green
CARLTON (76436) Hamilton(56), Comanche(40), Erath(2)
CARMINE (78932) Fayette(95), Washington(4)
CARRIZO SPRINGS Dimmit
CARROLLTON Dallas
CARTHAGE Panola
CASON Morris
CASTELL (76831) Llano(50), Mason(50)
CASTROVILLE Medina
CAT SPRING (78933) Austin(69), Colorado(30)
CATARINA Dimmit
CAYUGA Anderson

CEDAR CREEK (78612) Bastrop(92), Travis(7)
CEDAR HILL Dallas
CEDAR LANE Matagorda
CEDAR PARK Williamson
CEE VEE Cottle
CELESTE (75423) Hunt(95), Fannin(4)
CELINA (75009) Collin(94), Denton(5)
CENTER Shelby
CENTER POINT Kerr
CENTERVILLE Leon
CENTRALIA Trinity
CHALK Cottle
CHANDLER (75758) Henderson(88), Van Zandt(11)
CHANNELVIEW Harris
CHANNING (79018) Hartley(60), Moore(39)
CHAPMAN RANCH Nueces
CHAPPELL HILL (77426) Washington(89), Austin(10)
CHARLOTTE Atascosa
CHATFIELD Navarro
CHEROKEE (76832) San Saba(99), Llano(1)
CHESTER (75936) Tyler(94), Polk(5)
CHICO (76431) Wise(97), Jack(2)
CHICOTA Lamar
CHILDRESS (79201) Childress(95), Cottle(2), Hall(1)
CHILLICOTHE (79225) Hardeman(93), Wilbarger(6)
CHILTON Falls
CHINA Jefferson
CHINA SPRING (76633) McLennan(89), Bosque(10)
CHIRENO Nacogdoches
CHRIESMAN Burleson
CHRISTINE Atascosa
CHRISTOVAL (76935) Tom Green(53), Schleicher(46)
CIBOLO (78108) Guadalupe(75), Bexar(24)
CISCO (76437) Eastland(93), Callahan(4), Stephens(2)
CLARENDON (79226) Donley(81), Armstrong(12), Briscoe(3), Hall(2)
CLARKSVILLE Red River
CLAUDE Armstrong
CLAY Burleson
CLAYTON Panola
CLEBURNE (76033) Johnson(98), Somervell(1)
CLEVELAND Liberty
CLIFTON Bosque
CLINT El Paso
CLUTE Brazoria
CLYDE Callahan
COAHOMA (79511) Howard(73), Borden(26)
COLDSPRING San Jacinto
COLEMAN Coleman
COLLEGE STATION Brazos
COLLEGEPORT Matagorda
COLLEYVILLE Tarrant
COLLINSVILLE (76233) Grayson(75), Cooke(24)
COLMESNEIL Tyler
COLORADO CITY Mitchell
COLUMBUS Colorado
COMANCHE Comanche
COMBES Cameron
COMFORT (78013) Kendall(82), Kerr(17)
COMMERCE Hunt
COMO Hopkins
COMSTOCK Val Verde
CONCAN Uvalde
CONCEPCION Duval
CONCORD Leon
CONE Crosby
CONROE Montgomery
CONVERSE Bexar
COOKVILLE Titus

COOLIDGE (76635) Limestone(60), McLennan(39)
COOPER Delta
COPEVILLE Collin
COPPELL Dallas
COPPERAS COVE (76522) Coryell(94), Lampasas(5)
CORPUS CHRISTI Nueces
CORRIGAN Polk
CORSICANA Navarro
COST Gonzales
COTTON CENTER Hale
COTULLA La Salle
COUPLAND (78615) Williamson(65), Travis(34)
COVINGTON Hill
COYANOSA Pecos
CRANDALL Kaufman
CRANE Crane
CRANFILLS GAP (76637) Bosque(97), Hamilton(2)
CRAWFORD McLennan
CRESSON (76035) Hood(65), Parker(24), Johnson(9)
CROCKETT Houston
CROSBY Harris
CROSBYTON Crosby
CROSS PLAINS (76443) Callahan(95), Brown(3)
CROWELL (79227) Knox(60), Foard(39)
CROWLEY (76036) Tarrant(79), Johnson(20)
CRYSTAL CITY Zavala
CUERO De Witt
CUMBY Hopkins
CUNEY Cherokee
CUNNINGHAM Lamar
CUSHING (75760) Nacogdoches(90), Rusk(9)
CYPRESS Harris
D HANIS Medina
DAINGERFIELD Morris
DAISETTA Liberty
DALE (78616) Caldwell(93), Bastrop(6)
DALHART (79022) Dallam(69), Hartley(30)
DALLARDSVILLE Polk
DALLAS Dallas
DAMON (77430) Fort Bend(55), Brazoria(44)
DANBURY Brazoria
DANCIGER Brazoria
DANEVANG Wharton
DARROUZETT Lipscomb
DAVILLA Milam
DAWN Deaf Smith
DAWSON (76639) McLennan(58), Navarro(41)
DAYTON (77535) Liberty(94), Chambers(5)
DE BERRY Panola
DE KALB Bowie
DE LEON Comanche
DE SOTO Dallas
DEANVILLE Burleson
DECATUR Wise
DEER PARK Harris
DEL RIO Val Verde
DEL VALLE (78617) Travis(74), Bastrop(25)
DELL CITY Hudspeth
DELMITA (78536) Starr(86), Hidalgo(13)
DENISON Grayson
DENNIS Parker
DENTON Denton
DENVER CITY (79323) Yoakum(94), Gaines(5)
DEPORT Lamar
DESDEMONA (76445) Eastland(87), Comanche(12)
DESOTO Dallas
DETROIT (75436) Red River(93), Lamar(6)
DEVERS Liberty
DEVINE Medina

DEWEYVILLE Newton
DIANA (75640) Upshur(67), Harrison(31), Marion(1)
DIBOLL Angelina
DICKENS Dickens
DICKINSON Galveston
DIKE Hopkins
DILLEY Frio
DIME BOX Lee
DIMMITT Castro
DINERO Live Oak
DOBBIN Montgomery
DODD CITY Fannin
DODGE Walker
DODSON (79230) Collingsworth(82), Childress(17)
DONIE (75838) Freestone(79), Limestone(19)
DONNA Hidalgo
DOOLE McCulloch
DOSS Gillespie
DOUCETTE Tyler
DOUGHERTY Floyd
DOUGLASS Nacogdoches
DOUGLASSVILLE Cass
DRIFTWOOD Hays
DRIPPING SPRINGS (78620) Hays(89), Travis(10)
DRISCOLL Nueces
DRYDEN Terrell
DUBLIN (76446) Erath(85), Comanche(14)
DUMAS Moore
DUMONT King
DUNCANVILLE Dallas
DUNN Scurry
DYESS AFB Taylor
EAGLE LAKE (77434) Colorado(98), Wharton(1)
EAGLE PASS Maverick
EARLY Brown
EARTH (79031) Lamb(71), Castro(23), Bailey(4)
EAST BERNARD (77435) Wharton(83), Fort Bend(15), Colorado(1)
EASTLAND Eastland
EASTON Gregg
ECLETO Karnes
ECTOR Fannin
EDCOUCH Hidalgo
EDDY McLennan
EDEN Concho
EDGEWOOD Van Zandt
EDINBURG Hidalgo
EDMONSON Hale
EDNA Jackson
EDROY San Patricio
EGYPT Wharton
EL CAMPO Wharton
EL INDIO Maverick
EL PASO El Paso
ELBERT Throckmorton
ELDORADO Schleicher
ELECTRA (76360) Wichita(88), Wilbarger(11)
ELGIN (78621) Bastrop(78), Travis(12), Lee(4), Williamson(4)
ELIASVILLE Young
ELKHART Anderson
ELLINGER Fayette
ELM MOTT McLennan
ELMATON Matagorda
ELMENDORF (78112) Bexar(97), Wilson(2)
ELMO Kaufman
ELSA Hidalgo
ELYSIAN FIELDS Harrison
EMORY Rains
ENCINAL La Salle
ENCINO Brooks
ENERGY Comanche
ENLOE Delta
ENNIS Ellis

ENOCHS Bailey
EOLA (76937) Tom Green(70), Concho(29)
ERA Cooke
ESTELLINE Hall
ETOILE Nacogdoches
EULESS Tarrant
EUSTACE (75124) Henderson(77), Van Zandt(22)
EVADALE Jasper
EVANT (76525) Coryell(90), Lampasas(8), Hamilton(1)
FABENS El Paso
FAIRFIELD Freestone
FALCON HEIGHTS Starr
FALFURRIAS (78355) Brooks(95), Jim Wells(4)
FALLS CITY (78113) Wilson(53), Karnes(46)
FANNIN Goliad
FARMERSVILLE (75442) Collin(96), Hunt(3)
FARNSWORTH Ochiltree
FARWELL (79325) Parmer(96), Bailey(3)
FATE Rockwall
FAYETTEVILLE (78940) Fayette(76), Austin(15), Colorado(8)
FENTRESS Caldwell
FERRIS (75125) Ellis(83), Dallas(16)
FIELDTON Lamb
FISCHER (78623) Hays(54), Comal(45)
FLAT Coryell
FLATONIA (78941) Fayette(94), Bastrop(5)
FLINT Smith
FLOMOT (79234) Motley(85), Floyd(14)
FLORENCE (76527) Williamson(97), Bell(2)
FLORESVILLE Wilson
FLOWER MOUND Denton
FLOYDADA (79235) Floyd(97), Crosby(2)
FLUVANNA (79517) Scurry(72), Borden(27)
FLYNN Leon
FOLLETT Lipscomb
FORESTBURG (76239) Cooke(54), Montague(45)
FORNEY (75126) Kaufman(97), Rockwall(2)
FORRESTON Ellis
FORSAN Howard
FORT DAVIS Jeff Davis
FORT HANCOCK Hudspeth
FORT MC KAVETT (76841) Menard(91), Kimble(4), Schleicher(4)
FORT STOCKTON Pecos
FORT WORTH Tarrant
FOWLERTON (78021) La Salle(77), Atascosa(11), McMullen(11)
FRANCITAS Jackson
FRANKLIN Robertson
FRANKSTON (75763) Henderson(54), Anderson(45)
FRED Tyler
FREDERICKSBURG (78624) Gillespie(87), Kendall(12)
FREDONIA (76842) Mason(56), San Saba(38), McCulloch(5)
FREEPORT Brazoria
FREER Duval
FRESNO Fort Bend
FRIENDSWOOD Galveston
FRIONA (79035) Parmer(96), Deaf Smith(3)
FRISCO Collin
FRITCH (79036) Hutchinson(94), Carson(5)
FROST (76641) Navarro(98), Ellis(1)
FRUITVALE Van Zandt
FULSHEAR Fort Bend
FULTON Aransas
GAIL Borden
GAINESVILLE Cooke
GALENA PARK Harris

GALLATIN Cherokee
GALVESTON Galveston
GANADO Jackson
GARCIASVILLE Starr
GARDEN CITY (79739) Glasscock(88),
    Reagan(11)
GARDENDALE Ector
GARLAND Dallas
GARRISON (75946) Nacogdoches(52),
    Rusk(47)
GARWOOD Colorado
GARY (75643) Panola(94), Shelby(5)
GATESVILLE Coryell
GAUSE Milam
GENEVA Sabine
GEORGE WEST Live Oak
GEORGETOWN Williamson
GERONIMO Guadalupe
GIDDINGS Lee
GILCHRIST Galveston
GILLETT Karnes
GILMER (75645) Upshur(98), Gregg(1)
GIRARD Kent
GIRVIN Pecos
GLADEWATER (75647) Gregg(57),
    Upshur(29), Smith(12)
GLEN FLORA Wharton
GLEN ROSE Somervell
GLIDDEN Colorado
GOBER Fannin
GODLEY Johnson
GOLDEN Wood
GOLDSBORO (79519) Taylor(42),
    Runnels(32), Coleman(26)
GOLDSMITH Ector
GOLDTHWAITE Mills
GOLIAD Goliad
GONZALES Gonzales
GOODFELLOW AFB Tom Green
GOODRICH Polk
GORDON (76453) Palo Pinto(88),
    Erath(11)
GORDONVILLE Grayson
GOREE (76363) Knox(96), Haskell(2)
GORMAN (76454) Eastland(82),
    Comanche(17)
GOULDBUSK Coleman
GRAFORD Palo Pinto
GRAHAM (76450) Young(92), Stephens(3),
    Palo Pinto(3)
GRANBURY (76049) Hood(96), Parker(2)
GRAND PRAIRIE Dallas
GRAND SALINE Van Zandt
GRANDFALLS Ward
GRANDVIEW (76050) Johnson(89),
    Ellis(5), Hill(4)
GRANGER Williamson
GRAPELAND (75844) Houston(78),
    Anderson(21)
GRAPEVINE Tarrant
GREENVILLE Hunt
GREENWOOD Wise
GREGORY San Patricio
GROESBECK Limestone
GROOM (79039) Carson(69), Gray(27),
    Armstrong(1), Donley(1)
GROVES Jefferson
GROVETON Trinity
GRULLA Starr
GRUVER (79040) Hansford(62),
    Sherman(37)
GUERRA (78360) Jim Hogg(80), Starr(20)
GUNTER Grayson
GUSTINE Comanche
GUTHRIE King
GUY (77444) Fort Bend(74), Brazoria(25)
HALE CENTER (79041) Hale(97), Lamb(2)
HALLETTSVILLE Lavaca
HALLSVILLE Harrison
HALTOM CITY Tarrant
HAMILTON Hamilton
HAMLIN (79520) Jones(96), Fisher(3)

HAMSHIRE (77622) Jefferson(86),
    Chambers(13)
HANKAMER Chambers
HAPPY (79042) Randall(40), Swisher(30),
    Castro(17), Armstrong(12)
HARDIN Liberty
HARGILL Hidalgo
HARKER HEIGHTS Bell
HARLETON (75651) Harrison(95),
    Marion(4)
HARLINGEN Cameron
HARPER (78631) Gillespie(79), Kimble(19)
HARROLD Wilbarger
HART (79043) Castro(80), Lamb(18),
    Hale(1)
HARTLEY Hartley
HARWOOD (78632) Caldwell(53),
    Gonzales(46)
HASKELL Haskell
HASLET (76052) Tarrant(85), Wise(8),
    Denton(5)
HASSE Comanche
HAWKINS Wood
HAWLEY Jones
HEARNE Robertson
HEBBRONVILLE Jim Hogg
HEDLEY Donley
HEIDENHEIMER Bell
HELOTES (78023) Bexar(88), Medina(7),
    Bandera(3)
HEMPHILL Sabine
HEMPSTEAD Waller
HENDERSON Rusk
HENRIETTA Clay
HEREFORD (79045) Deaf Smith(96),
    Castro(3)
HERMLEIGH (79526) Scurry(95), Fisher(3)
HEWITT McLennan
HEXT (76848) Menard(94), Mason(5)
HICO (76457) Hamilton(46), Erath(46),
    Bosque(6)
HIDALGO Hidalgo
HIGGINS (79046) Lipscomb(87),
    Hemphill(12)
HIGH ISLAND Galveston
HIGHLANDS Harris
HILLISTER Tyler
HILLSBORO Hill
HITCHCOCK Galveston
HOBSON Karnes
HOCHHEIM De Witt
HOCKLEY (77447) Harris(46), Waller(38),
    Montgomery(15)
HOLLAND Bell
HOLLIDAY Archer
HONDO Medina
HONEY GROVE Fannin
HOOKS Bowie
HOUSTON Harris
HOWE Grayson
HUBBARD (76648) Hill(91), Navarro(5),
    Limestone(2)
HUFFMAN Harris
HUFSMITH Harris
HUGHES SPRINGS (75656) Cass(89),
    Morris(10)
HULL (77564) Liberty(97), Hardin(2)
HUMBLE Harris
HUNGERFORD Wharton
HUNT (78024) Kerr(98), Real(2)
HUNTINGTON Angelina
HUNTSVILLE Walker
HURST Tarrant
HUTCHINS Dallas
HUTTO Williamson
HYE Blanco
IDALOU Lubbock
IMPERIAL Pecos
INDUSTRY Austin
INEZ Victoria
INGLESIDE San Patricio
INGRAM Kerr

IOLA Grimes
IOWA PARK Wichita
IRA (79527) Scurry(78), Borden(21)
IRAAN Pecos
IREDELL (76649) Bosque(86), Erath(13)
IRENE Hill
IRVING Dallas
ITALY Ellis
ITASCA Hill
IVANHOE Fannin
JACKSBORO Jack
JACKSONVILLE Cherokee
JARRELL Williamson
JASPER Jasper
JAYTON (79528) Kent(84), Stonewall(15)
JEFFERSON (75657) Marion(87), Cass(9),
    Harrison(2)
JERMYN (76459) Jack(94), Young(5)
JEWETT (75846) Leon(85), Limestone(14)
JOAQUIN (75954) Shelby(91), Panola(8)
JOHNSON CITY Blanco
JOINERVILLE Rusk
JONESBORO (76538) Hamilton(53),
    Coryell(46)
JONESVILLE (75659) Harrison(75),
    Rusk(25)
JOSEPHINE Collin
JOSHUA Johnson
JOURDANTON Atascosa
JUDSON Gregg
JUNCTION Kimble
JUSTICEBURG Garza
JUSTIN (76247) Denton(98), Wise(1)
KAMAY Wichita
KARNACK Harrison
KARNES CITY Karnes
KATY (77494) Fort Bend(83), Harris(14),
    Waller(1)
KAUFMAN Kaufman
KEENE Johnson
KELLER Tarrant
KEMAH Galveston
KEMP (75143) Henderson(64),
    Kaufman(35)
KEMPNER (76539) Lampasas(88),
    Coryell(9), Bell(1)
KENDALIA Kendall
KENDLETON Fort Bend
KENEDY Karnes
KENNARD (75847) Houston(53),
    Trinity(46)
KENNEDALE Tarrant
KENNEY Austin
KERENS Navarro
KERMIT Winkler
KERRICK Dallam
KERRVILLE Kerr
KILDARE Cass
KILGORE Gregg
KILLEEN (76549) Bell(98), Burnet(1)
KINGSBURY (78638) Guadalupe(98),
    Gonzales(1)
KINGSLAND (78639) Llano(87), Burnet(12)
KINGSVILLE Kleberg
KIRBYVILLE Jasper
KIRKLAND Childress
KIRVIN Freestone
KLONDIKE Delta
KNICKERBOCKER Tom Green
KNIPPA Uvalde
KNOTT (79748) Howard(92), Martin(7)
KNOX CITY (79529) Knox(96), Haskell(2)
KOPPERL Bosque
KOSSE (76653) Limestone(54),
    McLennan(41), Falls(2), Robertson(1)
KOUNTZE Hardin
KRESS (79052) Swisher(94), Hale(5)
KRUM Denton
KURTEN Brazos
KYLE (78640) Hays(96), Caldwell(3)
LA BLANCA Hidalgo
LA COSTE (78039) Medina(87), Bexar(12)

LA FERIA Cameron
LA GRANGE Fayette
LA JOYA Hidalgo
LA MARQUE Galveston
LA PORTE Harris
LA PRYOR Zavala
LA SALLE Jackson
LA VERNIA (78121) Wilson(74),
    Guadalupe(25)
LA VILLA Hidalgo
LA WARD Jackson
LADONIA Fannin
LAIRD HILL Rusk
LAKE CREEK Delta
LAKE DALLAS Denton
LAKE JACKSON Brazoria
LAKEVIEW Hall
LAMESA (79331) Dawson(98), Martin(1)
LAMPASAS Lampasas
LANCASTER (75146) Dallas(98), Ellis(1)
LANE CITY Wharton
LANEVILLE Rusk
LANGTRY Val Verde
LAREDO Webb
LARUE Henderson
LASARA Willacy
LATEXO Houston
LAUGHLIN A F B Val Verde
LAVON Collin
LAWN (79530) Taylor(94), Runnels(5)
LAZBUDDIE Parmer
LEAGUE CITY Galveston
LEAKEY Real
LEANDER Williamson
LEDBETTER (78946) Fayette(67),
    Washington(18), Lee(13)
LEESBURG (75451) Camp(90), Wood(5),
    Upshur(4)
LEESVILLE Gonzales
LEFORS Gray
LEGGETT Polk
LELIA LAKE Donley
LEMING Atascosa
LENORAH Martin
LEON JUNCTION Coryell
LEONA Leon
LEONARD (75452) Fannin(68), Collin(17),
    Hunt(14)
LEROY McLennan
LEVELLAND Hockley
LEWISVILLE Denton
LEXINGTON Lee
LIBERTY Liberty
LIBERTY HILL (78642) Williamson(98),
    Burnet(1)
LILLIAN Johnson
LINCOLN Lee
LINDALE Smith
LINDEN Cass
LINDSAY Cooke
LINGLEVILLE Erath
LINN (78563) Hidalgo(75), Starr(25)
LIPAN (76462) Hood(46), Palo Pinto(20),
    Parker(15), Erath(12)
LIPSCOMB Lipscomb
LISSIE Wharton
LITTLE ELM Denton
LITTLE RIVER Bell
LITTLEFIELD (79339) Lamb(92),
    Hockley(7)
LIVERPOOL Brazoria
LIVINGSTON Polk
LLANO Llano
LOCKHART Caldwell
LOCKNEY (79241) Floyd(97), Swisher(1)
LODI Marion
LOHN (76852) McCulloch(98), Concho(1)
LOLITA Jackson
LOMETA (76853) Lampasas(98), Mills(1)
LONDON (76854) Kimble(75), Menard(23)
LONE OAK (75453) Hunt(77), Rains(20),
    Hopkins(1)

LONE STAR (75668) Morris(84), Marion(13), Henderson(2)
LONG BRANCH (75669) Panola(98), Rusk(1)
LONG MOTT Calhoun
LONGVIEW Gregg
LOOP Gaines
LOPENO Zapata
LORAINE (79532) Mitchell(93), Scurry(3), Nolan(2)
LORENA McLennan
LORENZO (79343) Crosby(69), Lubbock(30)
LOS EBANOS Hidalgo
LOS FRESNOS Cameron
LOS INDIOS Cameron
LOTT Falls
LOUISE (77455) Wharton(90), Jackson(8)
LOVELADY (75851) Houston(77), Trinity(22)
LOVING Young
LOWAKE Concho
LOZANO Cameron
LUBBOCK Lubbock
LUEDERS (79533) Jones(57), Shackelford(37), Haskell(5)
LUFKIN Angelina
LULING (78648) Caldwell(92), Guadalupe(5), Gonzales(1)
LUMBERTON Hardin
LYFORD (78569) Willacy(97), Hidalgo(2)
LYONS Burleson
LYTLE (78052) Atascosa(76), Medina(14), Bexar(8)
MABANK (75147) Henderson(56), Kaufman(22), Van Zandt(21)
MACDONA Bexar
MADISONVILLE Madison
MAGNOLIA (77355) Montgomery(98), Waller(1)
MAGNOLIA SPRINGS Jasper
MALAKOFF Henderson
MALONE Hill
MANCHACA (78652) Travis(74), Hays(25)
MANOR Travis
MANSFIELD (76063) Tarrant(92), Johnson(7)
MANVEL Brazoria
MAPLE Bailey
MARATHON Brewster
MARBLE FALLS Burnet
MARFA Presidio
MARIETTA Cass
MARION (78124) Guadalupe(91), Bexar(8)
MARKHAM Matagorda
MARLIN Falls
MARQUEZ Leon
MARSHALL Harrison
MART (76664) McLennan(91), Limestone(5), Falls(2)
MARTINDALE (78655) Caldwell(84), Guadalupe(15)
MARTINSVILLE Nacogdoches
MARYNEAL Nolan
MASON (76856) Mason(98), Menard(1)
MASTERSON (79058) Moore(61), Potter(38)
MATADOR Motley
MATAGORDA Matagorda
MATHIS (78368) San Patricio(96), Live Oak(3)
MAUD Bowie
MAURICEVILLE Orange
MAXWELL (78656) Caldwell(96), Hays(3)
MAY Brown
MAYDELLE Cherokee
MAYPEARL Ellis
MAYSFIELD Milam
MC CAMEY Upton
MC CAULLEY Fisher
MC COY Atascosa
MC DADE Bastrop

MC GREGOR (76657) McLennan(97), Coryell(2)
MC KINNEY Collin
MC LEOD Cass
MC NEIL Travis
MC QUEENEY Guadalupe
MCADOO (79243) Dickens(55), Crosby(44)
MCALLEN Hidalgo
MCFADDIN Victoria
MCLEAN (79057) Gray(62), Wheeler(30), Donley(6)
MEADOW (79345) Terry(92), Lynn(6)
MEDINA Bandera
MEGARGEL Archer
MELISSA Collin
MELVIN (76858) McCulloch(50), Concho(49)
MEMPHIS (79245) Hall(97), Collingsworth(2)
MENARD (76859) Menard(78), Kimble(21)
MENTONE Loving
MERCEDES Hidalgo
MERETA Tom Green
MERIDIAN Bosque
MERIT Hunt
MERKEL (79536) Taylor(75), Jones(23)
MERTENS (76666) Hill(96), Navarro(4)
MERTZON Irion
MESQUITE Dallas
MEXIA (76667) Limestone(97), Freestone(2)
MEYERSVILLE (77974) De Witt(65), Victoria(34)
MIAMI (79059) Roberts(94), Gray(5)
MICO Medina
MIDFIELD Matagorda
MIDKIFF Upton
MIDLAND Midland
MIDLOTHIAN Ellis
MIDWAY (75852) Madison(97), Walker(1)
MILAM Sabine
MILANO Milam
MILES (76861) Tom Green(51), Runnels(45), Concho(2)
MILFORD (76670) Ellis(90), Navarro(8), Hill(1)
MILLERSVIEW Concho
MILLICAN Brazos
MILLSAP (76066) Parker(93), Palo Pinto(6)
MINDEN Rusk
MINEOLA (75773) Wood(91), Smith(7)
MINERAL Bee
MINERAL WELLS Palo Pinto
MINGUS (76463) Erath(75), Palo Pinto(23)
MIRANDO CITY Webb
MISSION Hidalgo
MISSOURI CITY (77489) Fort Bend(95), Harris(4)
MOBEETIE (79061) Wheeler(93), Gray(3), Hemphill(3)
MONAHANS Ward
MONT BELVIEU Chambers
MONTAGUE Montague
MONTALBA (75853) Anderson(98), Henderson(1)
MONTGOMERY (77356) Montgomery(98), Grimes(1)
MOODY (76557) McLennan(64), Bell(34)
MOORE (78057) Medina(95), Frio(4)
MORAN (76464) Shackelford(81), Stephens(10), Callahan(6)
MORGAN Bosque
MORGAN MILL Erath
MORSE (79062) Hutchinson(75), Hansford(25)
MORTON (79346) Cochran(95), Bailey(4)
MOSCOW Polk
MOULTON Lavaca
MOUND Coryell
MOUNT CALM (76673) Hill(86), Limestone(9), McLennan(3)
MOUNT ENTERPRISE Rusk

MOUNT PLEASANT Titus
MOUNT VERNON Franklin
MOUNTAIN HOME Kerr
MUENSTER Cooke
MULDOON Fayette
MULESHOE (79347) Bailey(85), Parmer(9), Lamb(4)
MULLIN Mills
MUMFORD Robertson
MUNDAY Knox
MURCHISON (75778) Henderson(65), Van Zandt(34)
MYRA Cooke
NACOGDOCHES Nacogdoches
NADA Colorado
NAPLES (75568) Morris(88), Cass(11)
NASH Bowie
NATALIA Medina
NAVAL AIR STATION/ JRB Tarrant
NAVASOTA Brazos
NAZARETH Castro
NECHES Anderson
NEDERLAND Jefferson
NEEDVILLE Fort Bend
NEMO (76070) Somervell(85), Johnson(14)
NEVADA Collin
NEW BADEN Robertson
NEW BOSTON Bowie
NEW BRAUNFELS Comal
NEW CANEY Montgomery
NEW DEAL Lubbock
NEW HOME Lynn
NEW LONDON Rusk
NEW SUMMERFIELD Cherokee
NEW ULM (78950) Colorado(51), Austin(48)
NEW WAVERLY (77358) Walker(49), San Jacinto(39), Montgomery(11)
NEWARK (76071) Wise(96), Tarrant(3)
NEWCASTLE (76372) Young(80), Throckmorton(19)
NEWGULF Wharton
NEWPORT Clay
NEWTON (75966) Newton(92), Jasper(7)
NIXON (78140) Gonzales(89), Wilson(6), Guadalupe(3)
NOCONA Montague
NOLAN Nolan
NOLANVILLE Bell
NOME Jefferson
NORDHEIM (78141) De Witt(94), Karnes(5)
NORMANGEE (77871) Leon(59), Madison(40)
NORMANNA Bee
NORTH HOUSTON Harris
NORTH RICHLAND HILLS Tarrant
NORTH ZULCH Madison
NORTON Runnels
NOTREES Ector
NOVICE (79538) Coleman(52), Runnels(47)
NURSERY Victoria
O BRIEN Haskell
OAKHURST San Jacinto
OAKLAND Colorado
OAKVILLE Live Oak
OAKWOOD (75855) Leon(78), Freestone(21)
ODELL Wilbarger
ODEM San Patricio
ODESSA Ector
ODONNELL (79351) Borden(50), Lynn(25), Dawson(23)
OGLESBY (76561) Coryell(85), McLennan(14)
OILTON Webb
OKLAUNION Wilbarger
OLD GLORY (79540) Stonewall(98), Haskell(1)
OLD OCEAN Brazoria
OLDEN Eastland

OLMITO Cameron
OLNEY (76374) Young(97), Archer(1), Throckmorton(1)
OLTON (79064) Lamb(76), Hale(23)
OMAHA Morris
ONALASKA Polk
ORANGE Orange
ORANGE GROVE Jim Wells
ORANGEFIELD Orange
ORCHARD Fort Bend
ORE CITY (75683) Upshur(75), Marion(24)
ORLA Reeves
OTTINE Gonzales
OTTO Falls
OVALO (79541) Taylor(91), Callahan(8)
OVERTON (75684) Rusk(87), Smith(12)
OZONA (76943) Crockett(78), Val Verde(21)
PADUCAH (79248) Cottle(92), King(5), Foard(2)
PAIGE (78659) Lee(71), Bastrop(28)
PAINT ROCK Concho
PALACIOS (77465) Matagorda(75), Jackson(24)
PALESTINE Anderson
PALMER Ellis
PALO PINTO Palo Pinto
PALUXY Hood
PAMPA Gray
PANDORA Wilson
PANHANDLE Carson
PANNA MARIA Karnes
PANOLA Panola
PARADISE Wise
PARIS Lamar
PASADENA Harris
PATTISON Waller
PATTONVILLE Lamar
PAWNEE Bee
PEACOCK Stonewall
PEAR VALLEY McCulloch
PEARLAND Brazoria
PEARSALL Frio
PEASTER Parker
PECAN GAP (75469) Delta(91), Hunt(8)
PECOS Reeves
PEGGY Atascosa
PENDLETON Bell
PENELOPE Hill
PENITAS Hidalgo
PENNINGTON (75856) Trinity(70), Houston(30)
PENWELL Ector
PEP (79353) Hockley(84), Cochran(15)
PERRIN (76486) Jack(45), Palo Pinto(27), Parker(26)
PERRY Falls
PERRYTON Ochiltree
PETERSBURG (79250) Hale(48), Lubbock(22), Floyd(17), Crosby(11)
PETROLIA Clay
PETTUS Bee
PETTY Lamar
PFLUGERVILLE Travis
PHARR Hidalgo
PICKTON (75471) Hopkins(82), Wood(17)
PIERCE Wharton
PILOT POINT (76258) Denton(91), Grayson(8)
PINEHURST Montgomery
PINELAND Sabine
PIPE CREEK (78063) Bandera(98), Kerr(1)
PITTSBURG (75686) Camp(87), Upshur(7), Titus(2), Morris(2)
PLACEDO Victoria
PLAINS Yoakum
PLAINVIEW Hale
PLANO Collin
PLANTERSVILLE (77363) Grimes(98), Waller(1)
PLEASANTON Atascosa
PLEDGER Matagorda

PLUM Fayette
POINT Rains
POINT COMFORT Calhoun
POINTBLANK San Jacinto
POLLOK Angelina
PONDER Denton
PONTOTOC (76869) Llano(61), Mason(26), San Saba(11)
POOLVILLE (76487) Parker(67), Wise(23), Jack(8)
PORT ARANSAS Nueces
PORT ARTHUR Jefferson
PORT BOLIVAR Galveston
PORT ISABEL Cameron
PORT LAVACA Calhoun
PORT MANSFIELD Willacy
PORT NECHES Jefferson
PORT O CONNOR Calhoun
PORTER (77365) Montgomery(98), Harris(1)
PORTLAND San Patricio
POST (79356) Garza(95), Lynn(3), Crosby(1)
POTEET Atascosa
POTH Wilson
POTTSBORO Grayson
POTTSVILLE Hamilton
POWDERLY Lamar
POWELL Navarro
POYNOR Henderson
PRAIRIE HILL Limestone
PRAIRIE LEA Caldwell
PRAIRIE VIEW Waller
PREMONT Jim Wells
PRESIDIO Presidio
PRICE Rusk
PRIDDY Mills
PRINCETON Collin
PROCTOR Comanche
PROGRESO Hidalgo
PROSPER (75078) Collin(93), Denton(6)
PURDON Navarro
PURMELA (76566) Coryell(75), Hamilton(24)
PUTNAM Callahan
PYOTE Ward
QUAIL Collingsworth
QUANAH Hardeman
QUEEN CITY Cass
QUEMADO (78877) Maverick(98), Kinney(1)
QUINLAN (75474) Hunt(96), Kaufman(3)
QUITAQUE (79255) Briscoe(56), Motley(26), Floyd(15), Hall(1)
QUITMAN Wood
RAINBOW Somervell
RALLS Crosby
RANDOLPH Fannin
RANGER (76470) Eastland(85), Stephens(14)
RANKIN Upton
RANSOM CANYON Lubbock
RATCLIFF Houston
RAVENNA Fannin
RAYMONDVILLE Willacy
RAYWOOD Liberty
REAGAN Falls
REALITOS Duval
RED OAK (75154) Ellis(82), Dallas(17)
RED ROCK Bastrop
REDFORD Presidio
REDWATER Bowie
REESE AIR FORCE BASE Lubbock
REFUGIO Refugio
REKLAW (75784) Rusk(50), Cherokee(49)
RHOME Wise
RICE (75155) Navarro(94), Ellis(5)
RICHARDS (77873) Montgomery(56), Grimes(32), Walker(11)
RICHARDSON Dallas
RICHLAND Navarro
RICHLAND SPRINGS San Saba

RICHMOND Fort Bend
RIESEL (76682) McLennan(96), Falls(3)
RINGGOLD (76261) Montague(87), Clay(12)
RIO FRIO Real
RIO GRANDE CITY Starr
RIO HONDO Cameron
RIO MEDINA Medina
RIO VISTA (76093) Johnson(92), Hill(7)
RISING STAR (76471) Eastland(89), Brown(7), Comanche(3)
RIVERSIDE Walker
RIVIERA Kleberg
ROANOKE Denton
ROANS PRAIRIE Grimes
ROARING SPRINGS (79256) Motley(54), Dickens(45)
ROBERT LEE (76945) Coke(80), Tom Green(19)
ROBSTOWN Nueces
ROBY Fisher
ROCHELLE McCulloch
ROCHESTER Haskell
ROCK ISLAND Colorado
ROCKDALE Milam
ROCKLAND Tyler
ROCKPORT Aransas
ROCKSPRINGS Edwards
ROCKWALL (75087) Rockwall(97), Collin(2)
ROCKWOOD Coleman
ROGERS (76569) Bell(84), Milam(15)
ROMA Starr
ROMAYOR Liberty
ROOSEVELT (76874) Sutton(61), Kimble(38)
ROPESVILLE (79358) Hockley(80), Lubbock(18), Terry(1)
ROSANKY (78953) Bastrop(52), Caldwell(47)
ROSCOE (79545) Nolan(93), Scurry(3), Fisher(3)
ROSEBUD (76570) Falls(86), Milam(12)
ROSENBERG Fort Bend
ROSHARON (77583) Brazoria(78), Fort Bend(21)
ROSS McLennan
ROSSER Kaufman
ROSSTON Cooke
ROTAN (79546) Fisher(97), Stonewall(1)
ROUND MOUNTAIN Blanco
ROUND ROCK Williamson
ROUND TOP Fayette
ROWENA (76875) Runnels(85), Concho(14)
ROWLETT (75089) Dallas(95), Rockwall(4)
ROXTON Lamar
ROYALTY Ward
ROYSE CITY (75189) Rockwall(49), Hunt(28), Collin(21)
RULE Haskell
RUNGE (78151) Karnes(94), De Witt(4)
RUSK Cherokee
RYE Liberty
SABINAL Uvalde
SABINE PASS Jefferson
SACUL Nacogdoches
SADLER Grayson
SAINT HEDWIG Bexar
SAINT JO (76265) Montague(81), Cooke(18)
SALADO Bell
SALINENO Starr
SALT FLAT (79847) Hudspeth(60), Culberson(39)
SALTILLO Hopkins
SAMNORWOOD Collingsworth
SAN ANGELO Tom Green
SAN ANTONIO Bexar
SAN AUGUSTINE San Augustine
SAN BENITO Cameron

SAN DIEGO (78384) Duval(81), Jim Wells(18)
SAN ELIZARIO El Paso
SAN FELIPE Austin
SAN ISIDRO Starr
SAN JUAN Hidalgo
SAN MARCOS Hays
SAN PERLITA Willacy
SAN SABA San Saba
SAN YGNACIO Zapata
SANDERSON Terrell
SANDIA (78383) Jim Wells(44), Nueces(44), Live Oak(10)
SANDY Blanco
SANFORD Hutchinson
SANGER Denton
SANTA ANNA Coleman
SANTA ELENA Starr
SANTA FE Galveston
SANTA MARIA Cameron
SANTA ROSA Cameron
SANTO Palo Pinto
SARAGOSA Reeves
SARATOGA Hardin
SARITA Kenedy
SATIN Falls
SAVOY Fannin
SCHERTZ (78154) Guadalupe(89), Bexar(8), Comal(2)
SCHULENBURG (78956) Fayette(88), Lavaca(10)
SCHWERTNER Williamson
SCOTLAND Archer
SCOTTSVILLE Harrison
SCROGGINS (75480) Franklin(93), Wood(6)
SCURRY Kaufman
SEABROOK Harris
SEADRIFT Calhoun
SEAGOVILLE (75159) Dallas(85), Kaufman(14)
SEAGRAVES (79359) Gaines(75), Terry(13), Yoakum(11)
SEALY Austin
SEBASTIAN Willacy
SEGUIN Guadalupe
SELMAN CITY Rusk
SEMINOLE Gaines
SEYMOUR (76380) Baylor(96), Knox(3)
SHAFTER Presidio
SHALLOWATER (79363) Lubbock(97), Hockley(1)
SHAMROCK Wheeler
SHEFFIELD Pecos
SHELBYVILLE Shelby
SHEPHERD San Jacinto
SHEPPARD AFB Wichita
SHERIDAN Colorado
SHERMAN Grayson
SHINER (77984) Lavaca(90), Gonzales(9)
SHIRO Grimes
SIDNEY (76474) Comanche(98), Brown(1)
SIERRA BLANCA Hudspeth
SILSBEE Hardin
SILVER Coke
SILVERTON (79257) Briscoe(98), Swisher(1)
SIMMS Bowie
SIMONTON Fort Bend
SINTON (78387) San Patricio(95), Bee(4)
SKELLYTOWN (79080) Hutchinson(80), Carson(19)
SKIDMORE Bee
SLATON (79364) Lubbock(96), Lynn(3)
SLIDELL Wise
SMILEY Gonzales
SMITHVILLE (78957) Bastrop(65), Fayette(34)
SMYER Hockley
SNOOK Burleson
SNYDER Scurry

SOMERSET (78069) Atascosa(70), Bexar(29)
SOMERVILLE Burleson
SONORA Sutton
SOUR LAKE Hardin
SOUTH BEND Young
SOUTH HOUSTON Harris
SOUTH PADRE ISLAND Cameron
SOUTH PLAINS Floyd
SOUTHLAKE Tarrant
SOUTHLAND Garza
SOUTHMAYD Grayson
SPADE Lamb
SPEAKS Lavaca
SPEARMAN (79081) Hansford(93), Hutchinson(3), Ochiltree(3)
SPICEWOOD (78669) Travis(73), Burnet(25), Blanco(1)
SPLENDORA (77372) Montgomery(88), Liberty(11)
SPRING Montgomery
SPRING BRANCH Comal
SPRINGLAKE (79082) Lamb(82), Castro(17)
SPRINGTOWN (76082) Parker(78), Wise(21)
SPUR (79370) Dickens(91), Crosby(4), Kent(3)
SPURGER (77660) Tyler(97), Hardin(2)
STAFFORD Fort Bend
STAMFORD (79553) Jones(93), Haskell(6)
STANTON (79782) Martin(77), Glasscock(19), Midland(2)
STAPLES Guadalupe
STAR Mills
STEPHENVILLE Erath
STERLING CITY (76951) Sterling(97), Glasscock(2)
STINNETT (79083) Hutchinson(66), Moore(32), Hansford(1)
STOCKDALE Wilson
STONEWALL (78671) Gillespie(96), Blanco(3)
STOWELL Chambers
STRATFORD (79084) Sherman(95), Dallam(4)
STRAWN (76475) Eastland(74), Palo Pinto(24)
STREETMAN (75859) Freestone(64), Navarro(35)
SUBLIME Lavaca
SUDAN (79371) Lamb(60), Bailey(39)
SUGAR LAND Fort Bend
SULLIVAN CITY Hidalgo
SULPHUR BLUFF Hopkins
SULPHUR SPRINGS Hopkins
SUMMERFIELD (79085) Castro(85), Parmer(14)
SUMNER Lamar
SUNDOWN Hockley
SUNNYVALE Dallas
SUNRAY (79086) Moore(55), Sherman(44)
SUNSET (76270) Wise(70), Montague(29)
SUTHERLAND SPRINGS Wilson
SWEENY (77480) Brazoria(97), Matagorda(2)
SWEET HOME Lavaca
SWEETWATER (79556) Nolan(96), Fisher(3)
SYLVESTER (79560) Fisher(89), Jones(10)
TAFT San Patricio
TAHOKA Lynn
TALCO (75487) Franklin(94), Titus(5)
TALPA (76882) Coleman(62), Runnels(37)
TARPLEY Bandera
TARZAN Martin
TATUM Rusk
TAYLOR Williamson
TEAGUE Freestone
TEHUACANA Limestone

TELEGRAPH (76883) Edwards(69), Kimble(30)
TELEPHONE Fannin
TELFERNER (77988) Lavaca(77), Victoria(22)
TELL (79259) Childress(74), Hall(25)
TEMPLE Bell
TENAHA (75974) Shelby(61), Panola(38)
TENNESSEE COLONY Anderson
TENNYSON Coke
TERLINGUA Brewster
TERRELL Kaufman
TEXARKANA Bowie
TEXAS CITY Galveston
TEXLINE Dallam
THE COLONY Denton
THICKET Hardin
THOMASTON De Witt
THOMPSONS Fort Bend
THORNDALE (76577) Milam(97), Williamson(2)
THORNTON (76687) Limestone(73), Robertson(26)
THRALL (76578) Williamson(94), Milam(5)
THREE RIVERS Live Oak
THROCKMORTON Throckmorton
TILDEN McMullen
TIMPSON (75975) Shelby(96), Panola(1), Rusk(1)
TIOGA (76271) Grayson(88), Cooke(11)
TIVOLI (77990) Refugio(65), Calhoun(34)
TOKIO (79376) Yoakum(71), Terry(28)
TOLAR Hood
TOM BEAN Grayson
TOMBALL Harris
TORNILLO El Paso
TOW Llano
TOYAH Reeves
TOYAHVALE Reeves
TRENT (79561) Taylor(42), Nolan(35), Fisher(12), Jones(9)
TRENTON (75490) Fannin(98), Grayson(1)
TRINIDAD Henderson
TRINITY (75862) Trinity(97), Walker(2)
TROUP (75789) Smith(86), Cherokee(11), Rusk(1)
TROY (76579) Bell(98), Falls(1)
TRUSCOTT Knox
TULETA Bee
TULIA (79088) Swisher(96), Castro(1), Briscoe(1)

TURKEY (79261) Hall(89), Briscoe(10)
TUSCOLA Taylor
TYE Taylor
TYLER Smith
TYNAN Bee
UMBARGER Randall
UNIVERSAL CITY Bexar
UTOPIA Uvalde
UVALDE Uvalde
VALENTINE (79854) Presidio(52), Jeff Davis(47)
VALERA Coleman
VALLEY MILLS (76689) Bosque(58), McLennan(29), Coryell(12)
VALLEY SPRING Llano
VALLEY VIEW (76272) Cooke(98), Denton(1)
VAN (75790) Van Zandt(97), Smith(2)
VAN ALSTYNE (75495) Grayson(55), Collin(44)
VAN HORN Culberson
VAN VLECK Matagorda
VANCOURT (76955) Tom Green(56), Concho(43)
VANDERBILT Jackson
VANDERPOOL Bandera
VEGA (79092) Oldham(59), Deaf Smith(40)
VENUS (76084) Johnson(71), Ellis(28)
VERA (76383) Knox(91), Baylor(8)
VERIBEST Tom Green
VERNON Wilbarger
VICTORIA (77905) Victoria(90), Goliad(9)
VIDOR Orange
VILLAGE MILLS Hardin
VOCA McCulloch
VON ORMY (78073) Bexar(84), Atascosa(15)
VOSS Coleman
VOTAW Hardin
VOTH Jefferson
WACO McLennan
WADSWORTH Matagorda
WAELDER (78959) Gonzales(68), Fayette(27), Bastrop(2), Caldwell(1)
WAKA Ochiltree
WALBURG Williamson
WALL Tom Green
WALLER (77484) Waller(74), Harris(19), Grimes(4)
WALLIS (77485) Austin(63), Fort Bend(36)
WALLISVILLE Chambers

WALNUT SPRINGS (76690) Bosque(74), Somervell(24), Erath(1)
WARDA Fayette
WARING Kendall
WARREN Tyler
WASHINGTON Washington
WASKOM Harrison
WATER VALLEY Tom Green
WAXAHACHIE Ellis
WAYSIDE Armstrong
WEATHERFORD Parker
WEBSTER Harris
WEESATCHE Goliad
WEIMAR (78962) Colorado(98), Fayette(1)
WEINERT Haskell
WEIR Williamson
WELCH (79377) Dawson(63), Terry(27), Gaines(9)
WELLBORN Brazos
WELLINGTON (79095) Collingsworth(94), Childress(5)
WELLMAN Terry
WELLS Cherokee
WESLACO Hidalgo
WEST (76691) McLennan(98), Hill(1)
WEST COLUMBIA Brazoria
WEST POINT Fayette
WESTBROOK Mitchell
WESTHOFF De Witt
WESTMINSTER Collin
WESTON Collin
WHARTON Wharton
WHEELER Wheeler
WHEELOCK Robertson
WHITE DEER (79097) Carson(95), Gray(4)
WHITE OAK Gregg
WHITEFACE Cochran
WHITEHOUSE Smith
WHITESBORO (76273) Grayson(69), Cooke(30)
WHITEWRIGHT (75491) Grayson(75), Fannin(24)
WHITHARRAL Hockley
WHITNEY Hill
WHITSETT Live Oak
WHITT (76490) Parker(55), Palo Pinto(44)
WHON Coleman
WICHITA FALLS (76310) Wichita(65), Archer(18), Clay(16)
WICKETT Ward
WIERGATE Newton

WILDORADO (79098) Deaf Smith(50), Oldham(21), Randall(21), Potter(6)
WILLIS (77378) Montgomery(81), San Jacinto(18)
WILLOW CITY Gillespie
WILLS POINT (75169) Van Zandt(82), Hunt(10), Kaufman(6)
WILMER Dallas
WILSON Lynn
WIMBERLEY Hays
WINCHESTER Fayette
WINDOM Fannin
WINDTHORST (76389) Archer(62), Clay(29), Jack(8)
WINFIELD Titus
WINGATE (79566) Taylor(59), Runnels(34), Nolan(5)
WINK Winkler
WINNIE (77665) Chambers(98), Jefferson(1)
WINNSBORO (75494) Wood(78), Franklin(19), Hopkins(1)
WINONA Smith
WINTERS (79567) Runnels(97), Taylor(2)
WODEN Nacogdoches
WOLFE CITY (75496) Hunt(87), Fannin(12)
WOLFFORTH Lubbock
WOODLAKE Trinity
WOODLAWN Harrison
WOODSBORO Refugio
WOODSON (76491) Throckmorton(96), Stephens(3)
WOODVILLE Tyler
WOODWAY McLennan
WORTHAM (76693) Freestone(95), Limestone(4)
WRIGHTSBORO Gonzales
WYLIE (75098) Collin(86), Dallas(11), Rockwall(2)
YANCEY Medina
YANTIS (75497) Wood(98), Rains(1)
YOAKUM (77995) Lavaca(55), De Witt(29), Victoria(15)
YORKTOWN De Witt
ZAPATA Zapata
ZAVALLA (75980) Angelina(98), Jasper(1)
ZEPHYR (76890) Brown(95), Mills(2), Comanche(1)

ZIP/City Cross Reference

73301-73344 AUSTIN	75068-75068 LITTLE ELM	75116-75116 DUNCANVILLE	75153-75153 POWELL
75001-75001 ADDISON	75069-75071 MC KINNEY	75117-75117 EDGEWOOD	75154-75154 RED OAK
75002-75002 ALLEN	75074-75075 PLANO	75118-75118 ELMO	75155-75155 RICE
75006-75008 CARROLLTON	75076-75076 POTTSBORO	75119-75120 ENNIS	75157-75157 ROSSER
75009-75009 CELINA	75077-75077 LEWISVILLE	75121-75121 COPEVILLE	75158-75158 SCURRY
75010-75011 CARROLLTON	75078-75078 PROSPER	75123-75123 DE SOTO	75159-75161 SEAGOVILLE
75013-75013 ALLEN	75080-75083 RICHARDSON	75123-75123 DESOTO	75160-75161 TERRELL
75014-75017 IRVING	75084-75084 IRVING	75124-75124 EUSTACE	75163-75163 TRINIDAD
75019-75019 COPPELL	75085-75085 RICHARDSON	75125-75125 FERRIS	75164-75164 JOSEPHINE
75020-75021 DENISON	75086-75086 PLANO	75126-75126 FORNEY	75165-75165 WAXAHACHIE
75022-75022 FLOWER MOUND	75087-75087 ROCKWALL	75127-75127 FRUITVALE	75166-75166 LAVON
75023-75026 PLANO	75088-75089 ROWLETT	75132-75132 FATE	75167-75168 WAXAHACHIE
75027-75028 FLOWER MOUND	75090-75092 SHERMAN	75134-75134 LANCASTER	75169-75169 WILLS POINT
75029-75029 LEWISVILLE	75093-75094 PLANO	75135-75135 CADDO MILLS	75172-75172 WILMER
75030-75030 ROWLETT	75097-75097 WESTON	75137-75138 DUNCANVILLE	75173-75173 NEVADA
75032-75032 ROCKWALL	75098-75098 WYLIE	75140-75140 GRAND SALINE	75180-75181 MESQUITE
75034-75035 FRISCO	75099-75099 COPPELL	75141-75141 HUTCHINS	75182-75182 SUNNYVALE
75037-75039 IRVING	75101-75101 BARDWELL	75142-75142 KAUFMAN	75185-75187 MESQUITE
75040-75049 GARLAND	75102-75102 BARRY	75143-75143 KEMP	75189-75189 ROYSE CITY
75050-75054 GRAND PRAIRIE	75103-75103 CANTON	75144-75144 KERENS	75200-75398 DALLAS
75056-75056 THE COLONY	75104-75104 CEDAR HILL	75146-75146 LANCASTER	75401-75404 GREENVILLE
75057-75057 LEWISVILLE	75105-75105 CHATFIELD	75147-75147 MABANK	75407-75407 PRINCETON
75058-75058 GUNTER	75106-75106 CEDAR HILL	75148-75148 MALAKOFF	75409-75409 ANNA
75060-75063 IRVING	75109-75110 CORSICANA	75149-75150 MESQUITE	75410-75410 ALBA
75065-75065 LAKE DALLAS	75114-75114 CRANDALL	75151-75151 CORSICANA	75411-75411 ARTHUR CITY
75067-75067 LEWISVILLE	75115-75115 DE SOTO	75152-75152 PALMER	75412-75412 BAGWELL

75413-75413 BAILEY	75563-75563 LINDEN	75788-75788 SACUL	76000-76007 ARLINGTON
75414-75414 BELLS	75564-75564 LODI	75789-75789 TROUP	76008-76008 ALEDO
75415-75415 BEN FRANKLIN	75565-75565 MC LEOD	75790-75790 VAN	76009-76009 ALVARADO
75416-75416 BLOSSOM	75566-75566 MARIETTA	75791-75791 WHITEHOUSE	76010-76019 ARLINGTON
75417-75417 BOGATA	75567-75567 MAUD	75792-75792 WINONA	76020-76020 AZLE
75418-75418 BONHAM	75568-75568 NAPLES	75797-75797 BIG SANDY	76021-76022 BEDFORD
75420-75420 BRASHEAR	75569-75569 NASH	75798-75799 TYLER	76023-76023 BOYD
75421-75421 BROOKSTON	75570-75570 NEW BOSTON	75801-75803 PALESTINE	76028-76028 BURLESON
75422-75422 CAMPBELL	75571-75571 OMAHA	75831-75831 BUFFALO	76031-76033 CLEBURNE
75423-75423 CELESTE	75572-75572 QUEEN CITY	75832-75832 CAYUGA	76034-76034 COLLEYVILLE
75424-75424 BLUE RIDGE	75573-75573 REDWATER	75833-75833 CENTERVILLE	76035-76035 CRESSON
75425-75425 CHICOTA	75574-75574 SIMMS	75834-75834 CENTRALIA	76036-76036 CROWLEY
75426-75426 CLARKSVILLE	75599-75599 TEXARKANA	75835-75835 CROCKETT	76039-76040 EULESS
75428-75429 COMMERCE	75601-75615 LONGVIEW	75838-75838 DONIE	76041-76041 FORRESTON
75431-75431 COMO	75630-75630 AVINGER	75839-75839 ELKHART	76043-76043 GLEN ROSE
75432-75432 COOPER	75631-75631 BECKVILLE	75840-75840 FAIRFIELD	76044-76044 GODLEY
75433-75433 CUMBY	75633-75633 CARTHAGE	75844-75844 GRAPELAND	76048-76049 GRANBURY
75434-75434 CUNNINGHAM	75636-75636 CASON	75845-75845 GROVETON	76050-76050 GRANDVIEW
75435-75435 DEPORT	75637-75637 CLAYTON	75846-75846 JEWETT	76051-76051 GRAPEVINE
75436-75436 DETROIT	75638-75638 DAINGERFIELD	75847-75847 KENNARD	76052-76052 HASLET
75437-75437 DIKE	75639-75639 DE BERRY	75848-75848 KIRVIN	76053-76054 HURST
75438-75438 DODD CITY	75640-75640 DIANA	75849-75849 LATEXO	76055-76055 ITASCA
75439-75439 ECTOR	75641-75641 EASTON	75850-75850 LEONA	76058-76058 JOSHUA
75440-75440 EMORY	75642-75642 ELYSIAN FIELDS	75851-75851 LOVELADY	76059-76059 KEENE
75441-75441 ENLOE	75643-75643 GARY	75852-75852 MIDWAY	76060-76060 KENNEDALE
75442-75442 FARMERSVILLE	75644-75645 GILMER	75853-75853 MONTALBA	76061-76061 LILLIAN
75443-75443 GOBER	75647-75647 GLADEWATER	75855-75855 OAKWOOD	76063-76063 MANSFIELD
75444-75444 GOLDEN	75650-75650 HALLSVILLE	75856-75856 PENNINGTON	76064-76064 MAYPEARL
75446-75446 HONEY GROVE	75651-75651 HARLETON	75858-75858 RATCLIFF	76065-76065 MIDLOTHIAN
75447-75447 IVANHOE	75652-75654 HENDERSON	75859-75859 STREETMAN	76066-76066 MILLSAP
75448-75448 KLONDIKE	75656-75656 HUGHES SPRINGS	75860-75860 TEAGUE	76067-76068 MINERAL WELLS
75449-75449 LADONIA	75657-75657 JEFFERSON	75861-75861 TENNESSEE COLONY	76070-76070 NEMO
75450-75450 LAKE CREEK	75658-75658 JOINERVILLE	75862-75862 TRINITY	76071-76071 NEWARK
75451-75451 LEESBURG	75659-75659 JONESVILLE	75865-75865 WOODLAKE	76073-76073 PARADISE
75452-75452 LEONARD	75660-75660 JUDSON	75880-75880 TENNESSEE COLONY	76077-76077 RAINBOW
75453-75453 LONE OAK	75661-75661 KARNACK	75882-75882 PALESTINE	76078-76078 RHOME
75454-75454 MELISSA	75662-75663 KILGORE	75884-75886 TENNESSEE COLONY	76082-76082 SPRINGTOWN
75455-75456 MOUNT PLEASANT	75666-75666 LAIRD HILL	75901-75915 LUFKIN	76084-76084 VENUS
75457-75457 MOUNT VERNON	75667-75667 LANEVILLE	75925-75925 ALTO	76085-76088 WEATHERFORD
75458-75458 MERIT	75668-75668 LONE STAR	75926-75926 APPLE SPRINGS	76092-76092 SOUTHLAKE
75459-75459 HOWE	75669-75669 LONG BRANCH	75928-75928 BON WIER	76093-76093 RIO VISTA
75460-75462 PARIS	75670-75672 MARSHALL	75929-75929 BROADDUS	76094-76094 ARLINGTON
75468-75468 PATTONVILLE	75680-75680 MINDEN	75930-75930 BRONSON	76095-76095 BEDFORD
75469-75469 PECAN GAP	75681-75681 MOUNT ENTERPRISE	75931-75931 BROOKELAND	76096-76096 ARLINGTON
75470-75470 PETTY	75682-75682 NEW LONDON	75932-75932 BURKEVILLE	76097-76097 BURLESON
75471-75471 PICKTON	75683-75683 ORE CITY	75933-75933 CALL	76098-76098 AZLE
75472-75472 POINT	75684-75684 OVERTON	75934-75934 CAMDEN	76099-76099 GRAPEVINE
75473-75473 POWDERLY	75685-75685 PANOLA	75935-75935 CENTER	76100-76116 FORT WORTH
75474-75474 QUINLAN	75686-75686 PITTSBURG	75936-75936 CHESTER	76117-76117 HALTOM CITY
75475-75475 RANDOLPH	75687-75687 PRICE	75937-75937 CHIRENO	76118-76126 FORT WORTH
75476-75476 RAVENNA	75688-75688 SCOTTSVILLE	75938-75938 COLMESNEIL	76127-76127 NAVAL AIR STATION/ JRB
75477-75477 ROXTON	75689-75689 SELMAN CITY	75939-75939 CORRIGAN	76129-76179 FORT WORTH
75478-75478 SALTILLO	75691-75691 TATUM	75941-75941 DIBOLL	76180-76180 NORTH RICHLAND HILLS
75479-75479 SAVOY	75692-75692 WASKOM	75942-75942 DOUCETTE	76181-76181 FORT WORTH
75480-75480 SCROGGINS	75693-75693 WHITE OAK	75943-75943 DOUGLASS	76182-76182 NORTH RICHLAND HILLS
75481-75481 SULPHUR BLUFF	75694-75694 WOODLAWN	75944-75944 ETOILE	76185-76199 FORT WORTH
75482-75483 SULPHUR SPRINGS	75701-75713 TYLER	75946-75946 GARRISON	76201-76210 DENTON
75485-75485 WESTMINSTER	75750-75750 ARP	75947-75947 GENEVA	76225-76225 ALVORD
75486-75486 SUMNER	75751-75752 ATHENS	75948-75948 HEMPHILL	76226-76226 ARGYLE
75487-75487 TALCO	75754-75754 BEN WHEELER	75949-75949 HUNTINGTON	76227-76227 AUBREY
75488-75488 TELEPHONE	75755-75755 BIG SANDY	75951-75951 JASPER	76228-76228 BELLEVUE
75489-75489 TOM BEAN	75756-75756 BROWNSBORO	75954-75954 JOAQUIN	76230-76230 BOWIE
75490-75490 TRENTON	75757-75757 BULLARD	75956-75956 KIRBYVILLE	76233-76233 COLLINSVILLE
75491-75491 WHITEWRIGHT	75758-75758 CHANDLER	75957-75957 MAGNOLIA SPRINGS	76234-76234 DECATUR
75492-75492 WINDOM	75759-75759 CUNEY	75958-75958 MARTINSVILLE	76238-76238 ERA
75493-75493 WINFIELD	75760-75760 CUSHING	75959-75959 MILAM	76239-76239 FORESTBURG
75494-75494 WINNSBORO	75762-75762 FLINT	75960-75960 MOSCOW	76240-76241 GAINESVILLE
75495-75495 VAN ALSTYNE	75763-75763 FRANKSTON	75961-75965 NACOGDOCHES	76244-76244 KELLER
75496-75496 WOLFE CITY	75764-75764 GALLATIN	75966-75966 NEWTON	76245-76245 GORDONVILLE
75497-75497 YANTIS	75765-75765 HAWKINS	75968-75968 PINELAND	76246-76246 GREENWOOD
75501-75507 TEXARKANA	75766-75766 JACKSONVILLE	75969-75969 POLLOK	76247-76247 JUSTIN
75550-75550 ANNONA	75770-75770 LARUE	75970-75970 ROCKLAND	76248-76248 KELLER
75551-75551 ATLANTA	75771-75771 LINDALE	75972-75972 SAN AUGUSTINE	76249-76249 KRUM
75554-75554 AVERY	75772-75772 MAYDELLE	75973-75973 SHELBYVILLE	76250-76250 LINDSAY
75555-75555 BIVINS	75773-75773 MINEOLA	75974-75974 TENAHA	76251-76251 MONTAGUE
75556-75556 BLOOMBURG	75778-75778 MURCHISON	75975-75975 TIMPSON	76252-76252 MUENSTER
75557-75557 MAGNOLIA SPRINGS	75779-75779 NECHES	75976-75976 WELLS	76253-76253 MYRA
75558-75558 COOKVILLE	75780-75780 NEW SUMMERFIELD	75977-75977 WIERGATE	76254-76254 NEWPORT
75559-75559 DE KALB	75782-75782 POYNOR	75978-75978 WODEN	76255-76255 NOCONA
75560-75560 DOUGLASSVILLE	75783-75783 QUITMAN	75979-75979 WOODVILLE	76258-76258 PILOT POINT
75561-75561 HOOKS	75784-75784 REKLAW	75980-75980 ZAVALLA	76259-76259 PONDER
75562-75562 KILDARE	75785-75785 RUSK	75990-75990 WOODVILLE	76261-76261 RINGGOLD

76262-76262	ROANOKE
76263-76263	ROSSTON
76264-76264	SADLER
76265-76265	SAINT JO
76266-76266	SANGER
76267-76267	SLIDELL
76268-76268	SOUTHMAYD
76270-76270	SUNSET
76271-76271	TIOGA
76272-76272	VALLEY VIEW
76273-76273	WHITESBORO
76299-76299	ROANOKE
76301-76310	WICHITA FALLS
76311-76311	SHEPPARD AFB
76351-76351	ARCHER CITY
76352-76352	BLUEGROVE
76354-76354	BURKBURNETT
76357-76357	BYERS
76359-76359	ELBERT
76360-76360	ELECTRA
76363-76363	GOREE
76364-76364	HARROLD
76365-76365	HENRIETTA
76366-76366	HOLLIDAY
76367-76367	IOWA PARK
76369-76369	KAMAY
76370-76370	MEGARGEL
76371-76371	MUNDAY
76372-76372	NEWCASTLE
76373-76373	OKLAUNION
76374-76374	OLNEY
76377-76377	PETROLIA
76379-76379	SCOTLAND
76380-76380	SEYMOUR
76383-76383	VERA
76384-76385	VERNON
76388-76388	WEINERT
76389-76389	WINDTHORST
76401-76402	STEPHENVILLE
76424-76424	BRECKENRIDGE
76426-76426	BRIDGEPORT
76427-76427	BRYSON
76429-76429	CADDO
76430-76430	ALBANY
76431-76431	CHICO
76432-76432	BLANKET
76433-76433	BLUFF DALE
76435-76435	CARBON
76436-76436	CARLTON
76437-76437	CISCO
76438-76438	ELIASVILLE
76439-76439	DENNIS
76442-76442	COMANCHE
76443-76443	CROSS PLAINS
76444-76444	DE LEON
76445-76445	DESDEMONA
76446-76446	DUBLIN
76448-76448	EASTLAND
76449-76449	GRAFORD
76450-76450	GRAHAM
76452-76452	ENERGY
76453-76453	GORDON
76454-76454	GORMAN
76455-76455	GUSTINE
76456-76456	HASSE
76457-76457	HICO
76458-76458	JACKSBORO
76459-76459	JERMYN
76460-76460	LOVING
76461-76461	LINGLEVILLE
76462-76462	LIPAN
76463-76463	MINGUS
76464-76464	MORAN
76465-76465	MORGAN MILL
76466-76466	OLDEN
76467-76467	PALUXY
76468-76468	PROCTOR
76469-76469	PUTNAM
76470-76470	RANGER
76471-76471	RISING STAR
76472-76472	SANTO
76474-76474	SIDNEY
76475-76475	STRAWN
76476-76476	TOLAR
76481-76481	SOUTH BEND
76483-76483	THROCKMORTON
76484-76484	PALO PINTO
76485-76485	PEASTER
76486-76486	PERRIN
76487-76487	POOLVILLE
76490-76490	WHITT
76491-76491	WOODSON
76501-76508	TEMPLE
76511-76511	BARTLETT
76513-76513	BELTON
76517-76517	BEN ARNOLD
76518-76518	BUCKHOLTS
76519-76519	BURLINGTON
76520-76520	CAMERON
76522-76522	COPPERAS COVE
76523-76523	DAVILLA
76524-76524	EDDY
76525-76525	EVANT
76526-76526	FLAT
76527-76527	FLORENCE
76528-76528	GATESVILLE
76530-76530	GRANGER
76531-76531	HAMILTON
76533-76533	HEIDENHEIMER
76534-76534	HOLLAND
76537-76537	JARRELL
76538-76538	JONESBORO
76539-76539	KEMPNER
76540-76547	KILLEEN
76548-76548	HARKER HEIGHTS
76549-76549	KILLEEN
76550-76550	LAMPASAS
76552-76552	LEON JUNCTION
76554-76554	LITTLE RIVER
76555-76555	MAYSFIELD
76556-76556	MILANO
76557-76557	MOODY
76558-76558	MOUND
76559-76559	NOLANVILLE
76561-76561	OGLESBY
76564-76564	PENDLETON
76565-76565	POTTSVILLE
76566-76566	PURMELA
76567-76567	ROCKDALE
76569-76569	ROGERS
76570-76570	ROSEBUD
76571-76571	SALADO
76573-76573	SCHWERTNER
76574-76574	TAYLOR
76576-76576	GATESVILLE
76577-76577	THORNDALE
76578-76578	THRALL
76579-76579	TROY
76596-76599	GATESVILLE
76621-76621	ABBOTT
76622-76622	AQUILLA
76623-76623	AVALON
76624-76624	AXTELL
76625-76625	BIROME
76626-76626	BLOOMING GROVE
76627-76627	BLUM
76628-76628	BRANDON
76629-76629	BREMOND
76630-76630	BRUCEVILLE
76631-76631	BYNUM
76632-76632	CHILTON
76633-76633	CHINA SPRING
76634-76634	CLIFTON
76635-76635	COOLIDGE
76636-76636	COVINGTON
76637-76637	CRANFILLS GAP
76638-76638	CRAWFORD
76639-76639	DAWSON
76640-76640	ELM MOTT
76641-76641	FROST
76642-76642	GROESBECK
76643-76643	HEWITT
76644-76644	CLIFTON
76645-76645	HILLSBORO
76648-76648	HUBBARD
76649-76649	IREDELL
76650-76650	IRENE
76651-76651	ITALY
76652-76652	KOPPERL
76653-76653	KOSSE
76654-76654	LEROY
76655-76655	LORENA
76656-76656	LOTT
76657-76657	MC GREGOR
76660-76660	MALONE
76661-76661	MARLIN
76664-76664	MART
76665-76665	MERIDIAN
76666-76666	MERTENS
76667-76667	MEXIA
76670-76670	MILFORD
76671-76671	MORGAN
76673-76673	MOUNT CALM
76675-76675	OTTO
76676-76676	PENELOPE
76677-76677	PERRY
76678-76678	PRAIRIE HILL
76679-76679	PURDON
76680-76680	REAGAN
76681-76681	RICHLAND
76682-76682	RIESEL
76684-76684	ROSS
76685-76685	SATIN
76686-76686	TEHUACANA
76687-76687	THORNTON
76689-76689	VALLEY MILLS
76690-76690	WALNUT SPRINGS
76691-76691	WEST
76692-76692	WHITNEY
76693-76693	WORTHAM
76700-76711	WACO
76712-76712	WOODWAY
76714-76799	WACO
76801-76801	BROWNWOOD
76802-76802	EARLY
76803-76804	BROWNWOOD
76820-76820	ART
76821-76821	BALLINGER
76823-76823	BANGS
76824-76824	BEND
76825-76825	BRADY
76827-76827	BROOKESMITH
76828-76828	BURKETT
76831-76831	CASTELL
76832-76832	CHEROKEE
76834-76834	COLEMAN
76836-76836	DOOLE
76837-76837	EDEN
76841-76841	FORT MC KAVETT
76842-76842	FREDONIA
76844-76844	GOLDTHWAITE
76845-76845	GOULDBUSK
76848-76848	HEXT
76849-76849	JUNCTION
76852-76852	LOHN
76853-76853	LOMETA
76854-76854	LONDON
76855-76855	LOWAKE
76856-76856	MASON
76857-76857	MAY
76858-76858	MELVIN
76859-76859	MENARD
76861-76861	MILES
76862-76862	MILLERSVIEW
76864-76864	MULLIN
76865-76865	NORTON
76866-76866	PAINT ROCK
76867-76867	PEAR VALLEY
76869-76869	PONTOTOC
76870-76870	PRIDDY
76871-76871	RICHLAND SPRINGS
76872-76872	ROCHELLE
76873-76873	ROCKWOOD
76874-76874	ROOSEVELT
76875-76875	ROWENA
76877-76877	SAN SABA
76878-76878	SANTA ANNA
76880-76880	STAR
76882-76882	TALPA
76883-76883	TELEGRAPH
76884-76884	VALERA
76885-76885	VALLEY SPRING
76886-76886	VERIBEST
76887-76887	VOCA
76888-76888	VOSS
76889-76889	WHON
76890-76890	ZEPHYR
76901-76906	SAN ANGELO
76908-76908	GOODFELLOW AFB
76909-76909	SAN ANGELO
76930-76930	BARNHART
76932-76932	BIG LAKE
76933-76933	BRONTE
76934-76934	CARLSBAD
76935-76935	CHRISTOVAL
76936-76936	ELDORADO
76937-76937	EOLA
76939-76939	KNICKERBOCKER
76940-76940	MERETA
76941-76941	MERTZON
76943-76943	OZONA
76945-76945	ROBERT LEE
76949-76949	SILVER
76950-76950	SONORA
76951-76951	STERLING CITY
76953-76953	TENNYSON
76955-76955	VANCOURT
76957-76957	WALL
76958-76958	WATER VALLEY
77000-77299	HOUSTON
77301-77306	CONROE
77315-77315	NORTH HOUSTON
77316-77316	MONTGOMERY
77318-77318	WILLIS
77320-77320	HUNTSVILLE
77325-77325	HUMBLE
77326-77326	ACE
77327-77328	CLEVELAND
77331-77331	COLDSPRING
77332-77332	DALLARDSVILLE
77333-77333	DOBBIN
77334-77334	DODGE
77335-77335	GOODRICH
77336-77336	HUFFMAN
77337-77337	HUFSMITH
77338-77339	HUMBLE
77340-77344	HUNTSVILLE
77345-77347	HUMBLE
77348-77349	HUNTSVILLE
77350-77350	LEGGETT
77351-77351	LIVINGSTON
77353-77355	MAGNOLIA
77356-77356	MONTGOMERY
77357-77357	NEW CANEY
77358-77358	NEW WAVERLY
77359-77359	OAKHURST
77360-77360	ONALASKA
77362-77362	PINEHURST
77363-77363	PLANTERSVILLE
77364-77364	POINTBLANK
77365-77365	PORTER
77367-77367	RIVERSIDE
77368-77368	ROMAYOR
77369-77369	RYE
77371-77371	SHEPHERD
77372-77372	SPLENDORA
77373-77373	SPRING
77374-77374	THICKET
77375-77375	TOMBALL
77376-77376	VOTAW
77377-77377	TOMBALL
77378-77378	WILLIS
77379-77383	SPRING
77384-77385	CONROE
77386-77393	SPRING
77396-77396	HUMBLE
77399-77399	LIVINGSTON
77401-77402	BELLAIRE

77404-77404 BAY CITY	77519-77519 BATSON	77835-77835 BURTON	78015-78015 BOERNE
77406-77406 RICHMOND	77520-77522 BAYTOWN	77836-77836 CALDWELL	78016-78016 DEVINE
77410-77410 CYPRESS	77530-77530 CHANNELVIEW	77837-77837 CALVERT	78017-78017 DILLEY
77411-77411 ALIEF	77531-77531 CLUTE	77838-77838 CHRIESMAN	78019-78019 ENCINAL
77412-77412 ALTAIR	77532-77532 CROSBY	77839-77839 CLAY	78021-78021 FOWLERTON
77413-77413 BARKER	77533-77533 DAISETTA	77840-77845 COLLEGE STATION	78022-78022 GEORGE WEST
77414-77414 BAY CITY	77534-77534 DANBURY	77850-77850 CONCORD	78023-78023 HELOTES
77415-77415 CEDAR LANE	77535-77535 DAYTON	77852-77852 DEANVILLE	78024-78024 HUNT
77417-77417 BEASLEY	77536-77536 DEER PARK	77853-77853 DIME BOX	78025-78025 INGRAM
77418-77418 BELLVILLE	77538-77538 DEVERS	77855-77855 FLYNN	78026-78026 JOURDANTON
77419-77419 BLESSING	77539-77539 DICKINSON	77856-77856 FRANKLIN	78027-78027 KENDALIA
77420-77420 BOLING	77541-77542 FREEPORT	77857-77857 GAUSE	78028-78029 KERRVILLE
77422-77422 BRAZORIA	77545-77545 FRESNO	77859-77859 HEARNE	78039-78039 LA COSTE
77423-77423 BROOKSHIRE	77546-77546 FRIENDSWOOD	77861-77861 IOLA	78040-78049 LAREDO
77426-77426 CHAPPELL HILL	77547-77547 GALENA PARK	77862-77862 KURTEN	78050-78050 LEMING
77428-77428 COLLEGEPORT	77549-77549 FRIENDSWOOD	77863-77863 LYONS	78052-78052 LYTLE
77429-77429 CYPRESS	77550-77555 GALVESTON	77864-77864 MADISONVILLE	78053-78053 MC COY
77430-77430 DAMON	77560-77560 HANKAMER	77865-77865 MARQUEZ	78054-78054 MACDONA
77431-77431 DANCIGER	77561-77561 HARDIN	77866-77866 MILLICAN	78055-78055 MEDINA
77432-77432 DANEVANG	77562-77562 HIGHLANDS	77867-77867 MUMFORD	78056-78056 MICO
77433-77433 CYPRESS	77563-77563 HITCHCOCK	77868-77869 NAVASOTA	78057-78057 MOORE
77434-77434 EAGLE LAKE	77564-77564 HULL	77870-77870 NEW BADEN	78058-78058 MOUNTAIN HOME
77435-77435 EAST BERNARD	77565-77565 KEMAH	77871-77871 NORMANGEE	78059-78059 NATALIA
77436-77436 EGYPT	77566-77566 LAKE JACKSON	77872-77872 NORTH ZULCH	78060-78060 OAKVILLE
77437-77437 EL CAMPO	77568-77568 LA MARQUE	77873-77873 RICHARDS	78061-78061 PEARSALL
77440-77440 ELMATON	77571-77572 LA PORTE	77875-77875 ROANS PRAIRIE	78062-78062 PEGGY
77441-77441 FULSHEAR	77573-77574 LEAGUE CITY	77876-77876 SHIRO	78063-78063 PIPE CREEK
77442-77442 GARWOOD	77575-77575 LIBERTY	77878-77878 SNOOK	78064-78064 PLEASANTON
77443-77443 GLEN FLORA	77577-77577 LIVERPOOL	77879-77879 SOMERVILLE	78065-78065 POTEET
77444-77444 GUY	77578-77578 MANVEL	77880-77880 WASHINGTON	78066-78066 RIO MEDINA
77445-77445 HEMPSTEAD	77580-77580 MONT BELVIEU	77881-77881 WELLBORN	78067-78067 SAN YGNACIO
77446-77446 PRAIRIE VIEW	77581-77581 PEARLAND	77882-77882 WHEELOCK	78069-78069 SOMERSET
77447-77447 HOCKLEY	77582-77582 RAYWOOD	77901-77905 VICTORIA	78070-78070 SPRING BRANCH
77448-77448 HUNGERFORD	77583-77583 ROSHARON	77950-77950 AUSTWELL	78071-78071 THREE RIVERS
77449-77450 KATY	77584-77584 PEARLAND	77951-77951 BLOOMINGTON	78072-78072 TILDEN
77451-77451 KENDLETON	77585-77585 SARATOGA	77954-77954 CUERO	78073-78073 VON ORMY
77452-77452 KENNEY	77586-77586 SEABROOK	77957-77957 EDNA	78074-78074 WARING
77453-77453 LANE CITY	77587-77587 SOUTH HOUSTON	77960-77960 FANNIN	78075-78075 WHITSETT
77454-77454 LISSIE	77588-77588 PEARLAND	77961-77961 FRANCITAS	78076-78076 ZAPATA
77455-77455 LOUISE	77590-77592 TEXAS CITY	77962-77962 GANADO	78101-78101 ADKINS
77456-77456 MARKHAM	77597-77597 WALLISVILLE	77963-77963 GOLIAD	78102-78104 BEEVILLE
77457-77457 MATAGORDA	77598-77598 WEBSTER	77964-77964 HALLETTSVILLE	78107-78107 BERCLAIR
77458-77458 MIDFIELD	77611-77611 BRIDGE CITY	77967-77967 HOCHHEIM	78108-78108 CIBOLO
77459-77459 MISSOURI CITY	77612-77612 BUNA	77968-77968 INEZ	78109-78109 CONVERSE
77460-77460 NADA	77613-77613 CHINA	77969-77969 LA SALLE	78111-78111 ECLETO
77461-77461 NEEDVILLE	77614-77614 DEWEYVILLE	77970-77970 LA WARD	78112-78112 ELMENDORF
77462-77462 NEWGULF	77615-77615 EVADALE	77971-77971 LOLITA	78113-78113 FALLS CITY
77463-77463 OLD OCEAN	77616-77616 FRED	77972-77972 LONG MOTT	78114-78114 FLORESVILLE
77464-77464 ORCHARD	77617-77617 GILCHRIST	77973-77973 MCFADDIN	78115-78115 GERONIMO
77465-77465 PALACIOS	77619-77619 GROVES	77974-77974 MEYERSVILLE	78116-78116 GILLETT
77466-77466 PATTISON	77622-77622 HAMSHIRE	77975-77975 MOULTON	78117-78117 HOBSON
77467-77467 PIERCE	77623-77623 HIGH ISLAND	77976-77976 NURSERY	78118-78118 KARNES CITY
77468-77468 PLEDGER	77624-77624 HILLISTER	77977-77977 PLACEDO	78119-78119 KENEDY
77469-77469 RICHMOND	77625-77625 KOUNTZE	77978-77978 POINT COMFORT	78121-78121 LA VERNIA
77470-77470 ROCK ISLAND	77626-77626 MAURICEVILLE	77979-77979 PORT LAVACA	78122-78122 LEESVILLE
77471-77471 ROSENBERG	77627-77627 NEDERLAND	77982-77982 PORT O CONNOR	78123-78123 MC QUEENEY
77473-77473 SAN FELIPE	77629-77629 NOME	77983-77983 SEADRIFT	78124-78124 MARION
77474-77474 SEALY	77630-77632 ORANGE	77984-77984 SHINER	78125-78125 MINERAL
77475-77475 SHERIDAN	77639-77639 ORANGEFIELD	77985-77985 SPEAKS	78130-78132 NEW BRAUNFELS
77476-77476 SIMONTON	77640-77643 PORT ARTHUR	77986-77986 SUBLIME	78133-78133 CANYON LAKE
77477-77477 STAFFORD	77650-77650 PORT BOLIVAR	77987-77987 SWEET HOME	78135-78135 NEW BRAUNFELS
77478-77479 SUGAR LAND	77651-77651 PORT NECHES	77988-77988 TELFERNER	78140-78140 NIXON
77480-77480 SWEENY	77655-77655 SABINE PASS	77989-77989 THOMASTON	78141-78141 NORDHEIM
77481-77481 THOMPSONS	77656-77656 SILSBEE	77990-77990 TIVOLI	78142-78142 NORMANNA
77482-77482 VAN VLECK	77657-77657 LUMBERTON	77991-77991 VANDERBILT	78143-78143 PANDORA
77483-77483 WADSWORTH	77659-77659 SOUR LAKE	77993-77993 WEESATCHE	78144-78144 PANNA MARIA
77484-77484 WALLER	77660-77660 SPURGER	77994-77994 WESTHOFF	78145-78145 PAWNEE
77485-77485 WALLIS	77661-77661 STOWELL	77995-77995 YOAKUM	78146-78146 PETTUS
77486-77486 WEST COLUMBIA	77662-77662 VIDOR	78001-78001 ARTESIA WELLS	78147-78147 POTH
77487-77487 SUGAR LAND	77663-77663 VILLAGE MILLS	78002-78002 ATASCOSA	78148-78150 UNIVERSAL CITY
77488-77488 WHARTON	77664-77664 WARREN	78003-78003 BANDERA	78151-78151 RUNGE
77489-77489 MISSOURI CITY	77665-77665 WINNIE	78004-78004 BERGHEIM	78152-78152 SAINT HEDWIG
77491-77494 KATY	77670-77670 VIDOR	78005-78005 BIGFOOT	78154-78154 SCHERTZ
77496-77496 SUGAR LAND	77700-77708 BEAUMONT	78006-78006 BOERNE	78155-78156 SEGUIN
77497-77497 STAFFORD	77709-77709 VOTH	78007-78007 CALLIHAM	78159-78159 SMILEY
77501-77508 PASADENA	77710-77710 BEAUMONT	78008-78008 CAMPBELLTON	78160-78160 STOCKDALE
77510-77510 SANTA FE	77711-77711 LUMBERTON	78009-78009 CASTROVILLE	78161-78161 SUTHERLAND SPRINGS
77511-77512 ALVIN	77713-77726 BEAUMONT	78010-78010 CENTER POINT	78162-78162 TULETA
77514-77514 ANAHUAC	77801-77808 BRYAN	78011-78011 CHARLOTTE	78163-78163 BULVERDE
77515-77516 ANGLETON	77830-77830 ANDERSON	78012-78012 CHRISTINE	78164-78164 YORKTOWN
77517-77517 SANTA FE	77831-77831 BEDIAS	78013-78013 COMFORT	78200-78299 SAN ANTONIO
77518-77518 BACLIFF	77833-77834 BRENHAM	78014-78014 COTULLA	78330-78330 AGUA DULCE

ZIP Range	City	ZIP Range	City	ZIP Range	City	ZIP Range	City
78332-78333	ALICE	78584-78584	ROMA	78691-78691	PFLUGERVILLE	79027-79027	DIMMITT
78335-78336	ARANSAS PASS	78585-78585	SALINENO	78700-78799	AUSTIN	79029-79029	DUMAS
78338-78338	ARMSTRONG	78586-78586	SAN BENITO	78801-78802	UVALDE	79031-79031	EARTH
78339-78339	BANQUETE	78588-78588	SAN ISIDRO	78827-78827	ASHERTON	79032-79032	EDMONSON
78340-78340	BAYSIDE	78589-78589	SAN JUAN	78828-78828	BARKSDALE	79033-79033	FARNSWORTH
78341-78341	BENAVIDES	78590-78590	SAN PERLITA	78829-78829	BATESVILLE	79034-79034	FOLLETT
78342-78342	BEN BOLT	78591-78591	SANTA ELENA	78830-78830	BIG WELLS	79035-79035	FRIONA
78343-78343	BISHOP	78592-78592	SANTA MARIA	78832-78832	BRACKETTVILLE	79036-79036	FRITCH
78344-78344	BRUNI	78593-78593	SANTA ROSA	78833-78833	CAMP WOOD	79039-79039	GROOM
78347-78347	CHAPMAN RANCH	78594-78594	SEBASTIAN	78834-78834	CARRIZO SPRINGS	79040-79040	GRUVER
78349-78349	CONCEPCION	78595-78595	SULLIVAN CITY	78835-78835	DEL RIO	79041-79041	HALE CENTER
78350-78350	DINERO	78596-78596	WESLACO	78836-78836	CATARINA	79042-79042	HAPPY
78351-78351	DRISCOLL	78597-78597	SOUTH PADRE ISLAND	78837-78837	COMSTOCK	79043-79043	HART
78352-78352	EDROY	78598-78598	PORT MANSFIELD	78838-78838	CONCAN	79044-79044	HARTLEY
78353-78353	ENCINO	78599-78599	WESLACO	78839-78839	CRYSTAL CITY	79045-79045	HEREFORD
78355-78355	FALFURRIAS	78602-78602	BASTROP	78840-78842	DEL RIO	79046-79046	HIGGINS
78357-78357	FREER	78603-78603	BEBE	78843-78843	LAUGHLIN A F B	79051-79051	KERRICK
78358-78358	FULTON	78604-78604	BELMONT	78847-78847	DEL RIO	79052-79052	KRESS
78359-78359	GREGORY	78605-78605	BERTRAM	78850-78850	D HANIS	79053-79053	LAZBUDDIE
78360-78360	GUERRA	78606-78606	BLANCO	78851-78851	DRYDEN	79054-79054	LEFORS
78361-78361	HEBBRONVILLE	78607-78607	BLUFFTON	78852-78853	EAGLE PASS	79056-79056	LIPSCOMB
78362-78362	INGLESIDE	78608-78608	BRIGGS	78860-78860	EL INDIO	79057-79057	MCLEAN
78363-78364	KINGSVILLE	78609-78609	BUCHANAN DAM	78861-78861	HONDO	79058-79058	MASTERSON
78368-78368	MATHIS	78610-78610	BUDA	78870-78870	KNIPPA	79059-79059	MIAMI
78369-78369	MIRANDO CITY	78611-78611	BURNET	78871-78871	LANGTRY	79061-79061	MOBEETIE
78370-78370	ODEM	78612-78612	CEDAR CREEK	78872-78872	LA PRYOR	79062-79062	MORSE
78371-78371	OILTON	78613-78613	CEDAR PARK	78873-78873	LEAKEY	79063-79063	NAZARETH
78372-78372	ORANGE GROVE	78614-78614	COST	78877-78877	QUEMADO	79064-79064	OLTON
78373-78373	PORT ARANSAS	78615-78615	COUPLAND	78879-78879	RIO FRIO	79065-79066	PAMPA
78374-78374	PORTLAND	78616-78616	DALE	78880-78880	ROCKSPRINGS	79068-79068	PANHANDLE
78375-78375	PREMONT	78617-78617	DEL VALLE	78881-78881	SABINAL	79070-79070	PERRYTON
78376-78376	REALITOS	78618-78618	DOSS	78883-78883	TARPLEY	79072-79073	PLAINVIEW
78377-78377	REFUGIO	78619-78619	DRIFTWOOD	78884-78884	UTOPIA	79077-79077	SAMNORWOOD
78379-78379	RIVIERA	78620-78620	DRIPPING SPRINGS	78885-78885	VANDERPOOL	79078-79078	SANFORD
78380-78380	ROBSTOWN	78621-78621	ELGIN	78886-78886	YANCEY	79079-79079	SHAMROCK
78381-78382	ROCKPORT	78622-78622	FENTRESS	78931-78931	BLEIBLERVILLE	79080-79080	SKELLYTOWN
78383-78383	SANDIA	78623-78623	FISCHER	78932-78932	CARMINE	79081-79081	SPEARMAN
78384-78384	SAN DIEGO	78624-78624	FREDERICKSBURG	78933-78933	CAT SPRING	79082-79082	SPRINGLAKE
78385-78385	SARITA	78626-78628	GEORGETOWN	78934-78934	COLUMBUS	79083-79083	STINNETT
78387-78387	SINTON	78629-78629	GONZALES	78935-78935	ALLEYTON	79084-79084	STRATFORD
78389-78389	SKIDMORE	78630-78630	CEDAR PARK	78938-78938	ELLINGER	79085-79085	SUMMERFIELD
78390-78390	TAFT	78631-78631	HARPER	78940-78940	FAYETTEVILLE	79086-79086	SUNRAY
78391-78391	TYNAN	78632-78632	HARWOOD	78941-78941	FLATONIA	79087-79087	TEXLINE
78393-78393	WOODSBORO	78634-78634	HUTTO	78942-78942	GIDDINGS	79088-79088	TULIA
78400-78480	CORPUS CHRISTI	78635-78635	HYE	78943-78943	GLIDDEN	79090-79090	SHAMROCK
78501-78505	MCALLEN	78636-78636	JOHNSON CITY	78944-78944	INDUSTRY	79091-79091	UMBARGER
78516-78516	ALAMO	78638-78638	KINGSBURY	78945-78945	LA GRANGE	79092-79092	VEGA
78520-78526	BROWNSVILLE	78639-78639	KINGSLAND	78946-78946	LEDBETTER	79093-79093	WAKA
78535-78535	COMBES	78640-78640	KYLE	78947-78947	LEXINGTON	79094-79094	WAYSIDE
78536-78536	DELMITA	78641-78641	LEANDER	78948-78948	LINCOLN	79095-79095	WELLINGTON
78537-78537	DONNA	78642-78642	LIBERTY HILL	78949-78949	MULDOON	79096-79096	WHEELER
78538-78538	EDCOUCH	78643-78643	LLANO	78950-78950	NEW ULM	79097-79097	WHITE DEER
78539-78540	EDINBURG	78644-78644	LOCKHART	78951-78951	OAKLAND	79098-79098	WILDORADO
78543-78543	ELSA	78645-78646	LEANDER	78952-78952	PLUM	79100-79189	AMARILLO
78545-78545	FALCON HEIGHTS	78648-78648	LULING	78953-78953	ROSANKY	79201-79201	CHILDRESS
78547-78547	GARCIASVILLE	78650-78650	MC DADE	78954-78954	ROUND TOP	79220-79220	AFTON
78548-78548	GRULLA	78651-78651	MC NEIL	78956-78956	SCHULENBURG	79221-79221	AIKEN
78549-78549	HARGILL	78652-78652	MANCHACA	78957-78957	SMITHVILLE	79222-79222	CAREY
78550-78553	HARLINGEN	78653-78653	MANOR	78959-78959	WAELDER	79223-79223	CEE VEE
78557-78557	HIDALGO	78654-78654	MARBLE FALLS	78960-78960	WARDA	79224-79224	CHALK
78558-78558	LA BLANCA	78655-78655	MARTINDALE	78961-78961	ROUND TOP	79225-79225	CHILLICOTHE
78559-78559	LA FERIA	78656-78656	MAXWELL	78962-78962	WEIMAR	79226-79226	CLARENDON
78560-78560	LA JOYA	78657-78657	MARBLE FALLS	78963-78963	WEST POINT	79227-79227	CROWELL
78561-78561	LASARA	78658-78658	OTTINE	78964-78964	WINCHESTER	79229-79229	DICKENS
78562-78562	LA VILLA	78659-78659	PAIGE	79001-79001	ADRIAN	79230-79230	DODSON
78563-78563	LINN	78660-78660	PFLUGERVILLE	79002-79002	ALANREED	79231-79231	DOUGHERTY
78564-78564	LOPENO	78661-78661	PRAIRIE LEA	79003-79003	ALLISON	79232-79232	DUMONT
78565-78565	LOS EBANOS	78662-78662	RED ROCK	79005-79005	BOOKER	79233-79233	ESTELLINE
78566-78566	LOS FRESNOS	78663-78663	ROUND MOUNTAIN	79007-79008	BORGER	79234-79234	FLOMOT
78567-78567	LOS INDIOS	78664-78664	ROUND ROCK	79009-79009	BOVINA	79235-79235	FLOYDADA
78568-78568	LOZANO	78665-78665	SANDY	79010-79010	BOYS RANCH	79236-79236	GUTHRIE
78569-78569	LYFORD	78666-78667	SAN MARCOS	79011-79011	BRISCOE	79237-79237	HEDLEY
78570-78570	MERCEDES	78669-78669	SPICEWOOD	79012-79012	BUSHLAND	79238-79238	KIRKLAND
78572-78573	MISSION	78670-78670	STAPLES	79013-79013	CACTUS	79239-79239	LAKEVIEW
78575-78575	OLMITO	78671-78671	STONEWALL	79014-79014	CANADIAN	79240-79240	LELIA LAKE
78576-78576	PENITAS	78672-78672	TOW	79015-79016	CANYON	79241-79241	LOCKNEY
78577-78577	PHARR	78673-78673	WALBURG	79018-79018	CHANNING	79243-79243	MCADOO
78578-78578	PORT ISABEL	78674-78674	WEIR	79019-79019	CLAUDE	79244-79244	MATADOR
78579-78579	PROGRESO	78675-78675	WILLOW CITY	79021-79021	COTTON CENTER	79245-79245	MEMPHIS
78580-78580	RAYMONDVILLE	78676-78676	WIMBERLEY	79022-79022	DALHART	79247-79247	ODELL
78582-78582	RIO GRANDE CITY	78677-78677	WRIGHTSBORO	79024-79024	DARROUZETT	79248-79248	PADUCAH
78583-78583	RIO HONDO	78680-78683	ROUND ROCK	79025-79025	DAWN	79250-79250	PETERSBURG

79251-79251 QUAIL	79368-79368 SOUTHLAND	79538-79538 NOVICE	79754-79754 MENTONE
79252-79252 QUANAH	79369-79369 SPADE	79539-79539 O BRIEN	79755-79755 MIDKIFF
79255-79255 QUITAQUE	79370-79370 SPUR	79540-79540 OLD GLORY	79756-79756 MONAHANS
79256-79256 ROARING SPRINGS	79371-79371 SUDAN	79541-79541 OVALO	79758-79758 GARDENDALE
79257-79257 SILVERTON	79372-79372 SUNDOWN	79542-79542 PEACOCK	79759-79759 NOTREES
79258-79258 SOUTH PLAINS	79373-79373 TAHOKA	79543-79543 ROBY	79760-79769 ODESSA
79259-79259 TELL	79376-79376 TOKIO	79544-79544 ROCHESTER	79770-79770 ORLA
79260-79260 TRUSCOTT	79377-79377 WELCH	79545-79545 ROSCOE	79772-79772 PECOS
79261-79261 TURKEY	79378-79378 WELLMAN	79546-79546 ROTAN	79776-79776 PENWELL
79311-79311 ABERNATHY	79379-79379 WHITEFACE	79547-79548 RULE	79777-79777 PYOTE
79312-79312 AMHERST	79380-79380 WHITHARRAL	79549-79550 SNYDER	79778-79778 RANKIN
79313-79313 ANTON	79381-79381 WILSON	79553-79553 STAMFORD	79779-79779 ROYALTY
79314-79314 BLEDSOE	79382-79382 WOLFFORTH	79556-79556 SWEETWATER	79780-79780 SARAGOSA
79316-79316 BROWNFIELD	79383-79383 NEW HOME	79560-79560 SYLVESTER	79781-79781 SHEFFIELD
79320-79320 BULA	79400-79464 LUBBOCK	79561-79561 TRENT	79782-79782 STANTON
79321-79321 CONE	79489-79489 REESE AIR FORCE BASE	79562-79562 TUSCOLA	79783-79783 TARZAN
79322-79322 CROSBYTON	79490-79499 LUBBOCK	79563-79563 TYE	79785-79785 TOYAH
79323-79323 DENVER CITY	79501-79501 ANSON	79565-79565 WESTBROOK	79786-79786 TOYAHVALE
79324-79324 ENOCHS	79502-79502 ASPERMONT	79566-79566 WINGATE	79788-79788 WICKETT
79325-79325 FARWELL	79503-79503 STAMFORD	79567-79567 WINTERS	79789-79789 WINK
79326-79326 FIELDTON	79504-79504 BAIRD	79600-79606 ABILENE	79821-79821 ANTHONY
79329-79329 IDALOU	79505-79505 BENJAMIN	79607-79607 DYESS AFB	79830-79832 ALPINE
79330-79330 JUSTICEBURG	79506-79506 BLACKWELL	79608-79699 ABILENE	79834-79834 BIG BEND NATIONAL PARK
79331-79331 LAMESA	79508-79508 BUFFALO GAP	79701-79712 MIDLAND	79835-79835 CANUTILLO
79336-79338 LEVELLAND	79510-79510 CLYDE	79713-79713 ACKERLY	79836-79836 CLINT
79339-79339 LITTLEFIELD	79511-79511 COAHOMA	79714-79714 ANDREWS	79837-79837 DELL CITY
79342-79342 LOOP	79512-79512 COLORADO CITY	79718-79718 BALMORHEA	79838-79838 FABENS
79343-79343 LORENZO	79516-79516 DUNN	79719-79719 BARSTOW	79839-79839 FORT HANCOCK
79344-79344 MAPLE	79517-79517 FLUVANNA	79720-79721 BIG SPRING	79842-79842 MARATHON
79345-79345 MEADOW	79518-79518 GIRARD	79730-79730 COYANOSA	79843-79843 MARFA
79346-79346 MORTON	79519-79519 GOLDSBORO	79731-79731 CRANE	79845-79845 PRESIDIO
79347-79347 MULESHOE	79520-79520 HAMLIN	79733-79733 FORSAN	79846-79846 REDFORD
79350-79350 NEW DEAL	79521-79521 HASKELL	79734-79734 FORT DAVIS	79847-79847 SALT FLAT
79351-79351 ODONNELL	79525-79525 HAWLEY	79735-79735 FORT STOCKTON	79848-79848 SANDERSON
79353-79353 PEP	79526-79526 HERMLEIGH	79738-79738 GAIL	79849-79849 SAN ELIZARIO
79355-79355 PLAINS	79527-79527 IRA	79739-79739 GARDEN CITY	79850-79850 SHAFTER
79356-79356 POST	79528-79528 JAYTON	79740-79740 GIRVIN	79851-79851 SIERRA BLANCA
79357-79357 RALLS	79529-79529 KNOX CITY	79741-79741 GOLDSMITH	79852-79852 TERLINGUA
79358-79358 ROPESVILLE	79530-79530 LAWN	79742-79742 GRANDFALLS	79853-79853 TORNILLO
79359-79359 SEAGRAVES	79532-79532 LORAINE	79743-79743 IMPERIAL	79854-79854 VALENTINE
79360-79360 SEMINOLE	79533-79533 LUEDERS	79744-79744 IRAAN	79855-79855 VAN HORN
79363-79363 SHALLOWATER	79534-79534 MC CAULLEY	79745-79745 KERMIT	79900-88595 EL PASO
79364-79364 SLATON	79535-79535 MARYNEAL	79748-79748 KNOTT	
79366-79366 RANSOM CANYON	79536-79536 MERKEL	79749-79749 LENORAH	
79367-79367 SMYER	79537-79537 NOLAN	79752-79752 MC CAMEY	

General Help Numbers:

Governor's Office
210 State Capitol   801-538-1000
Salt Lake City, UT 84114   Fax 801-538-1528
www.governor.utah.gov   8AM-5PM

Attorney General's Office
236 State Capitol   801-538-9600
Salt Lake City, UT 84114   Fax 801-538-1121
http://attorneygeneral.utah.gov   8AM-5:30PM

State Court Administrator
450 S State   801-578-3800
Salt Lake City, UT 84114   Fax 801-578-3843
http://courtlink.utcourts.gov   8AM-5PM

State Archives
PO Box 141021   801-538-3012
Salt Lake City, UT 84114-1021   Fax 801-538-3354
www.archives.state.ut.us   8AM-5PM M-F

State Specifics:

Capital: Salt Lake City
Salt Lake County

Time Zone: MST

Number of Counties: 29

Population: 2,269,789

Web Site: www.utah.gov

State Agencies

Criminal Records

Bureau of Criminal Identification, Box 148280, Salt Lake City, UT 84114-8280 (Courier: 3888 West 5400 South, Salt Lake City, UT 84119); 801-965-4445, 801-965-4749 (Fax), 8AM-5PM.

http://bci.utah.gov

Note: Sex offender data is available online at http://corrections.utah.gov/asp-bin/sexoffendersearchform.asp

Indexing & Storage: Records are available back to 1950's. It takes 3 to 7 days before new records are available for inquiry. Records are indexed on inhouse computer. Records are normally destroyed after (records maintained indefinitely unless expunged). 62% of all arrests in database have final dispositions recorded, approximately 75% for those arrests within last 5 years.

Searching: Records are not open to the public nor to employers without fingerprints and without the subject's notarized signature. Those agencies authorized by law do not need to submit fingerprints, but still must have subject's notarized signature. Include the following in your request: name, DOB, SSN, driver's license number, notarized signature of subject, fingerprints. Records are 100% fingerprint-supported. All records are released, including those without dispositions.

Access by: mail.

Fee & Payment: The fee is $10.00 per name (authorization required); $15.00 for fingerprint searches. Statutorily-required searches may include an FBI fingerprint search, additional $24.00 fee. Fee payee: Utah Bureau of Criminal Investigation Personal checks accepted.

Mail search: Turnaround time is 7-10 days. Records are available by mail with submission of proper form.

Corporation Records
Limited Liability Company
Records
Fictitious Name
Limited Partnership Records
Assumed Name
Trademarks/Servicemarks

Commerce Department, Corporate Division, PO Box 146705, Salt Lake City, UT 84114-6705 (Courier: 160 E 300 S, 2nd fl, Salt Lake City, UT 84111); 801-530-4849 (Call Center), 801-530-6111 (Fax), 8AM-5PM.

www.commerce.utah.gov

Indexing & Storage: Records are available for active entities only. Records are indexed on inhouse computer and via the Internet.

Searching: Include the following in your request: full name of business. In addition to the articles of incorporation, corporation records include the following information: Annual Reports, Officers, Directors, DBAs, Prior (merged) names and Reserved names.

Access by: mail, phone, fax, in person, online.

Fee & Payment: Certified records are $10.00 per record. Copies are $.30 per page. Fax transmittals are $5.00 for the first page and $1.00 each page after. There are higher fees for other specific reports. Fee payee: State of Utah. Prepayment required. Personal checks accepted. Credit cards accepted: MasterCard, Visa.

Mail search: Turnaround time: 5-10 days. A self addressed stamped envelope is requested. Copies cost $.30 per page.

Phone search: Copies cost $.30 per page. They will answer questions on name availability, status, agent and officer information.

Fax search: Turnaround time is 5-10 days. There ia an additional fee of $5.00 for the first page and $1.00 for each add'l.

In person search: Copies cost $.30 per page.

Online search: A business entity/principle search service is available at www.utah.gov/government/onlineservices.html. Basic information (name, address, agent) is free, detailed data is a available for minimal fees, but registration is required. The web site also offers an Unclaimed Property search page.

Other access: State allows e-mail access for orders of Certification of Existence at orders@br.state.ut.us.

Expedited service: Expedited service is available. Turnaround time: 24 hours. Add $75.00 per business name.

Uniform Commercial Code

Department of Commerce, UCC Division, Box 146705, Salt Lake City, UT 84114-6705 (Courier: 160 E 300 South, Heber M Wells Bldg, 2nd Floor, Salt Lake City, UT 84111); 801-530-4849, 801-530-6438 (Fax), 8AM-5PM.

www.commerce.utah.gov/cor/index.html

Indexing & Storage: Records are available from 1965. Records are computerized since 1995. It takes 24 hours or less before new records are available for inquiry.

Searching: Use search request form UCC-11. All tax liens are filed at the county level. Include the following in your request: debtor name. File number(s) and/or debtor name(s), name and address of requesting party, and daytime phone number are required.

Access by: mail, fax, in person, online.

Fee & Payment: For a certified search, the fee is $10.00 per file number certified, copies are $.30 per page. For uncertified searches, the fee is only $.30 per page. Fee payee: State of Utah. They will bill for copy charges. Personal checks accepted. Credit cards accepted: MasterCard, Visa.

Mail search: Turnaround time: ten working days. A self addressed stamped envelope is requested.

Fax search: Same fees and turnaround time as mail search apply. They will invoice.

In person search: Searching is available in person.

Online search: UCC records are available free online at www.utah.gov/uccsearch/searchby.html. Search by debtor individual name or organization, or by filing number. There is also a pay system and it is the same system used for corporation records. User fee is $10.00 per month. There is no additional fee at this time; however, the state is considering a certification fee. Open 24 hours daily. E-mail requests are accepted at orders@br.state.ut.us.

Other access: Records are available on CD-ROM. Call 801-530-2267 for details.

Expedited service: Expedited service is available for mail and phone searches. Add $75.00 per name. Turnaround time is 24 hours.

Federal Tax Liens
State Tax Liens

Records not maintained by a state level agency.

Note: Records are found at the local level.

Sales Tax Registrations

Tax Commission, Taxpayer Services, 210 N 1950 W, Salt Lake City, UT 84134; 801-297-2200, 801-297-7697 (Fax), 8AM-5PM.

www.tax.ex.state.ut.us

Note: General forms and tax law information can be downloaded from the web site.

Indexing & Storage: Records are available for 15 years for business records, for 10 years for individual records.

Searching: Requester must have written consent. This agency will only confirm that a business is registered and active if a tax permit number is provided. They will provide no other information. Records are not accessible by the public; access is limited to the owner(s) of the account(s). You can show power of attorney to access, also. Requests must be in writing.

Access by: mail, in person.

Fee & Payment: Copies are $6.50 per record. Fee payee: Utah Tax Commission. Prepayment required. Personal checks accepted. No credit cards accepted.

Mail search: Turnaround time: 1 to 2 weeks. No self addressed stamped envelope is required.

In person search: Turnaround time is 24 hours.

Birth Certificates

Department of Health, Office of Vital Records & Statistics, Box 141012, Salt Lake City, UT 84114-1012 (Courier: 288 N 1460 W, Salt Lake City, UT 84114); 801-538-6105, 801-538-6380 (Voice, credit card orders), 801-538-9467 (Fax), 9AM-5PM (walk-in counter closes at 4:30 PM).

www.health.state.ut.us/bvr

Note: Must have a signed release from person of record or immediate family member.

Indexing & Storage: Records are available from 1905 on. Index computer files go back to 1978. Indexes are not available to the public. New records are available for inquiry immediately.

Searching: At the web site you can download an application at the Forms link on the navigation bar. Follow the instructions on the application and mail it or bring it to the Service Window in-person. Or, you may write a letter. Include the following in your request: full name, names of parents, mother's maiden name, date of birth, place of birth, relationship to person of record, reason for information request. Be sure to sign the request and include a daytime phone number. You may phone, fax or email to request an application form. The following data is not released: medical records.

Access by: mail, phone, fax, in person.

Fee & Payment: Search fee is $9.00 or specify a 5-year period to search for $12.00 (add'l 5-year periods are add'l charge of $12.00). Fee is $50.00 if the entire index must be searched. Add $5.00 per name for second copies. Fee payee: Vital Records. Prepayment required. Personal checks accepted. Credit cards accepted: MasterCard, Visa, AmEx, Discover.

Mail search: Turnaround time: 2 to 3 weeks. No self addressed stamped envelope is required.

Phone search: See expedited service.

Fax search: See expedited service.

In person search: Turnaround time 15 to 30 minutes.

Expedited service: Expedited service is available for mail, phone and fax searches. Turnaround time: overnight delivery. Add $10.00. Also, you must use a credit card which is an additional $5.00. Overnight return is $14.50 for FedEx or $10.50 express mail.

Death Records

Department of Health, Office of Vital Records & Statistics, Box 141012, Salt Lake City, UT 84114-1012 (Courier: 288 N 1460 W, Salt Lake City, UT 84114); 801-538-6105, 801-538-6380 (Voice, credit card orders), 801-538-9467 (Fax), 9AM-5PM (walk-in counter closes at 4:30 PM).

http://hlunix.state.ut.us/bvr/html/certificates.html

Note: Certificates can be obtained by an immediate family member or with written permission from the immediate family.

Indexing & Storage: Records are available from 1905 on. Index computer files go back since 1978. Indexes are not available to the public. New records are available for inquiry immediately.

Searching: At the web site you can download an application at the Forms link on the navigation bar. Follow the instructions on the application and mail it or bring it to the Service Window in-person. Or, you may write a letter. Include the following in your request: full name, date of death, place of death, relationship to person of record, reason for information request. If you do not know the date of death, include last known date alive. You may phone, fax or email to request an application form.

Access by: mail, phone, fax, in person, online.

Fee & Payment: Search fee is $9.00, add $5.00 per name for second copies. Fee payee: Vital Records. Prepayment required. Personal checks accepted. Credit cards accepted: MasterCard, Visa, AmEx, Discover.

Mail search: Turnaround time: 2 weeks. No self addressed stamped envelope is required.

Phone search: See expedited service.

Fax search: See expedited service.

In person search: Turnaround time 15 to 30 minutes.

Online search: Orders can be placed via a state designated vendor. Go to www.vitalcheck.com. Extra fees are involved.

Expedited service: Expedited service is available for mail, phone and fax searches. Turnaround time: overnight delivery. Expedite fee is $10.00 plus you must use a credit card which is an additional $5.00. Add fees for express mail for overnight service.

Marriage Certificates

Department of Health, Office of Vital Records & Statistics, Box 141012, Salt Lake City, UT 84114-1012 (Courier: 288 N 1460 W, Salt Lake City, UT 84114); 801-535-6105, 801-538-6380 (Voice, credit card orders), 801-538-9467 (Fax), 9AM-5PM (walk-in counter closes at 4:30 PM).

http://hlunix.state.ut.us/bvr/html/certificates.html

Note: Certification of marriage occurring in Utah from 1978 through 2001 are issued in this office. Requests for certified copies of marriage prior to 1978 are issued by the county where the marriage occurred.

Searching: Records are certification summaries and not copies of the original records. Download an application at the Forms link on the web site navigation bar. Mail or bring the application to the Service Window in-person, or you may write a letter. Include the following in your request: date & place of occurrence, groom's name, bride's maiden name. You may phone, fax or email to request an application form.

Access by: mail, phone, in person, online.

Fee & Payment: $9.00 is for the abstract certificate. Fee payee: Vital Records. Prepayment required Personal checks accepted Credit cards accepted: MasterCard, Visa, AmEx, Discover.

Mail search: Turnaround time: 2-3 weeks.

Phone search: See expedited service.

In person search: Turn in your order form for a certificate before 4:30 p.m., and wait while it is processed. Requests received at the counter after 4:30 p.m. are processed the following day.

Online search: Orders can be placed via a state designated vendor. Go to www.vitalcheck.com. Extra fees are involved.

Expedited service: Expedited service is available for mail, phone and fax searches. Turnaround time: same day service. You must use a credit card which is an additional $15.00. For express mail or FedEx, add current fee.

Divorce Records

Department of Health, Office of Vital Records & Statistics, Box 141012, Salt Lake City, UT 84114-1012 (Courier: 288 N 1460 W, Salt Lake City, UT 84114); 801-538-6101, 801-538-6380 (Credit card orders), 801-538-9467 (Fax), 9AM-5PM (walk-in counter closes at 4:30 PM).

http://hlunix.state.ut.us/bvr/html/certificates.html

Note: The offices releases certificates of abstract. Actual copies can only be obtained from the state by an immediate family member or with written permission from the immediate family.

Indexing & Storage: Records are available from 1978 to present. Requests for certified copies of divorce prior to 1978 are issued by the county where the divorce occurred.

Searching: Records are certification summaries and not copies of the original records. Download an application at the Forms link on the web site navigation bar. Mail or bring the application to the Service Window in-person, or you may write a letter. Include the following in your request: date and place of occurrence, date and place of marriage, husband's name, wife's name. You may phone or fax to request an application form.

Access by: mail, phone, in person, online.

Fee & Payment: $9.00 for an abstract only. Fee payee: Vital Records. Prepayment required Credit card orders, add $15.00 Personal checks accepted Credit cards accepted: Visa, MasterCard, Discover, AmEx.

Mail search: Turnaround time: 2-3 weeks.

Phone search: See expedited service.

In person search: Turn in your order form for a certificate before 4:30 p.m., and wait while it is processed the same day.

Online search: Orders can be placed via a state designated vendor. Go to www.vitalcheck.com. Extra fees are involved.

Expedited service: For phone credit card phone orders only. Turnaround time: 1-2 days. For express mail or FedEx, add their current fee.

Workers' Compensation Records

Labor Commission, Division of Industrial Accidents, PO Box 146610, Salt Lake City, UT 84114-6610 (Courier: 160 E 300 S, 3rd Floor, Salt Lake City, UT 84114); 801-530-6800, 801-530-6804 (Fax), 8AM-5PM.

www.labor.state.ut.us

Indexing & Storage: Records are available from 1970 to 1988 on microfiche, from 1989 to present on computer.

Searching: Must have a notarized release from claimant (not over 90 days old). If a conditional job has been offered, then include a statement of such with employer's signature. Include the following in your request: Social Security Number, date of birth. Phone or fax to request form.

Access by: mail, fax, in person.

Fee & Payment: The search fee is $15.00 per name, copies are $.50 per page. Fee payee: Division of Industrial Accidents. Prepayment required. Personal checks accepted. No credit cards accepted.

Mail search: Turnaround time: 2 to 3 days. Include your telephone number so they can call

with the total charge, which must be paid before records are released. No self addressed stamped envelope is required.

Fax search: Prepayment is required.

In person search: Same criteria as mail requests.

Accident Reports

Driver's License Division, Accident Reports Section, PO Box 30560, Salt Lake City, UT 84130-0560 (Courier: 4501 South 2700 West, 3rd Floor South, Salt Lake City, UT 84119); 801-965-4428, 8AM-5PM.

Indexing & Storage: Records are available for 7 years to present and are indexed on microfilm. It takes 2 weeks or more before new records are available for inquiry.

Searching: Include the following in your request: full name, date of accident, location of accident. The following data is not released: medical records, Social Security Numbers or addresses.

Access by: mail, fax, in person.

Fee & Payment: The fee is $5.00 per record. Fee payee: Department of Public Safety. Prepayment required. The state will allow ongoing requesters to pre-pay with an account. Personal checks accepted. No credit cards accepted.

Mail search: Turnaround time: 2 weeks. A self addressed stamped envelope is requested.

Fax search: Money must be received up front before records can be returned by fax.

In person search: Records will be mailed, or can be picked up if pre-paid.

Driver Records

Department of Public Safety, Driver License Division, Customer Service Section, PO Box 30560, Salt Lake City, UT 84130-0560 (Courier: 4501 South 2700 West, 3rd Floor South, Salt Lake City, UT 84119); 801-965-4437, 801-965-4496 (Fax), 8AM-5PM.

http://driverlicense.utah.gov/

Note: Copies of tickets can be purchased for $5.00 per record. However, if the ticket information came to the state via magnetic tape, the state will refer the requester to the court.

Indexing & Storage: Records are available for 3 years for moving violations, 6 years for DWIs and 3 years for suspensions (alcohol related suspensions are 6 years). Records on commercial drivers are kept for 10 years. It takes 2 weeks to 6 months before new records are available for inquiry.

Searching: Interstate speeding convictions less than 10 mph over are not shown unless there is written consent. Accidents are reported only if driver had citation. Addresses removed from report to comply with DPPA. Requests must comply with DPPA permissible uses. The driver's full name and DOB and/or license number are needed when ordering. Also helpful: SSN. The following data is not released: medical records or addresses.

Access by: mail, in person, online.

Fee & Payment: The fee is $4.25 per record. Fee payee: Department of Public Safety. Prepayment required. Personal checks accepted. No credit cards accepted.

Mail search: Turnaround time: approx. 1 week. Will FedEx if requester has account or submits pre-paid envelope. A self addressed stamped envelope is requested.

In person search: Up to 10 requests can be processed immediately; any additional requests are available the next day. Driving records can be obtained at any one of 17 branch offices throughout the state.

Online search: Driving records are available to eligible organizations through the eUtah. The system is available 24 hours daily. The fee per driving record is $5.75, there is an annual $50.00 subscription fee, also. For more information, visit the website at www.utah.gov/government/onlineservices.html

Other access: Magnetic tape inquiry is available for high volume users. The state will not sell its DL file to commercial vendors.

Vehicle Ownership & Identification
Vessel Ownership & Registration

State Tax Commission, Motor Vehicle Records Section, 210 North 1950 West, Salt Lake City, UT 84134; 801-297-3507, 801-297-3578 (Fax), 8AM-5PM.

www.dmv-utah.com

Indexing & Storage: Records are available from 1979. All boats 1985 or newer must be titled. All motors over 25 HP must be titled. All boats, except canoes, must be registered. It takes 2 weeks before new records are available for inquiry.

Searching: Access is not open to casual requesters without consent of subject. The name or the vehicle ID or registration number or hull ID is needed to search. The following data is not released: medical records or Social Security Numbers.

Access by: mail, phone, in person, online.

Fee & Payment: The current fee is $2.00 per record and $6.50 for each microfilm record requested. State has established accounts for dealerships and financial institutions requesting lien-holder information. Fee payee: State Tax Commission. Prepayment required. Personal checks accepted. No credit cards accepted.

Mail search: Turnaround time: 2 days. Boat records can take as long as 1 week to process. A self addressed stamped envelope is requested.

Phone search: Searching is available for pre-approved, established accounts.

In person search: Turnaround time while you wait for small amounts.

Online search: Motor Vehicle Dept. titles, liens, and registration searches are available at www.utah.gov/government/onlineservices.html; registration is required.

Other access: Utah offers a bulk or batch format for obtaining registration information on magnetic

tape or paper. A written request stating the purpose of the usage is required. Call 801-297-2700 for further information.

Legislation Records

Utah Legislature, Research and General Counsel, 436 State Capitol, Salt Lake City, UT 84114, 801-538-1588 (Bill Room), 801-538-1032 (Older Passed Bills), 801-538-1712 (Fax), 8AM-5PM.

www.le.state.ut.us

Note: Sessions start 3rd Monday in January.

Indexing & Storage: Records are available from 1980 to 1989 on microfiche and from 1990 forward on computer.

Searching: Bill room only has current bills. Include the following in your request: bill number, topic of bill.

Access by: mail, phone, fax, in person, online.

Fee & Payment: There is no search fee, copy fee is $.10 per page if over 10 pages. Fee payee: State of Utah. Personal checks accepted. No credit cards accepted.

Mail search: Turnaround time: variable. No self addressed stamped envelope is required.

Phone search: Records are available by phone.

Fax search: The fee is $1.00 per page.

In person search: It is necessary to call first and make an appointment.

Online search: Web site contains bill information and also the Utah Code.

Voter Registration
Access to Records is Restricted

Office of Lt Governor, Elections Office, 115 State Capitol, Salt Lake City, UT 84114; 801-538-1041, 801-538-1133 (Fax), 8AM-5PM.

http://elections.utah.gov

Note: Individual record requests are referred to the county clerk offices. Records that have not been secured by the registrant are open to the public; however, the counties will not release the SSN or DL. The entire state voter registration database (current records only) can be purchased from this office for approximately $1,000.

GED Certificates

State Office of Education, GED Testing, Attn Records, PO Box 144200, Salt Lake City, UT 84114-4200; 801-538-7921, 801-538-7868 (Fax), 8AM-5PM.

www.usoe.k12.ut.us/adulted/ged/index.html

Note: Records prior to 1989 may need to be obtained from the testing sites. Testing sites may have fees to verify or release records.

Indexing & Storage: Records are available from 1989 to present. It takes 1 to 3 months before new records are available for inquiry.

Searching: Include the following in your request: Social Security Number, signed release (for content of reocrds), name at time of testing, current name if different. The following information is not required to search, but is very helpful: date/year of test, date of birth, and city of test.

Access by: mail, phone, fax, in person.

Fee & Payment: There is no fee for verification.

Mail search: Turnaround time: 1 to 2 days. No self addressed stamped envelope is required.

Phone search: They will only confirm records available, and will not release content without signed release.

Fax search: Same criteria as phone searching.

In person search: Searchers should call first.

Hunting License Information
Fishing License Information

Utah Division of Wildlife Resources, PO Box 146301, Salt Lake City, UT 84114-6301 (Courier: 1594 West North Temple, #2110, Salt Lake City, UT 84116); 801-538-4700, 801-538-4709 (Fax), 8AM-5PM.

www.nr.state.ut.us?dwr/dwr.htm

Indexing & Storage: Records are available from 1988 on. the last 3 previous years are kept on computer. Records are indexed on inhouse computer.

Searching: Must use the official request form supplied by this agency. You must show a reasonable purpose in order to obtain information. Include the following in your request: name. DOB and SSN are helpful. The following data is not released: telephone numbers.

Access by: mail.

Fee & Payment: Fees are based upon actual cost of computer time, personnel time plus copy fee of $.25 per page. Fee payee: Utah Division of Wildlife Resources. Prepayment required. Personal checks accepted. No credit cards accepted.

Mail search: Turnaround time: variable. No self addressed stamped envelope is required.

Other access: Draw lists are provided for a small fee at the time of big game drawing.

Utah State Licensing Agencies

Licenses Searchable Online

Accounting Firm #5 .... https://secure.e-utah.org/llv
Acupuncturist #5 .... https://secure.e-utah.org/llv
Alarm Company #5 .... https://secure.e-utah.org/llv
Alarm Company Agent/Response Runner #5 .... https://secure.e-utah.org/llv
Animal Euthanasia Agency #5 .... https://secure.e-utah.org/llv
Arbitrator, Alternate Dispute Resolution #5 .... https://secure.e-utah.org/llv
Architect #5 .... https://secure.e-utah.org/llv
Athletic Judge #5 .... https://secure.e-utah.org/llv
Attorney #9 .... www.utahbar.org/html/find_a_lawyer.html
Bank #10 .... www.dfi.state.ut.us/Banks.htm (site may be down)
Boxer #5 .... https://secure.e-utah.org/llv
Building Inspector/Trainee #5 .... https://secure.e-utah.org/llv
Building Trades, General #5 .... https://secure.e-utah.org/llv
Burglar Alarm Agent #5 .... https://secure.e-utah.org/llv
Chiropractor #5 .... https://secure.e-utah.org/llv
Consumer Lender #10 .... www.dfi.state.ut.us/consumer.htm (site may be down)
Contractor #5 .... https://secure.e-utah.org/llv
Controlled Substance Precursor Distributor #5 .... https://secure.e-utah.org/llv
Cosmetologist #5 .... https://secure.e-utah.org/llv
Cosmetology School/Instructor #5 .... https://secure.e-utah.org/llv
Counselor Trainee, Professional #5 .... https://secure.e-utah.org/llv
Counselor, Professional #5 .... https://secure.e-utah.org/llv
Credit Union #10 .... www.dfi.state.ut.us/CreditUn.htm (site may be down)
Deception Detection Examiner/Intern #5 .... https://secure.e-utah.org/llv
Dental Hygienist #5 .... https://secure.e-utah.org/llv
Dental Hygienist/Local Anesthesia #5 .... https://secure.e-utah.org/llv
Dentist #5 .... https://secure.e-utah.org/llv
Dietitian #5 .... https://secure.e-utah.org/llv
Electrician (Residential) Trainee/Journeyman/Master #5
.... https://secure.e-utah.org/llv
Electrician, Apprentice/Journeyman/Master #5 .... https://secure.e-utah.org/llv
Electrologist #5 .... https://secure.e-utah.org/llv
Employee Leasing Company #5 .... https://secure.e-utah.org/llv
Employment Provider, Professional #5 .... https://secure.e-utah.org/llv
Engineer #5 .... https://secure.e-utah.org/llv
Engineer, Structural Professional #5 .... https://secure.e-utah.org/llv
Environmental Health Specialist/Specialist-In-Training #5
.... https://secure.e-utah.org/llv
Escrow Agent #10 .... www.dfi.state.ut.us/OtherInt.htm (site may be down)
Funeral Service Establishment #5 .... https://secure.e-utah.org/llv
Genetic Counselor #5 .... https://secure.e-utah.org/llv
Health Care Assistant #5 .... https://secure.e-utah.org/llv
Health Facility Administrator #5 .... https://secure.e-utah.org/llv
Hearing Aid Specialist #5 .... https://secure.e-utah.org/llv
Hearing Instrument Prof./Intern #5 .... https://secure.e-utah.org/llv
Industrial Loan #10 .... www.dfi.state.ut.us/IndustLn.htm (site may be down)
Insurance Agent #8 .... www.insurance.state.ut.us/companies.html
Insurance Establishment #8 .... www.insurance.state.ut.us/companies.html
Laboratory, Analytical #5 .... https://secure.e-utah.org/llv
Landscape Architect #5 .... https://secure.e-utah.org/llv
Lien Recovery Fund Member #5 .... https://secure.e-utah.org/llv
Manufactured Housing Dealer/Salesman #5 .... https://secure.e-utah.org/llv
Marriage & Family Therapist/Trainee #5 .... https://secure.e-utah.org/llv
Massage Technician/Apprentice #5 .... https://secure.e-utah.org/llv
Mediator, Alternate Dispute Resolution #5 .... https://secure.e-utah.org/llv
Medical Doctor/Surgeon #5 .... https://secure.e-utah.org/llv
Midwife Nurse #5 .... https://secure.e-utah.org/llv
Mortgage Broker, Residential #2 .... www.commerce.state.ut.us/dre/database.html
Mortgage Lender #10 .... www.dfi.state.ut.us/mortgage.htm (site may be down)
Naturopath #5 .... https://secure.e-utah.org/llv
Naturopathic Physician #5 .... https://secure.e-utah.org/llv
Negotiator, Alternate Dispute Resolution #5 .... https://secure.e-utah.org/llv

Nuclear Pharmacy #5 ....https://secure.e-utah.org/llv
Nurse #5 ....https://secure.e-utah.org/llv
Nurse-LPN #5 ....https://secure.e-utah.org/llv
Occupational Therapist/Assistant #5 ....https://secure.e-utah.org/llv
Optometrist #5 ....https://secure.e-utah.org/llv
Osteopathic Physician #5 ....https://secure.e-utah.org/llv
Pharmaceutical Admin. Facility #5 ....https://secure.e-utah.org/llv
Pharmaceutical Dog Trainer #5 ....https://secure.e-utah.org/llv
Pharmaceutical Researcher #5...............................https://secure.e-utah.org/llv
Pharmaceutical Teaching Org. #5 ....https://secure.e-utah.org/llv
Pharmaceutical Whse./Dist./Mfg. #5 ....https://secure.e-utah.org/llv
Pharmacist/Pharmacist Intern #5 ....https://secure.e-utah.org/llv
Pharmacy Out-of-State Mail Svc. #5.......................https://secure.e-utah.org/llv
Pharmacy Retail/Branch #5 ....https://secure.e-utah.org/llv
Pharmacy Technician #5 ....https://secure.e-utah.org/llv
Pharmacy, Institutional/Hospital #5.........................https://secure.e-utah.org/llv
Physical Therapist #5 ....https://secure.e-utah.org/llv
Physician Assistant #5..https://secure.e-utah.org/llv
Plumber (Residential) Journeyman/Apprentice #5...https://secure.e-utah.org/llv
Plumber Apprentice/Journeyman #5........................https://secure.e-utah.org/llv
Podiatrist #5...https://secure.e-utah.org/llv
Preneed Provider/Sales Agent #5...........................https://secure.e-utah.org/llv
Probation Provider, Private #5 ....https://secure.e-utah.org/llv
Psychologist #5...https://secure.e-utah.org/llv
Public Accountant-CPA #5.....................................https://secure.e-utah.org/llv
Radiology Practical Technician #5 ....https://secure.e-utah.org/llv
Radiology Technologist #5.....................................https://secure.e-utah.org/llv
Real Estate Appraiser #2 ....www.commerce.state.ut.us/dre/database.html
Real Estate Broker/Agent #2 ....www.commerce.state.ut.us/dre/database.html
Real Estate Establishment #5 ....https://secure.e-utah.org/llv
Recreational Therapist #5......................................https://secure.e-utah.org/llv
Recreational Vehicle Dealer #5 ....https://secure.e-utah.org/llv
Respiratory Care Practitioner #5.............................https://secure.e-utah.org/llv
Sanitarian #5...https://secure.e-utah.org/llv
Security Company #5...https://secure.e-utah.org/llv
Security Officer, Armed/Unarmed Private #5 ....https://secure.e-utah.org/llv
Shorthand Reporter #5 ....https://secure.e-utah.org/llv
Social Service Aide/Worker/Trainee #5 ....https://secure.e-utah.org/llv
Social Worker #5 ....https://secure.e-utah.org/llv
Social Worker, Clinical #5......................................https://secure.e-utah.org/llv
Speech Pathologist/Audiologist #5 ....https://secure.e-utah.org/llv
Substance Abuse Counselor #5 ....https://secure.e-utah.org/llv
Surveyor, Land #5 ....https://secure.e-utah.org/llv
Trade Instructor #5 ....https://secure.e-utah.org/llv
Veterinarian/Veterinary Intern #5 ....https://secure.e-utah.org/llv
Veterinary Pharmaceutical Outlet #5 ....https://secure.e-utah.org/llv

Licensing Quick Finder

Accounting Firm #5 801-530-6628
Acupuncturist #5 801-530-6628
Alarm Company #5 801-530-6628
Alarm Company Agent/Response Runner #5
....801-530-6628
Animal Euthanasia Agency #5 801-530-6628
Arbitrator, Alternate Dispute Resolution #5
....801-530-6628
Architect #5.......................................801-530-6628
Athletic Event Promoter #5..................801-530-6628
Athletic Judge #5 801-530-6628
Athletic Manager #5...........................801-530-6628
Attorney #9 801-531-9077
Bank #10...801-538-8835
Barber #5 801-530-6628
Barber School/Instructor #5.................801-530-6628
Beekeeper #3 801-538-7184
Boxer #5..801-530-6628
Brand Inspector #3 801-538-7161
Building Inspector/Trainee #5...............801-530-6628

Building Trades, General #5.................801-530-6628
Burglar Alarm Agent #5 801-530-6964
Chiropractor #5..................................801-530-6628
Consumer Lender #10.........................801-538-8830
Contractor #5.....................................801-530-6628
Controlled Substance Precursor Distributor #5
....801-530-6964
Cosmetologist #5...............................801-530-6628
Cosmetology School/Instructor #5.......801-530-6628
Counselor Trainee, Professional #5.....801-530-6628
Counselor, Professional #5 801-530-6628
Credit Union #10................................801-538-8840
Deception Detection Examiner/Intern #5
....801-530-6628
Dental Hygienist #5 801-530-6628
Dental Hygienist/Local Anesthesia #5..801-530-6628
Dentist #5..801-530-6628
Dietitian #5..801-530-6628
Egg & Poultry Inspector #3.................801-538-7124

Electrician (Residential) Trainee/Journeyman/Master
#5...801-530-6628
Electrician, Apprentice/Journeyman/Master #5
....801-530-6628
Electrologist #5..................................801-530-6628
Employee Leasing Company #5 801-530-6628
Employment Provider, Professional #5. 801-530-6628
Endowment Care/Cemetery #5............801-530-6628
Engineer #5.......................................801-530-6628
Engineer, Structural Professional #5 ... 801-530-6628
Environmental Health Specialist/Specialist-In-Training
#5...801-530-6628
Escrow Agent #10 801-538-8842
Feed #3 801-538-7183
Food & Dairy Inspector #3 801-538-7124
Funeral Service Director/Apprentice #5 801-530-6628
Funeral Service Establishment #5 801-530-6628
Genetic Counselor #5 801-530-6628
Geologist #7 801-537-3300
Grain & Seed #3................................801-538-7183

Health Care Assistant #5 801-530-6628	Nurse #5 801-530-6628	Real Estate Appraiser #2 801-530-6747
Health Facility Administrator #5 801-530-6628	Nurse-LPN #5 801-530-6628	Real Estate Broker/Agent #2 801-530-6747
Hearing Aid Specialist #5 801-530-6964	Occupational Therapist/Assistant #5 801-530-6628	Real Estate Establishment #5 801-530-6628
Hearing Instrument Prof./Intern #5 801-530-6628	Optometrist #5 801-530-6628	Recreational Therapist #5 801-530-6628
Industrial Loan #10 801-538-8841	Osteopathic Physician #5 801-530-6628	Recreational Vehicle Dealer #5 801-530-6628
Insurance Agent #8 801-538-3855	Pesticide Dealer/Applicator #3 801-538-7188	Referee #5 801-530-6628
Insurance Establishment #8 801-538-3855	Pharmaceutical Admin. Facility #5 801-530-6628	Respiratory Care Practitioner #5 801-530-6628
Interpreter for the Deaf #12 801-263-4860	Pharmaceutical Dog Trainer #5 801-530-6628	Sanitarian #5 801-530-6628
Laboratory, Analytical #5 801-530-6628	Pharmaceutical Researcher #5 801-530-6628	Savings & Loan #10 801-538-8842
Landscape Architect #5 801-530-6628	Pharmaceutical Teaching Org. #5 801-530-6628	School Administrator #6 801-538-7751
Lien Recovery Fund Member #5 801-530-6628	Pharmaceutical Whse./Dist./Mfg. #5 801-530-6628	School Librarian #6 801-538-7751
Liquor License #1 801-977-6800	Pharmacist/Pharmacist Intern #5 801-530-6628	Securities Broker/Dealer #5 801-530-6628
Liquor Store (Retail Liquor License) #1 . 801-977-6800	Pharmacy Out-of-State Mail Svc. #5 801-530-6628	Security Company #5 801-530-6628
Manufactured Housing Dealer/Salesman #5	Pharmacy Retail/Branch #5 801-530-6628	Security Officer, Armed/Unarmed Private #5
.... 801-530-6628	Pharmacy Technician #5 801-530-6628	 801-530-6964
Marriage & Family Therapist/Trainee #5 801-530-6628	Pharmacy, Institutional/Hospital #5 801-530-6628	Shorthand Reporter #5 801-530-6964
Massage Technician/Apprentice #5 801-530-6964	Physical Therapist #5 801-530-6628	Social Service Aide/Worker/Trainee #5 801-530-6628
Meat Inspector #3 801-538-7161	Physician Assistant #5 801-530-6628	Social Worker #5 801-530-6628
Mediator, Alternate Dispute Resolution #5	Plumber (Residential) Jouneyman/Apprentice #5	Social Worker, Clinical #5 801-530-6628
.... 801-530-6628	 801-530-6628	Speech Pathologist/Audiologist #5 801-530-6628
Medical Doctor/Surgeon #5 801-530-6628	Plumber Apprentice/Journeyman #5 801-530-6628	Substance Abuse Counselor #5 801-530-6628
Midwife Nurse #5 801-530-6628	Podiatrist #5 801-530-6628	Surveyor, Land #5 801-530-6628
Mortgage Broker, Residential #2 801-530-6747	Polygraph Examiner #5 801-530-6964	Teacher #6 801-538-7751
Mortgage Lender #10 801-538-8830	Preneed Provider/Sales Agent #5 801-530-6628	Third Party Payment Issuer #10 801-538-8842
Naturopath #5 801-530-6628	Probation Provider, Private #5 801-530-6628	Trade Instructor #5 801-530-6628
Naturopathic Physician #5 801-530-6628	Psychological Assistant #5 801-530-6628	Veterinarian/Veterinary Intern #5 801-530-6628
Negotiator, Alternate Dispute Resolution #5	Psychologist #5 801-530-6628	Veterinary Pharmaceutical Outlet #5 ... 801-530-6628
.... 801-530-6628	Public Accountant-CPA #5 801-530-6628	Weights & Measures #3 801-538-7158
Notary Public #4 801-530-6078	Radiology Practical Technician #5 801-530-6628	
Nuclear Pharmacy #5 801-530-6628	Radiology Technologist #5 801-530-6628	

Licensing Agency Information

#1 Alcoholic Beverage Control Department, 1625 S 900 W, Salt Lake City, UT 84130; 801-977-6800, Fax: 801-977-6888.
www.alcbev.state.ut.us
Agency email: abcmain.hotline@state.ut.us.
Search database at www.alcbev.state.ut.us

#2 Commerce Department, Real Estate Division, 160 E 300 S, 2nd Fl, Salt Lake City, UT 84145-0806; 801-530-6747, Fax: 801-530-6749.
www.commerce.utah.gov/dre
Agency email: realest@br.state.ut.us.
Search database at www.commerce.state.ut.us/dre/database.html

#3 Department of Agriculture, PO Box 146500, Salt Lake City, UT 84114-6500; 801-538-7100, Fax: 801-538-7126.

#4 Div of Cooperations & Commercial Code, 160 E 300 S, Salt Lake City, UT 84114-6705; 801-530-4849.
www.commerce.state.ut.us/corporat/notarypublic.htm. Agency email: kbachman@br.stateut.us.

#5 Department of Commerce, Division of Occupational & Professional Licensing, PO Box 146741 (160 E 300 S, Heber M Wells Bldg, 84111), Salt Lake City, UT 84114-6741; 801-530-6628, Fax: 801-530-6511.
www.commerce.state.ut.us/dopl
Agency email: brdopl.dblake@e-mail.state.ut.us.
Search database at https://secure.e-utah.org/llv

#6 Educator Licensing, Office of Education, PO Box 144200 (250 E 500 S), Salt Lake City, UT 84114; 801-538-7751, Fax: 801-538-7973.
www.usoe.k12.ut.us The CACTUS teacher information system at www.uen.org/training/free/cactus.cgi?c_id=11341&a_id requires user name and password.

#7 Geological Survey Department, PO Box 146100, Salt Lake City, UT 84114-6100; 801-537-3300, Fax: 801-537-3400.

#8 Insurance Department, 3110 State Office Bldg, Salt Lake City, UT 84114-6901; 801-538-3855, Fax: 801-538-3829.
www.insurance.state.ut.us

Search database at www.insurance.state.ut.us/companies.html. Online license search "coming soon."

#9 State Bar Association, 645 S 200 E, Salt Lake City, UT 84111; 801-531-9077, Fax: 801-531-0660.
www.utahbar.org
Agency email: jbaldwin@utahbar.org.
Search database at www.utahbar.org/html/find_a_lawyer.html

#10 Department of Financial Institutions, 324 S State #201, PO Box 89, Salt Lake City, UT 84110-0089; 801-538-8830, Fax: 801-538-8894.

#12 Division of Services for the Deaf & Hard of Hearing, Interpreter Svcs, 5709 S 1500 W, Salt Lake City, UT 84123; 801-263-4870, Fax: 801-263-4865.
www.usor.state.ut.us/dsdhh

Utah Federal Courts

County/Court Cross Reference

All counties report to Salt Lake City.

US District Court

District of Utah

Division Clerk's Office, Room 150, 350 S Main St, Salt Lake City, UT 84101-2180 (Courier Address: Use mail address for courier delivery), 801-524-6100, Fax: 801-526-1175.

www.utd.uscourts.gov

Counties: All counties in Utah. Although all cases are heard here, the district is divided into Northern and Central Divisions. The Northern Division includes the counties of Box Elder, Cache, Rich, Davis, Morgan and Weber, and the Central Division includes allother counties.

Indexing & Storage: Cases are indexed by defendant, plaintiff, and case number. New cases are available in the index 1 day after filing date. Older records are on microfiche. Open records are located at this court.

Fee & Payment Notes: Payment may be made by money order, cashier check, personal check, Visa, Mastercard. Payee: Clerk, US District Court. You are allowed to make your own copies. These copies cost $.15 per page. Public terminals are available.

Phone Search: Only limited information will be released over the telephone.

Mail Search: A stamped self addressed envelope is not required.

In Person Search: In person searching available.

PACER:. Case records are available back to July 1, 1989. Records are never purged. New records are available online after 1 day. PACER is available online at http://pacer.utd.uscourts.gov. Document images available.

US Bankruptcy Court

District of Utah

Division Clerk of Court, Frank E Moss Courthouse, 350 S Main St, Room 301, Salt Lake City, UT 84101 (Courier Address: Use mail address for courier delivery), 801-524-6687, Fax: 801-524-4409.

www.utb.uscourts.gov

Counties: All counties in Utah. Although all cases are handled here, the court divides itself into two divisions. The Northern Division includes the counties of Box Elder, Cache, Rich, Davis, Morgan and Weber, and the Central Division includes the remainingcounties. Court is held once per week in Ogden for Northern cases.

Indexing & Storage: Cases are indexed by debtor and creditors as well as by case number. New cases are available in the index as soon as the work load permits after filing date. Open records are located at this court.

Fee & Payment Notes: Payment may be made by money order, cashier check, personal check. Debtor's checks are not accepted. Payee: Clerk, US Bankruptcy Court.

Phone Search: Only docket information is available by phone. An automated voice case information service (VCIS) is available. Call VCIS at 800-733-6740 or 801-524-3107.

Fax Search: The court has a contract with a copy service that will accept fax requests. Call for more information. The court has a contract with a copy service that will fax docket listings for a fee. Call for more information.

In Person Search: In person searching available.

PACER:. Case records are available back to January 1985. Records are purged after 12 months. New civil records are available online after 2 days or more. PACER is available online at http://pacer.utb.uscourts.gov. Document images available.

Electronic Filing: Recent case filings reports are free. Information is available online at https://ecf.utb.uscourts.gov

Opinions Online: Court opinions are available online at www.utb.uscourts.gov/OPINIONS/opin.htm

Standards for Federal Courts: The search fee is $20.00 per item (one party name or case number). Certification fee is $7.00 per document. Copy fee is $.50 per page. All fees standard unless noted in profile. Mail Search: always enclose a stamped self addressed envelope unless otherwise noted. Before releasing records, all courts require prepayment unless noted in profile.

Open records are located at the court unless otherwise noted. District courts index by defendant and plaintiff as well as by case number. Bankruptcy courts usually index by debtor and case number. While most courts now have their indexes on computer, many still maintain index card files as well.

The universal PACER sign-up number is 800-676-6856. Find PACER and the Party/Case Index on the Web at http://pacer.psc.uscourts.gov. PACER dial-up access is $.60 per minute. Also, courts offering internet access via RACER, PACER, Web-PACER or the new CM-ECF charge $.07 per page fee unless noted as free.

Utah County Courts

Court	Jurisdiction	No. of Courts	How Organized
District Courts*	General	41	8 Districts
Justice Courts	Limited	128	128 Cities/ Counties
Juvenile Courts	Special		8 Juvenile Districts

* Profiled in this Sourcebook.

CIVIL									
Court	Tort	Contract	Real Estate	Min. Claim	Max. Claim	Small Claims	Estate	Eviction	Domestic Relations
District Courts*	X	X	X	$20,000	No Max	$2000	X	X	X
Justice Courts	X	X		$0	$1000	$2000			
Juvenile Courts									

CRIMINAL					
Court	Felony	Misdemeanor	DWI/DUI	Preliminary Hearing	Juvenile
District Courts*	X	X	X	X	
Justice Courts		X	X		
Juvenile Courts					X

ADMINISTRATION   Court Administrator, 450 S State Street, Salt Lake City, UT, 84114; 801-578-3800, Fax: 801-578-3843. http://courtlink.utcourts.gov

COURT STRUCTURE   41 District Courts are arranged in eight judicial districts. Effective July 1, 1996, each Circuit Court (the lower court) was combined with District Court (the higher court) in each county. It is reported that branch courts in larger counties such as Salt Lake which were formerly Circuit Courts have been elevated to District Courts, with full jurisdiction over felony as well as misdemeanor cases. Many misdemeanors are handled at Justice Courts, which are limited jurisdiction.

ONLINE ACCESS   Case information from all Utah District Court locations is available through XChange. Fees include $25.00 registration and $30.00 per month plus $.10 per minute for usage, over 120 minutes. Information about XChange and the subscription agreement can be found at http://courtlink.utcourts.gov/howto/access or call 801-238-7877. Records go back seven to ten years.

ADDITIONAL INFORMATION   UT Code Rule 4-202.08 sets fees for record searches (including above) at $21.00 per hour, billed on 15 minute increments, with the first 15 minutes free and the copy fee at $.25 per page. But, at the county level, there is a wide variance of per hour charges statewide. In 2002, the standard hourly search fee depends on which office person does the search; the basic clerk is $15.00. Yet, many courts still report their search fee as $10.00 per hour, many without the first 15 minutes free.

Salt Lake, Ogden, Roy, Provo and Orem District Courts have automated information phone lines that provide court appearance look-up, outstanding fine balance look-up, and judgment/divorce decree lookup. Use these numbers:

Salt Lake District Court - 801-238-7830

Ogden & Roy District Court - 801-395-1111

Provo & Orem District Court - 801-429-1000

Beaver County

5th Judicial District Court PO Box 1683, Beaver, UT 84713; 435-438-5309; Fax: 435-438-5395. Hours: 8AM-5PM (MST). *Felony, Misdemeanor, Civil, Eviction, Probate.*

Civil Records: Access: Fax, mail, in person, online. Both court and visitors may perform in person searches.

Search fee: $13.00 per hour. Required to search: name, years to search. Civil cases indexed by defendant, plaintiff. Civil records archived from 1800s, are on computer back to 1997. Online access available through Xchange, see http://courtlink.utcourts.gov. Also, see state introduction.

Criminal Records: Access: Fax, mail, in person, online. Both court and visitors may perform in person

searches. Search fee: $13.00 per hour. Required to search: name, years to search, DOB. Criminal records archived from 1896, are on computer back to 1997. Online access available through Xchange, see http://courtlink.utcourts.gov. Also, see state introduction.

General Information: No adoption, juvenile, sealed records released. SASE required. Turnaround time 2-7 days. Fax notes: Fee to fax results is $.25 per page. Copy fee: $.25 per page. Certification fee: $4.00 plus $.50 per page. Fee payee: 5th District Court. Personal checks accepted. Prepayment is required.

Box Elder County

1st District Court 43 N Main, PO Box 873, Brigham City, UT 84302; 435-734-4600; Fax: 435-734-4610. Hours: 8AM-5PM (MST). *Felony, Misdemeanor, Civil, Eviction, Small Claims, Probate.*

Civil Records: Access: Phone, fax, mail, online, in person. Both court and visitors may perform in person searches. Search fee: $13.00 per name. Required to search: name, years to search. Civil cases indexed by defendant, plaintiff. Civil records on computer from 3/87, books, microfiche, archived from 1856. Online access available through Xchange, see http://courtlink.utcourts.gov. Also, see state introduction.

Criminal Records: Access: Fax, mail, online, in person. Both court and visitors may perform in person searches. Search fee: $13.00 per name. Required to search: name, years to search; also helpful: DOB, SSN. Criminal records on computer from 3/87, books, microfiche, archived from 1856. Online access available via Xchange, see http://courtlink.utcourts.gov. Also, see state introduction.

General Information: Public access terminal is available. No adoptions, sealed records released. SASE required. Turnaround time 1 week. Fax notes: Fee to fax results is $.50 per page. Copy fee: $.25 per page. Certification fee: $2.00. Fee payee: 1st District Court. Personal checks accepted. Credit cards accepted: Visa, MasterCard. Prepayment is required.

Cache County

1st District Court 140 N. 100 W., Logan, UT 84321; 435-750-1300; Fax: 435-750-1355. Hours: 8AM-5PM (MST). *Felony, Misdemeanor, Civil, Eviction, Small Claims, Probate.*

Civil Records: Access: Phone, mail, online, in person. Both court and visitors may perform in person searches. Search fee: $10.00 per hour. Required to search: name, years to search. Civil cases indexed by defendant, plaintiff. Civil records on computer from 11-87, archived from 1983, microfiche in Salt Lake City. Online access available through Xchange, see http://courtlink.utcourts.gov. Also see state introduction.

Criminal Records: Access: Phone, mail, online, in person. Both court and visitors may perform in person searches. Search fee: $10.00 per hour. Required to search: name, years to search; also helpful: DOB, SSN. Criminal records on computer from 11-87, archived from 1983, microfiche in Salt Lake City. Online access available via Xchange, see http://courtlink.utcourts.gov. Also see state introduction.

General Information: Public access terminal is available. No sealed records released. SASE required. Turnaround time 2 weeks. Fax notes: Fee to fax results is $2.00 per page. Copy fee: $.25 per page. Certification fee: $4.00 plus $.50 per page. Fee payee: 1st Judicial District. Personal checks accepted. Credit cards accepted: Visa, MasterCard. Prepayment is required.

Carbon County

7th District Court 149 E. 100 South, Price, UT 84501; 435-636-3400; Fax: 435-637-7349. Hours: 8AM-5PM (MST). *Felony, Misdemeanor, Civil, Eviction, Small Claims, Probate.*

Civil Records: Access: Phone, mail, online, in person. Both court and visitors may perform in person searches. Search fee: $10.00 per hour. First 20 minutes no charge. Required to search: name, years to search. Civil cases indexed by defendant, plaintiff. Civil records on computer from 1988, on microfiche from 1985, archived prior to 1988. Online access available through Xchange, see http://courtlink.utcourts.gov. Also see state introduction.

Criminal Records: Access: Phone, mail, online, in person. Both court and visitors may perform in person searches. Search fee: $10.00 per hour. First 20 minutes no charge. Required to search: name, years to search, DOB; also helpful: SSN. Criminal records on computer from 1988, on microfiche from 1985, archived prior to 1988. Online access available through Xchange, see http://courtlink.utcourts.gov. Also see state introduction.

General Information: Public access terminal is available. No sealed records released. SASE required. Turnaround time 48 hrs after receipt. Fax notes: Fee to fax results is $2.00 1st page, $1.00 each add'l. Copy fee: $.25 per page. Certification fee: $2.00 plus $.50 per page. Fee payee: 7th District Court. Personal checks accepted. Credit cards accepted: Visa. Will bill fax fees.

Daggett County

8th District Court PO Box 219, Manila, UT 84046; 435-784-3154; Fax: 435-784-3335. Hours: 9AM-Noon, 1-5PM (MST). *Felony, Misdemeanor, Civil, Eviction, Probate.*

Civil Records: Access: Phone, fax, mail, in person, online. Both court and visitors may perform in person searches. No search fee. Required to search: name, years to search. Civil cases indexed by defendant, plaintiff. Civil records archived from 1918. Online access available through Xchange, see http://courtlink.utcourts.gov. Also see state introduction. Fax access requires prior approval.

Criminal Records: Access: Fax, mail, in person, online. Both court and visitors may perform in person searches. No search fee. Required to search: name, years to search, DOB, signed release. Criminal records archived from 1918. Online access available through Xchange, see http://courtlink.utcourts.gov. Also see state introduction.

General Information: No sealed records released. SASE required. Turnaround time 10 days. Signature and record request form required. Fax notes: Fee to fax results is $.50 per page. Copy fee: $.25 per page. Certification fee: $4.00 plus $.50 per page. Fee payee: Daggett County. Personal checks accepted. Prepayment is required.

Davis County

2nd District Court PO Box 769, Farmington, UT 84025; 801-447-3800; Fax: 801-447-3881. Hours: 8AM-5PM (MST). *Felony, Class A Misdemeanor, Civil, Probate.*

Civil Records: Access: Phone, mail, online, in person. Both court and visitors may perform in person searches. Search fee: $13.00 per hour. First 15 minutes no charge. Required to search: name, years to search. Civil cases indexed by defendant, plaintiff. Civil records on computer back to 1982, prior on microfiche and archived to 1896. Online access available through Xchange, see http://courtlink.utcourts.gov. Also see state introduction.

Criminal Records: Access: Phone, mail, online, in person. Both court and visitors may perform in person searches. Search fee: $13.00 per hour. First 15 minutes no charge. Required to search: name, years to search, DOB; also helpful: SSN. Criminal records on computer back to 1989, prior on microfiche and archived to 1896. Online access available through Xchange, see http://courtlink.utcourts.gov. Also see state introduction.

General Information: Public access terminal is available. No adoption, criminal pre-sentence investigation records released. SASE required. Turnaround time 2-3 days. Fax notes: Will fax results; no fee indicated. Copy fee: $.25 per page. Certified copies $.50 per page. Certification fee: $4.00. Fee payee: 2nd District Court. Personal checks accepted. Prepayment is required.

2nd District Court - Bountiful Department

805 South Main, Bountiful, UT 84010; 801-397-7008; Fax: 801-397-7010. Hours: 8AM-5PM (MST). *Felony, Misdemeanor, Civil, Eviction, Small Claims, Probate.*

Civil Records: Access: Phone, mail, online, in person. Both court and visitors may perform in person searches. No search fee. Required to search: name, years to search; also helpful: address. Civil cases indexed by defendant, plaintiff. Civil records on computer since 10/86. Online access available through Xchange, see http://courtlink.utcourts.gov. Also see state introduction. For in person searching, call ahead.

Criminal Records: Access: Phone, mail, online, in person. Both court and visitors may perform in person searches. No search fee. Required to search: name, years to search, DOB, signed release. Criminal records on computer since 10/86. Online access available through Xchange, see http://courtlink.utcourts.gov. Also see state introduction. For in person searching, call ahead.

General Information: Public access terminal is available. SASE required. Turnaround time 5 days. Copy fee: $.25 per page. Certification fee: $4.50. Fee payee: District Court. Personal checks accepted. Prepayment is required.

2nd District Court - Layton Department

425 Wasatch Dr, Layton, UT 84041; 801-444-4300. Hours: 8AM-5PM (MST). *Felony, Misdemeanor, Civil, Eviction, Small Claims, Probate.*

Civil Records: Access: Online, in person. Visitors must perform in person searches for themselves. No search fee. Required to search: name, years to search. Civil cases indexed by defendant, plaintiff. Civil records on computer from 1988, archived from start of court. Computer index alpha and case number, archives by alpha from 1982, prior to 1982 not indexed. Online access available through Xchange, see http://courtlink.utcourts.gov. Also see state introduction.

Criminal Records: Access: Mail, online, in person. Both court and visitors may perform in person searches. No search fee. Required to search: name, years to search; also helpful: DOB, SSN. Criminal records on computer from 1988, archived from start of court. Computer index alpha and case number, archives by alpha from 1982, prior to 1982 not indexed. Online access available through Xchange, see http://courtlink.utcourts.gov. Also see state introduction.

General Information: Public access terminal is available. No confidential records, probation reports, sealed records released. SASE requested. Turnaround time 1 day. Copy fee: $.25 per page. Certification fee: $4.00 plus $.50 per each add'l page. Fee payee: Layton Circuit Court. Personal checks accepted.

Duchesne County

8th District Court PO Box 990, Duchesne, UT 84021; 435-738-2753; Fax: 435-738-2754. Hours: 8AM-5PM (MST). *Felony, Misdemeanor, Civil, Eviction, Small Claims, Probate.*

Civil Records: Access: Phone, mail, fax, online, in person. Both court and visitors may perform in person searches. Search fee: $10.00 per hour. First 20 minutes no charge. Required to search: name, years to search. Civil cases indexed by defendant, plaintiff. Civil records on computer back to 6/1993, civil on microfiche back to 1912. Online access available through Xchange, see http://courtlink.utcourts.gov. Also see state introduction.

Criminal Records: Access: Phone, mail, fax, online, in person. Both court and visitors may perform in person searches. Search fee: $10.00 per hour. First 20 minutes no charge. Required to search: name, years to search. Criminal records on computer back to 1993; index books back to 1912. Online access available through Xchange-Online Access; for information contact Jolene Cox 578-3831. Also, see state introduction.

General Information: Public access terminal is available. No confidential records released. SASE required. Turnaround time 1-5 days. Fax notes: Fee to fax results is $1.00 per page. Copy fee: $.25 per page; $.50 if certified. Certification fee: $2.00. Fee payee: 8th District Court. Personal checks accepted. Prepayment is required.

8th District Court - Roosevelt Department
PO Box 1286, Roosevelt, UT 84066; 435-722-0235; Fax: 435-722-0236. Hours: 8AM-5PM. *Felony, Misdemeanor, Civil, Eviction, Probate.*

Civil Records: Access: Mail, online, in person. Both court and visitors may perform in person searches. Search fee: $13.00 per hour. First 15 minutes no charge. Required to search: name, years to search. Civil cases indexed by defendant, plaintiff. Civil records on computer since 1993. Online access available through Xchange, see http://courtlink.utcourts.gov. Also see state introduction.

Criminal Records: Access: Mail, online, in person. Both court and visitors may perform in person searches. Search fee: $13.00 per hour. First 15 minutes no charge. Required to search: name, years to search; also helpful: DOB. Criminal records on computer since 1994. Online access available through Xchange, see http://courtlink.utcourts.gov. Also see state introduction.

General Information: Public access terminal is available. No confidential, sealed, expunged or juvenile records released. Turnaround time 2-5 days. Copy fee: $.25 per page. Certification fee: $4.00 plus $.50 per page. Personal checks accepted. Prepayment is required.

Emery County

7th District Court PO Box 635, Castle Dale, UT 84513; 435-381-2619; Fax: 435-381-5625. Hours: 8AM-5PM (MST). *Felony, Misdemeanor, Civil, Eviction, Probate.*

Note: Phone for hearing impaired is 800-992-0172.

Civil Records: Access: Phone, fax, mail, in person, online. Both court and visitors may perform in person searches. Search fee: $10.00 per hour. First 20 minutes no charge. Required to search: name, years to search. Civil cases indexed by defendant, plaintiff. Civil records on computer from 1997, microfiche and archived from start of district court. Online access available through Xchange, see http://courtlink.utcourts.gov. Also see state introduction.

Criminal Records: Access: Phone, fax, mail, in person, online. Both court and visitors may perform in person searches. Search fee: $10.00 per hour. First 20 minutes no charge. Required to search: name, years to search, DOB. Criminal records on computer from 1997, microfiche and archived from start of district court. Online access available through Xchange, see http://courtlink.utcourts.gov. Also see state introduction.

General Information: Public access terminal is available. No adoption, sealed records released. SASE required. Turnaround time 1 week unless large request. Fax notes: $2.00 for first page, $1.00 each add'l. Copy fee: $.25 per page. Certification fee: $2.00 plus $.50 per page. Fee payee: 7th District Court. Personal checks accepted. Prepayment is required.

Garfield County

6th District Court PO Box 77, Panguitch, UT 84759; 435-676-8826 X104; Fax: 435-676-8239. Hours: 9AM-5PM (MST). *Felony, Misdemeanor, Civil, Eviction, Small Claims, Probate.*

Civil Records: Access: Phone, fax, mail, in person, online. Only the court performs in person searches; visitors may not. Search fee: $13.00 per hour. Required to search: name, years to search. Civil cases indexed by defendant, plaintiff. Civil records archived for 100 years; on computer back to 2000. Online access

available via Xchange, see http://courtlink.utcourts.gov. Also see state introduction.

Criminal Records: Access: Fax, mail, in person, online. Only the court performs in person searches; visitors may not. Search fee: $13.00 per hour. Required to search: name, years to search. Criminal records archived for 100 years; on computer back to 2000. Online access available through Xchange, see http://courtlink.utcourts.gov. Also see state introduction.

General Information: No adoption records released. SASE not required. Turnaround time 1 day. Fax notes: Fee to fax results is $1.00 for 1st page, $.50 each add'l. Copy fee: $.25 per page. Certification fee: $2.00 plus $.50 per page. Fee payee: 6th District Court. Personal checks accepted. Prepayment is required.

Grand County

7th District Court 125 E. Center, Moab, UT 84532; 435-259-1349; Fax: 435-259-4081. Hours: 8AM-5PM (MST). *Felony, Misdemeanor, Civil, Eviction, Probate.*

Civil Records: Access: Phone, mail, online, in person. Both court and visitors may perform in person searches. No search fee. Required to search: name, years to search. Civil cases indexed by defendant. District records on computer from Spring 1990, Circuit from spring 1989, archived since court started. Online access available via Xchange, see http://courtlink.utcourts.gov. Also see state introduction.

Criminal Records: Access: Phone, mail, online, in person. Both court and visitors may perform in person searches. Search fee: None for 1st 20 minutes; $13.00 per hour thereafter. Required to search: name, years to search; also helpful: DOB, SSN. District records on computer from spring 1990, Circuit from spring 1989, archived since court started. Online access available through Xchange, see http://courtlink.utcourts.gov. Also see state introduction.

General Information: Public access terminal is available. No adoption, expunged records released. SASE required. Turnaround time same day. Fax notes: $2.00 for 1st page; $1.00 each add'l. Copy fee: $.25 per page. Certification fee: $400 plus $.50 per page. Fee payee: 7th District Court. Personal checks accepted. Credit cards accepted: Visa, MasterCard. Prepayment is required.

Iron County

5th District Court 40 North 100 East, Cedar City, UT 84720; 435-586-7440; Fax: 435-586-4801. Hours: 8AM-5PM (MST). *Felony, Misdemeanor, Civil, Eviction, Small Claims, Probate.*

Note: Hearing location also in Parawon, but records held here.

Civil Records: Access: Mail, phone, online, in person. Both court and visitors may perform in person searches. Search fee: $13.00 per hour, 1st 15 minutes free. Required to search: name. Civil cases indexed by defendant, plaintiff. District records on computer from 4/89, former Circuit Court records on computer from 1987, archived from 1900. Online access available through Xchange, see http://courtlink.utcourts.gov. Also see state introduction.

Criminal Records: Access: Mail, phone, online, in person. Both court and visitors may perform in person searches. Search fee: $13.00 per hour, 1st 15 minutes free. Required to search: name, years to search, DOB, SSN. District records on computer from 4/89, former Circuit Court records on computer from 1987, archived from 1900. Online access available through Xchange, see http://courtlink.utcourts.gov. Also see state introduction.

General Information: Public access terminal is available. No sealed records released. SASE required. Turnaround time 2-3 days. Copy fee: $.25 per page. Certification fee: $4.00 plus $.50 per page. Fee payee:

5th District Court. Personal checks accepted. Prepayment is required.

Juab County

4th District Court 160 N. Main, PO Box 249, Nephi, UT 84648; 435-623-0901; Fax: 435-623-0922. Hours: 8AM-5PM (MST). *Felony, Misdemeanor, Civil, Eviction, Probate.*

Civil Records: Access: Phone, mail, online, in person. Both court and visitors may perform in person searches. Search fee: $13.00 per hour. First 15 minutes are no charge. Required to search: name, years to search. Civil cases indexed by defendant, plaintiff. Civil records on computer from 11/94, archived since court started. Online access available through Xchange, see http://courtlink.utcourts.gov. Also see state introduction.

Criminal Records: Access: Phone, mail, online, in person. Both court and visitors may perform in person searches. Search fee: $13.00 per hour. First 15 minutes are no charge. Required to search: name, years to search. Criminal records on computer from 11/94, archived since court started. Online access available through Xchange, see http://courtlink.utcourts.gov. Also see state introduction.

General Information: Public access terminal is available. All records must be viewed in this office. SASE required. Turnaround time 1 week. Copy fee: $.25 per page. Certification fee: $4.00 plus $.50 per page. Fee payee: 4th District Court. Personal checks accepted. Prepayment is required.

Kane County

6th District Court 76 North Main, Kanab, UT 84741; 435-644-2458; Fax: 435-644-2052. Hours: 8AM-5PM (MST). *Felony, Misdemeanor, Civil, Eviction, Small Claims, Probate.*

Civil Records: Access: Phone, fax, mail, in person, online. Only the court performs in person searches; visitors may not. Search fee: First 15 minutes of search is free, thereafter $25.00 per hour. Required to search: name, years to search. Civil cases indexed by defendant, plaintiff. Civil records on computer from 1985, archived since court started. Online access available through Xchange, see http://courtlink.utcourts.gov. Also see state introduction.

Criminal Records: Access: Phone, fax, mail, in person, online. Only the court performs in person searches; visitors may not. Search fee: First 15 minutes of search is free, thereafter $25.00 per hour. Required to search: name, years to search. Criminal records on computer from 1985, archived since court started. Online access available through Xchange, see http://courtlink.utcourts.gov. Also see state introduction.

General Information: No sealed, expunged records released. SASE requested. Turnaround time 2-3 days. Fax notes: Fee to fax results is $.50 per page. Copy fee: $.25 per page. Certification fee: $4.00 plus $.50 per page. Fee payee: Kane County. Personal checks accepted. Prepayment is required.

Millard County

4th District Court 765 S Highway 99, #6, Fillmore, UT 84631; 435-743-6223; Fax: 435-743-6923. Hours: 8AM-5PM (MST). *Felony, Misdemeanor, Civil, Eviction, Small Claims, Probate.*

Civil Records: Access: Phone, mail, online, in person. Both court and visitors may perform in person searches. Search fee: $10.00 per hour. Required to search: name, years to search. Civil cases indexed by defendant, plaintiff. Civil records on computer from 1988, archived from 1896. Online access available through Xchange, see http://courtlink.utcourts.gov. Also see state introduction.

Criminal Records: Access: Phone, mail, online, in person. Both court and visitors may perform in person searches. Search fee: $10.00 per hour. Required to search: name, years to search. Criminal records on computer from 1988, archived from 1896. Online access available through Xchange, see http://courtlink.utcourts.gov. Also see state introduction.

General Information: Public access terminal is available. No pre-sentence, expunged or sealed records released. SASE required. Turnaround time 1 day. Copy fee: $.50 per page. Certification fee: $4.00. Fee payee: 4th District Court. Business checks accepted. Prepayment is required.

Morgan County

2nd District Court PO Box 886, Morgan, UT 84050; 801-845-4020; Fax: 801-829-6176. Hours: 8AM-5PM (MST). *Felony, Misdemeanor, Civil, Eviction, Small Claims, Probate.*

Civil Records: Access: Phone, fax, mail, online, in person. Both court and visitors may perform in person searches. Search fee: $25.00 per name. Required to search: name, years to search. Civil cases indexed by defendant, plaintiff. Civil records on computer since 1990; on microfiche, books, archived from 1862. Online access available through Xchange, see http://courtlink.utcourts.gov. Also see state introduction.

Criminal Records: Access: Phone, fax, mail, online, in person. Both court and visitors may perform in person searches. Search fee: $25.00 per name. Required to search: name, years to search, DOB; also helpful: SSN. Criminal records on computer since 1990, prior in books. Online access available through Xchange, see http://courtlink.utcourts.gov. Also see state introduction.

General Information: Public access terminal is available. No sealed records released. Turnaround time same day. Fax notes: No fee to fax results. Copy fee: $.25 per page. Certification fee: $4.00 plus $.50 per page. Fee payee: Morgan District or Circuit Court. Personal checks accepted. Prepayment is required.

Piute County

6th District Court PO Box 99, Junction, UT 84740; 435-577-2840; Fax: 435-577-2433. Hours: 9AM-Noon, 1-5PM (MST). *Felony, Misdemeanor, Civil, Eviction, Small Claims, Probate.*

Civil Records: Access: Mail, in person, online. Both court and visitors may perform in person searches. Search fee: $10.00 per hour. Required to search: name, years to search. Civil cases indexed by defendant, plaintiff. Civil records archived from 1889. Online access available through Xchange, see http://courtlink.utcourts.gov. Also see state introduction.

Criminal Records: Access: Mail, in person, online. Both court and visitors may perform in person searches. Search fee: $10.00 per hour. Required to search: name, years to search. Criminal records archived from 1889. Online access available through Xchange, see http://courtlink.utcourts.gov. Also see state introduction.

General Information: No sealed records released. SASE required. Turnaround time 2-3 days. Copy fee: $.50 per page. Certification fee: $2.00. Fee payee: Piute County District Court. Personal checks accepted. Search fees may be billed if prior arrangements have been made.

Rich County

1st District Court PO Box 218, Randolph, UT 84064; 435-793-2415; Fax: 435-793-2410. Hours: 9AM-5PM (MST). *Felony, Misdemeanor, Civil, Eviction, Probate.*

Civil Records: Access: Phone, fax, mail, in person, online. Both court and visitors may perform in person searches. Search fee: $10.00 per hour. Required to search: name, years to search; also helpful: address. Civil cases indexed by defendant, plaintiff. Civil records ago back to 1896; computerized records since 1999. Online access available through Xchange, see http://courtlink.utcourts.gov. Also see state introduction.

Criminal Records: Access: Phone, fax, mail, in person, online. Both court and visitors may perform in person searches. Search fee: $10.00 per hour. Required to search: name, years to search; also helpful: address, DOB, SSN. Criminal records go back to 1896; computerized records since 1999. Online access available through Xchange, see http://courtlink.utcourts.gov. Also see state introduction.

General Information: No sealed records released. SASE required. Turnaround time 2-3 days. Copy fee: $.25 per page. Certification fee: $2.00. Fee payee: Rich County. Personal checks accepted. Prepayment is required.

Salt Lake County

3rd District Court 450 South State Street, Salt Lake City, UT 84111; 801-238-7300; Civil phone: 801-238-7480; Criminal phone: 801-238-7321; Fax: 801-238-7404. Hours: 8AM-5PM (MST). *Felony, Misdemeanor, Civil, Eviction, Small Claims, Probate.*

Note: An automated court information line allows phone access to court dates, fine balances, and judgment/divorce decrees (case or citation number required) at 801-238-7830.

Civil Records: Access: Phone, mail, online, in person. Both court and visitors may perform in person searches. Search fee: $13.00 per hour. First 15 minutes no charge. Required to search: name, years to search. Civil cases indexed by defendant, plaintiff. Civil records on computer from 1988, microfiche from 1940, archived from 1800s. Online access available through Xchange, see http://courtlink.utcourts.gov. Also see state introduction.

Criminal Records: Access: Phone, mail, online, in person. Both court and visitors may perform in person searches. Search fee: $13.00 per hour. First 15 minutes no charge. Required to search: name, years to search, DOB, SSN. Criminal records on computer from 1988, microfiche from 1940, archived from 1800s. Online access available through Xchange, see http://courtlink.utcourts.gov. Also see state introduction.

General Information: Public access terminal is available. No juvenile or adoption records released. Turnaround time 2-3 days. Copy fee: $1.00 per page. Certification fee: $4.00 plus $.50 per page. Fee payee: 3rd District Court. Personal checks accepted. Prepayment is required.

3rd District Court - Murray Department 5022 S. State St, Murray, UT 84107; 801-281-7700; Fax: 801-281-7736. Hours: 8AM-5PM (MST). *Felony, Misdemeanor, Civil, Eviction, Small Claims.*

Civil Records: Access: Fax, mail, online, in person. Both court and visitors may perform in person searches. Search fee: $10.00 per name. Required to search: name, years to search. Civil cases indexed by defendant, plaintiff. Civil records on computer from 1985, archived from 1979. Online access available through Xchange, see http://courtlink.utcourts.gov. Also see state introduction. Fax access requires pre-arrangement.

Criminal Records: Access: Fax, mail, online, in person. Both court and visitors may perform in person searches. Search fee: $10.00 per name. Required to search: name, years to search, DOB. Criminal records on computer from 1985, archived from 1979. Online access available through Xchange, see http://courtlink.utcourts.gov. Also see state introduction.

General Information: Public access terminal is available. No sealed records released. SASE required. Turnaround time 1 week. Fax notes: No fee to fax results. Copy fee: $.25 per page. Certification fee: $2.00 plus $.50 per page. Fee payee: Murray District Court. Personal checks accepted. Prepayment is required.

3rd District Court - Salt Lake City 450 South State St, Salt Lake City, UT 84111; 801-238-7480; Fax:

801-238-7396. Hours: 8AM-5PM (MST). *Felony, Misdemeanor, Civil, Eviction, Small Claims, Probate.*

Note: An automated court information line allows phone access to court dates, fine balances, and judgment/divorce decrees (case or citation number required) at 801-238-7830.

Civil Records: Access: Mail, online, in person. Both court and visitors may perform in person searches. No search fee. Required to search: name, years to search. Civil cases indexed by defendant, plaintiff. Civil records on computer from 1986, archived after satisfaction or dismissal, destroyed prior to 1985. Online access available via Xchange, see http://courtlink.utcourts.gov. Also see state introduction.

Criminal Records: Access: Mail, online, in person. Both court and visitors may perform in person searches. Search fee: First 20 minutes no charge. Required to search: name, years to search, DOB; also helpful: SSN. Criminal records on computer from 1986, archived after satisfaction or dismissal, destroyed prior to 1985. Online access available through Xchange, see http://courtlink.utcourts.gov. Also see state introduction.

General Information: Public access terminal is available. No confidential records released. Turnaround time 2-3 days. Copy fee: $.50 per page. Certification fee: $2.00. Fee payee: 3rd Circuit Court. Business checks accepted. Credit cards accepted: Visa, MasterCard.

3rd District Court - Sandy Department 210 West 10,000 South, Sandy, UT 84070-3282; 801-565-5714; Fax: 801-565-5703. Hours: 8AM-5PM (MST). *Felony, Misdemeanor, Civil, Eviction, Small Claims.*

Civil Records: Access: Phone, mail, online, in person. Both court and visitors may perform in person searches. Search fee: $13.00 per hour. Required to search: name, years to search. Civil cases indexed by defendant, plaintiff. Civil records on computer from 1986, civil archived from 1985. Online access available through Xchange, see http://courtlink.utcourts.gov. Also see state introduction.

Criminal Records: Access: Phone, mail, online, in person. Both court and visitors may perform in person searches. Search fee: $13.00 per hour. Required to search: name, years to search. Criminal records on computer from 1986, civil archived from 1985. Online access available through Xchange, see http://courtlink.utcourts.gov. Also see state introduction.

General Information: Public access terminal is available. (Available by appointment.) No police reports, pre-sentence records released. SASE required. Turnaround time 1-2 weeks. Copy fee: $.50 per page. Certification fee: $2.00. Fee payee: 3rd District Court-Sandy Dept. Personal checks accepted. No two-party checks. Credit cards accepted: Visa, MasterCard. Prepayment is required.

3rd District Court - West Valley Dept. 3636 S. Constitution Blvd, West Valley, UT 84119; 801-982-2400; Fax: 801-967-9857. Hours: 8AM-5PM (MST). *Felony, Misdemeanor, Civil, Eviction, Small Claims, Probate.*

Civil Records: Access: Mail, online, in person. Both court and visitors may perform in person searches. Search fee: First 15 minutes free; $13.00 per hour thereafter is assisted by staff clerk. Mail requests may send blank check. Required to search: name, years to search. Civil cases indexed by defendant, plaintiff. Civil records on computer since 1986, archived from 1983. Online access available through Xchange, see http://courtlink.utcourts.gov. Also see state introduction.

Criminal Records: Access: Mail, online, in person. Both court and visitors may perform in person searches. Search fee: First 15 minutes free; $13.00 per hour thereafter is assisted by staff clerk. Mail requests may send blank check. Required to search: name, years to search. Criminal records on computer since 1986, archived from 1983. Online access available through Xchange, see http://courtlink.utcourts.gov. Also see state introduction.

General Information: Public access terminal is available. No sealed records released. SASE required. Turnaround time 1 week. Copy fee: $.25 per page. Certification fee: $2.00 plus $.50 per page. Fee payee: 3rd District Court. Personal checks accepted. Prepayment is required.

San Juan County

7th District Court PO Box 68, Monticello, UT 84535; 435-587-2122; Fax: 435-587-2372. Hours: 8AM-5PM (MST). *Felony, Misdemeanor, Civil, Eviction, Probate.*

Civil Records: Access: Phone, mail, fax, online, in person. Both court and visitors may perform in person searches. Search fee: $13.00 per hour. Required to search: name, years to search. Civil cases indexed by defendant, plaintiff. Civil records on computer since 1991; on index books from 1919 to 1991. Online access available through Xchange, see http://courtlink.utcourts.gov. Also see state introduction.

Criminal Records: Access: Mail, fax, online, in person. Both court and visitors may perform in person searches. Search fee: $13.00 per hour. Required to search: name, years to search. Criminal records on computer since 1991; on index books from 1919 to 1991. Online access available through Xchange, see http://courtlink.utcourts.gov. Also see state introduction.

General Information: Public access terminal is available. No juvenile records released. SASE required. Turnaround time 1 week. Fax notes: Fee to fax results is $1.00 per page. Copy fee: $.25 per page. Certification fee: $4.00 plus $.50 per page. Fee payee: 7th District Court. Personal checks accepted. Credit cards accepted: Visa, MasterCard. Visa, MC accepted in person and by phone. Prepayment is required.

Sanpete County

6th District Court 160 N. Main, Manti, UT 84642; 435-835-2131; Fax: 435-835-2135. Hours: 8:30AM-5PM (MST). *Felony, Misdemeanor, Civil, Eviction, Small Claims, Probate.*

Civil Records: Access: Phone, fax, mail, in person, online. Both court and visitors may perform in person searches. Search fee: $13.00 per hour after first 15 minutes free. Required to search: name, years to search. Civil cases indexed by defendant, plaintiff. Civil records on computer from 1986. Online access available through Xchange, see http://courtlink.utcourts.gov. Also see state introduction.

Criminal Records: Access: Phone, fax, mail, in person, online. Both court and visitors may perform in person searches. Search fee: $13.00 per hour. Required to search: name, years to search; also helpful: DOB. Criminal records on computer from 1986. Online access available via Xchange, see http://courtlink.utcourts.gov. Also see state introduction.

General Information: Public access terminal is available. No criminal, expunged, or sealed records released. SASE requested. Turnaround time 10 days. Fax notes: $3.50 for first page, $2.50 each add'l. Copy fee: $.25 per page. Certification fee: $2.00 plus $.50 per page. Fee payee: 6th District Court. Personal checks accepted. Prepayment is required.

Sevier County

6th District Court 895 E 300 N, Richfield, UT 84701-2345; 435-896-2700; Fax: 435-896-8047. Hours: 8AM-5PM (MST). *Felony, Misdemeanor, Civil, Eviction, Probate.*

Civil Records: Access: Fax, mail, online, in person. Visitors must perform in person searches. Search fee: $13.00 per hour. For search requiring 15 minutes or less, no charge. Required to search: name, years to

search. Civil cases indexed by defendant, plaintiff. Circuit records on computer from 1989, District on computer from 1991. Online access available through Xchange, see http://courtlink.utcourts.gov. Also see state introduction.

Criminal Records: Access: Fax, mail, online, in person. Visitors must perform in person searches. Search fee: $13.00 per hour. For search requing 15 minutes or less, no charge. Required to search: name, years to search, DOB, SSN. Circuit records on computer from 1989, District on computer from 1991. Online access available through Xchange, see http://courtlink.utcourts.gov. Also see state introduction.

General Information: Public access terminal is available. No sealed records released. Turnaround time 2-3 days. Fax notes: $2.50 for first page, $.50 each add'l. Copy fee: $.25 per page. Certification fee: $4.00. Fee payee: 6th District Court. Personal checks accepted. Prepayment is required.

Summit County

3rd District Court PO Box 128, 6300 N Silvercreek Dr, Park City, UT 84098, Coalville, UT 84017; 435-336-4451 X3205; Fax: 435-336-3030. Hours: 8AM-5PM (MST). *Felony, Misdemeanor, Civil, Eviction, Probate.*

Civil Records: Access: Phone, in person, online. Both court and visitors may perform in person searches. Search fee: $10.00 per hour. Required to search: name, years to search. Civil cases indexed by defendant, plaintiff. All indexes on computer back to 1993, records archived back to 1900's. Online access available through Xchange, see http://courtlink.utcourts.gov. Also, see state introduction.

Criminal Records: Access: Mail, online, in person. Both court and visitors may perform in person searches. Search fee: $10.00 per hour. Required to search: name, years to search. Criminal records indexes on computer back to 1993, records archived back to 1900's. Online access available through Xchange, see http://courtlink.utcourts.gov. Also, see state introduction.

General Information: Public access terminal is available. No sealed probate records released. SASE required. Turnaround time 2-3 days. Copy fee: $.25 per page. Certification fee: $2.00 plus $.50 each additional page. Fee payee: 3rd District Court. Personal checks accepted. Prepayment is required.

3rd District Court - Park City Department, 6300 N Silver Creek, Park City, UT 84098; 435-615-4300. *Felony, Misdemeanor, Civil, Eviction, Small Claims.*

Note: 6/1/2001 merged with Coalville Dept. address above, Park City, Utah, 435-615-4300.

Tooele County

3rd District Court 47 S. Main, Tooele, UT 84074; 435-843-3210; Fax: 435-882-8524. Hours: 8AM-5PM (MST). *Felony, Misdemeanor, Civil, Eviction, Small Claims, Probate.*

Civil Records: Access: Fax, mail, online, in person. Both court and visitors may perform in person searches. Search fee: $10.00 per hour. First 20 minutes no charge. Required to search: name, years to search. Civil cases indexed by defendant, plaintiff. Civil records on computer from 1982, archived since court started. Online access available through Xchange, see http://courtlink.utcourts.gov. Also see state introduction.

Criminal Records: Access: Fax, mail, online, in person. Both court and visitors may perform in person searches. Search fee: $10.00 per hour. First 20 minutes no charge. Required to search: name, years to search; also helpful: SSN. Criminal records on computer back to 1989, archived since court started. Online access

available via Xchange, see http://courtlink.utcourts.gov. Also see state introduction.

General Information: Public access terminal is available. No adoption records released. SASE required. Turnaround time 2-3 days. Fax notes: Fee to fax results is $.25 per page. Copy fee: $.25 per page. Certification fee: $4.00. Fee payee: 3rd District Court. Personal checks accepted. Prepayment is required.

Uintah County

8th District Court 920 E Hway 40, Vernal, UT 84078; 435-781-9300; Fax: 435-789-0564. Hours: 8AM-5PM (MST). *Felony, Misdemeanor, Civil, Eviction, Probate.*

Civil Records: Access: Mail, online, in person. Both court and visitors may perform in person searches. Search fee: $10.00 per hour. First 20 minutes no charge. Required to search: name, years to search. Civil cases indexed by defendant, plaintiff. Circuit records on computer from 1987, everything else from 1989, archived since court started. Online access available through Xchange, see http://courtlink.utcourts.gov. Also see state introduction.

Criminal Records: Access: Mail, online, in person. Both court and visitors may perform in person searches. Search fee: $10.00 per hour. First 20 minutes no charge. Required to search: name, years to search. Circuit records on computer from 1987, everything else from 1989, archived since court started. Online access available through Xchange, see http://courtlink.utcourts.gov. Also see state introduction.

General Information: Public access terminal is available. No sealed records released. SASE required. Turnaround time 2-3 days. Copy fee: $.25 per page. Certification fee: $2.00 plus $.50 per page. Fee payee: 8th District Court. Personal checks accepted. Prepayment is required.

Utah County

4th District Court 125 North, 100 West, Provo, UT 84601; 801-429-1000; Fax: 801-429-1033. Hours: 8AM-5PM (MST). *Felony, Misdemeanor, Civil, Eviction, Small Claims, Probate.*

Civil Records: Access: Phone, mail, fax, in person. Both court and visitors may perform in person searches. Search fee: $13.00 per hour. Required to search: name, years to search. Civil cases indexed by defendant, plaintiff. Civil and probate on computer from 1986, judgments, tax liens, and divorce decrees on microfiche from 1900 to 1975, archived from 1900s. Online access available via Xchange, see http://courtlink.utcourts.gov. Also see state introduction.

Criminal Records: Access: Phone, mail, fax, in person. Both court and visitors may perform in person searches. Search fee: $13.00 per hour. Required to search: name, years to search, DOB. Felony on computer from 1989; archived from 1900s. Online access available through Xchange, see http://courtlink.utcourts.gov. Also see state introduction.

General Information: Public access terminal is available. No sealed records released. SASE required. Turnaround time 7-10 days. Fax notes: Will not fax results. Copy fee: $.25 per page. Certification fee: $4.00 for 1st page and $.50 per page thereafter. Fee payee: 4th District Court. Personal checks accepted. Credit cards accepted: Visa, MasterCard. Accepted in person only. Prepayment is required.

4th District Court - Orem Department 97 E Center, Orem, UT 84057; 801-764-5865/5864; Fax: 801-226-5244. Hours: 8AM-5PM (MST). *Misdemeanor, Civil, Eviction, Small Claims.*

Civil Records: Access: Mail, online, in person. Both court and visitors may perform in person searches. Search fee: $15.00 per hour. First 20 minutes no charge. Required to search: name, years to search. Civil cases indexed by defendant, plaintiff. Civil records on computer since 1988. Online access available through Xchange, see http://courtlink.utcourts.gov. Also see state introduction.

Criminal Records: Access: Mail, online, in person. Both court and visitors may perform in person searches. Search fee: $15.00 per hour. First 20 minutes no charge. Required to search: name, years to search; also helpful: DOB. Criminal records on computer since 1988. Online access available through Xchange, see http://courtlink.utcourts.gov. Also see state introduction.

General Information: Public access terminal is available. No sealed, expunged or confidential records released. Turnaround time 5-7 days. Copy fee: $.25 per page. Certification fee: $4.00 plus $.50 per page. Fee payee: 4th District Court. Personal checks accepted. Credit cards accepted: Visa, MasterCard. Prepayment is required.

4th District Court - Spanish Forks Department
40 S Main St, Spanish Forks, UT 84660; 801-798-8674; Fax: 801-798-1377. Hours: 8AM-5PM (MST). *Felony, Misdemeanor, Civil, Eviction, Small Claims.*

Civil Records: Access: Phone, fax, mail, online, in person. Both court and visitors may perform in person searches. Search fee: $13.00 per hour. First 15 minutes no charge. Required to search: name, years to search. Civil cases indexed by defendant, plaintiff. Civil records on computer since 1988. Online access available through Xchange, see http://courtlink.utcourts.gov. Also see state introduction.

Criminal Records: Access: Phone, fax, mail, online, in person. Both court and visitors may perform in person searches. Search fee: $13.00 per hour. First 15 minutes no charge. Required to search: name, years to search; also helpful: DOB. Criminal records on computer since 1988. Online access available through Xchange, see http://courtlink.utcourts.gov. Also see state introduction.

General Information: Public access terminal is available. No sealed, expunged or confidential records released. Turnaround time 5-7 days. Fax notes: No fee to fax results. Fax requires prior arrangement. Copy fee: $.25 per page. Certification fee: $4.00 plus $.50 per page. Fee payee: 4th District Court. Personal checks accepted. Credit cards accepted: Visa, MasterCard. Prepayment is required.

4th District Court - American Fork Department
98 N Center St, American Fork, UT 84003-1626; 801-756-9654; Fax: 801-763-0153. Hours: 8AM-5PM (MST). *Misdemeanor, Civil, Eviction, Small Claims.*

Civil Records: Access: Mail, online, in person. Both court and visitors may perform in person searches. Search fee: $10.00 per hour. First 20 minutes no charge. Required to search: name, years to search. Civil cases indexed by defendant, plaintiff. Civil records on computer since 1988. Online access available through Xchange, see http://courtlink.utcourts.gov. Also see state introduction.

Criminal Records: Access: Mail, online, in person. Both court and visitors may perform in person searches. Search fee: $10.00 per hour. First 20 minutes no charge. Required to search: name, years to search; also helpful: DOB. Online access available through Xchange, see http://courtlink.utcourts.gov. Also see state introduction.

General Information: Public access terminal is available. No sealed, expunged or confidential records released. SASE required. Turnaround time 5-7 days. Copy fee: $.25 per page. Certification fee: $2.00 plus $.50 per page. Fee payee: 4th District Court. Personal

checks accepted. Credit cards accepted: Visa, MasterCard. Prepayment is required.

Wasatch County

4th District Court PO Box 730, Heber City, UT 84032; 435-654-4676; Fax: 435-654-5281. Hours: 8AM-5PM (MST). *Felony, Misdemeanor, Civil, Eviction, Small Claims, Probate.*

Civil Records: Access: Phone, fax, mail, online, in person. Both court and visitors may perform in person searches. No search fee. Required to search: name, years to search. Civil cases indexed by defendant, plaintiff. Civil records on computer since 01/95; records archived since court started. Online access available through Xchange, see http://courtlink.utcourts.gov. Also see state introduction.

Criminal Records: Access: Phone, fax, mail, online, in person. Both court and visitors may perform in person searches. No search fee. Required to search: name, years to search; also helpful: DOB, signed release. Criminal records on computer since 01/95; records archived since court started. Online access available through Xchange, see http://courtlink.utcourts.gov. Also see state introduction.

General Information: Public access terminal is available. No adoption records released. SASE required. Turnaround time 1-2 days. Fax notes: Fee to fax results is $1.00 plus $.25 per page. Copy fee: $.25 per page. Certification fee: $2.00 plus $.50 per page. Fee payee: 4th District Court. Personal checks accepted. Prepayment is required.

Washington County

5th District Court 220 North 200 East, St. George, UT 84770; Civil phone: 435-986-5701; Criminal phone: 435-986-5700; Fax: 435-986-5723. Hours: 8AM-5PM (MST). *Felony, Misdemeanor, Civil, Eviction, Small Claims, Probate.*

Civil Records: Access: Mail, online, in person, fax. Both court and visitors may perform in person searches. No search fee. Required to search: name. Civil cases indexed by defendant, plaintiff. District Court records on computer from April, 1990; Circuit Court on computer from 1987. Online access available through Xchange, see http://courtlink.utcourts.gov. Also see state introduction.

Criminal Records: Access: Mail, online, in person, fax. Both court and visitors may perform in person searches. No search fee. Required to search: name, years to search. District Court records on computer from April, 1990; Circuit Court on computer from 1987. Online access available through Xchange, see http://courtlink.utcourts.gov. Also see state introduction.

General Information: Public access terminal is available. No mental health, adoption records released. SASE required. Turnaround time 2-3 days. Fax notes: Fee to fax results is extra $.25 per page. Copy fee: $.25 per page. Certification fee: $2.00 plus $.50 per page. Fee payee: 5th District Court. Personal checks accepted. Credit cards accepted: Visa, MasterCard. Prepayment is required.

Wayne County

6th District Court PO Box 189, Loa, UT 84747; 435-836-2731; Fax: 435-836-2479. Hours: 9AM-5PM (MST). *Felony, Misdemeanor, Civil, Eviction, Small Claims, Probate.*

Civil Records: Access: Phone, mail, fax, in person, online. Both court and visitors may perform in person searches. Search fee: $13.00 per hour. Required to search: name, years to search. Civil cases indexed by defendant, plaintiff. Civil records archived since court

started; computerized from Oct. 2000. Online access available through Xchange, see http://courtlink.utcourts.gov. Also see state introduction.

Criminal Records: Access: Phone, mail, fax, in person, online. Both court and visitors may perform in person searches. Search fee: $13.00 per hour. Required to search: name, years to search; also helpful: SSN. Criminal records archived since court started; computerized from Oct 2000. Online access available through Xchange, see http://courtlink.utcourts.gov. Also see state introduction.

General Information: No sealed records released. SASE required. Turnaround time 2-3 days. Fax notes: Fee to fax results is $1.00 per page. Copy fee: $.25 per page. Certification fee: $4.00. Fee payee: 6th District Court. Personal checks accepted. Prepayment required.

Weber County

2nd District Court 2525 Grant Ave, Ogden, UT 84401; Civil phone: 801-395-1091; Criminal phone: 801-395-1102; Probate phone: 801-395-1173. Hours: 8AM-5PM (MST). *Felony, Misdemeanor, Civil, Eviction, Small Claims, Probate.*

Note: An automated court information line allows phone access to court dates, fine balances, and judgment/divorce decrees (case or citation number required) at 801-395-1111.

Civil Records: Access: Phone, mail, online, in person. Both court and visitors may perform in person searches. Search fee: $13.00 per hour. First 15 minutes no charge. Required to search: name, years to search. Civil cases indexed by defendant, plaintiff. Civil records on computer the past 10 years, books prior to that. Online access available through Xchange, see http://courtlink.utcourts.gov. Also see state introduction.

Criminal Records: Access: Phone, mail, online, in person. Both court and visitors may perform in person searches. Search fee: $13.00 per hour. First 15 minutes no charge. Required to search: name, years to search, DOB, SSN. Criminal records on computer the past 10 years, books prior to that. Online access available through Xchange, see http://courtlink.utcourts.gov. Also see state introduction.

General Information: Public access terminal is available. No adoption, voluntary commitments, expunged criminal records released. SASE required. Turnaround time 2-9 days. Copy fee: $.25 per page. Certification fee: $4.00 plus $.50 per page. Fee payee: Ogden District Court. Personal checks accepted. Credit cards accepted: Visa, MasterCard. Prepayment is required.

2nd District Court - Roy Department
5051 South 1900 West, Roy, UT 84067; 801-774-1051; Fax: 801-774-1060. Hours: 8AM-5PM (MST). *Felony, Misdemeanor.*

Note: Civil and small claims records are are maintained in Ogden.

Criminal Records: Access: Mail, online, in person. Both court and visitors may perform in person searches. Search fee: $10.00 per hour. First 20 minutes no charge. Required to search: name, years to search, signed release; also helpful: address, DOB. Criminal records on computer since January 1987. Online access available through Xchange, see http://courtlink.utcourts.gov. Also see state introduction.

General Information: No sealed, expunged or juvenile records released. Turnaround time 5 days. Copy fee: $.25 per page. Certification fee: $4.00 plus $.50 per page. Fee payee: Roy District Court. Personal checks accepted. Credit cards accepted: Visa, MasterCard. Prepayment is required.

Utah Recording Offices

ORGANIZATION: 29 counties 29 recording offices. The recording officers are County Recorder and Clerk of District Court (state tax liens). The entire state is in the Mountain Time Zone (MST).

REAL ESTATE RECORDS: County Recorders will not perform real estate searches. Copy fees vary, and certification fees are usually $2.00 per document.

UCC RECORDS: Financing statements are filed at the state level, except for real estate related collateral, which are filed with the Register of Deeds (and at the state level in certain cases). Many filing offices will not perform UCC searches. Copy fees vary, but is usually $1.00. Certification usually costs $2.00 per document.

TAX LIEN RECORDS: All federal tax liens are filed with the County Recorder. They do not perform searches. All state tax liens are filed with Clerk of District Court, many of which have on-line access. Refer to the County Court section for information about Utah District Courts.

ONLINE ACCESS: A number of counties offer online access, some are fee-based.

Beaver County

County Recorder, PO Box 431, Beaver, UT 84713. 435-438-6480; Fax 435-438-6481.
Will search UCC records. UCC search does not include federal tax liens. Will not search real estate records. **Other Phones:** Assessor 435-438-6400; Treasurer 435-438-6410; Appraiser/Auditor 435-438-6460.

Box Elder County

County Recorder, 1 S. Main, Brigham City, UT 84302-2599. 435-734-2031; Fax 435-734-2038.
This agency will not search real estate or UCC records. **Other Phone Numbers:** Assessor 435-734-3333; Treasurer 435-734-3333; Appraiser/Auditor 435-734-3317; Elections 435-734-3391.

Cache County

County Recorder, 179 N. Main St, Logan, UT 84321. County Recorder, R/E and UCC Recording 435-716-7180; Fax 435-716-7159.
Call 435-755-9837 for more information regarding online access. Will search UCC records. Will not search real estate records. **Other Phone Numbers:** Assessor 435-716-7100; Treasurer 435-716-8394; Appraiser/Auditor 435-716-7123.

Carbon County

County Recorder, Courthouse Building, 120 E. Main, Price, UT 84501. County Recorder, R/E and UCC Recording 435-636-3244; Fax 435-637-6757.
This agency will not search real estate or UCC records. **Other Phone Numbers:** Assessor 435-636-3249; Treasurer 435-636-3258; Appraiser/Auditor 435-636-3227; Elections 435-636-3220.

Daggett County

County Recorder, PO Box 219, Manila, UT 84046-0219. 435-784-3210; Fax 435-784-3335.
This agency will not search real estate or UCC records. **Other Phone Numbers:** Assessor 435-784-3222; Treasurer 435-784-3154; Appraiser/Auditor 435-784-3210; Elections 435-784-5154.

Davis County

County Recorder, PO Box 618, Farmington, UT 84025. 801-451-3225 R/E Recording: 385-451-3225; www.co.davis.ut.us
Will not search UCC or tax lien records. Will not search real estate records. **Online Access:** Real Estate, Lien Records. Access to the county land records database requires written registration and $15.00 per month fee plus $.10 per transaction. Records go back to 1981. For information and sign-up, contact Janet at 801-451-3347. **Other Phones:** Assessor 385-451-3252; Treasurer 385-451-3243; Appraiser/Auditor 385-451-3214; Elections 385-451-3213; Vital Records 801-451-3337.

Duchesne County

County Recorder, PO Box 916, Duchesne, UT 84021. County Recorder, R/E and UCC Recording 435-738-1160; Fax 435-738-5522.
This agency will not search real estate or UCC records. **Other Phone Numbers:** Assessor 435-738-1115; Treasurer 435-738-1193; Appraiser/Auditor 435-738-1123; Elections 435-738-1101.

Emery County

County Recorder, PO Box 698, Castle Dale, UT 84513-0698. 435-381-2414; Fax 435-381-2614. www.emerycounty.com
This agency will not search real estate or UCC records. **Other Phone Numbers:** Assessor 435-381-2474; Treasurer 435-381-2510; Appraiser/Auditor 435-381-5106; Elections 435-381-5106.

Garfield County

County Recorder, PO Box 77, Panguitch, UT 84759. 435-676-1112 x112; Fax 435-676-8239.
Will search UCC records. Will not search real estate records. **Other Phone Numbers:** Assessor 435-676-1107; Treasurer 435-676-1109; Appraiser/Auditor 435-676-8826 x100.

Grand County

County Recorder & Deputies, 125 E. Center St., Moab, UT 84532. County Recorder & Deputies, R/E and UCC Recording 435-259-1331; Fax 435-259-1320.
This agency will not search real estate or UCC records. **Other Phone Numbers:** Assessor 435-295-1329; Treasurer 435-295-1337,8,9; Appraiser/Auditor 435-259-1322.

Iron County

County Recorder, PO Box 506, Parowan, UT 84761. 435-477-8350.
This agency will not perform searches. **Other Phone Numbers:** Assessor 435-477-8311; Treasurer 435-477-8360; Appraiser/Auditor 435-477-8331.

Juab County

County Recorder, 160 N. Main, Nephi, UT 84648. 435-623-3430.
Will search UCC records. This agency will not do a federal tax lien search. Will not search real estate records. **Other Phone Numbers:** Assessor 435-623-3425; Treasurer 435-623-0096; Appraiser/Auditor 435-623-3410.

Kane County

County Recorder, 76 N. Main #14, Kanab, UT 84741. 435-644-2360.
Will not search UCC records. This agency will not do a federal tax lien search. Will not search real estate records. **Other Phones:** Assessor 435-644-2649; Treasurer 435-644-5659; Appraiser/Auditor 644-2458.

Millard County

County Recorder, 50 S. Main, Fillmore, UT 84631. County Recorder, R/E and UCC Recording 435-743-6210; Fax 435-743-4221.
This agency will not search real estate or UCC records. **Other Phone Numbers:** Assessor 435-743-5719; Treasurer 435-743-5322; Appraiser/Auditor 743-5227.

Morgan County

County Recorder, PO Box 886, Morgan, UT 84050. 385-829-3277 UCC Recording: 385-845-4036; Fax 385-829-6176.
Will search UCC records. Will not search real estate records. **Other Phones:** Assessor 385-845-4000; Treasurer 385-845-4030; Appraiser/Auditor 845-4011.

Piute County

County Recorder, PO Box 116, Junction, UT 84740. 435-577-2505; Fax 435-577-2433.
Will search UCC records. Will not search tax lien records as a practice; if so, fee is $10.00 per search. Will not search real estate records as a practice. **Other Phone Numbers:** Assessor 435-577-2988; Treasurer 435-577-2505; Appraiser/Auditor 435-577-2840.

Rich County

County Recorder, PO Box 322, Randolph, UT 84064. 435-793-2005.
Will search UCC records. This agency will not do a federal tax lien search. Will not search real estate records. **Other Phones:** Assessor 435-793-5215; Treasurer 435-793-5155; Appraiser/Auditor 793-2415.

Salt Lake County

County Recorder, 2001 S. State St, Room N-1600, Salt Lake City, UT 84190-1150. 801-468-3391; www.co.slc.ut.us
Will search UCC records. This agency will not do a federal tax lien search. Will not search real estate records. **Online Access:** Assessor, Property Tax, Land Records. Two sources are available. Records on the county Truth-In-Tax Information web site are available free online at www.slpropertyinfo.org. Also, Assessor, real estate, appraisal, abstracts, and GIS mapping are available for $150.00 fee on the online system at http://rec.co.slc.ut.us/polaris/default.cfm. Search by

GIS, name, or property information. Register online or call 801-468-3013. **Other Phone Numbers:** Assessor 801-468-2165; Treasurer 801-468-3140; Appraiser/Auditor 801-468-3389.

San Juan County

County Recorder, PO Box 789, Monticello, UT 84535. 435-587-3228; Fax 435-587-2425.

This agency will not perform searches. **Other Phone Numbers:** Assessor 435-587-3221; Treasurer 435-547-3237; Appraiser/Auditor 435-587-3223.

Sanpete County

County Recorder, 160 N. Main, Manti, UT 84642. 435-835-2181 R/E Recording: 435-835-2181; Fax 435-835-2182.

Will not search UCC records. This agency will not do a federal tax lien search. Will not search real estate records. **Other Phone Numbers:** Assessor 435-835-2111; Treasurer 435-835-2101; Appraiser/Auditor 435-835-2142.

Sevier County

County Recorder, 250 N. Main, Richfield, UT 84701. 435-896-9262 x210; Fax 435-896-8888.

This agency will not search real estate or UCC records. **Other Phone Numbers:** Assessor 435-896-9262 x230; Treasurer 435-896-9262 x240; Appraiser/Auditor 435-896-9262 x203.

Summit County

County Recorder, PO Box 128, Coalville, UT 84017. 435-336-3238; Fax 435-336-3055.

This agency will not search real estate or UCC records. **Other Phones:** Assessor 435-336-3248; Treasurer 435-336-3266; Appraiser/Auditor 435-336-3254.

Tooele County

County Recorder, 47 S. Main St, Courthouse, Tooele, UT 84074-2194. County Recorder, R/E and UCC Recording 435-843-3180; Fax 435-882-7317. www.co.tooele.ut.us

Will search UCC records. Will not search real estate records. **Online Access:** Property Tax Records. Access to the property information database may be operational at www.co.tooele.ut.us/taxinfo.html. **Other Phone Numbers:** Assessor 435-843-3101; Treasurer 435-843-3191; Appraiser/Auditor 435-843-3130; Elections 435-843-3140; Vital Records 435-843-2300.

Uintah County

County Recorder, 147 E. Main St., County Building, Vernal, UT 84078. 435-781-5461 R/E Recording: 435-781-5398; Fax 435-781-5319. www.co.uintah.ut.us

This agency will not perform searches. **Online Access:** Property Records. Access to the counrty recorder's land records is available free at www.co.uintah.ut.us/recorder/landinfo.html. This site may be off temporarily; the URL may be changed. **Other Phones:** Assessor 435-781-5349; Treasurer 435-781-5362; Appraiser/Auditor 435-781-5360.

Utah County

County Recorder, PO Box 122, Provo, UT 84603. County Recorder, R/E and UCC Recording 801-370-8179; Fax 801-370-8181. www.co.utah.ut.us

Will search UCC records. This agency will not do a federal tax lien search. Will not search real estate records. **Online Access:** Real Estate, Lien, Assessor Records. Access to the land records database and also map searching is available free at www.co.utah.ut.us/omninet/land. Indexes go back to 1978; parcel indexes back to 1981. Document images go back to 1994. Building and GIS information is also available online. **Other Phone Numbers:** Assessor 801-370-8275; Treasurer 801-370-8255;

Appraiser/Auditor 801-370-8108; Elections 801-370-8226; Vital Records 801-370-4526.

Wasatch County

County Recorder, 25 N. Main, Heber, UT 84032. 435-654-3211; www.co.wasatch.ut.us/d/

This agency will not perform searches. **Online Access:** Real Property Records. The county GIS Dept. plans to have "metadata" (property information) available free online from its GIS mapping site at www.co.wasatch.ut.us/d/dpgis.html. **Other Phones:** Assessor 435-654-3211 x302; Treasurer 435-654-3211 x306; Appraiser/Auditor 435-654-3211 x309.

Washington County

County Recorder, 197 E. Tabernacle, St. George, UT 84770. County Recorder, R/E and UCC Recording 435-634-5709; Fax 435-634-5718.

This agency will not search real estate or UCC records. **Other Phones:** Assessor 435-634-5703; Treasurer 435-652-5856; Appraiser/Auditor 435-634-5712.

Wayne County

County Recorder, PO Box 187, Loa, UT 84747-0187. 435-836-2765; Fax 435-836-2479.

Will search UCC records. **Other Phone Numbers:** Assessor 435-836-2709; Treasurer 435-836-2765; Clerk/Auditor 435-836-2731.

Weber County

County Recorder, 2380 Washington Blvd, Suite 370, Ogden, UT 84401. 385-399-8441; www.co.weber.ut.us

Will search UCC records. UCC search includes federal tax liens if requested. Real estate record owner searches available. **Online Access:** Real Estate Records. Property records on the County Parcel Search site are available free online at www.co.weber.ut.us/netapps/Parcel/main.htm. **Other Phone Numbers:** Assessor 385-399-8122; Treasurer 385-399-8480; Appraiser/Auditor 385-399-8573.

Utah County Locator

You will usually be able to find the city name in the City/County Cross Reference below. In that case, it is a simple matter to determine the county from the cross reference. However, only the official US Postal Service city names are included in this index. There are an additional 40,000 place names that people use in their addresses. Therefore, we have also included a ZIP/City Cross Reference immediately following the City/County Cross Reference.

If you know the ZIP Code but the city name does not appear in the City/County Cross Reference index, look up the ZIP Code in the ZIP/City Cross Reference, find the city name, then look up the city name in the City/County Cross Reference. For example, you want to know the county for an address of Menands, NY 12204. There is no "Menands" in the City/County Cross Reference. The ZIP/City Cross Reference shows that ZIP Codes 12201-12288 are for the city of Albany. Looking back in the City/County Cross Reference, Albany is in Albany County.

City/County Cross Reference

ALPINE Utah
ALTAMONT Duchesne
ALTON Kane
ALTONAH Duchesne
AMERICAN FORK Utah
ANETH San Juan
ANNABELLA Sevier
ANTIMONY Garfield
AURORA Sevier
AXTELL Sanpete
BEAR RIVER CITY Box Elder
BEAVER Beaver
BERYL Iron
BICKNELL Wayne
BINGHAM CANYON Salt Lake
BLANDING San Juan
BLUEBELL Duchesne
BLUFF San Juan
BONANZA Uintah
BOULDER Garfield
BOUNTIFUL Davis
BRIAN HEAD Iron
BRIDGELAND Duchesne
BRIGHAM CITY Box Elder
BRYCE Garfield
BRYCE CANYON Garfield
CACHE JUNCTION Cache
CANNONVILLE Garfield
CASTLE DALE Emery
CEDAR CITY Iron
CEDAR VALLEY Utah
CENTERFIELD Sanpete
CENTERVILLE Davis
CENTRAL Washington
CHESTER Sanpete
CIRCLEVILLE Piute
CISCO Grand
CLARKSTON Cache
CLAWSON Emery
CLEARFIELD Davis
CLEVELAND Emery
COALVILLE Summit
COLLINSTON Box Elder
CORINNE Box Elder
CORNISH Cache
CROYDON Morgan
DAMMERON VALLEY Washington
DELTA Millard
DEWEYVILLE Box Elder
DRAPER Salt Lake
DUCHESNE Duchesne
DUCK CREEK VILLAGE Kane
DUGWAY Tooele
DUTCH JOHN Daggett
EAST CARBON Carbon
ECHO Summit
EDEN Weber
ELBERTA Utah
ELMO Emery
ELSINORE Sevier
EMERY Emery
ENTERPRISE Washington
EPHRAIM Sanpete
ESCALANTE Garfield

EUREKA Juab
FAIRVIEW Sanpete
FARMINGTON Davis
FAYETTE Sanpete
FERRON Emery
FIELDING Box Elder
FILLMORE Millard
FORT DUCHESNE Uintah
FOUNTAIN GREEN Sanpete
FRUITLAND Duchesne
GARDEN CITY Rich
GARLAND Box Elder
GARRISON Millard
GLENDALE Kane
GLENWOOD Sevier
GOSHEN Utah
GRANTSVILLE Tooele
GREEN RIVER Emery
GREENVILLE Beaver
GREENWICH Piute
GROUSE CREEK Box Elder
GUNLOCK Washington
GUNNISON Sanpete
GUSHER Uintah
HANKSVILLE Wayne
HANNA Duchesne
HATCH Garfield
HEBER CITY Wasatch
HELPER Carbon
HENEFER Summit
HENRIEVILLE Garfield
HIAWATHA Carbon
HILDALE Washington
HILL AFB Davis
HINCKLEY Millard
HOLDEN Millard
HONEYVILLE Box Elder
HOOPER (84315) Weber(93), Davis(6)
HOWELL Box Elder
HUNTINGTON Emery
HUNTSVILLE Weber
HURRICANE Washington
HYDE PARK Cache
HYRUM Cache
IBAPAH Tooele
IVINS Washington
JENSEN Uintah
JOSEPH Sevier
JUNCTION Piute
KAMAS Summit
KANAB Kane
KANARRAVILLE Iron
KANOSH Millard
KAYSVILLE Davis
KENILWORTH Carbon
KINGSTON Piute
KOOSHAREM Sevier
LA SAL San Juan
LA VERKIN Washington
LAKE POWELL San Juan
LAKETOWN Rich
LAPOINT Uintah
LAYTON Davis
LEAMINGTON Millard

LEEDS Washington
LEHI Utah
LEVAN Juab
LEWISTON Cache
LINDON Utah
LOA Wayne
LOGAN Cache
LYMAN Wayne
LYNNDYL Millard
MAGNA Salt Lake
MANILA Daggett
MANTI Sanpete
MANTUA Box Elder
MAPLETON Utah
MARYSVALE Piute
MAYFIELD Sanpete
MEADOW Millard
MENDON Cache
MEXICAN HAT San Juan
MIDVALE Salt Lake
MIDWAY Wasatch
MILFORD Beaver
MILLVILLE Cache
MINERSVILLE Beaver
MOAB Grand
MODENA Iron
MONA Juab
MONROE Sevier
MONTEZUMA CREEK San Juan
MONTICELLO San Juan
MONUMENT VALLEY San Juan
MORGAN Morgan
MORONI Sanpete
MOUNT CARMEL Kane
MOUNT PLEASANT Sanpete
MOUNTAIN HOME Duchesne
MYTON (84052) Duchesne(75), Uintah(24)
NEOLA Duchesne
NEPHI Juab
NEW HARMONY Washington
NEWCASTLE Iron
NEWTON Cache
NORTH SALT LAKE Davis
OAK CITY Millard
OAKLEY Summit
OASIS Millard
OGDEN Weber
ORANGEVILLE Emery
ORDERVILLE Kane
OREM Utah
PANGUITCH Garfield
PARADISE Cache
PARAGONAH Iron
PARK CITY Summit
PARK VALLEY Box Elder
PAROWAN Iron
PAYSON Utah
PEOA Summit
PINE VALLEY Washington
PLEASANT GROVE Utah
PLYMOUTH Box Elder
PORTAGE Box Elder
PRICE Carbon
PROVIDENCE Cache

PROVO Utah
RANDLETT Uintah
RANDOLPH Rich
REDMOND Sevier
RICHFIELD Sevier
RICHMOND Cache
RIVERSIDE Box Elder
RIVERTON Salt Lake
ROCKVILLE Washington
ROOSEVELT (84066) Duchesne(94), Uintah(5)
ROY Weber
RUSH VALLEY Tooele
SAINT GEORGE Washington
SALEM Utah
SALINA Sevier
SALT LAKE CITY Salt Lake
SANDY Salt Lake
SANTA CLARA Washington
SANTAQUIN Utah
SCIPIO Millard
SEVIER Sevier
SIGURD Sevier
SMITHFIELD Cache
SNOWVILLE Box Elder
SOUTH JORDAN Salt Lake
SPANISH FORK Utah
SPRING CITY Sanpete
SPRINGDALE Washington
SPRINGVILLE Utah
STERLING Sanpete
STOCKTON Tooele
SUMMIT Iron
SUNNYSIDE Carbon
SYRACUSE Davis
TABIONA Duchesne
TALMAGE Duchesne
TEASDALE Wayne
THOMPSON Grand
TOOELE Tooele
TOQUERVILLE Washington
TORREY Wayne
TREMONTON Box Elder
TRENTON Cache
TRIDELL Uintah
TROPIC Garfield
VERNAL Uintah
VERNON Tooele
VEYO Washington
VIRGIN Washington
WALES Sanpete
WALLSBURG Wasatch
WASHINGTON Washington
WELLINGTON Carbon
WELLSVILLE Cache
WENDOVER Tooele
WEST JORDAN Salt Lake
WHITEROCKS Uintah
WILLARD Box Elder
WOODRUFF Rich
WOODS CROSS Davis

ZIP/City Cross Reference

84001-84001 ALTAMONT	84078-84079 VERNAL	84523-84523 FERRON	84715-84715 BICKNELL
84002-84002 ALTONAH	84080-84080 VERNON	84525-84525 GREEN RIVER	84716-84716 BOULDER
84003-84003 AMERICAN FORK	84082-84082 WALLSBURG	84526-84526 HELPER	84717-84717 BRYCE CANYON
84004-84004 ALPINE	84083-84083 WENDOVER	84527-84527 HIAWATHA	84718-84718 CANNONVILLE
84006-84006 BINGHAM CANYON	84084-84084 WEST JORDAN	84528-84528 HUNTINGTON	84719-84719 BRIAN HEAD
84007-84007 BLUEBELL	84085-84085 WHITEROCKS	84529-84529 KENILWORTH	84720-84721 CEDAR CITY
84008-84008 BONANZA	84086-84086 WOODRUFF	84530-84530 LA SAL	84722-84722 CENTRAL
84010-84011 BOUNTIFUL	84087-84087 WOODS CROSS	84531-84531 MEXICAN HAT	84723-84723 CIRCLEVILLE
84012-84012 BRIDGELAND	84088-84088 WEST JORDAN	84532-84532 MOAB	84724-84724 ELSINORE
84013-84013 CEDAR VALLEY	84089-84089 CLEARFIELD	84533-84533 LAKE POWELL	84725-84725 ENTERPRISE
84014-84014 CENTERVILLE	84090-84094 SANDY	84534-84534 MONTEZUMA CREEK	84726-84726 ESCALANTE
84015-84016 CLEARFIELD	84095-84095 SOUTH JORDAN	84535-84535 MONTICELLO	84728-84728 GARRISON
84017-84017 COALVILLE	84097-84097 OREM	84536-84536 MONUMENT VALLEY	84729-84729 GLENDALE
84018-84018 CROYDON	84098-84098 PARK CITY	84537-84537 ORANGEVILLE	84730-84730 GLENWOOD
84020-84020 DRAPER	84100-84199 SALT LAKE CITY	84539-84539 SUNNYSIDE	84731-84731 GREENVILLE
84021-84021 DUCHESNE	84201-84244 OGDEN	84540-84540 THOMPSON	84732-84732 GREENWICH
84022-84022 DUGWAY	84301-84301 BEAR RIVER CITY	84542-84542 WELLINGTON	84733-84733 GUNLOCK
84023-84023 DUTCH JOHN	84302-84302 BRIGHAM CITY	84601-84606 PROVO	84734-84734 HANKSVILLE
84024-84024 ECHO	84304-84304 CACHE JUNCTION	84620-84620 AURORA	84735-84735 HATCH
84025-84025 FARMINGTON	84305-84305 CLARKSTON	84621-84621 AXTELL	84736-84736 HENRIEVILLE
84026-84026 FORT DUCHESNE	84306-84306 COLLINSTON	84622-84622 CENTERFIELD	84737-84737 HURRICANE
84027-84027 FRUITLAND	84307-84307 CORINNE	84623-84623 CHESTER	84738-84738 IVINS
84028-84028 GARDEN CITY	84308-84308 CORNISH	84624-84624 DELTA	84739-84739 JOSEPH
84029-84029 GRANTSVILLE	84309-84309 DEWEYVILLE	84626-84626 ELBERTA	84740-84740 JUNCTION
84030-84030 GUSHER	84310-84310 EDEN	84627-84627 EPHRAIM	84741-84741 KANAB
84031-84031 HANNA	84311-84311 FIELDING	84628-84628 EUREKA	84742-84742 KANARRAVILLE
84032-84032 HEBER CITY	84312-84312 GARLAND	84629-84629 FAIRVIEW	84743-84743 KINGSTON
84033-84033 HENEFER	84313-84313 GROUSE CREEK	84630-84630 FAYETTE	84744-84744 KOOSHAREM
84034-84034 IBAPAH	84314-84314 HONEYVILLE	84631-84631 FILLMORE	84745-84745 LA VERKIN
84035-84035 JENSEN	84315-84315 HOOPER	84632-84632 FOUNTAIN GREEN	84746-84746 LEEDS
84036-84036 KAMAS	84316-84316 HOWELL	84633-84633 GOSHEN	84747-84747 LOA
84037-84037 KAYSVILLE	84317-84317 HUNTSVILLE	84634-84634 GUNNISON	84749-84749 LYMAN
84038-84038 LAKETOWN	84318-84318 HYDE PARK	84635-84635 HINCKLEY	84750-84750 MARYSVALE
84039-84039 LAPOINT	84319-84319 HYRUM	84636-84636 HOLDEN	84751-84751 MILFORD
84040-84041 LAYTON	84320-84320 LEWISTON	84637-84637 KANOSH	84752-84752 MINERSVILLE
84042-84042 LINDON	84321-84323 LOGAN	84638-84638 LEAMINGTON	84753-84753 MODENA
84043-84043 LEHI	84324-84324 MANTUA	84639-84639 LEVAN	84754-84754 MONROE
84044-84044 MAGNA	84325-84325 MENDON	84640-84640 LYNNDYL	84755-84755 MOUNT CARMEL
84046-84046 MANILA	84326-84326 MILLVILLE	84642-84642 MANTI	84756-84756 NEWCASTLE
84047-84047 MIDVALE	84327-84327 NEWTON	84643-84643 MAYFIELD	84757-84757 NEW HARMONY
84049-84049 MIDWAY	84328-84328 PARADISE	84644-84644 MEADOW	84758-84758 ORDERVILLE
84050-84050 MORGAN	84329-84329 PARK VALLEY	84645-84645 MONA	84759-84759 PANGUITCH
84051-84051 MOUNTAIN HOME	84330-84330 PLYMOUTH	84646-84646 MORONI	84760-84760 PARAGONAH
84052-84052 MYTON	84331-84331 PORTAGE	84647-84647 MOUNT PLEASANT	84761-84761 PAROWAN
84053-84053 NEOLA	84332-84332 PROVIDENCE	84648-84648 NEPHI	84762-84762 DUCK CREEK VILLAGE
84054-84054 NORTH SALT LAKE	84333-84333 RICHMOND	84649-84649 OAK CITY	84763-84763 ROCKVILLE
84055-84055 OAKLEY	84334-84334 RIVERSIDE	84650-84650 OASIS	84764-84764 BRYCE
84056-84056 HILL AFB	84335-84335 SMITHFIELD	84651-84651 PAYSON	84765-84765 SANTA CLARA
84057-84059 OREM	84336-84336 SNOWVILLE	84652-84652 REDMOND	84766-84766 SEVIER
84060-84060 PARK CITY	84337-84337 TREMONTON	84653-84653 SALEM	84767-84767 SPRINGDALE
84061-84061 PEOA	84338-84338 TRENTON	84654-84654 SALINA	84770-84771 SAINT GEORGE
84062-84062 PLEASANT GROVE	84339-84339 WELLSVILLE	84655-84655 SANTAQUIN	84772-84772 SUMMIT
84063-84063 RANDLETT	84340-84340 WILLARD	84656-84656 SCIPIO	84773-84773 TEASDALE
84064-84064 RANDOLPH	84341-84341 LOGAN	84657-84657 SIGURD	84774-84774 TOQUERVILLE
84065-84065 RIVERTON	84400-84415 OGDEN	84660-84660 SPANISH FORK	84775-84775 TORREY
84066-84066 ROOSEVELT	84501-84501 PRICE	84662-84662 SPRING CITY	84776-84776 TROPIC
84067-84067 ROY	84510-84510 ANETH	84663-84663 SPRINGVILLE	84779-84779 VIRGIN
84068-84068 PARK CITY	84511-84511 BLANDING	84664-84664 MAPLETON	84780-84780 WASHINGTON
84069-84069 RUSH VALLEY	84512-84512 BLUFF	84665-84665 STERLING	84781-84781 PINE VALLEY
84070-84070 SANDY	84513-84513 CASTLE DALE	84667-84667 WALES	84782-84782 VEYO
84071-84071 STOCKTON	84515-84515 CISCO	84701-84701 RICHFIELD	84783-84783 DAMMERON VALLEY
84072-84072 TABIONA	84516-84516 CLAWSON	84710-84710 ALTON	84784-84784 HILDALE
84073-84073 TALMAGE	84518-84518 CLEVELAND	84711-84711 ANNABELLA	84790-84791 SAINT GEORGE
84074-84074 TOOELE	84520-84520 EAST CARBON	84712-84712 ANTIMONY	
84075-84075 SYRACUSE	84521-84521 ELMO	84713-84713 BEAVER	
84076-84076 TRIDELL	84522-84522 EMERY	84714-84714 BERYL	

Vermont

General Help Numbers:

Governor's Office
Pavillion Office Bldg
109 State St
Montpelier, VT 05609-0101
www.gov.state.vt.us

802-828-3333
Fax 802-828-3339
7:45AM-4:30PM

Attorney General's Office
109 State St
Montpelier, VT 05609-1001
www.state.vt.us/atg

802-828-3171
Fax 802-828-2154
7:45AM-4:30PM

State Court Administrator
Administrative Office of Courts
111 State St
Montpelier, VT 05609-0701
www.state.vt.us/courts/admin.htm

802-828-3278
Fax 802-828-3457
8AM-4:30PM

State Archives
State Archives Division
26 Terrace-Redstone Bldg
Montpelier, VT 05609-1103
http://vermont-archives.org

802-828-2308
Fax 802-828-1135
7:45AM-4:30PM

State Specifics:

Capital:

Montpelier
Washington County

Time Zone:

EST

Number of Counties:

14

Population:

613,090

Web Site:

www.state.vt.us

State Agencies

Criminal Records

Access to Records is Restricted

State Repository, Vermont Criminal Info. Center, 103 S. Main St., Waterbury, VT 05671-2101; 802-244-8727, 802-241-5552 (Fax), 8AM-4:30PM.

www.dps.state.vt.us

Note: Records are not publicly available and can only be access by those authorized by law and the subject for personal review. Those authorized include employers with employees working with children, the elderly, or disabled. Otherwise, search at the county level. 35% of records are fingerprint supported. 96% of records have dispositions. A sex offender registry is not available online to the public. Search only the current incarcerated offenders database at www.doc.state.vt.us:81/cgi-bin/public.cgi.

Corporation Records
Limited Liability Company Records
Limited Liability Partnerships
Limited Partnerships
Trademarks/Servicemarks

Secretary of State, Corporation Division, 81 River St, Drawer 9, Montpelier, VT 05609-1101; 802-828-2386, 802-828-2853 (Fax), 7:45AM-4:30PM.

www.sec.state.vt.us/soshome.htm

Indexing & Storage: Records are available from beginning of record keeping. Records are on computer if active. Inactive records are indexed by a card file.

Searching: Include the following in your request: full name of business.

Access by: mail, phone, fax, in person, online.

Fee & Payment: There is no search fee. Copies are $.10 per page or $.25 per page if on microfiche. The fee for certification is $5.00, or $1.00 per page when copies pulled. Fee payee: Secretary of State. Personal checks accepted. No credit cards accepted.

Mail search: Turnaround time: 3 to 5 days.

Phone search: They will only confirm if business is active.

Fax search: Same criteria as mail searching. They will return a page or two by fax, if local number, otherwise results are mailed.

In person search: Searching is available in person.

Online search: Corporate and trademark records can be accessed from the Internet for no fee. All records are available. Also, the web site offers a "Trade Name Finder."

Other access: There is an option on the Internet to download the entire corporation (and tradename) database.

Uniform Commercial Code

UCC Division, Secretary of State, 81 River St, Drawer 4, Montpelier, VT 05609-1101; 802-828-2386, 802-828-2853 (Fax), 7:45AM-4:30PM.

www.sec.state.vt.us/corps/corpindex.htm

Indexing & Storage: Records are available from 1967. All active records are computerized. It takes 3 to 5 days before new records are available for inquiry.

Searching: Use search request form UCC-11. All tax liens are filed at the town/city level. Include the following in your request: debtor name, business name.

Access by: mail, fax, in person, online.

Fee & Payment: Searches are $10.00 per name. The copy fee is $2.00 per page. If there are attachments, they are an additional $5.00 per page. If results are to be returned by fax, add $2.00 per page. Fee payee: Secretary of State. Personal checks accepted. No credit cards accepted.

Mail search: Turnaround time: 4 days. A self addressed stamped envelope is requested.

Fax search: Same criteria as mail searching.

In person search: Turnaround time depends on workload, may not be immediate.

Online search: Searches are available from the Internet site. You can search by debtor or business name, there is no fee.

Federal Tax Liens
State Tax Liens

Records not maintained by a state level agency.

Note: Records are found at the local town level.

Sales Tax Registrations

Administrative Agency/Tax Department, Business Tax Division, 109 State St, Montpelier, VT 05609-1401; 802-828-2551, 802-828-5787 (Fax), 7:45AM-4:30PM.

www.state.vt.us/tax

Indexing & Storage: Records are available for 4 years on computer database, then records archived.

Searching: This agency will only confirm that a business is registered. Records are considered confidential. They will provide no other information. Include the following in your request: business name or tax permit number or owner name or federal tax ID.

Access by: mail, phone, fax.

Mail search: Turnaround time: 7 to 10 days. A self addressed stamped envelope is requested. No fee for mail request.

Phone search: No fee for telephone request.

Fax search: Requests may be faxed.

Birth Certificates

Reference & Research, Vital Records Section, US Rte 2, Drawer 33, Montpelier, VT 05633-7601; 802-828-3286, 802-828-3710 (Fax), 8AM-4PM.

www.bgs.state.vt.us/gsc/pubrec/referen

Note: For records for the past 5 years only, contact the Department of Health at 802-863-7300.

Indexing & Storage: Records are available from 1760 to 1995. New records are available for inquiry immediately. Records are indexed on index cards, inhouse computer.

Searching: The records are open to the public. Include the following in your request: full name, names of parents, mother's maiden name, date of birth, place of birth.

Access by: mail, phone, fax, in person.

Fee & Payment: The search fee is $7.00 per name. Fee payee: VT Vital Records. Prepayment required. Use of credit card is only for expedited service. Personal checks accepted. Credit cards accepted: MasterCard, Visa, AmEx, Discover.

Mail search: Turnaround time: 2 to 3 days. A self addressed stamped envelope is requested.

Phone search: See expedited service.

Fax search: See expedited service.

In person search: You may view the records for no charge.

Expedited service: Expedited service is available for fax searches. Turnaround time: 1 to 2 days. Add $5.00 for use of credit card and $15.50 for overnight shipping.

Death Records

Reference & Research, Vital Records, US Rte 2, Drawer 33, Montpelier, VT 05633-7601; 802-828-3286, 8AM-4PM.

www.bgs.state.vt.us/gsc/pubrec/referen

Note: For records up to 5 years old, contact the Department of Health at 802-863-7300.

Indexing & Storage: Records are available from 1760 to 1995. New records are available for inquiry immediately. Records are indexed on index cards, inhouse computer.

Searching: Records are open to the public. Include the following in your request: full name, date of death, place of death, names of parents.

Access by: mail, phone, in person.

Fee & Payment: The search fee is $7.00 per name. Fee payee: VT Vital Records. Prepayment required. Credit card for expedited service only. Personal checks accepted. No credit cards accepted.

Mail search: Turnaround time: 2 to 3 days. A self addressed stamped envelope is requested.

Phone search: See expedited service.

In person search: You may view records at no charge.

Marriage Certificates

Reference & Research, Vital Records Section, US Rte 2, Drawer 33, Montpelier, VT 05633-7601; 802-828-3286, 8AM-4PM.

www.bgs.state.vt.us/gsc/pubrec/referen

Note: For records up to 5 years old, contact the VT Department of Health at 802-863-7300.

Indexing & Storage: Records are available from 1760 to 1995. New records are available for inquiry immediately. Records are indexed on index cards, inhouse computer.

Searching: Records are open. Include the following in your request: names of husband and wife, date of marriage, place or county of marriage, names of parents.

Access by: mail, in person.

Fee & Payment: The search fee is $7.00 per name. Fee payee: VT Vital Records. Prepayment required. Personal checks accepted. No credit cards accepted.

Mail search: Turnaround time: 2 to 3 days. A self addressed stamped envelope is requested.

In person search: Records may be viewed in person at no charge.

Divorce Records

Research & Reference, Vital Records Section, US Rte 2, Drawer 33, Montpelier, VT 05633-7601; 802-828-3286, 8AM-4PM.

www.bgs.state.vt.us/gsc/pubrec/referen

Note: For records less than 5 years old, contact the VT Department of health at 802-863-7300.

Indexing & Storage: Records are available from 1760 to 1995. New records are available for inquiry immediately. Records are indexed on index cards, inhouse computer.

Searching: Records are open. Include the following in your request: names of husband and wife, date of divorce, place of divorce.

Access by: mail, in person.

Fee & Payment: The search fee is $7.00 per name. Fee payee: VT Vital Records. Prepayment required. Personal checks accepted. No credit cards accepted.

Mail search: Turnaround time: 2 to 3 days. A self addressed stamped envelope is requested.

In person search: There is no fee to view records.

Workers' Compensation Records

Labor and Industry, Workers Compensation Division, Drawer 20, Montpelier, VT 05620-3401 (Courier: National Life Bldg, Montpelier, VT 05620); 802-828-2286, 802-828-2195 (Fax), 7:45AM-4:30PM.

www.state.vt.us/labind/wcindex.htm

Indexing & Storage: Records are available from 1997 on. Records prior to 1997 are in the State Archives. New records are available for inquiry immediately. Records are indexed on inhouse computer.

Searching: Must have a signed release from the claimant. You also will get only the employer's first report of injury. Include the following in your request: claimant name, Social Security Number, place of employment at time of accident. The following data is not released: medical records.

Access by: mail, phone, fax, in person.

Fee & Payment: No search fee, copy fee is $.04 per page. Fee payee: State of Vermont. Personal checks accepted. No credit cards accepted.

Mail search: Turnaround time: 2 weeks. A self addressed stamped envelope is requested.

Phone search: No fee for telephone request. They will indicate if there was a first report filed. They will release no additional information.

Fax search: Turnaround time is 2 weeks.

In person search: Turnaround time is while you wait if staff is available.

Driver Records
Driver License Information

Department of Motor Vehicles, DI - Records Unit, 120 State St, Montpelier, VT 05603-0001; 802-828-2050, 802-828-2098 (Fax), 7:45AM-4:30PM.

www.aot.state.vt.us/dmv/dmvhp.htm

Note: This office is closed on Wed. mornings. Ticket information is available from the Vermont Judicial Bureau, PO Box 607, White River Junction, VT 05001, 802-295-8869. There is no charge, but no information is given over the phone.

Indexing & Storage: Records are available for convictions and accidents. Records are sold as 3 year records or as complete (8+ years) records. It takes 5-7 days normally before new records are available for inquiry.

Searching: Ongoing permissible users must use Form TA-VG-118. Otherwise, use TA-VG-116 for written authorization from the subject to release personal information to the requester. Include the following in your request: name, DOB, signed release, if necessary. Mail or walk-in requesters need the driver's full name and DOB; the license number is optional. Online requesters need only the license number, but the last name and DOB are helpful. The following data is not released: addresses, Social Security Numbers, medical information or personal information (height, weight, sex, eye color, etc.).

Access by: mail, in person, online.

Fee & Payment: The charge is $8.00 for 3 year record and $16.00 for the "complete" record. There is a full charge for a "no record found." Fee payee: Vermont Department of Motor Vehicles. Prepayment required. Personal checks accepted. No credit cards accepted.

Mail search: Turnaround time: 5 to 7 days. A self addressed stamped envelope is requested.

In person search: Normal turnaround time is while you wait.

Online search: Online access costs $8.00 per 3 year record. The system is called "GovNet." Two methods are offered-single inquiry and batch mode. The system is open 24 hours a day, 7 days a week (except for file maintenance periods). Only the license number is needed when ordering, but it is suggested to submit the name and DOB also.

Other access: The state will sell its license file to approved requesters, but customization is not available.

Accident Reports

Department of Motor Vehicles, Accident Report Section, 120 State St, Montpelier, VT 05603; 802-828-2050, 7:45AM-4PM.

Note: The office is closed Wednesday mornings.

Indexing & Storage: Records are available for 5 years to present. Only records involving damage in excess of $1,000 or if injuries involved are reportable. It takes 45 days after the incident before new records are available for inquiry.

Searching: Include the following in your request: full name, date of accident, location of accident. If accident involves a criminal action it may take up to 3 months after accident date to get the report. The following data is not released: Social Security Numbers.

Access by: mail, in person.

Fee & Payment: The fee is $12.00 for the police report and $6.00 for a copy of the individual's report. For insurance information of the accident the fee is $4.00. Fee payee: Vermont Department of Motor Vehicles. Prepayment required. Personal checks accepted. No credit cards accepted.

Mail search: Turnaround time: 3 weeks. A self addressed stamped envelope is requested.

In person search: Searching is available.

Vehicle Ownership & Identification
Vessel Ownership & Registration

Department of Motor Vehicles, Registration & License Information/Records, 120 State St, Montpelier, VT 05603; 802-828-2000, 7:45AM-4:30PM (on Wed only 1PM-4:30PM).

www.dmv.state.vt.us

Indexing & Storage: Records are available from 1971 to present. Vessel records go back to the late 1970s and are removed after 14 years of inactivity. All motorized boats must be registered. It takes 1 to 3 weeks before new records are available for inquiry.

Searching: Ongoing permissible users must be authorized first. Occasional requesters must use form TA-VG 116. If record use is not "permissible" per DPPA, written authorization is needed from subject. Otherwise, records with no personal data are released. You must have name and DOB or plate # or VIN. To receive personal information, you must include signed release by individual, unless ongoing account. The following data is not released: Social Security Numbers, residence addresses, bulk information or lists for commercial purposes or medical information.

Access by: mail, in person.

Fee & Payment: $4.00 for each group (1-4) of registration records and $15.00 for an ownership (lien) search. Vessel fees are diffeent: registration check is $4.00, title search with lien is $7.50. Statsitical research is $25.00 per hour. Fee payee: Vermont Department of Motor Vehicles. Prepayment required. Personal checks accepted. No credit cards accepted.

Mail search: Turnaround time: 7 to 10 days. A self addressed stamped envelope is requested.

In person search: The turnaround time is generally 30 minutes for vehicle records. Vessel records are returned by mail.

Other access: High volume requesters can obtain records via magnetic tape. Bulk release of the database is not available except for statistical purposes. Apply to the Commissioner's Office.

Legislation Records

Vermont General Assembly, State House-Legislative Council, 115 State Street, Drawer 33, Montpelier, VT 05633; 802-828-2231, 802-828-2424 (Fax), 8AM-4:30PM.

www.leg.state.vt.us

Indexing & Storage: Records are available from 1940 at Legislative Council. Records are indexed on inhouse computer.

Searching: Include the following in your request: bill number.

Access by: mail, phone, fax, in person, online.

Fee & Payment: There is no fee.

Mail search: Turnaround time: same day. No self addressed stamped envelope is required.

Phone search: Records are available by phone.

Fax search: Fax searching available.

In person search: No fee for request. A public access terminal is available in the public lobby of the legislature.

Online search: The web site offers access to bill information.

Other access: A subscription service is available for bill text.

Voter Registration
Records not maintained by a state level agency.

Note: There is no statewide database. All records are kept at the municipal level.

GED Certificates

Department of Education, GED Testing, 120 State Street, Montpelier, VT 05620; 802-828-5161, 802-828-3146 (Fax), 8AM-4:30PM.

www.vermontcareers.org

Searching: Include the following in your request: date of birth, Social Security Number, signed release.

Access by: mail, fax, in person.

Fee & Payment: The fee is $3.00 for a transcript copy. Fee payee: Treasurer, State of Vermont. Prepayment required. No credit cards accepted.

Mail search: Turnaround time: 1 week.

Fax search: Same criteria as mail searching.

In person search: Searching is available in person.

Hunting License Information
Fishing License Information
Records not maintained by a state level agency.

Note: Although they maintain a central database on computer the records are not open to the public. Vendors forward records on a yearly basis (July).

Vermont State Licensing Agencies

Licenses Searchable Online

Accounting Firm #15...www.sec.state.vt.us/seek/lrspseek.htm
Acupuncturist #15..www.sec.state.vt.us/seek/lrspseek.htm
Architect #15...www.sec.state.vt.us/seek/lrspseek.htm
Auctioneer #15..www.sec.state.vt.us/seek/lrspseek.htm
Bank #5 ....www.bishca.state.vt.us/consumpubs/Bankpubs/AnnReport/banks.htm
Barber #15...www.sec.state.vt.us/seek/lrspseek.htm
Boxing Manager/Promoter #15 ....www.sec.state.vt.us/seek/lrspseek.htm
Chiropractor #15..www.sec.state.vt.us/seek/lrspseek.htm
Cosmetologist #15...www.sec.state.vt.us/seek/lrspseek.htm
Credit Union #5..www.bishca.state.vt.us/consumpubs/Bankpubs/AnnReport/credunions.htm
Dental Assistant #15..www.sec.state.vt.us/seek/lrspseek.htm
Dental Hygienist #15..www.sec.state.vt.us/seek/lrspseek.htm
Dentist #15 ....www.sec.state.vt.us/seek/lrspseek.htm
Dietitian #15...www.sec.state.vt.us/seek/lrspseek.htm
Embalmer #12 ....www.sec.state.vt.us/seek/lrspseek.htm
Engineer #15 ....www.sec.state.vt.us/seek/lrspseek.htm
Esthetician #15 ....www.sec.state.vt.us/seek/lrspseek.htm
Funeral Director #12 ....www.sec.state.vt.us/seek/lrspseek.htm
Hearing Aid Dispenser #15 ....www.sec.state.vt.us/seek/lrspseek.htm
Lobbyist #15 ....www.sec.state.vt.us/seek/lbylseek.htm
Manicurist #15 ....www.sec.state.vt.us/seek/lrspseek.htm
Marriage & Family Therapist #15.............................www.sec.state.vt.us/seek/lrspseek.htm
Medical Doctor/Surgeon #15 ....www.docboard.org/vt/df/vtsearch.htm
Mental Health Counselor, Clinical #15....................www.sec.state.vt.us/seek/lrspseek.htm
Naturopathic Physician #15 ....www.sec.state.vt.us/seek/lrspseek.htm
Notary Public #15 ....www.sec.state.vt.us/seek/not_seek.htm
Nurse/Nurse Practitioner/LNA #15..........................www.sec.state.vt.us/seek/lrspseek.htm
Nursing Home Administrator #15.............................www.sec.state.vt.us/seek/lrspseek.htm
Occupational Therapist #15.....................................www.sec.state.vt.us/seek/lrspseek.htm
Optician #15...www.sec.state.vt.us/seek/lrspseek.htm
Optometrist #15 ....www.sec.state.vt.us/seek/lrspseek.htm
Osteopathic Physician #15 ....www.sec.state.vt.us/seek/lrspseek.htm
Pharmacist #15..www.sec.state.vt.us/seek/lrspseek.htm
Pharmacy #15..www.sec.state.vt.us/seek/lrspseek.htm
Physical Therapist/Assistant #15 ....www.sec.state.vt.us/seek/lrspseek.htm
Physician Assistant #15...www.docboard.org/vt/df/vtsearch.htm
Podiatrist #15...www.docboard.org/vt/df/vtsearch.htm
Private Investigator #15 ....www.sec.state.vt.us/seek/lrspseek.htm
Psychoanalyst #15...www.sec.state.vt.us/seek/lrspseek.htm
Psychologist #15..www.sec.state.vt.us/seek/lrspseek.htm
Psychotherapist #15 ....www.sec.state.vt.us/seek/lrspseek.htm
Public Accountant-CPA #15.....................................www.sec.state.vt.us/seek/lrspseek.htm
Racing Promoter #15..www.sec.state.vt.us/seek/lrspseek.htm
Radiologic Technologist #15....................................www.sec.state.vt.us/seek/lrspseek.htm
Real Estate Appraiser #12 ....www.sec.state.vt.us/seek/lrspseek.htm
Real Estate Broker/Agent #12 ....www.sec.state.vt.us/seek/lrspseek.htm
Real Estate Salesperson #12 ....www.sec.state.vt.us/seek/lrspseek.htm
Security Guard #15..www.sec.state.vt.us/seek/lrspseek.htm
Social Worker, Clinical #15......................................www.sec.state.vt.us/seek/lrspseek.htm
Surveyor, Land #15 ....www.sec.state.vt.us/seek/lrspseek.htm
Tattoo Artist #15 ....www.sec.state.vt.us/seek/lrspseek.htm
Veterinarian #15 ....www.sec.state.vt.us/seek/lrspseek.htm

Licensing Quick Finder

Accounting Firm #15 802-828-2363
Acupuncturist #15 802-828-2373
Alcohol & Drug Abuse Counselor #18... 802-878-7776
Architect #15 802-828-2373
Armed Courier #15 802-828-2837
Asbestos Abatement Contractor/Worker #19
.... 802-863-7231
Attorney #2 802-828-3281
Auctioneer #15 802-828-3183
Bank #5 802-828-3307
Barber #15 802-828-2837
Boiler & Pressure Vessel Inspector #9 .. 802-879-2107
Boxing Manager/Promoter #15 802-828-2363
Chiropractor #15 802-828-2363
Cosmetologist #15 802-828-2363
Credit Union #5 802-828-3307
Dealer/Repairer Weighing & Measuring Devices #4
.... 802-244-2436
Dental Assistant #15 802-828-2363
Dental Hygienist #15 802-828-2363
Dentist #15 802-828-2363
Dietitian #15 802-828-2363
Driver Training Instructor #11 802-828-2114
Driving Instructor/School, Commercial #11
.... 802-828-2114
Electrician #8 802-828-2107
Embalmer #12 802-828-3183
Emergency Care Attendant #7 802-863-7310
Emergency Medical Technician #7 802-863-7310
Engineer #15 802-828-2363
Esthetician #15 802-828-2363
Fire Alarm System Installer/Dealer #8... 802-828-2107
Funeral Director #12 802-828-3183
Guard Dog Handler #15 802-828-2363
Hearing Aid Dispenser #15 802-828-2363

Horse Racing Trainers/Owners/Professional #17
.... 802-786-5050
Insurance Adjuster #5 802-828-3303
Insurance Agent/Consultant #5 802-828-3303
Insurance Appraiser #5 802-828-3303
Insurance Broker #5 802-828-3303
Investment Advisor #5 802-828-3420
Issuer Agent #5 802-828-3420
Lead Abatement Contr./Worker #19 802-863-7231
Lightning Rod Installer/Dealer #8 802-828-2107
Liquor, Retail/Wholesale #10 802-828-2339
Livestock Dealer #4 802-828-2421
Lobbyist #15 802-828-2464
Lottery Retailer #16 802-479-5686
Manicurist #15 802-828-2363
Marriage & Family Therapist #15 802-828-2363
Meat Inspection Laboratory #4 802-244-4510
Medical Doctor/Surgeon #15 802-828-2673
Mental Health Counselor, Clinical #15 .. 802-828-2363
Milk & Cream Tester #4 802-244-4510
Naturopathic Physician #15 802-828-2363
Notary Public #15 802-828-2464
Nurse/Nurse Practitioner/LNA #15 802-828-2396
Nursing Home Administrator #15 802-828-2363
Occupational Therapist #15 802-828-2363
Optician #15 802-828-2363
Optometrist #15 802-828-2373
Osteopathic Physician #15 802-828-2373
Pari-Mutuel Seller #17 802-786-5050
Peddler #15 802-828-2363
Pediatrist #15 802-828-2673
Pesticide Applicator #4 802-244-2431
Pharmacist #15 802-828-2363
Pharmacy #15 802-828-2363
Photographer, Itinerant #15 802-828-2363

Physical Therapist/Assistant #15 802-828-2363
Physician Assistant #15 802-828-2673
Plumber #8 802-828-2107
Podiatrist #15 802-828-2363
Polygraph Examiner #3 802-244-8781
Private Investigator #15 802-828-2363
Psychoanalyst #15 802-828-2373
Psychologist #15 802-828-2373
Psychotherapist #15 802-828-2363
Public Accountant-CPA #15 802-828-2363
Public Adjuster #5 802-828-3303
Race Driver/Track Personnel #15 802-828-2363
Racing Promoter #15 802-828-2363
Radiologic Technologist #15 802-828-2363
Real Estate Appraiser #12 802-828-3183
Real Estate Broker/Agent #12 802-828-3228
Real Estate Salesperson #12 802-828-3228
School Guidance Counselor #6 802-828-2445
School Librarian/Media Specialist #6... 802-828-2445
School Principal/Superintendent #6 802-828-2445
Securities Broker/Dealer #5 802-828-3420
Securities Sales Rep. #5 802-828-3420
Security Guard #15 802-828-2363
Social Worker, Clinical #15 802-828-2363
Surveyor, Land #15 802-828-3183
Tattoo Artist #15 802-828-2363
Teacher #6 802-828-2445
Vehicle Dealer #11 802-828-2038
Vendor, Itinerant #15 802-828-2363
Veterinarian #15 802-828-2363
Vocational Education Teacher #6 802-828-2445
Waste Water Treatment Plant Operator #1
.... 802-241-3822
Well Driller #1 802-241-3400

Licensing Agency Information

#1 Agency of Natural Resources, Department of Environmental Conservation, 103 S Main St, The Sewing Bldg, Waterbury, VT 05671-0405; 802-241-3822, Fax: 802-241-2596.
www.anr.state.vt.us
Agency email: carolef@dec.anr.state.vt.us.

#2 Board of Bar Examiners, 109 State St, Montpelier, VT 05609-0702; 802-828-3281, Fax: 802-828-3457.
www.state.vt.us/courts
Agency email: joann@supreme.crt.state.vt.us.

#3 Commission of Public Safety, 103 S Main St, Waterbury State Complex, Waterbury, VT 05671-2101; 802-244-8781, Fax: 802-244-1106.

#4 Department of Agriculture, Consumer Assurance, 103 S Main St, Waterbury, VT 05671; 802-244-4510, Fax: 802-241-3008.
www.state.vt.us/agric/pidconsumer.htm

#5 Department of Banking, Securities, Insurance & Health Care Admin., 89 Main St, City Ctr, Drawer 20, Montpelier, VT 05620-3101; 802-828-3301, Fax: 802-828-2896.
www.bishca.state.vt.us

#6 Department of Education, Licening Professional Standards, 120 State St, Montpelier, VT 05620-2501; 802-828-2445, Fax: 802-828-5107.
www.state.vt.us/educ/license

#7 Department of Health, Emergency Medical Services Division, 108 Cherry St, Burlington, VT 05402; 802-863-7310, Fax: 802-863-7577.
www.state.vt.us/health/ems

#8 Department of Labor & Industry, Fire Prevention Division, Drawer 20, National Life Bldg, Montpelier, VT 05620-3401; 802-828-2107, Fax: 802-828-2195.
www.state.vt.us/labind/fpindex.htm

#9 Department of Labor & Industry, Fire Prevention Division - Boiler Inspector, 372 Hurricane Ln #102, Williston, VT 05495-2080; 802-879-2304, Fax: 802-879-2312.
www.state.vt.us/labind/Fire/Boiler.htm. Agency email: malcolm.wheel@labind.state.vt.us.

#10 Department of Liquor Control, PO Drawer 20, Montpelier, VT 05620-4501; 802-828-2339, Fax: 802-828-2803.
www.sec.state.vt.us

#11 Department of Motor Vehicles, 120 State St, Montpelier, VT 05603; 802-828-2114, Fax: 802-828-2092.
www.dmv.state.vt.us

#12 Real Estate Commission, 81 Riverside St. Heritage Bldg, Montpelier, VT 05609-1106; 802-828-3228, Fax: 802-828-2368.
www.sec.state.vt.us
Agency email: real_estate@sec.state.vt.us.

Search database at
www.sec.state.vt.us/seek/lrspseek.htm

#15 Secretary of State, 109 State St, Montpelier, VT 05609; 802-828-2673, Fax: 802-828-5450.
www.vtprofessionals.org
Agency email: Nick@sec.state.vt.us.
Search database at
www.sec.state.vt.us/seek/lrspseek.htm

#16 Lottery Commission, PO Box 420 (379 S Barre Rd), South Barre, VT 05670-0429; 802-479-5686, Fax: 802-479-4294.
www.vtlottery.com

#17 Racing Commission, 128 Merchants Row, Rutland, VT 05701; 802-786-5050, Fax: 802-786-5051.

#18 Alcohol & Drug Abuse Certification Board, PO Box 135, St. Albans, VT 05478-0135; 802-878-7776, Fax: 802-879-6211.
www.vtboard.org/vtboard
Agency email: vadacb@together.net.

#19 Department of Health, Environmental Health, PO Box 70, Burlington, VT 05402; 802-863-7231, Fax: 802-863-7483.
www.state.vt.us/health

Vermont Federal Courts

The following list indicates the district and division name for each county in the state. If the bankruptcy court location is different from the district court, then the location of the bankruptcy court appears in parentheses.

County/Court Cross Reference

Addison	Rutland	Lamoille	Burlington (Rutland)
Bennington	Rutland	Orange	Rutland
Caledonia	Burlington (Rutland)	Orleans	Burlington (Rutland)
Chittenden	Burlington (Rutland)	Rutland	Rutland
Essex	Burlington (Rutland)	Washington	Burlington (Rutland)
Franklin	Burlington (Rutland)	Windham	Rutland
Grand Isle	Burlington (Rutland)	Windsor	Rutland

Standards for Federal Courts: The search fee is $20.00 per item (one party name or case number). Certification fee is $7.00 per document. Copy fee is $.50 per page. All fees standard unless noted in profile. Mail Search: always enclose a stamped self addressed envelope unless otherwise noted. Before releasing records, all courts require prepayment unless noted in profile.

Open records are located at the court unless otherwise noted. District courts index by defendant and plaintiff as well as by case number. Bankruptcy courts usually index by debtor and case number. While most courts now have their indexes on computer, many still maintain index card files as well.

The universal PACER sign-up number is 800-676-6856. Find PACER and the Party/Case Index on the Web at http://pacer.psc.uscourts.gov. PACER dial-up access is $.60 per minute. Also, courts offering internet access via RACER, PACER, Web-PACER or the new CM-ECF charge $.07 per page fee unless noted as free.

US District Court

District of Vermont

Burlington Division Clerk's Office, PO Box 945, Burlington, VT 05402-0945 (Courier Address: Room 506, 11 Elmwood Ave, Burlington, VT 05401), 802-951-6301.

www.vtd.uscourts.gov

Counties: Caledonia, Chittenden, Essex, Franklin, Grand Isle, Lamoille, Orleans, Washington. However, cases from all counties in the state are assigned randomly to either Burlington or Brattleboro. Brattleboro is a hearing location only, not listed here.

Indexing & Storage: Cases are indexed by defendant, plaintiff, and case number. New cases are available in the index 1 working day after filing date. New cases filed January 1, 1991 to present are on the automated in house system. Pre-1991 cases are indexed on microfiche or microfilm. Open records are located at this court.

Fee & Payment Notes: Payment may be made by money order, cashier check, personal check. Payee: Clerk, US District Court. You are allowed to make your own copies. These copies cost $.50 per page.

Phone Search: Only general information which can be accessed by computer will be released over the phone.

In Person Search: In person searching available.

PACER: Toll-free dial-up access: 800-263-9396. Local dial-up access: 802-951-6623. Case records are available back to January 1991. Records are never purged. New records are available online after 1 day.

Other Online Access: Search records on the Internet using the RACER link at www.vtd.uscourts.gov.

Rutland Division PO Box 607, Rutland, VT 05702-0607 (Courier Address: 151 West St, Rutland, VT 05701), 802-773-0245.

www.vtd.uscourts.gov

Counties: Addison, Bennington, Orange, Rutland, Windsor, Windham. However, cases from all counties in the state are randomly assigned to either Burlington or Brattleboro. Rutland is a hearing location only, not listed here.

Indexing & Storage: Cases are indexed by defendant, plaintiff, and case number. New cases are available in the index 1 day after filing date. New cases filed January 1, 1991 to present are on the automated in house system. Pre-1991 cases are indexed on microfiche or microfilm. There is no judge sitting in Rutland itself, but one is in Brattleboro.

Fee & Payment Notes: Payment may be made by money order, cashier check, personal check. Payee: Clerk, US District Court. You are allowed to make your own copies. These copies cost $.50 per page.

Phone Search: Only docket information is available by phone.

In Person Search: In person searching available.

PACER: Toll-free dial-up access: 800-263-9396. Local dial-up access: 802-951-6623. Case records are available back to January 1991. Records are never purged. New records are available online after 1 day.

Other Online Access: Search records on the Internet using the RACER link at www.vtd.uscourts.gov.

US Bankruptcy Court

District of Vermont

Rutland Division PO Box 6648, Rutland, VT 05702-6648 (Courier Address: 67 Merchants Row, Rutland, VT 05701), 802-776-2000, Fax: 802-776-2020.

www.vtb.uscourts.gov

Counties: All counties in Vermont.

Indexing & Storage: Cases are indexed by debtor and creditors as well as by case number. New cases are available in the index immediately after filing date. Open records are located at this court.

Fee & Payment Notes: Payment may be made by money order, cashier check, personal check, Visa or Mastercard. Payee: US Bankruptcy Court.

Phone Search: Docket information is available by phone. An automated voice case information service (VCIS) is available. Call VCIS at 800-260-9956 or 802-776-2007.

Fax Search: Will accept fax searches with credit card. Copy fees apply to faxed dockets.

Mail Search: A stamped self addressed envelope is not required.

In Person Search: In person searching available.

PACER:. Case records are available back to 1992 (limited information prior). Records are never purged. New civil records are available online after 1 day. PACER is available online at http://pacer.vtb.uscourts.gov. Document images available.

Electronic Filing: Information is available online at https://ecf.vtb.uscourts.gov

Vermont County Courts

Court	Jurisdiction	No. of Courts	How Organized
Superior Courts*	General	11	14 Counties
District Courts*	Limited	11	3 Circuits
Combined Courts*		3	
Probate Courts*	Probate	18	
Family Courts	Special	14	14 Counties
Environmental Court	Special	1	

* Profiled in this Sourcebook.

Court	CIVIL								
	Tort	Contract	Real Estate	Min. Claim	Max. Claim	Small Claims	Estate	Eviction	Domestic Relations
Superior Courts*	X	X	X	$0	No Max	$3500		X	
District Courts*									
Probate Courts*							X		
Family Courts									X

Court	CRIMINAL				
	Felony	Misdemeanor	DWI/DUI	Preliminary Hearing	Juvenile
Superior Courts*					
District Courts*	X	X	X	X	
Probate Courts*					
Family Courts					X

ADMINISTRATION Administrative Office of Courts, Court Administrator, 109 State St, Montpelier, VT, 05609-0701; 802-828-3278, Fax: 802-828-3457. www.vermontjudiciary.org

COURT STRUCTURE As of September, 1996, all small claims came under the jurisdiction of Superior Court, the court of general jurisdiction. All counties have a diversion program in which first offenders go through a process that includes a letter of apology, community service, etc. and, after 2 years, the record is expunged. These records are never released.

The Vermont Judicial Bureau has jurisdiction over Traffic, Municipal Ordinance, and Fish and Game, Minors in Possession, and hazing.

ONLINE ACCESS There is no online computer access to the public; however, some courts offer calendar data over the Internet. Supreme Court opinions are maintained by the Vermont Department of Libraries at http://dol.state.vt.us

ADDITIONAL INFORMATION There are statewide certification and copy fees, as follows: Certification Fee - $5.00 per document plus copy fee; Copy Fee - $.25 per page with a $1.00 minimum.

Addison County

Superior Court 7 Mahady Ct, Middlebury, VT 05753; 802-388-7741. Hours: 8:30AM-4:30PM (EST). *Civil, Eviction, Small Claims.*

Civil Records: Access: Mail, in person. Only the court performs in person searches; visitors may not. No search fee. Required to search: name, years to search. Civil cases indexed by defendant, plaintiff. Civil records on index cards and recording books; computer to 1995. **General Information:** No sealed or unserved records released. Turnaround time 2-3 days. Copy fee: $.25 per page. Certification fee: $5.00. Fee payee: Addison

Superior Court. Personal checks accepted. Prepayment is required.

District Court 7 Mahady Ct, Middlebury, VT 05753; 802-388-4237. Hours: 8AM-4:30PM (EST). *Felony, Misdemeanor.*

Criminal Records: Access: Phone, mail, in person. Only the court performs in person searches; visitors may not. Search fee: $1.00 per name. Required to search: name, years to search, DOB. Criminal records on computer since mid 1991; prior on dockets and index cards. **General Information:** No adoptions, juvenile, sealed, or expunged records released. Turnaround time up to 1

week. Copy fee: $.25 per page, $1.00 minimum. Certification fee: $5.00 per document. Fee payee: Addison District Court. Personal checks accepted. Prepayment is required.

Probate Court 7 Mahady Court, Middlebury, VT 05753; 802-388-2612. 8AM-4:30PM (EST). *Probate.*

Bennington County

Superior Court 207 South St, PO Box 4157, Bennington, VT 05201; 802-447-2700; Fax: 802-447-2703. 8AM-4:30PM *Civil, Eviction, Small Claims.*

Civil Records: Access: Phone, mail, in person. Both court and visitors may perform in person searches. No search fee. Required to search: name, years to search. Civil cases indexed by defendant, plaintiff. Civil records on computer from 1989, index from 1968.

General Information: No deposition, adoption, juvenile, sealed or expunged records released. Turnaround time 2-3 days. Copy fee: $.25 per page. Certification fee: $5.00. Fee payee: Bennington County. Personal checks accepted. Prepayment is required.

District Court 200 Veterans Memorial Dr #13, Bennington, VT 05201; 802-447-2727; Fax: 802-447-2750. Hours: 7:45AM-4:30PM *Felony, Misdemeanor.*

Criminal Records: Access: Phone, mail, in person. Both court and visitors may perform in person searches. No search fee. Required to search: name, years to search, DOB. Criminal records on index cards and docket books.

General Information: No sealed, diversion case records released. SASE requested. Turnaround time varies. Copy fee: $.25 per page. $1.00 minimum. Certification fee: $5.00. Fee payee: District Court or Vermont District Court. Personal checks accepted. Prepayment is required.

Probate Court - Bennington District 207 South St, PO Box 65, Bennington, VT 05201; 802-447-2705; Fax: 802-447-2703 (Attn: Probate Court). Hours: 8:30 am-Noon, 1:00-4:30pm (EST). *Probate.*

Probate Court - Manchester District PO Box 446, Manchester, VT 05254; 802-362-1410. Hours: 8AM-Noon, 1-4:20PM (EST). *Probate.*

Caledonia County

Superior Court 1126 Main St #1, St Johnsbury, VT 05819; 802-748-6600; Fax: 802-748-6603. Hours: 8AM-4:30PM (EST). *Civil, Eviction, Small Claims.*

Civil Records: Access: Phone, fax, mail, in person. Only the court performs in person searches; visitors may not. No search fee. Required to search: name, years to search. Civil cases indexed by defendant, plaintiff. Civil records on computer from 1992, in archives before 1985, index from 1985, all other records on index cards.

General Information: No adoption, juvenile, sealed or expunged records released. SASE requested. Turnaround time 1 week. Fax notes: $2.00 per page. Copy fee: Superior Court $1.00 minimum; Family Court $.25 per page, $1.00 minimum. Certification fee: $5.00 plus $.25 per page. Payee: Caledonia Superior Court. Personal checks accepted. Prepayment required.

District Court 1126 Main St #1, St Johnsbury, VT 05819; 802-748-6600; Fax: 802-748-6603. Hours: 8AM-4:30PM (EST). *Felony, Misdemeanor.*

Criminal Records: Access: Fax, mail, in person. Both court and visitors may perform in person searches. No search fee. Required to search: name, years to search; also helpful: DOB. Criminal records on computer since 1991, prior on index cards to 1950.

General Information: Public access terminal is available. No adoptions, juvenile, sealed or expunged records released. SASE not required. Turnaround time less than a week. Fax notes: $2.00 per page. Copy fee: $.25 per page. $1.00 minimum. Certification fee: $5.00. Payee: Caledonia Dist. Court. Personal checks accepted.

Probate Court 27 Main St, PO Box 406, St Johnsbury, VT 05819; 802-748-6605; Fax: 802-748-6603. Hours: 8AM-4:30PM (EST). *Probate.*

Chittenden County

Superior Court 175 Main St.(PO Box 187), Burlington, VT 05402; 802-863-3467. Hours: 8AM-4:30PM (EST). *Civil, Eviction, Small Claims.*

http://vbimail.champlain.edu/superior

Civil Records: Access: Phone, mail, in person. Only the court performs in person searches; visitors may not.

No search fee. Required to search: name, years to search. Civil cases indexed by defendant, plaintiff. Civil records on computer back to 1983, small claims since 1996, prior records on books from 1800s.

General Information: No adoption, juvenile, sealed or expunged records released. Turnaround time 1 week. Fax notes: Will not fax results. Copy fee: $.25 per page. $1.00 minimum. Certification fee: $5.00. Fee payee: Chittenden County Superior Court. Personal checks accepted. Prepayment is required.

District Court 32 Cherry St #300, Burlington, VT 05401; 802-651-1800. Hours: 8AM-4:30PM (EST). *Felony, Misdemeanor.*

Criminal Records: Access: Mail, in person. Both court and visitors may perform in person searches. No search fee. Required to search: name, years to search; also helpful: DOB. Criminal records on new computer from 6/90, on old computer from 6/85 to 06/90, books by alpha name from 12/69 to 1980, on index cards to 1970.

General Information: Public access terminal is available. No adoption, juvenile, sealed or expunged records released. Turnaround time 1-2 days. Copy fee: $.25 per page. Certification fee: $5.00. Fee payee: Vermont District Court. Personal checks accepted. Prepayment is required.

Probate Court PO Box 511, Burlington, VT 05402; 802-651-1518. 8AM-4:30PM (EST). *Probate.*

Essex County

District & Superior Court Box 75, Guildhall, VT 05905; 802-676-3910; Fax: 802-676-3463. Hours: 8AM-4:30PM (EST). *Felony, Misdemeanor, Civil, Eviction, Small Claims.*

www.state.vt.us/courts

Civil Records: Access: Phone, fax, mail, in person. Only the court performs in person searches; visitors may not. No search fee. Required to search: name, years to search. Civil cases indexed by defendant, plaintiff. Civil records indexed from 1974; on computer from 5/94. Calendar information on web site. Will not accept phone requests for more than 2 names.

Criminal Records: Access: Phone, fax, mail, in person. Only the court performs in person searches; visitors may not. No search fee. Required to search: name, years to search, DOB. Criminal records indexed from 1974; on computer from 5/94. Calendar information on web site. Will not accept phone requests for more than 2 names.

General Information: No adoptions, juvenile, sealed or expunged records released. Turnaround time 1 week. Fax notes: $1.00 per page. Copy fee: $.25 per page. $1.00 minimum. Certification fee: $5.00 plus $.25 per page. Fee payee: Depends on court (superior or district). Only cashiers checks and money orders accepted. Prepayment is required.

Probate Court PO Box 426, Island Pond, VT 05846; 802-723-4770; Fax: 802-723-4770. Hours: 8:30AM-Noon, 1-3:30PM (EST). *Probate.*

Franklin County

Superior Court Box 808 Church St, St Albans, VT 05478; 802-524-3863; Fax: 802-524-7996. Hours: 8AM-4:30PM (EST). *Civil, Eviction, Small Claims.*

Civil Records: Access: Phone, fax, mail, in person. Only the court performs in person searches; visitors may not. No search fee. Required to search: name, years to search. Civil cases indexed by defendant, plaintiff. Civil records on computer since 1996; prior on index cards from 1840.

General Information: No adoption, juvenile, sealed or expunged records released. SASE required. Turnaround time 1 week. Fax notes: $2.00 per page. Copy fee: $.25 per page. $1.00 minimum. Certification fee: $5.00. Fee

payee: Franklin Superior Court. Personal checks accepted. Prepayment is required.

District Court 36 Lake St, St Albans, VT 05478; 802-524-7997; Fax: 802-524-7946. Hours: 8AM-4:30PM (EST). *Felony, Misdemeanor.*

Criminal Records: Access: Phone, mail, in person. Both court (time permitting) and visitors may perform in person searches. No search fee. Required to search: name, years to search; also helpful: DOB, SSN. Criminal records on computer since 1987.

General Information: Public access terminal is available. No adoption, juvenile, sealed or expunged records released. Turnaround time 7-10 days. Fax notes: Fee to fax results is $1.00 per document and $.25 per page. Copy fee: $.25 per page. Certification fee: $5.00. Fee payee: Vermont District Court. Personal checks accepted. Prepayment is required.

Franklin Probate Court 17 Church St, St Albans, VT 05478; 802-524-4112. Hours: 8AM-Noon, 1-4:30PM (EST). *Probate.*

Grand Isle County

District & Superior Court PO Box 7, North Hero, VT 05474; 802-372-8350; Fax: 802-372-3221. Hours: 8AM-4:30PM (EST). *Felony, Misdemeanor, Civil, Eviction, Small Claims.*

Civil Records: Access: Phone, fax, mail, in person. Both court and visitors may perform in person searches. No search fee. Required to search: name, years to search. Civil cases indexed by defendant, plaintiff. Civil records on computer from 1990, on index 1940.

Criminal Records: Access: Phone, fax, mail, in person. Both court and visitors may perform in person searches. No search fee. Required to search: name, years to search; also helpful: DOB, SSN. Criminal records on computer from 1990, on index from 1940.

General Information: No adoption, juvenile, sealed or expunged records released. Turnaround time 1-2 days. Fax notes: Do not fax. Copy fee: $.25 per page. $1.00 minimum. Certification fee: $5.00. Fee payee: Grand Isle Superior or District Court. Personal checks accepted. Prepayment is required.

Probate Court PO Box 7, North Hero, VT 05474; 802-372-8350; Fax: 802-372-3221. Hours: 8AM-4:30PM (EST). *Probate.*

Lamoille County

Superior Court Box 490, Hyde Park, VT 05655; 802-888-2207. Hours: 8AM-4:30PM (EST). *Civil, Eviction, Small Claims.*

Civil Records: Access: Mail, in person. Only the court performs in person searches; visitors may not. No search fee. Required to search: name, years to search. Civil cases indexed by defendant, plaintiff. Civil records on computer from 1989, index from 1970s.

General Information: No adoption, juvenile, sealed or expunged records released. SASE required. Turnaround time 1 week. Copy fee: $.25 per page. Certification fee: $5.00. Fee payee: Lamoille Superior Court. Personal checks accepted.

District Court PO Box 489, Hyde Park, VT 05655-0489; 802-888-3887; Fax: 802-888-2591. Hours: 8AM-4:30PM (EST). *Felony, Misdemeanor.*

Criminal Records: Access: Fax, mail, in person. Only the court performs in person searches; visitors may not. No search fee. Required to search: name, DOB; also helpful: years to search. Criminal records on computer since 06/88; prior on index cards.

General Information: No adoption, juvenile, sealed or expunged records released. SASE required. Turnaround time 3 days if record on-site, 1 week if off-site. Fax notes: No fee to fax results. They will only fax returns to toll free calls. Copy fee: $.25 per page. $1.00 minimum.

Certification fee: $5.00. Fee payee: Vermont District Court. Personal checks accepted. Prepayment required.

Probate Court PO Box 102, Hyde Park, VT 05655-0102; 802-888-3306; Fax: 802-888-1347. Hours: 8AM-noon, 12;30-4:30PM (EST). *Probate.*

Orange County

District & Superior Court 5 Court St, Chelsea, VT 05038-9746; 802-685-4870; Fax: 802-685-3246. Hours: 8AM-4:30PM (EST). *Felony, Misdemeanor, Civil, Eviction, Small Claims.*

Civil Records: Access: Fax, mail, in person. Only the court performs in person searches; visitors may not. No search fee. Required to search: name, years to search; also helpful: address. Civil cases indexed by defendant, plaintiff. Civil records on computer from 7/94, on index from 1967.

Criminal Records: Access: Phone, fax, mail, in person. Only the court performs in person searches; visitors may not. No search fee. Required to search: name, years to search, DOB; also helpful: address. Criminal records on computer from 1990, on index from 1967.

General Information: No adoption, juvenile, sealed or expunged records released. Turnaround time 1 week. Fax notes: Fee to fax results is $1.00 per page. Copy fee: $.25 per page. $1.00 minimum. Certification fee: $5.00. Fee payee: Clerk of Court. Personal checks accepted. Prepayment is required.

Probate Court 5 Court Street, Chelsea, VT 05038-9746; 802-685-4610; Fax: 802-685-3246. Hours: 8AM-Noon, 1-4:30PM (EST). *Probate.*

The Bradford and Randolph Districts were consolidated into this one probate court as of June 1, 1994.

Orleans County

Superior Court 247 Main St #1, Newport, VT 05855-1203; 802-334-3344; Fax: 802-334-3385. 8AM-4:30PM (EST). *Civil, Eviction, Small Claims.*

Civil Records: Access: Phone, fax, mail, in person. Only the court performs in person searches; visitors may not. No search fee. Required to search: name; also helpful: years to search. Civil cases indexed by defendant, plaintiff. Civil records on computer since 1994; prior records on index from 1800s.

General Information: No juvenile records released. SASE required. Turnaround time 1 week. Fax notes: $2.00 per page. Copy fee: $.25 per page. $1.00 minimum. Certification fee: $5.00. Fee payee: Orleans Superior Court. Personal checks accepted. Prepayment is required.

District Court 217 Main St, #4, Newport, VT 05855; 802-334-3325. Hours: 8AM-4:30PM (EST). *Felony, Misdemeanor.*

Criminal Records: Access: Phone, mail, in person. Both court and visitors may perform in person searches. No search fee. Required to search: name, years to search, DOB. Criminal records on computer since 01/91; prior on index cards back to 1971. History checks of three or more names must be in writing.

General Information: No adoption, juvenile, sealed or expunged records released. SASE required. Turnaround time 1 week. Fax notes: Will not fax results. Copy fee: $.25 per page. $1.00 minimum; Add $4.00 if copies retrieved from public records. Certification fee: $5.00. Fee payee: District Court of Vermont. Personal checks accepted. Prepayment is required.

Probate Court 247 Main St, Newport, VT 05855; 802-334-3366. 8AM-Noon, 1-4:30PM (EST). *Probate.*

Rutland County

Superior Court 83 Center St, Rutland, VT 05701; 802-775-4394. Hours: 8AM-4:30PM (EST). *Civil, Eviction, Small Claims.*

Civil Records: Access: Mail, in person. Only the court performs in person searches; visitors may not. No search fee. Required to search: name, years to search. Civil cases indexed by defendant, plaintiff. Civil records on computer from 1987, on index from late 1700s.

General Information: No adoption, juvenile, sealed or expunged records released. SASE required. Turnaround time 1 week. Copy fee: $.25 per page. $1.00 minimum. Certification fee: $5.00. Fee payee: Rutland Superior Court. Personal checks accepted. Prepayment required.

District Court 92 State St, Rutland, VT 05701-2886; 802-786-5880. Hours: 8AM-4:30PM (EST). *Felony, Misdemeanor.*

Criminal Records: Access: Phone, mail, in person. Both court and visitors may perform in person searches. No search fee. Required to search: name, years to search, DOB; also helpful: SSN. Criminal records on computer the past 10 years.

General Information: Public access terminal is available. No sealed, expunged records released. SASE required. Turnaround time 1 week. Copy fee: $.25 per page. $1.00 minimum. Certification fee: $5.00. Payee: District Court of Vermont. Personal checks accepted.

Probate Court - Fair Haven District 3 North Park Place, Fair Haven, VT 05743; 802-265-3380. Hours: 8AM-4PM (EST). *Probate.*

Probate Court - Rutland District 83 Center St, Rutland, VT 05701; 802-775-0114. Hours: 8AM-4:30PM (EST). *Probate.*

Washington County

Superior Court 65 State St, Montpelier, VT 05602-3594; 802-828-2091. Hours: 8AM-4:30PM (EST). *Civil, Eviction, Small Claims.*

Civil Records: Access: Phone, mail, in person. Only the court performs in person searches; visitors may not. No search fee. Required to search: name, years to search; also helpful: address. Civil cases indexed by defendant, plaintiff. Civil records on computer from 1987, archives from 1900s.

General Information: No adoption, juvenile or expunged records released. SASE requested. Turnaround time 1-2 days. Copy fee: $.25 per page. $1.00 minimum. Cert fee: $5.00. Fee payee: Washington County Superior Court. Personal checks accepted.

District Court 255 N Main, Barre, VT 05641; 802-479-4252. 8AM-4:30PM *Felony, Misdemeanor.*

Criminal Records: Access: Phone, mail, in person. Both court and visitors may perform in person searches. No search fee. Required to search: name, years to search; also helpful: DOB. Criminal records on computer since 1989; prior records in index form 1970s.

General Information: No adoption, juvenile, sealed or expunged records released. SASE requested. Turnaround time 3-5 days. Copy fee: $.25 per page. $1.00 minimum. Certification fee: $5.00. Fee payee: Washington District Court. Personal checks accepted.

Probate Court 10 Elm Street #2, Montpelier, VT 05602; 802-828-3405. Hours: 8AM-Noon, 1-4:30PM M-Th; 8AM-Noon, 1-4PM F (EST). *Probate.*

Windham County

Superior Court Box 207, Newfane, VT 05345; 802-365-7979; Fax: 802-365-4360. Hours: 9AM-4PM (EST). *Civil, Eviction, Small Claims.*

Civil Records: Access: Phone, fax, mail, in person. Both court and visitors may perform in person searches. No search fee. Required to search: name, years to search. Civil cases indexed by defendant, plaintiff. Civil records on computer from 1994, on index from 1919. Fax available only in emergency.

General Information: No adoption, juvenile, sealed or expunged records released. SASE required. Turnaround time 1-2 days. Fax notes: No fee to fax results. Copy fee: $.25 per page. $1.00 minimum. Certification fee: $5.00. Fee payee: Windham Superior Court. Personal checks accepted. Prepayment is required.

District Court 30 Putney Rd #2, Brattleboro, VT 05301; 802-257-2800; Fax: 802-257-2853. Hours: 8AM-4:30PM (EST). *Felony, Misdemeanor, Civil.*

www.vermontjudiciary.org/courts/district/

Criminal Records: Access: Phone, fax, mail, in person. Both court and visitors may perform in person searches. No search fee. Required to search: name, years to search; also helpful: address, DOB, SSN. Criminal record go back to 1970's; computer since 1990; prior on index cards and docket books.

General Information: Public access terminal is available. No adoption, juvenile, sealed or expunged records released. SASE requested. Turnaround time 5-7 days. Fax notes: Fee to fax results is $.25 per page. Copy fee: $.25 per page. Certification fee: $5.00. Fee payee: Vermont District Court. Personal checks accepted. Prepayment is required.

Probate Court - Marlboro District PO Box 523, Brattleboro, VT 05302; 802-257-2898. Hours: 8AM-Noon, 1-4:30PM (EST). *Probate.*

Probate Court - Westminster District PO Box 47, Bellows Falls, VT 05101-0047; 802-463-3019. Hours: 8AM-Noon,1-4:30PM (EST). *Probate.*

Windsor County

Superior Court Box 458, Woodstock, VT 05091; 802-457-2121; Fax: 802-457-3446. Hours: 8AM-4:30PM (EST). *Civil, Eviction, Small Claims.*

Civil Records: Access: Phone, mail, in person. Only the court performs in person searches; visitors may not. No search fee. Required to search: name, years to search. Civil cases indexed by defendant, plaintiff. Civil records on computer since 1990.

General Information: No adoption, juvenile, sealed or expunged records released. SASE required. Turnaround time 1-2 weeks. Fax notes: $.25 per page. Copy fee: $.25 per page. $1.00 minimum. Certification fee: $5.00. Fee payee: Windsor County Clerk or Windsor Superior Court. Personal checks accepted. Prepayment required.

District Court Windsor Circuit Unit 1, 82 Railroad Row, White River Junction, VT 05001-1962; 802-295-8865. 8AM-4:30PM (EST). *Felony, Misdemeanor.*

Criminal Records: Access: Phone, mail, in person. Only the court performs in person searches; visitors may not. No search fee. Required to search: name, years to search; also helpful: DOB, SSN. Criminal records on computer from 1989, index from 1968.

General Information: No adoption, juvenile, sealed or expunged records released. SASE requested. Turnaround time 7 days. Copy fee: $.25 per page. $1.00 minimum. Cert fee: $5.00. Fee payee: Vermont District Court. Personal checks accepted. Prepayment required.

Probate Court - Hartford District PO Box 275, Woodstock, VT 05091; 802-457-1503; Fax: 802-457-3446. 8AM-Noon, 1-4:30PM (EST). *Probate.*

Probate Court - Windsor District PO Box 402, Rt. 106, Cota Fuel Bldg, North Springfield, VT 05150; 802-886-2284; Fax: 802-886-2285. Hours: 8AM-Noon, 1-4:30PM (EST). *Probate.*

Vermont Recording Offices

ORGANIZATION: 14 counties and 246 towns/cities, 246 recording offices. The recording officer is Town/City Clerk. There is no county administration in Vermont. Many towns are so small that their mailing addresses are in different towns. Four towns/cities have the same name as counties - Barre, Newport, Rutland, and St. Albans. The entire state is in the Eastern Time Zone (EST).

REAL ESTATE RECORDS: Most towns/cities will not perform real estate searches. Copy fees and certification fees vary. Certified copies are generally very expensive at $6.00 per page total. Deed copies usually cost $2.00 flat.

UCC RECORDS: This was a dual filing state until 12/31/94. From 01/01/95, only consumer goods and real estate related collateral were filed with Town/City Clerks. Starting 07/01/2001, only real estate collateral is filed at the local level. Most recording offices will perform UCC searches. Use search request form UCC-11. Search fees are usually $10.00 per name, and copy fees vary.

TAX LIEN RECORDS: All federal and state tax liens on personal property and on real property are filed with the Town/City Clerk in the lien/attachment book and indexed in real estate records. Most towns/cities will not perform tax lien searches.

OTHER LIENS: Mechanics, local tax, judgment, foreclosure.

ONLINE ACCESS: While there is virtually no online access to county recorded documents, state recorded UCC data is available online from the Vermont Secretary of State.

Addison Town

Town Clerk, 7099 VT Rte 22A, Addison, VT 05491. 802-759-2020; Fax 802-759-2233.
Will search UCC records. Will not search real estate records.

Albany Town

Town Clerk, PO Box 284, Albany, VT 05820-0284. 802-755-6100.
Will search UCC records. Will not search real estate records.

Alburg Town

Town Clerk, PO Box 346, Alburg, VT 05440-0346. 802-796-3468; Fax 802-796-3939.
Will search UCC records. Will not search real estate records. **Other Phone Numbers:** Assessor 802-796-4061.

Andover Town

Town Clerk, 953 Weston-Andover Rd., Andover, VT 05143. 802-875-2765; Fax 802-875-6647.
This agency will not search real estate or UCC records. **Other Phone Numbers:** Assessor 802-875-2765.

Arlington Town

Town Clerk, PO Box 304, Arlington, VT 05250. 802-375-2332; Fax 802-375-6474.
Will search UCC records. Will not search real estate records. **Other Phone Numbers:** Assessor 802-375-9022; Treasurer 802-375-1260.

Athens Town

Town Clerk, 56 Brookline Rd., Athens, VT 05143. 802-869-3370; Fax 802-869-3370.
Will search UCC records. Tax liens not included in UCC search. Will not search real estate records. **Other Phone Numbers:** Assessor 802-869-2246.

Bakersfield Town

Town Clerk, Box 203, Bakersfield, VT 05441. 802-827-4495; Fax 802-527-3106.
Will search UCC records.

Baltimore Town

Town Clerk, 1902 Baltimore Rd., Baltimore, VT 05143. 802-263-5419; Fax 802-263-9423.
Will search UCC records. Will not search real estate records.

Barnard Town

Town Clerk, PO Box 274, Barnard, VT 05031-0274. 802-234-9211.
This agency will not perform searches.

Barnet Town

Town Clerk, Box 15, Barnet, VT 05821-0015. 802-633-2256; Fax 802-633-4315.
Will search UCC records. Will not do tax lien searches. Will not search real estate records.

Barre City

Town Clerk, Box 418, Barre, VT 05641. Town Clerk, R/E and UCC Recording 802-476-0242; Fax 802-476-0264.
Will search UCC records. Will not search real estate records. **Other Phone Numbers:** Assessor 802-476-0244; Treasurer 802-476-0242; Appraiser/Auditor 802-476-0244; Elections 802-476-0242; Vital Records 802-476-0242.

Barre Town

Town Clerk, PO Box 124, Websterville, VT 05678-0124. Town Clerk, R/E and UCC Recording 802-479-9391; Fax 802-479-9332.
Will search UCC records. Will not search real estate records. **Other Phone Numbers:** Assessor 802-479-2595; Treasurer 802-479-9391; Appraiser/Auditor 802-479-2595; Elections 802-479-9391; Vital Records 802-479-9391; Town Manager 802-479-9331 802-479-9391.

Barton Town

Town Clerk, PO Box 657, Barton, VT 05822-1386. Town Clerk, R/E and UCC Recording 802-525-6222; Fax 802-525-8856.
Will search UCC records. **Other Phone Numbers:** Assessor 802-525-6222; Treasurer 802-525-6222; Appraiser/Auditor 802-525-6222; Elections 802-525-6222; Vital Records 802-525-6222.

Belvidere Town

Town Clerk, 3996 Vermont Rt 109, Belvidere Center, VT 05492. 802-644-2498.
This agency will not perform searches.

Bennington Town

Town Clerk, 205 South St, Bennington, VT 05201. 802-442-1043; Fax 802-442-1068. www.bennington.com/local.html
Will search UCC records. Will not search real estate records. **Online Access:** Property, Assessor Records. Access to the Grand List search program is available free at www.bennington.com/government/grandlist/index.html. No name searching at this time; site is under construction and data is incomplete. **Other Phone Numbers:** Assessor 802-442-1043; Appraiser/Auditor 802-442-1042.

Benson Town

Town Clerk, PO Box 163, Benson, VT 05731-0163. 802-537-2611; Fax 802-537-2611.
Will search UCC records. Will not search real estate records.

Berkshire Town

Town Clerk, RFD 1, Box 2560, Enosburg Falls, VT 05450. 802-933-2335; Fax 802-933-5913.
Will search UCC records. This agency will not do a tax lien search. Will not search real estate records.

Berlin Town

Town Clerk, 108 Shed Rd., Berlin, VT 05602. Town Clerk, R/E and UCC Recording 802-229-9298.
Will search UCC records. This agency will not do a tax lien search. Will not search real estate records. **Other Phone Numbers:** Assessor 802-229-4880; Treasurer 802-229-9298; Elections 802-229-9298; Vital Records 802-229-9298.

Bethel Town

Town Clerk, RD 2, Box 85, Bethel, VT 05032. Town Clerk, R/E and UCC Recording 802-234-9722; Fax 802-234-6840.
Will search UCC records. Will not search real estate records. **Other Phone Numbers:** Assessor 802-234-9722; Treasurer 802-234-9722; Elections 802-234-9722; Vital Records 802-234-9722.

Bloomfield Town

Town Clerk, PO Box 336, No. Stratford, NH, VT 03590. 802-962-5191; Fax 802-962-5191.
Will search UCC records. Will not search real estate records.

Bolton Town

Town Clerk, RD 1, Box 445, Waterbury, VT 05676. Town Clerk, R/E and UCC Recording 802-434-3064; Fax 802-434-6404.

This agency will not search real estate or UCC records. **Other Phones:** Assessor 802-434-3064; Treasurer 802-434-5075; Appraiser/Auditor 802-434-3064; Elections 802-434-5075; Vital Records 802-434-5075.

Bradford Town

Town Clerk, PO Box 339, Bradford, VT 05033-0339. 802-222-4727; Fax 802-222-3520.

Will search UCC records. Will not search real estate records.

Braintree Town

Town Clerk, RD 1, Box 361A, Randolph, VT 05060. 802-728-9787; Fax 802-728-9787.

Will search UCC records. This agency will not do a tax lien search. Will not search real estate records. **Other Phone Numbers:** Assessor 802-728-9787.

Brandon Town

Town Clerk, 49 Center St, Brandon, VT 05733. Town Clerk, R/E and UCC Recording 802-247-5721; Fax 802-247-5481. www.town.brandon.vt.us

Will search UCC records. Will not search real estate records. **Other Phones:** Assessor 802-247-0226; Treasurer 802-247-5721; Appraiser/Auditor 802-247-0226; Elections 247-5721; Vital Records 247-5721.

Brattleboro Town

Town Clerk, 230 Main St, Brattleboro, VT 05301-2885. 802-254-4541; Fax 802-257-2312. www.brattleboro.org

Will search UCC records. Will not search real estate records. **Other Phone Numbers:** Assessor 802-254-4541 x119.

Bridgewater Town

Town Clerk, PO Box 14, Bridgewater, VT 05034. Town Clerk, R/E and UCC Recording 802-672-3334; Fax 802-672-5395.

Will search UCC records. **Other Phone Numbers:** Assessor 802-672-3334; Treasurer 802-672-3334.

Bridport Town

Town Clerk, Box 27, Bridport, VT 05734-0027. Town Clerk, R/E and UCC Recording 802-758-2483.

Town clerk will perform searches as a private contractor. Will search UCC records. This agency will not do a tax lien search. Will not search real estate records. **Other Phone Numbers:** Assessor 802-758-2483; Treasurer 802-758-2483.

Brighton Town

Town Clerk, PO Box 377, Island Pond, VT 05846. Town Clerk, R/E and UCC Recording 802-723-4405; Fax 802-723-4405.

Will search UCC records. **Other Phone Numbers:** Assessor 802-723-4405; Treasurer 802-723-4405; Appraiser/Auditor 802-723-6672; Elections 802-732-4405; Vital Records 802-732-4405.

Bristol Town

Town Clerk, Box 249, Bristol, VT 05443. 802-453-2486; Fax 802-453-5188.

This agency will not search real estate or UCC records. **Other Phone Numbers:** Assessor 802-453-2486.

Brookfield Town

Town Clerk, PO Box 463, Brookfield, VT 05036-0463. 802-276-3352; Fax 802-276-3926.

Will search UCC records. This agency will not do a tax lien search. Will not search real estate records. **Other Phone Numbers:** Treasurer 802-728-2118.

Brookline Town

Town Clerk, PO Box 403, Brookline, VT 05345. 802-365-4648.

Will search UCC records. This agency will not do a tax lien search. Will not search real estate records. **Other Phone Numbers:** Assessor 802-365-4232.

Brownington Town

Town Clerk, 509 Dutton Brook Ln, Orleans, VT 05860. 802-754-8401; Fax 802-754-8401.

Will search UCC records. UCC search includes tax liens if requested. Real estate owner, mortgage, and property transfer searches available. **Other Phone Numbers:** Treasurer 802-754-6559.

Brunswick Town

Town Clerk, 4495 Vermont Rte. 102, RFD 1, Box 470, Brunswick, VT 05905. Town Clerk, R/E and UCC Recording 802-962-5283.

Will search UCC records. UCC search includes tax liens. Real estate owner, mortgage, and property transfer searches available. **Other Phone Numbers:** Assessor 802-962-3450; Treasurer 802-962-5283; Elections 802-962-5283; Vital Records 802-962-5283.

Burlington City

Town Clerk, City Hall, Room 20, 149 Church St., Burlington, VT 05401. 802-865-7135 R/E Recording: 802-865-7133; Fax 802-865-7014.

Will search UCC records. Will not search real estate records. **Other Phone Numbers:** Assessor 802-865-7111; Treasurer 802-865-7000; Appraiser/Auditor 802-865-7111; Elections 802-865-7136; Vital Records 802-865-7000.

Cabot Town

Town Clerk, PO Box 36, Cabot, VT 05647-0036. Town Clerk, R/E and UCC Recording 802-563-2279; Fax 802-563-2423.

Will search UCC records. Will not search real estate records. **Other Phone Numbers:** Assessor 802-563-2279; Treasurer 802-563-2279; Appraiser/Auditor 802-563-2279; Elections 802-563-2279; Vital Records 802-563-2279.

Calais Town

Town Clerk, 668 W. County Rd., Calais, VT 05648. Town Clerk, R/E and UCC Recording 802-223-5952 UCC Recording: 802-223-5952

802-223-5952.

Will search UCC records. This agency will not do a tax lien search. Will not search real estate records. **Other Phone Numbers:** Assessor 802-223-5952; Treasurer 802-223-5952; Appraiser/Auditor 802-223-5952; Elections 802-223-5952; Vital Records 802-223-5952.

Cambridge Town

Town Clerk, PO Box 127, Jeffersonville, VT 05464. Town Clerk, R/E and UCC Recording 802-644-2251; Fax 802-644-8348.

Will search UCC records. **Other Phone Numbers:** Appraiser/Auditor 802-644-2200; Vital Records 802-644-2251.

Canaan Town

Town Clerk, PO Box 159, Canaan, VT 05903-0159. Town Clerk, R/E and UCC Recording 802-266-3370; Fax 802-266-7085.

Will search UCC records. UCC search includes tax liens if requested. Real estate owner, mortgage, and property transfer searches available. **Other Phone Numbers:** Assessor 802-266-3370; Treasurer 802-266-3370; Appraiser/Auditor 802-266-3370; Elections 802-266-3370.

Castleton Town

Town Clerk, PO Box 727, Castleton, VT 05735. Town Clerk, R/E and UCC Recording 802-468-2212; Fax 802-468-5482.

Will search UCC records. **Other Phone Numbers:** Treasurer 802-468-5319; Appraiser/Auditor 802-468-2751; Elections 802-468-2212; Vital Records 802-468-2212.

Cavendish Town

Town Clerk, PO Box 126, Cavendish, VT 05142-0126. Town Clerk, R/E and UCC Recording 802-226-7292; Fax 802-226-7790.

Will search UCC records. Will not search real estate records. **Other Phone Numbers:** Assessor 802-226-7292; Treasurer 802-226-7292; Appraiser/Auditor 802-226-7292; Elections 802-226-7292; Vital Records 802-226-7292.

Charleston Town

Town Clerk, 5063 Vermont Rt 105, West Charleston, VT 05872-7902. 802-895-2814; Fax 802-895-2814. This agency will not search real estate or UCC records.

Charlotte Town

Town Clerk, PO Box 119, Charlotte, VT 05445-0119. Town Clerk, R/E and UCC Recording 802-425-3071; Fax 802-425-4241.

Will search UCC records. **Other Phone Numbers:** Assessor 802-425-3855; Treasurer 802-425-3071; Appraiser/Auditor 802-425-3855; Elections 802-425-3071; Vital Records 802-425-3071; Planning & Zoning 802-425-3533.

Chelsea Town

Town Clerk, PO Box 266, Chelsea, VT 05038. 802-685-4460; Fax 802-685-4460.

Will search UCC records. UCC search includes tax liens if requested. Real estate owner, mortgage, and property transfer searches available. **Other Phone Numbers:** Assessor 802-685-4460.

Chester Town

Town Clerk, PO Box 370, Chester, VT 05143. 802-875-2173; Fax 802-875-2237. Will search UCC records.

Chittenden Town

Town Clerk, Holden Road, Town Hall, Chittenden, VT 05737. 802-483-6647.

Chittenden is in Rutland County, not Chittenden County. Uninformed secured parties continue to attempt filings at the county level here even though there is no county filing in Vermont. Will search UCC records. This agency will not do a tax lien search. Will not search real estate records. **Other Phone Numbers:** Treasurer 802-483-647.

Clarendon Town

Town Clerk, PO Box 30, North Clarendon, VT 05759-0030. Town Clerk, R/E and UCC Recording 802-775-4274; Fax 802-775-4274.

Will search UCC records. Will not search real estate records. **Other Phone Numbers:** Assessor 802-775-1536; Treasurer 802-775-1536; Appraiser/Auditor 802-775-1536; Elections 802-775-4274; Vital Records 802-775-4274.

Colchester Town

Town Clerk, PO Box 55, Colchester, VT 05446. 802-655-0812 UCC Recording: 802-654-0700; Fax 802-654-0757. www.colchestervt.org

Will search UCC records. Will not search real estate records. **Other Phone Numbers:** Assessor 802-655-0863; Treasurer 802-655-0812; Elections 203-654-0700; Vital Records 203-654-0700.

Concord Town

Town Clerk, PO Box 317, Concord, VT 05824-0317. Town Clerk, R/E and UCC Recording 802-695-2220; Fax 802-695-2220.
Will search UCC records. Will not search real estate records. **Other Phone Numbers:** Assessor 802-695-2220; Treasurer 802-695-2220; Appraiser/Auditor 802-695-2220; Elections 802-695-2220; Vital Records 802-695-2220.

Corinth Town

Town Clerk, PO Box 461, Corinth, VT 05039. Town Clerk, R/E and UCC Recording 802-439-5850; Fax 802-439-5850.
This agency will not search real estate or UCC records. **Other Phone Numbers:** Assessor 802-439-5098; Treasurer 802-439-5850; Elections 802-439-5850; Vital Records 802-439-5850.

Cornwall Town

Town Clerk, 2629 Route 30, Cornwall, VT 05753-9299. 802-462-2775; Fax 802-462-2606.
Will search UCC records. **Other Phone Numbers:** Assessor 802-462-2855.

Coventry Town

Town Clerk, PO Box 104, Coventry, VT 05825. 802-754-2288; Fax 802-754-2288.
Will search UCC records. Will not search real estate records.

Craftsbury Town

Town Clerk, Box 55, Craftsbury, VT 05826. 802-586-2823; Fax 802-586-2823.
Will search UCC records. **Other Phone Numbers:** Assessor 802-586-2835.

Danby Town

Town Clerk, Box 231, Danby, VT 05739-0231. Town Clerk, R/E and UCC Recording 802-293-5136; Fax 802-293-5311.
Will search UCC records. **Other Phone Numbers:** Assessor 802-293-5136; Treasurer 802-293-5136; Appraiser/Auditor 802-293-5136; Elections 802-293-5136; Vital Records 802-293-5136.

Danville Town

Town Clerk, PO Box 183, Danville, VT 05828. 802-684-3352; Fax 802-684-9606.
Will search UCC records. Will not search real estate records.

Derby Town

Town Clerk, PO Box 25, Derby, VT 05829. 802-766-4906; Fax 802-766-2027.
Will search UCC records. Will not search real estate records. **Other Phone Numbers:** Assessor 802-766-4906; Treasurer 802-766-4906; Appraiser/Auditor 802-766-2012; Elections 802-766-4906; Vital Records 802-766-4906.

Dorset Town

Town Clerk, Mad Tom Road, Town Hall, East Dorset, VT 05253. 802-362-1178; Fax 802-362-5156.
Will search UCC records. Will not search real estate records. **Other Phones:** Assessor 802-362-0162.

Dover Town

Town Clerk, PO Box 527, Dover, VT 05356-0527. Town Clerk, R/E and UCC Recording 802-464-5100; Fax 802-464-8721. http://170.222.200.76/dover/
Will search UCC records. Will not search real estate records. **Other Phone Numbers:** Assessor 802-464-8720; Treasurer 802-464-5100; Appraiser/Auditor 802-464-8720; Elections 802-464-5100; Vital Records 802-464-5100.

Dummerston Town

Town Clerk, 1523 Middle Rd., E. Dummerston, VT 05346. 802-257-1496; Fax 802-257-4671.
Will search UCC records. Will not search real estate records.

Duxbury Town

Town Clerk, 3316 Crossett Hill Road, Waterbury, VT 05676. 802-244-6660; Fax 802-244-5442.
This agency will not perform searches.

East Haven Town

Town Clerk, PO Box 10, East Haven, VT 05837-0010. Town Clerk, R/E and UCC Recording 802-467-3772.
Will search UCC records. This agency will not do a tax lien search. Will not search real estate records. **Other Phone Numbers:** Assessor 802-467-3772; Treasurer 802-467-3772; Appraiser/Auditor 802-467-3772; Elections 802-467-3772; Vital Records 802-467-3772.

East Montpelier Town

Town Clerk, PO Box 157, East Montpelier, VT 05651-0157. Town Clerk, R/E and UCC Recording 802-223-3313; Fax 802-223-3314.
Will search UCC records. This agency will not do a tax lien search. Will not search real estate records. **Other Phone Numbers:** Assessor 802-223-3313; Treasurer 802-223-3313; Appraiser/Auditor 802-223-3313; Elections 802-223-3313.

Eden Town

Town Clerk, 71 Old Schoolhouse Rd., Eden Mills, VT 05653. 802-635-2528; Fax 802-635-1724.
Will search UCC records. Will not search real estate records. **Other Phone Numbers:** Assessor 802-635-2528; Vital Records 802-635-2528.

Elmore Town

Town Clerk, PO Box 123, Lake Elmore, VT 05657. 802-888-2637; Fax 802-888-2637.
Will search UCC records. This agency will not do a tax lien search. Will not search real estate records. **Other Phone Numbers:** Assessor 802-888-2637.

Enosburg Town

Town Clerk, PO Box 465, Enosburg Falls, VT 05450. Town Clerk, R/E and UCC Recording 802-933-4421; Fax 802-933-4832.
Will search UCC records. Will not search real estate records. **Other Phones:** Assessor 802-933-4421; Treasurer 802-933-4421; Appraiser/Auditor 802-933-4421; Elections 933-4421; Vital Records 933-4421.

Essex Town

Town Clerk, 81 Main St, Essex Junction, VT 05452. Town Clerk, R/E and UCC Recording 802-879-0413; Fax 802-878-1353. www.essex.org
Will search UCC records. Will not search real estate records. **Other Phone Numbers:** Assessor 802-878-1345; Treasurer 802-879-0413; Appraiser/Auditor 802-878-1345; Elections 802-879-0413; Vital Records 802-879-0413.

Fair Haven Town

Town Clerk, 3 N. Park Place, Fair Haven, VT 05743. 802-265-3610; Fax 802-265-2158.
Will search UCC records. Will not search real estate records. **Other Phones:** Treasurer 802-265-3010.

Fairfax Town

Town Clerk, PO Box 27, Fairfax, VT 05454. Town Clerk, R/E and UCC Recording 802-849-6111.
Will search UCC records. This agency will not do a tax lien search. Will not search real estate records. **Other Phone Numbers:** Assessor 802-849-6111; Treasurer 802-849-6111; Vital Records 802-849-6111.

Fairfield Town

Town Clerk, PO Box 5, Fairfield, VT 05455. 802-827-3261.
Will search UCC records. This agency will not do a tax lien search. Will not search real estate records.

Fairlee Town

Town Clerk, PO Box 95, Fairlee, VT 05045-0095. Town Clerk, R/E and UCC Recording 802-333-4363; Fax 802-333-9214.
Will search UCC records. Will not search real estate records. **Other Phone Numbers:** Assessor 802-333-4363; Treasurer 802-333-4363.

Fayston Town

Town Clerk, 866 N. Fayston Rd., No. Fayston, VT 05660. 802-496-2454.
Will search UCC records. This agency will not do a tax lien search. Will not search real estate records. **Other Phone Numbers:** Assessor 802-496-9849.

Ferrisburgh Town

Town Clerk, PO Box 6, Ferrisburgh, VT 05456-0006. 802-877-3429; Fax 802-877-6757.
Will search UCC records. Will not search real estate records.

Fletcher Town

Town Clerk, 2141 Cambridge Rd, Cambridge, VT 05444. 802-849-6616; Fax 802-849-2500.
Will search UCC records. Will not search real estate records.

Franklin Town

Town Clerk, PO Box 82, Franklin, VT 05457-0082. Town Clerk, R/E and UCC Recording 802-285-2101.
Will search UCC records. This agency will not do a tax lien search. Will not search real estate records. **Other Phone Numbers:** Assessor 802-285-2101; Treasurer 802-285-2101; Appraiser/Auditor 802-285-2101; Elections 802-285-2101; Vital Records 802-285-2101.

Georgia Town

Town Clerk, 47 Town Common Road North, St. Albans, VT 05478. Town Clerk, R/E and UCC Recording 802-524-3524; Fax 802-524-3543.
Will search UCC records. **Other Phone Numbers:** Assessor 802-524-3543; Treasurer 802-524-3524; Appraiser/Auditor 802-524-3543; Elections 802-524-3524; Vital Records 802-524-3524; Town Administrator 802-524-9794.

Glover Town

Town Clerk, 51 Bean Hill, Glover, VT 05839. 802-525-6227 R/E Recording: 802-525-6226 UCC Recording: 802-525-6226; Fax 802-525-6227.
Will search UCC records. Will not search real estate records. **Other Phone Numbers:** Assessor 802-525-6226; Treasurer 802-525-6226; Appraiser/Auditor 802-525-6226; Elections 802-525-6226; Vital Records 802-525-6226.

Goshen Town

Town Clerk, 50 Carlisle Hill Rd., Goshen, VT 05733. 802-247-6455; Fax none.
Will search UCC records. This agency will not do a tax lien search. Will not search real estate records. **Other Phone Numbers:** Assessor 802-247-6455.

Grafton Town

Town Clerk, PO Box 180, Grafton, VT 05146. 802-843-2419.
Will search UCC records. This agency will not do a tax lien search. Will not search real estate records.

Granby Town

Town Clerk, PO Box 56, Granby, VT 05840. 802-328-3611; Fax 802-328-3611.
Will search UCC records. **Other Phone Numbers:** Assessor 802-328-2683.

Grand Isle Town Clerk

Town Clerk, PO Box 49, Grand Isle, VT 05458. 802-372-8830; Fax 802-372-8815.
Will search UCC records. Will not search real estate records.

Granville Town

Town Clerk, PO Box 66, Granville, VT 05747-0066. 802-767-4403; Fax 802-767-3968.
Will search UCC records. This agency will not do a tax lien search. Will not search real estate records. **Other Phone Numbers:** Assessor 802-767-4403.

Greensboro Town

Town Clerk, Box 119, Greensboro, VT 05841. 802-533-2911.
Will search UCC records. This agency will not do a tax lien search. Will not search real estate records.

Groton Town

Town Clerk, 314 Scott Highway, Groton, VT 05046. Town Clerk, R/E and UCC Recording 802-584-3276; Fax 802-584-3276.
Will search UCC records. Will not search real estate records. **Other Phone Numbers:** Assessor 802-584-3276; Treasurer 802-584-3276; Appraiser/Auditor 802-584-3131; Elections 802-584-3276; Vital Records 802-584-3276.

Guildhall Town

Town Clerk, PO Box 10, Guildhall, VT 05905. 802-676-3797; Fax 802-676-3518.
Will search UCC records. Will not search real estate records.

Guilford Town

Town Clerk, 236 School Rd., Guilford, VT 05301-8319. 802-254-6857; Fax 802-257-5764.
Will search UCC records. Will not search real estate records.

Halifax Town

Town Clerk, PO Box 45, West Halifax, VT 05358. 802-368-7390; Fax 802-368-7390.
Will search UCC records. This agency will not do a tax lien search. Will not search real estate records. **Other Phone Numbers:** Treasurer 802-368-7698.

Hancock Town

Town Clerk, PO Box 100, Hancock, VT 05748. 802-767-3660; Fax 802-767-3660.
Will search UCC records. This agency will not do a tax lien search. Will not search real estate records. **Other Phone Numbers:** Assessor 802-767-3301; Treasurer 802-767-3660; Appraiser/Auditor 802-767-3660; Elections 802-767-3660; Vital Records 802-767-3660.

Hardwick Town

Town Clerk, Box 523, Hardwick, VT 05843. Town Clerk, R/E and UCC Recording 802-472-5971; Fax 802-472-6865.
Will search UCC records. Will not search real estate records. **Other Phone Numbers:** Assessor 802-472-5971; Treasurer 802-472-5971; Appraiser/Auditor 802-472-5971; Elections 802-472-5971.

Hartford Town

Town Clerk, 171 Bridge St, White River Junction, VT 05001-1920. Town Clerk, R/E and UCC Recording 802-295-2785; www.hartford-vt.org

Will search UCC records. This agency will not do a tax lien search. Will not search real estate records. **Other Phone Numbers:** Assessor 802-295-9353; Treasurer 802-295-9353; Appraiser/Auditor 802-295-3077; Elections 802-295-2785; Vital Records 802-295-2785.

Hartland Town

Town Clerk, PO Box 349, Hartland, VT 05048-0349. Town Clerk, R/E and UCC Recording 802-436-2444; Fax 802-436-2444.
Will search UCC records. **Other Phone Numbers:** Assessor 802-436-2464; Treasurer 802-436-2464; Elections 802-436-2444; Vital Records 802-436-2444.

Highgate Town

Town Clerk, PO Box 67, Highgate Center, VT 05459. 802-868-4697; Fax none.
This agency will not perform searches. **Other Phone Numbers:** Assessor 802-868-2741.

Hinesburg Town

Town Clerk, PO Box 133, Hinesburg, VT 05461. 802-482-2281; Fax 802-482-5404.
Will search UCC records. Will not search real estate records. **Other Phone Numbers:** Assessor 802-482-3619.

Holland Town

Town Clerk, 120 School Rd., Holland/Derby Line, VT 05830. 802-895-4440; Fax 802-895-4440.
Will search UCC records. Will not search real estate records.

Hubbardton Town

Town Clerk, 1831 Monument Hill Rd, Castleton, VT 05735. 802-273-2951; Fax 802-273-3729.
Will search UCC records. UCC search includes tax liens if requested. Real estate owner, mortgage, and property transfer searches available.

Huntington Town

Town Clerk, 4930 Main Rd., Huntington, VT 05462. Town Clerk, R/E and UCC Recording 802-434-2032; Fax 802-434-4779.
Will search UCC records. This agency will not do a tax lien search. Will not search real estate records. **Other Phone Numbers:** Assessor 802-434-5783; Treasurer 802-434-2032; Appraiser/Auditor 802-434-5783; Elections 802-434-2032; Vital Records 802-434-2032; Administrator 802-434-4779.

Hyde Park Town

Town Clerk, PO Box 98, Hyde Park, VT 05655-0098. Town Clerk, R/E and UCC Recording 802-888-2300; Fax 802-888-6878.
Will search UCC records. **Other Phone Numbers:** Assessor 802-888-2300; Treasurer 802-888-2300; Appraiser/Auditor 802-888-2300; Elections 802-888-2300; Vital Records 802-888-2300.

Ira Town

Town Clerk, 808 Route 133, West Rutland, VT 05777. 802-235-2745 R/E Recording: 802-235-2247 UCC Recording: 802-235-2247.
Will search UCC records. This agency will not do a tax lien search. Will not search real estate records. **Other Phone Numbers:** Assessor 802-235-2247; Treasurer 802-235-2747; Appraiser/Auditor 802-235-2747; Elections 802-235-2747; Vital Records 802-235-2747.

Irasburg Town

Town Clerk, Box 51, Irasburg, VT 05845. 802-754-2242.
Will search UCC records. This agency will not do a tax lien search. Will not search real estate records.

Isle La Motte Town

Town Clerk, PO Box 250, Isle La Motte, VT 05463. 802-928-3434; Fax 802-928-3002.
Will search UCC records. Will not search real estate records.

Jamaica Town

Town Clerk, PO Box 173, Jamaica, VT 05343. 802-874-4681.
Will search UCC records. This agency will not do a tax lien search. Will not search real estate records. **Other Phone Numbers:** Assessor 802-874-4908.

Jay Town

Town Clerk, 1036 Vermont Rte. 242, Jay, VT 05859-9820. 802-988-2996.
Will search UCC records. This agency will not do a tax lien search. Will not search real estate records.

Jericho Town

Town Clerk, PO Box 67, Jericho, VT 05465. Town Clerk, R/E and UCC Recording 802-899-4936; Fax 802-899-5549.
This agency will not search real estate or UCC records. **Other Phone Numbers:** Assessor 802-899-2640; Treasurer 802-899-4936; Appraiser/Auditor 802-899-2640; Elections 802-899-4936; Vital Records 802-899-4936.

Johnson Town

Town Clerk, PO Box 383, Johnson, VT 05656. 802-635-2611; Fax 802-635-9523.
Will search UCC records. Will not search real estate records.

Killington Town

Town Clerk, PO Box 429, Killington, VT 05751-0429. 802-422-3243; Fax 802-422-3030. www.killingtontown.com/staff.htm
Formerly known as the Town of Sherburne. Will search UCC records. Will not search real estate records. **Other Phone Numbers:** Treasurer 802-422-3241.

Kirby Town

Town Clerk, Town of Kirby, 346 Town Hall Rd., Lyndonville, VT 05851-9802. Town Clerk, R/E and UCC Recording 802-626-9386; Fax 802-626-9386.
Will search UCC records. **Other Phone Numbers:** Assessor 802-626-9386; Treasurer 802-626-9386; Appraiser/Auditor 802-626-9386; Elections 802-626-9386; Vital Records 802-626-9386.

Landgrove Town

Town Clerk, Box 508, Londonderry, VT 05148. 802-824-3716; Fax 802-824-3716.
Will search UCC records. Will not search real estate records. **Other Phone Numbers:** Assessor 802-824-3716.

Leicester Town

Town Clerk, 44 Schoolhouse Rd., Leicester, VT 05733. 802-247-5961.
Will search UCC records. This agency will not do a tax lien search. Will not search real estate records.

Lemington Town

Town Clerk, 2549 RIver Rd., VT 102, Lemington, VT 05903. 802-277-4814.
Will not search UCC records. Will not search tax liens. Real estate owner, mortgage, and property transfer searches available.

Lincoln Town

Town Clerk, 62 Quaker St., Lincoln, VT 05443. 802-453-2980; Fax 802-453-2975.
Will search UCC records.

Londonderry Town

Town Clerk, PO Box 118, South Londonderry, VT 05155-0118. 802-824-3356.
Will search UCC records. UCC search includes tax liens if requested. Real estate owner, mortgage, and property transfer searches available.

Lowell Town

Town Clerk, 2170 VT Rt. 100, Lowell, VT 05847-0007. 802-744-6559; Fax 802-744-2357.
This agency will not search real estate or UCC records.

Ludlow Town

Town Clerk, PO Box 307, Ludlow, VT 05149. 802-228-3232; Fax 802-228-8399.
Will search UCC records. Will not search real estate records. **Other Phone Numbers:** Assessor 802-228-7206; Treasurer 802-228-2828; Appraiser/Auditor 802-228-7206; Vital Records 802-228-3232.

Lunenburg Town

Town Clerk, PO Box 54, Lunenburg, VT 05906. Town Clerk, R/E and UCC Recording 802-892-5959 UCC Recording: 802-892-5954; Fax 802-892-5100.
Will search UCC records. This agency will not do a tax lien search. Will not search real estate records. **Other Phone Numbers:** Assessor 802-892-1162; Treasurer 802-892-5954; Appraiser/Auditor 802-892-1162; Elections 802-892-5954; Vital Records 802-892-5954.

Lyndon Town

Town Clerk, PO Box 167, Lyndonville, VT 05851. Town Clerk, R/E and UCC Recording 802-626-5785; Fax 802-626-1265.
Will search UCC records. Will not search real estate records. **Other Phone Numbers:** Assessor 802-626-5785; Treasurer 802-626-5785; Appraiser/Auditor 802-626-5785; Elections 802-626-5785; Vital Records 802-626-5785.

Maidstone Town

Town Clerk, PO Box 118, Maidstone, VT 05905-0118. Town Clerk, R/E and UCC Recording 802-676-3210; Fax 802-676-3210.
Will search UCC records. **Other Phone Numbers:** Elections 802-676-3210; Vital Records 802-676-3210.

Manchester Town

Town Clerk, PO Box 830, Manchester Center, VT 05255. 802-362-1315; Fax 802-362-1315.
Will search UCC records. Will not search real estate records. **Other Phone Numbers:** Assessor 802-362-1373; Treasurer 802-362-1197; Town Manager 802-362-1313; Planning/Zoning 802-362-4824;

Marlboro Town

Town Clerk, PO Box E, Marlboro, VT 05344-0305. 802-254-2181; Fax 802-257-2447.
Will search UCC records. This agency will not do a tax lien search. Will do minor checking on specifically-named records at clerk's discretion.

Marshfield Town

Town Clerk, 122 School St., Room 1, Marshfield, VT 05658. 802-426-3305; Fax 802-426-3045.
Will search UCC records. **Other Phone Numbers:** Assessor 802-426-3798.

Mendon Town

Town Clerk, 34 US Route 4, Mendon, VT 05701. Town Clerk, R/E and UCC Recording 802-775-1662; Fax 802-773-9682.
Will search UCC records. Will not search real estate records. **Other Phone Numbers:** Assessor 802-496-9689; Treasurer 802-775-1662; Elections 802-775-1662; Vital Records 802-775-1662.

Middlebury Town

Town Clerk, Municipal Building, 94 Main St., Middlebury, VT 05753-1334. 802-388-4041 R/E Recording: 802-388-8102 UCC Recording: 802-388-8102.
This agency will not perform searches. **Other Phones:** Assessor 802-388-8108; Treasurer 802-388-8102; Elections 802-388-8102; Vital Records 802-388-8102.

Middlesex Town

Town Clerk, 5 Church St., Middlesex, VT 05602. Town Clerk, R/E and UCC Recording 802-223-5915 UCC Recording: 802-223-5915

802-223-5915; Fax 802-223-0569.
Will search UCC records. Will not search real estate records. **Other Phone Numbers:** Assessor 802-223-5915; Treasurer 802-223-5915; Appraiser/ Auditor 802-223-5915; Elections 802-223-5915; Vital Records 802-223-5915.

Middletown Springs Town

Town Clerk, PO Box 1232, Middletown Springs, VT 05757-1197. 802-235-2220; Fax 802-235-2066.
Will search UCC records. This agency will not do a tax lien search. Will not search real estate records.

Milton Town

Town Clerk, PO Box 18, Milton, VT 05468. 802-893-4111; Fax 802-893-1005. www.miltonvt.org
Will search UCC records. Will not search real estate records. **Other Phone Numbers:** Assessor 802-893-4325; Appraiser/Auditor 802-893-4325.

Monkton Town

Town Clerk, RR 1, Box 2015, North Ferrisburg, VT 05473-9509. Town Clerk, R/E and UCC Recording 802-453-3800.
Will search UCC records. This agency will not do a tax lien search. Will not search real estate records. **Other Phone Numbers:** Assessor 802-453-4515; Treasurer 802-453-3800; Appraiser/Auditor 802-453-3800; Elections 802-453-3800; Vital Records 802-453-3800.

Montgomery Town

Town Clerk, PO Box 356, Montgomery Center, VT 05471-0356. Town Clerk, R/E and UCC Recording 802-326-4719; Fax 802-326-4939.
Will search UCC records. **Other Phone Numbers:** Assessor 802-326-4719; Treasurer 802-326-4719; Appraiser/Auditor 802-326-4719; Elections 802-326-4719; Vital Records 802-326-4719.

Montpelier City

Town Clerk, 39 Main St, City Hall, Montpelier, VT 05602. 802-223-9500; Fax 802-223-9518.
Will search UCC records. **Other Phone Numbers:** Assessor 802-223-9504.

Moretown Town

Town Clerk, PO Box 666, Moretown, VT 05660. 802-496-3645.
Will search UCC records. This agency will not do a tax lien search. Will not search real estate records.

Morgan Town

Town Clerk, PO Box 45, Morgan, VT 05853-0045. 802-895-2927; Fax 802-895-4204.
Will search UCC records. This agency will not do a tax lien search. Will do simple real estate searches.

Morristown Town

Town Clerk, PO Box 748, Morrisville, VT 05661-0748. 802-888-6370; Fax 802-888-6375.
Will search UCC records. Will not search real estate records. **Other Phone Numbers:** Assessor 802-888-6371.

Mount Holly Town

Town Clerk, PO Box 248, Mount Holly, VT 05758. Town Clerk, R/E and UCC Recording 802-259-2391; Fax 802-259-2391.
Will search UCC records. Will not search real estate records. **Other Phone Numbers:** Assessor 802-259-2391; Treasurer 802-259-2391; Appraiser/Auditor 802-259-2391; Elections 802-259-2391; Vital Records 802-259-2391.

New Haven Town

Town Clerk, 78 North St., New Haven, VT 05472. 802-453-3516.
Will search UCC records. Tax liens not included in UCC search. Real estate record owner searches available.

Newark Town

Town Clerk, 1336 Newark St, Newark, VT 05871. 802-467-3336.
This agency will not perform searches.

Newbury Town

Town Clerk, PO Box 126, Newbury, VT 05051. 802-866-5521; Fax 802-866-5301. www.cohase.org
Will search UCC records. UCC search includes tax liens if requested. Real estate owner, mortgage, and property transfer searches available.

Newfane Town

Town Clerk, PO Box 36, Newfane, VT 05345-0036. 802-365-7772; Fax 802-365-7692.
Will search UCC records. Will not search real estate records.

Newport City

Town Clerk, 222 Main St, Newport, VT 05855. Town Clerk, R/E and UCC Recording 802-334-2112; Fax 802-334-2964.
Will search UCC records. Will not search real estate records. **Other Phone Numbers:** Assessor 802-334-6992; Treasurer 802-334-2112; Appraiser/Auditor 802-334-6992; Elections 802-334-2112; Vital Records 802-334-2112.

Newport Town

Town Clerk, PO Box 85, Newport Center, VT 05857. 802-334-6442; Fax 802-334-6442.
Will search UCC records. Will not search real estate records.

North Hero Town

Town Clerk, PO Box 38, North Hero, VT 05474-0038. Town Clerk, R/E and UCC Recording 802-372-6926; Fax 802-372-3806.
Will search UCC records. **Other Phone Numbers:** Assessor 802-372-6926; Treasurer 802-372-6926; Appraiser/Auditor 802-372-6926; Elections 802-372-6926; Vital Records 802-372-6926.

Northfield Town

Town Clerk, 51 S. Main St, Northfield, VT 05663. 802-485-5421; Fax 802-485-8426.
Will search UCC records. **Other Phone Numbers:** Assessor 802-485-6004; Treasurer 802-485-5421; Elections 802-485-5421; Vital Records 802-485-5421.

Norton Town

Town Clerk, PO Box 148, Norton, VT 05907. Town Clerk, R/E and UCC Recording 802-822-9935.
This agency will not perform searches. **Other Phone Numbers:** Treasurer 802-822-9935; Elections 802-822-9935; Vital Records 802-822-9935.

Norwich Town

Town Clerk, PO Box 376, Norwich, VT 05055. 802-649-1419; Fax 802-649-0123.
Will search UCC records. Will not search real estate records. **Other Phone Numbers:** Assessor 802-649-1116.

Orange Town

Town Clerk, PO Box 233, East Barre, VT 05649. 802-479-2673; Fax 802-479-2673.
Will search UCC records. Will not search real estate records.

Orwell Town

Town Clerk, PO Box 32, Orwell, VT 05760-0032. 802-948-2032.
Will search UCC records. UCC search includes tax liens if requested. Will not search real estate records. **Other Phone Numbers:** Assessor 802-948-2032.

Panton Town

Town Clerk, PO Box 174, Vergennes, VT 05491-0174. 802-475-2333; Fax 802-475-2785.
Will search UCC records. This agency will not do a tax lien search. Will not search real estate records. **Other Phone Numbers:** Assessor 802-496-9689.

Pawlet Town

Town Clerk, PO Box 128, Pawlet, VT 05761-0128. Town Clerk, R/E and UCC Recording 802-325-3309 UCC Recording: 802-335-3309; Fax 802-325-6109.
Will search UCC records. Will not search real estate records. **Other Phone Numbers:** Assessor 802-325-3309; Treasurer 802-335-3309; Elections 802-335-3309; Vital Records 802-335-3309.

Peacham Town

Town Clerk, Box 244, Peacham, VT 05862. 802-592-3218.
Will search UCC records. This agency will not do a tax lien search. Will not search real estate records.

Peru Town

Town Clerk, Box 127, Peru, VT 05152. 802-824-3065; Fax 802-824-3065.
Will search UCC records. Will not search real estate records.

Pittsfield Town

Town Clerk, PO Box 556, Pittsfield, VT 05762-0556. 802-746-8170.
Will search UCC records. UCC search includes tax liens if requested. Real estate owner, mortgage, and property transfer searches available. **Other Phone Numbers:** Assessor 802-746-8113; Treasurer 802-746-8050.

Pittsford Town

Town Clerk, PO Box 10, Pittsford, VT 5763. 802-483-2931 R/E Recording: 802-483-2931 x12 UCC Recording: 802-483-2931 x12; Fax 802-483-6612.
Will search UCC records. **Other Phone Numbers:** Assessor 802-483-2275; Treasurer 802-483-2931 x12; Appraiser/Auditor 802-483-2931 x12; Elections 802-483-2931 x12; Vital Records 802-483-2931 x12.

Plainfield Town

Town Clerk, PO Box 217, Plainfield, VT 5667. 802-454-8461; Fax 802-454-8461.
This agency will not search real estate or UCC records.

Plymouth Town

Town Clerk, 68 Town Office Rd., Plymouth, VT 05056. 802-672-3655; Fax 802-672-5466.
This agency will not perform searches. **Other Phone Numbers:** Assessor 802-672-3655.

Pomfret Town

Town Clerk, PO Box 286, North Pomfret, VT 05053. 802-457-3861; Fax none.
This agency will not perform searches. **Other Phone Numbers:** Assessor 802-457-3861; Elections 802-457-3861.

Poultney Town

Town Clerk, 9 Main St., Suite 2, Poultney, VT 05764. 802-287-5761.
Husband and wife considered as one debtor for searching fee computation. Partnership name plus two partner names considered one name on filing for fee computation. See Filing Facts for further clarification. Will search UCC records. This agency will not do a tax lien search. Will not search real estate records. **Other Phone Numbers:** Assessor 802-287-5761.

Pownal Town

Town Clerk, PO Box 411, Pownal, VT 05261. Town Clerk, R/E and UCC Recording 802-823-7757; Fax 802-823-0116.
Will search UCC records. **Other Phone Numbers:** Assessor 802-823-5644.

Proctor Town

Town Clerk, 45 Main St, Proctor, VT 05765. 802-459-3333; Fax 802-459-2356.
Will search UCC records. Will not search real estate records.

Putney Town

Town Clerk, PO Box 233, Putney, VT 05346. 802-387-5862.
Will search UCC records. This agency will not do a tax lien search. Will not search real estate records.

Randolph Town

Town Clerk, Drawer B, Randolph, VT 05060. 802-728-5682; Fax 802-728-5818.
Will search UCC records. Will not search real estate records.

Reading Town

Town Clerk, PO Box 72, Reading, VT 05062. Town Clerk, R/E and UCC Recording 802-484-7250; Fax 802-454-7250.
Will search UCC records. Will not search real estate records. **Other Phone Numbers:** Assessor 802-484-7250; Treasurer 802-484-7250; Appraiser/Auditor 802-484-7250; Elections 802-484-7250; Vital Records 802-484-7250.

Readsboro Town

Town Clerk, PO Box 246, Readsboro, VT 05350. 802-423-5405; Fax 802-423-5423.
Will search UCC records. Will not search real estate records.

Richford Town

Town Clerk, PO Box 236, Richford, VT 05476-0236. Town Clerk, R/E and UCC Recording 802-848-7751; Fax 802-848-7752. www.richfordvt.com
Will search UCC records. Will not search real estate records. **Other Phone Numbers:** Assessor 802-848-7751; Treasurer 802-848-7751; Appraiser/Auditor 802-848-7751; Elections 802-848-7751; Vital Records 802-848-7751.

Richmond Town

Town Clerk, PO Box 285, Richmond, VT 05477. 802-434-2221; Fax 802-434-5570.
Will search UCC records. Will not search real estate records.

Ripton Town

Town Clerk, Box 10, Ripton, VT 05766-0010. 802-388-2266.
This agency will not perform searches. **Other Phone Numbers:** Assessor 802-388-2266.

Rochester Town

Town Clerk, PO Box 238, Rochester, VT 05767-0238. 802-767-3631; Fax 802-767-6028.
Will search UCC records. Will not search real estate records. **Other Phone Numbers:** Assessor 802-767-9872; Treasurer 802-767-3631; Elections 802-767-3631; Vital Records 802-767-3631.

Rockingham Town

Town Clerk, PO Box 339, Bellows Falls, VT 05101-0339. Town Clerk, R/E and UCC Recording 802-463-4336; Fax 802-463-1228.
Will search UCC records. This agency will not do a tax lien search. Will not search real estate records. **Other Phone Numbers:** Assessor 802-463-1229; Treasurer 802-463-3964; Elections 802-463-4336; Vital Records 802-463-4336; Health & Zoning 802-463-3964.

Roxbury Town

Town Clerk, Box 53, Roxbury, VT 05669. Town Clerk, R/E and UCC Recording 802-485-7840; Fax 802-485-7860.
Will search UCC records. **Other Phone Numbers:** Assessor 802-485-7840; Treasurer 802-485-7860; Appraiser/Auditor 802-485-7840; Elections 802-485-7840; Vital Records 802-485-7860.

Royalton Town

Town Clerk, PO Box 680, South Royalton, VT 05068-0680. 802-763-7207; Fax 802-763-7967.
Will search UCC records. Will not search real estate records. **Other Phone Numbers:** Assessor 802-763-2202; Second phone 802-763-7967.

Rupert Town

Town Clerk, Box 140, West Rupert, VT 05776. Town Clerk, R/E and UCC Recording 802-394-7728; Fax 802-394-7728.
Will search UCC records. This agency will not do a tax lien search. Will not search real estate records. **Other Phone Numbers:** Assessor 802-394-7728; Treasurer 802-394-7728; Elections 802-394-7728; Vital Records 802-394-7728.

Rutland City

Town Clerk, PO Box 969, Rutland, VT 05702. 802-773-1801 R/E Recording: 802-773-1800 UCC Recording: 802-773-1800.
Will search UCC records. This agency will not do a tax lien search. Will not search real estate records. **Other Phone Numbers:** Assessor 802-773-1800; Treasurer 802-773-1800; Elections 802-773-1800.

Rutland Town

Town Clerk, PO Box 225, Center Rutland, VT 05736. Town Clerk, R/E and UCC Recording 802-773-2528; Fax 802-773-7295.
Will search UCC records. Will not search real estate records. **Other Phone Numbers:** Assessor 802-773-2528; Treasurer 802-773-2528.

Ryegate Town

Town Clerk, PO Box 332, Ryegate, VT 05042. Town Clerk, R/E and UCC Recording 802-584-3880; Fax 802-584-3880.
Will search UCC records. Will not search real estate records. **Other Phone Numbers:** Assessor 802-584-3880; Treasurer 802-584-3880; Appraiser/Auditor 802-584-3880; Elections 802-584-3880; Vital Records 802-584-3880.

Salisbury Town

Town Clerk, PO Box 66, Salisbury, VT 05769-0066. 802-352-4228; Fax 802-352-9832.
Will search UCC records.

Sandgate Town

Town Clerk, 3266 Sandgate Rd., Sandgate, VT 05250. 802-375-9075; Fax 802-375-8350.
Will search UCC records. This agency will not do a tax lien search. Will not search real estate records. **Other Phone Numbers:** Assessor 802-375-9075; Treasurer 802-375-9075; Appraiser/Auditor 802-375-9075; Elections 802-375-9075; Vital Records 802-375-9075.

Searsburg Town

Town Clerk, PO Box 157, Wilmington, VT 05363. Town Clerk, R/E and UCC Recording 802-464-8081.
Will search UCC records. Tax liens not included in UCC search. Real estate owner, mortgage, and property transfer searches available. **Other Phone Numbers:** Assessor 802-464-8081; Treasurer 802-464-8081; Elections 802-464-8081; Vital Records 802-464-8081.

Shaftsbury Town

Town Clerk, PO Box 409, Shaftsbury, VT 05262. 802-442-4038; Fax 802-442-0955.
Will search UCC records. Will not search real estate records. **Other Phone Numbers:** Assessor 802-442-5740; Treasurer 802-442-6242.

Sharon Town

Town Clerk, PO Box 250, Sharon, VT 05065. 802-763-8268; Fax 802-763-7392.
Will search UCC records. This agency will not do a tax lien search. Will not search real estate records.

Sheffield Town

Town Clerk, Box 165, Sheffield, VT 05866-0165. 802-626-8862.
Will search UCC records. This agency will not do a tax lien search. Will not search real estate records. **Other Phone Numbers:** Assessor 802-626-9273.

Shelburne Town

Town Clerk, PO Box 88, Shelburne, VT 05482. Town Clerk, R/E and UCC Recording 802-985-5116; Fax 802-985-9550.
Will search UCC records. Will not search real estate records. **Other Phone Numbers:** Assessor 802-985-5115; Treasurer 802-985-5116; Elections 802-985-5116; Vital Records 802-985-5116; 802-985-5117.

Sheldon Town

Town Clerk, PO Box 66, Sheldon, VT 05483. 802-933-2524; Fax 802-933-4951.
Will search UCC records. This agency will not do a tax lien search. Real estate record owner searches available.

Shoreham Town

Town Clerk, 297 Main St., Shoreham, VT 05770-9759. Town Clerk, R/E and UCC Recording 802-897-5841; Fax 802-897-2545.
Will search UCC records. This agency will not do a tax lien search. **Other Phone Numbers:** Assessor 802-897-5542; Treasurer 802-897-5841; Vital Records 802-897-5841.

Shrewsbury Town

Town Clerk, 9823 Cold River Rd., Shrewsbury, VT 05738. 802-492-3511; Fax 802-492-3511.
Will search UCC records. Will not search real estate records. **Other Phone Numbers:** Treasurer 802-492-3558.

South Burlington City

Town Clerk, 575 Dorset St, South Burlington, VT 05403. Town Clerk, R/E and UCC Recording 802-846-4105; www.south-burlington.com
Will search UCC records. Will not search real estate records. **Other Phone Numbers:** Assessor 802-846-4103; Treasurer 802-846-4119; Appraiser/Auditor 802-846-4103; Elections 802-846-4105; Vital Records 802-846-4105; Taxes 802-846-4109.

South Hero Town

Town Clerk, PO Box 175, South Hero, VT 05486. Town Clerk, R/E and UCC Recording 802-372-5552.
Will search UCC records. This agency will not do a tax lien search. Will not search real estate records. **Other Phone Numbers:** Assessor 802-372-5552; Treasurer 802-372-5552; Elections 802-372-5552; Vital Records 802-372-5552.

Springfield Town

Town Clerk, 96 Main St, Springfield, VT 05156. Town Clerk, R/E and UCC Recording 802-885-2104; Fax 802-885-1617.
Will search UCC records. **Other Phone Numbers:** Assessor 802-885-2104; Treasurer 802-885-2104.

St. Albans City

Town Clerk, PO Box 867, St. Albans, VT 05478-0867. Town Clerk, R/E and UCC Recording 802-524-1501.
Will search UCC records. This agency will not do a tax lien search. Will not search real estate records. **Other Phone Numbers:** Assessor 802-524-1502; Treasurer 802-524-1501; Appraiser/Auditor 802-524-1502; Elections 802-524-1501; Water/Sewer 802-524-1504; Accounting 802-524-1506;

St. Albans Town

Town Clerk, PO Box 37, St. Albans Bay, VT 05481. 802-524-2415; Fax 802-524-9609.
Will search UCC records. Will not search real estate records. **Other Phones:** Assessor 802-524-7589.

St. George Town

Town Clerk, 1 Barber Rd., St. George, VT 05495. 802-482-5272; Fax 802-482-5548.
Will search UCC records. **Other Phone Numbers:** Assessor 802-496-9689.

St. Johnsbury Town

Town Clerk, 1187 Main St., Suite 2, St. Johnsbury, VT 05819-2288. 802-748-4331; Fax 802-748-1268.
Will search UCC records. Will not search real estate records. **Other Phones:** Assessor 802-748-4272.

Stamford Town

Town Clerk, 986 Main Rd., Stamford, VT 05352-9601. Town Clerk, R/E and UCC Recording 802-694-1361.
Will search UCC records. This agency will not do a tax lien search. Will not search real estate records. **Other Phone Numbers:** Assessor 802-694-1361; Treasurer 802-694-1361; Appraiser/Auditor 802-694-1361; Elections 802-694-1361; Vital Records 802-694-1361.

Stannard Town

Town Clerk, PO Box 94, Greensboro Bend, VT 05842-0094. 802-533-2577.
Will search UCC records. This agency will not do a tax lien search. Will not search real estate records.

Starksboro Town

Town Clerk, PO Box 91, Starksboro, VT 05487-0091. Town Clerk, R/E and UCC Recording 802-453-2639; Fax 802-453-7293.
Will search UCC records. Will not search real estate records. **Other Phone Numbers:** Assessor 802-453-6364; Treasurer 802-453-2639; Elections 802-453-2639; Vital Records 802-453-2639.

Stockbridge Town

Town Clerk, PO Box 39, Stockbridge, VT 05772-0039. 802-234-9371; Fax 802-234-9371.
Will search UCC records. Will not search real estate records. **Other Phone Numbers:** Assessor 802-234-9371.

Stowe Town

Town Clerk, PO Box 248, Stowe, VT 05672. Town Clerk, R/E and UCC Recording 802-253-6133; Fax 802-253-6143.
Will search UCC records. Will not search real estate records. **Other Phone Numbers:** Assessor 802-253-6144; Treasurer 802-253-6133; Appraiser/Auditor 802-253-6144; Elections 802-253-6133; Vital Records 802-253-6133.

Strafford Town

Town Clerk, PO Box 27, Strafford, VT 05072. 802-765-4411; Fax 802-765-9621.
This agency will not perform searches. **Other Phone Numbers:** Assessor 802-765-4411.

Stratton Town

Town Clerk, PO Box 166, West Wardsboro, VT 05360. Town Clerk, R/E and UCC Recording 802-896-6184; Fax 802-896-6630.
Will search UCC records. **Other Phone Numbers:** Assessor 802-896-6184; Treasurer 802-896-6184; Appraiser/Auditor 802-896-6184; Elections 802-896-6184; Vital Records 802-896-6184.

Sudbury Town

Town Clerk, 4694 Route 30, Sudbury, VT 05733. Town Clerk, R/E and UCC Recording 802-623-7296; Fax 802-623-7296.
Will search UCC records. Will do a tax lien search. Will not search real estate records. **Other Phone Numbers:** Assessor 802-623-7296; Treasurer 802-623-7296; Appraiser/Auditor 802-623-7296; Elections 802-623-7296; Vital Records 802-623-7296.

Sunderland Town

Town Clerk, PO Box 295, East Arlington, VT 05252. 802-375-6106.
Will search UCC records. This agency will not do a tax lien search. Will not search real estate records. **Other Phone Numbers:** Assessor 802-362-2284.

Sutton Town

Town Clerk, Box 106, Sutton, VT 05867. 802-467-3377; Fax 802-467-1052.
Will search UCC records.

Swanton Town

Town Clerk, PO Box 711, Swanton, VT 05488. Town Clerk, R/E and UCC Recording 802-868-4421; Fax 802-868-4957.
Will search UCC records. Will not search real estate records. **Other Phone Numbers:** Assessor 802-868-4421; Treasurer 802-868-4421; Appraiser/Auditor 802-868-4421; Elections 802-868-4421; Vital Records 802-868-4421.

Thetford Town

Town Clerk, PO Box 126, Thetford Center, VT 05075-0126. Town Clerk, R/E and UCC Recording 802-785-2922; Fax 802-785-2031.
Will search UCC records. Will not search real estate records. **Other Phone Numbers:** Assessor 802-785-2922 x4927; Treasurer 802-785-2922; Appraiser/Auditor 802-785-2922 x4927; Elections 802-785-2922; Vital Records 802-785-2922.

Tinmouth Town

Town Clerk, 515 North End Rd., Tinmouth, VT 05773. Town Clerk, R/E and UCC Recording 802-446-2498; Fax 802-446-2498.
Will search UCC records. Will not search real estate records. **Other Phone Numbers:** Assessor 802-446-2498; Treasurer 802-446-2498; Appraiser/Auditor 802-446-2498; Elections 802-446-2498; Vital Records 802-446-2498.

Topsham Town

Town Clerk, PO Box 69, Topsham, VT 05076. Town Clerk, R/E and UCC Recording 802-439-5505; Fax 802-439-5505.
This agency will not perform searches. **Other Phone Numbers:** Assessor 802-439-5505; Treasurer 802-439-5505; Elections 802-439-5505; Vital Records 802-439-5505.

Town of Burke

Town Clerk, 212 School St, West Burke, VT 05871. Town Clerk, R/E and UCC Recording 802-467-3717; Fax 802-467-8623.
Will search UCC records. Will not search real estate records. **Other Phone Numbers:** Assessor 802-467-3717; Treasurer 802-467-3717.

Town of Mount Tabor

Town Clerk, PO Box 245, Mt. Tabor, VT 05739. 802-293-5282; Fax 802-293-5287.
Will search UCC records. **Other Phone Numbers:** Treasurer 802-293-5741.

Townshend Town

Town Clerk, PO Box 223, Townshend, VT 05353-0223. 802-365-7300; Fax none.
This agency will not perform searches. **Other Phone Numbers:** Assessor 802-365-7300.

Troy Town

Town Clerk, PO Box 80, North Troy, VT 05859. 802-988-2663; Fax 802-988-2663.
Will search UCC records. UCC search includes tax liens if requested. Will not search real estate records.

Tunbridge Town

Town Clerk, PO Box 6, Tunbridge, VT 05077. Town Clerk, R/E and UCC Recording 802-889-5521; Fax 802-889-3744.
Will search UCC records. Will not search real estate records. **Other Phone Numbers:** Assessor 802-889-5521; Treasurer 802-889-5521; Appraiser/Auditor 802-889-3571; Elections 802-889-5521; Vital Records 802-889-5521.

Underhill Town

Town Clerk, PO Box 32, Underhill, VT 05490. Town Clerk, R/E and UCC Recording 802-899-4434; Fax 802-899-2137.
Will search UCC records. Will not search real estate records. **Other Phone Numbers:** Assessor 802-899-4434; Treasurer 802-899-4434; Appraiser/Auditor 802-899-4434; Elections 802-899-4434; Vital Records 802-899-4434.

Vergennes City

Town Clerk, PO Box 35, Vergennes, VT 05491-0035. Town Clerk, R/E and UCC Recording 802-877-2841; Fax 802-877-1157.
Will not search UCC records. **Other Phone Numbers:** Assessor 802-877-2841; Treasurer 802-877-2841; Appraiser/Auditor 802-877-2841; Elections 802-877-2841; Vital Records 802-877-2841.

Vernon Town

Town Clerk, 567 Governor Hunt Rd., Vernon, VT 05354. Town Clerk, R/E and UCC Recording 802-257-0292; Fax 802-254-3561.
Will search UCC records. Will not search real estate records. **Other Phone Numbers:** Assessor 802-257-0292; Treasurer 802-257-0292; Appraiser/Auditor 802-257-0292; Elections 802-257-0292; Vital Records 802-257-0292.

Vershire Town

Town Clerk, 6894 Vermont Rte. 113, Vershire, VT 05079. Town Clerk, R/E and UCC Recording 802-685-2227.
Will search UCC records. UCC search includes tax liens if requested. Will not search real estate records. **Other Phone Numbers:** Assessor 802-685-2227; Treasurer 802-685-2227.

Victory Town

Town Clerk, PO Box 609, North Concord, VT 05858. 802-328-2400; Fax 802-328-2400.
This agency will not perform searches.

Waitsfield Town

Town Clerk, 9 Bridge St, Bridge St, Waitsfield, VT 05673-0390. 802-496-2218; Fax 802-496-9284.
Will search UCC records. This agency will not do a tax lien search. Will not search real estate records. **Other Phone Numbers:** Assessor 802-496-9689.

Walden Town

Town Clerk, 12 Vt. Rte. 215, West Danville, VT 05873. 802-563-2220; Fax 802-563-3008.
Will search UCC records. This agency will not do a tax lien search. Will not search real estate records.

Wallingford Town

Town Clerk, PO Box 327, Wallingford, VT 05773. 802-446-2336;   Fax   802-446-3174. www.wallingfordvt.com
Will search UCC records. This agency will not do a tax lien search. Will not search real estate records. **Other Phone Numbers:** Assessor 802-446-2336.

Waltham Town

Town Clerk, PO Box 175, Vergennes, VT 05491. 802-877-3641; Fax 802-877-3641.
Will search UCC records. UCC search includes tax liens if requested. Will not search real estate records.

Wardsboro Town

Town Clerk, PO Box 48, Wardsboro, VT 05355-0048. 802-896-6055; Fax 802-896-1000.
Will search UCC records. Will search real estate records. **Other Phone Numbers:** Assessor 802-896-6055.

Warren Town

Town Clerk, PO Box 337, Warren, VT 05674. 802-496-2709; Fax 802-496-2418.
This agency will not perform searches. **Other Phone Numbers:** Assessor 802-496-2709.

Washington Town

Town Clerk, Clerk's Office, Rte. 100, Washington, VT 05675. 802-883-2218.
Will search UCC records. UCC search includes tax liens if requested. Real estate record owner searches available.

Waterbury Town

Town Clerk, 51 S. Main St, Waterbury, VT 05676. Town Clerk, R/E and UCC Recording 802-244-8447; Fax 802-244-1014.

Will search UCC records. Will not search real estate records. **Other Phone Numbers:** Assessor 802-244-8447; Treasurer 802-244-8447; Appraiser/Auditor 802-244-8447; Elections 802-244-8447; Vital Records 802-244-8447.

Waterford Town

Town Clerk, PO Box 56, Lower Waterford, VT 05848. Town Clerk, R/E and UCC Recording 802-748-2122; Fax 802-748-8196.
This agency will not search real estate or UCC records. **Other Phone Numbers:** Assessor 802-748-2122; Treasurer 802-748-2122; Appraiser/Auditor 802-748-2122; Elections 802-748-2122; Vital Records 802-748-2122.

Waterville Town

Town Clerk, PO Box 31, Waterville, VT 05492. Town Clerk, R/E and UCC Recording 802-644-8865; Fax 802-644-8865.
Will search UCC records. Will not search real estate records. **Other Phone Numbers:** Assessor 802-644-8865; Treasurer 802-644-8865; Appraiser/Auditor 802-644-8865; Elections 802-644-8865; Vital Records 802-644-8865.

Weathersfield Town

Town Clerk, PO Box E, Weathersfield, VT 05030-0304. 802-674-2626.
Will search UCC records. This agency will not do a tax lien search. Will not search real estate records. **Other Phone Numbers:** Assessor 802-674-2626.

Wells Town

Town Clerk, PO Box 585, Wells, VT 05774. 802-645-0486; Fax 802-645-0464.
Will search UCC records. UCC search includes tax liens if requested. Will search real estate records. **Other Phone Numbers:** Treasurer 802-645-0188.

West Fairlee Town

Town Clerk, Box 615, West Fairlee, VT 05083. 802-333-9696; Fax 802-333-9611.
This agency will not search real estate or UCC records. **Other Phone Numbers:** Assessor 802-333-9696; Elections 802-333-9696.

West Haven Town

Town Clerk, 2919 Main Rd., Fair Haven, VT 05743-9610. 802-265-4880; Fax 802-265-4880.
Will search UCC records. **Other Phone Numbers:** Assessor 802-265-7996; Treasurer 802-265-3675; Vital Records 802-265-4880.

West Rutland Town

Town Clerk, 35 Marble St., West Rutland, VT 05777. 802-438-2204; Fax 802-438-5133.
Will search UCC records. **Other Phone Numbers:** Assessor 802-438-2263.

West Windsor Town

Town Clerk, Box 6, Brownsville, VT 05037. Town Clerk, R/E and UCC Recording 802-484-7212; Fax 802-484-3518.
Will search UCC records. Will not search real estate records. **Other Phone Numbers:** Assessor 802-484-7212; Treasurer 802-484-7212; Appraiser/Auditor 802-484-7212.

Westfield Town

Town Clerk, 1257 Vermont Rte. 100, Westfield, VT 05874. 802-744-2484; Fax 802-744-2484.
Will search UCC records. UCC search includes tax liens if requested. Will not search real estate records. **Other Phone Numbers:** Assessor 802-744-2484; Treasurer 802-744-2484.

Westford Town

Town Clerk, 1713 Vermont Route 128, Westford, VT 05494. 802-878-4587; Fax 802-879-6503.
Will not search UCC records and tax lien records. Will not search real estate records.

Westminster Town

Town Clerk, PO Box 147, Westminster, VT 05158-0147. 802-722-4091; Fax 802-722-9816.
Will search UCC records. Will not search real estate records. **Other Phone Numbers:** Assessor 802-722-9516; Treasurer 802-722-4091; Appraiser/Auditor 802-722-9516; Elections 802-722-4091; Vital Records 802-722-4091.

Westmore Town

Town Clerk, 54 Hinton Hill Rd., Orleans, VT 05860. 802-525-3007; Fax 802-525-3007.
Will search UCC records. Will not search real estate records.

Weston Town

Town Clerk, PO Box 98, Weston, VT 05161. 802-824-6645; Fax 802-824-4121.
Will search UCC records. Will not search real estate records.

Weybridge Town

Town Clerk, 1727 Quaker Village Rd., Weybridge, VT 05753. Town Clerk, R/E and UCC Recording 802-545-2450; Fax 802-545-2450.
Will search UCC records. Will not search real estate records. **Other Phone Numbers:** Assessor 802-545-2450; Treasurer 802-545-2450; Appraiser/Auditor 802-545-2450; Elections 802-545-2450; Vital Records 802-545-2450.

Wheelock Town

Town Clerk, PO Box 1328, Lyndonville, VT 05851-0428. Town Clerk, R/E and UCC Recording 802-626-9094; Fax 802-626-9094.
Will search UCC records. UCC search includes tax liens if requested. Real estate record owner searches available. **Other Phone Numbers:** Assessor 802-626-8311; Treasurer 802-626-9094; Elections 802-626-9094; Vital Records 802-626-9094.

Whiting Town

Town Clerk, 29 S. Main St., Whiting, VT 05778. Town Clerk, R/E and UCC Recording 802-623-7813.
Will search UCC records. UCC search includes tax liens if requested. Real estate owner, mortgage, and property transfer searches available. **Other Phone Numbers:** Assessor 802-623-7813; Treasurer 802-623-7813.

Whitingham Town

Town Clerk, PO Box 529, Jacksonville, VT 05342. Town Clerk, R/E and UCC Recording 802-368-7887; Fax 802-368-7519.
Will search UCC records. UCC search includes tax liens if requested. Real estate owner, mortgage, and property transfer searches available. **Other Phone Numbers:** Assessor 802-368-2400; Treasurer 802-368-2801; Appraiser/Auditor 802-368-2400; Elections 802-368-7887; Vital Records 802-368-7887.

Williamstown Town

Town Clerk, PO Box 646, Williamstown, VT 05679. 802-433-5455; Fax 802-433-2160.
Will search UCC records as time permits. UCC search includes tax liens if requested. Will not search real estate records. **Other Phone Numbers:** Assessor 802-433-5455.

Williston Town

Town Clerk, 7900 Williston Rd., Williston, VT 05495. 802-878-5121.
St. George is a separate town with a Williston mailing address. Will search UCC records. This agency will not do a tax lien search. Will not search real estate records. **Other Phone Numbers:** Assessor 802-878-1091; Appraiser/Auditor 802-878-1091.

Wilmington Town

Town Clerk, PO Box 217, Wilmington, VT 05363-0217. Town Clerk, R/E and UCC Recording 802-464-5836; Fax 802-464-1238.
Will search UCC records. Will not search real estate records. **Other Phone Numbers:** Assessor 802-464-8591; Treasurer 802-464-8591; Appraiser/Auditor 802-464-8591; Elections 802-464-5836; Vital Records 802-464-5836.

Windham Town

Town Clerk, 5976 Windham Hill Rd, Windham, VT 05039. 802-874-4211; Fax 802-874-4144.
This office's jurisdiction includes ONLY Windham Town; do not confuse Windham Town with Windham County. Will search UCC records. This agency will not do a tax lien search. Will not search real estate records.

Windsor Town

Town Clerk, PO Box 47, Windsor, VT 05089. Town Clerk, R/E and UCC Recording 802-674-5610; Fax 802-674-1017.
Will search UCC records. Will not search real estate records. **Other Phone Numbers:** Assessor 802-674-5414; Treasurer 802-674-6788; Appraiser/Auditor 802-674-5414; Elections 802-674-5610; Vital Records 802-674-5610.

Winhall Town

Town Clerk, Box 389, Bondville, VT 05340. 802-297-2122.
Will search UCC records. This agency will not do a tax lien search. Will not search real estate records. **Other Phone Numbers:** Assessor 802-297-2119; Treasurer 802-297-1994.

Winooski City

Town Clerk, 27 W. Allen St, Winooski, VT 05404. 802-655-6419; Fax 802-655-6414.
Will search UCC records. Will not search real estate records. **Other Phone Numbers:** Assessor 802-655-6410.

Wolcott Town

Town Clerk, PO Box 100, Wolcott, VT 05680-0100. 802-888-2746; Fax 802-888-2746.
Will search UCC records. **Other Phone Numbers:** Assessor 802-888-2746; Treasurer 802-888-2746; Appraiser/Auditor 802-888-6858.

Woodbury Town

Town Clerk, PO Box 123, Woodbury, VT 05681. 802-456-7051.
Will search UCC records. This agency will not do a tax lien search. Will not search real estate records. **Other Phone Numbers:** Assessor 802-456-8836.

Woodford Town

Town Clerk, HRC 65 Box 600, Bennington, VT 05201. 802-442-4895; Fax 802-442-4895.
Will search UCC records. Will not search real estate records.

Woodstock Town

Town Clerk, 31 The Green, Woodstock, VT 05091. 802-457-3611; Fax 802-457-2329.
Will search UCC records. Will not search real estate records. **Other Phone Numbers:** Assessor 802-457-2607.

Worcester Town

Town Clerk, Drawer 161, Worcester, VT 05682-0161. 802-223-6942; Fax 802-229-5216.
Will search UCC records. Will not search real estate records.

Vermont County Locator

You will usually be able to find the city name in the City/County Cross Reference below. In that case, it is a simple matter to determine the county from the cross reference. However, only the official US Postal Service city names are included in this index. There are an additional 40,000 place names that people use in their addresses. Therefore, we have also included a ZIP/City Cross Reference immediately following the City/County Cross Reference.

City/County Cross Reference

ADAMANT Washington
ALBANY Orleans
ALBURG Grand Isle
ARLINGTON Bennington
ASCUTNEY Windsor
AVERILL Essex
BAKERSFIELD Franklin
BARNARD Windsor
BARNET Caledonia
BARRE Washington
BARTON Orleans
BEEBE PLAIN Orleans
BEECHER FALLS Essex
BELLOWS FALLS Windham
BELMONT Rutland
BELVIDERE CENTER Lamoille
BENNINGTON Bennington
BENSON Rutland
BETHEL Windsor
BOMOSEEN Rutland
BONDVILLE Bennington
BRADFORD Orange
BRANDON (05733) Rutland(94),
    Addison(5)
BRATTLEBORO Windham
BRIDGEWATER Windsor
BRIDGEWATER CORNERS Windsor
BRIDPORT Addison
BRISTOL Addison
BROOKFIELD Orange
BROWNSVILLE Windsor
BURLINGTON Chittenden
CABOT (05647) Washington(98),
    Caledonia(1)
CALAIS Washington
CAMBRIDGE (05444) Chittenden(94),
    Franklin(3), Lamoille(2)
CAMBRIDGEPORT Windham
CANAAN Essex
CASTLETON Rutland
CAVENDISH Windsor
CENTER RUTLAND Rutland
CHARLOTTE Chittenden
CHELSEA Orange
CHESTER Windsor
CHESTER DEPOT Windsor
CHITTENDEN Rutland
COLCHESTER Chittenden
CONCORD Essex
CORINTH Orange
COVENTRY Orleans
CRAFTSBURY Orleans
CRAFTSBURY COMMON Orleans
CUTTINGSVILLE Rutland
DANBY Rutland
DANVILLE Caledonia
DERBY Orleans
DERBY LINE Orleans
DORSET Bennington
EAST ARLINGTON Bennington
EAST BARRE (05649) Washington(93),
    Orange(6)
EAST BERKSHIRE Franklin
EAST BURKE Caledonia
EAST CALAIS Washington
EAST CHARLESTON Orleans
EAST CORINTH Orange
EAST DORSET (05253) Bennington(98),
    Rutland(1)
EAST DOVER Windham
EAST FAIRFIELD Franklin

EAST HARDWICK Caledonia
EAST HAVEN Essex
EAST MIDDLEBURY Addison
EAST MONTPELIER Washington
EAST POULTNEY Rutland
EAST RANDOLPH Orange
EAST RYEGATE Caledonia
EAST SAINT JOHNSBURY Caledonia
EAST THETFORD Orange
EAST WALLINGFORD Rutland
EDEN Lamoille
EDEN MILLS Lamoille
ELY Orange
ENOSBURG FALLS Franklin
ESSEX Chittenden
ESSEX JUNCTION Chittenden
FAIR HAVEN Rutland
FAIRFAX (05454) Chittenden(93),
    Franklin(6)
FAIRFIELD Franklin
FAIRLEE Orange
FERRISBURG Addison
FLORENCE Rutland
FOREST DALE Rutland
FRANKLIN Franklin
GAYSVILLE Windsor
GILMAN Essex
GLOVER Orleans
GRAFTON Windham
GRANBY Essex
GRAND ISLE Grand Isle
GRANITEVILLE (05654) Washington(87),
    Orange(12)
GRANVILLE Addison
GREENSBORO Orleans
GREENSBORO BEND Orleans
GROTON Caledonia
GUILDHALL Essex
HANCOCK Addison
HARDWICK Caledonia
HARTFORD Windsor
HARTLAND Windsor
HARTLAND FOUR CORNERS Windsor
HIGHGATE CENTER Franklin
HIGHGATE SPRINGS Franklin
HINESBURG Chittenden
HUNTINGTON Chittenden
HYDE PARK Lamoille
HYDEVILLE Rutland
IRASBURG Orleans
ISLAND POND Essex
ISLE LA MOTTE Grand Isle
JACKSONVILLE Windham
JAMAICA Windham
JEFFERSONVILLE Lamoille
JERICHO Chittenden
JOHNSON Lamoille
JONESVILLE Chittenden
KILLINGTON Rutland
LAKE ELMORE Lamoille
LONDONDERRY Windham
LOWELL Orleans
LOWER WATERFORD Caledonia
LUDLOW Windsor
LUNENBURG Essex
LYNDON Caledonia
LYNDON CENTER Caledonia
LYNDONVILLE Caledonia
MANCHESTER Bennington
MANCHESTER CENTER Bennington
MARLBORO Windham

MARSHFIELD Washington
MC INDOE FALLS Caledonia
MIDDLEBURY Addison
MIDDLETOWN SPRINGS Rutland
MILTON (05468) Chittenden(96),
    Franklin(3)
MONKTON Addison
MONTGOMERY Franklin
MONTGOMERY CENTER (05471)
    Franklin(97), Orleans(2)
MONTPELIER Washington
MORETOWN Washington
MORGAN Orleans
MORRISVILLE Lamoille
MOSCOW Lamoille
MOUNT HOLLY Rutland
NEW HAVEN Addison
NEWBURY Orange
NEWFANE Windham
NEWPORT Orleans
NEWPORT CENTER Orleans
NORTH BENNINGTON Bennington
NORTH CLARENDON Rutland
NORTH CONCORD Essex
NORTH FERRISBURG Addison
NORTH HARTLAND Windsor
NORTH HERO Grand Isle
NORTH HYDE PARK Lamoille
NORTH MONTPELIER Washington
NORTH POMFRET Windsor
NORTH POWNAL Bennington
NORTH SPRINGFIELD Windsor
NORTH THETFORD Orange
NORTH TROY Orleans
NORTHFIELD Washington
NORTHFIELD FALLS Washington
NORTON Essex
NORWICH Windsor
ORLEANS Orleans
ORWELL (05760) Addison(97), Rutland(2)
PASSUMPSIC Caledonia
PAWLET (05761) Rutland(98),
    Bennington(1)
PEACHAM Caledonia
PERKINSVILLE Windsor
PERU Bennington
PITTSFIELD (05762) Rutland(98),
    Windsor(1)
PITTSFORD Rutland
PLAINFIELD Washington
PLYMOUTH Windsor
POST MILLS Orange
POULTNEY Rutland
POWNAL Bennington
PROCTOR Rutland
PROCTORSVILLE Windsor
PUTNEY Windham
QUECHEE Windsor
RANDOLPH Orange
RANDOLPH CENTER Orange
READING Windsor
READSBORO Bennington
RICHFORD Franklin
RICHMOND Chittenden
RIPTON Addison
ROCHESTER (05767) Windsor(98),
    Addison(1)
ROXBURY (05669) Addison(91),
    Washington(7), Orange(1)
RUPERT Bennington
RUTLAND Rutland

SAINT ALBANS Franklin
SAINT ALBANS BAY Franklin
SAINT JOHNSBURY Caledonia
SAINT JOHNSBURY CENTER Caledonia
SALISBURY Addison
SAXTONS RIVER Windham
SHAFTSBURY Bennington
SHARON Windsor
SHEFFIELD Caledonia
SHELBURNE Chittenden
SHELDON Franklin
SHELDON SPRINGS Franklin
SHOREHAM Addison
SOUTH BARRE Washington
SOUTH BURLINGTON Chittenden
SOUTH HERO Grand Isle
SOUTH LONDONDERRY Windham
SOUTH NEWFANE Windham
SOUTH POMFRET Windsor
SOUTH ROYALTON Windsor
SOUTH RYEGATE Caledonia
SOUTH STRAFFORD Orange
SOUTH WOODSTOCK Windsor
SPRINGFIELD Windsor
STARKSBORO Addison
STOCKBRIDGE Windsor
STOWE Lamoille
STRAFFORD Orange
SUTTON Caledonia
SWANTON Franklin
TAFTSVILLE Windsor
THETFORD Orange
THETFORD CENTER Orange
TOWNSHEND Windham
TROY Orleans
TUNBRIDGE Orange
UNDERHILL Chittenden
UNDERHILL CENTER Chittenden
VERGENNES Addison
VERNON Windham
VERSHIRE Orange
WAITSFIELD Washington
WALLINGFORD Rutland
WARDSBORO Windham
WARREN Washington
WASHINGTON Orange
WATERBURY (05676) Washington(98),
    Chittenden(1)
WATERBURY CENTER Washington
WATERVILLE Lamoille
WEBSTERVILLE Washington
WELLS Rutland
WELLS RIVER Orange
WEST BURKE Caledonia
WEST CHARLESTON Orleans
WEST DANVILLE Caledonia
WEST DOVER Windham
WEST DUMMERSTON Windham
WEST FAIRLEE Orange
WEST GLOVER Orleans
WEST HALIFAX Windham
WEST HARTFORD Windsor
WEST NEWBURY Orange
WEST PAWLET (05775) Rutland(97),
    Bennington(2)
WEST RUPERT Bennington
WEST RUTLAND Rutland
WEST TOPSHAM Orange
WEST TOWNSHEND Windham
WEST WARDSBORO Windham
WESTFIELD Orleans

WESTFORD Chittenden
WESTMINSTER Windham
WESTMINSTER STATION Windham
WESTON Windsor
WHITE RIVER JUNCTION Windsor

WHITING (05778) Addison(96), Rutland(3)
WHITINGHAM Windham
WILDER Windsor
WILLIAMSTOWN Orange
WILLIAMSVILLE Windham

WILLISTON Chittenden
WILMINGTON Windham
WINDSOR Windsor
WINOOSKI Chittenden
WOLCOTT Lamoille

WOODBURY Washington
WOODSTOCK Windsor
WORCESTER Washington

ZIP/City Cross Reference

05001-05009 WHITE RIVER JUNCTION	05250-05250 ARLINGTON	05481-05481 SAINT ALBANS BAY	05758-05758 MOUNT HOLLY
05030-05030 ASCUTNEY	05251-05251 DORSET	05482-05482 SHELBURNE	05759-05759 NORTH CLARENDON
05031-05031 BARNARD	05252-05252 EAST ARLINGTON	05483-05483 SHELDON	05760-05760 ORWELL
05032-05032 BETHEL	05253-05253 EAST DORSET	05485-05485 SHELDON SPRINGS	05761-05761 PAWLET
05033-05033 BRADFORD	05254-05254 MANCHESTER	05486-05486 SOUTH HERO	05762-05762 PITTSFIELD
05034-05034 BRIDGEWATER	05255-05255 MANCHESTER CENTER	05487-05487 STARKSBORO	05763-05763 PITTSFORD
05035-05035 BRIDGEWATER CORNERS	05257-05257 NORTH BENNINGTON	05488-05488 SWANTON	05764-05764 POULTNEY
05036-05036 BROOKFIELD	05260-05260 NORTH POWNAL	05489-05489 UNDERHILL	05765-05765 PROCTOR
05037-05037 BROWNSVILLE	05261-05261 POWNAL	05490-05490 UNDERHILL CENTER	05766-05766 MIDDLEBURY
05038-05038 CHELSEA	05262-05262 SHAFTSBURY	05491-05491 VERGENNES	05766-05766 RIPTON
05039-05039 CORINTH	05301-05304 BRATTLEBORO	05492-05492 WATERVILLE	05767-05767 ROCHESTER
05040-05040 EAST CORINTH	05340-05340 BONDVILLE	05494-05494 WESTFORD	05768-05768 RUPERT
05041-05041 EAST RANDOLPH	05341-05341 EAST DOVER	05495-05495 WILLISTON	05769-05769 SALISBURY
05042-05042 EAST RYEGATE	05342-05342 JACKSONVILLE	05601-05633 MONTPELIER	05770-05770 SHOREHAM
05043-05043 EAST THETFORD	05343-05343 JAMAICA	05640-05640 ADAMANT	05772-05772 STOCKBRIDGE
05044-05044 ELY	05344-05344 MARLBORO	05641-05641 BARRE	05773-05773 WALLINGFORD
05045-05045 FAIRLEE	05345-05345 NEWFANE	05647-05647 CABOT	05774-05774 WELLS
05046-05046 GROTON	05346-05346 PUTNEY	05648-05648 CALAIS	05775-05775 WEST PAWLET
05047-05047 HARTFORD	05350-05350 READSBORO	05649-05649 EAST BARRE	05776-05776 WEST RUPERT
05048-05048 HARTLAND	05351-05351 SOUTH NEWFANE	05650-05650 EAST CALAIS	05777-05777 WEST RUTLAND
05049-05049 HARTLAND FOUR CORNERS	05352-05352 READSBORO	05651-05651 EAST MONTPELIER	05778-05778 WHITING
05050-05050 MC INDOE FALLS	05353-05353 TOWNSHEND	05652-05652 EDEN	05819-05819 SAINT JOHNSBURY
05051-05051 NEWBURY	05354-05354 VERNON	05653-05653 EDEN MILLS	05820-05820 ALBANY
05052-05052 NORTH HARTLAND	05355-05355 WARDSBORO	05654-05654 GRANITEVILLE	05821-05821 BARNET
05053-05053 NORTH POMFRET	05356-05356 WEST DOVER	05655-05655 HYDE PARK	05822-05822 BARTON
05054-05054 NORTH THETFORD	05357-05357 WEST DUMMERSTON	05656-05656 JOHNSON	05823-05823 BEEBE PLAIN
05055-05055 NORWICH	05358-05358 WEST HALIFAX	05657-05657 LAKE ELMORE	05824-05824 CONCORD
05056-05056 PLYMOUTH	05359-05359 WEST TOWNSHEND	05658-05658 MARSHFIELD	05825-05825 COVENTRY
05058-05058 POST MILLS	05360-05360 WEST WARDSBORO	05660-05660 MORETOWN	05826-05826 CRAFTSBURY
05059-05059 QUECHEE	05361-05361 WHITINGHAM	05661-05661 MORRISVILLE	05827-05827 CRAFTSBURY COMMON
05060-05060 RANDOLPH	05362-05362 WILLIAMSVILLE	05662-05662 MOSCOW	05828-05828 DANVILLE
05061-05061 RANDOLPH CENTER	05363-05363 WILMINGTON	05663-05663 NORTHFIELD	05829-05829 DERBY
05062-05062 READING	05401-05402 BURLINGTON	05664-05664 NORTHFIELD FALLS	05830-05830 DERBY LINE
05065-05065 SHARON	05403-05403 SOUTH BURLINGTON	05665-05665 NORTH HYDE PARK	05832-05832 EAST BURKE
05067-05067 SOUTH POMFRET	05404-05404 WINOOSKI	05666-05666 NORTH MONTPELIER	05833-05833 EAST CHARLESTON
05068-05068 SOUTH ROYALTON	05405-05406 BURLINGTON	05667-05667 PLAINFIELD	05836-05836 EAST HARDWICK
05069-05069 SOUTH RYEGATE	05407-05407 SOUTH BURLINGTON	05669-05669 ROXBURY	05837-05837 EAST HAVEN
05070-05070 SOUTH STRAFFORD	05439-05439 COLCHESTER	05670-05670 SOUTH BARRE	05838-05838 EAST SAINT JOHNSBURY
05071-05071 SOUTH WOODSTOCK	05440-05440 ALBURG	05671-05671 WATERBURY	05839-05839 GLOVER
05072-05072 STRAFFORD	05441-05441 BAKERSFIELD	05672-05672 STOWE	05840-05840 GRANBY
05073-05073 TAFTSVILLE	05442-05442 BELVIDERE CENTER	05673-05673 WAITSFIELD	05841-05841 GREENSBORO
05074-05074 THETFORD	05443-05443 BRISTOL	05674-05674 WARREN	05842-05842 GREENSBORO BEND
05075-05075 THETFORD CENTER	05444-05444 CAMBRIDGE	05675-05675 WASHINGTON	05843-05843 HARDWICK
05076-05076 EAST CORINTH	05445-05445 CHARLOTTE	05676-05676 WATERBURY	05845-05845 IRASBURG
05077-05077 TUNBRIDGE	05446-05446 COLCHESTER	05677-05677 WATERBURY CENTER	05846-05846 ISLAND POND
05079-05079 VERSHIRE	05447-05447 EAST BERKSHIRE	05678-05678 WEBSTERVILLE	05847-05847 LOWELL
05081-05081 WELLS RIVER	05448-05448 EAST FAIRFIELD	05679-05679 WILLIAMSTOWN	05848-05848 LOWER WATERFORD
05083-05083 WEST FAIRLEE	05449-05449 COLCHESTER	05680-05680 WOLCOTT	05849-05849 LYNDON
05084-05084 WEST HARTFORD	05450-05450 ENOSBURG FALLS	05681-05681 WOODBURY	05850-05850 LYNDON CENTER
05085-05085 WEST NEWBURY	05451-05451 ESSEX	05682-05682 WORCESTER	05851-05851 LYNDONVILLE
05086-05086 WEST TOPSHAM	05452-05453 ESSEX JUNCTION	05701-05702 RUTLAND	05853-05853 MORGAN
05088-05088 WILDER	05454-05454 FAIRFAX	05730-05730 BELMONT	05855-05855 NEWPORT
05089-05089 WINDSOR	05455-05455 FAIRFIELD	05731-05731 BENSON	05857-05857 NEWPORT CENTER
05091-05091 WOODSTOCK	05456-05456 FERRISBURG	05732-05732 BOMOSEEN	05858-05858 NORTH CONCORD
05101-05101 BELLOWS FALLS	05457-05457 FRANKLIN	05733-05733 BRANDON	05859-05859 NORTH TROY
05141-05141 CAMBRIDGEPORT	05458-05458 GRAND ISLE	05734-05734 BRIDPORT	05860-05860 ORLEANS
05142-05142 CAVENDISH	05459-05459 HIGHGATE CENTER	05735-05735 CASTLETON	05861-05861 PASSUMPSIC
05143-05143 CHESTER	05460-05460 HIGHGATE SPRINGS	05736-05736 CENTER RUTLAND	05862-05862 PEACHAM
05144-05144 CHESTER DEPOT	05461-05461 HINESBURG	05737-05737 CHITTENDEN	05863-05863 SAINT JOHNSBURY Ctr
05146-05146 GRAFTON	05462-05462 HUNTINGTON	05738-05738 CUTTINGSVILLE	05866-05866 SHEFFIELD
05148-05148 LONDONDERRY	05463-05463 ISLE LA MOTTE	05739-05739 DANBY	05867-05867 SUTTON
05149-05149 LUDLOW	05464-05464 JEFFERSONVILLE	05740-05740 EAST MIDDLEBURY	05868-05868 TROY
05150-05150 NORTH SPRINGFIELD	05465-05465 JERICHO	05741-05741 EAST POULTNEY	05871-05871 WEST BURKE
05151-05151 PERKINSVILLE	05466-05466 JONESVILLE	05742-05742 EAST WALLINGFORD	05872-05872 WEST CHARLESTON
05152-05152 PERU	05468-05468 MILTON	05743-05743 FAIR HAVEN	05873-05873 WEST DANVILLE
05153-05153 PROCTORSVILLE	05469-05469 MONKTON	05744-05744 FLORENCE	05874-05874 WESTFIELD
05154-05154 SAXTONS RIVER	05470-05470 MONTGOMERY	05745-05745 FOREST DALE	05875-05875 WEST GLOVER
05155-05155 SOUTH LONDONDERRY	05471-05471 MONTGOMERY CENTER	05746-05746 GAYSVILLE	05901-05901 AVERILL
05156-05156 SPRINGFIELD	05472-05472 NEW HAVEN	05747-05747 GRANVILLE	05902-05902 BEECHER FALLS
05158-05158 WESTMINSTER	05473-05473 NORTH FERRISBURG	05748-05748 HANCOCK	05903-05903 CANAAN
05159-05159 WESTMINSTER STATION	05474-05474 NORTH HERO	05750-05750 HYDEVILLE	05904-05904 GILMAN
05161-05161 WESTON	05476-05476 RICHFORD	05751-05751 KILLINGTON	05905-05905 GUILDHALL
05201-05201 BENNINGTON	05477-05477 RICHMOND	05753-05753 MIDDLEBURY	05906-05906 LUNENBURG
	05478-05479 SAINT ALBANS	05757-05757 MIDDLETOWN SPRINGS	05907-05907 NORTON

General Help Numbers:

Governor's Office

Capitol Bldg, 3rd Floor
Richmond, VA 23219
www.governor.state.va.us

804-786-2211
Fax 804-371-6351
8:30AM-5:30PM

Attorney General's Office

900 E Main St
Richmond, VA 23219
www.oag.state.va.us

804-786-2071
Fax 804-786-1991
8:30AM-5PM

State Court Administrator

Administrative Office of Courts
100 N 9th St, 3rd Floor
Richmond, VA 23219
www.courts.state.va.us

804-786-6455
Fax 804-786-4542
8AM-5PM

State Archives

800 E. Broad St
Richmond, VA 23219-8000
www.lva.lib.va.us

804-692-3500
Fax 804-692-3556
9AM-5PM M-SA

State Specifics:

Capital:

Richmond
Richmond City County

Time Zone:

EST

Number of Counties:

95

Population:

7,187,734

Web Site:

www.myvirginia.org

State Agencies

Criminal Records

Virginia State Police, CCRE, PO Box 85076, Richmond, VA 23261-5076 (Courier: 7700 Midlothian Turnpike, Richmond, VA 23235); 804-674-2084, 8AM-5PM.

www.vsp.state.va.us

Note: The state maintains a sexual offender registry at http://sex-offender.vsp.state.va.us/cool-ICE/

Indexing & Storage: Records are available from 1966. It takes 1 to 3 days before new records are available for inquiry. Records are indexed on inhouse computer. 83% of all arrests in database have final dispositions recorded.

Searching: Section 19.2-389 Code of Virginia outlines the non-criminal entities that can receive conviction only records. Certain state agencies may receive complete records. The web site gives complete details. Include the following in your request: full name, date of birth, Social Security Number, sex, race. Turnaround time is 4-6 weeks. The general public and employers not covered by statute must have a signed release form from person of record, including notarized signatures for both subject and requester. These requesters must use form "SP-167" which is downloadable from web site. Certain agencies receive complete records; non-criminal justice entities receive conviction only records.

Access by: mail, online.

Fee & Payment: The fee is $15.00 per name. Statutorily-required fingerprint checks are $13.00; $37 if the FBI fingerpirnt check is also required. Statutorily-required name search only turnaround time is 72 hours. Fee payee: Virginia State Police. Prepayment required. Pay by certified check or money order. MasterCard and Visa are accepted.

Mail search: Turnaround time: 4 to 6 weeks. A self addressed stamped envelope is requested.

Online search: Certain entities, including screening companies, are entitled to online access. The system is ONLY available to IN-STATE accounts. Fees are same as manual submission with exception of required software package purchase. The system is windows oriented, but will not handle networks. The PC user must be a stand alone system. There is a minimum usage requirement of 25 requests per month. Turnaround time is 24-72 hours. Fee is $15.00 per record.

Corporation Records
Limited Liability Company
Records
Fictitious Name
Limited Partnership Records

State Corporation Commission, Clerks Office, PO Box 1197, Richmond, VA 23218-1197 (Courier: Tyler Bldg, 1st Floor, 1300 E Main St, Richmond, VA 23219); 804-371-9733, 804-371-9133 (Fax), 8:15AM-5PM.

www.state.va.us/scc/division/clk/index.htm

Indexing & Storage: Records are available for all active entities on computer. Older inactive records must be researched from the State Library.

Searching: Records are public and are open for inspection. Include the following in your request: full name of business. In addition to the articles of incorporation, corporation records, the following information is available: Annual Reports, Officers, Directors, DBAs, Prior (merged) names, Inactive (back to 1976 on computer) and Reserved names, and Registered Agents.

Access by: mail, phone, fax, in person, online.

Fee & Payment: Plain copies cost $1.00 per page for the first two pages and $.50 for each additional page thereafter. Certification is $3.00. Fee payee: Treasurer of Virginia. Prepayment required. Requesters with billing accounts are encouraged to fax orders. Personal checks accepted. No credit cards accepted.

Mail search: Turnaround time: 3 to 5 days. Be sure to include your phone number and contact person with all written requests. No self addressed stamped envelope is required.

Phone search: No fee for telephone request. Agency will provide only limited information (screen data only) and name availability over the phone.

Fax search: Turnaround time is 3-5 days.

In person search: Information is available via public access terminals. Certificates for Fact and Good Standing are generally available in 1-3 days.

Online search: Their system is called Clerk's Information System and is available at www.state.va.us/scc/division/clk/diracc.htm. There are no fees. A wealth of information is available on this system.

Other access: Magnetic tape purchase is offered to those who wish the entire database.

Trademarks/Servicemarks

State Corporation Commission, Virginia Securities Division, PO Box 1197 (1300 Main St, 9th Fl), Richmond, VA 23218; 804-371-9051, 804-371-9911 (Fax), 8:15AM-5PM.

www.state.va.us/scc/index.html

Indexing & Storage: Records are available from as early as the 1920s. Records are computerized since the 1970s. Records are normally destroyed after they have been inactive for 1 year.

Access by: mail, phone, fax, in person.

Fee & Payment: There is no search fee. The copy fee is $2.00 for the first 2 pages and $.50 each additional page. Fee payee: Treasurer of Virginia.

Prepayment required. Personal checks accepted. No credit cards accepted.

Mail search: Turnaround time: 1 to 2 days.

Phone search: Limited to 1 or 2 searches per call.

Fax search: Fax searching available.

In person search: You may make copies at $.50 per page.

Uniform Commercial Code
Federal Tax Liens

UCC Division, State Corporation Commission, PO Box 1197, Richmond, VA 23218-1197 (Courier: 1300 E Main St, 1st Floor, Richmond, VA 23219); 804-371-9733, 804-371-9744 (Fax), 8:15AM-5PM.

www.state.va.us/scc/division/clk/index.htm

Indexing & Storage: Records are available from the 1960s on microfiche and from mid 1992 on computer.

Searching: Use search request form UCC-11. The search includes federal tax liens on businesses if specifically requested. Federal tax liens on individuals and all state tax liens are filed at the local level, which may be a county or independent city. Include the following in your request: debtor name. Turnaround time for copies of UCC searches is generally 5 days.

Access by: mail, phone, fax, in person, online.

Fee & Payment: Search request - $7.00; copies - $1.00 for each of the first 2 pages and $.50 for each additional page; certification - $1.00. Fee payee: State Corporation Commission. Prepayment required. Personal checks accepted. No credit cards accepted.

Mail search: A self addressed stamped envelope is requested.

Phone search: No fee for telephone request. They will do limited verification on a yes or no basis.

Fax search: Only available to those with billing accounts. Limit of 10 pages on return.

In person search: Cut-off time for same day service for Good Standings and Certificates is 3 PM if research not required.

Online search: Their system is called Clerk's Information System and is available at www.state.va.us/scc/division/clk/diracc.htm. There are no fees. A wealth of information is available on this system.

State Tax Liens
Records not maintained by a state level agency.

Note: All information is found at the local city or county level.

Sales Tax Registrations

Taxation Department, Sales - Taxpayer Assistance, PO Box 1115, Richmond, VA 23218-1115 (Courier: 2220 W Broad St, Richmond, VA 23220); 804-367-8037, 804-786-2670 (Fax), 8:30AM-4:30PM.

www.tax.state.va.us/tax.html

Note: Registration information of businesses is available from the Corporation Commission.

Indexing & Storage: Records are available for three years on computer, then put on microfilm for ten years, then purged.

Searching: This agency will provide no information without a written, signed, notarized authorization from the business itself; they will then provide the business name, address, phone, and tax permit number. Include the following in your request: business name, tax permit number.

Access by: mail.

Mail search: Turnaround time: 1 week to 10 days. No self addressed stamped envelope is required. No fee for mail request.

Birth Certificates

State Health Department, Office of Vital Records, PO Box 1000, Richmond, VA 23218-1000 (Courier: 1601 Willow Lawn Drive, #275, Richmond, VA 23220); 804-662-6200, 804-644-2550 (Fax), 8AM-4:45PM, Closed on major holidays.

www.vdh.state.va.us/vitalrec/f_08.htm

Note: An application for certification may be downloaded from the web site.

Indexing & Storage: Records are available from 1912 on. Records from 1853 to 1896 are located at the State Archives. New records are available for inquiry immediately. Records are indexed on microfiche, inhouse computer.

Searching: Vital records are available to immediate family members only. Birth records are public information 100 years after the date of the event. Include the following in your request: name at birth, date of birth, place of birth, mother's maiden name, father's name, relationship to the person on the certificate. Include your area code and daytime phone number, your return address, and be sure to sign your request and provide copy of ID.

Access by: mail, phone, fax, in person.

Fee & Payment: The fee is $10.00 per certificate. If certificate needs to be authorized, fee is additional $10.00 per authentication. The payee for authentication is the Secretary of the Commonwealth. Fee payee: The State Health Department. Prepayment required. Personal checks accepted. Credit cards accepted: MasterCard, Visa, AmEx, Discover.

Mail search: Turnaround time is 4-6 weeks, unless birth occurred between 1940-1978, then time is 2-5 days. No self addressed stamped envelope is required.

Phone search: You must use a credit card. See Expedited Service.

Fax search: You must use a credit card. See Expedited Service.

In person search: Turnaround time 15 minutes.

Expedited service: Expedited service is available from VitalChek Express Service. Phone 877-572-6333, select option #2. Web site: www.vitalchek.com; e-mail: vitals.reply@vitalchek.com. Turnaround time: 2 - 5 days. Provider: Federal Express $22.50 plus $8.00/1st copy and $8.00 each copy thereafter. Add $10.00 for authentication.

Death Records

State Health Department, Office of Vital Records, PO Box 1000, Richmond, VA 23218-1000 (Courier: 1601 Willow Lawn Drive, #275, Richmond, VA 23220); 804-662-6200, 804-644-2550 (Fax), 8AM-4:45PM, Closed on major holidays.

www.vdh.state.va.us/vitalrec/f_08.htm

Note: An application for certification may be downloaded form web site.

Indexing & Storage: Records are available from 1912 on. Records from 1853 to 1896 are located at the State Archives. New records are available for inquiry immediately. Records are indexed on microfiche, inhouse computer.

Searching: Vital records are available to immediate family members only. Death records are public information 50 years after the date of the event. Include the following in your request: name of deceased, date of death, place of death, relationship to the deceased, reason for the certificate. Include your area code and daytime phone number, your return address, and be sure to sign your requestand provide copy of ID.

Access by: mail, phone, fax, in person.

Fee & Payment: The fee is $10.00 per certificate. Fee payee: The State Health Department. Prepayment required. Personal checks accepted. Credit cards accepted: MasterCard, Visa, AmEx, Discover.

Mail search: Turnaround time: 4 to 6 weeks. No self addressed stamped envelope is required.

Phone search: You must use a credit card. See Expedited Service.

Fax search: You must use a credit card. See Expedited Service.

In person search: Turnaround time 15 minutes.

Expedited service: Expedited service is available from VitalChek Express Service. Phone 877-572-6333, select option #2. Web site: www.vitalchek.com; e-mail: vitals.reply@vitalchek.com. Turnaround time: 2 - 5 days. Provider: Federal Express $22.50 plus $8.00/1st copy and $8.00 each copy thereafter. Add $10.00 for authentication.

Marriage Certificates

State Health Department, Office of Vital Records, PO Box 1000, Richmond, VA 23218-1000 (Courier: 1601 Willow Lawn Drive, #275, Richmond, VA 23220); 804-662-6200, 804-644-2550 (Fax), 8AM-4:45PM, Closed on major holidays.

www.vdh.state.va.us/vitalrec/f_08.htm

Note: An application for certification may be downloaded form web site.

Indexing & Storage: Records are available from 1853 to present. New records are available for inquiry immediately. Records are indexed on microfiche, inhouse computer.

Searching: Vital records are available to immediate family members only. Marriage records are public information 50 years after the date of the event. Include the following in your request: name, date of marriage, place of marriage, relationship to the person on the certificate, reason for the certificate. Include your area code and daytime phone number, your return address, and be sure to sign your request.

Access by: mail, phone, fax, in person.

Fee & Payment: The fee is $8.00 per certificate. If certificate needs to be authorized, fee is additional $10.00 per authentication. The payee for authentication is the Secretary of the Commonwealth. Fee payee: The State Health Department. Prepayment required. Personal checks accepted. Credit cards accepted: MasterCard, Visa, AmEx, Discover.

Mail search: Turnaround time: 4 to 6 weeks. No self addressed stamped envelope is required.

Phone search: You must use a credit card. See Expedited Service.

Fax search: You must use a credit card. See Expedited Service.

In person search: Turnaround time 15 minutes.

Expedited service: Expedited service is available from VitalChek Express Service. Phone 877-572-6333, select option #2. Web site: www.vitalchek.com; e-mail: vitals.reply@vitalchek.com. Turnaround time: 2 - 5 days. Provider: Federal Express $22.50 plus $8.00/1st copy and $8.00 each copy thereafter. Add $10.00 for authentication.

Divorce Records

State Health Department, Office of Vital Records, PO Box 1000, Richmond, VA 23218-1000 (Courier: 1601 Willow Lawn Drive, #275, Richmond, VA 23220); 804-662-6200, 804-644-2550 (Fax), 8AM-4:45PM, Closed on major holidays.

www.vdh.state.va.us/vitalrec/f_08.htm

Note: An application for certification may be downloaded form web site.

Indexing & Storage: Records are available 1918 to present. New records are available for inquiry immediately. Records are indexed on microfiche, inhouse computer.

Searching: Vital records are available to immediate family members only. Divorce records are public information 50 years after the date of the event. Include the following in your request: name, date of divorce, place of divorce, relationship to the person on the certificate, reason for the certificate. Include your area code and daytime phone number, your return address, and be sure to sign your request and provide copy of ID.

Access by: mail, phone, fax, in person.

Fee & Payment: The fee is $10.00 per certificate, plus $10.00 per authentication. The payee for authentication is the Secretary of the Commonweatlh. Fee payee: The State Health Department. Prepayment required. Personal checks accepted. Credit cards accepted: MasterCard, Visa, AmEx, Discover.

Mail search: Turnaround time: 4 to 6 weeks. No self addressed stamped envelope is required.

Phone search: You must use a credit card. See Expedited Service.

Fax search: You must use a credit card. See Expedited Service.

In person search: Turnaround time 15 minutes.

Expedited service: Expedited service is available from VitalChek Express Service. Phone 877-572-6333, select option #2. Webside: www.vitalchek.com; e-mail: vitals.reply@vitalchek.com. Turnaround time: 2 - 5 days. Provider: Federal Express $22.50 plus $8.00/1st copy and $8.00 each copy thereafter. Add $10.00 for authentication.

Workers' Compensation Records

Workers' Compensation Commission, 1000 DMV Dr, Richmond, VA 23220; 804-367-8633, 804-367-9740 (Fax), 8:15AM-5PM.

Indexing & Storage: Records are available from 1977 on. New records are available for inquiry immediately. Records are indexed on microfilm, inhouse computer.

Searching: To receive file copies, you must have a notarized release from the claimant. They will release a "yes or no" answer when presented with a list. Awards issued are public information. Include the following in your request: claimant name, Social Security Number, claim number. All requests must be in writing. The following data is not released: sealed records.

Access by: mail, in person.

Fee & Payment: The search fee is $10.00. No copy fee for first 10 pages, then $.50 per page. Fee payee: Treasurer - State of Virginia. Prepayment required. Personal checks accepted. No credit cards accepted.

Mail search: Turnaround time: 1 to 4 days.

In person search: Request must be in writing.

Accident Reports

Department of Motor Vehicles, Driver Records Work Center, Rm 517, PO Box 27412, Richmond, VA 23269; 804-367-0538, 804-367-0390 (Fax), 8:30AM-5:30PM M-F; 8:30AM-12:30PM S.

www.dmv.state.va.us

Indexing & Storage: Records are available for 40 months to present. Records are indexed on computer.

Searching: All requests must be in writing. Records are only released to those involved or with a tangible interest. Include the following in your request: full name, date of accident, location of accident.

Access by: mail, fax, in person.

Fee & Payment: The fee is $6.00 per report. Fee payee: Department of Motor Vehicles. Prepayment required. Personal checks accepted. Credit cards accepted: MasterCard, Visa.

Mail search: Turnaround time: 5 days.

Fax search: Must pay with a credit card.

In person search: Turnaround time is while you wait, if personnel available.

Driver Records

Motorist Records Services, Attn: Records Request Work Center, PO Box 27412, Richmond, VA 23269; 804-367-0538, 8:30AM-5:30PM M-F; 8:30AM-12:30PM S.

www.dmv.state.va.us

Note: Copies of tickets from non-computerized courts are available at this address for $6.00 per record only to driver or driver's authorized representative. Ticket information from computerized courts must be obtained from each court.

Indexing & Storage: Records are available for 3 years for moving violations & misc convictions, 5 years for speeding & unauthorized use of a motor vehicle, 11 years for 3 reckless driving offenses and DWI, and 24 months from the complied date for suspensions. It takes 12 days from receipt before new records are available for inquiry. Records are indexed on inhouse computer.

Searching: Access to records follows DPPA guidelines. Casual requesters can only obtain records with consent using from CRD93 (formerly form DL93). Include the following in your request: full name, date of birth, sex. Insurance records display 5 years, employment records the last 7 years. Surrendered licenses are purged after 5 years.

Access by: mail, in person, online.

Fee & Payment: The current fee is $6.00 for mail or walk-in requests and $5.00 for online or tape requests. Add $5.00 for certification. Fee payee: Department of Motor Vehicles. Prepayment required. Personal checks accepted. No credit cards accepted.

Mail search: Turnaround time: 5 days. The driver's name, DOB, and sex must "match" to get a record. Request must be on a DMV form or on letterhead. A self addressed stamped envelope is requested.

In person search: Normal turnaround time is while you wait. There are 72 field offices where records can be requested.

Online search: Online service is provided by the Virginia Information Providers Network (VIPNet). Online reports are provided via the Internet on an interactive basis 24 hours daily. There is a $75 annual administrative fee and records are $5.00 each. Go to www.vipnet.org for more information or call 804-786-4718.

Other access: Magnetic tape ordering for batch requests is available from VIPnet. No records are sold for marketing purposes.

Vehicle Ownership
Vehicle Identification

Department of Motor Vehicles, Vehicle Records Work Center, PO Box 27412, Richmond, VA 23269; 804-367-0538, 8:30AM-5:30PM M-F; 8:30AM-12:30PM S.

www.dmv.state.va.us

Note: Lien information is only released to lending institutions, collection agencies, and businesses.

Indexing & Storage: It takes 12 days from receipt before new records are available for inquiry.

Searching: Casual requesters cannot obtain records without consent. High volume requesters must sign an agreement or contract and will be assigned a user number. Records cannot be purchased and resold for marketing purposes. Private investigators who are registered as compliance agents by the Department of Justice Services may obtain address information by submitting a license plate number.

Access by: mail, phone, in person, online.

Fee & Payment: The fee is $6.00 for vehicle ownership and registration information or $6.00 per vehicle on a name search. There is a full charge for a "no record found." Add $5.00 for verification. Fee payee: Department of Motor Vehicles. Prepayment required. Personal checks accepted. No credit cards accepted.

Mail search: Turnaround time: 5 days. A self addressed stamped envelope is requested.

Phone search: Phone requesting is available for pre-approved accounts. There is a limit of 5 requests a day.

In person search: Turnaround time: while you wait, usually limited to five at one time.

Online search: The online system, managed by the Virginia Information Providers Network (VIPNet), is an interactive system open 24 hours daily. There is an annual $75.00 administration fee and records are $5.00 each. All accounts must be approved by both the DMV and VIPNet. Call 804-786-4718 to request an information use agreement application. The URL is www.vipnet.org

Other access: Bulk release of vehicle or ownership information is not available except for statistical and vehicle recall purposes.

Vessel Ownership
Vessel Registration

Game & Inland Fisheries Dept, 4010 W Broad St, Richmond, VA 23230; 804-367-6135, 877-898-2628, 804-367-1064 (Fax), 8:15AM-5PM.

www.dgif.state.va.us

Indexing & Storage: Records are available from 1960 to the present. Records are indexed on computer from 1984 to the present. All motorized boats must be registered. All motorboats, or sailboats if over 18 ft are titled. Lien information will show on record.

Searching: All requests must be in writing. One of the following is required for a search: name, SSN, title #, hull #.

Access by: mail, in person, online.

Fee & Payment: If history or extensive research is required, there is a fee of $15.00 per boat. For simple record searches there is no fee, unless over 5 records are requested then the fee is $5.00 per record. Fee payee: Game & Inland Fisheries Dept. Prepayment required. No credit cards accepted.

Mail search: Turnaround time: 3 to 4 working days. No self addressed stamped envelope is required.

In person search: Turnaround time is usually immediate.

Online search: The VA boat registration database may be searched on the web at www.vipnet.org. There is both a free service and a more advanced pay service, but both require a subscription which is $75.00 a year. Other motor vehicle records are available.

Legislation Records

House of Delegates, Information & Public Relations, PO Box 406, Richmond, VA 23218 (Courier: 1st Floor, State Capitol Bldg, 9th and Grace Streets, Richmond, VA 23219); 804-698-1500, 877-391-3228 (Toll Free), 804-786-3215 (Fax), 8AM-5PM.

http://legis.state.va.us/

Indexing & Storage: Records are available from 1994 on computer. Final disposition reports and patron reports are on microfiche from 1975 to 1996.

Searching: A request in writing to the Clerk of the House of Delegates is necessary to obtain a member's voting record and statements of economic interests. Include the following in your request: bill number, topic of bill, year. The name of the bill sponsor (patron) and topic of bill are helpful.

Access by: mail, phone, in person, online.

Fee & Payment: There is no search fee. The copy fee is $.50 per page over 10 and additional charges for other records. Fee payee: Treasurer of Virginia. Personal checks accepted. No credit cards accepted.

Mail search: Turnaround time: 1 to 2 days. No self addressed stamped envelope is required.

Phone search: Records are available by phone.

In person search: Searching is available in person.

Online search: Information can be found on the web site. There is no fee.

Other access: Lists of General Assembly members, information on General Assembly, documents summarizing bills introduced and enacted are all available through this office.

Voter Registration
Access to Records is Restricted

State Board of Elections, 200 N 9th Street, #101, Richmond, VA 23219; 804-786-6551, 804-371-0194 (Fax), 8:30AM-5PM.

www.sbe.state.va.us

Note: Individual searches must be done at the county or city level with the General Registrars. The state will sell all or portions of its statewide database (95 counties, 40 cities) to organizations promoting voter registration and participation.

GED Certificates

Virginia Dept of Education, GED Services, PO Box 2120, Richmond, VA 23218-2120; 804-225-2075, 804-786-7243 (Fax), 8:15AM-5PM.

www.pen.k12.va.us

Indexing & Storage: Records are available from 1942. It takes 6 weeks before new records are available for inquiry.

Searching: To search, all of the following is required: a signed release, name, DOB, SSN, and year of test.

Access by: mail, fax, in person.

Fee & Payment: There is a $5.00 fee for a verification or for a transcript. Add $5.00 for certification. Fee payee: VA Department of Education - GED Srvs. Prepayment required. Only money orders and cashier's checks are accepted. No credit cards accepted.

Mail search: Turnaround time: 5 to 10 days. No self addressed stamped envelope is required.

Fax search: Same criteria as mail searching.

In person search: Turnaround time is typically immediate.

Hunting License Information
Fishing License Information
Records not maintained by a state level agency.

Note: They do not have a central database.

Virginia State Licensing Agencies

Licenses Searchable Online

Accountant/Accounting Firm/Sponsor #10..............www.boa.state.va.us/
Acupuncturist #6...www.vipnet.org/dhp/cgi-bin/search_publicdb.cgi
Air Conditioning Contractor #10..............................www.dpor.state.va.us/regulantlookup/
Architect #10...www.dpor.state.va.us/regulantlookup/
Asbestos Related Occupation #10...........................www.dpor.state.va.us/regulantlookup/
Auctioneer/Auction Company #10 ....www.dpor.state.va.us/regulantlookup/
Barber/Barber School/Business #10.......................www.dpor.state.va.us/regulantlookup/
Boxer #10..www.dpor.state.va.us/regulantlookup/
Carpenter #10..www.dpor.state.va.us/regulantlookup/
Cemetery #10...www.dpor.state.va.us/regulantlookup/
Cemetery Company #10..www.dpor.state.va.us/regulantlookup/
Cemetery Seller #10..www.dpor.state.va.us/regulantlookup/
Chiropractor #6..www.vipnet.org/dhp/cgi-bin/search_publicdb.cgi
Clinical Nurse Specialist #6 ....www.vipnet.org/dhp/cgi-bin/search_publicdb.cgi
Contractor #10...www.dpor.state.va.us/regulantlookup/
Cosmetologist/Cosmetology School/Entity #10........www.dpor.state.va.us/regulantlookup/
Dental Hygienist #6...www.vipnet.org/dhp/cgi-bin/search_publicdb.cgi
Dentist #6...www.vipnet.org/dhp/cgi-bin/search_publicdb.cgi
Electrical Contractor #10 ....www.dpor.state.va.us/regulantlookup/
Embalmer #6 ....www.vipnet.org/dhp/cgi-bin/search_publicdb.cgi
Engineer #10 ....www.dpor.state.va.us/regulantlookup/
Funeral Director #6..www.vipnet.org/dhp/cgi-bin/search_publicdb.cgi
Gas Fitter #10..www.dpor.state.va.us/regulantlookup/
Geologist #10...www.dpor.state.va.us/regulantlookup/
Hearing Aid Specialist #10.......................................www.dpor.state.va.us/regulantlookup/
Heating & Air Conditioning Mechanic #10..............www.dpor.state.va.us/regulantlookup/
Heating Contractor #10...www.dpor.state.va.us/regulantlookup/
Interior Designer #10 ....www.dpor.state.va.us/regulantlookup/
Landscape Architect #10 ....www.dpor.state.va.us/regulantlookup/
Lead-Related Occupation #10 ....www.dpor.state.va.us/regulantlookup/
Lobbyist #11 ....www.soc.state.va.us/databa.htm
Marriage & Family Therapist #6...............................www.vipnet.org/dhp/cgi-bin/search_publicdb.cgi
Medical Doctor #6..www.vipnet.org/dhp/cgi-bin/search_publicdb.cgi
Medical Equipment Supplier #6 ....www.vipnet.org/dhp/cgi-bin/search_publicdb.cgi
Nail Technician #10 ....www.dpor.state.va.us/regulantlookup/
Nurse/Nurse's Aide #6..www.vipnet.org/dhp/cgi-bin/search_publicdb.cgi
Nurse-LPN -- Nurse-RN #6.......................................www.vipnet.org/dhp/cgi-bin/search_publicdb.cgi
Nursing Home Administrator/Preceptor #6 ....www.vipnet.org/dhp/cgi-bin/search_publicdb.cgi
Occupational Therapist #6..www.vipnet.org/dhp/cgi-bin/search_publicdb.cgi
Optician #10...www.dpor.state.va.us/regulantlookup/
Optometrist #6 ....www.odfinder.org/LicSearch.asp
Osteopathic Physician #6 ....www.vipnet.org/dhp/cgi-bin/search_publicdb.cgi
Pharmacist/Pharmacy #6...www.vipnet.org/dhp/cgi-bin/search_publicdb.cgi
Physical Therapist #6 ....www.vipnet.org/dhp/cgi-bin/search_publicdb.cgi
Physician #6 ....www.vipnet.org/dhp/cgi-bin/search_publicdb.cgi
Pilot, Branch #10 ....www.dpor.state.va.us/regulantlookup/
Plumber #10 ....www.dpor.state.va.us/regulantlookup/
Podiatrist #6...www.vipnet.org/dhp/cgi-bin/search_publicdb.cgi
Polygraph Examiner #10..www.dpor.state.va.us/regulantlookup/
Property Association #10 ....www.dpor.state.va.us/regulantlookup/
Psychologist, Clinical/Applied #6 ....www.vipnet.org/dhp/cgi-bin/search_publicdb.cgi
Psychology School #6..www.vipnet.org/dhp/cgi-bin/search_publicdb.cgi
Public Accountant-CPA #10......................................www.dpor.state.va.us/regulantlookup/
Real Estate Agent/Business/School #10..............www.dpor.state.va.us/regulantlookup/
Real Estate Appraiser/Appraiser Business #10 ....www.dpor.state.va.us/regulantlookup/
Respiratory Care Practitioner #6...............................www.vipnet.org/dhp/cgi-bin/search_publicdb.cgi
Social Worker, Clinical #6...www.vipnet.org/dhp/cgi-bin/search_publicdb.cgi
Soil Scientist #10 ....www.dpor.state.va.us/regulantlookup/
Speech Pathologist/Audiologist #6 ....www.vipnet.org/dhp/cgi-bin/search_publicdb.cgi
Substance Abuse Treatment Practitioner #6 ....www.vipnet.org/dhp/cgi-bin/search_publicdb.cgi
Surveyor, Land #10 ....www.dpor.state.va.us/regulantlookup/
Tradesman #10...www.dpor.state.va.us/regulantlookup/
Veterinarian/Veterinary Technician #6.....................www.vipnet.org/dhp/cgi-bin/search_publicdb.cgi

Waste Management Facility Operator #10..............www.dpor.state.va.us/regulantlookup/
Waste Water Treatment Plant Operator #10 ....www.dpor.state.va.us/regulantlookup/
Wrestler #10 ....www.dpor.state.va.us/regulantlookup/

Licensing Quick Finder

Accountant/Accounting Firm/Sponsor #10
....804-367-8500
Acupuncturist #6.....................................804-662-9908
Air Conditioning Contractor #10 804-367-8511
Alcoholic Beverage Distributor #1 804-213-4400
Architect #10...804-367-8506
Asbestos-Related Occupation #10.......804-367-8595
Attorney/Attorney Associate #14 804-775-0500
Auctioneer/Auction Company #10........804-367-8506
Barber/Barber School/Business #10 804-367-8509
Boxer #10 804-367-0186
Cardiac Technical Professional #15.....804-371-3500
Carpenter #10...804-367-8511
Cemetery #10 804-367-2039
Cemetery Company #10.......................804-367-2039
Cemetery Seller #10..............................804-367-2039
Chiropractor #6.......................................804-662-9908
Clinical Nurse Specialist #6 804-662-9909
Contractor #10..804-367-8511
Cosmetologist/Cosmetology School/Business #10
....804-367-8509
Counselor, Professional #6 804-662-9912
Dental Hygienist #6................................804-662-9906
Dentist #6..804-662-9906
Electrical Contractor #10 804-367-8511
Embalmer #6 804-662-9907
Emergency Medical Technician #15 804-371-3500
Engineer #10...804-367-8506
Funeral Director #6.................................804-662-9907
Gas Fitter #10 804-367-8511
Geologist #10..804-367-2406
Hearing Aid Specialist #10 804-367-8509
Heating & Air Conditioning Mechanic #10
....804-367-8511
Heating Contractor #10 804-367-8511
Horse Racing #13...................................804-966-7400

Insurance Agent/Agency #2 804-371-9631
Interior Designer #10.............................804-367-8506
Investment Advisor/Advisor Agcy. #12..804-371-9686
Landscape Architect #10.......................804-367-8506
Lead-Related Occupation #10 804-367-8595
Lobbyist #11...804-786-2441
Marriage & Family Therapist #6 804-662-9912
Medical Doctor #6...................................804-662-9908
Medical Equipment Supplier #6 804-662-9921
Nail Technician #10................................804-367-8505
Notary Public #9.....................................804-786-2441
Nurse/Nurse's Aide #6...........................804-662-9909
Nurse-LPN #6..804-662-9909
Nurse-RN #6..804-662-9900
Nursing Home Administrator/Preceptor #6
....804-662-9111
Occupational Therapist #6 804-662-9908
Optician #10 804-367-8509
Optometrist #6...804-662-9910
Osteopathic Physician #6......................804-662-9908
Paramedic #15..804-371-3500
Personal Protection Specialist #5 804-786-0460
Pesticide Applicator (Private) #4 804-786-3798
Pesticide Applicator/Company (Commercial) #4
....804-786-3798
Pharmacist/Pharmacy #6.......................804-662-9921
Physical Therapist #6.............................804-662-9908
Physician #6..804-662-9968
Pilot, Branch #10....................................804-367-8514
Plumber #10..804-367-8511
Podiatrist #6..804-662-9908
Polygraph Examiner #10........................804-367-8506
Private Investigator #5...........................804-786-0460
Property Association #10........................804-367-8500
Psychologist, Clinical/Applied #6 804-662-9913
Psychology School #6............................804-662-9913

Public Accountant-CPA #10.................804-367-8505
Real Estate Agent/Business/School #10
....804-367-8526
Real Estate Appraiser/Appraiser Business #10
....804-367-2039
Rehabilitation Provider #6 804-662-9912
Respiratory Care Practitioner #6..........804-662-9908
School Guidance Counselor #8 804-225-2022
School Library Media Specialist #8......804-225-2022
School Principal/Superintendent #8.....804-225-2022
Securities Broker/Dealer/Dealer Agent #12
....804-371-9686
Securities Brokerage #12.....................804-371-9187
Security Officer, Unarmed/Armed #5....804-786-0460
Security Technician (Electronic Security) #5
....804-786-0460
Shock/Trauma Professional #15...........804-371-3500
Shorthand Reporter #3...........................703-768-8122
Social Worker, Clinical #6 804-662-9914
Soil Scientist #10....................................804-367-2785
Speech Pathologist/Audiologist #6 804-662-9111
Substance Abuse Counselor #6 804-662-9912
Substance Abuse Treatment Practitioner #6
....804-662-9912
Surveyor, Land #10................................804-367-8506
Teacher #8 804-225-2022
Tradesman #10..804-367-8511
Veterinarian/Veterinary Technician #6..804-662-9915
Veterinary Facility #6..............................804-662-9915
Waste Management Facility Operator #10
....804-367-8595
Waste Water Treatment Plant Operator #10
....804-367-8505
Wrestler #10..804-367-0186

Licensing Agency Information

#1 Alcoholic Beverage Control Board, 2901 Hermitage Rd, Richmond, VA 23220; 804-213-4400, Fax: 804-213-4586.
www.abc.state.va.us

#2 Bureau of Insurance, Financial Regulation, PO Box 1157, Richmond, VA 23209; 804-371-9801, Fax: 804-371-9511.
www.state.va.us/sec

#3 CSR Contact Person, 2404 Belle Haven Meadows, Alexandria, VA 22306; 703-768-8122, Fax: 703-768-8921.

#4 Department of Agriculture & Consumer Services, Office of Pesticide Services, PO Box 1163, Richmond, VA 23218; 804-786-3798, 371-6558, Fax: 804-371-8598 Admin ofc.; 786-9149 lic. app.
www.vdacs.state.va.us/pesticides
Agency email: rgilliam@vdacs.state.va.us.

#5 Department of Criminal Justice, Private Security, 805 E Broad St, 9th Fl, Richmond, VA 23219; 804-786-4000, Fax: 804-786-6344.
www.dcjs.state.va.us

#6 Department of Health Professions, 6606 W Broad St, 4th Fl, Richmond, VA 23230-1717; 804-662-9900, Fax: 804-662-9943.
www.dhp.state.va.us
Agency email: webmaster@dhp.state.va.us.
Search database at www.vipnet.org/dhp/cgi-bin/search_publicdb.cgi

#8 Office of Professional Licensure, Division of Teacher Licensure, PO Box 2120 (101 N 14th St, James Monroe Bldg.), Richmond, VA 23218-2120; 804-225-2022, Fax: 804-225-2031.
www.pen.k12.va.us

#9 Office of Secretary of Commonwealth, Notary Public Division, PO Box 1795, Richmond, VA 23218; 804-786-2441, Fax: 804-371-0017.
www.soc.state.va.us
Agency email: mford@gov.state.va.us.

#10 Department of Professional & Occupation Regulation, 3600 W Broad St, Richmond, VA 23230-4917; 804-367-8500, Fax: 804-367-2475.
www.state.va.us/dpor
Agency email: waters@dpor.state.va.us.
Search database at www.dpor.state.va.us/regulantlookup. Board of Accountancy is Suite #696.

#11 Secretary of the Commonwealth, PO Box 2454, Richmond, VA 23219-2454; 804-781-2441, Fax: 804-371-0017.
www.soc.state.va.us
Agency email: lobbyist@gov.state.va.us.
Search database at www.soc.state.va.us/databa.htm

#12 Corporation Commission, Securities Division, PO Box 1197 (1300 E Main, 9th Fl), Richmond, VA 23218; 804-371-9187, Fax: 804-371-9911.
www.state.va.us/sec/division/SRF/webpages/homepageJavaB.htm

#13 Virginia Racing Commission, 10700 Horsemans Road, PO Box 208, New Kent, VA 23124; 804-966-7400, Fax: 804-966-7418.
www.vrc.state.va.us
Agency email: shorland@vrc.state.va.us.

#14 State Bar Association, 707 E Main St, #1500, Richmond, VA 23219-2800; 804-775-0500, Fax: 804-775-0501.
www.vsb.org.

#15 Department of Health, Emergency Medical Services, 1538 E Parham Rd, Richmond, VA 23228; 804-371-3500, Fax: 804-371-3543.
www.voh.state.va.us/oems

Virginia Federal Courts

The following list indicates the district and division name for each county in the state. If the bankruptcy court location is different from the district court, then the location of the bankruptcy court appears in parentheses.

County/Court Cross Reference

County	District	Division
Accomack	Eastern	Norfolk
Albemarle	Western	Charlottesville (Lynchburg)
Alexandria City	Eastern	Alexandria
Alleghany	Western	Roanoke (Harrisonburg)
Amelia	Eastern	Richmond
Amherst	Western	Lynchburg
Appomattox	Western	Lynchburg
Arlington	Eastern	Alexandria
Augusta	Western	Harrisonburg
Bath	Western	Harrisonburg
Bedford	Western	Lynchburg
Bedford City	Western	Lynchburg
Bland	Western	Roanoke
Botetourt	Western	Roanoke
Bristol City	Western	Abingdon (Roanoke)
Brunswick	Eastern	Richmond
Buchanan	Western	Abingdon (Roanoke)
Buckingham	Western	Lynchburg
Buena Vista City	Western	Lynchburg (Harrisonburg)
Campbell	Western	Lynchburg
Caroline	Eastern	Richmond
Carroll	Western	Roanoke
Charles City	Eastern	Richmond
Charlotte	Western	Danville (Lynchburg)
Charlottesville City	Western	Charlottesville (Lynchburg)
Chesapeake City	Eastern	Norfolk
Chesterfield	Eastern	Richmond
Clarke	Western	Harrisonburg
Clifton Forge City	Western	Roanoke (Harrisonburg)
Colonial Heights City	Eastern	Richmond
Covington City	Western	Roanoke (Harrisonburg)
Craig	Western	Roanoke
Culpeper	Western	Charlottesville (Lynchburg)
Cumberland	Western	Lynchburg
Danville City	Western	Danville (Lynchburg)
Dickenson	Western	Big Stone Gap (Roanoke)
Dinwiddie	Eastern	Richmond
Emporia City	Eastern	Richmond
Essex	Eastern	Richmond
Fairfax	Eastern	Alexandria
Fairfax City	Eastern	Alexandria
Falls Church City	Eastern	Alexandria
Fauquier	Eastern	Alexandria
Floyd	Western	Roanoke
Fluvanna	Western	Charlottesville (Lynchburg)
Franklin	Western	Roanoke
Franklin City	Eastern	Norfolk
Frederick	Western	Harrisonburg
Fredericksburg City	Eastern	Richmond
Galax City	Western	Roanoke
Giles	Western	Roanoke
Gloucester	Eastern	Newport News
Goochland	Eastern	Richmond
Grayson	Western	Roanoke
Greene	Western	Charlottesville (Lynchburg)
Greensville	Eastern	Richmond
Halifax	Western	Danville (Lynchburg)
Hampton City	Eastern	Newport News
Hanover	Eastern	Richmond
Harrisonburg City	Western	Harrisonburg
Henrico	Eastern	Richmond
Henry	Western	Danville (Lynchburg)
Highland	Western	Harrisonburg
Hopewell City	Eastern	Richmond
Isle of Wight	Eastern	Norfolk
James City	Eastern	Newport News
King George	Eastern	Richmond
King William	Eastern	Richmond
King and Queen	Eastern	Richmond
Lancaster	Eastern	Richmond
Lee	Western	Big Stone Gap (Roanoke)
Lexington City	Western	Lynchburg (Harrisonburg)
Loudoun	Eastern	Alexandria
Louisa	Western	Charlottesville (Lynchburg)
Lunenburg	Eastern	Richmond
Lynchburg City	Western	Lynchburg
Madison	Western	Charlottesville (Lynchburg)
Manassas City	Eastern	Alexandria
Manassas Park City	Eastern	Alexandria
Martinsville City	Western	Lynchburg
Mathews	Eastern	Newport News
Mecklenburg	Eastern	Richmond
Middlesex	Eastern	Richmond
Montgomery	Western	Roanoke
Nelson	Western	Charlottesville (Lynchburg)
New Kent	Eastern	Richmond
Newport News City	Eastern	Newport News
Norfolk City	Eastern	Norfolk
Northampton	Eastern	Norfolk
Northumberland	Eastern	Richmond
Norton City	Western	Big Stone Gap (Roanoke)
Nottoway	Eastern	Richmond
Orange	Western	Charlottesville (Lynchburg)
Page	Western	Harrisonburg
Patrick	Western	Danville (Lynchburg)
Petersburg City	Eastern	Richmond
Pittsylvania	Western	Danville (Lynchburg)
Poquoson City	Eastern	Newport News
Portsmouth City	Eastern	Norfolk
Powhatan	Eastern	Richmond
Prince Edward	Eastern	Richmond
Prince George	Eastern	Richmond
Prince William	Eastern	Alexandria
Pulaski	Western	Roanoke
Radford City	Western	Roanoke
Rappahannock	Western	Charlottesville (Harrisonburg)
Richmond	Eastern	Richmond
Richmond City	Eastern	Richmond
Roanoke	Western	Roanoke
Roanoke City	Western	Roanoke
Rockbridge	Western	Lynchburg (Harrisonburg)
Rockingham	Western	Harrisonburg
Russell	Western	Abingdon (Roanoke)
Salem City	Western	Roanoke
Scott	Western	Big Stone Gap (Roanoke)
Shenandoah	Western	Harrisonburg
Smyth	Western	Abingdon (Roanoke)
South Boston City	Western	Danville (Lynchburg)
Southampton	Eastern	Norfolk
Spotsylvania	Eastern	Richmond
Stafford	Eastern	Alexandria
Staunton City	Western	Harrisonburg
Suffolk City	Eastern	Norfolk
Surry	Eastern	Richmond
Sussex	Eastern	Richmond
Tazewell	Western	Abingdon (Roanoke)
Virginia Beach City	Eastern	Norfolk
Warren	Western	Harrisonburg
Washington	Western	Abingdon (Roanoke)
Waynesboro City	Western	Harrisonburg
Westmoreland	Eastern	Richmond
Williamsburg City	Eastern	Newport News
Winchester City	Western	Harrisonburg
Wise	Western	Big Stone Gap (Roanoke)
Wythe	Western	Roanoke
York	Eastern	Newport News

Standards for Federal Courts: The search fee is $20.00 per item (one party name or case number). Certification fee is $7.00 per document. Copy fee is $.50 per page. All fees standard unless noted in profile. Mail Search: always enclose a stamped self addressed envelope unless otherwise noted. Before releasing records, all courts require prepayment unless noted in profile.

Open records are located at the court unless otherwise noted. District courts index by defendant and plaintiff as well as by case number. Bankruptcy courts usually index by debtor and case number. While most courts now have their indexes on computer, many still maintain index card files as well.

The universal PACER sign-up number is 800-676-6856. Find PACER and the Party/Case Index on the Web at http://pacer.psc.uscourts.gov. PACER dial-up access is $.60 per minute. Also, courts offering internet access via RACER, PACER, Web-PACER or the new CM-ECF charge $.07 per page fee unless noted as free.

US District Court

Eastern District of Virginia

Alexandria Division 401 Courthouse Square, Alexandria, VA 22314 (Courier Address: Use mail address for courier delivery), 703-299-2100.

www.vaed.uscourts.gov

Counties: Arlington, Fairfax, Fauquier, Loudoun, Prince William, Stafford, City of Alexandria, City of Fairfax, City of Falls Church, City of Manassas, City of Manassas Park.

Indexing & Storage: Cases are indexed by defendant, plaintiff, and case number. New cases are available in the index 1 day after filing date. Records are indexed and stored in numerical order. Open records are located at this court.

Fee & Payment Notes: Payment may be made by money order, cashier check, personal check. Payee: Clerk, US District Court.

Phone Search: Only docket information is available by phone.

In Person Search: In person searching available.

PACER: Toll-free dial-up access: 800-852-5186. Local dial-up access: 703-299-2158. Case records are available back to June 1990. New records are available online after 1 day. PACER is available online at http://pacer.vaed.uscourts.gov.

Newport News Division Clerk's Office, PO Box 494, Newport News, VA 23607 (Courier Address: US Post Office Bldg, Room 201, 101 25th St, Newport News, 23607), 757-223-4600.

www.vaed.uscourts.gov

Counties: Gloucester, James City, Mathews, York, City of Hampton, City of Newport News, City of Poquoson, City of Williamsburg.

Indexing & Storage: Cases are indexed by defendant, plaintiff, and case number. New cases are available in the index 1 day after filing date. Open records are located at this court.

Fee & Payment Notes: Payment may be made by money order, cashier check, personal check. Payee: Clerk, US District Court.

Phone Search: Only docket information is available by phone. The court will not honor requests for lists of names over the phone.

In Person Search: In person searching available.

PACER: Toll-free dial-up access: 800-852-5186. Local dial-up access: 703-299-2158. Case records are available back to June 1990. New records are available online after 1 day. PACER is available online at http://pacer.vaed.uscourts.gov.

Norfolk Division US Courthouse, Room 193, 600 Granby St, Norfolk, VA 23510 (Courier Address: Use mail address for courier delivery), 757-222-7204.

www.vaed.uscourts.gov

Counties: Accomack, City of Chesapeake, City of Franklin, Isle of Wight, City of Norfolk, Northampton, City of Portsmouth, City of Suffolk, Southampton, City of Virginia Beach.

Indexing & Storage: Cases are indexed by defendant, plaintiff, and case number. New cases are available in the index 1 day after filing date. Records are also indexed by microfiche from January 1981 to June 1991. Records prior to 1981 are in the card index. Open records are located at this court.

Fee & Payment Notes: Payment may be made by money order, cashier check, business check. Personal checks are not accepted. Payee: Clerk, US District Court.

Phone Search: Searching not available by phone. Only limited docket information is available by phone.

In Person Search: In person searching available.

PACER: Toll-free dial-up access: 800-852-5186. Local dial-up access: 703-299-2158. Case records are available back to June 1990. New records are available online after 1 day. PACER is available online at http://pacer.vaed.uscourts.gov.

Richmond Division Lewis F Powell, Jr Courthouse Bldg, 1000 E Main St, Room 305, Richmond, VA 23219-3525 (Courier Address: Use mail address for courier delivery), 804-916-2200.

www.vaed.uscourts.gov

Counties: Amelia, Brunswick, Caroline, Charles City, Chesterfield, Dinwiddie, Essex, Goochland, Greensville, Hanover, Henrico, King and Queen, King George, King William, Lancaster, Lunenburg, Mecklenburg, Middlesex, New Kent, Northumberland, Nottoway, City ofPetersburg, Powhatan, Prince Edward, Prince George, Richmond, City of Richmond, Spotsylvania, Surry, Sussex, Westmoreland, City of Colonial Heights, City of Emporia, City of Fredericksburg, City of Hopewell.

Indexing & Storage: Cases are indexed by defendant, plaintiff, and case number. New cases are available in the index 1 day after filing date. Records are indexed by case number and stored at the court. Open records are located at this court.

Fee & Payment Notes: Payment may be made by money order, cashier check, personal check. Payee: Clerk's Office, US District Court.

Phone Search: Only docket information is available by phone. The court will not honor requests for lists of names over the phone.

Mail Search: A stamped self addressed envelope is not required.

In Person Search: In person searching available.

PACER: Toll-free dial-up access: 800-852-5186. Local dial-up access: 703-299-2158. Case records are available back to June 1990. New records are available online after 1 day. PACER is available online at http://pacer.vaed.uscourts.gov.

US Bankruptcy Court

Eastern District of Virginia

Alexandria Division PO Box 19247, Alexandria, VA 22320-0247 (Courier Address: Suite 100, 200 S Washington St, Alexandria, VA 22314), 703-258-1200.

www.vaeb.uscourts.gov

Counties: City of Alexandria, Arlington, Fairfax, City of Fairfax, City of Falls Church, Fauquier, Loudoun, City of Manassas, City of Manassas Park, Prince William, Stafford.

Indexing & Storage: Cases are indexed by debtor as well as by case number. New cases are available in the index 2 days after filing date. A creditor register is also kept for each case. Index card are for cases prior to December 1989. Open records are located at this court.

Fee & Payment Notes: Payment may be made by money order, cashier check, personal check. Debtor's checks are not accepted. Payee: Clerk, US Bankruptcy Court.

Phone Search: Docket information is available by phone. An automated voice case information service (VCIS) is available. Call VCIS at 800-326-5879 or 804-771-2736.

In Person Search: In person searching available.

PACER: Toll-free dial-up access: 800-890-2858. Local dial-up access: 703-258-1234. Use of PC Anywhere v4.0 suggested. Case records are available back to mid 1989. Records are never purged. New civil records are available online after 1 day. PACER access is available online through CM/ECF at the web site. This replaces the free NIBS system.

Electronic Filing: Information is available online at http://ecf.vaeb.uscourts.gov

Other Online Access: Free online searching discontinued 8/1/2002. Court does not participate in the U.S. party case index.

Newport News Division Norfolk Bankruptcy Court, PO Box 1938, Norfolk, VA 23501-1938 (Courier Address: Walter E Hoffman US Courthouse, Room 400, 600 Granby St, Norfolk, VA 23510), 757-222-7500.

www.vaeb.uscourts.gov

Counties: Newport News City. Records are at the Norfolk Bankruptcy Court.

Indexing & Storage: Cases are indexed by debtor as well as by case number. New cases are available in the index 2 days after filing date. Open records are located at this court.

Fee & Payment Notes: Payment may be made by money order, cashier check, personal check. The search fee checks should be made to the clerk. Debtor checks are not accepted. Payee: Clerk, US Bankruptcy Court. The fee for copies made by court personnel is $.31 per page.

Phone Search: Call for name, case number, chapter, filing date, judge, attorney for debtor, trustee, Social Security number and date discharged. An automated voice case information service (VCIS) is available. Call VCIS at 800-326-5879 or 804-771-2736.

In Person Search: In person searching available.

PACER: Toll-free dial-up access: 800-890-2785. Local dial-up access: 757-595-1365. New civil records are available online after 7 days. PACER access is available online through CM/ECF at the web site. This replaces the free NIBS system.

Electronic Filing: Information is available online at http://ecf.vaeb.uscourts.gov

Other Online Access: Free online searching discontinued 8/1/2002. Court does not participate in the U.S. party case index.

Norfolk Division PO Box 1938, Norfolk, VA 23501-1938 (Courier Address: Walter E Hoffman US Courthouse, Room 400, 600 Granby St, Norfolk, VA 23510), 757-222-7500.

www.vaeb.uscourts.gov

Counties: Accomack, City of Cape Charles, City of Chesapeake, City of Franklin, Gloucester, City of Hampton, Isle of Wight, James City, Matthews, City of Norfolk, Northampton, City of PoquosonCity of Portsmouth, Southampton, City of Suffolk,City of Virginia Beach, City of Williamsburg, York.

Indexing & Storage: Cases are indexed by debtor as well as by case number. New cases are available in the index 2 days after filing date. Open records are located at this court.

Fee & Payment Notes: Payment may be made by money order, cashier check, personal check. The search fee checks should be made to the clerk. The searcher must use Ikon Manag

Mgmt Svcs for copies. The copy fee checks should be made to Ikon Mgmt Svcs. Debtor checks are not accepted. Payee: Clerk, US Bankruptcy Court. The fee for copies made by court personnel is $.31 per page.

Phone Search: Call for name, case number, chapter, filing date, judge, attorney for debtor, trustee, Social Security number and date discharged. An automated voice case information service (VCIS) is available. Call VCIS at 800-326-5879 or 804-771-2736.

In Person Search: In person searching available.

PACER: Toll-free dial-up access: 800-890-2954. Local dial-up access: 757-222-7441. New civil records are available online after 7 days. PACER access is available online through CM/ECF at the web site. This replaces the free NIBS system.

Electronic Filing: Information is available online at http://ecf.vaeb.uscourts.gov

Other Online Access: Free online searching discontinued 8/1/2002. Court does not participate in the U.S. party case index.

Richmond Division Office of the clerk, 1100 E Main St, Room 310, Richmond, VA 23219-3515 (Courier Address: 1100 E Main St, Room 301, Richmond, VA 23219), 804-916-2400.

www.vaeb.uscourts.gov

Counties: Amelia, Brunswick, Caroline, Charles City, Chesterfield, City of Colonial Heights, Dinwiddie, City of Emporia, Essex, City of Fredericksburg, Goochland, Greensville, Hanover, Henrico, City of Hopewell, King and Queen, King George, King William,Lancaster, Lunenburg, Mecklenburg, Middlesex, New Kent, Northumberland, Nottoway, City of Petersburg, Powhatan, Prince Edward, Prince George, Richmond, City of Richmond, Spotsylvania, Surry, Sussex, Westmoreland.

Indexing & Storage: Cases are indexed by debtor as well as by case number. New cases are available in the index 1 day after filing date. Open records are located at this court.

Fee & Payment Notes: Payment may be made by money order, cashier check, personal check. The court will not send statements. Debtor checks are not accepted. Dave Jones & Assoc Copy. Svc handles search requests. You must fax your request to them at 804-780-0652. They will call you back with the fees. Payee: Clerk, US Bankruptcy Court.

Phone Search: Only docket information is available by phone. An automated voice case information service (VCIS) is available. Call VCIS at 800-326-5879 or 804-771-2736.

In Person Search: In person searching available.

PACER: Sign-up number is. Access fee is. Toll-free dial-up access: 800-890-2829. Local dial-up access: 804-916-2484. PACER access is available online through CM/ECF at the web site. This replaces the free NIBS system.

Electronic Filing: Information is available online at http://ecf.vaeb.uscourts.gov

Other Online Access: Free online searching discontinued 8/1/2002. Court does not participate in the U.S. party case index.

US District Court

Western District of Virginia

Abingdon Division Clerk's Office, PO Box 398, Abingdon, VA 24212 (Courier Address: 180 W Main St, Abingdon, VA 24210), 276-628-5116, Fax: 276-628-1028.

www.vawd.uscourts.gov

Counties: Buchanan, City of Bristol, Russell, Smyth, Tazewell, Washington.

Indexing & Storage: Cases are indexed by defendant, plaintiff, and case number. New cases are available in the index immediately after filing date. Open records are located at this court.

Fee & Payment Notes: Payment may be made by money order, cashier check, personal check. Court will bill for searches and copies. Payee: Clerk, US District Court. You are allowed to make your own copies. These copies cost $.10 per page.

Phone Search: Docket information available by phone.

Fax Search: Will accept fax for searches from 1992 to present only.

Mail Search: A stamped self addressed envelope is not required.

In Person Search: In person searching available.

PACER: Access fee is. Toll-free dial-up access: 888-279-7848. Local dial-up access: 540-857-5140. Case records are available back to Mid 1990. Records are never purged. New records are available online after 1 day. PACER is available online at http://pacer.vawd.uscourts.gov.

Big Stone Gap Division PO Box 490, Big Stone Gap, VA 24219 (Courier Address: 322 Wood Ave E, Room 203, Big Stone Gap, VA 24219), 276-523-3557, Fax: 276-523-6214.

www.vawd.uscourts.gov

Counties: Dickenson, Lee, Scott, Wise, City of Norton.

Indexing & Storage: Cases are indexed by defendant, plaintiff, and case number. New cases are available in the index immediately after filing date. The style of the case is needed to conduct a search. A civil action number is very helpful. A

microfilm index is also maintained for older cases. Open records are located at this court.

Fee & Payment Notes: Payment may be made by money order, cashier check, personal check. Payee: Clerk, US District Court. You are allowed to make your own copies. These copies cost $.50 per page.

Phone Search: Only docket information is available by phone.

In Person Search: In person searching available.

PACER: Access fee is. Toll-free dial-up access: 888-279-7848. Local dial-up access: 540-857-5140. Case records are available back to Mid 1990. Records are never purged. New records are available online after 1 day. PACER is available online at http://pacer.vawd.uscourts.gov.

Charlottesville Division Clerk, Room 304, 255 W Main St, Charlottesville, VA 22902 (Courier Address: Use mail address for courier delivery), 434-296-9284.

www.vawd.uscourts.gov

Counties: Albemarle, Culpeper, Fluvanna, Greene, Louisa, Madison, Nelson, Orange, Rappahannock, City of Charlottesville.

Indexing & Storage: Cases are indexed by defendant, plaintiff, and case number. New cases are available in the index immediately after filing date. Records are indexed on microfiche from 1981 to 1991, and on card prior to that. District wide searches are available from this court for any information within the district.

Fee & Payment Notes: Payment may be made by money order, cashier check, personal check. Payee: Clerk, US District Court. You are allowed to make your own copies. These copies cost $.50 per page. Court only searches computer index. You may search microfiche index.

Phone Search: Searching not available by phone.

In Person Search: In person searching available.

PACER: Access fee is. Toll-free dial-up access: 888-279-7848. Local dial-up access: 540-857-5140. Case records are available back to Mid 1990. Records are never purged. New records are available online after 1 day. PACER is available online at http://pacer.vawd.uscourts.gov.

Danville Division PO Box 52, Danville, VA 24543-0053 (Courier Address: Dan Daniel Post Office Bldg, Room 202, 700 Main St, Danville, VA 24541), 434-793-7147, Fax: 434-793-0284.

www.vawd.uscourts.gov

Counties: Charlotte, Halifax, Henry, Patrick, Pittsylvania, City of Danville, City of Martinsville, City of South Boston. .

Indexing & Storage: Cases are indexed by defendant, plaintiff, and case number. New cases are available in the index immediately after filing date. Open records are located at this court.

Fee & Payment Notes: Payment may be made by money order, cashier check, personal check. Payee: Clerk, US District Court.

Phone Search: If there is an expedited request and the $15.00 search fee is prepaid, the court will call to give the information, and follow with a written response.

Mail Search: A stamped self addressed envelope is not required.

In Person Search: In person searching available.

PACER: Access fee is. Toll-free dial-up access: 888-279-7848. Local dial-up access: 540-857-5140. Case records are available back to Mid 1990. Records are never purged. New records are available online after 1 day. PACER is available online at http://pacer.vawd.uscourts.gov.

Harrisonburg Division Clerk, PO Box 1207, Harrisonburg, VA 22801 (Courier Address: Post Office Bldg, 116 N Main St, Room 314, Harrisonburg, VA 22801), 540-434-3181.

www.vawd.uscourts.gov

Counties: Augusta, Bath, Clarke, Frederick, Highland, Page, Rockingham, Shenandoah, Warren, City of Harrisonburg, City of Staunton, City of Waynesboro, City of Winchester.

Indexing & Storage: Cases are indexed by defendant, plaintiff, and case number. New cases are available in the index 1-2 days after filing date. Records are indexed on computer for civil cases from 1991 and criminal cases from 1993. District wide searches are available from this court 1-2 days after it is filed, but the court prefers that searches be conducted where the case is filed.

Fee & Payment Notes: Payment may be made by money order, cashier check, personal check. Payee: Clerk, US District Court.

Phone Search: Limited information available by phone.

Mail Search: A stamped self addressed envelope is not required.

In Person Search: In person searching available.

PACER: Access fee is. Toll-free dial-up access: 888-279-7848. Local dial-up access: 540-857-5140. Case records are available back to Mid 1990. Records are never purged. New records are available online after 1 day. PACER is available online at http://pacer.vawd.uscourts.gov.

Lynchburg Division Clerk, PO Box 744, Lynchburg, VA 24505 (Courier Address: Room 212, 1100 Main St, Lynchburg, VA 24504), 434-847-5722.

www.vawd.uscourts.gov

Counties: Amherst, Appomattox, Bedford, Buckingham, Campbell, Cumberland, Rockbridge, City of Bedford, City of Buena Vista, City of Lexington, City of Lynchburg.

Indexing & Storage: Cases are indexed by defendant, plaintiff, and case number. New cases are available in the index immediately after filing date. The computer index goes back to 1989. Open records are located at this court.

Fee & Payment Notes: Payment may be made by money order, cashier check, personal check. Payee: Clerk, US District Court.

Phone Search: Only docket information is available by phone.

Mail Search: A stamped self addressed envelope is not required.

In Person Search: In person searching available.

PACER: Access fee is. Toll-free dial-up access: 888-279-7848. Local dial-up access: 540-857-5140. Case records are available back to Mid 1990. Records are never purged. New records are available online after 1 day. PACER is available online at http://pacer.vawd.uscourts.gov.

Roanoke Division Clerk, PO Box 1234, Roanoke, VA 24006 (Courier Address: 210 Franklin Rd SW, Roanoke, VA 24011), 540-857-5100, Fax: 540-857-5110.

www.vawd.uscourts.gov

Counties: Alleghany, Bland, Botetourt, Carroll, Craig, Floyd, Franklin, Giles, Grayson, Montgomery, Pulaski, Roanoke, Wythe, City of Covington, City of Clifton Forge, City of Galax, City of Radford, City of Roanoke, City of Salem.

Indexing & Storage: Cases are indexed by defendant, plaintiff, and case number. New cases are available in the index immediately after filing date. Records are also indexed on microfiche. The automated in house system is available for records from 1992. District wide searches are available for all records from this court.

Fee & Payment Notes: Payment may be made by money order, cashier check, personal check. Payee: Clerk, US District Court.

Phone Search: If there is an expedited request and the $15.00 search fee is prepaid, the court will call to give the information. However, a written response will follow.

Mail Search: A stamped self addressed envelope is not required.

In Person Search: In person searching available.

PACER: Access fee is. Toll-free dial-up access: 888-279-7848. Local dial-up access: 540-857-5140. Case records are available back to Mid 1990. Records are never purged. New records are available online after 1 day. PACER is available online at http://pacer.vawd.uscourts.gov.

US Bankruptcy Court

Western District of Virginia

Harrisonburg Division PO Box 1407, Harrisonburg, VA 22803 (Courier Address: 116 N Main St, Harrisonburg, VA 22801), 540-434-8327, Fax: 540-434-9715.

www.vawb.uscourts.gov

Counties: Alleghany, Augusta, Bath, City of Buena Vista, Clarke, City of Clifton Forge, City of Covington, Frederick, City of Harrisonburg, Highland, City of Lexington, Page, Rappahannock, Rockbridge, Rockingham, Shenandoah, City of Staunton, Warren, City ofWaynesboro, City of Winchester.

Indexing & Storage: Cases are indexed by debtor as well as by case number. New cases are available in the index immediately after filing date. The computer index goes back to 1986. Older cases are on a card index. Open records are located at this court.

Fee & Payment Notes: Payment may be made by money order, cashier check, business check. Personal checks are not accepted. Payee: Clerk, US Bankruptcy Court.

Phone Search: Only docket information is available by phone, and only if it is available from the computer.

In Person Search: In person searching available.

PACER: Toll-free dial-up access: 800-248-0329. Local dial-up access: 540-434-8373. Case records

are available back to March 1986. Records are never purged. New civil records are available online after 1 day. PACER is available online at https://pacer.vawb.uscourts.gov.

Lynchburg Division PO Box 6400, Lynchburg, VA 24505 (Courier Address: 1100 Main St, Room 226, Lynchburg, VA 24504), 434-845-0317.

www.vawb.uscourts.gov

Counties: Albemarle, Amherst, Appomattox, Bedford, City of Bedford, Buckingham, Campbell, Charlotte, City of Charlottesville, Culpeper, Cumberland, City of Danville, Fluvanna, Greene, Halifax, Henry, Louisa, City of Lynchburg, Madison, City of Martinsville,Nelson, Orange, Patrick, Pittsylvania, City of South Boston.

Indexing & Storage: Cases are indexed by debtor as well as by case number. New cases are available in the index 24 hours after filing date. The computer index goes back to 1986. Open records are located at this court.

Fee & Payment Notes: Payment may be made by money order, cashier check, business check. Personal checks are not accepted. Payee: Clerk, US Bankruptcy Court.

Phone Search: Only the name, date filed and chapter will be released over the phone.

In Person Search: In person searching available.

PACER: Toll-free dial-up access: 800-248-2469. Case records are available back to 1986. New civil records are available online after 1 day. PACER is available at https://pacer.vawb.uscourts.gov.

Roanoke Division PO Box 2390, Roanoke, VA 24010 (Courier Address: Commonwealth Bldg, 210 Church Ave, Roanoke, VA 24011), 540-857-2391, Fax: 540-857-2873.

www.vawb.uscourts.gov

Counties: Bland, Botetourt, City of Bristol, Buchanan, Carroll, Craig, Dickenson, Floyd, Franklin, City of Galax, Giles, Grayson, Lee, Montgomery, City of Norton, Pulaski, City of Radford, Roanoke, City of Roanoke, Russell, City of Salem, Scott, Smyth, Tazewell,Washington, Wise, Wythe.

Indexing & Storage: Cases are indexed by debtor and creditors as well as by case number. New cases are available in the index same day if possible after filing date. Records are indexed numerically (for example: 7-92-00123 = office number, year and 5 digit case number). Open records are located at this court.

Fee & Payment Notes: Payment may be made by money order, cashier check. Business checks are not accepted. Personal checks are not accepted. Only firm checks will be accepted. Payee: Clerk, US Bankruptcy Court.

Phone Search: Searching not available by phone. Only the number of pages of the requested items will be given over the phone.

In Person Search: In person searching available.

PACER: Toll-free dial-up access: 800-249-9839. Local dial-up access: 540-857-2319. Case records are available back to 1988. Records are never purged. New civil records are available online after 1 day. PACER is available online at https://pacer.vawb.uscourts.gov.

Virginia County Courts

Court	Jurisdiction	No. of Courts	How Organized
Circuit Courts*	General	123	31 Circuits
District Courts*	Limited	123	
Combined Courts*		5	

* Profiled in this Sourcebook.

Court	Tort	Contract	Real Estate	Min. Claim	Max. Claim	Small Claims	Estate	Eviction	Domestic Relations
									CIVIL
Circuit Courts*	X	X	X	$15,000	No Max		X		X
District Courts*	X	X	X	$0	$15,000			X	X

Court	Felony	Misdemeanor	DWI/DUI	Preliminary Hearing	Juvenile
					CRIMINAL
Circuit Courts*	X				
District Courts*		X	X	X	X

ADMINISTRATION Executive Secretary, Administrative Office of Courts, 100 N 9th St 3rd Fl, Supreme Court Building, Richmond, Virginia, 23219; 804-786-6455, Fax: 804-786-4542. www.courts.state.va.us

COURT STRUCTURE 123 Circuit Courts in 31 districts are the courts of general jurisdiction. There are 123 District Courts of limited jurisdiction. Please note that a district can comprise a county or a city. Records of civil action from $3000 to $15,000 can be at either the Circuit or District Court as either can have jurisdiction. It is necessary to check both record locations as there is no concurrent database nor index.

ONLINE ACCESS 130 General District Courts (many are combined courts) may be searched free at http://208.210.219.132/courtinfo/vadistrict/select.jsp?court=. Here you will have to search both active and inactive cases.

Also, Virginia has the growing "Circuit Court Case Information Pilot Project" with free access to Circuit Court records. Also, you may select among 80 courts at http://208.210.219.132/courtinfo/vacircuit/select.jsp?court=

Another option is the statewide public access computer system: the Law Office Public Access System (LOPAS). The system allows remote access to the court case indexes and abstracts from most of the state's courts. Searching is by specific court; there is no combined index. as well as criminal and civil case information from Circuit and District Courts. There are no sign-up or other fees to use LOPAS. Access is granted on a request-by-request basis. Anyone wishing to establish an account or receive information on LOPAS must contact Ken Mittendorf, CIO, Supreme Court of Virginia, 100 N 9th St, Richmond VA 23219 or by phone at 804-786-6455 or Fax at 804-786-4542.

The www.courts.state.va.us site offers access to Supreme Court and Appellate opinions.

ADDITIONAL INFORMATION In many jurisdictions, the certification fee is $2.00 per document plus copy fee. The copy fee is $.50 per page.

Accomack County

2nd Circuit Court PO Box 126, Accomac, VA 23301; 757-787-5776; Fax: 757-787-1849. 9AM-5PM *Felony, Civil Actions Over $15,000, Probate.*

Civil Records: Access: Fax, mail, online, in person. Both court and visitors may perform in person searches. No search fee. Required to search: name, years to search. Civil cases indexed by defendant, plaintiff. Civil records on microfiche and archived from 1663; on computer back to 1984. Remote online access to court case indexes is via LOPAS; call 804-786-6455 to apply.

Criminal Records: Access: Fax, mail, online, in person. Both court and visitors may perform in person searches. No search fee. Required to search: name, years to search, DOB; also helpful: SSN. Criminal records on microfiche and archived from 1663; on computer back to 1984. Remote online access to court case indexes is via LOPAS; call 804-786-6455 to apply. **General Information:** Public access terminal is available. No juvenile, sealed, probate, tax return or adoption records released. SASE not required. Turnaround time 1-2 days. Fax notes: Fee to fax results is $2.00 1st page, $.50 each add'l. Copy fee: $.50 per

page. Certification fee: $2.00. Fee payee: Samuel H Cooper Jr, Clerk of Court. Personal checks accepted.

2A General District Court PO Box 276, Accomac, VA 23301; 757-787-0923. Hours: 9AM-5PM (EST). *Misdemeanor, Civil Actions Under $15,000, Eviction, Small Claims.*

Civil Records: Access: Phone, mail, online, in person. Both court and visitors may perform in person searches. No search fee. Required to search: name, years to search. Civil cases indexed by defendant. Civil records retained ten years. Select and search District Courts at http://208.210.219.132/courtinfo/vadistrict/select.jsp?co

urt=. For information about the statewide online systems, see the state introduction.

Criminal Records: Access: Phone, mail, online, in person. Both court and visitors may perform in person searches. No search fee. Required to search: name, years to search, DOB; also helpful: SSN. Criminal records retained ten years. Online access to criminal records is the same as civil.

General Information: Public access terminal is available. No juvenile, sealed, adoption records released. SASE required. Turnaround time 1-3 days. Copy fee: $1.00 for first 2 pages. Add $.50 per page thereafter. Fee payee: Accomack District Court. Personal checks accepted. Credit cards accepted: Visa, MasterCard. Prepayment is required.

Albemarle County

16th Circuit & District Court 501 E Jefferson St, Charlottesville, VA 22902; 434-972-4085; Fax: 434-972-4071. Hours: 8:30AM-4:30PM (EST). *Felony, Misdemeanor, Civil, Eviction, Probate.*

Civil Records: Access: Mail, online, in person. Both court and visitors may perform in person searches. Search fee: $5.00 per name. Required to search: name, years to search. Civil records on microfiche from 1980 to present and archived from 1700s to 1990. Remote online access to court case indexes is via LOPAS; call 804-786-6455 to apply.

Criminal Records: Access: Mail, online, in person. Both court and visitors may perform in person searches. Search fee: $5.00 per name. Required to search: name, years to search. Criminal records on microfiche from 1980 to present and archived from 1700s to 1990. Remote online access to court case indexes is via LOPAS; call 804-786-6455 to apply.

General Information: No juvenile, sealed records released. Turnaround time 7-10 days. Copy fee: $.50 per page. Certification fee: $2.00. Fee payee: Albemarle Clerk of Court. Personal checks accepted. Prepayment is required.

Alexandria City

18th Circuit Court 520 King St. #307, Alexandria, VA 22314. 703-838-4044. Hours: 9AM-5PM (EST). *Felony, Civil Actions Over $15,000, Probate.*

http://ci.alexandria.va.us/courts/courts_index.html

Civil Records: Access: In person only. Visitors must perform in person searches for themselves. No search fee. Required to search: name, years to search. Civil cases indexed by defendant, plaintiff. Civil records on computer from 1983 to present, microfiche from 1970s to present.

Criminal Records: Access: In person only. Visitors must perform in person searches for themselves. No search fee. Required to search: name, years to search; also helpful: DOB. Criminal records on computer since 7/87.

General Information: Public access terminal is available. No juvenile, sealed, adoption or expunged records released. Copy fee: $.50 per page. Certification fee: $2.00. Fee payee: Clerk of Court. Only cashiers checks and money orders okay. Prepayment required.

18th District Court 520 King St #201, PO Box 20206, Alexandria, VA 22314; 703-838-4041 (traffic); Civil phone: 703-838-4021; Criminal phone: 703-838-4030. Hours: 8AM-4PM (EST). *Misdemeanor, Civil Actions Under $15,000, Eviction, Small Claims.*

Civil Records: Access: Online, in person. Visitors must perform in person searches for themselves. No search fee. Required to search: name, years to search. Civil cases indexed by defendant. Civil records on computer from 1991 to present, index cards prior to 1986. Select and search District Courts at http://208.210.219.132/courtinfo/vadistrict/select.jsp?court=. For information

about the statewide online systems, see the state introduction.

Criminal Records: Access: Online, in person. Visitors must perform in person searches for themselves. No search fee. Required to search: name. Criminal records on computer from 1991 to present. Online access to criminal records is the same as civil.

General Information: Public access terminal is available. Copy fee: $1.00 first 2 pages, $.50 each addl.

Alleghany County

25th Circuit Court PO Box 670, Covington, VA 24426; 540-965-1730; Fax: 540-965-1732. Hours: 8:30AM-5PM M-F; 9AM-Noon Sat (EST). *Felony, Civil Actions Over $15,000, Probate.*

www.alleghanycountyclerk.com

Civil Records: Access: Online, in person. Visitors must perform in person searches for themselves. No search fee. Required to search: name. Civil cases indexed by plaintiff. Civil records available from 1822, some on microfilm. Select and search Circuit Courts online at http://208.210.219.132/courtinfo/vacircuit/select.jsp?court=. For information about the statewide online systems, see the state introduction.

Criminal Records: Access: Online, in person. Visitors must perform in person searches for themselves. No search fee. Required to search: name. Criminal records available from 1822, some on microfilm. Online access to criminal records is the same as civil.

General Information: No juvenile, adoption or sealed records released. Copy fee: $.50 per page. Certification fee: $2.00. Fee payee: Michael D Wolfe, Clerk of Court. Personal checks accepted. Prepayment required.

25th General District Court PO Box 139, Covington, VA 24426; 540-965-1720; Fax: 540-965-1722. Hours: 9AM-5PM (EST). *Misdemeanor, Civil Actions Under $15,000, Eviction, Small Claims.*

Civil Records: Access: Fax, mail, online, in person. Both court and visitors may perform in person searches. No search fee. Required to search: name, years to search. Civil cases indexed by defendant, plaintiff. Civil records on computer from 1/90, prior on index cards. Select and search District Courts at http://208.210.219.132/courtinfo/vadistrict/select.jsp?court=. For information about the statewide online systems, see the state introduction.

Criminal Records: Access: Fax, mail, online, in person. Both court and visitors may perform in person searches. No search fee. Required to search: name, years to search; also helpful: DOB, SSN. Criminal records on computer from 1/90, prior on index cards. Online access to criminal records is the same as civil.

General Information: Public access terminal is available. No juvenile, sealed records released. SASE requested. Turnaround time 1-2 days. Fax notes: No fee to fax results. Copy fee: $1.00 each for first 2 pages; $.50 each add'l. Personal checks accepted. Credit cards accepted: Visa, MasterCard. Acepted for fines and cost only.

Amelia County

11th Circuit Court PO Box 6309 (1 E Main St, B-5), PO Box 237, Amelia, VA 23068; 804-561-2128. Hours: 8:30AM-4:30PM (EST). *Felony, Civil Actions Over $15,000, Probate.*

www.governdata.com/amelia.htm

Note: Will search on telephone request if not busy.

Civil Records: Access: Mail, online, in person. Both court and visitors may perform in person searches. No search fee. Required to search: name, years to search. Civil cases indexed by defendant, plaintiff. Civil records on microfiche 1735 to present, indexed on books. Select and search Circuit Courts online at http://208.210.219.132/courtinfo/vacircuit/select.jsp?co

urt=. For information about the statewide online systems, see the state introduction.

Criminal Records: Access: Mail, online, in person. Both court and visitors may perform in person searches. No search fee. Required to search: name, years to search, DOB; also helpful: SSN. Criminal records on microfiche 1735 to present, indexed on books. Online access to criminal records is the same as civil.

General Information: No juvenile, sealed records released. SASE required. Turnaround time 3-5 days. Copy fee: $.50 per page. Certification fee: $3.00. Fee payee: Amelia County Circuit Court. Personal checks accepted. Prepayment is required.

11th General District Court PO Box 24, Amelia, VA 23002; 804-561-2456; Fax: 804-561-6956. Hours: 8:30AM-4:30PM (EST). *Misdemeanor, Civil Actions Under $15,000, Eviction, Small Claims.*

Civil Records: Access: Mail, online, fax, in person. Both court and visitors may perform in person searches. No search fee. Required to search: name, years to search. Civil cases indexed by defendant, plaintiff. Civil records on computer since 12/20/92, prior records on index cards. Select and search District Courts at http://208.210.219.132/courtinfo/vadistrict/select.jsp?co urt=. For information about the statewide online systems, see the state introduction.

Criminal Records: Access: Mail, online, fax, in person. Both court and visitors may perform in person searches. No search fee. Required to search: name, years to search, DOB; also helpful: SSN. Criminal records on computer since 12/20/92, prior records on index cards. Online access to criminal records is the same as civil.

General Information: Public access terminal is available. No juvenile, sealed records released. SASE required. Turnaround time 1-14 days. Copy fee: $1.00 for 1st two pages, $.50 each add'l page. Fee payee: Amelia District Court. Personal checks accepted. Prepayment is required.

Amherst County

24th Circuit Court PO Box 462, Amherst, VA 24521; 434-946-9321; Fax: 434-946-9323. 8AM-5PM (EST). *Felony, Civil Actions Over $15,000, Probate.*

Civil Records: Access: Online, in person. Visitors must perform in person searches for themselves. No search fee. Required to search: name, years to search. Civil cases indexed by defendant, plaintiff. Civil records on index books from 1761; on computer back to 1997. Remote online access to court case indexes is via LOPAS; call 804-786-6455 to apply.

Criminal Records: Access: Online, in person. Visitors must perform in person searches for themselves. No search fee. Required to search: name, years to search, date of offense. Criminal records on index books back to 1761; on comptuer back to 1997. Remote online access to court case indexes is via LOPAS; call 804-786-6455 to apply.

General Information: Public access terminal is available. No juvenile, sealed or adoption records released. Copy fee: $.50 per page. Certification fee: $2.00. Fee payee: Clerk of Circuit Court. Personal checks accepted. Prepayment is required.

24th General District Court PO Box 513, Amherst, VA 24521; 434-946-9351; Fax: 434-946-9359. Hours: 8AM-4:30PM (EST). *Misdemeanor, Civil Actions Under $15,000, Eviction, Small Claims.*

Note: Has handled misdemeanor cases since 1985.

Civil Records: Access: Online, in person. Visitors must perform in person searches for themselves. Required to search: name, years to search. Civil cases indexed by defendant, plaintiff. Civil records on computer 10 years prior. Select and search District Courts at http://208.210.219.132/courtinfo/vadistrict/select.jsp?co

urt=. For information about the statewide online systems, see the state introduction.

Criminal Records: Access: Online, in person. Visitors must perform in person searches for themselves. Required to search: name, years to search, DOB, SSN. Criminal records on computer 10 years prior. Online access to criminal records is same as civil.

General Information: Public access terminal is available. No sealed records released. Copy fee: $1.00 per page. Fee payee: Clerk of Court. Personal checks accepted. Credit cards accepted: Visa, MasterCard. Prepayment is required.

Appomattox County

10th Circuit Court PO Box 672, Appomattox, VA 24522; 434-352-5275; Fax: 434-352-2781. Hours: 8:30AM-4:30PM (EST). *Felony, Civil Actions Over $15,000, Probate.*

Civil Records: Access: Online, in person. Visitors must perform in person searches for themselves. No search fee. Required to search: name, years to search. Civil cases indexed by defendant, plaintiff. Civil records on books from 1892 to present; on computer since. Select and search Circuit Courts online at http://208.210.219.132/courtinfo/vacircuit/select.jsp?co urt=. For information about the statewide online systems, see the state introduction.

Criminal Records: Access: Online, in person. Visitors must perform in person searches for themselves. No search fee. Required to search: name, years to search. Criminal records on books from 1892 to present; on computer since. Online access to criminal records is the same as civil.

General Information: Public access terminal is available. No juvenile, sealed records released. Copy fee: $.50 per page. Fee payee: Clerk of Circuit Court. Personal checks accepted. Prepayment is required.

10th General District Court PO Box 187, Appomattox, VA 24522; 434-352-5540; Fax: 434-352-0717. Hours: 8:30AM-4:30PM (EST). *Misdemeanor, Civil Actions Under $15,000, Eviction, Small Claims.*

Civil Records: Access: Fax, mail, online, in person. Both court and visitors may perform in person searches. No search fee. Required to search: name, years to search. Civil cases indexed by defendant, plaintiff. Civil records on card file from 1985 to present, prior to 1985 in Circuit Court. Select and search District Courts at http://208.210.219.132/courtinfo/vadistrict/select.jsp?co urt=. For information about the statewide online systems, see the state introduction.

Criminal Records: Access: Fax, mail, online, in person. Both court and visitors may perform in person searches. No search fee. Required to search: name, years to search; also helpful: SSN. Criminal records on card file from 1985 to present, prior to 1985 in Circuit Court. Online access to criminal records is the same as civil.

General Information: Public access terminal is available. No juvenile, sealed records released. Turnaround time 1-5 days. Fax notes: No fee to fax results. Copy fee: $1.00 1st page; $.50 each add'l. Fee payee: General District Court. Personal checks accepted. Credit cards accepted: Visa, MasterCard.

Arlington County

17th Circuit Court 1425 N Courthouse Rd, Arlington, VA 22201; 703-358-7010. Hours: 8AM-5PM *Felony, Civil Actions Over $15,000, Probate.*

http://158.59.15.115/arlington

Civil Records: Access: Online, in person. Visitors must perform in person searches for themselves. No search fee. Required to search: name, years to search. Civil cases indexed by defendant, plaintiff. Civil records on computer from 1987; prior on books from mid-1930 to present. Online access available free at

http://208.210.219.132/courtinfo/vacircuit/select.jsp?co urt=. For information about the statewide online systems, see the state introduction.

Criminal Records: Access: Online, in person. Visitors must perform in person searches for themselves. No search fee. Required to search: name, years to search. Criminal records on computer from 1987; prior on books from mid-1930 to present. Online access to criminal records is the same as civil.

General Information: Public access terminal is available. (Criminal only.) No juvenile, adoption or sealed records released. Mail requests not accepted. Copy fee: $.50 per page. Certification fee: $2.00. Fee payee: Clerk of Court. Personal checks accepted. Prepayment is required.

17th General District Court 1425 N Courthouse Rd, Rm 2500, Arlington, VA 22201; 703-228-4485; Fax: 703-228-4593. Hours: 8AM-4PM (EST). *Misdemeanor, Civil Actions Under $15,000, Eviction, Small Claims.*

Note: Phone access limited to 4 requests.

Civil Records: Access: Phone, mail, online, in person. Both court and visitors may perform in person searches. No search fee. Required to search: name, years to search. Civil cases indexed by defendant. Civil records on computer back to 1990, books from early 1970s. Select and search District Courts at http://208.210.219.132/courtinfo/vadistrict/select.jsp?co urt=. For information about the statewide online systems, see the state introduction.

Criminal Records: Access: Phone, mail, online, in person. Both court and visitors may perform in person searches. No search fee. Required to search: name, years to search, DOB; also helpful-SSN, case number. Criminal records on computer back to 1990, books from early 1970s. Online access to criminal records is the same as civil.

General Information: Public access terminal is available. No juvenile, sealed records released. Turnaround time 1-2 days. Fax notes: Will not fax results. Copy fee: $.50 per page. Certification fee: $2.00. Fee payee: Clerk of Court. Personal checks accepted. Prepayment is required.

Augusta County

25th Circuit Court PO Box 689, Staunton, VA 24402-0689; 540-245-5321; Fax: 540-245-5318. Hours: 8AM-5PM (EST). *Felony, Civil Actions Over $15,000, Probate.*

Note: Court prefers that searches be done in person. Mail access is limited; they will only search back to 1987. Phone available for very short search only.

Civil Records: Access: Fax, mail, online, in person. Both court and visitors may perform in person searches. No search fee. Required to search: name, years to search. Civil cases indexed by defendant, plaintiff. Civil records on computer from 1987 to present, books from 1745 to 1986. Online access available free at http://208.210.219.132/courtinfo/vacircuit/select.jsp?co urt=. For information about the statewide online systems, see the state introduction.

Criminal Records: Access: Fax, mail, online, in person. Both court and visitors may perform in person searches. No search fee. Required to search: name, years to search; also helpful: DOB, SSN. Criminal records go back to 1987 felonies only. Online access to criminal records is the same as civil.

General Information: Public access terminal is available. No juvenile, adoption or sealed records released. SASE required. Turnaround time 1-2 days. Copy fee: $.50 per page. Certification fee: $2.00. Fee payee: Clerk, Augusta County Circuit Court. Personal checks accepted.

25th General District Court 6 E Johnson St, 2nd Floor, Staunton, VA 24401; 540-245-5300; Fax:

540-245-5302. 8:30AM-4:30PM (EST). *Misdemeanor, Civil Actions Under $15,000, Eviction, Small Claims.*

Note: This court also handles traffic infractions.

Civil Records: Access: Mail, online, in person. Both court and visitors may perform in person searches. No search fee. Required to search: name, years to search. Civil cases indexed by defendant, plaintiff. Civil records kept for 10 years on computer, then archived or destroyed. Select and search District Courts at http://208.210.219.132/courtinfo/vadistrict/select.jsp?co urt=. For information about the statewide online systems, see the state introduction.

Criminal Records: Access: Mail, online, in person. Both court and visitors may perform in person searches. No search fee. Required to search: name, years to search. Criminal records kept for 10 years on computer, then archived or destroyed. Online access to criminal records is the same as civil.

General Information: Public access terminal is available. No juvenile, sealed records released. SASE requested. Turnaround time 2-3 days. Copy fee: $.50 per page. Fee payee: Augusta General District Court. Personal checks accepted. Credit cards accepted: Visa, MasterCard. Prepayment is required.

Bath County

25th Circuit Court PO Box 180, Warm Springs, VA 24484; 540-839-7226; Fax: 540-839-7222. Hours: 8:30AM-4:30PM (EST). *Felony, Civil Actions Over $15,000, Probate.*

Civil Records: Access: Mail, online, in person. Both court and visitors may perform in person searches. No search fee. Required to search: name, years to search. Civil cases indexed by defendant, plaintiff. Civil records on books from 1791 to present. Remote online access to court case indexes is via LOPAS; call 804-786-6455 to apply.

Criminal Records: Access: Online, in person. Visitors must perform in person searches for themselves. No search fee. Required to search: name, years to search; also helpful: DOB, SSN. Criminal records on books from 1791 to present. Online access to criminal records is the same as civil.

General Information: No juvenile, sealed or adoption records released. Turnaround time 1-2 days. Copy fee: $.50 per page. Certification fee: $2.00. Fee payee: Bath County Circuit Court. Personal checks accepted. Prepayment is required.

25th General District Court PO Box 96, Warm Springs, VA 24484; 540-839-7241; Fax: 540-839-7248. Hours: 8:30AM-4:30PM (EST). *Misdemeanor, Civil Actions Under $15,000, Eviction, Small Claims.*

Civil Records: Access: Phone, fax, mail, online, in person. Both court and visitors may perform in person searches. No search fee. Required to search: name, years to search. Civil cases indexed by defendant, plaintiff. Civil records on files from 1985 to present, Prior records in Circuit Court. Select and search District Courts at http://208.210.219.132/courtinfo/vadistrict/select.jsp?court=. For information about the statewide online systems, see the state introduction.

Criminal Records: Access: Phone, fax, mail, online, in person. Both court and visitors may perform in person searches. No search fee. Required to search: name, years to search, DOB; also helpful: SSN. Criminal records on files back 10 years, Prior records in Circuit Court. Online access to criminal records is the same as civil.

General Information: Public access terminal is available. No juvenile, sealed records released. SASE requested. Turnaround time 2 days, will give immediate response on phone if not an extensive search. Copy fee: $.50 per page. Fee payee: Bath County Combined Court. Personal checks accepted. Credit cards accepted: Visa, MasterCard.

Bedford County

County Circuit Court 123 E Main St #201, Bedford, VA 24523; 540-586-7632; Fax: 540-586-6197. Hours: 8:30AM-5PM (EST). *Felony, Civil Actions Over $15,000, Probate.*

Civil Records: Access: Online, in person. Visitors must perform in person searches for themselves. No search fee. Required to search: name, years to search. Civil cases indexed by defendant, plaintiff. Civil records on computer from 1988, index books. Online access available free at http://208.210.219.132/courtinfo/vacircuit/select.jsp?court=. For information about the statewide online systems, see the state introduction.

Criminal Records: Access: Online, in person. Visitors must perform in person searches for themselves. No search fee. Required to search: name, years to search, DOB; also helpful: SSN, race, sex. Criminal records on computer from 1988, index books. Remote online access to court case indexes is via LOPAS; call 804-786-6455 to apply.

General Information: Public access terminal is available. No juvenile, sealed records released. Copy fee: $.50 per page. Certification fee: $.50 per page. Fee payee: Bedford Clerk of Court. Personal checks accepted. Prepayment is required.

24th General District Court 123 E Main St #202, Bedford, VA 24523; 540-586-7637; Fax: 540-586-7684. Hours: 8AM-4PM (EST). *Misdemeanor, Civil Actions Under $15,000, Eviction, Small Claims.*

Civil Records: Access: Mail, online, in person. Visitors must perform in person searches for themselves. Search fee: $5.00 per name. Required to search: name, years to search, SSN. Civil cases indexed by defendant. Civil records on computer for ten years. Date of birth or SSN also helpful in searching. Select and search District Courts at http://208.210.219.132/courtinfo/vadistrict/select.jsp?court=. For information about the statewide online systems, see the state introduction.

Criminal Records: Access: Mail, online, in person. Both court and visitors may perform in person searches. Search fee: $5.00 per name. Required to search: name, years to search; also helpful: DOB, SSN. Criminal records on computer for ten years. Date of birth or SSN also helpful in searching. Online access to criminal records is the same as civil.

General Information: Public access terminal is available. No sealed records released. SASE required. Turnaround time 1-5 days. Copy fee: $1.00 1st 2 pages, $.50 each additional page. Fee payee: Bedford General District Court. Personal checks accepted. Credit cards accepted: Visa, MasterCard. Prepayment is required.

Bedford City

Circuit & District Courts, VA.

Note: See Bedford County

Bland County

27th Circuit Court PO Box 295, Bland, VA 24315; 276-688-4562; Fax: 276-688-4562. Hours: 8AM-6PM (EST). *Felony, Civil Actions Over $15,000, Probate.*

Civil Records: Access: Phone, fax, mail, online, in person. Both court and visitors may perform in person searches. Search fee: $10.00 per name. Required to search: name, years to search. Civil cases indexed by defendant, plaintiff. Civil records on books from 1861 to present. Select and search Circuit Courts online at http://208.210.219.132/courtinfo/vacircuit/select.jsp?court=. For information about the statewide online systems, see the state introduction.

Criminal Records: Access: Phone, fax, mail, online, in person. Both court and visitors may perform in person searches. Search fee: $10.00 per name. Required to search: name, years to search, signed release; also

helpful: SSN. Criminal records on books from 1861 to present. Online access to criminal records is the same as civil.

General Information: No juvenile, sealed or adoption records released. Turnaround time 2 days. Fax notes: $1.00 per page. Copy fee: $.50 per page. Certification fee: $2.00. Fee payee: Clerk of Court. Personal checks accepted. Prepayment is required.

27th General District Court PO Box 157, Bland, VA 24315; 276-688-4433; Fax: 276-688-4789. Hours: 8AM-5PM (EST). *Misdemeanor, Civil Actions Under $15,000, Eviction, Small Claims.*

Civil Records: Access: Phone, fax, mail, online, in person. Both court and visitors may perform in person searches. No search fee. Required to search: name, years to search. Civil cases indexed by defendant. Civil records on computer from 4/23/92, card index back to 1985. Select and search District Courts at http://208.210.219.132/courtinfo/vadistrict/select.jsp?court=. For information about the statewide online systems, see the state introduction.

Criminal Records: Access: Phone, fax, mail, online, in person. Both court and visitors may perform in person searches. No search fee. Required to search: name, years to search; also helpful: DOB, SSN. Criminal records on computer from 4/23/92, card index back to 1985. Online access to criminal records is the same as civil. Phone access limited to specific cases only.

General Information: Public access terminal is available. No juvenile, sealed or adoption records released. SASE requested. Turnaround time 1-2 days. Copy fee: $1.00 1st 2 pages, $.50 each additional page. Fee payee: General District Court. Personal checks accepted. Credit cards accepted: Visa, MasterCard.

Botetourt County

25th Circuit Court PO Box 219, Fincastle, VA 24090; 540-473-8274; Fax: 540-473-8209. Hours: 8:30AM-4:30PM (EST). *Felony, Civil Actions Over $15,000, Probate.*

Civil Records: Access: Mail, online, in person. Both court and visitors may perform in person searches. No search fee. Required to search: name, years to search. Civil cases indexed by defendant, plaintiff. Civil records on computer 7/1/91 to present, books back to 1770. Select and search Circuit Courts online at http://208.210.219.132/courtinfo/vacircuit/select.jsp?court=. For information about the statewide online systems, see the state introduction.

Criminal Records: Access: Mail, online, in person. Both court and visitors may perform in person searches. No search fee. Required to search: name, years to search, DOB, SSN. Criminal records on computer 7/1/91 to present, books back to 1770. Online access to criminal records is the same as civil.

General Information: No juvenile, sealed or adoption records released. SASE required. Turnaround time same day. Copy fee: $.50 per page. Certification fee: $2.00. Fee payee: Clerk of Court. Personal checks accepted. Prepayment is required.

25th General District Court PO Box 858, Fincastle, VA 24090-0205; 540-473-8244; Fax: 540-473-8344. Hours: 8AM-4PM (EST). *Misdemeanor, Civil Actions Under $15,000, Eviction, Small Claims.*

Civil Records: Access: Mail, online, in person. Both court and visitors may perform in person searches. No search fee. Required to search: name, years to search. Civil cases indexed by defendant, plaintiff. Civil records on computer from 1992 to present. Civil records on files back to 1964, others back to 1974. Select and search District Courts at http://208.210.219.132/courtinfo/vadistrict/select.jsp?court=. For information about the statewide online systems, see the state introduction.

Criminal Records: Access: Mail, online, in person. Both court and visitors may perform in person searches.

No search fee. Required to search: name, years to search. Criminal records on computer from 1992 to present. Civil records on files back to 1964, others back to 1974. Online access to criminal records is the same as civil.

General Information: Public access terminal is available. No juvenile, sealed records released. SASE requested. Turnaround time 1-2 days. No copy fee. Personal checks accepted. Checks that require verification calls not accepted. Credit cards accepted: Visa, MasterCard.

Bristol City

28th Circuit Court 497 Cumberland St, Bristol, VA 24201; 276-645-7321; Fax: 276-645-7345. 9AM-5PM *Felony, Civil Actions Over $15,000, Probate.*

Civil Records: Access: Mail, online, in person. Visitors must perform in person searches for themselves. No search fee. Required to search: name, years to search. Civil cases indexed by defendant, plaintiff. Civil records indexed from 1890 to present. Select and search Circuit Courts online at http://208.210.219.132/courtinfo/vacircuit/select.jsp?court=. For information about the statewide online systems, see the state introduction.

Criminal Records: Access: Online, in person. Visitors must perform in person searches for themselves. No search fee. Required to search: name, years to search. Criminal records indexed from 1890 to present. Online access to criminal records is the same as civil.

General Information: No juvenile, sealed or adoption records released. SASE required. Turnaround time up to 1 week. Copy fee: $.50 per page. Certification fee: $2.00. Fee payee: Clerk of Circuit Court. Personal checks accepted. Prepayment is required.

28th General District Court 497 Cumberland St, Bristol, VA 24201; 276-645-7341; Fax: 276-645-7342. Hours: 8AM-5PM (EST). *Misdemeanor, Civil Actions Under $15,000, Eviction, Small Claims.*

Civil Records: Access: Mail, fax, online, in person. Both court and visitors may perform in person searches. No search fee. Required to search: name, years to search. Civil cases indexed by defendant, plaintiff. Civil records on computer from 1989, card file 1983 to 1988. Select and search District Courts at http://208.210.219.132/courtinfo/vadistrict/select.jsp?court=. For information about the statewide online systems, see the state introduction.

Criminal Records: Access: Mail, fax, online, in person. Visitors must perform in person searches for themselves. No search fee. Required to search: name, years to search, DOB, SSN. Criminal records on computer from 1989, card file 1983 to 1988. Online access to criminal records is the same as civil.

General Information: Public access terminal is available. No juvenile, sealed records released. SASE requested. Turnaround time 1-2 days. Copy fee: $.50 per page. Certification fee: $2.00. Fee payee: General District Court. Personal checks accepted. Credit cards accepted: Visa, MasterCard.

Brunswick County

6th Circuit Court 216 N Main St, Lawrenceville, VA 23868; 434-848-2215; Fax: 434-848-4307. Hours: 8:30AM-5PM (EST). *Felony, Civil, Probate.*

Civil Records: Access: In person, online. Visitors must perform in person searches for themselves. Search fee: No search fee. Required to search: name, years to search. Civil cases indexed by defendant, plaintiff. Civil records in books back to 1732; on computer since 1992 (office use only). Select and search Circuit Courts online at http://208.210.219.132/courtinfo/vacircuit/select.jsp?court=. For information about the statewide online systems, see the state introduction.

Criminal Records: Access: In person, online. Visitors must perform in person searches for themselves. Search fee: No search fee. Required to search: name, years to search. Criminal records in books back to 1732; on computer back to 1992 (office use only). Online access to criminal records is the same as civil.

General Information: Public access terminal is available. (However, it is available for land records and wills; no case information.) No juvenile, sealed or adoption records released. Fax notes: Will fax results to 800 number and to accounts. Copy fee: $.50 per page. Certification fee: $2.00. Fee payee: Clerk of Court. Personal checks accepted.

6th General District Court, 202 Main St, Lawrenceville, VA 23868-0066; 434-848-2315; Fax: 434-848-2550. 8:30AM-4:30PM (EST). *Misdemeanor, Civil Actions Under $15,000, Eviction, Small Claims.*

Civil Records: Access: Mail. Both court (as time permits) and visitors may perform in person searches. No search fee. Required to search: name, years to search. Civil cases indexed by defendant, plaintiff. Civil records computerized since 1988, records go back to 1988. Select and search District Courts at http://208.210.219.132/courtinfo/vadistrict/select.jsp?court=. For information about the statewide online systems, see the state introduction.

Criminal Records: Access: Mail, in person, online. Both court (as time permits) and visitors may perform in person searches. No search fee. Required to search: name, years to search, DOB; also helpful: SSN, signed release. Criminal records computerized since 1991; records go back ten years. Online access to misdemeanor records is the same as civil.

General Information: Public access terminal is available. No juvenile, sealed records released. SASE required. Turnaround time 1-2 days. No copy fee.

Buchanan County

29th Circuit Court PO Box 929, Grundy, VA 24614; 276-935-6575. 8:30AM-5PM (EST). *Felony, Misdemeanor, Civil Actions Over $15,000, Probate.*

Civil Records: Access: Phone, mail, online, in person. Both court and visitors may perform in person searches. No search fee. Required to search: name, years to search; also helpful: address. Civil cases indexed by defendant, plaintiff. Civil records on computer back to 1991, in books back to 1923. Remote online access to court case indexes is via LOPAS; call 804-786-6455 to apply.

Criminal Records: Access: Phone, mail, online, in person. Visitors must perform in person searches for themselves. No search fee. Required to search: name, years to search, DOB; also helpful: address, SSN. Criminal records on computer back to 1991; in books back to 1928. Remote online access to court case indexes is via LOPAS; call 804-786-6455 to apply.

General Information: Public access terminal is available. No juvenile, sealed records released. Turnaround time 1-2 days. Fax notes: Fee to fax results is $3.00 per document. Copy fee: $.50 per page. Certification fee: $.50. Fee payee: Clerk of Circuit Court. Personal checks accepted.

29th Judicial District Court PO Box 654, Grundy, VA 24614; 276-935-6526; Fax: 276-935-5479. Hours: 8AM-4PM (EST). *Civil Actions Under $15,000, Eviction, Small Claims.*

Civil Records: Access: Fax, mail, in person, phone, online. Both court and visitors may perform in person searches. No search fee. Required to search: name; also helpful: years to search. Civil cases indexed by defendant, plaintiff. Civil Records are indexed for 10 years, computerized back to 1993. Select and search District Courts at http://208.210.219.132/courtinfo/vadistrict/select.jsp?court=. For information about the statewide online systems, see the state introduction.

General Information: Public access terminal is available. Turnaround time is 1 week. Fax notes: Will

fax back to toll-free or local numbers only. Copy fee: No search fee. Fee payee: General District Court. Personal checks accepted. Credit cards accepted: Visa, MasterCard.

Buckingham County

10th Circuit Court Route 60, PO Box 107, Buckingham, VA 23921; 434-969-4734; Fax: 434-969-2043. Hours: 8:30AM-4:30PM (EST). *Felony, Civil Actions Over $15,000, Probate.*

Civil Records: Access: Mail, online, in person. Both court and visitors may perform in person searches. No search fee. Required to search: name, years to search. Civil cases indexed by defendant, plaintiff. Civil records on books from 1869 to present. Remote online access to court case indexes is via LOPAS; call 804-786-6455 to apply.

Criminal Records: Access: Mail, online, in person. Both court and visitors may perform in person searches. No search fee. Required to search: name, years to search; also helpful: DOB. Criminal records on books from 1869 to present. Remote online access to court case indexes is via LOPAS; call 804-786-6455 to apply.

General Information: No juvenile, sealed or adoption records released. Copy fee: $.50 per page. Certification fee: $2.00. Fee payee: Clerk of Court. Personal checks accepted.

Buckingham General District Court PO Box 127, Buckingham, VA 23921; 434-969-4755; Fax: 434-969-1762. Hours: 8:30AM-4:30PM (EST). *Misdemeanor, Civil Actions Under $15,000, Eviction, Small Claims.*

Civil Records: Access: Mail, online, in person, fax. Only the court performs in person searches; visitors may not. No search fee. Required to search: name, years to search. Civil cases indexed by defendant. Civil records on computer or hard copy from 1993, prior records on index cards. Select and search District Courts at http://208.210.219.132/courtinfo/vadistrict/select.jsp?court=. For information about the statewide online systems, see the state introduction.

Criminal Records: Access: Mail, online, in person, fax. Only the court performs in person searches; visitors may not. No search fee. Required to search: name, years to search, DOB, SSN, signed release. Criminal records on computer or hard copy from 1993, prior records on index cards. Online access to criminal records is the same as civil.

General Information: No juvenile, sealed records released. Turnaround time 2 weeks. Copy fee: No search fee. Fee payee: Buckingham. Personal checks accepted. Credit cards accepted: Visa, MasterCard.

Buena Vista City

25th Circuit & District Court 2039 Sycamore Ave, Buena Vista, VA 24416; 540-261-8627 X626/627; Fax: 540-261-8625. Hours: 8:30AM-5PM (EST). *Felony, Misdemeanor, Civil, Eviction, Probate.*

Civil Records: Access: Mail, online, in person. Both court and visitors may perform in person searches. No search fee. Required to search: name, years to search. Civil cases indexed by defendant, plaintiff. Civil records on manual records 1892 to present, computerized since 1996. Select and search Circuit Courts online at http://208.210.219.132/courtinfo/vacircuit/select.jsp?court=. Search District courts at http://208.210.219.132/courtinfo/vadistrict/select.jsp?court=.

Criminal Records: Access: Mail, online, in person. Both court and visitors may perform in person searches. No search fee. Required to search: name, years to search. Criminal records on manual records 1892 to present, computerized since 1996. Online access to criminal records is the same as civil.

General Information: Public access terminal is available. No juvenile, sealed records released. SASE

required. Turnaround time 1 day. Fax notes: $.50 per page. Copy fee: $.50 per page. Certification fee: $3.00. Fee payee: Buena Vista Circuit Court. Personal checks accepted. Prepayment is required.

Campbell County

24th Circuit Court 732 Village Hwy, PO Box 7, Rustburg, VA 24588; 434-592-9517. 8:30AM-4:30PM (EST). *Felony, Civil Actions Over $15,000, Probate.*

Civil Records: Access: Mail, online, in person. Both court and visitors may perform in person searches. No search fee. Required to search: name, years to search. Civil cases indexed by defendant, plaintiff. Civil records on index books. Remote online access to court case indexes is via LOPAS; call 804-786-6455 to apply.

Criminal Records: Access: Mail, online, in person. Both court and visitors may perform in person searches. No search fee. Required to search: name, years to search; also helpful: DOB. Criminal records on index books. Remote online access to court case indexes is via LOPAS; call 804-786-6455 to apply.

General Information: No juvenile, sealed or adoption records released. SASE required. Turnaround 2-10 days. Copy fee: $.50 per page. Certification fee: $2.00. Fee payee: Clerk of Court. Personal checks accepted.

24th General District Court 1st Floor, New Courthouse Bldg, PO Box 97, Rustburg, VA 24588; 434-332-9546; Fax: 434-332-9694. Hours: 8AM-4PM (EST). *Misdemeanor, Civil Actions Under $15,000, Eviction, Small Claims.*

Civil Records: Access: Online, in person. Visitors must perform in person searches for themselves. No search fee. Required to search: name, years to search. Civil cases indexed by defendant, plaintiff. Civil records on computer for 10 years. Select and search District Courts at http://208.210.219.132/courtinfo/vadistrict/select.jsp?court=. For information about the statewide online systems, see the state introduction.

Criminal Records: Access: Online, in person. Visitors must perform in person searches for themselves. No search fee. Required to search: name, years to search. Criminal records on computer for 10 years. Online access to criminal records is the same as civil.

General Information: Public access terminal is available. (Not available for criminal or civil information.) Copy fee: $1.00 for 1st 2 copies then $.50 per copy thereafter. Fee payee: Clerk of Court. Prepayment is required.

Caroline County

15th Circuit Court Main St & Courthouse Ln, PO Box 309, Bowling Green, VA 22427-0309; 804-633-5800. Hours: 8:30AM-5PM (EST). *Felony, Civil Actions Over $15,000, Probate.*

Civil Records: Access: Online, in person. Visitors must perform in person searches for themselves. No search fee. Required to search: name, years to search. Civil cases indexed by defendant, plaintiff. Civil records on books from early 1800s to present. Remote online access to court case indexes is via LOPAS; call 804-786-6455 to apply.

Criminal Records: Access: Online, in person. Visitors must perform in person searches for themselves. No search fee. Required to search: name, years to search; also helpful: DOB. Criminal records on books from early 1800s to present, computerized since 1992. Remote online access to court case indexes is via LOPAS; call 804-786-6455 to apply.

General Information: Public access terminal is available. No juvenile, sealed, adoption records released. Copy fee: $.50 per page. Certification fee: $2.00. Fee payee: Clerk of Court. Personal checks accepted. Accepted for payment of fines & costs only. Not accepted over the phone. Prepayment is required.

15th General District Court PO Box 511, Bowling Green, VA 22427; 804-633-5720; Fax: 804-633-3033. Hours: 8AM-4PM (EST). *Misdemeanor, Civil Actions Under $15,000, Eviction, Small Claims.*

Civil Records: Access: Mail, online, fax, in person. Both court and visitors may perform in person searches. No search fee. Required to search: name, years to search. Civil cases indexed by defendant, plaintiff. Civil records on computer from 1/92, index cards from 1991. Select and search District Courts at http://208.210.219.132/courtinfo/vadistrict/select.jsp?court=. For information about the statewide online systems, see the state introduction.

Criminal Records: Access: Mail, online, in person. Both court and visitors may perform in person searches. No search fee. Required to search: name, years to search, SSN. Criminal records on computer from 1/92, index cards from 1991. Online access to criminal records is the same as civil.

General Information: Public access terminal is available. Fax notes: Will not fax results.

Carroll County

27th Circuit Court PO Box 218, Hillsville, VA 24343; 276-728-3117. Hours: 8AM-5PM (EST). *Felony, Civil Actions Over $15,000, Probate.*

Civil Records: Access: Online, in person. Visitors must perform in person searches themselves. Required to search: name, years to search, also helpful: SSN. Civil cases indexed by defendant, plaintiff. Civil records on books from 1842 to present, on computer back to 1985. Select and search Circuit Courts online at http://208.210.219.132/courtinfo/vacircuit/select.jsp?court=. For information about the statewide online systems, see the state introduction.

Criminal Records: Access: Online, in person. Visitors must perform in person searches themselves. Required to search: name, years to search; also helpful: SSN. Criminal records on books from 1842 to present; on computer back to 1985. Online access to criminal records is the same as civil.

General Information: Public access terminal is available. No juvenile, sealed, adoption records released. Fax notes: Fee to fax results is $2.50 per page. Copy fee: $.50 per page. Certification fee: $2.00. Fee payee: Clerk of Court. Personal checks accepted. Prepayment is required.

Carroll Combined District Court PO Box 698, Hillsville, VA 24343; 276-728-7751; Fax: 276-728-2582. Hours: 8AM-4:30PM (EST). *Misdemeanor, Civil Actions Under $15,000, Eviction, Small Claims.*

Civil Records: Access: In person only. Visitors must perform in person searches for themselves. No search fee. Required to search: name, years to search. Civil cases indexed by defendant, plaintiff. Civil records on books from 1800s, on computer from 1988; no plaintiff index prior to computerization. Select and search District Courts at http://208.210.219.132/courtinfo/vadistrict/select.jsp?court=. For information about the statewide online systems, see the state introduction.

Criminal Records: Access: In person, online. Visitors must perform in person searches for themselves. No search fee. Criminal records on books from 1800s, on computer from 1988; no plaintiff index prior to computerization. Online assess to misdemeanor records is the same as civil.

General Information: Public access terminal is available. No juvenile, sealed records released. No copy fee. Fee payee: General District Court. Personal checks accepted. Credit cards accepted: Visa, MasterCard. Prepayment is required.

Charles City

9th Circuit Court 10700 Courthouse Rd, PO Box 86, Charles City, VA 23030-0086; 804-829-9212; Fax: 804-829-5647. Hours: 8:30AM-4:30PM (EST). *Felony, Civil Actions Over $15,000, Probate.*

Civil Records: Access: Mail, online, in person. Both court and visitors may perform in person searches. No search fee. Required to search: name, years to search. Civil cases indexed by defendant, plaintiff. Civil records on computer from 1990, on books from 1789. Select and search Circuit Courts online at http://208.210.219.132/courtinfo/vacircuit/select.jsp?court=. For information about the statewide online systems, see the state introduction.

Criminal Records: Access: Mail, online, in person. Both court and visitors may perform in person searches. No search fee. Required to search: name, years to search, DOB, SSN, signed release. Criminal records on computer from 1990, on books from 1789. Online access to criminal records is the same as civil.

General Information: No juvenile, sealed records released. Turnaround time 2-5 days. Fax notes: Fee to fax results is $.50 per page. Copy fee: $.50 per page. Certification fee: $2.00. Fee payee: Clerk of Circuit Court. Personal checks accepted. Prepayment required.

9th General District Court Charles City Courthouse, 10700 Courthouse Rd, Charles City, VA 23030; 804-829-9224; Fax: 804-829-5109. Hours: 8:30AM-4PM (EST). *Misdemeanor, Civil Actions Under $15,000, Eviction, Small Claims.*

Civil Records: Access: Mail, online, in person. Both court and visitors may perform in person searches. No search fee. Required to search: name, years to search. Civil cases indexed by defendant, plaintiff. Civil records on computer back to 1989; on books from 1700s. Select and search District Courts at http://208.210.219.132/courtinfo/vadistrict/select.jsp?court=. For information about the statewide online systems, see the state introduction.

Criminal Records: Access: Mail, online, in person. Both court and visitors may perform in person searches. No search fee. Required to search: name, years to search, DOB, SSN. Criminal records on computer back to 1989; on books from 1700s. Online access to criminal records is the same as civil.

General Information: Public access terminal is available. No juvenile, sealed records released. Turnaround time 3 days. Fax notes: Will not fax results. No copy fee. Certification fee: $2.00. Fee payee: Circuit Court. Personal checks accepted. Prepayment required.

Charlotte County

10th Circuit Court 115 LeGrande Ave PO Box 38, Charlotte Courthouse, VA 23923; 434-542-5147. Hours: 8:30AM-4:30PM (EST). *Felony, Civil Actions Over $15,000, Probate.*

Civil Records: Access: In person only. Visitors must perform in person searches for themselves. No search fee. Required to search: name, years to search. Civil cases indexed by defendant, plaintiff. Civil records on books from 1765, in folders by case number.

Criminal Records: Access: In person only. Visitors must perform in person searches for themselves. No search fee. Required to search: name, years to search, DOB. Criminal records on books from 1765, in folders by case number.

General Information: No juvenile, sealed records released. Copy fee: $.50 per page. Certification fee: $2.00. Fee payee: Clerk of Circuit Court. Personal checks accepted. Prepayment required.

Charlotte General District Court PO Box 127, Charlotte Courthouse, VA 23923; 434-542-5600; Fax: 434-542-5902. Hours: 8:30AM-4:30PM (EST).

Misdemeanor, Civil Actions Under $15,000, Eviction, Small Claims.

Civil Records: Access: Online, in person. Visitors must perform in person searches for themselves. No search fee. Required to search: name, years to search. Civil cases indexed by defendant, plaintiff. Civil records on computer back to 5/95, on books from 1988. Select and search District Courts at http://208.210.219.132/courtinfo/vadistrict/select.jsp?court=. For information about the statewide online systems, see the state introduction.

Criminal Records: Access: Online, in person. Visitors must perform in person searches for themselves. No search fee. Required to search: name, years to search, DOB; also helpful-SSN, signed release. Criminal records on computer back to 5/95, on books from 1988. Online access to criminal records is the same as civil.

General Information: Public access terminal is available. No juvenile, sealed records released. Fax notes: Fee to fax results is $.50 per page. Copy fee: $.50 per page. Fee payee: Clerk of General District Court. Personal checks accepted. Credit cards accepted: Visa, MasterCard.

Charlottesville City

16th Circuit Court 315 E High St, Charlottesville, VA 22902; 434-295-3182. Hours: 8:30AM-4:30PM (EST). *Felony, Civil Actions Over $15,000, Probate.*

Civil Records: Access: Online, in person. Visitors must perform in person searches for themselves. No search fee. Required to search: name, years to search. Civil cases indexed by defendant, plaintiff. Civil records on books from 1888 to present. Remote online access to court case indexes is via LOPAS; call 804-786-6455 to apply.

Criminal Records: Access: Online, in person. Visitors must perform in person searches for themselves. No search fee. Required to search: name, years to search; also helpful: DOB. Criminal records on books from 1888 to present. Remote online access to court case indexes is via LOPAS; call 804-786-6455 to apply.

General Information: No juvenile, sealed or adoption records released. Copy fee: $.50 per page. Certification fee: $2.00. Fee payee: Charlottesville Circuit Court Clerk's Office. Personal checks accepted. No out of state checks accepted. Prepayment is required.

Charlottesville General District Court 606 E Market St, PO Box 2677, Charlottesville, VA 22902; 434-970-3385; Fax: 434-970-3387. Hours: 8:30AM-4:30PM (EST). *Misdemeanor, Civil Actions Under $15,000, Eviction, Small Claims.*

Civil Records: Access: Mail, online, in person. Both court and visitors may perform in person searches. No search fee. Required to search: name, years to search. Civil cases indexed by defendant, plaintiff. Civil records kept for 10 years. Select and search District Courts at http://208.210.219.132/courtinfo/vadistrict/select.jsp?court=. For information about the statewide online systems, see the state introduction.

Criminal Records: Access: Mail, online, in person. Both court and visitors may perform in person searches. No search fee. Required to search: name, years to search; also helpful: DOB, SSN. Criminal records kept for 10 years. Online access to criminal records is the same as civil.

General Information: Public access terminal is available. No juvenile, sealed, confidential records released. SASE required. Turnaround time 3 days. Copy fee: $1.00 for first page, $.50 each add'l. Fee payee: General District Court. Personal checks accepted. Prepayment is required.

Chesapeake City

1st Circuit Court 307 Albemarle Dr, #300A, Chesapeake, VA 23322-5579; 757-382-3000; Fax: 757-

382-3035. Hours: 8:30AM-5PM (EST). *Felony, Civil Actions Over $15,000, Probate.*

Civil Records: Access: Mail, fax, online, in person. Visitors must perform in person searches for themselves. No search fee. Required to search: name, years to search. Civil cases indexed by defendant, plaintiff. Civil records on books from 1637, on computer from 1989. Online access available free at http://208.210.219.132/courtinfo/vacircuit/select.jsp?court=. For information about the statewide online systems, see the state introduction.

Criminal Records: Access: Mail, fax, online, in person. Visitors must perform in person searches for themselves. Search fee: $5.00. Required to search: name, years to search, DOB; also helpful: SSN, sex, signed release. Criminal records on books from 1800's; on computer from 1989. Online access to criminal records is the same as civil.

General Information: Public access terminal is available. No juvenile, sealed records released. SASE required. Turnaround time 1 week. Fax notes: Fee to fax results is $.50 per page. Copy fee: $.50 per page. Certification fee: $2.50. Fee payee: Clerk of Circuit Court. Personal checks accepted. Prepayment is required.

1st General District Court 307 Albemarle Dr #100, Chesapeake, VA 23322; Civil phone: 757-382-3143; Criminal phone: 757-382-3134; Fax: 757-382-3171. Hours: 8AM-4PM (EST). *Misdemeanor, Civil Actions Under $15,000, Eviction, Small Claims.*

Note: Indicate division (civil, criminal or traffic) in address.

Civil Records: Access: Mail, online, in person. Both court and visitors may perform in person searches. Search fee: $15.00 per name. Required to search: name, years to search. Civil cases indexed by defendant, plaintiff. Civil records on computer back to 1990; prior on books. Select and search District Courts at http://208.210.219.132/courtinfo/vadistrict/select.jsp?court=. For information about the statewide online systems, see the state introduction.

Criminal Records: Access: Mail, online, in person. Both court and visitors may perform in person searches. No search fee. Required to search: name, years to search, DOB; also helpful: SSN. Civil records on computer back to 1990; prior on books. Online access to criminal records is the same as civil.

General Information: Public access terminal is available. No juvenile, sealed records released. Turnaround time 2-14 days. Copy fee: $1.00 per page. Certification fee: $2.00. Fee payee: General District Court. Personal checks accepted. Credit cards accepted: Visa, MasterCard. Prepayment is required.

Chesterfield County

12th Circuit Court 9500 Courthouse Rd, PO Box 125, Chesterfield, VA 23832; 804-748-1241; Fax: 804-796-5625. Hours: 8:30AM-5PM (EST). *Felony, Civil Actions Over $15,000, Probate.*

www.co.chesterfield.va.us/JusticeAdministration/CircuitCourtClerk/clerhome.asp

Civil Records: Access: Mail, in person. Both court and visitors may perform in person searches. Search fee: No search fee. Required to search: name, years to search. Civil cases indexed by defendant, plaintiff. Civil records on computer go back to 1989; prior on index books.

Criminal Records: Access: Mail, in person. Only the court performs in person searches; visitors may not. Search fee: $3.00 per name. Required to search: name, years to search; also helpful: DOB, SSN. Criminal records on computer go back to 1989, prior on index books.

General Information: Public access terminal is available. (Civil only.) No juvenile, adoption, sealed records released. SASE required. Turnaround time 1-2

days. Copy fee: $.50 per page. Certification fee: $2.00. Fee payee: Chesterfield Circuit Court. Personal checks accepted. Prepayment is required.

12th General District Court PO Box 144, Chesterfield, VA 23832; 804-748-1231. Hours: 8AM-4PM (EST). *Misdemeanor, Civil Actions Under $15,000, Eviction, Small Claims.*

Civil Records: Access: Mail, online, in person. Both court and visitors may perform in person searches. No search fee. Required to search: name, years to search. Civil cases indexed by defendant, plaintiff. Civil records on computer from 1986 to present, index books from 1975 to 1986. Select and search District Courts at http://208.210.219.132/courtinfo/vadistrict/select.jsp?court=. For information about the statewide online systems, see the state introduction.

Criminal Records: Access: Mail, online, in person. Both court and visitors may perform in person searches. No search fee. Required to search: name, years to search, DOB, SSN. Criminal records on computer from 1986 to present, index books from 1975 to 1986. Online access to criminal records is the same as civil.

General Information: Public access terminal is available. No sealed records released. Turnaround time 2 days. Copy fee: $.50 per page. Certification fee: $2.00. Personal checks accepted. Credit cards accepted: Visa, MasterCard.

Clarke County

26th Circuit Court PO Box 189, Berryville, VA 22611; 540-955-5116; Fax: 540-955-0284. Hours: 9AM-5PM (EST). *Felony, Civil Actions Over $15,000, Probate.*

Civil Records: Access: Phone, mail, fax, online, in person. Both court and visitors may perform in person searches. No search fee. Required to search: name, years to search. Civil cases indexed by defendant, plaintiff. Civil records on books from 1920s. Remote online access to court case indexes is via LOPAS; call 804-786-6455 to apply.

Criminal Records: Access: Online, in person. Visitors must perform in person searches for themselves. No search fee. Required to search: name, years to search, signed release. Criminal records on books from 1920s. Remote online access to court case indexes is via LOPAS; call 804-786-6455 to apply.

General Information: No juvenile, sealed or adoption records released. No criminal records by mail. SASE requested. Turnaround time 1-2 days. Fax notes: Fee to fax results is $.50 per page. Copy fee: $.50 per page. Fee payee: Clerk of Court. Personal checks accepted. Prepayment is required.

General District Court 104 N Church St (PO Box 612), Berryville, VA 22611; 540-955-5128; Fax: 540-955-1195. Hours: 8:30AM-4:30PM (EST). *Misdemeanor, Civil Actions Under $15,000, Eviction, Small Claims.*

www.co.clarke.va.us

Civil Records: Access: Online, in person. Visitors must perform in person searches for themselves. No search fee. Required to search: name, years to search. Civil cases indexed by defendant, plaintiff. Civil records on computer from 1992, on index cards for 1991. Select and search District Courts at http://208.210.219.132/courtinfo/vadistrict/select.jsp?court=. For information about the statewide online systems, see the state introduction.

Criminal Records: Access: Online, in person. Visitors must perform in person searches for themselves. No search fee. Required to search: name, years to search, DOB, SSN, date of conviction, charge; also helpful: docket number, defendant's name. Criminal records on computer from 1992, on index cards for 1991. Online access to criminal records is the same as civil.

General Information: Public access terminal is available. Copy fee: $.50 per page. Fee payee: Clarke County General District Court. Personal checks accepted. Personal checks require name and address. Prepayment is required.

Clifton Forge City

25th Circuit Court PO Box 670, Covington, VA 24426; 540-965-1730. Hours: 9AM-5PM (EST). *Felony, Civil Actions Over $15,000, Probate.*

Note: This court closed 7/1/01 and was combined with the Alleghany County Circuit Court.

25th General District Court PO Box 139, Covington, VA 24426; 540-965-1720; Fax: 540-965-1720. Hours: 9AM-5PM (EST). *Misdemeanor, Civil Actions Under $15,000, Eviction, Small Claims.*

Note: As of 7/1/2001, the Clifton Forge Court is combined with the Alleghany County District Court to form the 25th Combined District Court.

Colonial Heights City

12th Circuit Court 401 Temple Ave, PO Box 3401, Colonial Heights, VA 23834; 804-520-9364. Hours: 8:30AM-5PM (EST). *Felony, Civil Actions Over $15,000, Probate.*

Civil Records: Access: Mail, online, in person. Both court and visitors may perform in person searches. Search fee: $5.00 per name. Required to search: name, years to search. Civil cases indexed by defendant, plaintiff. Civil records on books from 1961, on computer from 1991. Remote online access to court case indexes is via LOPAS; call 804-786-6455 to apply.

Criminal Records: Access: Mail, online, in person. Both court and visitors may perform in person searches. Search fee: $5.00 per name. Required to search: name, years to search; also helpful: DOB, SSN. Criminal records on books from 1961, on computer from 1991. Remote online access to court case indexes is via LOPAS; call 804-786-6455 to apply.

General Information: No juvenile, sealed or adoption records released. SASE required. Turnaround time 2 days. Copy fee: $.50 per page. Certification fee: $2.00. Fee payee: Clerk of Circuit Court. Personal checks accepted. Prepayment is required.

12th General District Court 401 Temple Ave, PO Box 279, Colonial Heights, VA 23834; 804-520-9346 (Dial 0); Fax: 804-520-9370. Hours: 8AM-4PM (EST). *Misdemeanor, Civil Actions Under $15,000, Eviction, Small Claims.*

Civil Records: Access: Mail, fax, online, in person. Both court and visitors may perform in person searches. No search fee. Required to search: name, years to search. Civil cases indexed by defendant, plaintiff. Civil records on computer from 1989 to present, index cards from 1985. Select and search District Courts at http://208.210.219.132/courtinfo/vadistrict/select.jsp?court=. For information about the statewide online systems, see the state introduction.

Criminal Records: Access: Mail, fax, online, in person. Both court and visitors may perform in person searches. No search fee. Required to search: name, years to search, DOB, SSN. Criminal records on computer from 1989 to present, index cards from 1985. Online access to criminal records is the same as civil.

General Information: Public access terminal is available. No juvenile, sealed records released. Turnaround time 1 week. Copy fee: $.50 per page. Fee payee: Colonial Heights Combined Court. Personal checks accepted. Credit cards accepted: Visa, MasterCard. Prepayment is required.

Covington City

Circuit & District Courts, VA.

Note: See Alleghany County.

Craig County

25th Circuit Court PO Box 185, New Castle, VA 24127-0185; 540-864-6141. Hours: 9AM-5PM (EST). *Felony, Civil Actions Over $15,000, Probate.*

Civil Records: Access: Online, in person. Visitors must perform in person searches for themselves. No search fee. Required to search: name, years to search. Civil cases indexed by defendant. Civil records on books from mid 1800s. Remote online access to court case indexes is via LOPAS; call 804-786-6455 to apply.

Criminal Records: Access: Online, in person. Visitors must perform in person searches for themselves. No search fee. Required to search: name, years to search; also helpful: SSN. Criminal records on books from mid 1800s. Online access to criminal records is the same as civil.

General Information: No juvenile, sealed or adoption records released. Copy fee: $.50 per page. Certification fee: $2.00. Fee payee: Clerk of Court. Personal checks accepted. Prepayment is required.

25th General District Court Craig County General District Court, PO Box 232, New Castle, VA 24127; 540-864-5989. Hours: 8:15AM-4:45PM (EST). *Misdemeanor, Civil Actions Under $15,000, Eviction, Small Claims.*

Civil Records: Access: Mail, online, in person. Visitors must perform in person searches for themselves. No search fee. Required to search: name, years to search. Civil cases indexed by defendant, plaintiff. Civil records in files 10 years back. Select and search District Courts at http://208.210.219.132/courtinfo/vadistrict/select.jsp?court=. For information about the statewide online systems, see the state introduction.

Criminal Records: Access: Mail, online, in person. Visitors must perform in person searches for themselves. No search fee. Required to search: name, years to search; also helpful: SSN. Criminal records in files 10 years back. Online access to criminal records is the same as civil. Lengthy searches must be performed in person.

General Information: Public access terminal is available. No juvenile, sealed records released. SASE Required. Copy fee: $1.00 per page. Fee payee: Craig County District Court. Personal checks accepted. Credit cards accepted: Visa, MasterCard.

Culpeper County

16th Circuit Court 135 W Cameron St, Culpeper, VA 22701-3097; 540-727-3438. Hours: 8:30AM-4:30PM *Felony, Civil Actions Over $15,000, Probate.*

Civil Records: Access: In person. Visitors must perform in person searches for themselves. No search fee. Required to search: name, years to search. Civil cases indexed by defendant, plaintiff. Civil records on computer from 1991, docket books from 1800s; records go back to 1950. Remote online access to court case indexes is via LOPAS; call 804-786-6455 to apply.

Criminal Records: Access: In person. Visitors must perform in person searches for themselves. No search fee. Required to search: name, years to search, signed release. Criminal records on computer from 1991, docket books from 1800s, roecords go back to 1950. Online access to criminal records is the same as civil.

General Information: Public access terminal is available. No juvenile, sealed records released. Copy fee: $.50 per page. Certification fee: $2.00. Fee payee: Clerk of Court. Personal checks accepted. Prepayment is required.

16th General District Court 135 W Cameron St, Culpeper, VA 22701; 540-727-3417; Fax: 540-727-3474. Hours: 8:30AM-4:30PM (EST). *Misdemeanor, Civil Actions Under $15,000, Eviction, Small Claims.*

Civil Records: Access: Mail, online, in person. Both court and visitors may perform in person searches. No

search fee. Required to search: name, years to search. Civil cases indexed by defendant, plaintiff. Civil records on computer from 1987 to present, prior on index cards. Select and search District Courts at http://208.210.219.132/courtinfo/vadistrict/select.jsp?court=. For information about the statewide online systems, see the state introduction.

Criminal Records: Access: Mail, online, in person. Both court and visitors may perform in person searches. No search fee. Required to search: name, years to search. Criminal records on computer from 1987 to present, prior on index cards. Online access to criminal records is the same as civil.

General Information: Public access terminal is available. No juvenile, sealed records released. SASE required. Turnaround time 1-5 days. Copy fee: $1.00 for 1st two copies, $.50 each add'l page. Fee payee: General District Court. Personal checks accepted. Prepayment is required.

Cumberland County

10th Circuit Court PO Box 8, Cumberland, VA 23040; 804-492-4442. Hours: 8:30AM-4:30PM (EST). *Felony, Civil Actions Over $15,000, Probate.*

Civil Records: Access: Online, in person. Visitors must perform in person searches for themselves. No search fee. Required to search: name, years to search. Civil cases indexed by defendant, plaintiff. Civil records in files. Select and search Circuit Courts online at http://208.210.219.132/courtinfo/vacircuit/select.jsp?court=. For information about the statewide online systems, see the state introduction. Phone access only available for simple requests.

Criminal Records: Access: Online, in person. Visitors must perform in person searches for themselves. No search fee. Required to search: name, years to search. Criminal records in files. Online access to criminal records is the same as civil.

General Information: No juvenile, sealed records released. Copy fee: $.50 per page. Certification fee: $.50 per page. Fee payee: Clerk of Circuit Court. Personal checks accepted. Prepayment is required.

10th General District Court PO Box 24, Cumberland, VA 23040; 804-492-4848; Fax: 804-492-9455. Hours: 8:30AM-4:30PM (EST). *Misdemeanor, Civil Actions Under $15,000, Eviction, Small Claims.*

Civil Records: Access: Phone, fax, mail, online, in person. Only the court performs in person searches; visitors may not. No search fee. Required to search: name, years to search. Civil cases indexed by defendant, plaintiff. Civil records on books from 1990, on computer from 1993. Select and search District Courts at http://208.210.219.132/courtinfo/vadistrict/select.jsp?court=. For information about the statewide online systems, see the state introduction.

Criminal Records: Access: Phone, fax, mail, online, in person. Only the court performs in person searches; visitors may not. No search fee. Required to search: name, years to search; also helpful: DOB, SSN, sex. Criminal records on books from 1990, on computer from 1993. Online access to criminal records is the same as civil.

General Information: No juvenile, sealed records released. SASE required. Turnaround time 2 days. Copy fee: $1.00 per page. Fee payee: Clerk of District Court. Personal checks accepted. Credit cards accepted: Visa, MasterCard.

Danville City

22nd Circuit Court PO Box 3300, Danville, VA 24543; 434-799-5168; Fax: 434-799-6502. Hours: 8:30AM-5PM (EST). *Felony, Civil Actions Over $15,000, Probate.*

Civil Records: Access: Online, in person. Visitors must perform in person searches for themselves. No search

fee. Required to search: name, years to search. Civil cases indexed by defendant, plaintiff. Civil records in index books from 1841, judgments on computer since 1990. Online access available free at http://208.210.219.132/courtinfo/vacircuit/select.jsp?court=. For information about the statewide online systems, see the state introduction.

Criminal Records: Access: Online, in person. Visitors must perform in person searches for themselves. No search fee. Required to search: name, years to search. Criminal records in index books from 1841. Criminal records on computer from 1988. Online access to criminal records is the same as civil.

General Information: No juvenile, sealed or adoption records released. Fax notes: Fee to fax results is $2.00 per page. Copy fee: $.50 per page. Certification fee: $2.00. Fee payee: Gerald A Gibson, Clerk. Personal checks accepted. Prepayment is required.

22nd General District Court PO Box 3300, Danville, VA 24543; 434-799-5179; Fax: 434-797-8814. Hours: 8:30AM-4:30PM (EST). *Misdemeanor, Civil Actions Under $15,000, Eviction, Small Claims.*

Civil Records: Access: Mail, online, in person. Both court and visitors may perform in person searches. No search fee. Required to search: name, years to search. Civil cases indexed by defendant, plaintiff. Civil records go back 10 years; on computer back to 1987. Select and search District Courts at http://208.210.219.132/courtinfo/vadistrict/select.jsp?court=. For information about the statewide online systems, see the state introduction.

Criminal Records: Access: Mail, online, in person. Both court and visitors may perform in person searches. No search fee. Required to search: name, years to search. Criminal records go back 10 years; on computer back to 1987. Select and search District Courts at http://208.210.219.132/courtinfo/vadistrict/select.jsp?court=.

General Information: Public access terminal is available. No juvenile, sealed records released. SASE requested. Turnaround time 2 days. Copy fee: $1.00 1st 2 pages, $.50 each additional page. Fee payee: General District Court. Personal checks accepted. Credit cards accepted: Visa, MasterCard.

Dickenson County

29th Circuit Court PO Box 190, Clintwood, VA 24228; 276-926-1616; Fax: 276-926-6465. Hours: 8:30AM-4:30PM (EST). *Felony, Civil Actions Over $15,000, Probate.*

Civil Records: Access: Phone, mail, online, in person. Both court and visitors may perform in person searches. No search fee. Required to search: name, years to search. Civil cases indexed by defendant, plaintiff. Civil records on computer from 1989, index book from 1880. Online access available free at http://208.210.219.132/courtinfo/vacircuit/select.jsp?court=. For information about the statewide online systems, see the state introduction.

Criminal Records: Access: Phone, mail, online, in person. Both court and visitors may perform in person searches. No search fee. Required to search: name, years to search, DOB; also helpful: SSN. Criminal records on computer from 1989, index book from 1880. Online access to criminal records is the same as civil.

General Information: Public access terminal is available. No juvenile, sealed, adoption, confidential records released. SASE requested. Turnaround time 1 week. Copy fee: $.50 per page. Certification fee: $2.00. Fee payee: Joe Tate, Clerk of Circuit Court. Personal checks accepted. Prepayment is required.

29th General District Court PO Box 128, Clintwood, VA 24228; 276-926-1630; Fax: 276-926-4815. Hours: 8:30AM-4:30PM (EST). *Misdemeanor, Civil Actions Under $15,000, Eviction, Small Claims.*

Civil Records: Access: Phone, mail, in person. Both court and visitors may perform in person searches. No search fee. Required to search: name, years to search. Civil cases indexed by defendant. Civil records on index cards 10 yrs back, on computer from 5/93. Select and search District Courts at http://208.210.219.132/courtinfo/vadistrict/select.jsp?court=. For information about the statewide online systems, see the state introduction.

Criminal Records: Access: Phone, mail, in person. Both court and visitors may perform in person searches. No search fee. Required to search: name, years to search. Criminal records on index cards 10 yrs back, on computer from 5/93. Online access to criminal records is the same as civil.

General Information: Public access terminal is available. No juvenile, sealed records released. SASE requested. Turnaround time 1 week. Copy fee: $.10 per page. Fee payee: Dickenson Combined Court or General District Court. Personal checks accepted. Credit cards accepted: Visa, MasterCard.

Dinwiddie County

11th Circuit Court PO Box 63, Dinwiddie, VA 23841; 804-469-4540. Hours: 8:30AM-4:30PM (EST). *Felony, Civil Actions Over $15,000, Probate.*

Civil Records: Access: Mail, online, in person. Both court and visitors may perform in person searches. No search fee. Required to search: name, years to search; also helpful: address. Civil cases indexed by defendant, plaintiff. Civil records on index cards from 1833; deeds on computer since 1989. Select and search Circuit Courts online at http://208.210.219.132/courtinfo/vadistrict/select.jsp?court=. For information about the statewide online systems, see the state introduction.

Criminal Records: Access: Mail, online, in person. Both court and visitors may perform in person searches. No search fee. Required to search: name, years to search; also helpful: DOB, SSN. Criminal records on index cards from 1833; deeds on computer since 1989. Online access to criminal records is the same as civil.

General Information: No juvenile, sealed or expunged records released. SASE requested. Turnaround time 3 days. Copy fee: $.50 per page. Certification fee: $2.00 plus $.50 per page. Fee payee: Clerk of Court. Personal checks accepted.

11th General District Court PO Box 280, Dinwiddie, VA 23841; 804-469-4533; Fax: 804-469-4412. Hours: 8:30AM-4:30PM (EST). *Misdemeanor, Civil Actions Under $15,000, Eviction, Small Claims.*

Civil Records: Access: Mail, online, in person. Only the court performs in person searches; visitors may not. No search fee. Required to search: name, years to search. Civil cases indexed by defendant, plaintiff. Civil records on index cards from 1800s, on computer from 1989. Select and search District Courts at http://208.210.219.132/courtinfo/vadistrict/select.jsp?court=. For information about the statewide online systems, see the state introduction.

Criminal Records: Access: Mail, online, in person. Only the court performs in person searches; visitors may not. No search fee. Required to search: name, years to search. Criminal records on index cards from 1800s, on computer from 1989. Online access to criminal records is the same as civil.

General Information: No juvenile, sealed records released. SASE required. Turnaround time 3 days. Copy fee: $1.00 per page. Certification fee: $2.00. Fee payee: District Court. Personal checks accepted. Credit cards accepted: Visa, MasterCard. Prepayment is required.

Emporia City

Circuit Court, VA.
Note: See Greensville County.

6th General District Court 315 S Main, Emporia, VA 23847; 434-634-5400. Hours: 8:30AM-4:30PM (EST). *Misdemeanor, Civil Actions Under $15,000, Eviction, Small Claims.*

Civil Records: Access: Online, in person. Visitors must perform in person searches for themselves. No search fee. Required to search: name, years to search. Civil cases indexed by defendant, plaintiff. Civil records on computer back to 1991. Select and search District Courts at http://208.210.219.132/courtinfo/vadistrict/select.jsp?court=. For information about the statewide online systems, see the state introduction.

Criminal Records: Access: Mail, online, in person. Only the court performs in person searches; visitors may not. No search fee. Required to search: name, years to search. Criminal records on computer back to 1991. Online access to criminal records is the same as civil.

General Information: Public access terminal is available. No juvenile records released. Turnaround time 1-2 days. No copy fee. Personal checks accepted.

Essex County

15th Circuit Court PO Box 445, 305 prince St, Tappahannock, VA 22560; 804-443-3541. Hours: 8:30AM-5PM (EST). *Felony, Civil Actions Over $15,000, Probate.*

Civil Records: Access: In person only. Visitors must perform in person searches for themselves. No search fee. Required to search: name, years to search. Civil cases indexed by defendant, plaintiff. Civil records on books from 1656; deed index on computer back to 1977. Remote online access to court case indexes is via LOPAS; call 804-786-6455 to apply.

Criminal Records: Access: In person only. Visitors must perform in person searches for themselves. No search fee. Required to search: name, years to search. Criminal records on books from 1656. Online access to criminal records is the same as civil.

General Information: No juvenile, sealed records released. Copy fee: $.50 per page. Certification fee: $2.00. Fee payee: Clerk of Court. Personal checks accepted. Prepayment is required.

15th General District Court PO Box 66, Tappahannock, VA 22560; 804-443-3744; Fax: 804-443-4122. Hours: 8AM-12:30PM, 1-4:30PM (EST). *Misdemeanor, Civil Actions Under $15,000, Eviction, Small Claims.*

Civil Records: Access: Mail, online, in person. Both court and visitors may perform in person searches. No search fee. Required to search: name, years to search. Civil cases indexed by defendant, plaintiff. Civil records on computer from 5/92, prior on index cards. Select and search District Courts at http://208.210.219.132/courtinfo/vadistrict/select.jsp?court=. For information about the statewide online systems, see the state introduction.

Criminal Records: Access: Online, in person. Visitors must perform in person searches for themselves. No search fee. Required to search: name, years to search, DOB, SSN. Criminal records on computer from 5/92, prior on index cards. Online access to criminal records is the same as civil.

General Information: Public access terminal is available. No juvenile, sealed records released. Turnaround time 1-2 days. No copy fee. Fee payee: General District Court. Personal checks accepted. Credit cards accepted: Visa, MasterCard. Prepayment is required.

Fairfax County

19th Circuit Court 4110 Chain Bridge Rd, Fairfax, VA 22030; Civil phone: 703-591-8507; Criminal phone: 703-246-2228. Hours: 8AM-4PM (EST). *Felony, Civil Actions Over $15,000, Probate.*
www.co.fairfax.va.us/courts

Civil Records: Access: In person, online. Visitors must perform in person searches for themselves. No search fee. Required to search: name, years to search. Civil cases indexed by defendant, plaintiff. Civil records on computer from 1979, index cards from 1940s. Remote online access to court case indexes is via LOPAS; call 804-786-6455 to apply.

Criminal Records: Access: In person, online. Visitors must perform in person searches for themselves. No search fee. Required to search: name, years to search, DOB; also helpful: SSN. Criminal records on computer from 1979, index cards from 1940s. Online access to criminal records is the same as civil.

General Information: No juvenile, sealed records released. Copy fee: $.50 per page. Certification fee: $2.00. Fee payee: Fairfax Circuit Court. Personal checks accepted. In-state personal checks accepted. Credit cards accepted: Visa, MasterCard. Prepayment is required.

19th General District Court 4110 Chain Bridge Rd, Fairfax, VA 22030; 703-246-2153; Civil phone: 703-246-3012; Criminal phone: 703-691-7320; Fax: 703-591-2349. 8AM-4PM (EST). *Misdemeanor, Civil Actions Under $15,000, Eviction, Small Claims.*
www.co.fairfax.va.us/courts

Note: Traffic division at 703-246-3764.

Civil Records: Access: Phone, in person, online. Visitors must perform in person searches for themselves. No search fee. Required to search: name, years to search. Civil cases indexed by defendant, plaintiff. Civil indexes for 10 years; onsite records held only 3 years before archiving; on computer back 10 years. Select and search District Courts at http://208.210.219.132/courtinfo/vadistrict/select.jsp?court=. For information about the statewide online systems, see the state introduction.

Criminal Records: Access: Phone, in person, online. Only the court performs in person searches; visitors may not. No search fee. Required to search: name, years to search; also helpful: DOB, SSN. Criminal records on computer for 10 years; onsite records held only 3 years before archiving. Online access to criminal records is the same as civil.

General Information: Public access terminal is available. No juvenile, sealed records released. Copy fee: $.50 per page. Fee payee: Fairfax General District Court. Personal checks accepted. Prepayment required.

Fairfax City

Circuit Court, VA.
Note: See Fairfax County.

19th General District Court 10455 Armstrong St #304, Fairfax, VA 22030; 703-385-7866; Fax: 703-352-3195. 8:30AM-4:30PM (EST). *Misdemeanor.*

Note: Find Circuit Court cases and General District civil cases for this city in the Fairfax County listing.

Criminal Records: Access: Mail, in person. Only the court performs in person searches; visitors may not. No search fee. Required to search: name, years to search; also helpful: SSN. Criminal records on computer and index from 1985.

General Information: No juvenile or sealed records released. SASE requested. Turnaround time same day. Copy fee: $1.00 for first 2 pages; each add'l page $.50. Fee payee: General District Court. Personal checks accepted. Credit cards accepted: Visa, MasterCard.

Falls Church City

Circuit Court, VA.
Note: See Arlington County.

17th District Courts Combined Falls Church District, 300 Park Ave, Falls Church, VA 22046-3305; 703-248-5096 (GDC); Civil phone: 703-248-5098; Fax:

703-241-1407. 8AM-4PM (EST). *Misdemeanor, Civil Actions Under $15,000, Eviction, Small Claims.*

www.ci.falls-church.va.us

Note: Small claims phone is 703-248-5157; juvenile and domestic relations is 703-248-5099.

Civil Records: Access: Fax, online. Only the court performs in person searches; visitors may not. No search fee. Required to search: name, years to search. Civil cases indexed by defendant, plaintiff. Civil records on computer from 1991, microfiche back to 1980. Select and search District Courts at http://208.210.219.132/courtinfo/vadistrict/select.jsp?court=. For information about the statewide online systems, see the state introduction.

Criminal Records: Access: Fax, online, in person. Only the court performs in person searches; visitors may not. No search fee. Required to search: name, years to search; also helpful: DOB, SSN. Criminal records on computer and microfiche back to 1991. Online access to criminal records is the same as civil.

General Information: No juvenile, sealed records released. Fax notes: No fee to fax results. Copy fee: $.50 per page. Fee payee: Falls Church District Court. Personal checks accepted. Credit cards accepted: Visa, MasterCard. Prepayment is required.

Fauquier County

20th Circuit Court 40 Culpeper St, Warrenton, VA 20186-3298; 540-347-8610. Hours: 8AM-4:30PM (EST). *Felony, Civil Actions Over $15,000, Probate.*

http://co.fauquier.va.us/services/ccc/index.html

Civil Records: Access: Online, in person. Visitors must perform in person searches for themselves. No search fee. Required to search: name, years to search. Civil cases indexed by defendant, plaintiff. Civil records on computer back to 1988. Online access available free at http://208.210.219.132/courtinfo/vacircuit/select.jsp?court=. For information about the statewide online systems, see the state introduction.

Criminal Records: Access: Online, in person. Visitors must perform in person searches for themselves. No search fee. Required to search: name, years to search. Criminal records on computer back to 1988. Online access to criminal records is the same as civil.

General Information: No juvenile, sealed, adoption records released. Copy fee: $.50 per page. Certification fee: $2.00. Fee payee: Clerk of Fauquier Circuit Court. Personal checks accepted. Prepayment is required.

20th General District Court 6 Court St, Warrenton, VA 20186; Civil phone: 540-347-8676; Criminal phone: 540-347-8624; Fax: 540-347-5756. Hours: 8:30AM-4:30PM (EST). *Misdemeanor, Civil Actions Under $15,000, Eviction, Small Claims.*

Civil Records: Access: Online, in person. Visitors must perform in person searches for themselves. No search fee. Required to search: name, years to search. Civil cases indexed by defendant, plaintiff. Civil records go back 10 years; civil records on computerized back 10 years, prior on file cards. Select and search District Courts at http://208.210.219.132/courtinfo/vadistrict/select.jsp?court=. For information about the statewide online systems, see the state introduction.

Criminal Records: Access: Online, in person. Visitors must perform in person searches for themselves. No search fee. Required to search: name, years to search. Criminal records computerized back 10 yeas, criminal records only go back 10 years. Online access to criminal records is the same as civil.

General Information: Public access terminal is available. No juvenile, sealed records released. Copy fee: $1.00 1st 2 pages, $.50 each additional page. Fee payee: General District Court. Personal checks accepted.

Floyd County

27th Circuit Court 100 East Main St, #200, Floyd, VA 24091; 540-745-9330. Hours: 8:30AM-4:30PM M-F, 8:30AM-Noon Sat (EST). *Felony, Civil Actions Over $15,000, Probate.*

Civil Records: Access: Online, in person. Visitors must perform in person searches for themselves. No search fee. Required to search: name, years to search. Civil cases indexed by defendant, plaintiff. Civil records on files from 1831. Select and search Circuit Courts online at http://208.210.219.132/courtinfo/vacircuit/select.jsp?court=. For information about the statewide online systems, see the state introduction.

Criminal Records: Access: Online, in person. Visitors must perform in person searches for themselves. No search fee. Required to search: name, years to search; also helpful: DOB, SSN. Criminal records on files from 1831. Online access to criminal records is the same as civil.

General Information: No juvenile, sealed records released. Copy fee: $.50 per page. Certification fee: $2.00. Fee payee: Clerk of Circuit Court. Personal checks accepted. Prepayment is required.

27th General District Court 100 East Main St, Floyd, VA 24091-2101; 540-745-9327; Fax: 540-745-9329. Hours: 8AM-4:30PM (EST). *Misdemeanor, Civil Actions Under $15,000, Eviction, Small Claims.*

Civil Records: Access: Online, in person. Visitors must perform in person searches. No search fee. Required to search: name, years to search. Civil cases indexed by defendant, plaintiff. Civil records computerized since 1993. Select and search District Courts at http://208.210.219.132/courtinfo/vadistrict/select.jsp?court=. Also, remote online access to court case indexes is via LOPAS; call 804-786-6455 to apply. Phone search results may be of limited content.

Criminal Records: Access: Online, in person. Visitors must perform in person searches for themselves. No search fee. Required to search: name, years to search, DOB. Criminal records computerized since 1993. Online access to criminal records is the same as civil. Phone search results may be of limited content.

General Information: Public access terminal is available. No juvenile, sealed records released. Copy fee: $.50 per page. Fee payee: Clerk of District Court. Prepayment is required.

Fluvanna County

16th Circuit Court PO Box 299, Palmyra, VA 22963; 434-589-8011; Fax: 434-589-6004. Hours: 8:30AM-4:30PM (EST). *Felony, Civil Actions Over $15,000, Probate.*

Civil Records: Access: Mail, in person. Both court and visitors may perform in person searches. Search fee: $5.00 per name. Required to search: name, years to search. Civil cases indexed by defendant, plaintiff. Civil records on index books from 1777; computerized back to 1985. Select and search Circuit Courts online at http://208.210.219.132/courtinfo/vacircuit/select.jsp?court=. For information about the statewide online systems, see the state introduction.

Criminal Records: Access: Mail, in person, online. Both court and visitors may perform in person searches. Search fee: $5.00 per name. Required to search: name, years to search, DOB; also helpful: SSN. Criminal records on index books from 1777; computerized back to 1985. Online access to criminal records is the same as civil.

General Information: Public access terminal is available. No juvenile or sealed records released. SASE required. Turnaround time same 1-2 days. Fax notes: Fee to fax results is $2.00 per document. Copy fee: $.50 per page. Certification fee: $2.00. Fee payee: Clerk of Circuit Court. Personal checks accepted. Prepayment is required.

16th General District Court Fluvanna County Courthouse, PO Box 417, Palmyra, VA 22963; 434-591-1980; Fax: 434-591-1981 press 4. Hours: 8:30AM-4:30PM (EST). *Misdemeanor, Civil Actions Under $15,000, Eviction, Small Claims.*

Civil Records: Access: Online, in person. Visitors must perform in person searches for themselves. No search fee. Required to search: name, years to search. Civil cases indexed by defendant, plaintiff. Civil records on computer since 12/91, on books since 1984. Select and search District Courts at http://208.210.219.132/courtinfo/vadistrict/select.jsp?court=. For information about the statewide online systems, see the state introduction.

Criminal Records: Access: Online, in person. Visitors must perform in person searches for themselves. No search fee. Required to search: name, years to search; also helpful: DOB, SSN. Criminal records on computer since 12/91, on books since 1984. Online access to criminal records is the same as civil.

General Information: Public access terminal is available. No juvenile records released. Copy fee: $.50 per page. Fee payee: Fluvanna District Court. Personal checks accepted. Prepayment is required.

Franklin City

5th Circuit Court PO Box 190, Courtland, VA 23837; 757-653-2200. Hours: 8:30AM-5PM (EST). *Felony, Civil Actions Over $15,000, Probate.*

Note: Southampton County serves as the Circuit Court for the city of Franklin.

Civil Records: Access: Mail, online, in person. Both court and visitors may perform in person searches. Search fee: $5.00 per name. Required to search: name, years to search. Civil cases indexed by defendant, plaintiff. Civil records on computer since 1990, prior on docket books since 1700s. Select and search Circuit Courts online at http://208.210.219.132/courtinfo/vacircuit/select.jsp?court=. For information about the statewide online systems, see the state introduction.

Criminal Records: Access: Mail, online, in person. Both court and visitors may perform in person searches. Search fee: $5.00 per name. Required to search: name, years to search; also helpful: SSN. Criminal records on computer since 1990, prior on docket books since 1700s. Online access to criminal records is the same as civil.

General Information: Public access terminal is available. No juvenile records released. Turnaround time 2-5 days. Copy fee: $.50 per page. Certification fee: $2.00. Fee payee: Clerk of the Circuit Court. Personal checks accepted. Credit cards accepted: Visa, MasterCard.

Circuit Court, VA.

Note: See Franklin County .

22nd General District Court PO Box 569, Rocky Mount, VA 24151; 540-483-3060; Fax: 540-483-3036. 8:30AM-4:30PM (EST). *Misdemeanor, Civil Actions Under $15,000, Eviction, Small Claims.*

Civil Records: Access: Online, in person. Visitors must perform in person searches for themselves. No search fee. Required to search: name, years to search. Civil cases indexed by defendant, plaintiff. Civil records file on computer from 1992. Select and search District Courts at http://208.210.219.132/courtinfo/vadistrict/select.jsp?court=. For information about the statewide online systems, see the state introduction.

Criminal Records: Access: Online, in person. Visitors must perform in person searches for themselves. No search fee. Required to search: name, years to search. Criminal records file on computer from 1992. Online access to criminal records is the same as civil.

General Information: Public access terminal is available. Copy fee: $.25 per page. Personal checks accepted. Credit cards accepted: Visa, MasterCard.

Frederick County

Circuit Court 5 North Kent St, Winchester, VA 22601; 540-667-5770. Hours: 9AM-5PM (EST). *Felony, Misdemeanor, Civil, Probate.*

www.winfredclerk.com

Civil Records: Access: Mail, in person. Both court and visitors may perform in person searches. No search fee. Required to search: name, years to search. Civil cases indexed by defendant, plaintiff. Civil records on books from 1970s. Select and search Circuit Courts online at http://208.210.219.132/courtinfo/vacircuit/select.jsp?court=. For information about the statewide online systems, see the state introduction. Mail access limited to simple requests.

Criminal Records: Access: In person only. Visitors must perform in person searches for themselves. No search fee. Required to search: name, years to search. Criminal records on books from 1970s. Online access to criminal records is the same as civil.

General Information: Public access terminal is available. No juvenile, sealed or adoption records released. Turnaround time 1-2 days. Copy fee: $.50 per page. Certification fee: $3.00. Fee payee: Clerk of Circuit Court. Personal checks accepted. Prepayment is required.

26th District Court 5 North Kent St, Winchester, VA 22601; 540-722-7208; Fax: 540-722-1063. Hours: 8AM-4PM (EST). *Misdemeanor, Civil Actions up to $15,000.*

Civil Records: Access: In person, online. Visitors must perform in person searches. No search fee. Required to search: name, years to search. Select and search District Courts at http://208.210.219.132/courtinfo/vadistrict/select.jsp?court=. For information about the statewide online systems, see the state introduction.

Criminal Records: Access: In person, online. Visitors must perform in person searches for themselves. No search fee. Required to search: name, years to search. Online access to criminal records is the same as civil.

General Information: Public access terminal is available. Copy fee: $.50 per page. Certification fee: $.50. Fee payee: Frederick District Court. Personal checks accepted. Prepayment is required.

Fredericksburg City

15th Circuit Court 815 Princess Anne St, PO Box 359, Fredericksburg, VA 22404-0359; 540-372-1066. Hours: 8AM-4PM (EST). *Felony, Civil Actions Over $15,000, Probate.*

Civil Records: Access: Online, in person. Visitors must perform in person searches for themselves. No search fee. Required to search: name, years to search. Civil cases indexed by defendant, plaintiff. Civil records on index books from 1765; computerized records since 1987. Online access available free at http://208.210.219.132/courtinfo/vacircuit/select.jsp?court=. For information about the statewide online systems, see the state introduction.

Criminal Records: Access: Online, in person. Visitors must perform in person searches for themselves. No search fee. Required to search: name, years to search, DOB; also helpful: SSN. Criminal records on index books from 1765; computerized records since 1987. Online access to criminal records is the same as civil.

General Information: Public access terminal is available. No juvenile, probate tax returns, sealed or adoption records released. Copy fee: $.50 per page. Certification fee: $2.00. Fee payee: Clerk of Circuit Court. Personal checks accepted.

15th General District Court PO Box 180, Fredericksburg, VA 22404; 540-372-1044; Civil phone:

540-372-1044; Criminal phone: 540-372-1043. Hours: 8AM-4PM (EST). *Misdemeanor, Civil Actions Under $15,000, Eviction, Small Claims.*

Civil Records: Access: Mail, online, in person. Both court and visitors may perform in person searches. No search fee. Required to search: name, years to search. Civil cases indexed by defendant, plaintiff. Civil records on computer the past 10 years, prior on index books. Select and search District Courts at http://208.210.219.132/courtinfo/vadistrict/select.jsp?court=. For information about the statewide online systems, see the state introduction.

Criminal Records: Access: Mail, online, in person. Both court and visitors may perform in person searches. No search fee. Required to search: name, years to search, DOB, SSN. Criminal records on computer the past 10 years, prior on index books. Online access to criminal records is the same as civil.

General Information: Public access terminal is available. No sealed records released. Turnaround time 1-10 days. Copy fee: $.50 per page. Certification fee: $2.00. Fee payee: Fredericksburg District Court. Personal checks accepted. Prepayment is required.

Galax City

Circuit Court, VA.

Note: See Carroll County for Hillsville area and Grayson County for Independence area.

27th General District Court 353 N Main St, PO Box 214, Galax, VA 24333-0214; 276-236-8731; Fax: 276-236-2754. Hours: 8:30AM-4:30PM (EST). *Misdemeanor, Civil Actions Under $15,000, Eviction, Small Claims.*

Note: Circuit Court jurisdiction for this city can be in Carroll County or Grayson County depending on side of the side the offense occurred.

Civil Records: Access: Mail, fax, online, in person. Both court and visitors may perform in person searches. No search fee. Required to search: name, years to search. Civil cases indexed by defendant, plaintiff. Civil records on computer since 1990, prior on index books. Select and search District Courts at http://208.210.219.132/courtinfo/vadistrict/select.jsp?court=. For information about the statewide online systems, see the state introduction.

Criminal Records: Access: Mail, fax, online, in person. Both court and visitors may perform in person searches. No search fee. Required to search: name, years to search. Criminal records on computer since 1990, prior on index books. Online access to criminal records is the same as civil.

General Information: Public access terminal is available. No juvenile, sealed records released. Turnaround time 1-5 days. Copy fee: $.25 per page. Fee payee: Clerk of District Court Galax District. Personal checks accepted. Credit cards accepted: Visa, MasterCard. Prepayment is required.

Giles County

27th Circuit Court 501 Wenonah Ave, PO Box 502, Pearisburg, VA 24134; 540-921-1722; Fax: 540-921-3825. Hours: 9AM-5PM (EST). *Felony, Civil Actions Over $15,000, Probate.*

Civil Records: Access: Mail, in person. Visitors must perform in person searches. No search fee. Required to search: name, years to search. Civil cases indexed by defendant, plaintiff. Civil records (financial) on computer since 1990, on index cards from 1985. Remote online access to court case indexes is via LOPAS; call 804-786-6455 to apply.

Criminal Records: Access: In person. Visitors must perform in person searches. No search fee. Required to search: name, years to search, DOB; also helpful: SSN. Criminal records (financial) on computer since 1990, on

index cards from 1985. Remote online access to court case indexes is via LOPAS; call 804-786-6455 to apply.

General Information: No juvenile, sealed records released. Turnaround time 1-2 days. Copy fee: $.50 per page. Certification fee: $3.00. Fee payee: Clerk of Circuit Court. Personal checks accepted. Prepayment is required.

27th General District Court 120 N Main St, #1, Pearisburg, VA 24134; 540-921-3533; Fax: 540-921-2752. Hours: 8:30AM-4:30PM (EST). *Misdemeanor, Civil Actions Under $15,000, Eviction, Small Claims.*

Civil Records: Access: Fax, mail, online, in person. Both court and visitors may perform in person searches. No search fee. Required to search: name, years to search. Civil cases indexed by defendant, plaintiff. Civil records on computer since 1990, prior on index cards back 10 years. Select and search District Courts at http://208.210.219.132/courtinfo/vadistrict/select.jsp?court=. For information about the statewide online systems, see the state introduction.

Criminal Records: Access: Fax, mail, online, in person. Both court and visitors may perform in person searches. No search fee. Required to search: name, years to search; also helpful: SSN. Criminal records on computer since 1990, prior on index cards back 10 years. Online access to criminal records is the same as civil.

General Information: Public access terminal is available. No juvenile, sealed records released. Turnaround time 3-7 days. Fax notes: Fee to fax results is $1.00 per page. Copy fee: $1.00 for first page, $.50 each add'l. Fee payee: General District Court. Personal checks accepted. Credit cards accepted: Visa, MC.

Gloucester County

9th Circuit Court PO Box 2118, Gloucester, VA 23061-0570; 804-693-2502; Fax: 804-693-2186. Hours: 8AM-4:30PM (EST). *Felony, Civil Actions Over $15,000, Probate.*

www.co.gloucester.va.us

Civil Records: Access: Phone, fax, mail, online, in person. Both court and visitors may perform in person searches. No search fee. Required to search: name, years to search. Civil cases indexed by defendant, plaintiff. Civil records on index books from 1862; on computer since 1990. Online access available free at http://208.210.219.132/courtinfo/vacircuit/select.jsp?court=. For information about the statewide online systems, see the state introduction.

Criminal Records: Access: Online, in person. Visitors must perform in person searches. No search fee. Required to search: name, years to search, DOB. Criminal records on index books from 1862; on computer since 1990. Online access to criminal records is the same as civil.

General Information: No juvenile, sealed or adoption records released. SASE requested. Turnaround time 1 day. Fax notes: $1.00 per page. Copy fee: $.50 per page. Certification fee: $2.00. Fee payee: Clerk of Circuit Court. Personal checks accepted.

9th General District Court PO Box 873, Gloucester, VA 23061; 804-693-4860; Fax: 804-693-6669. Hours: 8:30AM-4:30PM (EST). *Misdemeanor, Civil Actions Under $15,000, Eviction, Small Claims.*

Civil Records: Access: Fax, mail, online, in person. Both court and visitors may perform in person searches. No search fee. Required to search: name, years to search. Civil cases indexed by defendant, plaintiff. Civil records on index books from 1865; computerized back to 1992. Select and search District Courts at http://208.210.219.132/courtinfo/vadistrict/select.jsp?court=. For information about the statewide online systems, see the state introduction.

Criminal Records: Access: Fax, mail, online, in person. Both court and visitors may perform in person searches. No search fee. Required to search: name, years to search; also helpful: DOB, SSN. Criminal records go back to 1992, criminal records on index books from 1865; computerized back to 1992. Online access to criminal records is the same as civil.

General Information: Public access terminal is available. No juvenile, sealed records released. SASE requested. Turnaround time 1 week. Fax notes: No fee to fax results. Copy fee: $.50 per page. Fee payee: Clerk of General District Court/Gloucester District Court. Personal checks accepted. Credit cards accepted: Visa, MasterCard. Prepayment is required.

Goochland County

16th Circuit Court PO Box 196, Goochland, VA 23063; 804-556-5353. Hours: 8:30AM-5PM (EST). *Felony, Civil Actions Over $15,000, Probate.*

Civil Records: Access: Online, in person. Visitors must perform in person searches for themselves. No search fee. Required to search: name, years to search. Civil cases indexed by defendant, plaintiff. Civil records on index books from 1850. Remote online access to court case indexes is via LOPAS; call 804-786-6455 to apply.

Criminal Records: Access: Online, in person. Visitors must perform in person searches for themselves. No search fee. Required to search: name, years to search. Criminal records on index books from 1850. Remote online access to court case indexes is via LOPAS; call 804-786-6455 to apply.

General Information: No juvenile, sealed or adoption records released. Copy fee: $.50 per page. Certification fee: $1.00. Fee payee: Clerk of Circuit Court. Personal checks accepted. Prepayment is required.

General District Court PO Box 47, Goochland, VA 23063; 804-556-5309. Hours: 8:30AM-4:30PM (EST). *Misdemeanor, Civil Actions Under $15,000, Eviction, Small Claims.*

Civil Records: Access: Online, in person. Visitors must perform in person searches for themselves. No search fee. Required to search: name, years to search. Civil cases indexed by defendant, plaintiff. Civil records on index books and computer back to 1989. Select and search District Courts at http://208.210.219.132/courtinfo/vadistrict/select.jsp?court=. For information on the statewide online systems, see state introduction.

Criminal Records: Access: Online, in person. Visitors must perform in person searches for themselves. No search fee. Required to search: name, years to search, DOB. Criminal records on index books and computer back to 1989. Online access to criminal records is the same as civil.

General Information: Public access terminal is available. No juvenile records released. No copy fee. Fee payee: Clerk of General District Court, Goochland District Court. Credit cards accepted: Visa, MasterCard. Prepayment is required.

Grayson County

27th Circuit Court PO Box 130, Independence, VA 24348; 276-773-2231; Fax: 276-773-3338. 8AM-5PM *Felony, Civil Actions Over $15,000, Probate.*

Civil Records: Access: Mail, online, in person. Both court and visitors may perform in person searches. No search fee. Required to search: name, years to search. Civil cases indexed by defendant, plaintiff. Civil records on index books since 1793. Select and search Circuit Courts online at http://208.210.219.132/courtinfo/vacircuitselect.jsp?court=. For information about the statewide online systems, see the state introduction.

Criminal Records: Access: Mail, online, in person. Both court and visitors may perform in person searches. No search fee. Required to search: name, years to search, DOB. Criminal records on index books since 1793. Online access to criminal records is the same as civil.

General Information: No juvenile, sealed or adoption records released. SASE requested. Turnaround time 2-3 days. Copy fee: $.50 per page. Certification fee: $2.00. Fee payee: Clerk of Circuit Court. Personal checks accepted. Prepayment is required.

27th General District Court PO Box 280, Independence, VA 24348; 276-773-2011. Hours: 8AM-4:30PM (EST). *Misdemeanor, Civil Actions Under $15,000, Eviction, Small Claims.*

Civil Records: Access: Mail, online, in person. Both court and visitors may perform in person searches. No search fee. Required to search: name, years to search. Civil cases indexed by defendant. Civil records on index books from 1800s, on computer from 1989. Select and search District Courts at http://208.210.219.132/courtinfo/vadistrict/select.jsp?court=. For information about the statewide online systems, see the state introduction.

Criminal Records: Access: Mail, online, in person. Both court and visitors may perform in person searches. No search fee. Required to search: name, years to search; also helpful: DOB, SSN. Criminal records on index books from 1800s, on computer from 1989. Online access to criminal records is the same as civil.

General Information: Public access terminal is available. No juvenile, sealed records released. Turnaround time 1 week. No copy fee.

Greene County

16th Circuit Court PO Box 386, Stanardsville, VA 22973; 434-985-5208; Fax: 434-985-6723. Hours: 8:15AM-4:30PM (EST). *Felony, Civil Actions Over $15,000, Probate.*

Civil Records: Access: Mail, online, in person. Both court and visitors may perform in person searches. No search fee. Required to search: name, years to search. Civil cases indexed by defendant, plaintiff. Civil records on index books from 1838. Remote online access to court case indexes is via LOPAS; call 804-786-6455 to apply.

Criminal Records: Access: Mail, online, in person. Both court and visitors may perform in person searches. Search fee: $10.00 per name. Required to search: name, years to search. Criminal records on index books from 1838. Remote online access to court case indexes is via LOPAS; call 804-786-6455 to apply.

General Information: No juvenile, sealed or adoption records released. SASE required. Turnaround time 7-10 days. Copy fee: $.50 per page. Fee payee: Clerk of Circuit Court or Green County Circuit. Personal checks accepted. Prepayment is required.

16th General District Court Greene County Courthouse (PO Box 245), Stanardsville, VA 22973; 434-985-5224; Fax: 434-985-1448. Hours: 8:30AM-4PM (EST). *Misdemeanor, Civil Actions Under $15,000, Eviction, Small Claims.*

Civil Records: Access: Fax, mail, online, in person. Both court and visitors may perform in person searches. No search fee. Required to search: name, years to search. Civil cases indexed by defendant, plaintiff. Civil records on index books from 1838, on computer back to 10/93. Select and search District Courts at http://208.210.219.132/courtinfo/vadistrict/select.jsp?court=. For information about the statewide online systems, see the state introduction.

Criminal Records: Access: In person only. Visitors must perform in person searches for themselves. No search fee. Required to search: name, years to search, DOB; also helpful: SSN. Criminal records on computer back to 1/92, prior on cards, books. Online access to criminal records is the same as civil.

General Information: Public access terminal is available. No juvenile, sealed records released. Turnaround time 1 week. Fax notes: No fee to fax results. Copy fee: $.50 per page. Fee payee: Clerk of

General District Court or Greene County Combined Court. Personal checks accepted. Credit cards accepted: Visa, MasterCard. Prepayment is required.

Greensville County

6th Circuit Court PO Box 631, Emporia, VA 23847; 434-348-4215. Hours: 9AM-5PM (EST). *Felony, Civil Actions Over $15,000, Probate.*

Civil Records: Access: Online, in person. Visitors must perform in person searches for themselves. No search fee. Required to search: name, years to search. Civil cases indexed by defendant, plaintiff. Civil records on index books from 1781; on computer since 1989. Select and search Circuit Courts online at http://208.210.219.132/courtinfo/vacircuit/select.jsp?court=. For information about the statewide online systems, see the state introduction.

Criminal Records: Access: Online, in person. Visitors must perform in person searches for themselves. Court does not conduct criminal searches. No search fee. Required to search: name, years to search. Criminal records on index books from 1781; on computer since 1989. Online access to criminal records is same as civil.

General Information: Public access terminal is available. No juvenile, sealed records released. Fax notes: Fee to fax results is $.50 per document. Copy fee: $.50 per page. Certification fee: $2.00. Fee payee: Clerk of Circuit Court. Business checks accepted. Prepayment is required.

Greenville/Emporia Combined Court 315 S Main, Emporia, VA 23847; 434-348-4266. Hours: 8:30AM-4:30PM (EST). *Misdemeanor, Civil Actions Under $15,000, Eviction, Small Claims.*

Civil Records: Access: Online, in person. Visitors must perform in person searches for themselves. No search fee. Required to search: name, years to search. Civil cases indexed by defendant, plaintiff. Civil records on index books from 1800s; on computer back 10 years. Select and search District Courts at http://208.210.219.132/courtinfo/vadistrict/select.jsp?court=. For information about the statewide online systems, see the state introduction.

Criminal Records: Access: Online, in person. Visitors must perform in person searches for themselves. No search fee. Required to search: name, years to search, DOB; also helpful: SSN. Criminal records on index books from 1800s; on computer back 10 years. Online access to criminal records is the same as civil.

General Information: Public access terminal is available. No juvenile, sealed records released. Copy fee: $.50 per page. Fee payee: Clerk of General District Court. Personal checks accepted.

Halifax County

10th Circuit Court PO Box 729, Halifax, VA 24558; 434-476-6211. Hours: 8:30AM-5PM (EST). *Felony, Civil Actions Over $15,000, Probate.*

Civil Records: Access: Online, in person. Visitors must perform in person searches for themselves. No search fee. Required to search: name, years to search. Civil cases indexed by defendant, plaintiff. Civil records on computer from 1988, on index books from 1752. Remote online access to court case indexes is via LOPAS; call 804-786-6455 to apply.

Criminal Records: Access: Mail, online, in person. Only the court performs in person searches; visitors may not. Search fee: $5.00 per name. Required to search: name, years to search. Criminal records on computer from 1988, on index books from 1752. Remote online access to court case indexes is via LOPAS; call 804-786-6455 to apply.

General Information: No juvenile, sealed records released. Turnaround time 1-5 days. Copy fee: $.50 per page. Certification fee: $.50 per page. Fee payee: Circuit Court. Personal checks accepted. Prepayment required.

10th General District Court Halifax County Courthouse, PO Box 458, Halifax, VA 24558; 434-476-3385; Fax: 434-476-3387. Hours: 8:30AM-4:30PM (EST). *Misdemeanor, Civil Actions Under $15,000, Eviction, Small Claims.*

Civil Records: Access: Fax, mail, online, in person. Both court and visitors may perform in person searches. No search fee. Required to search: name, years to search, address. Civil cases indexed by defendant, plaintiff. Civil records on computer from 1991. Select and search District Courts at http://208.210.219.132/courtinfo/vadistrict/select.jsp?court=. For information about the statewide online systems, see the state introduction.

Criminal Records: Access: Fax, mail, online, in person. Both court and visitors may perform in person searches. No search fee. Required to search: name. Criminal records on computer from 1991. Online access to criminal records is the same as civil.

General Information: Public access terminal is available. (Available Tues, Thurs & Fri all day, also Wed afternoons.) No juvenile, sealed records released. Turnaround time within 7 days. Fax notes: Fax fee only charged for excessive number of pages. Copy fee: $.50 per page. Fee payee: General District Court. Personal checks accepted. Prepayment is required.

Hampton City

8th Circuit Court 101 King's Way, PO Box 40, Hampton, VA 23669-0040; 757-727-6105. Hours: 8:30AM-5PM (EST). *Felony, Civil Actions Over $15,000, Probate.*

Civil Records: Access: Phone, mail, fax, in person. Both court and visitors may perform in person searches. Search fee: $10.00 per name. Required to search: name, years to search. Civil cases indexed by defendant, plaintiff. Computerized records back to 1991, civil records on index books since 1834. Online access available free at http://208.210.219.132/courtinfo/vacircuit/select.jsp?court=. For information about the statewide online systems, see the state introduction.

Criminal Records: Access: Mail, online, in person. Both court and visitors may perform in person searches. Search fee: $10.00 per name. Required to search: name, years to search. Computerized records back to 1991, criminal records on index books since 1949. Online access to criminal records is the same as civil.

General Information: No pre-sentence, criminal correspondence, chancery, judges notes or medical records released. SASE preferred. Turnaround time 3 days. Copy fee: $.50 per page. Certification fee: $2.00. Fee payee: Clerk of Court. Personal checks accepted. No out of state checks accepted. Prepayment is required.

8th General District Court Courthouse, PO Box 70, Hampton, VA 23669-0070; Civil phone: 757-727-6480; Criminal phone: 757-727-6260/6262. Hours: 8AM-4PM (EST). *Misdemeanor, Civil Actions Under $15,000, Eviction, Small Claims.*

Civil Records: Access: Online, in person. Visitors must perform in person searches for themselves. No search fee. Required to search: name, years to search. Civil cases indexed by defendant, plaintiff. Civil records on index books from early 1900s, on computer from 1992. Select and search District Courts at http://208.210.219.132/courtinfo/vadistrict/select.jsp?court=. For information about the statewide online systems, see the state introduction. Mail access limited to specific case and two names.

Criminal Records: Access: Online, in person. Visitors must perform in person searches for themselves. No search fee. Required to search: name, years to search. Criminal records on index books from early 1900s, on computer from 1992. Online access to criminal records is the same as civil.

General Information: Public access terminal is available. No sealed records released. Copy fee: $.50 each. Fee payee: Hampton District Court. Personal checks accepted. Credit cards accepted. Accepted for fines only. Prepayment is required.

Hanover County

15th Circuit Court 7507 Library Dr, PO Box 39, Hanover, VA 23069; 804-365-6151; Fax: 804-365-6278. Hours: 8:30AM-4:30PM (EST). *Felony, Civil Actions Over $15,000, Probate.*

Civil Records: Access: Online, in person. Visitors must perform in person searches for themselves. No search fee. Required to search: name, years to search. Civil cases indexed by defendant, plaintiff. Civil records index in books, older records date from 1865. Remote online access to court case indexes is via LOPAS; call 804-786-6455 to apply.

Criminal Records: Access: Online, in person. Visitors must perform in person searches for themselves. No search fee. Required to search: name, years to search. Criminal records index in books, older records date from 1850. Remote online access to court case indexes is via LOPAS; call 804-786-6455 to apply.

General Information: Public access terminal is available. No juvenile, sealed records released. Copy fee: $.50 per page. Certification fee: $2.00. Fee payee: Clerk of Circuit Court. Personal checks accepted. Prepayment is required.

15th General District Court Hanover County Courthouse, PO Box 176, Hanover, VA 23069; 804-365-6191; Fax: 804-365-6290. Hours: 8AM-4PM (EST). *Misdemeanor, Civil Actions Under $15,000, Eviction, Small Claims.*

Civil Records: Access: Mail, online, in person. Both court and visitors may perform in person searches. No search fee. Required to search: name, years to search. Civil cases indexed by defendant, plaintiff. Civil records on index books back to 1991; on computer back to 1992. Select and search District Courts at http://208.210.219.132/courtinfo/vadistrict/select.jsp?court=. For information about the statewide online systems, see the state introduction.

Criminal Records: Access: Online, in person. Visitors must perform in person searches for themselves. No search fee. Required to search: name, years to search, DOB; also helpful: SSN. Criminal records on index books back to 1991; on computer back to 1992. Online access to criminal records is the same as civil.

General Information: Public access terminal is available. Copy fee: $1.00 for first page, $.50 each add'l. Fee payee: Hanover General District Court. Personal checks accepted. Credit cards accepted: Visa, MasterCard.

Harrisonburg City

Circuit & District Courts, VA.

Note: See Rockingham County

Henrico County

14th Circuit Court PO Box 27032, Richmond, VA 23273-7032; Civil phone: 804-501-5422; Criminal phone: 804-501-4758. Hours: 8AM-4:30PM (EST). *Felony, Civil Actions Over $15,000, Probate.*

Civil Records: Access: Mail, online, in person. Visitors must perform in person searches for themselves. No search fee. Required to search: name, years to search. Civil cases indexed by defendant, plaintiff. Civil records on computer from 11/88, on index cards from 1850. Remote online access to court case indexes is via LOPAS; call 804-786-6455 to apply.

Criminal Records: Access: Mail, online, in person. Visitors must perform in person searches for themselves. No search fee. Required to search: name, years to search, DOB. Criminal records on computer

from 11/88, on index cards from 1850. Remote online access to court case indexes is via LOPAS; call 804-786-6455 to apply.

General Information: Public access terminal is available. No juvenile, judges notes, adoption sealed records released. SASE required. Turnaround time 3-5 days. Copy fee: $.50 per page. Certification fee: $2.00 per document. Fee payee: Clerk of Circuit Court. Personal checks accepted. Prepayment is required.

14th General District Court PO Box 27032, Richmond, VA 23273; Civil phone: 804-501-4727; Criminal phone: 804-501-4723; Fax: 804-501-4141. Hours: 8AM-4PM (EST). *Misdemeanor, Civil Actions Under $15,000, Eviction, Small Claims.*

Civil Records: Access: Online, in person. Visitors must perform in person searches for themselves. No search fee. Required to search: name, years to search. Civil cases indexed by defendant. Civil records on computer from 07/85. Select and search District Courts at http://208.210.219.132/courtinfo/vadistrict/select.jsp?court=. For information about the statewide online systems, see the state introduction.

Criminal Records: Access: Online, in person. Visitors must perform in person searches for themselves. No search fee. Required to search: name, years to search, DOB. Criminal records on computer from 1992. Online access to criminal records is the same as civil.

General Information: Public access terminal is available. No juvenile, sealed records released. Copy fee: $1.00 per page. Fee payee: Clerk of General District Court. Personal checks accepted. Credit cards accepted. Not accepted over the phone. Prepayment is required.

Henry County

21st Circuit Court 3160 Kings Mountain Rd #B, Martinsville, VA 24112; 276-634-4880. Hours: 9AM-5PM *Felony, Civil Actions Over $15,000, Probate.*

www.courts.state.va.us

Civil Records: Access: Online, in person. Visitors must perform in person searches for themselves. No search fee. Required to search: name, years to search. Civil cases indexed by defendant, plaintiff. Civil records on computer since 4/92, index back to 1777. Online access available free at http://208.210.219.132/courtinfo/vacircuit/select.jsp?court=. For information about the statewide online systems, see the state introduction.

Criminal Records: Access: Online, in person. Visitors must perform in person searches for themselves. No search fee. Required to search: name, years to search, DOB; also helpful: SSN. Criminal records computerized since 7/92, index back to 1777. Online access to criminal records is the same as civil.

General Information: Public access terminal is available. No juvenile, expungments, sealed or adoption records released. Fax notes: Fee to fax results is $.50 per page. Copy fee: $.50 per page. Certification fee: $2.00. Fee payee: Clerk of Circuit Court. Personal checks accepted. Prepayment is required.

21st General District Court 3160 King's Mountain Rd Ste A, Martinsville, VA 24112; 276-634-4815; Fax: 276-634-4825. Hours: 9AM-5PM (EST). *Misdemeanor, Civil Actions Under $15,000, Eviction, Small Claims.*

www.courts.state.va.us

Civil Records: Access: Online, in person. Visitors must perform in person searches for themselves. No search fee. Required to search: name, years to search; also helpful: address. Civil cases indexed by defendant, plaintiff. Civil records on computer from 1991. Select and search District Courts at http://208.210.219.132/courtinfo/vadistrict/select.jsp?court=. For information about the statewide online systems, see the state introduction.

Criminal Records: Access: Online, in person. Visitors must perform in person searches for themselves. No search fee. Required to search: name, years to search, DOB; also helpful: address, SSN. Criminal records on computer from 1992. Online access to criminal records is the same as civil.

General Information: Public access terminal is available. No sealed records released. Copy fee: $.50 per page.

Highland County

25th Circuit Court PO Box 190, Monterey, VA 24465; 540-468-2447; Fax: 540-468-3447. Hours: 8:45AM-4:30PM (EST). *Felony, Civil Actions Over $15,000, Probate.*

Civil Records: Access: Mail, online, in person. Both court and visitors may perform in person searches. No search fee. Required to search: name, years to search. Civil cases indexed by defendant, plaintiff. Civil records on index books from 1868. Remote online access to court case indexes is via LOPAS; call 804-786-6455 to apply.

Criminal Records: Access: Mail, online, in person. Both court and visitors may perform in person searches. No search fee. Required to search: name, years to search. Criminal records on index books from 1868. Online access to criminal records is the same as civil.

General Information: No juvenile, sealed records released. Turnaround time up to 1 week. Copy fee: $.50 per page. Certification fee: $2.00. Fee payee: Clerk of Circuit Court. Personal checks accepted. Prepayment is required.

25th General District Court Highland County Courthouse, PO Box 88, Monterey, VA 24465; 540-468-2445; Fax: 540-468-3449. Hours: 8:30AM-5:00PM (EST). *Misdemeanor, Civil Actions Under $15,000, Eviction, Small Claims.*

Civil Records: Access: Fax, mail, online, in person. Both court and visitors may perform in person searches. No search fee. Required to search: name, years to search. Civil cases indexed by defendant, plaintiff. Civil records on index books from 1991; computerized back to 1993. Select and search District Courts at http://208.210.219.132/courtinfo/vadistrict/select.jsp?court=. For information about the statewide online systems, see the state introduction.

Criminal Records: Access: Fax, mail, online, in person. Both court and visitors may perform in person searches. No search fee. Required to search: name, years to search; also helpful: DOB, SSN, signed release. Criminal records on index books from 1991; computerized back to 1993. Online access to criminal records is the same as civil.

General Information: Public access terminal is available. No juvenile, sealed records released. SASE requested. Turnaround time 2-3 days. Copy fee: $1.00 copy fee for first 2 pages. Add $.50 per page thereafter. Fee payee: General District Court. Personal checks accepted. Prepayment is required.

Hopewell City

6th Circuit Court 100 E Broadway, PO Box 354, 2nd Fl, Room 251, Hopewell, VA 23860; 804-541-2239; Fax: 804-541-2438. Hours: 8:30AM-4:30PM (EST). *Felony, Civil Actions Over $15,000, Probate.*

Civil Records: Access: Mail, online, in person. Both court and visitors may perform in person searches. No search fee. Required to search: name, years to search. Civil cases indexed by defendant, plaintiff. Civil records on index books since 1916. Select and search Circuit Courts online at http://208.210.219.132/courtinfo/vacircuit/select.jsp?court=. For information about the statewide online systems, see the state introduction.

Criminal Records: Access: Online, in person. Visitors must perform in person searches for themselves. No

search fee. Required to search: name, years to search, DOB. Criminal records on index books since 1916. Online access to criminal records is the same as civil.

General Information: Public access terminal is available. No juvenile, sealed records released. SASE required. Turnaround time 1 week. Copy fee: $.50 per page. Certification fee: $2.00. Fee payee: Clerk of Circuit Court. Personal checks accepted. Prepayment is required.

Hopewell District Court 100 E Broadway, Hopewell, VA 23860; 804-541-2257; Fax: 804-541-2364. Hours: 8:30AM-4:30PM (EST). *Misdemeanor, Civil Actions Under $15,000, Eviction, Small Claims.*

Civil Records: Access: Mail, online, in person. Both court and visitors may perform in person searches. No search fee. Required to search: name, years to search. Civil cases indexed by defendant, plaintiff. Civil records on computer from 1988, older case records archived. Select and search District Courts at http://208.210.219.132/courtinfo/vadistrict/select.jsp?court=. For information about the statewide online systems, see the state introduction.

Criminal Records: Access: Mail, online, in person. Both court and visitors may perform in person searches. No search fee. Required to search: name, years to search, DOB; also helpful: SSN. Criminal records on computer from 1988, older case records are archived. Online access to criminal records is the same as civil.

General Information: Public access terminal is available. No juvenile, sealed or domestic relations records released. SASE requested. Turnaround time 3-5 days. Copy fee: $1.00 per page first 2 pages, then $.50 each. Certification fee: $2.00. Fee payee: Clerk of General District Court. Personal checks accepted. Credit cards accepted: Visa, MasterCard.

Isle of Wight County

5th Circuit Court 17122 Monument Circle, PO Box 110, Isle of Wight, VA 23397; 757-365-6233. Hours: 9AM-5PM (EST). *Felony, Civil Actions Over $15,000, Probate.*

Note: The Clerk can be reached at 757-365-6233.

Civil Records: Access: Online, in person. Visitors must perform in person searches for themselves. No search fee. Required to search: name, years to search. Civil cases indexed by defendant, plaintiff. Civil records on index books from 1800s; on computer back to 1988. Online access available free at http://208.210.219.132/courtinfo/vacircuit/select.jsp?court=. For information about the statewide online systems, see the state introduction.

Criminal Records: Access: Online, in person. Visitors must perform in person searches for themselves. No search fee. Required to search: name, years to search, DOB. Criminal records on index books from 1800s; on computer back to 1988. Online access to criminal records is the same as civil.

General Information: Public access terminal is available. No juvenile, sealed records released. Copy fee: $.50 per page. Certification fee: $2.00. Fee payee: Clerk of Circuit Court. Personal checks accepted. Prepayment is required.

5th General District Court Isle of Wight Courthouse, PO Box 122, Isle of Wight, VA 23397; 757-365-6243; Fax: 757-365-6246. Hours: 8AM-4PM (EST). *Misdemeanor, Civil Actions Under $15,000, Eviction, Small Claims.*

Note: The Clerk can be reached at 757-365-6244.

Civil Records: Access: Online, in person. Visitors must perform in person searches for themselves. No search fee. Required to search: name, years to search. Civil cases indexed by defendant, plaintiff. Civil records on index books back to 1800s; on computer since 1994. Select and search District Courts at http://208.210.219.132/courtinfo/vadistrict/select.jsp?court=.

For information about the statewide online systems, see the state introduction.

Criminal Records: Access: Online, in person. Visitors must perform in person searches for themselves. No search fee. Required to search: name, years to search. Criminal records on index books back to 1800s; on computer since 1994. Online access to criminal records is the same as civil.

General Information: Juvenile, sealed, adoption records not released. Copy fee: $.50 per page. Certification fee: $2.00. Fee payee: Clerk of GDC. Personal checks accepted. Credit cards accepted: Visa, MasterCard. Prepayment is required.

James City

Williamsburg-James City Circuit Court 5201 Monticello Ave #6, Williamsburg, VA 23188-8218; 757-564-2242; Fax: 757-564-2329. Hours: 8:30AM-4:00PM (EST). *Felony, Civil Actions Over $15,000, Probate.*

Civil Records: Access: Mail, online, in person. Both court and visitors may perform in person searches. Search fee: $2.00 per name. Required to search: name, years to search. Civil cases indexed by defendant, plaintiff. Civil records on computer since 1987, archived from 1970, prior on index books. Online access available free at http://208.210.219.132/courtinfo/vacircuit/select.jsp?court=. For information about the statewide online systems, see the state introduction.

Criminal Records: Access: Mail, online, in person. Both court and visitors may perform in person searches. Search fee: $2.00 per name. Required to search: name, years to search, DOB; also helpful: SSN. Criminal records on computer since 1987, archived from 1970, prior on index books. Online access to criminal records is the same as civil.

General Information: Public access terminal is available. No juvenile, sealed, adoption records released. SASE required. Turnaround time 1-2 days. Fax notes: Fee to fax results is $1.00 per page. Copy fee: $.50 per page. Certification fee: $2.00. Fee payee: Clerk of Circuit Court. Personal checks not accepted. Prepayment is required.

9th General District Court James City County Courthouse, 5201 Monticello Ave #2, Williamsburg, VA 23188-8218; 757-564-2400; Fax: 757-564-2410. Hours: 7:30AM-4PM (EST). *Misdemeanor, Civil Actions Under $15,000, Eviction, Small Claims.*

Civil Records: Access: Fax, mail, in person. Both court and visitors may perform in person searches. No search fee. Required to search: name, years to search. Civil cases indexed by defendant, plaintiff. Civil records on index books from 1991, on computer from 1991. Select and search District Courts at http://208.210.219.132/courtinfo/vadistrict/select.jsp?court=. For information about the statewide online systems, see the state introduction.

Criminal Records: Access: Fax, mail, in person. Both court and visitors may perform in person searches. No search fee. Required to search: name, years to search, DOB; also helpful: SSN. Criminal records on index books from 1991, on computer from 1991. Online access to criminal records is the same as civil.

General Information: Public access terminal is available. No juvenile, sealed records released. SASE requested. Turnaround time 10 days. Copy fee: Charges will be incurred if extensive searching or copies are needed. Fee payee: General District Court. Personal checks accepted. Credit cards accepted: Visa, MasterCard.

King and Queen County

9th Circuit Court PO Box 67, King & Queen Court House, VA 23085; 804-785-5984; Fax: 804-785-5698. Hours: 9AM-5PM (EST). *Felony, Civil Actions Over $15,000, Probate.*

Civil Records: Access: Online, in person. Visitors must perform in person searches for themselves. No search fee. Required to search: name, years to search. Civil cases indexed by plaintiff. Civil records archived from 1864. Remote online access to court case indexes is via LOPAS; call 804-786-6455 to apply.

Criminal Records: Access: Online, in person. Visitors must perform in person searches for themselves. No search fee. Required to search: name, years to search. Criminal records archived from 1864. Remote online access to court case indexes is via LOPAS; call 804-786-6455 to apply.

General Information: Public access terminal is available. No juvenile, sealed or adoption records released. Copy fee: $.50 per page. Certification fee: $1.00. Fee payee: Clerk of Circuit Court. Personal checks accepted. Prepayment is required.

King & Queen General District Court PO Box 86, King & Queen Courthouse, VA 23085-0086; 804-785-5982; Fax: 804-785-5694. Hours: 8:30AM-4:30PM (EST). *Misdemeanor, Civil Actions Under $15,000, Eviction.*

Civil Records: Access: Fax, mail, online, in person. Both court and visitors may perform in person searches. No search fee. Required to search: name, years to search. Civil cases indexed by defendant, plaintiff. Civil records on computer back to 1991. Select and search District Courts at http://208.210.219.132/courtinfo/vadistrict/select.jsp?court=. For information about the statewide online systems, see the state introduction.

Criminal Records: Access: Fax, mail, online, in person. Both court and visitors may perform in person searches. No search fee. Required to search: name, years to search, DOB; also helpful: SSN, signed release. Criminal records on computer back to 1991. Online access to criminal records is the same as civil.

General Information: Public access terminal is available. Turnaround time 1-5 days. Fax notes: No fee to fax results. Copy fee: $1.00 for first page, $.50 each add'l. Fee payee: General District Court. Personal checks accepted. Prepayment is required.

King George County

15th Circuit Court 9483 Kings Highway #3, King George, VA 22485; 540-775-3322. Hours: 8:30AM-4:30PM *Felony, Civil Actions Over $15,000, Probate.*

Civil Records: Access: Mail, online, in person. Both court and visitors may perform in person searches. Search fee: $10.00 per name. Required to search: name, years to search. Civil cases indexed by defendant, plaintiff. Civil records on index books from 1800s; computerized records since 1990. Select and search Circuit Courts online at http://208.210.219.132/courtinfo/vacircuit/select.jsp?court=. For information about the statewide online systems, see the state introduction.

Criminal Records: Access: Mail, online, in person. Both court and visitors may perform in person searches. Search fee: $10.00 per name. Required to search: name, years to search. Criminal records on index books from 1800s; computerized records since 1990. Online access to criminal records is the same as civil.

General Information: Public access terminal is available. No sealed records released. SASE required. Turnaround time 1-2 days. Copy fee: $.50 per page. Certification fee: $2.00. Fee payee: Clerk of Circuit court. Personal checks accepted. Prepayment required.

15th Judicial District King George Combined Court County Courthouse PO Box 279, King George, VA 22485; 540-775-3573. Hours: 8AM-4:30PM (EST). *Misdemeanor, Civil Actions Under $15,000, Eviction, Small Claims.*

Civil Records: Access: Mail, online, in person. Both court and visitors may perform in person searches. No search fee. Required to search: name, years to search. Civil cases indexed by defendant, plaintiff. Civil records on index books from early 1900s; computerized records since 1992. Select and search District Courts at http://208.210.219.132/courtinfo/vadistrict/select.jsp?court=. For information about the statewide online systems, see the state introduction.

Criminal Records: Access: Mail, online, in person. Both court and visitors may perform in person searches. No search fee. Required to search: name, years to search, DOB; also helpful: SSN. Criminal records on index books from early 1900s; computerized records since 1992. Online access to criminal records is the same as civil.

General Information: Public access terminal is available. No juvenile, sealed records released. Turnaround time 1-5 days. Copy fee: $1.00 per page for the 1st two pages, $.50 each add'l page. Certification fee: $2.00. Fee payee: Clerk of General District Court. Personal checks accepted. Credit cards accepted: Visa, MasterCard. Prepayment is required.

King William County

9th Circuit Court 227 Courthouse Lane, PO Box 216, King William, VA 23086; 804-769-4938. Hours: 8:30AM-4:30PM (EST). *Felony, Civil Actions Over $15,000, Probate.*

Civil Records: Access: Mail, in person, online. Both court and visitors may perform in person searches. No search fee. Required to search: name, years to search. Civil cases indexed by defendant, plaintiff. Civil records on index books from 1800s. Select and search Circuit Courts online at http://208.210.219.132/courtinfo/vacircuit/select.jsp?court=. For information about the statewide online systems, see the state introduction.

Criminal Records: Access: Mail, in person, online. Both court and visitors may perform in person searches. No search fee. Required to search: name, years to search, DOB; also helpful: SSN. Criminal records on index books from 1800s, computerized records from 1999. Online access to criminal records is the same as civil.

General Information: Public access terminal is available. No juvenile, sealed records released. SASE required. Turnaround time 1 week. Copy fee: $.50 per page. Certification fee: $1.00. Fee payee: Clerk of Circuit Court. Personal checks accepted. Prepayment is required.

King William General District Court PO Box 5, King William, VA 23086; 804-769-4948; Fax: 804-769-4971. 8:30AM-4:30PM (EST). *Misdemeanor, Civil Actions Under $15,000, Eviction, Small Claims.*

Civil Records: Access: Fax, mail, online, in person. Both court and visitors may perform in person searches. No search fee. Required to search: name, years to search. Civil cases indexed by defendant, plaintiff. Civil records on computer since 1992. Select and search District Courts at http://208.210.219.132/courtinfo/vadistrict/select.jsp?court=. For information about the statewide online systems, see the state introduction.

Criminal Records: Access: Fax, mail, online, in person. Both court and visitors may perform in person searches. No search fee. Required to search: name, years to search, DOB; also helpful: signed release, SSN. Criminal records on computer back to 1992. Online access to criminal records is the same as civil.

General Information: Public access terminal is available. No juvenile, sealed records released. SASE requested. Turnaround time 1-5 days. Fax notes: No fee to fax results. Copy fee: $1.00 for first page, $.50 each add'l. Fee payee: General District Court. Personal checks accepted.

Lancaster County

15th Circuit Court Courthouse Building, PO Box 99, Lancaster, VA 22503; 804-462-5611. Hours: 8:30AM-4:30PM (EST). *Felony, Civil Actions Over $15,000, Probate.*

Civil Records: Access: Mail, online, in person. Both court and visitors may perform in person searches. No search fee. Required to search: name, years to search. Civil cases indexed by defendant, plaintiff. Civil records on index books from 1845. Select and search Circuit Courts online at http://208.210.219.132/courtinfo/vacircuit/select.jsp?court=. For information about the statewide online systems, see the state introduction.

Criminal Records: Access: Mail, online, in person. Both court and visitors may perform in person searches. No search fee. Required to search: name, years to search. Criminal records on index books from 1845. Online access to criminal records is the same as civil.

General Information: Public access terminal is available. No juvenile, sealed records released. Turnaround time same day. Copy fee: $.50 per page. Certification fee: $2.00. Fee payee: Clerk of Circuit Court. Personal checks accepted. Out of state checks not accepted. Prepayment is required.

15th General District Court PO 129, Lancaster, VA 22503; 804-462-0012. Hours: 8:30AM-4:30PM (EST). *Misdemeanor, Civil Actions Under $15,000, Eviction, Small Claims.*

Civil Records: Access: Mail, online, in person. Both court and visitors may perform in person searches. No search fee. Required to search: name, years to search. Civil cases indexed by defendant. Civil records on computer from 11/93. Select and search District Courts at http://208.210.219.132/courtinfo/vadistrict/select.jsp?court=. For information about the statewide online systems, see the state introduction.

Criminal Records: Access: Mail, online, in person. Both court and visitors may perform in person searches. No search fee. Required to search: name, years to search, DOB; also helpful: SSN. Criminal records on computer from 11/93. Online access to criminal records is the same as civil.

General Information: Public access terminal is available. No sealed records released. Copy fee: $1.00 per page. Fee is for excessive number of pages. Fee payee: Clerk of General District Court. Personal checks accepted. Prepayment is required.

Lee County

30th Circuit Court PO Box 326, Jonesville, VA 24263; 276-346-7763; Fax: 276-346-3440. Hours: 8:30AM-5PM M-F, 9AM-Noon (EST). *Felony, Civil Actions Over $15,000, Probate.*

Civil Records: Access: Phone, fax, mail, online, in person. Both court and visitors may perform in person searches. No search fee. Required to search: name, years to search. Civil cases indexed by defendant, plaintiff. Civil records on index books from 1800s. Select and search Circuit Courts online at http://208.210.219.132/courtinfo/vacircuit/select.jsp?court=. For information about the statewide online systems, see the state introduction. Phone & fax access limited to short searches.

Criminal Records: Access: Phone, fax, mail, online, in person. Both court and visitors may perform in person searches. No search fee. Required to search: name, years to search, DOB; also helpful: SSN. Criminal records on index books from 1800s. Online access to criminal records is the same as civil.

General Information: Public access terminal is available. No juvenile, sealed records released. Turnaround time 1-3 days. Copy fee: $.50 per page.

Certification fee: $2.00. Fee payee: Clerk of Circuit Court. Personal checks accepted. Prepayment required.

30th General District Court
Lee County Courthouse, PO Box 306, Jonesville, VA 24263; 276-346-7729; Fax: 276-346-7701. Hours: 8AM-4:30PM (EST). *Misdemeanor, Civil Actions Under $15,000, Eviction, Small Claims.*

Civil Records: Access: Mail, online, in person. Both court and visitors may perform in person searches. No search fee. Required to search: name, years to search. Civil cases indexed by defendant, plaintiff. Civil records on index books from 1800s, on computer from 11/7/90. Select and search District Courts at http://208.210.219.132/courtinfo/vadistrict/select.jsp?court=. For information about the statewide online systems, see the state introduction.

Criminal Records: Access: Mail, online, in person. Both court and visitors may perform in person searches. No search fee. Required to search: name, years to search. Criminal records on index books from 1800s, on computer from 11/7/90. Online access to criminal records is the same as civil.

General Information: Public access terminal is available. No juvenile, sealed records released. Turnaround time 1-2 days. Copy fee: $1.00 for first page, $.50 each add'l. Fee payee: Clerk of General District Court. Personal checks accepted. Prepayment is required.

Lexington City

Circuit & District Courts, VA.
Note: See Rockbridge County

Loudoun County

20th Circuit Court
18 E Market Street, Leesburg, VA 20178; 703-777-0386; Fax: 703-777-0676. 9AM-5PM *Felony, Civil Actions Over $15,000, Probate.*

Civil Records: Access: Phone, mail, online, in person. Both court and visitors may perform in person searches. No search fee. Required to search: name, years to search. Civil cases indexed by defendant, plaintiff. Civil records on computer since 1986; prior on index books from 1700s. Remote online access to court case indexes is via LOPAS; call 804-786-6455 to apply. Also, docket lists are available free online at www.loudoun.gov/clerk/docs/dockets_/index.htm. Phone access limited to simple requests. Mail access for deeds & wills only.

Criminal Records: Access: Online, in person. Both court and visitors may perform in person searches. No search fee. Required to search: name, years to search, DOB; also helpful: SSN. Criminal records on computer since 1986; prior on index books from 1700s. Remote online access to court case indexes is via LOPAS; call 804-786-6455 to apply. Also, docket lists are available free online at www.loudoun.gov/clerk/docs/dockets_/index.htm.

General Information: No juvenile, sealed or adoption records released. Turnaround time 1 week. Copy fee: $.50 per page. Certification fee: $2.50. Fee payee: Clerk of Circuit Court. Business checks accepted. Personal checks accepted if in-state. Prepayment is required.

20th General District Court
18 E Market St, Leesburg, VA 20176; 703-777-0312; Fax: 703-777-0311. Hours: 8AM-4PM (EST). *Misdemeanor, Civil Actions Under $15,000, Eviction.*

Civil Records: Access: Mail, fax, online, in person. Both court and visitors may perform in person searches. No search fee. Required to search: name, years to search. Civil cases indexed by defendant, plaintiff. Civil records on computer back 10 years. Select and search District Courts at http://208.210.219.132/courtinfo/vadistrict/select.jsp?court=. For information about the statewide online systems, see the state introduction.

Criminal Records: Access: Mail, fax, online, in person. Both court and visitors may perform in person

searches. No search fee. Required to search: name, years to search. Criminal records on computer back 10 years. Online access to criminal records is the same as civil.

General Information: Public access terminal is available. SASE required. Turnaround time 7-10 days. Copy fee: $.50 per page. Personal checks accepted. Credit cards accepted: Visa, MasterCard. Prepayment is required.

Louisa County

16th Circuit Court
Box 37, Louisa, VA 23093; 540-967-5312; Fax: 540-967-2705. Hours: 8:30AM-5PM (EST). *Felony, Civil Actions Over $15,000, Probate.*

Civil Records: Access: Online, in person. Visitors must perform in person searches for themselves. No search fee. Required to search: name, years to search. Civil cases indexed by defendant, plaintiff. Civil records archived from 1742; on computer back to 1989. Select and search Circuit Courts online at http://208.210.219.132/courtinfo/vacircuit/select.jsp?court=. For information about the statewide online systems, see the state introduction.

Criminal Records: Access: Online, in person. Both court and visitors may perform in person searches. No search fee. Required to search: name, years to search, DOB or SSN. Criminal records archived from 1742; on computer back to 1989. Online access to criminal records is the same as civil.

General Information: No juvenile, sealed records released. Copy fee: $.50 per page. Certification fee: $2.00. Fee payee: Clerk of Circuit Court. Personal checks accepted. Prepayment is required.

16th General District Court
PO Box 452, Louisa, VA 23093; 540-967-5330; Fax: 540-967-2369. Hours: 8:30AM-4:30PM (EST). *Misdemeanor, Civil Actions Under $15,000, Eviction, Small Claims.*

Civil Records: Access: Online, in person. Visitors must perform in person searches for themselves. No search fee. Required to search: name, years to search. Civil cases indexed by defendant, plaintiff. Civil records on computer from 1991. Select and search District Courts at http://208.210.219.132/courtinfo/vadistrict/select.jsp?court=. For information about the statewide online systems, see the state introduction.

Criminal Records: Access: Online, in person. Visitors must perform in person searches for themselves. No search fee. Required to search: name, years to search. Criminal records on computer from 1991. Online access to criminal records is the same as civil.

General Information: Public access terminal is available. No juvenile, sealed records released. Copy fee: $1.00 for first page, $.50 each add'l. Fee payee: Louisa District Court. Personal checks accepted. Prepayment is required.

Lunenburg County

10th Circuit Court
11435 Courthouse Rd, Lunenburg, VA 23952; 434-696-2230; Fax: 434-696-3931. Hours: 8:30AM-4:30PM (EST). *Felony, Civil Actions Over $15,000, Probate.*

Civil Records: Access: Online, in person. Visitors must perform in person searches. No search fee. Required to search: name, years to search. Civil cases indexed by defendant, plaintiff. Civil records on index books from 1700s; computerized records since 2002. Select and search Circuit Courts online at http://208.210.219.132/courtinfo/vacircuit/select.jsp?court=. For information about the statewide online systems, see the state introduction.

Criminal Records: Access: Fax, mail, online, in person. Visitors must perform in person searches. No search fee. Required to search: name, years to search. Criminal records on index books from 1700s;

computerized records since 2002. Online access to criminal records is the same as civil.

General Information: No juvenile, sealed records released. Turnaround time 1-2 days. Fax notes: No fee to fax results. Copy fee: $.50 per page. Certification fee:50 per page. Fee payee: Clerk of Circuit Court. Personal checks accepted. Prepayment is required.

10th General District Court
11413 Courthouse Road, Lunenburg, VA 23952; 434-696-5508; Fax: 434-696-3665. 8:30AM-4:30PM (EST). *Misdemeanor, Civil Actions Under $15,000, Eviction, Small Claims.*

Civil Records: Access: Mail, online, in person. Both court and visitors may perform in person searches. No search fee. Required to search: name, years to search. Civil cases indexed by defendant, plaintiff. Civil records computerized since 1995, on index books and cards from 1991, prior to 1985 at Circuit Court: Select and search District Courts at http://208.210.219.132/courtinfo/vadistrict/select.jsp?court=. For information on the statewide online systems, see state introduction.

Criminal Records: Access: Mail, online, in person. Both court and visitors may perform in person searches. No search fee. Required to search: name, years to search, DBO, SSN. Criminal records computerized since 1995, on index books and cards from 1991, prior to 1985 at Circuit Court: Online access to criminal records is the same as civil.

General Information: Public access terminal is available. No juvenile records released. SASE required. Turnaround time 3 days. Personal checks accepted. Credit cards accepted: Visa, MasterCard.

Lynchburg City

24th Circuit Court
900 Court St, PO Box 4, Lynchburg, VA 24505-0004; 434-847-1590; Fax: 434-847-1864. Hours: 8:15AM-4:45PM (EST). *Felony, Civil Actions Over $15,000, Probate.*

Civil Records: Access: Online, in person. Both court and visitors may perform in person searches. No search fee. Required to search: name, years to search. Civil cases indexed by defendant, plaintiff. Civil records on index books from 1800s, on computer since 1993. Select and search Circuit Courts online at http://208.210.219.132/courtinfo/vacircuit/select.jsp?court=. For information about the statewide online systems, see the state introduction.

Criminal Records: Access: Online, in person. Both court and visitors may perform in person searches. No search fee. Required to search: name, years to search; also helpful: DOB, SSN. Criminal records on index books from 1800s, on computer since 1993. Online access to criminal records is the same as civil.

General Information: Public access terminal is available. No juvenile, sealed records released. Copy fee: $.50 per page. Certification fee: $2.00. Fee payee: Clerk of Circuit Court. Personal checks accepted. Prepayment is required.

24th General District Court - Civil Division
905 Court St, Lynchburg, VA 24504; 434-847-1639; Fax: 434-847-1779. 8AM-4PM (EST). *Civil Actions Under $15,000, Eviction, Small Claims.*

Civil Records: Access: Mail, online, in person. Both court and visitors may perform in person searches. No search fee. Required to search: name, years to search; also helpful: address. Civil cases indexed by defendant, plaintiff. On computer since 1987. Select and search District Courts at http://208.210.219.132/courtinfo/vadistrict/select.jsp?court=. For information about the statewide online systems, see the state introduction.

General Information: Public access terminal is available. No juvenile, sealed records released. Turnaround time 1-2 weeks. Copy fee: $1.00 for first 2 pages, $.50 each add'l. Fee payee: Lynchburg General District Court. Personal checks accepted.

24th General District Court - Criminal Division 905 Court St, Lynchburg, VA 24504; 434-847-1560; Fax: 434-847-1779. Hours: 8AM-4PM (EST). *Misdemeanor.*

Criminal Records: Access: Online, in person. Visitors must perform in person searches for themselves. No search fee. Required to search: name, years to search. Criminal records on index books and computer go back 10 years. For information about the statewide online systems, see the state introduction. Select and search General District Courts at http://208.210.219.132/courtinfo/vadistrict/select.jsp?court=. Mail access limited to specific cases only, not name searches.

General Information: Public access terminal is available. No juvenile, sealed records released. Copy fee: $1.00 for first 2 pages, $.50 each add'l. Fee payee: Lynchburg General District Court. Personal checks accepted.

Madison County

16th Circuit Court 100 Court Square, Main St (PO Box 220), Madison, VA 22727; 540-948-6888; Fax: 540-948-3759. Hours: 8:30AM-4:30PM (EST). *Felony, Civil Actions Over $15,000, Probate.*

Civil Records: Access: Mail, online, in person. Visitors must perform in person searches for themselves. No search fee. Required to search: name, years to search. Civil cases indexed by defendant, plaintiff. Civil records on index books from 1792, on computer since 1989. Select and search Combined Courts online at http://208.210.219.132/courtinfo/vacircuit/select.jsp?court=. For information about the statewide online systems, see the state introduction.

Criminal Records: Access: Mail, online, in person. Visitors must perform in person searches for themselves. No search fee. Required to search: name, years to search, DOB; also helpful: SSN. Criminal records on index books from 1792, on computer since 1989. Online access to criminal records is the same as civil.

General Information: Public access terminal is available. No juvenile, sealed records released. Turnaround time 1 week. Copy fee: $.50 per page. Certification fee: $2.00. Fee payee: Clerk of Circuit Court. Personal checks accepted. Prepayment is required.

16th General District Court Madison County Courthouse, PO Box 470, Madison, VA 22727; 540-948-4657; Fax: 540-948-5649. Hours: 8:30AM-4:30PM (EST). *Misdemeanor, Civil Actions Under $15,000, Eviction, Small Claims.*

Civil Records: Access: Phone, fax, mail, online, in person. Only the court performs in person searches; visitors may not. No search fee. Required to search: name, years to search. Civil cases indexed by defendant, plaintiff. Civil records on index books and computer back to 1992. Select and search District Courts at http://208.210.219.132/courtinfo/vadistrict/select.jsp?court=. For information about the statewide online systems, see the state introduction.

Criminal Records: Access: Phone, fax, mail, online, in person. Only the court performs in person searches; visitors may not. No search fee. Required to search: name, years to search, DOB; also helpful: address, SSN. Criminal records on index books and computer back to 1992. Online access to criminal records is the same as civil.

General Information: No juvenile, sealed or pre-trial records released. Turnaround time 3-4 days. Fax notes: No fee to fax results. No copy fee.

Manassas City

Circuit & District Courts, VA.
Note: See Prince William County

Manassas Park City

Circuit & District Courts, VA.
Note: See Prince William County

Martinsville City

21st Circuit Court PO Box 1206, Martinsville, VA 24114-1206; 276-656-5106; Fax: 276-656-5232. Hours: 9AM-5PM (EST). *Felony, Civil Actions Over $15,000, Probate.*

www.ci.martinsville.va.us/crms

Civil Records: Access: Online, in person. Visitors must perform in person searches for themselves. No search fee. Required to search: name, years to search. Civil cases indexed by defendant, plaintiff. Civil records on computer since 1988, on index books from 1942. Online access available free at http://208.210.219.132/courtinfo/vacircuit/select.jsp?court=. For information about the statewide online systems, see the state introduction. Also, judgments are available free online at www.ci.martinsville.va.us/crms/.

Criminal Records: Access: Online, in person. Visitors must perform in person searches for themselves. No search fee. Required to search: name, years to search; also helpful: DOB, SSN. Criminal records on computer since 1988, on index books from 1942. Online access to criminal records is the same as civil.

General Information: Public access terminal is available. No juvenile, sealed records released. Copy fee: $.50 per page. Certification fee: $2.00. Fee payee: Clerk of Circuit Court. Personal checks accepted.

21st General District Court PO Box 1402, Martinsville, VA 24112; 276-656-5125; Fax: 276-638-8584. Hours: 9AM-5PM (EST). *Misdemeanor, Civil Actions Under $15,000, Eviction, Small Claims.*

www.courts.state.va.us

Civil Records: Access: Online, in person. Visitors must perform in person searches for themselves. No search fee. Required to search: name, years to search. Civil cases indexed by defendant, plaintiff. Civil records on computer since 1992. Select and search District Courts at http://208.210.219.132/courtinfo/vadistrict/select.jsp?court=. For information about the statewide online systems, see the state introduction.

Criminal Records: Access: Online, in person. Visitors must perform in person searches for themselves. No search fee. Required to search: name, years to search. Criminal records on computer since 1992. Online access to criminal records is the same as civil.

General Information: No sealed or expunged records released. Copy fee: $.50 per copy.

Mathews County

9th Circuit Court PO Box 463, Mathews, VA 23109; 804-725-2550. Hours: 8AM-4PM (EST). *Felony, Civil Actions Over $15,000, Probate.*

www.courts.state.va.us/courts/circuit/Mathews/home.html

Civil Records: Access: Online, in person. Visitors must perform in person searches for themselves. No search fee. Required to search: name, years to search. Civil cases indexed by defendant, plaintiff. Civil records on index books from 1800s. Remote online access to court case indexes is via LOPAS; call 804-786-6455 to apply.

Criminal Records: Access: Online, in person. Visitors must perform in person searches for themselves. No search fee. Required to search: name, years to search; also helpful: DOB, SSN. Criminal records on index books from 1800s. Remote online access to court case indexes is via LOPAS; call 804-786-6455 to apply.

General Information: No juvenile, sealed records released. SASE required. Copy fee: $.50 per page. Certification fee: $2.00. Fee payee: Clerk of Circuit Court. Personal checks accepted. Prepayment required.

9th General District Court PO Box 169, Saluda, VA 23149; 804-758-4312. Hours: 8:30AM-4:30PM (EST). *Misdemeanor, Civil Actions Under $15,000, Eviction, Small Claims.*

Civil Records: Access: Mail, online, in person. Both court and visitors may perform in person searches. No search fee. Required to search: name, years to search. Civil cases indexed by defendant. Civil records on index books from 1800s; on computer 10 years back. Select and search District Courts at http://208.210.219.132/courtinfo/vadistrict/select.jsp?court=. For information about the statewide online systems, see the state introduction.

Criminal Records: Access: Mail, online, in person. Both court and visitors may perform in person searches. No search fee. Required to search: name, years to search, DOB, date of offense; also helpful: SSN. Criminal records on index books from 1800s; on computer 10 years back. Online access to criminal records is the same as civil.

General Information: Public access terminal is available. No juvenile, sealed records released. SASE required. Turnaround time 7-10 days. Copy fee: $.50 per page. Fee payee: Clerk of General District Court. Personal checks accepted. Prepayment is required.

Mecklenburg County

10th Circuit Court PO Box 530, Boydton, VA 23917; 434-738-6191; Fax: 434-738-6861. Hours: 8:30AM-4:30PM (EST). *Felony, Civil Actions Over $15,000, Probate.*

Civil Records: Access: Online, in person. Visitors must perform in person searches for themselves. No search fee. Required to search: name, years to search. Civil cases indexed by defendant, plaintiff. Civil records on index books from 1800s, on computer from 1987. Remote online access to court case indexes is via LOPAS; call 804-786-6455 to apply.

Criminal Records: Access: Online, in person. Visitors must perform in person searches for themselves. No search fee. Required to search: name, years to search. Criminal records on index books from 1800s, on computer from 1987. Remote online access to court case indexes is via LOPAS; call 804-786-6455 to apply.

General Information: Public access terminal is available. No juvenile, sealed or direct indictments (drug offenses) records released. Copy fee: $.50 per page. Certification fee: $2.00. Fee payee: Clerk of Circuit Court. Personal checks accepted. Prepayment is required.

10th General District Court 1294 Jefferson Street (PO Box 306), Boydton, VA 23917; 434-738-6191 X223; Fax: 434-738-0761. Hours: 8:30AM-4:30PM (EST). *Misdemeanor, Civil Actions Under $15,000, Eviction, Small Claims.*

Civil Records: Access: Fax, mail, online, in person. Both court and visitors may perform in person searches. Search fee: $5.00. Required to search: name, years to search. Civil cases indexed by defendant, plaintiff. Civil records on computer since 1992. Select and search District Courts at http://208.210.219.132/courtinfo/vadistrict/select.jsp?court=. For information on the statewide online systems, see state introduction.

Criminal Records: Access: Fax, mail, online, in person. Both court and visitors may perform in person searches. Search fee: $5.00. Required to search: name, years to search; also helpful: DOB, SSN. Criminal records on computer since 1992. Online access to criminal records is the same as civil.

General Information: Public access terminal is available. Sealed, and adoption records not released. Copy fee: $.50 per page. Fee payee: Clerk of General District Court. Personal checks accepted. Credit cards accepted: Visa, MasterCard.

Middlesex County

9th Circuit Court PO Box 158, Saluda, VA 23149; 804-758-5317; Fax: 804-758-0792. Hours: 8:30AM-4:30PM (EST). *Felony, Civil Actions Over $15,000, Probate.*

Civil Records: Access: Online, in person. Visitors must perform in person searches for themselves. No search fee. Required to search: name, years to search. Civil cases indexed by defendant, plaintiff. Civil records on index books from 1672; on computer back to 1992. Online access available free at http://208.210.219.132/courtinfo/vacircuit/select.jsp?court=. For information about the statewide online systems, see the state introduction.

Criminal Records: Access: Online, in person. Visitors must perform in person searches for themselves. No search fee. Required to search: name, years to search, DOB, SSN. Criminal records on index books from 1674; on computer back to 1992. Online access to criminal records is the same as civil.

General Information: No juvenile, sealed records released. Fax notes: Will not fax results. Copy fee: $.50 per page. Certification fee: $2.00. Fee payee: Clerk of Circuit Court. Personal checks accepted. Prepayment is required.

9th General District Court PO Box 169, Saluda, VA 23149; 804-758-4312. Hours: 8:30AM-4:30PM (EST). *Misdemeanor, Civil Actions Under $15,000, Eviction, Small Claims.*

Civil Records: Access: Mail, online, in person. Both court and visitors may perform in person searches. No search fee. Required to search: name, years to search. Civil cases indexed by defendant. Civil records on index books from 1800s; on computer back 10 years. Select and search District Courts at http://208.210.219.132/courtinfo/vadistrict/select.jsp?court=. For information about the statewide online systems, see the state introduction.

Criminal Records: Access: Mail, online, in person. Both court and visitors may perform in person searches. No search fee. Required to search: name, years to search. Criminal records on index books from 1800s; on computer back 10 years. Online access to criminal records is the same as civil.

General Information: Public access terminal is available. No juvenile, sealed records released. SASE required. Turnaround time 2-3 days. Copy fee: $.50 per page. Fee payee: Clerk of General District Court. Personal checks accepted. Prepayment is required.

Montgomery County

27th Circuit Court PO Box 6309, Christiansburg, VA 24068; 540-382-5760; Fax: 540-382-6937. Hours: 8:30AM-4:30PM (EST). *Felony, Civil Actions Over $15,000, Probate.*

Civil Records: Access: Phone, mail, online, in person. Both court and visitors may perform in person searches. No search fee. Required to search: name, years to search. Civil cases indexed by defendant, plaintiff. Civil records on index books from 1800s, on computer from 1/94. Online access available free at http://208.210.219.132/courtinfo/vacircuit/select.jsp?court=. For information about the statewide online systems, see the state introduction. Phone & mail access limited to cases filed 7/93-present.

Criminal Records: Access: Online, in person. Visitors must perform in person searches for themselves. No search fee. Required to search: name, years to search; also helpful: DOB, SSN. Criminal records on computer since 9/93, prior in books. Online access to criminal records is the same as civil.

General Information: Public access terminal is available. No juvenile, sealed records released. SASE requested. Copy fee: $.50 per page. Certification fee:

$2.00. Fee payee: Clerk of Circuit Court. Personal checks accepted. Prepayment is required.

27th General District Court Montgomery County Courthouse, 1 E Main St, Suite 201, Christiansburg, VA 24073; 540-382-5735; Fax: 540-382-6988. 8:30AM-4:30PM (EST). *Misdemeanor, Civil Actions Under $15,000, Eviction, Small Claims.*

Civil Records: Access: Online, in person. Visitors must perform in person searches for themselves. No search fee. Required to search: name, years to search. Civil cases indexed by defendant, plaintiff. Civil records on computerized records go back ten years. Select and search District Courts at http://208.210.219.132/courtinfo/vadistrict/select.jsp?court=. For information on the statewide online systems, see state introduction.

Criminal Records: Access: Fax, mail, online, in person. Visitors must perform in person searches for themselves. No search fee. Required to search: name, years to search. Computerized records go back ten years. Online access to criminal records is the same as civil.

General Information: Public access terminal is available. No juvenile records released. Turnaround time 5 days. Copy fee: $.50 per page. Fee payee: Clerk General District Court. Personal checks accepted.

Nelson County

24th Circuit Court PO Box 10, Lovingston, VA 22949; 434-263-4069; Fax: 434-263-8313. Hours: 8AM-5PM (EST). *Felony, Civil Actions Over $15,000, Probate.*

Civil Records: Access: Online, in person. Visitors must perform in person searches for themselves. No search fee. Required to search: name, years to search. Civil cases indexed by defendant, plaintiff. Civil records on index books from 1800s, deeds on computer from 7/93. Online access available free at http://208.210.219.132/courtinfo/vacircuit/select.jsp?court=. For information about the statewide online systems, see the state introduction.

Criminal Records: Access: Online, in person. Visitors must perform in person searches for themselves. No search fee. Required to search: name, years to search; also helpful- DOB, SSN. Criminal records on index books from 1800s, deeds on computer from 7/93. Online access to criminal records is the same as civil.

General Information: Public access terminal is available. (Deeds and marriage licenses from 6/30/93 and financing statements from 06/30/94 are on terminal.) No juvenile, sealed records released. Copy fee: $.50 per page. Certification fee: $2.00. Fee payee: Clerk of Circuit Court. Personal checks accepted. Prepayment is required.

24th General District Court Nelson County Courthouse, 84 Courthouse Square, PO Box 55, Lovingston, VA 22949; 434-263-4245; Fax: 434-263-4264. Hours: 8AM-4:30PM (EST). *Misdemeanor, Civil Actions Under $15,000, Eviction, Small Claims.*

Civil Records: Access: Fax, mail, online, in person. Both court and visitors may perform in person searches. No search fee. Required to search: name, years to search. Civil cases indexed by defendant, plaintiff. Civil records on computer from 1993, indexed from 1992. Select and search District Courts at http://208.210.219.132/courtinfo/vadistrict/select.jsp?court=. For information about the statewide online systems, see the state introduction.

Criminal Records: Access: Fax, mail, online, in person. Both court and visitors may perform in person searches. No search fee. Required to search: name, years to search. Criminal records on computer from 1993, indexed from 1992. Online access to criminal records is the same as civil.

General Information: Public access terminal is available. No sealed records released. SASE required.

Turnaround time 3-4 days. Fax notes: No fee to fax results. Copy fee: $.50 per page. Fee payee: Clerk of General District Court. Personal checks accepted. Prepayment is required.

New Kent County

9th Circuit Court PO Box 98, 2001 Court House Circle, New Kent, VA 23124; 804-966-9520; Fax: 804-966-9528. Hours: 8:30AM-4:30PM (EST). *Felony, Civil Actions Over $15,000, Probate.*

Civil Records: Access: Online, in person. Visitors must perform in person searches for themselves. No search fee. Required to search: name, years to search. Civil cases indexed by defendant, plaintiff. Civil records on index books from 1865, some on cards; computerized back to 1992. Online access available free at http://208.210.219.132/courtinfo/vacircuit/select.jsp?court=. For information about the statewide online systems, see the state introduction.

Criminal Records: Access: Online, in person. Visitors must perform in person searches for themselves. No search fee. Required to search: name, years to search, DOB, SSN. Criminal records on index books from 1865, some on cards; computerized back to 1992. Online access to criminal records is the same as civil.

General Information: Public access terminal is available. No juvenile, sealed, adoption records released. Copy fee: $.50 per page. Certification fee: $2.00. Fee payee: Circuit Court. Personal checks accepted. Prepayment is required.

9th General District Court PO Box 127, New Kent, VA 23124; 804-966-9530; Fax: 804-966-9535. Hours: 8:30AM-4:30PM (EST). *Misdemeanor, Civil Actions Under $15,000, Eviction, Small Claims.*

Civil Records: Access: Mail, online, in person. Both court and visitors may perform in person searches. No search fee. Required to search: name, years to search. Civil cases indexed by defendant, plaintiff. Civil records go back to 1992 and on computer since 1993. Select and search District Courts at http://208.210.219.132/courtinfo/vadistrict/select.jsp?court=. For information on the statewide online systems, see state introduction.

Criminal Records: Access: Mail, online, in person. Both court and visitors may perform in person searches. No search fee. Required to search: name, years to search; also helpful: DOB, SSN and signed release. Criminal records go back to 1992 and on computer since 1993. Online access to criminal records is the same as civil.

General Information: Public access terminal is available. No juvenile, sealed records released. SASE required. Turnaround time 5 days. Copy fee: $1.00 per page. Fee payee: General District Court. Personal checks accepted. Credit cards accepted: Visa, MasterCard. Prepayment is required.

Newport News City

7th Circuit Court 2500 Washington Ave, Newport News, VA 23607; 757-926-8561; Fax: 757-926-8531. Hours: 8AM-4:45PM (EST). *Felony, Civil Actions Over $15,000, Probate.*

Civil Records: Access: Mail, online, in person. Both court and visitors may perform in person searches. No search fee. Required to search: name, years to search. Civil cases indexed by defendant, plaintiff. Civil records on computer from 1987, prior on index books. Online access available free at http://208.210.219.132/courtinfo/vacircuit/select.jsp?court=. For information about the statewide online systems, see the state introduction. Mail access only available for old records.

Criminal Records: Access: Online, in person. Visitors must perform in person searches for themselves. No search fee. Required to search: name, years to search. Criminal records on computer from 1987, on index books from 1985 to 1987, prior on judgment books. Online access to criminal records is the same as civil.

General Information: Public access terminal is available. No adoption, juvenile, sealed records released. SASE requested. Turnaround time 1 day. Copy fee: $.50 per page. Certification fee: $2.00. Fee payee: Clerk of Circuit Court. Personal checks accepted. In state checks only. Prepayment is required.

7th General District Court 2500 Washington Ave, Newport News, VA 23607; Civil phone: 757-926-3520; Criminal phone: 757-926-8811; Fax: 757-926-8496. Hours: 7:30AM-4PM (EST). *Misdemeanor, Civil Actions Under $15,000, Eviction, Small Claims.*

Civil Records: Access: Phone, fax, mail, in person. Visitors must perform in person searches for themselves. No search fee. Required to search: name, years to search. Select and search District Courts at http://208.210.219.132/courtinfo/vadistrict/select.jsp?court=. For information about the statewide online systems, see the state introduction.

Criminal Records: Access: Phone, fax, mail, online, in person. Both court and visitors may perform in person searches. No search fee. Required to search: name, years to search. Criminal records on computer on index cards since 1985, prior records at Circuit Court. Online access to criminal records is the same as civil.

General Information: Public access terminal is available. No juvenile, sealed records released. Turnaround time 1-2 days. Copy fee: $1.00 for first page, $.50 each add'l. Fee payee: General District Court. Personal checks accepted. Credit cards accepted: Visa, MasterCard (criminal only). Prepayment is required.

Norfolk City

4th Circuit Court 100 St Paul's Blvd, Norfolk, VA 23510; 757-664-4380; Fax: 757-664-4581. 9AM-5PM (EST). *Felony, Civil Actions Over $15,000, Probate.*

Civil Records: Access: Online, in person. Both court and visitors may perform in person searches. Search fee: $10.00. Required to search: name, years to search. Civil cases indexed by defendant, plaintiff. Civil records on computer back to 1993, docket books back to 1800s. Online access available free at http://208.210.219.132/courtinfo/vacircuit/select.jsp?court=. For information about the statewide online systems, see the state introduction.

Criminal Records: Access: Online, in person. Both the court and visitors may perform in person searches. Search fee: $10.00. Required to search: name, years to search, DOB, SSN, signed release. Criminal records go back to 1972; on computer back to 1993, docket books back to 1800s. Online access to dockets is available free at http://208.210.219.132/courtinfo/vacircuit/select.jsp?court=.

General Information: Public access terminal is available. No juvenile, sealed records released. Copy fee: $.50 per page. Certification fee: $2.00. Fee payee: Clerk of Circuit Court. Personal checks accepted. Prepayment required.

4th General District Court 811 E City Hall Ave, Norfolk, VA 23510; 757-664-4910; Civil phone: 757-664-4913/4; Criminal phone: 757-664-4915/6. Hours: 8AM-4PM (EST). *Misdemeanor, Civil Actions Under $15,000, Eviction, Small Claims.*

Civil Records: Access: Mail, online, in person. Visitors must perform in person searches. Search fee: $10.00 per name. Required to search: name, years to search. Civil cases indexed by defendant, plaintiff. Civil records in files, on computer from 1992. Select and search District Courts at http://208.210.219.132/courtinfo/vadistrict/select.jsp?court=. For information about the statewide online systems, see the state introduction.

Criminal Records: Access: Online, in person. Visitors must perform in person searches. No search fee. Required to search: name, years to search. Criminal

records in files, on computer from 1992. Online access to criminal records is the same as civil.

General Information: Public access terminal is available. No juvenile, sealed, or adoption records released. Turnaround time within 1-2 weeks. Copy fee: $1.00 per page. Certification fee: $1.00. Fee payee: Norfolk General District Court. Personal checks accepted. Prepayment is required.

Northampton County

2nd Circuit Court PO Box 36 (16404 Courthouse Rd), Eastville, VA 23347-0036; 757-678-0465; Fax: 757-678-5410. Hours: 9AM-4:30PM (EST). *Felony, Civil Actions Over $15,000, Probate.*

Note: Oldest continuous records in the USA.

Civil Records: Access: Phone, fax, mail, online, in person. Both court and visitors may perform in person searches. No search fee. Required to search: name, years to search. Civil cases indexed by defendant, plaintiff. Civil records on index books from 1632; on computer back to 1993. Select and search Circuit Courts online at http://208.210.219.132/courtinfo/vacircuit/select.jsp?court=. For information about the statewide online systems, see the state introduction.

Criminal Records: Access: Phone, fax, mail, online, in person. Both court and visitors may perform in person searches. No search fee. Required to search: name, years to search, DOB. Criminal records on index books from 1632; on computer back to 1993, some previous. Online access to court index records is the same as civil.

General Information: Public access terminal is available. (Index goes back to 7/1997.) No juvenile, sealed records released. SASE required. Turnaround time 1 week. Fax notes: Fee to fax results is $.75 per page. Copy fee: $.50 per page. Certification fee: $1.00. Fee payee: Clerk of Circuit Court. Personal checks accepted. Credit cards accepted (for full payments only): Visa. Prepayment is required.

Northampton General District Court PO Box 125, Eastville, VA 23347; 757-678-0466. Hours: 8AM-5PM (EST). *Misdemeanor, Civil Actions Under $15,000, Eviction, Small Claims.*

Civil Records: Access: Mail, online, in person. Only the court performs in person searches; visitors may not. No search fee. Required to search: name, years to search. Civil cases indexed by defendant, plaintiff. Civil records on computer since 1990. Select and search District Courts at http://208.210.219.132/courtinfo/vadistrict/select.jsp?court=. For information about the statewide online systems, see the state introduction.

Criminal Records: Access: Mail, online, in person. Only the court performs in person searches; visitors may not. No search fee. Required to search: name, years to search, DOB or SSN. Criminal records on computer since 1990. Online access to criminal records is the same as civil.

General Information: No juvenile, sealed records released. SASE required. Turnaround time 1-2 days. Copy fee: $.50 per page. Fee payee: General District Court. Personal checks accepted.

Northumberland County

15th Circuit Court PO Box 217, Heathsville, VA 22473; 804-580-3700; Fax: 804-580-2261. Hours: 8:30AM-4:45PM (EST). *Felony, Civil Actions Over $15,000, Probate.*

Civil Records: Access: Mail, online, in person. Both court and visitors may perform in person searches. No search fee. Required to search: name, years to search. Civil cases indexed by defendant, plaintiff. Civil records on index books from 1650. Online access available free at http://208.210.219.132/courtinfo/vacircuit/select.jsp?court=. For information about the statewide online systems, see the state introduction.

Criminal Records: Access: Mail, online, in person. Both court and visitors may perform in person searches. No search fee. Required to search: name, years to search, DOB. Criminal records on index books from 1650. Online access to criminal records is the same as civil.

General Information: No juvenile, sealed records released. Turnaround time 1-2 days. Copy fee: $.50 per page. Fee payee: Clerk of Circuit Court. Personal checks accepted.

15th General District Court Northumberland Courthouse, PO Box 114, Heathsville, VA 22473; 804-580-4323; Fax: 804-580-6702. Hours: 8AM-4:30PM (EST). *Misdemeanor, Civil Actions Under $15,000, Eviction, Small Claims.*

Civil Records: Access: Online, in person. Visitors must perform in person searches for themselves. No search fee. Required to search: name, years to search. Civil cases indexed by defendant, plaintiff. Civil records on index books; on computer since 1994. Select and search District Courts at http://208.210.219.132/courtinfo/vadistrict/select.jsp?court=. For information about the statewide online systems, see the state introduction.

Criminal Records: Access: Online, in person. Visitors must perform in person searches for themselves. No search fee. Required to search: name, years to search, DOB; also helpful: SSN. Criminal records on index books back to 1991; on computer since 1995. Online access to criminal records is the same as civil.

General Information: Public access terminal is available. No juvenile, sealed records released. Copy fee: $1.00 for first page, $.10 each add'l. Fee payee: Clerk of District Court. Personal checks accepted. Credit cards accepted: Visa, MasterCard. Prepayment is required.

Norton City

Circuit & District Courts, VA.

Note: See Wise County

Nottoway County

11th Circuit Court Courthouse, PO Box 25, Nottoway, VA 23955; 434-645-9043; Fax: 434-645-2201. Hours: 8:30AM-4:30PM (EST). *Felony, Civil Actions Over $15,000, Probate.*

Civil Records: Access: Mail, online, in person. Both court and visitors may perform in person searches. No search fee. Required to search: name, years to search. Civil cases indexed by defendant, plaintiff. Civil records on index books from late 1700s; on computer back to 2000. Select and search Circuit Courts online at http://208.210.219.132/courtinfo/vacircuit/select.jsp?court=. For information about the statewide online systems, see the state introduction.

Criminal Records: Access: Online, in person. Visitors must perform in person searches for themselves. No search fee. Required to search: name, years to search; also helpful: DOB, SSN. Criminal records on index books from late 1700s; on computer back to 2000. Online access to criminal records is the same as civil.

General Information: Public access terminal is available. No juvenile, sealed records released. SASE required. Turnaround time 1-2 days. Fax notes: Fee to fax results is $1.00 per document. Copy fee: $.50 per page. Certification fee: $2.00. Fee payee: Clerk's Office. Personal checks accepted. Prepayment is required.

11th General District Court PO Box 25, Nottoway, VA 23955; 434-645-9312. Hours: 8AM-4:15PM (EST). *Misdemeanor, Civil Actions Under $15,000, Eviction, Small Claims.*

Civil Records: Access: Mail, online, in person. Both court and visitors may perform in person searches. No search fee. Required to search: name, years to search. Civil cases indexed by defendant, plaintiff. Civil records on index cards from 1986, on computer the past 10

Criminal Records: Access: Mail, online, in person. Both court and visitors may perform in person searches. No search fee. Required to search: name, years to search, DOB. Criminal records on index books from 1650. Online access to criminal records is the same as civil.

General Information: No juvenile, sealed records released. Turnaround time 1-2 days. Copy fee: $.50 per page. Fee payee: Clerk of Circuit Court. Personal checks accepted.

years. Only court can search prior to 1989. Select and search District Courts at http://208.210.219.132/courtinfo/vadistrict/select.jsp?court=. For information on the statewide online systems, see state introduction.

Criminal Records: Access: Mail, online, in person. Both court and visitors may perform in person searches. No search fee. Required to search: name, years to search; also helpful: DOB, SSN. Criminal records on index cards from 1986, on computer the past 10 years Only court can search prior to 1989. Online access to criminal records is the same as civil.

General Information: Public access terminal is available. No juvenile records released. SASE required. Turnaround time 2-3 days. Copy fee: $1.00 for first page, $.50 each add'l. Fee payee: Nottoway District Court. Personal checks accepted. Prepayment is required.

Orange County

16th Circuit Court PO Box 230, Orange, VA 22960; 540-672-4030; Fax: 540-672-2939. Hours: 8:30AM-4:30PM (EST). *Felony, Civil Actions Over $15,000, Probate.*

Civil Records: Access: Online, in person. Both court and visitors may perform in person searches. No search fee. Required to search: name, years to search. Civil cases indexed by defendant, plaintiff. Civil records on computer since 1989, in index books from 1734 for deeds, from 1853 for births, from 1912 for marriages. Select and search Circuit Courts online at http://208.210.219.132/courtinfo/vacircuit/select.jsp?court=. For information about the statewide online systems, see the state introduction.

Criminal Records: Access: Phone, fax, mail, online, in person. Both court and visitors may perform in person searches. No search fee. Required to search: name, years to search, DOB; also helpful: SSN. Criminal records on computer since 1989, in index books from 1734. Online access to criminal records is the same as civil.

General Information: Public access terminal is available. No juvenile, sealed records released. Turnaround time 1 week-10 days. Fax notes: No fee to fax results. Copy fee: $.50 per page. Fee payee: Clerk of Circuit Court. Personal checks accepted. Prepayment is required.

16th General District Court Orange County Courthouse, PO Box 821, Orange, VA 22960; 540-672-3150; Fax: 540-672-9438. Hours: 8:30AM-4:30PM (EST). *Misdemeanor, Civil Actions Under $15,000, Eviction, Small Claims.*

Civil Records: Access: Mail, online, in person. Only the court performs in person searches; visitors may not. No search fee. Required to search: name, years to search. Civil cases indexed by defendant, plaintiff. Civil records on index books from 1800s, on computer from 1990. Select and search District Courts at http://208.210.219.132/courtinfo/vadistrict/select.jsp?court=. For information about the statewide online systems, see the state introduction.

Criminal Records: Access: Mail, online, in person. Only the court performs in person searches; visitors may not. No search fee. Required to search: name, years to search, DOB; also helpful: SSN. Criminal records on index books from 1800s, on computer from 1990. Online access to criminal records is the same as civil.

General Information: No juvenile, sealed records released. Turnaround time 1-2 days. Copy fee: $1.00 for first page, $.50 each add'l. Certification fee: $1.00 for fist page, $.50 each add'l. Fee payee: Clerk of District Court. In-state checks accepted. Credit cards accepted: Visa, MasterCard. Prepayment is required.

Page County

26th Circuit Court 116 S Court St, #A, Luray, VA 22835; 540-743-4064; Fax: 540-743-2338. 9AM-5PM (EST). *Felony, Civil Actions Over $15,000, Probate.*

Civil Records: Access: Online, in person. Visitors must perform in person searches for themselves. No search fee. Required to search: name, years to search. Civil cases indexed by defendant, plaintiff. Civil records on index books from 1831. Computerized records go back to 1995. Online access available free at http://208.210.219.132/courtinfo/vacircuit/select.jsp?court=. For information about the statewide online systems, see the state introduction.

Criminal Records: Access: Online, in person. Visitors must perform in person searches for themselves. No search fee. Required to search: name, years to search, DOB; also helpful: SSN. Criminal records on index books from 1831. Computerized records go back to 1995. Online access to criminal records is the same as civil.

General Information: No juvenile, sealed records released. Copy fee: $.50 per page. Certification fee: $2.00. Fee payee: Ron Wilson, Clerk. Personal checks accepted. No second party checks accepted. Prepayment is required.

26th General District Court 116 S Court St, Luray, VA 22835; 540-743-5705. Hours: 8AM-4:30PM (EST). *Misdemeanor, Civil Actions Under $15,000, Eviction, Small Claims.*

Civil Records: Access: Mail, online, in person. Both court and visitors may perform in person searches. No search fee. Required to search: name, years to search. Civil cases indexed by defendant, plaintiff. Civil records on computer back to 1/90. Select and search District Courts at http://208.210.219.132/courtinfo/vadistrict/select.jsp?court=. For information about the statewide online systems, see the state introduction.

Criminal Records: Access: Mail, online, in person. Both court and visitors may perform in person searches. No search fee. Required to search: name, years to search; also helpful: DOB, SSN. Criminal records on computer back to 1/90. Online access to criminal records is the same as civil.

General Information: Public access terminal is available. No sealed records released. SASE requested. Turnaround time 7-10 days. Certification fee: $1.00. Fee payee: District Court. Personal checks accepted.

Patrick County

21st Circuit Court PO Box 148, Stuart, VA 24171; 276-694-7213. Hours: 9AM-5PM (EST). *Felony, Civil Actions Over $15,000, Probate.*

Civil Records: Access: In person only. Visitors must perform in person searches for themselves. No search fee. Required to search: name, years to search. Civil cases indexed by plaintiff. Civil records on index books from 1791. Online access available free at http://208.210.219.132/courtinfo/vacircuit/select.jsp?court=. For information about the statewide online systems, see the state introduction.

Criminal Records: Access: Online, in person. Visitors must perform in person searches for themselves. No search fee. Required to search: name, years to search; also helpful: DOB, SSN. Criminal records on index books from 1791. Online access to criminal records is the same as civil.

General Information: No juvenile, sealed records released. Copy fee: $.50 per page. Certification fee: $2.00. Fee payee: Clerk of Circuit Court. Personal checks accepted. Prepayment is required.

21st General District Court PO Box 149, Stuart, VA 24171; 276-694-7258; Fax: 276-694-5614. Hours: 8:30AM-5PM (EST). *Misdemeanor, Civil Actions Under $15,000, Eviction, Small Claims.*

Civil Records: Access: Mail, fax, online, in person. Both court and visitors may perform in person searches. No search fee. Required to search: name, years to search. Civil cases indexed by defendant, plaintiff. Civil recordsgo back to 1992; on computer from 10/94. Select and search District Courts at http://208.210.219.132/courtinfo/vadistrict/select.jsp?court=. For information about the statewide online systems, see the state introduction.

Criminal Records: Access: Mail, online, in person. Both court and visitors may perform in person searches. No search fee. Required to search: name, years to search, DOB; also helpful: SSN. Criminal records go back to 1992; on computer from 10/94. Online access to criminal records is the same as civil.

General Information: Public access terminal is available. No juvenile, sealed records released. SASE requested. Turnaround time 1 week. No copy fee. Personal checks accepted.

Petersburg City

11th Circuit Court 7 Courthouse Ave, Petersburg, VA 23803; 804-733-2367; Fax: 804-732-5548. Hours: 8AM-4:30PM (EST). *Felony, Civil Actions Over $15,000, Probate.*

Civil Records: Access: Online, in person. Visitors must perform in person searches for themselves. Search fee: No search fee. Required to search: name, years to search. Civil cases indexed by defendant, plaintiff. Civil records on index books back to 1784; on computer back to 1988. Online access available free at http://208.210.219.132/courtinfo/vacircuit/select.jsp?court=. For information about the statewide online systems, see the state introduction.

Criminal Records: Access: Online, in person. Visitors must perform in person searches for themselves. Search fee: No search fee. Required to search: name, years to search; also helpful: DOB, SSN. Criminal records go back to 1970; on computer back to 1996. Online access to criminal records is the same as civil.

General Information: No juvenile, sealed or adoption records released. Copy fee: $.50 per page. Certification fee: $2.00. Fee payee: Petersburg Circuit Court Clerk. Personal checks accepted. Out of state checks not accepted. Prepayment is required.

11th Judicial District Court 35 E Tabb St, Petersburg, VA 23803; 804-733-2374; Civil phone: X4153; Criminal phone: X4152; Fax: 804-733-2375 (Attn: Civil or Crimnal). Hours: 8AM-4PM (EST). *Misdemeanor, Civil Actions Under $15,000, Eviction, Small Claims.*

Civil Records: Access: Fax, mail, online, in person. Both court and visitors may perform in person searches. No search fee. Required to search: name, years to search. Civil cases indexed by defendant, plaintiff. Civil records on index books back to 1980. Select and search District Courts at http://208.210.219.132/courtinfo/vadistrict/select.jsp?court=. For information about the statewide online systems, see the state introduction.

Criminal Records: Access: Fax, mail, online, in person. Both court and visitors may perform in person searches. No search fee. Required to search: name, years to search, DOB; also helpful: SSN. Criminal records indexed on books for 10 years; on computer back to 1988. Online access to criminal records is the same as civil.

General Information: Public access terminal is available. No sealed records released. Turnaround time 1 week. Copy fee: $1.00 for first 2 pages. Add $.50 per page thereafter. Certification fee: $1.00 plus $.50 per page after second. Fee payee: General District Court.

Personal checks accepted. In state checks accepted. Prepayment is required.

Pittsylvania County

22nd Circuit Court PO Drawer 31, Chatham, VA 24531; 434-432-7887. Hours: 8:30AM-5PM (EST). *Felony, Civil Actions Over $15,000, Probate.*

Civil Records: Access: Online, in person. Visitors must perform in person searches for themselves. No search fee. Required to search: name, years to search. Civil cases indexed by defendant, plaintiff. Civil records on index books back to 1767; computerized records since 1995. Remote online access to court case indexes is via LOPAS; call 804-786-6455 to apply.

Criminal Records: Access: Online, in person. Visitors must perform in person searches for themselves. No search fee. Required to search: name, years to search, DOB, SSN. Criminal records on index books back to 1767; computerized records since 1995. Remote online access to court case indexes is via LOPAS; call 804-786-6455 to apply.

General Information: No juvenile, sealed records released. Copy fee: $.25 per page. Certification fee: $2.00. Fee payee: Clerk of Circuit Court. Personal checks accepted. Prepayment is required.

22nd General District Court Pittsylvania Courthouse Annex 2nd Flr, PO Box 695, Chatham, VA 24531; 434-432-7879; Fax: 434-432-7915. Hours: 8:30AM-4:30PM (EST). *Misdemeanor, Civil Actions Under $15,000, Eviction, Small Claims.*

www.courts.state.va.us/courts/gd/Pittsylvania/home.html

Civil Records: Access: Online, in person. Visitors must perform in person searches for themselves. No search fee. Required to search: name, years to search. Civil cases indexed by defendant, plaintiff. Civil records on computer since 1992. Select and search District Courts at http://208.210.219.132/courtinfo/vadistrict/select.jsp?court=. For information about the statewide online systems, see the state introduction.

Criminal Records: Access: Online, in person. Visitors must perform in person searches for themselves. No search fee. Required to search: name, years to search. Criminal records on computer since 1992. Online access to criminal records is the same as civil.

General Information: Public access terminal is available. No juvenile, sealed records released. Fax notes: Fee to fax results is $.25 per page. Copy fee: $.25 per page. Fee payee: General District Court. Personal checks accepted.

Poquoson City

Circuit & District Courts, VA.
Note: See York County

Portsmouth City

Circuit Court PO Drawer 1217, Portsmouth, VA 23705; 757-393-8671; Fax: 757-399-4826. 8AM-6PM (EST). *Felony, Civil Actions Over $15,000, Probate.*

Civil Records: Access: Mail, online, in person. Visitors must perform in person searches for themselves. Search fee: $10.00 per name. Required to search: name, years to search. Civil cases indexed by defendant, plaintiff. Civil records on computer back to 6/1987, prior on index books back to 1858. Online access available free at http://208.210.219.132/courtinfo/vacircuit/select.jsp?court=. For information about the statewide online systems, see the state introduction. Phone access limited to simple requests.

Criminal Records: Access: Mail, online, in person. Both court and visitors may perform in person searches. Search fee: $5.00 per name. Required to search: name, years to search, DOB; also helpful: SSN. Criminal records on computer back to 6/1987, prior indexed on books back to 1858. Online access to criminal records is the same as civil.

General Information: Public access terminal is available. No juvenile, sealed records released. Copy fee: $.50 per page. Certification fee: $2.00. Fee payee: Cynthia P Morris, Clerk. Business checks accepted. No credit cards accepted. Prepayment is required.

General District Court PO Box 129, Portsmouth, VA 23705; Civil phone: 757-393-8624; Criminal phone: 757-393-8681; Fax: 757-393-8634. Hours: 8:30AM-4:30PM (EST). *Misdemeanor, Civil Actions Under $15,000, Eviction, Small Claims.*

Note: Traffic Division: 757-393-8506.

Civil Records: Access: Online, in person. Visitors must perform in person searches for themselves. No search fee. Required to search: name, years to search. Civil cases indexed by defendant, plaintiff. Civil records on computer from 4/87, from 1981 to 4/87 paper files only. Select and search District Courts at http://208.210.219.132/courtinfo/vadistrict/select.jsp?court=. For information about the statewide online systems, see the state introduction.

Criminal Records: Access: Mail, fax, online, in person. Both court and visitors may perform in person searches. Search fee: $7.00 per name. Required to search: name, years to search; also helpful: DOB, SSN. Criminal records on computer and case (paper files) maintained for 10 years. Online access to criminal records is the same as civil.

General Information: Public access terminal is available. Juvenile, sealed records not released. SASE required. Turnaround time within 14 days. No copy fee. Fee payee: Clerk of General District Court. Personal checks accepted. Credit cards accepted: Visa, MasterCard.

Powhatan County

11th Circuit Court PO Box 37, Powhatan, VA 23139-0037; 804-598-5660; Fax: 804-598-5608. Hours: 8:30AM-5PM (EST). *Felony, Civil Actions Over $15,000, Probate.*

Civil Records: Access: Mail, in person, online. Visitors must perform in person searches for themselves. No search fee. Required to search: name, years to search. Civil cases indexed by defendant, plaintiff. Civil records on index books from 1777, on computer from 1993. Remote online access to court case indexes is via LOPAS; call 804-786-6455 to apply.

Criminal Records: Access: In person, online. Visitors must perform in person searches for themselves. No search fee. Required to search: name, years to search, signed release; also helpful: SSN. Criminal records on index books from 1777, on computer from 1993. Remote online access to court case indexes is via LOPAS; call 804-786-6455 to apply.

General Information: Public access terminal is available. No juvenile, sealed records released. SASE required. Turnaround time 1-2 weeks. Copy fee: $.50 per page. Certification fee: $2.00. Fee payee: Clerk of Court. Personal checks accepted. Will bill copy fees.

11th Judicial District Court Courthouse, 3880 D Old Buckingham Rd, Powhatan, VA 23139; 804-598-5665; Fax: 804-598-5648. Hours: 8:30AM-5PM (EST). *Misdemeanor, Civil Actions Under $15,000, Eviction, Small Claims.*

Civil Records: Access: Phone, fax, mail, online, in person. Only the court performs in person searches; visitors may not. No search fee. Required to search: name, years to search. Civil cases indexed by defendant. Civil records on index cards for 10 yrs, on computer from 1992. Select and search District Courts at http://208.210.219.132/courtinfo/vadistrict/select.jsp?court=. For information about the statewide online systems, see the state introduction.

Criminal Records: Access: Phone, fax, mail, online, in person. Only the court performs in person searches; visitors may not. No search fee. Required to search:

name, years to search, DOB; also helpful: SSN. Criminal records on index cards for 10 yrs, on computer from 1993. Online access to criminal records is the same as civil.

General Information: No juvenile, sealed records released. Turnaround time 1 week. Fax notes: No fee to fax results. Local faxing only. Copy fee: $.50 each for 1st two; $25. Each add'l. Fee payee: Powhatan District Court. Personal checks accepted.

Prince Edward County

Circuit Court PO Box 304, Court House, 111 South St, Farmville, VA 23901-0304; 434-392-5145. Hours: 8:30AM-4:30PM (EST). *Felony, Civil Actions Over $15,000, Probate.*

Civil Records: Access: Online, in person. Visitors must perform in person searches for themselves. No search fee. Required to search: name, years to search. Civil cases indexed by defendant, plaintiff. Civil records on computer from 1990, books from 1930s. Remote online access to court case indexes is via LOPAS; call 804-786-6455 to apply.

Criminal Records: Access: Online, in person. Visitors must perform in person searches for themselves. No search fee. Required to search: name, years to search, DOB; also helpful: SSN. Criminal records on computer from 1990, books from 1930s. Online access to criminal records is the same as civil.

General Information: Public access terminal is available. No juvenile, sealed records released. Copy fee: $.50 per page; court will charge for the time to make copies. Certification fee: $2.00. Fee payee: Clerk of Circuit Court. Personal checks accepted. Prepayment is required.

General District Court PO Box 41, Farmville, VA 23901-0041; 434-392-4024; Fax: 434-392-3800. Hours: 8:30AM-4:30PM (EST). *Misdemeanor, Civil Actions Under $15,000, Eviction, Small Claims.*

Civil Records: Access: Phone, mail, online, in person. Visitors must perform in person searches for themselves. No search fee. Required to search: name, years to search; also helpful: address. Civil cases indexed by defendant, plaintiff. Civil records on computer go back 10 years. Select and search District Courts at http://208.210.219.132/courtinfo/vadistrict/select.jsp?court=. For information about the statewide online systems, see the state introduction.

Criminal Records: Access: Mail, online, in person. Visitors must perform in person searches for themselves. No search fee. Required to search: name, years to search; also helpful: DOB, SSN. Criminal records on computer go back 10 years. Online access to criminal records is the same as civil.

General Information: Public access terminal is available. No juvenile, sealed records released. SASE required. Turnaround time 1 week. Copy fee: $1.00 per page. Fee payee: Clerk of District Court. Personal checks accepted. Prepayment is required.

Prince George County

6th Circuit Court PO Box 98, Prince George, VA 23875; 804-733-2640; Fax: 804-861-5721. Hours: 8:30AM-5PM (EST). *Felony, Civil Actions Over $15,000, Probate.*

Civil Records: Access: Mail, online, in person. Both court and visitors may perform in person searches. Search fee: $5.00 per name. Required to search: name, years to search. Civil cases indexed by defendant, plaintiff. Civil records on index books since 1930s, computerized since 04/96. Select and search Circuit Courts online at http://208.210.219.132/courtinfo/vacircuit/select.jsp?court=. For information about the statewide online systems, see the state introduction.

Criminal Records: Access: Mail, online, in person. Both court and visitors may perform in person searches.

Search fee: $5.00 per name. Required to search: name, years to search, DOB; also helpful: SSN. Criminal records on index books since 1930s, computerized since 04/96. Online access to criminal records is the same as civil.

General Information: Public access terminal is available. No juvenile or sealed records released. SASE required. Turnaround time 1-2 days. Copy fee: $.50 per page. Fee payee: Clerk of the Circuit Court. Personal checks accepted. Prepayment is required.

6th General District Court P.C. Courthouse, PO Box 187, Prince George, VA 23875; 804-733-2783. Hours: 8:30AM-4:30PM (EST). *Misdemeanor, Civil Actions Under $15,000, Eviction, Small Claims.*

Civil Records: Access: Online, in person. Both court and visitors may perform in person searches. No search fee. Required to search: name, years to search. Civil cases indexed by defendant, plaintiff. Civil records on computer since 1991, prior on books since 1985. Select and search District Courts at http://208.210.219.132/courtinfo/vadistrict/select.jsp?court=. For information on the statewide online systems, see state introduction.

Criminal Records: Access: Online, in person. Both court and visitors may perform in person searches. No search fee. Required to search: name, years to search; also helpful: SSN. Criminal records on computer since 1991, prior on books since 1985. Online access to criminal records is the same as civil.

General Information: Public access terminal is available. No juvenile records released. No copy fee. Fee payee: Prince George Combined Court. Personal checks accepted.

Prince William County

31st Circuit Court 9311 Lee Ave, Manassas, VA 20110; 703-792-6015; Fax: 703-792-4721. Hours: 8:30AM-5PM (EST). *Felony, Civil Actions Over $15,000, Probate.*

www.pwcgov.org/ccourt

Civil Records: Access: In person only. Visitors must perform in person searches for themselves. No search fee. Required to search: name, years to search. Civil cases indexed by defendant, plaintiff. Civil records on computer since 1989; prior on microfiche or books to 1981.

Criminal Records: Access: Mail, in person. Both court and visitors may perform in person searches. Search fee: $10.00 per name. Required to search: name, years to search, DOB; also helpful: SSN. Criminal records on computer since 1989; prior on microfiche or books to 1981.

General Information: Public access terminal is available. No juvenile records released. Turnaround time 1 week. Copy fee: $.50 per page. Certification fee: $2.00. Fee payee: Clerk of Circuit Court. Personal checks accepted.

31st General District Court 9311 Lee Ave, Manassas, VA 20110; Civil phone: 703-792-6149; Criminal phone: 703-792-6141; Fax: 703-792-6121. Hours: 8AM-4PM (EST). *Misdemeanor, Civil Actions Under $15,000, Eviction, Small Claims.*

www.courts.state.va.us/courts/gd/Prince_William/home.html

Civil Records: Access: Mail, fax, online, in person. Both court and visitors may perform in person searches. No search fee. Required to search: name, years to search. Civil cases indexed by defendant, plaintiff. Civil records on computer go back 10 years, on index cards since 1985. Select and search District Courts at http://208.210.219.132/courtinfo/vadistrict/select.jsp?court=. For information about the statewide online systems, see the state introduction.

Criminal Records: Access: Mail, fax, online, in person. Both court and visitors may perform in person

searches. No search fee. Required to search: name, years to search. Criminal records on computer go back 10 years. Online access to criminal records is the same as civil.

General Information: Public access terminal is available. No juvenile or sealed records released. SASE required. Turnaround time 10 days. Copy fee: $1.00 copy fee for first 2 pages. Add $.50 per page thereafter. Fee payee: Clerk G.D.C. Personal checks accepted. Prepayment required.

Pulaski County

27th Circuit Court 45 3rd St NW #101, Pulaski, VA 24301; 540-980-7825; Fax: 540-980-7835. Hours: 8:30AM-4:30PM (EST). *Felony, Civil Actions Over $15,000, Probate.*

www.pulaskicircuitcourt.com

Civil Records: Access: Online, in person. Visitors must perform in person searches for themselves. No search fee. Required to search: name, years to search. Civil cases indexed by defendant, plaintiff. Civil records on index books from 1839, online since 1998. Online access to court records available free at http://records.pulaskicircuitcourt.com/splash.jsp. Registration required; search by name, document type or number. Also, online access is available free at http://208.210.219.132/courtinfo/vacircuit/select.jsp?court=.

Criminal Records: Access: Online, in person. Visitors must perform in person searches for themselves. No search fee. Required to search: name, years to search, DOBV; also helpful: SSN. Criminal records on index books from 1839, online since 1998. Online access to criminal records is the same as civil. This agency will perform no record checks and refer all requests to the State Police.

General Information: No juvenile, sealed records released. Copy fee: $.50 per page. Certification fee: $1.00. Fee payee: Clerk of Court. Personal checks accepted. Prepayment is required.

27th General District Court 45 3rd St NW Ste 102, Pulaski, VA 24301; 540-980-7470; Fax: 540-980-7792. Hours: 8:30AM-4:30PM (EST). *Misdemeanor, Civil Actions Under $15,000, Eviction, Small Claims.*

Civil Records: Access: Online, in person. Visitors must perform in person searches for themselves. No search fee. Required to search: name, years to search. Civil cases indexed by defendant, plaintiff. Civil records on computer since 1987; no records prior due to courthouse fire. Select and search District Courts at http://208.210.219.132/courtinfo/vadistrict/select.jsp?court=. For information about the statewide online systems, see the state introduction.

Criminal Records: Access: Online, in person. Visitors must perform in person searches for themselves. No search fee. Required to search: name, years to search, DOB; also helpful: SSN. Criminal records on computer since 1987; no records prior due to courthouse fire. Online access to criminal records is the same as civil.

General Information: Public access terminal is available. No juvenile, sealed records released. Copy fee: $.50 per page. Fee payee: Clerk of General District Court. Personal checks accepted. Credit cards accepted: Visa, MasterCard. Credit cards accepted for fines & costs only. Prepayment is required.

Radford City

27th Circuit Court 619 2nd St, Radford, VA 24141; 540-731-3610; Fax: 540-731-3612. Hours: 8AM-5PM (no machine receipts after 4:30PM) (EST). *Felony, Civil Actions Over $15,000, Probate.*

Civil Records: Access: Fax, mail, online, in person. Both court and visitors may perform in person searches. No search fee. Required to search: name, years to search. Civil cases indexed by defendant, plaintiff. Civil records on books from 1892; on computer back to

6/2000. Select and search Circuit Courts online at http://208.210.219.132/courtinfo/vacircuit/select.jsp?court=. For information about the statewide online systems, see the state introduction.

Criminal Records: Access: Fax, mail, online, in person. Both court and visitors may perform in person searches. No search fee. Required to search: name, years to search, DOB, signed release; also helpful: SSN. Criminal records on books from 1892; on computer back to 6/2000. Online access to criminal records is the same as civil.

General Information: Public access terminal is available. No juvenile, sealed or adoption records released. SASE required. Turnaround time same day. Fax notes: $.50 per page. Copy fee: $.50 per page. Certification fee: $2.00. Fee payee: Radford Circuit Court. Personal checks accepted. Prepayment is required.

27th General District Court 619 2nd St, Radford, VA 24141; 540-731-3609; Fax: 540-731-3692. Hours: 8:30AM-4:30PM (EST). *Misdemeanor, Civil Actions Under $15,000, Eviction, Small Claims.*

Civil Records: Access: Mail, online, in person. Both court and visitors may perform in person searches. Search fee: A search fee may be required. Required to search: name, years to search. Civil cases indexed by defendant, plaintiff. Select and search District Courts at http://208.210.219.132/courtinfo/vadistrict/select.jsp?court=. For information about the statewide online systems, see the state introduction.

Criminal Records: Access: Fax, mail, online, in person. Both court and visitors may perform in person searches. Search fee: None, unless it is a lengthy search. Required to search: name, years to search, DOB, SSN, signed release. Criminal records on computer since 1989. Online access to criminal records is the same as civil.

General Information: Public access terminal is available. No juvenile, sealed records released. Turnaround time 7 days or longer. Fax notes: $.50 per page. Copy fee: $.50 per page. Fee payee: District Court. Personal checks accepted. Prepayment is required.

Rappahannock County

20th Circuit Court 238 Gay Street (PO Box 517), Washington, VA 22747; 540-675-3621. Hours: 8:30AM-4:30PM (EST). *Felony, Civil Actions Over $15,000, Probate.*

Civil Records: Access: Mail, online, in person. Both court and visitors may perform in person searches. No search fee. Required to search: name, years to search. Civil cases indexed by defendant, plaintiff. Civil records computerized since 1995, on index cards from 1833, early records archived. Select and search Circuit Courts online at http://208.210.219.132/courtinfo/vacircuit/select.jsp?court=. For information about the statewide online systems, see the state introduction. Mail access limited to specific cases only. Court will only do searches as time permits.

Criminal Records: Access: Mail, online, in person. Both court and visitors may perform in person searches. Search fee: Searches performed only as time permits. Required to search: name, years to search; also helpful: DOB, SSN. Criminal records computerized since 1995, on index cards from 1833, early records archived. Online access to criminal records is the same as civil. Mail access limited to specific cases only.

General Information: Public access terminal is available. No juvenile, sealed records released. SASE required. Turnaround time 1-2 days. Copy fee: $.50 per page. Fee payee: Clerk of the Circuit Court. Personal checks accepted. Prepayment is required.

20th Combined District Court PO Box 206, Washington, VA 22747; 540-675-3518. Hours:

8:30AM-4:30PM (EST). *Misdemeanor, Civil Actions Under $15,000, Eviction, Small Claims.*

Civil Records: Access: Mail, online, in person. Both court and visitors may perform in person searches. No search fee. Required to search: name, years to search. Civil cases indexed by defendant, plaintiff. Civil records on computer back to 1994, on index cards back to 1990, prior in Circuit Court. Select and search District Courts at http://208.210.219.132/courtinfo/vadistrict/select.jsp?court=. For information about the statewide online systems, see the state introduction.

Criminal Records: Access: Mail, online, in person. Both court and visitors may perform in person searches. No search fee. Required to search: name, years to search, DOB; also helpful: SSN, signed release. Criminal records on computer back to 1994, index cards back to 1985, prior in Circuit Court. Online access to criminal records is the same as civil.

General Information: No juvenile, sealed records released. SASE requested. Turnaround time up to 2 weeks. Copy fee: $.25 per page. Fee payee: Clerk of General District Court. Personal checks accepted. Credit cards accepted: Visa, MasterCard.

Richmond County

15th Circuit Court 101 Court Circle, PO Box 1000, Warsaw, VA 22572; 804-333-3781; Fax: 804-333-5396. Hours: 9AM-5PM (EST). *Felony, Civil Actions Over $15,000, Probate.*

Civil Records: Access: Phone, mail, in person, online. Both court and visitors may perform in person searches. No search fee. Required to search: name, years to search; also helpful: address, SS#. Civil cases indexed by defendant, plaintiff. Civil records archived from 1692. Select and search Circuit Courts online at http://208.210.219.132/courtinfo/vacircuit/select.jsp?court=. For information about the statewide online systems, see the state introduction.

Criminal Records: Access: Mail, in person, online. Both court and visitors may perform in person searches. No search fee. Required to search: name, years to search, DOB; also helpful: address. Criminal records archived from 1692, computerized since 1994. Online access to criminal records is the same as civil.

General Information: No juvenile, sealed records released. SASE requested. Turnaround time same day. Copy fee: $.50 per page; $1.00 per page if genealogy records. Certification fee: $2.00. Fee payee: Clerk of Circuit Court. Personal checks accepted. Prepayment is required.

15th Judicial District Court Richmond County Courthouse, PO Box 1000, Warsaw, VA 22572; 804-333-4616; Fax: 804-333-3741. Hours: 8AM-4:30PM (EST). *Misdemeanor, Civil Actions Under $15,000, Eviction, Small Claims.*

Civil Records: Access: Mail, online, in person. Both court and visitors may perform in person searches. No search fee. Required to search: name, years to search. Civil cases indexed by defendant, plaintiff. Civil records archived 10 years back; on computer from 1994. Select and search District Courts at http://208.210.219.132/courtinfo/vadistrict/select.jsp?court=. For information about the statewide online systems, see the state introduction.

Criminal Records: Access: Mail, online, in person. Both court and visitors may perform in person searches. No search fee. Required to search: name, years to search; also helpful: DOB, SSN. Criminal records archived 10 years back; on computer from 1994. Online access to criminal records is the same as civil.

General Information: Public access terminal is available. No juvenile, sealed records released. SASE requested. Turnaround time 2 days. Personal checks accepted.

Richmond City

13th Circuit Court - Division I John Marshall Courts Building, 400 N 9th St, Richmond, VA 23219; 804-646-6505; Civil phone: 804-646-6536; Criminal phone: 804-646-6553. Hours: 8:45AM-4:45PM (EST). *Felony, Civil Actions Over $15,000, Probate.*

www.courts.state.va.us/courts/circuit/Richmond/home.html

Note: A second web site is www.vipnet.org/vipnet/clerks/richmondjohnmarshall.html. Also search for felony records at the Manchester Courthouse location, 10th & Hull St.

Civil Records: Access: Mail, online, in person. Both court and visitors may perform in person searches. No search fee. Required to search: name, years to search. Civil cases indexed by defendant, plaintiff. Civil records on computer from 1987. On microfilm from 1980, on card index from 1970s, on index books from 1600s. Online access available free at http://208.210.219.132/courtinfo/vacircuit/select.jsp?court=. For information about the statewide online systems, see the state introduction.

Criminal Records: Access: Mail, online, in person. Both court and visitors may perform in person searches. No search fee. Required to search: name, years to search; also helpful: DOB, SSN. Criminal records on computer from 1987. On microfilm from 1980, on card index from 1970s, on index books from 1600s. Online access to criminal records is the same as civil.

General Information: Public access terminal is available. No juvenile, sealed records released. Copy fee: $.50 per page. Certification fee: $2.00. Fee payee: Bevill M Dean, Clerk. Personal checks accepted. Prepayment is required.

13th General District Court - Civil Division 400 N 9th St Rm 203, Richmond, VA 23219; 804-646-6461. Hours: 8AM-4PM (EST). *Civil Actions Under $15,000, Eviction, Small Claims.*

Civil Records: Access: Phone, mail, online, in person. Both court and visitors may perform in person searches. No search fee. Required to search: name, years to search. Civil cases indexed by defendant, plaintiff. Civil records computerized since 1994 in index books from 1973. Records destroyed after 20 years & 10 years after 1985. Select and search District Courts at http://208.210.219.132/courtinfo/vadistrict/select.jsp?court=. For information about the statewide online systems, see the state introduction.

General Information: Public access terminal is available. No juvenile, sealed records released. SASE required. Turnaround time 1-2 days. Copy fee: $.50 per page. Fee payee: Clerk of General District Court, Civil Division. Business checks accepted. Prepayment is required.

13th General District Court - Division II 905 Decatur St, Richmond, VA 23224; 804-646-8990; Fax: 804-646-0387. Hours: 8AM-4PM (EST). *Misdemeanor, Traffic.*

Criminal Records: Access: Mail, online, in person. Both court and visitors may perform in person searches. No search fee. Required to search: name, years to search, DOB; also helpful: SSN. Criminal records on computer from 1986, records prior to 1980 destroyed. For information about the statewide online systems, see the state introduction. Select and search General District Courts at http://208.210.219.132/courtinfo/vadistrict/select.jsp?court=.

General Information: Public access terminal is available. No juvenile, sealed records released. Turnaround time 1-5 days. Copy fee: $1.00 per page. Certification fee: $2.00. Fee payee: Clerk of General District Court. Personal checks accepted. Prepayment is required.

Richmond City - Manchester County

13th Circuit Court Manchester Courthouse, 10th and Hull St, Richmond, VA 23224-4070; 804-646-8470; Fax: 804-646-8122. Hours: 8:45AM-4:45PM (EST). *Felony.*

www.vipnet.org/vipnet/clerks/richmondmanchester.html

Note: Also search for felony records at the Division I location.

Civil Records: Access: Mail, online, in person. Only the court performs in person searches; visitors may not. No search fee. Required to search: name, years to search. Civil cases indexed by defendant, plaintiff. Civil records on computer from 1989, on index cards from 1961 to 1988, prior archived in Richmond. Online access available free at http://208.210.219.132/courtinfo/vacircuit/select.jsp?court=. For information on the statewide online systems, see the state introduction.

Criminal Records: Access: Mail, online, in person. Only the court performs in person searches; visitors may not. No search fee. Required to search: name, years to search. Criminal records on computer from 1989, on index cards from 1961 to 1988, prior archived in Richmond. Online access to criminal records is the same as civil.

General Information: Public access terminal is available. No juvenile, sealed, adoption records released. SASE required. Turnaround time 1-2 days. Copy fee: $.50 per page. Certification fee: $2.00. Fee payee: Clerk of Circuit Court. Business checks accepted. Prepayment is required.

Roanoke County

23rd Circuit Court PO Box 1126, Salem, VA 24153-1126; 540-387-6261. Hours: 8:30AM-4:30PM (EST). *Felony, Civil Actions Over $15,000, Probate.*

www.co.roanoke.va.us

Civil Records: Access: Online, in person. Visitors must perform in person searches for themselves. No search fee. Required to search: name, years to search. Civil cases indexed by defendant, plaintiff. Civil records on computer from 1986, on index books from 1838 to 1986, prior records to Botetourt County. Online access available free at http://208.210.219.132/courtinfo/vacircuit/select.jsp?court=. For information about the statewide online systems, see the state introduction.

Criminal Records: Access: Online, in person. Visitors must perform in person searches for themselves. No search fee. Required to search: name, years to search, DOB; also helpful: SSN. Criminal records on computer from 1986, on index books from 1838 to 1986, prior records to Botetourt County. Online access to criminal records is the same as civil.

General Information: Public access terminal is available. No juvenile, sealed records released. Copy fee: $.50 per page. Certification fee: $2.00. Fee payee: Clerk of Circuit Court. Personal checks accepted. Prepayment is required.

23rd General District Court PO Box 997, Salem, VA 24153; 540-387-6168; Fax: 540-387-6066. Hours: 8:15AM-4:30PM (EST). *Misdemeanor, Civil Actions Under $15,000, Eviction, Small Claims.*

www.co.roanoke.va.us

Civil Records: Access: Mail, online, in person. Both court and visitors may perform in person searches. No search fee. Required to search: name, years to search. Civil cases indexed by defendant, plaintiff. Computerized records the past 10 years, on index cards from 1980. Prior at Circuit Court or Archives. Select and search District Courts at http://208.210.219.132/courtinfo/vadistrict/select.jsp?court=. For information about the statewide online systems, see the state introduction.

Criminal Records: Access: Mail, online, in person. Both court and visitors may perform in person searches.

No search fee. Required to search: name, years to search, DOB; also helpful: SSN. Computerized records the past 10 years, on index cards from 1980. Prior at Circuit Court or Archives. Online access to criminal records is the same as civil.

General Information: Public access terminal is available. No sealed records released. SASE required. Turnaround time 5 days. Copy fee: $.50 per page. Fee payee: General. Personal checks accepted. Credit cards accepted: Visa, MasterCard. Not accepted for copy fees.

Roanoke City

23rd Circuit Court PO Box 2610, Roanoke, VA 24010-2610; Civil phone: 540-853-6702; Criminal phone: 540-853-6723. Hours: 8:30AM-4:30PM (EST). *Felony, Civil Actions Over $15,000, Probate.*

www.co.roanoke.va.us

Civil Records: Access: Mail, online, in person. Visitors must perform in person searches for themselves. No search fee. Required to search: name, years to search. Civil cases indexed by defendant, plaintiff. Civil records on computer from 1986, civil on microfiche from 1884, criminal on index books from 1800s, prior archived. Online access available free at http://208.210.219.132/courtinfo/vacircuit/select.jsp?court=. For information about the statewide online systems, see the state introduction.

Criminal Records: Access: Mail, online, in person. Visitors must perform in person searches for themselves. No search fee. Required to search: name, years to search, DOB; also helpful: SSN. Criminal records on computer from 1986, civil on microfiche from 1884, criminal on index books from 1800s, prior archived. Online access to criminal records is the same as civil.

General Information: Public access terminal is available. No juvenile, sealed records released. Copy fee: $.50 per page. Certification fee: $2.00. Fee payee: Clerk of Circuit Court. Personal checks accepted. Prepayment is required.

General District Court 315 W Church Ave, 2nd Flr, Roanoke, VA 24016-5007; Civil phone: 540-853-2364; Criminal phone: 540-853-2361. Hours: 8AM-4PM (EST). *Misdemeanor, Civil Actions Under $15,000, Eviction, Small Claims.*

Civil Records: Access: Mail, online, in person. Both court and visitors may perform in person searches. Search fee: $1.00 per name. Required to search: name, years to search. Civil cases indexed by defendant, plaintiff. Civil records on computer from 1986, prior on index cards. Select and search District Courts at http://208.210.219.132/courtinfo/vadistrict/select.jsp?court=. For information about the statewide online systems, see the state introduction.

Criminal Records: Access: Online, in person. Visitors must perform in person searches for themselves. No search fee. Required to search: name, years to search, DOB; also helpful: SSN. Criminal records on computer from 1986, prior on index cards. Online access to criminal records is the same as civil.

General Information: Public access terminal is available. (Records available from past 10 years.) No juvenile, sealed, adoptions records released. SASE required. Turnaround time 5 days. Copy fee: $1.00 per page. Fee payee: General District Court. Business checks accepted. Credit cards accepted: Visa, MasterCard. Prepayment is required.

Rockbridge County

25th Circuit Court Courthouse Square, 2 S Main St, Lexington, VA 24450; 540-463-2232; Fax: 540-463-3850. Hours: 8:30AM-4:30PM (EST). *Felony, Civil Actions Over $15,000, Probate.*

Civil Records: Access: Phone, mail, online, in person. Both court and visitors may perform in person searches.

No search fee. Required to search: name, years to search. Civil cases indexed by defendant, plaintiff. Civil records on computer from 1985, on index books from 1778. Criminal records are easily obtained from the late 1960s. Prior records are not easily accessible. Select and search Circuit Courts online at http://208.210.219.132/courtinfo/vacircuit/select.jsp?court=. For information on the statewide online systems, see the state introduction.

Criminal Records: Access: Online, in person. Visitors must perform in person searches for themselves. No search fee. Required to search: name, years to search, DOB; also helpful: SSN. Criminal records on computer from 1985, on index books from 1778. Criminal records are easily obtained from the late 1960s. Prior records are not easily accessible. Online access to criminal records is the same as civil.

General Information: Public access terminal is available. No juvenile, sealed records released. Turnaround time 2-3 days. Copy fee: $.50 per page. Certification fee: $2.50. Fee payee: Clerk of Circuit Court. Personal checks accepted. Prepayment required.

District Court 150 S Main St, Lexington, VA 24450; 540-463-3631. Hours: 8:30AM-4:30PM (EST). *Misdemeanor, Civil Actions Under $15,000, Eviction, Small Claims.*

Lexington-Rockbridge is a combined district court.

Civil Records: Access: Mail, online, in person. Both court and visitors may perform in person searches. No search fee. Required to search: name, years to search. Civil cases indexed by defendant, plaintiff. Civil records on computer from 1989, on index cards from 1985 to 1989, prior to 1985 at Circuit Court. Records destroyed after 10 years. Select and search District Courts at http://208.210.219.132/courtinfo/vadistrict/select.jsp?court=. For information about the statewide online systems, see the state introduction.

Criminal Records: Access: Mail, online, in person. Both court and visitors may perform in person searches. No search fee. Required to search: name, years to search, DOB; also helpful: SSN. Criminal records on computer from late 1989, on index cards from 1985 to 1989, prior to 1985 at Circuit Court. Online access to criminal records is the same as civil.

General Information: Public access terminal is available. No juvenile, sealed records released. SASE required. Turnaround time 5-7 days. Copy fee: $1.00 each for 1st two; $.50 each add'l.

Rockingham County

26th Circuit Court Courthouse, Court Square, Harrisonburg, VA 22801; Civil phone: 540-564-3114; Criminal phone: 540-564-3118; Fax: 540-564-3127. Hours: 9AM-5PM (EST). *Felony, Civil Actions Over $15,000, Probate.*

Civil Records: Access: Online, in person. Visitors must perform in person searches for themselves. No search fee. Required to search: name, years to search. Civil cases indexed by defendant, plaintiff. Civil records on index cards from the beginning of the county. Online access available free at http://208.210.219.132/courtinfo/vacircuit/select.jsp?court=. For information on the statewide online systems, see the state introduction.

Criminal Records: Access: Online, in person. Visitors must perform in person searches for themselves. No search fee. Required to search: name, years to search. Criminal records on index cards from the beginning of the county. Online access to criminal records is the same as civil.

General Information: Public access terminal is available. (Deeds only.) No juvenile, sealed records released. Copy fee: $.50 per page. Certification fee: $2.00. Fee payee: Clerk of Circuit Court. Personal checks accepted. Prepayment required.

26th General District Court 53 Court Square, Harrisonburg, VA 22801; Civil phone: 540-564-3135;

Criminal phone: 540-564-3130; Fax: 540-564-3096. Hours: 8AM-4PM (EST). *Misdemeanor, Civil Actions Under $15,000, Eviction, Small Claims.*

Civil Records: Access: Phone, mail, online, in person. Both court and visitors may perform in person searches. Search fee: $3.50 per each 15 minutes. Required to search: name, years to search. Civil cases indexed by defendant, plaintiff. Civil records on computer the past 10 years, on index cards from 1978, prior at Circuit Court. Select and search District Courts at http://208.210.219.132/courtinfo/vadistrict/select.jsp?court=. For information about the statewide online systems, see the state introduction.

Criminal Records: Access: Phone, mail, online, in person. Both court and visitors may perform in person searches. No search fee. Required to search: name, years to search, DOB; also helpful: SSN. Criminal records on computer from the past 10 years, on index cards from 1985, prior at Circuit Court. Online access to criminal records is the same as civil.

General Information: Public access terminal is available. No juvenile, sealed, adoption records released. SASE required. Turnaround time up to 1 week. Copy fee: $.50 per page. Certification fee: Cert fee included in copy fee. Fee payee: General District Court. Personal checks accepted. Credit cards accepted: Visa, MasterCard. Prepayment is required.

Russell County

29th Circuit Court PO Box 435, Lebanon, VA 24266; 276-889-8023; Fax: 276-889-8003. Hours: 8AM-5PM (EST). *Felony, Civil Actions Over $15,000, Probate.*

Civil Records: Access: Fax, mail, online, in person. Both court and visitors may perform in person searches. No search fee. Required to search: name, years to search. Civil cases indexed by defendant, plaintiff. Civil records on computer from 1990, archived from 1809. Select and search Circuit Courts online at http://208.210.219.132/courtinfo/vacircuit/select.jsp?court=. For information about the statewide online systems, see the state introduction. Fax access limited to short searches.

Criminal Records: Access: Fax, mail, online, in person. Both court and visitors may perform in person searches. No search fee. Required to search: name, years to search, signed release. Criminal records on computer from 1990, archived from 1809. Online access to criminal records is the same as civil.

General Information: No juvenile, sealed records released. Turnaround time 1-5 days. Copy fee: $.50 per page. Fee payee: Clerk of Circuit Court. Personal checks accepted. Prepayment is required.

29th General District Court Russell County Courthouse, PO Box 65, Lebanon, VA 24266; 276-889-8051; Fax: 276-889-8091. Hours: 8:30AM-4:30PM (EST). *Misdemeanor, Civil Actions Under $15,000, Eviction, Small Claims.*

Civil Records: Access: Phone, fax, mail, online, in person. Both court and visitors may perform in person searches. No search fee. Required to search: name. Civil cases indexed by defendant, plaintiff. Civil records on computer back to 1993. Select and search District Courts at http://208.210.219.132/courtinfo/vadistrict/select.jsp?court=. For information about the statewide online systems, see the state introduction.

Criminal Records: Access: Phone, fax, mail, online, in person. Both court and visitors may perform in person searches. No search fee. Required to search: name, DOB; also helpful: SSN. Criminal records on computer back to 1993; other records back to 1990. Online access to criminal records is the same as civil.

General Information: Public access terminal is available. No juvenile, sealed records released. Turnaround time 2-5 days. Fax notes: No fee to fax results. No copy fee. Personal checks accepted. Credit cards accepted: Visa, MasterCard.

Salem City

23rd Circuit Court 2 E Calhoun St, PO Box 891, Salem, VA 24153; 540-375-3067; Fax: 540-375-4039. Hours: 8:30AM-5PM (EST). *Felony, Civil Actions Over $15,000, Probate.*

Civil Records: Access: Mail, online, in person. Both court and visitors may perform in person searches. No search fee. Required to search: name, years to search. Civil cases indexed by defendant, plaintiff. Civil records on computer from 1985, on index books from 1968, prior at Roanoke Circuit Court. Select and search Circuit Courts online at http://208.210.219.132/courtinfo/vacircuit/select.jsp?court=. For information on the statewide online systems, see the state introduction.
Criminal Records: Access: Online, in person. Visitors must perform in person searches for themselves. No search fee. Required to search: name, years to search, DOB; also helpful: SSN. Criminal records on computer from 1985, on index books from 1968, prior at Roanoke Circuit Court. Online access to criminal records is the same as civil.
General Information: Public access terminal is available. No juvenile, sealed or adoption records released. SASE required. Turnaround time 2 weeks. Copy fee: $.50 per page. Certification fee: $2.00. Fee payee: Clerk of Circuit Court. Personal checks accepted. Prepayment is required.

23rd General District Court 2 E Calhoun St, Salem, VA 24153; 540-375-3044; Fax: 540-375-4024. Hours: 8AM-4PM (EST). *Misdemeanor, Civil Actions Under $15,000, Eviction, Small Claims.*

Civil Records: Access: Online, in person. Visitors must perform in person searches for themselves. No search fee. Required to search: name, years to search. Civil cases indexed by defendant, plaintiff. Civil records on computer from 1987, on index cards from 1986, prior records at City of Salem Circuit Court. Select and search District Courts at http://208.210.219.132/courtinfo/vadistrict/select.jsp?court=. For information about the statewide online systems, see the state introduction.
Criminal Records: Access: Online, in person. Visitors must perform in person searches for themselves. No search fee. Required to search: name, years to search, DOB, SSN. Criminal records on computer from 1987, on index cards from 1986, prior records at City of Salem Circuit Court. Online access to criminal records is the same as civil.
General Information: Public access terminal is available. No juvenile, sealed records released. Copy fee: $1.00 per page. Certification fee: $1.00 per page. Fee payee: General District Court. Personal checks accepted. Prepayment is required.

Scott County

30th Circuit Court 104 E Jackson St, #2, Gate City, VA 24251; 276-386-3801. Hours: 8:30AM-5PM (EST). *Felony, Civil Actions Over $15,000, Probate.*
Civil Records: Access: Phone, mail, online in person. Both court and visitors may perform in person searches. Search fee: $10.00 per name. Required to search: name, years to search. Civil cases indexed by defendant, plaintiff. Civil records on index books back to 1815; on computer back to 1999. Select and search Circuit Courts online at http://208.210.219.132/courtinfo/vacircuit/select.jsp?court=. For information about the statewide online systems, see the state introduction.
Criminal Records: Access: Mail, online, in person. Both court and visitors may perform in person searches. Search fee: $10.00 per name. Required to search: name, years to search, DOB; also helpful: SSN. Criminal

records on index books back to 1815; on computer back to 1999. Online access to criminal is the same as civil.
General Information: Public access terminal is available. No juvenile, sealed records released. SASE required. Turnaround time 3-4 days. Fax notes: Fee to fax results is $2.50 per page. Copy fee: $.50 per page. Certification fee: $1.50. Fee payee: Mark A. "Bo" Taylor, Clerk. Personal checks accepted. Will bill phone requests.

30th General District Court 104 E Jackson St, #9, Gate City, VA 24251; 276-386-7341. Hours: 8:15AM-4:45PM (EST). *Misdemeanor, Civil Actions Under $15,000, Eviction, Small Claims.*

Civil Records: Access: Mail, online, in person. Only the court performs in person searches; visitors may not. No search fee. Required to search: name, years to search. Civil cases indexed by plaintiff. Civil records on index books, on computer from 1990. Select and search District Courts at http://208.210.219.132/courtinfo/vadistrict/select.jsp?court=. For information about the statewide online systems, see the state introduction.
Criminal Records: Access: Mail, online, in person. Only the court performs in person searches; visitors may not. No search fee. Required to search: name, years to search, DOB; also helpful: SSN. Criminal records on index books, on computer from 1990. Online access to criminal records is the same as civil.
General Information: No juvenile, sealed records released. SASE required. Turnaround time up to 1-2 days. Copy fee: $1.00 per page. Fee payee: General District Court. Personal checks accepted. Prepayment is required.

Shenandoah County

26th Circuit Court 112 S Main St, PO Box 406, Woodstock, VA 22664; 540-459-6150; Fax: 540-459-6155. Hours: 9AM-5PM (EST). *Felony, Civil Actions Over $15,000, Probate.*

Civil Records: Access: Mail, online, in person. Only the court may perform in person searches. No search fee. Required to search: name, years to search. Civil cases indexed by defendant, plaintiff. Civil records on computer from 1996, on index cards from 1772. Select and search Circuit Courts online at http://208.210.219.132/courtinfo/vacircuit/select.jsp?court=. For information about the statewide online systems, see the state introduction. Mail access limited to specific cases only.
Criminal Records: Access: Online, in person. Visitors must perform in person searches for themselves. No search fee. Required to search: name, years to search, DOB; also helpful: SSN. Criminal records on computer from 1996, on index cards from 1772. Online access to criminal records is the same as civil.
General Information: No juvenile, sealed records released. SASE required. Turnaround time 1-2 days. Copy fee: $.50 per page. Certification fee: $2.00. Fee payee: Clerk of Circuit Court. Personal checks accepted. Prepayment is required.

26th General District Court 103 N Main St, PO Box 189, Woodstock, VA 22664; 540-459-6130; Fax: 540-459-6139. Hours: 8:30AM-4:30PM (EST). *Misdemeanor, Civil Actions Under $15,000, Eviction, Small Claims.*

Civil Records: Access: Mail, online, in person. Visitors must perform in person searches for themselves. No search fee. Required to search: name, years to search. Civil cases indexed by defendant, plaintiff. Civil records on computer from 1992, on index cards from 1985, prior at Circuit Court. Select and search District Courts at http://208.210.219.132/courtinfo/vadistrict/select.jsp?court=. For information about the statewide online systems, see the state introduction.
Criminal Records: Access: Online, mail, in person. Visitors must perform in person searches for

themselves. No search fee. Required to search: name, years to search, DOB; also helpful: SSN. Criminal records on computer from 1992, on index cards from 1985, prior at Circuit Court. Online access to criminal records is the same as civil. This agency will not do criminal record checks and refer all requesters to the State Police or the online system.
General Information: Public access terminal is available. No sealed or adoption records relapsed. Copy fee: No search fee. Fee payee: General District Court. Personal checks accepted. Visa/MC credit cards accepted. Accepted for criminal fines only. Prepayment is required.

Smyth County

28th Circuit Court PO Box 1025, Marion, VA 24354; 276-782-4044; Fax: 276-782-4045. 9AM-5PM (EST). *Felony, Civil Actions Over $15,000, Probate.*

Civil Records: Access: Mail, fax, online, in person. Both court and visitors may perform in person searches. Search fee: $10.00 per name. Required to search: name, years to search. Civil cases indexed by defendant, plaintiff. Civil records on index cards from 1832, most are computerized since 01/90. Select and search Circuit Courts online at http://208.210.219.132/courtinfo/vacircuit/select.jsp?court=. For information about the statewide online systems, see the state introduction.
Criminal Records: Access: Mail, fax, online, in person. Both court and visitors may perform in person searches. Search fee: $10.00 per name. Required to search: name, years to search; also helpful: DOB, SSN. Criminal records on index cards from 1832, most are computerized since 01/90. Online access to criminal records is the same as civil.
General Information: Public access terminal is available. (Not available for criminal or civil information.) No juvenile, sealed or adoption records released. SASE requested. Turnaround time 1 week. Fax notes: Fee to fax results is $1.oo per page. Copy fee: $.50 per page. Certification fee: $2.00. Fee payee: Clerk of Circuit Court. Personal checks accepted. Prepayment is required.

28th General District Court Smythe County Courthouse, Rm 231, 109 W Main St, Marion, VA 24354; 276-782-4047; Fax: 276-782-4048. Hours: 8:30AM-4:30PM (EST). *Misdemeanor, Civil Actions Under $15,000, Eviction, Small Claims.*

Civil Records: Access: Phone, mail, online, in person. Both court and visitors may perform in person searches. No search fee. Required to search: name, years to search; also helpful: address. Civil cases indexed by defendant, plaintiff. Civil records on computer back to 7/90. Select and search District Courts at http://208.210.219.132/courtinfo/vadistrict/select.jsp?court=. For information about the statewide online systems, see the state introduction.
Criminal Records: Access: Phone, mail, online, in person. Both court and visitors may perform in person searches. No search fee. Required to search: name, years to search, DOB; also helpful: SSN. Criminal records on computer back to 7/90. Online access to criminal records is the same as civil.
General Information: Public access terminal is available. No juvenile, sealed records released. Turnaround time 1-2 days. Copy fee: $.50 per page. Fee payee: General District Court. Personal checks accepted. Credit cards accepted: Visa, MasterCard. Prepayment is required.

South Boston City

Circuit & District Courts, VA.
Note: See Halifax County

Southampton County

5th Circuit Court PO Box 190, Courtland, VA 23837; 757-653-2200. Hours: 8:30AM-5PM (EST). *Felony, Civil Actions Over $15,000, Probate.*

Civil Records: Access: Mail, online, in person. Both court and visitors may perform in person searches. Search fee: $5.00 per name. Required to search: name, years to search. Civil cases indexed by defendant, plaintiff. Civil records on index books from 1749; on computer back to 1990. Select and search Circuit Courts online at http://208.210.219.132/courtinfo/vacircuit/select.jsp?court=. For information about the statewide online systems, see the state introduction. Will not certify searches.

Criminal Records: Access: Mail, online, in person. Both court and visitors may perform in person searches. Search fee: $5.00. Required to search: name, years to search. Criminal records on index books from 1749; on computer back to 1990. Online access to criminal records is the same as civil. Will not certify searches.

General Information: Public access terminal is available. No juvenile, sealed, adoption records released. Turnaround time 1-5 days. Fax notes: Will not fax results. Copy fee: $.50 per page. Fee payee: Clerk of Circuit Court. Personal checks accepted. Prepayment is required.

5th General District Court PO Box 347, Courtland, VA 23837; 757-653-2673. Hours: 8:30AM-4:30PM (EST). *Misdemeanor, Civil Actions Under $15,000, Eviction, Small Claims.*

Civil Records: Access: Mail, online, in person. Both court and visitors may perform in person searches. No search fee. Required to search: name, years to search. Civil cases indexed by defendant. Civil records on index cards, docket books and computer from 1985, prior records at Circuit Court. Select and search District Courts at http://208.210.219.132/courtinfo/vadistrict/select.jsp?court=. For information about the statewide online systems, see the state introduction.

Criminal Records: Access: Mail, online, in person. Both court and visitors may perform in person searches. No search fee. Required to search: name, years to search, DOB; also helpful: SSN. Criminal records on index cards, docket books and computer from 1985, prior records at Circuit Court. Online access to criminal records is the same as civil.

General Information: Public access terminal is available. No juvenile, sealed, adoption records released. Turnaround time 1-5 days. Fax notes: Fee to fax results is $2.00 per document. Copy fee: $1.00 1st 2 pages; $.50 each add'l page. Fee payee: Clerk of General District Court. Personal checks accepted. Credit cards accepted. Prepayment is required.

Spotsylvania County

15th Circuit Court 9113 Courthouse Rd, PO Box 96, Spotsylvania, VA 22553; 540-582-7090; Fax: 540-582-2169. Hours: 8AM-4:30PM (EST). *Felony, Civil Actions Over $15,000, Probate.*

Civil Records: Access: Online, in person. Visitors must perform in person searches for themselves. No search fee. Required to search: name, years to search. Civil cases indexed by defendant, plaintiff. Civil records on computer from 1996, on index books from late 1700s. Remote online access to court case indexes is via LOPAS; call 804-786-6455 to apply. Mail access limited to specific case only.

Criminal Records: Access: Online, in person. Visitors must perform in person searches for themselves. No search fee. Required to search: name, years to search, DOB, SSN. Criminal records on computer from 1996, on index books from late 1700s. Remote online access to court case indexes is via LOPAS; call 804-786-6455 to apply.

General Information: Public access terminal is available. No juvenile, sealed, adoption records released. Copy fee: $.50 per page. Certification fee: $2.00. Fee payee: Clerk of Circuit Court. Personal checks accepted. Prepayment is required.

15th General District Court Judicial Center, PO Box 339, Spotsylvania, VA 22553; 540-582-7110. Hours: 8AM-4PM (EST). *Misdemeanor, Civil Actions Under $15,000, Eviction, Small Claims.*

Civil Records: Access: Mail, online, in person. Visitors must peform in person searches for themselves. No search fee. Required to search: name, years to search. Civil cases indexed by defendant, plaintiff. Civil records go back 10 years; on computer back to 1988. Select and search District Courts at http://208.210.219.132/courtinfo/vadistrict/select.jsp?court=. For information on the statewide online systems, see state introduction.

Criminal Records: Access: Mail, online, in person. Visitors must peform in person searches for themselves. No search fee. Required to search: name, years to search. Criminal records go back 10 years; on computer back to 1988. Select and search District Courts at http://208.210.219.132/courtinfo/vadistrict/select.jsp?court=. For information about the statewide online systems, see the state introduction.

General Information: Public access terminal is available. No juvenile, sealed records released. Turnaround time 5 days. Copy fee: $.50 per page. Certification fee: $2.00. Fee payee: Clerk of General District Court. Personal checks accepted. Prepayment is required.

Stafford County

15th Circuit Court PO Box 69, Stafford, VA 22554; 540-658-8750. Hours: 8AM-4PM (EST). *Felony, Civil Actions Over $15,000, Probate.*

Civil Records: Access: Mail, online, in person. Both court and visitors may perform in person searches. No search fee. Required to search: name, years to search. Civil cases indexed by defendant, plaintiff. Civil records in index books from 1699, back on computer to 1992. Select and search Circuit Courts online at http://208.210.219.132/courtinfo/vacircuit/select.jsp?court=. For information about the statewide online systems, see the state introduction.

Criminal Records: Access: Mail, online, in person. Both court and visitors may perform in person searches. No search fee. Required to search: name, years to search, DOB; also helpful: SSN. Criminal records in index books from 1699, back on computer to 1992. Online access to criminal records is the same as civil.

General Information: Public access terminal is available. No juvenile, sealed records released. Turnaround time up to 10 days. Copy fee: $.50 per page. Certification fee: $2.00. Fee payee: Clerk of Circuit Court. Personal checks accepted.

15th General District Court 1300 Courthouse Rd, PO Box 940, Stafford, VA 22555; 540-658-8763; Fax: 540-658-4834. Hours: 8:AM-4PM (EST). *Misdemeanor, Civil Actions Under $15,000, Eviction, Small Claims.*

Civil Records: Access: Fax, mail, online, in person. Both court and visitors may perform in person searches. No search fee. Required to search: name, years to search. Civil cases indexed by defendant, plaintiff. Civil records on computer since 1986, prior at Circuit Court. Select and search District Courts at http://208.210.219.132/courtinfo/vadistrict/select.jsp?court=. For information about the statewide online systems, see the state introduction.

Criminal Records: Access: Fax, mail, online, in person. Both court and visitors may perform in person searches. No search fee. Required to search: name, years to search. Criminal records on computer since 1986, prior at Circuit Court. Online access to criminal records is the same as civil.

General Information: Public access terminal is available. No sealed records released. SASE requested. Turnaround time 2-7 days. Fax notes: No fee to fax results. Copy fee: $.50 per page. Fee payee: Clerk of General District Court. Personal checks accepted. Credit cards accepted: Visa, M/C. Prepayment required.

Staunton City

25th Circuit Court PO Box 1286, Staunton, VA 24402-1286; 540-332-3874; Fax: 540-332-3970. Hours: 8:30AM-5PM (EST). *Felony, Civil Actions Over $15,000, Probate.*

Civil Records: Access: Mail, online, in person. Both court and visitors may perform in person searches. No search fee. Required to search: name, years to search. Civil cases indexed by defendant, plaintiff. Civil records on index books since 1802; on computer back to 1988. Select and search Circuit Courts online at http://208.210.219.132/courtinfo/vacircuit/select.jsp?court=. For information about the statewide online systems, see the state introduction.

Criminal Records: Access: Online, in person. Both court and visitors may perform in person searches. No search fee. Required to search: name, years to search. Criminal records on index books since 1802; on computer back to 1988. Online access to criminal records is the same as civil.

General Information: Public access terminal is available. No juvenile, sealed or adoption records released. Fax notes: Fee to fax results is $.50 per page. Copy fee: $.50 per page. Certification fee: $2.00. Fee payee: Clerk of Circuit Court. Personal checks accepted. Prepayment is required.

Staunton General District Court 113 E Beverly St, Staunton, VA 24401-4390; 540-332-3878; Fax: 540-332-3985. Hours: 8:30AM-4:30PM (EST). *Misdemeanor, Civil Actions Under $15,000, Eviction, Small Claims.*

Civil Records: Access: Mail, online, in person. Both court and visitors may perform in person searches. No search fee. Required to search: name, years to search; also helpful: address. Civil cases indexed by defendant, plaintiff. Civil records on computer from 11/94, on index cards from 1952. Select and search District Courts at http://208.210.219.132/courtinfo/vadistrict/select.jsp?court=. For information about the statewide online systems, see the state introduction.

Criminal Records: Access: Mail, online, in person. Both court and visitors may perform in person searches. No search fee. Required to search: name, years to search, DOB. Criminal records indexed on computer since 1991. Online access to criminal records is the same as civil.

General Information: Public access terminal is available. Turnaround time 1-5 days. Copy fee: $.50 per page. Fee payee: Staunton General District Court. Personal checks accepted. Credit cards accepted: Visa, MasterCard. Credit cards accepted for criminal & traffic cases only. Prepayment is required.

Suffolk City

Suffolk Circuit Court PO Box 1604, Suffolk, VA 23439-1604; 757-923-2251; Fax: 757-934-3490. Hours: 8:30AM-5PM (EST). *Felony, Civil Actions Over $15,000, Probate.*

Civil Records: Access: Online, in person. Visitors must perform in person searches for themselves. No search fee. Required to search: name, years to search. Civil cases indexed by defendant, plaintiff. Civil records on computer from 1989, on index books from 1866. Select and search Circuit Courts online at http://208.210.219.132/courtinfo/vacircuit/select.jsp?court=.

For information about the statewide online systems, see the state introduction.

Criminal Records: Access: Online, in person. Visitors must perform in person searches for themselves. No search fee. Required to search: name, years to search. Criminal records on computer from 1989, on index books from 1866. Online access to criminal records is the same as civil.

General Information: No juvenile, sealed, adoption records released. Copy fee: $.50 per page. Certification fee: $1.50. Fee payee: Clerk of Circuit Court. Personal checks accepted. Credit cards accepted: Visa, MasterCard. Prepayment is required.

5th General District Court

150 N Main St, PO Box 1648, Suffolk, VA 23434; 757-923-2281; Fax: 757-925-1790. 8AM-4PM (EST). *Misdemeanor, Civil Actions up to $15,000, Eviction, Small Claims.*

Civil Records: Access: Mail, online, in person. Both court and visitors may perform in person searches. No search fee. Required to search: name, years to search. Civil cases indexed by defendant, plaintiff. Civil records on computer from 1992 prior on index cards. Records destroyed after 10 years. Select and search District Courts at http://208.210.219.132/courtinfo/vadistrict/select.jsp?court=. For information about the statewide online systems, see the state introduction.

Criminal Records: Access: Online, mail, in person. Visitors must perform in person searches for themselves. No search fee. Required to search: name, years to search, DOB; also helpful: SSN. Criminal records on computer from 1992, prior on index cards. Online access to criminal records is the same as civil.

General Information: Public access terminal is available. No juvenile, sealed, adoptions records released. SASE required. Turnaround time 1 week. Copy fee: $1.00 1st page, $.50 each add'l page. Fee payee: Suffolk General District Court. Personal checks accepted. Credit cards accepted: Visa, MasterCard. Prepayment is required.

Surry County

6th Circuit Court

28 Colonial Trail East, PO Box 203, Surry, VA 23883; 757-294-3161; Fax: 757-294-0471. Hours: 9AM-5PM (EST). *Felony, Civil Actions Over $15,000, Probate.*

Civil Records: Access: In person, online. Visitors must perform in person searches for themselves. No search fee. Required to search: name, years to search. Civil cases indexed by defendant, plaintiff. Civil records on cards. Remote online access to court case indexes is via LOPAS; call 804-786-6455 to apply.

Criminal Records: Access: In person, online. Visitors must perform in person searches for themselves. No search fee. Required to search: name, years to search, DOB; also helpful: SSN. Criminal records on cards. Online access to criminal records is the same as civil.

General Information: Juvenile, sealed records not released. Copy fee: $.50 per page. Certification fee: $2.00. Fee payee: Circuit Clerk. Business checks accepted.

6th General District Court

Hwy 10 and School St, PO Box 332, Surry, VA 23883; 757-294-5201; Fax: 757-294-0312. 8:30AM-4:30PM (EST). *Misdemeanor, Civil Actions Under $15,000, Eviction, Small Claims.*

Civil Records: Access: Online, in person. Visitors must perform in person searches for themselves. No search fee. Required to search: name, years to search. Civil cases indexed by defendant, plaintiff. Civil records on computer since 11/93, on books from 1985, prior at Circuit Court. Select and search District Courts at http://208.210.219.132/courtinfo/vadistrict/select.jsp?court=. For information about the statewide online systems, see the state introduction.

Criminal Records: Access: Online, in person. Visitors must perform in person searches for themselves. No

search fee. Required to search: name, years to search, DOB; also helpful: SSN. Criminal records on computer since 11/93, on books from 1985, prior at Circuit Court. Online access to criminal records is the same as civil.

General Information: Public access terminal is available. No juvenile, sealed, adoption records released. No copy fee.

Sussex County

6th Circuit Court

PO Box 1337, Sussex, VA 23884; 434-246-5511 X3276; Fax: 434-246-2203. Hours: 9AM-5PM (EST). *Felony, Civil Actions Over $15,000, Probate.*

Civil Records: Access: Mail, online, in person. Only the court performs in person searches; visitors may not. No search fee. Required to search: name, years to search. Civil cases indexed by defendant, plaintiff. Civil records on index books from 1754; on computer back to 1991. Remote online access to court case indexes is via LOPAS; call 804-786-6455 to apply.

Criminal Records: Access: Mail, online, in person. Visitors must perform in person searches for themselves. No search fee. Required to search: name, years to search, DOB, SSN, signed release. Criminal records on index books from 1754; on computer back to 1991. Online access to criminal records is the same as civil.

General Information: No juvenile, sealed, adoption, confidential, or probate records released. Turnaround time 1-2 days. Fax notes: Fee to fax results is $1.00 per page. Copy fee: $.50 per page. Certification fee: $2.00. Fee payee: Clerk of Circuit Court. Personal checks accepted. Prepayment is required.

6th Judicial District Court

Sussex Cnty Courthouse 15098 Courthouse Rd Rt 735, PO Box 1315, Sussex, VA 23884; 434-246-5511; Fax: 434-246-6604. Hours: 8:30AM-4:30PM (EST). *Misdemeanor, Civil Actions Under $15,000, Eviction, Small Claims.*

Civil Records: Access: Online, in person. Both court and visitors may perform in person searches. No search fee. Required to search: name, years to search. Civil cases indexed by defendant, plaintiff. Civil records on computer from 9/88, on index cards from 1985, prior in Circuit Court. Select and search District Courts at http://208.210.219.132/courtinfo/vadistrict/select.jsp?court=. For information about the statewide online systems, see the state introduction.

Criminal Records: Access: Online, in person. Visitors must perform in person searches for themselves. No search fee. Required to search: name, years to search, DOB; also helpful: SSN. Criminal records on computer from 9/88, on index cards from 1985, prior in Circuit Court. Online access to criminal records is same as civil.

General Information: Public access terminal is available. No juvenile, sealed, adoption records released. Copy fee: $1.00 minimum for first 2 pages, thereafter $.50 per page. Fee payee: Sussex District Court. Personal checks accepted. Credit cards accepted: Visa, MasterCard. Prepayment is required.

Tazewell County

29th Circuit Court

PO Box 968, Tazewell, VA 24651-0968; 276-988-7541 X311-312; Fax: 276-988-7501. Hours: 8AM-4:30PM (EST). *Felony, Civil Actions Over $15,000, Probate.*

Civil Records: Access: Mail, online, in person. Both court and visitors may perform in person searches. No search fee. Required to search: name, years to search. Civil cases indexed by defendant, plaintiff. Civil records on index cards from 1800s. Online access available free at http://208.210.219.132/courtinfo/vacircuit/select.jsp?court=. For information about the statewide online systems, see the state introduction.

Criminal Records: Access: Mail, online, in person. Both court and visitors may perform in person searches. No

No search fee. Required to search: name, years to search, signed release. Criminal records on computer from 1992. Online access to criminal records is the same as civil.

General Information: No juvenile, sealed records released. Turnaround time 1-3 days. Copy fee: $.50 per page. Certification fee: $2.00. Fee payee: Clerk of Circuit Court. Personal checks accepted. Prepayment is required.

29th General District Court

PO Box 566, Tazewell, VA 24651; 276-988-9057; Fax: 276-988-6202. Hours: 8AM-4:30PM (EST). *Misdemeanor, Civil Actions Under $15,000, Eviction, Small Claims.*

Civil Records: Access: Mail, fax, online, in person. Both court and visitors may perform in person searches. No search fee. Required to search: name, years to search. Civil cases indexed by defendant, plaintiff. Civil records on computer back to 1991, prior records to 1985 at Circuit Court. Select and search District Courts at http://208.210.219.132/courtinfo/vadistrict/select.jsp?court=. For information about the statewide online systems, see the state introduction.

Criminal Records: Access: Mail, fax, online, in person. Both court and visitors may perform in person searches. No search fee. Required to search: name, years to search, DOB; also helpful: SSN, signed release. Criminal records on computer back to 1991, prior records to 1985 at Circuit Court. Online access to criminal records is the same as civil.

General Information: Public access terminal is available. No juvenile, sealed, adoption records released. SASE requested. Turnaround time 1-3 days. Fax notes: Fee to fax results is $1.00 per document and $1.00 per page. Copy fee: $.50 per page. Fee payee: Clerk of General District Court. Personal checks accepted. Credit cards accepted: Visa, MasterCard.

Virginia Beach City

2nd Circuit Court

2425 Nimmo Parkway, Virginia Beach, VA 23456-9017; 757-427-4181; Fax: 757-426-5686. Hours: 8:30AM-5PM (EST). *Felony, Civil Actions Over $15,000, Probate.*

www.virginia-beach.va.us/courts

Civil Records: Access: Online, in person. Visitors must perform in person searches for themselves. No search fee. Required to search: name, years to search. Civil cases indexed by defendant, plaintiff. Civil records on computer from 1986, on files from 1960s. Online access available free at http://208.210.219.132/courtinfo/vacircuit/select.jsp?court=. For information on the statewide online systems, see the state introduction.

Criminal Records: Access: Online, in person. Visitors must perform in person searches for themselves. No search fee. Required to search: name, years to search, DOB; also helpful: SSN. Criminal records on computer from 1986, on files from 1960s. Online access to criminal records is the same as civil.

General Information: Public access terminal is available. No juvenile, sealed, presentencing probation report, judges notes or adoption records released. Copy fee: $.50 per page. Certification fee: $2.00. Fee payee: Clerk of Circuit Court. Personal checks accepted. Prepayment is required.

2nd General District Court

2425 Nimmo Parkway, Judicial Center, Virginia Beach, VA 23456-9057; 757-427-8531 Court Info Line; Civil phone: 757-427-4277; Criminal phone: 757-427-4707; Fax: 757-426-5672. Hours: 8:30AM-4PM (EST). *Misdemeanor, Civil Actions Under $15,000, Eviction, Small Claims.*

www.vbgov.com

Note: Records may be available online in 2002; check web site.

Civil Records: Access: Phone, fax, mail, online, in person. Both court and visitors may perform in person searches. Search fee: $10.00 per name. Required to search: name, years to search. Civil cases indexed by defendant, plaintiff. Civil cases on computer from 1987, on docket books and cards from 1978. Select and search District Courts at http://208.210.219.132/courtinfo/vadistrict/select.jsp?court=. For information on the statewide online systems, see state introduction.

Criminal Records: Access: Phone, fax, mail, online, in person. Both court and visitors may perform in person searches. Search fee: $10.00 per name. Required to search: name, years to search, DOB; also helpful: SSN. Criminal records on computer back ten years, then destroyed. Online access to criminal records is the same as civil.

General Information: Public access terminal is available. No juvenile, sealed, adoption or mental records released. Turnaround time 3-4 weeks. Fax notes: No fee to fax results. Copy fee: $.50 per page. Fee payee: Clerk of General District Court. Personal checks accepted. Prepayment is required.

Warren County

Circuit Court 1 East Main St, Front Royal, VA 22630; 540-635-2435; Fax: 540-636-3274. 9AM-5PM (EST). *Felony, Civil Actions Over $15,000, Probate.*

www.courts.state.va.us/courts/circuit/warren/home.html

Civil Records: Access: Phone, fax, mail, online, in person. Both court and visitors may perform in person searches. No search fee. Required to search: name, years to search. Civil cases indexed by defendant, plaintiff. Civil records on archives from 1836; on computer since 1986. Online access available free at http://208.210.219.132/courtinfo/vacircuit/select.jsp?court=. For information about the statewide online systems, see the state introduction. Phone access limited to specific case only.

Criminal Records: Access: Phone, fax, mail, online, in person. Both court and visitors may perform in person searches. No search fee. Required to search: name, years to search, DOB; also helpful: SSN. Criminal records on archives from 1836; on computer since 1986. Online access to criminal is the same as civil.

General Information: Public access terminal is available. No juvenile, sealed, adoption records released. SASE required. Turnaround time 1-2 days. Copy fee: $.50 per page. Certification fee: $2.00. Fee payee: William Hall, Clerk. Personal checks accepted.

26th General District Court 1 East Main St, Front Royal, VA 22630; 540-635-2335; Fax: 540-636-8233. Hours: 8:15AM-4:15PM (EST). *Misdemeanor, Civil Actions Under $15,000, Eviction, Small Claims.*

Civil Records: Access: Mail, fax, online, in person. Both court and visitors may perform in person searches. No search fee. Required to search: name, years to search. Civil cases indexed by defendant. Civil records in archives back to 1800's, on computer from 1989. Select and search District Courts at http://208.210.219.132/courtinfo/vadistrict/select.jsp?court=. For information about the statewide online systems, see the state introduction.

Criminal Records: Access: Mail, fax, online, in person. Both court and visitors may perform in person searches. No search fee. Required to search: name, years to search; also helpful: SSN. Criminal records in archives back to 1836, on computer from 1989. Online access to criminal records is the same as civil.

General Information: Public access terminal is available. No juvenile, sealed records released. SASE required. Turnaround time 2-3 days. Copy fee: $.50 per page. Fee payee: General District Court. Personal checks accepted. Credit cards accepted: Visa, MasterCard.

Washington County

Circuit Court PO Box 289, Abingdon, VA 24212-0289; 276-676-6224/6226; Fax: 276-676-6218. Hours: 7:30AM-5PM; Recording Hours: 8:30AM-4PM (EST). *Felony, Civil Actions Over $15,000, Probate.*

Civil Records: Access: Mail, online, in person. Both court and visitors may perform in person searches. Search fee is determined by time involved. No search fee. Required to search: name, years to search. Civil cases indexed by defendant, plaintiff. Civil records on archives from 1777, on computer from 1991. Remote online access to court case indexes is via LOPAS; call 804-786-6455 to apply.

Criminal Records: Access: Online, in person. Visitors must perform in person searches for themselves. There is no search fee. No search fee. Required to search: name, years to search. Criminal records on archives from 1777, on computer from 1991. Remote online access to court case indexes is via LOPAS; call 804-786-6455 to apply.

General Information: Public access terminal is available. No juvenile, sealed or adoption records released. SASE required. Turnaround time 1 week. Copy fee: $.50 per page. Certification fee: $2.00. Fee payee: Clerk, Circuit Court. Personal checks accepted. Will bill copy fees.

28th General District Court 191 E Main St, Abingdon, VA 24210; 276-676-6279; Fax: 276-676-6293. Hours: 8:30AM-5PM (EST). *Misdemeanor, Civil Actions Under $15,000, Eviction, Small Claims.*

Civil Records: Access: Mail, online, in person. Both court and visitors may perform in person searches. No search fee. Required to search: name, years to search. Civil cases indexed by defendant, plaintiff. Civil records on archives from 1777, on computer from 1992. Select and search District Courts at http://208.210.219.132/courtinfo/vadistrict/select.jsp?court=. For information about the statewide online systems, see the state introduction.

Criminal Records: Access: Mail, online, in person. Both court and visitors may perform in person searches. No search fee. Required to search: name, years to search. Criminal records on archives from 1777, on computer from 1992. Online access to criminal records is the same as civil.

General Information: Public access terminal is available. No sealed records released. SASE required. Turnaround time 1-2 days. Copy fee: $1.00 for first page, $.50 each add'l. Certification fee: $2.00. Fee payee: General District Court. Personal checks accepted. Credit cards accepted: Visa, MasterCard. Prepayment is required.

Waynesboro City

25th Circuit Court 250 S Wayne Ave, PO Box 910, Waynesboro, VA 22980; 540-942-6616; Fax: 540-942-6774. Hours: 8:30AM-5PM (EST). *Felony, Civil Actions Over $15,000, Probate.*

Civil Records: Access: Online, in person. Visitors must perform in person searches for themselves. No search fee. Required to search: name, years to search. Civil cases indexed by defendant, plaintiff. Civil records on computer from 11/88 (some), all on index books from 5/48. Online access available free at http://208.210.219.132/courtinfo/vacircuit/select.jsp?court=. For information about the statewide online systems, see the state introduction.

Criminal Records: Access: Online, in person. Visitors must perform in person searches for themselves. No search fee. Required to search: name, years to search, DOB; also helpful: SSN. Criminal records on computer from 11/88 (some), all on index books from 5/48. Online access to criminal records is the same as civil.

General Information: No juvenile, sealed, adoptions released. Copy fee: $.50 per page. Certification fee:

$2.00. Fee payee: Clerk of Circuit Court. Personal checks accepted. Prepayment is required.

25th General District Court - Waynesboro 250 S Wayne, PO Box 1028, Waynesboro, VA 22980; 540-942-6636; Fax: 540-942-6666. Hours: 8:30AM-4:30PM (EST). *Misdemeanor, Civil Actions Under $15,000, Eviction, Small Claims.*

Civil Records: Access: Mail, fax, online, in person. Visitors must perform in person searches. No search fee. Required to search: name, years to search. Civil cases indexed by defendant, plaintiff. Civil records on computer 10 years. Select and search District Courts at http://208.210.219.132/courtinfo/vadistrict/select.jsp?court=. For information about the statewide online systems, see the state introduction.

Criminal Records: Access: Mail, fax, online, in person. Visitors must perform in person searches. No search fee. Required to search: name, years to search. Criminal records on computer for 10 years. Online access to criminal records is the same as civil.

General Information: Public access terminal is available. Turnaround time up to 1 week. No copy fee. Fee payee: General District. Personal checks accepted. Credit cards accepted: Visa, MasterCard.

Westmoreland County

15th Circuit Court PO Box 307, Montross, VA 22520; 804-493-0108; Fax: 804-493-0393. Hours: 9AM-5PM (EST). *Felony, Civil Actions Over $15,000, Probate.*

Civil Records: Access: In person. Visitors must perform in person searches for themselves. No search fee. Required to search: name, years to search. Civil cases indexed by defendant, plaintiff. Civil records on index books from 1653.

Criminal Records: Access: In person. Visitors must perform in person searches for themselves. No search fee. Required to search: name, years to search, DOB; also helpful: SSN. Criminal records on index books from 1653; o.

General Information: No juvenile, sealed, adoption records released. Copy fee: $.50 per page. Certification fee: $3.00. Fee payee: Clerk of Circuit Court. No personal checks accepted. Will bill copy fees.

15th General District Court PO Box 688, Montross, VA 22520; 804-493-0105. Hours: 8AM-4:30PM (EST). *Misdemeanor, Civil Actions Under $15,000, Small Claims.*

Civil Records: Access: Mail, online, in person. Both court and visitors may perform in person searches. No search fee. Required to search: name, years to search. Civil cases indexed by defendant, plaintiff. Civil records on index books/cards for 10 years; on computer back to 5/93. Select and search District Courts at http://208.210.219.132/courtinfo/vadistrict/select.jsp?court=. For information about the statewide online systems, see the state introduction.

Criminal Records: Access: Mail, online, in person. Both court and visitors may perform in person searches. No search fee. Required to search: name, years to search; also helpful: DOB, SSN, date of offense. Criminal records on index books/cards for 10 years; on computer back to 5/93. Online access to criminal records is the same as civil.

General Information: Public access terminal is available. All records public. SASE required. Turnaround time 1 week. Copy fee: $1.00 for first page, $.50 each add'l. Fee payee: General District Court. Personal checks accepted. Attorney checks accepted. Credit cards accepted: Visa, MasterCard. Prepayment is required.

Williamsburg City

Circuit & District Courts, VA.
Note: See James City/County.

Winchester City

26th Circuit Court 5 N Kent St, Winchester, VA 22601; 540-667-5770; Fax: 540-667-6638. 9AM-5PM (EST). *Felony, Civil Actions Over $15,000, Probate.*
www.winfredclerk.com

Note: The Winchester Court and the Frederick County Court Clerks are housed in the same judicial center. The offices share microfilming and deed indexing systems.

Civil Records: Access: Online, in person. Visitors must perform in person searches for themselves. No search fee. Required to search: name, years to search. Civil cases indexed by defendant, plaintiff. Civil records on computer from 1985 to present, on index books from 1790. Online access available free at http://208.210.219.132/courtinfo/vacircuit/select.jsp?court=. For information about the statewide online systems, see the state introduction.
Criminal Records: Access: Mail, online, in person. Both court and visitors may perform in person searches. No search fee. Required to search: name, years to search; also helpful: DOB, SSN. Criminal records on computer from 1985 to present, on index books from 1790. Online access to criminal records is same as civil.
General Information: No juvenile, sealed, adoption records released. SASE required. Turnaround time same day. Copy fee: $.50 per page. Certification fee: $2.00. Fee payee: Clerk of Circuit Court. Personal checks accepted. Prepayment is required.

26th General District Court 5 N Kent St, PO Box 526, Winchester, VA 22604; 540-722-7208; Fax: 540-722-1063. 8AM-4PM (EST). *Misdemeanor, Civil Actions Under $15,000, Eviction, Small Claims.*

Civil Records: Access: Online, in person. Visitors must perform in person searches for themselves. No search fee. Required to search: name, years to search. Civil cases indexed by defendant, plaintiff. Civil records on computer from 1992, on index cards from 1985 to 1987, prior at Circuit Court. Select and search District Courts at http://208.210.219.132/courtinfo/vadistrict/select.jsp?court=. For information about the statewide online systems, see the state introduction.
Criminal Records: Access: Online, in person. Visitors must perform in person searches. No search fee. Required to search: name, years to search, DOB, SSN, signed release. Criminal records on computer from 1992, on index cards from 1985 to 1987, prior at Circuit Court. Online access to criminal records is the same as civil. Forms for criminal searches available from State Police.
General Information: Public access terminal is available. No sealed records released. Copy fee: $.50 per page. Certification fee: $2.00. Fee payee: Clerk of General District Court. Personal checks accepted. Prepayment is required.

Wise County

30th Circuit Court PO Box 1248, Wise, VA 24293-1248; 276-328-6111; Fax: 276-328-0039. Hours: 8:30AM-5PM (EST). *Felony, Civil Actions Over $15,000, Probate.*

Civil Records: Access: Phone, fax, mail, online, in person. Both court and visitors may perform in person searches. Search fee: $10.00 per name. Required to search: name, years to search; also helpful: address. Civil cases indexed by defendant, plaintiff. Civil records on archives from 1856. Online access available free at http://208.210.219.132/courtinfo/vacircuit/select.jsp?court=. For information about the statewide online systems, see the state introduction. Also, court indexes are available at www.courtbar.org. Registration and a fee is required. Records go back to June, 2000.

Criminal Records: Access: Phone, fax, mail, online, in person. Both court and visitors may perform in person searches. Search fee: $10.00 per name. Required to search: name, years to search, DOB; also helpful: SSN. Criminal records on archives from 1856. Online access to criminal records is the same as civil.
General Information: Public access terminal is available. No juvenile, sealed or adoption records released. Turnaround time 2-3 days. Copy fee: $.50 per page. Certification fee: $2.00 plus copy fee. Fee payee: Clerk of Circuit Court. Personal checks accepted. Prepayment is required.

30th General District Court Wise County Courthouse, PO Box 829, Wise, VA 24293; 276-328-3426; Fax: 276-328-4576. Hours: 8AM-4PM (EST). *Misdemeanor, Civil Actions Under $15,000, Eviction, Small Claims.*

Civil Records: Access: Phone, mail, online, in person. Both court and visitors may perform in person searches. No search fee. Required to search: name, years to search. Civil cases indexed by defendant, plaintiff. Civil records on computer back 10 years. Select and search District Courts at http://208.210.219.132/courtinfo/vadistrict/select.jsp?court=. For information about the statewide online systems, see the state introduction.
Criminal Records: Access: Phone, mail, online, in person. Both court and visitors may perform in person searches. No search fee. Required to search: name, years to search; also helpful: DOB, SSN. Criminal records on computer back 10 years. Online access to criminal records is the same as civil.
General Information: Public access terminal is available. No juvenile, sealed records released. Turnaround time 5 days. Copy fee: $.50 per page. Fee payee: General District Court. Personal checks accepted. Credit cards accepted. Prepayment required.

Wythe County

27th Circuit Court 225 S Fourth St, Rm 105, Wytheville, VA 24382; 276-223-6050; Fax: 276-223-6057. Hours: 8:30AM-5PM (EST). *Felony, Civil Actions Over $15,000, Probate.*

Civil Records: Access: Online, in person. Both court and visitors may perform in person searches. No search fee. Required to search: name, years to search. Civil cases indexed by defendant, plaintiff. Civil records on computer from 1989, on index cards/books from 1950s (some back to 1790s). Remote online access to court case indexes is via LOPAS; call 804-786-6455 to apply.
Criminal Records: Access: Online, in person. Both court and visitors may perform in person searches. No search fee. Required to search: name, years to search; also helpful: DOB, SSN. Criminal records on computer from 1989, on index cards/books from 1950s (some back to 1790s). Remote online access to court case indexes is via LOPAS; call 804-786-6455 to apply.
General Information: No juvenile, sealed, adoption records released. Copy fee: $.50 per page. Fee payee: Clerk of Circuit Court. Personal checks accepted. Credit cards accepted: Visa, MasterCard. Prepayment is required.

Wythe General District Court 245 S. Fourth St., # 205, Wytheville, VA 24382-2595; 276-223-6075; Fax: 276-223-6087. Hours: 8AM-4:30PM (EST). *Misdemeanor, Civil Actions Under $15,000, Eviction, Small Claims.*

Civil Records: Access: Phone, mail, fax, in person, online. Visitors must perform in person searches for themselves. No search fee. Required to search: name, years to search. Civil cases indexed by defendant, plaintiff. Civil records on computer from 1/92, prior at Circuit Court. Select and search District Courts at http://208.210.219.132/courtinfo/vadistrict/select.jsp?court=. For information about the statewide online systems, see the state introduction.
Criminal Records: Access: Online, in person. Visitors must perform in person searches. No search fee. Required to search: name, years to search; also helpful: DOB, SSN. Criminal records on computer from 1/92. They expunge after 10 years. Online access to criminal records is the same as civil.
General Information: Public access terminal is available. Copy fee: $.50 per page. Fee is only applied to requests for excessive amounts of information. Fee payee: General District Court. Personal checks accepted. Credit cards accepted: Visa, MasterCard.

York County

9th Circuit Court PO Box 371, Yorktown, VA 23690; 757-890-3350; Fax: 757-890-3364. Hours: 8:15AM-5PM (EST). *Felony, Civil Actions Over $15,000, Probate.*

Note: Also includes city of Poquoson.

Civil Records: Access: Online, in person. Visitors must perform in person searches for themselves. No search fee. Required to search: name, years to search. Civil cases indexed by defendant, plaintiff. Civil records on index books from 1950, computerized since 1986. Online access available free at http://208.210.219.132/courtinfo/vacircuit/select.jsp?court=. For information on the statewide online systems, see the state introduction.
Criminal Records: Access: Mail, online, in person. Both court and visitors may perform in person searches. Search fee: $5.00 per name. Required to search: name, years to search, DOB; also helpful: SSN. Criminal records on index books from 1950, computerized since 1986. Online access to criminal records is the same as civil.
General Information: Public access terminal is available. No juvenile, sealed, adoption records released. SASE required. Turnaround time 1 week. Copy fee: $.50 per page. Certification fee: $2.00. Fee payee: Clerk of Circuit Court. Personal checks accepted. Prepayment is required.

9th Judicial District Court York County GDC, PO Box 316, Yorktown, VA 23690-0316; 757-890-3450; Fax: 757-890-3459. Hours: 8:30AM-4:30PM (EST). *Misdemeanor, Civil Actions Under $15,000, Eviction, Small Claims.*
www.yorkcounty.gov

Civil Records: Access: Fax, mail, online, in person. Both court and visitors may perform in person searches. No search fee. Required to search: name, years to search. Civil cases indexed by defendant, plaintiff. Civil records on computer back to 1992; prior to 1985 at Circuit Court. Select and search District Courts at http://208.210.219.132/courtinfo/vadistrict/select.jsp?court=. For information about the statewide online systems, see the state introduction.
Criminal Records: Access: Fax, mail, online, in person. Both court and visitors may perform in person searches. No search fee. Required to search: name, years to search, DOB, SSN. Criminal records on computer back to 1992; prior to 1985 at Circuit Court. Online access to criminal records is the same as civil.
General Information: Public access terminal is available. No juvenile, sealed, adoption records released. Turnaround time 5 days. Fax notes: $1.00 for first page, $.50 each add'l. Copy fee: $1.00 for first page, $.50 each add'l.

Virginia Recording Offices

ORGANIZATION: 95 counties and 41 independent cities, 123 recording offices. The recording officer is Clerk of Circuit Court. Fifteen independent cities share the Clerk of Circuit Court with the county - Bedford, Covington (Alleghany County), Emporia (Greenville County), Fairfax, Falls Church (Arlington or Fairfax County), Franklin (Southhampton County), Galax (Carroll County), Harrisonburg (Rockingham County), Lexington (Rockbridge County), Manassas and Manassas Park (Prince William County), Norton (Wise County), Poquoson (York County), South Boston (Halifax County), and Williamsburg (James City County. Charles City and James City are counties, not cities. The City of Franklin is not in Franklin County, the City of Richmond is not in Richmond County, and the City of Roanoke is not in Roanoke County. The entire state is in the Eastern Time Zone (EST).

REAL ESTATE RECORDS: Only a few Clerks of Circuit Court will perform real estate searches. Copy fees and certification fees vary. The independent cities may have separate Assessor Offices.

UCC RECORDS: This was a dual filing state. Until 07/2001, financing statements were filed at the state level and with the Clerk of Circuit Court, except for consumer goods, farm and real estate related collateral, which were filed only with the Clerk of Circuit Court. Now, only real estate related collateral is filed at the county level. Some recording offices will perform UCC searches. Use search request form UCC-11. Searches fees and copy fees vary.

TAX LIEN RECORDS: Federal tax liens on personal property of businesses are filed with the State Corporation Commission. Other federal and all state tax liens are filed with the county Clerk of Circuit Court. They are usually filed in a "Judgment Lien Book." Most counties will not perform tax lien searches.

OTHER LIENS: Judgment, mechanics, hospital, lis pendens.

ONLINE ACCESS: A growing number of Virginia counties and cities provide free access to real estate related information via the Internet.

A limited but growing private company network named VamaNet provides free residential, commercial and vacant property and tax records for nine Virginia jurisdictions at www.vamanet.com/cgi-bin/LOCS. At the web site, click on the county name at left.

Accomack County

Clerk of Circuit Court, PO Box 126, Accomac, VA 23301-0126. 757-787-5776; Fax 757-787-1849.
Will search UCC records. This agency will not do a tax lien search. Will not search real estate records. **Other Phone Numbers:** Assessor 757-787-5729.

Albemarle County

Clerk of Circuit Court, 501 E. Jefferson St., Room 225, Charlottesville, VA 22902-5176. 434-972-4083; Fax 434-293-0298.
Will search UCC records. Will not search real estate records. **Other Phone Numbers:** Assessor 434-296-5856.

Alexandria City

Clerk of Circuit Court, 520 King St, Room 307, Alexandria, VA 22314. 703-838-4070 R/E Recording: 703-838-4066 UCC Recording: 703-838-4066; www.ci.alexandria.va.us
Will search UCC records. This agency will not do a tax lien search. Will not search real estate records. **Online Access:** Assessor, Prooperty Records. Access to city real estate assessments is available free at www.ci.alexandria.va.us/city/reasearch. No name searching. **Other Phone Numbers:** Assessor 703-838-4646; Treasurer 703-838-6420; Appraiser/Auditor 703-838-4646; Elections 703-838-4050; Vital Records 703-838-4400.

Alleghany County

Clerk of Circuit Court, PO Box 670, Covington, VA 24426-0670. Clerk of Circuit Court, R/E & UCC Recording 540-965-1730; Fax 540-965-1732. www.alleghanycountyclerk.com
This agency will not search real estate or UCC records. **Other Phone Numbers:** Assessor 540-965-1640; Treasurer 540-965-1630.

Alleghany County

Clerk of Circuit Court, PO Box 670, Clifton Forge, VA 24426. 540-965-1730; Fax 540-965-1732.
As of July 1, 2001, all Clifton Forge governmental functions were transferred to Alleghany County.

Amelia County

Clerk of Circuit Court, PO Box 237, Amelia Court House, VA 23002-0237. 804-561-2128.
This agency will not perform searches. **Other Phone Numbers:** Assessor 804-561-2158; Treasurer 804-561-2145; Elections 804-561-3460.

Amherst County

Clerk of Circuit Court, PO Box 462, Amherst, VA 24521. 434-946-9321.
Will search UCC records. This agency will not do a tax lien search. Will not search real estate records. **Other Phone Numbers:** Assessor 434-946-9310; Treasurer 434-946-9318.

Appomattox County

Clerk of Circuit Court, PO Box 672, Appomattox, VA 24522. 434-352-5275; Fax 434-352-2781.
Will search UCC records. Will not search real estate records. **Other Phone Numbers:** Assessor 434-352-7450; Treasurer 434-352-5200.

Arlington County

Clerk of Circuit Court, 1425 N. Courthouse Rd 6th Floor, Arlington, VA 22201. 703-228-7242.
Will search UCC records. This agency will not do a tax lien search. Will not search real estate records. **Online Access:** Real Estate, Assessor, Trade Name Records. Property records on the County assessor database are available free at www.co.arlington.va.us/REAssessments/Scripts/DreaDefault.asp. **Other Phone Numbers:** Assessor 703-228-3920.

Augusta County

Clerk of Circuit Court, PO Box 689, Staunton, VA 24402-0689. 540-245-5321; Fax 540-245-5318.
Will search UCC records. This agency will not do a tax lien search. Will not search real estate records. **Online Access:** Property, Appraisal, Most Wanted Records. Click on Augusta County to search property data for free at www.vamanet.com/cgi-bin/LOCS. Search the sheriff's most wanted list for free at www.augustacountyvirginia.com/sheriff/wanted.htm. **Other Phone Numbers:** Assessor 540-245-5647; Treasurer 540-245-5660.

Bath County

Clerk of Circuit Court, PO Box 180, Warm Springs, VA 24484. 540-839-7226.
Will search UCC records. This agency will not do a tax lien search. Will not search real estate records. **Other Phone Numbers:** Assessor 540-839-7231; Treasurer 540-839-7256.

Bedford County

Clerk of Circuit Court, 123 E Main St, Bedford, VA 24523. 540-586-7632; Fax 540-586-6197.
This agency will not perform searches. **Online Access:** Property Tax Records. County real estate records on the Bedford County Commissioner of the Revenue site are available free online at http://208.206.84.33/realestate2. Records on the City of Bedford (www.ci.bedford.va.us) Property Tax database are available free online at www.ci.bedford.va.us/taxf.shtml. Search by name, address or tax map reference number. **Other Phone Numbers:** Assessor 540-586-7626; Treasurer 540-586-7670.

Bland County

Clerk of Circuit Court, PO Box 295, Bland, VA 24315-0295. 276-688-4562; Fax 276-688-4562.
Will search UCC records. This agency will not do a tax lien search. Will not search real estate records. **Other Phone Numbers:** Assessor 276-688-4291; Treasurer 276-688-3741.

Botetourt County

Clerk of Circuit Court, PO Box 219, Fincastle, VA 24090. 540-473-8274.
Will search UCC records. This agency will not do a tax lien search. Will not search real estate records. **Other Phone Numbers:** Assessor 540-473-8254; Treasurer 540-473-8254.

Bristol City

Clerk of Circuit Court, 497 Cumberland St, Room 210, Bristol, VA 24201. 276-645-7321; Fax 276-645-7345.
Will search UCC records. Will not search real estate records. **Other Phone Numbers:** Assessor 276-645-7316; Treasurer 276-645-7311.

Brunswick County

Clerk of Circuit Court, 216 N. Main St., Lawrenceville, VA 23868. 434-848-2215; Fax 434-848-4307.
This agency will not search real estate or UCC records. **Other Phone Numbers:** Assessor 434-848-2313; Treasurer 434-848-2512.

Buchanan County

Clerk of Circuit Court, PO Box 929, Grundy, VA 24614. Clerk of Circuit Court, R/E and UCC Recording 276-935-6567; Fax 276-935-6574.
Will search UCC records. Will search real estate records. **Other Phone Numbers:** Assessor 276-935-6542; Treasurer 276-935-6551; Elections 276-935-6534; Vital Records 276-935-6575.

Buckingham County

Clerk of Circuit Court, PO Box 107, Buckingham, VA 23921. 434-969-4734; Fax 434-959-2043.
Will search UCC records. Will not search real estate records. **Other Phone Numbers:** Assessor 434-969-4181; Treasurer 434-969-4744.

Buena Vista City

Clerk of Circuit Court, 2039 Sycamore Ave., Buena Vista, VA 24416. 540-261-8627 R/E Recording: 540-261-8623 UCC Recording: 540-261-8626; Fax 540-261-8623.
Will search UCC records. This agency will not do a tax lien search. Will not search real estate records. **Other Phone Numbers:** Assessor 540-261-8611; Treasurer 540-261-8621; Elections 540-261-8605.

Campbell County

Clerk of Circuit Court, PO Box 7, Rustburg, VA 24588. 434-592-9517.
Will search UCC records. Tax liens not included in UCC search. Will not search real estate records. **Other Phone Numbers:** Treasurer 434-332-9590.

Caroline County

Clerk of Circuit Court, PO Box 309, Bowling Green, VA 22427-0309. 804-633-5800.
This agency will not perform searches. **Online Access:** Appraiser, Property Records. Click on Caroline County to search property records for free at www.vamanet.com/cgi-bin/LOCS.

Carroll County

Clerk of Circuit Court, PO Box 218, Hillsville, VA 24343-0218. Clerk of Circuit Court, R/E and UCC Recording 276-728-3117; Fax 276-728-0255.
Will search UCC records. Will not search real estate records. **Online Access:** Real Estate Records. Access to Carroll county property information is available free on the gis mapping site at http://arcims.webgis.net/webgis/carroll_grayson. No name searching at this time. Access to Town of Hillsville property information is available on the GIS mapping site at http://arcims.webgis.net/webgis/hillsville. **Other Phone Numbers:** Assessor 276-728-3281; Treasurer 276-728-9421; Appraiser/Auditor 276-728-3281; Elections 276-728-2332.

Charles City County

Clerk of Circuit Court, PO Box 86, Charles City, VA 23030-0086. Clerk of Circuit Court, R/E and UCC Recording 804-829-9212; Fax 804-829-5647.
This agency will not search real estate or UCC records. **Other Phone Numbers:** Assessor 804-829-9216; Elections 804-829-9210.

Charlotte County

Clerk of Circuit Court, PO Box 38, Charlotte Court House, VA 23923. 434-542-5147; Fax 434-542-4336.
Will search UCC records. Will not search real estate records. **Other Phone Numbers:** Assessor 434-542-5546; Treasurer 434-542-5725.

Charlottesville City

Clerk of Circuit Court, 315 E. High St, Charlottesville, VA 22902. 434-295-3182.
Will search UCC records. This agency will not do a tax lien search. Will not search real estate records. **Other Phone Numbers:** Assessor 434-970-3136; Treasurer 434-296-5851.

Chesapeake City

Clerk of Circuit Court, 307 Albemarle Dr, #300, Chesapeake, VA 23322. Clerk of Circuit Court, R/E and UCC Recording 757-382-3026 UCC Recording: 757-382-3031; Fax 757-436-3034.
Will search UCC records. Will not search real estate records. **Other Phone Numbers:** Assessor 757-382-6235; Treasurer 757-382-6281.

Chesterfield County

Clerk of Circuit Court, PO Box 40, Chesterfield, VA 23832-0125. Clerk of Circuit Court, R/E and UCC Recording 804-748-1241; Fax 804-796-5625.
This agency will not search real estate or UCC records. **Online Access:** Assessor, Property Tax, Property Sales Records. Search the real estate assessment data for free at www.co.chesterfield.va.us/ManagementServices/RealEstateAssessments/Rea_Search_Home.asp. **Other Phone Numbers:** Assessor 804-748-1321; Treasurer 804-748-1201; Elections 804-748-1471.

Clarke County

Clerk of Circuit Court, PO Box 189, Berryville, VA 22611. 540-955-5116; Fax 540-955-0284.
Will search UCC records. Will not search real estate records. **Online Access:** Property, Appraiser Records. Click on Clarke County to search property data for free at www.vamanet.com/cgi-bin/LOCS. **Other Phones:** Assessor 540-955-5108; Treasurer 540-955-5160.

Colonial Heights City

Clerk of Circuit Court, PO Box 3401, Colonial Heights, VA 23834. 804-520-9364.
This agency will not perform searches. **Other Phone Numbers:** Assessor 804-520-9272.

Craig County

Clerk of Circuit Court, PO Box 185, New Castle, VA 24127-0185. 540-864-6141.
Will search UCC records. This agency will not do a tax lien search. Will not search real estate records. **Other Phone Numbers:** Assessor 540-864-6241; Treasurer 540-864-5641.

Culpeper County

Clerk of Circuit Court, 135 W. Cameron St., Room 103, Culpeper, VA 22701. Clerk of Circuit Court, R/E and UCC Recording 540-727-3438.
Will search UCC records. This agency will not do a tax lien search. Will not search real estate records. **Other Phone Numbers:** Assessor 540-727-3443; Treasurer 540-727-3442.

Cumberland County

Clerk of Circuit Court, PO Box 8, Cumberland, VA 23040. 804-492-4442; Fax 804-492-4876.
Will search UCC records. **Other Phone Numbers:** Assessor 804-492-4280; Treasurer 804-492-4297.

Danville City

Clerk of Circuit Court, PO Box 3300, Danville, VA 24543. 434-799-5168; Fax 434-799-6502. www.ci.danville.va.us/clerk
Will search UCC records. This agency will not do a tax lien search. Will not search real estate records. **Online Access:** Real Estate, Lien Records. Access to Danville City online records is free; signup is required. Records date back to 1993. Lending agency information is available. For information, contact Leigh Ann Thomas at 804-799-5168. **Other Phone Numbers:** Assessor 434-799-5120; Treasurer 434-799-5140; Elections 434-799-6560.

Dickenson County

Clerk of Circuit Court, PO Box 190, Clintwood, VA 24228. Clerk of Circuit Court, R/E and UCC Recording 276-926-1616; Fax 276-926-6465.
Will search UCC records. **Other Phone Numbers:** Assessor 276-926-1646; Treasurer 276-926-1610.

Dinwiddie County

Clerk of Circuit Court, PO Box 63, Dinwiddie, VA 23841. 804-469-4540.
Will search UCC records. This agency will not do a tax lien search. Will not search real estate records. **Other Phone Numbers:** Assessor 804-469-4507; Treasurer 804-469-4510.

Essex County

Clerk of Circuit Court, PO Box 445, Tappahannock, VA 22560. Clerk of Circuit Court, R/E and UCC Recording 804-443-3541; Fax 804-445-1216.
This agency will not perform searches. **Other Phone Numbers:** Assessor 804-443-2661; Treasurer 804-443-4371; Elections 804-443-4611.

Fairfax County

Clerk of Circuit Court, 4110 Chain Bridge Rd, 3rd Floor, Fairfax, VA 22030. 703-246-4100; www.co.fairfax.va.us
As of 1/1/88, Falls Church filings for zip codes 22041, 22042, 22043 and 22044 are filed in Fairfax County. Will search UCC records. This agency will not do a tax lien search. Will not search real estate records. **Online Access:** Real Estate, Property Tax, Tax Sales Records. Records on the Dept. of Tax Administration Real Estate Assessment database are available free online at www.co.fairfax.va.us/dta/re. Also, the Automated Information System operates Monday-Saturday 7AM-7PM at 703-222-6740. Hear about property descriptions, assessed values and sales prices. Fax-back service is available. Also, the list of properties to be

auctioned is available free at www.co.fairfax.va.us/dta/auction.htm. **Other Phone Numbers:** Assessor 703-222-8234.

Fauquier County

Clerk of Circuit Court, First Floor, 40 CulpeperSt., Warrenton, VA 20186. 540-347-8608 R/E Recording: 540-347-8697; www.co.fauquier.va.us/government/departments/circuitcourt
This agency will not perform searches. **Other Phones:** Assessor 540-347-8614; Treasurer 540-347-8691.

Floyd County

Clerk of Circuit Court, 100 E. Main St, Room 200, Floyd, VA 24091. 540-745-9330.
This agency will not perform searches. **Online Access:** Real Estate Records. Access to county property information is available free at the gis mapping site at http://arcims.webgis.net/webgis/floyd/default.asp. No name searching at this time. **Other Phone Numbers:** Assessor 540-745-9345; Treasurer 540-745-9357.

Fluvanna County

Clerk of Circuit Court, PO Box 299, Palmyra, VA 22963-0299. Clerk of Circuit Court, R/E and UCC Recording 434-589-8011; Fax 434-589-6004.
This agency will not perform searches. **Online Access:** Appraiser, Property Records. Click on Fluvanna County to serach property data for free at www.vamanet.com/cgi-bin/LOCS. **Other Phone Numbers:** Assessor 434-589-8322; Treasurer 434-589-8012; Appraiser/Auditor 434-589-8322; Elections 434-589-3593; Vital Records 434-589-8021.

Franklin County

Clerk of Circuit Court, PO Box 567, Rocky Mount, VA 24151. 540-483-3065; Fax 540-483-3042.
Will search UCC records. Will not search real estate records. **Other Phones:** Assessor 757-562-8547.

Frederick County

Clerk of Circuit Court, 5 N. Kent St, Winchester, VA 22601. 540-667-5770; Fax 540-545-8711. www.winfredclerk.com/standard.htm
Do not confuse this county with Fredericksburg, VA or Frederick, MD. Also, the City of Winchester has a separate filing office. Will search UCC records. Tax liens not included in UCC search. Will not search real estate records. **Other Phone Numbers:** Assessor 540-662-5303; Treasurer 540-662-6611.

Fredericksburg City

Clerk of Circuit Court, PO Box 359, Fredericksburg, VA 22404. 540-372-1066.
Many Fredericksburg addresses are outside the city limits, in Stafford County or Spotsylvania County. Many residents are not themselves aware of this. Check debtor location carefully. Will search UCC records. This agency will not do a tax lien search. Will not search real estate records. **Other Phone Numbers:** Assessor 540-372-1004.

Giles County

Clerk of Circuit Court, 501 Wenonah Ave, Pearisburg, VA 24134-0501. 540-921-1722; Fax 540-921-3825.
Will search UCC records. Will not search real estate records. **Online Access:** Appraiser, Property Records. Click on Fluvanna County to search for property records for free at www.vamanet.com/cgi-bin/LOCS. **Other Phone Numbers:** Assessor 540-921-3321; Treasurer 540-921-1240.

Gloucester County

Clerk of Circuit Court, PO Box 2118, Gloucester, VA 23061-0570. Clerk of Circuit Court, R/E and UCC Recording 804-693-2502; Fax 804-693-2186. www.courts.state.va.us

Will search UCC records. **Online Access:** Judgment Records. Access to Law and Chancery cases is free at http://208.210.219.132/courtinfo/vacircuit/select.jsp?court=. **Other Phone Numbers:** Assessor 804-693-3451; Treasurer 804-693-2141.

Goochland County

Clerk of Circuit Court, PO Box 196, Goochland, VA 23063. 804-556-5353.
Will search UCC records. This agency will not do a tax lien search. Will not search real estate records. **Other Phone Numbers:** Assessor 804-556-5307.

Grayson County

Clerk of Circuit Court, PO Box 130, Independence, VA 24348-0130. 276-773-2231; Fax 276-773-3338.
Will search UCC records. This agency will not do a tax lien search. Will not search real estate records. **Online Access:** Real Estate Records. Access to Grayson county property information is available free on the gis mapping site at http://arcims.webgis.net/webgis/carroll_grayson. No name searching at this time. **Other Phone Numbers:** Assessor 276-773-3022; Treasurer 276-773-2571.

Greene County

Clerk of Circuit Court, PO Box 386, Stanardsville, VA 22973-0386. 434-985-5208; Fax 434-985-6723.
Will search UCC records. Will not search real estate records. **Other Phone Numbers:** Assessor 434-985-5211; Treasurer 434-985-5214.

Greensville County

Clerk of Circuit Court, PO Box 631, Emporia, VA 23847. Clerk of Circuit Court, R/E and UCC Recording 434-348-4215; Fax 434-348-4020.
Will search UCC records. Will not search real estate records. **Online Access:** Appraiser, Property Records. Click on Grennsville County to search property data for free at www.vamanet.com/cgi-bin/LOCS. **Other Phone Numbers:** Assessor 434-348-4229; Treasurer 434-348-4208.

Halifax County

Clerk of Circuit Court, PO Box 729, Halifax, VA 24558. 434-476-6211; Fax 434-476-2890.
Will search UCC records. Will not search real estate records. **Other Phone Numbers:** Assessor 434-476-2773; Treasurer 434-476-2025.

Hampton City

Clerk of Circuit Court, PO Box 40, Hampton, VA 23669-0040. 757-727-6896; Fax 757-728-3505.
Will search UCC records. This agency will not do a tax lien search. Will not search real estate records. **Other Phone Numbers:** Assessor 757-727-6363; Treasurer 757-727-6374.

Hanover County

Clerk of Circuit Court, PO Box 39, Hanover, VA 23069-0039. 804-537-6150 R/E Recording: 804-537-6120 UCC Recording: 804-537-6120.
Will search UCC records. This agency will not do a tax lien search. Will not search real estate records. **Other Phone Numbers:** Assessor 804-537-6029; Treasurer 804-537-6050; Registrar 804-537-6080

Henrico County

Clerk of Circuit Court, PO Box 27032, Richmond, VA 23273. 804-501-4202 R/E Recording: 804-501-4979 UCCs: 804-501-5468; www.co.henrico.va.us/clerk/
Will not search UCC records. This agency will not do a tax lien search. Will check book & page for name and date for real estate. **Other Phone Numbers:** Assessor 804-501-5580.

Henry County

Clerk of Circuit Court, 3160 Kings Mountain Rd. #B, Martinsville, VA 24112. Clerk of Circuit Court, R/E and UCC Recording 276-634-4880; http://henrycounty.neocom.net
This agency will not perform searches. **Online Access:** Real Estate, Assessor Records. Access to county porperty information is available free at the gis mapping site at www.webgis.net/henry. **Other Phone Numbers:** Assessor 276-634-4610; Treasurer 276-624-4675; Appraiser/Auditor 276-634-4610; Elections 276-634-4697; Vital Records 276-634-4880.

Highland County

Clerk of Circuit Court, PO Box 190, Monterey, VA 24465-0190. 540-468-2447; Fax 540-468-3447.
Will search UCC records. Will not search real estate records. **Other Phone Numbers:** Assessor 540-468-2142; Treasurer 540-465-2265.

Hopewell City

Clerk of Circuit Court, PO Box 354, Hopewell, VA 23860. 804-541-2239.
Will search UCC records. This agency will not do a tax lien search. Will not search real estate records. **Other Phone Numbers:** Assessor 804-541-2234; Treasurer 804-541-2240.

Isle of Wight County

Clerk of Circuit Court, PO Box 110, Isle of Wight, VA 23397. 757-357-3191 x233.
Will search UCC records. This agency will not do a tax lien search. Will not search real estate records. **Online Access:** Judgment Records. Access to Law and Chancery case judgments is available free at http://208.210.219.132/courtinfo/vacircuit/select2.jsp. **Other Phone Numbers:** Assessor 757-365-6219; Treasurer 757-357-3191.

James City County

Clerk of Circuit Court, 5201 Monticello Ave #6, Williamsburg, VA 23188. 757-564-2242 R/E Recording: 757-564-2349; www.regis.state.va.us/jcc/
This office also handles filings for the City of WIlliamsburg. Will search UCC records. This agency will not do a tax lien search. Will not search real estate records. **Online Access:** Real Estate Records. Records on the James City County Property Information database are available free online at www.regis.state.va.us/jcc/public/disclaimer.htm. Also, search the City of Williamsburg property assessor data for free at www.ci.williamsburg.va.us/realestate/disclaimer.html. **Other Phone Numbers:** Assessor 757-253-6650; Treasurer 757-229-6705.

King and Queen County

Clerk of Circuit Court, PO Box 67, King and Queen Court House, VA 23085. Clerk of Circuit Court, R/E and UCC Recording 804-785-5984; Fax 804-785-5698.
This agency will not search real estate or UCC records. **Other Phone Numbers:** Assessor 804-785-5976; Treasurer 804-785-5978; Elections 804-785-5980.

King George County

Clerk of Circuit Court, 9483 Kings Highway, #3, King George, VA 22485. Clerk of Circuit Court, R/E and UCC Recording 540-775-3322.
Will search UCC records. UCC search includes tax liens if requested. Real estate owner, mortgage, and property transfer searches available. **Other Phone Numbers:** Assessor 540-775-4664; Treasurer 540-775-2571.

King William County

Clerk of Circuit Court, PO Box 216, King William, VA 23086. 804-769-4936; Fax 804-769-4991.
Will search UCC records. This agency will not do a tax lien search. Real estate owner, mortgage, and property transfer searches available. **Online Access:** Land Records. Access to property and deeds indexes and images is available via a private company at http://auth.titlesearcher.com/ts/ts.asp or support@TitleSearcher.com. Fee/registration required; Monthly and per day available. **Other Phones:** Assessor 804-769-4942; Treasurer 804-769-4931.

Lancaster County

Clerk of Circuit Court, PO Box 99, Lancaster, VA 22503. 804-462-5611; Fax 804-462-9978.
Will search UCC records. This agency will not do a tax lien search. Will not search real estate records. **Other Phone Numbers:** Assessor 804-462-7920; Treasurer 804-462-5630; Elections 804-462-5277.

Lee County

Clerk of Circuit Court, PO Box 326, Jonesville, VA 24263. 276-346-7763; Fax 276-346-3440.
Will search UCC records. Will not search real estate records. **Other Phone Numbers:** Assessor 276-346-7722; Treasurer 276-346-7716.

Loudoun County

Clerk of Circuit Court, PO Box 550, Leesburg, VA 20178. Clerk of Circuit Court, R/E and UCC Recording 703-777-0270; www.loudoun.gov/government/
Will search UCC records. This agency will not do a tax lien search. Will not search real estate records. **Online Access:** Property, Assessor Records. Search the proeprty assessor data for free at http://inter1.loudoun.gov/webpdbs. No name searching; search by address, number, or ID only. **Other Phones:** Assessor 703-777-0260; Treasurer 703-777-0280.

Louisa County

Clerk of Circuit Court, PO Box 37, Louisa, VA 23093. 540-967-5312.
Will search UCC records. This agency will not do a tax lien search. Will not search real estate records. **Other Phone Numbers:** Assessor 540-967-3450.

Lunenburg County

Clerk of Circuit Court, Courthouse, Lunenburg, VA 23952. 434-696-2230.
Will search UCC records. This agency will not do a tax lien search. Will not search real estate records. **Other Phone Numbers:** Assessor 434-696-2516.

Lynchburg City

Clerk of Circuit Court, PO Box 4, Lynchburg, VA 24505. 434-847-1590; Fax 434-847-1864.
Will search UCC records. This agency will not do a tax lien search. Will not search real estate records. **Other Phone Numbers:** Assessor 434-847-1510; Treasurer 434-847-1520.

Madison County

Clerk of Circuit Court, PO Box 220, Madison, VA 22727-0220. 540-948-6888; Fax 540-948-3759.
Will search UCC records. Will not search real estate records. **Other Phone Numbers:** Assessor 540-948-4421; Treasurer 540-948-4409.

Martinsville City

Clerk of Circuit Court, PO Box 1206, Martinsville, VA 24114-1206. Clerk of Circuit Court, R/E and UCC Recording 276-656-5106; Fax 276-656-5232. www.ci.martinsville.va.us/crms/
Will search UCC records. This agency will not do a tax lien search. Will not search real estate records. **Online Access:** Property, Deed, Judgment, Wills, Marriage Records. Access to the Martinsville Circuit Court records is available free at www.ci.martinsville.va.us/crms. You may also search the tax map and for personal property. **Other Phone Numbers:** Assessor 276-656-5131.

Mathews County

Clerk of Circuit Court, PO Box 463, Mathews, VA 23109-0463. Clerk of Circuit Court, R/E and UCC Recording 804-725-2550.
This agency will not perform searches. **Other Phones:** Assessor 804-725-7168; Treasurer 804-725-2341.

Mecklenburg County

Clerk of Circuit Court, PO Box 530, Boydton, VA 23917-0530. 434-738-6191; Fax 434-738-6861.
Will search UCC records. This agency will not do a tax lien search. Will not search real estate records.

Middlesex County

Clerk of Circuit Court, PO Box 158, Saluda, VA 23149. Clerk of Circuit Court, R/E and UCC Recording 804-758-5317.
Will search UCC records. This agency will not do a tax lien search. Will not search real estate records. **Other Phone Numbers:** Assessor 804-758-5331; Treasurer 804-758-5302; Appraiser/Auditor 804-758-5331; Elections 804-758-4420.

Montgomery County

Clerk of Circuit Court, PO Box 6309, 1 E. Main #B5, Christiansburg, VA 24068. 540-382-5760; Fax 540-382-6937. www.montva.com
This agency will not search real estate or UCC records. **Online Access:** Real Estate, Property Tax Records. Access to the county Tax Parcel Information System database is available free online at www.webgis.net/montgomery/index.htm. Select what to search and click next. Records on the Town of Blackburg GIS site are available free online at www.webgis.net/blacksburg. Use map or enter an owner name. Find owner name, address, land or building value. **Other Phones:** Assessor 540-382-5717; Treasurer 540-382-5723; Appraiser/Auditor 540-382-5715; Elections 540-382-5741; Vital Records 540-382-5760; Public Information Office 540-381-6887.

Nelson County

Clerk of Circuit Court, PO Box 10, Lovingston, VA 22949. 434-263-4069; Fax 434-263-8313.
Will search UCC records. This agency will not do a tax lien search. Will not search real estate records. **Other Phone Numbers:** Assessor 434-263-4009; Treasurer 434-263-4079.

New Kent County

Clerk of Circuit Court, PO Box 98, New Kent, VA 23124-0098. Clerk of Circuit Court, R/E and UCC Recording 804-966-9520; Fax 804-966-9528.
This agency will not search real estate or UCC records. **Other Phone Numbers:** Assessor 804-966-9610; Treasurer 804-966-9615.

Newport News City

Clerk of Circuit Court, 2500 Washington Ave, Courthouse, Newport News, VA 23607. 757-926-8561 R/E Recording: 757-926-8355 UCC Recording: 757-926-8349; Fax 757-926-8531. www.newport-news.va.us
Will search UCC records. Will not search real estate records. **Online Access:** Assessor, Real Estate Records. Access to the City's "Real Estate on the Web" database is available free at http://216.54.20.244/reisweb1. Search by address or parcel number; new "advanced search" may include name searching. **Other Phones:** Assessor 757-247-8671; Treasurer 757-247-8731.

Norfolk City

Clerk of Circuit Court, 100 St. Paul's Blvd., Norfolk, VA 23510-2773. 757-664-4380; http://norfolkgov.com/home.asp
Will search UCC records. UCC search includes tax liens if requested. Real estate owner, mortgage, and property transfer searches available. **Online Access:** Real Estate, Assessor Records. Records on the City of Norfolk Real Estate Property Assessment database are available free at www.norfolkgov.com/RealEstate/index.html. **Other Phone Numbers:** Assessor 757-64-4732; Treasurer 757-441-2931.

Northampton County

Clerk of Circuit Court, PO Box 36, Eastville, VA 23347-0036. 757-678-0465; Fax 757-678-5410.
Will search UCC records. Will not search real estate records. **Other Phone Numbers:** Assessor 757-678-0446; Treasurer 757-678-0450.

Northumberland County

Clerk of Circuit Court, PO Box 217, Heathsville, VA 22473. 804-580-3700.
Will search UCC records. This agency will not do a tax lien search. Real estate record owner searches available. **Other Phone Numbers:** Assessor 804-580-4600; Treasurer 804-580-5201.

Nottoway County

Clerk of Circuit Court, PO Box 25, Nottoway, VA 23955. Clerk of Circuit Court, R/E and UCC Recording 434-645-9043; Fax 434-645-2201.
Will search UCC records. Will not search real estate records. **Other Phone Numbers:** Assessor 434-645-9317; Treasurer 434-645-9318; Appraiser/Auditor 434-645-9317; Vital Records 434-645-9043.

Orange County

Clerk of Circuit Court, PO Box 230, Orange, VA 22960. Clerk of Circuit Court, R/E and UCC Recording 540-672-4030; Fax 540-672-2939.
Will search UCC records. Will not search real estate records. **Other Phone Numbers:** Assessor 540-672-4441; Treasurer 540-672-2656.

Page County

Clerk of Circuit Court, 116 S. Court St, Suite A, Luray, VA 22835. Clerk of Circuit Court, R/E and UCC Recording 540-743-4064; Fax 540-743-2338.
This agency will not search real estate or UCC records. **Other Phone Numbers:** Assessor 540-743-3840; Treasurer 540-743-3975; Elections 540-743-3986.

Patrick County

Clerk of Circuit Court, PO Box 148, Stuart, VA 24171-0148. Clerk of Circuit Court, R/E and UCC Recording 276-694-7213; Fax 276-694-6943.
This agency will not search real estate or UCC records. **Other Phone Numbers:** Assessor 276-694-7131; Treasurer 276-694-7257; Elections 276-694-7206.

Petersburg City

Clerk of Circuit Court, 7 Courthouse Ave., Petersburg, VA 23803. 804-733-2367; Fax 804-732-5548.
Will search UCC records. Will not search real estate records. **Other Phone Numbers:** Assessor 804-733-2315; Treasurer 804-733-2321.

Pittsylvania County

Clerk of Circuit Court, PO Drawer 31, Chatham, VA 24531. 434-432-7887 R/E Recording: 434-432-7888; Fax 434-432-7913.
Will search UCC records. This agency will not do a tax lien search. Will not search real estate records. **Online Access:** Real Estate Records. See Danville City for Real Estate and Lien records online for Danville City. **Other**

Phone Numbers: Assessor 434-432-7949; Treasurer 434-432-7961; Elections 434-432-7971.

Portsmouth City

Clerk of Circuit Court, PO Drawer 1217, Portsmouth, VA 23705. 757-393-8671 R/E Recording: 757-393-8530; Fax 757-399-4826.
Will search UCC records. This agency will not do a tax lien search. Will not search real estate records. **Other Phone Numbers:** Assessor 757-393-8631; Treasurer 757-393-8651; Appraiser/Auditor 757-393-8771; Elections 757-393-8644.

Powhatan County

Clerk of Circuit Court, PO Box 37, Powhatan, VA 23139-0037. Clerk of Circuit Court, R/E and UCC Recording 804-598-5660.
Will search UCC records. This agency will not do a tax lien search. Will not search real estate records. **Online Access:** Appraiser, Property Records. Click on Powhatan County to search property data for free at www.vamanet.com/cgi-bin/LOCS. **Other Phone Numbers:** Assessor 804-598-5617; Treasurer 804-598-5626; Appraiser/Auditor 804-598-5617.

Prince Edward County

Clerk of Circuit Court, PO Box 304, Farmville, VA 23901. 434-392-5145.
Will search UCC records. This agency will not do a tax lien search. Will not search real estate records. **Other Phone Numbers:** Assessor 434-392-3231; Treasurer 434-392-3404.

Prince George County

Clerk of Circuit Court, PO Box 98, Prince George, VA 23875-0098. 804-733-2640.
Will search UCC records. This agency will not do a tax lien search. Will not search real estate records. **Other Phone Numbers:** Assessor 804-733-2616; Treasurer 804-733-2620.

Prince William County

Clerk of Circuit Court, 9311 Lee Ave, Room 300, Manassas, VA 20110-5598. 703-792-6035; Fax 703-792-6083. www.pwcgov.org/ccourt
Will search UCC records. Will not search real estate records. **Online Access:** Property Records. Records on the county Property Information database are available free at www.pwcgov.org/realestate/LandRover.asp. **Other Phone Numbers:** Assessor 703-792-6780; Vital Records 703-792-6045 (marriage only).

Pulaski County

Clerk of Circuit Court, Suite 101, 45 3rd St. NW, Pulaski, VA 24301. Clerk of Circuit Court, R/E and UCC Recording 540-980-7825; Fax 540-980-7835.
This agency will not perform searches. **Other Phone Numbers:** Assessor 540-980-7753; Treasurer 540-980-7785.

Radford City

Clerk of Circuit Court, 619 Second St, Courthouse, Radford, VA 24141. 540-731-3610; Fax 540-731-3612.
Will search UCC records. This agency will not do a tax lien search. Will not search real estate records. **Other Phone Numbers:** Treasurer 540-731-3661; Elections 540-731-3639.

Rappahannock County

Clerk of Circuit Court, PO Box 517, Washington, VA 22747-1517. Clerk of Circuit Court, R/E and UCC Recording 540-675-5350.
Will search UCC records. This agency will not do a tax lien search. Will not search real estate records. **Other Phone Numbers:** Assessor 540-675-5370; Treasurer 540-675-5360.

Richmond City

Clerk of Circuit Court, 400 N. 9th St., Richmond, VA 23219. 804-780-6520.
The City of Richmond is not in Richmond County. It is bordered by Henrico and Chesterfield Counties. Will search UCC records. This agency will not do a tax lien search. Will not search real estate records. **Online Access:** Property, Assessor Records. Search the city's Accessing Property & Real Estate Assessment Information for free at www.ci.richmond.va.us/accessingGIS.asp. Follow direction; name searching is available. **Other Phone Numbers:** Assessor 804-780-5600; Treasurer 804-646-6474; Appraiser/Auditor 804-646-5616; Elections 804-646-5950; City Clerk 804-646-7955; Sheriff 804-646-0930;

Richmond County

Clerk of Circuit Court, PO Box 1000, Warsaw, VA 22572-1000. 804-333-3781; Fax 804-333-5396. www.co.richmond.va.us/
The City of Richmond is a separate filing office and is not located in this county. The following ZIP Codes are the only ones for this county: 22572, 22460, 22472, 22548, and part of 22435. Will search UCC records. Tax liens included with UCC search if requested. Real estate record owner searches available. **Other Phone Numbers:** Assessor 804-333-5062; Treasurer 804-333-3555; Appraiser/Auditor 804-333-5062; Elections 804-333-4772; Vital Records 804-333-3781.

Roanoke City

Clerk of Circuit Court, Box 2610, Roanoke, VA 24010-2610. Clerk of Circuit Court, R/E and UCC Recording 540-853-6702.
Will search UCC records. This agency will not do a tax lien search. **Online Access:** Property Records. Access to Roanoke City property records are available free at www.webgis.net/RoanokeCity. **Other Phone Numbers:** Treasurer 540-853-2561.

Roanoke County

Clerk of Circuit Court, PO Box 1126, Salem, VA 24153-1126. 540-387-6205; Fax 540-387-6145.
Will search UCC records. Will not search real estate records. **Other Phone Numbers:** Assessor 703-772-2035.

Rockbridge County

Clerk of Circuit Court, 2 S. Main St, Court House, Lexington, VA 24450-2599. Clerk of Circuit Court, R/E and UCC Recording 540-463-2232; Fax 540-463-3850.
Will search UCC records. Will not search real estate records. **Online Access:** Appraiser, Property Records. Click on City of Lexington to search the city property data for free at www.vamanet.com/cgi-bin/LOCS. **Other Phone Numbers:** Assessor 540-463-2613; Treasurer 540-772-2056; Appraiser/Auditor 540-463-3431; Elections 540-463-7203.

Rockingham County

Clerk of Circuit Court, Courthouse, Harrisonburg, VA 22801. 540-564-3110 UCC Recording: 540-564-3126; Fax 540-564-3127.
Will search UCC records. Will not search real estate records. **Other Phone Numbers:** Assessor 540-564-3086.

Russell County

Clerk of Circuit Court, PO Box 435, Lebanon, VA 24266. 276-889-8023; Fax 276-889-8003.
Will search UCC records. Will not search real estate records. **Other Phone Numbers:** Assessor 276-889-8014; Treasurer 276-889-8028.

Salem City

Clerk of Circuit Court, PO Box 891, Salem, VA 24153. 540-375-3067 R/E Recording: 540-375-3058; Fax 540-375-4039.
This agency will not search real estate or UCC records. **Other Phone Numbers:** Elections 540-375-3058.

Scott County

Clerk of Circuit Court, 104 E. Jackson St, Courthouse, Suite 2, Gate City, VA 24251-3417. 276-386-3801.
Will search UCC records. UCC search includes tax liens if requested. Will not search real estate records. **Online Access:** Deed, Property, Recording Records. Access to Circuit Court records is available for a fifteen day trial demo. After, a username, password, and monthly fee is required. For information and sign-up, see http://auth.titlesearcher.com/ts/ts.asp or support@titlesearcher.com. **Other Phone Numbers:** Assessor 276-386-3801; Treasurer 276-386-7742; Registrar 276-386-6691.

Shenandoah County

Clerk of Circuit Court, PO Box 406, Woodstock, VA 22664-0406. 540-459-6150; Fax 540-459-6155.
Will search UCC records. Will not search real estate records. **Other Phone Numbers:** Assessor 540-459-6170; Treasurer 540-459-6180.

Smyth County

Clerk of Circuit Court, PO Box 1025, Marion, VA 24354. Clerk of Circuit Court, R/E and UCC Recording 276-782-4044; Fax 276-783-4045.
This agency will not search real estate or UCC records. **Other Phone Numbers:** Assessor 276-782-4040; Treasurer 276-782-4059.

Southampton County

Clerk of Circuit Court, PO Box 190, Courtland, VA 23837. 757-653-9245.
This agency will not perform searches. **Other Phones:** Assessor 757-653-3030; Treasurer 757-653-3025.

Spotsylvania County

Clerk of Circuit Court, PO Box 96, Spotsylvania, VA 22553-0096. 540-582-7090 R/E Recording: 540-582-7046 UCC Recording: 540-582-7090 X233; Fax 540-582-2169.
Will search UCC records. Will not search real estate records. **Other Phones:** Assessor 540-582-7132.

Stafford County

Clerk of Circuit Court, PO Box 69, Stafford, VA 22555. 540-659-8752 R/E Recording: 540-658-8752 UCC Recording: 540-658-8758.
Will search UCC records. This agency will not do a tax lien search. Will not search real estate records. **Other Phone Numbers:** Assessor 540-658-4132; Treasurer 540-659-8700.

Staunton City

Clerk of Circuit Court, PO Box 1286, Staunton, VA 24402-1286. Clerk of Circuit Court, R/E and UCC Recording 540-332-3874; Fax 540-332-3970. www.staunton.va.us/cityhall/spinhall.htm
This agency will not search real estate or UCC records. **Other Phone Numbers:** Assessor 540-332-3827; Treasurer 540-332-3833; Appraiser/Auditor 540-332-3827; Elections 540-332-3840.

Suffolk City

Clerk of Circuit Court, PO Box 1604, Suffolk, VA 23439-1604. 757-923-2251 R/E Recording: 757-923-2264 UCC Recording: 757-923-2347.
Will search UCC records. This agency will not do a tax lien search. Will not search real estate records. **Other Phone Numbers:** Assessor 757-923-2400.

Surry County

Clerk of Circuit Court, PO Box 203, Surry, VA 23883-0203. 757-294-3161.
Will search UCC records. This agency will not do a tax lien search. Will not search real estate records. **Other Phone Numbers:** Assessor 757-294-3000; Treasurer 757-294-5206.

Sussex County

Clerk of Circuit Court, PO Box 1337, Sussex, VA 23884. Clerk of Circuit Court, R/E and UCC Recording 434-246-5511 x3274.
Will search UCC records. This agency will not do a tax lien search. Will not search real estate records. **Other Phone Numbers:** Assessor 434-246-5511 x3222; Treasurer 434-246-5511 x3223.

Tazewell County

Clerk of Circuit Court, PO Box 968, Tazewell, VA 24651-0968. 276-988-7541; Fax 276-988-7501.
Will search UCC records. **Other Phone Numbers:** Assessor 276-988-7541 x305; Treasurer 276-988-7541 x315.

Virginia Beach City

Clerk of Circuit Court, Judicial Center, 2305 Judicial Blvd., Virginia Beach, VA 23456-9017. 757-427-8818; Fax 757-426-5686. www.vbgov.com
Will search UCC records. Will not search real estate records. **Online Access:** Real Estate Assessor Records. Search the assessor database for free at www.vbgov.com/dept/realestate. No name searching. **Other Phones:** Assessor 757-427-4601; Treasurer 757-427-4445; Elections 757-427-8683; Public Info Office 757-427-4111; City Clerk 757-427-4303;

Warren County

Clerk of Circuit Court, 1 E. Main St, Front Royal, VA 22630-3382. Clerk of Circuit Court, R/E and UCC Recording 540-635-2435; Fax 540-636-3274. www.courts.state.va.us
Will search UCC records. Will not search real estate records. **Other Phones:** Assessor 540-635-2651; Treasurer 540-635-2215; Elections 540-635-4327.

Washington County

Clerk of Circuit Court, PO Box 289, Abingdon, VA 24212. 276-676-6226 UCC Recording: 276-676-6265; Fax 276-676-6218.
Will search UCC records. Will not search real estate records. **Online Access:** Real Estate, Assessor Records. Search the county GIS-mapping site for free at http://arcims2.webgis.net/washington/default.asp. No name searching, but property and address information is available. **Other Phone Numbers:** Assessor 276-676-6270; Treasurer 276-676-6272; Vital Records 276-676-6265.

Waynesboro City

Clerk of Circuit Court, PO Box 910, Waynesboro, VA 22980. 540-942-6616.
Will search UCC records. This agency will not do a tax lien search. Will not search real estate records. **Other Phone Numbers:** Assessor 540-942-6621/5513; Treasurer 540-942-6606.

Westmoreland County

Clerk of Circuit Court, PO Box 307, Montross, VA 22520. 804-493-0108.
This agency will not perform searches. **Other Phones:** Assessor 804-493-0113; Treasurer 804-493-0124.

Winchester City

Clerk of Circuit Court, 5 N. Kent St, Winchester, VA 22601. Clerk of Circuit Court, R/E and UCC Recording 540-667-5770; Fax 540-667-6638. www.winfredclerk.com
This agency will not perform searches. **Other Phone Numbers:** Assessor 540-667-1815.

Wise County

Clerk of Circuit Court, PO Box 1248, Wise, VA 24293. 276-328-6111; Fax 276-328-0039. www.courtbar.org
This agency will not search real estate or UCC records. **Online Access:** Assessor, Real Estate, Lien, Probate, Marriage Records. Includes City of Norton. Premium User fee is $395 annually or $39 per month. Genealogists have two plans: the 150-year marriage and probate database is $99 annually or $10 per month. Database index and images include the Court's orders, land documents from 1970 including links to real estate tax assessments, fifty-year real estate transfer histories, tax maps, plat maps, delinquent taxes, and permit images. Probate and marriage records, with recent document images from probate. Access the judgment lien index for the past 20 years; UCC-1 indices for the past five years. Also, property information is available free at http://arcims.webgis.net/webgis/wise. **Other Phone Numbers:** Assessor 276-328-3556; Treasurer 276-328-3666.

Wythe County

Clerk of Circuit Court, 225 S. Fourth St, Room 105, Wytheville, VA 24382. Clerk of Circuit Court, R/E and UCC Recording 276-223-6050; Fax 276-223-6057.
Will search UCC records. Will not search real estate records. **Other Phone Numbers:** Assessor 276-223-6015; Treasurer 276-223-6070; Appraiser/Auditor 276-223-6015; Elections 276-223-6038.

York County

Clerk of Circuit Court, PO Box 371, Yorktown, VA 23690. 757-890-3350; Fax 757-890-3364. www.yorkcounty.gov/circuitcourt
Will search UCC records. Will not search real estate records. **Online Access:** Property Records. Property records from the County GIS site are available free online at http://206.246.204.37. **Other Phone Numbers:** Assessor 757-890-3270; Treasurer 757-890-3420.

Virginia County Locator

You will usually be able to find the city name in the City/County Cross Reference below. In that case, it is a simple matter to determine the county from the cross reference. However, only the official US Postal Service city names are included in this index. There are an additional 40,000 place names that people use in their addresses. Therefore, we have also included a ZIP/City Cross Reference immediately following the City/County Cross Reference.

If you know the ZIP Code but the city name does not appear in the City/County Cross Reference index, look up the ZIP Code in the ZIP/City Cross Reference, find the city name, then look up the city name in the City/County Cross Reference. For example, you want to know the county for an address of Menands, NY 12204. There is no "Menands" in the City/County Cross Reference. The ZIP/City Cross Reference shows that ZIP Codes 12201-12288 are for the city of Albany. Looking back in the City/County Cross Reference, Albany is in Albany County.

City/County Cross Reference

ABINGDON Washington
ACCOMAC Accomack
ACHILLES Gloucester
AFTON (22920) Nelson(64), Albemarle(31), Augusta(3)
ALBERTA Brunswick
ALDIE Loudoun
ALEXANDRIA Alexandria City
ALFONSO Lancaster
ALTAVISTA Campbell
ALTON Halifax
AMELIA COURT HOUSE Amelia
AMHERST Amherst
AMISSVILLE Rappahannock
AMMON Dinwiddie
AMONATE Tazewell
ANDERSONVILLE Buckingham
ANDOVER Wise
ANNANDALE Fairfax
APPALACHIA Wise
APPOMATTOX (24522) Appomattox(97), Buckingham(1), Charlotte(1)
ARARAT Patrick
ARCOLA Loudoun
ARK Gloucester
ARLINGTON Arlington
ARODA Madison
ARRINGTON (22922) Nelson(95), Amherst(4)
ARVONIA Buckingham
ASHBURN Loudoun
ASHLAND Hanover
ASSAWOMAN Accomack
ATKINS Smyth
ATLANTIC Accomack
AUGUSTA SPRINGS Augusta
AUSTINVILLE (24312) Carroll(56), Wythe(43)
AXTON (24054) Henry(66), Pittsylvania(33)
AYLETT King William
BACOVA Bath
BANCO Madison
BANDY Tazewell
BANK AMERICARD Roanoke City
BARBOURSVILLE (22923) Orange(52), Greene(24), Albemarle(22)
BARHAMSVILLE New Kent
BARREN SPRINGS (24313) Wythe(98), Pulaski(1)
BASKERVILLE Mecklenburg
BASSETT (24055) Henry(95), Franklin(4)
BASTIAN (24314) Bland(93), Tazewell(6)
BASYE Shenandoah
BATESVILLE Albemarle
BATTERY PARK Isle of Wight
BAVON Mathews
BEALETON Fauquier
BEAUMONT Goochland
BEAVERDAM (23015) Hanover(72), Caroline(14), Spotsylvania(11), Louisa(1)
BEAVERLETT Mathews
BEDFORD (24523) Bedford(74), Bedford City(25)

BEE Dickenson
BELLAMY Gloucester
BELLE HAVEN Accomack
BELSPRING Pulaski
BEN HUR Lee
BENA Gloucester
BENT MOUNTAIN Roanoke
BENTONVILLE (22610) Warren(98), Page(1)
BERGTON Rockingham
BERRYVILLE Clarke
BIG ISLAND Bedford
BIG ROCK Buchanan
BIG STONE GAP (24219) Wise(97), Lee(2)
BIRCHLEAF Dickenson
BIRDSNEST Northampton
BISHOP Tazewell
BLACKSBURG Montgomery
BLACKSTONE (23824) Nottoway(92), Brunswick(7)
BLACKWATER (24221) Lee(63), Scott(36)
BLAIRS Pittsylvania
BLAKES Mathews
BLAND Bland
BLOXOM Accomack
BLUE GRASS Highland
BLUE RIDGE (24064) Botetourt(62), Bedford(37)
BLUEFIELD Tazewell
BLUEMONT Loudoun
BOHANNON Mathews
BOISSEVAIN Tazewell
BOONES MILL (24065) Franklin(80), Roanoke(19)
BOSTON (22713) Culpeper(85), Rappahannock(14)
BOWLING GREEN Caroline
BOYCE Clarke
BOYDTON Mecklenburg
BOYKINS Southampton
BRACEY (23919) Mecklenburg(94), Brunswick(5)
BRANCHVILLE Southampton
BRANDY STATION Culpeper
BREAKS Dickenson
BREMO BLUFF Fluvanna
BRIDGEWATER (22812) Rockingham(80), Augusta(19)
BRIGHTWOOD Madison
BRISTOL Bristol City
BRISTOW Prince William
BROAD RUN Fauquier
BROADFORD (24316) Tazewell(60), Smyth(40)
BROADWAY (22815) Rockingham(97), Shenandoah(2)
BRODNAX (23920) Brunswick(76), Mecklenburg(21), Lunenburg(2)
BROOKE Stafford
BROOKNEAL (24528) Campbell(79), Charlotte(20)
BROWNSBURG Rockbridge
BRUCETOWN Frederick

BRUINGTON King and Queen
BUCHANAN Botetourt
BUCKINGHAM Buckingham
BUENA VISTA (24416) Buena Vista City(77), Rockbridge(22)
BUFFALO JUNCTION (24529) Mecklenburg(98), Halifax(1)
BUMPASS (23024) Louisa(82), Spotsylvania(14), Hanover(3)
BURGESS Northumberland
BURKE Fairfax
BURKES GARDEN Tazewell
BURKEVILLE (23922) Nottoway(90), Prince Edward(9)
BURR HILL Orange
CALLANDS (24530) Pittsylvania(98), Henry(1)
CALLAO (22435) Northumberland(98), Westmoreland(1)
CALLAWAY Franklin
CALVERTON Fauquier
CANA Carroll
CAPE CHARLES Northampton
CAPEVILLE Northampton
CAPRON Southampton
CARDINAL Mathews
CARET (22436) Essex(98), Caroline(1)
CARROLLTON Isle of Wight
CARRSVILLE Isle of Wight
CARSON (23830) Prince George(56), Dinwiddie(30), Sussex(13)
CARTERSVILLE Cumberland
CASANOVA Fauquier
CASCADE Pittsylvania
CASTLETON (22716) Rappahannock(95), Culpeper(4)
CASTLEWOOD Russell
CATAWBA (24070) Roanoke(71), Montgomery(26), Craig(1)
CATHARPIN Prince William
CATLETT Fauquier
CAUTHORNVILLE King and Queen
CEDAR BLUFF (24609) Russell(96), Tazewell(3)
CENTER CROSS Essex
CENTREVILLE Fairfax
CERES (24318) Smyth(68), Bland(31)
CHAMPLAIN (22438) Essex(90), Caroline(9)
CHANCE Essex
CHANTILLY Fairfax
CHARLES CITY Charles City
CHARLOTTE COURT HOUSE (23923) Charlotte(97), Prince Edward(2)
CHARLOTTESVILLE Albemarle
CHASE CITY (23924) Mecklenburg(93), Lunenburg(4), Charlotte(2)
CHATHAM Pittsylvania
CHECK Floyd
CHERITON Northampton
CHESAPEAKE Chesapeake City
CHESTER Chesterfield
CHESTER GAP Rappahannock

CHESTERFIELD Chesterfield
CHILHOWIE (24319) Smyth(73), Washington(26)
CHINCOTEAGUE Accomack
CHINCOTEAGUE ISLAND Accomack
CHRISTCHURCH Middlesex
CHRISTIANSBURG Montgomery
CHURCH ROAD (23833) Dinwiddie(89), Amelia(10)
CHURCH VIEW Middlesex
CHURCHVILLE Augusta
CITY OFFICES Roanoke City
CLAREMONT Surry
CLARKSVILLE Mecklenburg
CLAUDVILLE Patrick
CLEAR BROOK Frederick
CLEVELAND (24225) Russell(96), Dickenson(3)
CLIFFORD Amherst
CLIFTON Fairfax
CLIFTON FORGE (24422) Clifton Forge City(62), Alleghany(34), Botetourt(3)
CLINCHBURG Washington
CLINCHCO Dickenson
CLINTWOOD Dickenson
CLOVER Halifax
CLOVERDALE Botetourt
CLUSTER SPRINGS Halifax
COBBS CREEK Mathews
COBHAM Albemarle
COEBURN (24230) Wise(90), Dickenson(8), Scott(1)
COLEMAN FALLS Bedford
COLES POINT Westmoreland
COLLINSVILLE Henry
COLOGNE King and Queen
COLONIAL BEACH Westmoreland
COLONIAL HEIGHTS (23834) Colonial Heights City(71), Chesterfield(28)
COLUMBIA (23038) Goochland(66), Cumberland(26), Fluvanna(7)
CONCORD (24538) Campbell(82), Appomattox(17)
COPPER HILL (24079) Floyd(96), Roanoke(2)
CORBIN Caroline
COURTLAND (23837) Southampton(96), Sussex(3)
COVESVILLE Albemarle
COVINGTON (24426) Covington City(50), Alleghany(49)
CRADDOCKVILLE Accomack
CRAIGSVILLE Augusta
CREWE Nottoway
CRIDERS Rockingham
CRIMORA Augusta
CRIPPLE CREEK Wythe
CRITZ Patrick
CROCKETT Wythe
CROSS JUNCTION Frederick
CROZET Albemarle
CROZIER Goochland
CRYSTAL HILL Halifax

CULLEN (23934) Charlotte(53), Prince Edward(46)
CULPEPER (22701) Culpeper(92), Orange(7)
CUMBERLAND (23040) Cumberland(91), Buckingham(8)
DABNEYS Louisa
DAHLGREN King George
DALEVILLE Botetourt
DAMASCUS Washington
DANTE (24237) Dickenson(68), Russell(31)
DANVILLE Danville City
DARLINGTN HTS Prince Edward
DARLINGTON HEIGHTS Prince Edward
DAVENPORT Buchanan
DAVIS WHARF Accomack
DAYTON Rockingham
DEERFIELD Augusta
DELAPLANE Fauquier
DELTAVILLE Middlesex
DENDRON Surry
DEWITT Dinwiddie
DIGGS Mathews
DILLWYN (23936) Buckingham(97), Cumberland(2)
DINWIDDIE Dinwiddie
DISPUTANTA (23842) Prince George(92), Sussex(7)
DOE HILL Highland
DOGUE King George
DOLPHIN Brunswick
DORAN Tazewell
DOSWELL (23047) Hanover(75), Caroline(24)
DRAKES BRANCH (23937) Charlotte(94), Lunenburg(5)
DRAPER Pulaski
DREWRYVILLE Southampton
DRY FORK Pittsylvania
DRYDEN Lee
DUBLIN Pulaski
DUFFIELD (24244) Scott(83), Lee(16)
DUGSPUR Carroll
DULLES Loudoun
DUMFRIES Prince William
DUNDAS (23938) Brunswick(59), Lunenburg(40)
DUNGANNON Scott
DUNN LORING Fairfax
DUNNSVILLE Essex
DUTTON (23050) Gloucester(50), Mathews(50)
DYKE (22935) Greene(64), Albemarle(35)
EAGLE ROCK (24085) Botetourt(98), Alleghany(1)
EARLYSVILLE Albemarle
EAST STONE GAP Wise
EASTVILLE Northampton
EBONY Brunswick
EDINBURG Shenandoah
EDWARDSVILLE Northumberland
EGGLESTON Giles
ELBERON Surry
ELK CREEK Grayson
ELKTON (22827) Rockingham(89), Page(10)
ELKWOOD Culpeper
ELLISTON (24087) Montgomery(95), Roanoke(4)
EMORY Washington
EMPORIA (23847) Greensville(67), Emporia City(29), Southampton(2), Sussex(1)
ESMONT Albemarle
ETLAN Madison
EVERGREEN Appomattox
EVINGTON (24550) Campbell(86), Bedford(13)
EWING Lee
EXETER Wise
EXMORE Northampton

FABER (22938) Nelson(96), Albemarle(3)
FAIRFAX Fairfax City
FAIRFAX STATION Fairfax
FAIRFIELD Rockbridge
FALLS CHURCH Fairfax
FALLS MILLS Tazewell
FANCY GAP Carroll
FARMVILLE Prince Edward
FARNHAM Richmond
FERRUM Franklin
FIELDALE Henry
FIFE Goochland
FINCASTLE Botetourt
FISHERS HILL Shenandoah
FISHERSVILLE Augusta
FLINT HILL Rappahannock
FLOYD Floyd
FONESWOOD Richmond
FORD (23850) Dinwiddie(85), Amelia(14)
FOREST (24551) Bedford(86), Campbell(12)
FORK UNION Fluvanna
FORT BELVOIR Fairfax
FORT BLACKMORE Scott
FORT DEFIANCE Augusta
FORT EUSTIS Newport News City
FORT LEE (23801) Prince George(98), Petersburg City(1)
FORT MITCHELL Lunenburg
FORT MONROE Hampton City
FORT VALLEY Shenandoah
FOSTER Mathews
FRANKLIN (23851) Franklin City(49), Southampton(43), Isle of Wight(7)
FRANKTOWN Northampton
FREDERICKSBURG Stafford
FREE UNION (22940) Albemarle(76), Greene(23)
FREEMAN (23856) Brunswick(95), Greensville(4)
FRIES (24330) Grayson(93), Carroll(6)
FRONT ROYAL Warren
FT MYER Arlington
FULKS RUN Rockingham
GAINESVILLE Prince William
GALAX (24333) Grayson(38), Carroll(35), Galax City(26)
GARRISONVILLE Stafford
GASBURG Brunswick
GATE CITY Scott
GLADE SPRING Washington
GLADEHILL Franklin
GLADSTONE (24553) Nelson(77), Appomattox(11), Buckingham(11)
GLADYS Campbell
GLASGOW Rockbridge
GLEN ALLEN Henrico
GLEN LYN Giles
GLEN WILTON Botetourt
GLOUCESTER Gloucester
GLOUCESTER POINT Gloucester
GOLDBOND Giles
GOLDVEIN Fauquier
GOOCHLAND Goochland
GOODE Bedford
GOODVIEW Bedford
GORDONSVILLE (22942) Orange(63), Louisa(33), Albemarle(3)
GORE Frederick
GOSHEN (24439) Rockbridge(78), Augusta(21)
GRAVES MILL Madison
GREAT AMERICAN MAGAZINE Hampton City
GREAT FALLS (22066) Fairfax(96), Loudoun(3)
GREEN BAY (23942) Prince Edward(67), Lunenburg(32)
GREENBACKVILLE Accomack
GREENBUSH Accomack
GREENVILLE Augusta
GREENWAY Fairfax

GREENWOOD Albemarle
GRETNA Pittsylvania
GRIMSTEAD Mathews
GROTTOES (24441) Rockingham(81), Augusta(18)
GRUNDY Buchanan
GUM SPRING (23065) Goochland(71), Louisa(28)
GWYNN Mathews
HACKSNECK Accomack
HADENSVILLE Goochland
HAGUE Westmoreland
HALIFAX Halifax
HALLIEFORD Mathews
HALLWOOD Accomack
HAMILTON Loudoun
HAMPDEN SYDNEY Prince Edward
HAMPTON Hampton City
HANDSOM Southampton
HANOVER (23069) Hanover(41), Caroline(34), King William(24)
HARBORTON Accomack
HARDY (24101) Franklin(92), Bedford(6)
HARDYVILLE Middlesex
HARMAN Buchanan
HARRISONBURG Harrisonburg City
HARTFIELD Middlesex
HARTWOOD Stafford
HAYES Gloucester
HAYMARKET Prince William
HAYNESVILLE Richmond
HAYSI (24256) Dickenson(89), Buchanan(10)
HAYWOOD Madison
HEAD WATERS Highland
HEATHSVILLE (22473) Northumberland(98), Lancaster(1)
HENRY (24102) Franklin(92), Henry(7)
HERNDON Fairfax
HIGHLAND SPRINGS Henrico
HIGHTOWN Highland
HILLSVILLE Carroll
HILTONS (24258) Scott(97), Washington(2)
HINTON Rockingham
HIWASSEE (24347) Pulaski(90), Montgomery(9)
HONAKER (24260) Russell(87), Buchanan(12)
HOOD Madison
HOPEWELL (23860) Hopewell City(81), Prince George(18)
HORNTOWN Accomack
HORSEPEN Tazewell
HOT SPRINGS (24445) Bath(56), Alleghany(43)
HOWARDSVILLE (24562) Albemarle(60), Buckingham(39)
HUDDLESTON Bedford
HUDGINS Mathews
HUME Fauquier
HUNTLY Rappahannock
HURLEY Buchanan
HURT Pittsylvania
HUSTLE Essex
HYACINTH Northumberland
INDEPENDENCE Grayson
INDIAN VALLEY Floyd
IRON GATE Alleghany
IRVINGTON Lancaster
ISLE OF WIGHT Isle of Wight
IVANHOE (24350) Wythe(59), Carroll(34), Grayson(6)
IVOR (23866) Southampton(58), Isle of Wight(41)
IVY Albemarle
JAMAICA Middlesex
JAMES STORE Gloucester
JAMESTOWN James City
JAMESVILLE Northampton
JARRATT Greensville
JAVA (24565) Pittsylvania(88), Halifax(11)

JEFFERSONTON Culpeper
JENKINS BRIDGE Accomack
JERSEY King George
JETERSVILLE (23083) Amelia(97), Nottoway(2)
JEWELL RIDGE (24622) Tazewell(64), Buchanan(35)
JONESVILLE Lee
JORDAN MINES Alleghany
KEELING Pittsylvania
KEEN MOUNTAIN Buchanan
KEENE Albemarle
KEEZLETOWN Rockingham
KELLER Accomack
KENBRIDGE Lunenburg
KENTS STORE (23084) Goochland(42), Louisa(31), Fluvanna(25)
KEOKEE Lee
KESWICK (22947) Albemarle(96), Louisa(2)
KEYSVILLE (23947) Charlotte(50), Lunenburg(39), Prince Edward(9)
KILMARNOCK (22482) Northumberland(63), Lancaster(36)
KING AND QUEEN COURT HOUS King and Queen
KING GEORGE King George
KING WILLIAM King William
KINSALE Westmoreland
LA CROSSE (23950) Mecklenburg(87), Brunswick(12)
LACEY SPRING Rockingham
LACKEY York
LADYSMITH Caroline
LAHORE Orange
LAMBSBURG Carroll
LANCASTER Lancaster
LANEVIEW (22504) Essex(96), Middlesex(3)
LANEXA (23089) New Kent(75), James City(24)
LAUREL FORK (24352) Carroll(98), Floyd(1)
LAWRENCEVILLE Brunswick
LEBANON Russell
LEE MONT Accomack
LEESBURG Loudoun
LEON Madison
LEWISETTA Northumberland
LEXINGTON (24450) Rockbridge(71), Lexington City(28)
LIGHTFOOT York
LIGNUM Culpeper
LINCOLN Loudoun
LINDEN (22642) Warren(84), Fauquier(15)
LINVILLE Rockingham
LITTLE PLYMOUTH King and Queen
LIVELY Lancaster
LOCUST DALE Madison
LOCUST GROVE (22508) Orange(92), Spotsylvania(7)
LOCUST HILL Middlesex
LOCUSTVILLE Accomack
LONG ISLAND (24569) Pittsylvania(93), Halifax(5)
LORETTO Essex
LORTON Fairfax
LOTTSBURG Northumberland
LOUISA (23093) Louisa(92), Goochland(7)
LOVETTSVILLE Loudoun
LOVINGSTON Nelson
LOW MOOR Alleghany
LOWRY Bedford
LUNENBURG Lunenburg
LURAY Page
LYNCH STATION Campbell
LYNCHBURG Lynchburg City
LYNDHURST (22952) Augusta(96), Nelson(2), Waynesboro City(1)
MACHIPONGO Northampton
MACON Powhatan
MADISON Madison

MADISON HEIGHTS Amherst
MADISON MILLS Madison
MAIDENS (23102) Goochland(79), Louisa(13), Hanover(6)
MANAKIN SABOT Goochland
MANASSAS Manassas Park City
MANGOHICK King William
MANNBORO Amelia
MANQUIN King William
MAPPSVILLE Accomack
MARION Smyth
MARIONVILLE Northampton
MARKHAM Fauquier
MARSHALL Fauquier
MARTINSVILLE Martinsville City
MARYUS Gloucester
MASCOT King and Queen
MASSIES MILL Nelson
MATHEWS Mathews
MATTAPONI King and Queen
MAURERTOWN Shenandoah
MAVISDALE Buchanan
MAX MEADOWS Wythe
MAXIE Buchanan
MC CLURE Dickenson
MC COY Montgomery
MC DOWELL Highland
MC GAHEYSVILLE Rockingham
MC KENNEY Dinwiddie
MC LEAN Fairfax
MEADOWS OF DAN (24120) Patrick(75), Floyd(16), Carroll(8)
MEADOWVIEW Washington
MEARS Accomack
MECHANICSVILLE Hanover
MEHERRIN (23954) Prince Edward(66), Lunenburg(33)
MELFA Accomack
MENDOTA Washington
MEREDITHVILLE Brunswick
MERRIFIELD Fairfax
MERRY POINT Lancaster
MIDDLEBROOK (24459) Augusta(91), Rockbridge(8)
MIDDLEBURG Loudoun
MIDDLETOWN Warren
MIDLAND Fauquier
MIDLOTHIAN Chesterfield
MILES Chesterfield
MILFORD Caroline
MILLBORO Bath
MILLERS TAVERN Essex
MILLWOOD Clarke
MINE RUN Orange
MINERAL (23117) Louisa(87), Spotsylvania(10), Goochland(2)
MINT SPRING Augusta
MITCHELLS Culpeper
MOBJACK Mathews
MODEST TOWN Accomack
MOLLUSK Lancaster
MONETA (24121) Bedford(64), Franklin(35)
MONROE Amherst
MONTEBELLO Nelson
MONTEREY Highland
MONTPELIER (23192) Hanover(93), Louisa(6)
MONTPELIER STATION Orange
MONTROSS Westmoreland
MONTVALE Bedford
MOON Mathews
MORATTICO Lancaster
MOSELEY (23120) Chesterfield(95), Powhatan(4)
MOUNT CRAWFORD (22841) Rockingham(97), Augusta(2)
MOUNT HOLLY Westmoreland
MOUNT JACKSON Shenandoah
MOUNT SIDNEY Augusta
MOUNT SOLON Augusta
MOUNT VERNON Fairfax

MOUTH OF WILSON Grayson
MUSTOE Highland
NARROWS (24124) Giles(98), Bland(1)
NARUNA Campbell
NASSAWADOX Northampton
NATHALIE Halifax
NATURAL BRIDGE Rockbridge
NATURAL BRIDGE STATION Rockbridge
NAXERA Gloucester
NELLYSFORD Nelson
NELSON Mecklenburg
NELSONIA Accomack
NEW CANTON (23123) Buckingham(94), Cumberland(5)
NEW CASTLE Craig
NEW CHURCH Accomack
NEW HOPE Augusta
NEW KENT (23124) New Kent(95), Hanover(4)
NEW MARKET (22844) Shenandoah(91), Rockingham(8)
NEW POINT Mathews
NEW RIVER Pulaski
NEWBERN Pulaski
NEWINGTON Fairfax
NEWPORT (24128) Giles(87), Craig(8), Montgomery(3)
NEWPORT NEWS Hampton City
NEWSOMS Southampton
NEWTOWN King and Queen
NICKELSVILLE (24271) Scott(98), Russell(1)
NINDE King George
NOKESVILLE Prince William
NORA Dickenson
NORFOLK Norfolk City
NORGE James City
NORTH (23128) Gloucester(68), Mathews(31)
NORTH GARDEN Albemarle
NORTH TAZEWELL Tazewell
NORTON (24273) Norton City(85), Wise(14)
NORWOOD Nelson
NOTTOWAY Nottoway
NUTTSVILLE Lancaster
OAK HALL Accomack
OAKPARK Madison
OAKTON Fairfax
OAKWOOD Buchanan
OCCOQUAN Prince William
OILVILLE (23129) Goochland(96), Hanover(3)
OLDHAMS Westmoreland
ONANCOCK Accomack
ONEMO Mathews
ONLEY Accomack
OPHELIA Northumberland
ORANGE (22960) Orange(97), Madison(2)
ORDINARY Gloucester
ORISKANY Botetourt
ORKNEY SPRINGS Shenandoah
ORLEAN Fauquier
OYSTER Northampton
PAEONIAN SPRINGS Loudoun
PAINT BANK Craig
PAINTER Accomack
PALMYRA Fluvanna
PAMPLIN (23958) Prince Edward(57), Appomattox(29), Charlotte(12)
PARIS Fauquier
PARKSLEY Accomack
PARROTT Pulaski
PARTLOW Spotsylvania
PATRICK SPRINGS Patrick
PEARISBURG Giles
PEMBROKE Giles
PENHOOK (24137) Franklin(81), Pittsylvania(18)
PENN LAIRD Rockingham
PENNINGTON GAP Lee
PETERSBURG Petersburg City

PHENIX Charlotte
PHILOMONT Loudoun
PILGRIMS KNOB Buchanan
PILOT (24138) Montgomery(50), Floyd(49)
PINEY RIVER Nelson
PITTSVILLE Pittsylvania
PLAIN VIEW King and Queen
PLEASANT VALLEY Rockingham
POCAHONTAS Tazewell
POQUOSON Poquoson City
PORT HAYWOOD Mathews
PORT REPUBLIC Rockingham
PORT ROYAL Caroline
PORTSMOUTH Portsmouth City
POUND Wise
POUNDING MILL Tazewell
POWHATAN (23139) Powhatan(98), Cumberland(1)
PRATTS Madison
PRINCE GEORGE Prince George
PROSPECT Prince Edward
PROVIDENCE FORGE (23140) New Kent(57), Charles City(42)
PULASKI Pulaski
PUNGOTEAGUE Accomack
PURCELLVILLE Loudoun
QUANTICO Stafford
QUICKSBURG Shenandoah
QUINBY Accomack
QUINQUE Greene
QUINTON New Kent
RADFORD Radford City
RADIANT Madison
RANDOLPH (23962) Charlotte(90), Halifax(9)
RAPHINE (24472) Rockbridge(68), Augusta(31)
RAPIDAN (22733) Culpeper(72), Orange(27)
RAPPAHANNOCK ACADEMY Caroline
RAVEN (24639) Tazewell(86), Buchanan(12)
RAWLINGS Brunswick
RECTORTOWN Fauquier
RED ASH Tazewell
RED HOUSE (23963) Charlotte(74), Campbell(21), Appomattox(4)
RED OAK (23964) Charlotte(88), Mecklenburg(11)
REDART Mathews
REDWOOD Franklin
REEDVILLE Northumberland
REGINA Lancaster
REMINGTON (22734) Fauquier(85), Culpeper(14)
REPUBLICAN GROVE Halifax
RESCUE Isle of Wight
RESTON Fairfax
REVA (22735) Culpeper(88), Madison(11)
RHOADESVILLE Orange
RICE (23966) Prince Edward(53), Amelia(46)
RICH CREEK Giles
RICHARDSVILLE Culpeper
RICHLANDS Tazewell
RICHMOND Richmond City
RIDGEWAY Henry
RILEYVILLE Page
RINER (24149) Montgomery(75), Floyd(24)
RINGGOLD Pittsylvania
RIPPLEMEAD Giles
RIXEYVILLE Culpeper
ROANOKE Botetourt
ROCHELLE Madison
ROCKBRIDGE BATHS Rockbridge
ROCKVILLE (23146) Hanover(74), Goochland(25)
ROCKY GAP Bland
ROCKY MOUNT Franklin
ROLLINS FORK King George
ROSE HILL Lee
ROSEDALE Russell

ROSELAND (22967) Nelson(90), Amherst(9)
ROUND HILL Loudoun
ROWE (24646) Buchanan(85), Russell(14)
RUBY Stafford
RUCKERSVILLE (22968) Greene(90), Albemarle(8)
RURAL RETREAT (24368) Smyth(64), Wythe(35)
RUSTBURG Campbell
RUTHER GLEN (22546) Caroline(98), Hanover(1)
RUTHVILLE Charles City
SAINT CHARLES Lee
SAINT PAUL (24283) Wise(95), Russell(2), Dickenson(1)
SAINT STEPHENS CHURCH (23148) King and Queen(69), Essex(30)
SALEM Salem City
SALTVILLE (24370) Smyth(76), Washington(23)
SALUDA (23149) Gloucester(50), Middlesex(49)
SANDSTON Henrico
SANDY HOOK Goochland
SANDY LEVEL Pittsylvania
SANDY POINT Westmoreland
SANFORD Accomack
SAXE Charlotte
SAXIS Accomack
SCHLEY Gloucester
SCHUYLER (22969) Nelson(59), Albemarle(40)
SCOTTSBURG Halifax
SCOTTSVILLE (24590) Albemarle(71), Buckingham(17), Fluvanna(10)
SEAFORD York
SEALSTON King George
SEAVIEW Northampton
SEDLEY (23878) Southampton(97), Sussex(2)
SELMA Alleghany
SEVEN MILE FORD Smyth
SEVERN Gloucester
SHACKLEFORDS King and Queen
SHADOW Mathews
SHARPS Richmond
SHAWSVILLE Montgomery
SHENANDOAH Page
SHILOH King George
SHIPMAN Nelson
SHORTT GAP Buchanan
SINGERS GLEN Rockingham
SKIPPERS Greensville
SKIPWITH Mecklenburg
SMITHFIELD Isle of Wight
SOMERSET (22972) Orange(98), Madison(1)
SOMERVILLE Fauquier
SOUTH BOSTON Halifax
SOUTH HILL (23970) Mecklenburg(93), Lunenburg(6)
SPARTA Caroline
SPEEDWELL Wythe
SPENCER (24165) Henry(92), Patrick(7)
SPERRYVILLE (22740) Rappahannock(83), Culpeper(15), Madison(1)
SPOTSYLVANIA Spotsylvania
SPOTTSWOOD (24475) Augusta(96), Rockbridge(3)
SPOUT SPRING Appomattox
SPRING GROVE (23881) Prince George(51), Surry(48)
SPRINGFIELD Fairfax
STAFFORD Stafford
STAFFORDSVILLE Giles
STANARDSVILLE Greene
STANLEY Page
STANLEYTOWN Henry
STAR TANNERY (22654) Frederick(74), Shenandoah(25)

STATE FARM Goochland
STAUNTON Augusta
STEELES TAVERN Augusta
STEPHENS CITY (22655) Frederick(98), Warren(1)
STEPHENSON Frederick
STERLING Loudoun
STERLING PARK Loudoun
STEVENSBURG Culpeper
STEVENSVILLE King and Queen
STONEGA Wise
STONY CREEK (23882) Sussex(72), Dinwiddie(27)
STRASBURG (22657) Shenandoah(84), Warren(15)
STRATFORD Westmoreland
STUART Patrick
STUARTS DRAFT Augusta
STUDLEY Hanover
SUFFOLK Suffolk City
SUGAR GROVE Smyth
SUMERDUCK Fauquier
SUPPLY Essex
SURRY Surry
SUSAN Mathews
SUSSEX Sussex
SUTHERLAND Dinwiddie
SUTHERLIN Pittsylvania
SWEET BRIAR Amherst
SWOOPE Augusta
SWORDS CREEK Russell
SYRIA Madison
TANGIER Accomack
TANNERSVILLE Tazewell
TAPPAHANNOCK Essex
TASLEY Accomack
TAZEWELL Tazewell
TEMPERANCEVILLE Accomack
THAXTON Bedford
THE PLAINS Fauquier
THORNBURG Spotsylvania

TIMBERVILLE (22853) Rockingham(95), Shenandoah(4)
TOANO James City
TOMS BROOK Shenandoah
TOPPING Middlesex
TOWNSEND Northampton
TRAMMEL Dickenson
TREVILIANS Louisa
TRIANGLE Prince William
TROUT DALE (24378) Grayson(89), Smyth(10)
TROUTDALE (24378) Grayson(89), Smyth(10)
TROUTVILLE Botetourt
TROY (22974) Fluvanna(44), Louisa(35), Albemarle(20)
TURBEVILLE Halifax
TYRO Nelson
UNION HALL Franklin
UNIONVILLE Orange
UNIVERSITY OF RICHMOND Richmond City
UPPERVILLE Fauquier
URBANNA Middlesex
VALENTINES Brunswick
VANSANT Buchanan
VERNON HILL (24597) Halifax(80), Pittsylvania(19)
VERONA Augusta
VESTA Patrick
VESUVIUS (24483) Rockbridge(59), Amherst(21), Nelson(18)
VICTORIA Lunenburg
VIENNA Fairfax
VIEWTOWN (22746) Culpeper(72), Rappahannock(27)
VILLAGE Richmond
VILLAMONT Bedford
VINTON (24179) Roanoke(50), Bedford(49)
VIRGILINA (24598) Halifax(84), Mecklenburg(15)

VIRGINIA BEACH Virginia Beach City
VOLNEY Grayson
WACHAPREAGUE Accomack
WAKE Middlesex
WAKEFIELD (23888) Sussex(51), Southampton(27), Surry(21)
WALKERTON (23177) King and Queen(57), King William(42)
WALLOPS ISLAND Accomack
WARDTOWN Northampton
WARE NECK Gloucester
WARFIELD Brunswick
WARM SPRINGS Bath
WARNER Middlesex
WARRENTON Fauquier
WARSAW (22572) Richmond(93), Westmoreland(6)
WASHINGTON Rappahannock
WATER VIEW Middlesex
WATERFORD Loudoun
WATTSVILLE Accomack
WAVERLY Sussex
WAYNESBORO (22980) Waynesboro City(71), Augusta(28)
WEBER CITY Scott
WEEMS Lancaster
WEIRWOOD Northampton
WEST AUGUSTA Augusta
WEST MCLEAN Fairfax
WEST POINT (23181) King William(88), New Kent(11)
WESTMORELAND Westmoreland
WEYERS CAVE (24486) Augusta(89), Rockingham(10)
WHITE HALL Albemarle
WHITE MARSH Gloucester
WHITE PLAINS Brunswick
WHITE POST (22663) Clarke(60), Frederick(35), Warren(3)
WHITE STONE Lancaster
WHITETOP Grayson

WHITEWOOD Buchanan
WICOMICO Gloucester
WICOMICO CHURCH Northumberland
WILLIAMSBURG (23188) James City(78), York(20), Williamsburg City(1)
WILLIAMSVILLE (24487) Bath(62), Highland(37)
WILLIS (24380) Floyd(93), Carroll(6)
WILLIS WHARF Northampton
WILSONS (23894) Dinwiddie(87), Nottoway(12)
WINCHESTER Frederick
WINDSOR Isle of Wight
WINGINA (24599) Nelson(84), Buckingham(15)
WIRTZ Franklin
WISE Wise
WITHAMS Accomack
WOLFORD Buchanan
WOLFTOWN Madison
WOODBERRY FOREST Madison
WOODBRIDGE Prince William
WOODFORD (22580) Caroline(92), Spotsylvania(7)
WOODLAWN Carroll
WOODS CROSS ROADS Gloucester
WOODSTOCK Shenandoah
WOODVILLE Rappahannock
WOOLWINE Patrick
WYLLIESBURG Charlotte
WYTHEVILLE Wythe
YALE Sussex
YARDS Tazewell
YORKTOWN York
ZACATA Westmoreland
ZANONI Gloucester
ZUNI (23898) Isle of Wight(69), Southampton(30)

ZIP/City Cross Reference

20101-20104 DULLES	20186-20188 WARRENTON	22069-22069 HAYMARKET	22170-22170 STERLING PARK
20105-20105 ALDIE	20189-20189 DULLES	22070-22070 RESTON	22171-22171 THE PLAINS
20106-20106 AMISSVILLE	20190-20191 RESTON	22071-22071 HERNDON	22172-22172 TRIANGLE
20107-20107 ARCOLA	20192-20192 HERNDON	22075-22075 LEESBURG	22176-22176 UPPERVILLE
20108-20113 MANASSAS	20193-20196 RESTON	22078-22078 PURCELLVILLE	22180-22185 VIENNA
20115-20116 MARSHALL	20197-20197 WATERFORD	22079-22079 LORTON	22186-22186 WARRENTON
20117-20118 MIDDLEBURG	20198-20198 THE PLAINS	22080-22080 LOVETTSVILLE	22190-22190 WATERFORD
20119-20119 CATLETT	20199-20199 DULLES	22081-22082 MERRIFIELD	22191-22195 WOODBRIDGE
20120-20122 CENTREVILLE	22001-22001 ALDIE	22090-22090 HERNDON	22199-22199 LORTON
20124-20124 CLIFTON	22002-22002 AMISSVILLE	22091-22091 RESTON	22200-22210 ARLINGTON
20128-20128 ORLEAN	22003-22003 ANNANDALE	22092-22092 HERNDON	22211-22211 FT MYER
20129-20129 PAEONIAN SPRINGS	22009-22009 BURKE	22093-22093 ASHBURN	22212-22246 ARLINGTON
20130-20130 PARIS	22010-22010 ARCOLA	22094-22095 HERNDON	22300-22336 ALEXANDRIA
20131-20131 PHILOMONT	22011-22011 ASHBURN	22096-22096 RESTON	22401-22412 FREDERICKSBURG
20132-20134 PURCELLVILLE	22012-22012 BLUEMONT	22101-22102 MC LEAN	22421-22421 ALFONSO
20135-20135 BLUEMONT	22013-22013 BRISTOW	22103-22103 WEST MCLEAN	22427-22428 BOWLING GREEN
20136-20136 BRISTOW	22014-22014 BROAD RUN	22106-22109 MC LEAN	22430-22430 BROOKE
20137-20137 BROAD RUN	22015-22015 BURKE	22110-22111 MANASSAS	22432-22432 BURGESS
20138-20138 CALVERTON	22016-22016 CALVERTON	22115-22115 MARSHALL	22433-22433 BURR HILL
20139-20139 CASANOVA	22017-22017 CASANOVA	22116-22116 MERRIFIELD	22435-22435 CALLAO
20140-20140 RECTORTOWN	22018-22018 CATHARPIN	22117-22117 MIDDLEBURG	22436-22436 CARET
20141-20142 ROUND HILL	22019-22019 CATLETT	22118-22120 MERRIFIELD	22437-22437 CENTER CROSS
20143-20143 CATHARPIN	22020-22020 CENTREVILLE	22121-22121 MOUNT VERNON	22438-22438 CHAMPLAIN
20144-20144 DELAPLANE	22021-22022 FAIRFAX	22122-22122 NEWINGTON	22439-22439 CHANCE
20146-20149 ASHBURN	22024-22024 CLIFTON	22123-22123 NOKESVILLE	22442-22442 COLES POINT
20151-20153 CHANTILLY	22025-22025 DELAPLANE	22124-22124 OAKTON	22443-22443 COLONIAL BEACH
20155-20156 GAINESVILLE	22026-22026 DUMFRIES	22125-22125 OCCOQUAN	22446-22446 CORBIN
20158-20159 HAMILTON	22027-22027 DUNN LORING	22128-22128 ORLEAN	22448-22448 DAHLGREN
20160-20160 LINCOLN	22030-22038 FAIRFAX	22129-22129 PAEONIAN SPRINGS	22451-22451 DOGUE
20163-20167 STERLING	22039-22039 FAIRFAX STATION	22130-22130 PARIS	22454-22454 DUNNSVILLE
20168-20169 HAYMARKET	22040-22047 FALLS CHURCH	22131-22131 PHILOMONT	22456-22456 EDWARDSVILLE
20170-20172 HERNDON	22060-22060 FORT BELVOIR	22132-22132 PURCELLVILLE	22460-22460 FARNHAM
20175-20178 LEESBURG	22065-22065 GAINESVILLE	22134-22135 QUANTICO	22461-22461 FONESWOOD
20180-20180 LOVETTSVILLE	22066-22066 GREAT FALLS	22140-22140 RECTORTOWN	22463-22463 GARRISONVILLE
20181-20182 NOKESVILLE	22067-22067 GREENWAY	22141-22141 ROUND HILL	22469-22469 HAGUE
20184-20185 UPPERVILLE	22068-22068 HAMILTON	22150-22161 SPRINGFIELD	22471-22471 HARTWOOD

22472-22472	HAYNESVILLE
22473-22473	HEATHSVILLE
22476-22476	HUSTLE
22477-22477	HYACINTH
22480-22480	IRVINGTON
22481-22481	JERSEY
22482-22482	KILMARNOCK
22485-22485	KING GEORGE
22488-22488	KINSALE
22501-22501	LADYSMITH
22502-22502	LAHORE
22503-22503	LANCASTER
22504-22504	LANEVIEW
22505-22505	LEWISETTA
22507-22507	LIVELY
22508-22508	LOCUST GROVE
22509-22509	LORETTO
22511-22511	LOTTSBURG
22513-22513	MERRY POINT
22514-22514	MILFORD
22517-22517	MOLLUSK
22520-22520	MONTROSS
22523-22523	MORATTICO
22524-22524	MOUNT HOLLY
22526-22526	NINDE
22528-22528	NUTTSVILLE
22529-22529	OLDHAMS
22530-22530	OPHELIA
22534-22534	PARTLOW
22535-22535	PORT ROYAL
22538-22538	RAPPAHANNOCK ACADEMY
22539-22539	REEDVILLE
22540-22540	REGINA
22542-22542	RHOADESVILLE
22544-22544	ROLLINS FORK
22545-22545	RUBY
22546-22546	RUTHER GLEN
22547-22547	SEALSTON
22548-22548	SHARPS
22549-22549	SHILOH
22552-22552	SPARTA
22553-22553	SPOTSYLVANIA
22554-22555	STAFFORD
22558-22558	STRATFORD
22559-22559	SUPPLY
22560-22560	TAPPAHANNOCK
22565-22565	THORNBURG
22567-22567	UNIONVILLE
22568-22568	MINE RUN
22570-22570	VILLAGE
22572-22572	WARSAW
22576-22576	WEEMS
22577-22577	WESTMORELAND
22577-22577	SANDY POINT
22578-22578	WHITE STONE
22579-22579	WICOMICO CHURCH
22580-22580	WOODFORD
22581-22581	ZACATA
22601-22604	WINCHESTER
22610-22610	BENTONVILLE
22611-22611	BERRYVILLE
22620-22620	BOYCE
22622-22622	BRUCETOWN
22623-22623	CHESTER GAP
22624-22624	CLEAR BROOK
22625-22625	CROSS JUNCTION
22626-22626	FISHERS HILL
22627-22627	FLINT HILL
22630-22630	FRONT ROYAL
22637-22637	GORE
22638-22638	WINCHESTER
22639-22639	HUME
22640-22640	HUNTLY
22641-22641	STRASBURG
22642-22642	LINDEN
22643-22643	MARKHAM
22644-22644	MAURERTOWN
22645-22645	MIDDLETOWN
22646-22646	MILLWOOD
22649-22649	MIDDLETOWN
22650-22650	RILEYVILLE

22651-22651	FRONT ROYAL
22652-22652	FORT VALLEY
22654-22654	STAR TANNERY
22655-22655	STEPHENS CITY
22656-22656	STEPHENSON
22657-22657	STRASBURG
22660-22660	TOMS BROOK
22663-22663	WHITE POST
22664-22664	WOODSTOCK
22701-22701	CULPEPER
22709-22709	ARODA
22711-22711	BANCO
22712-22712	BEALETON
22713-22713	BOSTON
22714-22714	BRANDY STATION
22715-22715	BRIGHTWOOD
22716-22716	CASTLETON
22718-22718	ELKWOOD
22719-22719	ETLAN
22720-22720	GOLDVEIN
22721-22721	GRAVES MILL
22722-22722	HAYWOOD
22723-22723	HOOD
22724-22724	JEFFERSONTON
22725-22725	LEON
22726-22726	LIGNUM
22727-22727	MADISON
22728-22728	MIDLAND
22729-22729	MITCHELLS
22730-22730	OAKPARK
22731-22731	PRATTS
22732-22732	RADIANT
22733-22733	RAPIDAN
22734-22734	REMINGTON
22735-22735	REVA
22736-22736	RICHARDSVILLE
22737-22737	RIXEYVILLE
22738-22738	ROCHELLE
22739-22739	SOMERVILLE
22740-22740	SPERRYVILLE
22741-22741	STEVENSBURG
22742-22742	SUMERDUCK
22743-22743	SYRIA
22746-22746	VIEWTOWN
22747-22747	WASHINGTON
22748-22748	WOLFTOWN
22749-22749	WOODVILLE
22801-22807	HARRISONBURG
22810-22810	BASYE
22811-22811	BERGTON
22812-22812	BRIDGEWATER
22815-22815	BROADWAY
22820-22820	CRIDERS
22821-22821	DAYTON
22824-22824	EDINBURG
22827-22827	ELKTON
22830-22830	FULKS RUN
22831-22831	HINTON
22832-22832	KEEZLETOWN
22833-22833	LACEY SPRING
22834-22834	LINVILLE
22835-22835	LURAY
22840-22840	MC GAHEYSVILLE
22841-22841	MOUNT CRAWFORD
22842-22842	MOUNT JACKSON
22843-22843	MOUNT SOLON
22844-22844	NEW MARKET
22845-22845	ORKNEY SPRINGS
22846-22846	PENN LAIRD
22847-22847	QUICKSBURG
22848-22848	PLEASANT VALLEY
22849-22849	SHENANDOAH
22850-22850	SINGERS GLEN
22851-22851	STANLEY
22853-22853	TIMBERVILLE
22900-22911	CHARLOTTESVILLE
22920-22920	AFTON
22922-22922	ARRINGTON
22923-22923	BARBOURSVILLE
22924-22924	BATESVILLE
22929-22929	COBHAM
22931-22931	COVESVILLE

22932-22932	CROZET
22935-22935	DYKE
22936-22936	EARLYSVILLE
22937-22937	ESMONT
22938-22938	FABER
22939-22939	FISHERSVILLE
22940-22940	FREE UNION
22942-22942	GORDONSVILLE
22943-22943	GREENWOOD
22945-22945	IVY
22946-22946	KEENE
22947-22947	KESWICK
22948-22948	LOCUST DALE
22949-22949	LOVINGSTON
22951-22951	ROSELAND
22952-22952	LYNDHURST
22953-22953	MADISON MILLS
22954-22954	MASSIES MILL
22957-22957	MONTPELIER STATION
22958-22958	NELLYSFORD
22959-22959	NORTH GARDEN
22960-22960	ORANGE
22963-22963	PALMYRA
22964-22964	PINEY RIVER
22965-22965	QUINQUE
22967-22967	ROSELAND
22968-22968	RUCKERSVILLE
22969-22969	SCHUYLER
22971-22971	SHIPMAN
22972-22972	SOMERSET
22973-22973	STANARDSVILLE
22974-22974	TROY
22976-22976	TYRO
22980-22980	WAYNESBORO
22987-22987	WHITE HALL
22989-22989	WOODBERRY FOREST
23001-23001	ACHILLES
23002-23002	AMELIA COURT HOUSE
23003-23003	ARK
23004-23004	ARVONIA
23005-23005	ASHLAND
23009-23009	AYLETT
23011-23011	BARHAMSVILLE
23013-23013	BAVON
23014-23014	BEAUMONT
23015-23015	BEAVERDAM
23016-23016	BEAVERLETT
23017-23017	BELLAMY
23018-23018	BENA
23020-23020	BLAKES
23021-23021	BOHANNON
23022-23022	BREMO BLUFF
23023-23023	BRUINGTON
23024-23024	BUMPASS
23025-23025	CARDINAL
23027-23027	CARTERSVILLE
23029-23029	CAUTHORNVILLE
23030-23030	CHARLES CITY
23031-23031	CHRISTCHURCH
23032-23032	CHURCH VIEW
23035-23035	COBBS CREEK
23037-23037	COLOGNE
23038-23038	COLUMBIA
23039-23039	CROZIER
23040-23040	CUMBERLAND
23042-23042	DABNEYS
23043-23043	DELTAVILLE
23045-23045	DIGGS
23047-23047	DOSWELL
23050-23050	DUTTON
23054-23054	FIFE
23055-23055	FORK UNION
23056-23056	FOSTER
23058-23060	GLEN ALLEN
23061-23061	GLOUCESTER
23062-23062	GLOUCESTER POINT
23063-23063	GOOCHLAND
23064-23064	GRIMSTEAD
23065-23065	GUM SPRING
23066-23066	GWYNN
23067-23067	HADENSVILLE
23068-23068	HALLIEFORD

23069-23069	HANOVER
23070-23070	HARDYVILLE
23071-23071	HARTFIELD
23072-23072	HAYES
23075-23075	HIGHLAND SPRINGS
23076-23076	HUDGINS
23079-23079	JAMAICA
23080-23080	JAMES STORE
23081-23081	JAMESTOWN
23083-23083	JETERSVILLE
23084-23084	KENTS STORE
23085-23085	KING AND QUEEN COURT HOUS
23086-23086	KING WILLIAM
23089-23089	LANEXA
23090-23090	LIGHTFOOT
23091-23091	LITTLE PLYMOUTH
23092-23092	LOCUST HILL
23093-23093	LOUISA
23101-23101	MACON
23102-23102	MAIDENS
23103-23103	MANAKIN SABOT
23104-23104	MANGOHICK
23105-23105	MANNBORO
23106-23106	MANQUIN
23107-23107	MARYUS
23108-23108	MASCOT
23109-23109	MATHEWS
23110-23110	MATTAPONI
23111-23111	MECHANICSVILLE
23112-23113	MIDLOTHIAN
23114-23114	MILES
23114-23114	MIDLOTHIAN
23115-23115	MILLERS TAVERN
23116-23116	MECHANICSVILLE
23117-23117	MINERAL
23118-23118	MOBJACK
23119-23119	MOON
23120-23120	MOSELEY
23122-23122	NAXERA
23123-23123	NEW CANTON
23124-23124	NEW KENT
23125-23125	NEW POINT
23126-23126	NEWTOWN
23127-23127	NORGE
23128-23128	NORTH
23129-23129	OILVILLE
23130-23130	ONEMO
23131-23131	ORDINARY
23137-23137	PLAIN VIEW
23138-23138	PORT HAYWOOD
23139-23139	POWHATAN
23140-23140	PROVIDENCE FORGE
23141-23141	QUINTON
23142-23142	REDART
23146-23146	ROCKVILLE
23147-23147	RUTHVILLE
23148-23148	SAINT STEPHENS CHURCH
23149-23149	SALUDA
23150-23150	SANDSTON
23153-23153	SANDY HOOK
23154-23154	SCHLEY
23155-23155	SEVERN
23156-23156	SHACKLEFORDS
23157-23157	SHADOW
23160-23160	STATE FARM
23161-23161	STEVENSVILLE
23162-23162	STUDLEY
23163-23163	SUSAN
23168-23168	TOANO
23169-23169	TOPPING
23170-23170	TREVILIANS
23173-23173	UNIVERSITY OF RICHMOND
23175-23175	URBANNA
23176-23176	WAKE
23177-23177	WALKERTON
23178-23178	WARE NECK
23179-23179	WARNER
23180-23180	WATER VIEW
23181-23181	WEST POINT
23183-23183	WHITE MARSH
23184-23184	WICOMICO

23185-23188 WILLIAMSBURG	23630-23630 NEWPORT NEWS	23935-23935 DARLINGTN HTS	24133-24133 PATRICK SPRINGS
23190-23190 WOODS CROSS ROADS	23630-23631 HAMPTON	23935-23935 DARLINGTON HEIGHTS	24134-24134 PEARISBURG
23191-23191 ZANONI	23632-23632 GREAT AMERICAN	23936-23936 DILLWYN	24136-24136 PEMBROKE
23192-23192 MONTPELIER	MAGAZINE	23937-23937 DRAKES BRANCH	24137-24137 PENHOOK
23200-23298 RICHMOND	23651-23651 FORT MONROE	23938-23938 DUNDAS	24138-24138 PILOT
23301-23301 ACCOMAC	23653-23661 HAMPTON	23939-23939 EVERGREEN	24139-24139 PITTSVILLE
23302-23302 ASSAWOMAN	23662-23662 POQUOSON	23941-23941 FORT MITCHELL	24141-24143 RADFORD
23303-23303 ATLANTIC	23663-23681 HAMPTON	23942-23942 GREEN BAY	24146-24146 REDWOOD
23304-23304 BATTERY PARK	23690-23693 YORKTOWN	23943-23943 HAMPDEN SYDNEY	24147-24147 RICH CREEK
23306-23306 BELLE HAVEN	23694-23694 LACKEY	23944-23944 KENBRIDGE	24148-24148 RIDGEWAY
23307-23307 BIRDSNEST	23696-23696 SEAFORD	23947-23947 KEYSVILLE	24149-24149 RINER
23308-23308 BLOXOM	23700-23709 PORTSMOUTH	23950-23950 LA CROSSE	24150-24150 RIPPLEMEAD
23310-23310 CAPE CHARLES	23801-23801 FORT LEE	23952-23952 LUNENBURG	24151-24151 ROCKY MOUNT
23313-23313 CAPEVILLE	23803-23806 PETERSBURG	23954-23954 MEHERRIN	24153-24157 SALEM
23314-23314 CARROLLTON	23821-23821 ALBERTA	23955-23955 NOTTOWAY	24161-24161 SANDY LEVEL
23315-23315 CARRSVILLE	23822-23822 AMMON	23958-23958 PAMPLIN	24162-24162 SHAWSVILLE
23316-23316 CHERITON	23824-23824 BLACKSTONE	23959-23959 PHENIX	24165-24165 SPENCER
23320-23328 CHESAPEAKE	23827-23827 BOYKINS	23960-23960 PROSPECT	24167-24167 STAFFORDSVILLE
23336-23336 CHINCOTEAGUE	23828-23828 BRANCHVILLE	23962-23962 RANDOLPH	24168-24168 STANLEYTOWN
23336-23336 CHINCOTEAGUE ISLAND	23829-23829 CAPRON	23963-23963 RED HOUSE	24171-24171 STUART
23337-23337 CHINCOTEAGUE	23830-23830 CARSON	23964-23964 RED OAK	24174-24174 THAXTON
23337-23337 WALLOPS ISLAND	23831-23831 CHESTER	23966-23966 RICE	24175-24175 TROUTVILLE
23341-23341 CRADDOCKVILLE	23832-23832 CHESTERFIELD	23967-23967 SAXE	24176-24176 UNION HALL
23345-23345 DAVIS WHARF	23833-23833 CHURCH ROAD	23968-23968 SKIPWITH	24177-24177 VESTA
23347-23347 EASTVILLE	23834-23834 COLONIAL HEIGHTS	23970-23970 SOUTH HILL	24178-24178 VILLAMONT
23350-23350 EXMORE	23836-23836 CHESTER	23974-23974 VICTORIA	24179-24179 VINTON
23354-23354 FRANKTOWN	23837-23837 COURTLAND	23976-23976 WYLLIESBURG	24184-24184 WIRTZ
23356-23356 GREENBACKVILLE	23838-23838 CHESTERFIELD	24000-24040 ROANOKE	24185-24185 WOOLWINE
23357-23357 GREENBUSH	23839-23839 DENDRON	24041-24041 BANK AMERICARD	24201-24209 BRISTOL
23358-23358 HACKSNECK	23840-23840 DEWITT	24042-24045 ROANOKE	24210-24212 ABINGDON
23359-23359 HALLWOOD	23841-23841 DINWIDDIE	24046-24046 CITY OFFICES	24215-24215 ANDOVER
23389-23389 HARBORTON	23842-23842 DISPUTANTA	24048-24050 ROANOKE	24216-24216 APPALACHIA
23395-23395 HORNTOWN	23843-23843 DOLPHIN	24053-24053 ARARAT	24217-24217 BEE
23396-23396 OAK HALL	23844-23844 DREWRYVILLE	24054-24054 AXTON	24218-24218 BEN HUR
23397-23397 ISLE OF WIGHT	23845-23845 EBONY	24055-24055 BASSETT	24219-24219 BIG STONE GAP
23398-23398 JAMESVILLE	23846-23846 ELBERON	24058-24058 BELSPRING	24220-24220 BIRCHLEAF
23399-23399 JENKINS BRIDGE	23847-23847 EMPORIA	24059-24059 BENT MOUNTAIN	24221-24221 BLACKWATER
23401-23401 KELLER	23850-23850 FORD	24060-24063 BLACKSBURG	24224-24224 CASTLEWOOD
23403-23403 LEE MONT	23851-23851 FRANKLIN	24064-24064 BLUE RIDGE	24225-24225 CLEVELAND
23404-23404 LOCUSTVILLE	23856-23856 FREEMAN	24065-24065 BOONES MILL	24226-24226 CLINCHCO
23405-23405 MACHIPONGO	23857-23857 GASBURG	24066-24066 BUCHANAN	24228-24228 CLINTWOOD
23407-23407 MAPPSVILLE	23859-23859 HANDSOM	24067-24067 CALLAWAY	24230-24230 COEBURN
23408-23408 MARIONVILLE	23860-23860 HOPEWELL	24068-24068 CHRISTIANSBURG	24236-24236 DAMASCUS
23409-23409 MEARS	23866-23866 IVOR	24069-24069 CASCADE	24237-24237 DANTE
23410-23410 MELFA	23867-23867 JARRATT	24070-24070 CATAWBA	24239-24239 DAVENPORT
23412-23412 MODEST TOWN	23868-23868 LAWRENCEVILLE	24072-24072 CHECK	24243-24243 DRYDEN
23413-23413 NASSAWADOX	23870-23870 JARRATT	24073-24073 CHRISTIANSBURG	24244-24244 DUFFIELD
23414-23414 NELSONIA	23872-23872 MC KENNEY	24076-24076 CLAUDVILLE	24245-24245 DUNGANNON
23415-23415 NEW CHURCH	23873-23873 MEREDITHVILLE	24077-24077 CLOVERDALE	24246-24246 EAST STONE GAP
23416-23416 OAK HALL	23874-23874 NEWSOMS	24078-24078 COLLINSVILLE	24248-24248 EWING
23417-23417 ONANCOCK	23875-23875 PRINCE GEORGE	24079-24079 COPPER HILL	24249-24249 EXETER
23418-23418 ONLEY	23876-23876 RAWLINGS	24082-24082 CRITZ	24250-24250 FORT BLACKMORE
23419-23419 OYSTER	23878-23878 SEDLEY	24083-24083 DALEVILLE	24251-24251 GATE CITY
23420-23420 PAINTER	23879-23879 SKIPPERS	24084-24084 DUBLIN	24256-24256 HAYSI
23421-23421 PARKSLEY	23881-23881 SPRING GROVE	24085-24085 EAGLE ROCK	24258-24258 HILTONS
23422-23422 PUNGOTEAGUE	23882-23882 STONY CREEK	24086-24086 EGGLESTON	24260-24260 HONAKER
23423-23423 QUINBY	23883-23883 SURRY	24087-24087 ELLISTON	24263-24263 JONESVILLE
23424-23424 RESCUE	23884-23884 SUSSEX	24088-24088 FERRUM	24265-24265 KEOKEE
23426-23426 SANFORD	23885-23885 SUTHERLAND	24089-24089 FIELDALE	24266-24266 LEBANON
23427-23427 SAXIS	23887-23887 VALENTINES	24090-24090 FINCASTLE	24269-24269 MC CLURE
23429-23429 SEAVIEW	23888-23888 WAKEFIELD	24091-24091 FLOYD	24270-24270 MENDOTA
23430-23431 SMITHFIELD	23889-23889 WARFIELD	24092-24092 GLADEHILL	24271-24271 NICKELSVILLE
23432-23439 SUFFOLK	23890-23891 WAVERLY	24093-24093 GLEN LYN	24272-24272 NORA
23440-23440 TANGIER	23893-23893 WHITE PLAINS	24094-24094 GOLDBOND	24273-24273 NORTON
23441-23441 TASLEY	23894-23894 WILSONS	24095-24095 GOODVIEW	24277-24277 PENNINGTON GAP
23442-23442 TEMPERANCEVILLE	23897-23897 YALE	24101-24101 HARDY	24279-24279 POUND
23443-23443 TOWNSEND	23898-23898 ZUNI	24102-24102 HENRY	24280-24280 ROSEDALE
23450-23479 VIRGINIA BEACH	23899-23899 CLAREMONT	24104-24104 HUDDLESTON	24281-24281 ROSE HILL
23480-23480 WACHAPREAGUE	23901-23909 FARMVILLE	24105-24105 INDIAN VALLEY	24282-24282 SAINT CHARLES
23481-23481 CARRSVILLE	23911-23911 ANDERSONVILLE	24111-24111 MC COY	24283-24283 SAINT PAUL
23482-23482 WARDTOWN	23915-23915 BASKERVILLE	24112-24115 MARTINSVILLE	24285-24285 STONEGA
23483-23483 WATTSVILLE	23917-23917 BOYDTON	24120-24120 MEADOWS OF DAN	24289-24289 TRAMMEL
23484-23484 WEIRWOOD	23919-23919 BRACEY	24121-24121 MONETA	24290-24290 WEBER CITY
23486-23486 WILLIS WHARF	23920-23920 BRODNAX	24122-24122 MONTVALE	24292-24292 WHITETOP
23487-23487 WINDSOR	23921-23921 BUCKINGHAM	24124-24124 NARROWS	24293-24293 WISE
23488-23488 WITHAMS	23922-23922 BURKEVILLE	24126-24126 NEWBERN	24301-24301 PULASKI
23500-23551 NORFOLK	23923-23923 CHARLOTTE COURT	24127-24127 NEW CASTLE	24311-24311 ATKINS
23600-23603 NEWPORT NEWS	HOUSE	24128-24128 NEWPORT	24312-24312 AUSTINVILLE
23604-23604 FORT EUSTIS	23924-23924 CHASE CITY	24129-24129 NEW RIVER	24313-24313 BARREN SPRINGS
23605-23628 NEWPORT NEWS	23927-23927 CLARKSVILLE	24130-24130 ORISKANY	24314-24314 BASTIAN
23629-23629 GREAT AMERICAN	23930-23930 CREWE	24131-24131 PAINT BANK	24315-24315 BLAND
MAGAZINE	23934-23934 CULLEN	24132-24132 PARROTT	24316-24316 BROADFORD

24317-24317	CANA	24426-24426	COVINGTON	24522-24522	APPOMATTOX	24593-24593	SPOUT SPRING
24318-24318	CERES	24430-24430	CRAIGSVILLE	24523-24523	BEDFORD	24594-24594	SUTHERLIN
24319-24319	CHILHOWIE	24431-24431	CRIMORA	24526-24526	BIG ISLAND	24595-24595	SWEET BRIAR
24321-24321	CLINCHBURG	24432-24432	DEERFIELD	24527-24527	BLAIRS	24596-24596	TURBEVILLE
24322-24322	CRIPPLE CREEK	24433-24433	DOE HILL	24528-24528	BROOKNEAL	24597-24597	VERNON HILL
24323-24323	CROCKETT	24435-24435	FAIRFIELD	24529-24529	BUFFALO JUNCTION	24598-24598	VIRGILINA
24324-24324	DRAPER	24437-24437	FORT DEFIANCE	24530-24530	CALLANDS	24599-24599	WINGINA
24325-24325	DUGSPUR	24438-24438	GLEN WILTON	24531-24531	CHATHAM	24601-24601	AMONATE
24326-24326	ELK CREEK	24439-24439	GOSHEN	24533-24533	CLIFFORD	24602-24602	BANDY
24327-24327	EMORY	24440-24440	GREENVILLE	24534-24534	CLOVER	24603-24603	BIG ROCK
24328-24328	FANCY GAP	24441-24441	GROTTOES	24535-24535	CLUSTER SPRINGS	24604-24604	BISHOP
24330-24330	FRIES	24442-24442	HEAD WATERS	24536-24536	COLEMAN FALLS	24605-24605	BLUEFIELD
24333-24333	GALAX	24444-24444	HIGHTOWN	24538-24538	CONCORD	24606-24606	BOISSEVAIN
24340-24340	GLADE SPRING	24445-24445	HOT SPRINGS	24539-24539	CRYSTAL HILL	24607-24607	BREAKS
24343-24343	HILLSVILLE	24448-24448	IRON GATE	24540-24544	DANVILLE	24608-24608	BURKES GARDEN
24347-24347	HIWASSEE	24449-24449	JORDAN MINES	24549-24549	DRY FORK	24609-24609	CEDAR BLUFF
24348-24348	INDEPENDENCE	24450-24450	LEXINGTON	24550-24550	EVINGTON	24612-24612	DORAN
24350-24350	IVANHOE	24457-24457	LOW MOOR	24551-24551	FOREST	24613-24613	FALLS MILLS
24351-24351	LAMBSBURG	24458-24458	MC DOWELL	24553-24553	GLADSTONE	24614-24614	GRUNDY
24352-24352	LAUREL FORK	24459-24459	MIDDLEBROOK	24554-24554	GLADYS	24618-24618	HARMAN
24354-24354	MARION	24460-24460	MILLBORO	24555-24555	GLASGOW	24619-24619	HORSEPEN
24360-24360	MAX MEADOWS	24463-24463	MINT SPRING	24556-24556	GOODE	24620-24620	HURLEY
24361-24361	MEADOWVIEW	24464-24464	MONTEBELLO	24557-24557	GRETNA	24622-24622	JEWELL RIDGE
24363-24363	MOUTH OF WILSON	24465-24465	MONTEREY	24558-24558	HALIFAX	24624-24624	KEEN MOUNTAIN
24366-24366	ROCKY GAP	24467-24467	MOUNT SIDNEY	24562-24562	HOWARDSVILLE	24627-24627	MAVISDALE
24368-24368	RURAL RETREAT	24468-24468	MUSTOE	24563-24563	HURT	24628-24628	MAXIE
24370-24370	SALTVILLE	24469-24469	NEW HOPE	24565-24565	JAVA	24630-24630	NORTH TAZEWELL
24373-24373	SEVEN MILE FORD	24471-24471	PORT REPUBLIC	24566-24566	KEELING	24631-24631	OAKWOOD
24374-24374	SPEEDWELL	24472-24472	RAPHINE	24569-24569	LONG ISLAND	24634-24634	PILGRIMS KNOB
24375-24375	SUGAR GROVE	24473-24473	ROCKBRIDGE BATHS	24570-24570	LOWRY	24635-24635	POCAHONTAS
24377-24377	TANNERSVILLE	24474-24474	SELMA	24571-24571	LYNCH STATION	24637-24637	POUNDING MILL
24378-24378	TROUT DALE	24475-24475	SPOTTSWOOD	24572-24572	MADISON HEIGHTS	24639-24639	RAVEN
24378-24378	TROUTDALE	24476-24476	STEELES TAVERN	24574-24574	MONROE	24640-24640	RED ASH
24379-24379	VOLNEY	24477-24477	STUARTS DRAFT	24576-24576	NARUNA	24641-24641	RICHLANDS
24380-24380	WILLIS	24479-24479	SWOOPE	24577-24577	NATHALIE	24646-24646	ROWE
24381-24381	WOODLAWN	24482-24482	VERONA	24578-24578	NATURAL BRIDGE	24647-24647	SHORTT GAP
24382-24382	WYTHEVILLE	24483-24483	VESUVIUS	24579-24579	NATURAL BRIDGE STATION	24649-24649	SWORDS CREEK
24401-24407	STAUNTON	24484-24484	WARM SPRINGS	24580-24580	NELSON	24651-24651	TAZEWELL
24411-24411	AUGUSTA SPRINGS	24485-24485	WEST AUGUSTA	24581-24581	NORWOOD	24656-24656	VANSANT
24412-24412	BACOVA	24486-24486	WEYERS CAVE	24585-24585	REPUBLICAN GROVE	24657-24657	WHITEWOOD
24413-24413	BLUE GRASS	24487-24487	WILLIAMSVILLE	24586-24586	RINGGOLD	24658-24658	WOLFORD
24415-24415	BROWNSBURG	24501-24515	LYNCHBURG	24588-24588	RUSTBURG	24659-24659	YARDS
24416-24416	BUENA VISTA	24517-24517	ALTAVISTA	24589-24589	SCOTTSBURG		
24421-24421	CHURCHVILLE	24520-24520	ALTON	24590-24590	SCOTTSVILLE		
24422-24422	CLIFTON FORGE	24521-24521	AMHERST	24592-24592	SOUTH BOSTON		

Virgin Islands County Locator

City/County Cross Reference

CHRISTIANSTED St. Croix
FREDERIKSTED St. Croix
KINGSHILL St. Croix
SAINT JOHN St. John
SAINT THOMAS St. Thomas

ZIP/City Cross Reference

00801-00805   SAINT THOMAS
00820-00824   CHRISTIANSTED
00830-00831   SAINT JOHN
00840-00841   FREDERIKSTED
00850-00851   KINGSHILL

Washington

General Help Numbers:

Governor's Office
PO Box 40002
Olympia, WA 98504-0002
www.governor.wa.gov

360-902-4111
Fax 360-753-4110
8AM-5PM

Attorney General's Office
PO Box 40100
Olympia, WA 98504-0100
www.wa.gov/ago

360-753-6200
Fax 360-586-7671
8AM-5PM

State Court Administrator
Temple of Justice
PO Box 41174
Olympia, WA 98504-1174
www.courts.wa.gov

360-357-2121
Fax 360-357-2127
8AM-5PM

State Archives
State Archives
PO Box 40238
Olympia, WA 98504-0238
www.secstate.wa.gov/archives

360-753-5485
Fax 360-664-8814
8:30AM-4:30PM

State Specifics:

Capital:	Olympia
	Thurston County
Time Zone:	PST
Number of Counties:	39
Population:	5,987,973
Web Site:	http://access.wa.gov

State Agencies

Criminal Records

Washington State Patrol, Identification Section, PO Box 42633, Olympia, WA 98504-2633 (Courier: 3000 Pacific Ave. SE #204, Olympia, WA 98501); 360-705-5100, 360-570-5275 (Fax), 8AM-5PM.

www.wa.gov/wsp/wsphome.htm

Note: Currently, sex offender registry information is available at a number of county web sites, though the state plans to have statewide data available in the future at the web site.

Indexing & Storage: Records are available from 1974. Criminal history information is retained at the Identification Section until the offender is age

seventy, or ten years from the last date of arrest, whichever is longer. It takes 30 to 45 days before new records are available for inquiry. Records are indexed on inhouse computer. 79% of all arrests in database have final dispositions recorded, 70% for those arrests within last 5 years.

Searching: Mail requests are directed to the WSP or e-mail to crimhis@wsp.gov. Include the following in your request: date of birth, Social Security Number, sex, race, name and address of subject. Fingerprints are optional. Records are 100% fingerprint-supported. Records without dispositions are not released, unless the arrest is less than 1 year old.

Access by: mail, in person, online.

Fee & Payment: The fee for a name check is $10.00 per individual. For a fingerprint check, the fee is $25.00 per individual. Will not conduct FBI fingerprint checks. Fee payee: Washington State Patrol. Money orders or cashier's checks preferred.

Mail search: Turnaround time: 2 to 3 weeks. No self addressed stamped envelope is required.

In person search: Searching is available in person.

Online search: WSP offers access through a system called WATCH, which can be accessed from their web site. The fee per search is $10.00. The DOB and name are required. Credit cards are accepted online. To set up a WATCH account, call

(360) 705-5100 or e-mail to watch.help@ swp.wa.gov.

Other access: The State Court Administrator's office maintains a criminal records database in JIS-Link. Records do not include arrests unless case is filed. There is a $100.00 set-up fee and a $25.00 per hour access charge. Call 360-357-2407 or visit www.courts.wa.gov for a packet.

Corporation Records
Trademarks/Servicemarks
Limited Partnerships
Limited Liability Company
Records

Secretary of State, Corporations Division, PO Box 40234, Olympia, WA 98504-0234 (Courier: Dolliver Bldg, 801 Capitol Way South, Olympia, WA 98501); 360-753-7115, 360-664-8781 (Fax), 8AM-5PM.

www.secstate.wa.gov/corps

Indexing & Storage: Records are available for initial filing documents. Annual reports for the past 5 years are on microfilm.

Searching: All of the information here is public record. Include the following in your request: full name of business, UBI number if available. The copies for a limited partnership are different than corporation documents. Any single document is $1.00 per page plus $.20 per copy.

Access by: mail, phone, in person, online.

Fee & Payment: Directors, Officers list is $5.00 per corporate name. Photocopies fee is $10.00 per document, $20.00 if the document needs to be certified. If file exceeds 100 pages, a surcharge of $13.00 per 50 pages is added. Trademark documents are $.50 per page. Fee payee: Secretary of State. Prepayment required. Personal checks accepted. No credit cards accepted.

Mail search: Turnaround time: variable.

Phone search: Information requests are available at this department for limited information.

In person search: Turnaround time is while you wait.

Online search: Free searching of corporation registrations is at www.secstate.wa.gov/corps/search.aspx. Information is updated weekly.

Expedited service: Expedited service is available for mail and phone searches. Turnaround time: 48 hours. Add $20.00 per document.

Trade Names

Master License Service, Business & Professions Div, PO Box 9034, Olympia, WA 98507-9034 (Courier: 405 Black Lake Blvd, Olympia, WA 98507); 360-664-1400, 900-463-6000 (Trade Name Search), 360-570-7875 (Fax), 8AM-5PM.

www.wa.gov/dol

Indexing & Storage: Records are available from 1984 (note that everyone re-registered trade names in 1984).

Searching: Searching may be done by business name, business address, owner's name, or UBI number. The following data is not released: Social Security Numbers, personal information (height, weight, sex, eye color, etc.), date of birth or addresses.

Access by: mail, phone, in person, online.

Fee & Payment: The search fee is $4.00, which includes 3 business/owner names. A name variation is considered a separate name. Certification costs an additional $2.00. Fee payee: Washington State Treasurer. Prepayment required. Personal checks accepted. No credit cards accepted.

Mail search: Response time is generally one week. No self addressed stamped envelope is required.

Phone search: The 900 number fee is $4.95 for the first minute and $.50 for each additional minute. Average search is 2 minutes.

In person search: Copies cost $.25 per page. Turnaround time is while you wait.

Online search:

Other access: Records can be purchased on cartridges or 9 track tapes. Information includes date of registration, owner name, state ID numbers, and cancel date if cancelled. Call same number and ask for Jody Miller.

Expedited service: Expedited service is available for fax searches. Must have an account with a deposit.

Uniform Commercial Code
Federal Tax Liens

Department of Licensing, UCC Records, PO Box 9660, Olympia, WA 98507-9660 (Courier: 405 Black Lake Blvd, Olympia, WA 98502); 360-664-1530, 360-586-4414 (Fax), 8AM-5PM.

wwws2.wa.gov/dol/ucc/

Indexing & Storage: Records are available from 1967. Records are computerized since 1985. However, only currently active plus 1 full year are accessible.

Searching: Use search request form UCC-11. The search includes all notices of federal tax liens. State tax liens are filed at the county level. Include the following in your request: debtor name.

Access by: mail, online.

Fee & Payment: A mail or inperson request for information is $18.80. A request for information withall copies is $26.57. Fee payee: Department of Licensing. Prepayment required. Credit cards are accepted for online searching only. Personal checks accepted. Credit cards accepted: MasterCard, Visa.

Mail search: Turnaround time: 2 days. No self addressed stamped envelope is required.

Online search: For online access, go to https://wws2.wa.gov/dol/ucc/. There is a $15.00 search fee.

Other access: The database may be purchased on magnetic tape or microfilm.

State Tax Liens

Records not maintained by a state
level agency.

Note: State tax liens are filed at the county level.

Sales Tax Registrations

Department fo Revenue, Taxpayer Services, PO Box 47498, Olympia, WA 98504-7478 (Courier: 415 Gen Admin Bldg, Olympia, WA 98501); 360-486-2345, 800-647-7706, 360-486-2159 (Fax), 8AM-5PM.

www.dor.wa.gov

Indexing & Storage: Records are available from 1992 and are indexed on microfiche and optical imaging.

Searching: This agency will provide disclosable information authorized by statute such as business name, owner name, address, opening date, DBA, owner type, account status, and SIC code. For confidential information, submit a signed release. Include the following in your request: business name or owner name. They will also search by tax registration or UBI number.

Access by: mail, phone, fax, online.

Mail search: Turnaround time: 5 business days. A self addressed stamped envelope is requested. No fee for mail request.

Phone search: No fee for telephone request. Only "public registration" information is available.

Fax search: Turnaround time is 5 business days.

Online search: The agency provides a state business records database with free access on the Internet. Lookups are by owner names, DBAs, and tax reporting numbers. Results show a myriad of data.

Birth Certificates

Department of Health, Center for Health Statistics, PO Box 9709, Olympia, WA 98507-9709 (Courier: 1112 S Quince St, 1st Fl, Olympia, WA 98501); 360-236-4300 (Main Number), 360-236-4313 (Credit Card Ordering), 360-352-2586 (Fax), 8AM - 4:30PM.

www.doh.wa.gov

Indexing & Storage: Records are available from July 1, 1907 to present. It takes 2-3 months before new records are available for inquiry. Records are indexed on microfiche, inhouse computer.

Searching: The data on the lower portion of form is confidential. Include the following in your request: full name, names of parents, mother's maiden name, date of birth, place of birth. Please specify if father is not listed on birth certificate.

Access by: mail, phone, fax, in person.

Fee & Payment: The search fee is $13.00 per record. Fee payee: Dept of Health. Prepayment required. Personal checks accepted.

Mail search: Turnaround time: 7 to 8 weeks. Must send your current address and daytime phone number with request. A self addressed stamped envelope is requested.

Phone search: You must use a credit card for a $11.00 additional fee. Phone ordering is from 9-12 and 1-4, M-F. next day processing and mail-out.

Fax search: Same criteria as phone searching. Certificate can be returned by fax for an additional $5.00 (non-certified).

In person search: There is no counter service, but there is a drop box. Requests are returned by mail.

Expedited service: Expedited service is available for phone searches. Turnaround time: next working day mail. You must use a credit card for an additional $11.00 fee and courier or Express Mail are additional costs.

Death Records

Department of Health, Vital Records, PO Box 9709, Olympia, WA 98507-9709 (Courier: 1112 S Quince St, 1st Fl, Olympia, WA 98501); 360-236-4300 (Main Number), 360-236-4313 (Credit Card Ordering), 360-352-2586 (Fax), 8 AM - 4:30 PM.

www.doh.wa.gov

Indexing & Storage: Records are available from July 1, 1907 to present. It takes 2-6 months before new records are available for inquiry. Records are indexed on microfiche, inhouse computer.

Searching: A written request is required, there is no public viewing. Include the following in your request: full name, date of death, place of death.

Access by: mail, phone, fax, in person.

Fee & Payment: The fee for a certified record in $13.00. Fee payee: Dept of Health. Prepayment required. Personal checks accepted.

Mail search: Turnaround time: 7 to 8 weeks. Must send your current address and daytime phone number with request. A self addressed stamped envelope is requested.

Phone search: You must use a credit card for an additional $11.00 fee. Records are processed the next day. Credit card orders are taken between 9-12 and 1-4.

Fax search: Same criteria as phone searching. Non-certified copies can be returned by fax for $5.00 per page.

In person search: There is no counter service, they have a drop box. Requests are returned by mail.

Expedited service: Expedited service is available for phone and in person searches. Turnaround time: overnight delivery. You must use a credit card for an additional $11.00 fee and courier or Express Mail are additional costs.

Marriage Certificates

Department of Health, Vital Records, PO Box 9709, Olympia, WA 98507-9709 (Courier: 1112 S Quince St, 1st Fl, Olympia, WA 98501); 360-236-4300 (Main Number), 360-236-4313 (Credit Card Ordering), 360-352-2586 (Fax), 8 AM - 4:30 PM.

www.doh.wa.gov

Indexing & Storage: Records are available from 1968 to present. It takes 2-4 months before new records are available for inquiry. Records are indexed on microfiche, inhouse computer.

Searching: Written request is required, there is no public viewing. Include the following in your request: names of husband and wife, date of marriage, place or county of marriage.

Access by: mail, phone, fax, in person.

Fee & Payment: The search fee is $13.00. Fee payee: Dept of Health. Prepayment required. Personal checks accepted.

Mail search: Turnaround time: 7 to 8 weeks. Must send your current address and daytime phone number with request. A self addressed stamped envelope is requested.

Phone search: You must use a credit card for an additional $11.00 fee. Turnaround time is next day. Credit card ordering is between 9-12 and 1-4.

Fax search: Same criteria as phone searching. Non-certified records can be returned by fax for an additional $5.00 per record.

In person search: There is no counter service, a drop box is available. Requests are returned by mail.

Expedited service: Expedited service is available for phone and in person searches. Turnaround time: overnight delivery. You must use a credit card for an additional $11.00 fee and courier or Express Mail are additional costs.

Divorce Records

Department of Health, Vital Records, PO Box 9709, Olympia, WA 98507-9709 (Courier: 1112 S Quince St, 1st Fl, Olympia, WA 98501); 360-753-4300 (Main Number), 360-753-4313 (Credit Card Ordering), 360-352-2586 (Fax), 8AM - 4:30PM.

www.doh.wa.gov

Indexing & Storage: Records are available from 1968 to present. It takes 2-4 months before new records are available for inquiry. Records are indexed on microfiche, inhouse computer.

Searching: Include the following in your request: names of husband and wife, date of divorce, place of divorce.

Access by: mail, phone, fax, in person.

Fee & Payment: The search fee is $13.00. Fee payee: Dept of Health. Prepayment required. Personal checks accepted.

Mail search: Turnaround time: 5 weeks. Must send your current address and daytime phone number with request. A self addressed stamped envelope is requested.

Phone search: Phone requesters are required to use a credit card for an additional $11.00 fee. The request is processed the next day. Credit card ordering between 9-12 and 1-4.

Fax search: Same criteria as phone searching. Non-certified documents can be returned for an additional $5.00 per record.

In person search: There is no counter service, a drop box is used. All requests are returned by mail.

Expedited service: Expedited service is available for phone and in person searches. Turnaround time: overnight delivery. You must use a credit card for an additional $11.00 fee and courier or Express Mail are additional costs.

Workers' Compensation Records

Labor and Industries, Public Disclosure Unit, PO Box 44632, Olympia, WA 98504-4632 (Courier: 7273 Linderson Way SW, Tumwater, WA 98501); 360-902-5542, 360-902-5529 (Fax), 8AM-5PM.

www.wa.gov/LNI

Indexing & Storage: Records are available for the past 3 years. Prior records are at the State Archives, but you must go through this office for those records. It takes 1 month before new records are available for inquiry. Records are indexed on microfiche.

Searching: Must have signed release from the claimant. Written request only. Claims information is not released except as provided under Title 51 of the Revised Code of Washington (RCW). No out-of-state subpoenas are honored. Include the following in your request: claimant name, Social Security Number, claim number. The DOB is helpful. The following data is not released: chemically-related illness.

Access by: mail, in person.

Fee & Payment: Fees depend on extensive of file and search. First $20.00 in duplication fees are free. Fee payee: L & I Cashier. Personal checks accepted. No credit cards accepted.

Mail search: Turnaround time: 2 to 3 days. The record information that they send back is taken from microfiche only. No hard file copies released.

In person search: Must schedule by appointment.

Driver Records

Department of Licensing, Driver Record Section, PO Box 9030, Olympia, WA 98507-9030 (Courier: 1125 Washington Street SE, Olympia, WA 98504); 360-902-3921, 360-902-3900 (General Information), 360-586-9044 (Fax), 8AM-4:30PM.

www.dol.wa.gov

Note: Records available include a 3-year insurance record and the "full" employment record. The 3-year record contains employment or non-employment convictions. The full record contains both. Detailed information on access and forms are found at the web.

Indexing & Storage: It takes 2 to 3 weeks or more before new records are available for inquiry.

Searching: All mail or walk-in requests require a signed authorization from the driver, exceptions are for ongoing, pre-approved accounts. Casual requesters cannot obtain records without written consent. Either the license number or name and DOB are needed for a request. The license number is based upon a code of the name and DOB. This code can be confusing (O or 0, *'s) so it is suggested you try name and DOB first. The following data is not released: Social Security Numbers.

Access by: mail, in person.

Fee & Payment: The fee is $5.00 per record. Copies of tickets may be requested by the driver or driver's authorized representative. The fee is $.75 per ticket; the first 5 are free. Fee payee: Department of Licensing Prepayment required. Personal checks accepted. No credit cards accepted.

Mail search: Turnaround time: 2 weeks. There is no charge for a no record found. A self addressed stamped envelope is requested.

In person search: Turnaround time is immediate for up to 5 requests. There is no charge for a no record found.

Other access: Tape retrieval is offered for high volume requesters.

Vehicle Ownership & Identification
Vessel Ownership & Registration

Department of Licensing, Vehicle Records, PO Box 2957, Olympia, WA 98507-2957 (Courier: 1125 S Washington MS-48001, Olympia, WA 98504); 360-902-3780, 360-902-3827 (Fax), 8AM-5PM.

www.dol.wa.gov

Note: It is recommended that on-going, high volume users enter into a disclosure agreement with this agency; contact: Susan at 360-902-3760.

Indexing & Storage: Records are available for 10 years to present. All motorized boats and sailboats must be titled. All boats must be registered unless under 16 ft with less than a 10 hp motor. It takes 2 to 3 weeks before new records are available for inquiry. Records are indexed on inhouse computer.

Searching: Washington has strict access guidelines that restrict casual requesters. Permitted requesters include attorneys, PI's, insurance companies, and business entities for use in the normal course of business. A special form is required. Include the following in your request: VIN, license plate number. Records cannot be searched by owner or driver name. Requests must be in writing.

Access by: mail, phone, in person, online.

Fee & Payment: The fee for microfilm or microfiche searches is $.75. Fee for photocopy or printouts is $.15 each; no charge under $4.50. There is no charge to "view" a record.

Mail search: Turnaround time: 2 weeks. No self addressed stamped envelope is required.

Phone search: VIPS (Vehicle/Vessel Information Processing System) is a touch-tone ordering available for pre-approved, high volume accounts. The system processes by plate number, VIN, WN# & HIN, and is open 24/7. For more information, call 360-902-3760.

In person search: Searching is available in person.

Online search: This is a commercial subscription service and all accounts must be pre-approved. Access is via the Internet. Known as IVIPS, the system processes requests much the phone search. A $25.00 deposit is required and there is a $.04 fee per hit. For more information, call 360-902-3760.

Other access: Large bulk lists cannot be released for any commercial purposes. Lists are released to non-profit entities and for statistical purposes. For more information, call 360-902-3760.

Accident Reports

State Patrol, Collision Reports, PO Box 42628, Olympia, WA 98504-2628; 360-570-5200, 360-570-5220 (Fax), 8AM-5PM.

www.wa.gov/wsp/wsphome.htm

Indexing & Storage: Records are available for 6 years plus the present year. It takes 2 to 3 weeks before new records are available for inquiry.

Searching: Include the following in your request: name, date of accident, location of accident. It is strongly suggested to use their request form - Form 300-345-008. The agency will fax a copy of the form, upon request.

Access by: mail, in person.

Fee & Payment: The fee is $5.00 per record. Fee payee: Washington State Patrol. Prepayment required. Personal checks accepted. No credit cards accepted.

Mail search: Turnaround time: 2 weeks. A self addressed stamped envelope is requested.

In person search: Walk-in requesters may receive the report with proper credentials, if personnel are available to do the search.

Legislation Records

Washington Legislature, State Capitol-Legislative Info Center, PO Box 40600, Olympia, WA 98504-0600; 360-753-5000 (Information), 800-562-6000 (Local Only), 360-786-7573 (Bill Room), 360-786-1293 (Fax), 9AM-5PM.

www.leg.wa.gov

Indexing & Storage: Records are available for past 2 years. Records are indexed on microfiche.

Searching: Include the following in your request: bill number, topic of bill, year.

Access by: mail, phone, fax, in person, online.

Fee & Payment: There is no search fee, unless extensive research is required.

Mail search: Turnaround time: 1 to 2 days. There is a limit of one copy per bill. No self addressed stamped envelope is required.

Phone search: Records are available by phone.

Fax search: Turnaround is 1 to 2 days.

In person search: Searching is available in person.

Online search: The web site offers bill text and status look-up.

Other access: There is an array of subscription services available from the legislative Bill Room. Data available includes bill sets, final digest, roll call transcripts, summaries, budget notes, and various reports. Call the Bill Room for a price list.

Voter Registration

Access to Records is Restricted

Secretary of State, Election Division, PO Box 40220, Olympia, WA 98504; 360-902-4152, 360-586-5629 (Fax), 8AM-5PM.

www.secstate.wa.gov/elections

Note: All voter information is kept at the local level by the County Auditor (except King County where records are kept by the Dept of Records and Elections). Individual look-ups will not receive SSNs, DOBs, or telephone numbers.

GED Certificates

State Board for Community & Technical Colleges, GED Records, PO Box 42495, Olympia, WA 98504-2495 (Courier: 319 7th Ave, Olympia, WA 98504); 360-753-6748, 360-664-8808 (Fax), 8AM-5PM.

www.sbctc.ctc.edu

Searching: Include the following in your request: name, Social Security Number, date of birth, signed release. Also, the city, date of test, and any previous name the record could be under are helpful.

Access by: mail, fax, in person.

Fee & Payment: There is no fee for either verification or a transcript.

Mail search: Turnaround time: 1 week. No self addressed stamped envelope is required.

Fax search: Same criteria as mail searching.

In person search: Verification is while you wait.

Hunting License Information
Fishing License Information

Department of Fish & Wildlife, Attn: Public Disclosure Officer, 600 Capitol Way, N, Olympia, WA 98501-1091; 360-902-2253, 360-902-2171 (Fax), 8AM-5PM.

www.wa.gov/wdfw

Indexing & Storage: Records are available for 3 years. It takes up to 3 months before new records are available for inquiry.

Searching: Records cannot be purchased for commercial list purposes. All requests must be in writing.

Access by: fax, in person, online.

Fee & Payment: There is no fee unless a lengthy list is presented, then $.10 per page. No self addressed stamped envelope is required. No searching by mail.

Fax search: Fax searching available.

In person search: Searching is available in person.

Online search: You may send an e-mail request; check the web site for the exact address.

Other access: The database can be purchased for non-commercial purposes only.

Washington State Licensing Agencies

Licenses Searchable Online

Acupuncturist #10	www.doh.wa.gov/A-Z.htm
Adult Family Home #30	www.aasa.dshs.wa.gov/Lookup/AFHRequestv2.asp
Animal Technician #10	www.doh.wa.gov/A-Z.htm
Announcer, Athletic Event (Ring) #27	https://wws2.wa.gov/dol/profquery
Architect #26	https://wws2.wa.gov/dol/profquery/
Architect Corporation #26	https://wws2.wa.gov/dol/profquery/
Athlete, Professional #27	https://wws2.wa.gov/dol/profquery
Athletic Inspector #27	https://wws2.wa.gov/dol/profquery
Athletic Judge/Timekeeper/Physician #27	https://wws2.wa.gov/dol/profquery
Athletic Manager #27	https://wws2.wa.gov/dol/profquery
Athletic Promoter/Matchmaker #27	https://wws2.wa.gov/dol/profquery
Attorney #23	www.wsba.org/directory/default.htm
Auction Company #33	https://wws2.wa.gov/dol/profquery
Auctioneer #33	https://wws2.wa.gov/dol/profquery
Bail Bond Agent/Agency #15	https://wws2.wa.gov/dol/profquery
Barber #18	https://wws2.wa.gov/dol/profquery
Barber Instructor/School #18	https://wws2.wa.gov/dol/profquery
Barber Shop/Mobile/Booth #18	https://wws2.wa.gov/dol/profquery
Beauty Shop/Salon/Mobile #18	https://wws2.wa.gov/dol/profquery
Boarding Homes #30	www.aasa.dshs.wa.gov/Lookup/BHRequestv2.asp
Boxer #27	https://wws2.wa.gov/dol/profquery
Bulk Hauler #14	https://wws2.wa.gov/dol/profquery
Cemetery #6	https://wws2.wa.gov/dol/profquery
Child Care Facility #29	https://wws2.wa.gov/dshs/clic/request.asp
Chiropractor #10	www.doh.wa.gov/A-Z.htm
Collection Agency #32	https://wws2.wa.gov/dol/profquery
Contractor, General, Company #12	https://wws2.wa.gov/lni/bbip/contractor.asp
Cosmetologist #18	https://wws2.wa.gov/dol/profquery
Cosmetology Instructor #18	https://wws2.wa.gov/dol/profquery
Cosmetology School #18	https://wws2.wa.gov/dol/profquery
Counselor #10	www.doh.wa.gov/A-Z.htm
Court Reporter #33	https://wws2.wa.gov/dol/profquery
Crematory #6	https://wws2.wa.gov/dol/profquery
Dental Hygienist #10	www.doh.wa.gov/A-Z.htm
Dentist #10	www.doh.wa.gov/A-Z.htm
Dietitian #10	www.doh.wa.gov/A-Z.htm
Electrical Contractor/Admin. #12	https://wws2.wa.gov/lni/bbip/contractor.asp
Electrician #12	https://wws2.wa.gov/lni/bbip/contractor.asp
Embalmer #6	https://wws2.wa.gov/dol/profquery
Emergency Medical Technician #10	www.doh.wa.gov/A-Z.htm
Employment Agency #32	https://wws2.wa.gov/dol/profquery
Engineer #35	https://wws2.wa.gov/dol/profquery/LicenseeSearch.asp
Engineering Geologist #34	https://wws2.wa.gov/dol/profquery
Engineering/Land Surveying Company #35	https://wws2.wa.gov/dol/profquery/LicenseeSearch.asp
Esthetician Shop/Salon/Booth/Mobile #18	https://wws2.wa.gov/dol/profquery
Esthetician/Esthetician Instructor #18	https://wws2.wa.gov/dol/profquery
Feedlot #3	www.wa.gov/agr/FoodAnimal/Livestock/CertifiedFeedlots.htm
Funeral Director #6	https://wws2.wa.gov/dol/profquery
Funeral Establishment #6	https://wws2.wa.gov/dol/profquery
Gaming Occupation #24	www.wsgc.wa.gov/LicSearch.asp
Gaming Operation #24	www.wsgc.wa.gov/LicSearch.asp
Geologist #34	https://wws2.wa.gov/dol/profquery
Health Care Assistant #10	www.doh.wa.gov/A-Z.htm
Home Health Care Agency #9	www.doh.wa.gov/Licensing.htm
Hospital #9	www.doh.wa.gov/Licensing.htm
Hydrogeologist #34	https://wws2.wa.gov/dol/profquery
Insurance Company #25	www.insurance.wa.gov/tableofcontents/annualreptins.htm
Kick Boxer #27	https://wws2.wa.gov/dol/profquery
Land Development Rep #16	https://wws2.wa.gov/dol/profquery
Land Surveyor/Surveyor-in-Training #35	https://wws2.wa.gov/dol/profquery/LicenseeSearch.asp
Landscape Architect #26	https://wws2.wa.gov/dol/profquery/
Limousine Carrier #14	https://wws2.wa.gov/dol/profquery
Liquor Store #19	www.liq.wa.gov/services/storesearch.asp
Livestock Market #3	www.wa.gov/agr/FoodAnimal/Livestock/PublicMarkets.htm

Manicure Shop/Mobile/Booth #18	https://wws2.wa.gov/dol/profquery
Manicurist/Manicurist Instructor #18	https://wws2.wa.gov/dol/profquery
Manufactured Home Dealer #14	https://wws2.wa.gov/dol/profquery
Marriage & Family Therapist #10	www.doh.wa.gov/A-Z.htm
Mental Health Counselor #10	www.doh.wa.gov/A-Z.htm
Mobile Home/Travel Trailer Dealer #14	https://wws2.wa.gov/dol/profquery
Notary Public #17	https://wws2.wa.gov/dol/profquery/
Nursing Homes #30	www.aasa.dshs.wa.gov/Professional/NFDir/directory.asp
Optometrist #11	www.odfinder.org/LicSearch.asp
Pharmacist #10	www.doh.wa.gov/A-Z.htm
Pharmacy Technician #10	www.doh.wa.gov/A-Z.htm
Plumber #12	https://wws2.wa.gov/lni/bbip/contractor.asp
Private Investigative Agency #15	https://wws2.wa.gov/dol/profquery
Private Investigative Trainer #15	https://wws2.wa.gov/dol/profquery
Private Investigator, Armed/Unarmed #15	https://wws2.wa.gov/dol/profquery
Real Estate Appraiser, Certi./Licensed #16	https://wws2.wa.gov/dol/profquery
Real Estate Broker #16	https://wws2.wa.gov/dol/profquery
Real Estate LLC, LLP, Corp./Partnership #16	https://wws2.wa.gov/dol/profquery
Real Estate Sales Occupation #16	https://wws2.wa.gov/dol/profquery
Referee #27	https://wws2.wa.gov/dol/profquery
Scrap Processor #14	https://wws2.wa.gov/dol/profquery
Security Guard, Private Armed/Unarmed #15	https://wws2.wa.gov/dol/profquery
Security Guard/Agency #15	https://wws2.wa.gov/dol/profquery
Snowmobile Dealer #14	https://wws2.wa.gov/dol/profquery
Social Worker #10	www.doh.wa.gov/A-Z.htm
Timeshare Seller/Company/Project #33	https://wws2.wa.gov/dol/profquery
Tow Truck Operator #14	https://wws2.wa.gov/dol/profquery
Travel Agency #33	https://wws2.wa.gov/dol/profquery
Travel Seller #33	https://wws2.wa.gov/dol/profquery
Vehicle Dealer, Miscellaneous #14	https://wws2.wa.gov/dol/profquery
Vehicle Dealer/Manufacturer #14	https://wws2.wa.gov/dol/profquery
Vehicle Transporter #14	https://wws2.wa.gov/dol/profquery
Vessel Dealer #14	https://wws2.wa.gov/dol/profquery
Veterinarian #10	www.doh.wa.gov/A-Z.htm
Veterinary Medical Clerk #10	www.doh.wa.gov/A-Z.htm
Wastewater System Designer, On-Site #35	https://wws2.wa.gov/dol/profquery/LicenseeSearch.asp
Wastewater System Inspector, On-Site #35	https://wws2.wa.gov/dol/profquery/LicenseeSearch.asp
Whitewater River Outfitter #32	https://wws2.wa.gov/dol/profquery
Wrecker #14	https://wws2.wa.gov/dol/profquery
Wrestler #27	https://wws2.wa.gov/dol/profquery

Licensing Quick Finder

Acupuncturist #10 ... 360-236-4800	Boxer #27 ... 360-664-6644	Electrician #12 ... 360-902-5269
Adult Family Home #30 ... 360-725-2300	Bulk Hauler #14 ... 360-664-6466	Embalmer #6 ... 360-664-1555
Animal Technician #10 ... 360-236-4800	Business Opportunity Offering #7 ... 360-902-8760	Emergency Medical Technician #10 ... 360-705-6700
Announcer, Athletic Event (Ring) #27 ... 360-664-6644	Cemetery #6 ... 360-664-1555	Employment Agency #32 ... 360-664-1389
Applicator, Commercial #5 ... 877-301-4555	Check Casher/Seller #7 ... 360-902-8703	Employment Directory Service #32 ... 330-664-1400
Applicator, Private Commercial #5 ... 877-301-4555	Child Care Facility #29 ... 360-413-3209	Engineer #35 ... 360-664-1575
Architect #26 ... 360-664-1388	Chiropractor #10 ... 360-236-4800	Engineering Geologist #34 ... 360-664-1497
Architect Corporation #26 ... 360-664-1388	Cigarette Retailer/Vender/Whlse #32 ... 330-664-1400	Engineering/Land Surveying Company #35
Athlete, Professional #27 ... 360-664-6644	Collection Agency #32 ... 360-664-1389	... 360-664-1575
Athletic Inspector #27 ... 360-664-6644	Commodities #7 ... 360-902-8760	ESA Pathology #20 ... 360-725-6400
Athletic Judge/Timekeeper/Physician #27	Concealed Weapon #15 ... 360-664-6616	Escrow Company/Officers #7 ... 360-902-8703
... 360-664-6644	Consumer Loan Company #7 ... 360-902-8703	Esthetician Shop/Salon/Booth/Mobile #18
Athletic Manager #27 ... 360-664-6644	Contractor, General, Company #12 ... 360-902-5226	... 360-664-6626
Athletic Promoter/Matchmaker #27 ... 360-664-6644	Contractor, General, Individual #32 ... 330-664-1400	Esthetician/Esthetician Instructor #18 .. 360-664-6626
Attorney #23 ... 206-727-8200	Cosmetologist #18 ... 360-664-6626	Feedlot #3 ... 360-902-1855
Auction Company #33 ... 360-664-6636	Cosmetology Instructor #18 ... 360-664-6626	Fertilizer Distributor, Bulk #32 ... 330-664-1400
Auctioneer #33 ... 360-664-6636	Cosmetology School #18 ... 360-664-6626	Firearms Dealer #15 ... 360-664-6616
Audiologist #11 ... 360-236-4800	Counselor #10 ... 360-236-4800	Fishing, Commercial #8 ... 360-902-2464
Bail Bond Agent/Agency #15 ... 360-664-6624	Court Reporter #33 ... 360-664-6633	Foster Home #31 ... 888-794-1794
Bank #7 ... 360-902-8704	Credit Union #7 ... 360-902-8701	Franchise #7 ... 360-902-8760
Barber #18 ... 360-664-6626	Crematory #6 ... 360-664-1555	Fruit/Vegetable Inspector #4 ... 360-902-1832
Barber Instructor/School #18 ... 360-664-6626	Dental Hygienist #10 ... 360-236-4800	Funeral Director #6 ... 360-664-1555
Barber Shop/Mobile/Booth #18 ... 360-664-6626	Dentist #10 ... 360-236-4800	Funeral Establishment #6 ... 360-664-1555
Battery Collector #32 ... 330-664-1400	Dietitian #10 ... 360-236-4800	Gaming Occupation #24 ... 360-438-7654
Beauty Shop/Salon/Mobile #18 ... 360-664-6626	Egg Handler/Dealer #32 ... 330-664-1400	Gaming Operation #24 ... 360-438-7654
Boarding Homes #30 ... 360-725-2300	Egg Inspector #4 ... 360-902-1830	Geologist #34 ... 360-664-1497
Boiler Inspector #13 ... 360-902-5270	Electrical Contractor/Admin. #12 ... 360-902-5269	Grain Inspector/Weigher/Sampler #28 .. 360-753-1484

Health Care Assistant #10.....................360-753-1230
Hearing Instrument Fitter/Dispenser #11360-236-4800
Home Health Care Agency #9..............360-705-6611
Horse Racing #22.....................................360-459-6462
Hospital #9...360-705-6611
Hydrogeologist #34.................................360-664-1497
Hypnotherapist #11.................................360-236-4800
Insurance Agent/Broker #25.................360-407-0341
Insurance Broker, Resident/Non-Resident #25
....360-407-0341
Insurance Company #25.........................360-407-0341
Insurance Corporation, Resident #25...360-407-0341
Investment Advisors #7.........................360-902-8760
Kick Boxer #27..360-664-6644
Land Development Rep #16.....................306-664-6500
Land Surveyor/Surveyor-in-Training #35360-664-1575
Landscape Architect #26.......................360-664-1388
Limousine Carrier #14...........................360-664-6466
Liquor Store #19.....................................360-664-1600
Livestock Brand Record #3..................360-902-1855
Livestock Market #3...............................360-902-1855
Lottery Retailer #32................................330-664-1400
Manicure Shop/Mobile/Booth #18........360-664-6626
Manicurist/Manicurist Instructor #18.....360-664-6626
Manufactured Home Dealer #14...........360-664-6466
Marriage & Family Therapist #10.........360-236-4800
Massage Therapist #11..........................360-236-4800
Medical Doctor #11.................................360-236-4800
Mental Health Counselor #10.................360-236-4800
Midwife #11..360-236-4800
Minor Worker #32....................................330-664-1400
Mobile Home/Travel Trailer Dealer #14 360-664-6466
Mortgage Broker #7...............................360-902-8703
Naturopathic Physician #11....................360-236-4800
Notary Public #17...................................360-664-1550
Nurse/Nursing Assistant #11................360-236-4800
Nurse-LPN #11...360-236-4800
Nursery Retailer/Whlse #32..................330-664-1400
Nursing Home Administrator #11..........360-236-4800
Nursing Homes #30................................360-725-2300
Occupational Therapist #11...................360-236-4800

Ocularist #11...360-236-4800
Optician #11...360-236-4800
Optometrist #11.......................................360-236-4800
Osteopathic Physician #11....................360-236-4800
Pest Control Operator/Consultant, Public #5
....877-301-4555
Pesticide Dealer/Manager #5..............877-301-4555
Pesticide Demo & Research Applicator #5
....877-301-4555
Pesticide Operator/Applicator #5.........877-301-4555
Pesticide Private Application #5...........877-301-4555
Pharmacist #10.......................................360-236-4800
Pharmacy Technician #10.....................360-236-4800
Physical Therapist #11..........................360-236-4800
Physician Assistant #11........................360-236-4800
Pilot, Marine, Commercial #2..............206-515-3904
Plumber #12...360-902-5207
Podiatrist #11...360-236-4800
Private Investigative Agency #15.........360-664-9070
Private Investigative Trainer #15..........360-664-9070
Private Investigator, Armed/Unarmed #15
....360-664-9070
Psychologist #11.....................................360-236-4800
Public Accountant-CPA #1....................360-753-2585
Radiologic Technologist #11................360-236-4800
Real Estate Appraiser, Cert./Licensed #16
....306-664-6504
Real Estate Broker #16..........................360-664-6500
Real Estate LLC, LLP, Corp./Partnership #16
....360-664-6500
Real Estate Sales Occupation #16......360-664-6488
Referee #27..360-664-6644
Refrigerated Locker #32.........................330-664-1400
Rental Car #32..330-664-1400
Respiratory Therapist #11.....................360-236-4800
Savings & Loan/Savings Bank #7........306-902-8704
School Counselor #20............................360-725-6400
School Nurse #20....................................360-725-6400
School Occ./Physical Therapist #20....360-725-6400
School Principal/Superintendent #20...360-725-6400
School Program Administrator #20......360-725-6400

School Psychologist/Social Worker #20 360-725-6400
Scrap Processor #14..............................360-664-6466
Securities Broker/Dealer #7.................360-902-8760
Securities Salesperson #7....................306-902-8760
Security Guard, Private Armed/Unarmed #15
....360-664-6611
Security Guard/Agency #15..................360-664-6611
Seed Dealer #32......................................330-664-1400
Sex Offender Treatment Provider #11.360-236-4800
Shopkeeper (non-prescription drug) #32330-664-1400
Snowmobile Dealer #14.........................360-664-6466
Social Worker #10...................................360-236-4800
Speech-Language Pathologist #11......360-236-4800
Sport Fishing #8.....................................360-902-2464
Teacher #21...360-753-6773
Telephone Solicitor #32.........................330-664-1400
Timeshare Seller/Company/Project #33 360-664-6632
Tow Truck Operator #14.........................360-664-6466
Travel Agency #33.................................360-664-6632
Travel Seller #33....................................360-664-6632
Trust Company #7..................................360-902-8704
Underground Storage Tank #32...........330-664-1400
Vehicle Dealer, Miscellaneous #14......360-664-6466
Vehicle Dealer/Manufacturer #14.........360-664-6466
Vehicle for Hire #32................................330-664-1400
Vehicle Sales/Disposal #32...................330-664-1400
Vehicle Transporter #14.........................360-664-6466
Vessel Dealer #14..................................360-664-6466
Veterinarian #10......................................360-236-4800
Veterinary Medical Clerk #10................360-236-4800
Waste Tire Carrier #32...........................330-664-1400
Waste Tire Site Owner #32...................330-664-1400
Wastewater System Designer, On-Site #35
....360-664-1575
Wastewater System Inspector, On-Site #3
5...360-664-1575
Weights & Measures #3.........................360-902-1857
Whitewater River Outfitter #32.............330-664-1400
Wrecker #14...360-664-6466
Wrestler #27..360-664-6644
X-ray Technician #11.............................360-236-4800

Licensing Agency Information

#1 Board of Accountancy, PO Box 9131, Olympia, WA 98507-9131; 360-753-2585, Fax: 360-664-9190.
www.cpaboard.wa.gov
Agency email: webmaster@cpaboard.wa.gov.

#2 Board of Pilotage Commissioners, 2911 2nd Ave, Seattle, WA 98121-1012; 206-515-3904, Fax: 206-515-3969. Agency email: larsonp@wsdot.wa.gov.

#3 Department of Agriculture, Livestock Division, PO Box 42560 (1111 Washington St), Olympia, WA 98504-2560; 360-902-1800, Fax: 360-902-2086.
www.wa.gov/agr
Agency email: livestockid@agr.wa.gov.

#4 Department of Agriculture, Food Safety & Animal Health Division, PO Box 42560 (1111 Washington St SE), Olympia, WA 98504-2560; 360-902-1800.
www.wa.gov/agr/food.htm

#5 Department of Agriculture, PO Box 42589, Olympia, WA 98504-2589; 360-902-2010, Fax: 360-902-2093.
www.wa.gov/agr/pmd/index.htm
Agency email: mtucker@agr.wa.gov.

#6 Department of Licensing, Funeral & Cemetery Licensing Program, PO Box 9012, Olympia, WA 98507-9012; 360-664-1555, Fax: 360-586-4414.
www.dol.wa.gov/unfc/funfront.htm. Agency email: funerals@dol.wa.gov.
Search database at
https://wws2.wa.gov/dol/profquery

#7 Department of Financial Institutions, PO Box 41200, Olympia, WA 98504-1200; 360-902-8700, Fax: 360-586-5068.
www.wa.gov/dfi

#8 Department of Fish & Wildlife, 600 Capitol Way N, Olympia, WA 98501-1091; 360-902-2253, Fax: 360-902-2171.
www.wa.gov/wdfw

#9 Department of Health, Facilities Services Licensing, PO Box 47852, Olympia, WA 98504; 360-705-6652, Fax: 360-705-6654.
www.doh.wa.gov/hsqa/fsl/default.htm. Agency email: information@doh.wa.gov.
Search database at
www.doh.wa.gov/Licensing.htm

#10 Department of Health, Licensing & Certification, 1112 SE Quince St PO Box 47890, Olympia, WA 98504; 360-236-4800, Fax: 360-236-4818.
www.doh.wa.gov/Topics/topics.htm#Licensing
Search database at www.doh.wa.gov/A-Z.htm

#11 Department of Health, PO Box 47865 (1300 SE Quince St), Olympia, WA 98504; 360-236-4800, Fax: 360-236-4818.
www.doh.wa.gov/Licensing.htm

#12 Department of Labor & Industries, PO Box 44000, Olympia, WA 98504-4000; 360-902-5800, Fax: 360-902-5292.
www.lni.wa.gov
Agency email: berp235@lni.wa.gov.
Search database at
www.lni.wa.gov/contractors/contractor.asp

#13 Department of Labor & Industries, Boiler Section, PO Box 44410, Olympia, WA 98504-4410; 360-902-5270, Fax: 360-902-5292.
www.wa.gov/lni

#14 Department of Licensing, Dealer Services, PO Box 9039, Olympia, WA 98507-9039; 360-664-6466, Fax: 360-586-0479.
www.dol.wa.gov/vs/dl-lic.htm
Agency email: dealers@dol.wa.gov.
Search database at
https://wws2.wa.gov/dol/profquery

#15 Licensing Dept, Public Protection Unit & Firearms Program, Private Investigator & Security Guard, PO Box 9649, Olympia, WA 98507-9649; 360-664-9070, Fax: 360-570-7888.
www.wa.gov/dol
Agency email: Security@dol.wa.gov.

#16 Department of Licensing, Real Estate & Appraiser Program, PO Box 9015 (2000 4th Ave. W), Olympia, WA 98507-9015; 360-664-6500, Fax: 360-586-0998.
www.wa.gov/dol/bpd/refront.htm
Agency email: RealEstate@dol.gov.
Search database at
https://wws2.wa.gov/dol/profquery

#17 Department of Licensing, Notary Section, PO Box 9027 (405 Black Wake Blvd SW), Olympia, WA 98507-9027; 360-664-1550, Fax: 360-586-4414.
www.wa.gov/dol
Agency email: intnotarie@dol.wa.gov.
Search database at
https://wws2.wa.gov/dol/profquery

#18 Department of Licensing, Cosmetology Division, PO Box 9026, Olympia, WA 98507-9026; 360-664-6626, Fax: 360-664-2550.
www.wa.gov/dol/bpd/cosfront.htm. Agency email: plssunit@dol.wa.gov.

#19 Liquor Control Board, 3000 Paciic Ave. SE, Olympia, WA 98504-3075; 360-664-1600.
www.liq.wa.gov/default.asp. Agency email: wslcb@liq.wa.gov.
Search database at
www.liq.wa.gov/services/storesearch.asp

#20 Superintendent of Public Instruction, Professional Certification, PO Box 47200 (Old Capitol Bldg), Olympia, WA 98504-7200; 360-725-6400, Fax: 360-586-0145.
www.k12.wa.us/cert
Agency email: cert@ospi.wednet.edu.

#21 Teacher Certification, PO Box 47200, Olympia, WA 98504-7200; 360-753-6773, Fax: 360-586-0145.
www.k12.wa.us/cert
Agency email: cert@ospi.wednet.edu.

#22 Horse Racing Commission, 7912 Martin Way, #D, Olympia, WA 98516-5703; 360-459-6462, Fax: 360-459-6461.
www.whrc.wa.gov/licensing/index.htm
Agency email: whrc@whrc.state.wa.us.

#23 Bar Association, 2101 4th Ave, 4th Fl, Seattle, WA 98121-2599; 206-727-8200, Fax: 206-727-8320.
www.wsba.org. Agency email: license@wsba.org.
Search database at
www.wsba.org/directory/default.htm

#24 Gambling Commission, PO Box 42400, Olympia, WA 98504-2400; 360-438-7654 x358, Fax: 360-438-7503.
www.wsgc.wa.gov/
Search database at
www.wsgc.wa.gov/LicSearch.asp

#25 Insurance Licensing, 4224 6th Ave SE, Rowesix Bldg 5, Olympia, WA 98504-0257; 360-407-0341, Fax: 360-438-7629.
www.insurance.wa.gov
Agency email: georgiac@oic.wa.gov.

#26 Department of Licensing, Architects & Landscape Architects, Business and Professions Division, PO Box 9045, Olympia, WA 98507-9045; 360-664-1388, Fax: 360-664-2551.
www.wa.gov/dol/bpd/arcfront.htm
Agency email: architects@dol.wa.gov.
Search database at
www.wa.gov/dol/bpd/licquery.htm

#27 Department of Licensing, Professional Boxing, Martial Arts and Wrestling Licensing Program, PO Box 9026, Olympia, WA 98507-9026; 360-664-6644, Fax: 360-570-4956.
www.dol.wa.gov/plss/pafront.htm
Agency email: plssunit@dol.wa.gov.
Search database at
https://wws2.wa.gov/dol/profquery

#28 Department of Agriculture, Commodity Inspection, 3939 Cleveland Av SE, Olympia, WA 98501; 360-902-1921, Fax: 360-586-5257.
www.wa.gov/agr/pmd/index.htm
Agency email: commodity@agr.wa.gov.

#29 Department of Child Care & Early Learning, PO Box 45480, Olympia, WA 98504; 360-413-3209.
www.wa.gov/dol/bpd/refront.htm
Search database at
https://wws2.wa.gov/dshs/clic/request.asp

#30 Aging & Adult Services Administration, PO Box 45600, Olympia, WA 98504; 360-725-2300.
www.aasa.dshs.wa.gov/default.htm

#31 Children's Administration, Dept of Social & Health Services, P.O. Box 45715, Olympia, WA 98504; 888-794-1794.
http://www1.dshs.wa.gov/ca/index.asp. Agency email: Children@dshs.wa.gov.

#32 Department of Licensing, Master License Service, PO Box 9034, Olympia, WA 98507-9034; 360-664-1400, Fax: 360-570-7875.
www.dol.wa.gov/mls/reglic.htm
Agency email: MLS@dol.wa.gov.

#33 Department of Licensing, Professional Licensing Support Services Unit, PO Box 9026 (1125 Washington St. SE), Olympia, WA 98507-9020; 360-902-3600.
www.dol.wa.gov/main.htm
Search database at
https://wws2.wa.gov/dol/profquery

#34 Department of Licensing, Geologist Licensing Program, PO Box 9045, Olympia, WA 98507-9045; 360-664-1497, Fax: 360-664-2551.
www.dol.wa.gov/design/geofront.htm
Agency email: geologist@dol.wa.gov.
Search database at
https://wws2.wa.gov/dol/profquery

#35 Department of Licensing, Professional Engineers and Land Surveyors Section, PO Box 9049, Olympia, WA 98507-9049; 360-664-1575, Fax: 360-664-2551.
www.dol.wa.gov/engineers/engfront.htm
Agency email: engineers@dol.wa.gov.
Search database at https://wws2.wa.gov/dol/profquery/LicenseeSearch.asp

Washington Federal Courts

The following list indicates the district and division name for each county in the state. If the bankruptcy court location is different from the district court, then the location of the bankruptcy court appears in parentheses.

County/Court Cross Reference

County	District	Division
Adams	Eastern	Spokane
Asotin	Eastern	Spokane
Benton	Eastern	Spokane
Chelan	Eastern	Spokane
Clallam	Western	Tacoma (Seattle)
Clark	Western	Tacoma
Columbia	Eastern	Spokane
Cowlitz	Western	Tacoma
Douglas	Eastern	Spokane
Ferry	Eastern	Spokane
Franklin	Eastern	Spokane
Garfield	Eastern	Spokane
Grant	Eastern	Spokane
Grays Harbor	Western	Tacoma
Island	Western	Seattle
Jefferson	Western	Tacoma (Seattle)
King	Western	Seattle
Kitsap	Western	Tacoma (Seattle)
Kittitas	Eastern	Yakima (Spokane)
Klickitat	Eastern	Yakima (Spokane)
Lewis	Western	Tacoma
Lincoln	Eastern	Spokane
Mason	Western	Tacoma
Okanogan	Eastern	Spokane
Pacific	Western	Tacoma
Pend Oreille	Eastern	Spokane
Pierce	Western	Tacoma
San Juan	Western	Seattle
Skagit	Western	Seattle
Skamania	Western	Tacoma
Snohomish	Western	Seattle
Spokane	Eastern	Spokane
Stevens	Eastern	Spokane
Thurston	Western	Tacoma
Wahkiakum	Western	Tacoma
Walla Walla	Eastern	Spokane
Whatcom	Western	Seattle
Whitman	Eastern	Spokane
Yakima	Eastern	Yakima (Spokane)

Standards for Federal Courts: The search fee is $20.00 per item (one party name or case number). Certification fee is $7.00 per document. Copy fee is $.50 per page. All fees standard unless noted in profile. Mail Search: always enclose a stamped self addressed envelope unless otherwise noted. Before releasing records, all courts require prepayment unless noted in profile.

Open records are located at the court unless otherwise noted. District courts index by defendant and plaintiff as well as by case number. Bankruptcy courts usually index by debtor and case number. While most courts now have their indexes on computer, many still maintain index card files as well.

The universal PACER sign-up number is 800-676-6856. Find PACER and the Party/Case Index on the Web at http://pacer.psc.uscourts.gov. PACER dial-up access is $.60 per minute. Also, courts offering internet access via RACER, PACER, Web-PACER or the new CM-ECF charge $.07 per page fee unless noted as free.

US District Court

Eastern District of Washington

Spokane Division PO Box 1493, Spokane, WA 99210-1493 (Courier Address: Room 840, W 920 Riverside, Spokane, WA 99201), 509-353-2150.

www.waed.uscourts.gov

Counties: Adams, Asotin, Benton, Chelan, Columbia, Douglas, Ferry, Franklin, Garfield, Grant, Lincoln, Okanogan, Pend Oreille, Spokane, Stevens, Walla Walla, Whitman. Also, some cases from Kittitas, Klickitat and Yakima are heard here.

Indexing & Storage: Cases are indexed by defendant, plaintiff, and case number. New cases are available in the index 2-3 days after filing date. Records are also indexed on microfiche. Search must be in Spokane Division for all cases before 1989. Judge McDonald's records are maintained in Yakima (Yakima County). All other cases are kept in the Spokane Division.

Fee & Payment Notes: Payment may be made by money order, cashier check, personal check. Payee: Clerk, US District Court.

Phone Search: Searching not available by phone.

Mail Search: A stamped self addressed envelope is not required.

In Person Search: In person searching available.

PACER: Toll-free dial-up access: 888-372-5706. Local dial-up access: 509-353-2395. Case records are available back to July 1989. Records are purged every six months. New records are available online after 2-3 days. PACER is available online at http://pacer.waed.uscourts.gov.

Yakima Division PO Box 2706, Yakima, WA 98907 (Courier Address: Room 215, 25 S 3rd St, Yakima, WA 98901), 509-575-5838.

www.waed.uscourts.gov

Counties: Kittitas, Klickitat, Yakima. Cases assigned primarily to Judge McDonald are here. Some cases from Kittitas, Klickitat and Yakima are heard in Spokane.

Indexing & Storage: Cases are indexed by defendant, plaintiff, and case number. New cases are available in the index 1 day after filing date. Search must be in Spokane Division for all cases before 1989. Judge McDonald's records are maintained in Yakima. All other cases are kept in the Spokane Division.

Fee & Payment Notes: Payment may be made by money order, cashier check, business check. Personal checks are not accepted. Payee: Clerk, US District Court.

Phone Search: Some docket information is available by phone.

In Person Search: In person searching available.

PACER: Toll-free dial-up access: 888-372-5706. Local dial-up access: 509-353-2395. Case records are available back to July 1989. Records are purged every six months. New records are available online after 2-3 days. PACER is available online at http://pacer.waed.uscourts.gov.

US Bankruptcy Court

Eastern District of Washington

Spokane Division PO Box 2164, Spokane, WA 99210-2164 (Courier Address: W 904 Riverside, Suite 304, Spokane, WA 99201), 509-353-2404.

www.waeb.uscourts.gov

Counties: Adams, Asotin, Benton, Chelan, Columbia, Douglas, Ferry, Franklin, Garfield, Grant, Kittitas, Klickitat, Lincoln, Okanogan, Pend Oreille, Spokane, Stevens, Walla Walla, Whitman, Yakima.

Indexing & Storage: Cases are indexed by debtor and creditors as well as by case number. New cases are available in the index immediately after filing date. Open records are located at this court.

Fee & Payment Notes: Payment may be made by money order, cashier check, business check. Personal checks are not accepted. Prepayment is not required for copy requests. Copies will be provided with a bill through the mail. Payee: Clerk, US Bankruptcy Court.

Phone Search: Only docket information is available by phone. Press extension 6. An automated voice case information service (VCIS) is available. Call VCIS at 509-353-2404.

In Person Search: In person searching available.

PACER: Access fee is. PACER is available online at http://pacer.waeb.uscourts.gov.

Other Online Access: Search records on the Internet free using RACER at http://204.227.177.194. Records go back to 1997. Access fee of $.07 per page is planned.

US District Court

Western District of Washington

Seattle Division Clerk of Court, 215 US Courthouse, 1010 5th Ave, Seattle, WA 98104 (Courier Address: Use mail address for courier delivery), 206-553-5598.

www.wawd.uscourts.gov

Counties: Island, King, San Juan, Skagit, Snohomish, Whatcom.

Indexing & Storage: Cases are indexed by defendant, plaintiff, and case number. New cases are available in the index 10 days after filing date. Records are also indexed on microfiche. Open records are located at this court.

Fee & Payment Notes: Payment may be made by money order, cashier check, personal check. Payee: Clerk, US District Court. You are allowed to make your own copies. These copies cost $.25 per page. An outside copy service will make copies for $.11 per page.

Phone Search: Docket information is available by phone for civil cases since 1988 and criminal cases since 1992.

Mail Search: A stamped self addressed envelope is not required.

In Person Search: In person searching available.

PACER: Toll-free dial-up access: 800-520-8604. Local dial-up access: 206-553-2288. Case records are available back to 1988. Records are never purged. New civil records are available online after 4 days. New criminal records are available online after 2 days. PACER is available online at http://pacer.wawd.uscourts.gov. Document images available.

Tacoma Division Clerk's Office, Room 3100, 1717 Pacific Ave, Tacoma, WA 98402-3200 (Courier Address: Use mail address for courier delivery), 253-593-6313.

www.wawd.uscourts.gov

Counties: Clallam, Clark, Cowlitz, Grays Harbor, Jefferson, Kitsap, Lewis, Mason, Pacific, Pierce, Skamania, Thurston, Wahkiakum.

Indexing & Storage: Cases are indexed by defendant, plaintiff, and case number. New cases are available in the index immediately after filing date. District wide searches are available for information from 1989. Microfiche and card indexes are available for older records. Open records are located at this court.

Fee & Payment Notes: Payment may be made by money order, cashier check, personal check. There is a $25.00 service fee if a check is returned. Payee: Clerk, US District Court.

Phone Search: Only docket information is available by phone.

In Person Search: In person searching available.

PACER: Toll-free dial-up access: 800-520-8604. Local dial-up access: 206-553-2288. Case records are available back to 1988. Records are never purged. New civil records are available online after 4 days. New criminal records are available online after 2 days. PACER is available online at http://pacer.wawd.uscourts.gov. Document images available.

US Bankruptcy Court

Western District of Washington

Seattle Division Clerk of Court, 315 Park Place Bldg, 1200 6th Ave, Seattle, WA 98101 (Courier Address: Use mail address for courier delivery), 206-553-7545, Fax: 206-553-0131.

www.wawb.uscourts.gov

Counties: Clallam, Island, Jefferson, King, Kitsap, San Juan, Skagit, Snohomish, Whatcom.

Indexing & Storage: Cases are indexed by debtor, creditors and case number. New cases are available in the index 1 day after filing. Open cases are stored by case number. Closed cases are stored by year closed and then by case number.

Fee & Payment Notes: Payment may be made by money order, cashier check, personal check. Payee: Clerk, US Bankruptcy Court. You are allowed to make your own copies. These copies cost $.15 per page. An outside copy service is available at $.35 per page.

Phone Search: An automated voice case information service (VCIS) is available. Call VCIS at 888-436-7477 or 206-553-8543.

Fax Search: Will accept fax search request if no copies requested.

In Person Search: In person searching available.

PACER: Toll-free dial-up access: 800-704-4492. Local dial-up access: 206-553-0060. Case records are available back to June 1995. Records are never purged. New civil records are available online after 2 days. PACER is available online at http://pacer.wawb.uscourts.gov.

Electronic Filing: Information is available online at https://ecf.wawb.uscourts.gov

Tacoma Division Suite 2100, 1717 Pacific Ave, Tacoma, WA 98402-3233 (Use mail address for courier delivery), 253-593-6310.

www.wawb.uscourts.gov

Counties: Clark, Cowlitz, Grays Harbor, Lewis, Mason, Pacific, Pierce, Skamania, Thurston, Wahkiakum.

Indexing & Storage: Cases are indexed by debtor as well as by case number. New cases are available in the index 1 day after filing date. Records can be searched by debtor's name from 1987 to the present. Open records are located at this court.

Fee & Payment Notes: Payment may be made by money order, cashier check. Business checks are not accepted. Personal checks are not accepted. Attorney checks are accepted. Payee: Clerk, US Bankruptcy Court. You are allowed to make your own copies. These copies cost $.15 per page. An outside copy service is available for $.10 per page.

Phone Search: An automated voice case information service (VCIS) is available. Call VCIS at 888-436-7477 or 206-553-8543.

Mail Search: A SASE is not required.

In Person Search: In person searching available.

PACER: Toll-free dial-up access: 800-704-4492. Local dial-up access: 206-553-0060. Case records are available back to June 1995. Records are never purged. New civil records are available online after 2 days. PACER is available online at http://pacer.wawb.uscourts.gov.

Electronic Filing: Information is available online at https://ecf.wawb.uscourts.gov

Washington County Courts

Court	Jurisdiction	No. of Courts	How Organized
Superior Courts*	General	39	29 Districts
District Courts*	Limited	65	39 Counties
Municipal Courts	Municipal	131	131 Cities

* Profiled in this Sourcebook.

Court	CIVIL								
	Tort	Contract	Real Estate	Min. Claim	Max. Claim	Small Claims	Estate	Eviction	Domestic Relations
Superior Courts*	X	X	X	$50,000	No Max		X	X	X
District Courts*	X	X		$0	$50,000	$2500			
Municipal Courts									

Court	CRIMINAL				
	Felony	Misdemeanor	DWI/DUI	Preliminary Hearing	Juvenile
Superior Courts*	X				X
District Courts*		X	X	X	
Municipal Courts		X	X		

ADMINISTRATION   Court Administrator, Temple of Justice, PO Box 41174, Olympia, WA, 98504; 360-357-2121, Fax: 360-357-2127. www.courts.wa.gov

COURT STRUCTURE   District Courts retain civil records for 10 years from date of final disposition, then the records are destroyed. District Courts retain criminal records forever.

Washington has a mandatory arbitration requirement for civil disputes for $35,000 or less. However, either party may request a trial in Superior Court if dissatisfied with the arbitrator's decision.

The limit for civil actions in District Court has been increased from $25,000 to $35,000.

ONLINE ACCESS   Appellate, Superior, and District Court records are available online. The Superior Court Management Information System (SCOMIS), the Appellate Records System (ACORDS) and the District/Municipal Court Information System (DISCIS) are on the Judicial Information System's JIS-Link. Case records available through JIS-Link from 1977 include criminal, civil, domestic, probate, and judgments. JIS-Link is generally available 24-hours daily. Minimum browser requirement is Internet Explorer 5.5 or Netscape 6.0. There is a one-time installation fee of $100.00 per site, and a connect time charge of $25.00 per hour (approximately $.42 per minute), plus a surcharge of $.85 per session. For information or a registration packet, contact JISLink Coordinator, Office of the Administrator for the Courts, 1206 S Quince St., PO Box 41170, Olympia WA 98504-1170, 360-357-3365 or visit www.courts.wa.gov/jislink

ADD'L INFORMATION   SASE is required in every jurisdiction that responds to written search requests.

📖 📖 📖 📖 📖 📖 📖

Adams County

Superior Court 210 W Broadway (PO Box 187), Ritzville, WA 99169-0187; 509-659-3257; Fax: 509-659-0118. Hours: 8:30AM-Noon, 1-4:30PM (PST). *Felony, Civil, Eviction, Probate.*

Civil Records: Access: Phone, fax, mail, online, in person. Only the court performs in person searches; visitors may not. Search fee: $20.00 per hour. Required to search: name, years to search; also helpful: address. Civil cases indexed by defendant, plaintiff. Civil records on computer from 1985, archived from 1900s. Index available remotely online from JIS-Link; see www.courts.wa.gov/jislink (also, see state introduction). **Criminal Records:** Access: Phone, fax, mail, online, in person. Only the court performs in person searches;

visitors may not. Search fee: $20.00 per hour. Required to search: name, years to search; also helpful: address, DOB, SSN. Criminal records on computer from 1985, archived from 1900s. Index available remotely online from JIS-Link; see www.courts.wa.gov/jislink (also, see state introduction).

General Information: No sealed, juvenile, adoption, paternity, mental health, sex offenders (victims) records released. SASE required. Turnaround time 1 week. Fax notes: $1.00 per page. Copy fee: $.50 per page. Certification fee: $2.00 plus $1.00 each additional page. Fee payee: Adams County Clerk. Business checks accepted. Prepayment is required.

Othello District Court 165 N 1st, Othello, WA 99344; 509-488-3935; Fax: 509-488-3480. Hours:

8:30AM-4:30PM (PST). *Misdemeanor, Civil Actions Under $50,000, Small Claims.*

Civil Records: Access: Phone, fax, mail, online, in person. Only the court performs in person searches; visitors may not. No search fee. Required to search: name, years to search; also helpful: address. Civil cases indexed by defendant, plaintiff. Civil records on computer from 1992, prior on index cards. Index available remotely online from JIS-Link; see www.courts.wa.gov/jislink (also, see state introduction). **Criminal Records:** Access: Phone, fax, mail, online, in person. Only the court performs in person searches; visitors may not. No search fee. Required to search: name, years to search, signed release; also helpful: address, DOB, SSN. Criminal records on computer from 1992, prior on index cards. Index available remotely online from JIS-Link; see www.courts.wa.gov/jislink (also, see state introduction).

General Information: No sealed, juvenile, adoption, paternity, mental health, sex offenders (victims) or (sometimes) DUI records released. SASE required. Turnaround time 1-3 days. Fax notes: No fee to fax results. Copy fee: $2.50 for first page, $1.00 each add'l. Certification fee: $6.00. Fee payee: Othello District Court. Personal checks accepted. Prepayment required.

Ritzville District Court 210 W Broadway, Ritzville, WA 99169; 509-659-1002; Fax: 509-659-0118. Hours: 8:30AM-4:30PM (PST). *Misdemeanor, Civil Actions Under $50,000, Small Claims.*

Civil Records: Access: Fax, mail, online, in person. Only the court performs in person searches; visitors may not. No search fee. Required to search: name, years to search; also helpful: address. Civil cases indexed by defendant, plaintiff. Civil records on computer from 10/90. Index available remotely online from JIS-Link; see www.courts.wa.gov/jislink (also, see state introduction).

Criminal Records: Access: Fax, mail, online, in person. Only the court performs in person searches; visitors may not. No search fee. Required to search: name, years to search, DOB; also helpful: address, SSN. Criminal records on computer from 10/90. Index available remotely online from JIS-Link; see www.courts.wa.gov/jislink (also, see state introduction).

General Information: No sealed, juvenile, adoption, paternity, mental health, sex offenders (victims) or (sometimes) DUI records released. SASE required. Turnaround time 2 days. Fax notes: No fee to fax results. Copy fee: $1.00 per page. Certification fee: $5.00. Fee payee: Ritzville District Court. Personal checks accepted. Prepayment is required.

Asotin County

Superior Court PO Box 159, Asotin, WA 99402-0159; 509-243-2081; Fax: 509-243-4978. Hours: 8AM-5PM (PST). *Felony, Civil, Eviction, Probate.*

Civil Records: Access: Phone, fax, mail, online, in person. Only the court performs in person searches; visitors may not. No search fee. Required to search: name, years to search; also helpful: address. Civil cases indexed by defendant, plaintiff. Civil records on computer from mid 1985, on microfiche from 1970s, archived from 1895. Index available remotely online from JIS-Link; see www.courts.wa.gov/jislink (also, see state introduction).

Criminal Records: Access: Phone, fax, mail, online, in person. Only the court performs in person searches; visitors may not. No search fee. Required to search: name, years to search, DOB; also helpful: address, SSN. Criminal records on computer from mid 1985, on microfiche from 1970s, archived from 1895. Index available remotely online from JIS-Link; see www.courts.wa.gov/jislink (also, see state introduction).

General Information: No sealed, juvenile, adoption, paternity, mental health, sex offenders (victims) or (sometimes) DUI records released. SASE required. Turnaround time 1 day. Copy fee: $2.00 for first page, $1.00 each add'l. Certification fee: Cert fee included in copy fee. Fee payee: Asotin County Clerk. Personal checks accepted. Prepayment is required.

District Court PO Box 429, Asotin, WA 99402-0429; 509-243-2027; Fax: 509-243-2091. Hours: 8AM-5PM (PST). *Misdemeanor, Civil Actions Under $50,000, Small Claims.*

Civil Records: Access: Fax, mail, online, in person. Only the court performs in person searches; visitors may not. Search fee: $6.00 per name. Required to search: name, years to search; also helpful: address. Civil cases indexed by defendant, plaintiff. Civil records on computer since 1993; prior records on log books.

Index available remotely online from JIS-Link; see www.courts.wa.gov/jislink (also, see state introduction).

Criminal Records: Access: Fax, mail, online, in person. Only the court performs in person searches; visitors may not. Search fee: $6.00 per name. Required to search: name, years to search; also helpful: address, DOB, SSN. Criminal records on computer from 1993. Index available remotely online from JIS-Link; see www.courts.wa.gov/jislink (also, see state introduction).

General Information: No sealed, juvenile, adoption, paternity, mental health, sex offenders (victims) or (sometimes) DUI records released. SASE required. Turnaround time up to 2 weeks. Fax notes: No fee to fax results. Copy fee: $.25 per page. Certification fee: $6.00. Fee payee: Asotin County District Court. Personal checks accepted. Prepayment is required.

Benton County

Superior Court 7320 W Quinault, Kennewick, WA 99336-7690; 509-735-8388. Hours: 8AM-Noon, 1-4PM (PST). *Felony, Civil, Probate.*

Civil Records: Access: Mail, in person. Only the court performs in person searches; visitors may not. Search fee: $20.00 per hour. Required to search: name, years to search; also helpful: address. Civil cases indexed by defendant, plaintiff. Civil records on computer from 1979, pre-1979 on index books. Index available remotely online from JIS-Link; see www.courts.wa.gov/jislink (also, see state introduction).

Criminal Records: Access: Mail, in person. Only the court performs in person searches; visitors may not. Search fee: $20.00 per hour. Required to search: name, years to search; also helpful: address, DOB, SSN. Criminal records on computer from 1979, pre-1979 on index books. Index available remotely online from JIS-Link; see www.courts.wa.gov/jislink (also, see state introduction).

General Information: No sealed, dependency, adoption, paternity, mental health, sex offenders (victims). SASE required. Turnaround time 10 days. Fax notes: $3.00 for first page, $1.00 each add'l. Copy fee: $.25 per page. Certification fee: $2.00 plus $1.00 per page after first. Fee payee: Benton County Clerk. Personal checks accepted. Prepayment is required.

District Court 7320 W Quinault, Kennewick, WA 99336; 509-735-8476; Fax: 509-736-3069. Hours: 7AM-Noon, 1-4PM (PST). *Misdemeanor, Civil Actions Under $50,000, Small Claims.*

Civil Records: Access: Mail, fax, online, in person. Both court and visitors may perform in person searches. Search fee: $10.00 per name. Required to search: name, years to search; also helpful: address. Civil cases indexed by defendant, plaintiff. Civil records on computer from 7/91. Index available remotely online from JIS-Link; see www.courts.wa.gov/jislink (also, see state introduction).

Criminal Records: Access: Mail, fax, online, in person. Both court and visitors may perform in person searches. Search fee: $10.00 per name. Required to search: name, years to search, DOB, signed release; also helpful: address, SSN. Criminal records on computer from 7/91. Index available remotely online from JIS-Link; see www.courts.wa.gov/jislink (also, see state introduction).

General Information: Public access terminal is available. No sealed, juvenile, adoption, paternity, mental health, sex offenders (victims) or (sometimes) DUI records released. SASE requested. Turnaround time 10 days. Fax notes: Will not fax results. Copy fee: First 50 copies free, then $.05 each. Certification fee: $5.00. Fee payee: Benton County District Court. Personal checks accepted. Credit cards accepted: Visa, MasterCard. Prepayment is required.

Chelan County

Superior Court 350 Orondo (PO Box 3025), Wenatchee, WA 98807-3025; 509-664-5380; Fax: 509-664-2611. Hours: 9AM-5PM (PST). *Felony, Civil, Eviction, Probate.*

www.co.chelan.wa.us

Civil Records: Access: Phone, fax, mail, online, in person. Both court and visitors may perform in person searches. Search fee: $20.00 per hour. Required to search: name, years to search. Civil cases indexed by defendant, plaintiff. Civil docket records on computer back to 1984; prior on microfilm to 1900. Index available online from JIS-Link; see www.courts.wa.gov/jislink (also, see state introduction). Clerk records may also be available at www.co.chelan.wa.us/scc/scc4.htm.

Criminal Records: Access: Phone, fax, mail, online, in person. Both court and visitors may perform in person searches. Search fee: $20.00 per hour. Required to search: full name, years to search; also helpful: address, DOB, SSN. Criminal records on computer back to 1984; prior on microfilm to 1900. Index available remotely online from JIS-Link; see www.courts.wa.gov/jislink (also, see state introduction).

General Information: Public access terminal is available. No sealed, juvenile, adoption, paternity, mental health, sex offenders (victims) records released. SASE required. Turnaround time 1 day. Fax notes: $3.00 for first page, $1.00 each add'l. Copy fee: $2.00 for first page, $1.00 each add'l. Certification fee: The certification fee is included in the copy fee. Fee payee: Chelan County Clerk. Personal checks and credit cards accepted. Prepayment is required.

Chelan County District Court PO Box 2182, Courthouse 4th Fl, Wenatchee, WA 98807; 509-667-6600; Fax: 509-667-6456. Hours: 8:30AM-4:30PM (PST). *Misdemeanor, Civil Actions Under $50,000, Small Claims.*

Civil Records: Access: Fax, mail, online, in person. Both court and visitors may perform in person searches. Search fee: $15.00 per name. Required to search: name; also helpful: years to search, address. Civil cases indexed by defendant, plaintiff. Civil records on computer from 1984. Records destroyed 10 years after date of last action. Index available remotely online from JIS-Link; see www.courts.wa.gov/jislink (also, see state introduction).

Criminal Records: Access: Fax, mail, online, in person. Both court and visitors may perform in person searches. Search fee: $15.00 per name. Required to search: name, DOB, signed release; also helpful: years to search, address, SSN, aliases. Criminal records on computer. Criminal files may be destroyed 5 years after close of case, infractions destroyed 3 years after close. Index available remotely online from JIS-Link; see www.courts.wa.gov/jislink (also, see state introduction).

General Information: Public access terminal is available. (For records since 1986.) No sealed, domestic violence victim info, alcohol/probation evaluation records released. SASE required. Turnaround time 1 week. Copy fee: $2.00 for first page, $1.00 each add'l. Certification fee: $5.00. Fee payee: Chelan County District Court. Personal checks accepted. Prepayment is required.

Clallam County

Superior Court 223 E Fourth St, (PO Box 863), Port Angeles, WA 98362-3098; 360-417-2386; Fax: 360-417-2581. Hours: 8AM-5PM (PST). *Felony, Civil, Eviction, Probate.*

www.clallam.net/scout

Civil Records: Access: Phone, mail, in person. Both court and visitors may perform in person searches. Search fee: $20.00 per hour. Required to search: name, years to search; also helpful: address. Civil cases indexed by defendant, plaintiff. Civil records on computer from 10/83, on microfiche from 1914, some records on index cards.

Criminal Records: Access: Phone, mail, online, in person. Both court and visitors may perform in person searches. Search fee: $20.00 per hour. Required to search: name, years to search; also helpful: address, DOB. Criminal records on computer from 10/95, on microfiche from 1914, some records on index cards. Criminal Index available remotely online from JIS-Link; see www.courts.wa.gov/jislink (also, see state introduction).

General Information: Public access terminal is available. No sealed, juvenile, adoption, paternity, mental health, sex offenders (victims) records released. SASE required. Turnaround time 1 week plus. Fax notes: Fee to fax results is $3.00 plus $1.00 per page. Copy fee: $.10 per page. Certification fee: $2.00 plus $1.00 per page after first. Fee payee: Clerk. Business checks accepted. Prepayment is required.

District One Court 223 E 4th St, Port Angeles, WA 98362; 360-417-2285; Fax: 360-417-2470. Hours: 8AM-5PM (PST). *Misdemeanor, Civil Actions Under $50,000, Small Claims.*

www.courts.wa.gov/directory/home.cfm?org=5

Civil Records: Access: Mail, fax, online, in person. Visitors must perform in person searches for themselves. No search fee. Required to search: name, years to search; also helpful: address. Civil cases indexed by defendant, plaintiff. Civil records on computer from 1986. Index available remotely online from JIS-Link; see www.courts.wa.gov/jislink (also, see state introduction).

Criminal Records: Access: Mail, fax, online, in person. Visitors must perform in person searches for themselves. No search fee. Required to search: name, years to search, DOB, signed release; also helpful: address, SSN, nationality. Criminal records on computer from 1986. Index available remotely online from JIS-Link; see www.courts.wa.gov/jislink (also, see state introduction).

General Information: Public access terminal is available. No sealed, juvenile, adoption, paternity, mental health, sex offenders (victims) or (sometimes) DUI records released. Turnaround time up to 1 week. Copy fee: $.10 per page. Certification fee: $5.00 per document. Fee payee: Clallam County Clerk, District 1 Court. Personal checks accepted. Prepayment is required.

District Two Court 502 E Division St, Forks, WA 98331; 360-374-6383; Fax: 360-374-2100. Hours: 8:30AM-4:30PM (PST). *Misdemeanor, Civil Actions Under $50,000, Small Claims.*

Civil Records: Access: Mail, online, in person. Both court and visitors may perform in person searches. No search fee. Required to search: name, years to search; also helpful: address. Civil cases indexed by defendant, plaintiff. Civil records on computer from 1989, records go back to 1988. Index available remotely online from JIS-Link; see www.courts.wa.gov/jislink (also, see state introduction).

Criminal Records: Access: Mail, online, in person. Only the court performs in person searches; visitors may not. No search fee. Required to search: name, years to search DOB; also helpful: address, SSN. Criminal records on computer from 1992 (some back to 1989), on index cards from 1982-1986. Index available remotely online from JIS-Link; see www.courts.wa.gov/jislink (also, see state introduction).

General Information: Public access terminal is available. (Criminal cases available only.) No sealed, juvenile, adoption, paternity, mental health, sex offenders (victims) or (sometimes) DUI records released. Turnaround time 1 week. Fax notes: Fee to fax

results in $1.00 per page. Copy fee: $.15 per page. Certification fee: $5.00. Fee payee: Clallam County District II Court. Personal checks accepted.

Clark County

Superior Court PO Box 5000 (1200 Franklin St.), Attention-County Clerk, Vancouver, WA 98666; 360-397-2049 Court Admin.; Civil phone: 360-397-2292; Criminal phone: 360-397-2295. Hours: 8AM-4:30PM (PST). *Felony, Civil, Eviction, Probate.*

www.co.clark.wa.us/law/supcourt.htm

Civil Records: Access: Phone, mail, online, in person, email. Both court and visitors may perform in person searches. Search fee: $20.00 per hour. Required to search: name, years to search. Civil cases indexed by defendant, plaintiff. Civil records on computer back to 1979 indexed, on microfiche from 1960, and index books prior to 1979. Index available remotely online from JIS-Link; see www.courts.wa.gov/jislink (also, see state introduction).

Criminal Records: Access: Phone, mail, online, in person, email. Both court and visitors may perform in person searches. Search fee: $20.00 per hour. Required to search: name, years to search, DOB; also helpful: address, signed release (if for employment). Criminal records on computer back to 1979, prior to 1988 on microfilm. Index available remotely online from JIS-Link; see www.courts.wa.gov/jislink (also, see state introduction).

General Information: Public access terminal is available. No sealed, juvenile, adoption, paternity, mental health, sex offenders (victims). Turnaround time 1-3 days. Copy fee: $2.00 for first page, $1.00 each add'l. Certification fee: $2.00. Fee payee: County Clerk. Only cashiers checks, money orders and attorney checks accepted. Prepayment is required.

District Court PO Box 9806, Vancouver, WA 98666; Civil phone: 360-397-2424; Criminal phone: 360-397-2424; Fax: 360-397-6044. Hours: 8AM-5PM (PST). *Misdemeanor, Civil Actions Under $50,000, Small Claims.*

www.co.clark.wa.us/law/distct.htm

Civil Records: Access: Fax, mail, online, in person. Only the court performs in person searches; visitors may not. No search fee. Required to search: name, years to search; also helpful: address. Civil cases indexed by defendant, plaintiff. Civil records on computer for approximately ten years. Index available remotely online from JIS-Link; see www.courts.wa.gov/jislink (also, see state introduction).

Criminal Records: Access: Fax, mail, online, in person. Only the court performs in person searches; visitors may not. No search fee. Required to search: name, DOB, signed release; also helpful: years to search, address, SSN. Criminal records on computer for approximately five years. Index available remotely online from JIS-Link; see www.courts.wa.gov/jislink (also, see state introduction).

General Information: No sealed, juvenile, adoption, paternity, mental health, sex offenders (victims) or (sometimes) DUI records released. Turnaround time 1 week. Fax notes: No fee to fax results. Copy fee: $.15 per page. Certification fee: $5.00. Fee payee: Clark County District Court. Personal checks accepted. Prepayment is required.

Columbia County

Superior Court 341 E Main St, Dayton, WA 99328; 509-382-4321; Fax: 509-382-4830. Hours: 8:30AM-Noon, 1-4:30PM (PST). *Felony, Civil, Eviction, Probate.*

Civil Records: Access: Phone, fax, mail, online, in person. Only the court performs in person searches; visitors may not. Search fee: $20.00 per hour. Required to search: name, years to search. Civil cases indexed by

defendant, plaintiff. Civil records on computer from 1987, some records on index cards and books, archived from 1900s. Index available remotely online from JIS-Link; see www.courts.wa.gov/jislink (also, see state introduction).

Criminal Records: Access: Phone, fax, mail, online, in person. Only the court performs in person searches; visitors may not. Search fee: $20.00 per hour. Required to search: name, years to search. Criminal records on computer from 1987, some records on index cards and books, archived from 1900s. Index available remotely online from JIS-Link; see www.courts.wa.gov/jislink (also, see state introduction).

General Information: No sealed, juvenile, adoption, paternity, mental health, sex offenders (victims). SASE required. Turnaround time 1 week. Copy fee: $1.00 per page. Certification fee: $2.00 plus $1.00 per page after first. Fee payee: Columbia County Clerk. Personal checks accepted. Prepayment is required.

District Court 341 E Main St, Dayton, WA 99328-1361; 509-382-4812; Fax: 509-382-4830. Hours: 8:30AM-4:30PM (PST). *Misdemeanor, Civil Actions Under $50,000, Small Claims.*

Civil Records: Access: Mail, online, in person. Both court and visitors may perform in person searches. No search fee. Required to search: name, years to search; also helpful: address. Civil cases indexed by plaintiff. Civil records on computer since 05/96; prior on index books. Index available remotely online from JIS-Link; see www.courts.wa.gov/jislink (also, see state introduction).

Criminal Records: Access: Mail, online, in person. Both court and visitors may perform in person searches. Search fee: Fee may be charged if more than 1 case. Required to search: name, years to search, DOB, signed release; also helpful: address, SSN. Criminal records on computer from 1993, on books prior. Index available remotely online from JIS-Link; see www.courts.wa.gov/jislink (also, see state introduction).

General Information: No sealed, juvenile, adoption, paternity, mental health, sex offenders (victims) or (sometimes) DUI records released. SASE required. Turnaround time 7-10 days. Copy fee: $1.00 per page. Certification fee: $5.00 per page. Fee payee: District Court. Personal checks accepted. Prepayment required.

Cowlitz County

Superior Court 312 SW First Ave, Attn: County Clerk, Kelso, WA 98626-1724; 360-577-3016; Fax: 360-577-2323. Hours: 8:30-4:30PM (PST). *Felony, Civil, Eviction, Probate.*

www.co.cowlitz.wa.us/clerk

Civil Records: Access: Phone, fax, mail, online, in person. Both court and visitors may perform in person searches. Search fee: $10.00 per name. Required to search: name, years to search; also helpful: address. Civil cases indexed by defendant, plaintiff. Civil records on computer back to 1982; on microfilm through 1990, hard copy files from 1990. Index available remotely online from JIS-Link; see www.courts.wa.gov/jislink (also, see state introduction).

Criminal Records: Access: Phone, fax, mail, online, in person. Both court and visitors may perform in person searches. Search fee: $10.00 per name. Required to search: name, years to search; also helpful: address, DOB, SSN. Criminal records on computer back to 1982, on microfilm through 1980, hard copy files from 1990. Index available remotely online from JIS-Link; see www.courts.wa.gov/jislink (also, see state introduction).

General Information: Public access terminal is available. No sealed, juvenile, adoption, paternity, mental health records released. SASE required. Turnaround time 2 days. Fax notes: Will fax if pre-payment received. Copy fee: $2.00 for first page, $1.00 each add'l. Certification fee: Included in copy fee. Fee payee: Cowlitz County Superior Court Clerk. Business checks accepted. Prepayment is required.

District Court 312 SW First Ave, Kelso, WA 98626-1724; 360-577-3073. Hours: 8:30AM-5PM (PST). *Misdemeanor, Civil Actions Under $50,000, Small Claims.*

Civil Records: Access: Phone, fax, mail, online, in person. Only the court performs in person searches; visitors may not. Search fee: $2 mailing fee. Required to search: name, years to search; also helpful: address. Civil cases indexed by defendant, plaintiff. Civil records on index cards back to 1990. Index available remotely online from JIS-Link; see www.courts.wa.gov/jislink (also, see state introduction).

Criminal Records: Access: Mail, fax, online, in person. Only the court performs in person searches; visitors may not. Search fee: None$2 mailing fee. Required to search: name, years to search, DOB; also helpful: address, SSN. Criminal records on index cards back to 1991. Index available remotely online from JIS-Link; see www.courts.wa.gov/jislink (also, see state introduction).

General Information: No sealed, adoption, paternity, mental health records released. Turnaround time 2 weeks. Copy fee: $.25 per page. Certification fee: $5.00. Fee payee: District Court. No personal checks accepted. Prepayment is required.

Douglas County

Superior Court PO Box 516, Waterville, WA 98858-0516; 509-745-9063; Fax: 509-745-8027. Hours: 8AM-5PM (PST). *Felony, Civil, Eviction, Probate.*

Note: Clerk is reached at 509-745-8529.

Civil Records: Access: Phone, fax, mail, online, in person. Both the court and visitors may performs in person searches. Search fee: $20.00 per hour. Required to search: name, years to search; also helpful: address. Civil cases indexed by defendant, plaintiff. Civil records on computer from 1985, archived and on microfiche from 1883, some records on index books. Index available remotely online from JIS-Link; see www.courts.wa.gov/jislink (also, see state introduction).

Criminal Records: Access: Phone, fax, mail, online, in person. Both the court and visitor may perform in person searches. Search fee: $20.00 per hour. Required to search: name, years to search, DOB; also helpful: address, SSN. Criminal records on computer from 1985, archived and on microfiche from 1883, some records on index books. Index available remotely online from JIS-Link; see www.courts.wa.gov/jislink (also, see state introduction).

General Information: No sealed, juvenile, adoption, paternity, mental health, sex offenders (victims). SASE required. Turnaround time 1 week. Fax notes: $2.00 for first page, $1.00 each add'l. Copy fee: $2.00 for first page, $1.00 each add'l. Certification fee: $2.00 plus $1.00 per page after first. Fee payee: Douglas County Clerk. Business checks accepted. Prepayment is required.

District Court - Bridgeport 1206 Columbia Ave (PO Box 730), Bridgeport, WA 98813-0730; 509-686-2034; Fax: 509-686-4671. Hours: 8:30AM-4:30PM (PST). *Misdemeanor, Small Claims.*

Note: If record not found in this court, request forwarded to East Wenatchee (South) court.

Civil Records: Access: Fax, mail, online, in person. Only the court performs in person searches; visitors may not. Please use the court's "Request for Information" form. Search fee: $10.00 per name. Required to search: name, years to search; also helpful: address. Civil cases indexed by defendant. Civil records on computer back to 02/95. Index available remotely online from JIS-Link; see www.courts.wa.gov/jislink (also, see state introduction).

Criminal Records: Access: Fax, mail, online, in person. Only the court performs in person searches; visitors may not. Please use the court's "Request for Information" form. Search fee: $10.00 per name. Required to search: name, years to search; also helpful: address, DOB, SSN. Criminal records on computer back to 02/95. Index available remotely online from JIS-Link; see www.courts.wa.gov/jislink (also, see state introduction).

General Information: No sealed, juvenile, adoption, paternity, mental health, sex offenders (victims) or (sometimes) DUI records released. SASE required. Turnaround time 10 days. Fax notes: Will not fax results. Copy fee: $1.00 per page. Certification fee: $5.00 per page. Fee payee: Douglas County District Court Bridgeport. Personal checks accepted. Prepayment is required.

District Court - East Wenatchee 110 3rd St NE, East Wenatchee, WA 98802; 509-884-3536; Fax: 509-884-5973. 8:30AM-4:30PM (PST). *Misdemeanor, Civil Actions Under $50,000, Small Claims.*

www.douglascountywa.net/departments/district_court/index.html

Note: If record not found in this court, request forwarded to Bridgeport Branch (North) County District Court.

Civil Records: Access: Fax, mail, online, in person. Only the court performs in person searches; visitors may not. Search fee: $10.00 per hour. Required to search: name, years to search; also helpful: address. Civil cases indexed by defendant, plaintiff. Civil records on index cards from 1982. Index available remotely online from JIS-Link; see www.courts.wa.gov/jislink (also, see state introduction).

Criminal Records: Access: Fax, mail, online, in person. Only the court performs in person searches; visitors may not. Search fee: $10.00 per hour. Required to search: name, years to search; also helpful: address, DOB, SSN. Criminal records on computer back 5 years. Index available remotely online from JIS-Link; see www.courts.wa.gov/jislink (also, see state introduction).

General Information: No sealed, juvenile, adoption, paternity, mental health, sex offenders (victims), DUI records, treatment reports released. SASE required. Turnaround time 1 week. Fax notes: $1.00 for first page, $1.00 each add'l. Local faxing only. Copy fee: $1.00 per page. Certification fee: $5.00. Fee payee: Douglas District Court. Personal checks accepted. Prepayment is required.

Ferry County

Superior Court 350 E Delaware #4, Republic, WA 99166; 509-775-5245. Hours: 8AM-4PM (PST). *Felony, Civil, Probate.*

Civil Records: Access: Phone, mail, online, in person. Only the court may perform in person searches. Search fee: $20.00 per hour. Required to search: name, years to search; also helpful: address. Civil cases indexed by defendant, plaintiff. Civil records on computer back to 1987; other records go back to 1900. Index available remotely online from JIS-Link; see www.courts.wa.gov/jislink (also, see state introduction).

Criminal Records: Access: Phone, mail, online, in person. Only the court may perform in person searches. Search fee: $20.00 per hour. Required to search: name, years to search; also helpful: address, DOB. Criminal records on computer back to 1987; other records go back to 1900. Index available remotely online from JIS-Link; see www.courts.wa.gov/jislink (also, see state introduction).

General Information: No sealed, adoption, paternity, mental health or sex offenders (victims). SASE required. Turnaround time 1-4 days. Copy fee: $2.00 for first page, $1.00 each add'l. Certification fee: $2.00 plus

$1.00 each additional page. Fee payee: Ferry County Clerk. Business checks accepted. Prepayment required.

District Court 350 E Delaware Ave #6, Republic, WA 99166-9747; 509-775-5244; Fax: 509-775-5221. Hours: 8AM-4PM (PST). *Misdemeanor, Civil Actions Under $50,000, Small Claims.*

Civil Records: Access: Fax, mail, online, in person. Only the court performs in person searches; visitors may not. No search fee. Required to search: name, years to search; also helpful: address. Civil cases indexed by case number. Civil records on computer back to 1995; others back to 1995. Index available remotely online from JIS-Link; see www.courts.wa.gov/jislink for information (also, see state introduction).

Criminal Records: Access: Mail, fax, online, in person. Only the court performs in person searches; visitors may not. No search fee. Required to search: name, years to search, DOB; also helpful: address, SSN, signed release. Criminal records on computer back to 1995; others back to 1995. Index available remotely online from JIS-Link; see www.courts.wa.gov/jislink (also, see state introduction).

General Information: No sealed, juvenile, adoption, paternity, mental health, sex offenders (victims) or (sometimes) DUI records released. SASE required. Turnaround time 1 week. Fax notes: No fee to fax results. Copy fee: $2.00 for first page, $1.00 each add'l. Certification fee: $5.00. Fee payee: Ferry County District Court. Personal checks accepted. Prepayment is required.

Franklin County

Superior Court 1016 N 4th St, Pasco, WA 99301; 509-545-3525; Fax: 509-545-2243. Hours: 8:30AM-5PM (PST). *Felony, Civil, Eviction, Probate.*

www.co.franklin.wa.us

Civil Records: Access: Mail, online, in person, email. Only the court performs in person searches; visitors may not. Search fee: $20.00 per hour. Required to search: name, years to search; also helpful: address. Civil cases indexed by defendant, plaintiff. Civil records on computer from 7/83, on index books, archived from 1900s. Index available remotely online from JIS-Link; see www.courts.wa.gov/jislink (also, see state introduction).

Criminal Records: Access: Mail, online, in person. Only the court performs in person searches; visitors may not. Search fee: $20.00 per hour. Required to search: name, years to search, DOB; also helpful: address, SSN. Criminal records on computer from 7/83, on index books, archived from 1900s. Index available remotely online from JIS-Link; see www.courts.wa.gov/jislink (also, see state introduction).

General Information: No sealed, juvenile, adoption, paternity, mental health, sex offenders (victims). SASE required. Turnaround time 1 week. Fax notes: Fee to fax results is $3.00 per page. Copy fee: $2.00 for first page, $1.00 each add'l. Certification fee: $2.00 plus $1.00 per page after first. Fee payee: Franklin County Superior Court Clerk. Business checks accepted. Prepayment is required.

District Court 1016 N 4th St, Pasco, WA 99301; 509-545-3593; Fax: 509-545-3588. Hours: 8:30AM-Noon, 1-5PM (PST). *Misdemeanor, Civil Actions Under $50,000, Small Claims.*

Civil Records: Access: Mail, online, in person. Only the court performs in person searches; visitors may not. Search fee: $10.00 per name. Required to search: name, years to search; also helpful: address. Civil cases indexed by defendant, plaintiff. Civil records on computer from 1993, prior on index cards. Index available remotely online from JIS-Link; see www.courts.wa.gov/jislink (also, see state introduction).

Criminal Records: Access: Mail, online, in person. Only the court performs in person searches; visitors may not. Search fee: $10.00 per name. Required to search: name, years to search, DOB; also helpful: address, SSN. Criminal records on computer from 1987, prior on index cards. Index available remotely online from JIS-Link; see www.courts.wa.gov/jislink (also, see state introduction).

General Information: No sealed, juvenile, adoption, paternity, mental health, sex offenders (victims) or (sometimes) DUI records released. SASE required. Turnaround time 2-3 days. Copy fee: $.25 per page. Certification fee: $5.00. Fee payee: Franklin District Court. Personal checks accepted. Prepayment required.

Garfield County

Superior Court PO Box 915, Pomeroy, WA 99347-0915; 509-843-3731; Fax: 509-843-1224. Hours: 8:30AM-Noon, 1-5PM (PST). *Felony, Civil, Eviction, Probate.*

Civil Records: Access: Phone, fax, mail, online, in person. Only the court performs in person searches; visitors may not. Search fee: $8.00 per hour. Required to search: name, years to search; also helpful: address. Civil cases indexed by defendant, plaintiff. Civil records on docket books, archived from 1882; on computer back to 1993. Index available remotely online from JIS-Link; see www.courts.wa.gov/jislink (also, see state introduction).

Criminal Records: Access: Fax, mail, online, in person, email. Only the court performs in person searches; visitors may not. Search fee: $8.00 per hour. Required to search: name, years to search, DOB; also helpful: address, SSN. Criminal records on docket books, archived from 1882; on comptuer back to 1993. Index available remotely online from JIS-Link; see www.courts.wa.gov/jislink (also, see state introduction).

General Information: No sealed, juvenile, adoption, paternity, mental health, sex offenders (victims). SASE requested. Turnaround time 1 week. Fax notes: $.50 per page. Copy fee: $1.00 per page. Certification fee: $2.00 plus $1.00 per page after first. Fee payee: Garfield County Clerk. Personal checks accepted. Prepayment is required.

District Court PO Box 817, Pomeroy, WA 99347-0817; 509-843-1002. Hours: 8:30AM-5PM (PST). *Misdemeanor, Civil Actions Under $50,000, Small Claims.*

Civil Records: Access: Mail, online, in person. Only the court performs in person searches; visitors may not. No search fee. Required to search: name, years to search; also helpful: address. Civil cases indexed by defendant. Civil records on index cards. Index available remotely online from JIS-Link; see www.courts.wa.gov/jislink (also, see state introduction).

Criminal Records: Access: Mail, online, in person. Only the court performs in person searches; visitors may not. No search fee. Required to search: name, years to search, DOB; also helpful: address, SSN. Criminal records on index cards. Index available remotely online from JIS-Link; see www.courts.wa.gov/jislink (also, see state introduction).

General Information: No sealed, juvenile, adoption, mental health, sex offenders (victims) or (sometimes) DUI records released. Turnaround time 1 week. Copy fee: $.25 per page. Certification fee: $5.00. Fee payee: Garfield County District Court. Personal checks accepted. Prepayment is required.

Grant County

Superior Court PO Box 37, Ephrata, WA 98823-0037; 509-754-2011 X448; Fax: 509-754-6568. Hours: 8AM-4:30PM (PST). *Felony, Civil, Eviction, Probate.*

Civil Records: Access: Phone, mail, online, in person. Both court and visitors may perform in person searches. Search fee: $10.00 per name. Required to search: name, years to search; also helpful: address. Civil cases

indexed by defendant, plaintiff. Civil records on computer from 1982, and some on index cards, archived from 1909. Index available remotely online from JIS-Link; see www.courts.wa.gov/jislink (also, see state introduction).

Criminal Records: Access: Phone, mail, online, in person. Both court and visitors may perform in person searches. Search fee: $10.00 per name. Required to search: name, years to search; also helpful: address, DOB, SSN. Criminal records on computer from 1982, and some on index cards, archived from 1909. Index available remotely online from JIS-Link; see www.courts.wa.gov/jislink (also, see state introduction).

General Information: Public access terminal is available. No sealed, juvenile, adoption, paternity, mental health, sex offenders (victims) records released. SASE required. Turnaround time 2 weeks. Copy fee: $2.00 for first page, $1.00 each add'l. Certification fee: $2.00 plus $1.00 per page after first. Fee payee: Grant County Clerk's Office. Business checks accepted. Prepayment is required.

District Court PO Box 37, Ephrata, WA 98823-0037; 509-754-2011 X318; Fax: 509-754-6099. Hours: 8AM-5PM (PST). *Misdemeanor, Civil Actions Under $50,000, Small Claims.*

Civil Records: Access: Mail, online, in person. Only the court performs in person searches; visitors may not. Search fee: $10.00 per name. Required to search: name, years to search; also helpful: address. Civil cases indexed by defendant, plaintiff. Civil records on computer from 3/91, on index cards. Index available remotely online from JIS-Link; see www.courts.wa.gov/jislink (also, see state introduction).

Criminal Records: Access: Mail, online, in person. Only the court performs in person searches; visitors may not. Search fee: $10.00 per name. Required to search: name, years to search, DOB; also helpful: address, SSN. Criminal records on computer from 3/91, on index cards. Index available remotely online from JIS-Link; see www.courts.wa.gov/jislink (also, see state introduction).

General Information: No sealed, probation, juvenile, adoption, paternity, mental health, sex offenders (victims) or (sometimes) DUI records released. Turnaround time up to 30 days. Copy fee: $2.00 for first page, $1.00 each add'l. Certification fee: $5.00 per page. Fee payee: Grant County District Court. Personal checks accepted. Prepayment is required.

Grays Harbor County

Superior Court 102 W Broadway, Rm 203, Montesano, WA 98563-3606; 360-249-3842; Fax: 360-249-6381. Hours: 8AM-5PM (PST). *Felony, Civil, Eviction, Probate.*

Civil Records: Access: Phone, fax, mail, online, in person. Both court and visitors may perform in person searches. Search fee: $20.00 per name. No fee for records before 1980. Required to search: name, years to search; also helpful: address. Civil cases indexed by defendant, plaintiff. Civil records on computer from 12/80, on microfiche from 1856, on index cards. Index available remotely online from JIS-Link; see www.courts.wa.gov/jislink (also, see state introduction).

Criminal Records: Access: Phone, fax, mail, online, in person. Both court and visitors may perform in person searches. Search fee: $20.00 per name. No fee for records before 1980. Required to search: name, years to search; also helpful: address, DOB, SSN. Criminal records on computer from 12/80, on microfiche from 1856, on index cards. Index available remotely online from JIS-Link; see www.courts.wa.gov/jislink (also, see state introduction).

General Information: No sealed, juvenile, adoption, paternity, mental health, sex offenders (victims). SASE required. Turnaround time 2 days. Fax notes: No fee to fax results. Fax available in emergency only. Copy fee:

$2.00 for first page, $1.00 each add'l. Certification fee: Included in copy fee. Fee payee: Grays Harbor County Clerk. Business checks accepted. Prepayment required.

District Court No 1 102 W Broadway, Rm 202, Montesano, WA 98563; 360-249-3441; Fax: 360-249-6382. 8AM-Noon, 1-5PM (PST). *Misdemeanor, Civil Actions Under $50,000, Small Claims.*

www.co.grays-harbor.wa.us/info/judicial

Civil Records: Access: Phone, fax, mail, online, in person. Only the court performs in person searches; visitors may not. No search fee. Required to search: name, years to search; also helpful: address. Civil cases indexed by defendant, plaintiff. Civil records on computer from 4/91, on index cards. Index available remotely online from JIS-Link; see www.courts.wa.gov/jislink (also, see state introduction).

Criminal Records: Access: Phone, fax, mail, online, in person. Only the court performs in person searches; visitors may not. No search fee. Required to search: name, years to search, DOB; also helpful: address, SSN. Criminal records on computer from 4/91, on index cards. Index available remotely online from JIS-Link; see www.courts.wa.gov/jislink (also, see state introduction).

General Information: No sealed, juvenile, adoption, paternity, mental health, sex offenders (victims) records released. SASE required. Turnaround time 1 week. Copy fee: $.25 per page. Certification fee: $5.00. Fee payee: Grays Harbor District Court #1. Personal checks accepted. Prepayment is required.

District Court No 2 PO Box 142, Aberdeen, WA 98520-0035; 360-532-7061; Fax: 360-532-7704. Hours: 8AM-Noon, 1-5PM (PST). *Misdemeanor, Civil Actions Under $50,000, Small Claims.*

www.co.grays-harbor.wa.us

Civil Records: Access: Phone, fax, mail, online, in person. Only the court performs in person searches; visitors may not. No search fee. Required to search: name, years to search; also helpful: address. Civil cases indexed by defendant, plaintiff. Civil records on computer from 4/91, on index cards. Index available remotely online from JIS-Link; see www.courts.wa.gov/jislink (also, see state introduction).

Criminal Records: Access: Phone, fax, mail, online, in person. Only the court performs in person searches; visitors may not. No search fee. Required to search: name, years to search, DOB; also helpful: address, SSN. Criminal records on computer from 4/91, on index cards. Index available remotely online from JIS-Link; see www.courts.wa.gov/jislink (also, see state introduction).

General Information: No sealed, juvenile, adoption, paternity, mental health, sex offenders (victims) or (sometimes) DUI records released. SASE required. Turnaround time 1 week. Fax notes: No fee to fax results. Copy fee: $.25 per page. Certification fee: $5.00. Fee payee: Grays Harbor District Court #2. Personal checks accepted. Prepayment is required.

Island County

Superior Court PO Box 5000, Coupeville, WA 98239-5000; 360-679-7359. Hours: 8AM-4:30PM (PST). *Felony, Civil, Eviction, Probate.*

Civil Records: Access: Phone, mail, online, in person. Both court and visitors may perform in person searches. Search fee: $20.00 per hour. Required to search: name, years to search; also helpful: address. Civil cases indexed by defendant, plaintiff. Civil records on computer from 7/1984, microfiche from 1889. Archived in Bellingham, WA. Index available remotely online from JIS-Link; see www.courts.wa.gov/jislink (also, see state introduction).

Criminal Records: Access: Phone, mail, online, in person. Both court and visitors may perform in person searches. Search fee: $20.00 per hour. Required to search: name, years to search; also helpful: address, DOB. Criminal records on computer from 7/1984, microfiche from 1889. Archived in Bellingham, WA. Index available remotely online from JIS-Link; see www.courts.wa.gov/jislink (also, see state introduction). **General Information:** No sealed, dependency, truancy, adoption, paternity, mental health, sex offenders (victims). SASE required. Turnaround time 1 week. Copy fee: $.25 per page. Certification fee: $2.00 first page and $1.00 each add'l. Fee payee: Island county Clerk. Business checks accepted. Prepayment required.

District Court 800 S 8th Ave, Oak Harbor, WA 98277; 360-675-5988; Fax: 360-675-8231. Hours: 8AM-4:30PM (PST). *Misdemeanor, Civil Actions Under $50,000, Small Claims.*

Note: Records requests are done as time permits. Bottom of priority list.

Civil Records: Access: Fax, mail, online, in person. Both court and visitors may perform in person searches. No search fee. Required to search: name, years to search; also helpful: address. Civil cases indexed by defendant. Civil records on computer from 1991, on index by alpha. Index available remotely online from JIS-Link; see www.courts.wa.gov/jislink (also, see state introduction).
Criminal Records: Access: Fax, mail, online, in person. Only the court performs in person searches; visitors may not. No search fee. Required to search: name, years to search, DOB; also helpful: address, SSN. Criminal records on computer from 1991, on index by alpha. Index available remotely online from JIS-Link; see www.courts.wa.gov/jislink (also, see state introduction).
General Information: No sealed, juvenile, adoption, paternity, mental health, sex offenders (victims) or (sometimes) DUI records released. SASE required. Turnaround time 1-7 days. Fax notes: $1.00 per page. Copy fee: $.25 per page. Certification fee: $5.00. Fee payee: Island District Court. Personal checks accepted. Prepayment is required.

Jefferson County

Superior Court PO Box 1220, Port Townsend, WA 98368-0920; 360-385-9125. Hours: 9AM-5PM (PST). *Felony, Civil, Eviction, Probate.*

Civil Records: Access: Phone, mail, online, in person. Both court and visitors may perform in person searches. Search fee: $8.00 per hour. Required to search: name, years to search. Civil cases indexed by defendant, plaintiff. Civil records on computer from 1983, on microfiche from 1890s. Archive in Bellingham, WA. Index available remotely online from JIS-Link; see www.courts.wa.gov/jislink (also, see state introduction).
Criminal Records: Access: Phone, mail, online, in person. Both court and visitors may perform in person searches. Search fee: $8.00 per hour. Required to search: name, years to search; also helpful: DOB. Criminal records on computer from 1983, on microfiche from 1890s. Archive in Bellingham, WA. Index available remotely online from JIS-Link; see www.courts.wa.gov/jislink (also, see state introduction).
General Information: No sealed, juvenile, adoption, paternity, mental health records released. SASE required. Turnaround time 2 days. Copy fee: $1.00 for first page, $.50 each add'l. Certification fee: $2.00 plus $1.00 per page after first. Fee payee: County Clerk. Personal checks accepted. Out of state checks not accepted. Prepayment is required.

District Court PO Box 1220, Port Townsend, WA 98368-0920; 360-385-9135; Fax: 360-385-9367. Hours: 8AM-5PM (PST). *Misdemeanor, Civil Actions Under $50,000, Small Claims.*

www.co.jefferson.wa.us

Civil Records: Access: Phone, fax, mail, online, in person. Only the court performs in person searches;

visitors may not. No search fee. Required to search: name, years to search; also helpful: address. Civil cases indexed by defendant. Civil records on DISCIS computer from 1993, on computer from '90-'93, on log books prior to 1990. Physical files kept 10 years from disposition per retention schedule. Index available remotely online from JIS-Link; see www.courts.wa.gov/jislink (also, see state introduction).
Criminal Records: Access: Phone, fax, mail, online, in person. Only the court performs in person searches; visitors may not. No search fee. Required to search: name, DOB; also helpful: years to search, address, SSN. Criminal records on DISCIS computer from 1993, on computer from '90-'93, on log books prior to 1990. Physical files kept 10 years from disposition per retention schedule. Index available remotely online from JIS-Link; see www.courts.wa.gov/jislink (also, see state introduction).
General Information: No sealed, juvenile, adoption, paternity, mental health, sex offenders (victims) records released. SASE required. Turnaround time 1 week. Copy fee: $.15 per page. Certification fee: $6.00. Personal checks accepted. Prepayment is required.

King County

Superior Court 516 Third Ave, E-609 Courthouse, Seattle, WA 98104-2386; 206-296-9300, 800-325-6165 in state. Hours: 8:30AM-4:30AM (PST). *Felony, Civil, Eviction, Probate.*

www.metrokc.gov/kcscc

Civil Records: Access: Mail, online, in person. Both court and visitors may perform in person searches. Search fee: $20.00 per hour. Fee $25.00 minimum including copies. Required to search: name, years to search; also helpful: address. Civil cases indexed by defendant, plaintiff. Civil records on computer since 1979; prior records on microfiche back to 1935. Index available remotely online from JIS-Link; see www.courts.wa.gov/jislink (also, see state introduction).
Criminal Records: Access: Mail, online, in person. Both court and visitors may perform in person searches. Search fee: $20.00 per hour. Fee is $25.00 if number of pages unknown. Required to search: name, years to search; also helpful: address, DOB, SSN. Criminal records on computer since 1979; prior records on microfiche back to 1938. Index available remotely online from JIS-Link; see www.courts.wa.gov/jislink (also, see state introduction).
General Information: Public access terminal is available. No sealed, juvenile, adoption, paternity, mental health, sex offenders (victims). SASE required. Turnaround time 2 weeks. Copy fee: $.15 per page (self serve). Microfiche/computer image copy fee: $.25 per page. Certification fee: $2.00 plus $1.00 per page after first. Fee payee: King County Superior Court Clerk. Personal checks accepted if in state. Prepayment is required.

District Court Aukeen Division 1210 S Central, Kent, WA 98032-7426; 206-296-7740; 800-325-6165 +59200; 206-205-9200. Hours: 8:30AM-4:30PM (PST). *Misdemeanor, Civil Actions Under $50,000, Small Claims.*

www.metrokc.gov/kcdc

Note: Civil Filing Area: Enumclaw, Auburn, Black Diamond, Maple Valley, Covington, Algona, Pacific, Ravensdale, Hobart.
Civil Records: Access: Mail, online, in person. Only the court performs in person searches; visitors may not. No search fee. Required to search: name, years to search; also helpful: address. Civil cases indexed by defendant, plaintiff. Civil records on computer 5 years back. Index available remotely online from JIS-Link; see www.courts.wa.gov/jislink (also, see state introduction).

Criminal Records: Access: Mail, online, in person. Only the court performs in person searches; visitors may not. No search fee. Required to search: name, years to search, DOB; also helpful: address, SSN. Criminal records on computer 5 years back. Index available remotely online from JIS-Link; see www.courts.wa.gov/jislink (also, see state introduction).
General Information: No sealed, juvenile, adoption, paternity, mental health, sex offenders (victims) or (sometimes) DUI records released. SASE required. Turnaround time 1 day. Copy fee: $.15 per page. Certification fee: $5.00. Fee payee: Aukeen District Court. Personal checks accepted. Prepayment required.

District Court Bellevue Division 585 112th Ave SE, Bellevue, WA 98004; 206-296-3650; 800-325-6165 +59200; 206-205-9200; Fax: 206-296-0589. Hours: 8:30AM-4:30PM (PST). *Misdemeanor, Civil Actions Under $50,000, Small Claims.*

www.metrokc.gov/kcdc

Note: Civil Filing Area: Bellevue, Eastgate, Factoria, Mercer Island, Clyde Hill, Beaux Arts.
Civil Records: Access: Phone, mail, online, in person. Both court and visitors may perform in person searches. No search fee. Required to search: name, years to search; also helpful: address. Civil cases indexed by defendant, plaintiff. Civil records on computer for past 10 years. Index available remotely online from JIS-Link; see www.courts.wa.gov/jislink (also, see state introduction).
Criminal Records: Access: Phone, mail, online, in person. Both court and visitors may perform in person searches. No search fee. Required to search: name, years to search, DOB; also helpful: address, SSN. Criminal records on computer from 1987. Criminal records may be removed after 5 years from disposition. Index available remotely online from JIS-Link; see www.courts.wa.gov/jislink (also, see state introduction).
General Information: No sealed, juvenile, adoption, paternity, mental health, sex offenders (victims) or (sometimes) DUI records released. Turnaround time cannot be guaranteed for written requests. Copy fee: $.15 per page. Certification fee: $5.00. Fee payee: KCDC, Bellevue Division. Personal checks accepted. Credit cards accepted: Visa, MasterCard. Prepayment is required.

District Court Federal Way Division 33506 10th Pl South, Federal Way, WA 98003-6396; 206-296-7784; 800-325-6165 +59200; 206-205-9200; Fax: 206-296-0590. Hours: 8:30AM-4:30PM (PST). *Misdemeanor, Civil Actions Under $50,000, Small Claims.*

www.metrokc.gov/kcdc

Note: Civil Filing Area: Federal Way.
Civil Records: Access: Phone, mail, online, in person. Only the court performs in person searches; visitors may not. No search fee. Required to search: name, years to search; also helpful: address. Civil cases indexed by defendant, plaintiff. Civil records on computer back 10 years. Index available remotely online from JIS-Link; see www.courts.wa.gov/jislink (also, see state introduction).
Criminal Records: Access: Phone, mail, online, in person. Only the court performs in person searches; visitors may not. No search fee. Required to search: name, years to search, DOB, signed release; also helpful: address. Criminal records on computer back 5 years. Index available remotely online from JIS-Link; see www.courts.wa.gov/jislink (see state introduction).
General Information: No sealed, adoption, paternity, mental health, sex offenders (victims) or (sometimes) DUI records released. SASE required. Turnaround time up to 7 days. Copy fee: $.15 per page. Certification fee: $5.00. Fee payee: Federal Way Division King County

District Court. Personal checks accepted. Credit cards accepted: Visa, MasterCard. Prepayment is required.

District Court Issaquah Division
5415 220th Ave SW, Issaquah, WA 98029-6839; 206-296-7688; 800-325-6165 +59200; 206-205-9200; Fax: 206-296-0591. Hours: 8:30AM-4:30PM (PST). *Misdemeanor, Civil Actions Under $50,000, Small Claims.*

www.metrokc.gov/kcdc

Note: Civil Filing Area: Issaquah, Sammamish, High Point, Preston, Fall City, Snoqualmie, North Bend, Cedar Falls, Tokul, Alpental.

Civil Records: Access: Mail, online, in person. Only the court performs in person searches; visitors may not. No search fee. Required to search: name, years to search; also helpful: address. Civil cases indexed by defendant, plaintiff. Civil records on computer back 10 years. Index available remotely online from JIS-Link; see www.courts.wa.gov/jislink (also, see state introduction).

Criminal Records: Access: Mail, online, in person. Only the court performs in person searches; visitors may not. No search fee. Required to search: name, years to search, DOB, signed release; also helpful: address. Criminal records on computer back 5 years. Index available remotely online from JIS-Link; see www.courts.wa.gov/jislink (also, see state introduction).

General Information: No sealed, juvenile, sex offenders (victims) or (sometimes) DUI records released. SASE required. Turnaround time 1-5 days. Copy fee: $.15 per page. Certification fee: $6.00. Fee payee: Issaquah Division. Personal checks accepted. Prepayment is required.

District Court Northeast Division
8601 160th Ave NE, Redmond, WA 98052-3548; 206-296-3667; 800-325-6165 +59200; 206-205-9200. Hours: 8:30AM-4:30PM (PST). *Misdemeanor, Civil Actions Under $50,000, Small Claims.*

www.metrokc.gov/kcdc

Note: Civil Filing Area: Redmond, Kirkland, Woodinville, Bothell, Duvall, Carnation, Juanita.

Civil Records: Access: Mail, online, in person. Both court and visitors may perform in person searches. No search fee. Required to search: name, years to search; also helpful: address. Civil cases indexed by defendant, plaintiff. Civil records on computer back 10 years. Index available remotely online from JIS-Link; see www.courts.wa.gov/jislink (also, see state introduction).

Criminal Records: Access: Mail, online, in person. Both court and visitors may perform in person searches. No search fee. Required to search: name, years to search, DOB; also helpful: address. Criminal records on computer back 5 years. Index available remotely online from JIS-Link; see www.courts.wa.gov/jislink (also, see state introduction).

General Information: Public access terminal is available. No sealed, juvenile, adoption, paternity, mental health, sex offenders (victims) or (sometimes) DUI records released. Turnaround time 1-2 weeks. Copy fee: $.15 per page. Certification fee: $5.00. Fee payee: King County District Court. Personal checks accepted. Credit cards accepted: Visa, MasterCard. Prepayment is required.

District Court Renton Division
3407 NE 2nd St, Renton, WA 98056-4193; 206-296-3532; 800-325-6165 +59200; 206-205-9200; Fax: 206-296-0593. Hours: 8:30AM-4:30PM (PST). *Misdemeanor, Civil Actions Under $50,000, Small Claims.*

www.metrokc.gov/kcdc

Note: Civil Filing Area: Renton, Newcastle, Tukwila.

Civil Records: Access: Phone, fax, mail, online, in person. Only the court performs in person searches; visitors may not. No search fee. Required to search: name, years to search; also helpful: address. Civil cases

indexed by defendant, plaintiff. Civil records on computer back 10 years. Index available remotely online from JIS-Link; see www.courts.wa.gov/jislink (also, see state introduction).

Criminal Records: Access: Phone, fax, mail, online, in person. Only the court performs in person searches; visitors may not. No search fee. Required to search: name, years to search, signed release; also helpful: address, DOB, SSN. Criminal records on computer back 5 years. Index available remotely online from JIS-Link; see www.courts.wa.gov/jislink (also, see state introduction).

General Information: No sealed, juvenile, adoption, paternity, mental health, sex offenders (victims) or (sometimes) DUI records released. SASE requested. Turnaround time 2-3 days. Copy fee: $.15 per page. Certification fee: $5.00. Fee payee: Renton District Court. Personal checks accepted. Credit cards accepted: Visa/MC. Prepayment is required.

District Court Seattle Division
516 Third Ave E-327 Courthouse, Seattle, WA 98104-3273; 206-296-3565; 800-325-6165 +59200; 206-205-9200. Hours: 8:30AM-4:30PM (PST). *Misdemeanor, Civil Actions Under $50,000, Small Claims.*

www.metrokc.gov/kcdc

Note: Civil Filing Area: Seattle.

Civil Records: Access: Mail, online, in person. Both court and visitors may perform in person searches. No search fee. Required to search: name, years to search; also helpful: address. Civil cases indexed by defendant, plaintiff. Civil records on computer from back 10 years. Index available remotely online from JIS-Link; see www.courts.wa.gov/jislink (also, see state introduction).

Criminal Records: Access: Mail, online, in person. Both court and visitors may perform in person searches. No search fee. Required to search: name, years to search, DOB, signed release; also helpful: address, SSN. Criminal records on computer from back 10 years. Index available remotely online from JIS-Link; see www.courts.wa.gov/jislink (also, see state introduction).

General Information: Public access terminal is available. (10 minute limit. 90% of info available to public, other 10% can only be searched by court staff.) No sealed, juvenile, adoption, paternity, mental health, sex offenders (victims), treatment plans or (sometimes) DUI records released. SASE required. Turnaround time 10 days. Copy fee: $.15 per page. Certification fee: $5.00. Fee payee: King County District Court, Seattle. Personal checks accepted. Prepayment is required.

District Court Shoreline Division
18050 Meridian Ave N, Shoreline, WA 98133-4642; 800-325-6165 +59200; 206-205-9200; Fax: 206-296-0594. Hours: 8:30AM-4:30PM (PST). *Misdemeanor, Civil Actions Under $50,000, Small Claims.*

www.metrokc.gov/kcdc

Note: Civil Filing Area: Shoreline, Kenmore, Lake Forest Park.

Civil Records: Access: Phone, fax, mail, online, in person. Both court and visitors may perform in person searches. No search fee. Required to search: name, years to search; also helpful: address. Civil cases indexed by defendant, plaintiff. Civil records on computer from 1985. Index available remotely online from JIS-Link; see www.courts.wa.gov/jislink (also, see state introduction).

Criminal Records: Access: Phone, fax, mail, online, in person. Both court and visitors may perform in person searches. No search fee. Required to search: name, years to search; also helpful: address, DOB, SSN. Criminal records on computer from 1987. Index available remotely online from JIS-Link; see www.courts.wa.gov/jislink (also, see state introduction).

General Information: Public access terminal is available. No sealed, juvenile, adoption, paternity, mental health, sex offenders (victims) or (sometimes) DUI records released. SASE required. Turnaround time 1 week. Fax notes: No fee to fax results. Copy fee: $.25 per page. Certification fee: $5.00. Fee payee: King County District Court. Personal checks accepted. Credit cards accepted: Visa, M/C. Prepayment required.

District Court Southwest Division
601 SW 149th St, Seattle, WA 98166; 800-325-6165 +59200; 206-205-9200; 206-296-0133; Fax: 206-296-0585. Hours: 8:30AM-4:30PM (PST). *Misdemeanor, Civil Actions Under $50,000, Small Claims.*

www.metrokc.gov/kcdc

Note: Civil Filing Area: Burien, DesMoines, Normandy Park, Vashon Island, SeaTac.

Civil Records: Access: Mail, online, in person. Only the court performs in person searches; visitors may not. No search fee. Required to search: name, years to search; also helpful: address. Civil cases indexed by defendant, plaintiff. Civil records on computer back 10 years. Index available remotely online from JIS-Link; see www.courts.wa.gov/jislink (see state introduction).

Criminal Records: Access: Mail, online, in person. Only the court performs in person searches; visitors may not. No search fee. Required to search: name, years to search, DOB, signed release; also helpful: address. Criminal records on computer back 5 years. Index available remotely online from JIS-Link; see www.courts.wa.gov/jislink (also, see state introduction).

General Information: No sealed, juvenile, sex offenders (victims) or (sometimes) DUI records released. SASE requested. Turnaround time 2-4 days. Copy fee: $.15 per page. Certification fee: $5.00. Fee payee: Southwest Division, King County District Court. Personal checks accepted. Credit cards accepted: Visa, MasterCard. Prepayment is required.

District Court Southwest Division - Vashon
19021 99th SW (PO Box 111), Vashon, WA 98070-0111; 206-296-3664; 800-325-6165 +59200; 206-205-9200; Fax: 206-296-0578. 8:30AM-Noon, 1:15-4:30PM 2nd & 4th F of the month *Misdemeanor, Civil Actions Under $50,000, Small Claims.*

www.metrokc.gov/kcdc

Civil Records: Access: Fax, mail, online, in person. Only the court performs in person searches; visitors may not. No search fee. Required to search: name, years to search; also helpful: address. Civil cases indexed by defendant, plaintiff. Civil records on computer back 5 years. Index available remotely online from JIS-Link; see www.courts.wa.gov/jislink (see state introduction).

Criminal Records: Access: Fax, mail, online, in person. Only the court performs in person searches; visitors may not. No search fee. Required to search: name, years to search; also helpful: address, DOB, SSN. Criminal records on computer from 1987. Index available remotely online from JIS-Link; see www.courts.wa.gov/jislink (also, see state introduction).

General Information: No sealed, juvenile, adoption, paternity, mental health, sex offenders (victims) or (sometimes) DUI records released. Turnaround time 1 day. Fax notes: No fee to fax results. Copy fee: $.15 per page. Certification fee: $5.00. Fee payee: Vashon District Court. Personal checks accepted. Prepayment is required.

Kitsap County

Superior Court 614 Division St, MS34, Port Orchard, WA 98366-4699; 360-337-7164; Fax: 360-337-4927. Hours: 8AM-4:30PM (PST). *Felony, Civil, Eviction, Probate.*

www.kitsapgov.com/sc

Civil Records: Access: Mail, online, in person. Both court and visitors may perform in person searches.

Search fee: $20.00 per hour. Fee is for up to 5 names. Required to search: name, years to search. Civil cases indexed by defendant, plaintiff. Civil records on computer from 1978, on microfiche and archived from 1857. Index available remotely online from JIS-Link; see www.courts.wa.gov/jislink (see state introduction).

Criminal Records: Access: Mail, online, in person. Both court and visitors may perform in person searches. Search fee: $20.00 per hour. Fee is for up to 5 names. Required to search: name, years to search; also helpful: address, DOB, SSN. Criminal records on computer from 1978, on microfiche and archived from 1857. Index available remotely online from JIS-Link; see www.courts.wa.gov/jislink (also, see state introduction).

General Information: Public access terminal is available. No dependencies, adoption or mental illness records released. SASE required. Turnaround time 2 weeks. Copy fee: $2.00 for first page, $1.00 each add'l. Certification fee: Certification fee included in copy fee. Fee payee: Kitsap County Clerk. Personal checks accepted. Out-of state personal checks not accepted. Prepayment is required.

District Court 614 Division St, MS 25, Port Orchard, WA 98366-4614; 360-337-7109; Fax: 360-337-4865. 8:30AM-4:30PM (PST). *Misdemeanor, Civil Actions Under $50,000, Small Claims.*

Civil Records: Access: Phone, fax, mail, online, in person. Only the court performs in person searches; visitors may not. No search fee. Required to search: name, years to search; also helpful: address. Civil cases indexed by defendant, plaintiff. Civil records on computer from 10/95, prior in archives. Index available remotely online from JIS-Link; see www.courts.wa.gov/jislink (also, see state introduction).

Criminal Records: Access: Phone, fax, mail, online, in person. Only the court performs in person searches; visitors may not. No search fee. Required to search: name, years to search; also helpful: address, DOB, SSN. Criminal records on computer from 6/89, prior in archives. Index available remotely online from JIS-Link; see www.courts.wa.gov/jislink (also, see state introduction).

General Information: No dependencies, adoption and mental illness records released. Turnaround time 1 week. Fax notes: No fee to fax results. Local faxing only. Copy fee: $.15 per page. Certification fee: $5.00. Fee payee: Kitsap County District Court. Personal checks accepted. Prepayment is required.

District Court North 614 Division St, MS-25, Port Orchard, WA 98366; 360-337-7109; Fax: 360-337-4865. Hours: 8:30AM-12:15PM; 1:15-4:30PM (PST). *Misdemeanor, Civil Actions Under $50,000, Small Claims.*

Note: The court physical address is 19050 Jensen Way NE, Poulsbo, WA.

Civil Records: Access: Mail, online, in person. Only the court performs in person searches; visitors may not. No search fee. Required to search: name, years to search. Civil cases indexed by defendant, plaintiff. Civil records on computer back 8 years, on index cards for 10 years. Index available remotely online from JIS-Link; see www.courts.wa.gov/jislink (also, see state introduction). Send all mail requests to Port Orchard District court.

Criminal Records: Access: Mail, online, in person. Only the court performs in person searches; visitors may not. No search fee. Required to search: name, signed release; also helpful: years to search, DOB. Criminal records on computer back 8 years, on index cards for 10 years. Index available remotely online from JIS-Link; see www.courts.wa.gov/jislink (also, see state introduction). Send all mail requests to Port Orchard District Court.

General Information: No dependencies, adoption and mental illness records released. Copy fee: $.15 per page.

Certification fee: $5.00. Fee payee: District Court North, Kitsap County. Only cashiers checks and money orders accepted. Prepayment is required.

Kittitas County

Superior Court 205 W 5th Rm 210, Ellensburg, WA 98926; 509-962-7531; Fax: 509-962-7667. Hours: 9AM-Noon, 1-5PM (PST). *Felony, Misdemeanor, Civil, Eviction, Probate.*

Civil Records: Access: Phone, fax, mail, online, in person. Only the court performs in person searches; visitors may not. Search fee: $10.00 per name. Required to search: name, years to search; also helpful: address. Civil cases indexed by defendant, plaintiff. Civil records on computer from 1982, on microfiche and archived from 1890. Some records on index cards. Index available remotely online from JIS-Link; see www.courts.wa.gov/jislink (also, see state introduction).

Criminal Records: Access: Phone, fax, mail, online, in person. Only the court performs in person searches; visitors may not. Search fee: $10.00 per name. Required to search: name, years to search; also helpful: address, DOB, SSN. Criminal records on computer from 1982, on microfiche and archived from 1890. Some records on index cards. Index available remotely online from JIS-Link; see www.courts.wa.gov/jislink (also, see state introduction).

General Information: No dependencies, adoption, and mental illness records released. Turnaround time 2 days. Fax notes: No fee to fax results. Fax available in emergency only. Copy fee: $.15 per page. Certification fee: $2.00 first page, $1.00 each addl. Fee payee: Kittitas County Clerk. Personal checks accepted. Prepayment is required.

District Court Lower Kittitas 205 W 5th, Rm 180, Ellensburg, WA 98926; 509-962-7511. Hours: 9AM-5PM (PST). *Misdemeanor, Civil Actions Under $50,000, Small Claims.*

Civil Records: Access: Mail, online, in person. Only the court performs in person searches; visitors may not. No search fee. Required to search: name, years to search. Civil cases indexed by defendant, plaintiff. Civil records on computer from 8/91, archived back 10 years, some on index cards. Records retained for 20 years. Index available remotely online from JIS-Link; see www.courts.wa.gov/jislink (also, see state introduction).

Criminal Records: Access: Mail, online, in person. Only the court performs in person searches; visitors may not. No search fee. Required to search: name, years to search, DOB. Criminal records on computer from 8/91, archived back 10 years, some on index cards. Records retained for 20 years. Index available remotely online from JIS-Link; see www.courts.wa.gov/jislink (also, see state introduction).

General Information: No dependencies, adoption, and mental illness records released. SASE required. Turnaround time 7-10 days. Copy fee: No search fee. Certification fee: $6.00. Fee payee: Lower Kittitas County District Court. Personal checks accepted. Prepayment is required.

District Court Upper Kittitas 618 E First, Cle Elum, WA 98922; 509-674-5533; Fax: 509-674-4209. Hours: 8AM-5PM (PST). *Misdemeanor, Civil Actions Under $50,000, Small Claims.*

Civil Records: Access: Mail, online, in person. Only the court performs in person searches; visitors may not. No search fee. Required to search: name, years to search. Civil cases indexed by defendant, plaintiff. Civil records on computer since 8/91; prior records archived from 1890, some on index cards. Records retained for 10 years. Index available remotely online from JIS-Link; see www.courts.wa.gov/jislink (also, see state introduction).

Criminal Records: Access: Mail, online, in person. Only the court performs in person searches; visitors

may not. No search fee. Required to search: name, years to search, DOB, signed release; also helpful: SSN. Criminal records on computer back to 1997; prior records archived from 1890, some on index cards. Records retained for 5 years. Index available remotely online from JIS-Link; see www.courts.wa.gov/jislink (also, see state introduction).

General Information: Public access terminal is available, but not accessible. No dependencies, adoption, and mental illness records released. Turnaround time 1 week. Fax notes: Fee to fax results is $1.00 per page. Copy fee: $.25 per page. Certification fee: $5.00. Fee payee: UKCDC. Personal checks accepted. Credit cards accepted: Visa, MasterCard. Prepayment is required.

Klickitat County

Superior Court Superior Court Clerk, 205 S Columbus, MS CH-O3, Goldendale, WA 98620; 509-773-5744. Hours: 9AM-5PM (PST). *Felony, Civil, Eviction, Probate.*

Civil Records: Access: Phone, mail, online, in person. Only the court performs in person searches; visitors may not. Search fee: $8.00 per hour. Required to search: name, years to search; also helpful: address. Civil cases indexed by defendant, plaintiff. Civil records on computer from 9/87. Index available remotely online from JIS-Link; see www.courts.wa.gov/jislink (also, see state introduction).

Criminal Records: Access: Phone, mail, online, in person. Only the court performs in person searches; visitors may not. Search fee: $8.00 per hour. Required to search: name, years to search; also helpful: address, DOB, SSN. Criminal records on computer from 9/87; prior on books back to 1886. Index available remotely online from JIS-Link; see www.courts.wa.gov/jislink (also, see state introduction).

General Information: No dependencies, adoption, and mental illness records released. SASE required. Turnaround time 2 weeks. Copy fee: $2.00 for first page, $1.00 each add'l. Certification fee: $2.00 plus $1.00 per page after first. Fee payee: Klickitat County Clerk. No personal checks accepted. Prepayment is required.

East District Court 205 S Columbus, MS-CH11, Goldendale, WA 98620-9290; 509-773-4670; Fax: 509-773-4653. Hours: 8AM-12, 1-5pm (PST). *Misdemeanor, Civil Actions Under $50,000, Small Claims.*

Civil Records: Access: Phone, mail, fax, online, in person. Both court and visitors may perform in person searches. No search fee. Required to search: name, years to search. Civil cases indexed by defendant, plaintiff. Civil records on computer from 4/93, on index cards prior. Retained for 10 years. Index available remotely online from JIS-Link; see www.courts.wa.gov/jislink (also, see state introduction).

Criminal Records: Access: Phone, mail, fax, online, in person. Both court and visitors may perform in person searches. No search fee. Required to search: name, years to search, DOB. Criminal records on computer from 4/93, on index cards prior. Retained for 10 years. Index available remotely online from JIS-Link; see www.courts.wa.gov/jislink (also, see state introduction).

General Information: No dependencies, adoption, and mental illness records released. SASE required. Turnaround time 1 week. Copy fee: 1st 10 pages free, each additional page $.15. Certification fee: $5.00. Fee payee: East District Court. Personal checks accepted. Prepayment is required.

West District Court PO Box 435, White Salmon, WA 98672-0435; 509-493-1190; Fax: 509-493-4469. Hours: 8AM-5PM (PST). *Misdemeanor, Civil Actions Under $50,000, Small Claims.*

Civil Records: Access: Mail, in person. Only the court performs in person searches; visitors may not. No search fee. Required to search: name, years to search. Civil cases indexed by defendant, plaintiff. Civil records on computer from 5/93, on docket books. Index available remotely online from JIS-Link; see www.courts.wa.gov/jislink (also, see state introduction).
Criminal Records: Access: Mail, in person. Only the court performs in person searches; visitors may not. No search fee. Required to search: name, years to search, DOB; also helpful: address. Criminal records on computer from 5/93, on docket books. Index available remotely online from JIS-Link; see www.courts.wa.gov/jislink (also, see state introduction).
General Information: No dependencies, adoption, sealed and mental illness records released. SASE required. Turnaround time 3-5 days. Copy fee: $2.00 for first page, $1.00 each add'l. Certification fee: $6.00. Fee payee: West District Court. Personal checks accepted. Prepayment is required.

Lewis County

Superior Court 360 NW North St, MS:CLK 01, Chehalis, WA 98532-1900; 360-740-2704; Fax: 360-748-1639. Hours: 8AM-5PM (PST). *Felony, Misdemeanor, Civil, Eviction, Probate.*
Civil Records: Access: Phone, mail, online, in person. Both the court and visitors may perform in person searches. Search fee: $8.00 per hour. Required to search: name, years to search; also helpful: address. Civil cases indexed by defendant, plaintiff. Civil records on computer from 1983, archived from 1900s. Index available remotely online from JIS-Link; see www.courts.wa.gov/jislink (also, see state introduction).
Criminal Records: Access: Phone, mail, online, in person. Both the court and visitors may perform in person searches. Search fee: $8.00 per hour. Required to search: name, years to search; also helpful: address, DOB, SSN. Criminal records on computer from 1983, archived from 1900s. Index available remotely online from JIS-Link; see www.courts.wa.gov/jislink (also, see state introduction).
General Information: Public access terminal is available. No dependencies, adoption, paternity, and mental illness records released. SASE required. Turnaround time up to 7 days. Fax notes: Fee to fax results is $.50 per page. Copy fee: $2.00 for first page, $1.00 each add'l. Certification fee: $3.00. Fee payee: Lewis County Clerk. Personal checks accepted. Prepayment is required.

District Court PO Box 336, Chehalis, WA 98532-0336; 360-740-1203; Fax: 360-740-2779. Hours: 8AM-5PM (PST). *Misdemeanor, Civil Actions Under $50,000, Small Claims.*
Civil Records: Access: Fax, mail, online, in person. Court may perform in person searches. No search fee. Required to search: name, years to search. Civil cases indexed by defendant, plaintiff. Civil records on computer from 1983, on index cards. Records retained 10 years. Index available remotely online from JIS-Link; see www.courts.wa.gov/jislink (also, see state introduction).
Criminal Records: Access: Fax, mail, online, in person. Court may perform in person searches. No search fee. Required to search: name, years to search, DOB, sex, signed release; also helpful: address, SSN. Criminal records on computer since 1981. Records retained for 5 years. Index available remotely online from JIS-Link; see www.courts.wa.gov/jislink (also, see state introduction).
General Information: No dependencies, adoption, and mental illness records released. SASE required. Turnaround time 1 week. Fax notes: No fee to fax results. Copy fee: $.25 per page. Certification fee: $5.00 per page. Fee payee: Lewis County District Court. Personal checks accepted. Prepayment is required.

Lincoln County

Superior Court Box 68, Davenport, WA 99122-0396; 509-725-1401; Fax: 509-725-1150. Hours: 8AM-5PM (PST). *Felony, Misdemeanor, Civil, Eviction, Probate.*
Civil Records: Access: Mail, online, in person. Only the court performs in person searches; visitors may not. No search fee. Required to search: name, years to search; also helpful: address. Civil cases indexed by defendant, plaintiff. Civil records on computer and microfiche from 11/82, archived from 1903. Index available remotely online from JIS-Link; see www.courts.wa.gov/jislink (also, see state introduction).
Criminal Records: Access: Mail, online, in person. Only the court performs in person searches; visitors may not. No search fee. Required to search: name, years to search; also helpful: address, DOB, SSN. Criminal records on computer and microfiche from 11/82, archived from 1903. Index available remotely online from JIS-Link; see www.courts.wa.gov/jislink (also, see state introduction).
General Information: No dependencies, adoption, and mental illness records released. SASE required. Turnaround time same day. Copy fee: $1.00 per page. Certification fee: $2.00 1st page, $1.00 each add'l page. Fee payee: Lincoln County Clerk. Business checks accepted. Prepayment is required.

District Court PO Box 329, Davenport, WA 99122-0329; 509-725-2281. Hours: 8AM-5PM (PST). *Misdemeanor, Civil Actions Under $35,000, Small Claims.*
Note: This is a small office with limited time allowable for searches.
Civil Records: Access: Mail, fax, online, in person. Both court and visitors may perform in person searches. Search fee: $25.00 per hour. Required to search: name, years to search. Civil cases indexed by defendant. Civil records on computer back to 6/93, in books from 1985. Index available remotely online from JIS-Link; see www.courts.wa.gov/jislink (also, see state introduction).
Criminal Records: Access: Mail, fax, online, in person. Both the court and visitors may perform in person searches. Search fee: $25.00 per hour. Required to search: name, years to search, DOB. Criminal records on computer back to 6/93; hard copy files back to 1990. Index available remotely online from JIS-Link; see www.courts.wa.gov/jislink (also, see state introduction).
General Information: Public access terminal is available. No dependencies, adoption, and mental illness records released. SASE required. Turnaround time 1 week. Copy fee: $2.00 for first page, $1.00 each add'l. Certification fee: $6.00 plus $1.00 per page after first. Fee payee: Lincoln County District Court. Business checks accepted. Prepayment is required.

Mason County

Superior Court PO Box 340, Shelton, WA 98584; 360-427-9670 X346. Hours: 8:30AM-5PM (PST). *Felony, Civil, Eviction, Probate.*
www.co.mason.wa.us/Clerk
Civil Records: Access: Phone, mail, online, in person. Both court and visitors may perform in person searches. Search fee: $20.00 per hour. Required to search: name, years to search; also helpful: address. Civil cases indexed by defendant, plaintiff. Civil records on computer from 1982, on microfiche and archived from 1890, on index or docket books prior to 1982. Index available remotely online from JIS-Link; see www.courts.wa.gov/jislink (also, see state introduction).
Criminal Records: Access: Phone, mail, online, in person. Both court and visitors may perform in person searches. Search fee: $20.00 per hour. Required to search: name, years to search; also helpful: address, DOB. Criminal records on computer from 1982, on microfiche and archived from 1890, on index or docket books prior to 1982. Index available remotely online from JIS-Link; see www.courts.wa.gov/jislink (also, see state introduction).
General Information: No dependencies, adoption, and mental illness records released. SASE required. Turnaround time 1 week. Fax notes: Will not fax results. Copy fee: $2.00 for 1st page, $1.00 each add'l. Certification fee: $2.00 plus $1.00 per page after first. Fee payee: Mason County Clerk. Attorney checks accepted. Prepayment is required.

District Court PO Box "O", Shelton, WA 98584-0090; 360-427-9670 X339; Fax: 360-427-7776. Hours: 8:30AM-5PM (PST). *Misdemeanor, Civil Actions Under $50,000, Small Claims.*
Civil Records: Access: Mail, in person. Only the court performs in person searches; visitors may not. Search fee: $20.00 per name. Fee is for extensive searching. Required to search: name, years to search; also helpful: address. Civil cases indexed by defendant, plaintiff. Civil records on computer from 12/92, prior on index book. Index available remotely online from JIS-Link; see www.courts.wa.gov/jislink (also, see state introduction).
Criminal Records: Access: Mail, in person. Only the court performs in person searches; visitors may not. Search fee: Will charge $20.00 for extensive search. Required to search: name, years to search, DOB, signed release; also helpful: address, SSN. Criminal records on computer from 12/92, prior on index book. Index available remotely online from JIS-Link; see www.courts.wa.gov/jislink (also, see state introduction).
General Information: No dependencies, adoption, and mental illness records released. SASE required. Turnaround time 1 week. Copy fee: $.25 per page. Certification fee: $5.00. Fee payee: Mason County District Court. Personal checks accepted. Prepayment is required.

Okanogan County

Superior Court PO Box 72, Okanogan, WA 98840; 509-422-7275; Fax: 509-422-7277. Hours: 8:30AM-5:00PM (PST). *Felony, Misdemeanor, Civil, Eviction, Probate.*
Civil Records: Access: Phone, fax, mail, online, in person. Both court and visitors may perform in person searches. No search fee. Required to search: name, years to search; also helpful: address. Civil cases indexed by defendant, plaintiff. Civil records on computer from 1994, on hand-written indexes from 1895. Index available remotely online from JIS-Link; see www.courts.wa.gov/jislink (also, see state introduction).
Criminal Records: Access: Phone, fax, mail, online, in person. Both court and visitors may perform in person searches. No search fee. Required to search: name, years to search; also helpful: address, DOB, SSN. Criminal records on computer from 1994, on hand-written indexes from 1895. Index available remotely online from JIS-Link; see www.courts.wa.gov/jislink (also, see state introduction).
General Information: No dependencies, adoption, and mental illness records released. SASE required. Turnaround time 1-7 days. Copy fee: $1.00 per page. Certification fee: $2.00 plus $1.00 per page after first. Fee payee: Okanogan County Clerk. Personal checks accepted. Prepayment is required.

District Court PO Box 980, Okanogan, WA 98840-0980; 509-422-7170; Fax: 509-422-7174. Hours: 8AM-5PM (PST). *Misdemeanor, Civil Actions Under $50,000, Small Claims.*
Civil Records: Access: Phone, fax, mail, in person, online. Both court and visitors may perform in person searches. No search fee. Required to search: name, years to search. Civil cases indexed by defendant,

plaintiff. Civil records on computer from 8/91, prior on index cards. Index available remotely online from JIS-Link; see www.courts.wa.gov/jislink (also, see state introduction).

Criminal Records: Access: Phone, fax, mail, in person, online. Both court and visitors may perform in person searches. No search fee. Required to search: name, years to search, DOB. Criminal records on computer from 8/91. Index available remotely online from JIS-Link; see www.courts.wa.gov/jislink (also, see state introduction).

General Information: Public access terminal is available. No dependencies, adoption, alcohol related evaluations, mental illness records released. SASE requested. Turnaround time 7 days. Fax notes: $1.00 for first page, $.50 each add'l. Copy fee: $1.00 for first page, $.50 each add'l. Certification fee: $5.00. Fee payee: Okanogan County District Court. Personal checks accepted. Prepayment is required.

Pacific County

Superior Court PO Box 67, South Bend, WA 98586; 360-875-9320; Fax: 360-875-9321. Hours: 8AM-4PM M-Th; 8AM-5PM F (PST). *Felony, Civil, Eviction, Probate.*

Civil Records: Access: Phone, mail, online, in person. Both court and visitors may perform in person searches. Search fee: $20.00 per hour. Required to search: name, years to search. Civil cases indexed by defendant, plaintiff. Civil records on computer from 2/84, archived from 1887, some on docket books. Index available remotely online from JIS-Link; see www.courts.wa.gov/jislink (also, see state introduction).

Criminal Records: Access: Phone, mail, online, in person. Both court and visitors may perform in person searches. Search fee: $20.00 per hour if searching before 1984. Required to search: name, years to search. Criminal records on computer from 2/84, archived from 1887, some on docket books. Index available remotely online from JIS-Link; see www.courts.wa.gov/jislink (also, see state introduction).

General Information: No dependencies, adoption, and mental illness records released. Turnaround time varies. Copy fee: $2.00 for first page, $1.00 each add'l; Non-certified: $.15 per page. Certification fee: $2.00 1st page, $1.00 each add'l page. Fee payee: Pacific County Clerk. Personal checks accepted. Prepayment required.

District Court North Box 134, South Bend, WA 98586-0134; 360-875-9354; Fax: 360-875-9351. Hours: 9AM-4PM (PST). *Misdemeanor, Civil Actions Under $50,000, Small Claims.*

Civil Records: Access: Phone, fax, mail, online, in person. Only the court may perform in person searches. No search fee. Required to search: name, years to search; also helpful: address. Civil cases indexed by defendant, plaintiff. Civil records on computer back to 3/93, prior on index cards. Depending on disposition date, civil records retained ten years. Index available remotely online from JIS-Link; see www.courts.wa.gov/jislink (also, see state introduction).

Criminal Records: Access: Phone, fax, mail, online, in person. Only the court may perform in person searches. No search fee. Required to search: name, DOB; also helpful: years to search, address, SSN. Criminal Records retained forever, on computer back to 3/93. Index available remotely online from JIS-Link; see www.courts.wa.gov/jislink (also, see state introduction).

General Information: No dependencies, MVRs, defendant case histories, adoption, and mental illness records released. SASE required. Turnaround time 1 week. Fax notes: No fee to fax results. Copy fee: $2.00 for first page, $1.00 each add'l. Certification fee: $5.00. Fee payee: North District Court. Personal checks accepted. Prepayment is required.

District Court South PO Box 794, Ilwaco, WA 98624; 360-642-9417; Fax: 360-642-9416. Hours: 8AM-Noon, 1-5PM (PST). *Misdemeanor, Civil Actions Under $50,000, Small Claims.*

Civil Records: Access: Phone, fax, mail, online, in person. Only the court performs in person searches; visitors may not. No search fee. Required to search: name, years to search; also helpful: address. Civil cases indexed by defendant, plaintiff. Civil records on computer for current and open cases. Records retained for 10 years. Index available remotely online from JIS-Link; see www.courts.wa.gov/jislink (also, see state introduction).

Criminal Records: Access: fax, mail, online, in person. Only the court performs in person searches; visitors may not. No search fee. Required to search: name; also helpful: years to search, address, DOB, SSN. Criminal records on computer for current and open cases. Records retained for 10 years. Index available remotely online from JIS-Link; see www.courts.wa.gov/jislink (also, see state introduction).

General Information: No dependencies, adoption, and mental illness records released. SASE required. Turnaround time 1 week. Fax notes: No fee to fax results. Copy fee: $1.00 for first page, $.10 each add'l. Fee payee: South District Court. Personal checks accepted. Prepayment is required.

Pend Oreille County

Superior Court 229 S Garden Ave (PO Box 5020), Newport, WA 99156-5020; 509-447-2435; Fax: 509-447-2734. Hours: 8AM-4:30PM (PST). *Felony, Civil, Eviction, Probate.*

Civil Records: Access: Mail, in person. Both court and visitors may perform in person searches. Search fee: $20.00 per hour. Required to search: name, years to search; also helpful: address. Civil cases indexed by defendant, plaintiff. Civil records on computer and microfiche from 9/82, archived from 1911, on docket books prior to 9/82. Index available remotely online from JIS-Link; see www.courts.wa.gov/jislink (also, see state introduction).

Criminal Records: Access: Phone, mail, in person. Both court and visitors may perform in person searches. No search fee. Required to search: name, years to search; also helpful: address, DOB, SSN. Criminal records on computer and microfiche from 9/82, archived from 1911, on docket books prior to 9/82. Index available remotely online from JIS-Link; see www.courts.wa.gov/jislink (also, see state introduction).

General Information: No dependencies, adoption, and mental illness records released. SASE required. Turnaround time same day. Fax notes: Fee to fax results is $3.00 for the 1st page and $1.00 per page thereafter. Copy fee: $2.00 for first page, $1.00 each add'l. Certification fee: $2.00. Fee payee: Pend Oreille County Clerk. Personal checks accepted. Prepayment required.

District Court PO Box 5030, 229 S Garden Ave, Newport, WA 99156-5030; 509-447-4110; Civil phone: 800-359-1506; Fax: 509-447-5724. Hours: 8AM-4:30PM (PST). *Misdemeanor, Civil Actions Under $50,000, Small Claims.*

Civil Records: Access: Phone, fax, mail, online, in person. Only the court performs in person searches; visitors may not. No search fee. Required to search: name, years to search; also helpful: address. Civil cases indexed by defendant, plaintiff. Civil records on DISCIS computer from 10/92, on computer from 1989, archived from 1972. Records retained for 10 years. Index available remotely online from JIS-Link; see www.courts.wa.gov/jislink (also, see state introduction).

Criminal Records: Access: Fax, mail, online, in person. Only the court performs in person searches; visitors may not. No search fee. Required to search: name, DOB; also helpful: years to search, address, SSN.

Criminal records on DISCIS computer from 10/92, on computer from 1989, archived from 1972. Records retained for 10 years. Index available remotely online from JIS-Link; see www.courts.wa.gov/jislink (also, see state introduction).

General Information: No dependencies, adoption, and mental illness records released. SASE required. Turnaround time 10 days. Fax notes: No fee to fax results. Copy fee: $.25 per page. Certification fee: $5.00. Fee payee: Pend Oreille County District Court. Personal checks accepted. Prepayment is required.

Pierce County

Superior Court 930 Tacoma Ave South, Rm 110, Tacoma, WA 98402; 253-798-7455; Fax: 253-798-3428. Hours: 8:30AM-4:30PM (PST). *Felony, Civil, Eviction, Probate.*

www.co.pierce.wa.us/abtus/ourorg/supct/abtussup.htm

Civil Records: Access: Mail, online, in person. Both court and visitors may perform in person searches. Search fee: $10.00 per hour. Required to search: name, years to search; also helpful: address. Civil cases indexed by defendant, plaintiff. Civil records on computer from 5/81, archived from 1890. Online Superior Court case information, inmates, attorneys, and scheduled proceedings available free at www.co.pierce.wa.us/cfapps/linx/headerindex.cfm?source=search.cfm&activeTab=search. Also, a statewide index is available remotely online (see state introduction).

Criminal Records: Access: Mail, online, in person. Both court and visitors may perform in person searches. Search fee: $10.00 per hour. Required to search: name, years to search, DOB; also helpful: address, SSN. Criminal records on computer from 5/81, archived from 1890. Online access to criminal records is the same as civil. Also, a statewide case index is available remotely online (see state introduction).

General Information: No sealed, juvenile, adoption, paternity, mental health, sex offenders (victims) or (sometimes) DUI records released. SASE required. Turnaround time same day. Fax notes: Will fax results; $5.00 minimum. Copy fee: $2.00 for first page, $1.00 each add'l. Certification fee: $2.00 plus $1.00 per page after first. Fee payee: Pierce County Clerk. Business checks accepted. Prepayment is required.

District Court #1 - Civil 1902 96th St S., Tacoma, WA 98444; 253-798-7474; Fax: 253-798-6310. Hours: 8:30AM-4:30PM M-Th (PST). *Civil Actions Under $50,000, Small Claims.*

www.co.pierce.wa.us/abtus/ourorg/distct/abtusd1.htm

Civil Records: Access: Phone, mail, online, in person. Both court and visitors may perform in person searches. No search fee. Required to search: name, years to search, DOB; also helpful: address. Civil cases indexed by defendant, plaintiff. Civil records on computer back to 1990; Records go back 5 years. Index available remotely online from JIS-Link; see www.courts.wa.gov/jislink (also, see state introduction).

General Information: No sealed, juvenile, adoption, paternity, mental health, sex offenders (victims) or some DUI records released. SASE required. Turnaround time 1-2 weeks. Copy fee: $1.00 for first page, $.50 each add'l. Certification fee: $5.00. Fee payee: Pierce County District Court #1. Personal checks accepted. Credit cards accepted: Visa, MasterCard.

District Court #1 - Criminal 930 Tacoma Ave S, Rm 601, Tacoma, WA 98402-2175; 253-798-7474; Fax: 253-798-6166. Hours: 8:30AM-4:30PM (PST). *Misdemeanor.*

www.co.pierce.wa.us/abtus/ourorg/distct/abtusd1.htm

Criminal Records: Access: Mail, fax, online, in person. Both court and visitors may perform in person searches. No search fee. Required to search: name, years to search, DOB; also helpful: address, SSN. Criminal records on computer from 8/1990. Criminal Index available remotely online from www.courts.wa.gov/jislink (also, see state introduction). **General Information:** No sealed, juvenile, adoption, paternity, mental health, sex offenders (victims) or some DUI records released. SASE required. Turnaround time 1-2 weeks. Copy fee: $1.00 for first page, $.50 each add'l. Certification fee: $5.00. Fee payee: Pierce County District Court #1. Personal checks accepted. Credit cards accepted: Visa, MasterCard.

District Court #2 6659 Kimball Dr, #E-503, Gig Harbor, WA 98335-1229; 253-798-6670; Fax: 253-858-2184. 8:30AM-4:30PM (PST). *Misdemeanor, Civil Actions Under $50,000, Small Claims.*

www.co.pierce.wa.us/abtus/ourorg/distct/abtusd2.htm

Civil Records: Access: Phone, fax, mail, in person. Both court and visitors may perform in person searches. Search fee: $10.00 per name. Fee if records retrieved from archives. Required to search: name, years to search; also helpful: address. Civil cases indexed by defendant, plaintiff. Civil records on computer from 8/92, log books prior. Index available remotely online from JIS-Link; see www.courts.wa.gov/jislink (also, see state introduction).

Criminal Records: Access: Phone, fax, mail, in person. Both court and visitors may perform in person searches. Search fee: $10.00 per name. Fee is charged if records retrieved from archives. Required to search: name, DOB; also helpful: years to search, address, SSN. Criminal records on computer from 1990, log books prior to 1989. Index available remotely online from JIS-Link; see www.courts.wa.gov/jislink (also, see state introduction).

General Information: No sealed, judge's notes, treatment or probation report records released. SASE required. Turnaround time 1-2 weeks if archive material needed. Fax notes: No fee to fax results. Copy fee: $1.00 for first page, $.50 each add'l. Certification fee: $6.00. Fee payee: District Court No 2. Personal checks accepted. Credit cards accepted: Visa, MasterCard.

District Court #3 PO Box 105 (201 Center St), Eatonville, WA 98328-0105; 360-832-6000; Fax: 360-832-8911. 8:30AM-4:30PM (PST). *Misdemeanor, Civil Actions Under $50,000, Small Claims.*

www.co.pierce.wa.us/abtus/ourorg/distct/abtusd3.htm

Civil Records: Access: Fax, mail, online, in person. Only the court performs in person searches; visitors may not. No search fee. Required to search: name, years to search; also helpful: address. Civil cases indexed by defendant, plaintiff. Civil records on computer from Aug 1992, on index cards. Index available remotely online from JIS-Link; see www.courts.wa.gov/jislink (also, see state introduction). Fax requests must be on letterhead.

Criminal Records: Access: Mail, online, in person. Only the court performs in person searches; visitors may not. No search fee. Required to search: name, DOB; also helpful: years to search, address, SSN. Criminal records on computer from Aug 1992, on index cards. Index available remotely online from JIS-Link; see www.courts.wa.gov/jislink (also, see state introduction).

General Information: No sealed, juvenile, adoption, paternity, mental health, sex offenders (victims) or (sometimes) DUI records released. Turnaround time 1-2 days. Fax notes: No fee to fax results. Copy fee: $.25 per page. Certification fee: $5.00. Fee payee: Pierce County District Court #3. Personal checks accepted. Prepayment is required.

District Court #4 PO Box 110 (811 Main St), Buckley, WA 98321-0110; 360-829-0411; Fax: 360-829-3098. Hours: 8:30AM-Noon; 1PM-4PM (PST).

Misdemeanor, Civil Actions Under $50,000, Small Claims.

www.co.pierce.wa.us/abtus/ourorg/distct/abtusd4.htm

Civil Records: Access: Phone, mail, online, in person. Both court and visitors may perform in person searches. No search fee. Required to search: name, years to search; also helpful: address. Civil cases indexed by defendant, plaintiff. Civil records on index cards; computerized since 1997. Index available remotely online from JIS-Link; see www.courts.wa.gov/jislink (also, see state introduction).

Criminal Records: Access: Phone, mail, online, in person. Both court and visitors may perform in person searches. No search fee. Required to search: name, years to search; also helpful: address, DOB, SSN. Criminal records on index cards; computerized since 1997. Index available remotely online from JIS-Link; see www.courts.wa.gov/jislink (see state introduction).

General Information: No unclosed case records released. SASE required. Turnaround time 1 week. Copy fee: $.05 per page. Certification fee: $5.00. Fee payee: Pierce County District Court #4. Personal checks accepted. Prepayment is required.

San Juan County

Superior Court 350 Court St, #7, Friday Harbor, WA 98250; 360-378-2163; Fax: 360-378-3967. Hours: 8AM-4:30PM (PST). *Felony, Misdemeanor, Civil, Eviction, Probate.*

www.co.san-juan.wa.us/suprcourt/indexnew.html

Civil Records: Access: Phone, fax, mail, online, in person. Both court and visitors may perform in person searches. Search fee: $20.00 per hour. Required to search: name, years to search; also helpful: case number. Civil cases indexed by defendant, plaintiff. Civil records on computer back to 1987, on microfiche and archived from 1890s. Index available remotely online from JIS-Link; see www.courts.wa.gov/jislink (also, see state introduction).

Criminal Records: Access: Phone, fax, mail, online, in person. Only the court may perform in person searches on computer. Search fee: $20.00 per hour. Required to search: name, years to search, DOB; also helpful: address, SSN, case number. Criminal records on computer back to 1987, on microfiche and archived from 1890s. Index available remotely online from JIS-Link; see www.courts.wa.gov/jislink (also, see state introduction).

General Information: No dependencies, adoption, and mental illness records released. SASE required. Turnaround time 3 days. Fax notes: $5.00 for first page, $1.00 each add'l. Copy fee: $2.00 for first page, $1.00 each add'l. Certification fee: $2.00. Fee payee: San Juan County Clerk. Personal checks accepted. Credit cards accepted. Prepayment is required.

District Court PO Box 127, Friday Harbor, WA 98250-0127; 360-378-4017; Fax: 360-378-4099. Hours: 8:30AM-4:30PM (PST). *Misdemeanor, Civil Actions Under $50,000, Small Claims.*

Civil Records: Access: Mail, in person. Only the court performs in person searches; visitors may not. No search fee. Required to search: name, years to search; also helpful: address. Civil cases indexed by defendant, plaintiff. Civil records on computer from 1993, on index cards prior. Records retained for 10 years. Index available remotely online from JIS-Link; see www.courts.wa.gov/jislink (also, see state introduction).

Criminal Records: Access: Mail, in person. Only the court performs in person searches; visitors may not. No search fee. Required to search: name, years to search, signed release; also helpful: address, DOB, SSN. Criminal records on computer from 1993, log book prior. Retained 5 years. Index available remotely online from JIS-Link; see www.courts.wa.gov/jislink (also, see state introduction).

General Information: No dependencies, adoption, confidential social files and mental illness records released. SASE required. Turnaround time 1-3 days. Copy fee: $2.00 for first page, $1.00 each add'l. Certification fee: $5.00. Fee payee: San Juan County District Court. Personal checks accepted. Credit cards are accepted through OfficialPayments.Com or 1-877-876-7619. You will need to provide them with your case # or ticket #. Prepayment is required.

Skagit County

Superior Court PO Box 837, Mount Vernon, WA 98273-0837; 360-336-9440. Hours: 8:30AM-4:30PM (PST). *Felony, Civil, Eviction, Probate.*

Civil Records: Access: Mail, online, in person. Both court and visitors may perform in person searches. Search fee: $20.00 per hour. Required to search: name, years to search. Civil cases indexed by defendant, plaintiff. Civil records on computer from 10/81, on microfilm and archived from 1878. Index available remotely online from JIS-Link; see www.courts.wa.gov/jislink (also, see state introduction).

Criminal Records: Access: Mail, online, in person. Both court and visitors may perform in person searches. Search fee: $20.00 per hour. Required to search: name, years to search. Criminal records on computer from 10/81, on microfilm and archived from 1878. Index available remotely online from JIS-Link; see www.courts.wa.gov/jislink (also, see state introduction).

General Information: Public access terminal is available. No dependencies, adoption, and mental illness, juvenile offender prior to 07/01/78 records released. SASE required. Turnaround time 5 days. Copy fee: $.15 each, do-it-yourself. Self made copies cannot be certified. Certification fee: copies are $2.00 for first page, $1.00 each add'l page. Fee payee: Skagit County Clerk. Only cashiers checks and money orders accepted. Prepayment is required.

District Court PO Box 340, Mount Vernon, WA 98273-0340; 360-336-9319; Fax: 360-336-9318. Hours: 8:30AM-4:30PM (PST). *Misdemeanor, Civil Actions Under $50,000, Small Claims.*

Civil Records: Access: Phone, fax, mail, online, in person. Both court and visitors may perform in person searches. No search fee. Required to search: name, years to search; also helpful: address. Civil cases indexed by defendant, plaintiff. Civil records on computer from 1986, archived for 12 years. Open records retained for 10 years. Index available remotely online from JIS-Link; see www.courts.wa.gov/jislink (also, see state introduction). Mail search requires special form.

Criminal Records: Access: Phone, fax, mail, online, in person. Both court and visitors may perform in person searches. No search fee. Required to search: name, years to search, DOB; also helpful: SSN. Criminal records prior to 1995 only retained for 5 years. Index available remotely online from JIS-Link; see www.courts.wa.gov/jislink (also, see state introduction).

General Information: No dependencies, alcohol, adoption, and mental illness records released. SASE required. Turnaround time 3-4 days. Copy fee: $.50 per page. Certification fee: $5.00. Fee payee: District Court, Skagit County. Personal checks accepted. Prepayment is required.

Skamania County

Superior Court PO Box 790, Stevenson, WA 98648; 509-427-9431; Fax: 509-427-7386. Hours: 8:30AM-5PM (PST). *Felony, Civil, Eviction, Probate.*

Civil Records: Access: Phone, mail, online, in person. Only the court performs in person searches; visitors may not. Search fee: $20.00 per hour. Required to search: name, years to search; also helpful: address. Civil cases indexed by defendant, plaintiff. Civil records on computer from 1984, on microfiche and archived from 1900. Index available remotely online from JIS-Link; see www.courts.wa.gov/jislink (also, see state introduction).

Criminal Records: Access: Phone, mail, online, in person. Only the court performs in person searches; visitors may not. Search fee: $20.00 per hour. Required to search: name, years to search; also helpful: address, DOB. Criminal records on computer from 1984, on microfiche and archived from 1900. Index available remotely online from JIS-Link; see www.courts.wa.gov/jislink (also, see state introduction).

General Information: No dependencies, adoption, and mental illness records released. SASE required. Turnaround time same day. Copy fee: $2.00 first page, $1.00 each add'l. Certification fee: Same as copy fee. Fee payee: Skamania County Clerk. Personal checks accepted. Prepayment is required.

District Court PO Box 790, Stevenson, WA 98648; 509-427-9430; Fax: 509-427-7386. Hours: 8:30AM-5PM (PST). *Misdemeanor, Civil Actions Under $50,000, Small Claims.*

Civil Records: Access: Phone, fax, mail, online, in person. Both the court and visitors may perform in person searches. Search fee: $10.00 per hour. Required to search: name, years to search; also helpful: address. Civil cases indexed by defendant, plaintiff. Civil records on computer go back 10 years. Records retained for 10 years. Index available remotely online from JIS-Link; see www.courts.wa.gov/jislink (also, see state introduction).

Criminal Records: Access: Phone, fax, mail, online, in person. Both the court and visitors may perform in person searches. Search fee: $10.00 per hour. Required to search: name, years to search; also helpful: address, DOB, signed release. Criminal records on computer go back 10 years. Records retained for 10 years. Index available remotely online from JIS-Link; see www.courts.wa.gov/jislink (also, see state introduction).

General Information: Public access terminal is available. No dependencies, adoption, and mental illness records released. SASE required. Turnaround time 7 days. Fax notes: No fee to fax results. Copy fee: $3.00 for 1st page, $1.00 each add'l. Certification fee: $6.00. Fee payee: Skamania County District Court. Personal checks accepted. Prepayment is required.

Snohomish County

Superior Court 3000 Rockefeller, MS 605, Everett, WA 98201; 425-388-3466. Hours: 8:30AM-5PM (PST). *Felony, Civil Actions, Eviction, Probate.*

www.co.snohomish.wa.us

Civil Records: Access: Phone, mail, online, in person. Both court and visitors may perform in person searches. Search fee: $20.00 per hour. Required to search: name, years to search. Civil cases indexed by defendant, plaintiff. Civil records on computer from 1978, prior on database index. Index available remotely online from JIS-Link; see www.courts.wa.gov/jislink (also, see state introduction).

Criminal Records: Access: Phone, mail, online, in person. Both court and visitors may perform in person searches. Search fee: $20.00 per hour. Required to search: name, years to search. Criminal records on computer from 1978, prior on database index. Index available remotely online from JIS-Link; see www.courts.wa.gov/jislink (also, see state introduction).

General Information: Public access terminal is available. No sealed, juvenile, adoption, paternity, mental health, sex offenders (victims). SASE requested. Turnaround time 1 week. Copy fee: $.10 per page. Certification fee: $2.00 plus $1.00 per page after first. Fee payee: County Clerk or Snohomish County Clerk's Office. Business checks accepted. No credit cards or personal checks. Prepayment is required.

Cascade Division District Court 415 E Burke St, Arlington, WA 98223; 360-652-9552; Fax: 360-435-0873. Hours: 8:30AM-5PM (PST). *Misdemeanor, Civil Actions Under $50,000, Small Claims.*

Civil Records: Access: Mail, online, in person. Both court and visitors may perform in person searches. Search fee: $5.00 per name. Required to search: name, years to search; also helpful: address. Civil cases indexed by defendant, plaintiff. Civil records on computer from 1985. Index available remotely online from JIS-Link; see www.courts.wa.gov/jislink (also, see state introduction).

Criminal Records: Access: Mail, online, in person. Both court and visitors may perform in person searches. Search fee: $5.00 per name. Required to search: name, years to search, DOB; also helpful: address, SSN. Criminal records on computer from 1987. Index available remotely online from JIS-Link; see www.courts.wa.gov/jislink (see state introduction).

General Information: Public access terminal is available. No sealed, juvenile, adoption, paternity, mental health, sex offenders (victims) or some DUI records released. Turnaround time 1 week. Copy fee: $.15 per page. Certification fee: $5.00. Fee payee: Cascade Division. Personal checks accepted. Credit cards accepted: Visa, M/C. Prepayment required.

Everett Division District Court 3000 Rockefeller Ave MS 508, Everett, WA 98201; 425-388-3331; Civil phone: 425-388-3595; Fax: 425-388-3565. Hours: 8:30AM-5PM (PST). *Misdemeanor, Civil Actions Under $50,000, Small Claims.*

Civil Records: Access: Fax, mail, online, in person. Both court and visitors may perform in person searches. No search fee. Required to search: complete name, years to search; also helpful: address. Civil cases indexed by defendant, plaintiff. Civil records on computer back to 1986. Index available remotely online from JIS-Link; see www.courts.wa.gov/jislink (also, see state introduction).

Criminal Records: Access: Fax, mail, online, in person. Only the court performs in person searches; visitors may not. No search fee. Required to search: complete name, years to search, DOB; also helpful: address, SSN. Criminal records on computer back to 1986. Index available remotely online from JIS-Link; see www.courts.wa.gov/jislink (see state introduction).

General Information: Public access terminal is available. Limited DUI records released. SASE required. Turnaround time 1 week. Fax notes: No fee to fax results. Copy fee: $.15 per page. Certification fee: $5.00. Fee payee: Everett District Court. Personal checks accepted. Credit cards accepted: Visa, MC, AmEx, Discover. Prepayment is required.

Evergreen Division District Court 14414 179th Ave SE, PO Box 625, Monroe, WA 98272-0625; 360-805-6776; Fax: 360-805-6755. Hours: 8:30AM-5PM (PST). *Misdemeanor, Civil Actions Under $50,000, Small Claims.*

Civil Records: Access: Mail, in person. Only the court performs in person searches; visitors may not. No search fee. Required to search: name, years to search; also helpful: address. Civil cases indexed by defendant, plaintiff. Civil records on computer back 10 years; file retained until closure. Index available remotely online from JIS-Link; see www.courts.wa.gov/jislink (also, see state introduction).

Criminal Records: Access: Mail, in person. Only the court performs in person searches; visitors may not. No search fee. Required to search: name, years to search; also helpful: address, DOB. Criminal records on computer archived 3 years after closure by state. Index available remotely online from JIS-Link; see www.courts.wa.gov/jislink (also, see state introduction).

General Information: No sealed, juvenile, adoption, paternity, mental health, sex offenders (victims) or some

DUI records released. SASE requested. Turnaround time 1 week. Copy fee: $.15 per page. Certification fee: $5.00. Fee payee: Evergreen District Court. Personal checks accepted. Prepayment is required.

South Division District Court 20520 68th Ave W, Lynnwood, WA 98036-7406; 425-774-8803; Fax: 425-744-6820. 8:30AM-5PM (PST). *Misdemeanor, Civil Actions Under $50,000, Small Claims.*

Civil Records: Access: Mail, online, in person. No search fee. Required to search: name, years to search. Civil cases indexed by case number. Civil records on computer since 1987. Index available remotely online from JIS-Link; see www.courts.wa.gov/jislink (also, see state introduction).

Criminal Records: Access: Mail, online, in person. Only the court performs in person searches; visitors may not. No search fee. Required to search: name, years to search. Criminal records on computer since 1989. Index available remotely online from JIS-Link; see www.courts.wa.gov/jislink (also, see state introduction).

General Information: No sealed, juvenile, adoption, paternity, mental health, sex offenders (victims) or some DUI records released. SASE requested. Turnaround time 2-4 days. Copy fee: $.15 per page. Certification fee: $5.00. Fee payee: South District Court. Personal checks accepted. Prepayment is required.

Spokane County

Superior Court W 1116 Broadway, Spokane, WA 99260; 509-477-2211. Hours: 8:30AM-5PM (PST). *Felony, Civil, Eviction, Probate.*

Civil Records: Access: Phone, mail, online, in person. Both court and visitors may perform in person searches. Search fee: $10.00 per hour. Required to search: name, years to search. Civil cases indexed by defendant, plaintiff. Civil records on computer from 1973, archives back to 1800s, docket books prior to computer. Index available remotely online from JIS-Link; see www.courts.wa.gov/jislink (also, see state introduction).

Criminal Records: Access: Phone, mail, online, in person. Both court and visitors may perform in person searches. Search fee: $10.00 per hour. Required to search: name, years to search; also helpful: DOB. Criminal records on computer from 1973, archives back to 1800s, docket books prior to computer. Index available remotely online from JIS-Link; see www.courts.wa.gov/jislink (also, see state introduction).

General Information: No sealed, juvenile dependency, adoption, paternity, mental health records released. SASE required. Turnaround time 1-3 days. Copy fee: $2.00 for first page, $1.00 each add'l. Certification fee: $2.00 plus $1.00 each additional page. Fee payee: Spokane County Clerk. Personal checks accepted. Prepayment is required.

District Court 1100 Mallon W, Spokane, WA 99260; 509-477-4770. Hours: 8:30AM-5PM (PST). *Misdemeanor, Civil Actions Under $50,000, Small Claims.*

www.spokanecounty.org/districtcourt

Civil Records: Access: Phone, mail, online, in person. Only the court performs in person searches; visitors may not. No search fee. Required to search: name, years to search; also helpful: address. Civil cases indexed by defendant, plaintiff. Civil records on computer go back 10 years. Index available remotely online from JIS-Link; see www.courts.wa.gov/jislink (also, see state introduction).

Criminal Records: Access: Phone, mail, online, in person. Only the court performs in person searches; visitors may not. No search fee. Required to search: name, years to search, signed release; also helpful: address, DOB. Criminal records are computer since 1984, but searches are only done for five years time. Index available remotely online from JIS-Link; see www.courts.wa.gov/jislink (also, see state introduction).

General Information: SASE required. Turnaround time 1 week. Copy fee: $1.00 per page. Certification fee: $5.00. Fee payee: Spokane County District Court. Business checks accepted. Personal checks accepted for civil records only. Prepayment is required.

Stevens County

Superior Court 215 S Oak Rm 206, Colville, WA 99114; 509-684-7575. Hours: 8AM-Noon, 1-4:30PM (PST). *Felony, Civil, Eviction, Probate.*

Civil Records: Access: Phone, mail, online, in person. Only the court performs in person searches; visitors may not. Search fee: $8.00 per hour. Required to search: name, years to search; also helpful: address. Civil cases indexed by defendant, plaintiff. Civil records on computer from 10-82, microfiche from 1889-1982, archives 1889, index cards prior to 1982. Index available remotely online from JIS-Link; see www.courts.wa.gov/jislink (also, see state introduction).
Criminal Records: Access: Mail, online, in person. Only the court performs in person searches; visitors may not. Search fee: $8.00 per hour. Required to search: name, years to search, DOB; also helpful: address, SSN. Criminal records on computer from 10-82, microfiche from 1889-1982, archives 1889, index cards prior to 1982. Index available remotely online from JIS-Link; see www.courts.wa.gov/jislink (also, see state introduction).
General Information: No sealed, juvenile, adoption, paternity, mental health, sex offenders (victims). SASE required. Turnaround time same day. Copy fee: $2.00 for 1st page, $1.00 each add'l pg. Certification fee: Included in copy fee. Fee payee: Stevens County Clerk. Personal checks accepted. Prepayment is required.

District Court 215 S Oak Rm 213, Colville, WA 99114; 509-684-5249; Fax: 509-684-7571. Hours: 8AM-Noon, 1-4:30PM (PST). *Misdemeanor, Civil Actions Under $50,000, Small Claims.*

www.co.stevens.wa.us/distcourt/departments.htm

Civil Records: Access: Mail, online, in person. Only the court performs in person searches; visitors may not. Search fee: No search fee. Required to search: name, years to search; also helpful: address. Civil cases indexed by defendant. Civil records on computer from 1/93, prior on docket books to 1988. Index available remotely online from JIS-Link; see www.courts.wa.gov/jislink (also, see state introduction).
Criminal Records: Access: Mail, online, in person. Only the court performs in person searches; visitors may not. Search fee: No search fee. Required to search: name, years to search, DOB; also helpful: address, SSN, signed request. Criminal records on computer from 07/93, prior on docket books to 1988. Index available remotely online from JIS-Link; see www.courts.wa.gov/jislink (also, see state introduction).
General Information: No sealed, juvenile, adoption, paternity, mental health, sex offenders (victims) or some DUI records released. Turnaround time 1 week. Fax notes: Fee to fax results is $1.00 per page. Copy fee: $.15 per page. Certification fee: $5.00. Fee payee: Stevens County District Court. Business checks accepted. Prepayment is required.

Thurston County

Superior Court 2000 Lakeridge Dr SW, Bldg 2, Olympia, WA 98502; 360-786-5430. 8AM-5PM (PST). *Felony, Misdemeanor, Civil, Eviction, Probate.*

www.co.thurston.wa.us/clerk

Civil Records: Access: Phone, mail, in person, e-mail. Both court and visitors may perform in person searches. Search fee: $20.00 per hour. Required to search: name, years to search; also helpful: address. Civil cases indexed by defendant, plaintiff. Civil records on computer from 07/78, archives back to 1850s. Index

available remotely online from JIS-Link; see www.courts.wa.gov/jislink (also, see state introduction).
Criminal Records: Access: Phone, mail, in person, E-mail. Both court and visitors may perform in person searches. Search fee: $20.00 per hour. Required to search: name, years to search, DOB, signed release; also helpful: address, SSN. Criminal records on computer from 07/78, archives back to 1850s. Index available remotely online from JIS-Link; see www.courts.wa.gov/jislink (also, see state introduction).
General Information: Public access terminal is available. No sealed, juvenile, adoption, paternity, mental health, sex offenders (victims). SASE required. Turnaround time 1-7 days. Copy fee: $2.00 for first page, $1.00 each add'l. Certification fee: Certification fee is $2.00 first page and $1.00 each additional. Fee payee: Thurston County Clerk. Business checks accepted. Prepayment is required.

District Court 2000 Lakeridge Dr SW, Bldg 3, Olympia, WA 98502; 360-786-5450; Fax: 360-754-3359. Hours: 8:30AM-4PM (PST). *Misdemeanor, Civil Actions Under $50,000, Small Claims.*

Civil Records: Access: Phone, fax, mail, online, in person. Both court and visitors may perform in person searches. No search fee. Required to search: name, years to search; also helpful: address. Civil cases indexed by defendant, plaintiff. Civil records on computer from 1983. Index available remotely online from JIS-Link; see www.courts.wa.gov/jislink (also, see state introduction).
Criminal Records: Access: Phone, fax, mail, online, in person. Both court and visitors may perform in person searches. No search fee. Required to search: name, years to search; also helpful: address, DOB, SSN. Criminal records on computer from 1988. Index available remotely online from JIS-Link; see www.courts.wa.gov/jislink (also, see state introduction).
General Information: No sealed, juvenile, adoption, paternity, mental health, sex offenders (victims) or some DUI records released. SASE required. Turnaround time 2 week. Copy fee: $.25 per page. Certification fee: $5.00. Fee payee: Thurston County District Court. Personal checks accepted. Prepayment is required.

Wahkiakum County

Superior Court PO Box 116, Cathlamet, WA 98612; 360-795-3558; Fax: 360-795-8813. Hours: 8AM-4PM (PST). *Felony, Misdemeanor, Civil, Eviction, Probate.*

Civil Records: Access: Mail, online, in person. Both court and visitors may perform in person searches. Search fee: $20.00 per hour. Required to search: name, years to search. Civil cases indexed by defendant, plaintiff. Civil records on computer from 1988, archives from 1850s. Index available remotely online from JIS-Link; see www.courts.wa.gov/jislink (also, see state introduction).
Criminal Records: Access: Mail, online, in person. Both court and visitors may perform in person searches. Search fee: $20.00 per hour. Required to search: name, years to search; also helpful: address, DOB. Criminal records on computer from 1988, archives from 1850s. Index available remotely online from JIS-Link; see www.courts.wa.gov/jislink (also, see state introduction).
General Information: No sealed, juvenile, adoption, paternity, mental health, sex offenders (victims). SASE required. Turnaround time 1 day. Fax notes: Fee to fax results is $1.00 per page. Copy fee: $1.00 per page. Certification fee: $2.00. Fee payee: County Clerk. Personal checks accepted. Prepayment is required.

District Court PO Box 144, Cathlamet, WA 98612; 360-795-3461; Fax: 360-795-6506. Hours: 8AM-4PM (PST). *Misdemeanor, Civil Actions Under $50,000, Small Claims.*

Civil Records: Access: Phone, fax, mail, online, in person. Both court and visitors may perform in person searches. No search fee. Required to search: name, years to search; also helpful: address. Civil cases indexed by defendant, plaintiff. Civil records on computer from 1997, index cards back 10 years, archived prior. Index available remotely online from JIS-Link; see www.courts.wa.gov/jislink (also, see state introduction).
Criminal Records: Access: Phone, fax, mail, online, in person. Both court and visitors may perform in person searches. No search fee. Required to search: name, years to search; also helpful: DOB. Criminal records on computer from 1997, index cards back 10 years, archived prior. Index available remotely online from JIS-Link; see www.courts.wa.gov/jislink (also, see state introduction).
General Information: No sealed, juvenile, adoption, paternity, mental health, sex offenders (victims) or some DUI records released. SASE required. Turnaround time 2 days. Fax notes: No fee to fax results. Copy fee: $.25 per page. Certification fee: $5.00. Fee payee: Wahkiakum District Court. Personal checks accepted. Prepayment is required.

Walla Walla County

Superior Court PO Box 836, Walla Walla, WA 99362; 509-527-3221; Fax: 509-527-3214. Hours: 9AM-4PM (PST). *Felony, Civil, Eviction, Probate.*

Civil Records: Access: Phone, mail, online, in person. Only the court performs in person searches; visitors may not. Search fee: $20.00 per hour. Required to search: name, years to search; also helpful: DOB. Civil cases indexed by defendant, plaintiff. Civil records on computer from 7/81, prior in docket books. Index available remotely online from JIS-Link; see www.courts.wa.gov/jislink (also, see state introduction).
Criminal Records: Access: Phone, mail, online, in person. Only the court performs in person searches; visitors may not. Search fee: $20.00 per hour. Required to search: name, years to search, DOB; also helpful: address, SSN. Criminal records on computer from 7/81, prior in docket books. Index available remotely online from JIS-Link; see www.courts.wa.gov/jislink (also, see state introduction).
General Information: No sealed, juvenile, adoption, paternity, mental health, sex offenders (victims). Personal checks not accepted. Turnaround time 1 day. Fax notes: Will not fax results. Copy fee: $2.00 for first page, $1.00 each add'l. Certification fee: $2.00 plus $1.00 each add'l page. Fee payee: Walla Walla County Clerk. Only cashiers checks and money orders accepted. Prepayment is required.

District Court 317 W Rose St, Walla Walla, WA 99362; 509-527-3236. Hours: 9AM-4PM (PST). *Misdemeanor, Civil Actions Under $50,000, Small Claims.*

Civil Records: Access: Mail, online, in person. Only the court performs in person searches; visitors may not. Search fee: $5.00 per name. Required to search: name, years to search. Civil cases indexed by defendant, plaintiff. Civil records on computer from 7/87, on index books. Records retained for 10 years. Index available remotely online from JIS-Link; see www.courts.wa.gov/jislink (also, see state introduction).
Criminal Records: Access: Mail, online, in person. Only the court performs in person searches; visitors may not. Search fee: $5.00 per name. Required to search: name, years to search, signed release; also helpful: address, DOB, SSN. Criminal records on computer from 7/87, on index books. Records retained for 10 years. Index available remotely online from JIS-Link; see www.courts.wa.gov/jislink (also, see state introduction).
General Information: No sealed, juvenile, adoption, paternity, mental health, sex offenders (victims) or some

DUI records released. SASE required. Turnaround time 1-3 days. Copy fee: $1.00 for first page, $.50 each add'l. Certification fee: $5.00. Fee payee: Walla Walla District Court. Personal checks accepted. Prepayment required.

Whatcom County

Superior Court PO Box 1144, Bellingham, WA 98227; 360-676-6777; Fax: 360-676-6693. Hours: 8:30-4:30PM (PST). *Felony, Civil, Eviction, Probate.*

Note: Extension 50014 for criminal; 50018 for civil.

Civil Records: Access: Phone, fax, mail, online, in person. Only the court performs in person searches; visitors may not. Search fee: No search fee if record is on computer. Required to search: name, years to search; also helpful: address. Civil cases indexed by defendant, plaintiff. Civil records on computer from 1980, archives back to 1800s, index cards. Index available remotely online from JIS-Link; see www.courts.wa.gov/jislink (also, see state introduction).

Criminal Records: Access: Phone, fax, mail, online, in person. Only the court performs in person searches; visitors may not. No search fee. Required to search: name, years to search; also helpful: address, DOB, SSN. Criminal records on computer from 1980, archives back to 1800s, index cards. Index available remotely online from JIS-Link; see www.courts.wa.gov/jislink (also, see state introduction).

General Information: No sealed, juvenile, adoption, paternity, mental health, sex offenders (victims). SASE required. Turnaround time up to 1 week. Copy fee: $2.00 for first page, $1.00 each add'l. Certification fee: Included in copy fee. Fee payee: Whatcom County Clerk. Only cashiers checks and money orders accepted. Prepayment is required.

District Court 311 Grand Ave, Bellingham, WA 98225; 360-676-6770; Fax: 360-738-2452. Hours: 8AM-4:30PM (PST). *Misdemeanor, Civil Actions Under $50,000, Small Claims.*

www.co.whatcom.wa.us

Civil Records: Access: Mail, online, in person. Only the court performs in person searches; visitors may not. No search fee. Required to search: name, years to search; also helpful: address. Civil cases indexed by defendant, plaintiff. Civil records on computer since 1984. Index available remotely online from JIS-Link; see www.courts.wa.gov/jislink (see state introduction).

Criminal Records: Access: Mail, online, in person. Only the court performs in person searches; visitors may not. No search fee. Required to search: name, years to search; also helpful: address, DOB, SSN. Criminal records on computer 10 years back, archived since 1984. Index available remotely online from JIS-Link; see www.courts.wa.gov/jislink (see state introduction).

General Information: No sealed, juvenile, adoption, paternity, mental health, sex offenders (victims) or some DUI records released. Turnaround time 2 days. Copy fee: $.25 per page. Certification fee: $5.00. Fee payee: Whatcom District Court. Personal checks accepted. Prepayment is required.

Whitman County

Superior Court Box 390, Colfax, WA 99111; 509-397-6240; Fax: 509-397-3546. Hours: 8AM-5PM (PST). *Felony, Civil, Eviction, Probate.*

Civil Records: Access: Phone, fax, mail, online, in person. Only the court performs in person searches; visitors may not. Search fee: $8.00 per hour. Required

to search: name, years to search; also helpful: address. Civil cases indexed by defendant, plaintiff. Civil records on computer from 1985, archives back to 1887. Index available remotely online from JIS-Link; see www.courts.wa.gov/jislink (also, see state introduction).

Criminal Records: Access: Phone, fax, mail, online, in person. Only the court performs in person searches; visitors may not. Search fee: $8.00 per hour. Required to search: name, years to search, signed release; also helpful: address, DOB, SSN. Criminal records on computer from 1985, archives back to 1887. Index available remotely online from JIS-Link; see www.courts.wa.gov/jislink (also, see state introduction).

General Information: No sealed, juvenile, adoption, paternity, mental health, sex offenders (victims). SASE required. Turnaround time 1 week. Fax notes: $4.00 for first page, $1.00 each add'l. Copy fee: $.15 per page. Certification fee: $2.00 plus $1.00 per page after first. Fee payee: Whitman County Clerk. Personal checks accepted. Prepayment is required.

District Court 400 N Main St, PO Box 230, Colfax, WA 99111; 509-397-6260; Fax: 509-397-5584. Hours: 8AM-5PM; Public Hours: 8:30AM-4:30PM (PST). *Misdemeanor, Civil Actions Under $50,000, Small Claims.*

Civil Records: Access: Phone, fax, mail, online, in person. Only the court performs in person searches; visitors may not. Search fee: $8.00 per hour. Required to search: name, years to search; also helpful: address. Civil cases indexed by defendant, plaintiff. Civil records on DISCIS computer system from 7/91, prior on index log. Index available remotely online from JIS-Link; see www.courts.wa.gov/jislink (also, see state introduction).

Criminal Records: Access: Phone, fax, mail, online, in person. Only the court performs in person searches; visitors may not. Search fee: $8.00 per hour. Required to search: name, years to search, DOB; also helpful: address, SSN. Criminal records on DISCIS computer system from 7/91, prior on index log. Index available remotely online from JIS-Link; see www.courts.wa.gov/jislink (also, see state introduction).

General Information: No sealed, juvenile, adoption, paternity, mental health, sex offenders (victims) or some DUI records released. SASE required. Turnaround time 1 week. Fax notes: Fee to fax results is $3.00. Copy fee: $.15 per page. Certification fee: $6.00. Fee payee: Whitman County. Personal checks accepted. Prepayment is required.

District Court 325 SE Paradise St, Pullman, WA 99163; 509-332-2065; Fax: 509-332-5740. Hours: 8AM-5PM (PST). *Misdemeanor, Civil Actions Under $50,000, Small Claims.*

Civil Records: Access: Fax, mail, online, in person. Only the court performs in person searches; visitors may not. Search fee: $8.00 per hour. Required to search: name, years to search; also helpful: address. Civil cases indexed by defendant, plaintiff. Civil records on DISCIS computer system from 7/91; '89-'91 on index. Index available remotely online from JIS-Link; see www.courts.wa.gov/jislink (also, see state introduction).

Criminal Records: Access: Fax, mail, online, in person. Only the court performs in person searches; visitors may not. Search fee: $8.00 per hour. Required to search: name, years to search; also helpful: address, DOB, SSN. Criminal records on DISCIS computer system from 7/91; '89-'91 on index. Index available

remotely online from JIS-Link; see www.courts.wa.gov/jislink (also, see state introduction).

General Information: No sealed, juvenile, adoption, paternity, mental health, sex offenders (victims) or some DUI records released. SASE required. Turnaround time 1 week. Fax notes: No fee to fax results. Copy fee: $.15 per page. Certification fee: $6.00. Fee payee: Whitman District Court. Personal checks accepted.

Yakima County

Superior Court 128 N 2nd St, Rm 314, Yakima, WA 98901; 509-574-1430. Hours: 8:30AM-4:30PM (PST). *Felony, Civil, Domestic Relations, Probate.*

www.pan.co.yakima.wa.us/clerk

Civil Records: Access: Phone, mail, in person. Only the court performs in person searches; visitors may not. Search fee: $20.00 per hour. Required to search: name, years to search. Civil cases indexed by defendant, plaintiff. Civil records on computer from 1978, archives back to 1890s. Index available remotely online from JIS-Link; see www.courts.wa.gov/jislink (also, see state introduction).

Criminal Records: Access: Phone, mail, in person. Only the court performs in person searches; visitors may not. Search fee: $20.00 per hour. Required to search: name, years to search; also helpful: DOB. Criminal records on computer from 1978, archives back to 1890s. Index available remotely online from JIS-Link; see www.courts.wa.gov/jislink (also, see state introduction).

General Information: No sealed, juvenile, adoption, paternity, mental health, sex offenders (victims). SASE required. Turnaround time varies. Copy fee: $.15 per page. Microfilm copies $.25 per page. $1.00 minimum. Certification fee: $2.00 plus $1.00 per page after first. Fee payee: Yakima County Clerk. Business checks accepted, no personal. Prepayment is required.

District Court 128 N 2nd St, Rm 225, Yakima, WA 98901-2631; 509-574-1800; Fax: 509-574-1831. Hours: 8:30AM-4:30PM (PST). *Misdemeanor, Civil Actions Under $50,000, Small Claims.*

www.co.yakima.wa.us/courts

Civil Records: Access: Phone, fax, mail, online, in person. Both court and visitors may perform in person searches. No search fee. Required to search: name, years to search; also helpful: address. Civil cases indexed by defendant, plaintiff. Civil records on computer from 1984, generally. Index available remotely online from JIS-Link; see www.courts.wa.gov/jislink (also, see state introduction).

Criminal Records: Access: Phone, fax, mail, online, in person. Both court and visitors may perform in person searches. No search fee. Required to search: name, years to search, DOB; also helpful: address, case number, DRL, SSN. Criminal records on computer from 1984, generally. Index available remotely online from JIS-Link; see www.courts.wa.gov/jislink (also, see state introduction).

General Information: No sealed or some DUI records released. SASE requested. Turnaround time 2 days. Fax notes: No fee to fax results. Copy fee: $.15 per page. Certification fee: $5.00. Fee payee: Yakima County District Court. Personal checks accepted. Credit cards accepted: Visa. Prepayment is required.

Washington Recording Offices

ORGANIZATION: 39 counties, 39 recording offices. The recording officer is County Auditor. County records are usually combined in a Grantor/Grantee index. The entire state is in the Pacific Time Zone (PST).

REAL ESTATE RECORDS: Many County Auditors will perform real estate searches, including record owner. Search fees and copy fees vary. Copies usually cost $1.00 per page and $2.00 for certification per document. If the Auditor does not provide searches, contact the Assessor for record owner information. Contact the Treasurer (Finance Department in King County) for information about unpaid real estate taxes.

UCC RECORDS: Financing statements are filed at the state level, except for real estate related collateral, which are filed with the County Auditor. Most recording offices will perform UCC searches. Use search request form UCC-11R. Searches fees vary, copy fee is usually $1.00.

TAX LIEN RECORDS: All federal tax liens on personal property are filed with the Department of Licensing. Other federal and all state tax liens are filed with the County Auditor. Most counties will perform tax lien searches. Search fees are usually $8.00 or $10.00 per hour.

ONLINE ACCESS: A number of counites offer onlice access to assessor or real estate records, including the larger population counties.

Asotin County

County Auditor, PO Box 129, Asotin, WA 99402. 509-243-2084 R/E Recording: 509-246-4164; Fax 509-243-2087. www.co.asotin.wa.us
Will search UCC records. Will search tax lien records. Will search real estate records. **Other Phone Numbers:** Assessor 509-243-2016; Treasurer 509-243-2014; Appraiser/Auditor 509-243-2084.

Benton County

County Auditor, PO Box 470, Prosser, WA 99350. County Auditor, R/E and UCC Recording 509-786-5616; Fax 509-786-5528.
The county also has a second recording office located at 5600 W. Canal, Ste B, Kenniwick, WA 99336. Will search UCC records. UCC search includes tax liens if requested. Will search tax liens separately. Will search real estate records. **Other Phone Numbers:** Assessor 509-786-2046; Treasurer 509-786-2255; Appraiser/Auditor 509-736-3085; Elections 509-786-5618; Vital Records 509-786-5616.

Chelan County

County Auditor, PO Box 400, Wenatchee, WA 98807. County Auditor, R/E and UCC Recording 509-664-5432 UCC Recording: 509-664-5439; Fax 509-664-5246. www.co.chelan.wa.us
Will search UCC records. **Online Access:** Grantor/Grantee, Property, Marriage Records. Access to the Auditor's iCRIS database is available free at www.co.chelan.wa.us/ad/ad5da.htm. Click on the "key" to get to free registration page. Images go back to 1997; marriage images to 1990; earlier online records show indexing information only. **Other Phone Numbers:** Assessor 509-664-5365; Treasurer 509-664-5405; Appraiser/Auditor 509-664-5431; Elections 509-664-5431; Vital Records 509-236-4300.

Clallam County

Chief Deputy Auditor, PO Box 3030, Port Angeles, WA 98362. Chief Deputy Auditor, R/E and UCC Recording 360-417-2220; Fax 360-417-2517. www.clallam.net
Will search UCC records. Will not search real estate records. **Other Phone Numbers:** Assessor 360-417-2204; Treasurer 360-417-2373; Appraiser/Auditor 360-417-2221; Elections 360-417-2217; Vital Records 360-417-2303.

Clark County

County Auditor, PO Box 5000, Vancouver, WA 98666-5000. County Auditor, R/E and UCC Recording 360-397-2208; fax 360-397-6007. www.co.clark.wa.us/auditor/
Will search UCC records. Will not search real estate records. **Online Access:** Real Estate, Lien, Vital Statistic, Recording Records. Access to County Auditor's database is available free at http://auditor.co.clark.wa.us/auditor_new/index.cfm. Court documents are excluded from this index. Also, search maps online for property data at www.rtc.wa.gov/ccgis/mol/property.htm. No name searching. **Other Phone Numbers:** Assessor 360-397-2391; Treasurer 360-397-2252; Appraiser/Auditor 360-397-2345; Elections 360-397-2345; Vital Records 360-397-2243; Auditor Main Line 360-397-2241.

Columbia County

County Auditor, 341 E. Main St., Dayton, WA 99328-1361. County Auditor, R/E and UCC Recording 509-382-4541; Fax 509-382-4830. www.columbiaco.com
Will search UCC records. UCC search includes tax liens if requested. Will search separately. Will not search real estate records. **Other Phones:** Assessor 509-382-2131; Treasurer 509-382-2641; Appraiser/Auditor 509-382-4541; Elections 509-382-4541.

Cowlitz County

County Auditor, 207 Fourth Ave North, Kelso, WA 98626. County Auditor, R/E and UCC Recording 360-577-3006; Fax 360-414-5552. www.co.cowlitz.wa.us/auditor/
Will search UCC records. UCC search includes tax liens if requested. Will search separately. Real estate record owner and mortgage searches available. **Online Access:** Most Wanted, Missing Person Records. Access to sheriff's most wanted and missing persons lists is available free at www.co.cowlitz.wa.us/sheriff. **Other Phone Numbers:** Assessor 360-577-3010; Treasurer 360-577-3060; Appraiser/Auditor 360-577-3005; Elections 360-577-3002.

Douglas County

County Auditor, PO Box 456, Waterville, WA 98858. 509-745-8826 R/E Recording: 509-745-8527 x204 UCC Recording: 509-745-8527 x204; Fax 509-745-8812.
Will search UCC records. Will search tax lien records. Will search real estate records. **Other Phone Numbers:** Assessor 509-745-8521; Treasurer 509-745-8525; Appraiser/Auditor 509-884-9403; Elections 509-745-8527 x203; Vital Records 509-745-8527 x204.

Ferry County

County Auditor, 350 E. Delaware #2, Republic, WA 99166. 509-775-5200 R/E Recording: 509-775-5202 UCC Recording: 509-775-5202; Fax 509-775-5208.
Will search UCC records. **Other Phone Numbers:** Assessor 509-775-5203; Treasurer 509-775-5238; Appraiser/Auditor 509-775-5208; Elections 509-775-5208; Vital Records 509-775-5200.

Franklin County

County Auditor, PO Box 1451, Pasco, WA 99301. County Auditor, R/E and UCC Recording 509-545-3536; Fax 509-545-2142.
Will search UCC records. This agency will not do a tax lien search. Will not search real estate records. **Online Access:** Assessor, Property, Sex Offender Records. Search for property information by address or parcel number at www.co.franklin.wa.us/assessor. Also, search for residential sales data. Also, search the level 2 sex offenders at www.co.franklin.wa.us/sheriff/?p=14&v=2. Level 3 sex offenders are at www.co.franklin.wa.us/sheriff/?p=14&v=3. **Other Phones:** Assessor 509-545-3506; Treasurer 509-545-3518; Appraiser/Auditor 509-545-3538; Elections 509-545-3538; Vital Records 509-586-0207 X229.

Garfield County

County Auditor, PO Box 278, Pomeroy, WA 99347-0278. County Auditor, R/E and UCC Recording 509-843-1411; Fax 509-843-3941.
Will search UCC records. UCC search includes tax liens if requested. Will not search real estate records. **Other Phones:** Assessor 509-843-3632; Treasurer 509-843-1531; Appraiser/Auditor 509-843-1411; Elections 509-843-1411; Vital Records 509-843-1411.

Grant County

County Auditor, PO Box 37, Ephrata, WA 98823. 509-754-2011 x333.
Will search UCC records. Will not perform tax lien searches. Will not search real estate records. **Other Phone Numbers:** Assessor 509-754-2011 x310; Treasurer 509-754-2011 x353; Appraiser/Auditor 509-754-2011 x377.

Grays Harbor County

County Auditor, 101 W. Broadway, Ste. 2, Montesano, WA 98563. 360-249-4232 x331 R/E Recording: 360-249-4232; Fax 360-249-3330.
Will search UCC records. Will not search real estate records. **Other Phone Numbers:** Assessor 360-249-4121; Treasurer 360-249-3751; Appraiser/Auditor 360-249-4232.

Island County

Deputy Auditor, PO Box 5000, Coupeville, WA 98239. Deputy Auditor, R/E and UCC Recording 360-679-7366; Fax 360-240-5553. www.islandcounty.net/auditor/index.htm

Will not search UCC records due to incompleteness of their records. Will not search real estate records. **Online Access:** Sex Offender Records. Search the sexual offenders and kidnappers list for free at www.islandcounty.net/sheriff/rsolist.htm. **Other Phone Numbers:** Assessor 360-679-7303; Treasurer 360-678-5111; Appraiser/Auditor 360-679-7366; Elections 360-679-7366.

Jefferson County

County Auditor, PO Box 563, Port Townsend, WA 98368. County Auditor, R/E and UCC Recording 360-385-9116; Fax 360-385-9228. www.co.jefferson.wa.us/departments.htm

Will search UCC records. Will search single real estate records (but not for a title company). **Online Access:** Assessor, Real Estate Records. Access to the "Recorded Document Search" database is available at www.co.jefferson.wa.us/_hidden/disclaimer.htm. Records on the County Property (Tax Parcel) Database Tool are also available as well as plats and survey images. **Other Phones:** Assessor 360-385-9105; Treasurer 360-385-9150; Appraiser/Auditor 360-385-9119.

King County

Superintendent of Records, 500 4th Ave, Room 311, Administration Building, Room 311, Seattle, WA 98104. Superintendent of Records, R/E and UCC Recording 206-296-1570; Fax 206-205-8396. www.metrokc.gov

Will search UCC records. Will search real estate records. **Online Access:** Real Estate, Lien, Marriage Records. Access to the county recorder's database is available free at www.metrokc.gov/recelec/records. also, property records on Dept. of Developmental and Environmental Resources database are available free online at www.metrokc.gov/ddes/gis/parcel. After the disclaimer page, search by parcel number, address, street intersection, or map. **Other Phones:** Assessor 206-296-7300; Treasurer 206-296-3850; Appraiser/Auditor 206-296-8683; Elections 206-296-1565; Vital Records 206-296-4768; Finance Dept 206-296-3850.

Kitsap County

County Auditor, 614 Division St, Room 106 /MS 31, Port Orchard, WA 98366. 360-337-4935 R/E Recording: 360-337-7133; Fax 360-337-4645. www.kitsapgov.com/aud/default.htm

Will search UCC records. UCC search includes tax liens if requested. Will not search real estate records. **Other Phone Numbers:** Assessor 360-876-7160; Treasurer 360-876-7135; Appraiser/Auditor 360-227-7129; Elections 360-337-7128.

Kittitas County

County Auditor, 205 W. 5th, Room 105, Ellensburg, WA 98926-3129. 509-962-7504 R/E Recording: 509-962-7557; Fax 509-962-7687.

Will search UCC records. **Other Phone Numbers:** Assessor 509-962-7501; Treasurer 509-962-7535; Appraiser/Auditor 509-962-7503; Elections 509-962-7503; Vital Records 509-962-7504; Health Department 509-962-7504.

Klickitat County

County Auditor, 205 S. Columbus Ave, MS-CH-2, Goldendale, WA 98620. County Auditor, R/E and UCC Recording 509-773-4001; Fax 509-773-4244. www.klickitatcounty.org

Will search UCC records. **Other Phone Numbers:** Assessor 509-773-3715; Treasurer 509-773-4664;

Appraiser/Auditor 509-773-4001; Elections 509-773-4001; Vital Records 509-773-4001; Toll Free Auditor 800-583-8050.

Lewis County

County Auditor, PO Box 29, Chehalis, WA 98532-0029. County Auditor, R/E and UCC Recording 360-740-1163; Fax 360-740-1421.

Will search UCC records. Will not search real estate records. **Other Phone Numbers:** Assessor 360-740-1392; Treasurer 360-740-1115; Appraiser/Auditor 360-740-1164.

Lincoln County

County Auditor, PO Box 28, Davenport, WA 99122. County Auditor, R/E and UCC Recording 509-725-4971; Fax 509-725-0820.

Will search UCC records. **Other Phone Numbers:** Assessor 509-725-7011; Treasurer 509-725-5061; Appraiser/Auditor 509-725-4971; Elections 509-725-4971; Vital Records 509-725-4971.

Mason County

County Auditor, PO Box 400, Shelton, WA 98584. 360-427-9670 R/E Recording: 360-427-9670 x468 UCC Recording: 360-427-9670 x467; Fax 360-427-8425. http://auditor.co.mason.wa.us

Will search UCC records. Will not search real estate records. **Other Phone Numbers:** Assessor 360-427-9670 x491; Treasurer 360-427-9670 x484; Appraiser/Auditor 360-427-9670 x470; Elections 360-427-9670 x469; Vital Records 360-427-9670 x467.

Okanogan County

County Auditor, PO Box 1010, Okanogan, WA 98840. 509-422-7240; Fax 509-422-7163.

Will search UCC records. This agency will not do a tax lien search. Will not search real estate records. **Other Phone Numbers:** Assessor 509-422-7190; Treasurer 509-422-7180; Appraiser/Auditor 509-422-7240.

Pacific County

County Auditor, PO Box 97, South Bend, WA 98586-9903. 360-875-9318 R/E Recording: 360-875-9309 x313; Fax 360-875-9333. www.co.pacific.wa.us/directory.htm

Will search UCC records. Tax liens not included in UCC search. Will not perform title searches of real estate records; will search for individual documents. **Other Phone Numbers:** Assessor 360-875-9301; Treasurer 360-875-9421; Appraiser/Auditor 360-875-9317 x313; Elections 360-875-9317; Vital Records 360-875-9318.

Pend Oreille County

County Auditor, PO Box 5015, Newport, WA 99156. 509-447-3185; Fax 509-447-2475.

Will search UCC records. Tax liens are filed with County Treasurer. Will not search real estate records. **Other Phones:** Assessor 509-447-4312; Treasurer 509-447-3612; Appraiser/Auditor 509-447-3185.

Pierce County

County Auditor, 2401 S. 35th St, Room 200, Tacoma, WA 98409. 253-798-7440 R/E Recording: 206-591-7440; Fax 253-798-2761.

Will search UCC records. **Online Access:** Assessor, Real Estate, Recording, Deed, Lien, Vital Statistic, Judgment Records. Search the auditor's recording database for free at www.co.pierce.wa.us/cfapps/auditor/documentsearch.cfm. Also, property records on County Assessor-Treasurer database are available free at www.co.pierce.wa.us/CFApps/atr/TIMSNet/index.htm. After the disclaimer page, search by parcel number or site address. Also, the county sexual offrende/kidnappers list is available for free at http://pso.co.pierce.wa.us. **Other Phone Numbers:**

Assessor 253-798-6111; Treasurer 253-798-6111; Appraiser/Auditor 253-798-7430.

San Juan County

County Auditor, PO Box 638, Friday Harbor, WA 98250. 360-378-2161; Fax 360-378-6256.

Will search UCC records. UCC search includes tax liens if requested. Will not search real estate records. **Other Phones:** Assessor 360-378-4729; Treasurer 360-378-2171; Appraiser/Auditor 360-378-3357.

Skagit County

County Auditor, PO Box 1306, Mount Vernon, WA 98273-1306. 360-336-9420; Fax 360-336-9429.

Will search UCC records. UCC search includes tax liens if requested. Will not search real estate records. **Other Phone Numbers:** Assessor 360-336-9370; Treasurer 360-336-9350; Appraiser/Auditor 360-336-9305.

Skamania County

County Auditor, PO Box 790, Stevenson, WA 98648-0790. County Auditor, R/E and UCC Recording 509-427-9420; Fax 509-427-4165. www.wacounties.org/waco/county/skamania.html

Will search UCC records. **Other Phone Numbers:** Assessor 509-427-9400; Treasurer 509-427-9410; Appraiser/Auditor 509-427-9420; Elections 509-427-9420; Vital Records 509-427-9420.

Snohomish County

County Auditor, Dept. R., M/S # 204, 3000 Rockefeller Ave, Everett, WA 98201. County Auditor, R/E and UCC Recording 425-388-3483; Fax 425-259-2777.

Will search UCC records. UCC search includes tax liens if requested. Mortgage and property transfer searches available. **Online Access:** Real Estate, Assessor, Recording, Marriage Records. Acccss to the Auditor's office database is available free at http://198.238.192.100/default1.htm. Search on the OPR, map, or marriage page. **Other Phone Numbers:** Assessor 425-388-3433; Treasurer 425-388-3366; Appraiser/Auditor 425-388-3444; Elections 425-388-3444.

Spokane County

County Auditor, West 1116 Broadway, Spokane, WA 99260. 509-477-2270 R/E Recording: 509-477-2258 UCC Recording: 509-477-2258; Fax 509-477-6451.

Will search UCC records. **Other Phone Numbers:** Treasurer 509-456-4713; Appraiser/Auditor 509-456-3696; Elections 509-477-2320.

Stevens County

County Auditor, 215 S. Oak St., Colville, WA 99114. County Auditor, R/E and UCC Recording 509-684-7512; Fax 509-684-8310.

Will search UCC records. Tax liens not included in UCC search. Real estate owner, mortgage, and property transfer searches available. **Other Phone Numbers:** Treasurer 509-684-2593; Appraiser/Auditor 509-684-7514; Elections 509-684-7514; Auditor 509-684-6161.

Thurston County

County Auditor, 2000 Lakeridge Drive SW, Olympia, WA 98502. County Auditor, R/E and UCC Recording 360-786-5405; Fax 360-786-5223. www.co.thurston.wa.us/auditor

Will search UCC records. Will search real estate records. **Online Access:** Assessor, Real Estate Records. Assessor and property information on Thurston GeoData database are available free online at www.geodata.org/scripts/esrimap.dll?name=TGCMAP&Cmd=Map. **Other Phone Numbers:** Assessor 360-786-5410; Treasurer 360-786-5550; Appraiser/Auditor 360-786-6410; Elections 360-786-5408; Vital Records 360-786-5481.

Wahkiakum County

County Auditor, PO Box 543, Cathlamet, WA 98612. 360-795-3219; Fax 360-795-0824.
Will search UCC records. UCC search includes tax liens if requested. Will not search real estate records. **Other Phones:** Assessor 360-795-3791; Treasurer 360-795-8005; Appraiser/Auditor 360-795-3219; Elections 360-795-3219; Vital Records 360-795-6207.

Walla Walla County

County Auditor, PO Box 1856, Walla Walla, WA 99362-0356. 509-527-3204; Fax 509-526-4806. www.co.walla-walla.wa.us/auditor1.htm
Will search UCC records. UCC search includes tax liens if requested. Will not search real estate records. **Other Phones:** Assessor 509-527-3216; Treasurer 509-527-3212; Appraiser/Auditor 509-527-3204.

Whatcom County

County Auditor, 311 Grand Ave #103, Bellingham, WA 98225. 360-676-6740 R/E Recording: 360-676-6740 x50061 UCC Recording: 360-676-6740 x50060; Fax 360-738-4556. www.co.whatcom.wa.us/auditor
Will search UCC records. Will search tax lien records. Will search real estate records. **Online Access:** Assessor, Real Estate Records. Search the assessor parcel database information system free at www.co.whatcom.wa.us/cgibin/db2www/assessor/search/RPSearch.ndt/disclaimer. Also, voter registration lists are available for political purposes only; information and requests to www.co.whatcom.wa.us/auditor/elections/elections.htm. **Other Phone Numbers:** Assessor 360-676-6790; Treasurer 360-676-6774; Appraiser/Auditor 360-676-6745; Elections 360-676-6742; Vital Records 360-676-6740.

Whitman County

County Auditor, PO Box 350, Colfax, WA 99111-0350. 509-397-6270 R/E Recording: 509-397-6270509-397-6270 UCC Recording: 509-392-6270; Fax 509-397-6351. www.whitmancounty.org
Will search UCC records. Will not search real estate records. **Other Phone Numbers:** Assessor 509-397-6220; Treasurer 509-397-6230; Appraiser/Auditor 509-397-6270; Elections 509-397-6270; Vital Records 509-397-6270.

Yakima County

County Auditor, 128 N. 2nd St., #117, Yakima, WA 98901. County Auditor, R/E and UCC Recording 509-574-1330; Fax 509-574-1341. www.pan.co.yakima.wa.us
Will search UCC records. Will not search real estate records. **Online Access:** Assessor, Real Estate Records. Assessor and property information on County Assessor database are available free online at www.co.yakima.wa.us/assessor/propinfo/asr_info.asp.
Other Phone Numbers: Assessor 509-574-1100; Treasurer 509-575-4091; Appraiser/Auditor 509-574-1340.

Washington County Locator

You will usually be able to find the city name in the City/County Cross Reference below. In that case, it is a simple matter to determine the county from the cross reference. However, only the official US Postal Service city names are included in this index. There are an additional 40,000 place names that people use in their addresses. Therefore, we have also included a ZIP/City Cross Reference immediately following the City/County Cross Reference.

If you know the ZIP Code but the city name does not appear in the City/County Cross Reference index, look up the ZIP Code in the ZIP/City Cross Reference, find the city name, then look up the city name in the City/County Cross Reference. For example, you want to know the county for an address of Menands, NY 12204. There is no "Menands" in the City/County Cross Reference. The ZIP/City Cross Reference shows that ZIP Codes 12201-12288 are for the city of Albany. Looking back in the City/County Cross Reference, Albany is in Albany County.

City/County Cross Reference

ABERDEEN Grays Harbor
ACME Whatcom
ADDY Stevens
ADNA Lewis
AIRWAY HEIGHTS Spokane
ALBION Whitman
ALLYN Mason
ALMIRA (99103) Lincoln(88), Grant(11)
AMANDA PARK Grays Harbor
AMBOY (98601) Clark(98), Cowlitz(1)
ANACORTES Skagit
ANATONE Asotin
ANDERSON ISLAND Pierce
APPLETON Klickitat
ARDENVOIR Chelan
ARIEL Cowlitz
ARLINGTON Snohomish
ASHFORD Pierce
ASOTIN Asotin
AUBURN (98092) King(94), Pierce(5)
BAINBRIDGE ISLAND Kitsap
BARING King
BATTLE GROUND Clark
BAY CENTER Pacific
BEAVER Clallam
BELFAIR Mason
BELLEVUE King
BELLINGHAM Whatcom
BELMONT Whitman
BENGE Adams
BENTON CITY Benton
BEVERLY Grant
BICKLETON (99322) Klickitat(96), Yakima(3)
BINGEN Klickitat
BLACK DIAMOND King
BLAINE Whatcom
BLAKELY ISLAND San Juan
BOTHELL King
BOW Skagit
BOYDS Ferry
BREMERTON Kitsap
BREWSTER Okanogan
BRIDGEPORT Douglas
BRINNON Jefferson
BROWNSTOWN Yakima
BRUSH PRAIRIE Clark
BUCKLEY Pierce
BUCODA Thurston
BUENA Yakima
BURBANK Walla Walla
BURLEY Kitsap
BURLINGTON Skagit
BURTON King
CAMANO ISLAND Island
CAMAS Clark
CAMP MURRAY Pierce
CARBONADO Pierce
CARLSBORG Clallam
CARLTON Okanogan
CARNATION King
CARROLLS Cowlitz
CARSON Skamania

CASHMERE Chelan
CASTLE ROCK Cowlitz
CATHLAMET Wahkiakum
CENTERVILLE Klickitat
CENTRALIA (98531) Lewis(95), Thurston(4)
CHATTAROY Spokane
CHEHALIS Lewis
CHELAN Chelan
CHELAN FALLS Chelan
CHENEY Spokane
CHEWELAH Stevens
CHIMACUM Jefferson
CHINOOK Pacific
CINEBAR Lewis
CLALLAM BAY Clallam
CLARKSTON Asotin
CLAYTON (99110) Stevens(71), Spokane(28)
CLE ELUM Kittitas
CLEARLAKE Skagit
CLINTON Island
COLBERT Spokane
COLFAX Whitman
COLLEGE PLACE Walla Walla
COLTON Whitman
COLVILLE Stevens
CONCONULLY Okanogan
CONCRETE Skagit
CONNELL (99326) Franklin(91), Adams(8)
CONWAY Skagit
COPALIS BEACH Grays Harbor
COPALIS CROSSING Grays Harbor
COSMOPOLIS (98537) Grays Harbor(98), Pacific(1)
COUGAR Cowlitz
COULEE CITY (99115) Grant(78), Douglas(21)
COULEE DAM (99116) Okanogan(82), Douglas(15), Grant(2)
COUPEVILLE Island
COWICHE Yakima
CRESTON Lincoln
CUNNINGHAM Adams
CURLEW Ferry
CURTIS Lewis
CUSICK Pend Oreille
CUSTER Whatcom
DALLESPORT Klickitat
DANVILLE Ferry
DARRINGTON (98241) Snohomish(80), Skagit(19)
DAVENPORT (99122) Lincoln(90), Stevens(9)
DAYTON Columbia
DEER HARBOR San Juan
DEER PARK (99006) Spokane(86), Stevens(11), Pend Oreille(1)
DEMING Whatcom
DIXIE Walla Walla
DOTY Lewis
DRYDEN Chelan
DUPONT Pierce

DUVALL King
EAST OLYMPIA Thurston
EAST WENATCHEE Douglas
EASTON Kittitas
EASTSOUND San Juan
EATONVILLE Pierce
EDMONDS Snohomish
EDWALL (99008) Lincoln(85), Spokane(14)
ELBE (98330) Pierce(78), Lewis(21)
ELECTRIC CITY Grant
ELK (99009) Spokane(76), Pend Oreille(23)
ELLENSBURG Kittitas
ELMA (98541) Grays Harbor(71), Mason(28)
ELMER CITY Okanogan
ELTOPIA Franklin
ENDICOTT Whitman
ENTIAT Chelan
ENUMCLAW (98022) King(96), Pierce(3)
EPHRATA Grant
ETHEL Lewis
EVANS Stevens
EVERETT Snohomish
EVERSON Whatcom
FAIRCHILD AIR FORCE BASE Spokane
FAIRFIELD Spokane
FALL CITY King
FARMINGTON Whitman
FEDERAL WAY King
FERNDALE Whatcom
FORD (99013) Stevens(50), Spokane(48), Lincoln(1)
FORKS Clallam
FOUR LAKES Spokane
FOX ISLAND Pierce
FREELAND Island
FREEMAN Spokane
FRIDAY HARBOR San Juan
FRUITLAND Stevens
GALVIN Lewis
GARFIELD Whitman
GEORGE Grant
GIFFORD Stevens
GIG HARBOR Pierce
GLENOMA Lewis
GLENWOOD Klickitat
GOLD BAR (98251) Snohomish(96), King(3)
GOLDENDALE Klickitat
GOOSE PRAIRIE Yakima
GRAHAM Pierce
GRAND COULEE (99133) Grant(90), Douglas(6), Lincoln(3)
GRANDVIEW Yakima
GRANGER Yakima
GRANITE FALLS Snohomish
GRAPEVIEW Mason
GRAYLAND Grays Harbor
GRAYS RIVER Wahkiakum
GREENACRES Spokane
GREENBANK Island
HAMILTON Skagit

HANSVILLE Kitsap
HARRAH Yakima
HARRINGTON Lincoln
HARTLINE Grant
HATTON Adams
HAY Whitman
HEISSON Clark
HOBART King
HOODSPORT Mason
HOOPER Whitman
HOQUIAM Grays Harbor
HUMPTULIPS Grays Harbor
HUNTERS Stevens
HUSUM Klickitat
ILWACO Pacific
INCHELIUM Ferry
INDEX Snohomish
INDIANOLA Kitsap
IONE Pend Oreille
ISSAQUAH King
JOYCE Clallam
KAHLOTUS Franklin
KALAMA Cowlitz
KAPOWSIN Pierce
KELLER (99140) Ferry(98), Stevens(1)
KELSO Cowlitz
KENMORE King
KENNEWICK Benton
KENT King
KETTLE FALLS (99141) Stevens(88), Ferry(11)
KEYPORT Kitsap
KINGSTON Kitsap
KIRKLAND King
KITTITAS Kittitas
KLICKITAT Klickitat
LA CENTER Clark
LA CONNER Skagit
LA GRANDE Pierce
LA PUSH Clallam
LACEY Thurston
LACROSSE Whitman
LAKE STEVENS Snohomish
LAKEBAY Pierce
LAKEWOOD Pierce
LAMONA Lincoln
LAMONT (99017) Whitman(98), Adams(1)
LANGLEY Island
LATAH Spokane
LAURIER Ferry
LEAVENWORTH Chelan
LEBAM Pacific
LIBERTY LAKE Spokane
LILLIWAUP Mason
LINCOLN Lincoln
LIND Adams
LITTLEROCK Thurston
LONG BEACH Pacific
LONGBRANCH Pierce
LONGMIRE Pierce
LONGVIEW Cowlitz
LOOMIS Okanogan
LOON LAKE Stevens

LOPEZ ISLAND San Juan
LUMMI ISLAND Whatcom
LYLE Klickitat
LYMAN Skagit
LYNDEN Whatcom
LYNNWOOD Snohomish
MABTON Yakima
MALAGA Chelan
MALDEN Whitman
MALO Ferry
MALONE Grays Harbor
MALOTT Okanogan
MANCHESTER Kitsap
MANSFIELD Douglas
MANSON Chelan
MAPLE FALLS Whatcom
MAPLE VALLEY King
MARBLEMOUNT Skagit
MARCUS Stevens
MARLIN (98832) Grant(97), Adams(2)
MARSHALL Spokane
MARYSVILLE Snohomish
MATLOCK Mason
MATTAWA Grant
MAZAMA Okanogan
MCCLEARY Grays Harbor
MCKENNA Pierce
MEAD Spokane
MEDICAL LAKE Spokane
MEDINA King
MENLO Pacific
MERCER ISLAND King
MESA Franklin
METALINE Pend Oreille
METALINE FALLS Pend Oreille
METHOW Okanogan
MICA Spokane
MILTON (98354) Pierce(92), King(7)
MINERAL Lewis
MOCLIPS Grays Harbor
MOHLER Lincoln
MONITOR Chelan
MONROE Snohomish
MONTESANO Grays Harbor
MORTON Lewis
MOSES LAKE Grant
MOSSYROCK Lewis
MOUNT VERNON Skagit
MOUNTLAKE TERRACE Snohomish
MOXEE Yakima
MUKILTEO Snohomish
NACHES Yakima
NAHCOTTA Pacific
NAPAVINE Lewis
NASELLE Pacific
NEAH BAY Clallam
NEILTON Grays Harbor
NESPELEM Okanogan
NEWMAN LAKE Spokane
NEWPORT (99156) Pend Oreille(50),
    Spokane(49)
NINE MILE FALLS (99026) Spokane(54),
    Stevens(45)
NOOKSACK Whatcom
NORDLAND Jefferson
NORTH BEND King
NORTH BONNEVILLE Skamania
NORTH LAKEWOOD Snohomish

NORTHPORT Stevens
OAK HARBOR Island
OAKESDALE Whitman
OAKVILLE (98568) Grays Harbor(97),
    Thurston(2)
OCEAN PARK Pacific
OCEAN SHORES Grays Harbor
ODESSA (99159) Lincoln(87), Adams(12)
OKANOGAN Okanogan
OLALLA Kitsap
OLD NATIONAL BANK Spokane
OLGA San Juan
OLYMPIA Thurston
OMAK Okanogan
ONALASKA Lewis
ORCAS San Juan
ORIENT Ferry
ORONDO Douglas
OROVILLE Okanogan
ORTING Pierce
OTHELLO (99344) Adams(77), Grant(17),
    Franklin(5)
OTIS ORCHARDS Spokane
OUTLOOK Yakima
OYSTERVILLE Pacific
PACIFIC King
PACIFIC BEACH Grays Harbor
PACKWOOD Lewis
PALISADES Douglas
PALOUSE Whitman
PARADISE INN Pierce
PARKER Yakima
PASCO Franklin
PATEROS Okanogan
PATERSON Benton
PE ELL Lewis
PESHASTIN Chelan
PLYMOUTH Benton
POINT ROBERTS Whatcom
POMEROY (99347) Garfield(92), Asotin(3),
    Columbia(3), Whitman(1)
PORT ANGELES Clallam
PORT GAMBLE Kitsap
PORT HADLOCK Jefferson
PORT LUDLOW Jefferson
PORT ORCHARD Kitsap
PORT TOWNSEND Jefferson
POULSBO Kitsap
PRESCOTT Walla Walla
PRESTON King
PROSSER (99350) Benton(95), Klickitat(4)
PULLMAN Whitman
PUYALLUP Pierce
QUILCENE Jefferson
QUINAULT Grays Harbor
QUINCY Grant
RAINIER Thurston
RANDLE Lewis
RAVENSDALE King
RAYMOND Pacific
REARDAN (99029) Lincoln(56),
    Spokane(43)
REDMOND King
REDONDO King
RENTON King
REPUBLIC (99166) Ferry(98),
    Okanogan(1)
RETSIL Kitsap

RICE Stevens
RICHLAND Benton
RIDGEFIELD Clark
RITZVILLE Adams
RIVERSIDE Okanogan
ROCHESTER Thurston
ROCK ISLAND Douglas
ROCKFORD Spokane
ROCKPORT Skagit
ROLLINGBAY Kitsap
RONALD Kittitas
ROOSEVELT Klickitat
ROSALIA (99170) Whitman(63),
    Spokane(36)
ROSBURG Wahkiakum
ROSLYN Kittitas
ROY Pierce
ROYAL CITY Grant
RYDERWOOD Cowlitz
SAINT JOHN Whitman
SALKUM Lewis
SAMMAMISH King
SATSOP Grays Harbor
SEABECK Kitsap
SEAHURST King
SEATTLE King
SEAVIEW Pacific
SEDRO WOOLLEY (98284) Skagit(95),
    Whatcom(4)
SEKIU Clallam
SELAH Yakima
SEQUIM (98382) Clallam(97), Jefferson(2)
SHAW ISLAND San Juan
SHELTON Mason
SILVANA Snohomish
SILVER CREEK Lewis
SILVERDALE Kitsap
SILVERLAKE Cowlitz
SKAMOKAWA Wahkiakum
SKYKOMISH King
SNOHOMISH Snohomish
SNOQUALMIE King
SNOQUALMIE PASS King
SOAP LAKE Grant
SOUTH BEND Pacific
SOUTH CLE ELUM Kittitas
SOUTH COLBY Kitsap
SOUTH PRAIRIE Pierce
SOUTHWORTH Kitsap
SPANAWAY Pierce
SPANGLE Spokane
SPOKANE Spokane
SPRAGUE Lincoln
SPRINGDALE Stevens
STANWOOD Snohomish
STARBUCK Columbia
STARTUP Snohomish
STEHEKIN Chelan
STEILACOOM Pierce
STEPTOE Whitman
STEVENSON Skamania
STRATFORD Grant
SULTAN Snohomish
SUMAS Whatcom
SUMNER Pierce
SUNNYSIDE Yakima
SUQUAMISH Kitsap
TACOMA Pierce

TAHOLAH Grays Harbor
TAHUYA Mason
TEKOA (99033) Spokane(75), Whitman(24)
TENINO Thurston
THE CRESCENT STORE Spokane
THORNTON Whitman
THORP Kittitas
TIETON Yakima
TOKELAND Pacific
TOLEDO Lewis
TONASKET Okanogan
TOPPENISH Yakima
TOUCHET Walla Walla
TOUTLE Cowlitz
TRACYTON Kitsap
TROUT LAKE Klickitat
TUMTUM Stevens
TUMWATER Thurston
TWISP Okanogan
UNDERWOOD Skamania
UNION Mason
UNIONTOWN Whitman
UNIVERSITY PLACE Pierce
USK (99180) Pend Oreille(85),
    Spokane(14)
VADER Lewis
VALLEY Stevens
VALLEYFORD Spokane
VANCOUVER Clark
VANTAGE Kittitas
VASHON King
VAUGHN Pierce
VERADALE Spokane
WAHKIACUS Klickitat
WAITSBURG (99361) Walla Walla(95),
    Columbia(4)
WALDRON San Juan
WALLA WALLA Walla Walla
WALLULA Walla Walla
WAPATO Yakima
WARDEN Grant
WASHOUGAL (98671) Clark(79),
    Skamania(20)
WASHTUCNA Adams
WATERVILLE Douglas
WAUCONDA Okanogan
WAUNA Pierce
WAVERLY Spokane
WELLPINIT Stevens
WENATCHEE Chelan
WEST RICHLAND Benton
WESTPORT Grays Harbor
WHITE SALMON Klickitat
WHITE SWAN Yakima
WILBUR Lincoln
WILKESON Pierce
WILSON CREEK Grant
WINLOCK Lewis
WINTHROP Okanogan
WISHRAM Klickitat
WOODINVILLE (98072) King(87),
    Snohomish(12)
WOODLAND (98674) Cowlitz(65),
    Clark(34)
YACOLT Clark
YAKIMA Yakima
YELM Thurston
ZILLAH Yakima

City/County Cross Reference

98001-98002 AUBURN	98248-98248 FERNDALE	98354-98354 MILTON	98557-98557 MCCLEARY
98003-98003 FEDERAL WAY	98249-98249 FREELAND	98355-98355 MINERAL	98558-98558 MCKENNA
98004-98009 BELLEVUE	98250-98250 FRIDAY HARBOR	98356-98356 MORTON	98559-98559 MALONE
98010-98010 BLACK DIAMOND	98251-98251 GOLD BAR	98357-98357 NEAH BAY	98560-98560 MATLOCK
98011-98012 BOTHELL	98252-98252 GRANITE FALLS	98358-98358 NORDLAND	98561-98561 MENLO
98013-98013 BURTON	98253-98253 GREENBANK	98359-98359 OLALLA	98562-98562 MOCLIPS
98014-98014 CARNATION	98255-98255 HAMILTON	98360-98360 ORTING	98563-98563 MONTESANO
98015-98015 BELLEVUE	98256-98256 INDEX	98361-98361 PACKWOOD	98564-98564 MOSSYROCK
98019-98019 DUVALL	98257-98257 LA CONNER	98362-98363 PORT ANGELES	98565-98565 NAPAVINE
98020-98020 EDMONDS	98258-98258 LAKE STEVENS	98364-98364 PORT GAMBLE	98566-98566 NEILTON
98021-98021 BOTHELL	98259-98259 LAKEWOOD	98365-98365 PORT LUDLOW	98568-98568 OAKVILLE
98022-98022 ENUMCLAW	98259-98259 NORTH LAKEWOOD	98366-98367 PORT ORCHARD	98569-98569 OCEAN SHORES
98023-98023 FEDERAL WAY	98260-98260 LANGLEY	98368-98368 PORT TOWNSEND	98570-98570 ONALASKA
98024-98024 FALL CITY	98261-98261 LOPEZ ISLAND	98370-98370 POULSBO	98571-98571 PACIFIC BEACH
98025-98025 HOBART	98262-98262 LUMMI ISLAND	98371-98375 PUYALLUP	98572-98572 PE ELL
98026-98026 EDMONDS	98263-98263 LYMAN	98376-98376 QUILCENE	98575-98575 QUINAULT
98027-98027 ISSAQUAH	98264-98264 LYNDEN	98377-98377 RANDLE	98576-98576 RAINIER
98028-98028 KENMORE	98266-98266 MAPLE FALLS	98378-98378 RETSIL	98577-98577 RAYMOND
98029-98029 ISSAQUAH	98267-98267 MARBLEMOUNT	98380-98380 SEABECK	98579-98579 ROCHESTER
98031-98032 KENT	98270-98271 MARYSVILLE	98381-98381 SEKIU	98580-98580 ROY
98033-98034 KIRKLAND	98272-98272 MONROE	98382-98382 SEQUIM	98581-98581 RYDERWOOD
98035-98035 KENT	98273-98274 MOUNT VERNON	98383-98383 SILVERDALE	98582-98582 SALKUM
98036-98037 LYNNWOOD	98275-98275 MUKILTEO	98384-98384 SOUTH COLBY	98583-98583 SATSOP
98038-98038 MAPLE VALLEY	98276-98276 NOOKSACK	98385-98385 SOUTH PRAIRIE	98584-98584 SHELTON
98039-98039 MEDINA	98277-98278 OAK HARBOR	98386-98386 SOUTHWORTH	98585-98585 SILVER CREEK
98040-98040 MERCER ISLAND	98279-98279 OLGA	98387-98387 SPANAWAY	98586-98586 SOUTH BEND
98041-98041 BOTHELL	98280-98280 ORCAS	98388-98388 STEILACOOM	98587-98587 TAHOLAH
98042-98042 KENT	98281-98281 POINT ROBERTS	98390-98390 SUMNER	98588-98588 TAHUYA
98043-98043 MOUNTLAKE TERRACE	98282-98282 CAMANO ISLAND	98392-98392 SUQUAMISH	98589-98589 TENINO
98045-98045 NORTH BEND	98283-98283 ROCKPORT	98393-98393 TRACYTON	98590-98590 TOKELAND
98046-98046 LYNNWOOD	98284-98284 SEDRO WOOLLEY	98394-98394 VAUGHN	98591-98591 TOLEDO
98047-98047 PACIFIC	98286-98286 SHAW ISLAND	98395-98395 WAUNA	98592-98592 UNION
98050-98050 PRESTON	98287-98287 SILVANA	98396-98396 WILKESON	98593-98593 VADER
98051-98051 RAVENSDALE	98288-98288 SKYKOMISH	98397-98397 LONGMIRE	98595-98595 WESTPORT
98052-98053 REDMOND	98290-98291 SNOHOMISH	98398-98398 PARADISE INN	98596-98596 WINLOCK
98054-98054 REDONDO	98292-98292 STANWOOD	98401-98424 TACOMA	98597-98597 YELM
98055-98059 RENTON	98293-98293 STARTUP	98430-98430 CAMP MURRAY	98599-98599 OLYMPIA
98060-98060 SEATTLE	98294-98294 SULTAN	98431-98439 TACOMA	98601-98601 AMBOY
98061-98061 ROLLINGBAY	98295-98295 SUMAS	98439-98439 LAKEWOOD	98602-98602 APPLETON
98062-98062 SEAHURST	98296-98296 SNOHOMISH	98442-98466 TACOMA	98603-98603 ARIEL
98063-98063 FEDERAL WAY	98297-98297 WALDRON	98467-98467 UNIVERSITY PLACE	98604-98604 BATTLE GROUND
98064-98064 KENT	98303-98303 ANDERSON ISLAND	98471-98492 TACOMA	98605-98605 BINGEN
98065-98065 SNOQUALMIE	98304-98304 ASHFORD	98492-98492 LAKEWOOD	98606-98606 BRUSH PRAIRIE
98068-98068 SNOQUALMIE PASS	98305-98305 BEAVER	98493-98497 TACOMA	98607-98607 CAMAS
98070-98070 VASHON	98310-98314 BREMERTON	98497-98497 LAKEWOOD	98609-98609 CARROLLS
98071-98071 AUBURN	98315-98315 SILVERDALE	98498-98499 TACOMA	98610-98610 CARSON
98072-98072 WOODINVILLE	98320-98320 BRINNON	98499-98499 LAKEWOOD	98611-98611 CASTLE ROCK
98073-98073 REDMOND	98321-98321 BUCKLEY	98501-98508 OLYMPIA	98612-98612 CATHLAMET
98074-98075 SAMMAMISH	98322-98322 BURLEY	98509-98509 LACEY	98613-98613 CENTERVILLE
98082-98082 BOTHELL	98323-98323 CARBONADO	98511-98511 TUMWATER	98614-98614 CHINOOK
98083-98083 KIRKLAND	98324-98324 CARLSBORG	98512-98516 OLYMPIA	98616-98616 COUGAR
98092-98092 AUBURN	98325-98325 CHIMACUM	98520-98520 ABERDEEN	98617-98617 DALLESPORT
98093-98093 FEDERAL WAY	98326-98326 CLALLAM BAY	98522-98522 ADNA	98619-98619 GLENWOOD
98100-98109 SEATTLE	98327-98327 DUPONT	98524-98524 ALLYN	98620-98620 GOLDENDALE
98110-98110 BAINBRIDGE ISLAND	98328-98328 EATONVILLE	98526-98526 AMANDA PARK	98621-98621 GRAYS RIVER
98111-98199 SEATTLE	98329-98329 GIG HARBOR	98527-98527 BAY CENTER	98622-98622 HEISSON
98200-98208 EVERETT	98330-98330 ELBE	98528-98528 BELFAIR	98623-98623 HUSUM
98220-98220 ACME	98331-98331 FORKS	98530-98530 BUCODA	98624-98624 ILWACO
98221-98221 ANACORTES	98332-98332 GIG HARBOR	98531-98531 CENTRALIA	98625-98625 KALAMA
98222-98222 BLAKELY ISLAND	98333-98333 FOX ISLAND	98532-98532 CHEHALIS	98626-98626 KELSO
98223-98223 ARLINGTON	98334-98334 SEQUIM	98533-98533 CINEBAR	98628-98628 KLICKITAT
98224-98224 BARING	98335-98335 GIG HARBOR	98535-98535 COPALIS BEACH	98629-98629 LA CENTER
98225-98228 BELLINGHAM	98336-98336 GLENOMA	98536-98536 COPALIS CROSSING	98631-98631 LONG BEACH
98230-98231 BLAINE	98337-98337 BREMERTON	98537-98537 COSMOPOLIS	98632-98632 LONGVIEW
98232-98232 BOW	98338-98338 GRAHAM	98538-98538 CURTIS	98635-98635 LYLE
98233-98233 BURLINGTON	98339-98339 PORT HADLOCK	98539-98539 DOTY	98637-98637 NAHCOTTA
98235-98235 CLEARLAKE	98340-98340 HANSVILLE	98540-98540 EAST OLYMPIA	98638-98638 NASELLE
98236-98236 CLINTON	98342-98342 INDIANOLA	98541-98541 ELMA	98639-98639 NORTH BONNEVILLE
98237-98237 CONCRETE	98343-98343 JOYCE	98542-98542 ETHEL	98640-98640 OCEAN PARK
98238-98238 CONWAY	98344-98344 KAPOWSIN	98544-98544 GALVIN	98641-98641 OYSTERVILLE
98239-98239 COUPEVILLE	98345-98345 KEYPORT	98546-98546 GRAPEVIEW	98642-98642 RIDGEFIELD
98240-98240 CUSTER	98346-98346 KINGSTON	98547-98547 GRAYLAND	98643-98643 ROSBURG
98241-98241 DARRINGTON	98348-98348 LA GRANDE	98548-98548 HOODSPORT	98644-98644 SEAVIEW
98243-98243 DEER HARBOR	98349-98349 LAKEBAY	98550-98550 HOQUIAM	98645-98645 SILVERLAKE
98244-98244 DEMING	98350-98350 LA PUSH	98552-98552 HUMPTULIPS	98647-98647 SKAMOKAWA
98245-98245 EASTSOUND	98351-98351 LONGBRANCH	98554-98554 LEBAM	98648-98648 STEVENSON
98246-98246 BOW	98352-98352 SUMNER	98555-98555 LILLIWAUP	98649-98649 TOUTLE
98247-98247 EVERSON	98353-98353 MANCHESTER	98556-98556 LITTLEROCK	98650-98650 TROUT LAKE

98651-98651 UNDERWOOD	98922-98922 CLE ELUM	99037-99037 VERADALE	99166-99166 REPUBLIC
98660-98668 VANCOUVER	98923-98923 COWICHE	99039-99039 WAVERLY	99167-99167 RICE
98670-98670 WAHKIACUS	98925-98925 EASTON	99040-99040 WELLPINIT	99169-99169 RITZVILLE
98671-98671 WASHOUGAL	98926-98926 ELLENSBURG	99101-99101 ADDY	99170-99170 ROSALIA
98672-98672 WHITE SALMON	98929-98929 GOOSE PRAIRIE	99102-99102 ALBION	99171-99171 SAINT JOHN
98673-98673 WISHRAM	98930-98930 GRANDVIEW	99103-99103 ALMIRA	99173-99173 SPRINGDALE
98674-98674 WOODLAND	98932-98932 GRANGER	99104-99104 BELMONT	99174-99174 STEPTOE
98675-98675 YACOLT	98933-98933 HARRAH	99105-99105 BENGE	99176-99176 THORNTON
98682-98687 VANCOUVER	98934-98934 KITTITAS	99107-99107 BOYDS	99179-99179 UNIONTOWN
98801-98801 WENATCHEE	98935-98935 MABTON	99109-99109 CHEWELAH	99180-99180 USK
98802-98802 EAST WENATCHEE	98936-98936 MOXEE	99110-99110 CLAYTON	99181-99181 VALLEY
98807-98807 WENATCHEE	98937-98937 NACHES	99111-99111 COLFAX	99185-99185 WILBUR
98811-98811 ARDENVOIR	98938-98938 OUTLOOK	99113-99113 COLTON	99200-99256 SPOKANE
98812-98812 BREWSTER	98939-98939 PARKER	99114-99114 COLVILLE	99257-99257 THE CRESCENT STORE
98813-98813 BRIDGEPORT	98940-98940 RONALD	99115-99115 COULEE CITY	99258-99258 SPOKANE
98814-98814 CARLTON	98941-98941 ROSLYN	99116-99116 COULEE DAM	99259-99259 OLD NATIONAL BANK
98815-98815 CASHMERE	98942-98942 SELAH	99117-99117 CRESTON	99260-99299 SPOKANE
98816-98816 CHELAN	98943-98943 SOUTH CLE ELUM	99118-99118 CURLEW	99301-99302 PASCO
98817-98817 CHELAN FALLS	98944-98944 SUNNYSIDE	99119-99119 CUSICK	99320-99320 BENTON CITY
98819-98819 CONCONULLY	98946-98946 THORP	99121-99121 DANVILLE	99321-99321 BEVERLY
98821-98821 DRYDEN	98947-98947 TIETON	99122-99122 DAVENPORT	99322-99322 BICKLETON
98822-98822 ENTIAT	98948-98948 TOPPENISH	99123-99123 ELECTRIC CITY	99323-99323 BURBANK
98823-98823 EPHRATA	98950-98950 VANTAGE	99124-99124 ELMER CITY	99324-99324 COLLEGE PLACE
98824-98824 GEORGE	98951-98951 WAPATO	99125-99125 ENDICOTT	99326-99326 CONNELL
98826-98826 LEAVENWORTH	98952-98952 WHITE SWAN	99126-99126 EVANS	99327-99327 CUNNINGHAM
98827-98827 LOOMIS	98953-98953 ZILLAH	99127-99127 SAINT JOHN	99328-99328 DAYTON
98828-98828 MALAGA	99001-99001 AIRWAY HEIGHTS	99128-99128 FARMINGTON	99329-99329 DIXIE
98829-98829 MALOTT	99003-99003 CHATTAROY	99129-99129 FRUITLAND	99330-99330 ELTOPIA
98830-98830 MANSFIELD	99004-99004 CHENEY	99130-99130 GARFIELD	99332-99332 HATTON
98831-98831 MANSON	99005-99005 COLBERT	99131-99131 GIFFORD	99333-99333 HOOPER
98832-98832 MARLIN	99006-99006 DEER PARK	99133-99133 GRAND COULEE	99335-99335 KAHLOTUS
98833-98833 MAZAMA	99008-99008 EDWALL	99134-99134 HARRINGTON	99336-99338 KENNEWICK
98834-98834 METHOW	99009-99009 ELK	99135-99135 HARTLINE	99341-99341 LIND
98836-98836 MONITOR	99011-99011 FAIRCHILD AIR FORCE	99136-99136 HAY	99343-99343 MESA
98837-98837 MOSES LAKE	BASE	99137-99137 HUNTERS	99344-99344 OTHELLO
98840-98840 OKANOGAN	99012-99012 FAIRFIELD	99138-99138 INCHELIUM	99345-99345 PATERSON
98841-98841 OMAK	99013-99013 FORD	99139-99139 IONE	99346-99346 PLYMOUTH
98843-98843 ORONDO	99014-99014 FOUR LAKES	99140-99140 KELLER	99347-99347 POMEROY
98844-98844 OROVILLE	99015-99015 FREEMAN	99141-99141 KETTLE FALLS	99348-99348 PRESCOTT
98845-98845 PALISADES	99016-99016 GREENACRES	99143-99143 LACROSSE	99349-99349 MATTAWA
98846-98846 PATEROS	99017-99017 LAMONT	99144-99144 LAMONA	99350-99350 PROSSER
98847-98847 PESHASTIN	99018-99018 LATAH	99146-99146 LAURIER	99352-99352 RICHLAND
98848-98848 QUINCY	99019-99019 LIBERTY LAKE	99147-99147 LINCOLN	99353-99353 WEST RICHLAND
98849-98849 RIVERSIDE	99020-99020 MARSHALL	99148-99148 LOON LAKE	99356-99356 ROOSEVELT
98850-98850 ROCK ISLAND	99021-99021 MEAD	99149-99149 MALDEN	99357-99357 ROYAL CITY
98851-98851 SOAP LAKE	99022-99022 MEDICAL LAKE	99150-99150 MALO	99359-99359 STARBUCK
98852-98852 STEHEKIN	99023-99023 MICA	99151-99151 MARCUS	99360-99360 TOUCHET
98853-98853 STRATFORD	99025-99025 NEWMAN LAKE	99152-99152 METALINE	99361-99361 WAITSBURG
98855-98855 TONASKET	99026-99026 NINE MILE FALLS	99153-99153 METALINE FALLS	99362-99362 WALLA WALLA
98856-98856 TWISP	99027-99027 OTIS ORCHARDS	99154-99154 MOHLER	99363-99363 WALLULA
98857-98857 WARDEN	99028-99028 SPANGLE	99155-99155 NESPELEM	99371-99371 WASHTUCNA
98858-98858 WATERVILLE	99029-99029 REARDAN	99156-99156 NEWPORT	99401-99401 ANATONE
98859-98859 WAUCONDA	99030-99030 ROCKFORD	99157-99157 NORTHPORT	99402-99402 ASOTIN
98860-98860 WILSON CREEK	99031-99031 SPANGLE	99158-99158 OAKESDALE	99403-99403 CLARKSTON
98862-98862 WINTHROP	99032-99032 SPRAGUE	99159-99159 ODESSA	
98901-98909 YAKIMA	99033-99033 TEKOA	99160-99160 ORIENT	
98920-98920 BROWNSTOWN	99034-99034 TUMTUM	99161-99161 PALOUSE	
98921-98921 BUENA	99036-99036 VALLEYFORD	99163-99165 PULLMAN	

West Virginia

General Help Numbers:

Governor's Office
Office of the Governor   304-558-2000
1900 Kanawha Blvd, East   Fax 304-342-7025
Charleston, WV 25305-0370   8AM-6PM M-TH;
                                8AM-5PM F

www.state.wv.us/governor

Attorney General's Office
1900 Kanawha Blvd. Rm 26E   304-558-2021
Charleston, WV 25305-9924   Fax 304-558-0140
www.state.wv.us/wvag   8:30AM-5PM

State Court Administrator
State Supreme Court of Appeals   304-558-0145
1900 Kanawha Blvd, Bldg 1, Rm E 100 Fax 304-558-1212
Charleston, WV 25305-0830   9AM-5PM
www.state.wv.us/wvsca/

State Archives
Archives & History Section   304-558-0220
1900 Kanawha Blvd E   Fax 304-558-2779
Charleston, WV 25305-0300 9AM-8PM M-TH, 9-6 F-SA
www.wvculture.org/history/wvsamenu.html

State Specifics:

Capital:	Charleston Kanawha County
Time Zone:	EST
Number of Counties:	55
Population:	1,801,916
Web Site:	www.state.wv.us

State Agencies

Criminal Records

State Police, Criminal Identification Bureau, Records Section, 725 Jefferson Rd, South Charleston, WV 25309; 304-746-2277, 304-746-2402 (Fax), 8:30AM-4:30PM.

www.wvstatepolice.com

Note: The state will also sell an "incident report" of a specific criminal action for $15.00, call 304-746-2178. Sex offender data is available online at www.wvstatepolice.com/sexoff

Indexing & Storage: Records are available from 1938 on computer. It takes 3 days before new records are available for inquiry. Records are indexed on in house computer (100% of names). Approximately 30% of arrest data is computerized. Records are normally destroyed after the person reaches age 80. 70% of all arrests in database have final dispositions recorded.

Searching: Certain statutorily-required searches require fingerprints, also FBI fingerprint checks; standard name searches do not. Include the following in your request: signed release of subject, SSN, DOB, race, sex, and thumbprint. You must use their "39A Card." All records are returned by mail. Search can be initiated in person, results mailed. 100% of the records are fingerprint-supported. All records are released, including those without dispositions.

Access by: mail.

Fee & Payment: The search fee is $20.00 per record. Certain statutorily-required searches are $10.00, plus an addition FBI fingercheck can be conducted for an additional $24.00. A total record check (fingerprints/FBI/arrest data) is $44.00. Fee payee: West Virginia State Police. Prepayment required. Personal checks accepted. No credit cards accepted.

Mail search: Turnaround time: 5 to 10 days.

Corporation Records
Limited Liability Company Records
Limited Partnerships
Trademarks/Servicemarks
Limited Liability Partnerships

Secretary of State, Corporation Division, State Capitol Bldg, Room W139, Charleston, WV 25305-0776; 304-558-8000, 304-558-0900 (Fax), 8:30AM-4:30PM.

www.wvsos.com/common/information.htm

Indexing & Storage: Records are available for current active companies. It takes 24 hours before new records are available for inquiry. Records are indexed on inhouse computer.

Searching: Include the following in your request: full name of business. In addition to the initial organizing documents, business records include: Annual Reports, Officers, Directors, Prior (merged) names, Reserved names, mergers and amendments, agents of process and capital stock allocation of corporations.

Access by: mail, phone, fax, in person, online.

Fee & Payment: For plain copies, the fee is $1.00 for the first page and $.50 each additional page, providing it takes less than 15 min. For certified documents, the fee is $15.00 plus $5.00 for each amendment. Officer search is $5.00 plus $.50 a page if over 5 pages. Fee payee: Secretary of State. Prepayment required. Personal checks accepted. Credit cards accepted: MasterCard, Visa, AmEx, Discover.

Mail search: Turnaround time: 24 hours. No self addressed stamped envelope is required.

Phone search: They will confirm if a company is active, they will only do three searches per phone call.

Fax search: Fax searching available.

In person search: Searching is available in person.

Online search: Corporation and business types records on the Secretary of State Business Organization Information System are available free online at www.state.wv.us/wvcorporations/verifylogon.asp. Search by organization name. Certified copies may be ordered online or via e-mail to business@wvsos.com.

Uniform Commercial Code

UCC Division, Secretary of State, Bldg 1, West Wing, Rm 157K, Charleston, WV 25305-0440; 304-558-6000, 304-558-0900 (Fax), 8:30AM-4:30PM.

www.wvsos.com/ucc/main.htm

Note: The agency may place limited information under the web site in the future.

Indexing & Storage: Records are available from July 1, 1964. Records are indexed on inhouse computer.

Searching: Use search request form UCC-11. All tax liens are filed at the county level. Terminated filings are researched upon request. Include the following in your request: debtor name.

Access by: mail, phone, fax, in person.

Fee & Payment: The fee is $5.00 per search and $.50 per copy. Fee payee: Secretary of State. Prepayment required. Pre-paid accounts are accepted, but do not send excess amount-search request may be returned. Personal checks accepted. Credit cards accepted: MasterCard, Visa, AmEx, Discover.

Mail search: Turnaround time: 1 day. A self addressed stamped envelope is requested.

Phone search: They will bill for telephone searches.

Fax search: Same fees as phone or mail searches. Turnaround time in 24 hours.

In person search: Searching is available in person.

Federal Tax Liens
State Tax Liens
Records not maintained by a state level agency.

Note: All tax liens are filed at the county level.

Sales Tax Registrations

WV State Tax Department, Office of Business Registration, PO Box 11425, Charleston, WV 25339 (Courier: 1001 E Lee St E, Charleston, WV 25330); 304-558-8500, 304-558-8733 (Fax), 8:30AM-4:30PM.

www.state.wv.us/taxrev

Indexing & Storage: Records are available for the current year plus four years. It takes 4 to 6 weeks before new records are available for inquiry.

Searching: This agency will provide only confirmation if permit is registered or not. They will provide no other data. Include the following in your request: business name. They will also search by tax permit number.

Access by: mail, phone, fax, in person.

Mail search: Turnaround time: 2 weeks or less. A self addressed stamped envelope is requested. No fee for mail request.

Phone search: No fee for telephone request.

Fax search: Fax searching available.

In person search: No fee for request. Records are still returned by mail.

Birth Certificates

Bureau of Public Health, Vital Records, 350 Capitol St, Rm 165, Charleston, WV 25305-3701; 304-558-2931, 304-343-2169 (Fax), 8AM-4PM.

www.wvdhhr.org/bph/oehp/hsc

Indexing & Storage: Records are available from 1917 to present. New records are available for inquiry immediately. Records are indexed on microfiche, inhouse computer.

Searching: Records released to immediate family members only. Include the following in your request: full name, names of parents, mother's maiden name, date of birth, place of birth.

Access by: mail, phone, in person, online.

Fee & Payment: The fee is $5.00 per name, add $10.00 for using credit card. Fee payee: Vital Registration. Prepayment required. Personal checks accepted. Credit cards accepted: MasterCard, Visa, AmEx, Discover.

Mail search: Turnaround time: 3 to 4 weeks. A self addressed stamped envelope is requested.

Phone search: See expedited service.

In person search: Turnaround time 15 minutes.

Online search: Online ordering is available at www.vitalchek.com

Expedited service: Expedited service is available for mail and phone searches. To order by credit card and have 1 week turnaround time add $15.00. Add overnight delivery fees if desired.

Death Records

Bureau of Public Health, Vital Records, 350 Capitol St, Rm 165, Charleston, WV 25305-3701; 304-558-2931, 302-343-2169 (Fax), 8AM-4PM.

www.wvdhhr.org/bph/oehp/hsc

Indexing & Storage: Records are available from 1917 on. New records are available for inquiry immediately. Records are indexed on microfiche, inhouse computer.

Searching: Record released to immediate family or anyone with a verifiable, specific interest only. Include the following in your request: full name, date of death, place of death, names of parents, Social Security Number.

Access by: mail, phone, fax, in person, online.

Fee & Payment: The fee is $5.00 per name. Add $10.00 for use of credit card. Fee payee: Vital Registration. Prepayment required. Personal checks accepted. Credit cards accepted: MasterCard, Visa, AmEx, Discover.

Mail search: Turnaround time: 4 to 6 weeks. A self addressed stamped envelope is requested.

Phone search: See expedited service.

Fax search: Access is provided by VitalChek. Use of credit card is required.

In person search: Turnaround time 15 minutes.

Online search: Order online at www.vitalchek.com

Expedited service: Expedited service is available for mail and phone searches. Add $15.00 for using a credit card and 1 week expedited service. Add overnight service fees if desired.

Marriage Certificates

Bureau of Public Health, Vital Records, 350 Capitol St, Rm 165, Charleston, WV 25305-3701; 304-558-2931, 304-343-2169 (Fax), 8AM-4PM.

www.wvdhhr.org/bph/oehp/hsc

Indexing & Storage: Records are available from 1921 on. Records certified from 1964 on. New records are available for inquiry immediately. Records are indexed on microfiche, inhouse computer.

Searching: You must be a family member or show cause to receive the record. Include the following in your request: names of husband and wife, date of marriage, place or county of marriage.

Access by: mail, phone, fax, in person.

Fee & Payment: The fee is $5.00 per name. Add $10.00 for use of credit card. Fee payee: Vital Registration. Prepayment required. Personal checks accepted. Credit cards accepted: MasterCard, Visa, AmEx, Discover.

Mail search: Turnaround time: 3 to 4 weeks. A self addressed stamped envelope is requested.

Phone search: See expedited service.

Fax search: Available from VitalChek. Use of credit card required.

In person search: Turnaround time 15 minutes.

Expedited service: Expedited service is available for mail and phone searches. Turnaround time: overnight delivery. $15.00 fee expedited service included using a credit card. Add overnight delivery fees, if desired.

Divorce Records

Records not maintained by a state level agency.

Note: Records are maintained by the Clerk of Court in the county of divorce.

Workers' Compensation Records

Workers Compensation Division, Records Management, 4510 Pennsylvania, Charleston, WV 25302; 304-558-5587, 304-558-1908 (Fax), 8AM-4:30PM.

www.state.wv.us/bep

Indexing & Storage: Records are available from 1916. New records are available for inquiry immediately. Records are indexed on microfiche.

Searching: Must have a signed release from claimant or be a representative of the employer. They suggest the use of their WC910 Form. You may call for a copy of this form, but they will release no information over the phone. Include the following in your request: claimant name, Social Security Number, date of accident, file number (if known). The following data is not released: psychiatric information.

Access by: mail, in person.

Fee & Payment: There are no fees unless extensive copies or searching is needed.

Mail search: Turnaround time: 5 to 10 days. Turnaround time is 1-2 days for microfiche copies and 5-10 days if paper copies are required. A self addressed stamped envelope is requested.

In person search: Turnaround time is usually 1 or more days.

Driver License Information
Driver Records

Division of Motor Vehicles, 1800 Kanawha Blvd, Building 3, Rm 118, State Capitol Complex, Charleston, WV 25317; 304-558-0238, 304-558-5362, 304-558-0037 (Fax), 8:30AM-4:30PM.

www.wvdot.com/6_motorists/dmv/6G_DMV.HTM

Note: Use ZIP Code 25305 for courier deliveries.

Indexing & Storage: Records are available for 3 years for all violations including DWIs and suspensions. A Conviction not shown on the record iis speeding 10 mph or less over limit on interstate. It takes 1 week to 3 months (DUIs immediately) before new records are available for inquiry.

Searching: Casual requesters receive records without personal information, unless the subject

has given written consent. The driver's license number and last name are required for a request. The following data is not released: accidents.

Access by: mail, in person, online.

Fee & Payment: The fee is $5.00 per record including no record founds. Fee payee: Division of Motor Vehicles. Prepayment required. Personal checks accepted. Credit cards accepted.

Mail search: Turnaround time: 24 hours. A self addressed stamped envelope is requested.

In person search: Up to seven requests may be received immediately at the counter. Branch offices in at least 15 cities can issue instant records.

Online search: Online access is available in either interactive or batch mode. The system is open 24 hours a day. Batch requesters receive return transmission about 3 AM. Users must access through AAMVAnet. A contract is required and accounts must pre-pay. Fee is $5.00 per record. For more information, call Lacy Morgan at (304) 558-3915.

Other access: The state will sell its DL file to commercial vendors, but records cannot be re-sold.

Vehicle Ownership
Vehicle Identification
Vessel Ownership
Vessel Registration

Division of Motor Vehicles, Information Services, 1606 Washington St East, Charleston, WV 25311; 304-558-0282, 304-558-1012 (Fax), 8:30AM-4:30PM.

www.wvdot.com/6_motorists/dmv/6g2_registratio n.htm

Note: This agency maintains records for unattached mobile homes.

Indexing & Storage: Records are available from 1959 for vehicles, from 1975 for boat registrations, and from 1980 for boat titles. All motorized boats and all sailboats must be registered and titled. It takes 1 to 3 days before new records are available for inquiry.

Searching: High volume requesters must be approved after stating purpose of requests. Casual requesters cannot receive personal information. If doing search by name, it is suggested to also submit address. Boat records can be searched by hull number or WV number. The following data is not released: Social Security Numbers or medical information.

Access by: mail, in person.

Fee & Payment: The fee is $1.00 for registration information, $2.00 per vehicle for lien information, $5.00 per title copy, $15.00 for a complete title history (which includes lien information), and $5.00 for message forwarding. Fee payee: Division of Motor Vehicles. Prepayment required. Do not overpay, they do not have the capacity to refund. Personal checks accepted. No credit cards accepted.

Mail search: Turnaround time: 3 to 5 days. Return address must appear clearly on the request. A self addressed stamped envelope is requested.

In person search: Turnaround time is while you wait if the record is on computer, or 2 days for photocopies.

Other access: The entire state's vehicle file can be purchased. Costs for customized runs depend on

programming time. Further resale is prohibited. Call 304-558-0282 for more information.

Accident Reports

Department of Public Safety, Traffic Records Section, 725 Jefferson Rd, South Charleston, WV 25309-1698; 304-746-2128, 304-746-2206 (Fax), 8:30AM-4:30PM.

www.wvstatepolice.com

Note: It is suggested to send a letter explaining purpose of request and state if involved in some manner.

Indexing & Storage: Records are available of incidents investigated by the state police for the past 10 years. It takes 1 to 3 weeks before new records are available for inquiry.

Searching: If the State Police did not investigate the incident, the report must be obtained from the local investigating jurisdiction. Include the following in your request: name, date of accident, location of accident. The following data is not released: juvenile records.

Access by: mail, phone, fax, in person.

Fee & Payment: The fee is $10.00 per record. If certified, the cost is $15.00. Fee payee: Superintendent, Division of Public Safety. Prepayment required. Personal checks accepted. No credit cards accepted.

Mail search: Turnaround time: 2 to 3 weeks. A self addressed stamped envelope is requested.

Phone search: Records are available by phone.

Fax search: For an extra $5.00 per record, the agency will send data by fax.

In person search: Turnaround time is same day, if record is readily available.

Legislation Records

West Virginia State Legislature, State Capitol, Documents, Charleston, WV 25305; 304-347-4830, 800-642-8650 (Local), 8:30AM-4:30PM.

www.legis.state.wv.us

Note: Sessions start 2nd Wed. in January.

Indexing & Storage: Records are available for current session only. Records are indexed on books (volumes).

Searching: Include the following in your request: bill number, topic of bill.

Access by: mail, phone, fax, in person, online.

Fee & Payment: There is no fee.

Mail search: Turnaround time: 2 days. There is a limit of 7 bills per mailing. Indicate if the bill is pending by House or Senate, or if bill is passed. No self addressed stamped envelope is required.

Phone search: Records are available by phone.

Fax search: Same criteria as mail searching.

In person search: Searching is available in person.

Online search: The Internet site allows one to search for status and/or text of bills.

Voter Registration

Records not maintained by a state level agency.

Note: Voter information is held by the county clerks. There is no statewide system. All information is public record.

GED Certificates

Dept of Education, GED Office, 1900 Kanawha Blvd E, Bldg 6, Rm 250, Charleston, WV 25305-0330; 304-558-6315, 304-558-6317.

http://wvabe.state.k12.wv.us/ged/index.htm

Searching: To search, all of the following is a required: a signed release, name, year of test, date of birth, Social Security Number, city of test, and a copy of or presentation of a photo ID and daytime phone number.

Access by: mail.

Fee & Payment: There is $5.00 fee for verification. Copies of transcripts are $5.00 each. Fee payee: WV DOE Vocational Division. Prepayment required. No credit cards accepted.

Mail search: Turnaround time: 7 to 10 days. No self addressed stamped envelope is required.

Hunting License Information
Fishing License Information

Natural Resources Department, Licensing Division, 1900 Kanawha Blvd E, Bldg 3, Room 624, Charleston, WV 25305; 304-558-2758, 304-558-6208 (Fax), 8:30AM-4:30PM.

www.wvweb.com/www/hunting

Indexing & Storage: Records are available for current year only. Records are indexed on inhouse computer.

Searching: All requests must be in writing. Records are considered public records. Include the following in your request: full name, driver's license number.

Access by: mail.

Fee & Payment: The search fee is $29.00, but only if a record is found. Fee payee: Natural Resources Department. Personal checks accepted. Credit cards accepted: MasterCard, Visa.

Mail search: Turnaround time: 5 to 10 working days. No self addressed stamped envelope is required.

Other access: The agency sells mailing lists. Request must be in writing and certain restrictions apply. Call the number above for further details.

West Virginia State Licensing Agencies

Licenses Searchable Online

Aesthetician #3	www.state.wv.us/wvbc/licensees.cfm
Architect #2	http://wvbrdarch.org/cgi-wvbrdarch/wvbrdarch_licdb/wvbrdarch/architects/query_form
Attorney #14	www.wvbar.org/barinfo/mdirectory/
Barber #3	www.state.wv.us/wvbc/licensees.cfm
Barber/Beauty Culture School #3	www.state.wv.us/wvbc/schools.htm
Cosmetologist #3	www.state.wv.us/wvbc/licensees.cfm
Lobbyist #39	www.state.wv.us/ethics/lobby.htm
Manicurist #3	www.state.wv.us/wvbc/licensees.cfm
Nurse-LPN #8	www.state.wv.us/lpnboard/
Optometrist #41	www.odfinder.org/LicSearch.asp
Public Accountant-CPA #1	www.state.wv.us/scripts/wvboa/default.cfm
Radiologic Technologist #9	www.state.wv.us/rtboe/RTLIST.pdf
Real Estate Appraiser #34	www.asc.gov/content/category1/appr_by_state.asp

Licensing Quick Finder

Aesthetician #3	304-558-2924	
Animal Technician #22	304-558-2016	
Architect #2	304-528-5825	
Asbestos Worker #42	304-558-6720/6768	
Athletic Trainer #26	304-558-7010	
Attorney #14	304-558-7815	
Barber #3	304-558-2924	
Barber/Beauty Culture School #3	304-558-2924	
Boat & Canoe Expedition Provider #29	304-558-2783	
Boating Business, Whitewater #29	304-558-2783	
Charitable Organization #36	304-558-6000	
Chiropractor #4	304-772-1424	
Contractor, General #24	304-558-7890x122	
Cosmetologist #3	304-558-2924	
Counselor LPC, Professional #10	304-746-2512	
Counselor, Professional #10	304-746-2512	
Credit Service Organization #36	304-558-6000	
Dental Hygienist #6	304-252-8266	
Dentist #6	304-252-8266	
Educational Audiologist #26	304-558-7010	
Electrician #40	304-558-2191	
Embalmer #5	304-558-0302	
Emergency Medical Technician-Paramedic #27	304-558-3956	
Engineer #33	304-558-3554	
First Responder #27	304-558-3956	
Fishing Guide #29	304-558-2783	
Forester #20	304-924-6266	
Forestry Technician #20	304-924-6266	
Fund Raiser, For-Profit, Professional #37	800-982-8297	
Funeral Director; Funeral Home #5	304-558-0302	
Hearing Aid Specialist #12	304-558-7886	
Insurance Agent #30	304-558-3354	
Insurance Solicitor #30	304-558-3354	
Investment Advisor/Repres. #38	304-558-2257	
Landscape Architect #13	304-293-2141	
Lobbyist #39	304-558-0664	
Manicurist #3	304-558-2924	
Medical Doctor #15	304-558-2921	
Midwife Nurse #8	304-558-3596	
Mine Electrician #32	304-558-1425	
Mine Surveyor/Foreman #32	304-558-1425	
Miner #32	304-558-1425	
Notary Public #36	304-558-6000	
Nurse #8	304-558-3596	
Nurse Anesthetist #8	304-558-3596	
Nurse-LPN #8	304-558-3572	
Nursing Home Administrator #31	304-759-0722	
Occupational Therapist/Assistant #16	304-329-0480	
Optometrist #41	304-627-2106	
Osteopathic Physician/Physician Assistant #17	304-723-4638	
Pesticide Applicator #25	304-558-2209	
Pharmacist #18	304-558-0558	
Physical Therapist/Assistant #19	304-627-2251	
Physician Assistant #15	304-558-2921	
Podiatrist #15	304-558-2921	
Polygraph Examiner #28	304-558-7890 x122	
Private Detective #36	304-558-6000	
Psychologist #11	304-558-0604	
Public Accountant-CPA #1	304-558-3557	
Radiologic Technologist #9	304-787-4398	
Rafting Outfitter, Whitewater #29	304-558-2783	
Real Estate Appraiser #34	304-558-3919	
Real Estate Broker/Salesperson #35	304-558-3555	
Sanitarian, Registered/In-Training #23	304-558-2981	
School Counselor #26	304-558-7010	
School Nurse #26	304-558-7010	
School Principal #26	304-558-7010	
School Psychologist #26	304-558-7010	
School Social Services/Attendance Investigator #26	304-558-7010	
School Superintendent #26	304-558-7010	
Securities Agent #38	304-558-2257	
Securities Broker/Dealer #38	304-558-2257	
Security Guard #36	304-558-6000	
Shooting Reserve #29	304-558-2783	
Shot Firer #32	304-558-1425	
Social Worker #21	304-558-8816	
Speech/Language Pathologist #26	304-558-7010	
Supervisor of Instruction #26	304-558-7010	
Surveyor, Land #7	304-765-0315	
Teacher #26	304-558-7010	
Telemarketer #37	800-982-8297	
Veterinarian #22	304-558-2016	

Licensing Agency Information

#1 Board of Accountancy, 122 Capitol St #100, Charleston, WV 25301; 304-558-3557, Fax: 304-558-1325.
www.state.wv.us/wvboa
Agency email: wvboa@mail.wvnet.edu.
Search database at
www.state.wv.us/scripts/wvboa/default.cfm

#2 Board of Architects, PO Box 589 (916 5th Ave #203, 25701), Huntington, WV 25710-0589; 304-528-5825, Fax: 304-528-5826.
http://wvbrdarch.org
Agency email: lewilex@wvnvm.wvnet.edu.
Search database at http://wvbrdarch.org/cgi-wvbrdarch/wvbrdarch_licdb/wvbrdarch/architects/query_form

#3 Board of Barbers & Cosmetologists, 1716 Pennsylvania Ave, #7, Charleston, WV 25302; 304-558-2924, Fax: 304-558-3450.
www.state.wv.us/wvbc
Agency email: sholley@state.wv.us.
Search database at
www.state.wv.us/wvbc/licensees.cfm

#4 Board of Chiropractic Examiners, PO Box 8532 (415 1/2 D St, #6), South Charleston, WV 25303; 304-746-7839, Fax: 304-746-0794.
www.state.wv.us/wvboc
Agency email: wvboc@citynet.net.

#5 Board of Embalmers & Funeral Directors, 179 Summers St, #305, Charleston, WV 25301-2131; 304-558-0302, Fax: 304-558-0660.

www.state.wv.us/funeraldirector. Agency email: boeafd@mailcity.com. The Funeral Directors Assn. member list is available at www.wvfda.org/members.cfm

#6 Board of Examiners for Dentists/Dental Hygienists, PO Drawer 1459, Beckley, WV 25802-1459; 304-252-8266, Fax: 304-252-2779.

#7 Board of Examiners for Land Surveyors, PO Box 390 (2298 Sutton Lane), Flatwoods, WV 26621; 304-765-0315, Fax: 304-765-0316.

#8 Board of Examiners for Reg. Prof. Nurses, 101 Dee Dr, Charleston, WV 25311-1620; 304-558-3596, Fax: 304-558-3666.
www.state.wv.us/nurses/rn. Agency email: westvirginiarn@ncsbn.org. The LPNs have a

separate board at the same address; 304-558-3572; fax: 305-558-4367.

#9 Board of Examiners for Radiologic Technology, PO Box 638, Cool Ridge, WV 25825; 304-787-4398, Fax: 304-787-4398. www.state.wv.us/rtboe Agency email: wvrtbo@wvnvm.wvnet.edu. Search database at www.state.wv.us/rtboe/RTLIST.pdf

#10 Board of Examiners in Counseling, 100 Angus E Peyton Dr, South Charleston, WV 25303-1600; 304-746-2512, Fax: 305-746-1942. www.marshall.edu/schoolcoun/boe.html Agency email: jajohnson@marshall.edu.

#11 Board of Examiners of Psychologists, PO Box 3955, Charleston, WV 25339-3955; 304-558-0604, Fax: 304-558-0608. Agency email: wvpsychbd@earth1.net.

#12 Board of Hearing-Aid Dealers, 701 Jefferson Rd, South Charleston, WV 25309-1638; 304-558-7886, Fax: 304-558-7886. www.state.wv.us/bep/lmi/license/liclist.htm

#13 Board of Landscape Architects, 1107 9th St, Vienna, WV 26105; 304-293-2141, Fax: 304-293-3752.

#14 Board of Law Examiners, 1900 Kanawha Blvd, Bldg 1, #E-400, Charleston, WV 25305-0837; 304-558-7815, Fax: 304-558-0831. www.wvbar.org Agency email: rubens@mail.wvnet.edu. Search database at www.wvbar.org/barinfo/mdirectory

#15 Board of Medicine, 101 Dee Dr, Charleston, WV 25311-1620; 304-558-2921 x224, Fax: 304-558-2084. www.wvdhhr.org/wvbom

#16 Board of Occupational Therapy, 119 S Price St, Kingwood, WV 26537; 304-329-0480, Fax: 304-329-0480. www.wvbot.org

#17 Board of Osteopathy, 334 Penco Rd, Weirton, WV 26062-3813; 304-723-4638, Fax: 304-723-6723.

#18 Board of Pharmacy, 232 Capitol St, Charleston, WV 25301-2206; 304-558-0558, Fax: 304-558-0572. www.wvop.com

#19 WV Board of Physical Therapy, 153 W Main St, #103, Clarksburg, WV 26301; 304-627-2251, Fax: 304-627-2253. www.wvbopt.com

#20 Board of Registration for Foresters, 8 Kepner St, Buckhannon, WV 26201; 304-924-6266, Fax: 304-924-6142. Agency email: wdof3@neumedia.net.

#21 Board of Social Work Examiners, PO Box 5459, Charleston, WV 25361; 304-558-8816, Fax: 304-558-4189. Agency email: williju@mail.wvnet.edu.

#22 Board of Veterinary Medicine, 1900 Kanawha Blvd E, Charleston, WV 25305-0119; 304-558-2016, Fax: 304-558-0891. Agency email: goodww@mail.wvnet.edu.

#23 Bureau of Public Health, 815 Quarrier St, Charleston, WV 25301-2616; 304-558-2981, Fax: 304-558-1071.

#24 Contractor Licensing Board, 1900 Kanawha Blvd E, Bldg 3, Rm 319, Charleston, WV 25305; 304-558-7890 x122. www.state.wv.us/labor

#25 Department of Agriculture, Pesticide Applicator Licensing, State Capitol Complex, Bldg1, Rm M28, Charleston, WV 25305; 304-558-2209, Fax: 304-558-3594. www.state.wv.us/agriculture

#26 Department of Education, 1900 Kanawha Blvd E, Charleston, WV 25305; 304-558-7010, Fax: 304-558-0882. http://wvde.state.wv.us Agency email: Jnodell@access.k12.wv.us.

#27 Office of EMS, Bureau of Public Health, 350 Capitol St #515, Charleston, WV 25301-3716; 304-558-3956, Fax: 304-558-1437.

#28 Department of Labor, State Capitol Complex, Bldg. 6, Rm 749B, Charleston, WV 25305; 304-558-7890 x122, Fax: 304-558-3797. www.state.wv.us/labor

#29 Division of Natural Resources, 1900 Kanawha Blvd, East Bldg 3, Rm 837, Charleston, WV 25305; 304-558-2783, Fax: 304-558-1170. www.dnr.state.wv.us

#30 Insurance Commissioner, 1124 Smith St, Charleston, WV 25301; 304-558-0610, Fax: 304-558-4966. www.state.wv.us/insurance Agency email: strotj@wvnvn.wvnet.edu No longer licenses insurance brokers.

#31 Nursing Home Administrators Licensing Board, 5303 Kensington Dr, Cross Lanes, WV 25313; 304-759-0722, Fax: 304-759-0724.

#32 Office of Miners Health Safety & Training, 1615 Washington St E, Charleston, WV 25311; 304-558-1425, Fax: 304-558-1282.

www.state.wv.us/mhst Agency email: MINEINFO@mines.state.wv.us.

#33 Board of Registration for Professional Engineers, 608 Union Bldg, Charleston, WV 25301-2703; 304-558-3554, Fax: 304-558-6232.

#34 Real Estate Appraiser Licensing & Certification Bd, 2110 Kanawah Blvd E, #101, Charleston, WV 25311; 304-558-3919, Fax: 304-558-3983. www.state.wv.us/appraise Agency email: wvappbd@wvnvm.wvnet.edu.

#35 Real Estate Commission, 1033 Quarrier St, #400, Charleston, WV 25301-2315; 304-558-3555, Fax: 304-558-6442. www.state.wv.us/wvrec Agency email: wvrec@wvrec.state.wv.us.

#36 Secretary of State, 1900 Kanawha Blvd, Bldg 1, #157-K, Charleston, WV 25305-0770; 304-558-6000, Fax: 304-558-0900. www.state.wv.us/sos. Agency email: wvsos@secretary.state.wv.us.

#37 Department of Tax & Revenue, Taypayer Services, Telemarketing Registration, PO Box 3784, Charleston, WV 25337; 304-558-0211. www.state.wv.us/taxrev/ Search database at www.state.wv.us/taxrev

#38 State Auditor's Office, State Capitol, Rm W110, Charleston, WV 25305; 304-558-2257, Fax: 304-558-4211. www.wvauditor.com Agency email: johns@wvauditor.com.

#39 Ethics Commission, 1207 Quarrier St, 4th Fl, Charleston, WV 25301; 304-558-0664, Fax: 304-558-2169. www.state.wv.us/ethics Agency email: lsuchy@gwmail.state.wv.us. Search database at www.state.wv.us/ethics/lobby.htm

#40 State Fire Marshall, 1207 Quarrier, 2nd Fl, Charleston, WV 25301; 304-558-2191, Fax: 304-558-2537. www.wvfiremarshal.org

#41 Board of Optometry, 101 Michael St, Clarksburg, WV 26301-3937; 304-627-2106, Fax: 304-627-2282. Agency email: wvbdopt@westvirginia.net. Search database at www.odfinder.org/LicSearch.asp

#42 Department of Health & Human Resources, Office of Environmental Health, 815 Quarrier St #418, Charleston, WV 25301; 304-558-2981, Fax: 304-558-1289.

West Virginia Federal Courts

The following list indicates the district and division name for each county in the state. If the bankruptcy court location is different from the district court, then the location of the bankruptcy court appears in parentheses.

County/Court Cross Reference

County	District	Division
Barbour	Northern	Elkins (Wheeling)
Berkeley	Northern	Martinsburg (Wheeling)
Boone	Southern	Charleston
Braxton	Northern	Clarksburg (Wheeling)
Brooke	Northern	Wheeling
Cabell	Southern	Huntington (Charleston)
Calhoun	Northern	Clarksburg (Wheeling)
Clay	Southern	Charleston
Doddridge	Northern	Clarksburg (Wheeling)
Fayette	Southern	Beckley (Charleston)
Gilmer	Northern	Clarksburg (Wheeling)
Grant	Northern	Elkins (Wheeling)
Greenbrier	Southern	Beckley (Charleston)
Hampshire	Northern	Martinsburg (Wheeling)
Hancock	Northern	Wheeling
Hardy	Northern	Elkins (Wheeling)
Harrison	Northern	Clarksburg (Wheeling)
Jackson	Southern	Parkersburg (Charleston)
Jefferson	Northern	Martinsburg (Wheeling)
Kanawha	Southern	Charleston
Lewis	Northern	Clarksburg (Wheeling)
Lincoln	Southern	Huntington (Charleston)
Logan	Southern	Charleston
Marion	Northern	Clarksburg (Wheeling)
Marshall	Northern	Wheeling
Mason	Southern	Huntington (Charleston)
McDowell	Southern	Bluefield (Charleston)
Mercer	Southern	Bluefield (Charleston)
Mineral	Northern	Elkins (Wheeling)
Mingo	Southern	Huntington (Charleston)
Monongalia	Northern	Clarksburg (Wheeling)
Monroe	Southern	Bluefield (Charleston)
Morgan	Northern	Martinsburg (Wheeling)
Nicholas	Southern	Beckley (Charleston)
Ohio	Northern	Wheeling
Pendleton	Northern	Elkins (Wheeling)
Pleasants	Northern	Clarksburg (Wheeling)
Pocahontas	Northern	Elkins (Wheeling)
Preston	Northern	Elkins (Wheeling)
Putnam	Southern	Charleston
Raleigh	Southern	Beckley (Charleston)
Randolph	Northern	Elkins (Wheeling)
Ritchie	Northern	Clarksburg (Wheeling)
Roane	Southern	Charleston
Summers	Southern	Bluefield (Charleston)
Taylor	Northern	Clarksburg (Wheeling)
Tucker	Northern	Elkins (Wheeling)
Tyler	Northern	Clarksburg (Wheeling)
Upshur	Northern	Elkins (Wheeling)
Wayne	Southern	Huntington (Charleston)
Webster	Northern	Elkins (Wheeling)
Wetzel	Northern	Wheeling
Wirt	Southern	Parkersburg (Charleston)
Wood	Southern	Parkersburg (Charleston)
Wyoming	Southern	Beckley (Charleston)

Standards for Federal Courts: The search fee is $20.00 per item (one party name or case number). Certification fee is $7.00 per document. Copy fee is $.50 per page. All fees standard unless noted in profile. Mail Search: always enclose a stamped self addressed envelope unless otherwise noted. Before releasing records, all courts require prepayment unless noted in profile. Open records are located at the court unless otherwise noted. District courts index by defendant and plaintiff as well as by case number. Bankruptcy courts usually index by debtor and case number. While most courts now have their indexes on computer, many still maintain index card files as well. The universal PACER sign-up number is 800-676-6856. Find PACER and the Party/Case Index on the Web at http://pacer.psc.uscourts.gov. PACER dial-up access is $.60 per minute. Also, courts offering internet access via RACER, PACER, Web-PACER or the new CM-ECF charge $.07 per page fee unless noted as free.

US District Court

Northern District of West Virginia

Clarksburg Division PO Box 2857, Clarksburg, WV 26302-2857 (Courier Address: 500 W Pike St, Rm 301, Clarksburg, WV 26301), 304-622-8513, Fax: 304-623-4551.

www.wvnd.uscourts.gov

Counties: Braxton, Calhoun, Doddridge, Gilmer, Harrison, Lewis, Marion, Monongalia, Pleasants, Ritchie, Taylor, Tyler.

Indexing & Storage: Cases are indexed by defendant, plaintiff, and case number. New cases are available in the index 1-2 days after filing date. Open records are located at this court.

Fee & Payment Notes: Payment may be made by money order, cashier check. Business checks are not accepted. Personal checks are not accepted. Money orders are preferred unless it is a known person or business. Payee: Clerk, US District Court.

Phone Search: Only docket information is available by phone.

Mail Search: A stamped self addressed envelope is not required.

In Person Search: In person searching available.

PACER: Toll-free dial-up access: 888-513-7959. Local dial-up access: 304-233-7424. Case records are available back to October 1994. Records are purged every 5 years. New records are available online after 1 day. PACER is available online at http://pacer.wvnd.uscourts.gov.

Elkins Division PO Box 1518, Elkins, WV 26241 (Courier: 2nd Floor, 300 3rd St, Elkins, WV 26241), 304-636-1445, Fax: 304-636-5746.

www.wvnd.uscourts.gov

Counties: Barbour, Grant, Hardy, Mineral, Pendleton, Pocahontas, Preston, Randolph, Tucker, Upshur, Webster.

Indexing & Storage: Cases are indexed by defendant, plaintiff, and case number. New cases are available in the index 1 day after filing date. Civil cases are indexed on computer from October 1994 forward, and criminal cases from October 1995 forward. District-wide searches are available from this court. A case number and cause of action will be released.

Fee & Payment Notes: Payment may be made by money order, cashier check. Business checks are not accepted. Personal checks are not accepted. Money orders are preferred unless it is a known person or business. Payee: Clerk, US District Court. You are allowed to make your own copies. These copies cost $.50 per page. If court personnel help, the search fee will be charged.

Phone Search: Only docket information is available by phone.

Fax Search: Will accept search requests by fax with $15.00 fee. The fee is $1.00 per page.

Mail Search: A stamped self addressed envelope is not required.

In Person Search: In person searching available.

PACER: Toll-free dial-up access: 888-513-7959. Local dial-up access: 304-233-7424. Case records are available back to October 1994. Records are purged every 5 years. New records are available online after 1 day. PACER is available online at http://pacer.wvnd.uscourts.gov.

Martinsburg Division Room 207, 217 W King St, Martinsburg, WV 25401 (Courier Address: Use mail address for courier delivery), 304-267-8225, Fax: 304-264-0434.

www.wvnd.uscourts.gov

Counties: Berkeley, Hampshire, Jefferson, Morgan.

Indexing & Storage: Cases are indexed by defendant, plaintiff, and case number. New cases are available in the index 2 days after filing date. The computer index is from 1994 forward. Open records are located at this court.

Fee & Payment Notes: Payment may be made by money order, cashier check. Business checks are not accepted. Personal checks are not accepted. Payee: Clerk, US District Court.

Phone Search: Limited docket information is available by phone.

In Person Search: In person searching available.

PACER: Toll-free dial-up access: 888-513-7959. Local dial-up access: 304-233-7424. Case records are available back to October 1994. Records are purged every 5 years. New records are available online after 1 day. PACER is available online at http://pacer.wvnd.uscourts.gov.

Wheeling Division Clerk, PO Box 471, Wheeling, WV 26003 (Courier Address: 12th & Chapline Sts, Wheeling, WV 26003), 304-232-0011, Fax: 304-233-2185.

www.wvnd.uscourts.gov

Counties: Brooke, Hancock, Marshall, Ohio, Wetzel.

Indexing & Storage: Cases are indexed by defendant, plaintiff, and case number. New cases are available in the index immediately after filing date. Civil cases on computer since October 1994, and criminal cases since October 1995. Records have not yet been sent to the Federal Records Center from this office.

Fee & Payment Notes: Payment may be made by money order, cashier check, personal check. Payee: Clerk, US District Court. You are allowed to make your own copies. These copies cost - current fee is not known - per page.

Phone Search: All information that is not sealed is available for release over the phone.

In Person Search: In person searching available.

PACER: Toll-free dial-up access: 888-513-7959. Local dial-up access: 304-233-7424. Case records are available back to October 1994. Records are purged every 5 years. New records are available online after 1 day. PACER is available online at http://pacer.wvnd.uscourts.gov.

US Bankruptcy Court

Northern District of West Virginia

Wheeling Division PO Box 70, Wheeling, WV 26003 (Courier Address: 12th & Chapline Sts, Wheeling, WV 26003), 304-233-1655.

www.wvnb.uscourts.gov

Counties: Barbour, Berkeley, Braxton, Brooke, Calhoun, Doddridge, Gilmer, Grant, Hampshire, Hancock, Hardy, Harrison, Jefferson, Lewis, Marion, Marshall, Mineral, Monongalia, Morgan, Ohio, Pendleton, Pleasants, Pocahontas, Preston, Randolph, Ritchie, Taylor, Tucker, Tyler, Upshur, Webster, Wetzel.

Indexing & Storage: Cases are indexed by debtor as well as by case number. New cases are available in the index 24 hours after filing date. Open records are located at this court.

Fee & Payment Notes: Payment may be made by money order, cashier check, personal check. Payee: Clerk, US Bankruptcy Court.

Phone Search: Only docket information is available by phone. An automated voice case information service (VCIS) is available. Call VCIS at 800-809-3028 or 304-233-7318.

In Person Search: In person searching available.

PACER: Toll-free dial-up access: 800-809-3016. Local dial-up access: 304-233-2871. Case records are available back to early 1990. Records are never purged. New civil records are available online after 1 day. PACER is available online at http://pacer.wvnb.uscourts.gov. Document images available.

Electronic Filing: (Currently in the process of implementing CM/ECF.)

US District Court

Southern District of West Virginia

Beckley Division PO Drawer 5009, Beckley, WV 25801 (Courier Address: 110 N. Heber, Beckley, WV 25801), 304-253-7481, Fax: 304-253-3252.

www.wvsd.uscourts.gov

Counties: Fayette, Greenbrier, Raleigh, Sumners, Wyoming.

Indexing & Storage: Cases are indexed by defendant, plaintiff, and case number. New cases are available in the index immediately after filing date. Open records are located at this court.

Fee & Payment Notes: Payment may be made by money order, cashier check, personal check. Payee: Clerk, US District Court. You are allowed to make your own copies. These copies cost $.50 per page.

Phone Search: Only docket information is available by phone.

Fax Search: There is no charge for information on names only.

In Person Search: In person searching available.

PACER: Local dial-up access: 304-347-5681. Case records are available back to 1991. New records are available online after 1 day. PACER is available online at http://pacer.wvsd.uscourts.gov. Document images available.

Bluefield Division Clerk's Office, PO Box 4128, Bluefield, WV 24701 (Courier Address: 601 Federal St, Bluefield, WV 24701), 304-327-9798.

www.wvsd.uscourts.gov

Counties: McDowell, Mercer, Monroe.

Indexing & Storage: Cases are indexed by defendant, plaintiff, and case number. New cases are available in the index immediately after filing date. Open records are located at this court.

Fee & Payment Notes: Payment may be made by money order, cashier check, personal check. Payee: Clerk, US District Court. You are allowed to make your own copies. These copies cost $.50 per page.

Phone Search: One name may be searched by phone.

Fax Search: Fax requests are accepted.

In Person Search: In person searching available.

PACER: Local dial-up access: 304-347-5681. Case records are available back to 1991. New records are available online after 1 day. PACER is available online at http://pacer.wvsd.uscourts.gov. Document images available.

Charleston Division PO Box 3924, Charleston, WV 25339 (Courier Address: 300 Virginia St E, #24, Charleston, WV 25339), 304-347-3000.

www.wvsd.uscourts.gov/

Counties: Boone, Clay, Jackson, Kanawha, Lincoln, Logan, Mingo, Nicholas, Putnam, Roane.

Indexing & Storage: Cases are indexed by defendant, plaintiff, and case number. New cases are available in the index immediately after filing date. The fee to retrieve a record that has been sent to the Records Center is $25.00.

Fee & Payment Notes: Payment may be made by money order, cashier check, personal check.

Payee: Clerk, US District Court. You are allowed to make your own copies. These copies cost $.50 per page.

Phone Search: Only docket information is available by phone.

Fax Search: The court plans to accept fax requests. Call for more information.

Mail Search: A stamped self addressed envelope is not required.

In Person Search: In person searching available.

PACER: Local dial-up access: 304-347-5681. Case records are available back to 1991. New records are available online after 1 day. PACER is available online at http://pacer.wvsd.uscourts.gov. Document images available.

Huntington Division Clerk of Court, PO Box 1570, Huntington, WV 25716 (Courier Address: Room 101, 845 5th Ave, Huntington, WV 25701), 304-529-5588, Fax: 304-529-5131.

www.wvsd.uscourts.gov

Counties: Cabell, Mason, Wayne.

Indexing & Storage: Cases are indexed by defendant, plaintiff, and case number. New cases are available in the index immediately after filing date. Open records are located at this court.

Fee & Payment Notes: Payment may be made by money order, cashier check, personal check. Payee: Clerk, US District Court. You are allowed to make your own copies. These copies cost $.50 per page.

Phone Search: Only docket information is available by phone.

Fax Search: Fax requests will be accepted, but for a maximum of 1-2 names.

In Person Search: In person searching available.

PACER: Local dial-up access: 304-347-5681. Case records are available back to 1991. New records are available online after 1 day. PACER is available online at http://pacer.wvsd.uscourts.gov. Document images available.

Parkersburg Division Clerk of Court, PO Box 1526, Parkersburg, WV 26102 (Courier Address: Room 5102, 425 Julianna St, Parkersburg, WV 26101), 304-420-6490, Fax: 304-420-6363.

www.wvsd.uscourts.gov

Counties: Wirt, Wood.

Indexing & Storage: Cases are indexed by defendant, plaintiff, and case number. New cases are available in the index immediately after filing date. Open records are located at this court.

Fee & Payment Notes: Payment may be made by money order, cashier check, personal check. Payee: Clerk, US District Court. You are allowed to make your own copies. These copies cost $.50 per page.

Phone Search: Only docket information is available by phone.

Fax Search: Fax requests are accepted, but for a maximum of 1-2 names only.

In Person Search: In person searching available.

PACER: Local dial-up access: 304-347-5681. Case records are available back to 1991. New records are available online after 1 day. PACER is available online at http://pacer.wvsd.uscourts.gov. Document images available.

US Bankruptcy Court

Southern District of West Virginia

Charleston Division PO Box 3924, Charleston, WV 25339 (Courier Address: 300 Virginia St E, Room 2400, Charleston, WV 25301), 304-347-3000.

www.wvsd.uscourts.gov

Counties: Boone, Cabell, Clay, Fayette, Greenbrier, Jackson, Kanawha, Lincoln, Logan, Mason, McDowell, Mercer, Mingo, Monroe, Nicholas, Putnam, Raleigh, Roane, Summers, Wayne, Wirt, Wood, Wyoming.

Indexing & Storage: Cases are indexed by debtor as well as by case number. New cases are available in the index 1-2 days after filing date. Card index is maintained to December 1, 1988 after which index is on computer. Open records are located at this court.

Fee & Payment Notes: Payment may be made by money order, cashier check, personal check, Visa or Mastercard. Credit cards accepted only from law firms. Payee: Clerk, US Bankruptcy Court.

Phone Search: Only docket information is available by phone. An automated voice case information service (VCIS) is available. Call VCIS at 304-347-5337.

Mail Search: A stamped self addressed envelope is not required.

In Person Search: In person searching available.

PACER: Local dial-up access: 304-347-5678, 304-347-5679. Case records are available back to 1988. Records are purged every 6 months. New civil records are available online after 1 day. PACER is available online at http://pacer.wvsb.uscourts.gov. Document images available.

Electronic Filing: (Currently in the process of implementing CM/ECF.)

West Virginia County Courts

Court	Jurisdiction	No. of Courts	How Organized
Circuit Courts*	General	55	31 Circuits
Magistrate Courts*	Limited	55	55 Counties
Family Courts	Limited	55	55 Counties
Municipal Courts	Municipal	122	

* Profiled in this Sourcebook.

Court	CIVIL								
	Tort	Contract	Real Estate	Min. Claim	Max. Claim	Small Claims	Estate	Eviction	Domestic Relations
Circuit Courts*	X	X	X	$300	No Max		X		X
Magistrate Courts*	X	X		$0	$5000	$3000		X	X
Family Courts									X
Municipal Courts									

Court	CRIMINAL				
	Felony	Misdemeanor	DWI/DUI	Preliminary Hearing	Juvenile
Circuit Courts*	X				X
Magistrate Courts*		X	X	X	
Family Courts					
Municipal Courts			X		

ADMINISTRATION Administrative Office, Supreme Court of Appeals, 1900 Kanawha Blvd, 1 E 100 State Capitol, Charleston, WV, 25305; 304-558-0145, Fax: 304-558-1212. www.state.wv.us/wvsca

COURT STRUCTURE The 55 Circuit Courts are the courts of general jurisdiction. Probate is handled by the Circuit Court. Records are held at the County Commissioner's Office.

Family Courts were created by constitutional amendment and were formed as of 01/01/02. Family courts hear cases involving such matters as divorce, annulment, separate maintenance, family support, paternity, child custody, and visitation. Family court judges also conduct final hearings in domestic violence cases.

ONLINE ACCESS The state is working towards a statewide system that will allow access to public records, but one is not yet available. Magistrate Courts are on a private system, see www.swcg-inc.com/courts.htm or call 800-795-8543 for information. Fees are involved. This same provider offers access to 6 Circuit Courts: Kanawha, Putnam, Hancock, Ohio, Nicholas and Mineral.

ADDITIONAL INFORMATION There is a statewide requirement that search turnaround times not exceed five business days. However, most courts do far better than that limit. Release of public information is governed by WV Code Sec.29B-1-1 et seq.

📖 📖 📖 📖 📖 📖 📖

Barbour County

Circuit Court 8 N Main St, Philippi, WV 26416; 304-457-3454; Fax: 304-457-2790. 8:30AM-4:30PM (EST). *Felony, Civil Actions Over $5,000, Probate.*

Note: Probate is handled by the County Clerk at this address.

Civil Records: Access: Phone, mail, in person. Both court and visitors may perform in person searches. No search fee. Required to search: name, years to search. Civil cases indexed by defendant, plaintiff. Civil records on microfiche from 1843 to 1980s on index cards back to 1862, on dockets back to 1843.

Criminal Records: Access: Phone, mail, in person. Both court and visitors may perform in person searches. No search fee. Required to search: name, years to search. Criminal records on microfiche from 1843 to 1980s on index cards back to 1862, on dockets back to 1843.

General Information: Public access terminal is available. No sealed, juvenile, adoptions, mental health, expunged records released. SASE requested.

Turnaround time 1 day. Fax notes: No fee to fax results if one or two pages only. Copy fee: $.50 per page. Certification fee: $1.00. Fee payee: Barbour County Circuit Clerk. Personal checks accepted. Prepayment is required.

Magistrate Court PO Box 541, Philippi, WV 26416; 304-457-3676; Fax: 304-457-4999. Hours: 8:30AM-4:30PM (EST). *Misdemeanor, Civil Actions Under $5,000, Eviction, Small Claims.*

Civil Records: Access: In person, mail. Both court and visitors may perform in person searches. No search fee. Phone access limited to one name searched from 8/93 on only.

Criminal Records: Access: In person, mail. Visitors must perform in person searches for themselves. No search fee. Required to search: name, years to search.

General Information: Turnaround time varies.

Berkeley County

Circuit Court 110 W King St, Martinsburg, WV 25401-3210; 304-264-1918; Probate phone: 304-264-1940. Hours: 9AM-5PM (EST). *Felony, Civil Actions Over $5,000, Probate.*

Note: Probate is handled by Fiduciary Records Clerk, 100 W King St, Room 2, Martinsburg, WV 25401.

Civil Records: Access: Fax, mail, in person. Both court and visitors may perform in person searches. No search fee. Required to search: name, years to search. Civil cases indexed by defendant, plaintiff. Civil records on computer from 1/1990, on index books from 1863. No divorce, child custody or child support information given out over phone; phone ID required or notarized copy of photo ID.

Criminal Records: Access: In person only. Visitors must perform in person searches for themselves. No search fee. Required to search: name, years to search; also helpful: DOB, SSN. Criminal records on computer from 1/1990, on index books from 1800s.

General Information: Public access terminal is available. No sealed, juvenile, adoptions, mental health, guardianship records released. SASE not required. Turnaround time 1 week. Fax notes: $2.00 per page. Copy fee: $.50 per page. Fee payee: Clerk of Circuit Court. Business checks accepted.

Magistrate Court 120 W John St, Martinsburg, WV 25401; 304-264-1956; Fax: 304-263-9154. Hours: 9AM-4PM (EST). *Misdemeanor, Civil Actions Under $5,000, Eviction, Small Claims.*

Civil Records: Access: Fax, mail, in person. Both court and visitors may perform in person searches. No search fee.

Criminal Records: Access: In person only. Both court and visitors may perform in person searches. No search fee. Required to search: name, years to search; also helpful: address, DOB, SSN.

General Information: Public access terminal is available.

Boone County

Circuit Court 200 State St, Madison, WV 25130; 304-369-3925; Probate phone: 304-369-7337; Fax: 304-369-7326. Hours: 8AM-4PM (EST). *Felony, Civil Actions Over $5,000, Probate.*

Note: Probate is handled by County Clerk, 200 State St, Madison, WV 25130.

Civil Records: Access: Phone, fax, mail, in person. Both court and visitors may perform in person searches. No search fee. Required to search: name, years to search. Civil cases indexed by defendant, plaintiff. Civil records on computer from 1984 to present, on index books 1956 to present, on dockets back to 1900.

Criminal Records: Access: Phone, fax, mail, in person. Both court and visitors may perform in person searches. No search fee. Required to search: name, years to search, signed release. Criminal records on computer from 1984 to present, on index books 1956 to present, on dockets back to 1864.

General Information: No sealed, guardianship, juvenile, adoptions, mental health, expunged records released. SASE requested. Turnaround time 1 day. Fax notes: Fee to fax results is $3.00 per document. Copy fee: $.50 per page. Fee payee: Circuit Clerk. Business checks accepted. Prepayment is required.

Magistrate Court 200 State St., Madison, WV 25130; 304-369-7364; Fax: 304-369-1932. Hours: 8AM-4PM (EST). *Misdemeanor, Civil Actions Under $5,000, Eviction, Small Claims.*

Civil Records: Access: In person. Both court and visitors may perform in person searches. No search fee. Civil records go back to 1977; computer since 1997.

Criminal Records: Access: In person. Visitors must perform in person searches for themselves. No search fee. Required to search: name, years to search; also helpful: DOB, SSN. Criminal records go back to 1977; computerized records since 1997.

General Information: Copy fee: $.25 per page.

Braxton County

Circuit Court 300 Main St, Sutton, WV 26601; 304-765-2837; Probate phone: 304-765-2833; Fax: 304-765-2947. Hours: 8AM-4PM (EST). *Felony, Civil Actions Over $5,000, Probate.*

Civil Records: Access: Phone, fax, mail, in person, email. Both court and visitors may perform in person searches. No search fee. Required to search: name, years to search. Civil cases indexed by defendant, plaintiff. Civil records on microfiche 1806 to 1910, on dockets back to 1810; on computer back to 1993. Probate is located across the hall in the same building.

Criminal Records: Access: Phone, fax, mail, in person. Both court and visitors may perform in person searches. No search fee. Required to search: name, years to search, signed release. Criminal records on microfiche 1806 to 1910, on dockets back to 1810.

General Information: No adoption, juvenile, mental hygiene records released. SASE required. Turnaround time 2-3 days. Fax notes: $3.00 for first page, $1.00 each add'l. Copy fee: $.50 per page. Fee payee: JW Morris, Clerk. Personal checks accepted. Prepayment is required.

Magistrate Court 307 Main St, Sutton, WV 26601; 304-765-5678; Fax: 304-765-3756. Hours: 8:30AM-4:30PM (EST). *Misdemeanor, Civil Actions Under $5,000, Eviction, Small Claims.*

Civil Records: Access: Mail, fax, in person. Both court and visitors may perform in person searches. Search fee: $.50 per page found. Records go back to 1977; on computer back to 1998.

Criminal Records: Access: Mail, fax, in person. Both court and visitors may perform in person searches. Search fee: $.50 per page found. Required to search: name, years to search, DOB; also helpful: address, SSN, signed release. Records go back to 1977; on computer back to 1998.

General Information: Turnaround time 1-2 weeks. Fax notes: Fee to fax results is $2.00 per page. Copy fee: $.50 per page. Certification fee: $.50. Fee payee: Braxton County Magistrate Ct. Prepayment required.

Brooke County

Circuit Court Brooke County Courthouse, PO Box 474, Wellsburg, WV 26070; 304-737-3662; Probate phone: 304-737-3661. Hours: 9AM-5PM (EST). *Felony, Civil Actions Over $5,000, Probate.*

Note: Probate is handled by County Clerk, 632 Main St, Courthouse, Wellsburg, WV 26070.

Civil Records: Access: Mail, in person. Both court and visitors may perform in person searches. Search fee: $5.00 per name. Required to search: name; also helpful: years to search. Civil cases indexed by defendant, plaintiff. Civil records on dockets and files from prior to 1960 to present, in boxes back to 1800s; computerized records since 1997.

Criminal Records: Access: Mail, in person. Both court and visitors may perform in person searches. Search fee: $5.00 per name. Required to search: name; also helpful: years to search, DOB, SSN. Criminal records on dockets and files from prior to 1960 to present, in boxes back to 1800s; computerized records since 1997.

General Information: No divorce, juvenile, mental hygiene, adoption records released. Turnaround time same day, unless in archives. Copy fee: $.50 per page. Certification fee: $.50 per document. Fee payee: Brooke County Circuit Clerk. Personal checks accepted. Prepayment is required.

Magistrate Court 632 Main St, Wellsburg, WV 26070; 304-737-1321; Fax: 304-737-1509. Hours: 9AM-4PM (EST). *Misdemeanor, Civil Actions Under $5,000, Eviction, Small Claims.*

Civil Records: Access: In person only. Visitors must perform in person searches for themselves. No search fee. Civil records go back to 1977; computerized back to 1996.

Criminal Records: Access: In person only. Visitors must perform in person searches for themselves. No search fee. Required to search: name; also helpful: DOB, SSN, signed release. Criminal records go back to 1977; computerized back to 1996.

Cabell County

Circuit Court PO Box 0545, Huntington, WV 25710-0545; 304-526-8622; Fax: 304-526-8699. Hours: 8:30AM-4:30PM (EST). *Felony, Civil Actions Over $5,000, Probate.*

Civil Records: Access: Mail, in person. Both court and visitors may perform in person searches. No search fee. Required to search: name, years to search. Civil cases indexed by defendant, plaintiff. Civil records on computer from 1990 to present. On index books back to 1854.

Criminal Records: Access: In person only. Visitors must perform in person searches for themselves. No search fee. Required to search: name, years to search; also helpful: address, DOB, SSN. Criminal records on computer from 1990 to present. On index books back to 1854. Requests are directed to the state Criminal Investigation Bureau.

General Information: Public access terminal is available. No sealed, juvenile, adoptions, mental health, guardianship records released. SASE required. Turnaround time 1 day. Copy fee: $.50 per page. Fee payee: Clerk of Circuit Court. Business checks accepted. Prepayment is required.

Magistrate Court 750 5th Ave, Basement, Rm B 113 Courthouse, Huntington, WV 25701; 304-526-8642; Fax: 304-526-8646. Hours: 8:30AM-4:30PM (EST). *Misdemeanor, Civil Actions Under $5,000, Eviction, Small Claims.*

Civil Records: Access: In person only. Visitors must perform in person searches for themselves. No search fee. Records go back to 1977 (1987-95 in storage); on computer back to 1991.

Criminal Records: Access: In person only. Visitors must perform in person searches for themselves. No search fee. Required to search: name. Records go back to 1977 (1987-95 in storage); computer back to 1991.

General Information: Public access terminal is available. Fax notes: Fee to fax results is $2.00 per page. Copy fee: $.25 per page. Certification fee: $.50 per page. Fee payee: Magistrate Court Clerk. Prepayment is required.

Calhoun County

Circuit Court PO Box 266, Grantsville, WV 26147; 304-354-6910; Fax: 304-354-6910. Hours: 8:30AM-4PM *Felony, Civil Actions Over $5,000, Probate.*

Civil Records: Access: Phone, fax, mail, in person. Both court and visitors may perform in person searches. No search fee. Required to search: name, years to search. Civil cases indexed by defendant, plaintiff. Civil records on index books from 1800s.

Criminal Records: Access: Phone, fax, mail, in person. Both court and visitors may perform in person searches. No search fee. Required to search: name, years to search; also helpful: DOB, SSN. Criminal records on dockets from 1900s.

General Information: No adoption, juvenile, divorce, domestic relations, guardianship/conservatorship records released. Turnaround time same day received. Fax notes: $3.00 for first page, $.50 each add'l. Copy fee: $.50 per page. Certification fee: $1.00. Fee payee: Circuit Clerk. Personal checks accepted.

Magistrate Court PO Box 186, Grantsville, WV 26147; 304-354-6698; Fax: 304-354-6698. Hours: 8:30AM-4PM (EST). *Misdemeanor, Civil Actions Under $5,000, Eviction, Small Claims.*

Civil Records: Access: In person, mail, phone. Both court and visitors may perform in person searches. No search fee. Civil records computerized since 1997.

Criminal Records: Access: In person, mail, phone. Both court and visitors may perform in person searches. No search fee. Required to search: name; also helpful: years to search, DOB, SSN. Criminal records computerized since 1997.

General Information: Public access terminal is available. Turnaround time 1 week. Copy fee: $.25 per page. Certification fee: $.50 per page.

Clay County

Circuit Court PO Box 129, Clay, WV 25043; 304-587-4256; Fax: 304-587-4346. Hours: 8AM-4PM (EST). *Felony, Civil Actions Over $5,000, Probate.*

Civil Records: Access: In person only. Visitors must perform in person searches for themselves. No search fee. Required to search: name, years to search, address. Civil cases indexed by defendant, plaintiff. Civil records on docket books and index books back to 1962, microfilm back to 1858; computerized back to 1998.

Criminal Records: Access: Phone, fax, mail, in person. Only the court performs in person searches; visitors may not. Court will do name only searches if time allows. No search fee. Required to search: name, years to search, address, DOB, SSN. Criminal records on docket books and index books back to 1962, microfilm back to 1858; computerized back to 1998.

General Information: Public access terminal is available. No juvenile, guardianship, conservatorship or mental health records released. SASE required. Turnaround time 3 days. Fax notes: Fee to fax results is $.50 per page. Copy fee: $.50 per page. Fee payee: Clerk of the Circuit Court. Personal checks accepted. Prepayment is required.

Magistrate Court PO Box 393, Clay, WV 25043; 304-587-2131; Fax: 304-587-2727. Hours: 8:30AM-4:30PM (EST). *Misdemeanor, Civil Actions Under $5,000, Eviction, Small Claims.*

Civil Records: Access: In person, mail. Both court and visitors may perform in person searches. No search fee. Civil records go back to 1978; computerized since 2000.

Criminal Records: Access: In person, mail. Both court and visitors may perform in person searches. No search fee. Required to search: name, offense; also helpful: years to search, DOB, SSN. Criminal records go back to 1978; computerized since 2000.

General Information: Public access terminal is available. Turnaround time 5 days. Copies: $.50 per pg.

Doddridge County

Circuit Court 118 E. Court St, West Union, WV 26456; 304-873-2331. Hours: 8:30AM-4PM (EST). *Felony, Civil Actions Over $5,000, Probate.*

Civil Records: Access: Phone, mail, in person. Both court and visitors may perform in person searches. No search fee. Required to search: name, years to search. Civil cases indexed by defendant, plaintiff. Civil records

on index books 1960 to present, archived from 1845 to 1960; computerized records go back to 1999.

Criminal Records: Access: Phone, mail, fax, in person. Both court and visitors may perform in person searches. No search fee. Required to search: name, years to search. Criminal records in index books and files from 1948; computerized records go back to 1999.

General Information: No juvenile, adoption, mental, domestic records released. SASE required. Turnaround time 1-5 days. Copy fee: $.50 per page. Fee payee: Clerk of Circuit Court. Personal checks accepted. Prepayment is required.

Magistrate Court PO Box 207, West Union, WV 26456; 304-873-2694; Fax: 304-873-2643. Hours: 8AM-4PM (EST). *Misdemeanor, Civil Actions Under $5,000, Eviction, Small Claims.*

Civil Records: Access: In person, mail. Both court and visitors may perform in person searches. No search fee. Civil records go back to 1977; computer back to 1999.

Criminal Records: Access: In person, mail. Both court and visitors may perform in person searches. No search fee. Required to search: name, years to search DOB, SSN, signed release; also helpful: offense. Criminal records go back to 1977; on computer back to 1999.

General Information: Public access terminal is available. Turnaround time 5 days. Copy fee: $.25 per page. Certification fee: $.50 per page. Check accepted. Prepayment is required.

Fayette County

Circuit Court 100 Court St, Fayetteville, WV 25840; Civil phone: 304-574-4249; Criminal phone: 304-574-4303/4250; Probate phone: 304-574-4226. Hours: 8AM-4PM (EST). *Felony, Civil Actions Over $5,000, Probate.*

Note: Probate is handled by County Clerk, PO Box 569, Fayetteville, WV 25840.

Civil Records: Access: Mail, in person. Both court and visitors may perform in person searches. No search fee. Required to search: name; also helpful: years to search. Civil cases indexed by defendant, plaintiff. Civil records on computer since 1995; prior records on file 1850 to present.

Criminal Records: Access: Mail, in person. Both court and visitors may perform in person searches. No search fee. Required to search: name, years to search; also helpful: DOB, SSN. Criminal records on computer since 1995; prior records on file 1850 to present.

General Information: No divorce, adoption, mental, juvenile records released. SASE not required. Turnaround time 1 week. Copy fee: $.50 per page. Certification fee: $2.00. Fee payee: Circuit Clerk of Fayette County. No personal checks accepted. Prepayment is required.

Magistrate Court 100 Church St, Fayetteville, WV 25840; 304-574-4279; Fax: 304-574-2458. Hours: 8AM-4PM (EST). *Misdemeanor, Civil Actions Under $5,000, Eviction, Small Claims.*

Civil Records: Access: In person only. Visitors must perform in person searches for themselves. No search fee. Civil records on computer back to 1997.

Criminal Records: Access: In person only. Visitors must perform in person searches for themselves. No search fee. Required to search: name, years to search. Criminal records on computer back to 1997.

General Information: Public access terminal is available. Copy fee: $.25.

Gilmer County

Circuit Court Gilmer County Courthouse, Glenville, WV 26351; 304-462-7241; Fax: 304-462-7038. Hours: 8AM-4PM (EST). *Felony, Civil Actions Over $5,000, Probate.*

Civil Records: Access: Phone, mail, fax, in person. Both court and visitors may perform in person searches. No search fee. Required to search: name, years to search. Civil cases indexed by defendant, plaintiff. Civil records on dockets and files from 1845 to present; computerized back to 1999.

Criminal Records: Access: Phone, mail, fax, in person. Both court and visitors may perform in person searches. No search fee. Required to search: name, years to search. Criminal records on dockets and files from 1845 to present; computerized back to 1999.

General Information: No juvenile, mental, confidential records released. SASE not required. Turnaround time 1 day. Fax notes: Fee to fax results is $1.50 per page with a $3.00 minimum. Copy fee: $.50 per page. Fee payee: Circuit Clerk. Personal checks accepted.

Magistrate Court Courthouse Annex, Glenville, WV 26351; 304-462-7812; Fax: 304-462-8582. Hours: 8:30AM-4PM (EST). *Misdemeanor, Civil Actions Under $5,000, Eviction, Small Claims.*

Civil Records: Access: In person, mail. Both court and visitors may perform in person searches. No search fee. Civil records on computer back to 2000; other records back to 1977.

Criminal Records: Access: In person, mail. Both court and visitors may perform in person searches. No search fee. Required to search: name, years to search; also helpful: DOB, SSN. Civil records on computer back to 2000; other records back to 1977.

General Information: Public access terminal is available. Turnaround time 1-5 days. Fax notes: Fee to fax results is $2.00 per document.

Grant County

Circuit Court 5 Highland Ave, Petersburg, WV 26847; 304-257-4545; Fax: 304-257-2593 (Attn: Circuit Court). Hours: 8:30AM-4:30PM (EST). *Felony, Civil Actions Over $5,000, Probate.*

Civil Records: Access: Fax, mail, in person. Both court and visitors may perform in person searches. No search fee. Required to search: name, years to search; also helpful: address. Civil cases indexed by defendant, plaintiff. Computerized records from 1999, civil records on index cards (current cases only), on index books back to 1866.

Criminal Records: Access: Fax, mail, in person. Both court and visitors may perform in person searches. No search fee. Required to search: name, years to search, DOB, SSN; also helpful: address. Computerized records from 1999, criminal records on index cards (current cases only), on index books back to 1866.

General Information: No juvenile, guardianship, adoptions, mental, domestic order records released. SASE required. Turnaround time 1-2 days. Fax notes: Fee to fax results is $1.50 for first page, $.75 each page thereafter. Copy fee: $.50 per page. Certification fee: $1.50. Fee payee: Circuit Clerk. Business checks accepted. In-state personal checks accepted. Prepayment is required.

Magistrate Court 5 Highland Ave (PO Box 216), Petersburg, WV 26847; 304-257-4637/1289; Fax: 304-257-9501. Hours: 8:30AM-4:30PM (EST). *Misdemeanor, Civil Actions Under $5,000, Eviction, Small Claims.*

Civil Records: Access: Phone, fax, mail, in person. Both court and visitors may perform in person searches. No search fee. Records on computer back to 1994; prior records go back to 1977.

Criminal Records: Access: Fax, mail, in person. Both court and visitors may perform in person searches. No search fee. Required to search: name, years to search, DOB, SSN. Records on computer back to 1994; prior back to 1977.

General Information: Public access terminal is available. Turnaround time 1-2 days. Fax notes: Will not fax results. Copy fee: $.50 per page. Certification fee: $.50 per page. Fee payee: Grant County Magistrate Court. Prepayment is required.

Greenbrier County

Circuit Court PO Drawer 751, Lewisburg, WV 24901; 304-647-6626; Fax: 304-647-6666. Hours: 8:30AM-4:30PM (EST). *Felony, Civil Actions Over $5,000, Probate.*

Civil Records: Access: Mail, in person. Both court and visitors may perform in person searches. Search fee: $5.00 per name. Required to search: name, years to search. Civil cases indexed by defendant, plaintiff. Civil records indexed by general and docket books from 1800s; computerized back to 1994.

Criminal Records: Access: Mail, in person. Both court and visitors may perform in person searches. Search fee: $5.00 per name. Required to search: name, years to search; also helpful: DOB, SSN, signed release. Criminal records indexed by general and docket books from 1800s; computerized back to 1994. No information given over the telephone on criminal matters except to authorized personnel.

General Information: No juvenile, adoptions, mental health records released. Turnaround time 1-2 days. Fax notes: Fee to fax results is $2.50 per page. Copy fee: $.50 per page. Certification fee: $1.00. Fee payee: Clerk of Circuit Court. Personal checks accepted.

Magistrate Court 200 North Court St, Lewisburg, WV 24901; 304-647-6632; Fax: 304-647-3612. Hours: 8:30AM-4:30PM (EST). *Misdemeanor, Civil Actions Under $5,000, Eviction, Small Claims.*

Civil Records: Access: Phone, mail, in person. Both court and visitors may perform in person searches. No search fee. Civil records on computer back to 1989; other records back to 1977.

Criminal Records: Access: Mail, in person. Both court and visitors may perform in person searches. No search fee. Required to search: name, years to search; also helpful: DOB, SSN. Civil records on computer back to 1989; other records back to 1977.

General Information: Public access terminal is available. Turnaround time 1-2 days. Fax notes: Fee to fax results is $2.00 per page. Certification fee: $.75 plus $.25 per page. Fee payee: Greenbrier County Magistrate Court. Prepayment is required.

Hampshire County

Circuit Court PO Box 343, Romney, WV 26757; 304-822-5022; Probate phone: 304-822-5112. Hours: 9AM-4PM M-F 5PM-8PM Friday evening (EST). *Felony, Civil Actions Over $5,000, Probate.*

Note: Probate handled by County Clerk, PO Box 806, Romney, WV 26757.

Civil Records: Access: Fax, mail, in person. Both court and visitors may perform in person searches. No search fee. Required to search: name, years to search. Civil cases indexed by defendant, plaintiff. Civil records on index files from 1957 to present, on index cards in storage 1885 to 1957.

Criminal Records: Access: Fax, mail, in person. Both court and visitors may perform in person searches. Search fee: $10.00 per name. Required to search: name, years to search. Criminal records on index files from 1957 to present, on index cards in storage 1885 to 1957.

General Information: No juvenile, divorce or adoption records released. SASE required. Turnaround time 2 days. Copy fee: $.50 per page. Certification fee: $1.50. Fee payee: Clerk of Circuit Court. Personal checks accepted. Will bill to attorneys.

Magistrate Court 239 W Birch Ln, PO Box 881, Romney, WV 26757; 304-822-4311; Fax: 304-822-

3981. Hours: 8:00AM-4PM (EST). *Misdemeanor, Civil Actions Under $5,000, Eviction, Small Claims.*

Civil Records: Access: Mail, fax, in person. Both court and visitors may perform in person searches. No search fee. Civil records go back to 1977; on computer back to 1993.

Criminal Records: Access: Mail, fax, in person. Both court and visitors may perform in person searches. No search fee. Required to search: name, years to search; also helpful: DOB, SSN. Criminal records go back to 1977; on computer back to 1993.

General Information: Public access terminal is available. Turnaround time 5 days. Fax notes: Will fax back to toll-free numbers no charge. Copy fee: $.25 per page. Certification fee: $.50 per page. Fee payee: Magistrate Court Clerk. Prepayment is required.

Hancock County

Circuit Court PO Box 428, New Cumberland, WV 26047; 304-564-3311; Fax: 304-564-5014. Hours: 8:30AM-4:30PM (EST). *Felony, Civil Actions Over $5,000, Probate.*

Note: Probate can be reached at PO Box 367.

Civil Records: Access: Fax, mail, in person, online. Both court and visitors may perform in person searches. Search fee: $5.00 per name. Required to search: name, years to search; also helpful: address. Civil cases indexed by defendant, plaintiff. Civil records on computer since 1972. Online access to court records available via a pay service, see www.swcg-inc.com/courts.htm or call 800-795-8543. $125 set-up fee plus a $38.00 or $120 monthly fee plan.

Criminal Records: Access: Fax, mail, in person, online. Both court and visitors may perform in person searches. Search fee: $5.00 per name. Required to search: name, years to search, signed release; also helpful: address, DOB, SSN. Criminal records on computer since 1972. Online access to criminal records is the same as civil.

General Information: Public access terminal is available. No adoption, juvenile, mental hygiene released. SASE required. Turnaround time same day. Fax notes: Fee to fax results is $2.00 per page. Copy fee: $.50 per page. Certification fee: $1.50. Fee payee: Clerk of Circuit Court. Personal checks accepted.

Magistrate Court 106 Court St, New Cumberland, WV 26047; 304-564-3355; Fax: 304-564-3852. Hours: 8:30-4:30PM M-F (EST). *Misdemeanor, Civil Actions Under $5,000, Eviction, Small Claims.*

Civil Records: Access: In person, mail. Both court and visitors may perform in person searches. No search fee. Civil records on computer since 1996. Phone, fax and mail access limited.

Criminal Records: Access: In person, mail. Both court and visitors may perform in person searches. No search fee. Required to search: name, years to search; also helpful: DOB, SSN. Criminal records on computer since 1996. Phone, fax and mail access limited.

General Information: Turnaround time 1-2 days. Copy fee: $.25 per page. Certification fee: $.50 per pg.

Hardy County

Circuit Court 204 Washington St, RM 237, Moorefield, WV 26836; 304-538-7869; Fax: 304-538-6197. Hours: 9AM-4PM (EST). *Felony, Civil Actions Over $5,000, Probate.*

Civil Records: Access: In person only. Both court and visitors may perform in person searches. No search fee. Required to search: name, years to search. Civil cases indexed by defendant, plaintiff. Civil records on docket books back to 1960 (chrono index in front of book). Computerized records go back to 1995.

Criminal Records: Access: Phone, in person. Both court and visitors may perform in person searches. No search fee. Required to search: name, years to search,

DOB; also helpful: SSN. Criminal records on docket books back to 1960 (chrono index in front of book). Computerized records go back to 1995.

General Information: No juvenile, mental, domestic records released. Copy fee: $.50 per page. Certification fee: $1.00. Fee payee: Clerk of Circuit Court. Personal checks accepted. Prepayment is required.

Magistrate Court 204 Washington St, Moorefield, WV 26836; 304-538-6836; Fax: 304-538-2072. Hours: 9AM-4PM (EST). *Misdemeanor, Civil Actions Under $5,000, Eviction, Small Claims.*

Civil Records: Access: Fax, mail, in person. Both court and visitors may perform in person searches. No search fee. Civil records on computer back to 1990; others back to 1977.

Criminal Records: Access: Fax, mail, in person. Both court and visitors may perform in person searches. No search fee. Required to search: name, years to search; also helpful: DOB, SSN. Criminal records on computer back to 1990; others back to 1977.

General Information: SASE required. Turnaround time 10 days, 5 days if records on computer. Fax notes: Fee to fax results is $2.00 per page. Certification fee: $.50 per page. Fee payee: Hardy County Magistrate Court. Prepayment is required.

Harrison County

Circuit Court 301 W. Main, #301, Clarksburg, WV 26301-2967; 304-624-8640; Probate phone: 304-624-8673; Fax: 304-624-8710. Hours: 8:30AM-4PM (EST). *Felony, Civil Actions Over $5,000, Probate.*

Note: Probate is handled by County Clerk, 301 W Main St, Courthouse, Clarksburg, WV 26301.

Civil Records: Access: In person only. Visitors must perform in person searches for themselves. No search fee. Required to search: name, years to search. Civil cases indexed by defendant, plaintiff. Civil records on computer from 1990 to present. On index books back to mid-1800s.

Criminal Records: Access: In person only. Visitors must perform in person searches for themselves. No search fee. Required to search: name, years to search; also helpful: DOB, SSN. Criminal records on computer from 1990 to present. On index books back to mid-1800s.

General Information: Public access terminal is available. No adoption, juvenile, guardianship, mental health records released. Copy fee: $.50 per page. Fee payee: Harrison County Circuit Clerk. Only cashiers checks and money orders accepted. Prepayment is required.

Magistrate Court 306 Washington Ave Rm 222, Clarksburg, WV 26301; 304-624-8645; Fax: 304-624-8740. Hours: 8AM-4PM (EST). *Misdemeanor, Civil Actions Under $5,000, Eviction, Small Claims.*

Civil Records: Access: In person, mail. Both court and visitors may perform in person searches. No search fee. Civil records go back to 1980's; computerized to 9/97.

Criminal Records: Access: In person, mail. Both court and visitors may perform in person searches. No search fee. Required to search: name, years to search; also helpful: DOB, SSN. Criminal records go back to 1980's; computerized since 9/97.

General Information: Public access terminal is available. Turnaround time 5 days. Copy fee: $.25 per page. Certification fee: $.50 per page.

Jackson County

Circuit Court PO Box 427, Ripley, WV 25271; 304-372-2011 X329; Fax: 304-372-6205. Hours: 9AM-4PM M-F, 9AM-Noon Sat (EST). *Felony, Civil Actions Over $5,000, Probate.*

Civil Records: Access: Phone, mail, in person. Both court and visitors may perform in person searches. No search fee. Required to search: name, years to search. Civil cases indexed by defendant, plaintiff. Civil records on index books back to 1800s. Computerized records back to 1999.

Criminal Records: Access: Phone, mail, in person. Both court and visitors may perform in person searches. No search fee. Required to search: name, years to search; also helpful: DOB, SSN. Criminal records on index books back to 1800s. Computerized records back to 1999.

General Information: No juvenile, mental, adoption, domestic records released. SASE required. Turnaround time 1-2 days. Fax notes: Fax back $2.50 per page. Copy fee: $.50 per page. Certification fee: $2.00. Fee payee: Clerk of Circuit Court. Only cashiers checks and money orders accepted. Prepayment is required.

Magistrate Court PO Box 368, Ripley, WV 25271; 304-372-2011; Fax: 304-372-7132. Hours: 9AM-4PM (EST). *Misdemeanor, Civil Actions Under $5,000, Eviction, Small Claims.*

Civil Records: Access: In person only. Visitors must perform in person searches for themselves. No search fee.

Criminal Records: Access: In person only. Visitors must perform in person searches for themselves. No search fee. Required to search: name, years to search; also helpful: DOB, SSN. Records computerized since 1998, on dockets since 1977.

General Information: Public access terminal is available. Certification fee: $.50.

Jefferson County

Circuit Court PO Box 584, Charles Town, WV 25414; 304-728-3231; Fax: 304-728-3398. Hours: 9AM-5PM (EST). *Felony, Civil Actions Over $5,000.*

Civil Records: Access: In person only. Visitors must perform in person searches for themselves. No search fee. Required to search: name, years to search. Civil cases indexed by defendant, plaintiff. Civil records on computer back to 01/85; on index books 1960 to 1985. On dockets back 1960 back to 1800s in storage.

Criminal Records: Access: In person only. Visitors must perform in person searches for themselves. No search fee. Required to search: name, years to search. Criminal records on computer back to 01/85; on index books 1960 to 1985. On dockets back 1960 back to 1800s in storage.

General Information: Public access terminal is available. No juvenile, guardianship, adoption, or mental health records released. Fax notes: Fee to fax results is $2.00 per page. Copy fee: $.50 per page. Certification fee: $.50 per page; triple seal $3.00. Fee payee: Circuit Clerk. Cash or money order. No personal checks accepted. Prepayment is required.

Magistrate Court PO Box 607, Charles Town, WV 25414; 304-728-3233; Fax: 304-728-3235. Hours: 7:30AM-4:30PM (EST). *Misdemeanor, Civil Actions Under $5,000, Eviction, Small Claims.*

Civil Records: Access: Mail, fax, in person. Both court and visitors may perform in person searches. No search fee. Civil records on computer back to 1996; others go back to 1977.

Criminal Records: Access: Mail, fax, in person. Both court and visitors may perform in person searches. No search fee. Required to search: name, years to search, DOB; also helpful: SSN, signed release. Criminal records on computer back to 1996; others back to 1977.

General Information: Turnaround time 5 days. Fax notes: No fee to fax results. Certification fee: $.50 per page. Payee: Magistrate Clerk. Prepayment is required.

Kanawha County

Circuit Court PO Box 2351, Charleston, WV 25328; 304-357-0440; Probate phone: 304-357-0130; Fax: 304-357-0473. Hours: 8AM-5PM (EST). *Felony, Civil Actions Over $5,000, Probate.*

Note: Probate is handled by County Clerk, 409 Virginia St East, Charleston, WV 25301.

Civil Records: Access: In person, online. Visitors must perform in person searches for themselves. No search fee. Required to search: name, years to search; also helpful: address. Civil cases indexed by defendant, plaintiff. Civil records on computer from 7/1989 to present. On microfiche back to 1800s. Online access to court records available via a pay service, see www.swcg-inc.com/courts.htm or call 800-795-8543. $125 set-up fee plus a $38.00 or $120 monthly fee plan.

Criminal Records: Access: In person, online. Visitors must perform in person searches for themselves. No search fee. Required to search: name, years to search; also helpful: address, DOB, SSN. Criminal records on computer from 7/1989 to present. On microfiche back to 1800s. Online access to criminal records is the same as civil.

General Information: Public access terminal is available. No juvenile, neglect, adoption, domestic, guardianship, mental health or conservatorship records released. Copy fee: $.50 per page. Certification fee: $.50 per page. Fee payee: Kanawha Circuit Clerk. Business checks accepted. Prepayment is required.

Magistrate Court 111 Court St, Charleston, WV 25333; 304-357-0400; Fax: 304-357-0205. Hours: 8:30AM-4:30PM (EST). *Misdemeanor, Civil Actions Under $5,000, Eviction, Small Claims.*

Civil Records: Access: In person, mail. Both court and visitors may perform in person searches. No search fee. Civil records go back to 1982; computerized records since 1996.

Criminal Records: Access: In person, mail. Both court and visitors may perform in person searches. No search fee. Required to search: name, years to search; also helpful: DOB, SSN. Criminal records go back to 1982; computerized records since 1991.

General Information: Public access terminal is available. Turnaround time 14 days. Copy fee: $.25 per page. Certification fee: $.50 per page.

Lewis County

Circuit Court PO Box 69, Weston, WV 26452; 304-269-8210; Fax: 304-269-8249. Hours: 8:30AM-4:30PM (EST). *Felony, Civil Actions Over $5,000, Probate.*

Civil Records: Access: Phone, fax, mail, in person. Only the court performs in person searches; visitors may not. No search fee. Required to search: name, years to search. Civil cases indexed by defendant, plaintiff. Civil records on index books 1977 to 1992; on computer back to 1984. No index for chancery books back to 1800s.

Criminal Records: Access: Phone, fax, mail, in person. Only the court performs in person searches; visitors may not. No search fee. Required to search: name, years to search; also helpful: SSN. Criminal records on index books 1977 to 1992; on computer back to 1984. No index for chancery books back to 1800s.

General Information: No adoption, juvenile, domestic records released. SASE not required. Turnaround time 2 days. Fax notes: Fee to fax results is $2.00 per page. Copy fee: $.50 per page. Certification fee: $.50 per page. Fee payee: Clerk of Circuit Court. Business checks accepted.

Magistrate Court 111 Court St, PO Box 260, Weston, WV 26452; 304-269-8230; Fax: 304-269-8239. Hours: 8:30AM-Noon, 1-4:30PM (EST).

Misdemeanor, Civil Actions Under $5,000, Eviction, Small Claims.

Civil Records: Access: In person, mail, fax. Both court and visitors may perform in person searches. No search fee. Civil records computerized since 1991.

Criminal Records: Access: In person, mail, fax. Both court and visitors may perform in person searches. No search fee. Required to search: name, years to search; also helpful: DOB, SSN. Criminal records computerized since 1991.

General Information: Turnaround time 5 days. Copy fee: $.25 per page. Certification fee: $.50 per page.

Lincoln County

Circuit Court PO Box 338, Hamlin, WV 25523; 304-824-7887; Fax: 304-824-7909. Hours: 9AM-4:30PM *Felony, Civil Actions Over $5,000, Probate.*

Civil Records: Access: Phone, mail, in person. Both court and visitors may perform in person searches. No search fee. Required to search: name, years to search. Civil cases indexed by defendant, plaintiff. Civil records computerized since 1991, on index books 1971 to present, on docket books back to 1909.

Criminal Records: Access: Phone, mail, in person. Both court and visitors may perform in person searches. No search fee. Required to search: name, years to search, DOB, SSN; also helpful: address. Criminal records computerized since 1991, on index books 1971 to present, on docket books back to 1909.

General Information: Public access terminal is available. No juvenile, adoption, divorce or mental hygiene records released. SASE not required. Turnaround time immediate to next day. Copy fee: No search fee. Fee payee: Clerk of Circuit Court. Personal checks accepted. Prepayment is required.

Magistrate Court PO Box 573, Hamlin, WV 25523; 304-824-5001 x235; Fax: 304-824-5280. Hours: 9AM-4PM (EST) *Misdemeanor, Civil Actions Under $5,000, Eviction, Small Claims.*

Note: Searches performed by court only on second and fourth Thursday of each month.

Civil Records: Access: In person, mail. Only the court performs in person searches; visitors may not. No search fee.

Criminal Records: Access: In person, mail. Only the court performs in person searches; visitors may not. No search fee. Required to search: name, years to search; also helpful: DOB, SSN.

General Information: Turnaround time 1-14 days.

Logan County

Circuit Court Logan County Courthouse, Rm 311, Logan, WV 25601; 304-792-8550; Fax: 304-792-8555. Hours: 8:30AM-4:30PM (EST). *Felony, Civil Actions Over $5,000, Probate.*

Civil Records: Access: In person. Visitors must perform in person searches for themselves. No search fee. Required to search: name, years to search. Civil cases indexed by defendant, plaintiff. Civil records on index books back to 1800s, on computer from 1995.

Criminal Records: Access: Mail, fax, in person. Both court and visitors may perform in person searches. No search fee. Required to search: name, years to search, SSN. Criminal records on index books back to 1800s, on computer from 1995.

General Information: No adoptions, juvenile, domestic records released. SASE not required. Turnaround time 1-2 days. Fax notes: Fee to fax results is $1.00 per page. Copy fee: $.50 per page. Certification fee: $1.50 plus $.50 per page after first 2. Fee payee: Clerk of Circuit Court. Only cashiers checks and money orders accepted. Will bill to attorneys.

Logan Magistrate Court Logan County Courthouse, 300 Stratton St, Logan, WV 25601; 304-

792-8651; Fax: 304-752-0790. Hours: 8:30AM-Noon; 1-4:30PM (EST). *Misdemeanor, Civil Actions Under $5,000, Eviction, Small Claims.*

Civil Records: Access: In person, mail, fax. Both court and visitors may perform in person searches. No search fee.

Criminal Records: Access: In person, mail, fax. Both court and visitors may perform in person searches. No search fee. Required to search: name, years to search; also helpful: address, DOB, SSN.

General Information: Turnaround time 5 days. Fax notes: Fee to fax back is $2.00first page and $1.50 each addl. Copy fee: $.50 per page. Certification fee: $.50 per page. Fee payee: Logan Magistrate Court. Prepayment is required. Prepayment required for copies.

Marion County

Circuit Court PO Box 1269, Fairmont, WV 26554; 304-367-5360; Fax: 304-367-5374. Hours: 8:30AM-4:30PM (EST). *Felony, Civil Actions Over $3,000.*

Civil Records: Access: Phone, fax, mail, in person. Both court and visitors may perform in person searches. No search fee. Required to search: name, years to search. Civil cases indexed by defendant, plaintiff. Civil records on computer from Jan. 1988 to present. On docket books from 1849 to 1988.

Criminal Records: Access: In person only. Visitors must perform in person searches for themselves. No search fee. Required to search: name, years to search; also helpful: DOB, SSN. Criminal records on computer from Jan. 1988 to present. On docket books from 1849 to 1988. The court refers all written requests to the Dept of Public Safety.

General Information: Public access terminal is available. No adoptions, juvenile, mental or guardianship records released. SASE not required. Turnaround time 2-3 days. Fax notes: $5.00 for first page, $2.00 each add'l. Fax fee: After 10 pages fee is $1.00 per page. Copy fee: $.50 per page. Certification fee: $.50 per page. Fee payee: Clerk of Circuit Court. Business checks accepted. Prepayment is required.

Magistrate Court 200 Jackson St, Fairmont, WV 26554; 304-367-5330; Fax: 304-367-5337. Hours: 8:30AM-4:30PM M-T-W-F; 8:30AM-9PM Th (EST). *Misdemeanor, Civil Actions Under $5,000, Eviction, Small Claims.*

Note: No record checks performed between 11:30AM and 1:30PM.

Civil Records: Access: In person, mail. Both court and visitors may perform in person searches. No search fee. Civil records go back to 1977; computerized since 1996.

Criminal Records: Access: In person, mail. Both court and visitors may perform in person searches. No search fee. Required to search: name, years to search; also helpful: DOB, SSN. Criminal records go back to 1977; computerized since 1996.

General Information: Turnaround time 5-15 days, ASAP for phone requests, time permitting. Copy fee: $.25 per copy. Certification fee: $.50 per page. Fee payee: Marion County Magistrate Clerk. Prepayment is required.

Marshall County

Circuit Court Marshall County Courthouse, 7th St, Moundsville, WV 26041; 304-845-2130; Fax: 304-845-3948. Hours: 8:30AM-4:30PM M-Th; 8:30AM-5:30PM F (EST). *Felony, Civil Actions Over $5,000.*

Civil Records: Access: Fax, mail, in person. Both court and visitors may perform in person searches. No search fee. Required to search: name, years to search. Civil cases indexed by defendant, plaintiff. Civil records on computer since 01/98; prior records on index books and in files from 1836 to present.

Criminal Records: Access: Fax, mail, in person. Both court and visitors may perform in person searches. No search fee. Required to search: name, years to search; also helpful: DOB, SSN. Criminal records on computer since 01/98; prior records on index books and in files from 1836 to present.

General Information: No juvenile, mental, adoption, sealed, conservatorship, guardianship or divorce records released. SASE not required. Turnaround time 1-2 days. Fax notes: Fee to fax results is $.50 per page. Copy fee: $.25 per page. Certification fee: $1.00. Fee payee: Clerk of Circuit Court. Personal checks accepted. Will bill to attorneys.

Mason County

Circuit Court Mason County Courthouse, Point Pleasant, WV 25550; 304-675-4400; Fax: 304-675-7419. Hours: 8:30AM-4:30PM (EST). *Felony, Civil Actions Over $5,000, Probate.*

Civil Records: Access: In person only. Visitors must perform in person searches for themselves. No search fee. Required to search: name, years to search. Civil cases indexed by defendant, plaintiff. Civil records on computer from 1994. No time limit on open cases. Index books with data back to 1800s.

Criminal Records: Access: In person only. Visitors must perform in person searches for themselves. No search fee. Required to search: name, years to search. Criminal records on computer from 1994. No time limit on open cases. Index books with data back to 1800s.

General Information: Public access terminal is available. No divorce or juvenile records released. Fax notes: Fee to fax results is $2.00 per page. Copy fee: $.50 per page. Fee payee: Circuit Court Clerk. Personal checks accepted. Will bill mail requests.

Magistrate Court 200 6th St, Point Pleasant, WV 25550; 304-675-6840; Fax: 304-675-5949. Hours: 8:30AM-4:30PM (EST). *Misdemeanor, Civil Actions Under $5,000, Eviction, Small Claims.*

Civil Records: Access: In person, mail. Both court and visitors may perform in person searches. No search fee. Civil records go back to 1977; computerized since 1998.

Criminal Records: Access: In person, mail. Both court and visitors may perform in person searches. No search fee. Required to search: name, years to search. Criminal records go back to 1977; computerized since 1998.

General Information: Public access terminal is available. Turnaround time 3-4 days. Copy fee: $.25 per page. Certification fee: $.50 per page.

McDowell County

Circuit Court PO Box 400, Welch, WV 24801; 304-436-8535; Probate phone: 304-436-8544. Hours: 9AM-5PM (EST). *Felony, Civil Actions Over $5,000, Probate.*

Note: Probate is handled by County Clerk, 90 Wyoming St, Ste 109, Welch, WV 24801.

Civil Records: Access: Mail, in person. Both court and visitors may perform in person searches. No search fee. Required to search: name, years to search. Civil cases indexed by defendant, plaintiff. Civil records on index books back to 1800s; on computer back to 1999.

Criminal Records: Access: Mail, in person. Both court and visitors may perform in person searches. No search fee. Required to search: name, years to search; also helpful: DOB, SSN. Criminal records on index books back to 1800s; on computer back to 1999.

General Information: No sealed, juvenile, adoption, mental health, guardianship records released. SASE required. Turnaround time 1 week. Copy fee: $.50 per page. Certification fee: $.50 per page. Fee payee: Clerk of Circuit Court. Business checks accepted. Prepayment is required.

Magistrate Court PO Box 447, Welch, WV 24801; 304-436-8588; Fax: 304-436-8575. Hours: 9AM-5PM (EST). *Misdemeanor, Civil Actions Under $5,000, Eviction, Small Claims.*

Civil Records: Access: Mail, fax, in person. Visitors must perform in person searches for themselves. Search fee: None; will search as time permits. Records on computer go back to 1999.

Criminal Records: Access: Mail, fax, in person. Both court and visitors may perform in person searches. Search fee: None; will search as time permits. Required to search: name, years to search, DOB, SSN. Records on computer go back to 1999.

General Information: Public access terminal is available. Turnaround time 5 days. Fax notes: Fee to fax results is $2 per page. Copy fee: $.25 per page. Certification fee: $.50 per page.

Mercer County

Circuit Court 1501 W. Main St, Princeton, WV 24740; 304-487-8369; Probate phone: 304-487-8336; Fax: 304-425-1598. Hours: 8:30AM-4:30PM (EST). *Felony, Civil Actions Over $5,000.*

Note: Probate Court records are at the same address but separate office.

Civil Records: Access: Phone, fax, mail, in person. Both court and visitors may perform in person searches. No search fee. Required to search: name, years to search. Civil cases indexed by defendant, plaintiff. Civil records on computer from Oct. 1989 to present. On index books from 1930 to 1989 (Cott System). On index cards back to 1890s.

Criminal Records: Access: Phone, fax, mail, in person. Both court and visitors may perform in person searches. No search fee. Required to search: name, years to search; also helpful: DOB, SSN. Criminal records on computer from Oct. 1989 to present. On index books from 1930 to 1989 (Cott System). On index cards back to 1890s.

General Information: No juvenile, adoption, mental health, guardianship or conservatorship records released. Turnaround time 1-2 days. Fax notes: $2.00 per page. Copy fee: $.50 per page. Certification fee: $.50 per page. Fee payee: Circuit Court Clerk. Business checks accepted.

Magistrate Court 1519 N Walker St, Princeton, WV 24740; 304-431-7115. Hours: 8:30AM-4:30PM (EST). *Misdemeanor, Civil Actions Under $5,000, Eviction, Small Claims.*

Civil Records: Access: In person only. Visitors must perform in person searches for themselves. No search fee. Civil records from 1977; computerized back to 1984.

Criminal Records: Access: In person only. Visitors must perform in person searches for themselves. No search fee. Required to search: name, years to search; also helpful: address, DOB, SSN. Criminal records from 1977; computerized back to 1984.

General Information: Public access terminal is available. Certification fee: $.50. Fee payee: Mercer County Magistrate Court. Prepayment is required.

Mineral County

Circuit Court 150 Armstrong St, Keyser, WV 26726; 304-788-1562; Fax: 304-788-4109. Hours: 8:30AM-5PM (EST). *Felony, Civil Actions Over $5,000, Probate.*

Note: Probate court is a separate office at the same address, 2nd Fl, 304-788-3924.

Civil Records: Access: Fax, mail, in person, online. Both court and visitors may perform in person searches. Search fee: $5.00 per name. Required to search: name, years to search. Civil cases indexed by defendant, plaintiff. Civil records on computer 1/1991 to present, on dockets from 1920s. Online access to court records available via a pay service, see www.swcg-inc.com/courts.htm or call 800-795-8543. $125 set-up fee plus a $38.00 or $120 monthly fee plan. Fax access not guaranteed.

Criminal Records: Access: Fax, mail, in person, online. Both court and visitors may perform in person searches. Search fee: $5.00 per name. Required to search: name, years to search; also helpful: DOB, SSN. Criminal records on computer 1/1991 to present, on dockets from 1920s. Online access to criminal records is the same as civil. Fax access not guaranteed.

General Information: No juvenile, adoption, divorce, mental hygiene, conservatorship or guardianship records released. SASE requested. Turnaround time 2-4 days. Fax notes: No fee to fax results. Copy fee: $.50 per page. Fee payee: Clerk of Circuit Court. Personal checks accepted.

Magistrate Court 105 West St, Keyser, WV 26726; 304-788-2625; Fax: 304-788-9835. Hours: 8:30AM-4:30PM (EST). *Misdemeanor, Civil Actions Under $5,000, Eviction, Small Claims.*

Civil Records: Access: Mail, in person. Both court and visitors may perform in person searches. Search fee: No search fee. Required to search: name, years to search. Civil records on computer back to 1991.

Criminal Records: Access: Mail, in person. Both court and visitors may perform in person searches. No search fee. Required to search: name, years to search; also helpful: DOB, SSN. Records on computer back to 1991; prior back to 1977.

General Information: Public access terminal is available. Turnaround time: time permitting. Certification fee: $.50 per page. Fee payee: Magistrate Court. Prepayment is required.

Mingo County

Circuit Court PO Box 435, Williamson, WV 25661; 304-235-0320; Probate phone: 304-235-0330. Hours: 8:30AM-4:30PM M-W,F, 8:30AM-6:30PM Th (EST). *Felony, Civil Actions Over $5,000, Probate.*

Note: Probate is handled by County Clerk, 75 E 2nd Ave, Williamson, WV 25661.

Civil Records: Access: Mail, in person. Only the court performs in person searches; visitors may not. Search fee: $10.00 per name. Required to search: name, years to search. Civil cases indexed by defendant, plaintiff. Civil records on computer from 1/1991 to present, civil on index books back to 1960, chancery books back to 1800s (written or in person only).

Criminal Records: Access: Mail, in person. Only the court performs in person searches; visitors may not. Search fee: $10.00 per name. Required to search: name, years to search; also helpful: DOB. Criminal records on computer since 1/91, Index books back to 1955.

General Information: No adoption, mental hygiene, juvenile records released. Turnaround time 1-2 days. Copy fee: $.50 per page. Fee payee: Mingo County Circuit Clerk. Personal checks accepted. Prepayment is required.

Magistrate Court PO Box 986, Williamson, WV 25661; 304-235-2445; Fax: 304-235-3179. Hours: 8:30AM-4:30PM (EST). *Misdemeanor, Civil Actions Under $5,000, Eviction, Small Claims.*

Civil Records: Access: Phone, mail, fax, in person. Only the court performs in person searches; visitors may not. No search fee. Required to search: name, years to search; also helpful: DOB. Civil records go back to 1977; on computer back to 1998.

Criminal Records: Access: Phone, mail, fax, in person. Only the court performs in person searches; visitors may not. No search fee. Required to search: name, years to search; also helpful: DOB, SSN. Criminal records go back to 1977; on computer back to 1998.

General Information: Turnaround time 1 week, sooner for phone requests. Fax notes: Fee to fax is $2.00 per page; will fax free to toll-free. Copy fee: $.25 per page. Certification fee: $.50 per page. Fee payee: Magistrate Court.

Monongalia County

Circuit Court County Courthouse, 243 High St Rm 110, Morgantown, WV 26505; 304-291-7240; Probate phone: 304-291-7230; Fax: 304-291-7273. Hours: 9AM-7PM M; 9AM-5PM T-F (EST). *Felony, Civil Actions Over $5,000, Probate.*

Note: A disclaimer for the Clerk must be included by mail requesters. Probate is handled by County Clerk, 243 High St, Room 123, Morgantown, WV 26505.

Civil Records: Access: Mail, in person. Both court and visitors may perform in person searches. Search fee: $5.00 per name. Required to search: name, years to search. Civil cases indexed by defendant, plaintiff. Civil records on computer from 1/90 to present, on index book separated by plaintiff and defendant back to 1865.

Criminal Records: Access: Mail, in person. Both court and visitors may perform in person searches. Search fee: $5.00 per name. Required to search: name, years to search; also helpful: DOB, SSN. Criminal records on computer from 1/90 to present, on index book separated by plaintiff and defendant back to 1865.

General Information: No juvenile, divorce, mental hygiene, divorce, adoption, guardianship, conservatorship or domestic records released. SASE required. Turnaround time 1 day. Fax notes: Fee to fax results is $1.00 per page. Copy fee: $.50 per page. Fee payee: Circuit Clerk. Business checks accepted. Prepayment is required.

Magistrate Court 265 Spruce St, Morgantown, WV 26505; 304-291-7296; Fax: 304-284-7313. Hours: 8AM-7PM (EST). *Misdemeanor, Civil Actions Under $5,000, Eviction, Small Claims.*

Civil Records: Access: Mail, fax, in person. Both court and visitors may perform in person searches. Search fee: No search fee. Required to search: name, years to search. Records on computer back to 1999; prior in books back to 1977.

Criminal Records: Access: Mail, fax, online, in person. Both court and visitors may perform in person searches. No search fee. Required to search: name, years to search; also helpful: DOB, SSN, signed release. Records on computer go back to 1999; prior in books back to 1977.

General Information: Public access terminal is available. Turnaround time 10-14 days. Fax notes: Will not fax results. Certification fee: $.50 per page. Fee payee: Magistrate Court. Prepayment is required.

Monroe County

Circuit Court PO Box 350, Union, WV 24983-0350; 304-772-3017; Fax: 304-772-4497. Hours: 8AM-4PM (EST). *Felony, Civil Actions Over $5,000.*

Civil Records: Access: Phone, mail, in person. Both court and visitors may perform in person searches. No search fee. Required to search: name, years to search. Civil cases indexed by defendant, plaintiff. Civil records on index books 1799 to present; on computer back to 2000.

Criminal Records: Access: Phone, mail, in person. Both court and visitors may perform in person searches. No search fee. Required to search: name, years to search; also helpful: DOB, SSN. Criminal records on index books 1799 to present; on computer back to 2000.

General Information: No juvenile, adoption, divorce records released. SASE requested. Turnaround time 1 week. Copy fee: $.50 per page. Include postage with copy fee. Certification fee: $1.00. Fee payee: Clerk of Circuit Court. Personal checks accepted. Prepayment is required.

Magistrate Court PO Box 4, Union, WV 24983; 304-772-3321/3176; Fax: 304-772-4357. Hours: 8:30AM-4:30PM (EST). *Misdemeanor, Civil Actions Under $5,000, Eviction, Small Claims.*

Civil Records: Access: In person, mail. Both court and visitors may perform in person searches. No search fee. Criminal records go back to 1977; computerized records since 2000.

Criminal Records: Access: In person, mail. Both court and visitors may perform in person searches. No search fee. Required to search: name, years to search; also helpful: DOB, SSN. Criminal records go back to 1977; computerized records since 2000.

General Information: Turnaround time 1-2 days. Fax notes: $2.00. Copy fee: $.25 per page. Certification fee: $.50 per page.

Morgan County

Circuit Court 77 Fairfax St, Ste 2A, Berkeley Springs, WV 25411-1501; 304-258-8554; Fax: 304-258-7319. Hours: 9AM-5PM MTTh, 9AM-1PM Wed, 9AM-7PM Fri (EST). *Felony, Civil Actions Over $5,000, Probate.*

Civil Records: Access: In person only. Visitors must perform in person searches for themselves. No search fee. Required to search: name, years to search. Civil cases indexed by defendant, plaintiff. Civil records on computer back to 1/93, index cards back to 1960; in person searching only on index books back to 1800s.

Criminal Records: Access: In person only. Visitors must perform in person searches for themselves. No search fee. Required to search: name, years to search; also helpful-DOB, SSN, signed release. Criminal records on computer back to 1/93, index cards back to 1960; in person searching only on index books back to 1800s.

General Information: Public access terminal is available. No juvenile, adoption, mental health, divorce records released. Copy fee: $.50 per page. Fee payee: Betty R Moss-Miller, Circuit Clerk. Only cashiers checks and money orders accepted. Will bill to attorneys.

Magistrate Court 77 Fairfax St, Berkeley Springs, WV 25411; 304-258-8631; Fax: 304-258-8639. Hours: 9AM-4:30PM (EST). *Misdemeanor, Civil Actions Under $5,000, Eviction, Small Claims.*

Civil Records: Access: In person only. Visitors must perform in person searches for themselves. No search fee. Civil records go back to 1977; computerized records since 1998.

Criminal Records: Access: In person only. Visitors must perform in person searches for themselves. No search fee. Required to search: name, years to search; also helpful: DOB, SSN. Criminal records go back to 1977; computerized records since 1998. Phone, fax and mail access limited.

General Information: Public access terminal is available. Copy fee: $.25 per page. Certification fee: $.50 per page.

Nicholas County

Circuit Court 700 Main St, Summersville, WV 26651; 304-872-7810; Probate phone: 304-872-7820. Hours: 8:30AM-4:30PM (EST). *Felony, Civil Actions Over $5,000, Probate.*

Note: Probate is handled by County Clerk, 700 Main St, Ste 2, Summersville, WV 26651.

Civil Records: Access: Mail, in person, online. Both court and visitors may perform in person searches. No search fee. Required to search: name, years to search. Civil cases indexed by defendant, plaintiff. Civil records on computer since 1994; prior records on index cards from 1976 to 1994 on dockets back to 1818. Online access to court records available via a pay service, see

www.swcg-inc.com/courts.htm or call 800-795-8543. $125 set-up fee plus a $38.00 or $120 monthly fee plan.
Criminal Records: Access: Mail, in person, online. Both court and visitors may perform in person searches. No search fee. Required to search: name, years to search; also helpful: DOB, SSN. Criminal records on computer since 1994; prior records on index cards from 1976 to 1994 on dockets back to 1818. Online access to criminal records is the same as civil.
General Information: Public access terminal is available. No divorce, juvenile, adoption, mental, guardianship records released. SASE required. Turnaround time 1 week. Copy fee: $.50 per page. Fee payee: Circuit Clerk. Personal checks accepted.

Magistrate Court 511 Church St, #206 2nd Flr, Summersville, WV 26651; 304-872-7829; Fax: 304-872-7888. Hours: 8:30AM-4:30PM (EST). *Misdemeanor, Civil Actions Under $5,000, Eviction, Small Claims.*
Civil Records: Access: Mail, in person. Visitors must perform in person searches for themselves. No search fee. Civil records on computer back to 1990. Must have a request in writing.
Criminal Records: Access: Mail, in person. Visitors must perform in person searches for themselves. No search fee. Required to search: name, years to search; also helpful: DOB, SSN. Criminal records on computer back to 1990. Must have a request in writing.
General Information: Public access terminal is available. Certification fee: $.50 per page. Fee payee: Magistrate Court.

Ohio County

Circuit Court 1500 Chapline St, City & County Bldg Rm 403, Wheeling, WV 26003; 304-234-3613; Fax: 304-232-0550. Hours: 8:30AM-5PM (EST). *Felony, Civil Actions Over $5,000, Probate.*
Civil Records: Access: Fax, mail, in person, online. Both court and visitors may perform in person searches. Search fee: $5.00 per name. Required to search: name, years to search. Civil cases indexed by defendant, plaintiff. Civil records on computer from Oct 1986 to present, on index books back to 1800s. Online access to court records available via a pay service, see www.swcg-inc.com/courts.htm or call 800-795-8543. $125 set-up fee plus a $38.00 or $120 monthly fee plan.
Criminal Records: Access: Fax, mail, in person, online. Both court and visitors may perform in person searches. Search fee: $5.00 per name. Required to search: name, years to search; also helpful: DOB, SSN. Criminal records on computer from Oct 1986 to present, on index books back to 1800s. Online access to criminal records is the same as civil.
General Information: Public access terminal is available. No domestic, juvenile, mental, adoption records released. SASE required. Turnaround time 1 week for accounts only. Fax notes: Fee to fax is $2.00 per page. Copy fee: $.50 per page. Certification fee: $1.50. Fee payee: Ohio County Circuit Court. Business checks accepted. Prepayment is required.

Magistrate Court Courthouse Annex, 26 15th St, Wheeling, WV 26003; 304-234-3709; Fax: 304-234-3898. Hours: 8:30AM-4:30PM (EST). *Misdemeanor, Civil Actions Under $5,000, Eviction, Small Claims.*
Civil Records: Access: In person, mail. Both court and visitors may perform in person searches. No search fee. Phone, fax and mail access limited.
Criminal Records: Access: In person, mail. Both court and visitors may perform in person searches. No search fee. Required to search: name, years to search; also helpful: DOB, SSN. Phone, fax and mail access limited.
General Information: Turnaround time 1 week.

Pendleton County

Circuit Court PO Box 846, Franklin, WV 26807; 304-358-7067; Fax: 304-358-2152. Hours: 8:30AM-4PM *Felony, Civil Actions Over $5,000, Probate.*
Civil Records: Access: Phone, fax, mail, in person. Both court and visitors may perform in person searches. No search fee. Required to search: name, years to search. Civil cases indexed by defendant, plaintiff. Civil records on index books back to 1800s.
Criminal Records: Access: Phone, fax, mail, in person. Both court and visitors may perform in person searches. No search fee. Required to search: name, years to search; also helpful: DOB, SSN. Criminal records on index books back to 1800s.
General Information: No juvenile, divorce records released. SASE required. Turnaround time 2-3 days. Fax notes: $2.00 per page. Copy fee: $.50 per page. Fee payee: Pendleton County Circuit Clerk. Personal checks accepted. Local checks accepted.

Magistrate Court PO Box 637, Franklin, WV 26807; 304-358-2343; Fax: 304-358-3870. Hours: 8:30AM-4PM (EST). *Misdemeanor, Civil Actions Under $5,000, Eviction, Small Claims.*
Civil Records: Access: In person, mail. Both court and visitors may perform in person searches. No search fee.
Criminal Records: Access: In person, mail. Both court and visitors may perform in person searches. No search fee. Required to search: name, years to search. Records computerized since 1993.
General Information: Turnaround time 5-10 days.

Pleasants County

Circuit Court 301 Court Lane, Rm 201, St. Mary's, WV 26170; 304-684-3513; Probate phone: 304-684-3542; Fax: 304-684-3514. Hours: 8:30AM-4:30PM (EST). *Felony, Civil Actions Over $5,000, Probate.*
Note: Probate is handled by County Clerk, 301 Court Lane, Room 101, St Mary's, WV 26170.
Civil Records: Access: In person only. Visitors must perform in person searches for themselves. No search fee. Required to search: name, years to search. Civil cases indexed by defendant, plaintiff. Civil records on computer from Jan 1960 to present, on index cards from 1960 to present, on index books back to 1800s.
Criminal Records: Access: In person only. Visitors must perform in person searches for themselves. No search fee. Required to search: name, years to search. Criminal records on computer from Jan 1960 to present, on index cards from 1960 to present, on index books back to 1800s.
General Information: No domestic, marriage, adoption, juvenile or mental health records released. Copy fee: $.50 per page. Certification fee: $.50 per page. Fee payee: Gail E Mote, Circuit Clerk. Personal checks accepted. Will bill to attorneys.

Magistrate Court 301 Court Lane, Rm B-6, St Mary's, WV 26170; 304-684-7197; Fax: 304-684-3882. Hours: 8:30AM-4:30PM (EST). *Misdemeanor, Civil Actions Under $5,000, Eviction, Small Claims.*
Civil Records: Access: Phone, mail, fax, in person. Both court and visitors may perform in person searches. Search fee: None, but there is a copy fee. Required to search: name, years to search; also helpful: DOB or SSN. Records go back to 1977, on computer since mid-2000. Will do some searches over the phone while caller holds.
Criminal Records: Access: Phone, mail, fax, in person. Both court and visitors may perform in person searches. Search fee: None, but there is a copy fee. Required to search: name, years to search; also helpful: DOB, SSN. Records go back to 1977, on computer since mid-2000. Will do some searches over the phone while caller holds.

General Information: Public access terminal is available. Turnaround time 1-2 days. Copy fee: $.25 per page. Fax notes: Fee to fax results is $2.00 per page. Certification fee: $.50 per page. Fee payee: Pleasants County Magistrate Court. Prepayment is required.

Pocahontas County

Circuit Court 900-D 10th Ave, Marlinton, WV 24954; 304-799-4604. Hours: 9AM-4:30PM (EST). *Felony, Civil Actions Over $5,000, Probate.*
Civil Records: Access: Phone, mail, in person. Only the court performs in person searches; visitors may not. No search fee. Required to search: name, years to search; also helpful: address. Civil cases indexed by defendant, plaintiff. Civil records on index books from 1948 to present, order books back to 1800s. Computerized records to 1995.
Criminal Records: Access: In person only, mail. Visitors must perform in person searches for themselves. No search fee. Required to search: name, years to search; also helpful: DOB, SSN. Criminal records on index books from 1948 to present, order books back to 1800s. Computerized records to 1995.
General Information: No juvenile, domestic cases involving finances, adoption, guardianship records released. SASE required. Turnaround time same day. Fax notes: Fax back $1.00 per document. Copy fee: $.50 per page. Fee payee: Clerk of Circuit Court. Personal checks accepted. Prepayment is required.

Magistrate Court 900 10th Ave, Marlinton, WV 24954; 304-799-6603/4200; Fax: 304-799-6331. Hours: 9AM-4:30PM (EST). *Misdemeanor, Civil Actions Under $5,000, Eviction, Small Claims.*
Civil Records: Access: In person only. Visitors must perform in person searches for themselves. No search fee.
Criminal Records: Access: In person only. Visitors must perform in person searches for themselves. No search fee. Required to search: name, years to search; also helpful: DOB, SSN.

Preston County

Circuit Court 101 W. Main St, Rm 301, Kingwood, WV 26537; 304-329-0047; Probate phone: 304-329-0070; Fax: 304-329-1417. Hours: 9AM-5PM M-Th, 9AM-7PM Fri (EST). *Felony, Civil Actions Over $5,000, Probate.*
Note: Probate is handled by County Clerk, 101 W Main St, Room 201, Kingwood, WV 26537.
Civil Records: Access: Phone, fax, mail, in person. Only the court performs in person searches; visitors may not. No search fee. Required to search: name, years to search. Civil cases indexed by defendant, plaintiff. Civil records on computer from 1/80 to present, on index books 1965 to 1980, chancery file from 1869 to 1965.
Criminal Records: Access: Phone, fax, mail, in person. Only the court performs in person searches; visitors may not. No search fee. Required to search: name, years to search; also helpful: DOB, SSN. Criminal records on docket books from 1869 to 1979, records on computer since 1979.
General Information: No juvenile, adoption, domestic, mental hygiene records released. SASE required. Turnaround time 1 week. Fax notes: Fee to fax results is $2.00 per page. Copy fee: $.50 per page. Fee payee: Betsy Castle, Circuit Clerk. Personal checks accepted. Prepayment is required.

Magistrate Court 328 Tunnelton St, Kingwood, WV 26537; 304-329-2764; Fax: 304-329-0855. Hours: 8:30AM-4:30PM (EST). *Misdemeanor, Civil Actions Under $5,000, Eviction, Small Claims.*
Civil Records: Access: In person, mail. Both court and visitors may perform in person searches. No search fee.

Civil records go back to 1977; computerized records since 1987.

Criminal Records: Access: In person, mail. Both court and visitors may perform in person searches. No search fee. Required to search: name, years to search; also helpful: DOB, SSN. Criminal records go back to 1977; computerized records since 1987.

General Information: Public access terminal is available. Turnaround time 1 week. Copy fee: $.25 per page. Certification fee: $.50 per page.

Putnam County

Circuit Court Putnam County Judicial Bldg, 3389 Winfield Rd, Winfield, WV 25213; 304-586-0203; Fax: 304-586-0221. Hours: 8AM-4PM M-W & F, 8AM-7PM Th (EST). *Felony, Civil Actions Over $5,000, Probate.*

Civil Records: Access: In person, online. Both court and visitors may perform in person searches. No search fee. Required to search: name, years to search. Civil cases indexed by defendant, plaintiff. Civil records on computer from 1989 to present, on index books back to 1800s. Online access to court records available via a pay service, see www.swcg-inc.com/courts.htm or call 800-795-8543. $125 set-up fee plus a $38.00 or $120 monthly fee plan.

Criminal Records: Access: In person, online. Visitors must perform in person searches for themselves. No search fee. Required to search: name, years to search; also helpful: DOB, SSN. Criminal records on computer from 1982 to present. Online access to criminal records is the same as civil.

General Information: Public access terminal is available. No divorce records released. Copy fee: $.50 per pg. Payee: Circuit Clerk. Business checks accepted.

Magistrate Court 3389 Winfield Rd, Winfield, WV 25213; 304-586-0234; Fax: 304-586-0234. Hours: 8:30AM-4:30PM (EST). *Misdemeanor, Civil Actions Under $5,000, Eviction, Small Claims.*

Civil Records: Access: In person, mail. Both court and visitors may perform in person searches. No search fee. records are computerized since 1996, overall records kept since 1977.

Criminal Records: Access: In person, mail. Both court and visitors may perform in person searches. No search fee. Required to search: name, years to search; also helpful: DOB, SSN.

General Information: Turnaround time 1 week. Certification fee: $.50.

Raleigh County

Circuit Court 215 Main St, Beckley, WV 25801; 304-255-9135; Probate phone: 304-255-9123; Fax: 304-255-9353. Hours: 8:30AM-4:30PM (EST). *Felony, Civil Actions Over $5,000, Probate.*

Note: Probate is handled by County Clerk, 215 Main St, Courthouse, Beckley, WV 25801.

Civil Records: Access: In person only. Visitors must perform in person searches for themselves. No search fee. Required to search: name, years to search. Civil cases indexed by defendant, plaintiff. Civil records on master index books from 1977; on computer back to 1997; on dockets back to 1800s.

Criminal Records: Access: Phone, mail, in person. Both court and visitors may perform in person searches. No search fee. Required to search: name, years to search; also helpful: DOB, SSN. Criminal records on master index books from 1977; on computer back to 1997; on dockets back to 1800s.

General Information: Public access terminal is available. No divorce, juvenile, adoption records released. SASE required. Fax notes: Fee to fax results is $2.00 per page. Copy fee: $.50 per page. Fee payee: Clerk of Circuit Court. Business checks accepted. Will bill to attorneys.

Magistrate Court 115 W Prince St, #A, Beckley, WV 25801; 304-255-9197; Fax: 304-255-9354. Hours: 8AM-4PM (EST). *Misdemeanor, Civil Actions Under $5,000, Eviction, Small Claims.*

Civil Records: Access: In person only. Visitors must perform in person searches for themselves. No search fee. Civil records go back to 1977.

Criminal Records: Access: In person only. Visitors must perform in person searches for themselves. No search fee. Required to search: name, years to search, offense, date of offense; also helpful: DOB, SSN. Criminal records go back to 1977, on computer back to 1992.

General Information: Public access terminal is available. (For records since 1996.) Certification fee: $.50 per page.

Randolph County

Circuit Court Courthouse, 2 Randolph Ave, Elkins, WV 26241; 304-636-2765; Fax: 304-637-3700. Hours: 8AM-4:30PM (EST). *Felony, Civil Actions Over $5,000, Probate.*

Civil Records: Access: In person only. Visitors must perform in person searches for themselves. No search fee. Required to search: name, years to search. Civil cases indexed by defendant, plaintiff. Civil records on computer from 1/91 to present. On index books back to late 1800s.

Criminal Records: Access: In person only. Visitors must perform in person searches for themselves. No search fee. Required to search: name, years to search. Criminal records on computer from 1/91 to present. On index books back to late 1800s.

General Information: Public access terminal is available. No juvenile, adoption, mental health, or guardianship records released. Copy fee: $.50 per page. Fee payee: Circuit Clerk. Personal checks accepted.

Magistrate Court #11 Randolph Ave, Elkins, WV 26241; 304-636-5885; Fax: 304-636-2510. Hours: 8AM-4:30PM (EST). *Misdemeanor, Civil Actions Under $5,000, Eviction, Small Claims.*

Civil Records: Access: In person, mail. Both court and visitors may perform in person searches. No search fee. Civil records go back to 1977; computerized records since 10/90.

Criminal Records: Access: In person, mail. Both court and visitors may perform in person searches. No search fee. Required to search: name, years to search; also helpful: DOB, SSN. Criminal records go back to 1977; computerized records since 10/90.

General Information: Public access terminal is available. Turnaround time 3 days. Copy fee: $.25 per page. Certification fee: $.50 per page.

Ritchie County

Circuit Court 115 E. Main St, Harrisville, WV 26362; 304-643-2164 x229; Probate phone: 304-643-2164 x247. Hours: 8AM-4PM (EST). *Felony, Civil Actions Over $5,000, Probate.*

Note: Probate office is located at the same address.

Civil Records: Access: Phone, mail, in person. Both court and visitors may perform in person searches. No search fee. Required to search: name, years to search. Civil cases indexed by defendant, plaintiff. Civil records on index cards from 1960 to present. On index books back to mid-1800s; on computer back to 2000.

Criminal Records: Access: Phone, mail, in person. Both court and visitors may perform in person searches. No search fee. Required to search: name, years to search; also helpful: DOB, SSN. Criminal records on index cards from 1960 to present. On index books back to mid-1800s; on computer back to 2000.

General Information: Public access terminal is available. No juvenile, mental health, adoption records released. SASE requested. Turnaround time 1-2 days.

Copy fee: $.50 per page. Fee payee: Circuit Clerk. Personal checks accepted. Prepayment is required.

Magistrate Court 319 E. Main St, Harrisville, WV 26362; 304-643-4409; Fax: 304-643-2098. Hours: 8AM-4PM (EST). *Misdemeanor, Civil Actions Under $5,000, Eviction, Small Claims.*

Civil Records: Access: In person, mail. Both court and visitors may perform in person searches. No search fee. Civil records go back to 1977; computerized from 1990. Phone, fax and mail access limited.

Criminal Records: Access: In person, mail. Both court and visitors may perform in person searches. No search fee. Required to search: name, years to search; also helpful: DOB, SSN. Criminal records go back to 1977; computerized from 1990. Phone, fax and mail access limited.

General Information: Public access terminal is available. Turnaround time 1-2 days, 1-2 hours for phone requests. Copy fee: $.25. Certification fee: $.50. Fee payee: Magistrate Court.

Roane County

Circuit Court PO Box 122, Spencer, WV 25276; 304-927-2750; Fax: 304-927-2164. Hours: 9AM-Noon, 1-4:30PM M-F; 9:30AM-Noon Sat (EST). *Felony, Civil Actions Over $5,000, Probate.*

Civil Records: Access: Phone, fax, mail, in person. Both court and visitors may perform in person searches. No search fee. Required to search: name, years to search. Civil cases indexed by defendant, plaintiff. Civil records on index books back to early 1900s; computerized records go back to 1998.

Criminal Records: Access: Phone, fax, mail, in person. Both court and visitors may perform in person searches. No search fee. Required to search: name, years to search; also helpful: DOB, SSN. Criminal records on index books back to early 1900s; computerized records go back to 1998.

General Information: Public access terminal is available. No sealed, juvenile, adoption records released. SASE not required. Turnaround time 1-2 days, less by phone. Fax notes: $1.50 for the 1st page; $1.00 per page thereafter. Copy fee: $.50 per page. Certification fee: $.50 per page. Fee payee: Beverly Greathouse. Personal checks accepted. Local checks accepted.

Magistrate Court 201 Main St, Spencer, WV 25276; 304-927-4750; Fax: 304-927-2754. Hours: 9AM-4PM (EST). *Misdemeanor, Civil Actions Under $5,000, Eviction, Small Claims.*

Note: Record requests can be directed to 304-746-2180.

Civil Records: Access: In person only. Visitors must perform in person searches for themselves. No search fee. Required to search: name, years to search. Records on computer back to 1997; prior records go back to 1976.

Criminal Records: Access: In person only. Visitors must perform in person searches for themselves. No search fee. Required to search: name, DOB; also helpful: years to search, SSN. Records on computer back to 1997; prior records go back to 1976.

General Information: Public access terminal is available. Copy fee: $.25 per page. Certification fee: $.50 per page. Fee payee: Roane County Magistrate Court. Will bill to attorneys.

Summers County

Circuit Court PO Box 1058, Hinton, WV 25951; 304-466-7103; Fax: 304-466-7124 (Attn:Circuit Court). Hours: 8:30AM-4:30PM (EST). *Felony, Civil Actions Over $5,000, Probate.*

Civil Records: Access: Phone, fax, mail, in person. Both court and visitors may perform in person searches. No search fee. Required to search: name, years to search. Civil cases indexed by defendant, plaintiff. Civil records on index books back to late 1800s; computerized records since 1998.

Criminal Records: Access: Phone, fax, mail, in person. Both court and visitors may perform in person searches. No search fee. Required to search: name, years to search; also helpful: DOB, SSN. Criminal records on index books back to 1878, computerized since 1998.

General Information: No juvenile, adoption, child abuse records released. SASE required. Turnaround time 1-2 days. Fax notes: $2.00 per page. Copy fee: $.50 per page. Certification fee: $1.00. Fee payee: Clerk of Circuit Court. Personal checks accepted. Prepayment is required.

Magistrate Court PO Box 1059, Hinton, WV 25951; 304-466-7108; Fax: 304-466-4912. Hours: 8:30AM-4:30PM (EST). *Misdemeanor, Civil Actions Under $5,000, Eviction, Small Claims.*

Civil Records: Access: Phone, fax, mail, in person. Both court and visitors may perform in person searches. No search fee. Civil records on docket books and computer back to 1998.

Criminal Records: Access: Phone, fax, mail, in person. Both court and visitors may perform in person searches. No search fee. Required to search: name, years to search; also helpful: DOB, SSN. Criminal records on docket books and computer back to 1998.

General Information: Public access terminal is available. Turnaround time 1-2 days. Certification fee: $.50 per page. Fee payee: Magistrate Court. Prepayment is required.

Taylor County

Circuit Court 214 W. Main St, Rm 104, Grafton, WV 26354; 304-265-2480. Hours: 8:30AM-Noon, 1-4:30PM (EST). *Felony, Civil Actions Over $5,000, Probate.*

Civil Records: Access: Phone, mail, in person. Both court and visitors may perform in person searches. No search fee. Required to search: name, years to search. Civil cases indexed by defendant, plaintiff. Civil records on index books back to 1844, computerized since 1996.

Criminal Records: Access: Phone, mail, in person. Both court and visitors may perform in person searches. No search fee. Required to search: name, years to search; also helpful: DOB, SSN. Criminal records on index books back to 1929, computerized since 1996.

General Information: No juvenile, adoptions, mental health records released. SASE required; any additional fee for postage is 3X the amount. Turnaround time 2 days. Fax notes: Fee to fax results is $2.00 per page. Copy fee: $.50 per page. Fee payee: Circuit Clerk. Prepayment is required.

Magistrate Court 214 W. Main St, Grafton, WV 26354; 304-265-1322; Fax: 304-265-5708. Hours: 8:30AM-4:30PM (EST). *Misdemeanor, Civil Actions Under $5,000, Eviction, Small Claims.*

Civil Records: Access: In person, mail. Both court and visitors may perform in person searches. No search fee. Overall records go back to 1976. Computerized records go back to 1992.

Criminal Records: Access: In person, mail. Both court and visitors may perform in person searches. No search fee. Required to search: name, years to search; also helpful: DOB, SSN, signed release. Overall records go back to 1976. Computerized records go back to 1992.

General Information: Public access terminal is available. Turnaround time 1-2 days.

Tucker County

Circuit Court 215 1st St #2, Parsons, WV 26287; 304-478-2606; Criminal phone: 304-746-2177; Fax: 304-478-4464. Hours: 8AM-4PM (EST). *Felony, Civil Actions Over $5,000.*

Civil Records: Access: Mail, in person. Both court and visitors may perform in person searches. No search fee. Required to search: name, years to search. Civil cases indexed by defendant, plaintiff. Civil records on index books to 1856, 1997 to present on computer.

Criminal Records: Access: Mail, in person. Both court and visitors may perform in person searches. Written requests must include a disclaimer to release clerk of responsibility. No search fee. Required to search: name, years to search, SSN; also helpful: DOB, case number. Criminal records on index books to 1956, 1997 to present on computer.

General Information: No juvenile, domestic, adoption or mental hygiene records released. SASE required. Fax notes: Fee to fax is $1.00 per page. Copy fee: $.50 per page. Fee payee: Circuit Court Clerk. Personal checks accepted. Prepayment is required.

Magistrate Court 201 Walnut St, Parsons, WV 26287; 304-478-2665; Fax: 304-478-4836. Hours: 8:30AM-4:00PM (EST). *Misdemeanor, Civil Actions Under $5,000, Eviction, Small Claims.*

Civil Records: Access: In person, mail. Both court and visitors may perform in person searches. No search fee. Civil records go back to 1977; computerized since 2/2000.

Criminal Records: Access: In person, mail. Both court and visitors may perform in person searches. No search fee. Required to search: name, years to search; also helpful: DOB, SSN. Criminal records go back to 1977; computerized since 2/2000.

General Information: Public access terminal is available. Turnaround time 3-4 days. Copy fee: $.25 per page. Certification fee: $.50 per page.

Tyler County

Circuit Court PO Box 8, Middlebourne, WV 26149; 304-758-4811; Fax: 304-758-4008. Hours: 8AM-4PM (EST). *Felony, Civil Actions Over $5,000.*

Civil Records: Access: Phone, mail, fax, in person. Both court and visitors may perform in person searches. No search fee. Required to search: name, years to search. Civil cases indexed by defendant, plaintiff. Civil records on index books back to 1800s; computerized back to 1997.

Criminal Records: Access: Phone, mail, fax, in person. Both court and visitors may perform in person searches. No search fee. Required to search: name, years to search; also helpful: DOB, SSN. Criminal records on index books back to 1864; computerized back to 1997.

General Information: No adoption, juvenile, or domestic records released. SASE required. Turnaround time 1-2 days. Fax notes: Fee to fax results is $5.00 per page. Copy fee: $.50 per page. Fee payee: Tyler County Circuit Clerk. Personal checks accepted. Prepayment is required.

Magistrate Court PO Box 127, Middlebourne, WV 26149; 304-758-2137. Hours: 9AM-4PM (EST). *Misdemeanor, Civil Actions Under $5,000, Eviction, Small Claims.*

Civil Records: Access: In person, mail. Only the court performs in person searches; visitors may not. Search fee: No search fee. Records go back to 1/1/77; on computer back to 1/1/2000.

Criminal Records: Access: In person, mail. Only the court sorforms in person searches; visitors may not. No search fee. Required to search: name, years to search; also helpful: DOB, SSN. Records go back to 1/1/77; on computer back to 1/1/2000.

General Information: Turnaround time 1 week. Copy fee: $.50 per page. Certification fee: $.50 per page.

Upshur County

Circuit Court 38 W. Main St, Rm 304, Buckhannon, WV 26201; 304-472-2370; Probate phone: 304-472-1068; Fax: 304-472-2168. Hours: 8AM-4:30PM (EST). *Felony, Civil Actions Over $5,000, Probate.*

Note: Probate is handled by County Clerk, 40 W Main, Courthouse, Room 101, Buckhannon, WV 26201.

Civil Records: Access: Fax, mail, in person. Visitors perform in person searches. No search fee. Required to search: name, years to search. Civil cases indexed by defendant, plaintiff. Civil records on index books from 1900 to present, on computer from 1/1990.

Criminal Records: Access: Fax, mail, in person. Both court and visitors may perform in person searches. Search fee: $5.00 per name. Required to search: name, years to search; also helpful: DOB, SSN. Criminal records on computer from 1/90 to present, on index books from 1947 to 1/1990, on dockets back to 1800s.

General Information: Public access terminal is available. No mental health, juvenile, adoption records released. SASE requested. Turnaround time 1-2 days. Fax notes: $2.00 per page. Copy fee: $.50 per page. Certification fee: $.50 per page. Fee payee: Circuit Clerk. Business checks accepted. Prepayment required.

Magistrate Court 38 W Main, Rm 204 Courthouse Annex, Buckhannon, WV 26201; 304-472-2053. Hours: 8AM-4PM (EST). *Misdemeanor, Civil Actions Under $5,000, Eviction, Small Claims.*

Civil Records: Access: Mail, in person. Both court and visitors may perform in person searches. No search fee. Civil records from 1977; computerized back to 1996.

Criminal Records: Access: Mail, in person. Both court and visitors may perform in person searches. No search fee. Required to search: name; also helpful: DOB, SSN. Criminal records from 1977; computer back to 1992.

General Information: Public access terminal is available. Turnaround time 1-2 days. Copy fee: $.25 + $.50 court costs. Fee payee: Magistrate Court. Prepayment is required.

Wayne County

Circuit Court PO Box 38, Wayne, WV 25570; 304-272-6359; Probate phone: 304-272-4372. Hours: 8AM-4PM M,T,W,F; 8AM-8PM Th (EST). *Felony, Civil Actions Over $5,000, Probate.*

Note: Probate is handled by County Clerk, PO Box 248, Wayne, WV 25570.

Civil Records: Access: Phone, mail, in person. Both court and visitors may perform in person searches. No search fee. Required to search: name, years to search. Civil cases indexed by defendant, plaintiff. Civil records on computer back to 1993; prior on index books from 1960 to present. Contact Circuit Clerk for books prior (to 1800s). The staff will not conduct genealogical searches.

Criminal Records: Access: In person only. Visitors must perform in person searches for themselves. No search fee. Required to search: name, years to search, SSN; also helpful: DOB. Criminal records on computer back to 1993; prior on index books from 1960 to present. Contact Circuit Clerk for books prior (to 1800s).

General Information: No juvenile, adoption, mental records released. SASE required. Turnaround time 1-2 days. Copy fee: $.50 per page. Fee payee: Clerk of Circuit Court. Business checks accepted. Prepayment is required.

Magistrate Court PO Box 667, Wayne, WV 25570; 304-272-5648/6388. Hours: 8AM-4PM (EST). *Felony, Misdemeanor, Civil Actions Under $5,000, Eviction, Small Claims.*

Civil Records: Access: phone, fax, mail, in person. Both court and visitors may perform in person searches. No search fee. Required to search: name; also helpful: years to search, DOB, SSN. Civil records go back to 1977; on computer back to 1996.

Criminal Records: Access: phone, fax, mail, in person. Both court and visitors may perform in person searches. No search fee. Required to search: name; also helpful: years to search, DOB, SSN. Criminal records go back to 1977; on computer back to 1996.

General Information: Public access terminal is available. Turnaround time 1-2 days, usually same day for phone requests. Fax notes: $2.00 per page. Certification fee: $.50 per page. Fee payee: Wayne County Magistrate Court. Prepayment is required.

Webster County

Circuit Court 2 Court Square, Rm G-4, Webster Springs, WV 26288; 304-847-2421; Fax: 304-847-2062. Hours: 8:30AM-4PM (EST). *Felony, Civil Actions Over $5,000, Probate.*

Civil Records: Access: Phone, fax, mail, in person. Both court and visitors may perform in person searches. No search fee. Required to search: name, years to search. Civil cases indexed by defendant, plaintiff. Civil records on index cards from 1977 to present.

Criminal Records: Access: Phone, fax, mail, in person. Both court and visitors may perform in person searches. No search fee. Required to search: name, years to search; also helpful: DOB, SSN. Felony dockets back to 1800s.

General Information: No mental health, juvenile, guardianship, adoption, paternity records released. SASE requested. Turnaround time 1-2 days. Fax notes: $1.00 per page. Copy fee: $.50 per page. Fee payee: Clerk of Circuit Court. Personal checks accepted.

Magistrate Court 2 Court Square, Rm B-1, Webster Springs, WV 26288; 304-847-2613; Fax: 304-847-7747. Hours: 8:30AM-4PM (EST). *Misdemeanor, Civil Actions Under $5,000, Eviction, Small Claims.*

Note: They recommend that criminal searches be directed to the Court Repository in Charleston, 304-746-2180.

Civil Records: Access: In person only. Visitors must perform in person searches for themselves. No search fee. Civil records go back to 1977; on computer since 2001.

Criminal Records: Access: In person only. Visitors must perform in person searches for themselves. No search fee. Required to search: name, years to search; also helpful: DOB, SSN. Criminal records go back to 1977; on computer since 2001.

General Information: Certification fee: $.50 per page. Fee payee: Magistrate Court Clerk.

Wetzel County

Circuit Court PO Box 263, New Martinsville, WV 26155; 304-455-8219; Fax: 304-455-1069. 9AM-4:30PM (EST). *Felony, Civil Actions Over $5,000.*

Civil Records: Access: Phone, mail, in person. Both court and visitors may perform in person searches. No search fee. Required to search: name, years to search. Civil cases indexed by defendant, plaintiff. Civil records on index books back to mid 1863; computerized back to 1996.

Criminal Records: Access: Phone, mail, in person. Both court and visitors may perform in person searches. No search fee. Required to search: name. Criminal records on index books back to mid 1863; computerized back to 1996.

General Information: No juvenile, domestic, adoption records released. SASE required. Turnaround time same day. Copy fee: $.50 per page. Fee payee: Circuit Clerk. Personal checks accepted.

Magistrate Court PO Box 147, New Martinsville, WV 26155; 304-455-5040\5171\2450; Fax: 304-455-2859. Hours: 8:30AM-4:30PM (EST). *Misdemeanor, Civil Actions Under $5,000, Eviction, Small Claims.*

Civil Records: Access: mail, fax, in person. Both court and visitors may perform in person searches. No search fee.

Criminal Records: Access: mail, fax, in person. Both court and visitors may perform in person searches. No search fee. Required to search: name, years to search; also helpful: DOB, SSN.

General Information: Turnaround time 1-2 days.

Wirt County

Circuit Court PO Box 465, Elizabeth, WV 26143; 304-275-6597; Fax: 304-275-5230. Hours: 8:30AM-4PM (EST). *Felony, Civil Actions Over $5,000, Probate.*

Note: Probate is located at a separate office at the same address, phone 304-275-4271.

Civil Records: Access: Phone, fax, mail, in person. Both court and visitors may perform in person searches. No search fee. Required to search: name, years to search. Civil cases indexed by defendant, plaintiff. Civil records on index cards from 1848 to present; computerized back to 9/2000.

Criminal Records: Access: Phone, fax, mail, in person. Both court and visitors may perform in person searches. No search fee. Required to search: name, years to search; also helpful: DOB, SSN. Criminal records on index cards from 1848 to present; computerized back to 9/2000.

General Information: No divorce, juvenile or adoption records released. SASE required. Turnaround time same day if possible. Fax notes: No fee to fax results. Copy fee: $.50 per page. Certification fee: $.50 per document. Fee payee: Wirt County Circuit Clerk. Personal checks accepted.

Magistrate Court PO Box 249, Elizabeth, WV 26143; 304-275-3641; Fax: 304-275-4882. Hours: 8:30AM-4PM (EST). *Misdemeanor, Civil Actions Under $5,000, Eviction, Small Claims.*

Civil Records: Access: Phone, in person. Both court and visitors may perform in person searches. No search fee. Civil records go back 10 years; computerized back to 9/2000.

Criminal Records: Access: Phone, in person. Both court and visitors may perform in person searches. No search fee. Required to search: name, years to search; also helpful: address, DOB, SSN. Criminal records go back 10 years; computerized back to 9/2000.

General Information: Public access terminal is available.

Wood County

Circuit Court Wood County Judicial, #2 Government Sq, Parkersburg, WV 26101-5353; 304-424-1700. Hours: 8:30AM-4:30PM (EST). *Felony, Civil Actions Over $5,000, Probate.*

Note: Probate is handled by County Clerk, PO Box 1474, Parkersburg, WV 26102.

Civil Records: Access: Phone, mail, in person. Both court and visitors may perform in person searches. No search fee. Required to search: name, years to search. Civil cases indexed by defendant, plaintiff. Civil records

on computer from 1978 to present, on index books back to 1885.

Criminal Records: Access: Mail, in person. Both court and visitors may perform in person searches. No search fee. Required to search: name, years to search, DOB, SSN. Criminal records on computer since 1979; prior records on index back to 1885.

General Information: Public access terminal is available. No juvenile, adoption, mental hygiene, guardianship records released. Turnaround time 2-3 days. Copy fee: $.50 per page. Fee payee: Carole Jones, Clerk. No checks accepted. Prepayment is required.

Magistrate Court 208 Avery St, Parkersburg, WV 26101; 304-422-3444; Fax: 304-422-2451. Hours: 8:30AM-4:30PM (EST). *Misdemeanor, Civil Actions Under $5,000, Eviction, Small Claims.*

Civil Records: Access: In person, mail. Both court and visitors may perform in person searches. No search fee. Civil records go back to 1977; computerized records since 1996. Fax and mail access limited.

Criminal Records: Access: In person, mail. Both court and visitors may perform in person searches. No search fee. Required to search: name, years to search, address; also helpful: DOB, SSN. Criminal records go back to 1997; computerized since 1996. Fax and mail access limited.

General Information: Turnaround time 10 days. Copy fee: $.25 per page. Certification fee: $.50 per page.

Wyoming County

Circuit Court PO Box 190, Pineville, WV 24874; 304-732-8000 X238; Fax: 304-732-7262. Hours: 9AM-4PM (EST). *Felony, Civil Actions Over $5,000.*

Civil Records: Access: Phone, mail, in person. Both court and visitors may perform in person searches. No search fee. Required to search: name, years to search. Civil cases indexed by defendant, plaintiff. Civil records on index books back to 1800s.

Criminal Records: Access: Phone, mail, in person. Both court and visitors may perform in person searches. No search fee. Required to search: name, years to search; also helpful: DOB, SSN. Criminal records on index books back to 1800s.

General Information: No juvenile, mental hygiene, adoption, or sealed records released. SASE preferred. Turnaround time 1-2 days, less for phone requests. Copy fee: $.50 per page. Certification fee: $.50 per page. Fee payee: Jack Lambert, Circuit Clerk. Business checks accepted. Prepayment is required.

Magistrate Court PO Box 598, Pineville, WV 24874; 304-732-8000 X218; Fax: 304-732-7247. Hours: 9AM-4PM M-Th, 9AM-6PM Fri (EST). *Misdemeanor, Civil Actions Under $5,000, Eviction, Small Claims.*

Civil Records: Access: Mail, in person. Both court and visitors may perform in person searches. No search fee. Civil records from 1977; computerized back to 1995.

Criminal Records: Access: Mail, in person. Both court and visitors may perform in person searches. No search fee. Required to search: name, years to search; also helpful: DOB, SSN. Criminal records from 1977; computerized back to 1995.

General Information: Public access terminal is available. Turnaround time 1-2 days. Fax notes: Fee to fax results is $2.00 per page. Copy fee: $.25 per copy. Certification fee: $.75. Fee payee: Wyoming County Magistrate Court. Prepayment is required.

West Virginia Recording Offices

ORGANIZATION: 55 counties, 55 recording offices. The recording officer is County Clerk. The entire state is in the Eastern Time Zone (EST).

REAL ESTATE RECORDS: Most County Clerks will not perform real estate searches. Copy fees are usually $1.50 up to two pages and $1.00 for each additional page. Certification usually costs $1.00 per document.

UCC RECORDS: Financing statements are filed at the state level, except for real estate related collateral, which are filed only with the Register of Deeds. Previous to 07/2001, collateral on consumer goods were are filed in both places, now they are only filed at the state level. Many recording offices will perform UCC searches. Use search request form UCC-11. Searches fees and copy fees vary.

TAX LIEN RECORDS: All federal and state tax liens are filed with the County Clerk. Most counties will not perform tax lien searches.

OTHER LIENS: Judgment, mechanics, lis pendens

ONLINE ACCESS: There is no statewide system open to public. One county – Monongalia – offers online access to assessor records.

Barbour County

County Clerk, 8 N. Main St, Courthouse, Philippi, WV 26416. 304-457-2232.
Will search UCC records. UCC search includes tax liens if requested. Property transfer searches available. **Other Phone Numbers:** Assessor 304-457-2336; Treasurer 304-457-2881.

Berkeley County

County Clerk, 100 W. King St, Room 1, Martinsburg, WV 25401. 304-264-1927; Fax 304-267-1794.
Will search UCC records. Will not search real estate records. **Other Phone Numbers:** Assessor 304-264-1901; Treasurer 304-264-1980; Sheriff 304-264-1980.

Boone County

County Clerk, 200 State St, Madison, WV 25130. 304-369-7337; Fax 304-369-7329.
Will search UCC records. Will not search real estate records. **Other Phone Numbers:** Assessor 304-369-7308; Treasurer 304-369-7391.

Braxton County

County Clerk, PO Box 486, Sutton, WV 26601-0728. 304-765-2833; Fax 304-765-2093.
Will search UCC records. **Other Phone Numbers:** Assessor 304-765-2805; Treasurer 304-765-2830; Elections 304-765-2833; Vital Records 304-765-2833.

Brooke County

County Clerk, 632 Main St, Courthouse, Wellsburg, WV 26070. 304-737-3661; Fax 304-737-4023.
Will search UCC records. Will not search real estate records. **Other Phone Numbers:** Assessor 304-737-3667; Treasurer 304-737-3663; Elections 304-737-3668; Vital Records 304-737-3661.

Cabell County

County Clerk, Cabell County Courthouse, 750 Fifth Ave., Room 108, Huntington, WV 25701-2083. County Clerk, R/E and UCC Recording 304-526-8625 UCC Recording: 304-526-8631; Fax 304-526-8632.
Will search UCC records. **Other Phone Numbers:** Assessor 304-526-8601; Treasurer 304-526-8672; Vital Records 304-526-8631.

Calhoun County

County Clerk, PO Box 230, Grantsville, WV 26147-0230. 304-354-6725; Fax 304-354-6725.
Will search UCC records. Will not search real estate records. **Other Phone Numbers:** Assessor 304-354-6958; Treasurer 304-354-6333.

Clay County

County Clerk, PO Box 190, Clay, WV 25043. 304-587-4259; Fax 304-587-7329.
Will search UCC records. Will not search real estate records. **Other Phone Numbers:** Assessor 304-587-4258; Treasurer 304-587-4260.

Doddridge County

County Clerk, 118 E. Court St, Room 102, West Union, WV 26456-1297. County Clerk, R/E and UCC Recording 304-873-2631.
Will search UCC records. This agency will not do a tax lien search. Will not search real estate records. **Other Phone Numbers:** Assessor 304-873-1261; Treasurer 304-873-1000; Elections 304-873-2631.

Fayette County

County Clerk, PO Box 569, Fayetteville, WV 25840. 304-574-4226.
This agency will not perform searches. **Other Phone Numbers:** Assessor 304-574-4244; Treasurer 304-574-4216.

Gilmer County

County Clerk, 10 Howard St, Courthouse, Glenville, WV 26351. County Clerk, R/E and UCC Recording 304-462-7641; Fax 304-462-5134.
Will search UCC records. Will not search real estate records. **Other Phone Numbers:** Assessor 304-462-7731; Treasurer 304-462-7441; Elections 304-462-7641; Vital Records 304-462-7641.

Grant County

County Clerk, 5 Highland Ave, Petersburg, WV 26847. County Clerk, R/E and UCC Recording 304-257-4550; Fax 304-257-2593.
Will search UCC records. Will not search real estate records. **Other Phone Numbers:** Assessor 304-257-1050; Treasurer 304-257-1818; Appraiser/Auditor 304-257-4550; Elections 304-257-4550; Vital Records 304-257-4550; Sheriff 304-257-1818.

Greenbrier County

County Clerk, PO Box 506, Lewisburg, WV 24901. County Clerk, R/E and UCC Recording 304-647-6602; Fax 304-647-6666.
Will search UCC records. This agency will not do a tax lien search. Will not search real estate records. **Other Phone Numbers:** Assessor 304-647-6615; Treasurer 304-647-6609; Elections 304-647-6606; Vital Records 304-647-6602.

Hampshire County

County Clerk, PO Box 806, Romney, WV 26757-0806. County Clerk, R/E and UCC Recording 304-822-5112; Fax 304-822-4039.
Will search UCC records. This agency will not do a tax lien search. Will not search real estate records. **Other Phone Numbers:** Assessor 304-822-3326; Treasurer 304-822-4720; Appraiser/Auditor 304-822-3326; Elections 304-822-5112; Vital Records 304-822-5112.

Hancock County

County Clerk, PO Box 367, New Cumberland, WV 26047. 304-564-3311 x281 R/E Recording: 304-564-3311 x267; Fax 304-564-5941.
This agency will not search real estate or UCC records. **Other Phone Numbers:** Assessor 304-564-3311 x212; Treasurer 304-564-3311 x239; Appraiser/Auditor 304-564-3311 x256; Elections 304-564-3311 x288; Vital Records 304-564-3311 x268.

Hardy County

County Clerk, 204 Washington St, Courthouse - Room 111, Moorefield, WV 26836. 304-538-2929; Fax 304-538-6832.
Will search UCC records. Will not search real estate records. **Other Phone Numbers:** Assessor 304-538-6139; Treasurer 304-538-2593.

Harrison County

County Clerk, 301 W. Main St, Courthouse, Clarksburg, WV 26301. 304-624-8612; Fax 304-624-8673.
Will search UCC records. Will not search real estate records. **Other Phone Numbers:** Assessor 304-624-8510; Treasurer 304-624-8550.

Jackson County

County Clerk, Court & Main Streets, PO Box 800, Ripley, WV 25271. 304-372-2011; Fax 304-372-5259.
Will search UCC records. **Other Phone Numbers:** Assessor 304-372-2011 x356; Treasurer 304-372-2011 x305.

Jefferson County

County Clerk, PO Box 208, Charles Town, WV 25414. 304-728-3215; Fax 304-728-1957.
Will search UCC records. This agency will not do a tax lien search. Will not search real estate records. **Other Phone Numbers:** Assessor 304-728-3224; Treasurer 304-728-3220; Elections 304-728-3246.

Kanawha County

County Clerk, PO Box 3226, Charleston, WV 25332. 304-357-0130 R/E Recording: 304-357-0244 UCC Recording: 304-357-0244; Fax 304-357-0585.
Will search UCC records. Will not search real estate records. **Other Phone Numbers:** Assessor 304-357-0250; Treasurer 304-357-0210; Elections 304-357-0110; Vital Records 304-357-0710.

Lewis County

County Clerk, PO Box 87, Weston, WV 26452. County Clerk, R/E and UCC Recording 304-269-8215; Fax 304-269-8202.
Will search UCC records. Will not search real estate records. **Other Phone Numbers:** Assessor 304-269-8205; Treasurer 304-269-8222; Elections 304-269-8215; Vital Records 304-269-8215; Second Phone Line 304-269-8216.

Lincoln County

County Clerk, PO Box 497, Hamlin, WV 25523. 304-824-3336; Fax 304-824-7972.
Will search UCC records. Will not search real estate records. **Other Phone Numbers:** Assessor 304-824-7878; Treasurer 304-824-3336.

Logan County

County Clerk, Stratton & Main St, Courthouse, Room 101, Logan, WV 25601. 304-792-8600; Fax 304-792-8621.
Will search UCC records. This agency will not do a tax lien search. Will not search real estate records. **Other Phone Numbers:** Assessor 304-792-8525.

Marion County

County Clerk, PO Box 1267, Fairmont, WV 26555-1267. 304-367-5441 R/E Recording: 304-367-5440 UCC Recording: 304-367-5440; Fax 304-367-5448.
Will search UCC records. This agency will not do a tax lien search. Will not search real estate records. **Other Phone Numbers:** Assessor 304-367-5410; Treasurer 304-367-5303; Appraiser/Auditor 304-367-5310; Elections 304-367-5447; Vital Records 304-367-5453.

Marshall County

County Clerk, PO Box 459, Moundsville, WV 26041. County Clerk, R/E and UCC Recording 304-845-1220; Fax 304-845-5891.
Will search UCC records. Will not search real estate records. **Other Phone Numbers:** Assessor 304-845-1490; Treasurer 304-845-1400; Elections 304-845-1220; Vital Records 304-845-1220.

Mason County

County Clerk, 200 6th St, Point Pleasant, WV 25550. County Clerk, R/E and UCC Recording 304-675-1997; Fax 304-675-2521.
Will search UCC records. **Other Phone Numbers:** Assessor 304-675-4480; Treasurer 304-675-3810; Elections 304-675-1997; Vital Records 304-675-1997.

McDowell County

County Clerk, 90 Wyoming St, Suite 109, Welch, WV 24801-2487. 304-436-8544 R/E Recording: 304-436-8549 UCC Recording: 304-436-8542; Fax 304-436-8576.
Will search UCC records. Will not search real estate records. **Other Phone Numbers:** Assessor 304-436-8564; Treasurer 304-436-8527; Appraiser/Auditor 304-436-8528; Elections 304-436-8543; Vital Records 304-436-8542.

Mercer County

County Clerk, 1501 Main St., Princeton, WV 24740. County Clerk, R/E and UCC Recording 304-487-8312; Fax 304-487-8351.

Will search UCC records. This agency will not do a tax lien search. Will not search real estate records. **Other Phone Numbers:** Assessor 304-487-8329; Treasurer 304-425-8366; Elections 304-487-8339; Vital Records 304-487-8313.

Mineral County

County Clerk, 150 Armstrong St, Keyser, WV 26726. 304-788-3924; Fax 304-788-4109.
Will search UCC records. This agency will not do a tax lien search. Will not search real estate records. **Other Phone Numbers:** Assessor 304-788-3753; Elections 304-788-3924.

Mingo County

County Clerk, PO Box 1197, Williamson, WV 25661. 304-235-0330; Fax 304-235-0565.
Will search UCC records. Will not search real estate records. **Other Phone Numbers:** Assessor 304-235-1850.

Monongalia County

County Clerk, 243 High St, Courthouse - Room 123, Morgantown, WV 26505-5491. 304-291-7230; Fax 304-291-7233.
Will search UCC records. **Online Access:** Assessor, Real Estate Records. Records on the County Parcel Search database are available free online at www.assessor.org/parcelweb. Search by a wide variety of criteria including owner name and address. **Other Phone Numbers:** Assessor 304-291-7222; Treasurer 304-291-7244.

Monroe County

County Clerk, PO Box 350, Union, WV 24983. 304-772-3096.
Will search UCC records. This agency will not do a tax lien search. Will not search real estate records. **Other Phone Numbers:** Assessor 304-772-3083; Treasurer 304-772-3018.

Morgan County

County Clerk, 77 Fairfax St, #1A, Suite 100, Berkeley Springs, WV 25411. County Clerk, R/E and UCC Recording 304-258-8547.
Will search UCC records. This agency will not do a tax lien search. Will not search real estate records. **Other Phone Numbers:** Assessor 304-258-8570; Treasurer 304-258-8562; Elections 304-258-8547; Vital Records 304-258-8547.

Nicholas County

County Clerk, 700 Main St, Suite 2, Summersville, WV 26651. County Clerk, R/E and UCC Recording 304-872-7820; Fax 304-872-9600.
Will search UCC records. Will not search real estate records. **Other Phone Numbers:** Assessor 304-872-3630 x42; Treasurer 304-872-3630 x42; Elections 304-872-7820; Vital Records 304-872-7820.

Ohio County

County Clerk, 205 City County Building, Wheeling, WV 26003-3589. 304-234-3656; Fax 304-234-3829.
This agency will not perform searches. **Other Phone Numbers:** Assessor 304-234-3626; Treasurer 304-234-3688.

Pendleton County

County Clerk, PO Box 1167, Franklin, WV 26807-0089. 304-358-2505; Fax 304-358-2473.
Will search UCC records. Will not search real estate records. **Other Phone Numbers:** Assessor 304-358-2563; Treasurer 304-358-2214.

Pleasants County

County Clerk, Courthouse, 301 Court Lane, Room 101, St. Marys, WV 26170. County Clerk, R/E and UCC Recording 304-684-3542; Fax 304-684-9315.
Will search UCC records. **Other Phone Numbers:** Assessor 304-684-3132; Treasurer 304-684-2285; Appraiser/Auditor 304-684-3542; Elections 304-684-3542; Vital Records 304-684-3542; Sheriff 304-684-2285.

Pocahontas County

County Clerk, 900C 10th Ave, Marlinton, WV 24954. 304-799-4549.
Will search UCC records. This agency will not do a tax lien search. Will not search real estate records. **Other Phone Numbers:** Assessor 304-799-4750; Treasurer 304-799-4710.

Preston County

County Clerk, 101 W. Main St, Room 201, Kingwood, WV 26537. 304-329-0070; Fax 304-329-0198.
Will search UCC records. This agency will not do a tax lien search. Will not search real estate records. **Other Phone Numbers:** Assessor 304-329-1220; Treasurer 304-329-0105.

Putnam County

County Clerk, 3389 Winfield Rd., Winfield, WV 25213-9705. 304-586-0202; Fax 304-586-0200.
Will search UCC records. This agency will not do a tax lien search. Will not search real estate records. **Other Phone Numbers:** Assessor 304-586-0206; Treasurer 304-586-0204.

Raleigh County

County Clerk, 215 Main St, Courthouse, Beckley, WV 25801. 304-255-9123 R/E Recording: 304-255-9125; Fax 304-255-9352.
Will search UCC records. Will not search real estate records. **Other Phone Numbers:** Assessor 304-255-9179; Treasurer 304-255-9300; Appraiser/Auditor 304-255-9177; Elections 304-255-9127; Vital Records 304-255-9123.

Randolph County

County Clerk, PO Box 368, Elkins, WV 26241. 304-636-0543.
Will search UCC records. This agency will not do a tax lien search. Will not search real estate records. **Other Phone Numbers:** Assessor 304-636-2114; Treasurer 304-636-2100; Sheriff 304-636-2100.

Ritchie County

County Clerk, 115 E. Main St, Courthouse - Room 201, Harrisville, WV 26362. 304-643-2164 R/E Recording: 304-643-2164 x227 UCC Recording: 304-643-2164 x227; Fax 304-643-2906.
Will search UCC records. This agency will not do a tax lien search. Will not search real estate records. **Other Phone Numbers:** Assessor 304-643-2164 x242; Treasurer 304-643-2164 x237; Appraiser/Auditor 304-643-2164 x242; Elections 304-643-2164 x228; Vital Records 304-643-2164 x227; Sheriff 304-643-2164 x237.

Roane County

County Clerk, PO Box 69, Spencer, WV 25276. County Clerk, R/E and UCC Recording 304-927-2860; Fax 304-927-2489.
Will search UCC records. Will not search real estate records. **Other Phone Numbers:** Assessor 304-927-3020; Treasurer 304-927-2540; Appraiser/Auditor 304-927-3020; Elections 304-927-2860; Vital Records 304-927-2860; Sheriff 304-927-2540.

Summers County

County Clerk, PO Box 97, Hinton, WV 25951-0097. County Clerk, R/E and UCC Recording 304-466-7104; Fax 304-466-7146.

This agency will not perform searches. **Other Phone Numbers:** Assessor 304-466-7126; Treasurer 304-466-7112; Sheriff 304-466-7112.

Taylor County

County Clerk, 214 W. Main St, Room 101, Courthouse, Grafton, WV 26354. 304-265-1401; Fax 304-265-3016. Will search UCC records. This agency will not do a tax lien search. Will not search real estate records. **Other Phone Numbers:** Assessor 304-265-2420; Treasurer 304-265-5766.

Tucker County

County Clerk, 215 First St. #3, 215 First St., Parsons, WV 26287. County Clerk, R/E and UCC Recording 304-478-2414; Fax 304-478-4464.

Will search UCC records. Will not search real estate records. **Other Phone Numbers:** Assessor 304-478-3727; Treasurer 304-478-2321; Elections 304-478-2414; Vital Records 304-478-2414.

Tyler County

County Clerk, PO Box 66, Middlebourne, WV 26149. County Clerk, R/E and UCC Recording 304-758-2102; Fax 304-758-2126.

Will search UCC records. Will not search real estate records. **Other Phone Numbers:** Assessor 304-758-4781; Treasurer 304-758-4551; Elections 304-758-2102; Vital Records 304-758-2102.

Upshur County

County Clerk, 40 W. Main St, Courthouse - Room 101, Buckhannon, WV 26201. County Clerk, R/E and UCC Recording 304-472-1068; Fax 304-472-1029.

Will search UCC records. Will not search real estate records. **Other Phone Numbers:** Assessor 304-472-4650; Treasurer 304-472-1180; Appraiser/Auditor 304-472-4650; Elections 304-472-1068; Vital Records 304-472-1068.

Wayne County

Clerk of County Commission, PO Box 248, Wayne, WV 25570. Clerk of County Commission, R/E and UCC Recording 304-272-5974; Fax 304-272-5318.

Will search UCC records. Will not search real estate records. **Other Phone Numbers:** Assessor 304-272-6357; Treasurer 304-272-6721; Vital Records 304-272-6371.

Webster County

County Clerk, Courthouse - Room G-1, 2 Court Square, Webster Springs, WV 26288-1054. 304-847-2508; Fax 304-847-5780.

Will search UCC records. This agency will not do a tax lien search. Will not search real estate records. **Other Phone Numbers:** Assessor 304-847-2110; Treasurer 304-847-2006.

Wetzel County

County Clerk, PO Box 156, New Martinsville, WV 26155-0156. County Clerk, R/E and UCC Recording 304-455-8224; Fax 304-455-5256.

Will search UCC records. Will not search real estate records. **Other Phone Numbers:** Assessor 304-455-8214; Treasurer 304-455-8218; Elections 304-455-8235; Vital Records 304-455-8224.

Wirt County

County Clerk, PO Box 53, Elizabeth, WV 26143. County Clerk, R/E and UCC Recording 304-275-4271; Fax 304-275-3418.

Will search UCC records. This agency will not do a tax lien search. Will not search real estate records. **Other Phone Numbers:** Assessor 304-275-3192; Treasurer 304-275-4222; Elections 304-275-4271; Vital Records 304-275-4271.

Wood County

County Clerk, PO Box 1474, Parkersburg, WV 26102-1474. 304-424-1850 R/E Recording: 304-424-1899 UCC Recording: 304-424-1899; Fax 304-424-1864. www.woodcountywv.com

Will search UCC records. This agency will not do a tax lien search. Will not search real estate records. **Online Access:** Recording, Deed, Wills, Death, Birth Records. Access is by dial-up modem; visit www.woodcountywv.com/modem.htm for instructions for free connection. Records go back to early 1990s. **Other Phone Numbers:** Assessor 304-424-1875; Treasurer 304-424-1910; Appraiser/Auditor 304-424-1875; Elections 304-424-1863; Vital Records 304-424-1844.

Wyoming County

County Clerk, PO Box 309, Pineville, WV 24874. 304-732-8000; Fax 304-732-9659.

Will search UCC records. Will not search real estate records. **Other Phone Numbers:** Assessor 304-732-8000; Treasurer 304-732-8000; Sheriff 304-732-8000.

West Virginia County Locator

You will usually be able to find the city name in the City/County Cross Reference below. In that case, it is a simple matter to determine the county from the cross reference. However, only the official US Postal Service city names are included in this index. There are an additional 40,000 place names that people use in their addresses. Therefore, we have also included a ZIP/City Cross Reference immediately following the City/County Cross Reference.

If you know the ZIP Code but the city name does not appear in the City/County Cross Reference index, look up the ZIP Code in the ZIP/City Cross Reference, find the city name, then look up the city name in the City/County Cross Reference. For example, you want to know the county for an address of Menands, NY 12204. There is no "Menands" in the City/County Cross Reference. The ZIP/City Cross Reference shows that ZIP Codes 12201-12288 are for the city of Albany. Looking back in the City/County Cross Reference, Albany is in Albany County.

City/County Cross Reference

ACCOVILLE Logan
ADRIAN Upshur
ADVENT Jackson
ALBRIGHT Preston
ALDERSON (24910) Greenbrier(71), Summers(18), Monroe(10)
ALKOL Lincoln
ALLEN JUNCTION Wyoming
ALLOY Fayette
ALMA Tyler
ALPOCA Wyoming
ALUM BRIDGE Lewis
ALUM CREEK (25003) Kanawha(62), Lincoln(37)
ALVY Tyler
AMEAGLE Raleigh
AMHERSTDALE Logan
AMIGO Wyoming
AMMA Roane
ANAWALT McDowell
ANMOORE Harrison
ANSTED Fayette
APPLE GROVE Mason
ARBOVALE Pocahontas
ARNETT Raleigh
ARNOLDSBURG Calhoun
ARTHUR Grant
ARTHURDALE Preston
ARTIE Raleigh
ASBURY Greenbrier
ASHFORD Boone
ASHLAND McDowell
ASHTON Mason
ATHENS Mercer
AUBURN Ritchie
AUGUSTA Hampshire
AURORA Preston
AUTO Greenbrier
AVONDALE McDowell
BAISDEN Mingo
BAKER Hardy
BAKERTON Jefferson
BALD KNOB Boone
BALLARD Monroe
BALLENGEE (24919) Summers(54), Monroe(45)
BANCROFT Putnam
BARBOURSVILLE Cabell
BARRACKVILLE Marion
BARRETT Boone
BARTLEY McDowell
BARTOW Pocahontas
BAXTER Marion
BAYARD Grant
BEARDS FORK Fayette
BEAVER Raleigh
BECKLEY Raleigh
BECKWITH Fayette
BEECH BOTTOM Brooke
BEESON Mercer
BELINGTON Barbour
BELLE Kanawha
BELLEVILLE (26133) Wood(98), Jackson(1)
BELMONT Pleasants
BELVA (26656) Nicholas(67), Fayette(25), Clay(6)

BENS RUN Tyler
BENTREE Clay
BENWOOD Marshall
BEREA Ritchie
BERGOO Webster
BERKELEY SPRINGS Morgan
BERWIND McDowell
BETHANY (26032) Brooke(97), Ohio(2)
BEVERLY Randolph
BICKMORE Clay
BIG BEND Calhoun
BIG CREEK Logan
BIG RUN Wetzel
BIG SANDY McDowell
BIG SPRINGS Calhoun
BIM Boone
BIRCH RIVER (26610) Nicholas(88), Webster(11)
BLACKSVILLE Monongalia
BLAIR Logan
BLANDVILLE Doddridge
BLOOMERY Hampshire
BLOOMINGROSE Boone
BLOUNT Kanawha
BLUE CREEK Kanawha
BLUE JAY Raleigh
BLUEFIELD Mercer
BOB WHITE Boone
BOGGS Webster
BOLT Raleigh
BOMONT Clay
BOOMER Fayette
BOOTH Monongalia
BORDERLAND Mingo
BOWDEN (26254) Tucker(66), Randolph(33)
BOZOO Monroe
BRADLEY Raleigh
BRADSHAW McDowell
BRAMWELL Mercer
BRANCHLAND (25506) Lincoln(96), Cabell(3)
BRANDONVILLE Preston
BRANDYWINE Pendleton
BREEDEN Mingo
BRENTON Wyoming
BRETZ Preston
BRIDGEPORT (26330) Harrison(94), Taylor(4)
BRISTOL (26332) Harrison(97), Doddridge(2)
BROHARD (26138) Wirt(90), Calhoun(9)
BROOKS Summers
BROWNTON Barbour
BRUCETON MILLS Preston
BRUNO Logan
BUCKEYE Pocahontas
BUCKHANNON (26201) Upshur(97), Lewis(1), Barbour(1)
BUD Wyoming
BUFFALO (25033) Kanawha(80), Putnam(19)
BUNKER HILL Berkeley
BURLINGTON (26710) Mineral(90), Hampshire(9)
BURNSVILLE (26335) Braxton(58), Gilmer(41)

BURNWELL (25034) Kanawha(50), Putnam(50)
BURTON (26562) Wetzel(67), Monongalia(32)
CABIN CREEK Kanawha
CABINS Grant
CAIRO Ritchie
CALDWELL (24925) Greenbrier(86), Monroe(13)
CALVIN Nicholas
CAMDEN Lewis
CAMDEN ON GAULEY (26208) Webster(94), Nicholas(5)
CAMERON Marshall
CAMP CREEK Mercer
CANABRAKE McDowell
CANEBRAKE McDowell
CANNELTON Fayette
CANVAS Nicholas
CAPELS McDowell
CAPON BRIDGE Hampshire
CAPON SPRINGS Hampshire
CARETTA McDowell
CAROLINA Marion
CASS Pocahontas
CASSVILLE Monongalia
CEDAR GROVE Kanawha
CEDARVILLE (26611) Braxton(53), Gilmer(46)
CENTER POINT Doddridge
CENTRALIA Braxton
CENTURY Barbour
CEREDO Wayne
CHAPMANVILLE (25508) Logan(88), Boone(11)
CHARLES TOWN Jefferson
CHARLESTON Kanawha
CHARLTON HEIGHTS Fayette
CHARMCO Greenbrier
CHATTAROY Mingo
CHAUNCEY Logan
CHESTER Hancock
CHLOE (25235) Calhoun(87), Clay(12)
CIRCLEVILLE Pendleton
CLARKSBURG Harrison
CLAY (25043) Clay(96), Nicholas(3)
CLEAR CREEK Raleigh
CLEAR FORK Wyoming
CLENDENIN (25045) Roane(50), Kanawha(46), Clay(3)
CLEVELAND (26215) Upshur(92), Webster(7)
CLIFTON Mason
CLINTONVILLE Greenbrier
CLIO Roane
CLOTHIER (25047) Boone(58), Logan(41)
COAL CITY Raleigh
COAL MOUNTAIN Wyoming
COALTON Randolph
COALWOOD McDowell
COLCORD Raleigh
COLFAX Marion
COLLIERS Brooke
COMFORT Boone
COOL RIDGE Raleigh
COPEN Braxton
CORA Logan

CORE Monongalia
CORINNE Wyoming
CORINTH Preston
COSTA Boone
COTTAGEVILLE (25239) Jackson(81), Mason(18)
COTTLE Nicholas
COVEL Wyoming
COWEN Webster
COXS MILLS (26342) Gilmer(97), Ritchie(2)
CRAB ORCHARD Raleigh
CRAIGSVILLE Nicholas
CRANBERRY Raleigh
CRAWFORD (26343) Lewis(77), Upshur(22)
CRAWLEY Greenbrier
CRESTON (26141) Wirt(72), Calhoun(27)
CRICHTON Greenbrier
CROWN HILL Kanawha
CRUM Wayne
CRUMPLER McDowell
CUCUMBER McDowell
CULLODEN (25510) Cabell(66), Putnam(21), Lincoln(11)
CUZZART Preston
CYCLONE Wyoming
DAILEY Randolph
DALLAS Marshall
DANESE Fayette
DANIELS Raleigh
DANVILLE Boone
DAVIN (25617) Logan(83), Wyoming(16)
DAVIS Tucker
DAVISVILLE Wood
DAVY (24828) McDowell(98), Wyoming(1)
DAWES Kanawha
DAWMONT Harrison
DEEP WATER Fayette
DELBARTON Mingo
DELLSLOW Monongalia
DELRAY Hampshire
DIANA Webster
DILLE (26617) Clay(86), Nicholas(13)
DINGESS Mingo
DIXIE (25059) Nicholas(93), Fayette(6)
DOROTHY Raleigh
DOTHAN Fayette
DRENNEN Nicholas
DRY CREEK Raleigh
DRYBRANCH Kanawha
DRYFORK (26263) Tucker(63), Randolph(36)
DUCK (25063) Clay(62), Braxton(37)
DUNBAR Kanawha
DUNLOW Wayne
DUNMORE Pocahontas
DURBIN Pocahontas
EAST BANK Kanawha
EAST LYNN Wayne
ECCLES Raleigh
ECKMAN McDowell
EDGARTON Mingo
EDMOND Fayette
EGLON Preston
ELBERT McDowell
ELEANOR Putnam

ELIZABETH (26143) Wirt(93), Wood(4), Jackson(1), Ritchie(1)
ELK GARDEN (26717) Mineral(79), Grant(20)
ELKHORN McDowell
ELKINS Randolph
ELKVIEW (25071) Kanawha(94), Roane(5)
ELLAMORE Randolph
ELLENBORO (26346) Ritchie(86), Pleasants(13)
ELMIRA Braxton
ELTON Summers
EMMETT Logan
ENGLISH McDowell
ENTERPRISE Harrison
ERBACON Webster
ESKDALE Kanawha
ETHEL Logan
EUREKA Pleasants
EVANS (25241) Jackson(93), Mason(6)
EVERETTVILLE Monongalia
EXCHANGE Braxton
FAIRDALE Raleigh
FAIRLEA Greenbrier
FAIRMONT Marion
FAIRVIEW (26570) Marion(80), Monongalia(19)
FALLING ROCK Kanawha
FALLING WATERS (25419) Berkeley(84), Jefferson(15)
FALLS MILL Braxton
FANROCK Wyoming
FARMINGTON Marion
FAYETTEVILLE Fayette
FENWICK Nicholas
FISHER Hardy
FIVE FORKS Calhoun
FLAT TOP Mercer
FLATWOODS Braxton
FLEMINGTON (26347) Taylor(74), Barbour(25)
FOLA Clay
FOLLANSBEE Brooke
FOLSOM Wetzel
FOREST HILL Summers
FORT ASHBY Mineral
FORT GAY (25514) Wayne(70), Logan(29)
FORT SEYBERT Pendleton
FORT SPRING Greenbrier
FOSTER (25081) Boone(91), Kanawha(8)
FOUR STATES Marion
FRAMETOWN (26623) Braxton(97), Gilmer(2)
FRANKFORD Greenbrier
FRANKLIN Pendleton
FRAZIERS BOTTOM (25082) Putnam(64), Mason(34)
FREEMAN Mercer
FRENCH CREEK Upshur
FRENCHTON Upshur
FRIARS HILL Greenbrier
FRIENDLY (26146) Tyler(94), Pleasants(5)
GALLAGHER (25083) Kanawha(96), Fayette(3)
GALLIPOLIS FERRY Mason
GALLOWAY Barbour
GANDEEVILLE Roane
GAP MILLS Monroe
GARY McDowell
GASSAWAY Braxton
GAULEY BRIDGE (25085) Fayette(65), Kanawha(35)
GAY (25244) Roane(54), Jackson(45)
GENOA Wayne
GERRARDSTOWN Berkeley
GHENT Raleigh
GILBERT Mingo
GILBOA Nicholas
GILMER Gilmer
GIVEN (25245) Jackson(88), Putnam(11)
GLACE Monroe
GLADY Randolph

GLASGOW Kanawha
GLEN Clay
GLEN DALE Marshall
GLEN DANIEL Raleigh
GLEN EASTON Marshall
GLEN FERRIS Fayette
GLEN FORK Wyoming
GLEN JEAN Fayette
GLEN MORGAN Raleigh
GLEN ROGERS Wyoming
GLEN WHITE Raleigh
GLENDON Braxton
GLENGARY Berkeley
GLENHAYES Wayne
GLENVILLE Gilmer
GLENWOOD (25520) Mason(53), Cabell(46)
GORDON Boone
GORMANIA Grant
GRAFTON Taylor
GRANT TOWN Marion
GRANTSVILLE Calhoun
GRANVILLE Monongalia
GRASSY MEADOWS Greenbrier
GREAT CACAPON Morgan
GREEN BANK Pocahontas
GREEN SPRING Hampshire
GREEN SULPHUR SPRINGS Summers
GREENVILLE Monroe
GREENWOOD (26360) Doddridge(58), Ritchie(31), Tyler(10)
GRIFFITHSVILLE Lincoln
GRIMMS LANDING Mason
GYPSY Harrison
HACKER VALLEY Webster
HALLTOWN Jefferson
HAMBLETON (26269) Tucker(93), Monongalia(6)
HAMLIN (25523) Lincoln(93), Putnam(6)
HAMPDEN Mingo
HANDLEY Kanawha
HANOVER Wyoming
HANSFORD Kanawha
HARMAN (26270) Randolph(83), Pendleton(16)
HARMONY (25246) Roane(94), Jackson(5)
HARPER Raleigh
HARPERS FERRY Jefferson
HARRISON Clay
HARRISVILLE Ritchie
HARTFORD Mason
HARTS (25524) Lincoln(80), Logan(15), Wayne(3)
HAVACO McDowell
HAYWOOD Harrison
HAZELGREEN Ritchie
HAZELTON Preston
HEATERS Braxton
HEDGESVILLE (25427) Berkeley(86), Morgan(13)
HELEN Raleigh
HELVETIA (26224) Randolph(65), Upshur(34)
HEMPHILL McDowell
HENDERSON Mason
HENDRICKS Tucker
HENLAWSON Logan
HENSLEY McDowell
HEPZIBAH Harrison
HERNDON Wyoming
HERNSHAW Kanawha
HEWETT (25108) Boone(95), Logan(4)
HIAWATHA Mercer
HICO Fayette
HIGH VIEW Hampshire
HILLSBORO Pocahontas
HILLTOP Fayette
HINES Greenbrier
HINTON Summers
HOLDEN Logan
HOMETOWN Putnam
HORNER Lewis

HUGHESTON Kanawha
HUNDRED (26575) Wetzel(88), Monongalia(11)
HUNTINGTON Cabell
HURRICANE Putnam
HUTTONSVILLE Randolph
IAEGER (24844) McDowell(80), Wyoming(19)
IDAMAY Marion
IKES FORK Wyoming
IMPERIAL JUNCTION (25034) Kanawha(50), Putnam(50)
INDEPENDENCE (26374) Preston(74), Taylor(15), Monongalia(10)
INDORE Clay
INDUSTRIAL Harrison
INSTITUTE Kanawha
INWOOD Berkeley
IRELAND (26376) Lewis(86), Braxton(13)
ISABAN McDowell
ITMANN Wyoming
IVYDALE Clay
JACKSONBURG (26377) Wetzel(61), Tyler(38)
JANE LEW (26378) Lewis(68), Harrison(31)
JEFFREY Boone
JENKINJONES McDowell
JESSE Wyoming
JODIE Fayette
JOLO McDowell
JONBEN Raleigh
JOSEPHINE Raleigh
JULIAN Boone
JUMPING BRANCH (25969) Summers(86), Raleigh(13)
JUNCTION Hampshire
JUNIOR Barbour
JUSTICE Mingo
KANAWHA FALLS Fayette
KANAWHA HEAD Upshur
KEARNEYSVILLE (25430) Jefferson(66), Berkeley(33)
KEGLEY Mercer
KELLYSVILLE Mercer
KENNA Jackson
KENOVA Wayne
KENTUCK Jackson
KERENS (26276) Randolph(68), Tucker(31)
KERMIT (25674) Mingo(70), Wayne(29)
KESLERS CROSS LANES Nicholas
KEYSER Mineral
KEYSTONE McDowell
KIAHSVILLE Wayne
KIEFFER Greenbrier
KILSYTH Fayette
KIMBALL McDowell
KIMBERLY Fayette
KINCAID Fayette
KINGMONT Marion
KINGSTON Fayette
KINGWOOD Preston
KIRBY (26729) Hampshire(82), Hardy(17)
KISTLER Logan
KOPPERSTON Wyoming
KYLE McDowell
LAHMANSVILLE Grant
LAKE Logan
LAKIN Mason
LANARK Raleigh
LANSING Fayette
LASHMEET Mercer
LAVALETTE Wayne
LAYLAND (25864) Raleigh(78), Fayette(21)
LE ROY (25252) Roane(50), Jackson(43), Wirt(6)
LECKIE McDowell
LEEWOOD Kanawha
LEFT HAND Roane
LEIVASY Nicholas
LENORE Mingo

LEON (25123) Mason(54), Putnam(45)
LERONA Mercer
LESAGE Cabell
LESLIE Greenbrier
LESTER Raleigh
LETART Mason
LETTER GAP Gilmer
LEVELS Hampshire
LEWISBURG Greenbrier
LIBERTY (25124) Putnam(89), Jackson(8), Kanawha(2)
LIMA Tyler
LINDEN Roane
LINDSIDE Monroe
LINN (26384) Gilmer(69), Lewis(30)
LITTLE BIRCH Braxton
LITTLETON Wetzel
LIZEMORES Clay
LOCHGELLY Fayette
LOCKBRIDGE Summers
LOCKNEY Gilmer
LOGAN Logan
LONDON Kanawha
LONG BRANCH Fayette
LOOKOUT Fayette
LOONEYVILLE Roane
LORADO Logan
LORENTZ Upshur
LOST CITY Hardy
LOST CREEK Harrison
LOST RIVER Hardy
LUMBERPORT Harrison
LUNDALE Logan
LYBURN Logan
LYNCO Wyoming
MABEN Wyoming
MABIE Randolph
MABSCOTT Raleigh
MAC ARTHUR Raleigh
MACFARLAN Ritchie
MADISON Boone
MAHAN Fayette
MAIDSVILLE Monongalia
MALLORY Logan
MAMMOTH Kanawha
MAN Logan
MANNINGTON (26582) Marion(95), Wetzel(3), Harrison(1)
MAPLEWOOD Fayette
MARIANNA Wyoming
MARLINTON Pocahontas
MARTINSBURG Berkeley
MASON Mason
MASONTOWN (26542) Preston(90), Monongalia(9)
MATEWAN Mingo
MATHENY Wyoming
MATHIAS Hardy
MATOAKA (24736) Mercer(88), Wyoming(11)
MAXWELTON Greenbrier
MAYBEURY McDowell
MAYSEL Clay
MAYSVILLE Grant
MC COMAS Mercer
MC GRAWS Wyoming
MC MECHEN Marshall
MC WHORTER Harrison
MEADOR Mingo
MEADOW BLUFF Greenbrier
MEADOW BRIDGE (25976) Fayette(53), Summers(42), Greenbrier(3)
MEADOW CREEK Summers
MEADOWBROOK Harrison
MEDLEY Grant
METZ (26585) Marion(74), Wetzel(25)
MIAMI Kanawha
MIDDLEBOURNE Tyler
MIDKIFF Lincoln
MIDWAY Raleigh
MILAM (26838) Hardy(78), Pendleton(21)
MILL CREEK Randolph

MILLSTONE Calhoun
MILLVILLE Jefferson
MILLWOOD Jackson
MILTON Cabell
MINDEN Fayette
MINERAL WELLS Wood
MINGO Randolph
MOATSVILLE (26405) Barbour(85),
   Preston(14)
MOHAWK McDowell
MONAVILLE Logan
MONTANA MINES Marion
MONTCALM Mercer
MONTCOAL Raleigh
MONTERVILLE Randolph
MONTGOMERY (25136) Fayette(64),
   Kanawha(35)
MONTROSE (26283) Randolph(78),
   Barbour(14), Tucker(7)
MOOREFIELD Hardy
MORGANTOWN Monongalia
MOUNDSVILLE Marshall
MOUNT ALTO (25264) Jackson(59),
   Mason(40)
MOUNT CARBON Fayette
MOUNT CLARE Harrison
MOUNT GAY Logan
MOUNT HOPE (25880) Raleigh(59),
   Fayette(40)
MOUNT LOOKOUT Nicholas
MOUNT NEBO Nicholas
MOUNT OLIVE Fayette
MOUNT STORM (26739) Grant(96),
   Berkeley(3)
MOUNT ZION Calhoun
MOUNTAIN Ritchie
MOYERS Pendleton
MULLENS Wyoming
MUNDAY (26152) Calhoun(72), Wirt(27)
MURRAYSVILLE (26153) Jackson(88),
   Wood(11)
MYRA Lincoln
MYRTLE Mingo
NALLEN (26680) Fayette(79),
   Greenbrier(16), Nicholas(4)
NAOMA Raleigh
NAPIER Braxton
NAUGATUCK Mingo
NEBO (25141) Clay(94), Calhoun(5)
NELLIS Boone
NEMOURS Mercer
NEOLA Greenbrier
NETTIE Nicholas
NEW CREEK (26743) Mineral(70),
   Grant(29)
NEW CUMBERLAND Hancock
NEW HAVEN Mason
NEW MANCHESTER Hancock
NEW MARTINSVILLE Wetzel
NEW MILTON (26411) Doddridge(89),
   Gilmer(10)
NEW RICHMOND Wyoming
NEWBERNE (26409) Gilmer(55),
   Ritchie(44)
NEWBURG Preston
NEWELL Hancock
NEWHALL McDowell
NEWTON Roane
NEWTOWN Mingo
NICUT (26633) Calhoun(62), Braxton(34),
   Gilmer(3)
NIMITZ Summers
NITRO (25143) Kanawha(75), Putnam(24)
NOLAN Mingo
NORMANTOWN (25267) Gilmer(90),
   Braxton(4), Calhoun(4)
NORTH MATEWAN Mingo
NORTH SPRING Wyoming
NORTHFORK McDowell
NORTON Randolph
OAK HILL Fayette
OAKVALE Mercer

OCEANA Wyoming
ODD (25902) Raleigh(91), Mercer(8)
OHLEY Kanawha
OLD FIELDS (26845) Hardy(88),
   Hampshire(11)
OMAR Logan
ONA Cabell
ONEGO Pendleton
ORGAS Boone
ORLANDO (26412) Lewis(72), Braxton(22),
   Gilmer(4)
ORMA Calhoun
OSAGE Monongalia
OTTAWA Boone
OVAPA (25150) Clay(50), Roane(50)
PADEN CITY (26159) Wetzel(64), Tyler(35)
PAGE Fayette
PAGETON McDowell
PALERMO Lincoln
PALESTINE Wirt
PANTHER McDowell
PARKERSBURG Wood
PARSONS (26287) Tucker(98), Preston(1)
PAW PAW (25434) Morgan(50),
   Hampshire(49)
PAX Fayette
PAYNESVILLE McDowell
PEACH CREEK Logan
PECKS MILL Logan
PEMBERTON Raleigh
PENCE SPRINGS Summers
PENNSBORO (26415) Ritchie(97), Tyler(2)
PENTRESS Monongalia
PERKINS Gilmer
PETERSBURG Grant
PETERSTOWN Monroe
PETROLEUM (26161) Ritchie(88),
   Wood(6), Wirt(4)
PEYTONA Boone
PHILIPPI Barbour
PICKENS (26230) Randolph(89),
   Webster(10)
PIEDMONT Mineral
PINCH Kanawha
PINE GROVE Wetzel
PINEVILLE Wyoming
PINEY VIEW Raleigh
PIPESTEM (25979) Summers(76),
   Mercer(23)
PLINY Putnam
POCA Putnam
POE Nicholas
POINT PLEASANT Mason
POINTS Hampshire
POND GAP Kanawha
POOL Nicholas
PORTERS FALLS Wetzel
POWELLTON Fayette
POWHATAN McDowell
PRATT Kanawha
PREMIER McDowell
PRENTER Boone
PRICHARD Wayne
PRINCE Fayette
PRINCETON Mercer
PRINCEWICK Raleigh
PROCIOUS (25164) Roane(52), Clay(47)
PROCTOR (26055) Marshall(83),
   Wetzel(16)
PROSPERITY Raleigh
PULLMAN Ritchie
PURGITSVILLE (26852) Hampshire(71),
   Hardy(21), Grant(3), Mineral(3)
PURSGLOVE Monongalia
QUINNIMONT Fayette
QUINWOOD (25981) Nicholas(51),
   Greenbrier(48)
RACHEL Marion
RACINE Boone
RAGLAND Mingo
RAINELLE (25962) Fayette(93),
   Greenbrier(6)

RALEIGH Raleigh
RAMAGE Boone
RAMSEY Fayette
RANGER (25557) Lincoln(98), Wayne(1)
RANSON Jefferson
RAVENCLIFF Wyoming
RAVENSWOOD (26164) Jackson(88),
   Wood(11)
RAWL Mingo
RAYSAL McDowell
READER Wetzel
RED CREEK Tucker
RED HOUSE (25168) Putnam(65),
   Kanawha(34)
RED JACKET Mingo
REDSTAR Fayette
REEDSVILLE Preston
REEDY Roane
RENICK Greenbrier
REYNOLDSVILLE Harrison
RHODELL Raleigh
RICHWOOD (26261) Nicholas(98),
   Greenbrier(1)
RIDGELEY (26753) Mineral(90), Marion(9)
RIDGEVIEW Boone
RIDGEWAY Berkeley
RIO (26755) Hampshire(89), Hardy(10)
RIPLEY Jackson
RIPPON Jefferson
RIVERTON Pendleton
RIVESVILLE (26588) Marion(84),
   Monongalia(15)
ROANOKE Lewis
ROBERTSBURG Putnam
ROBSON Fayette
ROCK Mercer
ROCK CASTLE Jackson
ROCK CAVE (26234) Upshur(96),
   Webster(4)
ROCK CREEK Raleigh
ROCK VIEW Wyoming
ROCKPORT Wood
RODERFIELD McDowell
ROMNEY Hampshire
RONCEVERTE (24970) Greenbrier(98),
   Monroe(1)
ROSEDALE (26636) Gilmer(46),
   Braxton(26), Calhoun(26)
ROSEMONT Taylor
ROSSMORE Logan
ROWLESBURG (26425) Preston(98),
   Tucker(1)
RUPERT Greenbrier
SABINE Wyoming
SAINT ALBANS Kanawha
SAINT GEORGE (26290) Tucker(95),
   Preston(4)
SAINT MARYS (26170) Pleasants(93),
   Ritchie(6)
SALEM (26426) Harrison(68),
   Doddridge(31)
SALT ROCK Cabell
SAND FORK Gilmer
SAND RIDGE Calhoun
SANDSTONE Summers
SANDYVILLE Jackson
SARAH ANN Logan
SARTON Monroe
SAULSVILLE Wyoming
SAXON (25180) Boone(86), Raleigh(13)
SCARBRO Fayette
SCOTT DEPOT Putnam
SECONDCREEK (24974) Monroe(89),
   Greenbrier(10)
SELBYVILLE (26236) Upshur(53),
   Randolph(46)
SENECA ROCKS Pendleton
SETH Boone
SHADY SPRING Raleigh
SHANKS Hampshire
SHARON Kanawha
SHARPLES Logan

SHENANDOAH JUNCTION Jefferson
SHEPHERDSTOWN Jefferson
SHERMAN Jackson
SHINNSTON (26431) Harrison(98),
   Taylor(1)
SHIRLEY Tyler
SHOALS Wayne
SHOCK (26638) Gilmer(94), Calhoun(5)
SHORT CREEK Brooke
SIAS Lincoln
SIMON Wyoming
SIMPSON Taylor
SINKS GROVE (24976) Monroe(91),
   Greenbrier(8)
SISTERSVILLE Tyler
SKELTON Raleigh
SKYGUSTY McDowell
SLAB FORK (25920) Raleigh(89),
   Wyoming(10)
SLANESVILLE Hampshire
SLATYFORK Pocahontas
SMITHBURG Doddridge
SMITHERS Fayette
SMITHFIELD (26437) Wetzel(91),
   Marion(8)
SMITHVILLE (26178) Ritchie(95), Gilmer(4)
SMOOT Greenbrier
SNOWSHOE Pocahontas
SOD Lincoln
SOPHIA Raleigh
SOUTHSIDE Mason
SPANISHBURG Mercer
SPELTER Harrison
SPENCER Roane
SPRAGUE Raleigh
SPRIGG Mingo
SPRING DALE Fayette
SPRINGFIELD Hampshire
SPURLOCKVILLE (25565) Lincoln(63),
   Boone(36)
SQUIRE McDowell
STANAFORD Raleigh
STATTS MILLS Jackson
STEPHENSON Wyoming
STIRRAT Logan
STOLLINGS Logan
STOUTS MILLS Gilmer
STRANGE CREEK (26639) Braxton(72),
   Clay(13), Nicholas(13)
STUMPTOWN (25280) Gilmer(55),
   Calhoun(44)
SUGAR GROVE Pendleton
SUMERCO Lincoln
SUMMERLEE Fayette
SUMMERSVILLE Nicholas
SUMMIT POINT Jefferson
SUNDIAL Raleigh
SUPERIOR McDowell
SURVEYOR Raleigh
SUTTON Braxton
SWEET SPRINGS Monroe
SWEETLAND Lincoln
SWISS Nicholas
SWITCHBACK McDowell
SWITZER Logan
SYLVESTER Boone
TAD Kanawha
TALCOTT Summers
TALLMANSVILLE Upshur
TANNER Gilmer
TAPLIN Logan
TARIFF Roane
TEAYS Putnam
TERRA ALTA Preston
TERRY Raleigh
THACKER Mingo
THOMAS Tucker
THORNTON (26440) Taylor(68),
   Preston(23), Barbour(7)
THORPE McDowell
THREE CHURCHES Hampshire
THURMOND Fayette

TIOGA (26691) Nicholas(84), Webster(15)
TORNADO (25202) Kanawha(60), Lincoln(39)
TRIADELPHIA Ohio
TROY (26443) Gilmer(84), Doddridge(15)
TRUE Summers
TUNNELTON Preston
TURTLE CREEK Boone
TWILIGHT Boone
TWIN BRANCH McDowell
UNEEDA Boone
UNION Monroe
UPPER TRACT Pendleton
UPPERGLADE Webster
VALLEY BEND Randolph
VALLEY CHAPEL Lewis
VALLEY FORK Clay
VALLEY GROVE (26060) Ohio(98), Brooke(1)
VALLEY HEAD (26294) Randolph(81), Pocahontas(18)
VAN Boone
VARNEY Mingo
VERDUNVILLE Logan
VERNER (25650) Mingo(71), Logan(28)
VICTOR Fayette
VIENNA Wood

VIVIAN McDowell
VOLGA (26238) Barbour(67), Upshur(31), Harrison(1)
VULCAN Mingo
WADESTOWN Monongalia
WAITEVILLE Monroe
WALKER (26180) Wood(93), Wirt(6)
WALKERSVILLE (26447) Lewis(96), Braxton(3)
WALLACE (26448) Harrison(93), Doddridge(4), Marion(1)
WALLBACK (25285) Clay(82), Roane(17)
WALTON Roane
WANA Monongalia
WAR McDowell
WARDENSVILLE (26851) Hardy(91), Hampshire(8)
WARRIORMINE McDowell
WASHINGTON Wood
WAVERLY (26184) Wood(85), Pleasants(13)
WAYNE Wayne
WAYSIDE (24985) Monroe(63), Summers(36)
WEBSTER SPRINGS Webster
WEIRTON (26062) Hancock(85), Brooke(14)

WELCH McDowell
WELLSBURG Brooke
WEST COLUMBIA Mason
WEST HAMLIN Lincoln
WEST LIBERTY Ohio
WEST MILFORD Harrison
WEST UNION (26456) Doddridge(92), Tyler(3), Ritchie(3)
WESTON Lewis
WHARNCLIFFE Mingo
WHARTON Boone
WHEELING Ohio
WHITE OAK (25989) Raleigh(98), Summers(1)
WHITE SULPHUR SPRINGS Greenbrier
WHITESVILLE (25209) Raleigh(82), Boone(17)
WHITMAN Logan
WHITMER Randolph
WICK Tyler
WIDEN Clay
WILCOE McDowell
WILEY FORD Mineral
WILEYVILLE Wetzel
WILKINSON Logan
WILLIAMSBURG Greenbrier
WILLIAMSON Mingo

WILLIAMSTOWN Wood
WILSIE Braxton
WILSONBURG Harrison
WILSONDALE (25699) Wayne(78), Mingo(12), Lincoln(9)
WINDSOR HEIGHTS Brooke
WINFIELD Putnam
WINIFREDE Kanawha
WINONA Fayette
WOLF PEN Wyoming
WOLF SUMMIT Harrison
WOLFCREEK Monroe
WOLFE Mercer
WOODVILLE (25572) Boone(83), Lincoln(16)
WORTH McDowell
WORTHINGTON (26591) Marion(96), Harrison(3)
WYATT Harrison
WYCO Wyoming
WYOMING Wyoming
YAWKEY Lincoln
YELLOW SPRING Hampshire
YOLYN Logan
YUKON McDowell

ZIP/City Cross Reference

24701-24701 BLUEFIELD	24848-24848 JENKINJONES	24927-24927 CASS	25028-25028 BOB WHITE
24710-24710 ALPOCA	24849-24849 JESSE	24928-24928 CLINTONVILLE	25030-25030 BOMONT
24712-24712 ATHENS	24850-24850 JOLO	24931-24931 CRAWLEY	25031-25031 BOOMER
24714-24714 BEESON	24851-24851 JUSTICE	24934-24934 DUNMORE	25033-25033 BUFFALO
24715-24715 BRAMWELL	24852-24852 KEYSTONE	24935-24935 FOREST HILL	25034-25034 BURNWELL
24716-24716 BUD	24853-24853 KIMBALL	24936-24936 FORT SPRING	25034-25034 IMPERIAL JUNCTION
24719-24719 COVEL	24854-24854 KOPPERSTON	24938-24938 FRANKFORD	25034-25034 BURNWELL
24724-24724 FREEMAN	24855-24855 KYLE	24939-24939 FRIARS HILL	25035-25035 CABIN CREEK
24726-24726 HERNDON	24856-24856 LECKIE	24941-24941 GAP MILLS	25036-25036 CANNELTON
24729-24729 HIAWATHA	24857-24857 LYNCO	24942-24942 GLACE	25039-25039 CEDAR GROVE
24731-24731 KEGLEY	24859-24859 MARIANNA	24943-24943 GRASSY MEADOWS	25040-25040 CHARLTON HEIGHTS
24732-24732 KELLYSVILLE	24860-24860 MATHENY	24944-24944 GREEN BANK	25043-25043 CLAY
24733-24733 LASHMEET	24861-24861 MAYBEURY	24945-24945 GREENVILLE	25044-25044 CLEAR CREEK
24735-24735 MC COMAS	24862-24862 MOHAWK	24946-24946 HILLSBORO	25045-25045 CLENDENIN
24736-24736 MATOAKA	24866-24866 NEWHALL	24950-24950 KIEFFER	25046-25046 CLIO
24737-24737 MONTCALM	24867-24867 NEW RICHMOND	24951-24951 LINDSIDE	25047-25047 CLOTHIER
24738-24738 NEMOURS	24868-24868 NORTHFORK	24954-24954 MARLINTON	25048-25048 COLCORD
24739-24739 OAKVALE	24869-24869 NORTH SPRING	24957-24957 MAXWELTON	25049-25049 COMFORT
24740-24740 PRINCETON	24870-24870 OCEANA	24958-24958 MEADOW BLUFF	25051-25051 COSTA
24747-24747 ROCK	24871-24871 PAGETON	24961-24961 NEOLA	25052-25052 CROWN HILL
24751-24751 WOLFE	24872-24872 PANTHER	24962-24962 PENCE SPRINGS	25053-25053 DANVILLE
24801-24801 WELCH	24873-24873 PAYNESVILLE	24963-24963 PETERSTOWN	25054-25054 DAWES
24808-24808 ANAWALT	24874-24874 PINEVILLE	24966-24966 RENICK	25057-25057 DEEP WATER
24810-24810 ASHLAND	24877-24877 POWHATAN	24970-24970 RONCEVERTE	25059-25059 DIXIE
24811-24811 AVONDALE	24878-24878 PREMIER	24973-24973 SARTON	25060-25060 DOROTHY
24813-24813 BARTLEY	24879-24879 RAYSAL	24974-24974 SECONDCREEK	25061-25061 DRYBRANCH
24815-24815 BERWIND	24880-24880 ROCK VIEW	24976-24976 SINKS GROVE	25062-25062 DRY CREEK
24816-24816 BIG SANDY	24881-24881 RODERFIELD	24977-24977 SMOOT	25063-25063 DUCK
24817-24817 BRADSHAW	24882-24882 SIMON	24980-24980 SWEET SPRINGS	25064-25064 DUNBAR
24818-24818 BRENTON	24883-24883 SKYGUSTY	24981-24981 TALCOTT	25067-25067 EAST BANK
24819-24819 CANEBRAKE	24884-24884 SQUIRE	24983-24983 UNION	25070-25070 ELEANOR
24819-24819 CANABRAKE	24886-24886 SUPERIOR	24984-24984 WAITEVILLE	25071-25071 ELKVIEW
24820-24820 CAPELS	24887-24887 SWITCHBACK	24985-24985 WAYSIDE	25075-25075 ESKDALE
24821-24821 CARETTA	24888-24888 THORPE	24986-24986 WHITE SULPHUR SPRINGS	25076-25076 ETHEL
24822-24822 CLEAR FORK	24889-24889 TWIN BRANCH	24991-24991 WILLIAMSBURG	25079-25079 FALLING ROCK
24823-24823 COAL MOUNTAIN	24891-24891 VIVIAN	24993-24993 WOLFCREEK	25080-25080 FOLA
24824-24824 COALWOOD	24892-24892 WAR	25002-25002 ALLOY	25081-25081 FOSTER
24825-24825 CRUMPLER	24894-24894 WARRIORMINE	25003-25003 ALUM CREEK	25082-25082 FRAZIERS BOTTOM
24826-24826 CUCUMBER	24895-24895 WILCOE	25004-25004 AMEAGLE	25083-25083 GALLAGHER
24827-24827 CYCLONE	24896-24896 WOLF PEN	25005-25005 AMMA	25085-25085 GAULEY BRIDGE
24828-24828 DAVY	24897-24897 WORTH	25007-25007 ARNETT	25086-25086 GLASGOW
24829-24829 ECKMAN	24898-24898 WYOMING	25008-25008 ARTIE	25088-25088 GLEN
24830-24830 ELBERT	24899-24899 YUKON	25009-25009 ASHFORD	25090-25090 GLEN FERRIS
24831-24831 ELKHORN	24901-24901 LEWISBURG	25010-25010 BALD KNOB	25093-25093 GORDON
24832-24832 ENGLISH	24902-24902 FAIRLEA	25011-25011 BANCROFT	25095-25095 GRIMMS LANDING
24834-24834 FANROCK	24910-24910 ALDERSON	25013-25013 BARRETT	25102-25102 HANDLEY
24836-24836 GARY	24915-24915 ARBOVALE	25014-25014 BEARDS FORK	25103-25103 HANSFORD
24839-24839 HANOVER	24916-24916 ASBURY	25015-25015 BELLE	25105-25105 HARRISON
24841-24841 HAVACO	24917-24917 AUTO	25018-25018 BENTREE	25106-25106 HENDERSON
24842-24842 HEMPHILL	24918-24918 BALLARD	25019-25019 BICKMORE	25107-25107 HERNSHAW
24843-24843 HENSLEY	24919-24919 BALLENGEE	25021-25021 BIM	25108-25108 HEWETT
24844-24844 IAEGER	24920-24920 BARTOW	25022-25022 BLAIR	25109-25109 HOMETOWN
24845-24845 IKES FORK	24923-24923 BOZOO	25024-25024 BLOOMINGROSE	25110-25110 HUGHESTON
24846-24846 ISABAN	24924-24924 BUCKEYE	25025-25025 BLOUNT	25111-25111 INDORE
24847-24847 ITMANN	24925-24925 CALDWELL	25026-25026 BLUE CREEK	25112-25112 INSTITUTE

25113-25113	IVYDALE
25114-25114	JEFFREY
25115-25115	KANAWHA FALLS
25118-25118	KIMBERLY
25119-25119	KINCAID
25120-25120	KINGSTON
25121-25121	LAKE
25122-25122	LEEWOOD
25123-25123	LEON
25124-25124	LIBERTY
25125-25125	LIZEMORES
25126-25126	LONDON
25130-25130	MADISON
25131-25131	MAHAN
25132-25132	MAMMOTH
25133-25133	MAYSEL
25134-25134	MIAMI
25135-25135	MONTCOAL
25136-25136	MONTGOMERY
25139-25139	MOUNT CARBON
25140-25140	NAOMA
25141-25141	NEBO
25142-25142	NELLIS
25143-25143	NITRO
25147-25147	OHLEY
25148-25148	ORGAS
25149-25149	OTTAWA
25150-25150	OVAPA
25152-25152	PAGE
25154-25154	PEYTONA
25156-25156	PINCH
25158-25158	PLINY
25159-25159	POCA
25160-25160	POND GAP
25161-25161	POWELLTON
25162-25162	PRATT
25163-25163	PRENTER
25164-25164	PROCIOUS
25165-25165	RACINE
25166-25166	RAMAGE
25168-25168	RED HOUSE
25169-25169	RIDGEVIEW
25172-25172	ROBERTSBURG
25173-25173	ROBSON
25174-25174	ROCK CREEK
25177-25177	SAINT ALBANS
25180-25180	SAXON
25181-25181	SETH
25182-25182	SHARON
25183-25183	SHARPLES
25185-25185	MOUNT OLIVE
25186-25186	SMITHERS
25187-25187	SOUTHSIDE
25189-25189	SUNDIAL
25193-25193	SYLVESTER
25201-25201	TAD
25202-25202	TORNADO
25203-25203	TURTLE CREEK
25204-25204	TWILIGHT
25205-25205	UNEEDA
25206-25206	VAN
25208-25208	WHARTON
25209-25209	WHITESVILLE
25211-25211	WIDEN
25213-25213	WINFIELD
25214-25214	WINIFREDE
25231-25231	ADVENT
25234-25234	ARNOLDSBURG
25235-25235	CHLOE
25237-25237	CLIFTON
25239-25239	COTTAGEVILLE
25241-25241	EVANS
25243-25243	GANDEEVILLE
25244-25244	GAY
25245-25245	GIVEN
25246-25246	HARMONY
25247-25247	HARTFORD
25248-25248	KENNA
25249-25249	KENTUCK
25250-25250	LAKIN
25251-25251	LEFT HAND
25252-25252	LE ROY
25253-25253	LETART
25255-25255	LETTER GAP
25256-25256	LINDEN
25258-25258	LOCKNEY
25259-25259	LOONEYVILLE
25260-25260	MASON
25261-25261	MILLSTONE
25262-25262	MILLWOOD
25264-25264	MOUNT ALTO
25265-25265	NEW HAVEN
25266-25266	NEWTON
25267-25267	NORMANTOWN
25268-25268	ORMA
25270-25270	REEDY
25271-25271	RIPLEY
25272-25272	ROCK CASTLE
25274-25274	SAND RIDGE
25275-25275	SANDYVILLE
25276-25276	SPENCER
25279-25279	STATTS MILLS
25280-25280	STUMPTOWN
25281-25281	TARIFF
25283-25283	VALLEY FORK
25285-25285	WALLBACK
25286-25286	WALTON
25287-25287	WEST COLUMBIA
25300-25396	CHARLESTON
25401-25402	MARTINSBURG
25410-25410	BAKERTON
25411-25411	BERKELEY SPRINGS
25413-25413	BUNKER HILL
25414-25414	CHARLES TOWN
25419-25419	FALLING WATERS
25420-25420	GERRARDSTOWN
25421-25421	GLENGARY
25422-25422	GREAT CACAPON
25423-25423	HALLTOWN
25425-25425	HARPERS FERRY
25427-25427	HEDGESVILLE
25428-25428	INWOOD
25429-25430	KEARNEYSVILLE
25431-25431	LEVELS
25432-25432	MILLVILLE
25434-25434	PAW PAW
25437-25437	POINTS
25438-25438	RANSON
25440-25440	RIDGEWAY
25441-25441	RIPPON
25442-25442	SHENANDOAH JUNCTION
25443-25443	SHEPHERDSTOWN
25444-25444	SLANESVILLE
25446-25446	SUMMIT POINT
25501-25501	ALKOL
25502-25502	APPLE GROVE
25503-25503	ASHTON
25504-25504	BARBOURSVILLE
25505-25505	BIG CREEK
25506-25506	BRANCHLAND
25507-25507	CEREDO
25508-25508	CHAPMANVILLE
25510-25510	CULLODEN
25511-25511	DUNLOW
25512-25512	EAST LYNN
25514-25514	FORT GAY
25515-25515	GALLIPOLIS FERRY
25517-25517	GENOA
25519-25519	GLENHAYES
25520-25520	GLENWOOD
25521-25521	GRIFFITHSVILLE
25523-25523	HAMLIN
25524-25524	HARTS
25526-25526	HURRICANE
25529-25529	JULIAN
25530-25530	KENOVA
25534-25534	KIAHSVILLE
25535-25535	LAVALETTE
25537-25537	LESAGE
25540-25540	MIDKIFF
25541-25541	MILTON
25544-25544	MYRA
25545-25545	ONA
25546-25546	PALERMO
25547-25547	PECKS MILL
25550-25550	POINT PLEASANT
25555-25555	PRICHARD
25557-25557	RANGER
25559-25559	SALT ROCK
25560-25560	SCOTT DEPOT
25562-25562	SHOALS
25563-25563	SIAS
25564-25564	SOD
25565-25565	SPURLOCKVILLE
25567-25567	SUMERCO
25568-25568	SWEETLAND
25569-25569	TEAYS
25570-25570	WAYNE
25571-25571	WEST HAMLIN
25572-25572	WOODVILLE
25573-25573	YAWKEY
25601-25601	LOGAN
25606-25606	ACCOVILLE
25607-25607	AMHERSTDALE
25608-25608	BAISDEN
25611-25611	BRUNO
25612-25612	CHAUNCEY
25614-25614	CORA
25617-25617	DAVIN
25620-25620	EMMETT
25621-25621	GILBERT
25623-25623	HAMPDEN
25624-25624	HENLAWSON
25625-25625	HOLDEN
25628-25628	KISTLER
25630-25630	LORADO
25631-25631	LUNDALE
25632-25632	LYBURN
25634-25634	MALLORY
25635-25635	MAN
25636-25636	MONAVILLE
25637-25637	MOUNT GAY
25638-25638	OMAR
25639-25639	PEACH CREEK
25643-25643	ROSSMORE
25644-25644	SARAH ANN
25645-25645	STIRRAT
25646-25646	STOLLINGS
25647-25647	SWITZER
25648-25648	TAPLIN
25649-25649	VERDUNVILLE
25650-25650	VERNER
25651-25651	WHARNCLIFFE
25652-25652	WHITMAN
25653-25653	WILKINSON
25654-25654	YOLYN
25661-25661	WILLIAMSON
25665-25665	BORDERLAND
25666-25666	BREEDEN
25667-25667	CHATTAROY
25669-25669	CRUM
25670-25670	DELBARTON
25671-25671	DINGESS
25672-25672	EDGARTON
25674-25674	KERMIT
25676-25676	LENORE
25678-25678	MATEWAN
25682-25682	MEADOR
25684-25684	MYRTLE
25685-25685	NAUGATUCK
25686-25686	NEWTOWN
25687-25687	NOLAN
25688-25688	NORTH MATEWAN
25690-25690	RAGLAND
25691-25691	RAWL
25692-25692	RED JACKET
25693-25693	SPRIGG
25694-25694	THACKER
25696-25696	VARNEY
25697-25697	VULCAN
25699-25699	WILSONDALE
25700-25779	HUNTINGTON
25801-25802	BECKLEY
25810-25810	ALLEN JUNCTION
25811-25811	AMIGO
25812-25812	ANSTED
25813-25813	BEAVER
25814-25814	BECKWITH
25816-25816	BLUE JAY
25817-25817	BOLT
25818-25818	BRADLEY
25820-25820	CAMP CREEK
25823-25823	COAL CITY
25825-25825	COOL RIDGE
25826-25826	CORINNE
25827-25827	CRAB ORCHARD
25828-25828	CRANBERRY
25831-25831	DANESE
25832-25832	DANIELS
25833-25833	DOTHAN
25836-25836	ECCLES
25837-25837	EDMOND
25839-25839	FAIRDALE
25840-25840	FAYETTEVILLE
25841-25841	FLAT TOP
25843-25843	GHENT
25844-25844	GLEN DANIEL
25845-25845	GLEN FORK
25846-25846	GLEN JEAN
25847-25847	GLEN MORGAN
25848-25848	GLEN ROGERS
25849-25849	GLEN WHITE
25851-25851	HARPER
25853-25853	HELEN
25854-25854	HICO
25855-25855	HILLTOP
25856-25856	JONBEN
25857-25857	JOSEPHINE
25859-25859	KILSYTH
25860-25860	LANARK
25862-25862	LANSING
25864-25864	LAYLAND
25865-25865	LESTER
25866-25866	LOCHGELLY
25867-25867	LONG BRANCH
25868-25868	LOOKOUT
25870-25870	MABEN
25871-25871	MABSCOTT
25873-25873	MAC ARTHUR
25874-25874	MAPLEWOOD
25875-25875	MC GRAWS
25876-25876	SAULSVILLE
25878-25878	MIDWAY
25879-25879	MINDEN
25880-25880	MOUNT HOPE
25882-25882	MULLENS
25901-25901	OAK HILL
25902-25902	ODD
25904-25904	PAX
25905-25905	PEMBERTON
25906-25906	PINEY VIEW
25907-25907	PRINCE
25908-25908	PRINCEWICK
25909-25909	PROSPERITY
25910-25910	QUINNIMONT
25911-25911	RALEIGH
25912-25912	RAMSEY
25913-25913	RAVENCLIFF
25914-25914	REDSTAR
25915-25915	RHODELL
25916-25916	SABINE
25917-25917	SCARBRO
25918-25918	SHADY SPRING
25919-25919	SKELTON
25920-25920	SLAB FORK
25921-25921	SOPHIA
25922-25922	SPANISHBURG
25926-25926	SPRAGUE
25927-25927	STANAFORD
25928-25928	STEPHENSON
25931-25931	SUMMERLEE
25932-25932	SURVEYOR
25934-25934	TERRY
25936-25936	THURMOND
25938-25938	VICTOR
25942-25942	WINONA
25943-25943	WYCO
25951-25951	HINTON
25957-25957	BROOKS
25958-25958	CHARMCO
25961-25961	CRICHTON
25962-25962	RAINELLE
25965-25965	ELTON
25966-25966	GREEN SULPHUR SPRINGS
25967-25967	HINES
25969-25969	JUMPING BRANCH
25971-25971	LERONA
25972-25972	LESLIE
25973-25973	LOCKBRIDGE
25976-25976	MEADOW BRIDGE
25977-25977	MEADOW CREEK
25978-25978	NIMITZ
25979-25979	PIPESTEM
25981-25981	QUINWOOD
25984-25984	RUPERT
25985-25985	SANDSTONE
25986-25986	SPRING DALE
25988-25988	TRUE
25989-25989	WHITE OAK
26003-26003	WHEELING
26030-26030	BEECH BOTTOM
26031-26031	BENWOOD
26032-26032	BETHANY
26033-26033	CAMERON
26034-26034	CHESTER
26035-26035	COLLIERS

ZIP Range	City
26036-26036	DALLAS
26037-26037	FOLLANSBEE
26038-26038	GLEN DALE
26039-26039	GLEN EASTON
26040-26040	MC MECHEN
26041-26041	MOUNDSVILLE
26047-26047	NEW CUMBERLAND
26050-26050	NEWELL
26055-26055	PROCTOR
26056-26056	NEW MANCHESTER
26058-26058	SHORT CREEK
26059-26059	TRIADELPHIA
26060-26060	VALLEY GROVE
26062-26062	WEIRTON
26070-26070	WELLSBURG
26074-26074	WEST LIBERTY
26075-26075	WINDSOR HEIGHTS
26101-26104	PARKERSBURG
26105-26105	VIENNA
26106-26106	PARKERSBURG
26120-26121	MINERAL WELLS
26133-26133	BELLEVILLE
26134-26134	BELMONT
26135-26135	BENS RUN
26136-26136	BIG BEND
26137-26137	BIG SPRINGS
26138-26138	BROHARD
26141-26141	CRESTON
26142-26142	DAVISVILLE
26143-26143	ELIZABETH
26144-26144	EUREKA
26145-26145	FIVE FORKS
26146-26146	FRIENDLY
26147-26147	GRANTSVILLE
26148-26148	MACFARLAN
26149-26149	MIDDLEBOURNE
26150-26150	MINERAL WELLS
26151-26151	MOUNT ZION
26152-26152	MUNDAY
26153-26153	MURRAYSVILLE
26155-26155	NEW MARTINSVILLE
26159-26159	PADEN CITY
26160-26160	PALESTINE
26161-26161	PETROLEUM
26162-26162	PORTERS FALLS
26164-26164	RAVENSWOOD
26167-26167	READER
26169-26169	ROCKPORT
26170-26170	SAINT MARYS
26173-26173	SHERMAN
26175-26175	SISTERSVILLE
26178-26178	SMITHVILLE
26179-26179	TANNER
26180-26180	WALKER
26181-26181	WASHINGTON
26184-26184	WAVERLY
26185-26185	WICK
26186-26186	WILEYVILLE
26187-26187	WILLIAMSTOWN
26201-26201	BUCKHANNON
26202-26202	FENWICK
26203-26203	ERBACON
26205-26205	CRAIGSVILLE
26206-26206	COWEN
26207-26207	COTTLE
26208-26208	CAMDEN ON GAULEY
26209-26209	SNOWSHOE
26210-26210	ADRIAN
26214-26214	CENTURY
26215-26215	CLEVELAND
26217-26217	DIANA
26218-26218	FRENCH CREEK
26219-26219	FRENCHTON
26222-26222	HACKER VALLEY
26224-26224	HELVETIA
26228-26228	KANAWHA HEAD
26229-26229	LORENTZ
26230-26230	PICKENS
26234-26234	ROCK CAVE
26236-26236	SELBYVILLE
26237-26237	TALLMANSVILLE
26238-26238	VOLGA
26241-26241	ELKINS
26250-26250	BELINGTON
26253-26253	BEVERLY
26254-26254	BOWDEN
26257-26257	COALTON
26259-26259	DAILEY
26260-26260	DAVIS
26261-26261	RICHWOOD
26263-26263	DRYFORK
26264-26264	DURBIN
26266-26266	UPPERGLADE
26267-26267	ELLAMORE
26268-26268	GLADY
26269-26269	HAMBLETON
26270-26270	HARMAN
26271-26271	HENDRICKS
26273-26273	HUTTONSVILLE
26275-26275	JUNIOR
26276-26276	KERENS
26278-26278	MABIE
26280-26280	MILL CREEK
26281-26281	MINGO
26282-26282	MONTERVILLE
26283-26283	MONTROSE
26285-26285	NORTON
26287-26287	PARSONS
26288-26288	WEBSTER SPRINGS
26289-26289	RED CREEK
26290-26290	SAINT GEORGE
26291-26291	SLATYFORK
26292-26292	THOMAS
26293-26293	VALLEY BEND
26294-26294	VALLEY HEAD
26296-26296	WHITMER
26298-26298	BERGOO
26299-26299	BOGGS
26301-26306	CLARKSBURG
26320-26320	ALMA
26321-26321	ALUM BRIDGE
26322-26322	ALVY
26323-26323	ANMOORE
26325-26325	AUBURN
26327-26327	BEREA
26328-26328	BLANDVILLE
26330-26330	BRIDGEPORT
26332-26332	BRISTOL
26334-26334	BROWNTON
26335-26335	BURNSVILLE
26337-26337	CAIRO
26338-26338	CAMDEN
26339-26339	CENTER POINT
26342-26342	COXS MILLS
26343-26343	CRAWFORD
26344-26344	DAWMONT
26346-26346	ELLENBORO
26347-26347	FLEMINGTON
26348-26348	FOLSOM
26349-26349	GALLOWAY
26350-26350	GILMER
26351-26351	GLENVILLE
26354-26354	GRAFTON
26360-26360	GREENWOOD
26361-26361	GYPSY
26362-26362	HARRISVILLE
26366-26366	HAYWOOD
26367-26367	HAZELGREEN
26369-26369	HEPZIBAH
26372-26372	HORNER
26374-26374	INDEPENDENCE
26375-26375	INDUSTRIAL
26376-26376	IRELAND
26377-26377	JACKSONBURG
26378-26378	JANE LEW
26383-26383	LIMA
26384-26384	LINN
26385-26385	LOST CREEK
26386-26386	LUMBERPORT
26401-26401	MC WHORTER
26404-26404	MEADOWBROOK
26405-26405	MOATSVILLE
26407-26407	MOUNTAIN
26408-26408	MOUNT CLARE
26409-26409	NEWBERNE
26410-26410	NEWBURG
26411-26411	NEW MILTON
26412-26412	ORLANDO
26415-26415	PENNSBORO
26416-26416	PHILIPPI
26419-26419	PINE GROVE
26421-26421	PULLMAN
26422-26422	REYNOLDSVILLE
26423-26423	ROANOKE
26424-26424	ROSEMONT
26425-26425	ROWLESBURG
26426-26426	SALEM
26430-26430	SAND FORK
26431-26431	SHINNSTON
26434-26434	SHIRLEY
26435-26435	SIMPSON
26436-26436	SMITHBURG
26437-26437	SMITHFIELD
26438-26438	SPELTER
26439-26439	STOUTS MILLS
26440-26440	THORNTON
26443-26443	TROY
26444-26444	TUNNELTON
26446-26446	VALLEY CHAPEL
26447-26447	WALKERSVILLE
26448-26448	WALLACE
26451-26451	WEST MILFORD
26452-26452	WESTON
26456-26456	WEST UNION
26461-26461	WILSONBURG
26462-26462	WOLF SUMMIT
26463-26463	WYATT
26501-26508	MORGANTOWN
26519-26519	ALBRIGHT
26520-26520	ARTHURDALE
26521-26521	BLACKSVILLE
26522-26522	BOOTH
26523-26523	BRANDONVILLE
26524-26524	BRETZ
26525-26525	BRUCETON MILLS
26527-26527	CASSVILLE
26529-26529	CORE
26530-26530	CUZZART
26531-26531	DELLSLOW
26533-26533	EVERETTVILLE
26534-26534	GRANVILLE
26535-26535	HAZELTON
26537-26537	KINGWOOD
26541-26541	MAIDSVILLE
26542-26542	MASONTOWN
26543-26543	OSAGE
26544-26544	PENTRESS
26546-26546	PURSGLOVE
26547-26547	REEDSVILLE
26554-26555	FAIRMONT
26559-26559	BARRACKVILLE
26560-26560	BAXTER
26561-26561	BIG RUN
26562-26562	BURTON
26563-26563	CAROLINA
26566-26566	COLFAX
26568-26568	ENTERPRISE
26570-26570	FAIRVIEW
26571-26571	FARMINGTON
26572-26572	FOUR STATES
26574-26574	GRANT TOWN
26575-26575	HUNDRED
26576-26576	IDAMAY
26578-26578	KINGMONT
26581-26581	LITTLETON
26582-26582	MANNINGTON
26585-26585	METZ
26586-26586	MONTANA MINES
26587-26587	RACHEL
26588-26588	RIVESVILLE
26589-26589	WADESTOWN
26590-26590	WANA
26591-26591	WORTHINGTON
26601-26601	SUTTON
26610-26610	BIRCH RIVER
26611-26611	CEDARVILLE
26612-26612	CENTRALIA
26615-26615	COPEN
26617-26617	DILLE
26618-26618	ELMIRA
26619-26619	EXCHANGE
26620-26620	FALLS MILL
26621-26621	FLATWOODS
26623-26623	FRAMETOWN
26624-26624	GASSAWAY
26626-26626	GLENDON
26627-26627	HEATERS
26629-26629	LITTLE BIRCH
26631-26631	NAPIER
26633-26633	NICUT
26634-26634	PERKINS
26636-26636	ROSEDALE
26638-26638	SHOCK
26639-26639	STRANGE CREEK
26641-26641	WILSIE
26651-26651	SUMMERSVILLE
26656-26656	BELVA
26660-26660	CALVIN
26662-26662	CANVAS
26667-26667	DRENNEN
26671-26671	GILBOA
26674-26674	JODIE
26675-26675	KESLERS CROSS LANES
26676-26676	LEIVASY
26678-26678	MOUNT LOOKOUT
26679-26679	MOUNT NEBO
26680-26680	NALLEN
26681-26681	NETTIE
26683-26683	POE
26684-26684	POOL
26690-26690	SWISS
26691-26691	TIOGA
26704-26704	AUGUSTA
26705-26705	AURORA
26707-26707	BAYARD
26710-26710	BURLINGTON
26711-26711	CAPON BRIDGE
26713-26713	CORINTH
26714-26714	DELRAY
26716-26716	EGLON
26717-26717	ELK GARDEN
26719-26719	FORT ASHBY
26720-26720	GORMANIA
26722-26722	GREEN SPRING
26726-26726	KEYSER
26729-26729	KIRBY
26731-26731	LAHMANSVILLE
26734-26734	MEDLEY
26739-26739	MOUNT STORM
26743-26743	NEW CREEK
26750-26750	PIEDMONT
26753-26753	RIDGELEY
26755-26755	RIO
26757-26757	ROMNEY
26761-26761	SHANKS
26763-26763	SPRINGFIELD
26764-26764	TERRA ALTA
26765-26765	THREE CHURCHES
26767-26767	WILEY FORD
26769-26769	EGLON
26801-26801	BAKER
26802-26802	BRANDYWINE
26804-26804	CIRCLEVILLE
26806-26806	FORT SEYBERT
26807-26807	FRANKLIN
26808-26808	HIGH VIEW
26810-26810	LOST CITY
26811-26811	LOST RIVER
26812-26812	MATHIAS
26813-26813	MOYERS
26814-26814	RIVERTON
26815-26815	SUGAR GROVE
26816-26816	ARTHUR
26817-26817	BLOOMERY
26818-26818	FISHER
26823-26823	CAPON SPRINGS
26824-26824	JUNCTION
26833-26833	MAYSVILLE
26836-26836	MOOREFIELD
26838-26838	MILAM
26845-26845	OLD FIELDS
26847-26847	PETERSBURG
26851-26851	WARDENSVILLE
26852-26852	PURGITSVILLE
26855-26855	CABINS
26865-26865	YELLOW SPRING
26866-26866	UPPER TRACT
26884-26884	SENECA ROCKS
26886-26886	ONEGO

Wisconsin

General Help Numbers:

Governor's Office
PO Box 7863
Madison, WI 53707-7863
www.wisgov.state.wi.us

608-266-1212
Fax 608-267-8983
8AM-5PM

Attorney General's Office
Justice Department
PO Box 7857
Madison, WI 53707-7857
www.doj.state.wi.us

608-266-1221
Fax 608-267-2779
8AM-5PM

State Court Administrator
Supreme Court
PO Box 1688
Madison, WI 53701-1688
www.courts.state.wi.us

608-266-6828
Fax 608-267-0980
8AM-5PM

State Archives
Archives Division
816 State St
Madison, WI 53706
www.shsw.wisc.edu/archives

608-264-6450
Fax 608-264-6486
8AM-5PM M-F, 9-4 SA

State Specifics:

Capital:	Madison Dane County
Time Zone:	CST
Number of Counties:	72
Population:	5,401,906
Web Site:	www.wisconsin.gov

State Agencies

Criminal Records

Wisconsin Department of Justice, Crime Information Bureau, Record Check Unit, PO Box 2688, Madison, WI 53701-2688 (Courier: 17 W Main St, Madison, WI 53703); 608-266-5764, 608-266-7780 (Online Questions), 608-267-4558 (Fax), 8AM-4:30PM.

www.doj.state.wi.us

Note: Sexual Offender registry is maintained by the Department of Corrections, searching is available at http://offender.doc.state.wi.us/public/.

Indexing & Storage: Records are available from July 1971 (when the agencies were required to save records) and are computerized. It takes 4 days before new records are available for inquiry. Records are indexed on inhouse computer. Records are normally destroyed after (records maintained indefinitely). 76% of all arrests in database have final dispositions recorded, 67% for those arrests within last 5 years.

Searching: Criminal record information is open to the public per statute 3-21-91. Certain statutorily-required searches require fingerprints. Include the following in your request: sex, race, full name, date of birth. Fingerprints are optional. All requests must be in writing. The following data is not released: juvenile records. All records are released, including those without dispositions.

Access by: mail, fax, in person, online.

Fee & Payment: The fee is $13.00 per individual for a name search, and only $10.00 if a fingerprint search. Non-profits made submit name saearches for $2.00 per record. If a statutorily-required search also requires an FBI fingerprint check, add $24.00. Fee payee: Wisconsin Department of Justice. Prepayment required. Personal checks accepted. Credit cards accepted at web site only.

Mail search: Turnaround time: 7 to 10 days. A self addressed stamped envelope is requested.

Fax search: Incoming fax permitted only for customers with accounts. There must be a supply of return envelopes on hand.

In person search: Records are returned by mail.

Online search: The agency offers Internet access at http://wi-recordcheck.org. An account is required. Also, there is a free Internet service for access to the state's Circuit Courts' records. However, not all counties participate. Visit http://ccap.courts.state.wi.us

Corporation Records
Limited Partnership Records
Limited Liability Company Records
Limited Liability Partnerships

Department of Financial Institutions, Division of Corporate & Consumer Services, PO Box 7846, Madison, WI 53707-7846 (Courier: 345 W Washington Ave, 3rd Floor, Madison, WI 53703); 608-261-7577, 608-267-6813 (Fax), 7:45AM-4:30PM.

www.wdfi.org

Indexing & Storage: Records are available from 1873. Any records that are not at this office are kept at the State Records Center or the State Archives, but you must go through this office for access. New records are available for inquiry immediately. Records are indexed on inhouse computer, microfilm.

Searching: Include the following in your request: full name of business. In addition to the articles of incorporation, corporation records include the following information: Annual Reports, Officers, Directors, Prior (merged) names, Reserved names and Name Changes.

Access by: mail, phone, in person, online.

Fee & Payment: ID reports are $5.00, simple copywork is $2.00 per document. Short form certificates of status are $5.00. Certified copies are $5.00 plus $.50 per page. In-person copies are $.10 do it yourself. Fee payee: Department of Financial Institutions. Prepayment required. Personal checks accepted. Credit cards accepted; Visa or MasterCard

Mail search: Turnaround time: 7 to 10 days. A self addressed stamped envelope is requested.

Phone search: No fee for telephone request. They will only give a verbal response from the on-screen information.

In person search: Turnaround time is while you wait.

Online search: Selected elements of the database ("CRIS" Corporate Registration System) are available online on the department's website at www.wdfi.org/corporations/crispix

Other access: Some data is released in database format and is available for purchase in print form, cartridge or diskette.

Expedited service: Expedited service is available for mail searches. Turnaround time: 2 days. Add $25.00 per item.

Trademarks/Servicemarks
Trade Names

Secretary of State, Tradenames/Trademarks Division, PO Box 7848, Madison, WI 53707-7848 (Courier: 30 W Mifflin St, 10th Floor, Madison, WI 53702); 608-266-5653, 608-266-3159 (Fax), 7:45AM-4:30PM.

http://badger.state.wi.us/agencies/sos

Indexing & Storage: Records are available for the past 20 years. It takes 7-14 working days before new records are available for inquiry. Records are indexed on index cards.

Searching: All information is considered public record and they will release any information they have. Note that the data is not computerized. Include the following in your request: trademark/servicemark name, name of owner, date of application.

Access by: mail, phone, fax, in person.

Fee & Payment: There is no fee to see if a mark is listed. Plain copies of one record costs $2.00. For certified copies, the cost is $6.00 minimum, depending on the number of pages in the file. Fee payee: Secretary of State. Prepayment required. Personal checks accepted. No credit cards accepted.

Mail search: Turnaround time: 7 to 10 days.

Phone search: They will pull the file and give all available information over the phone.

Fax search: Same fees apply, $2.00 per copy if returned by fax. Turnaround time in 2-3 days.

In person search: There is no public access to copier. Staff will pull cards and forms for free inspection; staff will make copies for fees listed.

Uniform Commercial Code
Federal Tax Liens
State Tax Liens

Department of Financial Institutions, CCS/UCC, PO Box 7847, Madison, WI 53707-7847 (Courier: 345 W Washington Ave 3rd Fl, Madison, WI 53703); 608-261-9548, 608-264-7965 (Fax), 7:45AM-4:30PM.

www.wdfi.org

Indexing & Storage: Records are available from 1965, if still in effect. Records 1977 to present maintained on microfiche. Records are indexed on inhouse computer.

Searching: Use search request form UCC-11. The search includes federal tax liens on businesses. Federal tax liens on individuals and state tax liens are filed at the county level, but will show up if entered on the statewide lien system. Include the following in your request: debtor name.

Access by: mail, phone, fax, in person, online.

Fee & Payment: The search fee is $10.00 per name, copies are $1.00 per page. Fee payee: Department of Financial Institutions. Prepayment required. Personal checks accepted. No credit cards accepted.

Mail search: Turnaround time: up to 5 days.

Phone search: Call for uncertified information, some data is given over the phone.

Fax search: Turnaround time is 2-7 days.

In person: Searching is available in person.

Online search: There is free Internet access for most records. Some records may require a $1.00 fee. You may do a free debtor name search at www.wdfi.org/ucc/search/.

Instant filings are available immediately.

Sales Tax Registrations

Revenue Department, Income, Sales, & Excise Tax Division, PO Box 8902, Madison, WI 53708-8902 (Courier: 125 S Webster, Madison, WI 53702); 608-266-2776, 608-267-1030 (Fax), 7:45AM-4:30PM.

www.dor.state.wi.us

Indexing & Storage: Records are available from 1963. Records are indexed on inhouse computer.

Searching: This agency will provide the data on the face of the tax permit-business name, address, tax permit number. Include the following in your request: business name, tax permit number.

Access by: mail, phone, in person.

Fee & Payment: There is no search fee, no copy fee.

Mail search: Turnaround time: 2 to 3 weeks. A self addressed stamped envelope is requested.

Phone search: Records are available by phone.

In person: Searching is available in person.

Birth Certificates

The Center of Health Statistics, Vital Records, PO Box 309, Madison, WI 53701-0309 (Courier: One W Wilson St, Room 158, Madison, WI 53702); 608-266-1373, 608-266-1371 (Recording), 608-267-7820 (Genealogy), 608-255-2035 (Fax), 8AM-4:15PM.

www.dhfs.state.wi.us/VitalRecords

Indexing & Storage: Records are available from 1907 on. This office has the original records. The county of issue has a copy. New records are available for inquiry immediately. Records are indexed on microfiche.

Searching: Must have a signed release from person of record or immediate family member and include the reason for the inquiry for certified copies. Uncertified copy requests do not require a release or a reason, but cannot be expedited. Include the following in your request: full name, names of parents, mother's maiden name, date of birth, place of birth, relationship to person of record, reason for information request.

Access by: mail, fax, in person.

Fee & Payment: The fee is $12.00 per name. Add $3.00 per name per copy for additional copies. Uncertified copies are the same price. Fee payee: Vital Records. Prepayment required. Credit cards are for fax service only. Personal checks accepted. Credit cards accepted: MasterCard, Visa, AmEx, Discover.

Mail search: Turnaround time: 2 weeks. A self addressed stamped envelope is requested.

Fax search: See expedited service.

In person search: Turnaround time 2 to 4 hours.

Expedited service: Expedited service is available for fax searches. There is an additional $6.00 for use of a credit card and $15.50 for overnight shipping.

Death Records

The Center of Health Statistics, Vital Records, PO Box 309, Madison, WI 53701-0309 (Courier: One W Wilson St, Room 158, Madison, WI 53702); 608-266-1373, 608-266-1371 (Recording), 608-267-7820 (Genealogy), 608-255-2035 (Fax), 8AM-4:15PM.

www.dhfs.state.wi.us/VitalRecords

Indexing & Storage: Records are available from 1907 on. This office has the original records. The county of issue has a copy. New records are available for inquiry immediately. Records are indexed on microfiche.

Searching: Must have a signed release from immediate family member for certified copies. Uncertified copy requests do not require a release. Include the following in your request: full name, date of death, place of death, relationship to person of record, reason for information request.

Access by: mail, fax, in person.

Fee & Payment: The fee is $7.00 per name search. Add $3.00 per name per copy for additional copies. Uncertified copies are the same fee, but cannot be expedited. Fee payee: Vital Records. Prepayment required. Credit cards fax service only. Personal checks accepted. Credit cards accepted: MasterCard, Visa, AmEx, Discover.

Mail search: Turnaround time: 5 to 10 working days. A self addressed stamped envelope is requested.

Fax search: See expedited service.

In person search: Turnaround time 2 to 4 hours.

Expedited service: Expedited service is available for fax searches. The credit card fee is $6.00 and the overnight shipping fee is $15.50.

Marriage Certificates

The Center of Health Statistics, Vital Records, PO Box 309, Madison, WI 53701-0309 (Courier: One W Wilson St, Room 158, Madison, WI 53702); 608-266-1373, 608-266-1371 (Recording), 608-267-7820 (Genealogy), 608-255-2035 (Fax), 8AM-4:15PM.

www.dhfs.state.wi.us/VitalRecords

Indexing & Storage: Records are available from 1907 on. This office has the original records. The county of issue has a copy. New records are available for inquiry immediately. Records are indexed on microfiche.

Searching: Must have a signed release from the named parties for certified copies. Requests for uncertified copies do not require a release. Include the following in your request: names of husband and wife, date of marriage, place or county of marriage, reason for information request.

Access by: mail, fax, in person.

Fee & Payment: The fee is $7.00 per name search. Add $3.00 per name per copy for additional copies. The fee is the same for uncertified copies, but cannot be expedited. Fee payee: Vital Records. Prepayment required. Credit cards accepted for fax service only. Personal checks accepted. Credit cards accepted: MasterCard, Visa, AmEx, Discover.

Mail search: Turnaround time: 5 to 10 working days. A self addressed stamped envelope is requested.

Fax search: See expedited service.

In person search: Turnaround time 2 to 4 hours.

Expedited service: Available for fax requests. Using a credit card ($6.00 extra) required. Overnight shipping is $15.50.

Divorce Records

The Center of Health Statistics, Vital Records, PO Box 309, Madison, WI 53701-0309 (Courier: One W Wilson St, Room 158, Madison, WI 53702); 608-266-1373, 608-266-1371 (Recording), 608-267-7820 (Genealogy), 608-255-2035 (Fax), 8AM-4:15PM.

www.dhfs.state.wi.us/VitalRecords

Indexing & Storage: Records are available from 1907. Please note that this office does not house records for the years 1987, 1988 and 1989. You must search at the county level for those years. New records are available for inquiry immediately. Records are indexed on microfiche.

Searching: Must have a signed release form from the persons of record for a certified copy. Requests for uncertified copies do not require a release. Include the following in your request: names of husband and wife, date of divorce, place of divorce, case number (if known), reason for information request.

Access by: mail, fax, in person.

Fee & Payment: The fee is $7.00 per name search. Add $3.00 per name per copy for additional copies. Uncertified copies are the same fee, but cannot be expedited. Fee payee: Vital Records. Prepayment required. Credit cards accepted for fax service only. Personal checks accepted. Credit cards accepted: MasterCard, Visa, AmEx, Discover.

Mail search: Turnaround time: 5 to 10 working days. A self addressed stamped envelope is requested.

Fax search: See expedited service.

In person search: Turnaround time 2 to 4 hours.

Expedited service: Expedited service is available for fax searches. Using a credit card (extra $6.00) is required. The overnight shipping fee is $15.50.

Workers' Compensation Records

Dept of Workforce Development, Worker's Compensation Division, PO Box 7901, Madison, WI 53707-7901 (Courier: 201 E Washington Ave, Madison, WI 53707); 608-266-1340, 7:45AM-4:30PM.

www.dwd.state.wi.us/wc

Indexing & Storage: Records are available for 12 years from last benefit payment. New records are available for inquiry immediately. Records are indexed on microfilm, inhouse computer. Records are normally destroyed after 12 years if they are inactive. May be on microfilm if there was activity in the last couple of years.

Searching: Must have release from claimant or be a party to the claim. Must also specify what records you request. Include the following in your request: claimant name, date of accident, employer. Also, submit either the claim number or the SSN. It is suggested to call first so that they can locate records.

Access by: mail, in person.

Fee & Payment: There is a $3.00 service fee plus $.20 per copy fee, $2.00 if certified. Fee payee: Workforce Department. Prepayment required. Personal checks accepted. No credit cards accepted.

Mail search: Turnaround time: 1 to 2 weeks. A self addressed stamped envelope is requested.

In person search: If you make the copies, the fee is $.10 per page, but you must BRING YOUR OWN DIMES. They will not make change. Certification is not available for walk-ins.

Driver Records

Division of Motor Vehicles, Records & Licensing Info. Section, PO Box 7995, Madison, WI 53707-7995 (Courier: 4802 Sheboygan Ave, Room 350, Madison, WI 53707); 608-266-2353, 608-267-3636 (Fax), 7:30AM-5:15PM.

www.dot.state.wi.us

Note: Copies of tickets may be obtained from this address for $3.50 per citation.

Indexing & Storage: Records are available for 5 years from date of conviction for moving violations and suspensions/revocations, 55 years from date of convictions for alcohol-related violations, and 20 years withdrawal based on damage judgment. It takes no more than 15 days before new records are available for inquiry.

Searching: Driver record information can be obtained per DPPA guidelines. Casual requesters must submit Form MV2896 which requires signature of the subject. This form amy be downloaded from the web. The driver license number, or full name, DOB and sex are required when ordering a record. The driver's address is included as part of the search for approved requesters. The following data is not released: ID card information, juvenile record entries, arrests and medical information.

Access by: mail, phone, online.

Fee & Payment: The fee is $5.00 per driving record. Fee payee: Division of Motor Vehicles. Prepayment required. Personal checks accepted. No credit cards accepted.

Mail search: Turnaround time: 5 business days. The Employer Notification program provides an employee's MVR when an accident conviction, suspension, revocation or out of service order occurs. Cost is $20.00 to sign up and $2.00 when record mailed. Call 608-266-2353 to set up the program.

Phone search: Pre-approved accounts may order driving records by phone or fax. The fee is $6.00 if a human operator reads back the record or $5.00 for a digitized computer readback of record.

Online search: Commercial online access is available for high volume users only, fee is $5.00 per record. Call 608-266-2353 for more information.

Other access: Wisconsin offers a magnetic tape retrieval system for high volume users. The state will, also, sell its license file without histories to qualified entities. For more information, call 608-266-1951.

Vehicle Ownership
Vehicle Identification

Department of Transportation, Vehicle Records Section, PO Box 7911, Madison, WI 53707-7911 (Courier: 4802 Sheboygan Ave, Room 205, Madison, WI 53707); 608-266-3666, 608-266-1466 (Registration Laws), 608-267-6966 (Fax), 7:30AM-4:30PM.

www.dot.state.wi.us

Indexing & Storage: Records are available for 7 years to present. It takes 10 to 15 days before new records are available for inquiry.

Searching: All DPPA restrictions apply. All casual or occasional requestors must submit a request form MV2896. If the request is not for a permissible use, the subject's signature is necessary. The state no longer offers in-person access to records. Depending on what record is required, records can be looked up by VIN, plate or by name & city or county.

Access by: mail.

Fee & Payment: The fee is $5.00 per record, including lien searches. An additional $5.00 is charged for certification. The photocopy fee is $.25 per page. Fee payee: Registration Fee Trust. Prepayment required. Personal checks accepted. No credit cards accepted.

Mail search: Turnaround time: 5 business days. A self addressed stamped envelope is requested.

Other access: The state offers a variety of methods of obtaining bulk registration lists on cartridge and microfiche. FTP output by a specific request list is available only to law enforcement. Call 608-266-2064 for more information. All DPPA restrictions apply.

Accident Reports

Division of Motor Vehicles, Traffic Accident Section, PO Box 7919, Madison, WI 53707-7919 (Courier: 4802 Sheboygan Ave, Room 804, Madison, WI 53707); 608-266-8753, 608-267-0606 (Fax), 7:30AM-4:30PM.

www.dot.state.wi.us

Indexing & Storage: Records are available for 4 years to present. It takes 30 days, on average, from receipt of report before new records are available for inquiry.

Searching: The information is public record. Records can be accessed by driver license number, by plate number, or by accident report number. If none of these items are available, the full name, DOB, and date of accident will be used. The following data is not released: juvenile records.

Access by: mail, in person.

Fee & Payment: The fees are $6.00 for operator reports and $6.00 for police reports. Fee payee: Registration Fee Trust. Prepayment is required if

charges are above $6.00. Personal checks accepted. No credit cards accepted.

Mail search: Turnaround time: 24 to 48 hours. No self addressed stamped envelope is required.

In person search: Normal turnaround time is immediate.

Vessel Ownership
Vessel Registration

Department of Natural Resources, Boat Registration, PO Box 7236, Madison, WI 53707-7924 (Courier: 101 S Webster, Madison, WI 53703); 608-266-2107, 608-264-6130 (Fax), 7:45AM-4:30PM.

www.dnr.state.wi.us

Indexing & Storage: Records are available from 1978 to present. Records are indexed on computer. All motorized boats and all sailboats must be registered. All motorized boats and all sailboats, if 16 ft or over, must be titled. Lien information shows on title records.

Searching: To search one of the following is required: name, hull ID #, or boat registration #.

Access by: mail, phone, fax, in person.

Fee & Payment: There is no search fee unless the search is really involved, in which case the fee is $5.00 per name. Fee payee: DNR. Personal checks accepted. No credit cards accepted.

Mail search: Turnaround time: 1 to 2 days. No self addressed stamped envelope is required.

Phone search: Records are available by phone.

Fax search: Same criteria as mail searching.

In person search: Unless the search is a simple record check, records are returned by mail the next day.

Legislation Records

Wisconsin Legislation, Legislative Reference Bureau, PO Box 2037, Madison, WI 53701-2037 (Courier: 100 N. Hamilton Street, Madison, WI 53703); 608-266-0341, 800-362-9472 (Bill Status), 608-266-5648 (Fax), 7:45AM-5PM.

www.legis.state.wi.us

Note: Call first if you need bill number or act number and they will find it for you. Then you must call or go to Legislative Document Room 608, 608-266-2400, for actual copies.

Indexing & Storage: Records are available from 1848 on. Records are computerized since 1995.

Searching: Drafts are not available. Include the following in your request: bill number, topic of bill.

Access by: mail, phone, in person, online.

Fee & Payment: There is no search fee. Fee payee: Wisconsin Legislature. Personal checks accepted. No credit cards accepted.

Mail search: Turnaround time: variable. No self addressed stamped envelope is required.

Phone search: There is a nominal fee for microfiche or paper copies.

In person search: Searching is available in person.

Online search: Information on current bills is available over the Internet. There is a Folio Program to search text of previous session bills.

Voter Registration
Records not maintained by a state level agency.

Note: All records are maintained at the municipal level. Although records are open to the public be advised that not all municipalities maintain voter lists. Not all voters are registered.

GED Certificates

Department of Public Instruction, GED Program, PO Box 7841, Madison, WI 53707-7841 (Courier: 125 S Webster, Madison, WI 53707); 608-267-9245, 800-441-4563, 608-264-9552 (Fax).

www.dpi.state.wi.us

Searching: To search, the SSN and DOB are required. For a transcript, include a signed release.

Access by: mail, phone, fax, in person.

Fee & Payment: There is no fee.

Mail search: Turnaround time: 1 week. No self addressed stamped envelope is required.

Phone search: A requester can leave a message, with all required data, and the agency will call back with verification.

Fax search: Same criteria as mail searching.

In person search: Searching is available in person.

Hunting License Information
Fishing License Information
Access to Records is Restricted

Fish & Game Licensing Division, Records Manager - CS/G3, PO Box 7924, Madison, WI 53707 (Courier: 101 S Webster St, Madison, WI 53703); 608-266-2621, 608-261-0770 (List Sales), 608-261-4380 (Fax), 8AM-4:30PM.

www.dnr.state.wi.us

Note: They do not provide name searching, but will sell lists by license type. There is an opt out provision in place, and 50% of the licensees have opted out.

Wisconsin State Licensing Agencies

Licenses Searchable Online

Accounting Firm #2 .... http://drlchq.state.wi.us/plsql/chq/cred_holder_query
Acupuncturist #4 .... http://165.189.238.43/plsql/plsql/Search_Ind_Health
Adjustment Service Company #6 .... www.wdfi.org/fi/lfs/licensee_lists
Aesthetics Establishment/Specialty School #2 .... http://drlchq.state.wi.us/plsql/chq/cred_holder_query
Aesthetics Instructor #1 .... http://165.189.238.43/plsql/plsql/Search_Ind_Bdp
Ambulance Service Provider #7 .... www.dhfs.state.wi.us/reg_licens/dohprog/ems/provider/wicounties.htm
Appraiser, General #1 .... http://165.189.238.43/plsql/plsql/Search_Ind_Bdp
Appraiser, Residential #1 .... http://165.189.238.43/plsql/plsql/Search_Ind_Bdp
Architect #1 .... http://165.189.238.43/plsql/plsql/Search_Ind_Bdp
Architectural Corporation #2 .... http://drlchq.state.wi.us/plsql/chq/cred_holder_query
Art Therapist #4 .... http://165.189.238.43/plsql/plsql/Search_Ind_Health
Attorney #16 .... www.wisbar.org
Auction Company #2 .... http://drlchq.state.wi.us/plsql/chq/cred_holder_query
Auctioneer #1 .... http://165.189.238.43/plsql/plsql/Search_Ind_Bdp
Audiologist #4 .... http://165.189.238.43/plsql/plsql/Search_Ind_Health
Bank #5 .... www.wdfi.org/fi/savings_institutions/licensee_lists/
Barber #1 .... http://165.189.238.43/plsql/plsql/Search_Ind_Bdp
Barber School #2 .... http://drlchq.state.wi.us/plsql/chq/cred_holder_query
Barber/Apprentice/Instructor/Manager #1 .... http://165.189.238.43/plsql/plsql/Search_Ind_Bdp
Boxer #1 .... http://165.189.238.43/plsql/plsql/Search_Ind_Bdp
Boxing Club (Amateur or Professional) #2 .... http://drlchq.state.wi.us/plsql/chq/cred_holder_query
Boxing Show Permit #2 .... http://drlchq.state.wi.us/plsql/chq/cred_holder_query
Cemetery Authority/Warehouse #2 .... http://drlchq.state.wi.us/plsql/chq/cred_holder_query
Cemetery Preneed Seller #1 .... http://165.189.238.43/plsql/plsql/Search_Ind_Bdp
Cemetery Salesperson #1 .... http://165.189.238.43/plsql/plsql/Search_Ind_Bdp
Charitable Organization #2 .... http://drlchq.state.wi.us/plsql/chq/cred_holder_query
Check Seller #6 .... www.wdfi.org/fi/lfs/licensee_lists
Chiropractor #4 .... http://165.189.238.43/plsql/plsql/Search_Ind_Health
Collection Agency #6 .... www.wdfi.org/fi/lfs/licensee_lists
Cosmetologist #1 .... http://165.189.238.43/plsql/plsql/Search_Ind_Bdp
Cosmetology Instructor/Mgr./Apprentice #1 .... http://165.189.238.43/plsql/plsql/Search_Ind_Bdp
Cosmetology School #2 .... http://drlchq.state.wi.us/plsql/chq/cred_holder_query
Counselor, Professional #4 .... http://165.189.238.43/plsql/plsql/Search_Ind_Health
Credit Service Organization #5 .... www.wdfi.org/fi/cu/chartered_lists/default.asp
Credit Union #5 .... www.wdfi.org/fi/cu/chartered_lists/default.asp
Currency Exchange #6 .... www.wdfi.org/fi/lfs/licensee_lists
Dance Therapist #4 .... http://165.189.238.43/plsql/plsql/Search_Ind_Health
Debt Collector #6 .... www.wdfi.org/fi/lfs/licensee_lists
Dental Hygienist #4 .... http://165.189.238.43/plsql/plsql/Search_Ind_Health
Dentist #4 .... http://165.189.238.43/plsql/plsql/Search_Ind_Health
Designer of Engineering Systems #1 .... http://165.189.238.43/plsql/plsql/Search_Ind_Bdp
Dietitian #4 .... http://165.189.238.43/plsql/plsql/Search_Ind_Health
Drug Distributor/Manufacturer #2 .... http://drlchq.state.wi.us/plsql/chq/cred_holder_query
Electrologist #1 .... http://165.189.238.43/plsql/plsql/Search_Ind_Bdp
Electrology Establishment/School #2 .... http://drlchq.state.wi.us/plsql/chq/cred_holder_query
Electrology Instructor #1 .... http://165.189.238.43/plsql/plsql/Search_Ind_Bdp
Engineer/Engineer in Training #1 .... http://165.189.238.43/plsql/plsql/Search_Ind_Bdp
Engineering Corporation #2 .... http://drlchq.state.wi.us/plsql/chq/cred_holder_query
Firearms Permit #2 .... http://drlchq.state.wi.us/plsql/chq/cred_holder_query
Fund Raiser, Professional #1 .... http://165.189.238.43/plsql/plsql/Search_Ind_Bdp
Fund Raising Counsel #2 .... http://drlchq.state.wi.us/plsql/chq/cred_holder_query
Funeral Director/Director Apprentice #1 .... http://165.189.238.43/plsql/plsql/Search_Ind_Bdp
Funeral Establishment #2 .... http://drlchq.state.wi.us/plsql/chq/cred_holder_query
Funeral Preneed Seller #1 .... http://165.189.238.43/plsql/plsql/Search_Ind_Bdp
Geologist #1 .... http://165.189.238.43/plsql/plsql/Search_Ind_Bdp
Geology Firm #2 .... http://drlchq.state.wi.us/plsql/chq/cred_holder_query
Hearing Instrument Specialist #4 .... http://165.189.238.43/plsql/plsql/Search_Ind_Health
Home Inspector #1 .... http://165.189.238.43/plsql/plsql/Search_Ind_Bdp

Hydrologist #1	http://165.189.238.43/plsql/plsql/Search_Ind_Bdp
Hydrology Firm #2	http://drlchq.state.wi.us/plsql/chq/cred_holder_query
Insurance Company #6	http://badger.state.wi.us/agencies/oci/dir_ins.htm
Insurance Premium Finance Company #6	www.wdfi.org/fi/lfs/licensee_lists
Interior Designer #1	http://165.189.238.43/plsql/plsql/Search_Ind_Bdp
Investment Advisor/Advisor Rep #10	www.wdfi.org/fi/securities/licensing/licensee_lists/default.asp
Land Surveyor #1	http://165.189.238.43/plsql/plsql/Search_Ind_Bdp
Landfill #18	www.dnr.state.wi.us/org/aw/wm/solid/landfill/licensed.htm
Landfill Operator #18	www.dnr.state.wi.us/org/aw/wm/solid/landfill/licensed.htm
Landscape Architect #1	http://165.189.238.43/plsql/plsql/Search_Ind_Bdp
Loan Company #6	www.wdfi.org/fi/lfs/licensee_lists
Loan Solicitor/Originator #5	www.wdfi.org/fi/mortbank/licensee_lists/default.asp
Lobbying Organization, Principal #11	http://ethics.state.wi.us/Scripts/OEL2000.asp
Lobbyist #11	http://ethics.state.wi.us/Scripts/Lobbyists2000.asp
Manicurist Establishment/Specialty School #2	http://drlchq.state.wi.us/plsql/chq/cred_holder_query
Manicurist/Manicurist Instructor #1	http://165.189.238.43/plsql/plsql/Search_Ind_Bdp
Marriage & Family Therapist #4	http://165.189.238.43/plsql/plsql/Search_Ind_Health
Massage Therapist/Bodyworker #4	http://165.189.238.43/plsql/plsql/Search_Ind_Health
Medical Doctor/Surgeon #4	http://165.189.238.43/plsql/plsql/Search_Ind_Health
Midwife Nurse #4	http://165.189.238.43/plsql/plsql/Search_Ind_Health
Mobile Home & RV Dealer #6	www.wdfi.org/fi/lfs/licensee_lists
Mortgage Banker/Broker #5	www.wdfi.org/fi/mortbank/licensee_lists/default.asp
Motorcycle Dealer #6	www.wdfi.org/fi/lfs/licensee_lists
Music Therapist #4	http://165.189.238.43/plsql/plsql/Search_Ind_Health
Nurse-RN/LPN #4	http://165.189.238.43/plsql/plsql/Search_Ind_Health
Nursing Home Administrator #1	http://165.189.238.43/plsql/plsql/Search_Ind_Bdp
Occupational Therapist/Assistant #4	http://165.189.238.43/plsql/plsql/Search_Ind_Health
Optometrist #4	http://165.189.238.43/plsql/plsql/Search_Ind_Health
Payday Lender #6	www.wdfi.org/fi/lfs/licensee_lists
Pesticide Applicator/Application Business #9	http://datcp.state.wi.us/arm/agriculture/pest-fert/pesticides/data/
Pesticide Dealer #9	http://datcp.state.wi.us/arm/agriculture/pest-fert/pesticides/data/
Pharmacist #4	http://165.189.238.43/plsql/plsql/Search_Ind_Health
Pharmacy #4	http://165.189.238.43/plsql/plsql/Search_Ind_Health
Physical Therapist #4	http://165.189.238.43/plsql/plsql/Search_Ind_Health
Physician Assistant #4	http://165.189.238.43/plsql/plsql/Search_Ind_Health
Podiatrist #4	http://165.189.238.43/plsql/plsql/Search_Ind_Health
Private Detective #1	http://165.189.238.43/plsql/plsql/Search_Ind_Bdp
Private Detective Agency #2	http://drlchq.state.wi.us/plsql/chq/cred_holder_query
Psychologist #4	http://165.189.238.43/plsql/plsql/Search_Ind_Health
Public Accountant #1	http://165.189.238.43/plsql/plsql/Search_Ind_Bdp
Real Estate Appraiser #1	http://165.189.238.43/plsql/plsql/Search_Ind_Bdp
Real Estate Broker/Salesperson #1	http://165.189.238.43/plsql/plsql/Search_Ind_Bdp
Real Estate Business Entity #2	http://drlchq.state.wi.us/plsql/chq/cred_holder_query
Respiratory Care Practitioner #4	http://165.189.238.43/plsql/plsql/Search_Ind_Health
Sales Finance/Loan Company #6	www.wdfi.org/fi/lfs/licensee_lists
Savings & Loan Sales Finance Company #6	www.wdfi.org/fi/lfs/licensee_lists
Savings Institution #5	www.wdfi.org/fi/savings_institutions/licensee_lists/
School Librarian/Media Specialist #15	www.dpi.state.wi.us/dpi/dlsis/tel/lisearch.html
School Psychology Private Practice #4	http://165.189.238.43/plsql/plsql/Search_Ind_Health
Securities Broker/Dealer/Agent #10	www.wdfi.org/fi/securities/licensing/licensee_lists/default.asp
Security Guard #1	http://165.189.238.43/plsql/plsql/Search_Ind_Bdp
Social Worker #4	http://165.189.238.43/plsql/plsql/Search_Ind_Health
Soil Science Firm #2	http://drlchq.state.wi.us/plsql/chq/cred_holder_query
Soil Scientist #1	http://165.189.238.43/plsql/plsql/Search_Ind_Bdp
Speech Pathologist/Audiologist #4	http://165.189.238.43/plsql/plsql/Search_Ind_Health
Teacher #15	www.dpi.state.wi.us/dpi/dlsis/tel/lisearch.html
Timeshare Salesperson #1	http://165.189.238.43/plsql/plsql/Search_Ind_Bdp
Veterinarian/Veterinary Technician #4	http://165.189.238.43/plsql/plsql/Search_Ind_Health

Licensing Quick Finder

Accounting Firm #2......................608-266-5511 X43
Acupuncturist #4.................................608-266-0145
Adjustment Counselor #6....................608-261-9555
Adjustment Service Company #6.........608-267-3776
Aesthetics Establ./Specialty School #2
....608-266-5511 X43
Aesthetics Instructor #1...............608-266-5511 X42
Ambulance Service Provider #7..........608-266-1568
Appraiser, General #1..................608-266-5511 X43
Appraiser, Residential #1..............608-266-5511 X43
Architect #1...............................608-266-5511 X42
Architectural Corporation #2.........608-266-5511 X43
Art Therapist #4..................................608-266-2811
Asbestos Worker #17..........................608-261-6876
Attorney #16.......................................608-257-3838
Auction Company #2...................608-266-5511 X43
Auctioneer #1.............................608-266-5511 X43
Audiologist #4....................................608-266-0145
Bank #5..608-261-7578
Barber #1...................................608-266-5511 X42
Barber School #2.........................608-266-5511 X43
Barber/Apprentice/Instructor/Manager #1
....608-266-5511 X43
Beer Wholesaler #8............................608-266-2776
Boiler Repairer #19............................608-261-8500
Boxer #1.....................................608-266-5511 X442
Boxing Club (Amateur or Professional) #2
....608-266-5511 X43
Boxing Show Permit #2................608-266-5511 X43
Building Inspector #19........................608-261-8500
Business Tax Registration #8.............608-266-2776
Cemetery Authority/Warehouse #2608-266-5511 X441
Cemetery Preneed Seller #1......608-266-5511 X441
Cemetery Salesperson #1...........608-266-5511 X441
Charitable Gaming #14........................608-270-2555
Charitable Organization #2.........608-266-5511 X441
Check Seller #6..................................608-267-3776
Chiropractor #4...................................608-266-0145
Cigarette & Tobacco Distributor/Vendor/Multiple
Retailer #8..608-266-2776
Cigarette & Tobacco Warehouser/Wholesaler/Jobber
#8..608-266-2776
Collection Agency #6..........................608-267-3776
Cosmetologist #1........................608-266-5511 X42
Cosmetology Instructor/Mgr./Apprentice #1
....608-266-5511 X43
Cosmetology School #2................608-266-5511 X43
Counselor, Professional #4..................608-266-0145
Credit Service Organization #5............608-266-9543
Credit Union #5...................................608-266-9543
Currency Exchange #6........................608-267-3776
Dance Therapist #4............................608-266-2811
Debt Collector #6................................608-267-3776
Dental Hygienist #4............................608-266-2811
Dentist #4...608-266-2811
Designer of Engineering Systems #1
....608-266-5511 X42

Dietitian #4...608-266-0145
Director of Instruction #15...................608-266-1027
Dog Racing Professional #14..............608-270-2555
Drug Distributor/Manufacturer #2...608-266-5511 X43
Electrical Inspector #19......................608-261-8500
Electrician #19...................................608-261-8500
Electrologist #1..........................608-266-5511 X43
Electrology Establ./School #2......608-266-5511 X43
Electrology Instructor #1.............608-266-5511 X43
Employee Benefits Plan Administrator #12
....608-267-1238
EMT/Paramedic #7.............................608-266-1568
Engineer/Engineer in Training #1...608-266-5511 X42
Engineering Corporation #2..........608-266-5511 X43
Excise Tax Permit #8..........................608-266-2776
Fertilizer #9.......................................608-224-4548
Firearms Permit #2......................608-266-5511 X43
Fireworks Manufacturer #19................608-261-8500
Fuel Tax Permit #8.............................608-266-2776
Fund Raiser, Professional #1......608-266-5511 X441
Fund Raising Counsel #2............608-266-5511 X441
Funeral Director/Director Apprentice #1
....608-266-5511 X442
Funeral Establishment #2.............608-266-5511 X43
Funeral Preneed Seller #1...........608-266-5511 X442
Geologist #1...............................608-266-5511 X42
Geology Firm #2.........................608-266-5511 X43
Hearing Instrument Specialist #4.........608-266-2811
Home Inspector #1.....................608-266-5511 X43
Hydrologist #1............................608-266-5511 X42
Hydrology Firm #2......................608-266-5511 X43
Indian Gaming Vendor #14..................608-270-2555
Insurance Company #6........................608-267-3776
Insurance Intermediary #12.................608-266-8699
Insurance Premium Finance Company #6
....608-267-3776
Interior Designer #1....................608-266-5511 X43
Investment Advisor/Advisor Rep #10...608-266-3693
Land Surveyor #1.......................608-266-5511 X43
Landfill #18..608-267-6744
Landfill Operator #18..........................608-267-6744
Landscape Architect #1...............608-266-5511 X42
Liquor, Wholesale #8..........................608-266-2776
Loan Company #6...............................608-267-1708
Loan Solicitor/Originator #5................608-261-7578
Lobbying Organization, Principal #11..608-266-8123
Lobbyist #11.......................................608-266-8123
Manicurist Establ./Specialty School #2
....608-266-5511 X43
Manicurist/Manicurist Instructor #1 608-266-5511 X43
Marriage & Family Therapist #4...........608-266-0145
Massage Therapist/Bodyworker #4......608-266-2811
Medical Doctor/Surgeon #4.................608-266-2811
Midwife Nurse #4................................608-266-0145
Mobile Home & RV Dealer #6..............608-267-3743
Mortgage Banker/Broker #5.................608-261-7578
Motorcycle Dealer #6..........................608-267-3743
Wine Distributor, Public #8..................608-266-2776

Music Therapist #4.............................608-266-2811
Notary Public #13...............................608-266-5594
Nurse-RN/LPN #4................................608-266-0145
Nursing Home Administrator #1....608-266-5511 X43
Occupational Therapist/Assistant #4 ... 608-266-2811
Optometrist #4....................................608-266-0145
Osteopathic Physician #4....................608-266-2811
Payday Lender #6...............................608-267-1708
Pesticide Applicator/Application Business #9
....608-224-4548
Pesticide Dealer #9............................608-224-4548
Pesticide Vet Clinic #9........................608-224-4548
Pharmacist #4....................................608-266-2811
Pharmacy #4......................................608-266-2811
Physical Therapist #4..........................608-266-2811
Physician Assistant #4.........................608-266-2811
Plumber #19.......................................608-261-8500
Podiatrist #4.......................................608-266-2811
Private Detective #1....................608-266-5511 X43
Private Detective Agency #2...608-266-5511 X43
Psychologist #4..................................608-266-0145
Public Accountant #1...................608-266-5511 X42
Racing/Racing Vendor #14..................608-270-2555
Real Estate Appraiser #1............608-266-5511 X42
Real Estate Broker/Salesperson #1608-266-5511 X43
Real Estate Business Entity #2....608-266-5511 X43
Respiratory Care Practitioner #4..........608-266-2811
Sales Finance/Loan Company #6........608-267-3743
Sales Withholding Tax Registration #8. 608-266-2776
Sanitarian #17....................................608-267-4784
Savings & Loan Sales Finance Company #6
....608-267-3743
Savings Institution #5.........................608-261-4335
School Counselor #15..........................608-266-1027
School Librarian/Media Specialist #15.. 608-266-1027
School Nurse #15................................608-266-1027
School Principal/Superintendent/Bus. Mgr #15
....608-266-1027
School Psychologist/Social Worker #15608-266-1027
School Psychology Private Practice #4 608-266-0145
Securities Broker/Dealer/Agent #10.....608-266-3693
Security Guard #1.......................608-266-5511 X43
Social Worker #4.................................608-266-0145
Soil Science Firm #2...................608-266-5511 X43
Soil Scientist #1.........................608-266-5511 X42
Soil Tester #19...................................608-261-8500
Speech Pathologist/Audiologist #4......608-266-2811
Teacher #15.......................................608-266-1027
Timeshare Salesperson #1..........608-266-5511 X43
Veterinarian/Veterinary Technician #4.. 608-266-2811
Viatical Settlement Broker #12............608-266-8699
Vocational Education Coordinator, Local #15
....608-266-1027
Welder #19...608-261-8500

Licensing Agency Information

#1 Department of Regulation and Licensing, Division of Business Professional Licensure & Regulation, PO Box 8935 (1400 E Washington), Madison, WI 53708-8935; 608-266-5511, Fax: 608-267-3816.
www.state.wi.us/agencies/drl
Agency email: dorl@drl.state.wi.us.
Search database at http://165.189.238.43/plsql/plsql/Search_Ind_Bdp

#2 Dept of Regulation & Licensing, Division of Business Licensure & Regulation, PO Box 8935, Madison, WI 53708-8935; 608-266-5511, Fax: 608-267-3816.
http://badger.state.wi.us/agencies/drl
Agency email: dorl@drl.state.wi.us.
Search database at http://drlchq.state.wi.us/plsql/chq/cred_holder_query

#4 Bureau of Health Services Professions, PO Box 8935 (1400 E Washington Ave), Madison, WI 53708-8935; 608-266-0483, Fax: 608-261-7083.
www.state.wi.us/agencies/drl
Agency email: dorl@drl.state.wi.us.
Search database at http://165.189.238.43/plsql/plsql/Search_Ind_Health. This Department recommends an internet search; if not, inquire by mail. Phone verifications may not be accepted.

#5 Department of Financial Institutions, Division of Banking, PO Box 7876 (345 W Washington Av, 4th Fl), Madison, WI 53707-7876; 608-261-9555, Fax: 608-261-7200.
www.wdfi.org
Search database at www.wdfi.org/fi/savings_institutions/licensee_lists. Division of Financial Inst. - dfi - offers both an online list system and telephone system for verifications.

#6 Department of Financial Institutions, Licensed Financial Services, PO Box 7876, Madison, WI 53707-7876; 608-261-9555, Fax: 608-267-6889.
www.wdfi.org/fi/lfs/
Search database at www.wdfi.org/fi/lfs/licensee_lists. Also offers an online list system for verifications.

#7 Division of Public Health, Bureau of EMS and IP, 1 W Wilson St, Rm 118, Madison, WI 53703; 608-267-9777, 266-1568, Fax: 608-261-6392.
www.dhfs.state.wi.us/DPH_EMSIP
Agency email: webmaildph@dhfs.state.wi.us.

#8 Department of Revenue, 2135 Rimtock Rd, Madison, WI 53713; 608-266-2772, Fax: 608-267-0834. www.dor.state.wi.us
Agency email: sales10@dor.state.wi.us.

#9 Department of Agriculture, Trade & Consumer Protection, Applicator Cert. & Licensing, 2811 Agriculture Dr, Madison, WI 53718; 608-224-4548, Fax: 608-224-4656.
http://datcp.state.wi.us/arm/agriculture/pest-fert/pesticides. Agency email:
brian.swingle@datcp.state.wi.us.
Search database at http://datcp.state.wi.us/arm/agriculture/pest-fert/pesticides/data

#10 Department of Financial Institutions, Division of Securities, PO Box 1768, Madison, WI 53701; 608-266-3693, 608-266-1064, Fax: 608-256-1259.
www.wdfi.org/fi/securities
Agency email: info@dfi.state.wi.us.
Search database at www.wdfi.org/fi/securities/licensing/licensee_lists/default.asp

#11 Ethics Board, 44 E Mifflin St, #601, Madison, WI 53703-2800; 608-266-8123, Fax: 608-264-9319.
http://ethics.state.wi.us
Agency email: ethics@ethics.state.wi.gov.
Search database at http://ethics.state.wi.us/LobbyingRegistrationReports/LobbyingOverview.htm

#12 Office of the Commissioner of Insurance, 121 E Wilson St, Madison, WI 53702; 608-266-3585, Fax: 608-266-9935.
http://badger.state.wi.us/agencies/oci/oci_home.htm
Agency email: agentlicensing@oci.state.wi.us.

#13 Office of Secretary of State, PO Box 7848, Madison, WI 53707-7848; 608-266-5594, Fax: 608-266-3159.
http://badger.state.wi.us/agencies/sos/

#14 Department of Administration, Division of Gaming/Racing, 2005 W Beltline Hwy, #201 (PO Box 8979), Madison, WI 53713; 608-270-2555, Fax: 608-270-2564.
www.doa.state.wi.us/gaming/racing/index.asp.
Agency email: racingweb@doa.state.wi.us.

#15 Teacher Education, Department of Public Instruction, PO Box 7841, Madison, WI 53707-7841; 608-266-1027, Fax: 608-264-9558.
www.dpi.state.wi.us/dpi/dlsis/tel
Agency email: tcert@dpi.state.wi.us.
Search database at
www.dpi.state.wi.us/dpi/dlsis/tel/lisearch.html. At the search page, enter the User Name "view" and the Password, "1234567" then click "ok".

#16 State Bar Association, PO Box 7158, Madison, WI 53707; 608-257-3838, Fax: 608-257-5502. www.wisbar.org
Search database at www.wisbar.org.

#17 Department of Health & Family Svcs, Occupational Health, 1 W Wilson St, Perry Manor, Madison, WI 53703; 608-267-2297, Fax: 608-266-9711.

#18 Department of Natural Resources, Waste Management Program, Managers/Operators Certification, 101 S Webster St, PO Box 7921, Madison, WI 53707-7921; 608-267-6744.
www.dnr.state.wi.us
Search database at www.dnr.state.wi.us/org/aw/wm/solid/landfill/licensed

#19 Department of Commerce, Safety & Buildings, 201 W Washington Ave, PO Box 2689, Madison, WI 53707-2689; 608-261-8500.
www.commerce.state.wi.us/SB/SB-HomePage.html

Wisconsin Federal Courts

The following list indicates the district and division name for each county in the state. If the bankruptcy court location is different from the district court, then the location of the bankruptcy court appears in parentheses.

County/Court Cross Reference

County	District	Location		County	District	Location
Adams	Western	Madison		Marathon	Western	Madison (Eau Claire)
Ashland	Western	Madison (Eau Claire)		Marinette	Eastern	Milwaukee
Barron	Western	Madison (Eau Claire)		Marquette	Eastern	Milwaukee
Bayfield	Western	Madison (Eau Claire)		Menominee	Eastern	Milwaukee
Brown	Eastern	Milwaukee		Milwaukee	Eastern	Milwaukee
Buffalo	Western	Madison (Eau Claire)		Monroe	Western	Madison (Eau Claire)
Burnett	Western	Madison (Eau Claire)		Oconto	Eastern	Milwaukee
Calumet	Eastern	Milwaukee		Oneida	Western	Madison (Eau Claire)
Chippewa	Western	Madison (Eau Claire)		Outagamie	Eastern	Milwaukee
Clark	Western	Madison (Eau Claire)		Ozaukee	Eastern	Milwaukee
Columbia	Western	Madison		Pepin	Western	Madison (Eau Claire)
Crawford	Western	Madison		Pierce	Western	Madison (Eau Claire)
Dane	Western	Madison		Polk	Western	Madison (Eau Claire)
Dodge	Eastern	Milwaukee		Portage	Western	Madison (Eau Claire)
Door	Eastern	Milwaukee		Price	Western	Madison (Eau Claire)
Douglas	Western	Madison (Eau Claire)		Racine	Eastern	Milwaukee
Dunn	Western	Madison (Eau Claire)		Richland	Western	Madison
Eau Claire	Western	Madison (Eau Claire)		Rock	Western	Madison
Florence	Eastern	Milwaukee		Rusk	Western	Madison (Eau Claire)
Fond du Lac	Eastern	Milwaukee		Sauk	Western	Madison
Forest	Eastern	Milwaukee		Sawyer	Western	Madison (Eau Claire)
Grant	Western	Madison		Shawano	Eastern	Milwaukee
Green	Western	Madison		Sheboygan	Eastern	Milwaukee
Green Lake	Eastern	Milwaukee		St. Croix	Western	Madison (Eau Claire)
Iowa	Western	Madison		Taylor	Western	Madison (Eau Claire)
Iron	Western	Madison (Eau Claire)		Trempealeau	Western	Madison (Eau Claire)
Jackson	Western	Madison (Eau Claire)		Vernon	Western	Madison (Eau Claire)
Jefferson	Western	Madison		Vilas	Western	Madison (Eau Claire)
Juneau	Western	Madison (Eau Claire)		Walworth	Eastern	Milwaukee
Kenosha	Eastern	Milwaukee		Washburn	Western	Madison (Eau Claire)
Kewaunee	Eastern	Milwaukee		Washington	Eastern	Milwaukee
La Crosse	Western	Madison (Eau Claire)		Waukesha	Eastern	Milwaukee
Lafayette	Western	Madison		Waupaca	Eastern	Milwaukee
Langlade	Eastern	Milwaukee		Waushara	Eastern	Milwaukee
Lincoln	Western	Madison (Eau Claire)		Winnebago	Eastern	Milwaukee
Manitowoc	Eastern	Milwaukee		Wood	Western	Madison (Eau Claire)

Standards for Federal Courts: The search fee is $20.00 per item (one party name or case number). Certification fee is $7.00 per document. Copy fee is $.50 per page. All fees standard unless noted in profile. Mail Search: always enclose a stamped self addressed envelope unless otherwise noted. Before releasing records, all courts require prepayment unless noted in profile.

Open records are located at the court unless otherwise noted. District courts index by defendant and plaintiff as well as by case number. Bankruptcy courts usually index by debtor and case number. While most courts now have their indexes on computer, many still maintain index card files as well.

The universal PACER sign-up number is 800-676-6856. Find PACER and the Party/Case Index on the Web at http://pacer.psc.uscourts.gov. PACER dial-up access is $.60 per minute. Also, courts offering internet access via RACER, PACER, Web-PACER or the new CM-ECF charge $.07 per page fee unless noted as free.

US District Court

Eastern District of Wisconsin

Milwaukee Division Clerk's Office, Room 362, 517 E Wisconsin Ave, Milwaukee, WI 53202 (Courier Address: Use mail address for courier delivery), 414-297-3372.

www.wied.uscourts.gov

Counties: Brown, Calumet, Dodge, Door, Florence, Fond du Lac, Forest, Green Lake, Kenosha, Kewaunee, Langlade, Manitowoc, Marinette, Marquette, Menominee, Milwaukee, Oconto, Outagamie, Ozaukee, Racine, Shawano, Sheboygan, Walworth, Washington, Waukesha, Waupaca,Waushara, Winnebago.

Indexing & Storage: Cases are indexed by defendant, plaintiff, and case number. New cases are available in the index immediately after filing date. The computer index for civil cases goes back to 1991 and for criminal cases back to 1993. Open records are located at this court.

Fee & Payment Notes: Payment may be made by money order, cashier check, personal check. Payee: Clerk, US District Court. You are allowed to make your own copies. These copies cost $.25 per page.

Phone Search: Docket information available by phone if you have the case number or party names.

In Person Search: In person searching available.

PACER: Access fee is. Toll-free dial-up access: 877-253-4862. Local dial-up access: 414-297-3361. Case records are available back to 1991. Records are never purged. New records are available online after 1 day. PACER is available online at http://pacer.wied.uscourts.gov.

Electronic Filing: (Currently in the process of implementing CM/ECF.)

US Bankruptcy Court

Eastern District of Wisconsin

Milwaukee Division Room 126, 517 E Wisconsin Ave, Milwaukee, WI 53202 (Courier Address: Use mail address for courier delivery), 414-297-3291.

www.wieb.uscourts.gov

Counties: Brown, Calumet, Dodge, Door, Florence, Fond du Lac, Forest, Green Lake, Kenosha, Kewaunee, Langlade, Manitowoc, Marinette, Marquette, Menominee, Milwaukee, Oconto, Outagamie, Ozaukee, Racine, Shawano, Sheboygan, Walworth, Washington, Waukesha, Waupaca,Waushara, Winnebago.

Indexing & Storage: Cases are indexed by debtor as well as by case number. New cases are available in the index 1-2 days after filing date. The computer index goes back to 1986. Open records are located at this court.

Fee & Payment Notes: Payment may be made by money order, cashier check, personal check.

Payee: Clerk, US Bankruptcy Court. You are allowed to make your own copies. These copies cost $.25 per page.

Phone Search: An automated voice case information service (VCIS) is available. Call VCIS at 877-781-7277 or 414-297-3582.

In Person Search: In person searching available.

PACER: Toll-free dial-up access: 877-467-5537. Local dial-up access: 414-297-1400. Case records are available back to 1991. Records are purged after case is closed. New civil records are available online after 1-2 days. PACER is available online at http://pacer.wieb.uscourts.gov.

Electronic Filing: (Currently in the process of implementing CM/ECF.)

US District Court

Western District of Wisconsin

Madison Division PO Box 432, Madison, WI 53701 (Courier Address: 120 N Henry St, Madison, WI 53703), 608-264-5156.

www.wiw.uscourts.gov

Counties: Adams, Ashland, Barron, Bayfield, Buffalo, Burnett, Chippewa, Clark, Columbia, Crawford, Dane, Douglas, Dunn, Eau Claire, Grant, Green, Iowa, Iron, Jackson, Jefferson, Juneau, La Crosse, Lafayette, Lincoln, Marathon, Monroe, Oneida, Pepin, Pierce, Polk,Portage, Price, Richland, Rock, Rusk, Sauk, Sawyer, St. Croix, Taylor, Trempealeau, Vernon, Vilas, Washburn, Wood.

Indexing & Storage: Cases are indexed by defendant, plaintiff, and case number. New cases are available in the index 24 hours after filing date. District wide searches are available from this court.

Fee & Payment Notes: Payment may be made by money order, cashier check, personal check. Payee: Clerk, US District Court.

Phone Search: Only docket information is available by phone.

In Person Search: In person searching available.

PACER:. Case records are available back to 1990. Records are never purged. New records are available online after 1 day. PACER is available online at http://pacer.wiwd.uscourts.gov.

US Bankruptcy Court

Western District of Wisconsin

Eau Claire Division PO Box 5009, Eau Claire, WI 54702-5009 (Courier Address: 500 S Barstow Commons, Eau Claire, WI 54701), 715-839-2980, Fax: 715-839-2996.

www.wiw.uscourts.gov

Counties: Ashland, Barron, Bayfield, Buffalo, Burnett, Chippewa, Clark, Douglas, Dunn, Eau Claire, Iron, Jackson, Juneau, La Crosse, Lincoln, Marathon, Monroe, Oneida, Pepin, Pierce, Polk,Portage, Price, Rusk, Sawyer, St. Croix, Taylor, Trempealeau, Vernon,Vilas, Washburn, Wood. Division has satellite offices in LaCrosse and Wausau.

Indexing & Storage: Cases are indexed by debtor as well as by case number. New cases are available in the index 1 day after filing date. All division records are maintained here until they are forwarded to the Chicago Federal Records Center.

Fee & Payment Notes: Payment may be made by money order, cashier check, business check. Personal checks are not accepted. Personal checks are accepted only from attorneys. Payee: Clerk, US Bankruptcy Court.

Phone Search: Only limited docket information is available by phone. An automated voice case information service (VCIS) is available. Call VCIS at 800-743-8247 or 608-264-5035.

Mail Search: A stamped self addressed envelope is not required.

In Person Search: In person searching available.

PACER: Case records are available back to April 1991. New civil records are available online after 1 day. WebPACER is available at http://pacer.wiwb.uscourts.gov/js_index.html. Document images available.

Electronic Filing: Information is available online at https://ecf.wiwb.uscourts.gov

Madison Division PO Box 548, Madison, WI 53701 (Courier Address: Room 340, 120 N Henry St, Madison, WI 53703), 608-264-5178.

www.wiw.uscourts.gov/bankruptcy

Counties: Adams, Columbia, Crawford, Dane, Grant, Green, Iowa, Jefferson, Lafayette, Richland, Rock, Sauk.

Indexing & Storage: Cases are indexed by debtor as well as by case number. New cases are available in the index 24 hours after filing date. Open records are located at this court.

Fee & Payment Notes: Payment may be made by money order, cashier check, business check. Personal checks are not accepted. Payee: Clerk, US Bankruptcy Court.

Phone Search: Only limited docket information is available by phone. An automated voice case information service (VCIS) is available. Call VCIS at 800-743-8247 or 608-264-5035.

Fax Search: Fax requests are accepted.

Mail Search: A stamped self addressed envelope is not required.

In Person Search: In person searching available.

PACER: Case records are available back to April 1991. New civil records are available online after 1 day. WebPACER is available at http://pacer.wiwb.uscourts.gov/js_index.html. Document images available.

Electronic Filing: Information is available online at https://ecf.wiwb.uscourts.gov

Wisconsin County Courts

Court	Jurisdiction	No. of Courts	How Organized
Circuit Courts*	General	74	69 Circuits
Municipal Courts	Municipal	226	
Probate Courts*	Probate	72	

* Profiled in this Sourcebook.

Court	CIVIL								
	Tort	Contract	Real Estate	Min. Claim	Max. Claim	Small Claims	Estate	Eviction	Domestic Relations
Circuit Courts*	X	X	X	$0	No Max	$5000	X	X	X
Municipal Courts									
Probate Courts*							X		

Court	CRIMINAL				
	Felony	Misdemeanor	DWI/DUI	Preliminary Hearing	Juvenile
Circuit Courts*	X	X	X	X	X
Municipal Courts			X		X
Probate Courts*					

ADMINISTRATION

Director of State Courts, Supreme Court, PO Box 1688, Madison, WI, 53701; 608-266-6828, Fax: 608-267-0980. www.courts.state.wi.us

COURT STRUCTURE

The Circuit Court is the court of general jurisdiction. The Register in Probate maintains guardianship and mental health records, most of which are sealed but may be opened for cause with a court order. In some counties, the Register also maintains termination and adoption records, but practices vary widely across the state.

Most Registers in Probate are putting pre-1950 records on microfilm and destroying the hard copies. This is done as "time and workloads permit," so microfilm archiving is not uniform across the state.

The small claims limit was raised to $5000 in mid-1995.

ONLINE ACCESS

Wisconsin Circuit Court Access (WCCA) allows users to view circuit court case information at http://ccap.courts.state.wi.us/internetcourtaccess which is the Wisconsin court system web site. Data is available from all counties except Outagamie and Walworth. Searches can be conducted statewide or county by county. WCCA provides detailed information about circuit cases and for civil cases, the program displays judgment and judgment party information. WCCA also offers the ability to generate reports. In addition, public access terminals are available at each court. Due to statutory requirements, WCCA users will not be able to view restricted cases. There are probate records for all counties except Outagamie, Milwaukee and Walworth. Portage County offers probate records only online.

ADDITIONAL INFORMATION

The statutory fee schedule for the Circuit Courts is as follows: Search Fee - $5.00 per name; Copy Fee - $1.25 per page; Certification Fee - $5.00. In about half the Circuit Courts, no search fee is charged if the case number is provided. There is normally no search fee charged for in-person searches.

The fee schedule for probate is as follows: Search Fee - $4.00 per name; Certification Fee - $3.00 per document plus copy fee; Copy Fee - $1.00 per page.

PROBATE COURTS

Probate filing is a function of the Circuit Court; however, each county has a Register in Probate who maintains and manages the probate records. Probate records are available online at http://ccap.courts.state.wi.us/internetcourtaccess for all counties except Outagamie, Milwaukee and Walworth.

Adams County

Circuit Court PO Box 220, Friendship, WI 53934; 608-339-4208; Fax: 608-339-4503. Hours: 8AM-4:30PM (CST). *Felony, Misdemeanor, Civil, Eviction, Small Claims.*

Civil Records: Access: Phone, mail, online, in person. Both court and visitors may perform in person searches. Search fee: $5.00 per name. Required to search: name, years to search. Civil records on computer from 1993, on index cards and books from 1950. Historical societies have previous records and indexes. Organized 1848. Civil court records are available free online at http://ccap.courts.state.wi.us/internetcourtaccess.

Criminal Records: Access: Phone, mail, online, in person. Both court and visitors may perform in person searches. Search fee: $5.00 per name. Required to search: name, years to search, DOB. Criminal records on computer from 1993, on index cards and books from 1950. Historical societies have previous records and indexes. Organized 1848. Online access to criminal records is available free at http://ccap.courts.state.wi.us/internetcourtaccess.

General Information: Public access terminal is available. No juvenile, paternity, financial, PSI reports released. SASE required. Turnaround time 1-2 days. Fax notes: Fee to fax results is $1.25 per page. Copy fee: $1.25 per page. Certification fee: $5.00. Fee payee: Clerk of Court. Personal checks accepted. Prepayment is required.

Register in Probate PO Box 200, Friendship, WI 53934; 608-339-4213; Fax: 608-339-6414. Hours: 8AM-4:30PM (CST). *Probate.*

Note: Probate records are available free online; see Circuit Court.

Ashland County

Circuit Court Courthouse, 210 W Main St Rm 307, Ashland, WI 54806; 715-682-7016; Fax: 715-682-7919. Hours: 8AM-Noon, 1-4PM (CST). *Felony, Misdemeanor, Civil, Eviction, Small Claims.*

Civil Records: Access: Phone, fax, mail, online, in person. Both court and visitors may perform in person searches. Search fee: $5.00 per name. Required to search: name, years to search. Civil cases indexed by defendant, plaintiff. Civil records on index cards and index books concurrently from 1960. Organized 1860. Civil court records available free online at http://ccap.courts.state.wi.us/internetcourtaccess.

Criminal Records: Access: Fax, mail, online, in person. Both court and visitors may perform in person searches. Search fee: $5.00 per name. Required to search: name, years to search, DOB. Criminal records on computer back to 1994. Online access to criminal records is available free at http://ccap.courts.state.wi.us/internetcourtaccess.

General Information: Public access terminal is available. No juvenile or paternity records released. SASE required. Turnaround time 1-2 days. Fax notes: $1.25 per page. Copy fee: $1.25 per page. Certification fee: $5.00. Fee payee: Clerk of Court. Personal checks accepted. Local or pre-approved checks accepted. Prepayment is required.

Register in Probate Courthouse Rm 203, 201 W Main, Ashland, WI 54806; 715-682-7009; Fax: 715-682-7919. Hours: 8AM-Noon, 1-4PM (CST). *Probate.*

Note: Probate records are available free online; see Circuit Court.

Barron County

Circuit Court Barron County Courthouse, 330 E LaSalle Ave Room 208, Barron, WI 54812; 715-537-6265; Fax: 715-537-6269. Hours: 8AM-4:30PM *Felony, Misdemeanor, Civil, Eviction, Small Claims.*

Civil Records: Access: Online, in person. Visitors must perform in person searches for themselves. No search fee. Required to search: name, years to search. Civil cases indexed by defendant, plaintiff. Civil records on computer, index cards from 1983. Organized 1859. Civil court records available free online at http://courts.state.wi.us.

Criminal Records: Access: Online, in person. Visitors must perform in person searches for themselves. No search fee. Required to search: name, years to search. Criminal records on computer, index cards from 1983. Organized 1859. Online access to criminal records is available free at http://ccap.courts.state.wi.us/internetcourtaccess.

General Information: Public access terminal is available. No expunged, paternity or sealed records released. Copy fee: $1.25 per page. Certification fee: $5.00. Fee payee: Clerk of Court. Personal checks accepted. Prepayment is required.

Register in Probate Courthouse Rm 218, Barron, WI 54812; 715-537-6261; Fax: 715-537-6277. Hours: 8AM-4PM (CST). *Probate.*

Note: Probate records are available free online; see Circuit Court.

Bayfield County

Circuit Court 117 E 5th, Washburn, WI 54891; 715-373-6108; Fax: 715-373-6153. Hours: 8AM-4PM (CST). *Felony, Misdemeanor, Civil, Eviction, Small Claims.*

Civil Records: Access: Mail, online, in person. Both court and visitors may perform in person searches. Search fee: $5.00 per name. Required to search: name, years to search. Civil cases indexed by defendant, plaintiff. Civil records on computer for all open cases since 1982, on index cards from 1979, index books in archives from 1845 to 1979. Civil court records available free online at http://ccap.courts.state.wi.us/internetcourtaccess.

Criminal Records: Access: Mail, online, in person. Both court and visitors may perform in person searches. Search fee: $5.00 per name. Required to search: name, years to search, DOB. Criminal records on computer since 03/93. Online access to criminal records is available free at http://ccap.courts.state.wi.us/internetcourtaccess.

General Information: Public access terminal is available. No sealed records released. SASE required. Turnaround time 1-2 days. Fax notes: Fee to fax results is $2.25 per page. Copy fee: $1.25 per page. Certification fee: $5.00. Fee payee: Clerk of Court. Personal checks accepted. Prepayment is required.

Register in Probate 117 E 5th, PO Box 86, Washburn, WI 54891; 715-373-6155; Fax: 715-373-6153. Hours: 8AM-4PM (CST). *Probate.*

Note: Probate records are available free online; see Circuit Court.

Brown County

Circuit Court PO Box 23600, Green Bay, WI 54305-3600; 920-448-4161; Fax: 920-448-4156. Hours: 8AM-4:30PM (CST). *Felony, Misdemeanor, Civil, Eviction, Small Claims.*

Civil Records: Access: Mail, online, in person. Both court and visitors may perform in person searches. Search fee: $5.00 per name. Required to search: name, years to search. Civil cases indexed by defendant, plaintiff. Civil records on computer since 1990, on

microfiche from 1987-1990, archives from 1962-1990. Crossed on index cards from 1972, index books from 1982. Civil court records available free online at http://ccap.courts.state.wi.us/internetcourtaccess.

Criminal Records: Access: Mail, online, in person. Both court and visitors may perform in person searches. Search fee: $5.00 per name. Required to search: name, years to search, DOB. Criminal records on computer since 1990, on microfiche from 1987-1990, archives from 1962-1990. Crossed on index cards from 1972, index books from 1982. Online access to criminal records is available free at http://ccap.courts.state.wi.us/internetcourtaccess.

General Information: Public access terminal is available. No juvenile or paternity records released. SASE required. Turnaround time 10 days. Copy fee: $1.25 per page. Certification fee: $5.00. Fee payee: Brown County Clerk of Court. Personal checks accepted. Prepayment is required.

Register in Probate PO Box 23600, Green Bay, WI 54305-3600; 920-448-4275; Fax: 920-448-6208. Hours: 8AM-4:30PM (CST). *Probate.*

Note: Probate records are available free online; see Circuit Court.

Buffalo County

Circuit Court 407 S 2nd, PO Box 68, Alma, WI 54610; 608-685-6212; Fax: 608-685-6211. Hours: 8AM-4:30PM (CST). *Felony, Misdemeanor, Civil, Eviction, Small Claims.*

Civil Records: Access: Phone, fax, mail, online, in person. Both court and visitors may perform in person searches. Search fee: $5.00 per name. Required to search: name, years to search. Civil cases indexed by defendant, plaintiff. Civil records on computer from 1994, on index cards from 1979. No civil records available before 1962. Civil court records available free online http://ccap.courts.state.wi.us/internetcourtaccess.

Criminal Records: Access: Phone, fax, mail, online, in person. Both court and visitors may perform in person searches. Search fee: $5.00 per name. Required to search: name, years to search. Criminal records on computer from 1994. Felonies retained 50 years; misdemeanors 20 years. No misdemeanors available before 1962. Online access to criminal records is available free at http://ccap.courts.state.wi.us/internetcourtaccess.

General Information: Public access terminal is available. No closed records released. SASE required. Turnaround time 1 week. Fax notes: Fee to fax results is $1.25 per page. Copy fee: $1.25 per page. Certification fee: $5.00. Fee payee: Buffalo County Clerk of Court. Personal checks accepted. Prepayment is required.

Register in Probate 407 S 2nd, PO Box 68, Alma, WI 54610; 608-685-6202; Fax: 608-685-6211. Hours: 8AM-4:30PM (CST). *Probate.*

Note: Probate records are available free online; see Circuit Court.

Burnett County

Circuit Court 7410 County Road K #115, Siren, WI 54872; 715-349-2147. Hours: 8:30AM-4:30PM (CST). *Felony, Misdemeanor, Civil, Eviction, Small Claims.*

Civil Records: Access: Mail, online, in person. Both court and visitors may perform in person searches. Search fee: $5.00 per name. Required to search: name, years to search. Civil cases indexed by defendant, plaintiff. Civil records on computer from 10/92, on index books from 1800s. Organized 1856. Civil court records available free online at http://ccap.courts.state.wi.us/internetcourtaccess.

Criminal Records: Access: Mail, online, in person. Both court and visitors may perform in person searches. Search fee: $5.00 per name. Required to search: name, years to search. Criminal records on computer from 10/92, on index books from 1800s. Organized 1856. Online access to criminal records is available free at http://ccap.courts.state.wi.us/internetcourtaccess.

General Information: Public access terminal is available. No paternity, juvenile, sealed or confidential records released. SASE required. Turnaround time 1-2 days. Copy fee: $1.25 per page. Certification fee: $5.00. Fee payee: Clerk of Courts. Personal checks accepted. Prepayment is required.

Register in Probate 7410 County Road K #110, Siren, WI 54872; 715-349-2177; Fax: 715-349-7659. Hours: 8:30AM-4:30PM (CST). *Probate.*

Note: Probate records are available free online; see Circuit Court. This court also holds Juvenile, Guardianship, mental Commitments, Adoptions, and Term. Of Parental Right.

Calumet County

Circuit Court 206 Court St, Chilton, WI 53014; 920-849-1414; Fax: 920-849-1483. Hours: 8AM-4:30PM (CST). *Felony, Misdemeanor, Civil, Eviction, Small Claims.*

Civil Records: Access: Mail, online, in person. Both court and visitors may perform in person searches. Search fee: $5.00 per name. Required to search: name, years to search. Civil cases indexed by defendant, plaintiff. Civil records on computer from 1992, index cards from 1978, index books from 1800s. Civil court records available free online at http://ccap.courts.state.wi.us/internetcourtaccess.

Criminal Records: Access: Mail, online, in person. Both court and visitors may perform in person searches. Search fee: $5.00 per name. Required to search: name, years to search, DOB. Criminal records on computer from 1992, index cards from 1978, index books from 1800s. Online access to criminal records is available free at http://ccap.courts.state.wi.us/internetcourtaccess.

General Information: Public access terminal is available. No juvenile or paternity records released. SASE required. Turnaround time 2 days. Copy fee: $1.25 per page. Certification fee: $5.00. Fee payee: Clerk of Court. Personal checks accepted. Prepayment is required.

Register in Probate 206 Court St, Chilton, WI 53014-1198; 920-849-1455; Fax: 920-849-1483. Hours: 8AM-Noon, 1-4:30PM (CST). *Probate.*

Note: Probate records are available free online; see Circuit Court.

Chippewa County

Circuit Court 711 N Bridge St, Chippewa Falls, WI 54729-1879; 715-726-7758; Fax: 715-726-7786. Hours: 8AM-4:30PM (CST). *Felony, Misdemeanor, Civil, Eviction, Small Claims.*

Civil Records: Access: Mail, fax, online, in person. Both court and visitors may perform in person searches. Search fee: $5.00 per name per case type. Required to search: name, years to search; also helpful: address. Civil cases indexed by defendant, plaintiff. Civil records on computer from 1990, index cards from 1979, index books from 1900s. Civil court records available free online at http://ccap.courts.state.wi.us/internetcourtaccess.

Criminal Records: Access: Mail, fax, online, in person. Both court and visitors may perform in person searches. Search fee: $5.00 per name. Required to search: name, years to search, DOB; also helpful: SSN. Criminal records on computer from 1990, index cards from 1979, index books from 1900s. Online access to criminal records is available free at http://ccap.courts.state.wi.us/internetcourtaccess.

General Information: Public access terminal is available. Paternity records released only to party or attorney of record, or with written authorization. SASE required. Turnaround time 10 days or less; up to 30 days if pre-1990. Fax notes: Fee to fax results is $2.00 for 1st page and $1.00 per page thereafter. Copy fee: $1.25 per page. Certification fee: $5.00. Fee payee: Chippewa County Clerk of Courts. Personal checks accepted. Prepayment is required.

Register in Probate 711 N Bridge St, Chippewa Falls, WI 54729; 715-726-7737; Fax: 715-738-2626. Hours: 8AM-4:30PM (CST). *Probate.*

Note: Probate records are available free online; see Circuit Court.

Clark County

Circuit Court 517 Court St, Neillsville, WI 54456-1971; 715-743-5181; Fax: 715-743-5120. Hours: 8AM-4:30PM (CST). *Felony, Misdemeanor, Civil, Eviction, Small Claims.*

Civil Records: Access: Mail, online, in person. Both court and visitors may perform in person searches. Search fee: $5.00 per name. Required to search: name, years to search. Civil cases indexed by defendant, plaintiff. Civil records on computer from 1994, on index cards from 1981, index books from 1900s. Civil court records available for free online at http://ccap.courts.state.wi.us/internetcourtaccess.

Criminal Records: Access: Mail, online, in person. Both court and visitors may perform in person searches. Search fee: $5.00 per name. Required to search: name, years to search. Criminal records on computer from 1994, on index cards from 1981, index books from 1900s. Online access to criminal records is available free at http://ccap.courts.state.wi.us/internetcourtaccess.

General Information: No sealed or paternity records released. SASE required. Turnaround time 1-2 weeks. Copy fee: $.15 per page. Certification fee: $5.00. Fee payee: Clerk of Court. Personal checks accepted. Prepayment is required.

Register in Probate 517 Court St, Rm 403, Neillsville, WI 54456; 715-743-5172; Fax: 715-743-5120. Hours: 8AM-4:30PM (CST). *Probate.*

Note: There is a $4.00 search fee. Probate records are available free online; see Circuit Court.

Columbia County

Circuit Court PO Box 587, Portage, WI 53901; 608-742-9642; Fax: 608-742-9601. Hours: 8AM-4:30PM (CST). *Felony, Misdemeanor, Civil, Eviction, Small Claims.*

Civil Records: Access: Mail, online, in person. Both court and visitors may perform in person searches. Search fee: $5.00 per name. Required to search: name, years to search. Civil cases indexed by defendant, plaintiff. Civil records on computer from 1994, on microfiche to 1960s, concurrent index cards/books from 1940s. Civil court records available free online at http://ccap.courts.state.wi.us/internetcourtaccess.

Criminal Records: Access: Mail, online, in person. Both court and visitors may perform in person searches. Search fee: $5.00 per name. Required to search: name, years to search, DOB. Criminal records on computer from 1994, on microfiche to 1960s, concurrent index cards/books from 1940s. Online access to criminal records is available free at http://ccap.courts.state.wi.us/internetcourtaccess.

General Information: Public access terminal is available. No juvenile or paternity records released. SASE required. Turnaround time 1 week. Fax notes: Fee to fax results is $1.25 per page. Copy fee: $1.25 per page. Certification fee: $5.00. Fee payee: Clerk of Court. Personal checks accepted. Prepayment required.

Register in Probate 400 DeWitt, PO Box 221, Portage, WI 53901; 608-742-9636, 742-9637; Fax: 608-742-9601. Hours: 8AM-4:30PM (CST). *Probate.*

Note: Probate records are available free online; see Circuit Court.

Crawford County

Circuit Court 220 N Beaumont Rd, Prairie Du Chien, WI 53821; 608-326-0211. Hours: 8AM-4:30PM (CST). *Felony, Misdemeanor, Civil, Eviction, Small Claims.*

Civil Records: Access: Mail, online, in person. Both court and visitors may perform in person searches. Search fee: $5.00 per name. Required to search: name, years to search. Civil cases indexed by defendant, plaintiff. Civil records on computer from 1993, on index cards from 1984, index books from 1900. Historical Society has archives. Civil court records available for free online at http://ccap.courts.state.wi.us/internetcourt access.

Criminal Records: Access: Mail, online, in person. Both court and visitors may perform in person searches. Search fee: $5.00 per name. Required to search: name, years to search. Criminal records on computer from 1993, on index cards from 1984, index books from 1900. Historical Society has archives. Online access to criminal records is available free at http://ccap.courts.state.wi.us/internetcourtaccess.

General Information: Public access terminal is available. No juvenile, paternity, mental records released. SASE required. Turnaround time 10 working days. Copy fee: $1.25 per page. Certification fee: $5.00. Fee payee: Clerk of Court. Personal checks accepted. Prepayment is required.

Register in Probate 220 N Beaumont Rd, Prairie Du Chien, WI 53821; 608-326-0206; Fax: 608-326-0288. Hours: 8AM-4:30PM (CST). *Probate.*

Note: Probate records are available free online; see Circuit Court.

Dane County

Circuit Court 210 Martin Luther King Jr Blvd, Rm GR10, Madison, WI 53703; 608-266-4311; Fax: 608-267-8859. Hours: 7:45AM-4:30PM (CST). *Felony, Misdemeanor, Civil, Eviction, Small Claims.*

www.co.dane.wi.us/clrkcort/clrkhome.htm

Civil Records: Access: Fax, mail, online, in person. Both court and visitors may perform in person searches. Search fee: $5.00 per name. Required to search: name, years to search. Civil cases indexed by defendant, plaintiff. Civil records on computer from 1981, on microfiche from 1976, defendant index books 1848. Civil court records available free online at http://ccap.courts.state.wi.us/internetcourtaccess.

Criminal Records: Access: Fax, mail, online, in person. Both court and visitors may perform in person searches. Search fee: $5.00 per name. Required to search: name, years to search, DOB. Criminal records on computer from 1983, index back to 1848. Online access to criminal records is available free at http://ccap.courts.state.wi.us/internetcourtaccess.

General Information: Public access terminal is available. No "confidential records" released. SASE required. Turnaround time 2-3 days. Fax notes: $.50 for 1st five pages, $.23 for each additional 5 pages or fraction thereof. Copy fee: $1.25 per page. Certification fee: $5.00. Fee payee: Dane County Clerk of Courts. Personal checks accepted. Prepayment is required.

Register in Probate 210 Martin Luther King Jr Blvd, Rm 305, Madison, WI 53703-3344; 608-266-4331. Hours: 7:45AM-4:30PM (CST). *Probate.*

Note: Probate records are available free online; see Circuit Court.

Dodge County

Circuit Court 210 W Center St, Juneau, WI 53039; 920-386-3820; Fax: 920-386-3587. 8AM-4:30PM *Felony, Misdemeanor, Civil, Eviction, Small Claims.*

Civil Records: Access: Mail, online, in person. Both court and visitors may perform in person searches. Search fee: $5.00 per name. Required to search: name, years to search. Civil cases indexed by defendant, plaintiff. Civil records on computer from 1993, on index cards from 1986, microfiche from 1972, index books from 1950s. Civil court records available free online at http://ccap.courts.state.wi.us/internetcourtaccess.

Criminal Records: Access: Mail, online, in person. Both court and visitors may perform in person searches. Search fee: $5.00 per name. Required to search: name, years to search, DOB. Criminal records on computer from 1993, on index cards from 1986, microfiche from 1972, index books from 1950s. Online access to criminal records is available for free at http://ccap.courts.state.wi.us/internetcourtaccess.

General Information: Public access terminal is available. No juvenile or John Doe records released. SASE required. Turnaround time 1-2 days. Fax notes: Fee to fax results is $1.50 per page. Copy fee: $1.25 per page. Certification fee: $5.00. Fee payee: Clerk of Courts. Personal checks accepted. Prepayment required.

Register in Probate 210 W Center St, Juneau, WI 53039-1091; 920-386-3550; Fax: 920-386-3933. Hours: 8AM-4:30PM (CST). *Probate.*

Note: $4.00 search fee; records computerized since 1992. Probate records are available free online; see Circuit Court.

Door County

Circuit Court PO Box 670, Sturgeon Bay, WI 54235; 920-746-2205; Fax: 920-746-2520. Hours: 8AM-4:30PM (CST). *Felony, Misdemeanor, Civil, Eviction, Small Claims.*

Civil Records: Access: Mail, online, in person. Both court and visitors may perform in person searches. Search fee: $5.00 per name. Required to search: name, years to search. Civil cases indexed by defendant, plaintiff. Civil records on computer from 4/93, on index cards from 1984, index books from 1900s. Civil court records available free online at http://ccap.courts.state.wi.us/internetcourtaccess.

Criminal Records: Access: Mail, online, in person. Both court and visitors may perform in person searches. Search fee: $5.00 per name. Required to search: name, years to search, DOB. Criminal records on computer from 4/93, on index cards from 1984, index books from 1900s. Online access to criminal records is available free at http://ccap.courts.state.wi.us/internetcourtaccess.

General Information: Public access terminal is available. No financial or paternity records released. SASE required. Turnaround time 2-3 days. Fax notes: Fee to fax results is $3.00 per document. Copy fee: $1.25 per page. Certification fee: $5.00. Fee payee: Clerk of Court. Personal checks accepted.

Register in Probate PO Box 670, 421 Nebraska St, Rm C375, Sturgeon Bay, WI 54235-2470; 920-746-2482; Fax: 920-746-2470. Hours: 8AM-4:30PM (CST). *Probate.*

Note: Probate records are available free online; see Circuit Court.

Douglas County

Circuit Court 1313 Belknap, Superior, WI 54880; Civil phone: 715-395-1237; Criminal phone: 715-395-1240; Fax: 715-395-1421. Hours: 8AM-4:30PM *Felony, Misdemeanor, Civil, Eviction, Small Claims.*

Civil Records: Access: Mail, online, in person. Both court and visitors may perform in person searches.

Search fee: $5.00 per name. Required to search: name, years to search. Civil cases indexed by defendant, plaintiff. Civil records on computer since 1994; prior records on index cards from 1976, index books from 1900s. Civil court records available free online at http://ccap.courts.state.wi.us/internetcourtaccess.

Criminal Records: Access: Mail, online, in person. Both court and visitors may perform in person searches. Search fee: $5.00 per name. Required to search: name, years to search; also helpful: DOB. Criminal records on computer since 1994; prior records on index cards from 1976, index books from 1900s. Online access to criminal records is available for free at http://ccap.courts.state.wi.us/internetcourtaccess.

General Information: Public access terminal is available. No juvenile or paternity records released. SASE required. Turnaround time 1-2 weeks. Copy fee: $1.25 per page. Certification fee: $5.00. Fee payee: Clerk of Courts. Only cashiers checks and money orders accepted. Douglas County personal checks accepted. Prepayment is required.

Register in Probate 1313 Belknap, Superior, WI 54880; 715-395-1229; Fax: 715-395-1421. Hours: 8AM-4:30PM (CST). *Probate.*

Note: Probate records are available free online; see Circuit Court.

Dunn County

Circuit Court Stokke Parkway #1500, Menomonie, WI 54751; 715-232-2611. Hours: 8AM-4:30PM (CST). *Felony, Misdemeanor, Civil, Eviction, Small Claims.*

http://ccap.courts.state.wi.us/internetcourtaccess

Civil Records: Access: Mail, online, in person. Both court and visitors may perform in person searches. Search fee: $5.00 per name. Required to search: name, years to search. Civil cases indexed by defendant, plaintiff. Civil records on computer from 1987, index cards from 1977, index books from 1900s, archives from 1970. Civil court records available free online at http://ccap.courts.state.wi.us/internetcourtaccess.

Criminal Records: Access: Mail, online, in person. Both court and visitors may perform in person searches. Search fee: $5.00 per name. Required to search: name, years to search, DOB. Criminal records on computer from 1987, index cards from 1977, index books from 1900s, archives from 1970. Online access to criminal records is available free at http://ccap.courts.state.wi.us/internetcourtaccess.

General Information: Public access terminal is available. No juvenile, family financial, sealed records released. SASE not required. Turnaround time 2-3 days. Copy fee: $1.25 per page. Certification fee: $5.00. Fee payee: Clerk of Court. Personal checks accepted. Prepayment is required.

Register in Probate 615 Stokke Parkway #1300, Menomonie, WI 54751; 715-232-6782; Fax: 715-232-6787. Hours: 8AM-4:30PM (CST). *Probate.*

Note: Probate records are available free online; see Circuit Court.

Eau Claire County

Circuit Court 721 Oxford Ave, Eau Claire, WI 54703; 715-839-4816; Fax: 715-839-4817. Hours: 8AM-5PM (CST). *Felony, Misdemeanor, Civil, Eviction, Small Claims.*

Civil Records: Access: Mail, online, in person. Both court and visitors may perform in person searches. Search fee: $5.00 per name. Required to search: name, years to search. Civil cases indexed by defendant, plaintiff. Civil records on computer from 7/92, on index cards from 1970, index books from 1968. Civil court records available free at http://ccap.courts.state.wi.us/internetcourtaccess.

Criminal Records: Access: Mail, online, in person. Both court and visitors may perform in person searches. Search fee: $5.00 per name. Required to search: name, years to search, DOB. Criminal records on computer from 7/92, on index cards from 1970, index books from 1968. Online access to criminal records is available free at http://ccap.courts.state.wi.us/internetcourtaccess.

General Information: Public access terminal is available. No paternity, financial disclosure, expungment or sealed records released. SASE required. Turnaround time 1-10 days. Copy fee: $1.25 per page. Certification fee: $5.00. Fee payee: Clerk of Court-Eau Claire County. Personal checks accepted. Prepayment is required.

Register in Probate 721 Oxford Ave, Eau Claire, WI 54703; 715-839-4823. 8AM-5PM (CST). *Probate.*

Note: Probate records are available free online; see Circuit Court.

Florence County

Circuit Court PO Box 410, Florence, WI 54121; 715-528-3205; Fax: 715-528-5470. Hours: 8:30AM-4PM (CST). *Felony, Misdemeanor, Civil, Eviction, Small Claims.*

Civil Records: Access: Mail, online, in person. Both court and visitors may perform in person searches. Search fee: $5.00 per name. Required to search: name, years to search. Civil cases indexed by defendant, plaintiff. Civil records on computer from 1991; prior records on index books from 1900s. Civil court records available for free online at http://ccap.courts.state.wi.us/internetcourtaccess.

Criminal Records: Access: Mail, online, in person. Both court and visitors may perform in person searches. Search fee: $5.00 per name. Required to search: name, years to search. Criminal records on computer from 1991; prior records on index books from 1900s. Online access to criminal records is available free at http://ccap.courts.state.wi.us/internetcourtaccess.

General Information: Public access terminal is available. No juvenile, mental health, adoption or guardianship records released. SASE required. Turnaround time 2 weeks. Copy fee: $1.25 per page. Certification fee: $4.00. Fee payee: Clerk of Courts. Personal checks accepted. Prepayment is required.

Register in Probate PO Box 410, Florence, WI 54121; 715-528-3205; Fax: 715-528-5470. Hours: 8:30AM-Noon, 1-4PM (CST). *Probate.*

Note: Probate records are available free online; see Circuit Court.

Fond du Lac County

Circuit Court PO Box 1355, Fond du Lac, WI 54936-1355; 920-929-3041; Fax: 920-929-3933. Hours: 8AM-4:30PM (CST). *Felony, Misdemeanor, Civil, Eviction, Small Claims.*

Civil Records: Access: Mail, online, in person. Both court and visitors may perform in person searches. Search fee: $5.00 per name. Required to search: name, years to search. Civil cases indexed by defendant, plaintiff. Civil records on computer from 1990, index cards from 1978, microfiche 1836 to 1978, archives prior to 1900s. Old files destroyed, on microfiche or in Historical Society. Civil court records available free online at http://ccap.courts.state.wi.us/internetcourtaccess.

Criminal Records: Access: Mail, online, in person. Both court and visitors may perform in person searches. Search fee: $5.00 per name. Required to search: name, years to search, DOB. Criminal records on computer from 1990, index cards from 1978, microfiche 1836 to 1978, archives prior to 1900s. Old files destroyed, on microfiche or in Historical Society. Online access to criminal records is available free online at http://ccap.courts.state.wi.us/internetcourtaccess.

General Information: Public access terminal is available. No juvenile or paternity records released. SASE required. Turnaround time 1-2 days. Fax notes: Fee to fax results is $2.00 per document. Copy fee: $1.25 per page. Certification fee: $5.00. Fee payee: Clerk of Circuit Court. Personal checks accepted. Prepayment is required.

Register in Probate PO Box 1355, Fond du Lac, WI 54936-1355; 920-929-3084; Fax: 920-929-7058. Hours: 8AM-4:30PM (CST). *Probate.*

Note: Probate records are available free online; see Circuit Court.

Forest County

Circuit Court 200 E Madison St, Crandon, WI 54520; 715-478-3323; Fax: 715-478-3211. Hours: 8:30AM-4:30PM (CST). *Felony, Misdemeanor, Civil, Eviction, Small Claims.*

Civil Records: Access: Mail, online, in person. Both court and visitors may perform in person searches. Search fee: $5.00 per name. Required to search: name, years to search. Civil cases indexed by defendant, plaintiff. Civil records on computer from 1994, on index cards from 1979, index books from 1920s. Civil court records available for free online at http://ccap.courts.state.wi.us/internetcourtaccess.

Criminal Records: Access: Mail, online, in person. Both court and visitors may perform in person searches. Search fee: $5.00 per name. Required to search: name, years to search, DOB. Criminal records on computer from 1994, on index cards from 1979, index books from 1920s. Online access to criminal records is available free at http://ccap.courts.state.wi.us/internetcourtaccess.

General Information: Public access terminal is available. No juvenile, paternity records released. SASE required. Turnaround time 1-2 days. Fax notes: Fee to fax results is $1.25 per page. Copy fee: $1.25 per page. Certification fee: $5.00. Fee payee: Clerk of Court. Personal checks accepted. Prepayment is required.

Register in Probate 200 E Madison St, Crandon, WI 54520; 715-478-2418; Fax: 715-478-2430. Hours: 8:30AM-4:30PM (CST). *Probate.*

Note: Probate records are available free online; see Circuit Court.

Grant County

Circuit Court PO Box 110, Lancaster, WI 53813; 608-723-2752; Fax: 608-723-7370. Hours: 8AM-4:30PM (CST). *Felony, Misdemeanor, Civil, Eviction, Small Claims.*

Civil Records: Access: Phone, mail, fax, online, in person. Both court and visitors may perform in person searches. No search fee. Required to search: name, years to search. Civil cases indexed by defendant, plaintiff. Civil records on computer from 10/93, on index books from 1900s. Civil court records available for free online at http://ccap.courts.state.wi.us/internetcourtaccess.

Criminal Records: Access: Phone, mail, fax, online, in person. Only the court performs in person searches; visitors may not. No search fee. Required to search: name, years to search. Criminal records on computer from 10/93, on index books from 1900s. Online access to criminal records is available free at http://ccap.courts.state.wi.us/internetcourtaccess.

General Information: Public access terminal is available. No juvenile, paternity records released. SASE required. Turnaround time 2 weeks. Copy fee: $1.25 per page. Certification fee: $5.00 plus $1.25 per page. Fee payee: Clerk of Court. Personal checks accepted. Prepayment is required.

Register in Probate 130 W Maple St, Rm A360, Lancaster, WI 53813; 608-723-2697; Fax: 608-723-7370. Hours: 8AM-4:30PM (CST). *Probate.*

Note: $4.00 search fee, records computerized since 1993. Probate records are available free online; see Circuit Court.

Green County

Circuit Court 1016 16th Ave, Monroe, WI 53566; 608-328-9433; Fax: 608-328-2835. Hours: 8AM-5PM (CST). *Felony, Misdemeanor, Civil, Eviction, Small Claims.*

Civil Records: Access: Mail, online, in person. Both court and visitors may perform in person searches. Search fee: $5.00 per name. Required to search: name, years to search; also helpful: address. Civil cases indexed by defendant, plaintiff. Civil records on index cards from 1984, index books from 1900s; computerized back to 1994. Civil court records available free online at http://ccap.courts.state.wi.us/internetcourtaccess.

Criminal Records: Access: Mail, online, in person. Both court and visitors may perform in person searches. Search fee: $5.00 per name. Required to search: name, years to search; also helpful: DOB. Criminal records on index cards from 1984, index books from 1900s; computerized back to 1994. Online access to criminal records is available free at http://ccap.courts.state.wi.us/internetcourtaccess.

General Information: Public access terminal is available. No juvenile, paternity or sealed records released. SASE required. Turnaround time 1-2 days. Copy fee: $1.25 per page. Certification fee: $5.00. Fee payee: Clerk of Court. Personal checks accepted. Prepayment is required.

Register in Probate 1016 16th Ave, Monroe, WI 53566; 608-328-9567; Fax: 608-328-2835. Hours: 8AM-12, 1PM-5PM (CST). *Probate.*

Note: Probate records are available free online; see Circuit Court.

Green Lake County

Circuit Court 492 Hill St, PO Box 3188, Green Lake, WI 54941; 920-294-4142; Fax: 920-294-4150. Hours: 8AM-4:30PM (CST). *Felony, Misdemeanor, Civil, Eviction, Small Claims.*

Civil Records: Access: Mail, online, in person. Both court and visitors may perform in person searches. Search fee: $5.00 per name. Required to search: name, years to search. Civil cases indexed by defendant, plaintiff. Civil records on computer from 4/93, on index cards since 1900s. Civil court records available free online at http://ccap.courts.state.wi.us/internetcourtaccess.

Criminal Records: Access: Mail, online, in person. Both court and visitors may perform in person searches. Search fee: $5.00 per name. Required to search: name, years to search. Criminal records on computer from 4/93, on index cards since 1900s. Online access to criminal records is available for free at http://ccap.courts.state.wi.us/internetcourtaccess.

General Information: Public access terminal is available. No paternity or juvenile ordinance records released. SASE required. Turnaround time 1-3 days. Copy fee: $1.25 per page. Certification fee: $5.00. Fee payee: Clerk of Circuit Clerk. Personal checks accepted. Prepayment is required.

Register in Probate 492 Hill St, PO Box 3188, Green Lake, WI 54941; 920-294-4044. Hours: 8AM-4:30PM (CST). *Probate.*

www.co.green-lake.wi.us

Note: Probate records are available free online; see Circuit Court.

Iowa County

Circuit Court 222 N Iowa St, Dodgeville, WI 53533; 608-935-0395; Fax: 608-935-0386. Hours: 8:30AM-4:30PM (CST). *Felony, Misdemeanor, Civil, Eviction, Small Claims.*

Civil Records: Access: Mail, online, in person. Both court and visitors may perform in person searches. Search fee: $5.00 per name. Required to search: name, years to search. Civil cases indexed by defendant, plaintiff. Civil records on computer from 1992, index cards from 1987, archives from 1917, index books from 1829. Civil court records available free online at http://ccap.courts.state.wi.us/internetcourtaccess.

Criminal Records: Access: Mail, online, in person. Both court and visitors may perform in person searches. Search fee: $5.00 per name. Required to search: name, years to search, DOB. Criminal records on computer from 1992, index cards from 1987, archives from 1917, index books from 1829. Online access to criminal records is available free at http://ccap.courts.state.wi.us/internetcourtaccess.

General Information: Public access terminal is available. No adoption, paternity or mental records released. SASE required. Turnaround time same day. Fax notes: Fee to fax results is $1.25 per page. Copy fee: $1.25 per page. Certification fee: $5.00. Fee payee: Clerk of Court. Personal checks accepted. Prepayment is required.

Register in Probate 222 N Iowa St, Dodgeville, WI 53533; 608-935-0347; Fax: 608-935-0386. Hours: 8:30AM-Noon, 12;30-4:30PM (CST). *Probate.*

Note: Probate records are available free online; see Circuit Court.

Iron County

Circuit Court 300 Taconite St, #207, Hurley, WI 54534; 715-561-4084; Fax: 715-561-4054. Hours: 8AM-4PM (CST). *Felony, Misdemeanor, Civil, Eviction, Small Claims.*

Civil Records: Access: Phone, mail, online, in person. Both court and visitors may perform in person searches. Search fee: $5.00 per name. Required to search: name, years to search. Civil cases indexed by defendant, plaintiff. Civil records on index cards from 1989, index books from 1920. Civil court records available free online at http://ccap.courts.state.wi.us/internetcourtaccess. Phone access for title companies only.

Criminal Records: Access: Mail, online, in person. Both court and visitors may perform in person searches. Search fee: $5.00 per name. Required to search: name, years to search, DOB. Criminal records on index cards from 1989, index books from 1920. Online access to criminal records is available free at http://ccap.courts.state.wi.us/internetcourtaccess.

General Information: Public access terminal is available. No juvenile or paternity records released. SASE required. Turnaround time 10 days. Copy fee: $1.25 per page. Certification fee: $5.00. Fee payee: Clerk of Court. Personal checks accepted.

Register in Probate 300 Taconite St, Hurley, WI 54534; 715-561-3434; Fax: 715-561-4054. Hours: 8AM-4PM (CST). *Probate.*

Note: Probate records are available free online; see Circuit Court.

Jackson County

Circuit Court 307 Main St, Black River Falls, WI 54615; 715-284-0208; Fax: 715-284-0270. Hours: 8AM-4:30PM (CST). *Felony, Misdemeanor, Civil, Eviction, Small Claims.*

www.co.jackson.wi.us

Civil Records: Access: Mail, online, in person. Both court and visitors may perform in person searches.

Search fee: $5.00 per name. Required to search: name, years to search. Civil cases indexed by defendant, plaintiff. Civil records on computer from 6/92, on index cards from 1979, index books to 1935, files and indexes prior to 1935 destroyed. Civil court records available free online at http://ccap.courts.state.wi.us/internetcourtaccess.

Criminal Records: Access: Mail, online, in person. Both court and visitors may perform in person searches. Search fee: $5.00 per name. Required to search: name, years to search, DOB. Criminal records on computer from 6/92, on index cards from 1979, index books to 1935, files and indexes prior to 1935 destroyed. Online access to criminal records is available free at http://ccap.courts.state.wi.us/internetcourtaccess.

General Information: Public access terminal is available. No juvenile or pre-judgment paternity records released. SASE required. Turnaround time 1-4 days. Copy fee: $1.25 per page. Certification fee: $5.00. Fee payee: Clerk of Court. Personal checks accepted. I. Prepayment is required. Prepayment required if over $5.00.

Register in Probate 307 Main St, Black River Falls, WI 54615; 715-284-0213; Fax: 715-284-0277. Hours: 8AM-4:30PM (CST). *Probate.*

Note: Probate records are available free online; see Circuit Court.

Jefferson County

Circuit Court 320 S Main St, Jefferson, WI 53549; 920-674-7150; Fax: 920-674-7425. Hours: 8AM-4:30PM (CST). *Felony, Misdemeanor, Civil, Eviction, Small Claims.*

Civil Records: Access: Mail, online, in person. Both court and visitors may perform in person searches. Search fee: $5.00 per name. Required to search: name, years to search. Civil cases indexed by defendant, plaintiff. Civil records on computer from 1992, on index cards from 1979, index books from late 1800s. Civil court records available free online at http://ccap.courts.state.wi.us/internetcourtaccess.

Criminal Records: Access: Mail, online, in person. Both court and visitors may perform in person searches. Search fee: $5.00 per name. Required to search: name, years to search, DOB. Criminal records on computer from 1992, on index cards from 1979, index books from late 1800s. Online access to criminal records is available free at http://ccap.courts.state.wi.us/internetcourtaccess.

General Information: No juvenile or mental health records released. SASE required. Turnaround time 2-3 days. Copy fee: $1.25 per page. Certification fee: $5.00. Fee payee: Clerk of Courts. Personal checks accepted. Prepayment is required.

Register in Probate 320 S Main St, Jefferson, WI 53549; 920-674-7245; Fax: 920-675-0134. Hours: 8AM-4:30PM (CST). *Probate.*

Note: Probate records are available free online; see Circuit Court.

Juneau County

Circuit Court 220 E State St, Mauston, WI 53948; 608-847-9356; Fax: 608-847-9360. Hours: 8AM-Noon, 12:30-4:30PM (CST). *Felony, Misdemeanor, Civil, Eviction, Small Claims.*

Civil Records: Access: Mail, online, in person. Both court and visitors may perform in person searches. Search fee: $5.00 per name. Fee is per case. Required to search: name, years to search. Civil cases indexed by defendant, plaintiff. Civil records on computer from 1988, index cards from 1977, index books from 1900, microfiche from 1856-1900. Civil court records available free online at http://ccap.courts.state.wi.us/internetcourtaccess.

Criminal Records: Access: Mail, online, fax, in person. Both court and visitors may perform in person searches. Search fee: $5.00 per name. Required to search: name, years to search, DOB. Criminal records on computer from 1988, index cards from 1977, index books from 1900, microfiche from 1856-1900. Online access to criminal records is available free at http://ccap.courts.state.wi.us/internetcourtaccess.

General Information: Public access terminal is available. No juvenile, confidential family or paternity records released. SASE required. Turnaround time 1 week. Copy fee: $1.25 per page. Certification fee: $5.00. Fee payee: Juneau County Clerk of Court. Personal checks accepted. Prepayment is required.

Register in Probate 220 E State St Rm 205, Mauston, WI 53948; 608-847-9346; Fax: 608-847-9349. Hours: 8AM-4:30PM (CST). *Probate.*

Note: Probate records are available free online; see Circuit Court.

Kenosha County

Circuit Court 912 56th St, Kenosha, WI 53140; 262-653-2664; Fax: 262-653-2435. Hours: 8AM-5PM (CST). *Felony, Misdemeanor, Civil, Eviction, Small Claims.*

Civil Records: Access: Mail, online, in person. Both court and visitors may perform in person searches. Search fee: $5.00 per name. Required to search: name, years to search. Civil cases indexed by defendant, plaintiff. Civil records on computer from 1989, index cards from 1960, microfiche from 1850. Civil court records available for free online at http://ccap.courts.state.wi.us/internetcourtaccess.

Criminal Records: Access: Mail, online, in person. Both court and visitors may perform in person searches. Search fee: $5.00 per name. Required to search: name, years to search; also helpful: DOB, SSN. Criminal records on computer from 1989, index cards from 1960, microfiche from 1850. Online access to criminal records is available for free online at http://ccap.courts.state.wi.us/internetcourtaccess.

General Information: Public access terminal is available. No juvenile or paternity records released. SASE required. Turnaround time 1-2 days. Copy fee: $1.25 per page. Certification fee: $5.00. Fee payee: Clerk of Court. Personal checks accepted. Prepayment is required.

Register in Probate Courthouse Rm 304, 912 56th St, Kenosha, WI 53140; 262-653-6678; Fax: 262-653-2435. Hours: 8AM-5PM (CST). *Probate.*

Note: $4.00 per search, records indexed on computer (1992) and cards. Probate records are available free online; see Circuit Court.

Kewaunee County

Circuit Court 613 Dodge St, Kewaunee, WI 54216; 920-388-7144; Fax: 920-388-3139. Hours: 8AM-4:30PM (CST). *Felony, Misdemeanor, Civil, Eviction, Small Claims.*

Civil Records: Access: Phone, mail, online, in person. Both court and visitors may perform in person searches. Search fee: $5.00 per name. Required to search: name, years to search. Civil cases indexed by defendant, plaintiff. Computerized records from 1993, civil records on index cards from 1950, index books from 1852. Civil court records available free online at http://ccap.courts.state.wi.us/internetcourtaccess.

Criminal Records: Access: Phone, mail, online, in person. Both court and visitors may perform in person searches. Search fee: $5.00 per name. Required to search: name, years to search, DOB. Computerized records from 1993, criminal records on index cards from 1950, index books from 1852. Online access to criminal records is available free at http://ccap.courts.state.wi.us/internetcourtaccess.

General Information: No paternity records released. SASE required. Turnaround time 1-2 days. Copy fee: $1.25 per page. Certification fee: $5.00. Fee payee: Clerk of Circuit Court. Personal checks accepted. Prepayment is required.

Register in Probate 613 Dodge St, Kewaunee, WI 54216; 920-388-4410; Fax: 920-388-3139. Hours: 8AM-4:30PM (CST). *Probate.*

Note: Probate records are available free online; see Circuit Court.

La Crosse County

Circuit Court 333 Vine St, La Crosse, WI 54601; 608-785-9590/9573; Fax: 608-789-7821. Hours: 8:30AM-5PM (CST). *Felony, Misdemeanor, Civil, Eviction, Small Claims.*

Civil Records: Access: Phone, mail, online, in person. Both court and visitors may perform in person searches. Search fee: $5.00 per name. Required to search: name, years to search. Civil cases indexed by defendant, plaintiff. Civil records on computer from 1993, on index cards from 1983, index books from 1917. Civil court records available for free online at http://ccap.courts.state.wi.us/internetcourtaccess.

Criminal Records: Access: Phone, mail, online, in person. Both court and visitors may perform in person searches. Search fee: $5.00 per name. Required to search: name, years to search; also helpful: DOB, SSN. Criminal records on computer from 1993, on index cards from 1983, index books from 1917. Online access to criminal records is available free at http://ccap.courts.state.wi.us/internetcourtaccess.

General Information: Public access terminal is available. No juvenile, paternity or finances in family records released. SASE required. Turnaround time 1-2 days. Fax notes: Fee to fax results is $1.25 per page. Copy fee: $1.25 per page. Certification fee: $5.00. Fee payee: Clerk of Courts. Personal checks accepted. Prepayment is required.

Register in Probate 333 Vine St, Rm 1201, La Crosse, WI 54601; 608-785-9882. Hours: 8:30AM-5PM (CST). *Probate.*

Note: Probate records are available free online; see Circuit Court.

Lafayette County

Circuit Court 626 Main St, Darlington, WI 53530; 608-776-4832. Hours: 8AM-4:30PM (CST). *Felony, Misdemeanor, Civil, Eviction, Small Claims.*

Civil Records: Access: Mail, online, in person. Both court and visitors may perform in person searches. Search fee: $5.00 per name. Required to search: name, years to search. Civil cases indexed by defendant. Civil records on index cards from 1973, index books from 1900; computerized back to 1993. Civil court records available free online at http://ccap.courts.state.wi.us/internetcourtaccess.

Criminal Records: Access: Mail, online, in person. Both court and visitors may perform in person searches. Search fee: $5.00 per name. Required to search: name, years to search. Criminal records on index cards from 1973, index books from 1900; computerized back to 1993. Online access to criminal records is available free at http://ccap.courts.state.wi.us/internetcourtaccess.

General Information: Public access terminal is available. No juvenile records released. SASE required. Turnaround time 2-3 days. Copy fee: $1.25 per page. Certification fee: $5.00. Fee payee: Clerk of Circuit Court. Personal checks accepted. Prepayment required.

Register in Probate 626 Main St, Rm 302, Darlington, WI 53530; 608-776-4811. Hours: 8AM-4:30PM (CST). *Probate.*

Note: Probate records are available free online; see Circuit Court.

Langlade County

Circuit Court 800 Clermont St, Antigo, WI 54409; 715-627-6215. Hours: 8:30AM-4:30PM (CST). *Felony, Misdemeanor, Civil, Eviction, Small Claims.*

Civil Records: Access: Mail, online, in person. Both court and visitors may perform in person searches. Search fee: $5.00 per name. Required to search: name, years to search. Civil cases indexed by defendant, plaintiff. Civil records on index books from 1905, computerized since 1993. Civil court records available free online at http://ccap.courts.state.wi.us/internetcourtaccess.

Criminal Records: Access: Mail, online, in person. Both court and visitors may perform in person searches. Search fee: $5.00 per name. Required to search: name, years to search. Criminal records on index books from 1905, computerized since 1993. Online access to criminal records is available free at http://ccap.courts.state.wi.us/internetcourtaccess.

General Information: Public access terminal is available. No confidential records released. SASE required. Turnaround time 2-3 days. Copy fee: $1.25 per page. Certification fee: $5.00. Fee payee: Clerk of Court. Personal checks accepted. Prepayment is required.

Register in Probate 800 Clermont St, Antigo, WI 54409; 715-627-6213; Fax: 715-627-6329. Hours: 8:30AM-4:30PM (CST). *Probate.*

Note: There is a $4.00 search fee. Probate records are available free online; see Circuit Court.

Lincoln County

Circuit Court 1110 E Main St, Merrill, WI 54452; 715-536-0319; Fax: 715-536-0361. Hours: 8:15AM-4:30PM (CST). *Felony, Misdemeanor, Civil, Eviction, Small Claims.*

Civil Records: Access: Mail, online, in person. Both court and visitors may perform in person searches. Search fee: $5.00 per name. Required to search: name, years to search. Civil cases indexed by defendant. Civil records on computer from 1990, index cards from 1982, index books from 1900s. Civil court records available free at http://ccap.courts.state.wi.us/internetcourtaccess.

Criminal Records: Access: Mail, online, in person. Both court and visitors may perform in person searches. Search fee: $5.00 per name. Required to search: name, years to search; also helpful: DOB, SSN. Criminal records on computer from 1990, index cards from 1982, index books from 1900s. Online access to criminal records is available free at http://ccap.courts.state.wi.us/internetcourtaccess.

General Information: No paternity or sealed records released. SASE required. Turnaround time 1-2 days. Copy fee: $1.25 per page. Certification fee: $5.00. Fee payee: Clerk of Court. Personal checks accepted. Local personal checks accepted. Prepayment is required.

Register in Probate 1110 E Main St, Merrill, WI 54452; 715-536-0342; 536-0378; Fax: 715-536-5230. Hours: 8:15AM-Noon, 1-4:30PM (CST). *Probate.*

Note: Probate records are available free online; see Circuit Court.

Manitowoc County

Circuit Court PO Box 2000, Manitowoc, WI 54221-2000; 920-683-4030. Hours: 8:30AM-5PM M; 8:30AM-4:30PM T-F (CST). *Felony, Misdemeanor, Civil, Eviction, Small Claims.*

Civil Records: Access: Phone, mail, online, in person. Both court and visitors may perform in person searches. Search fee: $5.00 per name. Required to search: name, years to search. Civil cases indexed by defendant, plaintiff. Civil records on computer from 1993, on index cards from 1962, index books from 1906, Historical Society has prior records. Civil court records available free online at http://ccap.courts.state.wi.us/internetcourtaccess. Prior written agreement with court required for phone access.

Criminal Records: Access: Phone, mail, online, in person. Both court and visitors may perform in person searches. Search fee: $5.00 per name. Required to search: name, years to search, DOB. Criminal records on computer from 1993, on index cards from 1962, index books from 1906, Historical Society has prior records. Online access to criminal records is available free at http://ccap.courts.state.wi.us/internetcourtaccess. Prior written agreement with court required for phone access.

General Information: Public access terminal is available. No confidential records released. SASE required. Turnaround time 2-3 days. Copy fee: $1.25 per page. Certification fee: $1.25 per page. Fee payee: Clerk of Circuit Court. Personal checks accepted. Prepayment is required.

Register in Probate 1010 S 8th St Rm 116, Manitowoc, WI 54220; 920-683-4016; Fax: 920-683-5182. Hours: 8:30AM-4:30PM T-F; 8:30AM-5PM M (CST). *Probate.*

Note: Probate records are available free online; see Circuit Court.

Marathon County

Circuit Court 500 Forest St, Wausau, WI 54403; 715-261-1300; Civil phone: 715-261-1300; Fax: 715-261-1319 Civ; 261-1280 Crim. Hours: 8AM-5PM (Summer hours 8AM-4:30PM Memorial-Labor Day) *Felony, Misdemeanor, Civil, Eviction, Small Claims.*

Note: Small claims phone is 261-1310; Traffic, 261-1270.

Civil Records: Access: Mail, online, in person. Both court and visitors may perform in person searches. Search fee: $5.00 per name. Required to search: name, years to search. Civil cases indexed by defendant, plaintiff. Civil records on computer from 1992, on index cards from 1979. Civil court records available free at http://ccap.courts.state.wi.us/internetcourtaccess. All requests must be in writing, using their form if possible.

Criminal Records: Access: Mail, online, in person. Both court and visitors may perform in person searches. Search fee: $5.00 per name. Required to search: name, years to search, DOB. Criminal records on computer from 1992, on index cards from 1979, index books from 1900s. Criminal court records are available free at http://ccap.courts.state.wi.us/internetcourtaccess. All requests must be in writing, using their form if possible.

General Information: No mental health or juvenile records released. SASE required. Turnaround time 1-3 days. Copy fee: $1.25 per page. Certification fee: $5.00. Fee payee: Clerk of Court. Personal checks accepted. Prepayment is required.

Register in Probate 500 Forest St, Wausau, WI 54403; 715-261-1260; Fax: 715-261-1269. Hours: 8AM-5PM (CST). *Probate.*

Note: Probate records are available free online; see Circuit Court.

Marinette County

Circuit Court 1926 Hall Ave, Marinette, WI 54143-1717; 715-732-7450. Hours: 8:30AM-4:30PM (CST). *Felony, Misdemeanor, Civil, Eviction, Small Claims.*

Civil Records: Access: Mail, online, in person. Both court and visitors may perform in person searches. Search fee: $5.00 per name. Required to search: name, years to search. Civil cases indexed by defendant, plaintiff. Civil records on computer from 1989, index cards from 1980, index books from 1906, prior records at Historical Society. Civil court records 1994 to present available free online at http://ccap.courts.state.wi.us/internetcourtaccess.

Criminal Records: Access: Mail, online, in person. Both court and visitors may perform in person searches. Search fee: $5.00 per name. Required to search: name, years to search, DOB. Criminal records on computer from 1989, index cards from 1980, index books from 1906, prior records at Historical Society. Online access to criminal records is available free at http://ccap.courts.state.wi.us/internetcourtaccess.

General Information: Public access terminal is available. No paternity records released. SASE required. Turnaround time 2-3 days. Copy fee: $1.25 per page. Certification fee: $5.00. Fee payee: Clerk of Courts. Personal checks accepted. Prepayment required.

Register in Probate 1926 Hall Ave, Marinette, WI 54143-1717; 715-732-7475; Fax: 715-732-7561. Hours: 8:30AM-4:30PM (CST). *Probate.*

Note: Probate records are available free online; see Circuit Court.

Marquette County

Circuit Court PO Box 187, Montello, WI 53949; 608-297-9102; Fax: 608-297-9188. Hours: 8AM-Noon, 12:30-4:30PM (CST). *Felony, Misdemeanor, Civil, Eviction, Small Claims.*

Civil Records: Access: Phone, mail, online, in person. Both court and visitors may perform in person searches. Search fee: $5.00 per name. Required to search: name, years to search. Civil cases indexed by defendant, plaintiff. Civil records on index books from 1900s, prior records at Historical Society; computerized back to 1996. Civil court records available free online at http://ccap.courts.state.wi.us/internetcourtaccess.

Criminal Records: Access: Phone, mail, online, in person. Both court and visitors may perform in person searches. Search fee: $5.00 per name. Required to search: name, years to search, DOB, full name. Criminal records on index books from 1900s, prior records at Historical Society; computerized back to 1996. Online access to criminal records is available free at http://ccap.courts.state.wi.us/internetcourtaccess.

General Information: Public access terminal is available. No adoption, juvenile, paternity, guardianship, mental or termination of parental right records released. SASE not required. Turnaround time 1-2 days. Fax notes: Fee to fax results is $2.00 per page. Copy fee: $1.25 per page. Certification fee: $5.00. Fee payee: Clerk of Circuit Court. Personal checks accepted. Prepayment is required.

Register in Probate 77 W Park St, PO Box 749, Montello, WI 53949; 608-297-9105; Fax: 608-297-9188. Hours: 8AM-4:30PM (CST). *Probate.*

Note: Probate records are available free online; see Circuit Court profile.

Menominee County

Circuit Court PO Box 279, Keshena, WI 54135; 715-799-3313; Fax: 715-799-1322. Hours: 8AM-4:30PM (CST). *Felony, Misdemeanor, Civil, Eviction, Small Claims.*

Civil Records: Access: Mail, online, in person. Both court and visitors may perform in person searches. Search fee: $5.00 per name. Required to search: name, years to search. Civil cases indexed by defendant, plaintiff. Civil records are indexed by cards, kept in files since 1979, computerized since 1992. Ollder records are at the Historical Society. Civil court records available free at http://ccap.courts.state.wi.us/internetcourtaccess.
Criminal Records: Access: Mail, online, in person. Both court and visitors may perform in person searches. Search fee: $5.00 per name. Required to search: name, years to search, DOB. Criminal records are indexed by cards, kept in files since 1979, computerized since 1992. Older records are at the Historical Society. Online access to criminal records is available free at http://ccap.courts.state.wi.us/internetcourtaccess.
General Information: Public access terminal is available. No juvenile, mental, adoption. Turnaround time 3-4 days. Copy fee: $1.25 per page. Certification fee: $5.00. Fee payee: Clerk of Court. Personal checks accepted.

Register in Probate 311 N Main St, RM 203, Shawano, WI 54166; 715-526-8631; Fax: 715-526-8622. Hours: 8AM-4:30PM (CST). *Probate.*

Note: Tribal probate records only in Keshena (Menominee Tribal Court); Non-tribal records are in Shawano County. Probate records are available free online; see Circuit Court.

Milwaukee County

Circuit Court - Civil 901 N. 9th Street Rm G-9, Milwaukee, WI 53233; 414-278-4128; Fax: 414-223-1256. 8AM-5PM (CST). *Civil, Eviction, Small Claims.*
http://204.194.250.11

Civil Records: Access: Mail, online, in person. Both court and visitors may perform in person searches. Search fee: $5.00 per name. Required to search: name, years to search; also helpful-DOB or SSN. Civil cases indexed by defendant, plaintiff. Civil records on computer from 1985, on microfiche from 1949, prior with County Historical Society. Civil court records available free online at http://ccap.courts.state.wi.us/internetcourtaccess.
General Information: Public access terminal is available. (Terminla if room 114 of Safety Building.) No paternity records released. SASE required. Turnaround time 1-2 weeks. Fax notes: Will not fax results. Copy fee: $1.25 per page. Certification fee: $5.00. Fee payee: Milwaukee County Clerk of Circuit Court. Personal checks accepted. Prepayment is required.

Circuit Court - Criminal Division 821 W State St, Milwaukee, WI 53233; 414-278-4538; Fax: 414-223-1262. 8AM-5PM *Felony, Misdemeanor.*
http://204.194.250.11/Service/organizationDetail.asp?id=2830

Criminal Records: Access: Fax, mail, online, in person. Both court and visitors may perform in person searches. Search fee: $5.00 per name. Required to search: name, years to search, DOB. Criminal records on computer from 10/86, index books and cards prior. Criminal court records are available free on the Internet at http://ccap.courts.state.wi.us/internetcourtaccess. Also, criminal case records on Milwaukee Municipal Court Case Information System database are available free online at www.court.ci.mil.wi.us/home.asp. Search by Case Number, by Citation Number, or by Name.

General Information: Public access terminal is available. No sealed records released. SASE required. Turnaround time 4 days. Fax notes: No additional fee to fax results, but search fees still apply. Copy fee: $1.25 per page. Certification fee: $5.00. Fee payee: Clerk of Circuit Court. Personal checks accepted. Prepayment is required.

Register in Probate 901 N 9th St Rm 207, Milwaukee, WI 53233; 414-278-4444; Fax: 414-223-1814. Hours: 8AM-4:30PM (CST). *Probate.*

Monroe County

Circuit Court 112 S Court St #203, Sparta, WI 54656-1764; 608-269-8745. Hours: 8AM-4:30PM (CST). *Felony, Misdemeanor, Civil, Eviction, Small Claims.*

Civil Records: Access: Fax, mail, online, in person. Both court and visitors may perform in person searches. Search fee: $5.00 per name. Required to search: name, years to search. Civil cases indexed by defendant, plaintiff. Civil records on computer and cards. Civil court records available free online at http://ccap.courts.state.wi.us/internetcourtaccess.
Criminal Records: Access: Fax, mail, online, in person. Both court and visitors may perform in person searches. Search fee: $5.00 per name. Required to search: name, years to search. Criminal records on computer and cards. Online access to criminal records is available free at http://ccap.courts.state.wi.us/internetcourtaccess.
General Information: Public access terminal is available. No paternity, medical or financial records released. SASE required. Turnaround time 1 week. Fax notes: $1.25 per page. No charge to toll free lines. Copy fee: $1.25 per page. Certification fee: $5.00. Fee payee: Clerk of Court. Local checks accepted. Prepayment is required.

Register in Probate 112 S Court, Rm 301, Sparta, WI 54656-1765; 608-269-8701; Fax: 608-269-8950. Hours: 8AM-4:30PM (CST). *Probate.*

Note: Probate records are available free online; see Circuit Court.

Oconto County

Circuit Court 301 Washington St, Oconto, WI 54153; 920-834-6855; Fax: 920-834-6867. Hours: 8AM-4PM (CST). *Felony, Misdemeanor, Civil, Small Claims.*

Civil Records: Access: Mail, online, in person. Both court and visitors may perform in person searches. Search fee: $5.00 per name. Required to search: name, years to search. Civil cases indexed by defendant, plaintiff. Civil records on computer since 1994; prior records on index books from 1930s, Historical Society has earlier records. Civil court records available free at http://ccap.courts.state.wi.us/internetcourtaccess.
Criminal Records: Access: Mail, online, in person. Both court and visitors may perform in person searches. Search fee: $5.00 per name. Required to search: name, years to search, DOB. Criminal records on computer since 1994; prior records on index books from 1930s; Historical Society has earlier records. Online access to criminal records is available free at http://ccap.courts.state.wi.us/internetcourtaccess.
General Information: Public access terminal is available. No juvenile or paternity records released. SASE required. Turnaround time 1-2 days. Copy fee: $1.25 per page. Certification fee: $5.00. Fee payee: Oconto County Clerk of Court. Personal checks accepted. Prepayment is required.

Register in Probate 301 Washington St, Oconto, WI 54153; 920-834-6839; Fax: 920-834-6867. Hours: 8AM-4PM (CST). *Probate.*

Note: Probate records are available free online; see Circuit Court.

Oneida County

Circuit Court PO Box 400, Rhinelander, WI 54501; 715-369-6120. Hours: 8AM-4:30PM (CST). *Felony, Misdemeanor, Civil, Eviction, Small Claims.*

Civil Records: Access: Mail, online, in person. Both court and visitors may perform in person searches. Search fee: $5.00 per name. Required to search: name, years to search. Civil cases indexed by defendant, plaintiff. Civil records on computer from 1992, index cards from 1980, index books from 1900s. Civil court records available free online at http://ccap.courts.state.wi.us/internetcourtaccess.
Criminal Records: Access: Mail, online, in person. Both court and visitors may perform in person searches. Search fee: $5.00 per name. Required to search: name, years to search, DOB. Criminal records on computer from 1992, index cards from 1980, index books from 1900s. Online access to criminal records is available free at http://ccap.courts.state.wi.us/internetcourtaccess.
General Information: Public access terminal is available. No paternity records released. SASE not required. Turnaround time 1 week. Copy fee: $1.25 per page. Certification fee: $5.00. Fee payee: Clerk of Court. Personal checks accepted. Prepayment required.

Register in Probate PO Box 400, Rhinelander, WI 54501; 715-369-6159. Hours: 8AM-12, 1-4:30PM (CST). *Probate.*

Note: Probate records are available free online; see Circuit Court.

Outagamie County

Circuit Court 320 S Walnut St, Appleton, WI 54911; 920-832-5130; Fax: 920-832-5115. Hours: 8:00AM-4:30PM (CST). *Felony, Misdemeanor, Civil, Eviction, Small Claims.*

Note: Small claims and eviction records at 920-832-5135.

Civil Records: Access: In person only. Visitors must perform in person searches for themselves. No search fee. Required to search: name, years to search. Civil cases indexed by defendant, plaintiff. Civil records on computer from 10/87, index cards from 1983, index books from 1901, some records on microfiche.
Criminal Records: Access: Mail, in person. Both court and visitors may perform in person searches. Search fee: $5.00 per name. Required to search: name, years to search, DOB. Criminal records on computer from 10/87, index cards from 1983, index books from 1901, some records on microfiche.
General Information: Public access terminal is available. No adoption or juvenile records released. SASE required. Turnaround time 2-3 days. Fax notes: Fax fee is $1.25 per page. Copy fee: $1.25 per page. Certification fee: $5.00. Fee payee: Clerk of Court. Personal checks accepted. Prepayment is required.

Register in Probate 320 S Walnut St, Appleton, WI 54911; 920-832-5601; Fax: 920-832-5115. Hours: 8:30AM-Noon, 1-5PM (CST). *Probate.*

Ozaukee County

Circuit Court 1201 S Spring St, Port Washington, WI 53074; 262-284-8409; Fax: 262-284-8491. Hours: 8:30AM-5PM (CST). *Felony, Misdemeanor, Civil, Eviction, Small Claims.*
www.co.ozaukee.wi.us/ClerkCourts/default.htm

Civil Records: Access: Mail, online, in person. Both court and visitors may perform in person searches.

Search fee: $5.00 per name. Required to search: name, years to search. Civil cases indexed by defendant, plaintiff. Civil records on computer from 1991, index cards from late 1950s. Civil court records available free at http://ccap.courts.state.wi.us/internetcourtaccess.

Criminal Records: Access: Mail, online, in person. Both court and visitors may perform in person searches. Search fee: $5.00 per name. Required to search: name, years to search, DOB. Criminal records on computer from 1989. Online access to criminal records is available free at http://ccap.courts.state.wi.us/internetcourtaccess.

General Information: Public access terminal is available. No paternity records released. SASE required. Turnaround time 1 week. Copy fee: $1.25 per page. Certification fee: $5.00. Fee payee: Clerk of Court. Business checks accepted. In-state personal checks accepted. Prepayment is required.

Register in Probate PO Box 994, Port Washington, WI 53074; 262-284-8370; Fax: 262-284-8491. Hours: 8:30AM-5PM (CST). *Probate.*

Note: Probate records are available free online; see Circuit Court.

Pepin County

Circuit Court PO Box 39, Durand, WI 54736; 715-672-8861; Fax: 715-672-8521. Hours: 8:30AM-Noon, 12:30-4:30PM (CST). *Felony, Misdemeanor, Civil, Eviction, Small Claims.*

Civil Records: Access: Mail, online, in person. Both court and visitors may perform in person searches. Search fee: $5.00 per name. Required to search: name, years to search. Civil cases indexed by plaintiff. Civil records on computer from 1995, index books from 1900s. Civil court records available free online at http://ccap.courts.state.wi.us/internetcourtaccess.

Criminal Records: Access: Mail, online, in person. Both court and visitors may perform in person searches. Search fee: $5.00 per name. Required to search: name, years to search, DOB. Criminal records on computer from 1995, index books from 1900s. Online access to criminal records is available free at http://ccap.courts.state.wi.us/internetcourtaccess.

General Information: Public access terminal is available. No minor or financial divorce records released. SASE required. Turnaround time 1 week. Copy fee: $1.25 per page. Certification fee: $5.00. Fee payee: Clerk of Court. Personal checks accepted. Prepayment is required.

Register in Probate PO Box 39, Durand, WI 54736; 715-672-8859 X672; Fax: 715-672-8521. Hours: 8:30AM-Noon, 1-4:30PM (CST). *Probate.*

Note: Probate records are available free online; see Circuit Court Profile.

Pierce County

Circuit Court PO Box 129, Ellsworth, WI 54011; 715-273-3531. Hours: 8AM-5PM (CST). *Felony, Misdemeanor, Civil, Eviction, Small Claims.*

Civil Records: Access: Mail, online, in person. Both court and visitors may perform in person searches. Search fee: $5.00 per name. Fee is by type of case. Required to search: name, years to search. Civil cases indexed by defendant, plaintiff. Civil records are retained 20 years; on computer back to 1994. Archives in River Falls. Civil court records available free online at http://ccap.courts.state.wi.us/internetcourtaccess.

Criminal Records: Access: Mail, online, in person. Both court and visitors may perform in person searches. Search fee: $5.00 per name. Required to search: name, years to search, DOB. Felony records are retained 50-75 years; misdemeanors for 20. Criminal records on computer back to 1994. Archives in River Falls. Online

access to criminal records is available free at http://ccap.courts.state.wi.us/internetcourtaccess.

General Information: Public access terminal is available. No sealed records released. SASE required. Turnaround time 2-3 days. Copy fee: $1.25 per page. Certification fee: $5.00. Fee payee: Clerk of Court. Personal checks accepted. Prepayment is required.

Register in Probate PO Box 97, Ellsworth, WI 54011; 715-273-3531 x460; Fax: 715-273-6855. Hours: 8AM-5PM (CST). *Probate.*

Note: Probate records are available free online; see Circuit Court.

Polk County

Circuit Court 100 Polk Plaza, PO Box 549, Balsam Lake, WI 54810; 715-485-9299; Fax: 715-485-9262. Hours: 8:30AM-4:30PM (CST). *Felony, Misdemeanor, Civil, Eviction, Small Claims.*

Civil Records: Access: Mail, online, in person. Both court and visitors may perform in person searches. Search fee: $5.00 per name per record/file. Required to search: name, years to search. Civil cases indexed by defendant, plaintiff. Civil records go back to 1970s; on computer back to 1992. Civil court records available free at http://ccap.courts.state.wi.us/internetcourtaccess.

Criminal Records: Access: Mail, online, in person. Both court and visitors may perform in person searches. Search fee: $5.00 per name. Fee is per record/file. Required to search: name, years to search, DOB. Criminal records go back to 1970s; on computer back to 1992. Online access to criminal records is available free at http://ccap.courts.state.wi.us/internetcourtaccess.

General Information: Public access terminal is available. No juvenile, paternity or confidential records released. SASE required. Turnaround time 2 days. Copy fee: $1.25 per page. Certification fee: $5.00. Fee payee: Clerk of Court. Personal checks accepted. Prepayment is required.

Register in Probate 100 Polk Plaza, #230, Balsam Lake, WI 54810; 715-485-9238; Fax: 715-485-9275. Hours: 8:30AM-4:30PM (CST). *Probate.*

Note: Probate records are available free online; see Circuit Court.

Portage County

Circuit Court (Branches 1, 2 & 3) 1516 Church St, Stevens Point, WI 54481; 715-346-1364; Fax: 715-346-1236. Hours: 7:30AM-4:30PM (CST). *Felony, Misdemeanor, Civil, Eviction, Small Claims.*

Civil Records: Access: Mail, in person. Both court and visitors may perform in person searches. Search fee: $5.00 per name. Required to search: name, years to search. Civil cases indexed by defendant, plaintiff. Civil records on computer from 6/91, index cards from 1980, index books from 1900s.

Criminal Records: Access: Mail, in person. Both court and visitors may perform in person searches. Search fee: $5.00 per name. Required to search: name, years to search, address, DOB, SSN, signed release. Criminal records on computer from 6/91, index cards from 1980, index books from 1900s.

General Information: Public access terminal is available. No expunged records released. SASE required. Turnaround time 10 working days. Copy fee: $1.25 per page. Certification fee: $5.00. Fee payee: Clerk of Court. Business checks accepted. Prepayment is required.

Register in Probate 1516 Church St, Stevens Point, WI 54481; 715-346-1362; Fax: 715-346-1486. Hours: 7:30AM-4:30PM (CST). *Probate.*

Note: Probate records are available free on the Internet at http://ccap.courts.state.wi.us/internetcourtaccess.

Price County

Circuit Court Courthouse, 126 Cherry St, Phillips, WI 54555; 715-339-2353; Fax: 715-339-3079. Hours: 8AM-Noon, 1-4:30PM (CST). *Felony, Misdemeanor, Civil, Eviction, Small Claims.*

Civil Records: Access: Mail, online, in person. Both court and visitors may perform in person searches. Search fee: $5.00 per name. Required to search: name, years to search. Civil cases indexed by defendant, plaintiff. Civil records on computer from 1997, prior on index books. Civil court records available free online at http://ccap.courts.state.wi.us/internetcourtaccess.

Criminal Records: Access: Mail, online, in person. Both court and visitors may perform in person searches. Search fee: $5.00 per name. Required to search: name, years to search, DOB; also helpful: SSN. Criminal records on computer from 1997, prior on index books. Online access to criminal records is available free at http://ccap.courts.state.wi.us/internetcourtaccess.

General Information: Public access terminal is available. No confidential records per statute or order released. SASE required. Turnaround time 1-2 days. Copy fee: $1.25 per page. Certification fee: $5.00. Fee payee: Clerk of Circuit Court. Personal checks accepted. Prepayment is required.

Register in Probate Courthouse, 126 Cherry St-Room209, Phillips, WI 54555; 715-339-3078; Fax: 715-339-3079. Hours: 8AM-4:30PM (CST). *Probate.*

Note: Probate records are available free online; see Circuit Court.

Racine County

Circuit Court 730 Wisconsin Ave, Racine, WI 53403; 262-636-3333; Fax: 262-636-3341. Hours: 8AM-5PM (CST). *Felony, Misdemeanor, Civil, Eviction, Small Claims, Probate.*

Civil Records: Access: Mail, online, in person. Both court and visitors may perform in person searches. Search fee: $5.00 per name. Required to search: name, years to search. Civil cases indexed by defendant, plaintiff. Civil records on computer from 1990, index cards from 1970, archives prior to 1970. Civil court records available free online at http://ccap.courts.state.wi.us/internetcourtaccess.

Criminal Records: Access: Mail, online, in person. Both court and visitors may perform in person searches. Search fee: $5.00 per name. Required to search: name, years to search, DOB. Criminal records on computer from 1990, index cards from 1970, archives prior to 1970. Online access to criminal records is available free at http://ccap.courts.state.wi.us/internetcourtaccess.

General Information: Public access terminal is available. No adoption, juvenile, paternity or mental commitment records released. SASE required. Turnaround time 1-2 weeks. Copy fee: $1.25 per page. Certification fee: $5.00. Fee payee: Clerk of Court. Personal checks accepted. Prepayment is required.

Register in Probate 730 Wisconsin Ave, Racine, WI 53403; 262-636-3137; Fax: 262-636-3870. Hours: 8AM-5PM (CST). *Probate.*

Note: Probate records are available free online; see Circuit Court.

Richland County

Circuit Court PO Box 655, Richland Center, WI 53581; 608-647-3956. Hours: 8:30AM-4:30PM (CST). *Felony, Misdemeanor, Civil, Eviction, Small Claims.*

Civil Records: Access: Mail, online, in person. Both court and visitors may perform in person searches. Search fee: $5.00 per name. Required to search: name, years to search. Civil cases indexed by defendant, plaintiff. Civil records on index cards from 1982, index books from 1972, archives prior to 1972, on computer back to 1993. Civil court records available free online at http://ccap.courts.state.wi.us/internetcourtaccess.

Criminal Records: Access: Mail, online, in person. Only the court performs in person searches; visitors may not. Search fee: $5.00 per name. Required to search: name, years to search, DOB. Criminal records on index cards from 1982, index books from 1972, archives prior to 1972, on computer back t0 1993. Online access to criminal records is available free at http://ccap.courts.state.wi.us/internetcourtaccess.

General Information: Public access terminal is available. No juvenile or paternity records released. SASE required. Turnaround time 1 week. Copy fee: $1.25 per page. Certification fee: $5.00. Fee payee: Clerk of Circuit Court. Personal checks accepted. Personal out-of-state checks not accepted. Prepayment is required.

Register in Probate PO Box 427, Richland Center, WI 53581; 608-647-2626; Fax: 608-647-6134. Hours: 8:30AM-Noon, 1-4:30PM (CST). *Probate.*

Note: Probate records are available free online; see Circuit Court.

Rock County

Circuit Court 51 S Main, Janesville, WI 53545; 608-743-2200; Fax: 608-743-2223. Hours: 8AM-5PM (CST). *Felony, Misdemeanor, Civil, Eviction, Small Claims.*

Civil Records: Access: Mail, online, in person. Both court and visitors may perform in person searches. Search fee: $5.00 per name. Required to search: name, years to search. Civil cases indexed by defendant, plaintiff. Civil records on computer from 6/93, on index cards from 6/91, index books from 1940, archives prior to 1940. Civil court records available free online at http://ccap.courts.state.wi.us/internetcourtaccess.

Criminal Records: Access: Mail, online, in person. Both court and visitors may perform in person searches. Search fee: $5.00 per name. Required to search: name, years to search, DOB. Criminal records on computer from 6/93, on index cards from 6/91, index books from 1940, archives prior to 1940. Online access to criminal records is available for free online at http://ccap.courts.state.wi.us/internetcourtaccess.

General Information: Public access terminal is available. No juvenile, paternity or sealed records released. SASE required. Turnaround time 2-3 days. Copy fee: $1.25 per page. Certification fee: $5.00. Fee payee: Clerk of Court. Personal checks accepted. Prepayment is required.

Circuit Court - South Janesville Courthouse, 51 S Main St, Janesville, WI 53545; 608-743-2200. Hours: 8AM-5PM (CST). *Felony, Misdemeanor, Civil, Eviction, Small Claims.*

Civil Records: Access: Mail, online, in person. Both court and visitors may perform in person searches. Search fee: $5.00 per name. Required to search: name, years to search. Civil cases indexed by defendant, plaintiff. Civil records on computer from mid-1993, on index cards from 1970s, index books from 1900s in vault. Civil court records available free online at http://ccap.courts.state.wi.us/internetcourtaccess.

Criminal Records: Access: Mail, online, in person. Both court and visitors may perform in person searches. Search fee: $5.00 per name. Required to search: name, years to search, DOB. Criminal records on computer from mid-1993, on index cards from 1970s, index books from 1900s in vault. Online access to criminal records is available free at http://ccap.courts.state. wi.us/internetcourtaccess.

General Information: Public access terminal is available. No paternity records released. SASE required. Turnaround time 1 week. Copy fee: $1.25 per page. Certification fee: $5.00. Fee payee: Clerk of Court. Personal checks accepted. Prepayment required.

Register in Probate 51 S Main, Janesville, WI 53545; 608-757-5635. 8AM-5PM (CST). *Probate.*

Note: Probate records are available free online; see Circuit Court.

Rusk County

Circuit Court 311 Miner Ave East, #L350, Ladysmith, WI 54848; 715-532-2108. Hours: 8AM-4:30PM *Felony, Misdemeanor, Civil, Small Claims.*

Civil Records: Access: Mail, online, in person, phone, fax. Both court and visitors may perform in person searches. Search fee: $5.00 per name, no charge for persons performing their own search. Required to search: name, years to search. Civil cases indexed by defendant, plaintiff. Civil records on computer from 1992, on index cards from 1978, index books from 1900. Civil court records 1992 to present available free at http://ccap.courts.state.wi.us/internetcourtaccess. Phone requests are accepted if the case number is known.

Criminal Records: Access: Mail, online, in person, online. Both court and visitors may perform in person searches. Search fee: $5.00 per name, no charge for persons performing their own search. Required to search: name, years to search, DOB. Criminal records on computer from 1992, on index cards from 1978, index books from 1900. Online access to criminal records is available for free online at http://ccap.courts.state.wi.us/internetcourtaccess. Phone requests are accepted if the case number is known.

General Information: Public access terminal is available. No juvenile or paternity records released. SASE required. Turnaround time 5 days. Copy fee: $1.25 per page. Certification fee: $5.00. Fee payee: Clerk of Court. Personal checks accepted. Prepayment is required.

Register in Probate 311 E Miner Ave, Ladysmith, WI 54848; 715-532-2147; Fax: 715-532-2266. Hours: 8AM-4:30PM (CST). *Probate.*

Note: Probate records are available free online; see Circuit Court.

Sauk County

Circuit Court 515 Oak Street, Baraboo, WI 53913; 608-355-3287. Hours: 8AM-4:30PM (CST). *Felony, Misdemeanor, Civil, Eviction, Small Claims.*

Civil Records: Access: Mail, online, in person. Both court and visitors may perform in person searches. Search fee: $5.00 per name. Required to search: name, years to search. Civil cases indexed by defendant, plaintiff. Civil records on computer from 1990, index cards from 1980, index books from 1967. Civil court records available free online at http://ccap.courts. state.wi.us/internetcourtaccess.

Criminal Records: Access: Fax, mail, online, in person. Both court and visitors may perform in person searches. Search fee: $5.00 per name. Required to search: name, years to search. Criminal records on computer from 1990, index cards from 1980, index books from 1967. Online access to criminal records is available free at http://ccap.courts.state.wi.us/internetcourtaccess.

General Information: Public access terminal is available. No paternity, juvenile records released. SASE required. Turnaround time 2-3 days. Fax notes: Fee to fax results is $5.00 1st page, $1.00 each add'l plus tax. Copy fee: $1.25 per page. Certification fee: $5.00. Fee payee: Clerk of Court. Personal checks accepted. Prepayment is required.

Register in Probate 515 Oak St, Baraboo, WI 53913; 608-355-3226; Fax: 608-355-3480. Hours: 8AM-4:30PM (CST). *Probate, Juvenile.*

Note: Probate records are available free online; see Circuit Court profile.

Sawyer County

Circuit Court PO Box 508, Hayward, WI 54843; 715-634-4887. Hours: 8AM-4PM (CST). *Felony, Misdemeanor, Civil, Eviction, Small Claims.*

Civil Records: Access: Mail, online, in person. Both court and visitors may perform in person searches. Search fee: $5.00 per name. Required to search: name, years to search. Civil cases indexed by defendant, plaintiff. Civil records on index cards from 7/85, prior on books. Civil court records available free online at http://ccap.courts.state.wi.us/internetcourtaccess.

Criminal Records: Access: Mail, online, in person. Both court and visitors may perform in person searches. Search fee: $5.00 per name. Required to search: name, years to search. Criminal records on index cards from 7/85, prior on books. Online access to criminal records is available free at http://ccap.courts.state.wi.us/internetcourtaccess.

General Information: Public access terminal is available. No juvenile, probate or paternity records released. SASE required. Turnaround time 1 day. Copy fee: $1.25 per page. Certification fee: $5.00. Fee payee: Clerk of Court. Personal checks accepted. Prepayment is required.

Register in Probate PO Box 447, Hayward, WI 54843; 715-634-7519. 8AM-4PM (CST). *Probate.*

Note: Probate records are available free online; see Circuit Court.

Shawano County

Circuit Court 311 N Main Rm 206, Shawano, WI 54166; 715-526-9347; Fax: 715-526-4915. Hours: 8AM-4:30PM (CST). *Felony, Misdemeanor, Civil, Eviction, Small Claims.*

www.co.shawano.wi.us

Civil Records: Access: Fax, mail, online, in person. Both court and visitors may perform in person searches. Search fee: $5.00 per name. Required to search: name, years to search. Civil cases indexed by defendant, plaintiff. Civil records on computer from 1993, on index books from 1930s, prior in archives. Civil court records available free online at http://ccap.courts.state.wi.us/internetcourtaccess.

Criminal Records: Access: Fax, mail, online, in person. Both court and visitors may perform in person searches. Search fee: $5.00 per name. Required to search: name, years to search, DOB. Criminal records on computer from 1993, on index books from 1930s, prior in archives. Online access to criminal records is available free at http://ccap.courts.state.wi.us/internetcourtaccess.

General Information: Public access terminal is available. No juvenile, closed files or mental records released. SASE required. Turnaround time 10-20 days. Fax notes: $1.25 per page, add $2.50 for long distance. Copy fee: $1.25 per page. Certification fee: $5.00. Fee payee: Clerk of Court. Personal checks accepted.

Register in Probate 311 N Main, Rm 203, Shawano, WI 54166; 715-526-8631; Fax: 715-526-8622. Hours: 8AM-4:30PM (CST). *Probate.*

Note: Probate records are available free online; see Circuit Court.

Sheboygan County

Circuit Court 615 N 6th St, Sheboygan, WI 53081; 920-459-3068; Fax: 920-459-3921. Hours: 8AM-5PM (CST). *Felony, Misdemeanor, Civil, Eviction, Small Claims.*

Civil Records: Access: Mail, online, in person. Both court and visitors may perform in person searches. Search fee: $5.00 per case. Required to search: name, years to search; also helpful: address. Civil cases indexed by defendant, plaintiff. Civil records on computer since 1992; prior records on index cards from 1960, index books from 1860s, archives prior to 1971. Civil court records available free online at http://ccap.courts.state.wi.us/internetcourtaccess.

Criminal Records: Access: Mail, online, in person. Both court and visitors may perform in person searches. Search fee: $5.00 per case. Required to search: name, years to search, DOB; also helpful: address. Criminal records on computer since 1992; prior records on index cards from 1960, index books from 1860s, archives prior to 1971. Online access to criminal records is available free at http://ccap.courts.state.wi.us/internetcourtaccess.

General Information: Public access terminal is available. No juvenile or paternity records released. SASE required. Turnaround time 2-3 days. Copy fee: $1.25 per page. Certification fee: $5.00. Fee payee: Clerk of Circuit Court. Personal checks accepted. Prepayment is required.

Register in Probate 615 N 6th St, Sheboygan, WI 53081; 920-459-3050, 459-3202, 459-3051; Fax: 920-459-0541. Hours: 8AM-5PM (CST). *Probate.*

Note: There is a $4.00 search fee. Probate records are available free online; see Circuit Court.

St. Croix County

Circuit Court 1101 Carmichael Rd, Hudson, WI 54016; 715-386-4630. Hours: 8AM-5PM (CST). *Felony, Misdemeanor, Civil, Eviction, Small Claims.*

Civil Records: Access: Mail, online, in person. Both court and visitors may perform in person searches. Search fee: $5.00 per name. Required to search: name, years to search. Civil cases indexed by defendant, plaintiff. Civil records on computer from 10/92, on index cards from 1982, index books from 1900s. Civil court records available free online at http://ccap.courts.state.wi.us/internetcourtaccess.

Criminal Records: Access: Mail, online, in person. Both court and visitors may perform in person searches. Search fee: $5.00 per name. Required to search: name, years to search, DOB. Criminal records on computer from 10/92, on index cards from 1982, index books from 1900s. Online access to criminal records is available free at http://ccap.courts.state.wi.us/internetcourtaccess.

General Information: Public access terminal is available. No juvenile forfeitures, paternity, some case specific documents or sealed records released. SASE required. Turnaround time 5-10 days. Copy fee: $1.25 per page. Certification fee: $5.00. Fee payee: Clerk of Court. Personal checks accepted. Prepayment required.

Register in Probate 1101 Carmichael Rd, Rm 2242, Hudson, WI 54016; 715-386-4618; Fax: 715-381-4401. Hours: 8AM-5PM (CST). *Probate.*

Note: Probate records are available free online; see Circuit Court.

Taylor County

Circuit Court 224 S 2nd St, Medford, WI 54451-1811; 715-748-1425; Fax: 715-748-2465. Hours: 8:30AM-4:30PM (CST). *Felony, Misdemeanor, Civil, Eviction, Small Claims.*

Civil Records: Access: Mail, online, in person. Both court and visitors may perform in person searches. Search fee: $5.00 per name. Required to search: name, years to search. Civil cases indexed by defendant, plaintiff. Civil records on computer from 1989; prior records index books from 1917. Civil court records available free online at http://ccap.courts.state.wi.us/internetcourtaccess.

Criminal Records: Access: Mail, online, in person. Both court and visitors may perform in person searches. Search fee: $5.00 per name. Required to search: name, years to search, DOB. Criminal records on computer

from 1989; prior records index books from 1917. Online access to criminal records is available free at http://ccap.courts.state.wi.us/internetcourtaccess.

General Information: Public access terminal is available. No sealed records released. SASE required. Turnaround time 1-2 days. Copy fee: $1.25 per page. Certification fee: $5.00. Fee payee: Clerk of Circuit Court. Personal checks accepted. Prepayment required.

Register in Probate 224 S 2nd, Medford, WI 54451; 715-748-1435; Fax: 715-748-1524. Hours: 8:30AM-4:30PM (CST). *Probate.*

http://ccap.courts.state.wi.us/internetcourtaccess

Note: Probate records are available free online; see Circuit Court.

Trempealeau County

Circuit Court 36245 Main St, Whitehall, WI 54773; 715-538-2311. Hours: 8AM-4:30PM (CST). *Felony, Misdemeanor, Civil, Eviction, Small Claims.*

Civil Records: Access: Fax, mail, online, in person. Both court and visitors may perform in person searches. Search fee: $5.00 per name. Required to search: name, years to search. Civil cases indexed by defendant, plaintiff. Civil records on computer from 1993, on index cards from 1987, index books from 1940, archives prior to 1940. Civil court records available free online at http://ccap.courts.state.wi.us/internetcourtaccess.

Criminal Records: Access: Fax, mail, online, in person. Both court and visitors may perform in person searches. Search fee: $5.00 per name. Required to search: name, years to search, DOB. Criminal records on computer from 1993, on index cards from 1987, index books from 1940, archives prior to 1940. Online access to criminal records is available free at http://ccap.courts.state.wi.us/internetcourtaccess.

General Information: Public access terminal is available. No juvenile, paternity or child support records released. SASE required. Turnaround time 2-3 days. Fax notes: $2.00 per page. Copy fee: $1.25 per page. Certification fee: $5.00. Fee payee: Clerk of Circuit Court. Personal checks accepted. Prepayment required.

Register in Probate 36245 Main St, PO Box 67, Whitehall, WI 54773; 715-538-2311 X238; Fax: 715-538-4123. Hours: 8AM-4:30PM (CST). *Probate.*

Note: Probate records are available free online; see Circuit Court.

Vernon County

Circuit Court PO Box 426, Viroqua, WI 54665; 608-637-5340; Fax: 608-637-5554. Hours: 8:30AM-4:30PM (CST). *Felony, Misdemeanor, Civil, Eviction, Small Claims.*

Civil Records: Access: Phone, fax, mail, online, in person. Both court and visitors may perform in person searches. Search fee: $5.00 per name. Required to search: name, years to search, DOB. Civil cases indexed by defendant, plaintiff. Civil records on computer back to 1993; on index books & cards 1950 to 1992. Civil court records available free online at http://ccap.courts.state.wi.us/internetcourtaccess.

Criminal Records: Access: Phone, fax, mail, online, in person. Both court and visitors may perform in person searches. Search fee: $5.00 per name. Required to search: name, years to search; also helpful: DOB. Criminal records on computer back to 1993; on index books & cards 1950 to 1992. Online access to criminal records is available free at http://ccap.courts.state.wi.us/internetcourtaccess.

General Information: Public access terminal is available. No paternity or juvenile records released. SASE required. Turnaround time 2-3 days. Copy fee: $1.25 per page. Certification fee: $5.00. Fee payee: Clerk of Court. Personal checks accepted. Will bill to attorneys & credit agencies.

Register in Probate PO Box 448, Viroqua, WI 54665; 608-637-5347; Fax: 608-637-5554. Hours: 8:30AM-4:30PM (CST). *Probate.*

Note: Probate records are available free online; see Circuit Court.

Vilas County

Circuit Court 330 Court St, Eagle River, WI 54521; 715-479-3632; Fax: 715-479-3740. Hours: 8AM-4PM (CST). *Felony, Misdemeanor, Civil, Eviction, Small Claims.*

Civil Records: Access: Mail, online, in person. Both court and visitors may perform in person searches. Search fee: $5.00 per name. Required to search: name, years to search. Civil records on computer back to 1992, index cards from 1978, index books from 1900s. Civil court records available free online at http://ccap.courts.state.wi.us/internetcourtaccess.

Criminal Records: Access: Mail, online, in person. Both court and visitors may perform in person searches. Search fee: $5.00 per name. Required to search: name, years to search, DOB. Criminal records on computer back to 1992; index cards from 1978, index books from 1900s. Online access to criminal records is available free at http://ccap.courts.state.wi.us/internetcourtaccess.

General Information: Public access terminal is available. No paternity records released. SASE required. Turnaround time 2 weeks. Fax notes: Fee to fax results is $1.25 per page. Copy fee: $1.25 per page. Certification fee: $5.00. Fee payee: Clerk of Circuit Court. Personal checks accepted. Prepayment required.

Register in Probate 330 Court St, Eagle River, WI 54521; 715-479-3642; Fax: 715-479-3740. Hours: 8AM-4PM (CST). *Probate.*

Note: Probate records are available free online; see Circuit Court.

Walworth County

Circuit Court PO Box 1001, Elkhorn, WI 53121-1001; 262-741-4224; Fax: 262-741-4379. 8AM-5PM *Felony, Misdemeanor, Civil, Eviction, Small Claims.*

www.co.walworth.wi.us

Civil Records: Access: Mail, in person. Both court and visitors may perform in person searches. Search fee: $5.00 per name. Required to search: name, years to search. Civil cases indexed by defendant, plaintiff. Civil records on computer from 1989, index cards/books from 1836.

Criminal Records: Access: Mail, in person. Both court and visitors may perform in person searches. Search fee: $5.00 per name. Required to search: name, years to search, DOB. Criminal records on computer from 1989, index cards/books from 1836 (organized).

General Information: Public access terminal is available. No sealed records released. SASE required. Turnaround time 1-2 days. Copy fee: $1.25 per page. Certification fee: $5.00. Fee payee: County Clerk of Courts. Business checks accepted. Credit cards accepted: Visa, MasterCard. Credit cards accepted in person only. Prepayment is required.

Register in Probate PO Box 1001, Elkhorn, WI 53121; 262-741-4256; Fax: 262-741-4182. Hours: 8AM-5PM (CST). *Probate.*

Washburn County

Circuit Court PO Box 339, Shell Lake, WI 54871; 715-468-4677; Fax: 715-468-4678. 8AM-4:30PM *Felony, Misdemeanor, Civil, Eviction, Small Claims.*

Civil Records: Access: Mail, online, in person. Both court and visitors may perform in person searches. Search fee: $5.00 per name. Required to search: name, years to search. Civil cases indexed by defendant, plaintiff. Civil records on computer since 1993 (civil money judgments back to 1/1/90); on index books from 1883. Civil court records available free online at http://ccap.courts.state.wi.us/internetcourtaccess.

Criminal Records: Access: Mail, online, in person. Both court and visitors may perform in person searches. Search fee: $5.00 per name. Required to search: name, years to search; also helpful: DOB. Criminal records on computer since 1993; on index books from 1883. Online access to criminal records is available free at http://ccap.courts.state.wi.us/internetcourtaccess.

General Information: Public access terminal is available. No sealed records released. SASE required. Turnaround time 2-3 days. Copy fee: $1.25 per page. Certification fee: $5.00. Fee payee: Clerk of Court. Personal checks accepted. Prepayment is required.

Register in Probate PO Box 316, Shell Lake, WI 54871; 715-468-4688; Fax: 715-468-4678. Hours: 8AM-4:30PM (CST). *Probate.*

Note: Probate records are available free online; see Circuit Court.

Washington County

Circuit Court PO Box 1986, West Bend, WI 53095-7986; 262-335-4341; Fax: 262-335-4776. Hours: 8AM-4:30PM (CST). *Felony, Misdemeanor, Civil, Eviction, Small Claims.*

www.co.washington.wi.us

Civil Records: Access: Mail, fax, online, in person. Both court and visitors may perform in person searches. Search fee: $5.00 per name. Required to search: name, years to search; also helpful: address. Civil cases indexed by defendant, plaintiff. Civil records on computer from 1986, index cards from 1976, index books from 1836. Civil court records available free at http://ccap.courts.state.wi.us/internetcourtaccess.

Criminal Records: Access: Mail, fax, online, in person. Both court and visitors may perform in person searches. Search fee: $5.00 per name. Required to search: name, years to search, DOB; also helpful: address. Criminal records on computer from 1986, index cards from 1976, index books from 1836. Online access to criminal records is available free at http://ccap.courts.state.wi.us/internetcourtaccess.

General Information: Public access terminal is available. No paternity records released prior to adjudication. SASE required. Turnaround time 1 week. Copy fee: $1.25 per page. Certification fee: $5.00. Fee payee: Clerk of Court. Personal checks accepted. Prepayment is required.

Register in Probate PO Box 82, West Bend, WI 53095-0082; 262-335-4334; Fax: 262-306-2224. Hours: 8AM-4:30PM (CST). *Probate.*

www.co.washington.wi.us

Note: Probate records are available free online; see Circuit Court.

Waukesha County

Circuit Court 515 W Moreland Blvd, Waukesha, WI 53188; Civil phone: 262-548-7525; Criminal phone: 262-548-7484; Fax: 262-896-8228. Hours: 8AM-4:30PM (CST). *Felony, Misdemeanor, Civil, Eviction, Small Claims.*

www.waukeshacounty.gov/departments/courts/cocadmin.asp

Civil Records: Access: Mail, online, in person. Both court and visitors may perform in person searches. Search fee: $5.00 per name. Required to search: name, years to search. Civil cases indexed by defendant, plaintiff. Civil records on computer back to 1994. Civil court records available free online at http://ccap.courts.state.wi.us/internetcourtaccess.

Criminal Records: Access: Mail, online, in person. Both court and visitors may perform in person searches.

Search fee: $5.00 per name. Required to search: name, years to search, DOB. Criminal records on computer back to 1994. Online access to criminal records is available free at http://ccap.courts.state.wi.us/internetcourtaccess.

General Information: Public access terminal is available. No paternity, mental commitment records released. SASE required. Turnaround time 2-3 days. Fax notes: Fee to fax is $3.00 per document plus $1.25 per page. Copy fee: $1.25 per page. Certification fee: $5.00. Fee payee: Clerk of Circuit Court. Personal checks accepted. Credit cards accepted. Accepted in person only. Prepayment is required.

Register in Probate 515 W Moreland, Rm 375, Waukesha, WI 53188; 262-548-7468. Hours: 8AM-4:30PM M-F (CST). *Probate.*

Note: Probate records are available free online; see Circuit Court.

Waupaca County

Circuit Court 811 Harding St, Waupaca, WI 54981; 715-258-6460. Hours: 8AM-4PM (CST). *Felony, Misdemeanor, Civil, Eviction, Small Claims.*

Civil Records: Access: Mail, in person. Both court and visitors may perform in person searches. Search fee: $5.00 per name. Required to search: name, years to search. Civil cases indexed by defendant, plaintiff. Civil records on computer from 1992. Civil court records available free online at http://ccap.courts.state.wi.us/internetcourtaccess.

Criminal Records: Access: Mail, online, in person. Both court and visitors may perform in person searches. Search fee: $5.00 per name. Required to search: name, years to search. Criminal records on computer from 1992. Online access to criminal records is available free at http://ccap.courts.state.wi.us/internetcourtaccess.

General Information: Public access terminal is available. No juvenile, JO, paternity excluding past judgments released. SASE required. Turnaround time 3-4 days. Copy fee: $1.25 per page. Computer document copy fee $.50 per page. Certification fee: $5.00. Fee payee: Clerk of Court. Business checks accepted. Personal in-state checks accepted. Prepayment is required.

Register in Probate 811 Harding St, Waupaca, WI 54981; 715-258-6429; Fax: 715-258-6440. Hours: 8AM-4PM (CST). *Probate.*

www.co.waupaca.wi.us

Note: Probate records are available free online; see Circuit Court profile.

Waushara County

Circuit Court PO Box 507, Wautoma, WI 54982; 920-787-0441; Fax: 920-787-0481. Hours: 8AM-4:30PM (CST). *Felony, Misdemeanor, Civil, Eviction, Small Claims.*

Civil Records: Access: Mail, fax, online, in person. Both court and visitors may perform in person searches. Search fee: $5.00 per name. fee only if court does search. Required to search: name, years to search. Civil cases indexed by defendant. Civil records on computer from 1992, index cards prior to 1978, index books from 1900s. Civil court records available free online at http://ccap.courts.state.wi.us/internetcourtaccess.

Criminal Records: Access: Mail, fax, online, in person. Both court and visitors may perform in person searches. Search fee: $5.00 per name. Fee applies if court does search. Required to search: name, years to search, DOB. Criminal records on computer from 1993, prior on cards and books. Online access to criminal e at http://ccap.courts.state.wi.us/internetcourtaccess.

General Information: Public access terminal is available. SASE required. Turnaround time 1-2 weeks. Copy fee: $1.25 per page. Certification fee: $5.00. Fee

payee: Clerk of Court. Personal checks accepted. Personal in-state checks accepted, money orders for out of state requests. Prepayment is required.

Register in Probate PO Box 508, Wautoma, WI 54982; 920-787-0448. 8AM-4:30PM (CST). *Probate.*

Note: Probate records are available free online; see Circuit Court.

Winnebago County

Circuit Court PO Box 2808, Oshkosh, WI 54903-2808; 920-236-4848; Fax: 920-424-7780. Hours: 8AM-4:30PM (CST). *Felony, Misdemeanor, Civil, Eviction, Small Claims.*

Civil Records: Access: Mail, fax, online, in person. Both court and visitors may perform in person searches. Search fee: $5.00 per name. Required to search: name, years to search. Civil cases indexed by defendant, plaintiff. Civil records are on computer since 1990, prior on books and cards to 1997. Historical Society has records to 1938. Civil court records available free online at http://ccap.courts.state.wi.us/internetcourtaccess.

Criminal Records: Access: Mail, fax, online, in person. Both court and visitors may perform in person searches. Search fee: $5.00 per name. Required to search: full name, years to search, DOB. Criminal records are on computer since 1990, prior on books and cards. organized since 1938. Online access to criminal records is available free at http://ccap.courts.state.wi.us/internetcourtaccess.

General Information: Public access terminal is available. No juvenile, paternity, financial records released. SASE required. Turnaround time 1 week. Fax notes: Fee to fax results is $1.25 per page. Copy fee: $1.25 per page. Certification fee: $5.00. Fee payee: Clerk of Courts. Personal checks accepted.

Register in Probate PO Box 2808, Oshkosh, WI 54903-2808; 920-236-4833; Fax: 920-424-7536. Hours: 8AM-Noon, 1-4:30PM (CST). *Probate.*

Note: There is a $4.00 search fee. Probate records are available free online; see Circuit Court.

Wood County

Circuit Court 400 Market St, Po Box 8095, Wisconsin Rapids, WI 54494-958095; 715-421-8490. Hours: 8AM-4:30PM (CST). *Felony, Misdemeanor, Civil, Eviction, Small Claims.*

Civil Records: Access: Mail, online, in person. Both court and visitors may perform in person searches. Search fee: $5.00 per name. Required to search: name, years to search. Civil cases indexed by defendant, plaintiff. Civil records on computer from 1983, microfiche from 1856-1980s. Court records available at http://ccap.courts.state.wi.us/internetcourtaccess.

Criminal Records: Access: Mail, online, in person. Both court and visitors may perform in person searches. Search fee: $5.00 per name. Required to search: name, years to search, DOB. Criminal records on computer from 1980; manual search required for pre-1980 records. Online access to criminal records is available free at http://ccap.courts.state.wi.us/internetcourtaccess.

General Information: Public access terminal is available. No paternity or sealed records released. SASE required. Turnaround time 2-3 days. Copy fee: $1.25 per page. Certification fee: $5.00. Fee payee: Clerk of Court. Personal checks accepted. Prepayment is required.

Register in Probate Wood County Courthouse, PO Box 8095, Wisconsin Rapids, WI 54495-8095; 715-421-8520, 421-8523; Fax: 715-421-8808. Hours: 8AM-4:30PM (CST). *Probate.*

Note: Court also holds guardianships, juveniles, mental and adoption records. Probate records are available free online; see Circuit Court.

Wisconsin Recording Offices

ORGANIZATION: 72 counties, 72 recording offices. The recording officers are Register of Deeds and Clerk of Court (state tax liens). The entire state is in the Central Time Zone (CST).

REAL ESTATE RECORDS: Registers will not perform real estate searches. Copy fees and certification fees vary. Assessor telephone numbers are for local municipalities or for property listing agencies. Counties do not have assessors. Copies usually cost $2.00 for the first page and $1.00 for each additional page. Certification usually costs $.25 per document. The Treasurer maintains property tax records.

UCC RECORDS: Financing statements are filed at the state level, except for real estate related collateral, which are filed with the Register of Deeds. However, prior to 07/2001, consumer goods and farm collateral were also filed at the Register of Deeds and these older records can be searched there. Nearly all recording offices will perform UCC searches, and many will accept a search by phone. Use search request form UCC-11 for mail-in searches. Searches fees are usually $10.00 per debtor name. Copy fees are usually $1.00 per page.

TAX LIEN RECORDS: Federal tax liens on personal property of businesses are filed with the Secretary of State. Other federal tax liens are filed with the county Register of Deeds. State tax liens are filed with the Clerk of Court. Refer to the County Court Records section for information about Wisconsin courts. Many Registers will perform federal tax lien searches. Search fees and copy fees vary.

OTHER LIENS: Judgment, mechanics, breeders.

ONLINE ACCESS: A number of cities and a few counties offer online access to assessor and property records.

Adams County

Register of Deeds, PO Box 219, Friendship, WI 53934-0219. 608-339-4206.
Will search UCC records. Will not search real estate records.

Ashland County

Register of Deeds, 201 W. Main St, Room 206, Ashland, WI 54806. 715-682-7008; Fax 715-682-7032. Will search UCC records. Will not search real estate records. **Other Phones:** Treasurer 715-682-7012; Elections 715-682-7000; Vital Records 715-682-7008.

Barron County

Register of Deeds, 330 E. LaSalle, Room 201, Barron, WI 54812. Register of Deeds, R/E and UCC Recording 715-537-6210; Fax 715-537-6277.
Will search UCC records. Will not search real estate records. **Other Phones:** Assessor 715-537-6313; Treasurer 715-537-6270; Vital Records 715-537-6210.

Bayfield County

Register of Deeds, PO Box 813, Washburn, WI 54891. 715-373-6119; Fax 715-373-6153.
This agency will not perform searches. **Other Phones:** Assessor 715-373-6131; Treasurer 715-373-6131.

Brown County

Register of Deeds, PO Box 23600, Green Bay, WI 54305-3600. 920-448-4470 R/E Recording: 920-448-4439 UCC Recording: 920-448-4468; Fax 920-448-4449. www.co.brown.wi.us/rod
Will search UCC records. Will not search real estate records. **Online Access:** Real Estate, Recording Records. Access to Register of Deeds real estate records is available by subscription at www.co.brown.wi.us/rod/LaredoTapestry/main.html. Registration and usage fees are required. Images are available for $.50. A more sophisticated subscription system, named Laredo, offers full access to land records for firms operating in Wisconsin. Alos, Brown County land records can be downloaded from their ftp site; contact the Land Information office at 920-448-6295 to register and user information. **Other Phone Numbers:** Treasurer 920-448-4074; Elections 920-448-4016; Vital Records 920-448-4474.

Buffalo County

Register of Deeds, PO Box 28, Alma, WI 54610-0028. 608-685-6230; Fax 608-685-6213.
This agency will not perform searches. **Other Phone Numbers:** Treasurer 608-685-6214.

Burnett County

Register of Deeds, 7410 County Road K #103, Siren, WI 54872. 715-349-2183.
Will search UCC records. UCC search does not include federal tax liens. Will not search real estate records. **Other Phone Numbers:** Treasurer 715-349-2187.

Calumet County

Register of Deeds, 206 Court St, Chilton, WI 53014. 920-849-1441 UCC Recording: 920-849-1441 x205; Fax 920-849-1469.
Will search UCC records. Will not search real estate records. **Other Phones:** Assessor 920-849-1457.

Chippewa County

Register of Deeds, 711 North Bridge St, Chippewa Falls, WI 54729-1876. 715-726-7994; Fax 715-726-4582. www.co.chippewa.wi.us
Will search UCC records. Will not do a title search; will search for one or two records. **Other Phone Numbers:** Treasurer 715-726-7965; Elections 715-726-7980.

Clark County

Registrar, PO Box 384, Neillsville, WI 54456-1989. 715-743-5162 R/E Recording: 715-743-5163 UCC Recording: 715-743-5163; Fax 715-743-5154.
Will search UCC records. Will not search real estate records. **Other Phones:** Treasurer 715-743-5155; Elections 715-743-5148; Vital Records 715-743-5163.

Columbia County

Register of Deeds, PO Box 133, Portage, WI 53901. 608-742-9677; Fax 608-742-9602.
Will search UCC records. Will not search real estate records. **Online Access:** Property Tax, Land, Tax Sales Records. Search the land records system for free at www.co.columbia.wi.us/landrecords. Also, search the treasurers property/tax sale list at www.co.columbia.wi.us/dept/treasurer/landsale.asp.

Other Phone Numbers: Assessor 608-742-9677; Treasurer 608-742-9613.

Crawford County

Register of Deeds, 220 N. Beaumont Road, Prairie du Chien, WI 53821. Register of Deeds, R/E and UCC Recording 608-326-0219; Fax 608-326-0220.
Will search UCC records. Will not search real estate records. **Other Phones:** Vital Records 608-326-0219.

Dane County

Register of Deeds, PO Box 1438, Madison, WI 53701. Register of Deeds, R/E and UCC Recording 608-266-4141 UCC Recording: 608-266-4143; Fax 608-267-3110. www.co.dane.wi.us/regdeeds/rdhome.htm
Will search UCC records. Will not search real estate records. **Online Access:** Assessor, Real Estate Records. Records on the geographic & land database are available free online at http://dc-web.co.dane.wi.us/dane. For fuller access, a subscription service is available. Also, parcel information is available free at http://dc-web.co.dane.wi.us/dane/html/parcelsearch.asp. Professional companies may register to use assessor/land record services at http://dc-web.co.dane.wi.us/dane/html/community.asp. Registration & login. Also, the City of Madison tax assessor database is at www.ci.madison.wi.us/assessor/property.html. Also, search property information for Towns of Cross Plains, Mazomanie, Berry, and Medina is at www.wendorffassessing.com/municipalities.htm.
Other Phone Numbers: Vital Records 608-266-4142.

Dodge County

Register of Deeds, 127 E. Oak St, Administration Building, Juneau, WI 53039-1391. Register of Deeds, R/E and UCC Recording 920-386-3720 UCC Recording: 920-386-3723; Fax 920-386-3902.
Will search UCC records. Will not search real estate records. **Other Phones:** Assessor 920-386-3770; Treasurer 414-386-3781; Vital Records 920-386-3720.

Door County

Register of Deeds, PO Box 670, Sturgeon Bay, WI 54235-0670. Register of Deeds, R/E and UCC Recording 920-746-2270 UCC Recording: 608-261-9548 (Madison); Fax 920-746-2525. www.wrda.org

Will not search real estate records. **Other Phone Numbers:** Assessor 920-746-2905; Treasurer 920-746-2286; Vital Records 920-746-2270.

Douglas County

Register of Deeds, PO Box 847, Superior, WI 54880. 715-395-1463 R/E Recording: 715-395-1350; Fax 715-395-1553. www.douglascountywi.org
Will search UCC records. Will not search real estate records. **Other Phones:** Treasurer 715-395-1348; Elections 715-395-1397; Vital Records 715-395-1463.

Dunn County

Register of Deeds, 800 Wilson Ave, Menomonie, WI 54751. 715-232-1228; Fax 715-232-1324.
Will search UCC records. Will not search real estate records. **Other Phone Numbers:** Assessor 715-232-1401; Treasurer 715-232-3789.

Eau Claire County

Register of Deeds, PO Box 718, Eau Claire, WI 54702. 715-839-4745.
This agency will not search real estate or UCC records. **Other Phone Numbers:** Treasurer 715-839-4805; Vital Records 715-839-4745.

Florence County

Register of Deeds, PO Box 410, Florence, WI 54121-0410. 715-528-4252; Fax 715-528-5470.
Will not search UCC records. This agency will not do a tax lien search.

Fond du Lac County

Register of Deeds, PO Box 509, Fond du Lac, WI 54935-0509. 920-929-3018 R/E Recording: 920-929-3021 UCC Recording: 920-929-3022; Fax 920-929-3293. www.co.fond-du-lac.wi.us
Will search UCC records. This agency will not do a federal tax lien search. Will not search real estate records. **Other Phone Numbers:** Assessor 920-929-3010; Treasurer 920-929-3010; Elections 920-929-3000; Vital Records 920-929-3019.

Forest County

Register of Deeds, 200 E. Madison St, Crandon, WI 54520. Register of Deeds, R/E and UCC Recording 715-478-3823.
Will search UCC records. UCC search does not include federal tax liens. Will not search real estate records. **Other Phone Numbers:** Treasurer 715-478-2412; Elections 715-478-2422; Vital Records 715-478-3823.

Grant County

Register of Deeds, PO Box 391, Lancaster, WI 53813-0391. Register of Deeds, R/E and UCC Recording 608-723-2727; Fax 608-723-4048.
Will search UCC records. Will not search real estate records. **Other Phone Numbers:** Assessor 608-723-2666; Treasurer 608-723-2604; Elections 608-723-2675; Vital Records 608-723-2727.

Green County

Register of Deeds, 1016 16th Ave, Courthouse, Monroe, WI 53566. 608-328-9439; Fax 608-328-2835.
This agency will not perform searches.

Green Lake County

Register of Deeds, PO Box 3188, Green Lake, WI 54941-3188. Register of Deeds, R/E and UCC Recording 920-294-4021; Fax 920-294-4165.
Will search UCC records. **Other Phone Numbers:** Treasurer 920-294-4018; Vital Records 920-294-4019.

Iowa County

Register of Deeds, 222 N. Iowa St, Dodgeville, WI 53533. Register of Deeds, R/E and UCC Recording 608-935-0396; Fax 608-935-3024.
This agency will not search real estate or UCC records. **Other Phone Numbers:** Treasurer 608-935-0397; Elections 608-935-0399; Vital Records 608-935-0396.

Iron County

Register of Deeds, 300 Taconite St, Hurley, WI 54534. Register of Deeds, R/E and UCC Recording 715-561-2945; Fax 715-561-2928.
Will search UCC records. Will not search real estate records. **Other Phone Numbers:** Assessor 715-561-2883; Treasurer 715-561-2883; Appraiser/Auditor 715-561-2883; Vital Records 715-561-2945.

Jackson County

Register of Deeds, 307 Main, Black River Falls, WI 54615. 715-284-0204; Fax 715-284-0278.
This agency will not perform searches. **Other Phone Numbers:** Assessor 715-284-0203.

Jefferson County

Register of Deeds, PO Box 356, Jefferson, WI 53549. 920-674-7235.
This agency will not search real estate or UCC records. **Other Phone Numbers:** Treasurer 920-674-7250; Elections 920-674-7140; Vital Records 920-674-7235.

Juneau County

Register of Deeds, PO Box 100, Mauston, WI 53948-0100. Register of Deeds, R/E and UCC Recording 608-847-9325; Fax 608-849-9369.
Will search UCC records. Will not search real estate records. **Other Phones:** Treasurer 608-847-9308; Elections 608-847-9302; Vital Records 608-847-9325.

Kenosha County

Register of Deeds, 1010 56 St., Kenosha, WI 53140. 262-653-2444 R/E Recording: 262-653-2441; Fax 262-653-2564.
Will search UCC records. Will not search real estate records. **Online Access:** Real Estate, Lien, Vital Statistic, Assessor Records. The set-up fee is $500, plus $6.00 per hour usage fee. The sytem operates 24 hours daily; records date back to 5/1986. Federal tax liens are listed. Lending agency information is available. For further information, contact Joellyn Storz at 262-653-2511. Also, search the Kenosha City Assessor's property database for free at www.kenosha.org/departments/assessor/search.html. No name searching. **Other Phone Numbers:** Assessor 262-653-2545; Treasurer 262-653-2542; Vital Records 262-653-2444.

Kewaunee County

Register of Deeds, 613 Dodge St, Kewaunee, WI 54216-1398. 920-388-7126 R/E Recording: 920-388-7126/7127/7128; Fax 920-388-7195.
Will search UCC records prior to 7/2001. Will not search real estate records. **Other Phone Numbers:** Treasurer 920-388-7152; Elections 920-388-7133; Vital Records 920-388-7126.

La Crosse County

Register of Deeds, 400 N. 4th St, Room 106, Administrative Center, La Crosse, WI 54601-3200. 608-785-9644 R/E Recording: 608-785-9652 UCC Recording: 608-785-9651; Fax 608-785-9704. www.co.la-crosse.wi.us/departments.htm
Will search UCC records. Will not search real estate records. **Other Phones:** Assessor 608-785-7525; Treasurer 608-785-9711; Vital Records 608-785-9652.

Lafayette County

Register of Deeds, PO Box 170, Darlington, WI 53530. Register of Deeds, R/E and UCC Recording 608-776-4838; Fax 608-776-4991.
Will search UCC records. **Other Phone Numbers:** Treasurer 608-776-4862; Elections 608-776-4850; Vital Records 608-776-4838.

Langlade County

Register of Deeds, 800 Clermont St, Antigo, WI 54409. 715-627-6209; Fax 715-627-6303.
This agency will not perform searches. **Other Phone Numbers:** Treasurer 715-627-6204.

Lincoln County

Register of Deeds, 1110 E. Main, Courthouse, Merrill, WI 54452. Register of Deeds, R/E and UCC Recording 715-536-0318; Fax 715-536-0360. www.co.lincoln.wi.us
Will search UCC records. Will not search real estate records. **Other Phone Numbers:** Assessor 715-536-0479; Treasurer 715-536-0315; Elections 715-536-0359; Vital Records 715-536-0318.

Manitowoc County

Register of Deeds, PO Box 421, Manitowoc, WI 54221-0421. 920-683-4010 R/E Recording: 920-683-4011; Fax 920-683-2702. www.manitowoc-county.com
Will search UCC records. Will not search real estate records. **Online Access:** Assessor, Real Estate Records. Records on the City of Manitowoc Assessor database are available free online at http://assessor.manitowoc.org/default.htm. No name searching. Also, search property data for the Villages of Mishicot and Valders as well as Town of Manitowoc at www.wendorffassessing.com/municipalities.htm.
Other Phone Numbers: Assessor 920-683-4425; Treasurer 920-683-4020; Vital Records 920-683-4509.

Marathon County

Register of Deeds, 500 Forest St, Courthouse, Wausau, WI 54403-5568. Register of Deeds, R/E and UCC Recording 715-261-1470; Fax 715-261-1488.
Will search UCC records. **Other Phone Numbers:** Assessor 715-843-1300; Treasurer 715-261-1150; Elections 715-261-1500; Vital Records 715-261-1470.

Marinette County

Register of Deeds, 1926 Hall Ave, Courthouse, Marinette, WI 54143. 715-732-7550; Fax 715-732-7532.
This agency will not search real estate or UCC records. **Other Phone Numbers:** Treasurer 715-732-7430.

Marquette County

Register of Deeds, PO Box 236, Montello, WI 53949-0236. 608-297-9132; Fax 608-297-7606.
This agency will not search real estate or UCC records. **Other Phone Numbers:** Assessor 608-297-9148; Treasurer 608-297-9148.

Menominee County

Register of Deeds, PO Box 279, Keshena, WI 54135-0279. Register of Deeds, R/E and UCC Recording 715-799-3312; Fax 715-799-1322.
Will search UCC records. **Other Phone Numbers:** Assessor 715-799-3315; Treasurer 715-799-3001; Appraiser/Auditor 715-799-3001; Elections 715-799-3311; Vital Records 715-799-3312.

Milwaukee County

Register of Deeds, 901 N. 9th St, Milwaukee, WI 53233. Register of Deeds, R/E and UCC Recording 414-278-4005 UCC Recording: 414-278-4006; Fax 414-223-1257. www.co.milwaukee.wi.us
Will search UCC records. **Online Access:** Assessor, Real Estate, Property Sale Records. Ownership, property and assessment data as well as sales data by year on the Milwaukee City (not county) Assessor Office database are available free online at www.ci.mil.wi.us/citygov/assessor/assessor.htm. No name searching. Also, search the City of Cudahy assessor;s property data for free at http://exch02.ci.cudahy.wi.us/Scripts/GVSWeb.dll/Search. No name searching. Also, search City of Franklin assessor data at www.ci.franklin.wi.us/dynamic/pagetemplate.cfm?template=assessmentSearch.cfm.
Other Phone Numbers: Assessor 414-286-3651; Treasurer 414-278-4033; Elections 414-278-4060; Vital Records 414-278-4003.

Monroe County

Register of Deeds, 202 S. "K" St, Rm 2, Sparta, WI 54656. Register of Deeds, R/E and UCC Recording 608-269-8716; Fax 608-269-8715. www.co.monroe.wi.us
Will not search UCC records. UCC search includes federal tax liens if requested. Real estate record owner searches available. **Other Phone Numbers:** Treasurer 608-269-8710; Vital Records 608-269-8716.

Oconto County

Register of Deeds, 301 Washington St, Room 2035, Oconto, WI 54153-1699. 920-834-6807; www.co.oconto.wi.us
Will search UCC records. UCC search includes federal tax liens if requested. Will not search real estate records. **Other Phone Numbers:** Treasurer 920-834-6813.

Oneida County

Register of Deeds, PO Box 400, Rhinelander, WI 54501. 715-369-6150; Fax 715-369-6222.
Will search UCC records. **Other Phone Numbers:** Assessor 715-369-6137; Treasurer 715-369-6137.

Outagamie County

Register of Deeds, 410 S. Walnut St., CAB 205, Appleton, WI 54911-5999. Register of Deeds, R/E and UCC Recording 920-832-5095 UCC Recording: 920-832-5097; Fax 920-832-2177. www.co.outagamie.wi.us
Will search UCC records. Will not search real estate records. **Other Phone Numbers:** Treasurer 414-832-5065; Elections 920-832-5077; Vital Records 920-832-5095; Abstracting Phone 920-832-5114; Tax Lister 920-832-5665;

Ozaukee County

Register of Deeds, PO Box 994, Port Washington, WI 53074-0994. Register of Deeds, R/E and UCC Recording 262-284-8260; Fax 262-284-8100. www.co.ozaukee.wi.us
Will search UCC records. **Other Phone Numbers:** Treasurer 262-284-8280; Vital Records 262-284-8260.

Pepin County

Register of Deeds, PO Box 39, Durand, WI 54736. 715-672-8856; Fax 715-672-8677.
This agency will not search real estate or UCC records. **Other Phone Numbers:** Treasurer 715-672-8850.

Pierce County

Register of Deeds, PO Box 267, Ellsworth, WI 54011-0267. Register of Deeds, R/E and UCC Recording 715-273-3531 x418; Fax 715-273-6861.
Will search UCC records. Will not search real estate records. **Other Phone Numbers:** Assessor 715-273-3531; Treasurer 715-273-3531 x307-8; Vital Records 715-273-3531 x418.

Polk County

Register of Deeds, 100 Polk County Plaza, Suite 160, Balsam Lake, WI 54810. 715-485-9249 R/E Recording: 715-485-9240 UCC Recording: 715-485-9240; Fax 715-485-9202.
Will search UCC records. Will not search real estate records. **Other Phone Numbers:** Assessor 715-485-3161 x254; Treasurer 715-485-3161 x273; Elections 715-485-9223; Vital Records 715-485-9240.

Portage County

Register of Deeds, 1516 Church St, County-City Building, Stevens Point, WI 54481. 715-346-1428; Fax 715-345-5361.
Will search UCC records. **Other Phone Numbers:** Assessor 715-346-1553; Treasurer 715-346-1428.

Price County

Register of Deeds, 126 Cherry, Phillips, WI 54555. 715-339-2515.
Will not search UCC records. UCC search includes federal tax liens if requested. Real estate owner, mortgage, and property transfer searches available.

Racine County

Register of Deeds, 730 Wisconsin Ave, Racine, WI 53403. 262-636-3208; Fax 262-636-3851. www.goracine.org
This agency will not search real estate or UCC records. **Other Phone Numbers:** Treasurer 262-636-3238.

Richland County

Register of Deeds, PO Box 337, Richland Center, WI 53581. Register of Deeds, R/E and UCC Recording 608-647-3011.
Will search UCC records. UCC search includes federal tax liens if requested. Will not search real estate records. **Other Phone Numbers:** Assessor 608-647-3658; Treasurer 608-647-3658.

Rock County

Register of Deeds, 51 S. Main St, Janesville, WI 53545. 608-757-5657 R/E Recording: 608-757-5650; www.co.rock.wi.us/departments/reg_deeds.htm
Will search UCC records. UCC search does not include federal tax liens. Will not search real estate records. **Online Access:** Assessor, Real Estate Records. Records on the City of Janesville Assessor database are available free at http://assessor.ci.janesville.wi.us/Government/Assessor/PropertySearch/query.asp. No name searching. Also, search Evanville property assessor records for free at www.wendorffassessing.com/municipalities.htm. No name searching. **Other Phone Numbers:** Vital Records 608-757-5656.

Rusk County

Register of Deeds, 311 Miner Ave, Ladysmith, WI 54848-0311. 715-532-2139; Fax 715-532-2194.
This agency will not perform searches.

Sauk County

Register of Deeds, 505 Broadway St., Baraboo, WI 53913. 608-355-3288; Fax 608-355-3292.
This agency will not search real estate or UCC records. **Online Access:** Property, Assessor Records. Search Village of Spring Green property data for free at www.wendorffassessing.com/Spring%20Green%20options.htm. No name searching. **Other Phone Numbers:** Assessor 608-355-5581; Treasurer 608-355-3276.

Sawyer County

Register of Deeds, PO Box 686, Hayward, WI 54843-0686. Register of Deeds, R/E and UCC Recording 715-634-4867; Fax 715-634-6839. http://sawyercountygov.org
Will search UCC records. Will not search real estate records. **Other Phone Numbers:** Assessor 715-634-4868; Treasurer 715-634-4868; Elections 715-634-4866; Vital Records 715-634-4867.

Shawano County

Register of Deeds, 311 N. Main, Shawano, WI 54166. 715-524-2129; Fax 715-524-5157.
Will search UCC records. Will not search real estate records. **Other Phone Numbers:** Assessor 715-524-9130; Treasurer 715-524-9130.

Sheboygan County

Register of Deeds, 508 New York Ave., 2nd Floor, Sheboygan, WI 53081. 920-459-3023.
Will search UCC records. UCC search includes federal tax liens if requested. Will not search real estate records. **Other Phone Numbers:** Treasurer 920-459-3015.

St. Croix County

Register of Deeds, 1101 Carmichael Rd., Hudson, WI 54016. 715-386-4652 UCC Recording: 715-386-4654; Fax 715-386-4687. www.co.saint-croix.wi.us
Will not search UCC records. **Other Phone Numbers:** Assessor 715-386-4677; Treasurer 715-386-4645; Vital Records 715-386-4653.

Taylor County

Register of Deeds, PO Box 403, Medford, WI 54451-0403. 715-748-1483.
Will search UCC records. UCC search includes federal tax liens. Real estate owner, mortgage, and property transfer searches available. **Other Phone Numbers:** Assessor 715-748-3131; Treasurer 715-748-1466.

Trempealeau County

Register of Deeds, PO Box 67, Whitehall, WI 54773. 715-538-2311; www.tremplocounty.com
Will search UCC records. UCC search includes federal tax liens. Will not search real estate records. **Online Access:** Real Estate, Assessor Records. Access to the county assessor's database is available free at www.tremplocounty.com/Search. **Other Phone Numbers:** Treasurer 715-538-2311 x219.

Vernon County

Register of Deeds, PO Box 46, Viroqua, WI 54665. Register of Deeds, R/E and UCC Recording 608-637-3571; Fax 608-637-5304.
Will search UCC records. UCC search includes federal tax liens if requested. Will not search real estate records. **Other Phone Numbers:** Assessor 608-637-3222; Treasurer 608-637-3222; Elections 608-637-3571; Vital Records 608-637-3572.

Vilas County

Register of Deeds, 330 Court St., Eagle River, WI 54521. Register of Deeds, R/E and UCC Recording 715-479-3660; Fax 715-479-3695. http://co.vilas.wi.us Will search UCC records. Will not search real estate records. **Other Phones:** Assessor 715-479-3609; Treasurer 715-479-3610; Vital Records 715-479-3660.

Walworth County

Register of Deeds, PO Box 995, Elkhorn, WI 53121-0995. 262-741-4214 R/E Recording: 262-741-4233 UCC Recording: 262-741-4237; Fax 262-741-4947. www.co.walworth.wi.us Will search UCC records. Will search real estate records with grantor/grantee system. **Online Access:** Property Tax, Recording, Grantor/Grantee, Deed Records. Search the Register of Deeds index for free on the county e-government web page at www.co.walworth.wi.us. Click on "Public Records." Online records go as far back as 1976. Also, search the treasurer's tax roll list under "Tax Roll Documents" on the county e-government web page. Also search the Village of Walworth property data for free at www.wendorffassessing.com/Walworth%20options.htm. **Other Phone Numbers:** Assessor 262-741-4251; Treasurer 262-741-4251; Elections 262-741-4241; Vital Records 262-741-4235.

Washburn County

Register of Deeds, PO Box 607, Shell Lake, WI 54871. 715-468-4616 R/E Recording: 715-468-4619 UCC Recording: 715-468-4615; Fax 715-468-4658. Will search UCC records. **Other Phone Numbers:** Assessor 715-468-7410; Treasurer 715-468-4650; Elections 715-468-4605; Vital Records 715-468-4615.

Washington County

Register of Deeds, PO Box 1986, West Bend, WI 53095-7986. 262-335-4318; Fax 262-335-6866. www.co.washington.wi.us/departments/default.htm Will search UCC records. Will not search real estate records. **Other Phones:** Assessor 262-335-4370; Treasurer 262-335-4325; Elections 262-335-4468.

Waukesha County

Register of Deeds, 1320 Pewaukee Rd., Room 110, Waukesha, WI 53188. 262-548-7590; www.waukeshacounty.gov/departments/register Will search UCC records. UCC search includes federal tax liens if requested. Real estate owner, mortgage, and property transfer searches available. **Online Access:** Property, Assessor Records. Search the City of Waukesha assessor property databse or sales lists free at www.ci.waukesha.wi.us/dept/assessor/index.htm. Property information may be temporarily down. **Other Phone Numbers:** Assessor 262-542-0455; Treasurer 262-548-7576.

Waupaca County

Register of Deeds, PO Box 307, Waupaca, WI 54981. Register of Deeds, R/E and UCC Recording 715-258-6250; Fax 715-258-6212. Will search UCC records. Will not search real estate records. **Other Phone Numbers:** Assessor 715-258-6215; Treasurer 715-258-6220; Elections 715-258-6200; Vital Records 715-258-6250.

Waushara County

Register of Deeds, PO Box 338, Wautoma, WI 54982. Register of Deeds, R/E and UCC Recording 920-787-0444; Fax 920-787-0425. Will search UCC records. Will not search real estate records. **Other Phones:** Assessor 920-787-4631; Treasurer 920-787-4631; Vital Records 920-787-0444.

Winnebago County

Register of Deeds, PO Box 2808, Oshkosh, WI 54903-2808. 920-236-4883 R/E Recording: 920-236-4881; Fax 920-303-3025. Will search UCC records. Federal tax liens included in UCC search if requested. Will not search real estate records. **Online Access:** Assessor, Real Estate Records. Records on the City of Menasha Tax Roll Information database are available free online at www.cityofmenasha.com/finance.htm. Property records on the City of Oshkosh assessor database are available free at www.ci.oshkosh.wi.us/assessor/ProcessSearch.asp?cmd=NewSearch. **Other Phone Numbers:** Assessor 920-236-4775; Treasurer 920-236-4777; Elections 920-236-4888; Vital Records 920-236-4882.

Wood County

Register of Deeds, PO Box 8095, Wisconsin Rapids, WI 54495. 715-421-8450. Will search UCC records. This agency will not do a federal tax lien search. Will not search real estate records. **Other Phone Numbers:** Assessor 715-421-8484; Treasurer 715-421-8484.

Wisconsin County Locator

You will usually be able to find the city name in the City/County Cross Reference below. In that case, it is a simple matter to determine the county from the cross reference. However, only the official US Postal Service city names are included in this index. There are an additional 40,000 place names that people use in their addresses. Therefore, we have also included a ZIP/City Cross Reference immediately following the City/County Cross Reference.

If you know the ZIP Code but the city name does not appear in the City/County Cross Reference index, look up the ZIP Code in the ZIP/City Cross Reference, find the city name, then look up the city name in the City/County Cross Reference. For example, you want to know the county for an address of Menands, NY 12204. There is no "Menands" in the City/County Cross Reference. The ZIP/City Cross Reference shows that ZIP Codes 12201-12288 are for the city of Albany. Looking back in the City/County Cross Reference, Albany is in Albany County.

City/County Cross Reference

ABBOTSFORD (54405) Clark(71), Marathon(28)
ABRAMS Oconto
ADAMS Adams
ADELL Sheboygan
AFTON Rock
ALBANY Green
ALGOMA Kewaunee
ALLENTON (53002) Washington(97), Dodge(2)
ALMA Buffalo
ALMA CENTER Jackson
ALMENA Barron
ALMOND (54909) Portage(89), Waushara(10)
ALTOONA Eau Claire
AMBERG Marinette
AMERY Polk
AMHERST Portage
AMHERST JUNCTION Portage
ANIWA (54408) Marathon(56), Shawano(39), Langlade(4)
ANTIGO (54409) Langlade(97), Marathon(1), Shawano(1)
APPLETON Outagamie
ARCADIA (54612) Trempealeau(88), Buffalo(11)
ARENA Iowa
ARGONNE Forest
ARGYLE (53504) Lafayette(74), Green(25)
ARKANSAW (54721) Pepin(88), Pierce(6), Dunn(5)
ARKDALE Adams
ARLINGTON (53911) Columbia(93), Dane(6)
ARMSTRONG CREEK (54103) Forest(82), Marinette(15), Florence(1)
ARPIN Wood
ASHIPPUN Dodge
ASHLAND (54806) Ashland(87), Bayfield(12)
ATHELSTANE (54104) Marinette(98), Oconto(1)
ATHENS (54411) Marathon(97), Taylor(2)
AUBURNDALE (54412) Wood(75), Marathon(24)
AUGUSTA Eau Claire
AVALON (53505) Rock(98), Walworth(1)
AVOCA Iowa
BABCOCK Wood
BAGLEY Grant
BAILEYS HARBOR Door
BALDWIN St. Croix
BALSAM LAKE Polk
BANCROFT (54921) Portage(89), Adams(8), Waushara(1)
BANGOR La Crosse
BARABOO Sauk
BARNEVELD (53507) Iowa(98), Dane(1)
BARRON Barron
BARRONETT (54813) Barron(51), Burnett(31), Washburn(17)
BASSETT Kenosha

BAY CITY Pierce
BAYFIELD Bayfield
BEAR CREEK (54922) Outagamie(52), Waupaca(47)
BEAVER DAM Dodge
BEETOWN Grant
BELDENVILLE Pierce
BELGIUM (53004) Ozaukee(98), Sheboygan(1)
BELLEVILLE (53508) Dane(73), Green(26)
BELMONT Lafayette
BELOIT Rock
BENET LAKE Kenosha
BENOIT Bayfield
BENTON Lafayette
BERLIN (54923) Green Lake(72), Waushara(24), Winnebago(3)
BIG BEND Waukesha
BIG FALLS Waupaca
BIRCHWOOD (54817) Washburn(40), Sawyer(32), Barron(24), Rusk(3)
BIRNAMWOOD (54414) Shawano(77), Marathon(22)
BLACK CREEK (54106) Outagamie(98), Shawano(1)
BLACK EARTH Dane
BLACK RIVER FALLS (54615) Jackson(98), Monroe(1)
BLAIR (54616) Trempealeau(96), Jackson(3)
BLANCHARDVILLE (53516) Lafayette(56), Green(20), Iowa(19), Dane(2)
BLENKER Wood
BLOOM CITY Richland
BLOOMER Chippewa
BLOOMINGTON Grant
BLUE MOUNDS (53517) Dane(62), Iowa(37)
BLUE RIVER (53518) Richland(70), Grant(23), Crawford(5)
BONDUEL (54107) Shawano(96), Outagamie(4)
BOSCOBEL (53805) Grant(68), Crawford(31)
BOULDER JUNCTION Vilas
BOWLER Shawano
BOYCEVILLE Dunn
BOYD (54726) Eau Claire(50), Chippewa(49)
BRANCH Manitowoc
BRANDON (53919) Fond du Lac(98), Green Lake(1)
BRANTWOOD Price
BRIGGSVILLE (53920) Marquette(68), Adams(31)
BRILL Barron
BRILLION (54110) Calumet(79), Manitowoc(18), Brown(2)
BRISTOL Kenosha
BRODHEAD (53520) Green(74), Rock(25)
BROKAW Marathon
BROOKFIELD Waukesha

BROOKLYN (53521) Green(44), Dane(32), Rock(22)
BROOKS Adams
BROWNSVILLE (53006) Dodge(71), Fond du Lac(28)
BROWNTOWN (53522) Green(92), Lafayette(7)
BRUCE Rusk
BRULE (54820) Douglas(69), Bayfield(30)
BRUSSELS Door
BRYANT Langlade
BURLINGTON (53105) Racine(62), Walworth(26), Kenosha(11)
BURNETT Dodge
BUTLER Waukesha
BUTTE DES MORTS Winnebago
BUTTERNUT (54514) Price(53), Ashland(37), Iron(9)
BYRON Fond du Lac
CABLE (54821) Bayfield(98), Sawyer(1)
CADOTT (54727) Chippewa(91), Eau Claire(8)
CALEDONIA Racine
CAMBRIA (53923) Columbia(87), Green Lake(12)
CAMBRIDGE (53523) Jefferson(51), Dane(48)
CAMERON Barron
CAMP DOUGLAS (54618) Juneau(61), Monroe(38)
CAMP LAKE Kenosha
CAMPBELLSPORT (53010) Fond du Lac(95), Washington(3)
CAROLINE Shawano
CASCADE (53011) Sheboygan(90), Fond du Lac(9)
CASCO (54205) Kewaunee(97), Door(2)
CASHTON (54619) Monroe(78), Vernon(20), La Crosse(1)
CASSVILLE Grant
CATARACT Monroe
CATAWBA Price
CATO Manitowoc
CAZENOVIA (53924) Richland(95), Sauk(4)
CECIL (54111) Shawano(90), Oconto(9)
CEDAR GROVE (53013) Sheboygan(81), Ozaukee(18)
CEDARBURG (53012) Ozaukee(95), Washington(4)
CENTURIA Polk
CHASEBURG Vernon
CHELSEA Taylor
CHETEK (54728) Barron(87), Rusk(11), Dunn(1)
CHILI (54420) Clark(96), Wood(3)
CHILTON (53014) Calumet(97), Manitowoc(1)
CHIPPEWA FALLS Chippewa
CLAM LAKE (54517) Ashland(93), Sawyer(6)
CLAYTON (54004) Polk(59), Barron(40)

CLEAR LAKE (54005) Polk(79), St. Croix(11), Dunn(5), Barron(4)
CLEVELAND (53015) Manitowoc(85), Sheboygan(14)
CLINTON (53525) Rock(97), Walworth(2)
CLINTONVILLE (54929) Waupaca(67), Shawano(31), Outagamie(1)
CLYMAN Dodge
COBB Iowa
COCHRANE Buffalo
COLBY (54421) Clark(74), Marathon(25)
COLEMAN (54112) Marinette(75), Oconto(24)
COLFAX (54730) Dunn(77), Chippewa(22)
COLGATE (53017) Washington(72), Waukesha(27)
COLLINS Manitowoc
COLOMA (54930) Waushara(83), Adams(14), Marquette(2)
COLUMBUS (53925) Columbia(81), Dodge(14), Dane(4)
COMBINED LOCKS Outagamie
COMSTOCK (54826) Barron(62), Polk(37)
CONOVER Vilas
CONRATH Rusk
COON VALLEY (54623) La Crosse(50), Vernon(50)
CORNELL Chippewa
CORNUCOPIA Bayfield
COTTAGE GROVE Dane
COUDERAY Sawyer
CRANDON Forest
CRIVITZ (54114) Marinette(91), Oconto(8)
CROSS PLAINS Dane
CUBA CITY (53807) Grant(83), Lafayette(16)
CUDAHY Milwaukee
CUMBERLAND (54829) Barron(90), Polk(9)
CURTISS (54422) Clark(94), Taylor(5)
CUSHING Polk
CUSTER (54423) Portage(98), Marathon(1)
DALE Outagamie
DALLAS Barron
DALTON (53926) Green Lake(72), Marquette(16), Columbia(11)
DANBURY (54830) Burnett(93), Douglas(6)
DANE Dane
DARIEN (53114) Walworth(80), Rock(19)
DARLINGTON Lafayette
DE FOREST (53532) Dane(98), Columbia(1)
DE PERE (54115) Brown(92), Outagamie(7)
DE SOTO (54624) Vernon(89), Crawford(10)
DEER PARK (54007) St. Croix(66), Polk(33)
DEERBROOK Langlade
DEERFIELD Dane
DELAFIELD Waukesha
DELAVAN Walworth
DELLWOOD Adams

DENMARK (54208) Brown(52), Kewaunee(39), Manitowoc(7)
DICKEYVILLE Grant
DODGE Trempealeau
DODGEVILLE Iowa
DORCHESTER (54425) Clark(83), Marathon(9), Taylor(6)
DOUSMAN (53118) Waukesha(96), Jefferson(3)
DOWNING (54734) Dunn(94), St. Croix(5)
DOWNSVILLE Dunn
DOYLESTOWN Columbia
DRESSER Polk
DRUMMOND Bayfield
DUNBAR Marinette
DURAND (54736) Pepin(82), Buffalo(17)
EAGLE (53119) Waukesha(93), Walworth(4), Jefferson(2)
EAGLE RIVER (54521) Vilas(78), Oneida(19), Forest(1)
EAST ELLSWORTH Pierce
EAST TROY (53120) Walworth(97), Racine(2)
EASTMAN Crawford
EAU CLAIRE (54703) Eau Claire(89), Chippewa(10)
EAU GALLE (54737) Dunn(96), Pepin(3)
EDEN Fond du Lac
EDGAR Marathon
EDGERTON (53534) Rock(84), Dane(13), Jefferson(2)
EDGEWATER Sawyer
EDMUND Iowa
EGG HARBOR Door
ELAND (54427) Marathon(67), Shawano(32)
ELCHO (54428) Langlade(96), Oneida(3)
ELDERON Marathon
ELDORADO Fond du Lac
ELEVA (54738) Eau Claire(59), Trempealeau(39), Buffalo(1)
ELK MOUND (54739) Dunn(60), Chippewa(39)
ELKHART LAKE (53020) Sheboygan(91), Manitowoc(6), Calumet(2)
ELKHORN Walworth
ELLISON BAY Door
ELLSWORTH Pierce
ELM GROVE Waukesha
ELMWOOD (54740) Pierce(80), Dunn(19)
ELROY (53929) Juneau(83), Monroe(11), Vernon(5)
ELTON Langlade
EMBARRASS Waupaca
EMERALD St. Croix
EMERALDX St. Croix
ENDEAVOR Marquette
EPHRAIM Door
ETTRICK (54627) Trempealeau(91), Jackson(8)
EUREKA Winnebago
EVANSVILLE (53536) Rock(95), Green(4)
EXELAND (54835) Sawyer(89), Rusk(10)
FAIRCHILD (54741) Jackson(51), Eau Claire(48)
FAIRWATER Fond du Lac
FALL CREEK Eau Claire
FALL RIVER (53932) Columbia(95), Dodge(4)
FENCE (54120) Florence(61), Marinette(38)
FENNIMORE Grant
FERRYVILLE (54628) Crawford(94), Vernon(5)
FIFIELD Price
FISH CREEK Door
FLORENCE Florence
FOND DU LAC Fond du Lac
FONTANA Walworth
FOOTVILLE Rock
FOREST JUNCTION Calumet

FORESTVILLE (54213) Door(84), Kewaunee(15)
FORT ATKINSON (53538) Jefferson(97), Rock(2)
FOUNTAIN CITY Buffalo
FOX LAKE Dodge
FOXBORO Douglas
FRANCIS CREEK Manitowoc
FRANKLIN Milwaukee
FRANKSVILLE Racine
FREDERIC (54837) Polk(80), Burnett(19)
FREDONIA (53021) Ozaukee(88), Washington(11)
FREEDOM Outagamie
FREMONT (54940) Waupaca(51), Waushara(30), Winnebago(13), Outagamie(4)
FRIENDSHIP Adams
FRIESLAND Columbia
GALESVILLE Trempealeau
GALLOWAY Marathon
GAYS MILLS Crawford
GENESEE DEPOT Waukesha
GENOA Vernon
GENOA CITY (53128) Walworth(80), Kenosha(19)
GERMANTOWN Washington
GILE Iron
GILLETT Oconto
GILMAN (54433) Taylor(80), Chippewa(19)
GILMANTON Buffalo
GLEASON (54435) Lincoln(68), Langlade(31)
GLEN FLORA Rusk
GLEN HAVEN Grant
GLENBEULAH (53023) Sheboygan(97), Fond du Lac(2)
GLENWOOD CITY St. Croix
GLIDDEN Ashland
GOODMAN (54125) Marinette(98), Forest(1)
GORDON Douglas
GOTHAM Richland
GRAFTON Ozaukee
GRAND MARSH Adams
GRAND VIEW Bayfield
GRANTON Clark
GRANTSBURG (54840) Burnett(98), Polk(1)
GRATIOT Lafayette
GREEN BAY Brown
GREEN LAKE Green Lake
GREEN VALLEY Shawano
GREENBUSH Sheboygan
GREENDALE Milwaukee
GREENLEAF (54126) Brown(96), Manitowoc(3)
GREENVILLE Outagamie
GREENWOOD Clark
GRESHAM Shawano
GURNEY Iron
HAGER CITY Pierce
HALES CORNERS Milwaukee
HAMMOND St. Croix
HANCOCK (54943) Waushara(81), Adams(18)
HANNIBAL Taylor
HANOVER Rock
HARSHAW Oneida
HARTFORD (53027) Washington(96), Dodge(3)
HARTLAND Waukesha
HATLEY Marathon
HAUGEN Barron
HAWKINS (54530) Rusk(71), Price(27)
HAWTHORNE Douglas
HAYWARD (54843) Sawyer(80), Washburn(19)
HAZEL GREEN (53811) Grant(94), Lafayette(5)
HAZELHURST Oneida
HEAFFORD JUNCTION Lincoln

HELENVILLE Jefferson
HERBSTER Bayfield
HERTEL Burnett
HEWITT Wood
HIGH BRIDGE Ashland
HIGHLAND (53543) Iowa(91), Grant(8)
HILBERT Calumet
HILLPOINT (53937) Sauk(62), Richland(37)
HILLSBORO (54634) Vernon(78), Richland(19), Juneau(1)
HILLSDALE Barron
HINGHAM Sheboygan
HIXTON Jackson
HOLCOMBE (54745) Chippewa(87), Rusk(12)
HOLLANDALE (53544) Iowa(97), Dane(2)
HOLMEN La Crosse
HONEY CREEK Walworth
HORICON Dodge
HORTONVILLE Outagamie
HOULTON St. Croix
HUBERTUS Washington
HUDSON St. Croix
HUMBIRD (54746) Clark(76), Jackson(23)
HURLEY Iron
HUSTISFORD Dodge
HUSTLER Juneau
INDEPENDENCE (54747) Trempealeau(81), Buffalo(18)
IOLA Waupaca
IRMA Lincoln
IRON BELT Iron
IRON RIDGE Dodge
IRON RIVER Bayfield
IXONIA (53036) Jefferson(73), Dodge(20), Waukesha(5)
JACKSON Washington
JANESVILLE Rock
JEFFERSON Jefferson
JIM FALLS Chippewa
JOHNSON CREEK Jefferson
JUDA Green
JUMP RIVER Taylor
JUNCTION CITY (54443) Portage(94), Marathon(2), Wood(2)
JUNEAU Dodge
KANSASVILLE (53139) Racine(85), Kenosha(14)
KAUKAUNA (54130) Outagamie(95), Brown(2), Calumet(2)
KELLNERSVILLE Manitowoc
KEMPSTER Langlade
KENDALL (54638) Monroe(88), Vernon(9), Juneau(2)
KENNAN Price
KENOSHA Kenosha
KESHENA Menominee
KEWASKUM (53040) Washington(71), Sheboygan(16), Fond du Lac(12)
KEWAUNEE Kewaunee
KIEL (53042) Manitowoc(95), Calumet(4)
KIELER Grant
KIMBERLY Outagamie
KING Waupaca
KINGSTON Green Lake
KNAPP (54749) Dunn(88), St. Croix(11)
KOHLER Sheboygan
KRAKOW (54137) Shawano(76), Oconto(23)
LA CROSSE La Crosse
LA FARGE (54639) Vernon(92), Richland(7)
LA POINTE Ashland
LA VALLE (53941) Sauk(97), Juneau(1)
LAC DU FLAMBEAU (54538) Vilas(88), Oneida(6), Price(4)
LADYSMITH Rusk
LAKE DELTON Sauk
LAKE GENEVA Walworth
LAKE MILLS Jefferson
LAKE NEBAGAMON Douglas

LAKE TOMAHAWK Oneida
LAKEWOOD Oconto
LANCASTER Grant
LAND O LAKES Vilas
LANNON Waukesha
LAONA Forest
LARSEN Winnebago
LEBANON Dodge
LENA (54139) Oconto(98), Marinette(1)
LEOPOLIS Shawano
LEWIS Polk
LILY Langlade
LIME RIDGE Sauk
LINDEN Iowa
LITTLE CHUTE Outagamie
LITTLE SUAMICO Oconto
LIVINGSTON (53554) Grant(71), Iowa(28)
LODI (53555) Columbia(92), Dane(7)
LOGANVILLE Sauk
LOMIRA (53048) Dodge(97), Fond du Lac(2)
LONE ROCK (53556) Richland(83), Sauk(16)
LONG LAKE (54542) Forest(65), Florence(34)
LOWELL Dodge
LOYAL Clark
LUBLIN (54447) Taylor(97), Clark(2)
LUCK (54853) Polk(94), Burnett(5)
LUXEMBURG (54217) Kewaunee(88), Door(5), Brown(5)
LYNDON STATION (53944) Juneau(88), Sauk(11)
LYNXVILLE Crawford
LYONS Walworth
MADISON Dane
MAIDEN ROCK Pierce
MALONE (53049) Fond du Lac(92), Calumet(7)
MANAWA Waupaca
MANCHESTER Green Lake
MANITOWISH WATERS (54545) Vilas(98), Iron(1)
MANITOWOC Manitowoc
MAPLE Douglas
MAPLEWOOD Door
MARATHON Marathon
MARENGO Ashland
MARIBEL (54227) Manitowoc(98), Brown(1)
MARINETTE Marinette
MARION (54950) Shawano(51), Waupaca(48)
MARKESAN (53946) Green Lake(97), Fond du Lac(2)
MARQUETTE Green Lake
MARSHALL (53559) Dane(98), Jefferson(1)
MARSHALL FIELDS Milwaukee
MARSHFIELD Wood
MASON (54856) Bayfield(97), Ashland(2)
MATHER Juneau
MATTOON Shawano
MAUSTON Juneau
MAYVILLE Dodge
MAZOMANIE (53560) Dane(96), Iowa(3)
MC FARLAND Dane
MC NAUGHTON Oneida
MEDFORD Taylor
MEDINA Outagamie
MELLEN Ashland
MELROSE Jackson
MENASHA (54952) Winnebago(89), Calumet(10)
MENOMONEE FALLS Waukesha
MENOMONIE Dunn
MEQUON Ozaukee
MERCER Iron
MERRILL (54452) Lincoln(88), Marathon(11)
MERRILLAN (54754) Jackson(85), Clark(14)

MERRIMAC (53561) Sauk(86), Columbia(13)
MERTON Waukesha
MIDDLETON Dane
MIKANA Barron
MILAN Marathon
MILLADORE (54454) Wood(87), Portage(12)
MILLSTON Jackson
MILLTOWN Polk
MILTON Rock
MILWAUKEE Milwaukee
MINDORO (54644) La Crosse(96), Jackson(3)
MINERAL POINT (53565) Iowa(87), Lafayette(12)
MINOCQUA (54548) Oneida(79), Vilas(20)
MINONG (54859) Washburn(88), Douglas(11)
MISHICOT Manitowoc
MONDOVI (54755) Buffalo(64), Eau Claire(12), Pepin(11), Dunn(10)
MONROE Green
MONTELLO (53949) Marquette(98), Green Lake(1)
MONTFORT (53569) Grant(64), Iowa(35)
MONTICELLO Green
MONTREAL Iron
MORRISONVILLE Dane
MOSINEE (54455) Marathon(97), Portage(2)
MOUNT CALVARY Fond du Lac
MOUNT HOPE Grant
MOUNT HOREB Dane
MOUNT STERLING Crawford
MOUNTAIN Oconto
MUKWONAGO (53149) Waukesha(90), Walworth(8), Racine(1)
MUSCODA (53573) Grant(52), Richland(40), Iowa(7)
MUSKEGO (53150) Waukesha(98), Racine(1)
NASHOTAH Waukesha
NECEDAH Juneau
NEENAH Winnebago
NEILLSVILLE Clark
NEKOOSA (54457) Wood(57), Adams(39), Juneau(3)
NELSON Buffalo
NELSONVILLE Portage
NEOPIT Menominee
NEOSHO Dodge
NESHKORO (54960) Marquette(58), Waushara(35), Green Lake(5)
NEW AUBURN (54757) Chippewa(65), Barron(17), Dunn(9), Rusk(7)
NEW BERLIN Waukesha
NEW FRANKEN Brown
NEW GLARUS (53574) Green(97), Dane(2)
NEW HOLSTEIN Calumet
NEW LISBON Juneau
NEW LONDON (54961) Waupaca(81), Outagamie(18)
NEW MUNSTER Kenosha
NEW RICHMOND (54017) St. Croix(98), Polk(1)
NEWBURG Washington
NEWTON Manitowoc
NIAGARA (54151) Marinette(80), Florence(19)
NICHOLS Outagamie
NORTH FREEDOM Sauk
NORTH LAKE Waukesha
NORTH PRAIRIE Waukesha
NORWALK Monroe
OAK CREEK Milwaukee
OAKDALE Monroe
OAKFIELD (53065) Fond du Lac(91), Dodge(8)
OCONOMOWOC (53066) Waukesha(94), Jefferson(3), Dodge(1)

OCONTO Oconto
OCONTO FALLS (54154) Oconto(97), Shawano(2)
ODANAH Ashland
OGDENSBURG Waupaca
OGEMA Price
OJIBWA Sawyer
OKAUCHEE Waukesha
OMRO Winnebago
ONALASKA La Crosse
ONEIDA (54155) Brown(58), Outagamie(41)
ONTARIO (54651) Vernon(61), Monroe(38)
OOSTBURG Sheboygan
OREGON Dane
ORFORDVILLE Rock
OSCEOLA Polk
OSHKOSH Winnebago
OSSEO (54758) Trempealeau(70), Eau Claire(17), Jackson(11)
OWEN (54460) Clark(96), Taylor(3)
OXFORD (53952) Marquette(50), Adams(49)
PACKWAUKEE Marquette
PALMYRA Jefferson
PARDEEVILLE (53954) Columbia(96), Marquette(3)
PARK FALLS (54552) Price(92), Iron(7)
PATCH GROVE Grant
PEARSON Langlade
PELICAN LAKE (54463) Oneida(95), Langlade(4)
PELL LAKE Walworth
PEMBINE Marinette
PEPIN Pepin
PESHTIGO (54157) Marinette(98), Oconto(10)
PEWAUKEE Waukesha
PHELPS Vilas
PHILLIPS Price
PHLOX Langlade
PICKEREL (54465) Langlade(60), Forest(40)
PICKETT (54964) Winnebago(80), Fond du Lac(19)
PIGEON FALLS Trempealeau
PINE RIVER (54965) Waushara(98), Waupaca(1)
PITTSVILLE (54466) Wood(79), Clark(10), Jackson(10)
PLAIN Sauk
PLAINFIELD (54966) Waushara(85), Portage(13), Adams(1)
PLATTEVILLE (53818) Grant(95), Lafayette(3)
PLEASANT PRAIRIE Kenosha
PLOVER Portage
PLUM CITY Pierce
PLYMOUTH Sheboygan
POPLAR Douglas
PORT EDWARDS Wood
PORT WASHINGTON Ozaukee
PORT WING Bayfield
PORTAGE Columbia
PORTERFIELD Marinette
POSKIN Barron
POTOSI Grant
POTTER Calumet
POUND (54161) Marinette(54), Oconto(45)
POWERS LAKE Kenosha
POY SIPPI Waushara
POYNETTE Columbia
PRAIRIE DU CHIEN (53821) Crawford(98), Grant(1)
PRAIRIE DU SAC (53578) Sauk(90), Columbia(9)
PRAIRIE FARM (54762) Barron(94), Dunn(5)
PRENTICE Price
PRESCOTT Pierce
PRESQUE ISLE Vilas

PRINCETON (54968) Green Lake(93), Marquette(6)
PULASKI (54162) Shawano(63), Brown(28), Oconto(8)
RACINE Racine
RADISSON Sawyer
RANDOLPH Columbia
RANDOM LAKE (53075) Sheboygan(93), Ozaukee(5), Washington(1)
READFIELD Waupaca
READSTOWN (54652) Vernon(96), Crawford(3)
REDGRANITE Waushara
REEDSBURG Sauk
REEDSVILLE Manitowoc
REESEVILLE Dodge
REWEY Iowa
RHINELANDER Oneida
RIB LAKE (54470) Taylor(96), Price(3)
RICE LAKE Barron
RICHFIELD Washington
RICHLAND CENTER Richland
RIDGELAND (54763) Dunn(91), Barron(8)
RIDGEWAY Iowa
RINGLE Marathon
RIO Columbia
RIPON (54971) Fond du Lac(82), Green Lake(14), Winnebago(3)
RIVER FALLS (54022) Pierce(73), St. Croix(26)
ROBERTS St. Croix
ROCHESTER Racine
ROCK FALLS Dunn
ROCK SPRINGS Sauk
ROCKFIELD Washington
ROCKLAND (54653) La Crosse(89), Monroe(10)
ROSENDALE Fond du Lac
ROSHOLT (54473) Portage(79), Marathon(20)
ROTHSCHILD Marathon
ROYALTON Waupaca
RUBICON Dodge
RUDOLPH (54475) Wood(85), Portage(14)
SAINT CLOUD (53079) Fond du Lac(92), Sheboygan(7)
SAINT CROIX FALLS Polk
SAINT FRANCIS Milwaukee
SAINT GERMAIN (54558) Vilas(89), Oneida(10)
SAINT JOSEPH St. Croix
SAINT NAZIANZ Manitowoc
SALEM Kenosha
SAND CREEK Dunn
SARONA (54870) Washburn(95), Barron(4)
SAUK CITY (53583) Sauk(85), Dane(13)
SAUKVILLE Ozaukee
SAXEVILLE Waushara
SAXON (54559) Iron(94), Ashland(5)
SAYNER Vilas
SCANDINAVIA (54977) Waupaca(95), Portage(4)
SCHOFIELD Marathon
SENECA Crawford
SEXTONVILLE Richland
SEYMOUR (54165) Outagamie(95), Shawano(3), Brown(1)
SHARON (53585) Walworth(96), Rock(3)
SHAWANO Shawano
SHEBOYGAN Sheboygan
SHEBOYGAN FALLS Sheboygan
SHELDON (54766) Rusk(59), Taylor(40)
SHELL LAKE (54871) Washburn(63), Burnett(36)
SHERWOOD Calumet
SHIOCTON (54170) Outagamie(93), Shawano(6)
SHULLSBURG Lafayette
SILVER LAKE Kenosha
SINSINAWA Grant
SIREN (54872) Burnett(97), Polk(2)
SISTER BAY Door

SLINGER Washington
SOBIESKI Oconto
SOLDIERS GROVE (54655) Crawford(60), Richland(33), Vernon(5)
SOLON SPRINGS (54873) Douglas(60), Bayfield(39)
SOMERS Kenosha
SOMERSET St. Croix
SOUTH MILWAUKEE Milwaukee
SOUTH RANGE Douglas
SOUTH WAYNE Lafayette
SPARTA Monroe
SPENCER (54479) Marathon(56), Clark(43)
SPOONER (54801) Washburn(83), Burnett(16)
SPRING GREEN (53588) Sauk(77), Iowa(21)
SPRING VALLEY (54767) Pierce(95), St. Croix(3), Dunn(1)
SPRINGBROOK Washburn
SPRINGFIELD Walworth
STANLEY (54768) Chippewa(72), Clark(16), Eau Claire(8), Taylor(2)
STAR LAKE Vilas
STAR PRAIRIE (54026) Polk(60), St. Croix(39)
STETSONVILLE (54480) Taylor(95), Marathon(4)
STEUBEN Crawford
STEVENS POINT Portage
STITZER Grant
STOCKBRIDGE Calumet
STOCKHOLM (54769) Pepin(81), Pierce(18)
STODDARD (54658) Vernon(89), La Crosse(10)
STONE LAKE (54876) Sawyer(61), Washburn(38)
STOUGHTON (53589) Dane(98), Rock(1)
STRATFORD Marathon
STRUM (54770) Trempealeau(75), Eau Claire(25)
STURGEON BAY Door
STURTEVANT (53177) Racine(91), Kenosha(8)
SUAMICO Brown
SULLIVAN Jefferson
SUMMIT LAKE Langlade
SUN PRAIRIE Dane
SUPERIOR Douglas
SURING (54174) Oconto(96), Menominee(3)
SUSSEX Waukesha
TAYLOR (54659) Jackson(91), Trempealeau(8)
THERESA (53091) Dodge(94), Washington(5)
THIENSVILLE Ozaukee
THORP (54771) Clark(93), Taylor(6)
THREE LAKES (54562) Oneida(95), Forest(4)
TIGERTON (54486) Shawano(92), Waupaca(7)
TILLEDA Shawano
TISCH MILLS Manitowoc
TOMAH Monroe
TOMAHAWK (54487) Lincoln(88), Oneida(11)
TONY Rusk
TOWNSEND Oconto
TREGO Washburn
TREMPEALEAU Trempealeau
TREVOR Kenosha
TRIPOLI (54564) Oneida(46), Lincoln(36), Price(16)
TUNNEL CITY Monroe
TURTLE LAKE (54889) Barron(73), Polk(26)
TWIN LAKES Kenosha
TWO RIVERS Manitowoc
UNION CENTER Juneau

UNION GROVE (53182) Racine(91), Kenosha(8)
UNITY (54488) Clark(68), Marathon(31)
UPSON Iron
VALDERS Manitowoc
VAN DYNE (54979) Fond du Lac(87), Winnebago(12)
VERONA Dane
VESPER Wood
VIOLA (54664) Richland(66), Vernon(33)
VIROQUA (54665) Vernon(98), Crawford(1)
WABENO (54566) Forest(98), Langlade(1)
WALDO Sheboygan
WALES Waukesha
WALWORTH Walworth
WARRENS (54666) Monroe(81), Jackson(18)
WASCOTT Douglas
WASHBURN Bayfield
WASHINGTON ISLAND Door
WATERFORD Racine

WATERLOO (53594) Jefferson(81), Dodge(14), Dane(3)
WATERTOWN Dodge
WAUKAU Winnebago
WAUKESHA Waukesha
WAUNAKEE Dane
WAUPACA (54981) Waupaca(91), Waushara(4), Portage(3)
WAUPUN (53963) Dodge(52), Fond du Lac(47)
WAUSAU Marathon
WAUSAUKEE Marinette
WAUTOMA (54982) Waushara(97), Marquette(2)
WAUZEKA Crawford
WEBSTER Burnett
WEST BEND Washington
WEST SALEM La Crosse
WESTBORO (54490) Taylor(95), Price(4)
WESTBY (54667) Vernon(98), La Crosse(1)

WESTFIELD (53964) Marquette(96), Adams(2), Waushara(1)
WEYAUWEGA (54983) Waupaca(89), Waushara(10)
WEYERHAEUSER Rusk
WHEELER Dunn
WHITE LAKE (54491) Langlade(91), Oconto(8)
WHITEHALL Trempealeau
WHITELAW Manitowoc
WHITEWATER (53190) Walworth(61), Rock(28), Jefferson(10)
WILD ROSE Waushara
WILLARD Clark
WILLIAMS BAY Walworth
WILMOT Kenosha
WILSON St. Croix
WILTON Monroe
WINDSOR Dane
WINNEBAGO Winnebago
WINNECONNE (54986) Winnebago(98), Waushara(1)

WINTER Sawyer
WISCONSIN DELLS (53965) Columbia(38), Sauk(29), Adams(24), Juneau(7)
WISCONSIN RAPIDS Wood
WITHEE (54498) Clark(90), Taylor(9)
WITTENBERG (54499) Shawano(70), Marathon(28), Portage(1)
WONEWOC (53968) Juneau(67), Sauk(24), Vernon(6), Richland(1)
WOODFORD Lafayette
WOODLAND Dodge
WOODMAN Grant
WOODRUFF (54568) Vilas(66), Oneida(33)
WOODVILLE St. Croix
WOODWORTH Kenosha
WRIGHTSTOWN Brown
WYEVILLE Monroe
WYOCENA Columbia
ZACHOW Shawano
ZENDA Walworth

ZIP/City Cross Reference

ZIP	City		ZIP	City		ZIP	City		ZIP	City
53001-53001	ADELL		53066-53066	OCONOMOWOC		53149-53149	MUKWONAGO		53526-53526	COBB
53002-53002	ALLENTON		53069-53069	OKAUCHEE		53150-53150	MUSKEGO		53527-53527	COTTAGE GROVE
53003-53003	ASHIPPUN		53070-53070	OOSTBURG		53151-53151	NEW BERLIN		53528-53528	CROSS PLAINS
53004-53004	BELGIUM		53072-53072	PEWAUKEE		53152-53152	NEW MUNSTER		53529-53529	DANE
53005-53005	BROOKFIELD		53073-53073	PLYMOUTH		53153-53153	NORTH PRAIRIE		53530-53530	DARLINGTON
53006-53006	BROWNSVILLE		53074-53074	PORT WASHINGTON		53154-53154	OAK CREEK		53531-53531	DEERFIELD
53007-53007	BUTLER		53075-53075	RANDOM LAKE		53156-53156	PALMYRA		53532-53532	DE FOREST
53008-53008	BROOKFIELD		53076-53076	RICHFIELD		53157-53157	PELL LAKE		53533-53533	DODGEVILLE
53009-53009	BYRON		53077-53077	ROCKFIELD		53158-53158	PLEASANT PRAIRIE		53534-53534	EDGERTON
53010-53010	CAMPBELLSPORT		53078-53078	RUBICON		53159-53159	POWERS LAKE		53535-53535	EDMUND
53011-53011	CASCADE		53079-53079	SAINT CLOUD		53167-53167	ROCHESTER		53536-53536	EVANSVILLE
53012-53012	CEDARBURG		53080-53080	SAUKVILLE		53168-53168	SALEM		53537-53537	FOOTVILLE
53013-53013	CEDAR GROVE		53081-53083	SHEBOYGAN		53170-53170	SILVER LAKE		53538-53538	FORT ATKINSON
53014-53014	CHILTON		53085-53085	SHEBOYGAN FALLS		53171-53171	SOMERS		53540-53540	GOTHAM
53015-53015	CLEVELAND		53086-53086	SLINGER		53172-53172	SOUTH MILWAUKEE		53541-53541	GRATIOT
53016-53016	CLYMAN		53088-53088	STOCKBRIDGE		53176-53176	SPRINGFIELD		53542-53542	HANOVER
53017-53017	COLGATE		53089-53089	SUSSEX		53177-53177	STURTEVANT		53543-53543	HIGHLAND
53018-53018	DELAFIELD		53090-53090	WEST BEND		53178-53178	SULLIVAN		53544-53544	HOLLANDALE
53019-53019	EDEN		53091-53091	THERESA		53179-53179	TREVOR		53545-53547	JANESVILLE
53020-53020	ELKHART LAKE		53092-53092	THIENSVILLE		53181-53181	TWIN LAKES		53549-53549	JEFFERSON
53021-53021	FREDONIA		53093-53093	WALDO		53182-53182	UNION GROVE		53550-53550	JUDA
53022-53022	GERMANTOWN		53094-53094	WATERTOWN		53183-53183	WALES		53551-53551	LAKE MILLS
53023-53023	GLENBEULAH		53095-53096	WEST BEND		53184-53184	WALWORTH		53553-53553	LINDEN
53024-53024	GRAFTON		53097-53097	MEQUON		53185-53185	WATERFORD		53554-53554	LIVINGSTON
53026-53026	GREENBUSH		53098-53098	WATERTOWN		53186-53189	WAUKESHA		53555-53555	LODI
53027-53027	HARTFORD		53099-53099	WOODLAND		53190-53190	WHITEWATER		53556-53556	LONE ROCK
53029-53029	HARTLAND		53101-53101	BASSETT		53191-53191	WILLIAMS BAY		53557-53557	LOWELL
53031-53031	HINGHAM		53102-53102	BENET LAKE		53192-53192	WILMOT		53558-53558	MC FARLAND
53032-53032	HORICON		53103-53103	BIG BEND		53194-53194	WOODWORTH		53559-53559	MARSHALL
53033-53033	HUBERTUS		53104-53104	BRISTOL		53195-53195	ZENDA		53560-53560	MAZOMANIE
53034-53034	HUSTISFORD		53105-53105	BURLINGTON		53200-53234	MILWAUKEE		53561-53561	MERRIMAC
53035-53035	IRON RIDGE		53108-53108	CALEDONIA		53235-53235	SAINT FRANCIS		53562-53562	MIDDLETON
53036-53036	IXONIA		53109-53109	CAMP LAKE		53237-53259	MILWAUKEE		53563-53563	MILTON
53037-53037	JACKSON		53110-53110	CUDAHY		53260-53260	MARSHALL FIELDS		53565-53565	MINERAL POINT
53038-53038	JOHNSON CREEK		53114-53114	DARIEN		53263-53295	MILWAUKEE		53566-53566	MONROE
53039-53039	JUNEAU		53115-53115	DELAVAN		53400-53490	RACINE		53569-53569	MONTFORT
53040-53040	KEWASKUM		53118-53118	DOUSMAN		53501-53501	AFTON		53570-53570	MONTICELLO
53042-53042	KIEL		53119-53119	EAGLE		53502-53502	ALBANY		53571-53571	MORRISONVILLE
53044-53044	KOHLER		53120-53120	EAST TROY		53503-53503	ARENA		53572-53572	MOUNT HOREB
53045-53045	BROOKFIELD		53121-53121	ELKHORN		53504-53504	ARGYLE		53573-53573	MUSCODA
53046-53046	LANNON		53122-53122	ELM GROVE		53505-53505	AVALON		53574-53574	NEW GLARUS
53047-53047	LEBANON		53125-53125	FONTANA		53506-53506	AVOCA		53575-53575	OREGON
53048-53048	LOMIRA		53126-53126	FRANKSVILLE		53507-53507	BARNEVELD		53576-53576	ORFORDVILLE
53049-53049	MALONE		53127-53127	GENESEE DEPOT		53508-53508	BELLEVILLE		53577-53577	PLAIN
53050-53050	MAYVILLE		53128-53128	GENOA CITY		53510-53510	BELMONT		53578-53578	PRAIRIE DU SAC
53051-53052	MENOMONEE FALLS		53129-53129	GREENDALE		53511-53512	BELOIT		53579-53579	REESEVILLE
53056-53056	MERTON		53130-53130	HALES CORNERS		53515-53515	BLACK EARTH		53580-53580	REWEY
53057-53057	MOUNT CALVARY		53132-53132	FRANKLIN		53516-53516	BLANCHARDVILLE		53581-53581	RICHLAND CENTER
53058-53058	NASHOTAH		53137-53137	HELENVILLE		53517-53517	BLUE MOUNDS		53582-53582	RIDGEWAY
53059-53059	NEOSHO		53138-53138	HONEY CREEK		53518-53518	BLUE RIVER		53583-53583	SAUK CITY
53060-53060	NEWBURG		53139-53139	KANSASVILLE		53520-53520	BRODHEAD		53584-53584	SEXTONVILLE
53061-53062	NEW HOLSTEIN		53140-53144	KENOSHA		53521-53521	BROOKLYN		53585-53585	SHARON
53063-53063	NEWTON		53146-53146	NEW BERLIN		53522-53522	BROWNTOWN		53586-53586	SHULLSBURG
53064-53064	NORTH LAKE		53147-53147	LAKE GENEVA		53523-53523	CAMBRIDGE		53587-53587	SOUTH WAYNE
53065-53065	OAKFIELD		53148-53148	LYONS		53525-53525	CLINTON		53588-53588	SPRING GREEN

Zip	Place		Zip	Place		Zip	Place		Zip	Place
53589-53589	STOUGHTON		53969-53969	WYOCENA		54175-54175	TOWNSEND		54449-54449	MARSHFIELD
53590-53591	SUN PRAIRIE		54001-54001	AMERY		54176-54176	GILLETT		54450-54450	MATTOON
53593-53593	VERONA		54002-54002	BALDWIN		54177-54177	WAUSAUKEE		54451-54451	MEDFORD
53594-53594	WATERLOO		54003-54003	BELDENVILLE		54180-54180	WRIGHTSTOWN		54452-54452	MERRILL
53595-53595	DODGEVILLE		54004-54004	CLAYTON		54182-54182	ZACHOW		54453-54453	MILAN
53596-53596	SUN PRAIRIE		54005-54005	CLEAR LAKE		54201-54201	ALGOMA		54454-54454	MILLADORE
53597-53597	WAUNAKEE		54006-54006	CUSHING		54202-54202	BAILEYS HARBOR		54455-54455	MOSINEE
53598-53598	WINDSOR		54007-54007	DEER PARK		54203-54203	BRANCH		54456-54456	NEILLSVILLE
53599-53599	WOODFORD		54009-54009	DRESSER		54204-54204	BRUSSELS		54457-54457	NEKOOSA
53700-53794	MADISON		54010-54010	EAST ELLSWORTH		54205-54205	CASCO		54458-54458	NELSONVILLE
53801-53801	BAGLEY		54011-54011	ELLSWORTH		54206-54206	CATO		54459-54459	OGEMA
53802-53802	BEETOWN		54012-54012	EMERALD		54207-54207	COLLINS		54460-54460	OWEN
53803-53803	BENTON		54012-54012	EMERALDX		54208-54208	DENMARK		54462-54462	PEARSON
53804-53804	BLOOMINGTON		54013-54013	GLENWOOD CITY		54209-54209	EGG HARBOR		54463-54463	PELICAN LAKE
53805-53805	BOSCOBEL		54014-54014	HAGER CITY		54210-54210	ELLISON BAY		54464-54464	PHLOX
53806-53806	CASSVILLE		54015-54015	HAMMOND		54211-54211	EPHRAIM		54465-54465	PICKEREL
53807-53807	CUBA CITY		54016-54016	HUDSON		54212-54212	FISH CREEK		54466-54466	PITTSVILLE
53808-53808	DICKEYVILLE		54017-54017	NEW RICHMOND		54213-54213	FORESTVILLE		54467-54467	PLOVER
53809-53809	FENNIMORE		54020-54020	OSCEOLA		54214-54214	FRANCIS CREEK		54469-54469	PORT EDWARDS
53810-53810	GLEN HAVEN		54021-54021	PRESCOTT		54215-54215	KELLNERSVILLE		54470-54470	RIB LAKE
53811-53811	HAZEL GREEN		54022-54022	RIVER FALLS		54216-54216	KEWAUNEE		54471-54471	RINGLE
53812-53812	KIELER		54023-54023	ROBERTS		54217-54217	LUXEMBURG		54472-54472	MARSHFIELD
53813-53813	LANCASTER		54024-54024	SAINT CROIX FALLS		54220-54221	MANITOWOC		54473-54473	ROSHOLT
53816-53816	MOUNT HOPE		54025-54025	SOMERSET		54226-54226	MAPLEWOOD		54474-54474	ROTHSCHILD
53817-53817	PATCH GROVE		54026-54026	STAR PRAIRIE		54227-54227	MARIBEL		54475-54475	RUDOLPH
53818-53818	PLATTEVILLE		54027-54027	WILSON		54228-54228	MISHICOT		54476-54476	SCHOFIELD
53820-53820	POTOSI		54028-54028	WOODVILLE		54229-54229	NEW FRANKEN		54479-54479	SPENCER
53821-53821	PRAIRIE DU CHIEN		54082-54082	SAINT JOSEPH		54230-54230	REEDSVILLE		54480-54480	STETSONVILLE
53824-53824	SINSINAWA		54082-54082	HOULTON		54231-54231	ALGOMA		54481-54482	STEVENS POINT
53825-53825	STITZER		54101-54101	ABRAMS		54232-54232	SAINT NAZIANZ		54484-54484	STRATFORD
53826-53826	WAUZEKA		54102-54102	AMBERG		54234-54234	SISTER BAY		54485-54485	SUMMIT LAKE
53827-53827	WOODMAN		54103-54103	ARMSTRONG CREEK		54235-54235	STURGEON BAY		54486-54486	TIGERTON
53901-53901	PORTAGE		54104-54104	ATHELSTANE		54240-54240	TISCH MILLS		54487-54487	TOMAHAWK
53910-53910	ADAMS		54106-54106	BLACK CREEK		54241-54241	TWO RIVERS		54488-54488	UNITY
53911-53911	ARLINGTON		54107-54107	BONDUEL		54245-54245	VALDERS		54489-54489	VESPER
53913-53913	BARABOO		54110-54110	BRILLION		54246-54246	WASHINGTON ISLAND		54490-54490	WESTBORO
53916-53917	BEAVER DAM		54111-54111	CECIL		54247-54247	WHITELAW		54491-54491	WHITE LAKE
53919-53919	BRANDON		54112-54112	COLEMAN		54300-54344	GREEN BAY		54492-54492	STEVENS POINT
53920-53920	BRIGGSVILLE		54113-54113	COMBINED LOCKS		54401-54403	WAUSAU		54493-54493	WILLARD
53921-53921	BROOKS		54114-54114	CRIVITZ		54404-54404	MARSHFIELD		54494-54495	WISCONSIN RAPIDS
53922-53922	BURNETT		54115-54115	DE PERE		54405-54405	ABBOTSFORD		54498-54498	WITHEE
53923-53923	CAMBRIA		54119-54119	DUNBAR		54406-54406	AMHERST		54499-54499	WITTENBERG
53924-53924	CAZENOVIA		54120-54120	FENCE		54407-54407	AMHERST JUNCTION		54501-54501	RHINELANDER
53925-53925	COLUMBUS		54121-54121	FLORENCE		54408-54408	ANIWA		54511-54511	ARGONNE
53926-53926	DALTON		54123-54123	FOREST JUNCTION		54409-54409	ANTIGO		54512-54512	BOULDER JUNCTION
53927-53927	DELLWOOD		54124-54124	GILLETT		54410-54410	ARPIN		54513-54513	BRANTWOOD
53928-53928	DOYLESTOWN		54125-54125	GOODMAN		54411-54411	ATHENS		54514-54514	BUTTERNUT
53929-53929	ELROY		54126-54126	GREENLEAF		54412-54412	AUBURNDALE		54515-54515	CATAWBA
53930-53930	ENDEAVOR		54127-54127	GREEN VALLEY		54413-54413	BABCOCK		54517-54517	CLAM LAKE
53931-53931	FAIRWATER		54128-54128	GRESHAM		54414-54414	BIRNAMWOOD		54519-54519	CONOVER
53932-53932	FALL RIVER		54129-54129	HILBERT		54415-54415	BLENKER		54520-54520	CRANDON
53933-53933	FOX LAKE		54130-54130	KAUKAUNA		54416-54416	BOWLER		54521-54521	EAGLE RIVER
53934-53934	FRIENDSHIP		54131-54131	FREEDOM		54417-54417	BROKAW		54524-54524	FIFIELD
53935-53935	FRIESLAND		54135-54135	KESHENA		54418-54418	BRYANT		54525-54525	GILE
53936-53936	GRAND MARSH		54136-54136	KIMBERLY		54419-54419	CHELSEA		54526-54526	GLEN FLORA
53937-53937	HILLPOINT		54137-54137	KRAKOW		54420-54420	CHILI		54527-54527	GLIDDEN
53939-53939	KINGSTON		54138-54138	LAKEWOOD		54421-54421	COLBY		54528-54528	GURNEY
53940-53940	LAKE DELTON		54139-54139	LENA		54422-54422	CURTISS		54529-54529	HARSHAW
53941-53941	LA VALLE		54140-54140	LITTLE CHUTE		54423-54423	CUSTER		54530-54530	HAWKINS
53942-53942	LIME RIDGE		54141-54141	LITTLE SUAMICO		54424-54424	DEERBROOK		54531-54531	HAZELHURST
53943-53943	LOGANVILLE		54143-54143	MARINETTE		54425-54425	DORCHESTER		54532-54532	HEAFFORD JUNCTION
53944-53944	LYNDON STATION		54149-54149	MOUNTAIN		54426-54426	EDGAR		54534-54534	HURLEY
53945-53945	MANCHESTER		54150-54150	NEOPIT		54427-54427	ELAND		54536-54536	IRON BELT
53946-53946	MARKESAN		54151-54151	NIAGARA		54428-54428	ELCHO		54537-54537	KENNAN
53947-53947	MARQUETTE		54152-54152	NICHOLS		54429-54429	ELDERON		54538-54538	LAC DU FLAMBEAU
53948-53948	MAUSTON		54153-54153	OCONTO		54430-54430	ELTON		54539-54539	LAKE TOMAHAWK
53949-53949	MONTELLO		54154-54154	OCONTO FALLS		54432-54432	GALLOWAY		54540-54540	LAND O LAKES
53950-53950	NEW LISBON		54155-54155	ONEIDA		54433-54433	GILMAN		54541-54541	LAONA
53951-53951	NORTH FREEDOM		54156-54156	PEMBINE		54434-54434	JUMP RIVER		54542-54542	LONG LAKE
53952-53952	OXFORD		54157-54157	PESHTIGO		54435-54435	GLEASON		54543-54543	MC NAUGHTON
53953-53953	PACKWAUKEE		54159-54159	PORTERFIELD		54436-54436	GRANTON		54545-54545	MANITOWISH WATERS
53954-53954	PARDEEVILLE		54160-54160	POTTER		54437-54437	GREENWOOD		54546-54546	MELLEN
53955-53955	POYNETTE		54161-54161	POUND		54439-54439	HANNIBAL		54547-54547	MERCER
53956-53957	RANDOLPH		54162-54162	PULASKI		54440-54440	HATLEY		54548-54548	MINOCQUA
53958-53959	REEDSBURG		54164-54164	GILLETT		54441-54441	HEWITT		54550-54550	MONTREAL
53960-53960	RIO		54165-54165	SEYMOUR		54442-54442	IRMA		54552-54552	PARK FALLS
53961-53961	ROCK SPRINGS		54166-54166	SHAWANO		54443-54443	JUNCTION CITY		54554-54554	PHELPS
53962-53962	UNION CENTER		54169-54169	SHERWOOD		54444-54444	KEMPSTER		54555-54555	PHILLIPS
53963-53963	WAUPUN		54170-54170	SHIOCTON		54445-54445	LILY		54556-54556	PRENTICE
53964-53964	WESTFIELD		54171-54171	SOBIESKI		54446-54446	LOYAL		54557-54557	PRESQUE ISLE
53965-53965	WISCONSIN DELLS		54173-54173	SUAMICO		54447-54447	LUBLIN		54558-54558	SAINT GERMAIN
53968-53968	WONEWOC		54174-54174	SURING		54448-54448	MARATHON		54559-54559	SAXON

54560-54560	SAYNER	
54561-54561	STAR LAKE	
54562-54562	THREE LAKES	
54563-54563	TONY	
54564-54564	TRIPOLI	
54565-54565	UPSON	
54566-54566	WABENO	
54568-54568	WOODRUFF	
54601-54603	LA CROSSE	
54610-54610	ALMA	
54611-54611	ALMA CENTER	
54612-54612	ARCADIA	
54613-54613	ARKDALE	
54614-54614	BANGOR	
54615-54615	BLACK RIVER FALLS	
54616-54616	BLAIR	
54617-54617	BLOOM CITY	
54618-54618	CAMP DOUGLAS	
54619-54619	CASHTON	
54620-54620	CATARACT	
54621-54621	CHASEBURG	
54622-54622	COCHRANE	
54623-54623	COON VALLEY	
54624-54624	DE SOTO	
54625-54625	DODGE	
54626-54626	EASTMAN	
54627-54627	ETTRICK	
54628-54628	FERRYVILLE	
54629-54629	FOUNTAIN CITY	
54630-54630	GALESVILLE	
54631-54631	GAYS MILLS	
54632-54632	GENOA	
54634-54634	HILLSBORO	
54635-54635	HIXTON	
54636-54636	HOLMEN	
54637-54637	HUSTLER	
54638-54638	KENDALL	
54639-54639	LA FARGE	
54640-54640	LYNXVILLE	
54641-54641	MATHER	
54642-54642	MELROSE	
54643-54643	MILLSTON	
54644-54644	MINDORO	
54645-54645	MOUNT STERLING	
54646-54646	NECEDAH	
54648-54648	NORWALK	
54649-54649	OAKDALE	
54650-54650	ONALASKA	
54651-54651	ONTARIO	
54652-54652	READSTOWN	
54653-54653	ROCKLAND	
54654-54654	SENECA	
54655-54655	SOLDIERS GROVE	
54656-54656	SPARTA	
54657-54657	STEUBEN	
54658-54658	STODDARD	
54659-54659	TAYLOR	
54660-54660	TOMAH	
54661-54661	TREMPEALEAU	
54662-54662	TUNNEL CITY	
54664-54664	VIOLA	
54665-54665	VIROQUA	
54666-54666	WARRENS	
54667-54667	WESTBY	
54669-54669	WEST SALEM	
54670-54670	WILTON	
54671-54671	WYEVILLE	
54701-54703	EAU CLAIRE	
54720-54720	ALTOONA	
54721-54721	ARKANSAW	
54722-54722	AUGUSTA	
54723-54723	BAY CITY	
54724-54724	BLOOMER	
54725-54725	BOYCEVILLE	
54726-54726	BOYD	
54727-54727	CADOTT	
54728-54728	CHETEK	
54729-54729	CHIPPEWA FALLS	
54730-54730	COLFAX	
54731-54731	CONRATH	
54732-54732	CORNELL	
54733-54733	DALLAS	
54734-54734	DOWNING	
54735-54735	DOWNSVILLE	
54736-54736	DURAND	
54737-54737	EAU GALLE	
54738-54738	ELEVA	
54739-54739	ELK MOUND	
54740-54740	ELMWOOD	
54741-54741	FAIRCHILD	
54742-54742	FALL CREEK	
54743-54743	GILMANTON	
54744-54744	HILLSDALE	
54745-54745	HOLCOMBE	
54746-54746	HUMBIRD	
54747-54747	INDEPENDENCE	
54748-54748	JIM FALLS	
54749-54749	KNAPP	
54750-54750	MAIDEN ROCK	
54751-54751	MENOMONIE	
54754-54754	MERRILLAN	
54755-54755	MONDOVI	
54756-54756	NELSON	
54757-54757	NEW AUBURN	
54758-54758	OSSEO	
54759-54759	PEPIN	
54760-54760	PIGEON FALLS	
54761-54761	PLUM CITY	
54762-54762	PRAIRIE FARM	
54763-54763	RIDGELAND	
54764-54764	ROCK FALLS	
54765-54765	SAND CREEK	
54766-54766	SHELDON	
54767-54767	SPRING VALLEY	
54768-54768	STANLEY	
54769-54769	STOCKHOLM	
54770-54770	STRUM	
54771-54771	THORP	
54772-54772	WHEELER	
54773-54773	WHITEHALL	
54774-54774	CHIPPEWA FALLS	
54801-54801	SPOONER	
54805-54805	ALMENA	
54806-54806	ASHLAND	
54810-54810	BALSAM LAKE	
54812-54812	BARRON	
54813-54813	BARRONETT	
54814-54814	BAYFIELD	
54816-54816	BENOIT	
54817-54817	BIRCHWOOD	
54818-54818	BRILL	
54819-54819	BRUCE	
54820-54820	BRULE	
54821-54821	CABLE	
54822-54822	CAMERON	
54824-54824	CENTURIA	
54826-54826	COMSTOCK	
54827-54827	CORNUCOPIA	
54828-54828	COUDERAY	
54829-54829	CUMBERLAND	
54830-54830	DANBURY	
54832-54832	DRUMMOND	
54834-54834	EDGEWATER	
54835-54835	EXELAND	
54836-54836	FOXBORO	
54837-54837	FREDERIC	
54838-54838	GORDON	
54839-54839	GRAND VIEW	
54840-54840	GRANTSBURG	
54841-54841	HAUGEN	
54842-54842	HAWTHORNE	
54843-54843	HAYWARD	
54844-54844	HERBSTER	
54845-54845	HERTEL	
54846-54846	HIGH BRIDGE	
54847-54847	IRON RIVER	
54848-54848	LADYSMITH	
54849-54849	LAKE NEBAGAMON	
54850-54850	LA POINTE	
54851-54851	LEWIS	
54853-54853	LUCK	
54854-54854	MAPLE	
54855-54855	MARENGO	
54856-54856	MASON	
54857-54857	MIKANA	
54858-54858	MILLTOWN	
54859-54859	MINONG	
54861-54861	ODANAH	
54862-54862	OJIBWA	
54864-54864	POPLAR	
54865-54865	PORT WING	
54866-54866	POSKIN	
54867-54867	RADISSON	
54868-54868	RICE LAKE	
54870-54870	SARONA	
54871-54871	SHELL LAKE	
54872-54872	SIREN	
54873-54873	SOLON SPRINGS	
54874-54874	SOUTH RANGE	
54875-54875	SPRINGBROOK	
54876-54876	STONE LAKE	
54880-54880	SUPERIOR	
54888-54888	TREGO	
54889-54889	TURTLE LAKE	
54890-54890	WASCOTT	
54891-54891	WASHBURN	
54893-54893	WEBSTER	
54895-54895	WEYERHAEUSER	
54896-54896	WINTER	
54901-54906	OSHKOSH	
54909-54909	ALMOND	
54911-54919	APPLETON	
54921-54921	BANCROFT	
54922-54922	BEAR CREEK	
54923-54923	BERLIN	
54926-54926	BIG FALLS	
54927-54927	BUTTE DES MORTS	
54928-54928	CAROLINE	
54929-54929	CLINTONVILLE	
54930-54930	COLOMA	
54931-54931	DALE	
54932-54932	ELDORADO	
54933-54933	EMBARRASS	
54934-54934	EUREKA	
54935-54937	FOND DU LAC	
54940-54940	FREMONT	
54941-54941	GREEN LAKE	
54942-54942	GREENVILLE	
54943-54943	HANCOCK	
54944-54944	HORTONVILLE	
54945-54945	IOLA	
54946-54946	KING	
54947-54947	LARSEN	
54948-54948	LEOPOLIS	
54949-54949	MANAWA	
54950-54950	MARION	
54951-54951	MEDINA	
54952-54952	MENASHA	
54956-54957	NEENAH	
54960-54960	NESHKORO	
54961-54961	NEW LONDON	
54962-54962	OGDENSBURG	
54963-54963	OMRO	
54964-54964	PICKETT	
54965-54965	PINE RIVER	
54966-54966	PLAINFIELD	
54967-54967	POY SIPPI	
54968-54968	PRINCETON	
54969-54969	READFIELD	
54970-54970	REDGRANITE	
54971-54971	RIPON	
54974-54974	ROSENDALE	
54975-54975	ROYALTON	
54976-54976	SAXEVILLE	
54977-54977	SCANDINAVIA	
54978-54978	TILLEDA	
54979-54979	VAN DYNE	
54980-54980	WAUKAU	
54981-54981	WAUPACA	
54982-54982	WAUTOMA	
54983-54983	WEYAUWEGA	
54984-54984	WILD ROSE	
54985-54985	WINNEBAGO	
54986-54986	WINNECONNE	
54990-54990	IOLA	

Wyoming

General Help Numbers:

Governor's Office

State Capitol Building, Rm 124   307-777-7434
Cheyenne, WY 82002-0010   Fax 307-632-3909
www.state.wy.us/governor/   8AM-5PM
governor_home.asp

Attorney General's Office

123 State Capitol, 200 W 24th St   307-777-7841
Cheyenne, WY 82002   Fax 307-777-6869
http://attorneygeneral.state.wy.us   8AM-5PM

State Court Administrator

Supreme Court Bldg   307-777-7480
2301 Capitol Ave   Fax 307-777-3447
Cheyenne, WY 82002   8AM-5PM
www.courts.state.wy.us

State Archives

Archives Division   307-777-7826
2301 Central Ave, Barrett Bldg   Fax 307-777-7044
Cheyenne, WY 82002   8AM-5PM M-F
                    (Research Area 8AM-4:45PM)
http://wyoarchives.state.wy.us/index.htm

State Specifics:

Capital: Cheyenne
                                           Laramie County

Time Zone: MST

Number of Counties: 23

Population: 494,423

Web Site: www.state.wy.us

State Agencies

Criminal Records

Division of Criminal Investigation, Criminal Record Unit, 316 W 22nd St, Cheyenne, WY 82002; 307-777-7523, 307-777-7252 (Fax), 8AM to 5PM.

http://attorneygeneral.state.wy.us/dci/index.html

Note: Access to limited information on sexual offenders is at http://attorneygeneral.state.wy.us/dci/so/so_registration.html

Indexing & Storage: Records are available from 1941 on. It takes up to 10 days before new records are available for inquiry. Records are indexed on inhouse computer. 79% of all arrests in database have final dispositions recorded, 65% for those arrests within last 5 years.

Searching: First, obtain a Request for Criminal Record Packet ($15.00) from address above or phone. Include the following in your request: notarized waiver from subject, name, set of fingerprints, date of birth, Social Security Number, number of years to search. Use the standard 8" x

8" orange fingerprint card. Must also fill out waiver that is on the back of this office's fingerprint card. The following data is not released: juvenile records. Records include all felony and major misdemeanor arrests and convictions.

Access by: mail, in person.

Fee & Payment: The search fee is $15.00 plus an additional $5.00 if this office must perform the fingerprinting. The fee is $10.00 if the applicant is providing volunteer services, plus the fingerprinting fee if applicable. The FBI fingerprint check is an add'l $24.00. Fee payee: Office of the Attorney General. Prepayment required. Money order, cash or certified checks only. No credit cards accepted.

Mail search: Turnaround time: 2 to 4 weeks. A self addressed stamped envelope is requested.

In person search: Proper forms are required to be filled out.

Corporation Records
Limited Liability Company Records
Limited Partnership Records
Fictitious Name
Trademarks/Servicemarks

Corporations Division, Secretary of State, State Capitol, Cheyenne, WY 82002; 307-777-7311, 307-777-5339 (Fax), 8AM-5PM.

http://soswy.state.wy.us

Indexing & Storage: Records are available from 1800s on. The records on microfilm are inactive records before 1983. Newer records are on computer. New records are available for inquiry immediately. Records are indexed on microfilm, inhouse computer.

Searching: The Annual Report financial information (Appendix I Worksheet filed with Annual Report) is not released. Include the following in your request: full name of business. In addition to the articles of incorporation, corporation records include the following information: Annual Reports, Officers, Directors, DBAs, Prior (merged) names, Inactive and Reserved names.

Access by: mail, phone, fax, in person, online.

Fee & Payment: Copy fees are $.50 per page for the first 10 pages and $.15 for each additional page. Certification is $3.00. Fee payee: Secretary of State. They will invoice for copies and certificates. Prepaid accounts are available. Personal checks accepted. No credit cards accepted.

Mail search: Turnaround time: 1 to 3 days. A self addressed stamped envelope is requested.

Phone search: You may call for information.

Fax search: Turnaround time is 24-48 hours.

In person search: You may request information in person.

Online search: Information is available through the Internet site listed above. You can search by corporate name or even download the whole file. Also, they have 2 pages of excellent searching tips.

Uniform Commercial Code
Federal Tax Liens

UCC Division, Secretary of State, The Capitol, Cheyenne, WY 82002-0020 (Courier: Capitol Bldg, RM 110, Cheyenne, WY 82002); 307-777-5372, 307-777-5988 (Fax), 8AM-5PM.

http://soswy.state.wy.us

Indexing & Storage: Records are available for five years on computer, since the "beginning" on microfiche. Records are indexed on inhouse computer and microfiche.

Searching: The search includes federal tax liens on businesses. Include the following in your request: debtor name.

Access by: mail, fax, in person, online.

Fee & Payment: The search fee is $5.00. Copies cost $.50 each for the first 10 pages and $.15 for each additional page. Fee payee: Secretary of State. Personal checks accepted. No credit cards accepted.

Mail search: Turnaround time: 7 days. Please include your phone number with all requests.

Fax search: Requests may be faxed in.

In person search: Searching is available in person.

Online search: There is a $50.00 annual registration, a $20.00 monthly fee, and long distant access fees of between $3.00 and $6.00 per hour. A word of caution, if user fails to log off the "clock" still keeps ticking and user is billed! The system is open 24 hours daily except 1:30AM to 5AM Mon. through Sun., and 4PM to 6PM on Sunday.

State Tax Liens
Records not maintained by a state level agency.

Note: There is no state income tax. All other state tax liens are filed at the county level.

Sales Tax Registrations

Department of Revenue, Excise Tax Division, Herscher Bldg, 122 W 25th St, Cheyenne, WY 82002-0110; 307-777-5200, 307-777-3652 (Fax), 8AM-5PM.

http://revenue.state.wy.us

Indexing & Storage: Records are available for at least two years: inactive files are purged every two years.

Searching: This agency will only confirm that the business is registered. They will provide no other information. Requests may be e-mailed, visit the web site for the proper e-mail address. Include the following in your request: business name. They will also search by tax permit number.

Access by: mail, phone, in person.

Fee & Payment: There may be a copy fee per page, if record is not considered confidential per statute. The fee depends on the type of record and how many copies are needed. Suggest to call first or to send a restrictive check.

Mail search: A self addressed stamped envelope is requested. No fee for mail request.

Phone search: No fee for telephone request.

In person search: No fee for request.

Birth Certificates

Wyoming Department of Health, Vital Records Services, Hathaway Bldg, Cheyenne, WY 82002; 307-777-7591, 307-635-4103 (Fax), 8AM-5PM.

http://wdhfs.state.wy.us/vital_records

Indexing & Storage: Records are available from 1909 to present. New records are available for inquiry immediately. Records are indexed on microfilm, inhouse computer.

Searching: Must have a signed release from person of record or parent or guardian. Include the following in your request: full name, names of parents, mother's maiden name, date of birth, place of birth, relationship to person of record. Must include signature on request and copy of photo ID.

Access by: mail, fax, in person.

Fee & Payment: Search fee is $12.00 per name per 5 years searched. Fee includes certification. Use of credit card is an additional $5.00 for expedited service. Fee payee: Vital Records Services. Prepayment required. Personal checks accepted. Credit cards accepted: MasterCard, Visa, AmEx, Discover.

Mail search: Turnaround time: 3 to 4 working days. No self addressed stamped envelope is required.

Fax search: See expedited services.

In person search: Turnaround time is 15 minutes.

Expedited service: Expedited service is available for fax searches. Turnaround time: next day. Credit card is required ($5.00), records are overnighted for an additional $11.75.

Death Records

Wyoming Department of Health, Vital Records Services, Hathaway Bldg, Cheyenne, WY 82002; 307-777-7591, 307-635-4103 (Fax), 8AM-5PM.

http://wdhfs.state.wy.us/vital_records

Indexing & Storage: Records are available from 1945 to present. For prior records, contact the State Archives at 307-777-7826. New records are available for inquiry immediately. Records are indexed on microfilm, inhouse computer.

Searching: Must have a signed release form from immediate family member. The agency will verify information to family member, such as aunts and uncles, but will not release copies. Include the following in your request: full name, date of death, place of death, relationship to person of record, reason for information request. Must include signature and copy of photo ID with request.

Access by: mail, fax, in person.

Fee & Payment: Search fee is $9.00 per name if year is known; fee is $12.00 per name per 5 years if date is unknown. All copies are certified. Use of credit card for expedited service an extra $5.00. Fee payee: Vital Records Services. Prepayment required. Personal checks accepted. Credit cards accepted: MasterCard, Visa, AmEx, Discover.

Mail search: Turnaround time: 3 to 4 working days. No self addressed stamped envelope is required.

Fax search: See expedited services.

In person search: Turnaround time is 15 minutes.

Expedited service: Expedited service is available for fax searches. Turnaround time: next day. Include credit card fee and funds for overnight delivery.

Marriage Certificates

Wyoming Department of Health, Vital Records Services, Hathaway Bldg, Cheyenne, WY 82002; 307-777-7591, 307-635-4103 (Fax), 8AM-5PM.

http://wdhfs.state.wy.us/vital_records

Indexing & Storage: Records are available from 1941 to present. New records are available for inquiry immediately. Records are indexed on microfilm, inhouse computer.

Searching: Must have a signed release from persons of record. Include the following in your request: names of husband and wife, date of marriage, place or county of marriage, relationship to person of record, reason for information request, wife's maiden name. Signature and copy of photo ID must be included in request.

Access by: mail, fax, in person.

Fee & Payment: The fee is $12.00 per record and an additional $5.00 if a credit card is used for expedited service. Fee payee: Vital Records Services. Prepayment required. Personal checks accepted. Credit cards accepted: MasterCard, Visa, AmEx, Discover.

Mail search: Turnaround time: 3 to 4 working days. No self addressed stamped envelope is required.

Fax search: See expedited services.

In person search: Turnaround time is 15 minutes.

Expedited service: Expedited service is available for fax searches. Turnaround time: next day. Include credit card fee and funds for overnight delivery.

Divorce Records

Wyoming Department of Health, Vital Records Services, Hathaway Bldg, Cheyenne, WY 82002; 307-777-7591, 307-635-4103 (Fax), 8AM-5PM.

http://wdhfs.state.wy.us/vital_records

Indexing & Storage: Records are available from 1941 to present. New records are available for inquiry immediately. Records are indexed on microfilm, inhouse computer.

Searching: Must have a signed release from person of record. Include the following in your request: names of husband and wife, date of divorce, place of divorce, relationship to person of record. Include copy of photo ID with request.

Access by: mail, phone, fax, in person.

Fee & Payment: Fee is $12.00 per record, add $5.00 if expedited service used. Fee payee: Vital Records Services. Prepayment required. Personal checks accepted. Credit cards accepted: MasterCard, Visa, AmEx, Discover.

Mail search: Turnaround time: 3 to 4 working days.

Fax search: See expedited services.

In person search: Turnaround time is 30 minutes.

Expedited service: Expedited service is available for fax searches. Turnaround time: next day. Include credit card fee ($5.00) and funds for overnight delivery.

Workers' Compensation Records

Employment Department, Workers Compensation Division, 1510 E Persing Blvd, Cheyenne, WY 82002 (Courier: Herschler Bldg, 2nd Floor E, 122 W 25th St, Cheyenne, WY 82002); 307-777-7159, 307-777-5946 (Fax), 8AM-4:30PM.

http://wydoe.state.wy.us/doe.asp?ID=9

Indexing & Storage: Records are available from 1987 on computer. Records are on microfiche from 1919 to 1987. Searches on microfiche must include the date of injury, county of injury, employer and body part affected.

Searching: Only the injured party, employer or legal counsel for either party can obtain records from this agency. Include the following in your request: claimant name, Social Security Number. The only information released is case #, date of injury, body part, employer at time of injury, or other information specifically authorized by claimant.

Access by: mail, fax.

Fee & Payment: No search fee, copy fee is $.25 per copy.

Mail search: Turnaround time: variable. Send release form with request to Gary Lord at address above. No self addressed stamped envelope is required.

Fax search: They will fax results with appropriate request.

Accident Reports

Department of Transportation, Accident Records Section, 5300 Bishop Blvd, Cheyenne, WY 82009-3340; 307-777-4450, 307-777-4250 (Fax), 8AM-5PM.

Note: The agency refers to these reports as "Crash Reports."

Indexing & Storage: Records are available from 1992 on. It takes 10 to 30 days before new records are available for inquiry.

Searching: Accident reports (done by the officer) are considered open public record reports. Reports compiled by individuals involved are closed. Include the following in your request: date of accident, location of accident, full name, date of birth.

Access by: mail, phone, in person.

Fee & Payment: The fee is $3.00 per record uncertified and $5.00 certified. If the specific year or location is not given, the fee is $25.00. Fee payee: Department of Transportation. Prepayment required. Personal checks accepted. No credit cards accepted.

Mail search: Turnaround time: 1 week to 10 days. A self addressed stamped envelope is requested.

Phone search: Searches may be done by phone, but no copies are sent until payment is received.

In person search: In-person requests are normally processed in a few of minutes.

Driver License Information
Driver Records

Wyoming Department of Transportation, Driver Services, 5300 Bishop Blvd, Cheyenne, WY 82009-3340; 307-777-4800, 307-777-4773 (Fax), 8AM-5PM.

http://wydotweb.state.wy.us

Note: Tickets may be obtained from the address above for a fee of $5.00 per citation.

Indexing & Storage: Records are available for 3 years from offense date for moving violations, 5 years from conviction date for DWIs, and 3 to 5 years based on original charge for suspensions. Accidents are shown only if driver has no insurance. It takes 5 to 10 days before new records are available for inquiry.

Searching: Companies requesting records must complete and file the FCRA form available on the web site. Casual requesters cannot obtain records with personal information without signed release from subject. The driver license number or name and DOB is needed when ordering. In addition, a SSN is required when requesting a Commercial Driver License (CDL) record. The following data is not released: medical information.

Access by: mail, in person, online.

Fee & Payment: The fee is $5.00 per record, $3.00 by tape. Fee payee: Department of Transportation. Prepayment required. Personal checks accepted. No credit cards accepted.

Mail search: Turnaround time: 2 days. A self addressed stamped envelope is requested.

In person search: Normal turnaround time is while you wait. Individual licensees may request a copy of their own record at any field office.

Online search: This method is available using FTP or RJE technology. Only approved vendors and permissible users are supported. Call Mark Briggs in Support Services at 307-777-3864 for details.

Other access: Magnetic tape retrieval is available at $3.00 per record. The entire driver license file may be purchased for $2,500. Call Support Services for more information.

Vehicle Ownership
Vehicle Identification

Wyoming Dept. of Transportation, Motor Vehicle Services, 5300 Bishop Blvd, Cheyenne, WY 82009-3340 (Courier: 5300 Bishop Blvd, Cheyenne, WY 82002); 307-777-4709, 307-777-4772 (Fax), 8AM-5PM.

http://wydotweb.state.wy.us/web/vehicle_services/index.html

Note: At the web site, click on "Vehicle Services" for detailed WY DOT vehicle information.

Indexing & Storage: Records are available for 40 years on titles and 80 years on registrations. It takes 3 to 15 days before new records are available for inquiry.

Searching: Requests must be for a permissible use per DPPA. A "Privacy Disclosure Agreement" may need to be signed. Casual requesters cannot obtain records unless written consent of subject is provided. Lien records are not available from the state and must be obtained from the one of the 23 Wyoming county clerk offices.

Access by: mail, in person.

Fee & Payment: The fee is $5.00 per record. Fee payee: Department of Transportation. Prepayment required. Personal checks accepted. No credit cards accepted.

Mail search: Turnaround time: 1 week. No self addressed stamped envelope is required.

In person search: Turnaround time is normally in a few minutes.

Other access: Bulk information is available, customized lists can be obtained. Records cannot be resold once purchased. For more information, call the Information Technology Section at 307-777-4201.

Vessel Ownership
Vessel Registration

Wyoming Game & Fish Dept, Watercraft Section, 5400 Bishop Blvd, Cheyenne, WY 82006; 307-777-4575, 307-777-4610 (Fax), 8AM-5PM M-F.

http://gf.state.wy.us

Indexing & Storage: Records are available for the last 3 years on computer. The state does not issue titles. All motorized boats with a 5 HP or larger motor must be registered.

Searching: To search you must provide one of the following: Name, Wyoming #, or Hull Id #.

Access by: mail, phone, fax, in person.

Fee & Payment: There is no search fee.

Mail search: Turnaround time: 2 to 3 days. Turnaround time is 1 week if archived info is needed.

Phone search: Records are available by phone.

Fax search: Information can be faxed back.

In person search: No fee for request. Turnaround time is immediate if the file is not archived.

Other access: Printed lists are available, call for further details.

Legislation Records

Wyoming Legislature, State Capitol, Room 213, Cheyenne, WY 82002; 307-777-7881, 8AM-5PM.

http://legisweb.state.wy.us

Note: General Session starts on the 2nd Tuesday in odd years is January. Budget session starts in February on second Monday in even years.

Indexing & Storage: Records are available for the current session and for past bills, only as introduced. Records archived from 1972 forward

can be searched. Records are indexed on books (volumes).

Searching: This office will not do general research. You must profide specifics. Include the following in your request: bill number, year, date of debate, topic of bill.

Access by: mail, phone, in person, online.

Fee & Payment: Copies are $.10 a page with a minimum fee of $1.00. Fee payee: Wyoming Legislative Service Office Personal checks accepted. No credit cards accepted.

Mail search: Turnaround time: variable. No self addressed stamped envelope is required.

Phone search: Records are available by phone.

In person search: Searching is available in person.

Online search: The Internet site contains a wealth of information regarding the legislature and bills.

Voter Registration

Secretary of State, Election Division, Wyoming State Capitol, Cheyenne, WY 82002-0020; 307-777-7186, 307-777-7640 (Fax), 8AM-5PM.

http://soswy.state.wy.us

Note: Individual look-ups can also be done at the county level. The SSN and DOB are not released. The state will sell all or part of its database, but only for political reasons. Commercial use is not permitted.

Indexing & Storage: Records are available for for the last 10 years, from this office. Previous records are archived.

Access by: mail, in person.

Fee & Payment: The fee is $.50 a page for first 10 pages and $.15 each add'l page. Fee payee: Wyoming Secretary of State.

Mail search: Turnaround time: variable. No self addressed stamped envelope is required.

In person search: Records are pulled within minutes, when personnel available.

GED Certificates

Deptment of WorkForce Services, GED Program, 1740-H Dell Range Blvd #511, Cheyenne, WY 82009; 307-777-6911, 307-777-7106 (Fax), 8AM-5PM M-F.

www.commission.wcc.edu

Indexing & Storage: Records are available from 1992 forward. It takes 2 weeks before new records are available for inquiry.

Searching: To request a verification or transcript, the following is required: signed relelase from subject, full name, Social Security Number, and date of birth.

Access by: mail, fax, in person.

Fee & Payment: There is no fee for verifications or transcripts.

Mail search: Turnaround time: 2 weeks. No self addressed stamped envelope is required.

Fax search: Same criteria as mail searching.

In person search: Turnaround time is typically 10 minutes for verifications if clerical help available, otherwise mailed. All transcript copies are mailed.

Hunting License Information
Fishing License Information

Game & Fish Department, License Section, 5400 Bishop Blvd, Cheyenne, WY 82006; 307-777-4600 (Licensing Section), 307-777-4679 (Fax), 8AM-5PM.

http://gf.state.wy.us

Note: They have a central database for lottery (big game, moose, big horn sheep, elk, deer & antelope) permits only.

Indexing & Storage: Records are available from 3 years present on computer, 10 years on microfiche.

Searching: Include the following in your request: full name, date of birth, Social Security Number. The following data is not released: Social Security Numbers.

Access by: mail, phone, fax, in person.

Fee & Payment: Fees are incurred if there is extensive searching or lists are involved. Call first. Fee payee: Wyoming Game and Fish. Prepayment required. Money orders and cashier's checks are preferred. No credit cards accepted.

Mail search: Turnaround time: 1 to 3 days. No self addressed stamped envelope is required.

Phone search: Records are available by phone.

Fax search: Fax searching available.

In person search: Searching is available in person.

Other access: They have mailing and label lists available. Call 800-548-9453 for more information.

Wyoming State Licensing Agencies

Licenses Searchable Online

Attorney #9 .... www.wyomingbar.org/lawyer_directory.asp
Bank #23 .... http://audit.state.wy.us/banking/banks.htm
Collection Agency #24 .... http://audit.state.wy.us/banking/CAB.htm
Engineer #27 .... www.wrds.uwyo.edu/wrds/borpe/roster/roster.html
Funeral Preneed Agent #8 .... http://insurance.state.wy.us/search/search.asp
Geologist #18 .... http://wbpgweb.uwyo.edu/roster_search.htm (site may be down)
Insurance Agent #8 .... http://insurance.state.wy.us/search/search.asp
Insurance Broker, Resident #8 .... http://insurance.state.wy.us/search/search.asp
Insurance Claims Adjuster #8 .... http://insurance.state.wy.us/search/search.asp
Insurance Consultant #8 .... http://insurance.state.wy.us/search/search.asp
Insurance Service Reps #8 .... http://insurance.state.wy.us/search/search.asp
Insurance Solicitor #8 .... http://insurance.state.wy.us/search/search.asp
Lobbyist #36 .... http://soswy.state.wy.us/election/lob-list.htm
Medical Doctor #10 .... http://wyomedboard.state.wy.us/roster.asp
Motor Club Agent #8 .... http://insurance.state.wy.us/search/search.asp
Optometrist #6 .... www.odfinder.org/LicSearch.asp
Outfitter & Guide #13 .... http://outfitte.state.wy.us/directory.html
Pharmacist #14 .... http://pharmacyboard.state.wy.us/search.asp
Pharmacy Technician #14 .... http://pharmacyboard.state.wy.us/search.asp
Physician Assistant #10 .... http://wyomedboard.state.wy.us/PARoster.asp
Public Accountant-CPA #29 .... http://cpaboard.state.wy.us/search.cfm
Public Accountant-CPA Firm #29 .... http://cpaboard.state.wy.us/search.cfm
Real Estate Appraiser #21 .... www.asc.gov/content/category1/appr_by_state.asp
Savings & Loan Association #23 .... http://audit.state.wy.us/banking/fsb.htm
Surplus Line Broker, Resident #8 .... http://insurance.state.wy.us/search/search.asp
Surveyor, Land #27 .... www.wrds.uwyo.edu/wrds/borpe/roster/roster.html

Licensing Quick Finder

Architect #30 307-777-7788	Insurance Service Reps #8 307-777-7344	Psychologist #16 307-777-6529
Attorney #9 307-632-9061	Insurance Solicitor #8 307-777-7344	Public Accountant-CPA #29 307-777-7551
Bank #23 307-777-6605	Jockey/Jockey Apprentice #38 307-777-5887	Public Accountant-CPA Firm #29 307-777-7551
Barber/Barber Shop #2 307-754-5237	Landscape Architect #30 307-777-7788	Racetrack Security Employee #38 307-777-5887
Bus Driver #41 307-777-4800	Law Enforcement Officer #39 307-777-7718	Racing Event #38 307-777-5887
Child Care Facility #22 307-777-6595	Lobbyist #36 307-777-7186	Racing Permittee/Employee/Official #38
Chiropractor #32 307-777-6529	Manicurist/Nail Technician #3 307-777-3534	 307-777-5887
Collection Agency #24 307-777-3497	Marriage & Family Therapist #30 307-777-7788	Radiation (Ionizing) Agent #17 307-777-3507
Coroner/Deputy Coroner #39 307-777-7718	Medical Doctor #10 307-778-7053	Radiologic Technologist/Technician #17 307-777-3507
Cosmetologist #3 307-777-3534	Mine Foreman #33 307-362-5222	Radiopharmaceutical Agent #17 307-778-2068
Cosmetologist Instructor #3 307-777-3534	Mine Inspector/Examiner #33 307-362-5222	Real Estate Agent #21 307-777-7142
Counselor, Professional #30 307-777-7788	Motor Club Agent #8 307-777-7344	Real Estate Appraiser #21 307-777-7142
Dental Hygienist #4 307-777-6529	Notary Public #36 307-777-5407	Savings & Loan Association #23 307-777-6605
Dentist #4 307-777-6529	Nurse #37 877-626-2681	School Counselor #35 307-777-6261
Detention Officer #39 307-777-7718	Nurse-LPN #37 877-626-2681	School Librarian #35 307-777-6261
Dispatchers #39 307-777-7718	Nursing Assistant #37 877-626-2681	School Principal #35 307-777-6261
Educational Diagnostician #35 307-777-6261	Nursing Home Administrator #12 307-432-0465	School Superintendent #35 307-777-6261
Electrical Apprentice #26 307-777-7991	Occupational Therapist #12 307-432-0488	Securities Agent #34 307-777-7370
Electrician, Master/Journeyman #26 307-777-7991	Occupational Therapist Assistant #12 307-432-0488	Securities Broker/Dealer #34 307-777-7370
Embalmer #5 307-777-7788	Optometrist #6 307-777-3507	Social Worker #30 307-777-7788
Emergency Medical Technician #40 307-777-7955	Outfitter & Guide #13 307-777-5323	Speech Pathologist/Audiologist #28 307-777-6529
Engineer #27 307-777-6155	Pari-Mutuel Employee/Official #38 307-777-5887	Surplus Line Broker, Resident #8 307-777-7344
Esthetician #3 307-777-3534	Peace Officer #39 307-777-7718	Surveyor, Land #27 307-777-6155
Funeral Director #5 307-777-7788	Pesticide Applicator, Commercial #1 307-777-6569	Teacher #35 307-777-6261
Funeral Preneed Agent #8 307-777-7344	Pharmacist #14 307-234-0294	Travel & Baggage Agent #8 307-777-7344
Geologist #18 307-766-2490	Pharmacy Technician #14 307-234-0294	Truck Driver #41 307-777-4800
Hearing Aid Specialist #7 307-777-6529	Physical Therapist #15 307-777-3507	Veterinarian #20 307-777-3507
Insurance Agent #8 307-777-7344	Physician Assistant #10 307-778-7053	Water Dist/Collection Operator #42 307-777-7781
Insurance Broker, Resident #8 307-777-7344	Podiatrist #19 307-777-3507	Water/Waste Water Treatment Plant Operator
Insurance Claims Adjuster #8 307-777-7344	Property Tax Appraiser #25 307-777-5239	#42 307-777-7781
Insurance Consultant #8 307-777-7344	Psychiatrist #10 307-778-7053	

Licensing Agency Information

#1 Board of Agriculture, 2219 Carey Ave, Cheyenne, WY 82002-0100; 307-777-6569, Fax: 307-777-6593. www.wyagric.state.wy.us

#2 Board of Barber Examiners, 441 Sunlight Dr, Powell, WY 82435; 307-754-5237, Fax: 307-7545580. http://soswy.state.wy.us/director/ag-bd/barber.htm

#3 Board of Cosmetology, 2515 Warren Ave, #302, Cheyenne, WY 82002; 307-777-3534, Fax: 307-777-3681. http://soswy.state.wy.us/director/ag-bd/cos met.htm. Agency email: babern@state.wy.us.

#4 Board of Dental Examiners, 2020 Carey Ave #201, Cheyenne, WY 82002; 307-777-6529, Fax: 307-777-3508. http://soswy.state.wy.us/director/ag-bd/dental.htm

#5 Board of Embalming, 2020 Carey Ave, #201, Cheyenne, WY 82002; 307-777-7788, Fax: 307-777-3508.

#6 Board of Examiners in Optometry, 2020 Carey Ave, #201, Cheyenne, WY 82002; 307-777-3507, Fax: 307-777-3508. http://soswy.state.wy.us/director/ag-bd/optometr.htm. Agency email: nbrown1@missc.wy.state.us. Search database at www.odfinder.org/LicSearch.asp

#7 Board of Hearing Aid Specialists, 2020 Carey Ave, #201, Cheyenne, WY 82002; 307-777-6529, Fax: 307-777-3508. http://soswy.state.wy.us

#8 Board of Insurance Agents Examiners, 122 W 25th St, Cheyenne, WY 82002-0040; 307-777-7344, Fax: 307-777-5895. http://insurance.state.wy.us Agency email: gnalde@state.wy.us. Search database at http://insurance.state.wy.us/search/search.asp

#9 Board of Law Examiners, PO Box 109 (500 Randall Ave.), Cheyenne, WY 82003; 307-632-9061, Fax: 307-630-3737. www.wyomingbar.org Search database at www.wyomingbar.org/lawyer_directory.asp

#10 Board of Medicine, 211 W 19th St, 2nd Fl, Cheyenne, WY 82002; 307-778-7053, 800-438-5784, Fax: 307-778-2069. http://wyomedboard.state.wy.us. Agency email: wyomedical@wyomedicalboard.org.

#12 Board of Occupational Therapy, 2020 Carey Ave, #201, Cheyenne, WY 82002; 307-432-0488, Fax: 307-432-0492. http://soswy.state.wy.us/director/boards.htm. Agency email: kspire@state.wy.us.

#13 Board of Outfitters & Professional Guides, 1750 Wland Rd, Cheyenne, WY 82002; 307-777-5323, Fax: 307-777-6715. http://outfitte.state.wy.us Agency email: outfitte@www.state.wy.us. Search database at http://outfitte.state.wy.us/directory.html

#14 Board of Pharmacy, 1720 S Poplar St, #4, Casper, WY 82601; 307-234-0294, Fax: 307-234-7226. http://pharmacyboard.state.wy.us Agency email: wypharmbd@wercs.com. Search database at http://pharmacyboard.state.wy.us/search.asp

#15 Board of Physical Therapy, 2020 Carey Ave, #201, Cheyenne, WY 82002; 307-777-3507, Fax: 307-777-3508. http://soswy.state.wy.us/director/ag-bd/pt.htm. Agency email: nbrown@missc.wy.state.us.

#16 Board of Psychology, 2020 Carey Ave, #201, Cheyenne, WY 82002; 307-777-6529, Fax: 307-777-3508. http://soswy.state.wy.us/director/boards.htm

#17 Board of Radiologic Technologists, 2020 Carey Ave, #201, Cheyenne, WY 82002; 307-777-3507, Fax: 307-777-3508. http://soswy.state.wy.us/director/ag-bd/radiolog.htm Agency email: nbrown@missc.wy.state.us.

#18 Board of Registration for Professional Geologists, PO Box 3008, Laramie, WY 82071-3008; 307-766-2490, Fax: 307-766-2713. http://wbpgweb.uwyo.edu Search database at http://wbpgweb.uwyo.edu/roster_search.htm (site may be down).

#19 Board of Registration in Podiatry, 2020 Carey Ave, #201, Cheyenne, WY 82002; 307-777-3507, Fax: 307-777-3508. http://soswy.state.wy.us/director/ag-bd/podiatry.htm Agency email: nbrown@missc.wy.state.us.

#20 Board of Veterinary Medicine, 2020 Carey Ave, #201, Cheyenne, WY 82002; 307-777-3507, Fax: 307-777-3508. http://soswy.state.wy.us/director/ag-bd/vet-med.htm Agency email: nbrown@missc.wy.state.us.

#21 Real Estate Appraiser Board, 2020 Carey Ave, #100, Cheyenne, WY 82002; 307-777-7142, Fax: 307-777-3796. http://realestate.state.wy.us

#22 Child Care Certification Board, 2300 Capitol Ave, Hathaway Bldg., 3rd Fl, Cheyenne, WY 82002-0490; 307-777-6595, Fax: 307-777-3659. http://soswy.state.wy.us/director/ag-bd/ch-care.htm

#23 Department of Audit, Division of Banking, 122 W 25th St, Herschler Bldg 3 E, Cheyenne, WY 82002; 307-777-7797, Fax: 307-777-3555. http://audit.state.wy.us/banking/default.htm Search database at http://audit.state.wy.us/banking/Links.htm

#24 Department of Audit, Collecting Agency Board, Herschler Bldg, 3rd Fl, Cheyenne, WY 82002; 307-777-3497, Fax: 307-777-3555. http://audit.state.wy.us/banking/CAB.htm Agency email: ssmith@audit.state.wy.us. Search database at http://audit.state.wy.us/banking/CAB.htm

#25 Department of Revenue, 122 W 25th St, Herschler Bldg, 2nd Fl W, Cheyenne, WY 82002-0110; 307-777-5239. http://soswy.state.wy.us/director/boards.htm. Agency email: jburtol@missc.state.wy.us.

#26 Electrical Board, Herschler Bldg, 1st Fl W, Cheyenne, WY 82002; 307-777-7288, Fax: 307-777-7119. http://soswy.state.wy.us/director/ag-bd/electric.htm. Agency email: jnoel@state.wy.us.

#27 Engineers & Professional Land Surveyors, 2424 Pioneer Ave, #400, Cheyenne, WY 82001; 307-777-6155, Fax: 307-777-3403.

www.wrds.uwyo.edu/wrds/borpe/borpe.html. Agency email: wyopepls@wyoming.com. Search database at www.wrds.uwyo.edu/wrds/borpe/roster/roster.html

#28 Examiners for Speech Pathology & Audiology, 2020 Carey Ave, #201, Cheyenne, WY 82002; 307-777-6529, Fax: 307-777-3508. http://soswy.state.wy.us/director/boards.htm

#29 Board of CPAs, Licensing Boards, 2020 Carey Ave, #100, Cheyenne, WY 82002; 307-777-7551, Fax: 307-777-3796. http://cpaboard.state.wy.us Agency email: pmorga@state.wy.us. Search database at http://cpaboard.state.wy.us/search.cfm

#30 Professional Licensing Boards, 2020 Carey Ave, #201, Cheyenne, WY 82002; 307-777-7788, Fax: 307-777-3508.

#32 Licensing Boards - Chiropractic Examiners, 2020 Carey Ave, #201, Cheyenne, WY 82002; 307-777-6529, Fax: 307-777-3508. http://soswy.state.wy.us/director/boards.htm

#33 Mining Council, PO Box 1094, Rock Springs, WY 82901; 307-362-5222, Fax: 307-362-5233. http://soswy.state.wy.us/director/ag-bd/mining.htm

#34 Securities Division, Office of Secretary of State, Joseph B Meyer, State Capitol Bldg, Cheyenne, WY 82002; 307-777-7370, Fax: 307-777-5339. http://soswy.state.wy.us/securiti/securiti.htm

#35 Professional Teaching Standards Board, 2300 Capitol Ave, Hathaway Bldg, Cheyenne, WY 82002; 307-777-6261, Fax: 307-777-6234. www.k12.wy.us/ptsb Agency email: lstowe@state.wy.us.

#36 Secretary of State, Elections/Notary Division, Joseph B Meyer, State Capitol Bldg, Cheyenne, WY 82002; 307-777-7378, Fax: 307-777-5466. http://soswy.state.wy.us. Agency email: secofstate@missc.state.wy.us.

#37 Board of Nursing, 2020 Carey Ave, #110, Cheyenne, WY 82002; 307-777-7601; voice verification 877-626-2681, Fax: 307-777-3519. http://nursing.state.wy.us. Agency email: lleven@missc.state.wy.us.

#38 Pari-Mutuel Commission, 2515 Warren Ave, #301, Cheyenne, WY 82002; 307-777-5887, Fax: 307-777-5700. http://paramutuel.state.wy.us

#39 P.O.S.T. Commission, 1710 Pacific Ave, Cheyenne, WY 82002; 307-777-7718, Fax: 307-638-9706.

#40 Office of Emergency Medical Svcs, 2300 Capital Ave, Hathaway Bldg 4th Fl, Cheyenne, WY 82002; 307-777-7955, Fax: 307-777-5639.

#41 Driver Svcs, 5300 Bishop Blvd, Cheyenne, WY 82009-3340; 307-777-4800, Fax: 307-777-4803. www.wydotwea.state.wy.us

#42 Department of Environmental Quality, Water Quality Division, 122 W 25th St, Herschler Bldg 4W, Cheyenne, WY 82002; 307-777-7781, Fax: 307-777-5973. http://deq.state.wy.us/wqd.htm

Wyoming Federal Courts

The following list indicates the district and division name for each county in the state.

County/Court Cross Reference

Albany	Cheyenne	Natrona	Cheyenne
Big Horn	Cheyenne	Niobrara	Cheyenne
Campbell	Cheyenne	Park	Cheyenne
Carbon	Cheyenne	Platte	Cheyenne
Converse	Cheyenne	Sheridan	Cheyenne
Crook	Cheyenne	Sublette	Cheyenne
Fremont	Cheyenne	Sweetwater	Cheyenne
Goshen	Cheyenne	Teton	Cheyenne
Hot Springs	Cheyenne	Uinta	Cheyenne
Johnson	Cheyenne	Washakie	Cheyenne
Laramie	Cheyenne	Weston	Cheyenne
Lincoln	Cheyenne		

US District Court

District of Wyoming

Cheyenne Division PO Box 727, Cheyenne, WY 82003 (Courier Address: Room 2131, 2120 Capitol Ave, Cheyenne, WY 82001), 307-772-2145.

www.ck10.uscourts.gov/wyoming/district

Counties: All counties in Wyoming. Some criminal records are held in Casper.

Indexing & Storage: Cases are indexed by defendant, plaintiff, and case number. New cases are available in the index 1-2 days after filing date. Records older than 1992 are on microfiche also. Open records are located at this court.

Fee & Payment Notes: Payment may be made by money order, cashier check, personal check. Payee: Clerk, US District Court.

Phone Search: Searching not available by phone.

Mail Search: A stamped self addressed envelope is not required.

In Person Search: In person searching available.

PACER: Toll-free dial-up access: 888-417-3560. Local dial-up access: 307-772-2808. Case records are available back to 1988. Records are purged once per year. New civil records are available online after 1-2 days. New criminal records are available online after 1 day. PACER is available online at http://pacer.wyd.uscourts.gov.

US Bankruptcy Court

District of Wyoming

Cheyenne Division PO Box 1107, Cheyenne, WY 82003 (Courier Address: 6th Floor, 2120 Capitol Ave, Cheyenne, WY 82001), 307-772-2191.

www.wyb.uscourts.gov

Counties: All counties in Wyoming.

Indexing & Storage: Cases are indexed by debtor as well as by case number. New cases are available in the index 24 hours after filing date. Open records are located at this court.

Fee & Payment Notes: Payment may be made by money order, cashier check, personal check. Payee: Clerk, US Bankruptcy Court.

Phone Search: An automated voice case information service (VCIS) is available. Call VCIS at 888-804-5537 or 307-772-2191.

In Person Search: In person searching available.

PACER:. Case records are available back one year. Records are purged annually. New civil records are available online after 1 day. PACER is available online at http://pacer.wyb.uscourts.gov. Document images available.

Electronic Filing: Information is available online at https://ecf.wyb.uscourts.gov

Opinions Online: Court opinions available online at www.wyb.uscourts.gov/opinion_search.htm

Standards for Federal Courts: The search fee is $20.00 per item (one party name or case number). Certification fee is $7.00 per document. Copy fee is $.50 per page. All fees standard unless noted in profile. Mail Search: always enclose a stamped self addressed envelope unless otherwise noted. Before releasing records, all courts require prepayment unless noted in profile.

Open records are located at the court unless otherwise noted. District courts index by defendant and plaintiff as well as by case number. Bankruptcy courts usually index by debtor and case number. While most courts now have their indexes on computer, many still maintain index card files as well.

The universal PACER sign-up number is 800-676-6856. Find PACER and the Party/Case Index on the Web at http://pacer.psc.uscourts.gov. PACER dial-up access is $.60 per minute. Also, courts offering internet access via RACER, PACER, Web-PACER or the new CM-ECF charge $.07 per page fee unless noted as free.

Wyoming County Courts

Court	Jurisdiction	No. of Courts	How Organized
District Courts*	General	23	9 Districts
Circuit Courts*	Limited	20	16 Counties
Justice of the Peace Courts*	Municipal	7	7 Counties
Municipal Courts	Municipal	80	

* Profiled in this Sourcebook.

Court	CIVIL								
	Tort	Contract	Real Estate	Min. Claim	Max. Claim	Small Claims	Estate	Eviction	Domestic Relations
District Courts*	X	X	X	$3000/ $7000	No Max		X		X
Circuit Courts*	X	X	X	$0	$7000	$3000		X	X
Justice of the Peace Courts*	X	X	X	$0	$3000	$3000			
Municipal Courts									

Court	CRIMINAL				
	Felony	Misdemeanor	DWI/DUI	Preliminary Hearing	Juvenile
District Courts*	X				X
Circuit Courts*		X	X	X	
Justice of the Peace Courts*		X	X	X	
Municipal Courts		X	X		

ADMINISTRATION

Court Administrator, 2301 Capitol Av, Supreme Court Bldg, Cheyenne, WY, 82002; 307-777-7480, Fax: 307-777-3447. www.courts.state.wy.us

COURT STRUCTURE

Prior to 2003, for their "lower" jurisdiction court some counties have Circuit Courts and others have Justice Courts. Thus each county has a District Court ("higher" jurisdiction) and either a Circuit or Justice Court. Circuit Courts handle civil claims up to $7,000 while Justice Courts handle civil claims up to $3,000. The District Courts take cases over the applicable limit in each county.

Effective January 1, 2003 all Justice Courts become Circuit Courts and follow Circuit Court rules.

Three counties have two Circuit Courts each: Fremont, Park, and Sweetwater. Cases may be filed in either of the two court offices in those counties, and records requests are referred between the two courts.

Probate is handled by the District Court.

ONLINE ACCESS

Wyoming's statewide case management system is for internal use only. Planning is underway for a new case management system that will ultimately allow public access.

Albany County

2nd Judicial District Court County Courthouse, 525 Grand, Rm 305, Laramie, WY 82070; 307-721-2508. Hours: 9AM-5PM (MST). *Felony, Civil Actions Over $7,000, Probate.*

Civil Records: Access: Phone, mail, in person. Only the court performs in person searches; visitors may not. No search fee. Required to search: name; also helpful: years to search. Civil cases indexed by defendant, plaintiff. Civil records on computer go back to 1988, prior records on card index to 1890. Limit calls to three names.

Criminal Records: Access: Mail, in person. Only the court performs in person searches; visitors may not. Search fee: $5.00 per name. Search results can be phoned back to a toll-free number only. Required to search: name, years to search, DOB. Criminal records on computer go back to 1988, prior records on card index to 1890.

General Information: No sex offenses records released, signed release required for child support cases. SASE required. Turnaround time same day. Copy fee: $1.00 for first page, $.50 each add'l. Fee payee: Clerk of District Court. Personal checks accepted. Prepayment is required.

Albany Circuit Court County Courthouse, 525 Grand, Rm 105, Laramie, WY 82070; 307-742-5747; Fax: 307-742-5610. Hours: 8AM-5PM (MST). *Misdemeanor, Civil Actions Under $7,000, Eviction, Small Claims.*

Civil Records: Access: Mail, in person. Both court and visitors may perform in person searches. Search fee: $20.00 per name. Required to search: name, years to search. Civil cases indexed by defendant, plaintiff. Civil records on computer from 1993, prior on docket books to 1984.

Criminal Records: Access: Mail, in person, fax. Both court and visitors may perform in person searches. Search fee: $20.00 per name. Required to search: name, years to search, DOB. Criminal records on computer from 1989, prior on docket books to 1984.

General Information: No SSN or family violence records released. SASE required. Turnaround time same day. Fax notes: Fee to fax results is $2 per document. Copy fee: $1.00 for 1st page, $.50 each add'l. Certification fee: $5.00 per document. Fee payee: Albany Circuit Court. Personal checks accepted. In-state checks only. Prepayment is required.

Big Horn County

5th Judicial District Court PO Box 670, Basin, WY 82410; 307-568-2381; Fax: 307-568-2791. Hours: 8AM-Noon, 1-5PM (MST). *Felony, Civil Actions Over $7,000, Probate.*

Civil Records: Access: Fax, mail, in person. Both court and visitors may perform in person searches. Search fee: $5.00 per name. Required to search: name, years to search. Civil cases indexed by defendant, plaintiff. Civil records on computer 1988, on microfiche 1982, 1970 to present on cards.

Criminal Records: Access: Fax, mail, in person. Both court and visitors may perform in person searches. Search fee: $5.00 per name. Required to search: name, years to search. Criminal records on computer 1989, on microfiche 1982, 1970 to present on cards.

General Information: Some confidential records not released. SASE required. Turnaround time 24 hours. Copy fee: $1.00 for first page, $.50 each add'l. Certification fee: $.50. Fee payee: Clerk of Court. Business checks accepted. Prepayment is required.

Big Horn Circuit Court PO Box 749, Basin, WY 82410; 307-568-2367; Fax: 307-568-2554. Hours: 8AM-5PM (MST). *Misdemeanor, Civil Actions Under $7,000, Small Claims.*

Civil Records: Access: Fax, mail, in person. Only the court performs in person searches; visitors may not. Search fee: $20.00 per name. Required to search: name, years to search; also helpful: address. Civil cases indexed by defendant. Civil records on microfiche 1985.

Criminal Records: Access: Fax, mail, in person. Only the court performs in person searches; visitors may not. Search fee: $20.00 per name. Required to search: name, DOB; also helpful: SSN. Criminal records on computer since 1990, microfiche 1985.

General Information: No sex or juvenile offenses released. Turnaround time 1 day. Fax notes: Fee to fax results is $2 per document. Copy fee: $1.00 for 1st page, $.50 each add'l. Certification fee: $5.00 per document. Fee payee: Big Horn Circuit Court. Personal checks accepted. Prepayment is required.

Campbell County

6th Judicial District Court PO Box 817, Gillette, WY 82717; 307-682-3424; Fax: 307-687-6209. Hours: 8AM-5PM (MST). *Felony, Civil Actions Over $7,000, Probate.*

Civil Records: Access: Fax, mail, in person. Visitors must perform in person searches for themselves. Search fee: $5.00 per name. Required to search: name, years to search. Civil cases indexed by defendant. Civil records archived from 1913; on computer back to 1983.

Criminal Records: Access: Fax, mail, in person. Visitors must perform in person searches for themselves. Search fee: $5.00 per name. Required to search: name, years to search. Criminal records archived from 1913; on computer back to 1983.

General Information: Public access terminal is available. Names of victims in sex cases, confidential records not released. SASE not required. Turnaround time 1-2 days. Fax notes: $1.00 per page. Copy fee: $1.00 for first page, $.50 each add'l. Fee payee: Clerk of District Court. Personal checks accepted. Out of state checks not accepted. Prepayment is required.

Campbell Circuit Court 500 S Gillette Ave #301, Gillette, WY 82716; 307-682-2190; Fax: 307-687-6214. Hours: 8AM-5PM (MST). *Misdemeanor, Civil Actions Under $7,000, Eviction, Small Claims.*

Civil Records: Access: Mail, in person. Only the court performs in person searches; visitors may not. Search fee: $20.00 per name. Required to search: name, years to search; also helpful: address. Civil cases indexed by defendant, plaintiff. Civil records on computer since 1983, archives from 1979.

Criminal Records: Access: Mail, in person. Only the court may perform in person searches. Search fee: $20.00 per name. Required to search: name, years to search, DOB; also helpful: address. Criminal records on computer since 1983, archives from 1979.

General Information: No sex related cases released. SASE requested. Turnaround time 1-2 days. Fax notes: Fee to fax results is $2 per document. Copy fee: $1.00 for 1st page, $.50 each add'l. Certification fee: $5.00 per document. Fee payee: Campbell County Court. Personal checks accepted. Prepayment is required.

Carbon County

2nd Judicial District Court PO Box 67, Rawlins, WY 82301; 307-328-2628; Fax: 307-328-2629. Hours: 8AM-5PM (MST). *Felony, Civil Actions Over $7,000, Probate.*

Civil Records: Access: Phone, fax, mail, in person. Both court and visitors may perform in person searches. Search fee: $5.00 per name. Required to search: name, years to search; also helpful: address. Civil cases indexed by defendant, plaintiff. Civil records on file from late 1800s, index cards, docket books, then computer.

Criminal Records: Access: Phone, fax, mail, in person. Both court and visitors may perform in person searches. Search fee: $5.00 per name. Required to search: name, years to search; also helpful: address, DOB, SSN. Criminal records on index cards and docket books; on computer since.

General Information: No juvenile or adoption records released. SASE required. Turnaround time 4-5 days. Fax notes: No fee to fax results. Fax available for 800 numbers only. Copy fee: $1.00 for first page, $.50 each add'l. Fee payee: Clerk 2nd Judicial District Court, Clerk of Court. Personal checks accepted. Prepayment is required.

Carbon Circuit Court Attn: Chief Clerk, Courthouse Bldg, 415 W Pine St, Rawlins, WY 82301; 307-324-6655; Fax: 307-324-9465. Hours: 8AM-5PM (MST). *Misdemeanor, Civil Actions Under $7,000, Eviction, Small Claims.*

Civil Records: Access: Mail, fax, in person. Only the court performs in person searches; visitors may not. Search fee: $20.00 per name. Required to search: name, years to search; also helpful: address. Civil cases indexed by defendant, plaintiff. Civil records on computer back to 3/95.

Criminal Records: Access: Mail, fax, in person. Only the court performs in person searches; visitors may not. Search fee: $20.00 per name. Required to search: name, years to search, DOB. Criminal records on computer back to 08/87.

General Information: Sex related cases not released. SASE required. Turnaround time 1 week. Fax notes: Fee to fax results is $2 per document. Copy fee: $1.00 for 1st page, $.50 each add'l. Certification fee: $5.00 per document. Fee payee: Circuit Court of Carbon County. Personal checks accepted. Prepayment is required.

Converse County

8th Judicial District Court Box 189, Douglas, WY 82633; 307-358-3165; Fax: 307-358-9783. Hours: 9AM-5PM (MST). *Felony, Civil Actions Over $7,000, Probate.*

Civil Records: Access: Phone, fax, mail, in person. Both court and visitors may perform in person searches. Search fee: $5.00 per name or case. Required to search: name, years to search; also helpful: address. Civil cases indexed by defendant, plaintiff. Civil records on card file from 1888.

Criminal Records: Access: Phone, fax, mail, in person. Both court and visitors may perform in person searches. Search fee: $5.00 per name or case. Required to search: name, years to search; also helpful: address, DOB, SSN. Criminal records on card file from 1800.

General Information: No juvenile, adoptions or mental cases released. Turnaround time usually same day. Fax notes: $2.00 per page. Copy fee: $.25 per page. Certification fee: $1.00 plus $.50 each add'l page. Fee payee: Clerk of District Court. Only cashiers checks and money orders accepted. Prepayment is required.

Converse Circuit Court 107 N 5th Street #231, PO Box 45, Douglas, WY 82633; 307-358-2196; Fax: 307-358-2501. Hours: 8AM-5PM (MST). *Misdemeanor, Civil Actions Under $7,000, Eviction, Small Claims.*

Civil Records: Access: Mail, in person. Both court and visitors may perform in person searches. Search fee: $20.00 per name. Required to search: name, years to search. Civil cases indexed by defendant, plaintiff. Civil records on computer from 1994, card file prior.

Criminal Records: Access: Mail, in person. Both court and visitors may perform in person searches. Search fee: $20.00 per name. Required to search: name, years

to search, DOB also helpful: address, SSN. Criminal records on computer from 1990, card file prior.

General Information: No sealed records released. Turnaround time 1-2 days. Fax notes: Fee to fax results is $2 per document. Copy fee: $1.00 for 1st page, $.50 each add'l. Certification fee: $5.00 per document. Fee payee: Circuit Court of Converse County. Prepayment is required.

Crook County

6th Judicial District Court Box 904, Sundance, WY 82729; 307-283-2523; Fax: 307-283-2996. Hours: 8AM-5PM (MST). *Felony, Civil Actions Over $7,000, Probate, High Misdemeanor pre-7/1/02.*

Note: High misdemeanor cases are no longer heard by this court effective 7/1/02; High misdemeanor records prior to that date can be found here.

Civil Records: Access: Mail, in person. Both court and visitors may perform in person searches. Search fee: $5.00 per name. Required to search: name, years to search; also helpful: address. Civil cases indexed by defendant, plaintiff. Civil records on card file from late 1800s; on computer back to 1999. The civil limit was raised from $3000 to $7000 effective 7/1/2002. Cases prior to that date will remain with this court.

Criminal Records: Access: Mail, in person. Both court and visitors may perform in person searches. Search fee: $5.00 per name. Required to search: name, years to search; also helpful: address, DOB, SSN. Criminal records on card file from late 1800s; on computer back to 1999. As of 7/1/2002, high misdemeanor cases are no longer heard by this court, however, cases prior to that date will remain here.

General Information: No sealed records released. SASE required. Turnaround time 2 days. Fax notes: $3.00 for 1-10 pgs, $6 for 11-25 pgs; $9 if 25 pgs or more. Free to toll-free numbers. Copy fee: $.50 per page. Certification fee: $1.00. Fee payee: Clerk of District Court. Business checks accepted. Prepayment is required.

Circuit Court PO Box 650, Sundance, WY 82729; 307-283-2929; Fax: 307-283-1091. Hours: 8AM-5PM (MST). *Misdemeanor, Civil Actions Under $7,000, Small Claims.*

Note: This former Justice Court became a Circuit Court on 7/1/2002.

Civil Records: Access: Mail, fax, in person. Only the court performs in person searches; visitors may not. Search fee: $20.00 per name. Required to search: name, years to search; also helpful: address. Civil cases indexed by defendant, plaintiff. Civil records on cards, archives back to 1977; on computer back to 1998.

Criminal Records: Access: Mail, fax, in person. Only the court performs in person searches; visitors may not. Search fee: $20.00 per name. Required to search: name, years to search, DOB, SSN. Criminal records go back to 1983; on computer back to 1992.

General Information: No sex related cases released. SASE required. Turnaround time 2 days. Fax notes: Fee to fax results is $2 per document; no charge if $20 search fee is paid. Copy fee: $1.00 for 1st page, $.50 each add'l. Certification fee: $5.00 per document. Fee payee: Crook County Justice Court. Personal checks accepted. Prepayment is required.

Fremont County

9th Judicial District Court PO Box 370, Lander, WY 82520; 307-332-1134; Fax: 307-332-1143. Hours: 8AM-Noon, 1-5PM (MST). *Felony, Civil Actions Over $7,000, Probate.*

Civil Records: Access: Phone, fax, mail, in person. Both court and visitors may perform in person searches. Search fee: $5.00 per name. Required to search: name, years to search; also helpful: address. Civil cases indexed by defendant, plaintiff. Civil records on

computer since 1992, in books since 1991, on microfiche since 1939 and on card file from 1898.

Criminal Records: Access: Phone, fax, mail, in person. Both court and visitors may perform in person searches. Search fee: $5.00 per name. Required to search: name, years to search; also helpful: address, DOB, SSN. Criminal records on computer since 1992, in books since 1991, on microfiche since 1939 and on card file from 1898.

General Information: Public access terminal is available. No juvenile, involuntary hospitalization or adoption records released. SASE required. Turnaround time same day. Fax notes: No fee to fax results. Copy fee: $.50 per page. Fee payee: Clerk of District Court. Personal checks accepted.

Dubois Circuit Court Box 952, Dubois, WY 82513; 307-455-2920; Fax: 307-455-2132. Hours: 8AM-2:00PM (MST). *Misdemeanor, Civil Actions Under $7,000, Eviction, Small Claims.*

Note: This is a satellite of the Lander Court.

Civil Records: Access: Mail, in person. Both court and visitors may perform in person searches. Search fee: $20.00 per name. Required to search: name, years to search. Civil cases indexed by defendant, plaintiff. Civil records on index.

Criminal Records: Access: Mail, in person. Both court and visitors may perform in person searches. Search fee: $20.00 per name. Required to search: name, years to search; also helpful: DOB. Criminal records on computer since 12/98; prior records on indexes.

General Information: No juvenile, sexual data released. SASE required. Turnaround time 2 days. Fax notes: Fee to fax results is $2 per document. Copy fee: $1.00 for 1st page, $.50 each add'l. Certification fee: $5.00 per document. Fee payee: Fremont County Court. Personal checks accepted. Prepayment is required.

Fremont Circuit Court 450 N. 2nd, Rm 230, Lander, WY 82520; 307-332-3239; Fax: 307-332-1152. Hours: 8AM-5PM (MST). *Misdemeanor, Civil Actions Under $7,000, Eviction, Small Claims.*

Civil Records: Access: Phone, fax, mail, in person. Both court and visitors may perform in person searches. Search fee: $20.00 per name. Required to search: name, years to search; also helpful: address. Civil cases indexed by defendant, plaintiff. Civil records on computer from 1988, archive back to 1979.

Criminal Records: Access: Phone, fax, mail, in person. Both court and visitors may perform in person searches. Search fee: $20.00 per name. Required to search: name, years to search; also helpful: address, DOB, SSN. Criminal records on computer from 1988, archive back to 1979.

General Information: No juvenile or sexual data released. SASE required. Turnaround time 2 days. Fax notes: Fee to fax results is $2 per document. Copy fee: $1.00 for 1st page, $.50 each add'l. Certification fee: $5.00 per document. Fee payee: Circuit Court. Personal checks accepted. In-state checks only. Prepayment is required.

Riverton Circuit Court 818 S Federal Blvd, Riverton, WY 82501; 307-856-7259; Fax: 307-857-3635. Hours: 8AM-5PM (MST). *Misdemeanor, Civil Actions Under $7,000, Eviction, Small Claims.*

www.courts.state.wy.us/Brochure_files/ccriv.htm

Civil Records: Access: Mail, in person. Only the court performs in person searches; visitors may not. Search fee: $20.00 per name. Required to search: name, years to search. Civil cases indexed by defendant, plaintiff. Civil records are computerized since 1997; prior in books to 1981.

Criminal Records: Access: Mail, in person. Only the court performs in person searches; visitors may not. Search fee: $20.00 per name. Required to search: name,

years to search, DOB; also helpful: SSN. Criminal records on computer since 1989; prior in books to 1981.

General Information: No sex released cases released. SASE required. Turnaround time 2 days. Fax to fax results is $2 per document. Copy fee: $1.00 for 1st page, $.50 each add'l. Certification fee: $5.00 per document. Fee payee: Fremont County Court. Personal checks accepted. In state checks only. Prepayment is required.

Goshen County

8th Judicial District Court Clerk of District Court, PO Box 818, Torrington, WY 82240; 307-532-2155; Fax: 307-532-8608. Hours: 7:30AM-4PM (MST). *Felony, Civil Actions Over $7,000, Probate.*

Civil Records: Access: Mail, in person. Both court and visitors may perform in person searches. Search fee: $5.00 per name. Required to search: name, years to search; also helpful: address. Civil cases indexed by defendant, plaintiff. Civil records on index file only since 1913.

Criminal Records: Access: Mail, in person. Both court and visitors may perform in person searches. Search fee: $5.00 per name. Required to search: name, years to search; also helpful: address, DOB, SSN. Criminal records on index file only since 1913.

General Information: No juvenile records released. SASE required. Turnaround time 3-4 days. Copy fee: $1.00 for first page, $.50 each add'l. Certification fee: $.50. Fee payee: Clerk of District Court. Personal checks accepted. In-state checks only. Prepayment is required.

Goshen Circuit Court Drawer BB, Torrington, WY 82240; 307-532-2938; Civil phone: X251; Criminal phone: X249; Fax: 307-532-5101. Hours: 7AM-4PM (MST). *Misdemeanor, Civil Actions Under $7,000, Eviction, Small Claims.*

Civil Records: Access: Mail, in person. Only the court performs in person searches; visitors may not. Search fee: $20.00 per name. Required to search: name, years to search; also helpful: address. Civil cases indexed by defendant. Civil records go back to 1988; on computer back to 3/1997, prior archived.

Criminal Records: Access: Mail, in person. Only the court performs in person searches; visitors may not. Search fee: $20.00 per name. Required to search: name, years to search, DOB; also helpful: address, SSN. Criminal records go back to 10/1992; on computer back to 4/1989, prior archived.

General Information: No juvenile records released. SASE required. Turnaround time 3-4 days. Fax notes: Fee to fax results is $2 per document. Copy fee: $1.00 for 1st page, $.50 each add'l. Certification fee: $5.00 per document. Fee payee: Circuit Court 8th Judicial District. Personal checks accepted. Prepayment is required.

Hot Springs County

5th Judicial District Court 415 Arapahoe St, Thermopolis, WY 82443; 307-864-3323; Fax: 307-864-3210. Hours: 8AM-5PM (MST). *Felony, Civil Actions Over $7,000, Probate.*

Civil Records: Access: Mail, in person. Both court and visitors may perform in person searches. Search fee: $5.00 per name. Required to search: name, years to search; also helpful: address. Civil cases indexed by defendant, plaintiff. Civil records on card index back to 1900s.

Criminal Records: Access: Mail, in person. Both court and visitors may perform in person searches. Search fee: $5.00 per name. Required to search: name, years to search, DOB, SSN; also helpful: address. Criminal records on card index back to 1900s.

General Information: No juvenile, adoption or sexual data released. SASE required. Turnaround time 1 day.

Copy fee: $.25 per page. Certification fee: $.50. Fee payee: Clerk of District Court. Personal checks accepted. Prepayment is required.

Hot Springs Circuit Court

417 Arapahoe St, Thermopolis, WY 82443; 307-864-5161; Fax: 307-864-2067. Hours: 8AM-5PM (MST). *Misdemeanor, Civil Actions Under $7,000, Small Claims.*

Civil Records: Access: Mail, in person. Only the court performs in person searches; visitors may not. Search fee: $20.00 per name. Required to search: name, years to search. Civil cases indexed by defendant, plaintiff. Civil records on computer from 1990, prior in card file.

Criminal Records: Access: Mail, in person. Only the court performs in person searches; visitors may not. Search fee: $20.00 per name. Required to search: name, years to search. Criminal records on computer from 1990, prior in card file to 1980.

General Information: No closed case records released. SASE required. Turnaround time 2-3 days. Fax notes: Fee to fax results is $2 per document. Copy fee: $1.00 for 1st page, $.50 each add'l. Certification fee: $5.00 per document. Fee payee: Circuit Court. Business checks accepted. Prepayment is required.

Johnson County

4th Judicial District Court

76 N Main, Buffalo, WY 82834; 307-684-7271; Fax: 307-684-5146. Hours: 8AM-5PM (MST). *Felony, Civil Actions Over $3,000, Probate.*

Civil Records: Access: Fax, mail, in person. Both court and visitors may perform in person searches. Search fee: $5.00 per name. Required to search: name, years to search; also helpful: address. Civil cases indexed by defendant, plaintiff. Civil records on computer from 1989, card index since 1892.

Criminal Records: Access: Fax, mail, in person. Both court and visitors may perform in person searches. Search fee: $5.00 per name. Required to search: name, years to search; also helpful: address, DOB, SSN. Criminal records on computer from 1989, card index since 1892.

General Information: No adoption or juvenile records released. SASE required. Turnaround time 1 week. Copy fee: $.50 per page. Certification fee: $.50. Fee payee: Clerk of District Court. Personal checks accepted. In-state checks only. Prepayment is required.

Justice Court

76 N Main St, Buffalo, WY 82834-1847; 307-684-5720; Fax: 307-684-5146. Hours: 8AM-5PM (MST). *Misdemeanor, Civil Actions Under $3,000, Small Claims.*

Note: All Wyo. Justice Courts are to become Circuit Courts by 1/2003.

Civil Records: Access: Mail, fax, in person. Both court and visitors may perform in person searches. Search fee: $20.00 per name. Required to search: name, years to search; also helpful: address. Civil cases indexed by defendant, plaintiff. Civil records on computer since 1995; prior records on index cards.

Criminal Records: Access: Mail, fax, in person. Both court and visitors may perform in person searches. Search fee: $20.00 per name. Required to search: name, years to search, DOB; also helpful: SSN. Criminal records on computer since 05/90, card index back 5 years.

General Information: No sex cases released. SASE required. Turnaround time 2 days. Fax notes: Fee to fax results is $2 per document. Copy fee: $1 for 1st page; $.50 each add'l. Certification fee: $5 per document. Fee payee: Justice of the Peace. Personal checks accepted. Prepayment is required.

Laramie County

1st Judicial District Court

309 W 20th St, #3205, PO Box 787, Cheyenne, WY 82001; 307-633-4270; Fax: 307-633-4277. Hours: 8AM-5PM (MST). *Felony, Misdemeanor, Civil Actions Over $7,000, Probate.*

http://webgate.co.laramie.wy.us/dc/dc.html

Civil Records: Access: Fax, mail, in person. Both court and visitors may perform in person searches. Search fee: $5.00 per name. Required to search: name. Civil cases indexed by defendant, plaintiff. Civil records on card index to 1890; on computer back to 1984.

Criminal Records: Access: Fax, mail, in person. Both court and visitors may perform in person searches. Search fee: $5.00 per name. Required to search: name, years to search, DOB, SSN. Criminal records on card index to 1890; on computer back to 1984.

General Information: Public access terminal is available. No juvenile or paternity records released. SASE required. Turnaround time 2 days. Fax notes: No fee to fax results. Fax available for 800 numbers only. Copy fee: $1.00 for first page, $.50 each add'l. Certification fee: $.50. Fee payee: Laramie County Clerk of District Court. Business checks accepted. Prepayment is required.

Laramie County Circuit Court

309 W 20th St Rm 2300, Cheyenne, WY 82001; 307-633-4298; Fax: 307-633-4392. Hours: 8AM-5PM (MST). *Misdemeanor, Civil Actions Under $7,000, Eviction, Small Claims.*

Civil Records: Access: Fax, mail, in person. Both court and visitors may perform in person searches. Search fee: $20.00 per name. Required to search: name, years to search; also helpful: address. Civil cases indexed by defendant, plaintiff. Civil records on computer from 1988, card index from late 1977.

Criminal Records: Access: Fax, mail, in person. Both court and visitors may perform in person searches. Search fee: $20.00 per name. Required to search: name, years to search; also helpful: address. Criminal records on computer from 1988, card index from late 1977.

General Information: Public access terminal is available. SASE required. Turnaround time 48 hours. Fax notes: Fee to fax results is $2 per document. Copy fee: $1.00 for 1st page, $.50 each add'l. Certification fee: $5.00 per document. Fee payee: Laramie County Circuit Court. Business checks accepted. In-state checks only. Prepayment is required.

Lincoln County

3rd Judicial District Court

PO Drawer 510, Kemmerer, WY 83101; 307-877-9056; Fax: 307-877-6263. Hours: 8AM-5PM (MST). *Felony, Civil Actions Over $7,000, Probate.*

Civil Records: Access: Fax, mail, in person. Both court and visitors may perform in person searches. Search fee: $5.00 per name. Required to search: name; also helpful: years to search, address. Civil cases indexed by defendant. Civil records on card index and computer back to 1916.

Criminal Records: Access: Fax, mail, in person. Both court and visitors may perform in person searches. Search fee: $5.00 per name. Required to search: name; also helpful: years to search, address, DOB, SSN. Criminal records on card index and computer back to 1916.

General Information: No juvenile, sexual or PD records released. Turnaround time same day. Fax notes: $5.00 per document. Copy fee: $1.00 for first page, $.50 each add'l. Certification fee: $2.50. Fee payee: 3rd Judicial District Court. Personal checks accepted.

Lincoln Circuit Court

PO Box 949, Kemmerer, WY 83101; 307-877-4431; Fax: 307-877-4936. Hours: 8AM-5PM (MST). *Misdemeanor, Civil Actions Under $7,000, Eviction, Small Claims.*

Civil Records: Access: Mail, in person. Both court and visitors may perform in person searches. Search fee: $20.00 per name. Required to search: name, years to search. Civil cases indexed by defendant, plaintiff. Civil records on computer from 1/90, on card index from 1984, prior data in archives. All search requests must be in writing.

Criminal Records: Access: Mail, in person. Both court and visitors may perform in person searches. Search fee: $20.00 per name. Required to search: name, years to search, DOB; also helpful: SSN. Criminal records on computer from 10/90, card index from 1984, prior in archives. All search requests must be in writing.

General Information: No sexual or PD records released. SASE requested. Turnaround time same day. Fax notes: Fee to fax results is $2 per document. Copy fee: $1.00 for 1st page, $.50 each add'l. Certification fee: $5.00 per document. Fee payee: Lincoln Circuit Court. Business checks accepted. Out of state checks not accepted. Prepayment is required.

Natrona County

7th Judicial District Court

Clerk of District Court, PO Box 2510, Casper, WY 82602; 307-235-9243; Fax: 307-235-9493. Hours: 8AM-5PM (MST). *Felony, Civil Actions Over $7,000, Probate.*

Civil Records: Access: Phone, fax, mail, in person. Both court and visitors may perform in person searches. Search fee: $5.00 per name. Required to search: name, years to search; also helpful: address. Civil cases indexed by defendant, plaintiff. Civil records on computer, microfiche from 1891.

Criminal Records: Access: Phone, fax, mail, in person. Both court and visitors may perform in person searches. Search fee: $5.00 per name. Required to search: name, years to search; also helpful: address, DOB, SSN. Criminal records on computer, microfiche from 1891.

General Information: No adoption, juvenile, paternity, mental health records released. SASE required. Turnaround time 5 days. Fax notes: $.30 per page. Copy fee: $1.00 for first page, $.50 each add'l. Certification fee: $.50. Fee payee: Clerk of District Court. Business checks accepted. Prepayment required.

Natrona Circuit Court

PO Box 1339, Casper, WY 82602; 307-235-9266; Fax: 307-235-9331. Hours: 8AM-5PM (MST). *Misdemeanor, Civil Actions Under $7,000, Eviction, Small Claims.*

Civil Records: Access: Fax, mail, in person. Only the court performs in person searches; visitors may not. Search fee: $20.00 per name. Required to search: name, years to search; also helpful: address. Civil cases indexed by defendant, plaintiff. Civil records on computer from 1994, on microfiche from 1891. All search requests must be in writing.

Criminal Records: Access: Fax, mail, in person. Only the court performs in person searches; visitors may not. Search fee: $20.00 per name. Required to search: name, years to search; also helpful: address, DOB, SSN. Criminal records on computer from 1989, microfiche from 1891. All search requests must be in writing.

General Information: No sexual, abuse records released. SASE required. Turnaround time 2 days. Fax notes: Statewide fee to fax results is $2 per document. Fax available for 800 numbers only. Copy fee: $1.00 for 1st page, $.50 each add'l. Certification fee: $5.00 per document. Fee payee: Natrona Circuit Court. Personal checks accepted. Prepayment is required.

Niobrara County

8th Judicial District Court Clerk of District Court, PO Box 1318, Lusk, WY 82225; 307-334-2736; Fax: 307-334-2703. Hours: 8AM-Noon, 1-4PM (MST). *Felony, Civil Actions Over $3,000, Probate.*

Civil Records: Access: Mail, in person. Visitors must perform in person searches for themselves. Search fee: $5.00 per name. Required to search: name, years to search; also helpful: address. Civil cases indexed by defendant, plaintiff. Civil records on card index from early 1900s.

Criminal Records: Access: Mail, in person. Both court and visitors may perform in person searches. Search fee: $5.00 per name. Required to search: name, years to search; also helpful: address, DOB, SSN. Criminal records on card index from 1913.

General Information: No juvenile or adoption related released, no PD released. SASE required. Turnaround time 2 days. Fax notes: Fee to fax results is $1.00 per page. Copy fee: $1.00 for first page, $.50 each add'l. Certification fee: $.50. Fee payee: Niobrara Clerk of District Court. Personal checks accepted. Prepayment is required.

Justice Court PO Box 209, Lusk, WY 82225; 307-334-3845; Fax: 307-334-3846. Hours: 9AM-Noon, 1-5PM (MST). *Misdemeanor, Civil Actions Under $3,000, Small Claims.*

Note: All Wyo. Justice Courts are to become Circuit Courts by 2003.

Civil Records: Access: Mail, in person. Both court and visitors may perform in person searches. Search fee: $20.00 per name. Required to search: name, years to search; also helpful: address. Civil cases indexed by plaintiff. Civil records on index cards.

Criminal Records: Access: Fax, mail, in person. Both court and visitors may perform in person searches. Search fee: $20.00 per name. Required to search: name, years to search, DOB, SSN, signed release; also helpful: address. Criminal records on computer from 1988, prior archived.

General Information: No juvenile data released. SASE required. Turnaround time 2 days. Fax notes: Fee to fax results is $2 per document. Copy fee: $1.00 for 1st page; $.50 each add'l. Certification fee: $5 per document. Fee payee: Niobrara Justice Court. Personal checks accepted. Prepayment is required.

Park County

5th Judicial District Court Clerk of District Court, PO Box 1960, Cody, WY 82414; 307-527-8690; Fax: 307-527-8687. Hours: 8AM-5PM (MST). *Felony, Civil Actions Over $7,000, Probate.*

www.wtp.net/parkco/districtcourt.htm

Civil Records: Access: Phone, fax, mail, in person. Both court and visitors may perform in person searches. Search fee: $5.00 per name. Required to search: name, years to search; also helpful: address. Civil cases indexed by defendant, plaintiff. Civil records on computer from 1989, card index back to 1911.

Criminal Records: Access: Phone, fax, mail, in person. Both court and visitors may perform in person searches. Search fee: $5.00 per name. Required to search: name, years to search; also helpful: address, DOB, SSN. Criminal records on computer from 1989, card index back to 1911.

General Information: Public access terminal is available. No juvenile, adoptions or PD released. SASE preferred. Turnaround time same day. Fax notes: Fee to fax results is $1.00 per page. Copy fee: $1.00 for first page, $.50 each add'l. Fee payee: Clerk of District Court. Personal checks accepted. Prepayment is required.

Cody Circuit Court 1002 Sheridan Ave., Cody, WY 82414; 307-527-8590; Fax: 307-527-8596. Hours:

8AM-5PM (MST). *Misdemeanor, Civil Actions Under $7,000, Eviction, Small Claims.*

Note: On January 2, 1995 this court changed status from a Justice Court to a Circuit Court.

Civil Records: Access: Mail, in person. Only the court performs in person searches; visitors may not. Search fee: $20.00 per name. Required to search: name, years to search; also helpful: address. Civil cases indexed by defendant, plaintiff. Civil records on computer since 8/95; limited records available prior to 8/95.

Criminal Records: Access: Mail, in person. Only the court performs in person searches; visitors may not. Search fee: $20.00 per name. Required to search: name, years to search; also helpful: address, DOB, SSN. Criminal records on computer since 1990; limited records available prior to 1990.

General Information: No sexual or confidential data released. SASE required. Turnaround time 5 days. Fax notes: Fee to fax results is $2 per document. Copy fee: $1.00 for 1st page, $.50 each add'l. Certification fee: $5.00 per document. Fee payee: Park County Circuit Court. Business checks accepted. Prepayment is required.

Powell Circuit Court 109 W. 14th, Powell, WY 82435; 307-754-8890; Fax: 307-754-8896. Hours: 8AM-Noon, 1-5PM (MST). *Misdemeanor, Civil Actions Under $7,000, Eviction, Small Claims.*

Civil Records: Access: Mail, in person. Only the court performs in person searches; visitors may not. Search fee: $20.00 per name. Required to search: name, years to search. Civil cases indexed by defendant, plaintiff. Civil records on computer from 1995; prior records very poor.

Criminal Records: Access: Mail, in person. Only the court performs in person searches; visitors may not. Search fee: $20.00 per name. Required to search: name, years to search, DOB. Criminal records on computer from 1991; prior records very poor.

General Information: No sexual, confidential records released. SSE required. Turnaround time 1 week. Fax notes: Fee to fax results is $2 per document. Copy fee: $1.00 for 1st page, $.50 each add'l. Certification fee: $5.00 per document. Fee payee: Park County Circuit Court. Personal checks accepted. Prepayment required.

Platte County

8th Judicial District Court PO Box 158, Wheatland, WY 82201; 307-322-3857; Fax: 307-322-5402. Hours: 8AM-5PM (MST). *Felony, Civil Actions Over $3,000, Probate.*

Civil Records: Access: Mail, fax, in person. Both court and visitors may perform in person searches. Search fee: $5.00 per name. Required to search: name, years to search; also helpful: address. Civil cases indexed by defendant. Civil records on card file index last 15 yrs, then to archives.

Criminal Records: Access: Mail, fax, in person. Both court and visitors may perform in person searches. Search fee: $5.00 per name. Required to search: name, years to search; also helpful: address, DOB, SSN. Criminal records on card file index last 15 yrs, then to archives.

General Information: No juvenile data released. SASE required. Turnaround time same day. Copy fee: $1.00 for first page, $.50 each add'l. Certification fee: $.50. Fee payee: Clerk of the Court. Personal checks accepted. Prepayment is required.

Circuit Court PO Box 306, Wheatland, WY 82201; 307-322-3441; Fax: 307-322-5402. Hours: 8AM-5PM (MST). *Misdemeanor, Civil Actions Under $3,000, Small Claims.*

Note: This former Justice Court became a Circuit Court as of July 2002.

Civil Records: Access: Phone, mail, fax, in person. Only the court performs in person searches; visitors may not. Search fee: $20.00 per name. Required to search: name, years to search; also helpful: address. Civil cases indexed by defendant. Civil records on computer since 11/95; on card index since 1976.

Criminal Records: Access: Phone, mail, fax, in person. Only the court performs in person searches; visitors may not. Search fee: $20.00 per name. Required to search: name, years to search, signed release, DOB; also helpful: address, SSN. Criminal records on computer from 11/92, card index from 1976.

General Information: No juvenile data released. SASE required. Turnaround time 2 days. Fax notes: Fee to fax results is $2 per document. Copy fee: $1.00 for 1st page, $.50 each add'l. Certification fee: $5.00 per document. Fee payee: Platte County Justice Court. Business checks accepted. Prepayment is required.

Sheridan County

4th Judicial District Court 224 S. Main, #B-11, Sheridan, WY 82801; 307-674-2960; Fax: 307-674-2909. Hours: 8AM-5PM (MST). *Felony, Civil Actions Over $7,000, Probate.*

Civil Records: Access: Phone, mail, fax, in person. Both court and visitors may perform in person searches. Search fee: $5.00 per name. Required to search: name, years to search. Civil cases indexed by defendant, plaintiff. Civil records archived from 1800s.

Criminal Records: Access: Phone, mail, fax, in person. Both court and visitors may perform in person searches. Search fee: $5.00 per name. Required to search: name, years to search, DOB, SSN. Criminal records archived from 1800s.

General Information: No sex related, juvenile or adoption cases released except by judges permission. SASE required. Turnaround time 1 week. Fax notes: Fee to fax results is $5.00 per document. Copy fee: $1.00 for first page, $.25 each add'l. Certification fee: $.50. Fee payee: Clerk of District Court. Personal checks accepted. Prepayment is required.

Circuit Court 224 S. Main, #B-7, Sheridan, WY 82801; 307-674-2940; Fax: 307-674-2944. Hours: 8AM-5PM (MST). *Misdemeanor, Civil Actions Under $7,000, Eviction, Small Claims.*

Civil Records: Access: Mail, in person. Only the court performs in person searches; visitors may not. Search fee: $20.00 per name. Required to search: name, years to search; also helpful: address. Civil cases indexed by defendant, plaintiff. Civil records on cards from 1983; computerized records go back to 1983.

Criminal Records: Access: Mail, in person. Only the court performs in person searches; visitors may not. Search fee: $20.00 per name. Required to search: name, years to search; also helpful: address, DOB, SSN. Criminal records on computer from 1983, on cards from 1983.

General Information: Identity of victims not released in sexual assault cases. SASE required. Turnaround time 2-3 days. Fax notes: Fee to fax results is $2 per document. Copy fee: $1.00 for 1st page, $.50 each add'l. Certification fee: $5.00 per document. Fee payee: Sheridan Circuit Court. Personal checks accepted. Prepayment is required.

Sublette County

9th Judicial District Court PO Box 764, Pinedale, WY 82941-0764; 307-367-4376; Fax: 307-367-6474. Hours: 8AM-5PM (MST). *Felony, Civil Actions Over $7,000, Probate.*

Civil Records: Access: Mail, in person. Both court and visitors may perform in person searches. Search fee: $5.00 per name. Required to search: name; also helpful: years to search, address. Civil cases indexed by defendant, plaintiff. Civil records on card file from 1923.

Criminal Records: Access: Mail, in person. Both court and visitors may perform in person searches. Search fee: $5.00 per name. Required to search: name, years to search; also helpful: address, DOB, SSN. Criminal records go back to 1993.

General Information: No PD or juvenile records released. SASE required. Turnaround time same day. Fax notes: $3.00 for first page, $1.00 each add'l. Copy fee: $1.00 for first page, $.50 each add'l. Fee payee: Clerk of District Court. Personal checks accepted.

Sublette Circuit Court PO Box 1796, Pinedale, WY 82941; 307-367-2556; Fax: 307-367-2658. Hours: 8AM-5PM (MST). *Misdemeanor, Civil Actions Under $7,000, Eviction, Small Claims.*

Civil Records: Access: Mail, in person. Only the court performs in person searches; visitors may not. Search fee: $20.00 per name. Required to search: name, years to search; also helpful: address. Civil cases indexed by defendant. Civil records go back forever, computerized from 1998.

Criminal Records: Access: Mail, in person. Only the court performs in person searches; visitors may not. Search fee: $20.00 per name. Required to search: name, years to search, DOB; also helpful: address, SSN. Criminal records go back 10 years.

General Information: SASE not required. Turnaround time 2 business days. Fax notes: Fee to fax results is $2 per document. Copy fee: $1.00 for 1st page, $.50 each add'l. Certification fee: $5.00 per document. Fee payee: Circuit Court of Sublette County. Only cashiers checks and money orders accepted. In-state checks only. Prepayment is required.

Sweetwater County

3rd Judicial District Court PO Box 430, Green River, WY 82935; 307-872-6440; Fax: 307-872-6439. Hours: 9AM-5PM (MST). *Felony, Civil Actions Over $7,000, Probate.*

Civil Records: Access: Phone, fax, mail, in person. Both court and visitors may perform in person searches. Search fee: $5.00 per name. Required to search: name, years to search. Civil cases indexed by defendant, plaintiff. Civil records on computer from 1985, on microfiche from 1960, archived from late 1800.

Criminal Records: Access: Phone, fax, mail, in person. Both court and visitors may perform in person searches. Search fee: $5.00 per name. Required to search: name, years to search. Criminal records on computer from 1985, on microfiche from 1960, archived from late 1800.

General Information: Public access terminal is available. No PD, juvenile, or adoption records released. SASE required. Turnaround time same day. Fax notes: $1.00 for first page, $.50 each add'l. Copy fee: $1.00 for first page, $.50 each add'l. Certification fee: First free, add'l documents are $.50. Fee payee: Clerk of District Court. Business checks accepted. Prepayment is required.

Green River Circuit Court PO Drawer 1720, Green River, WY 82935; 307-872-6460; Fax: 307-872-6375. Hours: 8AM-5PM (MST). *Misdemeanor, Civil Actions Under $7,000, Eviction, Small Claims.*

Civil Records: Access: Mail, in person. Both court and visitors may perform in person searches. Search fee: $20.00 per name. Required to search: name, years to search. Civil cases indexed by defendant, plaintiff. Civil records on computer from 1994, in card file from 1978-1994, archived prior to 1978.

Criminal Records: Access: Mail, in person. Both court and visitors may perform in person searches. Search fee: $20.00 per name. Required to search: name, years to search, DOB; also helpful: SSN. Criminal Records

computerized since 1990, on card file from 1978 to 1990.

General Information: No sealed, sexual assault records released. Turnaround time same day. Fax notes: Fee to fax results is $2 per document. Copy fee: $1.00 for 1st page, $.50 each add'l. Certification fee: $5.00 per document. Fee payee: Sweetwater County Circuit Court. Business checks accepted. In-state checks only. Prepayment is required.

Sweetwater Circuit Court PO Box 2028, Rock Springs, WY 82902; 307-352-6817; Fax: 307-352-6758. Hours: 8AM-5PM (MST). *Misdemeanor, Civil Actions Under $7,000, Eviction, Small Claims.*

Civil Records: Access: Fax, mail, in person. Only the court performs in person searches; visitors may not. Search fee: $20.00 per name. Required to search: name, years to search; also helpful: address. Civil cases indexed by defendant, plaintiff. Civil records on computer from 1995, archived to 1981.

Criminal Records: Access: Fax, mail, in person. Only the court performs in person searches; visitors may not. Search fee: $20.00 per name. Required to search: name, years to search; also helpful: address, DOB, SSN. Criminal records on computer from 1989, archived to 1981.

General Information: No sexual assault, sealed records released. SASE required. Turnaround time 2 days. Fax notes: Fee to fax results is $2 per document. Copy fee: $1.00 for 1st page, $.50 each add'l. Certification fee: $5.00 per document. Fee payee: Sweetwater Circuit Court. Personal checks accepted. Prepayment is required.

Teton County

9th Judicial District Court PO Box 4460, Jackson, WY 83001; 307-733-2533; Fax: 307-734-1562. Hours: 8AM-5PM (MST). *Felony, Civil Actions Over $3,000, Probate.*

Note: E-mail record search requests are accepted at clerk-of-district-court@tetonwyo.org.

Civil Records: Access: Phone, fax, mail, in person. Both court and visitors may perform in person searches. Search fee: $5.00 per name. Required to search: name, years to search; also helpful: address. Civil cases indexed by defendant, plaintiff. Civil records on computer since 1990, card index back to 1920s.

Criminal Records: Access: Phone, fax, mail, in person. Both court and visitors may perform in person searches. Search fee: $5.00 per name. Required to search: name, years to search; also helpful: address, DOB, SSN. Criminal records on computer since 1990, card index back to 1920s.

General Information: Public access terminal is available. No juvenile or adoption records released. SASE required. Turnaround time 2 days. Copy fee: $1.00 for first page, $.50 each add'l. Certification fee: $.50. Fee payee: Clerk of District Court. Personal checks accepted. Prepayment is required.

Justice Court PO Box 2906 (180 S King St), Jackson, WY 83001; 307-733-7713; Fax: 307-733-8694. Hours: 8AM-5PM (MST). *Misdemeanor, Civil Actions Under $3,000, Small Claims.*

Note: All Wyo. Justice Courts are to become Circuit Courts by 2003.

Civil Records: Access: Mail, in person. Only the court performs in person searches; visitors may not. Search fee: $20.00 per name. Required to search: name, years to search; also helpful-DOB, SSN. Civil cases indexed by defendant, plaintiff. Civil records on docket books back to 1979. Actual files 5 years.

Criminal Records: Access: Mail, in person. Only the court performs in person searches; visitors may not. Search fee: $20.00 per name. Required to search: name, years to search, DOB, SSN. Criminal records citations

on computer from 1991. No citation record older than 5 years. On docket books and files back to 1979.

General Information: No juvenile, sexual or PD released. SASE requested. Turnaround time 3-4 days (may be longer for pre-1992 criminal records). Fax notes: Fee to fax results is $2.00 per document. Copy fee: $1.00 for 1st page, $.50 each add'l. Certification fee: $5 per document. Fee payee: Teton County Justice Court. Personal checks accepted. Prepayment required.

Uinta County

3rd Judicial District Court PO Drawer 1906, Evanston, WY 82931; 307-783-0456; Fax: 307-783-0400. Hours: 8AM-5PM (MST). *Felony, Civil Actions Over $7,000, Probate.*

www.uintacounty.com

Civil Records: Access: Mail, in person. Visitors must perform in person searches for themselves. Search fee: $5.00 per name. Required to search: name, years to search; also helpful: address. Civil cases indexed by defendant, plaintiff. Civil records on microfiche from the late 1800s.

Criminal Records: Access: Phone, fax, mail, in person. Visitors must perform in person searches for themselves. Search fee: $5.00 per name. Required to search: name, years to search, DOB, SSN; also helpful: address. Criminal records on microfiche since 1938.

General Information: Signed notarized release necessary on confidential cases. SASE required. Turnaround time 1 day. Fax notes: Fee to fax results is $1.00 per page. Copy fee: $.25 per page; $.50 if civil. First page is always double price. Certification fee: $.50 per seal. Fee payee: Clerk of District Court. Personal checks accepted. Will bill copy & fax fees.

Uinta Circuit Court 225 9th St, 2nd Fl, Evanston, WY 82931; 307-789-2471; Fax: 307-789-5062. Hours: 8AM-5PM (MST). *Misdemeanor, Civil Actions Under $7,000, Eviction, Small Claims.*

Civil Records: Access: Mail, in person. Only the court performs in person searches; visitors may not. Search fee: $20.00 per name. Required to search: name, years to search; also helpful: address. Civil cases indexed by defendant. Civil records on computer from 1994, prior on card index.

Criminal Records: Access: Mail, in person. Only the court performs in person searches; visitors may not. Search fee: $20.00 per name. Required to search: name, years to search; also helpful: address, DOB, SSN. Criminal records on computer since 1989, prior on index cards.

General Information: No juvenile records released. SASE requested. Turnaround time 1 week. Fax notes: Fee to fax results is $2 per document. Copy fee: $1.00 for 1st page, $.50 each add'l. Certification fee: $5.00 per document. Fee payee: Uinta County Court. Only cashiers checks and money orders accepted. Out of state checks not accepted. Prepayment is required.

Washakie County

5th Judicial District Court PO Box 862, Worland, WY 82401; 307-347-4821; Fax: 307-347-4325. Hours: 8AM-5PM (MST). *Felony, Civil Actions Over $3,000, Probate.*

Civil Records: Access: Fax, mail, in person. Both court and visitors may perform in person searches. Search fee: $5.00 per name. Required to search: name; also helpful: years to search, address. Civil cases indexed by defendant. Civil records on computer back to 1985, prior on file index.

Criminal Records: Access: Phone, fax, mail, in person. Both court and visitors may perform in person searches. Search fee: $5.00 per name. Required to search: name, years to search; also helpful: address, DOB, SSN. Criminal records on computer back to 1985, prior on file index.

General Information: No juvenile, sexual or PD released. SASE required. Turnaround time same day when possible. Fax notes: $1.00 per page. Copy fee: $1.00 for first page, $.50 each add'l. Certification fee: $.50. Fee payee: Clerk of Court. Personal checks accepted. Prepayment is required.

Justice Court PO Box 927, Worland, WY 82401; 307-347-2702; Fax: 307-347-4325. Hours: 8AM-5PM (MST). *Misdemeanor, Civil Actions Under $3,000, Small Claims.*

Note: All Wyoming Justice Courts are to become Circuit Courts by 2003.

Civil Records: Access: Mail, fax. Only the court performs in person searches; visitors may not Search fee: $20.00 per name. Required to search: name, years to search. Civil cases indexed by defendant. Civil records on computer since 1998, on card index from late 1970, prior archived.

Criminal Records: Access: Mail, fax, in person. Only the court performs in person searches; visitors may not Search fee: $20.00 per name. Required to search: name, years to search, DOB; also helpful: SSN. Criminal records on computer since 1995, on card index from late 1970, prior archived.

General Information: No juvenile or PD released; criminal only. SASE not required. Turnaround time

same day. Copy fee: $1.00 for 1st page; $.50 each add'l. Certification fee: $5 per document. Fee payee: Justice Court. Personal checks accepted. Prepayment required.

Weston County

6th Judicial District Court 1 W Main, Newcastle, WY 82701; 307-746-4778; Fax: 307-746-4778. Hours: 8AM-5PM (MST). *Felony, Civil Actions Over $3,000, Probate.*

Civil Records: Access: Mail, fax, in person. Both court and visitors may perform in person searches. Search fee: $5.00 per name. Required to search: name; also helpful: years to search, address. Civil cases indexed by defendant, plaintiff. Civil records on card index from 1913; computerized back to 1999.

Criminal Records: Access: Phone, fax, mail, in person. Both court and visitors may perform in person searches. Search fee: $5.00 per name. Required to search: name; also helpful: years to search, address, DOB, SSN. Criminal records on card index from 1913; computerized back to 1999.

General Information: No juvenile, sexual or PD released. SASE required. Turnaround time same day. Fax notes: Fee to fax results is $2.00 per document. Copy fee: $1.00 for first page, $.50 each add'l. Certification fee: $.50. Fee payee: Clerk of District

Court. Personal checks accepted. Prepayment is required.

Justice Court 6 W Warwick, Newcastle, WY 82701; 307-746-3547; Fax: 307-746-3558. Hours: 8:30AM-4:30PM (MST). *Misdemeanor, Civil Actions Under $3,000, Small Claims.*

Note: All Wyo. Justice Courts are to become Circuit Courts by 2003.

Civil Records: Access: Mail, fax, in person. Only the court performs in person searches; visitors may not. Search fee: $20.00. Required to search: name, years to search; also helpful: address. Civil cases indexed by defendant. Civil records in files back to 1970s; on computer back to 1998.

Criminal Records: Access: Fax, mail, in person. Only the court performs in person searches; visitors may not. Search fee: $20.00. Required to search: name, years to search, DOB; also helpful: address, offense, date of offense, SSN. Criminal records in files back to 1970s; on computer back to 1996.

General Information: Turnaround time is minimum 1 day. Fax notes: Fee to fax results is $2 per document. Copy fee: $1.00 first page; $.50 each add'l. Certification fee: $5.00 per document. Fee payee: Justice Court. Business checks accepted.

Wyoming Recording Offices

ORGANIZATION: 23 counties, 23 recording offices. The recording officer is County Clerk. The entire state is in the Mountain Time Zone (MST).

REAL ESTATE RECORDS: County Clerks will not perform real estate searches. Copy fees are usually $1.00 per page, and certification fees are usually $2.00 per document. The Assessor maintains property tax records.

UCC RECORDS: Since 07/1/2001, all filings have been centralized at the state. Prior, financing statements were usually filed with the County Clerk and accounts receivable and farm products require dula filing at the state level as well. All recording offices will perform UCC searches. Use search request form UCC-11. Searches fees are usually $10.00 per debtor name. Copy fees vary.

TAX LIEN RECORDS: Federal tax liens on personal property of businesses are filed with the Secretary of State. Other federal and all state tax liens are filed with the County Clerk. Most counties will perform tax lien searches. Search fees are usually $10.00 per name.

ONLINE ACCESS: Teton county offers online access to the County Clerk's database of recorded documents.

Albany County

County Clerk, 525 Grand Ave. Room 202, Laramie, WY 82070. County Clerk, R/E and UCC Recording 307-721-2547 UCC Recording: 307-721-2541; Fax 307-721-2544.
Will search UCC records. Will not search real estate records. **Other Phone Numbers:** Assessor 307-721-2511; Treasurer 307-721-2502; Appraiser/Auditor 307-721-2511; Elections 307-721-2546; Vital Records 307-777-7591.

Big Horn County

County Clerk, PO Box 31, Basin, WY 82410. County Clerk, R/E and UCC Recording 307-568-2357; Fax 307-568-9375. www.state.wy.us
Will search UCC records. Will not search real estate records. **Other Phone Numbers:** Assessor 307-568-2547; Treasurer 307-568-2578; Elections 307-568-2357; Vital Records 307-568-2357.

Campbell County

County Clerk, PO Box 3010, Gillette, WY 82717-3010. 307-682-7285; Fax 307-687-6455.
Will search UCC records. UCC search includes tax liens. Will not search real estate records. **Other Phone Numbers:** Assessor 307-682-7266.

Carbon County

County Clerk, 415 W. Pine, PO Box 6, Courthouse, Rawlins, WY 82301. 307-328-2679 R/E Recording: 307-328-2677 UCC Recording: 307-328-2667; Fax 307-328-2690.
Will search UCC records. Will not search real estate records. **Other Phone Numbers:** Assessor 307-328-2637; Treasurer 307-328-2662; Elections 307-328-2650; Vital Records 307-328-2670.

Converse County

County Clerk, 107 North 5th St, Ste 114, Douglas, WY 82633-0990. 307-358-2244; Fax 307-358-5998.
Will search UCC records. Will not search real estate records. **Other Phone Numbers:** Assessor 307-358-2741; Treasurer 307-358-3120; Elections 307-358-2244.

Crook County

County Clerk, PO Box 37, Sundance, WY 82729. 307-283-1323; Fax 307-283-3038.
Will search UCC records. Will not search real estate records. **Other Phone Numbers:** Assessor 307-283-2054; Treasurer 307-283-1244.

Fremont County

County Clerk, 450 N. 2nd St, Room 220, Lander, WY 82520. 307-332-2405; Fax 307-332-1132.
Will search UCC records. **Other Phone Numbers:** Assessor 307-332-1188; Treasurer 307-322-1105.

Goshen County

County Clerk, PO Box 160, Torrington, WY 82240. County Clerk, R/E and UCC Recording 307-532-4051; Fax 307-532-7375. www.state.wy.us
Will search UCC records. Will not search real estate records. **Other Phone Numbers:** Assessor 307-532-2349; Treasurer 307-532-5151; Elections 307-532-4051.

Hot Springs County

County Clerk, 415 Arapahoe St, Courthouse, Thermopolis, WY 82443-2783. 307-864-3515; Fax 307-864-3333.
Will search UCC records. Will not search real estate records. **Other Phone Numbers:** Assessor 307-864-3414; Treasurer 307-864-3616.

Johnson County

County Clerk, 76 N. Main St, Buffalo, WY 82834. 307-684-7272; Fax 307-684-2708.
Will search UCC records. Will not search real estate records. **Other Phone Numbers:** Assessor 307-684-7392; Treasurer 307-684-7302.

Laramie County

County Clerk, PO Box 608, Cheyenne, WY 82003. 307-633-4351 R/E Recording: 307-633-4350; Fax 307-633-4240. www.laramiecountyclerk.com
Will search UCC records. Will not search real estate records. **Other Phone Numbers:** Assessor 307-633-4307; Treasurer 307-633-4225; Elections 307-633-4242; Vital Records 307-777-7591.

Lincoln County

County Clerk, PO Box 670, Kemmerer, WY 83101-0670. 307-877-9056 R/E Recording: 307-877-9056 x305 UCC Recording: 307-877-9056 x304; Fax 307-877-3101.
Will search UCC records. Tax liens are a separate search. Will not search real estate records. **Other Phone Numbers:** Assessor 307-877-9056 x330; Treasurer 307-877-9056 x345; Elections 307-877-9056 x303.

Natrona County

County Clerk, PO Box 863, Casper, WY 82602. County Clerk, R/E and UCC Recording 307-235-9206 UCC Recording: 307-235-9207; Fax 307-235-9367. www.natrona.net
Will search UCC records. Will not search real estate records. **Other Phone Numbers:** Assessor 307-235-9444; Treasurer 307-235-9370; Elections 307-235-9217; Vital Records 307-777-7591.

Niobrara County

County Clerk, PO Box 420, Lusk, WY 82225. County Clerk, R/E and UCC Recording 307-334-2211; Fax 307-334-3013.
Will search UCC records. Will not search real estate records. **Other Phone Numbers:** Assessor 307-334-3201; Treasurer 307-334-2432; Elections 307-334-2211; Vital Records 307-334-2211.

Park County

County Clerk, Courthouse, 1002 Sheridan Ave., Cody, WY 82414. County Clerk, R/E and UCC Recording 307-527-8600; Fax 307-527-8626.
Will search UCC records. Will not search real estate records. **Other Phone Numbers:** Assessor 307-527-8650; Treasurer 307-527-8630; Elections 307-527-8620.

Platte County

County Clerk, PO Drawer 728, Wheatland, WY 82201. 307-322-2315 R/E Recording: 307-322-1306; Fax 307-322-2245.
Will search UCC records. Will not search real estate records. **Other Phone Numbers:** Assessor 307-322-2858; Treasurer 307-322-2092; Elections 307-322-1307.

Sheridan County

County Clerk, 224 S. Main St, Suite B-2, Sheridan, WY 82801-9998. 307-674-2500; Fax 307-674-2529.
Will search UCC records. Will not search real estate records. **Other Phone Numbers:** Assessor 307-674-2535; Treasurer 307-674-6522; Elections 307-674-2515.

Sublette County

County Clerk, PO Box 250, Pinedale, WY 82941-0250. County Clerk, R/E and UCC Recording 307-367-4372; Fax 307-367-6396.
Will search UCC records. Will not search real estate records. **Other Phone Numbers:** Assessor 307-367-4374; Treasurer 307-367-4373; Elections 307-367-4372.

Sweetwater County

County Clerk, PO Box 730, Green River, WY 82935. 307-872-6400 R/E Recording: 307-872-6409 UCC Recording: 307-872-6409; Fax 307-872-6337. www.co.sweet.wy.us/clerk

Will search UCC records. Will not search real estate records. **Other Phone Numbers:** Assessor 307-872-6416; Treasurer 307-872-6389; Appraiser/Auditor 307-872-6400.

Teton County

County Clerk, PO Box 1727, Jackson, WY 83001. 307-733-4433 R/E Recording: 307-733-4430; Fax 307-739-8681. www.tetonwyo.org/clerk/

Will search UCC records. Will not search real estate records. **Online Access:** Real Estate, Lien, Recording Records. Access to the Clerk's database of scanned images is available free at www.tetonwyo.org/clerk/query. Search for complete documents back to 7/1996; partial documents back to 4/1991. **Other Phone Numbers:** Assessor 307-733-4960; Treasurer 307-733-4770; Elections 307-733-7733; Vital Records 307-777-7591.

Uinta County

County Clerk, PO Box 810, Evanston, WY 82931. 307-783-0308 R/E Recording: 307-783-0304; Fax 307-783-0511.

Will search UCC records. UCC search includes tax liens. Will not search real estate records. **Other Phone Numbers:** Assessor 307-789-1780 x338; Treasurer 307-783-0333; Elections 307-783-0423; Vital Records 307-777-7591.

Washakie County

County Clerk, Box 260, Worland, WY 82401-0260. County Clerk, R/E and UCC Recording 307-347-3131; Fax 307-347-9366.

Will search UCC records. UCC search includes tax liens if requested. Will not search real estate records. **Other Phone Numbers:** Assessor 307-347-2831; Treasurer 307-347-2031; Elections 307-347-3131; Vital Records 307-347-3131.

Weston County

County Clerk, 1 W. Main, Newcastle, WY 82701. 307-746-4744; Fax 307-746-9505.

Will search UCC records. UCC search includes tax liens. Will not search real estate records. **Other Phone Numbers:** Assessor 307-746-4633.

Wyoming County Locator

You will usually be able to find the city name in the City/County Cross Reference below. In that case, it is a simple matter to determine the county from the cross reference. However, only the official US Postal Service city names are included in this index. There are an additional 40,000 place names that people use in their addresses. Therefore, we have also included a ZIP/City Cross Reference immediately following the City/County Cross Reference.

If you know the ZIP Code but the city name does not appear in the City/County Cross Reference index, look up the ZIP Code in the ZIP/City Cross Reference, find the city name, then look up the city name in the City/County Cross Reference. For example, you want to know the county for an address of Menands, NY 12204. There is no "Menands" in the City/County Cross Reference. The ZIP/City Cross Reference shows that ZIP Codes 12201-12288 are for the city of Albany. Looking back in the City/County Cross Reference, Albany is in Albany County.

City/County Cross Reference

AFTON Lincoln
ALADDIN Crook
ALBIN Laramie
ALCOVA Natrona
ALPINE Lincoln
ALVA Crook
ARAPAHOE Fremont
ARMINTO Natrona
ARVADA (82831) Campbell(37), Sheridan(32), Johnson(29)
AUBURN Lincoln
BAGGS Carbon
BAIROIL Sweetwater
BANNER (82832) Sheridan(82), Johnson(17)
BASIN Big Horn
BEDFORD Lincoln
BEULAH Crook
BIG HORN Sheridan
BIG PINEY Sublette
BILL Converse
BONDURANT Sublette
BOSLER Albany
BOULDER Sublette
BUFFALO Johnson
BUFORD (82052) Albany(68), Laramie(31)
BURLINGTON (82411) Big Horn(97), Park(2)
BURNS Laramie
BYRON Big Horn
CARLILE Crook
CARPENTER Laramie
CASPER Carbon
CENTENNIAL Albany
CHEYENNE Laramie
CHUGWATER (82210) Platte(89), Goshen(10)
CLEARMONT Sheridan
CODY Park
COKEVILLE Lincoln
CORA Sublette
COWLEY Big Horn
CROWHEART Fremont
DANIEL Sublette
DAYTON Sheridan
DEAVER (82421) Big Horn(85), Park(14)
DEVILS TOWER Crook
DIAMONDVILLE Lincoln
DIXON Carbon

DOUGLAS Converse
DUBOIS Fremont
EDGERTON Natrona
ELK MOUNTAIN Carbon
EMBLEM Big Horn
ENCAMPMENT Carbon
ETNA Lincoln
EVANSTON Uinta
EVANSVILLE (82636) Natrona(97), Converse(2)
FAIRVIEW Lincoln
FARSON Sweetwater
FE WARREN AFB Laramie
FORT BRIDGER Uinta
FORT LARAMIE Goshen
FORT WASHAKIE Fremont
FOUR CORNERS Weston
FRANNIE Park
FREEDOM Lincoln
FRONTIER Lincoln
GARRETT Albany
GILLETTE Campbell
GLENDO (82213) Platte(98), Converse(1)
GLENROCK Converse
GRANGER Sweetwater
GRANITE CANON Laramie
GREEN RIVER Sweetwater
GREYBULL Big Horn
GROVER Lincoln
GUERNSEY Platte
HAMILTON DOME Hot Springs
HANNA Carbon
HARTVILLE Platte
HAWK SPRINGS Goshen
HILAND (82638) Natrona(87), Fremont(12)
HILLSDALE Laramie
HORSE CREEK Laramie
HUDSON Fremont
HULETT Crook
HUNTLEY Goshen
HYATTVILLE Big Horn
IRON MOUNTAIN Laramie
JACKSON Teton
JAY EM Goshen
JEFFREY CITY Fremont
JELM Albany
KAYCEE (82639) Johnson(92), Natrona(7)
KEELINE Niobrara
KELLY Teton

KEMMERER Lincoln
KINNEAR Fremont
KIRBY Hot Springs
LA BARGE Lincoln
LAGRANGE Goshen
LANCE CREEK Niobrara
LANDER Fremont
LARAMIE Albany
LEITER Sheridan
LINCH Johnson
LINGLE Goshen
LITTLE AMERICA Sweetwater
LONETREE Uinta
LONTETREE Uinta
LOST SPRINGS (82224) Converse(85), Niobrara(14)
LOVELL Big Horn
LUSK Niobrara
LYMAN Uinta
LYSITE Fremont
MANDERSON (82432) Park(75), Big Horn(24)
MANVILLE Niobrara
MC FADDEN Carbon
MC KINNON Sweetwater
MEDICINE BOW (82329) Carbon(72), Albany(27)
MEETEETSE Park
MERIDEN Laramie
MIDWEST Natrona
MILLS Natrona
MOORCROFT (82721) Crook(58), Campbell(41)
MOOSE Teton
MORAN Teton
MOUNTAIN VIEW Uinta
NATRONA Natrona
NEWCASTLE Weston
NODE Niobrara
OPAL Lincoln
OSAGE Weston
OSHOTO (82724) Crook(77), Campbell(22)
OTTO Big Horn
PARKMAN Sheridan
PAVILLION Fremont
PINE BLUFFS Laramie
PINEDALE Sublette
POINT OF ROCKS Sweetwater
POWDER RIVER Natrona

POWELL Park
RALSTON Park
RANCHESTER Sheridan
RAWLINS Carbon
RECLUSE Campbell
RELIANCE Sweetwater
RIVERTON Fremont
ROBERTSON Uinta
ROCK RIVER (82083) Carbon(55), Albany(44)
ROCK SPRINGS Sweetwater
ROZET Campbell
SADDLESTRING Johnson
SAINT STEPHENS Fremont
SARATOGA Carbon
SAVERY Carbon
SHAWNEE Converse
SHELL Big Horn
SHERIDAN Sheridan
SHOSHONI Fremont
SINCLAIR Carbon
SMOOT Lincoln
STORY Sheridan
SUNDANCE (82729) Crook(96), Weston(3)
SUPERIOR Sweetwater
TEN SLEEP Washakie
TETON VILLAGE Teton
THAYNE Lincoln
THERMOPOLIS Hot Springs
TIE SIDING Albany
TORRINGTON Goshen
UPTON (82730) Weston(86), Crook(13)
VAN TASSELL Niobrara
VETERAN Goshen
WALCOTT Carbon
WAMSUTTER Sweetwater
WAPITI Park
WESTON (82731) Campbell(96), Crook(3)
WHEATLAND (82201) Platte(98), Albany(1)
WILSON Teton
WOLF Sheridan
WORLAND Washakie
WRIGHT Campbell
WYARNO Sheridan
YELLOWSTONE NATIONAL PARK Park
YODER Goshen

ZIP/City Cross Reference

82001-82003 CHEYENNE	82310-82310 JEFFREY CITY	82620-82620 ALCOVA	82845-82845 WYARNO
82005-82005 FE WARREN AFB	82321-82321 BAGGS	82630-82630 ARMINTO	82901-82902 ROCK SPRINGS
82006-82010 CHEYENNE	82322-82322 BAIROIL	82631-82631 BILL	82922-82922 BONDURANT
82050-82050 ALBIN	82323-82323 DIXON	82633-82633 DOUGLAS	82923-82923 BOULDER
82051-82051 BOSLER	82324-82324 ELK MOUNTAIN	82635-82635 EDGERTON	82925-82925 CORA
82052-82052 BUFORD	82325-82325 ENCAMPMENT	82636-82636 EVANSVILLE	82926-82926 ROCK SPRINGS
82053-82053 BURNS	82327-82327 HANNA	82637-82637 GLENROCK	82929-82929 LITTLE AMERICA
82054-82054 CARPENTER	82329-82329 MEDICINE BOW	82638-82638 HILAND	82930-82931 EVANSTON
82055-82055 CENTENNIAL	82331-82331 SARATOGA	82639-82639 KAYCEE	82932-82932 FARSON
82057-82057 LARAMIE	82332-82332 SAVERY	82640-82640 LINCH	82933-82933 FORT BRIDGER
82058-82058 GARRETT	82334-82334 SINCLAIR	82642-82642 LYSITE	82934-82934 GRANGER
82059-82059 GRANITE CANON	82335-82335 WALCOTT	82643-82643 MIDWEST	82935-82935 GREEN RIVER
82060-82060 HILLSDALE	82336-82336 WAMSUTTER	82644-82644 MILLS	82936-82936 LONETREE
82061-82061 HORSE CREEK	82401-82401 WORLAND	82646-82646 NATRONA	82936-82936 LONTETREE
82062-82062 IRON MOUNTAIN	82410-82410 BASIN	82648-82648 POWDER RIVER	82937-82937 LYMAN
82063-82063 JELM	82411-82411 BURLINGTON	82649-82649 SHOSHONI	82938-82938 MC KINNON
82070-82073 LARAMIE	82412-82412 BYRON	82701-82701 NEWCASTLE	82939-82939 MOUNTAIN VIEW
82080-82080 MC FADDEN	82414-82414 CODY	82710-82710 ALADDIN	82941-82941 PINEDALE
82081-82081 MERIDEN	82420-82420 COWLEY	82711-82711 ALVA	82942-82942 POINT OF ROCKS
82082-82082 PINE BLUFFS	82421-82421 DEAVER	82712-82712 BEULAH	82943-82943 RELIANCE
82083-82083 ROCK RIVER	82422-82422 EMBLEM	82713-82713 CARLILE	82944-82944 ROBERTSON
82084-82084 TIE SIDING	82423-82423 FRANNIE	82714-82714 DEVILS TOWER	82945-82945 SUPERIOR
82190-82190 YELLOWSTONE NATIONAL PARK	82426-82426 GREYBULL	82715-82715 FOUR CORNERS	83001-83002 JACKSON
	82427-82427 HAMILTON DOME	82716-82718 GILLETTE	83011-83011 KELLY
82201-82201 WHEATLAND	82428-82428 HYATTVILLE	82720-82720 HULETT	83012-83012 MOOSE
82210-82210 CHUGWATER	82430-82430 KIRBY	82721-82721 MOORCROFT	83013-83013 MORAN
82212-82212 FORT LARAMIE	82431-82431 LOVELL	82723-82723 OSAGE	83014-83014 WILSON
82213-82213 GLENDO	82432-82432 MANDERSON	82724-82724 OSHOTO	83025-83025 TETON VILLAGE
82214-82214 GUERNSEY	82433-82433 MEETEETSE	82725-82725 RECLUSE	83101-83101 KEMMERER
82215-82215 HARTVILLE	82434-82434 OTTO	82727-82727 ROZET	83110-83110 AFTON
82217-82217 HAWK SPRINGS	82435-82435 POWELL	82729-82729 SUNDANCE	83111-83111 AUBURN
82218-82218 HUNTLEY	82440-82440 RALSTON	82730-82730 UPTON	83112-83112 BEDFORD
82219-82219 JAY EM	82441-82441 SHELL	82731-82731 WESTON	83113-83113 BIG PINEY
82220-82220 KEELINE	82442-82442 TEN SLEEP	82732-82732 WRIGHT	83114-83114 COKEVILLE
82221-82221 LAGRANGE	82443-82443 THERMOPOLIS	82801-82801 SHERIDAN	83115-83115 DANIEL
82222-82222 LANCE CREEK	82450-82450 WAPITI	82831-82831 ARVADA	83116-83116 DIAMONDVILLE
82223-82223 LINGLE	82501-82501 RIVERTON	82832-82832 BANNER	83118-83118 ETNA
82224-82224 LOST SPRINGS	82510-82510 ARAPAHOE	82833-82833 BIG HORN	83119-83119 FAIRVIEW
82225-82225 LUSK	82512-82512 CROWHEART	82834-82834 BUFFALO	83120-83120 FREEDOM
82227-82227 MANVILLE	82513-82513 DUBOIS	82835-82835 CLEARMONT	83121-83121 FRONTIER
82228-82228 NODE	82514-82514 FORT WASHAKIE	82836-82836 DAYTON	83122-83122 GROVER
82229-82229 SHAWNEE	82515-82515 HUDSON	82837-82837 LEITER	83123-83123 LA BARGE
82240-82240 TORRINGTON	82516-82516 KINNEAR	82838-82838 PARKMAN	83124-83124 OPAL
82242-82242 VAN TASSELL	82520-82520 LANDER	82839-82839 RANCHESTER	83126-83126 SMOOT
82243-82243 VETERAN	82523-82523 PAVILLION	82840-82840 SADDLESTRING	83127-83127 THAYNE
82244-82244 YODER	82524-82524 SAINT STEPHENS	82842-82842 STORY	83128-83128 ALPINE
82301-82301 RAWLINS	82601-82615 CASPER	82844-82844 WOLF	

Guam County Locator

ZIP/City Cross Reference

96910-96910 AGANA	96915-96915 SANTA RITA
96910-96910 HAGATNA	96916-96916 MERIZO
96911-96911 TAMUNING	96917-96917 INARAJAN
96912-96912 DEDEDO	96918-96918 UMATAC
96913-96913 BARRIGADA	96919-96919 AGANA HEIGHTS
96914-96914 YONA	96921-96921 BARRIGADA

96922-96922 ASAN	96928-96928 AGAT
96923-96923 MANGILAO	96929-96929 YIGO
96924-96924 CHALAN PAGO	96930-96930 TALOFOFO
96925-96925 PITI	96931-96931 TAMUNING
96926-96926 SINAJANA	96932-96932 AGANA
96927-96927 MONGMONG	96932-96932 HAGATNA

Guam

Guam Department of Revenue & Taxation

Clerk, PO Box 23605, GMF, GU 96921. 671-475-5000 x815; Fax 671-472-2643.
Will search UCC records. This agency will not do a tax lien search. Will not search real estate records.

Puerto Rico County Locator

ZIP/City Cross Reference

00601-00601 ADJUNTAS	00664-00664 JAYUYA	00721-00721 PALMER	00778-00778 GURABO
00602-00602 AGUADA	00667-00667 LAJAS	00723-00723 PATILLAS	00780-00780 COTO LAUREL
00603-00605 AGUADILLA	00669-00669 LARES	00725-00727 CAGUAS	00782-00782 COMERIO
00606-00606 MARICAO	00670-00670 LAS MARIAS	00728-00728 PONCE	00783-00783 COROZAL
00610-00610 ANASCO	00674-00674 MANATI	00729-00729 CANOVANAS	00784-00785 GUAYAMA
00611-00611 ANGELES	00676-00676 MOCA	00730-00734 PONCE	00786-00786 LA PLATA
00612-00614 ARECIBO	00677-00677 RINCON	00735-00735 CEIBA	00791-00792 HUMACAO
00616-00616 BAJADERO	00678-00678 QUEBRADILLAS	00736-00737 CAYEY	00794-00794 BARRANQUITAS
00617-00617 BARCELONETA	00680-00682 MAYAGUEZ	00738-00738 FAJARDO	00795-00795 JUANA DIAZ
00622-00622 BOQUERON	00683-00683 SAN GERMAN	00739-00739 CIDRA	00901-00933 SAN JUAN
00623-00623 CABO ROJO	00685-00685 SAN SEBASTIAN	00740-00740 PUERTO REAL	00934-00934 FORT BUCHANAN
00624-00624 PENUELAS	00687-00687 MOROVIS	00741-00741 PUNTA SANTIAGO	00935-00940 SAN JUAN
00627-00627 CAMUY	00688-00688 SABANA HOYOS	00742-00742 ROOSEVELT ROADS	00949-00951 TOA BAJA
00631-00631 CASTANER	00690-00690 SAN ANTONIO	00744-00744 RIO BLANCO	00952-00952 SABANA SECA
00636-00636 ROSARIO	00692-00692 VEGA ALTA	00745-00745 RIO GRANDE	00953-00954 TOA ALTA
00637-00637 SABANA GRANDE	00693-00694 VEGA BAJA	00751-00751 SALINAS	00955-00955 SAN JUAN
00638-00638 CIALES	00698-00698 YAUCO	00754-00754 SAN LORENZO	00956-00961 BAYAMON
00641-00641 UTUADO	00703-00703 AGUAS BUENAS	00757-00757 SANTA ISABEL	00962-00963 CATANO
00646-00646 DORADO	00704-00704 AGUIRRE	00765-00765 VIEQUES	00964-00964 SAN JUAN
00647-00647 ENSENADA	00705-00705 AIBONITO	00766-00766 VILLALBA	00965-00971 GUAYNABO
00650-00650 FLORIDA	00707-00707 MAUNABO	00767-00767 YABUCOA	00975-00975 SAN JUAN
00652-00652 GARROCHALES	00714-00714 ARROYO	00769-00769 COAMO	00976-00977 TRUJILLO ALTO
00653-00653 GUANICA	00715-00715 MERCEDITA	00771-00771 LAS PIEDRAS	00978-00978 SAINT JUST
00656-00656 GUAYANILLA	00716-00717 PONCE	00772-00772 LOIZA	00978-00978 ST JUST
00659-00659 HATILLO	00718-00718 NAGUABO	00773-00773 LUQUILLO	00978-00978 SAINT JUST CONTRACT
00660-00660 HORMIGUEROS	00719-00719 NARANJITO	00775-00775 CULEBRA	00979-00999 CAROLINA
00662-00662 ISABELA	00720-00720 OROCOVIS	00777-00777 JUNCOS	

Virgin Islands County Locator

City/County Cross Reference

CHRISTIANSTED St. Croix
FREDERIKSTED St. Croix
KINGSHILL St. Croix
SAINT JOHN St. John
SAINT THOMAS St. Thomas

ZIP/City Cross Reference

00801-00805   SAINT THOMAS
00820-00824   CHRISTIANSTED
00830-00831   SAINT JOHN
00840-00841   FREDERIKSTED
00850-00851   KINGSHILL

Additional Resource Tools

Notes